The New
CENTURY DICTIONARY

The New

CENTURY DICTIONARY

[Reg. U. S. Pat. Off.]

OF THE

ENGLISH LANGUAGE

Based on matter selected from the original Century Dictionary and entirely rewritten, with the addition of a great amount of new material, and containing the great mass of words and phrases in ordinary use. 12,000 quotations. 4,000 pictorial illustrations.

EDITED BY

H. G. Emery and K. G. Brewster

Revision Editor, Charles H. Fitch

With supplements of synonyms and antonyms, foreign words and phrases, biographical names, geographical names, etc.

VOLUME ONE

A–pocket veto

D. APPLETON-CENTURY COMPANY

NEW YORK LONDON

414

PRINTED IN THE UNITED STATES OF AMERICA

PREFACE

The New Century Dictionary had its origin in numerous requests made to the publishers for a dictionary based on their original *Century Dictionary*, but more moderate in compass and more popular in character. The original work, in its latest editions, runs to more than 8,500 three-column pages, and is bound, in the usual form, in ten large quarto volumes. It aims to define fully not only all the ordinary words and phrases of the English language, including obsolete words, dialectal and provincial words, and colloquial and slang words, but also the technical terms of all the various sciences, arts, trades, and professions; and it supplements the definitions proper by a great amount of related encyclopedic matter. The present work aims to define all the words of the language that are in ordinary use, or are likely to be met with in general speech or writing, a large number of the common phrases, and, in addition, the more important of the scientific and technical terms, or any of them that may be met with from time to time by the general reader. It is intended to meet the needs of the ordinary dictionary-user of the widest range of requirements, though not to be all-inclusive; and while it endeavors to deal with its entries briefly and simply, it does not hesitate to go into detail when a word or sense seems to merit the more extended treatment proper to the larger work. In making the new dictionary, the material for all the words of the original work falling within the scope of the new was taken as a basis; this material was then condensed and rewritten in accordance with the most recent information available; and finally thousands of new words and senses of all kinds, originating since the period of the World War, were added, these being gathered through a systematic reading of current periodicals and other literature, and defined, wherever necessary, with the help of experts in their particular fields. Thus the present dictionary may be said to be an abridged, condensed, and popular rendering of the original *Century Dictionary*, making available to a wider public the substance of the great mass of accumulated learning of the original work, as contributed by its large corps of scholars and experts; but it may also, because of the thorough rewriting of the original material, and of the great mass of new material added, be said to be a new work.

In this new dictionary, the established principles and preferences of the original dictionary, with respect to spelling, pronunciation, etc., have in the main been adhered to; but close attention has been paid throughout to the tendencies, preferences, and accepted usages of recent years, and where a ruling or method of the original work has been found to be at variance with the best usage of the present day, it has been modified or discarded in favor of what is more in accordance with the most recent developments of the language.

The vocabulary, while a selected one, is intended, as has been said, to answer a wide range of requirements. It includes the mass of the ordinary words of the language, a large proportion of the scientific and technical terms (although the ultratechnical terms have been regularly omitted), a great many of the common dialectal and provincial words, and numerous colloquial and slang words. The requirements of the scholar and the student have throughout been borne in mind, and to answer the needs of these, and of the general reader of the English classics, the more important obsolete and historical words and senses have been included. Much attention has been paid to words and senses of recent origin, in all fields, including war words, scientific terms, names of inventions, proprietary names adopted into general use, and borrowings from foreign languages. In dealing with all proprietary names, care has been taken to indicate that they are private property, and not ordinary words of the language.

In writing the definitions, the constant aim has been exactness and clearness, with avoidance, as far as possible, of the use of uncommon and technical terms. In the effort to make clear the definitions, especially of general words, and more particularly of those having a number of different senses, extensive use has been made of illustrative phrases and sentences showing ordinary usage, and, in addition to these, of illustrative quotations from British and American authors. Such phrases, sentences, and quotations are an important feature of the large *Century Dictionary* (in which the quotations alone aggregate about 200,000); but while a number of these have been retained in the present work, the greater part of those used are new, being invented or selected for the purposes of this work. Of the quotations, a few belong to the period from Chaucer down to the Elizabethan age; many to the period from the Elizabethan age to the close of the 18th century; a still larger number to the 19th century; and a fairly large number to the present century. The quotations in the first and second of these groups are intended primarily as an aid to the scholar and the student, although the general reader will be helped to a better understanding of many terms still in use by the extracts from the Bible, Shakspere, Milton, Dryden, Pope, Cowper, and the other classics of the 17th and 18th centuries; the quotations in the third group are nearly all for still existing senses, and will, it is hoped, be of practical value to the general reader; the quotations in the last group are from a number of the best-known writers of recent years, and illustrate, in part, words and senses of late origin, toward an understanding of which they should prove useful. It may be added that every quotation employed has been verified from its source for its use in this work.

In general, the senses of each word are arranged, as far as possible, in the order of their derivation and development from the original source; and to make plain the course of development, a historical sense no longer in use, and of no particular importance otherwise, has often been retained to show the connection with the original source, or between one sense and another. It is thus possible, ordinarily, in running through a word, to trace the development from sense to sense, or from one group of senses to another group. The chief variation from this principle occurs with respect to technical senses preceded by an italic designation, these senses, for the most part, being placed after all the general senses.

The pronunciation system of the large *Century Dictionary* has met with favor because of its simplicity, and of the comparative ease with which the user is enabled to grasp the significance of its indications. This system has been adhered to in the present work, with a few slight modifications designed to make it even more useful. An abstract of the system is given across the foot of the pages of the Dictionary, and a more detailed *Key to Pronunciation* appears at the beginning of the work.

The etymologies of the original *Century Dictionary* are notable for their fullness; in them effort is directed to the presentation of a complete history of the words, which are traced back through earlier forms to their remotest known origin. In the present work the same elaboration of treatment has not been possible, but the aim has been to give an adequate, trustworthy, and useful statement of the origin and relations of many words of importance, and to give for most words at least an indication of any known or probable source. Where the derivation of a word is unknown, this is stated; where there are several suggested derivations, none of which bears unmistakable evidence of being the correct one, the origin is stated to be uncertain or obscure. For additional aid in this field, numerous prefixes, suffixes, and combining-forms have been entered in the vocabulary, to throw light on words already in existence and on new coinages that may appear hereafter, or to furnish guidance in the formation of new words that may be required to serve particular needs.

The pictorial illustrations in the text are in the main selected from the great collection used in the original work, which has been noted for its accuracy and general excellence. They have been chosen primarily for the help that they afford toward a better understanding of the definitions, each illustration being placed beside its definition, or as near as possible, and reference being made when necessary from the definition to the illustration. In addition to their usefulness in supplementing the definitions, it is felt that they possess a considerable degree of independent suggestiveness and artistic value.

The Century Dictionary, in its original and revised editions, was the work of a large staff of trained lexicographers assisted by many specialists representing all fields of knowledge. The new dictionary has been prepared by a staff trained in the methods of the makers of the original work, and endeavoring to maintain the traditions of their predecessors. To the labors of their predecessors they are under great obligation, for they have drawn heavily upon the materials of the original work in all departments of learning.

To all of the many persons who have served on the office staff of the new dictionary, and by their faithful and conscientious efforts have contributed to the production of the work, grateful acknowledgment is made. Of these, mention should be made in particular of Mr. Charles H. Fitch, who has had the general oversight of the scientific definitions, and has written much of the scientific matter; of Mr. Leo A. Kelly, who has given valuable aid in writing the definitions of the common words of the language; of Mr. O. F. Theis, who has contributed much to the definitions of both the common and the scientific words; and of Mr. Joseph M. Bachelor, who has aided most helpfully in various departments of the work.

A number of other persons connected with The Century Co. have been consulted from time to time during the making of the new dictionary, and have contributed special items of information or otherwise aided in the work of the editorial office. To these thanks are given: in particular, to Mr. W. Morgan Shuster, Mr. Gardner Hazen, Mr. George F. Thomson, Mr. J. L. Worley, Mr. Innis Brown, and Mr. F. V. Morley.

In connection with the definitions of words and senses of recent origin, valuable assistance has been received from a large number of scientists, inventors, manufacturers, original coiners of terms, and other authorities, to whose help is largely due such accuracy as may have been obtained. To give credit here to all of these would be impossible, but mention should be made of the assistance received from Professor Henry Norris Russell, of Princeton University; from Dr. George F. Kunz; from Dr. Henry D. Dakin; from Dr. Winford Lee Lewis; from Dr. F. G. Banting, of the University of Toronto; from Dr. A. A. Brill; from Professor Henry H. Goddard, of Ohio State University; from Dr. Frank H. Chittenden, Mr. Robert A. Young, and Mr. H. N. Vinall, of the United States Department of Agriculture; from Mr. Emile Berliner; from Mr. Elmer A. Sperry; from Dr. Lee de Forest; from Rear-Admiral Bradley A. Fiske; from Colonel B. W. Dunn, formerly of the United States Army; from Commander Charles Dennistoun Burney, formerly of the British Navy; from various officials of the Bell Telephone Laboratories, of E. I. du Pont de Nemours & Company, and of the General Electric Company; from the Holt Manufacturing Company; from the International Nickel Company; from the Bausch & Lomb Optical Company; from Messrs. Vickers, Limited; from Mr. Rudyard Kipling; from Mr. C. N. Chadbourn, of Minneapolis, Minn.; from Dr. Robert Underwood Johnson; from Rev. Henry H. Parker, of Honolulu; from Mr. D. Knickerbacker Boyd; from Mr. John Spargo; from Mr. A. Hamilton Gibbs; from Mr. Philip Moeller, of the Theatre Guild, of New York City; from Mr. Frank J. Wilstach; from Mr. Chesley R. Perry, secretary of the Rotary International; and from Mr. Fred. C. W. Parker, secretary of the Kiwanis Club International. To these, and to the many other persons who have contributed material or information, both the publishers and the editors of this work wish to express their sense of indebtedness and their thanks.

After the main vocabulary, or the Dictionary proper, there follow a number of separate sections of the work containing matter supplementary to the main vocabulary. These supplements, which have all been specially compiled for use in this work, have been based in part on material from the original *Century Dictionary* and its supplementary volume *The Century Cyclopedia of Names*, but they contain also a large amount of new matter.

The supplements appearing without designation as to compiler or editor were prepared by the editors of the main work and their associates. Of these, the supplement of *Abbreviations in Common Use* aims to give a practical selection, containing the abbreviations of a general nature which are met with most frequently. The supplement of *Foreign Words, Phrases, etc.*, lists and explains a large number of foreign words, phrases, sentences, and quotations which occur occasionally in English use, but are for the most part scarcely adapted for inclusion in the Dictionary proper. Of the longer sentences and quotations, many are often quoted in various fragments, so that the complete form of the original sometimes seems desirable to make the subject clear. For a number of legal entries in this list, thanks are due to Mr. Ira H. Brainerd. The supplement of *Biographical Names* gives brief records of a large number of celebrities of all periods of history and in all fields of human activity, including many of those of the present day. The supplement of *Tables of Measures, Weights, etc.*, lists in convenient form a number of tables useful for general reference.

The other supplements have been prepared by persons unconnected with the staff of the main work, but selected by the publishers because of special fitness for their tasks; to them the publishers have delegated full authority with regard to the selection and handling of the material in their respective sections of the work. Of these, the supplement of *Synonyms, Antonyms, and Discriminations* was compiled by Dr. Albert C. Baugh and Dr. Paul C. Kitchen, of the University of Pennsylvania. This supplement is by its nature intimately connected with the main vocabulary, and in its preparation the compilers have sought to provide material which will form a useful addition to the definitions of the Dictionary proper, both in lists of synonyms and antonyms and in discriminations of the senses of groups of words. The supplement of *Business Terms* was edited by Professor Edward Jones Kilduff, of the School of Commerce, Accounts, and Finance, of New York University. It aims to supply a glossary of common terms in the business field which will amplify and supplement the treatment of such terms in the Dictionary proper. The supplement of *Proper Names* was compiled under the direction of Mr. James Abbott. Its purpose is to give concise information concerning a large number of proper names exclusive of those in the fields of biography and geography. Some of these names might be placed equally well either here or in the main vocabulary, but the far greater number are by their nature marked off from the ordinary terms of the language; collectively they form a convenient group separate from the main vocabulary and from the biographical and geographical proper names which follow. The supplement of *Geographical Names* was prepared by Dr. Stephen Sargent Visher, of Indiana University. Its purpose is to give the spelling and pronunciation of all important names in its field, together with the location, size, and other facts of interest for the places, rivers, mountains, etc., themselves. Dr. Visher's own introduction to his supplement will be found at the beginning of the supplement itself.

Finally, sincere thanks are given to the J. S. Cushing Company, of Norwood, Mass., for the care and efficiency shown in the composition and proof-reading of the work, and for the unfailing courtesy with which members of that organization have met the long-continued demands made on their patience by the editors.

H. G. E.
K. G. B.

CONTENTS OF VOLUME I

LIST OF COLOR-PLATES

CONTENTS OF VOLUME II

LIST OF COLOR-PLATES

ABBREVIATIONS USED IN THIS DICTIONARY

a.	adjective.
abbr.	abbreviated; abbreviation.
abl.	ablative.
acc.	accusative.
act.	active.
A.D.	anno Domini (in the year of our Lord; after Christ).
adj.	adjective.
adv.	adverb.
AF.	Anglo-French.
Afr.	Africa; African.
agric.	agriculture.
AL.	Anglo-Latin.
alg.	algebra.
Amer.	America; American.
anat.	anatomy.
anc.	ancient.
Anglo-Ind.	Anglo-Indian.
anthropol.	anthropology.
antiq.	antiquities; antiquity.
appar.	apparently.
Ar.	Arabic.
Aram.	Aramaic.
arch.	architecture.
archæol.	archæology.
arith.	arithmetic.
art.	article.
AS.	Anglo-Saxon.
astrol.	astrology.
astron.	astronomy.
attrib.	attributive; attributively.
at. wt.	atomic weight.
aug.	augmentative.
aux.	auxiliary.
bact.	bacteriology.
B.C.	before Christ.
biol.	biology.
Bohem.	Bohemian.
bot.	botany.
Bret.	Breton.
Brit.	British.
Bulg.	Bulgarian.
cap.	capital.
caps.	capitals.
carp.	carpentry.
Cath.	Catholic.
cent.	century.
ceram.	ceramics.
cf.	Latin *confer*, compare.
ch.	chapter; church.
chem.	chemical; chemistry.
chem. sym.	chemical symbol.
class.	classical.
colloq.	colloquial; colloquially.
com.	commerce; commercial.
comp.	composition; compound.
compar.	comparative.
conch.	conchology.
conj.	conjunction.
contr.	contracted; contraction.
craniol.	craniology.
craniom.	craniometry.
crystal.	crystallography.
D.	Dutch.
Dan.	Danish.
dat.	dative.
def.	definite; definition.
defs.	definitions.
demonst.	demonstrative.
deriv.	derivation; derivative.
dial.	dialect; dialectal.
dim.	diminutive.
E.	East; English.
eccles.	ecclesiastical.
econ.	economics; economy.
ed.	edition.
Egypt.	Egyptian.
E. Ind.	East Indian.
elect.	electricity.
embryol.	embryology.
Encyc. Brit.	Encyclopædia Britannica.
Eng.	England; English.
engin.	engineering.
entom.	entomology.
erron.	erroneous; erroneously.
esp.	especially.
etc.	et cetera (and others; and so forth).
ethnol.	ethnology.
etym.	etymology.
F.	French.
fem.	feminine.
fig.	figurative; figuratively; figure.
Flem.	Flemish.
fort.	fortification.
freq.	frequentative.
Fries.	Friesic.
fut.	future.
G.	German.
Gael.	Gaelic.
gen.	genitive.
geog.	geography.
geol.	geology.
geom.	geometry.
Goth.	Gothic.
Gr.	Greek.
gram.	grammar.
Gr. Brit.	Great Britain.
gun.	gunnery.
Heb.	Hebrew.
her.	heraldry.
Hind.	Hindustani.
hist.	historical; history.
horol.	horology.
hort.	horticulture.
Hung.	Hungarian.
Icel.	Icelandic (usually meaning Old Icelandic, otherwise called Old Norse).
ichth.	ichthyology.
imit.	imitative.
impers.	impersonal.
impf.	imperfect.
impv.	imperative.
ind.	indicative.
Ind.	Indian.
indef.	indefinite.
inf.	infinitive.
interj.	interjection.
interrog.	interrogative.
intr.	intransitive.
introd.	introduction.
Ir.	Ireland; Irish.
irreg.	irregularly.
It.	Italian.
Jap.	Japanese.
L.	Latin.
l. c.	lower-case.
LG.	Low German.
LGr.	Late Greek.
lit.	literal; literally; literature.
Lith.	Lithuanian.
LL.	Late Latin.
mach.	machinery.
manuf.	manufacturing.
masc.	masculine.
math.	mathematics.
MD.	Middle Dutch.
ME.	Middle English.
mech.	mechanical; mechanics.
med.	medicine.
metal.	metallurgy.
metaph.	metaphysics.
meteor.	meteorology.
Mex.	Mexican.
MF.	Middle French.
MGr.	Middle Greek.
MHG.	Middle High German.
milit.	military.
mineral.	mineralogy.
ML.	Middle Latin.
MLG.	Middle Low German.
mod.	modern.
Mongol.	Mongolian.
myth.	mythology.
n.	noun.
N.	North.
N. Amer.	North American.
nat.	natural.
naut.	nautical.
neut.	neuter.
NGr.	New Greek.
NL.	New Latin.
nom.	nominative.
north.	northern.
Norw.	Norwegian.
numis.	numismatics.
O.	Old.
obj.	objective.
obs.	obsolete.
obstet.	obstetrics.
OD.	Old Dutch.
ODan.	Old Danish.
OF.	Old French.
OFries.	Old Friesic.
OGael.	Old Gaelic.
OHG.	Old High German.
OIr.	Old Irish.
OL.	Old Latin.
OPers.	Old Persian.
orig.	original; originally.

ornith.	ornithology.	pres.	present.	specif.	specific; specifically.
OS.	Old Saxon.	pret.	preterit.	sp. gr.	specific gravity.
OSw.	Old Swedish.	priv.	privative.	subj.	subjunctive.
p.	page.	prob.	probable; probably.	superl.	superlative.
p. a.	participial adjective.	pron.	pronoun; pronounced; pronunciation.	surg.	surgery.
paleon.	paleontology.	prop.	properly.	surv.	surveying.
pass.	passive.	pros.	prosody.	Sw.	Swedish.
pathol.	pathology.	prov.	provincial.	Syr.	Syriac.
perf.	perfect.	psychol.	psychology.	teleg.	telegraphy.
pers.	person.	redupl.	reduplicated; reduplication.	teleph.	telephony.
Pers.	Persian.	ref.	reference.	Teut.	Teutonic.
petrog.	petrography.	refl.	reflexive; reflexively.	theat.	theatrical.
Pg.	Portuguese.	rel.	relative.	theol.	theology.
phar.	pharmacy.	repr.	represented; representing.	tr.	transitive; translating; translation.
philol.	philology.	rhet.	rhetoric.	trigon.	trigonometry.
philos.	philosophy.	Rom.	Roman.	Turk.	Turkish.
photog.	photography.	Russ.	Russian.	typog.	typography.
phren.	phrenology.	S.	South.	ult.	ultimate; ultimately.
phys.	physical.	S. Amer.	South American.	U. S.	United States.
physiol.	physiological; physiology.	Sc.	Scotch, or Scottish; Scotland.	v.	verb.
phytogeog.	phytogeography.	Scand.	Scandinavian.	var.	variant; variety.
pl.	plural.	sculp.	sculpture.	vet.	veterinary.
Pol.	Polish.	sing.	singular.	v. i.	intransitive verb.
polit.	political.	Skt.	Sanskrit.	voc.	vocative.
poss.	possessive.	Slav.	Slavic.	v. t.	transitive verb.
pp.	past participle.	sociol.	sociology.	W.	Welsh; West.
ppr.	present participle.	Sp.	Spanish.	W. Ind.	West Indian.
Pr.	Provençal.			zoögeog.	zoögeography.
pred.	predicate.			zoöl.	zoölogy.
prep.	preposition.				

ABBREVIATIONS FOR BOOKS OF BIBLE AND APOCRYPHA

Gen.	Genesis.	Jer.	Jeremiah.	Phil.	Philippians.
Ex.	Exodus.	Lam.	Lamentations.	Col.	Colossians.
Lev.	Leviticus.	Ezek.	Ezekiel.	1 Thes.	I. Thessalonians.
Num.	Numbers.	Dan.	Daniel.	2 Thes.	II. Thessalonians.
Deut.	Deuteronomy.	Hos.	Hosea.	1 Tim.	I. Timothy.
Josh.	Joshua.	Obad.	Obadiah.	2 Tim.	II. Timothy.
1 Sam.	I. Samuel.	Hab.	Habakkuk.	Phile.	Philemon.
2 Sam.	II. Samuel.	Zeph.	Zephaniah.	Heb.	Hebrews.
1 Chron.	I. Chronicles.	Hag.	Haggai.	Jas.	James.
2 Chron.	II. Chronicles.	Zech.	Zechariah.	1 Pet.	I. Peter.
Neh.	Nehemiah.	Mal.	Malachi.	2 Pet.	II. Peter.
Ps.	Psalms.	Mat.	Matthew.	Rev.	Revelation.
Prov.	Proverbs.	Rom.	Romans.	Ecclus.	Ecclesiasticus.
Eccl.	Ecclesiastes.	1 Cor.	I. Corinthians.	Bar.	Baruch.
Cant.	Canticles (Song of Solomon).	2 Cor.	II. Corinthians.	1 Mac.	I. Maccabees.
Isa.	Isaiah.	Gal.	Galatians.	2 Mac.	II. Maccabees.
		Eph.	Ephesians.		

For other abbreviations, see lists at head of the various supplements, and also supplement of Abbreviations (page 2406)

KEY TO PRONUNCIATION

a as in fat, man, pang, parrot.
ā as in fate, mane, dale.
ä as in far, father, palm, guard.
â as in fall, talk, naught.
ȧ as in ask, fast, ant.
ã as in fare, hair, bear.

e as in net, pen, bless.
ē as in me, meet, meat.
ė as in her, fern, herd, hurt.

i as in pin, it, biscuit.
ī as in pine, fight, file.

o as in not, on, gloss, forest, dog, god (a variable sound: in the speech of some, or in some words, approaching ä; in other cases, approaching ô).
ō as in note, poke, floor.
ö as in move, spoon, room.
ô as in nor, song, off.

u as in up, son, blood.
ū as in mute, few, lute, tube (in many words, after l, t, etc., replaced in common speech by ö).
u̇ as in pull, book, could.

oi as in oil, joint, boy.
ou as in out, proud, now.

A single dot under a vowel in an unaccented syllable indicates shortening and lightening, without absolute loss of the distinctive quality. Thus:

ạ̄ as in aviary, prelate, captain.
ẹ̄ as in elect, ablegate, episcopal.
ọ̄ as in agony, abrogate, democrat.
ọ̈ as in into, injury.
ụ̄ as in unite, singular, educate.

Two dots under a vowel in an unaccented syllable indicate that its sound is obscured. Thus:

a̤ as in errant, publican, rural.
ä̤ as in opera, peninsular.
e̤ as in ardent, prudence, towel.
o̤ as in actor, valor, idiot.
ṳ̄ as in nature, feature, natural.

ch as in chip, much.
g as in go, bag.
s as in say, yes, vice.
th as in thin.
ᴛʜ as in then.
y as in you, yet.

A mark (˘) under the consonants d, s, t, z, indicates that they are variable to j, sh, ch, zh. Thus:

d̮ as in arduous, educate.
s̮ as in nausea, appreciation.
t̮ as in nature, adventure.
z̮ as in aphasia, usury.

o as in French cloche, German schloss (a short or medium open o-sound, intermediate in character between ō and ô: not an English sound).
ü as in French menu, German kümmel, Müller.
ċh as in Scotch loch, German ach.
ṅ nasal n, as in French bonbon.
ʙ as in Spanish Habana, Córdoba (sounded almost like v).
ʜ as in Spanish jacal, gitana (a strongly aspirated, guttural h-sound).
ʼ as in French faille, Swedish Strindberg (to indicate an obscure vowel-sound following a consonantal y-sound).

′ denotes a primary accent, ″ a secondary accent. (A secondary accent is not ordinarily marked if at its regular interval of two syllables from the primary, or from another secondary.)

In the pronunciation of French words (except such as are regarded as at least partially Anglicized) no accents are indicated; such being the usage of French dictionaries, and better suited to the light, nearly uniform accentuation of French words than the use of marks customarily denoting the heavier tonic accent of English words.

SIGNS

† obsolete.
< from; derived from.
+ and; compounded with.
= equals; equivalent to.

GREEK CHARACTERS

For transliteration of the Greek characters used in the etymologies and elsewhere, see list under the entry *Greek*, on page **683**.

SPECIAL EXPLANATIONS

The title-words of the Dictionary begin with a small (lower-case) letter, or with a capital, according to usage. When usage differs with the different senses of a word or entry, "[*cap.*]" for *capital* or "[*l. c.*]" for *lower-case* is inserted to indicate the fact, such an indication being understood to apply to all senses following, up to a differing indication or to a closing period.

Similarly, "*pl.*" for *plural* or "*sing.*" for *singular*, when preceding particular senses of a word, is understood to have force up to a differing indication or to a closing period.

Similarly, also, an italicized designation such as *arch.*, *med.*, *physics*, is understood to apply to following senses of a word up to some indication of change or to a closing period.

A single hyphen (-) in a title-word in the Dictionary proper is used to indicate syllabication only; a double hyphen (=) in a title-word in the Dictionary proper, or a single hyphen (-) in the supplements, is used for a hyphen that is intended to be retained in the word.

DICTIONARY

OF THE

ENGLISH LANGUAGE

a[1], a[1] (ā); pl. *A's, a's* (āz). A vowel, the 1st letter of the English alphabet.—**A 1,** in shipping registers, a symbol indicating a vessel of the highest grade; fig., first-class or first-rate (colloq.).

a[2] (ā or ạ), *prep.* [AS. *a*, for *an, on*: see *on*.] On; in; into; to; in course of: now used chiefly in certain combinations, as *a*bed, *a*field, *a*glow, nowadays, (to go) *a*-fishing, (the house is) *a*-building.

a[3] (ā or ạ), *indef. art.* [ME. *a*, for AS. *ān*: see *an*[1].] The form of *an* used before initial consonant-sounds. See *an*[1].

a[4] (ạ), *pron.* Obs. or prov. form of *I*, or of *he, she*, or *they*.

a[5] (ạ), *v.* Colloq. or prov. form of *have*.

a-[1]. [Gr. ἀ- ('alpha privative'), before a vowel ἀν-, akin to L. *in-*, not (see *in-*[2]), and E. *un-*[1].] A prefix of Greek origin, meaning 'without,' 'not,' sometimes used (before a consonant) as an English formative, as in *acaulescent, aplacental, asexual*. See *an-*.

Aardvark.

a-[2]. See *a*[2], *prep.*

aard-vark (ärd′-värk), *n.* [S. Afr. D., 'earth pig.'] The South African ground-hog or ant-bear, a burrowing, insect-eating edentate quadruped of the genus *Orycteropus*.

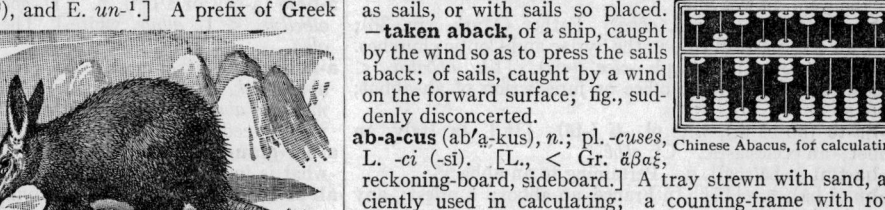

aard-wolf (ärd′-wůlf), *n.* [S. Afr. D., 'earth wolf.'] A hyena-like South African animal, *Proteles lalandi*.

Aardwolf.

Aa-ron-ic (a-ron′-ik), *a.* Pertaining to Aaron, the first Jewish high priest, or to the Jewish priestly order; also, pertaining to the second or lesser order of Mormon priests.

Aar-on's=beard (ar′ọnz-bērd′ or ãr′ọnz-), *n.* [Cf. Ps. cxxxiii. 2.] A dwarf evergreen shrub, *Hypericum calycinum*, with conspicuous hair-like stamens; also, the smoke-tree, *Cotinus cotinus*.

Aar-on's=rod (ar′ọnz-rod′ or ãr′ọnz-), *n.* [Cf. Ex. vii. 10; Num. xvii. 8.] An architectural ornament consisting of a rod with leaves sprouting on either side, or with one serpent twined about it; also, one of several plants with tall flowering stems, as the goldenrod.

Ab (ab), *n.* [Heb.] In the Jewish calendar, the eleventh month (30 days) of the civil year and the fifth of the ecclesiastical year, beginning in July or in the first part of August.

ab-. [L. *ab-*, repr. *ab*, prep., from; akin to Gr. ἀπό, Skt. *apa*, from, and E. *of* and *off*.] A prefix meaning 'from,' 'away,' 'off,' occurring orig. in words from the Latin, but now used occasionally as an English formative.

ab-a (ab′ä), *n.* [Ar.] A woolen fabric, usually striped, made in Arabia, Syria, and neighboring countries; also, an outer garment of this fabric, worn by Arabs.

a-ba-ca (ä-bä-kä′), *n.* [Philippine.] The Manila hemp plant, *Musa textilis*, or its fiber.

a-back (ạ-bak′), *adv.* Toward or at the back; backward; back; *naut.*, back against the mast, as sails, or with sails so placed. —**taken aback,** of a ship, caught by the wind so as to press the sails aback; of sails, caught by a wind on the forward surface; fig., suddenly disconcerted.

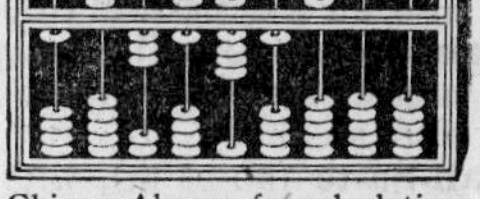

Chinese Abacus, for calculating.

ab-a-cus (ab′ạ-kus), *n.*; pl. *-cuses*, L. *-ci* (-sī). [L., < Gr. ἄβαξ, reckoning-board, sideboard.] A tray strewn with sand, anciently used in calculating; a counting-frame with rows of beads sliding on wires; in *arch.*, a rectangular slab, tablet, or shelf; a slab forming the uppermost member of the capital of a column and supporting the architrave.

Capital of the Parthenon.
A, abacus.

A-bad-don (ạ-bad′ọn), *n.* [Heb., 'destruction.'] "The angel of the bottomless pit" (Rev. ix. 11); Apollyon; also, hell.

a-baft (ạ-båft′). [ME. *on baft* (< AS. *bæftan, be æftan*, 'by aft').] *Naut.*: **I.** *adv.* At or toward the rear or stern; aft. **II.** *prep.* In the rear of; behind.

ab-a-lo-ne (ab-ạ-lō′nē), *n.* [Sp.] Any of various species of ear-shell (family *Haliotidæ*), esp. of the Pacific coasts, whose shell yields a richly colored kind of mother-of-pearl.

a-ban-don (ạ-ban′dọn), *v. t.* [OF. *abandoner* (F. *abandonner*), < *a bandon*, under one's jurisdiction: *a* (< L. *ad*), to; *bandon*, proclamation, authority, < ML. *bandum, bannum*, proclamation, = E. *ban*[1], *n.*] To give up wholly, as to another; yield or relinquish utterly; renounce; forsake or desert; also, to banish†.—**a-ban-don** (ạ-ban′dọn, F. â-bäṅ-dôṅ), *n.* [F.] Abandonment to naturalness of action or manner; freedom from conventional restraint; dash.—**a-ban′doned,** *p. a.* Forsaken; deserted; also, given over to evil courses; profligate; recklessly bad. —**a-ban′doned-ly,** *adv.*—**a-ban-don-ee′** (-ē′), *n.* In *law*, one to whom a thing is abandoned.—**a-ban′don-er,** *n* —**a-ban′don-ment,** *n.* The act of abandoning, or the state of being abandoned; relinquishment; surrender; desertion; freedom from constraint; abandon.

fat, fāte, fär, fâll, åsk, fãre; net, mē, hėr; pin, pīne; not, nōte, möve, nôr; up, lūte, pụll; oi, oil; ou, out; (lightened) aviāry, ẹlect, agōny, intọ̄, ūnite; (obscured) errạnt, operạ, ardẹnt, actọr, natụre; ch, chip; g, go; th, thin; ꟈʜ, then; y, you; (variable) ḍ as d or j, ș as s or sh, ṭ as t or ch, ẓ as z or zh; *o*, F. cloche; ü, F. menu; ċh, Sc. loch; ṅ, F. bonbon; ′, primary accent; ″, secondary accent; †, obsolete; <, from; +, and; =, equals. See also lists at beginning of book.

à bas (ä bä). [F.: *à* (< L. *ad*), to; *bas*, < LL. *bassus*, low.] Down! down with (the person or thing named)!

a-base (ạ-bās′), *v. t.*; *abased*, *abasing*. [OF. *abaissier* (F. *abaisser*), bring down, < L. *ad*, to, + LL. *bassus*, low, E. *base*[1].] To bring down; lower in position, rank, dignity, etc.; degrade; humble.—**a-base′ment,** *n.* The act of abasing; abased condition; degradation; humiliation.

a-bash (ạ-bash′), *v. t.* [AF. *abair* (*abaiss-*), OF. *esbahir* (F. *ébahir*), astonish, < *es-* (< L. *ex*, out of) + *bah*, exclamation of surprise.] To embarrass with awe or shame; confuse with a sense of inferiority, error, etc.—**a-bash′less,** *a.* Unabashed.—**a-bash′ment,** *n.* Confusion from awe or shame.

a-bat-a-ble (ạ-bā′tạ-bl), *a.* Capable of being abated.

a-bate (ạ-bāt′), *v.*; *abated*, *abating*. [OF. *abatre* (F. *abattre*), < L. *ad*, to (or *ab*, from), + *battere*, for *battuere*, beat.] **I.** *tr.* To bring down; reduce in amount, intensity, etc.; diminish; curtail; also, to deduct or subtract; omit; also, in *law*, to put down or suppress (a nuisance); suspend or extinguish (an action); annul (a writ). **II.** *intr.* To go down; decrease; subside; in *law*, to fail; become void. —**a-bat-ed** (ạ-bā′ted), *p. a.* Beaten down, or cut away, as the background of a decorative pattern in relief.—**a-bate′-ment,** *n.* The act of abating, or the resulting state; reduction; mitigation; also, an amount abated; a deduction; in *law*, annulment or failure; also, intrusion on a freehold before the entry of the heir; in *her.*, a mark of dishonor. —**a-bat′er,** *n.*

ab-a-tis (ab′ạ-tis, F. å-bå-tē), *n.* [F., < *abattre*, beat down, fell: see *abate*.] In *fort.*, a barricade of felled trees with sharpened branches directed toward the enemy.

a-ba-tor (ạ-bā′tọr), *n.* In *law*, one who abates.

a-bat-toir (å-bå-twor), *n.* [F.] A public slaughter-house.

abb (ab), *n.* [AS. *āb*, *āweb*: see *woof*.] The woof, or yarn for the woof, in weaving.

ab-ba (ab′ä), *n.* [Aram. *abbā*.] Father (Mark, xiv. 36); also, an ecclesiastical title in the Syriac and Coptic churches.

ab-ba-cy (ab′ạ-si), *n.*; pl. *-cies* (-siz). [LL. *abbatia*, < *abbas*: see *abbot*.] The office or jurisdiction of an abbot; also, an abbey.

ab-ba-te (äb-bä′tā), *n.*; pl. *-ti* (-tē). [It.] In Italy, an abbot; an ecclesiastic. Cf. *abbé*.

ab-ba-tial (a-bā′shạl), *a.* Pertaining to an abbacy.

ab-bé (å-bā), *n.* [F.] In France, an abbot; a priest; any ecclesiastic.

ab-bess (ab′es), *n.* [OF. *abbesse*, < LL. *abbatissa*, fem. of *abbas*, abbot.] The female superior of an abbey of nuns or other religious sisterhood.

ab-bey (ab′i), *n.*; pl. *abbeys* (-iz). [OF. *abaie*, < LL. *abbatia*.] The religious body or establishment under an abbot or abbess; a monastery or convent; also, the monastic buildings (sometimes used later for other purposes); also, an abbatial church.

ab-bot (ab′ọt), *n.* [AS. *abbod*, < LL. *abbas*, < LGr. ἀββᾶς, < Aram. *abbā*, father: see *abba*.] The father superior of an abbey of monks.—**ab′bot-ship,** *n.*

ab-bre-vi-ate (ạ-brē′vi-āt), *v. t.*; *-ated*, *-ating*. [LL. *abbreviatus*, pp. of *abbreviare*, < L. *ad*, to, + *breviare*, shorten, < *brevis*, short, brief.] To make briefer; abridge; shorten, esp. by omission of a part.—**ab-bre-vi-a′tion** (-ā′shọn), *n.* [LL. *abbreviatio*(*n-*).] Reduction in length; abridgment; also, a reduced or shortened form; esp., part of a word or phrase used as a symbol for the whole.—**ab-bre′vi-a-tor,** *n.*—**ab-bre′vi-a-to-ry** (-ạ-tō-ri), *a.* Serving to abbreviate.

a-b-c (ā-bē-sē′), *n.* [First three letters of the alphabet.] The alphabet; hence, the rudiments of any subject.—**a-b-c book,** a primer.

A. B. C. powers. The South American republics of Argentina, Brazil, and Chile, which entered into a treaty or alliance of peace in 1915.

Ab-de-rite (ab′dẹ-rīt), *n.* An inhabitant of Abdera, a town in ancient Thrace, as Democritus, the philosopher (born about 460 B.C.); also (from the proverbial stupidity of the Abderites), a stupid person.

ab-di-ca-ble (ab′di-kạ-bl), *a.* That may be abdicated.

ab-di-cate (ab′di-kāt), *v.*; *-cated*, *-cating*. [L. *abdicatus*, pp. of *abdicare*, < *ab*, from, + *dicare*, declare.] **I.** *tr.* To renounce (sovereignty, office, etc.); relinquish formally; resign; in *civil law*, to disown or disinherit. **II.** *intr.* To renounce office or power.—**ab-di-ca′tion** (-kā′shọn), *n.* [L. *abdicatio*(*n-*).] The act of abdicating; renunciation, esp. of sovereign power.—**ab′di-ca-tive** (-kạ-tiv), *a.* Involving abdication.—**ab′di-ca-tor** (-kā-tọr), *n.*

ab-do-men (ab-dō′men or ab′dọ-men), *n.* [L.] The belly; the visceral cavity; in insects, etc., the posterior division of the body, usually more or less distinctly marked off from the thorax.—**ab-dom′i-nal** (-dom′i-nạl), *a.* Pertaining to the abdomen.—**ab-dom′i-nal-ly,** *adv.*—**ab-dom′i-nous,** *a.* Pot-bellied.

ab-duce (ab-dūs′), *v. t.*; *-duced*, *-ducing*. [L. *abducere* (pp. *abductus*), < *ab*, from, + *ducere*, lead: cf. *abduct*.] To lead away; abduct.—**ab-du′cent** (-dū′sẹnt), *a.* In *physiol.*, drawing away: applied to muscles, etc.

ab-duct (ab-dukt′), *v. t.* [L. *abductus*, pp. of *abducere*: see *abduce*.] To lead away illegally; carry off; kidnap; in *physiol.*, to draw away from the main axis (opposed to *adduct*).—**ab-duc′tion** (-duk′shọn), *n.* [L. *abductio*(*n-*).] The act of abducting.—**ab-duc′tor,** *n.* One who abducts; in *physiol.*, an abducting muscle.

a-beam (ạ-bēm′), *adv.* *Naut.*, in the direction of the beam or greatest breadth of a ship; directly opposite to the middle part of a ship's side.

a-be-ce-da-ri-an (ā″bē-sē-dā′ri-ạn). [LL. *abecedarius*, < (the letters) *a*, *b*, *c*, *d*.] **I.** *a.* Pertaining to or concerned with the alphabet; alphabetical; hence, primary; rudimentary. **II.** *n.* A teacher or a learner of the alphabet. —**a″be-ce-da′ri-um** (-um), *n.*; pl. *-ria* (-ri-ä). [LL.] An a-b-c book; a primer.—**a-be-ce′da-ry** (-dạ-ri). **I.** *a.* Abecedarian. **II.** *n.*; pl. *-ries* (-riz). An abecedarium; hence, a rudiment.

a-bed (ạ-bed′), *adv.* In or to bed.

a-bele (ạ-bēl′ or ā′bẹl), *n.* [D. *abeel*, < OF. *abel*, < ML. *albellus*, < L. *albus*, white.] The white poplar, *Populus alba*.

a-bel-mosk (ā′bẹl-mosk), *n.* [NL. *Abelmoschus*, < Ar. *abu'l-misk*, 'father of musk.'] A malvaceous plant, *Abelmoschus abelmoschus*, of warm countries, cultivated for its musky seed, which is used in perfumery, etc.

a-ber-glau-be (ä′bėr-glou″bė), *n.* [G.] Belief beyond what is justified by knowledge; superstition.

ab-er-rant (ab-er′ạnt), *a.* Straying away; deviating from what is regular or normal; exhibiting aberration.—**ab-er′rance, ab-er′ran-cy,** *n.*

ab-er-rate (ab′ẹ-rāt), *v. i.*; *-rated*, *-rating*. [L. *aberratus*, pp. of *aberrare*, < *ab*, from, + *errare*, stray.] To go astray; exhibit aberration.—**ab-er-ra′tion** (-ẹ-rā′shọn), *n.* [L. *aberratio*(*n-*).] Deviation from the right course, or from a standard or type; abnormal procedure or character; lapse from a sound mental state; in *optics*, deviation of refracted or reflected light-rays from a single focus, or their convergence to different foci, due to the spherical shape of the lens or mirror, and resulting in the formation of a blurred image ('spherical aberration'); an analogous phenomenon depending on the different refrangibilities of the rays composing white light, and resulting in a prismatic coloring around the edge of the image ('chromatic aberration'); in *astron.*, apparent displacement of a heavenly body, due to the motion of the earth and of light.—**ab-er-ra′tion-al,** *a.*

a-bet (ạ-bet′), *v. t.*; *abetted*, *abetting*. [OF. *abeter*, < *a* (< L. *ad*), to, + *beter*, bait, as a bear: cf. Icel. *beita*, E. *bait*, *v.*] To encourage by approval or aid, esp. in wrongdoing; urge or help on mischievously; instigate; foment. —**a-bet′ment, a-bet′tal,** *n.* The act of abetting.— **a-bet′ter, a-bet′tor,** *n.*

a-bey-ance (ạ-bā′ạns), *n.* [AF. *abeiance*, OF. *abeance*, < *abeer*, be eager for, < *a* (< L. *ad*), to, + *beer*, < LL. *badare*, gape.] A state of expectancy legally as to ownership (as, a title in *abeyance*, or awaiting a possessor); hence, suspension; dormancy. Also **a-bey′an-cy.**—**a-bey′ant,** *a.* Being in abeyance.

ab-hor (ab-hôr′), *v. t.*; *-horred*, *-horring*. [L. *abhorrere*, < *ab*, from, + *horrere*, bristle, shudder.] To regard with horror or utter repugnance; loathe; abominate; also, to affect with horror†.—**ab-hor′rence** (-hor′ẹns), *n.* Horror; detestation; also, a thing abhorred.—**ab-hor′rent,** *a.*

Abhorring; feeling horror (*of*); also, exciting horror; detestable; repugnant (*to*); remote in character (*from*).—**ab-hor′rent-ly,** *adv.*—**ab-hor′rer** (-hôr′ėr), *n.*

a-bid-ance (ạ-bī′dạns), *n.* The act of abiding; abode.

a-bide[1] (ạ-bīd′), *v. t.* [For *aby.*] To pay or suffer for. [Obs. or archaic.]

a-bide[2] (ạ-bīd′), *v.*; *abode, abiding.* [AS. *ābīdan,* < *ā-*, away, on, + *bīdan,* bide.] **I.** *tr.* To wait for; await; also, to endure; tolerate. **II.** *intr.* To remain; stay; dwell or reside; continue; stand firm.—**to abide by,** to remain by; stand by; adhere or conform to.—**a-bid-er** (ạ-bī′dėr), *n.*—**a-bid′ing,** *p. a.* Continuing; lasting.—**a-bid′ing-ly,** *adv.*—**a-bid′ing-ness,** *n.*

ab-i-gail (ab′i-gạl), *n.* [From *Abigail,* the "waiting gentlewoman" in Beaumont and Fletcher's play, "The Scornful Lady." See also 1 Sam. xxv. 23–42.] A waiting-woman; a lady's-maid.

a-bil-i-ty (ạ-bil′i-ti), *n.*; pl. *-ties* (-tiz). [OF. *abilite,* < L. *habilitas,* < *habilis*: see *able.*] The quality of being able; power to do something; capability; competence; also, a faculty or talent.

ab-i-o-gen-e-sis (ab″i-ọ-jen′e-sis), *n.* [Gr. ἀ- priv. + βίος, life, + γένεσις, genesis.] In *biol.*, the (hypothetical) production of living things from inanimate matter; spontaneous generation.—**ab″i-o-ge-net′ic** (-jẹ-net′ik), *a.* Pertaining to abiogenesis.—**ab″i-o-ge-net′i-cal-ly,** *adv.*

ab-i-og-e-nist (ab-i-oj′e-nist), *n.* [Gr. ἀ- priv. + βίος, life, + γεν-, bear, produce.] A believer in the doctrine of spontaneous generation, or abiogenesis.—**ab-i-og′e-nous,** *a.* Produced by spontaneous generation.—**ab-i-og′e-ny,** *n.* Abiogenesis.

ab-i-o-log-i-cal (ab″i-ọ-loj′i-kạl), *a.* [See *a-*[1].] Not biological; not connected with biology.

ab-ir-ri-tate (ab-ir′i-tāt), *v. t.*; *-tated, -tating.* [See *ab-*.] In *med.*, to make less irritable.—**ab-ir-ri-ta′tion** (-tā′shọn), *n.* In *med.*, removal or absence of irritability; also, asthenia.

ab-ject (ab′jekt). [L. *abjectus,* pp. of *abjicere,* throw away or down, < *ab,* from, + *jacere,* throw.] **I.** *a.* Brought low; fallen or degraded; base; mean; wretched. **II.**† *n.* An outcast; a degraded person; an abject slave.—**ab-jec′tion** (-jek′shọn), *n.* [L. *abjectio(n-)*.] Abasement; abject condition; also, rejection†.—**ab′ject-ly,** *adv.*—**ab′ject-ness,** *n.*

ab-ju-ra-tion (ab-jö̤-rā′shọn), *n.* [LL. *abjuratio(n-)*.] The act of abjuring; renunciation upon oath; repudiation.—**ab-ju′ra-to-ry** (-jö′rạ-tọ-ri), *a.* Expressing abjuration.

ab-jure (ab-jör′), *v. t.*; *-jured, -juring.* [L. *abjurare,* < *ab,* from, + *jurare,* swear.] To renounce upon oath or with great solemnity; forswear; repudiate; recant; profess to abandon.—**ab-jur′er, ab-jur′or,** *n.*

ab-ka-ri (äb-kä′rẹ), *n.* [Hind. and Pers.] In India, the manufacture and sale of spirituous liquors; the government excise upon liquors; the licensing of dealers in strong drink.

ab-lac-ta-tion (ab-lak-tā′shọn), *n.* [L. *ablactatio(n-)*, < *ablactare,* wean, < *ab,* from, + *lactare,* suckle, < *lac,* milk.] The weaning of a child from the breast; in *hort.*, grafting by inarching (see *inarch*).

ab-la-tion (ab-lā′shọn), *n.* [L. *ablatio(n-)*, < *ablatus,* pp. of *auferre,* take away.] The act of taking away; removal; in *geol.*, a process of wearing, washing, or melting away.

ab-la-ti-tious (ab-lạ-tish′us), *a.* [L. *ablatus*: see *ablation.*] Tending to remove, as a force which diminishes the gravitation of a satellite toward its planet.

ab-la-tive (ab′lạ-tiv). [F. *ablatif,* < L. *ablativus,* < *ablatus*: see *ablation.*] In *gram.*: **I.** *a.* Expressing removal or separation: applied to a case in declension in Latin and some other languages, or to its forms or constructions. **II.** *n.* The ablative case, or a word in that case.

ab-laut (äp′lout), *n.* [G., < *ab,* off, + *laut,* sound.] In *philol.*, a substitution of one root-vowel for another, accompanying a modification of use or meaning, as in *bind, band, bond*; esp., change of a vowel to indicate tense-change in a verb, as in *get, gat, got.*

a-blaze (ạ-blāz′), *adv.* In a blaze, as of fire, light, ardor, etc.

a-ble (ā′bl), *a.*; compar. *abler,* superl. *ablest.* [OF. *able, abille, habile* (F. *habile*), < L. *habilis,* fit, apt, expert, < *habere,* have.] Having sufficient power, strength, or qualifications; competent; qualified; also, having superior powers or faculties.—**a′ble**†, *v. t.* To enable; also, to warrant.

-able. [OF. F. *-able,* < L. *-abilis,* suffix forming adjectives from verbs with infinitive in *-are,* being one form of the suffix *-bilis*: see *-ble,* and cf. *-ible.*] An adjective suffix meaning, in a passive signification, 'capable or susceptible of being,' 'liable to be,' 'fit or worthy to be,' 'that is to be,' as in *bearable, curable, deposable, enjoyable, laudable, lovable, payable, punishable, regrettable,* also, with active or neuter signification, 'able to,' 'such as to,' 'adapted for,' 'characterized by,' as in *comfortable, durable, peaceable, serviceable, suitable*: forming derivatives commonly from verbs, less often from nouns, and attached freely (now usually with passive force) to stems of any origin, Latin, Anglo-Saxon, or other. See *-ble* and *-ible.*

a-ble=bod-ied (ā′bl-bod′id), *a.* Sound of body; physically competent.

ab-le-gate (ab′lẹ-gāt), *n.* [L. *ablegatus,* pp. of *ablegare,* send away, < *ab,* from, + *legare,* send as legate.] A papal envoy to a newly appointed dignitary.

a-blins, ai-blins (ā′blinz), *adv.* [See *able.*] Possibly; perhaps. [Sc. and north. Eng.]

a-bloom (ạ-blöm′), *adv.* In bloom.

ab-lu-ent (ab′lö-ẹnt). [L. *abluens* (*-ent-*), ppr. of *abluere*: see *ablution.*] **I.** *a.* Washing away; cleansing; detergent. **II.** *n.* A cleansing lotion or medicine.

ab-lu-tion (ab-lö′shọn), *n.* [L. *ablutio(n-)*, < *abluere* (pp. *ablutus*), wash away, < *ab,* from, + *luere,* wash.] The act of washing; a cleansing with water or other liquid, as in ceremonial purification; also, the liquid used.—**ab-lu′tion-a-ry** (-ā̤-ri), *a.*

a-bly (ā′bli), *adv.* In an able manner; competently.

ab-ne-gate (ab′nẹ-gāt), *v. t.*; *-gated, -gating.* [L. *abnegatus,* pp. of *abnegare,* < *ab,* from, + *negare,* deny.] To refuse or deny to one's self; renounce.—**ab-ne-ga′tion** (-gā′shọn), *n.* [LL. *abnegatio(n-)*.] Denial; self-denial; renunciation.

ab-nor-mal (ab-nôr′mạl), *a.* [Earlier *anormal,* < F. *anormal* < ML. *anormalus,* for LL. *anomalus,* E. *anomalous,* but confused with L. *abnormis,* < *ab,* from, + *norma,* rule.] Not conforming to rule; deviating from the standard or type; irregular; anomalous.—**ab-nor-mal′i-ty** (-mal′i-ti), *n.*; pl. *-ties* (-tiz). Abnormal character; an abnormal form or feature.—**ab-nor′mal-ly,** *adv.*—**ab-nor′mi-ty,** *n.*; pl. *-ties* (-tiz). [LL. *abnormitas,* < L. *abnormis.*] Abnormality; irregularity; monstrosity; also, something abnormal.—**ab-nor′mous,** *a.* [L. *abnormis.*] Abnormal.

a-board (ạ-bōrd′). **I.** *adv.* On board; on or in a ship, railroad-car, etc.; also, alongside. **II.** *prep.* On board of.

a-bode[1] (ạ-bōd′). Preterit and past participle of *abide*[2].—**a-bode′**[1], *n.* [ME.; < *abide*[2].] Stay; sojourn; residence; also, place of residence; dwelling-place.

a-bode[2]† (ạ-bōd′), *n.* [AS. *ābēodan,* announce.] A prognostication; a foreboding.—**a-bode′**[2]†, *v. t.* To presage; forebode.—**a-bode′ment**†, *n.* Foreboding; omen.

a-boil (ạ-boil′), *adv.* In a boiling state.

a-bol-ish (ạ-bol′ish), *v. t.* [OF. F. *abolir* (*aboliss-*), < L. *abolere* (pp. *abolitus*), destroy, remove, abolish.] To do away with; put an end to; suppress.—**a-bol′ish-a-ble,** *a.* Capable of being abolished.—**a-bol′ish-er,** *n.*—**a-bol′ish-ment,** *n.* Abolition.—**ab-o-li-tion** (ab-ọ-lish′ọn), *n.* [L. *abolitio(n-)*.] The act of abolishing, or the resulting state; suppression; esp., the suppression of negro slavery.—**ab-o-li′tion-ism,** *n.* The principle or policy of abolition, esp. of negro slavery.—**ab-o-li′tion-ist,** *n.* An advocate of abolition, esp., formerly, the abolition of negro slavery in the U. S.

ab-o-ma-sum (ab-ọ-mā′sum), *n.*; pl. *-sa* (-sā̤). [NL., < L. *ab,* from, + NL. *omasum*: see *omasum.*] The fourth or true stomach of ruminating animals, lying next to the omasum.

a-bom-i-na-ble (ạ-bom′i-nạ-bl), *a.* [L. *abominabilis.*] Deserving to be abominated; detestable; odious.—**a-bom′i-na-ble-ness,** *n.*—**a-bom′i-na-bly,** *adv.*

a-bom-i-nate (ạ-bom′i-nāt), *v. t.*; *-nated, -nating.* [L. *abominatus,* pp. of *abominari,* < *ab,* from, + *ominari,* forebode, < *omen,* omen.] To regard with intense aversion; abhor; detest; loathe.—**a-bom-i-na′tion** (-nā′shọn), *n.* [LL. *abominatio(n-)*.] Intense aversion; abhorrence; detestation; also, an abominable thing or practice.—**a-bom'i-na-tor,** *n.*

ab-or-i-gen, ab-or-i-gin (ab-or'i-jen, -jin), **ab-o-rig-i-ne** (ab-ǫ-rij'i-nē), *n.* Assumed singular of *aborigines.*

ab-o-rig-i-nal (ab-ǫ-rij'i-nạl). **I.** *a.* Belonging to aborigines; also, existing from the beginning; original; primitive; native; indigenous. **II.** *n.* An original inhabitant; a native.—**ab-o-rig'i-nal-ly,** *adv.*

ab-o-rig-i-nes (ab-ǫ-rij'i-nēz), *n. pl.* [L., < *ab,* from, + *origo* (*origin-*), origin, beginning.] The primitive inhabitants of a country; also, the original fauna or flora of a region.

a-bort (ạ-bôrt'), *v. i.* [L. *abortus,* pp. of *aboriri,* < *ab,* from, + *oriri,* arise.] To miscarry in giving birth; also, to fail of development.—**a-bor-ti-cide** (ạ-bôr'ti-sīd), *n.* [L. *abortus,* miscarriage (< *aboriri*): see *-cide.*] Destruction of a fetus in the uterus; also, an abortifacient.—**a-bor-ti-fa'cient** (-fā'shẹnt). [L. *abortus,* miscarriage, + *faciens* (*facient-*), ppr. of *facere,* do, make.] **I.** *a.* Causing abortion. **II.** *n.* Any agent serving to cause abortion.—**a-bor'tion** (-shọn), *n.* [L. *abortio*(*n-*).] The act of aborting; the expulsion of a fetus before it is viable; miscarriage; also, arrested development; also, an imperfectly developed birth or product.—**a-bor'tion-al,** *a.*—**a-bor'tion-ist,** *n.* One who produces criminal abortion.—**a-bor'tive.** [L. *abortivus.*] **I.** *a.* Exhibiting abortion; imperfectly developed; rudimentary; failing to mature or succeed; also, causing abortion. **II.** *n.* An abortive birth; also, a drug causing abortion.—**a-bor'tive-ly,** *adv.*—**a-bor'tive-ness,** *n.*

a-bou-li-a (a-bö'li-ạ), etc. See *abulia,* etc.

a-bound (ạ-bound'), *v. i.* [OF. *abunder* (F. *abonder*), < L. *abundare,* < *ab,* from, + *undare,* rise in waves, overflow, < *unda,* a wave.] To be in great plenty; be rich (*in*); teem (*with*).

a-bout (ạ-bout'). [AS. *abūtan,* for *onbūtan,* < *on,* on, + *būtan,* outside: see *but.*] **I.** *adv.* Along the outside; on or to all or various sides; hither and thither; here and there; astir, or in action or operation; in the vicinity, or near; approximately (as, *about* a hundred miles); nearly (as, *about* finished); on the point of, or going (to do something); around or round; in rotation (as, turn and turn *about*); in a circuit; to pass (as, to bring or come *about*); so as to change or reverse the direction, etc. (as, to face *about*). **II.** *prep.* Along the outside of; around; here and there in; in the space surrounding; on or near (as, have you a pencil *about* you?); not far from (as, *about* one o'clock); in relation to, or concerning (as, to know *about* a matter); at or on (as, to set *about* a task; "I must be *about* my Father's business," Luke, ii. 49).—**a-bout'=face',** *n.* A facing about in the opposite direction, as by a soldier in drilling; hence, a change in action, etc., to the exact opposite; a complete reversal of procedure.—**a-bout'=face',** *v. i.*; *-faced, -facing.* To execute an about-face.

a-bove (ạ-buv'). [AS. *abufan,* < *a* (for *on,* on) + *bufan,* above, < *be,* by, + *ufan,* above.] **I.** *adv.* On high; aloft; overhead; on top; higher in place, rank, etc.; before. Often used elliptically as an adjective or noun: as, the *above* list; see the *above.* **II.** *prep.* Over or on the top of; higher in place or rank than; too high in dignity or character for; superior to; more than; beyond.—**a-bove'board',** *adv.* In open sight; without tricks or disguise.

A B R A C A D A B R A
A B R A C A D A B R
A B R A C A D A B
A B R A C A D A
A B R A C A D
A B R A C A
A B R A C
A B R A
A B R
A B
A

ab-ra-ca-dab-ra (ab''rạ-kạ-dab'rạ), *n.* [L.] A mystical word used in incantations, or written in triangular form as a charm on an amulet; hence, any mysterious jargon.

a-brad-ant (ạ-brā'dạnt). **I.** *a.* Abrading; scraping. **II.** *n.* An abrading substance, as emery or sand.

a-brade (ạ-brād'), *v. t.*; *abraded, abrading.* [L. *abradere* (pp. *abrasus*), < *ab,* from, + *radere,* scrape.] To scrape off; wear off or down by friction.—**a-brad-er** (ạ-brā'dėr), *n.*

a-bran-chi-ate (a-brang'ki-āt or ā-), *a.* [See *a-*[1].] Not branchiate; having no gills.

a-bra-sion (ạ-brā'zhọn), *n.* [L. *abrasio*(*n-*).] The act of abrading; wear by friction; also, an abraded surface; also, matter rubbed off.—**a-bra'sive** (-siv). **I.** *a.* Causing abrasion; tending to abrade. **II.** *n.* An abradant.

a-bras-tol (a-bras'tol or -tōl), *n.* [Gr. ἀ- priv. + βράζειν, boil, ferment.] A white powder, a naphthol derivative containing calcium, used as a preservative in wine and as a remedy for rheumatism etc.

ab-raum (ab'râm, G. äp'roum) **salts.** [G. *abraumsalze,* salts to be removed (as being thought worthless).] A mixture of salts of potassium, sodium, magnesium, etc., found in association with deposits of rock-salt at Stassfurt, Prussia, and vicinity.

Abraxas.

A-brax-as (ạ-brak'sạs), *n.* [Said to represent the Gr. numeral letters α, β, ρ, α, ξ, α, ς, amounting to the mystical number 365.] A mystical Gnostic word, or an amulet inscribed with it or with some symbolical Gnostic device.

a-breast (ạ-brest'), *adv.* With breasts in a line; side by side; equally advanced (*with*); alongside (*of*) in progress or attainment.

a-bri (â-brē), *n.*; pl. *abris* (F. â-brē). [F.] A shelter, or place of shelter: esp. in military use.

a-bridge (ạ-brij'), *v. t.*; *abridged, abridging.* [OF. *abregier* (F. *abréger*), < LL. *abbreviare*: see *abbreviate.*] To make shorter; shorten; curtail; reduce; bring to a shorter written form by condensation or omission; deprive (*of*).—**a-bridg'er,** *n.*—**a-bridg'ment, a-bridge'ment,** *n.* The act of abridging, or an abridged condition; curtailment; reduction, esp. to a shorter written form; also, a condensed form of a book, etc.; an epitome.

a-broach (ạ-brōch'), *adv.* Broached, as a cask; hence, running; going; in circulation.

a-broad (ạ-brâd'), *adv.* Over a broad area; broadly; wide; also, away from home; out of doors; in a foreign land; also, at large; in circulation; also, wide of the truth; 'at sea.'

ab-ro-ga-ble (ab'rǫ-gạ-bl), *a.* That may be abrogated.

ab-ro-gate (ab'rǫ-gāt), *v. t.*; *-gated, -gating.* [L. *abrogatus,* pp. of *abrogare,* < *ab,* from, + *rogare,* ask.] To make void by authoritative act; annul by an enactment that repeals or invalidates; abolish.—**ab-ro-ga'tion** (-gā'shọn), *n.* [L. *abrogatio*(*n-*).] The act of abrogating; authoritative annulment.—**ab'ro-ga-tive** (-gạ-tiv), *a.* Serving to abrogate.—**ab'ro-ga-tor** (-gā-tọr), *n.*

ab-rupt (ạ-brupt'). [L. *abruptus,* pp. of *abrumpere,* break off, < *ab,* from, + *rumpere,* break.] **I.** *a.* Broken off; terminating or changing suddenly; precipitous or steep; blunt; unceremonious (as, an *abrupt* entrance); disconnected (as, an *abrupt* literary style). **II.** *n.* A precipice or chasm: as, "Upborne with indefatigable wings, Over the vast *abrupt*" (Milton's "Paradise Lost," ii. 409). [Poetic.]—**ab-rup-tion** (ạ-brup'shọn), *n.* [L. *abruptio*(*n-*).] The act of breaking off; a sudden break or termination.—**ab-rupt'ly,** *adv.*—**ab-rupt'ness,** *n.*

ab-scess (ab'ses), *n.* [L. *abscessus,* < *abscedere,* go away, < *abs,* from, + *cedere,* go.] A collection of pus in the tissues of the body.

ab-scind (ab-sind'), *v. t.* [L. *abscindere* (pp. *abscissus*), < *ab,* from, + *scindere,* cut.] To cut off. [Archaic.]

ab-scis-sa (ab-sis'ạ), *n.*; pl. *abscissas,* L. *abscissæ* (-ē). [L., fem. of *abscissus,* pp. of *abscindere*: see *abscind.*] In conic sections, that part of a transverse axis which lies between its vertex and a perpendicular ordinate drawn to it from a given point of the conic. See also *coördinate.*

ab-scis-sion (ab-sizh'ọn), *n.* [L. *abscissio*(*n-*), < *abscindere*: see *abscind.*] A cutting off; sudden termination; in *rhet.,* a sudden break or reticence in discourse.

ab-scond (ab-skond'), *v. i.* [L. *abscondere,* hide, depart from, < *abs,* from, + *condere,* lay up: see *condiment.*] To go off into hiding; depart suddenly and secretly, esp. to avoid a legal process; decamp.—**ab-scond'er,** *n.*

ab-sence (ab'sẹns), *n.* [OF. F. *absence,* < L. *absentia.*] The state or period of being absent; also, a being wanting or lacking; also, absent-mindedness (usually 'absence of mind').

ab-sent (ab'sẹnt), *a.* [OF. F. *absent,* < L. *absens* (*absent-*), ppr. of *abesse,* be away, < *ab,* from, + *esse,* be.] Being away; not present; also, wanting; lacking; also, absent-minded.—**ab-sent** (ab-sent′), *v. t.* [F. *absenter*, < LL. *absentare*, < L. *absens.*] To make absent; take or keep (one's self) away.—**ab-sen-ta′tion** (-sen-tā′shọn), *n.* The act of absenting one's self.—**ab-sen-tee′** (-tē′), *n.* One who absents himself or remains absent, esp. from his country, estate, office, or post.—**ab-sen-tee′ism,** *n.* The practice of being an absentee.—**ab-sent′er,** *n.*—**ab′-sent-ly,** *adv.*—**ab′sent=mind′ed,** *a.* Forgetful of present surroundings; inattentive; abstracted; preoccupied.—**ab′sent=mind′ed-ly,** *adv.*—**ab′sent=mind′ed-ness,** *n.*—**ab′sent-ness,** *n.*

ab-sinth (ab′sinth), *n.* [F. *absinthe*, < L. *absinthium*, < Gr. *ἀψίνθιον*, wormwood.] Wormwood; also, absinthe. —**ab-sinthe** (ab′sinth, F. ȧp-sañt), *n.* [F.] A bitter green aromatic liqueur made with wormwood and other herbs.—**ab-sin′thi-al** (-sin′thi-ạl), *a.* Of or like wormwood.—**ab-sin′thi-ate** (-āt), *v. t.*; *-ated, -ating.* To impregnate with wormwood.—**ab′sinth-ism,** *n.* In *pathol.*, a morbid condition due to the use of absinthe.—**ab-sin′thi-um** (-um), *n.* [L.] The common wormwood, *Artemisia absinthium.*

ab-so-lute (ab′sọ-lūt), *a.* [L. *absolutus*, pp. of *absolvere*: see *absolve.*] Free from restriction or limitation; unconditioned or unconditional; unqualified; perfect; pure (as, *absolute* alcohol, ethyl alcohol containing not more than one per cent by weight of water); thorough; positive; independent; arbitrary or despotic (as, an *absolute* monarchy); viewed independently; not comparative or relative; self-existent; ultimate; in *gram.*, syntactically independent; forming an element in a sentence but not grammatically connected with it (as, the ablative *absolute* in Latin); of an adjective, having its noun understood, not expressed; of a transitive verb, used without its object being expressed; in *physics*, independent, or accepted as independent, of arbitrary standards (as, the *absolute* zero of temperature; *absolute* units); based on an absolute zero or unit (as, *absolute* temperature; *absolute* velocity or pressure); of or pertaining to absolute units.—**absolute system of units,** a system of units based on certain units (esp. those of mass, length, and time) of invariable value which are taken as fundamental: esp. as contrasted with any system of units based partly on some arbitrary unit, as of gravitation, whose value varies with latitude, altitude, or the like.—**absolute temperature,** temperature measured from the absolute zero, esp. on a scale depending upon certain thermodynamic principles.—**absolute unit,** any of the units in an absolute system of units.—**absolute zero,** the lowest possible temperature which the nature of matter admits, or that temperature at which the particles whose motion constitutes heat would be at rest: being a hypothetical point 273 degrees below the zero of the centigrade scale.—**ab′so-lute,** *n.* In *metaph.*, with *the*, that which is unconditioned or non-relative; the ultimate ground of all things; God.—**ab′so-lute-ly,** *adv.*—**ab′so-lute-ness,** *n.*

ab-so-lu-tion (ab-sọ-lū′shọn), *n.* [L. *absolutio(n-)*, < *absolvere*: see *absolve.*] The act of absolving, or the state of being absolved; release; discharge; forgiveness; remission, as of sin or of its penal consequences; the formula declaring this remission; also, a form of prayer for pardon, as over the dead in the burial service.

ab-so-lut-ism (ab′sọ-lūt-izm), *n.* The principle or the exercise of absolute power in government; in *metaph.*, the doctrine of an absolute or non-relative being.—**ab′so-lut-ist,** *n.* An advocate of absolutism.—**ab″so-lut-is′tic,** *a.*

ab-sol-u-to-ry (ab-sol′ū-tọ-ri), *a.* Giving absolution.

ab-solv-a-ble (ab-sol′vạ-bl), *a.* Capable of being absolved; deserving of absolution.

ab-solve (ab-solv′), *v. t.*; *-solved, -solving.* [L. *absolvere* (pp. *absolutus*), < *ab*, from, + *solvere*, loosen.] To set free from obligation or liability; release from a charge or penalty; acquit; pardon; also, to grant pardon for; *eccles.*, to grant or pronounce remission of sins to; also, to remit (sin).—**ab-solv′ent,** *a.* Absolving.—**ab-solv′er,** *n.*

ab-so-nant (ab′sọ-nạnt), *a.* [L. *ab*, from, + *sonans* (*sonant-*), ppr. of *sonare*, sound.] Discordant; abhorrent (*from* or *to*); incongruous: opposed to *consonant.*

ab-sorb (ab-sôrb′), *v. t.* [L. *absorbere* (pp. *absorptus*), < *ab*, from, + *sorbere*, suck in.] To suck or drink in; take in through pores or interstices; take up by chemical or molecular action; also, to swallow up; appropriate; incorporate; also, to occupy mentally; engross (*in*).—**ab-sorb′a-ble,** *a.* Capable of being absorbed.—**ab-sorb-a-bil′i-ty** (-bil′i-ti), *n.*—**ab-sorb′ed-ly,** *adv.*—**ab-sor-be-fa′cient** (-sôr-bẹ-fā′shẹnt). [L. *absorbere* + *faciens* (*facient-*), ppr. of *facere*, do, make.] **I.** *a.* Causing absorption. **II.** *n.* An agent that causes absorption.—**ab-sorb′ent.** **I.** *a.* Absorbing; taking up fluids, etc. **II.** *n.* An absorbent substance or vessel.—**ab-sorb′er,** *n.*—**ab-sorb′ing-ly,** *adv.*—**ab-sorp′tion** (-sôrp′shọn), *n.* [L. *absorptio(n-).*] The act of absorbing, or the state of being absorbed.—**ab-sorp′tive,** *a.* Having power to absorb.

ab-squat-u-late (ab-skwot′ū-lāt), *v. i.*; *-lated, -lating* [A made word, simulating Latin.] To run off; decamp. [Slang, U. S.]

ab-stain (ab-stān′), *v. i.* [OF. F. *abstenir*, < L. *abstinere* (pp. *abstentus*), < *abs*, from, + *tenere*, hold.] To hold back, as from doing or enjoying something; refrain.—**ab-stain′er,** *n.* One who abstains, esp. from the use of intoxicating liquors.

ab-ste-mi-ous (ab-stē′mi-us), *a.* [L. *abstemius*, < *abs*, from, + *tem-*, as in *temetum*, strong drink.] Sparing in diet; moderate in the use of food and drink; temperate in habit; abstinent.—**ab-ste′mi-ous-ly,** *adv.*—**ab-ste′mi-ous-ness,** *n.*

ab-sten-tion (ab-sten′shọn), *n.* [F. *abstention*, < LL. *abstentio(n-).*] The act of abstaining.—**ab-sten′tious** (-shus), *a.* Characterized by abstention; abstinent.

ab-sterge (ab-stėrj′), *v. t.*; *-sterged, -sterging.* [L. *abstergere* (pp. *abstersus*), < *abs*, from, + *tergere*, wipe.] To wipe off; cleanse; purge.—**ab-ster′gent** (-stėr′jẹnt). **I.** *a.* Cleansing; detergent. **II.** *n.* A cleansing agent; a detergent.—**ab-ster′sion** (-shọn), *n.* The act of absterging.—**ab-ster′sive** (-siv). **I.** *a.* Abstergent; cleansing. **II.** *n.* An abstergent.—**ab-ster′sive-ness,** *n.*

ab-sti-nence (ab′sti-nẹns), *n.* [OF. F. *abstinence*, < L. *abstinentia.*] The state of being abstinent; the act or practice of abstaining; abstention, esp. from the use of alcoholic beverages. Also **ab′sti-nen-cy.**

ab-sti-nent (ab′sti-nẹnt), *a.* [OF. F. *abstinent*, < L. *abstinens* (*-ent-*), ppr. of *abstinere*: see *abstain.*] Abstaining, esp. from self-indulgence; temperate; abstemious. —**ab′sti-nent-ly,** *adv.*

ab-stract (ab-strakt′), *v.* [L. *abstractus*, pp. of *abstrahere*, < *abs*, from, + *trahere*, draw.] **I.** *tr.* To take away; withdraw; remove; divert; separate in thought; conceive apart from matter or from particular instances; derive as an idea; summarize or epitomize. **II.** *intr.* To withdraw or depart (*from*); turn aside in thought; form abstractions. —**ab′stract.** **I.** *a.* Conceived apart from matter or from particular instances; pertaining to that which is so conceived (as, an *abstract* term or name); not concrete; concerned with general concepts or ideas rather than realities or actual instances; ideal or theoretical; profound or abstruse; general as opposed to particular; in *arith.*, noting a number which does not relate to a particular object or thing (as, 4 and 6 are *abstract* numbers, while in '4 trees,' '6 cats,' the numbers are concrete). **II.** *n.* A concise embodiment of essential features; a compendium; an epitome; a summary, as of facts or statements; also, an abstract idea or term; in *phar.*, a dry powder prepared from a drug by obtaining a solid extract of it and mixing this with milk-sugar until the final product is twice as strong as the original drug.—**ab-stract′ed,** *p. a.* Withdrawn; apart; also, lost in thought; absent in mind; also, abstract; ideal.—**ab-stract′ed-ly,** *adv.*—**ab-stract′ed-ness,** *n.*—**ab-stract′er,** *n.*—**ab-strac′tion** (-strak′shọn), *n.* [LL. *abstractio(n-).*] The act of abstracting, or an abstracted state; withdrawal; removal; separation; the formation of an abstract or general concept, or the concept formed; a mere idea; also, the state of being lost in thought; reverie; absence of mind. —**ab-strac′tion-ist,** *n.* One who occupies himself with abstractions; an idealist.—**ab-strac′tive,** *a.* Abstracting; pertaining to abstraction.—**ab′stract-ly,** *adv.*—**ab′stract-ness,** *n.*

ab-stric-tion (ab-strik′shọn), *n.* [L. *ab*, from, + LL. *strictio(n-)*, a drawing together, E. *striction.*] In *bot.*, a method of spore-formation in which successive portions of the sporophore are cut off through the growth of septa.

ab-struse (ab-strös′), *a.* [L. *abstrusus*, pp. of *abstrudere*, thrust away, < *abs*, from, + *trudere*, thrust.] Remote from comprehension; difficult to be understood; profound; recondite; esoteric.—**ab-struse′ly,** *adv.*—**ab-struse′ness,** *n.*—**ab-stru′si-ty** (-strö′si-ti), *n.*; pl. *-ties* (-tiz). Abstruse character; also, an abstruse point.

ab-surd (ab-sėrd′), *a.* [L. *absurdus*, discordant, irrational, absurd.] Contrary to reason or common sense; obviously false or foolish; logically contradictory; ridiculous; nonsensical.—**ab-sur′di-ty** (-sėr′di-ti), *n.*; pl. *-ties* (-tiz). The state or quality of being absurd; also, something absurd, as an action or statement.—**ab-surd′ly,** *adv.*—**ab-surd′ness,** *n.*

a-bu-li-a (a-bö′li-ạ or a-bū′-), *n.* [NL., < Gr. ἀ- priv. + βούλεσθαι, to will.] In *pathol.*, a form of mental derangement in which volition is impaired or lost.—**a-bu′lic,** *a.*

a-bun-dance (ạ-bun′dạns), *n.* [OF. *abundance* (F. *abondance*), < L. *abundantia.*] Abundant quantity or supply; overflowing plenty; copious or ample sufficiency; profusion; affluence.

a-bun-dant (ạ-bun′dạnt), *a.* [OF. *abundant* (F. *abondant*), < L. *abundans (-ant-)*, ppr. of *abundare*: see *abound.*] Present in great quantity; plentiful; copious; ample; also, abounding or rich in something (as, "the Lord . . . *abundant* in goodness and truth": Ex. xxxiv. 6).—**a-bun′dant-ly,** *adv.*

a-buse (ạ-būz′), *v. t.*; *abused, abusing.* [OF. F. *abuser*, < L. *abuti* (pp. *abusus*), use up, misuse, < *ab*, from, + *uti*, use.] To use improperly or ill; misuse; ill-treat or maltreat; violate or ravish; revile or vituperate; mislead† or deceive†.—**a-buse** (ạ-būs′), *n.* [OF. F. *abus*, < L. *abusus*, < *abuti.*] Wrong or improper use; misuse; a corrupt practice; ill treatment, as of a person; violation or defilement; revilement or vituperation; deception† or delusion†.—**a-bus-er** (ạ-bū′zėr), *n.*—**a-bu-sive** (ạ-bū′siv), *a.* Characterized by abuse; wrong; corrupt; harsh; injurious; rudely reproachful; vituperative; deceptive†.—**a-bu′sive-ly,** *adv.*—**a-bu′sive-ness,** *n.*

a-but (ạ-but′), *v. i.*; *abutted, abutting.* [OF. *abouter*, < *a* (< L. *ad*), to, + *bout*, end, < *bouter*, strike, thrust: see *butt*[1].] To touch at the end or border (*on*, *upon*, or *against*); rest in contact; border.

a-bu-ti-lon (ạ-bū′ti-lọn), *n.* [NL. *Abutilon*; from Ar.] Any plant of the malvaceous genus *Abutilon*, of tropical or warm regions, which includes species cultivated for their bell-shaped flowers and variegated leaves.

a-but-ment (ạ-but′mẹnt), *n.* [See *abut.*] The fact, state, or place of abutting; hence, an abutting part; also, that on which something abuts, as the part of a pier which receives the thrust of an arch; a part for sustaining or resisting pressure.—**a-but′tal,** *n.* The fact or state of abutting; also, an abutting part, as of land (chiefly in *pl.*).—**a-but′ter,** *n.* One whose property abuts.—**a-but′ting,** *p. a.* That abuts.

Abutment.
A, A, arch-abutments; *B, B*, current- or ice-abutments.

a-by, a-bye (ạ-bī′), *v. t.*; pret. and pp. *abought.* [AS. *ābycgan*, < *ā-*, away, on, up, + *bycgan*, E. *buy.*] To pay for; expiate; also, to suffer in expiation. [Archaic.]

a-bysm (ạ-bizm′), *n.* [OF. *abisme* (F. *abîme*), a superl. form < L. *abyssus*: see *abyss.*] An abyss: as, "the dark backward and *abysm* of time" (Shakspere's "Tempest," i. 2. 50).—**a-bys-mal** (ạ-biz′mạl), *a.* Of or like an abysm or abyss; immeasurably deep; most profound; abyssal.—**a-bys′mal-ly,** *adv.*

a-byss (ạ-bis′), *n.* [L. *abyssus*, < Gr. ἄβυσσος, < ἀ- priv. + βυσσός, depth, bottom.] A bottomless or immeasurably deep space; the primal chaos; the bottomless pit (hell); an unfathomable gulf; the lowest depths of anything (often in *pl.*).—**a-bys′sal,** *a.* Pertaining to or resembling an abyss; also, belonging to the lowest depths of the ocean.

Ab-ys-sin-i-an (ab-i-sin′i-ạn). **I.** *a.* Of or pertaining to Abyssinia, a country of eastern Africa. **II.** *n.* A native of Abyssinia.

a-ca-cia (ạ-kā′shiạ̈), *n.* [L., < Gr. ἀκακία.] Any tree or shrub of the mimosaceous genus *Acacia*, native in warm regions; also, the inspissated juice of certain species of *Acacia*; gum arabic; also, one of several other plants, as the locust-tree, *Robinia pseudacacia* ('false acacia'), and *R. hispida* ('rose-acacia').—**ac-a-cin, ac-a-cine** (ak′ạ-sin), *n.* Gum arabic.

Ac-a-deme (ak-ạ-dēm′), *n.* [L. *Academia*: see *academy.*] The Academy of Athens; [*l. c.*] any place for instruction; an academy.

ac-a-dem-ic (ak-ạ-dem′ik). [L. *academicus.*] **I.** *a.* [*cap.*] Pertaining to the Academy of Athens, or to Plato and his followers; [*l. c.*] pertaining to any academy; concerned with general collegiate rather than technical or professional study; scholarly; also, theoretical; formal; conventional. **II.** *n.* [*cap.*] A Platonist; [*l. c.*] a college student; also, an academician.—**ac-a-dem′i-cal. I.** *a.* Academic. **II.** *n.* A member of an academy; *pl.*, the college cap and gown.—**ac-a-dem′i-cal-ly,** *adv.*—**a-cad-e-mi-cian** (ạ-kad-ẹ-mish′ạn), *n.* A member of an academy or society for promoting literature, science, or art.

a-cad-e-mist (ạ-kad′ẹ-mist), *n.* An academician.

a-cad-e-my (ạ-kad′ẹ-mi), *n.*; pl. *-mies* (-miz). [F. *académie*, < L. *Academia*, < Gr. Ἀκαδήμεια, < Ἀκάδημος, Academus, an Attic hero.] [*cap.*] A public pleasure-ground of Athens, in which Plato taught; the Platonic school of philosophy; [*l. c.*] a place for instruction, esp. in an art or science; a superior school ranking below a college; also, a society of adepts for the promotion of literature, science, or art (as, the French *Academy*, a body, established in 1635, which now constitutes one of the five academies composing the Institute of France, and which consists of forty members, selected from among literary and other personages of eminence in France, who themselves fill vacancies occurring in their number, and whose chief duties are the regulation and purification of the French language and the encouragement of French literature).

A-ca-di-an (ạ-kā′di-ạn). **I.** *a.* Belonging to Acadia or Acadie, a former French territory in eastern North America, including what is now Nova Scotia; belonging to Nova Scotia. **II.** *n.* A native or inhabitant of Acadia or of Nova Scotia.

ac-a-jou (ak′ạ-zhö), *n.* [F.; from Brazilian name.] The cashew-tree, or its fruit; also, a gum or resin from the bark.

ac-a-leph (ak′ạ-lef), *n.* [NL. *acalepha*, < Gr. ἀκαλήφη, nettle.] One of the *Acalephæ*, a group of cœlenterate marine animals including the sea-nettles or jellyfishes. Also **ac-a-le′phan** (-lē′fạn), **ac′a-lephe** (-lēf).—**ac-a-le′phoid,** *a.* Like an acaleph.

Acaleph.

ac-a-na-ceous (ak-ạ-nā′shius), *a.* [Gr. ἄκανος, kind of thistle, < ἀκή, point.] In *bot.*, prickly.

a-can-tha (a-kan′thạ̈), *n.*; pl. *-thæ* (-thē). [NL., < Gr. ἄκανθα, thorn, spine, < ἀκή, point.] In *bot.*, a prickle; in *zoöl.*, a spine or prickly fin; in *anat.*, a spinous process of a vertebra; also, the vertebral column.

ac-an-tha-ceous (ak-an-thā′shius), *a.* [See *acanthus.*] Belonging to the *Acanthaceæ*, or acanthus family of plants.

a-can-tho-ceph-a-lan (a-kan-thọ-sef′ạ-lạn), *n.* [NL. *Acanthocephala*, pl., < Gr. ἄκανθα (see *acantha*) + κεφαλή, head.] Any of the *Acanthocephala*, a class or group of nemathelminths comprising internal parasitic worms having a protrusile proboscis with recurved hooks, but having no alimentary canal and absorbing their food through the body-wall.

a-can-thoid (a-kan′thoid), *a.* [See *acantha* and *-oid.*] Shaped like a spine; spiny; spinous.

a-can-thop-te-ryg-i-an (a-kan″thop-tẹ-rij′i-ạn). [NL. *Acanthopterygii*, pl., < Gr. ἄκανθα (see *acantha*) + πτερύγιον, fin, dim. of πτέρυξ, wing.] **I.** *a.* Belonging to the *Acanthopterygii*, a group of fishes with spiny fins, as the bass and perch. **II.** *n.* One of the *Acanthopterygii.*

a-can-thus (a-kan′thus), *n.*; pl. *-thuses*, L. *-thi* (-thī). [L., < Gr. ἄκανθος: cf. *acantha.*] A plant of the genus *Acanthus*, of

Leaf of Acanthus.

the Mediterranean regions, with large spiny or toothed leaves; also, an architectural ornament resembling the foliage of this plant, as in the Corinthian capital.

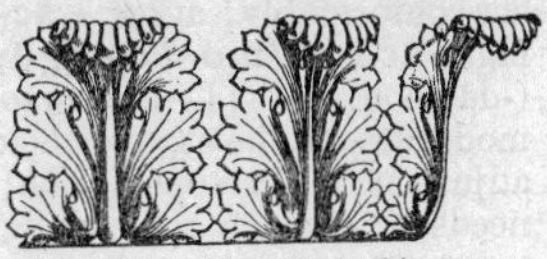

Acanthus in Roman Architecture.

ac-a-ri (ak′ạ-rī), *n.* Plural of *acarus.*

a-ca-ri-an (a-kā′ri-ạn), *a.* Belonging to or resembling the acari; acaridan.

ac-a-ri-a-sis (ak-ạ-rī′ạ-sis), *n.* [NL.] A skin-disease caused by an acarian parasite.

ac-a-rid (ak′ạ-rid), *n.* [NL. *Acarida*, pl., < *Acarus*: see *acarus.*] Any animal belonging to the *Acarida*, an order of arachnids including the acarus and other mites, ticks, etc. —**a-car-i-dan** (a-kar′i-dạn). **I.** *a.* Belonging to the *Acarida* or acarids. **II.** *n.* An acarid.

ac-a-roid (ak′ạ-roid), *a.* Resembling an acarus or mite.

a-car-pous (a-kär′pus), *a.* [Gr. ἄκαρπος, < ἀ- priv. + καρπός, fruit.] In *bot.*, unfruitful; sterile.

ac-a-rus (ak′ạ-rus), *n.*; pl. *-ri* (-rī). [NL., < Gr. ἄκαρι, kind of mite, < ἀκαρής, short, tiny.] An animal of the genus *Acarus*; a mite.

a-cat-a-lec-tic (a-kat-ạ-lek′tik or ā-), *a.* [LL. *acatalecticus*, < Gr. ἀ- priv. + καταληκτικός, E. *catalectic.*] In *pros.*, not catalectic; complete.

a-cau-date, a-cau-dal (a-kâ′dāt, -dạl), *a.* [See *a-*¹.] Not caudate; tailless.

ac-au-les-cent (ak-â-les′ẹnt), *a.* [See *a-*¹.] In *bot.*, not caulescent; stemless; without visible stem.—**ac-au-les′-cence,** *n.*—**a-cau-line** (a-kâ′lin), **a-cau′lose** (-lōs), **a-cau′-lous,** *a.* Same as *acaulescent.*

Ac-ca′di-an, *a.* and *n.* See *Akkadian.*

ac-cede (ak-sēd′), *v. i.*; *-ceded, -ceding.* [L. *accedere* (pp. *accessus*), < *ad*, to, + *cedere*, go.] To come (*to*); attain, as to an office or dignity; also, to give adhesion or assent; conform; agree.—**ac-ced-ence** (ak-sē′dẹns), *n.* The act of acceding.—**ac-ced′er,** *n.*

ac-ce-le-ran-do (ak-sel-ẹ-ran′dō, It. ät-chā-lā-rän′dō), *a.* [It.] In *music*, gradually increasing in speed.

ac-cel-er-ate (ak-sel′ẹ-rāt), *v.*; *-ated, -ating.* [L. *acceleratus*, pp. of *accelerare*, < *ad*, to, + *celerare*, quicken, < *celer*, quick.] **I.** *tr.* To make quicker or faster; bring about more quickly; hasten; also, to antedate; in *physics*, to increase or otherwise change the velocity of (a body) or the rate of (motion); cause to undergo acceleration. **II.** *intr.* To become faster; increase in speed.—**ac-cel′er-at-ed-ly,** *adv.*—**ac-cel-er-a′tion** (-ẹ-rā′shọn), *n.* [L. *acceleratio(n-)*.] The act of accelerating; increase in speed or velocity; in *physics*, a change in velocity or speed, esp. the rate of change of the velocity of a moving body (as, positive *acceleration*, when the velocity is increasing; negative *acceleration*, when the velocity is decreasing; *acceleration* of gravity, the acceleration of a falling body due to gravity, which is a little more than 32 feet per second per second at sea-level, varying in different latitudes, and is represented by the letter *g*); sometimes, in a broader sense, any change in velocity, as a change in the direction of the motion of a body. —**ac-cel′er-a-tive** (-ẹ-rạ-tiv), *a.* Tending to accelerate.—**ac-cel′er-a-tor** (-ẹ-rā-tọr), *n.* One who or that which accelerates; in an automobile, a device for opening and closing the throttle, esp. when operated by the foot; in *photog.*, any substance, device, or the like, that shortens the time of exposure or development.—**ac-cel′er-a-to-ry** (-ẹ-rạ-tō-ri), *a.* Accelerative.

ac-cent (ak′sent), *n.* [F. *accent*, < L. *accentus*, < *ad*, to, + *canere*, sing.] A special effort of utterance making one syllable more prominent than others, as by a change of pitch or by stress of voice; stress; a mark indicating stress or some other distinction in pronunciation or value; a letter or type bearing such a mark, as *á, à, ê, ç, ñ*; stress in verse, music, etc.; manner of utterance; characteristic mode of pronunciation; tone; an utterance; *pl.*, words as spoken; in *math.*, etc., a mark, or one of a number of marks, placed after a letter or figure to distinguish similar algebraic magnitudes which differ in value, as in a′, a″, a‴, etc. (called *a prime, a second, a third*, etc., respectively), or to indicate a particular unit or measure, as feet (′) or inches (″) (5′ 3″, for example, meaning 5 feet, 3 inches), or as minutes (′) or seconds (″) of time or of a degree (18′ 25″, for example, meaning 18 minutes, 25 seconds).—**ac-cent′,** *v. t.* [F. *accenter.*] To pronounce with an accent or stress; mark with an accent; accentuate; emphasize; also, to utter.—**ac-cen′tu-al** (-sen′tṳ̄-ạl), *a.* Pertaining to accent.—**ac-cen′tu-al-ly,** *adv.*

ac-cen-tu-ate (ak-sen′tṳ̄-āt), *v. t.*; *-ated, -ating.* [ML. *accentuatus*, pp. of *accentuare*, < L. *accentus*, E. *accent.*] To pronounce or mark with an accent; accent; emphasize. —**ac-cen-tu-a′tion** (-ā′shọn), *n.* Pronunciation or marking with an accent; mode of accenting; distinction by emphasis.

ac-cept (ak-sept′), *v.* [OF. F. *accepter*, < L. *acceptare*, freq. of *accipere*, take to one's self, < *ad*, to, + *capere*, take.] **I.** *tr.* To take (something offered); receive with favor or acquiescence; accede or assent to; also, to receive as to meaning; understand; in *com.*, to acknowledge, by signature, as calling for payment, and thus to agree to pay, as a draft. **II.** *intr.* To accept a gift, proposal, invitation, suggestion, etc.—**ac-cept′a-ble,** *a.* Capable or worthy of being accepted; satisfactory; agreeable; welcome. —**ac-cept-a-bil′i-ty** (-bil′i-ti), **ac-cept′a-ble-ness,** *n.*—**ac-cept′a-bly,** *adv.*—**ac-cept′ance,** *n.* The act of accepting, or the state of being accepted; favorable reception; favor; agreement to terms, whether expressly or by some act constituting a virtual acknowledgment, as of a contract; in *com.*, an engagement to pay an order, draft, or bill of exchange when it becomes due, as by the person on whom it is drawn; also, an order, draft, etc., which a person has accepted as calling for payment and has thus promised to pay (as, a trade *acceptance*, a draft of definite maturity drawn by the seller of goods on the purchaser of them, on which the purchaser has put the word "accepted" and his signature, thereby agreeing to pay at the date of maturity, as then due on the goods, the amount for which the draft is drawn, the draft being then returned to the seller of the goods, to become payable at maturity like any other draft, and to be discounted by him in advance if he so desires).—**ac-cept′ant,** *a.* Accepting; receptive.—**ac-cep-ta′tion** (-sep-tā′shọn), *n.* [LL. *acceptatio(n-)*.] Acceptance; favorable reception; favor; assent; belief; also, received meaning.—**ac-cept′ed-ly,** *adv.*—**ac-cept′er,** *n.* One who accepts. Also (esp. in *com.*) **ac-cep′tor.**

ac-cess (ak′ses or ak-ses′), *n.* [OF. *acces* (F. *accès*), < L. *accessus*, < *accedere*: see *accede.*] The act or privilege of coming to; admittance; approach; also, way or means of approach; also, accession or addition; also, an attack, as of disease; also, a fit or outburst, as of anger.

ac-ces-sa-ry (ak-ses′ạ-ri or ak′se-sā̤-ri), *a.* and *n.* Same as *accessory.* [Chiefly legal.]—**ac-ces′sa-ri-ly,** *adv.*—**ac-ces′-sa-ri-ness,** *n.*

ac-ces-si-ble (ak-ses′i-bl), *a.* [LL. *accessibilis*, < L. *accedere*: see *accede.*] Capable of being approached or reached; easy of access; approachable; attainable.—**ac-ces-si-bil′i-ty** (-bil′i-ti), *n.*—**ac-ces′si-bly,** *adv.*

ac-ces-sion (ak-sesh′ọn), *n.* [L. *accessio(n-)*, < *accedere*: see *accede.*] The act of acceding; attainment to an office, right, or dignity; adhesion or assent; addition or increase; something added; in *law*, addition to property by growth or improvement; in *med.*, the onset of disease; an attack. —**ac-ces′sion,** *v. t.* To enter in an accession-book.—**ac-ces′sion-al,** *a.* Additional.—**ac-ces′sion=book,** *n.* A blank-book in which the titles of books received by a library are entered, with all necessary details.—**ac-ces′sion=num″-ber,** *n.* The number given to a volume when it is entered in an accession-book.

ac-ces-so-ri-al (ak-se-sō′ri-ạl), *a.* Of or pertaining to an accessory; accessory.

ac-ces-so-ry (ak-ses′ọ-ri or ak′se-sō-ri). [ML. *accessorius*, < L. *accedere*: see *accede.*] **I.** *a.* Additional or auxiliary (*to*); subsidiary; contributory; in *law*, giving aid as an accessory. **II.** *n.*; pl. *-ries* (-riz). Something additional or contributory; a subordinate part or detail; an adjunct; an accompaniment; in *law*, one who is guilty of aiding or abetting a felony without being present at its commission.—**ac-ces′so-ri-ly,** *adv.*—**ac-ces′so-ri-ness,** *n.*

ac-ciac-ca-tu-ra (ät-chäk-kä-tö′rä), *n.* [It., < *acciaccare*, crush.] In *music*, a short grace-note one half-step below, and struck at the same time with, a principal note; also, a short appoggiatura.

Acciaccatura.

ac-ci-dence (ak′si-dẹns), *n.* [For *accidents*, or < L. *accidentia*, neut. pl. of *accidens*: see *accident.*] That part of grammar which treats of accidents or inflections; the rudiments of grammar, or of any subject.

ac-ci-dent (ak′si-dẹnt), *n.* [OF. F. *accident*, < L. *accidens* (*-ent-*), ppr. of *accidere*, fall on, happen, < *ad*, to, + *cadere*, fall.] A casual or undesigned occurrence; a fortuitous event; the operation of chance; a mischance or mishap; a casualty; an irregularity of surface, as of the ground; any incidental or non-essential circumstance or attribute; in *gram.*, an inflectional variation of a word.—**ac-ci-den′tal** (-den′tạl). **I.** *a.* Of the nature of an accident; happening or present as if by chance; casual; fortuitous; non-essential; incidental. **II.** *n.* An accidental circumstance or feature; in *music*, a sign, as the sharp, flat, or natural, placed before a particular note in the course of a piece or passage to indicate a change of pitch.—**ac-ci-den′tal-ly,** *adv.*—**ac-ci-den′tal-ness,** *n.*—**ac′ci-dent-ed** (-den-ted), *a.* Characterized by accidents or irregularities of surface, as ground.

ac-cip-i-ter (ak-sip′i-tėr), *n.*; pl. *-tres* (-trēz). [L., hawk, appar. < *accipere*, take to one's self: see *accept.*] Any bird of the genus *Accipiter*, which comprises short-winged, long-tailed hawks of small or moderate size, as the European sparrow-hawk, *A. nisus*; also, any bird of the order *Accipitres*, or *Raptores*; a raptorial bird; a bird of prey.—**ac-cip′i-tral** (-trạl), *a.* Hawk-like: accipitrine.—**ac-cip′i-trine** (-trin), *a.* Belonging to the *Accipitres*; hawk-like; raptorial.

ac-claim (a-klām′), *v.* [L. *acclamare* (pp. *acclamatus*), < *ad*, to, + *clamare*, cry out.] **I.** *tr.* To salute, applaud, or proclaim with shouts. **II.** *intr.* To make acclamation; shout applause.—**ac-claim′,** *n.* A shout of greeting; acclamation.—**ac-claim′er,** *n.*—**ac-cla-ma-tion** (ak-lạ-mā′shọn), *n.* [L. *acclamatio(n-)*.] The act of acclaiming; a shout of welcome or good-will; loud applause; also, a unanimous oral vote.—**ac-clam-a-to-ry** (a-klam′ạ-tọ-ri), *a.* Acclaiming.

ac-cli-mate (a-klī′mạt), *v. t.* or *i.*; *-mated, -mating.* [F. *acclimater*, < *à* (< L. *ad*), to, + *climat*, climate.] To habituate (persons, etc.), or to become habituated, to a new climate; acclimatize.—**ac-cli′mat-a-ble** (-mạ-tạ-bl), *a.*—**ac-cli-ma-ta′tion** (-mạ-tā′shọn), **ac-cli-ma-tion** (ak-li-mā′shọn), *n.*

ac-cli-ma-tize (a-klī′mạ-tīz), *v.*; *-tized, -tizing.* [F. *acclimater*: see *acclimate.*] **I.** *tr.* To habituate to a new climate; esp., to adapt (plants or animals) for permanent existence and propagation in a foreign climate. **II.** *intr.* To become habituated to a new climate.—**ac-cli″ma-ti-za′tion** (-ti-zā′shọn), *n.*—**ac-cli′ma-tiz-er** (-tī-zėr), *n.*

ac-cliv-i-ty (a-kliv′i-ti), *n.*; pl. *-ties* (-tiz). [L. *acclivitas*, < *acclivis*, sloping upward, < *ad*, to, + *clivus*, slope.] An upward slope, as of ground; an ascent: opposed to *declivity.*—**ac-cliv′i-tous,** *a.*—**ac-cli-vous** (a-klī′vus), *a.* [L. *acclivus*, for *acclivis.*] Sloping upward.

ac-co-lade (ak-ọ-läd′ or -läd′), *n.* [F., < It. *accollata*, < *accollare*, embrace, < L. *ad*, to, + *collum*, neck.] An embrace, a kiss, or, later, a blow on the shoulder with the flat of a sword, given in conferring knighthood; in *music*, a brace joining several staves; in *arch.*, a curved molding above an arched opening.

Accolade.

ac-com-mo-date (ạ-kom′ọ-dāt), *v.*; *-dated, -dating.* [L. *accommodatus*, pp. of *accommodare*, < *ad*, to, + *commodare*, adapt, supply, < *commodus*, fit.] **I.** *tr.* To make suitable; adapt or conform (*to*); adjust satisfactorily; reconcile; also, to provide suitably (*with*); provide for; serve; convenience; oblige. **II.** *intr.* To become or be conformable; act conformably; agree.—**ac-com′mo-dat-ing,** *p. a.* Obliging.—**ac-com′mo-dat-ing-ly,** *adv.*—**ac-com-mo-da′tion** (-dā′shọn), *n.* [L. *accommodatio(n-)*.] The act of accommodating, or the state of being accommodated; adaptation; adjustment; reconciliation; conformity; provision for needs or convenience; obligingness; whatever is provided to supply a want or to afford convenience; *pl.*, quarters or lodgings; *sing.*, an accommodation train (see below); in *com.*, a loan or pecuniary favor; in *physiol.*, the automatic adjustment by which the eye adapts itself to distinct vision at different distances.—**accommodation bill, draft, note,** etc., in *com.*, a bill, draft, note, etc., drawn, accepted, or indorsed by one person for another without consideration and merely as an accommodation to enable the second person to obtain credit or raise money thereon.—**accommodation ladder,** a ladder or stairway hung from a ship's side to connect with boats below.—**accommodation train,** a railroad-train which stops at all or nearly all stations.—**ac-com′mo-da-tive,** *a.* Tending to accommodate.—**ac-com′mo-da-tive-ness,** *n.*—**ac-com′mo-da-tor,** *n.*

Accommodation Ladder.

ac-com-pa-ni-er (ạ-kum′pạ-ni-ėr), *n.* One who or that which accompanies.

ac-com-pa-ni-ment (ạ-kum′pạ-ni-mẹnt), *n.* Something with which a thing is accompanied; an attendant circumstance; a concomitant; in *music*, any subsidiary part or parts added to a solo or concerted composition to enhance the effect.

ac-com-pa-nist (ạ-kum′pạ-nist), *n.* In *music*, one who plays an accompaniment.

ac-com-pa-ny (ạ-kum′pạ-ni), *v. t.*; *-nied, -nying.* [OF. *acompaignier* (F. *accompagner*), < *a* (< L. *ad*), to, + *compain*, companion: see *companion*².] To be or go in company with; go with as a companion or concomitant; attend; also, to cause to be attended (*with*); provide with some concomitant; in *music*, to play or sing an accompaniment to.—**ac-com′pa-ny-ist,** *n.* An accompanist.

ac-com-plice (ạ-kom′plis), *n.* [Extended form of *complice.*] A partner or associate, esp. in crime; any participator in an offense, whether as principal or as accessory.

ac-com-plish (ạ-kom′plish), *v. t.* [OF. *acomplir* (*acompliss-*) (F. *accomplir*), < L. *ad*, to, + *complere*, complete.] To bring to completion; achieve; fulfil; carry out; finish; perfect.—**ac-com′plish-a-ble,** *a.* Capable of being accomplished.—**ac-com′plished,** *p. a.* Completed; finished; consummate; perfected in the graces and attainments of polite society.—**ac-com′plish-er,** *n.*—**ac-com′plish-ment,** *n.* The act of accomplishing, or the state of being accomplished; achievement; fulfilment; perfection; also, a perfecting or polite attainment; an acquired art or grace.

ac-compt (ạ-kount′), **ac-compt-ant** (ạ-koun′tạnt), etc. Old forms of *account*, etc.

ac-cord (ạ-kôrd′), *v.* [OF. *acorder* (F. *accorder*), < ML. *accordare*, < L. *ad*, to, + *cor* (*cord-*), heart.] **I.** *intr.* To agree; concur; harmonize (*with*). **II.** *tr.* To bring into agreement; reconcile; adjust harmoniously; also, to agree to; also, to grant.—**ac-cord′,** *n.* [OF. *acord* (F. *accord*).] Agreement in sentiment or purpose; concurrence; consent; assenting will; hence, voluntary impulse (as, of one's own *accord*); also, agreeable correspondence of things, parts, sounds, etc.; harmony; concord; also, a musical chord; also, an amicable arrangement between parties.—**ac-cord′a-ble,** *a.* Capable of being accorded; reconcilable.—**ac-cord′ance,** *n.* The act of according; a state of accord; agreement; conformity; harmony; concession or grant.—**ac-cord′ant,** *a.* According or agreeing; conformable (*to*); consonant (*with*).—**ac-cord′ant-ly,** *adv.*—**ac-cord′er,** *n.*—**ac-cord′ing. I.** *p. a.* Agreeing; accordant; harmonious. **II.** *adv.* Conformably (*to* or *as*); agreeably; proportionately.—**ac-cord′ing-ly,** *adv.* In accordance; agreeably; conformably; correspondingly; also, hence; thus; so.

ac-cor-di-on (ą-kôr′di-ǫn). [G., < It. *accordare*, accord, harmonize.] **I.** *n.* A portable, keyed, bellows-like wind-instrument sounded by means of metallic reeds. **II.** *a.* Having folds like the bellows of an accordion.—**ac-cor′di-on-ist,** *n.* A player on the accordion.

ac-cost (ą-kôst′), *v. t.* [F. *accoster*, < ML. *accostare*, < L. *ad*, to, + *costa*, rib, side.] To approach, esp. with a greeting or remark; address; also, to adjoin†.—**ac-cost′,** *n.* Greeting; address.

ac-couche-ment (å-kösh-moṅ), *n.* [F., < *accoucher*, be brought to bed, also deliver.] Delivery in childbed.—**ac-cou-cheur** (å-kö-shėr), *n.* [F.] A man who acts as midwife; an obstetrician.—**ac-cou-cheuse** (-shėz), *n.* [F., fem. of *accoucheur*.] A midwife.

ac-count (ą-kount′), *v.* [OF. *aconter*, < L. *ad*, to, + *computare*, count, compute.] **I.** *tr.* To count†, calculate†, or compute†; also, to count or reckon as; esteem; deem; consider; also, to credit or impute (*to*). **II.** *intr.* To hold a reckoning (*with*); render a reckoning (*to*); answer (*for*); furnish a reason or explanation (*for*).—**ac-count′,** *n.* A reckoning or computation; a statement of pecuniary transactions; a record or a course of business dealings between parties; any detailed or explanatory statement; a narrative or recital; an explanation; reason or ground (as, postponed on *account* of rain); estimation, esteem, or consequence (as, of no *account*); interest or advantage (as, to turn a thing to good *account*); behalf or sake (as, do not go on my *account*).—**ac-count′a-ble,** *a.* Liable to be called to account; responsible; answerable; also, explicable.—**ac-count-a-bil′i-ty** (-bil′i-ti), **ac-count′a-ble-ness,** *n.*—**ac-count′a-bly,** *adv.*—**ac-count′ant,** *n.* One who keeps or examines accounts.—**ac-count′an-cy, ac-count′ant-ship,** *n.*—**ac-count′=book,** *n.* A book in which accounts are recorded.—**ac-count′ing,** *n.* A reckoning up or balancing of accounts; a statement of accounts; the art or science of keeping accounts.

ac-cou-tre, ac-cou-ter (ą-kö′tėr), *v. t.*; *-tred* or *-tered*, *-tring* or *-tering*. [F. *accoutrer*, OF. *acoutrer*; origin uncertain.] To equip; array; esp., to equip with military accoutrements.—**ac-cou′tre-ment, ac-cou′ter-ment,** *n.* Equipment; array; *pl.*, articles of equipment; trappings; esp., the equipments of a soldier other than arms and clothing.

ac-cred-it (a-kred′it), *v. t.* [F. *accréditer*, < *à* (< L. *ad*), to, + *crédit*, credit.] To bring into credit; invest with credit or authority; also, to send with credentials; also, to give credence to; believe; trust; also, to credit with something ascribed.

ac-cre-men-ti-tion (ak″rē-men-tish′ǫn), *n.* [Irreg. < L. *accrescere*: see *accrete*.] In *biol.*, production of a new individual by development and separation of a part of the parent; gemmation.

ac-cres-cent (a-kres′ęnt), *a.* [L. *accrescens* (*-ent-*), ppr. of *accrescere*: see *accrete*.] Growing; increasing; in *bot.*, growing larger after flowering.—**ac-cres′cence,** *n.*

ac-crete (a-krēt′), *v.*; *-creted*, *-creting*. [L. *accretus*, pp. of *accrescere*, < *ad*, to, + *crescere*, grow.] **I.** *intr.* To grow together; adhere (*to*). **II.** *tr.* To add as by growth.—**ac-crete′,** *a.* Accreted; grown together.—**ac-cre-tion** (a-krē′shǫn), *n.* [L. *accretio*(*n-*).] Growth in size or extent; increase by natural growth or by gradual external addition; adhesion or gradual addition of new matter or parts; also, something adhering or gradually added; an accession; in *law*, increase of property by external accessions, as of land by alluvium; in *pathol.*, the growing together of parts normally separate.—**ac-cre′tive,** *a.* Pertaining to accretion.

ac-croach (a-krōch′), *v. t.* [OF. *acrochier* (F. *accrocher*), < *a* (< L. *ad*), to, + *croc*, hook.] To take to one's self (power, etc.); usurp. [Archaic.]—**ac-croach′ment,** *n.*

ac-cru-al (a-krö′ąl), *n.* The act of accruing.

ac-crue (a-krö′), *n.* [OF. *acreue* (F. *accrue*), growth, increase, orig. pp. fem. of *acreistre* (F. *accroître*), < L. *accrescere*: see *accrete*.] An accession†; a reinforcement†; a loop forming an extra mesh in network.—**ac-crue′,** *v. i.*; *-crued*, *-cruing*. To arise as by natural growth; come as a natural product or result; fall as an increment or accession.—**ac-crue′ment,** *n.* The act of accruing; also, that which accrues.

ac-cu-ba-tion (ak-ū-bā′shǫn), *n.* [L. *accubatio*(*n-*), < *accubare*, lie near, < *ad*, to, + *cubare*, lie.] The act or

Accubation.—An ancient dinner.

posture of reclining, as at meals among the ancients; in *med.*, accouchement.

ac-cum-bent (a-kum′bęnt), *a.* [L. *accumbens* (*-ent-*), ppr. of *accumbere*, recline, < *ad*, to, + *-cumbere*, lie.] Reclining, as at table; in *bot.*, lying against something.

ac-cu-mu-late (ą-kū′mū-lāt), *v.*; *-lated*, *-lating*. [L. *accumulatus*, pp. of *accumulare*, < *ad*, to, + *cumulare*, heap up, < *cumulus*, a heap.] **I.** *tr.* To heap up; gather as into a mass; collect; amass. **II.** *intr.* To grow into a heap or mass; form an increasing quantity.—**ac-cu′mu-late** (-lāt), *a.* Accumulated; aggregate.—**ac-cu-mu-la′tion** (-lā′shǫn), *n.* [L. *accumulatio*(*n-*).] The act of accumulating, or the state of being accumulated; also, an accumulated mass or quantity.—**ac-cu′mu-la-tive** (-lą-tiv), *a.* Tending to accumulate; collective; cumulative.—**ac-cu′mu-la-tive-ly,** *adv.*—**ac-cu′mu-la-tive-ness,** *n.*—**ac-cu′mu-la-tor** (-lā-tǫr), *n.* [L.] One who or that which accumulates; a device or apparatus for collecting and storing energy, etc.

ac-cu-rate (ak′ū-rąt), *a.* [L. *accuratus*, pp. of *accurare*, < *ad*, to, + *curare*, care for, < *cura*, care.] Carefully conforming to truth or the standard; precise; exact; correct.—**ac′cu-ra-cy** (-rą-si), **ac′cu-rate-ness,** *n.*—**ac′cu-rate-ly,** *adv.*

ac-curse (ą-kėrs′), *v. t.* [Earlier *acurse*, < *a-* + *curse*.] To curse: now used only as in *accursed*, *accurst*, *p. a.*—**ac-cursed, ac-curst** (ą-kėrst′ or ą-kėr′sed, ą-kėrst′), *p. a.* Cursed; laid under a curse; blasted; ruined; also, execrable; damnable.—**ac-curs′ed-ly,** *adv.*—**ac-curs′ed-ness,** *n.*

ac-cus-a-ble (ą-kū′zą-bl), *a.* Liable to be accused.

ac-cu-sal (ą-kū′ząl), *n.* Accusation.

ac-cu-sa-tion (ak-ū-zā′shǫn), *n.* [L. *accusatio*(*n-*).] The act of accusing; a charge of wrong-doing; the offense charged.

ac-cu-sa-tive (ą-kū′zą-tiv). [L. *accusativus*.] **I.** *a.* Accusing; accusatory; in *gram.*, indicating the direct object of a verb or the goal of action or motion (applied to a case in declension in Latin and other languages, corresponding to the objective in English, or to its forms or constructions). **II.** *n.* In *gram.*, the accusative case, or a word in that case.—**ac-cu-sa-ti′val** (-tī′vąl), *a.*—**ac-cu′sa-tive-ly,** *adv.*

ac-cu-sa-to-ri-al (ą-kū-zą-tō′ri-ąl), *a.* [L. *accusatorius*.] Pertaining to an accuser.—**ac-cu-sa-to′ri-al-ly,** *adv.*—**ac-cu′sa-to-ry** (-tǫ-ri), *a.* Making or implying accusation; accusing.

ac-cuse (ą-kūz′), *v. t.*; *-cused*, *-cusing*. [L. *accusare* (pp. *accusatus*), call to account, accuse, < *ad*, to, + *causa*, cause, judicial proceeding: cf. *excuse*.] To bring a charge against; charge with the fault or crime (*of*); also, to betray or reveal (now rare).—**ac-cus-er** (ą-kū′zėr), *n.*—**ac-cus′ing-ly,** *adv.*

ac-cus-tom (ą-kus′tǫm), *v. t.* [OF. *acostumer* (F. *accoutumer*), < *a* (< L. *ad*), to, + *costume*, custom.] To make (something) customary or habitual (now only in *accustomed*, *p. a.*); also, to habituate to something; render used.—**ac-cus′tomed,** *p. a.* Customary, habitual, or wonted; also, habituated or used.—**ac-cus′tomed-ness,** *n.*

ace (ās), *n.* [OF. F. *as*, < L. *as*, unit.] A single pip on a card or die; a card, or the side of a die, with one pip; a single point, as a point won in certain games; a particle or atom; a hair's-breadth (as, to be within an *ace* of hitting the mark); also, the foremost or best; something first-class; esp., a combatant aviator who has brought down five or more enemy machines.

A-cel-da-ma (a-sel′dą-mą), *n.* [Gr. Ἀκελδαμά, repr. an Aramaic phrase meaning 'field of blood.'] The "field of blood," near Jerusalem, purchased with the bribe Judas took for betraying Jesus (Mat. xxvii. 8; Acts, i. 19); hence, any place stained by slaughter.

-aceous. [L. *-aceus.*] An adjective suffix meaning 'of the nature, kind, or class of,' 'like,' 'containing,' as in *arenaceous, cretaceous, herbaceous, sebaceous*: specif. used, in *bot.*, as a termination of adjectives accompanying New Latin names ending in *-aceæ* for the various families of plants, as *liliaceous* (NL. *Liliaceæ*, the lily family), *rosaceous* (NL. *Rosaceæ*, the rose family), *ulmaceous* (NL. *Ulmaceæ*, the elm family).

a-ceph-a-lan (a-sef'ą-ląn). [NL. *Acephala*, neut. pl. of LL. *acephalus*, < Gr. ἀκέφαλος, headless, < ἀ- priv. + κεφαλή, head.] **I.** *a.* Belonging to the *Acephala*, a class of mollusks, including the bivalves, without a distinct head. **II.** *n.* One of the *Acephala*.

a-ceph-a-lous (a-sef'ą-lus), *a.* [LL. *acephalus*: see *acephalan.*] Headless; lacking a distinct head, as the acephalan mollusks; having no leader or chief; defective at the beginning, as verse; in *bot.*, having the style springing from the base instead of the apex, as an ovary.

a-ce-qui-a (ä-sā'kē-ą), *n.* [Sp.] An irrigating canal.

a-ce-ra-ceous (as-ę-rā'shius), *a.* [L. *acer*, maple.] Belonging to the *Aceraceæ*, or maple family of trees and shrubs.

a-cerb (ą-sėrb'), *a.* [L. *acerbus*, < *acer*, sharp.] Sour, with astringency or bitterness, as unripe fruit; sharp; harsh; austere.

a-cer-bate (as'ėr-bāt), *v. t.*; *-bated, -bating.* [L. *acerbatus*, pp. of *acerbare*, < *acerbus*, E. *acerb.*] To sour; embitter; hence, to exasperate.—**a'cer-bate,** *a.* Acerbated; embittered.

a-cer-bi-ty (ą-sėr'bi-ti), *n.*; pl. *-ties* (-tiz). Acerb quality; sourness and astringency or bitterness of taste; sharpness; harshness.

a-cerb-ly (ą-sėrb'li), *adv.* In an acerb manner.

a-cer-ose (as'ę-rōs), *a.* [In form < L. *acerosus*, chaffy, < *acus*, chaff, but with sense < L. *acus*, needle.] In *bot.*, needle-shaped, as the leaves of the pine.

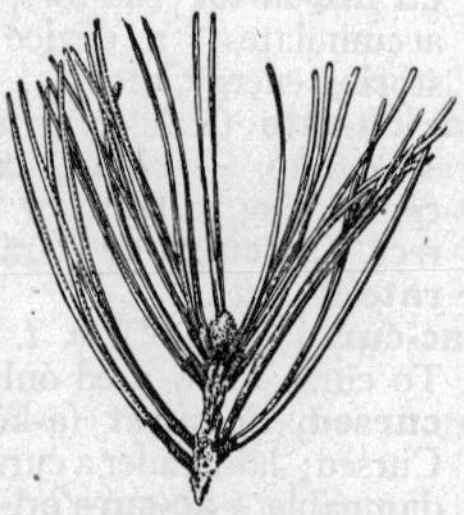

Acerose Leaves (Pine).

a-cer-ous (as'ę-rus), *a.* [Gr. ἄκερος, < ἀ- priv. + κέρας, horn.] In *zoöl.*, having no horns, tentacles, or antennæ.

a-cer-vate (a-sėr'vāt), *a.* [L. *acervatus*, pp. of *acervare*, heap up, < *acervus*, a heap.] Heaped; growing in heaps, or in closely compacted clusters.—**a-cer'vate-ly,** *adv.*

a-ces-cent (a-ses'ęnt), *a.* [L. *acescens* (*-ent-*), ppr. of *acescere*, become sour, < *acere*, be sour.] Turning sour; slightly sour; acidulous.—**a-ces'cence, a-ces'cen-cy,** *n.*

a-ce-tab-u-lum (as-ē-tab'ū-lum), *n.*; pl. *-la* (-lą). [L., vinegar-cup, < *acetum*, vinegar.] A cup-like part, process, or organ; a socket, esp. that in the hip-bone which receives the head of the femur; a sucker, as of a cuttlefish.—**a-ce-tab'u-lar** (-ląr), *a.*

a-cet-am-ide (as-et-am'īd or -id), *n.* In *chem.*, the amide of acetic acid, a white crystalline solid.

a-cet-an-i-lide (as-et-an'i-līd or -lid), *n.* A substance formed by the action of glacial acetic acid upon aniline: used as a remedy for fever, headache, rheumatism, etc.

a-ce-tate (as'ē-tāt), *n.* In *chem.*, a salt of acetic acid.—**a'ce-tat-ed** (-tā-ted), *a.* Formed into an acetate; combined with acetic acid.

a-ce-tic (a-sē'tik or a-set'ik), *a.* [L. *acetum*, vinegar.] Pertaining to or derived from vinegar: as, *acetic* acid (a colorless liquid, $CH_3CO.OH$, with a strongly acid smell and taste).—**a-cet-i-fi-ca-tion** (a-set"i-fi-kā'shǫn), *n.* Conversion into vinegar; acetous fermentation.—**a-cet'i-fy** (-fī), *v. t.* or *i.*; *-fied, -fying.* [See *-fy.*] To turn into vinegar; make or become acetous.—**a-cet'i-fi-er** (-fī-ėr), *n.*—**a-ce-tim-e-ter, a-ce-tom-e-ter** (as-ē-tim'e-tėr, -tom'e-tėr), *n.* [See *-meter.*] An instrument for ascertaining the strength of vinegar or acetic acid.—**a-ce-tim'e-try,** *n.* [See *-metry.*] The process of ascertaining the strength of vinegar or acetic acid.—**a-ce-tone** (as'ē-tōn), *n.* In *chem.*, a colorless, inflammable liquid, $(CH_3)_2CO$, formed in the distillation of acetates, etc.: used as a solvent.—**a-ce-to-nu-ri-a** (as"ē-tǫ-nū'ri-ą), *n.* [NL. (Gr. οὖρον, urine).] Excess of acetone in the urine, as in diabetes.—**a"ce-to-phe'none** (-fē'nōn), *n.* In *chem.*, a crystalline ketone formed by the distillation of a mixture of calcium acetate and benzoate: used as a hypnotic, etc.—**a-ce-tous** (a-sē'tus or as'ē-tus), *a.* Of or like vinegar; containing or producing acetic acid.—**a-cet-phe-net-i-din** (as"et-fē-net'i-din), *n.* Same as *phenacetin.*—**a-ce-tum** (a-sē'tum), *n.* [L.] Vinegar; in *phar.*, a preparation made with vinegar or dilute acetic acid.—**a-ce-tyl** (as'ē-til), *n.* [See *-yl.*] In *chem.*, a radical, CH_3CO, present in acetic acid.—**a-cet-y-lene** (a-set'i-lēn or as'ē-ti-lēn), *n.* A colorless gas, C_2H_2, prepared by the action of water on calcium carbide, and used as an illuminant and to increase the illuminating value of coal-gas and water-gas.—**a-ce-tyl'ic,** *a.* Of or pertaining to acetyl.

A-chæ-an, A-cha-ian (ą-kē'ąn, ą-kā'yąn). [L. *Achæus, Achaius*, < Gr. Ἀχαιός.] **I.** *a.* Belonging to the Achæi, one of the principal races of ancient Greece, or to the district of Achæa (Achaia), in the northern Peloponnesus; hence, Greek. **II.** *n.* A member of the Achæan race; an inhabitant of Achæa; hence, a Greek.

Ach-æ-me-ni-an (ak-ē-mē'ni-ąn). [L. *Achæmenius*, adj., < *Achæmenes*, < Gr. Ἀχαιμένης, < OPers. *Hakhāmani*, name of the reputed founder of the line.] **I.** *a.* Of or pertaining to the Achæmenidæ, an ancient royal family of Persia, historically beginning with Cyrus the Great, about 558 B.C., and ending with Darius III., who was overthrown by Alexander the Great in 330 B.C.; pertaining to the Persian language of their period. **II.** *n.* One of the Achæmenidæ, or a Persian of their period; also, the Persian language of this period.

a-char-né (å-shär-nā), *a.* [F., pp. of *acharner*, flesh (dogs, etc.), < L. *ad*, to, + *caro* (*carn-*), flesh.] Bloodthirsty; sanguinary; furious.—**a-char-ne-ment** (å-shär-nė-moṅ), *n.* Bloodthirsty fury; eagerness for slaughter; ferocity.

A-cha-tes (ą-kā'tēz), *n.* [From the companion and friend (L. "*fidus Achates*," faithful Achates) of Virgil's Æneas.] A faithful comrade.

ache (āk), *v. i.*; *ached, aching.* [Prop. *ake*, < ME. *aken*, < AS. *acan.*] To suffer pain; have a continued wearying pain.—**ache,** *n.* [ME. *ache*, < AS. *æce*, < *acan.*] A continued wearying pain, often local.

A-che-an (ą-kē'ąn), *a.* and *n.* See *Achæan.*

a-chene (a-kēn'), *n.* [NL. *achenium, achænium*, < Gr. ἀ- priv. + χαίνειν, gape.] In *bot.*, a small, dry, hard, one-seeded, indehiscent fruit. Also **a-che-ni-um** (a-kē'ni-um); pl. *-nia* (-ni-ą).

Ach-e-ron (ak'ę-ron), *n.* [L., < Gr. Ἀχέρων.] In *Gr.* and *Rom. myth.*, a river in Hades, over which the souls of the dead were ferried by Charon; hence, the lower world.

a-chiev-a-ble (ą-chē'vą-bl), *a.* That may be achieved.

a-chieve (ą-chēv'), *v. t.*; *achieved, achieving.* [OF. F. *achever*, < *a* (< L. *ad*), to, + *chef*, head, end: see *chief.*] To bring to a successful end; carry through; accomplish; also, to attain, as an end sought; gain.—**a-chieve'ment,** *n.* The act of achieving; a success achieved; a feat; in *her.*, a hatchment.—**a-chiev'er,** *n.*

Ach-il-le-an (ak-i-lē'ąn), *a.* Of or pertaining to Achilles, the Greek legendary hero in the war against Troy (as described in Homer's "Iliad"), noted for his valor, his invulnerability (save in the heel), and his unrelenting wrath.—**A-chil-les'** (ą-kil'ēz) **ten'don.** See *tendon of Achilles*, under *tendon.*

ach-ing (ā'king), *p. a.* That aches; suffering pain; painful.—**ach'ing-ly,** *adv.*

a-chlam-y-date (a-klam'i-dāt), *a.* [See *a-*[1].] In *zoöl.*, not chlamydate; having no mantle or pallium.

ach-la-myd-e-ous (ak-lą-mid'ę-us), *a.* [See *a-*[1].] In *bot.*, not chlamydeous; having no floral envelop.

ach-ro-mat (ak'rǫ-mat), *n.* [G., < Gr. ἀχρώματος: see *achromatic.*] In *optics*, a lens or a system of lenses corrected for chromatic aberration.

ach-ro-mat-ic (ak-rǫ-mat'ik). [Gr. ἀχρώματος, colorless, < ἀ- priv. + χρῶμα (χρωματ-), color.] **I.** *a.* Colorless; uncolored; not taking color; in *optics*, free from the color due to the decomposition of light in chromatic aberration (as, an *achromatic* lens, one sensibly free from chromatic aberration). **II.** *n.* A telescope with an achromatic object-glass.—**ach-ro-mat'i-cal-ly,** *adv.*—**a-chro-ma-ti-ci-ty**

(a-krō-mą-tis′i-ti), *n.* Achromatism.—**a-chro′ma-tism,** *n.* The quality of being achromatic; freedom from chromatic aberration.—**a-chro′ma-tize,** *v. t.*; *-tized, -tizing.* To render achromatic.

a-chro-ma-top-si-a (a-krō-mą-top′si-ä), *n.* [NL., < Gr. ἀ- priv. + χρῶμα (χρωματ-), color, + ὄψις, sight.] Color-blindness.

a-chro-ma-tous (a-krō′mą-tus), *a.* [Gr. ἀχρώματος: see *achromatic.*] Without color; of a lighter color than is normal.

a-ci-cle (as′i-kl), *n.* Same as *acicula.*

a-cic-u-la (a-sik′ū-lä), *n.*; pl. *-læ* (-lē). [L., dim. of *acus,* needle.] A needle-shaped part or process; a spine, prickle, or bristle; a needle-like crystal.—**a-cic′u-lar** (-lär), *a.* Needle-shaped.—**a-cic′u-lar-ly,** *adv.*—**a-cic′u-late** (-lāt), **a-cic′u-lat-ed** (-lā-ted), *a.* Having aciculæ; marked as with needle-scratches; also, needle-shaped; acicular.—**a-cic′u-lum** (-lum), *n.*; pl. *-la* (-lä). [NL.] Same as *acicula.*

a-cid (as′id). [L. *acidus,* < *acere,* be sour, akin to *acer,* sharp.] **I.** *a.* Sour; tart; in *chem.,* belonging or pertaining to acids; acidic; having only a part of the hydrogen of an acid replaced by a metal or its equivalent (as, an *acid* phosphate, salt, etc.: see *salt*², *n.*). **II.** *n.* A substance with a sour taste; in *chem.,* a compound (usually having a sour taste and capable of neutralizing alkalis and reddening blue litmus-paper) containing hydrogen which can be replaced by a metal or an electropositive radical to form a salt.—**a-cid-ic** (a-sid′ik), *a.* Pertaining to an acid; forming the acid (non-basic) element in a salt; of rocks, containing a large amount of the acid element or constituent (silicon or silica).—**a-ci-dif-er-ous** (as-i-dif′ę-rus), *a.* [See *-ferous.*] Yielding an acid.—**a-cid′i-fi-a-ble** (-i-fī-ą-bl), *a.* Capable of being acidified.—**a-ci-dif′ic,** *a.* [See *-fic.*] Making acid.—**a-cid″i-fi-ca′tion** (-fi-kā′shǫn), *n.* The process of acidifying.—**a-cid′i-fy** (-fī), *v. t.* or *i.*; *-fied, -fying.* [See *-fy.*] To make or become acid.—**a-cid′i-fi-er** (-fī-ėr), *n.*—**a-ci-dim′e-ter** (-dim′e-tėr), *n.* [See *-meter.*] An instrument for determining the strength of acids.—**a-ci-dim′e-try,** *n.* [See *-metry.*] Measurement of the strength of acids; determination of the amount of acid in a solution.—**a-cid′i-ty,** *n.* The quality of being acid; sourness; tartness.—**a′cid-ly,** *adv.*—**a′cid-ness,** *n.*—**a-ci-do′sis** (-dō′sis), *n.* [NL.] In *pathol.,* poisoning by acids formed within the body under morbid conditions.

a-cid-u-late (a-sid′ū-lāt), *v. t.*; *-lated, -lating.* [See *acidulous.*] To make acidulous.—**a-cid-u-la′tion** (-lā′shǫn), *n.*

a-cid-u-lous (a-sid′ū-lus), *a.* [L. *acidulus,* dim. of *acidus,* E. *acid.*] Slightly sour or acid; subacid.—**a-cid′u-lous-ly,** *adv.*—**a-cid′u-lous-ness,** *n.*

a-ci-er-age (as′i-ę-rāj), *n.* [F. *aciérage,* < *acier,* steel.] The process of depositing a layer of iron on another metal by electrical action.

a-ci-er-ate (as′i-ę-rāt), *v. t.*; *-ated, -ating.* [= F. *aciérer,* < *acier,* steel.] To convert (iron) into steel.—**a″ci-er-a′tion** (-ę-rā′shǫn), *n.*

a-ci-form (as′i-fôrm), *a.* [L. *acus,* needle: see *-form.*] Needle-shaped; acicular.

Acinaciform Leaf.

a-ci-na-ci-form (as-i-nas′i-fôrm), *a.* [L. *acinaces,* simitar: see *-form.*] In *bot.,* simitar-shaped, as a leaf.

a-cin-i-form (a-sin′i-fôrm), *a.* [L. *acinus,* grape: see *-form.*] Clustered like grapes; acinose.

a-ci-nose (as′i-nōs), *a.* [L. *acinosus,* < *acinus,* grape.] Consisting of acini; having clustered or granular subdivisions. Also **a′ci-nous.**

a-ci-nus (as′i-nus), *n.*; pl. *-ni* (-nī). [L., berry, grape, grape-stone.] In *bot.,* a drupel, as of a blackberry, or its seed; a grape-stone; in *anat.,* a minute lobule; the smallest saccular subdivision of a gland.

-acious. [L. *-aci-,* nom. *-ax,* forming adjectives from verbs, + E. *-ous.*] An adjective suffix meaning 'inclined or given to,' 'doing (as indicated) often or much,' 'being very,' as in *capacious, pugnacious, tenacious, vivacious, voracious.*

-acity. [L. *-acitas.*] Suffix of nouns of quality, etc., accompanying adjectives in *-acious,* as in *capacity, pugnacity.*

ac-know† (ak-nō′), *v. t.* [ME. *aknowen,* < AS. *oncnāwan,* < *on,* in, on, + *cnāwan,* E. *know.*] To recognize; acknowledge; admit; confess.—**to be acknown,** to make acknowledgment or admission.

ac-knowl-edge (ak-nol′ej), *v. t.*; *-edged, -edging.* [Appar. < *knowledge,* with prefix as in *acknow.*] To admit one's knowledge or recognition of; own as true, genuine, or authoritative; confess; avow; also, to express recognition or appreciation of (a favor, letter, salute, etc.) by some appropriate response; also, to avow or certify (a deed, etc.) in legal form.—**ac-knowl′edge-a-ble,** *a.* That may be acknowledged.—**ac-knowl′edg-ment, ac-knowl′edge-ment,** *n.* The act of acknowledging; confession; avowal; express recognition; an expression or token of recognition or appreciation; in *com.,* a receipt; in *law,* an official certificate of a formal acknowledging.

a-clas-tic (a-klas′tik), *a.* [Gr. ἄκλαστος, unbroken, < ἀ- priv. + κλαστός, broken, < κλᾶν, break.] In *physics,* not refracting.

a-clin-ic (a-klin′ik), *a.* [Gr. ἀκλινής, not bending, < ἀ- priv. + κλίνειν, incline.] Free from inclination or dip of the magnetic needle: applied to an imaginary line near the earth's equator.

ac-me (ak′mē), *n.* [Gr. ἀκμή, point, top.] The highest or culminating point; the climax or crisis.

ac-ne (ak′nē), *n.* [Perhaps for *acme,* < Gr. ἀκμή, point.] In *pathol.,* an inflammatory disease of the sebaceous glands, characterized by an eruption (often pustular) of the skin, esp. of the face.

ac-node (ak′nōd), *n.* [L. *acus,* needle, + *nodus,* E. *node.*] In *math.,* a point belonging to a curve, but separated from other real points of the curve.—**ac-no′dal** (-nō′dąl), *a.*

a-cock (ą-kok′), *adv.* In a cocked position.—**a-cock′bill,** *adv. Naut.,* with bills or ends cocked or turned upward, as an anchor hanging ready to be dropped, or as yards tilted at an angle with the deck.

a-cold (ą-kōld′), *a.* [Orig. pp. of AS. *ācōlian,* grow cold.] Chilled; cold. [Archaic.]

ac-o-lyte (ak′ǫ-līt), *n.* [LL. *acolytus, acoluthus,* < Gr. ἀκόλουθος, attendant.] An altar attendant of minor rank, esp., in the Roman Catholic Church, a member of the highest of the four minor orders, ranking next below a subdeacon; in general, an assistant or follower; in *astron.,* an attendant star; a satellite.

Aconite (*A. napellus*). *a,* flower; *b,* same, calyx removed.

ac-o-nite (ak′ǫ-nīt), *n.* [L. *aconitum,* < Gr. ἀκόνιτον.] Any plant of the ranunculaceous genus *Aconitum,* which includes herbs with poisonous and medicinal properties, as monk's-hood or wolf's-bane; also, the medicinal dried root of certain species of this genus, or an extract or tincture made from such a root.—**ac-o-nit′ic** (-nit′ik), *a.*—**a-con-i-tin, a-con-i-tine** (a-kon′i-tin), *n.* In *chem.,* a highly poisonous narcotic alkaloid from aconite.—**ac-o-ni′tum** (-nī′-tum), *n.* [L.] Same as *aconite.*

a-corn (ā′kôrn), *n.* [AS. *æcern,* < *æcer,* field: see *acre.*] The fruit of the oak, a nut in a hardened scaly cup.—**a′corn=shell,** *n.* A sessile cirriped of the family *Balanidæ.* See *barnacle*¹.

Acorns.

Acorn-shells.

a-cos-mism (a-koz′mizm), *n.* [Gr. ἀ- priv. + κόσμος, world.] Denial of the existence of a universe as distinct from God.—**a-cos′mist,** *n.*

a-cot-y-le-don (a-kot-i-lē′dǫn), *n.* [See *a-*¹.] In *bot.,* a plant without cotyledons; a cryptogam.—**a-cot-y-le′don-ous,** *a.*

a-cou-chy (ą-kö′shi), *n.* [F. *acouchi*; from native Guiana name.] A species of agouti, *Dasyprocta acouchy.*

a-cou-me-ter (ą-kö′me-tėr or ą-kou′-), *n.* [Gr. ἀκούειν, hear: see *-meter.*] An instrument for measuring the power of the sense of hearing.

a-cous-tic (ą-kös′tik or ą-kous′-), *a.* [Gr. ἀκουστικός, < ἀκούειν, hear.] Pertaining to hearing, or to the science of sound. Also **a-cous'ti-cal.**—**a-cous'ti-cal-ly,** *adv.*—**ac-ous-ti-cian** (ak-ös-tish'ạn or ak-ous-), *n.* One versed in acoustics.—**a-cous'tics,** *n.* The science of sound; also (construed as *pl.*), acoustic properties, as of an auditorium.

ac-quaint (ạ-kwānt'), *v. t.* [OF. *acointier* (F. *accointer*), < L. *ad*, to, + *cognitus*, pp. of *cognoscere*, come to know: see *cognition*, and cf. *quaint*.] To bring into relations of personal knowledge or cognizance (*with*); make more or less familiar or conversant.—**ac-quaint'ance,** *n.* The state of being acquainted; personal knowledge or conversance (falling short of intimacy or close familiarity); also, a person or the persons with whom one is acquainted.—**ac-quaint'ance-ship,** *n.* The state of having acquaintance; the relation between acquaintances.

ac-quest (ạ-kwest'), *n.* [F. *acquest* (now *acquêt*), < L. *acquirere*: see *acquire*.] Acquirement; an acquisition; in *civil law*, property acquired otherwise than by succession.

ac-qui-esce (ak-wi-es'), *v. i.*; *-esced, -escing.* [L. *acquiescere*, < *ad*, to, + *quiescere*, be at rest, < *quies*, rest.] To submit quietly; assent without demur; concur (*in*).—**ac-qui-es'cence** (-es'ẹns), *n.* Acquiescent action or state; quiet submission; passive assent; concurrence.—**ac-qui-es'cent,** *a.* Acquiescing; submissive; yielding.—**ac-qui-es'cent-ly,** *adv.*—**ac-qui-es'cing-ly,** *adv.*

ac-quir-a-ble (ạ-kwīr'ạ-bl), *a.* That may be acquired.

ac-quire (ạ-kwīr'), *v. t.*; *-quired, -quiring.* [L. *acquirere* (pp. *acquisitus*), < *ad*, to, + *quærere*, seek.] To get as one's own; gain as a possession, right, faculty, attribute, etc.; become possessed of.—**ac-quire'ment,** *n.* The act of acquiring; also, something acquired, esp. a faculty or aptitude; an attainment.—**ac-quir'er,** *n.*

ac-qui-si-tion (ak-wi-zish'ọn), *n.* [L. *acquisitio(n-)*.] The act of acquiring; also, something acquired, esp. a material possession; a gain.—**ac-quis-i-tive** (ạ-kwiz'i-tiv), *a.* Tending to make acquisitions.—**ac-quis'i-tive-ly,** *adv.*—**ac-quis'i-tive-ness,** *n.* Propensity to acquire possessions: in *phren.*, a special faculty.

ac-quist (ạ-kwist'), *n.* Same as *acquest.* [Archaic.]

ac-quit (ạ-kwit'), *v. t.*; *-quitted, -quitting.* [OF. *aquiter* (F. *acquitter*), < L. *ad*, to, + ML. *quietare*, release, discharge: see *quit*[1], *v.*] To settle (a claim, debt, etc.); also, to discharge (a person) from an obligation; also, to relieve from a charge of fault or crime; pronounce not guilty (*of*); also, to discharge (one's self) of a duty; also, to conduct (one's self).—**ac-quit'ment,** *n.* Acquittal.—**ac-quit'tal,** *n.* The act of acquitting, or the state of being acquitted; discharge; release; esp., judicial deliverance from a charge of offense by a verdict of not guilty.—**ac-quit'tance,** *n.* The act of acquitting; discharge of or from debt or obligation; release; also, a receipt or quittance.—**ac-quit'ter,** *n.*

a-cra-ni-al (a-krā'ni-ạl), *a.* [Gr. ἀ- priv. + κρανίον, skull.] Having no skull.

a-cre (ā'kėr), *n.* [AS. *æcer* = G. *acker* = Icel. *akr* = Goth. *akrs*, field; akin to L. *ager*, Gr. ἀγρός, field.] A field; a piece of land; also, a measure of land (160 square rods, or 43,560 square feet), 640 of which make a square mile.—**a'cre-age** (-āj), *n.* Extent in acres.—**a-cred** (ā'kėrd), *a.* Having acres; landed.—**a'cre=foot,** *n.* A unit of volume of water in irrigation, the amount covering one acre to a depth of one foot (43,560 cubic feet).

ac-rid (ak'rid), *a.* [L. *acer* (gen. *acris*), sharp.] Sharp or irritating to the tongue, skin, mucous membrane, etc.; severely pungent; caustic; corrosive; acrimonious; extremely harsh.—**a-crid-i-ty** (a-krid'i-ti), **ac'rid-ness,** *n.*—**ac'rid-ly,** *adv.*

ac-ri-mo-ni-ous (ak-ri-mō'ni-us), *a.* Full of acrimony; acrid; biting; irritatingly sharp.—**ac-ri-mo'ni-ous-ly,** *adv.*—**ac-ri-mo'ni-ous-ness,** *n.*

ac-ri-mo-ny (ak'ri-mọ-ni), *n.*; pl. *-nies* (-niz). [L. *acrimonia*, < *acer*, sharp.] Acrid or biting quality; irritating or angry sharpness.

ac-ri-tan (ak'ri-tạn). [NL. *Acrita* (see def.), < Gr. ἄκριτος, indistinguishable, < ἀ- priv. + κρίνειν, separate.] **I.** *a.* Belonging to the *Acrita*, a group comprising the low forms of animal life in which no nervous system is discernible. **II.** *n.* One of the *Acrita*.

a-crit-i-cal (a-krit'i-kạl or ā-), *a.* [See *a-*[1].] In *med.*, not critical.

acro-. Form of Gr. ἄκρος, at the end or top, highest, topmost, extreme, or ἄκρον, end, top, used in combination.

ac-ro-a-mat-ic (ak″rọ-ạ-mat'ik), *a.* [Gr. ἀκροαματικός, < ἀκροᾶσθαι, hear.] Addressed to hearers or disciples only, as Aristotle's esoteric works; esoteric; abstruse.

ac-ro-bat (ak'rọ-bat), *n.* [F. *acrobate*, < Gr. ἀκρόβατος, walking on tiptoe, < ἄκρος, at the end, + βαίνειν, go.] One who practises rope-dancing, trapeze performing, tumbling, or other like feats.—**ac-ro-bat'ic,** *a.* Pertaining to an acrobat.—**ac-ro-bat'i-cal-ly,** *adv.*—**ac'ro-bat-ism,** *n.* The feats or profession of an acrobat.

ac-ro-car-pous (ak-rọ-kär'pus), *a.* [Gr. ἀκρόκαρπος, < ἄκρος, at the end, + καρπός, fruit.] In *bot.*, having the fruit at the end of the primary axis.

ac-ro-drome (ak'rọ-drōm), *a.* Same as *acrodromous.*

a-crod-ro-mous (a-krod'rọ-mus), *a.* [Gr. ἄκρον, end, top, + -δρομος, < δραμεῖν, run.] In *bot.*, running to a point: said of a nervation with the nerves terminating in, or curving inward to, the point of a leaf.

ac-ro-gen (ak'rọ-jen), *n.* [Gr. ἄκρος, at the top, + -γενής, produced: see *-gen*.] In *bot.*, a plant that grows at the apex, as ferns and mosses.—**ac-ro-gen'ic, a-crog-e-nous** (a-kroj'e-nus), *a.*

ac-ro-lith (ak'rọ-lith), *n.* [Gr. ἀκρόλιθος, with ends made of stone, < ἄκρος, at the end, + λίθος, stone.] A sculptured figure having only the head and extremities made of stone or marble.—**ac-ro-lith'ic,** *a.*

ac-ro-meg-a-ly (ak-rọ-meg'ạ-li), *n.* [Gr. ἄκρος, at the end, + μέγας (μεγαλ-), great.] In *pathol.*, a chronic nervous disease characterized by enlargement of the head and extremities.

a-cro-mi-on (a-krō'mi-on), *n.*; pl. *-mia* (-mi-ạ). [NL., < Gr. ἀκρώμιον, < ἄκρος, at the end, + ὦμος, shoulder.] In *anat.*, the outward end of the spine of the scapula or shoulder-blade.—**a-cro'mi-al,** *a.*

a-cron-ych, a-cron-y-chal (a-kron'ik, -i-kạl), *a.* [Gr. ἀκρόνυχος, at nightfall, < ἄκρος, at the end, + νύξ, night.] In *astron.*, occurring at sunset, as the rising or setting of a star.—**a-cron'y-chal-ly,** *adv.*

a-crop-e-tal (a-krop'e-tạl), *a.* [Gr. ἄκρον, top, + L. *petere*, seek.] In *bot.*, developing from the base toward the apex; basifugal.

a-crop-o-lis (a-krop'ọ-lis), *n.* [Gr. ἀκρόπολις, < ἄκρος, highest, + πόλις, city.] The citadel of a Grecian city; [*cap.*] with *the*, the citadel of Athens.—**ac-ro-pol-i-tan** (ak-rọ-pol'i-tạn), *a.*

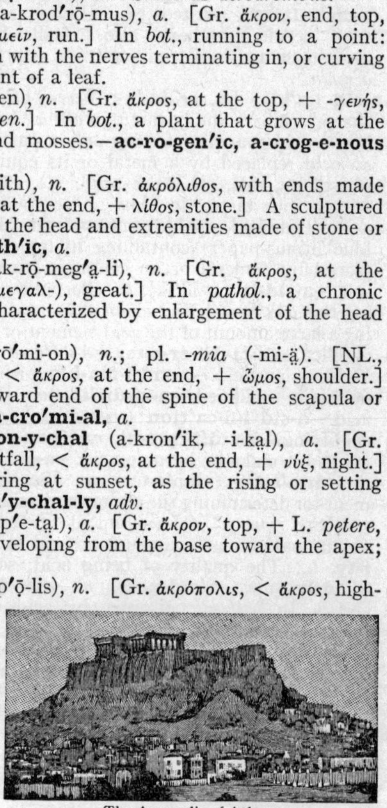

The Acropolis of Athens.

ac-ro-spire (ak'rọ-spīr), *n.* [Gr. ἄκρος, at the end, + σπεῖρα, E. *spire*[2].] The first sprout appearing in the germination of grain.

ac-ro-spore (ak'rọ-spōr), *n.* [Gr. ἄκρος, at the end, + σπορά, seed, E. *spore*.] In *bot.*, a spore borne at the end of a sporophore, as in fungi.

a-cross (ạ-krôs'). **I.** *adv.* In the form of a cross; crosswise; also, in a direction crossing the length of something; transversely; hence, from side to side; to the other side; also, on the other side. **II.** *prep.* So as to cross, intersect, or meet; crosswise or transversely over; also, on the other side of; beyond.

a-cros-tic (ạ-kros'tik). [Gr. ἀκροστιχίς, < ἄκρος, at the end, + στίχος, row, line.] **I.** *n.* A series of lines or verses in which the first, last, or other particular letters form a word, phrase, the alphabet, etc. **II.** *a.* Pertaining to or forming an acrostic.—**a-cros'ti-cal-ly,** *adv.*—**a-cros'ti-cism** (-sizm), *n.* Acrostic character.

ac-ro-tism (ak'rọ-tizm), *n.* [Gr. ἀ- priv. + κρότος, beat.] In *pathol.*, absence or weakness of the pulse.—**a-crot-ic** (a-krot'ik), *a.*

act (akt), *n.* [L. *actum*, a thing done, *actus*, a doing, < *agere*, drive, do, act: see *agent*.] A deed, performance, or proceeding; the process of doing; action; one of the main divisions of a play or opera; an individual performance, as in a variety entertainment; an authoritative decision or enactment; a statute or law; a deed or instrument recording a transaction; the public maintaining of a thesis by a candidate for a degree, as in certain English universities; *pl.* [*cap.*], the book of the New Testament called in full "The Acts of the Apostles."—**act of God,** in *law*, a direct, sudden, and irresistible action of natural forces, such as could not humanly have been foreseen or prevented.—**act,** *v.* [L. *actus*, pp. of *agere.*] **I.** *tr.* To actuate†; also, to do or perform; carry out; also, to perform, enact, or represent as on the stage; play; also, to simulate or feign. **II.** *intr.* To do something; exert power or influence; produce an effect; also, to perform functions; also, to play a part, as an actor; hence, to pretend; also, to conduct one's self; behave.—**ac-ta** (ak′tạ̈), *n. pl.* [L.] Acts; deeds; proceedings; records.—**act′a-ble,** *a.* That may be acted.

Ac-tian (ak′shiạn), *a.* Of or pertaining to Actium, an ancient town and a promontory of Acarnania in Greece. —**Actian games,** orig., certain games held at Actium every three years in honor of Apollo; later, certain games founded on the preceding by the Roman emperor Augustus to be celebrated at Actium every four years in commemoration of his naval victory near there over Antony and Cleopatra (Sept. 2, 31 B.C.).

ac-ti-nal (ak′ti-nạl or ak-tī′-), *a.* [Gr. ἀκτίς (ἀκτιν-), ray.] In *zoöl.*, noting or pertaining to that part of a sea-anemone, etc., containing the mouth and tentacles; noting or pertaining to that side or surface of a starfish, etc., which contains the mouth.—**ac′ti-nal-ly,** *adv.*

act-ing (ak′ting), *p. a.* That acts; performing functions; officiating or serving, esp. temporarily or in place of another (as, an *acting* governor or mayor).

ac-tin-i-a (ak-tin′i-ạ̈), *n.*; pl. *-iæ* (-i-ē). [NL. *Actinia*, < Gr. ἀκτίς (ἀκτιν-), ray.] A marine animal of the genus *Actinia* (class *Actinozoa*), with circles of ray-like tentacles about the mouth; hence, any sea-anemone.—**ac-tin′i-an,** *a.* and *n.*

ac-tin-ic (ak-tin′ik), *a.* [See *actinism.*] Pertaining to actinism; of radiation, chemically active.—**ac-tin′i-cal-ly,** *adv.*

ac-tin-i-form (ak-tin′i-fôrm), *a.* [See *actinia* and *-form.*] Resembling an actinia; having a radiate form.

ac-ti-nism (ak′ti-nizm), *n.* [Gr. ἀκτίς (ἀκτιν-), ray.] The action or the property of radiant energy of producing chemical change, as in photography.

ac-tin-i-um (ak-tin′i-um), *n.* [NL., < Gr. ἀκτίς (ἀκτιν-), ray.] In *chem.*, a radioactive substance found in the residue from pitchblende after the extraction of the uranium.

actino-, actin-. Forms of Gr. ἀκτίς (ἀκτιν-), ray, used in combination, esp. with reference to radiate structure, radiation, or actinism.—**ac-tin-o-gram** (ak-tin′ọ̄-gram), *n.* [+ *-gram.*] A record made by an actinograph.—**ac-tin′o-graph** (-gråf), *n.* [+ *-graph.*] A recording actinometer.—**ac″ti-no-graph′ic** (-ti-nọ̄-graf′ik), *a.*—**ac-ti-nog′ra-phy** (-nog′rạ-fi), *n.* [+ *-graphy.*] The recording of actinic power by the actinograph.—**ac′ti-noid,** *a.* [+ *-oid.*] Ray-like; radiate, as a starfish.—**ac-ti-nol′o-gy** (-nol′ọ̄-ji), *n.* [+ *-logy.*] The science of actinism.—**ac-ti-nom′e-ter** (-nom′e-tėr), *n.* [+ *-meter.*] An instrument for measuring the intensity of radiation, whether by the chemical effects or otherwise.—**ac-ti-nom′e-try,** *n.* [+ *-metry.*] Measurement of the intensity of radiation. —**ac″ti-no-met′ric** (-met′rik), *a.*—**ac″ti-no-mor′phic** (-môr′fik), **ac″ti-no-mor′phous,** *a.* [+ Gr. μορφή, form.] Having radial symmetry; of certain flowers, as the buttercup, divisible vertically into similar halves by each of a number of planes.

ac-ti-no-my-ces (ak″ti-nọ̄-mī′sēz), *n.*; pl. *-mycetes* (-mī-sē′tēz). [NL., < Gr. ἀκτίς (ἀκτιν-), ray, + μύκης, fungus.] The ray-fungus, a minute parasitic organism of the genus *Actinomyces*, found on grain and causing tumors in animals and man.—**ac″ti-no-my-co′sis** (-mī-kō′sis), *n.* [NL.] An infectious inflammatory disease of cattle and other animals and of man, due to the actinomyces and other parasites, and causing lumpy, often suppurating tumors, esp. about the jaws.—**ac″ti-no-my-cot′ic** (-kot′ik), *a.*

ac-ti-no-zo-ön (ak″ti-nọ̄-zō′on), *n.*; pl. *-zoa* (-zō′ạ̈). [NL., < Gr. ἀκτίς (ἀκτιν-), ray, + ζῷον, animal.] Any member of the *Actinozoa*, a class of cœlenterate marine animals including the sea-anemones, corals, sea-pens, etc.—**ac″ti-no-zo′an,** *a.* and *n.*

ac-tion (ak′shọn), *n.* [OF. F. *action*, < L. *actio(n-)*, < *agere*: see *agent.*] The process of acting; activity; operation; the production of an effect; performance of functions; mode of acting; movement, gesture, or behavior; procedure; also, a particular act, or series of acts; a deed, performance, or proceeding; the series of events forming the subject of a drama, etc.; a legal proceeding instituted by one party against another; a minor military engagement; also, the mechanism by which something is operated.—**ac′tion-a-ble,** *a.* Furnishing ground for an action at law. —**ac′tion-a-bly,** *adv.*—**ac′tion-less,** *a.* Without action; inert.

ac-tion-naire (åk-syọ-nãr), *n.* [F., < *action*, share of stock.] A shareholder; a stockholder.

ac-ti-vate (ak′ti-vāt), *v. t.*; *-vated, -vating.* To make active; in *physics*, to render radioactive.—**ac-ti-va′tion** (-vā′shọn), *n.*

ac-tive (ak′tiv). [OF. F. *actif*, < L. *activus*, < *agere*: see *agent.*] **I.** *a.* Engaged in or concerned with action; acting; working; operative; effective; practical; also, acting freely or quickly; energetic; agile; brisk; busy; in *gram.*, representing the subject as acting (as, the *active* voice, comprising those forms of transitive verbs which represent the subject as acting, as *broke* in 'John broke the window,' and also all forms of intransitive verbs; an *active* verb-form: opposed to *passive*); also, transitive. **II.** *n.* In *gram.*, the active voice, or a verb-form belonging to it.—**ac′tive-ly,** *adv.*—**ac′tive-ness,** *n.*—**ac-tiv′i-ty** (-tiv′i-ti), *n.*; pl. *-ties* (-tiz). The state or quality of being active; active operation; energy; agility; also, a mode or course of action.

ac-ton (ak′tọn), *n.* [OF. *aqueton*, < Sp. *alcoton*, now *algodón*, < Ar. *al-qutun*, 'the cotton.'] A quilted jacket anciently worn under armor; also, a jacket plated with metal.

ac-tor (ak′tọr), *n.* [L.] One who acts; a doer; a performer, esp. on the stage; a player.—**ac′tress,** *n.* A female actor.

ac-tu-al (ak′ṭū-ạl), *a.* [OF. F. *actuel*, < LL. *actualis*, < L. *actus*: see *act, n.*] Pertaining to or exhibited in action; existing in act or fact; being in reality or now; real; present; not merely potential, possible, nominal, ideal, or future.—**ac′tu-al-ist,** *n.* One who deals with actualities; a realist. —**ac-tu-al′i-ty** (-al′i-ti), *n.*; pl. *-ties* (-tiz). Actual existence; reality; also, something actual; a fact.—**ac′tu-al-ize,** *v. t.*; *-ized, -izing.* To make actual; realize in action or fact.—**ac″tu-al-i-za′tion** (-i-zā′shọn), *n.*—**ac′tu-al-ly,** *adv.* As an actual fact; in reality; really.—**ac′tu-al-ness,** *n.*

ac-tu-a-ry (ak′ṭū-ạ̄-ri), *n.*; pl. *-ries* (-riz). [L. *actuarius*, clerk, keeper of accounts, < *actus*: see *act, n.*] A clerk or registrar; in insurance companies, etc., an officer who computes risks, rates, and the like according to probabilities indicated by recorded facts.—**ac-tu-a′ri-al** (-ā′ri-ạl), *a.*

ac-tu-ate (ak′ṭū-āt), *v. t.*; *-ated, -ating.* [ML. *actuatus*, pp. of *actuare*, < L. *actus*: see *act, n.*] To put into action; move; impel.—**ac-tu-a′tion** (-ā′shọn), *n.*—**ac′tu-a-tor,** *n.*

ac-u-ate (ak′ū-āt), *a.* [L. *acus*, needle.] Needle-shaped.

a-cu-i-ty (ạ-kū′i-ti), *n.* [F. *acuité*, < ML. *acuitas*, < L. *acuere*, sharpen.] Sharpness; acuteness.

a-cu-le-ate (ạ-kū′lẹ̄-ạ̄t), *a.* [L. *aculeatus.*] In *zoöl.*, having an aculeus or sting, as an insect; in *bot.*, prickly; fig., stinging; pungent; sharp; keen. Also **a-cu′le-at-ed** (-ā-ted).—**a-cu′le-o-late** (-ọ̄-lạ̄t), *a.* In *bot.*, having small prickles.

a-cu-le-us (ạ-kū′lẹ̄-us), *n.*; pl. *-lei* (-lẹ̄-ī). [L., dim. of *acus*, needle.] In *zoöl.*, the sting of a wasp, bee, etc.; in *bot.*, a prickle.

a-cu-men (ạ-kū′men), *n.* [L., point, sharpness, < *acuere*, sharpen.] Sharpness or keenness of insight; mental acuteness.—**a-cu′mi-nate** (-mi-nāt), *v. t.*; *-nated, -nating.* [L. *acuminatus*, pp. of *acuminare*, < *acumen.*] To make sharp or pointed; render acute or keen. —**a-cu′mi-nate** (-nạ̄t), *a.* In *bot., zoöl.*, etc., pointed; tapering to a point.—**a-cu-mi-na′tion** (-nā′shọn), *n.* The act or the result of acuminating; sharpness; a sharp

Acuminate Leaf.

(variable) ḍ as d or j, ṣ as s or sh, ṭ as t or ch, ẓ as z or zh; ọ, F. cloche; ü, F. menu; ċh, Sc. loch; ṅ, F. bonbon; ′, primary accent; ″, secondary accent; †, obsolete; <, from; +, and; =, equals. See also lists at beginning of book.

or tapering point.—**a-cu′mi-nous,** *a.* Characterized by acumen; acute.—**ac-u-min-u-late** (ak-ū-min′ū-lāt), *a.* In *bot.*, having a small terminal point.

ac-u-pres-sure (ak′ū-presh-ụr), *n.* [L. *acus*, needle, + *pressura*, pressure.] In *surg.*, compression of a blood-vessel with a needle or wire inserted into the tissues to check the flow of blood, as during amputation.

ac-u-punc-ture (ak′ū-pungk-tụr), *n.* [L. *acus*, needle, + *punctura*, puncture.] In *surg.*, puncture or pricking with needles, as in the treatment of neuralgia.

a-cush-la (ạ-kush′lạ), *n.* [Ir., lit. 'O pulse' (of the heart).] Darling. [Ir.]

a-cute (ạ-kūt′). [L. *acutus*, pp. of *acuere*, sharpen.] **I.** *a.* Sharp in form; sharp-pointed; of an angle, being less than a right angle (or than 90°); sharp in action, effect, etc.; keen in intellect, perception, or sensibility; poignant; intense; brief and severe, as disease (opposed to *chronic*); high in pitch, as sound (opposed to *grave*); noting or having a particular accent (′) indicating orig. a raised pitch (as in ancient Greek), later stress (as in the Spanish *adiós*), quality of sound (as in the French *résumé*), vowel-length (as in Hungarian), etc. **II.** *n.* The acute accent. —**a-cute′=an″gled,** *a.* Having angles less than right angles. —**a-cute′ly,** *adv.*—**a-cute′ness,** *n.*

Acute Leaves.

a-cu-ti-fo-li-ate (ạ-kū-ti-fō′li-āt), *a.* [L. *acutus*, sharp, + *folium*, leaf.] In *bot.*, having sharp-pointed leaves.

-acy. [L. *-acia* and *-atia.*] A suffix of nouns of quality, state, office, etc., many of which accompany adjectives in *-acious* or nouns or adjectives in *-ate*, as in *contumacy, efficacy, fallacy*, etc., *advocacy, curacy, primacy*, etc., *accuracy, delicacy, legitimacy*, etc.

a-cyc-lic (a-sik′lik), *a.* [See *a-*¹.] In *bot.*, not cyclic; not arranged in whorls.

ad (ad), *n.* Shortened form of *advertisement.* [Colloq.]

ad-. [L. *ad-* (also, by assimilation to a following consonant, *ac-, af-, ag-, al-, an-, ap-*, etc.), repr. *ad*, prep., to, toward, at, about; akin to E. *at.*] A prefix meaning primarily 'to,' and implying motion, direction, change, intensification, addition, etc., occurring orig. in words from the Latin, but now sometimes used as an English formative.

-ad. [L. *ad*, to, toward.] An adverbial suffix meaning 'toward,' used in anatomical and other scientific terms, as *caudad, dextrad, dorsad.*

a-dac-ty-lous (a-dak′ti-lus), *a.* [Gr. ἀ- priv. + δάκτυλος, finger, toe.] In *zoöl.*, without fingers or toes.

ad-age (ad′āj), *n.* [F. *adage*, < L. *adagium*, < *ad*, to, + *-agium*, akin to *aio*, I say.] A pithy saying in current use; a proverb.

a-da-gio (ạ-dä′jō). [It., < *ad*, to, + *agio*, ease.] In *music*: **I.** *adv.* In a leisurely manner; slowly; when repeated (*adagio, adagio*), very slowly. **II.** *a.* Slow. **III.** *n.*; pl. *-gios* (-jōz). An adagio movement or piece.

Ad-am (ad′ạm), *n.* [Heb., 'man.'] The first human being (Gen. ii. 19); hence, 'original sin,' as inherited from him.—**Adam and Eve,** the puttyroot (plant). [U. S.]—**Adam's ale,** water. [Colloq.]—**Adam's apple,** a projection of the thyroid cartilage at the front of the (male) throat; also, a kind of lime (*Citrus medica*); the plantain, the fruit of *Musa paradisiaca*; the crape jasmine, *Tabernæmontana coronaria.*—**Adam's needle and thread,** a species of yucca, *Yucca filamentosa*, much cultivated for ornament.

ad-a-mant (ad′ạ-mant), *n.* [OF. *adamant*, < L. *adamas* (*adamant-*), < Gr. ἀδάμας (ἀδαμαντ-), 'unconquerable,' < ἀ- priv. + δαμᾶν, conquer: see *tame.*] In ancient times, some impenetrably hard substance: variously identified later, esp. as the diamond or a lodestone. Also fig.—**ad″a-man-te′an**† (-man-tē′ạn), *a.* Adamantine.—**ad-a-man′-tine** (-tin), *a.* Of or like adamant; impenetrably hard; unyielding; in *mineral.*, like a diamond in luster.

A-dam-ic (a-dam′ik), *a.* Of or pertaining to Adam.

Ad-am-ite (ad′ạ-mīt), *n.* A descendant of Adam; a human being; also, an imitator of Adam in going naked. —**Ad-am-it-ic** (ad-ạ-mit′ik), *a.*

a-dapt (ạ-dapt′), *v. t.* [L. *adaptare*, < *ad*, to, + *aptare*, adjust, fit, < *aptus*: see *apt.*] To make suitable to requirements; adjust or modify fittingly; accommodate or conform (*to*).—**a-dapt′a-ble,** *a.* Capable of being adapted.—**a-dapt-a-bil′i-ty** (-bil′i-ti), **a-dapt′a-ble-ness,** *n.*—**ad-ap-ta-tion** (ad-ap-tā′shọn), *n.* [ML. *adaptatio(n-).*] The act of adapting, or the resulting state; something produced by adapting.—**a-dap-ta-tive** (ạ-dap′tạ-tiv), *a.* Adaptive. —**a-dapt′ed-ness,** *n.*—**a-dapt′er,** *n.* One who or that which adapts; a connecting or accommodating piece in an apparatus.—**a-dap′tive,** *a.* Serving to adapt; showing adaptation.—**a-dap′tive-ly,** *adv.*—**a-dap′tive-ness,** *n.*

A-dar (ạ-där′), *n.* [Heb.] In the Jewish calendar, the sixth month (29 or 30 days) of the civil year and the twelfth of the ecclesiastical year, beginning in February or in the first part of March.

add (ad), *v.* [L. *addere*, < *ad*, to, + *-dere*, put: see *do*¹.] **I.** *tr.* To join, as one thing to another or to an aggregate; put or give by way of augmentation or supplement; also, to say further; in *math.*, to find the sum of (quantities). **II.** *intr.* To make or form an addition; in *math.*, to find the sum of quantities. —**add′a-ble,** *a.* Capable of being added.

Addax.

ad-dax (ad′aks), *n.* [L.; of African origin.] A large antelope, *Addax nasomaculatus*, of north-eastern Africa and Arabia, with loosely spiral horns.

ad-den-dum (a-den′dum), *n.*; pl. *-da* (-dạ). [L., neut. gerundive of *addere*, E. *add.*] A thing to be added; an addition; in *mach.*, that part of a tooth which projects beyond the pitch-circle or pitch-line of a toothed wheel or rack.—**ad-den′dum=cir″cle,** *n.* In *mach.*, an imaginary circle touching the ends of the teeth of a toothed wheel.

add-er¹ (ad′ėr), *n.* One who adds; a machine for adding.

ad-der² (ad′ėr), *n.* [For *nadder* (*a nadder* being taken as *an adder*), < AS. *nædre.*] The common European viper, *Vipera* (or *Pelias*) *berus*, a small venomous serpent; also, any of various other serpents, venomous or harmless.—**ad′der's=mouth,** *n.* Either of two small terrestrial orchids, *Achroanthes monophylla* and *A. unifolia*, natives of North America, bearing a terminal raceme of minute white or greenish flowers.—**ad′der's=tongue,** *n.* A fern of the genus *Ophioglossum* (so called from the form of its fruiting spike); also, any of certain other plants, as the American species of dog-tooth violet.

Adder (*Vipera berus*).

add-i-ble (ad′i-bl), *a.* See *addable.*

ad-dict (ạ-dikt′), *v. t.* [L. *addictus*, pp. of *addicere*, adjudge, deliver, devote, < *ad*, to, + *dicere*, say.] To give over, as to a habit or pursuit; apply or devote habitually (*to*), esp. through taste or inclination: chiefly reflexive or in the passive.—**ad-dict′,** *n.* One who is addicted to some habit or practice, as to the use of a drug.—**ad-dict′ed-ness,** *n.*—**ad-dic-tion** (ạ-dik′shọn), *n.* [L. *addictio(n-).*] The state of being addicted; inclination.

ad-di-o (äd-dē′ō), *interj.* [It.] Adieu; farewell.

Ad-di-so-ni-an (ad-i-sō′ni-ạn), *a.* Pertaining to or characteristic of the English author Joseph Addison (1672–1719) or his style of writing.

Ad-di-son's (ad′i-sọnz) **dis-ease′.** [From T. *Addison* (1793–1860), English physician, who first described it.] In *pathol.*, a disease characterized by asthenia, digestive disturbances, and (usually) a brownish coloration of the skin: due to disturbance of function of the suprarenal glands.

ad-di-ta-ment (ad′i-tạ-mẹnt), *n.* [L. *additamentum*, < *addere*, E. *add.*] An addition; an adjunct.

ad-di-tion (a-dish′ọn), *n.* [OF. *addicion* (F. *addition*), < L. *additio(n-)*, < *addere*, E. *add.*] The process of adding; the uniting of quantities in one sum, or the branch of arithmetic which treats of it; also, something added; an accession; an adjunct; in *law*, a particularizing designation added to a person's name (as, John Doe, *Plaintiff*); in *her.*, a charge added to a coat of arms as a mark of honor.—**ad-di′tion-al,** *a.* Added; supplementary.—**ad-di′tion-al-ly,** *adv.*

ad-di-tive (ad′i-tiv), *a.* [LL. *additivus.*] Added; involving addition.—**ad′di-tive-ly,** *adv.*

ad-dle (ad′l), *a.* [AS. *adela*, liquid filth, mud.] Bad or rotten, as eggs; hence, muddled, as the brain; mentally weak; witless.—**ad′dle,** *v. t.* or *i.*; *-dled, -dling.* To make or become addle.—**ad′dle=brain, ad′dle=head, ad′dle=pate,** *n.* One whose brain is muddled; a foolish or witless person.—**ad′dle=brained, ad′dle=head″ed, ad′dle=pat″ed** (-pā″ted), *a.*

ad-dress (ạ-dres′), *v.* [OF. *adrecier* (F. *adresser*), ult. < L. *ad*, to, + *directus*, straight, direct.] **I.** *tr.* To direct (*to*); aim, turn, send, or consign (*to*); apply (one's self) in action or speech (*to*); utter or write (*to*); inscribe as to be sent (*to*); also, to accost with words; direct speech or writing to; pay one's addresses or court to. **II.**† *intr.* To address one's self; appeal; also, to prepare.—**ad-dress′,** *n.* The act or the manner of addressing; personal bearing in intercourse; accost; also, speech or writing addressed, esp. a formal discourse or a petition; also, a direction as to name and abode, as inscribed on a letter, etc.; also, the place at which one may be reached by letter or otherwise; also, attention paid in courtship (usually in *pl.*); also, ready skill; adroitness; dexterity.—**ad-dress-ee′** (-ē′), *n.* One to whom something is addressed.—**ad-dress′er, ad-dress′or,** *n.*

ad-duce (a-dūs′), *v. t.*; *-duced, -ducing.* [L. *adducere* (pp. *adductus*), < *ad*, to, + *ducere*, lead: cf. *adduct.*] To bring forward in argument; cite as pertinent or conclusive. —**ad-du-cent** (a-dū′sẹnt), *a.* In *physiol.*, drawing toward; adducting: applied to muscles, etc.—**ad-du′cer,** *n.*—**ad-du′ci-ble,** *a.* Capable of being adduced.

ad-duct (a-dukt′), *v. t.* [L. *adductus*, pp. of *adducere*: see *adduce.*] In *physiol.*, to draw toward the main axis: opposed to *abduct.*—**ad-duc-tion** (a-duk′shọn), *n.* [ML. *adductio(n-)*.] The act of adducting or of adducing.—**ad-duc′tive,** *a.* Serving to draw or bring toward or to something.—**ad-duc′tor,** *n.* In *physiol.*, an adducting muscle.

-ade. [F. *-ade*, < Pr., Sp., or Pg. *-ada*, It. *-ata*, < L. *-ata*, fem.; also Sp. or Pg. *-ado*, It. *-ato*, < L. *-atus*, masc.] A suffix of nouns denoting action or process, the product or result of action, the person or persons acting, etc., as in *accolade, ambuscade, barricade, brigade, lemonade, renegade.*

a-deem (a-dēm′), *v. t.* [L. *adimere* (pp. *ademptus*), take to one's self from another, < *ad*, to, + *emere*, take.] To take away; in *law*, to revoke (a legacy), as by a different disposition of the bequest, or as by delivery in advance of the thing bequeathed or its equivalent.

a-de-lan-ta-do (ä″ᴛʜā-län-tä′ᴛʜō), *n.* [Sp.] Formerly, in Spanish use, the governor of a province.

-adelphous. An adjective termination from Gr. ἀδελφός, brother, in botanical terms denoting the number of bundles or sets of united stamens, as in *diadelphous, monadelphous, polyadelphous.*

a-demp-tion (a-demp′shọn), *n.* [L. *ademptio(n-)*, < *adimere*: see *adeem.*] The act of adeeming.

aden-, adeni-, adeno-. Forms of Gr. ἀδήν (ἀδεν-), gland, used in combination.—**ad-e-nal-gia** (ad-ẹ-nal′jiạ), *n.* [NL. (Gr. ἄλγος, pain).] In *pathol.*, pain in a gland.—**a-den-i-form** (a-den′i-fôrm or ad′ẹ-ni-), *a.* [+ *-form.*] Gland-like. —**ad-e-ni′tis** (-nī′tis), *n.* [NL.] In *pathol.*, inflammation of a gland.—**ad′e-noid.** [Gr. ἀδενοειδής: see *-oid.*] **I.** *a.* Gland-like; glandular; pertaining to the lymphatic glands (as, *adenoid* tissue, lymphoid tissue). **II.** *n.* In *pathol.*, a hypertrophied mass of adenoid tissue in the upper pharynx, as in children, preventing nasal breathing: usually in *pl.*—**ad-e-noi′dal** (-noi′dạl), *a.*—**ad-e-nol′ọ-gy** (-nol′ọ-ji), *n.* [+ *-logy.*] The science of the glands.—**ad-e-no′ma** (-nō′mạ), *n.*; pl. *-mas* or *-mata* (-mạ-tạ). [NL.: see *-oma.*] In *pathol.*, a tumor originating in a gland; a tumor of gland-like structure.—**ad-e-nom′a-tous** (-nom′ạ-tus), *a.*—**ad-e-nop′a-thy** (-nop′ạ-thi), *n.* [+ *-pathy.*] Disease of glands.—**ad″e-no-path′ic** (-nọ-path′ik), *a.*—**ad-e-not′o-my** (-not′ọ-mi), *n.* [+ *-tomy.*] Dissection or incision of a gland.

a-dept (ạ-dept′). [L. *adeptus*, pp. of *adipisci*, attain, < *ad*, to, + *apisci*, reach.] **I.** *a.* Thoroughly versed; proficient. **II.** *n.* One who is adept; a proficient; formerly, a master of occult science.—**a-dept′ness,** *n.*

ad-e-quate (ad′ẹ-kwạt), *a.* [L. *adæquatus*, pp. of *adæquare*, make or be equal to, < *ad*, to, + *æquare*, make equal, E. *equate.*] Equal to requirement; commensurate; sufficient; competent; suitable; fitting: often with *to.*—**ad′e-qua-cy** (-kwạ-si), **ad′e-quate-ness,** *n.*—**ad′e-quate-ly,** *adv.*

a-des-my (a-des′mi), *n.* [Gr. ἀ- priv. + δεσμός, bond.] In *bot.*, abnormal division or separation of organs.

ad-fect-ed (ad-fek′ted), *a.* [L. *adfectus*, later *affectus*, pp.: see *affect*[1].] In *alg.*, containing different powers of the unknown quantity.

ad-here (ad-hēr′), *v. i.*; *-hered, -hering.* [L. *adhærere* (pp. *adhæsus*), < *ad*, to, + *hærere*, stick.] To stick fast (*to*); cleave; cling; fig., to hold firmly; remain attached or faithful; also, to belong; also, to be consistent†; agree†.—**ad-her′ence** (-hēr′ẹns), *n.* The act or state of adhering (usually fig.); attachment; fidelity.—**ad-her′ent. I.** *a.* Adhering; attached; in *bot.*, adnate. **II.** *n.* One who adheres, as to a leader, party, or cause; a follower; a partizan.—**ad-her′ent-ly,** *adv.*—**ad-her′er,** *n.*—**ad-he′sion** (-hē′zhọn), *n.* [L. *adhæsio(n-)*.] The act or state of adhering; a holding fast; attachment; assent; also, something that adheres; in *physics*, molecular attraction exerted between the surfaces of bodies in contact.—**ad-he′sion-al,** *a.* —**ad-he′sive** (-siv), *a.* Tending to adhere; sticking or holding fast.—**ad-he′sive-ly,** *adv.*—**ad-he′sive-ness,** *n.* Adhesive quality; in *phren.*, the faculty of forming attachments, as of friendship.

ad-hib-it (ad-hib′it), *v. t.* [L. *adhibitus*, pp. of *adhibere*, < *ad*, to, + *habere*, have, hold.] To put or give (*to*); affix; apply; administer; also, to admit.—**ad-hi-bi′tion** (-hi-bish′ọn), *n.*

ad-i-a-bat-ic (ad″i-ạ-bat′ik), *a.* [Gr. ἀδιάβατος, impassable, < ἀ- priv. + διαβατός, passable, < διαβαίνειν, pass over: see *diabetes.*] In *physics*, without transmission (gain or loss) of heat; noting or pertaining to a change in the volume of a gas during which no heat enters or leaves it. —**ad″i-a-bat′i-cal-ly,** *adv.*

ad-i-an-tum (ad-i-an′tum), *n.* [L., < Gr. ἀδίαντον, maidenhair, lit. 'unwetted,' < ἀ- priv. + διαίνειν, to wet.] A maidenhair fern.

ad-i-aph-o-ra (ad-i-af′ọ-rạ), *n. pl.* [NL., < Gr. ἀδιάφορα, neut. pl. of ἀδιάφορος, indifferent, < ἀ- priv. + διάφορος, different, < διαφέρειν, differ.] Things morally indifferent; non-essentials in faith or conduct.—**ad-i-aph′o-rism,** *n.* Indifferentism; religious tolerance.—**ad-i-aph′o-rous,** *a.* Indifferent or non-essential, esp. morally; neutral.

ad-i-a-ther-ma-nous (ad″i-ạ-thėr′mạ-nus), *a.* [See *a-*[1].] In *physics*, not diathermanous; impermeable by radiant heat.—**ad″i-a-ther′man-cy** (-mạn-si), *n.*

a-dieu (ạ-dū′, F. à-dyė). [F., 'to God,' < L. *ad*, to, and *Deus*, God.] **I.** *interj.* A parting salutation commending one to the divine care; good-by; farewell. **II.** *n.*; pl. *adieus*, F. *adieux* (à-dyė). A farewell.

a-di-ós (ä-dē-ōs′), *interj.* [Sp.] Adieu; farewell.

ad-i-po-cere (ad′i-pọ-sēr″), *n.* [L. *adeps* (*adip-*), fat, + *cera*, wax.] A waxy substance sometimes formed from dead animal bodies in moist burial-places or under water.—**ad-i-po′cer-ous** (-pos′ẹ-rus), *a.*

ad-i-po-ma (ad-i-pō′mạ), *n.*; pl. *-mas* or *-mata* (-mạ-tạ). [NL., < L. *adeps* (*adip-*), fat: see *-oma.*] In *pathol.*, a fatty tumor; a lipoma.—**ad-i-pom′a-tous** (-pom′ạ-tus), *a.*

ad-i-pose (ad′i-pōs). [L. *adeps* (*adip-*), fat.] **I.** *a.* Fatty; fat. **II.** *n.* Animal fat.—**ad′i-pose-ness, ad-i-pos′i-ty** (-pos′i-ti), *n.*—**ad-i-po′sis** (-pō′sis), *n.* [NL.] The accumulation of fat; obesity.

a-dip-si-a (a-dip′si-ạ̈), *n.* [NL., < Gr. ἄδιψος, not thirsty, < ἀ- priv. + δίψα, thirst.] In *med.*, absence of thirst.

ad-it (ad′it), *n.* [L. *aditus*, < *adire*, approach, < *ad*, to, + *ire*, go.] An approach or entrance; a nearly horizontal passage leading into a mine; also, access; admission.

ad-ja-cence (ạ-jā′sẹns), *n.* The state of being adjacent; adjacency.—**ad-ja′cen-cy,** *n.*; pl. *-cies* (-siz). The state of being adjacent; contiguity; proximity; also, that which is adjacent (chiefly in *pl.*).

ad-ja-cent (ạ-jā′sẹnt), *a.* [L. *adjacens* (*-ent-*), ppr. of *adjacere*, lie near, < *ad*, to, + *jacere*, lie.] Lying near (*to*); neighboring; contiguous.—**ad-ja′cent-ly,** *adv.*

ad-jec-ti-val (aj-ek-tī′vạl or aj′ek-ti-vạl), *a.* Pertaining to or used as an adjective.—**ad-jec-ti′val-ly,** *adv.*

ad-jec-tive (aj′ek-tiv). [L. *adjectivus*, < *adjicere*, put to, add, < *ad*, to, + *jacere*, throw.] **I.** *a.* Additional; subsidiary; dependent; in *gram.*, used with a substantive to qualify its meaning; adjectival; in *law*, pertaining to procedure, the subsidiary part of law (as, *adjective* law); in *dyeing*, of colors, requiring a mordant or the like to render them permanent (opposed to *substantive*). **II.** *n.* In *gram.*, a word used to qualify the meaning of a substantive, as by expressing an attribute.—**ad′jec-tive-ly,** *adv.*

ad-join (ạ-join′), *v.* [OF. *ajoindre* (F. *adjoindre*), < L. *adjungere* (pp. *adjunctus*), < *ad*, to, + *jungere*, join.] **I.** *tr.* To join (*to*); attach; annex; also, to be in connection or contact with; abut on; be contiguous to. **II.** *intr.* To be contiguous.—**ad-join′ing,** *p. a.* Abutting; contiguous.

ad-journ (ạ-jėrn′), *v.* [OF. *ajorner* (F. *ajourner*), < L. *ad*, to, + *diurnus*, daily, < *dies*, day.] **I.** *tr.* To put off to another day; postpone; suspend until later; also, to transfer for procedure elsewhere. **II.** *intr.* To postpone, suspend, or transfer proceedings.—**ad-journ′ment,** *n.* The act of adjourning, or the state or period of being adjourned.

ad-judge (ạ-juj′), *v. t.*; *-judged*, *-judging.* [OF. *ajuger* (F. *adjuger*), < L. *adjudicare*: see *adjudicate.*] To award or assign judicially; also, to sentence or condemn (as, "rebel spirits *adjudged* to hell": Milton's "Paradise Lost," iv. 823); also, to pronounce or decree by judicial sentence (as, he was *adjudged* guilty); also, to settle judicially; adjudicate; also, to judge† or deem†.—**ad-judge′a-ble,** *a.* That may be adjudged.—**ad-judg′ment,** *n.* Adjudication.

ad-ju-di-cate (ạ-jö′di-kāt), *v.*; *-cated*, *-cating.* [L. *adjudicatus*, pp. of *adjudicare*, < *ad*, to, + *judicare*, E. *judge*, *v.*] **I.** *tr.* To adjudge; pronounce or decree by judicial sentence; settle judicially; try and determine; pass judgment upon. **II.** *intr.* To sit in judgment; pass judgment (*upon*).—**ad-ju-di-ca′tion** (-kā′shọn), *n.* [L. *adjudicatio*(*n-*).] The act of adjudicating; also, a judicial decision or sentence.—**ad-ju′di-ca-tor,** *n.*

ad-junct (aj′ungkt). [L. *adjunctus*, pp. of *adjungere*: see *adjoin.*] **I.** *a.* Joined to a thing or person, esp. subordinately; associated; auxiliary. **II.** *n.* Something joined, annexed, or pertaining; an accompaniment; an accessory; also, a subordinate colleague; an associate or assistant; in *gram.*, a qualifying word, phrase, etc., depending on a particular member of a sentence.—**ad-junc-tion** (a-jungk′shọn), *n.* [L. *adjunctio*(*n-*), < *adjungere.*] The act of joining (*to*); addition.—**ad-junc′tive,** *a.* Forming an adjunct.—**ad′junct-ly,** *adv.*

ad-ju-ra-tion (aj-ọ̈-rā′shọn), *n.* [L. *adjuratio*(*n-*).] The act of adjuring; a solemn charge or appeal.—**ad-ju-ra-to-ry** (ạ-jö′rạ-tọ̄-ri), *a.* Making adjuration.

ad-jure (ạ-jör′), *v. t.*; *-jured*, *-juring.* [L. *adjurare*, < *ad*, to, + *jurare*, swear.] To charge as on oath or under some grave penalty; entreat solemnly.—**ad-jur′er, ad-jur′or,** *n.*

ad-just (ạ-just′), *v. t.* [OF. *ajuster*, orig. 'put beside' (< L. *ad*, to, + *juxta*, near), but later associated with L. *justus*, just.] To dispose or arrange properly; regulate; settle; also, to arrange conformably (*to*); accommodate; adapt.—**ad-just′a-ble,** *a.* Capable of being adjusted.—**ad-just′a-bly,** *adv.*—**ad-just′er,** *n.*—**ad-just′ive,** *a.* Serving to adjust.—**ad-just′ment,** *n.* The act of adjusting, or the state of being adjusted; also, a means of adjusting.

ad-ju-tage (aj′ọ̈-tāj), *n.* See *ajutage.*

ad-ju-tant (aj′ọ̈-tạnt), *n.* [L. *adjutans* (*-ant-*), ppr. of *adjutare*: see *aid.*] An assistant; an aid; *milit.*, a staff-officer appointed to assist the commanding officer in details of duty; in *zoöl.*, the adjutant-bird.—**ad′ju-tan-cy,** *n.*—**ad′ju-tant=bird,** *n.* A large East Indian stork, *Leptoptilus argala.*—**ad′ju-tant=gen′er-al,** *n.*; pl. *adjutant-generals* or *adjutants-general. Milit.*, an executive officer on the staff of a commanding general or a commander-in-chief.—**ad′ju-tant-ship,** *n.*

ad-ju-vant (aj′ọ̈-vạnt). [L. *adjuvans* (*-ant-*), ppr. of *adjuvare*: see *aid.*] **I.** *a.* Aiding; auxiliary. **II.** *n.* An aid; an auxiliary; a subsidiary ingredient in a medical prescription.

ad-meas-ure (ad-mezh′ụ̈r), *v. t.*; *-ured*, *-uring.* [OF. *amesurer*, < L. *ad*, to, + *mensurare*, measure.] To measure off or out; apportion; assign a portion to (a person, etc.); measure.—**ad-meas′ure-ment,** *n.* Measurement; apportionment; measure.—**ad-meas′ur-er,** *n.*

ad-min-i-cle (ad-min′i-kl), *n.* [L. *adminiculum*, a prop, stay, support, aid.] An aid; an auxiliary; in *law*, a corroborative evidence.—**ad-mi-nic′u-lar** (-mi-nik′ụ̄-lạ̈r), *a.* Auxiliary; corroborative.

ad-min-is-ter (ad-min′is-tėr), *v.* [L. *administrare* (pp. *administratus*), < *ad*, to, + *ministrare*, serve, E. *minister*, *v.*] **I.** *tr.* To manage (affairs, a government, an estate, etc.); have executive charge of; conduct; also, to dispense, apply, or give (*to*). **II.** *intr.* To serve as administrator; also, to contribute; minister.—**ad-min′is-tra-ble** (-trạ-bl), *a.* Capable of being administered.—**ad-min′is-trant** (-trạnt). **I.** *a.* Administering. **II.** *n.* An administrator.—**ad-min′is-trate** (-trāt), *v. t.* or *i.*; *-trated*, *-trating.* [L. *administratus*, pp.] To administer.—**ad-min-is-tra′tion** (-trā′shọn), *n.* [L. *administratio*(*n-*).] The act of administering; esp., the administering of public affairs by executive officers; government; also, the officers, collectively, or their period of service; in *law*, authorized management of the estate of a deceased person.—**ad-min′is-tra-tive** (-trạ-tiv), *a.* Pertaining to administration; executive.—**ad-min′is-tra-tive-ly,** *adv.*—**ad-min′is-tra-tor** (-trā-tọr), *n.* [L.] One who administers; in *law*, a person appointed, as by a court, to take charge of the estate of a deceased person.—**ad-min′is-tra-tor-ship,** *n.*—**ad-min-is-tra′trix** (-triks), *n.*; pl. *administratrices* (ad-min″is-trạ-trī′sēz). [NL.] A female administrator.

ad-mi-ra-ble (ad′mi-rạ-bl), *a.* [L. *admirabilis.*] Wonderful†; also, worthy to be admired; fine; excellent.—**ad′mi-ra-ble-ness,** *n.*—**ad′mi-ra-bly,** *adv.*

ad-mi-ral (ad′mi-rạl), *n.* [OF. F. *amiral*, < Ar. *amīr-al-bahr*, commander of the sea.] A naval officer of the highest rank; a naval officer of a high rank, of which there are different grades (as, in the U. S. navy, admiral, vice-admiral, and rear-admiral); the commander-in-chief of a fleet; the officer in charge of a fleet of merchant vessels or the like; also, the flag-ship of an admiral; the most considerable ship of a fleet of merchantmen or the like; also, any of various handsome butterflies, as *Vanessa atalanta* ('red admiral').—**ad′mi-ral-ship,** *n.* The office or position of an admiral.—**ad′mi-ral-ty** (-ti), *n.*; pl. *-ties* (-tiz). [OF. *amiraulte* (F. *amirauté*).] The office or jurisdiction of an admiral, or of an official board presiding over maritime affairs; the officials or the department of state having charge of naval affairs, as in Great Britain; maritime law, or a tribunal administering it; [*cap.*] the official building, at London, of the British commissioners for naval affairs.

ad-mi-ra-tion (ad-mi-rā′shọn), *n.* [L. *admiratio*(*n-*).] The act of admiring; wonder (archaic); a feeling of wonder, pleasure, and approbation; the object of this feeling.

ad-mire (ad-mīr′), *v.*; *-mired*, *-miring.* [L. *admirari*, < *ad*, to, at, + *mirari*, wonder.] **I.** *tr.* To wonder or marvel at (archaic); regard with wonder, pleasure, and approbation. **II.** *intr.* To wonder (archaic); feel admiration.—**ad-mir′er,** *n.* One who admires; a lover.—**ad-mir′ing-ly,** *adv.*

ad-mis-si-ble (ad-mis′i-bl), *a.* [ML. *admissibilis.*] Capable or worthy of being admitted.—**ad-mis-si-bil′i-ty** (-bil′i-ti), **ad-mis′si-ble-ness,** *n.*—**ad-mis′si-bly,** *adv.*

ad-mis-sion (ad-mish′ọn), *n.* [L. *admissio*(*n-*).] The act of admitting, or the state or privilege of being admitted; access; entrance; reception, as into an office; a fee charged for entrance; allowance; acknowledgment; an acknowledgment of the truth of something.—**Admission Day,** in some States of the U. S., a legal holiday commemorating the day of admission of the individual State into the Union: it is Feb. 14 in Arizona, Sept. 9 in California, and Oct. 31 in Nevada.

ad-mis-sive (ad-mis′iv), *a.* Tending to admit.

ad-mit (ad-mit′), *v.*; *-mitted, -mitting.* [L. *admittere* (pp. *admissus*), < *ad,* to, + *mittere,* send.] **I.** *tr.* To grant or afford entrance to; let in; also, to let attain to a position, right, privilege, etc.; also, to permit or allow; also, to grant to be true; concede; acknowledge or confess. **II.** *intr.* To afford entrance; also, to give allowance or opportunity, or afford possibility (with *of*).—**ad-mit′tance,** *n.* The act of admitting; permission or right to enter; in *elect.*, the reciprocal of impedance.—**ad-mit′ted-ly,** *adv.* By admission; confessedly.—**ad-mit′ter,** *n.*

ad-mix (ad-miks′), *v. t.* [L. *admixtus,* pp. of *admiscere,* < *ad,* to, + *miscere,* mix.] To add in mixing; mix in.—**ad-mix′ture** (-ṭụr), *n.* Addition by mixing; also, an added ingredient in a mixture.

ad-mon-ish (ad-mon′ish), *v. t.* [OF. *amonester* (F. *admonester*), < L. *admonere* (pp. *admonitus*), advise, < *ad,* to, + *monere,* remind.] To remind, as of duty; advise or caution as to conduct; warn; reprove gently.—**ad-mon′ish-er,** *n.*—**ad-mon′ish-ing-ly,** *adv.*—**ad-mon′ish-ment,** *n.* Admonition.—**ad-mo-ni′tion** (-mọ-nish′ọn), *n.* [L. *admonitio(n-)*.] The act of admonishing; counsel; warning; gentle reproof.—**ad-mon′i-tor,** *n.* [L.] One who admonishes; a monitor.—**ad-mon′i-to-ry** (-tọ-ri), *a.* Serving to admonish.

Adnate Stipules.

ad-nate (ad′nāt), *a.* [L. *adnatus,* pp. of *adnasci,* grow to, < *ad,* to, + *nasci,* be born, grow.] In *bot.*, *zoöl.*, etc., grown fast to something; congenitally attached.—**ad-na′tion** (-nā′shọn), *n.* Adnate condition.

a-do (ạ-dö′), *n.* [Orig. inf., ME. *ado, at do,* to do.] Doing; activity; fuss; trouble; to-do.

a-do-be (ạ-dō′bẹ). [Sp.] **I.** *n.* A sun-dried brick; also, clay for making such bricks. **II.** *a.* Made of or suitable for making adobes.

ad-o-les-cence (ad-ọ-les′ẹns), *n.* The adolescent state or period; youth: extending from about fourteen to twenty-five years of age in man, and from about twelve to twenty-one in woman. Also **ad-o-les′cen-cy.**

ad-o-les-cent (ad-ọ-les′ẹnt). [L. *adolescens* (*-ent-*), ppr. of *adolescere,* grow up.] **I.** *a.* Growing to manhood or womanhood; youthful. **II.** *n.* An adolescent person.

Ad-o-na-i (ad-ọ-nā′ī or a-dō′nī), *n.* [Heb. *adōnāi,* lit. 'my lords,' < *adōn,* lord.] A Hebrew name of God, reverentially used in reading as a substitute for the 'ineffable name,' Heb. JHVH, commonly rendered in English by *Jehovah.* See *Jehovah.*

A-don-ic (ạ-don′ik). [F. *adonique.*] **I.** *a.* Of or pertaining to Adonis, a beautiful youth of Greek mythology; in *pros.*, noting a verse consisting of a dactyl and a spondee or trochee, said to have been so designated because of its use in songs at the festival of Adonis. **II.** *n.* An Adonic verse or line.

A-do-nis (ạ-dō′nis), *n.* [From *Adonis,* in Greek mythology, a beautiful youth loved by Aphrodite (Venus).] A beautiful youth or man; a dandy; a beau.

a-dopt (ạ-dopt′), *v. t.* [L. *adoptare,* < *ad,* to, + *optare,* choose.] To take (a person) into a particular relationship, as of heir, friend, or citizen; esp., to take as one's own child, specif. by a formal legal act; in general, to take as one's own; take up and use as one's own, as a method, idea, policy, etc.; esp., to accept formally, as by voting, as a resolution, constitution, etc.—**a-dopt′a-ble,** *a.* That may be adopted.—**a-dopt′er,** *n.*—**a-dop-tion** (ạ-dop′shọn), *n.* [L. *adoptio(n-)*.] The act of adopting, or the state of being adopted.—**a-dop′tion-ism,** *n.* In *eccles. hist.*, the doctrine that Christ as man is the Son of God by adoption only.—**a-dop′tion-ist,** *n.*—**a-dop′tive,** *a.* [L. *adoptivus.*] Tending to adopt; related by adoption; adopted.—**a-dop′tive-ly,** *adv.*

a-dor-a-ble (ạ-dōr′ạ-bl), *a.* [F. *adorable,* < L. *adorabilis.*] Worthy of being adored.—**a-dor-a-bil′i-ty** (-bil′i-ti), **a-dor′a-ble-ness,** *n.*—**a-dor′a-bly,** *adv.*

ad-o-ra-tion (ad-ọ-rā′shọn), *n.* [F. *adoration,* < L. *adoratio(n-)*.] The act of adoring; worship; reverent and fervent homage or love.

a-dore (ạ-dōr′), *v.*; *adored, adoring.* [OF. F. *adorer,* < L. *adorare,* < *ad,* to, + *orare,* speak, pray.] **I.** *tr.* To offer worship to; pay divine honors to; venerate; regard with the utmost respect and love; idolize. **II.** *intr.* To render adoration; worship.—**a-dor′er,** *n.*—**a-dor′ing-ly,** *adv.*

a-dorn (ạ-dôrn′), *v. t.* [OF. *adorner,* < L. *adornare,* < *ad,* to, + *ornare,* equip, deck.] To deck with ornaments; be an ornament to; ornament.—**a-dorn′er,** *n.*—**a-dorn′ing-ly,** *adv.*—**a-dorn′ment,** *n.* Ornamentation; ornament.

a-down (ạ-doun′), *adv.* and *prep.* [AS. *adūne, of dūne,* 'from (the) hill.'] Down. [Now poetic.]

ad-re-nal (ad-rē′nạl), *a.* [L. *ad,* to, at, + *ren,* kidney.] Situated near or on the kidney; suprarenal.—**ad-ren-a-lin, ad-ren-a-line** (ad-ren′ạ-lin or ad-rē′nạ-), *n.* In *physiol. chem.* and *phar.*, a white crystalline substance, the active principle of the suprarenal glands: obtained from the sheep, etc., and used as a hemostatic, etc. [Proprietary name of commercial product, *adrenalin.*]

a-drift (ạ-drift′), *adv.* Afloat without guidance; drifting.

a-drip (ạ-drip′), *adv.* In a dripping state.

a-droit (ạ-droit′), *a.* [F. *adroit,* < L. *ad,* to, + *directus,* straight, direct.] Skilful and ready in action; dexterous; clever.—**a-droit′ly,** *adv.*—**a-droit′ness,** *n.*

a-dry (ạ-drī′), *a.* [With *a-* as in *athirst.*] Dry; thirsty.

ad-sci-ti-tious (ad-si-tish′us), *a.* [L. *adscitus,* pp. of *adsciscere,* accept, take, < *ad,* to, + *sciscere,* learn, approve, < *scire,* know.] Derived from without; adventitious; extrinsic.—**ad-sci-ti′tious-ly,** *adv.*

ad-script (ad′skript), *a.* [L. *adscriptus,* pp. of *adscribere,* usually *ascribere*: see *ascribe.*] Written after: distinguished from *subscript* (as, in *Gr. gram.*, an iota *adscript*).

ad-scrip-tion (ad-skrip′shọn), *n.* Same as *ascription.*

ad-sorb (ad-sôrb′), *v. t.* [L. *ad,* to, + *sorbere,* suck in.] To gather (a gas, liquid, or dissolved substance) on a surface in a condensed layer.—**ad-sorp′tion** (-sôrp′shọn), *n.*—**ad-sorp′tive,** *a.*

ad-su-ki (ad-sö′ki) **bean.** See *adzuki bean.*

ad-u-la-ri-a (aḍ-ū-lā′ri-ạ), *n.* [From the *Adula* mountain group in Switzerland.] A transparent or translucent variety of orthoclase, often pearly or opalescent, as the moonstone.

ad-u-late (aḍ′ū-lāt), *v. t.*; *-lated, -lating.* [L. *adulatus,* pp. of *adulari,* fawn upon.] To flatter servilely.—**ad-u-la′tion** (-lā′shọn), *n.* [L. *adulatio(n-)*.] Servile flattery; hypocritical and fulsome praise.—**ad′u-la-tor,** *n.*—**ad′u-la-to-ry** (-lạ-tọ-ri), *a.* Characterized by adulation.

A-dul-lam-ite (ạ-dul′ạm-īt), *n.* [In allusion to the "cave of Adullam," to which the discontented followed David (1 Sam. xxii. 1, 2).] One of a group of British Liberals who seceded from their party in 1866.

a-dult (ạ-dult′). [L. *adultus,* pp. of *adolescere,* grow up.] **I.** *a.* Grown up; full-grown; mature. **II.** *n.* A person who is grown up or of age; a full-grown animal or plant.

a-dul-ter-ant (ạ-dul′tėr-ạnt). **I.** *a.* Adulterating. **II.** *n.* A substance used for adulterating.

a-dul-ter-ate (ạ-dul′tėr-āt), *v. t.*; *-ated, -ating.* [L. *adulteratus,* pp. of *adulterare,* commit adultery, debauch, also falsify, adulterate: see *adulterer.*] To debase by adding inferior elements; make impure by admixture.—**a-dul′ter-ate** (-ạt), *a.* Adulterated; adulterous.—**a-dul-ter-a′tion** (-ā′shọn), *n.* [L. *adulteratio(n-)*.] The act of adulterating; adulterated state; something adulterated.—**a-dul′ter-a-tor,** *n.*

a-dul-ter-er (ạ-dul′tėr-ėr), *n.* [From obs. *adulter,* v., < L. *adulterare,* commit adultery, < *adulter,* an adulterer, perhaps < *ad,* to, + *alter,* other.] A man guilty of adultery.—**a-dul′ter-ess,** *n.* A woman guilty of adultery.—**a-dul′ter-ine** (-in or -īn), *a.* [L. *adulterinus,* < *adulter,* an adulterer.] Born of or involving adultery; also, adulterated; impure.—**a-dul′ter-ous,** *a.* [L. *adulter.*] Characterized by or given to adultery; illicit; spurious.—**a-dul′ter-ous-ly,** *adv.*—**a-dul′ter-y,** *n.*; pl. *-ies* (-iz). [L. *adulterium,* < *adulter.*] Voluntary sexual intercourse on the part of a married person with any person of the opposite sex other than the lawful spouse; unchastity; also, adulteration† or sophistication†.

a-dult-ness (a̤-dult′nes), *n.* The state of being adult.
ad-um-brate (ad-um′brāt), *v. t.*; *-brated, -brating.* [L. *adumbratus*, pp. of *adumbrare*, < *ad*, to, + *umbrare*, shade, < *umbra*, a shadow.] To shade; overshadow; also, to shadow forth; indicate in a shadowy form.—**ad-um-bra′-tion** (-brā′sho̤n), *n.* [L. *adumbratio(n-)*.] The act of adumbrating; a shadowy or faint image.—**ad-um′bra-tive** (-bra̤-tiv), *a.* Shadowing forth; indicative.—**ad-um′bra-tive-ly,** *adv.*
a-dunc, a-dun-cous (a-dungk′, a-dung′kus), *a.* [L. *aduncus*, < *ad*, to, + *uncus*, hook.] Hooked; curved inward. Also **a-dun′cal, a-dun′cate** (-kāt).—**a-dun-ci-ty** (a-dun′si-ti), *n.* Hooked form.
a-dusk (a̤-dusk′), *adv.* In the dusk; in gloom.
a-dust[1] (a̤-dust′), *a.* Dusty.
a-dust[2] (a̤-dust′), *a.* [L. *adustus*, pp. of *adurere*, burn, scorch, < *ad*, to, + *urere*, burn.] Burned; parched; dried or darkened as by heat; sunburned; sallow; in the old physiology, affected by excess of bodily heat.—**a-dust′**[2]†, *v. t.* To burn; scorch; parch.
ad va-lo-rem (ad va-lō′rem). [L.] According to value: a phrase used, often adjectively, of duties or charges representing a fixed percentage of the certified value of goods. Cf. *specific duty*, under *specific*, *a.*
ad-vance (a̤d-vȧns′), *v.*; *-vanced, -vancing.* [OF. *avancier* (F. *avancer*), < LL. *abante*, from before, < L. *ab*, from, + *ante*, before.] **I.** *tr.* To move, put, or bring forward; bring onward in progress; further; promote; raise, as in rank or in rate; bring forward in time; make earlier; furnish beforehand or on credit; also, to adduce or propose. **II.** *intr.* To go forward; proceed; progress; rise.—**ad-vance′,** *n.* Forward movement or course; progress; advancement; rise, as in price or value; an approach or overture (usually in *pl.*); position forward or ahead; precedence; anticipation; that which is forward or ahead; a furnishing of money, goods, etc., beforehand; a loan.—**ad-vanced′,** *p. a.* Placed or being in advance; having gone beyond others or beyond the average; far on in progress, time, etc.—**ad-vance′-guard,** *n.* *Milit.*, a body of troops going before the main body to clear the way, guard against surprise, etc.—**ad-vance′ment,** *n.* The act of advancing; advanced state; furtherance; promotion; progress.—**ad-van′cer,** *n.*—**ad-van′cing-ly,** *adv.*
ad-van-tage (a̤d-vȧn′tāj), *n.* [OF. F. *avantage*, < *avant*, before, forward, < LL. *abante*: see *advance*.] A position affording special superiority; superiority, as of one over another; any means of prevailing or succeeding; a favorable circumstance; a benefit; a help; in *lawn-tennis*, the first point scored after deuce, or the resulting state of the score.—**ad-van′tage,** *v. t.*; *-taged, -taging.* [F. *avantager*.] To give or be an advantage to; benefit; profit; help.—**ad-van-ta-geous** (ad-va̤n-tā′jus), *a.* [F. *avantageux*.] Of advantage; favorable; beneficial; profitable.—**ad-van-ta′geous-ly,** *adv.*—**ad-van-ta′geous-ness,** *n.*
ad-vene (ad-vēn′), *v. i.*; *-vened, -vening.* [L. *advenire* (pp. *adventus*), come to, < *ad*, to, + *venire*, come.] To come (*to*); be present as something extraneous or adventitious; supervene.
ad-vent (ad′vent), *n.* [L. *adventus*, n., < *advenire*: see *advene*.] Coming or arrival; *eccles.*, [*l. c.* or *cap.*] the coming of Christ into the world; [*cap.*] a season (including four Sundays) preceding Christmas, commemorative of Christ's coming.—**Advent Sunday,** the first Sunday in Advent, being the Sunday nearest to St. Andrew's Day (Nov. 30).—**Ad′vent-ism,** *n.* The belief or doctrine that the expected second coming of Christ is near at hand.—**Ad′vent-ist,** *n.* A member of any of certain Christian denominations which maintain that the expected second coming of Christ is near at hand. Also called *Second Adventist.* See *Millerite*[1].
ad-ven-ti-tious (ad-ven-tish′us), *a.* [L. *adventicius*, < *advenire*: see *advene*.] Coming from without; foreign; extraneous; extrinsic; accidentally or casually present; in *bot.* and *zoöl.*, appearing in an abnormal or unusual position or place, as a root.—**ad-ven-ti′tious-ly,** *adv.*—**ad-ven-ti′tious-ness,** *n.*
ad-ven-tive (ad-ven′tiv), *a.* [L. *adventus*, pp. of *advenire*: see *advene*.] Extraneous; adventitious; in *bot.* and *zoöl.*, not indigenous, or not thoroughly naturalized, as exotic plants or animals.
ad-ven-ture (ad-ven′tu̇r), *n.* [OF. F. *aventure*, < ML. *adventura*, < L. *advenire*: see *advene*.] That which comes or happens to one†; chance†; hazard† or risk†; a hazardous or daring enterprise; an exciting experience; the undertaking of daring enterprises; a pecuniary venture; a commercial or other speculation.—**ad-ven′ture,** *v.*; *-tured, -turing.* [OF. F. *aventurer*.] **I.** *tr.* To risk; hazard; also, to venture on; dare. **II.** *intr.* To venture.—**ad-ven′tur-er,** *n.* One who adventures; a seeker of fortune in daring enterprises; one who lives by hazardous or equivocal methods; one who undertakes a commercial venture; a speculator.—**ad-ven′ture-some** (-sum), *a.* Adventurous.—**ad-ven′tur-ess,** *n.* A female adventurer, esp. one who goes about with a view to winning fortune, position, or the like by scheming or equivocal methods.—**ad-ven′tur-ous,** *a.* [OF. *aventuros* (F. *aventureux*).] Disposed to or involving adventure; boldly enterprising; daring; hazardous.—**ad-ven′tur-ous-ly,** *adv.*—**ad-ven′tur-ous-ness,** *n.*
ad-verb (ad′vėrb), *n.* [F. *adverbe*, < L. *adverbium*, < *ad*, to, + *verbum*, word, verb.] In *gram.*, a word used to qualify the meaning of a verb, adjective, or other adverb.—**ad-ver′bi-al** (-vėr′bi-a̤l), *a.* Pertaining to or used as an adverb.—**ad-ver′bi-al-ly,** *adv.*
ad-ver-sa-ry (ad′vėr-sa̤-ri). [L. *adversarius*, < *adversus*: see *adverse*.] **I.** *a.* Opposite; opposed. [Archaic.] **II.** *n.*; pl. *-ries* (-riz). An opponent; an antagonist; an enemy; [*cap.*] with *the*, the devil; Satan.
ad-ver-sa-tive (ad-vėr′sa̤-tiv). [LL. *adversativus*, < L. *adversari*, oppose, < *adversus*: see *adverse*.] **I.** *a.* Expressing opposition or contrariety, as the conjunction *but.* **II.** *n.* An adversative word or proposition.—**ad-ver′sa-tive-ly,** *adv.*
ad-verse (ad′vėrs, sometimes ad-vėrs′), *a.* [OF. *advers* (F. *adverse*), < L. *adversus*, pp. of *advertere*: see *advert*.] Opposed in position or course; opposite; opposing; contrary; hostile; unfavorable; untoward; in *bot.*, turned toward the axis, as a leaf.—**ad′verse-ly,** *adv.*—**ad′verse-ness,** *n.*—**ad-ver′si-ty** (-vėr′si-ti), *n.*; pl. *-ties* (-tiz). [OF. *adversite* (F. *adversité*), < L. *adversitas*.] Adverse or ill fortune; a misfortune; a trial.
ad-vert (ad-vėrt′), *v. i.* [OF. *advertir*, *avertir* (F. *avertir*), < L. *advertere*, turn to, < *ad*, to, + *vertere*, turn.] To turn the mind (*to*); direct the attention, as in the course of thought or discourse.—**ad-vert′ence,** *n.* Attention; regard; heed. Also **ad-vert′en-cy.**—**ad-vert′ent,** *a.* Attentive; heedful.—**ad-vert′ent-ly,** *adv.*
ad-ver-tise (ad′vėr-tīz or ad-vėr-tīz′), *v.*; *-tised, -tising.* [OF. *advertir* (*advertiss-*): see *advert*.] **I.** *tr.* To notify, inform, or warn (*of*); also, to give notice of; call public attention to, as by printed announcements. **II.** *intr.* To issue a public notice or request; place advertisements, as in newspapers or magazines.—**ad-ver-tise-ment** (ad-vėr′tiz-me̤nt or ad-vėr-tīz′me̤nt), *n.* [OF. *advertissement* (F. *avertissement*).] Notification; announcement; public notice, esp. in print; also, a printed announcement, as of goods for sale, in a newspaper, magazine, etc.—**ad-ver-tis-er** (ad′vėr-tī-zėr or ad-vėr-tī′zėr), *n.*
ad-vice (ad-vīs′), *n.* [OF. F. *avis*, opinion, < L. *ad*, to, + *visus*, pp. of *videre*, see, passive *videri*, seem, seem good.] Opinion†; an opinion recommending a course to be followed; counsel; deliberation†; also, information given; intelligence; notice.
ad-vis-a-ble (ad-vī′za̤-bl), *a.* Proper to be advised; expedient; also, open to advice.—**ad-vis-a-bil′i-ty** (-bil′i-ti), **ad-vis′a-ble-ness,** *n.*—**ad-vis′a-bly,** *adv.*
ad-vise (ad-vīz′), *v.*; *-vised, -vising.* [OF. F. *aviser*, < L. *ad*, to, + *visere*, look at, < *videre*, see.] **I.** *tr.* To look at†; consider (now only as in *advised*, *p. a.*); bethink (one's self)†; also, to give advice to; counsel; also, to recommend by advice; urge as expedient; also, to give (a person, etc.) information or notice (*of*); inform; notify; apprise. **II.** *intr.* To reflect; also, to take counsel; consult; also, to give advice.—**ad-vised′,** *p. a.* Having, or having been, duly considered; guided by forethought or judgment: now chiefly in *ill-advised* and *well-advised.*—**ad-vis′ed-ly** (-vī′zed-li), *adv.* After due consideration; deliberately.—**ad-vis′ed-ness,** *n.*—**ad-vise′ment,** *n.* Consideration; deliberation; consultation; advice (archaic).—**ad-vis′er,** *n.*

—ad-vi′so-ry (-vī′zọ-ri), *a.* Pertaining to or giving advice.

ad-vo-ca-cy (ad′vọ-kạ-si), *n.* The office or work of an advocate; the pleading of a cause.

ad-vo-cate (ad′vọ-kāt), *n.* [OF. F. *avocat*, < L. *advocatus*, orig. pp. of *advocare*, summon, call to one's aid, < *ad*, to, + *vocare*, call.] One who pleads the cause of another in a court of law; a lawyer; a pleader or champion of any cause; [*cap.*] often with *the*, Christ (cf. 1 John, ii. 1).—**ad′vo-cate,** *v. t.*; *-cated, -cating.* [L. *advocatus*, pp.] To plead in favor of; support or urge by argument, etc.; champion.—**ad′vo-cate-ship,** *n.* The office of an advocate.—**ad-vo-ca′tion** (-kā′shọn), *n.* [L. *advocatio(n-)*.] The act of advocating; advocacy.—**ad′vo-ca-tor,** *n.*—**ad′vo-ca-to-ry** (-kạ-tọ-ri), *a.* Of or pertaining to an advocate.

ad-vow-ee (ad-vou-ē′), *n.* [OF. *avoe*, < L. *advocatus*: see *advocate.*] In *Eng. law*, one who has a right of advowson.

ad-vow-son (ad-vou′zọn), *n.* [OF. *avoeson*, < L. *advocatio(n-)*, < *advocare*: see *advocate.*] In *Eng. law*, the right of presentation to a benefice.

ad-y-na-mi-a (ad-i-nā′mi-ạ), *n.* [NL., < Gr. ἀδυναμία, < ἀ- priv. + δύναμις, power.] In *pathol.*, weakness; debility.—**ad-y-nam′ic** (-nam′ik), *a.* In *pathol.*, pertaining to adynamia; in *physics*, characterized by absence of force.

ad-y-tum (ad′i-tum), *n.*; pl. *-ta* (-tạ). [L., < Gr. ἄδυτον, < ἀ- priv. + δύειν, enter.] In ancient worship, a sacred place which the public might not enter; an inner shrine; a sanctuary; in general, a sanctum.

Cooper's Adz.

adz, adze (adz), *n.* [AS. *adesa.*] A tool resembling an ax but with the blade set across the end of the handle and curving downward: used for dressing timber.—**adz, adze,** *v. t.*; *adzed, adzing.* To dress with an adz.

ad-zu-ki (ad-zö′ki) **bean.** [Jap. *adzuki.*] A variety of the gram (bean), *Phaseolus mungo*, cultivated in Japan, etc.

ae (ā), *a.* [= Sc. *ane*, E. *one.*] One. [Sc.]

æ-dile (ē′dīl), *n.* [L. *ædilis*, < *ædes*, a building.] In ancient Rome, a magistrate in charge of buildings, streets, markets, games, etc.—**æ′dile-ship,** *n.*

Æ-ge-an (ẹ-jē′ạn), *a.* [L. *Ægæus*, < Gr. Αἰγαῖος.] Pertaining to the Ægean Sea, an arm of the Mediterranean lying east of Greece; esp., noting or pertaining to the civilization which preceded the historic Hellenic period, and which flourished in various islands in, and lands adjacent to, the Ægean Sea, as Crete, Argolis, etc.

Æ-gi-ne-tan (ē-ji-nē′tạn). [L. *Ægineta*, < Gr. Αἰγινήτης, inhabitant of Ægina (Gr. Αἴγινα).] **I.** *a.* Of or pertaining to the island of Ægina (off the eastern coast of Greece) or its inhabitants: as, the *Æginetan* sculptures or marbles (a collection of sculptures dating from the 5th century B.C., discovered in 1811 on the island of Ægina). **II.** *n.* An inhabitant of Ægina.

æ-gis (ē′jis), *n.* [L., < Gr. αἰγίς.] The fabled shield or defensive piece (sometimes explained as a goatskin) of the Greek god Zeus, used also by the goddess Athene; fig., a protection; protecting influence or care.

æ-lu-ro-pho-bi-a (ẹ-lū-rọ-fō′bi-ạ), *n.* [NL., < Gr. αἴλουρος, cat, + -φοβία, fear: see *-phobia.*] A morbid fear or dread of cats.—**æ-lu′ro-phobe** (-fōb), *n.*

-æmia. See *-emia.*

a-ë-ne-ous (ā-ē′nẹ-us), *a.* [L. *aëneus*, < *æs*, copper, bronze.] In *zoöl.*, bronze-colored.

Æ-o-li-an[1] (ẹ-ō′li-ạn), *a.* Pertaining to Æolus, the Greek god of the winds; [*l. c.*] pertaining to the wind; sounded by the wind or by air, as a musical instrument (the *æolian harp* or *lyre*); borne by or due to the wind, as masses of detritus.

Æ-o-li-an[2] (ẹ-ō′li-ạn). **I.** *a.* Belonging to a branch of the Greek race named from Æolus, the legendary founder, or to Æolis or Æolia, a district in Asia Minor colonized by them. **II.** *n.* An Æolian Greek; also, Æolic.

Æ-ol-ic (ẹ-ol′ik). **I.** *a.* Æolian. See *Æolian*[2], *a.* **II.** *n.* The Æolian dialect of Greek.

æ-o-li-pile (ē′ọ-li-pīl or ẹ-ol′i-pīl), *n.* [L. *æolipila*, for *Æoli pila*, 'ball of Æolus.'] An instrument consisting essentially of a round vessel rotated by the force of steam generated within and escaping through bent arms.

æ-o-lo-trop-ic (ē″ọ-lọ-trop′ik), *a.* [Gr. αἰόλος, changeful: see *-tropic.*] In *physics*, varying with respect to some property in different directions; anisotropic.—**æ-o-lot-ro-pism** (ē-ọ-lot′rọ-pizm), **æ-o-lot′ro-py,** *n.*

æ-on, e-on (ē′ọn), *n.* [L. *æon*, < Gr. αἰών, lifetime, age.] An indefinitely long period of time; an age; in the Gnostic doctrine, one of a class of powers or beings existing from eternity, conceived as emanating from the Supreme Being and performing various parts in the operations of the universe.—**æ-o-ni-an, e-o-ni-an** (ẹ-ō′ni-ạn), *a.* Lasting or existing for ages; eternal.

æ-ra-ri-an (ẹ-rā′ri-ạn). [L. *ærarius*, monetary, fiscal, < *æs*, copper, bronze, money.] In *Rom. hist.*: **I.** *a.* Of or pertaining to the public treasury; fiscal. **II.** *n.* One of the lowest class of Roman citizens, who paid only a poll-tax and had no right to vote.

a-ër-ate (ā′ẹ-rāt), *v. t.*; *-ated, -ating.* [L. *aër*, air: see *air*[3].] To expose to air; charge or treat with air or a gas (as carbon dioxide); oxygenate (the blood) in respiration.—**aërated bread,** bread baked from dough into which carbon dioxide has been forced mechanically, instead of being generated within it as by fermentation.—**a-ër-a-tion** (ā-ẹ-rā′shọn), *n.* The act of aërating, or the state of being aërated.—**a′ër-a-tor,** *n.*

aëri-. Form of L. *aër*, air, used in combination, as in *aëriform.* Cf. *aëro-.*

a-ë-ri-al (ā-ē′ri-ạl; âr′i-ạl), *a.* [L. *aërius*, < *aër*, air.] Of or in the air; like air; airy; ethereal; visionary; lofty or elevated; growing in the air, as certain roots.—**aërial perspective.** See under *perspective, n.*—**a-ë′ri-al,** *n.* In *wireless teleg.* and *teleph.*, an antenna.—**a-ë′ri-al-ly,** *adv.*—**a-ë′ri-al-ness,** *n.*

Aërial Roots of the Banian.

ae-rie (ā′ri or ē′ri), *n.* See *aery*[2].

a-ër-if-er-ous (ā-ẹ-rif′ẹ-rus), *a.* [L. *aër*, air: see *-ferous.*] Conveying air.

a-ër-i-fi-ca-tion (ā″ẹ-ri-fi-kā′shọn), *n.* The act of aërifying; aërified state.

a-ër-i-form (ā′ẹ-ri-fôrm), *a.* [L. *aër*, air: see *-form.*] Air-like; gaseous; hence, unreal.

a-ër-i-fy (ā′ẹ-ri-fī), *v. t.*; *-fied, -fying.* [L. *aër*, air: see *-fy.*] To make aëriform; convert into vapor; also, to aërate.

aëro-. Form of Gr. ἀήρ (ἀερ-), air, used in combination, now esp. in aëronautical terms, and hence sometimes used, in composition or as a separate word, for some term of this class, as in *aëro-club* (or *aëro club*), *aëro-engine, aëro-gun.*

a-ër-o (ā′ẹ-rō), *n.*; pl. *aëros* (-rōz). [See *aëro-.*] An aëroplane or other aëronautical machine.

a-ër-o-bat-ics (ā″ẹ-rọ-bat′iks), *n.* [Gr. ἀήρ (ἀερ-), air, + -βατος, going, < βαίνειν, go: cf. *acrobat.*] The art or science of flying in aëroplanes or other machines or vehicles for aërial travel; aëronautics.—**a″ër-o-bat′ic,** *a.*

a-ër-obe (ā′ẹ-rōb), *n.* One of the aërobia.

a-ër-o-bi-a (ā-ẹ-rō′bi-ạ), *n. pl.* [NL., < Gr. ἀήρ (ἀερ-), air, + βίος, life.] Bacteria and other micro-organisms whose existence requires, or is not destroyed by, the presence of free oxygen: opposed to *anaërobia.*—**a-ër-o′bic,** *a.* Of bacteria, etc., requiring, or not destroyed by, the presence of free oxygen; also, pertaining to or caused by aërobia (as, *aërobic* fermentation).—**a-ër-o′bi-cal-ly,** *adv.*

a-ër-o-boat (ā′ẹ-rọ-bōt″), *n.* [See *aëro-.*] A flying-boat.—**a′ër-o-bus″,** *n.*; pl. *-buses.* A large aëroplane (with a cabin) that carries a number of passengers.—**a′ër-o-car″,** *n.* A conveyance for traveling in the air; a flying-machine; an airship.—**a′ër-o=club″,** *n.* A club or society devoted to aëronautics.—**a′ër-o=craft″,** *n.* An aircraft; also, aircraft collectively.—**a′ër-o-curve″,** *n.* A broad, thin, curved member (plane) affording a supporting surface in a flying-machine or gliding-machine. See *aëroplane.*

a-ër-o-done (ā′ẹ-rọ-dōn″), *n.* [Cf. Gr. ἀεροδόνητος, air-tossed, soaring, < ἀήρ (ἀερ-), air, + δονεῖν, shake, drive about.] A gliding-machine.—**a″ër-o-do-net′ics** (-dọ-net′-

(variable) ḑ as d or j, ş as s or sh, ţ as t or ch, ẓ as z or zh; *o*, F. cloche; ü, F. menu; ċh, Sc. loch; ṅ, F. bonbon; ′, primary accent; ″, secondary accent; †, obsolete; <, from; +, and; =, equals. See also lists at beginning of book.

ïks); *n.* The study of gliding or soaring flight; the science dealing with aërodones.—**a″ër-o-do-net′ic,** *a.*

a-ër-o-drome (ā′ę-rǭ-drōm″), *n.* [In the first sense, < Gr. ἀεροδρόμος, traversing the air, < ἀήρ (ἀερ-), air, + δραμεῖν, run; in later uses, < Gr. ἀήρ + δρόμος, a running, course, race-course.] A flying-machine or aëroplane (esp. Langley's); also, an aviation course or ground; also, a hangar.—**a″ër-o-drom′ic, a″ër-o-drom′i-cal** (-drom′ik, -i-kąl), *a.*

a-ër-o-dy-nam-ics (ā″ę-rǭ-dī-nam′iks), *n.* [See *aëro-*.] The dynamics of air or gases.—**a″ër-o-dy-nam′ic, a″ër-o-dy-nam′i-cal,** *a.*

a-ër-o=en-gine (ā′ę-rǭ-en″jin), *n.* [See *aëro-*.] An engine for use in an aëroplane.

a-ër-o-foil (ā′ę-rǭ-foil″), *n.* [See *aëro-* and *foil*[1].] A supporting plane (flat or curved) of a flying-machine or gliding-machine.

a-ër-o-go-ni-om-e-try (ā″ę-rǭ-gō-ni-om′e-tri), *n.* [See *aëro* and *goniometry*.] Radiogoniometric measurement done from aircraft.

a-ër-o-gram (ā′ę-rǭ-gram″), *n.* [See *aëro-* and *-gram*.] An aërographed message.—**a′ër-o-graph″** (-gråf″), *v. t.* [See *-graph*.] To telegraph by the wireless system.—**a-ër-og-ra-phy** (ā-ę-rog′rą-fi), *n.* [See *-graphy*.] Description of the air or atmosphere.—**a-ër-og′ra-pher,** *n.*—**a″ër-o-graph′ic, a″ër-o-graph′i-cal** (-graf′ik, -i-kąl), *a.*

a-ër-o=gun (ā′ę-rǭ-gun″), *n.* [See *aëro-*.] A gun for shooting at flying aëroplanes, etc.

a-ër-o-hy-dro-plane (ā″ę-rǭ-hī′drǭ-plān), *n.* Same as *hydro-aëroplane.*

a-ër-o-lite (ā′ę-rǭ-līt″), *n.* [= F. *aérolithe,* < Gr. ἀήρ (ἀερ-), air, + λίθος, stone.] A meteoric stone; a meteorite consisting mainly of stony matter. Also **a′ër-o-lith″** (-lith″).—**a″ër-o-li-thol′o-gy** (-li-thol′ǭ-ji), *n.* [See *-logy*.] The science of aërolites.—**a″ër-o-lit′ic** (-lit′ik), *a.*

a-ër-ol-o-gy (ā-ę-rol′ǭ-ji), *n.* [See *aëro-* and *-logy*.] The science of the air.—**a-ër-o-log-ic, a-ër-o-log-i-cal** (ā″ę-rǭ-loj′ik, -i-kąl), *a.*—**a-ër-ol′o-gist,** *n.*

a-ër-om-a-chy (ā-ę-rom′ą-ki), *n.*; pl. *-chies* (-kiz). [Gr. ἀερομαχία, < ἀήρ (ἀερ-), air, + μάχεσθαι, fight.] Fighting or a fight or battle in the air.

a-ër-o-man-cy (ā′ę-rǭ-man″si), *n.* [F. *aéromancie,* < LL. *aëromantia,* < Gr. ἀήρ (ἀερ-), air, + μαντεία, divination.] Divination by the air or atmospheric phenomena; also, the forecasting of the weather.

a-ër-o-me-chan-ics (ā″ę-rǭ-mę-kan′iks), *n.* [See *aëro-*.] The mechanics of air or gases.—**a″ër-o-me-chan′ic, a″ër-o-me-chan′i-cal,** *a.*

a-ër-om-e-ter (ā-ę-rom′e-tėr), *n.* [See *aëro-* and *-meter*.] An instrument for finding the weight, density, etc., of air or other gases.—**a-ër-om′e-try,** *n.* [See *-metry*.] The science of measuring air; the science of pneumatics.—**a-ër-o-met-ric** (ā″ę-rǭ-met′rik), *a.*

a-ër-o-mo-tor (ā′ę-rǭ-mō″tǫr), *n.* [See *aëro-*.] A motor for propelling an aëroplane or the like; also, any motor-driven aircraft.

a-ër-o-nat (ā′ę-rǭ-nat″), *n.* [F. *aéronat,* < Gr. ἀήρ (ἀερ-), air, + L. *natare,* swim, float.] A dirigible or motor-driven balloon.

a-ër-o-naut (ā′ę-rǭ-nât″), *n.* [F. *aéronaute,* < Gr. ἀήρ (ἀερ-), air, + ναύτης, sailor.] One who navigates the air, as in an airship or flying-machine.—**a″ër-o-nau′tic, a″ër-o-nau′ti-cal,** *a.* Pertaining to an aëronaut, or to aëronautics.—**a″ër-o-nau′ti-cal-ly,** *adv.*—**a″ër-o-nau′tics,** *n.* The science or art of aërial navigation.—**a′ër-o-naut″ism,** *n.* Aërial navigation.

a-ër-o-nef (ā′ę-rǭ-nef″), *n.* [F. *aéronef,* < Gr. ἀήρ (ἀερ-), air, + F. *nef,* < L. *navis,* ship.] An airship; a flying-machine.

a-ër-o-phyte (ā′ę-rǭ-fīt″), *n.* [See *aëro-* and *-phyte*.] In *bot.*, an air-plant or epiphyte.

a-ër-o-plane (ā′ę-rǭ-plān″; also, ār′ǭ-plān), *n.* [See *aëro-* and *plane*[2].] A plane (flat or curved) forming part of a flying-machine or gliding-machine and supporting it in the air; also, a flying-machine thus supported in flight and driven by a motor. — **a′ër-o-plane″,** *v. i.*; *-planed, -planing.* To aviate in an aëroplane. — **a′ër-o-plan″er, a′ër-o-plan″ist** (-plā″nėr, -nist), *n.*

a-ër-o-scep-sis (ā″ę-rǭ-skep′sis), *n.* [NL., < Gr. ἀήρ (ἀερ-), air, + σκέψις, viewing, perception.] In *zoöl.*, the faculty of aëroscopy. Also **a′ër-o-scep″sy.**

a-ër-os-co-py (ā-ę-ros′kǭ-pi), *n.* [Gr. ἀεροσκοπία, < ἀήρ (ἀερ-), air, + -σκοπία: see *-scopy*.] In *zoöl.*, perception of atmospheric conditions, as by insects and snails.—**a-ër-o-scop-ic** (ā″ę-rǭ-skop′ik), *a.*

a-ër-o-sid-er-ite (ā″ę-rǭ-sid′ę-rīt), *n.* [See *aëro-* and *siderite*.] A meteorite consisting essentially of metallic iron.—**a″ër-o-sid′er-o-lite** (-ę-rǭ-līt), *n.* [See *siderolite*.] A meteorite containing both iron and stone.

a-ër-o-stat (ā′ę-rǭ-stat″), *n.* [F. *aérostat,* < Gr. ἀήρ (ἀερ-), air, + στατός, standing.] An apparatus, as a balloon or a flying-machine, capable of floating in the air; also, an aëronaut.—**a″ër-o-stat′ic, a″ër-o-stat′i-cal,** *a.* Pertaining to aërostatics or to aërostation.—**a″ër-o-stat′ics,** *n.* The science of the equilibrium of air and other elastic fluids, and of the equilibrium of bodies sustained in them.—**a″ër-o-sta′tion** (-stā′shǫn), *n.* [F. *aérostation*.] Aërial navigation.

a-ër-o-tech-ni-cal (ā″ę-rǭ-tek′ni-kąl), *a.* [See *aëro-*.] Pertaining to the art that deals with machines or appliances for navigating the air and with the problems connected with their use.

a-ër-o-ther-a-peu-tics (ā″ę-rǭ-ther-ą-pū′tiks), *n.* [See *aëro-*.] That branch of therapeutics which deals with the curative use of air or of artificially prepared atmospheres.

æ-ru-gi-nous (ę-rö′ji-nus), *a.* [L. *æruginosus,* < *ærugo,* verdigris, < *æs,* copper.] Of or like verdigris.

a-ër-y[1] (ā′ėr-i), *a.* Aërial; airy; ethereal. [Poetic.]

ae-ry[2] (ā′ri or ē′ri), *n.*; pl. *aeries* (-riz). [OF. F. *aire,* prob. < L. *area,* open space.] The nest of a bird of prey; hence, any nest, habitation, or position aloft; also, a brood, as in a nest.

æs-cu-la-ceous (es-kū-lā′shius), *a.* [NL. *Æsculus,* the typical genus, L. *æsculus,* kind of oak.] Belonging to the *Æsculaceæ,* the buckeye or horse-chestnut family of trees and shrubs.

Æs-cu-la-pi-an (es-kū-lā′pi-ąn). **I.** *a.* Pertaining to Æsculapius, god of medicine, or to the healing art; medical. **II.** *n.* A physician.

Æs-cu-la-pi-us (es-kū-lā′pi-us), *n.* [L., = Gr. Ἀσκληπιός.] The Roman god of medicine and healing; hence, in general, a medical man; a physician.

Æ-sir (ē′sėr or ā′sir), *n. pl.* [Icel., pl. of *āss,* god.] The gods of the Scandinavian mythology, dwelling in Asgard.

æs-the-sia (es-thē′zią), *n.* [NL., < Gr. αἴσθησις, perception, sensation, < αἰσθάνεσθαι, perceive.] Perception; feeling; sensibility. Also **æs-the′sis.**

æs-the-si-om′e-ter, æs′thete, etc. See *esthesiometer, esthete,* etc.

æs′ti-val, etc., **æs′tu-a-ry,** etc. See *estival,* etc., *estuary,* etc.

æth-el-ing (ath′el-ing), *n.* Same as *atheling.*

æ′ther, etc. See *ether,* etc.

æ-thri-o-scope (ē′thri-ǭ-skōp or eth′ri-), *n.* [Gr. αἰθρία, open sky, + σκοπεῖν, view.] An instrument for measuring minute variations of temperature due to different conditions of the sky.

æ-ti-ol-o-gy, e-ti-ol-o-gy (ē-ti-ol′ǭ-ji), *n.* [LL. *ætiologia,* < Gr. αἰτιολογία, < αἰτία, cause, + λέγειν, speak.] The assigning of a cause; a theory of the cause of a phenomenon, as disease; the science of causes.—**æ″ti-o-log′i-cal, e″ti-o-log′i-cal** (-ǭ-loj′i-kąl), *a.*

a-far (ą-fär′), *adv.* [ME. *a fer,* earlier *of feor,* 'of far.'] From far; far; far away; far off.

a-feard, a-feared (ą-fērd′), *p. a.* [AS. *āfǣred,* pp. of *āfǣran,* affect with fear.] Frightened; afraid. [Now prov.]

a-feb-rile (a-feb′ril), *a.* [See *a-*[1].] Not febrile; without fever.

af-fa-ble (af′ą-bl), *a.* [L. *affabilis,* < *affari,* speak to, < *ad,* to, + *fari,* speak.] Easy of conversation or approach; gracious or complaisant in conversation or intercourse.—**af-fa-bil′i-ty** (-bil′i-ti), **af′fa-ble-ness,** *n.*—**af′fa-bly,** *adv.*

af-fair (ą-fãr′), *n.* [OF. *afaire* (F. *affaire*), orig. *a faire,* to do, < L. *ad,* to, and *facere,* do.] Something to do; a matter for action or attention; a concern; a performance or occurrence; a minor military engagement; indefinitely, a matter or thing.

af-fect[1] (a̤-fekt′), *v. t.* [L. *affectus*, pp. of *afficere*, < *ad*, to, + *facere*, do.] To act upon; produce an effect on; also, to move in mind or feelings; touch; also, to assign; allot. —**af-fect′**[1], *n.* Affection†; disposition†; in *psychol.*, the felt or affective component of a stimulus or motive to action.

af-fect[2] (a̤-fekt′), *v. t.* [OF. F. *affecter*, < L. *affectare*, freq. of *afficere*: see *affect*[1].] To aim at or strive after; tend toward; assume, use, or frequent by preference; fancy or like; also, to pretend or feign; imitate.—**af-fec-ta-tion** (af-ek-tā′sho̤n), *n.* [L. *affectatio(n-)*.] The act of affecting, striving after, or pretending; effort to present the appearance of something; studied or false show; pretense; artificiality of manner; an affected mannerism.

af-fect-ed[1] (a̤-fek′ted), *p. a.* Acted upon by something, esp. injuriously; impaired, as by disease; moved or touched in feelings; disposed or inclined; in *alg.*, adfected.

af-fect-ed[2] (a̤-fek′ted), *p. a.* Assumed; pretended; artificial; also, displaying affectation, as a person.—**af-fect′ed-ly,** *adv.*—**af-fect′ed-ness,** *n.*

af-fect-er (a̤-fek′tėr), *n.* One who affects (assumes, uses, likes, pretends, etc.).

af-fect-ing (a̤-fek′ting), *p. a.* Moving; touching; pathetic. —**af-fect′ing-ly,** *adv.*

af-fec-tion (a̤-fek′sho̤n), *n.* [OF. F. *affection*, < L. *affectio(n-)*, < *afficere*: see *affect*[1].] The act of affecting, or the resulting state; disposition or state of mind; a feeling; inclination; warm or tender attachment; fondness; love; also, an effect of action upon a thing; a modification; an attribute; a disease or malady.—**af-fec′tion-al,** *a.* Pertaining to the affections.—**af-fec′tion-ate** (-a̤t), *a.* Having or showing affection; loving; fond.—**af-fec′tion-ate-ly,** *adv.*—**af-fec′tion-ate-ness,** *n.*—**af-fec′tioned,** *a.* Disposed. [Archaic.]

af-fec-tive (a̤-fek′tiv), *a.* [F. *affectif*, < ML. *affectivus*, < L. *afficere*: see *affect*[1].] Affecting†; also, pertaining to the affections; emotional.

af-feer (a-fēr′), *v. t.* [OF. *afeurer*, < L. *ad*, to, + *forum*, market.] To assess (an amercement); also, to confirm. [Obs. or archaic.]—**af-feer′ment,** *n.*—**af-feer′or,** *n.*

af-fer-ent (af′e̤-re̤nt), *a.* [L. *afferens* (*-ent-*), ppr. of *afferre*, bring to, < *ad*, to, + *ferre*, bear.] In *physiol.*, bringing to a central organ or point: opposed to *efferent*.

af-fet-tu-o-so (äf-fet-tö̤-ō′sō), *a.* [It.] In *music*, tender; affecting.

af-fi-ance (a̤-fī′a̤ns), *n.* [OF. *afiance*, < *afier*: see *affy*.] Trust; faith; the pledging of faith; betrothal; intimate relations.—**af-fi′ance,** *v. t.*; *-anced, -ancing.* To pledge; betroth.—**af-fi′an-cer,** *n.*

af-fi-ant (a̤-fī′a̤nt), *n.* [F., ppr. of *affier*: see *affy*.] In *law*, one who makes an affidavit. [U. S.]

af-fiche (â-fēsh), *n.* [F., < *afficher*, affix.] A posted notice; a placard; a poster.

af-fi-da-vit (af-i-dā′vit), *n.* [ML., 3d pers. sing. perf. ind. of *affidare*, make oath: see *affy*.] A written declaration upon oath, esp. one made before an authorized official.

af-fil-i-a-ble (a̤-fil′i-a̤-bl), *a.* That may be affiliated.

af-fil-i-ate (a̤-fil′i-āt), *v.*; *-ated, -ating.* [ML. *affiliatus*, pp. of *affiliare*, < L. *ad*, to, + *filius*, son.] **I.** *tr.* To take or bring into relationship, as by adoption or formal association; associate; ally; unite (*to* or *with*); also, to fix the paternity of; father (*upon*). **II.** *intr.* To associate one's self.—**af-fil′i-ate. I.** *a.* Affiliated. **II.** *n.* An affiliated person, society, etc.—**af-fil-i-a′tion** (-ā′sho̤n), *n.* [ML. *affiliatio(n-)*.] The act of affiliating, or the state of being affiliated; association; alliance; relationship.

af-fine (a̤-fīn′), *n.* [OF. *affin*, < L. *affinis*, neighboring, related, < *ad*, to, + *finis*, border, end.] A relative by marriage; a connection.—**af-fined′,** *a.* Related; connected; also, bound†.

af-fin-i-ta-tive (a̤-fin′i-tā̤-tiv), *a.* Of the nature of affinity. —**af-fin′i-ta-tive-ly,** *adv.*

af-fin-i-tive (a̤-fin′i-tiv), *a.* Characterized by affinity.

af-fin-i-ty (a̤-fin′i-ti), *n.*; pl. *-ties* (-tiz). [OF. *affinite* (F. *affinité*), < L. *affinitas*, < *affinis*: see *affine*.] Relationship by marriage or by other ties than those of blood (distinguished from *consanguinity*); in general, relation; connection; inherent likeness; also, a natural or instinctive mutual attraction; one toward whom such an attraction is felt; in *chem.*, the attractive force holding elements together in combination.

af-firm (a̤-fėrm′), *v.* [OF. *afermer* (F. *affirmer*), < L. *affirmare*, < *ad*, to, + *firmare*, make firm, < *firmus*, firm.] **I.** *tr.* To state positively; aver; assert; also, to confirm; ratify. **II.** *intr.* To make a positive statement; make a legal affirmation.—**af-firm′a-ble,** *a.* Capable of being affirmed.—**af-firm′a-bly,** *adv.*—**af-firm′ance,** *n.* Affirmation; confirmation.—**af-firm′ant,** *n.* One who affirms.—**af-fir-ma-tion** (af-ėr-mā′sho̤n), *n.* [F. *affirmation*, < L. *affirmatio(n-)*.] The act of affirming; a positive or affirmative statement; a solemn declaration accepted in law instead of a statement under oath.—**af-fir-ma-tive** (a̤-fėr′ma̤-tiv). [F. *affirmatif*, < LL. *affirmativus*.] **I.** *a.* Serving to affirm; affirming; confirmative or ratifying; positive (as opposed to *negative*). **II.** *n.* An affirmative word or statement; the affirmative form of statement; the affirmative side of a question in debate: opposed to *negative*.—**af-fir′ma-tive-ly,** *adv.*—**af-fir′ma-to-ry** (-tō̤-ri), *a.* Affirmative.—**af-firm′er,** *n.*

af-fix (a̤-fiks′), *v. t.* [ML. *affixare*, freq. of L. *affigere* (pp. *affixus*), affix, fasten to, < *ad*, to, + *figere*, fix.] To fix, fasten, or join (*to*); attach; append.—**af-fix** (af′iks), *n.* [F. *affixe*, < L. *affixus*, pp.] Something affixed; a part or piece attached; a prefix or suffix in word-formation.—**af-fix′al,** *a.*—**af-fix′er,** *n.*—**af-fix′ture** (-t̤ūr), *n.* An affixing; something affixed.

af-flate (a-flāt′), *v. t.*; *-flated, -flating.* [L. *afflatus*, pp. of *afflare*, < *ad*, to, + *flare*, blow.] To blow or breathe on; inspire. [Obs. or rare.]—**af-fla-tion** (a-flā′sho̤n), *n.*—**af-fla′tus** (-tus), *n.* [L.] A blowing or breathing on; inspiration; a divine or preternatural inspiring influence.

af-flict (a̤-flikt′), *v. t.* [L. *afflictus*, pp. of *affligere*, < *ad*, to, + *fligere*, strike.] To cast down†; humble†; also, to subject to grievous trouble; trouble or distress grievously; torment.—**af-flict′er,** *n.*—**af-flict′ing-ly,** *adv.*—**af-flic-tion** (a̤-flik′sho̤n), *n.* [L. *afflictio(n-)*.] The state of being afflicted; grievous trouble or distress; also, something that afflicts; a grievous ill.—**af-flic′tive,** *a.* Afflicting; distressing.—**af-flic′tive-ly,** *adv.*

af-flu-ence (af′lö-e̤ns), *n.* [L. *affluentia*, < *affluens*: see *affluent*.] A flowing toward a point; afflux; also, affluent condition; abundance; profusion; wealth; an abundant supply.

af-flu-ent (af′lö-e̤nt). [L. *affluens* (*-ent-*), ppr. of *affluere*, flow to, < *ad*, to, + *fluere*, flow.] **I.** *a.* Flowing to; also, abounding; abundant; rich; wealthy. **II.** *n.* A tributary stream.—**af′flu-ent-ly,** *adv.*

af-flux (af′luks), *n.* [ML. *affluxus*, < L. *affluere*: see *affluent*.] A flow, as of a liquid, to a point; an accession.

af-force (a-fōrs′), *v. t.*; *-forced, -forcing.* [OF. *aforcier*, < L. *ad*, to, + *fortis*, strong.] To fortify† or strengthen†; strengthen or reinforce (a jury, court, etc.) by the addition of other or of specially qualified members.—**af-force′ment,** *n.*

af-ford (a̤-fōrd′), *v. t.* [AS. *geforthian*, further, accomplish; akin to E. *forth*.] To yield as a product or result; be the source of; furnish; give; also (with *may, can*, etc.), to give or spare without undue loss; meet the cost of; stand; manage (often with an infinitive).—**af-ford′a-ble,** *a.* That may be afforded.

af-for-est (a-for′est), *v. t.* [ML. *afforestare*, < L. *ad*, to, + ML. *foresta, forestis*, forest.] To convert (land) into forest. —**af-for-es-ta′tion** (-es-tā′sho̤n), *n.* The act of afforesting; the territory afforested.—**af-for′est-ment,** *n.*

af-fran-chise (a-fran′chīz or -chiz), *v. t.*; *-chised, -chising.* [OF. *afranchir* (*afranchiss-*) (F. *affranchir*), < *a* (< L. *ad*), to, + *franc*, free.] To enfranchise.

af-fray (a̤-frā′), *v. t.* [OF. *esfreer* (F. *effrayer*), < L. *ex*, out of, + ML. *fridus*, peace (from Teut.: cf. OHG. *fridu*, G. *friede*).] To frighten; alarm; disturb: now chiefly as in *afraid*.—**af-fray′,** *n.* [OF. *esfrei* (F. *effroi*).] Fright† or alarm†; a commotion† or tumult†; a public fight or brawl, constituting a disturbance of the peace.

af-freight (a-frāt′), *v. t.* [F. *affréter*, < *à* (< L. *ad*), to, + *fréter*, let by charter, akin to E. *freight*.] To hire, as a ship, for the transportation of goods or freight.—**af-freight′er,** *n.*—**af-freight′ment,** *n.*

af-fri-cate (af′ri-kāt), *n.* [L. *affricatus*, pp. of *affricare*, rub on or against, < *ad*, to, + *fricare*, rub.] In *phonetics*, an intimate combination of a stop with an immediately following spirant or fricative in the same position of the vocal organs, as German *pf* in *pfennig*, penny.

af-fright (a̤-frīt′), *v. t.* [AS. *āfyrhtan*, < *ā-* (intensive) + *fyrhtan*, frighten.] To impress with sudden fear; frighten; terrify.—**af-fright′**, *n.* A frightening; a cause or source of fright; sudden or startling fear; fright. — **af-fright′ed-ly,** *adv.*—**af-fright′ment,** *n.*

af-front (a̤-frunt′), *v. t.* [OF. *afronter* (F. *affronter*), < ML. *affrontare*, < L. *ad*, to, + *frons*, forehead, E. *front.*] To meet face to face; confront; also, to insult to one's face; slight or offend openly.—**af-front′**, *n.* A meeting face to face†; also, a direct or open insult; a deliberate slight or indignity.—**af-front′er**, *n.*—**af-front′ing-ly,** *adv.*—**af-fron′tive,** *a.* Affronting; insulting. [Obs. or archaic.]

af-fuse (a-fūz′), *v. t.*; *-fused, -fusing.* [L. *affusus*, pp. of *affundere*, < *ad*, to, + *fundere*, pour.] To pour (water, etc.) on something.—**af-fu-sion** (a-fū′zhọn), *n.* The pouring on of water or other liquid, as in baptism or for therapeutic purposes.

af-fy (a̤-fī′), *v. t.*; *-fied, -fying.* [OF. *afier* (F. *affier*), < ML. *affidare*, trust, pledge, make oath, < L. *ad*, to, + *fides*, faith.] To trust†; pledge, engage, or betroth (archaic); affirm on one's faith†.

Af-ghan (af′ga̤n). **I.** *n.* A native of Afghanistan; also, a language of Aryan affinity, spoken in Afghanistan; Pushtu; [*l. c.*] a blanket or covering of knitted or crocheted wool. **II.** *a.* Pertaining to Afghanistan.

a-field (a̤-fēld′), *adv.* In or to the field; abroad; away; astray.

a-fire (a̤-fīr′), *adv.* On fire.

a-flame (a̤-flām′), *adv.* In a flaming state; ablaze.

a-float (a̤-flōt′), *adv.* In a floating condition; on the water; at sea; adrift; in circulation; also, flooded.

a-flush[1] (a̤-flush′), *adv.* In a flushed state; aglow.

a-flush[2] (a̤-flush′), *adv.* On a level; even; flush.

a-flut-ter (a̤-flut′ėr), *adv.* In a flutter; in commotion.

a-foot (a̤-fůt′), *adv.* On foot; astir; about; in progress.

a-fore (a̤-fōr′), *adv.*, *prep.*, and *conj.* [AS. *onforan*, < *on*, on, + *foran*, before.] Before. [Now chiefly prov. or naut.] —**a-fore′hand,** *adv.* and *a.* Beforehand. [Archaic.]—**a-fore′said,** *a.* Said before; forementioned.—**a-fore′-thought. I.** *a.* Premeditated; prepense. **II.** *n.* Premeditation.—**a-fore′time,** *adv.* In time past; formerly.

a-foul (a̤-foul′), *adv.* In collision or entanglement.

a-fraid (a̤-frād′), *a.* [Orig. pp. of *affray.*] Frightened; fearful; apprehensive.

a-freet (a̤-frēt′ or af′rēt), *n.* See *afrit.*

a-fresh (a̤-fresh′), *adv.* Anew; again.

Af-ri-can (af′ri-ka̤n). **I.** *a.* Of or from Africa; belonging to the black race of Africa; negro. **II.** *n.* A native of Africa; a member of the black race of Africa; a negro.

Af-ri-can-der (af-ri-kan′dėr), *n.* [S. Afr. D. *Afrikaander.*] One born in South Africa but of European, esp. Dutch, descent.—**Af-ri-can′der-ism,** *n.* A word, expression, usage, etc., peculiar to or originating among the Africanders.

a-frit, a-frite (a̤-frēt′ or af′rēt), *n.* [Ar. *'ifrīt.*] In *Arabian myth.*, a powerful evil demon or monster.

Af-ro- (af′rọ-). Form of L. *Afer* (*Afr-*), African, used in combination, as in *Afro-American* (African and American, American of African descent), *Afro-European.*

a-front (a̤-frunt′), *adv.* In front; face to face; abreast.

aft (ȧft), *adv.* and *a.* [AS. *æftan*, behind, a superl. form related to *æfter*, E. *after.*] *Naut.*, at or toward the stern.

af-ter (ȧf′tėr). [AS. *æfter*, a compar. form related to *of*, E. *of*, *off.*] **I.** *adv.* Behind; later; afterward. **II.** *prep.* Behind; following; next to; in pursuit or imitation of; in accordance with; in reference to, or concerning (as, to ask *after* a person); also, later than; subsequently to; also, considering or notwithstanding (something past). **III.** *conj.* Subsequently to the time when.—**af′ter,** *a.* [AS. *æftera.*] Hinder; rear; following; subsequent; later; *naut.*, further aft.—**af′ter-birth,** *n.* The placenta and other parts expelled from the uterus after childbirth. —**af′ter-brain,** *n.* The metencephalon.—**af′ter-clap,** *n.* A subsequent and unexpected stroke, as of misfortune.—**af′ter-crop,** *n.* A second crop from land in the same year. —**af′ter=damp,** *n.* An irrespirable gas consisting chiefly of carbon dioxide and nitrogen, left in a coal-mine after an explosion of fire-damp.—**af′ter=din′ner,** *a.* Following dinner; postprandial: as, an *after-dinner* speech; an *after-dinner* nap.—**af′ter-feed,** *n.* Grass that grows after the first crop has been mowed, and is fed off instead of being cut.—**af′ter-glow,** *n.* A glow often seen in the sky after sunset.—**af′ter-grass,** *n.* A second growth of grass in a mowed field, or grass growing among the stubble after harvest.—**af′ter-growth,** *n.* A subsequent or later growth; an aftermath.—**af′ter=im″age,** *n.* A visual image or other sense-impression that persists after the withdrawal of the exciting stimulus.—**af′ter-math** (-màth), *n.* [See *math.*] A second mowing or crop of grass from land in the same season; fig., a later product or result.—**af′ter-most,** *a. superl.* Hindmost; *naut.*, furthest aft.—**af-ter-noon′,** *n.* The time from noon until evening.—**af′ter=pains,** *n. pl.* Uterine pains following childbirth.—**af′ter-piece,** *n.* A short dramatic piece performed after a play.—**af′ter-shaft,** *n.* In *ornith.*, a supplementary feather, usually small, arising from the under side of certain feathers in many birds; the shaft of such a supplementary feather.—**af′ter=taste,** *n.* A taste that remains in the mouth when the cause of it is no longer present. Also fig.—**af′ter-thought,** *n.* A later or subsequent thought; something thought of afterward. —**af′ter-time,** *n.* Subsequent, later, or future time.—**af′ter-ward, af′ter-wards** (-wa̤rd, -wa̤rdz), *adv.* Later; subsequently.

aft-most (ȧft′mōst), *a. superl.* *Naut.*, furthest aft.

a-ga, a-gha (a̤-gä′), *n.* [Turk. *aghā.*] In Turkey, a chief; a commander; also, a title of respect.

a-gain (a̤-gen′, also, esp. Brit., a̤-gān′). [AS. *ongegn*, *ongēan*, adv. and prep., < *on*, on, in, + *-gegn*, *-gēan*, akin to G. *gegen*, toward, against.] **I.** *adv.* Back; in return; also, once more; anew; also, moreover; besides; also, on the other hand. **II.** *prep.* and *conj.* Same as *against.* [Now prov.]

a-gainst (a̤-genst′, also, esp. Brit., a̤-gānst′). [Extended form of *again*, with *-s*, AS. *-es*, adverbial genitive ending, and a later excrescent *-t.*] **I.** *prep.* In an opposite position, direction, or course to; opposite to; facing; in front of; so as to meet, collide with, or bear upon; in opposition or resistance to; adversely, contrary, or counter to; so as to offset; in anticipation of; in preparation for. **II.** *conj.* Against the time that; by the time that; before. [Now colloq. or prov.]

a-gal-loch, a-gal-lo-chum (a-gal′ọk, a-gal′ọ-kum), *n.* [NL. *agallochum*, < Gr. ἀγάλλοχον.] The fragrant wood of a large thymelæaceous East Indian tree, *Aquilaria agallocha*: the aloes of the Bible.

Agama.

ag-al-mat-o-lite (ag-al-mat′ọ-līt), *n.* [Gr. ἄγαλμα (ἀγαλματ-), image, + λίθος, stone.] A soft grayish or greenish stone, used by the Chinese for cutting into images, etc.

ag-a-ma (ag′a̤-mä), *n.*; pl. *-mas.* [Caribbean name.] Any lizard of the family *Agamidæ*, of warm old-world regions, allied to the iguanas and including large and brilliantly colored species.

ag-a-mi (ag′a̤-mi), *n.*; pl. *-mis.* [Native name.] The golden-breasted trumpeter, *Psophia crepitans*, of Guiana and Brazil, a crane-like bird with little power of flight and easily tamed.

a-gam-ic (a-gam′ik), *a.* [Gr. ἄγαμος: see *agamous.*] In *biol.*, asexual; occurring without sexual union; germinating without impregnation; not gamic; in *bot.*, cryptogamic. —**a-gam′i-cal-ly,** *adv.*

ag-a-mo-gen-e-sis (ag″a̤-mọ-jen′e-sis), *n.* [Gr. ἄγαμος, unmarried, + γένεσις, genesis.] In *biol.*, asexual reproduction.—**ag″a-mo-ge-net′ic** (-jẹ-net′ik), *a.*

ag-a-mous (ag′ạ-mus), *a.* [Gr. ἄγαμος, unmarried, < ἀ- priv. + γάμος, marriage.] In *zoöl.*, having no distinguishable sexual organs; asexual; agamic; in *bot.*, cryptogamous.

Ag-a-nip-pe (ag-ạ-nip′ē), *n.* [L., < Gr. Ἀγανίππη.] A spring on Mount Helicon, in Bœotia, Greece, sacred to the Muses and regarded as a source of poetic inspiration.

ag-a-pan-thus (ag-ạ-pan′thus), *n.* [NL., < Gr. ἀγάπη, love, + ἄνθος, flower.] Any of several African liliaceous plants constituting the genus *Agapanthus* (or *Tulbaghia*), with umbels of blue or white flowers.

a-gape[1] (ạ-gäp′ or ạ-gāp′), *adv.* In a gaping state.

ag-a-pe[2] (ag′ạ-pē), *n.*; pl. *-pæ* (-pē). [LL., < Gr. ἀγάπη, love, pl. ἀγάπαι, love-feast.] Among the primitive Christians, a love-feast.

a-gar (ä′gär), *n.* Same as *agar-agar.*

a-gar=a-gar (ä′gär-ä′gär), *n.* [Malay.] Asiatic seaweed of several species, used for making soups, etc.; also, a gelatinous product from certain seaweeds, used as a medium in bacteria-culture.

ag-a-ric (ag′ạ-rik or a-gar′ik), *n.* [L. *agaricum*, < Gr. ἀγαρικόν, a tree-fungus used for tinder.] An old name for species of *Polyporus*, cork-like fungi growing on trees; also, any fungus of the genus *Agaricus* or family *Agaricaceæ*, which includes various edible species (mushrooms).—**a-gar-i-ca-ceous** (a-gar-i-kā′shius), *a.* Belonging to the *Agaricaceæ*, a large family of fungi including the mushrooms.

a-gate[1] (ạ-gāt′), *adv.* [See *a*[2] and *gate*[2].] On the way; in motion or progress; going. [Sc. and prov. Eng.]

ag-ate[2] (ag′ạt), *n.* [F. *agate*, < L. *achates*, < Gr. ἀχάτης.] A kind of quartz (chiefly chalcedony) showing variously colored bands or other markings (clouded, moss-like, etc.); a piece of this quartz, or something made of it; a playing-marble made of or resembling it; also, a printing-type (5½ point) of a size between pearl and nonpareil (see *type*).—**ag′ate=ware,** *n.* Pottery variegated to resemble agate; also, a kind of enameled iron or steel household ware of similar appearance.

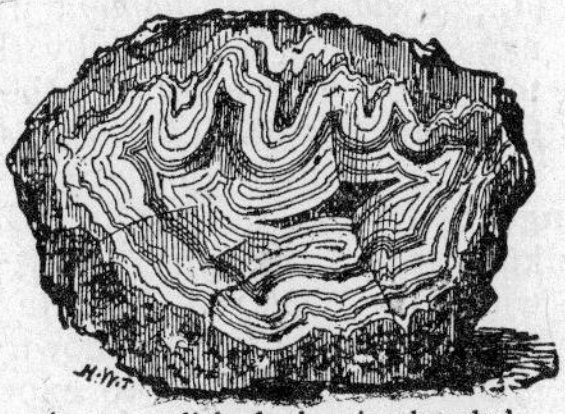

Agate, polished, showing banded structure.

ag-a-tho-de-mon, ag-a-tho-dæ-mon (ag″ạ-thọ-dē′mọn), *n.* [Gr. ἀγαθοδαίμων, < ἀγαθός, good, + δαίμων, spirit.] A good spirit; a good genius. Cf. *cacodemon.*

ag-a-tif-er-ous (ag-ạ-tif′ẹ-rus), *a.* [See *-ferous.*] Containing or yielding agate.

ag-at-ize (ag′ạ-tīz), *v. t.*; *-ized, -izing.* To change into agate; make agate-like: as, *agatized* (silicified) wood.

a-ga-ve (a-gā′vē), *n.* [NL., < Gr. ἀγαυή, fem. of ἀγαυός, noble.] Any plant of the American (chiefly Mexican) amaryllidaceous genus *Agave*, species of which yield useful fibers (Sisal hemp, etc.), a fermented beverage (pulque), a distilled spirit (mescal), or a soap substitute (amole), or are cultivated for ornament, as the century-plant.

a-gaze (ạ-gāz′), *adv.* In the attitude of gazing.

age (āj), *n.* [OF. *aage* (F. *âge*), < L. *ætas*, < *ævum*, age, lifetime, eternity.] Length of existence attained; actual time or measure of life; full or average term of life; a particular point or stage in life, as of physical maturity, legal capacity, or other qualification; a particular period of life (as youth); the final period ('old age'); a period of the world's or the earth's history; an era; an epoch; a century or generation; a long time; in *card-playing*, the first player to the left of the dealer; the eldest hand.—**ages in archæology,** the stone, bronze, and iron ages: with reference to the material used for implements.—**ages in history,** the dark ages (from about A.D. 476 to about 1000, or, according to some, to the Renaissance), the middle ages (from about 476 to about 1450 or 1500, or to about 1300 or the Renaissance), and the feudal ages (from about 900 to about 1500, or, in a more limited acceptation, to about 1300).—**ages in mythology,** the golden, silver, brazen, heroic, and iron ages: a poetic division ascribed to Hesiod. Cf. *golden age, silver age,* etc., under *golden, silver,* etc.—**age,** *v.*; *aged, aging* or *ageing.* **I.** *intr.* To grow old; take on characteristics of age. **II.** *tr.* To make old in years, appearance, etc.; mature (wine, etc.).

-age. [OF. F. *-age*, < L. *-aticum*, neut. of *-aticus*, adj. suffix: cf. E. *savage*, < L. *silvaticus.*] A suffix of nouns denoting a thing belonging or pertaining, such things collectively, or state, rank, action, service, cost, etc., as in *appendage, baggage, damage, foliage, marriage, peerage, postage, voyage.*

a-ged (ā′jed), *p. a.* Of advanced age; very old; pertaining to old age; also (pron. ājd), of the age of (as, *aged* ten years).—**a′ged-ly,** *adv.*—**a′ged-ness,** *n.*

a-gee (ạ-jē′), *adv.* [Cf. *gee*[1].] To one side; awry. [Prov.]

ag-e-last (aj′ẹ-last), *n.* [Gr. ἀγέλαστος, not laughing, < ἀ- priv. + γελᾶν, laugh.] One who never laughs.

age-less (āj′les), *a.* Exempt from age; never old.

age-long (āj′lông), *a.* Long as an age; lasting for an age.

a-gen-cy (ā′jẹn-si), *n.*; pl. *-cies* (-siz). [ML. *agentia.*] The action, function, or position of an agent; activity; operation; instrumentality; an active force or means; the business, establishment, or district of an agent; a commercial or other bureau furnishing some form of service for the public.

a-gen-dum (ạ-jen′dum), *n.*; pl. *-da* (-dạ). [L., neut. gerundive of *agere*: see *agent.*] A thing to be done; an item to be attended to; also, *pl.* (construed as *sing.*), a memorandum-book.

a-gent (ā′jẹnt). [L. *agens* (*agent-*), ppr. of *agere*, drive, do, act, akin to Gr. ἄγειν, lead, Skt. *aj-*, drive.] **I.** *a.* Acting. [Archaic.] **II.** *n.* One who or that which acts; the operating cause of a result; the producer of an effect; an acting representative; a factor or deputy; an official charged with special functions.—**a-gen-tial** (ā-jen′shạl), *a.* Pertaining to an agent or to agency.—**a′gent=noun′,** *n.* A noun that indicates an agent, or person or thing acting; esp., a noun that indicates the person or thing doing the act expressed by a verb, as *binder, creator, runner, sleeper*, in relation to *bind, create, run, sleep.*

a-gent pro-vo-ca-teur (ȧ-zhoṅ pro-vo-kȧ-tėr); pl. *agents provocateurs* (F. ȧ-zhoṅ pro-vo-kȧ-tėr). [F., 'provocatory agent.'] A secret agent of the police or the government, employed to incite persons, esp. suspected persons, to some offense, outbreak, or the like, in order to afford a pretext for police or governmental proceedings against them; hence, any secret agent employed to incite persons to some action, for the purpose of rendering them liable to punishment.

a-ger-a-tum (a-jer′ạ-tum, commonly aj-ẹ-rā′tum), *n.* [NL., < Gr. ἀγήρατον, kind of plant, < ἀ- priv. + γῆρας, old age.] Any plant of the asteraceous genus *Ageratum*, as *A. conyzoides*, a garden annual with small, dense blue or white flower-heads.

ag-glom-er-ate (ạ-glom′ẹ-rāt), *v. t.* or *i.*; *-ated, -ating.* [L. *agglomeratus*, pp. of *agglomerare*, < *ad*, to, + *glomerare*, form into a ball, < *glomus*, ball.] To collect or gather into a mass.—**ag-glom′er-ate** (-ẹ-rạt). **I.** *a.* Massed or packed together; in *bot.*, densely clustered. **II.** *n.* An agglomerate mass or formation, as of angular volcanic fragments.—**ag-glom-er-a′tion** (-ẹ-rā′shọn), *n.* The act of agglomerating; agglomerated state; an indiscriminately formed mass.—**ag-glom′er-a-tive** (-ẹ-rạ-tiv), *a.* Tending to agglomerate.

ag-glu-ti-nant (ạ-glö′ti-nạnt). **I.** *a.* Agglutinating; causing adhesion. **II.** *n.* An agglutinating agent.

ag-glu-ti-nate (ạ-glö′ti-nāt), *v. t.*; *-nated, -nating.* [L. *agglutinatus*, pp. of *agglutinare*, < *ad*, to, + *glutinare*, glue fast, < *gluten*, glue.] To join as with glue; cause to adhere.—**ag-glu′ti-nate** (-nạt), *a.* Joined or formed by agglutination.—**ag-glu-ti-na′tion** (-nā′shọn), *n.* The act of agglutinating; an agglutinated state or formation; a mass of cohering parts; in *philol.*, word-formation by the joining of elements retaining individual form and sense.—**ag-glu′ti-na-tive** (-nạ-tiv), *a.* Tending to agglutinate; characterized by agglutination.

ag-grade (ạ-grād′), *v. t.*; *-graded, -grading.* [L. *ad*, to, + *gradus*, E. *grade.*] In *geol.*, to raise the grade or level of (a river valley, etc.), as by the depositing of detritus: opposed to *degrade.*—**ag-gra-da-tion** (ag-rạ-dā′shọn), *n.*

ag-gran-dize (ag′ran-dīz), *v. t.*; *-dized, -dizing.* [F. *agrandir* (*agrandiss-*), < L. *ad*, to, + *grandire*, make great, <

grandis, great.] To make greater; extend; advance; exalt; enrich; magnify or exaggerate.—**ag′gran-diz-a-ble,** *a.*—**ag-gran-dize-ment** (ạ-gran′diz-mẹnt or ag′ran-dīz-mẹnt), *n.* The act of aggrandizing; aggrandized state; advancement; exaltation.—**ag′gran-diz-er** (-dī-zėr), *n.*

ag-gra-vate (ag′rạ-vāt), *v. t.*; *-vated, -vating.* [L. *aggravatus*, pp. of *aggravare*, < *ad*, to, + *gravare*, load, weigh down, < *gravis*, heavy.] To add weight to†; increase the gravity or grievousness of; make worse, more severe, or more heinous; exaggerate†; weigh down† or oppress†; provoke or irritate (colloq.).—**ag′gra-vat-ing-ly,** *adv.* —**ag-gra-va′tion** (-vā′shọn), *n.* [LL. *aggravatio(n-)*.] The act of aggravating, or the state of being aggravated; also, something that aggravates.—**ag′gra-va-tive** (-vạ-tiv). **I.** *a.* Tending or serving to aggravate. **II.** *n.* Something that tends or serves to aggravate.—**ag′gra-va-tor,** *n.*

ag-gre-gate (ag′rẹ-gāt), *v.*; *-gated, -gating.* [L. *aggregatus*, pp. of *aggregare*, < *ad*, to, + *gregare*, collect into a flock, < *grex* (*greg-*), flock.] **I.** *tr.* To collect into a body, mass, or whole; also, to unite to a body; also, to form as a total (as, the sums collected will *aggregate* a thousand dollars). **II.** *intr.* To form a mass or whole.—**ag′gre-gate** (-gạt). **I.** *a.* Formed of particulars collected into a whole; collective; total; in *bot.*, of a flower, formed of florets collected in a dense cluster but not cohering as in composite plants; of a fruit, composed of a cluster of carpels belonging to the same flower, as the raspberry (cf. *collective*); in *geol.*, composed of different mineral substances separable by mechanical means, as granite. **II.** *n.* An assemblage of particulars; a collective mass or whole; a total; also, any hard material used in small fragments for mixing with mortar or cement to form concrete.—**ag′gre-gate-ly,** *adv.* Collectively.—**ag-gre-ga′tion** (-gā′shọn), *n.* [LL. *aggregatio(n-)*.] The act of aggregating; aggregated state; an aggregate mass, body, or whole.—**ag′gre-ga-tive** (-gạ-tiv), *a.* Tending to aggregate; collective; gregarious.—**ag′gre-ga-tor** (-gā-tọr), *n.*

ag-gress (ạ-gres′), *v. i.* [L. *aggressus*, pp. of *aggredi*, < *ad*, to, + *gradi*, walk, go, < *gradus*, step.] To make an attack; commit the first act of hostility or offense; begin a quarrel. —**ag-gres-sion** (ạ-gresh′ọn), *n.* [L. *aggressio(n-)*.] The act of aggressing; an aggressive action or course; an act of offense.—**ag-gres-sive** (ạ-gres′iv), *a.* Tending to aggress or attack; offensive (as opposed to *defensive*); active in initiating movements in any cause.—**ag-gres′sive-ly,** *adv.* —**ag-gres′sive-ness,** *n.*—**ag-gres′sor,** *n.* [L.] One who aggresses; the beginner of a quarrel.

ag-grieve (ạ-grēv′), *v. t.*; *-grieved, -grieving.* [OF. *agrever*, < L. *aggravare*: see *aggravate*.] To oppress or wrong grievously; injure by injustice; distress† or grieve†: now commonly in the passive (as, to be or feel *aggrieved*).

a-gha (ạ-gä′), *n.* See *aga.*

a-ghast (ạ-gást′), *a.* [ME. *agast*, pp. of *agasten*, < AS. *ā-* (intensive) + *gǣstan*, terrify.] Struck with horror and amazement; filled with consternation.

ag-ile (aj′il), *a.* [F. *agile*, < L. *agilis*, < *agere*, act.] Quick and light in movement; nimble; active.—**ag′ile-ly,** *adv.* —**ag′ile-ness, a-gil-i-ty** (ạ-jil′i-ti), *n.*

ag-i-o (aj′i-ō or ā′ji-ō), *n.* [It. *aggio*, exchange, premium, = *agio*, ease.] Premium on money in exchange; allowance for the difference in value of two currencies; also, agiotage. —**ag′i-o-tage** (-ọ-tạj), *n.* The business of exchange; also, financial speculation.

a-gist (a-jist′), *v. t.* [OF. *agister*, < *a* (< L. *ad*), to, + *gister*, lodge, < *giste*, resting-place, bed: see *joist*.] To feed or pasture, as the cattle or horses of others, for a compensation: used orig. of the feeding of cattle in the king's forests.—**a-gist′ment,** *n.*—**a-gist′or, a-gist′er,** *n.*

ag-i-tate (aj′i-tāt), *v.*; *-tated, -tating.* [L. *agitatus*, pp. of *agitare*, < *agere*, drive: see *agent*.] **I.** *tr.* To move to and fro; put into commotion; also, to disturb; perturb; excite; also, to revolve in thought; also, to discuss; debate. **II.** *intr.* To argue or appeal persistently and publicly in behalf of a cause: with *for*.—**ag′i-tat-ed-ly,** *adv.*—**ag-i-ta′tion** (-tā′shọn), *n.* [L. *agitatio(n-)*.] The act of agitating; agitated state; commotion; perturbation; discussion; persistent urging of a cause before the public.—**a-gi-ta-to** (ä-jē-tä′tō), *a.* [It.] In *music*, agitated; restless or hurried in movement or style.—**ag′i-ta-tor,** *n.* [L.] One who or that which agitates; often, one who strives to rouse public discontent with existing conditions.

a-gleam (ạ-glēm′), *adv.* In a gleaming state.

ag-let (ag′let), *n.* [OF. *aguillette*, F. *aiguillette*: see *aiguillette*.] A metal tag at the end of a lace, etc.; a tagged lace or cord; an aiguillette.

a-gley, a-glee (ạ-glī′ or ạ-glē′, ạ-glē′), *adv.* [See *gley*.] Off the right line; awry; wrong. [Chiefly Sc.]

a-glim-mer (ạ-glim′ėr), *adv.* In a glimmering state.

a-glit-ter (ạ-glit′ėr), *adv.* In a glitter; glittering.

a-glos-sal (a-glos′ạl), *a.* [Gr. ἄγλωσσος, < ἀ- priv. + γλῶσσα, tongue.] Having no tongue. Also **a-glos-sate** (a-glos′āt).

a-glow (ạ-glō′), *adv.* In a glow; glowing.

ag-mi-nate (ag′mi-nāt), *a.* [L. *agmen* (*agmin-*), troop.] Clustered; grouped. Also **ag′mi-nat-ed** (-nā-ted).

ag-nail (ag′nāl), *n.* [AS. *angnægl*, < *ang-*, narrow, painful, + *nægl*, nail.] A whitlow†; a hangnail.

ag-nate (ag′nāt). [L. *agnatus*, pp. of *agnasci*, be born to, < *ad*, to, + *nasci*, be born.] **I.** *n.* A kinsman whose connection is traceable exclusively through males; sometimes, any male relation by the father's side. **II.** *a.* Related through males exclusively or by the father's side; also, allied or akin.—**ag-nat′ic** (-nat′ik), *a.*—**ag-na′tion** (-nā′shọn), *n.* [L. *agnatio(n-)*.] The relationship of agnates; kinship.

ag-nize (ag-nīz′), *v. t.*; *-nized, -nizing.* [L. *agnoscere*, < *ad*, to, + *gnoscere*, *noscere*, know: cf. *recognize*.] To recognize; acknowledge. [Archaic.]

ag-no-men (ag-nō′men), *n.*; pl. *agnomina* (ag-nom′i-nạ). [L., < *ad*, to, + *nomen*, name.] An additional (fourth) name given to a person by the ancient Romans in allusion to some achievement or other circumstance, as in 'Publius Cornelius Scipio *Africanus*' (cf. *prænomen*, *nomen*, *cognomen*); any added appellative.—**ag-nom′i-nal** (-nom′i-nạl), *a.*

ag-nos-tic (ag-nos′tik). [Gr. ἄγνωστος, unknown, unknowable, < ἀ- priv. + γιγνώσκειν, know.] **I.** *n.* One who holds that the ultimate cause (God) and the essential nature of things are unknown or unknowable, or that human knowledge is limited to experience. **II.** *a.* Of or belonging to agnostics.—**ag-nos′ti-cal-ly,** *adv.*—**ag-nos′ti-cism** (-sizm), *n.* The doctrine or the intellectual attitude of agnostics.

ag-nus cas-tus (ag′nus kas′tus). [L. *agnus* (< Gr. ἄγνος), the shrub, and *castus*, chaste.] A strongly aromatic verbenaceous shrub or small tree, *Vitex agnus-castus*, native in the Mediterranean regions, with spikes of purplish-blue or white flowers; the chaste-tree.

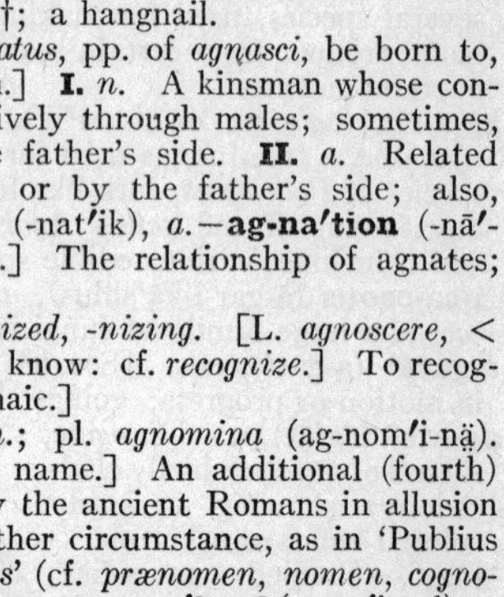

Agnus Dei. (From the Campanile of Giotto, Florence.)

Ag-nus De-i (ag′nus dē′ī). [LL., 'Lamb of God': see John, i. 29.] *Eccles.*, a figure of a lamb as emblematic of Christ; in the *Rom. Cath. Ch.*, a wax medallion stamped with this figure and blessed by the Pope; also, a prayer in the service of the mass, beginning with "Agnus Dei," or a musical setting for it; in the *Anglican Ch.*, a prayer beginning "O Lamb of God," often sung as an anthem, or a musical setting for this.

a-go (ạ-gō′). [Orig. pp. of ME. *agon*, < AS. *āgān*, go away, pass.] **I.** *a.* Gone; past. **II.** *adv.* In past time; since: used in the phrase *long ago*.

a-gog (ạ-gog′), *adv.* [Cf. OF. *gogue*, mirth, glee.] In eager desire or expectancy; in excitement.

a-go-ing (ạ-gō′ing), *adv.* In the act of going; in motion.

a-gone[1] (ạ-gôn′), *a.* and *adv.* Ago. [Archaic.]

ag-one[2] (ag′ōn), *n.* [Gr. ἄγωνος, without angles, < ἀ- priv. + γωνία, angle.] An agonic line.—**a-gon-ic** (a-gon′ik), *a.* Not forming an angle: as, an *agonic* line (an imaginary line connecting points on the earth's surface where the magnetic needle points to the true north).

ag-o-nist (ag'ǫ-nist), *n.* [Gr. ἀγωνιστής, < ἀγωνίζεσθαι: see *agonize*.] A contender in public games; a combatant. —**ag-o-nis'tic,** *a.* Pertaining to athletic or other contests; combative; also, displaying effort; strained.—**ag-o-nis'ti-cal-ly,** *adv.*—**ag-o-nis'tics,** *n.* Athletics.

ag-o-nize (ag'ǫ-nīz), *v.*; *-nized, -nizing.* [Gr. ἀγωνίζεσθαι, contend, < ἀγών, contest, assembly, < ἄγειν, lead.] **I.** *intr.* To strive painfully; struggle; writhe with pain; suffer agony. **II.** *tr.* To subject to agony; distress extremely.—**ag'o-niz-ed-ly,** *adv.*—**ag'o-niz-er,** *n.*—**ag'o-niz-ing-ly,** *adv.*

ag-o-ny (ag'ǫ-ni), *n.*; pl. *-nies* (-niz). [Gr. ἀγωνία, < ἀγών, contest: see *agonize*.] A violent or painful struggle; the death-struggle; intense suffering of body or mind; excruciating pain; a paroxysm; also, painful effort to produce a fine or elegant effect (often in *pl.*: colloq.).

ag-o-ra (ag'ǫ-rą), *n.*; pl. *-ræ* (-rē). [Gr. ἀγορά, < ἀγείρειν, assemble.] In ancient Greece, an assembly; the place of assembly; esp., the market-place.

Agouti.

a-gou-ta (ą-gö'tą), *n.* [Native name.] The solenodon or opossum-shrew of Haiti, *Solenodon paradoxus.*

a-gou-ti (ą-gö'ti), *n.* [Native Guiana name.] Any of several rabbit-like rodents of the genus *Dasyprocta*, of South and Central America and the West Indies.

a-gra (ą-grä'), *n.* [Ir., 'O love.'] Darling. [Ir.]

a-graffe (ą-graf'), *n.* [F. *agrafe*, OF. *agrape*, < *a*, to, + *grape*, hook: see *grape*.] A clasp for hooking together parts of clothing, etc.; a device for checking vibration in a piano-string; a small cramp-iron.

Ag-ra-pha (ag'rą-fą), *n. pl.* [NL., < Gr. ἄγραφα, neut. pl. of ἄγραφος, unwritten, < ἀ- priv. + γράφειν, write.] Sayings ascribed to Jesus which have been preserved in documents other than the canonical Gospels.

a-graph-i-a (a-graf'i-ą), *n.* [NL., < Gr. ἀ- priv. + γράφειν, write.] In *pathol.*, a cerebral disorder marked by inability to write.—**a-graph'ic,** *a.*

a-gra-ri-an (ą-grā'ri-ąn). [L. *agrarius*, < *ager*, land.] **I.** *a.* Pertaining to land, land-tenure, or the division of landed property; also, agricultural; rural; of plants, growing in fields; wild. **II.** *n.* One who favors the equal division of land or other regulation of the holding of landed property.—**a-gra'ri-an-ism,** *n.* The doctrines, methods, or practices of agrarians.

a-gree (ą-grē'), *v.*; *agreed, agreeing.* [OF. *agreer* (F. *agréer*), < *a gre*, to one's pleasure, < L. *ad*, to, and *gratus*, pleasing.] **I.** *tr.* To please†; regard with favor†; consent to, or arrange or settle by common consent (now only in the passive: see *agreed*); settle or adjust (differences, etc.) harmoniously (archaic). **II.** *intr.* To consent or accede (often with *to*); come to terms (often with *with*); make a bargain or agreement; be in accord or harmony, as in opinion, feeling, character, action, etc.; concur; accord; comport; correspond; get on together; of food, etc., to act favorably (*with*); in *gram.*, to correspond in number, case, gender, or person.—**a-gree'a-ble,** *a.* [OF. *agreable* (F. *agréable*).] Pleasing or pleasant; also, favorably inclined, or willing (colloq.); also, conformable (*to*); according; corresponding.—**a-gree-a-bil'i-ty** (-bil'i-ti), **a-gree'a-ble-ness,** *n.*—**a-gree'a-bly,** *adv.*—**a-greed',** *p. a.* Arranged or fixed by common consent (as, an *agreed* sum); also, being in accord; of like mind.—**a-gree'ment,** *n.* The act or state of agreeing; consent; mutual arrangement; a bargain, compact, or contract; accordance; accord; harmony; mutual correspondence; correspondence.

a-gré-ments (å-grā-moṅ), *n. pl.* [F.] Agreeable features or accessories; ornaments.

a-gres-tial (ą-gres'tiąl), *a.* [L. *agrestis*, < *ager*, land.] Pertaining to the fields; in *bot.*, growing wild in cultivated land.

a-gres-tic (ą-gres'tik), *a.* [L. *agrestis*: see *agrestial*.] Rural; rustic.

ag-ri-cul-tur-al (ag-ri-kul'ţūr-ąl), *a.* Of or pertaining to agriculture.—**ag-ri-cul'tur-al-ist,** *n.* An agriculturist.—**ag-ri-cul'tur-al-ly,** *adv.*

ag-ri-cul-ture (ag'ri-kul-ţūr), *n.* [L. *agricultura*, < *ager*, land, + *cultura*, culture.] The cultivation of land, as in the raising of crops; husbandry; tillage; farming: in a broad sense, including horticulture, forestry, stock-raising, etc.—**ag-ri-cul'tur-ist,** *n.* One engaged or versed in agriculture.

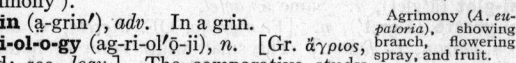

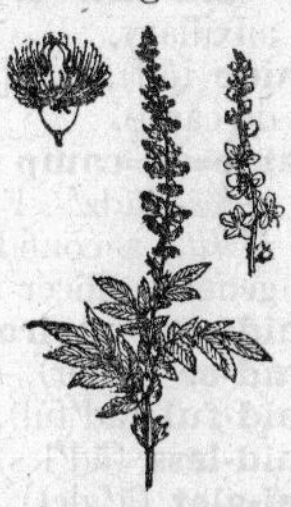
Agrimony (*A. eupatoria*), showing branch, flowering spray, and fruit.

ag-ri-mo-ny (ag'ri-mǫ-ni), *n.* [L. *agrimonia*, < Gr. ἀργεμώνη.] Any plant of the rosaceous genus *Agrimonia*, esp. *A. eupatoria*, a perennial herb with pinnate leaves and slender racemes of small yellow flowers; also, any of certain other plants, as *Eupatorium cannabinum* ('hemp-agrimony') or *Bidens cernua* (bur-marigold, or 'water-agrimony').

a-grin (ą-grin'), *adv.* In a grin.

ag-ri-ol-o-gy (ag-ri-ol'ǫ-ji), *n.* [Gr. ἄγριος, wild: see *-logy*.] The comparative study of the customs of uncivilized man.—**ag-ri-ol'o-gist,** *n.*

ag-ro-nom-ic, ag-ro-nom-i-cal (ag-rǫ-nom'ik, -i-kąl), *a.* Of or pertaining to agronomy.—**ag-ro-nom'ics,** *n.* The science of agronomy.

a-gron-o-my (ą-gron'ǫ-mi), *n.* [Gr. ἀγρονόμος, overseer of lands, < ἀγρός, field, + νέμειν, deal out, manage.] The art or science of the management of farming lands or farms: a branch of agriculture.—**a-gron'o-mist,** *n.*

ag-ros-tol-o-gy (ag-ros-tol'ǫ-ji), *n.* [Gr. ἄγρωστις, kind of grass: see *-logy*.] The part of botany that treats of grasses. —**ag-ros-tol'o-gist,** *n.*

ag-ro-tech-ny (ag'rǫ-tek-ni), *n.* [Gr. ἀγρός, field, + τέχνη, art.] The branch of agricultural science that deals with the conversion of raw farm-products into manufactured commodities, as in dairying, canning, etc.

a-ground (ą-ground'), *adv.* On the ground; stranded.

ag-ryp-not-ic (ag-rip-not'ik). [Gr. ἄγρυπνος, sleepless, banishing sleep, < ἀγρεῖν, hunt, + ὕπνος, sleep.] **I.** *a.* Preventing sleep. **II.** *n.* Something, as a drug, that prevents sleep.

a-guar-dien-te (ä-gwär-dyen'tā), *n.* [Sp., 'burning water.'] A brandy made in Spain and Portugal; hence, in Spanish-speaking countries, any spirituous liquor for drinking.

a-gue (ā'gū), *n.* [OF. *ague*, < ML. *acuta*, prop. fem. of L. *acutus*, acute.] An acute fever†; an intermittent malarial fever with periodic chills; chills and fever; a chill.—**a'gue,** *v. t.*; *agued, aguing.* To affect as with ague.—**a'gu-ish,** *a.* Of or like ague; conducive or subject to ague.—**a'gu-ish-ly,** *adv.*

ag-y-nous (aj'i-nus), *a.* [Gr. ἀ- priv. + γυνή, woman.] In *bot.*, having no female organs.

ah (ä), *interj.* An exclamation of pain, surprise, pity, joy, etc., according to the manner of utterance.

a-ha (ä-hä'), *interj.* An exclamation of triumph, derision, surprise, etc.

a-head (ą-hed'), *adv.* At or to the front; in advance; before; forward; onward.

a-heap (ą-hēp'), *adv.* In a heap.

a-hem (ą-hem'), *interj.* An utterance designed to attract attention, express doubt, etc.

a-hoy (ą-hoi'), *interj.* [Cf. *hoy*².] *Naut.*, a call used in hailing.

Ah-ri-man (ä'ri-mąn), *n.* [Pers.] In the Zoroastrian religion, the spirit or principle of evil. Cf. *Ormazd.*

a-hull (ą-hul'), *adv.* *Naut.*, with sails furled and helm lashed to the lee side.

a-hun-gered (ą-hung'gėrd), *a.* [Cf. AS. *ofhyngred.*] Affected with hunger; hungry. [Archaic.]

a-i (ä'ē), *n.* [Brazilian.] The three-toed sloth, *Bradypus tridactylus*, of South America: so called from its feeble, plaintive cry.

ai-blins (ā'blinz), *adv.* See *ablins.*

aid (ād), *v.* [OF. *aidier* (F. *aider*), < L. *adjutare*, freq. of *adjuvare*, give aid to, < *ad*, to, + *juvare*, help.] **I.** *tr.* To help; assist; afford support or relief to; second (efforts); facilitate (a process). **II.** *intr.* To give help or assistance. —**aid,** *n.* [OF. F. *aide.*] Help; assistance; succor; also, a helper or assistant; an auxiliary; a subordinate military or naval officer who acts as a confidential assistant to a superior officer; an aide-de-camp; also, a contribution from a feudal tenant or vassal to his lord; hence, a grant to the crown; a subsidy.—**aid′ance,** *n.* Assistance; aid. —**aid′ant.** **I.** *a.* Aiding; helpful. **II.** *n.* An assistant; an auxiliary.

aide (ād), *n.* [F.] An aid (subordinate officer); an aide-de-camp.

aide=de=camp (ād′dẹ-kamp′, F. ād-dė-käṅ), *n.*; pl. *aides-* (ādz′-, F. ād-). [F. *aide de camp,* 'camp assistant.'] *Milit.*, a confidential officer who transmits the orders of a general officer and otherwise assists him.

aide=mé-moire (ād-mā-mwor), *n.* [F.] A memorandum.

aid-er (ā′dėr), *n.* One who or that which aids.

aid-ful (ād′fụl), *a.* Helpful.

aid-less (ād′les), *a.* Unaided; helpless.

ai-glet (ā′glet), *n.* Same as *aglet.*

ai-grette (ā-gret′), *n.* [F. *aigrette,* OF. *aigrete,* < *aigron* = *hairon,* E. *heron.*] The small white egret or heron of Europe; also, a tuft or plume of heron's or other feathers used as a head-ornament, in millinery, etc.; a jeweled or other head-ornament of similar form; in *bot.*, an egret.

ai-guille (ā-gwēl′, F. ā-gwē-y′), *n.* [F. *aiguille,* OF. *aguille,* needle, < ML. *acucula,* dim. of L. *acus,* needle.] A slender drill for boring holes in blasting; also, a needle-like rock-mass or mountain peak.

ai-guil-lette (ā-gwi-let′), *n.* [F. *aiguillette,* OF. *aguillette,* dim. of *aguille*: see *aiguille.*] A metal tag (see *aglet*); now, usually, an ornamental tagged cord or braid on a uniform.

ail (āl), *v.* [AS. *eglan.*] **I.** *tr.* To affect with pain or uneasiness; trouble. **II.** *intr.* To be indisposed or unwell. —**ail,** *n.* Pain or disease; a bodily ill; an ailment.

ai-lan-tus, ai-lan-thus (ā-lan′tus, -thus), *n.* [NL., < Amboyna *ailanto,* 'tree of heaven.'] A tree of the simarubaceous genus *Ailantus,* with pinnate leaves and ill-scented greenish flowers, native in eastern Asia and planted in Europe and America as a shade-tree.—**ai-lan′tic, ai-lan′thic,** *a.*

ai-le-ron (ā′lẹ-ron), *n.* [F., dim. of *aile,* wing.] In an aëroplane, a small supplementary plane at the extremity of a main plane.

ail-ment (āl′mẹnt), *n.* A state or mode of ailing; a bodily disorder; a complaint.

aim (ām), *v.* [OF. *esmer,* or *aesmer* (with *a-* < L. *ad,* to), < L. *æstimare,* estimate.] **I.** *tr.* To estimate†; guess†; intend†; direct (a weapon, shot, stroke, action, effort, etc.) at a mark or object; point or level (*at*). **II.** *intr.* To direct one's course, purpose, efforts, etc. (with *at, for,* or an infinitive); take aim, as with a weapon.—**aim,** *n.* Estimation† or guess†; intention or purpose, or the thing intended; the act or direction of aiming a weapon, etc.; the mark aimed at.—**aim′er,** *n.*—**aim′less,** *a.* Lacking aim or purpose.—**aim′less-ly,** *adv.*—**aim′less-ness,** *n.*

ain (ān), *a.* Scotch form of *own.*

aî-né (ā-nā), *a.* [F.] Elder; senior.

ain't (ānt). A vulgar contraction of *am not* and of *are not*: often used for *is not, have not,* and *has not.*

air[1] (ãr), *n.* [F. *air,* appar. = OF. *air,* E. *air*[3].] Characteristic look, manner, or bearing; appearance; aspect; *pl.*, affected or pretentious manners.

air[2] (ãr), *n.* [F. *air,* < It. *aere* (now *aria*), < L. *aër*: see *air*[3].] In *music,* a tune; a melody; also, an aria; also, the soprano or treble part.

air[3] (ãr), *n.* [OF. F. *air,* < L. *aër,* < Gr. ἀήρ, < ἄηναι, breathe, blow: see *wind*[2].] The respirable fluid, a mixture of oxygen and nitrogen, which surrounds the earth and forms its atmosphere; also, any aëriform fluid; a gas; also, a breeze; also, space overhead or at large; fig., circulation; currency; publicity.—**in the air,** in circulation, as a rumor; also, without firm basis; uncertain; visionary; *milit.*, in an unsupported or unduly exposed position.—**to take the air,** to enjoy the fresh air in walking, driving, etc.—**air**[3], *v.* **I.** *tr.* To expose to the air; ventilate; also, to expose publicly; display. **II.** *intr.* To take the air: now chiefly in *airing, n.*—**air′=bed,** *n.* An inflatable air-tight mattress.—**air′=blad″der,** *n.* A vesicle or sac containing air; the swimming-bladder of fishes.—**air′=bound,** *a.* Stopped up by an accumulation of air, as a pipe.—**air′=brake,** *n.* A railroad brake, or system of continuous railroad brakes, operated by compressed air.—**air′=brush,** *n.* A kind of atomizer for spraying liquid paint upon a surface.—**air′-bus,** *n.* Same as *aërobus.*—**air′=cas″tle,** *n.* A castle in the air; a visionary project.—**air′=cell,** *n.* A cell containing air; an air-sac.—**air′=cham″ber,** *n.* A chamber containing air, as in a pump or a life-boat, or in an organic body.—**air′craft,** *n.* The art of aërial navigation; also, any vessel, vehicle, or machine for navigating the air; also, such vessels, etc., collectively.—**air′=cush″ion,** *n.* An inflatable air-tight cushion; also, a mechanical device using air to resist pressure.—**air′=cyl″in-der,** *n.* A cylinder containing air, esp. (with a piston) as a device for checking the recoil of a gun.—**air′=drain,** *n.* A space below a building to prevent dampness; an air passage.

Airacobra. A U. S. medium-altitude fighter plane (Bell).

Aire-dale (ãr′dāl) **ter′ri-er.** [From *Airedale* in Yorkshire, England.] A large, heavy kind of terrier with a rough brown or tan coat which is black or grizzled over the back.

air=en-gine (ãr′en″jin), *n.* A motor driven by the force of heated or compressed air.

air=gas (ãr′gas), *n.* An illuminating gas made by charging air with combustible vapor.

air=gun (ãr′gun), *n.* A gun operated by compressed air.

air=hole (ãr′hōl), *n.* A hole for the passage of air, or due to air; a natural opening in the ice on a river or pond; in *aëronautics,* a localized region in the atmosphere where a downward current or other cause deprives an aëroplane of a portion of its air-support, thus causing a drop or fall.

air-i-ly (ãr′i-li), *adv.* In an airy manner.—**air′i-ness,** *n.*

air-ing (ãr′ing), *n.* The act of one who airs; a walk, drive, etc., to take the air.

air=jack-et (ãr′jak″et), *n.* An inflatable jacket rendering the wearer buoyant in water; also, an envelop of inclosed air about part of a machine, as for checking radiation of heat.

air-less (ãr′les), *a.* Lacking air, or fresh air.

air=line (ãr′līn), *n.* A direct line, as if through the air.

air=lock (ãr′lok), *n.* An air-tight chamber in a caisson under water, for regulating the air-pressure between the chamber in which the men work and the entrance-shaft.

air=mail (ãr′māl), *n.* Mail service by aëroplane; mail so transmitted.—**air′=mail,** *v. t.* To send by air-mail.

air-man (ãr′mạn), *n.*; pl. *-men.* An aviator.—**air′man-ship,** *n.* Skill in aviation.

air-om-e-ter (ãr-om′e-tėr), *n.* [See *-meter.*] A gasometer for holding air; also, an apparatus for measuring the quantity or rate of flow of air.

air-plane (ãr′plān), *n.* An aëroplane.—**air′plane,** *v. i.*; *-planed, -planing.* To aëroplane.

air=plant (ãr′plant), *n.* A plant unconnected with the ground and apparently living on air, as many orchids; an aërophyte or epiphyte.

air=pock-et (ãr′pok″et), *n.* In *aëronautics,* a localized region of the air marked by atmospheric conditions different from those about it, and affecting the action of an aëroplane. Cf. *air-hole.*

air-port (ãr′pōrt), *n.* A landing-station for aircraft.

air=post (ãr′pōst), *n.* An aërial post; a mail service by aëroplane.

air=pres-sure (ãr′presh″ụr), *n.* Pressure exerted by air; esp., the pressure of the atmosphere.

air=proof (ãr′pröf), *a.* Impervious to air.

air=pump (ãr′pump), *n.* An apparatus for the exhaustion, compression, or transmission of air.

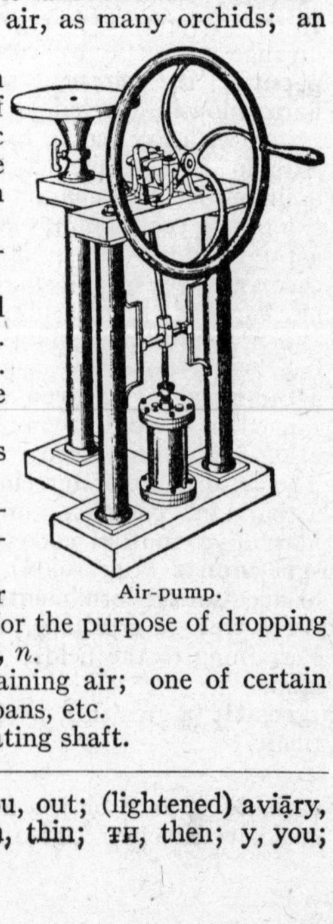

Air-pump.

air=raid (ãr′rād), *n.* A raid or incursion by hostile aircraft, esp. for the purpose of dropping bombs on a place.—**air′=raid″er,** *n.*

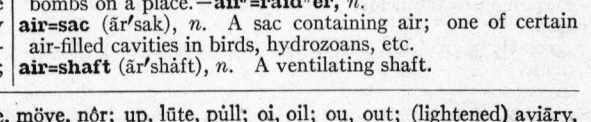

air=sac (ãr′sak), *n.* A sac containing air; one of certain air-filled cavities in birds, hydrozoans, etc.

air=shaft (ãr′shāft), *n.* A ventilating shaft.

air-ship (âr′ship), *n.* A vessel for navigating the air; esp., a dirigible balloon.
air-sick (âr′sik), *a.* Sick or ill as the result of traveling in the air.—**air′sick″ness,** *n.*
air=slaked (âr′slākt), *a.* Slaked by moist air, as lime.
air=spring (âr′spring), *n.* Any device for resisting sudden pressure by means of the elasticity of air.
air=stove (âr′stōv), *n.* A stove for heating air to be led off for warming purposes.
air=tight (âr′tīt), *a.* Impermeable to air.
air=trunk (âr′trungk), *n.* A large pipe or conduit for air, as for ventilating a public building.
air=ves-sel (âr′ves″ẹl), *n.* A vessel containing or conducting air; an air-chamber; a respiratory duct.
air-way (âr′wā), *n.* A passage for air, as for ventilating a mine; also, a route for aërial navigation.
air-wom-an (âr′wům″ạn), *n.*; pl. *-women* (-wim″en). A female aviator; an aviatress.
air-wor-thy (âr′wėr″ᴛʜi), *a.* Fit, well adapted, or safe for service in the air, as an aëroplane or airship.—**air′wor″thi-ness,** *n.*
air-y (âr′i), *a.*; compar. *airier,* superl. *airiest.* Of or like air; aëriform; unsubstantial; visionary; in or exposed to the air; aërial; breezy; light as air; buoyant; sprightly; also, full of airs; affected.
aisle (īl), *n.* [OF. *ele* (F. *aile*), < L. *ala,* wing.] A lateral division of a church, separated from the nave by piers or columns; a similar division at the side of the choir or a transept; sometimes, any of the divisions, as the nave; also, a passageway between seats in a church, hall, etc.; a long space between trees, etc., as in a forest.—**aisled,** *a.* Having aisles.

Aisle of Rouen Cathedral.

ait (āt), *n.* [ME. *æit*: cf. AS. *īggath,* < *īg,* island.] A small island; an islet in a river; an eyot. [Eng.]
aitch (āch), *n.* The letter H, h.
aitch-bone (āch′bōn), *n.* [For *nache-bone* (OF. *nache,* < L. *natis,* buttock).] The rump-bone, as of beef; a cut of beef including this bone.
a-jar[1] (ạ-jär′), *adv.* In a jarring state; in discord.
a-jar[2] (ạ-jär′), *adv.* On the jar or turn; slightly open, as a door.
a-jee (ạ-jē′), *adv.* See *agee.*
aj-o-wan (aj′ǫ-wạn), *n.* [E. Ind.] The fruit or seed of an Oriental apiaceous plant, *Ptychotis coptica,* used as a condiment and a carminative and yielding an aromatic oil.
aj-u-tage (aj′ǫ-tạj), *n.* [F., < OF. *ajuster*: see *adjust.*] A short tube adjusted to an orifice as a nozzle or spout.
a-kim-bo (ạ-kim′bō), *adv.* [ME. *in kenebowe,* appar. 'in keen bow,' in a sharp bend.] At an acute angle, as the arms when the hands are on the hips.
a-kin (ạ-kin′), *adv.* or *a.* Of kin; related; allied, as by nature or character: often with *to.*
ak-i-ne-sia (ak-i-nē′ẓiạ), *n.* [NL., < Gr. ἀκινησία, quiescence, rest, < ἀ- priv. + κινεῖν, move.] In *pathol.,* loss of the power of motion.
Ak-ka-di-an (a-kā′di-ạn). [From *Akkad,* city of ancient Babylonia.] **I.** *a.* Noting or pertaining to the primitive inhabitants of Babylonia or the non-Semitic language ascribed to them (see *Sumerian, a.*); also, noting or pertaining to the (later) Semitic language of Babylonia. **II.** *n.* One of the Akkadian people; also, the Akkadian language (in either sense).
-al[1]. [L. *-alis,* neut. *-ale*: cf. *-ar.*] A suffix meaning 'of or pertaining to,' 'connected with,' 'of the nature of,' 'like,' 'befitting,' etc., occurring in numerous adjectives and in many nouns of adjectival origin, as *annual, choral, equal, regal, rival.*
-al[2]. [OF. *-aille,* < L. *-alia,* neut. pl. of *-alis,* E. *-al*[1].] A suffix forming nouns of action from verbs, as in *espousal, refusal, reprisal.*
-al[3]. In *chem.,* a suffix representing *alcohol* or *aldehyde,* as in *bromal, chloral, citral.*
a-la (ā′lạ), *n.*; pl. *alæ* (ā′lē). [L., wing.] A wing; a wing-like part, process, or expansion, as of a bone, a shell, a seed, a stem, etc.; one of the two side petals of a papilionaceous flower.
à la (ä lä). [F.] To the; according to the; in the; often (with omission of F. *mode*), in the mode, manner, or style (specified): used in many phrases, as *à la mode* (in the fashion: see *à la mode*); *à la française* (in the French manner); *à la créole* (in the creole style; with a creole sauce: see *creole*); *à la carte* (see *à la carte*).
al-a-bas-ter (al′ạ-bås-tėr), *n.* [L., < Gr. ἀλάβαστρος, for ἀλάβαστος, an alabaster box.] A marble-like mineral, a finely granular variety of gypsum, often white and translucent, used for cutting into ornamental objects or work; also, a variety of calcite, often with a banded structure, used for similar purposes ('Oriental alabaster').—**al-a-bas′trine** (-trin), *a.*
à la carte (ä lä kärt). [F.] According to the bill of fare; with a stated price for each dish: as, dinner *à la carte.* Cf. *table d'hôte.*
a-lack (ạ-lak′), *interj.* [Perhaps for *ah, lack!*] An exclamation of sorrow. Also **a-lack′a-day′** (-ạ-dā′).
a-lac-ri-ty (ạ-lak′ri-ti), *n.* [L. *alacritas,* < *alacer,* lively.] Briskness; cheerful readiness; promptitude.—**a-lac′ri-tous,** *a.*
a-læ (ā′lē), *n.* Plural of *ala.*
a-la-me-da (ä-lä-mā′dä), *n.* [Sp., < *álamo,* poplar.] In Spanish use, a public walk shaded with poplars or other trees.
a-la-mo (ä′lä-mō), *n.* [Sp. *álamo.*] In Spanish use, a poplar; in the southwestern U. S., a cottonwood.
à la mode (ä lä mod). [F.] In the fashion; in a particular fashion (as, beef *à la mode,* beef larded and braised or stewed with vegetables, herbs, etc., and served with a rich brown gravy; pie *à la mode,* pie served with a portion of ice-cream on each piece): a phrase often used adjectively, and sometimes (esp. formerly) written *alamode.*—**al-a-mode** (al′ạ-mōd), *n.* A thin, glossy silk fabric formerly in use.
al-a-mort (al-ạ-môrt′), *a.* [F. *à la mort,* 'to the death.'] In a half-dead condition; melancholy. Also (as F.) **à la mort** (ä lä môr). [Archaic.]
a-lan-nah (ạ-lan′ạ), *n.* [Ir.] My child: used in familiar or affectionate address. [Ir.]
a-lar (ā′lạr), *a.* [L. *alaris,* < *ala,* wing.] Pertaining to wings or alæ; wing-like; alary; in *anat.* and *bot.,* axillary.
a-larm (ạ-lärm′), *n.* [OF. *alarme,* for *a l'arme,* 'to the arm!'—a cry calling to arms: see *arm*[2].] A call to arms, as on the approach of an enemy; a warning notice, as of danger; a signal; a mechanical contrivance for giving a warning or signal; also, a sudden attack or assault†; also, painful excitement due to sudden apprehension of danger; sudden fear.—**a-larm′,** *v. t.* To call to arms; warn of danger; also, to disturb with sudden fear; fill with alarm.—**a-larm′a-ble,** *a.* Liable to be alarmed.—**a-larm′ing-ly,** *adv.*—**a-larm′ism,** *n.* The habit or tendency of alarmists.—**a-larm′ist,** *n.* One given to raising alarms, esp. without sufficient reason, as by exaggerating dangers, prophesying calamities, etc.
a-lar-um (ạ-lar′um or ạ-lär′um), *n.* Same as *alarm.* [Now poetic, except as applied to a mechanical device.]
a-la-ry (ā′lạ-ri), *a.* [L. *alarius,* < *ala,* wing.] Pertaining to wings or alæ; alar.
a-las (ạ-lås′), *interj.* [OF. *a las, ha las* (F. *hélas*), < *a, ha,* ah, and *las,* miserable, < L. *lassus,* weary.] An exclamation of sorrow, pity, concern, etc.: sometimes followed by *for.*
A-las-kan (ạ-las′kạn). **I.** *a.* Of or pertaining to Alaska. **II.** *n.* A native or inhabitant of Alaska.
a-las-tor (ạ-las′tǫr), *n.* [Gr. ἀλάστωρ, < ἀ- priv. + λανθάνεσθαι, forget.] [Also *cap.*] A relentless avenging deity or spirit.

a-late (ā′lāt), *a.* [L. *alatus*, < *ala*, wing.] Having wings; winged; having alæ or wing-like parts. Also **a-lat-ed** (ā′lā-ted).—**a-la-tion** (ą̄-lā′-shǫn), *n.* Alate condition or form; manner of formation or disposition of the wings, as in insects.

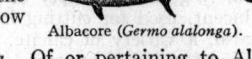

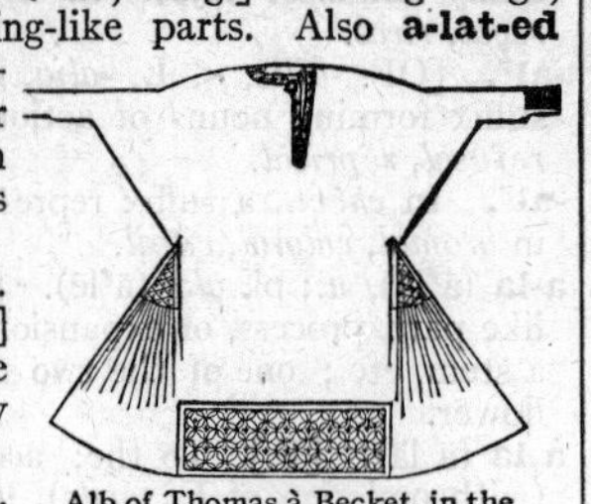
Alb of Thomas à Becket, in the cathedral at Sens.

alb (alb), *n.* [ML. *alba*, prop. fem. of L. *albus*, white.] *Eccles.*, a white linen robe with close sleeves, worn by an officiating priest.

al-ba-core (al′bą-kōr), *n.* [Pg. *albacor*, < Ar. *al*, the, + *bukr*, young camel, heifer.] A name for various fishes of the tunny kind; esp., the long-finned tunny, *Germo alalonga*, common in the Mediterranean and elsewhere.

Albacore (*Germo alalonga*).

Al-ba-ni-a (al-bā′ni-ą̈), *n.* [Cf. *Albion.*] An ancient name of the Highlands of Scotland. [Now poetic.]

Al-ba-ni-an (al-bā′ni-ąn). **I.** *a.* Of or pertaining to Albania, in the western part of the Balkan Peninsula, or its inhabitants. **II.** *n.* A native or inhabitant of Albania; the Albanian language.

al-ba-ta (al-bā′tą̈), *n.* [NL., < L. *albus*, white.] An alloy of nickel, zinc, and copper, used as a substitute for silver.

Albatross.

al-ba-tross (al′bą-trôs), *n.* [Pg. *alcatraz*; prob. from Ar.] Any of various large web-footed sea-birds related to the petrels, esp. of the genus *Diomedea*, of the Pacific and southern waters, noted for their powers of flight; also, a thin woolen fabric (also called *albatross cloth*).

al-be-it (âl-bē′it), *conj.* [ME. *al* (all, even) *be it.* Cf. *although.*] Even though it be; even though; although.

al-bert-ite (al′bėrt-īt), *n.* A pitch-like bituminous product from the Albert mine in New Brunswick.

al-ber-type (al′bėr-tīp), *n.* [From J. *Albert*, the inventor: see *-type.*] A method of printing in ink from a gelatin photographic plate; a print so made.

al-bes-cent (al-bes′ęnt), *a.* [L. *albescens* (*-ent-*), ppr. of *albescere*, become white, < *albus*, white.] Becoming white; whitish; blanched.—**al-bes′cence,** *n.*

al-bi-core (al′bi-kōr), *n.* See *albacore.*

Al-bi-gen-ses (al-bi-jen′sēz), *n. pl.* [ML., < *Albiga*, Albi, town in southern France.] The members of several anti-sacerdotal sects in the south of France in the 11th, 12th, and 13th centuries.—**Al-bi-gen′sian** (-şiąn), *a.* and *n.*

al-bi-no (al-bī′nō or al-bē′nō), *n.*; pl. *-nos* (-nōz). [Pg., < L. *albus*, white.] A person with a pale, milky skin, light hair, and pink eyes; hence, an animal or plant with a like defective coloring.—**al′bi-nism** (-bi-nizm), **al-bi′-no-ism,** *n.*

Al-bi-on (al′bi-ǫn), *n.* [L.; from Celtic.] An ancient name of England. [Now poetic.]

al-bite (al′bīt), *n.* [L. *albus*, white.] A white sodium feldspar, occurring in many crystalline rocks.

al-bo-lene (al′bǫ-lēn), *n.* [L. *albus*, white, + *oleum*, oil.] An oily liquid derived from petroleum, used as a spray for the nose, throat, etc.

al-bu-gin-e-a (al-bū-jin′ḗ-ą̈), *n.* [NL., < L. *albugo*, whiteness, < *albus*, white.] In *anat.*, any of several white membranes, as the sclerotic coat of the eye.—**al-bu-gin′e-ous,** *a.* Pertaining to or resembling an albuginea, as that of the eye; also, pertaining to or of the nature of the white of an egg.

al-bum (al′bum), *n.* [L., tablet, prop. neut. of *albus*, white.] A book of blank leaves for receiving autographs, photographs, etc.; also, a more or less ornate printed volume of selections of prose or verse.

al-bu-men (al-bū′men), *n.* [L., < *albus*, white.] The white of an egg; in *chem.*, albumin; in *bot.*, nutritive matter about the embryo in a seed.—**al-bu′min** (-min), *n.* In *chem.*, any of a class of substances composed of nitrogen, carbon, hydrogen, oxygen, and sulphur, occurring in animal and vegetable juices and tissues.—**al-bu′min-ate** (-āt), *n.* A compound resulting from the action of an alkali or an acid upon albumin; also, a compound formed by the union of an albumin with a metal, etc.—**al-bu′min-ize,** *v. t.*; *-ized, -izing.* To convert into albumin; treat with albumin.—**al-bu′mi-noid. I.** *a.* Resembling albumen or albumin. **II.** *n.* One of a class of albuminoid substances occurring in organic matter.—**al-bu-mi-noi′dal,** *a.*—**al-bu′mi-nose** (-nōs), **al-bu′mi-nous,** *a.* Containing albumen; pertaining to or resembling albumin.—**al-bu-mi-nu′-ri-a** (-nū′ri-ą̈), *n.* [NL. (Gr. οὖρον, urine).] In *pathol.*, the presence of albumin in the urine.—**al-bu-mi-nu′ric,** *a.*—**al′bu-mose** (-bų-mōs), *n.* [See *-ose*².] In *physiol. chem.*, any of a class of compounds derived from albumins, etc., by the action of proteolytic enzymes.

al-bur-num (al-bėr′num), *n.* [L., < *albus*, white.] In *bot.*, the lighter-colored, softer part of the wood of exogenous plants, between the inner bark and the heart-wood.

al-ca-hest (al′ką-hest), etc. See *alkahest*, etc.

Al-ca-ic (al-kā′ik). [L. *Alcaicus*, < Gr. Ἀλκαϊκός, < Ἀλκαῖος, Alcæus.] **I.** *a.* Pertaining to Alcæus, a Greek lyric poet of Mytilene in Lesbos (about 600 B.C.), or to certain meters or a form of strophe or stanza used by or named after him. **II.** *n.* An Alcaic verse; *pl.*, Alcaic verses or strophes.

al-caide (al-kād′, Sp. äl-kī′ᴛʜā), *n.* [Sp., < Ar. *al*, the, + *qāïd*, governor.] In Spanish use, the governor of a fortress; also, the warden of a prison.

al-cal-de (äl-käl′dā), *n.* [Sp., < Ar. *al*, the, + *qādī*, judge: cf. *cadi.*] In Spanish use, a chief municipal officer with judicial powers.—**al-cal-dí-a** (äl-käl-dē′ä), *n.* [Sp.] The office, jurisdiction, or official quarters of an alcalde.

al-can-na (al-kan′ą̈), *n.* [Sp. *alcana, alheña*, < Ar. *al*, the, + *hennā*, henna.] Same as *henna.*

al-cayde′, *n.* Same as *alcaide.*

al-ca-zar (al-kä′zär, Sp. äl-kä′thär), *n.* [Sp. *alcázar*, < Ar. *al*, the, + *qaçr*, castle.] A castle or palace of the Spanish Moors; hence, a name sometimes given to a public building in the Moorish style.

al-chem-ic (al-kem′ik), *a.* Of or pertaining to alchemy. Also **al-chem′i-cal.**—**al-chem′i-cal-ly,** *adv.*

al-che-mist (al′ke-mist), *n.* One who practises alchemy.—**al-che-mis′tic, al-che-mis′ti-cal,** *a.*

al-che-mize (al′ke-mīz), *v. t.*; *-mized, -mizing.* To transmute, as by alchemy.

al-che-my (al′ke-mi), *n.* [OF. *alkimie* (F. *alchimie*), < ML. *alchimia*, < Ar. *al*, the, + *kīmīa*, prob. < LGr. χημεία, for χυμεία, fusion (of metals), < Gr. χεῖν, pour, melt, smelt.] Medieval chemistry, an art which sought in particular to transmute baser metals into gold, also to find a universal solvent (alkahest) and an 'elixir of life'; hence, any magical power or process of transmutation; also, formerly, a mixed metal resembling brass.

al-co-gas (al′kǭ-gas), *n.* [From *alco*(*hol*) + *gas*(*oline*).] A fuel containing alcohol, benzol, gasoline, etc., for aëroplanes, automobiles, and the like, recommended as more efficient than gasoline, esp. at low temperatures. [Proprietary name.]

al-co-hol (al′kǭ-hol), *n.* [ML., orig. fine powder, < Ar. *al*, the, + *koh'l*, powdered antimony, kohl.] A colorless, inflammable liquid ('ethyl alcohol,' C_2H_5OH), the intoxicating principle of fermented liquors, formed from certain sugars (esp. glucose) by fermentation, and now usually prepared from grain by treating this with malt and causing the maltose and dextrin so formed to ferment by the addition of yeast; hence, any alcoholic liquor; in *chem.*, any of a class of chemical compounds analogous to ethyl alcohol.—**al-co-hol′ic,** *a.* Of or containing alcohol; also, suffering from alcoholism.—**al″co-hol-i′ci-ty** (-is′i-ti), *n.* Alcoholic quality or strength.—**al′co-hol-ism,** *n.* The morbid effects of excessive use of alcoholic beverages.—**al′co-hol-ize,** *v. t.*; *-ized, -izing.* To convert into alcohol; rectify (a spirit); also, to treat or affect with alcohol.—**al″co-hol-i-za′tion** (-i-zā′shǫn), *n.*—**al″co-hol-om′e-ter** (-om′e-tėr), *n.* [See *-meter.*] An instrument for finding the percentage of alcohol in a liquid. Also **al-co-hom′e-ter** (-hom′e-tėr).

Al-co-ran (al-kọ̄-rän′ or al′kọ̄-rạn), *n.* [Ar. *al-qurān*, 'the reading.'] Same as *Koran*.

al-cove (al′kōv or al-kōv′), *n.* [F. *alcôve*, < Sp. *alcoba*, < Ar. *al*, the, + *qobbah*, vaulted space.] A recess opening out of a room; any recessed space, as in a library or a garden.

al-cy-on (al′si-ọn), *n.* and *a.* See *halcyon*.

al-de-hyde (al′dẹ̄-hīd), *n.* [For NL. *alcohol dehydrogenatum*, alcohol deprived of hydrogen.] In *chem.*, a transparent colorless liquid, CH_3CHO, produced by the oxidation of ordinary alcohol; also, one of a class of analogous compounds derived from corresponding primary alcohols.—**al-de-hy′dic** (-hī′dik), *a.*

Alder (*Alnus glutinosa*).

al-der (âl′dėr), *n.* [AS. *alor*, *aler*, akin to G. *erle*.] Any shrub or tree of the betulaceous genus *Alnus*, growing in moist places in northern temperate or colder regions; also, any of various other shrubs or trees resembling this genus.

al-der-man (âl′dėr-mạn), *n.*; pl. *-men*. [AS. *aldormann*, *ealdormann*, < *aldor*, chief, elder, + *mann*, man.] In Anglo-Saxon times, a chief or lord; later, the chief magistrate of a territorial division; also, the head of a gild; now, one of a body of municipal officers, ranking below the mayor, with powers (executive, judicial, or legislative) varying according to locality.—**al′der-man-ate** (-āt), *n.* The office or dignity of alderman; the body of aldermen.—**al′der-man-cy, al′der-man-ship,** *n.* The office of alderman.—**al-der-man′ic** (-man′ik), *a.* Of or befitting an alderman.

Device of Aldus.

Al-der-ney (âl′dėr-ni), *n.*; pl. *-neys* (-niz). One of a breed of small cattle, usually fawn-colored, originating on the island of Alderney, in the English Channel, and noted for their milk.

Al-dine (âl′dīn or âl′dēn), *a.* Of or from the press of Aldus Manutius and his family, of Venice (about 1490–1597), as certain choice editions of the classics: hence used as a name for various editions of printed works and for styles of type.

ale (āl), *n.* [AS. *ealu*.] A light-colored beer made from malt dried at a low heat; an ale-drinking festival†; an ale-house†.

a-leak (ạ-lēk′), *adv.* In a leaking state.

a-le-a-to-ry (ā′lẹ̄-ạ-tọ̄-ri), *a.* [L. *aleatorius*, < *aleator*, gamester, < *alea*, game with dice.] Dependent on a contingent event.

ale=con-ner (āl′kon″ėr), *n.* [See *conner*[1].] Orig., an officer appointed to test ale and beer and see that they were good and wholesome; later, an officer chosen to inspect the measures used in public houses. [Eng.]

a-lec-try-o-man-cy (a-lek′tri-ọ̄-man″si), *n.* [Gr. ἀλεκτρυών, cock: see *-mancy*.] Divination by means of a cock picking up grains of corn.

A-lec-try-on (a-lek′tri-ọn), *n.* [Gr. ἀλεκτρυών.] A name for the domestic cock. [Poetic.]

a-lee (ạ-lē′), *adv.* *Naut.*, on or to the lee side: opposed to *aweather*.

al-e-gar (al′ẹ̄-gär or ā′lẹ̄-), *n.* [From *ale* + *-egar* as in *vinegar*.] Ale vinegar; sour ale.

ale=house (āl′hous), *n.* A house where ale is retailed.

a-lem-bic (ạ-lem′bik), *n.* [OF. F. *alambic*, < Ar. *al*, the, + *anbīq*, still, < Gr. ἄμβιξ, cup.] A vessel with a beaked cap or head, formerly used in distilling; fig., something that transforms or refines.

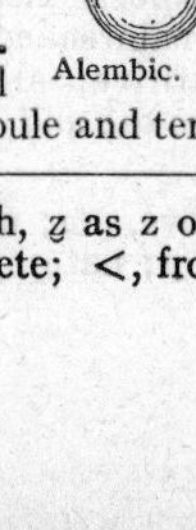
Alembic.

a-lep-i-dote (a-lep′i-dōt), *a.* [Gr. ἀλεπίδωτος, < ἀ- priv. + λεπίς (λεπιδ-), scale.] Having no scales, as some fishes.

A-lep-po (ạ-lep′ọ̄) **boil, but′ton,** or **ul′cer.** [From *Aleppo*, in Syria.] In *pathol.*, a local cutaneous affection beginning as a small red papule and terminating in an ulcer and leaving a permanent scar: endemic in Syria, Egypt, India, etc.

a-lert (ạ-lėrt′). [F. *alerte*, < It. *all' erta*, on the lookout (*erta*, lit. 'raised place,' prop. fem. pp. of *ergere*, < L. *erigere*, E. *erect*, *v.*).] **I.** *a.* On the lookout; vigilantly attentive or ready; prompt; active. **II.** *n.* The attitude of vigilance; lookout; watch; guard; *milit.*, an alarm; a sudden attack.—**a-lert′ly,** *adv.*—**a-lert′ness,** *n.*

a-leu-ro-nat (a-lū′rọ̄-nat), *n.* Flour made of aleurone: used esp. in making bread for diabetic persons.

a-leu-rone (a-lū′rōn), *n.* [Gr. ἄλευρον, flour.] Minute albuminoid granules (protein) found, in connection with starch and oily matter, in the endosperm of ripe seeds, and in a special layer of cells in grains of wheat, etc.—**al-eu-ron-ic** (al-ụ̄-ron′ik), *a.*

ale-wife (āl′wīf), *n.*; pl. *-wives* (-wīvz). A woman who keeps an ale-house; also, a North American fish, *Pomolobus pseudoharengus*, resembling a small shad but inferior as food.

Al-ex-an-dri-an (al-eg-zan′dri-ạn), *a.* Of or pertaining to the city of Alexandria in Egypt, founded by Alexander the Great; also, of or pertaining to Alexander the Great; in *pros.*, noting the verse known as an Alexandrine.

Al-ex-an-drine (al-eg-zan′drin), *n.* [From *Alexandre* Paris, an old French poet, or from his or some other poem in this meter on *Alexander* the Great.] In *pros.*, a verse of six iambic feet.

al-ex-an-drite (al-eg-zan′drīt), *n.* [From *Alexander* II. of Russia.] A variety of chrysoberyl appearing dark-green by daylight and red by artificial light or by daylight transmitted through the stone: used as a gem.

a-lex-i-a (a-lek′si-ạ̈), *n.* [NL., < Gr. ἀ- priv. + λέξις, a speaking, < λέγειν, speak.] In *pathol.*, a cerebral disorder marked by inability to read, or to read aloud.

a-lex-in (a-lek′sin), *n.* [Gr. ἀλέξειν, ward off.] In *physiol. chem.*, any of certain substances present in normal blood-serum which are capable of destroying bacteria, etc.

a-lex-i-phar-mic (a-lek-si-fär′mik). [Gr. ἀλεξιφάρμακος, < ἀλέξειν, ward off, + φάρμακον, poison.] **I.** *a.* Warding off poisoning or infection; antidotal; prophylactic. **II.** *n.* An alexipharmic agent; esp., an internal antidote.

a-lex-i-py-ret-ic (a-lek″si-pī-ret′ik), *a.* and *n.* [Gr. ἀλέξειν, ward off, + πυρετός, fever.] Same as *febrifuge*.

a-lex-i-ter-ic (a-lek-si-ter′ik). [Gr. ἀλεξητήριος, < ἀλεξητήρ, defender, < ἀλέξειν, ward off.] **I.** *a.* Warding off poisoning; counteracting venom. **II.** *n.* An alexiteric remedy, esp. an external application.

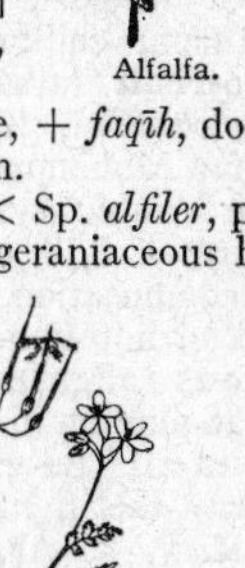
Alfalfa.

al-fal-fa (al-fal′fạ̈), *n.* [Sp.; from Ar.] The forage-plant lucerne, *Medicago sativa*, esp. as grown in the western U. S.

al-fa-qui (al-fạ-kē′), *n.* [Sp., < Ar. *al*, the, + *faqīh*, doctor of theology.] A Mohammedan theologian.

al-fi-le-ri-a (al″fi-lẹ-rē′ạ̈), *n.* [Amer. Sp., < Sp. *alfiler*, pin.] The pin-grass, *Erodium cicutarium*, a low geraniaceous herb with long-beaked fruit, native in Europe but widely naturalized elsewhere, and valued as a forage-plant. Also **al″fi-le-ril′la** (-rē′ạ̈). [Western U. S.]

al fres-co (äl fres′kō). [It., 'in the fresh.'] In the open air: a phrase often used adjectively (as, an *al-fresco* dinner).

al-ga (al′gạ̈), *n.*; pl. *-gæ* (-jē). [L., seaweed.] A seaweed; any plant belonging to a division or aggregate of chlorophyllous thallophytes comprising the seaweeds and various fresh-water forms.—**al′gal,** *a.*

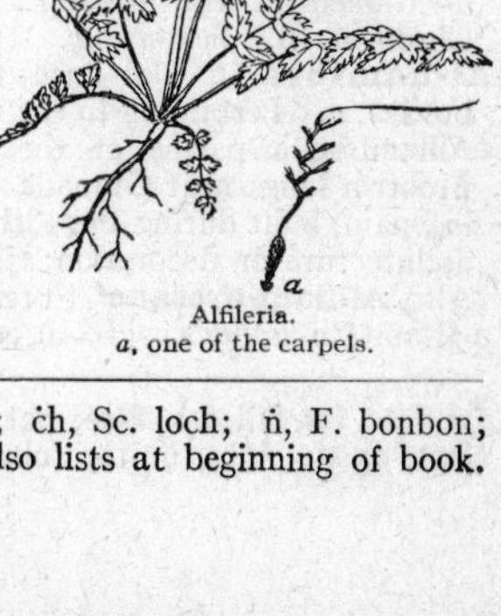
a
Alfileria.
a, one of the carpels.

al-gar-ro-ba (al-gạ-rō′bạ̈), *n.* [Sp., < Ar. *al*, the, + *kharrūbah*, E. *carob*.] The carob (fruit or tree); also, the mesquite, *Prosopis glandulosa*, or its sweet, bean-like pods; also, a large cæsalpiniaceous tree, *Hymenæa courbaril*, of the West Indies, etc.

Algarroba (*Hymenæa courbaril*).

al-gate, al-gates (âl′gāt, -gāts), *adv.* [From *all*, *a.*, + *gate*².] Always; in every way; everywhere; at all events, or in any case; however or nevertheless. [Now prov. Eng.]

al-ge-bra (al′je-brạ̈), *n.* [ML., < Ar. *al-jebr*, *al-jabr*, redintegration, bone-setting, algebraic reduction, < *al*, the, + *jabr*, < *jabara*, reunite.] The mathematical art of reasoning about (quantitative) relations by means of a systematized notation including letters and other symbols; the analysis of equations; also, a treatise on this subject.—**al-ge-bra′ic** (-brā′ik), *a.* Of or pertaining to algebra. Also **al-ge-bra′i-cal.**—**al-ge-bra′i-cal-ly,** *adv.*—**al′ge-bra-ist** (-brā-ist), **al′ge-brist,** *n.* One versed in algebra.

Al-ge-ri-an (al-jē′ri-ạn). **I.** *a.* Of or pertaining to Algiers or Algeria. **II.** *n.* A native or inhabitant of Algiers or Algeria; an Algerine.

Al-ge-rine (al-je-rēn′). **I.** *a.* Algerian. **II.** *n.* A native or inhabitant of Algiers or Algeria, esp. one of the indigenous Berber or Arab inhabitants.

-algia. [NL.] Noun termination from Gr. ἄλγος, pain, used in pathological terms, as *cardialgia*, *gastralgia*, *neuralgia*.

al-gid (al′jid), *a.* [L. *algidus*, < *algere*, be cold.] Cold; chilly.—**al-gid′i-ty,** *n.*

al-goid (al′goid), *a.* Resembling algæ.

al-gol-o-gy (al-gol′ọ̄-ji), *n.* [L. *alga*, seaweed: see *-logy*.] The part of botany that treats of algæ.—**al-gol′o-gist,** *n.*

al-gom-e-ter (al-gom′e-tėr), *n.* [Gr. ἄλγος, pain: see *-meter*.] A device for determining sensitiveness to pain due to pressure.—**al-go-met′ric** (-gọ̄-met′rik), *a.*

Al-gon-ki-an (al-gong′ki-ạn). **I.** *a.* Algonquian; in *geol.*, noting or pertaining to a geological era or period, or a group or system of rocks, immediately preceding the Cambrian in North America. **II.** *n.* In *geol.*, the Algonkian period or system.

Al-gon-qui-an (al-gong′ki-ạn), *a.* Belonging to or constituting a linguistic stock of North American Indians formerly extending from Labrador and the northern half of the U. S. eastern coast westward to the Rocky Mountains, and including the Algonquin, Cheyenne, Cree, Delaware, Micmac, Mohican, Ojibwa, Shawnee, and many other tribes.

al-gor (al′gọr), *n.* [L., < *algere*, be cold.] In *pathol.*, coldness; chill, esp. at the onset of fever.

al-go-rism (al′gọ̄-rizm), *n.* [OF. *algorisme*, < Ar. *al-Khowārazmī*, 'the native of *Khwārazm* (Khiva),' Abu Ja'far Mohammed ben Musa, an Arabian mathematician.] The Arabic system of arithmetical notation (with the figures 1, 2, 3, etc.); hence, arithmetic; also, any method of computation, esp. with a special notation.

Court of the Lions, Alhambra.

al-gous (al′gus), *a.* Of, like, or abounding in algæ.

al-gua-zil (al-gwạ-zēl′, Sp. äl-gwä-thēl′), *n.* [Sp., now *alguacil*, < Ar. *al*, the, + *wazīr*, vizier, officer.] In Spanish use, an officer of justice; a constable.

al-gum (al′gum), *n.* [Heb. *algūm*.] An unidentified tree mentioned in the Bible (2 Chron. ii. 8). See *almug*.

Al-ham-bra-ic (al-ham-brā′ik), *a.* Pertaining to the Alhambra, a palace of the Moorish kings near Granada in Spain, built during the 13th and 14th centuries, or to its architecture or decoration; in the style of the Alhambra. Also **Al-ham-bresque′** (-bresk′).

a-li-as (ā′li-ạs), *adv.* [L., at another time or place, < *alius*, other.] Otherwise; otherwise called: used in giving an alternative or assumed name.—**a′li-as,** *n.*; pl. *aliases.* An alternative or assumed name.

al-i-bi (al′i-bī), *n.*; pl. *-bis* (-bīz). [L., elsewhere, < *alius*, other.] In *law*, the plea or the fact of having been elsewhere at the time of an offense charged; also, in general use, an excuse (colloq.).

al-i-ble (al′i-bl), *a.* [L. *alibilis*, < *alere*, nourish.] Nutritive.—**al-i-bil′i-ty** (-bil′i-ti), *n.*

al-i-dade (al′i-dād), *n.* [F., < Ar. *al-'idādah*.] A movable arm passing over a graduated circle and carrying a vernier or an index: attached to instruments for measuring angles.

al-ien (āl′yẹn). [OF. *alien*, < L. *alienus*, < *alius*, other.] **I.** *a.* Belonging to others or elsewhere; not native or naturalized in the place of residence; foreign; strange; remote (*from*); adverse (*to*). **II.** *n.* A foreign-born resident not admitted to rights of citizenship; a foreigner; a stranger. Also fig.—**al′ien,** *v. t.* [OF. *aliener* (F. *aliéner*), < L. *alienare* (pp. *alienatus*), < *alienus*.] To alienate; transfer; estrange.—**al′ien-a-ble,** *a.* Subject to alienation.—**al″ien-a-bil′i-ty** (-bil′i-ti), *n.*—**al′ien-age** (-ā̤j), *n.* The state or status of an alien.

al-ien-ate (āl′yẹn-āt), *v. t.*; *-ated*, *-ating*. [L. *alienatus*, pp.: see *alien*, *v.*] To transfer (property, etc.) to another; fig., to turn away in feeling or affection; estrange (*from*).—**al′ien-ate,** *a.* Alienated; estranged. [Obs. or archaic.]—**al-ien-a′tion** (-ā′shọn), *n.* [L. *alienatio(n-)*.] The act of alienating; alienated state; transfer of title; estrangement; mental derangement.—**al′ien-a-tor,** *n.*

al-ien-ee (āl-yẹn-ē′), *n.* One to whom property is aliened.

al-ien-er (āl′yẹn-ėr), *n.* Same as *alienor*.

al-ien-ism (āl′yẹn-izm), *n.* Alienage; also, the study or treatment of mental diseases.—**al′ien-ist,** *n.* One engaged in the study or treatment of mental diseases.

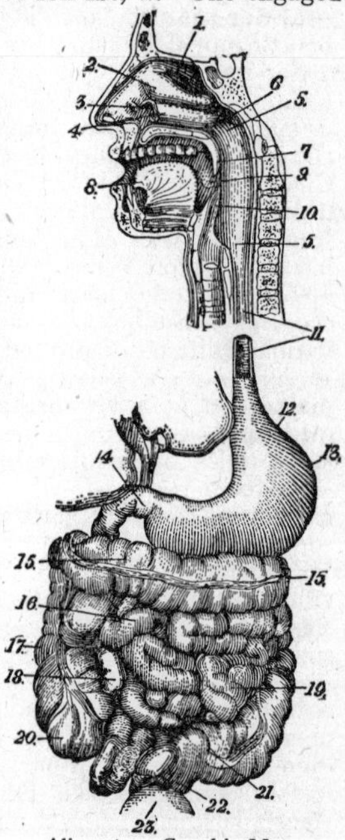

Alimentary Canal in Man.

1, superior turbinated bone; 2, middle turbinated bone; 3, opening of the nasal duct; 4, inferior turbinated bone; 5, 5, pharynx; 6, opening of Eustachian tube; 7, uvula; 8, tongue; 9, tonsil; 10, epiglottis; 11, esophagus; 12, cardiac portion (left side) of stomach; 13, fundus of stomach; 14, pylorus (right side of stomach), resting on right lobe of liver, partly shown in outline; 15, transverse colon; 16, duodenum; 17, ascending colon; 18, ileum; 19, jejunum; 20, cæcum; 21, sigmoid flexure of colon; 22, beginning of rectum; 23, fundus of urinary bladder.

al-ien-or (āl′yẹn-ọr), *n.* One who transfers property.

al-i-form (al′i-fôrm), *a.* [L. *ala*, wing: see *-form*.] Wing-shaped; wing-like; alar.

a-light¹ (ạ-līt′), *adv.* or *a.* [See *light*¹.] In a lighted state; illuminated; burning.

a-light² (ạ-līt′), *v. i.* [AS. *ālīhtan*, < *ā-*, away, + *līhtan*, E. *light*³.] To get down as from a horse or a vehicle; descend; come to rest (*on*); light or happen (*on*).

a-lign (ạ-līn′), etc. See *aline*, etc.

a-like (ạ-līk′), *a.* [AS. *gelīc*, or, with different prefix, *anlīc*, Icel. *ālīkr*: see *like*¹.] Like one another; similar: used regularly of a plural substantive or idea, and only rarely attributively.—**a-like′,** *adv.* In the same manner or degree; equally.

al-i-ment (al′i-mẹnt), *n.* [L. *alimentum*, < *alere*, nourish: see *old*.] Food; nutriment; sustenance; support.—**al′i-ment** (-ment), *v. t.* To furnish with aliment.—**al-i-men′tal** (-men′tạl), *a.* Of or pertaining to aliment.—**al-i-men′tal-ly,** *adv.*—**al-i-men′ta-ry** (-men′tạ-ri), *a.* [L. *alimentarius*.] Pertaining to aliment or to nutrition: as, the *alimentary* canal (the food-passage in any animal, from mouth to anus).—**al″i-men-ta′tion** (-tā′shọn), *n.* Nourishment; nutrition; also, maintenance; support.—**al-i-men′ta-tive** (-tạ-tiv), *a.* Nutritive; alimentary.—**al-i-men′tive-ness,** *n.* Propensity to eat and drink: in *phren.*, a special faculty.

al-i-mo-ny (al′i-mọ̄-ni), *n.* [L. *alimonia*, sustenance, < *alere*, nourish.] In *law*, an allowance paid to a woman by her husband or former husband for her maintenance, granted by a court on a legal separation or a divorce, or while action is pending.

a-line, a-lign (ạ-līn′), *v.*; *alined* or *aligned*, *alining* or *aligning*. [F. *aligner*, < *à* (< L. *ad*), to, + *ligne*, < L. *linea*, line.] **I.** *tr.* To adjust to a line; range in line. **II.** *intr.* To come into or be in line.—**a-line′ment, a-lign′ment,** *n.* Adjustment to a line; arrangement in line; the line or lines formed; in *archæol.*, a line or an arrangement of parallel or converging lines of upright stones (menhirs); in *engin.*, a ground-plan, as of a railroad or a field-work.—**a-lin′er, a-lign′er,** *n.*

al-i-ped (al′i-ped), *a.* [L. *alipes* (*aliped-*), having winged feet, < *ala*, wing, + *pes* (*ped-*), foot.] Having the toes connected by a wing-like membrane, as the bats.

al-i-quant (al′i-kwạnt), *a.* [L. *aliquantus*, some, < *alius*, other, + *quantus*, how great.] In *math.*, contained in a number or quantity, but not dividing it evenly: as, 5 is an *aliquant* part of 16.

al-i-quot (al′i-kwọt), *a.* [L., some, < *alius*, other, + *quot*, how many.] In *math.*, forming an exact divisor: as, 5 is an *aliquot* part of 15.

al-i-sphe-noid (al-i-sfē′noid). [L. *ala*, wing, + E. *sphenoid*.] In *anat.*: **I.** *a.* Noting or pertaining to either of two bones of the skull forming the greater wings of the sphenoid. **II.** *n.* An alisphenoid bone.—**al″i-sphe-noi′dal** (-sfẹ-noi′dạl), *a.*

a-li-tur-gic, a-li-tur-gi-cal (a-li-tėr′jik, -ji-kạl), *a.* [See *a-*[1].] *Eccles.*, not liturgical; having no connection with the official services of the church; esp., noting certain days on which the eucharistic service is not to be celebrated.

a-li-un-de (ā-li-un′dē), *adv.* [L.] From another source.

a-live (ạ-līv′), *a.* [AS. *on līfe*, in life.] In life or existence; living; hence, unextinguished, as fire, a memory, etc.; also, full of life; lively; animated; also, awake or sensitive (*to*: as, to be *alive* to one's own interests, or to the beauties of nature); also, swarming (*with*): rarely used attributively.—**a-live′ness,** *n.*

al-i-za-ri (al-i-zä′ri), *n.* [F. and Sp.; prob. from Ar.] The commercial name of madder in the Levant.—**a-liz-a-rin** (ạ-liz′ạ-rin), *n.* A coloring matter orig. obtained from madder and yielding red, but now made from anthracene and serving to form various colors.

al-ka-hest (al′kạ-hest), *n.* [Prob. coined by Paracelsus.] The universal solvent sought by the alchemists.—**al-ka-hes′tic,** *a.*

al-ka-les-cent (al-kạ-les′ẹnt), *a.* [See *-escent*.] Tending to become alkaline; slightly alkaline.—**al-ka-les′cence, al-ka-les′cen-cy,** *n.*

al-ka-li (al′kạ-lī or -li), *n.*; pl. *-lis* or *-lies* (-līz or -liz). [OF. *alcali*, < Ar. *al*, the, + *qalī*, saltwort ashes, < *qalay*, roast.] Orig., the soda derived from the ashes of plants; now, any of various compounds, the hydroxides of sodium, potassium, lithium, rubidium, and cæsium (the 'alkali metals'), and of ammonium, which neutralize acids to form salts and turn red litmus-paper blue; any of various other more or less active bases, as calcium hydroxide; also, any of various other compounds, as the carbonates of sodium and potassium; also, a soluble mineral salt, or a mixture of soluble salts, occurring in soils, etc.—**alkali flat,** a sterile plain at the bottom of an undrained basin, containing an excess of alkali in its soil.—**alkali soil,** any of various soils in poorly drained or arid regions, containing an unusually large amount of soluble mineral salts (chiefly of sodium) which during dry weather appear on the surface in the form of a (usually white) crust or powder.—**al-ka-lif′er-ous** (-lif′ẹ-rus), *a.* [See *-ferous*.] Yielding an alkali.—**al′ka-li-fy** (-li-fī), *v. t.* or *i.*; *-fied*, *-fying*. [See *-fy*.] To convert into or become an alkali.—**al-ka-lig′e-nous** (-lij′e-nus), *a.* [See *-genous*.] Generating an alkali.—**al-ka-lim′e-ter** (-lim′e-tėr), *n.* [See *-meter*.] An instrument for determining the quantity of an alkali in substances or solutions.—**al-ka-lim′e-try,** *n.*—**al′ka-line** (-lin or -līn), *a.* Of, like, or containing an alkali.—**alkaline earths,** in *chem.*, the oxides of barium, strontium, calcium, and sometimes magnesium.—**al-ka-lin′i-ty** (-lin′i-ti), *n.*—**al′ka-lize** (-līz), *v. t.*; *-lized*, *-lizing*. To make alkaline; alkalify.—**al″ka-li-za′tion** (-li-zā′shọn), *n.*—**al′ka-loid. I.** *a.* Resembling an alkali; alkaline. **II.** *n.* A substance resembling an alkali; esp., one of a class of basic nitrogenous organic compounds occurring in plants; sometimes, a leucomaine or a ptomaine.—**al-ka-loi′dal** (-loi′dạl), *a.*

al-ka-net (al′kạ-net), *n.* [Sp. *alcaneta*, dim. of *alcana*, henna: see *alcanna*.] A European boraginaceous plant, *Alkanna tinctoria*, whose root yields a red dye; also, the root, or the dye; also, any of several similar plants, as the bugloss (*Anchusa officinalis*) and the puccoon (genus *Lithospermum*).

al-ke-ken-gi (al-kẹ-ken′ji), *n.* [ML., < Ar. *al-kākanj*, < *al*, the, + Pers. *kākanj*, kind of resin.] A solanaceous herb, *Physalis alkekengi*, bearing an edible, slightly acid scarlet fruit, loosely inclosed in a large red calyx; also, the fruit.

Al-ko-ran′, *n.* See *Alcoran* and *Koran*.

all (âl), *a.* [AS. *all*, *eall*, = OHG. *al* (G. *all*) = Icel. *allr* = Goth. *alls*, all.] The whole quantity, extent, or number of; every (now only with *kind*, *manner*, etc.); any whatever (as, "Things without *all* remedy Should be without regard": Shakspere's "Macbeth," iii. 2. 11): placed before *the* or a possessive or demonstrative pronoun when used with such a word.—**All Fools' Day,** April 1, as observed with tricks or jests intended to make an 'April fool' of any unwary person.—**All Saints' Day,** Nov. 1, observed in the Roman Catholic and Anglican churches in commemoration of all the saints.—**All Souls' Day,** Nov. 2, observed (chiefly) in the Roman Catholic Church in commemoration of all the faithful dead.—**all. I.** *pron.* The whole quantity, extent, or number; all parts, things, or persons; everything. Used in various phrases, as *after all* (all things considered; notwithstanding everything; nevertheless); *all but* (everything but; almost); *all in all* (everything collectively); *at all* (in any degree or respect; under any circumstances). **II.** *n.* A whole; a totality; one's whole fortune, property, etc. (as, to risk one's *all*).—**all,** *adv.* Wholly; entirely; completely; altogether; quite; also, even or just (now poetic: cf. *albeit*, *although*).

Al-lah (al′ä̤), *n.* [Ar. *Allāh*, < *al*, the, + *ilāh*, God.] The Mohammedan name of the Supreme Being.

all=a-mort (âl-ạ-môrt′), *a.* See *alamort* and *amort*.

al-lan-to-ic (al-an-tō′ik), *a.* Pertaining to the allantois.

al-lan-toid (a-lan′toid). [Gr. ἀλλαντοειδής, < ἀλλᾶς, sausage, + εἶδος, form.] **I.** *a.* Sausage-like; allantoic. **II.** *n.* The allantois.—**al-lan-toi-dal** (al-an-toi′dạl), *a.* Allantoid.—**al-lan′to-is** (-tọ̄-is), *n.* [NL., earlier *allantoides*, < Gr. ἀλλαντοειδής.] A fetal appendage of mammals, birds, and reptiles, developing as a membranous sac from the posterior portion of the intestinal cavity.

al-lay[1] (ạ-lā′), *v.* and *n.* Same as *alloy*. [Obs. or archaic.]

al-lay[2] (ạ-lā′), *v.*; *-layed*, *-laying*. [AS. *ālecgan*, < *ā-*, away, + *lecgan*, lay.] **I.** *tr.* To put at rest; quiet (tumult, fear, suspicion, etc.); appease (wrath); assuage (pain, etc.); abate. **II.** *intr.* To become allayed; subside. [Obs. or archaic.]—**al-lay′er,** *n.*—**al-lay′ment,** *n.* The act of allaying; appeasement; assuagement.

al-le-ga-tion (al-ẹ-gā′shọn), *n.* [L. *allegatio(n-)*, < *allegare*: see *allege*.] The act of alleging; also, something alleged; an assertion made by a party in a legal proceeding, which he undertakes to prove; an averment; sometimes, a mere assertion, without proof.

al-lege (ạ-lej′), *v. t.*; *-leged*, *-leging*. [AF. *alegier*, in form = OF. *esligier*, < L. *ex*, out of, + *litigare*, sue, but with sense < L. *allegare*, adduce, < *ad*, to, + *legare*, send.] To declare or plead before a court; also, to assert or adduce in argument; sometimes, to declare as true, but without proving.—**al-lege′a-ble,** *a.* That may be alleged.—**al-leg′er,** *n.*

al-le-giance (ạ-lē′jạns), *n.* [ME. *alegeaunce*, for *legeaunce*, < OF. *ligeance*, < *lige*, liege.] The obligation of a subject or citizen to his sovereign or government; duty owed to a sovereign or state; hence, in general, fidelity; devotion.—**al-le′giant** (-jạnt). **I.** *a.* Loyal. **II.** *n.* One who owes allegiance.

al-le-gor-ic, al-le-gor-i-cal (al-ẹ-gor′ik, -i-kạl), *a.* [LL. *allegoricus*, < Gr. ἀλληγορικός.] Pertaining to or involving allegory.—**al-le-gor′i-cal-ly,** *adv.*—**al-le-gor′i-cal-ness,** *n.*

al-le-go-rist (al′ẹ-gọ̄-rist), *n.* One who allegorizes.—**al″-le-go-ris′tic,** *a.*

al-le-go-rize (al′ẹ-gọ̄-rīz), *v.*; *-rized, -rizing.* [LL. *allegorizare.*] **I.** *tr.* To turn into allegory; also, to understand or interpret as allegory. **II.** *intr.* To use allegory.—**al″le-go-ri-za′tion** (-ri-zā′shọn), *n.*—**al′le-go-riz-er** (-rī-zėr), *n.*

al-le-go-ry (al′ẹ-gọ̄-ri), *n.*; pl. *-ries* (-riz). [L. *allegoria,* < Gr. ἀλληγορία, < ἄλλος, other, + ἀγορεύειν, speak, < ἀγορά, assembly.] Figurative treatment of one subject under the guise of another; a presentation of an abstract or spiritual meaning under concrete or material forms; a symbolical narrative.

al-le-gret-to (äl-lā-gret′tō). [It., dim. of *allegro.*] In *music*: **I.** *a.* Quicker than andante, but not so quick as allegro. **II.** *n.*; pl. *-tos* (-tōz). An allegretto movement.

al-le-gro (äl-lā′grō). [It., < L. *alacer,* lively, brisk.] In *music*: **I.** *a.* Brisk; rapid. **II.** *n.*; pl. *-gros* (-grōz). An allegro movement (the quickest except presto).

al-lel-o-morph (a-lel′ọ̄-môrf or a-lē′lọ̄-), *n.* [Gr. ἀλλήλων, of one another, + μορφή, form.] In Mendelian phraseology, either of any pair of mutually incompatible characters or qualities, as tallness and dwarfishness, which are present potentially in the germ-cells of hybrids, and are exhibited among the hybrids and their offspring. See *Mendelism.* —**al-lel-o-mor′phic,** *a.*—**al-lel-o-mor′phism,** *n.*

al-le-lu-ia (al-ẹ-lö′yä̤), *interj.* and *n.* Same as *halleluiah.*

alle-mande (âl-mäṅd), *n.* [F., fem. of *allemand,* German.] Either of two German dances; a piece of music based on a dance rhythm; a movement in the suite, after the prelude.

al-ler-gen (al′ėr-jen), *n.* [See *allergy* and *-gen.*] In *med.*, a substance causing allergy or making it manifest.

al-ler-gic (a-lėr′jik), *a.* Pertaining to or affected with allergy.

al-ler-gy (al′ėr-ji), *n.*; pl. *-gies* (-jiz). [NL. *allergia,* < Gr. ἄλλος, other, + -εργός, working.] In *med.*, altered susceptibility due to a first inoculation, treatment, or the like, as exhibited in reaction to a subsequent one of the same nature (cf. *anaphylaxis*); also, an unusual or exaggerated natural sensitiveness to a particular substance, as a pollen, an article of food, a drug, a serum, etc., or to a particular physical agent, as light, heat, etc.

al-le-vi-ate (ạ-lē′vi-āt), *v. t.*; *-ated, -ating.* [LL. *alleviatus,* pp. of *alleviare,* < L. *ad,* to, + *levis,* light.] To make lighter, or less grave or distressing; lessen; mitigate; relieve.—**al-le-vi-a′tion** (-ā′shọn), *n.* [L. *alleviatio(n-).*] The act of alleviating; also, something that alleviates; an alleviative.—**al le′vi-a-tive** (-ạ̄-tiv). **I.** *a.* Serving to alleviate. **II.** *n.* Something that alleviates.—**al-le′vi-a-tor** (-ā-tọr), *n.*—**al-le′vi-a-to-ry** (-ạ̄-tọ̄-ri), *a.* Alleviative.

al-ley[1] (al′i), *n.*; pl. *alleys* (-iz). [Abbr. of *alabaster.*] A choice playing-marble, white or colored.

al-ley[2] (al′i), *n.*; pl. *alleys* (-iz). [OF. *alee* (F. *allée*), < *aler* (F. *aller*), go.] A narrow passageway between rows of seats, houses, etc.; also, a long, narrow inclosure for playing at bowls, etc.—**al′ley-way,** *n.* An alley, as between houses.

All=fa-ther (âl′fä″ᴛʜėr), *n.* Father of all: applied orig. to Odin, later to Jupiter and to God.

all=fours (âl′fōrz′), *n.* The card-game of seven-up.

all hail (âl hāl). An exclamation of salutation or welcome. See *hail*[2], *n.*[1]—**all=hail′,** *n.* A salutation of 'all hail!'—**all=hail′,** *v. t.* To salute with 'all hail!'

All-hal-low-mas (âl-hal′ọ̄-mạs), *n.* [See *-mas.*] The feast of All-hallows.

All=hal-lows (âl-hal′ōz), *n.* [See *hallow.*] All saints (as, the feast of *All-hallows,* or All Saints, celebrated on Nov. 1); All Saints' Day (see under *all, a.*).—**All-hal′low-tide** (-tīd), *n.* The time or season of All-hallows.

all-heal (âl′hēl), *n.* The valerian, *Valeriana officinalis;* also, the self-heal, *Prunella vulgaris.*

al-li-a-ble (ạ-lī′ạ-bl), *a.* Capable of being allied.

al-li-a-ceous (al-i-ā′shius), *a.* [L. *allium,* garlic.] Garlic-like; of the garlic kind; belonging to the genus *Allium,* which includes the garlic, onion, leek, etc.

al-li-ance (ạ-lī′ạns), *n.* [OF. *aliance* (F. *alliance*).] A becoming or being allied; a union formed by agreement, as a marriage or a league between states; also, association; connection; affinity; also, the persons or parties allied; in *zoöl.*, a group of related families.

al-lied (ạ-līd′), *p. a.* [See *ally, v.*] United by agreement, kinship, or other ties; associated; related; also [*cap.*], of the Allies of the World War (as, the *Allied* navies).

al-lies (ạ-līz′, often al′īz), *n.* Plural of *ally.*

al-li-ga-tion (al-i-gā′shọn), *n.* [L. *alligatio(n-),* a binding to, < *alligare*: see *ally.*] In *arith.*, a method of finding the relations between the proportions and prices of ingredients of a mixture and the cost of the mixture itself.

al-li-ga-tor (al′i-gā-tọr), *n.* [Sp. *el lagarto,* 'the lizard' (L. *lacertus,* lizard).] Any of the large lizard-like reptiles constituting the genus *Alligator* or family *Alligatoridæ* (order *Crocodilia*), chiefly of warm regions of America, having a shorter and broader head than the true crocodile; also, a scaly leather prepared from its skin.

al-li-ga-tor=pear (al′i-gā-tọr-pãr′), *n.* [Said to be a corruption of *avocado-pear.*] Same as *avocado.*

al-lit-er-ate (ạ-lit′ẹ-rāt), *v.*; *-ated, -ating.* [L. *ad,* to, + *litera,* letter.] **I.** *intr.* To agree in the initial letter or sound; also, to use alliteration. **II.** *tr.* To compose or arrange with alliteration.—**al-lit-er-a′tion** (-ẹ-rā′shọn), *n.* Constant or frequent repetition of the same initial letter or sound, as in verse.—**al-lit′er-a-tive** (-ẹ-rạ̄-tiv), *a.* Pertaining to or characterized by alliteration.—**al-lit′er-a-tive-ly,** *adv.*—**al-lit′er-a-tive-ness,** *n.*—**al-lit′er-a-tor** (-ẹ-rā-tọr), *n.* One who uses alliteration.

all-ness (âl′nes), *n.* Totality; universality.

allo-. Form of Gr. ἄλλος, other, used in combination, as in *allochromatic, allograph, allomerism.*

al-lo-cate (al′ọ̄-kāt), *v. t.*; *-cated, -cating.* [ML. *allocatus,* pp. of *allocare,* < L. *ad,* to, + *locare,* place, locate.] To assign or allot; distribute; also, to fix the place of.—**al-lo-ca′tion** (-kā′shọn), *n.* [ML. *allocatio(n-).*] Assignment; allotment; also, location.

al-lo-chro-mat-ic (al″ọ̄-krọ̄-mat′ik), *a.* [Gr. ἄλλος, other, + χρῶμα (χρωματ-), color.] Exhibiting variety of color, as a gem.

al-loch-ro-ous (a-lok′rọ̄-us), *a.* [Gr. ἀλλόχροος, < ἄλλος, other, + χρόα, color.] Of various colors, as a mineral.

al-lo-cu-tion (al-ọ̄-kū′shọn), *n.* [L. *allocutio(n-),* < *alloqui,* speak to, < *ad,* to, + *loqui,* speak.] A formal or official address, esp. by the Pope.

al-lod (al′od), *n.* Same as *allodium.*

al-lo-di-um (a-lō′di-um), *n.*; pl. *-dia* (-di-ạ̈). [ML.; from Teut. (cf. OHG. *al,* all, *ōt,* property).] Freehold estate; land held as absolute property, not subject to any rent, service, or acknowledgment.—**al-lo′di-al,** *a.*

al-log-a-my (a-log′ạ-mi), *n.* [Gr. ἄλλος, other, + γάμος, marriage.] In *bot.*, fecundation of the ovules of one flower by pollen from another (on the same or another plant); cross-fertilization: opposed to *autogamy.*

al-lo-graph (al′ọ̄-gráf), *n.* [Gr. ἄλλος, other, + γράφειν, write.] A writing made by one person on behalf of another: opposed to *autograph.*

al-lom-er-ism (a-lom′ẹ-rizm), *n.* [Gr. ἄλλος, other, + μέρος, part.] Variability in chemical constitution without change in crystalline form.—**al-lom′er-ous,** *a.*

al-lo-morph (al′ọ̄-môrf), *n.* [Gr. ἄλλος, other, + μορφή, form.] A variety, as of a mineral, differing in form but not in chemical constitution.—**al-lo-mor′phic,** *a.*—**al-lo-mor′phism,** *n.* Variability in form without change in chemical constitution.

al-lo-nym (al′ọ̄-nim), *n.* [Gr. ἄλλος, other, + ὄνυμα, name.] The name of a person as author assumed for a work not by him; also, a work thus published under another's name.—**al-lon-y-mous** (a-lon′i-mus), *a.*

al-lo-path (al′ọ̄-path), *n.* [See *allopathy.*] An allopathist. —**al-lo-path′ic,** *a.* Pertaining to allopathy.—**al-lo-path′-i-cal-ly,** *adv.*—**al-lop-a-thist** (a-lop′ạ-thist), *n.* One who practises or favors allopathy.

al-lop-a-thy (a-lop′ạ-thi), *n.* [Gr. ἄλλος, other, + παθεῖν, suffer.] The method of treating disease by the use of agents producing effects different from those of the disease treated: opposed to *homeopathy.*

al-lo-phane (al′ọ̄-fān), *n.* [Gr. ἀλλοφανής, appearing otherwise, < ἄλλος, other, + φαίνεσθαι, appear (with reference to its change of appearance under the blowpipe).] A mineral, a hydrous silicate of aluminium, occurring in various colors and usually in an amorphous state.

al-lo-phyl-i-an (al-ọ-fil'i-ạn), *a.* [Gr. ἀλλόφυλος, < ἄλλος, other, + φυλή, tribe.] Of another race; not Aryan or Semitic; Turanian. Also **al-lo-phyl'ic.**

al-lot (ạ-lot'), *v. t.*; *-lotted, -lotting.* [OF. *aloter*, < *a* (< L. *ad*), to, + *lot*, lot.] To distribute as by lot; parcel out in portions or shares; also, to assign as a portion (*to*); apportion; hence, in general, to appropriate to a special purpose; appoint.—**al-lot'ment,** *n.* Distribution as by lot; apportionment; also, a portion or thing allotted.

al-lot-ri-oph-a-gy (a-lot-ri-of'ạ-ji), *n.* [Gr. ἀλλότριος, strange (< ἄλλος, other), + -φαγία, < φαγεῖν, eat.] A depraved appetite for substances unsuitable for food.

al-lo-trope (al'ọ-trōp), *n.* [Gr. ἀλλότροπος, in another manner, < ἄλλος, other, + τρόπος, turn, way, guise: see *trope.*] One of two or more existing forms of a chemical element: as, charcoal, graphite, and the diamond are *allotropes* of carbon.—**al-lo-trop'ic, al-lo-trop'i-cal** (-trop'-ik, -i-kạl), *a.* Pertaining to or characterized by allotropism.—**al-lo-trop'i-cal-ly,** *adv.*—**al-lot-ro-pism, al-lot-ro-py** (a-lot'rọ-pizm, -pi), *n.* A property of certain chemical elements, as carbon, sulphur, and phosphorus, of existing in two or more distinct forms.

al-lot-ta-ble (ạ-lot'ạ-bl), *a.* That may be allotted.

al-lot-tee (al-o-tē'), *n.* One to whom something is allotted.

al-lot-ter (ạ-lot'ėr), *n.* One who allots.

all=out (âl'out'), *a.* Complete; total: as, *all-out* aid.

all=o-ver (âl'ō''vėr). **I.** *a.* Extending or repeated all over, as a decorative pattern on embroidered or lace fabrics; having a pattern of this kind. **II.** *n.* An embroidered or lace fabric with an all-over pattern.

al-low (ạ-lou'), *v.* [OF. *alouer*, assign (< ML. *allocare*: see *allocate*), confused with *alouer*, commend, approve, < L. *allaudare*, give praise to, < *ad*, to, + *laus*, praise.] **I.** *tr.* To assign, grant, or give; let have; also, to grant to be just or true; concede; admit; also, to grant permission to or for; permit; also, to concede for addition or deduction, as in an account; also, to say or think (prov.); commend†; approve or sanction (archaic). **II.** *intr.* To admit or permit (*of*); also, to make some concession or allowance (*for*).—**al-low'a-ble,** *a.* That may be allowed; admissible; permissible; proper.—**al-low'a-bly,** *adv.*—**al-low'ance,** *n.* The act of allowing; allotment or grant; an amount granted, esp. regularly or periodically; concession, admission, or permission; a concession made in consideration of something; an addition or deduction conceded in an account; approval or sanction (archaic).—**al-low'ance,** *v. t.*; *-anced, -ancing.* To put upon an allowance; limit to a fixed regular amount.—**al-low'ed-ly,** *adv.* Admittedly.—**al-low'er,** *n.*

al-loy (ạ-loi'), *v.* [F. *aloyer*, OF. *aloier*, *aliier*, < L. *alligare*: see *ally.*] **I.** *tr.* To mix (metals) so as to form an alloy; reduce in fineness by an admixture of a less valuable metal; fig., to modify, impair, or debase as by admixture. **II.** *intr.* To combine in an alloy.—**al-loy** (ạ-loi', also al'oi), *n.* [F. *aloi.*] A substance composed of two or more metals (or, sometimes, a metal and a non-metal) which have been intimately mixed by fusion, electrolytic deposition, or the like; also, an inferior metal mixed with a more valuable one; fig., a deleterious admixture.—**al-loy'age** (-āj), *n.* The process or practice of alloying.

all=round (âl'round'), *a.* Extending all round; hence, not narrow or specialized; having ability in all or many departments.

all-seed (âl'sēd), *n.* Any of various many-seeded plants, as a goosefoot, *Chenopodium polyspermum*, and the knotgrass, *Polygonum aviculare.*

all-spice (âl'spīs), *n.* [So named because thought to combine the flavors of various spices.] The berry of a West Indian myrtaceous tree, *Pimenta pimenta*, used as a spice; also, any of various aromatic or fragrant shrubs, as the strawberry-shrub ('Carolina allspice').

al-lude (ạ-lūd'), *v. i.*; *-luded, -luding.* [L. *alludere* (pp. *allusus*), play with, < *ad*, to, + *ludere*, play.] To refer indirectly, covertly, or casually (*to*).

al-lu-mette (al-ū-met'), *n.* [F.] A match for lighting.

al-lure¹ (ȧ-lür), *n.* [F., < *aller*, go.] Gait; bearing; air.

al-lure² (ạ-lūr'), *v. t.*; *-lured, -luring.* [OF. *alurer*, < *a* (< L. *ad*), to, + *loire*, a lure.] To draw or attract as by a lure; tempt by inherent charm; appeal to invitingly or seductively.—**al-lure'ment,** *n.* The act or the means of alluring; attraction; temptation; charm.—**al-lur'er,** *n.*—**al-lur'ing,** *p. a.* That allures; tempting; inviting; seductive; charming.—**al-lur'ing-ly,** *adv.*—**al-lur'ing-ness,** *n.*

al-lu-sion (ạ-lū'zhọn), *n.* [L. *allusio(n-).*] The act of alluding; an indirect reference, as by implication rather than express mention; any slight, casual mention.—**al-lu'-sive** (-siv), *a.* Making or involving allusion; containing allusions.—**al-lu'sive-ly,** *adv.*—**al-lu'sive-ness,** *n.*

al-lu-vi-al (ạ-lū'vi-ạl), *a.* Of or pertaining to alluvium.—**alluvial cone** or **fan,** in *phys. geog.*, a fan-shaped alluvial deposit formed by a stream where it issues from a ravine into a plain.—**al-lu'vi-al,** *n.* Alluvial soil; esp., gold-bearing alluvial soil (Australia).

al-lu-vi-on (ạ-lū'vi-ọn), *n.* [F., < L. *alluvio(n-)*, < *alluere*, wash against, < *ad*, to, + *luere*, wash.] The wash of water against a shore; overflow or flood; also, matter washed along and deposited; alluvium; in *law*, addition to land by deposits made by water.

al-lu-vi-um (ạ-lū'vi-um), *n.*; pl. *-via* (-vi-ä̤). [LL., neut. of *alluvius*, alluvial, < L. *alluere*: see *alluvion.*] A deposit of sand, mud, etc., formed by flowing water; in *geol.*, the sedimentary matter deposited thus within recent times, esp. in the valleys of large rivers.

all-where (âl'hwãr), *adv.* Everywhere. [Archaic.]

al-ly (ạ-lī'), *v.*; *-lied, -lying.* [OF. *alier*, *aliier* (F. *allier*), < L. *alligare*, bind to, < *ad*, to, + *ligare*, bind.] **I.** *tr.* To unite (*to* or *with*) by formal agreement, as by marriage, treaty, or league; connect by some relation, as of kinship, resemblance, etc. **II.** *intr.* To enter into alliance.—**al-ly** (ạ-lī', often al'ī), *n.*; pl. *allies* (ạ-līz', often al'īz). One allied with another, esp. by treaty or league; an allied sovereign, state, etc.; an auxiliary, associate, or confederate; a relative†; a related form or thing; in *zoöl.*, a member of the same alliance.—**the Allies,** in the World War, the powers of the Triple Entente (Great Britain, France, and Russia), with the powers or nations allied with them (Belgium, Serbia, Japan, Italy, etc., not including the United States), or, in loose use, with all the powers or nations allied or associated with them (including the United States), as opposed to the Central Powers (Germany, Austria-Hungary, etc.). Cf. *Central Powers*, under *central*, *a.*, and see *World War*, under *world.*

al-lyl (al'il), *n.* [L. *allium*, garlic: see *-yl.*] In *chem.*, a univalent organic radical, C_3H_5, occurring in the oil of garlic and in other compounds.—**al-lyl-ic** (a-lil'ik), *a.*

al-ma-cén (äl-mä-thān'), *n.* [Sp.] A warehouse.

Al-ma-gest (al'mạ-jest), *n.* [OF. *almageste*, < Ar. *al-majistī*, < *al*, the, + Gr. μεγίστη, fem. of μέγιστος, greatest, superl. of μέγας, great.] The famous Greek work on astronomy by the Alexandrian astronomer Ptolemy (flourished 127–151); [*l. c.*] any of various great medieval works, as on astrology or alchemy.

al-mah, al-ma (al'mä̤), *n.* [Ar. *'almah*, learned, < *'alama*, know.] In Egypt, a professional singing-girl.

al-ma ma-ter (al'mä̤ mā'tėr). [L., 'fostering mother.'] The university, college, or school at which one has been educated. Cf. *alumnus.*

al-ma-nac (âl'mạ-nak), *n.* [ML. *almanac*, *almanach*; appar. from Ar.] A calendar of the days of the year, in weeks and months, indicating the time of various events or phenomena during the period, as anniversaries, sunrise and sunset, changes of the moon and tides, etc., or giving other pertinent information.

al-man-dine (al'mạn-din), *n.* [ML. *alamandina*, for *alabandina*, < L. *Alabanda*, name of a city in Asia Minor.] The garnet (mineral). Also **al'man-dite** (-dīt).

al-meh, al-me (al'mė), *n.* Same as *almah.*

al-might-y (âl-mī'ti), *a.* [AS. *ælmihtig*, *ealmihtig.*] Possessing all might; omnipotent; also, great or extreme (colloq.).—**the Almighty,** the omnipotent God.—**al-might'i-ly,** *adv.*—**al-might'i-ness,** *n.*

al-mi-qui (äl-mē'kē), *n.* [Native name.] The solenodon or opossum-shrew of Cuba, *Solenodon cubanus.*

al-mond (ä′mǫnd), *n.* [OF. *almande, alemandle* (F. *amande*), < L. *amygdala*, < Gr. ἀμυγδάλη, almond.] The stone (nut) or kernel (sweet or bitter) of the fruit of an amygdalaceous tree, *Amygdalus communis*, of warm regions; the tree itself; also, something almond-shaped; a tonsil (usually 'almond of the throat': archaic).—**al′mond=eyed,** *a.* Having almond-shaped eyes, as the Mongolians. —**al′mond=shaped,** *a.* Of a long or narrow oval shape, tending to a point at the ends.

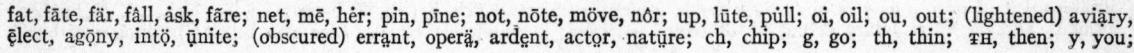

Almond.

al-mon-er (al′mǫn-ėr), *n.* [OF. *almosnier* (F. *aumônier*), < ML. *eleemosynarius*, < LL. *eleemosyna*: see *alms*.] A dispenser of alms, esp. for a religious house, a princely household, etc.—**al′mon-ry,** *n.*; pl. *-ries* (-riz). The place where an almoner resides, or where alms are distributed.

al-most (âl′mōst), *adv.* [AS. *ealmǣst*, mostly all.] Mostly or nearly all†; also, all but; very nearly.

alms (ämz), *n. sing.* or *pl.* [AS. *ælmysse*, < LL. *eleemosyna*, < Gr. ἐλεημοσύνη, compassion, alms, < ἔλεος, pity.] Charitable aid or relief, as for the poor; something given as charity.—**alms′=deed,** *n.* A charitable deed.—**alms′-giv″ing,** *n.* The giving of alms.—**alms′house,** *n.* A house for the poor, maintained at the public expense or, as in Great Britain, by private endowment.—**alms′-man** (-mạn), *n.*; pl. *-men.* One who lives on alms; also, a giver of alms.—**alms′wom″an,** *n.*; pl. *-women* (-wim″en).

al-mug (al′mug), *n.* [Heb. *almūg*, appar. = *algūm*: see *algum*.] An unidentified tree mentioned in the Bible (1 Kings, x. 11, 12). See *algum*.

al′od, a-lo′di-um, etc. See *allod*, etc.

al-oe (al′ō), *n.* [L., < Gr. ἀλόη.] Any plant of the liliaceous genus *Aloë*, chiefly African, various species of which yield a drug (aloes) and a fiber; also, the century-plant ('American aloe'). —**al′oes** (-ōz), *n.* A bitter purgative drug, the inspissated juice of several species of aloe; also, a fragrant resin or wood ('aloes wood') from an East Indian tree, *Aquilaria agallocha*.—**al-o-ët′ic** (-ǭ-et′ik), *a.* Pertaining to or containing the drug aloes.

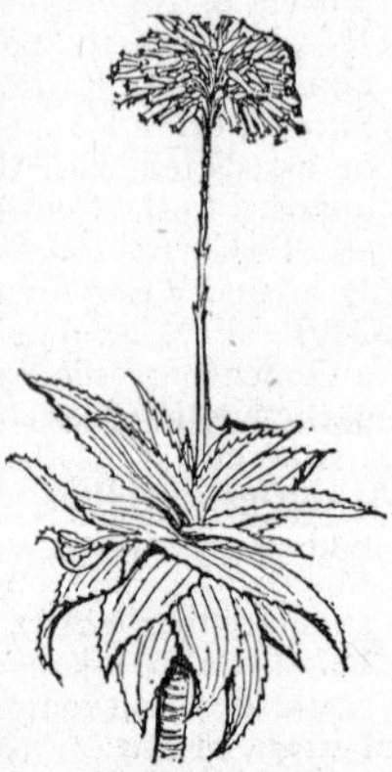
Aloe (*A. vulgaris*).

a-loft (ạ-lôft′), *adv.* [See *loft*.] Up in the air; high up; on high; *naut.*, at or toward the masthead; in the upper rigging.

al-o-in (al′ǭ-in), *n.* In *chem.*, an intensely bitter, crystalline, purgative substance obtained from aloes.

a-lone (ạ-lōn′), *a.* [ME. *al one*, 'all (wholly) one.'] Apart from others; unaccompanied or unaided; solitary; also, to the exclusion of all others or all else (as, "Man shall not live by bread *alone*": Luke, iv. 4); also, sole or exclusive (now rare); also, unique†: now rarely used attributively.—**to let alone.** See under *let*[1]. —**a-lone′,** *adv.* Only; exclusively; solely; merely.—**a-lone′-ness,** *n.*

a-long[1] (ạ-lông′), *adv.* [AS. *gelang*, belonging, owing.] On account (*of*), because (*of*). [Now prov.]

a-long[2] (ạ-lông′). [AS. *andlang*, < *and-*, against (see *anti-*), + *lang*, long.] **I.** *prep.* Through or by the length of; lengthwise over or beside. **II.** *adv.* Lengthwise; in a line; onward (as, to move *along*); on the way (*with*); in association or conjunction (*with*); in company.—**all along,** throughout; continuously.—**a-long′shore′,** *adv.* and *a.* Along by or on the shore.—**a-long′side′.** **I.** *adv.* Along or by the side. **II.** *prep.* Beside.

a-loof (ạ-löf′), *adv.* [Orig. naut.: see *loof*[2], *luff*.] To windward†; also, off; at a distance; intentionally apart from others, as from want of sympathy or favor (as, to stand, hold, or keep *aloof*).—**a-loof′ness,** *n.*

al-o-pe-cia (al-ǭ-pē′ṣiạ̈), *n.* [L., < Gr. ἀλωπεκία, < ἀλώπηξ, fox.] In *pathol.*, loss of hair, as from disease; baldness.

al-o-pe-coid (al-ǭ-pē′koid), *a.* [Gr. ἀλώπηξ, fox: see *-oid*.] Fox-like; of the fox kind; vulpine.

a-loud (ạ-loud′), *adv.* With loud, full, or unrepressed voice; loudly; audibly.

a-low[1] (ạ-lou′), *adv.* [See *low*[2].] On fire; ablaze. [Sc.]

a-low[2] (ạ-lō′), *adv.* [See *low*[4].] Low down; below. [Archaic or naut.]

alp (alp), *n.* [L. *Alpes*, pl., the Alps; perhaps from Celtic.] [*cap.*] A mountain of the range in Switzerland and neighboring countries (orig. and usually in *pl.*, 'the Alps'); [*l. c.*] a high mountain; also, a mountain pasture in the Alps.

Alpaca.

al-pac-a (al-pak′ạ̈), *n.* [Sp., for Peruvian *paco*.] A sheep-like South American ruminant animal of the genus *Lama* (or *Auchenia*), allied to the llama and like it considered a variety of the guanaco, and having long, soft, silky hair or wool; also, the hair, or a fabric made of it or of some substitute; esp., a glossy, wiry, commonly black woolen fabric with cotton warp.

al-pen-glow (al′pen-glō), *n.* [For G. *alpenglühen*.] A reddish glow often seen on the summits of mountains before sunrise and after sunset.

al-pen-horn (al′pen-hôrn), *n.* [G.] A long, powerful horn curving up and widening toward its extremity, used in the Alps, as by cowherds.

al-pen-stock (al′pen-stok), *n.* [G.] A long, stout staff pointed with iron, used by Alpine mountaineers and by mountain-climbers in general.

al-pes-trine (al-pes′trin), *a.* [ML. *alpestris*, < L. *Alpes*, the Alps.] Pertaining to mountain regions; in *bot.*, growing on mountains, below the alpine region; subalpine.

al-pha (al′fạ̈), *n.* [L., < Gr. ἄλφα.] The first letter (Α, α, = English A, a) of the Greek alphabet; the first of any series (esp. in scientific classification).—**alpha and omega,** the first and the last (omega being the last letter of the Greek alphabet); the beginning and the end, as determining the whole. See Rev. i. 8; i. 11.—**alpha rays.** See under *ray*[3], *n.*

al-pha-bet (al′fạ-bet), *n.* [LL. *alphabetum*, < Gr. ἄλφα, alpha, + βῆτα, beta.] The letters of a language in their customary order; also, any system of characters or signs for use in representing sounds or ideas; also, first elements; rudiments.—**al′pha-bet,** *v. t.*; *-beted, -beting.* To arrange alphabetically; alphabetize.—**al″pha-be-ta′ri-an** (-be-tā′-ri-ạn), *n.* A learner of the alphabet.—**al-pha-bet′ic, al-pha-bet′i-cal,** *a.* Pertaining to or using an alphabet; arranged by letters in the order of the alphabet.—**al-pha-bet′i-cal-ly,** *adv.* In the manner or order of the alphabet. —**al′pha-bet-ize,** *v. t.*; *-ized, -izing.* To arrange alphabetically; also, to express by an alphabet.

alp=horn (alp′hôrn), *n.* Same as *alpenhorn*.

al-pho-sis (al-fō′sis), *n.* [NL., < Gr. ἀλφός, kind of leprosy.] In *pathol.*, lack of pigment in the skin, as in albinism.

al-pine (al′pin or -pīn), *a.* [L. *Alpinus*, < *Alpes*, the Alps.] [*cap.*] Of or pertaining to the Alps; [*l. c.*] pertaining to high mountains; living or growing on mountains, above the limit of tree-growth.—**al′pin-ist,** *n.* A mountain-climber.

al-read-y (âl-red′i), *adv.* [ME. *al redy*, 'all ready.'] In anticipation or advance; before or by this time.

Al-sa-tia (al-sā′shiạ̈), *n.* [ML. (F. *Alsace*, G. *Elsass*), a province west of the Rhine, long a debatable ground between France and Germany.] A cant name for Whitefriars, a district in London formerly having privileges of sanctuary that made it a resort of debtors and criminals; hence, any asylum or resort of lawless persons.—**Al-sa′-tian.** **I.** *a.* Pertaining to Alsace (province west of the Rhine), or to Alsatia or Whitefriars (district in London). **II.** *n.* A native or inhabitant of Alsace; also, an inhabitant of Alsatia or Whitefriars; a debtor or criminal in sanctuary.

al-sike (al'sik), *n.* [From *Alsike*, in Sweden.] A European clover, *Trifolium hybridum*, with whitish or pink flowers, much grown in the U. S. for forage.

al-so (âl'sō), *adv.* [ME. *also*, < AS. *alswā*, *ealswā*, 'all (wholly or quite) so': cf. *as*[1].] Quite so†, or even thus†; likewise† or similarly†; hence, in addition; too.

alt (alt). [It. *alto*, high.] In *music*: **I.** *a.* High. **II.** *n.* The octave above the treble staff, beginning with G: usually in the phrase 'in alt' (notes in the octave above those 'in alt' being said to be 'in altissimo').

Al-tai-an (al-tā'ạn). **I.** *a.* Of or pertaining to the Altai Mountains, in central Asia; also, noting or pertaining to the Ural-Altaic languages or peoples. **II.** *n.* A member of a Tatar tribe of the Altai Mountains; also, a person belonging to any of the Ural-Altaic peoples.—**Al-ta'ic,** *a.* Altaian.

al-tar (âl'tạr), *n.* [L. *altare*, prob. < *altus*, high.] An elevated place or structure on which sacrifices are offered or at which any religious rites are performed; in most Christian churches, the communion-table; [*cap.*] in *astron.*, the southern constellation Ara.—**al'tar-age** (-āj), *n.* Money offered at an altar, or received by a priest for services at an altar.—**al'tar=cloth,** *n.* A cloth for covering an altar in a Christian church.—**al'tar-piece,** *n.* A decorative screen-like piece behind and above an altar; a reredos.

Ancient High Altar of Notre Dame, Paris, 13th century.

alt-az-i-muth (alt-az'i-muth), *n.* [From *alt*(*itude*) + *azimuth*.] An instrument for determining altitudes and azimuths of heavenly bodies.

al-ter (âl'tėr), *v.* [LL. *alterare* (pp. *alteratus*), < L. *alter*, other: see *other*.] **I.** *tr.* To make other or different; change in form, character, etc.; also, to exchange†. **II.** *intr.* To become different; undergo change.—**al'ter-a-ble,** *a.* Capable of being altered; admitting of alteration.—**al''ter-a-bil'i-ty** (-bil'i-ti), **al'ter-a-ble-ness,** *n.*—**al'ter-a-bly,** *adv.*—**al'ter-ant. I.** *a.* Causing alteration. **II.** *n.* Something that causes alteration.—**al-ter-a'tion** (-ā'shọn), *n.* [LL. *alteratio*(*n*-).] The act of altering; altered state; a change made in a thing; a modification.—**al'ter-a-tive** (-ạ-tiv). **I.** *a.* Serving to alter; in *med.*, gradually restoring healthy bodily functions. **II.** *n.* In *med.*, an alterative remedy.

al-ter-cate (al'tėr-kāt or âl'-), *v. i.*; *-cated*, *-cating*. [L. *altercatus*, pp. of *altercari*, < *alter*, other: cf. *alter*.] To dispute, one with another, with heat or anger; wrangle.—**al-ter-ca'tion** (-kā'shọn), *n.* [L. *altercatio*(*n*-).] The act of altercating; a heated or angry dispute; a wrangle.

al-tern (al'tėrn or âl'-), *a.* [L. *alternus*, one after the other, alternate, < *alter*, other: cf. *alter*.] Alternate.

al-ter-nant (al-tėr'nạnt or âl-), *a.* Alternating; of rocks, etc., composed of alternate layers.

al-ter-nate (al'tėr-nāt or âl'-), *v.*; *-nated*, *-nating*. [L. *alternatus*, pp. of *alternare*, < *alternus*: see *altern*.] **I.** *tr.* To perform by turns; cause to take turns; interchange successively (one with another). **II.** *intr.* To succeed by turns; take turns; change about by turns between points, states, actions, etc.—**al-ter'nate** (-nạt). **I.** *a.* Forming or having an alternating series; succeeding by turns; recurring as one of an alternating series; appearing in turn or as every other; in *bot.*, of leaves, etc., placed singly and at different heights on the axis, first on one side and then on the other, or at definite angular distances from one another; in *geom.*, noting two non-adjacent angles made by the crossing of two lines by a third line, both angles being either interior or exterior, and one being on one side of the third line and the other on the other side. **II.** *n.* Something that alternates; an official substitute, as at a political convention.—**al-ter'nate-ly,** *adv.*—**al-ter'nate-ness,** *n.*—**al'ter-nat-ing,** *p. a.* That alternates; in *elect.*, periodically reversing direction, as a current.—**al'ter-nat-ing-ly,** *adv.*—**al-ter-na'tion** (-nā'shọn), *n.* [L. *alternatio*(*n*-).] The act of alternating; the state of being alternate; appearance, occurrence, or change by turns.—**alternation of generations,** in *biol.*, alternation, in a line of reproduction, between generations unlike and generations like a given progenitor; the alternation of asexual with sexual reproduction.—**al-ter'na-tive** (-nạ-tiv). **I.** *a.* Affording or requiring a choice between things; involving mutually exclusive possibilities; constituting one of such possibilities. **II.** *n.* A choice between things; a possibility of one out of two (or, less strictly, more) things; one of the things thus open to choice, or possible; a remaining possibility.—**al-ter'na-tive-ly,** *adv.*—**al'ter-na-tor** (-nā-tọr), *n.* In *elect.*, an alternating-current dynamo or generator.

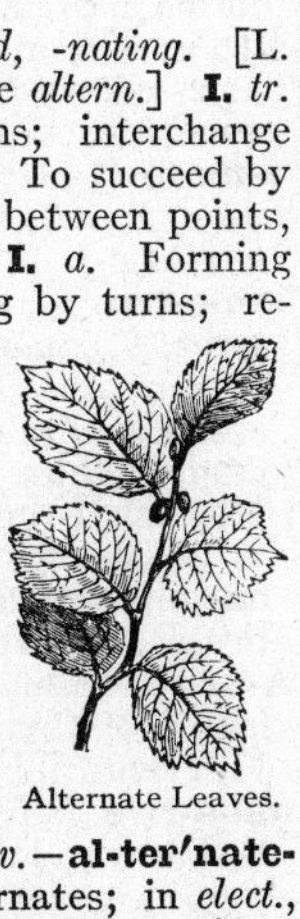
Alternate Leaves.

al-thæ-a, al-the-a (al-thē'ạ), *n.* [L. *althæa*, < Gr. ἀλθαία, wild mallow.] Any plant of the malvaceous genus *Althæa*, as the hollyhock, *A. rosea*, or the marsh-mallow, *A. officinalis*; also, a malvaceous flowering garden shrub, *Hibiscus syriacus*; the rose of Sharon.

al-tho, al-tho' (âl-ᴛʜō'), *conj.* See *although*.

alt-horn (alt'hôrn), *n.* [See *alt*.] The tenor saxhorn.

al-though (âl-ᴛʜō'), *conj.* [See *all*, *adv.*] Even though: practically equivalent to *though*, and preferred to it only for euphonic or metrical reasons.

al-tim-e-ter (al-tim'e-tėr), *n.* [L. *altus*, high: see *-meter*.] An instrument for measuring altitudes, as a quadrant or sextant; in *aëronautics*, an aneroid barometer on an aircraft, used to indicate height above the surface of the earth.—**al-tim'e-try,** *n.* [See *-metry*.] The art of measuring altitudes, as with an altimeter.

al-ti-scope (al'ti-skōp), *n.* [L. *altus*, high: see *-scope*.] An instrument consisting of an extensible telescopic tube with elbows and mirrors so arranged that the observer can look over or around intervening objects.

al-tis-o-nant (al-tis'ọ-nạnt), *a.* [L. *altus*, high, + *sonans* (*sonant*-), ppr. of *sonare*, sound.] High-sounding, as words.

al-tis-si-mo (al-tis'i-mō), *n.* [It., superl. of *alto*, high.] See *alt*, *n.*

al-ti-tude (al'ti-tūd), *n.* [L. *altitudo* (*altitudin*-), < *altus*, high.] Extent or distance upward; height; elevation; also, a high point or region; in *astron.*, etc., angular distance above the horizon.—**al-ti-tu'di-nal** (-tū'di-nạl), *a.*

al-to (al'tō). [It., < L. *altus*, high.] In *music*: **I.** *n.*; pl. *-tos* (-tōz). The highest male voice or voice-part; the counter-tenor; also, the lowest female voice or voice-part; the contralto; also, a singer with a counter-tenor or a contralto voice; also, the viola, or tenor violin. **II.** *a.* Of or pertaining to the alto; having the compass of the alto.

al-to=cu-mu-lus (al-tọ-kū'mụ-lus), *n.* [L. *altus*, high: see *cumulus*.] A cloud, a form of cumulus of great altitude, appearing in clumps or globular masses variously grouped.

al-to-geth-er (âl-tọ-geᴛʜ'ėr). [ME. *altogedere*, 'all together.'] **I.** *adv.* Wholly; entirely; completely; quite. **II.** *n.* A whole; the tout ensemble.

al-to=ri-lie-vo (äl''tō-rē-lyā'vō), *n.*; pl. *-vos* (-vōz). [It.] High relief; sculpture in high relief, in which the figures project at least one half from the background.

al-to=stra-tus (al-tọ-strā'tus), *n.* [L. *altus*, high: see *stratus*.] A comparatively high, veil-like or sheet-like cloud.

al-tru-ism (al'trö-izm), *n.* [F. *altruisme*, < *autrui*, another, others, < L. *alter*, other.] The principle or the practice of seeking the welfare of others: opposed to *egoism*.—**al'tru-ist,** *n.* One who practises altruism.—**al-tru-is'tic,** *a.* Of or like an altruist; exhibiting altruism.—**al-tru-is'ti-cal-ly,** *adv.*

al-u-del (al'ụ-del), *n.* [F. *aludel*, < Sp. *aludel*, < Ar. *al-uthāl*.] In *chem.*, one of a series of pear-shaped pots of earthenware or glass, open at both ends, used as a condenser in sublimation.

al-u-la (al'ụ-lạ), *n.*; pl. *-læ* (-lē). [NL., dim. of L. *ala*, wing.] In *ornith.*, the packet of small feathers which grows upon the thumb of a bird's wing.

Alula (the shaded part in the figure).

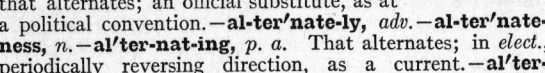

al-um (al′um), *n.* [OF. *alum* (F. *alun*), < L. *alumen*, alum.] An astringent crystalline substance, a double sulphate of aluminium and potassium, used in medicine, dyeing, and many other technical processes; in *chem.*, one of a class of double sulphates analogous to the potassium alum.

a-lu-mi-na (a-lū′mi-nạ̈), *n.* [NL., < L. *alumen*, alum.] The oxide of aluminium, occurring in nature as corundum (in the ruby and sapphire, emery, etc.); also, aluminium (in phrases, as 'silicate of alumina').

a-lu-mi-nate (a-lū′mi-nāt), *n.* In *chem.*, a salt formed from aluminium hydroxide when it acts as a weak acid.

a-lu-mi-nif-er-ous (a-lū-mi-nif′ẹ-rus), *a.* [See *alum* and *-ferous.*] Yielding alum, alumina, or aluminium.

al-u-min-i-um (al-ụ̄-min′i-um), *n.* [NL., earlier *aluminum*, < *alumina*: see *alumina.*] Chem. sym., Al; at. wt., 27.1; sp. gr., 2.56. A silver-white metallic element, light in weight, ductile, malleable, and not readily oxidized or tarnished, occurring combined in nature in rocks, clays, and most soils: much used in alloying, and for making utensils, instruments, etc.

alumino-. Form of *aluminum* or *aluminium* used in combination.—**a-lu-mi-nog-ra-phy** (a-lū-mi-nog′rạ-fi), *n.* [See *-graphy.*] The art or process of producing and of printing from aluminium plates instead of lithographic stone.—**a-lu″mi-no-ther′mics** (-nǫ-thėr′miks), *n.* [+ Gr. θέρμη, heat.] The processes in which high temperatures are produced by the chemical combination of oxygen and aluminium, as in the reactions produced by thermit, etc.; the science dealing with such processes.—**a-lu″mi-no-ther′mic,** *a.*—**a-lu′mi-no-ther″my,** *n.* Aluminothermics.

a-lu-mi-nous (a-lū′mi-nus), *a.* Of the nature of or containing alum or alumina.

a-lu-mi-num (a-lū′mi-num), *n.* Same as *aluminium.*

a-lum-na (ạ-lum′nạ̈), *n.*; pl. *-næ* (-nē). [L.] Feminine of *alumnus.*

a-lum-nus (ạ-lum′nus), *n.*; pl. *-ni* (-nī). [L., foster-child, pupil, < *alere*, nourish.] A pupil; usually, a graduate of an educational institution. Cf. *alma mater.*

al-um=root (al′um-röt), *n.* Any of several plants of the saxifragaceous genus *Heuchera*, with astringent roots, esp. *H. americana*; also, the root; also, the crane's-bill, *Geranium maculatum*, or its astringent root.

al-u-nite (al′ụ̄-nīt), *n.* [F., < *alun*, alum.] A mineral, a hydrous sulphate of potassium and aluminium, occurring in finely granular masses or sometimes in crystals.

al-ve-o-lar (al-vē′ǫ-lạ̈r or al′vẹ-ǫ-lạ̈r), *a.* Pertaining to an alveolus or to alveoli.

al-ve-o-late, al-ve-o-lat-ed (al-vē′ǫ-lāt or al′vẹ-ǫ-lāt, -lā-ted), *a.* Having alveoli; deeply pitted, as a honeycomb.—**al-ve-o-la′tion** (-lā′shǫn), *n.* Alveolate formation or structure.

al-ve-o-lus (al-vē′ǫ-lus), *n.*; pl. *-li* (-lī). [L., dim. of *alveus*, hollow, cavity.] A little cavity, pit, or cell, as a cell of a honeycomb; the socket of a tooth.

al-vine (al′vin or -vīn), *a.* [L. *alvus*, belly.] Pertaining to the belly; intestinal.

al-way (âl′wā), *adv.* [ME., 'all (the) way.'] Always. [Now poetic.]

al-ways (âl′wạ̄z), *adv.* [From *alway* + *-s*³.] All the time; continually; perpetually; ever; also, every time; at all times.

a-lys-sum (ạ-lis′um), *n.* [NL., < Gr. ἄλυσσον, kind of plant.] Any of the herbs constituting the brassicaceous genus *Alyssum*, characterized by small yellow or white racemose flowers.—**sweet alyssum,** a brassicaceous garden plant with racemes of small white flowers, sometimes regarded as a species of alyssum, *Alyssum maritimum*, and sometimes as a species of a different genus, *Königa maritima* or *Lobularia maritima.*

am (am). [AS. *am, eom*, akin to L. *sum*, Gr. εἰμί, Skt. *asmi.*] A verb-form, first person singular, present indicative, used as a part of *be.*

am-a-da-vat (am″ạ-dạ-vat′), *n.* [E. Ind.] A small finch-like East Indian bird, *Estrelda amandava*, exported as a cage-bird.

am-a-dou (am′ạ-dö), *n.* [F.] A soft, spongy substance prepared from fungi (*Polyporus fomentarius* and allied species) growing on trees: used as tinder and in surgery.

a-mah (ä′mạ̈), *n.* [Pg. *ama.*] In India, China, etc., a nurse or maid.

a-main (ạ-mān′), *adv.* With might and main; furiously.

am-al-dar, am-il-dar (am′ạl-där, am′il-), *n.* [Hind. and Pers. '*amaldār.*] In India, a manager or agent; a revenue-collector.

a-mal-gam (ạ-mal′gạm), *n.* [OF. F. *amalgame*, appar. < L. *malagma*, < Gr. μάλαγμα, poultice, < μαλακός, soft.] An alloy of mercury with another metal or other metals; fig., a mixture or combination.—**a-mal′ga-ma-ble** (-gạ-mạ-bl), *a.* Capable of being amalgamated.—**a-mal′ga-mate** (-māt), *v.*; *-mated, -mating.* **I.** *tr.* To form into an amalgam; combine; unite. **II.** *intr.* To form an amalgam; blend; coalesce.—**a-mal-ga-ma′tion** (-mā′shǫn), *n.* The act of amalgamating, or the resulting state; combination; union; fusion; in *metal.*, extraction of the precious metals from their ores by treatment with mercury.—**a-mal′-ga-ma-tive** (-mạ̄-tiv), *a.* Tending to amalgamate.—**a-mal′-ga-ma-tor** (-mā-tǫr), *n.*

am-a-ni-ta (am-ạ-nī′tạ̈), *n.* [NL., < Gr. ἀμανῖται, pl., kind of fungi.] Any fungus of the agaricaceous genus *Amanita*, which comprises both edible and highly poisonous species.

a-man-u-en-sis (ạ-man-ụ̄-en′sis), *n.*; pl. *-enses* (-en′sēz). [L., < *a*, from, + *manus*, hand.] One who does writing for another, as from dictation or by transcribing.

a-mar-a-cus (a-mar′ạ-kus), *n.* [L., < Gr. ἀμάρακος, kind of plant.] The plant dittany of Crete.

am-a-ran-ta-ceous (am″ạ-ran-tā′shius), *a.* Belonging to the *Amarantaceæ*, or amaranth family of plants.

am-a-ranth (am′ạ-ranth), *n.* [L. *amarantus*, < Gr. ἀμάραντος, unfading, < ἀ- priv. + μαραίνειν, waste, wither.] A fabled unfading flower; also, any plant of the genus *Amarantus*, which includes species cultivated for their showy flowers, as the love-lies-bleeding, or their colored foliage (green, purple, red, etc.); also, a purple color; also, a purplish-red coloring matter.—**am-a-ran′thine** (-ran′thin), *a.* Of or like the amaranth; unfading; also, purplish.

am-a-ryl-li-da-ceous (am-ạ-ril-i-dā′shius), *a.* Belonging to the *Amaryllidaceæ*, or amaryllis family of plants, which includes the amaryllis, narcissus, snowdrop, agave, etc.

Am-a-ryl-lis (am-ạ-ril′is), *n.* [L., < Gr. Ἀμαρυλλίς.] A name for a country girl in classical and later pastoral poetry; [*l. c.*] a bulbous plant, *Amaryllis belladonna*, the belladonna lily, with large, lily-like, normally rose-colored flowers; any of several related plants once referred to the genus *Amaryllis.*

Amaryllis (*A. belladonna*).

a-mass (ạ-mȧs′), *v.* [F. *amasser*, < ML. *amassare*, < L. *ad*, to, + *massa*, mass.] **I.** *tr.* To collect as into a mass; accumulate. **II.** *intr.* To gather; assemble.—**a-mass′a-ble,** *a.* Capable of being amassed.—**a-mass′er,** *n.*—**a-mass′ment,** *n.* The act of amassing; a quantity amassed; an accumulation.

a-mate (ạ-māt′), *v. t.*; *amated, amating.* [OF. *amater*, < *a* (< L. *ad*), to, + *mater*, E. *mate*².] To daunt; dismay. [Archaic.]

am-a-teur (am′ạ-tūr or am-ạ-tėr′). [F., < L. *amator*, lover, < *amare*, love.] **I.** *n.* One who cultivates any art or pursuit for the love or enjoyment of it, instead of professionally or for gain: often implying desultory action or crude results. **II.** *a.* Of or being an amateur.—**am-a-teur′ish** (-tūr′ish), *a.* Like or suggestive of an amateur, as in crudeness or other faults.—**am-a-teur′ish-ly,** *adv.*—**am-a-teur′ish-ness,** *n.*—**am′a-teur-ism,** *n.* The practice or character of an amateur.—**am′a-teur-ship,** *n.*

A-ma-ti (ä-mä′tē), *n.* A violin made by the Amati family of Cremona, Italy, who flourished in the 16th and 17th centuries.

am-a-tive (am′ạ-tiv), *a.* [L. *amare* (pp. *amatus*), love.] Disposed to love; amorous; amatory.—**am′a-tive-ness,** *n.* Propensity to (sexual) love: in *phren.*, a special faculty.

am-a-to-ri-al (am-ạ-tō′ri-ạl), *a.* Amatory.

am-a-to-ry (am′ạ-tō̤-ri), *a.* [L. *amatorius*, < *amator*: see *amateur.*] Of or pertaining to a lover or love-making; pertaining to or expressive of love.

am-au-ro-sis (am-â-rō′sis), *n.* [NL., < Gr. ἀμαύρωσις, < ἀμαυρός, dim.] In *pathol.*, partial or total loss of sight without apparent lesion.—**am-au-rot′ic** (-rot′ik), *a.*

a-maze (ạ-māz′), *v. t.*; *amazed, amazing.* [AS., in *āmasod*, pp.: cf. *maze.*] To stupefy† or stun†; confound†; overwhelm with surprise; astonish greatly.—**a-maze′**, *n.* Amazement. [Chiefly poetic.]—**a-maz-ed-ly** (ạ-mā′zed-li), *adv.*—**a-maz′ed-ness**, *n.*—**a-maze′ment**, *n.* Amazed condition; stupefaction†; consternation†; overwhelming surprise or astonishment.—**a-maz′ing-ly**, *adv.*

Am-a-zon (am′ạ-zon), *n.* [L., < Gr. Ἀμαζών; origin uncertain. The name of the river *Amazon* refers to female warriors seen in its vicinity.] One of a race of female warriors said in Greek legend to dwell near the Black Sea; [*cap.* or *l. c.*] a warlike or masculine woman; a virago.—**Am-a-zo′ni-an** (-zō′ni-ạn), *a.* Of, like, or befitting an Amazon; warlike; masculine; also, pertaining to the river Amazon, in South America.—**am′a-zon-ite** (-īt), *n.* [From the river *Amazon.*] A beautiful green variety of microcline found near the Amazon River and in other parts of the world. Also **Am′a-zon stone.**

Amazon.
(Statue in the Vatican.)

am-bage (am′bāj), *n.*; pl. *ambages* (am′bā-jez, L. am-bā′jēz). [L. *ambages*, < *ambi-*, around, + *agere*, drive.] A roundabout course or performance; a circumlocution; an equivocation.—**am-ba′gious** (-bā′jus), *a.* Roundabout; circumlocutory.—**am-ba′gious-ly**, *adv.*—**am-ba′gious-ness**, *n.*

am-ba-ry (am-bä′ri), *n.* [E. Ind.] An East Indian plant, a species of hibiscus, *Hibiscus cannabinus*, yielding a useful fiber; also, the fiber itself.

am-bas-sade (am-bạ-sād′), *n.* [OF. F., through Sp. or It. < ML. *ambasciata, ambaxiata*, < *ambasciare*, go on a mission, < *ambascia, ambaxia, ambactia*, charge, office, < L. *ambactus*, servant, retainer; prob. from Celtic.] The mission or function of an ambassador; an embassy. [Obs. or archaic.]

am-bas-sa-dor, em-bas-sa-dor (am-bas′ạ-dọr, em-), *n.* [OF. F. *ambassadeur*, < ML. *ambasciator*, < *ambasciare*: see *ambassade.*] A diplomatic agent of the highest rank, sent by one sovereign or government to another either as resident representative or on extraordinary or special service; in general, an accredited agent or messenger.—**am-bas-sa-do′ri-al** (-dō′ri-ạl), *a.*—**am-bas′sa-dor-ship**, *n.*—**am-bas′sa-dress**, *n.* [= F. *ambassadrice.*] A female ambassador; also, an ambassador's wife.

am-bas-sage (am′bạ-sạj), *n.* Same as *embassage.* [Obs. or archaic.]

am-bas-sy (am′bạ-si), *n.* [OF. *ambassee, embascee*, < ML. *ambasciata*: cf. *ambassade.*] Same as *embassy.* [Obs. or archaic.]

am-ber (am′bėr). [OF. F. *ambre*, < Ar. *'anbar*, ambergris.] **I.** *n.* Ambergris†; also, a hard, translucent yellow substance, a resin of extinct pine-trees, found mostly on the shores of the Baltic, which becomes electric with friction; the yellow color of this resin. **II.** *a.* Of or like amber; of the color of amber.

am-ber-gris (am′bėr-grēs), *n.* [F. *ambre gris*, 'gray amber.'] An opaque, ash-colored substance, a morbid secretion of the sperm-whale, fragrant when heated, usually found floating on the ocean or cast ashore: used chiefly in perfumery.

am-ber-ite (am′bėr-īt), *n.* [From *amber* + *-ite.*] An explosive, a variety of smokeless powder.

am-ber=seed (am′bėr-sēd), *n.* The seed of the abelmosk; ambrette.

am-bi-dex-ter (am-bi-deks′tėr). [ML., < L. *ambi-*, on both sides, + *dexter*, right.] **I.** *a.* Using both hands with equal facility; fig., double-dealing. **II.** *n.* One who uses both hands equally well; fig., a double-dealer.—**am″bi-dex-ter′i-ty** (-ter′i-ti), *n.* Ambidextrous facility; fig., duplicity.—**am-bi-dex′trous**, *a.* Using both hands equally well; hence, doubly dexterous; facile; fig., double-dealing.—**am-bi-dex′trous-ly**, *adv.*—**am-bi-dex′trous-ness**, *n.*

am-bi-ent (am′bi-ẹnt), *a.* [L. *ambiens* (*-ent-*), ppr. of *ambire* (pp. *ambitus*), go around, < *ambi-*, around, + *ire*, go.] Surrounding; encompassing: used esp. of the air.

am-bi-gu-i-ty (am-bi-gū′i-ti), *n.*; pl. *-ties* (-tiz). The quality of being ambiguous; also, an ambiguous expression.

am-big-u-ous (am-big′ṳ̄-us), *a.* [L. *ambiguus*, < *ambigere*, wander, be uncertain, < *ambi-*, around, + *agere*, drive.] Of doubtful nature or meaning; uncertain; having a double meaning; open to various interpretations; equivocal.—**am-big′u-ous-ly**, *adv.*—**am-big′u-ous-ness**, *n.*

am-bit (am′bit), *n.* [L. *ambitus*, < *ambire*: see *ambient.*] Circuit; compass; precincts; scope or range.

am-bi-tion (am-bish′ọn), *n.* [OF. F. *ambition*, < L. *ambitio(n-)*, the going about of a candidate to solicit votes, < *ambire*: see *ambient.*] Eager desire for preferment, power, fame, etc.; also, aspiration toward any object; also, the object of aspiring desire.—**am-bi′tion**, *v. t.* To desire or seek as the object of ambition.—**am-bi′tion-less**, *a.* Devoid of ambition.—**am-bi′tious** (-bish′us), *a.* [L. *ambitiosus.*] Having or showing ambition; aspiring; pretentious; strongly desirous (*of*).—**am-bi′tious-ly**, *adv.*—**am-bi′tious-ness**, *n.*

am-biv-a-lence (am-biv′ạ-lẹns), *n.* [L. *ambi-*, on both sides, + *valentia*, strength: see *valence.*] Coexistence of contrary tendencies or feelings, as in the mind.

am-bi-vert (am′bi-vėrt), *n.* [L. *ambi-*, on both sides, + *vertere*, turn.] In *psychol.*, a person of a type between the introvert and the extrovert.

am-ble (am′bl), *v. i.*; *-bled, -bling.* [OF. F. *ambler*, < L. *ambulare*, walk.] To move with the gait of a horse when it lifts first the two legs on one side and then the two on the other; hence, to go at an easy pace.—**am′ble**, *n.* The gait of a horse or like animal when it ambles; an easy or gentle pace.—**am′bler**, *n.*—**am′bling-ly**, *adv.*

am-blyg-o-nite (am-blig′ọ̄-nīt), *n.* [G. *amblygonit*, < Gr. ἀμβλυγώνιος, obtuse-angled, < ἀμβλύς, blunt, obtuse, + γωνία, angle.] A mineral, a phosphate of aluminium and lithium containing fluorine, varying in color from white to pale shades of violet, gray, green, and yellow.

am-bly-o-pi-a (am-bli-ō′pi-ạ̈), *n.* [NL., < Gr. ἀμβλυωπία, < ἀμβλύς, blunt, dull, + ὤψ, eye.] In *pathol.*, dimness of sight, without apparent organic defect.—**am-bly-op′ic** (-op′ik), *a.*

am-bo (am′bō), *n.*; pl. *ambos* (-bōz), L. *ambones* (-bō′nēz). [ML., < Gr. ἄμβων.] A raised desk or pulpit, as in early Christian churches, used in the reading of the epistle and the gospel and in making announcements to the people.

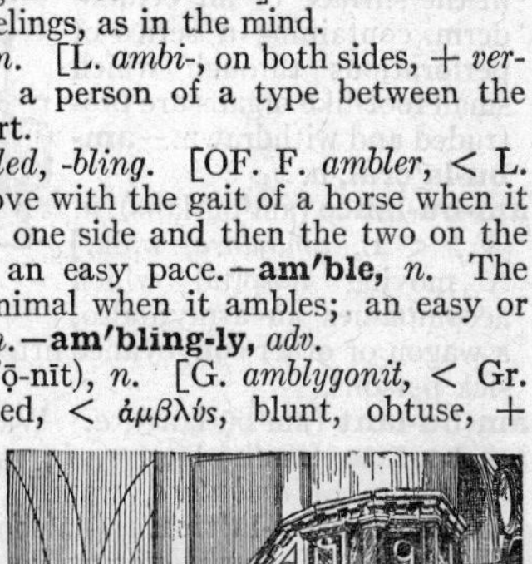
Ambo.
(Church of S. Maria in Ara Cœli, Rome.)

Am-boy-na (am-boi′nạ̈) **but′ton.** [From *Amboyna*, one of the Molucca Islands.] In *pathol.*, in the Molucca Islands, etc., same as *frambœsia.*—**Am-boy′na wood.** Kiabooca-wood.

am-brette (am-bret′), *n.* [F., < *ambre*, amber.] The musky seed of the abelmosk, used in perfumery, etc.

am-broid (am′broid), *n.* [See *-oid.*] Amber in large masses, produced from small fragments with the aid of heat and pressure.

am-bro-sia (am-brō′ẓiạ̈), *n.* [L., < Gr. ἀμβροσία, fem. of ἀμβρόσιος, < ἄμβροτος, immortal, < ἀ- priv. + βροτός = μορτός, mortal, akin to L. *mors*, death: see *mortal*, and cf. *amrita.*] The food of the gods of classical mythology, imparting immortality; the drink or the unguent of the gods; hence, something especially delicious; a dish made of mixed cut-up fruits, as oranges, bananas, pineapple, etc., with sugar and grated cocoanut.

am-bro-si-a-ceous (am-brō-zi-ā′shius), *a.* [NL. *Ambrosia*, the typical genus, < L. *ambrosia*: see *ambrosia.*] Belonging to the *Ambrosiaceæ*, or ragweed family of plants, which includes the ragweed, marsh-elder (genus *Iva*), etc.

am-bro-sial (am-brō′ziạl), *a.* Of or like ambrosia; divine; delicious; fragrant.—**am-bro′sial-ly,** *adv.*

am-bro-sian[1] (am-brō′ziạn), *a.* Ambrosial.

Am-bro-sian[2] (am-brō′ziạn), *a.* Of, pertaining to, instituted by, or named from St. Ambrose, bishop of Milan in the 4th century.

am-bro-type (am′brọ-tīp), *n.* [From James *Ambrose* Cutting (1814–67), the inventor: see *-type.*] In *photog.*, a picture or positive made from a glass negative by combining it with a dark background.

am-bry (am′bri), *n.*; pl. *-bries* (-briz). [OF. *almarie, armaire* (F. *armoire*), < L. *armarium*, < *arma*, arms, implements.] A closet, cupboard, or locker. [Archaic or prov.]

ambs=ace (āmz′ās or amz′-), *n.* [OF. *ambesas*, < *ambes* (< L. *ambo*), both, + *as*, ace.] The double ace, the lowest throw at dice; hence, the poorest chance or luck; also, the least possible amount or distance (as, within *ambs-ace* of succeeding). [Archaic.]

am-bu-la-crum (am-bū-lā′krum), *n.*; pl. *-cra* (-krạ̈). [L., a walk, alley, < *ambulare*, walk.] One of the radial areas in the surface of an echinoderm, containing a series of perforations through which small foot-like organs are protruded and withdrawn.—**am-bu-la′cral,** *a.*

Ambulance.

am-bu-lance (am′bū-lạns), *n.* [F., < L. *ambulare*, walk.] A moving hospital which accompanies an army; also, a wagon or other conveyance fitted for carrying wounded or sick persons.

am-bu-lant (am′bū-lạnt), *a.* Walking; ambulatory.

am-bu-late (am′bū-lāt), *v. i.*; *-lated, -lating.* [L. *ambulatus*, pp. of *ambulare*, walk.] To walk; travel; move about.—**am-bu-la′tion** (-lā′shọn), *n.*—**am′bu-la-to-ry** (-lạ-tọ-ri). [L. *ambulatorius* (as n., ML. *ambulatorium*).] **I.** *a.* Pertaining to or capable of walking; moving about; not stationary. **II.** *n.*; pl. *-ries* (-riz). A place for walking, as in a church or a monastery.

am-bus-cade (am-bus-kād′), *n.* [F. *embuscade*, < It. *imboscata*, < ML. *imboscata*, < *imboscare*: see *ambush.*] An ambushment or ambush; also, a place of ambush; also, a force lying in ambush.—**am-bus-cade′,** *v.*; *-caded, -cading.* **I.** *intr.* To lie in ambush. **II.** *tr.* To conceal in ambush; also, to attack from ambush.—**am-bus-cad′er** (-kā′dėr), *n.*—**am-bus-ca′do** (-kā′dō), *n.* Same as *ambuscade.* [Obs. or archaic.]

am-bush (am′bủsh), *v.* [OF. *embuscher*, < ML. *imboscare*, < L. *in*, in, + ML. *boscus*, wood.] **I.** *tr.* To station (troops, etc.) in concealment to await and attack an enemy by surprise; conceal in or as in ambush; also, to attack from ambush; waylay. **II.** *intr.* To lie in or as in ambush.—**am′bush,** *n.* An arrangement of troops or other persons in concealment for the purpose of attacking by surprise; the position or station of the attacking force, or the force itself.—**am′bush-er,** *n.*—**am′bush-ment,** *n.* The act or position of ambushing; an ambush.

a-me-ba (a-mē′bạ̈), etc. See *amœba*, etc.

a-meer (ạ-mēr′), *n.* See *amir.*

am-el-corn (am′ẹl-kôrn), *n.* [G. *amelkorn.*] A kind of wheat (*Triticum dicoccum*, or a race of *T. sativum*), resembling spelt, somewhat cultivated in Europe, esp. for its starch.

a-me-lio-ra-ble (ạ-mē′lyọ-rạ-bl), *a.* Capable of being ameliorated.

a-me-lio-rate (ạ-mē′lyọ-rāt), *v. t.* or *i.*; *-rated, -rating.* [= F. *améliorer*, < L. *ad*, to, + LL. *meliorare*, make better, E. *meliorate.*] To make or become better; improve; meliorate.—**a-me-lio-ra′tion** (-rā′shọn), *n.* The act of ameliorating, or the resulting state; an improvement.—**a-me′lio-ra-tive** (-rạ-tiv), *a.* Tending to ameliorate.—**a-me′lio-ra-tor** (-rā-tọr), *n.*

a-men (ā′men′ or ä′men′). [LL., < Gr. ἀμήν, < Heb. *āmēn*, firm or true, truth, truly, < *āman*, strengthen, confirm.] **I.** *adv.* or *interj.* Truly; verily: esp. used as a solemn expression of concurrence, or a concluding formula, as after a prayer. **II.** *n.* An utterance of 'amen'; an expression of concurrence; a concluding word or act; [*cap.*] the "faithful and true witness" (Rev. iii. 14); Christ.—**amen corner,** a place in a church, usually at one side of the pulpit, where formerly the deacons sat who led the responsive amens during the service.—**a′men′,** *v. t.* To say amen to; sanction or approve; also, to end or finish.

a-me-na-ble (ạ-mē′nạ-bl), *a.* [F. *amener*, bring to, < *à* (< L. *ad*), to, + *mener*, bring, lead, < L. *minare*, drive.] Accountable, responsible, or subject to some jurisdiction or authority; answerable (*to*); also, responsive or submissive.—**a-me-na-bil′i-ty** (-bil′i-ti), **a-me′na-ble-ness,** *n.*—**a-me′na-bly,** *adv.*

a-mend (ạ-mend′), *v.* [OF. F. *amender*, < L. *emendare*, correct, E. *emend.*] **I.** *tr.* To remove or correct faults in; change for the better; esp., to alter (a motion, bill, constitution, etc.) by due formal procedure. **II.** *intr.* To become better, as by reform or by regaining health.—**a-mend′,** *n.* [Sing. of *amends.*] Reparation; compensation: usually in *pl.* See *amends.*—**a-mend′a-ble,** *a.* Capable of being amended.—**a-men-da-to-ry** (ạ-men′dạ-tọ-ri), *a.* Serving to amend.

a-mende (ạ-mend′, F. å-moṅd), *n.* [F. and OF.: see *amends.*] Reparation, as for wrong done; a penalty or fine.—**amende honorable** (å-moṅd *o-no-*räbl). [F., 'honorable amend.'] An old French form of punishment involving a humiliating public appearance and confession by the person condemned; hence, in general, an open or formal apology and reparation.

a-mend-er (ạ-men′dėr), *n.* One who or that which amends.

a-mend-ment (ạ-mend′mẹnt), *n.* The act of amending; correction; improvement; esp., alteration of a motion, bill, constitution, etc., in due parliamentary or legislative form; also, that which is substituted or added in such alteration.

a-mends (ạ-mendz′), *n. pl.* or *sing.* [OF. *amendes*, pl. of *amende*, reparation, < *amender*, E. *amend*, *v.*: cf. *amende.*] Reparation, as for wrong or injury; atonement; satisfaction; compensation.

a-mene (ạ-mēn′), *a.* [F. *amène*, < L. *amœnus*, akin to *amare*, love.] Pleasant; agreeable.—**a-men-i-ty** (ạ-men′i-ti), *n.*; pl. *-ties* (-tiz). [F. *aménité*, < L. *amœnitas.*] The quality of being pleasant or agreeable (as, *amenity* of situation, scenery, or climate; *amenity* of manners); *pl.*, agreeable features, circumstances, ways, etc.; civilities.

a-men-or-rhe-a, a-men-or-rhœ-a (a-men-ọ-rē′ạ̈), *n.* [NL., < Gr. ἀ- priv. + μήν, month, + ῥοία, a flow, < ῥεῖν, flow.] In *pathol.*, absence or suppression of the menses.

am-ent (am′ent), *n.* [L. *amentum*, strap, thong.] In *bot.*, a spike of unisexual apetalous flowers with scaly bracts, usually deciduous; a catkin.—**am-en-ta′ceous** (-en-tā′shius), *a.*

Aments.
Willow (*Salix fragilis*), with separate flowers, male (upper figure) and female (lower figure).

a-men-tia (a-men′shiạ̈), *n.* [L., < *amens*, out of one's mind, < *a*, from, + *mens*, mind.] In *pathol.*, imbecility; idiocy.

a-merce (ạ-mėrs′), *v. t.*; *amerced, amercing.* [AF. *amercier*, < OF. *a* (< L. *ad*), to, at, + *merci*, E. *mercy.*] To punish by a discretionary fine; mulct; also, to deprive by way of penalty.—**a-merce′a-ble,** *a.* Liable to amercement.—**a-merce′ment,** *n.* The act of amercing; a discretionary pecuniary penalty (as distinguished from a fine fixed by statute).—**a-mer-cer** (ạ-mėr′sėr), *n.*

A-mer-i-can (ạ-mer′i-kạn), *a.* [From *Americus* Vespucius (Amerigo Vespucci), 1451–1512, Italian merchant and adventurer.] Of or pertaining to the continent of America; often, of or pertaining to the United States; also, noting or pertaining to the so-called 'red' race, characterized by a reddish or brownish skin, dark eyes, black hair, and prominent cheek-bones, and embracing the aborigines of North and South America (sometimes excluding the Eskimos), known as American Indians.—**American eagle,** the bald eagle (see *eagle*).—**American Legion,** a society, organized in 1919, composed of men who were in the military or naval service of the U. S. during the period in which the U. S. was a participant in the World War (between April 6, 1917, and Nov. 11, 1918), or who, being citizens of the U. S. at the time of enlistment, were in the military or naval service of any of the governments with which the U. S. was associated in the World War, its objects being to preserve ties of comradeship and to promote mutual helpfulness and service to the country.—**American plan,** that method of conducting a hotel according to which the fixed charge per day covers lodging, service, and board. Cf. *European plan.*—**A-mer′i-can,** *n.* A native or inhabitant of America; orig., a member of the aboriginal American (Indian) race; later, a person of European descent born or resident in America; esp., a citizen of the United States.—**A-mer-i-ca′na** (-kā′nạ), *n. pl.* [NL.: see *-ana.*] Books, papers, etc., relating to America, esp. to its history and geography. —**A-mer′i-can-ism,** *n.* American sympathies, nationality, or citizenship; an American trait or usage; a word or idiom considered to have originated in or gained currency from American use: in all senses referring particularly to the United States.—**A-mer′i-can-ize,** *v. t.* or *i.*; *-ized, -izing.* To make or become American; conform to the American character or type.—**A-mer″i-can-i-za′tion** (-i-zā′shọn), *n.*

Am-er-ind (am′ẹ-rind), *n.* [From *Amer(ican)* + *Ind(ian).*] An American Indian.—**Am-er-in′di-an,** *a.* and *n.*—**Am-er-in′dic,** *a.*

A-mer-i-pol (ạ-mer′i-pōl), *n.* [*Ameri(can)* + *pol(ymer).*] The trade-mark name for a synthetic rubber or its products.

am-e-thyst (am′ẹ̄-thist), *n.* [OF. *ametiste* (F. *améthyste*), < L. *amethystus,* < Gr. ἀμέθυστος, amethyst, so called because supposed to be a remedy for drunkenness, < ἀ- priv. + μεθύειν, be drunken, < μέθυ, wine.] A purple or violet variety of quartz, used in jewelry; also, the violet sapphire ('oriental amethyst'); also, a purple or violet color. —**am-e-thys′tine** (-this′tin), *a.* Of or like amethyst.

am-e-tro-pi-a (am-e-trō′pi-ạ̈), *n.* [NL., < Gr. ἄμετρος, without measure, disproportionate, + ὤψ, eye.] In *pathol.,* an abnormal condition of the eye with respect to refraction, as in astigmatism, myopia, etc. — **am-e-trop′ic** (-trop′ik), *a.*

Am-har-ic (am-har′ik). **I.** *a.* Of or pertaining to Amhara, a province of Abyssinia; also, noting or pertaining to the Semitic language spoken in Amhara, which is the official and court language of Abyssinia. **II.** *n.* The Amharic language.

a-mi (ȧ-mē), *n.* [F., < L. *amicus.*] A friend.

a-mi-a-ble (ā′mi-ạ-bl), *a.* [OF. *amiable* (< L. *amicabilis*: see *amicable*), confused with OF. *amable,* F. *aimable,* < L. *amabilis,* lovable, lovely.] Amicable or friendly; kindly in disposition or attitude; disposed to like or please; good-natured; sweet-tempered; also, lovable or lovely (archaic); pleasing; agreeable.—**a″mi-a-bil′i-ty** (-bil′i-ti), **a′mi-a-ble-ness,** *n.*—**a′mi-a-bly,** *adv.*

am-i-an-thus (am-i-an′thus), *n.* [L. *amiantus,* < Gr. ἀμίαντος, unstained, < ἀ- priv. + μιαίνειν, stain.] A fine variety of asbestos, with delicate, flexible filaments.

am-i-ca-ble (am′i-kạ-bl), *a.* [L. *amicabilis,* < *amicus,* friend, < *amare,* love.] Friendly; peaceable; harmonious; free from enmity or disagreement.—**am″i-ca-bil′i-ty** (-bil′i-ti), **am′i-ca-ble-ness,** *n.*—**am′i-ca-bly,** *adv.*

am-ice[1] (am′is), *n.* [ME. *amyse,* < OF. *amit,* < L. *amictus,* cloak, < *amicire,* throw about.] *Eccles.,* an oblong piece of linen worn about the neck and shoulders under the alb, or, formerly, on the head.

1 2

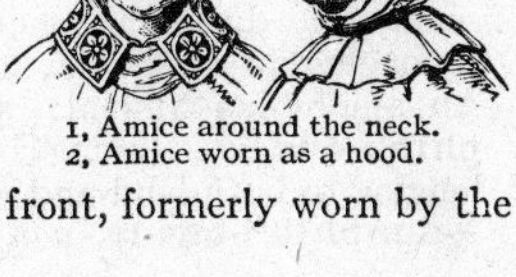

1, Amice around the neck.
2, Amice worn as a hood.

am-ice[2] (am′is), *n.* [ME. *amisse,* < OF. *aumuce* (F. *aumusse*), < ML. *almucia, almutium*; origin uncertain: cf. *mutch* and *mozzetta.*] *Eccles.,* a furred hood or hooded cape, with long ends hanging down in front, formerly worn by the clergy.

a-mid (ạ-mid′), *prep.* [ME. *amidde,* < AS. *on middan,* in the middle.] In the midst of; surrounded by; among.

am-ide (am′īd or -id), *n.* [From *ammonia.*] In *chem.,* a compound produced by replacing one or more of the hydrogen atoms of ammonia by univalent acid radicals.—**a-mid-ic** (a-mid′ik), *a.*—**am-i-do-** (am′i-dō-, also ạ-mē′dō-). A form of *amide* in compounds. Also **am′i-do,** *a.*—**a-mid′o-gen** (-ọ-jen), *n.* [See *-gen.*] In *chem.,* a hypothetical radical, NH_2, composed of one atom of nitrogen and two atoms of hydrogen.—**am′i-dol** (-dol or -dōl), *n.* A phenol derivative used as a photographic developer.

a-mid-ships (ạ-mid′ships), *adv.* *Naut.,* in or toward the middle of a ship, or the part midway between stem and stern; also, in the middle line, lengthwise, of a ship.

a-midst (ạ-midst′), *prep.* [Extended form of *amid,* with *-s,* AS. *-es,* adverbial genitive ending, and a later excrescent *-t.*] In the midst of; amid.

a-mie (ȧ-mē), *n.* [F., fem. of *ami.*] A woman friend; sometimes, a mistress.

a-mi-go (ä-mē′gō), *n.* [Sp., < L. *amicus.*] A friend.

am-il-dar (am′il-där), *n.* See *amaldar.*

am-ine (am′in; also, ạ-mēn′), *n.* [From *ammonia.*] In *chem.,* a compound produced by replacing one or more of the hydrogen atoms of ammonia by univalent hydrocarbon radicals.—**a-mi-no-** (am′i-nō-, also ạ-mē′nō-). A form of *amine* in compounds. Also **am′i-no,** *a.*

a-mir (ạ-mēr′), *n.* [Ar. *amīr,* < *amara,* command.] In Mohammedan countries, a commander or ruler; a chieftain; a lord; the title of the ruler of Afghanistan.

Am-ish (am′ish or ä′mish). **I.** *a.* Pertaining to Jakob Ammann (Ammon, or Amen), a Swiss Mennonite of the 17th century, or to his followers or their sect. **II.** *n. pl.* The Amish Mennonites.

a-miss (ạ-mis′), *adv.* and *a.* [See *miss*[1], *n.*] At fault; wrong; at variance with right, propriety, one's wishes, etc.; ill.—**a-miss′**†, *n.* A fault or wrong.

am-i-to-sis (am-i-tō′sis), *n.* [NL.: see *a-*[1] and *mitosis.*] In *biol.,* the direct method of cell-division, characterized by simple cleavage of the nucleus, without the formation of chromosomes. Cf. *mitosis.*—**am-i-tot′ic** (-tot′ik), *a.* Pertaining to or characterized by amitosis.—**am-i-tot′i-cal-ly,** *adv.*

am-i-ty (am′i-ti), *n.*; pl. *-ties* (-tiz). [OF. *amite, amiste* (F. *amitié*), < L. *amicus,* friend.] Friendly relations; friendship; good understanding, esp. between nations.

am-me-ter (am′ẹ̄-tėr or am′mē″tėr), *n.* [For *amperemeter.*] An instrument for measuring the strength of electric currents in amperes.

am-mo-nal (am′ọ-nal), *n.* [From *ammon(ium)* + *al(uminium).*] A high explosive consisting of a mixture of ammonium nitrate and aluminium.

am-mo-ni-a (a-mō′ni-ạ̈), *n.* [NL.; so called as being obtained from sal *ammoniac*: see *ammoniac, a.,* def.] The 'volatile alkali,' a colorless, pungent, suffocating gas, NH_3, a compound of nitrogen and hydrogen, very soluble in water and thus forming 'ammonia water' or 'aqueous ammonia'; hence, loosely, ammonia water.

am-mo-ni-ac (a-mō′ni-ak). [L. *ammoniacus* (as n., *ammoniacum,* Gr. ἀμμωνιακόν), applied to a salt and a gum said to come from near the shrine of *Ammon* in Libya.] **I.** *a.* Of or named from Ammon, the Egyptian deity, as a salt ('sal ammoniac,' ammonium chloride) and a medicinal gum-resin ('gum ammoniac,' perhaps orig. that from the plant *Ferula tingitana* of northern Africa, but now esp. that from *Dorema ammoniacum* of Persia, India, etc.); also, of or pertaining to ammonia. **II.** *n.* Gum ammoniac.—**am-mo-ni-a-cal** (am-ọ-nī′ạ-kạl), *a.* Of, containing, or using ammonia.

am-mo-ni-at-ed (a-mō′ni-ā-ted), *a.* Combined with ammonia.

am-mon-ic (a-mon′ik), *a.* Of or pertaining to ammonia or ammonium.

am-mon-i-fi-ca-tion (a-mon″i-fi-kā′shọn), *n.* The act of ammonifying, or the resulting state.

am-mon-i-fy (a-mon′i-fī), *v.*; *-fied, -fying.* [See *-fy.*] **I.** *tr.* To combine or impregnate with ammonia; form into ammonia or ammonium compounds. **II.** *intr.* To become ammonified; produce ammonification.

am-mon-ite (am'ọn-īt), *n.* [NL. *Ammonites*, for L. *cornu Ammonis*, horn of Ammon, the deity being represented with ram's horns.] One of the coiled, chambered fossil shells of the cephalopod mollusks of the extinct genus *Ammonites*, allied to the pearly nautilus.

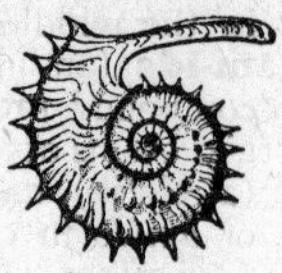
Ammonite.

am-mo-ni-um (a-mō'ni-um), *n.* [NL., < *ammonia*.] In *chem.*, a radical, NH_4, which plays the part of a metal in the compounds ('ammonium salts') formed when ammonia reacts with acids.

am-mu-ni-tion (am-ū-nish'ọn), *n.* [F. (obs.) *amunition*, for *munition*: see *munition*.] Military stores; in modern use, powder, shot, balls, etc., for firearms or ordnance.—**am-mu-ni'tion,** *v. t.* To supply with ammunition.

am-ne-sia (am-nē'ziạ), *n.* [NL., < Gr. ἀμνησία, < ἀ- priv. + μνᾶσθαι, remember: cf. *amnesty*.] In *pathol.*, loss of memory; esp., a form of aphasia marked by inability to remember words or their meaning.—**am-ne'sic** (-zik), **am-nes'tic** (-nes'tik), *a.*

am-nes-ty (am'nes-ti), *n.*; pl. *-ties* (-tiz). [L. *amnestia*, < Gr. ἀμνηστία, < ἀ- priv. + μνᾶσθαι, remember: see *mind*[2].] A forgetting or overlooking of offense, etc.; a general pardon of offenses against a government; also, oblivion.—**am'nes-ty,** *v. t.*; *-tied, -tying.* To grant an amnesty to.

am-ni-on (am'ni-on), *n.*; pl. *amnia* (-ạ). [NL., < Gr. ἀμνίον, < ἀμνός, lamb.] In *anat.*, a membrane lining the sac which incloses a fetus.—**am-ni-ot'ic** (-ot'ik), *a.*

a-mœ-ba (a-mē'bạ), *n.*; pl. *-bæ* (-bē) or *-bas.* [NL., < Gr. ἀμοιβή, change, < ἀμείβειν, to change.] An animalcule of the genus *Amœba*, which comprises microscopic rhizopodous protozoans existing as masses of protoplasm capable of changing form: common in ponds, etc.

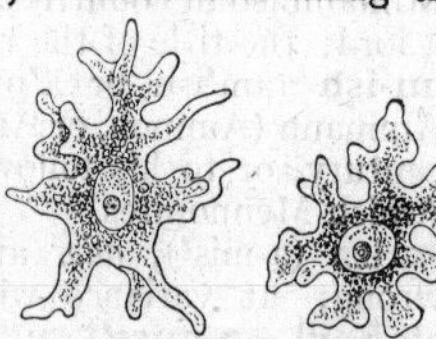
Amœbæ (much magnified).

am-œ-bæ-an, am-œ-be-an (am-ẹ-bē'ạn), *a.* [L. *amœbæus*, < Gr. ἀμοιβαῖος, alternate, < ἀμοιβή, change: see *amœba*.] Alternately responsive, as verses in dialogue form.

a-mœ-bic (a-mē'bik), *a.* [See *amœba*.] Of, pertaining to, or resembling an amœba; characterized by or due to the presence of amœbæ, as certain diseases.—**a-mœ'bi-cide** (-bi-sīd), *n.* [See *-cide*.] An agent that destroys amœbæ.—**a-mœ'bi-form** (-fôrm), *a.* Amœba-like; varying in form like an amœba.—**a-mœ'boid,** *a.* Like an amœba; related or pertaining to amœbæ.

a-mok (ạ-mok'), *a.* or *adv.* See *amuck*.

a-mo-le (ä-mō'lā), *n.* [Mex.] The roots, etc., of various plants, as Mexican species of *Agave*, used as a substitute for soap; also, any such plant.

a-mong (ạ-mung'), *prep.* [AS. *onmang*, for *ongemang*, < *on*, in, + *gemang*, mingling, crowd.] In the assemblage or group of; in the midst of; amid; also, in the number or class of (as, "Blessed art thou *among* women": Luke, i. 28); also, by the joint action of; also, by or for distribution to (as, divide these *among* you).—**a-mongst',** *prep.* [Extended form of *among*, with *-s*, AS. *-es*, adverbial genitive ending, and a later excrescent *-t*.] Same as *among*.

a-mon-til-la-do (ạ-mon-ti-lä'dō), *n.* [Sp.] A variety of sherry wine.

a-mor-al (ā-mor'ạl or a-), *a.* [See *a-*[1].] Non-moral; having no relation to morality; neither moral nor immoral.—**a-mo-ral-i-ty** (ā-mọ-ral'i-ti or am-ọ-), *n.*

a-mo-ret-to (ä-mō-ret'tō), *n.*; pl. *-ti* (-tē). [It.] An amorino.

a-mo-ri-no (ä-mō-rē'nō), *n.*; pl. *-ni* (-nē). [It., dim. of *amore*, < L. *amor*, love.] A little love; a cupid.

am-o-rist (am'ọ-rist), *n.* [L. *amor*, love.] One devoted to love or love-making; a gallant.—**am-o-ris'tic,** *a.*

a-mo-ro-so (ä-mō-rō'sō). [It., = E. *amorous*.] **I.** *a.* In *music*, loving; tender. **II.** *n.*; pl. *-si* (-sē). A lover.

am-o-rous (am'ọ-rus), *a.* [OF. *amorous* (F. *amoureux*), < ML. *amorosus*, < L. *amor*, love.] Inclined to love; also, affected with love; in love; also, due to or showing love; also, pertaining to love.—**am'o-rous-ly,** *adv.*—**am'o-rous-ness,** *n.*

a-mor-phism (ạ-môr'fizm), *n.* Amorphous condition; absence of definite form or crystalline structure; also, the anarchistic doctrine of the Russian writer Bakunin; nihilism.

a-mor-phous (ạ-môr'fus), *a.* [Gr. ἄμορφος, < ἀ- priv. + μορφή, form.] Lacking definite form; shapeless; formless; non-crystalline, as glass; also, of no particular kind or character; indeterminate; heterogeneous; unorganized.—**a-mor'phous-ly,** *adv.*—**a-mor'phous-ness,** *n.*

a-mort (ạ-môrt'), *a.* [From *alamort*, taken as *all amort*.] Lifeless; spiritless; melancholy. [Archaic.]

a-mor-tise (ạ-môr'tiz), etc. See *amortize*, etc.

a-mor-tize (ạ-môr'tiz), *v. t.*; *-tized, -tizing.* [OF. F. *amortir* (*amortiss-*), < L. *ad*, to, + *mors* (*mort-*), death.] To make dead†; in *law*, to alienate in mortmain; in *finance*, to extinguish (debt), as by a sinking-fund.—**a-mor'tiz-a-ble** (-ti-zạ-bl), *a.*—**a-mor-ti-za'tion** (-ti-zā'shọn), **a-mor'tize-ment,** *n.*

a-mo-tion (ạ-mō'shọn), *n.* [L. *amotio(n-)*, < *amovere*: see *amove*.] Removal; ejection, as from a position or office.

a-mount (ạ-mount'), *v. i.* [OF. *amonter*, < *amont*, upward, < L. *ad*, to, + *mons* (*mont-*), mountain.] To mount or go up†; come up (*to*) in the sum or aggregate; be equivalent in quantity, value, force, effect, etc.; be tantamount.—**a-mount',** *n.* Total sum; aggregate; full extent, value, or import; a sum or quantity.

a-mour (ạ-mör', F. å-mör), *n.* [F., < L. *amor*, love.] A love-affair; esp., an illicit love-affair.

a-mou-rette (å-mọ-ret'), *n.* [F., dim. of *amour*.] A petty amour.

a-mour=propre (å-mör-propr), *n.* [F.] Self-love; self-esteem.

a-move (ạ-möv'), *v. t.*; *amoved, amoving.* [L. *amovere*, < *a*, from, + *movere*, E. *move*.] To remove, esp. from a position or office.

am-pe-lop-sis (am-pe-lop'sis), *n.* [NL., < Gr. ἄμπελος, vine, + ὄψις, appearance.] Any plant of the vitaceous genus *Ampelopsis*, comprising climbing woody vines or shrubs, as the pepper-vine; also, some allied plant, as the Japanese ivy or the Virginia creeper.

am-per-age (am-pãr'ạj or am'pēr-ạj), *n.* The strength of an electric current measured in amperes.

am-pere (am-pãr' or am'pēr), *n.* [From A. M. *Ampère* (1775–1836), French physicist.] In *elect.*, the unit of current strength, the current produced by an electromotive force of one volt acting through a resistance of one ohm.—**am-pere'=hour,** *n.* In *elect.*, the quantity of electricity (3,600 coulombs) transferred by a current of one ampere in one hour: used as a unit.—**am-pere'=me"ter, am-pe-rom'e-ter** (-pe-rom'e-tėr), *n.* An ammeter.—**am-pere'=turn,** *n.* In *elect.*, one complete turn or convolution of a conducting coil, through which one ampere of current passes; the magnetomotive force produced by one ampere passing through one complete turn or convolution of a coil.

am-per-sand (am'pėr-sand"), *n.* [For *and per se—and*, '& by itself (as a mere symbol given after the letters of the alphabet, and called) *and*.'] The character &. See *and, n.*

amphi-. [Gr. ἀμφι-, repr. ἀμφί, prep. and adv., about, around, on both sides (of), akin to L. *ambi-*, around, on both sides.] A prefix meaning 'around,' 'on both sides,' and hence 'in two ways,' 'of two kinds,' occurring orig. in words from the Greek, but now used occasionally as an English formative.

am-phi-ar-thro-sis (am"fi-är-thrō'sis), *n.*; pl. *-throses* (-thrō'sēz). [NL.: see *amphi-* and *arthrosis*.] In *anat.*, a form of articulation which permits slight motion, as that between the bodies of the vertebræ.

am-phib-i-a (am-fib'i-ạ), *n. pl.* [NL., neut. pl. of *amphibius*, < Gr. ἀμφίβιος, amphibious, < ἀμφί, on both sides, + βίος, life.] Animals living both on land and in water, as frogs, turtles, crocodiles, seals, beavers, etc.; [*cap.*] a class of vertebrates, including the frogs, newts, and salamanders, more or less fish-like in the larval forms and at some time during life having gills.—**am-phib'i-an. I.** *a.* Belonging to amphibia, or to the class *Amphibia*. **II.** *n.* An amphibian animal; also, an amphibious plant.—**am-phib'i-ous,** *a.* Living both on land and in water; belonging to both land and water; hence, of a twofold nature.—**am-phib'i-ous-ly,** *adv.*—**am-phib'i-ous-ness,** *n.*

am-phi-bole (am′fi-bōl), *n.* [F., < Gr. ἀμφίβολος, ambiguous: see *amphibolous.*] A silicate mineral of varying composition, usually consisting of a silicate of calcium, magnesium, and one or more other metals, and having numerous varieties, including tremolite, common hornblende, etc.—**amphibole group,** a group of minerals consisting of amphibole and allied minerals.

am-phi-bol-ic (am-fi-bol′ik), *a.* Pertaining to or characterized by amphiboly; ambiguous; uncertain.

am-phib-o-lite (am-fib′ǫ-līt), *n.* [From *amphibole.*] A metamorphic rock consisting essentially of amphibole or hornblende.

am-phi-bol-o-gy (am-fi-bol′ǫ-ji), *n.*; pl. *-gies* (-jiz). [LL. *amphibologia,* < Gr. ἀμφίβολος, ambiguous (see *amphibolous*), + -λογία, < λέγειν, speak.] Ambiguity of speech, esp. from uncertainty of the grammatical construction rather than of the meaning of the words; also, a phrase, sentence, etc., capable of being construed in more than one way.

am-phib-o-lous (am-fib′ǫ-lus), *a.* [LL. *amphibolus,* < Gr. ἀμφίβολος, ambiguous, < ἀμφί, on both sides, + βάλλειν, throw.] Ambiguous, as in meaning; equivocal; characterized by amphibology.—**am-phib′o-ly,** *n.* [L. *amphibolia,* < Gr. ἀμφιβολία.] Amphibolous character or speech; ambiguity; amphibology.

am-phi-brach (am′fi-brak), *n.* [L. *amphibrachys,* < Gr. ἀμφίβραχυς, short on both sides, < ἀμφί, on both sides, + βραχύς, short.] In *pros.,* a foot of three syllables, short, long, and short.

am-phi-car-pous (am-fi-kär′pus), *a.* [Gr. ἀμφί (see *amphi-*) + καρπός, fruit.] In *bot.,* bearing two classes of fruit, differing in form or in time of ripening.

am-phi-chro-ic (am-fi-krō′ik), *a.* [Gr. ἀμφί (see *amphi-*) + χρόα, color.] In *chem.,* reacting both as an acid and as an alkali upon colors used as chemical tests. Also **am″phi-chro-mat′ic** (-krǫ-mat′ik).

am-phi-cœ-lous (am-fi-sē′lus), *a.* [Gr. ἀμφί (see *amphi-*) + κοῖλος, hollow.] In *anat.* and *zoöl.,* concave on both sides, as the bodies of the vertebræ of fishes.

am-phic-ty-on (am-fik′ti-ǫn), *n.* [Gr. ἀμφικτύονες, pl., = ἀμφικτίονες, dwellers around, neighbors.] [Often *cap.*] A deputy to the council of a league of ancient Greek states, esp. a league whose council met alternately at Delphi and Thermopylæ.—**am-phic-ty-on′ic** (-on′ik), *a.*—**am-phic′-ty-on-y** (-ǫn-i), *n.*; pl. *-ies* (-iz). A league of states represented by amphictyons.

am-phi-ge-an (am-fi-jē′ạn), *a.* [Gr. ἀμφί, around, + γῆ, earth.] In *bot.,* extending around the earth, as species of plants found throughout the same latitude.

am-phi-go-ry (am′fi-gǫ-ri), *n.*; pl. *-ries* (-riz). [F. *amphigouri;* origin unknown.] A meaningless tissue of words; a nonsensical rigmarole, esp. as a form of literary composition. Also (F.) **am-phi-gou-ri** (äṅ-fē-gö-rē).—**am-phi-gor′ic** (-gor′ik), *a.*

am-phim-a-cer (am-fim′ạ-sėr), *n.* [L. *amphimacrus,* < Gr. ἀμφίμακρος, long on both sides, < ἀμφί, on both sides, + μακρός, long.] In *pros.,* a foot of three syllables, long, short, and long.

am-phi-ox-us (am-fi-ok′sus), *n.* [NL., < Gr. ἀμφί, on both sides, + ὀξύς, sharp.] Any lancelet of the genus *Amphioxus* (or *Branchiostoma*).

am-phi-pod (am′fi-pod), *n.* [NL. *Amphipoda,* pl., < Gr. ἀμφί, on both sides, + πούς (ποδ-), foot.] One of the *Amphipoda,* a division of crustaceans, as the beach-fleas, having the anterior pairs of legs directed forward and the rest backward.—**am-phip′o-dous** (-fip′ǫ-dus), *a.*

am-phi-pro-style (am-fi-prō′stīl or am-fip′rǫ-). [L. *amphiprostylos,* < Gr. ἀμφιπρόστυλος, < ἀμφί, on both sides, + πρόστυλος, E. *prostyle.*] In *arch.*: **I.** *a.* Having a portico in both front and rear, as a temple. **II.** *n.* An amphiprostyle building.

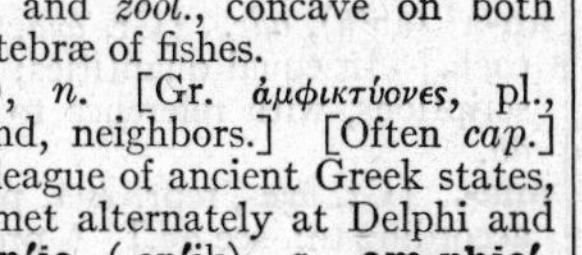

Amphisbæna.

am-phis-bæ-na (am-fis-bē′nạ), *n.* [L., < Gr. ἀμφίσβαινα, < ἀμφίς, on both sides, + βαίνειν, go.] A fabulous venomous serpent having a head at each end and able to move in either direction; also, a snake-like lizard of the genus *Amphisbæna,* of tropical America, with obtuse head and tail and moving forward or backward with equal ease.—**am-phis-bæ′nic,** *a.*

am-phi-the-a-ter, am-phi-the-a-tre (am-fi-thē′ạ-tėr), *n.* [L. *amphitheatrum,* < Gr. ἀμφιθέατρον, < ἀμφί, around, + θέατρον, theater.] A building or place of exhibition with seats in oval or circular tiers rising one behind another about an arena or central area; hence, any similar formation, as a hollow among hills; also, the uppermost gallery of a modern theater.—**am″phi-the-at′ric, am″phi-the-at′-ri-cal** (-thē-at′rik, -ri-kạl), *a.* Of, like, or in an amphitheater.—**am″phi-the-at′ri-cal-ly,** *adv.*

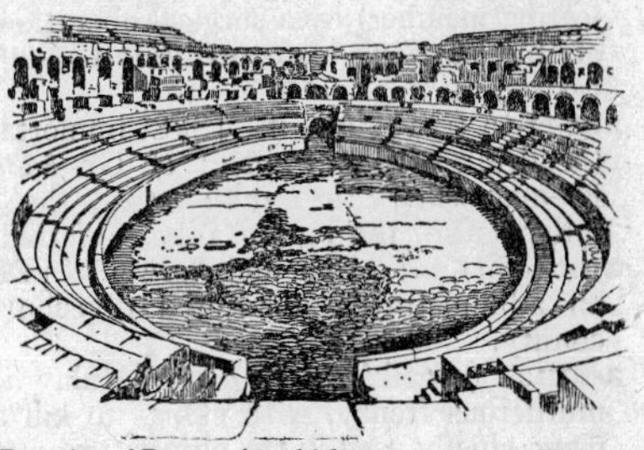

Remains of Roman Amphitheater at Nîmes, France.

Am-phit-ry-on (am-fit′ri-ǫn), *n.* [From *Amphitryon* in Molière's comedy of that name, who gives a dinner.] [Also *l. c.*] The host at a dinner.

am-pho-ra (am′fǫ-rạ̈), *n.*; pl. *-ræ* (-rē). [L., < Gr. ἀμφορεύς, for ἀμφιφορεύς, < ἀμφί, on both sides, + φέρειν, bear.] A two-handled, narrow-necked vessel, commonly pointed at the base, used by the Greeks and Romans for holding wine, oil, etc.—**am-phor′ic** (-for′ik), *a.* In *pathol.,* resembling the sound made by blowing across the mouth of a flask.

Amphoræ.

am-ple (am′pl), *a.*; compar. *ampler,* superl. *amplest.* [OF. F. *ample,* < L. *amplus.*] Of great extent, size, or amount; large; broad; big; full; in full or abundant measure; copious; liberal; fully sufficient for the purpose or for needs.—**am′ple-ness,** *n.*

am-plex-i-caul (am-plek′si-kâl), *a.* [L. *amplexus,* pp. of *amplecti,* embrace, + *caulis,* stem.] In *bot.,* clasping the stem, as some leaves do at their base.

Amplexicaul Leaves.

am-pli-a-tion (am-pli-ā′shǫn), *n.* [L. *ampliatio(n-),* < *ampliare,* enlarge, < *amplus,* E. *ample.*] Amplification.—**am′pli-a-tive** (-ạ-tiv), *a.*

am-pli-fi-ca-tion (am″pli-fi-kā′shǫn), *n.* [L. *amplificatio(n-).*] The act of amplifying; enlargement; extension; expansion of a statement, narrative, etc., as for rhetorical purposes; also, a statement, narrative, etc., so expanded; also, an addition made in expanding.—**am′pli-fi-ca-tive** (-kā-tiv), **am′pli-fi-ca-to-ry** (-kā-tǫ-ri), *a.*

am-pli-fi-er (am′pli-fī-ėr), *n.* One who or that which amplifies; any of various devices for enlarging, increasing, or extending something; a lens in a microscope, for enlarging the field of vision; an amplifying device used in radio.

am-pli-fy (am′pli-fī), *v.*; *-fied, -fying.* [OF. F. *amplifier,* < L. *amplificare,* < *amplus,* ample, large, + *facere,* make.] **I.** *tr.* To make larger or greater; enlarge; extend; expand in stating or describing, as by means of details, illustrations, etc.; develop rhetorically; specif., to increase the magnitude or intensity of (radio impulses, signals, etc.). **II.** *intr.* To discourse at length; expatiate or dilate (*on*).

am-pli-tude (am′pli-tūd), *n.* [L. *amplitudo.*] The state of being ample; great size or extent; wide range; large or full measure; abundance; the range of a projectile; in *physics,* the distance from one extremity of a vibration (properly) to the middle point, or (commonly) to the other extremity; in *astron.,* the arc of the horizon intercepted between the east or west point and the center of the sun or of a star at its rising or setting.

am-ply (am′pli), *adv.* In an ample manner or measure.

am-pul-la (am-pul′ạ̈), *n.*; pl. *ampullæ* (-ē). [L.] A two-handled bottle with a nearly globular body used by the Romans for holding oil, etc.; *eccles.,* a vessel for holding consecrated oil; a cruet for the wine and water used at the altar; in *anat.*, a dilated portion of a canal or duct.—**am-pul-la′ceous** (-pu-lā′shius), *a.* Bottle-shaped; inflated. Also **am-pul′lar** (-pul′ạ̈r).

am-pu-tate (am′pū-tāt), *v. t.*; *-tated, -tating.* [L. *amputatus*, pp. of *amputare*, < *ambi-*, around, + *putare*, lop, prune: see *putative.*] To cut off (a limb or other projecting member) by a surgical operation; remove all or part of by cutting.—**am-pu-ta′tion** (-tā′shọn), *n.*—**am′pu-ta-tor,** *n.*

am-ri-ta (am-rē′tạ̈), *n.* [Skt., immortal, as n. immortality, the drink of immortality: cf. Gr. ἄμβροτος, immortal, and E. *ambrosia.*] In *Hindu myth.*, the beverage of immortality; also, the immortality conferred by it.

amt (ämt), *n.* [Dan. and Norw.] In Denmark and Norway, an administrative territorial division corresponding to a county.

a-muck (ạ-muk′), *a.* or *adv.* [Malay *amoq.*] In a state of murderous frenzy, with efforts to kill all who come in the way: chiefly used in the phrase 'to run amuck' (orig. of frenzied Malays, later also of any one making wild, indiscriminate attacks).

am-u-let (am′ū-let), *n.* [L. *amuletum*; origin unknown.] Some object superstitiously worn to ward off evil; a protecting charm.

Amulets: 1, from the Vatican; 2, from a private collection.

a-muse (ạ-mūz′), *v. t.*; *amused, amusing.* [OF. F. *amuser*, occupy with trifles, beguile, divert, < OF. *a* (< L. *ad*), to, + *muser*, trifle: see *muse*[2].] To occupy or divert the attention of with something that beguiles or deceives (archaic); also, to occupy the attention of agreeably; entertain; divert; excite mirth in; also, to engross†; also, to puzzle†.—**a-mus′a-ble,** *a.*—**a-muse′ment,** *n.* Beguilement or deception (archaic); also, pleasant entertainment; diversion; mirth, as at something ludicrous; also, a form or means of entertainment; a pastime.—**a-mus′er,** *n.*—**a-mus′ing,** *p. a.* That amuses; entertaining; diverting.—**a-mus′ing-ly,** *adv.*—**a-mu-sive** (ạ-mū′ziv), *a.* Amusing; entertaining.

a-myg-da-la (ạ-mig′dạ-lạ̈), *n.*; pl. *-læ* (-lē). [L., < Gr. ἀμυγδάλη, almond: cf. *almond.*] An almond; in *anat.*, an almond-shaped part; a tonsil.

a-myg-da-la-ceous (ạ-mig-dạ-lā′shius), *a.* [L. *amygdalaceus*, almond-like, < *amygdala*: see *amygdala.*] Belonging to the *Amygdalaceæ*, or almond family of plants, which includes the almond, peach, plum, cherry, etc.

a-myg-da-lin (ạ-mig′dạ-lin), *n.* [L. *amygdala*: see *amygdala.*] In *chem.*, a glucoside existing in bitter almonds.

a-myg-da-loid (ạ-mig′dạ-loid). [Gr. ἀμυγδάλη, almond: see *-oid.*] **I.** *a.* Almond-like; of rocks, containing amygdules. **II.** *n.* An igneous rock in which rounded cavities formed by the expansion of steam have later become filled with various minerals.—**a-myg-da-loi′dal,** *a.*—**a-myg′dule** (-dūl), *n.* One of the mineral nodules in amygdaloid.

An Amygdaloid (Diabase) with calcite nodules or amygdules.

am-yl (am′il), *n.* [L. *am(ylum)*, starch, + E. *-yl.*] In *chem.*, a hypothetical radical, C_5H_{11}, believed to exist in many compounds, as 'amyl alcohol' ($C_5H_{11}OH$, the chief constituent of fusel-oil) and 'amyl nitrite' (a yellowish liquid of fruity odor and aromatic taste, inhaled as a remedy in asthma, etc.).

am-y-la-ceous (am-i-lā′shius), *a.* [L. *amylum*, starch: see *amylum.*] Of the nature of starch; starchy.

am-y-lene (am′i-lēn), *n.* [From *amyl.*] In *chem.*, any of certain unsaturated isomeric hydrocarbons with the formula C_5H_{10}.

a-myl-ic (a-mil′ik), *a.* Of or pertaining to amyl.

a-myl-o-gen (a-mil′ọ-jen), *n.* [L. *amylum*, starch: see *-gen.*] In *chem.*, that part of granulose which is soluble in water.—**a-myl-o-gen′ic,** *a.* Of or pertaining to amylogen; also, of leucoplasts, forming starch.

am-y-loid (am′i-loid). [L. *amylum*, starch: see *-oid.*] **I.** *a.* Starch-like; starchy. **II.** *n.* A starch-like substance; in *pathol.*, a proteid substance formed in the tissues in lardaceous degeneration.—**am-y-loi′dal,** *a.*

am-y-lol-y-sis (am-i-lol′i-sis), *n.* [NL., < L. *amylum*, starch, + Gr. λύσις, a loosing.] The conversion of starch into sugar in digestion.—**am″y-lo-lyt′ic** (-lọ-lit′ik), *a.*

am-y-lop-sin (am-i-lop′sin), *n.* [L. *amylum*, starch, + Gr. ὄψις, appearance.] In *chem.*, an enzyme of the pancreatic juice, capable of converting starch into sugar.

am-y-lose (am′i-lōs), *n.* [L. *amylum*, starch.] In *chem.*, any of a group of carbohydrates, as starch, dextrin, cellulose, etc., having the formula $C_6H_{10}O_5$, or some multiple thereof.

am-y-lum (am′i-lum), *n.* [L., starch, < Gr. ἄμυλον, fine flour, prepared otherwise than by the usual grinding, < ἀ- priv. + μύλη, mill.] Starch.

an[1], **a**[3] (an or ạn, ā or ạ), *indef. art.* [AS. *ān*, one, E. *one.*] One; some single; distributively, each or every (as, once *a* day; five cents *an* hour): *a* being now regularly used before initial consonant-sounds (including the ū-sound, as in *use* and *eulogy*, and the h-sound), *an* before initial vowel-sounds, and sometimes still, as formerly, before an initial h-sound in an unaccented syllable (as, *an* historian, but *a* history).

an[2] (an or ạn), *conj.* [Reduced form of *and.*] And (in this sense usually *an'*: colloq.); also, if (archaic or prov.).

an-. [Gr. ἀν-: see *a-*[1].] The form of *a-*, 'without,' 'not,' used before a vowel (or *h*), as in *anelectric.*

-an. [L. *-anus.*] A suffix meaning 'belonging to,' 'pertaining or relating to,' 'adhering to,' and commonly expressing connection with a place, person, leader, class, order, sect, system, doctrine, or the like, serving to form adjectives, many of which are also used as nouns, as *American, Babylonian, Christian, Dominican, Elizabethan, hydrozoan, lepidopteran, presbyterian, republican*, and hence serving to form other nouns of the same type, as *historian, theologian.*

a-na[1] (ā′nạ̈ or an′ạ̈), *n. pl.* [Noun use of *-ana*, as in *Shaksperiana*, etc.: see *-ana.*] Sayings, anecdotes, writings, etc., in connection with a particular person or subject.

an-a[2] (an′ạ̈), *adv.* [Gr. ἀνά, prep., at the rate of (so much) each.] In equal quantities; of each: used in medical prescriptions, with reference to ingredients, and often written *āā.*

ana-. [Gr. ἀνα-, repr. ἀνά, prep., up, upon, throughout, by, according to: see *on.*] A prefix meaning 'up,' 'throughout,' 'again,' 'back,' occurring orig. in words from the Greek, but used also in modern words (English and other) formed after the Greek type.

-ana. [L. *-ana*, neut. pl. of *-anus*, E. *-an.*] A suffix meaning 'things relating to,' used in collective plural nouns formed from the names of persons, places, or other subjects of interest, and denoting sayings, anecdotes, items of information, writings, etc., in connection with them, as in *Americana, Shaksperiana.*

an-a-bæ-na (an-ạ-bē′nạ̈), *n.* [NL., < Gr. ἀναβαίνειν, go up: see *anabasis.*] Any of the fresh-water algæ constituting the genus *Anabæna*, commonly occurring in masses, and often contaminating water, giving it a fishy odor and taste and sometimes a cloudy appearance; a mass of such algæ.

an-a-bap-tism (an-ạ-bap′tizm), *n.* [LGr. ἀναβαπτισμός, < ἀναβαπτίζειν, baptize again, < Gr. ανα-, again, + βαπτίζειν, E. *baptize.*] A second baptism; [*cap.*] the doctrine or practices of the Anabaptists.—**An-a-bap′tist,** *n.* A member of any of various sects arising in Germany, Switzerland, etc., early in the 16th century, that denied the validity of infant baptism and required the baptism of adults on entrance into communion: also applied, more or less opprobriously, to members of later sects or religious bodies holding the same doctrine.

an-a-bas (an′ạ-bas), *n.* [NL., < Gr. ἀναβάς, second aorist part. of ἀναβαίνειν, go up: see *anabasis.*] Any fish of the acanthopterygian genus *Anabas* of southern Asia, etc., as the climbing-fish, *A. scandens.*

a-nab-a-sis (a-nab′ạ-sis), *n.*; pl. *-ases* (-ạ-sēz). [Gr. ἀνάβασις, < ἀναβαίνειν, go up, < ἀνά, up, + βαίνειν, go.] A going up; a military advance or expedition, as that of Cyrus the Younger and his Greek mercenaries in 401 B.C., against Artaxerxes II. of Persia, described by Xenophon in his "Anabasis."

a-nab-o-lism (a-nab′ọ-lizm), *n.* [Gr. ἀναβολή, ascent, < ἀναβάλλειν, throw up, < ἀνά, up, + βάλλειν, throw.] In *biol.*, ascending or constructive metabolism: opposed to *catabolism.* See *metabolism.*—**an-a-bol-ic** (an-ạ-bol′ik), *a.*

an-a-branch (an′ạ-brȧnch), *n.* [For *anastomosing branch.*] A branch of a river which leaves it and enters it again. [Australia.]

an-a-car-di-a-ceous (an-ạ-kär-di-ā′shius), *a.* [NL. *Anacardium*, genus including the cashew, < Gr. ἀνά, according to, + καρδία, heart.] Belonging to the *Anacardiaceæ*, a family of trees and shrubs including the cashew, mango, pistachio, sumac, etc.

a-nach-o-rism (a-nak′ọ-rizm), *n.* [Gr. ἀνα-, back, against, + χώρα, place, country.] Something not properly belonging to the country to which it is referred.

an-a-chron-ic (an-ạ-kron′ik), *a.* Anachronistic.

a-nach-ro-nism (a-nak′rọ-nizm), *n.* [Gr. ἀναχρονισμός, < ἀναχρονίζεσθαι, refer to a wrong time, < ἀνα-, back, against, + χρόνος, time.] A misplacing in time; a crediting of a person or thing to a time other, esp. earlier, than the actual period; also, something placed or occurring out of its proper time.—**a-nach-ro-nis′tic, a-nach′ro-nous,** *a.* Placed or occurring out of the proper time; involving an anachronism.—**a-nach′ro-nous-ly,** *adv.*

a-nac-la-sis (a-nak′lạ-sis), *n.* [NL., < Gr. ἀνάκλασις, < ἀνακλᾶν, bend back, break off, < ἀνα-, back, + κλᾶν, break.] In *pros.*, a change of place between a short syllable and a preceding long one.—**an-a-clas-tic** (an-ạ-klas′tik), *a.* [Gr. ἀνάκλαστος, bent back, < ἀνακλᾶν.] Pertaining or due to the refraction of light; in *pros.*, pertaining to or characterized by anaclasis.—**an-a-clas′tics,** *n.* Same as *dioptrics.*

an-a-cli-nal (an-ạ-klī′nạl), *a.* [Gr. ἀνα-, against, + κλίνειν, incline.] In *geol.*, transverse to the dip, as a valley.

an-a-co-lu-thon (an″ạ-kọ-lū′thon), *n.*; pl. *-tha* (-thạ̈). [NL., < Gr. ἀνακόλουθον, neut. of ἀνακόλουθος, inconsequent, < ἀν- priv. + ἀκόλουθος, following.] In *gram.*, a construction or a sentence involving a break in grammatical sequence. See Luke, v. 14.—**an″a-co-lu′thic,** *a.*

an-a-con-da (an-ạ-kon′dạ̈), *n.* [Singhalese?] Orig., some large serpent or python of Ceylon; later, a large South American serpent, *Eunectes murinus*, of the boa family; hence, any boa-constrictor.

A-nac-re-on-tic (a-nak-rẹ-on′tik). **I.** *a.* [Also *l. c.*] Pertaining to or in the manner of the Greek lyric poet Anacreon (about 563–about 478 B.C.), who wrote of love and wine; amatory; convivial. **II.** *n.* [*l. c.*] A poem in the manner of Anacreon.

an-a-cru-sis (an-ạ-krö′sis), *n.* [NL., < Gr. ἀνάκρουσις, < ἀνακρούειν, strike up, < ἀνά, up, + κρούειν, strike.] In *pros.*, an unaccented syllable (or two) prefixed to a verse beginning with an accented syllable.—**an-a-crus′tic** (-krus′tik), *a.*

an-a-dem (an′ạ-dem), *n.* [L. *anadema*, < Gr. ἀνάδημα, < ἀναδεῖν, bind up, < ἀνά, up, + δεῖν, bind.] A headband; a wreath; a garland. [Poetic.]

an-a-di-plo-sis (an″ạ-di-plō′sis), *n.* [L., < Gr. ἀναδίπλωσις, < ἀναδιπλοῦν, make double, < ἀνά, up, + διπλοῦν, double.] In *rhet.*, repetition in the first part of one clause of a prominent word in the latter part of the preceding clause. See Rom. viii. 16, 17.

a-nad-ro-mous (a-nad′rọ-mus), *a.* [Gr. ἀνάδρομος, < ἀνά, up, + δραμεῖν, run.] Of fishes, going from the sea up a river to spawn. Cf. *catadromous.*

a-næ-mi-a (a-nē′mi-ạ̈), etc. See *anemia*, etc.

an-a-ër-obe (an-ā′ẹ-rōb), *n.* One of the anaërobia.

an-a-ër-o-bi-a (an-ā-ẹ-rō′bi-ạ), *n. pl.* [NL., < Gr. ἀν- priv. + ἀήρ (ἀερ-), air, + βίος, life.] Bacteria and other micro-organisms whose existence requires, or is not destroyed by, the absence of free oxygen: opposed to *aërobia.*—**an-a-ër-o′bic,** *a.* Of bacteria, etc., requiring, or not destroyed by, the absence of free oxygen; pertaining to anaërobia.—**an-a-ër-o′bi-cal-ly,** *adv.*

an-æs-the-sia (an-es-thē′ziạ̈), *n.* [NL., < Gr. ἀναισθησία, < ἀν- priv. + αἰσθάνεσθαι, perceive.] Loss of the sense of touch or feeling; esp., general or local insensibility, as to pain, induced by certain drugs. Also **an-æs-the′sis** (-sis).—**an-æs-thet′ic** (-thet′ik), etc. See *anesthetic*, etc.

an-a-glyph (an′ạ-glif), *n.* [Gr. ἀνάγλυφος, also ἀνάγλυπτος, wrought in low relief, < ἀνά, up, + γλύφειν, carve.] Something executed in low relief, as a cameo or an embossed ornament.—**an-a-glyph′ic, an-a-glyp′tic** (-glip′tik), *a.*—**an-a-glyp′tics,** *n.* [Gr. ἀνάγλυπτος.] The art of carving or decorating in low relief.

an-a-go-ge (an-ạ-gō′jẹ̄), *n.* [LL., < Gr. ἀναγωγή, < ἀνάγειν, lead up, raise, < ἀνά, up, + ἄγειν, lead.] Spiritual meaning or interpretation, as of Scripture.—**an-a-gog′ic, an-a-gog′i-cal** (-goj′ik, -i-kạl), *a.* Pertaining to anagoge; spiritual; mystical.—**an-a-gog′i-cal-ly,** *adv.*

an-a-gram (an′ạ-gram), *n.* [F. *anagramme*, < Gr. ἀνα-, back, again, + γράμμα, letter, < γράφειν, write.] A word or phrase formed by transposing the letters of another word or phrase.—**an″a-gram-mat′ic, an″a-gram-mat′-i-cal** (-grạ-mat′ik, -i-kạl), *a.*—**an″a-gram-mat′i-cal-ly,** *adv.*—**an-a-gram′ma-tism** (-gram′ạ-tizm), *n.* The making of anagrams.—**an-a-gram′ma-tist,** *n.*—**an-a-gram′-ma-tize,** *v. t.*; *-tized, -tizing.* To transpose into an anagram.

a-nal (ā′nạl), *a.* Of, pertaining to, or near the anus.

a-nal-cite (a-nal′sīt), *n.* [Gr. ἀναλκής, weak, < ἀν- priv. + ἀλκή, strength.] A white or slightly colored mineral, a hydrous silicate of aluminium and sodium, generally found in crystalline form.

an-a-lec-ta (an-ạ-lek′tạ̈), *n. pl.* [NL., < Gr. ἀνάλεκτα, neut. pl. of ἀνάλεκτος, adj. < ἀναλέγειν, pick up, gather, collect, < ἀνά, up, + λέγειν, pick.] Literary extracts or fragments forming a collection. Also **an′a-lects.**

an-a-lep-tic (an-ạ-lep′tik). [Gr. ἀναληπτικός, < ἀναλαμβάνειν, take up, recover, restore.] In *med.*: **I.** *a.* Promoting the recovery of strength after disease; strengthening; restorative. **II.** *n.* An analeptic remedy.

a-nal-gen, a-nal-gene (a-nal′jen, -jēn), *n.* [Gr. ἀν- priv. + ἄλγος, pain.] In *phar.*, a colorless crystalline derivative of quinoline, used as an antipyretic, analgesic, etc.

an-al-ge-sia (an-al-jē′ziạ̈), *n.* [NL., < Gr. ἀναλγησία, < ἀν- priv. + ἀλγεῖν, feel pain.] In *med.*, absence of sensibility to pain.—**an-al-ge′sic** (-zik), **an-al-get′ic** (-jet′ik). In *med.*: **I.** *a.* Pertaining to or causing analgesia. **II.** *n.* A remedy that removes pain.

an-a-log-ic, an-a-log-i-cal (an-ạ-loj′ik, -i-kạl), *a.* [See *analogy.*] Pertaining to, involving, or having analogy; analogous.—**an-a-log′i-cal-ly,** *adv.*—**a-nal-o-gist** (ạ-nal′ọ-jist), *n.* One who analogizes, or deals with analogies.—**a-nal′o-gize** (-jīz), *v.*; *-gized, -gizing.* **I.** *tr.* To explain by analogy; represent as analogous. **II.** *intr.* To use analogy; be analogous.

a-nal-o-gous (ạ-nal′ọ-gus), *a.* [L. *analogus*, < Gr. ἀνάλογος, proportionate, < ἀνά, according to, + λόγος, proportion, due relation: see *Logos.*] Corresponding or comparable (*to*) in some respect, though unlike as a whole; having analogy; in *biol.*, corresponding in function but not in type of structure and in origin (as, the wing of a bird and the wing of a butterfly are *analogous*).—**a-nal′o-gous-ly,** *adv.*—**a-nal′o-gous-ness,** *n.*

an-a-logue (an′ạ-log), *n.* [F., < L. *analogus*: see *analogous.*] Something analogous; in *biol.*, an organ or part which is analogous to another.

a-nal-o-gy (ạ-nal′ọ-ji), *n.*; pl. *-gies* (-jiz). [L. *analogia*, < Gr. ἀναλογία, < ἀνάλογος: see *analogous.*] A mathematical proportion, or equality of ratios; hence, a correspondence between things unlike in themselves (as, to trace an *analogy* between the heart and a machine); a ground of comparison in some respect, without actual or complete resemblance; the relation of being analogous; in *biol.*, analogous relation or correspondence.

an-al-pha-bete (an-al′fạ-bēt), *n.* [Gr. ἀναλφάβητος, not knowing one's a-b-c, < ἀν- priv. + ἄλφα, alpha (a), + βῆτα, beta (b).] A totally illiterate person.—**an-al-pha-bet′ic** (-bet′ik), *a.*

an-a-lyse (an′ạ-līz), etc. See *analyze*, etc.

a-nal-y-sis (ạ-nal′i-sis), *n.*; pl. *-yses* (-i-sēz). [ML., < Gr. ἀνάλυσις, < ἀναλύειν, unloose, undo, < ἀνά, up, + λύειν, loose.] Resolution or separation of a whole, whether a material substance or any matter of thought, into its constituent elements (opposed to *synthesis*); esp., this process as a method of studying the nature of a thing or of determining its essential features; also, a brief presentation of essential features; an outline or summary, as of a book; a synopsis; in *math.*, algebraic reasoning, esp. as applied to geometry; also, treatment by the calculus; in *chem.*, intentionally produced decomposition or separation of a substance into its ingredients or elements, as to find their kind or quantity; hence, the ascertainment of the kind or amount of one or more of the constituents of a substance, whether actually obtained in separate form or not.

an-a-lyst (an′ạ-list), *n.* [F. *analyste*, < *analyser*, E. *analyze.*] One who analyzes; one versed in analysis.

an-a-lyt-ic, an-a-lyt-i-cal (an-ạ-lit′ik, -i-kạl), *a.* [Gr. ἀναλυτικός.] Pertaining to or proceeding by analysis (opposed to *synthetic*); in *math.*, treated by algebra (as geometry: see *geometry*) or by the calculus; in *philol.*, characterized by the use of separate particles and auxiliary words rather than inflections, as some languages, expressions, etc. (see *synthetic*).—**an-a-lyt′i-cal-ly,** *adv.*—**an-a-lyt′ics,** *n.* Mathematical or algebraic analysis.

an-a-lyz-a-ble, an-a-lys-a-ble (an′ạ-lī-zạ-bl), *a.* Capable of being analyzed.

an-a-lyze, an-a-lyse (an′ạ-līz), *v. t.*; *-lyzed* or *-lysed*, *-lyzing* or *-lysing.* [F. *analyser*, < *analyse*, analysis, < ML. *analysis*: see *analysis.*] To resolve into elements or constituent parts; determine the elements or essential features of; examine by analysis; in *math.*, to treat algebraically or by the calculus.—**an″a-ly-za′tion, an″a-ly-sa′tion** (-li-zā′shọn), *n.* —**an′a-lyz-er, an′a-lys-er** (-lī-zėr), *n.*

an-am-ne-sis (an-am-nē′sis), *n.* [NL., < Gr. ἀνάμνησις, < ἀνα-, back, + μνᾶσθαι, remember.] The recalling of things past; recollection; reminiscence.—**an-am-nes′tic** (-nes′tik), *a.*—**an-am-nes′ti-cal-ly,** *adv.*

an-a-mor-pho-scope (an-ạ-môr′fọ-skōp), *n.* [See *anamorphosis* and *-scope.*] A device, as a curved mirror, for giving a correct image of a picture or the like that is distorted by anamorphosis.

an-a-mor-pho-sis (an-ạ-môr′fọ-sis), *n.*; pl. *-phoses* (-fọ-sēz). [NL., < Gr. ἀναμόρφωσις, a forming anew, < ἀναμορφοῦν, form anew: cf. *metamorphosis.*] A kind of drawing presenting a distorted image which appears in natural form under certain conditions, as when reflected from a curved mirror; the method of producing such drawings; in *bot.*, anomalous change of form; in *bot.* and *zoöl.*, gradual change of form, generally ascending, in successive members of a group of plants or animals.

an-an-drous (an-an′drus), *a.* [Gr. ἀν- priv. + ἀνήρ (ἀνδρ-), man.] In *bot.*, having no stamens.

An-a-ni-as (an-ạ-nī′ạs), *n.* [From *Ananias*, in Acts, v. 1–10, who was struck dead for lying.] A liar.

an-an-thous (an-an′thus), *a.* [Gr. ἀν- priv. + ἄνθος, flower.] In *bot.*, destitute of flowers.

an-a-nym (an′ạ-nim), *n.* [Gr. ἀνα-, back, + ὄνυμα, name.] A name written or spelled backward.

an-a-pæst, an-a-pest (an′ạ-pest), *n.* [L. *anapæstus*, < Gr. ἀνάπαιστος, struck back, reversed (as compared with a dactyl), < ἀνα-, back, + παίειν, strike.] In *pros.*, a foot of three syllables, two short followed by one long.—**an-a-pæs′tic, an-a-pes′tic. I.** *a.* Pertaining to or consisting of anapæsts. **II.** *n.* An anapæstic verse, as in Byron's "Destruction of Sennacherib."

a-naph-o-ra (a-naf′ọ-rạ̈), *n.* [L., < Gr. ἀναφορά, < ἀναφέρειν, bring up, < ἀνά, up, + φέρειν, bear.] In *rhet.*, repetition of the same word or words at the beginning of two or more successive verses, clauses, or sentences. See 1 Cor. i. 20.

an-aph-ro-dis-i-ac (an-af-rọ-diz′i-ak). [See *an-* and *aphrodisiac.*] In *med.*: **I.** *a.* Capable of diminishing sexual desire. **II.** *n.* An anaphrodisiac agent.

an-a-phy-lax-is (an″ạ-fi-lak′sis), *n.* [NL., < Gr. ἀνα-, back, against, + φυλάσσειν, guard.] In *pathol.*, increased susceptibility to the action of a foreign protein as the result of a first injection of the substance, as in serum treatment.

an-a-plas-tic (an-ạ-plas′tik), *a.* [Gr. ἀνάπλαστος, plastic, < ἀναπλάσσειν, form anew, < ἀνα-, again, + πλάσσειν, form.] Reparative: noting surgery which replaces lost tissue or parts, or remedies natural defects, as by transplanting.—**an′a-plas-ty,** *n.* Anaplastic surgery.

an-ap-tot-ic (an-ap-tot′ik), *a.* [Gr. ἀνα-, back, again, + ἄπτωτος, indeclinable: see *aptote.*] In *philol.*, designating languages, such as English, which have a tendency to lose, or have already lost, the use of inflections.

an-arch (an′ärk), *n.* [Gr. ἄναρχος, without a head or chief, < ἀν- priv. + ἀρχός, leader.] One who opposes government or law; an anarchist.

a-nar-chic, a-nar-chi-cal (a-när′kik, -ki-kạl), *a.* Of, like, or tending to anarchy; advocating anarchy.—**a-nar′chi-cal-ly,** *adv.*

an-ar-chism (an′ạ̈r-kizm), *n.* The principle of anarchy; the doctrine (advocated under various forms) urging the abolition of government and governmental restraint as the indispensable condition of political and social liberty; the methods or practices of anarchists; anarchy.—**an′ar-chist,** *n.* An advocate of anarchism; popularly, one who would overturn by violence all constituted forms and institutions of society and government, with no purpose of establishing any other system of order.—**an-ar-chis′tic,** *a.*

an-ar-chy (an′ạ̈r-ki), *n.* [Gr. ἀναρχία, < ἄναρχος: see *anarch.*] Absence of government or governmental restraint; a state of society without government or law; political and social disorder due to absence of governmental control; in general, disorder due to want of a controlling and regulating agency.

an-ar-throus (an-är′thrus), *a.* [Gr. ἄναρθρος, < ἀν- priv. + ἄρθρον, joint, article.] In *zoöl.*, without joints or articulated limbs; in *Gr. gram.*, used without the article.

an-a-sar-ca (an-ạ-sär′kạ̈), *n.* [Gr. ἀνά, up, + σάρξ (σαρκ-), flesh.] In *pathol.*, dropsy, of considerable extent, in the subcutaneous connective tissue.—**an-a-sar′cous,** *a.*

an-as-tig-mat (an-as′tig-mat), *n.* [G.] A system of lenses in which astigmatic defects are overcome.

an-as-tig-mat-ic (an-as-tig-mat′ik), *a.* [See *an-.*] Not astigmatic: applied esp. to a lens, or a system of lenses, in which astigmatic defects are overcome.

a-nas-to-mose (a-nas′tọ-mōz), *v. i.*; *-mosed*, *-mosing.* To communicate or be connected by anastomosis.

a-nas-to-mo-sis (a-nas-tọ-mō′sis), *n.*; pl. *-moses* (-mō′sēz). [NL., < Gr. ἀναστόμωσις, an opening, < ἀναστομοῦν, furnish with a mouth, < ἀνά, up, + στόμα, mouth.] In *anat.*, *zoöl.*, and *bot.*, communication between veins or other vessels; connection between parts of any branching system. Also fig.—**a-nas-to-mot′ic** (-mot′ik), *a.*

a-nas-tro-phe (a-nas′trọ-fẹ), *n.* [L., < Gr. ἀναστροφή, < ἀναστρέφειν, turn up or back, < ἀνά, up, + στρέφειν, turn.] In *rhet.*, inversion of the usual order of words.

a-nath-e-ma (a-nath′ẹ-mạ̈), *n.*; pl. *-mas* (-mạ̈z). [LL., < Gr. ἀνάθεμα, something devoted (to evil), < ἀνατιθέναι, dedicate, < ἀνά, up, + τιθέναι, set.] A person or thing accursed; also, a formal ecclesiastical curse involving excommunication; hence, in general, an imprecation or malediction.—**anathema maranatha** (mar-ạ-nā′thạ̈), in 1 Cor. xvi. 22, the term *anathema* supplemented by a phrase (Syr. *māran ethā*) meaning 'the Lord hath come,' apparently added for solemnity: hence used as an intensified form of *anathema.*—**a-nath′e-ma-tize** (-mạ-tīz), *v.*; *-tized*, *-tizing.* **I.** *tr.* To pronounce an anathema against; curse. **II.** *intr.* To utter anathemas.—**a-nath″e-ma-ti-za′tion** (-ti-zā′shọn), *n.*—**a-nath′e-ma-tiz-er** (-tī-zėr), *n.*

an-a-tine (an′ạ-tin), *a.* [L. *anatinus*, < *anas*, duck.] Of, pertaining to, or resembling a duck; duck-like.

An-a-to-li-an (an-ạ-tō′li-ạn), *a.* [Gr. ἀνατολή, rising, sunrise, the east, < ἀνατέλλειν, rise up.] Of or pertaining to Anatolia, or Asia Minor.

an-a-tom-ic, an-a-tom-i-cal (an-ạ-tom′ik, -i-kạl), *a.* [Gr. ἀνατομικός.] Of or pertaining to anatomy; structural. —**an-a-tom′i-cal-ly,** *adv.*

a-nat-o-mist (ạ-nat′ọ-mist), *n.* One versed in anatomy.

a-nat-o-mize (ạ-nat′ọ-mīz), *v. t.*; *-mized*, *-mizing.* To dissect, as for anatomical study; fig., to analyze.—**a-nat″o-mi-za′tion** (-mi-zā′shọn), *n.*

a-nat-o-my (ạ-nat′ọ-mi), *n.*; pl. *-mies* (-miz). [OF. F. *anatomie*, < LL. *anatomia*, < LGr. ἀνατομία, for Gr. ἀνατομή, < ἀνατέμνειν, cut up, < ἀνά, up, + τέμνειν, cut.] The dissection of organized bodies in order to study their structure; fig., analysis (as in the title of Burton's "*Anatomy* of Melancholy"); also, the science of the structure of animals and plants, or a treatise on the subject; also, bodily structure; physique; also, an anatomical subject or model; also, a skeleton, or a person reduced almost to a skeleton (as, "A hungry lean-faced villain, A mere *anatomy*": Shakspere's "Comedy of Errors," v. 1. 238).

a-nat-ro-pous (a-nat′rọ-pus), *a.* [Gr. ἀνά, up, + -τροπος, < τρέπειν, turn.] In *bot.*, of an ovule, inverted at an early stage of growth, so that the micropyle is turned toward the funicle, the chalaza being situated at the opposite end.

a-nat-to (a-nat′ō), *n.* Same as *arnotto.*

-ance. [F. *-ance*, < L. *-antia*, *-entia*, < *-ans*, *-ens*, ppr. ending (see *-ant*); or directly from L. *-antia.*] A suffix of nouns denoting action, state, or quality, or something exemplifying one of these, often accompanying adjectives in *-ant* or formed directly from verbs, as in *assistance, assonance, defiance, distance, hindrance, riddance.* Cf. *-ancy* and *-ence.*

an-ces-tor (an′ses-tọr), *n.* [OF. *ancestre* (F. *ancêtre*), < L. *antecessor*, predecessor, < *antecedere*: see *antecede.*] One from whom a person is descended; a forefather or progenitor; in *law*, one from whom an inheritance is derived.—**an-ces′tral** (-trạl), *a.* Pertaining to or derived from ancestors.—**an-ces′tral-ly,** *adv.*—**an′ces-tress,** *n.* A female ancestor.—**an′ces-try,** *n.*; pl. *-tries* (-triz). Descent from ancestors; lineage; honorable parentage or birth; a line of ancestors; ancestors collectively.

an-chor[1]† (ang′kọr), *n.* An anchoret; a hermit: as, "An *anchor's* cheer in prison be my scope!" (Shakspere's "Hamlet," iii. 2. 229).

an-chor[2] (ang′kọr), *n.* [AS. *ancor*, < L. *ancora*, < Gr. ἄγκυρα.] A device attached to a cable and sunk in water to hold a vessel in a particular place; typically, an iron implement with a shank having at one end a crosspiece or stock, and at the other two incurved arms, each terminating in a fluke; hence, some similar device, as for holding fast or for checking motion; fig., a means of stability.—**an′chor**[2], *v.* **I.** *tr.* To secure by an anchor; hence, to fix firmly; make fast. **II.** *intr.* To cast anchor; hence, to become or be stationary.—**an′chor-age** (-āj), *n.* The act of anchoring, or the state of being anchored; a place for anchoring; means of anchoring or making fast; a charge for anchoring.

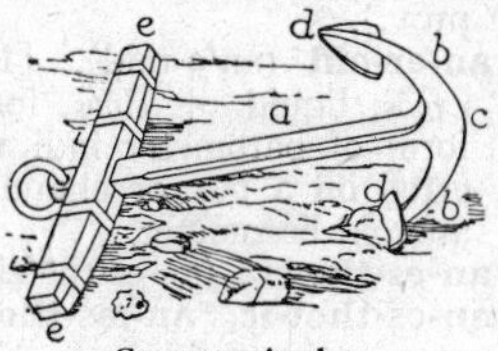

Common Anchor.
a, shank; *b, b*, arms; *c*, crown; *d, d*, flukes; *e, e*, stock.

an-chor-ess (ang′kọr-es), *n.* A female anchoret.

an-cho-ret, an-cho-rite (ang′kọ-ret, -rīt), *n.* [LL. *anachoreta*, ML. *anachorita*, < Gr. ἀναχωρητής, < ἀναχωρεῖν, retire, < ἀνα-, back, + χωρεῖν, give place, < χῶρος, place.] One who has retired to a solitary place for a life of religious seclusion; a hermit.—**an-cho-ret′ic,** *a.*

an-chor-less (ang′kọr-les), *a.* Without an anchor; drifting; not fixed or settled.

an-cho-vy (an-chō′vi or an′chọ-vi), *n.*; pl. *-vies* (-viz). [Sp. and Pg. *anchova*, It. dial. *anciova.*] A small herring-like fish, *Engraulis encrasicholus*, abundant in the Mediterranean, much used pickled and in the form of a salt paste; also, any of various related fishes.—**an-cho′vy=pear′,** *n.* The fruit of a West Indian tree, *Grias cauliflora*, often pickled, and somewhat resembling the mango; also, the tree.

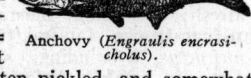

Anchovy (*Engraulis encrasicholus*).

an-chu-sin (ang′kụ-sin), *n.* [L. *anchusa*, < Gr. ἄγχουσα, alkanet.] A red coloring matter obtained from the root of the alkanet, *Alkanna tinctoria.*

an-chy-lose (ang′ki-lōz), etc. See *ankylose*, etc.

an-cient[1]† (ān′shẹnt), *n.* A corruption of *ensign.*

an-cient[2] (ān′shẹnt), *a.* [OF. F. *ancien*, < ML. *antianus*, < L. *ante*, before.] Of or in time long past, esp. before the fall of the Western Roman Empire (A.D. 476); dating from a remote period; of great age (archaic as applied to living beings); venerable (archaic); former or past.—**ancient régime.** Same as *ancien régime*, under *régime.*—**an′cient**[2], *n.* One who lived in ancient times (usually in *pl.*); an ancient classical author (usually in *pl.*); also, a very old person; a patriarch; also, an elder, or senior dignitary (archaic).—**Ancient of Days,** the Supreme Being, in reference to his existence from eternity. See Dan. vii. 9.—**an′cient-ly,** *adv.* In ancient times; of old.—**an′cient-ness,** *n.*—**an′cient-ry,** *n.* Ancient character or style (archaic); ancient times (archaic); ancient lineage†; old people† (see Shakspere's "Winter's Tale," iii. 3. 63).

an-cil-la-ry (an′si-lạ-ri), *a.* [L. *ancillaris*, < *ancilla*, handmaid.] Pertaining to or serving as a handmaid; fig., subservient (often with *to*); auxiliary; subordinate.

an-cip-i-tal (an-sip′i-tạl), *a.* [L. *anceps* (*ancipit-*), < *an-*, for *ambi-*, on both sides, + *caput*, head.] In *bot.* and *zoöl.*, two-edged. Also **an-cip′i-tous.**

an-cis-troid (an-sis′troid), *a.* [Gr. ἀγκιστροειδής, < ἄγκιστρον, hook, + εἶδος, form.] Hook-shaped.

an-cle (ang′kl), etc. See *ankle*, etc.

an-con (ang′kon), *n.*; pl. *ancones* (ang-kō′nēz). [L., < Gr. ἀγκών.] In *anat.*, the elbow; in *arch.*, any projection, as a console, supporting a cornice or the like.—**an-co-nal** (ang′kọ-nạl), **an-co′ne-al** (-kō′nẹ-ạl), *a.*

-ancy. An extended form of *-ance*, chiefly in nouns denoting state or quality, as in *ascendancy, buoyancy, redundancy.*

an-cy-los-to-mi-a-sis (an″si-los-tọ-mī′ạ-sis), *n.* [NL., < *Ancylostoma*, genus of hookworms, < Gr. ἀγκύλος, bent, hooked, + στόμα, mouth.] Hookworm disease. See *hookworm.*

An-cy-rene (an′si-rēn), *a.* Of or pertaining to Ancyra (now Angora), a city of ancient Galatia in Asia Minor: as, the *Ancyrene* inscription (an inscription in the temple of Augustus at Ancyra, a copy of a statement prepared by the Roman emperor of his own acts and policy).

and (and). [AS. *and*, akin to G. *und.*] **I.** *conj.* A particle used to connect words, phrases, clauses, or sentences, or to add or introduce further matter; sometimes, also or even (obs. or archaic); also, as expressing a condition, if (archaic or prov.). See *an*[2]. **II.** *n.* The character &, *&* (orig. formed by combining the letters of the Latin *et*, 'and'), used as a symbol for the conjunction *and*: sometimes called 'short and.' Cf. *ampersand.*

an-da-lu-site (an-dạ-lū′sīt), *n.* [From *Andalusia*, division of southern Spain.] A mineral consisting of a silicate of aluminium, first discovered in Andalusia, Spain.

an-dan-te (an-dan′tẹ, It. än-dän′tā). [It., ppr. of *andare*, walk.] In *music*: **I.** *a.* Proceeding with a moderate, even, graceful movement. **II.** *n.* An andante movement.—**an-dan-ti′no** (-tē′nō). [It., dim. of *andante.*] In *music*: **I.** *a.* Somewhat slower than andante; also, somewhat less slow than andante. **II.** *n.*; pl. *-nos* (-nōz). An andantino movement.

An-de-an (an′dẹ-ạn or an-dē′ạn), *a.* Of, pertaining to, or resembling the Andes.

an-des-ite (an′dẹz-īt), *n.* [From the *Andes* Mountains.] A widespread igneous rock occurring in various colors and resembling trachyte.

and-i-ron (and′ī″ėrn), *n.* [OF. *andier*; origin unknown. The E. form is due to association with *iron.*] One of a pair of metallic supports for wood burning on a hearth.

Andirons.

An-dre-a Fer-ra-ra (an′drẹ-ạ fe-rä′rạ). [From a Venetian sword-maker of this name.] A sword or sword-blade of a kind greatly esteemed in Scotland toward the end of the 16th century and later.

andro-, andr-. Forms of Gr. ἀνήρ (ἀνδρ-), man, male (hence used, in *bot.*, for 'male organ,' 'stamen'), in combination.—**an-dro-ceph-a-lous** (an-drọ-sef′ạ-lus), *a.* [+ Gr. κεφαλή, head.] Having a human head, as a sphinx.—**an-dro-clin′i-um** (-klin′i-um), *n.*; pl. *-ia* (-i-ạ). [NL. (Gr. κλίνη, bed).] In *bot.*, same as *clinandrium.*—**an-drœ′cium** (-drē′shium), *n.*; pl. *-cia* (-shiạ). [NL. (Gr. οἶκος, house).] In *bot.*, the stamens of a flower collectively. Cf. *gynœcium.*—**an-drœ′cial** (-shạl), *a.*

an-dro-gyne (an′drọ-jin), *n.* [L. *androgynus*, < Gr. ἀνδρόγυνος, < ἀνήρ (ἀνδρ-), man, + γυνή, woman.] A hermaphrodite; in *bot.*, an androgynous plant.—**an-drog′y-nous** (-droj′i-nus), *a.* Being both male and female;

hermaphrodite; in *bot.*, having male and female flowers in the same inflorescence.—**an-drog′y-ny,** *n.*

an-droid, an-droi-des (an′droid, an-droi′dēz), *n.* [Gr. ἀνδροειδής, like a man, < ἀνήρ (ἀνδρ-), man, + εἶδος, form.] An automaton in the form of a human being.

An-dro-med, An-dro-mede (an′drọ-med, -mēd), *n.* Same as *Andromedid.*

An-drom-e-did (an-drom′e-did), *n.* In *astron.*, any of a shower of meteors occurring about Nov. 27, and appearing to radiate from a point in the constellation Andromeda.

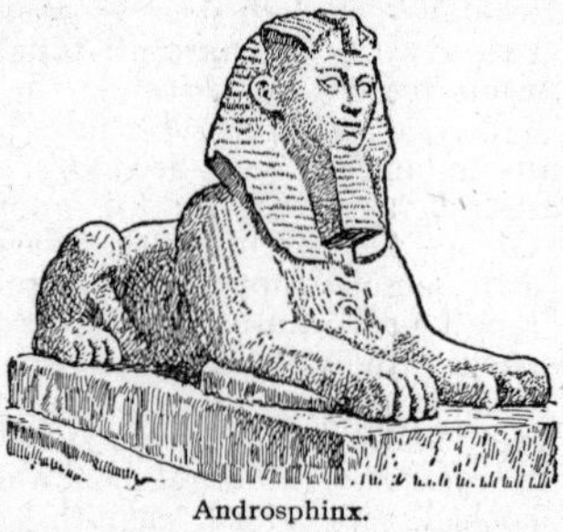
Androsphinx.

an-dro-sphinx (an′drọ-sfingks), *n.* [Gr. ἀνδρόσφιγξ, < ἀνήρ (ἀνδρ-), man, + σφίγξ, sphinx.] A sphinx with the head of a man.

-androus. [Gr. -ανδρος, < ἀνήρ (ἀνδρ-), man.] An adjective termination involving the idea of 'man,' 'husband,' 'male,' and hence used in botanical terms to imply 'male organ,' 'stamen,' as in *monandrous, polyandrous.* Cf. *-gynous.*

ane (ān). Sc. and north. Eng. form of *one.*

-ane. Noun suffix used in chemical terms, esp. names of hydrocarbons of the methane or paraffin series, as *decane, pentane, propane.*

a-near (ạ-nēr′), *adv.* and *prep.* Near. [Poetic or prov.]

an-ec-do-tage (an′ek-dō-tạj), *n.* Anecdotic matter; anecdotes; also, old age marked by fondness for telling anecdotes (humorous).—**an′ec-do-tal,** *a.* Anecdotic.

an-ec-dote (an′ek-dōt), *n.* [F., < Gr. ἀνέκδοτος, unpublished, < ἀν- priv. + ἔκδοτος, verbal adj. of ἐκδιδόναι, give out, < ἐκ, out of, + διδόναι, give.] Orig., as *pl.*, unpublished or little-known details of history; hence, as *sing.*, a short narrative of some more or less interesting incident, often one in connection with a particular person or thing; also, anecdotic matter.—**an-ec-dot′ic, an-ec-dot′i-cal** (-dot′ik, -i-kạl), *a.* Pertaining to or consisting of anecdotes; abounding in or given to anecdotes.—**an′-ec-dot-ist** (-dō-tist), *n.* A relater of anecdotes.

a-nele (ạ-nēl′), *v. t.*; *aneled, aneling.* [ME. *anelien*, < AS. *an*, on, + *ele*, oil.] To anoint; specif., to administer extreme unction to. [Archaic.]

an-e-lec-tric (an-ẹ-lek′trik). [See *an-*.] **I.** *a.* Non-electric; having no electric properties; not capable of being electrified by friction (cf. *idioelectric*). **II.** *n.* An anelectric substance; a conductor.

an-e-lec-trode (an-ẹ-lek′trōd), *n.* [Gr. ἀνά, up, + E. *electrode.*] In *elect.*, the anode.

a-ne-mi-a, a-næ-mi-a (a-nē′mi-ạ), *n.* [NL., < Gr. ἀναιμία, < ἀν- priv. + αἷμα, blood.] In *pathol.*, deficiency of the blood, or of certain of its constituents, in the living body, causing pallor, weakness, palpitation of the heart, etc. —**a-ne-mic, a-næ-mic** (a-nē′mik or a-nem′ik), *a.* Pertaining to or affected with anemia.

anemo-. Form of Gr. ἄνεμος, wind, used in combination.—**a-nem-o-gram** (a-nem′ọ-gram), *n.* [+ *-gram.*] A record made by an anemograph.—**a-nem′-o-graph** (-gråf), *n.* [+ *-graph.*] An instrument for measuring and recording the velocity, force, or direction of the wind.—**an-e-mo-graph-ic** (an″e-mọ-graf′ik), *a.* Of or pertaining to anemography.—**an-e-mog′ra-phy** (-mog′rạ-fi), *n.* [+ *-graphy.*] The art of measuring and recording the velocity, force, and direction of the wind.—**an-e-mol′o-gy** (-mol′ọ-ji), *n.* [+ *-logy.*] The science of the wind.—**an-e-mom′e-ter** (-mom′e-tėr), *n.* [+ *-meter.*] An instrument for indicating the velocity or pressure of the wind.—**an″e-mo-met′ric, an″e-mo-met′ri-cal** (-met′rik, -ri-kạl), *a.* Pertaining to anemometry.—**an″e-mo-met′ro-graph** (-rọ-gråf), *n.* [See *-graph.*] An instrument for measuring and recording the velocity, force, and direction of the wind. —**an-e-mom′e-try,** *n.* [+ *-metry.*] Determination of the velocity or pressure of the wind by an anemometer.

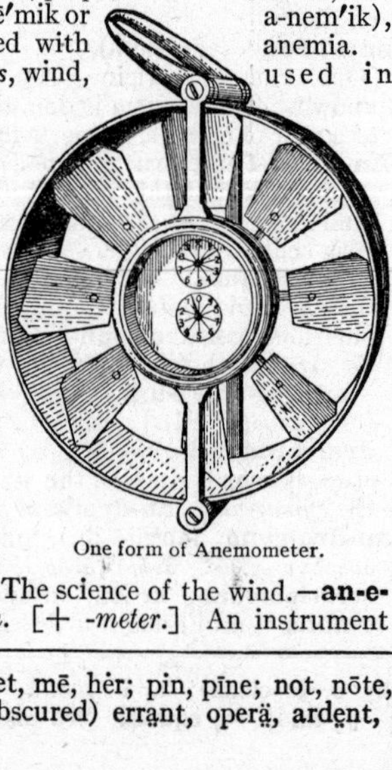
One form of Anemometer.

a-nem-o-ne (ạ-nem′ọ-nẹ), *n.* [L., < Gr. ἀνεμώνη, < ἄνεμος, wind.] Any plant of the ranunculaceous genus *Anemone*, as *A. quinquefolia*, a familiar spring wild flower of the woods with slender stem and delicate white blossoms, or as other species with variously colored flowers frequent in cultivation; a wind-flower; also, an actinia or sea-anemone.

Wood-anemone (*A. quinquefolia*).

an-e-moph-i-lous (an-e-mof′i-lus), *a.* [Lit. 'wind-loving': see *anemo-* and *-philous.*] In *bot.*, fertilized by wind-borne pollen, as a plant.—**an-e-moph′i-ly,** *n.*

a-nem-o-scope (a-nem′ọ-skōp), *n.* [See *anemo-* and *-scope.*] Any device for showing the direction of the wind.

an-e-mo-sis (an-e-mō′sis), *n.* [NL., < Gr. ἄνεμος, wind.] A condition of the wood of some trees, in which the annual layers are separated from one another: supposed by some to be due to the action of strong winds upon the trunk, and by others to the action of frost or of lightning.

a-nent, a-nenst (ạ-nent′, ạ-nenst′), *prep.* [AS. *on efen*, 'on even.'] In a line with (now prov.); over against (now prov.); with respect to, concerning, or about (archaic or prov.).

an-er-oid (an′ẹ-roid). [F. *anéroïde*, < Gr. ἀ- priv. + νηρός, liquid, + εἶδος, form.] **I.** *a.* Using no fluid, as a form of barometer indicating atmospheric pressure as exerted on a box or chamber exhausted of air. **II.** *n.* An aneroid barometer.

an-es-the-sia (an-es-thē′ziạ), etc. See *anæsthesia*, etc.

an-es-thet-ic, an-æs-thet-ic (an-es-thet′ik). [Gr. ἀναίσθητος, insensible, < ἀν- priv. + αἰσθητός, sensible, < αἰσθάνεσθαι, perceive.] **I.** *a.* Pertaining to or causing physical insensibility. **II.** *n.* An anesthetic agent, as chloroform, ether, cocaine, etc.—**an-es-thet′i-cal-ly, an-æs-thet′i-cal-ly,** *adv.*

an-es-the-tist, an-æs-the-tist (an-es′thẹ-tist), *n.* One who administers anesthetics.

an-es-the-tize, an-æs-the-tize (an-es′thẹ-tīz), *v. t.*; *-tized, -tizing.* [Gr. ἀναίσθητος, insensible: see *anesthetic.*] To render physically insensible, as by an anesthetic.—**an-es″-the-ti-za′tion, an-æs″the-ti-za′tion** (-ti-zā′shọn), *n.*—**an-es′the-tiz-er, an-æs′the-tiz-er** (-tī-zėr), *n.*

an-eu-rysm, an-eu-rism (an′ū-rizm), *n.* [Gr. ἀνεύρυσμα, < ἀνευρύνειν, dilate, < ἀνά, up, + εὐρύνειν, widen, < εὐρύς, wide.] In *pathol.*, a localized dilatation of an artery, due to the pressure of the blood acting on a part weakened by disease or injury.—**an-eu-rys′mal, an-eu-ris′mal** (-riz′mạl), *a.*

a-new (ạ-nū′), *adv.* [ME. *anewe*, earlier *of new.*] Newly; afresh; over again; once more.

an-frac-tu-ose (an-frak′tụ-ōs), *a.* [L. *anfractuosus*, < *anfractus*, a winding, < *an-*, for *ambi-*, around, + *frangere*, break.] Anfractuous; winding; in *bot.*, sinuous or twisted, as anthers.—**an-frac-tu-os′i-ty** (-os′i-ti), *n.*; pl. *-ties* (-tiz). Anfractuous state; sinuosity; a winding, or winding passage; in *anat.*, one of the sulci or fissures separating the convolutions of the brain.—**an-frac′tu-ous,** *a.* [L. *anfractuosus.*] Winding; sinuous; tortuous; circuitous.

an-gel (ān′jẹl), *n.* [OF. *angele* or AS. *engel*, < LL. *angelus*, < Gr. ἄγγελος, messenger.] A messenger, esp. of God; in theological use, one of a class of spiritual beings, attendants of God, conventionally represented in human form, with wings (in medieval angelology divided, according to their rank, into nine orders, ranging from highest to lowest as follows: seraphim, cherubim, thrones, dominations or dominions, virtues, powers, principalities or princedoms, archangels, angels); in general, a spirit, good or bad; also, a person of heavenly virtues or charms; a financial backer of a theatrical or other enterprise or the like (colloq.); also, an English gold coin, struck from 1465 to 1634, in value

Obverse. Reverse.
Angel of Edward IV., in the British Museum.

from 6*s.* 8*d.* to 10*s.* sterling.—**an′gel=cake,** *n.* A kind of delicate white sweet cake, made with the whites of many eggs but without shortening. Also called *white sponge-cake.*—**an′gel-et,** *n.* A half-angel (coin); also, a little angel.—**an′gel=fish,** *n.* A shark, *Squatina squatina*, of Atlantic waters, with large, wing-like pectoral fins; also, any of several fishes with beautiful coloration.—**an′gel-hood** (-hůd), *n.* The character or condition of an angel.

Angel-fish (*Squatina squatina*).

an-gel-ic (an-jel′ik), *a.* [LL. *angelicus*, < Gr. ἀγγελικός.] Of or belonging to angels; like or befitting an angel; also, pertaining to angelica.

an-gel-i-ca (an-jel′i-kạ̈), *n.* [ML., 'angelic (herb).'] Any plant of the apiaceous genus *Angelica*, esp. *A. officinalis*, cultivated in Europe for its aromatic odor and medicinal root, and for its stalks, which are candied as a sweetmeat; also [*cap.*], a kind of sweet white wine made in California.

an-gel-i-cal (an-jel′i-kạl), *a.* Angelic.—**an-gel′i-cal-ly,** *adv.*

an-gel-i-ca=tree (an-jel′i-kạ̈-trē), *n.* The Hercules'-club.

an-gel=light (ān′jẹl-līt), *n.* [Appar. for *angle-light.*] In *arch.*, a small triangular light at the head of a window in the perpendicular style, as next to the springing of the arch.

an-gel-ol-a-try (ān-jẹl-ol′ạ-tri), *n.* [See *-latry.*] The worship of angels.

an-gel-ol-o-gy (ān-jẹl-ol′ọ̄-ji), *n.* [See *-logy.*] The (or a) doctrine concerning angels.

an-gel-oph-a-ny (ān-jẹl-of′ạ-ni), *n.*; pl. *-nies* (-niz). [See *-phany.*] The appearing of angels to men.

An-ge-lus (an′je-lus), *n.* [LL. (the first word of the recitation): see *angel.*] [Also *l. c.*] In the *Rom. Cath. Ch.*, a devotion in memory of the angel Gabriel's annunciation to the Virgin Mary; also, a bell tolled in the morning, at noon, and at night, as a signal for the devotion.

an-ger (ang′gėr), *n.* [Icel. *angr*, grief, trouble.] Grief† or trouble†; also, painful inflammation (now prov. Eng.); also, strong mental irritation at something that offends; warm and resentful displeasure; wrath; ire.—**an′ger,** *v. t.* or *i.* To make or become angry.—**an′ger-ly,** *adv.* In an angry manner. [Now poetic.]

An-ge-vin (an′jẹ-vin). [F.] **I.** *a.* Of or from Anjou, a former western province of France, as the royal Plantagenet family of England. **II.** *n.* A native or inhabitant of Anjou; also, a member of an Angevin royal house, esp. that of the Plantagenets in England. Also **An′ge-vine** (-vin or -vīn), *a.* and *n.*

an-gi-na (an′ji-nạ̈, commonly an-jī′nạ̈), *n.* [L., akin to *angere*, constrict, distress.] In *pathol.*, any inflammatory affection of the throat or fauces, as quinsy, croup, mumps, etc.; also, angina pectoris.—**angina pectoris** (pek′tọ̄-ris). [NL., 'angina of the chest.'] A disease characterized by paroxysms of acute pain in the chest, with sense of suffocation, associated usually with morbid conditions of the heart or arteries.—**an-gi-nal** (an′ji-nạl), *a.* Pertaining to angina. Also **an′gi-nose** (-nōs), **an′gi-nous.**

angio-. Form of Gr. ἀγγεῖον, vessel, used in combination.—**an-gi-og-ra-phy** (an-ji-og′rạ-fi), *n.* [+ *-graphy.*] Anatomical description of the blood-vessels and lymphatics.—**an-gi-ol′o-gy** (-ol′ọ̄-ji), *n.* [+ *-logy.*] The part of anatomy that treats of the blood-vessels and lymphatics.

an-gi-o-ma (an-ji-ō′mạ̈), *n.*; pl. *-mas* or *-mata* (-mạ-tạ̈). [NL., < Gr. ἀγγεῖον, vessel: see *-oma.*] In *pathol.*, a tumor consisting chiefly of dilated or newly formed blood or lymph vessels.—**an-gi-om′a-tous** (-om′ạ-tus), *a.*

an-gi-o-sperm (an′ji-ọ̄-spėrm), *n.* [NL. *angiospermus*, < Gr. ἀγγεῖον, vessel, + σπέρμα, seed.] A plant having its seeds inclosed in an ovary: opposed to *gymnosperm.*—**an″gi-o-sper′mous,** *a.* Of the angiosperm class; having seeds inclosed in an ovary.

an-gi-ot-o-my (an-ji-ot′ọ̄-mi), *n.* [See *angio-* and *-tomy.*] Dissection of the blood-vessels and lymphatics.

an-gle[1] (ang′gl), *n.* [AS. *angel*; prob. akin to *Angle*[2] and *angle*[3].] A fish-hook: sometimes including also the line and rod. [Archaic.]—**an′gle**[1], *v. i.*; *-gled, -gling.* To fish with hook and line; hence, to seek (*for*) by any artful means of catching or obtaining.

An-gle[2] (ang′gl), *n.* [L. *Anglus*, from the Teut. form repr. by AS. *Angle, Engle*, the people of *Angel*, a district of what is now Schleswig, said to be named from its hook-like shape: cf. *angle*[1].] A member of a Low German tribe that crossed over to Britain in the 5th century and founded there the kingdoms of East Anglia, Mercia, and Northumbria, and from whom the name *England* is derived.

an-gle[3] (ang′gl), *n.* [OF. F. *angle*, < L. *angulus*, corner, angle.] A corner, viewed from within or without; a recess or part within two or more sides diverging from a common point or line; in *geom.*, the space within lines (straight or curved) or planes so diverging, or the figure formed (as, a right *angle*, one of four angles so formed by two intersecting lines as to be equal, each measuring 90°; acute, obtuse, or oblique *angles*, see the adjectives; a straight *angle*, an angle of 180°; a solid *angle*, formed by three or more planes intersecting in a common point, as seen in a cube; a spherical *angle*, formed by arcs of great circles of a sphere; rectilinear or curvilinear *angles*, formed, respectively, by straight or curved lines); the amount of divergence of two lines, measured by the intercepted arc of a circle whose center is the meeting-point of the lines.—**angle of incidence.** See *incidence.*—**angle of reflection.** See *reflection.*—**an′gle**[3], *v. t.*; *-gled, -gling.* To move or bend in angles; also, to place at an angle or angles.—**an′gled,** *a.* Having an angle or angles.—**an′gle=i″ron,** *n.* A bar of iron in the form of an angle, esp. a rolled iron or steel bar with an L-shaped cross-section, used in iron constructions.—**an′gle=me″ter,** *n.* Any of various instruments used for measuring angles; esp., a clinometer.—**an′gle=pod,** *n.* An asclepiadaceous plant, *Vincetoxicum gonocarpos*, of the southern U. S., having an angled pod; also, any of certain other plants of the same genus.

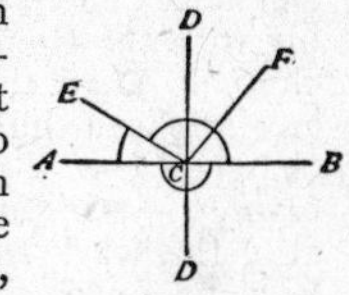

Angles.
BCD, right angle; *BCE*, obtuse angle; *ACE*, acute angle; *ACB*, straight angle.

an-gler (ang′glėr), *n.* One who angles; a fisher with hook and line; also, a fish, *Lophius piscatorius*, of the coasts of Europe and America, which is said to attract small fish, its prey, by the movement of filaments attached to its head and mouth; also, any of various fishes with a modified free dorsal spine above the mouth.

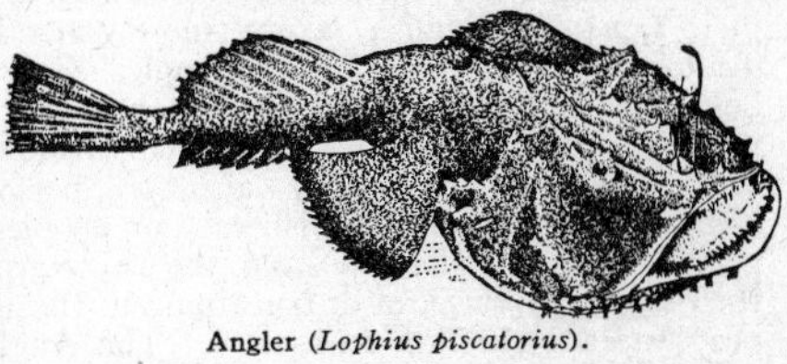

Angler (*Lophius piscatorius*).

an-gle-site (ang′glẹ-sīt), *n.* [From *Anglesey*, Wales.] A mineral consisting of sulphate of lead, found in massive forms or in colorless or variously tinted orthorhombic crystals: sometimes mined as an ore of lead.

an-gle-smith (ang′gl-smith), *n.* A blacksmith skilled in forging angle-irons, beams, etc., into the various forms used in ship-building.

an-gle-worm (ang′gl-wėrm), *n.* A worm used for bait in angling; an earthworm.

An-gli-an (ang′gli-ạn). **I.** *a.* Of or pertaining to the Angles. **II.** *n.* An Angle; the dialect of the Angles.

An-gli-can (ang′gli-kạn). [ML. *Anglicanus*, < *Anglicus*: see *Anglicè.*] **I.** *a.* Of or pertaining to England; English;

specif., of or pertaining to the Church of England (the 'Anglican Church'); in communion or accord with the Church of England, as various episcopal churches in other parts of the world; also, of or pertaining to the High-church party. **II.** *n.* A member of the Church of England or of a church in communion with it; also, a High-churchman.—**An'gli-can-ism,** *n.* Anglican principles; the Anglican Church system.

An-gli-cè (ang'gli-sē), *adv.* [ML. *Anglice,* < *Anglicus,* English, < L. *Anglus:* see *Angle*[2].] In English.

An-gli-cism (ang'gli-sizm), *n.* [ML. *Anglicus:* see *Anglicè.*] Characteristic English quality or usage; an English idiom; a word or expression peculiar to the English.

An-gli-cize (ang'gli-sīz), *v. t.* or *i.*; *-cized, -cizing.* [ML. *Anglicus:* see *Anglicè.*] [Also *l. c.*] To make or become English; conform to the English usage.—**An"gli-ci-za'tion** (-si-zā'shọn), *n.*

An-gli-fy (ang'gli-fī), *v. t.*; *-fied, -fying.* [L. *Anglus,* Angle (used to mean 'English'): see *-fy.*] To make English; Anglicize.—**An"gli-fi-ca'tion** (-fi-kā'shọn), *n.*

An-glo- (ang'glō-). Form of L. *Anglus,* Angle, used in combination, often in the sense of 'English,' as in *Anglo-African, Anglo-American, Anglo-Asiatic, Anglo-Australian, Anglo-Chinese, Anglo-Irish, Anglo-Japanese.*—**An'glo=Cath'o-lic. I.** *a.* Catholic according to the teachings of the Anglican Church; maintaining the Catholic character of the Anglican Church (as a branch of the Catholic Church, ranking with the Roman Catholic and Greek branches); High-church. **II.** *n.* A member of the Church of England or any Anglican church; esp., one who maintains the Catholic character of the Anglican Church.—**An'glo=Ca-thol'i-cism,** *n.*—**An'glo=French'. I.** *a.* English and French; also, English French, as the dialect of French developed in England under the Norman conquerors and later. **II.** *n.* The Anglo-French dialect.—**An'glo=In'di-an. I.** *a.* Of both England and India; also, of British India; also, pertaining to or used by the English in India. **II.** *n.* An English person born or resident in India.—**An-glo-ma'ni-a** (-mā'ni-ạ), *n.* A craze for English institutions or customs, and esp. for imitating them.—**An-glo-ma'ni-ac** (-ak), *n.* —**An'glo=Nor'man. I.** *a.* English and Norman; also, English Norman, as the Norman conquerors who settled in England, or their descendants, or their dialect. **II.** *n.* An English Norman; also, the Anglo-Norman dialect.—**An'glo-phil, An'glo-phile** (-fil). [+ *-phil, -phile.*] **I.** *a.* Friendly to England or the English; fond of English ways, institutions, etc. **II.** *n.* A friend or admirer of England or the English.—**An'glo-phobe** (-fōb), *n.* [+ *-phobe.*] One who fears or hates England or the English.—**An-glo-pho'bi-a** (-fō'bi-ạ), *n.* [+ *-phobia.*] Fear or hatred of England or anything English.—**An-glo-pho'bic,** *a.*

An-glo=Sax-on (ang'glō-sak'sọn). [ML. *Anglo-Saxones,* pl.] **I.** *n.* An English Saxon; more generally, one of the Teutonic inhabitants of Britain (Angles, Saxons, and others) before the Norman Conquest; also, their language, comprising several dialects (Old Northumbrian, Midland or Mercian, West Saxon, and Kentish); also, *pl.,* persons of English birth or descent; the English race or peoples. **II.** *a.* Of, pertaining to, or derived from the early Anglo-Saxons or their language; also, of or pertaining to the English race or peoples.—**An'glo=Sax'on-ism,** *n.* The Anglo-Saxon character, spirit, tendencies, etc.; an Anglo-Saxon trait or usage.

an-go-la (ang-gō'lạ), *n.* Corruption of *angora.*

an-gor (ang'gọr), *n.* [L., < *angere,* constrict.] In *pathol.,* a feeling of painful constriction at the epigastrium, with extreme anxiety and often palpitation.

an-go-ra (ang-gō'rạ), *n.*; pl. *-ras.* [From *Angora,* city and province in Asia Minor: cf. *Ancyrene.*] Any of various fabrics made of Angora wool or some substitute; [*cap.*] an Angora goat; also, an Angora cat.

An-go-ra (ang-gō'rạ) **cat.** [See *angora.*] A long-haired variety of the domestic cat, orig. from Angora.—**An-go'ra goat.** A variety of goat, orig. from Angora, extensively reared for its long, silky hair (or wool).—**An-go'ra wool.** The hair of the Angora goat; mohair.

An-gos-tu-ra (ang-gọs-tö'rạ) **bark.** [From *Angostura,* town in Venezuela.] The bitter aromatic bark of a South American rutaceous tree of the genus *Cusparia* (or *Galipea*), with tonic properties.—**An-gos-tu'ra bit'ters.** A bitter tonic prepared with Angostura bark.

an-gry (ang'gri), *a.*; compar. *angrier,* superl. *angriest.* [From *anger.*] Grievous†; also, grieved†; also, painfully inflamed, as a sore; also, feeling or showing anger or warm displeasure; incensed; wrathful; irate; also, raging or stormy, as waves; also, sharp, as appetite.—**an'gri-ly,** *adv.* —**an'gri-ness,** *n.*

an-guil-li-form (ang-gwil'i-fôrm), *a.* [L. *anguilla,* eel, < *anguis,* snake: see *-form.*] Eel-like.

an-guine (ang'gwin), *a.* [L. *anguinus,* < *anguis,* snake.] Pertaining to snakes; snake-like.

an-guish (ang'gwish), *n.* [OF. *anguisse* (F. *angoisse*), < L. *angustia,* straitness, pl. straits, distress, < *angustus,* strait, narrow, < *angere,* constrict.] Excruciating pain of body or mind; acute distress; agony.—**an'guish,** *v. t.* or *i.* To affect with or suffer anguish.

an-gu-lar (ang'gū-lạr), *a.* [L. *angularis,* < *angulus,* E. *angle*[3].] Of, pertaining to, or measured by an angle; also, having angles; pointed; sharp-cornered; hence, lacking graceful curves of figure; awkward; also, stiff; unaccommodating.—**an-gu-lar'i-ty** (-lar'i-ti), *n.*; pl. *-ties* (-tiz). Angular state or form; also, an angular part; an angle. —**an'gu-lar-ly,** *adv.*—**an'gu-lar-ness,** *n.*

an-gu-late (ang'gū-lāt), *v. t.*; *-lated, -lating.* [L. *angulatus,* pp. of *angulare,* < *angulus,* E. *angle*[3].] To form with angles.—**an'gu-late** (-lạt), *a.* Angled; angular.—**an'gu-late-ly,** *adv.*—**an-gu-la'tion** (-lā'shọn), *n.* Angular formation.

an-gus-tate (ang-gus'tāt), *a.* [L. *angustatus,* pp. of *angustare,* < *angustus,* narrow.] Narrowed or contracted, as leaves narrowed at the base.

an-gus-ti-fo-li-ate (ang-gus-ti-fō'li-ạt), *a.* [L. *angustus,* narrow, + *folium,* leaf.] In *bot.,* having narrow leaves.

an-he-la-tion (an-hẹ-lā'shọn), *n.* [L. *anhelatio(n-),* < *anhelare,* pant.] Panting; shortness of breath; asthma. [Archaic.]

an-his-tous (an-his'tus), *a.* [Gr. ἀν- priv. + ἱστός, web.] In *anat.,* having no recognizable structure.

an-hun-gered (ạn-hung'gėrd), *a.* [Cf. *ahungered.*] Hungry. See Mat. xxv. 35. [Archaic.]

an-hy-dride, an-hy-drid (an-hī'drīd or -drid, -drid), *n.* [Gr. ἄνυδρος: see *anhydrous.*] In *chem.,* one of a class of compounds consisting of oxides capable of reacting with water to form acids, and made by removing water from acids.

an-hy-drite (an-hī'drīt), *n.* [Gr. ἄνυδρος: see *anhydrous.*] A mineral consisting of anhydrous sulphate of calcium, usually whitish or slightly colored.

Ani.

an-hy-drous (an-hī'drus), *a.* [Gr. ἄνυδρος, without water, < ἀν- priv. + ὕδωρ, water.] Without water; in *chem.,* containing no water, esp. no water of crystallization.

a-ni (ä'nē), *n.* [Brazilian.] Any of certain birds of the cuckoo family constituting the genus *Crotophaga,* inhabiting the warmer parts of America.

a-nigh (ạ-nī'), *adv.* and *prep.* Nigh; near. [Prov. Eng. or pseudo-archaic.]

a-night, a-nights (ạ-nīt', ạ-nīts'), *adv.* At night; by night. [Archaic or prov. Eng.]

an-il (an'il), *n.* [F. and Pg., < Ar. *al,* the, + *nīl,* < Skt. *nīlī,* indigo, < *nīla,* dark-colored, dark-blue: cf. *lilac.*] A West Indian fabaceous shrub, *Indigofera anil,* one of the plants which yield indigo; also, indigo.

an-ile (an'il or -īl), *a.* [L. *anilis,* < *anus,* old woman.] Of, like, or befitting a (weak or doting) old woman.

an-i-line (an'i-lin). [See *anil.*] **I.** *n.* An oily liquid, $C_6H_5NH_2$, obtained first from indigo but now prepared from the benzene of coal-tar, and serving as the basis of many brilliant dyes. **II.** *a.* Pertaining to or derived from aniline.

a-nil-i-ty (a-nil′i-ti), *n.*; pl. *-ties* (-tiz). Anile state; feminine dotage; also, an anile notion or procedure.

an-i-mad-ver-sion (an″i-mad-vėr′shọn), *n.* [L. *animadversio(n-).*] The act of animadverting; critical or censuring comment; a criticism; a stricture.

an-i-mad-vert (an″i-mad-vėrt′), *v. i.* [L. *animadvertere*, < *animus*, mind, + *advertere*, turn to: see *advert.*] To take notice†; take judicial cognizance (archaic); make critical observations or comments (*on*); pass criticisms or strictures.—**an″i-mad-vert′er,** *n.*

an-i-mal (an′i-mạl), *a.* [L. *animalis*, living, < *anima*, air, breath, life, soul.] Living† or animate†; also, characterized by or pertaining to sentient life; pertaining to the merely sentient part of a living being, or to those parts of man's nature which he shares with the lower animals; also, of or pertaining to animals (as, the *animal* kingdom).—**animal magnetism,** mesmerism.—**an′i-mal,** *n.* [L. *animal*, living being.] A sentient living being; a member of the animal kingdom (including man), as distinguished from a vegetable or a mineral; also, an irrational sentient being ('lower animal'), as distinguished from man; a brute; a beast; also, a human being in whom the animal nature has the ascendancy.

an-i-mal-cule (an-i-mal′kūl), *n.* [NL. *animalculum*, dim. of L. *animal*, E. *animal*, *n.*] A small, usually a minute or microscopic animal.—**an-i-mal′cu-lar** (-kū-lạr), **an-i-mal′cu-line** (-lin), *a.*—**an-i-mal′cu-lum** (-lụm), *n.*; pl. *-la* (-lạ̈). [NL.] Same as *animalcule.*

an-i-mal=flow-er (an′i-mạl-flou″ėr), *n.* A flower-like animal, as the sea-anemone; a zoöphyte.

an-i-mal-hood (an′i-mạl-hu̇d), *n.* The condition of an animal.

an-i-mal-ism (an′i-mạl-izm), *n.* Animal existence, nature, or enjoyment; sensualism; also, a mere animal.—**an′i-mal-ist,** *n.* A sensualist; also, a painter, sculptor, or other artist whose chief subject is animal life.

an-i-mal-i-ty (an-i-mal′i-ti), *n.* Animal nature; also, animal life.

an-i-mal-ize (an′i-mạl-īz), *v. t.*; *-ized, -izing.* To make animal; brutalize; sensualize; also, to convert into animal matter, as food by assimilation.—**an″i-mal-i-za′tion** (-i-zā′shọn), *n.*

an-i-mal-ly (an′i-mạl-i), *adv.* Physically.

an-i-mate (an′i-māt), *v. t.*; *-mated, -mating.* [L. *animatus*, pp. of *animare*, < *anima*: see *animal, a.*] To give life to; make alive; vivify; hence, to make lively, vivacious, or vigorous; also, to inspirit or encourage; also, to move to action; actuate; inspire.—**an′i-mate** (-mạt), *a.* Living; alive; also, lively or animated.—**an′i-mat-ed** (-mā-ted), *p. a.* Animate or living; also, lively; vivacious; spirited; sprightly.—**an′i-mat-ed-ly,** *adv.*—**an′i-mat-er,** *n.* Same as *animator.*—**an′i-mat-ing-ly,** *adv.*—**an-i-ma′tion** (-mā′shọn), *n.* [L. *animatio(n-).*] The act of animating; animated state; life; liveliness; vivacity; spirit.—**an′i-ma-tive** (-mạ-tiv), *a.* Serving to animate.—**a-ni-ma-to** (ä-nē-mä′tō), *a.* [It.] In *music*, animated; lively; somewhat quick and with spirit.—**an′i-ma-tor** (-mā-tọr), *n.* [L.] One who or that which animates.

an-i-mé (an′i-mā or -mẹ), *n.* [F.; origin uncertain.] Any of various resins or copals, esp. that from *Hymenæa courbaril*, a tree of tropical America, used in making varnish, scenting pastilles, etc.

an-i-mism (an′i-mizm), *n.* [L. *anima*, soul.] The doctrine of a soul as existing in the material universe; also, the doctrine of the soul as constituting the principle of life and health; also, belief in spiritual beings or agencies.—**an′i-mist,** *n.* An adherent of some form of animism.—**an-i-mis′tic,** *a.*

an-i-mos-i-ty (an-i-mos′i-ti), *n.*; pl. *-ties* (-tiz). [L. *animositas*, < *animosus*, spirited, < *animus*: see *animus.*] Spirit† or courage†; also, warmly hostile spirit; a feeling of ill-will or enmity animating the conduct, or tending to display itself in action.

an-i-mus (an′i-mus), *n.* [L., mind, feeling, will; akin to *anima*, air, breath, soul, and Gr. ἄνεμος, wind.] Spirit; temper; esp., hostile spirit; animosity.

an-i-on (an′ī-ọn or an′i-ọn), *n.* [Gr. ἀνιόν, ppr. neut. of ἀνιέναι, go up, < ἀνά, up, + ἰέναι, go.] The product freed at the anode in electrolysis; an electronegative ion.

an-ise (an′is), *n.* [OF. F. *anis*, < L. *anisum*, < Gr. ἄνισον.] An apiaceous plant, *Pimpinella anisum*, of Mediterranean regions, yielding aniseed.—**an′i-seed** (-i-sēd), **an′ise=seed,** *n.* The aromatic seed of the anise, used in medicine and in cordials; also, any preparation of this seed.

Anise.

an-is-ei-ko-ni-a (an″is-ī-kō′ni-ạ̈), *n.* [Gr. ἀν-, not, + ἴσος, equal, + εἰκών, image.] A serious eye defect in which the perceptual image formed by one eye is not equal in size or shape, or both, to that formed by the other: corrected by lenses.

an-i-sette (an-i-set′), *n.* [F.] A cordial flavored with aniseed.

an-i-som-er-ous (an-ī-som′ẹ-rus), *a.* [See *an-.*] In *bot.*, not isomerous.

an-i-so-met-ric (an-ī-sọ-met′rik), *a.* [See *an-.*] Not isometric; of unequal measurement: applied to crystals developed dissimilarly in the three axial directions.

an-i-so-me-tro-pi-a (an-ī″sọ-me-trō′pi-ạ̈), *n.* [See *an-* and *isometropia.*] Inequality of the eyes in refractive power.

an-i-so-trop-ic (an-ī-sọ-trop′ik), *a.* [See *an-.*] In *physics*, not isotropic; æolotropic.—**an-i-sot′ro-py** (-sot′rọ-pi), *n.*

an-ker (ang′kėr), *n.* [D.] A Dutch liquid measure.

an-ker-ite (ang′kėr-īt), *n.* [From M. J. *Anker*, of Styria.] A mineral closely related to dolomite in composition, but containing relatively large quantities of iron.

ankh (angk), *n.* [Egypt.] In *Egyptian art*, a tau-cross with a loop at the top, used as a symbol of generation or enduring life.

Ankh, carried by Egyptian gods.

an-kle (ang′kl), *n.* [ME. *ankel* (also *anclee*, < AS. *anclēow*): cf. Icel. *ökkla*, Sw. and Dan. *ankel.*] The joint connecting the foot with the leg; the slender part of the leg above the foot.—**an′kle=bone,** *n.* The astragalus.—**an-klet** (ang′klet), *n.* A ring or band for the ankle, as an ornament, a fetter, or a brace.

an-kus (ang′kus), *n.* [Hind.] In India, an elephant-goad combining a sharp hook and a straight point or spike.

an-ky-lose (ang′ki-lōz), *v. t.* or *i.*; *-losed, -losing.* To unite or become united by ankylosis.

an-ky-lo-sis (ang-ki-lō′sis), *n.* [NL., < Gr. ἀγκύλωσις, < ἀγκυλοῦν, bend, crook, < ἀγκύλος, bent, crooked.] In *anat.*, union or consolidation of two or more bones into one; in *pathol.*, morbid adhesion of the bones of a joint.

an-ky-los-to-mi-a-sis (ang″ki-los-tọ-mī′ạ-sis), *n.* Same as *ancylostomiasis.*

an-ky-lot-ic (ang-ki-lot′ik), *a.* Pertaining to ankylosis.

an-lace (an′lạs), *n.* [Origin uncertain.] A dagger broad at the hilt and tapering to a point, formerly in use.

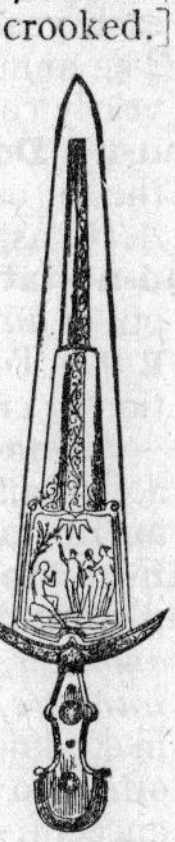
Anlace.

an-na (an′ạ̈), *n.* [Hind. *ānā.*] An East Indian money of account, the sixteenth part of a rupee; a nickel coin of this value: equivalent to about 2 U. S. cents.

an-na-berg-ite (an′ạ-bėrg-īt), *n.* [From *Annaberg*, town in Saxony.] A mineral consisting of hydrous arsenate of nickel, occurring in apple-green masses or (occasionally) capillary crystals.

an-nal (an′ạl), *n.* [Occasional sing. of *annals.*] The record of a single year in annals; also, a record chronicling a single event or fact.

an-nal-ist (an′ạl-ist), *n.* A writer of annals.—**an-nal-is′tic,** *a.*

an-nals (an′ạlz), *n. pl.* [L. *annales*, pl. of *annalis*, yearly, < *annus*, year.] Records of events or proceedings year by year; chronicles; historical records generally.

an-nates (an′āts), *n. pl.* [ML. *annata*, < L. *annus*, year.] *Eccles.*, formerly, the first year's revenue of a see or benefice, payable to the Pope as first-fruits.

an-nat-to (a-nat′ō), *n.* Same as *arnotto.*

an-neal (ạ-nēl′), *v. t.* [AS. *anǣlan*, < *an*, on, + *ǣlan*, burn; perhaps in part < OF. *neeler*, enamel, ult. < L. *niger*, black: cf. *niello*.] To treat with fire or heat; heat (glass, earthenware, metals, etc.) in order to fix colors; toughen (glass, metals, etc.) by heating and gradually cooling; fig., to bring to due condition; temper.—**an-neal′er,** *n.*

an-nec-tent (ạ-nek′tẹnt), *a.* [L. *annectens* (*-ent-*), ppr. of *annectere*: see *annex*.] Joining one to another; affording a connecting link, as between groups of animals.

an-ne-lid (an′e-lid). [F. *annélide*, < L. *anellus*, dim. of *anulus*, ring: see *annulus*.] **I.** *n.* A member of the phylum or division *Annelida*, comprising red-blooded worms, as the earthworms, leeches, various marine worms, etc., having the body made up of numerous segments. **II.** *a.* Of or pertaining to the *Annelida*.—**an-nel-i-dan** (a-nel′i-dạn), *a.* and *n.*

an-nex (ạ-neks′), *v. t.* [OF. F. *annexer* (ML. *annexare*), < L. *annectere* (pp. *annexus*), < *ad*, to, + *nectere*, bind.] To attach, join, or add, as to something larger or more important; unite; append; subjoin; attach as an attribute, concomitant, or consequence.—**an-nex** (ạ-neks′ or an′eks), *n.* [OF. F. *annexe*.] Something annexed; an added part; a supplementary building, department, etc.—**an-nex′a-ble,** *a.* That may be annexed.—**an-nex-a-tion** (an-ek-sā′shọn), *n.* [ML. *annexatio*(*n*-).] The act of annexing, or the fact of being annexed; attachment; addition or appropriation, as of territory; also, something annexed.—**an-nex-a′-tion-ist,** *n.* One who favors annexation, as of territory.—**an-nexe** (ạ-neks′), *n.* [F.] An annex, esp. to a building. —**an-nex′ment,** *n.* The act of annexing; also, something annexed. [Rare.]

an-ni-hi-la-ble (ạ-nī′hi-lạ-bl), *a.* That may be annihilated.

an-ni-hi-late (ạ-nī′hi-lāt), *v. t.*; *-lated, -lating.* [LL. *annihilatus*, pp. of *annihilare*, < L. *ad*, to, + *nihil*, nothing.] To reduce to nothing; deprive of existence; extinguish utterly; also, to bring to ruin or confusion; overthrow; demolish; destroy.—**an-ni-hi-la′tion** (-lā′shọn), *n.* The act of annihilating, or the resulting state; extinction; destruction.—**an-ni-hi-la′tion-ism,** *n.* The doctrine of the annihilation of the soul at death, or of annihilation as the ultimate doom of the wicked.—**an-ni-hi-la′tion-ist,** *n.* —**an-ni′hi-la-tive** (-lạ-tiv), *a.* Tending to annihilate; destructive.—**an-ni′hi-la-tor** (-lā-tọr), *n.*

an-ni-ver-sa-ry (an-i-vėr′sạ-ri). [L. *anniversarius*, < *annus*, year, + *vertere*, turn.] **I.** *a.* Returning or recurring each year; commemorated yearly. **II.** *n.*; pl. *-ries* (-riz). The annually recurring date of some past event; a day of yearly commemoration; a yearly commemoration.

an-no Dom-i-ni (an′ō dom′i-nī). [ML.] In the year of the (or our) Lord, that is, of the Christian era: abbreviated *A.D.*, as, A.D. (or A.D.) 1775.

an-no-tate (an′ọ-tāt), *v.*; *-tated, -tating.* [L. *annotatus*, pp. of *annotare*, < *ad*, to, + *notare*, mark, write, E. *note*, *v.*] **I.** *tr.* To furnish (a text, etc.) with notes, as of explanation or criticism. **II.** *intr.* To make notes or annotations. —**an-no-ta′tion** (-tā′shọn), *n.* [L. *annotatio*(*n*-).] The act of annotating; also, an explanatory or critical note.—**an′no-ta-tor,** *n.*

an-not-to (a-not′ō), *n.* Same as *arnotto*.

an-nounce (ạ-nouns′), *v. t.*; *-nounced, -nouncing.* [OF. *anoncier* (F. *annoncer*), < L. *annuntiare*, < *ad*, to, + *nuntiare*, announce, declare, < *nuntius*, messenger.] To make known formally; give notice of; proclaim; publish; often, to make known the presence or approaching appearance of.—**an-nounce′ment,** *n.* The act of announcing; a formal notice.—**an-noun′cer,** *n.*

an-noy (ạ-noi′), *n.* [OF. *anoi, enoi* (F. *ennui*), < L. *in odio*, in hatred (*odio*, abl. of *odium*: see *odium*).] A disturbed or resentful feeling caused by something unpleasant; vexation; annoyance; also, something annoying. [Now poetic.]—**an-noy′,** *v. t.* [OF. *anoier* (F. *ennuyer*).] To disturb by something displeasing or troublesome; vex, irritate, or offend; harass or molest.—**an-noy′ance,** *n.* The act of annoying; the state or feeling of being annoyed; vexation; irritation; also, something annoying.—**an-noy′er,** *n.*—**an-noy′ing,** *p. a.* That annoys; vexatious. —**an-noy′ing-ly,** *adv.*—**an-noy′ing-ness,** *n.*

an-nu-al (an′ū-ạl). [OF. F. *annuel*, < LL. *annualis*, < L. *annus*, year.] **I.** *a.* Of or for a year or each year; yearly; of plants, insects, etc., living but one year or season. **II.** *n.* A publication issued yearly; also, a plant or animal living but one year or season.—**an′nu-al-ly,** *adv.* Yearly; each year; year by year.

an-nu-i-tant (ạ-nū′i-tạnt), *n.* One who receives an annuity.

an-nu-i-ty (ạ-nū′i-ti), *n.*; pl. *-ties* (-tiz). [OF. *annuite* (F. *annuité*), < ML. *annuitas*, < L. *annuus*, yearly, < *annus*, year.] A yearly sum or income payable for a fixed or a contingent period, often for the recipient's life, either as a gift or in consideration of a gross sum received; the right to receive such a yearly sum.

an-nul (ạ-nul′), *v. t.*; *-nulled, -nulling.* [OF. *anuller* (F. *annuler*), < LL. *annullare*, < L. *ad*, to, + *nullus*, none, E. *null*.] To reduce to nothing; bring to naught; nullify; esp., to make null or void by authoritative decree.

an-nu-lar (an′ū-lạ̈r), *a.* [L. *annularis*, < *annulus*, ring: see *annulus*.] Ring-like; ring-shaped; ringed; annulate.—**an′nu-lar-ly,** *adv.*

an-nu-late (an′ū-lạ̄t), *a.* [L. *annulatus*, < *annulus*, ring: see *annulus*.] Having rings or ring-like parts or bands; formed of ring-like segments, as an annelid worm. Also **an′nu-lat-ed** (-lā-ted).—**an-nu-la′tion** (-lā′shọn), *n.* Formation with or into rings; also, a ring-like formation or part.

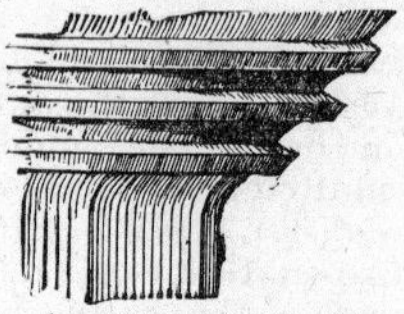
Annulets of the Doric Capital.

an-nu-let (an′ū-let), *n.* [Dim. < L. *annulus*: see *annulus*.] A little ring; in *arch.*, etc., an encircling band, molding, or fillet, as about a column.

an-nul-la-ble (ạ-nul′ạ-bl), *a.* [See *annul*.] That may be annulled.

an-nul-ler (ạ-nul′ėr), *n.* One who annuls.

an-nul-ment (ạ-nul′mẹnt), *n.* The act of annulling, or the state or fact of being annulled; a making null or void.

an-nu-lose (an′ū-lōs), *a.* [NL. *annulosus*, < L. *annulus*: see *annulus*.] Composed of ring-like parts.

an-nu-lus (an′ū-lus), *n.*; pl. *-li* (-lī). [L., prop. *anulus*, dim. of *anus*, ring.] A ring; a ring-like part, band, or space.

an-nun-ci-ate (ạ-nun′ṣi-āt), *v. t.*; *-ated, -ating.* [L. *annuntiatus*, pp. of *annuntiare*: see *announce*.] To announce. —**an-nun-ci-a′tion** (-ā′shọn), *n.* [LL. *annuntiatio*(*n*-).] The act of announcing; announcement; *eccles.*, [*cap.* or *l. c.*] the announcement by the angel Gabriel to the Virgin Mary of the incarnation of Christ; [*cap.*] a festival, held on March 25, in commemoration of the announcement.—**Annunciation lily,** the common white lily, *Lilium candidum*: so called from its frequent introduction in pictures of the Annunciation.—**an-nun′ci-a-tive** (-ạ-tiv), *a.* Making announcement.—**an-nun′ci-a-tor** (-ā-tọr), *n.* [LL. *annuntiator*.] One who or that which announces; a mechanical, electrical, or other signaling apparatus; an indicator.

a-no-ci-as-so-ci-a-tion (a-nō″si-ạ-sō-ṣi-ā′shọn), *n.* [From *a*-[1] + L. *nocere*, harm, + E. *association*.] A method of treatment before, during, and after a surgical operation, for preventing shock and other harmful effects: consisting principally in a combination of general and local anæsthesia (whereby the brain is entirely cut off from the field of operation), and in shielding the patient from alarming mental impressions. Also **a-no-ci-a′tion** (-ā′shọn).

an-ode (an′ōd), *n.* [Gr. ἄνοδος, way up, < ἀνά, up, + ὁδός, way.] The positive pole of a battery or other electric source; that terminal at which the current enters an electrolytic cell or the like: opposed to *cathode*.—**a-nod-ic** (a-nod′ik), *a.*

an-o-dyne (an′ọ-dīn). [L. *anodynus*, < Gr. ἀνώδυνος, < ἀν- priv. + ὀδύνη, pain.] **I.** *a.* Relieving pain; fig., soothing. **II.** *n.* A medicine that relieves pain. Also fig.

a-noint (ạ-noint′), *v. t.* [OF. *enoint*, pp. of *enoindre*, < L. *inunguere*, < *in*, in, on, + *unguere*, smear.] To put oil on; apply an unguent or liquid to; esp., to consecrate by applying oil.—**a-noint′er,** *n.*—**a-noint′ment,** *n.* The act of anointing; consecration; also, an ointment†.

a-nom-a-lism (ạ-nom′ạ-lizm), *n.* Anomalous character; also, something anomalous; an anomaly.—**a-nom-a-lis′tic**

(-lis′tik), *a.* Of or pertaining to an anomaly; in *astron.*, pertaining to the anomaly or angular distance of a planet from its perihelion.—**a-nom-a-lis′ti-cal-ly,** *adv.*

a-nom-a-lous (ạ-nom′ạ-lus), *a.* [LL. *anomalus*, < Gr. ἀνώμαλος, uneven, < ἀν- priv. + ὁμαλός, even, < ὁμός, same.] Deviating from the common rule, type, or form; irregular; abnormal.—**a-nom′a-lous-ly,** *adv.*—**a-nom′a-lous-ness,** *n.*—**a-nom′a-ly** (-li), *n.*; pl. *-lies* (-liz). [L. *anomalia*, < Gr. ἀνωμαλία.] Anomalous condition or character; deviation from the common rule; irregularity; also, something anomalous; in *astron.*, an angular quantity defining the position of a point in a planetary orbit; esp., the angular distance of a planet from its perihelion, as observed from the sun.

a-non (ạ-non′), *adv.* [AS. *on ān*, 'in one,' in a straight course, straightway.] Straightway or immediately (archaic); also, presently or soon (as, "Get you away; I'll send for you *anon*": Shakspere's "Othello," iv. 1. 270); also, presently again, or now again (as, ever and *anon*: see under *ever*).

an-o-na-ceous (an-ọ-nā′shius), *a.* [NL. *Anona*, genus including the custard-apple, < Sp. *anona*.] Belonging to the *Anonaceæ*, a family of trees and shrubs, mostly tropical, including the custard-apple, sour-sop, sweet-sop, and papaw (*Asimina*).

an-o-nym (an′ọ-nim), *n.* [F. *anonyme*, < Gr. ἀνώνυμος, nameless, < ἀν- priv. + ὄνυμα, name.] An anonymous person or publication; also, a pseudonym.

a-non-y-mous (ạ-non′i-mus), *a.* [Gr. ἀνώνυμος: see *anonym*.] Having or bearing no name; nameless; also, of unknown name or authorship.—**an-o-nym-i-ty** (an-ọ-nim′i-ti), **a-non′y-mous-ness,** *n.*—**a-non′y-mous-ly,** *adv.*

a-noph-e-les (a-nof′ẹ-lēz), *n.* [NL., < Gr. ἀνωφελής, useless, hurtful, < ἀν- priv. + ὄφελος, advantage.] A mosquito of the genus *Anopheles*, which, when infected with the organisms causing malaria, may transmit the disease to human beings by biting.

an-or-thic (an-ôr′thik), *a.* [Gr. ἀν- priv. + ὀρθός, straight.] In *mineral.*, having unequal oblique axes; triclinic.—**an-or′thite** (-thīt), *n.* A kind of feldspar containing calcium, forming a constituent of many igneous rocks.—**an-or-thit′ic** (-thit′ik), *a.*—**an-or′tho-site** (-thọ-sīt), *n.* A granular igneous rock composed largely of labradorite or a similar feldspar.

an-os-mi-a (an-os′mi-ạ̈), *n.* [NL., < Gr. ἀν- priv. + ὀσμή, smell.] In *pathol.*, loss of the sense of smell.—**an-os′mic,** *a.*

an-oth-er (ạ-nuᴛʜ′ėr), *a.* and *pron.* [Prop. two words.] An other; a second, additional, or different: with a substantive expressed or understood.—**one another.** See under *one*, *pron.*—**an-oth′er=gates** (-gāts), *a.* [See *gate*^{2}.] Of another or different kind. Also **an-oth′er=guess** (-ges). [Archaic or prov. Eng.]

a-not-ta, a-not-to (a-not′ạ̈, -ō), *n.* Same as *arnotto*.

an-sa (an′sạ̈), *n.*; pl. *ansæ* (-sē). [L., handle.] A handle or handle-like part; *pl.*, in *astron.*, the parts of Saturn's rings which, when seen obliquely, seemed, in the earlier telescopes, to project like handles on each side of the planet.—**an′sate, an′sat-ed** (-sāt, -sā-ted), *a.* [L. *ansatus*.] Having a handle or handle-like part.

an-schluss (än′shlùs), *n.* [G.] Joining; union; specif. [*cap.*], the political union of Austria with Germany in 1938.

an-ser-ine (an′sẹ-rin), *a.* [L. *anserinus*, < *anser*, goose.] Of or pertaining to a goose; goose-like; fig., stupid; silly.

an-ser-ous (an′sẹ-rus), *a.* [L. *anser*, goose.] Goose-like; silly.

an-swer (ȧn′sėr), *n.* [AS. *andswaru*, < *and-*, against (see *anti-*), + *-swaru*, akin to *swerian*, E. *swear*.] A reply to a charge or accusation, or to any statement, question, demand, etc.; a response in words or in act; the solution of a problem.—**an′swer,** *v.* [AS. *andswarian*, < *andswaru*.] **I.** *intr.* To make answer; reply by word or act; respond; give assurance or guaranty (*for*); be responsible, meet consequences, pay, or suffer (*for*); be satisfactory or serve (*for*); correspond (*to*). **II.** *tr.* To say in answer; reply; also, to make answer to; speak, write, or act in response to; hence, to attend to or meet by some response or return; also, to give satisfaction for; also, to satisfy, serve, or suit (as, this will *answer* the purpose); also, to conform or correspond to.—**an′swer-a-ble,** *a.* Capable of being answered; also, liable to be called to answer or give account; accountable or responsible; also, answering, conformable, or correspondent.—**an′swer-a-ble-ness,** *n.*—**an′swer-a-bly,** *adv.* Conformably; correspondingly.—**an′swer-er,** *n.*—**an′swer-less,** *a.* Without an answer; also, unanswerable.

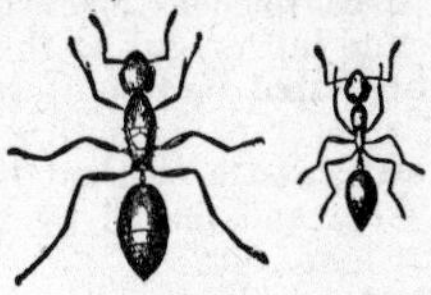

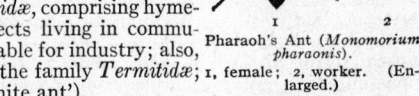

1 2
Pharaoh's Ant (*Monomorium pharaonis*). 1, female; 2, worker. (Enlarged.)

ant (ȧnt), *n.* [AS. *æmete*, akin to G. *ameise*.] Any member of the family *Formicidæ*, comprising hymenopterous insects living in communities and notable for industry; also, any insect of the family *Termitidæ*; a termite ('white ant').

ant-. A form of *anti-*, 'opposite to,' 'against,' commonly used before a vowel or *h*.

-ant. [F. *-ant*, < L. *-ant-*, *-ent-*, nom. *-ans*, *-ens*, ppr. ending, corresponding to E. *-ing*^{2}; or directly from L. *-ant-*.] A suffix of adjectives, orig. participial, with the general sense of doing or being something, as in *ascendant*, *distant*, *dormant*, *pleasant*, *relevant*, or of nouns of like origin, denoting a person or thing doing or being something, as in *pendant*, *pretendant*, *servant*, *tenant*. Cf. *-ance* and *-ent*.

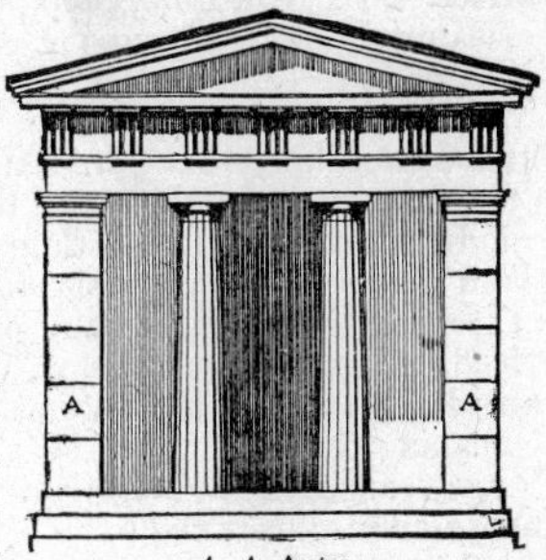

A, *A*, Antæ.

an-ta (an′tạ̈), *n.*; pl. *antæ* (-tē). [L. *antæ*, pl., perhaps < *ante*, before.] In *arch.*, a square or rectangular pier or pillar, formed by thickening a wall at its extremity: often furnished with a base and a capital.

ant-a-cid (ant-as′id). [See *ant-*.] **I.** *a.* Neutralizing acids; counteracting acidity, as of the stomach. **II.** *n.* An antacid agent or remedy.

An-tæ-an (an-tē′ạn), *a.* Of, like, or suggestive of Antæus, a giant of Greek legend who was invincible when in contact with the earth (his mother, Gæa), but was lifted into the air by Hercules and crushed.

an-tag-o-nism (an-tag′ọ-nizm), *n.* [Gr. ἀνταγώνισμα, < ἀνταγωνίζεσθαι: see *antagonize*.] The activity or the relation of contending parties or conflicting forces; active opposition; antagonistic spirit or tendency.—**an-tag′o-nist,** *n.* [Gr. ἀνταγωνιστής.] One who contends against another; an opponent; an adversary; in *physiol.*, a muscle which acts in opposition to another.—**an-tag-o-nis′tic,** *a.* Of or like an antagonist; opposing; conflicting; counteractive; adverse. Also **an-tag-o-nis′ti-cal.**—**an-tag-o-nis′ti-cal-ly,** *adv.*

an-tag-o-nize (an-tag′ọ-nīz), *v.*; *-nized*, *-nizing*. [Gr. ἀνταγωνίζεσθαι, < ἀντί, against, + ἀγωνίζεσθαι, contend: see *agonize*.] **I.** *tr.* To contend against; oppose; hence, to counteract; also, to render antagonistic. **II.** *intr.* To act in opposition or antagonism.—**an-tag″o-ni-za′tion** (-ni-zā′shọn), *n.*—**an-tag′o-niz-er** (-nī-zėr), *n.*

an-tal-gic (an-tal′jik). [Gr. ἀντί, against, + ἄλγος, pain.] In *med.*: **I.** *a.* Relieving pain; anodyne. **II.** *n.* An anodyne.

ant-al-ka-li (ant-al′kạ-lī or -li), *n.*; pl. *-lis* or *-lies* (-līz or -liz). [See *ant-*.] Something that neutralizes alkalis or counteracts alkalinity, as within the body.—**ant-al′ka-line** (-lin or -līn), *a.* and *n.*

ant-arc-tic (ant-ärk′tik). [OF. F. *antarctique*, < L. *antarcticus*, < Gr. ἀνταρκτικός, < ἀντί, opposite to, + ἀρκτικός, E. *arctic*.] **I.** *a.* Opposite to the arctic pole; of, at, or near the south pole: as, the *antarctic* circle (the northern boundary of the south frigid zone, everywhere distant 23° 28′ from the south pole). **II.** *n.* The antarctic region.

ant-ar-thrit-ic (ant-är-thrit′ik). [See *ant-* and *arthritic*.] In *med.*: **I.** *a.* Efficacious against gout. **II.** *n.* An antarthritic agent.

ant-asth-mat-ic (ant-as-mat′ik or ant-az-). [See *ant-*.] In *med.*: **I.** *a.* Efficacious against asthma. **II.** *n.* An antasthmatic agent.

ant=bear (ȧnt′bãr), *n.* A South American edentate quadruped, the tamanoir, or great or maned ant-eater, *Myrmecophaga jubata*, having a shaggy gray coat marked with a conspicuous black band which is broad across the chest and tapers back to the loins; also, the aardvark.

ant=bird (ȧnt′bėrd), *n.* Any of various birds that feed on ants; esp., a South American ant-thrush.

ant=cat-tle (ȧnt′kat″l), *n.* Aphids or plant-lice which are kept and tended by ants for the sake of their honeydew. Cf. *ant-cow.*

ant=cow (ȧnt′kou), *n.* An aphid or plant-louse from which ants obtain honeydew. Cf. *ant-cattle.*

an-te (an′tę̄), *n.* [Cf. L. *ante*, before.] In *poker*, a stake put into the pool by each player after seeing his hand but before drawing new cards, or, sometimes, as in jack-pots, before seeing his hand.—**an′te,** *v. i.* or *t.*; *ante'd* or *anteed, anteing.* To put (one's stake) into the pool in the game of poker; fig., to pay (one's share): often with *up.*

ante-. [L., repr. *ante*, prep. and adv.: see *anti-.*] A prefix meaning 'before,' occurring orig. in words from the Latin, but now freely used as an English formative, as in *antedate, ante-election, ante-Renaissance.* Cf. *pre-* and *post-.*

ant=eat-er (ȧnt′ē″tėr), *n.* Any of various edentates, as the South American ant-bear, the tamandua, the aardvark, and the pangolin, subsisting entirely or largely upon ants, and characterized by a slender, elongated head and a long, extensile tongue; also, any of certain other animals which feed on ants, as the echidna, the ant-thrush, etc.

an-te bel-lum (an′tę̄ bel′um). [L.] Before the war (often meaning the U. S. Civil War): a phrase often used adjectively (as, *ante-bellum* days).

an-te-cede (an-tę̄-sēd′), *v. t.* or *i.*; *-ceded, -ceding.* [L. *antecedere* (pp. *antecessus*), < *ante*, before, + *cedere*, go.] To go before, as in place, time, or order; precede.—**an-te-ced′ence** (-sē′dẹns), *n.* A going before; precedence; in *astron.*, an apparent motion of a planet from east to west.—**an-te-ced′en-cy,** *n.* Antecedent state; priority.—**an-te-ced′ent. I.** *a.* Going or being before; preceding; prior (*to*); previous. **II.** *n.* Something antecedent; a preceding circumstance, event, etc.; *pl.*, the facts of one's past; previous record; *sing.*, in *gram.*, the noun or its equivalent to which a relative pronoun refers; in *math.*, the first term of a ratio; in *logic*, the conditional member of a hypothetical proposition. See *consequent, n.*—**an-te-ced′ent-ly,** *adv.* Previously; in advance.

an-te-ces-sor (an-tę̄-ses′ọr), *n.* [L., < *antecedere*, E. *antecede.*] A predecessor; also, an ancestor†.

an-te-cham-ber (an′tę̄-chām″bėr), *n.* [F. *antichambre*, < *anti-*, for *ante-*, before, + *chambre*, chamber.] A room leading into a chamber or chief apartment; an anteroom.

an-te-chap-el (an′tę̄-chap″ẹl), *n.* [See *ante-.*] An apartment, vestibule, porch, or the like, before the entrance to a chapel.

an-te-choir (an′tę̄-kwīr), *n.* [See *ante-.*] A space, more or less inclosed, in front of the choir of a church.

an-te-com-mu-nion (an″tę̄-kọ-mū′nyọn), *n.* [See *ante-.*] *Eccles.*, that part of the Anglican communion office which precedes the communion service proper, and is used on holy days though there be no communion.

an-te-date (an′tę̄-dāt), *n.* [See *ante-.*] A prior date; a date earlier than the true date.—**an′te-date,** *v. t.*; *-dated, -dating.* To give an earlier date to than the true date; make earlier in date; also, to precede in time; also, to take or have in advance; anticipate.

an-te-di-lu-vi-an (an″tę̄-di-lū′vi-ạn). [L. *ante*, before, + *diluvium*, deluge.] **I.** *a.* Belonging to times before the Flood (see Gen. vii.–viii.); hence, antiquated. Cf. *postdiluvian.* **II.** *n.* One who lived before the Deluge; hence, an old fogy.

an-te-fix (an′tę̄-fiks), *n.* [L. *antefixum*, prop. neut. of *antefixus*, fixed before, < *ante*, before, + *fixus*, pp. of *figere*, E. *fix.*] In *class. arch.*, an upright ornament, as of terra-cotta, at the eaves of a tiled roof, to conceal the foot of a row of convex tiles which cover the joints of the flat tiles.—**an-te-fix′al,** *a.*

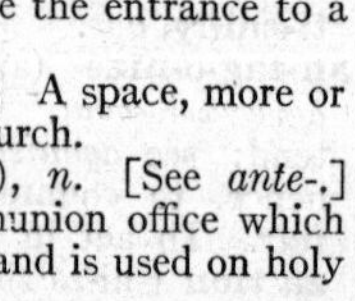
Antefix.

an-te-flex-ion (an-tę̄-flek′shọn), *n.* [L. *ante*, before, + *flexio(n-)*, a bending.] In *pathol.*, a bending forward, esp. of the body of the uterus. Cf. *retroflexion.*

an-te-lope (an′tę̄-lōp), *n.* [OF. *antelop*, < ML. *antalopus*, < LGr. ἀνθόλοψ.] Any animal of the subfamily *Antilopinæ*, comprising hollow-horned ruminants allied to cattle, sheep, and goats, found chiefly in Africa and Asia, and widely diverse in size and appearance.

an-te-lu-can (an-tę̄-lū′kạn), *a.* [L. *antelucanus*, < *ante*, before, + *lux*, light.] Before daylight.

an-te-me-rid-i-an (an″tę̄-mę̄-rid′i-ạn), *a.* [L. *antemeridianus*, < *ante*, before, + *meridies*, midday.] Before noon; of or pertaining to the forenoon. Cf. *postmeridian.*

an-te me-rid-i-em (an′tę̄ mę̄-rid′i-em). [L.] Before noon: used in specifying the hour of the day, usually in the abbreviated form *A.M.*, as, 10 A.M. (or A.M.).

an-te=mor-tem (an′tę̄-môr′tem), *a.* [L. *ante mortem*, before death.] Previous to death: as, an *ante-mortem* statement. Cf. *post-mortem.*

an-te-mun-dane (an-tę̄-mun′dān), *a.* [L. *ante*, before, + *mundus*, world.] Being before the creation of the world.

an-te-na-tal (an-tę̄-nā′tạl), *a.* [L. *ante*, before, + *natus*, born.] Previous to birth: as, "memories of an *antenatal* life" (Shelley's "Prince Athanase," i.).

an-ten-na (an-ten′ạ̈), *n.*; pl. *antennæ* (-ē). [L., a sail-yard.] One of the lateral articulated appendages occurring in pairs on the head of insects, crustaceans, etc.; a feeler, horn, or tentacle; in *wireless teleg.* and *teleph.*, the conductor by which the electric or Hertzian waves are sent out or received, consisting commonly of a wire or set of wires supported in the air at an elevation or otherwise.—**an-ten′nal, an-ten-na-ry** (ȧn-ten′ạ-ri or an′te-nạ-ri), *a.*—**an-ten-nule** (an-ten′ūl), *n.* A small antenna; esp., one of a pair of anterior and lesser antennæ of crustaceans.

an-te-nup-tial (an-tę̄-nup′shạl), *a.* [LL. *antenuptialis*, < L. *ante*, before, + *nuptiæ*, marriage.] Before marriage.

an-te-pas-chal (an-tę̄-pas′kạl), *a.* [See *ante-.*] Before the paschal season; previous to the Passover, or to Easter.

an-te-past (an′tę̄-pȧst), *n.* [L. *ante*, before, + *pastus*, food, < *pascere*, feed.] A foretaste. [Archaic.]

an-te-pen-di-um (an-tę̄-pen′di-um), *n.*; pl. *-diums* or *-dia* (-di-ạ̈). [ML., < L. *ante*, before, + *pendere*, hang.] *Eccles.*, a movable covering, as of silk or velvet, for the front of an altar; a frontal.

an-te-pe-nult (an″tę̄-pę̄-nult′ or -pē′nult), *n.* [L. *antepænultima*, < *ante*, before, + *pænultima*, penult.] The last syllable but two in a word. Also **an″te-pe-nul′ti-ma** (-nul′ti-mạ̈).—**an″te-pe-nul′ti-mate** (-mạt). **I.** *a.* Immediately preceding the penult; the last but two. **II.** *n.* The antepenult.

an-te-pran-di-al (an-tę̄-pran′di-ạl), *a.* [L. *ante*, before, + *prandium*, luncheon, meal.] Before dinner.

an-te-ri-or (an-tē′ri-ọr), *a.* [L., compar. adj. < *ante*, before.] More toward the front, head, or beginning (opposed to *posterior*); front; fore; also, going before, as in order or time; earlier; prior; also, antecedent (*to*), as in order or time.—**an-te-ri-or′i-ty** (-or′i-ti), *n.* Anterior position or date.—**an-te′ri-or-ly,** *adv.* In front; also, previously.

antero-. A positive form, meaning 'front,' 'fore,' assumed for use in combination from the comparative adjective L. *anterior*, anterior. Cf. *postero-* and *posterior.*—**an-te-ro-lat-er-al** (an″tẹ-rọ̄-lat′ẹ-rạl), *a.* In front, at one side.

an-te-room (an′tę̄-röm), *n.* [See *ante-.*] A room leading into a chief apartment; an adjoining waiting-room.

an-te-ro-pos-te-ri-or (an″tẹ-rọ̄-pos-tē′ri-ọr), *a.* [See *antero-.*] In *zoöl.*, in the direction from front to back or from head to tail; in *bot.*, median.

an-te-type (an′tę̄-tīp), *n.* [See *ante-.*] An earlier type; a prototype.

an-te-vert (an-tę̄-vėrt′), *v. t.* [L. *ante*, before, + *vertere*, turn.] In *pathol.*, to turn forward; displace (the uterus) as by tipping forward. Cf. *retrovert.*—**an-te-ver′sion** (-vėr′shọn), *n.*

ant-he-li-on (ant-hē′li-ọn or an-thē′-), *n.*; pl. *-lia* (-li-ạ̈). [Gr. ἀνθήλιον, neut. of ἀνθήλιος, opposite to the sun, < ἀντί, opposite to, + ἥλιος, sun.] A luminous ring seen around the shadow of the observer's head as thrown by the sun on a cloud, fog-bank, or moist surface.

ant-he-lix (ant-hē′liks), *n.* Same as *antihelix.*
an-thel-min-tic (an-thel-min′tik). [Gr. ἀντί, against, + ἕλμινς (ἑλμινθ-), worm.] In *med.*: **I.** *a.* Destroying or expelling intestinal worms. **II.** *n.* An anthelmintic remedy.
an-them (an′them), *n.* [AS. *antefen,* < ML. *antiphona*: see *antiphon.*] Orig., a hymn sung in alternate parts; now, a piece of sacred vocal music, with words taken usually from the Scriptures; in general, a hymn, as of praise, devotion, or patriotism.—**an′-them,** *v. t.* To celebrate or salute with an anthem: as, "sweet birds *antheming* the morn" (Keats's "To Fancy").

Anthemion-molding.—Frieze of the Erechtheum, Athens.

an-the-mi-on (an-thē′mi-ọn), *n.*; pl. *-mia* (-mi-a̤). [NL., < Gr. ἀνθέμιον, < ἄνθος, flower.] An ornament of floral or foliar forms arranged in a flat radiating cluster, as in architectural decoration, vase-painting, etc.

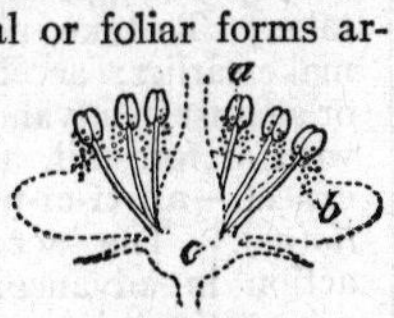

Anthers.
a, anther; *b*, pollen; *c*, filament.

an-ther (an′thėr), *n.* [NL. *anthera,* < Gr. ἀνθηρός, flowery, < ἄνθος, flower.] In *bot.*, the pollen-bearing part of a stamen.—**an′ther-al,** *a.*
an-ther-id-i-um (an-thẹ-rid′i-um), *n.*; pl. *-ia* (-i-a̤). [NL., < *anthera*: see *anther.*] In *bot.*, the male reproductive organ in ferns, mosses, etc. Also **an′ther-id.**—**an-ther-id′i-al,** *a.*
an-ther-if-er-ous (an-thẹ-rif′ẹ-rus), *a.* [See *-ferous.*] In *bot.*, producing or supporting anthers.
an-ther-less (an′thėr-les), *a.* Without anthers.
ant=hill (ȧnt′hil), *n.* A mound or hillock of earth, leaves, etc., formed by a colony of ants for, or in the process of constructing, their habitation.
antho-. Form of Gr. ἄνθος, flower, used in combination.
an-tho-clin-i-um (an-thọ-klin′i-um), *n.*; pl. *-ia* (-i-a̤). [NL., < Gr. ἄνθος, flower, + κλίνη, bed.] In *bot.*, same as *clinanthium.*
an-tho-di-um (an-thō′di-um), *n.*; pl. *-dia* (-di-a̤). [NL., < Gr. ἀνθώδης, flower-like, < ἄνθος, flower, + εἶδος, form.] In *bot.*, a flower-head or capitulum; esp., the head (or so-called compound flower) of a composite plant.
an-thog-ra-phy (an-thog′rạ-fi), *n.* [See *antho-* and *-graphy.*] The botanical description of flowers.
an-thol-o-gy (an-thol′ọ-ji), *n.*; pl. *-gies* (-jiz). [Gr. ἀνθολογία, lit. 'a flower-gathering,' < ἄνθος, flower, + λέγειν, pick, gather.] A collection of 'flowers of verse' from various authors; any collection of literary selections.—**an-tho-log′i-cal** (-thọ-loj′i-kạl), *a.*—**an-thol′o-gist,** *n.*
an-tho-ma-ni-a (an-thọ-mā′ni-a̤), *n.* [See *antho-.*] A mania or extravagant fondness for flowers.—**an-tho-ma′-ni-ac** (-ak), *n.*
an-thoph-a-gous (an-thof′ạ-gus), *a.* [See *antho-* and *-phagous.*] Flower-eating, as various beetles.
an-thoph-i-lous (an-thof′i-lus), *a.* [See *antho-* and *-philous.*] Flower-loving, as the bee.

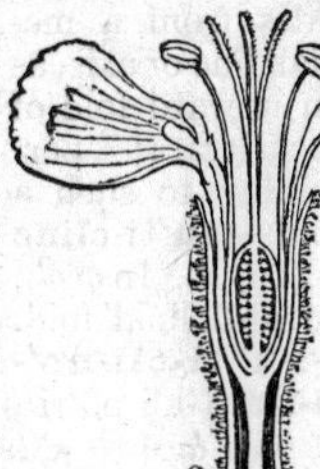

Anthophore.
Section of the flower of *Silene caroliniana,* enlarged, showing the anthophore (*a*) within the calyx, bearing the petals, stamens, and ovary.

an-tho-phore (an′thọ-fōr), *n.* [Gr. ἀνθοφόρος, flower-bearing, < ἄνθος, flower, + φέρειν, bear.] In *bot.*, a form of floral stipe, produced by the elongation of the internode between the calyx and the corolla, and bearing the corolla, stamens, and pistil, as in the catchfly (genus *Silene*).—**an-thoph′o-rous** (-thof′ọ-rus), *a.* Flower-bearing.
an-tho-tax-is (an-thọ-tak′sis), *n.* [NL.: see *antho-* and *-taxis.*] In *bot.*, the arrangement of flowers on the axis of growth; inflorescence. Also **an′tho-tax-y.**
-anthous. Adjective termination from Gr. ἄνθος, flower, as in *hapaxanthous, monanthous.*

an-tho-zo-ön (an-thọ-zō′on), *n.*; pl. *-zoa* (-zō′a̤). [NL., < Gr. ἄνθος, flower, + ζῷον, animal.] Any of the *Anthozoa,* a class of marine animals corresponding inexactly to the *Actinozoa*; an animal-flower or zoöphyte.—**an-tho-zo′an,** *a.* and *n.*
an-thra-cene (an′thrạ-sēn), *n.* [Gr. ἄνθραξ (ἀνθρακ-), coal.] In *chem.*, a hydrocarbon, $C_{14}H_{10}$, found in coal-tar, important commercially as a source of alizarin.
an-thra-cic (an-thras′ik), *a.* Pertaining to anthrax.
an-thra-cite (an′thrạ-sīt), *n.* [Gr. ἀνθρακῖτις, kind of coal, < ἄνθραξ, coal.] A variety of mineral coal containing but little of the volatile hydrocarbons, and therefore burning almost without flame; hard coal.—**an-thra-cit′ic** (-sit′ik), *a.*
an-thrac-nose (an-thrak′nōs), *n.* [F., < Gr. ἄνθραξ (ἀνθρακ-), coal, + νόσος, disease.] A destructive disease of grape-vines, in which brown spots appear on the shoots, leaves, and berries, due to the fungus *Sphaceloma ampelinum*; also, any of various other plant-diseases due to fungi.
an-thra-coid (an′thrạ-koid), *a.* Resembling anthrax.
an-thra-quin-one (an-thrạ-kwin′ōn), *n.* [From *anthra(cene)* + *quinone.*] In *chem.*, a yellow crystalline substance obtained from anthracene by oxidation, used in the preparation of alizarin.
an-thrax (an′thraks), *n.*; pl. *anthraces* (an′thrạ-sēz). [L., carbuncle, < Gr. ἄνθραξ, coal, carbuncle.] In *pathol.*, a carbuncle; also, a malignant infectious disease of cattle, sheep, and other animals and of man, associated with *Bacillus anthracis.*
an-throp-ic (an-throp′ik), *a.* [Gr. ἀνθρωπικός, < ἄνθρωπος, man.] Pertaining to man; human. Also **an-throp′i-cal.**
anthropo-. Form of Gr. ἄνθρωπος, man, human being, used in combination.—**an-thro-po-cen-tric** (an″thrọ-pọ-sen′trik), *a.* Regarding man as the central fact of the universe; assuming man to be the final aim and end of the universe.—**an″thro-po-gen′e-sis** (-jen′e-sis), *n.* The genesis or development of the human race, esp. as a subject of scientific study. Also **an-thro-pog′e-ny** (-poj′e-ni), **an-thro-pog′o-ny** (-pog′ọ-ni).—**an″thro-po-ge-og′ra-phy** (-jẹ-og′rạ-fi), *n.* Geography as concerned with man and the conditions of his habitat or environment.—**an-thro-pog′ra-phy** (-pog′rạ-fi), *n.* [+ *-graphy.*] The branch of anthropology that describes the varieties of mankind and their geographical distribution.
an-thro-poid (an′thrọ-poid). [Gr. ἀνθρωποειδής, < ἄνθρωπος, man, + εἶδος, form.] **I.** *a.* Resembling man: as, the *anthropoid* apes (see *ape, n.*). **II.** *n.* An anthropoid ape.—**an-thro-poi′dal,** *a.*
an-thro-pol-a-try (an-thrọ-pol′ạ-tri), *n.* [Gr. ἀνθρωπολατρεία, < ἄνθρωπος, man, + λατρεία, worship.] The worship of a human being as divine.—**an″thro-po-lat′ric** (-pọ-lat′rik), *a.*
an-thro-pol-o-gy (an-thrọ-pol′ọ-ji), *n.* [See *anthropo-* and *-logy.*] The science of man, or of the human kind; the science that treats of the origin, development (physical, intellectual, moral, etc.), characters, and varieties, and sometimes esp. the cultural development, customs, beliefs, etc., of mankind.—**an″thro-po-log′ic, an″thro-po-log′i-cal** (-pọ-loj′ik, -i-kạl), *a.*—**an-thro-pol′o-gist,** *n.*
an-thro-pom-e-try (an-thrọ-pom′e-tri), *n.* [See *anthropo-* and *-metry.*] Measurement of the human body, as in the Bertillon system; the branch of anthropology that deals with the measurements of the human body.—**an″thro-po-met′ric, an″thro-po-met′ri-cal** (-pọ-met′rik, -ri-kạl), *a.*—**an-thro-pom′e-trist,** *n.*
an-thro-po-mor-phic (an″thrọ-pọ-môr′fik), *a.* [Gr. ἀνθρωπόμορφος, having a human form, < ἄνθρωπος, man, + μορφή, form.] Ascribing human form or attributes to beings or things not human, esp. to a deity; characterized by or involving such ascription.—**an″thro-po-mor′phi-cal-ly,** *adv.*—**an″thro-po-mor′phism,** *n.* Anthropomorphic conception or representation, as of a deity.—**an″thro-po-mor′phist,** *n.*—**an″thro-po-mor′phize,** *v. t.*; *-phized, -phizing.* To ascribe human form or attributes to.—**an″thro-po-mor′pho-sis** (-fọ-sis), *n.* Transformation into human form.—**an″thro-po-mor′phous,** *a.* [Gr. ἀνθρωπόμορφος.] Having or resembling the human form; also, anthropomorphic.—**an″thro-po-mor′phous-ly,** *adv.*

an-thro-pon-o-my (an-thrǫ-pon′ǫ-mi), *n.* [Gr. ἄνθρωπος, man, + νόμος, law.] The science that treats of the laws regulating the development of the human organism in relation to other organisms and to environment. Also **an″thro-po-nom′ics** (-pǫ-nom′iks).—**an″thro-po-nom′i-cal,** *a.*

an-thro-pop-a-thy (an-thrǫ-pop′ą-thi), *n.* [Gr. ἀνθρωποπάθεια, the possession of human passions, < ἄνθρωπος, man, + παθεῖν, suffer.] Ascription of human passions or feelings to beings not human, esp. to God. Also **an-thro-pop′a-thism.**—**an″thro-po-path′ic** (-pǫ-path′ik), *a.*—**an″-thro-po-path′i-cal-ly,** *adv.*

an-thro-poph-a-gi (an-thrǫ-pof′ą-jī), *n. pl.* [L., pl. of *anthropophagus,* < Gr. ἀνθρωποφάγος, man-eating, < ἄνθρωπος, man, + φαγεῖν, eat.] Man-eaters; cannibals. —**an″thro-po-phag′ic, an″thro-po-phag′i-cal** (-pǫ-faj′ik, -i-kąl), *a.* Pertaining to or practising anthropophagy. —**an-thro-poph′a-gism,** *n.* Anthropophagy.—**an-thro-poph′a-gist, an-thro-poph′a-gite** (-jīt), *n.* A man-eater; a cannibal.—**an-thro-poph′a-gous** (-gus), *a.* Man-eating; cannibal.—**an-thro-poph′a-gus** (-gus), *n.* [L.] Singular of *anthropophagi.* A cannibal.—**an-thro-poph′-a-gy** (-ji), *n.* [Gr. ἀνθρωποφαγία.] The eating of human flesh; cannibalism.

an-thro-poph-u-ism (an-thrǫ-pof′ū-izm), *n.* [Gr. ἀνθρωποφυής, having a human nature, < ἄνθρωπος, man, + φυή, nature.] The ascription of human nature, functions, desires, etc., to gods.—**an″thro-poph-u-is′tic,** *a.*

an-thro-pot-o-my (an-thrǫ-pot′ǫ-mi), *n.* [See *anthropo-* and *-tomy.*] The anatomy of the human body.—**an″thro-po-tom′i-cal** (-pǫ-tom′i-kąl), *a.*—**an-thro-pot′o-mist,** *n.*

an-thro-po-zo-ic (an″thrǫ-pǫ-zō′ik), *a.* [Gr. ἄνθρωπος, man, + ζωή, life.] In *geol.,* belonging to the time of man's existence.

an-thu-ri-um (an-thū′ri-um), *n.* [NL., < Gr. ἄνθος, flower, + οὐρά, tail.] Any plant of the tropical American araceous genus *Anthurium,* including species cultivated in greenhouses, some for the showy, often richly colored spathes out of which the fleshy flower-spikes rise, others for the handsomely veined or colored foliage.

ant-hyp-not-ic (ant-hip-not′ik), *a.* and *n.* Same as *antihypnotic.*

anti-. [Gr. ἀντι-, repr. ἀντί, prep., opposite to, against, in return for, instead of, akin to L. *ante,* before, Skt. *anti,* opposite, in front, before, AS. *and-,* against: see *ante-, along*[2], and *answer.*] A prefix meaning 'opposite to,' 'opposing,' 'counter-,' 'rival' (and hence 'pseudo-'), 'the reverse of,' occurring orig. in words from the Greek, but now freely used as an English formative, as in *antidiphtheritic, antifat, anti-Jacobin, antimalarial, anti-Pelagian, anti-Sabbatarian, anti-unionist,* and many other words, largely self-explanatory. Cf. *pro-.*

an-ti (an′ti or -tī), *n.*; pl. *antis* (-tiz or -tīz). [Short for some compound of *anti-.*] One who is opposed to some course, measure, policy, or party. [Colloq.]

Antic, Amiens Cathedral, 13th century.

an-ti=air-craft (an″ti-ãr′kråft), *a.* Opposing or serving to oppose aëroplanes and other aircraft: as, *anti-aircraft* guns.

an-ti-ar (an′ti-är), *n.* [Javanese.] The upas-tree, *Ipo* (or *Antiaris*) *toxicaria,* of Java; also, an arrow-poison prepared from its sap.

an-ti-bod-y (an′ti-bod″i), *n.*; pl. *-ies* (-iz). [See *anti-.*] In *pathol.,* any of various substances existing in the blood or developed in immunization which counteract toxins or bacterial poisons in the system.

an-tic (an′tik). [F. *antique:* see *antique.*] **I.** *a.* Ancient†, antique†, or antiquated†; also, odd, fantastic, grotesque, or ludicrous (archaic). **II.** *n.* A ludicrous gesture or performance; a caper; also, a grotesque theatrical piece†; also, a clown or buffoon (archaic); in *art,* a grotesque figure or head, or a fantastic combination of incongruous figures, foliage, etc., as in sculpture (obs. or archaic).—**an′tic,** *v. i.*; *-ticked, -ticking.* To perform antics; caper.

an-ti-cath-ode (an-ti-kath′ōd), *n.* [See *anti-.*] The plate, often of platinum, opposite to the cathode in a vacuum-tube, on which the cathode rays impinge, thus producing the Röntgen rays.

an-ti-chlor (an′ti-klōr), *n.* [From *anti-* and *chlorine.*] In *chem.,* any of various substances, esp. sodium thiosulphate, used for removing the excess of chlorine from paper-pulp, cotton-fiber, etc., after bleaching.—**an″ti-chlo-ris′tic** (-klǭ-ris′tik), *a.*

an-ti-christ (an′ti-krīst), *n.* [LL. *antichristus,* < Gr. ἀντίχριστος.] An opponent of Christ; esp. [*cap.*], a particular personage or power (variously identified or explained) conceived as appearing in the world as a mighty antagonist of Christ.—**an-ti-chris′tian** (-kris′chąn). **I.** *a.* Of or like an antichrist; antagonistic to Christ; also, opposed to what is Christian. **II.** *n.* One opposed to the Christian religion.—**an-ti-chris′tian-ism,** *n.*

an-ti-ci-pant (an-tis′i-pąnt). **I.** *a.* Anticipating; anticipative (*of*). **II.** *n.* One who anticipates.

an-ti-ci-pate (an-tis′i-pāt), *v. t.*; *-pated, -pating.* [L. *anticipatus,* pp. of *anticipare,* < *ante,* before, + *capere,* take.] To take, use, have, or realize beforehand; also, to make earlier; accelerate; also, to take measures concerning or against in advance, as a thing or an action; be beforehand with or forestall, as a person; also, to look forward to or expect.—**an-ti-ci-pa′tion** (-pā′shǫn), *n.* [L. *anticipatio(n-).*] The act of anticipating; use, realization, or action in advance; foretaste; preconception; prevision; expectation; in *music,* the introduction into a chord of one or more of the component notes of the chord which follows, producing a passing discord.—**an-ti′ci-pa-tive** (-pą-tiv), *a.* Given to or involving anticipation; having anticipation (*of*).—**an-ti′ci-pa-tive-ly,** *adv.*—**an-ti′ci-pa-tor** (-pā-tǫr), *n.*—**an-ti′ci-pa-to-ry** (-pą-tǭ-ri), *a.* Anticipative.—**an-ti′ci-pa-to-ri-ly,** *adv.*

an-ti-civ-ic (an-ti-siv′ik), *a.* [F. *anticivique.*] Contrary to what is civic or befits a citizen.—**an-ti-civ′ism,** *n.* [F. *anticivisme.*] The reverse of civism; bad citizenship.

an-ti-clas-tic (an-ti-klas′tik), *a.* [Gr. ἀντί, opposite to, + κλαστός, adj. < κλᾶν, break, deflect.] Noting or pertaining to a surface (such as that of a saddle) which is curved convexly in its length and concavely in its breadth, or vice versa: opposed to *synclastic.*

an-ti-cler-i-cal (an-ti-kler′i-kąl), *a.* [See *anti-.*] Opposed to the clerical party; esp., opposed to the influence of the clergy in public affairs.—**an-ti-cler′i-cal-ism,** *n.*

an-ti-cli-max (an-ti-klī′maks), *n.* [See *anti-.*] The reverse of climax; a noticeable or ludicrous descent in discourse from lofty ideas or expressions to what is much less impressive; fig., an abrupt descent in dignity; an inglorious conclusion.

an-ti-cli-nal (an-ti-klī′nąl), *a.* [Gr. ἀντί, against, + κλίνειν, incline.] In *geol.,* inclining downward on both sides from a median line or axis, as an upward fold of rock-strata; pertaining to such a fold.—**an′ti-cline** (-klīn), *n.* In *geol.,* an anticlinal fold. —**an″ti-cli-no′ri-um** (-kli-nō′ri-um), *n.*; pl. *-ria* (-ri-ą) or *-riums.* [NL., < Gr. ἀντί + κλίνειν + ὄρος, mountain.] In *geol.,* a compound anticline, consisting of a series of subordinate anticlines and synclines, the whole formation having the general contour of an arch: opposed to *synclinorium.*

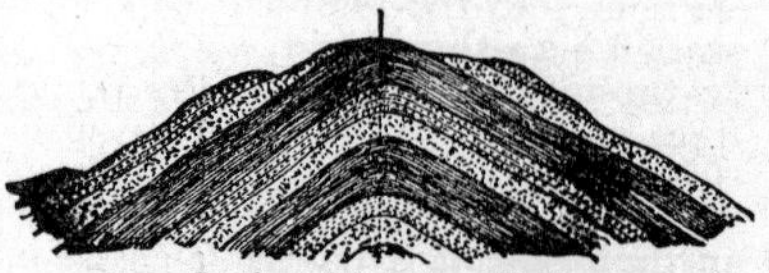

Section of Anticlinal Fold.

an-tic-ly (an′tik-li), *adv.* In an antic manner; oddly; grotesquely. [Obs. or archaic.]

an-ti-co-her-er (an″ti-kǫ-hēr′ėr), *n.* [See *anti-.*] In *elect.,* a device which, like a coherer, is used as a detector of Hertzian waves, its electrical resistance, however, being increased instead of decreased by them.

an-ti-creep (an-ti-krēp′), *a.* [See *anti-.*] In *mech.,* preventing creeping: applied specif. to various devices, as one for keeping rails from moving lengthwise.—**an-ti-creep′-ing,** *a.*

an-ti-cy-clone (an′ti-sī″klōn), *n.* An extensive horizontal movement of the atmosphere spirally around and away

from a gradually progressing central region of **high** barometric pressure. Cf. *cyclone*.—**an″ti-cy-clon′ic** (-klon′ik), *a.*
an-ti-dote (an′ti-dōt), *n.* [L. *antidotum*, < Gr. ἀντίδοτος, verbal adj. of ἀντιδιδόναι, give against, < ἀντί, against, + διδόναι, give.] A medicine or other remedy for counteracting the effects of poison, disease, etc.; hence, any means of counteracting; a corrective: with *against*, *to*, or *for*.—**an′ti-do-tal,** *a.*—**an′ti-do-tal-ly,** *adv.*
an-ti-feb-rile (an-ti-feb′ril or -fē′bril). [See *anti-*.] In *med.*: **I.** *a.* Efficacious against fever; febrifuge; antipyretic. **II.** *n.* An antifebrile agent.—**an-ti-feb′rine** (-feb′rin or -fē′brin), *n.* Acetanilide.
an-ti-fed-er-al (an-ti-fed′ėr-al), *a.* [See *anti-*.] Opposed to federalism, or to a federal constitution or party: esp. applied [*caps.*, as *Anti-Federal*] to a political party in early U. S. history.—**an-ti-fed′er-al-ism,** *n.* Opposition to federalism; the principles of the Anti-Federal party in U. S. history.—**an-ti-fed′er-al-ist,** *n.* One opposed to federalism; esp. [*caps.*, as *Anti-Federalist*], a member or supporter of the Anti-Federal party in U. S. history.
an-ti-fer-ment (an-ti-fėr′ment), *n.* [See *anti-*.] Any substance or agent that prevents or counteracts fermentation.
an-ti-fric-tion (an-ti-frik′shon). [See *anti-*.] **I.** *a.* Preventing or reducing friction. **II.** *n.* Something that prevents or reduces friction; a lubricant.
an-ti-he-lix (an-ti-hē′liks), *n.*; pl. *-helices* (-hel′i-sēz). [See *anti-*.] In *anat.*, the inner curved ridge of the pinna of the ear. Cf. *helix*.
an-ti-hyp-not-ic (an″ti-hip-not′ik). [See *anti-*.] In *med.*: **I.** *a.* Preventive of sleep. **II.** *n.* An antihypnotic agent.
an-ti=im-pe-ri-al-ism (an″ti-im-pē′ri-al-izm), *n.* [See *anti-*.] Opposition to imperialism or the spirit and methods of empire, esp. as in the acquisition and government of dependencies: with reference to the United States, used chiefly since the Spanish-American War of 1898.—**an″ti=im-pe′ri-al-ist,** *n.* An opponent of imperialism.—**an″ti=im-pe″ri-al-is′tic,** *a.*
an-ti-le-gom-e-na (an″ti-le-gom′e-nä), *n. pl.* [NL., < Gr. ἀντιλεγόμενα, neut. pl. ppr. pass. of ἀντιλέγειν, speak against: see *antilogy*.] Certain books of the New Testament (Hebrews, James, Jude, 2 Peter, 2 and 3 John, and Revelation) whose inspiration was not universally acknowledged in the early church.
an-ti-lith-ic (an-ti-lith′ik). [Gr. ἀντί, against, + λίθος, stone.] In *med.*: **I.** *a.* Preventive of or efficacious against urinary calculus. **II.** *n.* An antilithic agent.
an-ti-log-a-rithm (an-ti-log′a-rithm or -riᴛʜm), *n.* [See *anti-*.] In *math.*, the number corresponding to a logarithm.
an-til-o-gy (an-til′ō-ji), *n.*; pl. *-gies* (-jiz). [Gr. ἀντιλογία, < ἀντιλέγειν, speak against, < ἀντί, against, + λέγειν, speak.] A contradiction in terms or ideas.
an-ti-ma-cas-sar (an″ti-ma-kas′är), *n.* [See *anti-* and *Macassar oil*.] A tidy to protect a chair, sofa, etc., as from oil from the hair.
an-ti-masque (an′ti-måsk), *n.* [See *anti-*.] A comic or grotesque interlude between the acts of a masque.
an-ti-mere (an′ti-mēr), *n.* [Gr. ἀντί, opposite to, + μέρος, part.] In *zoöl.*, a segment or division of the body in the direction of one of the secondary or transverse axes, as either half of a bilaterally symmetrical animal, or one of the radiating parts of a radially symmetrical animal.—**an-ti-mer′ic** (-mer′ik), *a.* Pertaining to or of the nature of an antimere; characterized by antimeres.—**an-tim′er-ism** (-tim′e-rizm), *n.* The quality of being antimeric.
an-ti-mo-nar-chic, an-ti-mo-nar-chi-cal (an″ti-mō-när′kik, -ki-kal), *a.* [See *anti-*.] Opposed to monarchy or monarchical principles.
an-ti-mo-ni-al (an-ti-mō′ni-al), *a.* [See *antimony*.] Pertaining to or containing antimony.—**an-ti-mo′ni-ate** (-āt), *n.* In *chem.*, a salt of antimonic acid.—**an-ti-mon′ic** (-mon′ik), *a.* Of or containing antimony (see *antimonious*): as, *antimonic* acid.—**an-ti-mo′ni-ous,** *a.* Containing antimony (in larger proportion than a corresponding antimonic compound): as, *antimonious* acid.
an-ti-mon-soon (an″ti-mon-sön′), *n.* [See *anti-*.] In *meteor.*, a current of air moving in a direction opposite to that of a given monsoon, and lying above it.
an-ti-mo-ny (an′ti-mō-ni), *n.* [ML. *antimonium*; origin unknown.] Chem. sym., Sb (see *stibium*); at. wt., 120.2; sp. gr., 6.7. A brittle, lustrous, white metallic element occurring free in nature or combined: used chiefly in alloys and (in the form of compounds) in medicine.—**an′ti-mo-ny=glance″,** *n.* Stibnite.—**an′ti-mo-nyl** (-nil), *n.* [See *-yl*.] In *chem.*, a univalent group composed of one atom of antimony and one of oxygen, and regarded as forming salts when combined with acid radicals.
an-ti-node (an′ti-nōd), *n.* [See *anti-*.] In *physics*, a point, line, or plane in a vibrating body at which the amplitude of vibration is greatest, situated half-way between two adjacent nodes.
an-ti-no-mi-an (an-ti-nō′mi-an). [ML. *antinomi*, antinomians, < Gr. ἀντί, against, + νόμος, law.] **I.** *a.* Denying the obligatoriness of the moral law; pertaining to antinomians. **II.** *n.* One who maintains that Christians are freed from the moral law by the dispensation of grace set forth in the gospel: an opinion held under several forms at various times.—**an-ti-no′mi-an-ism,** *n.*
an-tin-o-my (an-tin′ō-mi), *n.*; pl. *-mies* (-miz). [L. *antinomia*, < Gr. ἀντινομία, < ἀντί, against, + νόμος, law.] Opposition between laws or principles; any law or principle opposed to another; in the philosophy of Kant, a contradiction in thought, unavoidable by the reason alone.
an-ti-o-pel-mous (an″ti-ō-pel′mus), *a.* [Gr. ἀντίος, set against, opposite, + πέλμα, sole of the foot.] In *ornith.*, having one of the two deep flexor tendons of the toes going to the third digit only, and the other dividing and going to the first, second, and fourth digits.
an-ti-pa-thet-ic (an″ti-pa-thet′ik), *a.* Having antipathy; naturally opposed; characterized by or rousing antipathy; repugnant: with *to*.—**an″ti-pa-thet′i-cal-ly,** *adv.*
an-ti-path-ic (an-ti-path′ik), *a.* Antipathetic; in *med.*, producing contrary symptoms; allopathic.
an-tip-a-thy (an-tip′a-thi), *n.*; pl. *-thies* (-thiz). [L. *antipathia*, < Gr. ἀντιπάθεια, < ἀντιπαθής, having opposite feelings, < ἀντί, against, + παθεῖν, suffer.] Instinctive opposition in feeling; natural or settled dislike; repugnance; aversion; also, an object of aversion; also, contrariety in nature†; also, a contrary†.
an-ti-pe-ri-od-ic (an″ti-pē-ri-od′ik). [See *anti-*.] In *med.*: **I.** *a.* Efficacious against periodic diseases, as intermittent fever. **II.** *n.* An antiperiodic agent.
an-ti-per-i-stal-sis (an″ti-per-i-stal′sis), *n.* [See *anti-*.] In *physiol.*, inverted peristaltic action of the intestines, by which their contents are carried upward.—**an″ti-per-i-stal′tic,** *a.*
an-ti-phlo-gis-tic (an″ti-flō-jis′tik). [See *anti-*.] **I.** *a.* Opposed to the old chemical theory of phlogiston; in *med.*, checking inflammation or fever. **II.** *n.* In *med.*, an antiphlogistic remedy.
an-ti-phon (an′ti-fon), *n.* [ML. *antiphona*, < Gr. ἀντίφωνος, sounding in answer, < ἀντί, against, + φωνή, sound.] *Eccles.*, a psalm, hymn, or prayer sung in alternate parts; also, an anthem; also, a verse sung in response; also, a verse or a series of verses sung as a prelude or conclusion to some part of the service.—**an-tiph′o-nal** (-tif′ō-nal). **I.** *a.* Pertaining to antiphons or antiphony; responsive. **II.** *n.* An antiphonary.—**an-tiph′o-nal-ly,** *adv.*—**an-tiph′o-na-ry** (-nā-ri). [ML. *antiphonarium*.] **I.** *n.*; pl. *-ries* (-riz). A book of antiphons. **II.** *a.* Antiphonal.—**an-ti-phon′ic** (-fon′ik), *a.* Antiphonal.—**an-tiph′o-ny,** *n.*; pl. *-nies* (-niz). Alternate or responsive singing by a choir in two divisions; also, a psalm or anthem so sung; an antiphon; also, a responsive musical utterance.
an-tiph-ra-sis (an-tif′ra-sis), *n.* [L., < Gr. ἀντίφρασις, < ἀντιφράζειν, express by the opposite, < ἀντί, against, + φράζειν, tell.] In *rhet.*, the use of words in a sense opposite to the proper meaning.—**an-ti-phras′tic** (-ti-fras′tik), *a.*
an-ti-pla-teau (an″ti-pla-tō′), *n.* [See *anti-*.] A sunken area in the floor of the ocean.
an-tip-o-dal (an-tip′ō-dal), *a.* [See *antipodes*.] Belonging to the antipodes; on the opposite side of the globe; in general, diametrically opposite.—**an′ti-pode** (-ti-pōd), *n.* One of the antipodes; a direct opposite.—**an-tip-o-de′an** (-dē′an). **I.** *a.* Of or pertaining to the antipodes. **II.** *n.* One of the antipodes.

an-tip-o-des (an-tip′ǫ-dēz), *n. pl.* [L., < Gr. ἀντίποδες, pl. of ἀντίπους, with feet opposite, < ἀντί, against, + πούς, foot.] Persons living at diametrically opposite points on the globe; persons who live on the side of the globe opposite to others; also, places diametrically opposite to each other on the globe; the place thus opposite to a given place; hence, direct opposites or contraries; the direct opposite of anything.—**an-tip′o-dism,** *n.* Antipodal state.

an-ti-pole (an′ti-pōl), *n.* [See *anti-*.] The opposite pole.

an-ti-pope (an′ti-pōp), *n.* [See *anti-*.] One who is elected pope in opposition to another held to be canonically chosen.

an-ti-py-ic (an-ti-pī′ik). [Gr. ἀντί, against, + πύον, pus.] In *med.*: **I.** *a.* Preventing or checking suppuration. **II.** *n.* An antipyic agent.

an-ti-py-ret-ic (an″ti-pī-ret′ik). [Gr. ἀντί, against, + πυρετός, fever.] In *med.*: **I.** *a.* Checking or preventing fever. **II.** *n.* An antipyretic agent.

an-ti-py-rine, an-ti-py-rin (an-ti-pī′rin), *n.* [See *antipyretic*.] A colorless crystalline substance, $C_{11}H_{12}N_2O$, used to reduce fever or relieve pain.

an-ti-qua-ri-an (an-ti-kwā′ri-ạn). [See *antiquary*.] **I.** *a.* Pertaining to the study of antiquities or antique relics, esp. as interesting curiosities rather than as a source of archæological knowledge. **II.** *n.* An antiquary.—**an-ti-qua′ri-an-ism,** *n.* Antiquarian pursuits or tastes.

an-ti-qua-ry (an′ti-kwạ-ri). [L. *antiquarius*, < *antiquus*: see *antique*.] **I.** *a.* Pertaining to antiquity. **II.** *n.*; pl. *-ries* (-riz). A student or collector of antiquities or antique relics.

an-ti-quate (an′ti-kwāt), *v. t.*; *-quated, -quating.* [L. *antiquatus*, pp. of *antiquare*, < *antiquus*: see *antique*.] To make antique or out of date.—**an′ti-quat-ed,** *p. a.* Old-fashioned; out of date; superannuated.—**an′ti-quat-ed-ness,** *n.*—**an-ti-qua′tion** (-kwā′shọn), *n.* [LL. *antiquatio(n-)*.] The act of rendering antiquated; antiquated state.

an-tique (an-tēk′). [F. *antique*, < L. *antiquus*, < *ante*, before.] **I.** *a.* Belonging to or dating from former or bygone times; ancient (often with reference to Greece or Rome); characteristic of former times; old-time; old-fashioned; antiquated. **II.** *n.* The antique (usually Greek or Roman) style, esp. in art; also, an antique relic, esp. an object of art; also, a style of type (see *type*).—**an-tique′ly,** *adv.*—**an-tique′ness,** *n.*—**an-ti′qui-ty** (-tik′wi-ti), *n.*; pl. *-ties* (-tiz). The quality of being ancient; ancient character; great age; also, ancient times; also, the ancients; also, something belonging to or remaining from ancient times (usually in *pl.*).

an-ti-rat-tler (an-ti-rat′lėr), *n.* [See *anti-*.] Any of various mechanical devices designed to prevent rattling, as of the parts of a carriage.

an-ti-rent (an-ti-rent′), *a.* [See *anti-*.] Opposed to the payment of rent; [also *cap.*] noting or pertaining to any of certain parties and movements advocating non-payment of rent, as a political party in the State of New York from 1839 to 1847 which resisted the collection of rent on certain manorial estates.—**an-ti-rent′er,** *n.*—**an-ti-rent′ism,** *n.*

an-ti-scor-bu-tic (an″ti-skôr-bū′tik). [See *anti-* and *scorbutic*.] In *med.*: **I.** *a.* Efficacious against scurvy. **II.** *n.* An antiscorbutic agent.

an-ti=Sem-ite (an″ti-sem′īt), *n.* [See *anti-*.] One hostile to the Jews (Semites).—**an″ti=Se-mit′ic** (-sẹ-mit′ik), *a.*—**an″ti=Sem′it-ism** (-sem′i-tizm), *n.*

an-ti-sep-sis (an-ti-sep′sis), *n.* [NL.: see *anti-* and *sepsis*.] Exclusion or destruction of the micro-organisms that produce sepsis or septic disease.—**an-ti-sep′tic. I.** *a.* Pertaining to or effecting antisepsis. **II.** *n.* An antiseptic agent, as carbolic acid.—**an-ti-sep′ti-cal-ly,** *adv.*—**an-ti-sep′ti-cism** (-ti-sizm), *n.* The principle or practice of using antiseptic measures or remedies, as in surgery.—**an-ti-sep′ti-cist,** *n.*—**an″ti-sep-ti′ci-ty** (-tis′i-ti), *n.* Antiseptic quality or character.—**an-ti-sep′ti-cize** (-sīz), *v. t.*; *-cized, -cizing.* To treat with antiseptics.

an-ti-slav-er-y (an-ti-slā′vėr-i), *a.* [See *anti-*.] Opposed to slavery.

an-ti-so-cial (an-ti-sō′shạl), *a.* [See *anti-*.] Opposed or averse to social intercourse or relations; also, opposed to social order, or to the principles on which society is constituted.—**an-ti-so′cial-ist,** *n.* One opposed to socialism.—**an″ti-so-cial-is′tic,** *a.*

an-ti-spas-mod-ic (an″ti-spaz-mod′ik). [See *anti-*.] In *med.*: **I.** *a.* Checking spasms. **II.** *n.* An antispasmodic agent.

an-tis-tro-phe (an-tis′trǫ-fẹ), *n.* [L., < Gr. ἀντιστροφή, < ἀντιστρέφειν, turn about, < ἀντί, against, + στρέφειν, turn.] The part of an ancient Greek choral ode, answering to a previous strophe, sung by the chorus when returning from left to right; also, the second of two metrically corresponding systems in a lyric poem (cf. *strophe* and *epode*).—**an-ti-stroph′ic** (-ti-strof′ik), *a.*

an-ti-the-ism (an-ti-thē′izm), *n.* [See *anti-*.] The doctrine opposed to theism, or denying the existence of a God.—**an-ti-the′ist,** *n.*

an-tith-e-sis (an-tith′e-sis), *n.*; pl. *-eses* (-e-sēz). [LL., < Gr. ἀντίθεσις, < ἀντιτιθέναι, set against, < ἀντί, against, + τιθέναι, set.] In *rhet.*, opposition or contrast of ideas by the setting of one clause or other member of a sentence against another (cf. Prov. x. 1); a clause or member thus set in opposition; hence, in general, opposition or contrast between things; something opposed, or forming a contrast.—**an-ti-thet′ic, an-ti-thet′i-cal** (-ti-thet′ik, -i-kạl), *a.* [Gr. ἀντιθετικός.] Of the nature of or involving antithesis; directly opposed; contrasted.—**an-ti-thet′i-cal-ly,** *adv.*

an-ti-tox-ic (an-ti-tok′sik), *a.* [See *anti-*.] Counteracting toxic influences; pertaining to or serving as an antitoxin.—**an-ti-tox′in** (-tok′sin), *n.* A substance formed in the body, capable of counteracting a specific toxin or infective agency; the antibody formed in immunization with a given toxin: used in treating certain infectious diseases or in producing immunity against them.

an-ti=trade (an′ti-trād), *n.* [See *anti-*.] Any of the upper tropical winds moving counter to and above the trade-winds, but descending to the surface beyond the trade-wind limits.

an-tit-ra-gus (an-tit′rạ-gus), *n.*; pl. *-gi* (-jī). [NL., < Gr. ἀντίτραγος.] In *anat.*, a process of the external ear, opposite to the tragus and behind the ear-passage.

an-ti-trust (an-ti-trust′), *a.* [See *anti-*.] Opposed to trusts, or large combinations of capital.

an-ti-type (an′ti-tīp), *n.* [Gr. ἀντίτυπος, corresponding as a stamp to the die, < ἀντί, against, + τύπτειν, strike.] Something corresponding to or represented by a type, as a New Testament event prefigured in the Old Testament.—**an′ti-ty-pal** (-tī-pạl), **an-ti-typ′ic, an-ti-typ′i-cal** (-tip′ik, -i-kạl), *a.*

an-ti-ve-nene, an-ti-ven-in (an″ti-ve-nēn′, an-ti-ven′in), *n.* [Gr. ἀντί, against, + L. *venenum*, poison.] An antitoxin produced in the blood by repeated injections of venom, as of snakes; also, the antitoxic serum obtained from such blood.

an-ti-viv-i-sec-tion-ist (an″ti-viv-i-sek′shọn-ist), *n.* [See *anti-*.] One who is opposed to vivisection.

an-ti-zym-ic (an-ti-zim′ik). [See *anti-*.] **I.** *a.* Preventive of fermentation. **II.** *n.* An antizymic agent.—**an″ti-zy-mot′ic** (-zī-mot′ik). **I.** *a.* Preventive of fermentation, or of zymotic disease. **II.** *n.* An antizymotic agent.

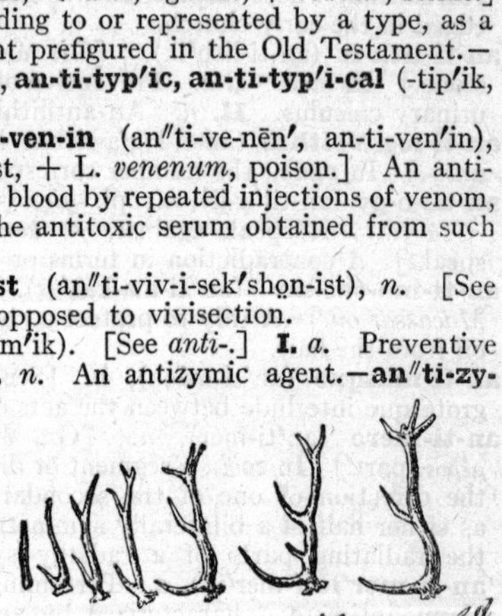

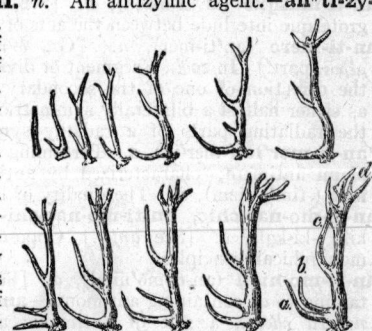

Stag's Antler in successive years.
a, brow-antler; *b*, bay-antler; *c*, royal antler; *d*, surroyal, or crown-antler.

ant-ler (ant′lėr), *n.* [OF. *antoillier* (F. *andouiller*), < L. *ante*, before, + *oculus*, eye.] The lowest branch or any branch of a deer's horn; also, one of the solid deciduous horns, usually branched, of an animal of the deer family.—**ant′lered,** *a.* Having antlers; also, decorated with antlers.

ant-li-a (ant′li-ạ̈), *n.*; pl. *antliæ* (-ē). [L., a pump, < Gr. ἀντλία, ship's hold, bilge-water.] In *entom.*, the spiral tubular proboscis of lepidopterous insects, with which they suck up plant-juices.—**ant′li-ate** (-āt), *a.* Furnished with an antlia.

ant=li-on (ȧnt′lī″ọn), *n.* A larval neuropterous insect of the genus *Myrmeleon*, which digs a pitfall in sand, where it lies in wait for ants, etc.; also, the adult insect.

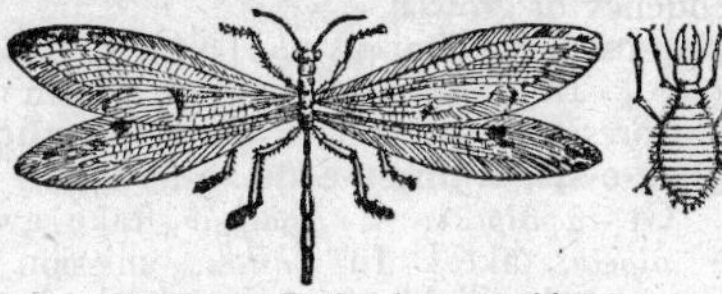

Ant-lion.—Perfect insect and larva.

an-ton-o-ma-sia (an″ton-ọ̄-mā′ziạ), *n.* [L., < Gr. ἀντονομασία, < ἀντονομάζειν, call instead, < ἀντί, instead of, + ὀνομάζειν, call, < ὄνομα, name.] In *rhet.*, the use of some epithet or appellative (as *his lordship*) instead of a person's name, or the use of a proper name out of its original application (as *a Shylock*).—**an″ton-o-mas′tic** (-mas′tik), *a.*

an-to-nym (an′tọ̄-nim), *n.* [Gr. ἀντί, against, + ὄνυμα, name.] A word that is an opposite in meaning of a particular word: as, 'sharp,' 'keen,' and 'acute' are *antonyms* of 'dull.' Opposed to *synonym.*

an-tre (an′tėr), *n.* [F., < L. *antrum*, < Gr. ἄντρον.] A cavern; a cave: as, "*antres* vast and deserts idle" (Shakspere's "Othello," i. 3. 140). [Archaic.]

an-trorse (an-trôrs′), *a.* [NL. *antrorsus*, < *antro-* (= E. *antero-*) + L. *versus*, toward: cf. *extrorse, introrse.*] Turned or directed forward or upward.—**an-trorse′ly,** *adv.*

Ant-thrush (family *Formicariidæ*).

an-trum (an′trum), *n.*; pl. *antra* (-trạ). [L.: see *antre.*] In *anat.*, a cavity.

an-trus-ti-on (an-trus′ti-ọn), *n.* [F., < ML. *antrustio(n-)*; from Teut.] Any of a body of men forming the body-guard or military household of Frankish kings.—**an-trus′ti-on-ship,** *n.*

ant=thrush (ȧnt′thrush), *n.* Any of the South American passerine birds (ant-birds) constituting the family *Formicariidæ*; also, any bird of the old-world family *Pittidæ*; a pitta.

a-nu-ran (a-nū′rạn), *n.* [NL. *Anura*, pl., < Gr. ἀν- priv. + οὐρά, tail.] One of the *Anura*, an order of amphibians comprising the batrachians proper (the frogs and toads), tailless when adult.—**a-nu′rous,** *a.* Tailless, as an anuran.

a-nus (ā′nus), *n.* [L.] The orifice at the end of the alimentary canal, through which the refuse of digestion is voided.

an-vil (an′vil), *n.* [AS. *anfilte.*] An iron block with a smooth face, usually of steel, on which metals are hammered and shaped; in *anat.*, a small bone of the ear, the incus.—**an′vil,** *v. t.*; *-viled* or *-villed, -viling* or *-villing.* To form or shape on or as on an anvil.

anx-i-e-ty (ang-zī′ẹ-ti), *n.*; pl. *-ties* (-tiz). [L. *anxietas.*] Anxious state or feeling; concern; solicitude; solicitous desire.

anx-ious (angk′shus), *a.* [L. *anxius*, < *angere*, constrict, distress.] Full of or attended with painful concern or solicitude, as for an uncertain future; painfully apprehensive; also, solicitously desirous (with an infinitive or *for*).—**anx′ious-ly,** *adv.*—**anx′ious-ness,** *n.*

an-y (en′i). [AS. *ǣnig*, < *ān*, one.] **I.** *a.* One, a or an, or (as *pl.*) some, whatever or whichever it may be; quantitatively, some, whether little or much, few or many (as, *any* money; *any* eggs): in affirmative sentences often practically equivalent to *every* or *all* (as, *any* child knows that). **II.** *pron.* Any person or persons; any individual, instance, or number (of several or more possible); also, either (of two: now prov. Eng.); also, any quantity or part.—**an′y,** *adv.* In any degree; to any extent; at all.—**an′y-bod″y,** *n.*; pl. *-ies* (-iz). Any person; any one (sometimes opposed in slight contempt to *somebody*); also, any one of importance (as, everybody who is *anybody* was present).—**an′y-how,** *adv.* In any way whatever; howsoever; also, with conjunctive force, in any case; at all events.—**an′y one.** Any person; anybody: sometimes as one word, *anyone.*—**an′y-thing. I.** *n.* Any thing, whatever it may be; a thing of any kind; something, no matter what. **II.** *adv.* To any extent; at all. [Archaic or prov. Eng.]—**an′y-way,** *adv.* In any way; anyhow; to any extent; also, conjunctively, in any case; at all events. Also (now colloq.) **an′y-ways.**—**an′y-when,** *adv.* At any time. [Chiefly prov. Eng.]—**an′y-where,** *adv.* In, at, or to any place.—**an′y-whith″er,** *adv.* To any place; in any direction. [Archaic.]—**an′y-wise,** *adv.* In any way, respect, or degree; at all.

An-zac (an′zak), *n.* [From the initials of the corps.] A member of the Australian and New Zealand Army Corps in Egypt, Gallipoli, and elsewhere, in the World War (during 1915 and later); a soldier from Australia or New Zealand.

A-o-ni-an (ạ-ō′ni-ạn), *a.* Of or pertaining to Aonia, a region of Bœotia in ancient Greece containing Mount Helicon and associated esp. with the Muses: as, "th' *Aonian* maids" (Pope's "Messiah," 4).

a-o-rist (ā′ọ̄-rist). [Gr. ἀόριστος, indefinite, < ἀ- priv. + ὁριστός, verbal adj. of ὁρίζειν, bound: see *horizon.*] In *gram.*: **I.** *n.* A tense of the Greek verb expressing action (in the indicative, past action) without further limitation or implication; a corresponding tense in some other language, as the Sanskrit. **II.** *a.* Of or in the aorist.—**a-o-ris′tic,** *a.* Indefinite; indeterminate; in *gram.*, pertaining to the aorist.

a-or-ta (ạ-ôr′tạ), *n.*; pl. *-tæ* (-tē). [NL., < Gr. ἀορτή, < ἀείρειν, raise.] In *anat.*, the main trunk of the arterial system, issuing from the left ventricle of the heart and conveying arterialized blood to all parts of the body except the lungs.—**a-or′tic,** *a.*—**a-or-ti-tis** (ā-ôr-tī′tis), *n.* [NL.] In *pathol.*, inflammation of the aorta.

Aoudad.

a-ou-dad (ä′ọ̄-dad), *n.* [Moorish name.] The wild sheep of northern Africa, *Ovis* (or *Ammotragus*) *tragelaphus.*

a-pace (ạ-pās′), *adv.* At a quick pace; rapidly; fast.

A-pach-e (ạ-pach′ẹ̄), *n.* One of a North American Indian people of the southern Athapascan stock; [*cap.* or *l. c.*] in French use (pron. ȧ-pȧsh), a predatory ruffian, esp. one of an organized band infesting city streets.

ap-a-go-ge (ap-ạ-gō′jẹ̄), *n.* [NL., < Gr. ἀπαγωγή, < ἀπάγειν, lead off, < ἀπό, from, + ἄγειν, lead.] In *logic*, demonstration of a proposition by showing the impossibility or absurdity of the contrary.—**ap-a-gog′ic, ap-a-gog′i-cal** (-goj′ik, -i-kạl), *a.*

ap-a-nage (ap′ạ-nāj), *n.* See *appanage.*

a-pa-re-jo (ä-pạ-rā′hō), *n.*; pl. *-jos* (-hōz, Sp. -hōs). [Sp.] A pack-saddle. [Spanish-American.]

a-part (ạ-pärt′), *adv.* [OF. *a part*, < L. *ad*, to, and *pars* (*part-*), part, side.] To one side; aside; off or away from others; separately or independently; separate or distinct (*from*); also, away from each other; also, to or in pieces; asunder; in separate parts.

a-part-ment (ạ-pärt′mẹnt), *n.* [F. *appartement*, < It. *appartamento*, ult. < L. *ad* + *pars*: see *apart.*] A room or a suite of rooms in a building; esp., a suite of rooms arranged for a single tenant or family in a building (*apartment-house*) divided into such suites.

a-part-ness (ạ-pärt′nes), *n.* The state of being apart.

ap-a-thet-ic (ap-ạ-thet′ik), *a.* Characterized by apathy; devoid of emotion; indifferent.—**ap-a-thet′i-cal-ly,** *adv.*

ap-a-thy (ap′ạ-thi), *n.*; pl. *-thies* (-thiz). [L. *apathia*, < Gr. ἀπάθεια, < ἀπαθής, without feeling, < ἀ- priv. + παθεῖν, suffer.] Absence of feeling, passion, or emotion;

insensibility to what ordinarily rouses feeling or interest; dull indifference.

ap-a-tite (ap′ạ-tīt), *n.* [Gr. ἀπάτη, deceit.] A native calcium phosphate containing fluorine or chlorine, occurring both crystallized and massive, and varying in color from white to green, blue, violet, or yellow or red: used in making fertilizers.

ape (āp), *n.* [AS. *apa*, akin to G. *affe*.] A monkey; esp., a tailless monkey or a monkey with a very short tail (as, the Barbary *ape*, a tailless monkey, *Inuus ecaudatus* or *Macacus inuus*, of northern Africa and the Rock of Gibraltar, closely related to the baboons and frequently trained by showmen); specif., a man-like or anthropoid monkey; a simian; one of the family *Simiidæ* ('anthropoid apes'), comprising the gorilla, chimpanzee, orang-utan, and gibbon, without cheek-pouches or developed tail; fig., an imitator or mimic (usually in contempt); also, a fool†.—**ape,** *v. t.*; *aped, aping.* To imitate like an ape; mimic unreasoningly or servilely.

Barbary Ape.

a-peak (ạ-pēk′), *adv.* [Cf. F. *à pic*, vertically.] *Naut.*, in a vertical position or direction, or nearly so.

a-pep-sia (a-pep′siạ), *n.* [NL., < Gr. ἀπεψία, < ἀ- priv. + πέπτειν, cook, digest.] Defective digestion; dyspepsia.

ap-er-çu (ap-ėr-sü′, F. à-per-sü), *n.*; pl. *-çus* (-süz′, F. -sü). [F., prop. pp. of *apercevoir*, perceive.] A glimpse; a hasty glance; a rapid survey; an outline or summary.

a-pe-ri-ent (ạ-pē′ri-ęnt). [L. *aperiens* (*-ent-*), ppr. of *aperire*, open, < *a*, from, + *-perire*, occurring also in *operire*, cover: see *overt*.] **I.** *a.* Opening the bowels; gently purgative; laxative. **II.** *n.* An aperient medicine or article of diet.

a-pe-ri-od-ic (a-pē-ri-od′ik), *a.* [See *a-*¹.] Not periodic, as a fever; of irregular occurrence; in *physics*, noting, pertaining to, or having an index needle or other moving part which comes to a stop with little or no recoil or oscillation.

a-pé-ri-tif (à-pā-rē-tēf), *n.* [F., prop. adj., orig. 'opening the passages of the body,' < L. *aperire*, open: see *aperient*.] A kind or a portion of alcoholic liquor (cordial, bitters, etc.) taken before a meal to stimulate the appetite.

a-per-i-tive (ạ-per′i-tiv), *a.* and *n.* Same as *aperient*.

a-pert (ạ-pėrt′), *a.* [OF. *apert*, < L. *apertus*, pp. of *aperire*, open: cf. *pert*.] Open, manifest, or unconcealed (obs. or archaic); also, bold†, forward†, or pert†.

ap-er-ture (ap′ėr-tụr), *n.* [L. *apertura*, < *aperire* (pp. *apertus*), open: see *aperient*.] An opening; an open space; a hole, gap, or orifice; in telescopes, etc., the diameter of the exposed part of the object-glass.—**ap′er-tured,** *a.*

ap-er-y (ā′pėr-i), *n.*; pl. *aperies* (-iz). Apish behavior or mimicry; an apish trick.

a-pet-a-lous (a-pet′ạ-lus), *a.* [See *a-*¹.] In *bot.*, having no petals.

a-pex (ā′peks), *n.*; pl. *apexes* or *apices* (ap′i-sēz). [L.] The tip, point, or vertex of anything; the summit.

a-phær-e-sis (a-fer′e-sis), etc. See *apheresis*, etc.

aph-a-nite (af′ạ-nīt), *n.* [Gr. ἀφανής, not apparent, obscure, < ἀ- priv. + φαίνεσθαι, appear.] A dark-colored, heavy variety of diorite, of such compact texture that the constituent minerals cannot be detected with the naked eye; also, any of various other rocks of similar texture.—**aph-a-nit′ic** (-nit′ik), *a.*

a-pha-sia (a-fā′ziạ), *n.* [NL., < Gr. ἀφασία, < ἀ- priv. + φάναι, say.] In *pathol.*, impairment or loss of the faculty of using or understanding spoken or written language, as from cerebral lesion.—**a-pha′si-ac** (-zi-ak), *n.* One affected with aphasia.—**a-pha′sic** (-zik). **I.** *a.* Pertaining to or affected with aphasia. **II.** *n.* An aphasiac.

a-phe-li-on (a-fē′li-ọn), *n.*; pl. *-lia* (-li-ạ). [NL., < Gr. ἀπό, from, + ἥλιος, sun.] In *astron.*, the point of a planet's or comet's orbit most distant from the sun: opposed to *perihelion*.

a-phe-li-o-trop-ic (a-fē″li-ọ-trop′ik), *a.* [Gr. ἀπό, from, + ἥλιος, sun, + E. *-tropic*.] In *bot.*, tending away from the light. Cf. *heliotropic*.—**a-phe″li-o-trop′i-cal-ly,** *adv.*—**a-phe-li-ot′ro-pism** (-ot′rọ-pizm), *n.* In *bot.*, apheliotropic tendency or growth.

a-phe-mi-a (a-fē′mi-ạ), *n.* [NL., < Gr. ἀ- priv. + φήμη, voice.] In *pathol.*, aphasia, esp. a form marked by inability to express ideas in spoken words.—**a-phem-ic** (a-fem′ik), *a.*

a-pher-e-sis, a-phær-e-sis (a-fer′e-sis), *n.* [L. *aphæresis*, < Gr. ἀφαίρεσις < ἀφαιρεῖν, take away, < ἀπό, from, + αἱρεῖν, take.] In *philol.*, omission of a letter or an unaccented syllable from the beginning of a word, as in *squire* for *esquire*.—**aph-e-ret-ic, aph-æ-ret-ic** (af-e-ret′ik), *a.*

aph-e-sis (af′e-sis), *n.* [NL., < Gr. ἄφεσις, a letting go, < ἀφιέναι, let go, < ἀπό, from, + ἱέναι, send.] In *philol.*, apheresis in which an unaccented initial vowel is gradually and unintentionally lost.—**a-phet-ic** (a-fet′ik), *a.* Pertaining or due to aphesis.—**aph′e-tize,** *v. t.*; *-tized, -tizing.* To shorten by aphesis.

aph-id (af′id), *n.* [NL. *aphis* (pl. *aphides*); origin uncertain.] Any of the plant-sucking insects of the genus *Aphis* or family *Aphididæ*; a plant-louse.—**a-phid-i-an** (a-fid′i-ạn), *a.* and *n.*

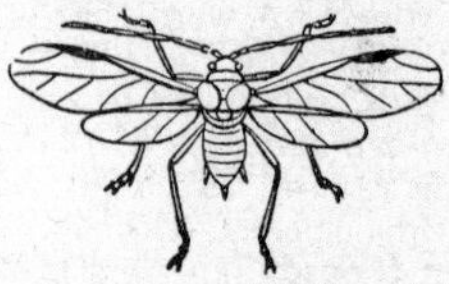

Apple-tree Aphid (*Aphis mali*). (Enlarged.)

a-phis (ā′fis), *n.*; pl. *aphides* (af′i-dēz). [NL.: see *aphid*.] An aphid; a plant-louse.—**a′phis=li′on,** *n.* Any of various insect larvæ, as those of the lacewings, that prey on plant-lice; also, the adult insect.—**a′phis=sug′ar,** *n.* Honeydew secreted by plant-lice.

aph-lo-gis-tic (af-lọ-jis′tik), *a.* [Gr. ἀφλόγιστος, < ἀ- priv. + φλογιστός, inflammable.] Flameless.—**aphlogistic lamp,** a lamp in which the illumination is produced by a coil of platinum wire kept at a red heat by the slow (flameless) combustion of alcohol vapor arising from a wick.

a-pho-ni-a (a-fō′ni-ạ), *n.* [NL., < Gr. ἀφωνία, < ἀ- priv. + φωνή, voice.] In *pathol.*, loss of voice, due to a morbid condition of the vocal organs.—**a-phon-ic** (a-fon′ik), *a.*

aph-o-rism (af′ọ-rizm), *n.* [F. *aphorisme*, < Gr. ἀφορισμός, < ἀφορίζειν, define, < ἀπό, from, + ὁρίζειν, bound: see *horizon*.] A concise statement of a principle; also, a detached sentence briefly setting forth a doctrine, rule, or general truth; often, a maxim.—**aph-o-ris′mic, aph″o-ris-mat′ic** (-riz′mik, -mat′ik), *a.*—**aph′o-rist,** *n.* A maker of aphorisms.—**aph-o-ris′tic,** *a.* Of, like, or containing aphorisms.—**aph-o-ris′ti-cal-ly,** *adv.*—**aph′o-rize,** *v. i.*; *-rized, -rizing.* To make or utter aphorisms.

aph-ro-dis-i-ac (af-rọ-diz′i-ak). [Gr. ἀφροδισιακός, < Ἀφροδίτη, Aphrodite.] **I.** *a.* Venereal; exciting venereal desire. **II.** *n.* An aphrodisiac drug or food.

Aphrodite of Cnidus.
(Copy in the Vatican of the statue by Praxiteles.)

Aph-ro-di-te (af-rọ-dī′tē), *n.* [Gr. Ἀφροδίτη.] The Greek goddess of love and beauty, identified by the Romans with Venus.

aph-tha (af′thạ), *n.*; pl. *-thæ* (-thē). [L. *aphthæ*, pl., < Gr. ἄφθαι, pl. of ἄφθα, < ἅπτειν, set on fire.] In *pathol.*, one of the small ulcerating vesicles, due to a parasitic fungus, occurring in the mouth and the intestinal canal in the disease thrush; also, a similar vesicle, esp. in the mouth, in some other disease; also, *pl.* or *sing.*, thrush, or some other aphthous disease.—**aph′thoid,** *a.* Resembling aphthæ.

aph-thong (af′thông), *n.* [Gr. ἄφθογγος, silent, < ἀ- priv. + φθόγγος, sound.] A silent letter or combination of letters in a word.—**aph-thon′gal** (-thông′gạl), *a.*

aph-thous (af′thus), *a.* Of, like, or characterized by aphthæ.

a-phyl-lous (a-fil′us), *a.* [Gr. ἄφυλλος, < ἀ- priv. + φύλλον, leaf.] In *bot.*, naturally leafless.—**a-phyl′ly,** *n.*

a-pi-a-ceous (ā-pi-ā'shius), *a.* [L. *apium*, parsley.] Belonging to the *Apiaceæ* (or *Umbelliferæ*), or parsley family of plants. See *umbelliferous.*
a-pi-an (ā'pi-ạn), *a.* [L. *apianus*, < *apis*, bee.] Of or pertaining to bees.
a-pi-a-ri-an (ā-pi-ā'ri-ạn), *a.* [See *apiary.*] Pertaining to beehives or bee-keeping.
a-pi-a-rist (ā'pi-ạ-rist), *n.* One who keeps an apiary; a bee-keeper.
a-pi-a-ry (ā'pi-ā-ri), *n.*; pl. *-ries* (-riz). [L. *apiarium*, < *apis*, bee.] A place in which bees are kept.
ap-i-cal (ap'i-kạl), *a.* Of, at, or forming the apex or tip.—**ap'i-cal-ly,** *adv.*
ap-i-ces (ap'i-sēz), *n.* Plural of *apex.*
A-pi-cian (a-pish'ạn), *a.* Of, like, or worthy of the ancient Roman epicure Apicius; epicurean.
a-pic-u-late (a-pik'ụ-lạt), *a.* [NL. *apiculus*, dim. of L. *apex*, point.] In *bot.*, tipped with a short, abrupt point, as a leaf. Also **a-pic'u-lat-ed** (-lā-ted).
a-pi-cul-ture (ā'pi-kul-ţụr), *n.* [L. *apis*, bee, + *cultura*, culture.] The rearing of bees; bee-keeping.—**a-pi-cul'-tur-ist,** *n.* A bee-keeper.
a-piece (ạ-pēs'), *adv.* For each piece, thing, or person; for each one; each.
ap-i-ol (ap'i-ol or ā'pi-ol, or -ōl), *n.* [L. *apium*, parsley.] The active principle of parsley-seed, obtained as white crystals and in an oleoresin ('green apiol'): used in medicine.
a-pi-ol-o-gy (ā-pi-ol'ọ-ji), *n.* [L. *apis*, bee: see *-logy.*] The scientific study of bees.—**a-pi-ol'o-gist,** *n.*
ap-ish (ā'pish), *a.* Of, like, or befitting an ape; senselessly imitative; foolishly affected; ridiculous.—**ap'ish-ly,** *adv.* —**ap'ish-ness,** *n.*
a-piv-o-rous (ā-piv'ọ-rus), *a.* [L. *apis*, bee, + *vorare*, devour.] Feeding on bees, as certain birds. Cf. *bee-eater.*
ap-la-cen-tal (ap-lạ-sen'tạl), *a.* [See *a-*¹.] Not placental; having no placenta, as the lowest mammals.
ap-la-nat-ic (ap-lạ-nat'ik), *a.* [Gr. ἀ- priv. + πλανᾶσθαι, wander.] In *optics*, free from aberration, esp. spherical aberration, as a lens.—**a-plan-a-tism** (a-plan'ạ-tizm), *n.*
a-pla-sia (a-plā'z̧iạ), *n.* [NL., < Gr. ἀ- priv. + πλάσσειν, form.] Defective development of a tissue or organ.—**a-plas-tic** (a-plas'tik), *a.* Characterized by aplasia.
ap-lite (ap'līt), etc. Same as *haplite*, etc.
a-plomb (à-plôṅ'), *n.* [F., < *à* (< L. *ad*), to, + *plomb*, E. *plumb.*] Perpendicular position; fig., imperturbable self-possession or assurance.
ap-nœa (ap-nē'ạ), *n.* [NL., < Gr. ἄπνοια, < ἄπνοος, breathless, < ἀ- priv. + πνεῖν, blow, breathe.] In *pathol.*, suspension of respiration.—**ap-nœ'al, ap-nœ'ic,** *a.*
apo-. [Gr. ἀπο-, repr. ἀπό, from: see *ab-.*] A prefix meaning 'from,' 'away,' 'off,' 'asunder,' occurring orig. in words from the Greek, but now used occasionally as an English formative, as in *apomorphine.*
a-poc-a-lypse (ạ-pok'ạ-lips), *n.* [L. *apocalypsis*, < Gr. ἀποκάλυψις, < ἀποκαλύπτειν, uncover, < ἀπό, from, + καλύπτειν, cover.] A revelation; esp., any of a class of writings ('apocalyptic literature'), Jewish and Christian, which appeared from about 200 B.C. to A.D. 350, assuming to make revelation of the ultimate divine purpose; [*cap.*] the book of Revelation, the last book of the New Testament. —**a-poc-a-lyp'tic** (-lip'tik). [Gr. ἀποκαλυπτικός.] **I.** *a.* Pertaining to or of the nature of an apocalypse; affording a revelation; esp., pertaining to the Apocalypse, or book of Revelation. **II.** *n.* The writer of the Apocalypse; also, apocalyptic writing or literature.—**a-poc-a-lyp'ti-cal,** *a.* Apocalyptic.—**a-poc-a-lyp'ti-cal-ly,** *adv.*—**a-poc-a-lyp'tist,** *n.* The writer or an interpreter of the Apocalypse.

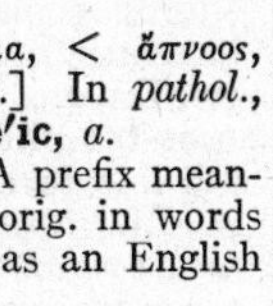
Apocarpous Fruit of Rue-anemone.

ap-o-car-pous (ap-ọ-kär'pus), *a.* [Gr. ἀπό, from, + καρπός, fruit.] In *bot.*, having the carpels separate.
a-poc-o-pate (a-pok'ọ-pāt), *v. t.*; *-pated, -pating.* To cut off or to shorten by apocope.—**a-poc'o-pate,** *a.* Apocopated.—**a-poc-o-pa'tion** (-pā'shọn), *n.*
a-poc-o-pe (a-pok'ọ-pē), *n.* [LL., < Gr. ἀποκοπή, < ἀποκόπτειν, cut off, < ἀπό, from, + κόπτειν, cut.] In *philol.*, the cutting off of the last letter or syllable of a word.

a-poc-ry-pha (ạ-pok'ri-fạ), *n. pl.* [LL., neut. pl. of *apocryphus*, < Gr. ἀπόκρυφος, hidden, < ἀποκρύπτειν, hide away, < ἀπό, from, + κρύπτειν, hide.] Writings or statements of doubtful authorship, authenticity, or authority; [*cap.*] fourteen books (1 and 2 Esdras, Tobit, Judith, part of Esther, Wisdom of Solomon, Ecclesiasticus, Baruch, Song of the Three Children, History of Susanna, Bel and the Dragon, Prayer of Manasses, and 1 and 2 Maccabees) formerly included in the Authorized Version of the Bible, but now generally omitted.—**a-poc'ry-phal,** *a.* Pertaining to or resembling apocrypha; of doubtful authenticity or authority; uncanonical; hence, spurious; fictitious; false. —**a-poc'ry-phal-ly,** *adv.*—**a-poc'ry-phal-ness,** *n.*
a-po-cy-na-ceous (a-pos-i-nā'shius), *a.* [NL. *Apocynum*, the dogbane genus, < Gr. ἀπόκυνον, kind of plant, < ἀπό, from, + κύων, dog.] Belonging to the *Apocynaceæ*, or dogbane family, which includes the dogbane, periwinkle, oleander, and various other plants, mostly tropical, some affording drugs and poisons, india-rubber, fiber, or wood.
ap-od, ap-ode (ap'od, -ōd). [Gr. ἄπους (ἀποδ-), < ἀ- priv. + πούς (ποδ-), foot.] **I.** *a.* Footless; apodal. **II.** *n.* An animal without feet; a fish without ventral fins.—**ap'o-dal** (-ọ-dạl), *a.* Having no distinct feet or foot-like members; lacking ventral fins; belonging to the *Apoda* or *Apodes* (names given to various groups of apodal animals).
ap-o-dic-tic, ap-o-deic-tic (ap-ọ-dik'tik, -dīk'tik), *a.* [L. *apodicticus*, < Gr. ἀποδεικτικός, < ἀποδεικνύναι, demonstrate, < ἀπό, from, + δεικνύναι, show.] Demonstrative; demonstrable; incontestable. Also **ap-o-dic'ti-cal, ap-o-deic'ti-cal.**—**ap-o-dic'ti-cal-ly, ap-o-deic'ti-cal-ly,** *adv.*
a-pod-o-sis (a-pod'ọ-sis), *n.* [L., < Gr. ἀπόδοσις, < ἀποδιδόναι, give back, < ἀπό, from, + διδόναι, give.] In *gram.*, the concluding clause of a conditional sentence: opposed to *protasis.*
ap-o-dous (ap'ọ-dus), *a.* [See *apod.*] Footless; apodal.
a-pog-a-my (a-pog'ạ-mi), *n.* [Gr. ἀπό, from, + γάμος, marriage.] In *bot.*, reproduction by processes other than sexual, as when a sporophyte is developed vegetatively from the prothallium of a fern; in *biol.*, mating or pairing at random; interbreeding of all varieties.—**ap-o-gam-ic** (ap-ọ-gam'ik), **a-pog'a-mous,** *a.*
ap-o-gee (ap'ọ-jē), *n.* [NL. *apogeum*, < Gr. ἀπόγειον, < ἀπό, from, + γῆ, earth.] In *astron.*, the point in the orbit of a heavenly body, now usually of the moon, that is most distant from the earth (opposed to *perigee*); fig., the furthest or highest point.—**ap-o-ge'al** (-jē'ạl), **ap-o-ge'an,** *a.*
ap-o-ge-o-trop-ic (ap"ọ-jē-ọ-trop'ik), *a.* [Gr. ἀπό, from, + γῆ, earth, + E. *-tropic.*] In *bot.*, tending away from the earth. Cf. *geotropic.*—**ap"o-ge-o-trop'i-cal-ly,** *adv.* —**ap"o-ge-ot'ro-pism** (-jē-ot'rọ-pizm), *n.* In *bot.*, apogeotropic tendency or growth.
ap-o-graph (ap'ọ-gráf), *n.* [Gr. ἀπόγραφον, < ἀπογράφειν, write off, < ἀπό, from, + γράφειν, write.] A copy or transcript, as of a manuscript.
a-po-lar (a-pō'lạr or ā-), *a.* [See *a-*¹.] Not polar; having no pole.
ap-o-laus-tic (ap-ọ-lâs'tik), *a.* [Gr. ἀπολαυστικός, < ἀπολαύειν, enjoy.] Pertaining or devoted to enjoyment.
A-pol-lo (ạ-pol'ō), *n.* [L., < Gr. Ἀπόλλων.] A Greek (and Roman) deity, the god of light, health and healing, music, poetry, prophecy, etc., represented as the highest type of youthful manly beauty; hence, an unusually well-formed, handsome young man.

Apollo Belvedere. (Statue in the Vatican.)

A-pol-lyon (ạ-pol'iọn), *n.* [Gr. Ἀπολλύων, lit. 'destroying,' < ἀπολλύναι, destroy.] "The angel of the bottomless pit" (Rev. ix. 11). Cf. *Abaddon.*
a-pol-o-get-ic (ạ-pol-ọ-jet'ik), *a.* [Gr. ἀπολογητικός, < ἀπολογεῖσθαι, speak in defense: cf. *apology.*] Making

apology; defending by speech or writing; excusing or acknowledging fault. Also **a-pol-o-get'i-cal.**—**a-pol-o-get'i-cal-ly,** *adv.*—**a-pol-o-get'ics,** *n.* The branch of theology concerned with the defense of Christianity.

ap-o-lo-gi-a (ap-ọ-lō'ji-ạ), *n.* [L.: see *apology.*] An apology, as in defense or justification.

a-pol-o-gist (ạ-pol'ọ-jist), *n.* One who makes an apology, or champions a cause by speech or writing.

a-pol-o-gize (ạ-pol'ọ-jīz), *v. i.*; *-gized, -gizing.* To make an apology; present defensive arguments; offer excuses or regrets for fault.—**a-pol'o-giz-er** (-jī-zėr), *n.*

ap-o-logue (ap'ọ-log), *n.* [F., < L. *apologus,* < Gr. ἀπόλογος, < ἀπό, from, + λέγειν, speak.] A moral fable; an allegorical story.

a-pol-o-gy (ạ-pol'ọ-ji), *n.*; pl. *-gies* (-jiz). [L. *apologia,* < Gr. ἀπολογία, < ἀπό, from, + λέγειν, speak.] A formal defense in speech or writing, as of a cause or doctrine; an excuse or explanation, or an expression of regret, offered for some fault; hence, a poor substitute; a makeshift.

ap-o-mor-phine (ap-ọ-môr'fin or -fēn), *n.* [See *apo-.*] In *chem.*, an artificial crystalline alkaloid prepared from morphine: used in the form of the hydrochloride as an emetic and expectorant.

ap-o-neu-ro-sis (ap″ọ-nụ-rō'sis), *n.*; pl. *-roses* (-rō'sēz). [NL., < Gr. ἀπονεύρωσις, < ἀπονευροῦσθαι, become a tendon, < ἀπό, from, + νεῦρον, tendon.] In *anat.*, a whitish fibrous membrane formed by the expansion of a tendon; a fascia-like tendon.—**ap″o-neu-rot'ic** (-rot'ik), *a.*

ap-o-pemp-tic (ap-ọ-pemp'tik), *a.* [Gr. ἀποπεμπτικός, < ἀποπέμπειν, send away, < ἀπό, from, + πέμπειν, send.] Pertaining to sending away; valedictory.

a-poph-a-sis (a-pof'ạ-sis), *n.* [LL., < Gr. ἀπόφασις, denial, < ἀποφάναι, deny, < ἀπό, from, + φάναι, say.] In *rhet.*, denial of an intention to speak of something which is at the same time hinted or insinuated.

ap-oph-thegm (ap'ọ-them), etc. See *apothegm*, etc.

a-poph-y-ge (a-pof'i-jē), *n.* [NL., < Gr. ἀποφυγή, < ἀποφεύγειν, flee from, < ἀπό, from, + φεύγειν, flee.] In *arch.*, the small, hollow outward spread given to the bottom of the shaft of a column to form the cincture by which it joins the base; also, a similar but slighter spread at the top of the shaft.

a-poph-yl-lite (a-pof'i-līt), *n.* [Gr. ἀπό, from, + φύλλον, leaf.] A mineral consisting of a hydrous potassium and calcium silicate (often with a small amount of fluorine), occurring in tetragonal crystals, usually transparent and colorless, but sometimes with a greenish or rose-red tint.

a-poph-y-sis (a-pof'i-sis), *n.*; pl. *-yses* (-i-sēz). [NL., < Gr. ἀπόφυσις, < ἀποφύειν, put forth, < ἀπό, from, + φύειν, produce.] In *anat.*, *bot.*, etc., an outgrowth; a process; a projection or protuberance.—**ap-o-phys-i-al** (ap-ọ-fiz'i-ạl), *a.*

ap-o-plec-tic (ap-ọ-plek'tik). [LL. *apoplecticus,* < Gr. ἀποπληκτικός.] **I.** *a.* Of or pertaining to apoplexy; stricken with or inclined to apoplexy. **II.** *n.* An apoplectic person.—**ap-o-plec'ti-cal-ly,** *adv.*

ap-o-plex-y (ap'ọ-plek-si), *n.* [L. *apoplexia,* < Gr. ἀποπληξία, < ἀποπλήσσειν, disable by a stroke, < ἀπό, from, + πλήσσειν, strike.] In *pathol.*, a sudden loss or impairment of consciousness and voluntary motion, due to cerebral hemorrhage, embolism. etc.; sometimes, hemorrhage into the tissue of any organ.

a-port (ạ-pōrt'), *adv.* *Naut.*, to port; to the left.

ap-o-si-o-pe-sis (ap″ọ-sī-ọ-pē'sis), *n.* [L., < Gr. ἀποσιώπησις, < ἀποσιωπᾶν, be silent.] In *rhet.*, a sudden breaking off in the midst of a sentence, as if from unwillingness to proceed.—**ap″o-si-o-pet'ic** (-pet'ik), *a.*

a-pos-ta-sy (ạ-pos'tạ-si), *n.*; pl. *-sies* (-siz). [LL. *apostasia,* < Gr. ἀποστασία, < ἀφίστασθαι, stand off, < ἀπό, from, + ἱστάναι, set up, stand.] Defection from one's faith, cause, or party; abandonment of professed religious or other principles.

a-pos-tate (ạ-pos'tāt). [LL. *apostata,* < Gr. ἀποστάτης, < ἀφίστασθαι: see *apostasy.*] **I.** *n.* One guilty of apostasy. **II.** *a.* Guilty of apostasy.—**ap-os-tat-ic, ap-os-tat-i-cal** (ap-ọs-tat'ik, -i-kạl), *a.*—**a-pos'ta-tize** (-tạ-tīz), *v. i.*; *-tized, -tizing.* To commit apostasy; withdraw as an apostate (*from* or *to*); forsake one's professed faith or principles.

a pos-te-ri-o-ri (ā pos-tē-ri-ō'rī or ä pos-tē-ri-ō'ri). [L.] From the latter or subsequent: a phrase used, often adjectively, of reasoning from effect to cause, or of knowledge derived from experience: opposed to *a priori.*

a-pos-til, a-pos-tille (a-pos'til), *n.* [F. *apostille.*] A marginal annotation or note.

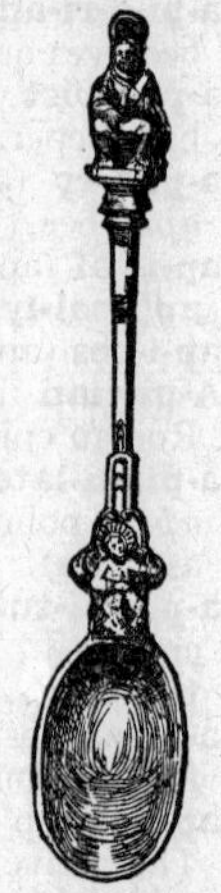
Apostle-spoon.

a-pos-tle (ạ-pos'l), *n.* [OF. *apostle* (F. *apôtre*), < LL. *apostolus,* < Gr. ἀπόστολος, messenger, < ἀποστέλλειν, send off, < ἀπό, from, + στέλλειν, send.] One sent to execute some mission; specif., one of the twelve disciples sent forth by Christ to preach the gospel; hence, any early Christian leader or missionary; a pioneer of Christianity in any country; also, the leader of any reform movement (as, Father Mathew, the *Apostle* of Temperance).—**Apostles' Creed,** a creed of universal acceptance in the Christian church, dating back in its present form to about A.D. 500, and traditionally ascribed to Christ's apostles.—**a-pos'tle-ship,** *n.* The office or function of an apostle.—**a-pos'tle=spoon',** *n.* One of a set of spoons, each having on its handle, usually at the end, the figure of one of Christ's apostles: formerly given by sponsors as a christening present.

a-pos-to-late (ạ-pos'tọ-lạt), *n.* [LL. *apostolatus.*] The office or dignity of an apostle; apostleship.

ap-os-tol-ic (ap-ọs-tol'ik), *a.* [LL. *apostolicus,* < Gr. ἀποστολικός.] Of, pertaining to, or derived from the apostles or their period; also, pertaining to the Pope as the successor of the apostle St. Peter; papal.—**apostolic succession,** *eccles.*, an uninterrupted succession of bishops in the church by regular ordination from Christ's apostles down to the present day, maintained by Roman Catholics, High-church Anglicans, and others to be historical and to be essential to the transmission of valid orders.—**ap-os-tol'i-cal,** *a.* Apostolic.—**ap-os-tol'i-cal-ly,** *adv.*—**ap-os-tol'i-cism** (-sizm), *n.* The quality of being apostolic; profession of or claim to apostolic principles or practices.—**a-pos-to-li-ci-ty** (ạ-pos-tọ-lis'i-ti), *n.* Apostolic character.

a-pos-tro-phe[1] (ạ-pos'trọ-fē), *n.* [L., < Gr. ἀποστροφή, < ἀποστρέφειν, turn away, < ἀπό, from, + στρέφειν, turn.] In *rhet.*, a turning aside from the subject in a discourse to address some person or thing (present or absent, real or imaginary); a digressive address.—**ap-os-troph-ic**[1] (ap-ọs-trof'ik), *a.*

a-pos-tro-phe[2] (ạ-pos'trọ-fē), *n.* [Prop. 3 syllables (with 4th due to confusion with *apostrophe*[1]), < F. *apostrophe,* < LL. *apostrophus,* < Gr. ἀπόστροφος, < ἀποστρέφειν: see *apostrophe*[1].] The omission of one or more letters from a word; also, a sign (') used to indicate such omission (as in *o'er* for *over, thro'* for *through*), or to mark the possessive case (as in *lion's, lions'*: see *possessive case,* under *possessive, a.*), or in forming certain plurals (as in *several M. D.'s, two a's, four 9's*), or for some other purpose, as (' or ") for a concluding mark of quotation.—**ap-os-troph-ic**[2] (ap-ọs-trof'ik), *a.*

a-pos-tro-phize (ạ-pos'trọ-fīz), *v.*; *-phized, -phizing.* **I.** *tr.* To address with a rhetorical apostrophe. **II.** *intr.* To utter an apostrophe; speak as in an apostrophe.

a-poth-e-ca-ry (ạ-poth'ẹ-kạ-ri), *n.*; pl. *-ries* (-riz). [LL. *apothecarius,* < L. *apotheca,* < Gr. ἀποθήκη, storehouse, < ἀπό, from, + τιθέναι, set.] One who prepares and sells drugs or medicines; a pharmacist; a druggist: in England and Ireland specially licensed to practise medicine also.—**apothecaries' measure,** the system of units used in the U. S. in compounding and dispensing liquid drugs: 60 minims (♏) = 1 fluid dram (f ʒ); 8 fluid drams = 1 fluid ounce (f ℥); 16 fluid ounces = 1 pint; 8 pints = 1 gallon (231 cubic inches). In Great Britain the pint (being the eighth part of a gallon of 277.274 cubic inches) is divided into 20 fluid ounces, with subdivisions corresponding to the U. S. use.—**apothecaries' weight,** a system of weights used in compounding and dispensing drugs: 20 grains = 1 scruple (℈); 3 scruples = 1 dram (ʒ); 8 drams = 1 ounce (℥); 12 ounces = 1 pound. The grain, ounce, and pound are the same as in troy weight, the grain alone being the same as in avoirdupois weight.

ap-o-thegm (ap′ǫ-them), *n.* [Gr. ἀπόφθεγμα, < ἀποφθέγγεσθαι, speak out, < ἀπό, from, + φθέγγεσθαι, utter a sound.] A short, pithy saying; a sententious precept or maxim.—**ap″o-theg-mat′ic** (-theg-mat′ik), *a.* Of or like an apothegm; containing or using apothegms. Also **ap″o-theg-mat′i-cal.**—**ap″o-theg-mat′i-cal-ly,** *adv.*—**ap-o-theg′ma-tist** (-mą-tist), *n.* A maker of apothegms.

ap-o-the-ke (äp-ō-tā′kė), *n.* [G.] An apothecary's shop; a drug-store.

ap-o-them (ap′ǫ-them), *n.* [Gr. ἀπό, from, + -θεμα, < τιθέναι, set.] In *geom.*, a perpendicular from the center of a regular polygon to one of its sides.

ap-o-the-o-sis (ap-ǫ-thē′ǫ-sis or ą-poth″ę-ō′sis), *n.*; pl. *apotheoses* (-sēz). [LL., < Gr. ἀποθέωσις, < ἀποθεοῦν, deify, < ἀπό, from, + θεοῦν, make a god of, < θεός, god.] Exaltation to the rank of a god; deification; hence, glorification; exaltation; also, a deified or glorified ideal.—**ap-o-the-o-size** (ap-ǫ-thē′ǫ-sīz or ą-poth′ę-ǫ-sīz), *v. t.*; *-sized, -sizing.* To deify; glorify.

ap-pal, ap-pall (ą-pâl′), *v.*; *appalled, appalling.* [OF. *apalir*, become or make pale, < *a* (< L. *ad*), to, + *pale*, E. *pale*².] **I.**† *intr.* To become pale; fail; lose strength or flavor; pall. **II.** *tr.* To make pale†; also, to weaken†; also, to overcome or confound with fear; fill with consternation and horror.

Ap-pa-lach-i-an (ap-ą-lach′i-ąn or -lā′chi-ąn), *a.* [From the *Apalachi* Indians.] Noting or pertaining to a system of mountains in eastern North America, extending from Cape Gaspé, in the province of Quebec, to northern Alabama, and divided into many ranges bearing separate names.—**Appalachian tea,** the leaves of any of certain plants of the aquifoliaceous genus *Ilex*, of the eastern U. S., as the shrub or small tree *I. vomitoria*, sometimes used as a tea; a plant yielding such leaves; also, a caprifoliaceous shrub, *Viburnum cassinoides*, of the eastern U. S.

ap-pal-ling (ą-pâ′ling), *p. a.* [See *appal.*] That appals; causing consternation and horror.—**ap-pal′ling-ly,** *adv.*—**ap-pal′ment,** *n.* The act of appalling, or the state of being appalled.

ap-pa-nage, ap-a-nage (ap′ą-nāj), *n.* [F. *apanage*, < OF. *apaner*, < ML. *appanare*, < L. *ad*, to, + *panis*, bread.] Land or some other source of revenue assigned for maintenance to a prince of a royal house; hence, one's allotted portion; also, an endowment or adjunct; also, a territorial dependency.

ap-pa-ra-tus (ap-ą-rā′tus), *n.*; pl. *-tuses* or *-tus.* [L., < *apparare*, prepare, < *ad*, to, + *parare*, make ready.] An equipment of things adapted as means to some end; esp., an assemblage of instruments, machinery, appliances, materials, etc., for a particular use; also, any complex appliance for a particular purpose.

ap-par-el (ą-par′ęl), *v. t.*; *-eled* or *-elled*, *-eling* or *-elling.* [OF. *apareillier* (F. *appareiller*), ult. < L. *ad*, to, + *par*, equal.] To fit out or equip (archaic); clothe, dress, or adorn; array.—**ap-par′el,** *n.* [OF. *apareil* (F. *appareil*).] Equipment or fittings (archaic); clothing; dress; array; garb.—**ap-par′el-ment,** *n.*

ap-par-ent (ą-pãr′ęnt or ą-par′-), *a.* [OF. *aparant* (F. *apparent*), < L. *apparens* (*-ent-*), ppr. of *apparere*: see *appear.*] Appearing plainly to the eye or the mind; visible; manifest; evident; also, seeming (as opposed to *actual* or *real*); ostensible.—**apparent noon.** See under *noon.*—**apparent solar time,** or **apparent time.** See under *time.*—**ap-par′ent-ly,** *adv.*—**ap-par′ent-ness,** *n.*

ap-pa-ri-tion (ap-ą-rish′ǫn), *n.* [OF. *aparicion* (F. *apparition*), < LL. *apparitio(n-)*, < L. *apparere*: see *appear.*] The act of appearing; appearance; also, that which appears, esp. a strange or supernatural sight or thing; a phenomenon; a ghost, specter, or phantom.—**ap-pa-ri′tion-al,** *a.*

ap-par-i-tor (ą-par′i-tǫr), *n.* [L., < *apparere*: see *appear.*] An attendant of a Roman magistrate; also, an officer of an ecclesiastical or, formerly, a civil court.

ap-pas-sio-na-to (äp-päs-syō-nä′tō), *a.* [It.] In *music*, impassioned; with passion or strong feeling.

ap-peach† (ą-pēch′), *v. t.* Same as *impeach.*

ap-peal (ą-pēl′), *v.* [OF. *apeler* (F. *appeler*), < L. *appellare*, approach, address, call upon, summon, accuse, also call, name, < *ad*, to, + *-pellare*, akin to *pellere*, drive.] **I.** *tr.* To call, summon, or challenge (archaic); in *law*, to accuse (archaic); also, to apply for the removal of (a cause) to a higher court. **II.** *intr.* To call in entreaty; make earnest request (*to* or *for*); apply or resort for aid, support, vindication, etc.; refer; fig., to offer a peculiar attraction, interest, enjoyment, etc.; in *law*, to refer a cause or a judicial decision to a higher court.—**ap-peal′,** *n.* [OF. *apel* (F. *appel*).] A summons or challenge (archaic); a call for aid, support, mercy, etc.; an earnest request or entreaty; application or reference to some person or authority for corroboration, vindication, decision, etc.; resort; recourse; in *law*, a formal charge or accusation (archaic); also, an application or proceeding for the removal of a cause to a higher tribunal, as for revision of a decision by a lower court; also, the right of such removal.—**ap-peal′a-ble,** *a.* That may be appealed; subject to appeal.—**ap-peal′er,** *n.*—**ap-peal′ing-ly,** *adv.*—**ap-peal′ing-ness,** *n.*

ap-pear (ą-pēr′), *v. i.* [OF. *apareir* (F. *apparoir*), < L. *apparere*, < *ad*, to, + *parere*, come forth.] To come or be in sight; show or present one's self, as before a court; come before the public; become or be evident to the mind; also, to seem or look (as, "They disfigure their faces, that they may *appear* unto men to fast": Mat. vi. 16).—**ap-pear′ance,** *n.* The act or fact of appearing, as to the eye, the mind, or the public; manner of appearing; aspect; outward show; semblance; look (often in *pl.*); also, a sight or object that appears; a phenomenon; an apparition; in *law*, the coming into court of a party to a suit.—**ap-pear′er,** *n.*

ap-peas-a-ble (ą-pē′zą-bl), *a.* That may be appeased.

ap-pease (ą-pēz′), *v. t.*; *-peased, -peasing.* [OF. *apaisier* (F. *apaiser*), < *a* (< L. *ad*), to, + *pais*, < L. *pax*, peace.] To bring to a state of peace, quiet, ease, or content; pacify; calm; allay; assuage; satisfy.—**ap-pease′ment,** *n.* The act of appeasing; the state of being appeased.—**ap-peas′er,** *n.*—**ap-peas′ing-ly,** *adv.*

ap-pel (ȧ-pel), *n.* [F., = E. *appeal, n.*] In *fencing*, a tap or stamp of the foot, formerly serving as a warning of one's intent to attack.

ap-pel-la-ble (ą-pel′ą-bl), *a.* [L. *appellare*: see *appeal.*] Appealable.

ap-pel-lant (ą-pel′ąnt). [F. *appelant*, < L. *appellans* (*-ant-*), ppr.] **I.** *a.* Appealing; appellate. **II.** *n.* One who appeals.

ap-pel-late (ą-pel′ąt), *a.* [L. *appellatus*, pp.] Appealed to; having cognizance of appeals.

ap-pel-la-tion (ap-e-lā′shǫn), *n.* [L. *appellatio(n-)*, < *appellare*: see *appeal.*] The act of appealing†; also, the act or mode of naming; nomenclature; also, a name, title, or designation.—**ap-pel-la-tive** (ą-pel′ą-tiv). [LL. *appellativus.*] **I.** *a.* Serving to name; denominative; designative; in *gram.*, of names or nouns, common (opposed to *proper*). **II.** *n.* A name, title, or appellation; in *gram.*, a common name or noun.—**ap-pel′la-tive-ly,** *adv.*

ap-pel-lee (ap-e-lē′), *n.* [OF. *apele*, pp.] In *law*, the defendant or respondent in an appeal.—**ap-pel′lor,** *n.* [OF. *apeleor.*] In *law*, one who appeals.

ap-pend (ą-pend′), *v. t.* [L. *appendere*, < *ad*, to, + *pendere*, hang.] To hang (*to*); attach as a pendant, supplementary part, or adjunct; annex; subjoin.—**ap-pen-dage** (ą-pen′dąj), *n.* Something appended, attached, or annexed; an external superadded part; an adjunct.—**ap-pend′ant.** [OF., ppr. of *appendre*, < ML. *appendere* (intr.).] **I.** *a.* Hanging or appended (*to*); attached; annexed; concomitant. **II.** *n.* Something appendant; an appendage.—**ap-pend′ance,** *n.*

ap-pen-dec-to-my (ap-en-dek′tǫ-mi), *n.* [NL. *appendix* (*vermiformis*) + Gr. ἐκ, out of, + -τομία, < τέμνειν, cut.] In *surg.*, excision of the vermiform appendix. Also **ap-pen-di-cec-to-my** (ą-pen-di-sek′tǫ-mi).

ap-pen-di-ces (ą-pen′di-sēz). Plural of *appendix.*

ap-pen-di-ci-tis (ą-pen-di-sī′tis), *n.* [NL.] In *pathol.*, inflammation of the vermiform appendix.

ap-pen-di-cle (ą-pen′di-kl), *n.* [L. *appendicula*, dim. of *appendix*: see *appendix.*] A small appendage.—**ap-pen-dic-u-lar** (ap-en-dik′ų-lãr), *a.* Pertaining to or forming an appendicle.—**ap-pen-dic′u-late** (-lāt), *a.* Having appendicles or appendages; also, appendicular.

ap-pen-dix (ą-pen′diks), *n.*; pl. *-dixes* or *-dices* (-di-sēz). [L.] Something appended; an appendage; esp., a part appended to a book, usually (as distinguished from a *supplement*) to give any relevant matter not essential to the completeness of the main work; in *anat.*, a process or projection; esp., the vermiform appendix.—**vermiform appendix,** in *anat.*, a narrow blind tube protruding from the cæcum: in man, situated in the lower right-hand part of the abdomen, and having no useful function, its diameter being about that of a goose-quill and its length 3 to 4 inches.—**ap-pen′dix ver-mi-for-mis** (vėr-mi-fôr′mis). [NL.] The vermiform appendix.

ap-per-ceive (ap-ėr-sēv′), *v. t.*; *-ceived, -ceiving.* [OF. F. *apercevoir*, < L. *ad*, to, + *percipere* (pp. *perceptus*), perceive.] To perceive; in *psychol.*, to be conscious of perceiving; comprehend.—**ap-per-cep′tion** (-sep′shǫn), *n.* Perception; apprehension; in *psychol.*, conscious perception; a voluntary mental activity accompanied with self-consciousness; also, the assimilation of a new perception or idea by a group or mass of ideas already present in the mind.—**ap-per-cep′tive,** *a.* Pertaining to apperception.—**ap-per-cep′tive-ly,** *adv.*

ap-per-tain (ap-ėr-tān′), *v. i.* [OF. *apartenir* (F. *appartenir*), < LL. *appertinere*, < L. *ad*, to, + *pertinere*, pertain.] To pertain (*to*); belong as a part, member, possession, attribute, etc.; relate.

ap-pe-tence, ap-pe-ten-cy (ap′ę-tęns, -tęn-si), *n.* [L. *appetentia*, < *appetere*: see *appetite*.] Strong desire; craving; appetite; natural inclination or tendency.

ap-pe-tite (ap′ę-tīt), *n.* [OF. *appetit* (F. *appétit*), < L. *appetitus*, < *appetere*, strive after, desire, < *ad*, to, + *petere*, seek.] Strong desire; craving; inclination; propensity; esp., an instinctive physical craving, as for food or drink; hunger; relish.—**ap-pet-i-tive** (ą-pet′i-tiv or ap′ę-tī-tiv), *a.* Pertaining to appetite.

ap-pe-tize (ap′ę-tīz), *v. t.*; *-tized, -tizing.* [Cf. F. *appétissant*, appetizing.] To excite or whet the appetite of: orig. and chiefly in *appetizing*, *p. a.*—**ap′pe-tiz-er,** *n.* Something that whets the appetite, or gives relish for food.—**ap′pe-tiz-ing-ly,** *adv.*

ap-plaud (ą-plâd′), *v.* [L. *applaudere* (pp. *applausus*), < *ad*, to, + *plaudere*, clap.] **I.** *tr.* To express approval of by hand-clapping or other significant signs; hence, to commend; praise. **II.** *intr.* To express approval by clapping or otherwise.—**ap-plaud′er,** *n.*—**ap-plaud′ing-ly,** *adv.*

ap-plause (ą-plâz′), *n.* [L. *applausus*, < *applaudere*, E. *applaud*.] Hand-clapping, shouting, or other demonstrations of approval; hence, laudation; commendation.—**ap-plau-sive** (ą-plâ′siv), *a.* Giving applause.—**ap-plau′sive-ly,** *adv.*

ap-ple (ap′l), *n.* [AS. *æppel*, akin to G. *apfel*.] The fruit of a malaceous tree, *Malus malus*, or the tree, cultivated in most temperate regions; the fruit of any of certain other species of the same genus, or any of these species; any of various other fruits, or fruit-like products, or plants, usually specially designated (as, custard-*apple*, love-*apple*, May-*apple*, oak-*apple*, pine*apple*); also, something globular or round.—**apple of discord,** the fabled golden apple inscribed "For the fairest," thrown by the goddess of discord among the Greek gods and awarded by Paris to Aphrodite, which led to the destruction of Troy; fig., a cause of envy and strife.—**apple of Peru,** a coarse solanaceous annual, *Physalodes physalodes*, bearing solitary pale-blue flowers, and a globose berry inclosed in the calyx.—**apple of Sodom,** or **Dead Sea apple,** a fruit described by ancient writers as fair to the eye but turning to smoke and ashes when plucked: fig., something specious but wholly disappointing.—**apple of the eye,** the pupil; fig., something most precious or dear.—**ap′ple=but′ter,** *n.* A kind of apple-sauce made by long stewing of the fruit, usually in cider.—**ap′ple=green′,** *n.* A clear light-green color.—**ap′ple=jack,** *n.* A liquor distilled from cider.—**ap′ple=sauce,** *n.* Apples stewed to a soft pulp; also (slang), nonsense; 'bunk.'

ap-pli-ance (ą-plī′ąns), *n.* The act of applying; application; also, something applied as a means to an end; an instrument, apparatus, device, or contrivance for a particular use; also, compliance†.

ap-pli-ca-ble (ap′li-ką-bl), *a.* [F. *applicable*, < L. *applicare*: see *apply*.] Capable of or suitable for being applied; appropriate; pertinent.—**ap″pli-ca-bil′i-ty** (-bil′-i-ti), **ap′pli-ca-ble-ness,** *n.*—**ap′pli-ca-bly,** *adv.*

ap-pli-cant (ap′li-kąnt), *n.* One who applies.

ap-pli-ca-tion (ap-li-kā′shǫn), *n.* [L. *applicatio(n-)*.] The act of applying; a putting to; a bringing to bear; use; appropriation; reference or relevancy; assiduous effort or attention; solicitation; a formal request; also, something applied, as an external remedy.—**ap′pli-ca-tive** (-kā-tiv), **ap′pli-ca-to-ry** (-tǫ-ri), *a.* Pertaining to application or use; practical.

ap-plied (ą-plīd′), *p. a.* Put or affixed to something (as, *applied* ornaments in needlework); also, put to practical use, as a science when its laws are employed and exemplified in dealing with concrete phenomena (distinguished from *abstract*, *theoretical*, or *pure*).

ap-pli-er (ą-plī′ėr), *n.* One who or that which applies.

ap-pli-qué (ap-li-kā′). [F.] **I.** *a.* Applied; formed with ornamentation of one material sewed or otherwise applied to another. **II.** *n.* Work so formed.—**ap-pli-qué′,** *v. t.*; *-quéd* (-kād′), *-quéing* (-kā′ing). To apply or form as in appliqué work.

ap-ply (ą-plī′), *v.*; *-plied, -plying.* [OF. *aplier*, < L. *applicare*, < *ad*, to, + *plicare*, fold: see *ply*.] **I.** *tr.* To put (*to*), esp. in order to effect some result; lay, administer, bring to bear, or use as effective or appropriate; put (a principle, etc.) into practical operation; appropriate, as to a purpose; use (a word, etc.) in reference (*to*); direct or address in effort (as, "*Apply* thine heart unto instruction": Prov. xxiii. 12); devote (one's self) assiduously. **II.** *intr.* To have a bearing or reference; be pertinent; also, to address one's self; make request or application; also, to give close attention; attend assiduously.

Appoggiatura: *a*, short; *b*, long.

ap-pog-gia-tu-ra (äp-pod-jä-tö′rä), *n.* [It., < *appoggiare*, prop, lean.] In *music*, a note of embellishment (short or long) preceding another note and taking a portion of its time.

ap-point (ą-point′), *v.* [OF. *apointier* (F. *appointer*), < ML. *appunctare*, < L. *ad*, to, + *punctum*, point.] **I.** *tr.* To fix, constitute, or ordain; prescribe; settle; also, to assign authoritatively to a particular use, task, or office; allot; designate; also, to equip or provide with requisites or accessories (now only in *appointed*, *pp.*). **II.** *intr.* To determine; resolve. [Archaic.]—**ap-point′a-ble,** *a.* That may be appointed.—**ap-point-ee** (ą-poin-tē′), *n.* A person appointed; a beneficiary under a legal appointment.—**ap-point′er,** *n.*—**ap-point′ive,** *a.* Pertaining to or dependent on appointment.—**ap-point′ment,** *n.* The act of appointing; ordainment, or an ordinance; designation to office, or the office; assignment, as, in law, of the use of an estate created under a preceding deed or will; engagement, as for a meeting; equipment, or a requisite or accessory of equipment (usually in *pl.*).—**ap-point′or,** *n.* One who has official or legal power of appointment.

ap-por-tion (ą-pôr′shǫn), *v. t.* [OF. *apportionner*, < L. *ad*, to, + *portio(n-)*, portion.] To assign as a portion or in portions; allot; portion out; distribute proportionally.—**ap-por′tion-er,** *n.*—**ap-por′tion-ment,** *n.* The act of apportioning; allotment or distribution in just proportion.

ap-pose (a-pōz′), *v. t.*; *-posed, -posing.* [F. *apposer*, < *à* (< L. *ad*), to, + *poser*, put (see *pose*[1]), but associated with derivatives of L. *apponere*: see *apposite*, *apposition*.] To put (*to*); apply; also, to place next, as one thing to another; place side by side, as two things.—**ap-pos′a-ble,** *a.*

ap-po-site (ap′ǫ-zit), *a.* [L. *appositus*, pp. of *apponere*, put to, < *ad*, to, + *ponere*, place.] Placed next or side by side (esp. in *bot.*); fig., well adapted (*to*); applicable; appropriate; suitable.—**ap′po-site-ly,** *adv.*—**ap′po-site-ness,** *n.*

ap-po-si-tion (ap-ǫ-zish′ǫn), *n.* [L. *appositio(n-)*, < *apponere*: see *apposite.*] A placing next or together; juxtaposition; in *gram.*, the relation between one noun (or some other word or words) and another to which it is added by way of explanation or characterization and with which it is in syntactic agreement (thus, in 'Cicero, the famous orator, died in 43 B.C.,' the noun *orator* is in apposition with *Cicero*). —**ap-po-si′tion-al,** *a.*—**ap-pos-i-tive** (ą-poz′i-tiv). In *gram.*: **I.** *a.* Placed in apposition. **II.** *n.* A word in apposition.—**ap-pos′i-tive-ly,** *adv.*

ap-praise (ą-prāz′), *v. t.*; *-praised, -praising.* [Appar. for *apprize*², with form due to *praise.*] To estimate or fix the value of; set a price upon officially, as under direction of law; in general, to estimate as to amount, quality, etc.—**ap-prais′a-ble,** *a.*—**ap-praise′ment, ap-prais′al,** *n.* The act of appraising; valuation, or the value fixed; estimation. —**ap-prais′er,** *n.* One who appraises; a person licensed and sworn to estimate and fix the value of goods or estate.

ap-pre-ci-a-ble (ą-prē′shi-ą-bl), *a.* Capable of being appreciated; perceptible.—**ap-pre′ci-a-bly,** *adv.*

ap-pre-ci-ate (ą-prē′shi-āt), *v.*; *-ated, -ating.* [LL. *appretiatus*, pp. of *appretiare*, appraise, < L. *ad*, to, + *pretium*, price.] **I.** *tr.* To appraise, estimate, or value; also, to value justly; recognize the worth or quality of; also, to be fully sensible of; perceive; also, to raise in value (opposed to *depreciate*). **II.** *intr.* To rise in value.—**ap-pre-ci-a′tion** (-ş̧i-ā′shǫn), *n.* The act of appreciating; estimation of value, worth, quality, etc.; just valuation or recognition; sympathetic understanding; also, rise in value.—**ap-pre′ci-a-tive** (-shi-ā̦-tiv), *a.* Having or showing appreciation.—**ap-pre′ci-a-tive-ly,** *adv.*—**ap-pre′ci-a-tive-ness,** *n.*—**ap-pre′ci-a-tor** (-ā-tǫr), *n.*—**ap-pre′ci-a-to-ry** (-ą-tǭ-ri), *a.* Appreciative.—**ap-pre′ci-a-to-ri-ly,** *adv.*

ap-pre-hend (ap-rę-hend′), *v.* [L. *apprehendere* (pp. *apprehensus*), < *ad*, to, + *prehendere*, seize.] **I.** *tr.* To seize, take prisoner, or arrest; also, to grasp mentally; become conscious of; perceive; understand; conceive; also, to anticipate or expect; dread; fear. **II.** *intr.* To have perception; understand; conceive; think; also, to fear.—**ap-pre-hend′er,** *n.*—**ap-pre-hen′si-ble** (-hen′si-bl), *a.* [LL. *apprehensibilis.*] Capable of being apprehended (by sense or intellect).—**ap-pre-hen-si-bil′i-ty** (-bil′i-ti), *n.* —**ap-pre-hen′sion** (-shǫn), *n.* [LL. *apprehensio(n-).*] The act of apprehending, or the fact of being apprehended; seizure or arrest; the faculty of apprehending; mental grasp; perception; understanding; a conception or notion; anticipation, esp. of coming evil; dread; fear.—**ap-pre-hen′sive** (-siv), *a.* Able or quick to apprehend; perceptive; intelligent; discerning; also, conscious or sensible of something (archaic); also, anticipative, esp. of coming evil; fearful; afraid.—**ap-pre-hen′sive-ly,** *adv.*—**ap-pre-hen′sive-ness,** *n.*

ap-pren-tice (ą-pren′tis), *n.* [OF. *aprentis*, < *aprendre*, learn, < L. *apprendere*, for *apprehendere*: see *apprehend.*] One bound by indenture to a master to learn some art or trade; a learner, novice, or tyro.—**ap-pren′tice,** *v. t.*; *-ticed, -ticing.* To bind as an apprentice.—**ap-pren′tice-ment,** *n.*—**ap-pren′tice-ship,** *n.*

ap-pressed (ą-prest′), *a.* [L. *appressus*, pp. of *apprimere*, press to, < *ad*, to, + *premere*, press.] Pressed close, as leaves to a stem, or as folds of strata.

ap-prise¹, **ap-prize**¹ (ą-prīz′), *v. t.*; *-prised* or *-prized, -prising* or *-prizing.* [F. *appris*, pp. of *apprendre*, OF. *aprendre*, learn, teach: see *apprentice.*] To inform; notify; advise: often with *of.*

ap-prize², **ap-prise**² (ą-prīz′), *v. t.*; *-prized* or *-prised, -prizing* or *-prising.* [OF. *aprisier*, < LL. *appretiare*: see *appreciate.*] Same as *appraise.*—**ap-prize′ment,** *n.* —**ap-priz-er** (ą-prī′zėr), *n.*

ap-proach (ą-prōch′), *v.* [OF. *aprochier* (F. *approcher*), < LL. *appropiare*, < L. *ad*, to, + *propius*, compar. of *prope*, near.] **I.** *intr.* To come nearer; draw near; fig., to come near (*to*) in character, amount, etc.; approximate. **II.** *tr.* To come nearer or near to; also, to approximate to; nearly equal; also, to bring near to something; also, to make advances or overtures to; *milit.*, to advance toward by means of approaches.—**ap-proach′,** *n.* The act of approaching; a drawing near; approximation; a passage or avenue for approaching; access; a movement, advance, or overture toward establishing personal, business, or other relations (usually in *pl.*); in *golf*, the stroke by which a player endeavors to get his ball on to the putting-green; *pl.*, *milit.*, works for protecting forces in an advance against a fortress or fortified position.—**ap-proach′a-ble,** *a.* Capable of being approached; easy of approach; accessible.—**ap-proach-a-bil′i-ty** (-bil′i-ti), **ap-proach′a-ble-ness,** *n.* —**ap-proach′less,** *a.* Without approach; inaccessible.

ap-pro-bate (ap′rǭ-bāt), *v. t.*; *-bated, -bating.* [L. *approbatus*, pp. of *approbare*: see *approve.*] To approve or sanction (now chiefly U. S.); also, to license (U. S.).—**ap-pro-ba′tion** (-bā′shǫn), *n.* [L. *approbatio(n-).*] Approval; sanction; commendation; also, probation†.—**ap′pro-ba-tive** (-tiv), *a.* Approving; expressing approbation.—**ap′pro-ba-tive-ness,** *n.* The quality of being approbative; in *phren.*, love of approbation.—**ap′pro-ba-to-ry** (-bą-tǭ-ri), *a.* Approving.

ap-proof (ą-pröf′), *n.* [See *approve*, and cf. *proof* and *prove.*] Proof; also, approval (as, "The self-same tongue, Either of condemnation or *approof*": Shakspere's "Measure for Measure," ii. 4. 174). [Archaic.]

ap-pro-pin-quate (ap-rǭ-ping′kwāt), *v. i.*; *-quated, -quating.* [L. *appropinquatus*, pp. of *appropinquare*, < *ad*, to, + *propinquus*, near.] To come near; approach. [Archaic.] —**ap″pro-pin-qua′tion** (-ping-kwā′shǫn), *n.*

ap-pro-pin-qui-ty (ap-rǭ-ping′kwi-ti), *n.* [L. *ad*, to, + *propinquitas*, nearness, E. *propinquity.*] Nearness, as of one to another; propinquity.

ap-pro-pri-a-ble (ą-prō′pri-ą-bl), *a.* Capable of being appropriated; applicable.

ap-pro-pri-ate (ą-prō′pri-āt), *v. t.*; *-ated, -ating.* [LL. *appropriatus*, pp. of *appropriare*, < L. *ad*, to, + *proprius*, one's own, E. *proper.*] To take to or for one's self; take possession of; also, to assign to a particular recipient; set apart for some purpose or use; allot specially; devote; also, to suit (archaic).—**ap-pro′pri-ate** (-ąt), *a.* Peculiarly belonging or suited (*to*); proper; fitting; suitable.—**ap-pro′pri-ate-ly,** *adv.*—**ap-pro′pri-ate-ness,** *n.*—**ap-pro-pri-a′tion** (-ā′shǫn), *n.* [LL. *appropriatio(n-).*] The act of appropriating to one's self or another or for any object or purpose; the fact of being appropriated; a thing or a sum appropriated.—**ap-pro′pri-a-tive** (-ą-tiv), *a.* Serving or tending to appropriate.—**ap-pro′pri-a-tor** (-ā-tǫr), *n.*

ap-prov-a-ble (ą-prö′vą-bl), *a.* Worthy of approval.

ap-prov-al (ą-prö′vąl), *n.* The act of approving, or the fact of being approved; sanction; favoring judgment; approbation.

ap-prove (ą-pröv′), *v.*; *-proved, -proving.* [OF. *aprover* (F. *approuver*), < L. *approbare*, < *ad*, to, + *probare*, try, E. *prove.*] **I.** *tr.* To make good or establish by proof†; demonstrate in practice (as, an opportunity to *approve* one's worth); show to be (as, to *approve* one's self worthy of confidence); corroborate† or attest†; also, to confirm or sanction officially; ratify; also, to pronounce or consider good; speak or think favorably of; commend; also, to present (one's self or itself) in a favorable light; recommend; also, to put to the proof†. **II.** *intr.* To speak or think favorably (*of*).—**ap-proved′,** *p. a.* Of proved truth or merit; sanctioned or recommended by experience; regarded with favor.—**ap-prov-ed-ly** (ą-prö′ved-li), *adv.*—**ap-prov′er,** *n.*—**ap-prov′ing-ly,** *adv.*

ap-prox-i-mate (ą-prok′si-māt), *v.*; *-mated, -mating.* [LL. *approximatus*, pp. of *approximare*, < L. *ad*, to, + *proximare*, come near, < *proximus*, superl. adj., < *prope*, near.] **I.** *intr.* To come near in position, character, amount, etc.; approach closely; be very like or nearly equal. **II.** *tr.* To come near to; approach closely to; also, to bring near.—**ap-prox′i-mate** (-mąt), *a.* Near; close together; very like; nearly equal, exact, or perfect; fairly accurate or correct.—**ap-prox′i-mate-ly,** *adv.* Nearly; closely; about. —**ap-prox-i-ma′tion** (-mā′shǫn), *n.* The act of approximating; close approach; also, continual approach to a true result, without absolute exactness; a result (sufficiently exact) so obtained.—**ap-prox′i-ma-tive** (-mą-tiv), *a.* Approximating; approximate.—**ap-prox′i-ma-tor** (-mā-tǫr), *n.*

ap-pui (à-pwē), *n.* [F., < *appuyer*, prop.] Support; a point or base of support, esp. in military operations.

ap-pulse (ạ-puls′ or ap′uls), *n.* [L. *appulsus*, < *appellere*, drive to, < *ad*, to, + *pellere*, drive.] A driving upon; approach; impact. Also **ap-pul-sion** (ạ-pul′shọn).—**ap-pul′sive** (-siv), *a.* Driving upon; impinging.

ap-pur-te-nance (ạ-pėr′tẹ-nạns), *n.* [AF. *apurtenance*, OF. *apartenance*, < ML. *appertinentia*, < LL. *appertinẹre*: see *appertain*.] The state or fact of appertaining; also, something appertaining; a belonging, adjunct, or accessory. —**ap-pur′te-nant.** [OF. *apartenant*, < LL. *appertinens* (*-ent-*), ppr. of *appertinere*.] **I.** *a.* Appertaining or belonging (*to*); pertaining; incident. **II.** *n.* An appurtenance.

ap-ri-cate (ap′ri-kāt), *v. i.* or *t.*; *-cated, -cating.* [L. *apricatus*, pp. of *apricari*, < *apricus*, sunny.] To bask in or expose to sunlight.—**ap-ri-ca′tion** (-kā′shọn), *n.*

a-pri-cot (ā′pri-kot or ap′ri-kọt), *n.* [F. *abricot* or Pg. *albricoque*, < Ar. *al*, the, + *burqūq*, < Gr. πραικόκιον, apricot, < L. *præcoquus*, for *præcox*, early ripe: see *precocious*.] The downy yellow fruit, somewhat resembling a small peach, of an amygdalaceous tree, *Prunus armeniaca*, of the plum genus; also, the tree; also, a pinkish-yellow or yellowish-pink color.

A-pril (ā′pril), *n.* [L. *Aprilis.*] The fourth month of the year, containing 30 days.—**April fool,** the victim of some trick or jest played in observance of April 1. See *All Fools' Day*, under *all*, *a.*

a pri-o-ri (ā prī-ō′rī or ä pri-ō′ri). [L.] From the former or antecedent: a phrase used, often adjectively, of reasoning from cause to effect or from a general law or notion to a particular instance, or of cognitions originating in the mind independently of experience: opposed to *a posteriori*.—**a-pri-or′i-ty** (-or′i-ti), *n.*

a-pron (ā′prọn), *n.* [For *napron* (*a napron* being taken as *an apron*), < OF. *naperon*, dim. of *nape*, < L. *mappa*, napkin, cloth.] A garment worn to protect the clothing, or for ornament or with official dress; any shielding piece or part, as a screen of leather fastened before the occupants of an open carriage, a covering for an opening in a grain-separator, or a platform to receive the water falling over a dam; in *geol.*, a deposit of gravel and sand extending forward from a moraine (also called 'frontal apron').—**a′pron,** *v. t.* To provide with or as with an apron.

Apse.—Cathedral of Pisa, Italy.

ap-ro-pos (ap-rọ-pō′). [F. *à propos*, 'to purpose': *à* (< L. *ad*), to; *propos*, < *proposer*, E. *propose*.] **I.** *adv.* To the purpose; pertinently; opportunely; also, as a pertinent circumstance (used to introduce an incidental remark); as to that (something just mentioned); in respect (*of*); with regard (*to*). **II.** *a.* Pertinent; opportune.

apse (aps), *n.* [L. *apsis*, < Gr. ἀψίς, loop, circle, bow, arch, apse, < ἅπτειν, fasten.] In *arch.*, a vaulted semicircular or polygonal recess in a building, esp. at the end of the choir of a church; in *astron.*, an apsis.—**ap-si-dal** (ap′si-dạl), *a.* Pertaining to an apsis or an apse.

ap-sis (ap′sis), *n.*; pl. *apsides* (ap′si-dēz). [L.: see *apse*.] In *astron.*, either of two points in the eccentric orbit of a planet, one ('higher apsis') at which it is furthest from the body about which it revolves, and the other ('lower apsis') at which it is nearest to it; in *arch.*, an apse.

apt (apt), *a.* [L. *aptus*, fastened, joined, fitted.] Fitted or adapted (*for*); suited to the purpose or occasion; suitable; appropriate; pertinent or apposite; also, disposed, prone, likely, or liable (with an infinitive); also, ready, quick, or intelligent; quick to learn.

ap-ter-al (ap′tẹ-rạl), *a.* [Gr. ἄπτερος, < ἀ- priv. + πτερόν, wing, row of columns.] Wingless; apterous; in *arch.*, without columns along the sides.—**ap′ter-ous,** *a.* Wingless, as some insects; in *bot.*, without membranous expansions, as a stem.

ap-ter-yx (ap′tẹ-riks), *n.* [NL., < Gr. ἀ- priv. + πτέρυξ, wing.] Any of several flightless ratite birds of New Zealand, constituting the genus *Apteryx*, allied to the extinct moas, and themselves approaching extinction. Also called *kiwi*.

Apteryx.

ap-ti-tude (ap′ti-tūd), *n.* [F., < ML. *aptitudo.*] The quality of being apt; special fitness; inclination or propensity; capacity for a thing; quick intelligence; readiness to learn.

apt-ly (apt′li), *adv.* In an apt manner.—**apt′ness,** *n.*

ap-tote (ap′tōt), *n.* [Gr. ἄπτωτος, indeclinable, < ἀ- priv. + πτωτός, verbal adj. of πίπτειν, fall.] In *gram.*, an indeclinable noun. — **ap-tot′ic** (-tot′ik), *a.* Having no grammatical inflections, as certain languages.

ap-y-ret-ic (ap-i-ret′ik), *a.* [Gr. ἀπύρετος, < ἀ- priv. + πυρετός, fever.] In *pathol.*, free from fever.

ap-y-rex-i-a (ap-i-rek′si-ạ̈), *n.* [NL., < Gr. ἀπυρεξία, < ἀ- priv. + πυρέσσειν, be feverish, < πυρετός, fever.] In *pathol.*, absence or intermission of fever.—**ap-y-rex′i-al,** *a.*

a-qua (ā′kwạ̈ or ak′wạ̈), *n.* [L., water.] Water; a liquid; a solution: esp. used in pharmacy.—**aqua ammoniæ** (a-mō′ni-ē). [NL., 'water of ammonia.'] A solution of gaseous ammonia in water: often popularly called *aqua ammonia*.—**aqua destillata** (des-ti-lā′tạ̈). [NL.] Distilled water.—**aqua fortis** (fôr′tis). [NL., 'strong water.'] Nitric acid.—**aqua pura** (pū′rạ̈). [L.] Pure water; distilled water.—**aqua regia** (rē′ji-ạ̈). [NL., 'royal water' (with allusion to its power to dissolve gold).] A mixture of one part of nitric acid and three to four parts of hydrochloric acid.—**aqua Tofana** (to-fä′nạ̈). [NL., = It. *acqua Tofana.*] A poisonous liquid (probably arsenical) to which many mysterious deaths in the 17th century were attributed: said to have been invented by a Sicilian woman named Tofana, who is reputed to have poisoned more than 600 persons.—**aqua vitæ** (vī′tē). [ML., 'water of life.'] Alcohol; spirituous liquor, as brandy or whisky.

a-qua-cul-ture (ā′kwạ-kul-tụ̄r), *n.* See *aquiculture*.

a-qua-ma-rine (ā″kwạ-mạ-rēn′ or ak″wạ-), *n.* [L. *aqua marina*, sea-water.] A transparent sea-green or bluish-green variety of beryl, used as a gem; also, its color.

a-qua-relle (ak-wạ-rel′), *n.* [F., < It. *acquerella*, < *acqua*, < L. *aqua*, water.] Water-color painting; also, a painting in water-colors.—**a-qua-rel′list,** *n.*

a-qua-ri-um (ạ-kwā′ri-um), *n.*; pl. *-riums* or *-ria* (-ri-ạ̈). [L., neut. of *aquarius*: see *Aquarius*.] A pond, tank, or establishment in which living aquatic animals or plants are kept, as for exhibition.

A-qua-ri-us (ạ-kwā′ri-us), *n.* [L., prop. adj., pertaining to water, < *aqua*, water.] The Water-bearer, a zodiacal constellation; also, the eleventh sign of the zodiac. See *zodiac*.

a-quat-ic (ạ-kwat′ik or ạ-kwot′-). [L. *aquaticus*, < *aqua*, water.] **I.** *a.* Of or belonging to the water. **II.** *n.* An aquatic plant or animal; *pl.*, sports practised on or in the water.—**a-quat′i-cal-ly,** *adv.*

a-qua-tint (ak′wạ-tint), *n.* [F. *aquatinte*, < It. *acqua tinta*, < L. *aqua tincta*, 'dyed water.'] An etching process in which spaces are bitten instead of lines; also, an etching made by this process.—**a′qua-tint,** *v. t.* or *i.* To etch in aquatint.

Aqueduct of Segovia, Spain, originally built by the Romans.

a-que-duct (ak′wẹ-dukt), *n.* [L. *aquæ ductus*, 'duct of water.'] A conduit or artificial channel for conducting water; esp., a structure for conducting a water-supply from a distance; in *anat.*, a canal or passage.

a-que-ous (ā'kwē̩-us), *a.* [L. *aqua*, water.] Of, like, or containing water; watery; of rocks, formed of matter deposited from water.—**aqueous humor,** in *anat.*, the limpid watery fluid which fills the space between the cornea and the crystalline lens in the eye.—**a'que-ous-ly,** *adv.*—**a'que-ous-ness,** *n.*

aqui-. Form of L. *aqua*, water, used in combination.—**a-quic-o-lous** (ā̩-kwik'ō̩-lus), *a.* [+ *-colous.*] Inhabiting water.—**a-qui-cul-ture** (ā'kwi-kul-t̩ū̩r), *n.* Culture of the natural inhabitants of water; fish-breeding; pisciculture.—**a-qui-cul'tur-al,** *a.*—**a-quif-er-ous** (ā̩-kwif'e̩-rus), *a.* [+ *-ferous.*] Conveying water.

a-qui-fo-li-a-ceous (ā″kwi-fō-li-ā'shius), *a.* [L. *aquifolium*, holly, < *acus*, needle, + *folium*, leaf.] Belonging to the *Aquifoliaceæ* (or *Ilicaceæ*), the holly family of plants.

a-qui-line (ak'wi-lin or -līn), *a.* [L. *aquilinus*, < *aquila*, eagle.] Of or like the eagle; of the nose, curved like an eagle's beak; hooked.

a-quiv-er (a̩-kwiv'ėr), *adv.* In a quivering state.

a-quose (ā̩-kwōs' or ā'kwōs), *a.* [L. *aquosus*, < *aqua*, water.] Abounding in water; watery; aqueous.—**a-quos-i-ty** (ā̩-kwos'i-ti), *n.* Wateriness.

-ar. [L. *-aris*, neut. *-are*, used for *-alis*, *-ale* (see *-al*[1]), after stems containing *l.*] An adjective suffix meaning 'of or pertaining to,' 'of the nature of,' 'like,' as in *alar*, *linear*, *polar*, *regular*.

Ar-ab (ar'a̩b). [L. *Arabs*, Gr. Ἄραψ, Ar. *'Arab.*] **I.** *n.* A native of Arabia, or a member of the Arabic race (now widespread in Asia and Africa, and formerly in southern Europe); also, an Arabian horse; also [sometimes *l. c.*], a wanderer or outcast, esp. a child, of the streets (commonly in 'street Arab'). **II.** *a.* Arabian; Arabic.

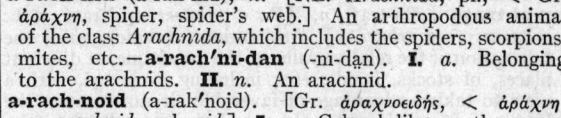

Moorish Arabesque.—Alhambra, Spain.

ar-a-besque (ar-a̩-besk'). [F., < It. *arabesco.*] **I.** *a.* In the Arabian style, esp. of ornamentation. **II.** *n.* A kind of ornament in which flowers, foliage, fruits, geometrical figures, etc. (in strict Mohammedan use, no animals), are represented in a fancifully combined pattern.

A-ra-bi-an (a̩-rā'bi-a̩n). [L. *Arabius.*] **I.** *a.* Pertaining to Arabia or the Arabs. **II.** *n.* An Arab.

Ar-a-bic (ar'a̩-bik). [L. *Arabicus.*] **I.** *a.* Belonging to or derived from Arabia or the Arabians: as, *Arabic* architecture; *Arabic* numerals or figures (the characters 1, 2, 3, 4, 5, 6, 7, 8, 9, 0). **II.** *n.* The language of the Arabians, a Semitic dialect which has contributed largely to many Oriental and other languages.

Arabic Architecture.—Tombs of the Califs, Cairo.

Ar-a-bist (ar'a̩-bist), *n.* One versed in the Arabic language, literature, or learning.

Ar-a-bize (ar'a̩-bīz), *v. t.*; *-bized*, *-bizing.* To render Arab; conform to the Arab type or ways.

ar-a-ble (ar'a̩-bl). [L. *arabilis*, < *arare*, plow.] **I.** *a.* Fit for plowing or tillage. **II.** *n.* Arable land.

a-ra-ceous (ā̩-rā'shius), *a.* [See *arum.*] Belonging to the *Araceæ*, or arum family of plants, which includes the arums, skunk-cabbage, sweet-flag, calla lily, taro, etc.

a-rach-nid (a-rak'nid), *n.* [NL. *Arachnida*, pl., < Gr. ἀράχνη, spider, spider's web.] An arthropodous animal of the class *Arachnida*, which includes the spiders, scorpions, mites, etc.—**a-rach'ni-dan** (-ni-da̩n). **I.** *a.* Belonging to the arachnids. **II.** *n.* An arachnid.

a-rach-noid (a-rak'noid). [Gr. ἀραχνοειδής, < ἀράχνη: see *arachnid* and *-oid.*] **I.** *a.* Cobweb-like, as the serous membrane (between the dura mater and the pia mater) enveloping the brain and spinal cord; pertaining to this membrane; in *bot.*, formed of or covered with long, delicate hairs or fibers; in *zoöl.*, spider-like; arachnidan. **II.** *n.* The arachnoid membrane; also, an arachnid.

ar-ach-nol-o-gy (ar-ak-nol'ō̩-ji), *n.* [Gr. ἀράχνη, spider: see *-logy.*] The part of zoölogy that treats of the arachnids.

ar-a-gon-ite (ar'a̩-go̩n-īt), *n.* [From *Aragon*, division of northeastern Spain.] A mineral consisting of calcium carbonate, chemically identical with calcite but differing in its orthorhombic crystallization, greater hardness and specific gravity, less marked cleavage, etc.

a-raise† (a̩-rāz'), *v. t.* Same as *raise.*

a-ra-li-a-ceous (a-rā-li-ā'shius), *a.* [NL. *Aralia*, genus including the American spikenard.] Belonging to the *Araliaceæ*, a family of plants including the American spikenard, ginseng, English ivy, etc.

Ar-a-ma-ic (ar-a̩-mā'ik). **I.** *a.* Pertaining to the Biblical country of Aram (Syria and Mesopotamia), or to a language, or group of dialects, spoken there and in neighboring regions. **II.** *n.* The Aramaic language, or group of dialects, belonging to the Semitic family and including the Syriac and the dialect spoken in Palestine at the time of Christ.

Ar-a-me-an, Ar-a-mæ-an (ar-a̩-mē'a̩n). [L. *Aramæus*, < Gr. Ἀραμαῖος.] **I.** *a.* Of or pertaining to Aram or its language; Aramaic. **II.** *n.* A Semite of the division associated with Aram; also, the Aramaic language.

a-ra-ne-id (a-rā'nē̩-id), *n.* [NL. *Araneida*, pl., < L. *aranea*, spider, spider's web: cf. *arachnid.*] An arachnid of the order *Araneida*; a spider.—**ar-a-ne-i-dan** (ar-ā̩-nē'i-da̩n), *a.* and *n.*

ar-a-ne-i-form (ar-ā̩-nē'i-fôrm), *a.* [L. *aranea*, spider: see *-form.*] Spider-like.

a-ra-ne-ol-o-gy (a-rā-nē̩-ol'ō̩-ji), *n.* [L. *aranea*, spider: see *-logy.*] The part of zoölogy that treats of spiders.

a-ra-ne-ose, a-ra-ne-ous (a-rā'nē̩-ōs, -us), *a.* [L. *araneosus*, < *aranea*, spider's web: cf. *araneid.*] Cobweb-like; arachnoid.

ar-a-pai-ma (ar-a̩-pī'mä̩), *n.* [Native name.] The largest known fresh-water fish, *Arapaima gigas*, of Brazil and Guiana, said to attain a length of 15 feet and a weight of 400 pounds.

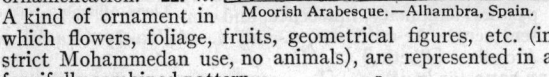

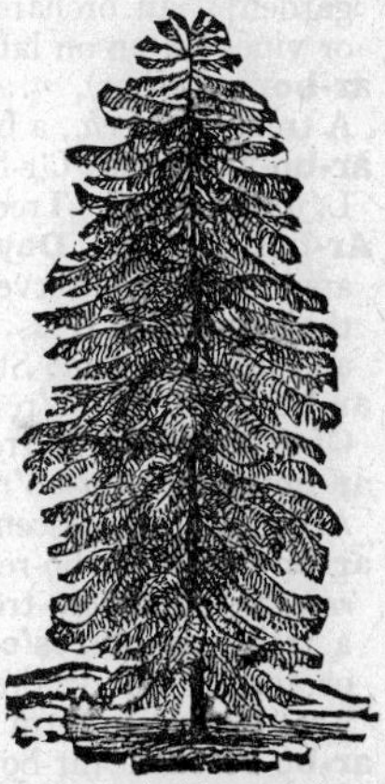
Araucaria (*A. excelsa*).

ar-a-ro-ba (ar-a̩-rō'bä̩), *n.* [Brazilian.] Goa powder.

ar-au-ca-ri-a (ar-â-kā'ri-ä̩), *n.* [NL.; named from *Arauco*, province of southern Chile.] Any tree of the pinaceous genus *Araucaria*, of South America, Australia, and Polynesia, which includes various species occurring native as very tall forest-trees, as *A. imbricata*, the monkey-puzzle, and *A. excelsa*, the Norfolk Island pine (sometimes over 200 feet high), but much smaller in cultivation, *A. excelsa* being familiar as a pot-plant.—**ar-au-ca'ri-an,** *a.* and *n.*

ar-ba-list, ar-ba-lest (är'ba̩-list, -lest), *n.* [OF. *arbaleste* (F. *arbalète*), < LL. *arcuballista*, < L. *arcus*, bow, + *ballista*: see *ballista.*] A powerful medieval crossbow, bent by a special mechanism and discharging arrows, balls, or stones.—**ar'ba-lis-ter, ar'ba-les-ter,** *n.* One armed with an arbalist.

Arbalister.

ar-bi-ter (är'bi-tėr), *n.* [L., < *ar-*, for *ad*, to, + *betere*, go.] One empowered to decide a point at issue; an arbitrator; also, one who has the sole or absolute power of determining.

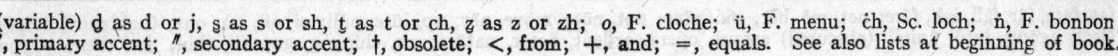

ar-bi-tra-ble (är′bi-tra̤-bl), *a.* Subject to arbitration.
ar-bi-trage (är′bi-trā̤j), *n.* [F., < *arbitrer*, arbitrate, < L. *arbitrari*: see *arbitrate*.] Arbitration (archaic); also, the calculation of the relative value at the same time, at different places, of stocks, bonds, etc., including exchange, with a view to taking advantage of favorable circumstances; the business founded on such calculations.—**ar′bi-trag-er, ar′bi-trag-ist** (-tra̤-jėr, -jist), *n.* One engaged in arbitrage.
ar-bi-tral (är′bi-tra̤l), *a.* Pertaining to an arbiter or to arbitration.
ar-bit-ra-ment (är-bit′ra̤-mẹnt), *n.* [OF. *arbitrement*, < *arbitrer*, < L. *arbitrari*: see *arbitrate*.] The power, decision, or sentence of an arbiter; decisive judgment.
ar-bi-tra-ry (är′bi-trā̤-ri), *a.* [L. *arbitrarius*, < *arbiter*, E. *arbiter*.] Decided or deciding according to judgment or will; independent of law or rule; discretionary; capricious; despotic.—**ar′bi-tra-ri-ly,** *adv.*—**ar′bi-tra-ri-ness,** *n.*
ar-bi-trate (är′bi-trāt), *v.*; *-trated, -trating.* [L. *arbitratus*, pp. of *arbitrari*, < *arbiter*, E. *arbiter*.] **I.** *intr.* To act as arbiter; decide between opposing parties or sides; also, to submit a matter to arbitration. **II.** *tr.* To act as arbiter of; determine; settle (a matter) by arbitration; submit (a matter) to arbitration.—**ar-bi-tra′tion** (-trā′shọn), *n.* [L. *arbitratio(n-)*.] The act of arbitrating; determination; settlement of a cause at issue by a person or a board of persons empowered to decide; also, arbitrage as concerned with exchange (commonly called *arbitration of exchange*).—**ar′bi-tra-tive** (-tra̤-tiv), *a.* Having the function of arbitrating; pertaining to arbitration.—**ar′bi-tra-tor** (-trā-tọr), *n.* [LL.] One who arbitrates; an arbiter; one specially empowered to arbitrate.—**ar′bi-tra-tor-ship,** *n.*
ar-bit-re-ment (är-bit′rẹ-mẹnt), *n.* See *arbitrament.*
ar-bi-tress (är′bi-tres), *n.* A female arbiter.
ar-blast (är′blast), etc. Same as *arbalist*, etc.
ar-bor[1] (är′bọr), *n.* [AF. *erber*, OF. *herbier*, < ML. *herbarium*, a garden, LL. a herbarium: see *herbarium*.] A garden†; an orchard†; a bower formed by trees, shrubs, or vines (often on latticework).
ar-bor[2] (är′bọr), *n.* [L., tree; in part through F. *arbre*.] A tree; in *mech.*, a beam, shaft, axis, or spindle.
ar-bo-ra-ceous (är-bọ-rā′shius), *a.* [NL. *arboraceus*, < L. *arbor*, tree.] Tree-like; arboreal.
Ar-bor (är′bọr) **Day.** [L. *arbor*, tree.] A day publicly appointed or observed in individual States of the U. S. for the planting of trees: varying in date according to the State, and being in some States a legal holiday.
ar-bo-re-al (är-bō′rẹ-a̤l), *a.* [L. *arboreus*: see *arboreous*.] Of or pertaining to trees; tree-like; living on or among trees.
ar-bo-re-ous (är-bō′rẹ-us), *a.* [L. *arboreus*, < *arbor*, tree.] Arboreal; arborescent; abounding in trees.
ar-bo-resce (är-bọ-res′), *v. i.*; *-resced, -rescing.* [L. *arborescere*, < *arbor*, tree: see *-esce*.] To take the form of a tree.—**ar-bo-res′cence** (-res′ẹns), *n.* Arborescent state or form; an arborescent formation.—**ar-bo-res′cent,** *a.* Tree-like, as in form or growth; branching; dendritic.
ar-bo-re-tum (är-bọ-rē′tum), *n.*; pl. *-tums* or *-ta* (-tä̤). [L., < *arbor*, tree.] A plantation of trees or shrubs, esp. for scientific purposes; a botanical tree-garden.
ar-bor-i-cole (är-bor′i-kōl), *a.* [L. *arbor*, tree: see *-cole*.] Inhabiting trees. Also **ar-bo-ric′o-lous** (-bọ-rik′ọ̄-lus).
ar-bo-ri-cul-ture (är′bọ-ri-kul″tūr), *n.* [L. *arbor*, tree, + *cultura*, culture.] Tree-culture; the cultivation of trees and shrubs.—**ar″bo-ri-cul′tur-ist,** *n.*
ar-bo-ri-form (är′bọ-ri-fôrm), *a.* [L. *arbor*, tree: see *-form*.] Having the form of a tree.
ar-bo-rist (är′bọ-rist), *n.* [L. *arbor*, tree.] One versed in the subject of trees.
ar-bo-rol-a-try (är-bọ-rol′a̤-tri), *n.* [L. *arbor*, tree: see *-latry*.] The worship of trees.
ar-bo-rous (är′bọ-rus), *a.* [L. *arbor*, tree.] Of or pertaining to trees.

Arbor-vitæ (*Thuja occidentalis*).

ar-bor=vi-tæ (är″bọr-vī′tē), *n.* [L. *arbor vitæ*, 'tree of life.'] An evergreen tree of the pinaceous genus *Thuja*, esp. *T. occidentalis*, planted for hedges, etc.; in *anat.*, a tree-like appearance in a vertical section of the cerebellum, due to the arrangement of the white and gray nerve-tissues.
ar-bour (är′bọr), *n.* British preferred form of *arbor*[1].
ar-bute (är′būt), *n.* The European arbutus. [Poetic.]
ar-bu-tus (är′bū̦-tus, U. S. är-bū′tus), *n.* [L., strawberry-tree.] Any of the evergreen shrubs or trees of the ericaceous genus *Arbutus*, esp. *A. unedo*, the strawberry-tree of southern Europe, with scarlet berries, cultivated for ornament; also, a creeping ericaceous plant, *Epigæa repens*, of the U. S., with fragrant white and pink flowers ('trailing arbutus'); the Mayflower.

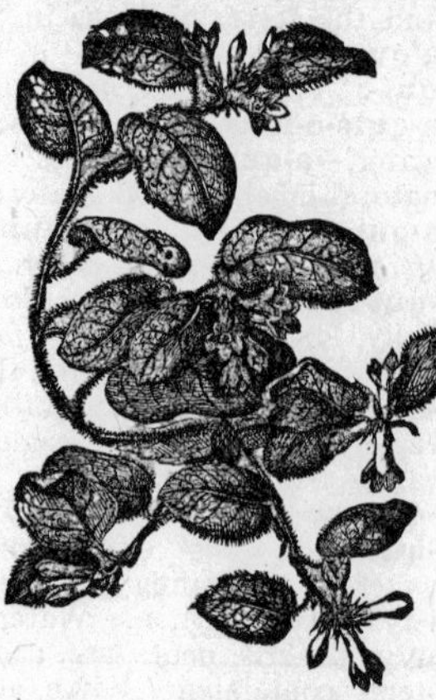

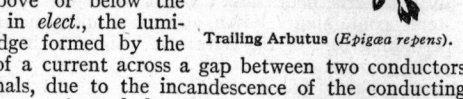

Trailing Arbutus (*Epigæa repens*).

arc (ärk), *n.* [OF. F. *arc*, < L. *arcus*, bow, arch, arc.] Something bow-shaped, as a rainbow; an architectural arch†; in *geom.*, any part of a circle or other curved line; in *astron.*, the part of a circle representing the apparent course of a heavenly body either above or below the horizon; in *elect.*, the luminous bridge formed by the passage of a current across a gap between two conductors or terminals, due to the incandescence of the conducting vapors.—**arc,** *v. i.*; *arcked, arcking.* In *elect.*, to form an arc.

Arcade.—Court of the Lions, Alhambra, Spain.

ar-cade (är-kād′), *n.* [F., < It. *arcata*, < ML. *arcata*, < L. *arcus*: see *arc*.] A series of arches supported on piers or pillars; an arched, roofed, or covered passageway; a building having an arched or covered passageway serving as a public thoroughfare.—**ar-cad′ed** (-kā′ded), *a.* Provided with an arcade.
Ar-ca-di-a (är-kā′di-a̤), *n.* [From *Arcadia*, a mountainous district in ancient Greece, proverbial for the contented pastoral simplicity of its people.] Any region (real or ideal) characterized by pastoral simplicity, innocence, and contentment.—**Ar-ca′di-an,** *a.* and *n.*—**Ar′ca-dy** (-ka̤-di), *n.* Arcadia. [Poetic.]
ar-cane (är-kān′), *a.* [L. *arcanus*, < *arcere*, keep, shut up: see *ark*.] Hidden; secret. [Now rare.]—**ar-ca′num** (-kā′-num), *n.*; pl. *-na* (-nä̤). [L., neut. of *arcanus*.] A secret; a mystery; esp., one of the great secrets that the alchemists sought to discover; hence, a sovereign remedy.
arch[1] (ärch), *n.* [OF. *arche*, a fem. form (due to confusion with *arche*, < L. *arca*, E. *ark*) for *arc*, < L. *arcus*: see *arc*.] Something bowed or curved; a bow-like part or form; an upward curving bend; a curved structure resting on supports at both extremities, used to sustain weight, to bridge or roof an open space, etc.; typically, a structure made up of separate blocks (voussoirs), each having the form of a truncated wedge, the central block being the keystone, so assembled on a curved line as to retain their position when the structure is supported only at its two extremities; an arched structure or place, or an archway (as, to pass through the *arch* of a bridge; a triumphal *arch*); in *aëronautics*, a downward curve, or a curve with the concave part downward, as at the end of a plane; a part or structure so curved.—**arch**[1], *v.* **I.** *tr.* To furnish, cover, or span with an

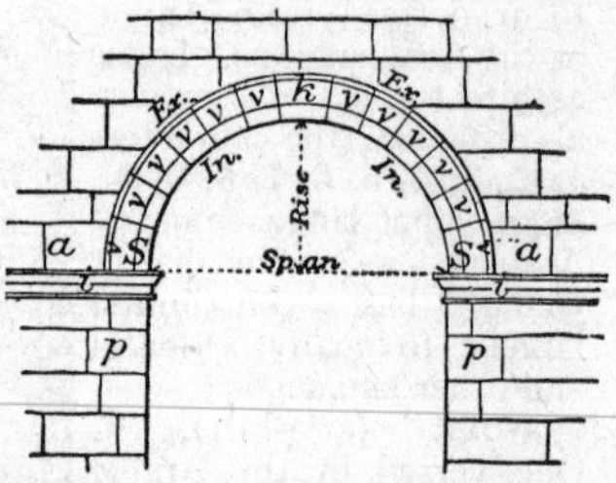

Arch.
a, abutments; *v*, voussoirs; *S*, springers; *i*, imposts; *In*, intrados; *p*, piers; *k*, keystone; *Ex*, extrados.

arch; also, to curve like an arch. **II.** *intr.* To form an arch.

arch² (ärch), *a.* [Separate use of *arch-*.] Chief, principal, or preëminent; also (from uses with *rogue, wag,* etc.), sly; cunning; roguish; playfully mischievous.

arch- (ärch-, also, in *archangel,* etc., ärk-). [AS. *arce-, erce-,* < L. *arch-, arche-, archi-,* < Gr. ἀρχ-, ἀρχε-, ἀρχι-, akin to ἀρχός, leader, chief, ἄρχειν, be first, begin, lead, rule.] A prefix meaning 'first,' 'chief,' occurring orig. in words from the Greek, but now freely used as an English formative, as in *arch-druid, arch-magician, arch-traitor, arch-villain.*

-arch. [Gr. -αρχος, -αρχης, < ἄρχειν, be first, lead, rule.] A noun termination meaning 'leader,' 'ruler,' as in *exarch, heptarch, monarch, oligarch, patriarch.* Cf. *-archy.*

Ar-chæ-an, Ar-che-an (är-kē′ạn). [Gr. ἀρχαῖος, primeval, ancient, < ἀρχή, beginning, < ἄρχειν, be first.] **I.** *a.* Noting or pertaining to the oldest geological period or system of rocks. **II.** *n.* The Archæan period or system.

archæo-, archeo-. Forms of Gr. ἀρχαῖος, primeval, ancient (see *Archæan*), used in combination.

ar-chæ-og-ra-phy (är-kẹ-og′rạ-fi), *n.* [See *archæo-* and *-graphy.*] The description of antiquities; descriptive archæology.

ar-chæ-o-log-ic, ar-che-o-log-ic (är″kẹ-ọ-loj′ik), *a.* Same as *archæological.*

ar-chæ-o-log-i-cal, ar-che-o-log-i-cal (är″kẹ-ọ-loj′i-kạl), *a.* Of or pertaining to archæology.—**ar″chæ-o-log′i-cal-ly, ar″che-o-log′i-cal-ly,** *adv.*

ar-chæ-ol-o-gist, ar-che-ol-o-gist (är-kẹ-ol′ọ-jist), *n.* One versed in archæology.

ar-chæ-ol-o-gy, ar-che-ol-o-gy (är-kẹ-ol′ọ-ji), *n.* [Gr. ἀρχαιολογία: see *archæo-* and *-logy.*] The science of antiquities; the branch of knowledge concerned with the remote past as studied from its records, monuments, or other remains.

ar-chæ-op-te-ryx (är-kẹ-op′tẹ-riks), *n.* [NL., < Gr. ἀρχαῖος, ancient, + πτέρυξ, wing, bird.] A bird of the extinct genus *Archæopteryx,* the oldest known avian type, occurring as a fossil, with teeth and a long reptilian vertebrate tail.

Ar-chæ-o-zo-ic (är″kẹ-ọ-zō′ik). [Gr. ἀρχαῖος, ancient, + ζωή, life.] In *geol.*: **I.** *a.* Noting or pertaining to the division of Archæan time characterized (supposedly) by the presence of organic life. Cf. *azoic.* **II.** *n.* The Archæozoic division of the Archæan.

ar-cha-ic (är-kā′ik), *a.* [Gr. ἀρχαϊκός, < ἀρχαῖος, ancient: see *Archæan.*] Proper to an earlier period; old-fashioned; antiquated; obsolescent.—**ar-cha′i-cal-ly,** *adv.*

ar-cha-ism (är′kạ-izm), *n.* [Gr. ἀρχαϊσμός.] The use of what is archaic, as in art or language; archaic quality or style; something archaic, as a word or expression.—**ar′cha-ist,** *n.* One who uses archaisms or affects an archaic style; also, an archæologist.—**ar-cha-is′tic,** *a.*

ar-cha-ize (är′kạ-īz), *v.*; *-ized, -izing.* [Gr. ἀρχαΐζειν.] **I.** *intr.* To use archaisms; affect archaism. **II.** *tr.* To render archaic; give an archaic appearance or quality to.—**ar′cha-iz-er,** *n.*

arch-an-gel (ärk′ān′jẹl), *n.* [LL. *archangelus,* < Gr. ἀρχάγγελος, 'chief angel.'] A chief or principal angel; one of a particular order of angels (see *angel*); also, a variety of domestic pigeon with lustrous metallic plumage.—**arch′-an-gel′ic** (-an-jel′ik), *a.*

arch-bish-op (ärch′bish′ọp), *n.* [AS. *arcebiscop,* < LL. *archiepiscopus,* < LGr. ἀρχιεπίσκοπος, 'chief bishop.'] A bishop of the highest rank; usually, a metropolitan.—**arch′bish′op-ric** (-rik), *n.* [AS. *arcebiscoprīce.*] The see, diocese, or office of an archbishop.

arch-dea-con (ärch′dē′kọn), *n.* [AS. *arcediacon,* < LL. *archidiaconus,* < LGr. ἀρχιδιάκονος, 'chief deacon.'] An ecclesiastic who has charge of the temporal and external administration of a diocese, with jurisdiction delegated from the bishop.—**arch′dea′con-ate** (-ạt), *n.* An archdeaconry. —**arch′dea′con-ry,** *n.*; pl. *-ries* (-riz). The jurisdiction, district, residence, or office of an archdeacon.—**arch′dea′-con-ship,** *n.*

arch-di-o-cese (ärch′dī′ọ-sēs), *n.* [See *arch-.*] An archbishop's diocese.

arch-du-cal (ärch′dū′kạl), *a.* Pertaining to an archduke.

arch-duch-ess (ärch′duch′es), *n.* [= F. *archiduchesse.*] The wife of an archduke; a princess of the imperial family of Austria.

arch-duch-y (ärch′duch′i), *n.*; pl. *-ies* (-iz). [= F. *archiduché.*] The territory of an archduke or archduchess.

arch-duke (ärch′dūk′), *n.* [From *arch-* + *duke,* after OF. *archeduc* (F. *archiduc*), < ML. *archidux,* 'chief duke.'] A title formerly borne by sovereign princes of Austrasia, Lorraine, Brabant, and Austria, but later only a titular dignity of princes of the house of Austria.—**arch′duke′dom** (-dọm), *n.* An archduchy.

Ar-che′an, *a.* and *n.* See *Archæan.*

arched (ärcht), *p. a.* Furnished with an arch or arches; curved like an arch.

ar-che-gone (är′kẹ-gōn), *n.* Same as *archegonium.*

ar-che-go-ni-um (är-kẹ-gō′ni-um), *n.*; pl. *-nia* (-ni-ạ). [NL., < Gr. ἀρχέγονος, first of a race, < ἀρχε- (see *arch-*) + -γονος, < γεν-, bear, produce.] In *bot.,* the female reproductive organ in ferns, mosses, etc.—**ar-che-go′ni-al,** *a.*—**ar-che-go′ni-ate** (-āt), *a.*

arch=en-e-my (ärch′en′ẹ-mi), *n.*; pl. *-mies* (-miz). [See *arch-.*] A chief enemy; with *the,* the devil; Satan.

ar-chen-te-ron (är-ken′tẹ-ron), *n.* [NL., < Gr. ἀρχ- (see *arch-*) + ἔντερον, E. *enteron.*] In *zoöl.,* the primitive enteron or digestive cavity of a gastrula.—**ar-chen-ter′ic** (-ter′ik), *a.*

archeo-, etc. See *archæo-,* etc.

ar-cher (är′chėr), *n.* [OF. *archier* (F. *archer*), < LL. *arcarius,* < L. *arcus,* bow.] One who shoots with a bow; also, an archer-fish; also [*cap.*], the zodiacal constellation or sign Sagittarius.—**ar′-cher-ess,** *n.* A female archer. —**ar′cher=fish,** *n.* Any of the small acanthopterygian fishes of the family *Toxotidæ,* of East Indian and Polynesian seas, said to bring down insects by shooting drops of water at them from the mouth.—**ar′cher-y,** *n.* The practice, art, or skill of an archer; archers' weapons; archers collectively.

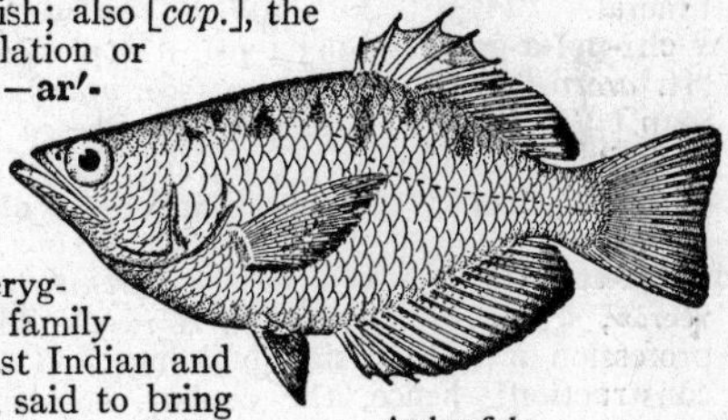
Archer-fish.

ar-che-spore (är′kẹ-spōr), *n.* [NL. *archesporium,* < Gr. ἀρχε- (see *arch-*) + σπορά, seed, E. *spore.*] In *bot.,* the primitive cell, or group of cells, which gives rise to the cells from which spores are derived.—**ar-che-spo′ri-al** (-spō′-ri-ạl), *a.*

ar-che-type (är′kẹ-tīp), *n.* [L. *archetypum,* < Gr. ἀρχέτυπον, neut. of ἀρχέτυπος, first-molded, original, < ἀρχε- (see *arch-*) + τύπτειν, strike.] An original form, model, or pattern; a prototype.—**ar′che-ty-pal** (-tī-pạl), **ar-che-typ′ic** (-tip′ik), *a.*

arch=fiend (ärch′fēnd′), *n.* [See *arch-.*] A chief fiend; with *the,* Satan.

archi-. [L. *archi-,* < Gr. ἀρχι-: see *arch-.*] A form of *arch-,* 'first,' 'chief,' in words derived from the Greek or formed after the Greek type: in biological and other scientific terms, commonly meaning 'primitive,' 'original.'—**ar-chi-blast** (är′ki-blast), *n.* [+ *-blast.*] In *biol.,* the formative yolk of an egg.—**ar′chi-carp** (-kärp), *n.* [+ *-carp.*] In *bot.,* an ascogonium.

ar-chi-di-ac-o-nal (är″ki-dī-ak′ọ-nạl), *a.* [LL. *archidiaconus,* E. *archdeacon.*] Pertaining to an archdeacon.—**ar″chi-di-ac′o-nate** (-nāt), *n.*

arch-ie (är′chi), *n.* [From *Archie,* for *Archibald,* man's name.] An anti-aircraft gun. [Soldiers' slang.]

ar-chi-e-pis-co-pal (är″ki-ẹ-pis′kọ-pạl), *a.* [LL. *archiepiscopus,* E. *archbishop.*] Pertaining to an archbishop.—**ar″chi-e-pis′co-pate** (-pāt), *n.*

ar-chil (är′kil), *n.* Same as *orchil.*

Ar-chi-lo-chi-an (är-ki-lō′ki-ạn), *a.* Of, pertaining to, or characteristic of the Greek poet Archilochus (flourished about 650 B.C.), noted for the bitterness and severity of his satire, and regarded as the originator of certain forms of verse.

ar-chi-mage (är′ki-māj), *n.* [NL. *archimagus*, < Gr. ἀρχίμαγος, 'chief mage.'] A chief or great magician. Also **ar-chi-ma′gus** (-mā′gus); pl. *-gi* (-jī).

ar-chi-man-drite (är-ki-man′drīt), *n.* [LGr. ἀρχιμανδρίτης, < Gr. ἀρχι- (see *arch-*) + μάνδρα, inclosed space, LGr. monastery.] In the *Greek Church*, the head of a monastery; an abbot; sometimes, a superior abbot, having superintendence of several monasteries.

Greek Archimandrite.

Ar-chi-me-de-an (är-ki-mē′dē-an or är″ki-mē-dē′an), *a.* Of or pertaining to the mathematician Archimedes (about 287–212 B.C.), of Syracuse, Sicily.—**Archimedean screw,** a device consisting essentially of a screw forming a spiral passage within an inclined cylinder, or of a tube wound spirally about an inclined axis, for raising water to a height when rotated.

Archimedean Screw.

ar-chi-mime (är′ki-mīm), *n.* [L. *archimimus*, < Gr. ἀρχίμιμος, 'chief mime.'] A chief mime; the hero of the Roman low comedy; the chief buffoon at a Roman funeral.

ar-chi-pel-a-go (är-ki-pel′a-gō), *n.*; pl. *-gos* or *-goes* (-gōz). [It. *arcipelago*, < Gr. ἀρχι- (see *arch-*) + πέλαγος, sea.] [*cap.*] The Ægean Sea, between Greece and Asia Minor, with its many islands; [*l. c.*] any body of water abounding with islands; also, the islands.—**ar″chi-pe-lag′ic** (-pe-laj′ik), *a.*

ar-chi-tect (är′ki-tekt), *n.* [L. *architectus*, < Gr. ἀρχιτέκτων, < ἀρχι- (see *arch-*) + τέκτων, builder.] One whose profession it is to design buildings and superintend their construction; hence, the deviser, constructor, maker, or creator of anything.—**ar′chi-tec-tive,** *a.* Serving for building.

ar-chi-tec-ton-ic (är″ki-tek-ton′ik). [L. *architectonicus*, < Gr. ἀρχιτεκτονικός, < ἀρχιτέκτων: see *architect.*] **I.** *a.* Pertaining to architecture, construction, or design; constructive; also, directive. **II.** *n.* The science of architecture; in *philos.*, the art of constructing systems.—**ar″chi-tec-ton′ics,** *n.* The science of architecture.

ar-chi-tec-tu-ral (är-ki-tek′tūr-al), *a.* Of or pertaining to architecture.—**ar-chi-tec′tur-al-ist,** *n.* A professed student of or connoisseur in architecture.—**ar-chi-tec′tur-al-ly,** *adv.*

ar-chi-tec-ture (är′ki-tek-tūr), *n.* [L. *architectura.*] The art or science of building, including design, construction, and decorative treatment; also, style of building; structure; also, the action or process of building; construction; also, architectural work; a building or structure.

ar-chi-trave (är′ki-trāv), *n.* [F., < It. *architrave*, < *archi-*, chief, + *trave*, < L. *trabs*, beam.] In *arch.*, the lowest division of an entablature, resting immediately on the columns; also, a band of moldings or other ornamentation about a (properly rectangular) door or other opening (cf. *archivolt*).

ar-chive (är′kīv), *n.* [F. *archives*, pl., < L. *archivum*, < Gr. ἀρχεῖον, public building, pl. records, < ἀρχή, rule, office, < ἄρχειν, be first.] A place in which public records are kept (now only in *pl.*); also, a public or other document preserved for evidence or for its historical interest (usually in *pl.*).—**ar-chi-val** (är-kī′val or är′ki-), *a.*—**ar-chi-vist** (är′kī-vist or är′ki-), *n.* A keeper of archives.

ar-chi-volt (är′ki-vōlt), *n.* [F. *archivolte*, < It. *archivolto*, appar. for *arcovolto* (= OF. *arvolt*, *arc vol*), arch, < *arco*, arch, + *volto*, turned, arched.] In *arch.*, a band of moldings or other ornamentation about an arched opening: corresponding to the architrave of a rectangular opening.

arch-ly (ärch′li), *adv.* In an arch manner; with playful mischievousness.—**arch′ness,** *n.*

ar-chon (är′kon), *n.* [Gr. ἄρχων, prop. ppr. of ἄρχειν, be first, rule.] A chief magistrate in an ancient Greek state, esp. Athens; in general, a magistrate, ruler, or president.—**ar′chon-ship, ar′chon-tate** (-tāt), *n.*—**ar-chon′tic,** *a.*

arch-priest (ärch′prēst′), *n.* [OF. *archeprestre* (F. *archiprêtre*), < LL. *archipresbyter*, < LGr. ἀρχιπρεσβύτερος, 'chief presbyter.'] A chief priest; a priest holding first rank, as among the members of a cathedral chapter (later called *dean*) or among the clergy of a district outside the episcopal city (later called *rural dean*); a priest acting as superior of the Roman Catholic secular clergy in England, first appointed in 1598 and superseded by a vicar apostolic in 1623.—**arch′priest′hood** (-hud), *n.*

arch-way (ärch′wā), *n.* An arched passageway.

-archy. [Gr. -αρχία, < -αρχος, -άρχης, E. *-arch.*] A noun termination meaning 'rule,' 'government,' as in *heptarchy*, *monarchy*, *oligarchy*. Cf. *-arch*.

ar-ci-form (är′si-fôrm), *a.* [L. *arcus*, bow: see *-form.*] Bow-shaped; arched.

arc=lamp (ärk′lamp), *n.* A form of lamp employing an electric arc.

arc=light (ärk′līt), *n.* A light produced by an electric arc.

ar-co-graph (är′kō-gråf), *n.* [L. *arcus*, bow, arc: see *-graph.*] An instrument for drawing arcs, having a flexible arc-shaped part adjustable at a required curve by an extensible straight bar connecting its ends.

arc-tic (ärk′tik). [OF. F. *arctique*, < L. *arcticus*, < Gr. ἀρκτικός, < ἄρκτος, a bear, the Great Bear (constellation), the north.] **I.** *a.* Of, near, or lying under the northern constellations of the Great and the Little Bear; of, at, or near the north pole; frigid: as, the *arctic* circle (the southern boundary of the north frigid zone, everywhere distant 23° 28′ from the north pole). **II.** *n.* The arctic region; *pl.*, warm waterproof overshoes.

Arc-to-gæ-a (ärk-tō-jē′ä), *n.* [NL., < Gr. ἄρκτος, the north, + γαῖα, land, earth.] In *zoögeog.*, a primary realm of the earth's surface, comprising Europe, Asia, Africa, and North America (exclusive of Central America).—**Arc-to-gæ′al, Arc-to-gæ′an, Arc-to-gæ′ic,** *a.*

Arc-tu-rus (ärk-tū′rus), *n.* [L., < Gr. Ἀρκτοῦρος, 'bear-ward,' < ἄρκτος, a bear, the Great Bear, + οὖρος, guard, keeper.] A bright star of the first magnitude in the constellation Boötes.—**Arc-tu′ri-an,** *a.*

ar-cu-ate (är′kū-āt), *a.* [L. *arcuatus*, pp. of *arcuare*, curve like a bow, < *arcus*, bow.] Curved like a bow; arched. Also **ar′cu-at-ed** (-ā-ted).—**ar′cu-ate-ly,** *adv.*—**ar-cu-a′-tion** (-ā′shon), *n.* Bow-like curvature; the use of arches in architecture; arched work.

ar-cu-ba-list (är′kū-ba-list), etc. Same as *arbalist*, etc.

-ard. [OF. F. *-ard*, *-art*; from Teut., and akin to E. *hard.*] A noun suffix, orig. intensive but now often depreciative or without special force, as in *coward*, *dotard*, *drunkard*, *mallard*, *wizard*.

ar-deb (är′deb), *n.* [Ar.] A measure of capacity in use in Egypt and neighboring countries, officially equivalent in Egypt to 5.62 U. S. bushels, but varying greatly in different localities.

ar-dent (är′dent), *a.* [OF. F. *ardent*, < L. *ardens* (*ardent-*), ppr. of *ardere*, burn.] Burning, fiery, or hot; also, inflammable (now only in *ardent spirits*, which see, below); also, glowing, as with feeling, eagerness, zeal, etc.; fervent.—**ardent spirits,** strong distilled alcoholic liquors, as whisky, brandy, gin, etc.—**ar′den-cy, ar′dent-ness,** *n.*—**ar′dent-ly,** *adv.*

Ar-dois (F. är-dwo) **sig′nal sys′tem.** [From proper name.] *Naut.*, a signaling system used by ships for sending messages at night, in which pairs of electric lights (each pair consisting of one red and one white light) are arranged vertically on a mast or stay and operated by a keyboard below.

ar-dor (är′dor), *n.* [OF. *ardour* (F. *ardeur*), < L. *ardor*, < *ardere*, burn: cf. *ardent.*] Burning heat; fig., warmth of feeling; fervor; eagerness; zeal.

ar-dour (är′dor), *n.* British preferred form of *ardor*.

ar-du-ous (är′dū-us), *a.* [L. *arduus*, lofty, steep, difficult.] Lofty; steep; hard to climb; hence, requiring or using great exertion; laborious; strenuous.—**ar′du-ous-ly,** *adv.*—**ar′du-ous-ness,** *n.*

are[1] (är). [AS. (Northumbrian) *aron*; from the stem seen in *art*[1] and *am*.] Present indicative plural of *be*.

are[2] (ãr), *n.* [F., < L. *area*: see *area*.] In the *metric system*, a surface measure equal to 100 square meters, or 119.6 square yards.

a-re-a (ā′rẹ̄-ạ̈), *n.*; pl. *areas*, L. *areæ* (-ē). [L., piece of level ground, open space.] A piece of unoccupied ground or surface; an open space; a particular extent of any surface; a tract; a yard or court of a building; a sunken space before a basement door; also, amount of surface (plane or curved), as within the lines of a geometrical figure; superficial extent; fig., extent, range, or scope.—**a′re-al,** *a.*

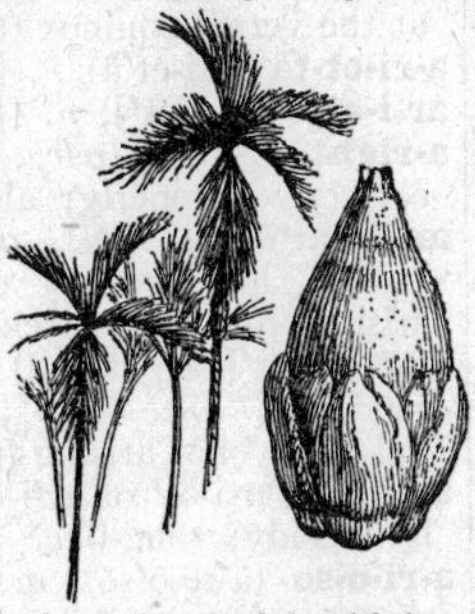

Areca (*A. catechu*), with its fruit, the Areca-nut.

ar-e-ca (ar′ẹ̄-kạ̈), *n.* [Pg.; from Dravidian name.] Any palm-tree of the genus *Areca*, of tropical Asia and the Malay Archipelago, esp. *A. catechu*, which bears a nut (the *areca-nut*, or betel-nut) used by the natives for chewing with lime and betel-leaves; the nut itself; also, any of various palms formerly referred to the genus *Areca*.

a-re-na (ạ-rē′nạ̈), *n.*; pl. *-nas*. [L., sand, sandy place.] The space, usually sanded, in a Roman amphitheater, in which the combats or other performances took place; a similar space in any amphitheater; the ground or scene of any contest; a field of conflict or endeavor.

ar-e-na-ceous (ar-ẹ̄-nā′shius), *a.* [L. *arenaceus*, < *arena*, sand.] Sand-like; sandy.

ar-e-na-tion (ar-ẹ̄-nā′shọn), *n.* [L. *arenatio(n-)*, < *arena*, sand.] Remedial application of (hot) sand to the body; a sand-bath.

a-re-nic (ạ-rē′nik), *a.* Of or pertaining to an arena.

ar-e-nic-o-lous (ar-ẹ̄-nik′ọ̄-lus), *a.* [L. *arena*, sand: see *-colous*.] Inhabiting sand.

ar-e-nose (ar′ẹ̄-nōs), *a.* [L. *arenosus*, < *arena*, sand.] Full of sand; sandy.

areo-. Form of Gr. Ἄρης, Ares, Mars, used in combination.—**a-re-o-cen-tric** (ā″rẹ̄-ọ̄-sen′trik or ar″ẹ̄-), *a.* Having the planet Mars as center.—**a-re-og′ra-phy** (-og′rạ-fi), *n.* [+ *-graphy*.] The description of or a treatise on the planet Mars.—**a-re-og′ra-pher,** *n.*—**a″re-o-graph′ic** (-graf′ik), *a.*

a-re-o-la (a-rē′ọ̄-lạ̈), *n.*; pl. *-læ* (-lē). [L., dim. of *area*: see *area*.] A small area or space; a small interstice, as between the fibers of cellular tissue; a ring of color, as about a pustule or the human nipple.—**a-re′o-lar** (-lạ̈r), *a.* Of or like an areola; containing areolæ, as tissue.—**a-re′o-late** (-lāt), *a.* Formed with areolæ. Also **a-re′o-lat-ed.**—**ar-e-o-la-tion** (ar″ẹ̄-ọ̄-lā′shọn), *n.* Areolate formation.—**ar′e-ole** (-ōl), *n.* An areola.

a-re-ol-o-gy (ā-rẹ̄-ol′ọ̄-ji or ar-ẹ̄-), *n.* [See *areo-* and *-logy*.] The scientific investigation of the planet Mars itself, not including its orbital motion and the like.

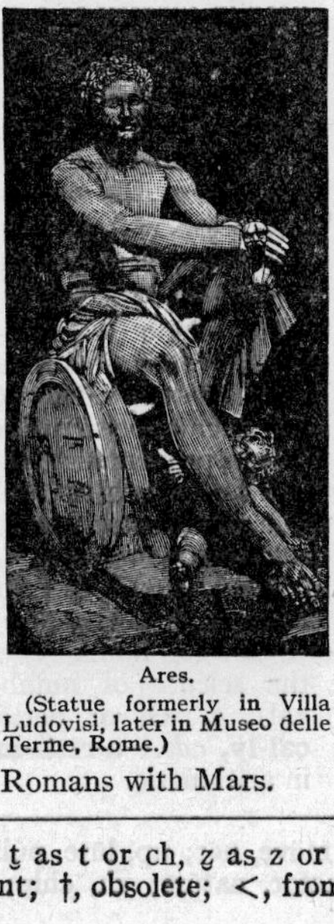

Ares.
(Statue formerly in Villa Ludovisi, later in Museo delle Terme, Rome.)

ar-e-om-e-ter (ar-ẹ̄-om′e-tėr), *n.* [Gr. ἀραιός, thin: see *-meter*.] An instrument for measuring density; a hydrometer.—**ar-e-om′e-try,** *n.*

Ar-e-op-a-gite (ar-ẹ̄-op′ạ-gīt or -jīt), *n.* [L. *Areopagites*, < Gr. Ἀρειοπαγίτης.] A member of the tribunal of the Areopagus.—**Ar-e-op-a-git′ic** (-git′ik or -jit′ik), *a.*

Ar-e-op-a-gus (ar-ẹ̄-op′ạ-gus), *n.* [L., < Gr. Ἀρειόπαγος, for Ἄρειος πάγος, hill of Ares (Mars): cf. Acts, xvii. 19, 22.] A hill in Athens, to the west of the Acropolis; also, the sovereign council or tribunal of ancient Athens, which held its sessions on this hill; hence, any high tribunal.

A-res (ā′rēz), *n.* [Gr. Ἄρης.] The Greek god of war, identified by the Romans with Mars.

a-rête (à-rāt), *n.* [F. *arête*, OF. *areste*, < L. *arista*, awn, spine: cf. *arris*.] A sharp ridge of a mountain.

ar-gal (är′gạl), *adv.* Corruption of *ergo*. See Shakspere's "Hamlet," v. 1. 21. [Archaic.]

ar-ga-la (är′gạ-lạ̈), *n.* [Hind. *hargīlā*.] The adjutant-bird of India; also, the African marabou.

ar-ga-li (är′gạ-li), *n.* [Mongol.] A large wild sheep of Asia, *Ovis argali* (or *ammon*), with long, thick, spirally curved horns; some other wild sheep, as the bighorn or the aoudad.

Argali (*Ovis argali*).

Ar-gand (är′gand) **lamp.** [From A. *Argand* (1755–1803), Swiss inventor.] A lamp with a tubular burner ('Argand burner'), admitting air to the flame both within and without.

ar-gent (är′jẹnt). [F. *argent*, < L. *argentum*, silver: cf. Gr. ἄργυρος, silver, ἀργός, bright, white.] **I.** *n.* Silver, or something resembling it (archaic or poetic); in *her.*, the tincture silver or white. **II.** *a.* Of or like silver; silvery.—**ar-gen′tal** (-jen′tạl), *a.* Of, pertaining to, containing, or resembling silver.—**ar′gen-tate** (-jẹn-tāt), *a.* [L. *argentatus*, silvered.] In *bot.*, silvery.—**ar-gen′te-ous** (-jen′tẹ̄-us), *a.* [L. *argenteus*.] Silvery.—**ar-gen′tic,** *a.* Of or containing silver. See *argentous*.—**ar-gen-tif′er-ous** (-jẹn-tif′ẹ-rus), *a.* [See *-ferous*.] Yielding silver.

ar-gen-tine[1] (är′jẹn-tin or -tīn). [F. *argentin*, < L. *argentum*, silver.] **I.** *a.* Of or like silver; silvery. **II.** *n.* A silver-like metal or substance; finely divided tin, used for plating and for printing on paper, etc.; a silvery slaty calcite; a silvery substance obtained from fish-scales, used in making artificial pearls.

Ar-gen-tine[2] (är′jẹn-tēn or -tīn). **I.** *a.* Of or pertaining to the South American republic of Argentina. **II.** *n.* A native or inhabitant of Argentina.—**Ar-gen-tin′e-an** (-tin′ẹ̄-ạn), *a.* and *n.*

ar-gen-tite (är′jẹn-tīt), *n.* [L. *argentum*, silver.] A native sulphide of silver, a dark lead-gray mineral occurring crystalline and massive: an important ore of silver.

ar-gen-tol (är′jẹn-tol or -tōl), *n.* [L. *argentum*, silver: see *-ol*.] A yellow organic compound of silver, derived from quinoline: used as an antiseptic and astringent.

ar-gen-tous (är-jen′tus), *a.* [L. *argentum*, silver.] Containing silver (in larger proportion than a corresponding argentic compound).

ar-gen-try (är′jẹn-tri), *n.* [F. *argenterie*, < *argent*: see *argent*.] Silver plate†; silvery appearance or light (poetic).

ar-gen-tum (är-jen′tum), *n.* [L.] Silver: in *chem.*, abbreviated *Ag* (without period).

ar-gil (är′jil), *n.* [F. *argile*, < L. *argilla*, < Gr. ἄργιλλα, < ἀργός, white.] Clay, esp. potters' clay.—**ar-gil-la′ceous** (-ji-lā′shius), *a.* [L. *argillaceus*.] Of the nature of or resembling clay; clayey.—**ar-gil-lif′er-ous** (-lif′ẹ-rus), *a.* [See *-ferous*.] Yielding clay.—**ar′gil-lite** (-līt), *n.* A schist or slate derived from clay.—**ar-gil′lous,** *a.* [L. *argillosus*.] Clayey.

Ar-give (är′giv or -jīv). [L. *Argivus*.] **I.** *a.* Of or pertaining to Argos, a leading city of ancient Greece, in the eastern Peloponnesus; hence, Greek. **II.** *n.* A native or inhabitant of Argos; hence, any Greek.

ar-gol (är′gol), *n.* [AF. *argoil*; origin unknown.] Crude tartar, gathering in a crust on the sides of vessels in which wine is fermented.

ar-gon (är′gon), *n.* [NL., < Gr. ἀργόν, neut. of ἀργός, idle, < ἀ- priv. + -εργός, working.] Chem. sym., A or Ar; at. wt., 39.88. A gaseous element existing in the atmosphere: named from its chemical inertness.

Ar-go-naut (är′gọ̄-nât), *n.* [L. *Argonauta*, < Gr. Ἀργοναύτης, < Ἀργώ, Argo, + ναύτης, sailor.] In Greek legend, one of those who sailed to Colchis with Jason in the ship Argo in quest of the golden fleece; hence, one of the fortune-seekers who went to California during the gold fever of

(variable) ḓ as d or j, ş as s or sh, ţ as t or ch, z̧ as z or zh; o, F. cloche; ü, F. menu; ċh, Sc. loch; ṅ, F. bonbon; ′, primary accent; ″, secondary accent; †, obsolete; <, from; +, and; =, equals. See also lists at beginning of book.

1849 and thereabouts; [*l. c.*] a dibranchiate cephalopod mollusk of the genus *Argonauta*; the paper-nautilus.—**Ar-go-nau′-tic,** *a.*

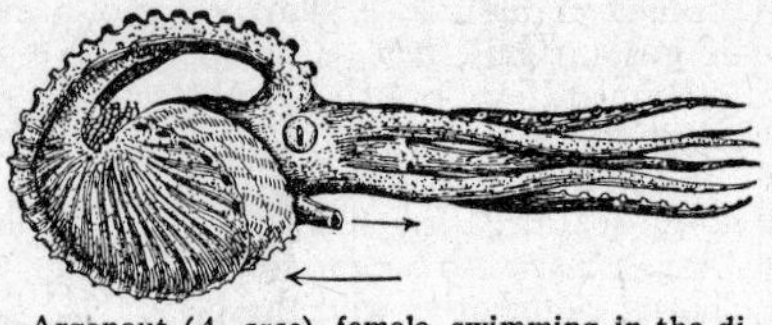

Argonaut (*A. argo*), female, swimming in the direction of the large arrow—the smaller showing the current from the siphon.

ar-go-sy (är′gǫ-si), *n.*; pl. *-sies* (-siz). [It. *Ragusea*, vessel of Ragusa (port in Dalmatia).] A large merchant vessel, esp. one carrying a rich freight: as, "Lombard and Venetian merchants with deep-laden *argosies*" (Longfellow's "Belfry of Bruges"). [Now poetic or fig.]

ar-got (är′gō or -gǫt), *n.* [F.; origin unknown.] The peculiar language or jargon of thieves and vagabonds; thieves' cant; hence, the cant of any class; slang.—**ar-got′ic** (-got′ik), *a.*

ar-gu-a-ble (är′gū-ą-bl), *a.* That may be argued.

ar-gue (är′gū), *v.*; *-gued, -guing.* [OF. F. *arguer*, < L. *argutare*, freq. of *arguere*, make clear, show, prove.] **I.** *intr.* To present reasons for or against a thing; contend in argument. **II.** *tr.* To treat by reasoning; discuss; debate; maintain in reasoning (as, to *argue* that something must be so); persuade, drive, etc., by reasoning; also, to accuse† or convict†; also, of reasons, evidence, etc., to show or prove; imply; indicate.—**ar′gu-er** (-gū-ėr), *n.*

ar-gu-fy (är′gū-fī), *v. i.* or *t.*; *-fied, -fying.* [From *argue* + *-fy.*] To argue or wrangle, or worry with argument; also, to signify or import. [Colloq. or prov.]

ar-gu-ment (är′gū-mẹnt), *n.* [OF. F. *argument*, < L. *argumentum*, < *arguere*: see *argue.*] A statement or fact tending to prove a point; a reason, evidence, or proof; an indication or manifestation; a process of reasoning; argumentation, debate, or controversy; the subject-matter of a discourse or writing; an abstract of contents, as prefixed to a book or a section of a book.—**ar″gu-men-ta′tion** (-men-tā′shǫn), *n.* [L. *argumentatio(n-)*, < *argumentari*, adduce proof, < *argumentum.*] The process of arguing; reasoning; discussion; debate.—**ar-gu-men′ta-tive** (-tą-tiv), *a.* Of or containing argument; also, given to arguing; disputatious.—**ar-gu-men′ta-tive-ly,** *adv.*—**ar-gu-men′ta-tive-ness,** *n.*

Ar-gus (är′gus), *n.* [L., < Gr. Ἄργος.] In Greek legend, a giant with a hundred eyes, set to guard the heifer Io (his eyes being transferred, after his death, to the peacock's tail); hence, any observant or vigilant person; [*l. c.*] a pheasant of the East Indian genus *Argus*, with very long feathers in wings and tail, marked with eye-like spots.—**Ar′gus=eyed,** *a.* Observant; vigilant.

ar-gute (är-gūt′), *a.* [L. *argutus*, pp. of *arguere*: see *argue.*] Clear; sharp; shrill; also, keen, acute, or subtle; shrewd. [Now rare.]—**ar-gute′ly,** *adv.*—**ar-gute′ness,** *n.*

ar-gyr-i-a (är-jir′i-ä), *n.* [Gr. ἄργυρος, silver: cf. *argent.*] In *pathol.*, discoloration of the skin or tissues from prolonged internal use of silver compounds.

ar-gyr-o-dite (är-jir′ǭ-dīt), *n.* [Gr. ἀργυρώδης, like silver, rich in silver, < ἄργυρος, silver, + εἶδος, form.] A rare mineral composed of silver, germanium, and sulphur, occurring in steel-gray crystals of a metallic luster.

ar-gy-rol (är′ji-rol or -rōl), *n.* [Gr. ἄργυρος, silver: see *-ol.*] A compound of silver and a proteid: used in the treatment of inflamed mucous membranes. [Proprietary name.]

a-ri-a (ä′ri-ä), *n.* [It.: see *air*².] In *music*, an air or melody; usually, an elaborate melody for a single voice, with accompaniment, in an opera, oratorio, etc., esp. one consisting of a principal section, a subordinate section, and a repetition of the first with or without alterations.

Ar-ian¹ (är′yąn or ar′i-ąn), *a.* and *n.* See *Aryan.*

A-ri-an² (ā′ri-ąn). **I.** *a.* Pertaining to Arius of Alexandria (died A.D. 336), who held that Christ the Son was subordinate to and not consubstantial with God the Father. **II.** *n.* An adherent of the Arian doctrine.—**A′ri-an-ism,** *n.*

-arian. [= *-ary* + *-an.*] A compound suffix of adjectives and nouns, often referring to pursuits, doctrines, etc., or to age, as in *antiquarian, humanitarian, millenarian, octogenarian.*

ar-id (ar′id), *a.* [L. *aridus*, < *arere*, be dry.] Dry; without moisture; fig., barren, bare, jejune, or uninteresting.—**a-rid-i-ty** (ą-rid′i-ti), **ar′id-ness,** *n.*—**ar′id-ly,** *adv.*

a-ri-el (ā′ri-ẹl), *n.* [Ar. *aryil*, var. of *ayyil*, stag.] An Arabian gazelle, *Gazella arabica.*

A-ri-es (ā′ri-ēz), *n.* [L.] The Ram, a zodiacal constellation; also, the first sign of the zodiac, which the sun enters at the vernal equinox (about March 21). See *zodiac.*

a-ri-et-ta (ä-ri-et′ä), *n.* [It., dim. of *aria.*] A short air or song.

ar-i-ette (ar-i-et′), *n.* [F.] Same as *arietta.*

a-right (ą-rīt′), *adv.* [AS. *ariht*, 'on right.'] Rightly; correctly; properly; also, to the right.

ar-il (ar′il), *n.* [NL. *arillus*, < ML. *arilli*, dried grapes.] In *bot.*, an accessory covering of certain seeds, esp. one arising from the placenta or the funicle.—**ar-il-late, ar-il-lat-ed** (ar′i-lāt, -lā-ted), *a.* Having an aril.—**ar-il-lode** (ar′-i-lōd), *n.* [See *-ode*².] In *bot.*, an aril-like covering, or 'false aril,' not arising from the placenta.

ar-i-ose (ar-i-ōs′ or ar′i-ōs), *a.* [See *arioso.*] Characterized by melody; song-like.

a-ri-o-so (ä-rē-ō′sō), *a.* [It., < *aria.*] In *music*, in the manner of an air or melody.

a-rise (ą-rīz′), *v. i.*; pret. *arose*, pp. *arisen*, ppr. *arising.* [AS. *ārīsan*, < *ā-*, up, + *rīsan*, rise.] To rise up; get up, as from sitting or lying; also, to move upward; mount or ascend; hence, to come into view, being, or action; appear; begin; originate; spring up.

a-ris-ta (ą-ris′tą), *n.*; pl. *-tæ* (-tē). [L.: cf. *arête.*] In *bot.*, a bristle-like appendage of grain, etc.; the awn.

ar-is-tarch (ar′is-tärk), *n.* [From *Aristarchus* of Alexandria (died about 145 B.C.), a severe critic of the Homeric poems.] A severe critic.

a-ris-tate (ą-ris′tāt), *a.* [LL. *aristatus.*] In *bot.*, having aristæ; awned.

ar-is-toc-ra-cy (ar-is-tok′rą-si), *n.*; pl. *-cies* (-siz). [OF. *aristocracie* (F. *aristocratie*), < Gr. ἀριστοκρατία, < ἄριστος, best, + κρατεῖν, rule.] Government by the best citizens; more commonly, government or a state in which the nobility or privileged upper class rule; also, a ruling body of nobles; the nobility and gentry of a country; the patrician class; any class ranking as socially or otherwise superior (as, the *aristocracy* of wealth or of culture).—**ar-is-to-crat** (ar′is-tǭ-krat or ą-ris′-), *n.* [F. *aristocrate.*] A member of the aristocracy; a patrician; one who has the tastes, opinions, manners, etc., of the aristocracy; also, one who favors an aristocratic form of government.—**ar″is-to-crat′ic,** *a.* [Gr. ἀριστοκρατικός.] Of or pertaining to government by an aristocracy; also, of, belonging to, or favoring the aristocracy or patrician class; resembling or befitting an aristocrat or patrician. Also **ar″is-to-crat′i-cal.**—**ar″is-to-crat′i-cal-ly,** *adv.*

ar-is-tol (ar′is-tol or -tōl), *n.* [Gr. ἄριστος, best: see *-ol.*] Thymol iodide, a brown powder containing 45% of iodine, used in surgery as a substitute for iodoform.

ar-is-to-lo-chi-a-ceous (ar″is-tǭ-lō-ki-ā′shius), *a.* [NL. *Aristolochia*, the birthwort genus, < Gr. ἀριστολόχεια, herb facilitating childbirth, < ἄριστος, best, + λοχεία, childbirth.] Belonging to the *Aristolochiaceæ*, a family of plants including birthwort, Dutchman's-pipe, Virginia snakeroot, etc.

Ar-is-to-te-lian (ar″is-tǭ-tē′liąn). **I.** *a.* Pertaining to Aristotle (384–322 B.C.), the Greek philosopher, or to his doctrines. **II.** *n.* A follower of Aristotle.

a-ris-to-type (a-ris′tǭ-tīp), *n.* [Gr. ἄριστος, best: see *-type.*] Orig., a process of photographic printing in which paper coated with silver chloride in gelatin is used; now, any such process using silver salts in gelatin or collodion; also, a print made by any such process.

a-ris-tu-late (a-ris′tų-lāt), *a.* [NL. *aristulatus*, < *aristula*, dim. of L. *arista*, awn.] In *bot.*, having a small or short awn.

a-rith-me-tic (ą-rith′mẹ-tik), *n.* [OF. *arismetique* (F. *arithmétique*), < L. *arithmetica*, < Gr. ἀριθμητική, prop. fem. of ἀριθμητικός, of or for reckoning, < ἀριθμεῖν, reckon, < ἀριθμός, number.] The art of computation with figures; the science of numbers.—**ar-ith-met-i-cal** (ar-ith-met′i-kąl), *a.* Of or pertaining to arithmetic.—**ar-ith-met′i-cal-ly,** *adv.*—**a-rith-me-ti′cian** (-tish′ąn), *n.* One versed in arithmetic.

ar-ith-mom-e-ter (ar-ith-mom′e-tėr), *n.* [Gr. ἀριθμός, number: see *-meter.*] Any of various devices or machines for performing one or more kinds of arithmetical operations, as addition, multiplication, etc.

-arium. [L., prop. neut. of *-arius*: see *-ary.*] A suffix of nouns denoting 'something connected with,' or 'a place for,' or 'a collection or assemblage of' (what is indicated by the preceding part of the word), as in *aquarium, herbarium, honorarium, insectarium, planetarium, polyzoarium.*

ark (ärk), *n.* [AS. *arc, earc,* < L. *arca,* < *arcere,* keep, akin to Gr. ἀρκεῖν, keep off.] A chest, box, bin, or like receptacle (archaic or prov.); the repository of the Jewish tables of the law ('ark of the covenant'); the vessel built by Noah for safety during the Flood; a flatboat (U. S.); any large, clumsy, or unwieldy boat, vehicle, etc. (colloq.).

arles (ärlz), *n.* [Appar. ult. < L. *arrha,* earnest.] Earnest-money; an earnest. [Sc. and north. Eng.]

arm[1] (ärm), *n.* [AS. *arm* = D. and G. *arm* = Icel. *armr* = Goth. *arms,* arm; akin to L. *armus,* shoulder, and Gr. ἁρμός, joint.] The upper limb of the human body from the shoulder to the hand; the fore limb of any vertebrate; hence, any limb-like or projecting part; a branch; also, a projecting support for the arm, as at the side of a chair or the end of a sofa; fig., a support or stay; strength; power; might.—**arm**[1], *v. t.* To take or lead by the arm; also, to clasp in the arms†.

arm[2] (ärm), *n.* [OF. F. *arme,* pl. *armes,* < L. *arma,* equipments, arms.] An offensive or defensive implement; a weapon (usually in *pl.*); *pl.*, armor; *sing.*, a branch of the military service, as the infantry, the cavalry, the artillery, or ('fourth arm') the air service; *pl.*, fighting, warfare, or war; also, heraldic bearings; distinctive device, as of a city or a corporation.—**arm**[2], *v.* [OF. F. *armer,* < L. *armare* (pp. *armatus*), < *arma.*] **I.** *tr.* To equip with arms; furnish with weapons, armor, or any means of offense or defense; provide with a protective covering; supply with requisite appliances, etc.; fit (a magnet) with an armature; equip for any specific purpose. **II.** *intr.* To take up arms; prepare for war.

ar-ma-da (är-mā′dạ or -mä′dạ), *n.* [Sp., < ML. *armata*: see *army.*] A fleet of war-ships: as, the Spanish or Invincible *Armada* (sent by Spain against England in 1588, but shattered and dispersed by storms).

Three-banded Armadillo (*Tolypeutes tricinctus*), walking, also rolled up.

ar-ma-dil-lo (är-mạ-dil′ō), *n.*; pl. *-dillos* (-ōz). [Sp., dim. of *armado,* < L. *armatus,* pp., armed: see *arm*[2], *v.*] Any of the edentate burrowing quadrupeds, mostly small, of the family *Dasypodidæ,* of South and southern North America, having an armor-like shell or carapace composed of bony plates and transverse movable bands, some species being able to roll themselves up into a ball with the armor on all sides.

Ar-ma-ged-don (är-mạ-ged′ọn), *n.* [See Rev. xvi. 16.] The place of some great and final conflict between the forces of good and of evil.

ar-ma-ment (är′mạ-mẹnt), *n.* [L. *armamenta,* pl., implements, equipments, ship's tackle, < *armare*: see *arm*[2], *v.*] Munitions of war; an equipment of guns, etc., as of a warship or a fortification; also, a land or naval force equipped for war; also, the process of equipping or arming for war.

ar-ma-men-ta-ri-um (är″mạ-men-tā′ri-um), *n.*; pl. *-ria* (-ri-ạ̈). [L., arsenal, armory, < *armamenta,* pl.: see *armament.*] An equipment of implements, appliances, or the like; esp., the equipment of instruments, drugs, therapeutic resources, etc., at the command of a surgeon or physician.

ar-ma-ture (är′mạ-ṭūr), *n.* [L. *armatura,* < *armare*: see *arm*[2], *v.*] Armor; defensive equipment; the protective covering of an animal or plant, or any part serving for defense or offense; any equipment or apparatus, as of organs of the body; in *magnetism,* a piece of soft iron applied to the poles of a magnet to close the circuit, or to those of an electromagnet to communicate the force; in *elect.*, that part of a dynamo or generator in which the induced current is developed; that part of a motor which receives and utilizes the current; also, the tin-foil linings of a Leyden jar.—**ar′ma-ture,** *v. t.*; *-tured, -turing.* To furnish with an armature.

arm=chair (ärm′chãr′). **I.** *n.* A chair with arms or side-pieces to support the elbows. **II.** *a.* Seated in an arm-chair; remaining, carried on, done, etc., in ease and comfort at home: as, *arm-chair* warriors or campaigns; *arm-chair* exploits.

armed (ärmd), *a.* Having arms: as, long-*armed.*

Ar-me-ni-an (är-mē′ni-ạn). **I.** *a.* Pertaining to Armenia, a region (anciently a kingdom) in western Asia, southeast of the Black Sea, or to the branch of the Christian church established there. **II.** *n.* A native of Armenia; an adherent of the Armenian Church; the Armenian language (belonging to the Aryan or Indo-European family).

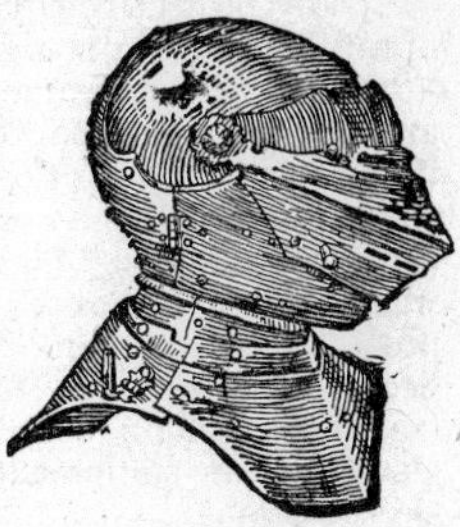

Steel Armet.

arm-er (är′mėr), *n.* One who arms, or equips with arms.

ar-met (är′met), *n.* [OF. F. *armet,* dim. of *arme,* E. *arm*[2], *n.*] A kind of helmet introduced about the year 1450.

arm-ful (ärm′fůl), *n.*; pl. *-fuls.* As much as the arm, or both arms, can hold.

arm-hole (ärm′hōl), *n.* The armpit (archaic or prov. Eng.); also, a hole for the arm in a garment.

ar-mi-ger (är′mi-jėr), *n.* [L., < *arma,* arms, + *gerere,* bear.] An armor-bearer to a knight; a squire; also, one entitled to armorial bearings.—**ar-mig′er-ous** (-mij′ẹ-rus), *a.* Entitled to armorial bearings.

ar-mil (är′mil), *n.* Same as *armilla.*

ar-mil-la (är-mil′ạ̈), *n.*; pl. *armillæ* (-ē). [L., appar. < *armus,* shoulder: see *arm*[1].] An armlet or bracelet; a hoop or ring; also, an ancient astronomical instrument consisting of a ring fixed in the plane of the equator ('equinoctial armilla'), and sometimes crossed at right angles by another ring fixed in the plane of the meridian ('solstitial armilla').—**ar′mil-la-ry** (-mi-lạ̄-ri), *a.* Resembling a bracelet; consisting of hoops or rings: as, an *armillary* sphere (an arrangement of rings, all circles of a single sphere, showing the relative positions of the principal circles of the celestial sphere).

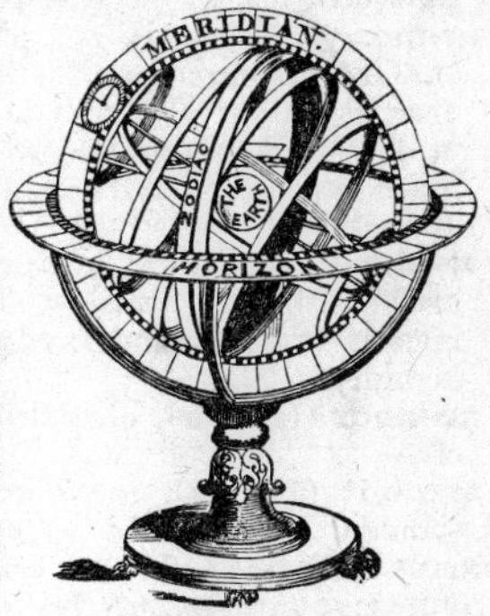

Armillary Sphere.

arm-ing (är′ming), *n.* The act of equipping with or taking up arms, or of furnishing with any requisite appliance or fitting; arms, appliances, etc., so supplied; the armature of a magnet; *naut.*, a piece of tallow at the lower end of a sounding-lead, for bringing up specimens of sand, etc., from the sea-bottom.

Ar-min-i-an (är-min′i-ạn). **I.** *a.* Of or pertaining to Jacobus Arminius, or Jacob Harmensen (1560–1609), a Dutch Protestant theologian, who opposed certain Calvinistic doctrines, esp. that of predestination; pertaining to or following the doctrines of Arminius. **II.** *n.* An adherent of the Arminian doctrines.—**Ar-min′i-an-ism,** *n.*

ar-mip-o-tent (är-mip′ọ-tẹnt), *a.* [L. *armipotens* (*-ent-*), < *arma,* arms, + *potens,* E. *potent.*] Mighty in arms or war.—**ar-mip′o-tence,** *n.*

ar-mi-stice (är′mi-stis), *n.* [F. *armistice,* < NL. *armistitium,* < L. *arma,* arms, + *sistere,* stand.] A temporary suspension of hostilities by agreement of the parties; a truce.—**Armistice Day,** Nov. 11, observed in commemoration of the day, Nov. 11, 1918, on which the armistice asked by Germany and granted by the Allies went into effect, at the close of the World War.

arm-less[1] (ärm′les), *a.* Without arms or limbs, etc.

arm-less² (ärm′les), *a.* Without arms or weapons, etc.
arm-let (ärm′let), *n.* A little arm or arm-like part; also, an ornamental band for the (upper) arm.

Persian. Egyptian.
Armlets.

ar-moire (är-mwor), *n.* [F.: see *ambry.*] A cupboard, closet, or wardrobe.
ar-mor (är′mọr), *n.* [OF. *armeure* (F. *armure*), < L. *armatura*: see *armature.*] Defensive arms; any covering of metal, leather, or other material, worn for protection in fighting; metallic sheathing or protective covering for war-vessels, fortifications, military trains and automobiles, etc.; any protective covering, as the scales of a fish or the water-tight dress of a diver. —**ar′mor,** *v. t.* To cover or protect with armor.—**ar′mor=bear″er,** *n.* A retainer bearing the armor or arms of a warrior. —**ar′mor=clad. I.** *a.* Protected with armor; armored. **II.** *n.* An armored war-vessel.—**ar′mored,** *p. a.* Covered or protected with armor.—**armored cruiser.** See under *cruiser.*—**ar′mor-er,** *n.* A maker or repairer of armor; also, one in charge of an equipment of arms, as of a ship.

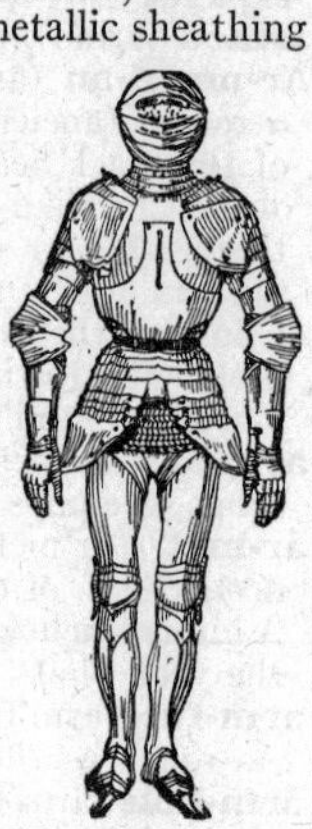

Suit of Plate-armor (about 1440).

ar-mo-ri-al (är-mō′ri-ạl). [From *armory*².] **I.** *a.* Pertaining to armory or heraldry. **II.** *n.* A book containing armorial bearings.
Ar-mor-ic (är-mor′ik). [L. *Armorica,* northwestern Gaul, Brittany; from Celtic.] **I.** *a.* Pertaining to Brittany, in northwestern France; Breton. **II.** *n.* The Breton language.—**Ar-mor′i-can** (-i-kạn). **I.** *a.* Breton. **II.** *n.* A Breton; also, the Breton language.
ar-mor=plate (är′mọr-plāt), *n.* A plate or plating of steel or iron for armoring war-ships, fortifications, etc.—**ar′mor=plat″ed** (-plā″ted), *a.*—**ar′mor=plat″ing,** *n.*
ar-mor-y¹ (är′mọr-i), *n.*; pl. *-ies* (-iz). [Appar. < *armor*: cf. OF. *armeurerie,* place where arms are kept.] Armor or arms collectively (archaic); a place where arms are kept; in the U. S., a building with drill-rooms, offices, etc., for State militia; also, a place where arms are made; an arsenal.
ar-mor-y² (är′mọr-i), *n.*; pl. *-ies* (-iz). [OF. *armoierie,* < *armoier,* blazon arms, < *armes,* arms.] Heraldic bearings or arms (archaic); also, the art of blazoning arms; heraldry.
ar-mour (är′mọr), etc. British preferred form of *armor,* etc.
arm-pit (ärm′pit), *n.* The hollow under the arm at the shoulder; the axilla.
arms (ärmz), *n. pl.* See *arm*², *n.*
arm=scye (ärm′sī), *n.* See *scye.*
ar-mure (är′mūr), *n.* [F.: see *armor.*] A silk or woolen fabric woven in a very small pattern.
ar-my (är′mi), *n.*; pl. *-mies* (-miz). [OF. *armee* (F. *armée*), < ML. *armata,* prop. fem. of L. *armatus,* pp. of *armare*: see *arm*², *v.*] An armed expedition†; also, an armed force; an organized body of men trained and equipped for war (a term usually applied to a body embracing all the land forces of a nation and divided into army-corps or other large units, but also applied to a portion of such a body, as a large force fighting in a particular region); hence, any body of persons organized or associated for a cause (as, the Salvation *Army*); also, a host; a great multitude.—**ar′my=corps** (-kōr), *n.* The largest unit of organization in an army, comprising two or more divisions.—**ar′my=worm,** *n.* A kind of caterpillar, the larva of a noctuid moth, *Leucania unipuncta,* which often travels in hosts over a region, destroying grass, grain, etc.; also, some similarly destructive larva.
ar-nat-to (är-nat′ō), *n.* Same as *arnotto.*
ar-ni-ca (är′ni-kạ̈), *n.* [NL.; origin unknown.] Any plant of the asteraceous genus *Arnica,* esp. *A. montana,* of Europe, the dried flowers and roots of which are used in medicine; also, a medicinal preparation of this species, esp. a tincture much used externally for bruises, sprains, etc.
ar-not-to (är-not′ō), *n.* [Native American name.] A small tree, *Bixa orellana,* of tropical America; also, a yellowish-red dye obtained from the pulp inclosing its seeds, used for coloring fabrics, butter, cheese, varnish, etc.
ar-oid (ar′oid or ā̆r′-). **I.** *a.* Arum-like; araceous. **II.** *n.* Any araceous plant.—**a-roi-de-ous** (a-roi′dẹ-us), *a.*
a-roint (ạ-roint′), *interj.* [Origin unknown.] In *aroint thee,* avaunt! begone! See Shakspere's "Macbeth," i. 3. 6. [Archaic.]—**a-roint′,** *v. t.* To bid 'aroint' or begone.
a-ro-ma (ạ-rō′mạ̈), *n.*; pl. *-mas.* [L., < Gr. ἄρωμα, spice, sweet herb.] Spice†; spicy odor; distinctive fragrance, flavor, or quality.—**ar-o-mat-ic** (ar-ọ-mat′ik), *a.* [Gr. ἀρωματικός.] Having aroma; spicy; fragrant; in *chem.,* noting or pertaining to a class of organic compounds comprising benzene and all its derivatives, many of which have an agreeable odor.—**aromatic vinegar.** See under *vinegar.* —**ar-o-mat′ic,** *n.* An aromatic plant or substance.—**ar-o-mat′i-cal-ly,** *adv.*—**a-ro′ma-tize** (-mạ-tīz), *v. t.*; *-tized, -tizing.* [Gr. ἀρωματίζειν.] To make aromatic, as in odor or flavor.
a-rose (ạ-rōz′). Preterit of *arise.*
a-round (ạ-round′). [See *a*² and *round*², *n.*] **I.** *adv.* In a round, circle, or circuit; circularly or spherically about; on every side (as, a dense mist lay *around*); here and there, or about (U. S.: as, to travel *around* from place to place); somewhere about or near (U. S.: as, to wait *around* for a person). **II.** *prep.* In a direction that turns about; so as to encircle or encompass; on all sides of; here and there in (U. S.: as, to roam *around* the country); somewhere in or near (U. S.: as, to stay *around* the house).
a-rouse (ạ-rouz′), *v.*; *aroused, arousing.* [With *a-* as in *arise.*] **I.** *tr.* To rouse up; awaken; excite. **II.** *intr.* To become aroused.—**a-rous′al,** *n.*—**a-rous′er,** *n.*
a-row (ạ-rō′), *adv.* In a row.
ar-peg-gio (är-ped′jō), *n.*; pl. *arpeggios* (-jōz). [It., < *arpeggiare,* play on the harp, < *arpa,* harp.] In *music,* the sounding of the notes of a chord in rapid succession instead of simultaneously; also, a chord thus sounded.
ar-pent (är′pẹnt, F. är-poṅ), *n.* [F., < L. *arepennis*; from Celtic.] An old French land-measure, varying in extent but averaging an acre (still used in Louisiana and Quebec); also, in Quebec, a linear measure equal to about 12 rods.
ar-que-bus (är′kẹ-bus or är′kwẹ-), etc. Same as *harquebus,* etc.
ar-rack (ar′ạk), *n.* [Said to be < Ar. *'araq,* sweat, juice.] Any of various spirituous liquors distilled in the East Indies and elsewhere in the East from palm toddy, fermented rice, molasses, or other materials.
ar-rah (ar′ạ̈), *interj.* [Ir.] An exclamation of surprise, indignation, etc. [Ir.]
ar-raign (ạ-rān′), *v. t.* [AF. *arainer,* OF. *araisnier,* < ML. *arrationare,* < L. *ad,* to, + ML. *rationare,* reason, discourse: see *reason, v.*] To call or bring before a court to answer to a charge or accusation; call to account as before a tribunal; call in question for fault; find fault with.—**ar-raign′er,** *n.*—**ar-raign′ment,** *n.*
ar-range (ạ-rānj′), *v.*; *-ranged, -ranging.* [OF. *arangier* (F. *arranger*), < *a* (< L. *ad*), to, + *rangier,* E. *range, v.*] **I.** *tr.* To range, marshal, or dispose in due order; place or adjust properly; settle, as relations between parties; prepare or plan; in *music,* to adapt (a composition) for a particular mode of rendering (by voices or instruments). **II.** *intr.* To make a settlement; come to an agreement; make preparations.—**ar-range′a-ble,** *a.* Capable of being arranged.—**ar-range′ment,** *n.* The act of arranging; the state or mode of being arranged; disposition; adjustment; settlement; agreement; preparation (usually in *pl.*); also, something arranged in a particular way, as a piece of music; any combination of parts.—**ar-ran-ger** (ạ-rān′jėr), *n.*
ar-rant (ar′ạnt), *a.* [Var. of *errant.*] Wandering†; vagrant†; good-for-nothing†; also, notorious; rank; unmitigated; downright; thorough.—**ar′rant-ly,** *adv.*
ar-ras (ar′ạs), *n.* [From *Arras,* city in northern France.] A kind of tapestry formerly in use; hangings or a curtain of tapestry.—**ar′rased,** *a.* Furnished or hung with arras.
ar-ra-sene (ar-ạ-sēn′), *n.* [From *arras.*] A kind of embroidery thread with a velvet-like pile.

ar-ras-tre (är-räs′trā), *n.* [Sp., < *arrastrar*, drag along the ground.] A rude apparatus used in Mexico and elsewhere for grinding and amalgamating ores containing free gold or silver, the grinding and mixing being done by heavy masses of rock which are dragged around a circular bed of flat stones.

Mexican Arrastre.

ar-ray (ạ-rā′), *v. t.* [OF. *areer*, < *a* (< L. *ad*), to, + *-reer* (also in OF. *desreer*, put out of order (see *deray*), *conreer*, put in order, E. *curry*²), from Teut., and ult. akin to E. *ready*.] To set in due order; draw up, as troops for battle; marshal; also, to prepare†; also, to deck out; adorn with dress; attire; dress; in *law*, to arrange or call (the jury) man by man at a trial.—**ar-ray′**, *n.* [OF. *arei*, *arroi*, < *areer*.] Orderly arrangement; order, as of troops drawn up for battle; a marshaled host; a muster or display; ordered state of things (archaic); condition†; attire or dress; in *law*, the arraying of a jury, or the jury or panel.—**ar-ray′al**, *n.* The act of arraying; muster; array.—**ar-ray′er**, *n.*—**ar-ray′ment**, *n.* Array; attire. Cf. *raiment*. [Obs. or archaic.]

ar-rear (ạ-rēr′). [OF. *arere* (F. *arrière*), < L. *ad*, to, + *retro*, backward.] **I.**† *adv.* Backward; behind; behindhand. **II.** *n.* The rear (archaic); the state of being behindhand; something behindhand or overdue; an amount due but unpaid (usually in *pl.*).—**in arrear** or **arrears**, behindhand; in debt.—**ar-rear′age** (-ạ̄j), *n.* The state of being behindhand; also, an amount overdue; *pl.*, arrears.

ar-rect (a-rekt′), *a.* [L. *arrectus*, pp. of *arrigere*, raise, < *ad*, to, + *regere*, direct.] Upright; erect; also, intent†; in *bot.*, stiffly erect; pointing upward.

ar-rest (ạ-rest′), *v. t.* [OF. *arester* (F. *arrêter*), < ML. *arrestare*, < L. *ad*, to, + *restare*, stay: see *rest*².] To bring to a standstill; stop; check; also, to seize by legal authority; take into custody; also, to catch and fix (the sight, attention, etc.).—**ar-rest′**, *n.* [OF. *arest* (F. *arrêt*), < *arester*.] The act of arresting, or the state or fact of being arrested; stoppage, check, halt, or stay; any device for arresting motion in a mechanism; seizure by legal authority or warrant; legal restraint, as in custody; a judgment† or decree†.—**ar-rest′a-ble**, *a.* Liable to be arrested.—**ar-res-ta-tion** (ar-es-tā′shọn), *n.* [F.] The act of arresting; arrest.—**ar-rest′er**, *n.*—**ar-res′tive**, *a.* Serving to arrest.—**ar-rest′ment**, *n.* The act of arresting; stoppage.

ar-rêt (ȧ-rā), *n.* [F.: see *arrest*, *n.*] In French use, a judgment or decision of a court; a decree of a sovereign authority.

ar-rhi-zal, ar-rhi-zous (a-rī′zạl, -zus), *a.* [Gr. ἄρριζος, < ἀ- priv. + ῥίζα, root.] In *bot.*, having no root.

ar-ride (a-rīd′), *v. t.*; *-rided*, *-riding*. [L. *arridere*, < *ad*, to, at, + *ridere*, laugh.] To laugh or smile at†; be agreeable or pleasing to (archaic).

ar-ri-ère=ban (ar′i-ãr-ban′, F. ȧ-ryãr-bäṅ), *n.* [F. (with form due to confusion with *arrière*, behind), = G. *heerbann*, < OHG. *hari*, *heri*, army, + *ban*, proclamation.] In feudal times, the summons of the sovereign to his vassals to take the field for military service; also, the force liable to the summons.

ar-rière=pen-sée (ȧ-ryãr-poṅ-sā), *n.* [F., < *arrière*, behind, + *pensée*, thought.] A thought kept back; a mental reservation.

ar-ris (ar′is), *n.* [OF. *areste*: see *arête*.] A sharp edge, as of squared stone; a sharp ridge, as between adjoining channels of a Doric column.

ar-ri-val (ạ-rī′vạl), *n.* The act of arriving; also, a person or thing that arrives.

ar-rive (ạ-rīv′), *v.*; *-rived*, *-riving*. [OF. F. *arriver*, < ML. *arripare*, < L. *ad*, to, + *ripa*, bank, shore.] **I.** *intr.* Orig., to come to shore; hence, to come to a certain point in any course of travel (often with *at*); reach one's destination; reach a point in any course or process; attain (with *at*, formerly *to*: as, to *arrive* at a decision); sometimes, to attain a position of success in the world (a French use: as, an artist or an author who has *arrived*); also, to come, as a time, opportunity, etc.; occur or happen. **II.** *tr.* To bring to shore or to any destination or point†; come to or reach (a port, place, point, etc.: archaic); happen to†.

ar-ro-ba (är-rō′bä), *n.* [Sp. and Pg., < Ar. *arrub*ʻ, < *al*, the, + *rub*ʻ, quarter.] A Spanish and Portuguese unit of weight of varying value, in Mexico, etc., equal to 25.36 pounds avoirdupois, and in Brazil to 32.38 pounds avoirdupois; also, a liquid measure of varying value, used in Spain, etc., and commonly equal (when used for wine) to 4.26 U. S. gallons.

ar-ro-gance (ar′ọ-gạns), *n.* [OF. F. *arrogance*, < L. *arrogantia*.] The quality of being arrogant; overbearing pride. Also **ar′ro-gan-cy.**

ar-ro-gant (ar′ọ-gạnt), *a.* [OF. F. *arrogant*, < L. *arrogans* (*-ant-*), ppr. of *arrogare*: see *arrogate*.] Making unwarrantable claims to superior importance or rights; overbearingly assuming; insolently proud; characterized by arrogance.—**ar′ro-gant-ly,** *adv.*

ar-ro-gate (ar′ọ-gāt), *v. t.*; *-gated*, *-gating*. [L. *arrogatus*, pp. of *arrogare*, < *ad*, to, + *rogare*, ask.] To claim unwarrantably or presumptuously; assume or appropriate to one's self without right; attribute or assign to another without just reason.—**ar-ro-ga′tion** (-gā′shọn), *n.* [L. *arrogatio*(*n*-).] The act of arrogating; a claiming or taking presumptuously and without right.—**ar′ro-ga-tor,** *n.*

ar-ron-disse-ment (ȧ-rôṅ-dēs-moṅ), *n.* [F.] In France, the largest administrative division of a department.

ar-row (ar′ō), *n.* [AS. *arwe*, *earh*.] A slender missile weapon for shooting from a bow; something like it in form, as a mark to show direction; the long flower-bearing joint of the sugar-cane; [*cap.*] in *astron.*, the northern constellation Sagitta.—**ar′row,** *v. i.* To shoot arrows (poetic); pass like an arrow; dart; of the sugar-cane, to form arrows.—**ar′row=head,** *n.* The head or tip of an arrow, typically of an elongated triangular shape with the base or short side often having a reëntrant angle; also, any plant of the aquatic genus *Sagittaria*, species of which have arrow-headed leaves.—**ar′row=head″ed,** *a.* Shaped like an arrow-head; sagittate; cuneiform.—**ar′row-root,** *n.* A tropical American plant, *Maranta arundinacea*, or some other species, whose rhizomes yield a nutritious starch much used in food-preparations; the starch itself, or a similar starch from some other plant; a food-preparation made of such starch.—**ar′row=shaped,** *a.* Shaped like an arrow; often, shaped like an arrow-head; sagittate.—**ar′row=wood,** *n.* Any of several shrubs and small trees, as the wahoo (*Euonymus atropurpureus*) and certain viburnums, with tough, straight shoots, formerly used for making arrows.—**ar′row-y,** *a.* Arrow-like; consisting of arrows.

Flowering Plant of Arrow-head.

Arrowroot (*Maranta arundinacea*).—*a*, *a*, rhizomes.

ar-roy-o (ạ-roi′ō), *n.*; pl. *-os* (-ōz). [Sp.] A watercourse; also, the dry bed of a stream; a gully. [Western U. S.]

arse (ärs), *n.* [AS. *ears* = G. *arsch*.] The buttocks; the rump. [Now prov. or vulgar.]

ar-se-nal (är′sẹ-nạl), *n.* [It. *arsenale*, < Ar. *dār-aççinā*ʻ*ah*, 'house of the construction.'] A dockyard†; a public establishment for the manufacture and storage of arms, ammunition, equipments, etc., for military and naval use; a magazine of arms and military stores; any repository or collection of weapons, etc.

ar-se-nate (är′sẹ-nāt), *n.* In *chem.*, a salt of arsenic acid.

ar-se-nic (är′sẹ-nik), *n.* [OF. F. *arsenic*, < L. *arsenicum*, < Gr. ἀρσενικόν, orpiment, < ἄρσην, male, strong.] Chem. sym., As; at. wt., 74.96; sp. gr., 5.727. A grayish-white element having a metallic luster, volatilizing when heated, and forming poisonous compounds; also, some one of the compounds, esp. the trioxide, As_2O_3, which is used in medicine and the arts and in poisons for vermin.—**ar-sen′ic** (-sen′ik), *a.* Of or containing arsenic. See *arsenious.* —**ar-sen′i-cal,** *a.* Pertaining to or containing arsenic.—**ar-sen′i-cate** (-i-kāt), *v. t.*; *-cated, -cating.* To combine or treat with arsenic.—**ar′se-nide** (-nīd or -nid), *n.* In *chem.*, a compound of arsenic and a metal or other positive element or radical.—**ar-se′ni-ous** (-sē′ni-us), *a.* Containing arsenic (in larger proportion than a corresponding arsenic compound). Also **ar′se-nous** (-se̤-nus).—**ar′se-nite** (-nīt), *n.* In *chem.*, a salt of arsenious acid.—**ar-se′niu-ret** (-sē′niṳ-ret), *n.* Same as *arsenide.*—**ar-se′niu-ret-ed, ar-se′niu-ret-ted,** *a.* In *chem.*, combined with arsenic so as to form an arseniuret or arsenide: as, *arseniureted* hydrogen (arsine).

ar-se-no-py-rite (är″se̤-nō̤-pī′rīt), *n.* [From *arsenic* + *pyrite.*] A silver-white or steel-gray mineral, a compound of iron, arsenic, and sulphur, occurring in orthorhombic crystals or in masses or grains: an important ore of arsenic. Also called *mispickel.*

ar-sine (är′sin or -sēn), *n.* [From *arsenic.*] In *chem.*, arseniureted hydrogen, AsH_3, a colorless, inflammable, highly poisonous gas, with a fetid garlic-like odor.

ar-sis (är′sis), *n.*; pl. *arses* (-sēz). [L., < Gr. ἄρσις, a raising (perhaps of the foot or hand in beating time), < αἴρειν, raise.] In *pros.*, orig. the unaccented, later the accented, part of a foot: opposed to *thesis.*

ar-son (är′so̤n), *n.* [OF. *arson*, < L. *ardere*, burn.] In *law*, the malicious burning of a house belonging to another, or a burning of other property (as fixed by statute).

art[1] (ärt). [AS. *eart*: see *are*[1].] Second person singular, present indicative, of *be*: now only in poetic or solemn use.

art[2] (ärt), *n.* [OF. F. *art*, < L. *ars* (*art-*), skill, art.] Skilled workmanship, execution, or agency (often opposed to *nature*); skill; knack; craft; cunning; an artifice or artful device (usually in *pl.*); the body of rules and methods for any department of work or performance; applied (as opposed to abstract) science; a department of skilled performance (as, the industrial *arts*; the fine *arts*; the healing *art*; decorative *art*; the *art* of angling); a branch of learning or university study (as, the liberal *arts*; master of *arts*); learning or science (archaic); the department of esthetic production, esp. as comprising painting, drawing, sculpture, etc.; the production or expression of what is beautiful or appeals to the faculty of taste; esthetic or artistic excellence. —**black art,** the pretended art, regarded as dark, sinister, or evil, of performing acts beyond mere human power by recourse to supernatural agencies, esp. evil spirits or the spirits of the dead; black magic; necromancy; sorcery.—**fine arts,** arts depending on taste and esthetic excellence, esp. architecture, sculpture, painting, and engraving.—**liberal arts** ('arts befitting a freeman'), branches of academic study, varying according to time and place, comprised in a university course.—**the arts,** the liberal arts; also, the fine arts; also, the industrial arts.

Artemis (Diana) of Versailles. (Statue in the Louvre, Paris.)

ar-tel (är-tel′), *n.* [Russ.] In Russia, a voluntary association of working-men for working together, with division of profits; a coöperative association.

Ar-te-mis (är′tē̤-mis), *n.* [L., < Gr. Ἄρτεμις.] A Greek goddess, sister of Apollo, represented as a virgin huntress and associated with the moon: identified by the Romans with Diana.

ar-te-ri-al (är-tē′ri-a̤l), *a.* Of, pertaining to, or resembling the arteries; noting or pertaining to the blood of the arteries which has become purified and charged with oxygen in passing through the lungs, and, in the higher animals, is bright-red in color.—**ar-te′ri-al-ize** (-īz), *v. t.*; *-ized, -izing.* To convert (venous blood) into the bright-red blood of the arteries by the action of oxygen in the lungs.—**ar-te″ri-al-i-za′tion** (-i-zā′sho̤n), *n.*—**ar-te′ri-al-ly,** *adv.*

arterio-. Form of Gr. ἀρτηρία, artery, used in combination. —**ar-te-ri-ol-o-gy** (är-tē-ri-ol′ō̤-ji), *n.* [+ *-logy.*] The science of the arteries.—**ar-te″ri-o-scle-ro′sis** (-ō̤-sklē̤-rō′sis), *n.* [NL.] In *pathol.*, sclerosis or hardening of the walls of the arteries, esp. of the intima, occurring chiefly in old age.—**ar-te″ri-o-scle-rot′ic** (-rot′ik), *a.*—**ar-te″ri-o-ste-no′sis** (-ste-nō′sis), *n.* [NL.] In *pathol.*, stenosis or contraction of an artery.—**ar-te-ri-ot′o-my** (-ot′ō̤-mi), *n.* [Gr. ἀρτηριοτομία: see *-tomy.*] The cutting of an artery, as in letting blood; dissection of the arteries.

ar-te-ri-tis (är-te̤-rī′tis), *n.* [NL.] In *pathol.*, inflammation of an artery.

ar-te-ry (är′te̤-ri), *n.*; pl. *-ries* (-riz). [L. *arteria*, < Gr. ἀρτηρία.] The windpipe†; also, one of the system of branching vessels or tubes conveying blood from the heart to all parts of the body; hence, a main channel in any branching system, as of streets.—**ar′te-ry,** *v. t.*; *-ried, -rying.* To supply with or traverse like arteries.

Artesian Well.
a, a, fault filled with clay and impervious to water; *b, b,* impermeable strata; *c,* permeable strata; *d,* artesian boring and well.

ar-te-sian (är-tē′zha̤n), *a.* Pertaining to Artois, a former province of northern France: applied to a kind of bored well from which water gushes up, forced by natural pressure due to strata conditions, and hence to any deep bored well.

art-ful (ärt′fu̇l), *a.* Characterized by or showing art; skilful; clever; crafty; cunning; also, artificial†.—**art′ful-ly,** *adv.*—**art′ful-ness,** *n.*

ar-thral-gia (är-thral′jiạ), *n.* [NL., < Gr. ἄρθρον, joint, + ἄλγος, pain.] In *pathol.*, pain, esp. neuralgic pain, in a joint.—**ar-thral′gic,** *a.*

ar-thrit-ic (är-thrit′ik), *a.* [L. *arthriticus*, < Gr. ἀρθριτικός, < ἄρθρον, joint.] Pertaining to or affecting the joints; also, pertaining to arthritis; gouty.

ar-thri-tis (är-thrī′tis), *n.* [L., < Gr. ἀρθρῖτις, < ἄρθρον, joint.] In *pathol.*, inflammation of a joint, as in gout or rheumatism.

arthro-. Form of Gr. ἄρθρον, joint, used in combination.—**ar-thro-mere** (är′thrō̤-mēr), *n.* [+ *-mere.*] In *zoöl.*, one of the segments or parts into which the body of articulate animals is divided.—**ar-throp′a-thy** (-throp′a̤-thi), *n.* [+ *-pathy.*] Disease of the joints.

ar-thro-pod (är′thrō̤-pod). [NL. *Arthropoda*, pl., < Gr. ἄρθρον, joint, + πούς (ποδ-), foot.] **I.** *n.* One of the *Arthropoda*, a phylum of articulate invertebrate animals, comprising those with jointed legs, as the insects, arachnids, crustaceans, and myriapods. **II.** *a.* Arthropodous.—**ar-throp′o-dous** (-throp′ō̤-dus), *a.* Having jointed legs; belonging to the *Arthropoda.*

ar-thro-sis (är-thrō′sis), *n.*; pl. *-throses* (-thrō′sēz). [NL., < Gr. ἄρθρωσις, < ἀρθροῦν, fasten by a joint, < ἄρθρον, a joint.] In *anat.*, an articulation or suture joining two bones or cartilages.

ar-thro-spore (är′thrō̤-spōr), *n.* [See *arthro-* and *spore.*] In *bact.*, an isolated vegetative cell which has passed into a resting state: occurring in species of bacteria, and not regarded as a true spore.—**ar-thros′po-rous** (-thros′pō̤-rus), *a.* In *bact.*, producing arthrospores.

Ar-thu-ri-an (är-thū′ri-a̤n), *a.* Of or pertaining to Arthur, a legendary king of ancient Britain, who, with his knights (cf. *Round Table*), formed the subject of a great body of romantic literature.

ar-ti-ad (är′ti-ad). [Gr. ἄρτιος, even.] In *chem.*: **I.** *n.* An atom or element whose valence is expressed by an even number: opposed to *perissad.* **II.** *a.* Having the valence expressed by an even number.

ar-ti-choke (är′ti-chōk), *n.* [It. *articiocco* = Sp. *alcachofa*, < Ar. *al*, the, + *kharshūf*, artichoke.] An asteraceous plant, *Cynara scolymus*, somewhat resembling a thistle, with a flower-head whose receptacle and also the fleshy bases of the involucral scales are used as food; also, the edible portion of this plant, esteemed as a table vegetable; also, any of several other plants with edible parts, as *Helianthus tuberosus*, a species of sunflower with an edible tuberous root ('Jerusalem artichoke': said to be a corruption of It. *girasole articiocco*, sunflower artichoke), or *Stachys sieboldi*, a plant of China and Japan with edible tubers.

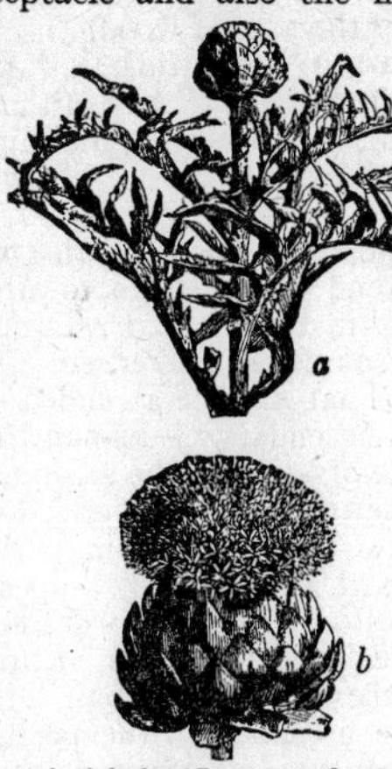

Artichoke (*Cynara scolymus*). *a*, top of plant; *b*, flowering head.

ar-ti-cle (är′ti-kl), *n.* [OF. F. *article*, < L. *articulus*, dim. of *artus*, joint, akin to Gr. ἄρθρον, joint.] A joint connecting parts†; a part connected by a joint; a distinct portion of a document or writing; a clause, as of a statute, a contract, etc.; a member of a series of propositions, stipulations, regulations, etc. (as, *articles* of faith, of impeachment, of agreement, of indenture, of war; the Thirty-nine *Articles* of doctrine of the Church of England); a literary composition published with others in a periodical or book; an item or particular; an individual piece or thing of a class (as, an *article* of food or of dress); a thing, indefinitely (as, what is that *article?*); a commodity; a matter† or subject†; juncture or moment (archaic: as, in the *article* of death); in *gram.*, one of the words *a* or *an* ('indefinite article') and *the* ('definite article'), or an equivalent in a foreign language, used before nouns to indicate the scope of their application.—**ar′ti-cle,** *v. t.*; *-cled, -cling.* To set forth in articles; charge or accuse specifically; bind by articles of agreement.—**ar-tic′u-lar** (-tik′ū-lạr), *a.* [L. *articularis.*] Of or pertaining to the joints.

ar-tic-u-late (är-tik′ū-lāt), *v.*; *-lated, -lating.* [L. *articulatus*, pp. of *articulare*, < *articulus*: see *article.*] **I.** *tr.* To unite by a joint or joints; utter in distinct syllables or speech; set forth in articles†. **II.** *intr.* To form a joint (*with*); utter distinct syllables or speech; make terms of agreement†.—**ar-tic′u-late** (-lạt). **I.** *a.* Articulated or jointed; uttered in distinct syllables or as intelligible speech; distinct or clear; in *zoöl.*, having a body composed of segments; belonging to the *Articulata*, a former division of invertebrates with segmented body, comprising the arthropods and the annelid worms. **II.** *n.* An articulate invertebrate.—**ar-tic′u-late-ly,** *adv.*—**ar-tic′u-late-ness,** *n.* —**ar-tic-u-la′tion** (-lā′shọn), *n.* [L. *articulatio(n-).*] The act of jointing; jointed state or formation; a joint; also, articulate utterance; speech; an articulate sound; in *bot.*, a joint or place between two parts where separation may take place spontaneously, as at the point of attachment of a leaf or of the pedicel of a flower; also, a node in a stem, or the space between two such nodes.—**ar-tic′u-la-tive** (-lạ-tiv), *a.* Pertaining to articulation.—**ar-tic′u-la-tor** (-lā-tọr), *n.*—**ar-tic′u-la-to-ry** (-lạ-tọ̄-ri), *a.* Pertaining to articulation (in speech).

ar-ti-fact (är′ti-fakt), *n.* [L. *ars* (*art-*), art, + *factus*, pp. of *facere*, make.] Anything made by art; an artificial product; in *biol.*, a substance, structure, or the like, not naturally present in tissue but formed by reagents, death, etc.

ar-ti-fice (är′ti-fis), *n.* [F. *artifice*, < L. *artificium*, art, handicraft, cunning, artifice, < *ars* (*art-*), art, + *facere*, make.] An art† or craft†; a product of art†; workmanship†; skilful or artful contrivance; craft; a crafty device or expedient; a shift, stratagem, or trick.—**ar-tif′i-cer** (-tif′i-sėr), *n.* A skilled workman; a craftsman; an artisan; also, a contriver, deviser, or inventor.

ar-ti-fi-cial (är-ti-fish′ạl), *a.* [L. *artificialis*, < *artificium*: see *artifice.*] Pertaining to art†; technical†; produced by art (opposed to *natural*); sown, not springing up spontaneously, as grasses; made as a substitute or imitation (opposed to *real*); factitious; feigned or assumed; affected, as a person; showing art or skill†; artful†.—**artificial horizon.** See under *horizon.*—**artificial selection.** See *selection.*—**ar-ti-fi-ci-al′i-ty** (-fish-i-al′i-ti), *n.*; pl. *-ties* (-tiz). The quality of being artificial; also, an artificial thing or characteristic.—**ar-ti-fi′cial-ize,** *v. t.*; *-ized, -izing.* To render artificial.—**ar-ti-fi′cial-ly,** *adv.*—**ar-ti-fi′cial-ness,** *n.*

ar-til-ler-ist (är-til′ẹ-rist), *n.* One versed in the subject of artillery; an artilleryman or gunner.

ar-til-ler-y (är-til′ẹ-ri), *n.* [OF. *artillerie*, implements of war (cf. *artillier*, maker of bows and other arms, *artiller*, provide with engines of war, *artil*, implement of war, *artillos*, skilful, artful); appar. < ML. *articulum*, artful device, dim. of L. *ars*, E. *art*².] Implements or engines of war†; munitions of war†; in modern use, mounted guns, movable or stationary, light or heavy, as distinguished from small arms; ordnance; cannon; also, the troops, or the branch of the army, concerned with the service of such guns; also, the science which treats of the use of such guns.—**ar-til′ler-y-man** (-mạn), *n.*; pl. *-men.* One who serves a piece of artillery; a gunner.

ar-ti-o-dac-tyl (är″ti-ọ̄-dak′til). [Gr. ἄρτιος, even, + δάκτυλος, finger or toe.] **I.** *a.* Having an even number of toes or digits on each foot; belonging to the *Artiodactyla*, a suborder of ungulate or hoofed mammals including the ox, sheep, hog, deer, camel, hippopotamus, etc.: opposed to *perissodactyl.* **II.** *n.* One of the *Artiodactyla.*—**ar″ti-o-dac′ty-lous** (-ti-lus), *a.*

ar-ti-san (är′ti-zạn, Brit. är-ti-zan′), *n.* [F. *artisan*, < It. *artigiano*, < L. *artitus*, pp. of *artire*, instruct in arts, < *ars*: see *art*².] One skilled in an industrial art; a handicraftsman; a mechanic; also, an artist†.

ar-tist (är′tist), *n.* [F. *artiste*, < ML. *artista*, < L. *ars*: see *art*².] One versed in the liberal arts†; a man of learning or science†; one trained or proficient in any art†; an artisan†; one who practises one of the fine arts, as painting; a member of any profession subject to esthetic standards, as an actor, a singer, or a dancer; one who exhibits art in his work, or makes an art of his employment; one who uses artifice or craft†.—**ar-tiste** (är-tēst), *n.* [F., masc. and fem.] An artist, esp. an actor, a singer, a dancer, or other public performer.—**ar-tis′tic,** *a.* [F. *artistique.*] Of, like, or befitting an artist; conformable to the standards of art; esthetically excellent or admirable. Also **ar-tis′ti-cal.** —**ar-tis′ti-cal-ly,** *adv.*—**ar′tist-ry,** *n.* The work or workmanship of an artist.

ar′ti-zan, *n.* See *artisan.*

art-less (ärt′les), *a.* Lacking art; unskilled; ignorant; inartistic; rude; also, natural; simple; ingenuous; guileless.—**art′less-ly,** *adv.*—**art′less-ness,** *n.*

ar-to-type (är′tọ̄-tīp), *n.* [See *art*² and *-type.*] A method of printing in ink from a gelatin photographic plate; also, a print so made.

art=square (ärt′skwãr), *n.* A square rug of ingrain carpet.

a-rum (ā′rum or ã′rum), *n.* [L., < Gr. ἄρον.] Any plant of the genus *Arum*, having a characteristic inflorescence consisting of a spadix inclosed in a large spathe, as the British wake-robin, *A. maculatum*; also, any of various allied plants, as *Peltandra virginica* ('arrow-arum'), *Arisæma dracontium* ('dragon-arum'), *Calla palustris* ('water-arum'), and the calla lily.

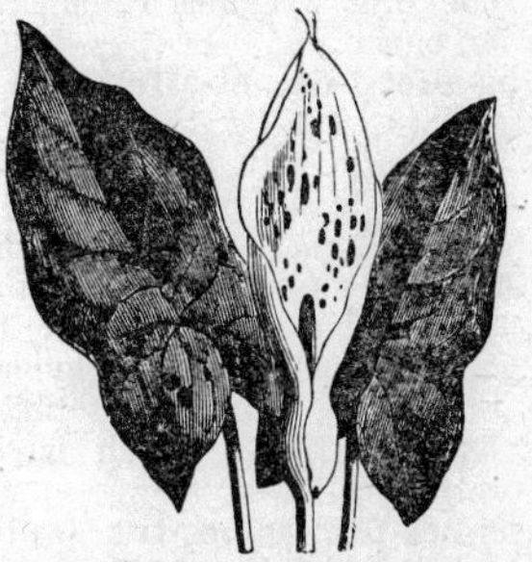
Arum (*A. maculatum*).

a-run-di-na-ceous (a-run-di-nā′shius), *a.* [L. *arundinaceus*, < *arundo*, *harundo*, reed.] Reed-like, as plants.

a-rus-pex (a-rus′peks), etc. Same as *haruspex*, etc.

Ar-val (är′vạl) **Breth′ren.** [L. *arvalis*, pertaining to plowed land, < *arvum*, plowed land.] In ancient Rome, a college of twelve priests who offered sacrifices for the fertility of the fields. Also **Ar′val Broth′ers.**

-ary. [L. *-arius*, neut. *-arium* (see *-arium*); sometimes, L. *-aris*, neut. *-are* (see *-ar*).] A suffix of adjectives meaning 'pertaining to or connected with' (something), as in *arbitrary, elementary, honorary, military, sumptuary,* or of nouns meaning 'one concerned with or engaged in,' or 'a thing connected with,' or 'a place for' (something), as in *antiquary, apothecary, dictionary, granary.*

Ar-yan (är'yạn or ar'i-ạn). [Skt. *Arya,* name by which the Sanskrit-speaking immigrants into India called themselves, = OPers. *Ariya,* name applied by the ancient Persians to themselves; origin obscure.] **I.** *a.* Pertaining to the Aryans or their speech. **II.** *n.* A member of the Asiatic division of the Indo-European family, occupying India and Persia, or of the whole Indo-European family, comprising (chiefly) the Hindus and Iranians (Persians) and the Greeks, Italians, Celts, Slavs, and Teutons, whose languages are all akin; also, the original Aryan speech.

ar-y-te-noid (ar-i-tē'noid). [Gr. ἀρυταινοειδής, < ἀρύταινα, ladle, cup, + εἶδος, form.] In *anat.*: **I.** *a.* Ladle-shaped: applied to two cartilages of the larynx, and hence to adjoining muscles and glands. **II.** *n.* An arytenoid cartilage. —**ar″y-te-noi'dal** (-tẹ-noi'dạl), *a.*

as[1] (az), *adv.* [ME. *als, alse, also,* < AS. *alswā, ealswā,* 'all so,' quite so, quite as, as: cf. *also.*] To such a degree or extent: the antecedent in the correlation *as . . . as* (as, *as* good as gold), the consequent being sometimes omitted (as, this is *as* good). See *so, adv.*—**as well as,** as much or as truly as; just as; as also: as, to give facts *as well as* opinions; good *as well as* beautiful. Hence, elliptically, *as well,* equally; also; too: as, beautiful, and good *as well.* —**as**[1], *conj.* The consequent in the correlations *as . . . as, so . . . as, such . . . as, same . . . as,* etc., noting degree, extent, manner, etc. (as, as good *as* gold; in the same way *as* before), or in the correlations *so as, such as,* noting purpose or result (with infinitive: as, to listen so *as* to hear; such *as* to please); also (without antecedent), in the degree, manner, etc., of or that (as, to be good *as* gold; to rank *as* major; do *as* we do); also, when or while; since; for instance; even or just (now chiefly in the phrase *as yet*); than (prov.); in dependent clauses, that (colloq.: as, I don't know *as* I do). —**as for, as to,** with respect to. —**as if, as though,** as it would be if.—**as it were,** as if it were; in some sort; so to speak.—**as**[1], *rel. pron.* That; who; which: after *such* or *same* (now prov. after other antecedents).

Obverse.

Reverse.
Roman As, in the British Museum.

as[2] (as), *n.*; pl. *asses* (L. as'ēz). [L.] In ancient Rome, a unit of weight, the pound, of 12 ounces (or about 5,050 grains); also, a monetary unit, a copper coin orig. weighing 12 ounces but gradually reduced to half an ounce.

as-a-fet-i-da, as-a-fœt-i-da (as-ạ-fet'i-dạ), *n.* [ML., < *asa* (< Pers. *azā,* mastic) + L. *fetida, fœtida,* fetid.] A gum-resin with a strong garlic-like odor, from the roots of several plants of Persia and Afghanistan, of the apiaceous genus *Ferula*: used in medicine.

A-saph-ic (a-saf'ik), *a.* Of or pertaining to Asaph, one of the chief singers in the Temple in the time of David and Solomon, and eponymous head of one of the gilds of singers, "sons of Asaph": as, *Asaphic* psalms (psalms 50 and 73–83, which have the name of Asaph superscribed).

as-bes-tos, as-bes-tus (as-bes'tọs, -tus, or az-), *n.* [L. *asbestos,* < Gr. ἄσβεστος, unquenchable, < ἀ- priv. + σβεστός, verbal adj. of σβεννύναι, quench.] A fabulous stone, unquenchable when burning†; a fibrous variety of amphibole or hornblende, used for making articles required to be incombustible or fireproof; also, the mineral chrysotile, which is similarly used.—**as-bes'ti-form,** *a.*—**as-bes'tine** (-tin), **as-bes'tous,** *a.*

as-bo-lin (as'bọ-lin or az'-), *n.* [Gr. ἄσβολος, soot.] In *phar.,* an acrid, brownish-yellow, oil-like liquid obtained from the soot of wood.

as-ca-rid (as'kạ-rid), *n.* [Gr. ἀσκαρίς (ἀσκαριδ-), an intestinal worm.] Any of the *Ascaridæ,* a family of nematoid worms including the roundworm and pinworm.

as-cend (ạ-send'), *v.* [L. *ascendere* (pp. *ascensus*), < *ad,* to, + *scandere,* climb.] **I.** *intr.* To climb or go upward (opposed to *descend*); rise to a higher point or degree; slope or tend upward; go toward the source or beginning; go back in time. **II.** *tr.* To climb; mount; go up; go toward the source of (a river, etc.).—**as-cend'a-ble, as-cend'i-ble,** *a.* That may be ascended.—**as-cend'ance, as-cend'ence,** *n.* Ascendancy.—**as-cend'an-cy, as-cend'en-cy,** *n.* The state of being in the ascendant; dominance.—**as-cend'ant, as-cend'ent.** [F. *ascendant,* < L. *ascendens* (*-ent-*), ppr.] **I.** *a.* Ascending; rising, esp. above the horizon or toward the zenith; superior; dominant. **II.** *n.* An ancestor (opposed to *descendant*); in *astrol.,* the point of the ecliptic or the sign of the zodiac rising above the horizon at the time of a birth, etc.; the horoscope; hence, fig. ('the ascendant'), the position of dominance or controlling influence; superiority; predominance.—**as-cend'er,** *n.*—**as-cend'ing,** *p. a.* That ascends; rising; tending upward; in *bot.,* growing or directed upward, esp. obliquely or in a curve from the base.

as-cen-seur (å-soṅ-sėr), *n.* [F.] An elevator or lift.

as-cen-sion (ạ-sen'shọn), *n.* [L. *ascensio(n-).*] The act of ascending; ascent; in *astron.,* the rising of a star or point above the horizon on the celestial sphere (as, right *ascension,* the arc of the celestial equator intercepted between the vernal equinox and the great circle of the celestial sphere passing through the celestial poles and a heavenly body whose position is in question, reckoned toward the east, and expressed in degrees or time); *eccles.,* [*l. c.* or *cap.*] the bodily passing of Christ from earth to heaven (Luke, xxiv. 51); also, [*cap.*] a day ('Ascension Day') on which it is annually commemorated, the fortieth day (counting forward) from Easter (also called *Holy Thursday*).—**as-cen'sion-al,** *a.*—**as-cen'sion-ist,** *n.* One who makes ascensions; a mountain-climber; also, a balloonist.

as-cen-sive (ạ-sen'siv), *a.* Ascending; rising; in *gram.,* intensive.

as-cent (ạ-sent'), *n.* [Formed from *ascend,* to parallel *descent.*] The act of ascending; upward movement; rise; procedure toward a source or beginning; also, an upward way or slope; an acclivity; also, the angle made by an ascending line or surface with the horizontal.

as-cer-tain (as-ėr-tān'), *v. t.* [OF. *acertener,* < *a* (< L. *ad*), to, + *certain,* E. *certain.*] To make certain, clear, or definitely known (archaic); find out with certainty; determine; insure as a certainty (archaic); fix the amount, extent, etc., of†; certify (one) of a thing†; assure†; inform†.—**as-cer-tain'a-ble,** *a.* Capable of being ascertained.—**as-cer-tain'a-ble-ness,** *n.*—**as-cer-tain'a-bly,** *adv.*—**as-cer-tain'ment,** *n.* The act of ascertaining; determination.

as-cet-ic (a-set'ik). [Gr. ἀσκητικός, < ἀσκητής, an ascetic, < ἀσκεῖν, practise.] **I.** *a.* Practising special forms of self-denial and devotion as a religious discipline; seeking holiness through self-mortification; rigorously abstinent; austere; pertaining to asceticism. **II.** *n.* In the early Christian church, one who practised unusual self-denial and devotion; in modern use, one who practises religious austerities; a hermit or recluse.—**as-cet'i-cal,** *a.* Of or pertaining to ascetic practice or discipline: as, *ascetical* theology.—**as-cet'i-cal-ly,** *adv.*—**as-cet'i-cism** (-sizm), *n.* The life or practice of an ascetic; ascetic discipline.—**as-cet'ics,** *n.* Ascetical theology.

as-ci (as'ī), *n.* Plural of *ascus.*

as-cid-i-an (a-sid'i-ạn), *n.* [NL. *Ascidia,* pl., < Gr. ἀσκίδιον, dim. of ἀσκός, bag, wine-skin.] One of the *Ascidia,* or *Tunicata,* a class of marine animals, simple or compound, fixed or free, with a leathery sac-like integument, connecting the molluscoid invertebrates with the vertebrates; a tunicate; a sea-squirt.—**as-cid'i-oid,** *a.* and *n.*

as-cid-i-um (a-sid′i-um), *n.*; pl. *-ia* (-i-ạ̈). [NL., < Gr. ἀσκίδιον: see *ascidian.*] In *bot.*, a bag-like or pitcher-like part, as of a pitcher-plant.

Ascidium.
Leaf of pitcher-plant (*Nepenthes*) with a winged petiole and terminating in an operculate pitcher.

as-cif-er-ous, as-cig-er-ous (a-sif′ẹ-rus, a-sij′ẹ-rus), *a.* [See *ascus* and *-ferous, -gerous.*] In *bot.*, bearing asci.

as-ci-tes (a-sī′tēz), *n.* [L., < Gr. ἀσκίτης, < ἀσκός, bag, belly.] In *pathol.*, dropsy of the belly or peritoneum.—**as-cit-ic** (a-sit′ik), *a.*

as-cle-pi-a-da-ceous (as-klē″pi-ạ-dā′shius), *a.* [NL. *Asclepias*, the milkweed genus, < Gr. ἀσκληπιάς, kind of plant, < Ἀσκληπιός, Æsculapius.] Belonging to the *Asclepiadaceæ*, or milkweed family of plants.

As-cle-pi-a-de-an (as-klē″pi-ạ-dē′ạn). In *anc. pros.*: **I.** *a.* Noting or pertaining to a kind of verse which according to some is logaœdic, but which according to others is choriambic and consists of a spondee, two (or three) choriambi, and an iambus: so called after the Greek poet Asclepiades. **II.** *n.* An Asclepiadean verse.

as-co-carp (as′kō-kärp), *n.* [NL. *ascus* (see *ascus*) + Gr. καρπός, fruit.] In *bot.*, in ascomycetous fungi, one of the spherical, saucer-shaped, or cup-shaped bodies inclosing the asci.

as-co-go-ni-um (as-kō-gō′ni-um), *n.*; pl. *-nia* (-ni-ạ̈). [NL., < *ascus* (see *ascus*) + *-gonium* as in *archegonium.*] In *bot.*, the female sexual organ in the gametophyte of ascomycetous fungi.—**as-co-go′ni-al,** *a.*

as-co-my-ce-tous (as″kō-mī-sē′tus), *a.* [NL. *Ascomycetes*, pl., < *ascus* (see *ascus*) + Gr. μύκης (μυκητ-), fungus.] In *bot.*, belonging or pertaining to the *Ascomycetes*, a class of fungi characterized by the formation of spores within an ascus, including the yeasts, mildews, truffles, morels, etc.

as-co-spore (as′kō-spōr), *n.* [See *ascus* and *spore.*] In *bot.*, a spore formed within an ascus.—**as-cos′po-rous** (-kos′pō-rus), *a.*

As-cot (as′kọt). **I.** *a.* Noting or pertaining to the celebrated race-course at Ascot, in Berkshire, England, or the horse-races held there annually in June. **II.** *n.* [*l. c.*] A kind of scarf or necktie with broad ends, tied and arranged so that the ends are laid flat, one across the other.

as-cribe (ạs-krīb′), *v. t.*; *-cribed, -cribing.* [L. *ascribere* (pp. *ascriptus*), < *ad*, to, + *scribere*, write.] To add in writing†; subscribe†; inscribe†; enroll†; also, to set down or impute as due, referable, or belonging (*to*); attribute; refer.—**as-crib′a-ble** (-krī′bạ-bl), *a.*—**as-crip′tion** (-krip′shọn), *n.* [L. *ascriptio(n-).*] The act of ascribing; a statement ascribing something.

as-cus (as′kus), *n.*; pl. *asci* (as′ī). [NL., < Gr. ἀσκός, bag, wine-skin.] In *bot.*, a sac or cell in certain fungi in which the spores are formed.

-ase. [From *diastase.*] A noun suffix used in *chem.*, in names of enzymes, as *glucase, inulase, lactase, pectase.*

a-sea (ạ-sē′), *adv.* On the sea; at sea; also, to the sea.

a-sep-sis (a-sep′sis or ā-), *n.* [NL.: see *a-*[1] and *sepsis.*] Absence of the micro-organisms that produce sepsis or septic disease; methods or treatment characterized by the absence of such micro-organisms, as in surgery.—**a-sep′tic,** *a.* Pertaining to, characterized by, or effecting asepsis.—**a-sep′ti-cal-ly,** *adv.*—**a-sep′ti-cism** (-sizm), *n.* Use of aseptic methods.—**a-sep′ti-cize** (-sīz), *v. t.*; *-cized, -cizing.* To render aseptic.

a-sex-u-al (a-sek′shū-ạl or ā-), *a.* [See *a-*[1].] Not sexual; having no sex, or no sexual organs; independent of sexual processes.—**a-sex-u-al′i-ty** (-al′i-ti), *n.*—**a-sex″u-al-i-za′tion** (-i-zā′shọn), *n.* The act of rendering sexually incompetent, as by castration.—**a-sex′u-al-ly,** *adv.*

As-gard (as′gärd), *n.* [Icel. *āsgardhr*, < *āss*, god, + *gardhr*, yard.] The abode of the Æsir, or Scandinavian gods, situated in the heavens, and connected with the earth by a rainbow bridge (Bifrost).

ash[1] (ash), *n.* [AS. *æsc* = G. *esche.*] Any tree of the oleaceous genus *Fraxinus*, esp. *F. excelsior* of Europe and Asia, or *F. americana* of North America ('white ash'); also, the wood, tough, straight-grained, and elastic, and valued as timber; also, one of various other trees or shrubs, as the mountain-ash.

ash[2] (ash), *n.* [AS. *asce* = G. *asche.*] The powdery incombustible residue of matter after burning (often in *pl.*); pulverized lava from a volcano in eruption; solid residue from evaporated wine; *pl.*, human remains, orig. as after cremation; ruins, as from destruction by burning.

a-shamed (ạ-shāmd′), *p. a.* [AS. *āscamod*, pp. of *āscamian*, < *ā-*, away, on, + *scamian*, E. *shame, v.*] Affected with shame; disconcerted or uncomfortable from a sense of fault, impropriety, or disgrace (often with *of* or a clause); reluctant through fear of shame (with infinitive).—**a-sham-ed-ly** (ạ-shā′med-li), *adv.*

ash=can (ash′kan), *n.* A can or metal receptacle for ashes; also (colloq.), a depth bomb (see under *depth*: so called from its appearance).

ash=col-ored (ash′kul″ọrd), *a.* Of the whitish-gray color of ashes; having a pale grayish tinge.

ash-en[1] (ash′n), *a.* Of or pertaining to the ash-tree or its timber; made of ash.

ash-en[2] (ash′n), *a.* Of or like ashes; ashy.

ash-er-y (ash′ėr-i), *n.*; pl. *asheries* (-iz). A place for ashes; also, a potash or pearlash manufactory.

ash-es (ash′ez), *n. pl.* See *ash*[2].

a-shine (ạ-shīn′), *adv.* In a shining state.

a-shiv-er (ạ-shiv′ėr), *adv.* In a shiver; aquiver.

Ash-ke-naz-im (ash-kē-naz′im), *n. pl.* [Heb., < *Ashkenaz*, a descendant of Japheth (Gen. x. 3), a people descended from him, also, in medieval use, Germany.] German-Polish Jews and their descendants, as distinguished from the Sephardim or Spanish-Portuguese Jews and their descendants, the two groups differing from each other in liturgy and in pronunciation of Hebrew, but not in doctrine.—**Ash-ke-naz′ic,** *a.*

ash=key (ash′kē), *n.* The winged fruit (samara) of the ash-tree.

ash-ler, ash-lar (ash′lėr, -lạ̈r), *n.* [OF. *aiseler*, ult. < L. *axis*, board, axle.] A squared block of building-stone, finished or rough; such stones collectively, or masonry made of them; in *carp.*, one of the studs or uprights in ashlering.—**ash′lered, ash′lared,** *a.* Faced with ashler, as a wall.—**ash′ler-ing, ash′lar-ing,** *n.* Masonry or a facing of ashler; in *carp.*, a short studding cutting off the angle between floor and roof in a garret and affording a wall of some height.

a-shore (ạ-shōr′), *adv.* On or to shore or land.

Ash-to-reth (ash′tō-reth), *n.*; pl. *Ashtaroth* (ash′tạ-roth or -rōth). The Hebrew name of an ancient Semitic goddess. See *Astarte.*

Ash Wednes-day (ash wenz′dā). The first day of Lent: named from the custom in the Western Church of sprinkling ashes on penitents' heads on that day.

ash-wort (ash′wėrt), *n.* A composite plant, *Senecio tomentosus*, of the southeastern U. S., covered with an ash-colored wool.

ash-y (ash′i), *a.* Of or like ashes; pale as ashes; sprinkled or strewn with ashes.

A-sian (ā′shiạn or ā′zhiạn). **I.** *a.* Of or pertaining to the continent of Asia. **II.** *n.* An Asiatic.

A-si-arch (ā′shi-ärk), *n.* [L. *Asiarcha*, < Gr. Ἀσιάρχης: see *-arch.*] An official in the ancient Roman province of Asia whose office it was to preside over the religious rites and the public games.

A-si-at-ic (ā-shi-at′ik or ā-zhi-). **I.** *a.* Of or pertaining to Asia or its inhabitants: as, *Asiatic* cholera (see *cholera*). **II.** *n.* A native of Asia.—**A-si-at′i-cal-ly,** *adv.*—**A-si-at′i-cize** (-i-sīz), *v. t.*; *-cized, -cizing.* To conform to the Asiatic character or type.

a-side (ạ-sīd′). **I.** *adv.* On or to one side; apart; away; off; of speaking, so as (ostensibly) not to be heard by others. **II.** *prep.* Beside (now prov. Eng. and Sc.); also, beyond†.

III. *n.* A remark, as on the stage, assumed not to be heard by persons present.
as-i-en-to (as-ẹ̄-en′tō), *n.* See *assiento.*
as-i-nine (as′i-nīn), *a.* [L. *asininus,* < *asinus,* ass.] Of, like, or suggestive of an ass; awkward; obstinate; stupid; silly.—**as′i-nine-ly,** *adv.*—**as-i-nin′i-ty** (-nin′i-ti), *n.*
-asis. See *-iasis.*
ask (ȧsk), *v.* [AS. *āscian,* also *ācsian,* = OHG. *eiscōn* (G. *heischen*).] **I.** *tr.* To seek by words to hear or learn; inquire; put (a question); make inquiry of (a person, etc.); interrogate or question; also, to seek by words to receive; make request for; solicit; demand; call for; require; also, to make request to; petition; invite; also, to publish (banns), or publish the banns of (persons). **II.** *intr.* To make inquiry; inquire (*about, after, for,* etc.); make request (often with *for*).
a-skance (ạ-skans′), *adv.* [Origin uncertain.] Sidewise; with a side glance; with a glance of disfavor and suspicion (often fig.). Also **a-skant′.**
ask-er (ȧs′kėr), *n.* One who asks.
a-skew (ạ-skū′). [See *skew.*] **I.** *adv.* Obliquely; sidelong; to one side; awry. **II.** *a.* Oblique; skew.
a-slant (ạ-slȧnt′). **I.** *adv.* At a slant; slantingly; obliquely. **II.** *prep.* Slantingly across; athwart.
a-sleep (ạ-slēp′), *adv.* or *a.* In or into a state of sleep; sleeping; hence, dormant; also, dead; also, of the foot, hand, etc., numb, as from pressure on a nerve-trunk.
a-slope (ạ-slōp′), *adv.* At a slope or inclination.
a-so-ma-tous (a-sō′mạ-tus), *a.* [Gr. ἀσώματος, < ἀ- priv. + σῶμα, body.] Without a body; incorporeal.
asp[1] (asp), *n.* [AS. *æspe* = G. *espe.*] A European poplar, *Populus tremula,* with leaves that tremble in the lightest breeze; any of several other species, as, in America, *P. tremuloides* ('quaking asp'), or *P. alba* ('white asp'): commonly called *aspen.*
asp[2] (asp), *n.* [L. *aspis,* < Gr. ἀσπίς.] Any of several venomous serpents, as that (prob. the horned viper, *Cerastes cornutus*) said to have caused Cleopatra's death, or as a kind of cobra, *Naja haje,* also found in Egypt; also, the common European viper or adder.

Asp (*Naja haje*).

as-par-a-gus (as-par′ạ-gus), *n.* [L., < Gr. ἀσπάραγος.] Any plant of the convallariaceous genus *Asparagus,* esp. *A. officinalis,* cultivated for its edible shoots; also, the shoots, esteemed as a table vegetable.
As-pa-sia (as-pā′shiạ̈), *n.* [From *Aspasia* (flourished about 445 B.C.), mistress of Pericles, the Athenian statesman.] A courtezan, esp. one of great talents and influence.
as-pect (as′pekt), *n.* [L. *aspectus,* < *aspicere,* look at, < *ad,* to, + *specere,* look at.] Look, glance, or gaze at anything (archaic); way of looking or appearing to observers; look; appearance; countenance; a way in which a thing may be viewed or regarded; view commanded; prospect, outlook, or exposure; in *astrol.,* the relative position of planets as determining their influence; in *aëronautics,* the appearance presented by a plane of an aëroplane when viewed in a given direction; the arrangement of a plane in relation to the direction of flight.
as-pen (as′pẹn). **I.** *a.* Of or pertaining to the asp (tree); hence, trembling or quivering, like the leaves of the asp. **II.** *n.* Any of various species of poplar. See *asp*[1].
as-per-ate (as′pẹ-rāt), *v. t.*; *-ated, -ating.* [L. *asperatus,* pp. of *asperare,* < *asper,* rough.] To make rough.
as-per-ges (as-pėr′jēz), *n.* [L., 'thou shalt sprinkle.'] In the *Rom. Cath. Ch.,* the rite of sprinkling the altar, clergy, and people with holy water before high mass on Sundays; [*cap.*] the anthem beginning "Asperges," sung while the priest performs this rite.
as-per-gil-lum (as-pėr-jil′um), *n.*; pl. *-gilla* (-jil′ạ̈). [ML., < L. *aspergere,* sprinkle: see *asperse.*] In the *Rom. Cath. Ch.,* a brush or instrument for sprinkling holy water.
as-per-i-fo-li-ate (as″pẹ-ri-fō′li-ạ̄t), *a.* [L. *asper,* rough, + *folium,* leaf.] In *bot.,* having rough leaves.
as-per-i-ty (as-per′i-ti), *n.*; pl. *-ties* (-tiz). [L. *asperitas,* < *asper,* rough.] Roughness; harshness; severity; acrimony; also, something rough or harsh.
as-per-mous (as-pėr′mus), *a.* [Gr. ἄσπερμος, < ἀ- priv. + σπέρμα, seed.] In *bot.,* destitute of seed.
as-perse (as-pėrs′), *v. t.*; *-persed, -persing.* [L. *aspersus,* pp. of *aspergere,* sprinkle, < *ad,* to, + *spargere,* scatter.] To sprinkle; bespatter; fig., to assail with damaging charges or insinuations; cast reproach upon by foul or false reports.—**as-pers′er,** *n.*—**as-per′sion** (-pėr′shọn), *n.* [L. *aspersio(n-).*] The act of aspersing; a sprinkling; fig., damaging or calumnious imputation; a derogatory or defamatory criticism.
as-per-soir (ȧs-per-swor), *n.* [F., < ML. *aspersorium*: see *aspersorium.*] An aspergillum.
as-per-so-ri-um (as-pėr-sō′ri-um), *n.*; pl. *-ria* (-ri-ạ̈). [ML., < L. *asperse,* sprinkle: see *asperse.*] In the *Rom. Cath. Ch.,* a vessel for holding holy water; also, an aspergillum.
as-phalt (as′falt, commonly as′fȧlt), *n.* [LL. *asphaltus,* < Gr. ἄσφαλτος.] Any of various dark-colored, solid bituminous substances, composed mostly of mixtures of hydrocarbons, occurring native in various parts of the earth; also, a mixture of such a substance with crushed rock, etc., used for pavements, roofing, etc.—**as-phalt** (as-falt′ or as′falt), *v. t.* To cover or pave with asphalt.—**as-phal′tic,** *a.*—**as-phal′-tum** (-tum), *n.* [NL.] Asphalt.

Asphodel (*Asphodelus ramosus*).

as-pho-del (as′fọ-del), *n.* [L. *asphodelus,* < Gr. ἀσφοδελός.] Any of various liliaceous plants of the genera *Asphodelus* and *Asphodeline,* native in southern Europe, with white or yellow flowers; also, a flower or plant, said to be *Asphodeline lutea,* associated by the ancient Greeks with the dead and the Elysian fields; also, any of various other plants, as the daffodil.
as-phyx-i-a (as-fik′si-ạ̈), *n.* [NL., < Gr. ἀσφυξία, stopping of the pulse, < ἀ- priv. + σφύζειν, throb.] The extreme condition caused by lack of oxygen and excess of carbon dioxide in the blood, brought about by any sufficient interference with respiration, as in choking.—**as-phyx′i-al,** *a.*—**as-phyx′i-ant. I.** *a.* Asphyxiating; producing asphyxia. **II.** *n.* An asphyxiating agent, as a gas.—**as-phyx′i-ate** (-āt), *v. t.*; *-ated, -ating.* To produce asphyxia in; suffocate.—**as-phyx-i-a′tion** (-ā′shọn), *n.*—**as-phyx′-i-a-tor,** *n.*
as-pic[1] (as′pik), *n.* [F., < L. *aspis,* E. *asp*[2].] An asp or serpent. [Chiefly poetic.]
as-pic[2] (as′pik), *n.* [F.; origin unknown.] A savory meat-jelly containing fowl, game, fish, etc.
a-spir-ant (ạ-spīr′ạnt or as′pi-rạnt). **I.** *a.* Aspiring. **II.** *n.* One who aspires, as to a position of honor.
as-pi-rate (as′pi-rāt), *v. t.*; *-rated, -rating.* [L. *aspiratus,* pp. of *aspirare*: see *aspire.*] To pronounce with a breathing, or *h*-sound; also, to draw or remove by suction.—**as′pi-rate** (-rạ̄t). **I.** *a.* Aspirated; pronounced with an *h*-sound. **II.** *n.* An aspirated sound, as that (originally) of the Greek χ, θ, or φ; a sound, as that of the English *f* (*ph*) or *th,* representable by an *h*-combination; the *h*-sound, or rough breathing; a character or a combination of characters representing any of these sounds.
as-pi-ra-tion (as-pi-rā′shọn), *n.* [L. *aspiratio(n-).*] The act of aspirating; breathing; suction; an aspirated sound; also, the act of aspiring; lofty or ambitious desire.
as-pi-ra-tor (as′pi-rā-tọr), *n.* [See *aspirate, v.*] An apparatus or device employing suction, as a winnowing-machine, a surgical instrument for removing fluids from the body, or a vessel for drawing off air or gas by means of a vacuum produced.—**a-spir-a-to-ry** (ạ-spīr′ạ-tọ-ri), *a.* Pertaining to aspiration.
a-spire (ạ-spīr′), *v.*; *aspired, aspiring.* [L. *aspirare,* < *ad,* to, + *spirare,* breathe.] **I.**† *tr.* To breathe on, in, or forth; pant or long for; attempt; attain. **II.** *intr.* To long, aim, or seek ambitiously (usually with *after, to,* or an infinitive); also, to rise, as an exhalation; mount; soar; tower.—**a-spir′er,** *n.*

as-pi-rin (as′pi-rin), *n.* [Arbitrary name, orig. used as a trade-mark.] A white crystalline substance, a derivative of salicylic acid, used in the treatment of rheumatism, gout, neuralgia, etc.

a-spir-ing (ạ-spīr′ing), *p. a.* That aspires; ambitious.—**a-spir′ing-ly,** *adv.*

a-squint (ạ-skwint′), *adv.* [ME.: cf. D. *schuinte,* slant, slope.] With an oblique glance; obliquely; with a squint.

ass (âs), *n.* [AS. *assa,* appar. < L. *asinus,* ass.] A long-eared, usually ash-colored quadruped, *Equus asinus,* of the horse family, when domesticated serving as a slow, patient, sure-footed beast of burden, and proverbial for obstinacy and stupidity; a donkey; also, any allied wild species; fig., a dull, stupid, or silly fellow; a ridiculous fool.—**asses′ bridge,** or **bridge of asses.** Same as *pons asinorum.* See under *pons.*

as-sa-fet′i-da, as-sa-fœt′i-da, *n.* See *asafetida.*

as-sa-gai (as′ạ-gī), *n.* [Pg. *azagaia,* Sp. *azagaya,* < Ar. *al,* the, + (Berber) *zaghāyah,* spear.] A spear or lance, orig. a weapon used in northern Africa; now, commonly, a javelin used by South African tribes; also, a South African cornaceous tree, *Curtisia faginea,* from whose wood such javelins are made.

as-sai[1] (äs-säi′), *adv.* [It., < L. *ad,* to, + *satis,* enough.] In *music,* very: as, allegro *assai* (very quick).

as-sai[2] (a-sī′), *n.* [Brazilian.] Any of several slender Brazilian palms of the genus *Euterpe,* esp. *E. edulis,* a species bearing a purple fruit from which a beverage is made by infusion; also, the beverage.

as-sail (ạ-sāl′), *v. t.* [OF. *asalir* (F. *assaillir*), < ML. *assalire, adsalire,* < L. *ad,* to, + *salire,* leap.] To set upon with violence; attack; assault; beset; set upon vigorously with arguments, importunities, abuse, etc.—**as-sail′a-ble,** *a.* Capable of being assailed.—**as-sail′ant. I.** *a.* Assailing; attacking. **II.** *n.* One who assails.—**as-sail′er,** *n.*—**as-sail′ment,** *n.* The act of assailing; assault; attack.

As-sam-ese (as-ạ-mēs′ or -mēz′). **I.** *a.* Of or pertaining to Assam, a province of eastern British India. **II.** *n.*; pl. *-ese.* A native of Assam; also, the language of Assam.

as-sart (a-särt′), *v. t.* [AF. *assarter,* OF. *essarter,* < ML. *exsartare,* < L. *ex,* out of, + *sarrire,* to hoe.] In *Eng. law,* to grub up (trees and bushes) from woodland; clear (woodland).—**as-sart′,** *n.* [AF. *assart,* OF. *essart.*] In *Eng. law,* the act of assarting; a grubbed-up tree or bush; a piece of land cleared of trees and bushes.

as-sas-sin (ạ-sas′in), *n.* [F. *assassin,* < ML. *assassinus,* < Ar. *hashshāshīn,* pl., 'hashish-eaters,' < *hashīsh,* hashish.] [*cap.*] One of an order of murderous fanatics (about 1090–1272) in Persia and Syria, who were especially hostile to the Crusaders; [*l. c.*] one who undertakes to murder, esp. from fanaticism or for a reward.—**as-sas′si-nate** (-nāt), *v. t.*; *-nated, -nating.* [ML. *assassinatus,* pp. of *assassinare,* < *assassinus.*] To kill by sudden or secret assault; murder.—**as-sas-si-na′tion** (-nā′shọn), *n.*—**as-sas′si-na-tor,** *n.*

as-sault (ạ-sâlt′), *n.* [OF. *asaut* (F. *assaut*), < ML. *assaltus,* < *assalire:* see *assail.*] The act of assailing; an attack; an onslaught; *milit.,* a sudden, vigorous attack on a fortified position; in *law,* an attempt or offer to do violence to another (with or without *battery,* or actual touching).—**as-sault′,** *v. t.* To make an assault upon; attack; assail.—**as-sault′a-ble,** *a.* Capable of being assaulted.—**as-sault′er,** *n.*

as-say (ạ-sā′), *n.* [OF. *assay, asai,* var. of *essai,* E. *essay, n.*] Trial or test; now, esp., trial of the fineness of a metallic substance; determination of the amount of a metal, esp. gold or silver, in an ore, alloy, etc.; also, the substance undergoing trial; also, trial of the strength, purity, etc., of a pharmaceutical substance or ingredient; formerly, the tasting of food or drink, as a formality, before presenting it to a personage at table; a taste†; an attempt or essay (archaic); an affliction†.—**as-say′,** *v. t.* [OF. *assaier,* var. of *essaier,* < *essai.*] To try or test; now, esp., to analyze (an ore, alloy, etc.) in order to determine the quantity of gold, silver, or other metal in it; also, to subject (a drug, etc.) to an assay; formerly, to take the assay of food before presenting it at table; taste†; attempt or essay (archaic); assail†.—**as-say′a-ble,** *a.* That may be assayed.—**as-say′er,** *n.*

as-se-gai (as′ẹ-gī), *n.* See *assagai.*

as-sem-blage (ạ-sem′blāj), *n.* [F.] The act of assembling, or the state of being assembled; also, a number of persons or things assembled; an assembly.

as-sem-ble (ạ-sem′bl), *v.*; *-bled, -bling.* [OF. F. *assembler,* < ML. *assimulare,* < L. *ad,* to, + *simul,* together.] **I.** *tr.* To bring together; gather into one place, company, body, or whole; put or fit (parts) together; put together the parts of (a mechanism, etc.). **II.** *intr.* To come together; gather; meet.—**as-sem′bler,** *n.*

as-sem-bly (ạ-sem′bli), *n.*; pl. *-blies* (-bliz). [OF. *assemblee* (F. *assemblée*).] The act of assembling, or the state of being assembled; a gathering; a concourse; a meeting; a convocation; a social gathering; a ball; a company of persons assembled; a deliberative council; a legislative body, sometimes esp. a lower house of a legislature; a collection of things†; *milit.,* a signal, as by drum or bugle, for troops to assemble and form in ranks.—**as-sem′bly-man** (-mạn), *n.*; pl. *-men.* A member of a legislative assembly, esp. of a lower house of a legislature. [U. S.]

as-sent (ạ-sent′), *v. i.* [OF. *assenter,* < L. *assentari,* freq. of *assentiri,* assent, < *ad,* to, + *sentire,* feel.] To agree, as to a proposal or a statement, by expressing acquiescence or admitting truth; express agreement or concurrence.—**as-sent′,** *n.* [OF.] Agreement, as to a proposal or statement; acquiescence; concurrence.

as-sen-ta-tion (as-ẹn-tā′shọn), *n.* [L. *assentatio(n-),* < *assentari:* see *assent.*] The practice of assenting; esp., obsequious assent; flattery.—**as′sen-ta-tor,** *n.* An obsequious assenter.

as-sent-er (ạ-sen′tėr), *n.* One who assents.

as-sen-tient (ạ-sen′shiẹnt). [L. *assentiens* (*-ent-*), ppr. of *assentiri:* see *assent.*] **I.** *a.* Assenting. **II.** *n.* One who assents.

as-sent-ing (ạ-sen′ting), *p. a.* That assents; giving assent.—**as-sent′ing-ly,** *adv.*

as-sent-or (ạ-sen′tọr), *n.* One who assents; esp., in *Eng. law,* one of those who, in addition to the proposer and seconder, indorse the nomination of a candidate in a parliamentary or other election.

as-sert (ạ-sėrt′), *v. t.* [L. *assertus,* pp. of *asserere,* < *ad,* to, + *serere,* join.] To support the cause of†; maintain (claims, rights, etc.); put (one's self) forward boldly and insistently; also, to maintain as true; state positively; affirm; aver.—**as-sert′a-ble, as-sert′i-ble,** *a.* That may be asserted.—**as-sert′er, as-sert′or,** *n.*—**as-ser-tion** (ạ-sėr′shọn), *n.* [L. *assertio(n-).*] The act of asserting; a positive declaration; an unsupported statement.—**as-ser′tive,** *a.* Making assertion; given to asserting; positive; dogmatic.—**as-ser′tive-ly,** *adv.*—**as-ser′tive-ness,** *n.*—**as-ser′to-ry** (-tọ-ri), *a.* Assertive; declaratory.

ass′es, *n.* Plural of *ass,* also of *as*[2].

as-sess (ạ-ses′), *v. t.* [OF. *assesser,* < ML. *assessare,* freq. of L. *assidere,* sit at or by, be an assessor, < *ad,* to, + *sedere,* sit.] To fix the amount of (a tax, fine, etc.); fix and impose (a tax, etc.); impose a tax or other charge on (a person, property, etc.); estimate the value of (property, etc.) for taxation.—**as-sess′a-ble,** *a.* That may be assessed; liable to assessment.—**as-sess′ment,** *n.* The act of assessing, or fixing or imposing a tax or other charge; an amount assessed as payable; an official valuation of taxable property, etc., or the value assigned.—**as-ses′sor,** *n.* [L., < *assidere.*] One who sits beside another (obs. or archaic); an advisory associate or assistant, as of a judge or magistrate; one appointed to make assessments for purposes of taxation.—**as-ses-so-ri-al** (as-e-sō′ri-ạl), *a.*—**as-ses′sor-ship,** *n.*

as-set (as′et), *n.* A single item of one's assets.

as-sets (as′ets), *n. pl.* [Orig. sing., AF. *asetz,* OF. *asez* (F. *assez*), enough, < L. *ad,* to, + *satis,* enough.] Orig., property sufficient to pay the debts or legacies of a deceased person; hence, any property available for paying debts, etc.; property or effects, as opposed to *liabilities.*

as-sev-er-ate (ạ-sev′ẹ-rāt), *v. t.*; *-ated, -ating.* [L. *asseveratus,* pp. of *asseverare,* < *ad,* to, + *severus,* serious, severe.] To declare earnestly or solemnly; affirm positively.—**as-sev′er-at-ing-ly,** *adv.*—**as-sev-er-a′tion** (-ẹ-rā′shọn), *n.* [L. *asseveratio(n-).*] The act of asseverating; an earnest declaration; an emphatic assertion.—**as-sev′er-a-tive** (-ẹ-rạ-tiv), *a.*

as-sib-i-late (a-sib'i-lāt), *v. t.*; *-lated, -lating.* [L. *assibilatus*, pp. of *assibilare*, hiss at, < *ad*, to, + *sibilare*, hiss.] In *phonetics*, to give a hissing sound to; make sibilant: as, 'church' is an *assibilated* form of 'kirk.'—**as-sib-i-la'tion** (-lā'shọn), *n.*

as-si-du-i-ty (as-i-dū'i-ti), *n.*; pl. *-ties* (-tiz). [L. *assiduitas.*] The quality of being assiduous; constant application; *pl.*, devoted or solicitous attentions.

as-sid-u-ous (ạ-sid'ū-us), *a.* [L. *assiduus*, < *assidere*, sit at or by: see *assess.*] Constant in application; unremittingly attentive; sedulous; devoted.—**as-sid'u-ous-ly,** *adv.*—**as-sid'u-ous-ness,** *n.*

as-si-en-to, as-i-en-to (as-ẹ-en'tō), *n.* [Sp. *assiento*, now *asiento*, contract, treaty.] Formerly, a contract between Spain and a foreign country for supplying African slaves to the Spanish colonies in America, esp. that in force with British merchants from 1713 to 1750.

as-sign (ạ-sīn'), *v.* [OF. F. *assigner*, < L. *assignare* (pp. *assignatus*), < *ad*, to, + *signare*, mark, E. *sign*, *v.*] **I.** *tr.* To allot or appropriate (*to*); make over or give as in distribution; appoint, as to a post or duty; ascribe, attribute, or refer; designate, specify, or show; in *law*, to transfer, esp. in trust for the benefit of creditors. **II.** *intr.* In *law*, to make an assignment of property, as in bankruptcy.—**as-sign',** *n.* [OF. *assigne* (F. *assigné*), pp.: cf. *assignee.*] One appointed to act for another†; also, an appurtenance† (see Shakspere's "Hamlet," v. 2. 157); in *law*, one to whom the property or interest of another is or may be transferred.—**as-sign'a-ble,** *a.* Capable of being assigned.—**as-sign-a-bil'i-ty** (-bil'i-ti), *n.*—**as-sign'a-bly,** *adv.*

as-sig-nat (as'ig-nat, F. ȧ-sē-nyä), *n.* [F., < L. *assignatus*, pp.: see *assign*, *v.*] One of the notes (paper currency) issued from 1789 to 1796 by the French revolutionary government on the security of confiscated lands.

as-sig-na-tion (as-ig-nā'shọn), *n.* [L. *assignatio(n-).*] The act of assigning; assignment; also, an appointment for a meeting, now esp. an illicit love-meeting.

as-sign-ee (as-i-nē'), *n.* [F. *assigné*, pp.: cf. *assign*, *n.*] In *law*, one to whom some right or interest is transferred, either for his own enjoyment or in trust.

as-sign-er (ạ-sī'nėr), *n.* One who assigns.

as-sign-ment (ạ-sīn'mẹnt), *n.* The act of assigning; allotment; appointment; designation; something assigned, as a duty; in *law*, transference of a right or interest, or the instrument of transfer; esp., a transference of property to assignees for the benefit of creditors.

as-sign-or (as-i-nôr'), *n.* In *law*, one who makes an assignment.

as-sim-i-la-ble (ạ-sim'i-lạ-bl), *a.* Capable of being assimilated.—**as-sim"i-la-bil'i-ty** (-bil'i-ti), *n.*

as-sim-i-late (ạ-sim'i-lāt), *v.*; *-lated, -lating.* [L. *assimilatus*, pp. of *assimilare*, < *ad*, to, + *similis*, like.] **I.** *tr.* To make like, accordant, or conformable (*to* or *with*); liken or compare; convert (food, etc.) into a substance suitable for absorption into the system; appropriate and absorb or incorporate, as the body does food. **II.** *intr.* To become or be like; conform; of food, etc., to be converted into the substance of the body; be absorbed into the system.—**as-sim-i-la'tion** (-lā'shọn), *n.* [L. *assimilatio(n-).*] The act of assimilating, or the resulting state; esp., the conversion of food into the substance of the body; in *phonetics*, change of a sound to make it like, or more in accord with, a neighboring sound in a word, as in L. *assimilare* for *adsimilare* (cf. *dissimilation*).—**as-sim'i-la-tive** (-lạ-tiv), **as-sim'i-la-to-ry** (-tọ-ri), *a.* Characterized by assimilation; assimilating.—**as-sim'i-la-tor** (-lā-tọr), *n.*

as-sist (ạ-sist'), *v.* [OF. F. *assister*, < L. *assistere*, stand at or by, < *ad*, to, + *sistere*, stand.] **I.** *intr.* To be present, as at a ceremony or other proceeding (now regarded as a French use); also, to take part in any performance; give aid. **II.** *tr.* To be present at or with†; attend†; also, to take part in or with; aid; help; be associated with as assistant.—**as-sist',** *n.* An act of assisting, as in making a put-out in baseball.—**as-sist'ance,** *n.* The act of assisting; presence, or the persons present, at a ceremony, etc. (now regarded as a French use); aid or help.—**as-sist'ant.** **I.** *a.* Assisting; auxiliary; associated with a superior in some office or work. **II.** *n.* A helper; an aid; an auxiliary; one who assists a superior in some office or work.—**as-sist'ant-ship,** *n.*—**as-sist'er,** (in *law*) **as-sist'or,** *n.*

as-size (ạ-sīz'), *n.* [OF. *asise*, prop. pp. fem. of *aseeir*, < L. *assidere*: see *assess.*] A session of a legislative body†; a legislative enactment†; an ordinance, esp. as to measures, weights, or prices†; the standard prescribed†; size†; also, a session of a judicial body; a judicial inquest; a trial by jury (now Sc.); a periodical session of court held in an English county by judges on circuit under royal commission (usually in *pl.*); judgment (as, the last or great *assize*).

as-so-cia-ble (ạ-sō'shạ-bl), *a.* Capable of being associated; in *pathol.*, liable to be affected sympathetically.—**as-so-cia-bil'i-ty** (-bil'i-ti), **as-so'cia-ble-ness,** *n.*

as-so-ci-ate (ạ-sō'shi-āt), *v.*; *-ated, -ating.* [L. *associatus*, pp. of *associare*, < *ad*, to, + *sociare*, join: see *sociable.*] **I.** *tr.* To join as a companion, partner, or ally (*with*); connect by some relation, as in thought; link; unite; combine; also, to accompany†; attend†. **II.** *intr.* To keep company (*with*), as a comrade or intimate; consort; enter into a league or union; unite.—**as-so'ci-ate** (-ạt). **I.** *a.* Associated, esp. as a companion or colleague; having the office or standing of an associate. **II.** *n.* A companion, comrade, or mate; a partner or ally; a colleague, as in office; one associated or classed with others in office or standing, but ranking somewhat below; one admitted to a subordinate degree of membership in a society or institution; an accompaniment or concomitant.—**as-so'ci-ate-ship,** *n.* The position or office of an associate.

as-so-ci-a-tion (ạ-sō-ṣi-ā'shọn), *n.* [ML. *associatio(n-).*] The act of associating, or the state of being associated; companionship or intercourse; connection or relation; the connection of ideas in thought, or an idea connected with or suggested by a subject of thought; alliance; combination; union; also, a body of persons associated together for the promotion of a common purpose; a society; also, Association football.—**Association football.** Same as *soccer.*—**as-so-ci-a'tion-al,** *a.*—**as-so-ci-a'tion-ism,** *n.* The psychological theory that the laws of the association of ideas are the fundamental laws of mental action; also, Fourierism.—**as-so-ci-a'tion-ist,** *n.*

as-so-ci-a-tive (ạ-sō'shi-ā-tiv), *a.* Tending to associate; pertaining to association.

as-so-ci-a-tor (ạ-sō'shi-ā-tọr), *n.* One who or that which associates.

as-soil (ạ-soil'), *v. t.* [OF. *assoldre* (*assoil-*), < L. *absolvere*: see *absolve.*] To absolve, acquit, or pardon (archaic); expiate (archaic); solve (a question, etc.)†. Also (Sc.) **as-soil'yie, as-soil'zie** (-yi).

as-so-nance (as'ọ-nạns), *n.* The quality of being assonant; correspondence in sound; agreement; in *pros.*, a substitute for rime, esp. common in Spanish poetry, in which the same vowel-sounds, though with different consonants, are used in the terminal words of lines, as in *penitent* and *reticence.*—**as'so-nanced,** *a.* Characterized by assonance.

as-so-nant (as'ọ-nạnt). [L. *assonans* (*-ant-*), ppr. of *assonare*, sound to, < *ad*, to, + *sonare*, sound.] **I.** *a.* Of words, etc., corresponding in sound; using the same vowel-sound; characterized by assonance. **II.** *n.* An assonant word or syllable.—**as-so-nan'tal** (-nan'tạl), *a.*

as-sort (ạ-sôrt'), *v.* [OF. *assorter*, < ML. *assortare*, distribute, < L. *ad*, to, + *sors*, lot.] **I.** *tr.* To distribute or arrange according to sort or kind; furnish with various sorts; also, to group or class (*with*); also, to suit (*to*); match. **II.** *intr.* To agree in sort or kind; match; comport; also, to consort or associate.—**as-sort'ment,** *n.* The act of assorting; a collection of various sorts; a group or class.

as-suage (ạ-swāj'), *v.*; *-suaged, -suaging.* [OF. *assuagier*, < L. *ad*, to, + *suavis*, sweet.] **I.** *tr.* To make milder or less severe; mitigate (pain, wrath, etc.); also, to mollify (a person); also, to appease (appetite, tumult, etc.); to allay. **II.** *intr.* To abate; subside. [Archaic.]—**as-suage'ment,** *n.* The act or the means of assuaging; an alleviative.—**as-sua-ger** (ạ-swā'jėr), *n.*

as-sua-sive (ạ-swā'siv). [Appar. a mixture of *assuage* and *persuasive.*] **I.** *a.* Soothing; alleviative. **II.** *n.* A soothing remedy.

as-sum-a-ble (ạ-sū'mạ-bl), *a.* Capable of being assumed.—**as-sum'a-bly,** *adv.* As may be assumed; presumably.

as-sume (ạ-sūm′), *v. t.*; *-sumed, -suming.* [L. *assumere* (pp. *assumptus*), < *ad*, to, + *sumere*, take.] To take up or in (archaic); take upon one's self; undertake; take on or put on; adopt, appropriate, or arrogate; also, to take for granted; suppose; also, to simulate, pretend, or feign. —**as-sum-ed-ly** (ạ-sū′med-li), *adv.* As is assumed, or taken for granted.—**as-sum′er,** *n.*—**as-sum′ing,** *p. a.* Taking upon one's self more than is fitting; arrogant; presuming.

as-sump-sit (ạ-sump′sit), *n.* [L., 'he undertook.'] In *law*, an action to recover damages for breach of a simple contract (a promise not under seal); also, an actionable promise.

as-sump-tion (ạ-sump′shọn), *n.* [L. *assumptio(n-)*.] The act of assuming; undertaking; adoption; appropriation; arrogation or arrogance; supposition, or a thing supposed; *eccles.*, [*l. c.* or *cap.*] the bodily taking up into heaven of the Virgin Mary after her death; [*cap.*] a feast commemorating it, celebrated on Aug. 15.

as-sump-tive (ạ-sump′tiv), *a.* [L. *assumptivus.*] Characterized by assumption; assuming; assumed.—**as-sump′tive-ly,** *adv.*

as-sur-a-ble (ạ-shör′ạ-bl), *a.* Capable of being assured; suitable for assurance or insurance.

as-sur-ance (ạ-shör′ạns), *n.* The act of assuring; a making sure or certain; positive demonstration; proof; legal evidence of title to property; a positive declaration intended to give confidence; pledge, guaranty, or surety; insurance, as of life or property; betrothal†; also, security; certainty; confidence; often, self-confidence; sometimes, presumptuous boldness.

as-sure (ạ-shör′), *v. t.*; *-sured, -suring.* [OF. *aseurer* (F. *assurer*), < ML. *assecurare*, < L. *ad*, to, + *securus*, E. *secure, sure.*] To make sure or confident; convince (*of*); inform or tell positively, as of something sure; declare earnestly; render certain, secure, safe, or stable; guarantee; insure, as against loss; betroth†.—**as-sured′,** *p. a.* Made sure; insured; sure; certain; confident; bold.—**as-sur′ed-ly,** *adv.* Surely; certainly; confidently.—**as-sur′ed-ness,** *n.*—**as-sur′er,** *n.*

as-sur-gent (a-sėr′jẹnt), *a.* [L. *assurgens* (*-ent-*), ppr. of *assurgere*, rise up, < *ad*, to, + *surgere*, rise.] Rising; ascending; in *bot.*, curving upward, as leaves.—**as-sur′gen-cy,** *n.*

As-syr-i-an (ạ-sir′i-ạn). **I.** *a.* Of or pertaining to Assyria, an ancient country or empire of western Asia, to the north of (and for a time dominating) Babylonia; pertaining to the Assyrians or their language. **II.** *n.* One of the Assyrian people; also, the Assyrian language, belonging to the Semitic family.

As-syr-i-ol-o-gy (ạ-sir-i-ol′ọ̄-ji), *n.* [See *-logy.*] The science of Assyrian antiquities.—**As-syr″i-o-log′i-cal** (-ọ̄-loj′i-kạl), *a.*—**As-syr-i-ol′o-gist,** *n.*

As-tar-te (as-tär′tē), *n.* [L., < Gr. Ἀστάρτη; from Phenician.] An ancient Semitic deity, goddess of fertility and reproduction (the female counterpart of Baal), as worshiped by the Phenicians: corresponding to the Hebrew *Ashtoreth* and the Babylonian and Assyrian *Ishtar*.

a-stat-ic (a-stat′ik), *a.* [Gr. ἄστατος, unstable, < ἀ- priv. + στατός, verbal adj. of ἱστάναι, stand.] Unstable; unsteady; having no tendency to take a definite position, as a magnetic needle whose directive power has been neutralized.—**a-stat′i-cal-ly,** *adv.*—**a-stat′i-cism** (-sizm), *n.*

as-tat-ki (as-tat′ki), *n.* [Russ.] A thick fluid residuum obtained in the distillation of Russian crude petroleum: much used as a fuel.

as-ter (as′tėr), *n.* [L., < Gr. ἀστήρ, star.] A star†; any plant of the widespread genus *Aster*, with flower-heads of the composite type, in characteristic forms having rays varying from white or pink to purple about a disk that is usually yellow; a plant of some allied genus, as *Callistephus chinensis* ('China aster'); in *biol.*, either of two star-shaped structures formed in a cell during mitosis (cf. *centrosphere*).

-aster. [L. *-aster*, used with diminutive force or expressing incomplete resemblance.] A suffix used to form nouns denoting something that imperfectly resembles or merely apes the true thing, or an inferior or petty instance of something, as in *criticaster, grammaticaster, oleaster, poetaster, theologaster*.

as-ter-a-ceous (as-tẹ-rā′shius), *a.* Belonging to the *Asteraceæ*, or aster family of plants.

as-te-ri-a (as-tē′ri-ạ̈), *n.* [L., < Gr. ἀστέριος, starry, < ἀστήρ, star.] A gem-stone, as a sapphire, that when cut as a cabochon shows a starlike luminous figure. See *asterism.* —**as-te′ri-at-ed** (-ā-ted), *a.* Exhibiting asterism, as a sapphire.

as-ter-id (as′tẹ-rid), *n.* An asteroid (starfish).

as-ter-isk (as′tẹ-risk), *n.* [LL. *asteriscus*, < Gr. ἀστερίσκος, dim. of ἀστήρ, star.] The figure of a star (*), used in writing and printing as a reference-mark or to indicate omission, doubtful matter, etc.—**as′ter-isk,** *v. t.* To mark with an asterisk.

as-ter-ism (as′tẹ-rizm), *n.* [Gr. ἀστερισμός, < ἀστερίζειν, mark with stars, < ἀστήρ, star.] A group of stars; also, three asterisks ($^*{}_*{}^*$ or ${}_*{}^*{}_*$) placed before a passage to direct attention to it; rarely, a single asterisk; also, a property of some crystallized minerals of showing a starlike luminous figure in reflected or transmitted light.

as-te-ri-um (as-tē′ri-um), *n.* [NL., < Gr. ἀστήρ, star.] A chemical element supposed by some to exist in the atmosphere of certain stars.

a-stern (ạ-stėrn′), *adv.* *Naut.*, at or toward the stern; to the rear (*of*); behind; backward.

as-ter-oid (as′tẹ-roid). [Gr. ἀστεροειδής, < ἀστήρ, star, + εἶδος, form.] **I.** *a.* Starlike. **II.** *n.* One of the many small planets revolving about the sun between the orbits (mostly) of Mars and Jupiter; a minor planet; a planetoid; also, one of the *Asteroidea*, a class or group of echinoderms containing the starfishes; a starfish.—**as-ter-oi′dal,** *a.*

as-the-ni-a (as-thē′ni-ạ̈ or as-the-nī′ạ̈), *n.* [NL., < Gr. ἀσθένεια, < ἀσθενής, weak, < ἀ- priv. + σθένος, strength.] In *pathol.*, want or loss of strength; debility.—**as-then′ic** (-then′ik), *a.*

as-the-no-pi-a (as-the-nō′pi-ạ̈), *n.* [NL., < Gr. ἀσθενής, weak, + ὤψ, eye.] In *pathol.*, weakness of the eyes or visual organs.—**as-the-nop′ic** (-nop′ik), *a.*

asth-ma (as′mạ̈, commonly az′mạ̈), *n.* [ML., < Gr. ἆσθμα, < ἄζειν, breathe hard, < ἄηναι, breathe, blow.] A paroxysmal disorder of respiration, with labored breathing, a feeling of constriction in the chest, and cough.—**asth-mat′ic** (-mat′ik). [L. *asthmaticus*, < Gr. ἀσθματικός.] **I.** *a.* Pertaining to or suffering from asthma. **II.** *n.* One suffering from asthma.—**asth-mat′i-cal-ly,** *adv.*

as-tig-mat-ic (as-tig-mat′ik), *a.* [Gr. ἀ- priv. + στίγμα (στιγματ-), prick, spot.] Pertaining to or exhibiting astigmatism.—**as-tig-mat′i-cal-ly,** *adv.*—**as-tig′ma-tism** (-mạ-tizm), *n.* A defect of the eye or of a lens whereby rays of light from an external point fail to converge to a focus, thus giving rise to imperfect vision or images.

a-stir (ạ-stėr′), *adv.* In a stir; in motion or activity.

as-tom-a-tous (as-tom′ạ-tus or as-tō′mạ-), *a.* [Gr. ἀ- priv. + στόμα (στοματ-), mouth.] In *zoöl.* and *bot.*, having no mouth, stoma, or stomata. Also **as′to-mous** (-tọ̄-mus).

a-ston-ied (ạ-ston′id). Preterit and past participle of *astony*.

a-ston-ish (ạ-ston′ish), *v. t.* [Earlier *astony*, (obs.) *astone* (ME. pp. *astoned, astouned*: see *astound, p. a.*); appar. < OF. *estoner* (F. *étonner*), stun, astonish, < L. *ex*, out of, + *tonare*, thunder: cf. *stun.*] To stun†; stupefy†; confound†; strike with sudden and overpowering wonder; surprise greatly; amaze.—**a-ston′ished-ly,** *adv.*—**a-ston′ish-er,** *n.*—**a-ston′ish-ing-ly,** *adv.*—**a-ston′ish-ment,** *n.* Stunned, stupefied, or benumbed condition†; consternation (archaic); overpowering wonder or surprise; amazement; also, an object of amazement.

a-ston-y (ạ-ston′i), *v. t.*; *astonied, astonying.* [See *astonish.*] To stun†; also, to confound or amaze (archaic: as, "Upright men shall be *astonied* at this," Job, xvii. 8).

a-stound (ạ-stound′), *p. a.* [ME. *astoned, astouned*, pp.: see *astonish.*] Stunned†; confounded or amazed (archaic). —**a-stound′,** *v. t.* To stun†; confound†; overwhelm with amazement; astonish greatly.—**a-stound′ing-ly,** *adv.*—**a-stound′ment,** *n.*

aṣ′tra-chan, *n.* See *astrakhan.*

a-strad-dle (ạ-strad′l), *adv.* In a straddle; astride.

as-tra-gal (as′tra̤-ga̤l), *n.* [L. *astragalus*: see *astragalus.*] In *arch.*, a small convex molding cut into the form of a string of beads; also, a plain convex molding; in *anat.*, the astragalus.

Astragal in Greek Architecture.

as-trag-a-lus (as-trag′a̤-lus), *n.*; pl. *-li* (-lī). [L., < Gr. ἀστράγαλος, ankle-bone, molding.] In *anat.*, the ankle-bo̤ne, or uppermost bone of the tarsus, on which the tibia rests.

as-tra-khan (as′tra̤-ka̤n), *n.* A kind of fur, the skin or pelt of young lambs, with closely curled wool, from Astrakhan in Russia; also, a woolen fabric of similar appearance.

as-tral (as′tra̤l), *a.* [LL. *astralis*, < L. *astrum*, < Gr. ἄστρον, star.] Of or pertaining to the stars; stellar; sidereal; associated with or inhabiting the stars (as, *astral* spirits); in *theosophy*, noting or pertaining to a supersensible substance or fluid supposed to pervade all space and form the substance of a second (astral) body belonging, like the material or physical body, to each individual.—**astral lamp,** a lamp with an annular oil-reservoir which encircles the burner and which connects by two small pipes with the wick-tube, designed to avoid the shadow cast upon the table by ordinary lamps having the oil-reservoir under the wick-tube.

a-strand (a̤-strand′), *adv.* On the strand; stranded.

a-stray (a̤-strā′), *adv.* and *a.* [OF. *estraie*, pp. of *estraier*, stray: see *stray.*] Out of the right way; straying.

as-trict (as-trikt′), *v. t.* [L. *astrictus*, pp. of *astringere*: see *astringe.*] To bind; constrict; restrict.—**as-tric′tion** (-trik′sho̤n), *n.* [L. *astrictio(n-).*] The act of binding; constriction; obligation; restriction.—**as-tric′tive,** *a.* Binding; astringent.

a-stride (a̤-strīd′), *adv.* In the posture of striding or bestriding; with one leg on each side (*of*).

as-tringe (as-trinj′), *v. t.*; *-tringed, -tringing.* [L. *astringere* (pp. *astrictus*), < *ad*, to, + *stringere*, draw tight.] To bind; constrict; contract; also, to oblige†.—**as-trin′gent** (-trin′je̤nt). **I.** *a.* Binding; constricting; contracting; styptic. **II.** *n.* A substance which contracts the tissues or canals of the body, thereby diminishing discharges, as of blood.—**as-trin′gen-cy,** *n.*—**as-trin′gent-ly,** *adv.*

astro-. Form of Gr. ἄστρον, star, used in combination.—**as-trog-e-ny** (as-troj′e-ni), *n.* [+ *-geny.*] Same as *astrogony.*—**as-trog′no-sy** (-trog′no̤-si), *n.* [+ *-gnosy.*] Knowledge of the stars; specif., the part of astronomy that treats of the fixed stars.—**as-trog′o-ny** (-o̤-ni), *n.* [+ *-gony.*] The genesis or origination of the stars.—**as-trog′ra-phy** (-ra̤-fi), *n.* [+ *-graphy.*] The science and art of mapping the stars, esp. by means of photography.—**as-tro-graph′ic** (-tro̤-graf′ik), *a.*

Sir Francis Drake's Astrolabe. (Royal Naval College, England.)

as-tro-labe (as′tro̤-lāb), *n.* [OF. *astrelabe* (F. *astrolabe*), < ML. *astrolabium*, < Gr. ἀστρολάβον, < ἄστρον, star, + λαμβάνειν, take.] An obsolete astronomical instrument for taking altitudes, etc.

as-trol-a-try (as-trol′a̤-tri), *n.* [See *astro-* and *-latry.*] Worship of the heavenly bodies.—**as-trol′a-ter,** *n.*

as-trol-o-ger (as-trol′o̤-jėr), *n.* [See *astrology.*] An astronomer†; also, one who practises astrology.

as-trol-o-gy (as-trol′o̤-ji), *n.* [OF. F. *astrologie*, < L. *astrologia*, < Gr. ἀστρολογία, < ἄστρον, star, + λέγειν, speak.] Formerly, practical astronomy, the earliest form of the science; now, an art which assumes, and professes to determine, the influence of the heavenly bodies on human affairs.—**as-tro-log′ic, as-tro-log′i-cal** (-tro̤-loj′ik, -i-ka̤l), *a.*—**as-tro-log′i-cal-ly,** *adv.*

as-tro-me-te-o-rol-o-gy (as″tro̤-mē-te̤-o̤-rol′o̤-ji), *n.* [See *astro-.*] Investigation of the (alleged) influence of the heavenly bodies upon the weather.

as-trom-e-try (as-trom′e-tri), *n.* [See *astro-* and *-metry.*] Measurement of the magnitudes, distances, motions, etc., of the heavenly bodies.—**as-tro-met′ri-cal** (-tro̤-met′ri-ka̤l), *a.*

as-tron-o-mer (as-tron′o̤-mėr), *n.* [See *astronomy.*] One versed in astronomy; also, an astrologer†.

as-tro-nom-ic, as-tro-nom-i-cal (as-tro̤-nom′ik, -i-ka̤l), *a.* [F. *astronomique*, < L. *astronomicus*, < Gr. ἀστρονομικός.] Of, pertaining to, or connected with astronomy.—**astronomical time,** mean solar time reckoned from noon through the twenty-four hours.—**astronomical year.** See *year.*—**as-tro-nom′i-cal-ly,** *adv.*

as-tron-o-my (as-tron′o̤-mi), *n.* [OF. F. *astronomie*, < L. *astronomia*, < Gr. ἀστρονομία, < ἄστρον, star, + νέμειν, distribute.] The science of the heavenly bodies, treating of their motions, positions, distances, magnitudes, etc.

as-tro-pho-tog-ra-phy (as″tro̤-fo̤-tog′ra̤-fi), *n.* [See *astro-.*] Photography of the heavenly bodies, as for astronomic purposes.—**as″tro-pho-to-graph′ic** (-fō-to̤-graf′ik), *a.*

as-tro-pho-tom-e-ter (as″tro̤-fo̤-tom′e-tėr), *n.* [See *astro-.*] A photometer for measuring the intensity of the light of heavenly bodies.—**as″tro-pho-tom′e-try,** *n.* Measurement of the intensity of the light of heavenly bodies.—**as″tro-pho-to-met′ri-cal** (-fō-to̤-met′ri-ka̤l), *a.*

as-tro-phys-ics (as-tro̤-fiz′iks), *n.* [See *astro-.*] Astronomical physics, treating of the physical properties and phenomena of the heavenly bodies.—**as-tro-phys′i-cal,** *a.*—**as-tro-phys′i-cist,** *n.*

as-tro-sphere (as′tro̤-sfēr), *n.* [See *aster* and *sphere.*] In *biol.*, the central portion of an aster, inclusive of the region in which the centrosome lies; also, the whole aster exclusive of the centrosome.

a-strut (a̤-strut′), *adv.* In a strut; with a strutting gait.

as-tu-cious (as-tū′shus), *a.* [F. *astucieux*, < *astuce*, < L. *astutia*, astuteness.] Astute.—**as-tu′ci-ty** (-si-ti), *n.*

as-tute (as-tūt′), *a.* [L. *astutus*, < *astus*, adroitness, cunning.] Sagacious; shrewd; cunning; crafty.—**as-tute′ly,** *adv.*—**as-tute′ness,** *n.*

a-sty-lar (a-stī′lär), *a.* [Gr. ἄστυλος, < ἀ- priv. + στῦλος, pillar, column.] In *arch.*, without columns.

a-sud-den (a̤-sud′n), *adv.* Suddenly. [Poetic.]

a-sun-der (a̤-sun′dėr), *adv.* [AS. *on sundran*, 'in sunder': see *sunder, n.*] In a sundered state; apart; in pieces.

a-swarm (a̤-swârm′), *adv.* In a state of swarming.

a-sway (a̤-swā′), *adv.* In the act of swaying.

a-swing (a̤-swing′), *adv.* In the act of swinging; asway.

a-swoon (a̤-swön′), *adv.* In a swoon.

a-sy-lum (a̤-sī′lum), *n.* [L., < Gr. ἄσυλον, neut. of ἄσυλος, inviolable, < ἀ- priv. + σύλη, right of seizure.] An inviolable refuge, as formerly for criminals and debtors; a sanctuary; inviolable shelter; any secure retreat; an institution for the maintenance and care of the blind, the insane, orphans, or some other class of unfortunate persons.

as-ym-met-ric, as-ym-met-ri-cal (as-i-met′rik, -ri-ka̤l), *a.* [See *a-*[1].] Not symmetrical; without symmetry.—**asymmetric carbon atom,** in *chem.*, a carbon atom combined directly with four different atoms or groups.—**as-ym-met′ri-cal-ly,** *adv.*—**a-sym-me-try** (a-sim′e-tri), *n.* Absence of symmetry.

as-ymp-tote (as′im-tōt), *n.* [Gr. ἀσύμπτωτος, not close, < ἀ- priv. + συμπίπτειν, fall together: see *symptom.*] In *math.*, a straight line that continually approaches a curve but does not meet it within finite distance.—**as-ymp-tot′ic, as-ymp-tot′i-cal** (-tot′ik, -i-ka̤l), *a.*—**as-ymp-tot′i-cal-ly,** *adv.*

a-syn-chro-nism (a-sing′kro̤-nizm), *n.* [See *a-*[1].] Want of synchronism, or coincidence in time.—**a-syn′chro-nous,** *a.* Not synchronous.

a-syn-de-ton (a-sin′de-ton), *n.* [LL., < Gr. ἀσύνδετον, neut. of ἀσύνδετος, unconnected, < ἀ- priv. + σύνδετος, verbal adj. of συνδεῖν, bind together: see *syndetic.*] In *rhet.*, the omission of conjunctions, as in Mat. x. 8. Cf. *polysyndeton.*—**as-yn-det-ic** (as-in-det′ik), *a.*—**as-yn-det′i-cal-ly,** *adv.*

at (at), *prep.* [AS. *æt*, akin to L. *ad*, to, at: see *ad-.*] A particle specifying a point occupied, attained, sought, or otherwise concerned, as in place, time, order, experience, etc., and hence used in many idiomatic phrases expressing circumstantial or relative position, degree or rate, action, manner, etc.: as, to stand *at* the door; to aim *at* a mark; to clutch *at* a straw; *at* home; *at* hand; *at* noon; *at* zero; *at* work; *at* ease; *at* daggers drawn; *at* length; *at* a risk; *at* cost; *at* one's best.

at-a-bal (at′ạ-bal), *n.* [Sp., < Ar. *al*, the, + *tabl*, drum.] A kind of drum used by the Moors.

a-tac-a-mite (ạ-tak′ạ-mīt), *n.* [From *Atacama*, province of Chile.] A mineral, a basic chloride of copper, occurring commonly in small prismatic crystals of various (usually dark) shades of green.

at-a-ghan (at′ạ-gan), *n.* Same as *yataghan.*

at-a-man (at′ạ-man), *n.*; pl. *-mans.* [Russ.: see *hetman.*] A chief of Cossacks; a hetman.

at-a-mas-co (at-ạ-mas′kō), *n.* [N. Amer. Ind.] An amaryllidaceous plant, *Atamosco atamasco*, of the southeastern U. S., bearing a single white lily-like flower; also, any species of this genus. Also called *atamasco lily.*

a-taunt (ạ-tânt′), *adv.* [F. *autant*, as much.] As much as possible†; *naut.*, in a fully rigged condition; with all sails set. Also (*naut.*) **a-taun-to** (ạ-tân′tō).

a-tav-ic (a-tav′ik), *a.* [L. *atavus*, remote ancestor: cf. *avus*, grandfather.] Of or pertaining to remote ancestors; also, atavistic.

at-a-vism (at′ạ-vizm), *n.* [L. *atavus*: see *atavic.*] In *biol.*, the recurrence in an individual of characteristics of some more or less remote ancestor that have been absent in intervening generations; loosely, reversion to an earlier type. —**at′a-vist,** *n.* An animal or plant exhibiting atavism.—**at-a-vis′tic,** *a.* Of or pertaining to atavism.—**at-a-vis′ti-cal-ly,** *adv.*

a-tax-i-a (a-tak′si-ạ̈), *n.* [NL., < Gr. ἀταξία, disorder, < ἀ- priv. + τάσσειν, arrange.] In *pathol.*, irregularity, as in bodily functions or muscular movements; inability to coördinate voluntary movements; often, locomotor ataxia (see under *locomotor*).—**a-tax-ic** (a-tak′sik), *a.*

ate[1] (āt or et). Pret. and pp. of *eat.* See *eat.*

A-te[2] (ā′tē), *n.* [Gr. ἄτη, infatuation, mad impulse, ruin.] In *Gr. myth.*, the goddess of reckless blindness and mischief: later regarded as an avenging deity.

-ate[1]. [L. *-atus*, pp. suffix of verbs with infinitive in *-are*, also adj. suffix forming derivatives from nouns.] An adjective suffix equivalent to *-ed*[2] (in participial and other adjectives), as in *accumulate, elaborate, prostrate, separate, serrate*: many adjectives of this class being used also as nouns, as *degenerate, reprobate.*

-ate[2]. [L. *-atus*, pp. and adj. suffix: see *-ate*[1].] A suffix of nouns denoting esp. persons charged with some duty or function or invested with some dignity, right, or special character, as in *advocate, candidate, curate, legate, licentiate, prelate.*

-ate[3]. [L. *-atum*, neut. of *-atus*, pp. suffix: see *-ate*[1].] A suffix of nouns denoting some product or result of action, as in *mandate* (lit. 'a thing commanded'): much used in *chem.*, esp. in the names of salts formed from acids, as in *acetate, benzoate, carbonate, cyanate, nitrate.*

-ate[4]. [L. *-atus*, pp. suffix: see *-ate*[1].] A suffix of verbs, orig. taken from Latin past participles but now formed from any Latin or other stem, as in *actuate, agitate, calibrate, castigate, imitate, methylate, pepsinate.*

-ate[5]. [L. *-atus* (stem *-atu-*).] A suffix of nouns denoting condition, estate, office, officials or an official, etc., as in *consulate, episcopate, magistrate, marquisate, senate, triumvirate.*

a-tech-nic (a-tek′nik or ā-). [Gr. ἄτεχνος, without art, < ἀ- priv. + τέχνη, art.] **I.** *a.* Without technical knowledge. **II.** *n.* A person without technical knowledge.

a-te-lier (à-tė-lyā), *n.* [F.] A workshop; a studio.

ath-a-na-sia (ath-ạ-nā′ẓiạ̈), *n.* [LL., < Gr. ἀθανασία, < ἀ- priv. + θάνατος, death.] Deathlessness; immortality.

Ath-a-na-sian (ath-ạ-nā′ẓiạn or -shiạn), *a.* Of or pertaining to Athanasius (died 373), bishop of Alexandria, an active opponent of the Arians.—**Athanasian Creed,** a creed or formulary of Christian faith, of unknown authorship, formerly ascribed to Athanasius.

a-than-a-sy (a-than′ạ-si), *n.* Same as *athanasia.*

Ath-a-pas-can (ath-ạ-pas′kạn), *a.* Belonging to or constituting a linguistic stock of North American Indians extending from Alaska to Hudson Bay and southward to Mexico, and including the Apache, Navajo, and other tribes.

a-the-ism (ā′thẹ̄-izm), *n.* [Gr. ἄθεος, without a god, < ἀ- priv. + θεός, god.] The doctrine that there is no God; disbelief in the existence of a God (or of gods); also, godlessness of life.—**a′the-ist,** *n.* One who denies, or disbelieves in, the existence of a God; also, a godless person. —**a-the-is′tic, a-the-is′ti-cal,** *a.*—**a-the-is′ti-cal-ly,** *adv.*

ath-e-ling (ath′ẹ-ling), *n.* [AS. *ætheling*, < *æthelu*, noble family.] In *Anglo-Saxon hist.*, a noble or prince; a crown-prince.

A-the′na, *n.* See *Athene.*

Ath-e-næ-um, Ath-e-ne-um (ath-ẹ-nē′um), *n.*; pl. *-næa, -nea* (-nē′ạ̈) or *-næums, -neums.* [L. *Athenæum*, < Gr. Ἀθήναιον.] A temple of Athene at Athens, frequented by poets and men of learning; [*l. c.*] an institution for the promotion of literary or other learning, as by means of a library, reading-room, lectures, etc.

Athene.
(Statue from Farnese collection, in the Museo Nazionale, Naples.)

A-the-ne, A-the-na (ạ-thē′nē, -nạ̈), *n.* [Gr. Ἀθήνη.] The Greek goddess of wisdom, arts and industries, and prudent warfare, identified by the Romans with Minerva.

A-the-ni-an (ạ-thē′ni-ạn). **I.** *a.* Pertaining to the city of Athens, in Greece. **II.** *n.* A native or citizen of Athens.

a-ther-ma-nous (a-thėr′mạ-nus), *a.* [Gr. ἀ- priv. + θερμαίνειν, heat: see *diathermanous.*] In *physics*, impermeable to or stopping radiant heat. Cf. *diathermanous.*—**a-ther′man-cy** (-mạn-si), *n.*

ath-e-to-sis (ath-e-tō′sis), *n.* [NL., < Gr. ἄθετος, without position or place, < ἀ- priv. + τιθέναι, set.] In *pathol.*, a condition in which the hands and feet continually perform involuntary, slow, irregular movements, occurring most frequently in children.

a-thirst (ạ-thėrst′), *a.* [AS. *ofthyrst, ofthyrsted*: cf. *ahungered.*] Thirsty; thirsting: as, "When thou art *athirst*, go unto the vessels, and drink" (Ruth, ii. 9).

ath-lete (ath′lēt), *n.* [L. *athleta*, < Gr. ἀθλητής, < ἀθλεῖν, contend, < ἆθλος, contest, ἆθλον, prize.] A contender in the public games of ancient Greece; hence, any one trained to exercises of agility and strength.—**ath-let′ic** (-let′ik), *a.* Of, like, or befitting an athlete; physically active and strong; also, of or pertaining to athletics. —**ath-let′i-cal-ly,** *adv.*—**ath-let′i-cism** (-sizm), *n.* The practice of athletics.—**ath-let′ics,** *n.* The practice of athletic exercises; the principles of athletic training; as *pl.*, athletic sports, as running, rowing, boxing, etc.

at=home (at-hōm′), *n.* A reception of visitors during certain hours for which a hostess or host has been announced to be 'at home.'

a-thrill (ạ-thril′), *adv.* In a thrill, or thrilled state.

a-throb (ạ-throb′), *adv.* In a throbbing condition.

a-thwart (ạ-thwârt′). [See *thwart*[1].] **I.** *adv.* Crosswise; transversely; obliquely; fig., wrong; awry. **II.** *prep.* Across; against; contrary to; *naut.*, across the line or course of.—**a-thwart′ships,** *adv.* *Naut.*, crosswise of the ship.

a-tilt (ạ-tilt′), *adv.* At a tilt or inclination; tilted; also, in a tilting encounter.

-ation. [F. *-ation*, < L. *-atio(n-)*, form of *-io(n-)* preceded by *-at-* of pp. stem: see *-ion* and *-ate*[1].] A suffix of nouns denoting action or process, state or condition, a product or result, or something producing a result, often accompanying verbs or adjectives of Latin origin ending in *-ate*, as in *agitation, decoration, elation, migration, separation*, but also formed in English from any stem, as in *botheration, flirtation, starvation.* See *-ion* and *-tion.*

-ative. [L. *-ativus*, form of *-ivus* preceded by *-at-* of pp. stem: see *-ive* and *-ate*[1].] A suffix of adjectives expressing tendency, disposition, function, bearing, etc., as in *affirmative, depreciative, locative, optative, talkative.* See *-ive.*

At-lan-te-an (at-lan-tē′ạn), *a.* [L. *Atlanteus.*] Pertaining to the god Atlas; also, pertaining to the island of Atlantis.

Atlantes.
(Otto Heinrich's Palace, Heidelberg Castle.)

at-lan-tes (at-lan′tēz), *n. pl.* [L., < Gr. Ἄτλαντες, pl. of Ἄτλας: see *Atlas.*] In *arch.*, figures of men used like supporting columns. Cf. *caryatid.*

At-lan-tic (at-lan′tik). [L. *Atlanticus,* < Gr. Ἀτλαντικός.] **I.** *a.* Pertaining to the god Atlas, or to Mount Atlas; being, or pertaining to, the ocean west of Africa and Europe. **II.** *n.* The Atlantic Ocean.

Atlantic Charter, the joint declaration of President Roosevelt and Prime Minister Churchill (Aug. 14, 1941) resulting from a meeting at sea.

At-lan-tis (at-lan′tis), *n.* [L., < Gr. Ἀτλαντίς.] A mythical island in the Atlantic Ocean, first mentioned by Plato, and said to have been finally overwhelmed by the sea: sometimes taken, after Plato, as a type of ideal state, as in Bacon's "New Atlantis," which describes a community notable for scientific enlightenment.

At-las (at′lạs), *n.* [L., < Gr. Ἄτλας (Ἀτλαντ-), akin to τλῆναι, bear.] A god (later a king) of classical mythology, charged with holding up the heavens, and associated with a mountain ('Mount Atlas') in northwestern Africa; hence, one who sustains the burden of anything; a mainstay; [*l. c.*] a bound collection of maps (from the figure of Atlas bearing a globe on his shoulders, as used in such works); also, a volume of plates or tables illustrating any subject; in *arch.*, a supporting male figure (see *atlantes*); in *anat.*, the first cervical vertebra, which supports the head.

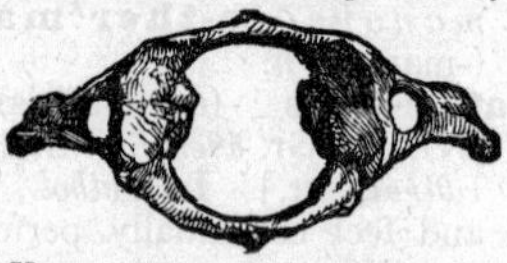

Human Atlas, which supports the head.

at-man (ät′mạn), *n.* [Skt. *ātman*, breath, spirit, soul.] The soul of the individual, or [*cap.*] of the universe, as conceived by the Brahman philosophers.

at-mi-dom-e-ter (at-mi-dom′e-tėr), *n.* [Gr. ἀτμίς (ἀτμιδ-), vapor: see *-meter.*] An atmometer.

atmo-. Form of Gr. ἀτμός, vapor, used in combination.

at-mol-o-gy (at-mol′ọ̄-ji), *n.* [See *atmo-* and *-logy.*] The science that treats of the laws and phenomena of aqueous vapor.—**at-mo-log′i-cal** (-mọ̄-loj′i-kạl), *a.*—**at-mol′o-gist,** *n.*

at-mol-y-sis (at-mol′i-sis), *n.* [See *atmo-* and *-lysis.*] Separation of mixed gases by partial diffusion through a porous substance.—**at′mo-lyze** (-mọ̄-līz), *v. t.*; *-lyzed, -lyzing.* [See *-lyze.*] To separate by atmolysis.—**at″mo-ly-za′tion** (-li-zā′shọn), *n.*—**at′mo-lyz-er** (-lī-zėr), *n.*

at-mom-e-ter (at-mom′e-tėr), *n.* [See *atmo-* and *-meter.*] An instrument for measuring evaporation.—**at-mo-met′ric** (-mọ̄-met′rik), *a.*—**at-mom′e-try,** *n.*

at-mo-sphere (at′mọs-fēr), *n.* [NL. *atmosphæra,* < Gr. ἀτμός, vapor, + σφαῖρα, E. *sphere.*] The aëriform fluid surrounding the earth; the air; hence, any gaseous envelop or medium; fig., environing or pervading influence; also, a conventional unit of atmospheric pressure, as the average pressure of the air to the square inch at sea-level, about 15 pounds (used for measuring steam-pressure, etc.), or, in English use, the pressure of a vertical column of 30 inches of mercury at the freezing-point at London.—**at-mo-spher′ic** (-mọs-fer′ik), *a.* Of or pertaining to the atmosphere. Also **at-mo-spher′i-cal.**—**at-mo-spher′i-cal-ly,** *adv.*

a-to-le (ä-tō′lā), *n.* [Mex. Sp.] In Spanish-American countries, a mush or gruel made of the meal of Indian corn.

a-toll (ạ-tol′ or at′ol), *n.* [E. Ind.] A ring-like coral island inclosing a lagoon.

Atoll.

at-om (at′ọm), *n.* [F. *atome,* < L. *atomus,* < Gr. ἄτομος, indivisible, < ἀ- priv. + τέμνειν, cut.] An indivisible or extremely minute particle of matter; an extremely small quantity or thing; in *chem.* and *physics,* one of the very small particles (formerly conceived as indivisible) by the aggregation or combination of which all forms of matter are assumed to be constituted.—**a-tom-ic** (ạ-tom′ik), *a.* Pertaining to atoms; minute; infinitesimal.—**atomic weight,** in *chem.*, the relative weight of the atom of an element according to some system, usually one in which the weight of the oxygen atom is taken as 16.—**a-tom′i-cal,** *a.*—**a-tom′i-cal-ly,** *adv.*—**at-o-mi-ci-ty** (at-ọ-mis′i-ti), *n.* In *chem.*, valence.—**at′om-ism,** *n.* The theory of atoms, as in philosophy or chemistry.—**at′om-ist,** *n.* An adherent of atomism.—**at-om-is′tic,** *a.*

at-om-ize (at′ọm-īz), *v. t.*; *-ized, -izing.* [From *atom* + *-ize.*] To reduce to fine particles or spray.—**at″om-i-za′tion** (-i-zā′shọn), *n.*—**at′om-iz-er** (-īz-ėr), *n.* One who or that which atomizes; an apparatus for reducing liquids to a fine spray, as for medicinal application.

at-om-y[1] (at′ọm-i), *n.*; pl. *-ies* (-iz). [For *atom.*] An atom; a mote; also, a pygmy. [Archaic.]

at-om-y[2] (at′ọm-i), *n.*; pl. *-ies* (-iz). [From *anatomy,* taken as *an atomy.*] A skeleton. [Archaic or prov.]

a-ton-a-ble (ạ-tō′nạ-bl), *a.* Admitting of atonement.

a-tone (ạ-tōn′), *v.*; *atoned, atoning.* [From *at one,* formerly written *atone.*] **I.** *tr.* To set at one, or bring into unity or concord (archaic); make amends to†; make amends for; expiate. **II.** *intr.* To be at one†; agree†; make amends or reparation, as for crime or sin; make up (*for*).—**a-tone′ment,** *n.* The act or the result of atoning; agreement†; reconciliation (now only as in *theol.*); amends; reparation; expiation; in *theol.*, the reconciliation of God and man by means of the life, sufferings, and death of Christ.—**Day of Atonement,** a Jewish fast-day: see *Yom Kippur.*—**a-ton-er** (ạ-tō′nėr), *n.*

a-ton-ic (a-ton′ik). [Gr. ἄτονος, relaxed, unaccented, < ἀ- priv. + τείνειν, stretch.] **I.** *a.* In *pathol.*, characterized by want of tone, esp. muscular tone; in *gram.*, unaccented; in *phonetics,* surd. **II.** *n.* In *gram.*, an unaccented syllable; in *phonetics,* a surd.—**at-o-ny** (at′ọ̄-ni), *n.* In *pathol.*, want of tone; muscular weakness, esp. in a contractile organ.

a-top (ạ-top′). **I.** *adv.* On or at the top. **II.** *prep.* On the top of.

at-ra-bi-la-ri-ous (at″rạ-bi-lā′ri-us), *a.* [ML. *atrabilarius,* < L. *atra bilis,* black bile.] Pertaining to or affected by 'black bile,' an imagined secretion of the renal glands; atrabilious.—**at-ra-bil′i-ar** (-bil′i-är), **at-ra-bil′i-a-ry** (-ạ̄-ri), *a.* Pertaining to or secreting black bile; atrabilious.—**at-ra-bil′ious,** *a.* Affected by black bile; melancholy; hypochondriac; splenetic.—**at-ra-bil′ious-ness,** *n.*

at-ra-ment (at′rạ-mẹnt), *n.* [L. *atramentum,* < *ater,* black.] Blacking; ink; any black fluid.—**at-ra-men′tal** (-men′tạl), **at-ra-men′tous,** *a.*

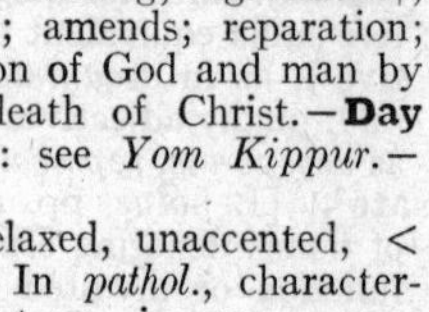

Atrium.—Restoration of a Pompeian interior.

a-trem-ble (ạ-trem′bl), *adv.* In a trembling state.

a-trip (ạ-trip′), *adv. Naut.*, of an anchor, just raised clear of the ground in weighing; of sails, hoisted up, sheeted home, and ready for trimming; of yards, hoisted up and ready to be swayed to a horizontal position.

a-tri-um (ā′tri-um), *n.*; pl. *atria* (-ạ̈). [L.] The entrance-hall and chief apartment of an ancient Roman house; hence, a hall or court; in *anat.*, an auricle, or the main part of an auricle, of the heart; also, any of various other chambers or cavities.

at-ro-ce-ru-le-ous (at″rọ-sẹ-rö′lẹ-us), *a.* [L. *ater*, black, + *cæruleus*, blue.] Of a blackish-blue color, as an insect.

a-tro-cious (ạ-trō′shus), *a.* [L. *atrox* (*atroc-*), < *ater*, black.] Outrageously wicked or cruel; heinous; also, shockingly bad (often used in colloquial exaggeration: as, an *atrocious* pun).—**a-tro′cious-ly,** *adv.*—**a-tro′cious-ness,** *n.*—**a-troc-i-ty** (ạ-tros′i-ti), *n.*; pl. *-ties* (-tiz). The quality of being atrocious; outrageous wickedness or cruelty; enormity; also, an atrocious deed or thing.

a-troph-ic (a-trof′ik), *a.* Pertaining to or characterized by atrophy.

at-ro-phy (at′rọ-fi), *n.* [LL. *atrophia*, < Gr. ἀτροφία, < ἀ- priv. + τρέφειν, nourish.] A wasting of the body or of an organ or part, as from defective nutrition or other causes; degeneration.—**at′ro-phy,** *v. t.* or *i.*; *-phied, -phying.* To affect with or undergo atrophy.

at-ro-pine, at-ro-pin (at′rọ-pin), *n.* [NL. *atropina*, < *Atropa*: see def.] A poisonous crystalline alkaloid obtained from the deadly nightshade, *Atropa belladonna*, and other solanaceous plants, having the property of dilating the pupil of the eye.—**at′ro-pism,** *n.* The morbid state induced by atropine.

a-trous (ā′trus), *a.* [L. *ater*.] Intensely black.

at′ta-ball, *n.* See *atabal*.

at-tac-ca (ät-täk′kä). [It., impv. of *attaccare*: see *attack*.] In *music*, attack, or begin, at once: a direction at the end of a movement to proceed with the following movement immediately.

at-tach (ạ-tach′), *v.* [OF. *atachier* (F. *attacher*), < *a* (< L. *ad*), to, + *-tachier*, akin to E. *tack*[1].] **I.** *tr.* To fasten (*to*); affix; join or connect; associate; assign; attribute; bind by ties of affection or regard; lay hold of†; seize†; in *law*, to take (persons or property) by legal authority. **II.** *intr.* To adhere (*to*); pertain; belong; rest (*upon*); also, to come into operation; take effect.—**at-tach′a-ble,** *a.* Capable of being attached.

at-ta-ché (ạ-tȧ′shā, F. ȧ-tȧ-shā), *n.* [F., prop. pp. of *attacher*, attach: see *attach*.] One attached to an official staff, esp. that of an embassy or legation.—**at-ta′ché-ship,** *n.*

at-tach-ment (ạ-tach′mẹnt), *n.* The act of attaching, or the state of being attached; connection; adherence; affection or regard; also, a means of attaching; a fastening or tie; also, something attached; an adjunct or supplementary device (as, *attachments* to a sewing-machine); in *law*, seizure by legal authority, or the writ or process commanding it.

at-tack (ạ-tak′), *v.* [F. *attaquer*, < It. *attaccare*, attach, attack (cf. *attaccare battaglia*, join battle), = F. *attacher*, E. *attach*.] **I.** *tr.* To set upon with force or arms; assault; begin hostilities against; fig., to assail with criticism, abuse, etc.; also, to set about (a task) or go to work on (a thing) vigorously; of disease, destructive agencies, etc., to begin to affect. **II.** *intr.* To make an attack; begin hostilities.—**at-tack′,** *n.* The act of attacking; assault; onslaught; onset; an offensive operation; the initial movement in a contest or performance; a seizure by disease.—**at-tack′a-ble,** *a.* That may be attacked.—**at-tack′er,** *n.*

at-tain (ạ-tān′), *v.* [OF. *ataindre* (F. *atteindre*), < L. *attingere*, < *ad*, to, + *tangere*, touch.] **I.** *tr.* To touch†; reach, as by effort or progress; arrive at in due course; gain; achieve. **II.** *intr.* To succeed in coming (*to* or *unto*).—**at-tain′a-ble,** *a.* Capable of being attained.—**at-tain-a-bil′i-ty** (-bil′i-ti), **at-tain′a-ble-ness,** *n.*

at-tain-der (ạ-tān′dėr), *n.* [OF. *ataindre*: see *attaint*.] An attainting; the legal consequence of judgment of death or outlawry for treason or felony, involving the loss of all civil rights; also, disgrace†; dishonor†.

at-tain-er (ạ-tā′nėr), *n.* One who attains.

at-tain-ment (ạ-tān′mẹnt), *n.* The act of attaining; also, something attained; a personal or mental acquirement.

at-taint (ạ-tānt′), *v. t.* [OF. *ataint*, pp. of *ataindre* (see *attain*); in part confused with E. *taint*.] To touch†; hit in tilting†; also, to convict†; condemn by a sentence or a bill or act of attainder (see *attainder*); accuse (archaic); also, to sully; disgrace; infect; taint.—**at-taint′,** *n.* A touch or hit, esp. in tilting (archaic); a wound on a horse's leg from overreaching; also, attainder; also, stain; disgrace; taint.—**at-taint′ment, at-tain-ture** (ạ-tān′tụ̄r), *n.*

at-tar (at′ạ̈r), *n.* [Pers. *'atar*, < Ar. *'atara*, smell sweet.] A perfume or essential oil obtained from flowers, esp. roses.—**at′tar=gul′** (-gůl′), *n.* [Pers. *'atar-gul*.] Attar of roses.

at-tem-per (ạ-tem′pėr), *v. t.* [OF. *atemprer* (F. *attremper*), < L. *attemperare*, < *ad*, to, + *temperare*, E. *temper*.] To temper, qualify, or regulate duly; accommodate or adapt (*to*); attune; modify as by admixture; moderate; mitigate; soften.

at-tempt (ạ-tempt′), *v. t.* [OF. *atempter*, < L. *attemptare*, < *ad*, to, + *temptare*, *tentare*, try, E. *tempt*.] To make an effort at; try; essay; undertake; seek (with infinitive); venture upon; also, to tempt (archaic); also, to make an effort against; try to take or destroy (life, etc.).—**at-tempt′,** *n.* A putting forth of effort to accomplish something; a trial or essay; an attack, as on one's life.—**at-tempt′a-ble,** *a.* That may be attempted.—**at-tempt-a-bil′i-ty** (-bil′i-ti), *n.*—**at-tempt′er,** *n.*

at-tend (ạ-tend′), *v.* [OF. *atendre* (F. *attendre*), < L. *attendere* (pp. *attentus*), < *ad*, to, + *tendere*, stretch, E. *tend*[1].] **I.** *tr.* To give heed to (archaic); devote one's services to; minister to; wait upon; tend; be present at (a meeting, etc.); accompany (a person, etc.); go with as a concomitant or result; await (archaic). **II.** *intr.* To give heed (*to*); apply one's self (*to*); wait (*on*) with service, etc.; be present (*at*); be consequent (*on*); wait† or stay†.—**at-tend′ance,** *n.* The act of attending; heed†; service; ministry; waiting; presence, or the company present; a retinue†.—**at-tend′ant. I.** *a.* Attending; present; accompanying; concomitant; consequent: often with *on*. **II.** *n.* One who attends another, as for service or company; also, one who is present, as at a meeting; also, an accompaniment or concomitant.—**at-tend′er,** *n.*

at-tent (ạ-tent′), *a.* [L. *attentus*, pp. of *attendere*, E. *attend*.] Attentive; intent: as, "with an *attent* ear" (Shakspere's "Hamlet," i. 2. 193). [Archaic.]

at-ten-tion (ạ-ten′shọn), *n.* [L. *attentio(n-)*, < *attendere*, E. *attend*.] The act or the faculty of attending; concentration of the mind upon an object; heed; consideration; care; civility or courtesy shown; a complimentary service; *pl.*, acts of courtesy or of devoted assiduity, as in courtship.

at-ten-tive (ạ-ten′tiv), *a.* [F. *attentif*, < L. *attendere*, E. *attend*.] Characterized by or giving attention; heedful; observant; assiduous in service or courtesy.—**at-ten′tive-ly,** *adv.*—**at-ten′tive-ness,** *n.*

at-ten-u-ant (ạ-ten′ụ̄-ạnt). **I.** *a.* Attenuating; making thin. **II.** *n.* A medicine that thins the humors.

at-ten-u-ate (ạ-ten′ụ̄-āt), *v.*; *-ated, -ating.* [L. *attenuatus*, pp. of *attenuare*, < *ad*, to, + *tenuare*, make thin, < *tenuis*, thin.] **I.** *tr.* To make thin; make slender or fine; reduce in density; dilute; fig., to weaken; lower; reduce. **II.** *intr.* To become thin, slight, or weak.—**at-ten′u-ate** (-ạt), *a.* Attenuated; thin; in *bot.*, tapering to a narrow extremity.—**at-ten-u-a′tion** (-ā′shọn), *n.* [L. *attenuatio(n-)*.] The act of attenuating, or the resulting state; reduction in thickness, density, strength, etc.; dilution; weakening.

at-test (ạ-test′), *v.* [L. *attestari*, < *ad*, to, + *testari*, bear witness, < *testis*, a witness.] **I.** *tr.* To bear witness to; certify; vouch for; authenticate, as by signature; give evidence of; also, to call to witness (archaic); also, to put upon oath. **II.** *intr.* To bear witness (*to*).—**at-test′,** *n.* Attestation; testimony; witness.—**at-tes-ta-tion** (at-es-tā′shọn), *n.* [LL. *attestatio(n-)*.] The act of attesting; an attesting declaration; testimony; evidence.—**at-test′er,** (in *law*) **at-test′or,** *n.*

At-tic (at′ik). [L. *Atticus*, < Gr. Ἀττικός, < Ἀττική, Attica.] **I.** *a.* Pertaining to Attica in Greece, or to its chief city, Athens; characteristic or worthy of Attica, as in refinement, elegance, or other merits: as, *Attic* salt (delicate, pungent wit); *Attic* faith (inviolable faith).

II. *n.* A native of Attica; also, the Attic dialect of Greek (regarded as the standard of the Greek language); [*l. c.*] a low story above an entablature or main cornice of a building; also, a garret. —**At-ti-cism** (at'i-sizm), *n.* [Gr. Ἀττικισμός.] Sympathy with Athens; also, a usage or idiom of Attic Greek; hence, an elegant expression, or turn of speech. —**At'ti-cist,** *n.* One who affects Attic style. —**At'ti-cize** (-sīz), *v.*; *-cized, -cizing.* [Gr. Ἀττικίζειν.] **I.** *intr.* To side or sympathize with Athens; also, to affect Attic style, usages, idioms, etc. **II.** *tr.* To make conformable to Attic usage.

Attic of St. Peter's, Rome.
A, attic of the main edifice; *B*, attic of the dome.

at-tire (ạ-tīr'), *v. t.*; *-tired, -tiring.* [OF. *atirer*, < *a* (< L. *ad*), to, + *tire*, row, order: see *tire*¹, *n.*] To put in order†; equip†; dress; apparel; array. —**at-tire',** *n.* Equipment†; dress; apparel; array; a costume†; a head-dress†; the horns of a deer. —**at-tire'ment,** *n.* Dress; attire. —**at-tir'er,** *n.*

at-ti-tude (at'i-tūd), *n.* [F., < It. *attitudine*, < ML. *aptitudo* (*aptitudin-*), E. *aptitude.*] The position of body appropriate to an action, purpose, emotion, etc.; a posture; fig., position or disposition with regard to a person or thing; in *aëronautics*, the inclination of the three principal axes of an aircraft to the relative wind or to the ground. —**at-ti-tu'di-nize** (-tū'di-nīz), *v. i.*; *-nized, -nizing.* To assume attitudes; pose for effect. —**at-ti-tu'di-niz-er** (-nī-zėr), *n.*

at-torn (ạ-tėrn'), *v.* [OF. *atorner*, transfer, appoint, < *a* (< L. *ad*), to, + *torner*, turn.] In *law*: **I.** *tr.* To turn over to another; transfer. **II.** *intr.* To transfer homage and service to a new feudal lord; acknowledge the relation of tenant to a new landlord.

at-tor-ney¹ (ạ-tėr'ni), *n.*; pl. *-neys* (-niz). [OF. *atorne*, pp. of *atorner*, appoint: see *attorn.*] One duly appointed or empowered by another to transact any business for him ('attorney in fact,' or 'private attorney'); a professional legal agent, qualified to act for others in legal proceedings ('attorney at law': cf. *counselor*); a deputy† or proxy†. —**at-tor'ney**², *n.* [OF. *atornee*, pp. fem.] The appointment of another to act in one's stead: as, a letter, warrant, or power of *attorney*. —**at-tor'ney=gen'er-al,** *n.*; pl. *attorneys-general* or *attorney-generals.* The chief law-officer of a state. —**at-tor'ney-ship,** *n.*

at-torn-ment (ạ-tėrn'mẹnt), *n.* In *law*, the act of attorning.

at-tract (ạ-trakt'), *v. t.* [L. *attractus*, pp. of *attrahere*, < *ad*, to, + *trahere*, draw.] To draw to one's self or itself; act upon by an inherent physical force compelling approach or union; fig., to draw by some moral force or influence; invite; allure; win. —**at-tract'a-ble,** *a.* Capable of being attracted. —**at-tract-a-bil'i-ty** (-bil'i-ti), *n.* —**at-tract'er,** *n.* —**at-trac'tile** (-til), *a.* Exerting attraction. —**at-trac'tion** (-shọn), *n.* [L. *attractio*(*n-*).] The act or the power of attracting; an inherent physical force through which bodies are drawn together and particles of matter tend to unite or cohere; fig., influence serving to draw or allure; an allurement; a charm. —**at-trac'tive,** *a.* Exerting attraction; drawing by inherent physical force; fig., engaging; alluring; pleasing; appealing to one's liking or admiration. —**at-trac'tive-ly,** *adv.* —**at-trac'tive-ness,** *n.* —**at-trac'tor,** *n.*

at-tra-hent (at'rạ-hẹnt), *a.* [L. *attrahens* (*-ent-*), ppr. of *attrahere*: see *attract.*] Drawing; attracting.

at-trib-ut-a-ble (ạ-trib'ū-tạ-bl), *a.* That may be attributed; ascribable; imputable.

at-trib-ute (ạ-trib'ūt), *v. t.*; *-uted, -uting.* [L. *attributus*, pp. of *attribuere*, < *ad*, to, + *tribuere*, grant, give, pay.] To grant or give as due†; also, to consider as belonging; regard as owing, as an effect to a cause; ascribe; impute; refer. —**at-tri-bute** (at'ri-būt), *n.* Something attributed as belonging; a quality, character, characteristic, or property; a symbol of office, character, or personality (as, the eagle is the *attribute* of Jupiter); reputation† or honor†; in *logic*, that which may be predicated of a subject, esp. an essential quality; in *gram.*, an attributive word or adjunct. —**at-tri-bu'tion** (-bū'shọn), *n.* [L. *attributio*(*n-*).] The act of attributing; ascription; also, an attribute; sometimes, authority or function assigned. —**at-trib'u-tive** (-ū-tiv). **I.** *a.* Pertaining to attribution; in *gram.*, expressing an attribute, as an adjective or an adjective equivalent; used adjectively before a substantive, as the adjective *bad* in 'a bad boy' or the noun *boy* in 'a boy singer' (distinguished from *predicate* and *appositive*). **II.** *n.* In *gram.*, an attributive word or adjunct. —**at-trib'u-tive-ly,** *adv.* In an attributive manner; as or like an adjective preceding its substantive. —**at-trib'u-tive-ness,** *n.* —**at-trib'u-tor,** *n.*

at-trite (ạ-trīt'), *a.* [L. *attritus*, pp. of *atterere*, rub against, < *ad*, to, + *terere*, rub.] Worn by rubbing or attrition (obs. or rare); in *theol.*, having attrition. —**at-trit-ed** (ạ-trī'ted), *a.* Worn by attrition. —**at-tri-tion** (ạ-trish'ọn), *n.* [LL. *attritio*(*n-*).] A rubbing against; friction; also, a wearing down or away by friction; abrasion; in *theol.*, imperfect contrition (see *contrition*). —**at-tri-tive** (ạ-trī'tiv), *a.* Characterized by attrition. —**at-tri'tus** (-tus), *n.* Matter reduced to particles by attrition.

at-tune (ạ-tūn'), *v. t.*; *-tuned, -tuning.* [With *at-* as in *attemper.*] To tune (*to*); adjust to tune or harmony; bring into accord; make tuneful or melodious. —**at-tune'-ment,** *n.*

a-twain (ạ-twān'), *adv.* In twain; in two; asunder. [Archaic.]

a-tween (ạ-twēn'), *prep.* and *adv.* Between. [Archaic or prov.]

a-typ-ic, a-typ-i-cal (a-tip'ik, -i-kạl, or ā-), *a.* [See *a-*¹.] Not typic or typical; not conforming to the type; irregular; abnormal. —**a-typ'i-cal-ly,** *adv.*

au-bade (ō-båd), *n.* [F., < Pr. *albada*, < *alba*, dawn, < L. *albus*, white.] An early morning song or other musical performance in the open air, esp. in compliment; a piece of music suitable for such performance. Cf. *serenade.*

au-baine (ō-bān), *n.* [F., < OF. *aubain*, alien, foreign, < L. *alibi*, elsewhere.] In *old French law*, succession to the goods of a resident alien at his death: as, the right of *aubaine* (F. *droit d'aubaine*), exercised by the kings and by Napoleon, but abolished in 1819.

au-berge (ō-berzh), *n.* [F.; from Teut., and akin to E. *harbor.*] An inn.

au-ber-gine (ō-ber-zhēn), *n.* [F.] The fruit of the egg-plant, or the plant; also, a dark-purple color, like that of the fruit.

au-burn (â'bėrn). [OF. *auborne*, < ML. *alburnus*, < L. *albus*, white.] **I.** *a.* Whitish†; flaxen†; reddish-brown: usually applied to hair. **II.** *n.* An auburn color.

Au-bus-son (ō-bü-sôṅ) **car'pet.** A choice kind of tapestry carpet made in one piece by hand at Aubusson, France, in elegant designs (usually with a central medallion) and fine material and coloring.

auc-tion (âk'shọn), *n.* [L. *auctio*(*n-*), < *augere*, increase: see *eke*¹.] Increase† or growth†; also, a public sale with increasing bids for property or goods to be awarded to the highest bidder; also, auction bridge (see under *bridge*²). —**auc'tion,** *v. t.* To sell by auction. —**auc-tion-eer'** (-ēr'), *n.* [See *-eer.*] One who conducts sales by auction. —**auc-tion-eer',** *v. t.* To auction.

au-cu-ba (â'kū-bạ), *n.*; pl. *-bas.* [NL.; from Jap.] Any plant of the cornaceous genus *Aucuba*, of eastern Asia, esp. *A. japonica*, with glossy leathery green leaves mottled with yellow, and red berries, much cultivated for ornament.

au-da-cious (â-dā'shus), *a.* [F. *audacieux*, < *audace*, < L. *audacia*, boldness, < *audax*, bold, < *audere*, dare.] Bold; daring; esp., recklessly or shamelessly bold; impudent. —**au-da'cious-ly,** *adv.* —**au-da'cious-ness,** *n.* —**au-da-ci-ty** (â-das'i-ti), *n.*; pl. *-ties* (-tiz). Boldness or daring; esp., reckless boldness; effrontery or impudence; also, something audacious.

au-di-ble (â'di-bl), *a.* [ML. *audibilis*, < L. *audire*, hear.] Capable of being heard. —**au-di-bil'i-ty** (-bil'i-ti), **au'di-ble-ness,** *n.* —**au'di-bly,** *adv.*

au-di-ence (â′di-ẹns), *n.* [OF. F. *audience*, < L. *audientia*, < *audire*, hear.] The act of hearing; attention; a formal hearing or interview, esp. as granted by a sovereign or high official; also, an assembly of hearers; an auditory.—**au′-di-ent,** *a.* [L. *audiens* (*-ent-*), ppr. of *audire.*] Hearing; listening.
au-dile (â′dil), *n.* [L. *audire*, hear.] In *psychol.*, one in whose mind auditory images are especially distinct.
au-di-o (â′di-ō) **fre′quen-cy.** See under *frequency*.
au-di-om-e-tėr (â-di-om′e-tėr), *n.* [L. *audire*, hear: see *-meter.*] An instrument for gaging and recording the power of hearing.—**au-di-om′e-try,** *n.*
au-di-on (â′di-on), *n.* [L. *audire*, hear.] A device somewhat resembling an incandescent electric-light bulb, used as a means of detecting or amplifying feeble electric waves or currents, as in wireless telegraphy, wireless telephony, long-distance telephoning by wire, etc.: invented by Dr. Lee de Forest. [Proprietary name.]
au-di-phone (â′di-fōn), *n.* [L. *audire*, hear: see *-phone.*] A kind of diaphragm held against the upper teeth to assist hearing by transmitting sound-vibrations to the auditory nerve.
au-dit (â′dit), *n.* [L. *auditus*, a hearing, < *audire*, hear.] A hearing, esp. a judicial hearing or examination (archaic); an official examination and verification of accounts (sometimes fig., as with reference to the Last Judgment); a statement of account.—**au′dit,** *v. t.* To make audit of; examine (accounts, etc.) officially.
au-di-tion (â-dish′ọn), *n.* [L. *auditio*(*n-*), < *audire*, hear.] The act or the sense of hearing.—**au-di-tive** (â′di-tiv), *a.* Pertaining to hearing; auditory.
au-di-tor (â′di-tọr), *n.* [L., < *audire*, hear.] A hearer; also, one authorized to audit accounts.—**au-di-to′ri-um** (-tō′ri-um), *n.*; pl. *-riums*, L. *-ria* (-ri-ạ̈). [L.] The space for the audience in a church, theater, or the like.—**au′di-tor-ship,** *n.* The office of auditor, as of accounts.—**au′di-to-ry** (-tọ-ri), *a.* [LL. *auditorius.*] Pertaining to hearing.—**au′di-to-ry,** *n.*; pl. *-ries* (-riz). [L. *auditorium.*] A place for hearing or hearers; an auditorium; also, an assembly of hearers; an audience.—**au′di-tress,** *n.* A female auditor.
auf-klä-rung (ouf′klä-rụ̂ng), *n.* [G.] Enlightenment: esp. applied [*cap.*] to the active 18th century movement in France and elsewhere toward intellectual light and freedom.
Au-ge-an (â-jē′ạn), *a.* Pertaining to Augeas, of Greek mythology, a king of Elis whose stables, sheltering 3,000 oxen, remained uncleaned for 30 years, until Hercules turned the river Alpheus through them; hence, filthy.

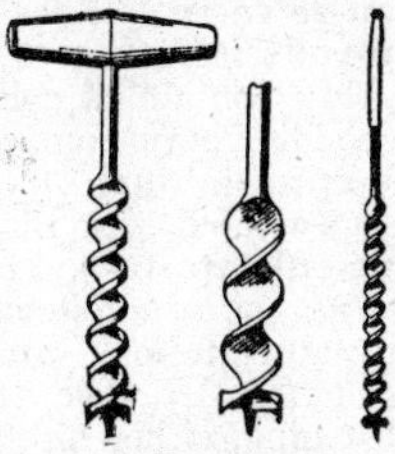
Augers.

au-ger (â′gėr), *n.* [For *nauger* (*a nauger* being taken as *an auger*), < AS. *nafogār*, < *nafu*, nave, hub, + *gār*, borer, spear.] A tool, larger than a gimlet, for boring holes in wood; also, an earth-boring instrument.
aught[1] (ât). [AS. *āwiht*, *ōwiht*, 'ever a whit,' < *ō*, *ā*, ever, + *wiht*, thing, E. *whit*: cf. *ought*[1].] **I.** *n.* Anything whatever; any part. **II.** *adv.* In any respect; in any degree; at all.
aught[2] (ât), *n.* [For *naught.*] A cipher (0). [Colloq.]
aught[3] (ât), *n.* [AS. *ǣht*, < *āgan*, have, own.] Possession; property. [Now Sc.]
au-gite (â′jīt), *n.* [L. *augites*, < Gr. αὐγή, light, gleam.] A mineral, a dark-green to black variety of pyroxene characteristic of basic eruptive rocks.—**au-git-ic** (â-jit′ik), *a.*
aug-ment (âg′ment), *n.* [OF. F. *augment*, < L. *augmentum*, < *augere*, increase: see *eke*[1].] Increase†; in *gram.*, in some Indo-European languages, an addition at the beginning of a past indicative verb-form (in Greek a prefixed ἐ- or a lengthening of an initial vowel: see *syllabic*, *a.*, and *temporal*[2], *a.*).—**aug-ment′,** *v.* [OF. F. *augmenter*, < LL. *augmentare*, < L. *augmentum.*] **I.** *tr.* To increase; add to; make greater; in *gram.*, to give an augment to. **II.** *intr.* To become greater.—**aug-ment′a-ble,** *a.* Capable of being augmented.—**aug-men-ta′tion** (-men-tā′shọn), *n.* [LL. *augmentatio*(*n-*).] The act of augmenting; augmented state; also, that by which anything is augmented; an increase; an addition; in *music*, modification of a theme, as in repetition, by increasing the time-value of all its notes.—**aug-men′ta-tive** (-tạ-tiv). **I.** *a.* Serving to augment; in *gram.*, increasing the force of the idea conveyed. **II.** *n.* In *gram.*, an augmentative word-form or affix.—**aug-ment′ed,** *p. a.* Increased; in *music*, of an interval, greater by a half-step than the corresponding perfect or major interval.—**aug-ment′er,** *n.*
au-gur (â′gėr), *n.* [L., perhaps < *avis*, bird.] One of a body of ancient Roman officials charged with observing and interpreting omens as afforded by birds or other animals, thunder and lightning, etc., for guidance in public affairs; in general, a prognosticator; a soothsayer; a prophet.—**au′gur,** *v.* [L. *augurari*, < *augur.*] **I.** *tr.* To divine or predict, as from omens; prognosticate; also, to afford an omen of; portend. **II.** *intr.* To conjecture from omens; presage; also, to give presage; bode (*well* or *ill*).—**au-gu-ral** (â′gū-rạl), *a.* Pertaining to an augur; affording an omen.—**au-gu-ri-al** (â-gū′ri-ạl), *a.* Pertaining to augurs or augury.—**au′gur-ship,** *n.*—**au-gu-ry** (â′gū-ri), *n.*; pl. *-ries* (-riz). [L. *augurium.*] The art or practice of an augur; divination; prognostication; a rite or observation of an augur; also, presage; promise; also, a prognostic or omen; a token or indication.

Augur.
(From a Roman bas-relief.)

au-gust[1] (â-gust′), *a.* [L. *augustus*, perhaps < *augur*, augur, but usually referred to *augere*, increase: cf. *augment.*] Inspiring reverence and admiration; of supreme dignity or grandeur; majestic; venerable; worshipful.
Au-gust[2] (â′gust), *n.* [From the Roman emperor *Augustus.*] The eighth month of the year, containing 31 days.
Au-gus-tan (â-gus′tạn). **I.** *a.* Pertaining to Augustus, the first Roman emperor, or to his reign (27 B.C.–A.D. 14): as, the *Augustan* age (the highest period) of Roman and hence of any national literature. **II.** *n.* A writer of the Augustan age in any literature.
Au-gus-tin-i-an (â-gus-tin′i-ạn). **I.** *a.* Pertaining to St. Augustine (354–430), bishop of Hippo in northern Africa, to his doctrines (esp. of divine grace, original sin, predestination, etc.), or to any religious order following his rule. **II.** *n.* One who adopts the views or doctrines of St. Augustine; also, a member of any of several religious orders deriving their name and rule from St. Augustine, esp. a member of the order of mendicant friars called 'Hermits of St. Augustine,' or 'Austin Friars.'—**Au-gus-tin′i-an-ism,** *n.*
au-gust-ly (â-gust′li), *adv.* In an august manner; majestically.—**au-gust′ness,** *n.*
auk (âk), *n.* [Icel. *ālka.*] Any of the short-winged diving birds constituting the family *Alcidæ*, of northern seas; specif., one of certain species of this family, as *Alca torda* ('razor-billed auk') or *Alca* (or *Plautus*) *impennis* ('great auk': now extinct).—**auk′let,** *n.* Any of various small species of the auk family of the genus *Simorhynchus* and allied genera, as *S. cristatellus* ('crested auklet').

Great Auk.

Crested Auklet.

auld (âld), *a.* Scotch form of *old.*—**auld lang syne** ('old long since'), old times, esp. as fondly remembered. [Sc.]

au-lic (â'lik), *a.* [L. *aulicus*, < Gr. αὐλικός, < αὐλή, court.] Pertaining to a royal court.—**Aulic Council,** in the old German Empire, or Holy Roman Empire, a personal council of the emperor, exercising chiefly judicial powers on his behalf, and constituting, like the Imperial Chamber which acted for the empire, one of the two supreme courts of justice.

aunt (änt, U. S. commonly ant), *n.* [OF. *ante*, < L. *amita.*] A sister of one's father or mother; an uncle's wife; a familiar term applied to any elderly woman; a procuress† or a prostitute†.—**aunt'y, aunt'ie,** *n.* Familiar diminutive of *aunt.*

au-ra (â'rä), *n.*; pl. *-ras*, L. *-ræ* (-rē). [L., < Gr. αὔρα, breeze, < ἀῆναι, blow.] A gentle breeze, esp. [*cap.*] as personified and represented in Greek art; [*l. c.*] a subtle emanation; a kind of influence, force, or supersensible fluid supposed to proceed from a body and sometimes conceived to surround it as an atmosphere; fig., a distinctive influence or atmosphere; in *pathol.*, a sensation, as of a current of cold air, preceding an attack of epilepsy, hysteria, etc.; in *elect.*, a supposed fluid formerly thought to surround an electrified body; also, a motion of the air at an electrified point.—**au'ral**[1], *a.*

Auræ (in art).

au-ral[2] (â'ral), *a.* [L. *auris*, ear.] Of, pertaining to, or perceived by the ear.—**au'ral-ly,** *adv.*

au-ran-ti-a-ceous (â-ran-ti-ā'shius), *a.* [NL. *aurantium*, orange.] Orange-like; allied to the orange; orange-colored.

au-rate (â'rāt), *n.* In *chem.*, a salt of auric acid.

au-re-ate (â'rē-āt), *a.* [LL. *aureatus*, < L. *aureus*, golden, < *aurum*, gold.] Gilded; golden; golden-yellow.

au-re-lia (â-rē'liä), *n.* [It., < L. *aurum*, gold.] In *entom.*, a chrysalis, as of a butterfly. [Archaic.]—**au-re'lian,** *n.* A student or collector of butterflies, moths, etc.; a lepidopterist. [Archaic.]

au-re-o-la (â-rē'ō-lä), *n.*; pl. *-las.* [L., fem. of *aureolus*, golden, dim. of *aureus*: see *aureate.*] A radiance surrounding the whole pictured figure of a sacred or glorified personage; also, any encircling ring of light or color; a halo; in *Rom. Cath. theol.*, a higher reward added to the essential bliss of heaven for a special spiritual victory.—**au-re-ole** (â'rē-ōl), *n.* An aureola; an encircling radiance; a halo.—**au're-oled,** *a.* Encircled with an aureole.

Aureola.—Figure of Christ, from tympanum of portal of St. Trophime, Arles, France; 12th century.

au-ric (â'rik), *a.* [L. *aurum*, gold.] Of or containing gold. See *aurous.*—**auric acid,** in *chem.*, a hydroxide of gold, which behaves as a weak acid and forms salts.

au-ri-cle (â'ri-kl), *n.* [L. *auricula*, dim. of *auris*, ear.] The projecting outer portion of the ear; the pinna; also, an ear-like part; a lobe; also, one of two chambers of the heart through which blood from the veins passes into the ventricles.—**au'ri-cled,** *a.* Having auricles.

au-ric-u-la (â-rik'ū-lä), *n.*; pl. *-las.* [NL. use of L. *auricula* (see *auricle*); from the leaf, likened to the furry ear of a bear.] A yellow primrose, *Primula auricula*, with thick, pubescent leaves, native in the Alps; bear's-ear; also, any of the many varieties of this species, with variously colored flowers, developed in cultivation.

au-ric-u-lar (â-rik'ū-lär). [ML. *auricularis*, < L. *auricula*: see *auricle.*] **I.** *a.* Of or pertaining to the ear; perceived by or addressed to the ear (as, *auricular* confession); dependent on hearing; aural; also, shaped like an ear; auriculate; also, pertaining to an auricle of the heart; in *ornith.*, noting certain feathers, usually of peculiar structure, which overlie and defend the outer opening of a bird's ear. **II.** *n.* In *ornith.*, an auricular feather: usually in *pl.*—**au-ric'u-lar-ly,** *adv.*

au-ric-u-late, au-ric-u-lat-ed (â-rik'ū-lāt, -lā-ted), *a.* [NL. *auriculatus*, < L. *auricula*: see *auricle.*] Having auricles, or ear-like parts; shaped like an ear.—**au-ric'u-late-ly,** *adv.*

au-rif-er-ous (â-rif'e-rus), *a.* [L. *aurifer*, < *aurum*, gold, + *ferre*, bear.] Yielding gold.—**au-rif'er-ous-ly,** *adv.*

au-ri-form (â'ri-fôrm), *a.* [L. *auris*, ear: see *-form.*] Having the form of an ear, esp. of the external human ear.

au-ri-lave (â'ri-lāv), *n.* [L. *auris*, ear, + *lavare*, wash.] An instrument for cleansing the external ear and auditory meatus.

au-ri-scope (â'ri-skōp), *n.* [L. *auris*, ear: see *-scope.*] An instrument for examining the ear.—**au-ris-co-py** (â-ris'kō-pi), *n.*

au-rist (â'rist), *n.* [L. *auris*, ear.] One skilled in treating diseases of the ear; an otologist.

au-rochs (â'roks), *n.* [G. *aurochs*, now *auerochs*, < OHG. *urohso*, < *ur*, urus, + *ohso*, ox.] A European wild ox, the urus, now extinct; also, the European bison, now found only in Lithuania and the Caucasus.

Aurochs (European bison).

au-ro-ra (â-rō'rä), *n.* [L.; akin to Gr. ἠώς, Skt. *ushas*, dawn, and E. *east.*] The rising light of morning; dawn, often personified [*cap.*], by the Romans and others, as a goddess (cf. *Eos*); also, a natural phenomenon, probably of electrical origin, consisting of streamers, bands, arcs, etc., of light appearing in the heavens at night in the higher northern or southern latitudes; the polar lights ('aurora borealis,' northern lights, or 'aurora australis,' southern lights); also, an electric glow-discharge appearing at very high voltages.—**au-ro'ral,** *a.* Of or like the dawn; roseate; also, pertaining to a polar aurora.—**au-ro'ral-ly,** *adv.*—**au-ro're-an** (-rē-an), *a.* Dawn-like; auroral. [Poetic.]

au-rous (â'rus), *a.* [L. *aurum*, gold.] Of or pertaining to gold; containing gold (in larger proportion than a corresponding auric compound).

au-rum (â'rum), *n.* [L.] Gold: in *chem.*, abbreviated *Au* (without period).

aus-cul-tate (âs'kul-tāt), *v. t.*; *-tated, -tating.* [L. *auscultatus*, pp. of *auscultare*, listen to.] To listen to; examine by auscultation.—**aus-cul-ta'tion** (-tā'shon), *n.* [L. *auscultatio(n-).*] The act of listening; in *pathol.*, the act of listening, either directly or through a stethoscope or other instrument, to sounds within the body, as a method of determining conditions within.—**aus-cul'ta-tive** (-ta-tiv), **aus-cul'ta-to-ry** (-tō-ri), *a.*—**aus'cul-ta-tor** (-tā-tor), *n.* One who auscultates; an instrument used in auscultation.

aus-gleich (ous'glĭch), *n.* [G.] An adjustment; an arrangement or compromise between parties; esp. [*cap.*], the agreement made between Austria and Hungary in 1867 regulating the relations between the countries.

aus-pex (âs'peks), *n.*; pl. *auspices* (âs'pi-sēz). [L., < *avis*, bird, + *specere*, look at.] In ancient Rome, a diviner who drew his prognostications from the movements, cries, etc., of birds; an augur.

aus-pi-cate (âs'pi-kāt), *v.*; *-cated, -cating.* [L. *auspicatus*, pp. of *auspicari*, take auspices, < *auspex*: see *auspex.*] **I.** *intr.* To take auspices†; augur or presage (obs. or rare). **II.** *tr.* To initiate with ceremonies calculated to insure good luck; begin or mark by some initial act, etc.; inaugurate; also, to augur or portend (obs. or rare).

aus-pice (âs'pis), *n.* [F. *auspice*, < L. *auspicium*, < *auspex*: see *auspex.*] A divination or prognostication, orig. from birds; a prognostic or omen; a propitious circumstance; a favoring influence, as of a patron (esp. in the phrase 'under the auspices of'): usually in *pl.*—**aus-pi′cial** (-pish′ạl), *a.* Of or pertaining to auspices; also, auspicious.

aus-pi-cious (âs-pish′us), *a.* [L. *auspicium*: see *auspice.*] Of good omen; favorable; also, favored by fortune; fortunate.—**aus-pi′cious-ly,** *adv.*—**aus-pi′cious-ness,** *n.*

Aus-ter (âs′tėr), *n.* [L.] The south wind personified (poetic); also, the south†.

aus-tere (âs-tēr′), *a.* [OF. *austere* (F. *austère*), < L. *austerus*, < Gr. αὐστηρός, < αὔειν, to dry.] Harsh in flavor or effect; sour; severe; rigid; strict; grave; severely simple.—**aus-tere′ly,** *adv.*—**aus-tere′ness,** *n.*—**aus-ter′i-ty** (-ter′i-ti), *n.*; pl. *-ties* (-tiz). Austere quality; severity of manner, life, etc.; rigor; *pl.*, austere practices.

Aus-tin (âs′tin), *a.* Augustinian: as, an *Austin* friar.

aus-tral (âs′trạl), *a.* [L. *australis*, < *auster*, the south wind, the south.] Southern; of or in the southern hemisphere; [*cap.*] Australian; Australasian.

Aus-tra-la-sian (âs-trạ-lā′shiạn or -zhiạn). [From *Australasia*, < F. *Australasie*, < L. *australis*, southern, + *Asia*, Asia.] **I.** *a.* Of or pertaining to Australasia, a division of Oceanica comprising Australia, Papua, Tasmania, New Zealand, and neighboring islands. **II.** *n.* A native or inhabitant of Australasia.

Aus-tra-lian (âs-trā′liạn). [F. *Australien*, < L. *australis*, southern, in *Terra Australis*, 'southern land.'] **I.** *a.* Of or pertaining to Australia; in *zoögeog.*, belonging to a division comprising Australia and other Pacific islands from Celebes eastward. **II.** *n.* A native or inhabitant of Australia; a member of the aboriginal race of Australia.—**Aus-tra′li-oid** (-li-oid), *a.* [See *-oid.*] Of the racial type of the Australian aborigines (perhaps allied to the Dravidian peoples of India). Also **Aus′tra-loid** (-trạ-loid).

Aus-tra-sian (âs-trā′shiạn or -zhiạn), *a.* [LL. *Austrasia*, also *Austria*; from Teut. (cf. OHG. *ostar*, eastern).] Of or pertaining to Austrasia, the eastern kingdom of the Franks, with its capital at Metz. Cf. *Neustrian.*

Aus-tri-an (âs′tri-ạn). [LL. *Austria*, 'eastern land': see *Austrasian.*] **I.** *a.* Of or pertaining to Austria. **II.** *n.* An inhabitant of Austria.

aus-tro-[1] (âs′trọ-). Form of L. *auster*, the south wind, the south, used in combination, as in *austrocentral* (south-central), *austro-occidental, austro-oriental.*

Aus-tro-[2] (âs′trọ-). Form of *Austrian* or *Austria* used in combination, as in *Austro-Hungarian.*

au-tar-chy[1] (â′tär-ki), *n.*; pl. *-chies* (-kiz). [Gr. αὐταρχία, < αὐτός, self, + ἄρχειν, rule.] Absolute sovereignty; despotism; also, self-government.—**au-tar′chic** (-kik), *a.*

au-tar-chy[2] (â′tär-ki), *n.* [For *autarcy*, < Gr. αὐτάρκεια, < αὐτός, self, + ἀρκεῖν, suffice.] Self-sufficiency, esp., in recent use, as a national policy.—**au-tar′chic** (-kik), *a.*

au-then-tic (â-then′tik), *a.* [OF. *autentique* (F. *authentique*), < LL. *authenticus*, < Gr. αὐθεντικός, < αὐθέντης, actual doer of a thing, < αὐτός, self, + -εντης as in συνέντης, co-worker.] Possessing original or inherent authority†; authoritative†; entitled to acceptance or belief; reliable; legally executed and attested, as a deed; being of the authorship or origin reputed; genuine; original†; own (archaic); in *Gregorian music*, having the final tone or keynote as the lowest tone of the scale, as a mode; in *modern music*, noting a cadence in which the chord of the tonic is preceded by that of the dominant.—**au-then′ti-cal-ly,** *adv.*

au-then-ti-cate (â-then′ti-kāt), *v. t.*; *-cated, -cating.* [ML. *authenticatus*, pp. of *authenticare*, < LL. *authenticus*, E. *authentic.*] To establish as authentic; make authoritative or valid; certify as reliable; prove genuine.—**au-then-ti-ca′tion** (-kā′shọn), *n.*—**au-then′ti-ca-tor,** *n.*

au-then-ti-ci-ty (â-then-tis′i-ti), *n.* The quality of being authentic; reliability; genuineness.

au-thor (â′thọr), *n.* [OF. *autor*, *auctor* (F. *auteur*), < L. *auctor*, < *augere*, increase.] The originator, beginner, or creator of anything; the composer of a literary production; the literary productions of a writer (as, to find a passage in an *author*); one who is the authority for a statement†.—**au′thor-ess,** *n.* A female author.—**au-tho-ri-al** (â-thō′ri-ạl), *a.* Of or pertaining to an author.

au-thor-i-ta-ri-an (â-thor-i-tā′ri-ạn). **I.** *a.* Favoring the principle of authority as opposed to that of individual freedom. **II.** *n.* One who favors the principle of authority.

au-thor-i-ta-tive (â-thor′i-tā-tiv), *a.* Characterized by or having authority; duly authorized; also, imperative or peremptory.—**au-thor′i-ta-tive-ly,** *adv.*—**au-thor′i-ta-tive-ness,** *n.*

au-thor-i-ty (â-thor′i-ti), *n.*; pl. *-ties* (-tiz). [OF. *auctorite* (F. *autorité*), < L. *auctoritas*, < *auctor*: see *author.*] Power or admitted right to command or act; title to respect or acceptance; commanding influence; weight, importance, or credit; the person or persons exercising power or control (usually in *pl.*); an accepted source of information; an expert; a warrant for action; a justification; a legal precedent.

au-thor-ize (â′thọr-īz), *v. t.*; *-ized, -izing.* [OF. *auctoriser* (F. *autoriser*), < ML. *auctorizare*, < L. *auctor*: see *author.*] To give authority, formal warrant, or legal power to (a person); empower (to do something); also, to give authority for (a thing); sanction; warrant; justify; also, to vouch for†; also, to make legal or valid†.—**Authorized Version** (of the Bible). See *version.*—**au″thor-i-za′tion** (-i-zā′shọn), *n.*—**au′thor-iz-er** (-ī-zėr), *n.*

au-thor-less (â′thọr-les), *a.* Having no author; not originated by any one; of unknown authorship; anonymous.

au-thor-ship (â′thọr-ship), *n.* The function of an author; also, origin as to author.

auto-. Form of Gr. αὐτός, self, in combination: sometimes used to represent *automatic* and *automobile.*

au-to (â′tō), *n.*; pl. *autos* (-tōz). Shortened form of *automobile.*—**au′to,** *v. i.*; *-toed, -toing.* To ride in an automobile. [Colloq.]

au-to-bi-og-ra-pher (â″tọ-bī-og′rạ-fėr), *n.* [See *auto-.*] One who writes a biography of himself.—**au″to-bi-og′ra-phy,** *n.*; pl. *-phies* (-fiz). Biography of one's self; an account of a person's life written by himself.—**au″to-bi-o-graph′ic, au″to-bi-o-graph′i-cal** (-ọ-graf′ik, -i-kạl), *a.*—**au″to-bi-o-graph′i-cal-ly,** *adv.*

au-to-boat (â′tọ-bōt″), *n.* [See *auto-.*] A motor-boat.—**au′to-boat″ing,** *n.*—**au′to-bus″,** *n.*; pl. *-buses.* An automobile omnibus.—**au′to-cab″,** *n.* An automobile cab.—**au′to-car″,** *n.* An automobile; a motor-car.—**au′to-car″riage,** *n.* An automobile carriage; a motor-car.

au-to-ceph-a-lous (â-tọ-sef′ạ-lus), *a.* [LGr. αὐτοκέφαλος, < Gr. αὐτός, self, + κεφαλή, head.] Of churches, bishops, etc., independent of jurisdiction.

au-toch-thon (â-tok′thọn), *n.*; pl. *-thons* (-thọnz) or *-thones* (-thọ-nēz). [Gr. αὐτόχθων, < αὐτός, self, + χθών, earth.] One sprung from the land he inhabits; an aboriginal inhabitant; one of the primitive animals or plants of a region.—**au-toch′tho-nal** (-thọ-nạl), **au-toch-thon′ic** (-thon′ik), *a.* Autochthonous.—**au-toch′thon-ism,** *n.* Autochthonous origin or condition.—**au-toch′tho-nous,** *a.* Pertaining to autochthons; aboriginal; indigenous; originating where found.—**au-toch′tho-nous-ly,** *adv.*—**au-toch′tho-ny,** *n.* Autochthonism.

au-to-clave (â′tọ-klāv), *n.* [F. *autoclave*, self-closing (as vessels made close by the pressure of steam within against the lid), < Gr. αὐτός, self, + L. *clavis*, key.] A strong closed vessel in which liquids may be heated above the boiling-point under pressure: used in digesting chemicals, in sterilizing, etc.

au-to-co-her-er (â″tọ-kọ-hēr′ėr), *n.* [See *auto-.*] In *elect.*, a coherer which spontaneously recovers its resistance after the passing of the Hertzian wave.

au-toc-ra-cy (â-tok′rạ-si), *n.*; pl. *-cies* (-siz). [= F. *autocratie*, < Gr. αὐτοκράτεια, < αὐτοκρατής, ruling by one's self, < αὐτός, self, + κρατεῖν, rule.] Self-derived or independent power†; absolute authority or rule; autocratic government.—**au-to-crat** (â′tọ-krat), *n.* [F. *autocrate*, < Gr. αὐτοκρατής.] An absolute ruler (as, 'the *autocrat* of all the Russias,' a title of the czars of Russia); one who exercises unlimited authority.—**au-to-crat′ic,** *a.* Of or like an autocrat; absolute in power or authority.—**au-to-crat′i-cal-ly,** *adv.*

au-to-cy-cle (â′tọ-sī″kl), *n.* [See *auto-.*] A motor-cycle.

au-to da fé (ou′tō dä fā); pl. *autos da fé* (ou′tōs). [Pg., 'act of the faith.'] The public declaration of the judgment passed on persons tried in the courts of the Spanish Inquisition; also, the execution (by the civil authorities) of the sentence of those condemned in these courts. Also (Sp.) **au′to de fe** (dā fā); pl. *autos de fe* (ou′tōs).

au-to-di-dact (â′tǫ-di-dakt″), *n.* [Gr. αὐτοδίδακτος, self-taught, < αὐτός, self, + διδάσκειν, teach.] One who is self-taught.—**au″to-di-dac′tic,** *a.*

au-to-di-ges-tion (â″tǫ-di-jes′chǫn or â″tǫ-dī-), *n.* [See *auto-*.] In *physiol.*, self-digestion; autolysis.

au-tœ-cious (â-tē′shus), *a.* [Gr. αὐτός, self, + οἶκος, house.] In *bot.*, passing through all stages of growth on the same host, as certain parasitic fungi.—**au-tœ′cism** (-sizm), *n.*

au-tog-a-my (â-tog′ą-mi), *n.* [Gr. αὐτός, self, + γάμος, marriage.] In *bot.*, fecundation of the ovules of a flower by its own pollen; self-fertilization: opposed to *allogamy.* —**au-tog′a-mous,** *a.*

au-to-gen-e-sis (â-tǫ-jen′e-sis), *n.* [See *auto-*.] Self-production; spontaneous generation.—**au″to-ge-net′ic** (-ję-net′ik), *a.* Pertaining to autogenesis; self-generated.—**au″to-ge-net′i-cal-ly,** *adv.*

au-to-gen-ic (â-tǫ-jen′ik), *a.* Autogenous.

au-tog-e-nous (â-toj′e-nus), *a.* [Gr. αὐτογενής, < αὐτός, self, + γεν-, bear, produce.] Self-produced; self-generated. —**autogenous soldering,** the process of uniting pieces of metal by fusing them together, without the use of a separate solder.—**au-tog′e-nous-ly,** *adv.*—**au-tog′e-ny,** *n.* Spontaneous generation; autogenesis.

au-to-gi-ro (â-tǫ-jī′rō), *n.*; pl. *-ros* (-rōz). [Sp.: cf. *auto-* and *gyre.*] A form of aëroplane with revolving wings or vanes (forming a sort of extra, horizontal propeller) on an upright axis projecting above the fuselage, which are wind-driven (except at the start), and which lift the machine and allow it to ascend and descend almost vertically. [Proprietary name.]

au-to-graph (â′tǫ-gråf). [L. *autographus,* < Gr. αὐτόγραφος, < αὐτός, self, + γράφειν, write.] **I.** *a.* Written by a person's own hand. **II.** *n.* A person's own handwriting; an autograph signature or manuscript.—**au′to-graph,** *v. t.* To write with one's own hand; also, to write one's autograph on or in; also, to reproduce as in the original writing or form.—**au-to-graph′ic** (-graf′ik), *a.* Pertaining to autograph writing or to autography; written in autograph; reproducing the original writing or form; also, self-recording, as an instrument; recorded by such an instrument, as a record.—**au-to-graph′i-cal-ly,** *adv.*—**au-tog-ra-phy** (â-tog′rą-fi), *n.* Autograph writing; a branch of diplomatics concerned with autographs; also, a lithographic process of reproducing writing, drawing, etc., in facsimile.

au-to-gra-vure (â″tǫ-grą-vūr′ or â-tǫ-grā′vųr), *n.* [Gr. αὐτός, self, + F. *gravure,* engraving.] A kind of photo-engraving.

au-to-gy-ro (â-tǫ-jī′rō), *n.* See *autogiro.*

au-to-harp (â′tǫ-härp″), *n.* [See *auto-*.] A musical instrument of the zither class, having across the strings bars with dampers, each of which, when pressed down, renders all strings mute except those of a particular chord.

au-to-hyp-no-sis (â″tǫ-hip-nō′sis), *n.* [See *auto-*.] Self-induced hypnosis or hypnotic state. Also **au-to-hyp′no-tism** (-nǫ-tizm).—**au″to-hyp-not′ic** (-not′ik), *a.*

au-to=in-fec-tion (â″tǫ-in-fek′shǫn), *n.* [See *auto-*.] In *pathol.*, infection of the body from within.—**au″to=in-oc-u-la′tion,** *n.* In *pathol.*, inoculation of a healthy part with virus from a diseased part of the same body.—**au″to=in-tox-i-ca′tion,** *n.* In *pathol.*, poisoning with toxic substances formed within the body, as during intestinal digestion.

au-to-ist (â′tǫ-ist), *n.* [See *auto, n.*] An automobilist.

au-to-ki-ne-sis (â″tǫ-ki-nē′sis), *n.* [NL., < Gr. αὐτοκίνησις, < αὐτοκινεῖν, move of itself, < αὐτός, self, + κινεῖν, move.] Voluntary or spontaneous motion.—**au″-to-ki-net′ic** (-net′ik), *a.* Self-moving; automatic.

au-tol-a-try (â-tol′ą-tri), *n.* [Gr. αὐτός, self, + λατρεία, worship.] Worship of self.

au-to-lu-mi-nes-cence (â″tǫ-lū-mi-nes′ęns), *n.* [See *auto-*.] The spontaneous emission of luminous rays, as by radioactive substances.—**au″to-lu-mi-nes′cent,** *a.*

au-tol-y-sis (â-tol′i-sis), *n.* [Gr. αὐτός, self, + λύσις, a loosing.] In *physiol.*, digestion or disintegration of tissue by ferments generated in its cells.—**au-to-lyt-ic** (â-tǫ-lit′ik), *a.*

au-to-mat (â′tǫ-mat), *n.* [G., 'automaton.'] An automatic apparatus for serving articles of food to customers upon the dropping of suitable coins or tokens into a slot; a restaurant using such apparatuses.

au-tom-a-ta (â-tom′ą-tą), *n.* Plural of *automaton.*

au-to-math (â′tǫ-math), *n.* [Gr. αὐτομαθής, having learned of one's self, < αὐτός, self, + μανθάνειν, learn.] One who is self-taught; an autodidact.

au-to-mat-ic (â-tǫ-mat′ik), *a.* [Gr. αὐτόματος, self-acting: see *automaton.*] Pertaining to or acting as an automaton; self-moving; self-acting; mechanical; of a firearm, pistol, etc., utilizing the recoil, or part of the force of the explosive, to eject the spent cartridge-shell, introduce a new cartridge, cock the arm, etc.; in *physiol.*, occurring independently of volition, as certain muscular actions; also, independent of external stimuli, as the beating of the heart.—**au-to-mat′i-cal-ly,** *adv.*—**au″to-ma-ti′ci-ty** (-mą-tis′i-ti), *n.*

au-tom-a-tism (â-tom′ą-tizm), *n.* The action or condition of an automaton; mechanical or involuntary action; also, the doctrine that animals are mere automata; in *physiol.*, automatic action.

au-tom-a-ton (â-tom′ą-ton), *n.*; pl. *-tons* or *-ta* (-tą). [L., < Gr. αὐτόματον, neut. of αὐτόματος, self-acting, < αὐτός, self, + -ματος, akin to ματεύειν, seek, strive.] Something capable of acting spontaneously or without external impulse; also, a mechanical figure or contrivance constructed to act as if spontaneously through power communicated; also, a person or animal whose actions are purely mechanical.

au-to-mo-bile (â-tǫ-mō′bil), *a.* [Gr. αὐτός, self, + L. *mobilis,* movable.] Self-moving; carrying its own source of motive power.—**au-to-mo-bile** (â-tǫ-mǫ-bēl′ or â-tǫ-mō′bēl), *n.* [F.] An automobile vehicle; a vehicle, esp. a car or carriage for passengers, carrying its own propelling mechanism, for travel on ordinary roads; a motor-car.—**au-to-mo-bile′,** *v. i.*; *-biled, -biling.* To ride or travel in an automobile. —**au-to-mo′bil-ism,** *n.* The use of automobiles.—**au-to-mo′bil-ist,** *n.* One who uses an automobile.

au-to-mor-phic (â-tǫ-môr′fik), *a.* [Gr. αὐτός, self, + μορφή, form.] Characterized by the ascription of one's own attributes to others.—**au-to-mor′phism,** *n.*

au-to-mo-tive (â-tǫ-mō′tiv), *a.* [See *auto-*.] Self-moving or self-propelled, as a vehicle; carrying its own source of motive power; also, pertaining to self-propelled vehicles.

au-to-nom-ic (â-tǫ-nom′ik), *a.* Of or pertaining to autonomy; autonomous.—**au-to-nom′i-cal-ly,** *adv.*

au-ton-o-mist (â-ton′ǫ-mist), *n.* An advocate of autonomy.

au-ton-o-mize (â-ton′ǫ-mīz), *v. t.*; *-mized, -mizing.* To make autonomous.

au-ton-o-mous (â-ton′ǫ-mus), *a.* [Gr. αὐτόνομος, < αὐτός, self, + νέμειν, deal out, manage.] Self-governing; independent; subject to its own laws only; also, pertaining to an autonomy; in *biol.*, existing as an independent organism and not as a mere form or stage of development of an organism; in *bot.*, spontaneous (as, *autonomous* movements). —**au-ton′o-mous-ly,** *adv.*—**au-ton′o-my** (-mi), *n.*; pl. *-mies* (-miz). [Gr. αὐτονομία, < αὐτόνομος.] The condition of being autonomous; self-government, or the right of self-government; independence; also, a self-governing community.

au-to-nym (â′tǫ-nim), *n.* [Gr. αὐτός, self, + ὄνυμα, name.] A person's, esp. an author's, own name (opposed to *pseudonym*); a work published under the author's own name; in *ethnol.*, the name by which a people calls itself.

au-to-ped (â′tǫ-ped), *n.* [See *auto-* and *-ped.*] A kind of low vehicle with two wheels, one in front of the other, and a tread or footboard between them, and sometimes with a saddle or seat, which is steered by a handle-bar, and propelled by an engine or motor. Also called *scooter.*

au-to-plas-ty (â′tǫ-plas-ti), *n.* [Gr. αὐτόπλαστος, self-formed, < αὐτός, self, + πλάσσειν, form.] In *surg.*, the repairing of lesions with tissue from another part of the patient.—**au-to-plas′tic,** *a.*

au-top-sy (â′top-si), *n.*; pl. *-sies* (-siz). [Gr. αὐτοψία, < αὐτός, self, + ὀπ-, see, as in ὄψις, sight, ὀπτικός, E. *optic.*] A seeing for one's self; personal observation; esp., dissection and inspection of a body after death, as for determination of the cause of death; a post-mortem examination.—**au-top′tic, au-top′ti-cal,** *a.* [Gr. αὐτοπτικός.] Pertaining to or based on personal observation.—**au-top′ti-cal-ly,** *adv.*

au-to-sug-ges-tion (â″tǫ-su-jes′chǫn), *n.* [See *auto-*.] Suggestion by the mind to itself of ideas that operate to produce actual or physical effects.

au-to-tox-e-mi-a, au-to-tox-æ-mi-a (â″tọ-tok-sē′mi-ạ̈), *n.* [See *auto-*.] Same as *auto-intoxication.*—**au-to-tox′in** (-tok′sin), *n.* In *pathol.*, a toxin or poisonous principle formed within the body and acting against it.—**au-to-tox′ic,** *a.*—**au-to-tox′is,** *n.* Same as *auto-intoxication.*

au-to-trans-form-er (â″tọ-trans-fôr′mėr), *n.* [See *auto-*.] In *elect.*, a transformer in which a part of the primary coil is used as a secondary coil, or a part of the secondary coil as a primary coil.

au-to-truck (â′tọ-truk″), *n.* [See *auto-*.] An automobile truck.

au-to-type (â′tọ-tīp), *n.* [See *auto-* and *-type.*] A facsimile; also, a photographic process for producing permanent prints in a carbon pigment; a picture so produced.—**au′to-type,** *v. t.*; *-typed, -typing.* To reproduce by the autotype process.—**au-to-typ′ic** (-tip′ik), *a.*—**au′to-ty-py** (-tī-pi), *n.*

au-tumn (â′tum), *n.* [OF. *autompne* (F. *automne*), < L. *autumnus*; origin uncertain.] The third season of the year, between summer and winter, in North America taken as comprising September, October, and November, in Great Britain August, September, and October; fall; fig., a season of maturity passing into decay.—**au-tum-nal** (â-tum′-nạl), *a.* Belonging to or suggestive of autumn; past maturity.—**au-tum′nal-ly,** *adv.*

au-tun-ite (â′tun-īt), *n.* [From *Autun*, city in eastern France.] A yellow mineral consisting of a hydrous phosphate of uranium and calcium, occurring in tabular crystals with a very nearly square outline.

aux-a-nom-e-ter (âk-sạ-nom′e-tėr), *n.* [Gr. *αὐξάνειν*, increase: see *-meter.*] An instrument for measuring the rate of growth in plants.

aux-e-sis (âk-sē′sis), *n.* [LL., < Gr. *αὔξησις*, < *αὔξειν*, increase.] In *rhet.*, amplification; hyperbole.

aux-il-iar (âg-zil′iạr), *a.* and *n.* Same as *auxiliary.* [Archaic.]—**aux-il′iar-ly,** *adv.*

aux-il-ia-ry (âg-zil′iạ-ri). [L. *auxiliarius*, < *auxilium*, aid, < *augere*, increase.] **I.** *a.* Helping or aiding; giving support; subsidiary or additional (as, *auxiliary* power, supplementary power, as steam on a sailing-vessel); hence, an *auxiliary* schooner, catboat, etc., one fitted with an engine or motor to supplement or replace the power furnished by the sails): often with *to.* **II.** *n.*; pl. *-ries* (-riz). A helper or aid; a confederate; an ally, as in war (usually in *pl.*); a tug, supply-ship, or the like, as distinguished from fighting craft, as in the U. S. navy ('naval auxiliary'); a schooner or other vessel carrying auxiliary power; in *gram.*, a verb, as *have, will, be, may, do,* etc., used in phrase-like tense, voice, mode, and other forms of other verbs; in *math.*, a quantity introduced to facilitate an operation.

a-va[1] (ä′vạ̈), *n.* Same as *kava.*

a-va[2], **a-va′** (ạ-vâ′ or ạ-vä′), *adv.* [For *of a′.*] Of all; at all. [Sc.]

a-vail (ạ-vāl′), *v.* [ME. *availen*, < OF. *a* (< L. *ad*), to, + *valoir*, < L. *valere*, be strong, have force or effect, be worth.] **I.** *intr.* To have force or efficacy; be of use; serve; be of value or profit; be worth (*much, little,* etc.); also, to derive profit†. **II.** *tr.* To be of use or value to; profit; advantage; also, to give (one's self) the advantage (*of*); also, to promote†.—**a-vail′,** *n.* Efficacy for a purpose; use; also, value, profit, or advantage (archaic); *pl.*, profits or proceeds.—**a-vail′a-ble,** *a.* Such as to avail; of use or service; efficacious; profitable; advantageous; also, suitable or ready for use.—**a-vail-a-bil′i-ty** (-bil′i-ti), **a-vail′a-ble-ness,** *n.*—**a-vail′a-bly,** *adv.*—**a-vail′ing-ly,** *adv.*

av-a-lanche (av′ạ-lȧnch), *n.* [F., < OF. *avaler*, go down, < *aval*, downward, < L. *ad*, to, + *vallis*, valley: cf. *amount.*] A large mass of snow, ice, etc., detached from a mountain-slope and sliding or falling suddenly downward. Also fig.

Av-a-lon (av′ạ-lon), *n.* In *Celtic myth.*, the Land of the Blessed, or Isle of Souls, represented as an earthly paradise in the western seas, to which King Arthur and other heroes were carried at death. Also **Av′al-lon, A-vil-ion** (a-vil′yọn).

a-vant=cou-ri-er (ạ-vänt′kö′ri-ėr), *n.* [F. *avant-courrier*, < *avant*, before, + *courrier*, E. *courier.*] One who goes in advance, as a herald; *pl.*, the advance-guard of an army†.

a-vant=garde (ȧ-väṅ-gärd), *n.* [F.] The vanguard.

a-vant=pro-pos (ȧ-väṅ-pro-pō), *n.* [F.] A preface.

av-a-rice (av′ạ-ris), *n.* [OF. F. *avarice*, < L. *avaritia*, < *avarus*, greedy, < *avere*, crave.] Greed of wealth; miserly desire of gain; cupidity; covetousness.—**av-a-ri′cious** (-rish′us), *a.* [OF. F. *avaricieux.*] Characterized by avarice; greedy of wealth; covetous.—**av-a-ri′cious-ly,** *adv.*—**av-a-ri′cious-ness,** *n.*

a-vast (ạ-vȧst′), *interj.* [Prob. < D. *houd vast*, 'hold fast.'] *Naut.*, hold! stop! stay!

av-a-tar (av-ạ-tär′), *n.* [Hind. *avatār*, < Skt. *avatāra*, descent.] In *Hindu myth.*, the descent of a deity to earth in an incarnate form; hence, in general, an incarnation; an embodiment; a concrete manifestation.

a-vaunt (ạ-vânt′ or ạ-vänt′), *interj.* [OF. *avant*, forward: see *advantage.*] Away! begone! as, "*Avaunt,* thou hateful villain, get thee gone!" (Shakspere's "King John," iv. 3. 77). [Archaic.]

a-ve (ā′vē or ä′vā). [L., impv. of *avere*, be or fare well.] **I.** *interj.* Hail! also, farewell! **II.** *n.*; pl. *aves* (ā′vēz or ä′vāz). The salutation 'ave,' as a greeting or a farewell; also, an Ave Maria.—**A-ve Ma-ri-a** (ä′vā mä-rē′ä). [ML.] The "Hail, Mary," a devotion or prayer in the Roman Catholic Church, based on the salutation of the angel Gabriel to the Virgin Mary (Luke, i. 28) and the words of Elizabeth (Luke, i. 42); also, a recitation of this devotion. Also **A-ve Ma-ry** (ā′vē mā′ri).

av-e-na-ceous (av-ẹ-nā′shius), *a.* [L. *avenaceus*, < *avena*, oats.] Of or like oats; of the oat kind.

a-venge (ạ-venj′), *v.*; *avenged, avenging.* [OF. *avengier*, < *a* (< L. *ad*), to, + *vengier*, E. *venge.*] **I.** *tr.* To take vengeance or exact atonement on behalf of (a person, etc., conceived as wronged); also, to take vengeance for (a wrong, etc.). **II.** *intr.* To take vengeance.—**a-venge′ment,** *n.* Vengeance.—**a-ven′ger,** *n.*—**a-ven′ging-ly,** *adv.*

Avenger. A U. S. torpedo bomber (Grumman).

av-ens (av′ẹnz), *n.* [OF. *avence.*] Any of the perennial rosaceous herbs constituting the genus *Geum*, esp. *G. urbanum* ('common avens,' or herb-bennet) or *G. rivale* ('water-avens,' or 'purple avens').

av-en-tail (av′ẹn-tāl), *n.* Same as *ventail.*

a-ven-tu-rine (ạ-ven′tụ-rin), *n.* [F., < It. *avventurino*, < *avventura*, chance, the glass having orig. been made by chance.] An opaque brown glass containing fine gold-colored particles; also, any of several minerals, varieties of quartz or feldspar, spangled with bright particles of mica or other minerals; also, a gold-flecked brown sealing-wax.

av-e-nue (av′ẹ-nū), *n.* [F., orig. pp. fem. of *avenir*, < L. *advenire*, come to: see *advene.*] A way of approach or passage; a road or walk leading through grounds, as to a house; also, a wide street, often bordered with trees.

a-ver[1] (ạ-vėr′), *v. t.*; *averred, averring.* [OF. *averer*, < ML. *adverare*, prove true, < L. *ad*, to, + *verus*, true.] To prove true†; confirm†; also, to assert as a fact; affirm or declare positively; avouch; also, to assert the existence of (archaic); in *law*, to allege as a fact; offer to verify.

a-ver[2] (ā′vėr), *n.* [OF. *aver, aveir:* see *havior.*] Property†; also, a beast of burden (north. Eng. and Sc.).

av-er-age (av′ẹ-rạj). [F. *avarie* = It. *avaria* = Sp. *avería*; origin obscure.] **I.** *n.* A duty or tax on goods†; some special charge or expense incurred in shipping (as, petty *averages*); an expense, partial loss, or damage, on ship or cargo, due to some accident of navigation, or the incidence of such expense on the owners or their insurers (as, general *average*, affecting all the owners of ship and cargo or their insurers; particular *average*, affecting a particular owner or his insurers); an equitable apportionment among all the parties interested of expense or loss incurred for the safety of ship and cargo; hence, determination of a quantity intermediate to a number of different quantities (as by adding them and dividing the sum by their number); a quantity intermediate to a set of quantities; an arithmetical mean; also, an estimate of the medium for any set of specific cases; the medium as estimated; also, the ordinary amount, rate, quality, kind, etc.; the common run. **II.** *a.* Of or pertaining to an average; estimated by average; forming an average; intermediate or medial in amount, rate, quality, etc.; medium; ordinary; usual.—**av′er-age,** *v.*; *-aged, -aging.* **I.** *tr.* To apportion (marine losses, etc.) by average; also, to find the average amount, rate, etc., of; fix at a particular average; also, to accomplish or have as an average; amount to as an average. **II.** *intr.* To have or show an average: as, to *average* as expected; to *average* well.—**av′er-age-ly,** *adv.*—**av′er-ag-er,** *n.*

a-ver-ment (ạ-vėr′mẹnt), *n.* The act of averring; positive assertion; affirmation; allegation; also, a positive statement.

A-ver-nus (ạ-vėr′nus), *n.* [L. (It. *Averno*).] A small lake near Naples, Italy, occupying the crater of an extinct volcano, anciently fabled to be the entrance to the infernal regions; hence, the infernal regions.

a-ver-ra-ble (ạ-vėr′ạ-bl), *a.* That may be averred.

Av-er-ro-ism (av-ẹ-rō′izm), *n.* The philosophy of Averroës (about 1126–98), consisting chiefly of a pantheistic interpretation of the doctrines of Aristotle.—**Av-er-ro′ist,** *n.* A follower of Averroës; an adherent of Averroism.—**Av″er-ro-is′tic** (-ẹ-rọ̄-is′tik), *a.*

a-verse (ạ-vėrs′), *a.* [L. *aversus*, pp. of *avertere*: see *avert.*] Turned away or back (now chiefly in *bot.*); also, disinclined, reluctant, or opposed (now usually with *to*, sometimes, as formerly, *from*); also, unfavorable.—**a-verse′ly,** *adv.*—**a-verse′ness,** *n.*

a-ver-sion (ạ-vėr′shọn), *n.* [L. *aversio(n-)*, < *avertere*: see *avert.*] A turning away†; also, repugnance, antipathy, or rooted dislike (now usually with *to* or *for*); also, an object of repugnance.

a-vert (ạ-vėrt′), *v. t.* [L. *avertere*, < *a*, from, + *vertere*, turn.] To turn away or aside; also, to alienate or render unfavorable (archaic); also, to ward off; prevent.—**a-vert′ed-ly,** *adv.*—**a-vert′er,** *n.*—**a-vert′i-ble, a-vert′a-ble,** *a.* That may be averted.

A-ves (ā′vēz), *n. pl.* [L., pl. of *avis*, bird.] In *zoöl.*, the class of vertebrates comprising the birds.

A-ves-ta (ạ-ves′tạ), *n.* The sacred writings of the ancient Zoroastrian religion, still in use by the Parsees.—**A-ves′tan. I.** *a.* Of or pertaining to the Avesta or its language. **II.** *n.* The language of the Avesta, an ancient Persian (Iranian) dialect. Cf. *Zend.*

a-vi-an (ā′vi-ạn), *a.* [L. *avis*, bird.] Of or pertaining to birds (the class *Aves*, of vertebrates); ornithic.

a-vi-a-ry (ā′vi-ā-ri), *n.*; pl. *-ries* (-riz). [L. *aviarium*, < *avis*, bird.] A large cage or a house or inclosure in which birds are kept.—**a′vi-a-rist,** *n.*

a-vi-ate (ā′vi-āt), *v. i.*; *-ated, -ating.* [L. *avis*, bird.] To fly by mechanical means; practise aviation.—**a-vi-at′ic** (-at′ik), *a.* Of or pertaining to aviation.—**a-vi-at′ics,** *n.* The art or science of aviation.—**a-vi-a′tion** (-ā′shọn), *n.* [= F. *aviation.*] The act, art, or science of flying by mechanical means, esp. with machines heavier than air; navigation of the air with flying-machines or aëroplanes.—**a′vi-a-tor,** *n.* [= F. *aviateur.*] One who practises aviation; also, a flying-machine or aëroplane.—**a″vi-a-to′ri-al** (-ạ-tō′ri-ạl), **a′vi-a-to-ry** (-tọ̄-ri), *a.*—**a′vi-a-tress** (-ā-tres), **a-vi-a′trix** (-ā′triks), *n.* [Cf. F. *aviatrice.*] A woman who practises aviation. Also **a′vi-a-trice** (-tris).

av-i-cide (av′i-sīd), *n.* [L. *avis*, bird: see *-cide.*] The slaying of birds.—**av′i-ci-dal** (-sī-dạl), *a.*

a-vi-cul-ture (ā′vi-kul-tụ̄r), *n.* [L. *avis*, bird, + *cultura*, culture.] The rearing or keeping of birds.—**a-vi-cul′tur-ist,** *n.*

av-id (av′id), *a.* [L. *avidus*, < *avere*, crave.] Eager; greedy: often with *of.*—**a-vid-i-ty** (ạ-vid′i-ti), *n.* Eagerness; greediness.—**av′id-ly,** *adv.*

a-vi-ette (ā-vi-et′), *n.* [F., dim. < L. *avis*, bird.] In *aëronautics*, a bicycle or the like equipped with a plane or planes, etc., and capable of making flights through the air for longer or shorter distances after attaining a sufficient speed in moving along the ground.—**a-vi-ette′,** *v. i.*; *-etted, -etting.*

a-vi-fau-na (ā′vi-fâ-nạ), *n.* [NL., < L. *avis*, bird, + NL. *fauna.*] The birds of a region.—**a′vi-fau-nal,** *a.*

av-i-ga-tion (av-i-gā′shọn), *n.* [See *aviate* and *navigation.*] Aërial navigation.—**av′i-gate,** *v. t.* or *i.*

a-vion (à-vyôn), *n.* [F., < L. *avis*, bird.] An aëroplane.—**avion de chasse** (dė shâs). [F.] A swift aëroplane for chasing or pursuing enemy aircraft.

av-o-ca-do (av-ọ̄-kä′dō), *n.*; pl. *-dos* (-dōz). [Corruption of Mex. *ahuacatl.*] A tropical American fruit resembling a large green or purplish pear, borne by a lauraceous tree, *Persea persea*, and eaten raw, esp. with salad dressing; the alligator-pear; also, the tree.

Avocado, or Alligator-pear.

av-o-ca-tion (av-ọ̄-kā′shọn), *n.* [L. *avocatio(n-)*, < *avocare*, call away, < *a*, from, + *vocare*, call.] A calling away†; diversion or distraction (archaic); also, something that calls or takes one away from his regular or proper business; a minor occupation; a distraction; less correctly, one's regular occupation, calling, or vocation.

av-o-cet, av-o-set (av′ọ̄-set), *n.* [F. *avocette*, < It. *avosetta*, said to be < L. *avis*, bird.] Any of the long-legged, web-footed shore-birds constituting the genus *Recurvirostra*, of both hemispheres, having a characteristic long, slender beak curving upward toward the end.

a-void (ạ-void′), *v.* [AF. *avoider*, OF. *esvuidier*, < *es-* (< L. *ex*, out of) + *vuidier*, empty, E. *void, v.*] **I.** *tr.* To empty out (a vessel, etc., or the contents)†; eject† or expel†; get rid of†; depart from†; keep away from; keep clear of; shun; eschew; evade; in *law*, to make void or of no effect; invalidate. **II.** *intr.* To depart (archaic); escape†; in *law*, to become void or vacant†.—**a-void′a-ble,** *a.* Capable of being avoided.—**a-void′a-bly,** *adv.*—**a-void′ance,** *n.* The act of avoiding; a keeping away from or shunning; in *law*, a making void, invalidating, or annulling; a becoming or being void or vacant; vacancy, as of an office or benefice.—**a-void′er,** *n.*—**a-void′less,** *a.* Unavoidable; inevitable. [Poetic.]

av-oir-du-pois (av″ọr-dụ̄-poiz′), *n.* [OF. *avoir de pois, aveir de peis*, 'goods of weight.'] Goods sold by weight†; avoirdupois weight (see below); weight (colloq.).—**avoirdupois weight,** the system of weights in British and U. S. use for goods other than gems, precious metals, and drugs: 16 drams = 1 ounce; 16 ounces = 1 pound; 112 pounds (Brit.) or 100 pounds (U. S.) = 1 hundredweight; 20 hundredweight = 1 ton (2,240 pounds, 'long ton'; 2,000 pounds, 'short ton'). The pound avoirdupois contains 7,000 grains, the grain being the samẹ as in the troy and apothecaries' weights (in which, however, the pound contains 5,760 grains).

av-o-set (av′ọ̄-set), *n.* See *avocet.*

a-vouch (ạ-vouch′), *v.* [OF. *avochier*, < L. *advocare*, summon: see *advocate.*] **I.** *tr.* To cite as warrant or proof†; prove†; warrant or guarantee; also, to affirm or declare as with warrant; assert; maintain; also, to acknowledge, own, or avow. **II.** *intr.* To give assurance; also, to affirm.—**a-vouch′,** *n.* Avouchment; assurance. [Archaic.]—**a-vouch′a-ble,** *a.* That may be avouched.—**a-vouch′er,** *n.*—**a-vouch′ment,** *n.* The act of avouching; declaration; assurance.

a-vow (ạ-vou′), *v. t.* [OF. *avoer* (F. *avouer*), < L. *advocare*: see *advocate.*] To acknowledge connection with or responsibility for (a person, action, etc.); own; acknowledge, confess, or admit; declare frankly or openly; avouch.—**a-vow′a-ble,** *a.* That may be avowed.—**a-vow′al,** *n.* The act of avowing; acknowledgment; open declaration.—**a-vowed′,** *p. a.* Acknowledged; declared; open.—**a-vow′ed-ly,** *adv.*—**a-vow′ed-ness,** *n.*—**a-vow′er,** *n.*—**a-vow′ry** (-ri), *n.*; pl. *-ries* (-riz). [OF. *avoerie.*] Patronage† or protection†; a patron†; a patron saint†; in *law*, avowal of an act, esp. that of a distrainer of goods who, in an action of replevin, avows and justifies the taking as done in his own right.

a-vul-sion (ạ-vul′shọn), *n.* [L. *avulsio(n-)*, < *avellere*, pluck off, < *a*, from, + *vellere*, pluck.] A plucking or tearing off; a part torn off†; in *law*, sudden removal of land, as by flood, to another's estate.

a-vun-cu-lar (ạ-vung′kụ̄-lạr), *a.* [L. *avunculus*, uncle, dim. of *avus*, grandfather.] Of or pertaining to an uncle.

a-wa (ạ-wâ′ or ạ-wä′), *adv.* Scotch form of *away.*

a-wait (ạ-wāt′), *v.* [OF. *awaitier*, < *a* (< L. *ad*), to, + *waitier*, watch, E. *wait.*] **I.** *tr.* To watch for†; lie in wait for†; wait for; stay or remain in expectation of; also, to be in store for. **II.** *intr.* To watch†; wait or attend (*on*)†; wait as in expectation.—**a-wait′er,** *n.*

a-wake (ạ-wāk′), *v.*; *awoke* or *awaked, awaking.* [AS. *āwacan* (earlier *onwacan*) (pret. *āwōc*, pp. *āwacen*), also *āwacian* (pret. *āwacode*, pp. *āwacod*), < *ā-* (*on-*) + *wacan, wacian*, E. *wake*[2].] **I.** *intr.* To wake up; come out of sleep; hence, to become roused to consciousness, attention, activity, etc.; also, to remain awake (archaic). **II.** *tr.* To rouse from sleep, inaction, etc.; arouse; excite.—**a-wake′,** *a.* [ME. *awake*, pp., for *awaken*, < AS. *āwacen*, pp.] Waking; not sleeping; hence, vigilant; alert.

a-wak-en (ạ-wā′kn), *v. i.* or *t.* [AS. *āwæcnan*, earlier *onwæcnan*, < *on-* + *wæcnan*, E. *waken.*] To awake; waken.—**a-wak′en-er,** *n.*—**a-wak′en-ment,** *n.* An awakening.

a-wane (ạ-wān′), *adv.* On the wane.

a-want-ing (ạ-won′ting), *a.* Wanting; lacking.

a-ward (ạ-wârd′), *v. t.* [AF. *awarder*, OF. *eswarder, esguarder*, observe, consider, decide, < *es-* (< L. *ex*, out of) + *warder, guarder*, watch, guard: see *guard.*] To decide or determine after consideration†; also, to appoint by judicial sentence; assign by deliberate judgment, as in arbitration; adjudge; allot; also, to sentence†.—**a-ward′,** *n.* [AF. *award*, OF. *eswart, esguart.*] A decision after consideration; a judicial sentence; the decision of arbitrators on points submitted to them, or the document containing it; also, something awarded.—**a-ward′a-ble,** *a.* That may be awarded.—**a-ward′er,** *n.*

a-ware (ạ-wãr′), *a.* [AS. *gewær*, < *ge-*, together, altogether, + *wær*, wary.] Watchful† or wary†; also, cognizant or conscious (often with *of*); sensible; apprised; informed.—**a-ware′ness,** *n.*

a-wash (ạ-wosh′), *adv.* At such a level as to be washed by the waves; washed over; also, washed about, as on the waves.

a-way (ạ-wā′), *adv.* [AS. *aweg*, earlier *on weg*, 'on way.'] Onward or along; on, continuously (as, to blaze *away*); to or at a distance; apart; aside; absent; off, as from a place or position; out of possession, notice, use, or existence. Sometimes used elliptically, with verb suppressed: as, we must *away*; whither *away?*

awe (â), *n.* [Icel. *agi* = AS. *ege*, fear.] Fear† or dread†; respectful or reverential fear; a feeling of wondering reverence, approaching fear, inspired by what is grand or sublime; also, power to inspire fear or reverence (archaic).—**awe,** *v. t.*; *awed, awing.* To inspire with awe; influence or restrain by awe.

a-wear-y (ạ-wẽr′i), *a.* Weary. [Now poetic.]

a-weath-er (ạ-weᴛʜ′ėr), *adv.* *Naut.*, on or to the weather side; toward the wind: opposed to *alee.*

a-weigh (ạ-wā′), *adv.* *Naut.*, raised just enough to be clear of the ground and hanging perpendicularly: said of an anchor.

awe-less (â′les), *a.* Without awe; fearless; not to be awed; devoid of reverence; also, inspiring no awe†.—**awe′less-ness,** *n.*

awe-some (â′sum), *a.* Inspiring awe; awful; also, characterized by awe; awed.—**awe′some-ly,** *adv.*—**awe′some-ness,** *n.*

awe=strick-en, awe=struck (â′strik″n, -struk), *a.* Struck or impressed with awe.

awe=strike (â′strīk), *v. t.*; pret. *-struck*, pp. *-struck* or *-stricken*, ppr. *-striking.* To strike with awe.

aw-ful (â′ful), *a.* [Cf. AS. *egefull.*] Such as to inspire fear; dreadful or terrible; also, full of fear or dread†; also, inspiring reverential awe; solemnly impressive; also, full of awe; reverential; also, extremely bad, unpleasant, ugly, etc. (colloq.); very great (colloq.).—**aw′ful-ly,** *adv.*—**aw′ful-ness,** *n.*

a-while (ạ-hwīl′), *adv.* [Prop. two words, *a while.*] For a while or time.

a-whirl (ạ-hwėrl′), *adv.* In a whirl.

a-wing (ạ-wing′), *adv.* On the wing.

awk-ward (âk′wạrd), *a.* [ME. *awke*, backhanded (prob. < Icel. *öfigr*, turning the wrong way, < *af*, = E. *off*), + *-ward*: see *-ward.*] Turned the wrong way†; untoward†; perverse†; unhandy, clumsy, or bungling; ungraceful or uncouth; embarrassed; also, embarrassing or trying; requiring caution.—**awk′ward-ly,** *adv.*—**awk′ward-ness,** *n.*

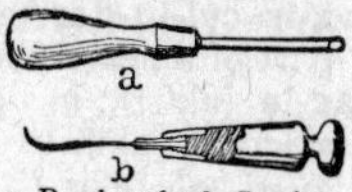

a, Brad-awl; *b*, Sewing-awl.

awl (âl), *n.* [AS. *āwel, āl, æl*, = G. *ahle.*] A pointed instrument for piercing small holes in leather, wood, etc.

aw-less (â′les), etc. See *aweless*, etc.

awl-wort (âl′wėrt), *n.* A small, stemless, aquatic brassicaceous plant, *Subularia aquatica*, with awl-shaped leaves.

awn (ân), *n.* [Appar. < Icel. *ögn*, chaff.] A bristle-like appendage of a plant, esp. on the glumes of grasses, or such appendages collectively, as those forming the beard of wheat, barley, etc.—**awned,** *a.* Having awns.

awn-ing (â′ning), *n.* [Prob. < F. *auvent*, penthouse; origin uncertain.] A roof-like shelter of canvas or other material before a window or door, over a deck, etc., as for protection from the sun.—**awn′inged,** *a.*

awn-less (ân′les), *a.* Without an awn.

awn-y (â′ni), *a.* Having awns; bearded, as grain.

a-woke (ạ-wōk′). Pret. and pp. of *awake.*

a-wry (ạ-rī′), *adv.* and *a.* In a wry state or manner; with a turn or twist to one side; askew; fig., amiss; wrong.

aw-some (â′sum), etc. See *awesome*, etc.

ax, axe (aks), *n.* [AS. *æx*, akin to G. *axt*, L. *ascia*, Gr. ἀξίνη, ax.] An instrument with a bladed head on a handle or helve, used for hewing, cleaving, chopping, etc.—**ax, axe,** *v. t.*; *axed, axing.* To cut, shape, or dress with an ax.

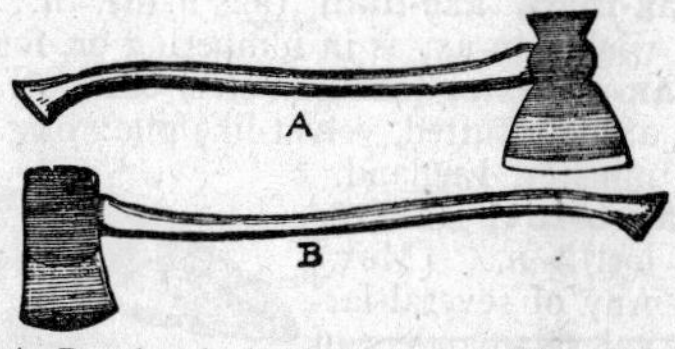

A, Broadax, for hewing; *B*, Ax for chopping.

ax=ham-mer (aks′-ham″ėr), *n.* An ax with two opposite cutting edges, for dressing rougher kinds of stone.—**ax′=ham″mered,** *a.* Of stone, dressed with an ax-hammer.

ax-i-al (ak′si-ạl), *a.* Of, pertaining to, or forming an axis.—**ax′i-al-ly,** *adv.* In the line or direction of the axis.

ax-il (ak′sil), *n.* [L. *axilla*, armpit.] In *bot.*, the angle between the upper side of a leaf or stem and the supporting stem or branch.

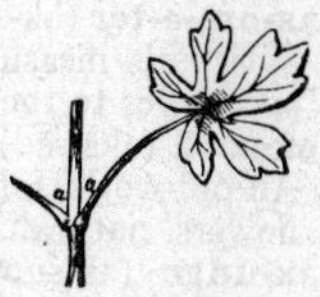
a, a, Axils.

ax-ile (ak′sil), *a.* Of or in an axis; axial.

ax-il-la (ak-sil′ä), *n.*; pl. *axillæ* (-ē). [L., armpit.] In *anat.*, the armpit; also, the corresponding region under a bird's wing; in *bot.*, an axil.—**ax-il-lar** (ak′si-lạ̈r). **I.** *a.* Axillary. **II.** *n.* One of the under wing-coverts of a bird, growing from the axilla: usually in *pl.*—**ax-il-la-ry** (ak′si-lạ̈-ri). **I.** *a.* Pertaining to the axilla or axil; situated in or growing from the axil of a plant. **II.** *n.*; pl. *-ries* (-riz). An axillar.

ax-i-nite (ak′si-nīt), *n.* [Gr. ἀξίνη, ax.] A mineral consisting essentially of an aluminium and calcium borosilicate, commonly occurring in flattened brown crystals edged like an ax.

ax-i-om (ak′si-ọm), *n.* [L. *axioma*, < Gr. ἀξίωμα, < ἀξιοῦν, think worthy, < ἄξιος, worthy, < ἄγειν, lead, weigh.] A self-evident proposition; a recognized truth; an established principle.—**ax″i-o-mat′ic** (-ọ-mat′ik), *a.* [Gr. ἀξιωματικός.] Pertaining to or of the nature of an axiom; self-evident; also, full of axioms. Also **ax″i-o-mat′i-cal.**—**ax″i-o-mat′i-cal-ly,** *adv.*

ax-is[1] (ak′sis), *n.*; pl. *axes* (-sēz). [L., axle, axis, board: cf. *axle.*] An axle; a piece or part on which something turns; an imaginary line about which a body rotates; a central or principal line in a symmetrical arrangement or in any system (as, the *axis* of a crystal, any of the imaginary lines assumed for convenience to define the position of the planes of the crystal, and to exhibit its symmetry); a central or principal animal or plant structure, about which something turns or is arranged; specif., in *anat.*, the second cervical vertebra, on which the atlas (supporting the head) turns; in *bot.*, the longitudinal support on which organs or parts are arranged; the stem; also [usually *cap.*], the alliance between Germany and Italy formed in Oct., 1936, or the parties to it (often attrib.).

ax-is[2] (ak′sis), *n.* [L.] An East Indian deer, *Cervus axis*, with white spots.

ax-is=cyl-in-der (ak′sis-sil′in-dėr), *n.* In *anat.*, the central part of a nerve-fiber.

ax-le (ak′sl), *n.* [ME. *axel-*, in *axeltre*, < Icel. *öxultrē*, axletree; akin to AS. *eaxl*, shoulder, and *eax*, L. *axis*, Gr. ἄξων, axle, axis.] The pin, bar, shaft, or the like, on which or together with which a wheel or wheels rotate; either end (spindle) of an axletree or the like; the whole (fixed) axletree, or a similar bar connecting and turning with two opposite wheels of a vehicle; also, the axis of rotation of a planet or the like (obs. or poetic).—**ax′le=box,** *n.* The box which contains the bearings for the spindle of an axle, or the journal of an axle, as of a car-wheel; also, a bushing which forms the rotatory bearing of an axle.—**ax′led,** *a.* Having an axle.—**ax′le=guard,** *n.* Those parts of a railroad-car in which the axle-box plays vertically under the action of the car-springs.—**ax′le-tree,** *n.* [ME. *axeltre*, < Icel. *öxultrē*.] A bar fixed crosswise under the body of a vehicle, with a rounded spindle at each end upon which a wheel rotates.

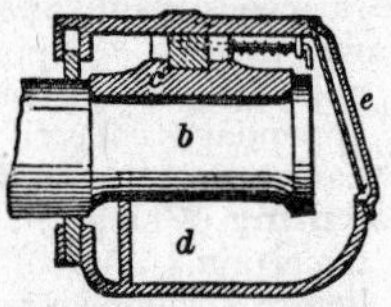

Railroad-car Axle-box.
b, journal; *c*, saddle, by means of which the weight of the car rests on the journal; *d*, chamber for a lubricating substance, having its lid at *e*.

ax-man, axe-man (aks′mạn), *n.*; pl. *-men*. One who wields an ax, as in lumbering or, formerly, in battle.

Ax-min-ster (aks′min-stėr) **car′pet.** A kind of carpet with a finely tufted, velvet-like pile: orig. made, by hand, at Axminster, England.

ax-o-lotl (ak′sọ-lotl), *n.* [Mex.] Any of several larval salamanders of the genus *Amblystoma*, of Mexico and the U. S., that usually retain their gills through life and breed in the larval state (hence formerly classed as a distinct genus, *Siredon*): in Mexico prized as food.

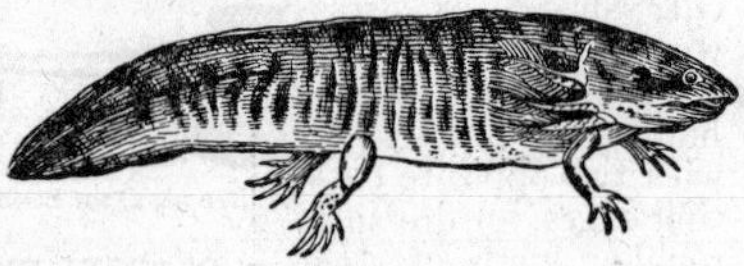
Axolotl.

ax-om-e-ter (ak-som′e-tėr), *n.* [See *axis*[1] and *-meter*.] An optician's measuring device used in adjusting the frames of spectacles to the centers of the eyes.

ax-seed (aks′sēd), *n.* [So called from the ax-shaped seed.] An old-world fabaceous plant, *Coronilla varia*, with pinkish flowers, naturalized in the U. S.

ax-unge (ak′sunj), *n.* [F. *axunge* (now *axonge*), < L. *axungia*, < *axis*, axle, + *ungere*, smear.] Fat or grease, esp. of hogs or geese; in *phar.*, lard prepared for use in medicine.

ay[1], **aye**[1] (ā), *adv.* [Icel. *ei* = AS. *ā* = G. *je* = Goth. *aiw*, akin to Gr. ἀεί, ever.] Ever; always. [Now poetic or prov.]

ay[2] (ā), *interj.* [ME. *ey*; with *ay me* cf. OF. *aimi*, It. *ahime*, Sp. *ay de mí*.] Ah! O!—an exclamation of surprise, interest, regret, etc.: now prov., except in *ay me* (poetic).

ay[3] (ī), *adv.* and *n.* See *aye*[2].

a-yah (ä′yä), *n.* [Hind. *āya*, < Pg. *aia*, fem. of *aio*, tutor.] In the East Indies, a native maid or nurse.

aye[1] (ā), *adv.* See *ay*[1].

aye[2], **ay**[3] (ī), *adv.* [Origin uncertain.] Yes: a word expressing assent.—**aye**[2], **ay**[3], *n.* An expression of assent; an affirmative vote or voter.

aye=aye (ī′ī), *n.* [Native name: prob. imit. of the cry.] A squirrel-like nocturnal animal, *Daubentonia madagascariensis*, of Madagascar, of the lemur kind.

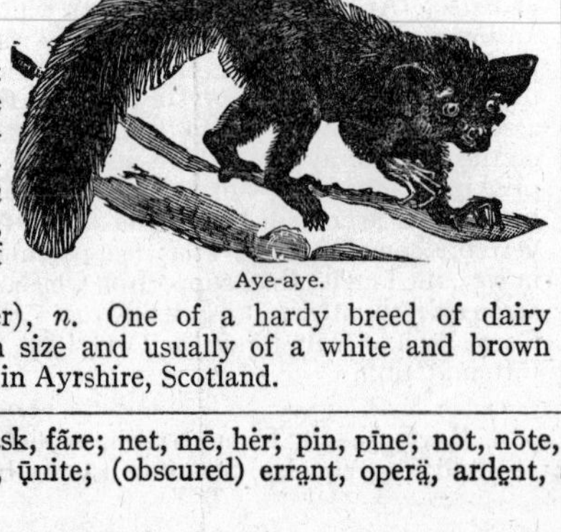
Aye-aye.

Ayr-shire (ãr′shėr), *n.* One of a hardy breed of dairy cattle of medium size and usually of a white and brown color, originating in Ayrshire, Scotland.

a-yun-ta-mien-to (ä-yön-tä-myen′tō), *n.*; pl. *-tos* (-tōs). [Sp.] In Spanish-speaking countries, a body of municipal magistrates; a town council; also, a town hall.

a-za-le-a (ạ-zā′lē-ạ̈), *n.* [NL. (so named as growing in dry soil), < Gr. ἀζαλέος, dry, < ἄζειν, parch.] Any plant of the ericaceous genus *Azalea*, allied to the rhododendron, comprising species with handsome, variously colored flowers, some of which are familiar in cultivation.

a-zan (ạ-zän′), *n.* [Ar.] In Mohammedan countries, the call to prayer, proclaimed by the muezzin from the minaret or the top of a mosque.

az-a-role (az′ạ-rōl), *n.* [F. *azerole*, < Ar. *al*, the, + *zu'rūr*, azarole.] The slightly acid, pleasantly flavored fruit, about the size of a cherry, of a malaceous tree, *Cratægus azarolus*, a species of hawthorn of southern Europe, or the tree itself; Neapolitan medlar.

a-zed-a-rach (ạ-zed′ạ-rak), *n.* [F. *azédarac*, < Pers. *āzād dirakht*, 'free (noble) tree.'] An East Indian meliaceous tree, *Melia azedarach*, cultivated elsewhere for ornament; the china-tree; also, the cathartic and emetic bark of its root.

az-i-muth (az′i-muth), *n.* [OF. *azimut*, < Ar. *al*, the, + *sumūt*, pl. of *samt*, way.] In *astron.*, an arc of the horizon intercepted between the meridian of a place and the vertical circle passing through the center of a celestial object.—**az′i-muth-al,** *a.*—**az′i-muth-al-ly,** *adv.*

az-in, az-ine (az′in), *n.* [From *azote*.] In *chem.*, any of a group of organic compounds containing a benzene ring with one or more of its carbon atoms replaced by nitrogen or by nitrogen and another element.

az-o- (az′ọ-). A form of *azote* in compounds: as, *azo*-dyes (coal-tar colors containing the diatomic group —N=N—, bound on either side to a benzene radical). Also **az′o,** *a.*

a-zo-ic (a-zō′ik), *a.* [Gr. ἄζωος, lifeless, < ἀ- priv. + ζωή, life.] Destitute of organic life; [*cap.*] in *geol.*, noting or pertaining to a division of Archæan time destitute of organic life (cf. *Archæozoic*).

az-o=im-ide (az-ọ-im′īd or -id), *n.* In *chem.*, hydrazoic acid.

az-ole (az′ōl), *n.* [From *azote*.] In *chem.*, any of a class of organic compounds containing a five-membered ring of atoms, at least one of which is nitrogen.

a-zon-ic (a-zon′ik), *a.* [Gr. ἀζωνικός, < ἀ- priv. + ζωνή, zone.] Not confined to any particular zone or region; not local.

a-zo-ni-um (a-zō′ni-um), *n.* [From *azote*.] In *chem.*, any of a class of organic compounds containing a pentavalent nitrogen atom together with a second nitrogen atom.

az-ote (az′ōt), *n.* [Gr. ἀ- priv. + ζώειν, var. of ζάειν, live (the gas being unfit to support life in respiration).] Nitrogen.—**az′ot-ed** (-ọ-ted), *a.* Nitrogenized.

az-oth (az′oth), *n.* [= F. *azoth, azoch*, < Ar. *al*, the, + *zāūq*, mercury.] In *alchemy*, mercury, as the assumed first principle of all metals; also, the universal remedy of Paracelsus.

a-zot-ic (a-zot′ik), *a.* Of or pertaining to azote; nitric.

az-o-tize (az′ọ-tīz), *v. t.*; *-tized, -tizing*. To nitrogenize.

Az-tec (az′tek). **I.** *n.* A member of an Indian people dominant in central Mexico at the time of the Spanish invasion (1519); also, their language, still spoken by Mexican Indians. **II.** *a.* Of or pertaining to the Aztecs or their language.—**Az′tec-an,** *a.*

az-ure (azh′ụr or ā′zhụr). [OF. F. *azur*, < Ar. *lāzward*, < Pers. *lājward*, lapis lazuli.] **I.** *n.* Lapis lazuli†; also, a blue pigment, now esp. cobalt blue; also, the clear blue color of the unclouded sky; sky-blue; also, the blue vault of heaven. **II.** *a.* Of the color of blue sky; blue.—**az′ure,** *v. t.*; *-ured, -uring*. To color blue.—**az′ure=stone,** *n.* Lapis lazuli; also, azurite.—**az-ur-ite** (azh′ụ-rīt), *n.* A blue mineral, a hydrous carbonate of copper: one of the ores of copper.—**az-urn**† (azh′ụrn or ā′zhụrn), *a.* Azure; blue.—**az′ur-y,** *a.* Bluish; blue.

az-y-gous (az′i-gus), *a.* [Gr. ἄζυγος, < ἀ- priv. + ζυγόν, yoke.] In *anat.*, not being one of a pair; single.

az-ym, az-yme (az′im), *n.* [LL. *azymus*, < Gr. ἄζυμος, unleavened, < ἀ- priv. + ζύμη, leaven.] A cake of unleavened bread, as that in Jewish use at the Passover.—**a-zym-ic** (a-zim′ik), **az-y-mous** (az′i-mus), *a.* Unleavened.

B

B, b (bē); pl. *B's, b's* (bēz). A consonant, the 2d letter of the English alphabet.

baa (bä), *v. i.*; *baaed, baaing.* [Imit.] To cry as a sheep; bleat.—**baa,** *n.* The cry of a sheep.

Ba-al (bā'a̦l), *n.*; pl. *Baalim* (bā'a̦-lim). [Heb. *ba'al,* possessor, lord.] The title of numerous local deities among the ancient Semitic peoples, typifying the productive forces of nature and worshiped with much sensuality; esp., a solar deity, the chief god of the Phenicians; in general, a false god. Cf. *Bel* and *Astarte.*—**Ba'al-ism,** *n.* Baal-worship; hence, gross idolatry.—**Ba'al-ist, Ba'al-ite** (-īt), *n.*

bab-bitt (bab'it), *n.* Babbitt metal.—**bab'bitt,** *v. t.* To line, face, or furnish with Babbitt metal.

Bab-bitt (bab'it) **met'al.** [From Isaac *Babbitt* (1799–1862), American inventor.] An antifriction metal, an alloy of tin, antimony, and copper, used for bearings, etc.; also, any of various similar alloys used for the same purpose.

bab-ble (bab'l), *v.*; *-bled, -bling.* [Cf. D. LG. *babbelen,* Icel. *babbla,* Dan. *bable,* F. *babiller*; all ult. imit.] **I.** *intr.* To utter words imperfectly, as a child; talk irrationally or foolishly; prattle; chatter; also, to make a murmuring sound. **II.** *tr.* To utter incoherently or foolishly; also, to reveal by talking too freely; blab.—**bab'ble,** *n.* Inarticulate speech; senseless or foolish prattle; murmuring sound.—**bab'ble-ment,** *n.* Babbling; babble.—**bab'bler,** *n.*—**bab'bling-ly,** *adv.*

babe (bāb), *n.* [ME.; prob. ult. < *ba,* syllable of infant utterance.] A young child; an infant; a baby; also, one who has the innocence, inexperience, etc., of an infant; also, a doll†.

Ba-bel (bā'be̦l), *n.* [Heb. *Bābel,* Babylon.] An ancient city (Babylon) where, according to Gen. xi. 4–9, the building of a tower intended to reach to heaven was begun and a confounding of the language of the people took place; fig., any excessively lofty structure or ambitious scheme; [usually *l. c.*] a scene of noise and confusion; a confusion of sounds.

ba-bies'=breath (bā'biz-breth'), *n.* See *baby's-breath.*

Bab-i-ism (bäb'ē̦-izm), *n.* Same as *Babism.*

bab-i-ru-sa (bab-i-rö'sa̦), *n.* [Malay *bābi rūsa,* 'hog deer.'] A wild, or sometimes domesticated, East Indian species of swine, *Babirusa alfurus,* the male being remarkable for its peculiar canines or tusks, of which the upper pair grow upward from their bases, pierce the skin of the face, and curve backward like horns, and the lower pair, shorter and less curved, protrude between the lips.

Babirusa.

Bab-ism (bäb'izm), *n.* [Pers. *bāb,* 'gate,' assumed as a title by the founder of the sect.] The belief and practice of a pantheistic Persian sect, founded about 1844 by Mirza Ali Mohammed, inculcating a high morality, recognizing the equality of the sexes, and forbidding polygamy.—**Bab'ist,** *n.*

ba-boo (bä'bö), etc. See *babu,* etc.

ba-boon (ba-bön'), *n.* [OF. *babuin*; origin uncertain.] Any of various (usually) large and ferocious monkeys, with a dog-like muzzle, large cheek-pouches, naked ischial callosities, and a short tail, which constitute the genus *Papio* or *Cynocephalus* (subfamily *Cynopithecinæ*) of Africa and Arabia, including the chacma, *P. porcarius,* and the drill, *P. leucophæus,* and the mandrill, *P. maimon*; also, any of certain monkeys of allied genera.—**ba-boon'er-y,** *n.* Baboonish condition or behavior.—**ba-boon'ish,** *a.* Like or befitting a baboon.

ba-boosh, ba-bouche (ba-bösh'), *n.* [F. *babouche,* < Ar. *bābūsh,* < Pers. *pāpūsh.*] A kind of slipper without heel or quarters, worn in Turkey and elsewhere.

ba-bu (bä'bö), *n.* [Hind. *bābū.*] A Hindu title, equivalent to *sir* or *Mr.*; a gentleman; in Anglo-Indian use, a native clerk who writes English; any native with a smattering of English culture, esp. as manifested in speech with ludicrous effect.—**ba'bu-ism,** *n.* The superficial English culture and peculiar English of babus.

ba-bul (bä-böl'), *n.* [Hind. *babūl.*] Any of several trees of the mimosaceous genus *Acacia,* which yield a gum, tannin, etc., esp. *A. arabica,* of India; also, the gum, pods, or bark of such a tree.

ba-by (bā'bi). [Dim. of *babe.*] **I.** *n.*; pl. *-bies* (-biz). A babe or infant; also, a babyish or childish person; also, a doll†; also, the minute reflection which a person sees of himself in the pupil of another's eye†. **II.** *a.* Of, like, or suitable for a baby; infantile; babyish; young; small; little.—**baby act,** an act of or befitting a baby; a babyish or childish act; an excusing or defending of one's self on the ground of legal infancy or of inexperience or the like; also, a statute releasing a person from liability for such a reason. [Colloq.]—**baby blue,** a soft, light blue.—**baby ribbon,** ribbon of a very narrow width.—**ba'by,** *v. t.*; *-bied, -bying.* To treat as a baby.—**ba'by=farm,** *n.* A place where babies are kept and cared for, for hire.—**ba'by=farm''er,** *n.*—**ba'by=farm''ing,** *n.*—**ba'by-hood** (-hu̇d), *n.* The state or period of being a baby; infancy; also, babies collectively.—**ba'by=house,** *n.* A toy house for dolls.—**ba'by-ish,** *a.* Like or befitting a baby; infantile; childishly simple, silly, or weak.—**ba'by-ish-ly,** *adv.*—**ba'by-ish-ness,** *n.*—**ba'by-ism,** *n.* Babyhood; babyish character; also, a babyish act or expression (as, "*babyisms,* and dear diminutives": Tennyson's "Aylmer's Field," 539).

Bab-y-lon (bab'i-lo̦n), *n.* [L., < Gr. Βαβυλών, = Heb. *Bābel.*] An ancient city of western Asia, on the river Euphrates, famed for its magnificence and culture, and the capital of a once mighty empire; hence, any great, rich, and luxurious or wicked city (cf. Rev. xviii.).—**Bab-y-lo'ni-an** (-lō'ni-a̦n). **I.** *a.* Of or pertaining to Babylon or Babylonia (the country of which Babylon was the capital): as, the *Babylonian* captivity or exile of the Jews (esp., that occurring after the capture of Jerusalem in 586 B.C., and lasting until about 536 B.C.). Cf. *Assyrian, a.* **II.** *n.* An inhabitant of Babylon; also, an astrologer; also, the Babylonian language, belonging to the Semitic family.—**Bab-y-lo'nish,** *a.* Babylonian.

ba-by's=breath (bā'biz-breth'), *n.* A tall silenaceous herb, *Gypsophila paniculata,* bearing numerous small, fragrant, white or pink flowers; also, any of certain other plants, as the grape-hyacinth.

bac-a-la-o (bak-a̦-lä'ō), *n.*; pl. *-os* (-ōz). [Sp., codfish.] A West Indian serranoid fish, *Mycteroperca falcata,* important as a food-fish.

bac-ca-lau-re-ate (bak-a̦-lâ'rē̦-a̦t). [ML. *baccalaureatus,* < *baccalaureus* (simulating L. *bacca,* berry, and *laureus,* of laurel), for *baccalarius,* E. *bachelor.*] **I.** *n.* The academic degree of bachelor; also, a baccalaureate sermon. **II.** *a.* Pertaining to the degree of bachelor: as, a *baccalaureate* sermon (in some American colleges, a farewell sermon delivered to a graduating class).

bac-ca-rat, bac-ca-ra (bak-a̦-rä'), *n.* [F.; origin unknown.] A gambling game at cards played by a banker and two or more punters.

bac-cate (bak'āt), *a.* [L. *baccatus,* < *bacca,* berry.] In *bot.,* berry-like and pulpy, as fruits; also, bearing berries.

Bac-chæ (bak'ē), *n. pl.* [L., pl. of *Baccha,* < Gr. Βάκχη.] The female attendants of Bacchus or Dionysus; also, the priestesses of Bacchus; also, the women who took part in the Bacchanalia.

bac-cha-nal (bak'a̦-na̦l). [L. *Bacchanalis,* < *Bacchus,* Bacchus.] **I.** *a.* Pertaining to Bacchus or his worship;

(variable) d̦ as d or j, ș as s or sh, ț as t or ch, z̦ as z or zh; *o,* F. cloche; ü, F. menu; ċh, Sc. loch; ṅ, F. bonbon; **'**, primary accent; **''**, secondary accent; †, obsolete; <, from; +, and; =, equals. See also lists at beginning of book.

bacchanalian. **II.** *n.* A votary of Bacchus; hence, a drunken reveler; also, an occasion of drunken revelry; *pl.* [*cap.*], the Bacchanalia.—**Bac-cha-na′lia** (-nā′liạ̈), *n. pl.* [L.] A Roman festival in honor of Bacchus; [*l. c.*] drunken orgies; riotous revelry.—**bac-cha-na′lian. I.** *a.* Belonging to or indulging in bacchanalia. **II.** *n.* A bacchanalian reveler.—**bac-cha-na′lian-ism,** *n.*

bac-chant (bak′ạnt). [L. *bacchans* (*bacchant-*), ppr. of *bacchari*, celebrate the festival of Bacchus.] **I.** *n.* A priest, priestess, or votary of Bacchus; a bacchanal. **II.** *a.* Bacchanal.—**bac-chante** (ba-kȧnt′, bak′ạnt, or ba-kan′tẹ̄), *n.* [F. *bacchante* = It. *baccante*, < L. *bacchans* (*bacchant-*).] A female bacchant; a mænad.—**bac-chan-tic** (ba-kan′tik), *a.*

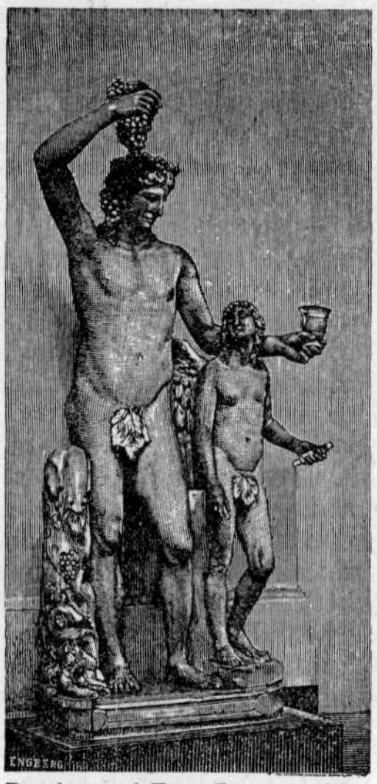

Bacchus and Eros (Love).—Museo Nazionale, Naples.

Bac-chus (bak′us), *n.* [L., < Gr. Βάκχος.] A name of Dionysus, the Greek god of wine: adopted as the current name of the god among the Romans.—**Bac′chic,** *a.*

bacci-. Form of L. *bacca*, berry, used in combination.—**bac-cif-er-ous** (bak-sif′ẹ-rus), *a.* [L. *baccifer*: see *-ferous.*] Berry-bearing.—**bac-ci-form** (bak′si-fôrm), *a.* [+ *-form.*] Berry-shaped.—**bac-civ-o-rous** (bak-siv′ọ̄-rus), *a.* [+ *-vorous.*] Feeding on berries.

Bach-a-rach (bak′ạ-rak), *n.* A white Rhine wine made at Bacharach, near Coblenz.

bach-e-lor (bach′ẹ-lọr), *n.* [OF. *bacheler* (F. *bachelier*), < ML. *baccalarius*, appar. orig. the holder of a small farm.] A young knight, not powerful enough to display his own banner, who followed the banner of another; a person who has taken the first or lowest degree at a college or university (as, *bachelor* of arts); a man of any age who has not married; also, the crappie (fish), *Pomoxys annularis*; also, a young male fur-seal kept from the breeding-grounds by the older males.—**bachelor's hall.** See under *hall.*—**knight bachelor.** See under *knight, n.*—**bach′e-lor-dom** (-dọm), *n.* The bachelor state.—**bach′e-lor-hood** (-hu̇d), *n.* The condition of a bachelor.—**bach′e-lor's=but′ton,** *n.* Any of various plants with round flower-heads, esp. double-flowered varieties (white or yellow) of ranunculus, or the cornflower, *Centaurea cyanus.*—**bach′e-lor-ship,** *n.*

ba-cil-lar (ba-sil′ạ̈r or bas′i-lạ̈r), *a.* Of or like a bacillus; rod-shaped; characterized by bacilli. Also **ba-cil-la-ry** (bas′i-lạ̄-ri).

bacilli-. Form of LL. *bacillus*, rod, E. *bacillus*, used in combination.—**ba-cil-li-cide** (ba-sil′i-sīd), *n.* [+ *-cide.*] An agent that destroys bacilli.—**ba-cil′li-form** (-fôrm), *a.* [+ *-form.*] Rod-shaped; bacillar.

ba-cil-lus (ba-sil′us), *n.*; pl. *bacilli* (-ī). [LL., dim. of L. *baculus*, rod.] Any of the rod-shaped or cylindrical bacteria constituting the genus *Bacillus*, species of which cause certain diseases; sometimes, any bacterium.

back[1] (bak), *n.* [D. *bak* = F. *bac*, tub, trough, ferry-boat.] A tub or vat; a flat-bottomed ferry-boat hauled by a chain or rope; a wooden vessel for carrying fuel (Sc.).

back[2] (bak). [AS. *bæc* = MD., LG., and Icel. *bak.*] **I.** *n.* The hinder part of the human body, extending from the neck to the end of the spine; the corresponding part of the body of animals; the corresponding portion of any part or organ of the body (as, the *back* of the head or of the hand); the whole body, with reference to clothing; anything resembling the human or animal back; the part opposite to or farthest from the face or front; the hinder side; the rear part; the side or part away from the spectator or the actor; the other or farther side; the part coming behind in the ordinary movements or use of a thing, as the thick edge of a knife; the upright hind part of a chair, etc., supporting a sitter's back; the ridge of a hill; in *football*, etc., a player behind the forward line (called *quarter-back, half-back*, etc., according to the distance from the line). **II.** *a.* Hinder; rear; remote from the front; backward; overdue, as pay.—**back**[2], *adv.* [Reduced from *aback.*] At, to, or toward the rear; behind; backward; in or toward the past; in return (as, to pay *back* a loan); away from the front, foreground, main region, proper destination, etc.; in reversal of the regular or expected course.—**back**[2], *v. t.* To furnish with a back; strengthen at the back; support or sustain, as with corroboration, authority, influence, or money (often with *up*); bet in favor of; get upon the back of; mount; write on the back of; indorse; move or send backward; reverse the action of.—**to back water,** *naut.*, to propel a boat in the opposite direction to that in which the prow is pointed, or to retard its progress, by reversing the action of the oars, propeller, or the like. Also fig.—**back**[2], *v. i.* To go backward; reverse the course; withdraw from an undertaking (with *out*); abandon an attempt or pretension (with *down*); *naut.*, of the wind, to change in direction by moving round the points of the compass in a manner contrary to the usual one (as, the wind *backs* in the north temperate regions when it moves counter-clockwise, as from east through north to west).—**to back and fill,** to proceed by catching the wind alternately in the front and in the back of a ship's sails; fig., to vacillate.

back-bite (bak′bīt), *v. t.* or *i.*; pret. *-bit*, pp. *-bitten* or *-bit*, ppr. *-biting.* To speak evil of (the absent).—**back′bit″er** (-bī″tėr), *n.*

back-board (bak′bōrd), *n.* A board placed at or forming the back of anything; also, a board worn to support or straighten the back.—**back′board,** *v. t.* To subject to the wearing of a backboard.

back-bone (bak′bōn′), *n.* The spinal or vertebral column; the spine; a spine-like part; also, strength of character.—**back′boned′,** *a.*—**back′bone′less,** *a.* Having no backbone; spineless.

back-cast (bak′kȧst), *n.* A cast backward; a reverse; a relapse. [Sc. and north. Eng.]

back-down (bak′doun), *n.* A backing down; the abandoning of an attempt or pretension.

back=draft (bak′drȧft), *n.* A draft or current, as of air or gas, going in a direction contrary to the normal, as in a furnace.

backed (bakt), *a.* Having a back: as, a high-*backed* chair.

back-er (bak′ėr), *n.* One who or that which backs; esp., one who backs a person or thing as in an enterprise or a contest.

back-fall (bak′fâl), *n.* A falling back; that which falls back; in *wrestling*, a fall in which a wrestler is thrown upon his back.

back-fire (bak′fīr′), *v. i.*; *-fired, -firing.* To check a fire, as in a forest, by burning off an area in advance; of an internal-combustion engine, to have a premature explosion in the cylinder or an explosion in the admission or exhaust passages.—**back′fire,** *n.* In fighting a fire by backfiring, the fire purposely started some distance in advance; also, the backfiring of an internal-combustion engine, or the resulting explosion.

back-fisch (bäk′fish), *n.* [G., orig. a fish for baking or frying.] A young girl; a half-grown school-girl. [Colloq.]

back-flash (bak′flash′), *v. i.* Of a flame which is consuming a combustible gas, to move back through the current of gas and burn at a point farther back than is desired.

back=for-ma-tion (bak′fôr-mā′shọn), *n.* Formation of a word from one that has the appearance of being its derivative, as of *greed* from *greedy*, *orate* from *oration*, *typewrite* from *typewriter*; also, a word so formed.

back-gam-mon (bak-gam′ọn or bak′gam″ọn), *n.* [Cf. *gammon*[1].] A game played by two persons on a board having two tables or parts, with pieces or men moved in accordance with throws of dice, the object of each player being to advance his men to the last six points, and then throw them off, or remove them entirely from the board; also, a victory at this game in which a player is not only gammoned, but still has at least one man on the opponent's home table.—**back-gam′mon,** *v. t.* To defeat at backgammon; esp., to win a backgammon over.

back-ground (bak′ground), *n.* The ground or parts situated, or represented as situated, in the rear; the more distant portion of a scene: opposed to *foreground*.—**back′ground,** *v. t.* To furnish with a background; form a background for.

back-hand (bak′hand). **I.** *n.* The hand turned backward in making a stroke, as in tennis; also, the position or play to the left of a right-handed player and to the right of a left-handed player; also, handwriting in which the upward slope of the letters is to the left. **II.** *a.* Backhanded.—**back′hand′ed,** *a.* With the back of the hand (as, a *backhanded* blow); done or effected with the hand turned backward, or with the back of the hand in the direction of the stroke; also, marked by a backward slope, as handwriting; also, awkward; being the opposite in meaning, as a compliment; indirect; insincere; also, of a rope, twisted in the opposite way from the usual or right-handed method.—**back′hand′ed-ly,** *adv.*—**back′hand′ed-ness,** *n.*—**back′hand′er,** *n.* A backhanded blow or stroke; also, a glass of wine out of turn, for which the bottle is passed back.

back-house (bak′hous), *n.* An outhouse at the back of a main building; hence, a privy; also, the back room or kitchen of a cottage (prov. Eng. and Sc.).

back-ing (bak′ing), *n.* The act of one who or that which backs; also, that which forms the back part of a thing; something placed at or attached to the back of anything to support or strengthen it; aid or support of any kind; supporters or backers collectively.

back-lash (bak′lash), *n.* The jarring reaction, or the play, between loosely fitting or worn parts of a machine or mechanical device. Also **back′lash″ing.**

back-less (bak′les), *a.* Having no back: as, *backless* benches.

back-log (bak′log), *n.* A large log placed at the back of an open wood-fire; fig., something serving as a basis or support.

back-most (bak′mōst), *a. superl.* Hindmost.

back-ped-al (bak′ped″ạl), *v. i.*; *-aled* or *-alled*, *-aling* or *-alling*. To work the pedals of a bicycle, etc., backward, or press down upon a pedal as it rises in order to retard speed. Also fig.

back-set (bak′set), *n.* A setback; a reverse; also, an eddy or counter-current.

back-sheesh (bak′shēsh), *n.* See *bakshish.*

back-side (bak′sīd′), *n.* The hind side; the back; the posteriors; the back premises of a house, etc. (prov. Eng. and Sc.).

back-sight (bak′sīt), *n.* In *surv.*, a sight or reading taken in a backward direction or toward a previous station.

back-slide (bak′slīd′), *v. i.*; pret. *-slid*, pp. *-slidden* or *-slid*, ppr. *-sliding.* To fall back in one's moral or religious course; relapse into error or sin.—**back′slid′er** (-slī′dėr), *n.*

back=spin (bak′spin), *n.* Backward rotation, as of a golf-ball.

back-stair, back-stairs (bak′stãr, -stãrz), *a.* Pertaining to or proceeding as by the back stairs or some private way; indirect; underhand; intriguing.

back-stay (bak′stā), *n.* A supporting or checking piece in a mechanism; *naut.*, a stay or supporting rope leading from a masthead to the ship's side.

back-stitch (bak′stich), *n.* Stitching or a stitch in which the thread doubles back each time on the preceding stitch.—**back′stitch,** *v. t.* or *i.* To sew by backstitch.

back=stroke (bak′strōk), *n.* A stroke or blow in return; a recoil; also, a backhanded stroke.

back=sword (bak′sōrd), *n.* A sword with only one sharp edge; also, a cudgel with a basket-hilt, used like a sword or foil in fencing; play or exercise with this.—**back′=sword′man, back′=swords′man** (-mạn), *n.*; pl. *-men.*

back-ward (bak′wạrd). **I.** *adv.* Toward the back, rear, or past; with the back foremost; in the reverse of the usual or right way; retrogressively. **II.** *a.* Directed toward the back or the past; reversed; behind in time or progress; late; slow; reluctant; bashful. **III.** *n.* The part (of time) that is behind or past: as, "the dark *backward* and abysm of time" (Shakspere's "Tempest," i. 2. 50). [Archaic.]—**back-war-da′tion** (-wạr-dā′shọn), *n.* A premium paid by a seller of stock to the buyer for the privilege of postponing its delivery. Cf. *contango.* [Eng.]—**back′ward-ly,** *adv.*—**back′ward-ness,** *n.*—**back′wards,** *adv.* Backward.

back-wash (bak′wosh), *n.* The water thrown back by oars, paddle-wheels, or the like.

back-wa-ter (bak′wâ″tėr), *n.* Water turned or held back, as by a dam; also, backwash.

back-woods (bak′wu̇dz′), *n. pl.* Uncleared or wild regions remote from towns.—**back′woods′man** (-mạn), *n.*; pl. *-men.*

ba-con (bā′kọn), *n.* [OF. *bacon*; from Teut., and akin to E. *back*[2].] The back and sides of the hog salted and dried, usually in smoke; also, pork†.—**to save one's bacon.** See under *save, v. t.*

Ba-co-ni-an (bạ-kō′ni-ạn), *a.* Of or pertaining to Francis Bacon ('Lord Bacon,' 1561–1626), the English philosopher and statesman, or his doctrines: as, the *Baconian* method (the method of induction, or procedure from particular instances to general principles, as in science); the *Baconian* theory (the theory that Bacon wrote the plays usually attributed to Shakspere).

bac-te-ri-a (bak-tē′ri-ạ̈), *n.* Plural of *bacterium.*

bac-te-ri-al (bak-tē′ri-ạl), *a.* Of, pertaining to, or caused by bacteria; of the nature of or consisting of bacteria. Also **bac-ter′ic** (-ter′ik).

bac-te-ri-cide (bak-tē′ri-sīd), *n.* [See *-cide.*] An agent that destroys bacteria.—**bac-te′ri-ci-dal** (-sī-dạl), *a.*

bac-te-ri-form (bak-tē′ri-fôrm), *a.* [See *-form.*] Having the form of bacteria.

bac-te-rin (bak′tẹ-rin), *n.* A vaccine prepared from bacteria.

bacterio-. Form of *bacterium* used in combination.

bac-te-ri-oid (bak-tē′ri-oid). [See *-oid.*] **I.** *a.* Resembling bacteria. **II.** *n.* One of the minute rod-like or branched organisms (regarded as forms of bacteria) found in the root-nodules of nitrogen-fixing plants, as the legumes.—**bac-te-ri-oi′dal,** *a.*

bac-te-ri-o-log-i-cal (bak-tē″ri-ọ-loj′i-kạl), *a.* Of or pertaining to bacteriology.—**bac-te″ri-o-log′i-cal-ly,** *adv.*

bac-te-ri-ol-o-gy (bak-tē-ri-ol′ọ-ji), *n.* [See *bacterio-* and *-logy.*] The science that deals with bacteria and other microbes.—**bac-te-ri-ol′o-gist,** *n.*

bac-te-ri-ol-y-sis (bak-tē-ri-ol′i-sis), *n.* [See *bacterio-* and *-lysis.*] The process of dissolution or destruction of bacteria.—**bac-te″ri-o-lyt′ic** (-lit′ik), *a.*

bac-te-ri-os-co-py (bak-tē-ri-os′kọ-pi), *n.* [See *bacterio-* and *-scopy.*] Microscopic investigation of bacteria.—**bac-te″ri-o-scop′ic** (-skop′ik), *a.*—**bac-te-ri-os′co-pist,** *n.*

bac-te-ri-o-ther-a-py (bak-tē″ri-ọ-ther′ạ-pi), *n.* [See *bacterio-* and *therapy.*] In *med.*, treatment of disease by the introduction of specific bacteria into the system.

bac-te-ri-um (bak-tē′ri-um), *n.*; pl. *-ria* (-ri-ạ̈). [NL., < Gr. βακτήριον, dim. of βάκτρον, stick.] Any of numerous microscopic vegetable organisms multiplying by fission and spore-formation, various species of which are concerned in fermentation and putrefaction, the production of disease, the fixing of atmospheric nitrogen, etc.; a schizomycete.

bac-te-roid (bak′tẹ-roid), *a.* and *n.* Same as *bacterioid.*

Bac-tri-an (bak′tri-ạn), *a.* Of or pertaining to Bactria, an ancient country in west-central Asia: as, the *Bactrian* camel (see *camel*).

ba-cu-li-form (ba-kū′li-fôrm), *a.* [L. *baculum*, rod: see *-form.*] Rod-shaped.

bac-u-line (bak′ū̦-lin), *a.* [L. *baculum*, rod.] Pertaining to the rod (for chastising).

bad (bad). [ME. *badde*; origin uncertain.] **I.** *a.*; compar. *worse*, superl. *worst.* Not good; having defects of quality or character; poor; worthless; incorrect or faulty; not valid; unfavorable or unfortunate; morally depraved; evil; wicked; vicious; causing displeasure, inconvenience, or pain; offensive; disagreeable; grievous; having an injurious or unfavorable tendency or effect; hurtful; noxious; also (colloq.), in ill health or unsound condition; sick; ill; in pain. **II.** *n.* That which is bad; bad condition, character, etc.; a bad thing, quality, etc.—**to the bad,** to a bad condition; to ruin; also, in arrear or deficit.—**bad,** *adv.* Badly. [Colloq.]—**bad′dish,** *a.* Rather bad.

bade (bad). Preterit of *bid.*

badge (baj), *n.* [ME. *bage*, *bagge*; origin unknown.] A token or device worn orig. to distinguish a knight and his followers and hence as a sign of principles, occupation.

authority, achievements, etc.; hence, an emblem; a distinctive mark.—**badge,** *v. t.*; *badged, badging.* To furnish with a badge; mark as with a badge.—**badge'less,** *a.* Without a badge.

badg-er[1] (baj'ėr), *n.* [Perhaps < *badge,* with allusion to the stripes on the head.] Any of various burrowing carnivorous mammals of the family *Mustelidæ,* as *Meles vulgaris,* a European species about two feet long, with gray fur, and with black and white stripes on the head, and *Taxidea americana,* a similar American species; any of certain other animals, as in Australia a wombat; also, a resident of Wisconsin (the 'Badger State'); also, a brush made of badgers' hair, as for artists' use.—**badg'er**[1], *v. t.* To harass, as if baiting a badger; worry; torment; pester; tease.

American Badger (*Taxidea americana*).

badg-er[2] (baj'ėr), *n.* [Perhaps akin to *bag.*] One who buys corn or other commodities to sell elsewhere; a huckster; a hawker. [Obs. or prov. Eng.]

ba-di-geon (bạ-dij'ọn), *n.* [F.; origin unknown.] A mixture of ground stone and plaster for filling up holes in stone for sculpture or masonry; also, a wash for giving plaster the appearance of stone.

bad-i-nage (bad'i-nāj, F. bȧ-dē-näzh), *n.* [F., < *badiner,* jest, < ML. *badare,* gape.] Banter; raillery.—**bad'i-nage,** *v. t.*; *-naged, -naging.* To drive or force by badinage.

bad-ly (bad'li), *adv.* In a bad manner; ill.

bad-min-ton (bad'min-tọn), *n.* [From *Badminton,* seat of the Duke of Beaufort in Gloucestershire, England.] [Also *cap.*] A beverage made of claret and soda-water sweetened and flavored; also, a game similar to lawn-tennis but played with a shuttlecock.

bad-ness (bad'nes), *n.* The quality or state of being bad.

Bae-de-ker (bā'dė-kėr, G. bā'dė-kėr), *n.* Any of the series of guide-books for travelers issued by the German publisher Karl Baedeker (1801–59) and his successors.

baff (baf), *v. i.* [Appar. imit.] To beat or strike (Sc.); in *golf,* to strike the ground with the club in making a stroke.—**baff,** *n.* A blow or stroke (Sc.); a thud (Sc.); in *golf,* a baffing stroke, unduly lofting the ball.

baf-fle (baf'l), *v.*; *-fled, -fling.* [Origin uncertain; cf. OF. *beffler,* mock, and Sc. *bauchle,* treat with contumely.] **I.** *tr.* To put to public shame†; mock†; cheat, confound, or confuse (now prov. Eng.); thwart or frustrate disconcertingly; foil; balk; check; of the wind, etc., to beat about (grass, etc.: prov. Eng.). **II.** *intr.* To shuffle† or quibble†; struggle ineffectually, as a ship in a gale.—**baf'fle,** *n.* A humiliation†; a discomfiture, balk, or check; also, an artificial obstruction for checking or deflecting the flow of a fluid; a baffle-plate.—**baf'fle-ment,** *n.* The act of baffling, or the state of being baffled.—**baf'fle=plate,** *n.* A plate used to direct or retard the flow of gases or the like, as in the flue of a boiler.—**baf'fler,** *n.*—**baf'fling-ly,** *adv.*

baff-y (baf'i), *n.*; pl. *baffies* (-iz). [See *baff.*] In *golf,* a short wooden club with a deeply pitched face, for lofting the ball. Also **baff'y=spoon.**

bag (bag), *n.* [ME. *bagge*: cf. Icel. *baggi,* bag, bundle, and OF. *bagues,* baggage.] A receptacle of leather, cloth, paper, etc., capable of being closed at the mouth; a sack; a pouch; a valise or other portable receptacle for carrying articles as in traveling; a purse or money-bag; a small silken pouch to hold the back hair of a wig; also, the contents of a bag or pouch; a sportsman's take of game, etc.; also, any of various measures of capacity; also, something resembling or suggesting a bag; a sac, as in an animal body; an udder; a baggy part; in *coal-mining,* a cavity filled with gas or water.—**bag,** *v.*; *bagged, bagging.* **I.** *intr.* To swell or bulge; hang loosely like an empty bag; also, to grow big with child†. **II.** *tr.* To cause to swell or bulge; distend; also, to put into a bag, as killed game; kill or catch, as in hunting; also, to catch, seize, or steal (colloq.).

ba-gasse (bạ-gas'), *n.* [F., < Sp. *bagazo.*] Crushed sugarcane or beet refuse from sugar-making.

bag-a-telle (bag-ạ-tel'), *n.* [F., < It. *bagattella.*] A trifle; a thing of no importance; also, a short and light musical composition, usually for the piano; also, a game played on a board having at one end holes into which balls are to be struck with a cue, or some variation of this game.

bag-ful (bag'fůl), *n.*; pl. *-fuls.* A quantity sufficient to fill a bag.

bag-gage (bag'āj), *n.* [OF. F. *bagage,* < OF. *baguer,* pack up, < *bagues,* pl., baggage: cf. *bag.*] The trunks, bags, etc., taken by a traveler on a journey (in Great Britain called *luggage*); the portable equipment of an army; rubbish†; a worthless woman; less severely, a hussy, minx, or flirt.—**bag'gage=car,** *n.* A railroad-car for carrying the baggage of the passengers on a train.—**bag'gage-man** (-man), *n.*; pl. *-men.* A man whose business it is to carry, check, or handle baggage.—**bag'gage=mas"ter,** *n.* The official in charge of a baggage department of a transportation company.—**bag'gage=smash"er,** *n.* A man employed to handle baggage, as in a railroad-station. [Colloq.]

bag-ging (bag'ing), *n.* Woven material, as of hemp or jute, for bags.

bag-gy (bag'i), *a.* Bag-like; hanging loosely.

bag-man (bag'mạn), *n.*; pl. *-men.* A commercial traveler. [Eng.]

ba-gnio (ban'yō), *n.*; pl. *bagnios* (-yōz). [It. *bagno,* < L. *balneum,* bath.] A bath† or bathing-house†; also, a prison, penal institution, or place of detention for slaves, as in the Orient; also, a house of prostitution; a brothel.

bag-pipe (bag'pīp), *n.* A musical wind-instrument of great antiquity, consisting of a bag which receives air from the player's mouth or from bellows, and of pipes (a chanter for the melody, and a drone or drones for the bass) into which the air is pressed from the bag: often in *pl.* with sense of *sing.*—**bag'pip"er** (-pī"pėr), *n.*

Old English Bagpipe.

bag=wig (bag'wig), *n.* A wig the back hair of which was inclosed in a bag.

bag=worm (bag'wėrm), *n.* The larva of a lepidopterous insect, *Thyridopteryx ephemeræformis,* of the northern U. S.: so called from the silken bag which it constructs and carries about for protection.

bah (bä), *interj.* [F.] An exclamation of contempt.

ba-ha-dur (bạ-hä'důr), *n.* [Hind. *bahādur,* brave, hero.] In India, a title of honor, commonly affixed to the names of European officers in Indian documents.

Ba-ha-ism (bạ-hä'izm), *n.* [Pers. *Bahā* (*u'llāh*), 'splendor (of God),' title of the leader.] Babism as accepted by the followers of Mirza Husayn Ali, who in 1863 proclaimed himself leader of the Babists.—**Ba-ha'ist,** *n.*

ba-hut (bạ-höt', F. bȧ-ü), *n.* [F.; origin uncertain.] A large chest or coffer, often with an arched top and sometimes richly ornamented, used in the middle ages and later for holding clothing, etc., as in traveling; also, an ornamental buffet or cabinet of antique style.

Bahut. — French 16th century work.

bai-gnoire (bā-nwor), *n.* [F., lit. 'bathtub.'] A theater box on the ground (main) floor.

bail[1] (bāl), *n.* [ME. *beyl*; prob. from Scand.] A hoop or ring; the semicircular handle of a kettle or pail; a hoop-like support, as for a wagon-cover.—**bail**[1], *v. t.* To provide with a bail.

bail[2] (bāl), *v. t.* [OF. *baillier*, deliver, < L. *bajulare*, carry, < *bajulus*, carrier.] In *law*, to deliver (goods, etc.) in trust, or without transfer of ownership; also, to grant or to obtain the liberty of (a person under arrest) on security given for his appearance when required, as in court for trial.—**bail**[2], *n.* [OF. *bail*, < *baillier.*] Custody†; the position or the privilege of being bailed; the security given in bailing, or the person or persons giving it; in general, security (as, to go *bail*, or to vouch, for a thing).

bail[3] (bāl), *n.* [OF. *bail*, *baile*, palisade, barrier, perhaps < L. *baculum*, rod, stick.] A palisade† or barrier†; also, the wall of an outer court of a feudal castle; the court itself; a bailey; also, a bar for separating horses in a stable; also, a framework for securing the head of a cow during milking (prov. Eng. and Australian); also, a cross-bar†; in *cricket*, either of the two small bars or sticks laid across the tops of the stumps which form the wicket.—**bail**[3], *v.* **I.** *tr.* To secure by means of a bail; secure the head of (a cow) in a bail during milking (with *up*: prov. Eng. and Australian); also, to stop, esp. by force in order to rob (with *up*: Australian). **II.** *intr.* To stop or surrender, esp. at the command of a robber: with *up.* [Australian.]

bail[4] (bāl), *n.* [F. *baille*, bucket.] A bucket or other vessel used for dipping water out of a boat.—**bail**[4], *v.* **I.** *tr.* To dip (water) out of a boat, as with a bucket; clear (a boat) of water by dipping: usually with *out.* **II.** *intr.* To bail water; also, to make a parachute drop (with *out*).

bail-a-ble (bā'lạ-bl), *a.* [See *bail*[2].] That may be bailed; also, admitting of bail, as an offense.

bail=bond (bāl'bond), *n.* A bond given to insure due appearance of one who is bailed.

bail-ee (bā-lē'), *n.* In *law*, one to whom goods are committed in bailment.

bail-er[1] (bā'lėr), *n.* See *bailor.*

bail-er[2] (bā'lėr), *n.* In *cricket*, a ball that strikes the bails.

bail-er[3] (bā'lėr), *n.* One who or that which bails out water from a boat.

bail-ey (bā'li), *n.*; pl. *baileys* (-liz). [Var. of *bail*[3].] The wall of defense about the outer court of a feudal castle, or any one of several circuits of walls surrounding the keep; also, the outer court, or any court between the circuits of walls.

bail-ie (bā'li), *n.* [OF. *bailli*, earlier *baillif*: see *bailiff.*] A bailiff†; in Scotland, a municipal officer or magistrate, corresponding to an English alderman.

bail-iff (bā'lif), *n.* [OF. *baillif*, < ML. *bajulivus*, < *bajulus*, administrator, L. carrier.] A person charged with local administrative authority, as any of various king's officers in England, the chief magistrate in certain towns, etc.; also, a sheriff's officer, esp. in England, employed to execute writs and processes, make arrests, etc.; also, an overseer or steward of an estate.

bail-i-wick (bā'li-wik), *n.* [See *wick*[2].] The district within which a bailie or bailiff has jurisdiction; also, the office of a bailie or bailiff.

bail-ment (bāl'mẹnt), *n.* [See *bail*[2].] In *law*, the act of bailing; delivery of goods, etc., in trust.—**bail'or, bail'er**[1], *n.* In *law*, one who delivers goods, etc., in bailment.—**bails'man** (-mạn), *n.*; pl. *-men.* In *law*, one who gives bail or security.

bain=ma-rie (baṅ-mä-rē), *n.*; pl. *bains-marie* (baṅ-). [F., earlier *bain de marie*, 'bath of Mary' (perhaps with allusion to the gentle heat).] A vessel containing hot water, in which another vessel is placed to heat its contents.

Bai-ram (bī-räm' or bī'räm), *n.* [Turk.] Either of two Mohammedan festivals, one of 3 days ('lesser Bairam'), immediately after the fast of Ramadan, the other of 4 days ('greater Bairam') occurring 70 days after this fast.

bairn (bãrn), *n.* [AS. *bearn*, < *beran*, E. *bear*[1].] A child. [North. Eng. and Sc.]

bait (bāt), *v.* [Icel. *beita*, cause to bite, feed, < *bīta*, = E. *bite.*] **I.** *tr.* To set dogs to attack and worry (a bull, bear, etc.) for sport; hence, to worry; torment; also, to give food and drink to (horses, etc.), esp. during a journey; also, to prepare (a hook or trap) with bait; also, to lure as with a bait. **II.** *intr.* To take food; stop for food or refreshment during a journey.—**bait**, *n.* [Icel. *beita*, food, bait.] Food, or some substitute, used as a lure in angling, trapping, etc.; an alluring inducement; also, a light repast; refreshment, or a halt for refreshment, during a journey.—**bait'er**, *n.*

baith (bāth). Scotch form of *both.*

baize (bāz), *n.* [Orig. pl. (formerly also *bays*), < obs. F. *baies*, pl., < *bai*, bay-colored, E. *bay*[5].] A thick woolen fabric with a nap, and now usually green or red, used esp. for curtains, table-covers, etc.; also, a curtain or other article of this fabric.

bake (bāk), *v.*; pret. *baked*, pp. *baked* (archaic *baken*), ppr. *baking.* [AS. *bacan* = G. *backen.*] **I.** *tr.* To cook (food) by dry heat in a closed place, as an oven; harden (bricks, pottery, etc.) by heat; in general, to harden or cake (earth, etc.: now chiefly prov.). **II.** *intr.* To bake bread, etc.; also, to become baked.—**bake**, *n.* A baking.—**baked'=ap'ple**, *n.* The cloudberry.—**bake'house**, *n.* A building or room to bake in; a bakery.

ba-ke-lite (bā'kẹ-līt), *n.* [From L. H. *Baekeland*, chemist and inventor.] A non-inflammable synthetic material produced by the action of formaldehyde on phenol, used in place of amber, hard rubber, etc., for making pipe-stems, beads, umbrella-handles, billiard-balls, electric insulators, etc., and employed also for cements, protective coatings, etc. [Proprietary name.]

bake=meat† (bāk'mēt), *n.* A dish of food prepared by baking.

bak-er (bā'kėr), *n.* One who bakes; one who makes and sells bread, cake, etc.; also, a small portable oven.—**baker's dozen.** See *dozen.*—**bak'er-y**, *n.*; pl. *-ies* (-iz). The trade or the establishment of a baker; a baker's shop.

bak-ing (bā'king), *n.* The act of one who or that which bakes; also, the quantity baked at one time; a batch.—**bak'ing=pow"der**, *n.* Any one of various powders (differing as to ingredients) used as a substitute for yeast in baking.—**bak'ing=so"da**, *n.* Sodium bicarbonate.

bak-shish, bakh-shish (bak'shēsh), *n.* [Pers. *bakhshīsh*, < *bakhshīdan*, give.] In the East, a gift of money, as to a beggar, a servant or employee, an official, etc.; a gratuity; a fee or tip.

bal-a-lai-ka (bal-ạ-lī'kạ̈), *n.* [Russ.] A musical instrument of the guitar kind, with a triangular body, of ancient Slavic origin.

bal-ance (bal'ạns), *n.* [OF. F. *balance*, < LL. *bilanx*, having two scales, < L. *bi-*, two, + *lanx*, scale.] An instrument for weighing, typically a bar poised or swaying on a central support according to the weights borne in scales (pans) suspended at the ends; hence, power to decide as by a balance; authoritative control; [*cap.*] the zodiacal constellation or sign Libra; [*l. c.*] either one of the scales of a balance; also, any apparatus for weighing, as a steelyard; a contrivance, now usually a balance-wheel, for regulating the beat of a watch or clock; also, a condition in which the counteracting weights in a balance are equal; a state of equilibrium or equipoise; equal distribution of weight, amount, etc.; harmonious arrangement or adjustment, esp. in the arts of design; equanimity or mental equipoise; composure; also, something used to produce equilibrium; a weight put into one scale of a balance to offset that in the other; a counterpoise; also, the turn of the balance; the preponderating weight, as of public opinion; also, an act of balancing; comparison as to weight, amount, importance, etc.; estimate; an adjustment of accounts; the excess of either side (debit or credit) of an account over the other; the remainder or the rest (colloq.); equality between the totals of the two sides of an account; also, a balancing movement in dancing.—**balance of power**, in *international law*, an even adjustment of power among nations, as in Europe.—**balance of trade**, the difference in amount or value between the exports and the imports of a country, said to be favorable or unfavorable according as the exports are greater or less than the imports.—**bal'ance**, *v.*; *-anced*, *-ancing.* **I.** *tr.* To weigh in or as in a balance; ponder over (a matter); compare (two or more things) as to relative weight, value, importance, etc.; bring to or hold in equilibrium; poise; adjust evenly; sway like a balance; furnish or be a counterpoise for; counterbalance or offset; use as a counterpoise; set off (one against another); reckon up, adjust, or settle (accounts). **II.** *intr.* To be in equilibrium; be even; move to and fro, esp. in dancing; sway; waver; reckon or adjust accounts.—**bal'ance-a-ble,** *a.* Capable of being balanced.—**bal'an-cer,** *n.*—**bal'ance=reef,** *n. Naut.*, the last reef in a sail; specif., a reef in which the reef-band starts at the throat and extends across the sail in such a manner as to reduce the sail to a triangle.—**bal'ance=reefed,** *a. Naut.*, having the balance-reef or last reef taken in.—**bal'ance=sheet,** *n.* A tabular statement of both sides of an account or set of accounts, in which the debit and credit balances foot up as equal. — **bal'ance=wheel,** *n.* A wheel for regulating motion; a wheel in a watch or chronometer which by the regularity of its motion determines the beat; a fly-wheel, as of an engine.

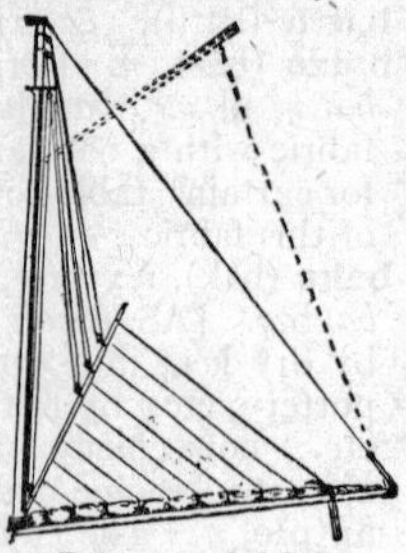
Balance-reefed Sail.

bal-a-noid (bal'ạ-noid), *a.* [Gr. βαλανοειδής, < βάλανος, acorn, + εἶδος, form.] Acorn-shaped.

bal-as (bal'ạs), *n.* [OF. F. *balais,* < Ar. *balakhsh,* < Pers. *Badakhshān,* name of a province in northeastern Afghanistan.] A variety of spinel ruby, of a pale rose-red color.

bal-a-ta (bal'ạ-tạ), *n.* [Amer. Sp.; of native origin.] The dried juice or gum obtained from the bully-tree, *Mimusops balata*: used as a substitute for gutta-percha and in making chewing-gum.

A Venetian Balcony.

ba-la-yeuse (bȧ-lạ-yėz), *n.* [F., fem. of *balayeur,* sweeper, < *balayer,* sweep.] A pleating or ruffle of silk, lace, etc., sewed on the inner side of a woman's (long) skirt just above the lower edge as a protection against dust or wear.

Bal-brig-gan (bal-brig'ạn), *a.* [Also *l. c.*] Noting hosiery of unbleached cotton made at Balbriggan, in eastern Ireland, and hence applied also to machine-knit garments of similar fabric or appearance made elsewhere.

bal-co-ny (bal'kọ-ni), *n.*; pl. *-nies* (-niz). [It. *balcone,* < *balco,* scaffold; from Teut., and akin to E. *balk.*] A balustraded or railed platform projecting from the wall of a building, within or without; also, a gallery in a theater.—**bal'co-nied** (-nid), *a.*

Double Baldachin.—Sainte Chapelle, Paris.

bald (bâld), *a.* [ME. *balled*; origin uncertain.] Lacking hair on some part of the scalp; also, destitute of some natural growth or covering; fig., bare; plain; meager; unadorned; also, having white on the head, as certain birds (as, the *bald* eagle: see *eagle*).—**bald rush,** any of the leafy-stemmed cyperaceous plants constituting the genus *Psilocarya.*

bal-da-chin (bal'dạ-kin), *n.* [It. *baldacchino,* orig. silk from Bagdad, < *Baldacco,* Bagdad.] A rich silk fabric (see *baudekin*); also, a canopy of silk, or of stone, metal, etc., as above an altar; often, a portable canopy carried in religious processions. Also **bal'da-quin** (-kin).

bal-der-dash (bâl'dėr-dash), *n.* [Origin unknown.] Froth†; a jumbled mixture of liquors†; a senseless jumble of words; trashy talk or writing; nonsense.

bald=faced (bâld'fāst), *a.* Of animals, having white on the face.

bald-head (bâld'hed), *n.* One who has a bald head.—**bald'=head''ed,** *a.*

bald-ly (bâld'li), *adv.* In a bald manner; barely; meagerly.—**bald'ness,** *n.*

bald-pate (bâld'pāt), *n.* One who has a bald head; also, a widgeon (duck), *Mareca americana.*—**bald'=pat''ed** (-pā''ted), *a.*

bal-dric (bâl'drik), *n.* [ME. *bawdrik, baudry*: cf. OF. *baldrei,* MHG. *balderich,* also L. *balteus,* belt.] A belt, sometimes richly ornamented, worn diagonally from shoulder to hip, and often supporting a sword, horn, etc.

bale[1] (bāl), *n.* [AS. *balu, bealo.*] Evil; harm; misfortune; woe. [Archaic.]

bale[2] (bāl), *n.* [AS. *bǣl.*] A bale-fire: as, "On Penchryst glows a *bale* of fire" (Scott's "Lay of the Last Minstrel," iii. 27). [Obs. or archaic.]

bale[3] (bāl), *n.* [OF. *bale, balle,* < OHG. *balla,* ball: cf. *ball*[1].] A large bundle or package of merchandise prepared for storage or transportation, esp. one closely compressed and secured by cords, wires, hoops, or the like, sometimes with a wrapping.—**bale**[3], *v. t.*; *baled, baling.* To make into bales.

bale[4] (bāl), *v.* See *bail*[4].

ba-leen (bạ-lēn'), *n.* [OF. F. *baleine,* < L. *balæna,* whale.] A whale†; also, whalebone.

bale=fire (bāl'fīr), *n.* [AS. *bǣlfȳr*: see *bale*[2].] A great fire; a bonfire; a signal-fire; a funeral pyre. [Archaic.]

bale-ful (bāl'fụl), *a.* [AS. *bealofull*: see *bale*[1].] Fraught with bale; evil; deadly; disastrous.—**bale'ful-ly,** *adv.*—**bale'ful-ness,** *n.*

balk (bâk), *n.* [AS. *balca,* ridge, = G. *balken,* beam: cf. *balcony.*] A ridge, as between furrows; a strip left unplowed; a miss, slip, or failure; an illegal deceptive motion of a baseball pitcher, as if to pitch; a thin place in a coal-bed; a check or hindrance; a large beam or timber; in *billiards,* any of the eight panels or compartments lying between the cushion of the table and the balk-lines.—**balk,** *v.* **I.** *tr.* To leave balks in, in plowing†; also, to miss; also, to evade or shirk; also, to hinder, thwart, or foil; disappoint. **II.** *intr.* To stop, as at an obstacle; of horses, to stop short and stubbornly refuse to go on.

Bal-kan (bâl'kạn), *a.* Noting or pertaining to a range of mountains ('the Balkans') in southeastern Europe, extending across Bulgaria from west to east; noting or pertaining to the peninsula of southeastern Europe lying between the Adriatic, Ægean, and Black Seas, or the countries of this peninsula.

balk-er (bâ'kėr), *n.* One that balks.

balk=line (bâk'līn), *n.* In *billiards,* a straight line drawn across the table near one end, behind which the cue-balls are placed in beginning a game; also, any of four lines, each near to and parallel with one side of the cushion, which divide the table into a large central panel or compartment and eight smaller compartments (balks) lying between this and the cushion.

balk-y (bâ'ki), *a.* Given to balking, as a horse.

ball[1] (bâl), *n.* [ME. *bal, balle*: cf. Icel. *böllr,* OHG. *ballo, balla,* ball, OF. *balle,* ball, bale (see *bale*[3]).] A spherical body; a sphere; a globe; a planetary or celestial body, esp. the earth; esp., a round or roundish body, of different materials and sizes, for use in various games, as baseball, football, tennis, or golf; such a ball in play or action, as tossed, thrown, struck, etc. (as, a low *ball*; a high *ball*; a curved *ball*); a ball in baseball too high or too low or not over the plate, and not struck at by the batter; a game played with a ball, esp. baseball; also, a missile or projectile to be thrown from an engine of war, orig. always spherical, but for modern firearms also conical or cylindrical; a solid projectile for a cannon, etc. (as distinguished from a *shell*); projectiles, esp. bullets, collectively; a globular mass of combustible ingredients, or a case filled with them, designed to set fire to something or to give forth light, etc.; also, a small spherical body of wood, ivory, etc., used in voting by ballot (cf. *blackball*); hence, any globular or rounded mass; a spherical piece of soap†; a globular mass made by winding thread, twine, yarn, etc.; a bolus, or quantity of medicine in the form of a large pill; a rounded package; a bale; a rounded mass or cushion, as of hair or wool covered with soft leather, formerly used for inking type; also, any rounded protuberant part of a thing, esp. of the human body, as on the palm of the hand at the base of the thumb or on the sole of the foot at the base of the great toe.—**ball=and=socket joint,** a natural or an artificial joint formed by a ball or knob working in a socket, and admitting, to a certain degree, of rotary movement in every direction.—**ball**[1], *v.* **I.** *tr.* To make into a ball; round out; clog, as a horse's hoofs with snow; confuse (with *up*: slang). **II.** *intr.* To form or gather into a ball; become clogged, as a horse's hoofs with snow or mud.

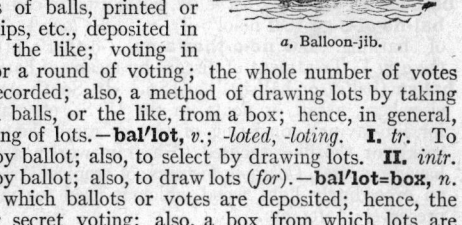

Ball-and-socket Joint.

ball[2] (bâl), *n.* [F. *bal*, < OF. *baler* (F. *baller*), < LL. *ballare*, dance.] A dance†; also, a social assembly for dancing.

bal-lad (bal′ạd), *n.* [OF. *balade* (F. *ballade*), < Pr. *ballada*, dancing-song, dance, < *ballar*, < LL. *ballare*, dance.] A song to accompany a dance†; also, any light, simple song, esp. one of sentimental or romantic character, having two or more stanzas, all sung to the same melody; also, a simple, often crude, narrative poem, of popular origin, composed in short stanzas, esp. one of romantic character and adapted for singing; any poem written in similar style.

bal-lade (bạ-läd′), *n.* [F.: see *ballad*.] A poem consisting commonly of 3 stanzas of 8 or 10 lines each, followed by an envoy of 4 or 5 lines, the last line of each stanza and of the envoy being the same, and the same rime-sounds recurring throughout.—**ballade royal,** a ballade in which each line consists of 10 syllables.

bal-lad-er, bal-lad-ist (bal′ạd-ėr, -ist), *n.* A maker of ballads.

bal-lad-mong-er (bal′ạd-mung″gėr), *n.* A dealer in or seller of ballads; also, an inferior poet; a poetaster.

bal-lad-ry (bal′ạd-ri), *n.* Ballad poetry.

bal-last (bal′ạst), *n.* [Cf. D., LG., Sw., and Dan. *ballast*, OSw. and ODan. *barlast*, appar. < *bar*, bare, mere, + *last*, load: cf. *last*[3].] Any heavy material carried by a ship or boat for insuring proper stability, so as to avoid capsizing and to secure the greatest effectiveness of the propelling power; something heavy, as bags of sand, placed in the car of a balloon to steady it; gravel, broken stone, slag, etc., used to give stability, as in road-building; anything that gives stability or steadiness.—**bal′last,** *v. t.* To furnish with ballast; fill in with ballast; give steadiness to; freight† or load†; load or weigh down (archaic).—**bal′last-ing,** *n.* The act or process of furnishing with ballast; also, material used for ballast.

ball=bear-ing (bâl′bãr″ing), *n.* A bearing in which the shaft or journal turns upon a number of steel balls running in an annular track; also, any of the steel balls so used.

ball=cock (bâl′kok), *n.* A device for regulating the supply of water in a tank, cistern, or the like, consisting essentially of an inlet cock or valve connected by a lever with a hollow metal ball which floats in the water and by its rise or fall causes the lever to shut or open the valve.

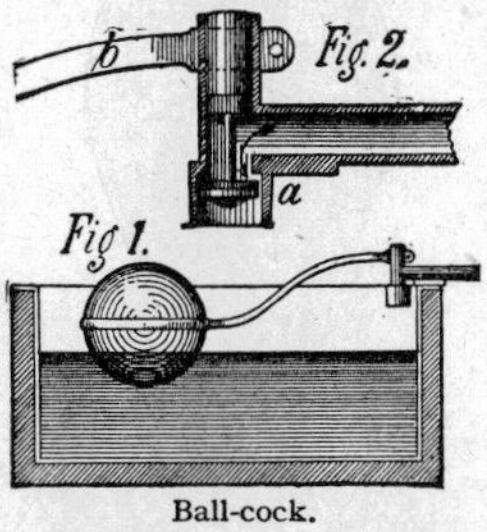

Ball-cock.
Fig. 1, Cistern with ball-cock attached. Fig. 2, Section of ball-cock on larger scale: *a*, valve shown open so as to admit water; *b*, arm of the lever which being raised shuts the valve.

bal-le-ri-na (bäl-lā-rē′nä), *n.*; pl. *-ne* (-nā). [It.] A female professional dancer.

bal-let (bal′ā), *n.* [F., < It. *balletto*, dim. of *ballo*, dance, ball.] A spectacular entertainment rendered by a company of dancers (chiefly women), either as a feature of an operatic or theatrical performance, or independently; also, the dancers.

ball=flow-er (bâl′flou″ėr), *n.* In *arch.*, an ornament resembling a ball placed in a circular flower, the three (or rarely four) petals of which form a cup around it: usually inserted in a hollow molding.

Ball-flowers.

bal-lis-ta (bạ-lis′tạ), *n.*; pl. *-tæ* (-tē). [L., < Gr. βάλλειν, throw.] An ancient military engine for throwing stones or other missiles.

bal-lis-tic (bạ-lis′tik), *a.* [From *ballista*: cf. F. *balistique*.] Pertaining to the throwing of missiles or projectiles, or to the science of ballistics.—**bal-lis′ti-cal-ly,** *adv.*—**bal-lis-ti-cian** (bal-is-tish′ạn), *n.* One versed in ballistics.—**bal-lis′tics,** *n.* The science of missiles or projectiles as thrown from engines or weapons of war.

bal-lis-tite (bal′is-tīt), *n.* [From *ballista*.] A smokeless powder containing nitroglycerin and guncotton.

bal-lon d'es-sai (bȧ-lôṅ dā-sā). [F., 'balloon of trial,' a small balloon sent up before an ascension, to determine the direction of the wind.] A statement, procedure, etc., designed to test public opinion.

bal-loon (bạ-lön′), *n.* [F. *ballon*, < *balle*, ball.] A large ball inflated with air, used in play†; a bag made of some material impermeable to air or gas and filled with some gas lighter than ordinary air, designed to rise and float in the atmosphere, and in the large forms (some of which are dirigible) having a car or compartment attached for passengers; also, in drawings, etc., a balloon-shaped figure inclosing words represented as issuing from the mouth of the speaker; in *arch.*, an ornamental ball, as on the top of a pillar; in *chem.*, a globular glass vessel.—**bal-loon′,** *v. i.* To go up or ride in a balloon; also, to swell or puff out like a balloon.—**bal-loon′er, bal-loon′ist,** *n.*—**bal-loon′=fish,** *n.* A globe-fish.—**bal-loon′=jib,** *n.* *Naut.*, a large triangular sail of light canvas used by yachts in light winds, instead of the ordinary jib.—**bal-loon′=vine,** *n.* A sapindaceous tropical climbing plant, *Cardiospermum halicacabum*, with bladder-like pods.

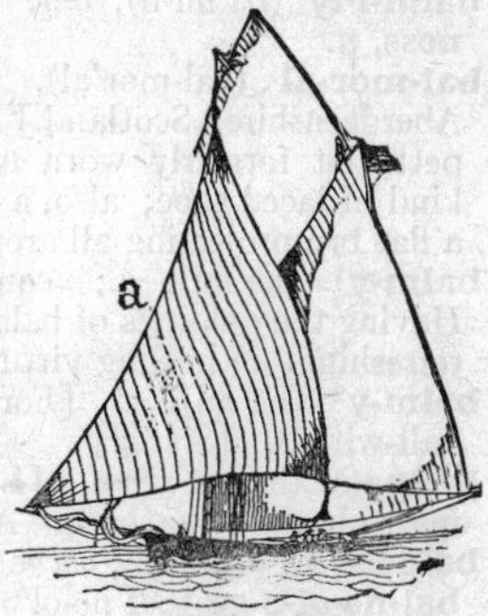

a, Balloon-jib.

bal-lot (bal′ọt), *n.* [It. *ballotta*, dim. of *balla*, = E. *ball*[1].] A little ball used in secret voting; a ticket, paper, etc., used in voting; the method of secret voting by means of balls, printed or written slips, etc., deposited in a box or the like; voting in general, or a round of voting; the whole number of votes cast or recorded; also, a method of drawing lots by taking out small balls, or the like, from a box; hence, in general, the drawing of lots.—**bal′lot,** *v.*; *-loted, -loting.* **I.** *tr.* To vote on by ballot; also, to select by drawing lots. **II.** *intr.* To vote by ballot; also, to draw lots (*for*).—**bal′lot=box,** *n.* A box in which ballots or votes are deposited; hence, the ballot, or secret voting; also, a box from which lots are drawn.—**bal′lot-er,** *n.*

bal-lotte-ment (ba-lot′mẹnt, F. bȧ-lot-moṅ), *n.* [F., < *ballotter*, toss as a ball, < *ballotte*, dim. of *balle*, ball.] In *med.*, a method of diagnosing pregnancy, in which a sudden shock is imparted to the fetus, as through the uterine wall, causing it to move suddenly upward and fall back again against the examining finger; also, a similar method employed in testing for floating kidney, etc.

ball=room (bâl′röm), *n.* A room for balls or dancing.

ball=valve (bâl′valv), *n.* A valve formed by a ball resting upon a concave circular part containing an aperture, and operated by the upward pressure of the fluid (which lifts the ball and opens the aperture), and by gravity or gravity and suction (which lowers the ball and closes the aperture) when such pressure is removed.

bal-ly (bal′i), *a.* [Origin obscure.] A word of indefinite meaning used humorously or for emphasis in place of some adjective of more definite (possibly profane) signification. [Slang, orig. Eng.]

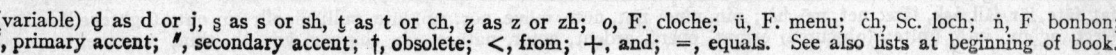

bal-ly-hoo (bal-i-hö′), *n.* [Origin obscure.] A barker, as at the door of a show or shop; hence, clamorous attempts to win customers or advance any cause; blatant advertising or publicity; in general, clamor or outcry. [Slang.]—**bal-ly-hoo′,** *v. i.* or *t.*; *-hooed, -hooing.* To use, or advertise or push by, ballyhoo. [Slang.]—**bal-ly-hoo′er,** *n.*

bal-ly-rag (bal′i-rag), *v. t.* See *bullyrag.*

balm (bäm), *n.* [OF. *basme* (F. *baume*), < L. *balsamum,* E. *balsam.*] Any of various oily, fragrant, resinous substances, often of medicinal value, exuding from certain plants, esp. tropical trees of the balsameaceous genus *Balsamea*; a plant or tree yielding such a substance; also, any of various aromatic menthaceous plants, esp. of the genus *Melissa,* as *M. officinalis,* a lemon-scented perennial herb; also, an aromatic preparation used in embalming the dead†; also, any aromatic or fragrant ointment; fig., aromatic fragrance; sweet odor; also, a healing or soothing ointment; fig., anything that heals, soothes, or mitigates.—**balm of Gilead,** an oleoresin obtained from a balsameaceous tree or shrub, *Balsamea opobalsamum,* and esteemed in the East for its fragrance and medicinal properties; some similar product; also, a variety of the balsam-poplar; also, the balsam-fir, *Abies balsamea.*—**balm,** *v. t.* To treat with balm; embalm; fig., to soothe or assuage. [Archaic.]

bal-ma-caan (bal-mạ-kän′), *n.* [From *Balmacaan,* estate of Bradley Martin in Glen Urquhart, Inverness, Scotland.] [Also *cap.*] Orig., a man's short, full-skirted overcoat of rough woolen cloth, unlined or only partly lined, with raglan shoulders and a high collar buttoned about the throat; hence, some variation of this garment, similar in material and general appearance, worn by either sex.

balm=crick-et (bäm′krik″et), *n.* [Earlier *baum-cricket,* appar. repr. G. *baumgrille,* 'tree cricket.'] The cicada. See Tennyson's "Dirge." [Obs. or archaic.]

balm-i-ly (bä′mi-li), *adv.* In a balmy manner.—**balm′i-ness,** *n.*

bal-mor-al (bal-mor′ạl), *n.* [From *Balmoral* Castle in Aberdeenshire, Scotland.] [Also *cap.*] A colored woolen petticoat formerly worn under a looped-up skirt; also, a kind of laced shoe; also, a kind of brimless Scotch cap with a flat top projecting all around the head.

balm-y[1] (bä′mi), *a.*; compar. *balmier,* superl. *balmiest.* Having the qualities of balm; aromatic; fragrant; soothing; refreshing; of healing virtue; also, producing balm.

balm-y[2] (bä′mi), *a.* [For *barmy.*] Silly; weak-minded; half-witted. [Slang.]

bal-ne-al (bal′nē-ạl), *a.* [L. *balneum,* bath.] Of or pertaining to baths or bathing. Also **bal′ne-a-ry** (-ā-ri).

balneo-. Form of L. *balneum,* bath, used in combination.—**bal-ne-ol-o-gy** (bal-nē-ol′ọ-ji), *n.* [+ *-logy.*] The science of bathing.—**bal″ne-o-ther′a-py** (-ọ-ther′ạ-pi), *n.* [+ *therapy.*] Treatment of disease by means of baths.

bal-sa (bal′sä or bâl′sä), *n.* [Sp.] In South America and elsewhere, a raft or float; in the U. S., etc., a raft (esp. for life-saving) consisting of two or more floats, air-tight casks, or the like, secured to a framework; also, a bombacaceous tree, *Ochroma lagopus,* of tropical America, with an exceedingly light wood which is used for making life-preservers, rafts, etc.

bal-sam (bâl′sạm), *n.* [L. *balsamum,* < Gr. βάλσαμον.] Any of various fragrant exudations from certain trees, esp. of the balsameaceous genus *Balsamea* (see *balm*), as the balm of Gilead ('balsam of Mecca'), and the product ('balsam of Peru') yielded by a leguminous tree, *Toluifera pereiræ,* of Central America; balm; an oleoresin; any of certain transparent turpentines, as that ('Canada balsam') obtained from a pinaceous tree, the balsam-fir, *Abies balsamea,* and used for mounting objects for the microscope; also, a plant or tree yielding a balsam; the balsam-fir; any of various plants of the balsaminaceous genus *Impatiens,* as *I. balsamina,* a common garden annual bearing ornamental flowers, and seed-vessels that burst with considerable force when ripe; also, any aromatic ointment, whether for ceremonial or for medicinal use; any healing or soothing agent or agency.—**bal′sam,** *v. t.* To treat with balsam.—**bal′sam=ap″ple,** *n.* A cucurbitaceous vine, *Momordica balsamina,* with a red or orange fruit; also, any of certain allied species.

bal-sa-me-a-ceous (bâl″sạ-mē-ā′shius or bal″-), *a.* [NL. *Balsamea,* the typical genus, < L. *balsamum,* E. *balsam.*] Belonging to the *Balsameaceæ,* a family of tropical trees and shrubs yielding important resinous products, as myrrh, frankincense, bdellium, etc.

bal-sam=fir (bâl′sạm-fėr), *n.* A species of fir, *Abies balsamea,* which yields Canada balsam (see *balsam*); also, any of certain other firs.

bal-sam-ic (bâl-sam′ik or bal-), *a.* Of, like, or containing balsam; balmy; fragrant; soothing; healing.—**bal-sam′i-cal-ly,** *adv.*

bal-sa-mif-er-ous (bâl-sạ-mif′ẹ-rus or bal-), *a.* [See *-ferous.*] Yielding balsam.

bal-sa-mi-na-ceous (bâl″sạ-mi-nā′shius or bal″-), *a.* [NL. *balsamina,* < Gr. βαλσαμίνη, balsam-plant, < βάλσαμον, E. *balsam.*] Belonging to the *Balsaminaceæ,* a family of plants with irregular flowers, including many tropical Asiatic species and also the balsams of the genus *Impatiens.*

bal-sam=pop-lar (bâl′sạm-pop″lạr), *n.* A species of poplar, *Populus balsamifera,* yielding tacamahac.

bal-sam=tree (bâl′sạm-trē), *n.* Any of various balsam-bearing trees, as the balsam-fir or the balsam-poplar.

bal-sa-mum (bâl′sạ-mum or bal′-), *n.* [L.] Balsam.

bal-sam-y (bâl′sạm-i), *a.* Balsam-like; balsamic.

Balt (bâlt). **I.** *n.* One of the inhabitants of the former Baltic provinces of Russia, to the east of the Baltic Sea; esp., one of the German inhabitants of this region, largely descendants of Germanic invaders who settled there in the 13th century. **II.** *a.* Of or pertaining to the Balts.

bal-ter, bol-ter[4] (bâl′tėr, bōl′-), *v. t.* or *i.* [Origin obscure.] To form into masses or lumps; clot; mat. See Shakspere's "Macbeth," iv. 1. 123. [Now prov. Eng.]

Bal-tic (bâl′tik), *a.* Noting, pertaining to, or situated on the sea which separates Sweden from Denmark, Germany, Lithuania, etc.

Bal-ti-more (bâl′ti-mōr) **o′ri-ole.** See *oriole.*

bal-us-ter (bal′us-tėr), *n.* [F. *balustre,* < It. *balaustro,* baluster, < L. *balaustium,* < Gr. βαλαύστιον, flower of the wild pomegranate.] One of a series of short, pillar-like supports for a railing, as of a staircase; *pl.,* a series of such supports, with the railing; *sing.,* a balustrade (archaic).

Balustrade.

Baluster.

bal-us-trade (bal-us-trād′), *n.* [F., < *balustre,* E. *baluster.*] A series of balusters supporting a railing.—**bal-us-trad′ed** (-trā′ded), *a.*

bam (bam), *v. t.* or *i.*; *bammed, bamming.* [Cf. *bamboozle.*] To bamboozle; humbug. [Slang or prov.]—**bam,** *n.* An imposition; a trick; a hoax. [Slang or prov.]

bam-bi-no (bäm-bē′nō), *n.*; pl. *-ni* (-nē). [It., dim. of *bambo,* simple.] A child or baby; esp., an image of the infant Jesus.

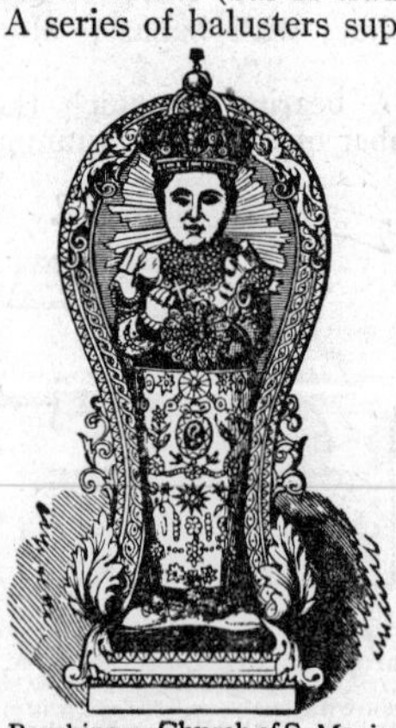
Bambino.—Church of S. Maria in Ara Cœli, Rome.

bam-boo (bam-bö′), *n.* [E. Ind. (Malay *bambu*).] Any of the woody or tree-like tropical and semitropical grasses of the genus *Bambos* (or *Bambusa*) and allied genera; also, the hollow woody stem of such a plant, used for building purposes and for making furniture, poles, etc.

Bamboo (*Bambos bambos*).

bam-boo-zle (bam-bö′zl), *v.*; *-zled, -zling.* [Origin obscure: cf. *bam.*] **I.** *tr.* To impose upon; cozen; delude; beguile; trick. **II.** *intr.* To practise imposition or trickery.—**bam-boo′zle-ment,** *n.*—**bam-boo′zler,** *n.*

bam-bu-sa-ceous (bam-bū̦-sā′shius), *a.* [NL. *Bambusa* (= *Bambos*), typical genus of bamboos.] Resembling the bamboo; belonging to the *Bambuseæ*, a tribe of grasses comprising the various species of bamboo.

ban[1] (ban), *v. t.*; *banned, banning.* [AS. *bannan*, summon, = Icel. *banna*, prohibit, curse; from Teut., and prob. akin to L. *fari*, Gr. *φάναι*, speak.] To summon†; curse, or invoke damnation upon (archaic); chide or scold (prov.); pronounce an ecclesiastical curse upon; anathematize; also, to prohibit, interdict, or proscribe.—**ban**[1], *n.* [Partly from *ban*[1], *v.*, partly from OF. F. *ban* (ML. *bannum*), proclamation, from the Teut. source of *ban*[1], *v.*] A public proclamation or edict; in feudal times, the summons of the sovereign's vassals for military service; the whole body liable to the summons; *pl.*, a proclamation or notice of an intended marriage (see *banns*); *sing.*, a malediction, curse, or execration; esp., a formal ecclesiastical denunciation; an anathema; excommunication; also, an authoritative prohibition or interdiction; a sentence of outlawry; fig., informal denunciation or prohibition, as by public opinion.

ban[2] (ban), *n.* [Hung., < Pers. *bān*, lord.] A title orig. given to the wardens of the southern marches of Hungary, later only to the governor of Croatia and Slavonia.

ban-al (ban′a̦l or bā′na̦l), *a.* [F. *banal*, < OF. *ban*: see *ban*[1], *n.*] Of or pertaining to compulsory feudal service; also, commonplace; hackneyed; trite; trivial.—**ba-nal-i-ty** (ba̦-nal′i-ti), *n.*; pl. *-ties* (-tiz). Banal character; commonplaceness; triteness; triviality; also, anything banal; a commonplace (as, "Bringing the decent praise, the due regret, And each *banality* prescribed of old": Browning's "Balaustion's Adventure").—**ban′al-ly,** *adv.*

Banana (*Musa sapientum*).

ba-nan-a (ba̦-nan′ä̦), *n.* [Pg. and Sp.; from native name.] Any plant of the tropical genus *Musa*, of which various species are cultivated for their nutritious finger-shaped fruit; also, the fruit, esp. that of *M. sapientum*, with yellow or red rind.

ban-at, ban-ate (ban′a̦t, -āt), *n.* The territory, jurisdiction, or term of office, of a ban, as of Croatia and Slavonia.

banc (bangk), *n.* [AF. and F. *banc* (ML. *bancus*), bench: see *bank*[2].] A bench of justice; a court.—**in banc,** with all or a quorum of the judges present.

ban-ca (bäng′kä), *n.* [Philippine Sp.] A kind of dugout or canoe used in the Philippines.

band[1] (band), *n.* [Icel. *band*; from the Teut. source of E. *bind.*] Something that serves to bind; a bond: as, "He was kept bound with chains and in fetters; and he brake the *bands*" (Luke, viii. 29). [Archaic.]

band[2] (band), *n.* [OF. F. *bande*; from the same (Teut.) source as E. *band*[1].] A thin, flat strip of some material, for binding, confining, trimming, or some other purpose; a fillet, belt, or strap; a stripe, as of color or decorative work; a kind of collar worn by men and women in the 17th century; a linen collar with two pendent strips ('bands') in front, worn esp. by clergymen.—**band**[2], *v. t.* To furnish or mark with bands; stripe.

band[3] (band), *n.* [OF. F. *bande* = It. *banda*; appar. from Teut., and akin to E. *band*[1], *band*[2].] A number of persons (or animals) joined or acting together; a company, party, or troop; esp., a company of musicians playing various instruments in combination, commonly such instruments as are suitable for marching or open-air performance.—**band**[3], *v. t.* or *i.* To unite in a band or company.

ban-dage (ban′dā̦j), *n.* [F. *bandage*, < *bander*, bind with a band, < *bande*, E. *band*[2].] A strip of cloth or other material used to bind up a wound, etc.; anything bound as a band about something.—**ban′dage,** *v. t.*; *-daged, -daging.* To bind or cover with a bandage.—**ban′dag-er** (-dā̦-jėr), *n.*

ban-dan-a, ban-dan-na (ban-dan′ä̦), *n.* [Hind. *bāndhnū*, a mode of dyeing in which the cloth is tied in spots to prevent parts from receiving the dye.] A large colored handkerchief with spots or figures due to absence or removal of dye.

band-box (band′boks), *n.* A light box of pasteboard, thin wood, etc., for holding a hat or bonnet (orig. bands or collars).

ban-deau (ban-dō′), *n.*; pl. *-deaux* (-dōz′). [F., dim. of *bande*, E. *band*[2].] A band worn about or on the head; a head-band; a fillet; a circular band of stiff material for fastening in or under a woman's hat to fit it to the head.

ban-de-ril-la (bän-dā-rēl′yä), *n.*; pl. *-las* (-yäs). [Sp. dim. of *bandera*, banner.] A barbed dart ornamented with a colored streamer, thrust into the bull in bull-fighting.—**ban″de-ril-le′ro** (-rēl-yā′rō), *n.*; pl. *-ros* (-rōs). [Sp.] A bull-fighter (on foot) who thrusts in the banderillas.

Australian Bandicoot (*Chœropus castanotis*).

ban-de-role, ban-de-rol (ban′de̦-rōl, -rōl or -rol), *n.* [F. *banderole*, dim. of *bandière* (also *bannière*), banner.] A small flag or streamer borne on a lance, at a masthead, etc.; also, a bannerol, or funeral flag; also, a band or ribbon-like scroll bearing a device or inscription.

ban-di-coot (ban′di-köt), *n.* [E. Ind.] A very large East Indian rat, *Nesokia bandicota*; also, any of various rat-like marsupials (family *Peramelidæ*) of Australia, etc.

ban-dit (ban′dit), *n.* [It. *bandito*, prop. pp. of *bandire*, proclaim, proscribe, akin to E. *ban*[1], *banish.*] An outlaw; hence, a brigand.—**ban′dit-ry,** *n.* The work or practice of bandits; also, bandits collectively; banditti.—**ban-dit′ti** (-dit′i), *n. pl.* [It. *banditi.*] Bandits; sometimes, as *sing.*, a company of bandits.

band=mas-ter (band′mȧs″tėr), *n.* The leader or conductor of a band (of musicians).

ban-dog (ban′dog), *n.* [For *band-dog.*] A dog kept tied or chained, as a mastiff or bloodhound. [Archaic or prov.]

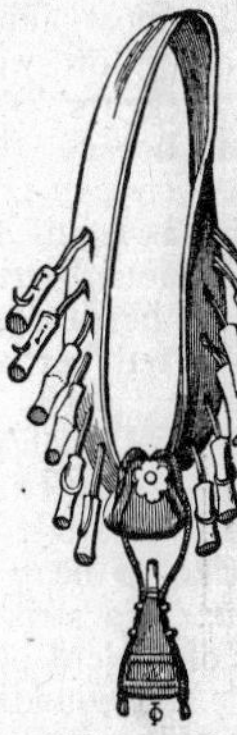
Bandoleer, with cases for ammunition.

ban-do-leer, ban-do-lier (ban-do̦-lēr′), *n.* [F. *bandoulière*, < Sp. *bandolera*, < *banda*, band, sash.] A broad belt worn over the shoulder and across the breast, as for suspending a wallet at the side†; *sing.* or *pl.*, such a belt worn by soldiers, having a number of small cases attached, each containing a charge of ammunition; *sing.*, one of these cases; also, a shoulder-belt having loops for carrying cartridges.

ban-do-line (ban′do̦-lin or -lēn), *n.* [F.] A mucilaginous preparation from quince-seeds, etc., used for keeping the hair smooth or in curls, waves, etc.

ban-dore (ban-dōr′), *n.* [Sp. *bandurria*, < LL. *pandura*: see *pandora*[2].] An old stringed musical instrument resembling the lute or the guitar.

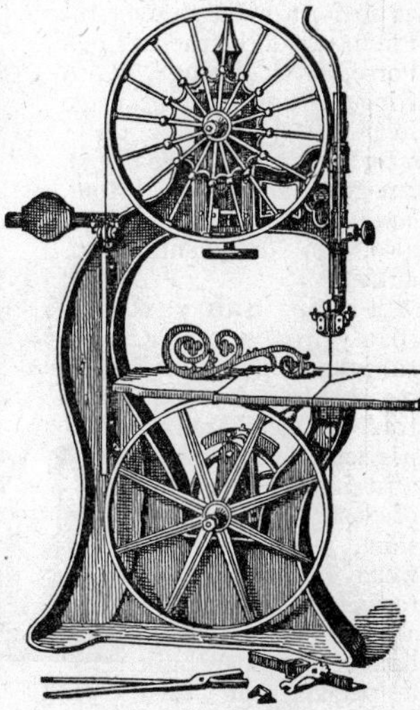
Band-saw.

band=saw (band′sâ), *n.* A saw consisting of an endless serrated steel band passing over two wheels.

(variable) d̦ as d or j, ș as s or sh, ț as t or ch, z̦ as z or zh; *o*, F. cloche; ü, F. menu; ċh, Sc. loch; ṅ, F. bonbon; ′, primary accent; ″, secondary accent; †, obsolete; <, from; +, and; =, equals. See also lists at beginning of book.

bands-man (bandz′mạn), *n.*; pl. *-men.* A musician who plays in a band.

band=wag-on (band′wag″ọn), *n.* A wagon carrying a band of music, as at the head of a procession or parade; hence, a figurative wagon of this kind humorously conceived as leading some movement or organized effort, as in a political campaign, and advancing confidently or triumphantly toward expected victory (colloq., U. S.: as, to climb aboard the Republican *band-wagon*).

ban-dy[1] (ban′di), *v.*; *-died, -dying.* [Origin obscure: cf. F. *bander*, bandy, perhaps < *bande*, E. *band*[2].] **I.** *tr.* To throw or strike to and fro, or from side to side, as a ball in tennis; pass from one to another, or back and forth; give and take, as blows, words, or compliments; exchange, as blow for blow; also, to league or band together (chiefly reflexive)†. **II.** *intr.* To be bandied; also, to form a band or league†; also, to contend or strive.—**ban′dy**[1], *n.*; pl. *-dies* (-diz). An old method of playing tennis†; a stroke in tennis†; the game of hockey or shinny; a hockey-club or shinny.

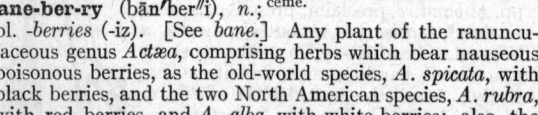

Red Baneberry (*Actæa rubra*), showing flowering plant and fruiting raceme.

ban-dy[2] (ban′di), *a.* [Appar. < *bandy*[1], *n.* (bent hockey-club).] Having a bend or crook outward, as a person's legs.—**ban′dy=legged** (-legd or -leg″ed), *a.*

bane (bān), *n.* [AS. *bana*, slayer.] A slayer†; something deadly, as poison; a thing that ruins or spoils (as, "Thoughts with better thoughts at strife, The most familiar *bane* of life": Wordsworth's "Sequel to 'Beggars' ").

bane-ber-ry (bān′ber″i), *n.*; pl. *-berries* (-iz). [See *bane.*] Any plant of the ranunculaceous genus *Actæa*, comprising herbs which bear nauseous poisonous berries, as the old-world species, *A. spicata*, with black berries, and the two North American species, *A. rubra*, with red berries, and *A. alba*, with white berries; also, the berry.

bane-ful (bān′fụl), *a.* Deadly; pernicious.—**bane′ful-ly,** *adv.*—**bane′ful-ness,** *n.*

bang[1] (bang), *v.* [Cf. Icel. *banga*, hammer.] **I.** *tr.* To strike or beat resoundingly; slam; surpass (colloq.). **II.** *intr.* To strike violently and noisily; make a loud noise as of violent blows; resound with clashing noises.—**bang**[1], *n.* A resounding stroke or blow; a loud, sudden noise.—**bang**[1], *adv.* With a bang; suddenly and loudly; abruptly.

bang[2] (bang), *v. t.* [Cf. *bang*[1], *adv.*] To cut (the hair) so as to form a fringe over the forehead; dock (the tail of a horse, etc.).—**bang**[2], *n.* A fringe of banged hair: often in *pl.*

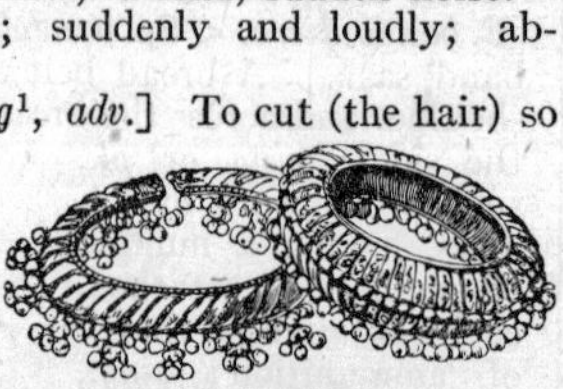

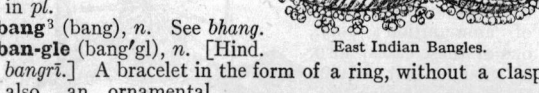

East Indian Bangles.

bang[3] (bang), *n.* See *bhang.*

ban-gle (bang′gl), *n.* [Hind. *bangrī.*] A bracelet in the form of a ring, without a clasp; also, an ornamental anklet.

Banian.

ban-ian, ban-yan (ban′yạn), *n.* [Pg. *banian*, < Skt. *vaṇij*, merchant.] A Hindu trader or merchant of a particular caste which abstains from the use of flesh; also, a loose shirt, jacket, or gown worn in India; also (orig. *banian tree*, from a tree under which banians or traders built a pagoda), an East Indian fig-tree, *Ficus bengalensis*, whose branches send out adventitious roots to the ground, sometimes causing the tree to spread over a wide area.—**banian days,** days when no meat is served (orig. *naut.*); days of meager fare.

ban-ish (ban′ish), *v. t.* [OF. *banir* (*baniss-*) (F. *bannir*); from Teut., and akin to E. *ban*[1].] To put under ban as an outlaw†; condemn to exile; expel from or relegate to a country or place by authoritative decree; compel to depart; send, drive, or put away.—**ban′ish-er,** *n.*—**ban′ish-ment,** *n.* Expulsion; exile.

ban-is-ter (ban′is-tėr), *n.* A corruption of *baluster*, esp., *pl.* and *sing.*, as meaning the balustrade of a staircase.

ban-jo (ban′jō), *n.*; pl. *-jos* (-jōz). [Corruption of *bandore.*] A musical instrument of the guitar class, having a circular body covered in front with tightly stretched parchment, and from 5 to 9 strings played with the fingers or a plectrum.—**ban′jo-ist,** *n.* A banjo-player.

ban-jo-rine (ban-jọ-rēn′), *n.* A variety of the banjo, smaller than the usual form and properly higher in pitch.

bank[1] (bangk), *n.* [ME. *banke*, prob. from Scand. (cf. Icel. *bakki*, river-bank, ridge, cloud-bank); ult. akin to E. *bench*: cf. *bank*[2], *bank*[3].] A long pile or heap, as of earth, snow, or cloud; a ridge, shelf, or embankment; the raised or rising ground beside a river or any depression; a slope or acclivity; an elevation in the bed of a body of water (as, the *banks* of Newfoundland); a shoal; in *billiards* and *pool*, the cushion of the table; in *aëronautics*, the lateral inclination of an aëroplane when going around a curve.—**bank**[1], *v.* **I.** *tr.* To border with or like a bank; embank; also, to raise in a bank; heap (*up*); also, to cover (a fire) with ashes, so that it will burn long and slowly; in *billiards* and *pool*, to drive (a ball) to the bank or cushion; pocket (the object-ball) by driving it against the bank; in *aëronautics*, to tip or incline (an aëroplane) laterally, inner side downward, when going around a curve. **II.** *intr.* To border (*on*)†; rise in or form banks, as clouds or snow; form a slope or acclivity.

bank[2] (bangk), *n.* [OF. F. *banc*, bench; from the Teut. source of E. *bench*: cf. *bank*[1], *bank*[3].] A bench, platform, table, or tier (now only in special uses); a bench for rowers in a galley; the rowers on one bench or to one oar; a row or tier of oars (ancient galleys sometimes having two or more tiers, one above another); a row of keys in an organ.

bank[3] (bangk), *n.* [F. *banque*, < It. *banca*, orig. bench, table; from Teut., and akin to E. *bank*[2], *bench*, and *bank*[1].] A money-changer's counter or shop†; a sum of money, esp. as a fund for use in business†; the fund of the manager or the dealer in gaming; the stock or fund of pieces from which the players draw in the game of dominoes, etc.; an institution for receiving and lending money (in some cases, issuing notes that serve as money) or transacting other financial business; the office or quarters of such an institution.—**bank discount.** See *discount*, *n.*—**bank rate,** the rate of discount fixed by a bank or banks.—**bank**[3], *v.* **I.** *intr.* To keep a bank; exercise the functions of a bank or banker; also, to keep money in, or have an account with, a bank; also, to form a bank in gaming; also, to rely or count (*on*: colloq.). **II.** *tr.* To deposit in a bank; also, to convert into money or cash.—**bank′a-ble,** *a.* Receivable by a bank.—**bank′=bill,** *n.* A note drawn by one bank on another, payable on demand or at a specified future date; also, a bank-note (chiefly U. S.).—**bank′=book,** *n.* A book held by a depositor in which a bank enters the credits and debits of his account.

banked[1] (bangkt), *a.* [See *bank*[1].] Having banks or raised margins: as, a high-*banked* river.

banked[2] (bangkt), *a.* [See *bank*[2].] Having a bank or banks, as of oars or of organ-keys.

bank-er[1] (bang′kėr), *n.* [See *bank*[1].] A vessel employed in the cod-fishery on the banks of Newfoundland.

bank-er[2] (bang′kėr), *n.* [See *bank*[3].] A money-changer†; a dealer in bills of exchange†; one who conducts or manages a bank; a banking corporation; in gaming establishments or games of chance, the keeper or holder of the bank.

bank-ing[1] (bang′king), *n.* [See *bank*[1].] The construction of banks or embankments; also, a bank or embankment.

bank-ing[2] (bang′king), *n.* [See *bank*[3].] The business of a bank or banker.

bank=note (bangk′nōt), *n.* A promissory note, payable on demand, issued by a bank and intended to circulate as money.

bank-rupt (bangk′rupt). [F. *banqueroute*, < It. *bancarotta*, bankruptcy, < *banca*, bench, bank, + *rotta*, pp. fem. of *rompere*, < L. *rumpere*, break.] **I.** *n.* Bankruptcy†; a person who upon his own petition or that of his creditors is adjudged insolvent by a court, and whose property is administered for and divided among his creditors, under a system of bankruptcy laws; in popular usage, any insolvent debtor; one hopelessly in debt; one unable to satisfy any just claims made upon him. **II.** *a.* Subject to, or under, legal process because of insolvency; unable to pay one's debts; insolvent; fig., at the end of one's resources; bereft or destitute (*of*); wanting (*in*); also, pertaining to bankrupts.—**bank′rupt,** *v. t.* To make bankrupt; also, to impoverish†.—**bank′rupt-cy** (-si), *n.*; pl. *-cies* (-siz). The state of being or the fact of becoming bankrupt; fig., utter wreck or ruin.

bank-si-a (bangk′si-ạ), *n.* [NL., < Sir Joseph *Banks* (1743–1820), English naturalist.] Any plant of the Australasian genus *Sirmuellera* (formerly *Banksia*), comprising shrubs and trees with leathery leaves and dense cylindrical heads of flowers.

Bank-swallow.

bank=swal-low (bangk′-swol″ō), *n.* A small swallow, *Cotile riparia*, which burrows in banks to build its nest.

ban-ner (ban′ėr). [OF. *banere* (F. *bannière*), < ML. *bandum*, standard; from Teut. (cf. Goth. *bandwo*, sign, token).] **I.** *n.* A piece of cloth, attached by one side to the upper part of a pole or staff, formerly used as the standard of a sovereign, lord, or knight, and serving as a rallying-point in battle; the flag of a country, army, troop, etc.; an ensign or the like bearing some device or motto, as one attached by its upper edge and borne in processions; fig., anything displayed as a profession of principles; in *bot.*, a vexillum. **II.** *a.* Leading or foremost in some respect: as, the *banner* county of the country in the production of cotton.—**ban′nered,** *a.* Furnished with or displaying a banner or banners; also, borne on a banner.

ban-ner-et[1] (ban′ėr-et), *n.* [OF. *baneret.*] Orig., a knight who could bring a company of followers into the field under his own banner; later (also *knight banneret*), the title of the members of an order of knighthood now extinct, or a member of this order.

ban-ner-et[2], **ban-ner-ette** (ban-ėr-et′), *n.* [OF. *banerette.*] A small banner.

ban-ne-rol (ban′ẹ-rōl or -rol), *n.* [= *banderole.*] A banderole, or small flag or streamer; also, a square banner borne at the funeral of a great man and placed over the tomb.

ban′nis-ter, *n.* See *banister*.

ban-nock (ban′ọk), *n.* [AS. *bannuc.*] A flat cake made of oatmeal, barley-meal, or the like, commonly cooked on a griddle. [Prov. Eng. and Sc.]

banns (banz), *n. pl.* [For *bans*, pl. of *ban*[1].] Notice of an intended marriage, given three times in church by the parish priest.

ban-quet (bang′kwet), *n.* [OF. F. *banquet*, < It. *banchetto*, dim. of *banco*, bench, a masc. form corresponding to *banca*, fem., E. *bank*[3].] A feast; esp., a feast of state; a ceremonious public dinner or supper.—**ban′quet,** *v. t.* or *i.*; *-queted*, *-queting*. To entertain (another) or regale one's self at or as at a banquet; feast.—**ban′quet-er,** *n.*—**ban′quet=ring,** *n.* A finger-ring with a very large and elaborate piece of ornamentation surmounting the hoop (often extending at the ends over the finger-joints), worn on state occasions; a dinner-ring.

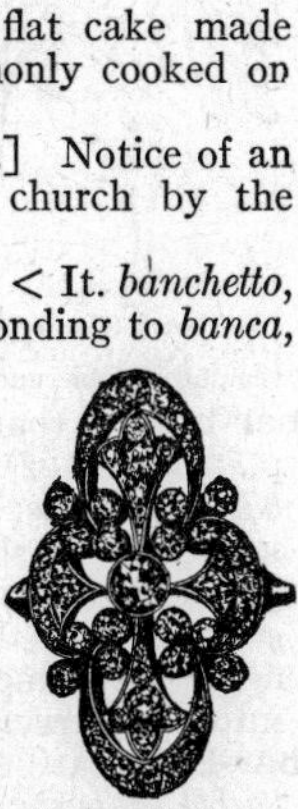
Banquet-ring.

ban-quette (bang-ket′), *n.* [F.] A platform along the inside of a parapet, for soldiers to stand on when firing; a raised footway on a bridge; a sidewalk (southern U. S.); a bench for passengers on top of a stage-coach.

ban-shee (ban′shē), *n.* [Ir. *bean sīdhe*, 'woman of the fairies.'] A supernatural being supposed to give warning by its wails of an approaching death in the family. [Ir. and Sc.]

bant (bant), *v. i.* To practise Bantingism. [Colloq.]

ban-tam (ban′tạm), *n.* [Prob. from *Bantam*, in western Java.] A domestic fowl of any of certain varieties or breeds characterized by very small size.—**ban′tam=weight,** *n.* A boxer of very light weight, lighter than a feather-weight.

ban-ter (ban′tėr), *v.* [Origin unknown.] **I.** *tr.* To address with mischievous or teasing raillery; rally; chaff; also, to impose upon as for sport (obs. or archaic); beat (*down*) in price, as by haggling (prov.); challenge, as to a contest (prov.). **II.** *intr.* To use banter.—**ban′ter,** *n.* Playfully teasing language; good-humored raillery; a jest or pleasantry (obs. or archaic); also, a challenge (prov.).—**ban′ter-er,** *n.*—**ban′ter-ing-ly,** *adv.*

Bant-ing-ism (ban′ting-izm), *n.* A method of reducing corpulence, recommended by William Banting, of London, in 1863, consisting chiefly in the avoidance of fat, starch, and sugar in the diet.—**Bant′ing-ize,** *v. i.*; *-ized*, *-izing.* To practise Bantingism.

bant-ling (bant′ling), *n.* [Perhaps < G. *bänkling*, bastard.] A young child; a brat.

Ban-tu (ban′tö). [Native word, meaning 'men,' 'people.'] **I.** *n. pl.* A large family of negro tribes inhabiting central and southern Africa; the languages of these tribes, constituting a linguistic family, characterized esp. by the use of prefixes (instead of suffixes) in derivation and inflection; *sing.* (pl. *-tus*), a member of any of these tribes. **II.** *a.* Of or pertaining to the Bantu (tribes or languages).

banx-ring (bangks′ring), *n.* [Javanese.] A squirrel-like insectivorous East Indian animal of the genus *Tupaia*.

ban′yan, *n.* See *banian*.

ban-zai (bän-zäi′), *interj.* [Jap., 'ten thousand years.'] A Japanese complimentary salutation or patriotic shout, as in honor of the emperor.

ba-o-bab (bā′ọ-bab), *n.* [Native African.] A bombacaceous tree of the genus *Adansonia*, esp. *A. digitata*, a native of tropical Africa, sometimes having a trunk 30 feet in diameter and a height of 70 feet, bearing a gourd-like fruit (monkey-bread) and affording a bark-fiber for making rope, cloth, etc.

Foliage, Fruit, and Flower of the Baobab (*Adansonia digitata*).

bap-tism (bap′tizm), *n.* [OF. *baptesme* (F. *baptême*), < LL. *baptisma*, < Gr. βάπτισμα, < βαπτίζειν: see *baptize*.] The act of baptizing; a ceremonial immersion in water, or application of water, as an initiatory rite or sacrament of the Christian church; hence, any like ceremony of initiation, dedication, christening, etc.—**bap-tis′mal** (-tiz′mạl), *a.*—**bap-tis′mal-ly,** *adv.*

bap-tist (bap′tist). [OF. *baptiste*, < LL. *baptista*, < Gr. βαπτιστής.] **I.** *n.* One who baptizes (as, John the *Baptist*); [*cap.*] a member of a Christian denomination which maintains that baptism (usually implying immersion) can be administered only upon a personal profession of Christian faith. **II.** *a.* [*cap.*] Of or pertaining to Baptists.

bap-tis-te-ry, bap-tis-try (bap′tis-tẹ-ri, -tri), *n.*; pl. *-ries* (-riz), *-tries* (-triz). [LL. *baptisterium*, < Gr. βαπτιστήριον.] A building, or a part of a church, in which baptism is administered; in Baptist churches, a tank containing water for baptism by immersion.

Baptistery of the Duomo, Pisa, Italy.

bap-tis-tic (bap-tis′tik), *a.* Pertaining to baptism or [*cap.*] to Baptists.

bap-tize (bap-tīz′), *v.*; *-tized*, *-tizing.* [OF. *baptizier* (F.

baptiser), < LL. *baptizare*, < Gr. βαπτίζειν, immerse, baptize, < βάπτειν, dip in water.] **I.** *tr.* To immerse in water, or sprinkle or pour water on, in the Christian rite of baptism; administer baptism to; also, to name in baptism; christen. Also fig. **II.** *intr.* To administer baptism.—**bap-tiz′er** (-tī′zėr), *n.*

bar (bär), *n.* [OF. F. *barre*, < ML. *barra*; origin unknown.] A relatively long and evenly shaped piece of some solid substance; esp., such a piece of wood or metal used as a guard or obstruction, or for some mechanical purpose (as, a crow*bar*); any barrier or obstruction; a bank of sand, etc., in water; a railing inclosing the space occupied by counsel in a court of justice; the legal profession; the place in court where prisoners are stationed; any tribunal; a counter or a place where liquors, etc., are served to customers; a band or stripe; in lace, a bride; in *her.*, a stripe, properly horizontal, crossing the field; in *music*, a vertical line marking off a measure on the staff; also, the measure; in *vet. science*, a toothless space in the mouth of a horse between the molar and canine teeth, in which the bit is fitted.—**bar sinister,** in *her.*, erroneously, a baton or a bend sinister.—**bar,** *v. t.*; *barred, barring.* [OF. F. *barrer.*] To provide, fasten, or obstruct with a bar or bars; shut in or out by or as by bars; block (a way, etc.), as with a barrier; prevent or hinder, as access; debar, as a person or an action; exclude or except (cf. *barring*); also, to mark with bars, stripes, or bands.—**bar,** *prep.* Barring; except.

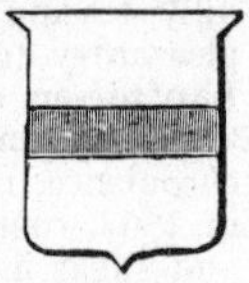
Heraldic Bar.

bar-ad (bar′ad), *n.* [Gr. βάρος, weight.] In the centimeter-gram-second system, the unit of pressure, equal to one dyne per square centimeter.

barb[1] (bärb), *n.* [OF. F. *barbe*, < L. *barba*, beard.] A beard†; a beard-like growth or part; one of the side processes of a feather; a point projecting backward from a main point, as of a fish-hook or an arrow-head; a linen covering for the throat and breast, formerly worn by women; a band or small scarf of lace, worn by women; in *vet. science*, a small protuberance under the tongue in horses and cattle, esp. when inflamed and swollen (usually in *pl.*).—**barb**[1], *v. t.* To trim or shave the beard of†; clip (coin, etc.); also, to furnish (a hook, etc.) with a barb or barbs.

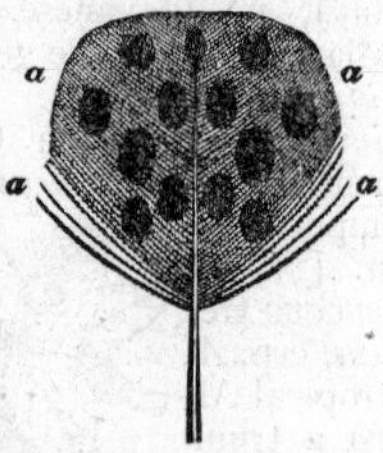

a, a, Barbs of a feather.

Barb, middle of 14th century.

barb[2] (bärb), *n.* [F. *barbe*, < *Barbarie*, Barbary.] A horse of a breed brought from Barbary to Spain by the Moors; also, one of a breed of domestic pigeons with a short, broad beak.

bar-ba-cue (bär′bạ-kū), *n.* and *v.* See *barbecue.*

Bar-ba-resque (bär-bạ-resk′), *a.* [F., < It. *Barbaresco.*] Of or pertaining to Barbary in northern Africa; [*l. c.*] barbarous in style, as forms of art.

bar-ba-ri-an (bär-bā′ri-ạn). [OF. *barbarien*, < L. *barbaria*, foreign country, barbarism, < *barbarus*: see *barbarous.*] **I.** *n.* A foreigner, orig. as compared with the Greeks; also, an uncultured person; also, an uncivilized person; a savage. **II.** *a.* Foreign; also, uncivilized; barbarous.—**bar-ba′ri-an-ism,** *n.*—**bar-ba′ri-an-ize,** *v. t.*; *-ized, -izing.* To render barbarian.

bar-bar-ic (bär-bar′ik), *a.* [L. *barbaricus*, < Gr. βαρβαρικός, foreign, barbaric, < βάρβαρος: see *barbarous.*] Of, like, or befitting a barbarous people; outlandish; bizarre; crudely rich or splendid.—**bar-bar′i-cal-ly,** *adv.*

bar-ba-rism (bär′bạ-rizm), *n.* [L. *barbarismus*, < Gr. βαρβαρισμός, < βαρβαρίζειν: see *barbarize.*] The use of words or idioms foreign to the accepted usage of a language; a word or idiom of this kind; also, barbarous or uncivilized condition; also, something belonging or proper to a barbarous condition; a barbarous act.

bar-bar-i-ty (bär-bar′i-ti), *n.*; pl. *-ties* (-tiz). Barbarous or uncivilized condition (obs. or archaic); also, barbarous character or style; a barbarism; also, barbarous or savage conduct or treatment; brutal cruelty; a barbarous act.

bar-ba-rize (bär′bạ-rīz), *v.*; *-rized, -rizing.* [Gr. βαρβαρίζειν, < βάρβαρος: see *barbarous.*] **I.** *intr.* To use barbarisms of speech; also, to become barbarous. **II.** *tr.* To render barbarous; esp., to debase (language, etc.) by departure from recognized classical standards.—**bar″ba-ri-za′tion** (-ri-zā′shọn), *n.*

bar-ba-rous (bär′bạ-rus), *a.* [L. *barbarus*, < Gr. βάρβαρος, foreign, outlandish, rude, barbarous; prob. orig. with reference to speech: cf. Skt. *barbara*, stammering, pl. foreigners, L. *balbus*, stammering.] Foreign, orig. as compared with the Greeks or their language, usages, etc.; hence, not conforming or conformed to classical standards or accepted usage, as language; also, uncultured or unpolished; rough; rude; also, uncivilized; savage; hence, savagely cruel; inhuman.—**bar′ba-rous-ly,** *adv.*—**bar′ba-rous-ness,** *n.*

bar-bate (bär′bāt), *a.* [L. *barbatus*, < *barba*, beard.] In *zoöl.* and *bot.*, bearded; tufted or furnished with hairs.

bar-be-cue (bär′bẹ-kū), *n.* [Haitian *barbacoa*, framework of sticks set upon posts.] A framework on which, in the West Indies, etc., meat or fish is dried or cured over a fire; a framework on which animals are broiled or roasted whole or in large pieces; a dressed ox or other animal roasted whole; a large social entertainment, usually in the open air, at which animals are roasted whole as part of a generous feast (U. S.); an open floor on which coffee-beans are spread to dry.—**bar′be-cue,** *v. t.*; *-cued, -cuing.* To dry or cure on a barbecue; also, to broil or roast (an animal) whole.

barbed[1] (bärbd), *a.* Furnished with a barb or barbs, as a fish-hook or an arrow-head; made with sharp points at intervals, as a kind of wire.

barbed[2] (bärbd), *p. a.* [Erron. for *barded*: see *bard*[1], *v.*] Armed with bards, as a horse. [Obs. or archaic.]

bar-bel (bär′bel), *n.* [OF. *barbel* (F. *barbeau*), < LL. *barbus*, barbel, < L. *barba*, beard.] Any of various cyprinoid fishes of the genus *Barbus*, esp. *B. vulgaris*, a large fresh-water fish of Europe; also, a slender, cylindrical tactile process appended to the head or mouth of certain fishes, as the barbel.

Barbel (*Barbus vulgaris*).

bar-bel-late (bär′be-lāt), *a.* [NL. *barbella*, dim. of L. *barbula*: see *barbule.*] In *bot.*, having short, stiff hairs.

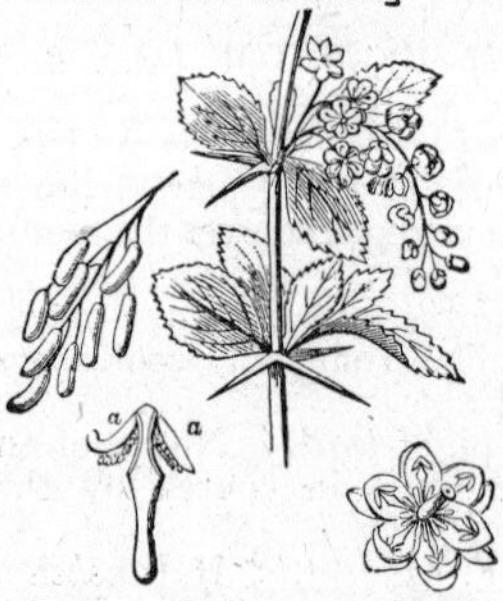

Barberry (*Berberis vulgaris*), with fruit, flower, and anther (*a a*) in the act of dehiscence.

bar-ber (bär′bėr), *n.* [AF. *barbour*, OF. *barbeor*, < L. *barba*, beard.] One whose occupation it is to shave or trim the beard and to cut and dress the hair of customers.—**bar′ber,** *v. t.* To trim or dress the beard and hair of.

bar-be-ra (bär-bā′rạ̈), *n.* [It.] An Italian red wine.

bar-ber-ry (bär′ber″i), *n.*; pl. *-berries* (-iz). [ML. *barbaris, berberis*; origin unknown.] A shrub of the genus *Berberis*, esp. *B. vulgaris*, or its red, elongated, acid fruit, sometimes made into a preserve.

Peruvian Barbet (family *Capitonidæ*).

bar-bet (bär′bet), *n.* [F. *barbet*, < *barbe*, < L. *barba*, beard.] A small dog with long curly hair; a poodle; also, any of the birds of the family *Capitonidæ* and the subfamily *Bucconinæ* (family *Galbulidæ*), characterized chiefly by large heads, and stout, often bristly bills.

bar-bette (bär-bet′), *n.* [F. *barbette*, < *barbe*: see *barbet.*] A platform or mound of earth within a fortification, from which guns may be fired over the parapet instead of through embrasures; also, an armored structure on a war-ship, protecting a gun platform.

bar-bi-can (bär′bi-kạn), *n.* [OF. *barbacane*; perhaps from Ar.] An outwork of a castle or fortified place, esp. a large tower, often a watch-tower, over a gate or bridge: as, "Within the *Barbican* a Porter sate, Day and night duely keeping watch and ward" (Spenser's "Faerie Queene," ii. 9. 25).

bar-bi-cel (bär′bi-sel), *n.* [NL. *barbicella*, dim. of L. *barba*, beard.] One of the minute processes fringing the barbules of certain feathers.

barb-less (bärb′les), *a.* Without barbs, as a fish-hook.

bar-bo-tine (bär′bọ-tin), *n.* [F. *barbotine*, < *barboter*, dabble.] In *ceram.*, same as *slip*[1].

bar-bu-do (bär-bö′dō) *n.*; pl. *-dos* (-dōz). [Sp., lit. 'bearded.'] A thread-fin of the genus *Polydactylus*, esp. *P. virginicus*, a small food-fish of Florida, the West Indies, etc.

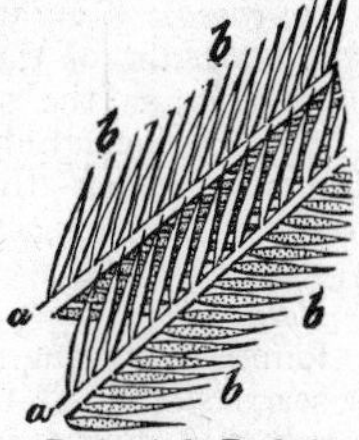

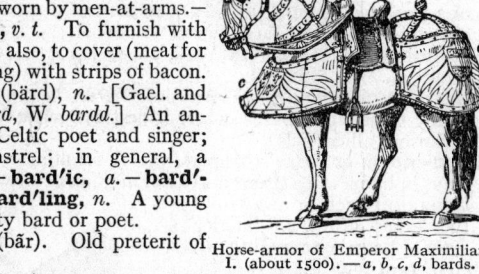

a, Barb; *b*, *b*, Barbules. (Highly magnified.)

bar-bule (bär′būl), *n.* [L. *barbula*, dim. of *barba*, beard.] A little barb; specif., one of the small processes fringing the barbs of a feather.

bar-ca-role, bar-ca-rolle (bär′kạ-rōl), *n.* [F. *barcarolle*, < It. *barcaruola*, < *barca*, boat.] A boating-song of the Venetian gondoliers; a piece of music composed in imitation of such songs.

bard[1] (bärd), *n.* [F. *barde*; perhaps from Ar.] Any of various pieces of defensive armor for a horse, or an ornamental covering, as of velvet, representing such a piece; *pl.*, armor of metal plates, formerly worn by men-at-arms.—**bard**[1], *v. t.* To furnish with bards; also, to cover (meat for roasting) with strips of bacon.

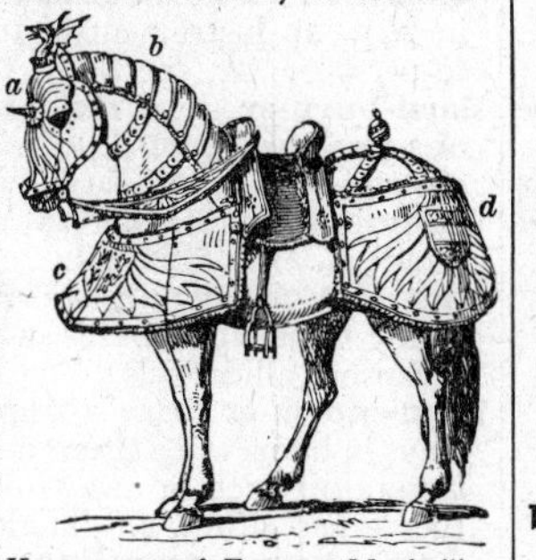

Horse-armor of Emperor Maximilian I. (about 1500).—*a*, *b*, *c*, *d*, bards.

bard[2] (bärd), *n.* [Gael. and Ir. *bard*, W. *bardd.*] An ancient Celtic poet and singer; a minstrel; in general, a poet.—**bard′ic,** *a.*—**bard′let, bard′ling,** *n.* A young or petty bard or poet.

bare[1] (bãr). Old preterit of *bear*[1].

bare[2] (bãr), *a.*; compar. *barer*, superl. *barest.* [AS. *bær* = G. *bar.*] Without covering or clothing; naked or nude; with the head uncovered; unconcealed, undisguised, or open to view; without the natural or usual covering, as of hair, wool, foliage, etc.; napless or threadbare; without the usual equipments, furnishings, contents, etc.; stripped or destitute (*of*); plain, bald, or unadorned; also, being such and no more; mere; also, paltry†.—**bare**[2], *v. t.*; *bared*, *baring.* To make bare; uncover; reveal; strip (*of*).—**bare′back,** *a.* and *adv.* With the back (of a horse, etc.) bare, or without saddle.—**bare′backed,** *a.*—**bare′boned,** *a.* Lean; emaciated.—**bare′faced,** *a.* With the face uncovered; not masked; hence, undisguised; boldly open; shameless.—**bare′faced″ly,** *adv.*—**bare′faced″ness,** *n.*—**bare′foot,** *a.* and *adv.* With the feet bare.—**bare′foot″ed,** *a.*

ba-rège (bạ-rāzh′), *n.* [F., < *Barèges*, town in the Pyrenees (France).] A thin fabric of wool, wool and silk, or wool and cotton, used for dresses, veils, etc.

bare-hand-ed (bãr′han″ded), *a.* [See *bare*[2].] With hands uncovered; also, with empty hands; without means.—**bare′head″ed,** *a.* With the head uncovered.—**bare′legged** (-legd or -leg″ed), *a.* With the legs bare.

bare-ly (bãr′li), *adv.* In a bare manner; nakedly; openly; plainly; baldly; meagerly or scantily; also, scarcely; merely; only just.

bare-necked (bãr′nekt), *a.* With the neck bare.

bare-ness (bãr′nes), *n.* The state of being bare.

bare-sark (bãr′särk). [For *berserk*, as if meaning 'bare sark,' that is, bare shirt (without armor).] **I.** *n.* Same as *berserk*. **II.** *adv.* In a shirt only, or without armor.

bar-ful (bär′fu̇l), *a.* Full of bars or impediments. See Shakspere's "Twelfth Night," i. 4. 41. [Obs. or rare.]

bar-gain (bär′gạn), *n.* [OF. *bargaigne*; origin uncertain.] Discussion of the terms of a proposed agreement or compact†; also, an agreement between parties settling what each shall give and take, or perform and receive, in a transaction; a compact; a contract; also, such an agreement as affecting one of the parties (as, a losing *bargain*); also, that which one of the parties has stipulated to give and take or perform and receive; also, that which is acquired by bargaining; a purchase considered as advantageous or the reverse; often, an advantageous purchase.—**into the bargain,** over and above what is stipulated; moreover; besides.—**bar′gain,** *v.* [OF. *bargaignier.*] **I.** *intr.* To discuss the terms of a bargain or compact; haggle over terms; also, to come to terms; make or strike a bargain; arrange (*for*) beforehand in or as in a bargain. **II.** *tr.* To arrange by bargain; stipulate; also, to agree to buy or sell†; also, to part with or lose as the result of a bargain (with *away*).—**bar-gain-ee′** (-ē′), *n.* In *law*, the recipient in a bargain.—**bar′gain-er,** *n.* One who bargains; in *law*, the party contracting to sell or deliver to the bargainee. Also (in *law*) **bar′gain-or.**

barge (bärj), *n.* [OF. F. *barge*, < ML. *barga*, perhaps for LL. *barca*, E. *bark*[3].] Formerly, any of various sea-going sailing-vessels; now, a comparatively large, usually flat-bottomed boat (towed by a tug or the like, or propelled by sail, etc.) used for transporting freight, etc.; a two-decked boat towed by another boat, used esp. for pleasure-excursions; a vessel of state, used in pageants, etc.; a large elegantly finished rowing-boat for the use of a flag-officer; a long, narrow racing-boat, somewhat wider and stronger than a shell; also, a large wagon or omnibus used for picnics, etc.—**barge,** *v. t.*; *barged*, *barging.* To carry or transport by barge.

Barge of State.

barge=board (bärj′bōrd), *n.* [Cf. ML. *bargus*, kind of gallows.] In *arch.*, a board, often ornamental, placed along the projecting sloping edge of a gable-roof, usually concealing or taking the place of a rafter.—**barge′=cou″ple,** *n.* In *arch.*, one of the pair of rafters in a gable, situated outside the end wall and carrying the overhanging portion of the roof.—**barge′=course,** *n.* In *arch.*, the range of tiles along the sloping edges of a gable-roof; the part of a gable-roof that projects beyond the end wall.

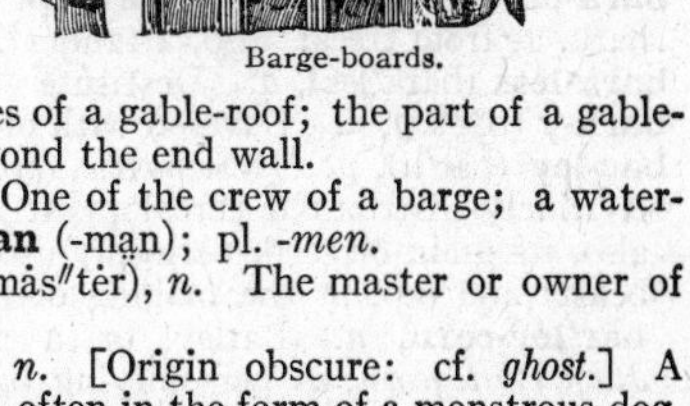
Barge-boards.

bar-gee (bär-jē′), *n.* One of the crew of a barge; a waterman. Also **barge′man** (-mạn); pl. *-men.*

barge=mas-ter (bärj′mȧs″tėr), *n.* The master or owner of a barge.

bar-ghest (bär′gest), *n.* [Origin obscure: cf. *ghost.*] A local specter or goblin, often in the form of a monstrous dog, believed to portend misfortune. [North. Eng. and Sc.]

bar-ic[1] (bar′ik), *a.* [Gr. βάρος, weight.] Of or pertaining to weight, esp. that of the atmosphere; barometric.

bar-ic[2] (bar′ik or bā′rik), *a.* Of or containing barium.

bar-ie (bar′i, F. bȧ-rē), *n.* [F. *barie*, < Gr. βαρεῖα, fem. of βαρύς, heavy.] In *physics*, a unit of gaseous pressure, equal to one dyne per square centimeter.

ba-ril-la (bą-ril′ä), *n.* [Sp. *barrilla.*] Either of two European saltworts, *Salsola kali* and *S. soda*, whose ashes yield an impure carbonate of soda; also, the alkali obtained from the ashes of these and certain other maritime plants.
bar-ish (bãr′ish), *a.* Somewhat bare.
ba-rite (bā′rīt), *n.* Native barium sulphate; barytes.
bar-i-tone (bar′i-tōn), *n.* and *a.* A common spelling (after It. *baritono*) of *barytone* as used in music.
ba-ri-um (bā′ri-um), *n.* [NL., < E. *barytes.*] Chem. sym., Ba; at. wt., 137.37; sp. gr., 3.6. A whitish, malleable metallic element occurring in combination in various minerals.
bark[1] (bärk), *v.* [AS. *beorcan.*] **I.** *intr.* To utter an abrupt, explosive cry or a series of such cries, as a dog; fig., to clamor; also, to cough (colloq.). **II.** *tr.* To utter or give forth with or as with a bark.—**bark**[1], *n.* The abrupt, explosive cry of a dog; a similar sound made by some other animal; a cough (colloq.).
bark[2] (bärk), *n.* [Icel. *börkr* = Sw. and Dan. *bark.*] The external covering of the woody stems or roots of plants (sometimes restricted to the rough outer part, but usually including the corky tissues and the phloëm or 'inner bark'); in *phar.*, cinchona ('Peruvian bark'); in *tanning*, tan-bark.—**bark**[2], *v. t.* To strip off the bark of; remove a circle of bark from; scrape off the dead bark of; scrape or rub off the skin from; also, to cover or inclose with or as with bark; incrust; also, to treat with an infusion of bark; tan.

Bark.

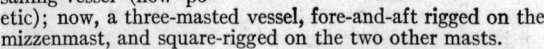

bark[3] (bärk), *n.* [F. *barque*, < It. *barca*, < LL. *barca.*] A boat or sailing-vessel (now poetic); now, a three-masted vessel, fore-and-aft rigged on the mizzenmast, and square-rigged on the two other masts.
bar-kan-tine, bar-ken-tine (bär′kąn-tēn, -kęn-tēn), *n.* [From *bark*[3], after *brigantine.*] A three-masted vessel with the foremast square-rigged and the mainmast and mizzenmast fore-and-aft rigged.

Barkantine.

bark=bee-tle (bärk′bē″tl), *n.* Any of the small beetles constituting the family *Scolytidæ*, nearly all of which make burrows between the bark and the wood of woody plants.
bark=bound (bärk′bound), *a.* Hindered in growth by rigidity or tightness of the bark.
bar-keep-er (bär′kē″pėr), *n.* One who tends a bar where liquors are served to customers.
bar′ken-tine, *n.* See *barkantine.*
bark-er[1] (bär′kėr), *n.* [See *bark*[1].] An animal or a person that barks; also, one who stands before a shop, etc., calling passers-by to enter (colloq.).
bark-er[2] (bär′kėr), *n.* [See *bark*[2].] One who strips off bark, as from trees; also, a tanner†.
bark-less (bärk′les), *a.* Destitute of bark.
bark-y (bär′ki), *a.* Covered with or resembling bark.
bar-ley (bär′li), *n.* [AS. *bærlic*, appar. < *bere*, E. *bear*[3].] A widely distributed cereal plant of the genus *Hordeum*; also, its grain or seed, variously used as food (for man and beast) and esp. in the making of beer, ale, whisky, etc.—**bar′ley-corn,** *n.* Barley, or a grain of barley (hence *John Barleycorn*, as personifying barley as used in making malt liquor, or malt liquor itself); also, a measure equal to the third part of an inch.—**bar′ley=sug″ar,** *n.* Sugar boiled, formerly in a decoction of barley, till it becomes brittle and candied.—**bar′ley=wa″ter,** *n.* A decoction of barley, used as a demulcent.
barm (bärm), *n.* [AS. *beorma* = G. *bärme.*] Yeast formed on malt liquors while fermenting. See Shakspere's "Midsummer Night's Dream," ii. 1. 38.
bar-maid (bär′mād), *n.* A female attendant at a bar, as of an inn or tavern.
Bar-me-cide (bär′mę-sīd). **I.** *n.* A member of a noble Persian family of Bagdad (the Barmecides, so called from Barmak, the founder), who, according to a tale in the "Arabian Nights' Entertainments," gave a beggar a pretended feast with empty dishes; hence, one who makes an empty pretense of hospitality, beneficence, etc. **II.** *a.* Like the Barmecide or his feast.—**Bar′me-ci-dal** (-sī-dąl), *a.*
barm-y (bär′mi), *a.* Full of barm; frothing; in a ferment; flighty, silly, or weak-minded (prov. or slang: cf. *balmy*[2]).
barn (bärn), *n.* [AS. *bern*, *berern*, < *bere*, barley, + *ærn*, place, house.] A building for storing hay, grain, etc., and often for stabling live stock.
bar-na-cle[1] (bär′nạ-kl), *n.* [ME. *bernacle* (earlier *bernak*) = F. *bernacle* (earlier *bernaque*); origin uncertain.] A wild goose, *Bernicla* (or *Branta*) *leucopsis*, chiefly of northern Europe (also called *barnacle-goose*); also, any of certain crustaceans of the group *Cirripedia*, as the stalked cirripeds of the family *Lepadidæ*, which attach themselves to ships' bottoms, etc., and the sessile cirripeds of the family *Balanidæ*, the acorn-shells, found incrusting rocks along seacoasts; fig., a thing or person that clings tenaciously.

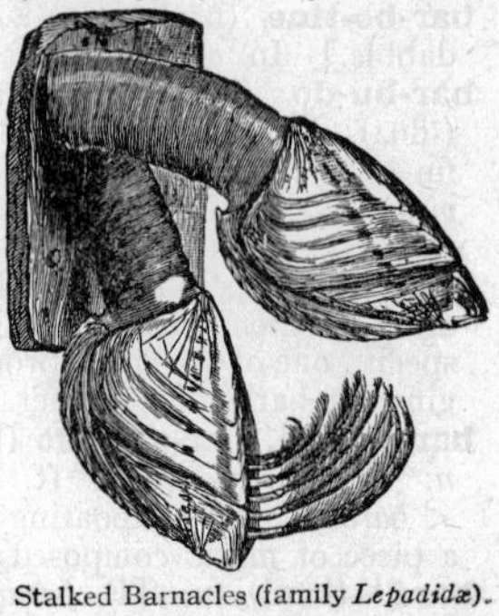
Stalked Barnacles (family *Lepadidæ*).

bar-na-cle[2] (bär′nạ-kl), *n.* [ME. *bernacle*, *bernak*, < OF. *bernac*; origin unknown.] An instrument with two hinged branches for confining the nose of an unruly horse (usually in *pl.*); an instrument of torture applied in a similar way to persons; *pl.*, spectacles (colloq.).
Barn-burn-er (bärn′bėr″nėr), *n.* [In allusion to the story of a farmer who burned his barn to get rid of rats.] Orig., a member of the radical reform section of the Democratic party in the State of New York, about 1845; hence [*l. c.*], a radical. Cf. *Hunker*[1].
barn=owl (bärn′oul), *n.* An owl, *Strix flammea*, commonly frequenting barns, where it destroys mice; also, any of various allied owls.
barn=storm-er (bärn′stôr″mėr), *n.* A strolling actor who plays in barns when theaters are lacking; an actor who plays in rural districts or away from the larger cities; an inferior actor.—**barn′=storm″ing,** *n.*
barn=swal-low (bärn′swol″ō), *n.* The common swallow of North America, *Hirundo erythrogastra*; in Great Britain, the chimney-swallow, *H. rustica.* See *swallow*[1].
barn-yard (bärn′yärd), *n.* A yard about a barn.
baro-. Form of Gr. βάρος, weight, used in combination.—**bar-o-cy-clo-nom-e-ter** (bar″ǫ-sī-klǫ-nom′e-tėr), *n.* [+ *cyclone* + *-meter.*] An aneroid barometer used with accompanying charts and diagrams to determine the existence of a storm at a considerable distance.—**bar′o-gram** (-gram), *n.* [+ *-gram.*] A record traced by a barograph or similar instrument.—**bar′o-graph** (-gråf), *n.* [+ *-graph.*] A self-registering instrument for recording variations in the pressure of the atmosphere.—**bar-o-graph′ic** (-graf′ik), *a.*—**ba-rol-o-gy** (bą-rol′ǫ-ji), *n.* [+ *-logy.*] The science of weight.

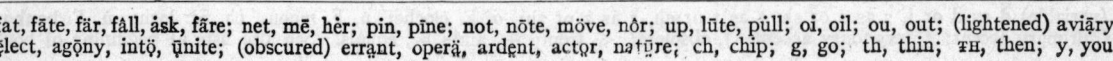

Barn-swallow (*Hirundo erythrogastra*).

ba-rom-e-ter (bą-rom′e-tėr), *n.* [See *baro-* and *-meter.*] An instrument (in various forms) for measuring the pressure of the atmosphere, and thus determining probable changes of weather, height above sea-level, etc.—**bar-o-met-ric, bar-o-met-ri-cal** (bar-ǫ-met′rik, -ri-kąl), *a.* Of, pertaining to, or indicated by the barometer.—**bar-o-met′ri-cal-ly,** *adv.*—**ba-rom′e-try,** *n.* [See *-metry.*] The art of measuring the pressure of the atmosphere.

bar-on (bar′ǫn), *n.* [OF. F. *baron*, < LL. *baro(n-)*, man; origin uncertain.] In England, formerly, a feudatory holding land by honorable service, esp. directly from the king; in Great Britain, a member of the lowest order of nobility, ranking immediately below a viscount; a member of a corresponding order in various other countries; a freeman of any of certain English cities, etc.†; the title of the judges of the English Court of Exchequer; a man of wealth possessing extensive influence over a particular commodity in trade (colloq.: as, a coal *baron*); in *law* and *her.*, a husband.—**baron of beef,** in *cookery*, a joint consisting of two sirloins not cut asunder. —**bar′on-age** (-ąj), *n.* The whole body of British barons; formerly, the nobility or peerage in general; also, the dignity or rank of a baron.—**bar′on-ess,** *n.* The wife of a baron; also, a lady holding a baronial title in her own right.

Coronet of a British Baron.

bar-on-et (bar′ǫn-et), *n.* [Dim. of *baron.*] A lesser or inferior baron†; a member of a British hereditary order of honor, ranking below the barons and above the knights, and made up of commoners (designated by *Sir* before the name, and *Baronet*, usually abbreviated *Bart.*, after, as in 'Sir John Smith, Bart.').—**bar′on-et,** *v. t.*; *-eted, -eting.* To raise to the rank of a baronet.—**bar′on-et-age** (-ąj), *n.* The order of baronets; the baronets as a body; also, the rank of a baronet.—**bar′on-et-cy** (-si), *n.*; pl. *-cies* (-siz). The rank or patent of a baronet.

ba-rong (bä-rong′), *n.* [Native name.] A large, broad-bladed knife or cleaver used by the Moros.

ba-ro-ni-al (bą-rō′ni-ąl), *a.* Of or pertaining to a baron or a barony.

ba-ronne (bȧ-ron), *n.* [F.] In French use, a baroness.

bar-on-y (bar′ǫn-i), *n.*; pl. *-ies* (-iz). [OF. *baronie* (F. *baronnie*).] The domain of a baron; in Ireland, a division of a county; in Scotland, any large freehold estate; also, the rank or dignity of a baron; formerly, the tenure by which a baron held of his superior.

ba-roque (bą-rōk′), *a.* [F., < Pg. *barroco* or Sp. *barrueco* = It. *barocco*; origin uncertain.] Irregular in shape, as some pearls; also, artistically irregular, incongruous, or fantastic, as a style of architectural and other decoration of the 18th century; tastelessly odd; bizarre; grotesque.

bar-o-scope (bar′ǭ-skōp), *n.* [See *baro-* and *-scope.*] An instrument for showing variations in the pressure or the density of the air; also, a physical apparatus used to demonstrate the upward pressure of the air.—**bar-o-scop′ic** (-skop′ik), *a.*

ba-rouche (bą-rösh′), *n.* [G. *barutsche*, < It. *baroccio*, < L. *birotus*, two-wheeled, < *bi-*, two, + *rota*, wheel.] A four-wheeled carriage with a seat in front for the driver, and seats inside for two couples, the forward one facing backward and the rear one forward, and with a falling or folding top over the back seat.

bar-quan-tine, bar-quen-tine (bär′kąn-tēn, -kęn-tēn), *n.* See *barkantine.*

barque (bärk), *n.* See *bark*³.

bar-ra-ble (bär′ą-bl), *a.* That may be barred.

bar-rack (bar′ąk), *n.* [F. *baraque*, < It. *baracca* = Sp. *barraca*; origin uncertain.] A building or range of buildings for lodging soldiers, esp. in garrison; also, a large, plain building, or a collection of huts or cabins, in which large numbers of men are lodged: usually in *pl.*—**bar′rack,** *v. t.* or *i.* To lodge in barracks.

bar-ra-coon (bar-ą-kön′), *n.* [Sp. *barracón*, < *barraca*, barrack.] A barrack or an inclosure containing sheds for the temporary detention of negro slaves, etc.

bar-ra-cou-ta (bar-ą-kö′tą), *n.* Same as *barracuda.*

bar-ra-cu-da (bar-ą-kö′dą), *n.* [W. Ind.] A large voracious fish, *Sphyræna barracuda*, of West Indian and neighboring seas ('great barracuda'); also, any of various related species.

bar-rage (bär′ąj, F. bȧ-räzh), *n.* [F. *barrage*, < *barrer*, E. *bar, v.*] The act of barring; the formation of an artificial obstruction in a watercourse, to increase the depth of the water, facilitate irrigation, etc.; the obstruction or bar thus formed, esp. one of those in the Nile; *milit.*, the formation of a barrier of artillery fire to prevent the enemy from advancing (and at the same time to enable troops behind it to operate more safely), or to cut off the enemy's retreat in one or more directions; the artillery fire so formed; also, captive balloons with nets, etc., to obstruct airplanes ('balloon barrage').—**bar-rage** (bär′ąj or bȧ-räzh′), *v. t.*; *-raged, -raging.* To subject to a barrage.

bar-ra-mun-da (bar-ą-mun′dą), *n.* [Native Australian.] A dipnoous fish, *Neoceratodus forsteri*, of rivers of Australia, attaining a length of 6 feet. Also **bar-ra-mun′di** (-di).

bar-ran-co (bä-räng′kō), *n.*; pl. *-cos* (-kōs). [Sp.] A ravine or mountain-gorge with steep sides.

bar-ra-tor (bar′ą-tǫr), *n.* [OF. *baratour*, fraudulent dealer, < *barater*, exchange, cheat: cf. *barter.*] In *law*, a trafficker in offices of state, ecclesiastical preferments, etc. (obs. or archaic); a judge who takes a bribe (Sc.); a ship's officer or seaman who commits any fraud against the owners, freighters, or insurers; one who incites to litigation or controversy.—**bar′ra-trous,** *a.* Of the nature of barratry.—**bar′ra-trous-ly,** *adv.*—**bar′ra-try,** *n.* [OF. *baraterie.*] In *law*, the conduct or offense of a barrator.

barred (bärd), *a.* Having bars: as, a five-*barred* gate.

bar-rel (bar′ęl), *n.* [OF. F. *baril*; origin uncertain.] A wooden vessel, approximately cylindrical, with slightly bulging sides made of staves hooped together, and with flat, parallel ends; the quantity which such a vessel of some standard size can hold (as 31½ gallons of liquid or 196 pounds of flour); also, any vessel, case, or part similar in form; a cylinder or drum; the tube of a gun.—**bar′rel,** *v. t.*; *-reled* or *-relled, -reling* or *-relling.* To put, pack, or store in a barrel or barrels.—**bar′reled, bar′relled,** *a.* Having a barrel or barrels: as, a double-*barreled* gun.—**bar′rel=or″gan,** *n.* A musical instrument in which air from a bellows is admitted to a set of pipes by means of a revolving barrel-like mechanism; a hand-organ.

bar-ren (bar′ęn). [OF. *baraine*, fem., *brehain*, masc.; origin unknown.] **I.** *a.* Incapable of producing, or not producing, offspring, fruit, or vegetation; sterile; unproductive; fruitless; bare; devoid (*of*). **II.** *n.* A tract of more or less unproductive land: often in *pl.*—**bar′ren-ly,** *adv.*—**bar′ren-ness,** *n.*

bar-ret (bar′et), *n.* [F. *barrette*, cap, = E. *biretta.*] A kind of small cap, esp. a biretta.

bar-rette (bä-ret′), *n.* [F. *barrette*, dim. of *barre*, bar.] A clasp for holding up a woman's hair, as when drawn up from the back of the neck.

bar-ri-cade (bar-i-kād′), *n.* [F. *barricade*, prob. < Pr. *barricada*, a barricade, orig. made of casks filled with earth, < *barrica*, cask.] A defensive barrier hastily constructed, as in a street, to stop the progress of an enemy; hence, any barrier or obstruction to passage.—**bar-ri-cade′,** *v. t.*; *-caded, -cading.* To obstruct or block with a barricade; render impassable; also, to shut in and defend with or as with a barricade.—**bar-ri-cad′er** (-kā′dėr), *n.*—**bar-ri-ca′do** (-kā′dō), *n.* and *v.* Same as *barricade.* [Obs. or archaic.]

bar-ri-er (bar′i-ėr), *n.* [OF. *barrere* (F. *barrière*), < *barre*, bar.] Anything built or serving to bar passage, as a stockade or fortress, a railing, or any natural bar; a dividing obstacle; a means of separation or restraint.—**bar′ri-er,** *v. t.* To shut in or off by a barrier.

bar-ring (bär′ing), *prep.* [Orig. ppr.] Excluding from consideration; excepting: as, *barring* accidents, it will be ready on time.

bar-ri-o (bär′rē-ō), *n.*; pl. *-os* (-ōs). [Sp.] In Spain and countries colonized by Spain, one of the divisions into which a town or city, together with the contiguous rural territory, is divided.

bar-ris-ter (bar′is-tėr), *n.* [See *bar.*] In England, a counselor or advocate at law admitted to plead at the bar in any court. Cf. *solicitor.*

bar=room (bär′röm), *n.* A room containing a bar for the sale of liquors.

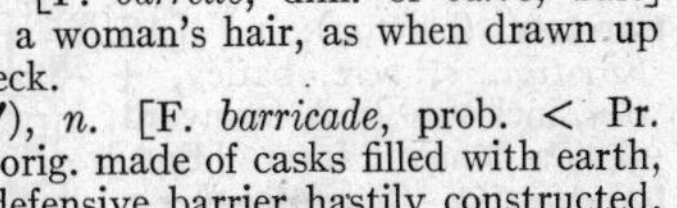
Barrow (tumulus).

bar-row¹ (bar′ō), *n.* [AS. *beorg*, *beorh*, hill, mound, = G. *berg*, hill, mountain.] A hill (now chiefly in Eng. place-names); also, a mound of earth or stones raised over a tomb (as, "grassy

(variable) d̹ as d or j, s̹ as s or sh, t̹ as t or ch, z̹ as z or zh; *o*, F. cloche; ü, F. menu; ċh, Sc. loch; ṅ, F. bonbon; **′**, primary accent; **″**, secondary accent; †, obsolete; <, from; +, and; =, equals. See also lists at beginning of book.

barrows of the happier dead": Tennyson's "Tithonus"); a tumulus.

bar-row[2] (bar′ō), *n.* [ME. *barewe*, prob. < AS. *beran*, E. *bear*[1].] A flat, rectangular frame used by two or more persons for carrying a load, esp. such a frame with projecting shafts at each end for handles; a hand-barrow; also, a modification of this, generally in the form of a shallow box with flaring sides supported in front by a wheel and having shafts at the rear by which one man may push it; a wheelbarrow; also, a push-cart or hand-cart; also, the load carried on or in a barrow.

bar-row[3] (bar′ō), *n.* [AS. *bearg, bearh.*] The castrated male of swine.

bar-row[4] (bar′ō), *n.* [Origin uncertain.] A long flannel garment for infants, wrapped about the body below the arms and turned up and pinned about the feet. Also **bar′row=coat.**

Barry of six.

bar-ru-let (bar′ö-let), *n.* [Dim. of *bar.*] In *her.*, a diminutive of the bar, usually one fourth of its width.

bar-ry (bär′i), *a.* [F. *barré*, pp. of *barrer*, E. *bar, v.*] In *her.*, divided into bars: said of the field.

bar=shot (bär′shot), *n.* A shot consisting of a bar with a ball at each end.

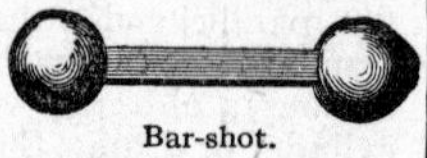
Bar-shot.

bar-tend-er (bär′ten″dėr), *n.* A barkeeper.

bar-ter (bär′tėr), *v.* [OF. *barater* (= It. *barattare*), exchange, barter, cheat: cf. *barrator.*] **I.** *tr.* To exchange in trade, as one commodity for another; trade (often with *away*). **II.** *intr.* To trade or traffic by exchange of commodities (rather than by the use of money).—**bar′ter,** *n.* The act of bartering; traffic by exchange of commodities; also, the thing bartered.—**bar′ter-er,** *n.*

bar-ti-zan (bär′ti-zạn), *n.* [Appar. a corruption of *brat-ticing.*] A small overhanging turret on a wall or tower: as, "On battlement and *bartizan* Gleam'd axe, and spear, and partisan" (Scott's "Lay of the Last Minstrel," iv. 20).—**bar′ti-zaned,** *a.* Furnished with a bartizan.

Bartizan. — Carcassonne, France. *A*, merlon; *B*, embrasure; *C*, loophole; *D*, machicolation.

bar-ton (bär′tọn), *n.* [AS. *bere-tūn*, < *bere*, barley, + *tūn*, inclosure.] A farmyard; also, a demesne farm. [Eng.]

bar-to-ni-a (bär-tō′ni-ạ̈), *n.* [NL.; named from B. S. *Barton* (1766–1815), American naturalist.] Any of several large-flowered plants of the family *Loasaceæ*, formerly regarded by some botanists as constituting a genus *Bartonia* but now generally referred to the genus *Mentzelia*, as *M. lindleyi*, which is commonly known in cultivation as *Bartonia aurea* ('golden bartonia'); also, any of the small-flowered plants constituting the gentianaceous genus *Bartonia*.

bar-wood (bär′wụ̇d), *n.* [Cf. *logwood.*] A red dyewood from a fabaceous tree, *Baphia nitida*, of western Africa.

bar-y-cen-tric (bar-i-sen′trik), *a.* [Gr. βαρύς, heavy, + κέντρον, E. *center*[2].] Of or pertaining to the center of gravity.

ba-ry-ta (ba-rī′tạ̈), *n.* [See *barytes.*] In *chem.*, barium oxide, BaO; also, barium (in phrases, as 'carbonate of baryta').

ba-ry-tes (ba-rī′tēz), *n.* [Gr. βαρύς, heavy.] Baryta†; also, native sulphate of barium; barite.

ba-ryt-ic (ba-rit′ik), *a.* Pertaining to or containing baryta.

bar-y-tone (bar′i-tōn). [= F. *baryton* = It. *baritono*, < Gr. βαρύτονος, deep-sounding, < βαρύς, heavy, + τόνος, tone.] **I.** *n.* In *music*, a male voice or voice-part intermediate between tenor and bass; a singer with such a voice; in *Gr. gram.*, a word having (theoretically) the grave accent, or having no accent, on the last syllable. **II.** *a.* In *music*, of or pertaining to the barytone; having the compass of the barytone; in *Gr. gram.*, without accent on the last syllable.

ba-sal (bā′sạl), *a.* Of, at, or forming the base; fundamental.—**ba′sal-ly,** *adv.*

ba-salt (bạ-sâlt′ or bas′âlt), *n.* [L. *basaltes.*] Any of various heavy, dark-colored, basic rocks of volcanic origin, containing various constituents (such as plagioclase, augite, olivine, and magnetite), occurring in porphyritic and coarse or fine crystalline forms, and sometimes displaying a remarkable columnar structure.—**ba-sal-tic** (bạ-sâl′tik), *a.* Of or like basalt.—**ba-sal′ti-form,** *a.* [See *-form.*] Having the form of basalt; columnar.—**ba-sal′toid,** *a.* [See *-oid.*] Resembling basalt.

Columnar Basalt.

bas-an (baz′ạn), *n.* [F. *basane*; from Ar.] Sheepskin tanned in oak-bark or larch-bark, used for bookbinding, etc.

bas-a-nite (bas′ạ-nīt), *n.* [L. *basanites*, < Gr. βάσανος, touchstone.] A black siliceous rock; touchstone.

bas=bleu (bä-blė), *n.* [F.] A blue-stocking.

bas-cule (bas′kūl), *n.* [F., a seesaw.] A device operating like a balance or seesaw, esp. an arrangement in drawbridges by which the rising floor or section is counterbalanced by a weight.—**bas′cule=bridge,** *n.*

base[1] (bās), *a.*; compar. *baser*, superl. *basest.* [OF. F. *bas*, < LL. *bassus*, short, low.] Of small height (archaic); low in place or position†; deep or grave in sound; of low or humble origin, grade, or station (archaic); of illegitimate birth; morally low; also, without dignity of sentiment; mean-spirited; selfish; cowardly; also, befitting or characteristic of an inferior person or thing; abject; unworthy; menial; also, held or holding by villeinage, as an estate or a tenant; also, coarse in quality; common, poor, or shabby; not classical or refined, as language; also, of little comparative value (as, *base* metals, those inferior to gold and silver); worthless; debased or counterfeit, as coin; in *bot.*, of low or lowly growth.

base[2] (bās), *n.* [OF. F. *base*, < L. *basis*: see *basis.*] The bottom of anything, considered as its support; that on which a thing stands or rests; fig., a fundamental principle or groundwork; also, formerly, a pleated skirt reaching from the waist to the knee, appended to the doublet; an imitation of this in armor; also, the principal element or ingredient of anything, considered as its fundamental part; esp., the stem of a word; also, that from which a commencement, as of action or reckoning, is made; a starting-point for racers, etc.; the goal in hockey and certain other games; any of the four corners of the diamond in baseball; also, the game of prisoners' base (see under *prisoner*); in *arch.*, the lowest member of a wall, monument, or the like; that part of a column on which the shaft rests, commonly consisting of a torus or tori and a plinth, and sometimes restricted to the parts between the shaft and the plinth; in *her.*, the lower part of a shield; in *bot.* and *zoöl.*, the part of an organ nearest its point of attachment; the point of attachment; in *geom.*, the line or surface forming that part of a figure on which it is supposed to stand; in *fort.*, the imaginary line drawn from the salient angle of one bastion to that of the next; in *math.*, the number which serves as a starting-point for a logarithmic or other system; in *surv.*, an accurately determined line forming one side of a triangle or serving as the starting-point for a system of triangles; *milit.*, a fortified or more or less protected tract or place from which the operations of an army proceed or from which supplies are obtained; in *chem.*, a compound which reacts with an acid to form a salt, as ammonia, calcium oxide, certain nitrogen-containing organic compounds (as the amines and alkaloids), etc.; esp., the hydroxide of a metal or of an electropositive element or radical.—**base**[2], *v. t.*; *based, basing.* To make or form a base or foundation for; place or establish on a base or basis; found (*on*); ground (*on*).

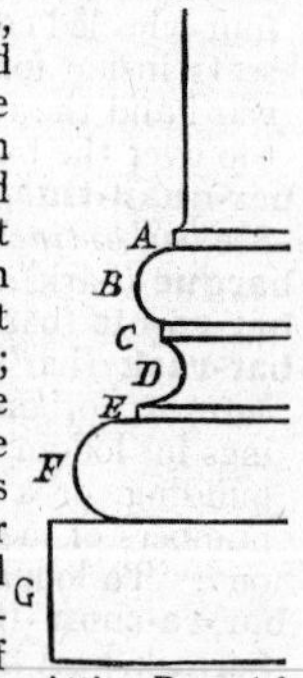

Attic Base (of column): *A, C, E*, fillets; *B*, upper torus; *D*, scotia; *F*, lower torus; *G*, plinth.

base-ball (bās′bâl′), *n.* A game of ball played by two sides of nine players each, on a 'diamond' inclosed by lines connecting four 'bases,' a complete circuit of which must be made by a player after batting, in order to score a 'run'; also, the ball used in playing this game.

base-board (bās′bōrd), *n.* A line of boarding around the interior walls of a room, next to the floor; also, a board forming the base of anything.

base=born (bās′bôrn), *a.* Of low or humble birth; of base origin; also, born out of wedlock; illegitimate.

base=burn-er (bās′bėr″nėr), *n.* A stove or furnace with a self-acting fuel-hopper over the fire-chamber.

based (bāst), *a.* Having a base: as, broad-*based*.

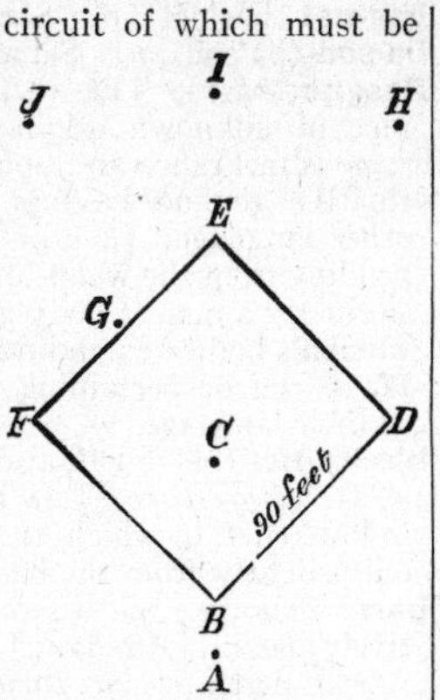

Baseball.
A, catcher; *B*, home; *C*, pitcher; *D*, first base; *E*, second base; *F*, third base; *G*, shortstop; *H*, *I*, *J*, right, center, and left fielders.

Ba-se-dow's (bä′zė-dōz) **dis-ease′.** [From *Basedow*, German physician, who first described it.] A disease characterized by exophthalmia, enlargement of the thyroid gland, and palpitation of the heart.

base=hit (bās′hit′), *n.* In *baseball*, a hit.

base-less (bās′les), *a.* Having no base; without foundation; groundless.—**base′less-ness**, *n.*

base=lev-el (bās′lev″ẹl), *n.* The ideal level to which a stream tends to erode its valley, as the level of the sea or of a lake.

bas-el-la-ceous (bas-ẹ-lā′shius), *a.* [NL. *Basella*, the typical genus.] Belonging to the *Basellaceæ*, a small family of tropical (usually) climbing herbs, including the Madeira-vine, etc.

base-ly (bās′li), *adv.* In a base manner; meanly.

base-man (bās′mạn), *n.*; pl. *-men.* In *baseball*, a player stationed at first, second, or third base.

base-ment (bās′mẹnt), *n.* A base or foundation; the lowest division of the wall of a building; a story partly or wholly below the ground-level.

base-ness (bās′nes), *n.* Base quality or conduct.

bash (bash), *v. t.* [Appar. imit.: cf. Sw. *basa*, whip, beat.] To strike with a crushing or smashing blow. [Prov. or slang.]—**bash**, *n.*

ba-shaw (bạ-shâ′), *n.* [Turk. *bāshā*, var. of *pāshā*, E. *pasha.*] A pasha; fig., an important personage.

bash-ful (bash′fụl), *a.* [Cf. *abash.*] Easily abashed; uncomfortably diffident or shy; timid and easily embarrassed in intercourse with others; also, indicative of, proceeding from, or accompanied with bashfulness.—**bash′ful-ly**, *adv.* —**bash′ful-ness**, *n.*

bash-i=ba-zouk (bash″i-bạ-zök′), *n.* [Turk.] One of a class of irregular mounted troops in the Turkish military service.

ba-sic (bā′sik), *a.* Of, pertaining to, or forming a base; fundamental; in *chem.*, pertaining to, of the nature of, or containing a base; alkaline; not having all of the hydroxyls of the base replaced by the acid radical, or having the metal or its equivalent united partly to the acid radical and partly to oxygen (as, a *basic* chloride, salt, etc.: see *salt*², *n.*); in *geol.*, of rocks, having a relatively small amount of the acid element or constituent (silicon or silica); in *metal.*, noting, pertaining to, or made by a steel-making process in which the furnace is lined with a basic or non-siliceous material, principally lime and magnesia.—**ba′si-cal-ly**, *adv.*—**ba-si-ci-ty** (bạ-sis′i-ti), *n.* In *chem.*, the state of being a base; the power of an acid to react with bases, dependent on the number of replaceable hydrogen atoms of the acid.

Basic English. A system of English speech with a vocabulary reduced to 850 essential words: devised by C. K. Ogden.

ba-sid-i-o-my-ce-tous (bạ-sid″i-ọ-mī-sē′tus), *a.* [NL. *Basidiomycetes*, pl., < *basidium* (see *basidium*) + Gr. μύκης (μυκητ-), fungus.] In *bot.*, belonging to the *Basidiomycetes*, a large group of fungi including the mushrooms.

ba-sid-i-um (bạ-sid′i-um), *n.*; pl. *-ia* (-i-ạ̈). [NL., dim. < Gr. βάσις, base: see *basis.*] In *bot.*, a special form of sporophore, characteristic of basidiomycetous fungi, producing by abstriction spores borne upon slender projections at its summit.

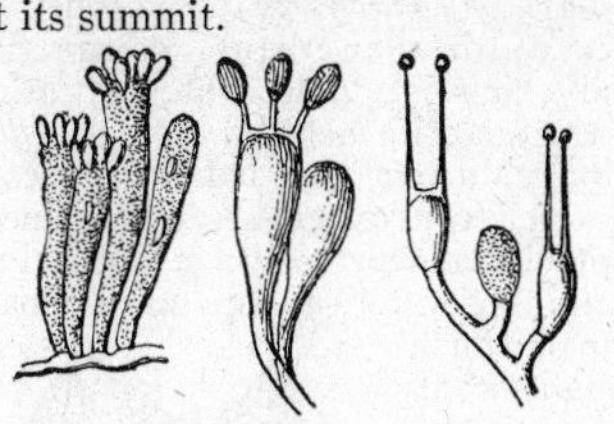

Basidia.

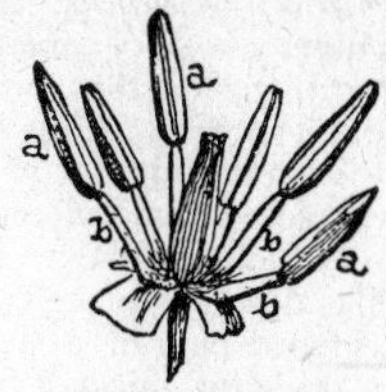

Basifixed Anthers.
a, a, anthers; *b, b*, filaments.

ba-si-fixed (bā′si-fikst), *a.* [L. *basis*, base, + E. *fixed.*] In *bot.*, attached by the base, as an anther.

ba-sif-u-gal (bạ-sif′ụ̄-gạl), *a.* [L. *basis*, base, + *fugere*, flee.] In *bot.*, developing from the base upward.

ba-si-fy (bā′si-fī), *v. t.*; *-fied*, *-fying.* [See *-fy.*] In *chem.*, to convert into a base.

bas-il¹ (baz′il), *n.* [OF. *basile*, *basilicon*, < LL. *basilicon*, < Gr. βασιλικόν: see *basilicon.*] A plant of the menthaceous genus *Ocimum*, as *O. basilicum* ('sweet basil'), a species whose leaves are used in cookery; also, any of various other menthaceous plants, as certain perennial herbs of the genus *Kœllia*.

bas-il² (baz′il), *n.* A corruption of *basan*.

bas-i-lar (bas′i-lạ̈r), *a.* [NL. *basilaris*, irreg. < L. *basis*, base.] Of, pertaining to, or situated at the base, esp. the base of the skull. Also **bas′i-la-ry** (-lạ̄-ri).

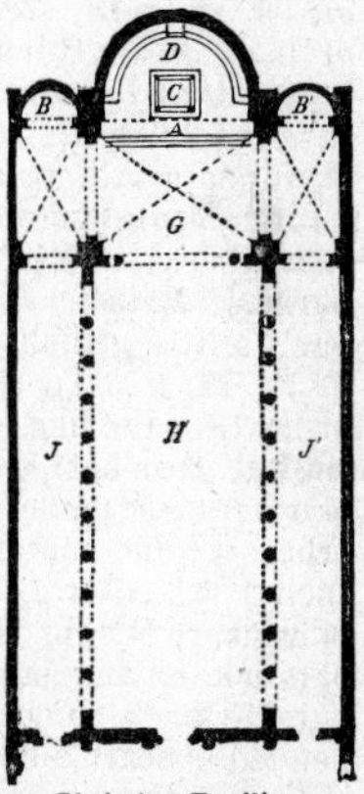

Christian Basilica.
S. Pietro in Vincoli, Rome: a typical plan with the addition of a transept and of secondary apses.—*AD*, apse; *B*, *B′*, secondary apses; *C*, high altar; *D*, bishop's throne; *G*, transept; *H*, nave; *J*, *J′*, aisles.

Ba-sil-i-an (ba-sil′i-ạn). **I.** *a.* Of, pertaining to, instituted by, or named from St. Basil (329–379), a Greek father of the Christian church. **II.** *n.* A member of a religious order deriving its name and rule from St. Basil.

ba-sil-ic (bạ-sil′ik), *a.* [F. *basilique*, < L. *basilicus*, < Gr. βασιλικός, kingly, royal, < βασιλεύς, king.] Royal; in *anat.*, noting a large vein on the inner side of the upper arm.

ba-sil-i-ca (bạ-sil′i-kạ̈), *n.* [L., < Gr. βασιλική, prop. fem. of βασιλικός, royal: see *basilic.*] A stoa or colonnaded building in ancient Athens in which justice was administered; also, among the ancient Romans, a large oblong building with a broad nave separated from side aisles by rows of columns, and often with a semicircular apse at one end, used as a hall of justice and a public meeting-place; hence, later, a Christian church having this form; also, an honorific title conferred by the Pope on a church without reference to its architectural form. —**ba-sil′i-can**, *a.*

ba-sil-i-con (bạ-sil′i-kọn), *n.* [L., < Gr. βασιλικόν, kind of plaster, also the herb basil, prop. neut. of βασιλικός, royal: see *basilic.*] Any of various ointments supposed to possess 'sovereign' virtues: as, "My mother imagined he had stepped down for lint and *basilicon*" (Sterne's "Tristram Shandy," v. 27).

Basilisk.

bas-i-lisk (bas′i-lisk), *n.* [L. *basiliscus*, < Gr. βασιλίσκος, kind of serpent, dim. of βασιλεύς, king.] A fabulous creature (serpent, lizard, or dragon) said by the ancients to kill by its breath or look; also, a tropical American lizard of the genus *Basiliscus*, of the iguana family, with an erectile crest along the back and a dilatable membranous pouch on the head; also, a large form of cannon†.

ba-sin (bā′sn), *n.* [OF. *bacin*, *bachin* (F. *bassin*), < ML. *bachinus*, *bacchinus*, appar. < *bacca*, water-vessel.] A circular vessel of greater width than depth, contracting toward the bottom, used chiefly to hold water or other liquid, esp. for washing; the quantity held by such a vessel; any vessel of similar shape, as a pan of a balance; a concave piece of metal on which convex glasses are formed; also, any basin-like receptacle or depression; a natural or artificial hollow place containing water, as a pond or a bay, a widened part of a river or canal, or a dock for ships; a roundish valley or hollow; a region draining into a lake, etc.; the tract of country drained by a river and its tributaries; in *geol.*, an area in which the strata dip from the sides toward a common center.—**ba′sined,** *a.* Inclosed in a basin.

Italian Basinet of 1380.

bas-i-net (bas′i-net), *n.* [OF. *bacinet* (F. *bassinet*), dim. of *bacin*, E. *basin*.] A steel cap of somewhat globular form, when used in battle commonly furnished with a vizor, except when worn under the heavy helmet.

ba-sip-e-tal (bā-sip′e-tạl), *a.* [L. *basis*, base, + *petere*, seek.] In *bot.*, developing from the apex toward the base.

ba-sis (bā′sis), *n.*; pl. *bases* (-sēz). [L. *basis*, < Gr. *βάσις*, a stepping, step, base, < *βαίνειν*, go.] The bottom or base of anything, or that on which it stands or rests; hence, that by which anything is sustained, or upon which it is established; a foundation or support; a groundwork or fundamental principle; also, the principal constituent; a fundamental ingredient; *milit.*, a base.

bask (bȧsk), *v.* [Prob. < Icel. *badhask*, refl. of *badha*, bathe.] **I.** *intr.* To bathe, esp. in warm water†; expose one's self to genial warmth or heat, as in the sunshine (also fig.). **II.** *tr.* To expose to or suffuse with genial warmth or heat, or the like.—**bask′er,** *n.*

bas-ket (bȧs′ket), *n.* [ME.; origin unknown.] A vessel or receptacle made of twigs, rushes, thin strips of wood, or other flexible material, woven together; the contents of such a vessel, or as much as it will hold; also, a protection of wickerwork for the handle of a sword or stick; a sword or stick having such a protection; also, an overhanging outside back compartment of a stage-coach; the car suspended beneath a balloon, for passengers, etc.; in *basket-ball*, either of the two basket-like goals.—**bas′ket,** *v. t.*; *-keted*, *-keting*. To put into a basket; hang up in a basket; cover or protect with basketwork; also, to throw into the waste-basket; reject.—**bas′ket=ball,** *n.* A game played, usually indoors, between two teams of players, with an inflated ball, the object being to throw the ball into elevated basket-like goals placed at opposite ends of the court; also, the ball used.—**bas′ket=fish,** *n.* Any of various ophiuroids of the genus *Astrophyton*, with rays divided into tendril-like branches.—**bas′ket-ful** (-fu̇l), *n.*; pl. *-fuls*.—**bas′ket=hilt,** *n.* A basket-like hilt of a sword, etc., as of narrow plates of steel, serving to cover and protect the hand.—**bas′ket=hilt″ed,** *a.*—**bas′ket-ry,** *n.* Basket-work; baskets; basket-making.—**bas′ket=stitch,** *n.* A stitch in embroidery in which the threads are interlaced as in basketry.—**bas′ket-work,** *n.* Work of the basket kind or weave; wickerwork; interwoven work.

Basket-fish.

Basket-hilt.

bask-ing=shark (bȧs′king-shärk), *n.* A large shark, *Cetorhinus maximus*, of northern seas, which frequently comes to the surface to bask in the sun.

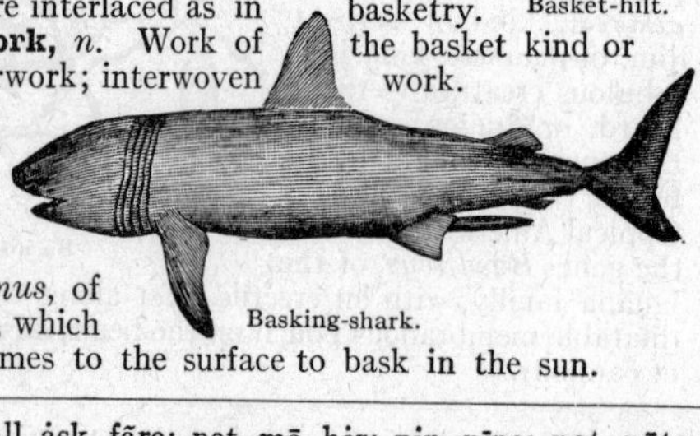

Basking-shark.

bas-net (bas′net), *n.* Same as *basinet*.

ba-son (bā′sọn), *n.* Same as *basin*.

Basque (bȧsk). [F., < L. *Vascones*, pl.] **I.** *n.* One of a race of unknown origin inhabiting the western Pyrenees regions in France and Spain; also, their language, an agglutinative tongue having no known connection with any other language; [*l. c.*] a short skirt or attached piece depending from the waist-line of a woman's (formerly a man's) body-garment; also, a woman's bodice extending over the hips. **II.** *a.* Of or pertaining to the Basques or their language.

Bas-relief. — Greek; 4th century B.C.

bas=re-lief (bä″rẹ-lēf′, also bȧs″-), *n.* [F., < It. *basso-rilievo*.] Low relief; sculpture in low relief, in which the figures project only slightly from the background.

bass[1] (bȧs), *n.*; pl. *basses* or (esp. collectively) *bass*. [AS. *bærs*.] Orig., the European perch, *Perca fluviatilis*; now, any of various similar fishes, as the black-bass, striped-bass, sea-bass, calico-bass, and rock-bass (see these words).

bass[2] (bȧs), *n.* [= *bast*.] Bast; also, a mat or other article made of bast; also, the basswood.

bass[3] (bās), *a.* [Var. of *base*[1], after It. *basso*.] In *music*, low in pitch; of the lowest pitch or range, as a (male) voice, voice-part, singer, or instrument; of or pertaining to the lowest part in harmonized music.—**bass viol.** See under *viol*.—**bass**[3], *n.* In *music*, the bass part; a bass voice, singer, or instrument. Cf. *double-bass*.

bas-set[1] (bas′et or ba-set′), *n.* [F. *bassette*, < It. *bassetta*.] An old card-game resembling faro.

bas-set[2] (bas′et), *n.* [Origin obscure.] In *mining* and *geol.*, an outcrop, as of the edges of strata.—**bas′set**[2], *v. i.*; *-seted*, *-seting*. In *mining* and *geol.*, to crop out.

bas-set[3] (bas′et), *n.* [F. *basset*, < *bas*, low.] A long-bodied, short-legged dog resembling a dachshund but larger and heavier.

bas-set=horn (bas′et-hôrn), *n.* [It. *bassetto*, dim. of *basso*, low.] A tenor clarinet.

bas-set=hound (bas′et-hound), *n.* Same as *basset*[3].

bas-si-net (bas′i-net), *n.* [F. *bassinet*: see *basinet*.] A wicker basket with a hood or canopy over one end, for use as a baby's cradle; also, a basket for holding clothing, toilet articles, etc., for a baby; also, a form of child's perambulator.

bas-so (bäs′sō), *n.*; pl. *-si* (-sē). [It.] Same as *bass*[3].

bas-soon (ba-sön′), *n.* [F. *basson*, < *basse*, bass.] A wind-instrument of the oboe class, of which it is the bass, having a doubled wooden tube or body and a long, curved metallic mouthpiece.—**double bassoon,** a bassoon an octave lower in pitch than the ordinary bassoon: the largest and deepest-toned instrument of the oboe class.—**bas-soon′-ist,** *n.* A performer on the bassoon.

bas-so=pro-fon-do (bäs″sō-prō-fōn′dō), *n.*; pl. *-dos* (-dōz). [It., 'deep bass.'] In *music*, the lowest bass voice or singer.

bas-so=ri-lie-vo (bäs″sō-rē-lyā′vō), *n.*; pl. *-vos* (-vōz). [It.] Same as *bas-relief*.

Bassoon.

bass-wood (bȧs′wu̇d), *n.* [See *bass*[2].] A linden, esp. *Tilia americana*; the wood of such a tree.

bast (bȧst), *n.* [AS. *bæst* = G. *bast*.] The inner bark of the linden, used in making matting, etc.; any fibrous bark, or its tissue or fiber; in *bot.*, phloëm.

bas-ta (bäs′tä), *interj.* [It.] Enough! stop! See Shakspere's "Taming of the Shrew," i. 1. 203.

bas-tard (bas′tạrd). [OF. *bastard* (F. *bâtard*), < *bast*, pack-saddle, E. *bat*[4].] **I.** *n.* A child begotten and born out of wedlock; fig., something irregular, inferior, spurious, or unusual; also, a kind of sweet Spanish wine†. **II.** *a.* Illegitimate in birth; hence, irregular; mongrel; inferior; spurious; not genuine; specif., of other than the standard form, size, style, etc.—**bastard title,** an abbreviated title of a book on an otherwise blank page preceding the full title-page.—**bastard wing.** Same as *alula*.—**bas′tard-ize** (-īz), *v.*; *-ized*, *-izing*. **I.** *tr.* To make a bastard of; declare or prove to be a bastard; hence, to debase. **II.** *intr.* To become debased; degenerate.—**bas″tard-i-za′tion** (-i-zā′shọn), *n.*—**bas′tard-y,** *n.* The condition of a bastard; illegitimacy; also, the begetting of bastards.

baste[1] (bāst), *v. t.*; *basted, basting.* [Origin uncertain: cf. Icel. *beysta,* bruise, beat.] To beat, as with a stick; thrash.

baste[2] (bāst), *v. t.*; *basted, basting.* [Origin uncertain.] To moisten (meat, etc., while cooking) with drippings, butter, etc.

baste[3] (bāst), *v. t.*; *basted, basting.* [OF. *bastir* (F. *bâtir*); prob. from Teut.] To sew slightly; sew with temporary stitches, as a garment in the first stages of making; tack.—**bast′er,** *n.*

bas-tile, bas-tille (bas-tēl′), *n.* [OF. F. *bastille,* < ML. *bastile,* < *bastire,* build.] A tower, as of a castle; a small fortress; a movable tower used for the protection of besieging troops; [*cap.*; spelled *Bastille*] a famous fortress in Paris, used as a prison, built in the 14th century and destroyed in 1789; [*l. c.*] any prison.

bas-ti-nade (bas-ti-nād′), *n.* and *v.* Same as *bastinado.* [Archaic.]

bas-ti-na-do (bas-ti-nā′dō), *n.*; pl. *-does* (-dōz). [Sp. *bastonada,* < *bastón,* stick, = E. *baton.*] A blow or a beating with a stick, etc.; an Oriental mode of punishment consisting in blows with a stick on the soles of the feet, or on the buttocks; also, a stick or cudgel.—**bas-ti-na′do,** *v. t.*; *-doed, -doing.* To beat with a stick, etc., esp. on the soles of the feet or on the buttocks as an Oriental mode of punishment.

bast-ing[1] (bās′ting), *n.* [See *baste*[1].] A beating.

bast-ing[2] (bās′ting), *n.* [See *baste*[2].] The moistening of meat, etc., while cooking, with drippings, butter, etc.; *pl.,* the drippings, etc., used.

bast-ing[3] (bās′ting), *n.* [See *baste*[3].] Sewing with slight or temporary stitches; *pl.,* the stitches taken, or the threads used.

bas-tion (bas′chọn), *n.* [F. *bastion,* < It. *bastione,* < *bastire,* < ML. *bastire,* build.] In *fort.,* a projecting portion of a rampart or fortification, in form an irregular pentagon attached at the base to the main work, with two faces forming the forward (salient) angle, and with two shorter, reëntrant flanks commanding adjacent parts of the work.—**bas′tioned,** *a.*

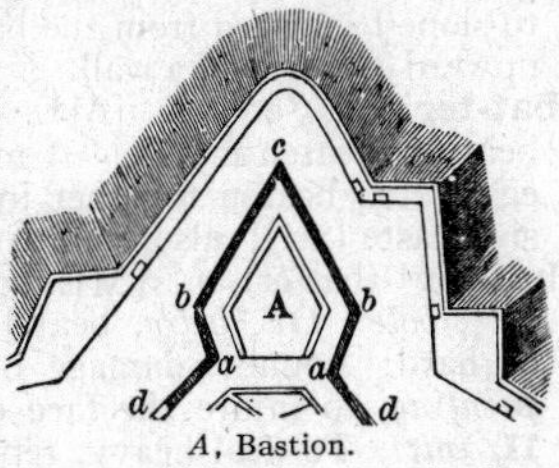

A, Bastion.
a, a, curtain-angles; *b, b,* shoulder-angles; *c,* salient angle; *ab, ab,* flanks; *bc, bc,* faces; *aa,* gorge; *ad, ad,* parts of curtains.

ba-syl, ba-syle (bā′sil), *n.* [Gr. βάσις, base, + ὕλη, matter.] In *chem.,* the electro-positive constituent of a salt.—**ba′sy-lous,** *a.*

bat[1] (bat), *n.* [ME. *batte*: cf. F. *batte,* implement for beating.] A heavy stick, club, or cudgel; a thick walking-stick (now prov. Eng.); the club used in certain games, as baseball and cricket, to strike the ball; the racket used in certain games; a batsman or batter; a piece of brick having one end entire; any fragment of brick; a sheet of matted cotton-wool; a felted mass of fur, or of hair and wool, as used in hat-making; a stroke or blow, as with a club; the act of batting in a game, or the right or turn to bat; rate of motion, or speed (prov. Eng. or colloq.); a spree, or fit of intoxication (slang, U. S.).—**bat**[1], *v.*; *batted, batting.* **I.** *tr.* To strike or hit with or as with a bat or club. **II.** *intr.* To use a bat or club; in *baseball,* etc., to strike at the ball with the bat.

Bat (*Synotus barbastellus*).

bat[2] (bat), *n.* [Corruption of ME. *bakke*; from Scand.] Any of the nocturnal and crepuscular flying mammals constituting the order *Chiroptera,* characterized by modified fore limbs which serve as wings and are covered with a membranous skin extending to the hind limbs.

bat[3] (bat), *v. t.*; *batted, batting.* [Var. of *bate*[1].] To wink (the eyes). [Colloq. or prov.]

bat[4] (bat or bä), *n.* [F. *bât,* < OF. *bast.*] A pack-saddle. See *bathorse, batman.*

Ba-ta-vi-an (bạ-tā′vi-ạn). [L. *Batavia,* country of the ancient Batavi (now included in Holland).] **I.** *a.* Of or pertaining to Holland or the Netherlands; Dutch. **II.** *n.* A native of Holland or the Netherlands; a Dutchman.

batch (bach), *n.* [ME. *batche,* < AS. *bacan,* bake.] The quantity of bread made at one baking; a quantity produced at one operation; the quantity of a thing prepared or required for one operation; a quantity or number coming at one time or taken together.

bate[1] (bāt), *v. t.* or *i.*; *bated, bating.* [OF. *batre* (F. *battre*), < L. *battere,* for *battuere,* beat.] To flap (the wings); flutter: said of hawks, etc.

bate[2] (bāt), *v.*; *bated, bating.* [For *abate.*] **I.** *tr.* To abate; reduce; lessen; restrain (the breath); deprive (*of*); also, to take away or deduct; also, to except. **II.** *intr.* To decrease; fall off.

bate[3] (bāt), *v. i.*; *bated, bating.* [For *debate.*] To contend; quarrel. [Now prov. Eng.]—**bate**[3], *n.* Contention; strife; debate. Cf. *makebate.* [Now prov. Eng.]

bate[4] (bāt), *v. t.*; *bated, bating.* [Cf. Sw. *beta,* tan, G. *beizen,* steep in lye.] To steep (hides) in a solution of dung.—**bate**[4], *n.* The solution used in bating hides.

ba-teau (ba-tō′), *n.*; pl. *-teaux* (-tōz′). [F. *bateau,* OF. *batel,* < ML. *batellus,* dim. of *batus, battus,* boat: cf. *boat.*] A light boat, esp. one having a flat bottom and tapering ends, used in Canada and Louisiana; also, a pontoon of a floating bridge.—**ba-teau′=bridge,** *n.*

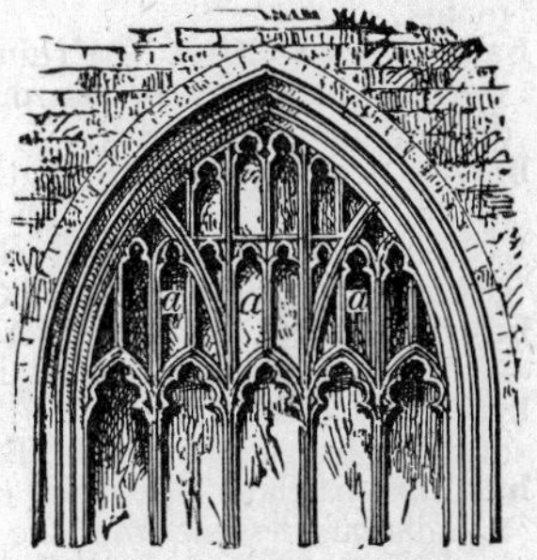

Head of Perpendicular Window.—*a, a, a,* batement-lights.

bate-ment=light (bāt′mẹnt-līt), *n.* [Cf. *bate*[2].] In *arch.,* a light or window having vertical sides and a curved or inclined bottom.

bat=fish (bat′fish), *n.* Any of the flat-bodied marine fishes (thought to resemble the bat) constituting the family *Ogcocephalidæ,* as *Ogcocephalus vespertilio,* which is common along the southern Atlantic coast of the U. S.; also, any of various other fishes, as the flying-gurnard, *Cephalacanthus volitans.*

Bat-fish (*Ogcocephalus vespertilio*), dorsal view.

bat=fowl (bat′-foul), *v. i.* [Prob. < *bat*[1] + *fowl.*] To catch birds at night by dazzling them with a light, and striking them down or taking them in a net.—**bat′=fowl″er,** *n.*

bath[1] (bȧth), *n.*; pl. *baths* (bȧTHz). [AS. *bæth* = G. *bad.*] An immersion of the body in, or an exposure of it to the action of, water or other liquid, or vapor, etc., as for cleansing, refreshment, or medical treatment; water or other agent prepared for this purpose; a vessel for containing this, as a bathtub; an apartment equipped for bathing; a building containing such apartments, or fitted up for bathing (often in *pl.,* esp. with reference to one of the elaborate bathing establishments of the ancients); a town or place resorted to for medical treatment by bathing, etc. (usually in *pl.*); a preparation, as an acid solution, in which something is immersed; the vessel containing such a preparation; a device for heating or cooling something by means of a surrounding medium such as sand, water, or the like; the mass of molten metal in a metallurgical furnace.—**Order of the Bath,** a high order of British knighthood, of which there are three classes: so called in allusion to an initiatory

Badge of the Order of the Bath.

bath of purification.—**bath¹,** *v. t.* To put into or wash in a bath.

bath² (bȧth), *n.* [Heb.] Either of two Hebrew liquid measures, equivalent to about 9½ and 7½ U. S. gallons respectively. See Ezek. xlv. 11.

Bath (bȧth) **brick.** [From *Bath*, England: see *Bath chair.*] A brick or compacted, molded mass of fine siliceous sand, used for scouring metal.

Bath (bȧth) **chair.** [From *Bath*, watering-place in southwestern England, noted for its hot springs.] An invalid's wheeled chair.

bathe (bāᴛʜ), *v.*; *bathed, bathing.* [AS. *bathian*, < *bæth*, E. *bath¹*.] **I.** *tr.* To immerse (the body, or any part of it) in water or other liquid for cleansing, refreshment, etc.; immerse in or surround with anything analogous to water; apply water or other liquid to with a sponge or the like; wash, moisten, or suffuse with any liquid. **II.** *intr.* To take a bath; be immersed in or as in water; disport one's self in the water, as at the seaside.—**bathe,** *n.* A bathing, as in the sea.—**bath-er** (bā'ᴛʜėr), *n.*

ba-thet-ic (bạ-thet'ik), *a.* Characterized by bathos.

bath=house (bȧth'hous), *n.* A house or building fitted up for bathing; also, a structure, as at the seaside, serving as a dressing-room for bathers or containing a number of such rooms.

bath-ing=ma-chine (bā'ᴛʜing-mạ-shēn″), *n.* A covered vehicle which may be run out into the water, used as a dressing-room for bathers.

bath-o-lite, bath-o-lith (bath'ọ-līt, -lith), *n.* [Gr. βάθος, depth, + λίθος, stone.] In *geol.*, a great mass of deep-seated, intrusive igneous rock, which may be exposed by erosion.—**bath-o-lit'ic** (-lit'ik), **bath-o-lith'ic,** *a.*

ba-thom-e-ter (ba-thom'e-tėr), *n.* [Gr. βάθος, depth: see *-meter.*] A device for ascertaining the depth of water.

bat-horse (bat'hôrs or bä'-), *n.* [See *bat⁴*.] A horse for carrying baggage, as in the British army.

ba-thos (bā'thos), *n.* [Gr. βάθος, depth, < βαθύς, deep.] A ludicrous descent from the elevated to the commonplace in writing or speech; anticlimax.

bath=robe (bȧth'rōb), *n.* A long, loose garment for wear in going to and from a bath.

bath-room (bȧth'röm), *n.* A room fitted up for bathing.

bath-tub (bȧth'tub), *n.* A tub to bathe in, esp. an elongated one forming a permanent fixture in a bathroom.

ba-thym-e-ter (ba-thim'e-tėr), *n.* [Gr. βαθύς, deep: see *-meter.*] A device for ascertaining the depth of water.—**bath-y-met-ric, bath-y-met-ri-cal** (bath-i-met'rik, -ri-kạl), *a.* Pertaining to bathymetry.—**ba-thym'e-try,** *n.* [See *-metry.*] The art of measuring depths, esp. in the sea.

bath-y-sphere (bath'i-sfēr), *n.* [Gr. βαθύς, deep: see *sphere.*] A spherical diving-apparatus from which to study deep-sea life.

ba-tik (bä-tēk'), *n.* [Malay *bātik*, Javanese *batik.*] A process of executing designs on a fabric, employed orig. in the Dutch East Indies, by covering with melted wax the portions forming the pattern, and dyeing the uncovered portions, the wax being then removed; also, the fabric.

bat-ing (bā'ting), *prep.* [Orig. ppr.: see *bate²*.] Deducting; excepting; except.

ba-tiste (ba-tēst'), *n.* [F., < *Baptiste*, name of the alleged first maker, said to have lived at Cambrai in the 13th century: cf. *cambric.*] A fine, light linen or cotton fabric.

bat-man (bat'mạn or bä'-), *n.*; pl. *-men.* [See *bat⁴*.] A man in charge of a bathorse and its load.

bat-on (bat'ọn, F. bä-tôṅ), *n.* [F. *bâton*, OF. *baston* = Sp. *bastón*, < ML. *basto(n-)*; origin uncertain.] A staff, club, or truncheon, esp. as a mark of office or authority; in *music*, the wand used by a conductor for beating time; in *her.*, an ordinary of one fourth the breadth of the bend sinister and extending in the same diagonal direction, but cut off at each end so as not to reach the edge of the field, borne in England as a mark of bastardy.

ba-tra-chi-an (ba-trā'ki-ạn). [NL. *Batrachia*, pl., < Gr. βατράχειος, frog-like, < βάτραχος, frog.] **I.** *a.* Belonging to the *Batrachia*, a division of vertebrates comprising all the amphibians (*Amphibia*), or, in a restricted sense, only the anurans (*Anura*), or frogs and toads; also, frog-like. **II.** *n.* A batrachian animal.

bat-ra-choid (bat'rạ-koid), *a.* [Gr. βάτραχος, frog: see *-oid.*] Frog-like.

bats-man (bats'mạn), *n.*; pl. *-men.* One who wields a bat, or the one whose turn it is to wield it, as in baseball, cricket, etc.

bat-tai-lous (bat'ẹ-lus), *a.* [OF. *bataillos*, < *bataille*, E. *battle¹*.] Warlike; bellicose. [Archaic.]

bat-ta-lia (ba-tā'liạ), *n.* [It. *battaglia*, < LL. *battalia*: see *battle¹*.] Battle array; also, an army, or a large division of it, in battle array or on the march; also, the main body or center of an army. [Archaic.]

bat-tal-ion (ba-tal'yọn), *n.* [F. *bataillon*, < It. *battaglione*, < *battaglia*: see *battalia.*] An army in battle array; also, one of the large subdivisions of an army; esp., a body of infantry composed of two or more companies and forming part of a regiment.—**bat-tal'ioned,** *a.* Formed into battalions.

bat-tel (bat'l), *n.* [Origin obscure.] At the University of Oxford, England, college accounts for board and provisions supplied from the kitchen and buttery; also, college accounts generally: used in *pl.*, except attributively.—**bat'tel,** *v. i.* To have a battel account at the University of Oxford.—**bat'tel-er,** *n.*

bat-ten¹ (bat'n), *v.* [Cf. Icel. *batna*, get better, improve.] **I.** *intr.* To thrive as by feeding; grow fat; feed gluttonously. **II.** *tr.* To cause to thrive as by feeding; fatten.

bat-ten² (bat'n), *n.* [Var. of *baton.*] A squared timber of a special size used for flooring, etc., usually 6 or more feet long, 7 inches wide, and 2½ inches thick; a strip of wood, as one used to secure the edges of a tarpaulin over a hatchway on a ship; a thin strip of wood sewed into a sail to keep it flat.—**bat'ten²,** *v. t.* To furnish with battens; fasten (*down*), as a ship's hatches, with battens and tarpaulins.—**bat'ten-ing,** *n.* Woodwork consisting of battens.

bat-ter¹ (bat'ėr), *n.* One who wields a bat, as in baseball or cricket; a batsman.

bat-ter² (bat'ėr), *v. i.* [Origin uncertain.] Of walls, etc., to slope backward from the base.—**bat'ter²,** *n.* A receding upward slope, as of a wall.

bat-ter³ (bat'ėr), *n.* [ME. *bater*, *batour*: cf. OF. *bature*, beating, beaten metal.] A mixture of flour, milk or water, eggs, etc., beaten together for use in cookery; also, adhesive paste (Sc.); also, mud (prov. Eng.).

bat-ter⁴ (bat'ėr), *v.* [ME. *bateren*, a freq. form akin to E. *bat¹*, *bate¹*, OF. *batre*, beat.] **I.** *tr.* To beat persistently or hard; pound; damage by beating or hard usage; in *printing*, to injure the face of (type, etc.), as by a blow. **II.** *intr.* To deal heavy, repeated blows; pound; also, to become damaged as by blows.—**bat'ter⁴,** *n.* A battering; in *printing*, a damaged spot on the face of type or a plate, or the resulting defect in print.—**bat'ter-er,** *n.*—**bat'tering=ram,** *n.* An ancient military engine with a heavy horizontal beam for battering down walls, etc.

bat-ter-y (bat'ėr-i), *n.*; pl. *-ies* (-iz). [F. *batterie*, < *battre*, beat: see *bate¹*.] The act of beating or battering; in *law*, an unlawful attack upon another by beating or wounding, or even by touching in a menacing manner; *milit.*, two or more pieces of artillery used for combined action; a tactical unit of artillery, usually consisting of four guns together with the artillerymen, equipment, etc.; also, a group of guns on, or the whole armament of, a vessel of war; also, a parapet or fortification equipped with artillery; in *mech.*, etc., a set or series of similar machines, parts, or the like, as a group of boilers; in *elect.*, a device ('voltaic battery') for generating electricity, consisting of one or more voltaic cells (see *cell*); also, a number of Leyden jars, dynamos, or the like, joined to give a united electrical effect; in *baseball*, the pitcher and catcher together.

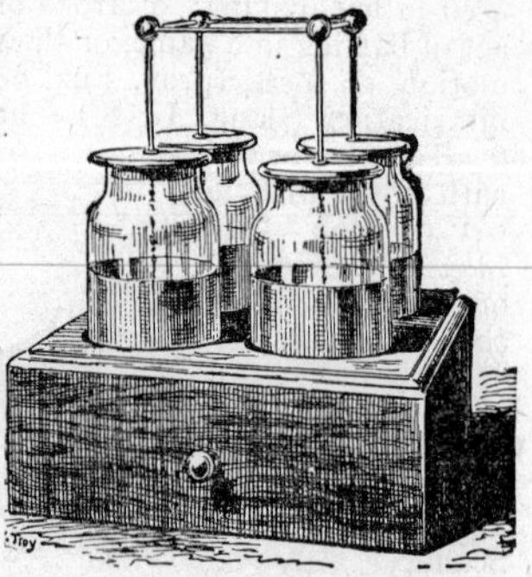

Leyden-jar Battery.

bat-ting (bat'ing), *n.* Cotton-wool in bats or sheets.

bat-tle[1] (bat'l), *n.* [OF. F. *bataille* = It. *battaglia*, < LL. *battalia*, for *battualia*, fighting exercises, < L. *battuere*, beat.] A hostile encounter or engagement between opposing forces on land or sea; a combat; a fight; an encounter between two persons; a fight between two animals, esp. when pitted against each other to provide sport; also, victory in a fight or encounter; also, actual conflict with enemies (as, wounds received in *battle*); warfare; hostile action; also, any conflict, contest, or struggle for mastery; also, a battalion (archaic); the main body of an army or fleet†.—**battle cruiser.** See under *cruiser*.—**battle royal,** a fight in which more than two combatants are engaged; a free fight.—**bat'tle**[1]**,** *v. i.*; *-tled, -tling.* [OF. F. *batailler.*] To strive in or as in battle; fight; contend.

bat-tle[2] (bat'l), *v. t.*; *-tled, -tling.* [OF. *bataillier*, < *bataille*, battlement.] To furnish with battlements; embattle: now only in *battled*, *p. a.* (as, "the *battled* tower": Tennyson's "Dream of Fair Women"). [Archaic.]

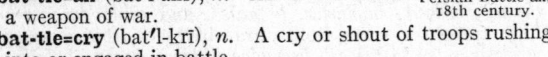

Persian Battle-ax, 18th century.

bat-tle=ax (bat'l-aks), *n.* An ax for use as a weapon of war.

bat-tle=cry (bat'l-krī), *n.* A cry or shout of troops rushing into or engaged in battle.

bat-tle-dore (bat'l-dōr), *n.* [Cf. Pr. *batedor*, beater.] A bat or beetle used in washing clothes, or for smoothing them out after being washed; hence, any of various similar implements; also, an instrument shaped like a racket, but smaller, used in striking a shuttlecock to and fro in play; also, a game played with such instruments by two persons ('battledore and shuttlecock').

bat-tle=field (bat'l-fēld), *n.* The field or ground on which a battle is fought. Also **bat'tle=ground.**

bat-tle-ment (bat'l-mẹnt), *n.* [See *battle*[2].] In *arch.*, an indented parapet, having a series of solid parts (merlons) alternating with openings (crenels), orig. for shooting through; a crenelated upper wall: often in *pl.*—**bat'tle-ment,** *v. t.* To furnish with battlements: chiefly in *battlemented*, *p. a.*

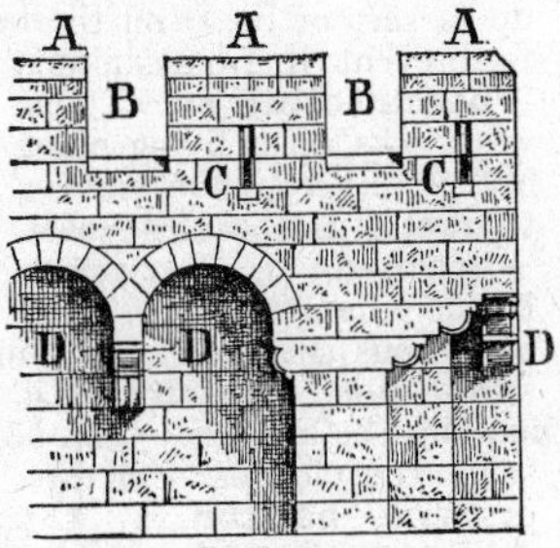

Battlement.
A, A, merlons; *B, B*, crenels; *C, C*, loopholes; *D, D*, machicolations.

bat-tle-plane (bat'l-plān), *n.* An aëroplane designed for fighting purposes; esp., one of a class of small, light, armed aëroplanes capable of great speed and suitable for pursuing enemy aircraft.

bat-tle=ship (bat'l-ship), *n.* A vessel of war; esp., one of a class of war-ships comprising those which are the largest and most heavily armored, and are equipped with the most powerful batteries.

bat-tue (ba-tū', F. bȧ-tü), *n.* [F., < *battre*, beat.] The beating or driving of game from cover, to be killed by sportsmen; a hunt in which this process is used; fig., a general hunting out, as of victims for slaughter.

bat-ty (bat'i), *a.* Of or like the bat.

bau-bee (bâ-bē'), *n.* See *bawbee*.

bau-ble (bâ'bl), *n.* [OF. *baubel*, toy; origin uncertain.] A toy, trinket, or gewgaw; also, a trifle; also, a jester's staff, usually topped with a hooded fool's head, and sometimes having at the other end a bladder or ball inflated with air.

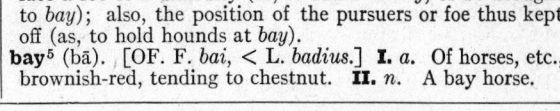

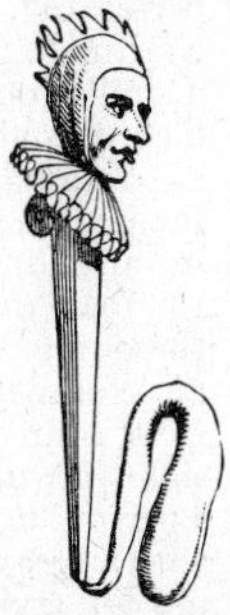
Jester's Bauble.

bau-de-kin, baud-kin (bâ'dẹ-kin, bâd'kin), *n.* [OF. *baudequin*, < It. *baldacchino*: see *baldachin*.] A rich brocaded silk fabric, orig. with a warp of gold. [Obs. or archaic.]

baud-rons (bâd'rọnz), *n.* [Origin unknown.] A name for the cat. [Sc.]

baulk (bâk), *n.* and *v.* See *balk*.

bau-son (bâ'sọn), *n.* [OF. *bausen*, *bausent*, *balcent* (= It. *balzano*), streaked or marked with white, < L. *balteus*, belt.] A badger (animal). [Archaic or prov. Eng.]—**bau'sond,** *a.* [OF. *bausent*.] Of animals, marked with white (as the badger is on the head); streaked or spotted with white. [Now Sc. and north. Eng.]—**bau'son=faced,** *a.* Marked with white on the face. [Sc. and north. Eng.]

baux-ite (bâk'sīt, popularly bok'sīt; also bō'zīt), *n.* [F.; from Les *Baux*, in southern France.] A mineral consisting essentially of a hydrated aluminium oxide: used as a source of alum and aluminium.

ba-var-dage (bȧ-vär-däzh), *n.* [F., < *bavarder*, chatter, < *bavard*, talkative, < *bave*, drivel.] Idle talk; chatter; prattle; prate.

Ba-va-ri-an (bạ-vā'ri-ạn). **I.** *a.* Of or pertaining to Bavaria, in southern Germany: as, the *Bavarian* Alps; *Bavarian* cream (a dessert, variously made, of whipped cream combined with chopped fruit or a custard or other ingredients, and stiffened with gelatin). **II.** *n.* A native or inhabitant of Bavaria.

Obverse. Reverse.
Bawbee of James V. — British Museum.

ba-vette (ba-vet'), *n.* [F., < *bave*, drivel.] A child's bib.

baw-bee (bâ-bē'), *n.* [Origin uncertain.] An old Scotch billon coin, worth about a halfpenny of English coin; hence, a halfpenny. [Sc.]

baw-cock (bâ'kok), *n.* [F. *beau coq*, 'fine cock.'] A fine fellow: used familiarly or ironically. See Shakspere's "Twelfth Night," iii. 4. 125. [Now prov. Eng.]

bawd (bâd), *n.* [ME. *bawde*; origin uncertain.] A pander; a procurer or procuress; a person, now esp. a woman, who keeps a house of prostitution.—**bawd'i-ly,** *adv.* In a bawdy manner.—**bawd'i-ness,** *n.*—**bawd'ry,** *n.* The business of a bawd; also, unchastity†; also, obscenity.—**bawd'y,** *a.* Lewd; obscene.

bawl (bâl), *v.* [Prob. < ML. *baulare*, bark as a dog.] **I.** *intr.* To bark or howl as a dog†; cry out with a loud, full sound; shout or wail lustily. **II.** *tr.* To utter by bawling. —**bawl,** *n.* A bawling cry.—**bawl'er,** *n.*

bax-ter (bak'stėr), *n.* [AS. *bæcestre*, fem. of *bæcere*, baker.] A baker; orig., a female baker. [Now Sc. and north. Eng.]

bay[1] (bā), *n.* [OF. F. *baie*, < L. *baca*, *bacca*, berry.] A berry, esp. of the laurel†; the European laurel, *Laurus nobilis* ('sweet-bay'); any of various laurel-like trees; *pl.*, the laurels (wreath, honor, or renown) rewarding achievement, esp. by a poet.

bay[2] (bā), *n.* [OF. F. *baie*, < LL. *baia*.] A recessed portion of a sea or other body of water, extending into the land; also, a recess of land, as between hills.

bay[3] (bā), *n.* [OF. *baee* (F. *baie*), an opening, < *baer*, < LL. *badare*, gape.] A space or division of a wall, building, etc., between two columns, piers, or other architectural features or members; the part of a window included between two mullions; a recessed space projecting outward from the line of a wall, as to contain a window; a compartment in a barn, as for storing hay; *naut.*, the forward part of a ship between decks on either side, formerly often used as a hospital.

Architectural Bays.
F, C, A, bays; *F, F*, window-bays; *C*, triforium-bay; *A*, arch of aisle.

bay[4] (bā), *v.* [OF. *baier*, also *abaier*, perhaps < LL. *badare*, gape: cf. *bay*[3].] **I.** *intr.* To bark, esp. with a deep, prolonged sound, as a hound in hunting. **II.** *tr.* To bark at; also, to express by barking; also, to bring to bay.—**bay**[4]**,** *n.* A deep, prolonged bark, as of a hound in hunting; also, a stand made by a hunted animal to face or repel pursuers, or, fig., by a person, etc., forced to face a foe or a difficulty (as, to stand at *bay*, or be brought to *bay*); also, the position of the pursuers or foe thus kept off (as, to hold hounds at *bay*).

bay[5] (bā). [OF. F. *bai*, < L. *badius*.] **I.** *a.* Of horses, etc., brownish-red, tending to chestnut. **II.** *n.* A bay horse.

bay[6] (bā), *n.* [Origin uncertain.] A dam or embankment to retain water or divert its course.—**bay**[6], *v. t.* To retain or obstruct (water) with a bay or dam.

ba-ya-dere (bā-yạ-dēr′, F. bä-yä-dãr). [F. *bayadère*, < Pg. *bailadeira*, < *bailar*, dance.] **I.** *n.* An East Indian dancing-girl. **II.** *a.* Of stripes on fabrics, running crosswise; transverse; of fabrics, having such stripes.

bay=ant-ler (bā′ant″lėr), *n.* [For *bez-antler*, < OF. *bes-* (< L. *bis*, twice) + E. *antler*.] The second branch (from the base) of a stag's horn.

bay-ard[1] (bā′ạrd), *n.* [OF., < *bai*, E. *bay*[5].] A bay horse; also, a name for a horse, esp. for a proverbial horse that was both blind and bold. [Archaic.]

Bay-ard[2] (bā′ạrd, F. bä-yär), *n.* [From Pierre Terrail, Seigneur de *Bayard* (about 1473–1524), the heroic French "knight without fear and without reproach."] A man of heroic courage, chivalrous spirit, and unstained honor.

bay-ber-ry (bā′ber″i), *n.*; pl. *-berries* (-iz). The fruit of the bay or laurel, *Laurus nobilis*; also, any of certain shrubs or trees of the genus *Myrica*, as *M. carolinensis*, a shrub common on seacoasts, and *M. cerifera* (see *wax-myrtle*); the berry of such a plant; also, a West Indian tree, *Pimenta acris*, whose leaves are used in making bay-rum.

bay-o-net (bā′ọ-net), *n.* [F. *baïonnette*, earlier *bayonnette*, prob. < *Bayonne*, town in southwestern France.] A short, flat dagger†; also, a short stabbing instrument of steel, for infantry soldiers, for attaching to the muzzle of a gun; also, a pin which plays in and out of holes, and serves to connect and disconnect parts of machinery.—**bay′o-net,** *v. t.*; *-neted, -neting.* To stab with a bayonet; drive or compel by the bayonet.

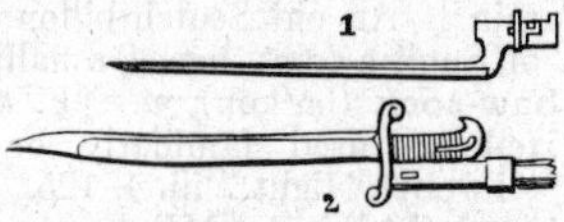

1, Common Bayonet; 2, Sword-bayonet.

bay-ou (bī′ö), *n.* [Louisiana F.; origin uncertain.] An arm or outlet of a lake, river, etc.; an extent of sluggish water connected with or left by a stream. [Southern U. S.]

bay=rum (bā′rum′), *n.* A fragrant liquid used as a cosmetic, etc., esp. by barbers, prepared by distilling the leaves of the bayberry, *Pimenta acris*, with rum, or by mixing the oil obtained from such leaves with alcohol, water, and other oils.

bay=salt (bā′sâlt′), *n.* Coarse-grained salt, esp. that obtained by evaporation of sea-water.

bay=tree (bā′trē), *n.* The European laurel, *Laurus nobilis*.

bay=win-dow (bā′win′dō), *n.* A window forming a recess or bay in a room and projecting outward from the wall of the building, esp. one rising from the ground or basement and having a rectangular or semi-polygonal plan. Cf. *bow-window* and *oriel*.

Bay-window.

bay=wood (bā′wu̇d), *n.* A kind of mahogany, esp. that found near the Gulf (or Bay) of Campeche.

ba-zaar, ba-zar (bạ-zär′), *n.* [Pers. *bāzār*.] An Oriental market-place, or quarter containing shops; any place or establishment for the sale of miscellaneous goods; also, a sale of miscellaneous articles, esp. fancy-work and other things contributed, for some charitable or other special object.

bdel-li-um (del′i-um), *n.* [L., < Gr. βδέλλιον.] Any of various fragrant gum-resins obtained from certain balsameaceous plants, as *Balsamea mukul*, an Asiatic tree; also, a plant yielding such a gum-resin.

be (bē), *v. i.*; ind. pres. 1 *am*, 2 *art*, 3 *is*, pl. *are*; pret. 1 *was*, 2 *wast* or *wert*, 3 *was*, pl. *were*; subj. *be, were, wert*; pp. *been*; ppr. *being*. [A defective verb, AS. *bēon*, inf. (akin to G. *bin*, am, L. *fui*, I was, Gr. φύεσθαι, come into being, Skt. *bhū-*, become), with parts supplied from two other verbs: see *am, is, was*.] **A.** *substantive verb.* To exist; have reality; live; take place; occur; remain as before: as, he *is* no more; it was not to *be*; think what might have *been*; the wedding *was* last week; to let *be* (to leave unmolested; let alone; hence, to desist from; cease). **B.** *copula.* A link connecting a subject with predicative or qualifying words in assertive, interrogative, and imperative sentences, or serving to form infinitive and participial phrases: as, you *are* late; he *is* much to blame; *is* he here? he *is* [here]; do *be* still; *be* it so; try to *be* just; the art of *being* agreeable. **C.** *auxiliary.* Used with the present participle of a principal verb to form a continuous present tense (as, I *am* waiting; the house *is* building, or being built), or with a past participle in passive forms, regularly of transitive verbs (as, the date *was* fixed; it must *be* done), and formerly, as still to some extent, of intransitives (as, I *am* done; he *is* come).

be-. [AS. *be-, bi-*, repr. *be, bī*, E. *by*.] A prefix of Anglo-Saxon origin, meaning 'about,' 'around,' 'all over,' and hence having an intensive and often disparaging force, much used as an English formative of verbs (and their derivatives), as in *begird, besiege, bestud, bespread, becloud, bethump, bedaub, beplaster, bepraise,* and often serving to form transitive verbs from intransitives or from nouns or adjectives, as in *bewail, begrudge, belabor, begem, befriend, befoul, belittle.*

beach (bēch), *n.* [Origin unknown.] The shingle, or loose water-worn pebbles, of the seashore; also, that part of the shore of the sea, or of a large river or a lake, which is washed by the tide or waves.—**beach,** *v. t.* or *i.* To run or haul up (a ship or boat) on the beach; run (a boat) ashore, as to prevent it from sinking.—**beach′=comb″er,** *n.* One who picks up a living along beaches, as from wreckage; a vagrant of the beach or coast.—**beached,** *a.* Having a beach.—**beach′=flea,** *n.* Any of various small hopping amphipods found on beaches; a sand-hopper.—**beach′less,** *a.* Without a beach.

Beach-flea (*Orchestia agilis*), enlarged.

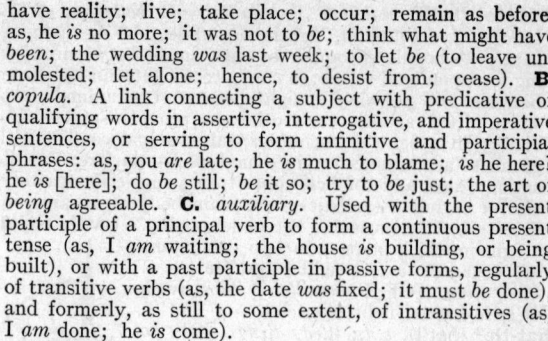

bea-con (bē′kọn), *n.* [AS. *bēacen*, sign.] A fire, a light, or some conspicuous structure or object designed to guide or warn.—**bea′con,** *v.* **I.** *tr.* To serve as a beacon to; guide; light; also, to mark with beacons. **II.** *intr.* To shine as a beacon: as, "Where the lighthouse *beacons* bright Far in the bay" (M. Arnold's "Southern Night").—**bea′con-age** (-āj), *n.* A system of beacons, or a charge for its maintenance.

Beacon, over a rock at sea.

bead (bēd), *n.* [ME. *bede*, < AS. *bed-, gebed*, prayer, akin to *biddan*, ask: see *bid*.] Prayer†, or a prayer†; one of the small, perforated, usually round or roundish objects threaded on a string to form a chaplet or rosary to keep count of prayers; a similar object used with others for ornament, as in a necklace; a small globule or drop, as of liquid; a bubble of foam; one of the bubbles in an effervescing liquor; the foam or head formed by these; a small projecting piece of metal near the muzzle of a firearm, serving as a sight (as, to draw a *bead* on a person, to take aim at him with a firearm); a glass globule for trying the strength of alcoholic spirits; in *chem.* and *mineral.*, a globule of borax or of some other flux, supported on a platinum wire, with which a small amount of some other substance is heated in a flame as a test for its constituents, etc.; in *arch.*, etc., a small globular ornament, esp. one of a series in a line or row; also, a narrow convex molding, usu-

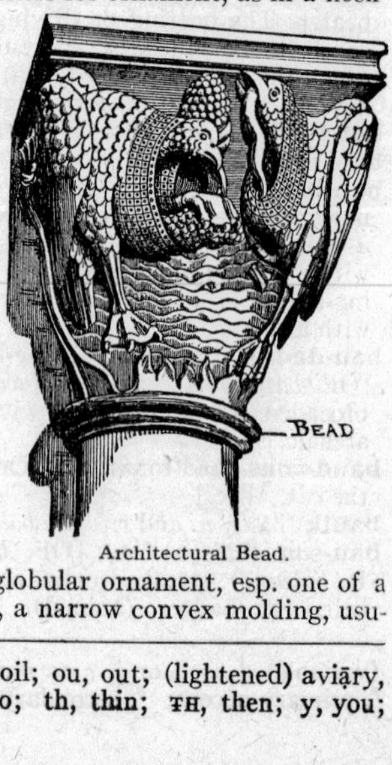

Architectural Bead.

ally more or less semicircular in section.—**bead,** *v.* **I.** *tr.* To furnish or adorn with beads or beading. **II.** *intr.* To form beads.—**bead′ed,** *p. a.* Adorned with or having beads; also, formed into or like beads.—**bead′house,** *n.* Formerly, an almshouse whose beneficiaries were to pray for the soul of the founder.—**bead′ing,** *n.* Narrow openwork trimming, as of lace or embroidery, through which ribbon may be run; in *arch.*, etc., the beads ornamenting an object; also, a narrow convex molding; a bead.

bea-dle (bē′dl), *n.* [Orig. < AS. *bydel*, akin to *bēodan*, announce (see *bid*), but later merged with forms from OF. *bedel* (F. *bedeau*), from Teut.] One who makes a proclamation†; a crier or messenger of a court (obs. or rare); in universities, one of certain officials, formerly executives, whose duties are now chiefly processional (see *bedel, bedell*); in England, a parish officer having various subordinate duties, as keeping order in church, punishing petty offenders, waiting on the clergyman, etc.—**bea′dle-ship,** *n.*

bead=roll (bēd′rōl), *n.* A list of persons to be prayed for; any list or catalogue (as, "Fames eternall *beadroll*": Spenser's "Faerie Queene," iv. 2. 32); also, a rosary. [Archaic.]

beads-man (bēdz′man), *n.*; pl. *-men.* One who prays for another; an inmate of a beadhouse. [Archaic.]—**beads′-wom″an,** *n.*; pl. *-women* (-wim″en).

bead-work (bēd′wėrk), *n.* Ornamental work made of or with beads; in *arch.*, etc., beading.

bead-y (bē′di), *a.* Bead-like; beaded.

bea-gle (bē′gl), *n.* [ME. *begle*; origin unknown.] One of a breed of small hounds with short legs and drooping ears, used in hunting hares; fig., one who scents out or hunts down; a spy, bailiff, or constable.

beak (bēk), *n.* [OF. F. *bec*; from Celtic.] The horny bill or neb of a bird; a similar (often horny) part in other animals, as in the turtle, duckbill, etc.; the rostrum, elongated head, or suctorial organ of certain insects; anything beak-like or ending in a point, as the tapering tube of a retort or the lip of a pitcher; *naut.*, a beak-like projection from the prow of a ship, esp. of an ancient war-vessel, as for ramming an enemy's ship.—**beaked,** *a.* Having a beak.

beak-er (bē′kėr), *n.* [Icel. *bikarr* = G. *becher.*] A large drinking-vessel with a wide mouth; also, an open-mouthed vessel of glass, etc., often with a lip for pouring, used chiefly in scientific experiments.

beak=i-ron (bēk′ī″ėrn), *n.* [Corruption of *bickern.*] The horn or tapering end of an anvil; an anvil with such a horn; a bickern.

beam (bēm), *n.* [AS. *bēam* = D. *boom* = G. *baum*, tree, beam: cf. *boom*[1].] A large, relatively long piece of timber, prepared for use (also fig., as in allusion to the mote and the beam spoken of in Mat. vii. 3–5); a similar piece of metal, stone, etc.; one of the principal horizontal timbers, etc., in a building or the like, as for supporting a floor; a roller or cylinder in a loom, on which the warp is wound before weaving; a similar cylinder on which cloth is wound as it is woven; the main piece of a plow, in which the plow-tail is fixed; also, the transverse bar of a balance from the ends of which the scales or pans are suspended; the balance itself; also, the main stem of a deer's horn, bearing the branches or tines; also, a lever of a steam-engine moving upon a center, and forming the medium of communication between the piston-rod and the crank or its equivalent; also, one of the strong transverse pieces of timber or metal stretching across a ship from side to side to support the deck, hold the sides in place, etc.; the greatest breadth of a ship; the side of a vessel, or the direction at right angles to the keel, with reference to the wind, sea, etc. (as, the weather *beam*, the side toward the wind; or, attributively, a *beam* sea, one rolling against a vessel's side); also, a ray, as of light; a collection of parallel rays of light or radiant energy.—**beam,** *v.* **I.** *tr.* To furnish with or as with beams; wind on a beam, as warp; emit in or as in beams or rays. **II.** *intr.* To emit beams, as of light; fig., to look or smile radiantly.—**beam′=com″pass,** *n.* An instrument consisting of a wooden or brass beam with sliding sockets that carry steel or pencil points, for describing large circles and for laying off distances.—**beam′i-ly,** *adv.* In a beamy manner; radiantly.—**beam′i-ness,** *n.*—**beam′ing,** *p. a.* Radiant.—**beam′ing-ly,** *adv.*—**beam′y,** *a.* Beam-like; massive; also, having antlers, as a stag; also, broad in the beam, as a ship; also, emitting beams, as of light; radiant.

bean (bēn), *n.* [AS. *bēan* = G. *bohne.*] The edible nutritious seed of various fabaceous plants; a plant producing such seeds, as *Vicia faba* (or *Faba vulgaris*), an old-world species cultivated since prehistoric times, or *Phaseolus vulgaris*, the common species of the U. S., occurring in numerous varieties, and used as a string-bean or snap-bean and also as a shell-bean, or *P. lunatus*, a species of which the Lima bean is a variety (see *Lima bean*); also, any of various other seeds or plants likened to the common bean.—**bean′=ca″per,** *n.* Any of the fleshy-leaved plants constituting the genus *Zygophyllum*, esp. *Z. fabago*, a small tree of the Levant, whose flower-buds are used as capers.—**bean′=meal,** *n.* Meal made from beans.—**bean′=tree,** *n.* Any of several trees bearing pods resembling those of a bean, as the catalpa and the carob-tree.

bear[1] (bār), *v.*; pret. *bore* (formerly *bare*), pp. *borne* or *born* (see *borne*), ppr. *bearing.* [AS. *beran*, akin to G. *gebären*, bring forth, L. *ferre*, Gr. *φέρειν*, Skt. *bhar-*, bear.] **I.** *tr.* To hold up or support; carry, fetch, or bring; press, push, or drive; afford (testimony, company, etc.); sustain in experience; undergo, esp. successfully or without giving way; endure (pain, loss, etc.); stand (annoyance, etc.); meet (expense); admit of; have (a name, aspect, etc.) as one's or its own; have (marks, traces, etc.) on one's self or itself; entertain (malice, etc.); wield or exercise (sway, etc.); deport or conduct (one's self); bring forth (young, fruit, etc.); produce or yield. **II.** *intr.* To hold, or remain firm, as under pressure (often with *up*); be patient (*with*); press (*on, against*, etc.); have an effect, reference, or bearing (with *on*); tend in course or direction; move or go; be situated (as, the land *bore* due west from the ship); bring forth young, fruit, etc.

bear[2] (bār). [AS. *bera* = G. *bär.*] **I.** *n.* Any of the plantigrade, carnivorous or omnivorous mammals of the family *Ursidæ*, esp. of the genus *Ursus*, having massive bodies, long shaggy hair, short limbs, and almost rudimentary tails; any of various animals resembling the bear (as, the ant-*bear*); fig., a rough, gruff, or surly person; in the stock-exchange, etc., one who endeavors to effect, or operates in the expectation of, a decline in the price of stock, etc. (cf. *bull*[1], *n.*); [*cap.*] with *the*, Russia (from the use of the bear as an emblem of Russia); also, in *astron.*, either of two northern constellations, Ursa Major ('Great Bear') and Ursa Minor ('Little Bear'). **II.** *a.* In the stock-exchange, etc., pertaining to the bears; marked by a decline in price.—**bear**[2], *v. t.* In the stock-exchange, etc., to attempt to lower the price of; operate in for a decline in price.

American Black Bear (*Ursus americanus*).

bear[3], **bere** (bēr), *n.* [AS. *bere.*] Barley. [Now north. Eng. and Sc.]

bear-a-ble (bār′a-bl), *a.* That may be borne; endurable.—**bear′a-ble-ness,** *n.*—**bear′a-bly,** *adv.*

bear=bait-ing (bār′bā″ting), *n.* The act or practice of baiting bears with dogs: a sport formerly popular in England, but now prohibited.

bear-ber-ry (bār′ber″i), *n.*; pl. *-berries* (-iz). A trailing, evergreen ericaceous shrub, *Arctostaphylos uva-ursi*, bearing small bright-red berries and tonic, astringent leaves; also, a related species, *A. alpina* (or, according to some botanists, *Mairania alpina*), bearing black berries ('alpine bearberry' or 'black bearberry'); also, any of certain other plants, as *Ilex decidua*, a species of holly of the southern U. S.

beard (bērd), *n.* [AS. *beard* = G. *bart.*] The growth of hair on the face of an adult man, sometimes exclusive of the mustache; a tuft, growth, or part resembling or suggesting this, as the tuft of long hairs on the lower jaw of a goat, or a cluster of fine, hair-like feathers at the base of the beak of

(variable) ḍ as d or j, ș as s or sh, ț as t or ch, ẓ as z or zh; ȯ, F. cloche; ü, F. menu; ċh, Sc. loch; ṅ, F. bonbon; **′, primary accent; ″, secondary accent; †, obsolete; <, from; +, and; =, equals. See also lists at beginning of book.**

certain birds; in *bot.*, a tuft or growth of awns or the like, as in wheat, barley, etc.; in *printing*, the part of a type which connects the face with the shoulder of the body.—**beard,** *v. t.* To seize, pluck, or pull the beard of, as in anger or contempt; hence, to oppose (a person, etc.) to his face, or openly; set at defiance; also, to furnish with a beard; also, to remove the beard from; also, to chip or plane (timber) to a desired shape.—**beard'ed,** *a.* Having a beard.—**beard'less,** *a.* Without a beard; hence, not yet arrived at manhood; of wheat, etc., without awns.—**beard'less-ness,** *n.*—**beard'=tongue,** *n.* Any plant of the scrophulariaceous genus *Pentstemon*, bearing a bearded sterile stamen.

bear-er (bãr'ėr), *n.* One who or that which bears; a supporting piece in a structure or mechanism; one who presents an order for money or goods; the presenter and ostensible payee of a check not limited to a specifically named payee.

bear=gar-den (bãr'gär"dn), *n.* A place for keeping or exhibiting bears, or for bear-baiting or other sports; hence, any place of tumult or disorder.

bear=grass (bãr'gràs), *n.* Any of several American plants of the liliaceous genus *Yucca*, having grass-like foliage; also, any of certain similar liliaceous plants, as the camass, *Quamasia quamash.*

bear-ing (bãr'ing), *n.* The act of a person or thing that bears; a supporting, carrying, pressing, undergoing, producing, etc.; carriage or deportment; reference or relation (with *on*); aspect; direction or relative position (often in *pl.*); also, a supporting part, as in a structure; also, a part resting on a support, or (of timbers, etc.) spanning the distance between supports; in *mach.*, a part in which a journal, pivot, or the like, turns or moves; in *her.*, any single device on a coat of arms; a charge.—**bear'ing=rein,** *n.* The rein by which the head of a horse is held up in driving; a check-rein.

bear-ish (bãr'ish), *a.* Bear-like; rough; surly; in the stock-exchange, etc., aiming at or tending to a decline in price.—**bear'ish-ness,** *n.*

bear=lead-er (bãr'lē"dėr), *n.* A person who leads about a trained bear for exhibition; hence, humorously, a tutor in charge of a young man of rank or wealth, as when on his travels (as, "young lords travelling with their *bear-leaders*": Thackeray's "Book of Snobs," vii.).

bear's=breech (bãrz'brēch), *n.* The acanthus plant.

bear's=ear (bãrz'ēr), *n.* A primrose, the auricula.

bear's=foot (bãrz'fůt), *n.* Any of various species of hellebore, esp. *Helleborus fœtidus*, a plant with digitate leaves and an offensive smell.

bear-skin (bãr'skin), *n.* The skin of a bear; also, a coarse, shaggy woolen cloth for overcoats; also, a tall black fur cap worn by soldiers.

bear-ward (bãr'wârd), *n.* A bear-keeper.

bear-wood (bãr'wůd), *n.* The buckthorn, *Rhamnus purshiana.*

beast (bēst), *n.* [OF. *beste* (F. *bête*), < L. *bestia.*] Any animal except man; hence, the animal nature in man; esp., a quadruped, as distinguished from birds, insects, reptiles, fishes, etc., as well as from man; also, an animal of the chase; also, a domesticated animal (in rural economy now usually restricted to cattle, esp. fatting cattle); sometimes, a horse, ass, etc.; in fig. use, a human being under the influence of animal propensities; a brutal man; a coarse, filthy, or degraded person.—**beast'hood** (-hůd), *n.* The nature or condition of a beast.—**beast'ie,** *n.* A little animal: esp. used in pity or endearment. [Orig. Sc.]—**beast'ly,** *a.*; compar. *beastlier*, superl. *beastliest.* Of or like a beast; bestial; low; vile.—**beast'li-ness,** *n.*

beat (bēt), *v.*; pret. *beat*, pp. *beaten* or *beat*, ppr. *beating.* [AS. *bēatan* = OHG. *bōzan* = Icel. *bauta.*] **I.** *tr.* To strike repeatedly, as in chastising, threshing, metal-working, making a batter, or driving out game; sound as on a drum, as a tattoo; break, forge, or make by blows; tread (a path, etc.); mark (time) by strokes, as with the hand; scour (cover) for game; exercise (the brains) severely; exhaust (a person, etc.), as by hard work; overcome in a contest; defeat; surpass or excel; swindle (slang). **II.** *intr.* To strike repeated blows; pound; throb or pulsate; dash (*against*, *on*, etc.); resound under blows, as a drum; win in a contest; *naut.*, to advance against the wind by alternate tacks; in *physics*, to make a beat or beats.—**to beat about the bush,** to approach a matter in a roundabout way; avoid coming to the point.—**beat,** *n.* The act of beating; a stroke or blow, or the sound produced by it; a throb or pulsation; the stroke made by the action of the escapement of a watch or clock; one's beaten path or habitual round; a subdivision of a county, as in Mississippi; the securing and publishing by a newspaper of some piece of news in advance or to the exclusion of its rivals, or the piece of news so published (journalistic slang); one who habitually evades paying for what he gets (slang); in *music*, a stroke of the hand, baton, etc., marking time-division or accent for music during performance; a time-unit or accent so indicated; in *physics*, a pulsation in sound due to interference of sound-waves; hence, a pulsation resembling this in other wave-motions, as of light.—**beat,** *p. a.* Beaten; exhausted. [Colloq.]—**beat'en,** *p. a.* Having undergone blows; hammered; much trodden; commonly used; defeated; baffled; exhausted.—**beat'er,** *n.* One who or that which beats; an implement or contrivance for beating something (as, an egg-*beater*).

be-a-tif-ic (bē-ạ-tif'ik), *a.* [L. *beatificus*, < *beatus*, blessed (pp. of *beare*, bless), + *facere*, make.] Rendering blessed; blissful: as, the *beatific* vision (the direct vision of God).—**be-a-tif'i-cal-ly,** *adv.*

be-at-i-fy (bẹ-at'i-fī), *v. t.*; *-fied*, *-fying.* [OF. *beatifier* (F. *béatifier*), < LL. *beatificare*, < L. *beatus*, blessed, + *facere*, make: cf. *beatific.*] To render blessed; in the *Rom. Cath. Ch.*, to declare (a deceased person) to be among the blessed, and thus entitled to specific religious honor.—**be-at"i-fi-ca'tion** (-fi-kā'shọn), *n.*

beat-ing (bē'ting), *n.* The act of a person or thing that beats; a striking, pounding, hammering, throbbing, etc.; an assaulting or chastising with blows; a thrashing; a defeat.

be-at-i-tude (bẹ-at'ĭ-tūd), *n.* [F. *béatitude*, < L. *beatitudo*, < *beatus*, blessed: see *beatific.*] The state of being blessed; supreme happiness; bliss; also, a declaration of blessedness, as those in Christ's Sermon on the Mount (Mat. v. 3–11).

beau (bō), *n.*; pl. *beaus* or *beaux* (bōz). [F., noun use of F. and OF. *beau*, also *bel* (fem. *belle*), fair, beautiful, fine, < L. *bellus*, pretty, handsome, fine: cf. *belle.*] A dandy; a fop; also, a lover or swain (as, "Her love was sought, I do aver, By twenty *beaux* and more": Goldsmith's "Elegy on Mrs. Mary Blaize").

beau=i-de-al (bō'ī-dē'ạl), *n.* [F. *beau idéal*, 'ideal beautiful.'] A conception of perfect beauty; a model of excellence; an ideally perfect type.

beau-ish (bō'ish), *a.* Like or characteristic of a beau.

beau monde (bō môṅd). [F., 'fine world.'] The fashionable world.

beau-te-ous (bū'tẹ-us), *a.* Beautiful. [Chiefly poetic.]—**beau'te-ous-ly,** *adv.*—**beau'te-ous-ness,** *n.*

beau-ti-fi-ca-tion (bū"ti-fi-kā'shọn), *n.* The act of beautifying.

beau-ti-fi-er (bū'ti-fī-ėr), *n.* One who or that which beautifies.

beau-ti-ful (bū'ti-fůl), *a.* Having beauty; delighting the eye; admirable to the taste or the mind.—**beau'ti-ful-ly,** *adv.*—**beau'ti-ful-ness,** *n.*

beau-ti-fy (bū'ti-fī), *v.*; *-fied*, *-fying.* [See *-fy.*] **I.** *tr.* To make beautiful; embellish. **II.** *intr.* To become beautiful.

beau-ty (bū'ti), *n.*; pl. *-ties* (-tiz). [OF. *bealte*, *beltet* (F. *beauté*), < ML. *bellitas*, < L. *bellus*, pretty, fine.] That quality of any object of sense or thought whereby it excites an admiring pleasure; qualification of a high order for delighting the eye or the esthetic, intellectual, or moral sense; also, something beautiful; a grace, charm, or pleasing excellence; a beautiful woman.—**beau'ty=sleep,** *n.* The sleep before midnight.—**beau'ty=spot,** *n.* A patch worn on the face or elsewhere to set off the fairness of the skin; hence, a mole or (humorously) any trifling spot or mark on the skin; also, any spot, place, or feature of especial beauty.

beaux (bōz), *n.* Plural of *beau.*

bea-ver[1] (bē′vėr), *n.* [AS. *beofor,* akin to G. *biber,* L. *fiber,* beaver, Skt. *babhrus,* ichneumon, as adj. brown.] An amphibious rodent quadruped of the genus *Castor,* of Europe, northern Asia, and North America, valued for its fur and for castor, and noted for its ingenuity in building houses and damming streams with trees, branches, stones, mud, etc.; also, its fur; also, a kind of furry hat-felt, or a hat made of it; a man's high silk hat; also, a heavy woolen cloth.

Beaver (*Castor fiber*).

bea-ver[2] (bē′vėr), *n.* [OF. *baviere,* orig. 'bib,' < *bave,* drivel.] A piece of armor for protecting the lower part of the face; also, a vizor.

B, Beaver, capable of being raised to cover the face.

bé-bé (bā-bā), *n.* [F., < E. *baby.*] A baby.

be-bee-rine (bē-bē′rin), *n.* In *chem.,* an alkaloid resembling quinine, obtained from the bark of the bebeeru and from other plants.

be-bee-ru, bi-bi-ru (bē-bē′rö), *n.* [Native name.] A large lauraceous tree, *Nectandra rodiœi,* of tropical America, the bark of which yields bebeerine.

be-calm (bē-käm′), *v. t.* To make calm; quiet; also, to halt (a ship, etc.) by a calm, or by lack of wind.

be-came (bē-kām′). Preterit of *become.*

be-cause (bē-kâz′). [ME. *bi cause,* 'by cause.'] **I.** *adv.* For the cause or reason (*that*: archaic); also, by reason (*of*); on account (*of*). **II.** *conj.* For the reason that; since; also, in order that†.

bec-ca-fi-co (bek-ạ-fē′kō), *n.*; pl. *-cos* (-kōz). [It., < *beccare,* peck, + *fico,* fig.] Any of various small birds esteemed in Italy for the table, as the warblers of the family *Sylviidæ,* esp. *Sylvia hortensis.*

Beccafico (*Sylvia hortensis*).

bé-cha-mel (bā-shȧ-mel), *n.* [F.; named from the inventor, Louis de *Béchamel,* Marquis de Nointel, steward of Louis XIV.] A white sauce made with cream.

be-chance (bē-châns′), *v. t.* or *i.* To befall.

be-charm (bē-chärm′), *v. t.* To charm; enchant.

bêche=de=mer (bāsh′dė-mãr′), *n.* [F., 'spade of (the) sea.'] A trepang; also, a mixed jargon used in Melanesia.

be-chic (bē′kik or bek′ik), *a.* [LL. *bechicus,* < Gr. βηχικός, < βήξ, cough.] In *med.,* pertaining to or relieving a cough.

beck[1] (bek), *n.* [Icel. *bekkr.*] A brook, esp. one with a stony bed or rugged course; also, the valley through which this flows. [Eng.]

beck[2] (bek), *v.* [Shortened form of *beckon.*] **I.** *intr.* To beckon; signal by a gesture; also, to nod, bow, or curtsy (chiefly Sc.). **II.** *tr.* To beckon to. —**beck**[2], *n.* A beckoning gesture (as, to be at one's *beck* and call, to be subject to one's summons or command); also, a nod, bow, or curtsy (chiefly Sc.).

beck[3] (bek), *n.* [Cf. *back*[1].] A vat, as used in dyeing, etc.

beck-et (bek′et), *n.* [Origin unknown.] *Naut.,* any of various contrivances for holding spars, etc., in position, as a short rope with a knot at one end which can be secured in a loop at the other end; also, a loop or ring of rope forming a handle, a means of attachment to the bottom of a block, or the like; also, a kind of bracket.

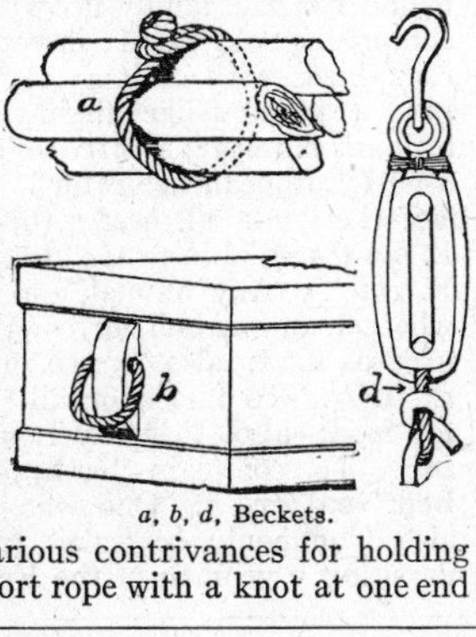

a, b, d, Beckets.

beck-on (bek′ọn), *v. i.* or *t.* [AS. *bīecnan, bēacnian,* < *bēacen,* sign, E. *beacon.*] To signal, summon, or direct by a gesture of the head or hand.—**beck′on,** *n.* A beckoning gesture.—**beck′on-er,** *n.*

be-cloud (bē-kloud′), *v. t.* To overcloud; obscure.

be-come (bē-kum′), *v.*; pret. *-came,* pp. *-come,* ppr. *-coming.* [AS. *becuman*: see *be-* and *come.*] **I.** *intr.* To come†; come about† or happen†; come into being; come or grow to be (as stated); be the fate (*of*), as to place, experience, etc. (with *what* as subject); be proper or fitting (now only as in *becoming, p. a.*). **II.** *tr.* To befit; suit; look well on.—**be-com′ing,** *p. a.* Fitting; seemly; appropriate; pleasingly suitable in appearance, as a garment to the wearer.—**be-com′ing-ly,** *adv.*—**be-com′ing-ness,** *n.*

Becque-rel (bek-rel) **rays.** See under *ray*[3], *n.*

be-curl (bē-kėrl′), *v. t.* To deck out with curls.

bed (bed), *n.* [AS. *bedd* = D. *bed* = G. *bett* = Goth. *badi,* bed.] That upon which or within which a person reposes or sleeps; a mattress; a mattress with the bedclothes; the mattress and bedclothes together with the bedstead; a bedstead alone; also, the use of a bed for the night; also, the bed as the place of conjugal union; matrimonial rights and duties; also, the bed as the place of childbirth; parental union; offspring or progeny; also, any resting-place; fig., the grave; the resting-place of an animal; also, something resembling a bed in form or position; a plat or piece of ground in a garden, usually raised somewhat, in which plants, esp. flowers, are grown; an extended mass of anything on or within the earth; a layer or stratum; a layer of shell-fish covering a tract of the bottom of the sea; the bottom of a body of water; that on which anything rests; the gravel, broken stone, etc., upon which the rails of a railroad are laid; in *printing,* the level surface in a printing-press on which the form of type is laid; in *mach.,* etc., a piece or part forming a foundation; in *building,* a layer of cement or mortar in which a stone or brick is embedded, or against which it bears; either of the horizontal surfaces of a stone in position; the under surface of a brick, shingle, slate, or tile in position.—**bed,** *v.*; *bedded, bedding.* **I.** *tr.* To provide with a bed; put to bed; go to bed with (archaic); plant in or as in a bed; lay flat, or in a bed or layer; embed, as in a substance. **II.** *intr.* To go to bed; share a bed; lie or rest on something; form a compact layer.

be-dab-ble (bē-dab′l), *v. t.* To dabble all over; soil by dabbling; bespatter.

be-dark-en (bē-där′kn), *v. t.* To darken completely.

be-dash (bē-dash′), *v. t.* To dash with water, etc.; cover with dashes of water, mud, color, etc.

be-daub (bē-dâb′), *v. t.* To daub all over; besmear.

be-daze (bē-dāz′), *v. t.* To daze completely; stupefy.

be-daz-zle (bē-daz′l), *v. t.* To dazzle completely; blind or confuse by dazzling.—**be-daz′zle-ment,** *n.*

bed=bolt (bed′bōlt), *n.* A bolt for fastening something, as a machine, to its bed or foundation.

Bedbug.
(Vertical line shows natural size.)

bed-bug (bed′bug), *n.* A small, blood-sucking hemipterous insect, *Cimex lectularius,* that infests houses and esp. beds.

bed-cham-ber (bed′chām″bėr), *n.* A chamber to sleep in; a bedroom.

bed-clothes (bed′klōᴛʜz), *n. pl.* Coverings for a bed.

bed-der (bed′ėr), *n.* One who beds; also, the under (stationary) stone of a mill (cf. *millstone*); also, a plant suitable for garden beds.

bed-ding (bed′ing), *n.* Materials or articles for a bed.

bede (bēd), etc. Archaic form of *bead,* etc.

be-deck (bē-dek′), *v. t.* To deck out; deck showily; adorn.

a, a, Bedegars.

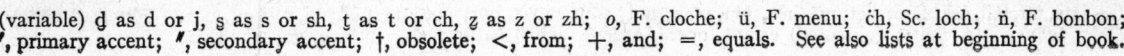

bed-e-gar, bed-e-guar (bed′ē-gär), *n.* [F. *bédegar, bédeguar,* < Pers. *bādāwar,* 'wind-brought.'] A spongy excrescence or gall produced on rose-bushes, esp. on the sweet-brier, by various gall-flies, as *Rhodites rosæ*, etc.

be-del, be-dell (bē'dl), *n.* Archaic forms of *beadle* used respectively at the universities of Oxford and Cambridge.

bede'=roll, bedes'man, etc. Archaic forms of *bead-roll, beadsman,* etc.

be-dev-il (bẹ-dev'l), *v. t.*; *-iled* or *-illed, -iling* or *-illing.* To treat diabolically; torment maliciously; also, to possess as with a devil; bewitch; also, to confound; muddle; spoil.—**be-dev'il-ment,** *n.*

be-dew (bẹ-dū'), *v. t.* To wet with or as with dew.

bed-fast (bed'fȧst), *a.* Confined to bed; bedridden.

bed-fel-low (bed'fel″ō), *n.* A sharer of one's bed.

Bed-ford (bed'fọrd) **cord.** [From *Bedford,* proper name.] A thick woolen or cotton fabric with heavy rounded ribs separated only by narrow lines of depression.

bed=gown (bed'goun), *n.* A nightgown; also, a short, loose jacket worn by women of the working class (prov. Eng.).

be-dight (bẹ-dīt'), *v. t.* [See *dight.*] To equip; array; deck out; bedeck: now usually in *bedight, pp.* (as, "Many a rare and sumptuous tome, In vellum bound, with gold *bedight*": Longfellow's "Wayside Inn," i., Prelude). [Archaic.]

be-dim (bẹ-dim'), *v. t.*; *-dimmed, -dimming.* To dim completely; obscure; darken.

be-diz-en (bẹ-diz'n or -dī'zn), *v. t.* [See *dizen.*] To deck out with clothes or finery; dress or adorn gaudily.—**be-diz'en-ment,** *n.*

bed-lam (bed'lạm), *n.* [Corruption of *Bethlehem.*] [*cap.*] The hospital of St. Mary of Bethlehem, in London, founded as a priory in 1247, but afterward used as an asylum for lunatics; [*l. c.*] any lunatic asylum; a madhouse; a scene of wild uproar and confusion; also, a lunatic†.—**bed'lam-ite** (-īt), *n.* A lunatic.

bed-less (bed'les), *a.* Without a bed.

bed=mold-ing (bed'mōl″ding), *n.* In *arch.,* the molding, or series of moldings, between the corona and the frieze of an entablature; also, any molding under a projection.

Bed-ou-in (bed'ö̩-in), *n.* [F. *Bédouin,* < Ar. *badawīn,* pl. of *badawīy,* dweller in the desert, < *badw,* desert.] An Arab of the desert, in Asia or Africa; a nomadic Arab; in general, a nomad; a wanderer; a vagrant.

bed=pan (bed'pan), *n.* A warming-pan; also, a chamber utensil for the use of persons confined to bed.

bed=plate (bed'plāt), *n.* A plate or foundation upon which a structure, as a machine, rests or is fixed.

bed-post (bed'pōst), *n.* One of the upright supports of a bedstead.

be-drab-ble (bẹ-drab'l), *v. t.* To render all drabbled, or wet and dirty; bedraggle.

be-drag-gle (bẹ-drag'l), *v. t.* To render all draggled, or limp and soiled as with wet and dirt.—**be-drag'gle-ment,** *n.*

be-drench (bẹ-drench'), *v. t.* To drench completely; soak.

bed-rid-den, bed-rid (bed'rid″n, -rid), *a.* [AS. *bedrida, bedreda,* 'bed rider.'] Confined (permanently or for a very long time) to one's bed, as by sickness or infirmity.

be-driz-zle (bẹ-driz'l), *v. t.* To wet with drizzling rain.

bed=rock (bed'rok'), *n.* Underlying rock; rocky or solid foundation.

bed-room (bed'röm), *n.* A sleeping-room.

bed-side (bed'sīd), *n.* The side of a bed, esp. as the place of one in attendance on the sick.

bed=sore (bed'sōr), *n.* A sore due to prolonged contact with a bed, as in a long illness.

bed-spread (bed'spred), *n.* An outer bed-cover.

Bedstaff. — From a French manuscript of the 15th century.

bed-staff (bed'stȧf), *n.*; pl. *-staves* (-stāvz) or *-staffs.* A staff or stick used in some way about a bed, as for tucking in the bedclothes. [Obs. or prov.]

bed-stead (bed'sted), *n.* A framework to support a bed.

bed-straw (bed'strâ), *n.* A rubiaceous plant, *Galium verum* ('our Lady's bedstraw'), or some allied species: formerly used like straw for beds.

bed-tick (bed'tik), *n.* The tick or cloth case holding the feathers, hair, straw, etc., of a bed.

bed-time (bed'tīm), *n.* The time to go to bed.

bed-ward (bed'wạrd), *adv.* To bed. Also **bed'wards.**

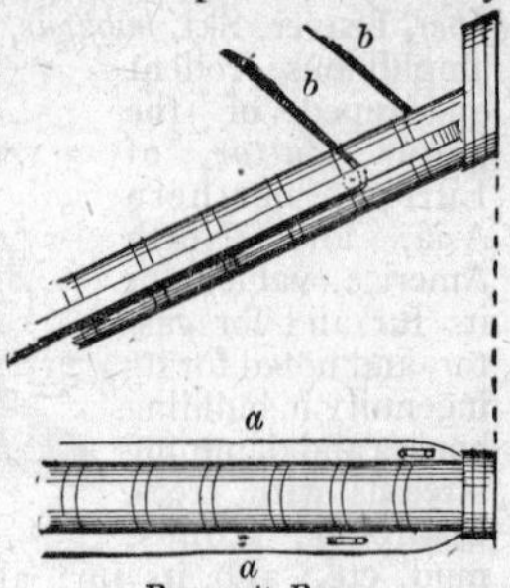

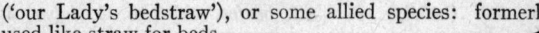

Bowsprit Bees.
a, a, bees; *b, b,* foretopmast stays.

bee[1] (bē), *n.* [AS. *bēag, bēah.*] A ring of metal, esp. as an ornament for the arm or neck†; *naut.,* a piece of hard wood bolted to the side of the bowsprit and used to reeve stays through.

bee[2] (bē), *n.* [AS. *bēo,* akin to G. *biene,* bee.] Any of various hymenopterous insects of the genus *Apis,* esp. *A. mellifica* (the common honey-bee), producing honey and wax, and forming highly organized colonies; any of various similar (social or solitary) insects of other genera; a figure or representation of a bee (used as a decorative emblem by Napoleon); a social gathering for joint work or amusement (chiefly U. S.: as, a husking-*bee*); a craze, mad notion, or tormenting desire for something (as, the presidential *bee*).—**bee'=balm,** *n.* The common balm, *Melissa officinalis,* of the gardens.—**bee'=bee″tle,** *n.* A European beetle, *Trichodes apiarius,* which sometimes infests bee-hives.

Honey-bee (*Apis mellifica*). Queen.

Neuter, or Worker.

Drone.

bee=block (bē'blok), *n.* *Naut.,* a bee. See *bee*[1].

bee=bread (bē'bred), *n.* A bitter brownish substance, consisting of pollen, or pollen and honey, stored up by bees as food for their young.

beech (bēch), *n.* [AS. *bēce,* also *bōc* (cf. *buckwheat*), akin to G. *buche* and L. *fagus,* beech, Gr. φηγός, oak.] Any tree of the genus *Fagus,* of temperate regions, having a smooth gray bark, and bearing small edible triangular nuts; the wood of such a tree; also, any of various similar trees.—**beech'=drops,** *n.* A low annual plant, *Leptamnium virginianum,* without green foliage, parasitic upon the roots of the beech.—**beech'en,** *a.* Of or pertaining to the beech or its wood.—**beech'=mast,** *n.* The mast or nuts of the beech, esp. as lying under the trees.—**beech'=nut,** *n.* The small triangular nut of the beech, serving as food for animals and yielding an oil.—**beech'y,** *a.* Of or pertaining to the beech; abounding in beeches.

bee=eat-er (bē'ē″tėr), *n.* Any member of the family *Meropidæ,* comprising old-world insectivorous birds with a long, slender bill, a swallow-like flight, and brilliant plumage, as *Merops apiaster* ('European bee-eater').

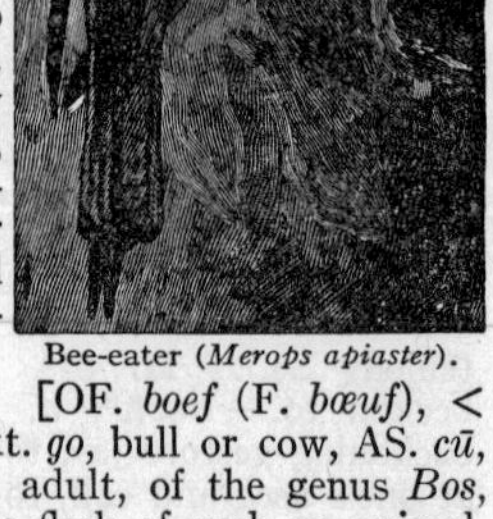

Bee-eater (*Merops apiaster*).

beef (bēf), *n.*; pl. *beeves* (bēvz). [OF. *boef* (F. *bœuf*), < L. *bos* (*bov-*), akin to Gr. βοῦς, Skt. *go,* bull or cow, AS. *cū,* E. *cow*[1].] Any animal, esp. an adult, of the genus *Bos,* whether an ox, bull, or cow; the flesh of such an animal, used as food; also, brawn or muscularity (colloq.).—**beef,** *v.* **I.** *tr.* To fatten or kill (an animal of the beef kind) for food; also, to apply raw beef to (a bruise, etc.). **II.** *intr.* To complain loudly; bluster; boast. [Slang.]—**beef'=eat″er,** *n.* One who eats beef; a well-fed fellow; also (commonly *beefeater,* without hyphen), the popular name for a yeoman of the English royal guard or a warder

of the Tower of London.—**beef′ing,** *n.* See *biffin.*—**beef′less,** *a.* Without beef: as, *beefless* days.
bee=fly (bē′flī), *n.*; pl. *-flies* (-flīz). A fly which more or less resembles a bee; esp., a fly of the family *Bombyliidæ.*
beef-steak (bēf′stāk′), *n.* A steak of beef for broiling, etc.
beef=wit-ted (bēf′wit″ed), *a.* Thick-witted; stupid. See Shakspere's "Troilus and Cressida," ii. 1. 14.
beef-y (bē′fi), *a.* Fleshy; brawny; solid; heavy.
bee=gum (bē′gum), *n.* A gum-tree, hollowed as by decay, in which bees live or from which hives are made; hence, a beehive. [Southern and western U. S.]
bee-hive (bē′hīv), *n.* A hive or receptacle, often dome-shaped, serving as a habitation for bees.
bee=kill-er (bē′kil″ėr), *n.* Any of the large, voracious, insectivorous dipterous flies constituting the family *Asilidæ,* which attack honey-bees on the wing and kill them.
bee=line (bē′līn′), *n.* A direct line, like the course of bees to the hive.
Be-el-ze-bub (bẹ-el′zẹ-bub), *n.* [Var. of *Baal-zebub,* name of a god of the Philistines mentioned in 2 Kings, i. 2, and commonly explained as meaning 'lord of flies': cf. *Baal.*] "The prince of the devils" (Mat. xii. 24); the devil; a devil; in Milton's "Paradise Lost," one of the fallen angels, second only to Satan himself.
bee=mar-tin (bē′mär″tin), *n.* The kingbird.
been (bin or, esp. Brit., bēn). Past participle of *be.*
bee=plant (bē′plant), *n.* Any plant which is especially useful in furnishing nectar to bees, as the cleome, *Cleome serrulata,* or the figwort, *Scrophularia californica.*
beer (bēr), *n.* [AS. *bēor* = G. *bier.*] An alcoholic beverage made by fermentation from cereals, usually malted barley, and flavored with hops, etc., to give a bitter flavor, in a broad sense including ale, but in a restricted sense distinguished from ale as being of lighter alcoholic content; also, any of various beverages made from roots, molasses or sugar, yeast, etc.—**beer′=gar″den,** *n.* A garden or place where beer is sold and served at tables.—**beer′y,** *a.* Of, like, or abounding in beer; affected by or suggestive of beer.—**beer′i-ness,** *n.*
beest-ings (bēs′tingz), *n. pl.* [AS. *bȳsting,* < *bēost,* beestings.] The first milk given by a mammal, esp. a cow, after parturition.
bees-wax (bēz′waks), *n.* The wax secreted by bees, of which they construct their honeycomb: used for various purposes in the arts, etc.—**bees′wax,** *v. t.* To rub, polish, or treat with beeswax.
bees-wing (bēz′wing), *n.* A thin film formed in port and some other wines after long keeping; also, old wine showing such a film.—**bees′winged,** *a.* Of such age as to show beeswing.
beet (bēt), *n.* [AS. *bēte,* < L. *beta.*] Any of various biennial plants of the chenopodiaceous genus *Beta,* esp. *B. vulgaris,* whose varieties include the common 'red beet,' which has a thick, fleshy edible root, and the 'sugar-beet' (see *sugar-beet*); also, the root of this plant.
bee-tle[1] (bē′tl), *n.* [AS. *bīetel,* < *bēatan,* E. *beat.*] A heavy hammering or ramming instrument, usually of wood, used to drive wedges, force down paving-stones, consolidate earth, etc.; also, any of various wooden instruments for beating linen, mashing potatoes, etc.; also, a beetling-machine.—**bee′tle**[1], *v. t.*; *-tled, -tling.* To use a beetle on; drive, ram, beat, or crush with a beetle; finish (cloth) by means of a beetling-machine.
bee-tle[2] (bē′tl), *n.* [AS. *bitela,* < *bītan,* E. *bite.*] Any insect of the order *Coleoptera,* with hard wing-covers (as, the Colorado *beetle,* the potato-beetle); a coleopter (see *coleopter*); also, popularly, any of various insects more or less resembling a beetle, as the common large black cockroach, *Stylopyga* (or *Periplaneta*) *orientalis* ('black beetle').

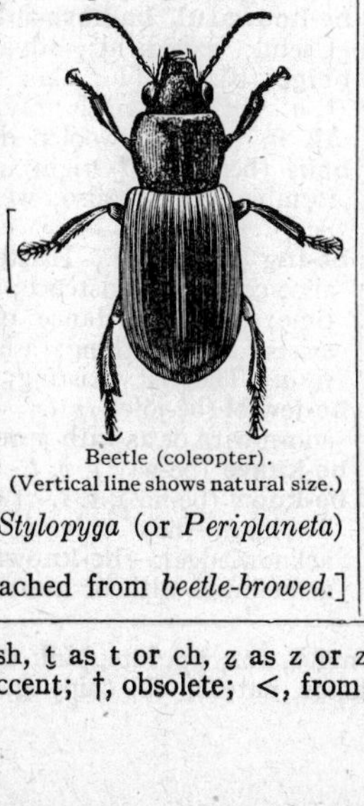

Beetle (coleopter).
(Vertical line shows natural size.)

bee-tle[3] (bē′tl), *a.* [Appar. detached from *beetle-browed.*] Of brows, projecting; overhanging.—**bee′tle**[3], *v. i.*; *-tled, -tling.* To project; overhang.
bee-tle=browed (bē′tl-broud), *a.* [Appar. < *beetle*[2].] Having projecting brows; scowling; sullen.
bee-tle=head (bē′tl-hed), *n.* [See *beetle*[1].] A stupid fellow; a blockhead.—**bee′tle=head″ed,** *a.*
bee-tling=ma-chine (bēt′ling-mạ-shēn″), *n.* A machine for finishing linen or cotton goods by a hammering process.
bee=tree (bē′trē), *n.* The basswood or American linden, *Tilia americana,* whose flowers are rich in honey; also, a hollow tree occupied by bees.
beet=root (bēt′röt), *n.* The root of the beet.
beeve (bēv), *n.* Erroneous singular of *beeves,* plural of *beef.*
bee=wolf (bē′wůlf), *n.*; pl. *-wolves* (-wůlvz). The bee-beetle, or its larva.
be-fall (bẹ-fâl′), *v.*; pret. *-fell,* pp. *-fallen.* [AS. *befeallan*: see *be-* and *fall.*] **I.** *intr.* To fall†; fall or come (*to*) by right (archaic); happen or occur. **II.** *tr.* To happen to.
be-fit (bẹ-fit′), *v. t.*; *-fitted, -fitting.* To be fitting, appropriate, or seemly for; be suited to; become.—**be-fit′ting-ly,** *adv.*
be-fog (bẹ-fog′), *v. t.*; *-fogged, -fogging.* To involve in fog or obscurity; confuse.
be-fool (bẹ-föl′), *v. t.* To fool; dupe; also, to call 'fool.'
be-fore (bẹ-fōr′). [AS. *beforan,* < *be,* by, + *foran,* before.] **I.** *adv.* In front; in advance; ahead; also, in time preceding; previously; also, earlier or sooner. **II.** *prep.* In front of; in advance of; ahead of; also, at a time preceding that of; previously to; earlier than; also, in precedence of, as in order or rank; also, in preference to; rather than; also, in the presence or sight of; also, in the view or opinion of (archaic).—**before the mast,** *naut.,* as a common sailor (the crew of a ship being berthed forward of the foremast).—**before the wind,** *naut.,* in the direction in which the wind blows; hence, fig., in prosperous circumstances; out of debt or difficulty.—**be-fore′,** *conj.* Previously to the time when; also, sooner than; rather than.—**be-fore′hand,** *adv.* or *a.* In advance; also, ahead financially; with something over and above one's needs.—**be-fore′time,** *adv.* Formerly. [Archaic.]
be-foul (bẹ-foul′), *v. t.* To make foul; defile; sully.
be-friend (bẹ-frend′), *v. t.* To act as a friend to; aid.
be-fringe (bẹ-frinj′), *v. t.* To adorn with or as with fringe.
be-fud-dle (bẹ-fud′l), *v. t.* To render fuddled, or stupid with intoxicating liquor; bemuse with drink.
beg (beg), *v.*; *begged, begging.* [ME. *beggen*; origin uncertain: see *beggar.*] **I.** *tr.* To ask for or supplicate in charity; ask as alms; also, to ask as a favor; hence, to ask for with humility or earnestness; crave; also, in argument, to take for granted without warrant (as, to *beg* the question, to assume indirectly the very point raised in it); also, to ask or entreat (a person), as to do something. **II.** *intr.* To ask alms or charity; live by asking alms; also, to make petition or entreaty.
be-gad (bẹ-gad′), *interj.* [For *by God.*] A minced oath or emphatic expletive.
be-gat (bẹ-gat′). Old preterit of *beget.*
be-gem (bẹ-jem′), *v. t.*; *-gemmed, -gemming.* To adorn with or as with gems.
be-get (bẹ-get′), *v. t.*; pret. *-got* (formerly *-gat*), pp. *-gotten* or *-got,* ppr. *-getting.* [AS. *begitan*: see *be-* and *get.*] To get† or acquire†; also, to procreate or generate (used chiefly of the male parent alone, sometimes of both parents); also, to cause to exist; produce as an effect.—**be-get′ter,** *n.*
beg-gar (beg′ạr), *n.* [ME. *beggare, beggere*; of uncertain origin, possibly < OF. *begard,* Beghard (a name said to have been assumed by numerous mendicants in the 13th century), and perhaps itself the source of *beg, v.*] One who begs alms, or lives by begging; a mendicant; also, a penniless person; also, a wretch or rogue (often playfully).—**beg′gar,** *v. t.* To reduce to beggary; impoverish; hence, to exhaust the resources of (as, to *beggar* description); also, to deprive wholly (*of*).—**beg′gar-dom** (-dọm), *n.* The class or fraternity of beggars.—**beg′gar-hood** (-hůd), *n.* The condition of a beggar; also, beggars collectively.—**beg′gar-ly,** *a.* Like or befitting a beggar; wretchedly poor; mean.—**beg′gar-li-ness,** *n.*—**beg′gar's=lice′,** *n. pl.* The burs or prickly or adhesive fruit or seeds of various plants, so

called because they stick to the clothing; as *sing.*, any of these plants. Also **beg′gar's=ticks′.**—**beg′gar=weed,** *n.* A plant of the fabaceous genus *Meibomia*, esp. *M. tortuosa* ('Florida beggar-weed') which is cultivated for fodder; also, any of certain other plants, as the knot-grass, dodder, etc.—**beg′gar-y,** *n.* The state of a beggar; utter poverty; penniless condition.

Beg-hard (beg′ärd), *n.* [OF. *begard*, also *beguin*: see *Beguine.*] A member of one of certain former religious communities of men which arose in Flanders in the 13th century, living after the manner of the Beguines.

be-gin (bē-gin′), *v.*; pret. *-gan*, pp. *-gun*, ppr. *-ginning.* [AS. *beginnan* (= D. and G. *beginnen*), < *be-* (see *be-*) + *-ginnan*, as in *onginnan*, *aginnan*, begin.] **I.** *intr.* To enter upon an action; take the first step; commence; start; also, to come into existence; arise; originate. **II.** *tr.* To enter upon the performance, execution, accomplishment, etc., of; take the first step in; commence; also, to bring into existence; give origin to; originate; be the first to do or practise.—**be-gin′ner,** *n.*—**be-gin′ning,** *n.* The act or fact of entering upon an action; the act of entering upon or of bringing into existence; commencement; origination; the point of time or space at which anything begins; the first part or initial stage of anything; that in which anything has its rise or origin; source.

be-gird (bē-gėrd′), *v. t.*; pret. and pp. *-girt* or *-girded.* [AS. *begyrdan*: see *be-* and *gird*[1].] To gird about; encompass.

be-gnaw (bē-nâ′), *v. t.* [AS. *begnagan*: see *be-* and *gnaw.*] To gnaw at. See Shakspere's "Richard III.," i. 3. 222.

be-gone (bē-gôn′). [Prop. two words.] Be gone; go away; depart: used interjectionally, as an imperative, and hence sometimes for other verb-forms (as, he charged them to *begone*; we must *begone*).

Begonia.

be-go-ni-a (bē-gō′ni-ạ), *n.* [NL. *Begonia* (see def.); named from Michel *Bégon* (1638–1710), French patron of science.] Any plant of the tropical genus *Begonia*, including species much cultivated for their handsome succulent, often varicolored leaves and waxy flowers.—**be-go-ni-a′ceous** (-ā′shius), *a.* Belonging to the *Begoniaceæ*, or begonia family of plants.

be-got (bē-got′). Preterit and past participle of *beget.*—**be-got′ten.** Past participle of *beget.*

be-grime (bē-grīm′), *v. t.* To make grimy.

be-grudge (bē-gruj′), *v. t.* To grudge; be reluctant to give, grant, or allow (something); be discontented at seeing (a person) have (something).

be-guile (bē-gīl′), *v. t.* To work upon by guile; delude; cheat; disappoint† or foil†; deprive artfully (*of*); draw (*into, out of*, etc.) as by wiles; charm or divert; while away (time) pleasantly.—**be-guile′ment,** *n.* The act of beguiling; the state of being beguiled; a beguiling agency or influence.—**be-guil′er** (-gī′lėr), *n.*—**be-guil′ing-ly,** *adv.*

Be-guin (beg′in, F. bā-gaṅ), *n.* [OF. *beguin* (F. *béguin*): see *Beguine.*] Same as *Beghard.*

be-guin-age (beg′in-āj, F. bā-gē-näzh), *n.* [F. *béguinage.*] A community of Beguines.

Be-guine (beg′in, F. bā-gēn), *n.* [OF. *beguine*, F. *béguine* (with masc., OF. *beguin*); named from Lambert le *Begue* ('the Stammerer'), the founder.] A member of one of certain communities of Roman Catholic women in Belgium, Holland, and elsewhere, who devote themselves to a religious life but retain the right of private property and are free to leave at any time. The first of these communities was founded at Liége in the 12th century.

be-gum (bē′gum), *n.* [Hind. *begam.*] In India, a queen or princess; a lady of high rank.

be-gun (bē-gun′). Past participle of *begin.*

be-half (bē-häf′ or -hȧf′), *n.* [ME. *behalve*, orig. phrase, AS. *be healfe*, by the side, but used as noun through confusion with (AS.) *on healfe*, on the side: see *half.*] Side or part (used in phrases after *on*, as, an ambassador speaks on *behalf* of his country, or on his country's *behalf*); interest, favor, or aid (after *in*, as, to plead in *behalf* of a person or a cause: sometimes also, less properly, after *on*); respect or matter (after *in*, as, in this or that *behalf*: archaic).

be-have (bē-hāv′), *v.*; *-haved*, *-having.* [Appar. < *be-* and *have.*] **I.** *tr.* To conduct (one's self or itself) in a specified way; deport; comport; also, to conduct (one's self) properly; also, to manage† or regulate†. **II.** *intr.* To conduct one's self or itself; act; also, to act properly.

be-hav-ior (bē-hāv′yọr), *n.* [From *behave.*] Manner of behaving or acting; conduct; deportment; mode or course of action; sometimes, proper deportment; specif., in *psychol.*, the actions or activities of the individual as matter of psychological study (cf. *behaviorism*).—**be-hav′ior-ism,** *n.* A theory or method of psychological procedure that regards objective facts of behavior or activity (in the broadest sense), of both man and animals, as the proper matter for study.—**be-hav′ior-ist,** *n.* An advocate of behaviorism; one who follows the method of behaviorism.—**be-hav-ior-is′tic,** *a.* Pertaining to behaviorists or behaviorism.—**be-hav-ior-is′ti-cal-ly,** *adv.*

be-hav-iour (bē-hāv′yọr), etc. British preferred form of *behavior*, etc.

be-head (bē-hed′), *v. t.* [AS. *behēafdian*, < *be-* priv. + *hēafod*, head.] To cut off the head of; decapitate; execute (a condemned person) by decapitation.—**be-head′al,** *n.* Beheading; execution by beheading.

be-held (bē-held′). Preterit and past participle of *behold.*

be-he-moth (bē-hē′mọth), *n.* [Heb. *b'hēmōth*, intensive pl. of *b'hēmah*, beast.] An animal, perhaps the hippopotamus, mentioned in Job, xl. 15; hence, any great and powerful beast.

be-hest (bē-hest′), *n.* [AS. *behæs*, promise: cf. *hest.*] Promise (as, the land of *behest*)†; bidding or injunction; a mandate or command (as, "But us he sends upon his high *behests* For state, as Sovran King": Milton's "Paradise Lost," viii. 238).

be-hind (bē-hīnd′). [AS. *behindan*, < *be*, by, + *hindan*, behind: see *hind*[3].] **I.** *adv.* At or toward the back; in the rear; also, in a place, state, or stage already passed; also, remaining; in reserve; still to come; also, in arrears; behindhand; also, slow, as a watch or clock. **II.** *prep.* At the back of; in the rear of; also, after; later than; also, less advanced than; inferior to; also, remaining after.—**be-hind′hand,** *adv.* or *a.* Behind others in progress; backward; also, behind time; late; also, in arrears; in debt.

be-hold (bē-hōld′), *v.*; pret. and pp. *-held.* [AS. *behealdan*: see *be-* and *hold*[2].] **I.** *tr.* To hold†; also, to hold in view; observe; look at; see. **II.** *intr.* To look; see: often used interjectionally, in the imperative, to call attention, or as a mere expletive due to surprise, etc.—**be-hold′en,** *p. a.* Held or bound by obligation; indebted; obliged.—**be-hold′er,** *n.*—**be-hold′ing,** *a.* Erroneous form of *beholden.*

be-hoof (bē-höf′), *n.* [AS. *behōf-* (in *behōflīc*, needful) (= G. *behuf*), < *be-* (see *be-*) + *-hōf-*, related to E. *heave.*] Use, advantage, or benefit: used chiefly in phrases after *to* or *for*, or sometimes (by confusion with *behalf*) *in* or *on.*

be-hoove, be-hove (bē-höv′, -hōv′ or -hōv′), *v.*; *-hooved*, *-hoved*, *-hooving*, *-hoving.* [AS. *behōfian*, < *behōf-*: see *behoof.*] **I.** *tr.* To need† or require†; also, to be needful or proper for or incumbent on (esp. used impersonally). **II.** *intr.* To be needful, proper, or due.

be-hoove-ful, be-hove-ful (bē-höv′fu̇l), *a.* [From *behoof.*] Useful; expedient; advantageous; necessary. [Archaic.]

beige (bāzh). [F., akin to *bis*, brownish-gray: see *bice.*] **I.** *a.* Of a brownish gray, as unbleached and undyed wool. **II.** *n.* A light woolen dress-fabric (orig. beige in color).

bein (bēn), *a.* [Origin unknown.] Well provided; comfortable; cozy; also, well-to-do; well off. [Now chiefly Sc.]

be-ing (bē′ing), *n.* Existence, as opposed to non-existence; also, conscious existence; life; also, mortal existence; lifetime; also, substance or nature; also, something that exists; a living thing; a human being or a person.—**be′ing,** *p. a.* That is; existing; present: as, for the time *being.*

be-jew-el (bē-jö′ẹl), *v. t.*; *-eled* or *-elled*, *-eling* or *-elling.* To adorn with or as with jewels.

be-knave (bē-nāv′), *v. t.* To call (one) 'knave.'

be-know (bē-nō′), *v. t.* [AS. *becnāwan*: see *be-* and *know.*] To know (now only as in *beknown*, *p. a.*); recognize†; acknowledge†.—**be-known′,** *p. a.* Known; that one is acquainted with or aware of. [Archaic or prov.]

Bel (bel), *n.* [= *Baal.*] A deity of the Babylonians and Assyrians, the god of the earth. Cf. *Baal.*
be-la-bor (bẹ-lā′bọr), *v. t.* To labor at†; beat vigorously; ply with heavy blows; fig., to assail persistently, as with ridicule or abuse.—**be-la′bour,** *v. t.* British preferred form of *belabor.*
be-late (bẹ-lāt′), *v. t.* To make late.—**be-lat′ed** (-lā′ted), *p. a.* Coming or being late or too late, esp. at night; overtaken by night.—**be-lat′ed-ly,** *adv.*—**be-lat′ed-ness,** *n.*
be-laud (bẹ-lâd′), *v. t.* To laud highly; bepraise.
be-lay (bẹ-lā′), *v. t.*; pret. and pp. (*naut.*) *-layed.* [AS. *belecgan*: see *be-* and *lay*[1].] To surround†; beset†; waylay†; *naut.*, to fasten (a rope) by winding around a pin or the like.—**belay there!** *naut.*, make fast (the rope)! fig., hold on! stop!—**be-lay′ing=pin,** *n. Naut.*, a pin for use in belaying.

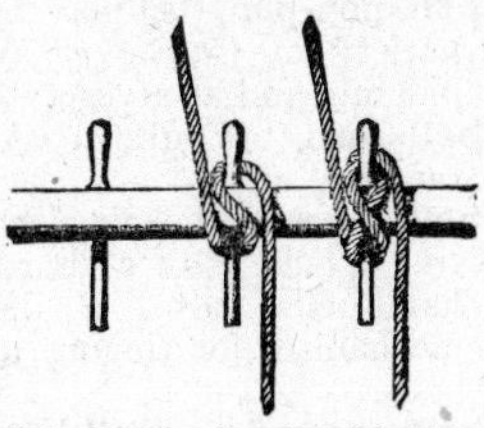
Belaying-pins in rail, with ropes belayed on them.

belch (belch), *v.* [AS. *bealcian.*] **I.** *intr.* To eject wind spasmodically and noisily from the stomach through the mouth; hence, to emit contents violently, as a volcano; also, to issue spasmodically, as flame. **II.** *tr.* To eject spasmodically and noisily from the stomach through the mouth; eructate; hence, to emit violently, as flame; cast forth; also, to vent with vehemence (as, to *belch* out one's fury); ejaculate.—**belch,** *n.* A belching; an eructation.—**belch′er**[1], *n.*
belch-er[2] (bel′chėr), *n.* [From Jim *Belcher*, an English pugilist.] A neckerchief having a dark-blue ground and large white spots with a blue spot in the center of each.
bel-dam, bel-dame (bel′dạm, -dạm or -dām), *n.* [ME., < *bel-* (< OF. *bel, belle*, fair), used like *grand-* in words expressing relationship, + *dame*, E. *dame.*] A grandmother†; an old woman; an old hag (as, "Our witches are no longer old And wrinkled *beldames*, Satan-sold": Whittier's "New England Legend").
be-lea-guer (bẹ-lē′gėr), *v. t.* [D. *belegeren*, < *be-*, about, + *leger*, camp.] To besiege.—**be-lea′guer-er,** *n.*—**be-lea′guer-ment,** *n.*

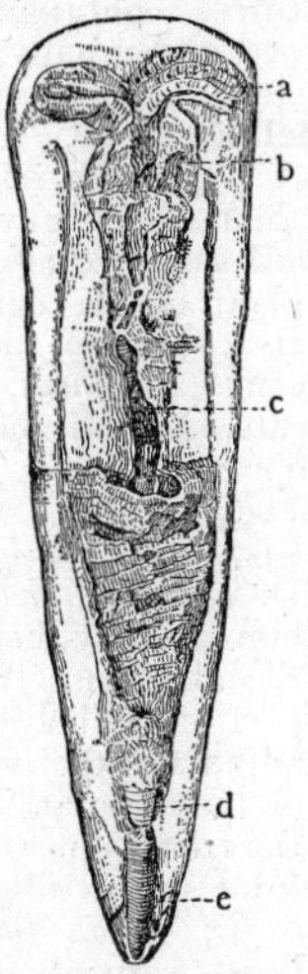

Belemnite, with remains of the animal.
a, arms with hooks; *b*, head; *c*, ink-bag; *d*, phragmocone; *e*, guard, or rostrum.

bel-em-nite (bel′ẹm-nīt or bẹ-lem′-), *n.* [Gr. βέλεμνον, dart.] A cylindrical fossil, several inches long, and tapering to a point at one end, consisting of the internal bone of an extinct animal allied to the cuttlefish; also, the animal itself.
bel-fried (bel′frid), *a.* Having a belfry.
bel-fry (bel′fri), *n.*; pl. *-fries* (-friz). [OF. *berfrei, berfroi* (F. *beffroi*); from Teut., = MHG. *bercvrit*, < OHG. *bergan*, protect, + *fridu*, peace, shelter.] A wooden tower, generally movable, used in medieval siege operations as a shelter for troops and as an engine of attack; a shed used as a shelter for cattle, etc. (now only local, Eng.); a watch-tower†; a bell-tower, generally one attached to a church or other building, but sometimes one standing apart; that part of a steeple or other structure in which a bell is hung.

Belfry used in the assault of a medieval fortress.

Bel-gian (bel′jiạn), *a.* [L. *Belgium*, country of the Belgæ: see *Belgic.*] Of or pertaining to Belgium, a small country of Europe, bordering on France, Germany, and Holland, formerly part of the Netherlands but erected into an independent kingdom in 1830.—**Belgian block,** a nearly cubical block of granite, etc., used for paving.—**Belgian hare,** one of a breed of domestic rabbits notable for large size.—**Belgian marble,** a dull-red marble marked with blue and white, obtained from Belgium.—**Bel′gian,** *n.* A native or inhabitant of Belgium.
Bel-gic (bel′jik), *a.* [L. *Belgicus*, < *Belgæ*: see def.] Of or pertaining to the Belgæ, an ancient warlike people of northern Gaul, probably of mixed Celtic and Teutonic stock; also, of or pertaining to Belgium; Belgian.
Bel-gra-vi-an (bel-grā′vi-ạn), *a.* Of or pertaining to Belgravia, a fashionable section of the western part of London; hence, aristocratic; fashionable.
Be-lial (bē′liạl), *n.* [Heb. *b'liya'al*, worthlessness.] The spirit of evil personified; the devil; Satan; in Milton's "Paradise Lost," one of the fallen angels.
be-lie (bẹ-lī′), *v. t.*; *-lied, -lying.* [AS. *belēogan*: see *be-* and *lie*[2].] To lie about; calumniate; misrepresent; also, to show to be false; also, to prove false to; fail to justify.—**be-li′er,** *n.*
be-lief (bẹ-lēf′), *n.* [ME. *bileafe* (with *bi-* for *ge-*), for AS. *gelēafa* = G. *glaube*, belief; akin to E. *lief* and *love.*] Confidence or trust; conviction of the truth or reality of a thing, based upon grounds insufficient to afford positive knowledge; that which is believed; an accepted opinion; a tenet or creed.
be-liev-a-ble (bẹ-lē′vạ-bl), *a.* That may be believed.—**be-liev′a-ble-ness,** *n.*
be-lieve (bẹ-lēv′), *v.*; *-lieved, -lieving.* [ME. *bileven*, for AS. *gelēfan* = G. *glauben*, believe: cf. *belief.*] **I.** *intr.* To have confidence (*in*); trust; rely through faith (*on*); be persuaded of the truth or reality of a thing (with *in*). **II.** *tr.* To have belief in; credit; accept as true; also, to think.—**be-liev′er,** *n.* One who believes; an adherent of some religious faith.—**be-liev′ing-ly,** *adv.*
be-like (bẹ-līk′), *adv.* [Appar. for *by like.*] Very likely; probably; perhaps: as, "Things that I know not of *belike* to thee are dear" (Wordsworth's "Pet-Lamb"). [Archaic or prov.]
be-lit-tle (bẹ-lit′l), *v. t.* To make little or less important; depreciate; disparage.—**be-lit′tle-ment,** *n.*—**be-lit′tler,** *n.*
bell[1] (bel), *n.* [AS. *belle* = D. *bel.*] A metallic sounding-instrument, typically cup-shaped with flaring rim, rung by the strokes of a tongue or clapper or a hammer; the stroke or sound of such an instrument (used on shipboard to indicate time); anything of the form of a bell, as the corolla of a flower.—**bell, book, and candle,** the accessories of an old form of excommunication in the Roman Catholic Church (the book being closed and candles extinguished); hence, the resources of the church against heretics or offenders; the terrors of excommunication; also, the accessories of religious ceremony (humorous).—**bell**[1], *v.* **I.** *tr.* To put a bell on; also, to cause to swell (*out*) like a bell. **II.** *intr.* To take or have the form of a bell.
bell[2] (bel), *v.* [AS. *bellan*, roar, = G. *bellen*, bark.] **I.** *intr.* To bellow; roar; now, chiefly, to utter the cry of a rutting deer (as, "The wild-buck *bells* from ferny brake": Scott's "Marmion," iv. 15). **II.** *tr.* To bellow. [Archaic.]—**bell**[2], *n.* The cry of a rutting deer.
bell[3] (bel), *n.* [ME. *belle* = D. *bel.*] A bubble, as in a liquid. [Now chiefly Sc.]—**bell**[3], *v. i.* To bubble. [Chiefly Sc.]
bel-la-don-na (bel-ạ-don′ạ̈), *n.* [It., 'fair lady.'] A poisonous solanaceous plant, *Atropa belladonna*; the deadly nightshade; also, a poisonous drug from this plant. See *atropine.*—**bel-la-don′na lil′y.** The amaryllis, *Amaryllis belladonna.*

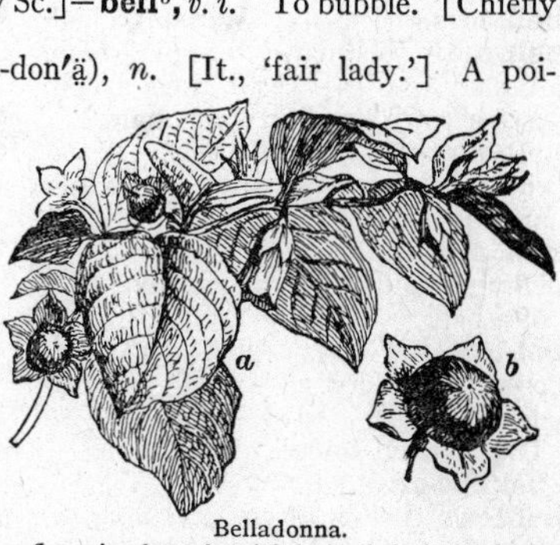

Belladonna.
a, flowering branch, with fruit; *b*, fruit, on larger scale.

bel-lar-mine (bel′är-min or -mēn), *n.* A large globular stoneware jug with a narrow neck, decorated with the face of a bearded man, orig. designed as a caricature of Cardinal Bellarmine (1542–1621).

Bell-cote.

bell=bird (bel′bėrd), *n.* A name for various birds of the southern hemisphere whose notes resemble the sound of a bell, as the honey-eater, *Manorhina melanophrys*, of Australia.

bell=boy (bel′boi), *n.* A boy who answers a bell; esp., an employee in a hotel who attends to the wants of guests in their rooms when summoned by a bell.

bell=cote, bell=cot (bel′kōt, -kot), *n.* In *arch.*, a small structure designed to contain one or more bells, often carried upon brackets projecting from a wall.

bell=crank (bel′krangk), *n.* A right-angled lever for communicating motion, as from one bell-wire to another lying at right angles to it.

Bell-crank. *F*, center about which arms oscillate.

belle (bel), *n.* [F., fem. of *beau*: see *beau*.] A woman or girl who is especially admired for her beauty; a recognized or reigning beauty.

belled (beld), *a.* Having a bell or bells.

bel-ler-ic (be-ler′ik), *n.* [F. *bellèric*, < Ar. *balīlaj*, < Pers. *balīlah*.] The astringent fruit of an East Indian tree, *Terminalia bellerica*: a variety of myrobalan.

belles=let-tres (bel-letr), *n. pl.* [F., 'fine letters.'] The finer or higher forms of literature; literature regarded as a fine art.

bel-let-rist (bel-let′rist), *n.* [By contraction from *belles-lettres*.] One devoted to belles-lettres.—**bel-let-ris-tic** (bel-let-ris′tik), *a.* Of or pertaining to belles-lettres.

bell=flow-er (bel′flou″ėr), *n.* A campanula.

bell=glass (bel′glȧs), *n.* A bell-shaped glass vessel or cover, as for protecting delicate instruments, bric-à-brac, etc., or for holding gases in chemical operations.

bell=hang-er (bel′hang″ėr), *n.* One whose business it is to put up and repair bells, bell-wires, etc.

bell=hop (bel′hop), *n.* A bell-boy. [Slang.]

bel-li-cose (bel′i-kōs or bel-i-kōs′), *a.* [L. *bellicosus*, < *bellum*, war.] Inclined to war; warlike; pugnacious.—**bel′li-cose-ly,** *adv.*—**bel-li-cos′i-ty** (-kos′i-ti), *n.*

bel-lied (bel′id), *a.* Having a belly: as, big-*bellied*.

bel-lig-er-ent (be-lij′ẹ-rẹnt). [F. *belligérant*, < L. *belligerans* (*-ant-*), ppr. of *belligerare*, wage war, < *bellum*, war, + *gerere*, bear, wage.] **I.** *a.* Waging war; warring; warlike; actively hostile; also, of or pertaining to belligerents. **II.** *n.* A nation, power, or person engaged in war; a combatant.—**bel-lig′er-ence, bel-lig′er-en-cy,** *n.*—**bel-lig′er-ent-ly,** *adv.*

Bellows for blowing a fire.—French, 17th century.

bel-lip-o-tent (be-lip′ọ-tẹnt), *a.* [L. *bellipotens* (*-ent-*), < *bellum*, war, + *potens*, E. *potent*.] Mighty in war.

bell=jar (bel′jär), *n.* A bell-glass.

bell=less (bel′les), *a.* Without a bell.

bell-man (bel′mạn), *n.*; pl. *-men*. A man who carries or rings a bell, esp. a town crier or watchman.

bell=met-al (bel′met″ạl), *n.* A variety of bronze, an alloy of copper and tin, of which bells are made.

bell=mouthed (bel′mouᴛʜd), *a.* Having a flaring mouth like that of a bell.

bel-low (bel′ō), *v. i.* or *t.* [AS. *bylgean*.] To cry as a bull, cow, or deer; roar; bawl.—**bel′low,** *n.* The act or sound of bellowing.—**bel′low-er,** *n.*

bel-lows (bel′ōz or -us), *n. sing.* or *pl.* [Orig. pl., < AS. *belg*, bag (*blǣst-belg*, 'blast-bag,' bellows): see *belly*.] An instrument or machine for producing a strong current of air, as for blowing a fire or sounding a musical instrument, consisting essentially of an air-chamber which can be alternately expanded to draw in air through a valve and contracted to expel the air through a tube; also, anything resembling or suggesting this, as the expansile part of a photographic camera.

bell=pep-per (bel′pep″ėr), *n.* The bell-shaped fruit of a variety of *Capsicum annuum* (see *capsicum*), used for pickling and as a vegetable.

bell=pull (bel′pụl), *n.* A handle for pulling a bell (attached by wire, etc.).

bell=ring-er (bel′ring″ėr), *n.* One whose business it is to ring a bell, as of a church; also, a performer with musical hand-bells; also, a device or mechanism for ringing a bell or bells.

Bell-turret.—Abbaye-aux-Hommes, Caen, Normandy.

bell=shaped (bel′shāpt), *a.* Shaped like a bell, or like a cup flaring more or less at the rim.

bell=tow-er (bel′tou″ėr), *n.* A tower built to contain a bell or bells.

bell=tur-ret (bel′tur″et), *n.* A turret containing a bell-chamber, and usually crowned with a spire or other ornamental feature.

bell=weth-er (bel′weᴛʜ″ėr), *n.* A wether or sheep which leads the flock, usually bearing a bell.

bell-wort (bel′wėrt), *n.* Any plant of the campanula family; also, a plant of the melanthiaceous genus *Uvularia*, bearing a delicate, slenderly bell-shaped yellow flower.

bel-ly (bel′i), *n.*; pl. *bellies* (-iz). [AS. *bælg*, *belg*, bag, = D. *balg*, skin, belly, = G. *balg*, skin, case.] The part of the human body, below the breast, which contains the bowels; the abdomen; the corresponding part of an animal; the part of the body which receives food; the stomach with its adjuncts; the inside or interior of anything; a protuberant or bulging part of anything; a concave or hollow surface; the front, inner, or under surface or part of something; the front surface of a violin or similar instrument.—**bel′ly,** *v. t.* or *i.*; *-lied*, *-lying*. To swell out.—**bel′ly=band,** *n.* A band worn about the belly, as of a harnessed or saddled horse.—**bel′ly-ful** (-fụl), *n.*; pl. *-fuls*. As much as fills the belly or stomach, or satisfies the appetite; hence, a great abundance; more than enough.—**bel′ly=god,** *n.* One who makes a god of his belly or appetite; a glutton.—**bel′ly=tim″ber,** *n.* Food: as, "Regions desolate . . . Where *belly-timber* above ground, Or under, was not to be found" (Butler's "Hudibras," i. 1). [Chiefly humorous.]

bel-o-man-cy (bel′ọ-man-si), *n.* [Gr. βέλος, arrow, dart, + μαντεία, divination.] Divination by means of arrows.

be-long (bẹ-lông′), *v. i.* [ME. *belongen*, < *be-* (E. *be-*) + *longen*, belong.] To be a possession, appurtenance, adjunct, or part (with *to*); pertain as a property, function, or concern (*to*); appertain as proper or due (*to*); bear the relation of a native or inhabitant, or an adherent, member, etc. (*to*); have one's or its proper place (*in*, *on*, *at*, or otherwise as specified).—**be-long′ing,** *n.* Something that belongs; *pl.*, possessions; appurtenances.

be-love (bẹ-luv′), *v. t.* To love: now only in the passive.—**be-lov′ed** (-luv′ed or -luvd′). **I.** *p. a.* Loved; dear. **II.** *n.* One who is beloved.

be-low (bẹ-lō′). [ME. *biloghe*, 'by low.'] **I.** *adv.* In or to a lower place; lower down; beneath; on earth; in the lower world or the infernal regions; downstairs; further down in a scale, as of rank, or in direction from the top, head, or beginning. **II.** *prep.* Lower down than; beneath; under; lower in rank, degree, amount, rate, etc., than.

belt (belt), *n.* [AS. *belt*, prob. < L. *balteus*, belt.] A band of flexible material for encircling the waist; a girdle; any encircling or transverse band, strip, or stripe; a zone-like tract with distinctive characteristics (as, the wheat *belt*); a thwack or blow (slang); in *mach.*, a flexible band or cord passing about two or more wheels, pulleys, or the like, to transmit motion.—**belt,** *v. t.* To gird or furnish with a belt; invest with a distinctive belt, as of an earl or knight; fasten on (a sword, etc.) by means of a belt; encircle like or as with a belt; mark with bands or stripes; beat with a belt, strap, etc.; give a thwack or blow to (slang).

Bel-tane (bel′tān), *n.* [Gael. and Ir.] May 1 (Old Style), anciently one of the quarter-days of Scotland; May Day; also, an ancient Celtic festival celebrated with bonfires, in Scotland on May Day, in Ireland on June 21.

belt-ed (bel′ted), *p. a.* Girded or furnished with a belt; invested with a distinctive belt, as a knight; fastened on by a belt, as a sword; encircled or marked by a belt or belts, as of color.—**belt′ing,** *n.* Material for belts; belts, or a belt.

be-lu-ga (be-lö′gä), *n.* [Russ.] The large white sturgeon, *Acipenser huso*, of the Caspian Sea and Black Sea and their tributary rivers; also, a cetacean, *Delphinapterus leucas*, chiefly of arctic seas, characterized by a rounded head and almost pure white color.

Beluga, or White Whale (*Delphinapterus leucas*).

bel-ve-dere (bel′vẹ-dēr, It. bel-vā-dā′rā), *n.* [It., 'beautiful view.'] An upper story or any structure or building designed to afford a fine view.—**bel′ve-dered,** *a.* Provided with a belvedere.

be-ma (bē′mä), *n.*; pl. *bemata* (-mạ-tä). [Gr. *βῆμα*, < *βαίνειν*, go.] In *Gr. antiq.*, a stage or platform from which a speaker addressed an assembly; in the *Gr. Ch.*, the inclosed space surrounding the altar; the sanctuary or chancel.

be-maul (bẹ-mâl′), *v. t.* To maul severely.

be-maze (bẹ-māz′), *v. t.* To daze; bewilder.

be-mean (bẹ-mēn′), *v. t.* To make mean; lower (one's self).

be-mire (bẹ-mīr′), *v. t.* To befoul with or sink in mire.

be-mist (bẹ-mist′), *v. t.* To cover or surround with mist; befog; obscure.

be-moan (bẹ-mōn′), *v.* [AS. *bemǣnan*: see *be-* and *moan*.] **I.** *tr.* To moan over; bewail; lament; also, to express pity for. **II.** *intr.* To lament; mourn.

be-mock (bẹ-mok′), *v. t.* To mock; deride; delude.

be-moil (bẹ-moil′), *v. t.* To befoul with mud or dirt. [Now prov. Eng.]

be-mud-dle (bẹ-mud′l), *v. t.* To muddle completely.

be-muse (bẹ-mūz′), *v. t.* To confuse or stupefy, as with drink; bemuddle; befuddle.

ben[1] (ben), *prep.* and *adv.* [AS. *binnan*.] Within (esp. with reference to an inner room). [Sc.]—**ben**[1], *n.* The inner room (parlor) of a cottage. Cf. *but*, *n.* [Sc.]

ben[2] (ben), *n.* [Ar. *bān*.] A tree of the genus *Moringa*, of Arabia, India, and elsewhere, bearing a winged seed (nut) which yields an oil ('oil of ben') used in extracting flower-perfumes, lubricating delicate machinery, etc. (cf. *horseradish-tree*); also, the seed of such a tree.

ben[3] (ben), *n.* [Gael. *beann*.] A mountain-peak: used chiefly in the names of Scottish mountains (as, *Ben* Lomond).

bench (bench), *n.* [AS. *benc*; from a Teut. source whence also E. *bank*[1], *bank*[2], and *bank*[3].] A long seat, as for several persons; the seat on which judges sit in court; the office or dignity of a judge; a court of justice; the body of persons sitting as judges; a seat occupied by persons in their official capacity, the office or dignity of those occupying it, or the persons themselves (as, the episcopal *bench*, the bishops having seats in the British House of Lords); the work-table of a carpenter or other mechanic; a platform on which animals are placed for exhibition, as at a dog-show; a raised, level tract of land, as between a river and hills.—**bench,** *v.* **I.** *tr.* To furnish with benches; also, to seat or place on a bench. **II.** *intr.* To seat one's self on a bench.—**bench′er,** *n.* One who sits on a bench; a frequenter of tavern benches; an idler; one occupying a bench officially, as a judge (archaic); in England, one of the senior members of an Inn of Court, who have the government of the society.—**bench′=mark,** *n.* In *surv.*, a mark cut into some durable material, as stone, to serve as a starting-point or guide in a line of levels for the determination of altitudes over any region.—**bench′=show,** *n.* An exhibition of animals, as dogs, arranged on benches, where awards are made for physical merits.

bend[1] (bend), *n.* [AS. *bend*, bond, band, head-band, fillet (see *bend*[3]); from the Teut. source of E. *bind*: cf. *band*[1].] A band†, bond†, or fetter†; *naut.*, a knot by which a rope is fastened to another rope or to something else.

bend[2] (bend), *v.*; *bent* or *bended*, *bending*. [AS. *bendan*, bind, bend (a bow), = Icel. *benda*, bend; from the same (Teut.) source as E. *bend*[1].] **I.** *tr.* To strain (a bow, etc.) into a state of tension as by a string; strain or brace tensely (archaic); render curved or angular; flex; crook; force into a different or particular shape, as by pressure; cause to bow or yield (as, to *bend* a man to one's will); bow (the head); turn in a particular direction; incline; direct or aim, as a bow†; direct or apply (the mind, efforts, etc.); in the passive, to be determined or resolved (usually with *on*); *naut.*, to fasten. **II.** *intr.* To become curved, crooked, or bent; stoop, or assume a bent posture; bow in submission or reverence; yield or submit; turn or incline in a particular direction; be directed; direct one's energies (as, to *bend* to a task).—**bend**[2], *n.* A bending, or a bent condition; an inclination of the body; a turning in a particular direction; inclination; a bent thing or part; a curve or flexure; a crook; *pl.*, caisson disease (colloq.); *pl.*, *naut.*, the wales of a ship.

bend[3] (bend), *n.* [Orig. < AS. *bend*, band, fillet (see *bend*[1]), but in part also < OF. *bende*, *bande*, E. *band*[2].] A band† or strip†; the half of a trimmed hide of sole-leather; in *her.*, a diagonal band extending from the dexter chief to the sinister base.—**bend sinister,** in *her.*, a diagonal band extending from the sinister chief to the dexter base: a mark of bastardy.

Heraldic Bend.

bend-a-ble (ben′dạ-bl), *a.* That may be bent.

bend-er (ben′dėr), *n.* One who or that which bends, as a pair of pliers; a sixpence (slang, Eng.); a spree (slang, U. S.); in *baseball*, a curve (slang).

bene (bēn), *n.* [AS. *bēn* = Icel. *bōn*, E. *boon*[1].] A prayer or petition: as, "a bootless *bene*" (Wordsworth's "Force of Prayer"). [Obs. or archaic.]

be-neath (bẹ-nēth′). [AS. *beneothan*, < *be*, by, + *neothan*, below, akin to E. *nether*.] **I.** *adv.* Below; underneath. **II.** *prep.* Below; under; lower than; below the level or dignity of; inferior to; unworthy of.

ben-e-di-ci-te (ben-ẹ-dis′i-tē). [L., 2d pers. pl. impv. of *benedicere*, bless: see *benediction*.] **I.** *interj.* A term used like 'bless you!' as expressing a wish, or like 'bless us!' or 'bless me!' as expressing surprise or remonstrance. [Archaic.] **II.** *n.* [*cap.*] The canticle or hymn beginning in Latin "Benedicite, omnia opera Domini," and in English "O all ye works of the Lord, bless ye the Lord"; a musical setting for this canticle; [*l. c.*] an invocation of a blessing.

ben-e-dick, ben-e-dict (ben′ẹ-dik, -dikt), *n.* [From *Benedick*, in Shakspere's "Much Ado about Nothing," for *Benedict*, < L. *benedictus*, pp. of *benedicere*, bless: see *benediction*.] A married man; usually, a newly married man, esp. one who has been long a bachelor.

Ben-e-dic-tine (ben-ẹ-dik′tin, also -tēn). **I.** *a.* Pertaining to St. Benedict of Nursia (about 480–543), to an order of monks founded by him, or to various congregations of nuns following his rule. **II.** *n.* A Benedictine monk or nun; also (pron. ben-ẹ-dik′tēn), a French liqueur orig. made by Benedictine monks.

ben-e-dic-tion (ben-ẹ-dik′shọn), *n.* [L. *benedictio(n-)*, < *benedicere*, praise, bless, < *bene*, well, + *dicere*, say.] The act of uttering a blessing; an invocation of divine blessing by a private person or by a church official; the form of blessing pronounced by an officiating minister, as at the close of divine service or at a marriage, etc.; the ceremony which accompanies any blessing; the rite of instituting an abbot or an abbess; a service in the Roman Catholic Church in which, after the solemn exposition and adoration of the eucharist inclosed in a monstrance, the priest makes the sign of the cross with the monstrance over the kneeling congregation ('Benediction of the Blessed Sacrament'); also, the advantage conferred by blessing; a mercy or benefit.—**ben-e-dic′tion-al,** *a.*—**ben-e-dic′tive,** *a.* Serving to bless; conveying a blessing.—**ben-e-dic′to-ry** (-tō̦-ri), *a.* Of, pertaining to, or expressing benediction.

Ben-e-dic-tus (ben-ē̦-dik′tus), *n.* [L., pp. of *benedicere,* bless: see *benediction.*] The short canticle or hymn beginning in Latin "Benedictus qui venit in nomine Domini," and in English "Blessed is He that cometh in the name of the Lord"; also, the canticle or hymn beginning in Latin "Benedictus Dominus Deus Israel," and in English "Blessed be the Lord God of Israel"; also, a musical setting of either of these canticles.

ben-e-fac-tion (ben-ē̦-fak′sho̦n), *n.* [LL. *benefactio(n-),* < L. *benefacere,* do good, < *bene,* well, + *facere,* do.] The act of conferring a benefit; a doing good; beneficence; also, a benefit conferred; a charitable donation; a grant or endowment.

ben-e-fac-tor (ben′ē̦-fak-to̦r), *n.* [LL., < L. *benefacere:* see *benefaction.*] A well-doer (rare); one who confers a benefit; a kindly helper; one who makes a benefaction, as to a charitable or religious institution; one who makes a bequest or endowment.—**ben′e-fac-tress,** *n.* A female benefactor.

be-nef-ic (bē̦-nef′ik), *a.* [L. *beneficus,* < *bene,* well, + *facere,* do.] Beneficent; benign; in *astrol.,* of good or favorable influence.

ben-e-fice (ben′ē̦-fis), *n.* [OF. *benefice* (F. *bénéfice*), < L. *beneficium,* benefit, favor, < *bene,* well, + *facere,* do.] A benefit† or favor†; also, a fief, or estate in land, granted by a feudal superior; also, an ecclesiastical living.—**ben′e-fice,** *v. t.*; *-ficed, -ficing.* To invest with a benefice or ecclesiastical living: chiefly in *beneficed, pp.*

be-nef-i-cence (bē̦-nef′i-se̦ns), *n.* [L. *beneficentia,* < *beneficent-,* for *beneficus:* see *benefic.*] The doing of good; active goodness or kindness; charity; also, a benefaction.—**be-nef′i-cent** (-se̦nt), *a.* Doing or effecting good; conferring benefits; kindly in action or purpose.—**be-nef-i-cen′tial** (-sen′sha̦l), *a.* Of or pertaining to beneficence.—**be-nef′i-cent-ly,** *adv.*

ben-e-fi-cial (ben-ē̦-fish′a̦l), *a.* [LL. *beneficialis,* < L. *beneficium:* see *benefice.*] Producing benefit; advantageous; salutary; in *law,* pertaining or entitled to the usufruct of property.—**ben-e-fi′cial-ly,** *adv.*—**ben-e-fi′cial-ness,** *n.*

ben-e-fi-ci-a-ry (ben-ē̦-fish′i-ā̦-ri). [L. *beneficiarius,* < *beneficium:* see *benefice.*] **I.** *a.* Pertaining to or conferred as a favor; also, feudatory. **II.** *n.*; pl. *-ries* (-riz). One who receives benefits, profits, or advantages; also, a feudatory or vassal; also, the holder of a benefice.

ben-e-fit (ben′ē̦-fit), *n.* [OF. F. *bienfait,* < L. *benefactum,* prop. pp. neut. of *benefacere:* see *benefaction.*] Good done or received; a kindness or favor; anything that is for the good of a person or thing; advantage or profit; a theatrical performance or other public entertainment given to raise money for a particular object.—**benefit of clergy,** the privilege of exemption from trial before a secular court and of appearing instead before an ecclesiastical one, accorded orig. to the clergy, and later, under certain conditions, to all who could read: no longer recognized by secular authority.—**benefit society,** an association of persons formed for the purpose of creating a fund (as by dues or assessments) for the assistance of members in sickness, etc., and of their families in case of death.—**ben′e-fit,** *v.*; *-fited, -fiting.* **I.** *tr.* To do good to; be of benefit, advantage, or service to. **II.** *intr.* To derive benefit.—**ben′e-fit-er,** *n.*

be-net (bē̦-net′), *v. t.*; *-netted, -netting.* To inclose in or as in a net; insnare.

be-nev-o-lence (bē̦-nev′ō̦-le̦ns), *n.* Benevolent disposition or action; kindness; charity; also, an act of kindness; a charitable gift; in *Eng. hist.,* a forced contribution or gratuity to the sovereign.

be-nev-o-lent (bē̦-nev′ō̦-le̦nt), *a.* [L. *benevolens* (*-ent-*), < *bene,* well, + *volens,* ppr. of *velle,* wish.] Wishing, disposed, or intended to do good; kindly; charitable.—**be-nev′o-lent-ly,** *adv.*

Ben-ga-lese (ben-ga̦-lēs′ or -lēz′). **I.** *a.* Of or pertaining to Bengal, a province or division of British India. **II.** *n.*; pl. *-lese.* A native of Bengal; a Bengali.

Ben-ga-li (ben-gâ′lē). **I.** *a.* Of or pertaining to Bengal; Bengalese. **II.** *n.* A native of Bengal; a Bengalese; also, the Bengali language.

ben-ga-line (beng′ga̦-lēn), *n.* [F.] A silk fabric with transverse cords, filled with wool or cotton, at small intervals; also, a similar woolen fabric.

be-night (bē̦-nīt′), *v. t.* To surround with the darkness of night, or, fig., of ignorance, etc.—**be-night′ed,** *p. a.* Overtaken by night; fig., involved in moral darkness; ignorant.—**be-night′ment,** *n.*

be-nign (bē̦-nīn′), *a.* [OF. *benigne* (F. *bénin*), < L. *benignus,* < *bene,* well, + *-gnus,* akin to *genus,* kind: cf. *malign.*] Kindly or gracious; favorable; propitious; of climate, salubrious; in *med.,* mild; not malignant (as, a *benign* tumor).—**be-nig′nant** (-nig′na̦nt), *a.* [Prob. < *benign,* after *malignant* as related to *malign, a.*] Kindly; gracious; benevolent; favorable.—**be-nig′nan-cy,** *n.*—**be-nig′nant-ly,** *adv.*—**be-nig′ni-ty** (-ni-ti), *n.*; pl. *-ties* (-tiz). [L. *benignitas.*] Benign quality or character; kindliness; graciousness; mildness; also, a gracious favor.—**be-nign′ly,** *adv.*

ben-i-son (ben′i-zo̦n or -so̦n), *n.* [OF. *beneison,* < L. *benedictio(n-):* see *benediction.*] A blessing pronounced, or benediction (as, "The priest had spoke his *benison*": Scott's "Lay of the Last Minstrel," vi. 6); also, a blessing or favor bestowed (as, "God's *benison* go with you": Shakspere's "Macbeth," ii. 4. 40). [Now chiefly poetic.]

Bénitier. — Villeneuve-le-Roi, France; 13th century.

bé-ni-tier (bā-nē-tyā), *n.* [F., < (*eau*) *bénite,* 'blessed (water).'] In Roman Catholic use, a vessel or receptacle for holy water.

Ben-ja-min[1] (ben′ja̦-min), *n.* [From *Benjamin,* son of Jacob: see Gen. xlii. 4, xliv. 20.] A tenderly loved youngest son.

ben-ja-min[2] (ben′ja̦-min), *n.* [Corruption of *benjoin,* earlier form of *benzoin.*] The resin benzoin.—**ben′ja-min=bush,** *n.* The spice-bush.

ben-ne (ben′ē̦), *n.* [Malay.] The sesame, *Sesamum indicum,* from the seeds of which a fixed oil ('oil of benne') is expressed.

ben-net (ben′et), *n.* Same as *herb-bennet.*

be-no (bē′nō), *n.* [Sp. *vino,* wine.] Aguardiente. [Philippines.]

be-north (bē̦-nôrth′), *prep.* [AS. *be northan,* 'by north.'] North of. [Now Sc.]

bent[1] (bent). Preterit and past participle of *bend*[2].—**bent**[1], *n.* Bent state or form; direction taken; inclination, leaning, or bias; extent of tension, as of an archer's bow; fig., capacity of endurance.

bent[2] (bent), *n.* [ME., akin to G. *binse.*] Any stiff, wiry grass, or grass-like plant, such as grows on waste ground or sandy shores; a stalk of such grass; a grassy tract, a moor, or a hillside (Sc. and north. Eng.).—**bent′=grass,** *n.*

ben-thal (ben′tha̦l), *a.* [See *benthos.*] Of or pertaining to depths of the sea of a thousand fathoms and more.

Ben-tham-ism (ben′tha̦m-izm), *n.* The doctrines of Jeremy Bentham (1748–1832), an English jurist and utilitarian philosopher.—**Ben′tham-ite** (-īt), *n.*

ben-thos (ben′thos), *n.* [Gr. βένθος, depth (of the sea).] The aggregate of the animals and plants that are fixed to or crawl upon the sea-bottom. Cf. *plankton* and *nekton.*—**ben′thic** (-thik), **ben-thon′ic** (-thon′ik), *a.*

bent=wood (bent′wůd), *n.* Wood in rods, bars, etc., bent, while softened by steam, into various forms, for use in boat-building, furniture-making, etc.

bent-y (ben′ti), *a.* Pertaining to, of the nature of, or abounding in bents or bent-grass.

be-numb (bē̦-num′), *v. t.* [Orig. pp., ME. *benome, benomen,* < AS. *benumen,* pp. of *beniman,* deprive: see *be-* and *numb.*] To deprive of sensation; make numb; deaden; dull.—**be-numbed′ness,** *n.*—**be-numb′ment,** *n.*

ben-zal-de-hyde (ben-zal′dē̦-hīd), *n.* [For *benzoic alde-*

hyde.] In *chem.*, an aldehyde obtained from natural oil of bitter almonds or other oils, or produced artificially, used in the manufacture of dyes, as a flavoring agent, etc.

ben-zene (ben′zēn or ben-zēn′), *n.* [From *benzoic.*] In *chem.*, a colorless, volatile, inflammable liquid hydrocarbon, C_6H_6, with an ethereal odor, obtained chiefly from coal-tar, and used as a solvent for resins, fats, etc., and in the manufacture of dyes, etc.—**benzene ring,** or **benzene nucleus,** in *chem.*, a ring of six carbon atoms assumed to be present in the molecule of benzene or a benzene derivative; the graphic representation of these six carbon atoms or of benzene, in the form of a hexagon.—**ben′zi-dine** (-zi-din), *n.* In *chem.*, a crystalline basic derivative of benzene, used in the preparation of dyes.—**ben-zine** (ben′zēn or ben-zēn′), **ben′zin** (-zin), *n.* A colorless, volatile, inflammable liquid, consisting of a mixture of various hydrocarbons, obtained in the distillation of petroleum, and used in cleaning, dyeing, etc. Cf. *gasoline.*

ben-zo-ate (ben′zọ-āt), *n.* In *chem.*, a salt of benzoic acid. —**ben′zo-at-ed,** *a.* Mixed or treated with benzoic acid or with benzoin.

ben-zo-ic (ben-zō′ik), *a.* [From *benzoin.*] Pertaining to or obtained from benzoin: as, *benzoic* acid (an acid obtained by sublimation from benzoin and other balsams, or prepared artificially, used in medicine, etc.).

ben-zo-in (ben′zọ-in or -zoin), *n.* [F. *benjoin*, through Sp. or Pg. < Ar. *lubān jāwī*, 'incense of Java' (the first syllable being perhaps taken as the definite article).] A balsamic resin obtained from species of *Styrax*, esp. *S. benzoin*, a tree of Java, Sumatra, etc., and used in perfumery, medicine, etc.; also, a crystalline compound obtained from benzaldehyde; also, any plant of the lauraceous genus *Benzoin*, which includes the spice-bush and other aromatic plants.—**flowers of benzoin,** benzoic acid.

ben-zol (ben′zol or -zōl), *n.* [From *benzoic.*] Benzene, C_6H_6; also, a clear, limpid, liquid mixture of homologous hydrocarbons, commonly containing about 70% of benzene and 20 to 30% of toluene. Also **ben′zole** (-zōl).—**ben′zo-yl** (-zọ-il), *n.* [See *-yl.*] In *chem.*, a univalent radical, C_6H_5-CO, present in benzoic acid and allied compounds.—**ben′zyl** (-zil), *n.* [See *-yl.*] In *chem.*, an organic radical, $C_6H_5CH_2$.

be-paint (bē-pānt′), *v. t.* To paint over; bedaub with paint; color as with paint.

be-pelt (bē-pelt′), *v. t.* To pelt soundly.

be-plas-ter (bē-plȧs′tėr), *v. t.* To plaster over.

be-pow-der (bē-pou′dėr), *v. t.* To powder over.

be-praise (bē-prāz′), *v. t.* To praise greatly or extravagantly; belaud.

be-puz-zle (bē-puz′l), *v. t.* To puzzle greatly.—**be-puz′zle-ment,** *n.*

be-queath (bē-kwēᴛʜ′), *v. t.* [AS. *becwethan*, < *be-* (see *be-*) + *cwethan*, say: see *quoth.*] To say†; assign or transfer (property)†; give or leave (esp. personal property) by will; hand down or leave to posterity; commit†, commend†, or devote†.—**be-queath′a-ble,** *a.* That may be bequeathed.—**be-queath′al,** *n.* The act of bequeathing.—**be-queath′er,** *n.*—**be-queath′ment,** *n.* The act of bequeathing; also, a bequest.

be-quest (bē-kwest′), *n.* [ME. *biqueste*, prob. < AS. *bi-* (see *be-*) + *cwis*, saying, < *cwethan*, say.] The act of bequeathing; also, something bequeathed; a legacy.

be-rate (bē-rāt′), *v. t.* To rate or scold roundly.

Ber-ber (bėr′bėr). **I.** *n.* A member of a primitive northern African race of Barbary and the Sahara; also, their language. **II.** *a.* Of or pertaining to the Berbers.

ber-be-ri-da-ceous (bėr″bẹ-ri-dā′shius), *a.* [NL. *Berberis*, the barberry genus.] Belonging to the *Berberidaceæ*, a family of plants including the barberry, May-apple, blue cohosh, etc.

ber-be-rine (bėr′bẹ-rin), *n.* [NL. *Berberis*: see *berberidaceous.*] In *chem.*, a yellow crystalline alkaloid obtained from the barberry and other plants: used in medicine as a tonic.

ber-ceuse (ber-sėz), *n.* [F.] A cradle-song or lullaby; also, a piece of instrumental music of similar character.

bere (bēr), *n.* See *bear*[3].

be-reave (bē-rēv′), *v. t.*; *-reaved* or *-reft*, *-reaving.* [AS. *berēafian*: see *be-* and *reave.*] To deprive (*of*) ruthlessly; rob; strip; render desolate through loss, esp. by death: also, to take away†.—**be-reave′ment,** *n.* The act of bereaving, or the fact or state of being bereaved.—**be-reav′er,** *n.*—**be-reft′** (-reft′). Pret. and pp. of *bereave.*

Ber-e-ni-ce's (ber-ẹ-nī′sēz) **Hair.** In *astron.*, the constellation Coma Berenices.

bé-ret (bā-rā), *n.* [F.: cf. *biretta.*] A soft woolen cap with a broad, flat crown, worn by peasants, sailors, and others.

berg (bėrg), *n.* [From *iceberg.*] An iceberg: as, "glittering *bergs* of ice" (Tennyson's "Princess," iv. 53).

ber-gall, bur-gall (bėr′gâl), *n.* [Origin uncertain.] The cunner (fish), *Tautogolabrus adspersus.*

ber-ga-mot[1] (bėr′gạ-mot), *n.* [Appar. < *Bergamo*, town and province in northern Italy.] A small tree of the citrus kind, *Citrus bergamia* or a variety of *C. aurantium*, the rind of whose fruit yields a fragrant essential oil ('essence of bergamot'); the oil or essence itself; also, any of various plants of the mint family, as *Monarda fistulosa*, yielding an oil resembling the essence of bergamot.

ber-ga-mot[2] (bėr′gạ-mot), *n.* [F. *bergamote*, < It. *bergamotta*, appar. < Turk. *begarmūdi*, 'prince's pear.'] A fine variety of pear.

ber-gère (ber-zhãr), *n.* [F.] A shepherdess; also, a deep, cushioned arm-chair.

berg-fall (berċh′fäl), *n.* [G., 'mountain fall.'] An avalanche of rock or stone.

berg-mehl (berċh′māl), *n.* [G., 'mountain meal.'] A fine, meal-like geological deposit, consisting almost entirely of the siliceous cell-walls of diatoms.

berg-schrund (berċh′shrůnt), *n.* [G., 'mountain fissure.'] A crevice or fissure in a glacier, near the rocky wall of its valley.

be-rhyme (bē-rīm′), *v. t.* See *berime.*

ber-i-ber-i (ber′i-ber′i), *n.* [Singhalese.] In *pathol.*, a form of multiple neuritis characterized by loss of muscular power with emaciation and exhaustion, found in China, Japan, the Philippines, etc.

be-rime (bē-rīm′), *v. t.* To make rimes about; celebrate or assail in verse.

ber-lin (bėr-lin′ or bėr′lin), *n.* [From *Berlin*, capital of Prussia.] A kind of four-wheeled carriage with a separate hooded seat behind; also, Berlin wool; also, a knitted glove; also, a dance resembling the polka.—**Ber′lin wool.** A soft woolen yarn used for knitting, needlework, etc.

berm (bėrm), *n.* [F. *berme*; from Teut., and perhaps akin to E. *brim*[2].] A narrow space or ledge; esp., in *fort.*, a space of ground of varying width, sometimes left between the moat and the base of the parapet.

ber-na-cle, ber-na-cle=goose (bėr′nạ-kl, -gös), *n.* The barnacle (wild goose). See *barnacle*[1].

Ber-nar-dine (bėr′nạ̈r-din). **I.** *a.* Pertaining to St. Bernard (1090–1153), abbot of Clairvaux, the most distinguished member of the Cistercian order and regarded as its second founder; hence, pertaining to the Cistercians. **II.** *n.* A Cistercian monk or nun.

ber-ni-cle, ber-ni-cle=goose (bėr′ni-kl, -gös), *n.* The barnacle (wild goose). See *barnacle*[1].

ber-ret-ta (be-ret′ạ̈), *n.* [It.] Same as *biretta.*

ber-ried (ber′id), *a.* Having berries; in the form of berries; also, of lobsters, etc., having eggs.

ber-ry (ber′i), *n.*; pl. *berries* (-iz). [AS. *berie, berige*, = G. *beere.*] Any small, (usually) stoneless, juicy fruit, irrespective of botanical structure, as the gooseberry, strawberry, hackberry, etc.; the hip of the rose; a dry seed or kernel, as of wheat; also, one of the eggs of lobsters, crabs, etc.; in *bot.*, a simple fruit having a pulpy pericarp in which the seeds are embedded, as the grape, gooseberry, currant, tomato, etc.—**ber′ry,** *v. i.*; *-ried, -rying.* To bear or produce berries; also, to gather berries.

ber-sa-glie-re (ber-sä-lyā′rā), *n.*; pl. *-ri* (-rē). [It., sharpshooter, < *bersaglio*, mark, target.] One of a class of riflemen or sharpshooters in the Italian army.

ber-seem (bėr-sēm′), *n.* [Egyptian Ar. *barsīm.*] An Egyptian clover, *Trifolium alexandrinum*, cultivated as a forage-plant in Egypt and elsewhere.

ber-serk (bėr′sėrk), *n.* Same as *berserker.*

ber-ser-ker (bėr′sėr-kėr), *n.* [Icel. *berserkr*, prob. meaning 'bear sark' (bearskin garment).] [Also *cap.*] One of a class of wild Norse warriors of great strength and courage, of heathen times, reputed to have fought with frenzied fury in battle. Also fig.

berth (bėrth), *n.* [Origin uncertain; prob. < *bear*[1].] Sea-room for a vessel; a space allowed for convenience or safety (often fig.: as, to give one a wide *berth*, to keep well away from him); a station for a vessel at anchor or at a wharf; an apartment in a ship where a number of officers or men mess and reside; a sleeping-place or bunk in a ship, railroad-car, etc.; in general, a place, position, or situation; a post of employment.—**berth,** *v.* **I.** *tr.* To place in or assign to a berth; provide with a berth or berths. **II.** *intr.* To have or occupy a berth.

ber-tha[1] (bėr′thạ̈), *n.* [F. *berthe,* < *Berthe,* Bertha, woman's name.] A kind of collar or trimming, as of lace, worn by women about the shoulders, as at the top of a low-necked waist.

Ber-tha[2] (bėr′thạ̈), *n.* [From *Bertha* (G. *Berta*) Krupp von Bohlen und Halbach, chief owner of the Krupp works at Essen, Prussia, where such guns were made.] A colloquial term for a German gun or cannon, esp. one of large size, as used during the World War: often occurring in phrases such as 'big Bertha,' 'busy Bertha,' 'fat Bertha,' etc.

berth-age (bėr′thạ̄j), *n.* Accommodation for berthing a vessel; also, berth dues.

ber-til-lon (bėr′ti-lọn, F. ber-tē-yôṅ), *v. t.* To take the measurements, fingerprints, etc., of, according to the Bertillon system.—**ber′til-lon-age** (-ạ̄j), *n.* Application of the Bertillon system.

Ber-til-lon (bėr′ti-lọn, F. ber-tē-yôṅ) **sys′tem.** [From the inventor, A. *Bertillon,* French anthropometrist (1853–1914).] A system of identifying persons, as criminals, by a record of individual measurements and physical peculiarities.

ber-yl (ber′il), *n.* [OF. *beril* (F. *béryl*), < L. *beryllus,* < Gr. *βήρυλλος.*] A mineral, a silicate of aluminium and beryllium (glucinum), occurring in various colors, esp. green, and in both opaque and transparent varieties, including the emerald and aquamarine; also, a clear, pale bluish green; sea-green.—**ber′yl-line** (-i-lin), *a.* Like beryl; of a pale bluish-green color.

be-ryl-li-um (be-ril′i-um), *n.* [NL.; so named as occurring in the beryl.] In *chem.,* same as *glucinum*: abbreviated *Be* (without period).

be-scat-ter (bē̦-skat′ėr), *v. t.* To scatter over something; also, to bestrew as with things scattered; besprinkle.

be-screen (bē̦-skrēn′), *v. t.* To cover or hide with or as with a screen.

be-seech (bē̦-sēch′), *v. t.*; pret. and pp. *-sought.* [ME. *bisechen,* var. of *biseken,* < *bi-* (E. *be-*) + *seken,* seek.] To seek after†; also, to beg eagerly for (a thing); entreat; also, to supplicate or implore (a person).—**be-seech′er,** *n.*—**be-seech′ing-ly,** *adv.*—**be-seech′ing-ness,** *n.*—**be-seech′ment,** *n.* Beseeching; entreaty.

be-seem (bē̦-sēm′), *v.* **I.** *intr.* To seem†; appear†; be seemly or fitting. **II.** *tr.* To befit; become; be suitable or proper for.—**be-seem′ing-ly,** *adv.*

be-seen (bē̦-sēn′), *pp.* [Pp. of *besee* (otherwise obs.), < AS. *besēon*: see *be-* and *see*[2].] Seen; looking or appearing; arrayed, appointed, or equipped; furnished; versed. [Obs. or archaic.]

be-set (bē̦-set′), *v. t.*; *-set, -setting.* [AS. *besettan*: see *be-* and *set.*] To set, stud, or surround with something; also, to surround as in a siege or attack; hem in; besiege; attack on all sides; assail.—**be-set′ment,** *n.* The act of besetting, or the state of being beset; also, something that besets; a besetting sin or tendency.—**be-set′ting,** *p. a.* That besets; habitually attacking: as, a *besetting* sin (see Heb. xii. 1).

be-show (bē̦-shō′), *n.* [N. Amer. Ind.] An acanthopterygian food-fish, *Anoplopoma fimbria,* of the western coast of North America.

be-shrew (bē̦-shrö′), *v. t.* [See *shrew*[2].] To make evil†; invoke evil on, or curse (now only in mild imprecations: archaic).

be-side (bē̦-sīd′). [AS. *be sīdan,* 'by side.'] **I.** *adv.* By the side, or near by (obs. or archaic); also, besides. **II.** *prep.* By or at the side of; near; hence, compared with; also, in addition to; over and above; also, aside from; apart or away from.—**beside one's self,** out of one's senses.—**be-sides′. I.** *adv.* Moreover; in addition; else. **II.** *prep.* In addition to; over and above; also, other than; except.

be-siege (bē̦-sēj′), *v. t.*; *-sieged, -sieging.* To lay siege to; beset with or as with a siege; beleaguer; assail persistently.—**be-siege′ment,** *n.* The act of besieging.—**be-sieg′er,** *n.*—**be-sieg′ing-ly,** *adv.*

be-slav-er (bē̦-slav′ėr), *v. t.* To slaver over; cover with or as with slaver; beslobber.

be-slob-ber (bē̦-slob′ėr), *v. t.* To slobber over; beslaver.

be-smear (bē̦-smēr′), *v. t.* [AS. *besmierwan*: see *be-* and *smear.*] To smear over; bedaub; befoul or sully as by smearing.

be-smirch (bē̦-smėrch′), *v. t.* To sully as by smirching.

be-smoke (bē̦-smōk′), *v. t.* To fill with smoke; make smoky; blacken with smoke.

be-smut (bē̦-smut′), *v. t.*; *-smutted, -smutting.* To blacken with smut; befoul with soot.

be-snow (bē̦-snō′), *v. t.* To cover with or as with snow.

be-som (bē′zọm), *n.* [AS. *besma* = G. *besen.*] A bunch of twigs for sweeping; a broom; anything that sweeps out or cleanses; also, a plant used for a besom, as the common European broom, *Cytisus scoparius.*—**be′som,** *v. t.* To sweep, as with a broom.

be-sot (bē̦-sot′), *v. t.*; *-sotted, -sotting.* To make sottish; cause to dote; infatuate; stupefy as with drink: often in *besotted, pp.*—**be-sot′ted-ly,** *adv.*—**be-sot′ted-ness,** *n.*

be-sought (bē̦-sôt′). Pret. and pp. of *beseech.*

be-south (bē̦-south′), *prep.* South of. [Now Sc.]

be-span-gle (bē̦-spang′gl), *v. t.* To adorn with or as with spangles.

be-spat-ter (bē̦-spat′ėr), *v. t.* To spatter about; also, to soil by spattering; fig., to asperse.—**be-spat′ter-er,** *n.*—**be-spat′ter-ment,** *n.*

be-speak (bē̦-spēk′), *v.*; pret. *-spoke* (archaic *-spake*), pp. *-spoken* or *-spoke.* [AS. *besprecan*: see *be-* and *speak.*] **I.** *tr.* To speak for beforehand; engage in advance; ask for, as a favor; also, to speak to or address (chiefly poetic); also, to give evidence of or indicate; foretell. **II.**† *intr.* To speak up or out; exclaim.—**be-speak′,** *n.* A bespeaking; also, a theatrical benefit for an actor or actress (Eng.).

be-speck-le (bē̦-spek′l), *v. t.* To mark with speckles.

be-spice (bē̦-spīs′), *v. t.* To season with spice.

be-splash (bē̦-splash′), *v. t.* To splash all over.

be-spoke (bē̦-spōk′). Preterit and past participle of *bespeak.*—**be-spok′en** (-spō′kn). Past participle of *bespeak.*

be-spot (bē̦-spot′), *v. t.*; *-spotted, -spotting.* To cover or mark with or as with spots.—**be-spot′ted-ness,** *n.*

be-spread (bē̦-spred′), *v. t.*; pret. and pp. *-spread.* To spread over with something; overspread; cover as by spreading over.

be-sprent (bē̦-sprent′), *pp.* [Pp. of *bespreng* (otherwise obs.), < AS. *besprengan,* besprinkle: cf. *sprent.*] Besprinkled; bestrewed: as, "The floor with tassels of fir was *besprent*" (Longfellow's "Saga of King Olaf," iv.). [Archaic.]

be-sprin-kle (bē̦-spring′kl), *v. t.* To sprinkle over with something; bestrew; bespatter; dot.

bes-se-mer-ize (bes′ẹ-mėr-īz), *v. t.*; *-ized, -izing.* To treat by the Bessemer process.

Bes-se-mer (bes′ẹ-mėr) **pro′cess.** [From Sir H. *Bessemer* (1813–98), English inventor.] A process of removing carbon (and other constituents) from molten iron in steel-making, by means of a blast of air.—**Bes′se-mer steel.** Steel made by the Bessemer process.

best (best), *a.*; superl. of *good.* [AS. *betst, betest,* = G. *best,* superl.: see *better*[2].] Of the highest or greatest excellence, merit, advantage, usefulness, suitability, etc.; most kind or beneficent; largest or most (as, the *best* part of a day); chief (as, the *best* man, the bridegroom's chief attendant, at a wedding).—**best seller,** something that sells best, or is most in demand among purchasers; esp., a book that attains the highest record of sale during a given period, or the author of such a book. [Colloq.]—**best,** *n.* The best thing or state; the advantage (with *the*: as, to get the *best* of one); one's highest, finest, utmost, etc. (as, to be at one's *best*; to look or do one's *best*).—**to make the best of,** to use to the best advantage; do as well as one may in (any adverse circumstances).—**best,** *adv.*; superl. of *well.* Most excellently or satisfactorily; most thoroughly; in the highest degree.—**best,** *v. t.* To get the best of; overreach; outdo; defeat; beat.

be-stain (bę̄-stān'), *v. t.* To mark with stains.

be-star (bę̄-stär'), *v. t.*; *-starred, -starring.* To stud or adorn with or as with stars.

be-stead[1] (bę̄-sted'), *v. t.*; pret. and pp. *-steaded* (pp. also *-stead, -sted*). [See *be-* and *stead, v.*] To help; assist; serve; avail. See Milton's "Il Penseroso," 3.

be-sted, be-stead[2] (bę̄-sted'), *a.* [ME. *bistad,* < *bi-* (E. *be-*) + Icel. *staddr,* pp. of *stedhja,* place, fix.] Placed, situated, or circumstanced: now chiefly with *ill, sore,* etc.

bes-tial (bes'tịal), *a.* [LL. *bestialis,* < L. *bestia,* E. *beast.*] Belonging to a beast or to the beasts; animal; also, having the qualities of a beast; brutish or irrational; carnal; degraded.—**bes-tial'i-ty** (-tịal'i-ti), *n.* Bestial character or conduct; also, unnatural connection with a beast.—**bes'tial-ize,** *v. t.*; *-ized, -izing.* To render bestial.—**bes'tial-ly,** *adv.*

bes-ti-a-ry (bes'ti-ą̄-ri), *n.* [ML. *bestiarium,* prop. neut. of L. *bestiarius,* pertaining to beasts, < *bestia,* E. *beast.*] A treatise on beasts or animals, such as those written in the middle ages.

be-stick (bę̄-stik'), *v. t.*; pret. and pp. *-stuck.* To stick all over; also, to pierce through.

be-stir (bę̄-stėr'), *v. t.*; *-stirred, -stirring.* To stir up; rouse to action; exert (one's self) vigorously.

best-ness (best'nes), *n.* The quality of being best.

be-stow (bę̄-stō'), *v. t.* To stow or put; deposit; store; lodge or quarter; also, to dispose of; apply to some use; confer on a recipient; give.—**be-stow'a-ble,** *a.* That may be bestowed.—**be-stow'al,** *n.* The act of bestowing.—**be-stow'er,** *n.*—**be-stow'ment,** *n.* Bestowal; also, something bestowed.

be-strad-dle (bę̄-strad'l), *v. t.* To straddle over.

be-streak (bę̄-strēk'), *v. t.* To mark with streaks.

be-strew (bę̄-strö'), *v. t.*; pret. *-strewed,* pp. *-strewed* or *-strewn.* [AS. *bestrēowian*: see *be-* and *strew.*] To strew over with something; also, to strew (things) about; scatter over a surface.

be-stride (bę̄-strīd'), *v. t.*; pret. *-strode* or *-strid,* pp. *-stridden* or *-strid,* ppr. *-striding.* [AS. *bestrīdan*: see *be-* and *stride.*] To get or be astride of; bestraddle; also, to stride over or across.

be-strow (bę̄-strō'), *v. t.* Same as *bestrew.* [Archaic.]

be-stuck (bę̄-stuk'). Pret. and pp. of *bestick.*

be-stud (bę̄-stud'), *v. t.*; *-studded, -studding.* To stud over; set with studs or other objects distributed over a surface; dot.

bet (bet), *v.*; *bet* (also *betted*), *betting.* [Prob. < *abet.*] **I.** *tr.* To pledge as a forfeit, against something similarly pledged by another, on some issue not yet determined; stake; wager. **II.** *intr.* To stake money, etc., upon a contingency; lay a wager.—**bet,** *n.* The act of betting; a wager; that which is bet or wagered; that about or on which something is wagered.

be-ta (bē'tą or bā'tą), *n.* [L., < Gr. βῆτα.] The second letter (Β, β, = English B, b) of the Greek alphabet; the second of any series (esp. in scientific classification).—**beta rays.** See under *ray*[3], *n.*

be-ta-ine (bē'tą-in), *n.* [L. *beta,* E. *beet.*] In *chem.,* a non-poisonous crystalline base, of sweetish taste, found in the sugar-beet, cotton-seed, the sprouts of wheat and barley, etc.

be-take (bę̄-tāk'), *v. t.*; pret. *-took,* pp. *-taken,* ppr. *-taking.* To take (one's self) to a place; address or apply (one's self) to anything.

bête (bāt), *n.* [F., < L. *bestia,* E. *beast.*] A beast; also, a stupid person.—**bête noire** (nwor). [F., 'black beast.'] A bugbear; an object of one's especial dread or aversion.

be-teem† (bę̄-tēm'), *v. t.* [Origin uncertain.] To vouchsafe; grant; permit. See Shakspere's "Hamlet," i. 2. 141.

be-tel (bē'tl), *n.* [Pg.; from Dravidian name.] An East Indian pepper-plant, *Piper betle,* the leaves of which are chewed in the East with areca-nut and lime.—**be'tel=nut,** *n.* The areca-nut.—**be'tel=palm,** *n.* The palm, *Areca catechu,* that bears the areca-nut or betel-nut.

beth-el (beth'el), *n.* [Heb. *bēth-ēl,* 'house of God.'] A hallowed spot, or a pillar or structure marking it (see Gen. xxviii. 10–22); a dissenters' chapel or meeting-house (Eng.); a church or chapel for seamen, often one afloat in a harbor.

Be-thes-da (be-thez'dą), *n.* [From the pool so named, of miraculous healing powers, at Jerusalem: see John, v. 2–4.] A pool or spring of healing waters; a source of spiritual relief or comfort; a chapel.

be-think (bę̄-thingk'), *v.*; pret. and pp. *-thought.* [AS. *bethencan*: see *be-* and *think*[2].] **I.** *tr.* To think of†; occupy (one's self) in thought (often with *of*); remind (one's self). **II.** *intr.* To think; consider.

be-thumb (bę̄-thum'), *v. t.* To thumb all over; mark (books, etc.) by thumbing.

be-thump (bę̄-thump'), *v. t.* To thump soundly.

be-thwack (bę̄-thwak'), *v. t.* To thwack soundly.

be-tide (bę̄-tīd'), *v.*; *-tided* (archaic or prov. *-tid*), *-tiding.* [Cf. *tide, v.*] **I.** *intr.* To befall; happen. **II.** *tr.* To befall; happen to; erroneously, to betoken.

be-time (bę̄-tīm'), *adv.* [ME. *bi time,* 'by time.'] In good time; early. [Archaic or prov. Eng.]—**be-times',** *adv.* Early; soon; also, at times (prov.).

bê-tise (bā-tēz), *n.* [F., < *bête,* beast.] Stupidity; also, a stupid thing; a foolish act or speech.

be-to-ken (bę̄-tō'kn), *v. t.* To be or afford a token of; indicate; show; foreshow; portend.

be-tol (bē'tol or -tōl), *n.* [From *beta* + (*naphth*)*ol.*] A white crystalline derivative of naphthol: used as an intestinal and urinary antiseptic, etc.

bet-on (bet'ǫn, F. bā-tôṅ), *n.* [F. *béton,* OF. *betun,* < L. *bitumen,* E. *bitumen.*] A kind of concrete composed of a mixture of cement, sand, and gravel.

bet-o-ny (bet'ǫ-ni), *n.* [OF. *betone* (F. *bétoine*), < L. *betonica, vettonica.*] A plant, *Betonica officinalis,* of the mint family, with spikes of purple flowers, formerly used in medicine and dyeing; also, any of various similar plants. Cf. *wood-betony.*

be-took (bę̄-tůk'). Preterit of *betake.*

be-toss (bę̄-tos'), *v. t.* To toss about.

be-tray (bę̄-trā'), *v. t.* [ME. *bitraien,* < *bi-* (E. *be-*) + *traien,* < OF. *trair,* < L. *tradere,* give over: cf. *traitor treason.*] To deliver to, or expose to the power of, an enemy by treachery or disloyalty; prove false to, be disloyal to, or disappoint the hopes or expectations of; deceive, mislead, or seduce; also, to reveal or disclose in violation of confidence; make known, against one's will or desire, the existence, identity, or true character of; hence, to give indication or evidence of; exhibit; show.—**be-tray'al,** *n.* The act of betraying, or the fact of being betrayed.—**be-tray'er,** *n.*

be-trim (bę̄-trim'), *v. t.*; *-trimmed, -trimming.* To trim up; deck out; bedeck.

be-troth (bę̄-trôth', -trōth', or -trōᴛʜ'), *v. t.* To pledge one's troth to marry (archaic); also, to contract to give in marriage; affiance; also, to pledge†.—**be-troth'al,** *n.* The act or ceremony of betrothing; the fact of being betrothed. Also **be-troth'ment.**

bet-ter[1] (bet'ėr), *n.* One who bets.

bet-ter[2] (bet'ėr). [AS. *betera* (= G. *besser*), compar., with positive lacking, superl. *betst,* E. *best.*] **I.** *a.* As comparative of *good,* of greater excellence, advantage, usefulness, fitness, etc.; superior; as comparative of *well,* more satisfactory; in an improved state, esp. of health. **II.** *n.* A better person, thing, or state; the advantage (with *the*: as, to get the *better* of one); *pl.,* one's superiors.—**bet'ter**[2], *adv.*; compar. of *well.* In a better manner; more satisfactorily; also, in a higher degree; more.—**better off,** in better circumstances.—**to think better of,** to reconsider, with consequent change of mind.—**bet'ter**[2], *v.* **I.** *tr.* To make better; improve; also, to render better off; advance the interests of; also, to improve on or surpass. **II.** *intr.* To become better.—**bet'ter-er,** *n.*—**bet'ter-ment,** *n.* A making or becoming better; improvement; in *law,* an improvement of real property, other than mere repairs (usually in *pl.*).—**bet'ter-most,** *a. superl.* Best. [Colloq. or prov.]—**bet'ter-ness,** *n.*

bet-tor (bet'ǫr), *n.* Same as *better*[1].

bet-ty (bet'i), *n.*; pl. *betties* (-iz). [From *Betty,* for *Elizabeth,* woman's name.] A man who concerns himself with matters proper to women; also, a burglar's jimmy†; also, a pear-shaped Italian olive-oil bottle.

bet-u-la-ceous (bet-ū-lā′shius), *a.* [L. *betula*, birch.] Belonging to the *Betulaceæ*, a family of trees and shrubs including the birch, alder, hornbeam, etc.

be-tween (bē-twēn′). [AS. *betwēonum*, < *be*, by, + *twēonum*, akin to *twā*, E. *two*.] **I.** *prep.* In the space separating (two points, objects, etc.); in the interval of time separating; intermediate to in degree, amount, character, etc. (as, *between* zero and 32°; *between* $5 and $6; *between* pink and red); connecting (as, a link *between* parts; relation *between* ideas); involving, concerning, or as to both of (as, war *between* states; comparison or choice *between* things); by joint action or possession of (as, they did it *between* them; they own the land *between* them): strictly referring to two objects, but sometimes used (for *among*) of more than two. **II.** *adv.* In the intervening space or time; in an intermediate position or relation.—**be-tween′-brain,** *n.* The thalamencephalon.

be-twixt (bē-twikst′), *prep.* and *adv.* [AS. *betweox*, < *be*, by, + *-tweox*, akin to *twā*, E. *two*.] Between.—**betwixt and between,** in an intermediate position; of intermediate quality, grade, etc.; neither one thing nor the other. [Colloq.]

bev-el (bev′el). [Prob. from OF. (cf. F. *biveau*).] **I.** *n.* An adjustable instrument used by mechanics for drawing angles or adjusting the surfaces of work to a particular inclination; also, the inclination which one line or surface makes with another when not at right angles; also, a surface or part making such an inclination. **II.** *a.* Oblique, sloping, or slant; inclined from a right angle, or from a horizontal or vertical position.—**bev′el,** *v. t.* or *i.*; *-eled* or *-elled, -eling* or *-elling*. To cut or slant at a bevel.

Mechanic's Bevel.

bev-er-age (bev′e-rāj), *n.* [OF. *bevrage* (F. *breuvage*), < *bevre, beivre*, < L. *bibere*, drink.] A liquid used or prepared for drinking.

bev-y (bev′i), *n.*; pl. *bevies* (-iz). [Perhaps orig. 'a drinking company,' < OF. *bevee*, a drinking, < *bevre*: see *beverage*.] A flock of birds, esp. larks or quails; a company of roes; any group or small band, usually of women or girls (as, "a lovely *bevy* of faire Ladies": Spenser's "Faerie Queene," ii. 9. 34).

be-wail (bē-wāl′), *v.* **I.** *tr.* To wail over; bemoan; lament. **II.** *intr.* To wail; lament.—**be-wail′er,** *n.*—**be-wail′ing-ly,** *adv.*—**be-wail′ment,** *n.* The act of bewailing; lamentation.

be-ware (bē-wãr′). **I.** [Prop. two words.] Be ware; be wary, cautious, or careful; take care: often followed by *of, lest, that not*, or *how*. **II.** *v. i.* or *t.*; *-wared, -waring*. To be ware, or wary, or be ware of: as, "*Beware* the awful avalanche!" (Longfellow's "Excelsior").

be-weep (bē-wēp′), *v. t.*; pret. and pp. *-wept*. [AS. *bewēpan*: see *be-* and *weep*.] To weep over or for; also, to wet with tears.

be-wil-der (bē-wil′dėr), *v. t.* [See *wilder*.] To confuse completely as to direction or course; render utterly confused in mind; perplex completely; daze.—**be-wil′dered-ly,** *adv.*—**be-wil′der-ing-ly,** *adv.*—**be-wil′der-ment,** *n.* Bewildered state; also, a bewildering maze or tangle.

be-witch (bē-wich′), *v. t.* To affect by witchcraft; put under a spell; fig., to enchant; charm; fascinate.—**be-witch′er,** *n.*—**be-witch′er-y,** *n.* Bewitching action or influence; witchery.—**be-witch′ing-ly,** *adv.*—**be-witch′ment,** *n.* The act of bewitching, or the resulting state; enchantment; fascination.

be-wray (bē-rā′), *v. t.* [ME. *bewreien*, < *be-* (E. *be-*) + *wreien*, < AS. *wrēgan*, accuse.] To accuse†; expose or betray, as a person (archaic); reveal or disclose, as secrets (archaic); reveal unintentionally the existence, identity, or true character of (archaic: as, "Thy speech *bewrayeth* thee," Mat. xxvi. 73).

bey (bā), *n.* [Turk.] The governor of a minor Turkish province; a Turkish title of respect for persons of rank; the title of the native head of Tunis.—**bey′lik** (-lik), *n.* [Turk.] The jurisdiction of a bey.

be-yond (bē-yond′). [AS. *begeondan*, < *be*, by, + *geondan*, beyond, < *geond*, across, through, beyond.] **I.** *adv.* On or to the farther side; farther away. **II.** *prep.* On or to the farther side of; farther away than; also, further on than; also, later than; past; also, outside the limit of; out of reach of; also, above or surpassing; also, more than; in addition to.—**be-yond′,** *n.* That which lies beyond, in space or time.

Obverse. Reverse.
Gold Bezant of Romanus III. — British Museum.

bey-ship (bā′ship), *n.* The office of a bey.

bez-ant (bez′ant or bē-zant′), *n.* [OF. *besant*, < L. *Byzantius*, Byzantine.] A gold coin of the Byzantine emperors, widely circulated in Europe during the middle ages; also, a Byzantine silver coin; also, in *arch.*, an ornament in the form of a flat disk, often one of a number in close succession or overlapping.

bez=ant-ler (bez′ant″lėr or bāz′-), *n.* Same as *bay-antler*.

bez-el (bez′el), *n.* [Prob. from OF. (cf. F. *biseau*).] A slope, or sloping face or edge, as of a cutting tool; the oblique sides or faces of a cut gem, esp. that part of a brilliant comprising all the facets or faces between the girdle and the table; the grooved ring or rim which holds a gem or the crystal of a watch in its setting.—**bez′el,** *v. t.*; *-eled* or *-elled, -eling* or *-elling*. To grind or cut to an edge.

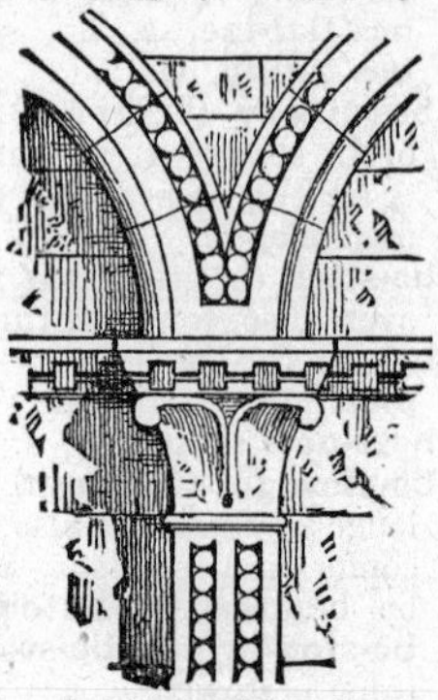

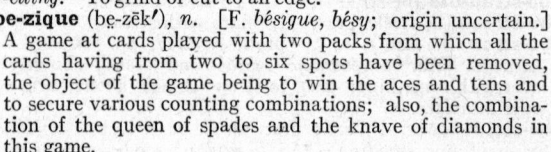

Architectural Bezants.

be-zique (be-zēk′), *n.* [F. *bésigue, bésy*; origin uncertain.] A game at cards played with two packs from which all the cards having from two to six spots have been removed, the object of the game being to win the aces and tens and to secure various counting combinations; also, the combination of the queen of spades and the knave of diamonds in this game.

be-zoar (bē′zōr), *n.* [Ar. *bāzahr*, < Pers. *pādzahr*, counter-poison.] A counterpoison† or antidote†; a calculus or concretion found in the stomach or intestines of certain animals, esp. ruminants, formerly reputed to be efficacious against poison, and still used medicinally in some Eastern countries.—**bez-o-ar-dic** (bez-ō-är′dik), *a.*

be-zo-ni-an (bē-zō′ni-an), *n.* [It. *bisogno*, want, need, hence formerly a needy fellow, esp. a raw recruit.] A needy or worthless fellow; a rascal. See Shakspere's "2 Henry VI.," iv. 1. 134. [Obs. or archaic.]

bhang (bang), *n.* [Hind., < Skt. *bhangā*, hemp.] The Indian hemp plant (see under *hemp*); also, a preparation of the leaves and capsules, used in India (by smoking or swallowing) as a narcotic and intoxicant. Cf. *hashish*.

bhees-ty, bhees-tie (bēs′ti), *n.* [Pers. *bihishtī*, < *bihisht*, paradise.] In India, a water-carrier.

bi-. [L. *bi-*, repr. *bis*, twice, doubly; akin to Gr. δι- (see *di-*[1]), Skt. *dvi-*, OHG. *zwi-*, AS. *twi-*: see *twi-*.] A prefix of Latin origin, meaning 'twice,' 'doubly,' 'two,' freely used as an English formative, as in *biconvex, bifold, biforked, bimetallic, biplane, bivalve, biweekly*, and, in chemical terms, denoting the presence of two parts or equivalents of a constituent indicated, as in *bicarbonate, bisulphide*.

bi-an-gu-lar (bī-ang′gū-lạr), *a.* [See *bi-*.] Having two angles. Also **bi-an′gu-lat-ed** (-lā-ted).

bi-an-nu-al (bī-an′ū-al), *a.* [See *bi-*.] Occurring twice a year; semiannual.—**bi-an′nu-al-ly,** *adv.*

bi-an-nu-late (bī-an′ū-lāt), *a.* [See *bi-*.] In *zoöl.*, having two rings or ring-like bands, as of color.

bi-as (bī′as). [F. *biais*, OF. *bies, bihais*; origin uncertain.] **I.** *n.*; pl. *biases*. An oblique or diagonal line of direction, esp. across a woven fabric (as, to cut cloth on the *bias*); also, the oblique course of a bowl, in the sport of bowling, due to shape or weighting; a bulge or a greater weight on one side of the bowl, that causes the oblique course; fig., a one-sided tendency of mind; a leaning or inclination; a bent. **II.** *a.* Oblique; diagonal; cut, set, folded, etc., diagonally to the texture of a fabric. **III.** *adv.* Obliquely; diagonally; on the bias.—**bi′as,** *v. t.*; *-ased* or *-assed, -asing* or *-assing.* To give a bias to; fig., to incline to one side; prejudice; warp.

bi-au-ric-u-lar (bī-â-rik′ū-lär), *a.* [See *bi-.*] Having two auricles; also, pertaining to the two ears.—**bi-au-ric′u-late** (-lāt), *a.* Having two auricles or ear-like parts.

bi-ax-i-al (bī-ak′si-al), *a.* [See *bi-.*] Having two axes; of a crystal, having two lines or directions in which no double refraction occurs.—**bi-ax-i-al′i-ty** (-al′i-ti), *n.*—**bi-ax′i-al-ly,** *adv.*

bib[1] (bib), *v. t.* or *i.*; *bibbed, bibbing.* [Origin uncertain: cf. L. *bibere,* drink.] To drink; tipple. [Archaic or prov.]

bib[2] (bib), *n.* [Appar. < *bib*[1].] A cloth, or article of clothing, worn under the chin by a child, esp. while eating, to protect the dress; also, the upper part of an apron, covering the breast.

bi-ba-cious (bi-bā′shus), *a.* [L. *bibax* (*bibac-*), < *bibere,* drink.] Addicted to drinking; bibulous.—**bi-ba′ci-ty** (-bas′i-ti), *n.*—**bi-ba′tion** (-bā′shon), *n.* Drinking; potation.

bi-ba-sic (bī-bā′sik), *a.* [See *bi-.*] In *chem.,* of an acid, having two atoms of hydrogen replaceable by one or two basic atoms or radicals.

bibb (bib), *n.* [= *bib*[2].] *Naut.,* a bracket of timber bolted to the hound of a mast, to support the trestletree.

bib-ber (bib′ėr), *n.* One who bibs; a tippler. [Archaic.]

bib-ble=bab-ble (bib′l-bab′l), *n.* [Varied redupl. of *babble.*] Mere babble; senseless chatter.

bib=cock (bib′kok), *n.* A cock or faucet having a nozzle bent downward.

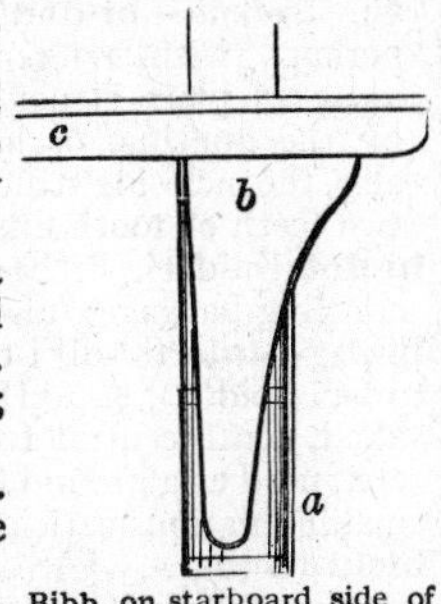

Bibb, on starboard side of mast. *a,* mast; *b,* bibb; *c,* trestletree.

bibe-lot (bēb-lō), *n.* [F.] Any small object of curiosity, beauty, or rarity.

bi-bi-ru (bē-bē′rö), *n.* See *bebeeru.*

Bi-ble (bī′bl), *n.* [OF. F. *Bible,* < LL. *biblia,* < Gr. βιβλία, pl. of βιβλίον, dim. of βίβλος, book, papyrus bark.] The collection of sacred writings of the Christian religion, comprising the Scriptures of the Old and the New Testament; the Old Testament as distinct from the New Testament (now only prov.); the Old Testament in the form received by the Jews ('Hebrew Bible'); a copy of the Scriptures; a particular version or edition of the Scriptures (cf. *version*); [*cap.* or *l. c.*] the sacred writings of any religion; [*l. c.*] any book accepted as an authority; also, any large book†.—**Bible Christian,** a Christian according to the Scriptural standard; also, one of a religious sect founded in 1816 by William O'Bryan, a Methodist preacher in Cornwall, England.—**Breeches Bible,** the Geneva Bible, so called because in Gen. iii. 7 occurs the expression "made themselves *breeches* [Authorized and Revised Versions *aprons*]."—**Geneva Bible,** an English Bible issued by several English divines at Geneva in 1560.—**Gutenberg Bible,** an edition of the Vulgate printed at Mainz before 1456, ascribed to Gutenberg and others.—**Mazarin Bible,** the Gutenberg Bible, the first known copy of which was discovered in the library of Cardinal Mazarin (1602–61).—**Treacle Bible,** an English Bible of the year 1568, in which Jer. viii. 22 reads, "Is there no *treacle* [Authorized and Revised Versions *balm*] in Gilead?"—**Vinegar Bible,** an English Bible printed at Oxford in 1717, with the heading to Luke, xx. as the "Parable of the *Vinegar* [instead of *Vineyard*]."—**Wicked Bible,** a Bible printed in 1631, in which the word *not* is omitted from the commandment "Thou shalt not commit adultery" (Ex. xx. 14).

Bib-li-cal (bib′li-kal), *a.* [ML. *biblicus.*] [Also *l. c.*] Of, pertaining to, or contained in the Bible; in accordance with the teachings of the Bible.—**Bib′li-cal-ly,** *adv.* [Also *l. c.*]—**Bib′li-cist** (-sist), *n.* A professed adherent of the letter of the Bible; also, a Biblical scholar.

biblio-. Form of Gr. βιβλίον, book (see *Bible*), used in combination.

bib-li-o-clasm (bib′li-ō-klazm), *n.* [From *biblio-* + *-clasm* as in *iconoclasm.*] Deliberate destruction of books, or of the Bible.—**bib′li-o-clast** (-klast), *n.* One who deliberately destroys books.

bib-li-og-nost (bib′li-og-nost), *n.* [From *biblio-* + *-gnost.*] One versed in the subject of books or bibliography.

bib-li-o-graph (bib′li-ō-gràf), *n.* [Gr. βιβλιογράφος, < βιβλίον, book, + γράφειν, write.] A bibliographer.—**bib-li-og′ra-pher** (-og′ra-fėr), *n.* A writer of books†; also, one versed in bibliography.—**bib″li-o-graph′ic, bib″li-o-graph′i-cal** (-graf′ik, -i-kal), *a.* Pertaining to bibliography.—**bib″li-o-graph′i-cal-ly,** *adv.*—**bib-li-og′ra-phy,** *n.*; pl. *-phies* (-fiz). [Gr. βιβλιογραφία: see *-graphy.*] The writing of books†; also, the science that treats of books, their authorship, editions, classification, etc.; also, a list of books or writings on a subject.

bib-li-o-klept (bib′li-ō-klept), *n.* [Gr. βιβλίον, book, + κλέπτης, thief.] One who steals books.—**bib″li-o-klep-to-ma′ni-ac,** *n.*

bib-li-ol-a-try (bib-li-ol′a-tri), *n.* [See *biblio-* and *-latry.*] Worship of books; also, excessive reverence for the letter of the Bible.—**bib-li-ol′a-ter,** *n.*—**bib-li-ol′a-trous,** *a.*

bib-li-ol-o-gy (bib-li-ol′ō-ji), *n.* [See *biblio-* and *-logy.*] Bibliography; also, Biblical literature or doctrine.—**bib-li-ol′o-gist,** *n.*

bib-li-o-man-cy (bib′li-ō-man″si), *n.* [See *biblio-* and *-mancy.*] Divination by means of a book, as the Bible, opened at random to some verse taken as significant.

bib-li-o-ma-ni-a (bib″li-ō-mā′ni-ä), *n.* [See *biblio-* and *mania.*] A mania for collecting books.—**bib″li-o-ma′ni-ac** (-ak), *n.* and *a.*—**bib″li-o-ma-ni′a-cal** (-ma-nī′a-kal), *a.*

bib-li-op-e-gy (bib-li-op′ē-ji), *n.* [Gr. βιβλίον, book, + -πηγία, < πηγνύναι, fasten.] The art of binding books.—**bib″li-o-peg′ic** (-pej′ik), *a.*—**bib-li-op′e-gist,** *n.*

bib-li-o-phile, bib-li-o-phil (bib′li-ō-fil), *n.* [F. *bibliophile,* < Gr. βιβλίον, book, + φίλος, loving.] A lover of books.—**bib″li-o-phil′ic,** *a.*—**bib-li-oph′i-lism** (-of′i-lizm), **bib-li-oph′i-ly,** *n.* The tastes or practices of a bibliophile; love of books.—**bib-li-oph′i-list,** *n.* A bibliophile.—**bib″li-oph-i-lis′tic,** *a.*—**bib-li-oph′i-lous,** *a.* Book-loving.

bib-li-o-pole (bib′li-ō-pōl), *n.* [L. *bibliopola,* < Gr. βιβλιοπώλης, < βιβλίον, book, + πωλεῖν, sell.] A bookseller; esp., a dealer in rare and curious books.—**bib″li-o-pol′ic** (-pol′ik), *a.*—**bib-li-op′o-lism** (-op′ō-lizm), **bib-li-op′o-ly,** *n.* The trade of a bibliopole; bookselling.—**bib-li-op′o-list,** *n.* A bibliopole.—**bib″li-op-o-lis′tic,** *a.*

bib-li-o-taph (bib′li-ō-tàf), *n.* [F. *bibliotaphe,* < Gr. βιβλίον, book, + τάφος, burial, tomb.] One who 'buries' books, as by shutting them up, away from use, or keeping them in closed or locked cases.—**bib″li-o-taph′ic** (-taf′ik), *a.*

bib-li-o-the-ca (bib″li-ō-thē′kä), *n.* [L., < Gr. βιβλιοθήκη, < βιβλίον, book, + θήκη, case.] A library.—**bib″li-o-the′cal,** *a.*—**bib″li-o-the-ca′ri-an** (-thē-kā′ri-an), *a.* Of or pertaining to a librarian.—**bib-li-oth′e-ca-ry** (-oth′ē-kā-ri), *n.*; pl. *-ries* (-riz). A librarian.

Bib-list (bib′list or bī′blist), *n.* One who regards the Bible as the sole rule of faith; also, a Biblical scholar.

bib-u-lous (bib′ū-lus), *a.* [L. *bibulus,* < *bibere,* drink.] Addicted to drinking; also, absorbent; spongy.—**bib′u-lous-ly,** *adv.*

bi-cal-lose (bī-kal′ōs), *a.* [See *bi-.*] In *bot.,* having two callosities.

bi-cam-er-al (bī-kam′ė-ral), *a.* [See *bi-* and *camera.*] Having two chambers, as a legislature.—**bi-cam′er-ist,** *n.* An advocate of a bicameral legislature.

bi-cap-su-lar (bī-kap′sū-lär), *a.* [See *bi-.*] In *bot.,* having two capsules; also, having a bilocular capsule.

bi-car-bo-nate (bī-kär′bo-nāt), *n.* [See *bi-.*] A carbonate in which one half of the hydrogen of the carbonic acid is replaced by a metal or its equivalent; an acid carbonate: as, *bicarbonate* of soda (sodium bicarbonate: see under *sodium*).

bi-car-i-nate (bī-kar′i-nāt), *a.* [See *bi-.*] In *bot.* and *zoöl.,* having two carinæ or keel-like ridges.

bi-car-pel-la-ry (bī-kär′pe-lā-ri), *a.* [See *bi-.*] In *bot.,* having two carpels.

bi-cau-date (bī-kâ′dāt), *a.* [See *bi-.*] In *entom.,* having two tail-like appendages.

bice (bīs), *n.* [OF. F. *bis,* dark-colored, brownish-gray, = It. *bigio,* gray: cf. *beige.*] A blue pigment, also a green pigment, variously prepared, as from native carbonates of copper.

bi-cen-te-na-ry (bī-sen′te-nā-ri). [See *bi-*.] **I.** *a.* Pertaining to two hundred; recurring once every two hundred years. **II.** *n.*; pl. *-ries* (-riz). A period of two hundred years; also, a two-hundredth anniversary; a bicentennial celebration.

bi-cen-ten-ni-al (bī-sen-ten′i-al). [See *bi-*.] **I.** *a.* Consisting of or completing two hundred years; recurring every two hundred years. **II.** *n.* A two-hundredth anniversary, or its celebration.

bi-ceph-a-lous (bī-sef′a-lus), *a.* [L. *bi-*, two, + Gr. *κεφαλή*, head.] Having two heads; dicephalous.

bi-ceps (bī′seps). [L. *biceps* (*bicipit-*), < *bi-*, two, + *caput*, head.] **I.** *a.* Having two heads or origins, as a muscle of the upper arm and one of the thigh. **II.** *n.* A biceps muscle, esp. that on the front of the upper arm, which bends the forearm.

bi-chlo-ride (bī-klō′rīd or -rid), *n.* [See *bi-*.] A compound in which two atoms of chlorine are combined with another element or radical; also, an abbreviation for 'bichloride of mercury,' or corrosive sublimate (see under *corrosive*).

bi-chro-mate (bī-krō′māt), *n.* [See *bi-*.] A salt of a theoretical acid, $H_2Cr_2O_7$, containing two atoms of chromium (as, *bichromate* of potassium, a reddish crystalline compound); also, an abbreviation for 'bichromate of potassium.'

bi-cip-i-tal (bī-sip′i-tal), *a.* Of, pertaining to, or having the form of a biceps; having two heads.

bi-cir-cu-lar (bī-sėr′kū-lär), *a.* [See *bi-*.] Composed of or resembling two circles.

bick-er (bik′ėr), *v. i.* [ME. *bikeren*; origin uncertain.] To skirmish† or fight†; quarrel, squabble, or wrangle; make a brawling, babbling, or rattling sound; also, to move lightly and rapidly; quiver; flash.—**bick′er,** *n.* A fight (obs. or Sc.); a quarrel or squabble; a babbling or rattling sound; also, a short, rapid run (Sc.).—**bick′er-er,** *n.*

bick-ern (bik′ėrn), *n.* [F. *bigorne*, < L. *bicornis*: see *bicorn*.] Orig., an anvil with two projecting, tapering ends; later, a tapering end of an anvil; also, any iron implement ending in a beak.

bi-col-or (bī′kul-or), *a.* [L., < *bi-*, two, + *color*, color.] Of two colors. Also **bi′col-ored.**

bi-con-cave (bī-kon′kāv), *a.* [See *bi-*.] Concave on both sides, as a lens.

bi-con-ic, bi-con-i-cal (bī-kon′ik, -i-kal), *a.* [See *bi-*.] Having the form of two cones placed base to base.

bi-con-ju-gate (bī-kon′jö-gāt), *a.* [See *bi-*.] In *bot.*, twice conjugate, as a forked petiole of which each branch bears a pair of leaflets.

bi-con-vex (bī-kon′veks), *a.* [See *bi-*.] Convex on both sides, as a lens.

bi-corn (bī′kôrn), *a.* [L. *bicornis*, < *bi-*, two, + *cornu*, horn.] Having two horns or horn-like parts. Also **bi′-corned, bi-cor′nous** (-kôr′nus), **bi-cor-nute′** (-nūt′).

bi-cor-po-ral (bī-kôr′pō-ral), *a.* [L. *bicorpor*, < *bi-*, two, + *corpus*, body.] Having two bodies. Also **bi-cor′po-rate** (-rāt).

bi-cus-pid (bī-kus′pid). [See *bi-*.] **I.** *a.* Having two cusps or points, as certain teeth. **II.** *n.* A bicuspid tooth; one of the teeth (eight in all) situated in pairs behind the canine teeth on each side of the upper and the lower jaw in man.—**bi-cus′pi-dal, bi-cus′pi-date** (-dāt), *a.*

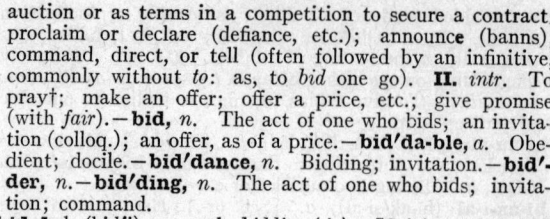

Man's Bicycle, chainless.

bi-cy-cle (bī′si-kl), *n.* [F. *bicycle*, < L. *bi-*, two, + Gr. *κύκλος*, circle, wheel.] A vehicle with two wheels, one in front of the other, and a saddle-like seat for the rider, steered by a handle-bar and driven by pedals or a motor: in some forms carrying more than one rider.—**bi′cy-cle,** *v. i.*; *-cled, -cling.* To ride a bicycle.—**bi′cy-cler, bi′cy-clist,** *n.*

Woman's Bicycle, chain-driven.

bid (bid), *v.*; pret. *bade* or *bid*, pp. *bidden* or *bid*, ppr. *bidding.* [AS. *biddan* = G. *bitten*, ask, pray; in part, also, AS. *bēodan*, offer, announce, command, = G. *bieten*, offer.] **I.** *tr.* To ask earnestly†, beseech†, or pray†; invite, as to a wedding (archaic or prov.); wish or say, as in greeting or leave-taking (as, to *bid* one good morning); offer, as a price at an auction or as terms in a competition to secure a contract; proclaim or declare (defiance, etc.); announce (banns); command, direct, or tell (often followed by an infinitive, commonly without *to*: as, to *bid* one go). **II.** *intr.* To pray†; make an offer; offer a price, etc.; give promise (with *fair*).—**bid,** *n.* The act of one who bids; an invitation (colloq.); an offer, as of a price.—**bid′da-ble,** *a.* Obedient; docile.—**bid′dance,** *n.* Bidding; invitation.—**bid′der,** *n.*—**bid′ding,** *n.* The act of one who bids; invitation; command.

bid-dy[1] (bid′i), *n.*; pl. *biddies* (-iz). [Origin uncertain.] A familiar name for a hen.

Bid-dy[2] (bid′i), *n.*; pl. *Biddies* (-iz). [Dim. of *Bridget*.] [Also *l. c.*] An Irish servant-girl. [Colloq.]

bide (bīd), *v.*; pret. *bode* or *bided*, pp. *bided*, ppr. *biding.* [AS. *bīdan* = G. *beiten*.] **I.** *intr.* To wait; remain; continue; dwell; abide. [Archaic or prov.] **II.** *tr.* To wait for (now chiefly in 'to bide one's time'); also, to encounter, endure, or bear (archaic or prov.).

bi-dent (bī′dent), *n.* [L. *bidens* (*bident-*), with two teeth, < *bi-*, two, + *dens*, tooth.] A two-pronged instrument. Cf. *trident*.—**bi-den′tal** (-den′tal), *n.* [L., < *bidens*, perhaps with reference to forked lightning.] In *Rom. antiq.*, a place struck by lightning, which was consecrated by the pontiffs, or later by the haruspices, and inclosed; also, the inclosing structure.—**bi-den′tate** (-tāt), *a.* Having two teeth or tooth-like processes.

bi-det (bi-det′, F. bē-dā), *n.* [F.] A small horse, as for carrying baggage; also, a kind of sitz-bath.

bi-dig-i-tate (bī-dij′i-tāt), *a.* [See *bi-*.] Having two digits.

bid-ri (bid′ri), *n.* [Hind. *bidrī*, < *Bidar*, town in Hyderabad, south-central India.] An alloy of copper, lead, zinc, etc., used as a ground for inlaying with gold or silver, and for making various articles; also, work or ware of this kind.

bield (bēld), *n.* [AS. *bieldo*, < *beald*, E. *bold*.] Boldness†; resource†; shelter, or a place of shelter (Sc. and north. Eng.).—**bield,** *v. t.* [AS. *bieldan*.] To embolden†; encourage†; shelter or protect (Sc. and north. Eng.).

Bie-lid (bē′lid), *n.* [From *Biela's* comet (1826).] In *astron.*, an Andromedid.

bien (bēn), *a.* See *bein*.

bi-en-ni-al (bī-en′i-al). [L. *biennis*, < *bi-*, two, + *annus*, year.] **I.** *a.* Lasting two years; also, occurring every two years. **II.** *n.* A plant that completes its normal term of life in two years, flowering and fruiting the second year; also, something that occurs every two years.—**bi-en′ni-al-ly,** *adv.*—**bi-en′ni-um** (-um), *n.*; pl. *-niums* or *-nia* (-ä). [L.] A period of two years.

bien-sé-ance (byan-sā-äns), *n.* [F., < *bienséant*, becoming, < *bien* (< L. *bene*), well, + *séant*, ppr. of *seoir*, < L. *sedere*, sit.] Propriety; decorum.

bier (bēr), *n.* [AS. *bǣr* = G. *bahre*; from the Teut. source of E. *bear*[1].] A frame for carrying loads on†; a framework on which a corpse (or the coffin) is laid before burial or carried to the grave.

biest-ings (bēs′tingz), *n. pl.* See *beestings*.

bi-fa-cial (bī-fā′shal), *a.* [See *bi-*.] Having two faces or fronts; having the opposite surfaces alike; in *bot.*, having the opposite surfaces unlike, as a leaf.

bi-fa-ri-ous (bī-fā′ri-us), *a.* [L. *bifarius*: see *bi-* and *-farious*.] Twofold; double; in two rows.—**bi-fa′ri-ous-ly,** *adv.*

bi-fer (bī′fėr), *n.* [L., bearing twice, < *bi-*, twice, + *ferre*, bear.] In *bot.*, a plant that bears flowers or fruit twice a year.—**bif-er-ous** (bif′e-rus), *a.*

biff (bif), *v. t.* [Imit.] To strike with a smart blow. [Colloq.]—**biff,** *n.* A smart blow. [Colloq.]—**biff′er,** *n.*

bif-fin (bif′in), *n.* [For *beefing*, < *beef* (from the color).] A red variety of winter apple, preserved by drying in the oven and often pressed flat. [Eng.]

bi-fid (bī′fid), *a.* [L. *bifidus*, < *bi-*, two, + *fid-*, stem of *findere*, cleave.] Cleft into two parts or lobes.

bi-fi-lar (bī-fī′lär). [L. *bi-*, two, + *filum*, thread.] **I.** *a.* Furnished or fitted with two filaments or threads. **II.** *n.* A form of micrometer in which measurements are made by means of two very fine filaments or threads.—**bi-fi′lar-ly,** *adv.*

bi-flo-rous (bī-flō′rus), *a.* [L. *bi-*, two, + *flos* (*flor-*), flower.] In *bot.*, bearing two flowers.

bi-fo-cal (bī-fō′kạl). [See *bi-*.] **I.** *a.* Having two foci; of spectacle or eye-glass lenses, having two parts or segments (upper and lower) so ground as to be adapted for two lengths of vision (far and near); pertaining to such lenses. **II.** *n.* A bifocal lens.

bi-fold (bī′fōld), *a.* [See *bi-*.] Twofold.

bi-fo-li-ate (bī-fō′li-ạt), *a.* [L. *bi-*, two, + *folium*, leaf.] In *bot.*, having two leaves.—**bi-fo′li-o-late** (-ọ-lāt), *a.* In *bot.*, having two leaflets.

bi-forked (bī′fôrkt), *a.* [See *bi-*.] Having two forks or branches; bifurcate.

bi-form (bī′fôrm), *a.* [L. *biformis*, < *bi-*, two, + *forma*, form.] Having or combining two forms, as a centaur. Also **bi′formed.**

bi-front (bī′frunt), *a.* [L. *bifrons* (*bifront-*), < *bi-*, two, + *frons*, forehead, front.] Having two fronts or faces.

bi-fur-cate (bī′fėr-kāt or bī-fėr′kāt), *v. t.* or *i.*; *-cated*, *-cating.* [ML. *bifurcatus*, two-forked, < L. *bi-*, two, + *furca*, fork.] To divide or fork into two branches.—**bi′fur-cate, bi′fur-cat-ed,** *a.* Divided into two branches; forked.—**bi-fur-ca′tion** (-kā′shọn), *n.* A forking; also, the point of forking; also, a fork or branch.

big[1] (big), *a.*; compar. *bigger*, superl. *biggest.* [ME.; origin uncertain.] Of great strength† or strong†; great in extent, bulk, or amount; large; grown up, as a person; great with young, or ready to give birth; filled or full as if ready to burst; full or loud, as the voice; great in importance or standing, as a person; haughty, pompous, or boastful.—**big stick,** a large stick or club, or, fig., some other manifestly effective means, with which to deal with offenders or aggressors: from Theodore Roosevelt's phrase, "Speak softly, but carry a big stick."—**big tree,** an extremely tall and large tree, a species of sequoia, *Sequoia washingtoniana*, of California.—**big**[1], *adv.* To a great extent, amount, or degree (colloq.: as, to pay *big*); finely or prosperously (colloq.: as, things are going *big*); also, pretentiously or boastfully (as, to talk *big*).

big[2], **bigg**[1] (big), *v. t.* [Icel. *byggja.*] To build. [Sc. and north. Eng.]

big[3], **bigg**[2] (big), *n.* [Icel. *bygg.*] A variety of barley of northern Europe. [Sc. and prov. Eng.]

big-a-mist (big′ạ-mist), *n.* One guilty of bigamy.

big-a-mous (big′ạ-mus), *a.* [LL. *bigamus*, < L. *bi-*, twice, + Gr. γάμος, marriage.] Having two wives or husbands at the same time; guilty of bigamy; also, involving bigamy.—**big′a-mous-ly,** *adv.*—**big′a-my,** *n.* The state or offense of having two or more wives or husbands at the same time.

big-ar-reau (big′ạ-rō), *n.*; pl. *-reaus* or *-reaux* (-rōz). [F. < *bigarrer*, variegate.] A kind of large heart-shaped cherry with sweet flavor and firm flesh. Also **big-a-roon′** (-ạ-rön′).

Big=end-i-an (big-en′di-ạn), *n.* [Also *l. c.*] In Swift's "Gulliver's Travels" (i. 4, 5, 7), a member of the heretical religious party in Lilliput who maintained that eggs should be broken at the big end (cf. *Little-endian*); hence, a member of any set of disputers about trifles.

bigg[1], **bigg**[2]. See *big*[2], *big*[3].

big-gin[1] (big′in), *n.* [OF. *beguin*, the cap worn by the Beguines.] A cap or coif; esp., a child's cap; also, a nightcap. [Now prov. Eng.]

big-gin[2] (big′in), *n.* [From *Biggin*, name of the inventor.] A kind of coffee-pot containing a strainer to retain the grounds during infusion.

big-ging (big′ing), *n.* [See *big*[2].] A building; a cottage, hut, or outbuilding. [Sc. and north. Eng.]

big-head (big′hed), *n.* A disease of horses, sheep, etc., characterized by enlargement or swelling of the head.

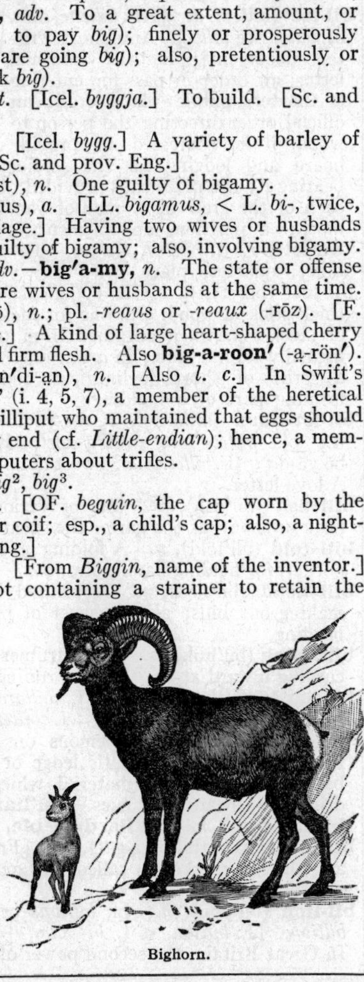

Bighorn.

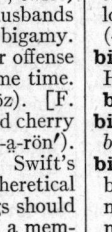

big-horn (big′hôrn), *n.* A wild sheep, *Ovis montana* (or *canadensis*), of the Rocky Mountains, with large, curving horns.

bight (bīt), *n.* [AS. *byht*, a bend, < *būgan*, E. *bow*[1].] A bend or bending; an angle, as in the human or animal body; esp., the loop or bent part of a rope, as distinguished from the ends; the part of a rope between the ends; also, an indentation or recess, as in the shore of the sea or a river; hence, the space between two headlands; a bay; esp., a slightly receding bay between comparatively distant headlands.

big-ly (big′li), *adv.* In a big manner; pretentiously; boastfully.—**big′ness,** *n.*

big-no-ni-a (big-nō′ni-ạ̈), *n.* [NL.; named from *Bignon*, librarian to Louis XV.] Any plant of the genus *Bignonia*, which comprises climbing shrubs, American and mostly tropical, including species much cultivated in gardens and greenhouses for their showy trumpet-shaped flowers.—**big-no-ni-a′ceous** (-ā′shius), *a.* Belonging to the *Bignoniaceæ*, a family of plants including the bignonia, trumpet-creeper, catalpa, etc.

big-ot (big′ọt), *n.* [F.; origin unknown.] A person who is obstinately and unreasonably attached to a particular creed, doctrine, opinion, etc., and intolerant of all others.—**big′ot-ed,** *a.* Obstinately and blindly attached to a creed, opinion, etc.; unreasonably devoted to a particular system of belief, a party, etc., and intolerant toward all others.—**big′ot-ed-ly,** *adv.*—**big′ot-ry,** *n.*; pl. *-ries* (-riz). The character, attitude, or action of a bigot.

big-wig (big′wig), *n.* [From the large wigs worn by British judges, etc.] A man of importance, officially or otherwise; a person of consequence.

bi-jou (bē′zhö), *n.*; pl. *bijoux* (-zhöz). [F., < Breton *bizou*, finger-ring.] A jewel; fig., something small and choice.—**bi-joute-rie** (bē-zhöt-rē), *n.* [F.] Jewelry.

bi-ju-gate (bī′jö-gāt), *a.* [L. *bi-*, two, + *jugum*, yoke.] In *bot.*, having two pairs of leaflets. Also **bi′ju-gous.**

bike[1] (bīk), *n.* [Origin unknown.] A nest of wild bees, hornets, or wasps; also, a crowd of persons. [Sc. and north. Eng.]

bike[2] (bīk), *n.* and *v.* Colloquial form of *bicycle.*

bi-la-bi-ate (bī-lā′bi-āt), *a.* [See *bi-*.] In *bot.*, two-lipped; having an upper and a lower lip, as a corolla.—**bi-la-bi-a′tion** (-ā′shọn), *n.* Bilabiate formation.

Bilabiate Calyx and Corolla of *Salvia* (sage).

bi-lam-el-late (bī-lam′ẹ-lāt), *a.* [See *bi-*.] Having two lamellæ or thin plates. Also **bi-lam′el-lat-ed** (-lā-ted).

bi-lam-i-nar, bi-lam-i-nate (bī-lam′i-när, -nāt), *a.* [See *bi-*.] Having two laminæ, thin plates, or layers.

bil-an-der (bil′ạn-dėr or bī′lạn-), *n.* [D. *bijlander*, < *bij*, by, + *land*, land.] A small merchant vessel with two masts, used on canals and along the coast in Holland, etc.

Bilander.

bi-lat-er-al (bī-lat′ẹ-rạl), *a.* [NL. *bilateralis*, < L. *bi-*, two, + *latus* (*later-*), side.] Pertaining to or affecting two or both sides; disposed on opposite sides of an axis; two-sided; of a contract, binding the parties to perform reciprocal obligations each toward the other.—**bi-lat′er-al-ism,** *n.* Bilateral symmetry.—**bi-lat′er-al-ly,** *adv.*—**bi-lat′er-al-ness,** *n.*

bil-ber-ry (bil′ber″i), *n.*; pl. *-berries* (-iz). [Prob. from Scand.: cf. Dan. *böllebær.*] The edible fruit (whortleberry) of the shrub *Vaccinium myrtillus*, or the shrub itself; also, the berry yielded by any of various allied shrubs, or any of these shrubs, as *V. uliginosum* ('bog-bilberry'), a low shrub whose berry is sometimes eaten.

bil-bo[1] (bil′bō), *n.*; pl. *-boes* (-bōz). [From *Bilbao*, city in northern Spain.] A sword, orig. one made at Bilbao. [Archaic.]

bil-bo² (bil′bō), *n.*; pl. *-boes* (-bōz). [Origin unknown.] A long iron bar with sliding shackles and a lock, formerly used to confine the feet of prisoners or offenders, esp. on shipboard: usually in *pl.* in same sense.

Bilboes, from the Tower of London.

bile (bīl), *n.* [F. *bile*, < L. *bilis.*] A bitter, viscid, yellow or greenish alkaline liquid secreted by the liver and aiding in digestion (one of the four humors of the old physiology: see *choler*); hence, ill humor; anger.—**black bile,** an imagined secretion of the renal glands, that one of the four humors of the old physiology supposed when predominant to cause dejection and gloom. Cf. *melancholy, n.*—**bile′-stone,** *n.* A biliary calculus, or gall-stone.

bilge (bilj), *n.* [Var. of *bulge.*] The widest part of a cask; *naut.*, the bottom or approximately flat under portion of a ship's hull; hence, the lowest portion of a ship's interior.—**bilge,** *v.*; *bilged, bilging.* *Naut.*: **I.** *intr.* To suffer fracture of the bilge; spring a leak in the bilge. **II.** *tr.* To stave in the bilge of.—**bilge′=keel,** *n.* Either of two keel-like projections extending longitudinally along the turn of a ship's bilge, one on each side, to retard rolling.—**bilge′=wa″ter,** *n.* Water that collects in a vessel's bilge.—**bilg′y,** *a.* Having the smell or other characteristic of bilge-water.

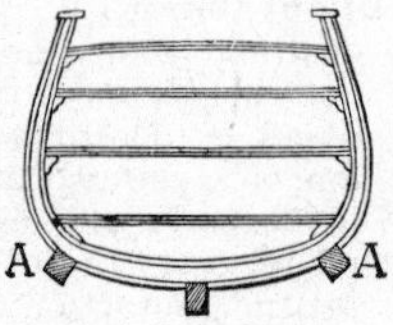

A, A, Bilge-keels.

bil-i-a-ry (bil′i-ā-ri), *a.* [NL. *biliaris.*] Of or pertaining to bile: as, a *biliary* calculus (a gall-stone).

bi-lim-bi (bi-lim′bi), *n.* [E. Ind.] A tree, *Averrhoa bilimbi*, of India, etc., yielding a juice esteemed by the natives as a cure for skin-diseases; also, the acid fruit of this tree. Also **bi-lim′bing.**

bi-lin-e-ar (bī-lin′ē-är), *a.* [L. *bi-*, two, + *linea*, line.] Of, pertaining to, or involving two lines.

bi-lin-gual (bī-ling′gwal), *a.* [L. *bilinguis*, < *bi-*, two, + *lingua*, tongue.] Using or involving two languages.—**bi-lin′gual-ism,** *n.* Habitual use of two languages.—**bi-lin′gual-ly,** *adv.*

bil-ious (bil′yus), *a.* [L. *biliosus.*] Pertaining to or associated with bile; biliary; also, suffering from, caused by, or attended with derangement of the biliary processes; fig., choleric, peevish, or testy.—**bil′ious-ly,** *adv.*—**bil′ious-ness,** *n.*

bi-lit-er-al (bī-lit′ē-ral), *a.* [L. *bi-*, two, + *litera*, letter.] Consisting of two letters, as a word-root.—**bi-lit′er-al-ism,** *n.* The use of biliteral roots.

bilk (bilk), *v. t.* [Origin obscure: cf. *balk.*] To balk or spoil the score of, at cribbage; fig., to disappoint; cheat; defraud; elude.—**bilk,** *n.* A bilking; a fraud; a cheat; also, a swindler.

bill¹ (bil), *n.* [AS. *bile.*] The horny sheath enveloping the jaws of a bird; a similar structure in other animals, as the turtle; a beak; also, a beak-like projection; a narrow promontory; the point of the fluke of an anchor.—**bill¹,** *v. i.* Of birds, to join bills, as if caressing. Also fig.

bill² (bil), *n.* [AS. *bil, bill*, sword, = G. *bille*, pick.] An obsolete military weapon consisting of a variously shaped cutting head affixed to a long handle; a similar cutting instrument, often with a hook-shaped point, used for pruning, etc.; also, a billman.

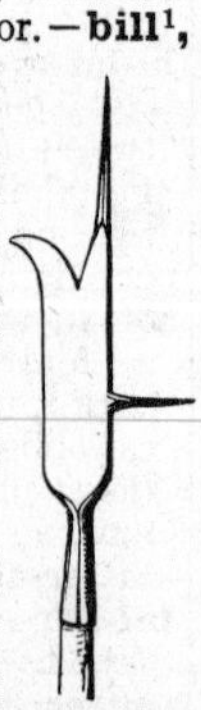

Old English Bill, time of Elizabeth.

bill³ (bil), *n.* [Cf. *bell².*] The cry of the bittern: as, "When first the bittern's hollow *bill* Was heard" (Wordsworth's "Evening Walk").

bill⁴ (bil), *n.* [AF. *bille*, < AL. *billa*, for ML. *bulla*, writing, document: see *bull², bulla.*] A writing of any kind, as a will, a medical prescription, etc.†; a written petition†; a formal written or printed declaration, as a statement of particulars; a written or printed public notice or advertisement, as a handbill, placard, or poster; an account of money due or claimed for goods supplied or services rendered; a promissory note†; a bank-note or other like piece of paper money; a bill of exchange (see below); a draft of a proposed statute, presented to a legislature for adoption; in *law*, a written statement, usually of complaint, presented to a court.—**bill of credit,** in *U. S. hist.*, a paper issued by a State, and based on its own credit, to be circulated as money: forbidden by the Constitution.—**bill of exchange,** an order in writing to pay a certain sum in money to a specified person or to his order.—**bill of fare,** a list of the dishes served at a meal, or of those that may be ordered, as at a restaurant.—**bill of lading,** a written receipt given by a carrier for goods delivered to the carrier for transportation.—**bill of rights,** a formal statement of the fundamental rights of the people of a nation.—**bill of sale,** a formal instrument for the conveyance or transfer of personal chattels.—**bill⁴,** *v. t.* To enter in a bill; charge in a bill; also, to announce by bill or public notice; cover with bills; post bills throughout (a town, etc.).

bil-la-bong (bil′a-bong), *n.* [Native Australian.] A branch of a river flowing away from the main stream, in some cases returning to it lower down. [Australia.]

bill=board¹ (bil′bōrd), *n.* *Naut.*, a projection placed abaft the cat-head, for the bill or fluke of an anchor to rest on.

bill=board² (bil′bōrd), *n.* A board for posting bills or advertisements on.

bill=book (bil′bu̇k), *n.* A book in which a merchant keeps a record of the details of his bills of exchange, promissory notes, etc., payable and receivable.

bill=brok-er (bil′brō″kėr), *n.* One who negotiates the discount of bills of exchange.

bill=bug (bil′bug), *n.* Any beetle of the genus *Sphenophorus*, as *S. sculptilis* ('corn bill-bug'), breeding in the roots and stems of grains and grasses.

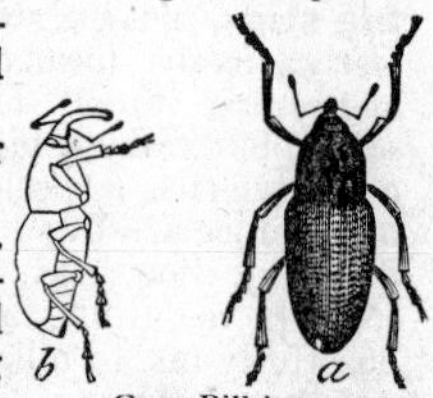

Corn Bill-bug.
a, adult beetle, dorsal view; *b*, adult beetle, side view in outline. (Somewhat enlarged.)

billed (bild), *a.* Having a bill or beak.

bil-let¹ (bil′et), *n.* [AF. *billette*, dim. of *bille*: see *bill⁴.*] Any short written document†; a brief informal letter; an order or pass for entering a theater, public place, etc.†; an official order directing the person to whom it is addressed to provide board and lodging for the soldier bearing it; the place thus provided; a place assigned, as to each of the crew of a man-of-war for slinging his hammock; a position, appointment, or situation (colloq.).—**bil′let¹,** *v. t.*; *-leted, -leting.* To assign to quarters by billet; quarter; place.

bil-let² (bil′et), *n.* [OF. F. *billette*, dim. of *bille*, log.] A thick stick of wood, esp. one for fuel; a bar or slab of iron or steel, esp. when obtained from an ingot by forging, etc.; in *arch.*, one of a series of short (cylindrical) rods forming part of a molding.

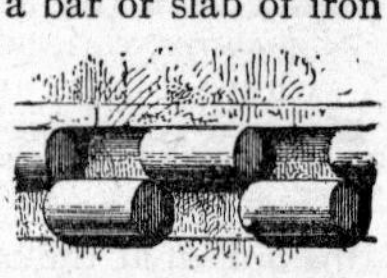

Architectural Billets.

bil-let=doux (bil′ā-dö′, F. bē-yā-dö), *n.*; pl. *billets-doux* (bil′ā-döz′, F. bē-yā-dö). [F. *billet doux*, 'sweet note.'] A love-letter.

bill=fish (bil′fish), *n.* One of various fishes with a long beak or snout, as the gar or the spear-fish.

bill=fold (bil′fōld), *n.* A folding leather case carried in the pocket, for holding bank-notes, etc.

bill=head (bil′hed), *n.* A printed heading on paper for making out bills; also, a sheet of paper with the heading.

bill=hook (bil′hu̇k), *n.* An instrument with a blade curving inward at the tip, for pruning or cutting.

Bill-hook.

bil-liards (bil′yärdz), *n.* [F. *billard*, OF. *billart*, billiard-cue, < *bille*, log: cf. *billet².*] A game played by two or more persons on a rectangular table inclosed by an elastic ledge or cushion, with balls of ivory or other material, which the players drive by means of cues.—**bil′liard=cue,** *n.*—**bil′liard-ist,** *n.*—**bil′liard=ta″ble,** *n.*

bil-lings-gate (bil′ingz-gāt), *n.* [From the ancient gate and the fish-market so called, in London.] Foul language; scurrilous abuse.

bil-lion (bil′yon), *n.*; pl. *billions* or (as after a numeral) *billion.* [F. *billion*, < L. *bi-*, two, + F. (*m*)*illion*, million.] In Great Britain, the second power of a million, represented by 1 followed by 12 ciphers; in France and the U. S., a thousand millions, represented by 1 followed by 9 ciphers. —**bil-lion-aire′** (-âr′), *n.* The owner of a billion dollars, or francs, pounds, etc.—**bil′lionth. I.** *a.* Coming last in a series of a billion; being one of a billion equal parts. **II.** *n.* The billionth member of a series; a billionth part.

bill-man (bil′mạn), *n.*; pl. *-men.* A soldier, etc., armed with a bill; also, a laborer using a bill.

bil-lon (bil′ọn), *n.* [F. and OF. *billon*, debased metal, ingot, < *bille*, log.] An alloy used in coinage, consisting of gold or silver with a preponderating admixture of some base metal; esp., an alloy of silver with copper or the like in very large proportion, used for coins of small denomination.

bil-low (bil′ō), *n.* [Prob. < Icel. *bylgja*, billow.] A great wave or surge of the sea; any wave. Also fig.—**bil′low,** *v. i.* To rise or roll in or like billows; surge.—**bil′low-y,** *a.* Full of billows; billowing; surging.

bill=post-er (bil′pōs″tėr), *n.* One whose business it is to post up bills or advertisements in public places. Also **bill′=stick″er.**

bil-ly[1] (bil′i), *n.*; pl. *billies* (-iz). [From *Billy*, for *William*, man's name.] A bludgeon, as one for carrying in the pocket; a policeman's club; also, in the Australian bush, a tin kettle, can, or pot, as for making tea.

bil-ly[2] (bil′i), *n.*; pl. *billies* (-iz). [Origin obscure.] A comrade or companion; a fellow; a brother. [Sc. and north. Eng.]

bil-ly-cock (bil′i-kok), *n.* [Cf. *bully*[1].] A round, low-crowned felt hat; a derby hat. [Eng.]

bil-ly=goat (bil′i-gōt), *n.* [See *billy*[1].] A he-goat. Cf. *nanny-goat.* [Colloq.]

bi-lo-bate (bī-lō′bāt), *a.* [See *bi-*.] Having two lobes. Also **bi′lobed** (-lōbd).—**bi-lob′u-lar** (-lob′ụ̄-lạ̈r), *a.* Having two lobules or small lobes.

bi-lo-ca-tion (bī-lọ-kā′shọn), *n.* [See *bi-*.] The fact or power of being in two places at the same time.

bi-loc-u-lar (bī-lok′ụ̄-lạ̈r), *a.* [See *bi-*.] Having two loculi, chambers, or cells.

bil-sted (bil′sted), *n.* [Origin uncertain.] The American liquidambar or sweet-gum tree, *Liquidambar styraciflua.*

bil-tong (bil′tong), *n.* [S. Afr. D.] Lean meat in strips dried in the open air. [South Africa.]

bim-a-nous (bim′ạ-nus), *a.* [NL. *bimanus*, < L. *bi-*, two, + *manus*, hand.] Two-handed.

bi-man-u-al (bī-man′ụ̄-ạl), *a.* [See *bi-*.] Involving the use of both hands.—**bi-man′u-al-ly,** *adv.*

bi-mes-tri-al (bī-mes′tri-ạl), *a.* [L. *bimestris*, < *bi-*, two, + *mensis*, month.] Lasting two months; also, occurring every two months; bimonthly.

bi-me-tal-lic (bī-me-tal′ik), *a.* [See *bi-*.] Pertaining to or using two metals; pertaining to bimetallism.—**bi-met′al-lism** (-met′ạl-izm), *n.* The use of two metals (gold and silver), at a fixed relative value, as the standard of money values.—**bi-met′al-list,** *n.* An advocate of bimetallism.

bi-month-ly (bī-munth′li). [See *bi-*.] **I.** *a.* Occurring or appearing every two months; also, semimonthly. **II.** *n.*; pl. *-lies* (-liz). A bimonthly publication. **III.** *adv.* Every two months; also, twice a month.

bin (bin), *n.* [AS. *binn.*] A box or inclosed place for holding grain, coal, or the like.—**bin,** *v. t.*; *binned, binning.* To store in a bin.

bin-. [Prob. suggested by words from L. *bini*, two at a time: see *binary.*] A form of *bi-*, 'twice,' 'two,' sometimes used before a vowel, as in *binoxide* (a dioxide).

bi-na-ry (bī′nạ-ri), *a.* [LL. *binarius*, < L. *bini*, two at a time, < *bis*, twice.] Consisting of or involving two; dual; twofold; double.—**binary compound,** in *chem.*, a compound containing only two elements; also, sometimes, a compound composed of an element and a radical, or of two radicals.—**binary star,** in *astron.*, a form of double star in which the two members are comparatively near together and revolve round a common center of gravity. See *double star*, under *double, a.*—**bi′na-ry,** *n.*; pl. *-ries* (-riz). A whole composed of two; a binary star.

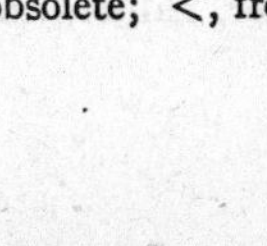
Binate Leaf.

bi-nate[1] (bī′nāt), *a.* [NL. *binatus*, < L. *bini*, two at a time: see *binary.*] In *bot.*, double; paired.

bi-nate[2] (bī′nāt), *v. i.*; *-nated, -nating.* [= F. *biner*, < ML. *binare*, < L. *bini*, two at a time: see *binary.*] In the *Rom. Cath. Ch.*, of a priest, to say two masses on the same day (Sunday or holy day of obligation).—**bi-na′tion** (-nā′-shọn), *n.*

bin-au-ral (bin-â′rạl), *a.* [L. *bini*, two at a time, + *auris*, ear.] Having two ears; also, of, with, or for both ears (as, *binaural* audition; a *binaural* stethoscope).

bind (bīnd), *v.*; pret. *bound*, pp. *bound* (archaic *bounden*), ppr. *binding.* [AS. *bindan* = G. *binden* = Icel. *binda* = Goth. *bindan*, bind; akin to Skt. *bandh-*, bind.] **I.** *tr.* To fasten by a band or bond; tie; wrap or cover with a band; bandage, swathe, or gird; make fast as a tie or band (*about, on*, etc.); fasten together or unite in a compact whole; secure within a cover, in book form; cause to cohere; unite as by some moral or legal tie; cover the edge of, as for protection or ornament; confine or constrict; restrain or restrict; make costive; constrain or oblige; put under legal obligation (often with *over*); indenture as an apprentice (often with *out*). **II.** *intr.* To cohere; become compact or solid; be obligatory.—**bind,** *n.* Something that binds; a twining or climbing plant-stem (now prov. Eng.); in *music*, a tie, slur, or brace; in *mining*, indurated clay.—**bind′er,** *n.* One who or that which binds; esp., an attachment to a harvester or reaper for tying the grain in bundles or sheaves; a machine that both cuts and binds grain.—**bind′er-y,** *n.*; pl. *-ies* (-iz). An establishment for binding books.—**bind′ing,** *n.* The act or work of one that binds; that which serves to bind; the covering within which the leaves of a book are bound; a protecting or finishing strip covering the edge of anything.—**bind′ing,** *p. a.* Fastening; constricting; astringent; obligatory.—**bind′ing-ly,** *adv.* —**bind′ing-ness,** *n.*—**bind′weed,** *n.* A name for various twining or vine-like plants, esp. certain common species of convolvulus.

bine (bīn), *n.* [For *bind.*] A twining plant-stem, as of the hop (as, "when burr and *bine* were gather'd": Tennyson's "Aylmer's Field," 113); also, some variety of hop.

bi-ner-vate (bī-nėr′vāt), *a.* [See *bi-*.] Two-nerved.

Bi-net (bē-nā) **test,** or **Bi-net=Si-mon** (sē-môṅ) **test.** [From Alfred *Binet* (1857–1911) and Thomas *Simon* (born 1873), French psychologists.] A test for determining the relative development of the intelligence of children and others, consisting of a series of questions and tasks graded with reference to the ability of the normal child to deal with them in the successive years of his age.

Binnacle.

bin-na-cle (bin′ạ-kl), *n.* [Earlier *bittacle*, through Sp. or Pg. < L. *habitaculum*, dwelling-place, < *habitare*, dwell.] A framework or case for holding a ship's compass, placed near the steersman.

bin-o-cle (bin′ọ-kl), *n.* [F. *binocle*, < L. *bini*, two at a time, + *oculus*, eye.] A telescope, field-glass, or the like, adapted for the use of both eyes at once.

bi-noc-u-lar (bi-nok′ụ̄-lạ̈r or bī-). [L. *bini*, two at a time, + *oculus*, eye.] **I.** *a.* Pertaining to or employing both eyes; suited for the simultaneous use of both eyes, as certain telescopes, etc. **II.** *n.* A binocular optical instrument, as a field-glass.—**bi-noc-u-lar′i-ty** (-lar′i-ti), *n.*—**bi-noc′u-lar-ly,** *adv.*

bi-no-mi-al (bī-nō′mi-ạl). [ML. *binomius*, for L. *binominis*, < *bi-*, two, + *nomen*, name.] **I.** *a.* In *alg.*, consisting of or pertaining to two terms connected by the sign + or −; in *zoöl.* and *bot.*, noting a name comprising two terms (designating genus and species), or characterized by the use of such names. **II.** *n.* In *alg.*, a binomial expression (as $a + b$); in *zoöl.* and *bot.*, a binomial name (as *Felis leo*, the lion).—**bi-no′mi-al-ism,** *n.* In *zoöl.* and *bot.*, the binomial method of nomenclature.—**bi-no′mi-al-ly,** *adv.*

bi-nom-i-nal (bī-nom′i-nạl), *a.* [L. *binominis*: see *binomial.*] Having or using two names, as of genus and species in scientific nomenclature.

bi-nu-cle-ar (bī-nū′klẹ-ạ̈r), *a.* [See *bi-*.] Having two nuclei. Also **bi-nu′cle-ate** (-āt).

bio-. Form of Gr. *βίος*, life, used in combination.

bi-o-blast (bī′ǫ-blast), *n.* [From *bio-* + *-blast.*] In *biol.*, a formative cell; also, according to some authorities, a hypothetical unit of protoplasm practically equivalent to a biophore.—**bi-o-blas′tic,** *a.*

bi-o-cel-late (bī-os′e-lāt), *a.* [See *bi-.*] Having two ocelli or eye-like spots.

bi-o-chem-is-try (bī-ǫ-kem′is-tri), *n.* [See *bio-.*] The chemistry of living matter; physiological chemistry.—**bi-o-chem′ic, bi-o-chem′i-cal,** *a.*—**bi-o-chem′ist,** *n.*

bi-o-dy-nam-ics (bī″ǫ-dī-nam′iks), *n.* [See *bio-.*] The branch of biology that treats of vital force or energy, or of the action of living organisms: opposed to *biostatics.*—**bi″o-dy-nam′ic, bi″o-dy-nam′i-cal,** *a.*

bi-o-gen (bī′ǫ-jen), *n.* [See *bio-* and *-gen.*] In *biol.*, one of the smallest theoretical units of living substance: a term practically equivalent to *biophore.*

bi-o-gen-e-sis (bī-ǫ-jen′e-sis), *n.* [See *bio-.*] The production of living beings from living beings (opposed to *abiogenesis*); also, the doctrine that life is produced only from living matter.—**bi″o-ge-net′ic** (-jẹ-net′ik), *a.* Pertaining to biogenesis.—**bi″o-ge-net′i-cal-ly,** *adv.*—**bi-og′e-ny** (-oj′e-ni), *n.* Biogenesis.

bi-o-ge-og-ra-phy (bī″ǫ-jẹ-og′rạ-fi), *n.* [See *bio-.*] The branch of biology that treats of the geographical distribution of living things.—**bi″o-ge-o-graph′ic, bi″o-ge-o-graph′i-cal** (-jē-ǫ-graf′ik, -i-kạl), *a.*

bi-o-graph (bī′ǫ-gråf), *n.* [See *bio-* and *-graph.*] An instrument for projecting moving pictures on a screen.

bi-og-ra-pher (bī-og′rạ-fėr), *n.* [See *biography.*] A writer of biography.—**bi-o-graph′ic, bi-o-graph′i-cal** (-ǫ-graf′ik, -i-kạl), *a.* Pertaining to biography.—**bi-o-graph′i-cal-ly,** *adv.*—**bi-og′ra-phist,** *n.* A biographer.—**bi-og′ra-phize** (-fīz), *v. t.*; *-phized, -phizing.* To write a biography of (a person, etc.).

bi-og-ra-phy (bī-og′rạ-fi), *n.*; pl. *-phies* (-fiz). [NL. *biographia*, < LGr. βιογραφία, < Gr. βίος, life, + γράφειν, write.] A written account of a person's life; also, writing that treats of individual lives.

bi-o-log-ic, bi-o-log-i-cal (bī-ǫ-loj′ik, -i-kạl), *a.* [See *biology.*] Pertaining to biology.—**bi-o-log′i-cal-ly,** *adv.*—**bi-ol′o-gist** (-ol′ǫ-jist), *n.* One versed in biology.

bi-ol-o-gy (bī-ol′ǫ-ji), *n.* [F. *biologie* or G. *biologie*, < Gr. βίος, life, + -λογία, < λέγειν, speak.] The science of life or living matter in all its forms and phenomena, often esp. with reference to origin, growth, reproduction, structure, etc.

bi-o-mag-net-ism (bī-ǫ-mag′ne-tizm), *n.* [See *bio-.*] Animal magnetism; mesmerism.—**bi″o-mag-net′ic,** *a.*

bi-o-met-ric, bi-o-met-ri-cal (bī-ǫ-met′rik, -ri-kạl), *a.* [See *biometry.*] Pertaining to biometry.—**bi-o-met′ri-cal-ly,** *adv.*—**bi″o-me-tri′cian** (-me-trish′ạn), **bi-o-met′ri-cist** (-sist), *n.* One versed in biometry.—**bi-o-met′rics,** *n.* Biometry.

bi-om-e-try (bī-om′e-tri), *n.* [See *bio-* and *-metry.*] The measurement of life; the calculation of the probable duration of human life; also, the branch of biological science concerned with quantitative statistics of the properties and phenomena of living things.

bi-on (bī′on), *n.* [G., < Gr. βίος, life.] In *biol.*, a unit or individual which is functionally or physiologically independent: contrasted with *morphon.*

bi-o-nom-ics (bī-ǫ-nom′iks), *n.* [See *bio-* and cf. *economics.*] That branch of biology which treats of the relations between organisms and their environment; ecology.—**bi-o-nom′ic, bi-o-nom′i-cal,** *a.*—**bi-on′o-mist** (-on′ǫ-mist), *n.*

bi-on-o-my (bī-on′ǫ-mi), *n.* [See *bio-* and *-nomy.*] The science of the laws of life, or of living functions.

bi-o-phore (bī′ǫ-fōr), *n.* [See *bio-* and *-phore.*] In *biol.*, the vital unit, as a cell, or as the hypothetical primary constituent of germ-plasm.

bi-o-plasm (bī′ǫ-plazm), *n.* [See *bio-* and *-plasm.*] In *biol.*, living or germinal matter; living protoplasm.—**bi-o-plas′mic** (-plaz′mik), *a.*—**bi′o-plast** (-plast), *n.* [See *-plast.*] In *biol.*, a particle of bioplasm; a germinal cell.—**bi-o-plas′tic,** *a.*

bi-o-scope (bī′ǫ-skōp), *n.* [See *bio-* and *-scope.*] A device for projecting moving pictures on a screen.

bi-o-stat-ics (bī-ǫ-stat′iks), *n.* [See *bio-* and *static.*] The branch of biology that treats of the structure of organisms in relation to their functions: opposed to *biodynamics.*—**bi-o-stat′ic, bi-o-stat′i-cal,** *a.*

bi-o-ta (bī-ō′tạ), *n.* [NL., < Gr. βίος, life.] The animal and plant life of a given region or period, taken collectively.

bi-o-tax-y (bī′ǫ-tak-si), *n.* [See *bio-* and *-taxy.*] The classification of living organisms.

bi-ot-ic, bi-ot-i-cal (bī-ot′ik, -i-kạl), *a.* [Gr. βιωτικός, < βίος, life: see *quick.*] Pertaining to life; vital.—**bi-ot′ics,** *n.* The science of vital activities and powers.

bi-o-tite (bī′ǫ-tīt), *n.* [From J. B. *Biot* (1774–1862), French physicist.] A black or dark-colored mica.—**bi-o-tit′ic** (-tit′ik), *a.*

bip-a-rous (bip′ạ-rus), *a.* [L. *bi-*, two, + *parere*, bring forth.] Bringing forth two at a birth.

bi-par-ti-ble (bī-pär′ti-bl), *a.* [See *bi-.*] Divisible into two parts. Also **bi-par′tile** (-til).

bi-par-tite (bī-pär′tīt), *a.* [L. *bipartitus*, pp. of *bipartire*, < *bi-*, two, + *partire*, divide.] Divided into two parts; in *bot.*, divided into two parts nearly to the base, as a leaf; in *law*, being in two corresponding parts, or counterparts, as a contract or indenture.—**bi-par-ti′tion** (-pär-tish′ǫn), *n.*

bi-par-ti-zan, bi-par-ti-san (bī-pär′ti-zạn), *a.* [See *bi-.*] Of or pertaining to two groups of partizans; representing two parties (as, a *bipartizan* candidate); composed of persons belonging some to one and some to the other of two parties (as, a *bipartizan* election-board).

bi-ped (bī′ped), *n.* [L. *bipes* (*biped-*), two-footed, < *bi-*, two, + *pes* (*ped-*), foot.] A two-footed animal.—**bi′ped-al** (-ped-ạl or -pē-dạl), *a.*

bi-pet-a-lous (bī-pet′ạ-lus), *a.* [See *bi-.*] In *bot.*, having two petals.

bi-pin-nate (bī-pin′āt), *a.* [See *bi-.*] In *bot.*, pinnate, as a leaf, with the divisions also pinnate.—**bi-pin-nat′i-fid** (-pi-nat′i-fid), *a.* In *bot.*, pinnatifid, as a leaf, with the divisions also pinnatifid.—**bi-pin-nat-i-lo′bate** (-lō′bāt), *a.* In *bot.*, of a leaf, pinnatilobate, with the divisions also pinnatilobate.—**bi-pin-nat-i-par′tite** (-pär′tīt), *a.* In *bot.*, of a leaf, pinnatipartite, with the divisions also pinnatipartite.—**bi-pin-nat′i-sect** (-sekt), *a.* In *bot.*, of a leaf, pinnatisect, with the divisions also pinnatisect.

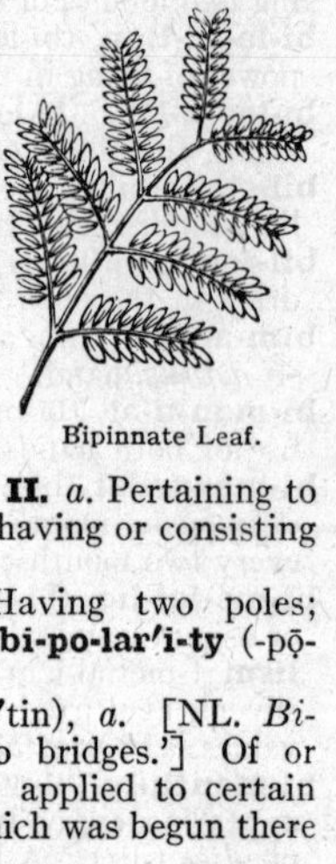

Bipinnate Leaf.

bi-plane (bī′plān). [See *bi-* and *plane*².] **I.** *n.* An aëroplane with two supporting planes, one above the other. **II.** *a.* Pertaining to a biplane or its two supporting planes; having or consisting of two supporting planes.

bi-po-lar (bī-pō′lạ̈r), *a.* [See *bi-.*] Having two poles; pertaining to or found at both poles.—**bi-po-lar′i-ty** (-pǫ-lar′i-ti), *n.*

Bi-pont, Bi-pon-tine (bī′pont, bī-pon′tin), *a.* [NL. *Bipontium*, tr. of G. *Zweibrücken*, 'two bridges.'] Of or pertaining to Zweibrücken in Bavaria: applied to certain editions of the classics the printing of which was begun there in 1779.

bi-py-ram-i-dal (bī-pi-ram′i-dạl), *a.* [See *bi-.*] In *crystal.*, having the form of two pyramids set base to base.

bi-quad-rate (bī-kwod′rāt), *n.* [See *bi-.*] In *math.*, the fourth power, or the square of the square.—**bi-quad-rat′ic** (-rat′ik). In *math.*: **I.** *a.* Of or pertaining to a fourth power: as, a *biquadratic* equation (one in which the highest power of the unknown quantity is the fourth). **II.** *n.* The fourth power of a number; also, a biquadratic equation.

bi-ra-di-ate, bi-ra-di-at-ed (bī-rā′di-āt, -ā-ted), *a.* [See *bi-.*] Having two rays.

bi-ra-mose, bi-ra-mous (bī-rā′mōs, -mus), *a.* [See *bi-* and *ramose.*] Having, or consisting of, two branches.

birch (bėrch), *n.* [AS. *birce* = G. *birke*; akin to Skt. *bhūrja*, kind of birch.] Any tree or shrub of the genus *Betula*, comprising species with smooth, laminated outer bark and close-grained wood; also, the wood; also, a rod or a bunch of twigs from the tree, for-

Branch of Low Birch (*Betula pumila*).

merly much used to chastise with, as in schools.—**birch,** *v. t.* To chastise with a birch rod.—**birch′en,** *a.* Of or pertaining to birch; consisting or made of birch; also, of or pertaining to the birch used in chastising (as, "unless you had the same *birchen* argument to convince me": Fielding's "Tom Jones," v. 11).

bird (bėrd), *n.* [AS. *brid*, young bird.] The young of any member of the feathered tribe†; the young of various other animals†; a young person (now rare); any of the *Aves*, a class of warm-blooded vertebrates having a body more or less completely covered with feathers, and the fore limbs so modified as to form wings by means of which most species fly in the air; among sportsmen, any of various game-birds, as a partridge; also, a clay pigeon; also, a person or thing notable on account of some characteristic, as excellence, eccentricity, etc. (slang).—**bird of paradise,** any bird of the family *Paradiseidæ*, of New Guinea, etc., noted for magnificent plumage, as *Paradisea apoda*, one of the most beautiful species.—**bird of passage,** a bird that migrates at the change of seasons. Also fig.—**bird of prey,** any of a group of predaceous, flesh-eating birds comprising the eagles, hawks, vultures, owls, etc., and commonly regarded as constituting the order *Raptores*.—**bird,** *v. i.* To catch or shoot birds.—**bird′=cage,** *n.* A cage for a bird.—**bird′=call,** *n.* The call or cry of a bird, or a sound in imitation of it; also, an instrument for imitating the call.—**bird′lime,** *n.* A viscous substance smeared on twigs to catch small birds that light on it. Also fig.—**bird′lime,** *v. t.* To smear or catch with or as with birdlime.—**bird′man** (-man), *n.*; pl. *-men*. An aviator.—**bird′=seed,** *n.* Small seed, esp. that of a grass, *Phalaris canariensis*, used as food for birds.—**bird's′=eye. I.** *a.* Seen comprehensively, as by a bird flying above; hence, general; not entering into details; also, having markings or spots resembling birds' eyes (as, *bird's-eye* maple; *bird's-eye* diaper). **II.** *n.* Any of various plants with small, round, bright-colored flowers, as a primrose, *Primula farinosa*, or the germander speedwell, *Veronica chamædrys*.—**bird's′=foot,** *n.* Any of various plants whose leaves, flowers, or pods resemble or suggest the foot or claw of a bird, esp. plants of the fabaceous genus *Ornithopus*, which have claw-like pods.—**bird's′=nest,** *n.* The nest of a bird; specif., the nest of swifts of the genus *Collocalia*, consisting largely of the inspissated saliva of the birds, used esp. by the Chinese for making soup ('edible bird's-nest'); also, a name for various plants, as the wild carrot.—**bird's′=nest,** *v. i.* To search for birds' nests.—**bird′ wom″an,** *n.*; pl. *-women* (-wim″en). An aviatress.

Bird of Paradise (*Paradisea apoda*).

Edible Bird's-nest.

bi-re-frin-gent (bī-rē-frin′jent), *a.* [See *bi-*.] Having the power of double refraction.—**bi-re-frin′gence,** *n.*

bi-reme (bī′rēm), *n.* [L. *biremis*, < *bi-*, two, + *remus*, oar.] A galley having two banks or tiers of oars.

bi-ret-ta (bi-ret′ạ), *n.* [It. *berretta*, < ML. *birretum*, < L. *birrus*, cloak.] A stiff, square cap with three (or four) upright projecting pieces extending from the center of the top to the edge, worn by Roman Catholic ecclesiastics.

Biretta.

birk-ie (bėr′ki), *n.* [Cf. Icel. *berkja*, bark, bluster.] A smart fellow. [Sc.]

birl[1] (bėrl), *v. t.* or *i.* [AS. *byrelian*, < *byrele*, cup-bearer.] To pour out (drink) or serve (a person) with drink, or to drink or carouse. [Now north. Eng. and Sc.]

birl[2] (bėrl), *v. t.* or *i.* [Imit.] To spin round; revolve or move with a whirring sound. [Sc. and north. Eng.]

bir-linn (bēr′lin), *n.* [Gael.] A kind of large rowing-vessel used in the Hebrides.

birr (bėr), *v. i.* [Imit.] To whir; move with a whirring sound. [Sc.]—**birr,** *n.* A whirring sound. [Sc.]

birth (bėrth), *n.* [ME.; from the Teut. source of E. *bear*[1], prob. through Scand. (cf. Icel. *burdhr*).] The fact of being born; nativity; entrance into existence; origin; also, the bearing of young; parturition; also, that which is born; something produced; also, parentage, extraction, or lineage; often, high or noble lineage; also, natural character†.—**birth′=con-trol″,** *n.* The control of births or child-bearing by deliberate measures to control or prevent conception.—**birth′day,** *n.* The day or the anniversary of one's birth.—**birth′dom**† (-dọm), *n.* Birthright.—**birth′=mark,** *n.* A congenital mark on the body; a nævus.—**birth′night,** *n.* The night of the day of one's birth; the night of a birthday.—**birth′place,** *n.* The place of birth or origin.—**birth′=rate,** *n.* The proportion of the number of births in a place in a given time to the total population.—**birth′right,** *n.* Right by birth; anything to which one is entitled by birth.—**birth′root,** *n.* A species of trillium, *Trillium erectum*, the roots of which are reputed to be astringent, tonic, and alterative, and to aid in parturition; also, any of certain other species of trillium.—**birth′=stone,** *n.* A precious or semiprecious stone traditionally associated with a particular month of the year, and supposed to bring good luck to persons born in that month: thus, by a commonly accepted list, the garnet is the birth-stone for January, the amethyst for February, the bloodstone (or the aquamarine) for March, the diamond for April, the emerald for May, the pearl (or the moonstone) for June, the ruby for July, the sardonyx (or the peridot) for August, the sapphire for September, the opal (or the tourmalin) for October, the topaz for November, the turquoise (or lapis lazuli) for December.—**birth′wort** (-wėrt), *n.* A plant, *Aristolochia clematitis*, a native of Europe, reputed to facilitate childbirth; also, any of certain other species of the same genus; also, the birthroot.

bis (bis), *adv.* [L.] Twice; a second time: used esp. to direct or request a repetition, as of a piece of music.

bis-cuit (bis′kit), *n.* [OF. *bescuit* (F. *biscuit*), < L. *bis*, twice, + *coctus*, pp. of *coquere*, cook.] A kind of dry and crisp or hard bread in thin, flat cakes, made without yeast or other raising agent; a cake of such bread; a cracker; also, a kind of bread in small, soft cakes, made with yeast or (commonly) baking-powder or the like; a cake of this kind; also, a pale-brown color; also, pottery after the first baking and before glazing.

bis-cuit gla-cé (bēs-kwē glȧ-sā). [F.] A rich ice-cream with powdered macaroons, etc., sprinkled over the top, and usually served in small paper cases.

bise (bēz), *n.* [F.] A dry, cold north or northeast wind in southeastern France, Switzerland, and adjoining regions.

bi-sect (bī-sekt′), *v. t.* [L. *bi-*, two, + *sectus*, pp. of *secare*, cut.] To divide into two (usually equal) parts.—**bi-sec′tion** (-sek′shọn), *n.* The act or the point of bisecting.—**bi-sec′tor,** *n.* A bisecting line.—**bi-sec′trix,** *n.* In *geom.*, a bisector; in *crystal.*, the line which bisects the angle of the optic axes in a biaxial crystal.

bi-seg-ment (bī-seg′mẹnt), *n.* [See *bi-*.] One of the segments or parts of a bisected line, etc.

bi-se-ri-al (bī-sē′ri-ạl), *a.* [See *bi-*.] Arranged in two series or rows. Also **bi-se′ri-ate** (-āt).

bi-ser-rate (bī-ser′āt), *a.* [See *bi-*.] In *bot.*, doubly serrate; notched like a saw, with the teeth also notched, as certain leaves; in *zoöl.*, serrate on both sides, as some antennæ.

bi-se-tose (bī-sē′tōs), *a.* [See *bi-*.] In *zoöl.* and *bot.*, having two bristles or bristle-like appendages.

bi-sex-u-al (bī-sek′shụ̈-a̤l), *a.* [See *bi-*.] Of both sexes; esp., combining both male and female organs in one individual, as an animal or a flower; hermaphrodite.

bish-op (bish′o̤p), *n.* [AS. *biscop*, < LL. *episcopus*, < Gr. ἐπίσκοπος, overseer, < ἐπί, on, + -σκοπος: see *-scope*.] A spiritual overseer; an officer in the early Christian church; an overseer over a number of local churches or a diocese, being in the Greek, Roman Catholic, Anglican, and other churches a member of the highest order in the ministry (cf. *priest* and *deacon*); also, a chessman with a top like a bishop's miter; also, a hot drink made of port wine, oranges, cloves, etc.—**bish′op,** *v. t.*; *-oped, -oping.* To appoint to the office of bishop; also, to administer the rite of confirmation to (now prov. Eng.).—**bish′op-ric** (-rik), *n.* [AS. *biscoprīce*.] The see, diocese, or office of a bishop.—**bish′op's=cap,** *n.* A plant of the genus *Mitella*; miterwort.

bisk[1], **bisk**[2]. See *bisque*[1], *bisque*[2].

Bis-kra (bis′krạ) **but′ton.** [From *Biskra*, town in Algeria.] Same as *Aleppo boil.*

bis-muth (biz′muth), *n.* [G., now *wismut*, earlier *wissmuth*; origin unknown.] Chem. sym., Bi; at. wt., 208; sp. gr., 9.8. A brittle metallic element, having compounds used in medicine.—**bis′muth-al,** *a.*—**bis′muth-ic,** *a.* Of or pertaining to bismuth; containing bismuth, esp. in the pentavalent state.—**bis′muth-ous,** *a.* Containing bismuth, esp. in the trivalent state.

bi-son (bī′so̤n), *n.* [L.; from Teut. (cf. G. *wisent*).] The aurochs, an old-world bovine quadruped, *Bos* (or *Bison*) *bonasus* ('European bison'), now nearly exterminated; also, a large North American bovine quadruped, *Bos* (or *Bison*) *americanus* or *Bos bison* ('American bison,' or buffalo), with long, shaggy hair on the fore parts, now nearly extinct.

American Bison.

bisque[1] (bisk), *n.* [F.; origin unknown.] A thick soup made of shell-fish or game stewed long and slowly; any smooth, creamy soup (as, *bisque* of tomato or asparagus).

bisque[2] (bisk), *n.* [F., also earlier *biscaye*; origin uncertain.] A point, extra turn, or the like, allowed to a player as odds in tennis and other games.

bisque[3] (bisk), *n.* [For *biscuit*.] Biscuit ware; also, a white unglazed porcelain used for statuettes, etc.; also, a kind of ice-cream containing powdered macaroons (cf. *biscuit glacé*).

bis-sex-tile (bi-seks′til). [LL. *bissextilis*, < L. *bissextus*, the intercalary day of the Julian calendar, lit. 'twice sixth' (the sixth day before the calends of March being reckoned twice every fourth year).] **I.** *a.* Containing or noting the intercalary or extra day of leap-year. **II.** *n.* A leap-year.

bis-son† (bis′o̤n), *a.* [AS. *bisene*.] Blind; purblind. See Shakspere's "Coriolanus," ii. 1. 70.

bis-ter, bis-tre (bis′tėr), *n.* [F. *bistre*; origin unknown.] A dark-brown pigment prepared from the soot of wood, esp. that of the beech; also, the color of this.—**bis′tered, bis′tred,** *a.* Browned, as with bister.

bis-tort (bis′tôrt), *n.* [NL. *bistorta*, < L. *bis*, twice, + *torta*, pp. fem. of *torquere*, twist.] A European perennial herb, *Polygonum bistorta*, with a twisted root which is sometimes used as an astringent; snakeweed; also, some allied species.

bis-tou-ry (bis′tö̤-ri), *n.*; pl. *-ries* (-riz). [F. *bistouri*; origin unknown.] A small, narrow surgical knife, as for minor incisions.

bi-sul-cate (bī-sul′kāt), *a.* [See *bi-*.] Having two sulci or grooves; also, cloven-footed; cloven-hoofed.

bi-sul-phate (bī-sul′fāt), *n.* [See *bi-*.] In *chem.*, a salt of sulphuric acid, in which one half of the hydrogen of the acid is replaced by a metal or its equivalent; an acid sulphate.—**bi-sul′phide** (-fīd or -fid), *n.* In *chem.*, a sulphide in which two atoms of sulphur are combined with the other element or radical.

bit[1] (bit), *n.* [AS. *bite*, a bite, < *bītan*, E. *bite*, *v.*] A bite†; the biting, cutting, or penetrating part of various tools; the movable boring or drilling part (in many forms) used in a carpenter's brace, a drilling-machine, or the like; the part of a key which enters the lock and acts on the bolt and tumblers; the metallic mouthpiece of a bridle, with the adjacent parts to which the reins are fastened; hence, anything that curbs or restrains.—**bit**[1], *v. t.*; *bitted, bitting.* To put a bit in the mouth of; bridle.

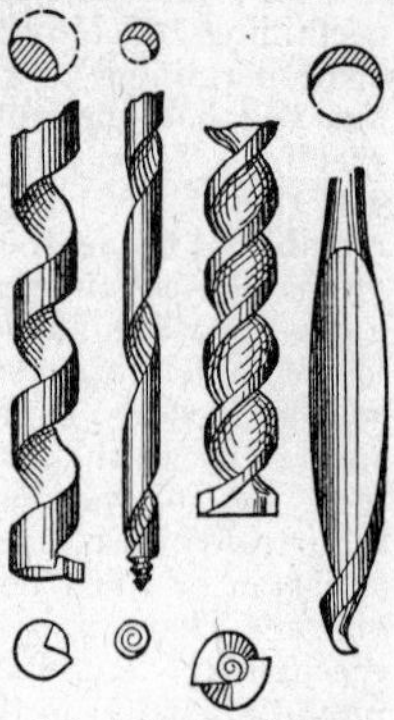

Spiral Bits for Boring.

bit[2] (bit), *n.* [AS. *bita*, bit, morsel, < *bītan*, E. *bite*, *v.*] A piece bitten off†; a small piece or quantity of anything; a small measure or degree (colloq.); a short time (colloq.); a small coin (as, a fourpenny-*bit*); a Spanish or Mexican silver coin worth 12½ cents, formerly current in parts of the U. S.; hence, the sum of 12½ cents (local, U. S.).—**long bit,** the sum of 15 cents. [Local, U. S.]—**short bit,** the sum of 10 cents. [Local, U. S.]

bit[3] (bit). Pret. and occasional pp. of *bite.*

bi-tar-trate (bī-tär′trāt), *n.* [See *bi-*.] In *chem.*, a tartrate in which one half of the hydrogen of the tartaric acid is replaced by a metal or its equivalent; an acid tartrate.

bitch (bich), *n.* [AS. *bicce*.] The female of the dog, or of other, esp. canine, animals, as the wolf and fox: sometimes applied opprobriously to a woman, esp. a lewd woman.

bite (bīt), *v.*; pret. *bit*, pp. *bitten* or *bit*, ppr. *biting.* [AS. *bītan* = G. *beissen* = Icel. *bīta*, bite; akin to L. *findere*, Skt. *bhid-*, cleave.] **I.** *tr.* To cut into or wound, or cut (*off*, *out*, etc.), with the teeth; cut or pierce, as a sharp instrument does; sting, as an insect does; nip; cause to smart; eat into or corrode, as an acid does; close the teeth tightly on; take firm hold or act effectively on (as, the anchor *bites* the ground; the wheels *bite* the rails); grip; cheat or trick (now only in the passive: colloq.). **II.** *intr.* To press the teeth (*into*, *on*, etc.); snap with the teeth (*at*); of fish, to take a bait; of insects, etc., to sting; of an acid, to eat (*in*); of anchors, cog-wheels, etc., to grip; hold; act effectively.—**bite,** *n.* The act of biting; a wound made by biting; cutting, stinging, or nipping effect; the corrosive action of an acid, etc.; grip or hold; also, a piece bitten off; a morsel of food.—**bit-er** (bī′tėr), *n.*—**bit′ing,** *p. a.* Cutting; nipping; pungent; sharp.—**bit′ing-ly,** *adv.*

bit=stock (bit′stok), *n.* The stock or handle by which a boring-bit is held and rotated; a brace.

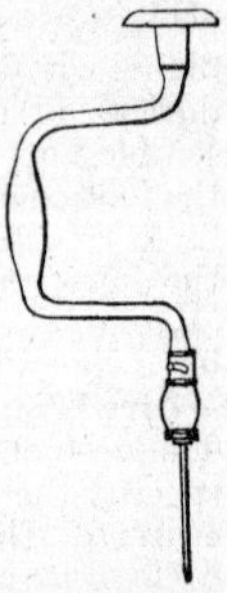

Bit-stock and Bit.

bitt (bit), *n.* [Origin uncertain: cf. Icel. *biti*, cross-beam.] *Naut.*, one of the strong posts of wood or iron projecting (usually in pairs) above the deck of a ship, and used for securing cables, lines for towing, etc.—**bitt,** *v. t.* To put (a cable, etc.) round the bitts.

bit-ten (bit′n). Past participle of *bite.*

bit-ter (bit′ėr), *a.* [AS. *biter* = D. and G. *bitter* = Icel. *bitr*; from the Teut. source of E. *bite*.] Having the harsh taste characteristic of aloes, quinine, etc.; unpalatable to the mind; hard to admit or receive; hard to be borne, grievous, or distressful; mournful or pitiable; evincing or betokening intense grief or misery (as, a *bitter* cry); causing pain or smart, as cold; harsh or cutting, as words; stern, severe, or cruel; characterized by intense animosity (as, *bitter* enmity).—**to the bitter end,** to the last and direst extremity; to death itself.—**bit′ter,** *n.* That which is bitter; bitterness; a bitter medicine (see *bitters*).—**bit′ter,** *adv.* In a bitter manner.—**bit′ter,** *v. t.* To make bitter.—**bit′ter=end′,** *a.* Characterized by persistence to the bitter end without yielding or compromising, as a person, party, course of action, etc.—**bit′ter=end′er,** *n.* One disposed to hold out or persist to the bitter end, without yielding or compromising.—**bit′ter=end′er-ism,** *n.*—**bit′ter-ing,** *n.* A very bitter compound of quassia and other substances, used for adulterating beer.—**bit′ter-ish,** *a.* Somewhat bitter.—**bit′ter-ly,** *adv.*

bit-tern[1] (bit′ėrn), *n.* [OF. F. *butor*; origin uncertain.] A European heron, *Botaurus stellaris*, living in marshes and having a characteristic 'booming' cry; also, any of various allied herons, as *B. lentiginosus*, of America.

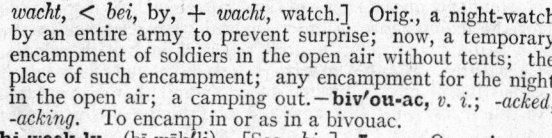

Bittern (*Botaurus stellaris*).

bit-tern[2] (bit′ėrn), *n.* [Cf. *bittering.*] A bitter, oily liquid remaining in salt-making after the salt has crystallized out of sea-water or brine, used as a source of bromine, etc.; also, bittering.

bit-ter-ness (bit′ėr-nes), *n.* The state or quality of being bitter.

bit-ter-nut (bit′ėr-nut), *n.* A species of hickory, *Hicoria minima*, growing in swamps and moist woods, and bearing thin-shelled nuts with a bitter kernel.

bit-ter=root (bit′ėr-röt), *n.* A plant, *Lewisia rediviva*, allied to the portulaca, having fleshy roots and handsome pink flowers, growing in the mountains of Idaho, Montana, etc.; also, the dogbane, *Apocynum androsæmifolium.*

bit-ters (bit′ėrz), *n. pl.* Bitter medicinal substances in general, as quinine, gentian, etc.; also, a liquid, usually alcoholic, impregnated with a bitter medicine, as gentian, quassia, etc., used as a stomachic, tonic, or the like.

bit-ter=sweet (bit′ėr-swēt). **I.** *a.* Being at once both bitter and sweet. Often fig. **II.** *n.* Something that is bitter-sweet.

bit-ter-sweet (bit′ėr-swēt), *n.* The woody nightshade, *Solanum dulcamara*, a climbing or trailing solanaceous plant with scarlet berries; also, a climbing celastraceous plant, *Celastrus scandens*, with orange capsules opening to expose red-coated seeds.

bit-ter=weed (bit′ėr-wēd), *n.* Any of various plants containing a bitter principle, as the ragweed, *Ambrosia artemisiæfolia*, and the horseweed, *Leptilon canadense.*

bit-ter=wood (bit′ėr-wůd), *n.* The wood of various American trees of the genus *Xylopia*; any such tree; also, quassia wood.

bit-ter-wort (bit′ėr-wėrt), *n.* A name for various species of gentian.

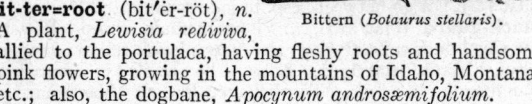

Bittersweet (*Solanum dulcamara*).

bit-tock (bit′ǫk), *n.* A little bit or portion. [Sc. and north. Eng.]

bi-tu-men (bi-tū′men or bit′ū-), *n.* [L.] Any of various natural substances, as asphalt, maltha, petroleum, naphtha, etc., consisting mainly of hydrocarbons; the typical or hydrocarbon constituents of such a substance, as distinguished from the earthy matter and other impurities it contains.—**bi-tu′mi-nize** (-mi-nīz), *v. t.*; *-nized, -nizing.* To convert into or treat with bitumen.—**bi-tu″mi-ni-za′tion** (-ni-zā′shǫn), *n.*—**bi-tu′mi-nous,** *a.* [L. *bituminosus.*] Of, like, or containing bitumen: as, *bituminous* shale (a shale impregnated with bitumen); *bituminous* coal (soft coal, a mineral coal which contains volatile hydrocarbons and tarry matter, and burns with a yellow smoky flame).—**bi-tu-mi-nos′i-ty** (-nos′i-ti), *n.*

bi-va-lent (bī-vā′lẹnt or biv′ạ-), *a.* [See *bi-* and *-valent.*] In *chem.*, having a valence of two.—**bi-va′lence,** *n.*

bi-valve (bī′valv). [See *bi-.*] **I.** *a.* Having two valves, as a shell or a seed-case. **II.** *n.* A mollusk, as the oyster, whose shell has two hinged valves.—**bi′valved, bi-val′vu-lar** (-val′vų-lạr), *a.* Bivalve.

biv-ou-ac (biv′ǫ-ak or biv′wak), *n.* [F., prob. < G. *beiwacht*, < *bei*, by, + *wacht*, watch.] Orig., a night-watch by an entire army to prevent surprise; now, a temporary encampment of soldiers in the open air without tents; the place of such encampment; any encampment for the night in the open air; a camping out.—**biv′ou-ac,** *v. i.*; *-acked, -acking.* To encamp in or as in a bivouac.

bi-week-ly (bī-wēk′li). [See *bi-.*] **I.** *a.* Occurring or appearing every two weeks; fortnightly; also, semiweekly. **II.** *n.*; pl. *-lies* (-liz). A biweekly publication. **III.** *adv.* Every two weeks; also, twice a week.

bi-zarre (bi-zär′), *a.* [F., < Sp. *bizarro*, brave, gallant.] Singular in appearance, style, or general character; whimsically strange; odd; fantastic.—**bi-zar-re-rie** (bi-zä′rẹ-ri, F. bē-zär-rē), *n.* [F.] Bizarre quality.

blab (blab), *n.* [ME. *blabbe*: cf. ME. *blaberen*, Dan. *blabbre*, G. *plappern*, babble, gabble; all ult. imit.] One who talks too freely; a blabber; a tattler; also, idle talk; babbling.—**blab,** *v. t.* or *i.*; *blabbed, blabbing.* [Appar. < *blab, n.*] To tell or talk indiscreetly; babble; tattle.—**blab′ber,** *n.*

black (blak), *a.* [AS. *blæc* = OHG. *blah-*, *blach-*, = Icel. *blakkr.*] Of the darkest possible color or hue, like soot or coal; absorbing all light, or incapable of reflecting it; also, of an extremely dark color; having the dark skin characteristic of negroes; noting or pertaining to the negro race; dark-complexioned (archaic); wearing black or dark clothing, armor, etc.; soiled or stained with dirt; characterized by the absence of light; involved or enveloped in darkness; dismal or gloomy; boding ill; sullen and forbidding; destitute of moral light or goodness; evil or wicked (as, the *black* art; *black* magic); causing or marked by ruin or desolation; calamitous or disastrous (as, *Black* Friday: see below); deadly, malignant, or baneful; indicating censure, disgrace, liability to punishment, etc. (as, a *black* mark on one's record).—**black and blue,** of a dark, livid color from a bruise, as the human body.—**black and tan,** having black hair upon the back, and tan or yellowish-brown upon the face, flanks, and legs, as a kind of terrier dog: sometimes used elliptically as a substantive.—**black art.** See under *art*[2].—**black bile.** See under *bile.*—**black book,** any of several books of a political character, so called either from the color of their binding or from the nature of their contents, as the book compiled under Henry VIII. of England containing official reports concerning abuses in the monasteries; also, a book containing the names of persons liable to censure or punishment (hence, fig., *to be in one's black books*, to be in disfavor with one).—**black canon,** an Augustinian canon (see *canon*[2]): so called from the black habit.—**black death,** a destructive plague which originated in Asia and spread over Asia and Europe in the 14th century, attaining its height about 1348.—**black diamond,** carbonado (diamond); also, coal.—**black dog,** in popular or nursery language, an evil creature or influence supposed to produce ill temper, the sulks, or the dumps: as, to have a *black dog* on one's back.—**black flag.** See *flag*[2], *n.*—**black friar,** a Dominican friar (from the distinctive black mantle); also, sometimes, a Benedictine monk.—**Black Friday,** any of various Fridays on which disastrous events occurred, as, in the U. S., Sept. 24, 1869, and Sept. 19, 1873, marked by financial panics.—**black grouse.** See *grouse*[1], *n.*—**Black Hand,** an anarchistic society in Spain, comprised of members of the laboring classes, repressed in 1883; in the U. S., a secret society, esp. of Italians, organized for purposes of blackmail and deeds of violence.—**black hole,** a military cell or lockup (as, the *Black Hole* of Calcutta, in Fort William, into which, in 1756, 146 Europeans were thrust for a night, only 23 of whom lived until morning); any place of confinement for punishment.—**black ivory,** negroes as an article of traffic for slave-traders in Africa.—**black Magellanic cloud.** See under *Magellanic.*—**black Maria,** a close vehicle used for jail prisoners; also, a smoke-producing explosive shell of the World War.—**black market,** an illegal market violating price ceilings, rationing, etc.—**black pope,** a popular name for the general, or head, of the Society of Jesus (the Jesuits): in allusion to his power and the color of the Jesuit habit.—**Black Rod,** the chief gentleman usher of the Lord Chamberlain's department of the English royal household, also usher of the Order of the Garter, whose principal duty is attendance on the House of Lords, in which he is responsible for the maintenance of order (named with reference to the black rod he carries); a similar official in British colonial legislatures.—**black vomit,** a dark-colored substance, consisting chiefly of altered blood, vomited in some cases of yellow fever, usually presaging a fatal issue of the disease; also, the disease itself.—**black walnut.** See *walnut*.—**black,** *n.* That which is black; black hue or color; a black pigment, paint, dye, etc.; a black part, as of a target; a black speck, flake, or spot; black clothing, esp. when worn as a sign of mourning; funereal hangings or drapery; also, a member of a black-skinned race; a negro.—**black,** *v. t.* To make black; put a black color on; clean and polish (shoes, etc.) with blacking; draw in black; stain, sully, or defame.

black-a-moor (blak′ạ-mör), *n.* [For *black Moor*.] A black man or woman, esp. an African negro; any very dark-complexioned person.

black-a-vised (blak′ạ-vīst or -vīzd), *a.* [From *black*, *a.*, + F. *vis*, face, visage.] Dark-complexioned. [Chiefly north. Eng. and Sc.]

black-ball (blak′bâl), *n.* A black ball deposited as in a ballot-box to signify an adverse vote; any secret adverse vote; also, the smut or the bunt of wheat.—**black′ball,** *v. t.* To cast a vote against by a blackball; vote against, esp. secretly; reject or exclude by adverse vote; ostracize.

black-band (blak′band), *n.* In *mining* and *metal.*, a kind of iron ore consisting essentially of carbonate of iron intimately mixed with coaly matter.

Small-mouthed Black-bass.

black=bass (blak′-bȧs′), *n.* An American fresh-water fish of the genus *Micropterus*, which comprises two species, the large-mouthed, *M. salmoides*, and the small-mouthed, *M. dolomieu*.

black-ber-ry (blak′ber″i), *n.*; pl. *-berries* (-iz). The fruit, black or very dark purple when ripe, of certain species of the rosaceous genus *Rubus* in which the receptacle falls off with the drupelets (being thus distinguished from the raspberry); also, the plant.—**blackberry lily,** a perennial iridaceous plant, *Gemmingia chinensis*, with orange-colored lily-like flowers, and clusters of black globose seeds resembling blackberries.—**black′ber″ry-ing,** *n.* The gathering of blackberries.

Common or High Blackberry (*Rubus nigrobaccus*).

black-bird (blak′bėrd), *n.* A European thrush, *Merula vulgaris*; the merle; also, one of various birds of the American family *Icteridæ*, as *Quiscalus purpureus* (the common crow-blackbird); also, a negro or other dark-skinned person seized as a slave.—**black′bird″ing,** *n.* The kidnapping of negroes or other dark-skinned people for slavery.—**black′bird″er,** *n.*

black-board (blak′bōrd), *n.* A dark, smooth surface, as of wood painted black, or of slate, etc., for writing or drawing on with chalk or crayons.

black-boy (blak′boi), *n.* The grass-tree (genus *Xanthorrhœa*).

black-cap (blak′kap), *n.* Any of several birds having the top of the head black, as the chickadee and certain warblers; also, the black raspberry.

Blackcock.

black-cock (blak′kok), *n.* The male of the European black grouse, *Lyrurus tetrix*.

black=damp (blak′damp), *n.* Same as *choke-damp*.

black=draft, black=draught (blak′dráft), *n.* A purgative medicine consisting of an infusion of senna, manna, fennel, and magnesium sulphate.

black-en (blak′n), *v. i.* or *t.* To become or make black. Often fig.—**black′en-er,** *n.*

black-er (blak′ėr), *n.* One who or that which blacks.

black=eyed (blak′īd), *a.* Having eyes with a black or blackish-brown iris.—**black=eyed Susan,** any of several plants having flowers or heads with a dark center, as the cone-flower or yellow daisy, *Rudbeckia hirta*, and the hibiscus, *Hibiscus trionum*.

black-fel-low (blak′fel″ō), *n.* An Australian aboriginal.

black-fin (blak′fin), *n.* A Lake Michigan whitefish, *Argyrosomus nigripinnis*; also, any of certain other whitefishes.

black-fish (blak′fish), *n.* Any of various dark-colored fishes, as the tautog, *Tautoga onitis*, or the sea-bass, *Centropristes striatus*, or a small fresh-water food-fish, *Dallia pectoralis*, of Alaska and Siberia, notable for its ability to revive after having been long frozen; also, the black-whale.

black=fly (blak′flī), *n.*; pl. *-flies* (-flīz). Any of several small, black-bodied flies of the genus *Simulium*, whose bite is very painful, esp. *S. venustum* of the wooded regions of the northern U. S. and Canada: the larvæ are aquatic.

Black-foot (blak′fůt), *n.* A member of a tribe of North American Indians (the Blackfeet) of Algonquian stock; also [*l. c.*], a go-between, esp. in love-making (Sc.).

black-guard (blag′ärd), *n.* Low menials, camp-followers, or vagabonds collectively†; also, a despicable fellow; a scoundrel.—**black′guard,** *v.* **I.** *tr.* To revile in scurrilous language. **II.** *intr.* To behave like a blackguard.—**black′guard-ism,** *n.* Blackguardly conduct or language.—**black′guard-ly,** *a.* Of, like, or befitting a blackguard.

black=gum (blak′gum), *n.* The tupelo (tree), *Nyssa sylvatica*.

black=haw (blak′hâ), *n.* A caprifoliaceous shrub or small tree, *Viburnum prunifolium*, of North America, bearing cymes of small white flowers and black drupes; also, a similar North American shrub or small tree, *V. lentago*.

black-head (blak′hed), *n.* Any of several birds having a black head, as the scaup, *Æthyia* (or *Aythya*) *marila*; also, a comedo; also, a malignant, infectious disease of turkeys, peacocks, etc., attacking esp. the intestines and liver.

black-heart (blak′härt), *n.* A kind of cherry bearing a somewhat heart-shaped fruit with a nearly black skin.

black=heart-ed (blak′här′ted), *a.* Having a wicked heart or malignant disposition.

black-ing (blak′ing), *n.* Any of various preparations for producing a black coating or finish, as on shoes, stoves, etc.

black-ish (blak′ish), *a.* Somewhat black.

black=jack (blak′jak), *n.* A large drinking-cup or jug for beer, ale, etc., orig. one made of leather coated externally with tar; the black flag of a pirate; native zinc sulphide, or blende; caramel or burnt sugar for coloring spirits, vinegar, coffee, etc.; candy made from dark molasses; a short bludgeon consisting of a heavy head, as of metal, on an elastic shaft; a small oak, *Quercus marilandica*, of the eastern U. S., with a nearly black bark and a wood of little value except for fuel.

Leather Black-jacks.

black=lead (blak′led′), *n.* Graphite; plumbago.—**black′-lead′,** *v. t.* To cover or treat with black-lead.

black-leg (blak′leg), *n.* An infectious, usually fatal disease of cattle, sheep, etc., characterized by painful swellings on the legs; also, a swindler, as in connection with racing or gambling; also, in opprobrium, a scab (workman).

black=let-ter (blak′let″ėr). **I.** *n.* The heavy-faced letter or type characteristic of early English (and other) printed books: also adapted for modern use. See *type*. **II.** *a.* Printed in black-letter.

black=list (blak′list), *n.* A list of persons who have incurred suspicion, disfavor, censure, punishment, etc.; a list of insolvents, defaulters, etc.; any list of bad cases.—**black′-list,** *v. t.* To place upon a black-list.

black-ly (blak′li), *adv.* In a black manner; with a black appearance; darkly; gloomily; wickedly.
black-mail (blak′māl), *n.* [See *mail*².] A tribute formerly exacted in the north of England and in Scotland by free-booting chiefs for protection from pillage; hence, any payment extorted by intimidation, as by threats of injurious revelations; also, the extortion of such payment.—**black′-mail,** *v. t.* To extort blackmail from.—**black′mail″er,** *n.*
black-ness (blak′nes), *n.* The quality or state of being black.
black=out (blak′out″), *n.* The extinguishing of all visible lights in a city, etc., as a war protection.
black-poll (blak′pōl), *n.* A North American warbler, *Dendrœca* (or *Dendroica*) *striata*, the adult male of which has the top of the head black.
black=root (blak′röt), *n.* Culver's-root.
black-smith (blak′smith), *n.* [Cf. *whitesmith.*] A smith who works in iron; one who makes horseshoes and shoes horses.—**black′smith″ing,** *n.*
black=snake (blak′snāk), *n.* Any of various snakes of a black or very dark color; esp., in the U. S., a non-venomous serpent, *Zamenis constrictor*, sometimes attaining a length of 5 to 6 feet, and possessing great strength and agility; also, a heavy, tapering, flexible whip of braided cowhide or the like.

Black-snake (*Zamenis constrictor*).

black=strap (blak′-strap), *n.* Any of various dark-colored beverages; a mixture of rum or whisky with molasses and vinegar.
black-tail (blak′tāl), *n.* The mule-deer.
black-thorn (blak′thôrn), *n.* A much-branched, thorny shrub, *Prunus spinosa*, bearing white flowers which appear before the leaves, and small, plum-like fruits; the sloe; also, a walking-stick or cudgel made from the stem of this shrub.
black-wa-ter (blak′wâ″tėr) **fe′ver.** A disease occurring in tropical and semitropical regions, characterized by febrile paroxysms, bloody urine, etc.
black=whale (blak′hwāl), *n.* A dolphin-like cetacean of the genus *Globicephalus.*
black=work (blak′wėrk), *n.* Iron wrought by blacksmiths: so called in distinction from that wrought by whitesmiths.
black-y (blak′i), *n.*; pl. *-ies* (-iz). A black person; a negro; also, any black bird or animal. [Colloq.]
blad (blad), *v. t.*; *bladded, bladding.* [Prob. imit.] To slap; strike; beat; maltreat; spoil. [Sc.]
blad-der (blad′ėr), *n.* [AS. *blǣdre*, bladder, blister, = G. *blatter*, blister; from the Teut. source of E. *blow*³.] A distensible sac with muscular and membranous walls, serving as a receptacle for the urine secreted by the kidneys; any similar sac or receptacle (see *gall-bladder*); a vesicle, blister, etc., filled with fluid or air; fig., anything inflated; a pretentious person; in *bot.*, a sac or the like containing air, as in certain seaweeds.—**blad′der=fern,** *n.* Any fern of the genus *Filix*, as *F. bulbifera*, the common species of the U. S.: so called from the bladder-like indusium.—**blad′der=fish,** *n.* Same as *globe-fish.*—**blad′der=nose,** *n.* A large seal, *Cystophora cristata*, of the northern Atlantic, the male of which has a large, distensible, hood-like sac upon the head.—**blad′der=nut,** *n.* The bladder-like fruit-capsule of any shrub or small tree of the genus *Staphylea*, as *S. trifolia* of the eastern U. S.; also, the shrub or tree itself.—**blad′der=worm,** *n.* The bladder-like encysted larva of a tapeworm; a cysticercus or hydatid.—**blad′der-wort** (-wėrt), *n.* Any of various herbs of the genus *Utricularia*, some floating free in water by means of small bladders on the leaves, and others rooting in mud.—**blad′der-y,** *a.* Of the nature of or like a bladder; thin, inflated, and hollow; also, containing bladders or vesicles.

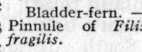

Bladder-fern. Pinnule of *Filix fragilis.*

blade (blād), *n.* [AS. *blæd* = G. *blatt*; from the Teut. source of E. *blow*².] The leaf of a plant, esp. of a grass or cereal; the broad part of a leaf, as distinguished from the stalk; a thin, flat part of something, as of an oar or a bone; the cutting part of an edged weapon or tool; hence, a sword; also, a swordsman; also, a smart or dashing fellow; also, in *phonetics*, the front flat part of the tongue.—**blade′=bone,** *n.* The shoulder-blade or scapula.—**blad-ed** (blā′ded), *a.* Having a blade or blades; also, blade-like.
blae (blā or blē), *a.* [Icel. *blār* = OHG. *blāo*: see *blue.*] Dark-blue; bluish-gray; livid. [Sc. and north. Eng.]—**blae′ber″ry,** *n.* The bilberry or whortleberry. [Sc. and north. Eng.]
blague (blåg), *n.* [F.] Empty, extravagant talk; pretentious lying; humbug.
blain (blān), *n.* [AS. *blegen.*] An inflammatory swelling or sore; a blister or pustule: as, "Botches and *blains* must all his flesh emboss" (Milton's "Paradise Lost," xii. 180).
blam-a-ble (blā′mạ-bl), *a.* Deserving of blame.—**blam′a-ble-ness,** *n.*—**blam′a-bly,** *adv.*
blame (blām), *v. t.*; *blamed, blaming.* [OF. *blasmer* (F. *blâmer*), < LL. *blasphemare*: see *blaspheme.*] To find fault with; censure; also, to lay the blame of (a fault, error, etc.) on a person (colloq.).—**blame,** *n.* Imputation of fault; censure; also, ground for censure; culpability; fault.—**blame′ful,** *a.* Meriting blame; also, imputing blame; censorious.—**blame′ful-ly,** *adv.*—**blame′ful-ness,** *n.*—**blame′less,** *a.* Free from blame; irreproachable; innocent; guiltless.—**blame′less-ly,** *adv.*—**blame′less-ness,** *n.*—**blam-er** (blā′mėr), *n.*—**blame′wor″thy,** *a.* Deserving of blame.—**blame′wor″thi-ness,** *n.*
blanch (blȧnch), *v.* [OF. F. *blanchir*, < *blanc*, white: see *blank.*] **I.** *tr.* To make white, esp. by depriving of color; bleach; whiten; give a white luster to (metals), as by means of acids; cover (sheet-iron) with a thin coating of tin; also, to make pale, as with sickness, fear, cold, etc.; also, to give a fair appearance to; palliate; in *cookery*, to deprive (almonds, etc.) of their skins by immersion in hot water; also, to scald (meat, etc.) by short, rapid boiling. **II.** *intr.* To become white; bleach; turn pale.—**blanch′er,** *n.*
blanc-mange (blạ-mänzh′), *n.* [OF. F. *blanc-manger*, 'white food.'] A jelly-like preparation of milk thickened with isinglass or gelatin, corn-starch, arrowroot, or the like, and flavored.
bland (bland), *a.* [L. *blandus.*] Smooth, suave, or agreeable, as persons or their speech, manner, etc.; soft, gentle, or balmy, as air; mild, as medicines.
blan-dil-o-quence (blan-dil′ọ-kwẹns), *n.* [L. *blandiloquentia*, < *blandiloquens*, speaking smoothly, < *blandus*, smooth, suave, + *loquens*, ppr. of *loqui*, speak.] Smooth speech; agreeable or flattering language.
blan-dish (blan′dish), *v. t.* [OF. *blandir* (*blandiss-*), < L. *blandiri*, < *blandus*, E. *bland.*] To treat in a caressing or flattering manner; coax; cajole.—**blan′dish-er,** *n.*—**blan′-dish-ment,** *n.* Caressing or flattering action or speech; cajolery; also, something that pleases or allures.
bland-ly (bland′li), *adv.* In a bland manner; suavely; mildly.—**bland′ness,** *n.*
blank (blangk), *a.* [OF. F. *blanc* (fem. *blanche*), white, < OHG. *blanch*, bright, shining.] White or pale; of paper, etc., left white, or free from marks; not written or printed on; not filled out, as a check or ballot; empty or unoccupied; without contents; void or bare; unrelieved or unbroken by ornament or opening, as a wall; lacking some usual or completing feature (as, a *blank* window, door, etc., one having the usual casings, etc., but no opening); void of interest, results, etc.; showing no attention, interest, or emotion, as a person's face or look; vacant in expression; disconcerted or nonplussed; complete, utter, or unmitigated (as, *blank* stupidity); unrimed (applied to verse, esp. to the iambic pentameter commonly adopted in English dramatic and epic poetry).—**blank cartridge.** See under *cartridge.*—**blank,** *n.* A small French coin, orig. of silver†; the white spot in the center of a target; anything aimed at; something left blank, or not written on, filled in, etc.; a written or printed form with blank spaces to be filled in; any of these spaces; provisional words printed in italics in a bill before a legislature; a dash put in place of an omitted

word or letter; any space from which something is omitted or absent; a void; a mere form without substance; anything insignificant; a lottery ticket which does not win a prize; a piece of metal prepared to be formed into some finished object by a further operation; an unstamped metal disk for a coin.—**blank,** *v. t.* To make white†; make blank or void; render void of result, etc.; keep (an opponent) from scoring in a game; disconcert (archaic); also, a euphemistic substitute for *damn.*—**blank′=book,** *n.* A book of blank leaves for accounts, memoranda, etc.

blan-ket (blang′ket). [OF. *blankete,* dim. of *blanc,* white: see *blank.*] **I.** *n.* A white or undyed woolen fabric, used for clothing†; a large rectangular piece of soft, loosely woven fabric, usually wool, serving as a bed-covering, a covering for a horse, etc.; a similar piece of cloth, etc., for various other uses. **II.** *a.* Covering or intended to cover a group or class of things, conditions, contingencies, etc.: as, a *blanket* mortgage; a *blanket* indictment.—**blan′ket,** *v. t.* To cover with or as with a blanket; toss in a blanket, as for punishment; *naut.,* to take the wind out of the sails of (a vessel) by passing to windward of it.—**blan′ket-ing,** *n.* Material for blankets; also, a supply or quantity of blankets.

blank-ly (blangk′li), *adv.* In a blank manner; vacantly. —**blank′ness,** *n.*

blan-quette (bläṅ-ket), *n.* [F., dim. of *blanc,* white: see *blank.*] A stew or fricassee, as of veal or chicken, with a white sauce.

blan-quil-lo (bläng-kēl′yō), *n.* [Sp., dim. of *blanco,* white.] Any of the food-fishes constituting the genus *Caulolatilus,* esp. *C. microps,* of the West Indies, etc., and *C. princeps,* of the coast of southern California.

Blanquillo (*Caulolatilus microps*).

blare (blãr), *v.*; *blared, blaring.* [ME. *bleren* = LG. *blaren* = G. *plärren*; prob. imit.] **I.** *intr.* To roar, bellow, or cry (now chiefly prov. Eng.); emit a loud sound as of a trumpet. **II.** *tr.* To utter with blaring.—**blare,** *n.* A blaring; the sound of a trumpet; any similar sound; also, glare or brilliance of color.

blar-ney (blär′ni), *n.* [From *Blarney* Castle, near Cork, Ireland; one who kisses the 'Blarney Stone,' in the castle wall, is said to acquire skill in cajoling.] Flattering or wheedling talk; cajolery.—**blar′ney,** *v. t.* or *i.*; *-neyed, -neying.* To ply or beguile with blarney, or use blarney; wheedle.—**blar′ney-er,** *n.*

bla-sé (blȧ-zā′), *a.* [F. (fem. *blasée*), pp. of *blaser,* exhaust, satiate.] Satiated with enjoyment; having one's capacity for pleasure or interest blunted or exhausted by experience.

blas-pheme (blȧs-fēm′), *v.*; *-phemed, -pheming.* [LL. *blasphemare,* < Gr. *βλασφημεῖν,* blaspheme, < *βλάσφημος,* speaking evil.] **I.** *tr.* To speak impiously or irreverently of (God or sacred things); in general, to speak evil of; calumniate. **II.** *intr.* To utter impious words; talk profanely; also, to utter abusive words†.—**blas-phem′er** (-fē′mėr), *n.*—**blas′phe-mous** (-fē-mus), *a.* [LL. *blasphemus,* < Gr. *βλάσφημος.*] Uttering or containing blasphemy; impiously irreverent; also, abusive† or defamatory†.—**blas′phe-mous-ly,** *adv.*—**blas′phe-mous-ness,** *n.* —**blas′phe-my,** *n.*; pl. *-mies* (-miz). [LL. *blasphemia,* < Gr. *βλασφημία,* < *βλάσφημος.*] Impious utterance concerning God or sacred things; impious irreverence; evil speaking against anything held sacred.

blast (blȧst), *n.* [AS. *blǣst* = OHG. *blāst* = Icel. *blāstr*; akin to E. *blaze*[2] and *blow*[3].] A blowing or gust of wind; a forcible stream of air, steam, etc.; the rush of gases outside a great gun upon its discharge, sometimes affecting the operation of neighboring guns; the blowing of a trumpet, etc.; the sound produced by this, or some similar sound; any pernicious or destructive influence on animals or plants; a blight; a curse; the product of a blight; a bud which never blossoms; blasted state or condition; the act of rending rock, etc., or an attempt to do this, by an explosive; the charge of explosive used for this; a smoke of tobacco (Sc.); in *metal.,* a current of air forced into a furnace to accelerate combustion; the operation of a blast-furnace with such a current (as, a furnace is *in blast* when in operation, and *out of blast* when stopped).—**blast,** *v.* **I.** *intr.* To puff† or breathe hard†; blow on a trumpet or the like; boast or brag (Sc.); smoke tobacco (Sc.); become blighted. **II.** *tr.* To blow forth†; proclaim†; blow (a trumpet, etc.); confound or stun as by a loud blast; smoke (tobacco: Sc.); blow or breathe on injuriously or destructively; cause to shrivel or wither; arrest in growth; blight; affect with any pernicious influence; ruin or destroy (hopes, happiness, reputation, etc.); strike with the wrath of heaven; curse; rend or attempt to rend (rock, etc.) by an explosive.

-blast. Noun termination from Gr. *βλαστός,* sprout, germ, used in biological and other scientific terms, as *archiblast, bioblast, meroblast, neuroblast.*

blast-ed (blȧs′ted), *p. a.* Affected with a blast or blight, or other destructive influence; withered or shriveled; blighted; also, damned (a euphemism).

blas-te-ma (blas-tē′mạ), *n.*; pl. *-mata* (-mạ-tạ). [NL., < Gr. *βλάστημα,* sprout.] In *biol.,* the formative substance of a germinating ovum; also, the initial point of growth from which an organ or part is developed.

blast-er (blȧs′tėr), *n.* One who or that which blasts.

blast=fur-nace (blȧst′fėr″nạs), *n.* A furnace in which ores are smelted by the aid of a blast of air.

blast-ment (blȧst′mẹnt), *n.* A blasting; a blast or blight.

blasto-. Form of Gr. *βλαστός,* sprout, germ, used in combination.—**blas-to-cyst** (blas′tọ-sist), *n.* In *embryol.,* the germinal vesicle; also, a vesicular blastoderm.—**blas′to-derm** (-dėrm), *n.* [+ *-derm.*] In *embryol.,* the primitive membrane or layer of cells which results from the segmentation of the ovum, and which in most metazoans becomes differentiated into the ectoderm, mesoderm, and endoderm. —**blas-to-der′mic,** *a.*—**blas′to-disk, blas′to-disc** (-disk), *n.* In *embryol.,* a disk-like aggregation of formative protoplasm appearing in an egg after fertilization.—**blas-to-gen′e-sis** (-jen′e-sis), *n.* In *biol.,* reproduction by gemmation or budding; also, the theory of the transmission of hereditary characters by germ-plasm.—**blas′to-mere** (-mēr), *n.* [+ *-mere.*] In *embryol.,* any of the cells or segments into which an ovum or egg first divides.—**blas′to-pore** (-pōr), *n.* In *embryol.,* the orifice of an archenteron.—**blas-to-por′ic** (-por′ik), *a.*—**blas′to-sphere** (-sfēr), *n.* In *embryol.,* a blastula; specif., the hollow spherical blastoderm of mammals, formed after gastrulation.

blas-tu-la (blas′tū-lạ), *n.*; pl. *-læ* (-lē). [NL., dim. < Gr. *βλαστός,* sprout, germ.] In *embryol.,* an embryo of a metazoan, consisting in typical cases of a sac or hollow sphere formed of a single layer of cells.

blat (blat), *v.*; *blatted, blatting.* [Imit.] **I.** *intr.* To cry as a calf; give forth a harsh sound; talk loudly and senselessly or indiscreetly. [Colloq.] **II.** *tr.* To utter loudly and indiscreetly; blurt out. [Colloq.]

bla-tant (blā′tạnt), *a.* [Appar. coined by Spenser: cf. L. *blatire,* babble, and E. *bleat.*] Clamorous; loud-mouthed; noisy; loud: orig. in *blatant beast* (in Spenser's "Faerie Queene," a monster with a thousand tongues, symbolizing calumny).—**bla′tan-cy** (-tạn-si), *n.*—**bla′tant-ly,** *adv.*

blate (blāt), *a.* [Cf. AS. *blāt,* pale.] Bashful; diffident; backward; dull. [Sc. and north. Eng.]

blath-er (blaᴛʜ′ėr), *v. i.* or *t.* [Orig. Sc., < Icel. *bladhra.*] To talk or utter volubly and foolishly.—**blath′er,** *n.* Voluble, foolish talk.—**blath′er-skite** (-skīt), *n.* One given to voluble, empty talk.

blat-ter (blat′ėr), *v.* [Cf. L. *blaterare,* talk foolishly.] **I.** *tr.* To utter volubly. **II.** *intr.* To speak or prate volubly; also, to clatter or patter.—**blat′ter,** *n.* A volley of clattering words; a rattling or clattering noise.—**blat′ter-er,** *n.*

blaud (blâd), *v. t.* Same as *blad.* [Sc.]

blauw-bok (blou′bok), *n.* [S. Afr. D., 'blue buck.'] A South African antelope (now extinct), *Hippotragus leucophæus,* with a bluish appearance, and rather large horns; also, any of various small South African antelopes of the genus *Cephalophus.*

blaze[1] (blāz), *n.* [Perhaps < Icel. *blesi* or D. *bles* = G. *blässe,* blaze on a horse's head.] A white spot on the face of a horse, cow, etc.; a white mark made on a tree, as by removing a piece of the bark, to indicate a boundary or a path in a forest; a path or trail indicated by such marks.—

blaze[1], *v. t.*; *blazed, blazing.* To mark (a tree) with a blaze; indicate (a spot, path, etc.) by blazes.

blaze[2] (blāz), *v. t.*; *blazed, blazing.* [ME. *blasen*, prob. < Icel. *blāsa* = G. *blasen*, blow, sound, ult. akin to E. *blow*[3]; in part confused with *blazon*.] To blow, as from a trumpet†; also, to proclaim; publish; make known; also, to blazon†.

blaze[3] (blāz), *n.* [AS. *blæse*, torch, flame, = MHG. *blas*, torch.] A torch†; a flame; a flaming fire; a glowing or glaring light; intense brightness; brilliance; a fiery or violent outburst, as of passion; *pl.*, hell (slang).—**blaze**[3], *v.*; *blazed, blazing.* **I.** *intr.* To flame; shine like flame, or with intense brightness; flare (*up*); burst (*out*); fire (*away*), as with a gun. **II.** *tr.* To cause to blaze; temper (steel) by coating with tallow or oil and then burning off.—**blaz-er** (blā'zėr), *n.* That which blazes; something intensely hot or bright; a bright-colored jacket worn by tennis-players and others.—**blaz'ing-ly,** *adv.*—**blaz'ing=star',** *n.* Any of certain American plants with showy flower-clusters, as the liliaceous herb *Aletris farinosa*, the melanthiaceous herb *Chamælirium luteum*, or the asteraceous herb *Laciniaria squarrosa*.

bla-zon (blā'zo̤n), *n.* [OF. *blazon*, shield, later armorial bearings, heraldry (F. *blason*).] A heraldic shield; armorial bearings; the heraldic description of armorial bearings; in general, a setting forth; description; display.—**bla'zon,** *v. t.* To describe in heraldic language; depict (heraldic arms, etc.) in due form and color; inscribe with arms or some ornament; embellish; also, to set forth conspicuously or publicly; display; proclaim.—**bla'zon-er,** *n.*—**bla'zon-ment,** *n.* The act of blazoning.—**bla'zon-ry,** *n.* The art of blazoning heraldic arms; armorial bearings; decoration in color, as with heraldic devices; brilliant decoration or display.

-ble. [L. *-bilis* (*-abilis, -ibilis*).] A suffix occurring in adjectives of Latin origin, as *noble, soluble, voluble*, but appearing most often, as a recognized English suffix, in the forms *-able* and *-ible*. See *-able* and *-ible*.

bleach (blēch), *v.* [AS. *blǣcan* = G. *bleichen* = Icel. *bleikja*; akin to E. *bleak*[2].] **I.** *tr.* To make white or whiter, as linen by exposure to sunlight or by chemical agents; deprive of color; make lighter in color; blanch. **II.** *intr.* To become white; whiten; become pale or colorless.—**bleach,** *n.* The act of bleaching; also, the color given by bleaching; also, any agent or preparation used for bleaching.—**bleach'er,** *n.* One who or that which bleaches; a vessel used in bleaching; an uncovered seat or stand for spectators at outdoor games, as baseball (usually in *pl.*).—**bleach'er-y,** *n.*; pl. *-ies* (-iz). A place or establishment where bleaching is carried on.—**bleach'ing=pow''der,** *n.* A powder used for bleaching; esp., chloride of lime.

bleak[1] (blēk), *n.* [ME. *bleke*: cf. *bleak*[2].] A small cyprinoid fish, *Alburnus lucidus*, of European rivers.

bleak[2] (blēk), *a.* [Earlier *blake*, < AS. *blāc* = G. *bleich* = Icel. *bleikr*, pale, orig. 'shining': cf. L. *fulgere*, shine, Gr. φλέγειν, burn, also E. *bleach*.] Pale†; bare of vegetation; exposed to cold and wind; desolate; cheerless; raw; cold.—**bleak'ly,** *adv.*—**bleak'ness,** *n.*

blear (blēr), *a.* [ME. *blere*; origin uncertain.] Dim from a watery discharge or other superficial affection, as the eyes; dim, misty, or indistinct.—**blear,** *v. t.* To render (the eyes) dim, as with tears, rheum, or inflammation; dim the vision of; blind or deceive; blur, as the face with weeping.—**bleared'ness,** *n.*—**blear'=eye,** *n.* Chronic catarrhal inflammation of the margins of the eyelids.—**blear'=eyed,** *a.* Having blear eyes; affected with blear-eye; dim-sighted; fig., having the mental vision dimmed; dull of perception.—**blear'y,** *a.* Somewhat blear.

bleat (blēt), *v.* [AS. *blǣtan*.] **I.** *intr.* To cry as a sheep, goat, or calf; make a similar sound. **II.** *tr.* To give forth with a bleat; also, to babble or prate.—**bleat,** *n.* The cry of a sheep, goat, or calf; any similar sound, as that made by a snipe.—**bleat'er,** *n.*

bleb (bleb), *n.* [Cf. *blob*.] A blister or pustule; a bubble, as in water or glass; a small vesicular body.—**bleb'by,** *a.* Full of blebs.

bled (bled). Preterit and past participle of *bleed*.

blee (blē), *n.* [AS. *blēo*.] Color; complexion: as, "white of *blee*" (Mrs. Browning's "Romaunt of the Page," xx.). [Archaic.]

bleed (blēd), *v.*; *bled, bleeding.* [AS. *blēdan*, < *blōd*, E. *blood*.] **I.** *intr.* To emit or shed blood; let blood, esp. surgically; exude sap, juice, etc.; leak; run, as color in dyeing; part with money, as under extortion (slang); fig., esp. of the heart, to feel anguish (*for*). **II.** *tr.* To emit, as blood or sap; shed; let blood from; draw sap, etc., from; extort money from (slang); trim the margin of (a book) so closely as to mutilate the text.—**bleed'er,** *n.* One who or that which bleeds; a person predisposed to bleeding.—**bleed'ing=heart',** *n.* Any of various plants of the genus *Dicentra* (or *Bikukulla*), esp. *D. spectabilis*, a common garden-plant with racemes of red heart-shaped flowers; also, the wallflower, *Cheiranthus cheiri* (Eng.); also, the wahoo, *Euonymus atropurpureus* (southern U. S.).

Bleeding-heart (*Dicentra spectabilis*).

blem-ish (blem'ish), *v. t.* [OF. *blemir* (*blemiss-*), *blesmir*, make livid or pale, wound (F. *blêmir*, grow pale), < *blesme* (F. *blême*), pale, wan; origin uncertain.] To damage or impair; destroy the perfection of; make defective; deface; mar; also, to impair morally; sully; stain.—**blem'ish,** *n.* That which blemishes; a defect, flaw, or imperfection; a moral defect or injury; a blot or stain.—**blem'ish-er,** *n.*—**blem'ish-ment,** *n.*

blench[1] (blench), *v.* [AS. *blencan*, deceive; perhaps akin to E. *blink*.] **I.** *tr.* To deceive† or cheat†; also, to draw back or flinch from; avoid; also, to disconcert† or foil†. **II.** *intr.* To start back or aside; shrink; flinch.

blench[2] (blench), *v. t.* or *i.* Same as *blanch*.

blench-er (blen'chėr), *n.* One who blenches or flinches.

blend (blend), *v.*; *blended* or *blent, blending.* [ME. *blenden*, appar. < Icel. *blanda* = AS. *blandan*, mix.] **I.** *tr.* To mix or mingle; mix thoroughly or intimately; combine so that the things mixed or the line of division cannot be distinguished; mix (different sorts of a commodity) in order to produce a particular kind or quality; confuse†; spoil† or corrupt†. **II.** *intr.* To become mixed or mingled; unite in a uniform or harmonious whole; pass or shade imperceptibly, as colors into one another.—**blend,** *n.* The act or the result of blending; a mixture or kind produced by blending.

blende (blend), *n.* [G., < *blenden*, blind, deceive.] A native sulphide of zinc, with a non-metallic luster and a color varying from black or brown to yellow or white; sphalerite; also, any of certain other native sulphides (as, manganese-*blende*, a sulphide of manganese).

blend-er (blen'dėr), *n.* One who or that which blends.

blend-ous (blen'dus), *a.* Of or containing blende.

Blen-heim (blen'e̤m), *n.* [From *Blenheim* Palace, in Oxfordshire, England, built as a public gift to the first Duke of Marlborough after his victory at Blenheim in Bavaria, in 1704.] One of a breed of small spaniels with short head and very long ears, kept as pets.

blen-ni-oid (blen'i-oid), *a.* Resembling a blenny; pertaining to the blennies.

blen-nor-rhe-a, blen-nor-rhœ-a (blen-o̤-rē'ạ̈), *n.* [NL., < Gr. βλέννος, slime, + ῥοία, a flow, < ῥεῖν, flow.] An excessive secretion and discharge of mucus; also, gonorrhea.

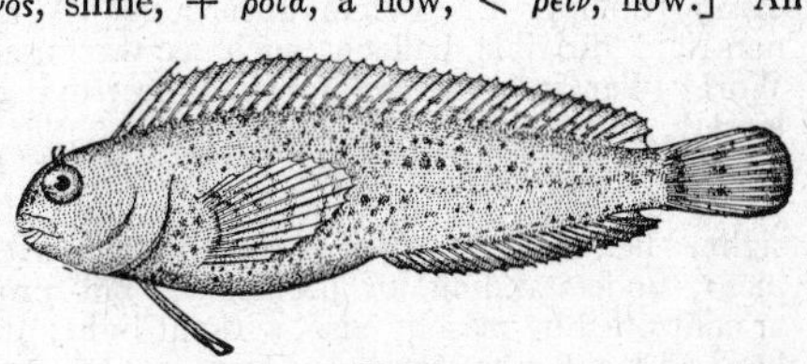

Blenny.

blen-ny (blen'i), *n.*; pl. *blennies* (-iz). [L. *blennius*, < Gr. βλέννος, blenny, orig. slime.] Any of various fishes of the genus *Blennius* and allied genera, with an elongated tapering body.

blent (blent). Preterit and past participle of *blend*.

bleph-a-ri-tis (blef-ạ-rī'tis), *n.* [NL., < Gr. βλέφαρον, eyelid.] In *pathol.*, inflammation of the eyelids.—**bleph-a-rit'ic** (-rit'ik), *a.*

(variable) d̦ as d or j, ș as s or sh, ț as t or ch, z̦ as z or zh; o, F. cloche; ü, F. menu; ḉh, Sc. loch; ṅ, F. bonbon; ', primary accent; '', secondary accent; †, obsolete; <, from; +, and; =, equals. See also lists at beginning of book.

bles-bok (bles′bok), *n.* [S. Afr. D., 'blaze buck.'] A large South African antelope, *Bubalis* (or *Damaliscus*) *albifrons*, having a blaze or white spot on the face.

Blesbok.

bless (bles), *v. t.*; *blessed* or *blest*, *blessing*. [AS. *blētsian*, *blēdsian*, consecrate, orig. with blood, < *blōd*, E. *blood*.] To consecrate by a religious rite, as of prayer; make the sign of the cross over, as for defense against evil; guard or save, as from evil†; invoke the divine favor or protection for; ask a blessing on; extol as holy or as divinely beneficent; glorify; thank devoutly; bestow divine favor on; bestow happiness or prosperity on; favor, as with some special benefit; congratulate or felicitate (one's self): sometimes used colloquially as a euphemistic substitute for *curse* or *confound*.—**bless-ed** (bles′ed or blest), *p. a.* Consecrated; sacred; holy; divinely or supremely favored; beatified; fortunate or happy: sometimes used colloquially as if for *cursed* or *confounded*, and hence also merely to lend emphasis.—**bless′ed-ly,** *adv.*—**bless′ed-ness,** *n.*—**bless′er,** *n.*—**bless′ing,** *n.* The act or the words of one who blesses; an invocation of divine favor; a benediction; a bestowal of divine favor; a special favor, mercy, or benefit; a boon; a source of happiness or peculiar advantage.—**blest,** *p. a.* Same as *blessed*.

blet (blet), *v. i.*; *bletted*, *bletting*. [F. *blettir*, < *blet*, soft from overripeness.] Of fruits, to become soft internally from incipient decay, as the medlar and persimmon.—**blet,** *n.* A soft spot due to bletting.

bleth-er (bleᴛʜ′ėr), *v.* and *n.* Same as *blather*.

blet-on-ism (blet′on-izm), *n.* [From *Bleton*, a Frenchman said to have had this faculty.] The alleged faculty of divining the presence of underground waters.—**blet′on-ist,** *n.*

blew¹, blew² (blö). Preterit of *blow²*, *blow³*.

blight (blīt), *n.* [Origin unknown.] Some influence, usually hidden or not conspicuous, that blasts or destroys plants, arrests their growth, etc.; a diseased state of plants resulting from this; smut, mildew, or other fungous plant-disease; any insect which blasts or destroys plants; any malignant influence of obscure or mysterious origin; anything which withers hope, blasts prospects, or checks prosperity; also, a blighting or being blighted.—**blight,** *v. t.* To affect with blight; blast; ruin or frustrate.—**blight′er,** *n.* One that blights; a person who causes trouble or makes himself obnoxious (slang, Eng.).—**blight′ing-ly,** *adv.*

blight-y (blī′ti), *n.* [Hind. *bilaiti*, < *bilait*, used in India to signify England, or Europe, < Ar. *wilāyat*, province, government: cf. *vilayet*.] England, or home, esp. as the destination of soldiers when wounded or on furlough; hence, a wound, furlough, or the like, that takes a soldier away from the front. [British army slang.]

blimp (blimp), *n.* [Origin uncertain.] A kind of small, non-rigid dirigible balloon, such as was used during the World War in searching for and destroying submarines; loosely, any dirigible. [Colloq.]

blind (blīnd), *a.* [AS. *blind* = D. and G. *blind* = Icel. *blindr* = Goth. *blinds*, blind.] Destitute of the sense of sight; fig., without mental perception; without discernment, understanding, or judgment; not proceeding from or controlled by reason; also, without light; dark; obscure; hard to make out; concealed from sight; secret†; without an opening or outlet (as, a *blind* wall or arch); closed at one end (as, a *blind* alley); abortive (as, a *blind* bud); also, of or pertaining to blind persons.—**blind spot,** a circular area on the retina, insensitive to light, at which the optic nerve enters the eye.—**blind tiger,** a place where intoxicating liquors are sold surreptitiously, without a license. [Slang, U. S.]—**blind,** *v. t.* To make blind; render unable to see, as by injuring, dazzling, or bandaging the eyes; deprive of discernment or judgment; render insensible (*to*); darken or dim; cover, conceal, or hide.—**blind,** *n.* Something that obstructs vision or keeps out light; a shade or shutter for a window; a blinker for a horse; a cover for masking action or purpose; a hiding-place or ambush, as for a hunter; *milit.*, a blindage; in *poker*, a compulsory stake placed in the pool by the age before the cards are dealt.—**blind′age** (-āj), *n.* *Milit.*, a screen or other structure as for protecting men in a trench; also, a mantelet.—**blind′er,** *n.* One who or that which blinds; a blinker for a horse.—**blind′=fish,** *n.* Any of several small fishes with rudimentary, functionless eyes, found in subterranean streams, as *Amblyopsis spelæus*, of the Mammoth Cave, in Kentucky.—**blind′fold,** *v. t.* [Altered from ME. *blindfellen* (pp. *blindfelled*), 'fell (strike) blind,' by confusion with *fold¹*.] To strike or make blind†; cover or bandage the eyes of, to prevent seeing.—**blind′fold,** *a.* Blindfolded; fig., blinded as to perception or judgment.—**blind′ing-ly,** *adv.*—**blind′ly,** *adv.*—**blind′-man's=buff′,** *n.* A game in which a blindfolded player is buffeted or pushed about until he can catch and identify one of the others, who must then take his place.—**blind′-man's hol′i-day.** The time just before the evening lights are lighted, when it is too dark to work, read, or the like.—**blind′ness,** *n.*—**blind′stitch,** *v. t.* To sew with stitches that do not show on the right side of the work.—**blind′=sto″ry,** *n.*; pl. *-ries* (-riz). In *arch.*, a story without windows or window-like openings; esp., the triforium of a medieval church, possessing no exterior windows.—**blind′worm,** *n.* A small, snake-like European lizard, *Anguis fragilis*, with minute eyes, popularly supposed to be blind; also, formerly, the adder.

Blind-fish (*Amblyopsis spelæus*).

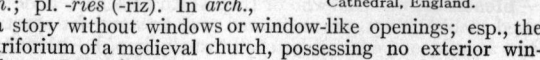

Blind-story. — Triforium of Lincoln Cathedral, England.

Blindworm (*Anguis fragilis*).

blink (blingk), *v.* [= D. and G. *blinken* = Sw. *blinka* = Dan. *blinke*.] **I.** *intr.* To wink, esp. rapidly and repeatedly; look with winking or half-shut eyes; glance with unsteady or dim vision; cast a glance; take a peep; look evasively or with indifference; also, to shine unsteadily or dimly; twinkle. **II.** *tr.* To cause to blink; also, to see dimly; also, to shut the eyes to; evade; shirk.—**blink,** *n.* A blinking; a glance or glimpse; the twinkling of an eye; a very short time; a gleam; glimmer; also, ice-blink.—**blink-ard** (bling′kärd), *n.* One who blinks habitually or who sees imperfectly; fig., one who lacks intellectual perception.—**blink′er,** *n.* One who or that which blinks; also, either of two flaps on a bridle, to prevent a horse from seeing sidewise or backward; a blinder; hence, any obstruction to sight or discernment; also, *pl.*, goggles; also, *sing.*, a device used, as at night, for flashing signals with electric lamps, as in the navy.—**blink′ing-ly,** *adv.*

bliss (blis), *n.* [AS. *bliss*, *blīths*, < *blīthe*, E. *blithe*.] Blitheness; gladness; lightness of heart; supreme happiness or delight; blessedness; the joy of heaven; also, a cause of great joy or happiness.—**bliss′ful,** *a.* Full of bliss; enjoying or conferring bliss; supremely joyful.—**bliss′ful-ly,** *adv.*—**bliss′ful-ness,** *n.*

blis-ter (blis′tėr), *n.* [ME. *blister, blester,* perhaps < OF. *blestre, blostre,* clod, lump, swelling.] A thin vesicle on the skin, containing watery matter or serum, due to friction, a burn, etc.; any similar swelling or cavity, as an air-bubble in a casting; also, something applied to the skin to raise a blister.—**blis′ter,** *v.* **I.** *tr.* To raise blisters on. **II.** *intr.* To develop blisters; become covered with blisters.—**blis′ter=bee″tle,** *n.* Any of various beetles of the family *Meloidæ,* certain species of which, as *Cantharis vesicatoria,* when dried and powdered, are used for raising blisters. See *cantharides.*—**blis′ter=cop″per,** *n.* A form of metallic copper in which gases have produced cavities or blisters.—**blis′ter-ing-ly,** *adv.*—**blis′ter=steel,** *n.* A kind of steel produced by cementation: so called from the blistered appearance of its surface.—**blis′ter-y,** *a.* Full of blisters.

blite (blīt), *n.* [L. *blitum,* < Gr. βλῖτον.] Any of various chenopodiaceous plants, as *Chenopodium bonus-henricus,* sometimes used as a pot-herb, or *Blitum capitatum* ('strawberry-blite'), with red fleshy clusters of fruit.

blithe (blīᴛʜ or blīth), *a.* [AS. *blīthe,* kind, pleasant, joyous, = D. *blijde,* joyous, = Icel. *blīdhr,* mild, pleasant, = Goth. *bleiths,* kind: cf. *bliss.*] Kind†; joyous or gay; glad; cheerful. [Now prov. or literary.]—**blithe′ful,** *a.* Blithesome. [Archaic.]—**blithe′ly,** *adv.*—**blithe′ness,** *n.*—**blithe′some** (-sum), *a.* Gladsome; blithe. [Now prov. or literary.]—**blithe′some-ly,** *adv.*—**blithe′some-ness,** *n.*

blitz-krieg (blits′krēg, G. blits′krēch), *n.* [G., 'lightning war.'] War waged by surprise, swiftly, and violently, as by the use of aircraft, tanks, etc.; hence, any swift, vigorous attack or onset.

bliz-zard (bliz′ärd), *n.* [Origin obscure; perhaps ult. < *blaze*³.] A violent storm of wind with dry, driving snow and intense cold, frequent on the plains of North America east of the Rocky Mountains.—**bliz′zard-ly,** *a.* Blizzard-like.

bloat (blōt), *a.* [Cf. Icel. *blautr,* soft, soaked, wet.] Soft†; cured by salting (orig. by steeping in brine) and smoking until half-dried, as herrings (obs. or prov. Eng.); swollen or bloated (archaic).—**bloat,** *v.* **I.** *tr.* To cure (herrings) as bloaters; also, to render swollen. **II.** *intr.* To become swollen.—**bloat′ed,** *p. a.* Cured as a bloater (as, a *bloated* herring); also, swollen, as with dropsy; having a sodden, puffy appearance, as from drinking or luxurious living; also, pampered; puffed up; also, inflated; overgreat.—**bloat′er,** *n.* A herring slightly salted and partially smoke-dried, but not split open; also, a whitefish, *Argyrosomus prognathus,* of the Great Lakes ('bloater whitefish').

blob (blob), *n.* [Prob. imit.: cf. *blubber.*] A bubble; a blister; a globule of liquid or viscid substance; a drop; a small, round mass or object.—**blob′by,** *a.* Abounding in blobs; blob-like.

bloc (blok), *n.* [F.: see *block.*] A block, or number of things or persons taken or acting as a unit; specif., a number of members of a legislative assembly acting as a unit and representing a particular interest (as, the agricultural *bloc* in the U. S. Congress).

block (blok), *n.* [ME. *blok,* appar. < OF. F. *bloc,* block, mass, from Teut. (cf. G. *block*).] A solid mass of wood, stone, or the like, usually with one or more plane or approximately plane faces; a log of wood; a stump of a tree; a blockhead; a solid mass of wood, etc., used for a particular purpose, as one on which meat is chopped, a slave placed for sale, or a condemned person beheaded; a piece of wood prepared for cutting, or as cut, by an engraver; a mold or piece on which something is shaped or kept in shape; the mold on which a hat is formed; the shape of a hat, or the hat itself; a head, as of wood, for a wig; the wig itself; the human head (slang); a device consisting of one or more grooved pulleys mounted in a casing or shell, to which a hook or the like is attached, used for transmitting power, or changing the direction of motion, by means of ropes or chains passing round the pulleys; a mass of wood, stone, etc., forming an obstruction; an obstacle or hindrance; a blocking or obstructing, or blocked or obstructed state or condition; a stoppage, as of traffic on a road; an animal of a stocky, stout, compact, and well-made form; any compact or connected mass; a large building divided into separate houses, shops, etc.; a connected mass of buildings; a portion of a city, town, etc., inclosed by (usually four) neighboring and intersecting streets; a square; the length of one side of this; a quantity, portion, or section taken as a unit or dealt with at one time; a large number of shares taken together, as in the stock-exchange; one of the short divisions into which a railroad is divided for signaling purposes, as for keeping an interval of space between successive trains.—**block,** *v. t.* [Partly < *block, n.,* partly appar. < F. *bloquer,* block up, blockade, < *bloc.*] To form into blocks; fit with blocks; mount on a block; shape or prepare on or with a block; sketch or outline roughly or in a general plan, without details; obstruct (a way, etc.); obstruct the way or course of; prevent passage to or from (a place, etc.); blockade; in *cricket,* etc., to stop (a ball) with the bat, without knocking it to a distance.

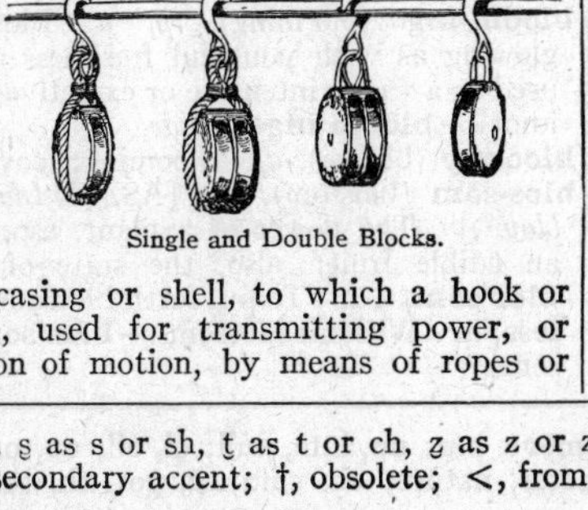

Single and Double Blocks.

block-ade (blo-kād′), *n.* [From *block, v.*] The shutting up of a place, esp. a port, harbor, or line of coast, by hostile ships or troops, so as to prevent ingress or egress; a blockading force; any obstruction of passage or progress.—**block-ade′,** *v. t.; -aded, -ading.* To subject to a blockade; prevent ingress to or egress from by warlike means; block up or obstruct.—**block-ad-er** (blo-kā′dėr), *n.*

block-age (blok′āj), *n.* The state of being blocked or obstructed; obstruction.

block=book (blok′bu̇k), *n.* A book printed by the old process of block-printing.

block-er (blok′ėr), *n.* One who or that which blocks; a tool or machine for some process of blocking.

block-head (blok′hed), *n.* A stupid person; a dolt.

block-house (blok′hous), *n.* Orig., a detached fort blocking passage; later, an edifice constructed chiefly of hewn timber, often with a projecting upper story, having loopholes for musketry and sometimes embrasures for cannon; also, a house built of squared logs.

Blockhouse.
a, a, loopholes for musketry.

block-ish (blok′ish), *a.* Like a block; stupid; dull; wooden.—**block′ish-ly,** *adv.*—**block′ish-ness,** *n.*

block=print-ing (blok′prin″ting), *n.* Printing from carved or engraved blocks of wood, as by the process used for producing books, etc., before the invention of movable types, or by a modern process for decorating calico, etc.

block=tin (blok′tin), *n.* Commercial tin cast into blocks.

block-y (blok′i), *a.* Marked by blocks or patches of unequally distributed light and shade, as a photograph.

bloke (blōk), *n.* [Origin unknown.] A man; a fellow. [Slang.]

blol-ly (blol′i), *n.* [Cf. *loblolly.*] A nyctaginaceous shrub or small tree, *Pisonia longifolia,* of Florida, the West Indies, etc., bearing oval leaves and bright-red fleshy fruit.

blond (blond), *a.* [OF. F. *blond,* masc.; origin unknown.] Light-colored, as golden or light-brown hair; fair-haired and fair-complexioned, as a person; light in hue, as the complexion.—**the blond beast.** [Tr. G. *die blonde Bestie*; in one passage, *die blonde germanische* (Germanic, Teutonic) *Bestie.*] In the writings of the German philosopher Nietzsche (see his "Genealogy of Morals," i. §11, published in 1887), a blond or fair type of man, the early Aryan ancestor of the modern European races during the period of the Aryan descent on the aboriginal inhabitants of Europe, or, more especially, the early Teutonic ancestor (as the Goth or the Vandal) of modern Teutonic peoples, looked upon as a "robber-animal," or beast of prey, "the splendid blond beast roving greedily after prey and victory" (cf. *superman,* Nietzsche's ideal superior being); a natural, non-moral man of prehistoric or primitive times, taken by Nietzsche as the progenitor of the superior races of modern times;

hence, the type of man, in any age or country, possessing, or credited with possessing, such characteristics (often applied, during the period of the World War, to the modern German, or to the type of German taken as the embodiment of German militarism).—**blond,** *n.* A blond person; also, a kind of silk lace, orig. made of unbleached silk (now commonly *blonde*).—**blonde** (blond), *a.* and *n.* [F.] Fem. of *blond.*—**blond'ness,** *n.*

blood (blud), *n.* [AS. *blōd* = D. *bloed* = G. *blut* = Icel. *blōdh* = Goth. *blōth,* blood.] The fluid that circulates in the arteries and veins or principal vascular system of animals, in man being of a red color and consisting of a pale-yellow plasma containing semisolid corpuscles, some red and some white; the vital fluid as shed from a wound; gore; bloodshed or slaughter; juice or sap, as of plants; the physical nature; temper or state of mind (as, to act in cold *blood;* there is bad *blood,* or hostile feeling, between them); also, the blood of a family or race looked upon as a characteristic or distinctive attribute of its members; birth, parentage, kinship, or breed, esp. good birth or breed; lineage; royal lineage (as, a prince of the *blood*); family, race, or kindred; offspring; also, a spirited or dashing fellow.—**blue blood.** See under *blue, a.*—**fresh blood.** See under *fresh, a.*—**full blood.** See under *full* [1], *a.*—**half blood,** relationship through one parent only, as distinguished from *whole blood,* or relationship through both parents. — **blood,** *v. t.* To draw blood from; bleed; stain with blood†; give (hounds, etc.) a first taste or sight of blood.—**blood'ed,** *a.* Having blood; of good blood or breed.

blood=feud (blud'fūd), *n.* A feud involving bloodshed or murder.

blood=guilt-y (blud'gil"ti), *a.* Guilty of bloodshed or murder.—**blood'=guilt"i-ness,** *n.*

blood=heat (blud'hēt), *n.* The normal temperature (about 98.6° F.) of human blood.

blood-hound (blud'hound), *n.* One of a breed of large, powerful dogs with a very acute sense of smell, used for tracking game, human fugitives, etc.; fig., a relentless pursuer.

Bloodhound.

blood-i-ly (blud'i-li), *adv.* In a bloody manner.—**blood'i-ness,** *n.*

blood-less (blud'les), *a.* Lacking blood; pale; spiritless; cold-hearted; also, without bloodshed. — **blood'less-ly,** *adv.*—**blood'less-ness,** *n.*

blood-let-ting (blud'let"ing), *n.* The act of letting blood or bleeding, as by opening a vein, as a remedial measure; phlebotomy.

blood=mon-ey (blud'mun"i), *n.* Money paid to procure or to compensate for the killing of a person.

blood=poi-son-ing (blud'poi"zn-ing), *n.* A morbid condition of the blood due to the presence of toxic matter or micro-organisms; toxemia; septicemia; pyemia.

blood=pres-sure (blud'presh"ūr), *n.* The pressure exerted by the blood against the inner walls of the blood-vessels, varying in different parts of the body, and with exertion, excitement, etc., and under different conditions of health.

blood=red (blud'red'), *a.* Of the deep-red color of blood; also, red with blood.

blood=re-la-tion (blud'rē-lā'shon), *n.* One related by birth; a kinsman. Also **blood'=rel'a-tive.**

blood-root (blud'röt), *n.* An old-world rosaceous plant, *Potentilla tormentilla,* with a reddish root; also, a North American papaveraceous plant, *Sanguinaria canadensis,* with red root and root-sap.

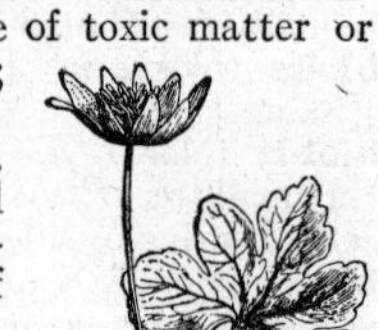

Bloodroot (*Sanguinaria canadensis*).

blood-shed (blud'shed), *n.* The shedding of blood; slaughter.—**blood'shed"ding,** *n.*

blood-shot (blud'shot), *a.* Of the eyes, red from inflamed blood-vessels.

blood-stone (blud'stōn), *n.* A greenish kind of quartz with small blood-like spots of red jasper scattered through it; heliotrope; also, a kind of hematite.

blood-suck-er (blud'suk"ėr), *n.* Any animal that sucks blood, esp. a leech; fig., an extortioner or sponger.

blood-thirst-y (blud'thėrs"ti), *a.* Eager to shed blood; sanguinary; murderous.—**blood'thirst"i-ly,** *adv.*—**blood'thirst"i-ness,** *n.*

blood=ves-sel (blud'ves"el), *n.* Any of the vessels of the body (arteries, veins, capillaries) through which the blood circulates.

blood-wite (blud'wīt), *n.* [AS. *blōdwīte,* 'blood punishment.'] In *old Eng. law,* a fine, in addition to the wergild, for the shedding of blood, to be paid to the king or other superior.

blood-wood (blud'wůd), *n.* Any of various trees with a red wood or red sap, as the logwood.

blood-wort (blud'wėrt), *n.* Any of the plants, with red roots, constituting the family *Hæmodoraceæ,* esp. the redroot, *Gyrotheca tinctoria,* of North America; also, any of various other plants with red roots, leaves, etc., as the bloodroot, *Sanguinaria canadensis,* or the dock, *Rumex sanguineus,* or the hawkweed, *Hieracium venosum.*

blood-y (blud'i), *a.;* compar. *bloodier,* superl. *bloodiest.* [AS. *blōdig.*] Of, like, or stained with blood; bleeding; blood-red; seeking or involving bloodshed; bloodthirsty; sanguinary; also, a vague term of vituperation often used merely for emphasis (low slang, chiefly Eng.: see *bloody, adv.*).—**blood'y,** *adv.* [First recorded in the phrase *bloody drunk,* possibly referring to the 17th century *bloods,* or men of fashion.] Exceedingly; very. [Low slang, chiefly Eng.] —**blood'y,** *v. t.; bloodied, bloodying.* To stain with blood. —**blood'y=mind'ed,** *a.* Bloodthirsty.

bloom[1] (blöm), *n.* [Icel. *blōm* = G. *blume,* flower; akin to E. *blow*[2].] The flower of a plant; a blossom; flowers collectively; the state of blossoming or flowering; a flourishing or the most flourishing state, as of beauty or vigor; freshness; the rosy hue of the cheek; flush; a powdery deposit or coating, as on the surface of certain fruits; any similar surface coating or appearance; the fluorescence of petroleum, etc.; any of certain minerals (as, cobalt *bloom,* a mineral containing cobalt and arsenic, usually of a rose-red color, and often occurring as a pulverulent incrustation).—**bloom**[1], *v.* **I.** *intr.* To produce blooms or blossoms; flower; be in a state of healthful beauty or vigor; flourish; glow with a warm color. **II.** *tr.* To cause to blossom; also, to impart a bloom or rosy hue to (as, "Barred clouds *bloom* the soft-dying day": Keats's "Ode to Autumn").

bloom[2] (blöm), *n.* [AS. *blōma.*] A roughly prepared (oblong) mass of wrought-iron, usually made by squeezing or hammering one of the ball-like pasty masses of iron obtained by puddling; any of various other masses of iron or steel, esp. a thick bar of steel obtained by hammering or rolling an ingot.

bloom-er (blö'mėr). **I.** *a.* [Orig. *cap.*] Noting or pertaining to a style of dress for women, advocated about 1850 by Mrs. Amelia Bloomer of New York, of which the distinctive features were a short skirt, loose trousers buttoned round the ankle, and a broad-brimmed, low-crowned hat. **II.** *n.* A bloomer dress or costume; a bloomer hat; *pl.,* loose trousers gathered at the knee, worn by women as part of gymnasium, riding, bathing, or other like dress.

bloom-er-y (blö'mėr-i), *n.;* pl. *-ies* (-iz). A bloom-making establishment where the wrought-iron is obtained directly from the ore by a crude primitive process.

bloom-ing (blö'ming), *p. a.* Blossoming; flourishing; glowing as with youthful freshness and vigor: sometimes used as a vague intensive or expletive (slang: as, a *blooming* idiot).—**bloom'ing-ly,** *adv.*

bloom-y (blö'mi), *a.* Blooming; covered with bloom.

blos-som (blos'om), *n.* [AS. *blōstma,* akin to *blōwan,* E. *blow*[2].] The flower of a plant, esp. of a plant producing an edible fruit; also, the state of flowering; bloom.—**blos'som,** *v. i.* To put forth blossoms; bloom.—**blos'som-less,** *a.* Without blossoms.—**blos'som-y,** *a.* Full of blossoms.

blot[1] (blot), *n.* [ME.; origin unknown.] A spot or stain, as of ink or mud; a disfiguring stain or mark; a blemish; any black or dark patch; a stain upon character or reputation; a reproach; imputed stain or disgrace; defamation; also, a striking out, obliterating, or erasing, as in a writing. —**blot**[1], *v.*; *blotted, blotting.* **I.** *tr.* To spot, stain, or bespatter, as with ink or mud; cast a blot upon (reputation, etc.); sully; obliterate with a blot, as writing; cancel; efface; annihilate or destroy; obscure or eclipse; write with blots; cover (paper) with worthless writing (archaic); paint coarsely, or daub; dry with blotting-paper or the like. **II.** *intr.* To make blots; also, to become blotted or stained.

blot[2] (blot), *n.* [Cf. Dan. *blot*, Sw. *blott*, bare.] In *backgammon*, an exposed piece liable to be taken or forfeited; the act of exposing the piece; fig., an exposed or weak point, as in an argument or a course of action.

blotch (bloch), *n.* [Origin obscure: cf. *blot*[1] and *botch*[1].] An inflamed eruption or discolored patch on the skin; any large irregular spot or blot; a daub.—**blotch,** *v. t.* To cover or mark with blotches.—**blotch'y,** *a.* Covered with blotches; blotched.

blot-ter (blot'ėr), *n.* One who or that which blots; something used to absorb superfluous ink, as a piece of blotting-paper; also, a book in which transactions or occurrences, as sales, arrests, etc., are recorded as they take place.

blot-tesque (blo-tesk'), *a.* [See *blot*[1] and *-esque.*] Executed with heavy blot-like touches, as painting.

blot-ting=pa-per (blot'ing-pā″pėr), *n.* A bibulous, unsized paper, used to absorb superfluous ink.

blouse (blouz, F. blöz), *n.* [F.; origin unknown.] A loose upper garment worn by peasants, workmen, and others in France and elsewhere; a loosely fitting outer garment belted in at the waist, worn by the Russians and others; a loosely fitting waist worn by women or children; also, a semifitting coat closing to the neck, worn as part of the undress uniform of the U. S. army.—**blouse,** *v. i.*; *bloused, blousing.* To project or hang loosely, as a blouse over the belt.—**bloused,** *a.* Wearing a blouse; also, full or hanging loosely, as a blouse above the belt.

blow[1] (blō), *n.* [ME. *blaw*: cf. D. *blouwen*, G. *bläuen*, beat with a beetle.] A stroke with the fist, a weapon, etc.; a knock, buffet, or thump; any adverse or offensive stroke; a severe shock or misfortune.

blow[2] (blō), *v.*; pret. *blew*, pp. *blown*, ppr. *blowing.* [AS. *blōwan* = G. *blühen*; akin to L. *florere*, bloom, *flos*, E. *flower.*] **I.** *intr.* To flower; blossom; bloom; open out, as a flower. **II.** *tr.* To cause to bloom.—**blow**[2], *n.* A yield of blossoms (as, "a *blow* of tulips": Addison, in "Tatler," 218); also, the blossoming state; bloom.

blow[3] (blō), *v.*; pret. *blew*, pp. *blown*, ppr. *blowing.* [AS. *blāwan*, blow, = G. *blähen*, blow up, swell; akin to L. *flare*, blow.] **I.** *intr.* To move in a current, as air or wind; be carried by the wind (as, to *blow* over, to pass over or away, as storm-clouds, or, fig., to pass away or be forgotten, as trouble); produce or drive a current of air, as from the mouth or a bellows; puff or pant; sound, as a wind-instrument, under the action of air; spout, as a whale; explode (with *up*); boast (colloq.). **II.** *tr.* To expel or drive (air, smoke, etc.) as in a current; drive air upon; drive or carry by or as by an air-current; sound by a blast of air; clear or empty by forcing air through; swell or puff (*up* or *out*) with or as with air; form or shape (glass, etc.) by inflation; put out of breath; put (*out*), as a light, by a current of air; force or burst (*out, up,* etc.) by explosion; scold (with *up*: colloq.); spend, or spend money on (slang); of flies, to deposit eggs in; in *photog.*, to enlarge (with *up*: colloq.). —**blow**[3], *n.* The act of one who or that which blows; a blast; a gale; the spouting of a whale; brag (colloq.); also, the deposited egg of a fly; also, in *metal.*, the time during which, or that part of a process in which, a blast is used; the operation of making a quantity of steel in a Bessemer converter, or the quantity of metal involved or made. —**blow'er,** *n.* One who or that which blows; a metal cover for an open fireplace, to aid the draft; a machine for forcing air into a furnace, building, mine, etc.

blow=fish (blō'fish), *n.* Any of various fishes capable of inflating the body; also, the wall-eyed pike-perch, *Stizostedion vitreum.*

blow=fly (blō'flī), *n.*; pl. *-flies* (-flīz). Any of various true flies which deposit their eggs or larvæ on flesh or in wounds, etc.

blow=gun (blō'gun), *n.* A long pipe or tube through which arrows, etc., are blown by the breath.

blow-hard (blō'härd), *n.* A boaster; a braggart. [Slang.]

blow=hole (blō'hōl), *n.* Either of two nostrils or spiracles, or a single one, at the top of the head in whales and other cetaceans, through which they breathe; any hole for the passage or escape of air; a hole in the ice to which whales, etc., come to breathe; in *metal.*, a defect in a casting, due to the imprisonment of a bubble of air or gas.

blow-ing (blō'ing), *n.* The act of one who or that which blows; also, a defect in china caused by the development of gas, by the reaction upon one another of the constituents of the glaze, or by a too strong firing.

blown (blōn), *p. a.* Carried or driven by the wind; swollen or puffed up or out; inflated; having the stomach distended by gorging green food, as cattle; put out of breath; fatigued; exhausted; stale, as from exposure to air; flyblown; tainted; unsavory.

blow=out (blō'out), *n.* A sudden or violent escape of air, steam, or the like; a rupture of the casing of an automobile-tire with the consequent bursting of the inner tube; the melting of an electric fuse, usually in a more or less explosive manner; also, a festive celebration (colloq.).

blow-pipe (blō'pīp), *n.* A tube through which a stream of air or gas is forced into a flame to concentrate and increase its heating action; also, a device in which two gases (as oxygen and hydrogen) under pressure are made to form a united current at an orifice, where they are kindled, thus producing an extremely hot flame; also, a blow-gun.

Blowpipes.
a, common blowpipe; *b*, blowpipe with chamber near the jet.

blow=torch (blō'tôrch), *n.* A small portable apparatus which gives an extremely hot gasoline-flame intensified by a blast: used in plumbing, etc.

blow=tube (blō'tūb), *n.* A blow-gun; also, a long iron tube used in glass-blowing to blow the semifluid glass into the required shape or size.

blow-y (blō'i), *a.* Windy.

blowze (blouz), *n.* [Origin unknown.] A beggar wench†; a fat, red-faced, and coarse-looking or untidy woman (now chiefly prov. Eng.); a blowzy condition (prov. Eng.).—**blowzed,** *a.* Blowzy: as, "I don't like to see my daughters trudging up to their pew all *blowzed* and red with walking" (Goldsmith's "Vicar of Wakefield," x.).—**blowz'y,** *a.* Red-faced; high-colored; coarse-looking; untidy.

blub-ber (blub'ėr), *v.* [Prob. imit.] **I.** *intr.* To bubble†; weep, esp. noisily or effusively (used chiefly in sarcasm or ridicule). **II.** *tr.* To disfigure with weeping; also, to utter with blubbering.—**blub'ber,** *n.* A bubble†; also, the fat of whales and other cetaceans, from which train-oil is obtained; also, a medusa; also, the act of blubbering.—**blub'ber=lip,** *n.* A swollen or thick, protruding lip.—**blub'ber=lipped,** *a.*—**blub'ber-y,** *a.* Abounding in or resembling blubber; fat, as a cetacean.

blu-cher (blö'chėr), *n.* [From Field-Marshal von *Blücher* (1742–1819), of the Prussian army.] A kind of strong leather half-boot; also, a shoe in which the vamp is continued up beneath the top, which laps over it from the sides.

bludg-eon (bluj'ọn), *n.* [Origin unknown.] A short, heavy club or weapon, with one end loaded, or thicker and heavier than the other.—**bludg'eon,** *v. t.* To strike or fell with a bludgeon.

blue (blö), *a.*; compar. *bluer*, superl. *bluest.* [OF. *blou, blau* (F. *bleu*); from Teut. (cf. OHG. *blāo*, G. *blau*).] Of a color like or approaching that of the clear sky; azure; cerulean; livid, as from cold or a bruise; depressed in spirits; dismal or unpromising (as, a *blue* outlook); strict or rigid, as in morals; of women, learned or pedantic (see *blue-stocking*); also, noting or pertaining to the south pole of a magnet.—**blue baby,** in *pathol.*, an infant affected with congenital cyanosis.—**blue blood,** aristocratic blood: a phrase of Spanish origin, said to refer to the blueness of the veins of people of fairer complexion than those having an admixture of Moorish or Jewish blood.—**blue devils,** low spirits; also, delirium tremens.—**blue jay.** See *jay.*—**blue laws,** severe or puritanic laws: from an alleged code said to have been adopted in the colonies of Connecticut and New Haven.—**blue mass,** in *phar.*, a preparation of metallic mercury with other ingredients, used for making blue pills.—**blue peter,** *naut.*, a blue flag with a white square in the center, hoisted as a signal for immediate sailing, to recall boats, etc.—**blue pill,** in *phar.*, a pill of blue mass, used as an alterative, cathartic, etc.—**blue ribbon,** a blue ribbon worn as a badge of honor, esp. that worn by members of the Order of the Garter; a member of this order; the greatest distinction or highest place; the first prize; a badge denoting a pledge of abstinence from intoxicating drinks.—**blue vitriol,** sulphate of copper, a compound occurring in large, transparent, deep-blue triclinic crystals: used in calico-printing, fluids for electric batteries, etc.—**blue water,** the deep or open sea.—**blue,** *n.* A blue color; a blue dye or pigment; bluing; something blue, as the sky or the sea; a member of a company, party, army, etc., wearing or having blue as its distinctive color; an athlete representing Cambridge University ('light blue') or Oxford University ('dark blue') in an inter-university contest; a blue-stocking; *pl.*, with *the*, low spirits; despondency.—**into the blue,** into the remote distance; out of sight and knowledge: as, to pass *into the blue.* [A French use.]—**blue,** *v. t.*; *blued, bluing.* To make blue; tinge with bluing.

Blue Peter.

blue-back (blö′bak), *n.* Any of various fishes with a bluish back, as a salmon of Alaska (*Oncorhynchus nerka*), a trout of Maine (*Salvelinus oquassa*), etc.

blue-bell (blö′bel), *n.* Any of various plants with blue bell-shaped flowers, as the harebell, *Campanula rotundifolia* ('bluebell of Scotland'), or a liliaceous plant, *Scilla non-scripta*, of England, or, usually in *pl.*, the lungwort, *Mertensia virginica*, of the U. S.

blue-ber-ry (blö′ber″i), *n.*; pl. *-berries* (-iz). The edible berry, usually bluish in color, of any of various shrubs of the genus *Vaccinium*, or any of these shrubs (some being locally known as *huckleberries*). Cf. *huckleberry.*

blue-bird (blö′bėrd), *n.* Any bird of the genus *Sialia*, comprising small North American passerine song-birds whose prevailing color is blue, esp. *S. sialis*, of the eastern U. S., which appears early in the spring; any of various other birds of which the predominant color is blue.

Common Eastern Bluebird (*Sialia sialis*).

blue=black (blö′blak′), *a.* Of a bluish-black color; of the darkest shade of blue, almost black.

blue-bon-net (blö′bon″et), *n.* A broad, flat bonnet or cap of blue woolen material, formerly much worn in Scotland; also, a person wearing such a bonnet; a Scotchman; also, a bird, the European blue titmouse, *Parus cæruleus*; also, the cornflower, *Centaurea cyanus.*

blue=book (blö′bu̇k), *n.* A British parliamentary or other official publication, bound in a blue cover; an official register of persons holding U. S. government offices; a blank-book with a blue cover, for replies to questions at an examination, as at certain American colleges; a register or directory of persons prominent socially.

blue-bot-tle (blö′bot″l), *n.* The cornflower, *Centaurea cyanus*; any of various plants with blue flowers; also, any of several species of large flies with blue abdomen.

blue-cap (blö′kap), *n.* Same as *bluebonnet* (in all senses).

blue-coat (blö′kōt), *n.* A person who wears a blue coat, esp. as part of a uniform or livery; often, a policeman.—**blue′=coat″ed,** *a.*

blue=curls (blö′kėrlz), *n.* Any plant of the menthaceous genus *Trichostema*, which comprises herbs with flowers varying from blue to pink or (rarely) white, and having long, curved filaments; also, the self-heal, *Prunella vulgaris.*

blue=eyed (blö′īd), *a.* Having eyes with a blue iris.—**blue=eyed grass,** any of numerous plants of the iridaceous genus *Sisyrinchium*, having grass-like leaves and small, usually blue, terminal flowers.

blue-fish (blö′fish), *n.* Any of various bluish or partly blue fishes, esp. *Pomatomus saltatrix*, a common food-fish of the Atlantic coast of the U. S.

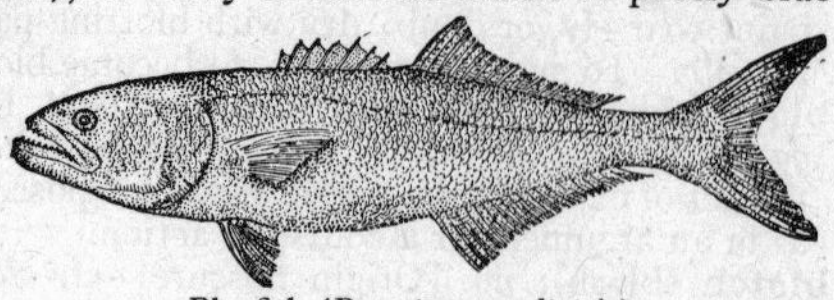
Bluefish (*Pomatomus saltatrix*).

blue-gill (blö′gil), *n.* A large fresh-water sunfish, *Lepomis pallidus*, of the Mississippi valley, much used for food.

blue=grass (blö′gràs), *n.* Any of various grasses with bluish-green stems, esp. species of *Poa*, as *P. pratensis* ('Kentucky blue-grass').

blue=gum (blö′gum), *n.* A tree, *Eucalyptus globulus*, native in Australia. See *eucalyptus.*

blue=hearts (blö′härts), *n.* A perennial American scrophulariaceous herb, *Buchnera americana*, with deep-purple flowers.

blue′ing, *n.* See *bluing.*

blue=jack (blö′jak), *n.* A small oak, *Quercus cinerea* (or *brevifolia*), of the southern U. S.

blue=jack-et (blö′jak″et), *n.* In the naval service, a sailor, often as distinguished from a marine.

blue-ly (blö′li), *adv.* With a blue color.—**blue′ness,** *n.*

blue=nose (blö′nōz), *n.* A native of Nova Scotia. [Colloq.]

blue=pen-cil (blö′pen′sil), *v. t.* To alter, abridge, or cancel with a pencil that makes a blue mark, as in editing a manuscript.

blue=point (blö′point), *n.* A small-sized oyster suitable for serving raw, orig. one from near Blue Point, on the south shore of Long Island.

Kentucky Blue-grass.

blue=print (blö′print), *n.* A print made, as from a mechanical tracing or a photographic negative, on sensitized paper which turns blue on exposure to light and washing in water.

blue=sky (blö′skī′) **law.** A law designed to prevent the sale of fraudulent securities.

blue=stock-ing (blö′stok″ing), *n.* A woman who affects literary or intellectual tastes: orig. applied to certain ladies of London who used to meet, about 1750, in plain dress, for literary or intellectual entertainment.—**blue′=stock″ing-ism,** *n.*

blue=stone (blö′stōn), *n.* Blue vitriol; also, a bluish argillaceous sandstone used for building purposes, flagging, etc.

blu-et (blö′et), *n.* [F. *bluet*, *bleuet*, dim. of *bleu*, blue.] Any of various plants with blue flowers, as the cornflower, *Centaurea cyanus*, or, often in *pl.*, any of various species of houstonia, esp. *Houstonia cærulea.*

blue-weed (blö′wēd), *n.* A bristly boraginaceous weed, *Echium vulgare*, with showy blue flowers, a native of Europe which has been naturalized in the U. S.

blue-wood (blö′wu̇d), *n.* A rhamnaceous shrub or small tree, *Condalia obovata*, of western Texas and northern Mexico, often forming dense chaparral.

bluff[1] (bluf), *v.* [Origin unknown.] **I.** *tr.* To blindfold†; in poker, to deceive by a show of confidence in the strength of one's cards; fig., to mislead or daunt by bold pretense. **II.** *intr.* To make a show of strength and confidence in order to mislead.—**bluff**[1], *n.* The act of bluffing; a bold pretense of strong resources, as for the purpose of daunting an opponent.

bluff[2] (bluf). [Origin obscure: cf. obs. D. *blaf*, flat, broad, as a face.] **I.** *a.* Of a ship, nearly vertical in the bows, or presenting a broad, flattened front; presenting a steep, nearly perpendicular front, as a coast; also, pompous or surly; abrupt or blunt; also, rough and hearty; plain and frank. **II.** *n.* A cliff, headland, etc., with a broad, steep face.—**bluff'ly,** *adv.*—**bluff'ness,** *n.*

blu-ing (blö'ing), *n.* A substance used to give a blue color or tinge, esp. in laundering.

blu-ish (blö'ish), *a.* Somewhat blue; tending to blue.—**blu'ish-ness,** *n.*

blun-der (blun'dėr), *v.* [ME. *blundren*, *blondren*; perhaps akin to *blend*.] **I.** *tr.* To mix up†, confuse†, or muddle†; do clumsily and wrong; bungle; also, to blurt out. **II.** *intr.* To move or proceed blindly and clumsily; flounder; also, to make a stupid or gross mistake; bungle.—**blun'der,** *n.* Confusion†; a stupid or gross mistake.

blun-der-buss (blun'dėr-bus), *n.* [Corruption of D. *donderbus*, 'thunder box.'] An obsolete short gun with a large bore and funnel-shaped muzzle, loaded with a number of balls or slugs, and used at a limited range without exact aim; also, a blunderhead.

Blunderbuss. — Armory, Tower of London.

blun-der-er (blun'dėr-ėr), *n.* One who blunders.

blun-der-head (blun'dėr-hed), *n.* A blundering, stupid person.

blun-der-ing (blun'dėr-ing), *p. a.* That blunders; bungling; clumsy.—**blun'der-ing-ly,** *adv.*

blunge (blunj), *v. t.*; *blunged, blunging.* [Origin obscure.] To mix (clay or the like) with water.—**blun'ger,** *n.* A shovel-like device, or a machine, for mixing or blunging clay or the like.

blunt (blunt). [ME.; origin unknown.] **I.** *a.* Obtuse, thick, or dull, as an angle or point; having an obtuse, thick, or dull edge or point, as a knife or sword; not sharp; dull, as the sight or other faculties; slow in perception or understanding; rude or unrefined (archaic); harsh† or unfeeling†; also, abrupt in manner or speech; unceremonious; plain-spoken. **II.** *n.* A needle shorter and less sharply pointed than a sharp; also, ready money (slang).—**blunt,** *v. t.* or *i.* To make or become blunt or less sharp; dull.—**blunt'ly,** *adv.*—**blunt'ness,** *n.*

blur (blėr), *v.*; *blurred, blurring.* [Origin uncertain; perhaps connected with *blear*.] **I.** *tr.* To obscure or sully as by smearing with ink, etc.; stain or blemish; obscure by making confused in form or outline; render indistinct; dim the perception or susceptibility of; make dull or insensible to impression. **II.** *intr.* To make blurs; also, to become blurred.—**blur,** *n.* A smudge or smear, such as that made by brushing writing before it is dry; a blot; a stain; also, a blurred condition; indistinctness.—**blur'ry,** *a.* Full of blurs; indistinct.

blurb (blėrb), *n.* [A made word.] An effusively laudatory statement or announcement concerning a book or other writing or an author, designed to win public favor; any public announcement of similar character. [Colloq.]

blurt (blėrt), *v. t.* [Appar. imit.] To utter abruptly, impulsively, or inadvertently: usually with *out.*—**blurt,** *n.* A blurting out of something; an abrupt or impulsive utterance.

blush (blush), *v.* [ME. *bluschen*: cf. AS. *blyscan*, glow.] **I.** *intr.* To shine†; glance†; redden as from embarrassment or shame; feel shame (*for*, etc.); of the sky, flowers, etc., to become rosy. **II.** *tr.* To make red; flush; also, to make known by a blush or flush.—**blush,** *n.* A glance or glimpse (as, at first *blush*); also, a reddening, as of the face; a flush; also, a rosy glow or hue.—**blush'er,** *n.*—**blush'ful,** *a.* Given to blushing; rosy.—**blush'ing-ly,** *adv.*—**blush'less,** *a.* Without a blush; unblushing; shameless.

blus-ter (blus'tėr), *v.* [Prob. akin to *blast* and *blow*[3].] **I.** *intr.* To blow boisterously, as the wind; roar and be tumultuous; talk in a bullying way; utter loud, empty threats or protests; swagger. **II.** *tr.* To utter with noise and violence; compel or force by blustering.—**blus'ter,** *n.* Boisterous noise and violence, as of the wind; a boisterous blast; a noisy commotion; a violent disturbance; noisy, empty menaces or protests; inflated talk; swaggering.—**blus'ter-er,** *n.*—**blus'ter-ing-ly,** *adv.*—**blus'ter-ous, blus'ter-y,** *a.* Blustering; tempestuous; bullying; truculent.

bo (bō), *interj.* An exclamation used to startle.

bo-a (bō'ą), *n.* [L. *boa*, *bova*, kind of serpent.] Any of various large, nonvenomous tropical serpents of the family *Boidæ*, notable for their power of constriction, as *Boa constrictor*, a common American species; any similar large serpent; also, a long, snake-shaped wrap of silk, feathers, or other material, worn about the neck by women.—**bo'a=con-stric'tor,** *n.* Any large serpent of the boa kind.

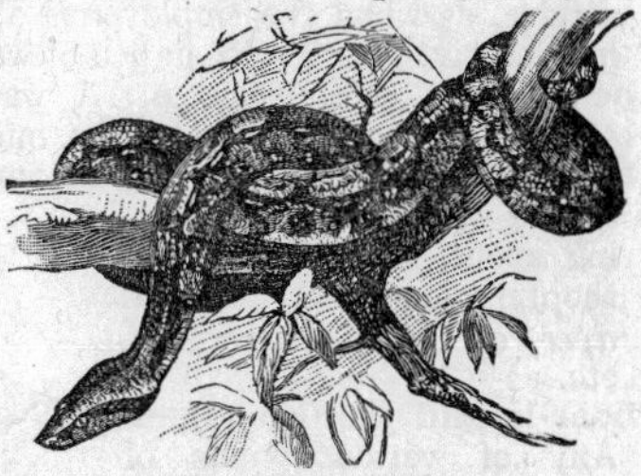
Boa (*B. constrictor*).

Bo-a-ner-ges (bō-ą-nėr'jēz), *n.* [From the (Aramaic) surname given by Christ to James and John, explained as meaning "sons of thunder" (Mark, iii. 17).] A vociferous preacher or orator.

boar (bōr), *n.* [AS. *bār*.] The uncastrated male of swine, wild or tame; also, a wild old-world species of swine, *Sus scrofa* ('wild boar'), the supposed original of most of the domestic hogs. See *swine*.

Wild Boar (*Sus scrofa*).

board (bōrd), *n.* [AS. *bord*, board, plank, and *bord*, side: two orig. distinct Teut. words.] A piece of timber sawed thin, and of considerable length and breadth compared with the thickness; *pl.*, the stage of a theater; *sing.*, a flat slab or surface of wood or other material used for a specific purpose (as, a black*board*; a bulletin-*board*; an ironing-*board*); a tablet or frame on which games are played (as, a checker-*board*; a chess-*board*); a kind of thick, stiff paper; pasteboard; a table, esp. to serve food on; food served on a table; daily meals, esp. as provided for pay; the condition of one boarding in another's house; a table at which a council is held; a meeting at such a table; the persons holding the meeting; a body of persons having the management or direction of some business (as, a *board* of trade; a *board* of health; a school-*board*); also, the border or edge of anything (cf. *seaboard*); *naut.*, the side of a ship (cf. *overboard* and *starboard*); also, the course a ship sails on one tack; a leg.—**board on board, board and board,** side by side, as ships.—**by the board,** over the ship's side; overboard. Also fig.—**on board,** on a ship, railroad-car, or other conveyance; aboard.—**board,** *v.* **I.** *tr.* To cover, close, inclose, lay, or furnish with boards; place (a card) on the board or table in a game; furnish with food, or with food and lodging, esp. for pay; place at board; also, to come up alongside of (a ship), as to attack or to go on board; go on board of or enter (a ship, train, etc.); approach† or accost†. **II.** *intr.* To take one's meals, or be supplied with food and lodging, in another's house at a fixed price.—**board'er,** *n.* One who boards; esp., one who has his meals, or both meals and lodging, in the house of another for pay.

board=foot (bōrd'fůt), *n.* A unit of measure equal to the cubic contents of a board one foot square and one inch thick (144 cubic inches): used in measuring logs and lumber.

board-ing (bōr'ding), *n.* The act of one that boards; also, boards collectively; a structure of boards, as a fence or floor.—**board'ing=house,** *n.* A house at which board, or a regular service of meals, is furnished, often with lodging.—**board'ing=school,** *n.* A school at which board and lodging are furnished for the pupils.

board=meas-ure (bōrd′mezh″ūr), *n.* A system of cubic measure in which the unit is the board-foot.
board=rule (bōrd′röl), *n.* A rule or measuring device having scales for finding the cubic contents of a board without calculation.
board=wa-ges (bōrd′wā′jez), *n. pl.* or *sing.* Money allowed to servants in lieu of board; also, low wages, nominally to pay for board, given to servants during intermission of service, as when the employer is absent; also, board and lodging given for service in lieu of wages in money.
board-walk (bōrd′wâk), *n.* A walk or promenade constructed of boards or planks, esp. one along a beach.
boar=fish (bōr′fish), *n.* Any of various fishes of different genera which have a projecting snout, as a small acanthopterygian fish, *Capros aper*, of the Mediterranean, etc.

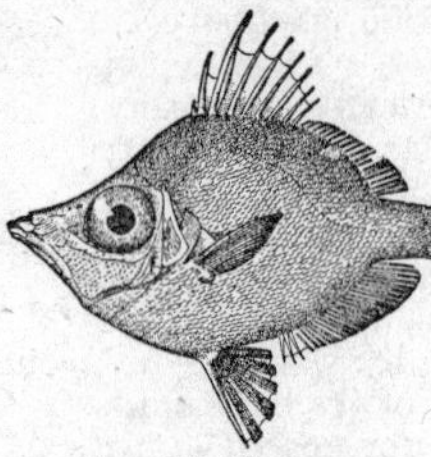
Boar-fish (*Capros aper*).

boar-hound (bōr′hound), *n.* Any of various kinds of large dogs used orig. for hunting wild boars, esp. a dog of a German breed ('German boarhound') or a great Dane.
boar-ish (bōr′ish), *a.* Boar-like; swinish; brutal.
boast[1] (bōst), *v. t.* [Origin unknown.] To dress or shape (stone, etc.) roughly.
boast[2] (bōst), *v.* [ME. *bosten*; origin unknown.] **I.** *intr.* To threaten†; also, to speak vaingloriously or ostentatiously; vaunt; brag; speak with pride (*of*); also, to have possession (*of*). **II.** *tr.* To threaten†; also, to speak of vaingloriously or ostentatiously; brag of; pride (one's self); also, to exult in possessing; be the proud possessor of.—**boast**[2], *n.* Loud noise†; also, threatening†; also, vainglorious or ostentatious speech; bragging; also, a cause of boasting; an occasion of pride or exultation.—**boast′er,** *n.*—**boast′ful,** *a.* Given to or characterized by boasting.—**boast′ful-ly,** *adv.*—**boast′ful-ness,** *n.*—**boast′ing-ly,** *adv.*
boat (bōt), *n.* [AS. *bāt* = Icel. *beit.*] A small (open) vessel for traveling on the surface of the water, propelled by oars, sail, motor, or the like; any vessel for navigation; a ship; also, a dish or other object resembling a boat in shape. —**to be in the same boat,** to be in the same (esp. unfortunate) position or circumstances.—**boat,** *v.* **I.** *tr.* To place or transport in a boat. **II.** *intr.* To go in a boat; also, to operate a boat.—**boat′a-ble,** *a.* Navigable by boat.—**boat-age** (bō′tạj), *n.* Carriage by boat, or a charge made for it.—**boat′bill,** *n.* A bird of the genus *Cancroma*, of the heron family, which is regarded by many authorities as containing the single species *C. cochlearia*, a tropical American bird having a large, broad bill shaped somewhat like an inverted boat. —**boat′er,** *n.*—**boat′-ful** (-fůl), *n.*; pl. *-fuls.*—**boat′=hook,** *n.* A metal hook fixed to a pole, for pulling or pushing a boat.—**boat′=house,** *n.* A house or shed for sheltering boats.—**boat′ing,** *n.* The act or practice of rowing or sailing, esp. as a means of exercise or amusement.—**boat′-man** (-mạn), *n.*; pl. *-men.* A man who manages a boat. —**boat′man-ship,** *n.* The art or skill of a boatman.—**boat-swain** (bōt′swān, naut. bō′sn), *n.* A subordinate officer or warrant-officer on a war-ship, or a seaman on a merchant vessel, in charge of rigging, anchors, cables, etc.; also, a name for various birds, as skuas and tropic-birds.

Boatbill (*Cancroma cochlearia*).

bob[1] (bob), *n.* [ME. *bobbe*, bunch; origin obscure.] A bunch or cluster, as of flowers or fruit (now Sc. and prov. Eng.); a small dangling or terminal object, as the weight on a pendulum or a plumb-line; a knob or knot of something, as hair; a knot of worms, rags, or the like, on a string, used in angling; a float for a fishing-line; a short sled (see *bobsled*); a short jerky motion; a curtsy; a set of changes in bell-ringing; a shilling (slang, Eng.); also, a very young calf (hence *bob veal*, veal too immature for use as food).—**bob**[1], *v.*; *bobbed, bobbing.* **I.** *tr.* To move jerkily; also, to cut short; dock. **II.** *intr.* To swing, toss, or play loosely or with jerks; make a jerky bow; also, to fish with a bob, as for eels.
bob[2] (bob), *v. t.*; *bobbed, bobbing.* [ME. *bobben*; perhaps imit.] To strike; tap; rap. [Now prov.]—**bob**[2], *n.* A stroke; a tap; a rap. [Now prov.]
bob[3] (bob), *v. t.*; *bobbed, bobbing.* [ME. *bobben*, < OF. *bober.*] To delude, trick, or cheat (obs. or prov. Eng.); get by trickery†; mock† or deride†.—**bob**[3]†, *n.* A trick; a mock; a taunt.
Bob-a-dil (bob′ạ-dil), *n.* [From *Bobadil*, a boastful character in Ben Jonson's play, "Every Man in His Humour."] A blustering braggart.
bob-ber-y (bob′ėr-i), *n.*; pl. *-ies* (-iz). [Prob. orig. Anglo-Ind., from Hind.] A hubbub; a disturbance. [Slang, chiefly Eng.]
bob-bin (bob′in), *n.* [F. *bobine.*] A reel or spool for holding thread, as for use in lace-making; a reel, cylinder, or spool upon which yarn or thread is wound, as used in spinning, weaving, machine-sewing, etc.; a reel round which wire is wound in certain electrical devices.
bob-bi-net (bob-i-net′ or bob′i-net), *n.* [Orig. *bobbin-net.*] A machine-made cotton netting.
bob-bish (bob′ish), *a.* [Cf. *bob*[1].] In good health and spirits; lively; well: as, "The cows is well, and the boys is *bobbish*" (Dickens's "Nicholas Nickleby," lvii.). [Prov. Eng. or slang.]
bob-ble (bob′l), *v. i.*; *-bled, -bling.* [Freq. of *bob*[1].] To move with a continual bobbing.—**bob′ble,** *n.* A bobbing movement.
bob-by (bob′i), *n.*; pl. *bobbies* (-iz). [From *Bobby*, for *Robert*, here Sir Robert Peel (1788–1850), who improved the police system of London: cf. *peeler*[2].] A policeman. [Slang, Eng.]
bob-cat (bob′kat), *n.* A lynx, *Lynx rufus*, the common wildcat of the eastern U. S., or some allied species.
bo-bèche (bǫ-bāsh′), *n.* [F.] A disk or shallow cup of glass, etc., with a central perforation, placed about a candle at the base to catch melted wax, etc.
bob-o-link (bob′ǫ-lingk), *n.* [Imit. of its note.] A common American passerine song-bird, *Dolichonyx oryzivorus*: in its fat season much esteemed for food. Also called *reed-bird* and *rice-bird.*

Bobolink.

bob=sled (bob′sled), *n.* [See *bob*[1].] A sled formed of two short sleds, one behind the other, with a coupling, plank, etc., between them; either of the short sleds. Similarly **bob′=sleigh.**
bob-stay (bob′stā), *n.* *Naut.*, a rope or chain extending from the cutwater to the outer end of the bowsprit.
bob-tail (bob′tāl). **I.** *n.* A short or docked tail; also, a bobtailed animal. Also fig. **II.** *a.* Bobtailed; cut short.—**bob′tail,** *v. t.* To cut short the tail of; dock; curtail.—**bob′tailed,** *a.* Having the tail short or docked; curtailed.
bob=white (bob′hwīt′), *n.* [Imit. of its note.] The common American quail, *Colinus virginianus.*
boche (bōsh, F. bosh). [F.; variously explained, but by many said to be a shortened form of F. *caboche*, head, pate, noddle, < L. *caput*, head.] [Also *cap.*] **I.** *n.* A term applied colloquially and more or less opprobriously to a German: first brought into general French use during the German invasion of France in 1914. **II.** *a.* Of or pertaining to a boche; characteristic of the boches.—**boch′ism,** *n.*
bock=beer (bok′bēr), *n.* [G. *bockbier*, for *Eimbecker bier*, beer of Eimbeck, or Einbeck, in Prussia.] A strong, dark beer, commonly drunk in the spring. Also called *bock.*

bod-dle (bod′l), *n.* See *bodle.*
bode[1] (bōd). Preterit of *bide.*
bode[2] (bōd), *n.* [AS. *boda,* < *bēodan,* announce: see *bid.*] A messenger; a herald. [Archaic.]—**bode**[2], *v.*; *boded, boding.* [AS. *bodian,* announce, proclaim, foretell, < *boda.*] **I.** *tr.* To foretell or predict (archaic); also, to foretoken or portend; also, to have a presentiment of. **II.** *intr.* To give presage; promise (*well* or *ill*); augur.—**bode′ful,** *a.* Boding; ominous.
bo-de-ga (bō-dā′gä), *n.* [Sp.] A wine-cellar or wine-shop.
bode-ment (bōd′ment), *n.* A boding or prediction (as, "This foolish, dreaming, superstitious girl Makes all these *bodements*": Shakspere's "Troilus and Cressida," v. 3. 80); also, an omen or presage; also, a foreboding. [Archaic.]
bod-ice (bod′is), *n.* [For *bodies,* pl. of *body.*] Stays† or a corset†; a woman's laced outer garment covering the waist and bust (common in peasant dress); a woman's fitted waist or dress-body.
bod-ied (bod′id), *a.* Having a body.
bod-i-less (bod′i-les), *a.* Having no body; incorporeal.
bod-i-ly (bod′i-li). **I.** *a.* Of or belonging to the body; corporeal; physical. **II.** *adv.* With respect to the body; in the flesh; corporeally; also, as a whole; entirely.
bod-ing (bō′ding), *p. a.* That bodes; presaging; ominous; foreboding.—**bod′ing-ly,** *adv.*
bod-kin (bod′kin), *n.* [ME. *boydekyn;* origin unknown.] A dagger†; a small pointed instrument for piercing holes in cloth, etc.; a blunt needle-like instrument for drawing tape, cord, etc., through a loop, hem, or the like; a long pin-shaped instrument used by women to fasten up the hair; a printers' tool for picking out letters in making corrections in type which has been set; also, a third person sitting between two others, as in a carriage, on a seat suited for two only (as, "He's too big to travel *bodkin* between you and me": Thackeray's "Vanity Fair," xl.).
bod-le (bod′l), *n.* [Said to be < *Bothwell,* name of a mint-master.] An old Scotch copper coin, orig. worth one sixth of an English penny; hence, any very small coin. [Sc.]

Obverse. Reverse.
Bodle of Charles II.—British Museum.

bod-y (bod′i), *n.*; pl. *bodies* (-iz). [AS. *bodig* = OHG. *botah,* MHG *botech,* body.] The physical structure or material organized substance of man or any animal; the material frame of a human being or an animal; also, the trunk or main mass of a thing; the bulk, or main portion; also, an organized or collective whole; an assemblage of persons or things; a systematic collection; a code, as of laws; also, any material thing; a separate portion of matter; a mass; a kind or form of matter; matter; consistence, density, or substance; substantial quality; also, a human being; a person; also, that part of a dress which covers the trunk, esp. above the waist; in *geom.,* a figure having the three dimensions, length, breadth, and thickness; a solid.—**body corporate,** a legally incorporated body of persons; a corporation.—**body politic,** a people as forming a political body under an organized government.—**bod′y,** *v. t.*; *bodied, bodying.* To invest with or as with a body; embody; set (*forth*) in bodily form or outward reality.—**bod′y=cav″i-ty,** *n.* In *zoöl., anat.,* etc., the general or common cavity of the body, as distinguished from special cavities or those of particular organs.—**bod′y=col″or,** *n.* A pigment possessing body or a high degree of consistence, substance, and covering power; a color rendered opaque by an admixture of white.—**bod′y=guard,** *n.* A personal or private guard, as for a sovereign; a retinue or escort.—**bod′y=snatch″er,** *n.* One who steals dead bodies, as for use in dissecting.—**bod′y=snatch″ing,** *n.*
Bœ-o-tian (bē-ō′shian). **I.** *a.* Pertaining to Bœotia, a district of ancient Greece, whose inhabitants were proverbial for dullness; hence, dull; stupid. **II.** *n.* A native of Bœotia; a stupid person.
Boer (bör). [D. *boer,* peasant, countryman, = E. *boor.*] **I.** *n.* A South African Dutch colonist or farmer; an inhabitant of either of the former Dutch republics of South Africa. **II.** *a.* Of or pertaining to the Boers: as, the *Boer* War (a war between Great Britain and the Transvaal, or South African Republic, 1880–81; also, esp., a war between Great Britain on the one side and the Transvaal and the Orange Free State on the other, 1899–1902).
bog (bog), *n.* [Ir. and Gael. *bog,* soft.] A piece of wet, spongy ground, with soil composed mainly of decayed vegetable matter; a moss; a quagmire; a marsh; also, ground of this kind; boggy soil.—**bog,** *v. t.* or *i.*; *bogged, bogging.* To sink or stick in or as in a bog.—**bog′=as′pho-del,** *n.* Either of two melanthiaceous plants, *Abama ossifraga,* of Europe, and *A. americana,* of the U. S., growing in boggy places, and resembling the true asphodel.—**bog′=bean,** *n.* Same as *buck-bean.*—**bog′ber″ry,** *n.* The European cranberry.
bo-gey[1] (bō′gi), *n.* [See *bogy*[1].] A bogy; a bugbear; in *golf,* the score of 'Colonel Bogey.'—**Colonel Bogey,** in *golf,* an imaginary player with an assigned score against which other players must contend.
bo-gey[2] (bō′gi), *n.* See *bogie*[2].
bog-gle[1] (bog′l), *n.* Variant of *bogle.* [Prov. Eng.]
bog-gle[2] (bog′l), *v.*; *-gled, -gling.* [Prob. < *boggle*[1], with sense in part due to *bungle.*] **I.** *intr.* To start with fright; shy, as a horse; hold back, hesitate, or demur; quibble or equivocate; also, to make clumsy attempts; bungle. **II** *tr.* To frighten†; embarrass or perplex; also, to bungle or botch.—**bog′gle**[2], *n.* A boggling; a bungle.—**bog′gler,** *n.*—**bog′gling-ly,** *adv.*
bog-gy (bog′i), *a.*; compar. *boggier,* superl. *boggiest.* Bog-like; marshy; swampy.
bo-gie[1] (bō′gi), *n.* See *bogy*[1].
bo-gie[2] (bō′gi), *n.* [Origin unknown.] A low, strongly built truck or cart; also, a pivoted truck for carrying one end of a locomotive or of a railroad-carriage.
bo-gle (bō′gl), *n.* [Orig. Sc.; prob. from Celtic: cf. *bogy*[1], *bug*[2].] A bogy or a specter (as, "Glow'ring round wi' prudent cares, Lest *bogles* catch him unawares": Burns's "Tam o' Shanter," 86); also, a bugbear.
bog=oak (bog′ōk), *n.* Oak (or other wood) found preserved in bogs.
bog=or-chis (bog′ôr″kis), *n.* A small old-world orchis, *Malaxis paludosa,* with inconspicuous flowers, growing in boggy places.
bog=ore (bog′ōr), *n.* A variety of limonite found in bogs or water.
bog=trot-ter (bog′trot″ėr), *n.* An Irish peasant.
bo-gus (bō′gus). [Origin obscure.] **I.**† *n.* An apparatus for coining counterfeit money. **II.** *a.* Counterfeit; spurious; sham.
bog=wood (bog′wu̇d), *n.* Bog-oak.
bo-gy[1] (bō′gi), *n.*; pl. *-gies* (-giz). [Cf. *bogle* and *bug*[2].] A fearsome specter; a hobgoblin; also, a bugbear; any object of dread; specif. [*cap.*], the devil (often called *old Bogy*).
bo-gy[2] (bō′gi), *n.* See *bogie*[2].
bo-hea (bō-hē′), *n.* [From the *Wu-yi* Hills, in Fu-kien province, China.] Tea, esp. an inferior black China tea.
Bo-he-mi-a (bō-hē′mi-ä), *n.* A country or region of central Europe; also, Gipsies collectively (formerly thought to come from Bohemia); also, a place where people, esp. artists or writers, lead a free, unconventional life; the community of such persons.—**Bo-he′mi-an. I.** *n.* A native of Bohemia; also, the (Slavic) language of Bohemia; Czech; also, a Gipsy; also [*cap.* or *l. c.*], any person, esp. an artist or a writer, who leads a free, unconventional life. **II.** *a.* Of or pertaining to Bohemia; [*cap.* or *l. c.*] pertaining to or characteristic of social Bohemians; free from social restraints; unconventional.—**Bo-he′mi-an-ism,** *n.*
bo-hunk (bō′hungk), *n.* A Bohemian or Czech. See Čapek's "Čechs in America," x. [Slang, U. S.]
boil[1] (boil), *n.* [AS. *bȳle* = G. *beule.*] A painful suppurating inflammatory sore forming a central core, caused by microbic infection; a furuncle.
boil[2] (boil), *v.* [OF. *buillir* (F. *bouillir*), < L. *bullire,* < *bulla,* bubble.] **I.** *intr.* To bubble up and emit vapor, as a liquid under the action of heat; undergo cooking or other treatment in liquid so heated; move in commotion or agitation; seethe; be violently agitated or incensed. **II.** *tr.* To cause (liquid) to boil; cook or treat in a boiling liquid; make by such cooking or treatment.—**boil**[2], *n.* The act

or state of boiling; the condition of being at the boiling-point.—**boil′er,** *n.* One who or that which boils; a vessel for boiling something in; a strong metallic structure in which steam is generated, as for heating purposes or for driving engines; a device in which water is heated; a tank for storing hot water; also, a fowl, vegetable, etc., suitable for boiling.—**boil′er-y,** *n.*; pl. *-ies* (-iz). A place, establishment, or apparatus for boiling.—**boil′ing=point,** *n.* The temperature at which a liquid boils: as, the *boiling-point* of water (212° F., 100° C., or 80° R., at the sea-level).

bois (bwo), *n.* [F.: see *bush*[1].] A wood; a tract of woodland; also, wood or timber.

bois-ter-ous (bois′tėr-us), *a.* [ME. *boistrous,* earlier *boistous;* origin unknown.] Coarse† or heavy†; rough; turbulent; tumultuous; rudely vigorous; roughly or noisily exuberant in spirits.—**bois′ter-ous-ly,** *adv.*—**bois′ter-ous-ness,** *n.*

bo-lar (bō′lạr), *a.* Of, pertaining to, or of the nature of bole or clay.

bo-las (bō′lạs), *n. pl.* or *sing.* [Sp., pl. of *bola,* ball.] A weapon of war and the chase, used by South American Indians and others, consisting of balls of stone or metal attached to the ends of a thong or connected thongs: thrown so as to wind about an object aimed at.

bold (bōld), *a.* [AS. *bald, beald,* = D. *boud,* akin to G. *bald,* soon.] Fearless; courageous; exhibiting or requiring courage; also, audacious or forward; impudent; using or showing freedom or license; also, striking or conspicuous; steep or bluff, as a shore; deep close to the shore, as water; also, confident† or certain†.—**bold′=face,** *n.* An impudent person; in *printing,* bold-faced type, such as that used for headings of entries in this dictionary. See *type.*—**bold′=faced,** *a.* Having a bold face; impudent; of type, having thick lines that make a heavy impression.—**bold′ly,** *adv.*—**bold′ness,** *n.*

bole[1] (bōl), *n.* [Icel. *bolr.*] The stem or trunk of a tree; something similar to this in shape, as a pillar.

bole[2] (bōl), *n.* [LL. *bolus,* < Gr. βῶλος, clod, lump.] Any one of a class of soft, more or less brittle, unctuous clays varying from yellow or red to nearly black and affording pigments.

bole[3] (bōl), *n.* [Origin unknown.] A small recess in the wall of a room, for holding articles; also, a small opening in a wall, for letting in light or air. [Sc.]

bo-lec-tion (bọ-lek′shọn), *n.* [Origin unknown.] In *arch.,* a molding which projects beyond the surface of the work which it decorates.

bo-le-ro (bọ-lā′rō), *n.*; pl. *-ros* (-rōz). [Sp.] A lively Spanish dance, or the music for it; also, a short jacket ending above or at the waist-line.

bo-lide (bō′lid or -līd, or bol′id), *n.* [F. *bolide,* < L. *bolis* (*bolid-*), < Gr. βολίς (βολιδ-), missile, < βάλλειν, throw.] A large, brilliant meteor, esp. one that explodes.

Bo-liv-i-an (bọ-liv′i-ạn). **I.** *a.* Of or pertaining to Bolivia, in South America. **II.** *n.* A native or inhabitant of Bolivia.

boll[1] (bōl), *n.* [AS. *bolla,* bowl: cf. *bowl*[1].] A bowl†; also, a rounded seed-vessel or pod of a plant, as of flax or cotton.—**boll**[1], *v. i.* To form into or produce bolls.

boll[2] (bōl), *n.* [Appar. < Icel. *bolli,* bowl, = AS. *bolla,* E. *boll*[1].] A measure for grain, etc., of varying capacity, but generally containing about six bushels. [Sc. and north. Eng.]

Bol-land-ist (bol′ạn-dist), *n.* Any of a series of Jesuit editors, beginning with Jean Bolland (1596–1665), engaged in the publication of the "Acta Sanctorum," a well-known collection of lives of the saints.

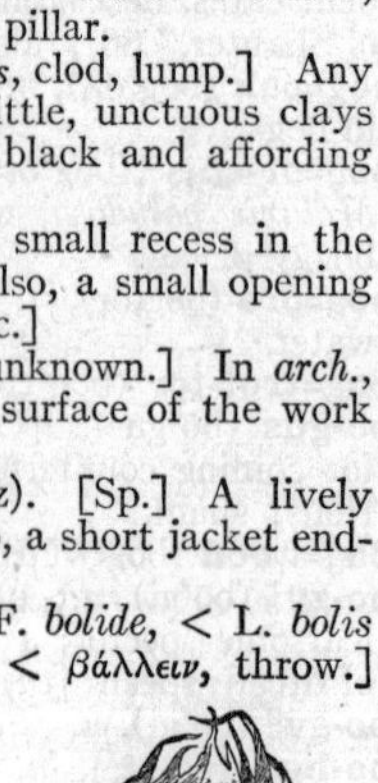

Cotton-bolls.
a, immature boll; *b,* mature and opened boll.

bol-lard (bol′ạrd), *n.* [Perhaps < *bole*[1].] *Naut.,* a post on which hawsers are made fast.

boll=wee-vil (bōl′wē″vl), *n.* A weevil, *Anthonomus grandis,* that attacks the bolls of cotton.

boll=worm (bōl′wėrm), *n.* The larva of a noctuid moth, *Heliothis armigera,* destructive to the bolls of cotton and to other plants.

bo-lo (bō′lō), *n.*; pl. *-los* (-lōz). [Native name.] A large, heavy knife resembling a machete, used in the Philippine Islands.

Bolo.

Bo-lo-gna (bọ-lō′nä, It. bō-lō′nyä) **sau′sage.** [From *Bologna,* city and province of northern Italy.] A large-sized variety of sausage containing a mixture of meats.

bo-lo-graph (bō′lọ-gräf), *n.* [Gr. βολή, a throw, ray: see *-graph.*] A record made by a bolometer.—**bo-lo-graph′ic** (-graf′ik), *a.*

bo-lom-e-ter (bọ-lom′e-tėr), *n.* [Gr. βολή, a throw, ray: see *-meter.*] An electrical instrument for measuring minute amounts of radiant heat.—**bo-lo-met-ric** (bō-lọ-met′rik), *a.*

Bol-she-vik (bol′she-vēk, Russ. bol-she-vēk′). [Russ., < *bolshe,* greater, larger, more: with allusion to the majority (Russ. *bolshinstvo*) or larger faction of the party.] **I.** *n.*; pl. *Bolsheviki* (bōl-she-vē′kẹ, Russ. bol-she-vē-kē′) or *-viks* (-vēks). In Russian politics, orig. (from 1903), a member of the more radical faction (the Bolsheviki) of the Social Democratic party, which demanded the carrying out of the whole socialistic program at once, including control of the means of production by the workers and distribution of the land among the peasants, by means of a revolution which should place the control of the government in the hands of the proletariat (as opposed to the Mensheviki, or less radical faction of the same party, which sought the gradual attainment of socialistic ends through measures suited to the existing conditions, and also as opposed to the Social Revolutionaries, or members of the Social Revolutionary party, the other of the two chief Russian socialistic parties); in later use, a member of the ultraradical communist party in control of Russia after the overthrow, on Nov. 7, 1917, by the former Bolsheviki group and new adherents, of the provisional revolutionary government under the moderate socialist Kerenski (the Kerenski government having come into power after the overthrowing of the Czar on March 15, 1917, and the taking over of the government by the Duma group and allied moderate socialist groups); hence [sometimes *l. c.*], a member of an ultraradical party or group in any country whose aims include the control of property and government by the working classes, effected by means of armed revolution or otherwise; one advocating a proposed international order to consist of a federation of national governments throughout the world, under the control of the working classes; in general, an ultraradical socialist; any political ultraradical. **II.** *a.* Of, pertaining to, or suggestive of the Bolsheviki or their doctrines or methods.—**Bol′she-vik-ism,** *n.* Same as *Bolshevism.*—**Bol-she-vism** (bol′she-vizm), *n.* The doctrines, methods, or procedure of the Bolsheviki (see *Bolshevik, n.*); [sometimes *l. c.*] the principles or practices of ultraradical socialists or political ultraradicals generally.—**Bol′she-vist** (-vist). **I.** *n.* A follower or advocate of the doctrines or methods of the Bolsheviki; a Bolshevik; in general [sometimes *l. c.*], an ultraradical socialist; any political ultraradical. **II.** *a.* Bolshevistic.—**Bol-she-vis′tic,** *a.* Pertaining to or characteristic or suggestive of Bolshevists or Bolshevism.—**Bol-she-vis′ti-cal-ly,** *adv.*—**Bol′she-vize** (-vīz), *v.*; *-vized, -vizing.* **I.** *tr.* To render Bolshevik or Bolshevistic; bring under the influence or domination of Bolshevists. **II.** *intr.* To become Bolshevik or Bolshevistic; act like a Bolshevik.—**Bol″she-vi-za′tion** (-vi-zā′shọn), *n.*

bol-ster (bōl′stėr), *n.* [AS. *bolster* = G. *polster.*] A pillow, esp. a long under-pillow for a bed; something resembling or suggesting this in form or use; a cushion or pad; a supporting piece in a structure or apparatus.—**bol′ster,** *v. t.* To support with or as with a bolster; prop; sustain; also to pad or stuff.—**bol′ster-er,** *n.*

bolt[1] (bōlt), *n.* [AS. *bolt,* akin to G. *bolz, bolzen.*] An arrow, esp. one for a crossbow or other engine; a shaft of lightning; a strong metal pin, often with a head at one end and with a screw-thread at the other to receive a nut; an appliance

Door-bolt.

for fastening a door, etc., consisting of a cylindrical or other sliding piece, as of metal, which can be pushed or shot into a socket; the part of a lock which is protruded from and drawn back into the case, as by the action of the key; a fetter†; some object or piece resembling or suggesting a metal bolt; a roll or (whole) piece of cloth; a bundle, as of osiers; also, an act of bolting; a sudden dash, run, or flight; in *U. S. politics*, a breaking away, as from a nominating convention or a party.—**bolt[1]**, *v.* **I.** *intr.* To move suddenly like a bolt or arrow; dart, dash, or run suddenly away; in *U. S. politics*, to break away, as from a party; refuse to support the policy or candidates of one's party. **II.** *tr.* To shoot like a bolt; blurt (*out*); swallow hurriedly or without chewing; fasten with a bolt or bolts; fetter† or shackle†; in *U. S. politics*, to break away from; refuse to support.—**bolt[1]**, *adv.* Like a bolt or arrow; straight (as, *bolt* upright); suddenly.

bolt[2] (bōlt), *v. t.* [OF. *buleter* (F. *bluter*), for *bureter*, < *bure*, coarse woolen cloth: see *bureau*.] To sift through a cloth or sieve; hence, to examine or separate as by sifting. —**bolt′age** (-ạj), *n.* The process of bolting; removal of bran or coarser particles from flour by bolting.

bolt-er[1] (bōl′tėr), *n.* One who or that which bolts; in *U. S. politics*, one who bolts from a party.

bolt-er[2] (bōl′tėr), *n.* One who bolts meal, etc.; also, a piece of cloth or a sieve used in sifting.

bol-ter[3] (bōl′tėr), *n.* [Earlier *boulter*; origin unknown: cf. *bultow*.] A long fishing-line on which a number of hooks are strung.

bol-ter[4] (bol′tėr), *v.* See *balter*.

bolt=head (bōlt′hed), *n.* The head of a bolt; in *chem.*, a glass vessel with a long, straight neck and a rounded body; a matrass.

bolt-ing=cloth (bōl′ting-klôth), *n.* Cloth, as of linen or silk, for bolting or sifting meal, etc.

bolt=rope (bōlt′rōp), *n.* A rope or the cordage sewed on the edges of a sail or the like to strengthen it.

bo-lus (bō′lus), *n.*; pl. *boluses*. [LL.: see *bole[2]*.] A round mass of medicine, larger than an ordinary pill, forming a dose; any small rounded mass.

bomb (bom or, chiefly Brit., bum), *n.* [F. *bombe*, < It. *bomba*, bomb, < L. *bombus*, < Gr. *βόμβος*, a booming sound.] A hollow (usually spherical) projectile for a mortar, etc., filled with a bursting charge, and exploded by means of a fuse, by impact, or otherwise; a shell; also, any similar missile or device (as, a dynamite *bomb*).—**bomb**, *v. t.* To hurl bombs at; drop bombs upon, as from an aëroplane; bombard.

bom-ba-ca-ceous (bom-bạ-kā′shius), *a.* [NL. *Bombax*, a silk-cotton genus, ML. *bombax*, cotton: see *bombast*.] Belonging to the *Bombacaceæ*, a family of trees including the silk-cotton trees and the baobab.

bom-bard (bom′bärd or bum′-), *n.* [OF. *bombarde*, < L. *bombus*: see *bomb*.] The earliest kind of cannon, orig. for throwing stone balls; a bomb-ketch; a leather jug or bottle for liquor†; a toper†; a former deep-toned musical instrument of the oboe family.—**bom-bard′** (-bärd′), *v. t.* To attack or batter with artillery; attack with bombs; assail vigorously and persistently.—**bom-bard′er**, *n.* —**bom-bar-dier′** (-bär-dēr′), *n.* [F.] A soldier in charge of a bombard or cannon; a cannoneer; in the British army, a non-commissioned officer in the artillery.—**bom-bard′-ment**, *n.* The act of bombarding; a prolonged attack with artillery; an attack with bombs.

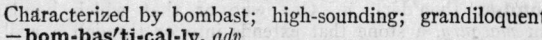

bom-bar-don (bom′bär-dọn or bom-bär′-), *n.* [It. *bombardone*, akin to E. *bombard*.] A large, deep-toned, valved brass wind-instrument, in tone not unlike an ophicleide.

Bombardon.

bom-ba-sine′, *n.* See *bombazine*.

bom-bast (bom′bast), *n.* [OF. *bombace*, < ML. *bombax*, cotton, for L. *bombyx*, cotton, silk, silkworm, < Gr. *βόμβυξ*, silk, silkworm.] Cotton†; padding†; inflated or high-sounding language; fustian.—**bom-bas′tic** (-bas′tik), *a.* Characterized by bombast; high-sounding; grandiloquent. —**bom-bas′ti-cal-ly**, *adv.*

bom-ba-zine (bom-bạ-zēn′ or bum-), *n.* [OF. *bombasin*, < L. *bombycinus*, of silk, < *bombyx*, silk: see *bombast*.] A cotton or part-cotton fabric†; a fine twilled fabric with a silk warp and worsted weft, formerly much used (in black) for mourning.

bombed (bomd or bom′bed), *a.* [F. *bombé*, rounded like a bomb.] Rounded; convex: as, "that *bombed* brow" (Browning's "Fifine at the Fair," lx.).

bomb-er (bom′ėr), *n.* A thrower of bombs, as a plane.

bom-bi-nate (bom′bi-nāt), *v. i.*; *-nated*, *-nating*. [LL. *bombinatus*, pp. of *bombinare*, < L. *bombus*, a booming or humming sound.] To hum; buzz.—**bom-bi-na′tion** (-nā′-shọn), *n.*

bomb=ketch (bom′kech), *n.* [See *bomb*.] A small ketch-rigged vessel carrying a mortar or mortars for bombarding.

bomb=plane (bom′plān), *n.* An aëroplane for dropping bombs.

bomb=proof (bom′pröf). **I.** *a.* Proof against bombs or shells. **II.** *n.* A bomb-proof structure.

bomb-shell (bom′shel), *n.* A bomb.

bom-by-cid (bom′bi-sid). [NL. *Bombycidæ*, pl., < *Bombyx*, the typical genus, < L. *bombyx*, silkworm: see *bombast*.] **I.** *n.* Any of the *Bombycidæ*, a family of moths containing the silkworm-moths of the genus *Bombyx* and allied genera. **II.** *a.* Belonging to the *Bombycidæ*.

bo-na fi-de (bō′nạ fī′dē). [L.] In good faith; in all sincerity; without make-believe or fraud: a phrase often used adjectively (as, a *bona-fide* offer).

bo-nan-za (bọ-nan′zạ), *n.* [Sp., fair weather, prosperity, < L. *bonus*, good.] A rich mass of ore, as found in mining; hence, any rich source of profit.

bo-na-si (bō-nä-sē′), *n.* [Cuban Sp.] Any of several food-fishes, groupers of the genus *Mycteroperca*, of Florida, the West Indies, etc., esp. *M. bonaci*.

bon-bon (bon′bon, F. bôṅ-bôṅ), *n.* [F., 'good-good.'] A sweetmeat or sugar-plum; a piece of confectionery; any dainty or delicacy.—**bon-bon-nière** (F. bôṅ-bo-nyãr), *n.* [F.] A box or receptacle for bonbons.

bond[1] (bond), *n.* [Var. of *band[1]*.] Something that binds; a band; a shackle or fetter; a link or tie; an obligation; an agreement or engagement; a legal instrument, under seal, binding the maker (and usually his heirs, etc.) to a specified course of action; a bondsman or security; the state of dutiable goods on which the duties are unpaid, when stored, under a bond, in charge of the government; an interest-bearing security issued by a government or corporation and based on a capital debt; in *masonry*, etc., the connection of the stones or bricks in a wall, etc., made by overlapping them in order to bind the whole into a compact mass; a particular method of so disposing stones or bricks; also, a stone or brick that binds; a bonder; in *carp.*, the fastening together of two or more pieces of timber; *pl.*, the timbers used for supporting or strengthening the walls of a building, etc.; *sing.*, in *chem.*, a unit of combining power equivalent to that of one hydrogen atom.—**bond[1]**, *v.* **I.** *tr.* To bind or join firmly together, as stones in a wall; also, to put under bonds; put (goods) in bond; issue bonds on, or mortgage, as a railroad; convert into bonds, as a debt. **II.** *intr.* To hold together firmly, as stones bonded in a wall.

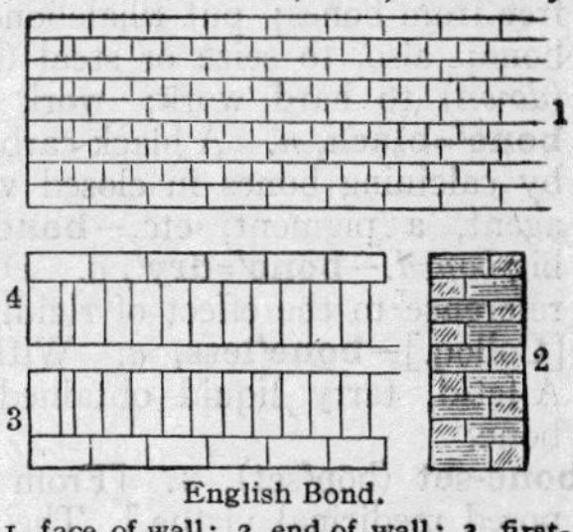

English Bond.

1, face of wall; 2, end of wall; 3, first-course bed; 4, second-course bed.

bond[2] (bond). [AS. *bonda*, householder, < Icel. *bōndi*, husbandman, < *būa*, dwell.] **I.**† *n.* A peasant; also, a serf. **II.** *a.* In bondage. [Archaic.]—**bond′age** (-ạj), *n.* Serfdom; involuntary servitude; slavery; subjection.

bond-ed (bon′ded), *p. a.* Subject to or secured by bonds; placed in bond, as goods; designed to hold goods in bond, as a warehouse.

bond·er (bon′dėr), *n.* One who or that which bonds; in *masonry*, a stone that extends into or through a wall, to bind it together.

bond·hold·er (bond′hōl″dėr), *n.* A holder of a bond; esp., one who holds or owns a bond or bonds issued by a government or corporation. —**bond′hold″ing,** *n.* and *a.*

bond·maid (bond′mād), *n.* [See *bond*[2].] A female slave. —**bond′man** (-mạn), *n.*; pl. *-men.* A male serf or slave. —**bond′=ser″vant,** *n.* One who serves in bondage. —**bond′=slave,** *n.* One who is in bondage or slavery.

bonds·man (bondz′mạn), *n.*; pl. *-men.* One who by bond becomes surety for another; also, a bondman.

bond=stone (bond′stōn), *n.* In *masonry*, a bonder.

bon·duc (bon′duk), *n.* [F., < Ar. *bunduq.*] A tropical shrub of the cæsalpiniaceous genus *Guilandina*, with hard gray seeds (nicker-nuts), which are used as beads.

Bonduc (*Guilandina crista*), showing prickly pods which inclose the nicker-nuts (shown separately).

bond·wom·an (bond′wu̇m″ạn), *n.*; pl. *-women* (-wim″en). A female slave.

bone[1], **born**[2], **bourn**[3] (bōn, bōrn), *v. t.* [Origin uncertain: cf. *bourn*[2].] To sight along (an object or objects) to see whether level or in line.

bone[2] (bōn), *n.* [AS. *bān* = G. *bein.*] Any one of the distinct pieces of which the skeleton or hard framework of the body of vertebrates is composed; a bone or piece of a bone with the meat adhering to it, as an article of food; *pl.*, the bones of the body collectively; the skeleton; the bodily frame; the mortal remains; *sing.*, the skeleton or bony structure considered as one of the components of the body; the hard substance of which bones are composed; any of various similar substances, as ivory, whalebone, etc.; something made of bone, ivory, etc.; *pl.*, dice; also, pieces of bone (or wood), used in pairs, held between the fingers and rattled, esp. by negro minstrels, to produce a kind of music, or to keep time to music; *pl.* (construed as *sing.*), an end-man in a minstrel-troupe, who performs on these; *sing.*, a strip of whalebone or other material used for stiffening a corset, bodice, etc. —**bone**[2], *v.*; *boned, boning.* **I.** *tr.* To free from bones; put whalebone into; manure with ground bone; also, to seize or steal (slang). **II.** *intr.* To settle (*down*) to hard work; work or study hard. [Slang.] —**bone′=black,** *n.* A black carbonaceous substance obtained by calcining bones in closed vessels, used as a decoloring agent, a pigment, etc. —**boned,** *a.* Having bones: as, big-*boned.* —**bone′=dry′,** *a.* Dry as a bone: used esp. with reference to the effect of rigidly enforced prohibition laws. [Colloq.] —**bone′less,** *a.* Without bones. —**bone′=oil,** *n.* A fetid, tarry liquid obtained in the dry distillation of bone.

bone·set (bōn′set), *n.* [From *bone* + *set*; from its supposed medicinal virtue.] The plant thoroughwort.

bon·fire (bon′fīr), *n.* [Earlier *bonefire.*] A fire of bones†; any fire built in the open air, as to burn rubbish or to celebrate some event.

bon·go (bong′gō), *n.*; pl. *-gos* (-gōz). [Native name.] A large antelope, *Boöcercus eurycerus*, of western Africa, of a chestnut color marked with white, the flesh of which is esteemed as food; also, a similar species, *B. isaaci*, of eastern Africa, regarded by some as a variety of the former.

bon·ho·mie (bon-ọ-mē′, F. bo-no-mē), *n.* [F., < *bonhomme*, 'good man.'] Good nature; unaffected affability.

Bon·i·face (bon′i-fās), *n.* [From *Boniface*, the landlord in Farquhar's play, "The Beaux' Stratagem."] [Also *l. c.*] The landlord of an inn or hotel.

bon·i·ness (bō′ni-nes), *n.* Bony quality.

bo·ni·to (bọ-nē′tō), *n.*; pl. *-tos* (-tōz). [Sp.] Any of various sea-fishes, esp. of the mackerel family, as *Sarda sarda*, a food-fish of northern Atlantic waters.

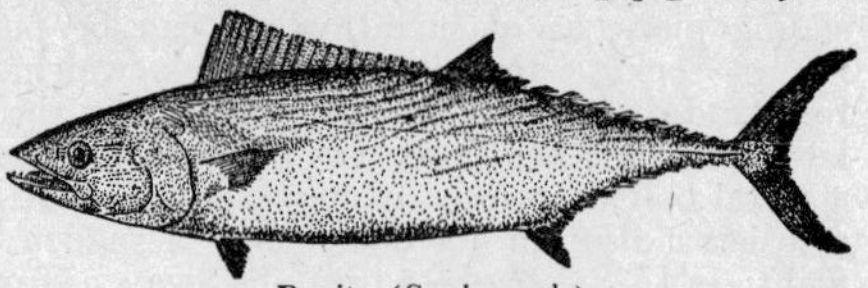

Bonito (*Sarda sarda*).

bon mot (bôṅ mō); pl. *bons mots* (bôṅ mōz, F. bôṅ mō). [F., 'good word.'] A clever saying; a witticism.

bonne (bon), *n.* [F., fem. of *bon*, good: see *bonny.*] A maid-servant; a child's nurse.

bonne bouche (bon bösh); pl. *bonnes bouches* (bon bö′shez, F. bon bösh). [F., an agreeable taste in the mouth, lit. 'good mouth.'] A choice morsel, esp. one kept for the last; a titbit.

bon·net (bon′et), *n.* [OF. *bonet* (F. *bonnet*), cap, orig. its material; origin unknown.] A man's or boy's cap (now chiefly Sc.); a woman's or child's outdoor head-covering, commonly fitting down over the hair and often tied on with strings; any of various hoods, covers, or protective devices, as the cowl of a chimney, or the movable covering inclosing the motor, etc., at the fore part of the chassis of an automobile; also, any person or thing serving as a cloak for something underhand; a decoy; *naut.*, an additional piece of canvas laced to the foot (formerly the top) of a jib or other sail. —**bon′net,** *v. t.*; *-neted, -neting.* To put a bonnet on; also, to force the hat down over the eyes of. —**bon′net=piece,** *n.* A gold coin issued by James V. of Scotland: so called from the representation of a bonnet on the king's head.

Obverse. Reverse.
Bonnet-piece. — British Museum.

bon·net rouge (bo-nā rözh); pl. *bonnets rouges* (bo-nā rözh). [F., 'red cap.'] A red liberty-cap, worn by extremists at the time of the French Revolution; hence, a wearer of such a cap; an extreme or radical republican.

bon′nie, *a.* See *bonny.*

bon·ny (bon′i), *a.*; compar. *bonnier*, superl. *bonniest.* [ME. *bonie*, appar. < OF. F. *bon* (fem. *bonne*), < L. *bonus*, good.] Pleasing to the eye; fair; comely; handsome; pretty; plump and healthy; cheerful or gay; excellent or fine. [Now chiefly Sc. and prov. Eng.] —**bon′ni·ly,** *adv.* —**bon′ni·ness,** *n.*

bon·ny·clab·ber (bon′i-klab″ėr), *n.* [Ir. *bainne*, milk, + *claba*, thick.] Sour, thick milk.

bon·spiel (bon′spēl), *n.* [Origin obscure.] A curling-match between two clubs, parishes, etc. [Sc.]

bon·te·bok (bon′tẹ-bok), *n.* [S. Afr. D., 'variegated buck.'] A large South African antelope, *Bubalis* (or *Damaliscus*) *pygargus*, of a red color, with a blaze on the face.

bon ton (bôṅ tôṅ). [F., 'good tone.'] Good or elegant style; good breeding; fashionable society.

bont=tick (bont′tik), *n.* [D. *bont*, variegated.] A South African tick (acarid), *Amblyomma hebræum*, with variegated coloring, found on cattle, etc.

bo·nus (bō′nus), *n.*; pl. *bonuses.* [L., good.] Something given or paid over and above what is due; a premium; an extra dividend; also, a bribe. —**bo′nus,** *v. t.*; *-nused, -nusing.* To give a bonus to; promote by the payment of bonuses.

bon vi·vant (bôṅ vē-väṅ); pl. *bons vivants* (bôṅ vē-väṅz, F. bôṅ vē-väṅ). [F. (fem. *bonne vivante*), 'good liver.'] One who lives well or luxuriously; one fond of good living.

bon·y (bō′ni), *a.*; compar. *bonier*, superl. *boniest.* Of or like bone; consisting chiefly of bone; having prominent bones.

bonze (bonz), *n.* [Jap. *bonzo*; from Chinese.] A Buddhist monk, esp. of Japan or China.

boo (bö), *interj.* [Cf. *bo.*] An exclamation used to express contempt, disapprobation, etc., or to frighten. —**boo,** *v.*; *booed, booing.* **I.** *intr.* To cry 'boo'; hoot. **II.** *tr.* To cry 'boo' at; hoot.

boo-by (bö′bi), *n.*; pl. *-bies* (-biz). [Prob. < Sp. *bobo*, fool, also the bird booby.] A stupid person; a dunce; the player who has failed most conspicuously, as in progressive euchre; also, any of various gannets, as *Sula leucogastra* of the southern Atlantic coast of the U. S.—**boo′by=hatch,** *n. Naut.*, a wooden hood over a small hatch or opening.—**boo′by-ish,** *a.* Booby-like; stupid.—**boo′by=trap,** *n.* Any device used to trap or discomfit unwary persons, as a pail of water so balanced on the top of a partly open door as to upset when the door is opened further, or some apparently harmless object left behind by a retreating enemy (as by the Germans in the World War) to explode with deadly effect when touched.

boo-dle (bö′dl), *n.* [Cf. D. *boedel*, goods, property.] The (whole) lot, pack, or crowd; also, spoils or illicit gains, as from defalcation, from bribes or collusive contracts in the public service, etc.; bribe-money; also, counterfeit money. [Slang, U. S.]—**boo′dle,** *v. i.*; *-dled, -dling.* To obtain money dishonestly, as by defalcation, corrupt political bargains, etc. [Slang, U. S.]—**boo′dler,** *n.*

boo-hoo (bö-hö′), *interj.* and *n.* A word imitating the sound of noisy weeping or laughter.—**boo-hoo′,** *v. i.*; *-hooed, -hooing.* To cry or weep noisily; shout; hoot.

book (bůk), *n.* [AS. *bōc* = G. *buch*, book, = Goth. *bōka*, letter of the alphabet, pl. writing, book.] A writing† or document†; a written or printed work of some length, as a treatise or other literary composition, esp. on sheets fastened or bound together; a volume; [*cap.*] the Bible; [*l. c.*] a libretto; a division of a literary work, esp. one of the larger divisions; a record of bets, as on a horse-race; any collection of sheets fastened or bound together; a number of sheets of writing-paper bound together and used for making entries, as of commercial transactions; a pile or package of leaves, as of tobacco; a trick at cards, or a number of cards forming a set; in *whist*, six tricks taken by one side.—**Book of Common Prayer,** the service-book of the Anglican churches.—**Book of the Dead,** among the ancient Egyptians, a collection of religious texts, etc., for the guidance of the soul on its journey to the next world, a copy of which, in whole or in part, was placed with the mummy in the tomb.—**to bring to book,** to bring to account.—**without book,** by memory; also, without authority.—**book,** *v.* **I.** *tr.* To enter in a book or list; record; register; also, to put down for a place, passage, etc.; issue a ticket to, or obtain one for (a person); also, to engage (a place, passage, etc.) in due manner; also, to enter (a theatrical company, a lecturer, etc.) for an engagement, or for the engagements of a tour. **II.** *intr.* To register one's name; engage a place, passage, etc.; make an engagement or engagements, as for public exhibition or appearance.

book-bind-er (bůk′bīn″dėr), *n.* One whose business or work it is to bind books.—**book′bind″er-y,** *n.*; pl. *-ies* (-iz). An establishment for binding books.—**book′bind″ing,** *n.*

book-case (bůk′kās), *n.* A case with shelves for holding books.

book=end (bůk′end), *n.* A support, often ornamental and of considerable weight, for placing at the end of a row of books in order to keep the volumes upright.

book-er (bůk′ėr), *n.* One who books, or enters in a book, list, or the like.

book-ie (bůk′i), *n.* In horse-racing, a book-maker. [Colloq.]

book-ish (bůk′ish), *a.* Pertaining to books; literary; given to reading or study; also, knowing books only.—**book′ish-ly,** *adv.*—**book′ish-ness,** *n.*

book-keep-er (bůk′kē″pėr), *n.* One who keeps account-books, as for a business house.—**book′keep″ing,** *n.* The work or art of keeping account-books or systematic records of pecuniary transactions.

book-land (bůk′land), *n.* [AS. *bōcland.*] In *old Eng. law*, land held by charter or deed, as distinguished from *folkland*, which was held by folkright or customary law. See Stubbs's "Constitutional Hist. of Eng.," v. § 36.

book-less (bůk′les), *a.* Without books; unlearned; ignorant.

book-let (bůk′let), *n.* A little book; esp., a small unbound, often paper-covered, book of printed matter, as for holiday greetings, advertising purposes, etc.

book=mak-er (bůk′mā″kėr), *n.* A maker of books; a compiler; a professional betting man who accepts the bets of others, as on horses in racing.—**book′=mak″ing,** *n.*

book-man (bůk′man), *n.*; pl. *-men.* A man interested or versed in books; a scholar or student; also, one concerned with the publishing or selling of books.

book=mark (bůk′märk), *n.* A ribbon or the like placed between the pages of a book to mark a place; also, a book-plate.

book=mus-lin (bůk′muz′lin), *n.* A wiry, sheer muslin, folded in book-like form when in the piece.

book=name (bůk′nām), *n.* In *zoöl.* and *bot.*, a name (other than the scientific name) of an animal or plant, used only in treatises, as when the popular name for a single species is used for all the animals or plants of the same genus, family, or the like.

book=plate (bůk′plāt), *n.* A label bearing the owner's name or crest or some other device, for pasting in or on a book.

book=rack (bůk′rak), *n.* A rack for supporting an open book; also, a rack for holding a number of books.

book=scor-pi-on (bůk′skôr″pi-on), *n.* Any of the minute arachnids, superficially resembling a tailless scorpion, which constitute the order *Pseudoscorpionida*, as *Chelifer cancroides*, a species found in old books, etc.

book-sell-er (bůk′sel″ėr), *n.* One whose business it is to sell books.—**book′sell″ing,** *n.*

book=shelf (bůk′shelf), *n.* A shelf for holding books.

book=shop (bůk′shop), *n.* A book-store.

book=stack (bůk′stak), *n.* A set of book-shelves one above another, as in a library.

book=stall (bůk′stâl), *n.* A stall at which books (usually second-hand) are sold.

book=stand (bůk′stand), *n.* A book-rack; also, a book-stall.

book=store (bůk′stōr), *n.* A store for the sale of books.

book-worm (bůk′wėrm), *n.* Any insect larva that gnaws books; also, a person closely addicted to reading or study.

boom[1] (böm), *n.* [D. *boom*, tree, beam: see *beam.*] A long pole or spar used to extend the foot of certain sails; a strong spar or beam projecting from the mast of a derrick, for supporting or guiding the weights to be lifted; an upright spar in water, for marking a channel, etc.; also, a chain or cable or a series of connected floating timbers or the like, serving to obstruct navigation, to confine floating timber, etc.; also, the area thus shut off.—**boom**[1], *v. t.* To extend (a sail) with a boom; shove or guide (a vessel) with a boom or pole; also, to furnish (a river, etc.) with a boom; confine (logs, etc.) with a boom.

boom[2] (böm), *v.* [Imit.] **I.** *intr.* To make a deep, prolonged, resonant sound; make a rumbling, humming, or droning noise; also, to move with a resounding rush or great impetus; also, to progress or flourish vigorously, as business. **II.** *tr.* To give forth with a booming sound; also, to push or urge (an enterprise, etc.) vigorously by calculated means.—**boom**[2], *n.* A booming sound; also, a booming rush; also, a sudden, rapid advance in commercial or other progress.—**boom′er,** *n.*

boo-me-rang (bö′me-rang), *n.* [Native name.] A bent or curved piece of hard wood used as a missile by the native Australians, which can be so thrown as to return to the thrower; fig., something that recoils on the user.

boon[1] (bön), *n.* [Icel. *bōn*, petition.] A petition†; a favor sought or granted; a great privilege; a blessing.

boon[2] (bön), *a.* [OF. F. *bon*, < L. *bonus*, good.] Good†; favorable† or prosperous†; kindly, gracious, or pleasant (poetic); jolly or convivial (as, *boon* companions).

boon-dog-gle (bön′dog-l), *n.* [Made word.] A cord of plaited leather (worn round the neck by Boy Scouts), or a belt, knife-sheath, ax-handle, or other product of simple manual skill; a gimcrack or gadget; also, an instance of boondoggling. [Colloq.]—**boon′dog-gle,** *v. i.*; *-gled, -gling.* To engage in boondoggling. [Colloq.]—**boon′dog-gler,** *n.*—**boon′dog-gling,** *n.* The making of boondoggles, esp. (orig. in 1935) as made work for the unemployed; hence, any relief work of little practical value; any work or projects of little or no real value financed by government funds; any useless work. [Colloq.]

boon-ga-ry (bông′ga-ri), *n.* [Native name.] A small arboreal kangaroo, *Dendrolagus lumholtzi*, of Queensland.

boor (bör), *n.* [Prob. < LG. *bur* or D. *boer*, peasant, countryman.] A peasant; a rustic; a clownish, rude, or unmannerly person.—**boor′ish,** *a.* Of or like a boor; rustic; clownish; rude; unmannerly.—**boor′ish-ly,** *adv.*—**boor′ish-ness,** *n.*

boose (böz), etc. See *booze*, etc.

boost (böst), *v. t.* [Origin obscure.] To lift by shoving up, as from behind; push up; fig., to advance or aid. [Colloq., U. S.]—**boost,** *n.* ^ boosting; an upward shove or push; an aid or help. [Colloq., U. S.]—**boost′er,** *n.*

boot[1] (böt), *n.* Booty; spoil: as, "September . . . laden with the spoyle Of harvests riches, which he made his *boot*" (Spenser's "Faerie Queene," vii. 7. 38). [Archaic.]

boot[2] (böt), *n.* [AS. *bōt*, advantage, help, amends; akin to E. *better*[2].] Advantage or profit (now chiefly in 'to boot,' into the bargain, in addition); something given into the bargain, or as an additional consideration (obs. or prov.); avail† or use†; help (archaic); resource† or alternative†.—**boot**[2], *v.* **I.**† *tr.* To give (something) to boot; present (one) with something to boot; help, relieve, or cure. **II.** *intr.* To be of profit, avail, or use (as, it *boots* not to complain; sometimes with indirect personal object and adverbial modifier, as, it *boots* us little to complain); also, to matter or signify (now prov. Eng.).

boot[3] (böt), *n.* [OF. *bote* (F. *botte*); origin unknown.] A covering, usually of leather, for the foot and leg, reaching at least to the middle of the calf, and often to the knee or higher; any shoe or outer foot-covering reaching above the ankle; a protective covering for the foot and part of the leg of a horse; something resembling or suggesting a boot; an instrument of torture for the leg; the external step on each side of a coach†, or an uncovered side seat or outside end compartment of old coaches†; a receptacle or place for baggage at either end of a coach; a protecting apron or cover for the driver's seat of a vehicle.—**boots and saddles,** *milit.*, a trumpet-call which is the first signal for mounted drill and other formations mounted.—**boot**[3], *v.* **I.** *tr.* To put boots on; torture with the boot; kick, or drive or compel by kicking (slang). **II.** *intr.* To put on one's boots.—**boot′=black,** *n.* One whose business it is to black or polish boots, etc.—**boot′ed,** *a.* Equipped with boots, as for riding; in *ornith.*, of the tarsus of certain birds, covered with a continuous horny, boot-like sheath.—**boot-ee** (bö-tē′), *n.* A kind of half-boot for women; also, a baby's knitted shoe.

Torture with the Boot.

Bo-ö-tes (bọ-ō′tēz), *n.* [L., < Gr. βοώτης, ox-driver, < βοῦς, ox.] In *astron.*, a northern constellation, behind Ursa Major, containing the bright star Arcturus and represented as a man holding a crook (as if driving the Great Bear).

booth (böᴛʜ or böth), *n.* [ME. *bothe*; prob. from Scand.] A temporary structure of boughs, canvas, boards, etc., as for shelter; a stall or light structure for the sale of goods, for exhibition purposes, etc., as at a market, fair, etc.

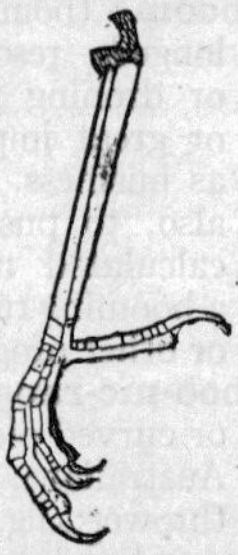
Booted Tarsus (Robin).

boot=hose (böt′hōz), *n. sing.* or *pl.* Outside hose worn instead of boots or with boots.

boot-i-kin (bö′ti-kin), *n.* [Dim. of *boot*[3].] A little boot; also, a kind of soft boot or mitten formerly worn as a cure for the gout; also, an instrument of torture, the boot.

boot-jack (böt′jak), *n.* A device to aid in pulling off boots.

boot-leg (böt′leg), *n.* That part of a boot which covers the leg.—**boot′leg,** *v. t.* or *i.* To carry (liquor) about secretly, as in a flask concealed in the bootleg, for illicit sale; deal in (liquor) illicitly.—**boot′leg″ger,** *n.*—**boot′leg″ging,** *n.*

boot-less (böt′les), *a.* Without boot, profit, or avail; unavailing; useless; also, without help or remedy†.—**boot′less-ly,** *adv.*—**boot′less-ness,** *n.*

boots (böts), *n.* A servant, as at a hotel, who blacks or polishes boots, etc.

boot=tree (böt′trē), *n.* An instrument inserted into a boot or shoe to stretch it or preserve its shape.

boo-ty (bö′ti), *n.*; pl. *-ties* (-tiz). [ME. *botye*, *buty*; akin to F. *butin* and G. *beute*.] Spoil taken, as in war or robbery; plunder; a prize.

booze (böz), *v. i.* or *t.*; *boozed, boozing.* [Var. of *bouse*[1].] To drink deeply, esp. to partial intoxication.—**booze,** *n.* Liquor or drink; also, a drinking-bout; a spree. [Colloq.]—**booz′er,** *n.*—**booz′y,** *a.* Showing the effects of liquor; somewhat intoxicated.—**booz′i-ly,** *adv.*—**booz′i-ness,** *n.*

bo=peep (bō-pēp′), *n.* [Cf. *bo* and *peep*[2].] An alternate withdrawing or concealing of the face or person and sudden peeping out again, often employed as an amusement for young children.

bo-ra (bō′rạ̈), *n.* [It., for *borea*, north wind, < L. *boreas*: see *Boreas*.] On the coasts of the Adriatic, a violent, dry, cold wind blowing from a northerly or northeasterly direction.

bo-ra-cic (bọ-ras′ik), *a.* Of or pertaining to borax: as, *boracic* acid (boric acid, H_3BO_3: prepared from borax).

bo-ra-cite (bō′rạ-sīt), *n.* A mineral, a borate and chloride of magnesium, occurring in translucent to transparent, white or colorless crystals, notable for their pyro-electric properties.

bor-age (bur′ạj), *n.* [ML. *borrago*, prob. < *burra*, wool.] A plant, *Borago officinalis*, native of southern Europe, with hairy leaves and stems and blue flowers, used in salads, in flavoring beverages, and sometimes medicinally; also, any of various allied or similar plants.—**bor′age-wort** (-wėrt), *n.* Any boraginaceous plant.

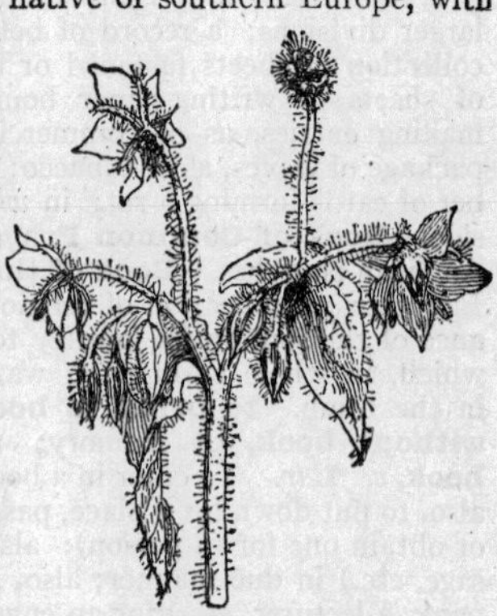
Borage (*B. officinalis*).

bo-rag-i-na-ceous (bọ-raj i-nā′shius), *a.* [NL. *Borago*, the typical genus, < ML. *borrago*: see *borage*.] Belonging to the *Boraginaceæ*, or borage family of plants, including borage, bugloss, comfrey, heliotrope, forget-me-not, etc.

bo-rate (bō′rāt), *n.* In *chem.*, a salt of boric acid.—**bo′rat-ed** (-rā-ted), *a.* Mixed or treated with boric acid or borax or with both.

bo-rax (bō′raks), *n.* [ML., < Ar. *būraq*, < Pers. *būrah*.] A white crystalline salt of sodium, $Na_2B_4O_7$, occurring native or prepared artificially: used as a flux, antiseptic, cleansing agent, etc. Cf. *boron*.

Bor-deaux (bôr-dō′), *n.* Wine of many varieties, red (claret) and white (Sauterne, etc.), produced in the region about Bordeaux, in southwestern France; also, any of various dyestuffs that produce a vinous red color.

Bor-deaux (bôr-dō′) **mix′ture.** In *hort.*, a fungicide consisting of a mixture of copper sulphate, lime, and water.

bor-der (bôr′dėr). [OF. *bordure*, *bordeure* (F. *bordure*), < ML. *bordatura*, < *bordus*, side, edge, from the Teut. source of AS. *bord*, side: see *board*.] **I.** *n.* A side, edge, or margin; a boundary; a frontier; the brink or verge; a marginal strip or finish; an edging. **II.** *a.* Pertaining to a border or frontier.—**bor′der,** *v.* **I.** *tr.* To furnish with a border; edge; also, to form a border to; also, to adjoin. **II.** *intr.* To touch or abut at the border; fig., to verge: with *on* or *upon*.

borde-reau (bôrd-rō), *n.*; pl. *-reaux* (-rōz, F. -rō). [F., < *bord*, edge.] A memorandum or note; a detailed list, as of documents.

bor-der-er (bôr′dėr-ėr), *n.* One who dwells on a border, or at the extreme part of a country, region, or district; also, one who makes borders or bordering.

bor-der-ing (bôr′dėr-ing), *n.* Material for or used as a border; also, a border or edging.

bor-der-land (bôr′dėr-land), *n.* Land forming a border or frontier; hence, an uncertain intermediate district or space.
bor-der-less (bôr′dėr-les), *a.* Without a border.
bor-dure (bôr′d̤ūr), *n.* Archaic form of *border.*
bore[1] (bōr), *v.*; *bored, boring.* [AS. *borian* = G. *bohren*; akin to L. *forare*, pierce.] **I.** *tr.* To pierce (a solid substance) or make (a hole, etc.) with an auger, drill, or other rotated instrument; perforate or penetrate as if with such an instrument; force or make as if by boring, as one's way; also, to trick†. **II.** *intr.* To make a hole, as with an auger or drill; also, to admit of being pierced with an auger or the like, as a substance; also, to force a way; push forward. —**bore**[1], *n.* A hole made by or as by boring; the cylindrical cavity of a tube, as a gun-barrel; the caliber or internal diameter of a tube.
bore[2] (bōr), *n.* [Prob. < Icel. *bāra*, wave, billow.] A high, abrupt tidal wave which breaks in an estuary, the water then rushing up the channel with great violence.
bore[3] (bōr), *n.* [Origin unknown.] Ennui† or a fit of ennui†; one who suffers from ennui†; a cause of ennui or annoyance; a dull, tiresome, or uncongenial person.—**bore**[3], *v. t.*; *bored, boring.* To weary by tedious iteration, by dullness, or by unwelcome attentions, etc.
bore[4] (bōr). Preterit of *bear*[1].
bo-re-al (bō′rḗ-a̤l), *a.* [LL. *borealis.*] Pertaining to Boreas, or the north wind (as, "the *Boreal* blast": Pope's tr. Homer's "Iliad," xxiii.); also, pertaining to the north; northern. Also **bo′re-an.**
Bo-re-as (bō′rḗ-a̤s), *n.* [L., < Gr. Βορέας.] The north wind, as personified or deified by the Greeks and Romans.
bore-cole (bōr′kōl), *n.* [Cf. D. *boerenkool*, 'peasant's cabbage.'] A variety of cabbage; kale.
bore-dom (bōr′do̤m), *n.* Bored condition; ennui; also, the quality of being a bore; also, bores collectively.
bor-el (bor′e̤l), *a.* See *borrel.*
bor-er (bōr′ėr), *n.* One who or that which bores; an instrument for boring; any of various mollusks, insects, etc., that bore into wood, etc.; also, the hag (cyclostome).
bo-ric (bō′rik), *a.* Of or containing boron: as, *boric* acid (any of certain acids containing boron, esp. a white crystalline acid, H_3BO_3, occurring in nature or prepared from borax).
bo-ride (bō′rīd or -rid), *n.* In *chem.*, a compound of boron with a more positive element or radical.
bor-ing (bōr′ing), *n.* The act or process of one who or that which bores or pierces; also, the hole made, or a chip, fragment, etc., produced, by such action or process.
born[1] (bôrn), *p. a.* [See *borne.*] Brought forth; being as specified by birth or native character (as, a *born* poet); natural or innate (as, *born* dignity).
born[2] (bōrn), *v. t.* See *bone*[1].
borne (bôrn). Past participle of *bear*[1], in all uses except, in the passive (when not followed by *by*), in the sense 'brought forth,' where *born* is now used: as, I have *borne* witness; to be *borne* by the tide; she has *borne* a son; a child was *borne* by her; but, a child was *born* yesterday.
bor-né (bôr-nā), *a.* [F., pp. of *borner*, bound, limit, < *borne*, a bound: see *bourn*[2].] Bounded; limited; contracted; narrow.
bor-ne-ol (bôr′nḗ-ol or -ōl), *n.* [From the island of *Borneo.*] A substance closely resembling common camphor, found in concrete masses in the trunk of *Dryobalanops aromatica*, a large tree of Borneo, Sumatra, etc.
born-ite (bôrn′īt), *n.* [From I. von *Born* (1742–91), Austrian mineralogist.] A native sulphide of copper and iron with a metallic appearance, usually found massive, and constituting a valuable ore of copper.
bo-ron (bō′ron), *n.* [NL., < ML. *borax*: see *borax.*] Chem. sym., B; at. wt., 11.0. A non-metallic element present in borax, etc., and obtained in either an amorphous or a crystalline form when reduced from its compounds.
bo-ro-sil-i-cate (bō-rō̤-sil′i-kāt), *n.* In *chem.*, a double salt of boric and silicic acids.
bor-ough (bur′ō̤), *n.* [AS. *burg, burh*, castle, fortified place, town, = Icel. *borg*, G. *burg*, castle, = LL. *burgus*, castle, later town, = F. *bourg*, town; all from Teut., prob. from the source of AS. *beorgan*, protect.] In England, a town with a municipal corporation and with privileges conferred by charter; also, a town that sends representatives to Parliament; in certain States of the U. S., an incorporated municipality smaller than a city; also, one of the five administrative divisions of the (enlarged) city of New York. —**bor′ough=Eng′lish,** *n.* In *law*, a customary descent of certain estates in England to the youngest son, or, if the owner leaves no son, to the youngest surviving brother.—**bor′ough-mon″ger** (-mung″gėr), *n.* One who buys or sells parliamentary seats for boroughs.—**bor′ough-mon″ger-ing,** *n.* and *a.*
bor-rel (bor′e̤l), *a.* [ME. *borel, burel*, appar. < *burel*, woolen cloth, < OF. *burel*: see *bureau.*] Lay or non-clerical (obs. or archaic); unlearned, rough, or rude (archaic or Sc.).
bor-row (bor′ō), *n.* [AS. *borg, borh*, pledge, surety, akin to *beorgan*, protect: see *borough.*] A pledge; bail; a surety (as, St. George to *borrow*, St. George as surety, or by St. George!); a tithing or frank-pledge; also, a borrowing. [Chiefly archaic or prov.]—**bor′row,** *v.* [AS. *borgian.*] **I.** *tr.* To take or receive (a thing) on pledge given for its return or on the understanding that it (or its equivalent) is to be returned; obtain temporary use of (something belonging to another); get from another or from a foreign source; appropriate or adopt; steal or plagiarize; assume or usurp, as something counterfeit or feigned; also, to be surety for†; ransom†; in *arith.*, in subtraction, to take from one denomination to add to the next lower. **II.** *intr.* To borrow something; in *golf*, when putting across sloping ground, to play the ball a little up the slope to counteract its effect.—**bor′row-a-ble,** *a.* That may be borrowed.—**bor′row-er,** *n.*—**bor′row-ing,** *n.* The act of one who borrows; also, a thing borrowed.
bors-hold-er (bôrs′hōl″dėr), *n.* [For ME. *borghes alder*, 'head of a borrow (tithing).'] In England, orig., the head or chief of a borrow or tithing; a headborough; later, a petty constable. [Now only hist.]
bort (bôrt), *n.* [Origin uncertain.] Material composed of imperfectly crystallized or inferior diamonds, or of fragments obtained in cutting diamonds.—**bort′y,** *a.*
bor-zoi (bôr′zoi), *n.* [Russ.] The Russian wolfhound.
bos-cage (bos′kāj), *n.* [OF. *boscage* (F. *bocage*), < ML. *boscus*: see *bush*[1].] Woodland; a wood; a grove, shrubbery, or thicket; sylvan scenery.
bosch, etc. See *boche*, etc.
bosch-bok (bosh′bok), *n.* [S. Afr. D., 'wood buck.'] A rather small South African antelope, *Tragelaphus sylvaticus*, frequenting forests and bushy regions; also, any of several related species, esp. of the same genus.

Boschbok (*Tragelaphus sylvaticus*).

bosch-vark (bosh′värk), *n.* [S. Afr. D., 'wood pig.'] A species of wild swine, *Potamochœrus chœropotamus*, of South Africa.
bosh[1] (bosh), *n.* [Turk., empty, vain.] Utter nonsense; absurd or foolish talk or opinions. [Colloq.]
bosh[2] (bosh), *n.* [Cf. G. *böschen*, slope.] A trough in which tools or ingots are cooled; *pl.*, the lower portion of a blast-furnace, extending from the widest part to the hearth.
bosk (bosk), *n.* [ME. *bosk*, var. of *busk*, bush: see *bush*[1].] A bush (now prov. Eng.); a thicket; a small wood.—**bos-kage** (bos′kāj), *n.* See *boscage.*—**bos′ket, bos′quet** (-ket), *n.* [F. *bosquet*, < It. *boschetto*, dim. of *bosco*, wood: see *bush*[1].] A grove; a thicket.—**bosk′y,** *a.* Abounding in bosks, thickets, or woodland; bushy; wooded; shady. —**bosk′i-ness,** *n.*
bos-om (bu̇z′o̤m). [AS. *bōsm* = G. *busen.*] **I.** *n.* The breast of a human being; the inclosure formed by the

breast and arms; affectionate embrace; that part of a garment which covers the breast, esp. a part of a shirt of different character from the rest of the garment, as in being made of finer material or in having pleats or the like; the breast as the seat of thought and emotion; inclination† or desire†; something likened to the breast, as a sustaining surface, a hollow interior, the inmost recess, etc. **II.** *a.* Of or pertaining to the bosom; cherished in the bosom; intimate or confidential.—**bos′om,** *v. t.* To take to the bosom; embrace; also, to inclose in the bosom; also, to conceal in the bosom.

bos′quet, *n.* See *bosket.*

boss[1] (bôs or bos). [D. *baas,* master.] **I.** *n.* A master; a foreman or superintendent; a manager; a politician who controls the machinery of his party, as in a particular district; also, the chief or champion (slang). [U. S.] **II.** *a.* Master; chief; also, champion or first-rate (slang). [U. S.]—**boss**[1], *v. t.* To be master of or over; control; manage; direct. [Colloq., U. S.]

boss[2] (bos or bôs), *n.* [OF. *boce* (F. *bosse*): cf. *botch*[1].] A protuberance or roundish excrescence on the body or on some organ of an animal or plant; hence, any knob-like prominence or mass; a knob-like mass of rock, esp. such an outcrop of eruptive rock; an ornamental protuberance of metal, ivory, etc.; in *arch.*, a knob-like projection of ornamental character, as at the intersection of ribs or groins.—**boss**[2], *v. t.* To furnish or ornament with bosses; emboss.

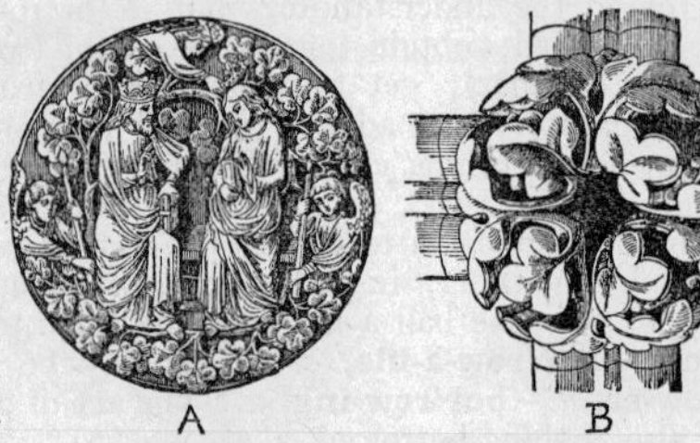

A B

Architectural Bosses. — French, 13th century. *A*, from collegiate church of Semur-en-Auxois. *B*, from refectory of former priory of St. Martin-des-Champs, Paris.

boss-ism (bôs′izm), *n.* Control by bosses, esp. political bosses.

boss-y[1] (bôs′i), *a.* Given to acting like a boss; domineering. [Colloq., U. S.]

boss-y[2] (bos′i), *a.* Studded with bosses; swelling in bosses; projecting, as decorative work (as, "*bossy* sculptures": Milton's "Paradise Lost," i. 716).

bos-ton (bôs′tọn), *n.* [From *Boston,* Mass.] A game at cards, played by four persons with two packs of cards, one dealt and the other cut to determine the trump; the first five tricks taken by a player in this game; also, a dance, a modification of the waltz.

Bos-well (boz′wel), *n.* [From James *Boswell* (1740–95), biographer of Samuel Johnson.] A devoted biographer.—**Bos-well′i-an,** *a.* Of, pertaining to, or suggestive of James Boswell or his biography of Dr. Johnson, which is characterized by great faithfulness and fullness, with minute details of the sayings and doings of its subject.—**Bos′well-ism,** *n.*

bot, bott (bot), *n.*; pl. *bots, botts.* [Origin unknown.] An insect larva infesting horses, cattle, etc. See *bot-fly.*

bo-tan-ic, bo-tan-i-cal (bọ-tan′ik, -i-kạl), *a.* [F. *botanique,* < Gr. βοτανικός, < βοτάνη, herb.] Pertaining to plants or to botany.—**bo-tan′i-cal-ly,** *adv.*

bot-a-nist (bot′ạ-nist), *n.* [F. *botaniste.*] One versed in botany.

bot-a-nize (bot′ạ-nīz), *v.*; *-nized, -nizing.* **I.** *intr.* To seek plants for botanical study; study plants botanically. **II.** *tr.* To explore botanically.—**bot′a-niz-er,** *n.*

bot-a-ny (bot′ạ-ni), *n.*; pl. *-nies* (-niz). [From *botanic.*] The science that treats of plants or the vegetable kingdom; also, a treatise on this science.

botch[1] (boch), *n.* [OF. *boche,* var. of *boce,* E. *boss*[2].] A swelling on the skin; a boil; an eruptive disease. [Now only prov. Eng.]

botch[2] (boch), *v. t.* [ME. *bocchen*; origin uncertain.] To patch; mend clumsily; bungle; spoil by poor work.—**botch**[2], *n.* A patch; a clumsy patch; a clumsy or poor piece of work; a bungle.—**botch′er,** *n.*—**botch′er-y,** *n.* Botching; clumsy work.—**botch′y,** *a.* Botched; poorly made or done.—**botch′i-ly,** *adv.*

bote (bōt), *n.* [AS. *bōt*: see *boot*[2].] In *old Eng. law,* the repair of buildings, bridges, etc., or an assessment levied for this; also, the right of a tenant to take timber, etc., for repairs, fuel, and other necessary purposes, from off the landlord's estate; also, compensation paid, as for an injury; amends; satisfaction.

bot=fly (bot′flī), *n.*; pl. *-flies* (-flīz). Any of various dipterous insects of the family *Œstridæ*, the larvæ of which are parasitic in horses, sheep, cattle, etc.

a *b*

Horse Bot-fly (*Gasterophilus equi*), about natural size. — *a*, lateral view; *b*, dorsal view.

both (bōth), *a.* and *pron.* [ME. *bothe, bathe,* prob. from Scand.: cf. Icel. *bādhir* = G. *beide,* akin to AS. *bā,* Goth. *bai,* L. *ambo,* Gr. ἄμφω, Skt. *ubha,* both.] The one and the other; the two together or alike.—**both,** *adv.* or *conj.* Together, alike, or equally: used with (commonly before, sometimes after) two (or sometimes more) coördinate words or phrases joined by *and* (as, he is *both* ready *and* willing).

both-er (boᴛʜ′ėr), *v.* [Appar. < Ir. *bodhar,* deaf.] **I.** *tr.* To deafen (Ir.); confuse or bewilder by noise (obs. or prov.); harass by clamor, importunities, or anything annoying; pester, worry, or trouble (sometimes used in the imperative in mild imprecation). **II.** *intr.* To cause annoyance or trouble; trouble one's self, as in the effort to do something. —**both′er,** *n.* Annoyance; worry; trouble; also, something that bothers.—**both-er-a′tion** (-ẹ-rā′shọn), *n.* Bother; annoyance; vexation: sometimes used interjectionally.—**both′er-er,** *n.*—**both′er-some,** *a.* Causing bother; troublesome.

both-y, both-ie (both′i), *n.*; pl. *-ies* (-iz). [Cf. *booth.*] A hut or cottage; a structure for lodging laborers, as on a farm. [Sc.]

bo=tree (bō′trē), *n.* [Singhalese *bo,* < Skt. *bodhi,* wisdom.] The pipal or sacred fig-tree, *Ficus religiosa,* of India, under which the founder of Buddhism is said to have attained the enlightenment which constituted him the Buddha.

bot-ry-oid, bot-ry-oi-dal (bot′ri-oid, bot-ri-oi′dạl), *a.* [Gr. βοτρυοειδής, < βότρυς, bunch of grapes, + εἶδος, form.] Having the form of a bunch of grapes.—**bot-ry-oi′dal-ly,** *adv.*

Botryoid Structure (Chalcedony).

bot-ry-ose (bot′ri-ōs), *a.* [Gr. βότρυς: see *botryoid.*] In *bot.,* botryoid; clustered; racemose.

bots (bots), *n. pl.*, **bott** (bot), *n.* See *bot.*

bot-tine (bo-tēn′), *n.* [F., dim. of *botte,* boot.] A half-boot; a woman's boot or shoe; also, a boot-like appliance to correct distortion of the legs.

bot-tle[1] (bot′l), *n.* [OF. *botel,* dim. of *botte,* bundle.] A bundle, esp. of hay. [Now chiefly prov. Eng.]

bot-tle[2] (bot′l), *n.* [OF. *botele* (F. *bouteille*), < ML. *buticula,* dim. of *buttis,* vessel, E. *butt*[3].] A vessel, now commonly of glass, with a neck or mouth that may be closed with a stopper, for holding liquids; the amount of liquid held by such a vessel; with *the,* strong drink.—**bot′tle**[2], *v. t.*; *-tled, -tling.* To put into bottles; fig., to store or shut (*up*).—**bot′tle=brush,** *n.* A brush for cleaning bottles, with bristles radiating from a central stem; also, any of various plants, as the mare's-tail, *Hippuris vulgaris,* or the field horsetail, *Equisetum arvense,* or any shrub of the Australian genus *Callistemon.*—**bot′tle-ful** (-fůl), *n.*; pl. *-fuls.*—**bot′tle=green′,** *n.* A dark-green color.—**bot′tle-head,** *n.* A bottlenose whale.—**bot′tle=hold″er,** *n.* A pugilist's attendant at a prize-fight.—**bot′tle=imp,** *n.* Same as *Cartesian devil.* See *Cartesian.*—**bot′tle-nose,** *n.* A swollen or inflamed nose, as from intemperate drinking; also, any of various cetaceans, as *Hyperoödon rostratus,* a member of the sperm-whale family, or a black-whale; also, the puffin.—**bot′tler,** *n.*—**bot′tle=tree,** *n.* Any Australian tree of the genus *Sterculia,* as *S. rupestris:* so called from the globular, bottle-like expansion of the trunk.

Bottle-tree (*Sterculia rupestris*).

bot-tom (bot′om). [AS. *botm* = G. *boden.*] **I.** *n.* The lowest or undermost part; the foot, base, or foundation; the underlying ground, as beneath water; low land adjacent to a river; grounds or sediment; the part of the body on which one sits; the seat of a chair; power of endurance; the part of a ship below the wales; also, a ship; also, a nucleus on which to wind thread†, or the thread so wound†. **II.** *a.* Lowest; undermost; underlying; fundamental.—**bot′tom,** *v.* **I.** *tr.* To furnish with a bottom; also, to base or found (*on* or *upon*); also, to get to the bottom of; fathom; also, to wind, as thread, on something†. **II.** *intr.* To be based; rest; also, to reach the bottom.—**bot′tomed,** *a.* Having a bottom: as, a flat-*bottomed* boat.—**bot′tom-less,** *a.* Without a bottom; baseless; fathomless; immeasurably deep.—**the bottomless pit,** hell. See Rev. ix. 1; xx. 1–3.—**bot′tom-most,** *a. superl.* Lowest.—**bot′tom-ry,** *n.* A contract, of the nature of a mortgage, by which the owner of a ship borrows money to make a voyage, pledging the ship as security for the money.

botts (bots), *n. pl.* See *bot.*

bot-u-li-form (bot′ū-li-fôrm), *a.* [L. *botulus,* sausage: see *-form.*] In *bot.,* sausage-shaped.

bot-u-lin, bot-u-line (bot′ū-lin), *n.* [L. *botulus,* sausage.] The toxin causing botulism.

bot-u-li-nus (bot-ū-lī′nus), *n.* [NL., < L. *botulus,* sausage.] The bacterium *Bacillus botulinus,* which forms the toxin causing botulism.

bot-u-lism (bot′ū-lizm), *n.* [L. *botulus,* sausage.] A form of poisoning produced by eating spoiled food (as sausages, canned meats and vegetables, etc.), and due to a toxin formed by the bacterium *Bacillus botulinus.* Also (NL.) **bot-u-lis′mus** (-liz′mus).

bou-clé (bö-klā). [F., pp. of *boucler,* curl.] **I.** *a.* Of fabrics, having small curly loops over the surface, formed by drawing up threads at intervals in weaving. **II.** *n.* A bouclé fabric (usually of wool).

bou-doir (bö′dwor), *n.* [F., 'place to sulk in,' < *bouder,* pout, sulk.] A lady's retiring-room or private sitting-room.

bouf-fant (bö′font, F. bö-fäṅ), *a.* [F. (fem. *bouffante*), ppr. of *bouffer,* swell, puff.] Puffed out; full, as sleeves or draperies.

bou-gain-vil-læ-a (bö″gān-vi-lē′ạ, commonly -vil′ē-ạ), *n.* [NL.; named from L. A. de *Bougainville* (1729–1811), French navigator.] Any plant of the nyctaginaceous South American genus *Bougainvillæa,* comprising shrubs with small flowers subtended by large colored bracts (red, purple, etc.), species of which are cultivated for ornament. Also **bou″gain-vil-le′a.**

bough (bou), *n.* [AS. *bōg, bōh,* shoulder, bough, = D. *boeg,* LG. *bug,* Icel. *bōgr,* shoulder, bow of a ship (cf. *bow*[3]), = G. *bug,* shoulder; akin to Gr. πῆχυς, Skt. *bāhu,* forearm.] A branch of a tree, esp. one of the larger or main branches; also, the gallows (archaic).—**boughed,** *a.* Having boughs; shaded with boughs.—**bough′=pot,** *n.* A pot or other vessel for holding boughs or flowers for ornament; also, a flower-pot; also, a bouquet.

bought[1] (bout), *n.* [Prob. var. of *bight,* under the influence of *bow*[1].] A bend or curve; a turn or loop, as in a rope; a coil (as, "The dragon-*boughts* . . . Began to move, seethe, twine, and curl": Tennyson's "Gareth and Lynette," 229); a fold, as of cloth. [Archaic or prov. Eng.]

bought[2] (bât). Preterit and past participle of *buy.*—**bought-en** (bât′n), *p. a.* Bought or purchased, esp. as opposed to *home-made.* [Prov. or poetic.]

bough-y (bou′i), *a.* Abounding in boughs.

bou-gie (bö′ji, F. bö-zhē), *n.* [F., < *Bougie,* town in Algeria from which wax was obtained.] A wax candle; also, a slender, flexible instrument for dilating or opening passages of the body; also, a pencil of medicated paraffin or other readily melting substance for introduction into the body.

bou-illa-baisse (bö-yȧ-bās), *n.* [F.; from Provençal.] A kind of stew or chowder made of fish and vegetables.

bou-illi (bö-yē), *n.* [F., pp. of *bouillir,* boil, = E. *boil*[2].] Boiled or stewed meat.

bou-illon (bö′lyon, F. bö-yôṅ), *n.* [F., < *bouillir:* see *bouilli.*] A clear, thin broth made by boiling meat, etc., long and slowly.

boul-der (bōl′dėr), *n.* [Short for *boulder-stone,* ME. *bulder ston:* cf. Sw. *bullersten.*] A detached and rounded or worn mass of rock, esp. one of some size; a large, detached rock rounded by the action of weather, water, etc.—**boul′der,** *v. t.* To make into boulders; also, to wear smooth, as an emery-wheel, by abrading with flint pebbles.—**boul′der=clay,** *n.* A stiff, tenacious, unlaminated clay, often containing boulders, deposited during the glacial epoch.—**boul′der-y,** *a.* Characterized by the presence of boulders.

boule[1] (böl), *n.* See *boulle* and *buhl.*

Bou-le[2] (bö′lē), *n.* [Gr. βουλή, will, counsel, legislative council in ancient Greece, < βούλεσθαι, will, wish.] The legislative assembly of modern Greece.

bou-le-vard (bö′le-värd, F. böl-vär), *n.* [F. *boulevard,* OF. *boulvert, bolvercq, bolluwercq;* from Teut., from the same source as E. *bulwark.*] A public walk or street on the site of demolished fortifications; hence, a broad, handsome avenue of a city.—**boule-var-dier** (F. böl-vär-dyā), *n.* [F.] One who frequents the boulevards.

boule-verse-ment (böl-vers-mоṅ), *n.* [F., < *bouleverser,* overturn.] A turning upside down or upsetting; subversion; complete disorder.

boulle, boule[1] (böl), *n.* Better (French) forms of *buhl.*

boul-ter (bōl′tėr), *n.* See *bolter*[3].

boun (boun), *a.* [ME. *boun, bun,* < Icel. *būinn,* pp. of *būa,* make ready, dwell: cf. *bound*[4].] Ready; prepared; ready or intending to go; bound; going to, or on the point of. [Now only prov.]—**boun,** *v.* [ME. *bounen,* < *boun.*] **I.** *tr.* To make ready; prepare. [Archaic or prov.] **II.** *intr.* To get ready; also, to betake one's self to a place; set out; go. [Archaic or prov.]

bounce (bouns), *v.; bounced, bouncing.* [ME. *bunsen:* cf. D. *bonzen,* bounce, knock, LG. *bunsen,* knock.] **I.** *tr.* To beat, knock, or bang (now only prov. Eng.); bully or scold (colloq.); cause to bound or rebound, as a ball; also, to eject or discharge summarily (slang, U. S.). **II.** *intr.* To knock loudly, as at a door†; make an explosive noise†; also, to bluster, brag, or exaggerate; also, to strike and rebound; bound; also, to come or go suddenly or unceremoniously.—**bounce,** *n.* A heavy or noisy blow; a loud noise, as of an explosion†; also, bluster or boasting; a boast; a boastful falsehood; a lie; also, a rebound or bound; a spring or leap; also, expulsion or discharge (slang, U. S.).—**bounce,** *adv.* With a bounce; suddenly.—**bounce′a-ble,** *a.* That may be bounced, as a ball; also, inclined to bluster, brag, or exaggerate.—**boun′cer,** *n.* One who or that which bounces; a blusterer, boaster, or liar; a bare-faced lie; something big of its kind; a large, strong, vigorous person; one employed in a place of public resort to eject disorderly or obnoxious persons (slang, U. S.).—**boun′cing,** *p. a.* That bounces; blustering or boastful; exaggerated or excessive; big; stout, strong, or vigorous.

bound[1] (bound), *n.* [OF. *bodne* (F. *borne*), < ML. *bodina,* earlier *butina,* bound, limit.] A limiting line, or boundary; that which limits, confines, or restrains; *pl.,* territory on or near a boundary; also, an area included within boundaries.—**bound**[1], *v.* **I.** *tr.* To limit as by bounds; also, to form the boundary or limit of; also, to name the boundaries of (as, to *bound* the State of Maine). **II.** *intr.* To have its boundary (*on*); abut.

bound[2] (bound), *v.* [F. *bondir,* leap, orig. resound, perhaps ult. < L. *bombus,* booming sound.] **I.** *intr.* To leap or spring; move by leaps or springs; also, to rebound, as a ball. **II.** *tr.* To cause to bound.—**bound**[2], *n.* A leap or spring upward or onward; also, a rebound.

bound[3] (bound). Preterit and past participle of *bind*.—**bound**[3], *p. a.* Made fast by or as by a band or bond; tied; in bonds; secured within a cover, as a book; costive, as a person; constrained or obliged; under obligation, legally or morally; destined or sure (as, it is *bound* to happen); determined or resolved (as, he is *bound* to go).—**bound up in,** inseparably connected with; also, having the affections centered in.

bound[4] (bound), *a.* [Later form of *boun*, *a.*, prob. regarded also as pp. of *bind*.] Ready or intending to go; having set out; directing one's course.

boun-da-ry (boun'dạ-ri), *n.*; pl. *-ries* (-riz). [From *bound*[1], *n.*] Something that indicates bounds or limits; a limiting line, or bound.

bound-ed (boun'ded), *p. a.* Having bounds or limits; having its bounds or limits marked; limited; circumscribed; narrow.—**bound'ed-ness,** *n.*

bound-en (boun'dn), *p. a.* [See *bind*.] Bound; obliged; beholden; also, obligatory. [Archaic.]

bound-er (boun'dėr), *n.* An obtrusive, ill-bred person; a vulgar upstart. [Colloq., orig. Eng.]

bound-less (bound'les), *a.* Without bounds; unlimited.—**bound'less-ly,** *adv.*—**bound'less-ness,** *n.*

boun-te-ous (boun'tẹ-us), *a.* [ME. *bountevous*, < OF. *bontif*, < *bonte*: see *bounty*.] Beneficently liberal; generous; bountiful.—**boun'te-ous-ly,** *adv.*—**boun'te-ous-ness,** *n.*

boun-ti-ful (boun'ti-fu̇l), *a.* Characterized by bounty; liberal or generous; abundant or ample.—**boun'ti-ful-ly,** *adv.*—**boun'ti-ful-ness,** *n.*

boun-ty (boun'ti), *n.*; pl. *-ties* (-tiz). [OF. *bonte* (F. *bonté*), < L. *bonitas*, < *bonus*, good.] Goodness†; also, beneficent liberality; generosity; munificence; also, a benevolent gift; a gratuity; also, a premium or reward, esp. one offered by a government.—**boun'ty=jump"er,** *n.* In *U. S. hist.*, one who, during the Civil War, enlisted as a soldier for the sake of the bounty offered, and then deserted.

bou-quet (bö-kā'), *n.* [F., bouquet, bunch, clump of trees, OF. *boquet*, *bosquet*, little wood, dim. of *bosc*, wood: see *bush*[1].] A bunch of flowers; a nosegay; also, a bunch of various herbs for seasoning in cookery; also, something resembling a bunch of flowers, as a cluster of precious stones, a piece or flight of fireworks, etc.; also, the characteristic perfume of wines, etc.

Bour-bon (bör'bọn), *n.* [From the seigniory of *Bourbon*, with castle at Bourbon-l'Archambault, in central France.] A member of the last royal family of France, or of any of its branches, as the former royal family of Spain; hence, an extreme conservative, or one devoted to ideas suited only to past conditions, as in U. S. politics (applied esp. to certain Southern Democrats); also [*l. c.*], a kind of whisky, orig. the corn-whisky made in Bourbon County, Kentucky.—**Bour'bon-ism,** *n.* Adherence to the Bourbons; also, extreme conservatism, as in U. S. politics.—**Bour'bon-ist,** *n.*

bour-don (bör'dọn), *n.* [F.: see *burden*[2].] The drone of a bagpipe; an invariable bass, as of a bagpipe; a low ground-melody.

bou-rette (bö-ret'), *n.* [Cf. F. *bourrette*, coarse silk.] A woolen fabric with small knots or lumps at intervals over the surface, due to irregularities in the yarn.

bourg (börg, F. bör), *n.* [F.: see *borough*.] A town: as, "Ye think the rustic cackle of your *bourg* The murmur of the world!" (Tennyson's "Marriage of Geraint," 276).

bour-geois[1] (bėr-jois'), *n.* [Said to be named from *Bourgeois*, a French type-founder.] A printing-type (9 point) of a size between brevier and long primer. See *type*.

bour-geois[2] (bör-zhwo). [F. *bourgeois* (fem. *bourgeoise*), OF. *burgeis*, citizen: see *burgess*.] **I.** *n.* In France and elsewhere, a member of the middle (esp. the mercantile) class of the people. **II.** *a.* Middle-class; common; wanting in refinement or elegance.—**bour-geoi-sie** (bör-zhwo-zē), *n.* [F.] The bourgeois class.

bour-geon (bėr'jọn), *n.* and *v.* See *burgeon*.

bourn[1], **bourne**[1] (bōrn), *n.* [Var. of *burn*[1].] A small stream; a brook; a burn.

bourn[2], **bourne**[2] (bōrn or börn), *n.* [F. *borne*, for OF. *bodne*: see *bound*[1].] A bound or limit (as, "The undiscover'd country from whose *bourn* No traveller returns": Shakspere's "Hamlet," iii. 1. 79); hence, a goal; also, a realm† or domain†.

bourn[3], **bourne**[3] (bōrn), *v. t.* See *bone*[1].

bourse (börs), *n.* [F., < ML. *bursa*, purse: see *bursa*.] An exchange where merchants transact business with one another; a stock-exchange, as that of Paris.

bouse[1] (böz or bouz), *v. i.* or *t.*; *boused*, *bousing*. [ME. *bousen*: cf. MD. *busen*, drink, *buise*, large drinking-vessel.] To drink, esp. to excess. Cf. *booze*.—**bouse**[1], *n.* Liquor or drink; also, a drinking-bout; a carouse. [Colloq.]

bouse[2], **bowse** (bous), *v. t.*; *boused* or *bowsed*, *bousing* or *bowsing*. [Origin unknown.] *Naut.*, to haul with tackle.

bou-stro-phe-don (bö-strọ-fē'dọn or bou-), *n.* [Gr. βουστροφηδόν, adv., with turning like that of oxen in plowing, < βοῦς, ox, + στρέφειν, turn.] An ancient method of writing in which the lines run alternately from right to left and from left to right.

bous-y (bö'zi or bou'zi), *a.* Intoxicated; boozy.

bout (bout), *n.* [Var. of *bought*[1].] A bend or loop; also, a turn at work or any action; a contest or set-to; a spell or fit of anything.

bou-ton-nière (bö-to-nyãr), *n.* [F., buttonhole, < *bouton*, button.] A buttonhole bouquet.

bouts=ri-més (bö-rē-mā), *n. pl.* [F., 'ends rimed.'] Riming words given out as line-endings to be filled out into verse.

bou-var-di-a (bö-vär'di-ạ̈), *n.* [NL.; named from Dr. Charles *Bouvard*, physician to Louis XIII. of France.] Any plant of the rubiaceous genus *Bouvardia*, chiefly of tropical America, with corymbs of red, pink, yellow, or white flowers, well known in cultivation.

bo-vid (bō'vid), *a.* [NL. *Bovidæ*, pl., < L. *bos* (*bov-*), ox.] Of or pertaining to the *Bovidæ*, or ox family, comprising the hollow-horned ruminants, as oxen, sheep, goats, and antelopes.

bo-vine (bō'vīn or -vin). [LL. *bovinus*, < L. *bos* (*bov-*), ox.] **I.** *a.* Of the ox kind; ox-like; hence, stolid; dull. **II.** *n.* A bovine animal.

bow[1] (bou), *v.* [AS. *būgan* = G. *biegen*, bend; prob. akin to L. *fugere*, Gr. φεύγειν, flee, Skt. *bhuj-*, bend.] **I.** *intr.* To bend or stoop; bend the head or body, as in respect or worship; incline the head in salutation; yield or submit. **II.** *tr.* To cause to bend; incline; express by an inclination of the head; usher (*out*, etc.) with a bow; cause to stoop, sink, or yield.—**bow**[1], *n.* An inclination of the head or body, as in respect or in salutation.

bow[2] (bō), *n.* [AS. *boga* = G. *bogen*; akin to E. *bow*[1].] A bend or curve; something curved or arc-shaped (as, a rain*bow*; an ox-*bow*; a saddle-*bow*); a weapon consisting of a strip of elastic wood or other material bent by a string stretched between its ends, used for shooting arrows; a bowman or archer; an implement, orig. curved but now almost straight, with horsehairs stretched upon it, for playing a violin or the like; a single stroke of such an implement; a ring-like part, as a key-handle or one of the two hoops of a pair of scissors fitted for the fingers; also, a looped knot, as of ribbon; a bow-knot.—**bow**[2], *v.* **I.** *tr.* To bend or bring into a curved form; curve; also, to play or perform with a bow. **II.** *intr.* To be curved; also, to use a bow on a stringed instrument.

bow[3] (bou), *n.* [From LG. or Scand., orig. meaning 'shoulder,' = E. *bough*.] The forward part of a ship, beginning where the sides trend inward, and terminating where they close or unite in the stem (often in *pl.*); any similar forward end or part, as of an airship; also, the bow-oar.—**bow'=chas"er** (-chā"sėr), *n.* A gun at the bow of a ship, for firing at vessels pursued.

bow=com-pass (bō'kum"pạs), *n.* Any of various forms of compasses for drawing small circles, arcs, etc., as one having the legs joined by a bow-shaped piece.

Bowd-ler-ism (boud'lėr-izm), *n.* [From Thomas *Bowdler*, who in 1818 published an expurgated edition of Shakspere.] The practice of omitting from an author's edited works words or passages considered indelicate or offensive.—**Bowd′ler-ize,** *v. t.*; *-ized, -izing.* To expurgate (a book, etc.).

bow-el (bou′el), *n.* [OF. *boel* (F. *boyau*), < L. *botellus,* dim. of *botulus,* sausage.] An intestine; usually *pl.*, the parts of the alimentary canal below the stomach; the intestines or entrails; also, inward or interior parts; also, feelings of pity or compassion; also, offspring†.—**bow′el,** *v. t.*; *-eled* or *-elled, -eling* or *-elling.* To disembowel.

bow-er[1] (bou′ėr), *n.* One who or that which bows, bends, etc.

bow-er[2] (bō′ėr), *n.* A bow-maker†; a player with the bow on a violin, etc.

bow-er[3] (bou′ėr), *n.* An anchor carried at a ship's bow.

bow-er[4] (bou′ėr), *n.* [G. *bauer,* peasant.] In *euchre,* the knave of trumps ('right bower') or the other knave of the same color ('left bower'): the highest cards in the game, unless the joker (often called the 'best bower') is used.

bow-er[5] (bou′ėr), *n.* [AS. *būr,* akin to *būan,* dwell.] A dwelling, esp. a rustic abode (poetic); a chamber, esp. a lady's private chamber (poetic); an arbor; a leafy shelter or recess.—**bow′er**[5], *v. t.* To embower.—**bow′er=bird,** *n.* Any of various Australian oscine birds, as *Ptilonorhynchus holosericeus,* which build bower-like structures, used, not as nests, but as places of resort to attract the females, and often decorated with feathers, shells, etc.—**bow′er=maid″en,** *n.* A maid or woman in waiting on a lady. Also **bow′er=wom″an;** pl. *-women* (-wim″en). [Archaic.]

Bower-bird (*Ptilonorhynchus holosericeus*).

bow-er-y[1] (bou′ėr-i), *n.*; pl. *-ies* (-iz). [D. *bouwerij,* < *bouwer,* farmer.] Among the Dutch settlers of New York, a farm or country-seat: as, "He had his little *bowerie,* or retreat in the country" (Irving's "Knickerbocker's New York," iv. 4).

bow-er-y[2] (bou′ėr-i), *a.* Bower-like; embowering; shady.

bow-fin (bō′fin), *n.* A North American fresh-water ganoid fish, *Amia calva.*

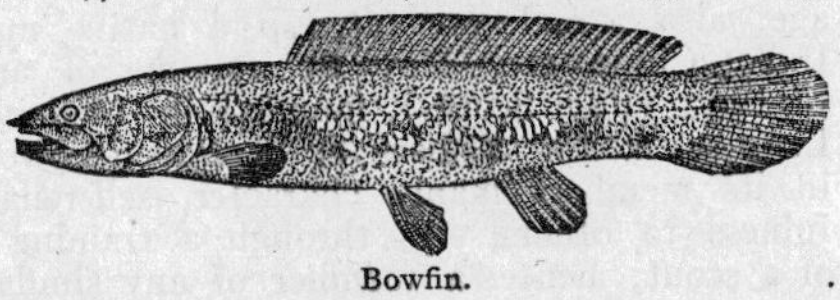

Bowfin.

bow=grace (bou′grās), *n.* A fender, as of junk, for protecting a ship's bows from floating ice, etc.

bow=hand (bō′hand), *n.* In *archery,* the hand that holds the bow, usually the left hand; in *music,* the hand that draws the bow; the right hand.

bow=head (bō′hed), *n.* The right whale, *Balæna mysticetus,* of arctic seas.

bow-ie (bou′i), *n.* [Origin uncertain.] A small barrel or cask with the head taken off; a tub; also, a wooden vessel for milk, porridge, etc. [Sc.]

bow-ie=knife (bō′i-nīf or bō′-), *n.*; pl. *-knives* (-nīvz). [From James *Bowie* (1796–1836), American pioneer, whose knife became famous.] A heavy sheath-knife having a long, single-edged blade with a straight back which slopes concavely toward the edge from a place near the point; hence, any large sheath-knife.

Bowie-knife and Sheath.

bow=knot (bō′not), *n.* A looped slip-knot, usually with two loops and two ends.

bowl[1] (bōl), *n.* [Var. of *boll*[1] (AS. *bolla*).] A vessel of greater width than depth, usually hemispherical or nearly so, for holding liquids, etc.; such a vessel used to drink from; a large drinking-cup or goblet; drink or drinking; the contents of a bowl; a rounded hollow part, as of a spoon or tobacco-pipe; any bowl-shaped formation or structure; an edifice with a bowl-like interior, as for athletic contests, etc. (as, the Yale *Bowl*).

bowl[2] (bōl), *n.* [OF. F. *boule,* ball, < L. *bulla,* bubble.] A ball† or globe†; one of the biased or weighted balls used in the game of bowls; one of the balls, having little or no bias, used in playing ninepins or tenpins; the disk sometimes used in playing skittles; also, a cast or delivery of the ball in bowling. See *bowls.*—**bowl**[2], *v.* **I.** *intr.* To play with bowls or at bowling; roll a bowl; move along smoothly and rapidly, as a carriage; in *cricket,* to deliver the ball to be played by the batsman. **II.** *tr.* To cause (a ball, hoop, etc.) to roll; carry or convey as in a wheeled vehicle; pelt with or as with bowls; knock or strike (*over* or *down*) as by the ball in bowling; in *cricket,* to deliver (the ball) to be played by the batsman; also, to put (*off, out,* etc.) by bowling.

bowl-der (bōl′dėr), etc. See *boulder,* etc.

bow=leg (bō′leg), *n.* Outward curvature of the legs, causing a separation of the knees when the ankles are in contact; a leg so curved.—**bow′=legged** (-legd or -leg″ed), *a.*

bowl-er (bō′lėr), *n.* One who bowls; also, a derby hat (Eng.).

bow-line (bō′lin or -līn), *n.* [ME. *bouline*: cf. D. *boeglijn,* Sw. *boglina,* Dan. *bovline,* bowline, and E. *bow*[3].] *Naut.*, a rope leading forward, fastened to the leech of a square sail to steady the weather edge and keep it forward when sailing close-hauled; also, a kind of knot used in making a loop ('bowline-knot').

bowl-ing (bō′ling), *n.* The sport of playing at bowls; the game played; esp., in the U. S. and Canada, tenpins, now chiefly as played on a bowling-alley ('American bowling').—**bowl′ing=al″ley,** *n.* A long inclosure for playing at bowls, etc.; a covered place with a long, narrow planked inclosure, for playing at tenpins, etc.—**bowl′ing=green″,** *n.* A level piece of greensward kept smooth for bowling.

bowls (bōlz), *n.* [See *bowl*[2].] A game, common in Great Britain, in which the players roll biased or weighted balls along the sward in an effort to bring them as near as possible to a stationary ball called the *jack*; sometimes, skittles, ninepins, or ('American bowls') tenpins.

bow-man[1] (bō′man), *n.*; pl. *-men.* One who shoots with a bow; an archer; a soldier armed with a bow.

bow-man[2] (bou′man), *n.*; pl. *-men.* The oarsman who sits nearest the bow of a boat; the bow-oar.

Bowman, 15th century.

bown (boun), *a.* and *v.* See *boun.*

bow=net (bō′net), *n.* A kind of wickerwork trap for catching lobsters, etc.

bow=oar (bou′ōr), *n.* In *rowing,* the foremost oar or oarsman, in the bow of the boat.

bow=pen (bō′pen), *n.* A bow-compass with a pen at the end of one leg. Similarly **bow′=pen″cil.**

bow=pot (bou′pot), *n.* See *bough-pot.*

bowse[1], **bowse**[2]. See *bouse*[1], *bouse*[2].

bow-shot (bō′shot), *n.* A shot from a bow; also, the distance over which a bow sends an arrow.

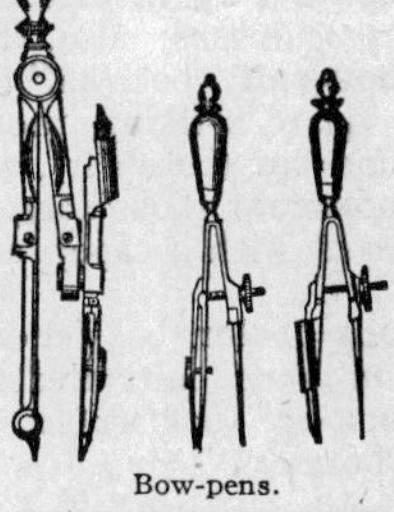

Bow-pens.

bow-sprit (bō′sprit or bou′-), *n.* [ME. *bouspret*: cf. D. *boegspriet*, LG. *boogspret*, Sw. *bogspröt*, bowsprit, and E. *bow*[3] and *sprit*.] *Naut.*, a large spar projecting forward from the stem of a ship or other vessel: used for extending the forward sail or sails.

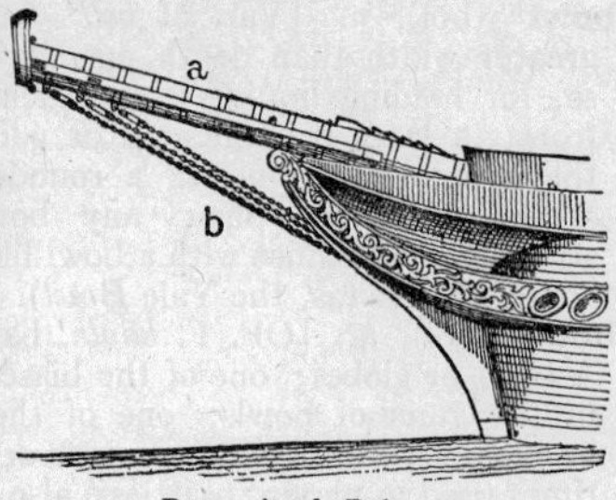

a, Bowsprit; *b*, Bobstays.

bow-string (bō′string), *n.* The string of a bow; also, a string used, as by the Turks, for strangling offenders.—**bow′string,** *v. t.* To strangle with a bowstring.

bow=win-dow (bō′win′dō), *n.* A rounded bay-window.

bow=wow (bou′wou′). [Imit.] **I.** *interj.* A word representing the bark of a dog. **II.** *n.* The bark of a dog; also (pron. bou′wou), a dog.—**bow′=wow′,** *v. i.* To bark.

bow-yer (bō′yėr), *n.* A maker or seller of bows; also, an archer.

box[1] (boks), *n.* [AS. *box*, < L. *buxus* = Gr. πύξος.] An evergreen shrub or small tree of the genus *Buxus*, esp. *B. sempervirens*, much used for ornamental borders, hedges, etc., and yielding a hard, durable wood; the wood itself (see *boxwood*); also, any of various other shrubs or trees, esp. species of eucalyptus.

Box (*Buxus sempervirens*).

box[2] (boks), *n.* [AS. *box*, < L. *buxus*, box-tree (see *box*[1]), perhaps through L. *buxum*, boxwood, something made of boxwood: cf. also ML. *buxis*, box, for L. *pyxis*, E. *pyx*.] A case or receptacle, as of metal, wood, or pasteboard, in many forms and sizes; a chest; the quantity contained in a box; also, a case or package containing a present or presents, as at Christmas; that which is contained in such a case; a present or gift (see *Christmas box*, under *Christmas*); also, a compartment or inclosure, as one for the separate accommodation of persons; a seated compartment in a theater, etc.; a small shelter (as, a sentry-*box*); a small house, as for use while following some sport (as, a shooting-*box*); the driver's seat on a coach; a space in a newspaper, etc., set off as by inclosing lines, in which news or other matter is featured, summarized, or the like; in *mach.*, an inclosing, protecting, or hollow part; a casing; a chamber; a bush; a socket; in *baseball*, the space where the pitcher stands to deliver the ball; also, that for the batter.—**box**[2], *v. t.* To put into a box; inclose or confine as in a box; furnish with a box; form into a box or the shape of a box; *naut.*, to veer (a sailing-vessel) round on her heel by manipulating the sails, etc. (often with *off*); boxhaul.—**to box the compass,** *naut.*, to name the points of the compass in their order; fig., to go or turn completely around.

box[3] (boks), *n.* [ME.; origin uncertain.] A blow, as with the hand or fist, esp. on the ear.—**box**[3], *v.* **I.** *tr.* To strike (esp. the ear) with the hand or fist. **II.** *intr.* To fight with the fists (bare or gloved); spar.

box=bed (boks′bed′), *n.* A bed boarded in and roofed over so as to resemble a box; also, a bed that folds up in the form of a box.

box-ber-ry (boks′ber″i), *n.* The checkerberry, *Gaultheria procumbens*; also, the partridge-berry, *Mitchella repens*.

box=calf (boks′käf′), *n.* A chrome-tanned calfskin with square markings produced by graining.

box=car (boks′kär), *n.* An inclosed and covered freight-car.

box=coat (boks′kōt), *n.* A coachman's overcoat; an overcoat with a cape; an outer coat with a straight, unfitted back.

box=el-der (boks′el′dėr), *n.* A North American maple, *Acer negundo*, cultivated for shade.

box-er[1] (bok′sėr), *n.* One who packs or puts up things in boxes.

box-er[2] (bok′sėr), *n.* One who boxes; a pugilist; [*cap.*] a member of a Chinese association, "The Righteousness, Harmony, and Fists Society," which in 1900 rose up against foreigners and native Christians, in the northern provinces of China, and besieged the legations at Peking for two months, until the uprising was suppressed by foreign military forces.

box-ful (boks′fu̇l), *n.*; pl. *-fuls*. A quantity sufficient to fill a box.

box-haul (boks′hâl), *v. t.* *Naut.*, to veer (a ship) round on her heel by bracing the head-yards flat aback, with other manipulations.

box-ing[1] (bok′sing), *n.* The act of one who boxes something; a putting into or furnishing with a box; also, material for boxes or casings; also, a structure or work of boxes; a box-like inclosure; a casing; also, the giving of a box or present, as at Christmas (hence *Boxing Day*, in England, the first week-day after Christmas, when Christmas boxes or presents are given to employees, postmen, etc.).

box-ing[2] (bok′sing), *n.* The act or art of fighting with the fists; sparring.—**box′ing=glove,** *n.* A padded glove worn in boxing.

box=kite (boks′kīt′), *n.* A kite consisting of a light frame in the form of a rectangular parallelepiped, covered with cloth or the like with the exception of the ends and a space about the middle.

box=of-fice (boks′of″is), *n.* In a theater, the office in which tickets are sold.

box=oys-ter (boks′ois″tėr), *n.* An oyster of large size and superior quality: orig. shipped to market in boxes instead of barrels.

box=plait, box=pleat (boks′plāt, -plēt), *n.* A double plait, with the material folded under at each side.—**box′=plait, box′=pleat,** *v. t.* To arrange in box-plaits.

box=stew (boks′stū), *n.* A stew made of large select oysters, orig. of box-oysters.

box=thorn (boks′thôrn), *n.* Any of the deciduous or evergreen plants constituting the solanaceous genus *Lycium*, species of which are cultivated for their ornamental foliage, flowers, and berries.

box-wood (boks′wu̇d), *n.* The hard, fine-grained, compact wood of the box (genus *Buxus*), much used for wood-engravers' blocks, musical and mathematical instruments, etc.; the tree or shrub itself; also, any of various shrubs or trees with a hard, compact wood, as *Cornus florida*, the flowering dogwood of the U. S.

boy (boi), *n.* [ME. *boy*, *boi*; prob. from LG.] A male child; a lad; also, a familiar term for a man of any age; also, a male servant, esp. a native male servant in India, China, etc.—**Boy Scout,** one of an organization of boys (Boy Scouts), founded in England in 1908 by Lieut.-Gen. Sir Robert S. S. Baden-Powell, to develop in its members manly character, self-reliance, and usefulness to others, esp. through a training in the duties of a scout; hence, a member of any similar society elsewhere.

boy-ar (boi′ä̤r or bō̤-yär′), *n.* [Russ.] A member of a former order or class of the Russian aristocracy; also, one of a privileged class in Rumania.

boy-au (bwo-yō), *n.*; pl. *boyaux* (-yōz, F. -yō). [F., lit. 'bowel,' 'gut': see *bowel*.] In *fort.*, a connecting trench; a passageway between parallel trenches or other parts of a trench system; also, a branch or small gallery of a mine.

boy-cott (boi′kot), *v. t.* [From Captain *Boycott*, the first victim (1880), agent of an Irish landlord.] To combine in abstaining from or preventing dealings with (a person, business house, etc.) as a means of intimidation or coercion; abstain from buying or using (commercial products, etc.).—**boy′cott,** *n.* A process of boycotting.—**boy′-cott-er,** *n.*

boy-hood (boi′hu̇d), *n.* The state or period of being a boy; also, boys collectively.

boy-ish (boi′ish), *a.* Of, like, or befitting a boy.—**boy′-ish-ly,** *adv.*—**boy′ish-ness,** *n.*

brab-ble (brab′l), *v. i.*; *-bled*, *-bling*. [Cf. *babble* and *brawl*[2].] To dispute noisily; wrangle; brawl. [Archaic or prov. Eng.]—**brab′ble,** *n.*—**brab′ble-ment,** *n.*

brac-cate (brak′āt), *a.* [L. *bracatus,* wearing breeches, < *bracæ,* breeches.] In *ornith.,* having the feet covered with feathers.

Braccate. — Foot of Snow-owl.

brace (brās), *n.* [OF. *brace,* the two arms (as outstretched or embracing), < L. *bracchia,* pl. of *bracchium,* arm.] The part of a suit of armor which covers the arms†; a state of defense†; something that holds parts together or in place, as a clasp or clamp; *pl.,* suspenders; *sing.,* an appliance for supporting a weak back, round shoulders, etc.; a device for producing or regulating tension in a drum; the character { or } for connecting written or printed lines, staves in music, etc.; also, two things taken together; a pair or couple; also, anything that imparts rigidity or steadiness; in *mech.,* a device for holding and turning tools for boring or drilling; a bit-stock; *naut.,* on a square-rigged ship, a rope by which a yard is swung about and secured horizontally; in *arch., building,* etc., a piece of timber, metal, etc., as across an angle, for strengthening or supporting a framework or the like.—**brace,** *v.*; *braced, bracing.* **I.** *tr.* To furnish, fasten, or strengthen with or as with a brace; encompass, clasp, or gird; make tight, as the skin of a drum; increase the tension of; give firmness to; bring to greater vigor, etc. (often with *up*); fix firmly; make steady; connect (lines, etc.) with a brace, in writing or printing; *naut.,* to move or turn by means of braces. **II.** *intr.* To acquire vigor; rouse one's strength or energy: often with *up.* [Colloq.]

Hand-brace, with Bit.

brace-let (brās′let), *n.* [OF. F. *bracelet,* dim. of OF. *bracel,* < L. *bracchiale,* armlet, < *bracchium,* arm.] An ornamental band or circlet for the wrist or arm; also, a handcuff (colloq.).—**brace′let-ed,** *a.*

Ancient Bracelets.

bra-cer (brā′sėr), *n.* One who or that which braces; a tonic or stimulating drink.

brach (brach or brak), *n.* [ME. *braches,* pl., < OF. *braches,* pl. of *brachet;* from Teut.] A kind of hound that hunts by scent†; in later use, a bitch of the hound kind.

brach-et (brach′et), *n.* See *bratchet.*

bra-chi-a (brā′ki-ạ̈ or brak′i-), *n.* Plural of *brachium.*

bra-chi-al (brā′ki-ạl or brak′i-), *a.* [L. *brachialis.*] Belonging to the arm, esp. the upper arm or brachium; arm-like, as an appendage.

bra-chi-ate (brā′ki-āt or brak′i-), *a.* [L. *brachiatus.*] In *zoöl.,* having brachia or arm-like appendages, as a crinoid; in *bot.,* having widely spreading branches in alternate pairs, or decussate.

brach-i-o-pod (brak′i-ọ-pod), *n.* [NL. *Brachiopoda,* pl., < Gr. βραχίων, arm, + πούς (ποδ-), foot.] One of the *Brachiopoda,* a class of mollusk-like animals with a pair of brachial appendages, one on each side of the mouth.

bra-chi-um (brā′ki-um or brak′i-), *n.*; pl. *brachia* (-ạ̈). [L., prop. *bracchium,* = Gr. βραχίων, arm.] The upper arm, from the shoulder to the elbow; the corresponding part of any fore limb, as in the wing of a bird; also, an arm-like part, appendage, or process.

brachy-. Form of Gr. βραχύς, short, used in combination.

brach-y-cat-a-lec-tic (brak″i-kat-ạ-lek′tik). [Gr. βραχυκατάληκτος, < βραχύς, short, + καταλήγειν, leave off: see *catalectic.*] In *pros.*: **I.** *a.* Wanting the last foot of the last dipody. **II.** *n.* A brachycatalectic verse.

brach-y-ce-phal-ic (brak″i-se-fal′ik), *a.* [Gr. βραχύς, short, + κεφαλή, head.] Short-headed; having a breadth of skull at least four-fifths as great as the length from front to back: opposed to *dolichocephalic.* Also **brach-y-ceph′a-lous** (-sef′ạ-lus).—**brach-y-ceph′a-ly,** *n.*

bra-chyg-ra-phy (bra-kig′rạ-fi), *n.* [See *brachy-* and *-graphy.*] Shorthand; stenography.

bra-chyl-o-gy (bra-kil′ọ-ji), *n.*; pl. *-gies* (-jiz). [Gr. βραχυλογία: see *brachy-* and *-logy.*] Brevity of diction; conciseness; also, a condensed expression.

bra-chyp-ter-ous (bra-kip′tẹ-rus), *a.* [Gr. βραχύπτερος: see *brachy-* and *-pterous.*] Short-winged; brevipennate.

brach-y-u-ran (brak-i-ū′rạn). [NL. *Brachyura,* pl., < Gr. βραχύς, short, + οὐρά, tail.] **I.** *a.* Belonging or pertaining to the *Brachyura,* a group of stalk-eyed decapod crustaceans with short tails, consisting of the common crabs. **II.** *n.* A brachyuran crustacean.—**brach-y-u′rous** (-ū′rus), *a.* Short-tailed, as the crabs: opposed to *macrurous.*

bra-cing (brā′sing), *n.* The act of one who or that which braces; also, a brace, or braces collectively.—**bra′cing,** *p. a.* That braces; strengthening; invigorating.—**bra′cing-ly,** *adv.*—**bra′cing-ness,** *n.*

brack[1] (brak), *n.* [= *break.*] A break, breach, or gap; a flaw. [Now prov.]

brack[2] (brak), *a.* [D. *brak.*] Salt; brackish. [Now prov.]

brack-en (brak′ẹn), *n.* [ME. *braken;* prob. from Scand. (cf. Sw. *bräken*).] A large fern or brake, esp. *Pteris aquilina;* also, such ferns collectively.

brack-et (brak′et), *n.* [Earlier *bragget:* cf. Sp. *bragueta,* ult. < L. *bracæ,* breeches.] A projection from the face of a wall, to support a statue, pier, etc.; a corbel; a shelf-like support to be attached to a wall; any projecting support, as for a shelf; a projecting fixture for gas or electricity; one of two marks, [ ], used in writing or printing to inclose parenthetic matter, interpolations, etc.; also, a brace for connecting lines.—**brack′et,** *v. t.*; *-eted, -eting.* To support with a bracket; inclose in brackets; couple with a brace; associate or mention together.—**brack′et-ing,** *n.* A series of brackets or bracket-like supports.

Bracket for Statue. — Cathedral of Rheims, France; 13th century.

brack-ish (brak′ish), *a.* [See *brack*[2].] Slightly salt, as water; having a saltish or briny flavor. Also fig.—**brack′ish-ness,** *n.*

bract (brakt), *n.* [L. *bractea,* thin plate of metal.] In *bot.,* a small leaf-like part, esp. at the base of a pedicel or a flower —**brac-te-al** (brak′tẹ-ạl), *a.* Pertaining to or of the nature of a bract.—**brac′-te-ate** (-āt), *a.* Having bracts. Also **bract′ed.**—**brac′te-o-late** (-ọ-lāt), *a.* Having bracteoles.—**brac′te-ole** (-ōl), *n.* [L. *bracteola,* dim. of *bractea.*] In *bot.,* a small or secondary bract, as on a pedicel. Also **bract′let.**

Bracts of Marigold: *a, a,* of pedicel; *b,* of flower.

brad (brad), *n.* [ME. *brad, brod:* cf. Icel. *broddr,* spike.] A thin, flat, usually small, nail of uniform thickness, but tapering in width, having instead of a head a slight projection at the top on one side; also, a wire nail with a small deep head; also, a small, flat wedge-shaped piece of tinplate or the like, as for holding glass in a sash.—**brad′=awl,** *n.* An awl for making holes for brads, etc.

brady-. Form of Gr. βραδύς, slow, used in combination.—**brad-y-car-di-a** (brad-i-kär′di-ạ̈), *n.* [NL. (Gr. καρδία, heart).] Abnormally slow heart-action.—**brad-y-pep′sia** (-pep′ṣiạ̈), *n.* [NL. (Gr. πέπτειν, cook, digest).] Slow digestion.—**brad-yp-nœ′a** (-ip-nē′ạ̈), *n.* [NL. (Gr. πνεῖν, blow, breathe).] Slow or labored breathing.

brad-y-pod (brad′i-pod), *n.* [Gr. βραδύπους (-ποδ-), slow-footed: see *brady-* and *-pod.*] Any animal of the sloth family (*Bradypodidæ*).

brae (brā), *n.* [Icel. *brā* = AS. *brǣw,* eyelid.] A slope; a declivity; a hillside: as, "Maxwelton *braes* are bonnie Where early fa's the dew" (Wm. Douglas's "Annie Laurie"). [Sc. and north. Eng.]

brag (brag), *v.*; *bragged, bragging.* [ME. *braggen;* origin uncertain; related F. forms are appar. later.] **I.** *intr.* To blare, as a trumpet†; also, to speak vaingloriously; boast (*of* or *about*); vaunt. **II.** *tr.* To boast of; vaunt; also, to challenge or defy (now Sc. and north. Eng.).—**brag,** *n.* [ME.] A boast or vaunt; bragging; also, a thing to brag of; also, a braggart; also, a game of cards resembling poker.

brag-ga-do-cio (brag-ạ-dō′shiō), *n.*; pl. *-cios* (-shiōz). [From *Braggadocchio*, a braggart in Spenser's "Faerie Queene."] A braggart; also, empty brag.

brag-gart (brag′ạ̈rt). [Cf. obs. F. *bragard*, boastful.] **I.** *n.* One given to bragging; a vainglorious boaster. **II.** *a.* Bragging; boastful.—**brag′gart-ism,** *n.*

brag-ger (brag′ėr), *n.* One who brags; a boaster.

brah-ma[1] (brä′mạ̈, often brā′mạ̈), *n.* [From *Brahmaputra*, river in northeastern India.] One of a breed of large domestic fowls, of Asiatic origin, with feathered legs and small wings and tail.

Brah-ma[2] (brä′mạ̈), *n.* [Skt. *brăhma*, neut., worship, prayer, the impersonal divinity, *brahmá*, masc., worshiper, priest, the divinity as personified.] In *Hindu religion*, the highest object of philosophic adoration; the impersonal and absolute divinity; later, the divinity personified, or conceived as a god, combined as Creator into a trinity with Vishnu as Preserver and Siva as Destroyer. Cf. *Trimurti.*—**Brah′man, Brah′min** (-mạn, -min), *n.*; pl. *-mans, -mins.* [Skt. *brāhmana.*] A member of the highest, or sacerdotal, caste among the Hindus.—**brah′ma-na** (-mạ-nạ̈), *n.* [Skt. *brāhmana.*] [Also *cap.*] In *Sanskrit lit.*, one of a class of prose writings, concerned chiefly with dogma and ritual, forming a part of the Vedic literature.—**Brah-man′ic, Brah-min′ic** (-man′ik, -min′ik), *a.* Pertaining to the Brahmans or to Brahmanism. Also **Brah-man′i-cal, Brah-min′i-cal.**—**Brah′man-ism, Brah′min-ism,** *n.* The religion or doctrines of the Brahmans; the social system of the Hindus, with the Brahmans as the highest caste.—**Brah′man-y, Brah′min-y,** *a.* Pertaining to the Brahmans; regarded as sacred by the Hindus (as, the *Brahmany* kite, a kite-like bird of prey, *Haliastur indus*, of India, etc.).

braid[1] (brād), *v. t.* [AS. *bregdan*, move quickly, move to and fro, weave, = OS. *bregdan*, OHG. *brettan*, Icel. *bregdha*, all orig. 'move quickly.'] To move quickly or suddenly†; jerk†, snatch†, or fling†; also, to weave together strips or strands of; plait; also, to form by weaving; also, to trim (garments, etc.) with braid; also, to confine (the hair) with a band or fillet (archaic or poetic).—**to braid St. Catharine's tresses,** of a woman, to remain unmarried; be an old maid.—**braid**[1], *n.* A sudden movement†; a start† or jerk†; a braided length, or plait, of hair, etc.; a woven band or strip, as of wool, silk, or cotton for trimming or binding garments, etc., or of linen thread for forming into lace patterns, or of straw or other fiber for making hats; a band or fillet for confining the hair (archaic or poetic: as, "The maiden's jet-black hair . . . Forth streaming from a *braid* of pearl," Tennyson's "Day-Dream," 82).

braid[2] (brād), *a.* Scotch form of *broad.*

braid-er (brā′dėr), *n.* One who or that which braids; a sewing-machine attachment for use in stitching braid on anything.—**braid′ing,** *n.* The act of one who or that which braids; also, braided work; trimming consisting of braid.

brail (brāl), *n.* [OF. *braiel*, cincture, orig. for holding up the breeches, < L. *bracæ*, breeches.] *Naut.*, one of the ropes sometimes fitted to a sail, by which it may be gathered up into a bunch, as against the mast and gaff, preparatory to or instead of furling.—**brail,** *v. t.* To gather or haul in (a sail) by means of brails: usually with *up.*

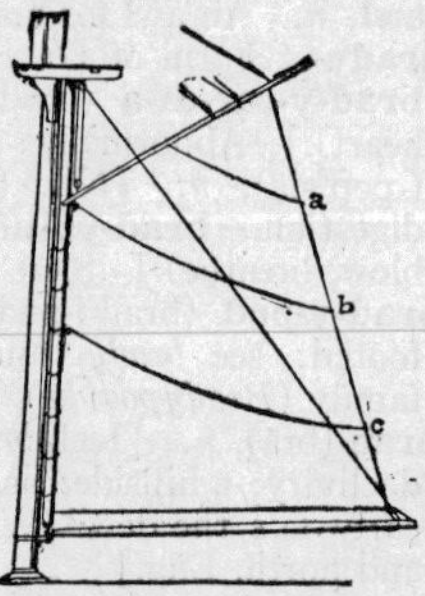

Sail set, showing Brails.—*a*, peak-brail; *b*, throat-brail; *c*, lower brail.

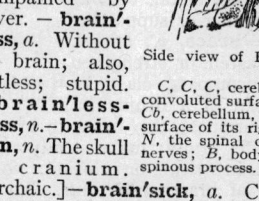

braille (brāl, F. brä-y'), *n.* [From Louis *Braille* (1809–52), the (French) inventor.] A system of writing or printing for the blind, in which combinations of tangible dots or points are used to represent letters, etc.

brain (brān), *n.* [AS. *brægen* = LG. *brägen* = D. *brein.*] The soft, convoluted mass of grayish and whitish nerve substance which fills the cranium of man and other vertebrates (sometimes in *pl.*); this organ considered as the center of sensation, and the seat of thought, memory, etc. (often in *pl.*); intellectual power (often in *pl.*); in many invertebrates, a part of the nervous system more or less corresponding to the brain of vertebrates.—**brain,** *v. t.* To dash out the brains of; also, to understand†; also, to furnish with a brain.—**brained,** *a.* Having a brain: as, mad-*brained.*—**brain′=fag,** *n.* Mental exhaustion, as from overwork.—**brain′=fe′ver,** *n.* Inflammation of the brain; encephalitis; also, any acute cerebral affection accompanied by fever.—**brain′less,** *a.* Without a brain; also, witless; stupid.—**brain′less-ness,** *n.*—**brain′pan,** *n.* The skull or cranium. [Archaic.]—**brain′sick,** *a.* Crazy; mad.—**brain′sick-ly,** *adv.*—**brain′sick-ness,** *n.*—**brain′=storm,** *n.* A sudden, violent, but temporary attack of mental disturbance.—**brain′=work,** *n.* Work requiring special use of the brain, as distinguished from ordinary manual or mechanical work; intellectual labor.—**brain′=work″er,** *n.* One who does brain-work, as a professional man, a teacher, a writer, or the like.—**brain′y,** *a.* Having brains; intelligent; clever.

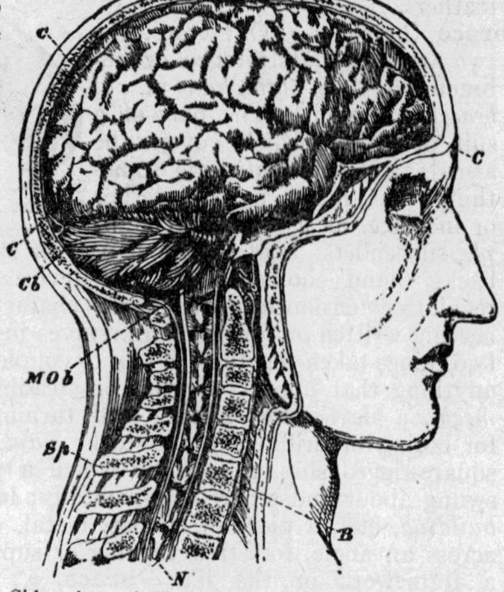

Side view of Human Brain and upper part of Spinal Cord.

C, C, C, cerebrum, or brain proper, showing the convoluted surface of the right cerebral hemisphere; *Cb,* cerebellum, or little brain, showing the striated surface of its right half; *MOb,* medulla oblongata; *N,* the spinal cord with beginnings of the spinal nerves; *B,* body of sixth cervical vertebra; *Sp,* its spinous process.

braise (brāz), *v. t.*; *braised, braising.* [F. *braiser*, < *braise*, hot charcoal, live coals; from Teut.] To cook (meat) long and slowly in a deep, covered pan.—**braise,** *n.* Braised meat.—**brais′er,** *n.* A pan or vessel for use in braising.

braize[1] (brāz), *n.* Same as *breeze*[2].

braize[2] (brāz), etc. Same as *braise*, etc.

brake[1] (brāk). Archaic preterit of *break.*

brake[2] (brāk), *n.* [ME. *brake*; prob. from LG., akin to E. *break.*] A tool or machine for breaking up flax or hemp, to separate the fiber; a machine for kneading or rolling dough; a heavy harrow for breaking clods; a basket-makers' tool for stripping the bark from willow wands; the handle or lever of a pump; a frame for holding a horse's foot while being shod; any mechanical device for arresting the motion of a wheel or a vehicle by means of friction; a kind of carriage (see *break, n.*).—**brake**[2], *v.*; *braked, braking.* **I.** *tr.* To use a brake on; break up (flax, etc.) with a brake; arrest the motion of (a wheel, etc.) as by a brake; also, to furnish with brakes. **II.** *intr.* To attend to a brake; act as brakeman.

brake[3] (brāk), *n.* [Cf. MLG. *brake*, bushes.] A place overgrown with bushes, shrubs, or brambles, or with cane; a thicket: as, "So thick entwined, As one continued *brake*, the undergrowth Of shrubs and tangling bushes" (Milton's "Paradise Lost," iv. 175).

brake[4] (brāk), *n.* [ME. *brake*: cf. *bracken.*] Any large or coarse fern, esp. *Pteris aquilina* (*Pteridium aquilinum*) or some allied species.

brake-age (brāk′ạ̄j), *n.* The action of a brake, as in stopping a vehicle; also, brakes collectively.

brake-man (brāk′mạn), *n.*; pl. *-men.* A man who operates brakes, as on a railroad-car. Also (Eng.) **brakes′man.**

brak-y (brā′ki), *a.* Of the nature of a brake or thicket; overgrown with bushes, shrubs, etc.

Bram-ah (bram′ạ̈ or brä′mạ̈) **lock.** [From J. *Bramah* (1748–1814), English inventor.] A form of lock whose chief characteristic is a series of notched sliding pieces which are moved by the key.—**Bram′ah press.** The hydraulic press.

bram-ble (bram′bl), *n.* [AS. *brēmel*; akin to E. *broom.*] Any plant of the rosaceous genus *Rubus*, as the blackberry; also, any rough, prickly shrub.—**bram′bled,** *a.* Overgrown with brambles.—**bram′bling,** *n.* An old-world finch, *Fringilla montifringilla*, closely related to and resembling the chaffinch, but larger.—**bram′bly,** *a.* Full of or resembling brambles.

Brambling.

bran (bran), *n.* [OF. *bran, bren* (F. *bran*); origin uncertain.] The ground husk of wheat or other grain, separated from flour or meal by bolting.

bran-card (brang′kąrd), *n.* [F., shaft, litter, akin to *branche*, branch.] A litter or stretcher for carrying wounded or sick persons.—**bran-car-dier** (F. bräṅ-kär-dyā), *n.* [F.] A stretcher-bearer.

branch (brȧnch). [OF. F. *branche*, < LL. *branca*, paw, claw.] **I.** *n.* An arm-like part diverging from a main stem or axis, as of a tree or any ramifying system; a limb, offshoot, or ramification; an extension; a division or department; a local operating division of a business house, a library, or the like; a line of family descent; a tributary stream. **II.** *a.* Forming a branch; of or pertaining to a branch.—**branch,** *v.* **I.** *intr.* To put forth branches; spread in branches, or ramify; issue or diverge as a branch from a main stem, etc. (with *from, out, off*, etc.). **II.** *tr.* To divide as into branches; also, to adorn with branches or sprays, as in needlework.—**branch′age** (-āj), *n.* Branches collectively.—**branched,** *a.* Having branches: as, many-*branched*.—**branch′er,** *n.* A young hawk or other bird when it first leaves the nest and takes to the branches of trees.—**branch′er-y,** *n.* Branches collectively.

bran-chi-a[1] (brang′ki-ạ), *n.* [LL.] Occasional singular of *branchiæ*.

bran-chi-a[2] (brang′ki-ạ), *n. pl.* [Gr. βράγχια.] Same as *branchiæ*.

bran-chi-æ (brang′ki-ē), *n. pl.* [L., < Gr. βράγχια, pl., gills (βράγχιον, sing., fin).] The respiratory organs or gills of fishes, etc.; also, the gill-like organs of other animals.—**bran′chi-al,** *a.* Of, pertaining to, or resembling branchiæ or gills.—**bran′chi-ate, bran′chi-at-ed** (-āt, -ā-ted), *a.* Having branchiæ.—**bran-chif′er-ous** (-kif′ẹ-rus), *a.* [See *-ferous.*] Bearing or having branchiæ.

bran-chi-o-pod (brang′ki-ọ-pod), *n.* [NL. *Branchiopoda*, pl., < Gr. βράγχια, gills, + πούς (ποδ-), foot.] One of the *Branchiopoda*, a group of crustaceans having branchiæ or gills on the feet.

bran-chi-os-te-gous (brang-ki-os′tẹ-gus), *a.* [Gr. βράγχια, gills, + στέγειν, cover.] Having or forming a membranous covering over the gills.

branch-less (brȧnch′les), *a.* Without branches.

branch-let (brȧnch′let), *n.* A little branch.

branch-y (brȧn′chi), *a.* Abounding in branches; branching; ramifying.

brand (brand), *n.* [AS. *brand, brond,* = D. and G. *brand* = Icel. *brandr*; from the Teut. verb represented by E. *burn*[2].] A burning or partly burned piece of wood; a sword (archaic); a mark made by burning with a hot iron, as on a convicted criminal, or on cattle to identify them; any mark of infamy, or stigma; a mark made by burning or otherwise to indicate kind, grade, make, etc.; kind, grade, or make, as indicated by a brand, stamp, trade-mark, or the like; an iron for branding; in *bot.*, a fungous disease in which the leaves and stems of plants appear as if burned, or any fungus producing such a disease.—**brand,** *v. t.* To mark with a hot iron or otherwise; mark or stamp indelibly; often, to mark with infamy; stigmatize.

bran-den-burg (bran′dẹn-bėrg), *n.* [From *Brandenburg*, in Germany.] An ornament of braid with loops, for fastening a garment; a frog.

brand-er (bran′dėr), *n.* One who or that which brands.

brand=goose (brand′gös), *n.* Same as *brant*[2].

bran-died (bran′did), *p. a.* Prepared with brandy.

brand=i-ron (brand′ī″ėrn), *n.* A gridiron, andiron, or trivet (now only prov.); also, an iron for branding.

bran-dish (bran′dish), *v. t.* [OF. F. *brandir* (*brandiss-*), < *brand*, sword; from Teut.: cf. *brand.*] To shake or wave (a weapon, etc.); flourish.—**bran′dish,** *n.* A wave or flourish, as of a weapon.—**bran′dish-er,** *n.*

brand-ling (brand′ling), *n.* A small earthworm, *Allolobophora fœtida*, used as bait by anglers; also, a young salmon, or parr.

brand=new (brand′nū′), *a.* New, as metal fresh from the fire; quite new.

bran-dy (bran′di), *n.*; pl. *-dies* (-diz). [Earlier *brandywine*, < D. *brandewijn*, 'burnt (or distilled) wine.'] Properly, an ardent spirit distilled from wine; also, some similar liquor, as from the fermented juice of the apple, peach, etc.—**bran′dy,** *v. t.*; *-died, -dying.* To mix, flavor, or preserve with brandy; supply or refresh with brandy.—**bran′dy=paw′nee** (-pâ′nē), *n.* [Hind. *pānī*, water.] Brandy and water, as a beverage. [Anglo-Ind.]—**bran′dy=smash′,** *n.* Brandy with crushed ice and sprigs of mint.—**bran′dy=snap,** *n.* A gingersnap made with or without brandy.

bran-gle (brang′gl), *v. i.* [Cf. *wrangle* and *brawl*[2].] To dispute contentiously; wrangle: as, "Thus wrangled, *brangled*, jangled they a month" (Browning's "Ring and the Book," i.). [Archaic or prov. Eng.]—**bran′gle,** *n.*

branks (brangks), *n. pl.* [Origin uncertain.] A kind of bridle formerly used in Scotland and England to punish a scold; also, a kind of bridle for horses and cows (Sc.).

Branks.

brank-ur-sine (brangk-ėr′sin), *n.* [ML. *branca ursina*, 'bear's claw.'] The bear's-breech, or acanthus plant.

bran=new (bran′nū′), *a.* Same as *brand-new.*

bran-ny (bran′i), *a.* Of, containing, or resembling bran.

brant[1] (brant), *a.* Same as *brent*[1]. [North. Eng.]

brant[2] (brant), *n.* [Cf. Icel. *brandgās*, Dan. *brandgaas*, 'brand goose,' applied to various wildfowl, appar. with reference to the coloring.] Any of several species of small, dark-colored geese of the genus *Bernicla*, esp. *B. brenta*, breeding in high northern latitudes and migrating south in the autumn. Also **brant′=goose;** pl. *-geese.*

Brant-goose (*Bernicla brenta*).

brash[1] (brash), *v.* [Origin obscure; perhaps from several sources.] **I.** *tr.* To assault or attack; also, to stir vigorously; churn. [Now prov.] **II.** *intr.* To move vigorously or hastily; rush headlong; dash. [Prov.]—**brash**[1], *n.* An assault†; an attack of illness; a rash or eruption; a watery eructation from a disordered stomach; a burst of wind, rain, etc.; a rush or dash. [Now prov.]—**brash**[1], *a.* Headlong; hasty; rash. [Prov. or colloq.]

brash[2] (brash). [Origin obscure.] **I.** *a.* Brittle: used esp. of timber. [Prov. Eng. and U. S.] **II.** *n.* Broken or refuse boughs, twigs, etc. (prov. Eng.); loose fragments of rock; small fragments of ice drifted together.—**brash′y,** *a.* Broken, fragmentary, crumbly.

bra-sier[1], **bra-sier**[2] (brā′zhėr). See *brazier*[1], *brazier*[2].
bras-i-lin (braz′i-lin), *n.* See *brazilin.*
brass (bràs). [AS. *bræs.*] **I.** *n.* A durable, malleable, and ductile yellow alloy, consisting essentially of copper and zinc; anything made of it, as a memorial tablet, etc.; a brass musical instrument, or such instruments collectively in a band or orchestra; brass, copper, or bronze coin†; money (colloq.); effrontery or impudence (colloq.); in *mach.*, a bearing, bush, or the like. **II.** *a.* Made of brass; brazen; brassy; also, using musical instruments made of brass (as, a *brass* band).

Memorial Brass of Eleanor Bohun (died 1399), in Westminster Abbey.

bras-sage (bras′ạj), *n.* [F., < *brasser*, stir (melted metal).] A charge for coining money. Cf. *seigniorage.*
bras-sard (bras′ạrd or bra-särd′), *n.* [F., < *bras*, arm.] A piece of armor for the arm; also, a band worn about the arm above the elbow as a badge, as by ambulance-corps men on the battle-field.

Brassard.

brasse-rie (bràs-rē), *n.* [F., < *brasser*, brew, stir.] A brewery; also, a beer-garden or a beer-saloon.
bras-si-ca-ceous (bras-i-kā′shius), *a.* [L. *brassica*, cabbage.] Allied to or resembling the cabbage; belonging to the *Brassicaceæ*, a family of plants including the cabbage, turnip, radish, mustard, cress, etc.
bras-si-ère (bras-i-ãr′, F. brà-syãr), *n.* [F., < *bras*, arm.] A short stiffened or boned waist or bust-support worn by women.
brass=wind (bràs′wind), *n.* See *wind*[2], *n.*
brass-y (bràs′i). **I.** *a.*; compar. *brassier*, superl. *brassiest.* Of or like brass; also, brazen or impudent. **II.** *n.*; pl. *-ies* (-iz). In *golf*, a wooden club with a brass sole.—**brass′i-ly,** *adv.*—**brass′i-ness,** *n.*
brat (brat), *n.* [Origin uncertain.] A child: now used only in contempt.
bratch-et (brach′et), *n.* [OF. *brachet*: see *brach.*] A brach (as, "Attentive as the *bratchet's* bay From the dark covert drove the prey": Scott's "Marmion," ii., Introd.); also, a little brat or child (in contemptuous or familiar use).
brat-tice (brat′is), *n.* [OF. *bretesche* (F. *bretêche*), parapet, gallery, balcony; perhaps from Teut. (cf. G. *brett*, board).] A wooden breastwork, parapet, or gallery erected on the battlement of a fortress†; also, a partition forming an air-passage, or a lining, as of planks, in a mine.—**brat′tice,** *v. t.*; *-ticed, -ticing.* To provide with a brattice; line with planks or bratticing.—**brat′ti-cing,** *n.* A wooden breast-work or parapet with its appurtenances†; also, a piece of ornamental openwork, as over a shrine; also, brattice-work in a mine.
brat-tle (brat′l), *v. i.*; *-tled, -tling.* [Imit.] To make a loud, clattering noise; clatter; move with a clatter. [Chiefly Sc. and north. Eng.]—**brat′tle,** *n.* A loud, clattering noise; a noisy rush (as, "Thou need na start awa sae hasty, Wi' bickering *brattle*!" Burns's "To a Mouse"). [Chiefly Sc. and north. Eng.]
braun-ite (broun′īt), *n.* [From M. *Braun*, of Gotha.] A native siliceous oxide of manganese, occurring in tetragonal crystals of brownish-black color.
bra-va (brä′vạ), *interj.* and *n.* [It.] Feminine form corresponding to *bravo*[1].
bra-va-do (brạ-vä′dō or brạ-vā′dō), *n.*; pl. *-does* or *-dos* (-dōz). [Sp. *bravada*, *bravata*, < It. *bravata*, < *bravare*, brave, defy, < *bravo*, E. *brave*, *a.*] Ostentatious boldness; swaggering defiance; a bold show of indifference.—**bra-va′do,** *v. i.*; *-doed, -doing.* To act or talk with bravado.
brave (brāv). [F. *brave*, < It. *bravo*, brave, bold, fine; origin uncertain.] **I.** *a.*; compar. *braver*, superl. *bravest.* Having or showing courage or fortitude; unswayed by fear; courageous; valiant; also, making a fine appearance; gay; gallant; splendid; also, excellent or fine (archaic). **II.** *n.* A brave person; a North American Indian warrior; a bravo or bully (obs. or archaic); a bold threat or defiance (archaic).—**brave,** *v. t.*; *braved, braving.* To meet or face with courage; dare; defy; also, to make fine†.—**brave′ly,** *adv.*—**brave′ness,** *n.*—**brav-er-y** (brā′vėr-i), *n.*; pl. *-ies* (-iz). Brave spirit or conduct; courage; valor; also, brave appearance; splendor; finery; an ornament (obs. or archaic).
bra-vo[1] (brä′vō). [It., prop. adj. (fem. *brava*): see *brave.*] **I.** *interj.* Fine! excellent! **II.** *n.*; pl. *-vos* (-vōz). A cry of 'bravo!'
bra-vo[2] (brä′vō), *n.*; pl. *-voes* or *-vos* (-vōz). [It., < *bravo*, adj.: see *brave.*] A daring villain; a murderous bully; a professional assassin.
bra-vu-ra (brä-vö′rạ), *n.* [It.] Display of daring; show of brilliant performance; dash; in *music*, a florid passage or piece, requiring great skill and spirit in the performer.
braw (brâ), *a.* [= *brave.*] Brave; fine: as, "a *braw* new coat" (Burns's "Brigs of Ayr," 81). [Sc.]
brawl[1]† (brâl), *n.* [F. *branle*, < *branler*, shake, swing.] A kind of dance.
brawl[2] (brâl), *v.* [ME.; origin uncertain.] **I.** *intr.* To quarrel noisily and indecently; wrangle; also, to be clamorous or noisy; also, to make a loud, babbling noise (as, "Now the late dimpling current began to *brawl* around them": Irving's "Knickerbocker's New York," ii. 4). **II.** *tr.* To wrangle about; also, to utter clamorously; also, to drive, force, etc., by brawling.—**brawl**[2], *n.* A noisy, turbulent quarrel; a squabble; also, clamor.—**brawl′er,** *n.*—**brawl′ing-ly,** *adv.*
brawn (brân), *n.* [OF. *braon*; from Teut. (cf. G. *braten*, roast meat).] The flesh of animals as food†; boar's or swine's flesh, esp. boiled and pickled; also, muscular tissue, esp. when firm and well developed; hence, muscular strength.—**brawn′y,** *a.*; compar. *brawnier*, superl. *brawniest.* Muscular; strong.—**brawn′i-ness,** *n.*
brax-y (brak′si), *n.* [Origin uncertain.] A fatal infectious disease of sheep, resembling anthrax; a sheep affected with this disease; its flesh; also, any of various other diseases of sheep.
bray[1] (brā), *v. t.* [OF. *breier* (F. *broyer*); prob. from Teut., and akin to E. *break.*] To pound or crush fine, as with an instrument; triturate.
bray[2] (brā), *v.* [OF. F. *braire*; prob. ult. imit.] **I.** *intr.* To utter a loud, harsh cry, as the ass; make any loud, harsh sound. **II.** *tr.* To utter or emit with a loud, harsh sound.—**bray**[2], *n.* The cry of an ass; any loud, harsh sound.
bray-er[1] (brā′ėr), *n.* One who or that which brays or triturates; in *printing*, an instrument employed for spreading ink.
bray-er[2] (brā′ėr), *n.* One who or that which brays like an ass.
braze[1] (brāz), *v. t.*; *brazed, brazing.* [AS. *brasian*, < *bræs*, E. *brass.*] To make of brass; cover or adorn with brass; make brass-like.
braze[2] (brāz), *v. t.*; *brazed, brazing.* [F. *braser*, < *braise*, live coals: see *braise.*] To solder with a solder of high melting-point; esp., to unite (pieces of brass, steel, etc.) by intensely heating the parts to be joined and applying zinc or an alloy of copper and zinc.
bra-zen (brā′zn), *a.* [AS. *bræsen.*] Of or as of brass; like brass, as in sound, color, strength, impenetrability, etc.; fig., shameless or impudent.—**brazen age,** one of the mythological ages of mankind, a period of war and violence. See *ages in mythology*, under *age*, *n.*—**brazen sea,** a large vessel of brass in Solomon's temple, for the priests to wash in before performing the service of the temple (also called *molten sea*). See 2 Kings, xxv. 13, also 1 Kings, vii. 23–26 and 2 Chron. iv. 2–5.—**bra′zen,** *v. t.* To face with brazen boldness or effrontery (usually with *out*); also, to make brazen or bold.—**bra′zen=faced,** *a.* Openly shameless; impudent.—**bra′zen-ly,** *adv.*—**bra′zen-ness,** *n.*
bra-zier[1] (brā′zhėr), *n.* [ME. *brasier.*] One who works in brass.

bra-zier[2] (brā′zhėr), *n.* [F. *brasier*, < *braise*, live coals.] A metal receptacle for holding burning charcoal or other fuel, as for heating a room.

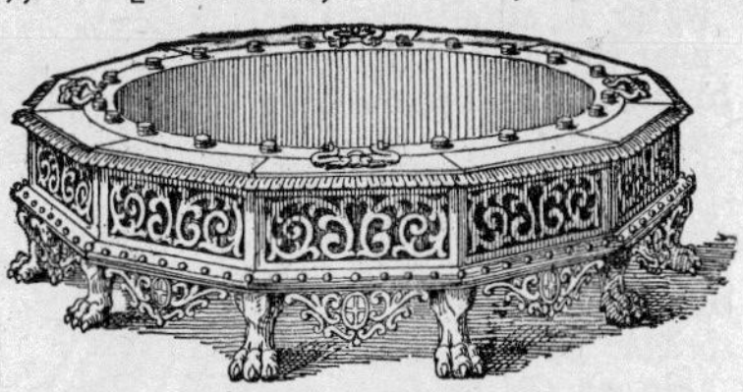

Bronze Brazier. — Spanish; 17th century.

bra-zil (brą-zil′), *n.* [ME. *brasile* = OF. *bresil* = Sp. and Pg. *brasil* = It. *brasile*; origin unknown.] Orig., a hard East Indian dyewood yielding a red color, from the tree *Biancæa sappan* (see *sapan-wood*); later, a dyewood from various tropical American trees of the genus *Cæsalpinia* (esp. *C. echinata*) and allied genera, yielding reds and purples.

Bra-zil-ian (brą-zil′ian). [From *Brazil*, orig. (Pg.) *terra de brasil*, 'land of brazil (dyewood).'] **I.** *a.* Of, pertaining to, or characteristic of Brazil or its inhabitants. **II.** *n.* A native or inhabitant of Brazil.

braz-i-lin (braz′i-lin), *n.* [From *brazil*.] In *chem.*, a coloring principle from brazil (dyewood from trees of the genus *Cæsalpinia*), crystallizing in yellow crystals.

Bra-zil=nut (brą-zil′nut), *n.* The triangular edible seed of the tree *Bertholletia excelsa*, of Brazil and other countries.

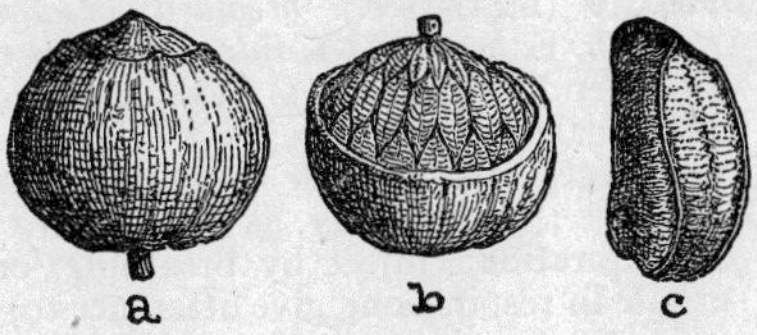

Brazil-nut.
a, fruit; *b*, same with portion of shell removed; *c*, a single seed or nut on larger scale.

bra-zil=wood (brą-zil′wůd), *n.* Same as *brazil*.

breach (brēch), *n.* [Partly < AS. *bryce*, < *brecan*, E. *break*, partly < OF. *breche* (F. *brèche*), from the same ult. (Teut.) source.] The act or the result of breaking; a break or rupture; a rift, fissure, or gap; a gap made in a fortification; a wound†; infraction or violation, as of the peace, of faith or trust, or of a promise to marry; severance of friendly relations; an irruption†, inroad†, or assault†; the breaking of waves; the dashing of surf; the springing of a whale from the water.—**breach,** *v.* **I.** *tr.* To make a breach or opening in. **II.** *intr.* Of a whale, to spring from the water.—**breach′y,** *a.* Apt to break fences, as cattle.

bread (bred), *n.* [AS. *brēad* = D. *brood* = G. *brot* = Icel. *braudh*.] A kind of food made of flour or meal, milk or water, etc., made into a dough or batter, with or without yeast or the like, and baked; hence, food; sustenance; livelihood.—**bread and butter,** bread spread with butter: commonly taken as the type of plain, wholesome food, the staple of diet of young people (as school-girls, or 'bread-and-butter misses'), or as representing the material essentials of life.—**bread line,** a line of needy persons assembled to receive bread and sometimes other food given gratuitously as a form of charity.—**bread,** *v. t.* In *cookery*, to cover or dress with bread-crumbs.—**bread′=bas″ket,** *n.* A basket for holding or carrying bread; a tray for holding bread at table; also, the stomach (slang).—**bread′=crumb,** *n.* A crumb of bread; also, the soft part of bread, as distinguished from the crust.—**bread′fruit,** *n.* A large, round starchy fruit yielded by a moraceous tree, *Artocarpus communis*, of the Pacific islands, etc., much used, baked or roasted, for food; the tree bearing this fruit; also, some similar fruit, as the jack.—**bread′less,** *a.* Without bread; foodless.—**bread′=nut,** *n.* The nut of a moraceous tree, *Brosimum alicastrum*, of Jamaica and Central America, which is roasted or boiled for use as food.—**bread′=root,** *n.* The edible farinaceous root of *Psoralea esculenta*, a fabaceous plant of central North America.—**bread′=stick,** *n.* A long, slender, cylindrical piece of bread-dough baked until dry and crisp.—**bread′stuff,** *n.* Grain, flour, or meal for making bread.

Branch of Breadfruit-tree (*Artocarpus communis*).

breadth (bredth), *n.* [Earlier *brede*, < AS. *brǣdu*, < *brād*, E. *broad*.] Measure from side to side; extent across; width; a piece, as of cloth, of definite or full width; an extent as measured by its breadth; also, broad extent or scope; largeness; freedom from narrowness; in *art*, broad or general effect due to subordination of details or non-essentials.—**breadth′wise, breadth′ways,** *adv.* In the direction of the breadth.

bread-win-ner (bred′win″ėr), *n.* One who earns his bread or living; one who earns a living for those dependent on him; also, a means of earning a living.—**bread′win″ning,** *n.*

break (brāk), *v.*; pret. *broke* (archaic *brake*), pp. *broken* (sometimes *broke*), ppr. *breaking*. [AS. *brecan* = D. and LG. *breken* = G. *brechen* = Goth. *brikan*, break; akin to L. *frangere*, break.] **I.** *tr.* To divide into parts violently, as by a blow or pull; reduce to pieces or fragments (often with *up*); shatter; crush; burst; disrupt (a bond, fetter, etc.); infringe or violate (a law, contract, promise, etc.); dissolve or annul (a connection or engagement: often with *off*); disperse (a household, meeting, etc.: usually with *up*); make a rupture or opening in the surface of; crack; bruise or abrade; dig or plow up (ground); destroy the unity or continuity of; make a gap in; discontinue abruptly; interrupt or suspend (one's fast, a blockade, etc.); disturb (sleep, silence, etc.); destroy the regularity or arrangement of (as, to *break* step; to *break* ranks); interrupt the uniformity or sameness of; relieve (monotony, dullness, etc.); cause (a line, a thrown ball, etc.) to change direction abruptly; destroy the completeness of (a set or other whole), as by taking out a part; sever or remove (a part) as by a blow or pull (with *away*, *off*, etc.); force (*in*, *down*, *open*, etc.) by violence; make (a hole, passage, way, etc.) by or as by forcing away obstructions; lay open (an inclosure); make a way through; penetrate; enter (a house, etc.) burglariously (obs. or archaic); make one's way out of (jail, cover, etc.); go beyond (a bound, etc.); exceed (a record); disclose or divulge (news, etc.), esp. with caution or delicacy; utter (a jest, a sigh, etc.); open† or begin†; disable or destroy by or as by shattering or crushing; ruin financially, or make bankrupt; degrade or cashier (an officer); impair or weaken in strength, spirit, force, or effect; train to obedience or discipline; tame; accustom or habituate, as to a method of procedure (often with *in*); train away from a habit or practice (with *of*); in *elect.*, to render (a circuit) incomplete and so stop the flow of the current, or to stop the flow of (a current) by so doing. **II.** *intr.* To become broken; become separated into parts or fragments, esp. suddenly and violently; burst or fall apart; part and disperse; crack; burst open, as a boil; become suddenly discontinuous or interrupted; leave (*off*) abruptly; become detached (with *off*, etc.); sever relations (*with*); break ranks or fall into disorder, as a band of soldiers; change suddenly, as in sound, movement, or direction; free one's self or escape suddenly, as from restraint (often with *away*); force a way (*in*, *through*, etc.); burst (*in*, *forth*, *from*, *out*, etc.); come suddenly, as into notice; dawn, as the day; give way or fail as under strain (often with *down*); become bankrupt; of plants, to bud, also to flower too soon.—**break,** *n.* A breaking; a fracture, rupture, or shattering; an opening made by breaking; a gap; an interruption of continuity; a suspension or stoppage; a severance of relations; an abrupt or marked change, as in sound or direction; a breaking forth or away, as from restraint; a sudden emergence; dawn (of day); a sequence of successful shots, as in billiards; an unlucky remark, or a breach of propriety, etiquette, or the like (colloq., U. S.); a large, high four-wheeled carriage or wagonette; in *elect.*, the rendering of a circuit incomplete; the discontinuance of the current when a circuit is rendered incomplete.—**break′a-ble,** *a.* That may be broken.—**break-age** (brā′kąj), *n.* The act of breaking; a break; damage or loss by breaking; allowance made for this; *naut.*, the leaving of empty space in stowing a ship's hold.—**break′a-way,** *n.* A breaking away; a start, as of competitors in a contest; a stampede of sheep, cattle, etc. (Australia); an animal which breaks away from a herd or flock (Australia).—**break'bone fe'ver.** Same as *dengue.* —**break'down,** *n.* A breaking down; a collapse; also, a noisy, lively dance; also, an analysis, as of a total.

break-er[1] (brā'kėr), *n.* One who or that which breaks; a structure in which coal is broken into sizes for the market; a wave that breaks or dashes into foam; a device for opening an electric circuit.

break-er[2] (brā'kėr), *n.* [Sp. *barrica*, cask.] A small water-cask for use in a boat.

break-fast (brek'fạst), *n.* [ME. *brekefast, brekfast.*] The first meal of the day, with which the fast of the night is broken; a morning meal.—**break'fast,** *v.* **I.** *intr.* To take breakfast. **II.** *tr.* To supply with breakfast; entertain at breakfast.—**break'fast-er,** *n.*—**break'fast-less,** *a.* Without breakfast.

break-neck (brāk'nek). **I.** *a.* Endangering the neck or life; headlong; precipitous. **II.** *n.* A breakneck fall; a dangerous business.

break=up (brāk'up), *n.* A breaking up; disintegration; disruption; dispersal.

break-wa-ter (brāk'wâ″tėr), *n.* Any barrier built or serving to break the force of waves, as before a harbor.

bream[1] (brēm), *n.*; pl. *breams* or (esp. collectively) *bream.* [OF. *bresme* (F. *brème*); from Teut.] Any of various fresh-water cyprinoid fishes of the genus *Abramis*, as *A. brama* of Europe, with compressed, rather deep body; also, any of various sparoid marine fishes, the sea-breams (see *sea-bream*); also, any of various fresh-water sunfishes of the genus *Eupomotis* and allied genera.

bream[2] (brēm), *v. t.* [Origin uncertain: cf. D. *brem*, broom, furze.] To clean (a ship's bottom) by applying burning furze, reeds, etc., to soften the pitch and loosen adherent matter.

breast (brest), *n.* [AS. *brēost*, akin to G. *brust.*] Either of the two soft protuberances on the thorax in females, containing the milk-secreting organs; the analogous rudimentary organ in males; also, the front of the thorax in either sex; the bosom; the chest; the bosom as the seat of thoughts and feelings; also, any surface or part resembling or likened to the human breast; the portion of a wall between a window and the floor; the portion of a chimney between the flues and the apartment; the face at which the working is going on in a mine.—**to make a clean breast of,** to make full confession of.—**breast,** *v. t.* To meet or oppose with the breast; face; advance against; stem.—**breast'=bone,** *n.* The sternum.—**breast'ed,** *a.* Having a breast: as, broad-*breasted.*—**breast'=high',** *a.* and *adv.* As high as the breast.

breast=hook (brest'hu̇k), *n.* One of the strong knee-shaped timbers set across the stem of a ship to strengthen the junction of the bows.

Breastplate, steel ornamented with gilding; 16th century.

breast-ing (bres'ting), *n.* The curved channel in which a breast-wheel turns.

breast-pin (brest'pin), *n.* A pin worn on the breast or at the throat; a brooch.

breast-plate (brest'plāt), *n.* A piece of armor for the breast; also, a plate which receives the butt-end of a boring-tool and against which the breast is set in working; also, the under shell of a tortoise; also, a square ornament worn on the breast by the Jewish high priest.

breast=plow (brest'plou), *n.* A kind of spade propelled by pressure of the breast on a cross-bar, for cutting turf.

breast=rail (brest'rāl), *n.* The upper rail of a balcony or parapet; a railing in front of a ship's quarter-deck.

breast=sum-mer (brest'sum″ėr), *n.* A summer or beam placed horizontally over a large opening, as a shop-window, to support the superstructure.

breast=wall (brest'wâl), *n.* A retaining wall.

breast=wheel (brest'hwēl), *n.* A water-wheel to which the water is admitted at or near the level of the axle.

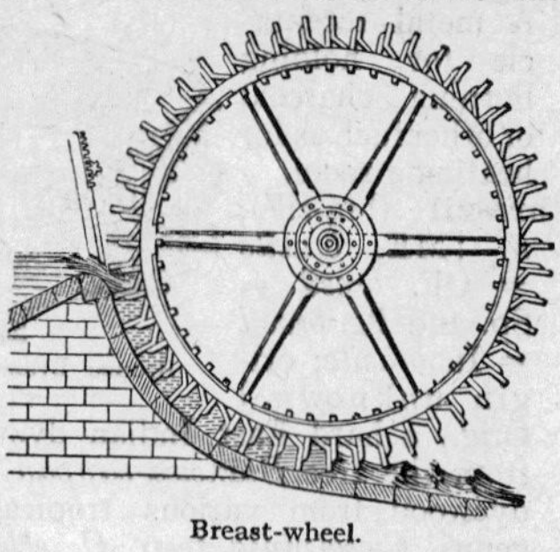

Breast-wheel.

breast-work (brest'wėrk), *n.* A defensive work of moderate height, hastily thrown up; also, a parapet, as of a building.

breath (breth), *n.* [AS. *brǣth*, odor, exhalation, akin to G. *brodem*, exhalation, vapor, steam.] Odor†; vapor†; an odorous exhalation, or the air impregnated by it; the air inhaled and exhaled in respiration; respiration, esp. as necessary to life; power of breathing freely (as, out of *breath*); time to breathe; pause or respite; a single respiration; the brief time required for it; an instant; an utterance; a whisper; a light current of air; in *phonetics*, voiceless expiration of air, producing a hiss, puff, or the like.—**under one's breath,** in a low voice or a whisper.

breath-a-ble (brē'ᴛʜạ-bl), *a.* That may be breathed; respirable.

breathe (brēᴛʜ), *v.*; *breathed, breathing.* [ME. *brethen*, < *breth*, E. *breath.*] **I.** *intr.* To pass off in vapor†; exhale an odor; be redolent (*of*); exhale air from the lungs; inhale and exhale air, or respire; live or exist; pause, as for breath; take rest; emit audible breath or sound; whisper, speak, sing, etc.; blow lightly, as air. **II.** *tr.* To exhale, or emit by expiration; inject by breathing, or infuse; inhale and exhale in respiration; give utterance to; whisper; express or manifest (as, language *breathing* the eloquence of truth); allow to rest, as to recover breath; exercise briskly; put out of breath; tire or exhaust; blow into, or cause to sound by the breath; open and bleed (a vein); in *phonetics*, to utter with the breath and not with the voice.

breathed (bretht), *a.* Having breath: as, sweet-*breathed.*

breath-er (brē'ᴛʜėr), *n.* One who or that which breathes; a pause, as for breath; something, as exercise, that stimulates breathing, or that exhausts the breath (colloq.).

breath-ing (brē'ᴛʜing), *n.* The act of one who or that which breathes; respiration; a single breath; the short time required for it; a pause, as for breath; physical exercise, as stimulating breathing; utterance or words; aspiration or longing; gentle blowing, as of wind; in *gram.*, aspiration; pronunciation with reference to the use or the omission of an *h*-sound, or a sign to indicate this (as, the rough or the smooth *breathing* in Greek, ʽ or ʼ, indicating respectively the *h*-sound or its absence).

breath-less (breth'les), *a.* Without breath; also, out of breath; panting; also, with the breath held, as in suspense. —**breath'less-ly,** *adv.*—**breath'less-ness,** *n.*

breath-y (breth'i), *a.* Of, pertaining to, or of the nature of breath; of vocal sounds, esp. singing, characterized by a conspicuous use of the breath; in *phonetics*, uttered with breath.

brec-cia (brech'ạ̈), *n.* [It.; from Teut., and akin to E. *break.*] In *geol.*, rock composed of angular fragments of older rocks cemented together.—**brec-ci-at-ed** (brech'i-ā-ted), *a.* Having the form of breccia. —**brec-ci-a'tion** (-ā'shọn), *n.* Brecciated formation.

Breccia. — Polished surface.

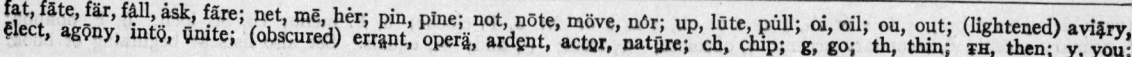

bred (bred). Preterit and past participle of *breed.*

brede (brēd), *n.* [Var. of *braid*[1].] A braid or plait; anything interwoven; embroidery. [Archaic.]

bree (brē), *n.* [Cf. AS. *brīw*, pottage.] Broth; liquor; juice. [Sc. and north. Eng.]

breech (brēch), *n.* [AS. *brēc*, pl., akin to D. *broek*, Icel. *brōk*: cf. L. *bracæ*, breeches (from Celtic).] A garment for the hips and thighs†; breeches†; also, the lower part of the trunk of the body behind; the posteriors or buttocks; also, the hinder or lower part of anything; the part of a cannon or other firearm behind the bore or barrel.—**breech** (brēch or brich), *v. t.* To clothe with breeches; whip on the breech; furnish (a gun) with a breech; secure (a gun) with a breeching.—**breech′=block** (brēch′-), *n.* A movable piece of metal which closes the breech end of the barrel in certain firearms.—**breech′=cloth, breech′=clout,** *n.* A cloth worn about the breech, as by uncivilized peoples.

breech-es (brich′ez, also brē′chez), *n. pl.* [Pl. of *breech* (itself orig. pl.).] A bifurcated garment worn by men (and by women for riding, etc.), covering the hips and thighs; also, trousers (colloq.).—**Breeches Bible.** See under *Bible.* —**breech′es=buoy,** *n.* A life-saving device consisting of a belt-like buoy from which hangs a support for the body resembling a pair of breeches, which travels on a rope, and is used to carry persons ashore from a wreck.

Breeches-buoy.

breech-ing (brē′ching or brich′ing), *n.* A whipping on the breech; the part of a harness which passes around a horse's breech; a rope securing the cascabel of a gun to a ship's side, for checking the recoil; the breech of a gun, or its mechanism.

breech-less (brēch′les), *a.* Without breeches.

breech=load-er (brēch′lō″dėr), *n.* A firearm, as a rifle, loaded at the breech. Cf. *muzzle-loader.*—**breech′=load″ing,** *a.* Of firearms, receiving the charge or load at the breech.

breech=plug (brēch′plug), *n.* A plug for closing the breech of a gun.

breed (brēd), *v.*; *bred, breeding.* [AS. *brēdan,* < *brōd,* E. *brood.*] **I.** *tr.* To produce (offspring); procreate; hence, to engender or cause (as, dirt *breeds* disease); also, to be the native place or the source of; also, to bring up, rear, or train; also, to procure by the mating of parents; raise (live stock, etc.). **II.** *intr.* To produce offspring; also, to be engendered or produced; grow; develop; also, to procure the birth of young, as in raising stock.—**breed,** *n.* The progeny or race from particular parents or stock; race; lineage; strain; in domestic animals (or cultivated plants), a group or variety distinguished by particular characteristics, developed and maintained in existence through the agency of man; hence, kind or sort (as, "This courtesy is not of the right *breed*": Shakspere's "Hamlet," iii. 2. 327); also, a brood†.—**breed′er,** *n.*—**breed′ing,** *n.* The act of a person or thing that breeds; nurture or training; the results of training as shown in behavior and manners; manners, esp. good manners.

breeks (brēks), *n. pl.* Sc. and north. Eng. form of *breeches.*

breese (brēz), *n.* See *breeze*[1].

breeze[1] (brēz), *n.* [AS. *briosa.*] A gadfly or horse-fly.

breeze[2] (brēz), *n.* [Prob. < F. *braise,* live coals, cinders.] Cinders; dust of charcoal, coke, or coal.

breeze[3] (brēz), *n.* [F. *brise* = Sp. *brisa* = Pg. *briza*: cf. *bise.*] A northeast wind†; also, a wind or current of air, esp. a light or moderate one; also, a disturbance or quarrel (colloq.).—**breeze**[3], *v. i.*; *breezed, breezing.* To blow gently, as a breeze; rise on the breeze, as a noise; become stronger, as a wind (with *up*); also, to run or move briskly (colloq.).—**breeze′less,** *a.* Without a breeze.—**breez′y,** *a.*; compar. *breezier,* superl. *breeziest.* Abounding in breezes; windy; fig., airy; fresh; sprightly.—**breez′i-ly,** *adv.*—**breez′i-ness,** *n.*

breg-ma (breg′mạ), *n.* [Gr. βρέγμα, front of the head.] In *craniol.,* the point of junction of the sagittal and coronal sutures of the skull.—**breg-mat′ic** (-mat′ik), *a.*

bre-hon (brē′hon), *n.* [OIr. *brithem.*] One of a class of judges in ancient Ireland.—**brehon law,** the ancient system of law of Ireland, not entirely superseded by English law among the native Irish until about 1650.

bre-loque (brė-lok), *n.* [F.] A trinket or small object worn suspended from a chain, ribbon, etc.

breme, brim[1] (brēm, brim), *a.* [ME. *breme, brim,* < AS. *brēme,* famous.] Famous†; fine†; bright†; clear† or loud†; fierce†; sharp, violent, or stormy, as weather, etc. (as, "The same to him glad summer or the winter *breme*": Thomson's "Castle of Indolence," ii. 7); bleak or windswept, as a place; keen or eager, as a person. [Now Sc. and north. Eng.]

brent[1] (brent), *a.* [AS. *brant,* lofty.] Steep; sheer; of the brow, smooth or unwrinkled (as, "Your bonnie brow was *brent*": Burns's "John Anderson My Jo"). [Sc. and north. Eng.]

brent[2], **brent=goose** (brent, brent′gös), *n.* Same as *brant*[2].

brer (brur), *n.* A dialectal contraction of the word *brother* in use among the negroes of the southern U. S.: as, *brer* Fox, *brer* Rabbit, etc.

brere (brēr), *n.* Same as *brier*[1]. See Shelley's "Adonais," xviii. [Prov. or poetic.]

brest=sum-mer (brest′sum″ėr), *n.* See *breast-summer.*

bre-telle (brẹ-tel′), *n.* [F., strap, suspender.] In *dressmaking,* one of a pair of suspender-like ornamental bands extending over the shoulders from front to back.

breth-ren (breᴛʜ′ren), *n.* Plural of *brother*: now usually denoting spiritual brotherhood. See *brother* and *Dunker.*

Bret-on (bret′ọn, F. brė-tôṅ). [F.: see *Briton.*] **I.** *n.* A native of Brittany, a former province in northwestern France; also, the language of Brittany, a dialect of Celtic. **II.** *a.* Of or pertaining to Brittany, the Bretons, or their language; Armorican.

breve (brēv), *n.* [Var. of *brief.*] A writ, as one issued by a court of law; also, a mark placed over a vowel to show that it is short, as in *ŭ*; in *music,* the longest modern note (rarely used), equivalent to two semibreves or whole-notes.

bre-vet (brẹ-vet′, also, chiefly Brit., brev′et). [OF., dim. of *bref*: see *brief.*] **I.** *n.* A patent conferring a privilege or rank; esp., a commission promoting a military officer to a higher rank without increase of pay. **II.** *a.* Conferred or appointed by brevet.—**bre-vet′,** *v. t.*; *-vetted, -vetting* (or, for pron. brev′et, *-eted, -eting*). To appoint or promote by brevet.—**bre-vet′cy** (-si), *n.* Brevet rank.

bre-vi-a-ry (brē′vi-ā-ri), *n.*; pl. *-ries* (-riz). [L. *breviarium,* abridgment, prop. neut. of *breviarius,* abridged, < *brevis,* short.] A summary†; a compendium†; a book of daily offices of the Roman Catholic Church, to be read by those in major orders; any similar book used in some other church.

bre-vier (brẹ-vēr′), *n.* [Said to be < G. *brevier,* breviary (as printed in this type).] A printing-type (8 point) of a size between minion and bourgeois. See *type.*

brev-i-ped (brev′i-ped), *a.* [L. *brevis,* short, + *pes* (*ped-*), foot.] Having short feet or legs, as a bird.

brev-i-pen-nate (brev-i-pen′āt), *a.* [L. *brevis,* short, + *penna,* feather.] Having short wings.

brev-i-ros-tral, brev-i-ros-trate (brev-i-ros′trạl, -trāt), *a.* [L. *brevis,* short, + *rostrum,* beak.] Having a short beak or bill.

brev-i-ty (brev′i-ti), *n.* [L. *brevitas,* < *brevis,* short.] Shortness; briefness; also, conciseness.

brew (brö), *v.* [AS. *brēowan* = D. *brouwen* = G. *brauen* = Icel. *brugga,* brew.] **I.** *tr.* To make (beer, ale, etc.) from malt, etc., by steeping, boiling, and fermentation; prepare (any beverage) by due process; also, to concoct or contrive; bring about. **II.** *intr.* To be in preparation; be forming or gathering.—**brew,** *n.* That which is brewed; a brewing. —**brew′age** (-āj), *n.* The process of brewing; also, that which has been brewed; a brewing.—**brew′er,** *n.* One who brews; a maker of malt liquors.—**brewers' grains,** the residue left from the grain in the manufacture of beer, used for feeding live stock.—**brew′er-y,** *n.*; pl. *-ies* (-iz). An establishment for brewing malt liquors.—**brew′house,** *n.* A brewery.—**brew′ing,** *n.* The act of one who brews; the making of malt liquors; also, a quantity brewed at once.

brew-is (brö′is), *n.* [OF. *broez, broet* (F. *brouet*), dim. of *bro,* < OHG. *brod,* = E. *broth.*] Broth; also, bread soaked in broth, gravy, hot milk, or the like. [Now chiefly prov.]

brew-ster (brö′stėr), *n.* [ME. *brewester.*] A brewer (orig. female). [Obs. or Sc. and north. Eng.]

(variable) ḍ as d or j, ș as s or sh, ț as t or ch, ẓ as z or zh; ọ, F. cloche; ü, F. menu; ċh, Sc. loch; ṅ, F. bonbon; **′, primary accent; ″, secondary accent; †, obsolete; <, from; +, and; =, equals. See also lists at beginning of book**

bri-ar¹, bri-ar² (brī'ä̤r), etc. See *brier¹*, *brier²*, etc.

Bri-a-re-an (brī-ā'rē-a̤n), *a.* Of or like Briareus, a giant of Greek mythology having a hundred hands; many-handed.

brib-a-ble (brī'ba̤-bl), *a.* That may be bribed.

bribe (brīb), *n.* [ME.: cf. OF. *bribe*, *brimbe*, piece of bread given to a beggar, *briber*, *brimber*, beg.] Something given or promised to (formerly, exacted by) a person, esp. an official, to influence improperly his judgment or conduct; hence, anything given or serving to persuade or induce; an allurement.—**bribe,** *v.*; *bribed, bribing.* **I.** *tr.* To steal†; extort†; also, to give or promise a bribe to; influence or corrupt by a bribe; also, to obtain by bribery (archaic). **II.** *intr.* To give bribes; practise bribery.—**brib-er** (brī'bėr), *n.*—**brib'er-y,** *n.*; pl. *-ies* (-iz). Robbery†; the act or practice of giving or accepting bribes; the exaction of a bribe (archaic).

bric=à=brac (brik'a̤-brak), *n.* [F.] Miscellaneous articles of antiquarian interest, decorative value, etc., esp. such as are used for ornament about a room.

brick (brik), *n.* [OF. *brike*, *bricque* (F. *brique*), brick; prob. from Teut., and perhaps akin to E. *break*.] A block of clay, usually rectangular, hardened by drying in the sun or burning in a kiln, and used for building, paving, etc.; such blocks collectively, or the material; hence, a similar block of other material, for building, etc. (usually with a qualifying term: as, a concrete *brick*); any similar block (as, a *brick* of ice-cream); also, a good fellow, or a person of genuine good qualities (colloq.).—**brick,** *v. t.* To lay, line, wall, or build with brick.—**brick'bat,** *n.* A piece of broken brick.—**brick'=kiln,** *n.* A kiln or furnace in which bricks are baked or burned; also, a pile of bricks for burning, laid loose, with arches underneath to receive the fuel.—**brick'-lay''er,** *n.* One whose occupation it is to lay bricks, as in building.—**brick'lay''ing,** *n.*

brick-le (brik'l), *a.* [ME. *brekyl*, < AS. *brecan*, E. *break*.] Easily broken; fragile; brittle. [Now prov. Eng. and Sc.]

brick-mak-er (brik'mā''kėr), *n.* One whose occupation it is to make bricks.—**brick'mak''ing,** *n.*

brick=red (brik'red'), *n.* A yellowish or brownish red.

brick=tea (brik'tē'), *n.* Tea molded into a brick-like mass.

brick-wise (brik'wīz), *adv.* In the manner of arrangement of bricks in a wall.

brick-work (brik'wėrk), *n.* Work made of bricks.

brick-y (brik'i), *a.* Consisting or made of bricks; abounding in bricks; brick-like; brick-red.

brick=yard (brik'yärd), *n.* A place where bricks are made.

bri-cole (bri-kōl' or brik'o̤l), *n.* [F. *bricole* = It. *briccola* = ML. *bricola*, catapult; origin uncertain.] A kind of catapult†; in *billiards*, a shot by which the cue-ball is made to strike the cushion first.

bri-dal (brī'da̤l). [AS. *brȳdealo*, 'bride ale.'] **I.** *n.* A wedding-feast†; a wedding. **II.** *a.* Of or pertaining to a bride or a wedding.—**bri'dal-ly,** *adv.*—**bri'dal=wreath',** *n.* A rosaceous shrub, *Spiræa hypericifolia*, bearing long sprays of small white flowers, much cultivated for ornament; also, a saxifragaceous shrub, *Francoa ramosa*, a native of Chile, with dense racemes of white flowers.

bride¹ (brīd), *n.* [F., bridle, string, tie.] In lace, a stitch or thread connecting parts of the pattern.

bride² (brīd), *n.* [AS. *brȳd* = G. *braut*.] A woman newly married, or about to be married.—**bride'=cake,** *n.* A cake served in honor of the bride at a wedding.—**bride'-groom,** *n.* [AS. *brȳdguma* (*guma*, man).] A man newly married, or about to be married.—**brides'maid,** *n.* A young unmarried woman who attends the bride at a wedding.—**brides'man** (-ma̤n), *n.*; pl. *-men.* A man who attends the bride and groom at a wedding.

bride-well (brīd'wel), *n.* [From a former penal workhouse near St. *Bride's* (Bridget's) *Well*, in London.] A house of correction for vagrants and disorderly persons; a jail. [Eng.]

bridge¹ (brij), *n.* [AS. *brycg* = G. *brücke*.] A structure spanning a river, chasm, road, or the like, and affording passage; any structure or part similar in form or use; the ridge or upper line of the nose; a piece raising the strings of a musical instrument above the sounding-board; a ridge or wall-like projection of fire-brick or the like, at either end of the hearth in a metallurgical furnace; *naut.*, a raised platform from side to side of a ship above the rail, for the officer in charge; in *dentistry*, a mounting for artificial teeth, secured to adjoining teeth; in *billiards*, a notched piece of wood with a long handle, sometimes used to support a cue; in *elect.*, an apparatus for measuring electrical resistance.—**bridge¹,** *v. t.*; *bridged, bridging.* To make a bridge over; span; also, to make (a way) by a bridge.

bridge² (brij), *n.* [Origin uncertain.] A card-game resembling whist, in which the dealer or his partner (the dummy) declares the trump, and the dealer plays both his own and his partner's hand.—**auction bridge,** a variety of bridge in which the players bid for the privilege of declaring the trump.—**contract bridge,** a modification of auction bridge.

bridge=board (brij'bōrd), *n.* A notched board at the side of a wooden stair, supporting the treads and risers.

bridge=head (brij'hed), *n.* In *fort.*, a defensive work covering or protecting the end of a bridge toward the enemy.

bridge-less (brij'les), *a.* Without a bridge; not bridged.

bridge=tow-er (brij'tou''ėr), *n.* A tower for the defense of a bridge, sometimes erected on the bridge, with the road passing through an archway in its lower story, sometimes separate from the bridge and defending the approach to it; also, a tower or raised structure on a bridge, for the support of cables, etc.

Bridge-tower. — Prague, Bohemia.

bridge=ward (brij'wârd), *n.* The principal ward of a key.

bridge-work (brij'wėrk), *n.* The fitting in of artificial teeth with bridges.

bridg-ing (brij'ing), *n.* In *arch.*, a piece or an arrangement of pieces fixed between timbers to keep them in place.

bri-dle (brī'dl), *n.* [AS. *brīdel* = D. *breidel*.] The part of the harness of a horse, etc., about the head, consisting usually of head-stall, bit, and reins, and used to restrain and guide the animal; anything that restrains or curbs; any of various devices or parts resembling a horse's bridle in form or use; also, a bridling, or drawing up the head, as in disdain.—**bri'dle,** *v.*; *-dled, -dling.* **I.** *tr.* To put a bridle on; control as with a bridle; curb. **II.** *intr.* To hold up the head in the manner of a spirited horse under a strong rein; draw up the head and draw in the chin as in disdain or resentment.—**bri'dle-less,** *a.* Without a bridle; unbridled.—**bri'dle=path,** *n.* A path adapted for riding on horseback.—**bri'dler,** *n.*—**bri'dle=wise,** *a.* Trained to obey the action of the bridle or reins, as a horse.

bri-doon (bri-dön'), *n.* [F. *bridon*, < *bride*, bridle.] A light snaffle or bit and a rein, used in certain military bridles in addition to the principal bit and its rein; also, a kind of simple snaffle.

Brie (brē) **cheese.** [From *Brie*, district east of Paris, France.] A kind of soft, salted, white cream-cheese.

brief (brēf). [OF. *brief*, *bref* (F. *bref*), < L. *brevis*, short, *breve*, a summary, ML. letter, brief.] **I.** *a.* Short, esp. in duration; lasting or occupying but a short time; concise or succinct; abrupt or curt. **II.** *n.* A short or concise writing or statement; a summary; a papal letter less formal than a bull, sealed with the Pope's signet-ring or stamped with the device borne on this ring; in *law*, a writ; also, a memorandum of points of fact or of law for use in conducting a case; in England, an abstract of the facts of a case drawn up by a solicitor for the instruction of the barrister who acts in court.—**in brief,** in a brief form or statement; in few words; in short.—**brief,** *adv.* In or after a brief time; also, in brief. [Obs. or poetic.]—**brief,** *v. t.* To summarize; make a brief of; also, to furnish with a brief; hence, to retain as counsel in a suit.—**brief'=case,** *n.* A flat, rectangular, expansible leather case, often with two or more lengthwise compartments, which opens along one edge, where it is closed by a flap strapped down or locked on one side, and which has a handle attached on the top of the flap: used by lawyers for carrying briefs, etc., and others for documents, manuscripts, etc.—**brief'less,** *a.* Having no brief, as a barrister without clients.—**brief'ly,** *adv.*—**brief'ness,** *n.*

bri-er[1] (brī'ėr), *n.* [AS. *brēr, brǣr.*] A prickly plant or shrub, esp. the sweetbrier or the greenbrier.

bri-er[2] (brī'ėr), *n.* [F. *bruyère,* heath; from Celtic.] The white heath, *Erica arborea,* of France and Corsica, whose woody root is used for making tobacco-pipes; also, a pipe made of this woody root.—**bri'er=root,** *n.*—**bri'er=wood,** *n.*

bri-er-y (brī'ėr-i), *a.* Full of briers; thorny.

brig[1] (brig), *n.* Sc. and north. Eng. form of *bridge*[1].

brig[2] (brig), *n.* [Short for *brigantine.*] A two-masted vessel square-rigged on both masts; also, the prison on a war-ship.—**hermaphrodite brig.** See under *hermaphrodite.*

bri-gade (bri-gād'), *n.* [F. *brigade,* < It. *brigata,* troop, < *brigare,* strive, contend, < *briga,* strife.] A large body of troops; esp., a unit of organization in an army, varying in different countries, but commonly consisting of two or more regiments; hence, any body of individuals organized for a special purpose (as, a fire-*brigade*).—**bri-gade',** *v. t.*; *-gaded, -gading.* To form into a brigade.

brig-a-dier (brig-ạ-dēr'), *n.* [F.] An officer in command of a brigade; a brigadier-general.—**brig-a-dier'=gen'er-al,** *n.*; pl. *-als.* An officer in command of a brigade or engaged in other duties, in the U. S. ranking next below a major-general.

brig-and (brig'ạnd), *n.* [OF. F. *brigand,* < It. *brigante,* < *brigare*: see *brigade.*] An irregular foot-soldier†; also, a plundering marauder; a bandit; esp., one of a gang of robbers in mountain or forest regions.—**brig'and-age** (-ạn-dāj), *n.* The practice of brigands; plundering; organized spoliation.

brig-an-dine (brig'ạn-dēn), *n.* [OF. *brigandine,* < *brigand,* foot-soldier.] A defensive coat of linen, leather, etc., reinforced by plates of steel.

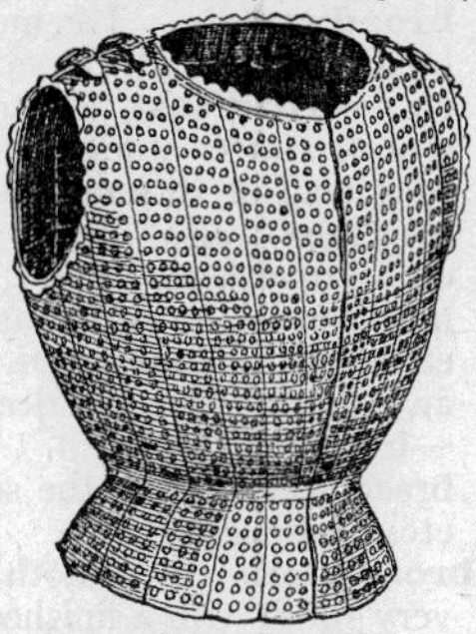

Brigandine.

brig-and-ish (brig'ạn-dish), *a.* Like or suggestive of a brigand.—**brig'and-ism,** *n.* Brigandage.

brig-an-tine (brig'ạn-tēn), *n.* [F. *brigantin,* < It. *brigantino,* < *brigante,* E. *brigand.*] A two-masted vessel in which the foremast is square-rigged and the mainmast bears a fore-and-aft mainsail and square topsails; also, commonly, a hermaphrodite brig.

bright (brīt). [AS. *bryht, beorht,* = OHG. *beraht* = Icel. *bjartr* = Goth. *bairhts,* bright: cf. Skt. *bhrāj-,* shine.] **I.** *a.* Radiating or reflecting light; luminous; shining; filled with light; vivid or brilliant, as color; clear or translucent, as liquids; manifest to the mind†; radiant or splendid (as, *bright* beauty); illustrious or glorious, as a period; quick-witted or intelligent, as a person; clever or witty, as a remark; animated, lively, or cheerful, as a person; characterized by happiness or gladness (as, *bright* days); favorable or auspicious (as, *bright* prospects). **II.** *n.* Brightness; splendor. [Archaic.]—**bright,** *adv.* In a bright manner.—**bright'en,** *v. i.* or *t.* To become or make bright or brighter.—**bright'en-er,** *n.*—**bright'ly,** *adv.*—**bright'ness,** *n.*

Bright's (brīts) **dis-ease'.** [From R. *Bright,* English physician, who described it in 1827.] Kidney disease, attended with albuminuria.

bright-some (brīt'sum), *a.* Bright. [Archaic.]

Brig-it-tine (brij'i-tin or -tēn), *n.* A member of an order of nuns and monks founded by St. Brigitta (or Bridget) of Sweden about 1346: a few houses of nuns of this order still exist, including one in England.

brill (bril), *n.* [Origin unknown.] A European flatfish, *Bothus* (or *Rhombus*) *lævis,* allied to the turbot.

bril-liant (bril'yạnt). [F. *brillant,* ppr. of *briller,* < It. *brillare,* shine, sparkle, < L. *beryllus,* E. *beryl.*] **I.** *a.* Shining brightly; sparkling; glittering; lustrous; vivid or intense, as color; splendid or distinguished, as an assemblage; striking or illustrious, as an achievement; characterized by or showing unusual mental keenness or cleverness; extremely favorable, as prospects. **II.** *n.* A diamond (or other gem) of a particular cut, typically shaped like two pyramids united at their bases, the top one cut off near the base and the bottom one close to the apex, with many facets on the slopes; also, a cotton fabric with a woven figure; also, a printing-type (about 3½ point), the smallest of the regular sizes (see *type*).—**bril'liance, bril'lian-cy,** *n.*

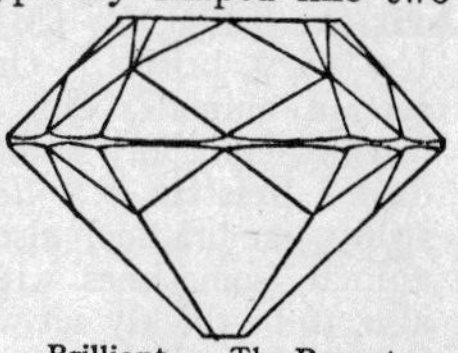

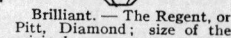

Brilliant. — The Regent, or Pitt, Diamond; size of the original.

bril-lian-tine (bril-yạn-tēn'), *n.* [F. *brillantine.*] A dress-fabric resembling alpaca; also, a toilet preparation for the hair.

bril-liant-ly (bril'yạnt-li), *adv.* In a brilliant manner.—**bril'liant-ness,** *n.*

brim[1] (brim), *a.* See *breme.*

brim[2] (brim), *n.* [ME. *brimme*: cf. G. *bräme,* Icel. *barmr,* brim, also AS. *brim,* surf, sea.] The edge or margin of the land bordering a body of water; the edge of the water (archaic); the upper edge of a cup, basin, or anything of similar shape; the rim; a projecting edge about something (as, the *brim* of a hat); the brink† or verge†; in general, edge† or margin†.—**brim**[2], *v.*; *brimmed, brimming.* **I.** *tr.* To fill to the brim. **II.** *intr.* To be full to the brim; run (*over*).—**brim'=full',** *a.* Full to the brim; completely full. Also **brim'ful'.**—**brim'less,** *a.* Without a brim, as a hat.—**brimmed,** *a.* Having a brim.—**brim'mer,** *n.* A cup or the like full to the brim.—**brim'ming-ly,** *adv.*

brim-stone (brim'stōn), *n.* [ME. *brinston,* < *brinnen,* burn, + *ston,* stone.] Sulphur; also, a virago.—**brim'ston-y,** *a.* Of, like, or containing brimstone.

brin (brin), *n.* [F., blade, shoot.] One of the radiating sticks of a fan.

brin-ded (brin'ded), *a.* [Earlier *brended,* prob. for *branded,* as if 'marked by branding.'] Of a gray or tawny color, with darker streaks or spots: as, "Thrice the *brinded* cat hath mew'd" (Shakspere's "Macbeth," iv. 1. 1).

brin-dle (brin'dl). [Prob. < *brindled.*] **I.** *a.* Brindled. **II.** *n.* A brindled coloring; also, a brindled animal.

brin-dled (brin'dld), *a.* [Var. of *brinded.*] Brinded; streaked; variegated.

brine (brīn), *n.* [AS. *brȳne* = MD. *brine.*] Water saturated or strongly impregnated with salt; also, the water of the sea; the sea or ocean; also, tears (poetic).—**brine,** *v. t.*; *brined, brining.* To treat with or steep in brine.

bring (bring), *v.*; *brought, bringing.* [AS. *bringan* = D. *brengen* = G. *bringen* = Goth. *briggan,* bring.] **I.** *tr.* To cause to come with one's self; take along to the place or person sought; convey or conduct; fetch; lead or induce; in general, to cause to come, as to a recipient or possessor, to the mind or knowledge, into a particular position or state, to a particular opinion or decision, or into existence, view, action, or effect (used in many phrases, as with *about, forth, on, out,* etc.). **II.** *intr.* With *up,* to come to a stop or halt.—**bring'er,** *n.*

brin-ish (brī'nish), *a.* Like brine; briny.

brink (bringk), *n.* [ME.; prob. from Scand. (cf. Dan. *brink*).] The edge or margin of a steep place or of land bordering water; the verge or extreme edge of anything; the brim of a vessel†; in general, edge† or margin†.

brin-y (brī'ni), *a.* Of or like brine; salt.

bri-o (brē'ō), *n.* [It.] Animation; spirit.

bri-oche (brē-osh), *n.* [F.] A kind of light raised bun or cake.

bri-o-lette (brē-ọ-let'), *n.* [F.] A pear-shaped diamond having its entire surface cut with triangular facets.

bri-o-ny (brī'ọ-ni), *n.* See *bryony.*

bri-quette, bri-quet (bri-ket'), *n.* [F. *briquette,* dim. of *brique,* brick.] A molded block of compacted coal-dust for fuel; also, a similar block of some other material.

brisk (brisk), *a.* [Origin uncertain: cf. W. *brysg,* quick.] Quick and active; lively; smart; vigorous; spirited; sprightly; of liquors, effervescing; sharp.—**brisk,** *v. t.* or *i.* To make or become brisk; liven (*up*). Also **brisk'en.**

bris-ket (bris′ket), *n.* [ME. *brusket*: cf. OF. *bruschet*, *brichet* (F. *brechet*).] The breast of an animal, or the part of the breast lying next to the ribs.

brisk-ly (brisk′li), *adv.* In a brisk manner; quickly; actively; smartly.—**brisk′ness,** *n.*

bris-tle (bris′l), *n.* [ME. *bristil*, < AS. *byrst* = G. *borste* = Icel. *burst*, bristle.] One of the short, stiff, coarse hairs of certain animals, esp. hogs, used extensively in making brushes, etc.; any similar short, stiff hair or hair-like appendage.—**bris′tle,** *v.*; *-tled, -tling.* **I.** *intr.* To stand or rise stiffly, like bristles; also, to erect the bristles, as an irritated animal (sometimes with *up*, and often fig., of persons); also, to be thickly set with something suggestive of bristles; be rough; also, to be visibly roused or stirred (*with*). **II.** *tr.* To erect like bristles; also, to furnish with a bristle or bristles; make bristly.—**bris′tled,** *a.* Having bristles; bristly.—**bris′tle-tail,** *n.* Any of various wingless insects of the order *Thysanura*, having long, bristle-like caudal appendages.—**bris-tly** (bris′li), *a.* Covered with bristles; rough with bristle-like hairs, etc.; also, resembling bristles. —**bris′tli-ness,** *n.*

Bris-tol (bris′tọl) **board.** [From *Bristol*, city in southwestern England.] A fine, smooth kind of pasteboard, sometimes glazed.—**Bris′tol brick.** Bath brick.—**Bris′tol di′a-mond, Bris′tol stone.** A rock-crystal from near Bristol, England.

brit, britt (brit), *n.* [Origin obscure.] A young herring of the common kind; also, the young of various other marine fishes.

Bri-tan-ni-a (bri-tan′i-ạ), *n.* [L., < *Britanni* (later *Britones*), the ancient Britons.] Britain, or Great Britain, or, in a broader sense, the British Empire; a feminine personification of either.—**Britannia metal,** a white alloy of tin, copper, and antimony, usually with small amounts of zinc, etc.—**Bri-tan′nic,** *a.* [L. *Britannicus*.] British.

Brit-i-cism (brit′i-sizm), *n.* A word, phrase, or idiom peculiar to the British rather than to English-speaking people generally.

Brit-ish (brit′ish). [AS. *Bryttisc*, < *Bryttas*, *Brettas*, pl., Britons; from Celtic.] **I.** *a.* Of or pertaining to the ancient Britons; also, of or pertaining to the whole island of Britain (more fully called Great Britain), or, in a broader sense, the British Empire, or the inhabitants. **II.** *n.* The British people, taken collectively; also, the ancient British tongue. —**Brit′ish-er,** *n.* A British subject. [Colloq.]

Brit-on (brit′ọn), *n.* [OF. *Breton* (usually, as in F., meaning a Breton: see *Breton*), < L. *Brito(n-)*, *Britto(n-)*, one of the people inhabiting Britain; from Celtic (cf. *British*).] One of the Celtic people which in early times occupied the southern part of the island of Britain; also, a native or inhabitant of Britain, or Great Britain, or, in a broader sense, of the British Empire.—**North Briton,** a Scot.

brits-ka, britz-ka (brits′kạ), *n.* [Pol. *bryczka*, dim. of *bryka*, freight-wagon.] An open carriage with a calash-top and space for reclining.

brit-tle (brit′l), *a.* [ME. *britel*, < AS. *brēotan*, break.] Breaking readily, with a comparatively smooth fracture, as glass; fragile; fig., perishable†; insecure, unstable, or changeable (archaic or prov.).—**brit′tle-ly,** *adv.*—**brit′tle-ness,** *n.*—**brit′tle=star,** *n.* Any of several ophiuroids: so called from their fragility.

britz′ka, britzs′ka, *n.* See *britska*.

broach (brōch), *n.* [OF. F. *broche*, < ML. *broca*, *brocca*, sharp stake or instrument: cf. L. *broccus*, *brocchus*, projecting, as teeth.] Any of various pointed instruments; a spear†; a spit for roasting meat; any of various tools or drills for boring or widening holes; a reamer; a gimlet for tapping casks; a tool for dressing stone; also, a brooch.—**broach,** *v.* **I.** *tr.* To pierce as with a spit; tap (a cask, etc.); draw (liquor, etc.) as by tapping; break into for the purpose of taking out something; mention or suggest (a subject) for the first time; dress (stone) with a broach. **II.** *intr.* *Naut.*, with *to*, of a ship, to veer to windward, esp. so as to be broadside to the wind.—**broach′er,** *n.*

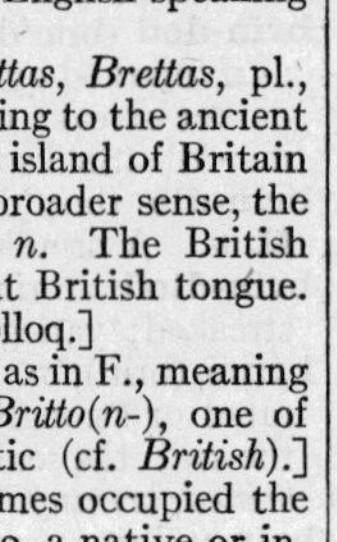

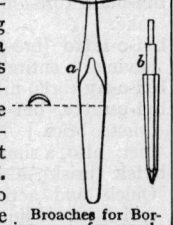

Broaches for Boring. — *a*, for wood; *b*, for metal.

broad (brôd), *a.* [AS. *brād* = D. *breed* = G. *breit* = Icel. *breidhr* = Goth. *braids*, broad.] Of great breadth; wide; of great extent; large; of extensive range or scope (as, *broad* principles); not limited or narrow (as, *broad* views); liberal (as, the *Broad*-church party in the Church of England); main or general (as, the *broad* outlines of a subject); unrestricted or full (as, *broad* daylight); unrestrained (as, *broad* farce); characterized by full, strong utterance (as, *broad* Scotch); plain or clear, as language; plain-spoken, as a person; indelicate or indecent, as a story; in *art*, marked by breadth.—**broad seal,** a great or official seal, as of a state.—**broad,** *n.* The broad part of a thing; also, an expanse of water formed by a river overflowing low, flat land (Eng.).

broad=ar-row (brôd′ar′ō), *n.* A mark of the shape of a broad arrow-head, placed upon British government stores.

Broad-arrow.

broad-ax (brôd′aks), *n.* An ax with a broad blade, as a battle-ax, or an ax for hewing timber.

broad-bill (brôd′bil), *n.* Any of various birds with a broad bill, as the scaup, shoveler, and spoonbill.—**broad′=billed,** *a.*

broad-brim (brôd′brim), *n.* A hat with a broad brim, as that worn by Quakers; hence [*cap.*], a Friend or Quaker (colloq.).—**broad′=brimmed,** *a.*

broad-cast (brôd′kȧst). **I.** *a.* Cast abroad or all over an area, as seed sown thus (rather than in drills or rows); performed by casting abroad (as, *broadcast* sowing); fig., widely spread or disseminated (as, *broadcast* discontent); also, specif., sent broadcast, or to an indefinite number of receiving stations or instruments in various directions, as radio messages, speeches, music, etc.; also, pertaining to such sending. **II.** *adv.* So as to be cast abroad over an area (as, seed sown *broadcast*); fig., so as to be spread or disseminated widely; also, specif., so as to reach an indefinite number of radio receiving stations or instruments in various directions.—**broad′cast,** *n.* The method of sowing by scattering seed broadcast; also, the broadcasting of radio messages, speeches, etc.—**broad′cast,** *v.*; *-casted* or *-cast, -casting.* **I.** *tr.* To cast or scatter abroad over an area, as seed in sowing; fig., to spread or disseminate widely (as, to *broadcast* seditious principles); also, specif., to send (messages, speeches, music, etc.) broadcast by radio. **II.** *intr.* To scatter or disseminate something broadcast, specif. radio messages, speeches, etc.—**broad′cast″er,** *n.* One who or that which broadcasts; an apparatus for broadcasting radio messages, speeches, etc. —**broad′cast″ing,** *n.* The act of one who or that which broadcasts; specif., the sending of radio messages, speeches, etc., broadcast.

broad-cloth (brôd′klôth), *n.* A fine woolen cloth (orig. very wide) with a finished surface.

broad-en (brô′dn), *v. i.* or *t.* To become or make broad; widen.

broad-ish (brôd′ish), *a.* Somewhat broad.

broad-ly (brôd′li), *adv.* In a broad manner.

broad=mind-ed (brôd′mīn′ded), *a.* Characterized by mental breadth; free from prejudice or bigotry; liberal; tolerant. —**broad′=mind′ed-ness,** *n.*

broad-ness (brôd′nes), *n.* The state or character of being broad.

broad=piece (brôd′pēs), *n.* An old English gold coin worth 20 shillings, first issued in 1619 by James I.: so called after the introduction, in 1663, of the guinea, which was narrower and thicker.

broad-sheet (brôd′shēt), *n.* A large sheet of paper forming a single page, or printed on one side only.

broad-side (brôd′sīd), *n.* The whole side of a ship above the water-line, from the bow to the quarter; any broad surface or side, as of a house, etc.; all the guns that can be fired to one side of a ship, or their simultaneous discharge; any comprehensive attack; also, a sheet of paper, esp. of large size, printed on one side only, as for distribution.—**broad′side,** *adv.* With the side turned (*to* or *on*).

broad-sword (brôd′sōrd), *n.* A sword with a broad, flat cutting blade.

broad-tail (brôd′tāl), *n.* The skin or fur of the young of the Persian breed of sheep, killed when a few days old, before the wool has had time to develop beyond a flat, wavy state, in which it resembles moiré silk.

broad-way (brôd′wā), *n.* A broad road or highway, often [*cap.*] the proper name of a street, as in New York City.
broad-wise, broad-ways (brôd′wīz, -wāz), *adv.* Breadthwise.
brob (brob), *n.* [Cf. *brad.*] A wedge-shaped spike driven in beside an abutting timber to keep it from slipping.

Brobs.

Brob-ding-nag-i-an (brob-ding-nag′i-ạn). **I.** *a.* Of or befitting the region of Brobdingnag, in Swift's "Gulliver's Travels," where everything was of enormous size; enormous; gigantic. **II.** *n.* A giant; a gigantic person.
bro-cade (brọ-kād′), *n.* [Sp. *brocado* = It. *broccato*, < ML. *brocare*, interweave with gold or silver, < *broca*: see *broach.*] A silk fabric with a woven, often elaborate pattern, orig. formed by interweaving threads of gold or silver; a similar fabric of wool or other material.—**bro-cade′**, *v. t.*; *-caded, -cading.* To weave with a design or figure.—**bro-cad′ed** (-kā′ded), *p. a.* Woven or wrought into a brocade.
bro-cage (brō′kạj), *n.* See *brokage.*
broc-ard (brok′ärd or brō′kärd), *n.* [F.; so called from *Burchard*, bishop of Worms (died 1025), compiler of ecclesiastical canons.] A legal or other maxim; a canon.
bro-ca-tel, bro-ca-telle (brō-kạ-tel′ or brok-ạ-), *n.* [F. *brocatelle*, < It. *broccatello*, dim. of *broccato*, = E. *brocade.*] An inferior kind of brocade, made of silk and wool, silk and cotton, wool, or cotton, used chiefly for upholstery; also, an ornamental marble with variegated coloring, from Italy, Spain, and elsewhere.
broc-co-li (brok′ọ-li), *n.* [It., pl. of *broccolo*, sprout.] A variety of cabbage resembling the cauliflower.

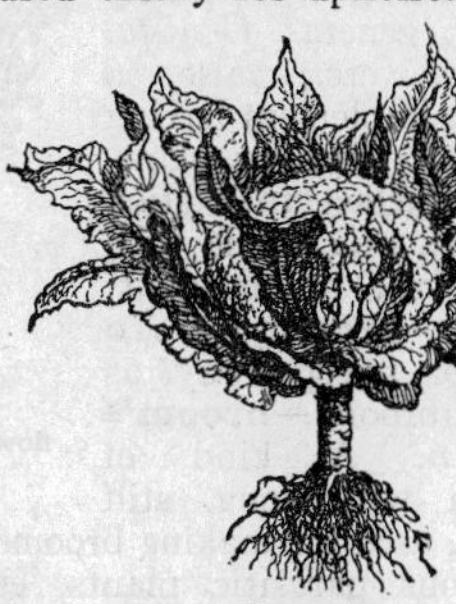
Broccoli.

bro-ché (brō-shā′), *a.* [F., pp. of *brocher*, weave with a pattern, stitch, < ML. *brocare*: see *brocade.*] Woven with a pattern; brocaded; also, stitched (but not bound), as a pamphlet.
bro-chette (brō-shet′), *n.* [F., dim. of *broche*, spit: see *broach.*] A skewer, for use in cookery.
bro-chure (brō-shör′, F. bro-shür), *n.* [F., < *brocher*, stitch: see *broché.*] A pamphlet.
brock (brok), *n.* [AS. *broc*; from Celtic.] A European badger. [Obs. or prov.]
Brock-en (brok′en) **spec′ter.** See *specter of the Brocken*, under *specter.*
brock-et (brok′et), *n.* [OF. *brocart*, < *broque*, var. of *broche*, broach, tine.] The male red deer in the second year, with the first growth of straight, spike-like horns; also, any of various small South and Central American deer of the genus *Mazama*, with straight, unbranched horns.
bro-gan (brō′gạn), *n.* [Ir. and Gael. *brōgan*, < *brōg*, E. *brogue*[1].] A coarse, stout shoe.
brogue[1] (brōg), *n.* [Ir. and Gael. *brōg.*] A rude shoe, commonly of untanned hide, worn, esp. formerly, in Ireland and Scotland; also, any coarse, stout shoe; in recent use, a strongly made, comfortable type of ordinary shoe, often with decorative perforations on the vamp and foxing.

Ancient Irish Brogues.

brogue[2] (brōg), *n.* [Origin unknown.] A dialectal, esp. Irish, mode of pronunciation; an Irish accent in the pronunciation of English.
broi-der (broi′dėr), *v. t.* [OF. *brouder*, *brosder* (F. *broder*); appar. from Teut.] To embroider; fig., to adorn (as, "The violet, Crocus, and hyacinth, with rich inlay *Broider'd* the ground": Milton's "Paradise Lost," iv. 702). [Archaic.]—**broi′der-y,** *n.* Embroidery; embroidered work. [Archaic.]
broil[1] (broil), *v.* [OF. F. *brouiller*, mix up, disorder, embroil; origin uncertain.] **I.** *tr.* To mix confusedly†; confuse†; disturb†; involve in discord or broils; embroil. **II.** *intr.* To engage in a broil; quarrel; fight.—**broil**[1], *n.* A state of confusion and discord or strife; an angry quarrel or struggle; a disturbance; a tumult.
broil[2] (broil), *v.* [OF. *bruiller*, *bruller*, *brusler* (F. *brûler*), burn.] **I.** *tr.* To cook by exposure to a clear fire, as on a gridiron; grill; also, to scorch; make very hot. **II.** *intr.* To be exposed to great or distressing heat; also, to burn with impatience, etc.—**broil**[2], *n.* A broiling; also, something broiled.—**broil′er,** *n.* One who or that which broils; a device for broiling meat, etc.; a fowl for broiling; a very hot day (colloq.).—**broil′ing,** *p. a.* Scorching; very hot.—**broil′ing-ly,** *adv.*
bro-kage (brō′kạj), *n.* Brokerage.
broke[1] (brōk). Preterit and past participle of *break.*
broke[2] (brōk), *v. i.*; *broked, broking.* [See *broker.*] To act as a broker.
brok-en (brō′kn), *p. a.* [See *break.*] That has been subjected to breaking; violently separated into parts; in pieces or fragments; burst; infringed or violated; interrupted or disconnected; uneven or irregular; fragmentary or incomplete; changing direction abruptly, as a line; imperfectly spoken, as language; destroyed, overwhelmed, or ruined; weakened in strength, spirit, etc.; reduced to submission; tamed; outlawed (Sc.).—**broken wind,** in *vet. science*, heaves.—**brok′en=down′,** *a.* Shattered or collapsed; ruined; having given way, as in health.—**brok′en=heart′ed,** *a.* Crushed by grief.—**brok′en-ly,** *adv.*—**brok′en-ness,** *n.*—**brok′en=wind′ed,** *a.* Affected with heaves, as a horse; breathing with spasmodic efforts.
bro-ker (brō′kėr), *n.* [AF. *brocour*, OF. *brokeor*, orig. broacher (of casks), tapster (hence retailer); akin to E. *broach.*] A middleman or agent; one who buys and sells stocks, bonds, etc., or other property, on commission; a pawnbroker; a pander†.—**bro′ker-age** (-ạj), *n.* The business, service, or commission of a broker.
bro-mal (brō′mạl), *n.* [From *brom*(*ine*) + *al*(*cohol*): cf. *chloral.*] A colorless, oily liquid, CBr_3COH, obtained by the action of bromine on alcohol: used in medicine.
bro-mate (brō′māt), *n.* In *chem.*, a salt of bromic acid.—**bro′mate,** *v. t.*; *-mated, -mating.* To combine with bromine.
brome=grass (brōm′gràs), *n.* [NL. *Bromus* (see def.), < Gr. βρόμος, kind of oats.] Any grass of the genus *Bromus*, as chess.
bro-me-li-a-ceous (brọ-mē-li-ā′shius), *a.* [NL. *Bromelia*, the typical genus; named from Olaf *Bromel* (1639–1705), Swedish botanist.] Belonging to the *Bromeliaceæ*, a family of plants, mostly of tropical America, including the pineapple.
bro-mic (brō′mik), *a.* Of or containing bromine: as, *bromic* acid, $HBrO_3$.
bro-mide, bro-mid (brō′mīd or -mid, -mid), *n.* A compound of bromine with an element or radical; a salt of hydrobromic acid (HBr), esp. any of certain salts (as potassium bromide, strontium bromide, etc.) that act as cerebral and cardiac depressants and are much used in medicine as sedatives and hypnotics; also, a person who is stupidly conventional in thought and speech, or given to uttering tedious platitudes (colloq.: cf. *sulphite*).—**bro-mid-ic** (brọ-mid′ik), *a.* Pertaining or proper to or being a bromide. [Colloq.]
bro-mine, bro-min (brō′min), *n.* [Gr. βρῶμος, stench.] Chem. sym., Br; at. wt., 79.92; sp. gr., 3.19. An element, a dark reddish fuming liquid, resembling chlorine and iodine in chemical properties.—**bro′min-ism, bro′mism,** *n.* A morbid condition due to excessive use of bromides.—**bro′mo-form** (-mọ-fôrm), *n.* In *chem.*, a colorless liquid, $CHBr_3$, analogous to chloroform: used in medicine.—**bro-mo-gel′a-tin** (-jel′ạ-tin), *a.* In *photog.*, formed from or prepared with certain bromides together with silver nitrate and gelatin, as the sensitive emulsions used for making dry plates; pertaining to such emulsions.—**bro′mol** (-mol or -mōl), *n.* A white crystalline substance, a bromine derivative of phenol, used as an antiseptic and disinfectant.
bron-chi (brong′kī), *n.* Plural of *bronchus.*
bron-chi-a (brong′ki-ä), *n. pl.* [LL., < Gr. βρόγχια, pl., < βρόγχος, windpipe.] In *anat.*, the ramifications of the

bronchi or two main branches of the trachea.—**bron'chi-al,** *a.* Pertaining to the bronchia or the bronchi.—**bronchial tubes,** the bronchi, or the bronchi and their ramifications.

bron-chi-tis (brong-kī'tis), *n.* [NL.] In *pathol.*, inflammation of the bronchial membrane.—**bron-chit'ic** (-kit'ik), *a.*

bron-cho (brong'kō), etc. See *bronco*, etc.

broncho-. Form of Gr. βρόγχος, windpipe, in combination: sometimes used also to represent *bronchia.*—**bron-cho-cele** (brong'kọ-sēl), *n.* [Gr. βρογχοκήλη: see *-cele.*] Goiter.—**bron"cho-pneu-mo'ni-a,** *n.* In *pathol.*, inflammation of the bronchia and lungs: a form of pneumonia.—**bron'cho-tome** (-tōm), *n.* [+ *-tome.*] A cutting instrument for use in bronchotomy.—**bron-chot-o-my** (brong-kot'ọ-mi), *n.* [+ *-tomy.*] Surgical incision into the windpipe.

bron-chus (brong'kus), *n.*; pl. *-chi* (-kī). [NL., < Gr. βρόγχος, windpipe.] In *anat.*, either of the two main branches of the trachea; also, any of the ramifications of these branches.

bron-co (brong'kō), *n.*; pl. *-cos* (-kōz). [Sp., rough, rude.] A pony or mustang of the western U. S., esp. one that is not broken, or is only imperfectly broken.—**bron'co=bust"er,** *n.* One who breaks broncos to the saddle. [Western U. S.]—**bron'co=grass,** *n.* A Mediterranean brome-grass, *Bromus maximus gussoni*, introduced into California.

bronto-. Form of Gr. βροντή, thunder, used in combination.—**bron-to-graph** (bron'tọ-grȧf), *n.* [+ *-graph.*] A brontometer, or the tracing or record produced by it.—**bron-tom'e-ter** (-tom'e-tėr), *n.* [+ *-meter.*] An instrument for recording the phenomena of thunder-storms.—**bron-to-sau'rus** (-sâ'rus), *n.* [NL.: see *-saur, -saurus.*] Any of the dinosaurs of the American genus *Brontosaurus*, which attained a length of 60 feet or over.

bronze (bronz). [F., < It. *bronzo*, said to be < L. *Brundisium* (It. *Brindisi*), town in southeastern Italy.] **I.** *n.* A durable brown alloy, consisting essentially of copper and tin; any of various similar alloys, as one of copper and aluminium; something made of bronze, as a statue or other work of art; a lustrous metallic brown coloring substance; a lustrous brown color; impudence†. **II.** *a.* Of, pertaining to, or like bronze; of the color of bronze.—**bronze age,** the age in the history of mankind (between the stone and iron ages) marked by the use of bronze implements. See *ages in archæology*, under *age, n.*—**bronze,** *v.*; *bronzed, bronzing.* **I.** *tr.* To give the appearance or color of bronze to; make brown, as by exposure to the sun; also, to make hard or unfeeling. **II.** *intr.* To take on a bronze color.—**bronz'ite** (-īt), *n.* A mineral consisting of a ferriferous silicate of magnesium, which is often characterized by a bronze-like luster.

brooch (brōch or brōch), *n.* [Var. of *broach.*] A clasp or ornament for the dress, having a pin at the back for passing through the clothing and a catch for securing the point of the pin.—**brooch,** *v. t.* To adorn as with a brooch.

brood (bröd), *n.* [AS. *brōd* = D. *broed* = G. *brut*: cf. *breed.*] A family of offspring or young; a number of young creatures produced or hatched at one time; a hatch, as of birds; also, breed or kind.—**brood,** *v.* **I.** *intr.* To sit as a bird over eggs to be hatched; rest fixedly; meditate with morbid persistence (*on* or *over*). **II.** *tr.* To sit as a bird over (eggs or young); incubate; cherish, as a bird her young; dwell persistently or moodily in thought on.—**brood'er,** *n.*—**brood'ing-ly,** *adv.*—**brood'=mare,** *n.* A mare kept for breeding.—**brood'y,** *a.* Inclined to brood.

brook[1] (bruk), *v. t.* [AS. *brūcan* = G. *brauchen*, use; akin to L. *frui*, enjoy.] To use†; possess†; also, to bear, suffer, or tolerate (now only in negative constructions: as, "Your son, sir, insulted me in a manner which my honour could not *brook*," Sheridan's "Rivals," v. 3).

brook[2] (bruk), *n.* [AS. *brōc*, stream, = G. *bruch*, marsh.] A natural stream of water, smaller than a river, flowing through a glen or through woods, meadows, etc.—**brook'let,** *n.* A small brook.

brook-lime (bruk'līm), *n.* [ME. *brokelemke*, < *broke*, brook, + AS. *hleomoc*, a kind of plant.] An old-world scrophulariaceous plant, *Veronica beccabunga*, with small racemose flowers, growing on the edge of brooks, etc.; an allied species, *V. americana*, of America; also, the water-cress, *Roripa nasturtium.*

brook=trout (bruk'trout), *n.* A fish, *Salvelinus fontinalis*, the common speckled trout of eastern North America.

Brook-trout.

brook-weed (bruk'wēd), *n.* Either of two primulaceous plants, *Samolus valerandi*, of the Old World, and *S. floribundus*, of North America, both bearing small white flowers.

brook-y (bruk'i), *a.* Abounding in brooks.

broom (bröm), *n.* [AS. *brōm*; akin to E. *bramble.*] Any of the shrubby fabaceous plants of the genus *Cytisus*, esp. *C.* (or *Genista*) *scoparius*, common in western Europe, which grows on uncultivated ground and has long, slender branches bearing yellow flowers; any of various allied or other plants of the genera *Genista, Spartium*, etc.; also, a sweeping implement having a brush of twigs or plant-stems attached to a stick or handle, orig. made with twigs of the broom-plant; a besom.—**broom,** *v.t.* To sweep, or sweep away, as with a broom.—**broom'=corn,** *n.* A kind of sorghum with long, stiff panicles, used for making brooms.—**broom'=rape,** *n.* Any of various parasitic plants, esp. of the genus *Orobanche*, living on the roots of broom and other plants.—**broom'stick,** *n.* The long stick forming the handle of a broom.—**broom'y,** *a.* Abounding in broom; broom-like.

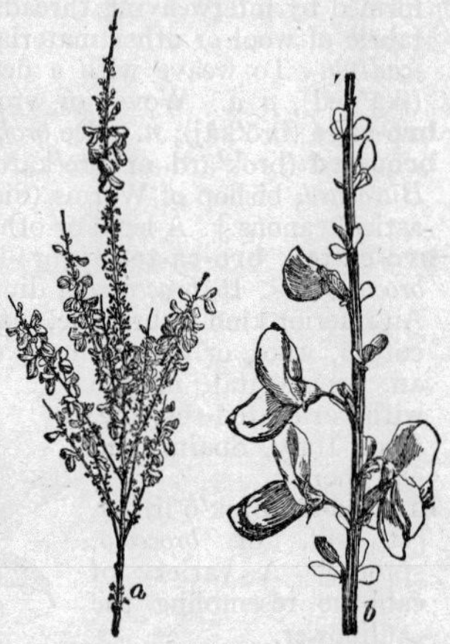

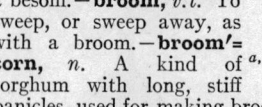

Broom (*Cytisus scoparius*). *a*, flowering branch; *b*, flowers, natural size.

broose (brōz), *n.* [Origin unknown.] At country weddings, a race by the young men, from the place of the marriage ceremony to the bridegroom's house. [Sc.]

brose (brōz), *n.* [= *brewis.*] A dish made by pouring boiling water, milk, or the like on oatmeal or other meal. [Sc.]

broth (brôth), *n.* [AS. *broth* = OHG. *brod* = Icel. *brodh*; from the root of E. *brew*: cf. *brewis.*] The liquor from boiled meat, etc.; thin soup.—**a broth of a boy,** the essence of what a boy should be; a first-rate fellow. [Ir.]

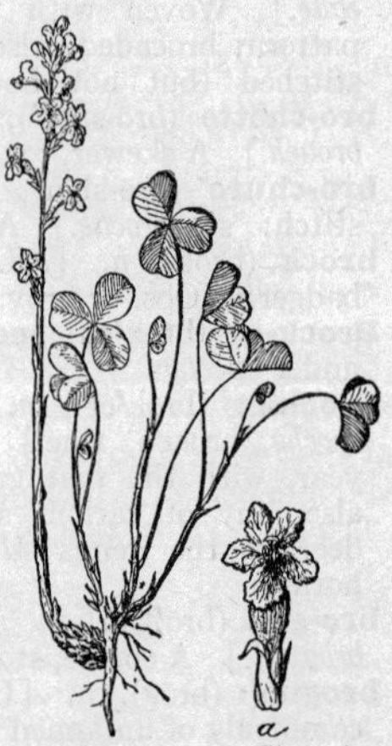

Broom-rape. — Flowering plant of *Orobanche minor*, parasitic on the root of white clover; *a*, a flower.

broth-el (broth'ẹl), *n.* [ME. *brothel*, worthless person (< AS. *brēothan*, ruin), confused with *bordel* (< OF. *bordel*), brothel.] A worthless or depraved man†; a lewd woman†; also, a house of prostitution or ill fame.

broth-er (bruᴛʜ'ėr). [AS. *brōthor* = D. *broeder* = G. *bruder* = Icel. *brōdhir* = Goth. *brōthar*; akin to L. *frater*, brother, Gr. φράτηρ, clansman, Skt. *bhrātar*, brother.] **I.** *n.*; pl. *brothers* or *brethren* (breᴛʜ'ren). A male relative, a son of the same parents or parent; a male member of a religious order; a member of a religious congregation of laymen, or a lay member of a community having priests; a member of any of various Christian organizations or sects using the plural form 'Brethren' in their titles; a male fellow-member of a church, or of any society, profession, or the like; a fellow or associate; a fellow-countryman, fellow-man, etc. **II.** *a.* Being a brother; related by brotherhood. —**broth′er,** *v. t.* To treat or address as a brother; admit to or join in brotherhood.—**broth′er-hood** (-hu̇d), *n.* The condition of a brother; a relation as between brothers; also, an association of persons joined as brothers; a fraternity; any group considered as brothers.—**broth′er=in=law″,** *n.*; pl. *brothers-in-law.* One's husband's or wife's brother; one's sister's husband.—**Broth′er Jon′a-than.** A name for the U. S. government or people.—**broth′er-less,** *a.* Without a brother.—**broth′er-ly,** *a.* Of, like, or befitting a brother.—**broth′er-li-ness,** *n.*—**broth′er-ly,** *adv.*

brough-am (brö′ạm, brō′ạm, or bröm), *n.* [From Lord *Brougham* (1778–1868), British statesman.] A four-wheeled close carriage for two or four persons.

Brougham.

brought (brôt). Preterit and past participle of *bring.*

brow (brou), *n.* [AS. *brū,* akin to Icel. *brūn,* Gr. *ὀφρύς,* Skt. *bhrū,* 'eyebrow.'] The ridge or prominence over the eye, or the hair growing upon it; *pl.* or *sing.*, the forehead; *sing.*, the countenance; also, the edge of a steep place; the upper part of a slope.—**brow,** *v. t.* To form the brow of (a slope, etc.).—**brow′=ant″ler,** *n.* The first or lowest tine of a stag's horn.

brow-beat (brou′bēt), *v. t.*; pret. *-beat,* pp. *-beaten,* ppr. *-beating.* [From *brow* + *beat.*] To intimidate by overbearing looks, words, etc.; bully.—**brow′beat″er,** *n.*

browed (broud), *a.* Having a brow or brows: as, low-*browed.*

brown (broun), *a.* [AS. *brūn* = D. *bruin* = G. *braun* = F. *brun.*] Of a dark or dusky color, inclining to red or yellow; having a brownish skin; sunburned or tanned; noting or pertaining to the Malay race.—**brown Bess,** the flintlock musket formerly used in the British army: probably so called from the brown walnut stock.—**brown betty,** a baked pudding made of layers of apples cut up and bread (or cake) in crumbs or small pieces, with sugar, bits of butter, spice, etc.—**brown bread,** any bread made of flour darker in color than the bolted wheat flour; esp., Graham bread; also, a dark-brown baked or steamed bread made of Indian meal and rye meal (or Graham or wheat flour), sweetened with molasses.—**brown coal,** lignite.—**brown study,** a fit of deep abstraction.—**brown sugar,** unrefined or partially refined sugar, as distinguished from 'white' or refined sugar.—**brown,** *n.* A brown color, pigment, or dye; something of a brown color.—**brown,** *v. i.* or *t.* To become or make brown.

Brown-i-an (broun′i-ạn), *a.* Pertaining to some person bearing the name of Brown; Brunonian.—**Brownian movement,** a rapid oscillatory motion often observed in very minute particles suspended in water or other liquid: first noticed (in 1827) by Robert Brown, a British botanist.

brown-ie (brou′ni), *n.* A little brown goblin, esp. one supposed to help secretly in household work. [Orig. Sc.]

brown-ing (brou′ning), *n.* A preparation, as of sugar, port wine, spices, etc., for coloring sauces, etc., brown.

brown-ish (brou′nish), *a.* Somewhat brown; tending to brown.

Brown-ism (broun′izm), *n.* The ecclesiastical system and doctrine advocated by Robert Browne (about 1550–about 1633), the English Puritan; Independency or Congregationalism.—**Brown′ist,** *n.*

brown-ness (broun′nes), *n.* Brown coloration.

brown-stone (broun′stōn), *n.* A reddish-brown variety of sandstone, extensively used as a building material.

brown=tailed (broun′tāld), *a.* Having a brown tail or posterior extremity: as, the *brown-tailed* moth (a moth, *Euproctis chrysorrhœa,* having white wings and, in the female, a brown-tipped abdomen: in the larval stage very destructive to trees).

browse (brouz), *n.* [Appar. < OF. *broust* (F. *brout*), young shoot, from Teut.] Tender shoots of shrubs or other plants, such as cattle eat; green food for cattle, deer, etc.; also, the act of browsing.—**browse,** *v.*; *browsed, browsing.* [Cf. OF. *brouster* (F. *brouter*).] **I.** *tr.* Of cattle, deer, etc., to crop and eat (tender shoots of shrubs, etc.); also, to pasture on; graze. **II.** *intr.* To feed on tender shoots of shrubs, etc.; also, to graze. Also fig., as of reading here and there at pleasure.—**brows′er,** *n.*

bru-cine, bru-cin (brö′sin), *n.* [From James *Bruce* (1730–94), Scottish explorer of Africa.] A bitter, poisonous alkaloid obtained from the nux vomica tree, *Strychnos nux-vomica,* and from other species of the same genus, resembling strychnine in action but less powerful.

bru-cite (brö′sīt), *n.* [From A. *Bruce,* American mineralogist.] A mineral consisting of magnesium hydroxide, usually found in thin foliated plates of white or greenish color and pearly luster.

Bru-in (brö′in), *n.* [MD. *bruin* = E. *brown.*] A name for the bear, orig. in the medieval epic of "Reynard the Fox"; [*l. c.*] a bear.

bruise (bröz), *v.*; *bruised, bruising.* [Partly < AS. *brȳsan,* crush, bruise, partly < OF. *bruisier, brisier* (F. *briser*), break.] **I.** *tr.* To injure by a blow or by pressure without laceration; contuse; also, to batter or dent; also, to crush fine or bray; fig., to crush, disable, or oppress. **II.** *intr.* To fight with the fists; box.—**bruise,** *n.* An injury due to bruising; a contusion.—**bruis′er,** *n.* One who or that which bruises; a pugilist; a bully.

bruit (bröt), *n.* [OF. F. *bruit,* < *bruire,* make a noise.] Noise or din (archaic); report or rumor; fame†; (F., pron. brwē) in *pathol.*, any sound heard within the body in auscultation.—**bruit,** *v. t.* To noise abroad; report; rumor; spread the fame of.

Bru-maire (brü-mãr), *n.* [F. *brumaire,* < *brume,* fog: see *brume.*] In the calendar of the first French republic, the second month of the year, extending from Oct. 22 to Nov. 20.

bru-mal (brö′mạl), *a.* [L. *brumalis,* < *bruma,* winter: see *brume.*] Belonging to winter; wintry.

brume (bröm), *n.* [F. *brume,* fog, < L. *bruma,* winter, winter solstice, lit. 'shortest day,' < *brevis,* short.] Fog; mist: as, "drifting *brume*" (Longfellow's "Saga of King Olaf," xix.).

brum-ma-gem (brum′ạ-jẹm). [For *Birmingham,* manufacturing city in England.] **I.** *a.* Of a cheap, showy make or kind; sham. [Colloq.] **II.** *n.* Any cheaply made, showy article; a sham. [Colloq.]

bru-mous (brö′mus), *a.* [See *brume.*] Foggy.

bru-net (brö-net′). [F., dim. of *brun,* brown; from Teut.: cf. *brown.*] In *anthropol.*: **I.** *a.* Of or pertaining to a dark type; having brown or dark skin, hair, and eyes. **II.** *n.* A person of the brunet type.

bru-nette (brö-net′). [F., fem. of *brunet*: see *brunet.*] **I.** *a.* Dark or brownish; having dark complexion, hair, and eyes; brown-haired. **II.** *n.* A girl or woman of dark complexion, hair, and eyes.

Bru-no-ni-an (brö-nō′ni-ạn), *a.* [ML. *Bruno(n-)*, Brown (proper name).] Pertaining to some person or thing bearing the name of Brown, as, in the U. S., to Brown University, at Providence, R. I.

brunt (brunt), *n.* [ME.; origin unknown.] A sharp blow†; an onset† or attack†; the shock or force of an attack, etc.; the main stress, force, or violence.

brush[1] (brush), *n.* [OF. *broche, broce, brouce*; origin uncertain: cf. *brush*[2].] A dense growth of bushes, shrubs, etc.; underwood; scrub; a thicket; also, lopped or broken branches; brushwood.

brush[2] (brush), *n.* [OF. *broisse, brosse* (F. *brosse*); prob. from Teut. (cf. G. *borste,* bristle).] An instrument of various forms, consisting of bristles, hair, or the like, set in or attached to a handle or stock, used for removing dirt or dust, polishing, smoothing, applying moisture or paint, etc.; also, something resembling or suggesting this, as the bushy tail of an animal, esp. of the fox; an agricultural contrivance made of small trees, etc., used instead of a harrow for drawing over the ground to cover grain, etc., after sowing; one of the pieces of carbon, copper, or the like, in a dynamo or motor, which are in contact with the commutator and connect it with the outside circuit or external current; a kind of electric discharge accompanied by diverging rays of pale-blue light; also, the art or skill of a painter of pictures; a painter; also, a brushing, or an application of a brush; a graze or abrasion, as on a horse's leg; also, a swift passage, as a quick ride across country; also, a hostile collision; a brief but smart encounter.—**brush²**, *v.* **I.** *tr.* To pass a brush over, as for removing dirt or smoothing the surface; brighten, polish, or improve by or as by the use of a brush (with *up*); wet or paint lightly with a brush (with *over*); strike or graze lightly, as in passing; injure by grazing; pass (a brush, etc.) over something; move or sweep away or along with or as with a brush; apply with or as with a brush. **II.** *intr.* To use a brush; refresh or revive one's acquaintance with some subject (with *up*); pass over or touch against something lightly like a brush; move quickly or in haste; make off or be gone with a rush.—**brush'er,** *n.* —**brush'=tongued,** *a.* Having the tongue set with long papillæ, as certain parrots.

brush=tur-key (brush'tėr″ki), *n.* A large gallinaceous bird, *Talegalla lathami*, of eastern Australia; also, any of various allied birds of New Guinea, etc.

Brush-turkey (*Talegalla lathami*).

brush=wheel (brush'hwēl), *n.* A toothless wheel used to turn a similar wheel by means of bristles, cloth, or the like, attached to the circumference; also, a circular rotary brush used for polishing or cleaning.

brush-wood (brush'wụd), *n.* Densely growing bushes, shrubs, etc.; brush; also, broken or lopped branches.

brush-y¹ (brush'i), *a.* Overgrown with or consisting of brush or brushwood.

brush-y² (brush'i), *a.* Resembling a brush (of bristles, etc.); shaggy.

brusk, etc. See *brusque*, etc.

brusque (brụsk or brusk), *a.* [F., < It. *brusco.*] Tart, as wine†; abrupt in manner; rudely offhand or blunt.—**brusque,** *v. t.*; *brusqued, brusquing.* To treat in a brusque manner.—**brusque'ly,** *adv.*—**brusque'ness,** *n.*—**brus-que-rie** (F. brüs-kė-rē), *n.* [F.] Brusque quality; abruptness of manner.

Brus-sels (brus'ẹlz) **car'pet.** [From *Brussels*, city in Belgium.] A kind of carpet, orig. made in Brussels, having a heavy linen web inclosing worsted yarns of different colors, which are raised in loops to form the pattern, the loops being left uncut, or (in the 'imperial Brussels carpet') cut only in the portions forming the pattern.

Brus-sels (brus'ẹlz) **sprouts.** A kind of cabbage originating in Belgium, having small edible heads or sprouts along the stalk, which resemble miniature cabbages.

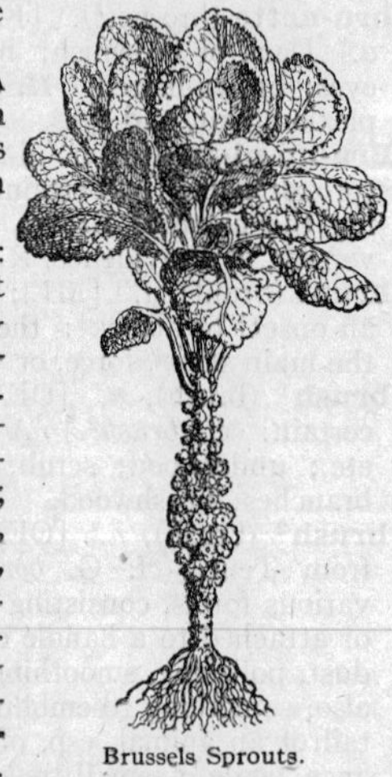

Brussels Sprouts.

brut (brüt), *a.* [F., < L. *brutus*: see *brute*.] Rough, as an uncut diamond; raw; crude; of champagne, containing little or no liqueur (for sweetening); not sweet.

bru-tal (brö'tąl), *a.* [ML. *brutalis.*] Of, pertaining to, characteristic of, or resembling brutes; irrational or unreasoning; rude, coarse, or unrefined; inhuman, savage, or cruel; gross or sensual. —**bru-tal'i-ty** (-tal'i-ti), *n.*; pl. *-ties* (-tiz). Brutal state, quality, or character; brutal conduct; also, a brutal act.—**bru'-tal-ize,** *v.*; *-ized, -izing.* **I.** *tr.* To make brutal; also, to treat as a brute or in a brutal manner. **II.** *intr.* To become brutal; live like a brute.—**bru″tal-i-za'tion** (-i-zā'shọn), *n.*—**bru'tal-ly,** *adv.*

brute (bröt). [L. *brutus*, heavy, dull, stupid, irrational.] **I.** *a.* Not possessing reason or understanding (as, *brute* beasts); of, pertaining to, or characteristic of animals as distinguished from man; dull or stupid; unintelligent or uninformed; lacking sensibility or refined feeling; rough or rude; crude or unpolished; savage or cruel; gross or sensual; also, not endowed or associated with sense or sensation; senseless; unconscious; merely material. **II.** *n.* A brute creature; an animal as distinguished from man, esp. one of the larger quadrupeds; the animal nature in man; a person resembling an animal in want of intelligence or in some other quality, as cruelty or sensuality; often, a general term of opprobrium.—**brute'hood** (-hụd), *n.* The character or condition of a brute.

bru-ti-fy (brö'ti-fī), *v. t.*; *-fied, -fying.* [See *-fy*.] To make brute-like; brutalize.

brut-ing (brö'ting), *n.* [From *brut.*] The process of cutting or shaping diamonds by rubbing one against another.

brut-ish (brö'tish), *a.* Of or pertaining to brutes or lower animals; brute-like; irrational; stupid; uncultured; savage; unfeeling; sensual.—**brut'ish-ly,** *adv.*—**brut'ish-ness,** *n.*

brut-ism (brö'tizm), *n.* The condition or behavior of a brute.

bry-ol-o-gy (brī-ol'ọ-ji), *n.* [Gr. βρύον, moss: see *-logy*.] The part of botany that treats of mosses.—**bry-o-log'i-cal** (-ọ-loj'i-kąl), *a.*—**bry-ol'o-gist,** *n.*

bry-o-ni-a (brī-ō'ni-ä), *n.* [L., bryony, < Gr. βρυωνία, < βρύειν, swell.] In *phar.*, the root of species of bryony (*Bryonia alba* and *B. dioica*): an active hydragogue cathartic.—**bry'o-nin** (-ọ-nin), *n.* In *chem.*, a white, amorphous, very bitter substance obtained from the root of bryony.—**bry'o-ny,** *n.* Any plant of the old-world cucurbitaceous genus *Bryonia*, comprising vines or climbers with acrid juice and emetic and purgative properties, as *B. dioica*, the common British species, with red berries, and *B. alba*, with black berries.

bry-o-phyte (brī'ọ-fīt), *n.* [NL. *Bryophyta*, pl., < Gr. βρύον, moss, + φυτόν, plant.] Any of the *Bryophyta*, a primary division or group of plants comprising the true mosses and liverworts.—**bry-o-phyt'ic** (-fit'ik), *a.*

bry-o-zo-ön (brī-ọ-zō'on), *n.*; pl. *-zoa* (-zō'ä). [NL., < Gr. βρύον, moss, + ζῷον, animal.] A polyzoön or sea-moss. —**bry-o-zo'an,** *a.* and *n.*

bub (bub), *n.* [Appar. a corruption of *brother.*] A childish term for a brother, also used in familiar address to any boy. Cf. *sis.*

bu-ba-line (bū'bą-lin), *a.* [L. *bubalinus*, < *bubalus*, buffalo, African antelope: see *buffalo*.] Pertaining to or resembling the buffalo; specif., belonging or pertaining to a genus (*Bubalis*) of antelopes, including the bubalis, hartebeest, blesbok, etc.

bu-ba-lis (bū'bą-lis), *n.* [NL., < Gr. βούβαλις.] A large antelope, *Bubalis bubalis*, of northern Africa, Arabia, etc. Cf. *bubaline.*

bub-ble (bub'l), *v.*; *-bled, -bling.* [Cf. *burble* (recorded earlier), also MLG. *bubbeln*, D. *bobbelen*, Dan. *boble*, bubble; all ult. imit.] **I.** *intr.* To emit slight explosive sounds caused by the formation and bursting of vesicles or globules of air or gas, as boiling water, etc.; make any similar sound, as a gurgle; form bubbles; rise in bubbles, as gas through a liquid, or water from a spring; arise or issue like bubbles; of a person, to be in a state of animation, gaiety, excitement, etc. **II.** *tr.* To cause to bubble; emit with the sound or in the form of bubbles; also, to delude with bubbles or fraudulent schemes; cheat or deceive.—**bub'ble,** *n.* A thin vesicle of water or other liquid inflated with air or gas; a small globule of air or gas in or rising through a liquid; the vesicle of air left in a spirit-level; a globule of air or gas, or a globular vacuum, in a solid substance cooled from fusion, as glass; one of the hollow glass beads formerly used for testing the strength of spirits or liquors; also, anything wanting firmness, permanence, substance, or reality (as, "A soldier . . . Seeking the *bubble* reputation Even in the cannon's mouth": Shakspere's "As You Like It," ii. 7. 152); a false show; a vain project; sometimes, a delusive commercial scheme; a financial fraud; also, a dupe† or gull†; also, the act, process, or sound of bubbling.—**bubble and squeak,** beef and cabbage fried together.—**bub'bling-ly,** *adv.*—**bub'bly,** *a.* Full of bubbles.

bub-by (bub'i), *n.* Same as *bub.*

bu-bo (bū'bō), *n.*; pl. *-boes* (-bōz). [ML. *bubo(n-)*, < Gr. βουβών, groin, swelling in the groin.] An inflammatory swelling of a lymphatic gland, esp. when in the groin.—**bu-bon-ic** (bū̦-bon′ik), *a.* Of or pertaining to a bubo; accompanied by or affected with buboes. Cf. *plague.*—**bu-bon′o-cele** (-ō̦-sēl), *n.* [Gr. βουβωνοκήλη: see *-cele.*] In *pathol.*, an inguinal hernia, esp. one in which the protrusion of the intestine is limited to the region of the groin.

buc-cal (buk′ạl), *a.* [L. *bucca*, cheek, mouth.] Of or pertaining to the cheek; pertaining to the sides of the mouth or to the mouth; oral.

buc-ca-neer (buk-ạ-nēr′), *n.* [F. *boucanier*, < *boucan*, frame for curing meat on; from Carib.] Orig., one who cured meat on a particular kind of frame (first used of French settlers in Haiti); later, one of the piratical adventurers who made depredations on the Spaniards in America; in general, any freebooter or pirate.—**buc-ca-neer′,** *v. i.* To act as a buccaneer.—**buc-ca-neer′ish,** *a.* Buccaneer-like.

buc-ci-nal (buk′si-nạl), *a.* [L. *buccina*, prop. *bucina*, a crooked horn or trumpet.] Shaped or sounding like a horn or trumpet; trumpet-like.

buc-ci-na-tor (buk′si-nā-tọr), *n.* [L., trumpeter, < *buccinare*, blow a trumpet, < *buccina*: see *buccinal.*] In *anat.*, a thin, flat muscle forming the wall of the cheek, assisting in mastication and in blowing wind-instruments.—**buc′ci-na-to-ry** (-nạ-tō̦-ri), *a.*

bu-cen-taur (bū̦-sen′târ), *n.* [It. *bucentoro, bucintoro*, said to be for *buzino d' oro*, 'bark of gold.'] The state barge of Venice, in which the doge and senate on Ascension Day performed the ceremonial marriage of the state with the Adriatic, by dropping a ring into the sea.

Bu-ceph-a-lus (bū̦-sef′ạ-lus), *n.* [L., < Gr. βουκέφαλος, ox-headed, < βοῦς, ox, + κεφαλή, head.] The war-horse of Alexander the Great; hence, any riding-horse (humorous).

bu-chu (bū′kū), *n.* [S. Afr.] The medicinal aromatic leaves of several shrubby South African plants (genus *Barosma*).

buck[1] (buk), *n.* [AS. *bucca*, he-goat, *buc*, male deer, = D. *bok* = G. *bock.*] A he-goat; the male of the deer, esp. of the fallow-deer; the male of the antelope, the rabbit, or the hare; any goat or antelope (South Africa); also, a gay or dashing fellow; a dandy or fop; a male person, as an American Indian or a negro (colloq.: often used attributively, as, a *buck* Indian; a *buck* negro; also, in recent army use, a *buck* private).—**buck**[1], *v.* **I.** *tr.* To strike with the head or horns; butt; also, to attempt to master or control, as a balking animal or a difficult affair (colloq.); dress (*up*: colloq.); brace (*up*: colloq.); in *football*, to charge into (the line of opponents) with the ball. **II.** *intr.* To butt; make obstinate opposition or resistance (colloq.); dress or tidy one's self (*up*: colloq.); pluck (*up*) courage (colloq.).

buck[2] (buk), *v.* [Appar. < *buck*[1].] **I.** *intr.* Of a horse or mule, to spring into the air, arching the back, and coming down with the fore legs perfectly stiff. **II.** *tr.* To throw or attempt to throw (a rider) by bucking.—**buck**[2], *n.* The act of bucking; the effort of a horse or mule to throw its rider by bucking.

Bucking Bronco.

buck[3] (buk), *v. t.* [ME. *bouken*; prob. from Teut. (cf. G. *beuchen*).] To steep, boil, or wash in lye or suds; clean by beating in water; wash. [Now chiefly prov.]—**buck**[3], *n.* Lye or suds in which to buck cloth, clothes, etc.; also, the quantity of cloth, clothes, etc., bucked at one time. [Archaic or prov.]

buck[4] (buk), *n.* [Cf. AS. *būc*, belly.] The body of a cart or wagon. [Prov. Eng.]

buck[5] (buk), *n.* A sawbuck; also, a kind of leather-covered frame used by gymnasts in vaulting exercises.

buck[6] (buk), *v. t.* [Cf. MD. and MLG. *boken*, beat.] To pulverize or break into small pieces, as ore.

buck[7] (buk), *n.* [Cf. *buck*[1].] In certain card-games, an article, as a penknife, passed from one player to another, as to indicate whose turn it is to deal or to ante for all the players; in poker, an article placed in a jack-pot and taken by the winner, serving to remind him that when the deal passes to him he must order another jack-pot.—**to pass the buck,** to pass a burden, as of responsibility or blame, to another. [Slang.]

buck=bas-ket (buk′bås″ket), *n.* A basket in which clothes are taken to be bucked or washed. See Shakspere's "Merry Wives of Windsor," iii. 5. 90.

buck=bean (buk′bēn), *n.* A plant, *Menyanthes trifoliata*, with white or pink flowers, growing in bogs.

buck-ber-ry (buk′ber″i), *n.*; pl. *-berries* (-iz). A huckleberry, *Gaylussacia ursina*, of the southern U. S.: so called because deer feed on it.

buck-board (buk′bōrd), *n.* [Cf. *buck*[4].] A four-wheeled carriage in which a long elastic board or frame is used in place of body and springs.

Buckboard.

buck-een (buk-ēn′), *n.* [See *-een.*] In Ireland, a young man of the poorer gentry or aristocracy, having no profession and trying to play the buck or dandy.

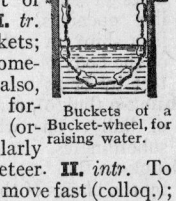

buck-er (buk′ėr), *n.* A horse that bucks.

buck-et (buk′et), *n.* [Appar. < OF. *buket*, pail, tub.] A vessel for drawing up water, as from a well; a pail or other vessel of wood, leather, metal, etc., for holding or carrying water, coal, etc.; also, anything resembling or suggesting this; one of the compartments on the circumference of a water-wheel into which the water falls in turning the wheel; a float-board of a paddle-wheel; a scoop of a dredging-machine; one of the scoops or cups attached to the endless chain or belt in certain forms of conveyers or elevators; the piston of a lifting-pump; a socket or rest for a whip, lance, etc.; also, as much as a bucket holds; esp., half a bushel; in *rowing*, the act of bucketing.—**buck′et,** *v.*; *-eted, -eting.* **I.** *tr.* To draw up or carry (water, etc.) in buckets; also, to pour buckets of water upon (something); also, to cheat or swindle (slang); also, to ride (a horse) hard; hence, to drive forward hurriedly (colloq.); also, to handle (orders, etc.) as in a bucket-shop, or irregularly or fraudulently in the manner of a bucketeer. **II.** *intr.* To use a bucket, as in drawing water; also, to move fast (colloq.); also, to conduct a bucket-shop; act as a bucketeer; also, in *rowing*, to hurry the forward swing of the body in preparation for a stroke.—**buck-et-eer′** (-ēr′), *n.* One who conducts a bucket-shop; a broker who handles his customers' orders or property irregularly or fraudulently.—**buck-et-eer′,** *v. i.* To act as a bucketeer; conduct a bucket-shop.—**buck′et-ful** (-fůl), *n.*; pl. *-fuls.*—**buck′et=shop,** *n.* An establishment conducted nominally for transacting a stock-exchange or similar business, but really for making bets on the rise and fall of the prices of stocks, grain, oil, etc., with no actual buying or selling; also, an establishment operating ostensibly for the transaction of a legitimate stock-exchange or similar business, but actually making a practice clandestinely of speculating on its own account against its customers' purchases and sales (or taking the other side of their trades), or of otherwise handling their orders or property irregularly or fraudulently.

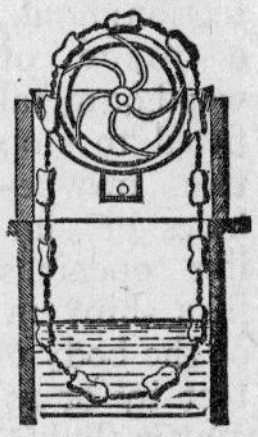
Buckets of a Bucket-wheel, for raising water.

buck-eye (buk′ī), *n.* Any of various trees or shrubs (genus *Æsculus*) allied to the horse-chestnut, as *A. glabra* ('Ohio buckeye'), a large tree with an ill-smelling bark; [*cap.*] an inhabitant of Ohio, the 'Buckeye State,' where such trees abound (colloq.).

Flowering Branch of Ohio Buckeye, with nut and dehiscing fruit.

buck-horn (buk′hôrn), *n.* The substance of the horns of bucks or deer, used for making knife-handles, etc.

buck-hound (buk′hound), *n.* A hound for hunting bucks, etc.: similar to the staghound, but smaller.

buck-ie (buk′i), *n.* [Origin obscure.] The spiral shell of a mollusk, esp. of the whelk; also, a perverse or refractory person. [Sc.]

buck-ish (buk′ish), *a.* Like a buck or gay young fellow.—**buck′ish-ly,** *adv.*—**buck′ish-ness,** *n.*

buck=jump (buk′jump), *n.* A leap like that of a buck or a bucking horse or mule.—**buck′=jump″er,** *n.*—**buck′=jump″ing,** *n.*

buck-le (buk′l), *n.* [OF. *bucle, boucle,* buckle, boss of a shield, F. *boucle,* buckle, ring, curl, < L. *buccula,* dim. of *bucca,* cheek, mouth.] A clasp consisting of a rectangular or curved rim with one or more movable tongues, used for fastening together two loose ends, as of a belt or strap; any similar contrivance used for such a purpose; an ornament, as of metal, beads, etc., of similar appearance; also, a bend, bulge, or kink, as in a saw-blade; a curl of hair†; the condition of being curled, as of hair†.—**buck′le,** *v.*; *-led, -ling.* **I.** *tr.* To fasten with a buckle; prepare for action; apply (one's self) vigorously to something; unite in marriage (chiefly prov.); also, to bend, bow, or warp; curl (the hair)†. **II.** *intr.* To apply one's self vigorously; grapple or contend (now prov.); marry (chiefly prov.); also, to bend, bow, or warp; submit or give way (now prov.).

buck-ler (buk′lėr), *n.* [OF. *boucler* (F. *bouclier*), shield, orig. one with a boss, < *boucle,* boss: see *buckle.*] A small, usually round shield, generally clasped by the hand only, but sometimes strapped to the arm; any means of defense; a protection; *naut.,* a piece of wood or metal fitted to stop the hawse-holes or similar openings in a ship; in *zoöl.,* a plate or protective covering on parts of the body of various animals.—**buck′ler,** *v. t.* To protect by or as a buckler; shield; protect.

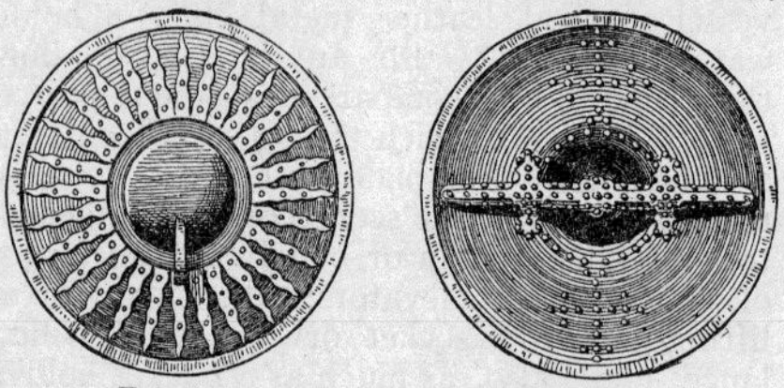

Exterior. Interior.
Buckler, beginning of 16th century.

buck-o (buk′ō), *n.*; pl. *-oes* (-ōz). [Cf. *buck*[1].] A blusterer or bully; one who domineers roughly or brutally over subordinates.

buck-ra (buk′rạ), *n.* [Prob. W. Afr.] A white man: used by the blacks of the African coast, the West Indies, and the southern U. S.

buck-ram (buk′rạm). [OF. *boquerant* (F. *bougran*); origin uncertain.] **I.** *n.* A fine linen or cotton fabric†; a coarse linen or cotton fabric sized with glue or gum, used for stiffening garments, binding books, etc.; also, a stiff, formal, or haughty manner; stiffness. **II.** *a.* Made of buckram; like buckram; stiff, formal, or haughty.—**buck′ram,** *v. t.*; *-ramed, -raming.* To stiffen with or as with buckram; make stiff (as, "his *buckramed* habit of clerical decorum": Hawthorne's "Scarlet Letter," xx.).

buck=saw (buk′sâ), *n.* A saw consisting of a blade set across an upright frame or bow, used with both hands in cutting wood on a sawbuck or sawhorse.

buck-shot (buk′shot), *n.* A large size of leaden shot used in shooting deer, etc.

buck-skin (buk′skin), *n.* The skin of a buck or deer; a kind of strong, soft leather of a yellowish or grayish color, orig. prepared from deerskins, but now usually from sheepskins; *pl.,* breeches made of this; *sing.,* a person dressed in it, esp. [*cap.*] an American soldier in the Revolutionary War.

buck-thorn (buk′thôrn), *n.* Any of the trees or shrubs (sometimes thorny) constituting the genus *Rhamnus,* as *R. cathartica,* a shrub whose berries were formerly much used in medicine and yield a coloring matter, and *R. purshiana,* a tree yielding cascara sagrada; also, a tree or shrub of the sapotaceous genus *Bumelia,* esp. *B. lycioides,* a tree common in the southern U. S.

buck=tooth (buk′tōth), *n.* A projecting tooth.

buck-wheat (buk′hwēt), *n.* [Cf. AS. *bōc,* beech, also D. *boekweit,* G. *buchweizen,* buckwheat, lit. 'beech wheat,' from its beechnut-shaped seed.] An herb, *Fagopyrum fagopyrum,* cultivated for its triangular seeds, which are used as a food for animals, and made into a flour used for making pancakes, etc.; also, the seeds or the flour.

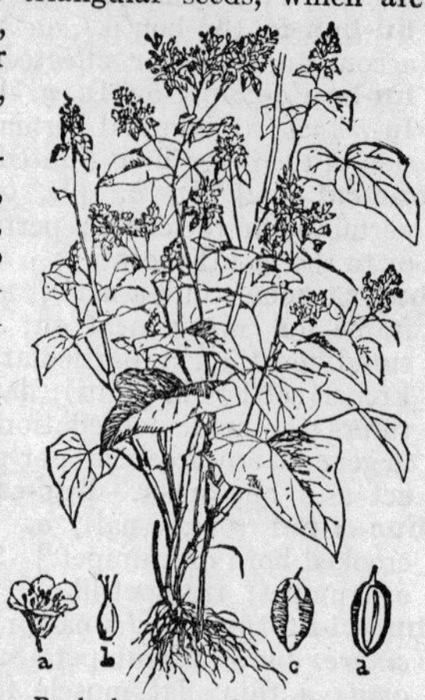

Buckwheat.—*a,* flower; *b,* ovary; *c,* fruit; *d,* section of same, showing embryo.

bu-col-ic (bū̦-kol′ik). [L. *bucolicus,* < Gr. βουκολικός, < βουκόλος, herdsman, < βοῦς, ox.] **I.** *a.* Of or pertaining to herdsmen or shepherds; pastoral; also, rustic, rural, or agricultural (humorous). **II.** *n.* A pastoral poem (chiefly in *pl.*: as, the "Bucolics," L. *Bucolica,* of Virgil, also called "Eclogues"); also, a writer of pastorals; also, a countryman or farmer (humorous).—**bu-col′i-cal,** *a.* Bucolic.—**bu-col′i-cal-ly,** *adv.*

bu-crane (bū̦-krān′), *n.* [F. *bucrâne,* < L. *bucranium,* < Gr. βουκράνιον, < βοῦς, ox, + κρανίον, skull.] An ornament, often sculptured, representing the skull of an ox. Also **bu-cra′ni-um** (-krā′ni-um); pl. *-nia* (-ni-ạ̈).

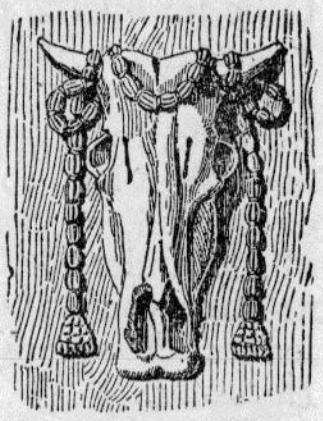

Bucrane, from frieze of Temple of Vespasian, Rome.

bud[1] (bud), *n.* [Reduced form of *brother.*] A familiar term for *brother*: also used as a familiar name for any small boy or any man, regardless of his actual name. [Colloq., U. S.]

bud[2] (bud), *n.* [ME. *budde*; origin uncertain.] An undeveloped or rudimentary stem or branch of a plant; a small axillary or terminal protuberance on a plant, containing rudimentary foliage ('leaf-bud'), the rudimentary inflorescence ('flower-bud'), or both ('mixed bud'); loosely, a leaf or flower not wholly expanded; in some cryptogamous plants, a body produced asexually which becomes detached and develops into a new plant; in certain animals of low organization, a prominence which develops into a new individual, sometimes permanently attached to the parent organism and sometimes becoming detached; a gemma; in general, some similar part or organ (as, a tactile *bud* or a gustatory *bud*: see under *tactile* and *gustatory*); fig., anything in an immature or undeveloped state; a child or young person; a young lady just introduced into society; also, the state of budding, or putting forth buds.—**bud**[2], *v.*; *budded, budding.* **I.** *intr.* To put forth or produce buds, as a plant; issue or push out, as a bud; fig., to begin to grow or develop; also, of birds, to eat buds. **II.** *tr.* To cause to bud; also, to put forth as buds; produce by means of buds or gemmæ which develop into new individuals; also, in *hort.,* to ingraft by inserting a bud of one plant into the stem of another.

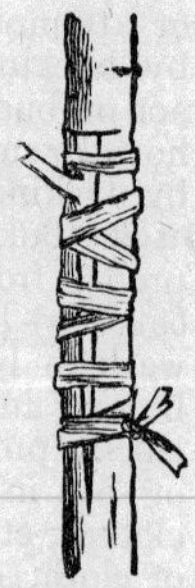

Horticultural Budding.

Bud-dha (bu̇d′ạ̈), *n.* [Skt., 'wise, enlightened.'] 'The Enlightened One,' a title applied esp. to a great religious teacher, variously known as Siddhartha, Gautama (Gotama), or Sakyamuni, who flourished in India about the 6th century B.C., regarded by his followers as the latest of a series of teachers (Buddhas) possessing perfect enlightenment and wisdom.—**Bud-dhism** (bu̇d′izm), *n.* The religious system founded by Buddha, which regards life as an evil, and the attainment of nirvana as the supreme felicity.—**Bud′dhist.** **I.** *n.* A follower of Buddha. **II.** *a.* Of or pertaining to Buddha or Buddhism.—**Bud-dhis′tic,** *a.*

bud-dle (bud′l), *n.* [Origin unknown.] A device for separating the metalliferous portion of an ore from the earthy or valueless part by means of running water.—**bud-dle,** *v. t.*; *-dled, -dling.* To treat (ore) in a buddle.

bud-dy, bud-die (bud′i), *n.*; pl. *buddies* (-iz). [From *bud*[1].] A familiar term for *brother*; also, a comrade or mate. [Colloq., U. S.]

Bude (būd) **burn′er.** [From *Bude*, town in Cornwall, England, near the home of the inventor, Sir G. Gurney (1793–1875).] A device for giving a powerful light, consisting essentially of two or more concentric Argand burners.—**Bude light.** A brilliant light produced by directing a current of oxygen into the interior of the flame of an Argand burner.

budge[1] (buj), *v. i.* or *t.*; *budged, budging.* [F. *bouger*, ult. < L. *bullire*, E. *boil*[2].] To stir; move: usually with a negative.

budge[2] (buj). [ME. *boge*, earlier *bugee*; origin uncertain.] **I.** *n.* Lambskin dressed with the wool outward, formerly much used as a fur for trimming. **II.** *a.* Trimmed or adorned with budge; also, solemn or pompous (now only prov. Eng.).

budg-et (buj′et), *n.* [OF. *bougette*, dim. of *bouge*, bag: see *bulge.*] A bag, pouch, or wallet (now chiefly prov.); the contents of a bag or wallet; a collection, stock, or store (sometimes used as a title for newspapers, etc., denoting a supply of news or the like); also, in Great Britain, the annual financial statement made by the chancellor of the Exchequer in the House of Commons, containing an estimate of the income and expenditure for the following year, and financial proposals based on this estimate; hence, any similar financial statement, estimate, or proposal.—**budg′et,** *v. i.*; *-eted, -eting.* To provide (*for*) in a financial budget.—**budg′et-a-ry** (-ạ-ri), *a.* Of or pertaining to a budget.—**budg-et-eer′** (-ēr′), *n.* One who makes up a budget.

bud-less (bud′les), *a.* Without buds.

bud-let (bud′let), *n.* A little bud; a secondary bud springing from a parent bud.

bud=worm (bud′wėrm), *n.* Any of various moth larvæ destructive to buds, as that of the noctuid moth *Chloridea virescens,* which attacks the tobacco-plant.

buff[1] (buf). [Appar. for earlier *buffle*, < F. *buffle*, buffalo.] **I.** *n.* A buffalo†; a kind of thick leather orig. and properly made of buffalo-skin but later also of other skins, having a fuzzy surface, and used for making belts, pouches, etc., and formerly in place of light armor ('buff-leather'); hence, military attire; a buff-coat; also, the bare skin (colloq.); also, a buff-stick or buff-wheel; also, the color of the leather, a pinkish yellow; in *med.*, the buffy coat. **II.** *a.* Made of buff-leather; also, pinkish-yellow.—**buff**[1], *v. t.* To impart to (something) a fuzzy surface like that of buff-leather; also, to polish with a buff.

buff[2] (buf), *n.* [Appar. < OF. *buffe*, a blow.] A blow, esp. with the hand; a box, cuff, or slap; a buffet; a stroke. Cf. *blindman's-buff.* [Now chiefly prov. Eng. and Sc.]—**buff**[2], *v. t.* To strike, cuff, or buffet (now prov. Eng. and Sc.); also, to resist or deaden the shock of, as a buffer does.

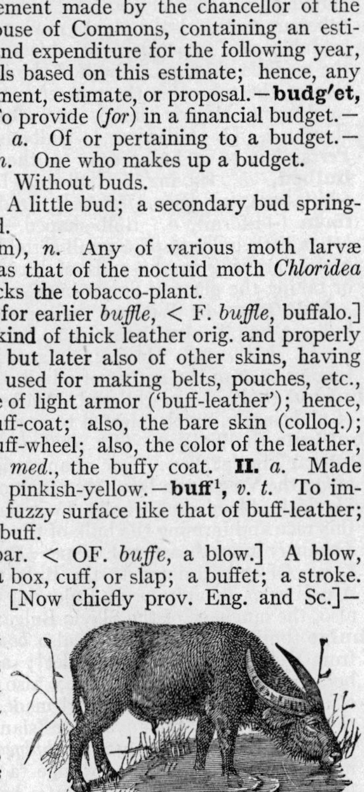

Common (Indian) Buffalo (*Bos bubalus*).

buf-fa-lo (buf′ạ-lō), *n.*; pl. *buffaloes* (-lōz) or (esp. collectively) *buffalo.* [Sp. *búfalo* = F. *buffle*, < LL. *bufalus*, L. *bubalus*, < Gr. βούβαλος, buffalo, African antelope.] Any of several mammals of the ox kind, as *Bos bubalus* or *Bubalus buffelus*, an old-world species, orig. from India, valued as a draft-animal, and *Bos caffer* or *Bubalus caffer* ('Cape buffalo'), a South African species, and *Bos* (or *Bison*) *americanus* or *Bos bison*, the American bison; also, a buffalo-robe; also, a buffalo-fish.—**buf′fa-lo,** *v. t.*; *-loed, -loing.* To render completely at a loss or helpless as by some sudden and disconcerting action. [Slang.]—**buf′fa-lo=ber″ry,** *n.* The edible red or yellowish berry of either of two shrubs, *Lepargyrea argentea* and *L. canadensis,* of the oleaster family, of the U. S. and Canada; also, either of these shrubs.—**buf′fa-lo=bug,** *n.* The carpet-beetle.—**buf′fa-lo=bush,** *n.* The buffalo-berry (shrub).—**buf′fa-lo=fish,** *n.* Any of several large North American fresh-water fishes of the subfamily *Ictiobinæ* of the sucker family (*Catostomidæ*), esp. those of the genus *Ictiobus.* See *carp-sucker.*—**buf′fa-lo=moth,** *n.* The carpet-beetle.—**buf′fa-lo=nut,** *n.* The oily drupaceous fruit of the North American santalaceous shrub *Pyrularia pubera*; also, the shrub.—**buf′fa-lo=robe,** *n.* The skin of an American bison, prepared with the hair on, used as a lap-robe.

Cape Buffalo (*Bos caffer*).

buff=coat (buf′kōt), *n.* A thick coat of buff-leather, worn esp. by soldiers; also, one who wears a buff-coat; a soldier.

buff-er[1] (buf′ėr), *n.* One who or that which buffs or polishes.

buff-er[2] (buf′ėr), *n.* An apparatus, as at the end of a railroad-car, for deadening the force of a concussion; anything serving to deaden or sustain a shock, or to neutralize or come between opposing forces (hence, *buffer state*, a smaller state lying between more or less opposed or hostile larger states).

buf-fer[3] (buf′ėr), *n.* [Origin obscure.] A chap or fellow: used esp. of elderly persons, generally with a slight degree of contempt. [Slang or colloq.]

buf-fet[1] (buf′et), *n.* [OF. *buffet*, dim. of *buffe*, a blow: see *buff*[2].] A blow, as with the fist; a box; a cuff; an adverse stroke.—**buf′fet**[1], *v.*; *-feted, -feting.* **I.** *tr.* To strike as with the fist; beat; contend against as with blows. **II.** *intr.* To deal blows; fight; struggle.

buf-fet[2] (bọ̈-fā′, also buf′et, F. bü-fā), *n.* [F. *buffet*; origin unknown.] A sideboard or cabinet for holding china, plate, etc.; also, a counter, bar, or the like, for lunch or refreshments; also, the space set apart for refreshments in public places.—**buf-fet=car** (bọ̈-fā′kär, also buf′et-), *n.* A railroad-car with a small compartment equipped for preparing light meals for serving to passengers.

buf-fet-er (buf′et-ėr), *n.* One who buffets.

buf-fle (buf′l), *n.* [F., = E. *buffalo.*] A buffalo†; also, a North American duck, *Bucephala albeola*, the male of which has a remarkable fullness of feathers on the head.—**buf′fle-head,** *n.* A blockhead or fool; a stupid fellow; also, the buffle (duck).

Buffle.

buf-fo (böf′fō), *n.*; pl. *-fi* (-fē). [It.] A comic actor or opera-singer.

buf-foon (bu-fön′), *n.* [F. *bouffon*, < It. *buffone*, jester, < *buffa*, a jest.] One who makes a practice of amusing others by tricks, odd gestures and postures, jokes, etc.; a clown; a jester; hence, one given to coarse or undignified joking.—**buf-foon′er-y,** *n.*; pl. *-ies* (-iz). The practice of a buffoon; ridiculous pranks; vulgar tricks; low or rude jesting.—**buf-foon′ish,** *a.* Of or like a buffoon.

buff=stick (buf′stik), *n.* A small stick covered with leather or the like, used in polishing.

buff=wheel (buf′hwēl), *n.* A wheel for polishing metal, etc., commonly one covered with leather and bearing a polishing-powder.

buff-y (buf′i), *a.* Buff-colored; approaching buff in color.—**buffy coat,** the buff-colored layer on the upper surface of a blood-clot, due to the settling of the red blood-corpuscles from delayed coagulation.

bug[1] (bug), *n.* [Origin unknown.] Any of various insects, arachnids, or the like, esp. of the crawling kind; often, a bedbug; in *entom.*, a heteropterous insect.

bug[2] (bug), *n.* [ME. *bugge*: cf. W. *bwg*, bogy, ghost, bugbear.] An object of terror, usually imaginary; a bugbear;

a hobgoblin: as, "*bugs* to fearen babes withall" (Spenser's "Faerie Queene," ii. 12. 25). [Now chiefly prov.]

bug-a-boo (bug'a-bö), *n.* [Cf. *bug*[2] and *boo, interj.*] A bugbear; a bogy.

bug-bane (bug'bān), *n.* Any of various tall, erect herbs of the ranunculaceous genus *Cimicifuga*, as *C. fœtida* of Europe and *C. racemosa* of North America, bearing elongated racemes of white flowers which are supposed to drive away bugs or insects.

bug-bear (bug'bãr), *n.* [See *bug*[2].] An imaginary being supposed to devour naughty children†; anything arousing terror, esp. groundless terror.

bug-ger (bug'ėr), *n.* [F. *bougre*, < ML. *Bulgarus*, a Bulgarian, a heretic; certain Bulgarian heretics being charged with this crime.] One guilty of the crime of bestiality or sodomy: in vulgar language often used abusively or playfully without reference to its meaning.—**bug'ger-y,** *n.* The crime of bestiality or sodomy.

bug-gy[1] (bug'i), *a.* Infested with bugs.

bug-gy[2] (bug'i), *n.*; pl. *buggies* (-iz). [Origin obscure: cf. *bogie*[2].] In England, a light two-wheeled vehicle without a top or hood; in India, a similar vehicle having a hood; in the U. S., a light four-wheeled vehicle with or without a top.

American Buggy.

bu-gle[1] (bū'gl), *n.* [F. *bugle*, < LL. *bugula*, kind of plant.] Any plant of the menthaceous genus *Ajuga*, esp. *A. reptans*, a low blue-flowered herb.

bu-gle[2] (bū'gl), *n.* [Origin unknown.] A tubular glass bead, usually black, used for ornamenting women's apparel.

bu-gle[3] (bū'gl), *n.* [OF. *bugle*, < L. *buculus*, dim. of *bos*, ox.] A wild ox†; a young bull (obs. or prov. Eng.); a hunting-horn, made orig. of the horn of a wild ox; a military wind-instrument of brass or copper, resembling a trumpet but shorter, being curved, and sometimes furnished with keys or valves.—**bu'gle**[3], *v.*; *bugled, bugling.* **I.** *intr.* To sound a bugle. **II.** *tr.* To sound forth as a bugle does; also, to call by bugle.—**bu'gle=horn,** *n.* A bugle or hunting-horn.—**bu'gler,** *n.* One who plays, or gives signals with, a bugle.—**bu'glet,** *n.* A small bugle.

bu-gle-weed (bū'gl-wēd), *n.* A plant of the menthaceous genus *Lycopus*, esp. *L. virginicus*, an herb with medicinal properties; also, the bugle (genus *Ajuga*).

bu-gloss (bū'glos), *n.* [F. *buglosse*, < L. *buglossa*, < Gr. βούγλωσσος, < βοῦς, ox, + γλῶσσα, tongue.] Any of various boraginaceous plants, as *Anchusa officinalis*, an old-world medicinal herb with rough leaves, and *Lycopsis arvensis*, a bristly, blue-flowered herb.

bug=seed (bug'sēd), *n.* An annual chenopodiaceous herb, *Corispermum hyssopifolium*, of northern temperate regions: so called from the flat, oval shape of its seeds.

buhl (böl), *n.* [An erroneous form of F. *boulle* or *boule*, < A. C. *Boulle* or *Boule* (1642–1732), French cabinet-maker.] Work made by inlaying wood with metal, tortoise-shell, ivory, etc., in elaborate patterns; furniture, etc., thus inlaid.—**buhl'=work,** *n.*

Buhl. — Commode executed by Boulle, in the Bibliothèque Mazarine, Paris.

buhr, buhr-stone (bėr, bėr'stōn). See *bur*[1], *burstone.*

buik (bük), *n.* Scotch form of *book.*

build (bild), *v.*; *built* (archaic *builded*), *building.* [AS. *byldan* (in pp. *gebyld*), < *bold*, dwelling, house.] **I.** *tr.* To construct or erect, as a house; form by uniting materials into a regular structure; hence, to form by art in any way; fashion; make; also, to establish by gradual means; also, to raise as on a support or foundation; rear; found; base. **II.** *intr.* To erect a dwelling or other edifice; practise the art or follow the business of a builder; make nests or the like, as birds, etc.; hence, to construct, rear, or establish anything; also, to base one's confidence, opinions, etc. (*on*); rely (*on*); also, to become built.—**build,** *n.* Style or manner of construction; form; make.—**build'er,** *n.* One who or that which builds; one who, as an employer of carpenters, masons, etc., directs or controls the building of houses or other structures.—**build'ing,** *n.* The act of one who or that which builds; the art of building houses or other structures; also, that which is built, esp. for use as a dwelling, barn, factory, store, etc.

bulb (bulb), *n.* [L. *bulbus*, < Gr. βολβός.] A large spheroidal leaf-bud, usually subterranean, in which the stem is reduced to a flat disk, rooting from the under side, and bearing above closely appressed fleshy leaves, in the form of broad, concentric coatings, as in the onion ('tunicated bulb'), or in the form of narrow, thick, imbricated scales, as in the lily ('scaly bulb'); less properly, a corm inclosed within the dry sheathing bases of a few leaves, as in the crocus ('solid bulb'); loosely, any of various rhizomes, tubers, or tuberous roots; also, a plant growing from a bulb; also, any protuberance, expansion, or object resembling a bulb, as the medulla oblongata ('bulb of the spinal cord'), the expansion of the tube of a thermometer, the glass case of an incandescent electric lamp, etc.—**bul-ba-ceous** (bul-bā'shius), *a.* [L. *bulbaceus.*] Bulbous.—**bul'bar** (-bär), *a.* Pertaining to a bulb, esp. to the medulla oblongata.—**bulbed,** *a.* Having a bulb or bulbs.—**bul-bif'er-ous** (-bif'e-rus), *a.* [See *-ferous.*] Producing bulbs.—**bul'bi-form** (-bi-fôrm), *a.* Bulb-shaped.—**bul'bil** (-bil), *n.* In *bot.*, a little bulb; esp., a small aërial bulb or bud with fleshy scales, growing in the axils of leaves, as in the tiger-lily, or taking the place of flower-buds, as in the common onion.—**bulb'less,** *a.* Without bulbs.—**bulb'let,** *n.* A little bulb; a bulbil.—**bul'bose** (-bōs), *a.* Bulbous.—**bul'bous,** *a.* [L. *bulbosus.*] Having, or growing from, bulbs; pertaining to or of the nature of a bulb; bulb-shaped.

bul-bul (bůl'bůl), *n.* [Pers.] An Asiatic song-bird, a kind of nightingale, much referred to in poetry.

bul-bule (bul'būl), *n.* [LL. *bulbulus.*] A little bulb

Bul-gar (bul'gär), *n.* One of an ancient Finnic race, living along the Volga, the Don, etc.; one of a people, now partly Slavic in blood and wholly so in language, derived from this race and forming the bulk of the population of Bulgaria, a country in southeastern Europe.—**Bul-ga'ri-an** (-gā'ri-an). **I.** *a.* Of or pertaining to the Bulgars or Bulgaria. **II.** *n.* A native or inhabitant of Bulgaria; esp., a Slavic Bulgar; also, the language of the Slavic Bulgars.

bulge (bulj), *n.* [OF. *boulge*, also *bouge*, < L. *bulga*, bag; from Celtic.] A bag† or wallet†; also, a rounded protuberance; a swelling; a hump; also, the bilge, or bottom of a ship's hull; also, the swirl made by a salmon rising to the surface; also, the advantage (slang: as, to get, or have, the *bulge* on one).—**bulge,** *v.*; *bulged, bulging.* **I.** *tr.* To make protuberant; also, to bilge (a ship)†. **II.** *intr.* To form a protuberance; swell out; bend outward; also, of a ship, to bilge†.—**bul'ger,** *n.* One who or that which bulges; in *golf*, a club with a convex face.—**bul'gy,** *a.* Bulging; swollen.—**bul'gi-ness,** *n.*

bu-lim-i-a (bū-lim'i-ä), *n.* [NL., < Gr. βουλιμία, < βοῦς, ox, + λιμός, hunger.] In *pathol.*, morbidly voracious appetite; a disease marked by constant and insatiable hunger.—**bu-lim'ic,** *a.*

bulk[1] (bulk), *n.* [ME. *bolke*, heap; prob. from Scand. (cf. Icel. *búlki*, heap, cargo).] A heap or pile; cargo, etc., lying loose, and not inclosed in bags, boxes, etc.; also, the body or mass of anything; a mass, esp. a large mass; the main body or greater part of anything; also, magnitude in three dimensions; volume; esp., great size or volume; also, the trunk of the body†; a body, esp. one of large size.—**bulk**[1], *v.* **I.** *intr.* To be of bulk or size; be of weight or importance; also, to increase in bulk; grow large; swell. **II.** *tr.* To pile in heaps; put into a bulk or mass; swell or stuff out; also, to ascertain the bulk of.

bulk[2] (bulk), *n.* [Origin uncertain: cf. *balk* (a beam).] A structure, as a stall, projecting from the front of a building.—**bulk'head,** *n.* The head or roof of a bulk or projecting structure; the structure itself; a box-like structure on a roof, floor, etc., covering the head of a staircase or other opening; a horizontal or inclined door leading from the outside of a house to the cellar; also, one of the upright partitions dividing a ship into water-tight compartments to prevent sinking, etc.; a resisting partition or wall.—**bulk′head″ed,** *a.* Furnished with or divided off by bulkheads.

bulk-y (bul′ki), *a.*; compar. *bulkier*, superl. *bulkiest*. Of great bulk or size; large; massive; hence, unwieldy or clumsy.—**bulk′i-ly,** *adv.*—**bulk′i-ness,** *n.*

bull[1] (bůl). [ME. *bule, bole* (cf. Icel. *boli*); appar. from an unrecorded AS. form implied in the dim. *bulluc*, E. *bullock*.] **I.** *n.* The male of a bovine animal, esp. of the domestic species *Bos taurus*; the male of various other animals, as the elephant, whale, etc.; a policeman or detective (slang); in the stock-exchange, etc., one who endeavors to effect, or operates in the expectation of, a rise in the price of stock, etc. (cf. *bear*[2], *n.*); [*cap.*] the zodiacal constellation or sign Taurus. **II.** *a.* Of or pertaining to a bull; also, male; in the stock-exchange, etc., pertaining to the bulls; marked by a rise in price.—**Bull Moose,** in *U. S. politics*, a member of the Progressive party (or 'Bull Moose party').—**bull**[1], *v. t.* In the stock-exchange, etc., to endeavor to raise the price of (stocks, etc.); operate in for a rise in price.

bull[2] (bůl), *n.* [ML. *bulla*, seal, writing furnished with a seal, document: see *bulla*.] A bulla or seal; a formal papal document having a bulla or leaden seal attached; an official letter or edict.

bull[3] (bůl), *n.* [Origin obscure.] A ludicrous blunder in language, involving a contradiction in terms: commonly regarded as esp. characteristic of the Irish, and often called *Irish bull*.

bul-la (bul′ạ̈ or bůl′ạ̈), *n.*; pl. *bullæ* (-ē). [L. *bulla*, bubble, round object, ML. seal, document.] A boss, knob, or stud; a locket-like ornament worn by children in ancient Rome; any ornament of rounded form, esp. if suspended; a seal attached to an official document, as a papal bull; in *pathol.*, a vesicle or elevation of the epidermis containing a watery fluid; in *anat.*, an inflated portion of the bony external meatus of the ear.

Bulla of Pope Alexander IV.

bul-lace (bůl′ạs), *n.* [ME. *bolace*: cf. OF. *beloce*, wild plum.] An old-world species of plum, *Prunus insititia*.

bul-la-ri-um (bu-lā′ri-um or bů-), *n.*; pl. *-ria* (-ri-ạ̈). [ML., < *bulla*: see *bull*[2].] A collection of papal bulls.

bul-late (bul′āt or bůl′-), *a.* [L. *bullatus*, < *bulla*: see *bulla*.] Having blister-like projections or elevations, as a leaf; blistered or puckered.

bull=bait-ing (bůl′bā″ting), *n.* The action or practice of baiting bulls with dogs: a sport formerly popular in England, but now prohibited.

bull-bri-er (bůl′brī″ėr), *n.* A smilacaceous plant, *Smilax pseudo-china*, with tuberous rootstocks.

bull-dog (bůl′dog). **I.** *n.* A large-headed, short-haired, heavily-built variety of dog, of comparatively small size but very muscular and courageous, formerly used for bull-baiting; also, a pistol; in recent use, a short-barreled revolver of large caliber. **II.** *a.* Like or characteristic of a bull-dog: as, *bulldog* courage or tenacity.

Bulldog.

bull-doze (bůl′dōz), *v. t.*; *-dozed, -dozing*. [Origin uncertain.] To flog severely; also, to coerce or intimidate, as by violence or threats. [Colloq.]—**bull′-doz-er,** *n.* One who bulldozes; also, a revolver. [Colloq.]

bul-let (bůl′et), *n.* [F. *boulette*, also *boulet*, dim. of *boule*, ball: see *bowl*[2].] A small, round ball; a cannon-ball†; a round, conical, or otherwise shaped piece of metal (commonly lead) used as a projectile or missile for small arms.—**bul′let=head,** *n.* A round head; a person having such a head; a thick-headed or stupid, obstinate person (colloq.).—**bul′let=head″ed,** *a.*

bul-le-tin (bůl′ẹ-tin), *n.* [F., < It. *bullettino*, < *bulletta*, dim. of *bulla, bolla*, < ML. *bulla*, writing, document: see *bull*[2].] A brief account or statement, as of news or events, issued for the information of the public, esp. by authority; also, a periodical publication, as of a learned society (sometimes used as the name of a newspaper).—**bul′le-tin,** *v. t.*; *-tined, -tining*. To make known by a bulletin.

bul-let=proof (bůl′et-pröf), *a.* Proof against bullets: as, *bullet-proof* armor.

bull=fight (bůl′fīt), *n.* A combat between men and a bull or bulls in an inclosed arena: a popular sport among Spaniards and peoples of Spanish origin.—**bull′=fight″er,** *n.*—**bull′=fight″ing,** *n.*

Bullfinch (*Pyrrhula vulgaris*).

bull-finch[1] (bůl′-finch), *n.* A European fringilline bird, *Pyrrhula vulgaris*, with a short, stout bill, valued as a cage-bird; any of various allied or similar birds.

bull-finch[2] (bůl′-finch), *n.* [Possibly for *bull fence* (as if for confining bulls).] A hedge high enough to impede hunters.

bull-frog (bůl′frog), *n.* A large frog, *Rana catesbiana*, producing a sound likened to the bellowing of a bull.

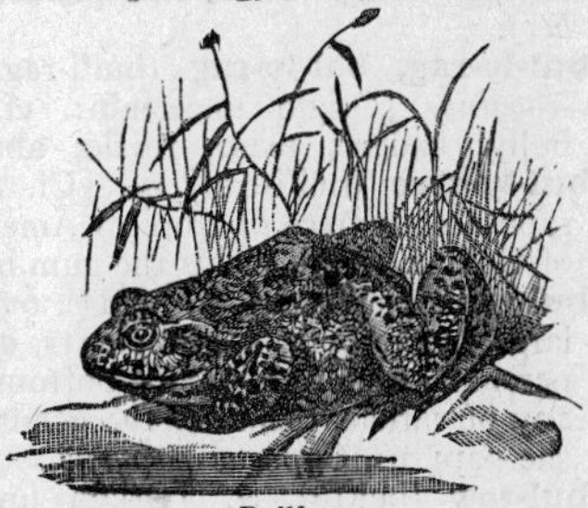
Bullfrog.

bull-head (bůl′hed), *n.* Any of various fishes with a large or broad head, esp. the horn-pout (see *pout*[1]); also, the golden plover, *Charadrius dominicus*; also, a stupid fellow.—**bull′=head″ed,** *a.* Having a large or broad head like that of a bull; also, stupid; obstinate; stupidly aggressive.—**bull′=head″ed-ness,** *n.*

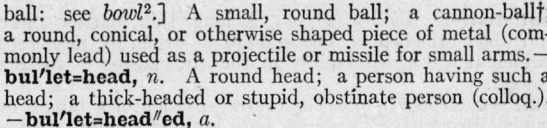

bul-lion (bůl′yọn), *n.* [AF. *bullion*, mint, appar. < OF. *bouillon*, a boiling (< ML. *bullio(n-)*, < L. *bullire*, boil), in part confused with OF. *billon*, debased metal.] A mint†; gold or silver in the mass; uncoined or unmanufactured gold or silver in the form of bars or ingots; coin, plate, etc., considered only with reference to metallic value; solid gold or silver; impure gold or silver†; also, a cord-like trimming made of twisted gold or silver wire, or a trimming of cord covered with gold or silver thread ('bullion-fringe'), used to ornament uniforms, etc.—**bul′lion-ism,** *n.* The doctrine or system of an exclusively metallic currency, or a metallic currency combined with a convertible paper currency.—**bul′lion-ist,** *n.*

bul′li-rag, *v. t.* See *bullyrag*.

bull-ish (bůl′ish), *a.* Of, pertaining to, or resembling a bull; in the stock-exchange, etc., aiming at or tending to a rise in price.

bull=neck (bůl′nek), *n.* A thick neck like that of a bull.—**bull′=necked,** *a.*

bull=net-tle (bůl′net″l), *n.* A silvery-leaved solanaceous weed, *Solanum elæagnifolium*, usually bearing prickles.

bul-lock (bůl′ọk), *n.* [AS. *bulluc*: see *bull*[1].] Orig., a young bull; now, an ox or castrated bull.—**bul′lock's=heart,** *n.* The custard-apple, *Anona reticulata*, or its fruit.

bull=pen (bůl′pen), *n.* A pen for a bull or bulls; also, an inclosure or place in which persons, as prisoners or suspects, are temporarily confined (colloq.).

bull-pout (bůl′pout), *n.* A horn-pout. See *pout*[1].

bull=roar-er (bu̇l′rōr″ėr), *n.* A long, thin, narrow piece of wood attached at one end to a string, by means of which it is whirled rapidly in the air, causing a roaring sound.

bull's=eye (bu̇lz′ī), *n.* The central division of a target, or a shot that hits it; a round, hard lump of candy; a thick disk or lens-like piece of glass inserted in a deck or the like to admit light; a plano-convex lens; a small lantern fitted with a convex lens to concentrate the light; a small circular opening or window; *naut.*, an oval or circular wooden block having a groove around it and a hole in the center through which to reeve a rope.

Nautical Bull's-eye.

bull=ter-ri-er (bu̇l′ter′i-ėr), *n.* One of a breed of dogs produced by crossing the bulldog and the terrier, exhibiting the courage of the former and the activity of the latter.

bull=trout (bu̇l′trout), *n.* Any of certain fishes of the salmon kind, as the salmon-trout, *Salmo trutta*; also, a large trout, *Salvelinus malma*, of the Pacific slope.

bul-ly[1] (bu̇l′i). [Origin uncertain: cf. D. *boel*, lover, brother, G. *buhle*, lover.] **I.** *n.*; pl. *bullies* (-iz). A sweetheart, of either sex†; of men, a good friend or fine fellow†; a brother, mate, or companion (prov. Eng.); also, a blustering, overbearing fellow; a swaggerer; esp., a coward who tyrannizes over the weak; also, a hired ruffian; also, a degraded fellow who protects prostitutes and lives on their gains. **II.** *a.* Good, worthy, or excellent; fine, capital, or first-rate; also, resembling or befitting a bully or ruffian. —**bul′ly**[1], *v.*; *-lied, -lying.* **I.** *tr.* To act the bully toward; treat overbearingly; overawe; intimidate. **II.** *intr.* To act the bully; bluster; be overbearing.

bul-ly[2] (bu̇l′i), *n.* [F. *bouilli*, boiled meat, prop. pp. of *bouillir*, boil.] Canned or pickled beef. Also called *bully beef*.

bul-ly-rag, bal-ly-rag (bu̇l′i-rag, bal′i-), *v. t.*; *-ragged, -ragging.* [Origin uncertain: cf. *bully*[1] and *rag*[3].] To bully; badger; tease; revile; abuse. [Prov. or slang.]

bul-ly=tree (bu̇l′i-trē), *n.* [Cf. *balata.*] Any of various sapotaceous trees of tropical America, as *Mimusops balata*, of Guiana, which yields the gum balata.

bul-rush (bu̇l′rush), *n.* [ME. *bulrysche.*] Any of various large rushes or rush-like plants, as *Scirpus lacustris*, a tall perennial from which mats, bottoms of chairs, etc., are made; any of various rushes of the genus *Juncus*; in Biblical use, the papyrus, *Cyperus papyrus*.

bul-tow (bu̇l′tō), *n.* [Origin uncertain: cf. *bolter*[3].] A trawl (line); a bolter; a mode of fishing by stringing a number of hooks on one line.

bul-wark (bu̇l′wạrk), *n.* [ME. *bulwerk*; from Teut. (cf. D. *bolwerk*, G. *bollwerk*, Dan. *bulværk*), appar. orig. 'bole (tree-trunk) work': cf. *boulevard.*] A defensive mound of earth or other material carried round a place; a rampart; a mole or breakwater; a confining wall or embankment, as of a river; any powerful defense or safeguard; *naut.*, a solid part of a ship's side extending like a fence above the level of the deck (usually in *pl.*).—**bul′wark,** *v. t.* To provide with bulwarks; also, to serve as a bulwark to.

bum[1] (bum), *v. i.*; *bummed, bumming.* [Imit.] To make a humming sound; hum; buzz: as, "Let the busy, grumbling hive *Bum* owre their treasure" (Burns's "To William Simpson," 96). [Now chiefly prov.]—**bum**[1], *n.*

bum[2] (bum), *v. i.*; *bummed, bumming.* [Origin obscure.] To drink†; sponge on others, as for drink (slang); lead the life of a drunken loafer (slang); go on a spree or debauch (slang); loaf (slang).—**bum**[2]. **I.** *n.* One who 'bums'; a drunken lounger; a loafer; also, the act of bumming; a drunken spree. [Slang.] **II.** *a.* Of poor quality; inferior; very unsatisfactory. [Slang.]

bum[3] (bum), *n.* [Origin obscure.] The buttocks. [Now vulgar.]

bum-bail-iff (bum′bā′lif), *n.* [Cf. *bum*[3].] A bailiff or under-bailiff employed in serving writs, making arrests, etc.: used in contempt.

bum-ble (bum′bl), *v. i.*; *-bled, -bling.* [Freq. of *bum*[1].] To hum; buzz. [Now prov.]

bum-ble-bee (bum′bl-bē), *n.* [See *bumble.*] Any of various large, hairy social bees of the genus *Bombus*.

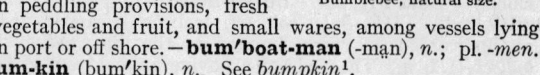

Bumblebee, natural size.

bum-ble-pup-py (bum′bl-pup″i), *n.* [Cf. obs. or prov. *bumble*, to bungle, blunder.] The game of whist played unscientifically.

bum-boat (bum′bōt), *n.* [Origin obscure.] A boat used in peddling provisions, fresh vegetables and fruit, and small wares, among vessels lying in port or off shore.—**bum′boat-man** (-mạn), *n.*; pl. *-men.*

bum-kin (bum′kin), *n.* See *bumpkin*[1].

bum-mer (bum′ėr), *n.* [See *bum*[2].] A 'bum' or loafer. [Slang.]

bump (bump), *v.* [Imit.] **I.** *tr.* To cause to come into more or less violent contact, as one heavy body with another; hurt (one's head, etc.) by striking it against something; strike the posteriors of (a person) against a wall, etc.; also, to strike heavily against (something); in English boat-racing, to overtake and touch (a boat ahead); also, to kill or murder (often with *off*: slang). **II.** *intr.* To come heavily into collision; go or move with a jolt or jolts.—**bump,** *n.* A dull, heavy impact or blow; a jolt; also, a swelling or protuberance, as from a collision or blow; popularly, one of the natural protuberances on the skull associated by phrenologists with faculties of the mind; in English boat-racing, the striking of one boat by the prow of another boat following it; in *aëronautics*, a rapidly rising current of air which when encountered by an aëroplane gives it a more or less dangerous jolt or upward thrust (cf. *air-hole*).—**bump′er. I.** *n.* One who or that which bumps; something used to prevent bumping; a buffer; a cup or glass filled to the brim, as for drinking a toast; something unusually large of its kind (colloq.); a marine fish, *Chloroscombrus chrysurus*, with a compressed body, common in the West Indies, etc. **II.** *a.* Brimming; abundant; very large. [Colloq.]

bump-kin[1], **bum-kin** (bump′kin, bum′-), *n.* [Appar. < *boom*[1] + *-kin.*] *Naut.*, a beam or spar projecting outward from the bow, side, or stern of a ship to extend a sail, secure blocks, or the like.

bump-kin[2] (bump′kin), *n.* [Origin uncertain: cf. *bumpkin*[1].] An awkward, ignorant rustic; a country lout: as, "The more bashful country *bumpkins* hung sheepishly back" (Irving's "Sketch-Book," Sleepy Hollow).

bump-tious (bump′shus), *a.* [Prob. < *bump.*] Offensively self-assertive; arrogant and domineering or quarrelsome.—**bump′tious-ly,** *adv.*—**bump′tious-ness,** *n.*

bump-y (bum′pi), *a.* Having bumps or protuberances; also, causing bumps or jolts; in *aëronautics*, characterized by bumps or the like, as the air or the weather.

bun[1] (bun), *n.* [ME. *bunne*; origin uncertain.] A kind of cake or bread-roll, variously shaped.

bun[2] (bun), *n.* [Origin unknown.] A squirrel or rabbit.

bu-na S (bū′nạ, or bö′nạ, es). [Prob. from *butadiene* and *styrene.*] A synthetic rubber made by copolymerizing butadiene and styrene: used in making passenger-car tires, etc.

bunch (bunch), *n.* [ME. *bunche*: origin uncertain.] A lump, protuberance, or hump; also, a cluster of things growing or held together; a collected mass; an assemblage, company, or lot (chiefly colloq.).—**bunch,** *v.* **I.** *intr.* To form a bunch; swell out; cluster. **II.** *tr.* To form into a bunch; gather into bunches; assemble in an aggregate.—**bunch′=ber″ry,** *n.* A dwarf species of cornel, *Cornus canadensis*, bearing dense clusters of bright-red berries.—**bunch′er,** *n.* A person or thing that bunches; an attachment to a mower for bunching the clover, grass, etc., as fast as it is cut.—**bunch′=flow″er,** *n.* A melanthiaceous plant, *Melanthium virginicum*, of the U. S., bearing grass-like leaves and a panicle of small greenish flowers; also, any other plant of the same genus.—**bunch′=grass,** *n.* Any of various grasses of the western U. S., usually growing in distinct clumps, as *Poa buckleyana*, an erect perennial grass of mountain slopes, etc.—**bunch′y,** *a.* Bulging or protuberant; full of protuberances; in or like a bunch; having bunches.—**bunch′i-ness,** *n.*

bun-co (bung′kō), etc. See *bunko*, etc.
bun-combe, bun-kum (bung′kum), *n.* [From a Congressional representative's phrase, "talking for *Buncombe*" (county of North Carolina).] Speech-making intended merely to please political constituents; insincere talk; claptrap; humbug.
bund[1] (bund), *n.* [Hind. *band.*] In India, China, Japan, etc., an embankment; an embanked quay; an embankment forming a promenade and carriageway along a water-front.
bund[2] (bůnt), *n.* [G., < *binden*, bind.] In German usage, a league, society, or association.
bun-der (bun′dėr), *n.* [Hind. and Pers. *bandar.*] In India, etc., a landing-place; a pier; a harbor.
Bun-des-rat, Bun-des-rath (bůn′des-rät), *n.* [G., < *bund*, league, + *rat*, *rath*, council.] The federal council of the former German Empire (previously to 1918), which was composed of members appointed to represent the various states, and exercised legislative functions in conjunction with the Reichstag; also, the federal council of Switzerland, composed of seven members chosen by the legislature and vested with the chief executive authority.
bun-dle (bun′dl), *n.* [ME. *bundel* = D. *bundel* = G. *bündel*; from the Teut. verb represented by E. *bind.*] A number of things bound or fastened together; a parcel or package; a roll; a collected mass of anything; a number of things considered together; a quantity of paper consisting of two reams; in *bot.*, an aggregation of strands of specialized tissue (as, a vascular *bundle*, an aggregation of conducting tissue traversing the body of a plant, and typically consisting of a woody portion or xylem and a bast portion or phloëm). —**bun′dle,** *v.*; *-dled, -dling.* **I.** *tr.* To tie in a bundle; make up into a bundle; wrap (*up*) warmly; also, to send (*off, out,* etc.) unceremoniously. **II.** *intr.* To depart hurriedly; also, to sleep or lie in the same bed without undressing (a former custom of men and women, esp. sweethearts, in Wales and New England: see Irving's "Knickerbocker's New York," iii. 7).—**bun′dler,** *n.*
bung (bung), *n.* [ME. *bunge*; perhaps ult. < L. *pungere*, prick, pierce.] A large stopper, esp. one for closing the hole in the side of a cask through which it is filled; also, a bung-hole.—**bung,** *v. t.* To stop with a bung; also, to shut or close, as by a blow (slang: as, to *bung* up one's eyes); bruise, exhaust, etc., by hard blows or strenuous effort (slang); also, to shut up in or as in a cask: in all senses commonly followed by *up*.
bun-ga-low (bung′gạ-lō), *n.* [Hind. *banglā*, lit. 'of Bengal.'] In India, etc., a one-story house with a low-peaked roof and a veranda; in the U. S., etc., a cottage of more or less similar appearance, commonly of one story, or a story and a half, esp. for country or seaside residence.

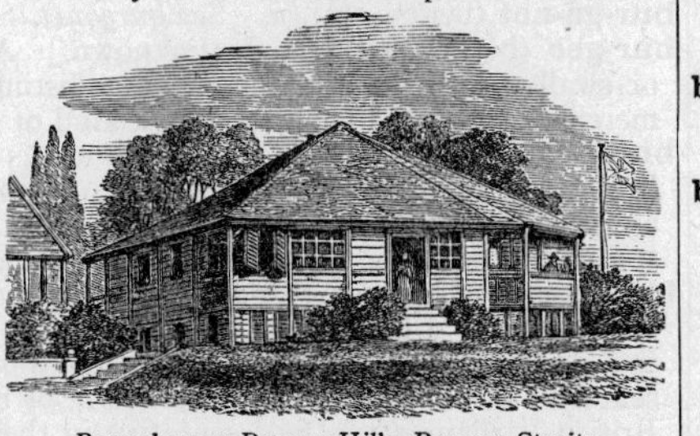
Bungalow on Penang Hills, Penang, Straits Settlements.

bung=hole (bung′hōl), *n.* The hole in a cask through which it is filled, closed by a bung.
bun-gle (bung′gl), *v.*; *-gled, -gling.* [Origin uncertain.] **I.** *tr.* To do, make, or mend clumsily or unskilfully; spoil by unskilful workmanship. **II.** *intr.* To work or act clumsily or unskilfully.—**bun′gle,** *n.* A clumsy or unskilful performance or piece of work.—**bun′gler,** *n.*—**bun′gle-some** (-sum), *a.* Bungling; clumsy; unskilful.—**bun′gling-ly,** *adv.*
bun-ion, bun-yon (bun′yọn), *n.* [Origin uncertain.] A swelling on the foot caused by the inflammation of a synovial bursa, esp. of the great toe.
bunk[1] (bungk), *n.* [Origin uncertain: cf. *bank*[1].] A raised recess, case, or frame serving for a bed, as in a ship or a sleeping-car, often one of two or more arranged one above another; any sleeping-place; also, a piece of timber across a sled, car, or truck, for sustaining the weight of logs (U. S.); also, a car or truck used in logging (U. S.).—**bunk**[1], *v.* **I.** *intr.* To occupy a bunk; sleep, esp. in rough quarters. **II.** *tr.* To place (logs) on bunks. [U. S.]
bunk[2] (bungk), *n.* [Abbr. of *bunkum*: see *buncombe.*] Claptrap; humbug; mere pretense. [Slang.]—**bunk**[2], *v. t.* To humbug; delude. [Slang.]
bunk-er (bung′kėr), *n.* [Cf. *bunk*[1].] A chest, a seat formed by a chest, or a settle (Sc.); a large bin or receptacle for coal, esp. on board ship; in *golf*, a sandy hollow or other rough place on the course, often artificial.—**bunk′er,** *v. t.* To load (coal) into a steamer's bunkers for its own use; in *golf*, to drive (a ball) into a bunker.
bunk-ie (bung′ki), *n.* [See *bunk*[1].] A berth-mate; a comrade. [Colloq., U. S.]
bun-ko (bung′kō), *n.* [Perhaps < Sp. *banco*, bank (for money dealings, etc.).] A swindle in which a person is lured to some place and there fleeced at a game or otherwise victimized; a confidence game; any swindle. [Slang, U. S.]—**bun′ko,** *v. t.*; *-koed, -koing.* To victimize by a bunko. [Slang, U. S.]—**bun′ko=game,** *n.* A bunko. [Slang, U. S.]—**bun′ko=joint,** *n.* A house or rendezvous to which victims are lured and in which they are swindled. [Slang, U. S.]—**bun′ko=man** (-man), *n.*; pl. *-men.* A man who practises the bunko swindle. [Slang, U. S.]—**bun′ko=steer″er,** *n.* One who lures victims to a rendezvous in a bunko. [Slang, U. S.]
bun-kum (bung′kum), *n.* See *buncombe.*
bunk-y (bung′ki), *n.* See *bunkie.*
bunn (bun), *n.* See *bun*[1].
bun-ny (bun′i), *n.*; pl. *bunnies* (-iz). [Dim. of *bun*[2].] A familiar name for the rabbit or the squirrel.
Bun-sen (bun′sẹn, G. bůn′zen) **burn′er.** A type of gas-burner invented by a German chemist, R. W. Bunsen (1811–99), with which a very hot, practically non-luminous flame is obtained by allowing air to enter at the base and mix with the gas.

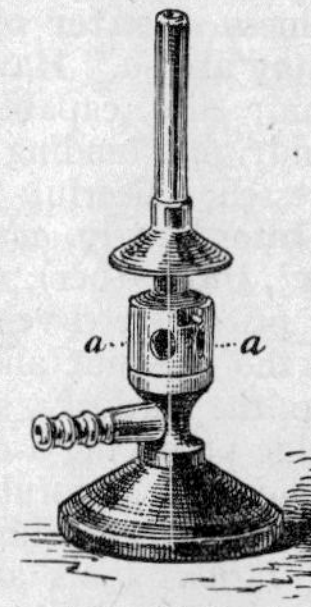

Bunsen Burner.
a, a, openings to admit air.

bunt[1] (bunt), *v. t.* or *i.* [Cf. *butt*[1].] To strike with the head or horns, as a goat does; push; in *baseball*, to block (the ball) with the bat so that it goes to the ground and rolls only a short distance.—**bunt**[1], *n.* A push or shove, as with the head; in *baseball*, an act of bunting; a bunted ball.
bunt[2] (bunt), *n.* [Origin uncertain.] The bagging part of a fishing-net or the like; also, the middle part of a square sail.—**bunt**[2], *v. i.* To swell out or belly, as a sail.
bunt[3] (bunt), *n.* [Origin uncertain.] A disease of wheat which destroys the kernels, due to the fungus *Tilletia tritici*; also, the fungus itself.—**bunt′ed,** *a.* Of wheat, affected with bunt.
bun-ting[1] (bun′ting), *n.* [Origin uncertain.] Any of various fringilline birds of the genus *Emberiza* and other genera, as *E. miliaria*, a common European species, and *Plectrophanes nivalis*, the snow-bunting; any of various non-fringilline birds, as the bobolink.

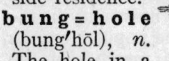

Bunting (*Emberiza miliaria*).

bun-ting[2] (bun′ting), *n.* [Origin uncertain.] A light woolen fabric of a plain, loose weave, used esp. for flags, gala draperies, etc.; flags, draperies, etc., of this fabric.
bunt-line (bunt′lin or -līn), *n.* [See *bunt*[2].] *Naut.*, one of the ropes attached to the foot of a square sail to haul it up to the yard for furling.
bun-ya=bun-ya (bun′yạ̈-bun′yạ̈), *n.* [Native Australian.] A large pinaceous tree, *Araucaria bidwillii*, of Australia, having a

strong, durable wood, and bearing edible seeds about two inches long.

bun-yip (bun′yip), *n.* [Native Australian.] A fabulous animal of native Australian tradition, usually described as of amphibious character and large size; hence, an impostor; a humbug. [Australia.]

bun-yon (bun′yọn), *n.* See *bunion.*

buoy (boi or böi), *n.* [MD. *boeye* (D. *boei*), buoy, fetter, or OF. *boyee, bouee* (F. *bouée*), buoy, = OF. *boie, buie,* bond, fetter, < L. *boia,* collar.] An upright spar, sheet-iron can, or other floating device, fixed in a certain place to indicate the position of a rock or other object beneath the water, or to mark a channel or the like; also, a buoyant object used to keep a person afloat.—**buoy,** *v.* **I.** *tr.* To furnish or mark with a buoy or buoys; also, to support by or as by a buoy; keep afloat in a fluid; bear up or sustain, as hope or courage does; also, to bring afloat (a sunken ship, etc.); raise or elevate (the heart or spirits). **II.** *intr.* To float; rise by reason of lightness.—**buoy′age** (-āj), *n.* The providing of buoys; also, a system of buoys.—**buoy′an-cy,** *n.* The quality of being buoyant; the power to float or rise in a fluid; relative lightness; also, the power of supporting a body so that it floats; the upward pressure exerted upon a body by the fluid in which it is immersed (equivalent to the weight of the fluid which the body displaces); also, tendency to rise, as in the price of stocks; also, elasticity of spirit; cheerfulness; hopefulness.—**center of buoyancy.** See under *center*², *n.*—**buoy′ant,** *a.* Having the quality of floating or rising in a fluid; also, capable of keeping another body afloat, as a fluid; fig., tending to keep up or rise; also, not easily depressed; cheerful; hopeful; also, cheering or invigorating.—**buoy′ant-ly,** *adv.*

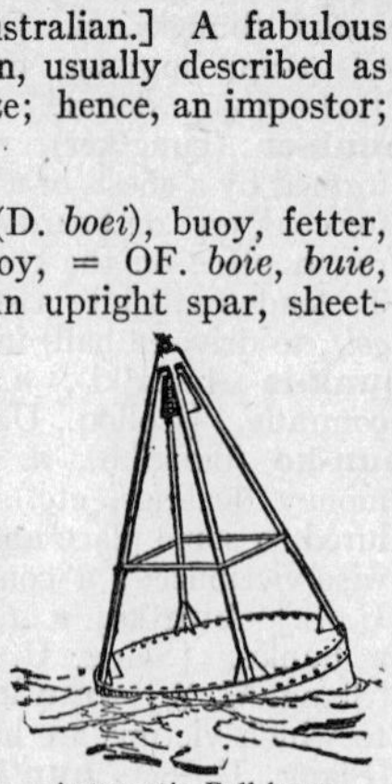
Automatic Bell-buoy.

bur¹, **burr**¹ (bėr), *n.* [ME. *burre* = Dan. *borre.*] A rough or prickly seed-vessel, receptacle, husk, or flower-head, as of the chestnut and burdock; an herb bearing such burs, esp. the burdock; something that adheres like a bur; something producing a choking sensation in the throat; a rough ridge, edge, protuberance, or area, as that left on metal after cutting, drilling, etc. (commonly spelled *burr*); any of various tools and mechanical devices, as a triangular chisel, a small circular saw, or a dentist's drill with a knob-like or expanded head (commonly spelled *burr*); also, burstone (commonly spelled *buhr* or *burr*).—**bur**¹, **burr**¹, *v. t.*; *burred, burring.* To extract burs and other extraneous matter from (wool).

bur² (bėr), *n.* and *v.* See *burr*².

bu-ran (bö-rän′), *n.* [Russ.] A violent storm of wind on the steppes of Russia and Siberia, esp. one accompanied by driving snow and intense cold.

bur-ble (bėr′bl), *v. i.*; *-bled, -bling.* [ME.; ult. imit.] To bubble; rise or flow with bubbles or with a sound as of bubbling; gurgle; purl.

bur-bot (bėr′bọt), *n.*; pl. *burbots* or (esp. collectively) *burbot.* [OF. *borbote, barbote,* appar. < L. *barba,* beard.] A fresh-water fish, *Lota maculosa,* of North America, with an elongated body, a depressed head, and two barbels on the nose and one on the chin; also, a similar European species, *Lota lota.*

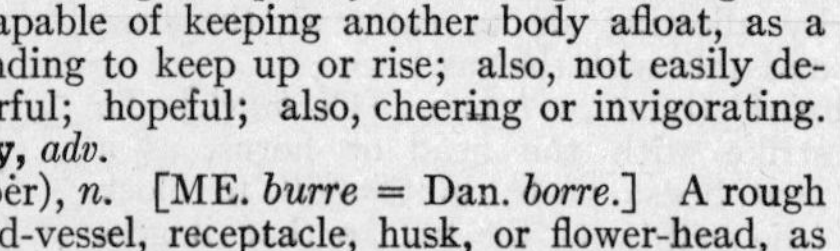
Burbot (*Lota maculosa*).

bur-den¹ (bėr′dn), *n.* [AS. *byrthen*; from the root of E. *bear*¹.] That which is borne or carried; a load; a responsibility or obligation; something borne with labor or difficulty; anything grievous, wearisome, or oppressive; a heavy lot or fate; an encumbrance; a load considered as a measure of quantity; the carrying capacity of a ship; the weight of a ship's cargo; also, the carrying of loads (as, a beast of *burden*).—**burden of proof,** in *law,* the obligation resting upon one of the parties to an action to establish an alleged fact by proof.—**bur′den**¹, *v. t.* To put a burden or load on; load; oppress; encumber.

bur-den² (bėr′dn), *n.* [ME. *burdoun,* < OF. (also F.) *bourdon,* a humming, the drone of a bagpipe; origin uncertain. Later E. senses show association with *burden*¹.] The bass or accompaniment in music†; the refrain or recurring chorus of a song; fig., something often repeated or much dwelt upon; the principal idea; the gist.

bur-den-some (bėr′dn-sum), *a.* Weighing like a heavy burden; heavy or hard to bear; oppressive; onerous.—**bur′den-some-ly,** *adv.*—**bur′den-some-ness,** *n.*

bur-dock (bėr′dok), *n.* A plant of the asteraceous genus *Arctium,* esp. *A. lappa,* a coarse, broad-leaved weed with prickly heads or burs which stick to the clothing.

bu-reau (bū′rō), *n.*; pl. *-reaus* or *-reaux* (-rōz). [F. *bureau,* desk, office, OF. *burel,* cloth-covered table, kind of woolen cloth, dim. of *bure,* coarse woolen cloth, perhaps < L. *burrus,* red.] A desk or writing-table with drawers for papers; a chest of drawers for holding clothing, etc., often surmounted by a mirror; an office for transacting business, giving out information, etc.; a department of government, or a subdivision of such a department, for the transaction of public business.

bu-reau-cra-cy (bū-rō′krạ-si, also bū-rok′rạ-), *n.*; pl. *-cies* (-siz). [See *-cracy.*] Government by bureaus; the concentration of power in administrative bureaus; a body of officials administering government bureaus: usually implying excessive formalism, red tape, or pretentious officialism.—**bu′reau-crat** (-rọ-krat), *n.* [See *-crat.*] A member of a bureaucracy; an official of a bureau, esp. one given to excessive formalism.—**bu-reau-crat′ic,** *a.*—**bu-reau-crat′i-cal-ly,** *adv.*—**bu-reau′crat-ism** (-rō′krạ-tizm), *n.* Government by bureaus; bureaucracy.—**bu-reau′crat-ist,** *n.* An advocate or supporter of bureaucracy.

bu-rette (bū-ret′), *n.* [F., cruet, dim. of *buire,* vessel for wine, etc.] In *chem.,* a graduated glass tube, commonly having a stop-cock at the bottom, used for accurately measuring, or measuring out, small quantities of liquid.

burg (bėrg), *n.* [AS.: see *borough.*] A fortress or fortified town of early and medieval times; also, a town or city (colloq., U. S.).—**burg′age** (-āj), *n.* In *law,* in England, a tenure whereby burgesses, citizens, or townsmen hold their lands or tenements of the king or other lord for a certain yearly rent; in Scotland, that tenure by which the property in royal burghs is held under the crown, proprietors being liable to the (nominal) service of watching and warding.

bur-gall (bėr′gâl), *n.* See *bergall.*

bur-ga-net (bėr′gạ-net), *n.* See *burgonet.*

bur-gee (bėr′jē), *n.* [Origin unknown.] A three-cornered or swallow-tailed pennant used as a distinguishing flag on merchant ships and yachts; also, a kind of small coal.

bur-geon (bėr′jọn), *n.* [ME. *burjon,* < OF. *burjon* (F. *bourgeon*); origin unknown.] A bud or sprout.—**bur′geon,** *v.* [OF. *burjuner* (F. *bourgeonner*).] **I.** *intr.* To bud; sprout; grow forth. **II.** *tr.* To put forth as buds.

bur-gess (bėr′jes), *n.* [OF. *burgeis* (F. *bourgeois*), < ML. *burgensis,* < LL. *burgus*: see *borough.*] An inhabitant, esp. a citizen or freeman, of an English borough; a representative of a borough, corporate town, or university in the British Parliament; a representative in the popular branch of the colonial legislature of Virginia; a member of the lower house in the colonial legislature of Maryland; a magistrate or a member of the governing body of an English borough (now obs.) or of a borough in the U. S.—**bur′gess-ship,** *n.*

burg-grave (bėrg′grāv), *n.* See *burgrave.*

burgh (bur′ọ), *n.* [Var. of *borough.*] A borough: now applied only to chartered towns in Scotland.—**burgh-al** (bėr′gạl), *a.* Pertaining to a burgh.—**burgh-er** (bėr′gėr), *n.* [= D. *burger* = G. *bürger.*] An inhabitant of a borough; a citizen; in South Africa, a citizen of one of the former Dutch republics.

bur-glar (bėr′glạr), *n.* [AL. *burglator* (later *burgulator*), for *burgator,* < LL. *burgus,* castle: see *borough,* and cf. AS. *burh-bryce,* a breaking into a castle or dwelling.] One who breaks into a house at night with intent to commit a felony; one guilty of burglary.—**bur-gla′ri-ous** (-glā′ri-us), *a.* Pertaining to or involving burglary.—**bur-gla′ri-ous-ly,**

Black Fox (melanistic form of *Vulpes* (*Canis*) *fulvus*)
Winter pelage

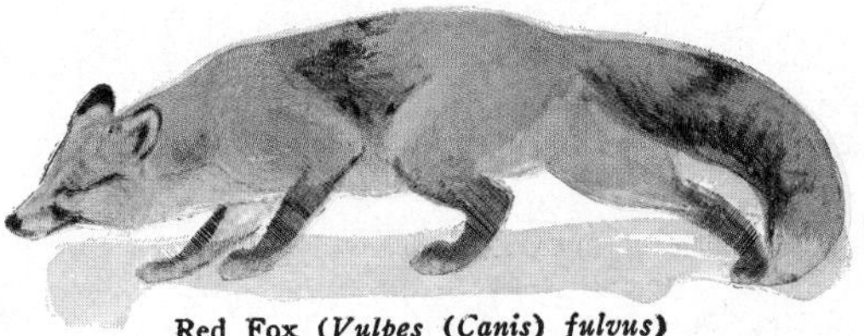

Red Fox (*Vulpes* (*Canis*) *fulvus*)
Winter pelage

Fur-seal (*Callorhinus ursinus*)
Summer pelage

Astrakhan Lamb (variety of *Ovis aries*)
Spring pelage

Russian Sable (*Mustela zibellina*)
Winter pelage

Canadian Lynx (*Lynx canadensis*)
Winter pelage

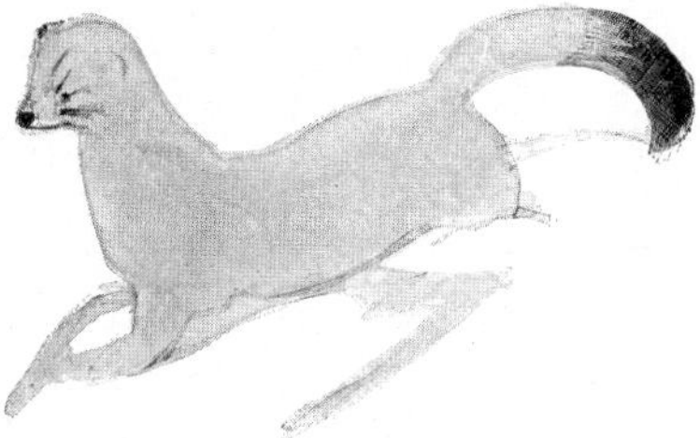

Ermine (*Putorius ermineus*)
Winter pelage

Blue Fox (*Vulpes* (*Canis*) *lagopus*)
Summer pelage

Beaver (*Castor canadensis*)
Winter pelage

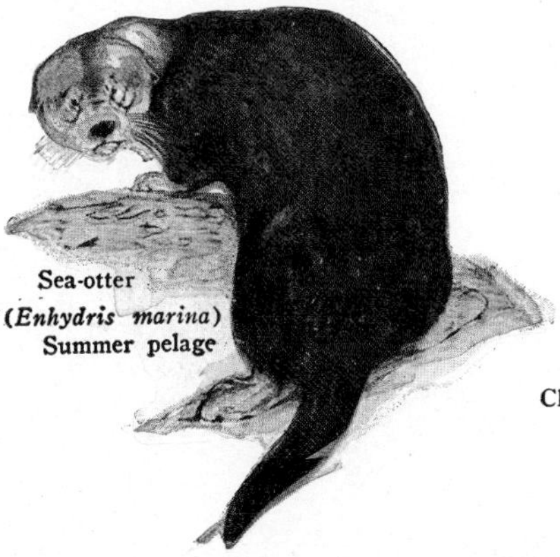

Sea-otter
(*Enhydris marina*)
Summer pelage

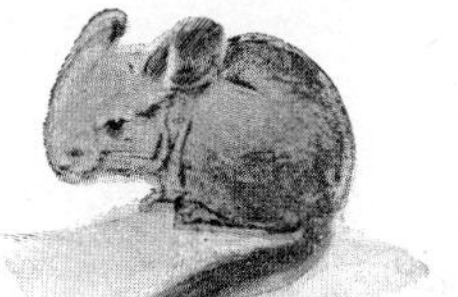

Chinchilla (*Chinchilla lanigera*)
Summer pelage

Mink (*Putorius vison*)
Summer pelage

FUR-BEARING ANIMALS

adv.—**bur′glar-ize,** *v. t.*; *-ized, -izing.* To commit burglary upon.—**bur′glar-y,** *n.*; pl. *-ies* (-iz). The crime of breaking into the house of another at night with felonious intent: sometimes extended by statute to cover the breaking and entering of any of various buildings, by night or day.

Burgomaster-gull.

bur-gle (bėr′gl), *v. i.* or *t.*; *-gled, -gling.* [Back-formation from *burglar.*] To commit burglary, or commit burglary upon. [Colloq.]

bur-go-mas-ter (bėr′gō-mȧs″tėr), *n.* [D. *burgemeester*, 'town master': cf. G. *bürgermeister.*] The chief magistrate of a municipal town of Holland, Flanders, or Germany, nearly corresponding to a mayor in England and the U. S.; also, a large, whitish gull, *Larus glaucus*, of the arctic regions.

bur-go-net (bėr′gō-net), *n.* [F. *bourguignotte*, < *Bourgogne*, Burgundy.] A steel cap or helmet, in two forms, one without and the other with a vizor.

Spanish Burgonet, 16th century.

bur-goo (bėr′gö or bėr-gö′), *n.* [Origin unknown.] A thick oatmeal gruel, esp. as used by seamen; also, a kind of thick, highly seasoned soup, or a picnic or feast at which it is served (local, U. S.).

bur-grave, burg-grave (bėr′-grāv, bėrg′-), *n.* [G. *burggraf*, 'castle (or town) count.'] Formerly, in some European countries, the hereditary governor of a castle or town.

Bur-gun-dy (bėr′gun-di), *n.* [Often *l. c.*] Wine, of many varieties, red and white, mostly still, full, and dry, produced in Burgundy, in eastern France; some similar wine made elsewhere.

bur-i-al (ber′i-a̤l), *n.* [AS. *byrgels*, tomb, < *byrgan*, bury.] A grave† or tomb†; also, the act of burying; interment; sepulture.—**bur′i-al=ground,** *n.* A burying-ground; a graveyard or cemetery.

bur-i-er (ber′i-ėr), *n.* One who or that which buries.

bu-rin (bū′rin), *n.* [F.; prob. from Teut., and akin to E. *bore*[1].] An engravers' tool of tempered steel, used for cutting furrows; the style of execution of an engraver; also, a similar tool used by marble-workers.—**bu′rin-ist,** *n.* An engraver.

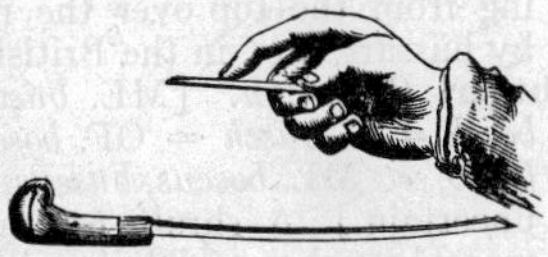

Engravers' Burins.

bu-ri-on (bū′ri-o̤n), *n.* [Origin uncertain.] A small fringilline bird, *Carpodacus frontalis*, of the southwestern U. S.

burke (bėrk), *v. t.*; *burked, burking.* [From W. *Burke*, hanged at Edinburgh in 1829 for murders of this kind.] To suffocate in order to sell the body for dissection; murder so as to leave no or few marks of violence; hence, to smother or suppress; get rid of by some indirect means.

burl (bėrl), *n.* [OF. *bourle*, dim. of *bourre*, hair or wool.] A small knot or lump in wool, thread, or cloth; also, a knot in wood.—**burl,** *v. t.* To remove burls from; pick out knots, etc., from (cloth) in finishing.

bur-lap (bėr′lap), *n.* [Origin obscure.] A coarse fabric of jute, hemp, or the like, used for sacking or wrappings, and, in finer grades, for upholstery, wall-coverings, etc.

bur-lesque (bėr-lesk′). [F. *burlesque*, < It. *burlesco*, < *burla*, jest, mockery.] **I.** *a.* Odd† or grotesque†; of the nature of derisive imitation; tending to excite laughter by extravagant representation, or by ludicrous contrast, as when a serious subject is treated ridiculously or a trifling one with mock solemnity; also, of or pertaining to the kind of theatrical entertainment known as 'burlesque' (as, a *burlesque* show; a *burlesque* theater). **II.** *n.* Burlesque imitation or representation; also, a burlesque literary or dramatic composition; a dramatic travesty with more or less music; theatrical entertainment consisting of such travesties or musical farces, with individual performances or 'acts' of singing, dancing, etc. (cf. *variety*); also, a gross perversion; a mockery.—**bur-lesque′,** *v.*; *-lesqued, -lesquing.* **I.** *tr.* To imitate grotesquely; ridicule by burlesque; caricature; travesty. **II.** *intr.* To use burlesque.—**bur-lesque′ly,** *adv.*—**bur-les′quer** (-les′kėr), *n.*

bur-ley (bėr′li), *n.* [Appar. < *Burley*, proper name.] An American variety of tobacco grown esp. in Kentucky and southern Ohio.

bur-ly (bėr′li), *a.*; compar. *burlier*, superl. *burliest.* [ME. *burli, borlich*; origin uncertain.] Stately†, noble†, or goodly†; also, great in bodily size, stout, or sturdy (as, "a *burly*, roaring, roistering blade . . . the hero of the country round": Irving's "Sketch-Book," Sleepy Hollow); also, bluff or brusque (archaic).—**bur′li-ly,** *adv.*—**bur′li-ness,** *n.*

bur=mar-i-gold (bėr′mar′i-gōld), *n.* Any of various herbs of the asteraceous genus *Bidens*, esp. those with conspicuous yellow flowers.

Bur-mese (bėr-mēs′ or -mēz′). **I.** *a.* Of or pertaining to Burma, a province of eastern British India. **II.** *n.*; pl. *-mese.* A native of Burma; also, the language of Burma.

burn[1] (bėrn), *n.* [AS. *burna, burne*, akin to G. *born, brunnen*, spring.] A brook or rivulet: as, "Tumbling brown, the *burn* comes down, And roars frae bank to brae" (Burns's "Winter"). [Sc. and north. Eng.]

burn[2] (bėrn), *v.*; *burned* or *burnt, burning.* [AS. *beornan*, intr., *bærnan*, tr.; akin to G. *brennen*, Icel. *brinna, brenna*, Goth. *brinnan, brannjan*, burn.] **I.** *intr.* Of fire, to be active or aglow; of a furnace, etc., to contain fire; of fuel, etc., to be on fire, or in process of consumption by fire; fig., to be fierce or vehement, as passion; be inflamed with passion, desire, etc., as a person; experience ardent desire; also, to be or become very hot; feel excess of heat; be affected with a sensation of heat; in certain games, of a person, to be very near a concealed object which is sought; hence, to be nearly right in a guess; also, to flame, or give light, as a candle, lamp, or the sun; glow like fire; also, to undergo destruction, injury, or change from exposure to fire or heat; become charred, singed, scorched, etc.; become discolored by the effect of fire or heat, as the skin on exposure to the sun; suffer death by fire; also, to make a way (*into*) by or as by burning; in *chem.*, to undergo combustion; oxidize. **II.** *tr.* To consume or destroy by fire; set on fire, or consign to the flames; make a burnt-offering of; put to death by fire; keep alight, as a candle or lamp; inflame with passion, desire, etc.; expose to the action of fire or heat (as, to *burn* clay); produce or make by means of fire; injure or change by fire or heat; char, singe, scorch, etc.; change the color of by fire or heat; wound or hurt by contact with fire or with something very hot; cauterize, as a wound; brand with a hot iron; produce an effect or a sensation like that of fire or heat on (something); in *chem.*, to cause to undergo combustion; oxidize.—**burn**[2], *n.* The act or effect of burning; a wound or hurt caused by burning; a mark made by burning; a burnt place; also, a disease of plants; brand.—**burn′a-ble,** *a.* Capable of being burned.—**burn′er,** *n.* One who or that which burns; a lamp for heating a painted surface so that the paint may be removed; that part of a lamp, gas-fixture, etc., from which the flame issues or in which it is produced.

bur-net (bėr′net), *n.* [OF. *burnet, brunet*, dim. of *brun*, brown.] A plant of the genus *Sanguisorba*, esp. *S. sanguisorba*, an erect herb whose leaves are used for salad.

bur-nett-ize (bėr′net-īz), *v. t.*; *-ized, -izing.* [From Sir W. *Burnett*, the patentee (1837).] To impregnate (timber, canvas, etc.) with a solution of zinc chloride, in order to prevent decay.

burn-ing (bėr′ning), *p. a.* That burns; glowing; raging; ardent; vehement; very hot; shining; scorching.—**burn′ing=bush′,** *n.* Any of various plants, esp. the strawberry-bush, *Euonymus americanus*, or the wahoo, *E. atropur-*

(variable) d̤ as d or j, s̤ as s or sh, t̤ as t or ch, z̤ as z or zh; o, F. cloche; ü, F. menu; ċh, Sc. loch; ṅ, F. bonbon; ′, primary accent; ″, secondary accent; †, obsolete; <, from; +, and; =, equals. See also lists at beginning of book.

pureus.—**burn′ing=glass,** *n.* A lens used to produce heat or ignite substances by bringing the direct rays of the sun to a focus.—**burn′ing-ly,** *adv.*

bur-nish (bėr′nish), *v. t.* [OF. *burnir* (*burniss-*), *brunir*, make brown, burnish, < *brun*, brown.] To make (metal) smooth and bright; polish (a surface) by friction; cause to glow or be resplendent.—**bur′nish,** *n.* Polish; luster.—**bur′nish-er,** *n.*

bur-nous (bėr-nös′ or bėr′nös), *n.* [F., < Ar. *burnus.*] A hooded mantle or cloak of a coarse woolen fabric, worn by Moors and Arabs.

burn-sides (bėrn′sīdz), *n. pl.* [From A.E. *Burnside* (1824–81), American general.] A style of beard consisting of side-whiskers and a mustache, the chin being clean-shaven.

burnt (bėrnt), *p. a.* Affected by, or as by, burning.—**burnt′=of′fer-ing,** *n.* An offering burnt upon an altar in sacrifice to a deity. See Lev. vi. 9.

burr[1] (bėr), *n.* and *v.* See *bur*[1].

burr[2] (bėr), *n.* [Imit.] A guttural or rough pronunciation of the letter *r*, esp. characteristic of the speech of Northumberland, England; any rough or dialectal pronunciation; also, a whirring noise.—**burr**[2], *v.* **I.** *intr.* To pronounce the letter *r* with a burr; speak roughly, indistinctly, or inarticulately; also, to make a whirring sound. **II.** *tr.* To pronounce (the letter *r*) with a burr.

bur=reed (bėr′rēd), *n.* Any plant of the genus *Sparganium*, whose species have ribbon-like leaves and bur-like heads of fruit.

bur-ro (bůr′ō or bur′ō), *n.*; pl. *burros* (-ōz). [Sp.] A donkey.

bur-row (bur′ō), *n.* [ME. *borow*: cf. AS. *beorg*, *beorh*, shelter.] A hole in the ground made by an animal, as a rabbit or a fox, for refuge and habitation; any similar habitation or place of retreat.—**bur′row,** *v.* **I.** *intr.* To make a burrow for habitation; work a way into or under something; lodge in or as in a burrow; hide one's self. **II.** *tr.* To make a burrow or burrows in; construct by burrowing; hide (one's self) in or as in a burrow.—**bur′row-er,** *n.*

burr-stone (bėr′stōn), *n.* See *burstone.*

bur-ry[1] (bėr′i), *a.* Full of burs; bur-like; prickly.

bur-ry[2] (bėr′i), *a.* Characterized by a burr, as speech.

bur-sa (bėr′sạ), *n.*; pl. *-sæ* (-sē). [ML., bag, purse, < Gr. βύρσα, skin, hide.] In *anat.* and *zoöl.*, a pouch, sac, or vesicle; esp., a sac containing synovia, placed between parts moving on each other, to facilitate motion, as between a tendon and a bone ('synovial bursa').—**bur′sal,** *a.* Of or pertaining to a bursa or bursæ.

bur-sar (bėr′sạr), *n.* [ML. *bursarius*, < *bursa*, purse: see *bursa.*] A treasurer, esp. of a college; also, a student who receives an allowance from a college endowment fund (Sc.).—**bur-sa′ri-al** (-sā′ri-ạl), *a.*—**bur′sar-ship,** *n.*—**bur′sa-ry** (-sạ-ri), *n.*; pl. *-ries* (-riz). [ML. *bursaria.*] A treasury, esp. of a college; also, an allowance given to a student from a college endowment fund (Sc.).

bursch-en-schaft (bůrsh′en-shäft), *n.*; pl. *-schaften* (-shäf″-ten). [G., < *bursch*, student.] Any of certain associations of students at the German universities, formed orig. to foster patriotism and Christian conduct and to promote liberal ideas, but later becoming purely social fraternities; also, an organization formed by affiliation of these.

burse (bėrs), *n.* [ML. *bursa*, purse: see *bursa*, and cf. *bourse.*] A purse; an exchange† or bourse†; a fund to provide allowances for students, or an allowance so provided; *eccles.*, a case or receptacle for the corporal.

bur-si-form (bėr′si-fôrm), *a.* [ML. *bursa*, bag, purse: see *-form.*] Pouch-shaped; saccate.

bur-si-tis (bėr-sī′tis), *n.* [NL.] In *pathol.*, inflammation of a bursa.

burst (bėrst), *v.*; *burst* (also, chiefly prov., *bursted*), *bursting.* [AS. *berstan* = G. *bersten.*] **I.** *intr.* To break or be broken suddenly, as with tension or with expansion of contents; fly to pieces; explode; break open; fly open suddenly, as a door; be extremely full, as if ready to break open; break or give way, or be on the verge of giving way, from violent pain or emotion; make a sudden display of activity, emotion, etc. (as, to *burst* into speech or tears); issue forth suddenly and forcibly from or as from confinement; become visible, audible, evident, etc., suddenly and clearly; spring forth, as a plant; force a way or passage; come or go suddenly and violently. **II.** *tr.* To cause to burst; break suddenly and violently; shatter; disrupt; cause or suffer the rupture of (as, to *burst* a blood-vessel); force open, as a door.—**burst,** *n.* The act of bursting, or the resulting state; a sudden disruption; an explosion; a sudden display of activity or energy; a sudden and violent issuing forth; an outburst; a sudden opening to sight or view; a sudden expression or manifestation of emotion, etc.; a spree (colloq.).—**burst′er,** *n.*—**burst′ing=charge,** *n.* In *ordnance*, the charge of explosive required for bursting a shell or the like.

bur-stone, burr-stone (bėr′stōn), *n.* Any of various cellular siliceous rocks used for making millstones; also, a millstone of such material.

bur-then (bėr′ᴛʜn). Var. of *burden*[1], *n.* and *v.*, and hence (less correctly) of *burden*[2]. [Archaic.]—**bur′then-some,** etc. Var. of *burdensome*, etc. [Archaic.]

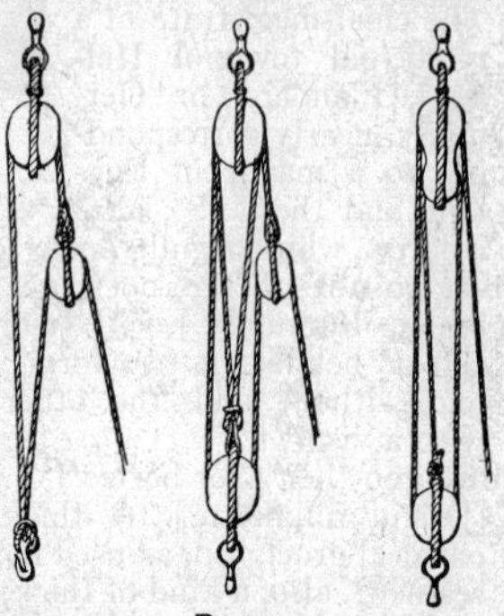
Burtons.

bur-ton (bėr′tọn), *n.* [Origin unknown.] *Naut.*, any of various kinds of tackle used for setting up rigging, raising sails, etc.

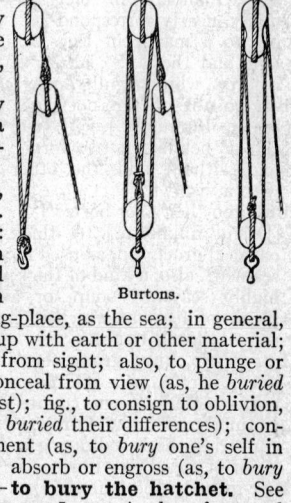

bur-weed (bėr′wēd), *n.* Any of various plants having a bur-like fruit, as the cocklebur, burdock, etc.

bur-y (ber′i), *v. t.*; *buried*, *burying.* [AS. *byrgan*, prob. akin to *beorgan*, protect: cf. *borough.*] To deposit in a grave or tomb, as a dead body; inter; entomb; consign (a corpse) to any final resting-place, as the sea; in general, to put under ground; cover up with earth or other material; cover over so as to conceal from sight; also, to plunge or sink in anything, so as to conceal from view (as, he *buried* the knife in his enemy's breast); fig., to consign to oblivion, abandon, or forget (as, they *buried* their differences); consign to obscurity or retirement (as, to *bury* one's self in solitude or in a monastery); absorb or engross (as, to *bury* one's self in one's work).—**to bury the hatchet.** See under *hatchet.*—**bur′y-ing=ground,** *n.* A plot of ground appropriated to the burial of the dead; a graveyard; a cemetery.

bus (bus), *n.*; pl. *buses*, also *busses.* [Abbr. of *omnibus.*] An omnibus (vehicle); also, a waiter's assistant, or a man or boy employed as a helper in a restaurant; also, an aëroplane. [Colloq.]

Busby.

bus-by (buz′bi), *n.*; pl. *-bies* (-biz). [Origin unknown.] A tall fur hat with a bag hanging from the top over the right side, worn by hussars, etc., in the British army.

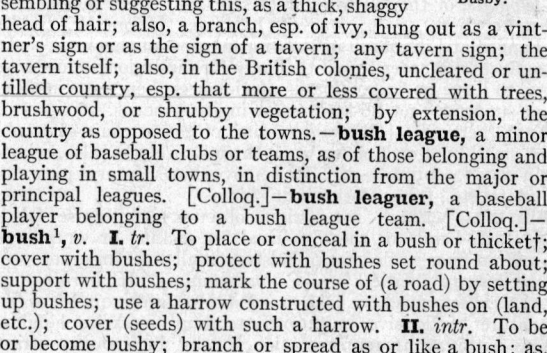

bush[1] (bůsh), *n.* [ME. *busch*, *busk*, = D. *bosch* = G. *busch* = OF. *bosc*, F. *bois*, = It. *bosco*, < ML. *boscus*, *buscus*, a wood: origin uncertain.] A shrub, esp. a low one with many branches, which usually arise from or near the ground; a small cluster of shrubs appearing as a single plant; also, something resembling or suggesting this, as a thick, shaggy head of hair; also, a branch, esp. of ivy, hung out as a vintner's sign or as the sign of a tavern; any tavern sign; the tavern itself; also, in the British colonies, uncleared or untilled country, esp. that more or less covered with trees, brushwood, or shrubby vegetation; by extension, the country as opposed to the towns.—**bush league,** a minor league of baseball clubs or teams, as of those belonging and playing in small towns, in distinction from the major or principal leagues. [Colloq.]—**bush leaguer,** a baseball player belonging to a bush league team. [Colloq.]—**bush**[1], *v.* **I.** *tr.* To place or conceal in a bush or thicket†; cover with bushes; protect with bushes set round about; support with bushes; mark the course of (a road) by setting up bushes; use a harrow constructed with bushes on (land, etc.); cover (seeds) with such a harrow. **II.** *intr.* To be or become bushy; branch or spread as or like a bush: as,

"She stood, Half spied, so thick the roses *bushing* round About her glow'd" (Milton's "Paradise Lost," ix. 426).

bush[2] (bůsh), *n.* [Cf. D. *bus*, box, bush of a wheel.] A lining of metal or the like let into an orifice to guard against wearing by friction, erosion, etc.; a metal lining, usually detachable, used as a bearing.—**bush**[2], *v. t.* To furnish with a bush; line with metal.

bush-buck (bůsh′buk), *n.* Same as *boschbok.*

bush=clo-ver (bůsh′klō″vėr), *n.* Any plant of the fabaceous genus *Lespedeza*, allied to the clover, often of an erect or ascending habit.

bush=dog (bůsh′dog), *n.* The potto, *Perodicticus potto.*

bushed (bůsht), *a.* Lost in the bush; hence, bewildered; at a loss.

bush-el[1] (bůsh′ẹl), *n.* [OF. *boissiel* (F. *boisseau*), dim. < ML. *buxta*, for *buxis*, box: see *box*[2].] A dry measure containing 4 pecks, equivalent in the U. S. (and formerly in England) to 2,150.42 cubic inches ('Winchester bushel'), and in Great Britain to 2,218.192 cubic inches ('imperial bushel'); a vessel of this capacity; also, an indefinitely large quantity (colloq.).

bush-el[2] (bůsh′ẹl), *v. t.* or *i.*; *-eled* or *-elled, -eling* or *-elling.* [Origin uncertain.] In *tailoring*, to alter or repair (a garment). [U. S.]—**bush′el-er, bush′el-ler,** *n.* One who bushels garments; a tailor's assistant who does altering or repairing. [U. S.] Also **bush′el-man** (-mạn); pl. *-men.*

bush-er (bůsh′ėr), *n.* A bush leaguer (see under *bush*[1], *n.*). [Colloq.]

bush=ham-mer (bůsh′ham″ėr), *n.* [Cf. G. *bosshammer.*] A hammer having a face studded with pyramidal points or the like for dressing stone.

bu-shi-do (bö′shē-dō), *n.* [Jap., 'military knight way.'] The code of moral principles which the knights and warriors of feudal Japan were required to put into practice in all the circumstances and relations of life; knightly spirit and conduct; chivalry.

bush-i-ness (bůsh′i-nes), *n.* Bushy state or form.

bush-ing (bůsh′ing), *n.* [See *bush*[2].] A lining of metal or the like, used to protect an orifice or to serve as a bearing; a bush.

Bush-man (bůsh′mạn), *n.*; pl. *-men.* One of an aboriginal tribe near the Cape of Good Hope, similar but inferior to the Hottentots; [*l. c.*] a settler in the Australian bush; one acquainted with the bush.

bush-mas-ter (bůsh′mȧs″tėr), *n.* A large venomous serpent, *Lachesis mutus*, of tropical South America.

bush=ran-ger (bůsh′rān″jėr), *n.* One who ranges in the bush or woods; esp., in Australia, a criminal, often an escaped convict, leading a predatory life in the bush.—**bush′=ran″ging,** *n.*

bush-whack-er (bůsh′hwak″ėr), *n.* One accustomed to go about among bushes; hence, a Confederate guerrilla in the American Civil War (a term used by the Federal forces); any guerrilla; also, a scythe for cutting bushes.—**bush′-whack″ing,** *n.*

bush-y (bůsh′i), *a.*; compar. *bushier*, superl. *bushiest.* Full of or overgrown with bushes; also, resembling a bush; thick and spreading like a bush.

bus-ied (biz′id). Preterit and past participle of *busy.*

bus-i-ly (biz′i-li), *adv.* In a busy manner.

busi-ness (biz′nes), *n.* [Cf. *busyness.*] The state of being busy† (see *busyness*); anxiety† or care†; also, that with which one is busy or occupied; a matter of special concern at a particular time; a particular mission, charge, purpose, etc.; something to be done or attended to; an affair in which one has the right to act or interfere, or the right itself (colloq.); any matter, affair, or thing (chiefly colloq.: as, this is a bad *business*; tired of the whole *business*); also, a matter of habitual concern or interest; one's occupation, profession, or trade; also, action which requires time, attention, and labor; serious employment as opposed to a pastime (as, *business* before pleasure); also, dealings or intercourse generally; esp., commercial dealings; mercantile pursuits collectively; trade; commercial transactions or engagements; also, a commercial enterprise or establishment; *theat.*, action as opposed to dialogue, esp. incidental action intended for realistic effect.—**busi′ness-like,** *a.* Suitable for, befitting, or conforming to the methods of business or trade; methodical; systematic.—**busi′ness-like-ness,** *n.*

busk[1] (busk), *v. t.* [Icel. *būask*, refl. of *būa*, make ready.] To prepare; get ready; equip; dress. [Now chiefly Sc.]

busk[2] (busk), *n.* [F. *busc*: origin uncertain.] A strip of wood, steel, whalebone, or other stiffening material placed in the front of a corset to keep it in form; also, the whole corset (now prov.).

bus-kin (bus′kin), *n.* [Appar. < OF. *bouzequin, brosequin*, F. *brodequin*: cf. MD. *broseken*, Sp. *borceguí*, It. *borzacchino.*] A half-boot, or outer covering for the foot and leg reaching to the calf or higher; specif., the cothurnus of ancient Greek and Roman tragic actors, sometimes taken as a symbol of tragedy (cf. *sock*); *pl.*, *eccles.*, the stockings belonging to a bishop's canonicals; also, a bishop's sandals.—**bus′kined,** *a.* Wearing buskins; esp., wearing the buskins of tragedy; hence, of or pertaining to tragedy; tragic; lofty or elevated, as language.

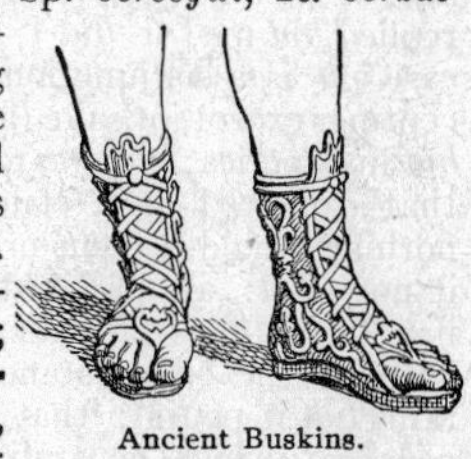

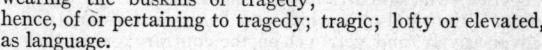

Ancient Buskins.

buss (bus), *v. t.* or *i.* [Origin uncertain; prob. imit.] To kiss. [Archaic or prov.]—**buss,** *n.* A kiss. [Archaic or prov.]

bust[1] (bust), *n.* [F. *buste*, < It. *busto.*] The chest or breast; the bosom; also, the human head, shoulders, and breast, sometimes with the upper arms, as represented in sculpture.

bust[2] (bust), *v.* and *n.* Prov. or vulgar form of *burst.*

bus-tard (bus′tạ̈rd), *n.* [OF. *bistarde*, < L. *avis tarda*, 'slow bird.'] Any of various old-world birds (family *Otididæ*) allied to both the cranes and the plovers, as *Otis tarda* ('great bustard'), a large bird of Europe and Africa.

Great Bustard.

bust-ed[1] (bus′ted), *a.* Having a bust (as, full-*busted*); also, adorned with busts.

bust-ed[2] (bus′ted), *p. a.* [See *bust*[2].] Broken; ruined; bankrupt. [Slang.]

bust-er (bus′tėr), *n.* One who or that which 'busts,' or bursts, breaks, etc. (as, a trust-*buster*; a bronco-*buster*); something very big, striking, or remarkable of its kind; a big, dashing fellow; a term applied to a small boy. [Slang.]

bus-tic (bus′tik), *n.* [Origin uncertain.] A sapotaceous tree, *Dipholis salicifolia*, of southern Florida and the West Indies, having a heavy, hard, close-grained wood.

bus-tle[1] (bus′l), *v.*; *-tled, -tling.* [Cf. Icel. *bustla*, splash about, bustle.] **I.** *intr.* To move or act with a great show of energy; stir about energetically; be in a busy commotion. **II.** *tr.* To cause to bustle; force, drive, etc., by bustling.—**bus′tle**[1], *n.* Activity with great show of energy; stir; commotion; also, a conflict, scuffle, or fray (archaic).

bus-tle[2] (bus′l), *n.* [Origin uncertain: cf. *bustle*[1].] A pad, cushion, or wire framework worn by women on the back part of the body below the waist, to expand and support the skirt.

bus-tler (bus′lėr), *n.* One who bustles, or makes a great show of energy.—**bus′tling,** *p. a.* That bustles; marked by activity or bustle; stirring.—**bus′tling-ly,** *adv.*

bus-y (biz′i), *a.*; compar. *busier*, superl. *busiest.* [AS. *bisig* = D. *bezig* = LG. *besig.*] Actively or attentively engaged; closely occupied; not at leisure; also, having much business; constantly or habitually occupied; in constant motion or activity; also, full of or indicating activity or business (as, a *busy* season; a *busy* street); pursued or carried on energetically (as, a *busy* trade); also, active in that which does not concern one; officious; meddlesome; prying.—**bus′y,** *v. t.*; *busied, busying.* [AS. *bisgian.*] To employ with constant attention; keep engaged; make or keep busy. —**bus'y-bod''y,** *n.*; pl. *-ies* (-iz). One who officiously or impertinently concerns himself with the affairs of others; a meddler.—**bus'y-ness,** *n.* The state or quality of being busy.

but (but). [AS. *būtan*, outside, < *be*, by, + *ūtan*, outside, < *ūt*, out.] **I.** *adv.* Outside†; in or to an outer room (Sc.); only or merely (as, he is *but* a boy; we can *but* try). **II.** *prep.* Outside of†; in or to the outer room of (Sc.); without, or with no (Sc.); also, with the exception of (as, no one replied *but* me [or '*but* I,' with *replied* understood: in which case *but* is a conjunction]); except; save. **III.** *conj.* Excepting, except, or save (as, right *but* for one thing; anywhere *but* in America; no one replied *but* I: cf. *but, prep.*); except that (followed by a clause, often with *that* expressed: as, nothing would do *but*, or *but that*, I should come in); were it not (*that*: as, I should come in *but that* it is impossible); if not, or unless (archaic: as, *but* he be dead he will hear); without the circumstance that, or that not (as, it never rains *but* it pours); that (esp. after *doubt, deny*, etc., with a negative, which neutralizes the negative force of *but*, and often with *that* also, in which case *but* is unnecessary); also, adversatively, and yet; yet on the contrary; nevertheless. Used in various idiomatic constructions, due chiefly to ellipsis: as, I cannot [choose] *but* hope; not [meaning to imply anything else] *but* that I was willing; not a man *but* [one who] knows; he did all *but* succeed (hence, he all *but* succeeded); I don't know *but* that (or, colloq., *but* what: see *what, conj.*) you are right.—**but,** *n.* The outer room (kitchen) of a cottage (Sc.: cf. *ben*[1], *n.*); also, the word 'but' as introducing an objection; hence, an objection.

bu-ta-di-ene (bū-tạ-dī'ēn), *n.* A hydrocarbon (C_4H_6).

bu-tane (bū'tān), *n.* [L. *butyrum*, butter.] In *chem.*, either of two gaseous isomeric hydrocarbons, C_4H_{10}.

butch-er (bu̇ch'ėr), *n.* [OF. *bochier* (F. *boucher*), < *boc, buc*, he-goat; from Teut., and akin to E. *buck*[1].] One who slaughters large domesticated animals, or dresses their flesh, for food or for market; one who deals in meat; also, one guilty of indiscriminate or brutal slaughter of men; a brutal murderer; an executioner† or torturer†; also, an unskilful worker or performer (colloq.).—**butch'er,** *v. t.* To slaughter (animals) or dress (meat) for food or for market; also, to murder indiscriminately or brutally; also, to treat bunglingly, or spoil by bad work (colloq.).—**butch'er=bird,** *n.* Any of various shrikes of the genus *Lanius*, which impale their excess prey upon thorns.—**butch'er-er,** *n.* —**butch'er-ly,** *a.* Like, or characteristic of, a butcher.—**butch'er=meat,** *n.* The flesh of animals, such as oxen, sheep, pigs, etc., slaughtered by butchers, as distinguished from poultry, game, fish, etc.—**butch'er's=broom',** *n.* A shrubby convallariaceous evergreen, *Ruscus aculeatus*, of England: used for making brooms.—**butch'er-y,** *n.*; pl. *-ies* (-iz). [OF. F. *boucherie.*] A slaughter-house or butcher's shop; also, the trade or business of a butcher; the act of butchering animals for food; hence, brutal slaughter; carnage.

Butcher-bird (*Lanius ludovicianus*).

but-ler (but'lėr), *n.* [OF. *butiller*, < ML. *buticularius*, < *buticula*: see *bottle*[2].] A man-servant having charge of the wines and liquors in a household; the head male servant of a household, who keeps the plate, etc.; also, an official of high rank nominally connected with the supply of wine for the royal table.—**but'ler-ship,** *n.*—**but'ler-y,** *n.*; pl. *-ies* (-iz). A butler's room or pantry; a buttery.

butt[1] (but), *v.* [OF. *buter, bouter*, strike, thrust, abut, touch; from Teut.] **I.** *tr.* To strike, thrust, or push, esp. with the head or horns. **II.** *intr.* To strike or push, as with head or horns; also, to pitch forward; also, to jut or project.—**butt**[1], *n.* A thrust or push with the head or horns.

butt[2] (but), *n.* [OF. *but*, goal, mark, *bout*, end, extremity, < *buter, bouter*: see *butt*[1]. With later E. senses cf. F. *pied bot*, clubfoot, D. *bot*, blunt, G. *butt*, Dan. *but*, short and thick, stumpy.] A mark or target for archery practice; an erection on which this is placed; a mound or embankment to receive shots fired in rifle or gunnery practice or experiments; *pl.*, a range for archery, rifle, or gunnery practice; *sing.*, an end, aim, or object; an object of ridicule, scorn, or abuse; a goal†, bound†, or limit†; also, the end or extremity of anything, esp. the thicker, larger, or blunt end, as of a musket, fishing-rod, whip-handle, arrow, etc.; the trunk of a tree, esp. just above the root; the base of a leafstalk; a buttock or the buttocks (colloq.); also, the end of a plank, timber, or plate, which exactly meets another endwise in a ship's side or bottom; the joint between two such pieces; a joint where two ends meet squarely; a hinge for a door or the like, secured to the butting parts instead of the adjacent sides; also, the thicker or hinder part of a hide or skin; the thick leather made from this.—**butt**[2], *v.* **I.** *tr.* To fix or mark the bounds or limits of†; also, to place (a timber, etc.) with its end against something; join (planks, etc.) end to end; also, to cut off the rough ends of (boards, logs, etc.). **II.** *intr.* To join at the end; abut; be contiguous; fit together end to end.

butt[3] (but), *n.* [OF. *botte, bote* (F. *botte*), = It. *botte*, < ML. *butta, buttis*, vessel, cask.] A large cask, esp. for wine or ale; also, a measure of capacity equivalent to two hogsheads; also, any cask or barrel.

butte (būt), *n.* [F. *butte*, hill, OF. *bute*, mound bearing a butt to shoot at, fem. of *but*: see *butt*[2].] A conspicuous isolated hill or mountain rising abruptly. [Western U. S. and Canada.]

butt-ed (but'ed), *a.* Having a butt: as, a thick-*butted* whip.

butt=end (but'end'), *n.* The butt, extremity, or thicker end of a thing; fig., the concluding part.

butt-er[1] (but'ėr), *n.* One who or that which butts.

but-ter[2] (but'ėr), *n.* [AS. *butere*, < L. *butyrum*, < Gr. *βούτυρον*; origin uncertain.] The fatty portion of milk, separating as a soft whitish or yellowish solid when milk or cream is agitated or churned; also, any of various substances of similar consistence, as various metallic chlorides, and certain vegetable oils solid at ordinary temperatures; also, a preparation of fruit, as apples, reduced to a thick consistence by long stewing; also, gross flattery (colloq.).—**but'ter**[2], *v. t.* To spread with butter; put butter on or in; also, to flatter grossly (colloq.). — **but'ter=and=eggs',** *n.* Any of certain plants whose flowers are of two shades of yellow, as the toad-flax, *Linaria linaria.*—**but'ter-ball,** *n.* The buffle (duck).—**but'ter=bean,** *n.* A kind of snap-bean or string-bean with a tender yellowish pod. — **but'ter-bur,** *n.* An asteraceous plant, *Petasites petasites*, with large, soft leaves which are said to have been used for wrapping up butter.—**but'ter-cup,** *n.* A plant of the genus *Ranunculus*, esp. *R. acris* or *R. bulbosus*, with yellow cup-shaped flowers. — **but'ter=fin''gered,** *a.* Apt to let things slip or fall through the fingers; failing to catch or stop a ball, as in baseball. [Colloq.]—**but'ter=fin''gers,** *n.* A butter-fingered person. [Colloq.]—**but'ter-fish,** *n.* Any of various fishes with a smooth, unctuous surface, as *Poronotus triacanthus*, a small silvery food-fish of the Atlantic coast of America.

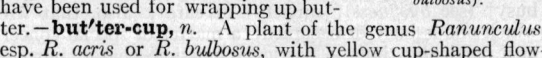

Buttercup (*Ranunculus bulbosus*).

Butterfish (*Poronotus triacanthus*).

but-ter-fly (but′ėr-flī), *n.*; pl. *-flies* (-flīz). [AS. *buttorflēoge* = D. *botervlieg* = G. *butterfliege*, 'butter fly'; perhaps orig. used of a butter-colored (yellow) species.] Any of a group (sometimes classed as the suborder *Rhopalocera*) of lepidopters, comprising diurnal species with large wings, clubbed antennæ, and (often) conspicuous colors or markings (cf. *moth*); fig., a pretty, fragile creature; a showily dressed, trifling, or giddy person; also, the guide for the reins on the front of a hansom.—**but′ter-fly=fish,** *n.* Any of various fishes suggestive of a butterfly, as the ocellated blenny, *Blennius ocellaris*, or any of the tropical marine fishes constituting the family *Chætodontidæ*, most of which are remarkable for their brilliant coloring.—**but′ter-fly=valve,** *n.* A kind of double clack-valve, in which there are two lid-like semicircular pieces hinged to a common crosspiece; also, a valve in a pipe, consisting of a disk which turns on one of its diameters.—**but′ter-fly=weed,** *n.* Either of two North American milkweeds, *Asclepias tuberosa* and *A. decumbens*, bearing orange-colored flowers.

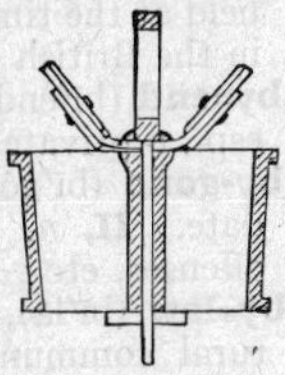

Butterfly-valve.

but-ter-ine (but′ėr-ēn), *n.* An artificial butter; oleomargarin.

but-ter-is (but′ėr-is), *n.* [Cf. F. *boutoir*, butteris.] A steel instrument for paring the hoofs of horses.

but-ter-less (but′ėr-les), *a.* Without butter.

but-ter-milk (but′ėr-milk), *n.* [= D. *botermelk* = G. *buttermilch*.] The more or less acidulous liquid remaining after the butter has been separated from milk.

but-ter-nut (but′ėr-nut), *n.* The edible oily nut of an American tree, *Juglans cinerea*, of the walnut family; also, the tree itself; also, the souari-nut; also, the brown color of homespun uniforms worn by Confederate soldiers in the American Civil War.

but-ter=scotch (but′ėr-skoch), *n.* A kind of taffy made with butter.

but-ter-weed (but′ėr-wēd), *n.* The horseweed, *Leptilon canadense*; also, a ragwort, *Senecio lobatus*.

but-ter-wort (but′ėr-wėrt), *n.* Any plant of the genus *Pinguicula*, comprising small herbs whose leaves secrete a viscid substance in which small insects are caught.

Butterwort (*Pinguicula vulgaris*).

but-ter-y[1] (but′ėr-i), *a.* Of the nature of, resembling, or containing butter; smeared with butter; also, given to gross flattery (colloq.); also, butter-fingered (colloq.).

but-ter-y[2] (but′ėr-i), *n.*; pl. *-ies* (-iz). [OF. *boterie* (cf. *boutier*, butler), < *bote*, *botte*, cask: see *butt*[3].] A room or apartment in which the wines, liquors, and provisions of a household are kept; a pantry; in some English colleges, a place where liquors, fruit, etc., are kept for disposal to students.

butt=joint (but′joint), *n.* A joint formed by two pieces of wood or metal united end to end so that they come exactly against each other, without overlapping.

but-tock (but′ọk), *n.* [Appar. < *butt*[2].] Either of the two protuberances which form the rump; *pl.*, the rump; *sing.* or *pl.*, the convex aftermost portion of a ship's body above the water-line.

but-ton (but′n), *n.* [OF. *butun*, *boton* (F. *bouton*), akin to *buter*, *bouter*, thrust: see *butt*[1].] A small knob or stud attached to another body; a knob, stud, or disk for attaching to a garment, etc., used generally for securing one part to another by passing through a buttonhole or a loop, but often merely for ornament; any of various objects of similar shape, function, etc., as the knob fixed to the point of a foil, or the knob or disk pressed to ring an electric bell; a knob on the cap of a Chinese official, indicating by its material or color his rank; a bud or other protuberant part of a plant; a young or undeveloped mushroom; an elongated piece of wood or metal, turning on a nail or screw fixed through its center, used to fasten a door, window, etc.; in *assaying*, etc., a globule or mass of metal lying at the bottom of a crucible or cupel after fusion.—**but′ton,** *v.* **I.** *tr.* To furnish or adorn with a button or buttons; also, to fasten or close with a button or buttons; in *fencing*, to touch with the button of the foil. **II.** *intr.* To be capable of being buttoned; also, of cauliflowers, etc., to come to a head prematurely.—**but′ton-ball,** *n.* The buttonwood or plane-tree.—**but′ton=bush,** *n.* A North American rubiaceous shrub, *Cephalanthus occidentalis*, with globular flower-heads.—**but′toned,** *a.* Furnished, adorned, or fastened with buttons: as, brass-*buttoned* uniforms.—**but′ton-er,** *n.*—**but′ton-hole,** *n.* The hole or slit through which a button is passed: commonly worked over the edge with a stitch ('buttonhole stitch') in which the individual stitches are laid side by side, each being linked at the edge with the one before it.—**but′ton-hole,** *v. t.*; *-holed*, *-holing*. To sew with the buttonhole stitch; also, to seize by the buttonhole, button, etc., and detain in conversation.—**but′ton-hol″er** (-hō″lėr), *n.*—**but′ton=hook,** *n.* A small hook for pulling the buttons of shoes, gloves, etc., through the buttonholes.—**but′ton-less,** *a.* Without buttons.—**but′ton=mold,** *n.* A shaped piece of wood or other material for covering with cloth, crochet-work, etc., to form a button.—**but′tons,** *n.* A page: in allusion to the buttons on his uniform. [Colloq.]—**but′ton=tree,** *n.* A tropical combretaceous tree or shrub, *Conocarpus erecta*, with heavy, hard, compact wood and button-like fruits; also, the buttonwood, *Platanus occidentalis*.—**but′ton-wood,** *n.* A tall, massive plane-tree, *Platanus occidentalis*, yielding a useful timber (so called from its small pendulous fruit); also, the button-tree, *Conocarpus erecta*.—**but′ton-y,** *a.* Button-like; also, having many buttons.

but-tress (but′res), *n.* [OF. *bouterez*, pl. of *bouteret*, adj. and n. (applied to arches and pillars), < *bouter*, thrust, abut: see *butt*[1].] A structure built against a wall or building for the purpose of giving it stability; something resembling such a structure in use or appearance; a prop or support.—**flying buttress,** in *arch.*, a structure of masonry, usually in the form of an inclined straight piece supported on a segment of an arch and springing from a solid mass of masonry, which abuts against a part of a structure to be buttressed.—**but′tress,** *v. t.* To support by a buttress; hence, to prop up; also, to conceal by a buttress (as, "Beside the portal doors, *Buttress'd* from moonlight, stands he": Keats's "Eve of St. Agnes," ix.).

Church of St. Denis, at St. Denis, France.
a, *a*, buttresses; *b*, *b*, flying buttresses.

butt=shaft (but′shȧft), *n.* A blunt or barbless arrow.

butt=weld (but′weld), *n.* A weld formed by joining the flattened ends of two pieces of iron at a white heat; a welded butt-joint.

bu-tyl (bū′til), *n.* [From *but*(*yric*) + *-yl*.] In *chem.*, a univalent hydrocarbon radical of the formula C_4H_9.—**bu′ty-lene** (-ti-lēn), *n.* In *chem.*, any of three gaseous isomeric hydrocarbons, of the formula C_4H_8, belonging to the ethylene series.

bu-ty-ra-ceous (bū-ti-rā′shius), *a.* [L. *butyrum*, butter.] Of the nature of, resembling, or containing butter.—**bu′ty-rate** (-rāt), *n.* In *chem.*, a salt or ester of butyric acid.—**bu-tyr-ic** (bụ-tir′ik), *a.* Pertaining to or derived from butter: as, *butyric* acid (either of two isomeric acids, esp. the one, a rancid liquid, present in butter, etc., as an ester and sometimes free).—**bu-ty-rin** (bū′ti-rin), *n.* In *chem.*, a yellowish liquid fat present in butter, and formed from glycerin and butyric acid.—**bu-ty-rom′e-ter** (-rom′e-tėr), *n.* [See *-meter*.] An apparatus for ascertaining the amount of fatty matter in milk.

bux-a-ceous (buk-sā′shius), *a.* [L. *buxus*, box: see *box*[1].] Belonging to the *Buxaceæ*, or box family of plants.

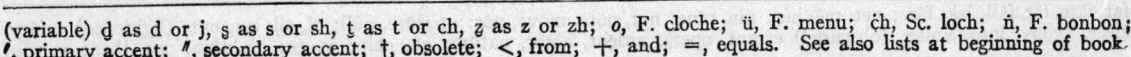

bux-om (buk′sọm), *a.* [ME. *buxum*, *buhsum*, < AS. *būgan*, bend, bow, + *-sum*, E. *-some*[1].] Obedient, tractable, or submissive (archaic); flexible† or pliant†; yielding to pressure†; also, blithe, lively, or gay (archaic); healthy and cheerful; plump and comely.—**bux'om-ly,** *adv.*—**bux'om-ness,** *n.*

buy (bī), *v.*; *bought, buying.* [AS. *bycgan* = OS. *buggean* = Goth. *bugjan.*] **I.** *tr.* To acquire the possession of, or the right to, by paying an equivalent, esp. in money; purchase; hence, to acquire or procure by any kind of equivalent, as by a sacrifice; also, to pay the penalty of†; also, to redeem or ransom (now only fig. in theological use); also, to win over by money or other consideration; hire or bribe; also, of things, to be sufficient to purchase or procure; serve as an equivalent in procuring. **II.** *intr.* To make a purchase or purchases.—**buy,** *n.* A buying; also, something bought or to be bought; a purchase; a bargain. [Colloq.] —**buy'a-ble,** *a.* That may be bought.—**buy'er,** *n.* One who buys; a purchaser; one employed, as in a mercantile house, to make purchases of goods.

buzz[1] (buz), *v.* [Imit.] **I.** *intr.* To make a continuous humming sound such as that of bees; fly or hover with or as with such a sound; fig., to move about busily; also, to speak in a low humming tone; make an indistinct murmuring sound, as a number of people talking together; be filled with such a sound, as a place; be uttered with a murmur, as words. **II.** *tr.* To utter or express by buzzing; tell in a murmur or whisper; spread with busy talk; also, to cause to buzz.—**buzz**[1], *n.* A continuous humming sound such as that of bees; also, a confused humming sound, as of a number of people busily engaged in conversation; the sound of bustling activity; hence, a state of activity or excitement; also, a report or rumor.

buzz[2] (buz), *v. t.* [Cf. *booze, bouse*[1].] To finish to the last drop the contents of (a bottle, etc.). [Eng.]

buz-zard[1] (buz'ạrd), *n.* [OF. *busart* (F. *busard*), < *buse*, buzzard, < L. *buteo*, kind of hawk.] Any of various more or less heavily built diurnal birds of prey of the hawk family, of the genus *Buteo* and allied genera, as *B. vulgaris*, a rather sluggish European species; also, any of various other birds of prey, as the turkey-buzzard.

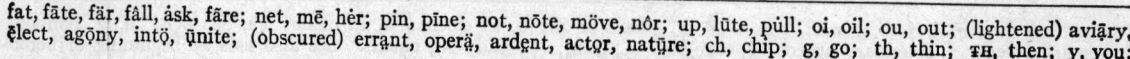

Rough-legged Buzzard (*Archibuteo lagopus*).

buz-zard[2] (buz'ạrd), *n.* Any buzzing insect, as a cockchafer; a moth; a butterfly. [Prov. Eng.]

buzz-er (buz'ėr), *n.* One who or that which buzzes; a device, esp. an electrical one, for making a buzzing noise as a signal; also, a talebearer†.

buzz=saw (buz'sâ), *n.* A circular saw.

buzz=wig (buz'wig), *n.* [Origin uncertain.] A large, bushy wig; a person wearing such a wig; a person of consequence.

by (bī). [AS. *bī, be,* = G. *bei*, by, near; perhaps akin to L. *ambi-*, Gr. ἀμφί, about, Skt. *abhi*, to.] **I.** *prep.* Beside or near; along beside, over, or through; toward (in naming points of the compass: as, east *by* south); before (in adjuration); through the act of; through the means, use, or efficacy of; combined with in multiplication or relative dimensions (as, five *by* four feet); in the measure of (as, eggs *by* the dozen); to the extent of (as, larger *by* half); according to (as, to work *by* rule); in relation to (now chiefly with *deal, do,* etc.); separately with (as, two *by* two); of time, during (as, *by* day; *by* night); not later than (as, *by* six o'clock). **II.** *adv.* Near, or at hand (as, near *by*); past, in place or time (as, days gone *by*); aside or away (as, to put or lay a thing *by*).—**by and by,** one by one†; in succession†; also, straightway† or at once†; also, before long; after a while.—**by and large,** *naut.*, to the wind and off it; fig., in every way or aspect (as, to take a matter *by and large*). —**by, bye. I.** *a.* Situated to one side or in an out-of-the-way place; hence, being aside from the main point, subject, course, procedure, etc.; secondary; incidental; private or secret. **II.** *n.* (In sporting use commonly spelled *bye.*) That which is aside from the main course or consideration; also, the condition of being odd instead of paired; in *golf*, the holes of a tipulated course remaining to be played after the match is finished; in *cricket*, a run made on a ball not struck by the batsman and missed by the wicket-keeper.—**by the by,** by the side (rather than the main) way or course†; also, aside from the main point, subject, etc.; incidentally speaking.

by=bid-der (bī'bid''ėr), *n.* A person employed at an auction to bid in order to raise the prices.

by=blow (bī'blō), *n.* A side blow; an indirect, incidental, or accidental blow; also, an illegitimate child.

by=by, bye=bye (bī'bī'), *interj.* A childish or colloquial form for *good-by*: as, "Well, you are going to be in a passion, I see, and I shall only interrupt you—so, *bye-bye*" (Sheridan's "School for Scandal," iii. 1).

bye (bī), *a.* and *n.* See *by.*

by=e-lec-tion (bī'ẹ-lek''shọn), *n.* A special election, not held at the time of a general election, as one to fill a vacancy in the British Parliament.

by=end (bī'end), *n.* A secondary or incidental aim or object; esp., a private end, or secret purpose or design.

by-gone (bī'gôn). **I.** *a.* Past; former; departed; out of date. **II.** *n.* That which is past; *pl.*, past occurrences, offenses, etc.; *sing.*, past time; the past.

by=law (bī'lâ), *n.* A law made by a municipality or by a rural community for the regulation of affairs within its authority; also, a standing rule, as of a corporation or society, made for the regulation of its internal organization and conduct; also, a secondary or accessory law.

by=name (bī'nām), *n.* A secondary name or appellation; a cognomen or surname; a nickname.

by=pass (bī'pȧs), *n.* A secondary pipe or other channel connected with a main passage as for conducting a fluid around an obstruction; in *elect.*, a shunt.

by-past (bī'pȧst), *a.* Bygone; past: as, "*by-past* perils" (Shakspere's "Lover's Complaint," 158).

by=path (bī'pȧth), *n.* A side path; a byway.

by=place (bī'plās), *n.* An out-of-the-way or retired place, spot, or situation.

by=play (bī'plā), *n.* Action carried on aside while the main action proceeds, esp. on the stage; something apart from the main purpose; a diversion.

by=prod-uct (bī'prod''ukt), *n.* A secondary or incidental product, as in a process of manufacture.

byre (bīr), *n.* [AS. *bӯre*, akin to *būr*, E. *bower*[5].] A cow-house: as, "From *byre* or field the kine were brought" (Wordsworth's "Prelude," viii. 21).

byr-la-dy (bīr-lā'di), *interj.* Contraction of *by our Lady*, used as an oath or expletive. [Archaic or prov. Eng.]

byr-nie (bėr'ni), *n.* [Var. of ME. *brynie*, < Icel. *brynja.*] A coat of mail; a hauberk.

by=road (bī'rōd), *n.* A side road; a road other than the main or usual road.

By-ron-ic (bī-ron'ik), *a.* Of or pertaining to Lord Byron (1788–1824), the English poet; possessing the characteristics of Byron or his poetry.—**By-ron'i-cal-ly,** *adv.*—**By-ron-ism** (bī'rọn-izm), *n.* The characteristics of Byron or his poetry; imitation of Byron.

bys-sa-ceous (bi-sā'shius), *a.* [L. *byssus*: see *byssus.*] In *bot.*, consisting of fine threads or filaments.

bys-sal (bis'ạl), *a.* In *zoöl.*, of or pertaining to the byssus of a mollusk.

bys-sif-er-ous (bi-sif'ẹ-rus), *a.* [See *-ferous.*] In *zoöl.*, having a byssus.

bys-sine (bis'in), *a.* [L. *byssinus.*] Of or like byssus or fine linen.

bys-sus (bis'us), *n.*; pl. *byssi* (-ī). [L., < Gr. βύσσος.] Among the ancients, orig., a fine yellowish flax, or the linen made from it, as the Egyptian mummy-cloth; later, also, cotton or silk; in *zoöl.*, a collection of silky filaments (secreted by a gland of the foot) by which certain mollusks attach themselves to rocks.

Mollusk (*Pinna flabellum*), with Byssus (*a*).

by-stand-er (bī'stan''dėr), *n.* One who stands by or near; one who is present without taking part; a chance spectator.

by=street (bī'strēt), *n.* A side street; a street other than a main thoroughfare.

by=talk (bī'tâk), *n.* Talk aside; incidental talk; small talk; gossip.

by-way (bī'wā), *n.* A way other than the highway; a by-road; an unfrequented, secluded, or obscure way.

by-word (bī′wėrd), *n.* [AS. *bīword.*] A proverb or proverbial saying; also, a person or thing that becomes proverbial as a type; esp., an object of derision or contempt; also, a nickname, esp. one of scorn.

by=work (bī′wėrk), *n.* Work done in addition to one's regular work, as in intervals of leisure.

By-zan-tian (bi-zan′shiạn). **I.** *a.* Pertaining to Byzantium; Byzantine. **II.** *n.* A Byzantine.

Byz-an-tine (biz′ạn-tin or bi-zan′tin, or -tīn). **I.** *a.* Of or pertaining to Byzantium, an ancient city, afterward Constantinople, which became the capital of the Eastern Empire (see under *eastern, a.*); noting or pertaining to the Eastern Empire after the fall of the Western Empire in A.D. 476; in *arch.*, noting or pertaining to a style developed from the classical under the Eastern or Byzantine Empire, characterized by the round arch, the cross, the circle, the dome supported on pendentives, and rich mosaic decoration. **II.** *n.* A native or inhabitant of Byzantium or Constantinople, esp. as the capital of the Byzantine Empire. — **Byz-an-tin-esque** (biz″ạn-tin-esk′ or bi-zan-), *a.* In the Byzantine style. — **Byz-an-tin-ism** (biz′ạn-tin-izm or bi-zan′-), *n.* The spirit, principles, and methods of the Byzantines, esp. with reference to literature and art; the manifestation of Byzantine characteristics, as in painting or sculpture.

Byzantine Architecture. — Church of St. Theodore, Athens.

C

C, c (sē); pl. *C's, c's* (sēz). A consonant, the 3d letter of the English alphabet.

ca' (kâ), *v.* Sc. form of *call* (esp. in the sense 'to drive'). — **to ca' canny,** to drive carefully; fig., to go cautiously; proceed in a leisurely manner. The phrase *ca' canny* is often used substantively to mean 'cautious procedure' or 'leisurely action,' and specif. 'deliberate restriction of production on the part of workers.' [Sc.]

Caa-ba (kä′bạ or kä′ạ-bạ), *n.* See *Kaaba.*

caa-ing=whale (kâ′ing-hwāl), *n.* [Sc. *caa, ca'*, for *call, v.*, drive (because the animals may be driven like cattle).] Any of various dolphin-like cetaceans of the genus *Globicephalus*, esp. *G. melas*, of the northern Atlantic, which is gregarious in habit and sometimes reaches a length of 20 feet; a black-whale.

cab[1] (kab), *n.* [Short for *cabriolet.*] Any of various one-horse vehicles for public hire, as one (the hansom) with two wheels and a seat for the driver behind, or one with four wheels and a seat for the driver in front; any of certain motor vehicles for public hire; also, the hooded part of a locomotive.

cab[2] (kab), *n.* [Heb. *qab.*] A Hebrew measure of capacity, equal to about two quarts.

ca-bal (kạ-bal′), *n.* [F. *cabale,* < ML. *cabbala*: see *cabala.*] Secret artifices of a few persons united in some design; a conjoint intrigue; also, a secret meeting, as of intriguers (archaic); also, a body of persons united in some close design or intrigue; a junto. — **ca-bal′,** *v. i.*; *-balled, -balling.* To form a cabal; intrigue.

cab-a-la (kab′ạ-lạ), *n.* [ML. *cabbala,* < Heb. *qabbālāh,* received or traditional doctrine.] Among Jewish rabbis and certain medieval Christians, a system of esoteric theosophy, based on a mystical interpretation of the Scriptures, at first handed down by oral tradition; hence, any occult or secret doctrine or science. — **cab′a-lism,** *n.* The system of the Jewish cabala; occult or mystic doctrine. — **cab′a-list,** *n.* One versed in the cabala or other secret doctrine; a mystic. — **cab-a-lis′tic, cab-a-lis′ti-cal,** *a.* Pertaining to the cabalists; mystic; occult. — **cab-a-lis′ti-cal-ly,** *adv.*

ca-bal-ler (kạ-bal′ėr), *n.* One who cabals.

ca-bal-le-ro (kä-bäl-yā′rō), *n.*; pl. *-ros* (Sp. -rōs). [Sp., = E. *cavalier.*] A horseman; a knight or gentleman.

cab-al-line (kab′ạ-lin), *a.* [L. *caballinus,* < *caballus,* horse.] Of or pertaining to a horse or horses: as, the *caballine* spring (the spring Hippocrene, produced by a stroke of the hoof of Pegasus).

ca-bane (kȧ-bȧn), *n.* [F., lit. 'cabin': see *cabin.*] In *aëronautics,* a mast-like structure on the top of an aëroplane, to which overhead bracing wires are attached.

cab-a-ret (kab′ạ-ret, F. kȧ-bȧ-rā), *n.* [F.; origin unknown.] A tavern, as in France; also, a restaurant providing musical or other entertainment; also, the entertainment; also, a small table, stand, or tray with a set of vessels forming a service for tea, coffee, or the like.

cab-as (kab′ạ, F. kȧ-bä), *n.* [F., basket, bag; from Provençal.] A bag of plaited straw or the like, or of silk, leather, or other material, carried by women to hold small purchases, articles for work, etc.

cab-bage[1] (kab′ạj), *v. t.* or *i.*; *-baged, -baging.* [Cf. F. *cabasser,* put into a basket, purloin, < *cabas*: see *cabas.*] To purloin or steal; esp., of a tailor, to appropriate (part of a customer's cloth) when making garments. — **cab′bage**[1], *n.* Something purloined, as cloth by a tailor when making garments.

cab-bage[2] (kab′ạj), *n.* [OF. *caboce* (F. *caboche*), head, < L. *caput,* head.] Any of various cultivated varieties of the cruciferous plant *Brassica oleracea,* esp. one of the ordinary varieties with short stem and leaves formed into a compact, edible head, but in a wider sense including also such plants as the cauliflower, Brussels sprouts, kale, etc.; the head of the ordinary cabbage; any of various similar plants; also, the terminal bud of certain palms. — **cabbages and kings,** miscellaneous subjects, as of conversation or discussion: in allusion to the lines, " 'The time has come,' the Walrus said, 'To talk of many things: Of shoes — and ships — and sealing-wax — Of cabbages — and kings,' " in "Through the Looking-Glass," iv., by C. L. Dodgson ("Lewis Carroll"). — **cab′bage**[2], *v. i.*; *-baged, -baging.* To form a head like a cabbage. — **cab′bage=rose,** *n.* A rose, *Rosa centifolia,* with a large, round, compact flower. — **cab′bage=tree,** *n.* Any of several palm-trees with large terminal leaf-buds which are eaten like cabbage, as *Livistona australis* or *L. inermis* of Australasia, *Inodes palmetto* of the southern U. S., or *Oreodoxa oleracea* of the West Indies; also, any of certain other trees and plants, as the Australasian loranthaceous tree *Nuytsia floribunda* or the tropical American fabaceous tree *Vouacapoua americana.*

cab-ba-la (kab′ạ-lạ), etc. See *cabala,* etc.

cab-by (kab′i), *n.*; pl. *cabbies* (-iz). A cabman. [Colloq.]

ca-ber (kā′bėr), *n.* [Gael. *cabar.*] A pole or beam, esp. one used for tossing as a trial of strength in the Highland exercise or game called 'tossing the caber.' [Sc.]

cab-in (kab′in), *n.* [OF. F. *cabane,* < ML. *capanna*; origin uncertain.] A temporary shelter, as a soldier's tent†; a small, rude house; a hut; a cell, as of an anchorite†; any small room or inclosed space†; an apartment or room in a boat or ship, as for officers or passengers; in a man-of-war, the apartment used by the commanding officer or the officer commanding the squadron; in a passenger-ship, a section comprising state-rooms, saloon, etc., allotted to the use of the higher class passengers (cf. *steerage*); one of two or more such sections, distinguished as 'first cabin,' 'second cabin,' etc., according to the grade of accommodations. — **cab′in,** *v.* **I.** *tr.* To confine as in a cabin. See Shakspere's "Macbeth," iii. 4. 24. **II.** *intr.* To live in a cabin. — **cab′in=boy,** *n.* A boy employed to wait on the officers and passengers in the cabin of a ship.

cab-i-net (kab′i-net). [Appar. dim. of *cabin*, with some senses from F. *cabinet*, < It. *cabinetto, gabinetto*, < ML. *capanna*: cf. *cabin*.] **I.** *n.* A little cabin†; a small room (archaic); a private room, esp. one in which a sovereign confers with his ministers, etc.; the council of a sovereign or executive; the body of ministers who direct the government of a nation or country; a case with compartments for holding various objects; a piece of furniture with shelves or drawers, commonly closed in, often with glass, as for holding or displaying objects of interest. **II.** *a.* Of or pertaining to a cabinet or private room; private; also, pertaining to a political cabinet; also, of such value, beauty, or size as to be fitted for a private chamber, or for keeping in a cabinet or case (as, a *cabinet* organ, a small, portable reed-organ; a *cabinet* photograph, one about 4½ by 6½ inches in size).—**cab′i-net=mak″er,** *n.* One who makes fine furniture, etc.—**cab′i-net=mak″ing,** *n.*—**cab′i-net=wood,** *n.* Wood suitable for cabinet-work.—**cab′i-net=work,** *n.* Cabinet-makers' work; the making of fine furniture, etc., or the product made.

ca-ble (kā′bl), *n.* [OF. *cable* (F. *câble*), < ML. *capulum*, halter, < L. *capere*, take.] A thick, strong rope of hemp, jute, or other fiber, esp. one 10 inches or more in circumference; a thick wire rope; the rope or chain used to hold a vessel at anchor; an insulated bundle of wires used as an electrical conductor, as in submarine telegraphy; an electrical conductor composed of a number of separately insulated wires, as for supplying different circuits; also, a cablegram.—**ca′ble,** *v.*; *-bled, -bling.* **I.** *tr.* To furnish with a cable or cables; fasten with or as with a cable; also, to transmit or communicate by submarine telegraph-cable. **II.** *intr.* To send a message by submarine telegraph-cable.—**ca′ble=car,** *n.* A car used on a cable-railroad.—**ca′ble-gram,** *n.* [See *-gram*.] A message sent by a submarine telegraph-cable.—**ca′ble=laid,** *a.* Of a rope, made by laying three plain-laid ropes together with a left-handed twist.—**ca′ble=rail′road,** *n.* A railroad on which the cars are moved by gripping an endless cable traveling under the roadway. Also **ca′ble=road′.**—**ca′ble's=length,** *n.* A nautical unit of length, approximately equivalent to either 100 or 120 fathoms.—**ca′blet,** *n.* A small cable, esp. a cable-laid rope less than 10 inches in circumference.—**ca′ble-way,** *n.* A conveying apparatus in which a wire cable supports or conveys the moving load.

Cable-laid Rope.

cab-man (kab′mạn), *n.*; pl. *-men.* A cab-driver.

ca-bob (kạ-bob′), *n.* [Ar. *kabāb*.] An Oriental dish consisting of small pieces of meat seasoned and roasted on a skewer: now only in *pl.*

ca-boched′, *a.* See *caboshed*.

ca-bo-chon (kȧ-bo-shôn), *n.* [F., < *caboche*, head: see *cabbage*².] A precious stone of convex rounded form, which has been polished but not cut into facets.

ca-boo-dle (kạ-bö′dl), *n.* [Cf. *boodle*.] The (whole) lot, pack, or crowd. [Slang, U. S.]

ca-boose (kạ-bös′), *n.* [D. *kabuis, kombuis*; perhaps akin to E. *cabin*.] A cook-room on the deck of a merchant ship; also, a car used by brakemen, workmen, etc., on a freight-train or construction-train (U. S.).

ca-boshed, ca-boched (kạ-bosht′), *a.* [F. *caboche*, head: see *cabbage*².] In *her.*, of the head of an animal, borne full-faced and with no part of the neck showing.

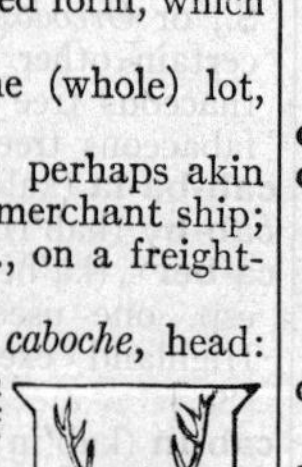
Stag's Head Caboshed.

cab-o-tage (kab′ọ-tạj), *n.* [F., < *caboter*, sail along the coast.] Coastwise navigation.

ca-bril-la (kä-brēl′yä or kạ-bril′ä), *n.* [Sp., dim. of *cabra*, goat.] Any of various serranoid food-fishes, as the grouper, *Epinephelus maculosus*, of the West Indies, etc., or the rock-bass, *Paralabrax clathratus*, of the coast of California.

cab-ri-ole (kab′ri-ōl), *n.* [F.: see *capriole*.] A caper† or leap†; also, a gracefully curving form of leg, often terminating in an animal's paw or some other ornamental finish, used for chairs and other articles of furniture, and seen esp. in the work of Chippendale and later makers.

cab-ri-o-let (kab″ri-ọ-lā′), *n.* [F., < *cabriole*, a leap, = E. *capriole*.] Orig., a light, hooded one-horse carriage with two wheels and a single seat; now, any of various one-seated or two-seated, two-wheeled or four-wheeled vehicles; a cab; also, a type of automobile somewhat like a coupé, having a folding top.

ca-ca-o (kạ-kā′ō or -kä′ō), *n.* [Sp.; from Mexican.] A small evergreen sterculiaceous tree, *Theobroma cacao*, a native of tropical America, cultivated for its seeds, which are used in making cocoa, chocolate, etc.; also, the seeds of this tree.—**ca-ca′o=but′ter,** *n.* A fatty substance expressed from the seeds of the cacao, used in making soaps, cosmetics, etc.

Fruiting Branch of Cacao.

cach-a-lot (kash′ạ-lot), *n.* [F.; origin uncertain.] The sperm-whale.

cache (kash), *n.* [F., < *cacher*, hide, ult. < L. *cogere*, collect: see *cogent*.] A hiding-place, esp. one in the ground or under a cairn for hiding a store of provisions, etc.; also, the store of provisions, etc., so hidden.—**cache,** *v. t.*; *cached, caching.* To put in a cache; conceal.

ca-chec-tic (ka-kek′tik), *a.* Pertaining to or characterized by cachexia.

cache=pot (kash′pot, F. kȧsh-pō), *n.* [F., 'hide-pot.'] An ornamental receptacle for a flower-pot.

ca-chet (kȧ-shā), *n.* [F., < *cacher*, hide: see *cache*.] A seal, as on a letter (see *lettre de cachet*); hence, a distinguishing mark or character; also, in *phar.*, a hollow wafer for inclosing an ill-tasting medicine.

ca-chex-i-a (ka-kek′si-ạ), *n.* [NL., < Gr. καχεξία, < κακός, bad, + ἕξις, habit, < ἔχειν, have.] General bodily ill health and malnutrition, due to chronic disease, as malaria, cancer, etc. Also **ca-chex′y.**

cach-in-nate (kak′i-nāt), *v. i.*; *-nated, -nating.* [L. *cachinnatus*, pp. of *cachinnare*; imit.] To laugh loudly or immoderately.—**cach-in-na′tion** (-nā′shọn), *n.* Loud or immoderate laughter.—**cach′in-na-to-ry** (-nạ-tọ-ri), *a.*

cach-o-long (kash′ọ-long), *n.* [Kalmuck.] A variety of opal, usually of a milky white color.

ca-chot (kȧ-shō), *n.* [F., < *cache*: see *cache*.] A dungeon cell, usually subterranean.

ca-chou (ka-shö′), *n.* [F., < Malay *kāchu*, catechu.] Catechu; also, a pill or pastille for sweetening the breath.

ca-chu-cha (kạ-chö′chạ), *n.* [Sp.] A lively Spanish dance; also, the music for it.

ca-cique (kạ-sēk′), *n.* [Sp.; from Haitian.] A native chief in the West Indies, Mexico, etc.

cack-le (kak′l), *v.*; *-led, -ling.* [ME. *kakelen* = D. *kakelen* = G. *kakeln*; imit.] **I.** *intr.* To utter a shrill, broken sound or cry, as a hen after laying an egg or a goose when excited or alarmed; also, to laugh brokenly; giggle; chuckle; also, to prate or chatter. **II.** *tr.* To utter with or express by cackling.—**cack′le,** *n.* The act or sound of cackling; idle talk; silly prattle.—**cack′ler,** *n.*

caco-, cac-. Forms of Gr. κακός, bad, used in combination.

cac-o-de-mon, cac-o-dæ-mon (kak-ọ-dē′mọn), *n.* [Gr. κακοδαίμων, < κακός, bad, + δαίμων, spirit.] An evil spirit; a devil: as, "Hie thee to hell for shame, and leave the world, Thou *cacodemon!*" (Shakspere's "Richard III.," i. 3. 144). Cf. *agathodemon*.

cac-o-dor-ous (kak-ō′dọr-us), *a.* [See *caco-*.] Having a bad odor; malodorous.

cac-o-dyl (kak′ọ-dil), *n.* [Gr. κακώδης, ill-smelling, < κακός, bad, + ὄζειν, smell: see *-yl*.] In *chem.*, an arsenical radical, $As(CH_3)_2$; also, a poisonous, ill-smelling liquid, $As_2(CH_3)_4$, which takes fire on exposure to air.—**cac-o-dyl′-ic,** *a.*

cac-o-ë-py (kak′ọ-e-pi or ka-kō′ẹ-pi), *n.* [Gr. κακοέπεια, faulty language, < κακός, bad, + ἔπος, word.] Bad pronunciation: opposed to *orthoëpy*.

cac-o-ë-thes (kak-ọ-ē′thēz), *n.* [L., < Gr. κακόηθες, < κακός, bad, + ἦθος, habit.] A bad habit; a morbid propensity, or mania, as for talking (L. *cacoëthes loquendi*) or for writing (L. *cacoëthes scribendi*).

cac-o-gen-ic (kak-ọ-jen′ik), *a.* [See *caco-*.] Same as *dysgenic*.

ca-cog-ra-phy (ka-kog′rạ-fi), *n.* [See *caco-* and *-graphy.*] Bad handwriting (opposed to *calligraphy*); also, bad spelling (opposed to *orthography*).—**ca-cog′ra-pher,** *n.*—**cac-o-graph-ic, cac-o-graph-i-cal** (kak-ǭ-graf′ik, -i-kạl), *a.*

ca-col-o-gy (ka-kol′ǭ-ji), *n.* [See *caco-* and *-logy.*] Bad choice of words; faulty diction; also, bad pronunciation.

cac-o-mix-l, cac-o-mis-tle (kak′ǭ-mik-sl, -mis-l), *n.* [Mex.] A carnivorous animal, *Bassariscus astutus,* of Mexico and the southwestern U. S., resembling the racoon but slenderer and with a sharper snout and longer tail.

Cacomixl.

ca-coph-o-nist (ka-kof′ǭ-nist), *n.* [From *cacophony.*] A composer or a lover of music marked by dissonances.

ca-coph-o-nous (ka-kof′ǭ-nus), *a.* [Gr. κακόφωνος, < κακός, bad, + φωνή, sound.] Ill-sounding; harsh-sounding; discordant.—**ca-coph′o-nous-ly,** *adv.*—**ca-coph′o-ny,** *n.*; pl. *-nies* (-niz). [Gr. κακοφωνία, < κακόφωνος.] The quality of being cacophonous; harsh sound; an arrangement of words which produces an inharmonious combination of sounds; dissonance; a discord.

cac-ta-ceous (kak-tā′shius), *a.* Belonging to the *Cactaceæ,* or cactus family of plants.

cac-toid (kak′toid), *a.* Resembling the cactus.

cac-tus (kak′tus), *n.*; pl. *-tuses,* L. *-ti* (-tī). [L., < Gr. κάκτος, kind of prickly plant.] Any of various fleshy-stemmed plants of the family *Cactaceæ,* usually leafless and spiny, and often producing showy flowers, chiefly natives of the hot and dry regions of America.

Flower of the Giant Cactus (*Cereus giganteus*).

ca-cu-mi-nal (ka-kū′mi-nạl), *a.* [L. *cacumen* (*cacumin-*), top.] Pertaining to the top or apex, as of a plant or a bodily organ; in *phonetics,* same as *cerebral.*

cad (kad), *n.* [Prob. short for *caddie.*] A messenger or assistant (Eng.); the conductor of an omnibus†; a hanger-on about a college, ready to do services for the students (Eng.); a vulgar, ill-bred fellow; one who falls short of his pretensions to good breeding.

ca-das-ter, ca-das-tre (kạ-das′tėr), *n.* [F. *cadastre,* prob. ult. < L. *caput,* head.] A register of the real property of a region, with the extent, value, and ownership of each holding or lot, serving as a basis of taxation.—**ca-das′tral,** *a.*—**cad-as-tra-tion** (kad-ạs-trā′shọn), *n.* The making of a cadaster.

ca-dav-er (kạ-dav′ėr or -dā′vėr), *n.* [L., < *cadere,* fall.] A dead body, esp. of a human being; a corpse.—**ca-dav′er-ic,** *a.* Of or pertaining to a dead body.—**ca-dav′er-ous,** *a.* Corpse-like; wan; ghastly.—**ca-dav′er-ous-ly,** *adv.*—**ca-dav′er-ous-ness,** *n.*

cad-dice[1], **cad-dice**[2] (kad′is), etc. See *caddis*[1], *caddis*[2], etc.

cad-die (kad′i), *n.* [F. *cadet:* see *cadet.*] A cadet (Sc.); a lad (Sc.); an errand-boy or messenger (Sc.); a golf-player's attendant, employed to carry the clubs during the game.—**cad′die=bag,** *n.* A bag for golf-clubs, etc.

cad-dis[1] (kad′is), *n.* [OF. *cadas;* origin unknown.] Wool, cotton-wool, or any similar fibrous matter; lint; woolen yarn; woolen braid. [Obs. or prov.]

cad-dis[2] (kad′is), *n.* [Origin uncertain.] The larva of the caddis-fly: used as bait in fishing.—**cad′dis=fly,** *n.* Any of various insects with four membranous, more or less hairy wings, considered as belonging to the neuropters or as constituting a separate order, the trichopterous insects: a term usually applied to the adult insect in contradistinction to the caddis-worm.

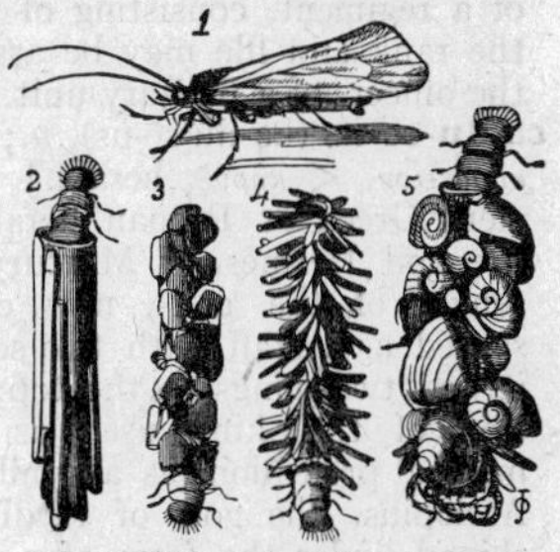

Caddis-fly and Worms.
1. Caddis-fly. 2. Larva in case formed of straw or dry grass-stalks. 3. In case formed of small stones. 4. In case formed of grass-roots. 5. In case formed of shells.

cad-dish (kad′ish), *a.* Like a cad; ill-bred; ungentlemanly.—**cad′dish-ly,** *adv.*—**cad′dish-ness,** *n.*

cad-dis=worm (kad′is-wėrm), *n.* Same as *caddis*[2].

cad-dy[1] (kad′i), *n.*; pl. *caddies* (-iz). See *caddie.*

cad-dy[2] (kad′i), *n.*; pl. *caddies* (-iz). [= *catty*[2].] A small box, can, or chest, esp. one for holding tea.

cade[1] (kād), *n.* [F., < L. *cadus,* < Gr. κάδος, jar.] A barrel, cask, or keg; also, a former measure for herrings or sprats, containing 500 (or 720) of the former or 1,000 of the latter.

cade[2] (kād), *n.* [F.; from Provençal.] A species of juniper, *Juniperus oxycedrus,* of the Mediterranean region, whose wood on destructive distillation yields an empyreumatic oily liquid ('oil of cade') used in the treatment of skin affections.

cade[3] (kād), *n.* [Origin unknown.] A pet lamb. Also **cade′=lamb.**

ca-dence (kā′dẹns), *n.* [ML. *cadentia,* < L. *cadens,* ppr. of *cadere,* fall.] A falling† or sinking†; also, a fall of the voice, as in speaking; the general modulation of the voice; also, rhythmic flow, as of verses or periods; rhythm; the beat of any rhythmical movement; *milit.,* rate of stepping in marching (as, a *cadence* of 120 steps per minute); in *music,* a sequence of chords expressing conclusion, finality, or repose, occurring at the end of a phrase, etc.; the concluding part of a melody or harmony; also, a cadenza.—**ca′dence,** *v. t.*; *-denced, -dencing.* To render in cadence.—**ca′den-cy,** *n.* Cadence; also, the descent of a younger branch from the main line of a family; the state of a cadet or younger son.—**ca′dent,** *a.* [L. *cadens* (*cadent-*), ppr.] Falling (archaic); also, having cadence.—**ca-den-tial** (kạ-den′shạl), *a.* Of or pertaining to cadence.

ca-den-za (kạ-den′tsä), *n.* [It., < ML. *cadentia,* E. *cadence.*] In *music,* an elaborate flourish or showy passage introduced near the end of an aria or concerto or as a connective between divisions of a movement.

ca-det (kạ-det′), *n.* [F. *cadet,* ult. < L. *caput,* head.] A younger son or brother; the youngest son; a gentleman, usually a younger son, who entered the army to prepare for a subsequent commission; a junior or a younger assistant in some service or profession; a student in a military or naval school; also, a young man who secures women for purposes of prostitution, or who prostitutes a woman and lives on what she earns as a prostitute.—**ca-det′cy** (-si), **ca-det′ship,** *n.*

cadge (kaj), *v. t.* or *i.*; *cadged, cadging.* [Origin uncertain.] To hawk or peddle; also, to beg; sponge. [Colloq. or prov.]—**cadg′er,** *n.*

ca-di (kä′di), *n.* [Ar. *qādī,* judge: cf. *alcalde.*] A judge in a Moslem community, whose decisions are based on Mohammedan canon law.

Cad-me-an (kad-mē′ạn), *a.* Pertaining to Cadmus, the legendary founder of Thebes, to whom the introduction of the Greek alphabet is attributed.—**Cadmean victory,** a victory in which the victor suffers as much as the vanquished.

cad-mi-um (kad′mi-um), *n.* [NL., < L. *cadmia,* < Gr. καδμεία, calamin (with which cadmium is usually associated).] Chem. sym., Cd; at. wt., 112.40; sp. gr., 8.55 to 8.67. A white, ductile metallic element resembling tin in appearance: used in the manufacture of certain alloys.—**cad′mic,** *a.*

cadre (kȧdr), *n.* [F., frame, < L. *quadrum*, a square.] A framework; *milit.*, the permanently organized skeleton of a regiment, consisting of the officers, etc., about which the rank and file may be assembled at short notice; also, the officers of a military unit.

ca-du-ce-us (kạ-dū′sẹ-us), *n.*; pl. *-cei* (-sẹ-ī). [L., = Gr. κηρύκειον, < κῆρυξ, herald.] The staff carried by an ancient Greek or Roman herald; esp., the wand borne by the god Hermes, or Mercury, as herald or messenger of the gods, now conventionally represented as a staff with two serpents twined about it and two wings at the top; also, a representation of this kind used as an emblem of the medical profession (as a symbol of Æsculapius, or Asclepius, the god of medicine, who was worshiped under the form of a serpent, and who is commonly represented with a staff having a single serpent coiled about it).—**ca-du′ce-an,** *a.*

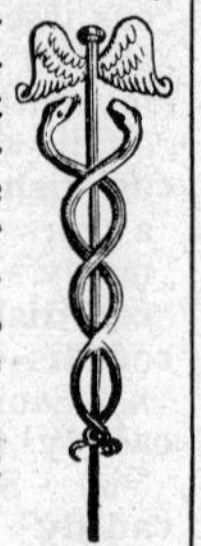

Caduceus.

ca-du-ci-ty (kạ-dū′si-ti), *n.* [See *caducous.*] Tendency to fall; frailty; esp., the infirmity of old age; senility.

ca-du-cous (kạ-dū′kus), *a.* [L. *caducus*, < *cadere*, fall.] Tending to fall; subject to shedding; deciduous; dropping off very early, as leaves; also, fleeting or transitory.

cæ-cal (sē′kạl), *a.* Of, pertaining to, or resembling the cæcum.—**cæ′cal-ly,** *adv.*

cæ-cil-ian (sē-sil′iạn), *n.* [L. *cæcilia*, kind of lizard, < *cæcus*, blind.] Any animal of the order *Gymnophiona*, which comprises blind, or nearly blind, limbless, worm-like amphibians of tropical countries.

cæ-cum (sē′kum), *n.*; pl. *cæca* (-kạ). [L., neut. of *cæcus*, blind.] In *anat.*, a cul-de-sac; esp., the one at the beginning of the human large intestine, bearing the vermiform appendix.

cæ-no-gen-e-sis (sē-nọ-jen′e-sis or sen-ọ-), etc. See *cenogenesis*, etc.

Cæ-no-zo-ic (sē-nọ-zō′ik or sen-ọ-), *a.* and *n.* See *Cenozoic.*

cæs-al-pin-i-a-ceous (ses″al-pin-i-ā′shius), *a.* [NL. *Cæsalpinia*, the typical genus; named from Andrea *Cesalpini* (1519–1603), Italian botanist.] Belonging to the *Cæsalpiniaceæ*, a family of plants including the cassia or senna plants, honey-locust, Judas-tree, bonduc, carob, copaiba trees, logwood, tamarind, etc.

Cæ-sar (sē′zạr), *n.* [L., family surname of Caius Julius *Cæsar*: cf. *czar*, *kaiser.*] A title of the Roman emperors from Augustus to Hadrian, and later of the heir presumptive; in general, an emperor.—**Cæ-sa-re-an, Cæ-sa-ri-an** (sẹ-zā′rẹ-ạn, -ri-ạn), *a.* Pertaining to Cæsar or the Cæsars.—**Cæsarean operation** or **section,** in *surg.*, the operation by which a fetus is taken from the uterus by cutting through the walls of the abdomen and uterus: said to have been performed at the birth of Julius Cæsar.—**Cæ′sar-ism,** *n.* Absolute government; imperialism.—**Cæ′sar-ist,** *n.*

cæ-si-ous (sē′zi-us), *a.* [L. *cæsius.*] Bluish-gray.

cæ-si-um (sē′zi-um), *n.* [NL., neut. of L. *cæsius*, E. *cæsious.*] Chem. sym., Cs; at. wt., 132.81; sp. gr., 1.8. A rare metallic element showing bluish lines in the spectrum.

cæs-pi-tose (ses′pi-tōs), etc. See *cespitose*, etc.

cæ-su-ra, ce-su-ra (sẹ-zū′rạ), *n.*; pl. *-ras*, L. *-ræ* (-rē). [L. *cæsura*, < *cædere*, cut.] In *Greek* and *Latin pros.*, a division made by the ending of a word within a foot (or sometimes at the end of a foot), esp. in certain recognized places near the middle of a verse; in *Eng. pros.*, a break, esp. a sense pause, usually occurring near the middle of a verse; in *music*, a pause or break at the end of a phrase or other rhythmic division.—**cæ-su′ral, ce-su′ral,** *a.*

ca-fard (kȧ-fär), *n.* [F., canting hypocrite, humbug, telltale, sneak, cockroach, cafard; origin obscure.] A condition of extreme morbid depression with indifference to or repugnance for surroundings and duties and a feeling of insurmountable fatigue, esp. among soldiers; also, one suffering from this condition. [Colloq.]

ca-fé (kȧ-fā′), *n.* [F., = E. *coffee.*] Coffee; also, a coffee-house; a restaurant; also, a bar-room.—**café au lait** (kȧ-fā ō lā). [F.] Coffee with milk; also, a deep brownish cream-color.—**café chantant** (shäṅ-täṅ). [F., 'singing café.'] A café in which musical entertainment is provided.—**café noir** (nwor). [F.] Black coffee (without milk or cream).

caf-e-te-ri-a (kaf″ẹ-tẹ-rē′ạ̈, often kaf-ẹ-tē′ri-ạ̈), *n.* [Sp. *cafetería.*] A kind of restaurant in which the patrons wait on themselves, carrying the food, as served out to them, to small tables where it is eaten.

caf-fe-ic (ka-fē′ik), *a.* [NL. *caffea*, *coffea*, coffee.] Of, pertaining to, or derived from coffee: as, *caffeic* acid (a yellowish crystalline organic acid obtained from coffee).—**caf-fe-ine** (kaf′ẹ-in or -ēn), *n.* A bitter crystalline alkaloid obtained from coffee, tea, and other sources: used in medicine as a stimulant, diuretic, etc.—**caf′fe-in-ism,** *n.* The morbid state caused by excessive use of caffeine or of substances containing it.—**caf′fe-ol** (-ol or -ōl), *n.* An aromatic oil developed in coffee by roasting.—**caf-fe-tan-nic** (kaf-e-tan′ik), *a.* Pertaining to coffee and resembling tannin: as, *caffetannic* acid (a tannin-like substance obtained from coffee).

Caf-fre (kaf′ėr), *n.* See *Kafir.*

caf-tan (kaf′tạn), *n.* [Turk. *qaftān.*] A long garment having long sleeves and confined at the waist by a girdle, worn under a coat in Turkey, Egypt, etc.—**caf′taned,** *a.*

cage (kāj), *n.* [OF. F. *cage*, < L. *cavea*, inclosure, < *cavus*, hollow.] A box-like receptacle or inclosure for confining birds or other animals, made with openwork of wires, bars, etc.; also, a prison or place of confinement for malefactors; a lockup; fig., anything that confines or imprisons; also, something suggestive of a cage in structure or purpose; an inclosing, confining, or protecting framework; a baseball catcher's mask; the car or inclosed platform of an elevator.—**cage,** *v. t.*; *caged, caging.* To confine in or as in a cage.—**cage′ling,** *n.* A caged bird.

Ca-got (kȧ-gō), *n.* [F.; origin uncertain.] One of a people, of remote but unknown origin, inhabiting the valleys of the Pyrenees, who were, until the French Revolution, political and social outcasts, but have since been practically absorbed in the general peasantry; hence, an outcast; a pariah.

ca-hier (kȧ-yā), *n.* [F.: see *quire*[2].] A number of sheets of paper or leaves of a book placed together, as for binding; also, a report of the proceedings of any body, as a legislature.

ca-hin-ca=root (kạ-hing′kạ̈-röt), *n.* [From Brazilian name.] The root of any of certain shrubs of the tropical American rubiaceous genus *Chiococca*, as that of *C. racemosa*, used as a purgative, diuretic, etc., or that of *C. anguifuga*, used as an antidote against the venom of snakes.

ca-hoot (kạ-höt′), *n.* [Cf. F. *cahute*, hut, cabin.] Partnership or league: used in *sing.* or *pl.*, and commonly after *in.* [Slang, U. S.]

cai-man (kā′mạn), *n.* See *cayman.*

Cain (kān), *n.* [From *Cain*, who slew his brother Abel: see Gen. iv. 1–15.] One who slays his brother or a brother man; a fratricide; a murderer.

Cai-no-zo-ic (kī-nọ-zō′ik), *a.* and *n.* See *Cenozoic.*

ca-ïque (kä-ēk′), *n.* [F., < Turk. *kāïk.*] A kind of long, narrow skiff or rowboat used on the Bosporus; also, a Levantine sailing-vessel.

Caïque.

caird (kārd), *n.* [Gael. *ceard.*] A traveling tinker; a tramp or vagrant; a gipsy. [Sc.]

cairn (kārn), *n.* [Gael. *carn.*] Any of certain monumental piles of stones erected by early inhabitants of Great Britain (as, "On many a *cairn's* grey pyramid, Where urns of mighty chiefs lie hid": Scott's "Lay of the Last Minstrel," iii. 29); also, a heap of stones set up as a landmark, etc.—**cairned,** *a.* Having a cairn.

cairn-gorm (kārn′gôrm), *n.* [From *Cairngorm* ('blue cairn'), mountain in Scotland.] A smoky-yellow or smoky-brown variety of rock-crystal or quartz, used in jewelry, etc.

cais-son (kā′sọn), *n.* [F. *caisson*, earlier *casson*, < It. *cassone*, aug. of *cassa*, < L. *capsa*, box: see *case*[2].] A wooden chest containing bombs or explosives, used as a mine; an ammunition-chest; an ammunition-wagon; a water-tight box or casing in which masonry is built and is sunk to the bottom of rivers, etc.; a structure in which men can work on river bottoms, etc., consisting essentially of an air-tight box or chamber with an open bottom, the water being kept out by the high air-pressure maintained within; a float or boat-like structure used as a flood-gate for a dock or the like; a camel (buoyant water-tight structure) for raising ships, etc.; a sunken panel in a ceiling.—**caisson disease,** a disease marked by paralysis and other nervous symptoms, developed in coming from an atmosphere of high pressure, as in a caisson, to air of ordinary pressure.

cai-tiff (kā'tif). [OF. *caitif*, < L. *captivus*, E. *captive*.] **I.** *a.* Captive†; also, wretched†; also, base; despicable; mean. **II.** *n.* A captive†; also, a wretched person†; also, a base, despicable person; a wretch; one who is mean and wicked.

caj-e-put (kaj'ẹ-put), *n.* See *cajuput.*

ca-jole (kạ-jōl'), *v. t.*; *-joled, -joling.* [F. *cajoler*; origin uncertain.] To beguile by flattery or fair words; wheedle; coax.—**ca-jole'ment,** *n.* Cajoling; cajolery.—**ca-jol'er** (-jō'lėr), *n.*—**ca-jol'er-y,** *n.*; pl. *-ies* (-iz). The act of cajoling; delusive wheedling.—**ca-jol'ing-ly,** *adv.*

ca-jon (kä-hōn'), *n.* [Sp. *cajón*, aug. of *caja*, < L. *capsa*, box: see *case*².] A narrow cañon or gorge with vertical sides. [Southwestern U. S.]

caj-u-put (kaj'ụ-put), *n.* [Malay *kāyū*, tree, + *pūtih*, white.] Any of various trees of the myrtaceous genus *Melaleuca*, esp. *M. leucadendron*, native in the Malay Archipelago, yielding an aromatic oil used in medicine as a stimulant, antispasmodic, and sudorific.

cake (kāk), *n.* [ME. *cake, kake*, prob. from Scand.: cf. Icel. and Sw. *kaka*, Dan. *kage*, cake, akin to D. *koek*, G. *kuchen*.] A mass of dough or batter baked or otherwise cooked in a definite form; a flat, comparatively thin mass of bread, esp. unleavened bread; an oat-cake (Sc.); a pan-cake or griddle-cake; a kind of sweet bread enriched with various ingredients and made in masses (large or small) of various forms, or one of these masses (as, sponge-*cake*; fruit-*cake*; a loaf-*cake*; a layer-*cake*); a shaped or molded mass of other food (as, a fish-*cake*; a meat-*cake*); a shaped or concreted mass, esp. a flat one, of any material, as tobacco, soap, wax, ice, etc.—**cakes and ale,** dainties; good things and enjoyments of life. See Shakspere's "Twelfth Night," ii. 3. 124.—**cake,** *v. t.* or *i.*; *caked, caking.* To form or become formed into a cake or compact mass.—**cake'walk,** *n.* A promenade or march, of American negro origin, in which couples walk, to musical accompaniment, in competition before judges and an audience, the most graceful, eccentric, or fantastic performers receiving cakes as prizes.—**cake'walk,** *v. i.* To walk in or as in a cakewalk.—**cake'walk"er,** *n.*—**cak-y** (kā'ki), *a.* Cake-like.

Cal-a-bar (kal-ạ-bär') **bean.** [From *Calabar*, region on the west coast of Africa.] The violently poisonous seed of a fabaceous African climbing plant, *Physostigma venenosum*, used as a remedy in diseases of the eye and in tetanus, neuralgia, rheumatic diseases, etc.

cal-a-bash (kal'ạ-bash), *n.* [F. *calebasse*, < Sp. *calabaza*, gourd, pumpkin; perhaps ult. from Pers.] Any of various gourds, esp. the fruit of the bottle-gourd, *Lagenaria vulgaris* (or *lagenaria*); any of the plants bearing them; also, the fruit of a bignoniaceous tree, *Crescentia cujete*, of tropical America, or the tree itself; also, the dried hollow shell of the calabash (in either sense) used as a vessel or otherwise; a bottle, kettle, tobacco-pipe bowl, or the like, made from the shell of a calabash.

Decorated Calabashes (shells).

cal-a-ba-zil-la (kal"ạ-bä-sēl'yạ), *n.* [Mex. Sp., dim. of Sp. *calabaza*: see *calabash*.] A wild squash, *Cucurbita fœtidissima*, of Mexico and the southwestern U. S., with a fruit whose pulp while unripe is used as a substitute for soap, and with an exceedingly large root which is macerated for use as a medicinal remedy.

cal-a-boose (kal-ạ-bös'), *n.* [Sp. *calabozo*.] A prison; a jail or lockup. [U. S.]

ca-la-di-um (kạ-lā'di-um), *n.* [NL.; from Malay.] A plant of the araceous genus *Caladium*, of Asia and the Pacific islands, as *C. colocasia*, the taro, well known also in cultivation as a large-leaved foliage-plant (often called *elephant's ear*); also, any of various cultivated species of the South American araceous genus *Cyrtospadix*, with large, handsomely variegated leaves.

Caladium (*C. colocasia*).

cal-a-man-co (kal-ạ-mang'kō), *n.* [Origin uncertain: cf. Sp. *calamaco*, D. *kalamink*, G. *kalmank*.] A glossy woolen fabric checkered or brocaded in the warp so that the pattern shows on one side only.

cal-a-man-der (kal-ạ-man'dėr), *n.* [Origin uncertain.] The hard wood of a tree, *Diospyros quæsita*, of Ceylon and India, used for cabinet-work.

cal-a-ma-ry (kal'ạ-mạ̄-ri), *n.*; pl. *-ries* (-riz). [L. *calamarius*, pertaining to a pen, < *calamus*, reed, pen.] A squid, esp. of the genus *Loligo* and related genera, with a pen-shaped internal skeleton; also, the skeleton.

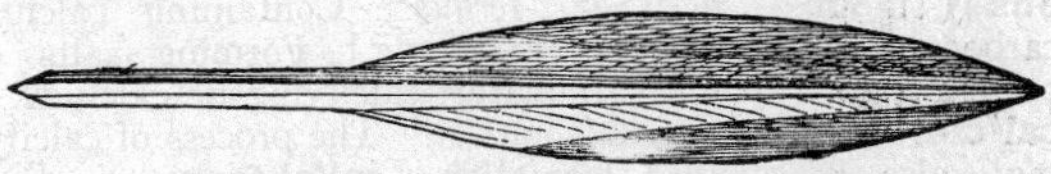

Calamary, Pen, or Skeleton of a Squid (*Loligo*).

cal-a-min, cal-a-mine (kal'ạ-min, -min or -mīn), *n.* [F. *calamine*, < ML. *calamina*, appar. for L. *cadmia*: see *cadmium*.] Native hydrous silicate of zinc; sometimes, native zinc carbonate.—**cal'a-min, cal'a-mine,** *v. t.*; *-mined, -mining.* To coat (pottery) with calamin.

cal-a-mint (kal'ạ-mint), *n.* [LL. *calaminthe*, < Gr. καλαμίνθη.] Any plant of the menthaceous genus *Clinopodium*, some of whose species are used for herb-teas.

ca-lam-i-tous (kạ-lam'i-tus), *a.* [L. *calamitosus*.] Fraught with or involving calamity; disastrous.—**ca-lam'i-tous-ly,** *adv.*—**ca-lam'i-tous-ness,** *n.*

ca-lam-i-ty (kạ-lam'i-ti), *n.*; pl. *-ties* (-tiz). [L. *calamitas*; perhaps connected with *incolumis*, unharmed.] A great (often a public) misfortune; a disaster; also, grievous affliction; adversity.

cal-a-mus (kal'ạ-mus), *n.*; pl. *-mi* (-mī). [L., < Gr. κάλαμος, reed: cf. *halm*.] A reed† or cane†; the sweet-flag, *Acorus calamus*, or its aromatic root; any palm of the genus *Calamus*, yielding ratan, canes, etc. (cf. *ratan* and *Malacca cane*); also, the quill of a feather.

ca-lash (kạ-lash'), *n.* [F. *calèche*; from Slavic.] A light, low-wheeled carriage, either with or without a folding top, sometimes (as in Canada) having a seat on the splash-board for the driver; the folding top ('calash-top') of such a vehicle; also, a kind of hood formerly worn by women.

Calash.

cal-a-thus (kal'ạ-thus), *n.*; pl. *-thi* (-thī). [L., < Gr. κάλαθος.] In *class. antiq.*, a vase-shaped basket; esp., one in which women kept their work: often employed as a symbol of maidenhood.

cal-ca-ne-um (kal-kā'nẹ-um), *n.*; pl. *-nea* (-nẹ-ạ). [L., heel, < *calx*, heel.] In *anat.*, in man, the largest bone of the tarsus, forming the prominence of the heel; also, the corresponding bone in other vertebrates.—**cal-ca'ne-al,** *a.*

cal-car (kal'kär), *n.*; pl. *calcaria* (kal-kā'ri-ạ). [L., < *calx*, heel.] In *bot.*, *zoöl.*, etc., a spur, or spur-like process.

—**cal′ca-rate** (-kạ-rāt), *a.* Furnished with a calcar or calcaria; spurred.

cal-ca-re-ous (kal-kā′rẹ-us), *a.* [Earlier, more correctly, *calcarious*, < L. *calcarius*, < *calx*, lime.] Of, containing, or like calcium carbonate; chalky.—**cal-ca′re-ous-ness,** *n.*

cal-ce-ate (kal′sẹ-āt), *a.* [L. *calceatus*, pp. of *calceare*, to shoe, < *calceus*, a shoe, < *calx*, heel.] Shod; wearing shoes: used esp. of certain religious orders (cf. *discalceate*). Also **calced** (kalst).

cal-ce-i-form (kal′sẹ-i-fôrm), *a.* [L. *calceus*, a shoe: see *-form.*] Having the form of a shoe or slipper, as the labellum of certain orchids.

Calcarate Foot of Pheasant.

cal-ce-o-la-ri-a (kal″sẹ-ọ-lā′ri-ạ̈), *n.* [NL., < L. *calceolus*, slipper, dim. of *calceus*: see *calceate.*] Any plant of the violaceous genus *Calceolaria*, comprising herbs and shrubs, chiefly tropical American, with inconspicuous white or greenish flowers; also, commonly, a plant of the scrophulariaceous genus *Jovellana* (or *Calceolaria*), native chiefly in South America, species of which are much cultivated for their slipper-like flowers, usually yellow or purple and handsomely spotted with darker color.

cal-ces (kal′sēz), *n.* Latin plural of *calx.*

cal-cic (kal′sik), *a.* [L. *calx* (*calc-*), lime.] Pertaining to or containing lime or calcium.—**cal-cic′o-lous** (-sik′ọ-lus), *a.* [See *-colous.*] Inhabiting calcareous soil.—**cal-cif′er-ous** (-sif′ẹ-rus), *a.* [See *-ferous.*] Containing calcium carbonate.—**cal-cif′ic,** *a.* [See *-fic.*] Forming salts of calcium, esp. calcium carbonate; calcifying or calcified.—**cal″ci-fi-ca′tion** (-si-fi-kā′shọn), *n.* The process of calcifying; also, a calcified formation.—**cal′ci-form,** *a.* [See *-form.*] Having the form of chalk or lime.—**cal′ci-fy** (-fī), *v. t.* or *i.*; *-fied, -fying.* [See *-fy.*] To make or become calcareous or bony; harden by the deposit of calcium salts. —**cal-cig′er-ous** (-sij′ẹ-rus), *a.* [See *-gerous.*] Producing or containing salts of calcium.

cal-ci-mine (kal′si-mīn or -min), *n.* [L. *calx* (*calc-*), lime: cf. *kalsomine.*] A white or tinted wash for walls, ceilings, etc.—**cal′ci-mine,** *v. t.*; *-mined, -mining.* To wash or cover with calcimine.

cal-ci-na-tion (kal-si-nā′shọn), *n.* The process of calcining; also, a product formed by calcining.—**cal-ci-na-to-ry** (kal′si-nạ-tọ-ri or kal-sin′ạ-), *a.*

cal-cine (kal-sīn′ or kal′sin), *v. t.* or *i.*; *-cined, -cining.* [ML. *calcinare*, < L. *calx*, lime.] To convert or be converted into calx by heat; burn to a friable substance; roast; oxidize.—**cal-cin-er** (kal-sī′nėr or kal′si-), *n.*

cal-cite (kal′sīt), *n.* [L. *calx* (*calc-*), lime.] Native calcium carbonate.—**cal-cit′ic** (-sit′ik), *a.*

cal-ci-um (kal′si-um), *n.* [NL., < L. *calx*, lime.] Chem. sym., Ca; at. wt., 40.07; sp. gr., about 1.57. A silver-white ductile metal, occurring combined in limestone, chalk, etc.—**calcium carbide,** a crystalline compound of calcium and carbon, CaC_2, which reacts with water to form acetylene gas.—**calcium carbonate,** a crystalline compound, $CaCO_3$, occurring in nature as calcite, etc.—**calcium light,** a brilliant white light produced by heating lime to incandescence in an oxyhydrogen or other hot flame. Cf. *limelight.*

calc=sin-ter (kalk′sin″tėr), *n.* [G. *kalksinter*, 'lime sinter.'] Travertin.—**calc′=spar,** *n.* Any crystallized and cleavable variety of calcite.—**calc′=tuff, calc′=tu″fa,** *n.* Calcareous tufa. See *tufa.*

cal-cu-la-ble (kal′kụ̄-lạ-bl), *a.* That may be calculated.

cal-cu-late (kal′kụ̄-lāt), *v.*; *-lated, -lating.* [LL. *calculatus*, pp. of *calculare*, < L. *calculus*, pebble, counter: see *calculus.*] **I.** *tr.* To ascertain by mathematical methods; compute; reckon; also, to plan, devise, or think out; also, to make suitable, adapt, or fit for a purpose (chiefly in *pp.*); also, to intend or purpose (local, U. S.); also, to think or guess (local, U. S.). **II.** *intr.* To make a computation; reckon; also, to count or rely (*on* or *upon*).—**cal-cu-la′tion** (-lā′shọn), *n.* [LL. *calculatio*(*n-*).] The act or result of calculating; computation; a reckoning; an estimate based on the various facts and circumstances in a case; a forecast.—**cal′cu-la-tive** (-lạ-tiv), *a.* Pertaining to calculation; given to calculating.—**cal′cu-la-tor** (-lā-tọr), *n.*

cal-cu-lous (kal′kụ̄-lus), *a.* Hard like a pebble; gritty; in *pathol.*, pertaining to, caused by, or affected with a calculus or calculi.

cal-cu-lus (kal′kụ̄-lus), *n.*; pl. *-luses*, L. *-li* (-lī). [L., pebble, stone used in counting, reckoning, dim. of *calx*, small stone, lime.] A pebble; in *pathol.*, a morbid concretion formed in the gall-bladder, kidneys, and other parts of the body; in *math.*, a method of calculation, esp. a highly systematic method of treating problems by means of some peculiar system of algebraic notation (as, differential *calculus*, which investigates differentials and their relations; integral *calculus*, which deals with the finding and the properties of integrals, etc.; infinitesimal *calculus*, or simply 'the calculus,' the differential calculus and the integral calculus considered together).

cal-da-ri-um (kal-dā′ri-um), *n.*; pl. *-ria* (-ri-ạ̈). [L., prop. neut. of *caldarius*: see *caldron.*] An apartment of the ancient Roman thermæ, in which water was heated to the highest temperature.

cal-de-ra (kal-dā′rạ̈), *n.* [Sp., < L. *caldaria*, kettle, prop. fem. of *caldarius*: see *caldron.*] A large bowl-like cavity or crater produced by violent volcanic action, as when the upper part of a cone is blown off; a volcanic crater which has been enlarged by subterranean disruptive forces.

cal-dron (kâl′drọn), *n.* [OF. *caudron*, < L. *caldarius*, serving to heat, < *caldus*, *calidus*, hot, < *calere*, be hot.] A large kettle or boiler.

Cal-e-do-ni-a (kal-ẹ-dō′ni-ạ̈), *n.* [L.] Scotland. [Chiefly poetic.]—**Cal-e-do′ni-an,** *a.* and *n.*

cal-e-fa-cient (kal-ẹ-fā′shẹnt). [L. *calefaciens* (*-ent-*), ppr. of *calefacere*, make hot, < *calere*, be hot, + *facere*, make.] **I.** *a.* Heating; warming. **II.** *n.* A substance which produces a sensation of heat when applied to the body, as mustard.—**cal-e-fac′tion** (-fak′shọn), *n.* [L. *calefactio*(*n-*).] The act of heating; heated state.—**cal-e-fac′tive, cal-e-fac′to-ry** (-tọ-ri), *a.* Serving to heat.

ca-lem-bour (kȧ-loṅ-bör), *n.* [F.] A pun.

cal-en-dar (kal′ẹn-dạ̈r), *n.* [L. *calendarium*, account-book, < *calendæ*, calends.] Any of various systems of reckoning time, esp. with reference to the beginning, length, and divisions of the year (as, the Julian *calendar*; the Gregorian *calendar*; the Jewish *calendar*: see the adjectives); a tabular or other arrangement of the days of each month and week in a year, sometimes combined with astronomical or other data; an almanac; any arrangement or contrivance for reckoning days, months, etc.; a guide† or example†; a list or register, esp. one arranged chronologically.—**calendar of the first French republic,** a calendar introduced in France Oct. 5, 1793, and reckoned from Sept. 22, 1792, by which the year was divided into 12 months of 30 days each, with 5 or 6 extra days called *sansculottides*: the names of the months, beginning at the autumnal equinox, were Vendémiaire, Brumaire, Frimaire, Nivôse, Pluviôse, Ventôse, Germinal, Floréal, Prairial, Messidor, Thermidor, and Fructidor.—**cal′en-dar,** *v. t.* To enter in a calendar; register.—**cal′en-dar-er,** *n.*—**cal-en-da′ri-al** (-dā′ri-ạl), *a.* Of or pertaining to a calendar.

Cal-en-der[1] (kal′ẹn-dėr), *n.* [Pers. *qalandar.*] [Also *l. c.*] One of an order of mendicant dervishes founded in the 14th century.

cal-en-der[2] (kal′ẹn-dėr), *n.* [F. *calandre*, < ML. *celendra*, < L. *cylindrus*, E. *cylinder.*] A machine in which cloth, paper, or the like is smoothed, glazed, etc., by pressing between revolving cylinders.—**cal′en-der**[2], *v. t.* To press or finish in a calender.—**cal′en-der-er,** *n.*

cal-ends, kal-ends (kal′endz), *n. pl.* [L. *calendæ*, *kalendæ.*] The first day of the month in the Roman calendar.—**on the Greek calends,** on a day that will never arrive (since the Greeks had no calends); never.

ca-len-du-la (kạ-len′dụ̄-lạ̈), *n.*; pl. *-las.* [NL., < L. *calendæ*, calends; so called as flowering almost every month of the year.] Any plant of the asteraceous genus *Calendula*, esp. *C. officinalis*, a common marigold; also, the dried florets of this plant, used in medicine as a vulnerary, etc.

cal-en-ture (kal′ẹn-tụ̄r), *n.* [F., < Sp. *calentura*, < L. *calere*, be hot.] A violent fever with delirium, affecting persons in the tropics, esp. on shipboard: as, "In this voyage . . . I was continually sick, being thrown into a violent *calenture* by the excessive heat of the climate" (Defoe's "Robinson Crusoe," i. 2).

ca-les-cent (ka̤-les′e̤nt), *a.* [L. *calescens (-ent-)*, ppr. of *calescere*, grow hot, < *calere*, be hot.] Growing warm; increasing in heat.—**ca-les′cence,** *n.*

calf[1] (käf or kȧf), *n.*; pl. *calves* (kävz or kȧvz). [ME.: cf. Icel. *kālfi.*] The fleshy hinder part of the human leg below the knee.

calf[2] (käf or kȧf), *n.*; pl. *calves* (kävz or kȧvz). [AS. *cealf* = G. *kalb.*] The young of the cow or of other bovine animals; the young of certain other animals, as the elephant, seal, and whale; a small island lying near a large one; a mass of ice detached from a glacier, iceberg, or floe; an awkward, silly, or meek or cowardly boy or man (colloq.); calfskin leather.—**golden calf.** See under *golden, a.*—**calf′=love,** *n.* Transitory affection or passion of a boy or a girl for a person of the opposite sex.—**calf′skin,** *n.* The skin or hide of a calf, or leather made from it.

Cal-i-ban (kal′i-ban), *n.* [From *Caliban*, "a savage and deformed slave" in Shakspere's play, "The Tempest."] A man of low, bestial nature.

cal-i-ber, cal-i-bre (kal′i-bėr), *n.* [F. *calibre*; origin uncertain.] The diameter of something of circular section, esp. that of the inside of a tube, as of the bore of a gun; sometimes, the diameter of the bore of a gun taken as a unit in stating its length (as, a fifty *caliber* 14-inch gun); in fig. use, degree of capacity or ability; personal character; degree of merit or importance; quality.—**cal′i-bered, cal′i-bred** (-bėrd), *a.* Having a caliber: as, large-*calibered* guns.—**cal′i-ber=rule′,** *n.* Same as *caliper-rule.*

cal-i-brate (kal′i-brāt), *v. t.*; *-brated, -brating.* [Cf. F. *calibrer.*] To ascertain the caliber of (the bore of a thermometer-tube, etc.); determine, check, or rectify the graduation of (a thermometer or other instrument, or any graduated scale).—**cal-i-bra′tion** (-brā′sho̤n), *n.*—**cal′i-bra-tor,** *n.*

cal-i-ces (kal′i-sēz), *n.* Plural of *calix.*

ca-li-che (kä-lē′chā), *n.* [Amer. Sp. use of Sp. *caliche*, pebble, flake of lime, < L. *calx*, lime.] Any of various mineral deposits, as native Chile saltpeter, containing from 48 to 75% of nitrate of sodium, or a calcareous deposit in Arizona, etc., sometimes yielding gold.

cal-i-cle (kal′i-kl), *n.* [L. *caliculus*, dim. of *calix*, cup.] A cup-like depression or formation, as in corals.

cal-i-co (kal′i-kō). [From *Calicut*, city in southwestern India.] **I.** *n.*; pl. *-coes* or *-cos* (-kōz). Orig., cotton cloth imported from India; now, white cotton cloth (Eng.); printed cotton cloth (U. S.). **II.** *a.* Made of calico; resembling printed calico, as a horse or other animal marked with patches of different colors.—**cal′i-co=bass′** (-bȧs′), *n.* A valuable fresh-water food-fish, *Pomoxys sparoides*, of the eastern and central parts of the U. S. Cf. *crappie.*—**cal′i-co=bush,** *n.* The mountain-laurel, *Kalmia latifolia.* See *laurel.*

ca-lic-u-lar (ka-lik′ū-lär), *a.* Pertaining to a calicle; cup-like.—**ca-lic′u-late** (-lāt), *a.* Having calicles.

ca-lif, ca-liph (kā′lif or kal′if), *n.* [OF. F. *calife*, < Ar. *khalīfah*, < *khalafa*, succeed.] Successor (of Mohammed): a title of the head of a Moslem state.—**ca-li-fate, ca-li-phate** (kā′li-fāt or kal′i-), *n.* The office or government of a calif.

cal-i-for-nite (kal-i-fôr′nīt), *n.* [From *California.*] A mineral, a compact variety of vesuvianite, of an olive-green to grass-green color, resembling certain kinds of jade.

ca-lig-i-nous (ka̤-lij′i-nus), *a.* [L. *caliginosus*, < *caligo*, mist.] Misty; dim; dark.—**ca-lig-i-nos′i-ty** (-nos′i-ti), *n.*

cal-i-pash (kal′i-pash or kal-i-pash′), *n.* [Origin uncertain: cf. *carapace, calipee.*] That part of a turtle next to the upper shield, consisting of a greenish gelatinous substance.

cal-i-pee (kal′i-pē or kal-i-pē′), *n.* [Cf. *calipash.*] That part of a turtle next to the lower shield, consisting of a yellowish gelatinous substance.

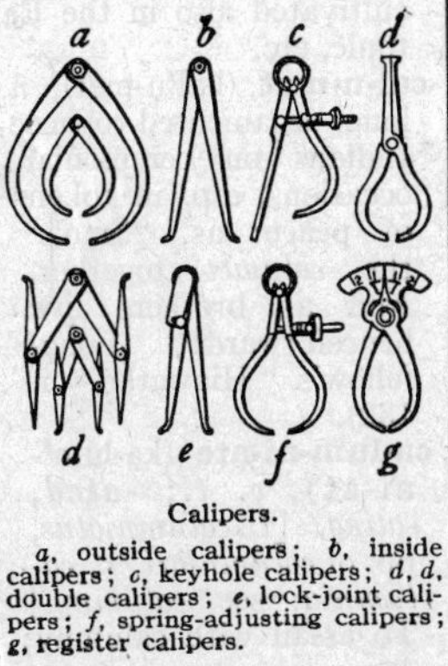

Calipers.
a, outside calipers; *b*, inside calipers; *c*, keyhole calipers; *d, d*, double calipers; *e*, lock-joint calipers; *f*, spring-adjusting calipers; *g*, register calipers.

cal-i-per (kal′i-pėr), *n.* [Corruption of *caliber.*] Usually *pl.*, an instrument, commonly having two legs and resembling a pair of compasses, for measuring outside and inside diameters, the thickness of objects, etc.—**cal′i-per,** *v. t.* To measure with calipers.—**cal′i-per=rule′,** *n.* A rule having a graduated slide with a projecting foot, used as calipers for measuring outside diameters.

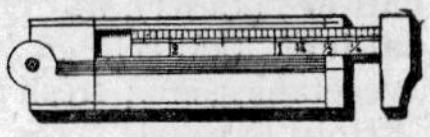
Caliper-rule.

ca′liph, etc. See *calif*, etc.

cal-i-sa-ya (kal-i-sā′yä̤), *n.* [S. Amer.] The medicinal bark of the tree *Cinchona calisaya.* See *cinchona.*

cal-is-then′ic, etc. See *callisthenic*, etc.

cal-i-ver (kal′i-vėr), *n.* [= *caliber.*] A former hand-firearm, lighter than a musket, fired without the use of a rest or support.

ca-lix (kā′liks), *n.*; pl. *calices* (kal′i-sēz). [L., cup: cf. *chalice* and *calyx.*] A cup-like part or organ; also, a calyx.

calk[1], **caulk** (kâk), *v. t.* [OF. *calquier*, < L. *calcare*, tread, press, < *calx*, heel.] To fill the seams of (a ship, etc.) with oakum, etc., to prevent leaking; fill or close the seams or crevices of (a tank, window, boiler, etc.) in order to make water-tight, air-tight, steam-tight, or the like; also, to fill or close (a seam, joint, etc.).

calk[2] (kalk), *v. t.* [F. *calquer*, < It. *calcare*, < L. *calcare*: see *calk*[1].] To copy or transfer by tracing.

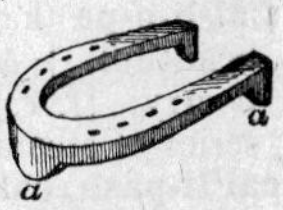

Horseshoe-calks, *a, a.*

calk[3] (kâk), *n.* [Appar. < *calkin.*] A projection on a horseshoe to prevent slipping; also, a similar device on the heel or sole of a shoe (U. S.).—**calk**[3], *v. t.* To fit with calks; also, to injure with a calk.

calk-er[1], **caulk-er** (kâ′kėr), *n.* One who calks ships, etc.

calk-er[2] (kâ′kėr), *n.* A calk. [Sc. and prov. Eng.]

calk-in (kâ′kin), *n.* [Cf. OF. *calcain*, heel, < L. *calcaneum*, < *calx*, heel.] A calk on a horseshoe.

call (kâl), *v.* [AS. *ceallian* = Icel. *kalla.*] **I.** *tr.* To utter in a loud voice; read over (as a roll or list) in a loud tone; announce or proclaim; attract the attention of by loudly uttering something; rouse from sleep as by a call; attract or lure (wild birds, etc.) by a particular cry or sound; command or request to come; summon; call for (as, the next case was then *called*); demand payment or fulfilment of (a loan, etc.); invoke, or appeal to (as, "I *call* heaven and earth to witness against you": Deut. iv. 26); convoke or convene, as a meeting or assembly; summon to an office, duty, etc.; invite to a pastorate; also, to name; designate as something specified; reckon or consider (as, to *call* a thing a success); apply abusive names to (now prov.); also, to drive (an animal, vehicle, etc.: Sc.); in *poker*, to require (a player) to show his hand, after equaling his bet; in *baseball*, to terminate (a game) because of darkness, rain, or the like (said of the umpire). **II.** *intr.* To speak loudly, as to attract attention; shout; cry; also, to make a demand; also, to make a short visit; stop at a place on some errand or business; also, to drive a horse, vehicle, etc. (Sc.); in *poker*, to demand a showing of hands.—**call,** *n.* The act of calling; a roll-call; a cry or shout; the cry of a bird or other animal; an instrument for imitating this and attracting or luring the animal; a note blown on a horn to encourage the hounds; a summons or bidding; a request or invitation, as to become pastor of a church; a summons or signal sounded upon a bugle, etc.; a whistle, etc., for sounding a signal; vocation† or occupation†; a demand or claim; the privilege of buying a certain amount of stock, etc., at a specified price, within a fixed time, as in the stock-exchange, etc.; a need or occasion; a short visit; a stop at a place on some business; in *poker*, a demand for the showing of hands.

cal-la (kal′ä̤), *n.* [L., kind of plant.] An araceous plant, *Calla palustris*, of cold marshes of Europe and North America, with heart-shaped leaves, an open white spathe, and red berries; also, a plant of the allied genus *Aroides* (or *Richardia*), native in Africa, esp. *A. æthiopicum*, which has a large white spathe inclosing a yellow spadix, and is familiar in cultivation ('calla lily').

cal-la-ble (kâ′la̤-bl), *a.* That may be called; subject to call or summons; subject to payment on demand, as money loaned; subject to redemption upon notice, as a bond.

cal-lant (kȧl′ạnt), *n.* [Flem. and D. *kalant* = F. *chaland*, customer.] A lad; a boy. [Sc. and north. Eng.]

call-er[1] (kâ′lėr), *n.* One that calls.

cal-ler[2] (kȧl′ėr), *a.* [Origin obscure.] Fresh, as fish, vegetables, etc.; fresh and cool (as, "the *caller* air": Burns's "Holy Fair," 4). [Sc. and north. Eng.]

cal-let (kal′et), *n.* [Origin uncertain.] A prostitute; a drab; a scold. [Obs. or prov.]

calli-. A form of Gr. καλός, beautiful, used in combination. Cf. *calo-*.

cal-li-graph (kal′i-gráf), *n.* [Gr. καλλιγράφος, a calligrapher, < καλός, beautiful, + γράφειν, write.] A calligrapher; also, a specimen of beautiful penmanship.—**cal′li-graph,** *v. t.* To write or transcribe beautifully.—**cal-lig-ra-pher** (ka-lig′rạ-fėr), *n.* One who does beautiful handwriting; a fine penman; a transcriber of manuscripts.—**cal-li-graph′ic** (-graf′ik), *a.* Of or pertaining to calligraphy.—**cal-lig′ra-phist,** *n.* A calligrapher.—**cal-lig′ra-phy,** *n.* [Gr. καλλιγραφία.] Beautiful handwriting; fine penmanship; in general, handwriting; penmanship.

call-ing (kâ′ling), *n.* The act of one that calls; summons; invitation; convocation; vocation, profession, or trade; a name† or appellation†.

Cal-li-o-pe (ka-lī′ọ̄-pē), *n.* [L., < Gr. Καλλιόπη, < καλός, beautiful, + ὄψ, voice.] The Muse of eloquence and heroic poetry; [*l. c.*] a harsh musical instrument consisting of a series of steam-whistles played by keys.

cal′li-pash, cal′li-pee. See *calipash, calipee*.

cal′li-per, *n.* and *v.* See *caliper*.

cal-lis-then-ic (kal-is-then′ik), *a.* [Gr. καλός, beautiful, + σθένος, strength.] Serving to promote bodily grace and strength, as muscular exercises.—**cal-lis-then′ics,** *n.* As *pl.*, callisthenic exercises; light gymnastics; as *sing.*, the practice or art of callisthenic exercises.

cal-li-thum-pi-an (kal-i-thum′pi-ạn). [A humorous formation < *calli-* + *thump*.] **I.** *a.* Noting or pertaining to a noisy concert, characterized by beating of tin pans, blowing of horns, shouts, groans, catcalls, etc., usually given as a mock serenade. [U. S.] **II.** *n.* A callithumpian concert; a charivari; also, one who takes part in it. [U. S.]

call=loan (kâl′lōn), *n.* A loan repayable on demand.

cal-los-i-ty (kạ-los′i-ti), *n.*; pl. *-ties* (-tiz). Callous condition; also, a callous part.

cal-lous (kal′us), *a.* [L. *callosus*, < *callum*, *callus*, hard skin.] Hard, as skin; indurated, as portions of the skin exposed to friction; fig., hardened in mind, feelings, etc.; unfeeling.—**cal-loused** (kal′ust), *a.* Made callous; hardened.—**cal′lous-ly,** *adv.*—**cal′lous-ness,** *n.*

cal-low (kal′ō), *a.* [AS. *calu*, prob. < L. *calvus*, bald.] Bald†; also, unfledged; fig., immature or inexperienced.—**cal′low-ness,** *n.*

cal-lus (kal′us), *n.*; pl. *calluses* or *calli* (-ī). [L.] A hardened or thickened portion of the skin; a callosity; a hard excrescence on a plant; the substance or tissue which forms over the wounds of plants, protecting the inner tissues and causing healing; a new growth of osseous matter at the ends of a fractured bone, serving to unite them.

calm (käm). [OF. F. *calme*, prob. (as if orig. 'heat of the day,' hence 'time for resting, quiet') < LL. *cauma*, < Gr. καῦμα, burning heat, < καίειν, burn.] **I.** *n.* Freedom from motion or disturbance; stillness; absence of wind; hence, freedom from agitation, excitement, or passion; tranquillity; serenity. **II.** *a.* Without motion; still; not windy; hence, tranquil; free from excitement or passion.—**calm,** *v. t.* or *i.* To make or become calm.—**cal-ma-tive** (kal′mạ-tiv or käm′ạ-). **I.** *a.* That calms; sedative. **II.** *n.* A calmative agent.—**calm′ly,** *adv.*—**calm′ness,** *n.*—**calm′y,** *a.* Calm: as, "A still And *calmy* bay" (Spenser's "Faerie Queene," ii. 12. 30). [Poetic.]

calo-. A form of Gr. καλός, beautiful, used in combination. Cf. *calli-*.

cal-o-mel (kal′ọ̄-mel), *n.* [Appar. < Gr. καλός, beautiful, + μέλας, black; various explanations are given.] Mercurous chloride, Hg_2Cl_2, a white, tasteless solid used in medicine as a mercurial, a purgative, etc.

cal-o-res-cence (kal-ọ̄-res′ẹns), *n.* [L. *calor*, heat: see *-escence*.] The change of non-luminous heat-rays into light-rays.

ca-lor-ic (kạ-lor′ik). [F. *calorique*, < L. *calor*, heat: see *calory*.] **I.** *a.* Pertaining to heat; of engines, driven by heated air. **II.** *n.* A supposed imponderable fluid to which the phenomena of heat were formerly attributed; hence, heat.—**cal-o-ri-ci-ty** (kal-ọ̄-ris′i-ti), *n.* The faculty in animals of generating and maintaining a uniform or nearly uniform body-temperature.

cal′o-rie, *n.* See *calory*.

cal-o-rif-ic (kal-ọ̄-rif′ik), *a.* [L. *calorificus*, < *calor*, heat, + *facere*, make.] Producing heat; also, pertaining to heat.—**ca-lor-i-fi-ca-tion** (kạ-lor″i-fi-kā′shọn), *n.* The production of heat, esp. animal heat.—**cal-o-rif′ics,** *n.* The science of heat.

cal-o-rim-e-ter (kal-ọ̄-rim′e-tėr), *n.* [L. *calor*, heat: see *-meter*.] An apparatus for measuring the quantity of heat given off by or present in a body.—**cal″o-ri-met′ric, cal″o-ri-met′ri-cal** (-ri-met′rik, -ri-kạl), *a.* Of or pertaining to the calorimeter or calorimetry.—**cal″o-ri-met′ri-cal-ly,** *adv.*—**cal-o-rim′e-try,** *n.* [See *-metry*.] The art of using the calorimeter; the quantitative measurement of heat.

cal-o-ry, cal-o-rie (kal′ọ̄-ri), *n.*; pl. *-ries* (-riz). [F. *calorie*, < L. *calor*, heat, < *calere*, be hot.] In *physics*, the quantity of heat necessary to raise the temperature of a kilogram of water one degree centigrade, esp. from 0° to 1° ('large calory'); also, the quantity of heat necessary to raise the temperature of a gram of water one degree centigrade, esp. from 0° to 1° ('small calory'); in *physiol.*, a unit corresponding to the large calory, used to express the fuel or energy value of food; also, a quantity of food capable of producing such a unit of energy.

ca-lotte (kạ-lot′), *n.* [F., < *cale*, cap: cf. *caul*.] A plain skullcap, as that worn by Roman Catholic ecclesiastics; also, anything having the form of a small cap.

cal-o-type (kal′ọ̄-tīp), *n.* [See *calo-* and *-type*.] An old process of producing a photograph by exposing a sensitized paper in the camera; also, the picture so made.—**cal′o-typ-ist,** *n.*

cal-o-yer (kal′ọ̄-yėr), *n.* [F., < LGr. καλόγηρος, < Gr. καλός, beautiful, + γῆρας, old age.] A monk of the Greek Church.

cal-pac (kal′pak), *n.* [Turki *qalpāq*.] A kind of cap of sheepskin or other material worn by Turks and others.

cal-te-tep-on (kal-te-tep′on), *n.* [Mex.] A venomous lizard, *Heloderma horridum*, of Mexico. See *Gila monster*.

cal-trop, cal-trap (kal′trọp, -trạp), *n.* [AS. *coltræppe*, *calcatrippe*, spiny plant, appar. < L. *calx*, heel, + ML. *trappa*, trap.] Any of various plants having spiny heads or fruit, as the star-thistle, *Centaurea calcitrapa* (also called *caltrops*); also, an iron ball with four projecting spikes so disposed that when the ball is placed on the ground one of them always points upward, used to obstruct the passage of cavalry, etc.; also, a four-armed sponge-spicule.

Caltrop.

ca-lum-ba (kạ-lum′bạ̈), *n.* [Prob. from native African name.] The root of *Jateorhiza palmata*, an African plant cultivated also in the East Indies: used in medicine as a tonic, etc.

cal-u-met (kal′ụ̄-met), *n.* [F., < L. *calamus*, reed.] A long, ornamented tobacco-pipe used by the North American Indians on ceremonial occasions, esp. in token of peace: as, "Smoke the *calumet* together, And as brothers live henceforward!" (Longfellow's "Hiawatha," i. 132).

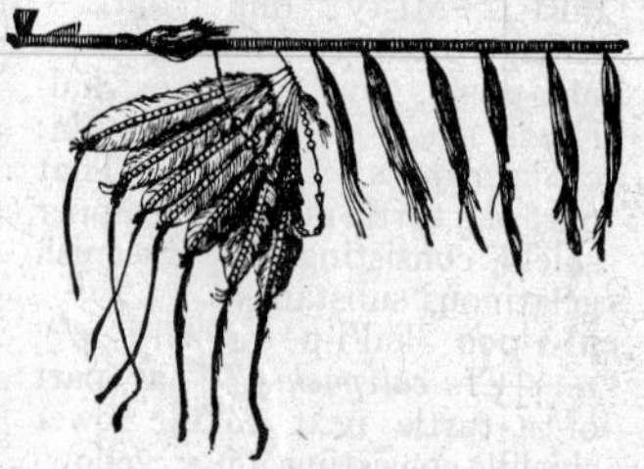

Calumet.

ca-lum-ni-ate (kạ-lum′ni-āt), *v. t.*; *-ated*, *-ating*. [L. *calumniatus*, pp. of *calumniari*, < *calumnia*: see *calumny*.] To assail with calumny; make malicious false statements concerning; slander; traduce.—**ca-lum-ni-a′tion** (-ā′shọn), *n.* The act of calumniating; slander; also, a calumny.—**ca-lum′ni-a-tor,** *n.*—**ca-lum′ni-a-to-ry** (-ạ-tō-ri), *a.* Calumnious.

ca-lum-ni-ous (kạ-lum′ni-us), *a.* [LL. *calumniosus.*] Of the nature of, involving, or using calumny; slanderous; defamatory.—**ca-lum′ni-ous-ly,** *adv.*

cal-um-ny (kal′um-ni), *n.*; pl. *-nies* (-niz). [L. *calumnia*, < *calvi*, intrigue against.] Malicious false statement tending to defame; slander; also, a slanderous report.

cal-va-ri-a (kal-vā′ri-ạ̈), *n.* [L.] Same as *calvarium.*

cal-va-ri-um (kal-vā′ri-um), *n.* [NL., < L. *calvaria*, skull: see *Calvary.*] In *anat.*, the upper domed part of the cranium, covering the brain.—**cal-va′ri-al, cal-va′ri-an,** *a.*

Cal-va-ry (kal′vạ-ri), *n.*; pl. *-ries* (-riz). [L. *calvaria*, skull (< *calvus*, bald), used to render the Aramaic name, lit. 'skull,' whence E. *Golgotha.*] Golgotha, the place where Christ was crucified (Luke, xxiii. 33); [*l. c.*] a sculptured representation of the Crucifixion, erected in the open air or in a church or chapel; also, a series of representations, as in a chapel, of scenes from the passion of Christ.

calve (käv or kȧv), *v.*; *calved, calving.* [AS. *cealfian*, < *cealf*, calf.] **I.** *intr.* To give birth to a calf; of a glacier, iceberg, etc., to give off a detached piece. **II.** *tr.* To give birth to (a calf); bring forth; give off.

Cal-vin-ism (kal′vin-izm), *n.* The doctrines of the French Protestant theologian John Calvin (1509–64) and his followers, or of later theologians and religious bodies accepting his teachings with various modifications; also, adherence to these doctrines.—**Cal′vin-ist,** *n.* An adherent of Calvinism.—**Cal-vin-is′tic,** *a.*

cal-vi-ti-es (kal-vish′i-ēz), *n.* [L., < *calvus*, bald.] In *pathol.*, baldness.

calx (kalks), *n.*; pl. *calxes*, L. *calces* (kal′sēz). [L., small stone, lime.] Lime; also, the oxide or ashy substance which remains after metals, minerals, etc., have been thoroughly roasted or burned; also, refuse glass for remelting.

cal-y-ces (kal′i-sēz), *n.* Latin plural of *calyx.*

ca-ly-ci-form (ka-lis′i-fôrm), *a.* [L. *calyx* (*calyc-*), calyx: see *-form.*] In *bot.*, having the form of a calyx.

cal-y-cine (kal′i-sin), *a.* Pertaining to or resembling a calyx. Also **ca-ly-ci-nal** (ka-lis′i-nạl).

cal-y-cle (kal′i-kl), *n.* [L. *calyculus*, dim. of *calyx*, calyx.] In *bot.*, a set of bracts resembling an outer calyx.—**ca-lyc-u-lar** (ka-lik′ū̦-lạ̈r), *a.* Of or pertaining to a calycle.—**ca-lyc′u-late, ca-lyc′u-lat-ed** (-lāt, -lā-ted), *a.* Having a calycle.

Cal-y-do-ni-an (kal-i-dō′ni-ạn), *a.* Of or pertaining to Calydon, an ancient city of Ætolia, in northern Greece: as, the *Calydonian* hunt (in Greek legend, the pursuit, by Meleager and a band of heroes, of a savage boar sent by Artemis to ravage Calydon, the boar being slain by Meleager).

ca-lyp-tra (ka-lip′trạ̈), *n.* [NL., < Gr. καλύπτρα, veil, < καλύπτειν, cover: see *hall.*] In *bot.*, a hood-like part connected with the organs of fructification in flowering plants; also, the hood which caps the spore-case in true mosses.

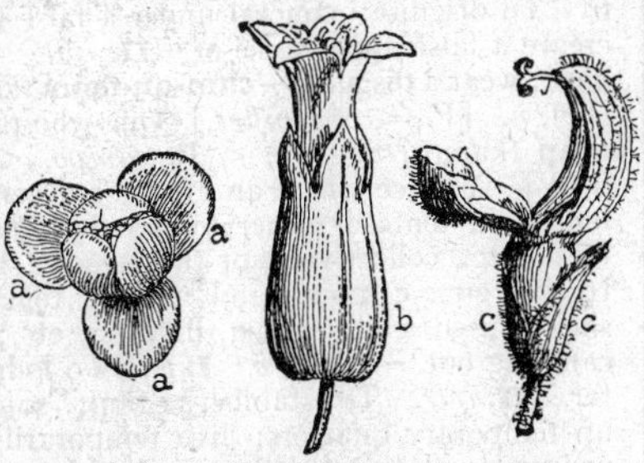

Floral Calyxes.
a, a, a, trisepalous calyx; *b*, gamosepalous calyx; *c, c*, bilabiate calyx.

ca-lyx (kā′liks), *n.*; pl. *calyxes*, L. *calyces* (kal′i-sēz). [L., < Gr. κάλυξ, covering, husk, calyx, < καλύπτειν, cover.] In *bot.*, the external, usually green, envelop of a flower; the sepals; in *anat.* and *zoöl.*, a cup-like part.

cam (kam), *n.* [Cf. D. and Dan. *kam*, G. *kamm*, comb, crest, cog, etc.] A device for converting regular rotary motion into irregular rotary or reciprocating motion, etc., commonly consisting of an oval, heart-shaped, or other specially shaped flat piece, an eccentric wheel, or the like, fastened on and revolving with a shaft, and engaging with other mechanism.

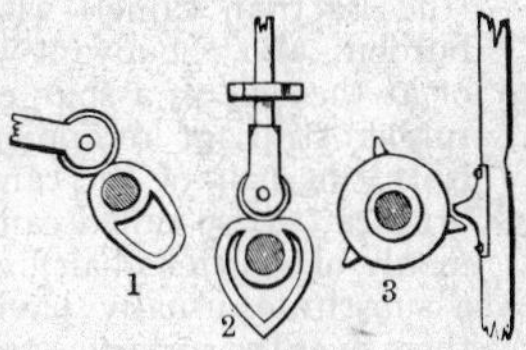

Cams.
1. Elliptical cam, used for giving motion to the levers of punching-machines. 2. The heart-cam, much used in cotton-machinery to produce a regular ascent and descent. 3. Form of cam much used in iron-works for setting in motion the tilt-hammers.

ca-ma-ïeu (kȧ-mȧ-yė), *n.* [F. *camaïeu.*] A cameo; also, a method of painting in monochrome, or a monochrome painting.

ca-mail (kạ-māl′), *n.* [F., < Pr. *capmalh*, < *cap* (< L. *caput*), head, + *malha*, = E. *mail*[1].] A piece of chain-mail for protecting the neck and shoulders, esp. one attached to the edge of the basinet or some other head-piece.—**ca-mailed′,** *a.*

Camails, 14th century.

ca-ma-rade-rie (kȧ-mȧ-rȧd-rē), *n.* [F.] Comradeship; friendly fellowship.

cam-a-ril-la (kam-ạ-ril′ạ̈, Sp. kä-mä-rēl′yä), *n.* [Sp., dim. of *cámara*, chamber.] A body of private advisers; a cabal; a clique.

cam-ass, cam-as (kam′as), *n.* [N. Amer. Ind.] Any of various plants of the liliaceous genus *Quamasia*, esp. *Q. quamash*, a species of western North America, with sweet, edible bulbs.

cam-ber (kam′bėr), *v. t.* or *i.* [F. *cambrer*, < L. *camerare*, < *camera*, arch.] To arch slightly; bend or curve upward in the middle.—**cam′ber,** *n.* A slight arching or convexity above, as of a ship's deck; also, a slightly arching piece of timber; in *aëronautics*, the convexity of a plane.

cam-bist (kam′bist), *n.* [F. *cambiste*, < It. *cambista*, < *cambio*, < ML. *cambium*, exchange.] One versed in the science of monetary exchange; a dealer in bills of exchange; also, a manual giving the moneys, weights, and measures of different countries, with their equivalents.—**cam′bist-ry,** *n.* The science or practice of the cambist.

cam-bi-um (kam′bi-um), *n.* [ML., exchange, < L. *cambire*, exchange, barter: cf. *change.*] In *bot.*, a layer of soft cellular tissue or meristem between the bark and wood (or phloëm and xylem) in trees and shrubs, from which new bark and new wood originate; also, phellogen, an analogous tissue from which cork arises ('cork cambium').

Cam-bri-a (kam′bri-ạ̈), *n.* [ML.: cf. *Cymry.*] Wales. [Chiefly poetic.]—**Cam′bri-an. I.** *a.* Pertaining to Cambria, or Wales; also, noting or pertaining to a geological period or a system of rocks preceding the Silurian and constituting the earliest principal division of the Paleozoic. **II.** *n.* A Welshman; in *geol.*, the Cambrian period or system.

cam-bric (kām′brik), *n.* [Flem. *Kameryk*, for F. *Cambrai*, town in northern France.] A fine, thin linen or cotton fabric.—**cambric tea,** a mixture of hot water and milk, with sugar and, sometimes, a little tea.

came[1] (kām). Preterit of *come.*

came[2] (kām), *n.* [Origin uncertain.] A slender grooved bar of lead for holding together the pieces of glass in windows of lattice-work or stained glass.

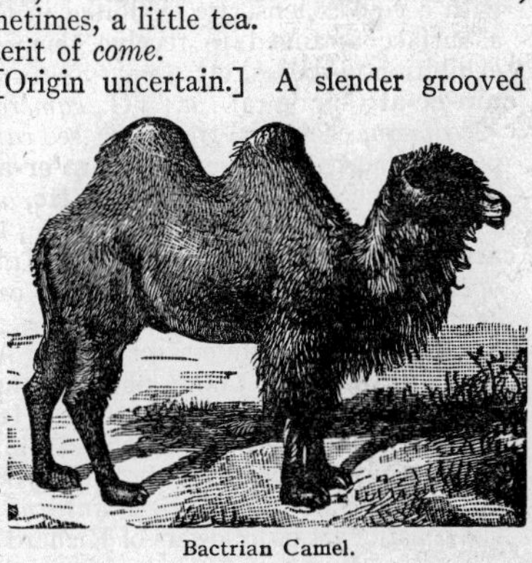
Bactrian Camel.

cam-el (kam′ẹl), *n.* [L. *camelus*, < Gr. κάμηλος; from Semitic.] Either of two large old-world ruminant quadrupeds of the genus *Camelus*, *C. dromedarius* (the Arabian camel, or dromedary) with one hump and *C. bactrianus* (the Bactrian camel) with two humps, used as beasts of burden; also, a buoyant water-tight structure placed under, or at the side of, a ship, etc., to raise it.—**camel back,** the rubber strip for recapping and retreading tires.—**camel's hair,** the hair of the camel, used for cloth, shawls, paint-brushes (the so-called camel's-hair brushes now being commonly of squirrel's hair), etc.; cloth made of this hair, or of a substitute, usually having long, flattened hairs here and there over the surface.—**to strain at a gnat and swallow a camel.** See under *gnat.*—**cam-el-eer'** (-ēr'), *n.* A camel-driver; a soldier on a camel.

ca-mel-lia (kạ-mel'iạ̈, also kạ-mē'liạ̈), *n.* [NL.; named from G. J. *Kamel*, Moravian Jesuit missionary.] A plant, *Thea* (or *Camellia*) *japonica*, native in Asia, with glossy evergreen leaves and white or pink waxy rose-like flowers, familiar in cultivation.

ca-mel-o-pard (kạ-mel'ọ-pärd or kam'ẹ-lọ-), *n.* [LL. *camelopardus*, L. *camelopardalis*, < Gr. καμηλοπάρδαλις, < κάμηλος, camel, + πάρδαλις, pard.] A giraffe; [*cap.*] in *astron.*, the northern constellation Camelopardalis.

cam-el-ry (kam'ẹl-ri), *n.* Soldiers mounted on camels.

Camellia.

Ca-mem-bert (kȧ-moṅ-bãr) **cheese.** [From *Camembert*, village in Normandy, France.] A rich, soft, yellowish variety of cream-cheese.

Ca-me-næ (ka-mē'nē), *n. pl.* [L., pl. of *Camena*, akin to *carmen*, song.] In *Rom. myth.*, prophetic nymphs, in later times often identified with the Greek Muses.

cam-e-o (kam'ẹ̄-ō), *n.*; pl. *-os* (-ōz). [It. *cammeo* = F. *camaïeu*; origin uncertain.] An engraving in relief upon a gem, stone, etc., esp. when differently colored layers of the stone are utilized to produce a background of one hue and a design of another; a gem, stone, etc., so engraved; also, the art of engraving small figures in relief.

cam-er-a (kam'ẹ-rạ̈), *n.*; pl. *cameras*, L. *cameræ* (-rē). [L., arch, vault, ML. chamber, treasury: cf. *chamber.*] An arched roof; a vault; also, a chamber; also, a camera obscura; esp., in *photog.*, a box-like device in which photographic plates, etc., are exposed, the image being formed by means of a lens.—**camera lucida** (lū'si-dä̤). [NL., 'light chamber.'] An instrument, as one consisting of a prismatic piece of glass, by which the image of an external object is made to appear as if on a sheet of paper, etc., upon which it may be traced.—**camera obscura** (ob-skū'rạ̈). [NL., 'dark chamber.'] A darkened box-like device in which images of external objects, received through an aperture, as with a convex lens, are exhibited in their natural colors on a surface arranged to receive them: used for sketching, exhibition purposes, etc.

cam-er-al (kam'ẹ-rạl), *a.* [G. *kameral*, < ML. *cameralis*, < *camera*, chamber, treasury: see *camera.*] Pertaining to public finances or revenue.—**cam'er-al-ist,** *n.* One versed in public finance.—**cam''er-al-is'tic,** *a.*—**cam''er-al-is'tics,** *n.* The science of public finance.

cam-er-a-man (kam'ẹ-rạ̈-mạn), *n.*; pl. *-men.* A man who operates a photographic camera, esp. a moving-picture camera.

cam-er-a-plane (kam'ẹ-rạ̈-plān), *n.* An aëroplane equipped with apparatus for taking photographs.

cam-er-lin-go (kam-ėr-ling'gō), *n.* [It.] The Pope's chamberlain, chosen from among the cardinals and having charge of the secular interests of the papacy.

Cam-er-o-ni-an (kam-ẹ-rō'ni-ạn), *n.* One of the Scotch Calvinistic sect of followers of Richard Cameron (died 1680), a Scotch Presbyterian minister and a leader of the Covenanters.

cam-ion (kam'iọn, F. kȧ-myôṅ), *n.* [F.; origin uncertain.] A strongly built cart or wagon for transporting heavy loads; a truck, as for carrying military supplies.

cam-i-sade (kam-i-sād'), *n.* [F., < It. *camiciata*, < *camicia*, shirt, = E. *chemise.*] *Milit.*, a night attack: so called because orig. the soldiers wore shirts over their armor as a means of recognition. Also **cam-i-sa'do** (-sā'dō). [Obs. or archaic.]

ca-mise (kạ-mēs'), *n.* [Ar. *qamīç.*] A loose shirt, smock, or tunic.

cam-i-sole (kam'i-sōl), *n.* [F., < It. *camiciola*, dim. of *camicia*: see *camisade.*] A woman's dressing-sack; also, an ornamental underbodice, worn under a thin outer bodice.

cam-let (kam'let), *n.* [F. *camelot*, prob. < Ar. *khamlat*, < *khaml*, nap.] A rich fabric, apparently orig. made of goat's hair, formerly in use; also, a durable waterproof cloth used for cloaks, etc.

cam-o-mile, cham-o-mile (kam'ọ-mīl), *n.* [OF. F. *camomille*, < L. *chamomilla*, *chamæmelon*, < Gr. χαμαίμηλον, < χαμαί, on the ground, + μῆλον, apple.] Any plant of the asteraceous genus *Anthemis*, esp. *A. nobilis* (the common camomile of Europe and of gardens elsewhere), an herb with strongly scented foliage and flowers that are used medicinally for their tonic and stomachic properties; also, any of various allied plants, as *Matricaria chamomilla* ('German camomile').

Camomile (*Anthemis nobilis*).

Ca-mor-ra (kạ-mor'ạ̈), *n.* [It.] A Neapolitan secret society, first publicly known about 1820, which developed into a powerful political organization, and has been associated with blackmail, robbery, etc.; hence [*l. c.*], some similar society or group.—**Ca-mor'rism,** *n.* The practices of the Camorra.—**Ca-mor'rist,** *n.*

cam-ou-flage (kam'ọ-fläzh, F. kȧ-mö-fläzh), *n.* [F., < *camoufler*, disguise, make up under a false semblance, < It. *camuffare*, muffle up, disguise.] The act of disguising, or giving a false appearance; the result of this, or the means of effecting it; disguise; deception; false pretense; esp., *milit.*, the act, art, result, or means of disguising things, or of giving them a false appearance, so as to deceive the enemy, as by painting or screening objects so that they are lost to view in the general background, or by making up objects so that they have a false appearance of fortifications, guns, roads, or the like.—**cam'ou-flage,** *v.*; *-flaged*, *-flaging.* **I.** *tr.* To disguise; conceal under a false semblance; also, to create a false appearance of. **II.** *intr.* To practise camouflage; wear a disguise.—**cam-ou-fleur** (kam'ọ-flėr, F. kȧ-mö-flėr), *n.* [F., < *camoufler.*] One who practises camouflage.

camp (kamp), *n.* [F., < It. *campo*, < L. *campus*, plain, field.] A place where an army or other body of persons is lodged in tents or other temporary means of shelter; the tents, etc., collectively, or the persons sheltered; a body of troops, etc., camping and moving together; a temporary shelter used while fishing, hunting, etc.; an encamping, or camping out.—**camp,** *v.* **I.** *tr.* To lodge in a camp; shelter. **II.** *intr.* To establish a camp; sojourn in a camp; take up temporary quarters; live temporarily in a tent or tents or in rude places of shelter, as for pleasure (often with *out*).

cam-paign (kam-pān'), *n.* [F. *campagne*, < It. *campagna*, < ML. *campania*, < L. *campus*, plain.] Level, open country†; the military operations of an army in the field during one season or enterprise; any course of aggressive operations, as to influence voters in an election.—**campaign',** *v. i.* To serve in or go on a campaign.—**campaign'er,** *n.*

cam-pa-ne-ro (kam-pạ-nā′rō), *n.*; pl. *-ros* (-rōz). [Sp., < *campana*, < ML. *campana*, bell.] A South American bell-bird, esp. *Chasmorhynchus niveus.*

Campanile of Giotto, Florence.

cam-pan-i-form (kam-pan′i-fôrm), *a.* [ML. *campana*, bell: see *-form.*] Bell-shaped.

cam-pa-ni-le (käm-pä-nē′lā), *n.*; pl. *-li* (-lē). [It., < ML. *campana*, bell.] A bell-tower (often a detached structure).

cam-pa-nol-o-gy (kam-pạ-nol′ọ-ji), *n.* [ML. *campana*, bell: see *-logy.*] The study of bells; the principles of bell-founding, bell-ringing, etc.—**cam-pa-nol′o-gist,** *n.*

cam-pan-u-la (kam-pan′ụ-lạ), *n.*; pl. *-las.* [ML., dim. of *campana*, bell.] Any plant of the genus *Campanula*, as the harebell or the canterbury-bell; a bell-flower.—**cam-pan-u-la′ceous** (-lā′shius), *a.* Belonging to the *Campanulaceæ*, or campanula family of plants.

cam-pan-u-late (kam-pan′ụ-lạt), *a.* [NL. *campanulatus*, < ML. *campanula*: see *campanula.*] Bell-shaped, as a corolla.

Camp-bell-ite (kam′bẹl-īt or kam′ẹl-), *n.* [From Alexander *Campbell* (1788–1866), founder of the body.] A member of the body of Christians known as Disciples of Christ. See under *disciple*, *n.*

camp=chair (kamp′chãr), *n.* A light folding chair.

Cam-pea-chy (kam-pē′chi) **wood.** [From *Campeachy* (*Campeche*), state of Mexico.] Logwood.

camp-er (kam′pėr), *n.* One who camps; one who sojourns in a camp.

cam-pes-tral (kam-pes′trạl), *a.* [L. *campester*, < *campus*, field.] Pertaining to or growing in the fields. Also **cam-pes′tri-an, cam-pes′trine** (-trin).

camp=fire (kamp′fīr), *n.* A fire in a camp for warmth or cooking; also, a social gathering or reunion of soldiers or former soldiers.

camp=fol-low-er (kamp′fol″ọ-ėr), *n.* One who follows a camp or an army without being officially connected with it, as a sutler, washerwoman, etc.

cam-phene (kam′fēn or kam-fēn′), *n.* [From *camphor.*] A hydrocarbon, $C_{10}H_{16}$, present in certain plants.

cam-phine (kam′fēn or kam-fēn′), *n.* [From *camphor.*] A purified oil of turpentine, formerly burned in lamps.

cam-phire (kam′fīr), *n.* [Old form of *camphor.*] Camphor (obs. or prov.); in the Bible (Authorized Version, Cant. i. 14), the henna-plant.

cam-phol (kam′fol or -fōl), *n.* [From *camphor.*] Same as *borneol.*—**cam-phol′ic** (-fol′ik), *a.*

cam-phor (kam′fọr), *n.* [F. *camphre*, < ML. *camphora*, < Ar. *kāfūr.*] A whitish, translucent, crystalline, aromatic substance, obtained chiefly from the tree *Cinnamomum camphora* (see *camphor-tree*), used in medicine, in the manufacture of celluloid, etc.; also, any of various similar substances.—**cam-pho-ra′ceous** (-fọ-rā′shius), *a.* Of the nature of or resembling camphor.—**cam′pho-rate** (-rāt), *v. t.*; *-rated*, *-rating.* To impregnate with camphor.—**cam′pho-rate,** *n.* In *chem.*, a salt of camphoric acid.—**cam-phor′ic** (-for′ik), *a.* Of, containing, or derived from camphor: as, *camphoric* acid (a dibasic crystalline acid obtained by the oxidation of camphor).—**cam′phor-ous,** *a.* Camphor-like.—**cam′phor=tree,** *n.* A lauraceous tree, *Cinnamomum camphora*, of Japan, China, etc., yielding the camphor of commerce; also, any of various similar trees, as *Dryobalanops aromatica* of Borneo, etc., which yields borneol.

cam-pim-e-ter (kam-pim′e-tėr), *n.* [L. *campus*, field: see *-meter.*] An apparatus for measuring range of color-sensitivity of the retina, and other visual properties.

cam-pi-on (kam′pi-ọn), *n.* [Origin uncertain.] Any of certain plants of the pink family, as *Lychnis coronaria*, a cultivated plant with crimson flowers ('rose-campion').

camp=meet-ing (kamp′mē″ting), *n.* A religious meeting, usually lasting for some days, held in an encampment formed for the purpose.

camp=stool (kamp′stöl), *n.* A light folding seat.

cam-pus (kam′pus), *n.* [L., field.] The grounds or yard of an American college or other school.

Campylotropous Seed.

cam-py-lot-ro-pous (kam-pi-lot′rọ-pus), *a.* [Gr. καμπύλος, curved, + -τροπος, < τρέπειν, turn.] In *bot.*, having the nucellus and its integuments so curved that the micropyle is brought near the hilum: said of an ovule or seed.

cam-wood (kam′wůd), *n.* [Prob. from native African name.] Same as *barwood.*

can[1] (kan), *v.*; pres. 1 *can*, 2 *canst*, 3 *can*, pl. *can*; pret. *could.* [AS. *cann*, *can*, 1st and 3d pers. sing. pres. ind. (pret. *cūthe*) of *cunnan* = G. *können* = Icel. *kunna*, know, be able, = Goth. *kunnan*, know: cf. *ken* and *know.*] **A.**† *tr.* or *intr.* To know; also, to be able to do. **B.** *auxiliary.* Know how to; am (is, are, etc.) able to; have the ability, power, right, qualifications, or means to; am liable to; may: as, he *can* speak French; I *can* hear; we *can* soon tell; you *can* scarcely refuse; it *can* (or *may*) be done.

can[2] (kan), *n.* [AS. *canne* = G. *kanne*, can, pot, mug.] A vessel for holding water, milk, oil, etc., now commonly one of tinned or other metal; a drinking-vessel; a tinned or other vessel in which food or the like is sealed up for keeping; an ash-can, or depth bomb (colloq.).—**can**[2], *v. t.*; *canned*, *canning.* To put or preserve in a can; also, to expel or dismiss, as from employment (slang).

Ca-naan (kā′nạn), *n.* The region, included in modern Palestine, lying between the Jordan and the Mediterranean, the land promised by God to Abraham (Gen. xii.); fig., any land of promise; heaven.—**Ca′naan-ite** (-īt), *n.* A descendant of Canaan, son of Ham (Gen. x.); one of the inhabitants of the land of Canaan before the Hebrews.—**Ca′naan-it-ish** (-ī-tish), *a.*

ca-ña-da (kä-nyä′dạ), *n.* [Sp.] A deep, narrow valley.

Can-a-da (kan′ạ-dạ) **bal′sam.** See *balsam.*—**Can′a-da goose.** The common wild goose, *Bernicla* (*Branta*) *canadensis*, of North America.—**Can′a-da grouse.** See *grouse*[1], *n.*—**Can′a-da hemp.** See *Indian hemp*, under *hemp.*—**Can′a-da rob′in.** The cedar-bird.

Canada Goose.

Ca-na-di-an (kạ-nā′di-ạn). **I.** *a.* Of or pertaining to Canada. **II.** *n.* A native or inhabitant of Canada.

ca-nai-gre (kạ-nā′gėr), *n.* [Mex. Sp.] A species of dock, *Rumex hymenosepalus*, of the southwestern U. S., whose root yields tannin.

Canaigre, with its fruit.

ca-naille (kȧ-nä-y′), *n.* [F., < It. *canaglia*, < L. *canis*, dog.] Riffraff; the rabble.

can-a-kin (kan′ạ-kin), *n.* See *cannikin.*

ca-nal (kạ-nal′), *n.* [F. *canal*, < L. *canalis*, pipe, groove, channel.] A pipe† or tube†; a tubular passage or cavity, as in an animal or plant body; a duct; a channel† or watercourse†; a long, narrow arm of the sea penetrating far inland (as, Lynn *Canal*, in Alaska); an artificial waterway for navigation, irrigation, etc.; a groove or furrow.—**canal rays.** See under *ray*[3], *n.*—**canals of Mars,** certain long, narrow dark lines on the surface of the planet Mars, formerly thought to be canals, but now supposed by some to be due to vegetation.—**ca-nal′,** *v. t.*; *-nalled*, *-nalling.* To make a canal through; furnish with canals.—**ca-nal′age** (-ạj), *n.* The construction of canals; canals as a means of transportation; a charge for the use of a canal.—**ca-nal′=boat,** *n.* A comparatively long and narrow boat used on canals and commonly moved by traction.

can-a-lic-u-lus (kan-ạ-lik′ụ-lus), *n.*; pl. *-li* (-lī). [L., dim. of *canalis*: see *canal.*] In *anat.* and *zoöl.*, a small canal or tubular passage, as in bone; a small channel, groove, or furrow.—**can-a-lic′u-lar** (-lạr), *a.*—**can-a-lic′u-late, can-a-lic′u-lat-ed** (-lāt, -lā-ted), *a.*

ca-nal-ize (kạ-nal′īz), *v. t.*; *-ized, -izing.* To make a canal or canals through; also, to convert into a canal.—**ca-nal″i-za′tion** (-i-zā′shọn), *n.*

ca-nal-ler, ca-nal-er (kạ-nal′ėr), *n.* One employed on a canal-boat or engaged in the business of canal transportation; also, a canal-boat.

can-a-pé (kan-ạ-pā′, F. kȧ-nȧ-pā), *n.* [F., = E. *canopy.*] A thin piece of fried or toasted bread covered with a fish, game, cheese, or other seasoned preparation and served hot.

ca-nard (kạ-närd′, F. kȧ-när), *n.* [F., lit. 'duck.'] A fabricated story or report circulated as true; a hoax.

Can-a-rese, Kan-a-rese (kan-ạ-rēs′ or -rēz′), *n.* A Dravidian language spoken in the districts of North and South Canara, or Kanara, in southwestern India.

ca-na-ry (kạ-nā′ri), *n.*; pl. *-ries* (-riz). Wine of the Canary Islands; a lively kind of dance†; a canary-bird; also, the color of the bird, a light, clear yellow.—**ca-na′ry†,** *v. i.* To dance the canary (dance). See Shakspere's "Love's Labour's Lost," iii. 1. 12.—**ca-na′ry=bird,** *n.* A well-known cage-bird, a kind of finch, *Serinus canarius* (or *Carduelis canaria*), native in the Canary Islands, and orig. of a brownish or greenish color, but through modification in the domesticated state now usually of a light, clear yellow.—**ca-na′ry=grass,** *n.* Any of various grasses of the genus *Phalaris*, as *P. canariensis*, native in the Canary Islands, which yields a seed used as food for cage-birds, or *P. arundinacea* ('reed canary-grass'), a widely diffused species of the northern hemisphere, which is used as fodder.—**ca-na′ry=seed,** *n.* The seed of the canary-grass, *Phalaris canariensis*, used as food for canaries and other cage-birds.

Canary-grass (*Phalaris canariensis*).—1, the plant; 2, the spike-like inflorescence; *a*, empty glumes; *b*, flowering glumes inclosing the flower.

ca-nas-ter (kạ-nas′tėr), *n.* [Sp. *canastro, canasta*, basket, < L. *canistrum*, E. *canister.*] A kind of tobacco for smoking, consisting of the dried leaves coarsely broken: so called from the rush baskets in which it was formerly imported.

can-can (kan′kan, F. käṅ-käṅ), *n.* [F.] A disorderly form of quadrille marked by extravagant leaping and kicking, which came into vogue about 1830 at the public balls of Paris; loosely, an indecorous dance.

can-cel (kan′sẹl), *v. t.*; *-celed* or *-celled, -celing* or *-celling.* [OF. F. *canceller*, < L. *cancellare* (pp. *cancellatus*), < *cancelli*, pl., bars, lattice.] To deface or obliterate, as writing, by drawing a line or lines over; strike out; efface or wipe out; annul or make void; suppress or omit, as some portion of a printed work; in *math.*, to eliminate by striking out (a factor common to both terms of a fraction, equivalent quantities on opposite sides of an equation, etc.); balance and eliminate (an equivalent opposed quantity); in general, to neutralize or counterbalance; compensate for.—**can′cel,** *n.* A canceling; also, a canceled part.—**can′cel-a-ble, can′cel-la-ble,** *a.* That may be canceled.—**can′cel-er, can′cel-ler,** *n.*—**can′cel-late, can′cel-lat-ed** (-lāt, -lā-ted), *a.* [L. *cancellatus*, pp.] Marked with crossing lines, like lattice-work; reticulated; also, of spongy or porous structure, as bone.—**can-cel-la′tion** (-lā′shọn), *n.* [L. *cancellatio(n-).*] The act or an act of canceling; also, something canceled; also, cancellate arrangement.—**can′cel-lous,** *a.* Cancellate.

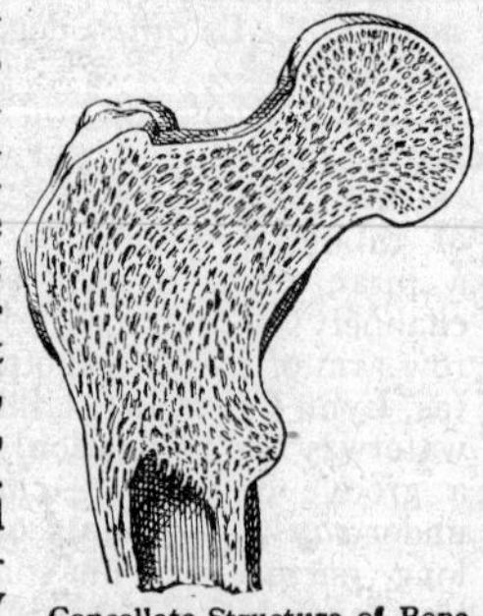

Cancellate Structure of Bone.—Upper part of femur, in section.

can-cer (kan′sėr), *n.* [L. *cancer* (*cancr-*), a crab, the Crab, also the tumor: cf. Gr. καρκίνος, Skt. *karkata*, crab.] [*cap.*] The Crab, a zodiacal constellation; also, the fourth sign of the zodiac (see *zodiac*); [*l. c.*] in *pathol.*, a malignant growth or tumor, esp. one originating in the epithelium and tending to recur after excision; fig., an evil likened to a malignant, corrosive sore.—**can′cer,** *v. t.* To eat into like a cancer; make (a way) slowly and persistently, as a cancer does.—**can′cer-ate** (-sẹ-rāt), *v. i.*; *-ated, -ating.* [L. *canceratus*, cancerous.] To become cancerous.—**can-cer-a′tion** (-sẹ-rā′shọn), *n.*—**can′cer-ous,** *a.* Cancer-like; affected with cancer.—**can′cer=root,** *n.* Any of several orobanchaceous plants parasitic upon the roots of trees, as the beech-drops, etc.

can-cri-form (kang′kri-fôrm), *a.* [L. *cancer* (*cancr-*): see *cancer* and *-form.*] Crab-like; also, cancerous.

can-cri-nite (kang′kri-nīt), *n.* [From Count *Cancrin* (1774–1845), Russian minister of finance.] A silicate and carbonate mineral containing sodium, calcium, and aluminium, occurring in various volcanic rocks and often bright yellow in color.

can-cri-zans (kang′kri-zạnz), *a.* [ML., ppr. of *cancrizare*, go backward like a crab, < L. *cancer*: see *cancer.*] Going or moving backward, like a crab; in *music*, designating a canon in which the theme or subject is repeated backward instead of forward.

can-croid (kang′kroid). [L. *cancer* (*cancr-*): see *cancer* and *-oid.*] **I.** *a.* Resembling a crab; in *pathol.*, resembling a cancer, as certain tumors. **II.** *n.* In *pathol.*, a form of cancer of the skin.

can-de-la-brum (kan-de-lā′brum), *n.*; pl. *-bra* (-brạ) or *-brums.* [L., < *candela*, candle.] Orig., a candlestick or lamp-stand used by the Romans; now, an ornamental branched candlestick. Also **can-de-la′bra** (properly *pl.*, but taken as *sing.*); pl. *-bras* (-brạz).

Candelabrum, time of Napoleon I.

can-dent (kan′dẹnt), *a.* [L. *candens* (*candent-*), ppr. of *candere*, shine.] Glowing with heat; at a white heat; white.

can-des-cent (kan-des′ẹnt), *a.* [L. *candescens* (*-ent-*), ppr. of *candescere*, begin to glow, < *candere*, shine.] Glowing; incandescent.—**can-des′cence,** *n.*—**can-des′cent-ly,** *adv.*

can-did (kan′did), *a.* [L. *candidus*, white, fair, clear, sincere, candid, < *candere*, shine.] White†; also, clear or pure; also, frank; outspoken; open and sincere; also, honest; impartial.

can-di-date (kan′di-dāt), *n.* [L. *candidatus*, clad in white, as a Roman candidate for office, < *candidus*, white: see *candid.*] One who seeks an appointment, honor, etc.; one who is selected by others as a contestant for an office or the like; an aspirant.—**can′di-da-cy** (-dạ-si), **can′di-da-ture** (-tụr), *n.*

can-did-ly (kan′did-li), *adv.* In a candid manner; frankly; fairly.—**can′did-ness,** *n.*

can-died (kan′did), *p. a.* Crystallized, as sugar; also, impregnated or incrusted with or as with sugar; fig., honeyed or sweet.

Can-di-ot, Can-di-ote (kan′di-ot, -ōt). [See *-ot* and *-ote.*] **I.** *n.* A native or inhabitant of Candia, or Crete; a Cretan. **II.** *a.* Cretan.

can-dle (kan′dl), *n.* [AS. *candel*, < L. *candela*, < *candere*, shine.] A stick of tallow, wax, or the like, inclosing a wick, burned to give light, and sometimes (in a fixed size and of special composition, etc.) used as a standard of illuminating power; also, something like or likened to this, as a pastille for burning in a sick-room.—**to hold a candle to,** to approach in excellence, merit, etc.; bear comparison with: used in negative expressions.—**can′dle,** *v. t.*; *-dled, -dling.* To examine, as eggs for freshness, by holding between the eye and a lighted candle or any light.—**can′dle-ber″ry,** *n.* The candlenut; also, the wax-myrtle (genus *Myrica*), or its berry.—**can′dle=coal,** *n.* Same as *cannel-*

coal.—**can′dle=fish,** *n.* An edible fish, *Thaleichthys pacificus,* of the northwestern coast of America, allied to the smelt, with flesh so oily that when the fish is dried and supplied with a wick it may be used as a candle.—**can′dle=foot,** *n.* The illumination of a standard candle at a distance of one foot: used as a unit.—**can′dle=light,** *n.* The light of a candle; hence, artificial light; also, the time during or at which candles are lighted.—**Can′dle-mas** (-mąs), *n.* [AS. *candelmæsse*: see *-mas.*] An ecclesiastical festival in honor of the presentation of the infant Christ in the Temple and the purification of the Virgin Mary, celebrated by lighted candles; also, the day on which it is held, Feb. 2 (cf. *ground-hog day*).—**can′dle-nut,** *n.* The oily fruit or nut of a euphorbiaceous tree, *Aleurites moluccana,* of the South Sea Islands, etc., the kernels of which, when strung together, are used as candles by the natives; also, the tree itself.—**can′dle=pow′er,** *n.* The illuminating power of a standard candle: used as a unit of measurement.—**can′dler,** *n.*—**can′dle-stick,** *n.* An instrument for holding a candle in the position for burning.—**can′dle-wood,** *n.* Any resinous wood used for torches, or as a substitute for candles; any of various trees or shrubs yielding such wood.

Candle-fish.

can-dor (kan′dǫr), *n.* [L., < *candere,* shine.] Whiteness†; also, purity, as of character or mind†; also, frankness, as of speech; sincerity; honesty.

can-dour (kan′dǫr), *n.* British preferred form of *candor.*

can-dy (kan′di), *n.*; pl. *-dies* (-diz). [F. *candi,* candied, < Ar. and Pers. *qand,* sugar; prob. from Skt.] A sweet, dry confection of many varieties, made of sugar, or of molasses, honey, etc., often with the addition of chocolate, fruit, nuts, or other ingredients; also, a single piece of such a confection; a bonbon.—**can′dy,** *v.*; *-died, -dying.* **I.** *tr.* To reduce (sugar, etc.) to a crystalline form, as by boiling down; also, to impregnate or incrust with sugar, etc., as by boiling in a sugary solution; fig., to incrust with any crystalline matter (as, "The cold brook, *Candied* with ice": Shakspere's "Timon of Athens," iv. 3. 226); also, to make sweet, palatable, or agreeable (as, to *candy* one's words; to *candy* an unpleasant task); give a pleasing aspect to. **II.** *intr.* To crystallize; become incrusted with sugar: as, the jelly has *candied* at the surface.—**can′dy=pull,** *n.* A gathering, as of young people, for the purpose of making molasses candy: so called from the 'pulling,' or drawing out, of the semisolid candy after boiling, in order to work it into the desired condition. [U. S.]

can-dy-tuft (kan′di-tuft), *n.* [From *Candy,* for *Candia* (Crete).] A plant of the brassicaceous genus *Iberis,* esp. *I. umbellata,* a cultivated annual with tufted flowers, orig. from the island of Candia.

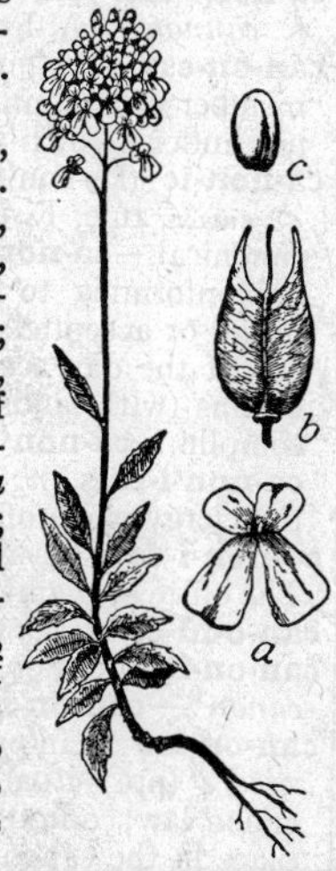

Candytuft (*Iberis umbellata*).—*a,* flower; *b,* fruit; *c,* seed.

cane (kān), *n.* [OF. *cane* (F. *canne*), < L. *canna,* < Gr. κάννα, reed: cf. Heb. *qāneh.*] A long, hollow or pithy, jointed woody stem, as that of bamboo, certain palms, etc.; such stems as a material; also, a plant having such a stem; the sugar-cane; any of various tall, woody, bamboo-like grasses, esp. of the genus *Arundinaria,* as *A. macrosperma* ('large cane') and *A. tecta* ('small cane'), of the southern U. S.; also, the stem of a bamboo, etc., used as a walking-stick or as a rod for chastising; hence, any walking-stick; also, a slender cylindrical stick or rod of various substances, as sealing-wax or glass.—**cane,** *v. t.*; *caned, caning.* To beat or chastise with a cane; also, to furnish or make with cane.—**cane′=brake,** *n.* A thicket of canes.

ca-nel-la (ką-nel′ą̈), *n.* [ML., cinnamon, < L. *canna,* E. *cane.*] The cinnamon-like bark of a West Indian tree, *Canella winterana*: used as a condiment and in medicine.—**can-el-la-ceous** (kan-e-lā′shius), *a.* Belonging to the *Canellaceæ,* a family of trees including the genus *Canella.*

ca-neph-o-ra (ka-nef′ǫ-rą̈), *n.*; pl. *-ræ* (-rē). [L., also *canephoros,* < Gr. κανηφόρος, < κάνεον, basket, + φέρειν, bear.] In ancient Greece, one of the maidens who bore upon their heads baskets containing the materials for sacrifice in certain religious festivals; in *arch.,* a representation of one of these; also, a caryatid having a basket-like cushion upon the head.

Canephora, from the frieze of the Parthenon, at Athens.

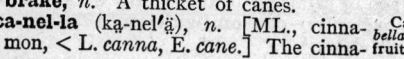

can-er (kā′nėr), *n.* One who canes something, as chairs.

ca-nes-cent (ką-nes′ęnt), *a.* [L. *canescens (-ent-),* ppr. of *canescere,* grow white, < *canus,* white.] Growing white; whitish; hoary; gray.—**ca-nes′cence,** *n.*

cane=sug-ar (kān′shůg′ą̈r), *n.* Sugar obtained from the sugar-cane; saccharose.

cangue (kang), *n.* [F., prob. < Pg. *canga,* yoke.] A kind of portable pillory worn about the neck by Chinese criminals.

Ca-nic-u-la (ką-nik′ū-lą̈), *n.* [L., dim. of *canis,* dog.] The dog-star, Sirius.—**ca-nic′u-lar,** *a.* Of or pertaining to the dog-star or its rising (as, the *canicular* days, the dog-days); pertaining to the dog-days.—**can-i-cule** (kan′i-kūl), *n.* [F.] The dog-days.

can′i-kin, *n.* See *cannikin.*

ca-nine (kā′nīn or ką-nīn′). [L. *caninus,* < *canis,* dog.] **I.** *a.* Of or like a dog; pertaining to or characteristic of dogs: as, *canine* madness (hydrophobia); *canine* teeth (the four pointed teeth, esp. prominent in dogs, situated one on each side of each jaw, next to the incisors). **II.** *n.* A dog; any animal of the dog family (*Canidæ*); also, a canine tooth.—**ca-nin-i-ty** (ką-nin′i-ti), *n.* Canine nature; also, the canine race; also, kindness to dogs.

can-ions (kan′yǫnz), *n. pl.* [Sp. *cañón,* tube: see *cañon.*] Ornamental rolls formerly worn round the lower ends of the legs of breeches.

Ca-nis Ma-jor (kā′nis mā′jǫr). [L., 'greater dog.'] The Great Dog, a southern constellation following Orion, and containing Sirius, the dog-star, the brightest of the fixed stars.—**Ca′nis Mi-nor** (mī′nǫr). [L., 'lesser dog.'] The Little Dog, a constellation south of Gemini and separated from Canis Major by the Milky Way, and containing the bright star Procyon.

can-is-ter (kan′is-tėr), *n.* [L. *canistrum,* < Gr. κάναστρον, basket, < κάννα, reed.] A basket (obs. or archaic: as, "White lilies in full *canisters* they bring," Dryden's tr. Virgil's "Pastorals," ii. 61); also, a box, usually of metal, for holding tea, coffee, etc.; also, the case of case-shot; hence, case-shot ('canister-shot').

can-ker (kang′kėr), *n.* [OF. *cancre,* < L. *cancer,* E. *cancer.*] A gangrenous or ulcerous sore, esp. in the mouth; any of various diseases of plants producing slow decay; a disease affecting horses' feet; a canker-worm; fig., anything that corrodes, corrupts, consumes slowly, or irritates; also, the dogrose (obs. or prov.).—**can′ker,** *v.* **I.** *tr.* To infect with canker; fig., to corrupt; consume slowly; irritate or fret. **II.** *intr.* To become infected with or as with canker; become malignant.—**can′kered,** *p. a.* Affected with canker; ulcerated; eaten by a canker-worm; fig., morally corrupt; depraved; also, malignant; ill-natured.—**can′ker-ous,** *a.* Of the nature of or resembling canker; causing canker.—**can′ker=rash,** *n.* A variety of scarlet fever complicated with ulcerations in the throat.—**can′ker=root,** *n.* Any of various plants with astringent or bitter roots, as the goldthread.—**can′ker=worm,** *n.* Any of various insect larvæ injurious to plants; esp., in the U. S., the larva of either of two geometrid moths, *Paleacrita vernata* ('spring canker-worm') and *Alsophila pometaria* ('fall canker-worm'), injurious to trees.—**can′ker-y,** *a.* Cankered.

can-na (kan'ạ), *n.* [L., reed: see *cane.*] Any plant of the tropical genus *Canna* (family *Cannaceæ*), various species of which are cultivated for their large, handsome leaves and showy flowers.

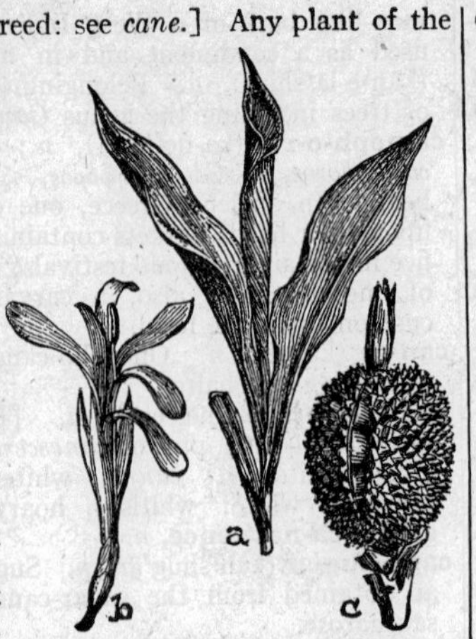

Canna (*C. indica*).—*a*, foliage; *b*, flower; *c*, fruit, dehiscing.

can-nab-ic (ka-nab'ik), *a.* [L. *cannabis*, < Gr. κάνναβις, hemp.] Of or pertaining to hemp.—**can-na-bin** (kan'ạ-bin), *n.* A poisonous resin extracted from Indian hemp (see under *hemp*). —**can'na-bism,** *n.* The morbid effects due to excessive use of Indian hemp.

canned (kand), *p. a.* Put up or preserved in a can; preserved on a phonographic record, as music (slang); in general, specially prepared in advance (slang).

can-nel=coal (kan'ẹl-kōl), *n.* [Appar. for *candle-coal.*] A compact coal burning readily with a bright flame.—**can'nel-oid,** *a.* [See *-oid.*] Resembling cannel-coal.

canne-lon (kån-lôñ), *n.* [F., a channeled mold.] In *cookery*, a hollow roll of puff-paste; also, a roll of minced and seasoned meat or the like, baked or fried.

can-ne-lure (kan'ẹ-lūr), *n.* [F., < *canneler*, to groove, channel.] A groove or channel in a surface.—**can'nelured,** *a.*

can-ner (kan'ėr), *n.* One who cans meat, fish, fruit, or the like, for preservation.—**can'ner-y,** *n.*; pl. *canneries* (-iz). An establishment for canning meat, fish, fruit, or the like.

can-ni-bal (kan'i-bạl). [Sp. *Caníbal*, for *Caríbal*, < *Caribe*, Carib.] **I.** *n.* A human being, esp. a savage, that eats human flesh; hence, any animal that eats its own kind. **II.** *a.* Pertaining to or characteristic of cannibals; given to cannibalism.—**can-ni-bal'ic** (-bal'ik), *a.*—**can'ni-bal-ism,** *n.* The practice of eating one's own kind.—**can''ni-bal-is'tic,** *a.*

can-nie (kan'i), *a.* and *adv.* See *canny.*

can-ni-kin (kan'i-kin), *n.* [Dim. of *can*².] A little can; a cup.

can-ni-ly (kan'i-li), *adv.* In a canny manner.—**can'ni-ness,** *n.*

can-non (kan'ọn), *n.*; pl. *cannons* or (esp. collectively) *cannon.* [OF. F. *canon*, < It. *cannone*, aug. of *canna*, tube, < L. *canna*: see *cane.*] A mounted gun for throwing heavy balls, etc., by the force of gunpowder; a piece of ordnance or artillery; a gun, howitzer, or mortar; also, a hollow cylinder fitted over a shaft and capable of revolving independently; the cannon-bone; the metal loop of a bell by which it is hung; the part of a bit that is let into the horse's mouth; a smooth round bit; also, in *billiards*, a carom (chiefly Eng.).

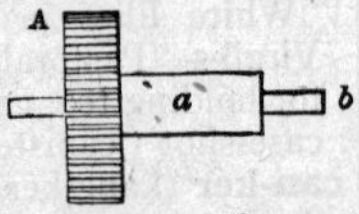

a, Cannon, being part of wheel *A* loose on shaft *b*.

—**can'non,** *v. i.* To discharge cannon; also, to make a carom in billiards (chiefly Eng.); strike and rebound; collide violently.—**can-non-ade'** (-ād'), *n.* A continued discharge of cannon, esp. during an attack.—**can-non-ade',** *v. t.* or *i.*; *-aded, -ading.* To attack with or discharge cannon.—**can'non=ball,** *n.* A missile, usually round and made of iron or steel, designed to be fired from a cannon.—**can'non=bone,** *n.* In hoofed quadrupeds, the bone extending from the tarsal or carpal joint to the fetlock-joint.—**can'noned,** *a.* Provided with cannon.—**can-non-eer'** (-ēr'), *n.* An artilleryman.—**can'non=fod''der,** *n.* [Tr. G. *kanonenfutter*, for the source of which see entry *kanonenfutter.*] Food for cannon; common soldiers as the material used up in war.—**can'non-ry,** *n.* Cannonading; also, artillery.—**can'non=shot,** *n.* The shooting of a cannon; a ball or shot for a cannon; the range of a cannon.

can-not (kan'ot). A common form of *can not.*

can-nu-la (kan'ū-lạ), *n.* [L., dim. of *canna*: see *cane.*] In *surg.*, a small tube of metal or the like for introduction into the body, as for drawing off fluid.—**can'nu-lar,** *a.* Tubular.—**can'nu-late, can'nu-lat-ed** (-lāt, -lā-ted), *a.* Hollow or tubular: as, a *cannulated* needle (a surgeon's needle made hollow to allow a wire, thread, etc., to pass through its entire length).

can-ny (kan'i), *a.*; compar. *cannier*, superl. *canniest.* [Appar. < *can*¹.] Knowing or sagacious; shrewd or astute; skilled or expert; having supernatural powers†; safe to deal or meddle with (chiefly with a negative); frugal or thrifty; careful or cautious; quiet or gentle; snug or cozy; pleasing or comely; good or worthy. [Chiefly Sc.]—**can'ny,** *adv.* In a canny manner; carefully; warily; gently. [Sc.]—**to ca' canny.** See under *ca'*.

ca-noe (kạ-nö'), *n.* [Sp. *canoa*; prob. from Carib.] Among primitive peoples, a boat hollowed out of the trunk of a tree, or made of birch-bark, skins, etc., and propelled by a paddle or paddles; hence, any light boat propelled by paddle.—**ca-noe',** *v. i.*; *-noed, -noeing.* To paddle a canoe; go in a canoe.—**ca-noe'ist,** *n.* One who paddles a canoe; one skilled in canoeing.

War-canoe of Alaska Indians.

can-on¹ (kan'ọn), *n.* [L., rule, canon, < Gr. κανών, straight rod, rule, standard.] An ecclesiastical rule or law enacted by a council or other competent authority; the body of ecclesiastical law ('canon law'); any rule or law; a fundamental principle; a standard or criterion; the books of the Bible recognized by the Christian church as genuine and inspired; any recognized set of sacred books; that part of the mass between the Sanctus and the Lord's Prayer; a catalogue or list, as of the saints acknowledged by the church; a large size of printing-type (48 point); the cannon of a bell; in *music*, a kind of composition in which the different participants begin the same melody one after another at regular intervals, either at the same or at a different pitch.

can-on² (kan'ọn), *n.* [OF. *canone* (F. *chanoine*), < LL. *canonicus*, n., earlier adj.: see *canonic.*] *Eccles.*, one of a body of dignitaries or prebendaries attached to a cathedral or a collegiate church; a member of the chapter of a cathedral or a collegiate church; also, one of the members ('canons regular') of certain Roman Catholic religious orders, as the order called 'Canons Regular of St. Augustine' ('Augustinian Canons,' 'Austin Canons,' or 'Black Canons') or that of the Premonstratensians ('White Canons').

ca-ñon (kan'yọn, Sp. kä-nyōn'), *n.* [Sp. *cañón*, tube, = E. *cannon.*] A deep valley with precipitous sides. [U. S.]

can-on-ess (kan'ọn-es), *n.* [Fem. of *canon*².] *Eccles.*, a member of a community of women living under a rule, but not under a vow; a member of a female chapter.

ca-non-ic (kạ-non'ik), *a.* [L. *canonicus*, < Gr. κανονικός, < κανών, rule, E. *canon*¹.] Pertaining to a canon or rule; canonical.—**ca-non'i-cal,** *a.* Pertaining to, established by, or conforming to a canon or canons; authorized, recognized, or accepted.—**canonical hours,** *eccles.*, certain periods of the day set apart for prayer and devotion, namely, matins (with lauds), prime, terce, sext, nones, vespers, and complin.—**ca-non'i-cal-ly,** *adv.*—**ca-non'i-cal-ness,** *n.*—**ca-non'i-cals,** *n. pl.* The dress prescribed by canon for the clergy when officiating; prescribed official costume.

ca-non-i-cate (kạ-non'i-kāt), *n.* [LL. *canonicus*, E. *canon*².] The office or dignity of a canon; a canonry.

can-o-ni-ci-ty (kan-ọ-nis'i-ti), *n.* Canonical character.

can-on-ist (kan'ọn-ist), *n.* One versed in canon law. See *canon*¹.—**can-on-is'tic, can-on-is'ti-cal,** *a.*

can-on-ize (kan'ọn-īz), *v. t.*; *-ized, -izing.* [ML. *canonizare* (pp. *-atus*).] To make canonical; include in the canon law; admit into the canon, as of Scripture; also, to place in the canon or catalogue of the saints; declare to be a saint; hence, to glorify.—**can''on-i-za'tion** (-i-zā'shọn), *n.*

can'on law. See *canon*¹.

can-on-ry (kan′ọn-ri), *n.*; pl. *-ries* (-riz). The office or benefice of a canon. Also **can′on-ship.**

Ca-no-pic (ka-nō′pik), *a.* Of or from Canopus, an ancient city of Egypt, as a kind of vase used to hold the entrails of embalmed bodies: hence applied also to vases used elsewhere to hold the ashes of the dead.

Etruscan Canopic Vases.

can-o-py (kan′ọ-pi), *n.*; pl. *-pies* (-piz). [OF. *canape* (F. *canapé*), < L. *conopeum*, < Gr. κωνωπεῖον, mosquito-net, < κώνωψ, gnat, mosquito.] A covering suspended or supported over a throne, bed, etc., or held over an exalted person, sacred object, etc.; hence, an overhanging protection or shelter; often, the sky; in *arch.*, an ornamental roof-like projection or covering.—**can′o-py,** *v. t.*; *-pied, -pying.* To cover with or as with a canopy.

Architectural Canopy. — Portal of the church of St. Père-sous-Vézelay, France.

ca-no-rous (kạ-nō′rus), *a.* [L. *canorus*, < *canor*, song, melody, < *canere*, sing.] Melodious; musical. —**ca-no′rous-ly,** *adv.*—**ca-no′rous-ness,** *n.*

cant¹ (kant), *n.* [Prob. < OF. *cant*, < ML. *cantus*, corner, side.] A nook† or corner†; a salient angle; also, an oblique line or surface, as one formed by cutting off the corner of a square or cube; an oblique or slanting face of anything; also, a slanting or tilted position; an inclination; also, a sudden movement tending to tilt a thing; also, a sudden pitch or toss.—**cant**¹, *v.* **I.** *tr.* To bevel; also, to put in an oblique position; tilt; turn over; also, to throw with a sudden jerk. **II.** *intr.* To take or have an inclined position; tilt; turn.

cant² (kant), *v.* [Prob. < L. *cantare*, sing, declaim in a singing tone, < *canere*, sing.] **I.** *intr.* To speak in the whining or singsong tone of a beggar; beg; also, to talk in a special jargon, as that of thieves or gipsies; also, to use the phraseology peculiar to a particular school, party, profession, etc.; also, to affect religious phraseology, esp. in a pharisaical or hypocritical manner; sham goodness or piety. **II.** *tr.* To utter or say in a whining tone, in some conventional phraseology, or in hypocritical phrases.—**cant**², *n.* Whining or singsong speech, as of beggars; the special language or jargon spoken by thieves, gipsies, etc.; the phraseology peculiar to a particular class, party, profession, etc. (with disparaging implication); a pet or stock phrase (archaic); insincere conventionality in speech, esp. conventional pretense of enthusiasm for high ideals; affected or insincere use of religious phraseology; an insincere assumption of goodness or piety (as, "Nor in the church with hypocritic face Supplied with *cant* the lack of Christian grace": Whittier's "Daniel Neall").

can't (känt or kant). Contraction of *cannot.*

can-ta-bi-le (kän-tä′bē-lā). [It., < LL. *cantabilis*, that may be sung, < L. *cantare*, sing.] In *music*: **I.** *a.* Song-like and flowing in style. **II.** *n.* Cantabile style; a cantabile passage or piece.

Can-ta-brig-i-an (kan-tạ-brij′i-ạn). [ML. *Cantabrigia*, Cambridge.] **I.** *a.* Of or pertaining to Cambridge, England, or Cambridge University. **II.** *n.* A native or inhabitant of Cambridge; a member or graduate of Cambridge University.

can-ta-liv-er (kan′tạ-liv-ėr), *n.* See *cantilever.*

can-ta-loup, can-ta-loupe (kan′tạ-löp or -lōp), *n.* [F. *cantaloup*; from *Cantalupo*, a former estate of the Pope near Rome.] A small, ribbed, delicately flavored variety of muskmelon.

can-tan-ker-ous (kan-tang′kẹ-rus), *a.* [Cf. ME. *contek*, contention, strife.] Ill-naturedly perverse or contrary, as in disposition; cross-grained: as, "There's not a more bitter *cantankerous* toad in all Christendom!" (Goldsmith's "She Stoops to Conquer," ii. 1).—**can-tan′ker-ous-ly,** *adv.*—**can-tan′ker-ous-ness,** *n.*

can-tar (kan-tär′), *n.* See *kantar.*

can-ta-ta (kan-tä′tạ), *n.*; pl. *-tas.* [It., < *cantare*, < L. *cantare*, sing.] Orig., a metrical narrative set to recitative, or alternate recitative and air, usually for a single voice, accompanied by one or more instruments; now, a choral composition, either sacred and resembling a short oratorio, or secular, as a lyric drama set to music but not to be acted.

can-ta-trice (F. käṅ-tȧ-trēs, It. kän-tä-trē′chā), *n.*; pl. F. *-trices* (-trēs), It. *-trici* (-trē′chē). [F. and It., < L. *cantatrix.*] A female singer.

can-teen (kan-tēn′), *n.* [F. *cantine*, < It. *cantina*, cellar, wine-cellar.] A place in a military camp, reservation, etc., for the sale, under military control, of liquors, provisions, etc., to enlisted men; any place, as in a city, where food and the like are furnished to soldiers, sailors, or others (esp. in governmental service), either for a price or without charge; also, a small vessel or flask, as of tin, used by soldiers and others for carrying water or liquor for drinking; also, a box or chest containing table utensils, etc., used by army officers and others.—**can-teen′er,** *n.*

can-ter¹ (kan′tėr), *n.* [Abbr. of *Canterbury gallop* (as of pilgrims to Canterbury, England).] An easy gallop.—**can′ter**¹, *v. i.* or *t.* To go or ride at a canter.

cant-er² (kan′tėr), *n.* One who uses or talks cant.

can-ter-bur-y (kan′tėr-ber-i), *n.*; pl. *-ies* (-iz). [From *Canterbury*, city in southeastern England.] A stand with divisions for holding music, papers, etc.

can-ter-bur-y=bell (kan′tėr-ber-i-bel′), *n.* A plant, *Campanula trachelium*, with bell-shaped flowers (so named because found about Canterbury, England); also, some other species of *Campanula*, esp. *C. medium*, much cultivated for its showy flowers.

Canterbury-bell (*Campanula medium*).

can-ter-er (kan′tėr-ėr), *n.* One who or that which canters.

can-thar-i-des (kan-thar′i-dēz), *n. pl.* [L., pl. of *cantharis*, < Gr. κανθαρίς, a blistering fly.] The blister-beetles of the genus *Cantharis*, dried and used in medicine, esp. externally for raising blisters and as a stimulant.—**can-thar′i-dism,** *n.* A morbid state due to the use of cantharides.—**can-thar′i-dize,** *v. t.*; *-dized, -dizing.* To treat with cantharides.

Cant-hook.

cant=hook (kant′hu̇k), *n.* A wooden lever with a movable iron hook near the lower end, used for grasping and canting or turning over logs, etc.

can-thus (kan′thus), *n.*; pl. *-thi* (-thī). [NL., < Gr. κανθός.] In *anat.*, the angle or corner on each side of the eye, formed by the junction of the upper and lower lids.

can-ti-cle (kan′ti-kl), *n.* [L. *canticulum*, dim. of *canticum*, song, < *canere*, sing.] A little song; a song; one of the non-metrical hymns or chants, chiefly from the Bible, used in church services; *pl.* [*cap.*], the book of the Old Testament called "The Song of Solomon."

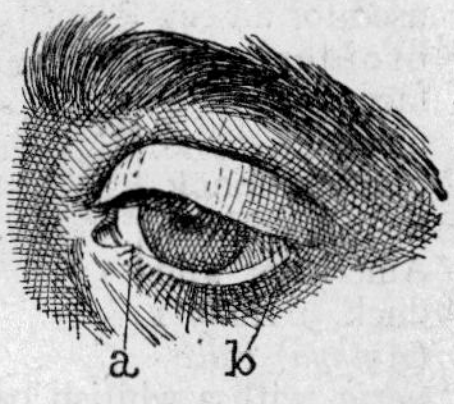

a, Inner Canthus; *b*, Outer Canthus.

can-ti-lev-er (kan′ti-lev-ėr or -lē-vėr), *n.* [Perhaps for *cantle lever.*] A large bracket, usually ornamental, for supporting a balcony, cornice, or the like; also, either of two bracket-like arms projecting toward each other from opposite banks or piers, serving to form the span of a bridge ('cantilever bridge') when united.

Cantilevers.

can-til-late (kan′ti-lāt), *v. t.* or *i.*; *-lated, -lating.* [L. *cantillatus*, pp. of *cantillare*, dim. of *cantare*, sing.] To recite in musical tones; chant or intone, as in Jewish synagogues.—**can-til-la′-tion** (-lā′shọn), *n.*

can-tle (kan′tl), *n.* [OF. *cantel*, dim. of *cant*, corner, E. *cant*[1].] A corner; a piece; a portion; the hind bow of a saddle.—**cant′let,** *n.* A small cantle; a bit.

can-to (kan′tō), *n.*; pl. *-tos* (-tōz). [It., < L. *cantus*, song.] One of the main or larger divisions of a long poem (as Spenser's "Faerie Queene," Scott's "Marmion," or Byron's "Childe Harold's Pilgrimage"); in *music*, the part to which the melody is assigned; the soprano part.

can-ton (kan′tọn or kan-ton′), *n.* [F., < It. *cantone*, aug. of *canto*, < ML. *cantus*, corner, E. *cant*[1].] A nook† or corner†; a corner† or angle†; a square division occupying an upper corner of an escutcheon, etc.; a division, part, or portion of anything; a small territorial district, esp. one of the states of the Swiss confederation.—**can′ton,** *v. t.* To divide into parts or portions; divide into cantons or territorial districts; also (pron. kan-ton′ or kan-tön′), to allot quarters to (soldiers, etc.).—**can′ton-al,** *a.* Of, pertaining to, or of the nature of a canton.

Canton of an Escutcheon.

Can-ton-ese (kan-tọn-ēs′ or -ēz′). **I.** *a.* Of or pertaining to Canton, China, its inhabitants, or their dialect. **II.** *n.*; pl. *-ese.* A native or inhabitant of Canton; the Chinese dialect spoken in Canton.

Can-ton (kan′tọn) **flan′nel.** See *flannel.*

can-ton-ment (kan′tọn-mẹnt, kan-ton′-, or kan-tön′-), *n.* The act of cantoning; also, the place allotted to a regiment or body of soldiers for quarters; esp., a camp (usually of large size and with wooden buildings) where men are trained for military service; *pl.*, military quarters.

can-tor (kan′tọr), *n.* [L., singer, < *canere*, sing.] A precentor.

can-trip (kan′trip), *n.* [Origin unknown.] A charm; a spell; a trick. [Chiefly Sc.]

cant-y (kȧn′ti), *a.* [ME. *cant*, bold.] Cheerful (as, "Oft have ye heard my *canty* strains": Burns's "Elegy on Capt. Matthew Henderson," 62); also, lively; brisk. [Sc. and north. Eng.]

Ca-nuck (kạ-nuk′), *n.* [N. Amer. Ind.] A Canadian. [Colloq.]

can-vas (kan′vạs), *n.* [OF. F. *canevas*, < L. *cannabis*, hemp.] A closely woven, heavy cloth of hemp, flax, or cotton, used for tents, sails, etc.; sail-cloth, or sails collectively; a piece of canvas for a particular purpose, as to receive an oil-painting; an oil-painting; also, any of various other fabrics, of linen, cotton, wool, silk, etc., of a distinct, open weave, used for an embroidery surface, for dress-material, etc.—**can′vas-back,** *n.* A North American wild duck, *Æthyia* (*Aythya*) *vallisneria*, with a whitish back: esteemed for the delicacy of its flesh.

Canvasbacks.

can-vass (kan′vạs), *v.* [From *canvas.*] **I.** *tr.* To toss in or as in canvas, for sport or punishment†; buffet†; criticize severely†; discuss or debate; examine carefully; investigate by inquiry; also, to apply to or address (persons), or traverse (a district), in soliciting votes, subscriptions, orders, etc. **II.** *intr.* To engage in discussion or debate; also, to go about soliciting votes, orders, etc.—**can′vass,** *n.* The act of canvassing; an investigation by inquiry; a soliciting of votes, orders, etc.—**can′vass-er,** *n.*

can-y (kā′ni), *a.* Made of cane; cane-like.

can-yon (kan′yọn), *n.* See *cañon.*

can-zo-ne (kän-tsō′nā), *n.*; pl. *-ni* (-nē). [It., < L. *cantio(n-)*, song: see *chanson.*] A form of lyric poem, of Provençal origin, developed esp. by the Italians.

can-zo-net (kan-zọ-net′), *n.* [It. *canzonetta*, dim. of *canzone*: see *canzone.*] A short song, esp. one of light and airy character. Also **can-zo-nette′.**

caout-chouc (kö′chůk or kou′-), *n.* [F.; of S. Amer. origin.] The gummy coagulated juice of certain tropical plants; india-rubber.

cap (kap), *n.* [AS. *cæppe*, < ML. *cappa*, *capa*, cap, hooded cloak, cape; origin uncertain.] A covering for the head, esp. one fitting closely and made of softer material than a hat, and having little or no brim; a special head-dress denoting rank, occupation, etc.; also, any object, part, or piece resembling a cap for the head in shape, use, or position; a cap-like covering or top; a percussion-cap; in general, the topmost part; fig., the acme; also, a name given (with distinctive qualifications) to several large sizes of writing-paper (cf. *foolscap*).—**cap of maintenance,** a kind of cap of state or official dignity formerly worn by high personages, and still carried before the sovereign and certain mayors in England, and also represented in heraldry.—**to set one's cap at** or **for,** to seek to win (a man) as a husband.—**cap,** *v.*; *capped, capping.* **I.** *tr.* To provide or cover with or as with a cap; also, to serve as a cap, covering, or top to; overlie; also, to complete; surpass; follow up with something as good or better; also, to salute by doffing the cap. **II.** *intr.* To uncover the head in respect.

ca-pa-bil-i-ty (kā-pạ-bil′i-ti), *n.*; pl. *-ties* (-tiz). The quality of being capable; capacity; ability; quality of admitting of certain treatment; also, a property or faculty capable of being developed or put to use (usually in *pl.*).

ca-pa-ble (kā′pạ-bl), *a.* [F. *capable*, < LL. *capabilis*, < L. *capere*, take, hold.] Able to be a container (*of*)†; capacious† or comprehensive†; open to the influence (*of*); admitting (*of*); having the power or possibility (with *of* or formerly an infinitive); able, efficient, or competent.—**ca′pa-ble-ness,** *n.*—**ca′pa-bly,** *adv.*

ca-pa-cious (kạ-pā′shus), *a.* [L. *capax* (*capac-*), < *capere*, take, hold.] Able to hold or contain†; also, capable of holding much; spacious; also, qualified or adapted for the reception (*of*: archaic).—**ca-pa′cious-ly,** *adv.*—**ca-pa′cious-ness,** *n.*

ca-pa-ci-tate (kạ-pas′i-tāt), *v. t.*; *-tated, -tating.* To endow with capacity or powers; make capable; qualify.—**ca-pa-ci-ta′tion** (-tā′shọn), *n.*

ca-pa-ci-tive (kạ-pas′i-tiv), *a.* In *elect.*, pertaining to capacity: as, a *capacitive* coupler (a coupler which joins circuits by means of a condenser).

ca-pa-ci-ty (kạ-pas′i-ti), *n.*; pl. *-ties* (-tiz). [F. *capacité*, < L. *capacitas*, < *capax*: see *capacious.*] The power of receiving or containing; cubic contents; volume; also, power of receiving impressions, knowledge, etc.; receptivity; mental ability; also, power, ability, or possibility of doing something; also, quality of admitting of certain treatment; also, legal qualification; also, position, character, or relation (as, in the *capacity* of legal adviser); specif., in *elect.*, capability; esp., the ability of a conductor, condenser, or the like, to hold charges of electricity; the ratio of the charge of a conductor or the like to its potential.

cap=a=pie (kap-ạ-pē′), *adv.* [OF. *cap a pie* (L. *caput*, head; *ad*, to; *pes*, foot).] From head to foot: as, "A figure like your father, Armed . . . *cap-a-pe*" (Shakspere's "Hamlet," i. 2. 200).

ca-par-i-son (kạ-par′i-sọn), *n.* [OF. *capparasson* (F. *caparaçon*), < Sp. *caparazón*, < ML. *capa*, E. *cape*[2].] A covering, usually ornamented, laid over the saddle or harness of a horse, etc.; hence, dress, equipment, or outfit.—**ca-par'i-son,** *v. t.* To cover with a caparison; hence, to dress finely; deck.

War-horse with Caparison.

cape[1] (kāp), *n.* [OF. F. *cap,* < Pr. *cap* or It. *capo,* < L. *caput,* head.] A piece of land jutting into the sea or some other body of water: as, the *Cape* of Good Hope (often called *the Cape*). —**Cape glove,** a cape-skin glove.

cape[2] (kāp), *n.* [F. *cape,* < ML. *capa*: see *cap.*] A sleeveless garment fitting round the neck and falling loosely over the shoulders: worn separately or attached to a coat, etc.—**caped,** *a.*

cap-e-lin (kap'ẹ-lin), *n.* See *caplin.*

ca-pell-meis-ter (kä-pel'-mīs″tėr), *n.* See *kapellmeister.*

Caper (*Capparis spinosa*).

ca-per[1] (kā'pėr), *v. i.* [Prob. < *capriole.*] To leap or skip about in a sprightly manner; prance.—**ca'per**[1], *n.* A frolicsome leap or spring; a capricious action; a prank.

ca-per[2] (kā'pėr), *n.* [L. *capparis,* < Gr. κάππαρις.] A shrub, *Capparis spinosa,* of Mediterranean regions, or its flower-bud, which is pickled and used as a condiment.

ca-per[3] (kā'pėr), *n.* [D. *kaper,* < *kapen,* seize.] A privateer; also, its captain. [Obs. or hist.]

Capercaillie.

cap-er-cail-lie, cap-er-cail-zie (kap-ėr-kāl'yi, -yi or -zi), *n.* [Gael. *capull-coille.*] The wood-grouse, *Tetrao urogallus,* a large gallinaceous bird of northern Europe.

ca-per-er (kā'pėr-ėr), *n.* One who or that which capers.

ca-per-some (kā'pėr-sum), *a.* Given to capering.

cape-skin (kāp'skin), *n.* A heavy, durable glove-skin from goats of the Cape district of South Africa; also, glove-skin of similar appearance from various sheep or lambs, made by special tannage processes.

cap-ful (kap'fụl), *n.*; pl. *-fuls.* As much as a cap will hold. —**capful of wind,** *naut.,* a light gust of wind: as, "I warrant you were frightened, weren't you, last night, when it blew but a *capful of wind?*" (Defoe's "Robinson Crusoe," i. 1).

ca-pi-as (kā'pi-as), *n.* [L., 'take thou.'] In *law,* a writ commanding an officer to take a person specified into custody. The term includes various writs specially named, for enforcing attendance in court, for imprisoning after judgment until a claim is satisfied, etc.

cap-i-ba-ra, cap-y-ba-ra (kap-i-bä'rạ), *n.*; pl. *-ras.* [Pg. *capibara*; from Brazilian name.] A South American rodent, *Hydrochœrus capibara,* 3 or 4 feet long, living along the banks of rivers.

Capibara.

cap-il-la-ceous (kap-i-lā'shius), *a.* [L. *capillaceus,* < *capillus,* hair.] Hair-like; capillary.

cap-il-lar-i-ty (kap-i-lar'i-ti), *n.* The state of being capillary; capillary action; capillary attraction or repulsion.

cap-il-la-ry (kap'i-lạ-ri). [L. *capillaris,* < *capillus,* hair.] **I.** *a.* Of or pertaining to hair; resembling a hair; very slender; having a very small bore; pertaining to or occurring in or as in a tube of fine bore (as, *capillary* action, the elevation or depression of the surface of liquids in fine tubes, etc., due to the forces of cohesion and adhesion; *capillary* attraction or repulsion, the apparent attraction or repulsion between a liquid and a tube, etc., observed in such phenomena); in *anat.,* pertaining to a capillary or capillaries. **II.** *n.*; pl. *-ries* (-riz). A tube with a very small bore; in *anat.,* one of the minute blood-vessels between the terminations of the arteries and the beginnings of the veins.

cap-i-tal[1] (kap'i-tạl), *n.* [L. *capitellum,* dim. of *caput,* head.] The head, or uppermost part, of a column, pillar, etc.

Medieval Capital, 13th century.—Abbey of Vézelay, France.

cap-i-tal[2] (kap'i-tạl). [OF. F. *capital,* < L. *capitalis,* pertaining to the head or to life, chief (as n., ML. *capitale,* wealth, stock), < *caput,* head.] **I.** *a.* Pertaining to the head or top†; involving the loss of the head or life, as punishment; punishable by death, as a crime; fatal or serious, as an error; of letters, of the large size regularly used at the head or beginning of a sentence, or as the first letter of a proper name; of a city, town, etc., chief, esp. as being the official seat of government of a country, state, etc.; of a war-ship, of the highest grade or class; in general, principal; highly important; excellent or first-rate; also, of or pertaining to capital (as, *capital* stock). **II.** *n.* A capital letter; also, the city or town which is the official seat of government in a country, state, etc.; also, any form of wealth employed or capable of being employed in the production of more wealth; an accumulated stock of such wealth; the wealth, whether in money or property, owned or employed in business by an individual, firm, corporation, etc.; fig., resources; any source of profit or advantage.—**cap'i-tal-ism,** *n.* Possession of capital; the concentration of capital in the hands of a few, or the resulting power or influence; a system favoring such concentration of wealth.—**cap'i-tal-ist,** *n.* One who has capital; esp., a person who has an extensive capital employed in business enterprises.—**cap″i-tal-is'tic,** *a.*—**cap″i-tal-i-za'tion** (-i-zā'shọn), *n.* The act of capitalizing; also, the capital stock of a corporation.—**cap'i-tal-ize** (-īz), *v. t.*; *-ized, -izing.* To write or print in capital letters, or with an initial capital; also, to convert into or use as capital; convert (a periodical payment, etc.) into an equivalent capital or lump sum; also, to fix the capital of (a corporation) at a certain sum for the purpose of issuing shares of stock accordingly.—**cap'i-tal-ly,** *adv.*

cap-i-tate (kap'i-tāt), *a.* [L. *capitatus,* < *caput,* head.] Having or forming a head; headed.

cap-i-ta-tion (kap-i-tā'shọn), *n.* [LL. *capitatio(n-),* < L. *caput,* head.] A numbering or assessing by the head; a poll-tax; a fee or payment of a uniform amount for each person.

Cap-i-tol (kap'i-tọl), *n.* [L. *Capitolium,* < *caput,* head.] The ancient temple of Jupiter at Rome, situated on a summit of the Capitoline Hill; the hill itself; a similar Roman edifice, as in ancient provincial cities; in the U. S., the edifice occupied by Congress at Washington (see cut on following page); also [often *l. c.*], a state-house.—**Cap'i-to-line** (-tọ-līn), *a.* [L. *Capitolinus.*] Of or pertaining to the

Capitol at Rome, the hill on which it stood, or the god Jupiter (of whose worship the Capitol was the seat).

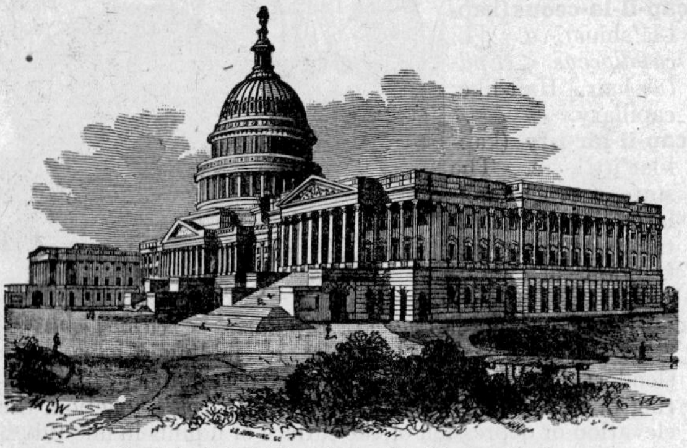

Capitol of the United States, Washington, D. C.

ca-pit-u-lar (ka̧-pit̨′ū̧-lä̧r). [ML. *capitularis*, < L. *capitulum*: see *capitulum*.] **I.** *a.* Pertaining to an ecclesiastical or other chapter; in *anat.* and *bot.*, pertaining to or forming a capitulum. **II.** *n.* A member of an ecclesiastical chapter; also, an act passed in a chapter; also, a Frankish capitulary.

ca-pit-u-la-ry (ka̧-pit̨′ū̧-lā̧-ri). [ML. *capitularius*, < L. *capitulum*: see *capitulum*.] **I.** *a.* Pertaining to a chapter. **II.** *n.*; pl. *-ries* (-riz). A member of a chapter; also, an ordinance or law of a Frankish sovereign (usually in *pl.*).

ca-pit-u-late (ka̧-pit̨′ū̧-lāt), *v. i.*; *-lated*, *-lating*. [ML. *capitulatus*, pp. of *capitulare*, < L. *capitulum*: see *capitulum*.] To draw up a writing under heads or in chapters†; arrange terms†; make terms of surrender; surrender on stipulated terms.—**ca-pit-u-la′tion** (-lā′sho̧n), *n.* The act of capitulating; a statement of the heads of a subject; summary; enumeration; a making of terms†; an agreement made, as the pledge sworn to by an emperor of the Holy Roman Empire before his coronation; a surrendering upon stipulated terms, or the instrument containing the terms.—**Capitulation Day,** the anniversary (Aug. 13) of the capitulation of Manila to the American troops in 1898, observed as a holiday in the Philippines.—**ca-pit′u-la-tor,** *n.*

ca-pit-u-lum (ka̧-pit̨′ū̧-lum), *n.*; pl. *-la* (-lä̧). [L., small head, capital of column, chapter, dim. of *caput*, head.] In *anat.*, the head of a bone; in *bot.*, a close head of sessile flowers; a flower-head.

cap-lin, cap-e-lin (kap′lin, -ȩ-lin), *n.* [F. *capelan*, *caplan*.] A small food-fish, *Mallotus villosus*, allied to the smelt: much used as bait for cod.

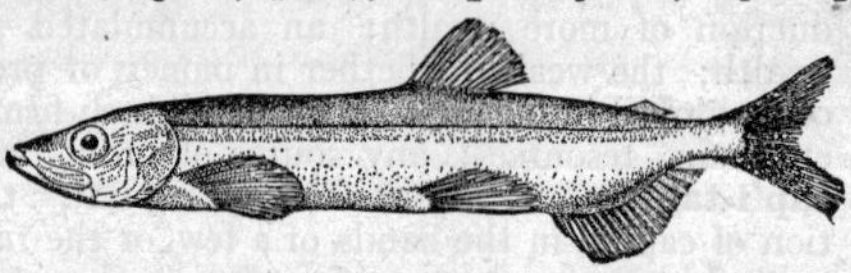

Caplin.

cap-no-man-cy (kap′nō̧-man-si), *n.* [Gr. καπνός, smoke, + μαντεία, divination.] Divination by means of smoke.

ca-pon (kā′po̧n), *n.* [AS. *capūn*, < L. *capo*(*n*-).] A cock castrated to improve the flesh for use as food.

cap-o-nier (kap-ō̧-nēr′), *n.* [F. *caponnière*, < It. *capponiera* or Sp. *caponera*, lit. 'coop for capons.'] In *fort.*, a work or covered passage in or across a ditch.

cap-o-ral (kȧp-ō̧-rȧl′ or kap′ō̧-ra̧l), *n.* [F., lit. 'corporal'; said to be so called because superior to the common (French) soldier's or canteen tobacco.] A kind of tobacco.

ca-pot (ka̧-pot′), *n.* [F.; origin uncertain.] In *piquet*, a winning of all the tricks.—**ca-pot′,** *v. t.*; *-potted*, *-potting*. In *piquet*, to win all the tricks from.

ca-po-tas-to (kä-pō-täs′tō), *n.* [It.] A device attached to fretted musical instruments, as the guitar, for the purpose of raising the pitch of all the strings at once.

ca-pote (ka̧-pōt′), *n.* [F., < ML. *capa*, E. *cape*[2].] A long cloak with a hood; also, a close, cap-like bonnet worn by women and children.

cap-pa-ri-da-ceous (kap″a̧-ri-dā′shius), *a.* [L. *capparis*: see *caper*[2].] Belonging to the *Capparidaceæ*, or caper family of plants.

capped (kapt), *a.* Wearing or having a cap: as, *white-capped*.

cap-per (kap′ėr), *n.* One who or that which caps; also, a stool-pigeon, as for gamblers (slang); a by-bidder at an auction (slang).—**cap′ping,** *n.* The act of one who or that which caps; also, that with which something is capped.

cap-re-o-late (kap′rȩ̄-ō̧-lāt), *a.* [L. *capreolus*, tendril.] In *bot.*, having tendrils.

cap-ric (kap′rik), *a.* [L. *caper*, goat.] In *chem.*, noting or pertaining to a fatty acid found in butter, cocoanut-oil, etc., and having a faint goat-like odor.

ca-pric-cio (ka̧-prich′iō, It. kä-prēt′chō), *n.*; pl. *capriccios* (-iōz), It. *capricci* (-chē). [It., appar. < *capro*, < L. *caper*, goat.] A caper; a prank; a caprice; a musical composition in a free, irregular style.—**ca-pric-cio-so** (kä-prēt-chō′sō), *a.* [It.] In *music*, capricious; fantastic in style.

ca-price (ka̧-prēs′), *n.* [F. *caprice*, < It. *capriccio*: see *capriccio*.] A sudden change of mind without apparent or adequate motive; a whim; also, mere fancy; susceptibility to varying or freakish impulses; freakishness; also, a fantastic production; in *music*, a capriccio.—**ca-pri′cious** (-prish′us), *a.* [F. *capricieux*, < It. *capriccioso*.] Subject to, led by, or indicative of caprice or fancy; whimsical; changeable; freakish.—**ca-pri′cious-ly,** *adv.*—**ca-pri′cious-ness,** *n.*

Cap-ri-corn (kap′ri-kôrn), *n.* [L. *Capricornus*, < *caper*, goat, + *cornu*, horn.] A zodiacal constellation between Sagittarius and Aquarius, represented by a figure with the fore part of a goat and the hind part of a fish, or sometimes as a goat; also, the tenth sign of the zodiac. See *zodiac*. Also (L.) **Cap-ri-cor′nus** (-kôr′nus).

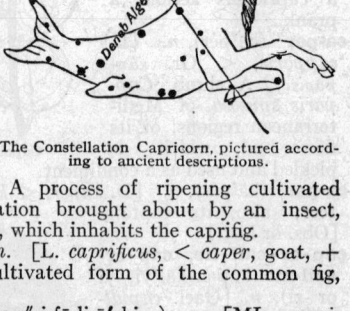

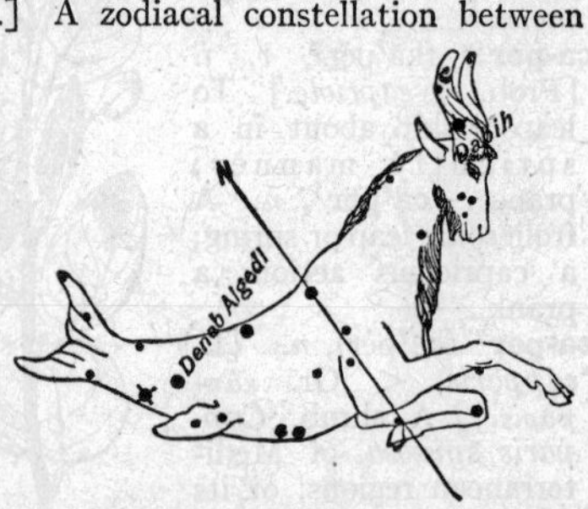

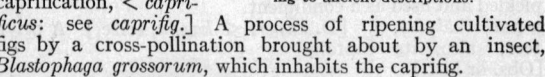

The Constellation Capricorn, pictured according to ancient descriptions.

cap-ri-fi-ca-tion (kap″ri-fi-kā′sho̧n), *n.* [L. *caprificatio*(*n*-), < *caprificare*, ripen by caprification, < *caprificus*: see *caprifig*.] A process of ripening cultivated figs by a cross-pollination brought about by an insect, *Blastophaga grossorum*, which inhabits the caprifig.

cap-ri-fig (kap′ri-fig), *n.* [L. *caprificus*, < *caper*, goat, + *ficus*, fig.] The uncultivated form of the common fig, *Ficus carica*.

cap-ri-fo-li-a-ceous (kap″ri-fō-li-ā′shius), *a.* [ML. *caprifolium*, honeysuckle, < L. *caper*, goat, + *folium*, leaf.] Belonging to the *Caprifoliaceæ*, a family of plants including the honeysuckle, elder, viburnum, snowberry, etc.

cap-ri-form (kap′ri-fôrm), *a.* [L. *caper*, goat: see *-form*.] Goat-like.

cap-ri-ole (kap′ri-ōl), *n.* [F. *capriole* (now *cabriole*), < It. *capriola*, < L. *caper*, goat.] A caper or leap; an upward spring made by a horse with all four feet and without advancing.—**cap′ri-ole,** *v. i.*; *-oled*, *-oling*. To execute a capriole.

ca-pro-ic (ka-prō′ik), *a.* [Cf. *capric*.] In *chem.*, noting or pertaining to a fatty acid found accompanying capric acid, and occurring as a clear, colorless oil with a faintly rancid odor.

cap-si-cum (kap′si-kum), *n.* [NL., < L. *capsa*, box, E. *case*[2].] Any plant of the solanaceous genus *Capsicum*, as *C. annuum*, the common pepper of the garden, in many varieties, with hot, pungent seeds inclosed in a podded or bell-shaped pericarp which also (except in the so-called 'sweet peppers') is of extreme pungency; also, the fruit of these plants, or some preparation of it, used as a condiment (see *cayenne*) and in medicine.

Capsicum (*C. annuum*).

cap-size (kap-sīz′), *v. i.* or *t.*; *-sized*, *-sizing*. [Origin unknown.] To upset or overturn, as a boat.—**cap-si′zal, cap-size′,** *n.*

cap-stan (kap′stąn), *n.* [F. and Pr. *cabestan*, prob. < L. *capistrare*, tie with a halter, < *capistrum*, halter, < *capere*, hold.] A device resembling a windlass but having a vertical axis, commonly turned by a bar or lever, and serving to wind a cable, as for raising weights (as an anchor).

Capstan.
a, capstan-head; *b*, barrel; *c*, pawl-rim and pawls; *d*, capstan-bar.

cap-stone (kap′stōn), *n.* A capping or finishing stone of a structure.
cap-su-lar (kap′sū-ląr), *a.* Of, pertaining to, or of the nature of a capsule. Also **cap′su-la-ry** (-lą-ri).
cap-su-late, cap-su-lat-ed (kap′sū-lāt, -lā-ted), *a.* Inclosed in or formed into a capsule.—**cap-su-la′tion** (-lā′shọn), *n.* Inclosure in a capsule.
cap-sule (kap′sūl), *n.* [L. *capsula*, dim. of *capsa*, box, E. *case*[2].] A small case, envelop, or covering; a thin metal covering for the mouth of a corked bottle; a gelatinous case inclosing a dose of medicine; in *anat.* and *zoöl.*, a membranous sac or integument; in *bot.*, a dry dehiscent fruit or seed-vessel, composed of two or more carpels; also, the theca of mosses; in *chem.*, a small shallow vessel, as of porcelain.

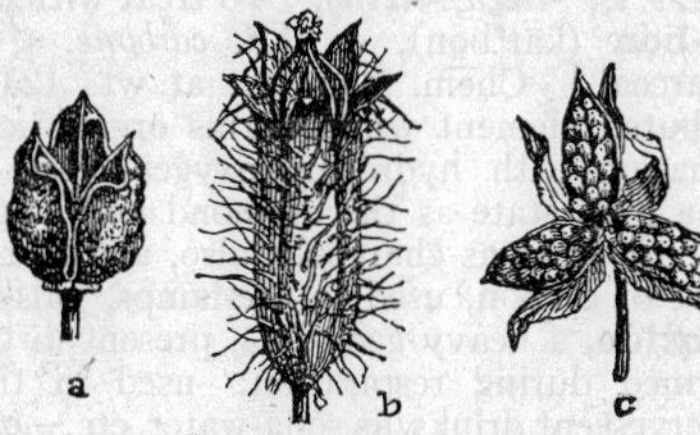

Capsules, after dehiscence.
a, asphodel; *b*, prickly poppy; *c*, violet.

cap-tain (kap′tąn), *n.* [OF. F. *capitaine*, < ML. *capitaneus*, < L. *caput*, head.] One who is at the head of or in authority over others; a chief or leader; a military leader; an officer in the army ranking below a major and above a lieutenant, and usually in command of a company, troop, or battery; an officer in the navy ranking below a rear-admiral and above a commander, and usually in command of a war-ship; the commander or master of a merchant ship or other vessel; the leader of a racing crew, baseball team, or the like.—**cap′tain,** *v. t.* To lead or command as captain.—**cap′tain-cy** (-si), *n.*; pl. *-cies* (-siz). The rank, post, or leadership of a captain.—**cap′tain=gen′er-al,** *n.*; pl. *-als*. The commander-in-chief of a military force.—**cap′tain-ship,** *n.* The office, authority, or skill of a captain.
cap-ta-tion (kap-tā′shọn), *n.* [L. *captatio(n-)*, < *captare*, strive to take: see *catch*.] The use of artful endeavors, appeals, etc., to secure or accomplish something.
cap-tion (kap′shọn), *n.* [L. *captio(n-)*, < *capere*, take.] A taking or seizing (now rare); caviling†; that part of a legal document which states time, place, etc., of execution or performance; also, a heading or title, as of a chapter or article.
cap-tious (kap′shus), *a.* [L. *captiosus*, < *captio(n-)*: see *caption*.] Apt to insnare or perplex, as in argument; also, apt to notice and make much of unimportant faults or defects; faultfinding; proceeding from a faultfinding or caviling disposition; also, capacious†.—**cap′tious-ly,** *adv.* —**cap′tious-ness,** *n.*
cap-ti-vate (kap′ti-vāt), *v. t.*; *-vated, -vating*. [LL. *captivatus*, pp. of *captivare*, < L. *captivus*: see *captive*.] To capture†; subjugate†; overpower and hold as by beauty or excellence; enchant; charm.—**cap′ti-vat-ing-ly,** *adv.* —**cap-ti-va′tion** (-vā′shọn), *n.* The act of captivating, or the state of being captivated.—**cap′ti-va-tor,** *n.*
cap-tive (kap′tiv), *a.* [L. *captivus*, < *capere*, take.] Made or held prisoner, as in war; kept in confinement or restraint; also, enslaved as by love or other passion; captivated; also, of or pertaining to a captive.—**captive balloon,** a balloon held in a particular station by means of a rope or cable, as for observation purposes.—**cap′tive,** *n.* A prisoner; also, one who is enslaved by love, beauty, etc.—**cap-tiv′i-ty,** *n.* The state or period of being captive: as, the Babylonian *captivity* of the Jews (see *Babylonian, a.*).
cap-tor (kap′tọr), *n.* [L., < *capere*, take.] One who takes or captures.—**cap′tress,** *n.* A female captor.
cap-ture (kap′tūr), *n.* [L. *captura*, < *capere*, take.] The act of taking as by force or stratagem; also, that which is so taken; a prize.—**cap′ture,** *v. t.*; *-tured, -turing*. To take by force or stratagem; win.—**cap′tur-er,** *n.*
ca-puche (ką-pösh′), *n.* [F. *capuche*, *capuce*, < It. *cappuccio*, hood, cowl, < ML. *capa*, E. *cape*[2].] A hood or cowl; esp., the long, pointed cowl of the Capuchins.
Cap-u-chin (kap′ū-chin or kap-ū-shēn′), *n.* [F. *capuchin*, now *capucin*, < It. *cappuccino*, < *cappuccio*: see *capuche*.] One of an order of Franciscan friars, a reformed branch of the Observants, wearing a long, pointed cowl; [*l. c.*] a hooded cloak for women; a variety of pigeon with a hood-like tuft of feathers on the back of the head; a tropical American monkey, *Cebus capucinus*, so called from the cowl-like appearance of the hair of the head, or any monkey of the same genus.

Capuchin (*Cebus capucinus*).

ca-put mor-tu-um (kā′put môr′tū-um). [L., 'dead head.'] In old chemistry, the residuum of chemicals after distillation or sublimation; fig., any worthless residue.
cap-y-ba-ra (kap-i-bä′rą), *n.* See *capibara*.
car (kär), *n.* [OF. *car*, *char* (F. *char*), < L. *carrus*, kind of two-wheeled vehicle for carrying loads; from Celtic.] A wheeled vehicle in many varieties, often one with two wheels; a chariot, as of war or triumph; a vehicle of state or solemnity; an automobile; a vehicle running on rails; the part of a balloon, elevator, or the like, for carrying the passengers, etc.
ca-ra-ba-o (kä-rą-bä′ō), *n.*; pl. *-os* (-ōz). [Philippine Sp.] In the Philippine Islands, the water-buffalo.

Carabao.

car-a-bi-neer, car-a-bi-nier (kar″ą-bi-nēr′), *n.* [F. *carabinier* (= It. *carabiniere*), < *carabine*: see *carbine*, and cf. *carbineer*.] A soldier, usually of the cavalry, armed with the carbine.
car-a-cal (kar′ą-kal), *n.* [F. *caracal*, < Turk. *qarah*, black, + *qulaq*, ear.] A small feline animal, *Lynx caracal*, of Asia and Africa, of a reddish-brown color, and having a tuft of long black hair at the tip of each ear.

Caracal.

ca-ra-ca-ra (kä-rą-kä′rą), *n.* [S. Amer. name; imit. of its cry.] Any of certain vulture-like birds of the falcon family (subfamily *Polyborinæ*) of the warmer parts of America.
car-ack, car-rack (kar′ąk), *n.* [OF. *carrake* (F. *caraque*), < ML. *carraca*; origin uncertain.] A large, armed merchant vessel, esp. Spanish or Portuguese, of former times.
car-a-cole (kar′ą-kōl), *n.* [F. *caracole*, < Sp. *caracol*, snail, winding staircase, wheeling movement.] A spiral staircase;

also, a half-turn executed by a horseman in riding.—**car′a-cole,** *v. i.*; *-coled, -coling.* To execute caracoles; wheel; prance: as, "Now *caracol'd* the steeds in air" (Scott's "Bridal of Triermain," ii. 19).

car-a-cul (kar′ạ-köl or -kul), *n.* [Russ.] The skin of the very young of certain Asiatic or Russian sheep, dressed as a fur, resembling astrakhan, but with a flatter, looser curl.

ca-rafe, ca-raffe (kạ-räf′), *n.* [F. *carafe,* < It. *caraffa*; prob. from Ar.] A glass water-bottle.

car′a-geen, car′a-gheen, *n.* See *carrageen.*

car-am-bo-la (kar-ạm-bō′lạ̈), *n.* [Pg.] The acid fruit of a small East Indian tree, *Averrhoa carambola*; also, the tree itself.

car-am-bole (kar′ạm-bōl), *n.* and *v.* See *carom.*

car-a-mel (kar′ạ-mel), *n.* [F. *caramel,* < Sp. *caramelo.*] Burnt sugar, used for coloring and flavoring food, etc.; also, a kind of candy, commonly in small blocks, made from sugar, butter, milk, etc.—**car′a-mel,** *v. t.* or *i.* To caramelize.—**car′a-mel-ize** (-īz), *v. t.* or *i.*; *-ized, -izing.* [= F. *caraméliser.*] To convert or be converted into caramel.—**car″a-mel-i-za′tion** (-i-zā′shọn), *n.*

ca-ran-goid (ka-rang′goid), *a.* [NL. *Caranx,* the typical genus (cf. Sp. *carangue,* a West Indian flatfish): see *-oid.*] Belonging to or resembling the *Carangidæ,* a family of fishes including the cavally, pompano, pilot-fish, etc.

car-a-pace (kar′ạ-pās), *n.* [F., < Sp. *carapacho.*] The shell of a turtle, etc., esp. the upper shell. Also **car′a-pax** (-paks).

car-at (kar′ạt), *n.* [F. *carat,* < It. *carato,* < Ar. *qīrāt,* < Gr. κεράτιον, carob bean, carat, dim. of κέρας, horn.] A twenty-fourth part (used in expressing the fineness of gold, pure gold being 24 carats fine); also, a unit of weight for precious stones (equal to about 3 grains troy).

car-a-van (kar′ạ-van or kar-ạ-van′), *n.* [F. *caravane,* < Pers. *kārwān.*] A company of merchants or others traveling together, as for safety, esp. over deserts, etc., in Asia or Africa; any similar band of travelers; also, a large covered vehicle for passengers or goods; a van; a house on wheels.

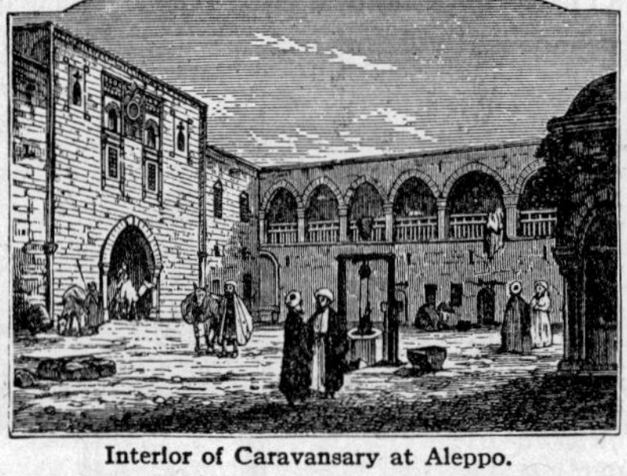
Interior of Caravansary at Aleppo.

car-a-van-sa-ry (kar-ạ-van′sạ-ri), *n.*; pl. *-ries* (-riz). [Pers. *kārwān-sarāī*: cf. *serai.*] In the East, a kind of inn for the accommodation of caravans; hence, any large inn or hotel. Also **car-a-van′se-rai** (-sẹ-rī).

car-a-vel (kar′ạ-vel), *n.* [Sp. and Pg. *caravela,* ult. < Gr. κάραβος, kind of light ship.] A kind of small ship formerly used by the Spaniards and Portuguese; also, a Turkish man-of-war.

Caravel, 15th century.

car-a-way (kar′ạ-wā), *n.* [Ar. *karawīyā*: cf. L. *careum,* Gr. κάρον.] An apiaceous plant, *Carum carui,* bearing aromatic seed-like fruit ('caraway-seeds') used in cookery and medicine and yielding a volatile oil; also, the fruit or seeds.

car-ba-mate (kär′bạ-māt), *n.* In *chem.,* a salt of carbamic acid.

car-bam-ic (kär-bam′ik), *a.* [From *carbonic* + *amide.*] In *chem.,* noting or pertaining to an organic acid, $CONH_2OH$, not occurring in the free state, but known in the form of salts, esp. that of ammonium.

car-ba-mide (kär′bạ-mīd or -mid), *n.* [From *carbon* + *amide.*] In *chem.,* urea.

car-bide (kär′bīd or -bid), *n.* In *chem.,* a compound of carbon with a more electropositive element or radical.

car-bine (kär′bīn), *n.* [F. *carabine* (= It. *carabina*), orig. a small harquebus, < *carabin,* a mounted soldier armed with this weapon: origin uncertain.] A short rifle (or, formerly, musket) adapted for cavalry.—**car-bi-neer′** (-bi-nēr′), *n.* [Cf. *carabineer.*] A soldier armed with a carbine.

carbo-. Form of *carbon* used in combination.

car-bo-hy-drate (kär-bō-hī′drāt), *n.* [See *carbo-.*] In *chem.,* any of a class of carbon compounds, including starch, sugar, and cellulose, which contain twice as many hydrogen as oxygen atoms.

car-bo-late (kär′bọ-lāt), *n.* In *chem.,* a salt of carbolic acid.—**car′bo-lat-ed** (-lā-ted), *a.* Containing carbolic acid.

car-bol-ic (kär-bol′ik), *a.* [L. *carbo,* coal, + *oleum,* oil.] Pertaining to or derived from carbon or coal: as, *carbolic* acid (C_6H_5OH, obtained from the heavy oil of coal-tar: used as a disinfectant, antiseptic, etc.).—**car′bo-lize** (-bọ-līz), *v. t.*; *-lized, -lizing.* To treat with carbolic acid.

car-bon (kär′bọn), *n.* [F. *carbone,* < L. *carbo(n-),* coal, charcoal.] Chem. sym., C; at. wt., 12.005. A widely distributed element which forms organic compounds in combination with hydrogen, oxygen, etc., and which occurs in a pure state as the diamond and as graphite, and in an impure state as charcoal; also, a rod or plate composed in part of carbon, used in arc-lamps, batteries, etc.—**carbon dioxide,** a heavy gas, CO_2, present in the atmosphere and formed during respiration: used in the manufacture of effervescent drinks, as soda-water, etc.—**carbon monoxide,** a colorless, odorless, very poisonous gas, CO, which burns with a pale-blue flame, and is formed when carbon burns with an insufficient supply of air.—**carbon process,** a method of making photographic prints by the use of a pigment, such as carbon, contained in sensitized gelatin.—**car-bo-na′ceous** (-bọ-nā′shius), *a.* Of, like, or containing carbon.

car-bo-na-do[1] (kär-bọ-nā′dō), *n.*; pl. *-does* or *-dos* (-dōz). [Sp. *carbonada,* < L. *carbo(n-),* coal.] A piece of meat or the like scored and broiled.—**car-bo-na′do**[1], *v. t.*; *-doed, -doing.* To score and broil; also, to slash or hack.

car-bo-na-do[2] (kär-bọ-nā′dō), *n.*; pl. *-does* (-dōz). [Pg., < *carbone,* carbon.] An opaque, dark-colored, massive form of diamond, found chiefly in Brazil, and used for drills; black diamond.

Car-bo-na-ro (kär-bọ-nä′rō), *n.*; pl. *-ri* (-rē). [It., 'charcoal-burner.'] A member of a former secret political society of revolutionary aims in Italy and France, originating in southern Italy early in the 19th century as a movement against the French rule: usually in *pl.*—**Car-bo-na′rism,** *n.*

car-bo-nate (kär′bọ-nāt), *n.* In *chem.,* a salt of carbonic acid.—**car′bo-nate,** *v. t.*; *-nated, -nating.* To form into a carbonate; charge or impregnate with carbonic-acid gas (carbon dioxide).—**car-bo-na′tion** (-nā′shọn), *n.*

car-bon-ic (kär-bon′ik), *a.* Of or containing carbon: as, *carbonic* acid (an acid, H_2CO_3, whose salts are carbonates; also, carbon dioxide); *carbonic*-acid gas (carbon dioxide).

car-bo-nif-er-ous (kär-bọ-nif′ẹ-rus). [L. *carbo(n-),* coal, + *ferre,* bear.] **I.** *a.* Coal-bearing; [*cap.*] noting or pertaining to a geological period or a system of rocks preceding the Permian. **II.** *n.* [*cap.*] The Carboniferous period or system.

car-bon-ite (kär′bọ-nīt), *n.* An explosive used in blasting, containing nitroglycerin and various other substances, such as powdered wood and sodium nitrate.

car-bon-ize (kär′bọ-nīz), *v. t.*; *-ized, -izing.* To convert into carbon, as by partial combustion; cover with carbon; combine with carbon.—**car″bon-i-za′tion** (-bọ-ni-zā′shọn), *n.*—**car′bon-iz-er** (-bọ-nī-zėr), *n.*

car-bon=pa-per (kär′bọn-pā″pėr), *n.* Paper faced with a preparation of carbon or other material, used between two sheets of plain paper in order to reproduce upon the lower sheet that which may be written upon the upper.

car-bon-yl (kär′bọ-nil), *n.* [From *carbon* + *-yl.*] In *chem.,* a bivalent radical, CO, composed of one atom of carbon and one of oxygen.—**carbonyl chloride,** in *chem.,* a gas, $COCl_2$, formed by the action of light on a mixture of carbon monoxide and chlorine.—**car-bon-yl′ic,** *a.*

car-bo-run-dum (kär-bo̤-run′dum), *n.* [From *carbon* + *corundum.*] Silicon carbide, SiC, an important abrasive produced in the electric furnace. [Proprietary name.]

car-box-yl (kär-bok′sil), *n.* [From *carb(on)* + *ox(ygen)* + *-yl.*] In *chem.*, a univalent radical or group containing carbon, oxygen, and hydrogen (COOH), present in organic acids.—**car-box-yl-a′tion** (-bok-si-lā′sho̤n), *n.* The introduction of a carboxyl group into a compound.—**car-box-yl′ic,** *a.*

car-boy (kär′boi), *n.* [Pers. *qarābah*, large flagon.] A large globular glass bottle, esp. one protected by basketwork or a wooden box, as for containing acids.

Carboy.

car-bun-cle (kär′bung-kl), *n.* [OF. *carbuncle,* < L. *carbunculus,* dim. of *carbo(n-),* (live) coal.] Formerly, a red gem, as a ruby or garnet; now, a garnet cut in a convex rounded form without facets; also, a painful circumscribed inflammation of the subcutaneous tissue, resulting in suppuration and sloughing, and having a tendency to spread (somewhat like a boil, but more serious in its effects); also, an inflamed spot or pimple, as on the nose, due to intemperance. — **car′-bun-cled,** *a.* Set with carbuncles; afflicted with a carbuncle; spotted or pimpled; red or glowing like a carbuncle.—**car-bun′cu-lar** (-bung′kṳ̄-lä̤r), *a.* Of or like a carbuncle; characterized by carbuncles; inflamed.

car-bu-rate (kär′bṳ̄-rāt), *v. t.*; *-rated, -rating.* [See *carburet.*] To impregnate or mix with hydrocarbons, as the air in an internal-combustion engine.—**car-bu-ra′tion** (-rā′sho̤n), *n.*

car-bu-ret (kär′bṳ̄-ret), *n.* [From *carbon.*] In *chem.*, a carbide.—**car′bu-ret,** *v. t.*; *-reted* or *-retted, -reting* or *-retting.* To combine with carbon; impregnate or mix with hydrocarbons.—**car′bu-ret-ant,** *n.* A hydrocarbon used for carbureting.—**car′bu-ret-er, car′bu-ret-or,** *n.* Any of various devices for impregnating air or gas with hydrocarbons: used for making an explosive mixture in an internal-combustion engine, or for adding hydrocarbons to a non-luminous gas in making illuminating gas.—**car-bu-re′tion** (-rē′sho̤n), *n.* The act of carbureting; the process of impregnating air with volatile hydrocarbons in an internal-combustion engine.

car-bu-rize (kär′bṳ̄-rīz), *v. t.*; *-rized, -rizing.* [F. *carbure,* a carbide, < *carbone,* E. *carbon.*] To combine with carbon.—**car″bu-ri-za′tion** (-ri-zā′sho̤n), *n.*—**car′bu-riz-er** (-rī-zėr), *n.*

car-ca-jou (kär′ka̤-zhö or -jö), *n.* [Canadian F.; of Indian origin.] The wolverene (animal).

car-ca-net (kär′ka̤-net), *n.* [OF. *carcant* (F. *carcan*); from Teut.] An ornamental collar or necklace, as of gold or jewels (archaic: see Tennyson's "Last Tournament," 6); also, a similar ornamental circlet or band worn on the head (obs. or hist.: as, "his high-crowned grey hat . . . encircled by a *carcanet* of large balas rubies," Scott's "Fortunes of Nigel," v.).

car-cass, car-case (kär′ka̤s), *n.* [AF. *carcois* (OF. *charcois*), also F. *carcasse* (< It. *carcassa*); ult. origin uncertain.] The dead body of an animal or (now only in contempt) of a human being; a living body (now chiefly in contempt or ridicule); anything from which the vital principle is gone; the decaying remains of anything (as, "a very dangerous flat . . . where the *carcases* of many a tall ship lie buried": Shakspere's "Merchant of Venice," iii. 1. 6); an unfinished framework or skeleton, as of a house or ship; an iron case containing combustibles, used as a missile, and intended to set fire to buildings, etc.

car-cel (kär-sel′ or kär′se̤l), *n.* [From B. G. *Carcel*: see *Carcel lamp.*] A French unit of illuminating power, based on the light emitted by a standard Carcel lamp.

Car-cel (kär-sel′ or kär′se̤l) **lamp.** [From B. G. *Carcel,* (French) inventor (1800) of the lamp.] A lamp in which the oil is fed to the wick by means of a pump operated by clockwork: used in lighthouses, etc., and (in a standard form) for testing illuminating power.

car-ci-no-ma (kär-si-nō′mä̤), *n.*; pl. *-mas* or *-mata* (-ma̤-tä̤). [L., < Gr. *καρκίνωμα,* < *καρκινοῦν,* affect with cancer, < *καρκίνος,* crab, cancer.] In *pathol.*, a malignant tumor that spreads and often recurs after excision; a cancer.—**car-ci-nom′a-tous** (-nom′a̤-tus), *a.*

card[1] (kärd), *n.* [OF. F. *carte,* < L. *charta*: see *chart.*] A chart†, map†, or plan†; the circular piece of paper, etc., on which the 32 points indicating direction are marked in a compass; one of a set of pieces of cardboard printed with spots, figures, etc., used in playing various games; a playing-card; *pl.*, a game or games played with such a set; card-playing; *sing.*, a piece of stiff paper or thin pasteboard, usually rectangular, for various uses; a small sheet of stiff paper for bearing a note, message, etc. (as, a postal *card*); a piece of thin cardboard or heavy paper bearing an invitation, or serving as a ticket or the like; a piece of cardboard with more or less elaborate ornamentation, bearing complimentary greetings (as, a Christmas *card*); a piece of thin cardboard bearing the name, or the name and address, of the person presenting it, used in making a call ('visiting-card'), announcing the nature and place of the person's business ('business card'), etc.; a short published notice or advertisement, as in a newspaper; a program of the events at races, etc.; a person of some indicated characteristic (slang: as, a queer *card*); also, a thin, flat piece or sheet, as of gingerbread.—**card**[1], *v. t.* To provide with a card; also, to fasten on a card.

card[2] (kärd), *n.* [OF. F. *carde,* teazel, wool-card, < L. *carduus,* thistle.] A wire-toothed brush or some similar implement, as used in disentangling and combing out fibers of wool, flax, etc., preparatory to spinning; also, a kind of currycomb.—**card**[2], *v. t.* To dress (wool, etc.) with a card; also, to mix†.

car-da-mom (kär′da̤-mo̤m), *n.* [L. *cardamomum,* < Gr. *καρδάμωμον,* < *κάρδαμον,* cress, + *ἄμωμον,* kind of spice-plant.] The aromatic seed-capsule of various zingiberaceous plants of the genera *Amomum* and *Elettaria,* native in the East Indies and elsewhere, used as a spice or condiment and in medicine; also, any of the plants.

card-board (kärd′bōrd), *n.* A thin, fine pasteboard.

card=case (kärd′kās), *n.* A small pocket-case for holding visiting-cards, etc.

card=cat-a-logue (kärd′kat′a̤-log), *n.* A catalogue in which each entry is made on a separate card, the cards being arranged in order, alphabetically or otherwise, in boxes or drawers.

card-er (kär′dėr), *n.* One who or that which cards wool, etc.; a machine for carding.

car-di-ac (kär′di-ak). [L. *cardiacus,* < Gr. *καρδιακός,* < *καρδία,* heart.] **I.** *a.* Of or pertaining to the heart; also, stimulating the heart, as a drug; invigorating; also, pertaining to the esophageal portion of the stomach. **II.** *n.* A cardiac remedy; a cordial.—**car-di′a-cal** (-dī′a̤-ka̤l), **car′di-al,** *a.* Cardiac.

car-di-al-gia (kär-di-al′jiä̤), *n.* [NL., < Gr. *καρδία,* heart, + *ἄλγος,* pain.] Heartburn.

car-di-gan (kär′di-ga̤n), *n.* [From the seventh Earl of *Cardigan* (1797–1868).] A close-fitting knitted woolen jacket. Also **car′di-gan jack′et.**

car-di-nal (kär′di-na̤l). [L. *cardinalis,* < *cardo,* hinge, critical point.] **I.** *a.* Pertaining to a hinge (of a bivalve shell); also, of prime importance; chief, principal, or fundamental (as, the *cardinal* virtues, see *virtue*; the four *cardinal* points of the compass, the north, south, east, and west points; the *cardinal* numbers, *one, two, three,* etc., as opposed to the *ordinal*); also, cardinal-red. **II.** *n.* One of the seventy members of the Sacred College of the Roman Catholic Church, ranking next to the Pope, and wearing a red hat and cassock; a cardinal-red color; a woman's short, hooded cloak (orig. red)†; a car-di̤nal-bird; mulled red wine; also, a cardinal number.—**car′di-nal-ate** (-āt), *n.*

Cardinal's Hat used heraldically as part of the armorial achievement of a cardinal.

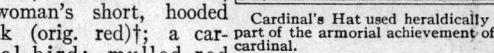

The office or rank of a cardinal.—**car′di-nal=bird,** *n.* An American song-bird, *Cardinalis virginianus,* with brilliant red plumage and a crested head; any of various similar birds.—**car′di-nal=flow″er,** *n.* A North American plant, *Lobelia cardinalis,* with showy red flowers.—**car′di-nal-ly,** *adv.*—**car′di-nal=red′,** *a.* Of a deep, rich red (darker than that of a cardinal's dress).—**car′di-nal-ship,** *n.*

Cardinal-bird (*Cardinalis virginianus*).

cardio-. Form of Gr. καρδία, heart, used in combination.—**car-di-o-gram** (kär′di-ǫ-gram), *n.* [+ *-gram.*] A tracing made by the cardiograph.—**car′di-o-graph** (-gråf), *n.* [+ *-graph.*] An instrument for recording by a tracing the movements of the heart.—**car″di-o-graph′ic** (-graf′ik), *a.*

car-di-oid (kär′di-oid), *n.* [Gr. καρδιοειδής, heart-shaped: see *cardio-* and *-oid.*] A somewhat heart-shaped mathematical curve, being the path of a point on the circumference of a circle which rolls on another circle of equal size.

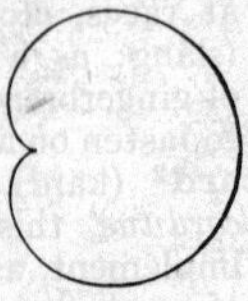

The Cardioid.

car-di-ol-o-gy (kär-di-ol′ǫ-ji), *n.* [See *cardio-* and *-logy.*] The science of the heart.

car-di-tis (kär-dī′tis), *n.* [NL., < Gr. καρδία, heart.] In *pathol.*, inflammation of the muscles of the heart.

car-doon (kär-dön′), *n.* [F. *cardon,* < L. *carduus,* thistle.] A perennial plant, *Cynara cardunculus,* native in Mediterranean regions, related to the artichoke and eaten as a vegetable.

care (kãr), *n.* [AS. *caru, cearu,* = Goth. *kara.*] Grief† or distress†; also, anxiety, concern, or solicitude; also, serious attention; heed; caution; also, watchful oversight; charge; also, an object of concern or attention.—**care,** *v. i.; cared, caring.* [AS. *carian, cearian.*] To be concerned or solicitous; have thought or regard; also, to be concerned so as to feel or express objection (with a negative: as, I don't *care* if I do); also, to be inclined (*to*); have an inclination or liking (*for*); have a fondness or affection (*for*); also, to make provision or look out (*for*).

ca-reen (kạ-rēn′), *n.* [F. *carine,* now *carène,* < L. *carina,* keel.] The position of a ship when laid over on one side; also, a careening.—**ca-reen′,** *v.* **I.** *tr.* To cause (a ship) to lie over on one side for repairing or the like; clean or repair (a ship in such a position); also, to cause (a ship) to heel over. **II.** *intr.* To careen a ship; also, to lean to one side, as a ship.—**ca-reen′age** (-āj), *n.* A place or a charge for careening a ship.

ca-reer (kạ-rēr′), *n.* [F. *carrière,* < L. *carrus,* E. *car.*] A race-course†; a path† or way†; a charge at full speed†; a course, esp. a swift one; (full) speed; general course of action or procedure, as of a person through life or in some profession or office, esp. a conspicuous course; a course of life or employment offering possibilities of advancement or fame.—**career diplomat, girl,** etc., one who has purposely prepared or studied for a desired career.—**ca-reer′,** *v. i.* To run or move rapidly along.—**ca-reer′er,** *n.*

care=free (kãr′frē′), *a.* Free from care; without anxiety.

care-ful (kãr′fụl), *a.* [AS. *carful.*] Full of care, trouble, or anxiety (archaic); attended with trouble or anxiety (archaic); also, full of care or concern for something; solicitously mindful (*of*); also, heedful; painstaking; watchful; cautious; also, performed with care, heed, or caution.—**care′ful-ly,** *adv.*—**care′ful-ness,** *n.*

care-less (kãr′les), *a.* [AS. *carlēas.*] Free from care or anxiety (archaic); also, having no care or concern; unconcerned; not caring or troubling; also, not taking due care; heedless; thoughtless; negligent; inaccurate; also, marked by lack of care; unconsidered or unstudied; done heedlessly or negligently; due to lack of proper care; also, uncared-for†.—**care′less-ly,** *adv.*—**care′less-ness,** *n.*

car-er (kãr′ėr), *n.* One who cares.

ca-ress (kạ-res′), *n.* [F. *caresse,* < It. *carezza,* < L. *carus,* dear.] An act of endearment; an expression of affection by touch.—**ca-ress′,** *v. t.* To bestow caresses on; fondle; fig., to treat with favor.—**ca-ress′ant, ca-res′sive** (-res′iv), *a.* Caressing.—**ca-ress′er,** *n.*—**ca-ress′ing-ly,** *adv.*

car-et (kar′et or kā′ret), *n.* [L., 'there is lacking.'] A mark (‸) made in written or printed matter to show the place of something to be inserted.

care-tak-er (kãr′tā″kėr), *n.* One who takes care of a thing, place, or person; a person put in charge of anything.

care=worn (kãr′wôrn), *a.* Showing marks of care or anxiety.

car-go (kär′gō), *n.*; pl. *-goes* or *-gos* (-gōz). [Sp., < *cargar,* load, = E. *charge, v.*] The lading or freight of a ship or other vessel; load.

car-goose (kär′gös), *n.*; pl. *-geese* (-gēs). [Cf. prov. Eng. *car, carr,* pool, marsh.] The crested grebe (bird), *Podiceps cristatus.*

Car-ib (kar′ib), *n.* [Sp. *Caribe:* cf. *cannibal.*] A member of an Indian people of northeastern South America, formerly dominant through the Lesser Antilles; also, their language.—**Car-ib-be-an** (kar-i-bē′ạn), *a.* Of or pertaining to the Caribs, or the Lesser Antilles, or the sea between the Lesser Antilles and South and Central America ('Caribbean Sea').

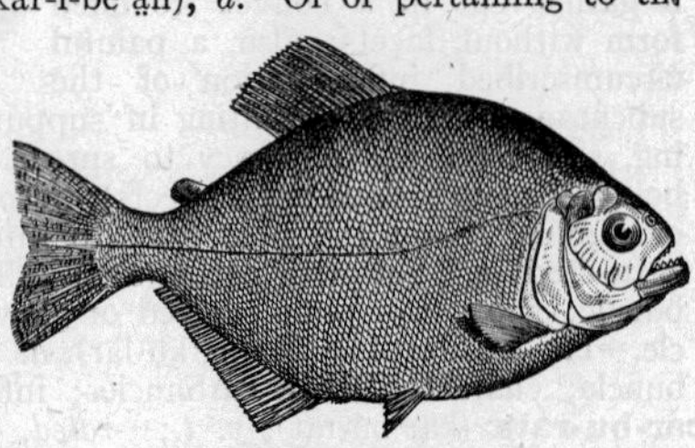

Caribe (*Serrasalmo piraya*).

ca-ri-be (kä-rē′bā), *n.* [Sp., cannibal, orig. Carib.] A voracious South American fresh-water fish, *Serrasalmo piraya;* also, any of various allied fishes.

car-i-bou (kar′i-bö), *n.*; pl. *-bous* or (esp. collectively) *-bou.* [Canadian F.; of Indian origin.] Any of several North American species or varieties of reindeer.

Caribou (*Rangifer caribou*).

car-i-ca-ture (kar′i-kạ-ţūr), *n.* [F., < It. *caricatura,* < *caricare,* load, overload, exaggerate, = E. *charge, v.*] A representation, pictorial or descriptive, ludicrously exaggerating the peculiarities or defects of persons or things; also, the art or process of making such representations; also, any mere travesty.—**car′i-ca-ture,** *v. t.; -tured, -turing.* To represent in caricature.—**car′i-ca-tur-ist,** *n.* One who makes caricatures.

ca-ri-es (kā′ri-ēz), *n.* [L.] Decay, as of bone or teeth, or of plant tissue.

car-il-lon (kar′i-lǫn), *n.* [F., chime of (orig. four) bells, < L. *quattuor,* four.] A set of stationary bells arranged for playing melodies, sounded by manual action or by machinery; also, a melody played on such bells; also, a musical instrument, or an attachment to one, to imitate a peal of bells.

ca-ri-na (ka-rī′nạ), *n.*; pl. *-næ* (-nē). [L., keel.] In *bot.* and *zoöl.*, a keel-like part or ridge.—**ca-ri′nal,** *a.* Pertaining to or resembling a carina.—**car-i-nate** (kar′i-nāt), *a.* [L. *carinatus.*] Formed with a carina; keel-like. Also **car′i-nat-ed.**—**car-i-na′tion** (-nā′shǫn), *n.* A carinate or keel-like formation.

car-i-ole, car-ri-ole (kar′i-ōl), *n.* [F. *carriole,* < It. *carriuola,* < L. *carrus,* E. *car.*] A small open carriage; also, a covered cart.

ca-ri-ous (kā′ri-us), *a.* [L. *cariosus.*] Affected with caries, as teeth; decayed.—**ca-ri-os′i-ty** (-os′i-ti), **ca′ri-ous-ness,** *n.*

cark (kärk), *v.* [OF. *carquier, cargier,* also *chargier:* see *charge.*] **I.** *tr.* To load†; oppress, trouble, or worry (archaic or prov.). **II.** *intr.* To have care or anxiety; worry; fret. [Archaic or prov.]—**cark,** *n.* A load†; also, care, trouble, or worry (archaic or prov.: as, "At night the swart mechanic comes to drown his *cark* and care, Quaffing ale from pewter tankards," Longfellow's "Nuremberg").

carl (kärl), *n.* [From Scand.: cf. Icel. *karl*, Sw. and Dan. *karl*, man, akin to E. *churl.*] A man; a fellow; a rustic; a churl. [Archaic or Sc. and north. Eng.]—**carl′=hemp,** *n.* [So called because, from its greater coarseness and robustness, it was supposed to be the male plant.] The female or pistillate plant of hemp, which is harvested after the male or staminate plant. Cf. *fimble.*

car-lin, car-line[1] (kär′lin), *n.* [From Scand.: cf. Icel. *kerling*, woman, esp. old woman, and E. *carl.*] An old woman (as, "that auld capricious *carlin*, Nature": Burns's "To James Smith," 13); a hag. [Archaic or Sc. and north. Eng.]

car-line[2] (kär′lin), *n.* [F.] A thistle-like plant of the European composite genus *Carlina*, as *C. vulgaris*, the common species, whose involucral scales are so hygroscopic as to serve for a natural weather-glass.

car-line[3], **car-ling** (kär′lin, -ling), *n.* [Origin uncertain: cf. Icel. *kerling.*] In a ship, one of the fore-and-aft timbers which form part of the deck framework.

Car-list (kär′list), *n.* A supporter of the claims of Don Carlos (1788–1855), second son of Charles IV. of Spain, or of his successors, to the Spanish throne; also, formerly, one of the partizans of Charles X. of France, and of the elder branch of the Bourbons, afterward called *Legitimists.* —**Car′lism,** *n.*

car-lot† (kär′lọt), *n.* [Dim. of *carl.*] A countryman. See Shakspere's "As You Like It," iii. 5. 108.

Car-lo-vin-gi-an (kär-lọ̄-vin′ji-ạn), *a.* Carolingian.

Car-ma-gnole (kär-mä-nyol), *n.* [F., orig. a kind of coat introduced into Paris by the revolutionists from Marseilles in 1792, later the dance and song; from *Carmagnola*, town in northwestern Italy.] A dance and song popular during the French Revolution.

car-man (kär′mạn), *n.*; pl. *-men.* One who drives a car; one of the crew of a street-car or the like.

Car-mel-ite (kär′mẹl-īt), *n.* A mendicant friar or a nun of a religious order founded at Mt. Carmel, Syria, in the 12th century; a white friar.

car-min-a-tive (kär-min′ạ-tiv). [F. *carminatif*, < L. *carminare* (pp. *-atus*), card (wool).] **I.** *a.* Expelling wind from the body; relieving flatulence. **II.** *n.* A carminative medicine.

car-mine (kär′min or -mīn). [F. *carmin* = Sp. *carmín*, ult. < Ar. *qirmiz*, E. *kermes.*] **I.** *n.* The coloring matter or principle of cochineal; also, a crimson pigment obtained from cochineal; also, a light crimson color. **II.** *a.* Of the color called carmine.—**car-min′ic** (-min′ik), *a.*

car-nage (kär′nạj), *n.* [F. *carnage*, < It. *carnaggio*, < L. *caro* (*carn-*), flesh.] The flesh of slain animals†; also, dead bodies, as of men slain in battle (archaic); also, the slaughter of a great number, as in battle; butchery; massacre.

car-nal (kär′nạl), *a.* [LL. *carnalis*, < L. *caro* (*carn-*), flesh.] Pertaining to the flesh; fleshly; bodily; sensual; also, not spiritual; worldly; also, flesh-eating†.—**car-nal′i-ty** (-nal′i-ti), *n.*; pl. *-ties* (-tiz). Fleshliness; sensuality; worldliness; also, a carnal thing, deed, etc.—**car′nal-ize,** *v. t.*; *-ized, -izing.* To make carnal.

car-nall-ite (kär′nạl-īt), *n.* [From R. von *Carnall* (1804–74), Prussian mining official.] A mineral consisting of a hydrous chloride of potassium and magnesium, occurring in transparent, deliquescent crystals, and forming a valuable source of potassium.

car-nal-ly (kär′nạl-i), *adv.* In a carnal manner.

car-nas-si-al (kär-nas′i-ạl). [F. *carnassier*, flesh-eating, < L. *caro* (*carn-*), flesh.] **I.** *a.* Noting or pertaining to teeth adapted for cutting and tearing flesh, esp. the last upper premolar or the first lower molar teeth in a typically carnivorous dentition. **II.** *n.* A carnassial tooth.

car-na-tion (kär-nā′shọn), *n.* [F. *carnation*, < L. *caro* (*carn-*), flesh.] Flesh-color†; pink; sometimes, red; also, any of numerous cultivated varieties of the clove-pink, *Dianthus caryophyllus*, with fragrant flowers of various colors.

car-na-u-ba (kär-nä-ö′bạ), *n.* [Brazilian Pg.] The Brazilian wax-palm.

car-ne-lian (kär-nē′lyạn), *n.* [Var. (due to association with L. *caro*, *carn-*, flesh) of earlier *cornelian*, *corneline*, < OF. *corneline* (F. *cornaline*), appar. < L. *cornu*, horn.] A red or reddish variety of chalcedony: used in jewelry, etc.

car-ne-ous (kär′nẹ̄-us), *a.* [LL. *carneus*, < L. *caro* (*carn-*), flesh.] Fleshy; also, flesh-colored.

car-ni-fy (kär′ni-fī), *v. t.* or *i.*; *-fied, -fying.* [L. *caro* (*carn-*), flesh: see *-fy.*] To turn into or form flesh; make or become flesh-like.—**car″ni-fi-ca′tion** (-fi-kā′shọn), *n.*

car-ni-val (kär′ni-vạl), *n.* [It. *carnevale*, prob. < L. *caro* (*carn-*), flesh, + *levare*, lighten, take away.] The season immediately preceding Lent, observed in Italy and elsewhere with merrymaking and revelry; the festivity of this season; in general, a large, usually public merrymaking, festivity, or entertainment; revelry.

car-ni-vore (kär′ni-vōr), *n.* [F. *carnivore*, flesh-eating, < L. *carnivorus*: see *carnivorous.*] A flesh-eating animal or plant; esp., one of the *Carnivora*, an order of mammals, chiefly flesh-eating, including the cats, dogs, bears, seals, etc.

car-niv-o-rous (kär-niv′ọ̄-rus), *a.* [L. *carnivorus*, < *caro* (*carn-*), flesh, + *vorare*, devour.] Flesh-eating, as certain animals; pertaining to the carnivores (mammals); of plants, digesting animal matter (insects).—**car-niv′o-rous-ly,** *adv.* —**car-niv′o-rous-ness,** *n.*

car-nose (kär′nōs or kär-nōs′), *a.* [L. *carnosus*, < *caro* (*carn-*), flesh.] Fleshy; pulpy.—**car-nos′i-ty** (-nos′i-ti), *n.*; pl. *-ties* (-tiz). Fleshiness†; also, a fleshy growth.

car-no-tite (kär′nọ̄-tīt), *n.* [From A. *Carnot* (born 1839), French inspector-general of mines.] A mineral, a yellow, earthy hydrous vanadate containing uranium, potassium, radioactive substances, etc., occurring in Colorado, and used as a source of radium.

car-ob (kar′ọb), *n.* [F. *carobe*, now *caroube*, < Ar. *kharrūbah.*] The fruit of a cæsalpiniaceous tree, *Ceratonia siliqua*, of the Mediterranean regions, a long pod containing hard seeds in a sweet pulp, used for feeding animals and sometimes eaten by man; the locust-bean; St. John's bread; also, the tree.

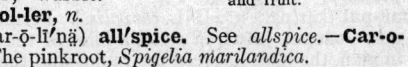

Branch of Carob-tree, with flower and fruit.

ca-roche (kạ-rōch′ or -rōsh′), *n.* [F. (obs.) *carroche* (now *carrosse*), through It. < L. *carrus*, E. *car.*] An old form of coach or carriage of a stately kind.

car-ol (kar′ọl), *n.* [OF. *carole*; origin uncertain.] A kind of dance†; a song, esp. of joy; a Christmas song.—**car′ol,** *v. t.* or *i.*; *-oled* or *-olled*, *-oling* or *-olling.* To sing, esp. in a lively or joyous manner; warble.—**car′ol-er, car′ol-ler,** *n.*

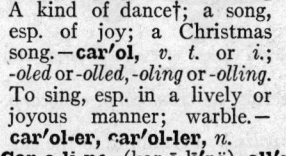

Car-o-li-na (kar-ọ̄-lī′nạ̈) **all′spice.** See *allspice.*—**Car-o-li′na pink.** The pinkroot, *Spigelia marilandica.*

Car-o-line (kar′ọ̄-lin or -līn), *a.* [ML. *Carolinus*, < *Carolus*, Charles.] Of or pertaining to some person named Charles, esp. Charles the Great (Charlemagne), or Charles I. or Charles II. of England.

Car-o-lin-gi-an (kar-ọ̄-lin′ji-ạn), *a.* [ML. *Carolingi*, pl., the Carolingian dynasty, < OHG. *Karling*, patronymic deriv. < *Karl*, Charles (Charles Martel, or perhaps Charlemagne).] Belonging to the Frankish dynasty which succeeded the Merovingian dynasty in 751, and which reigned in France until 987 and in Germany until 911.

Car-o-lin-i-an (kar-ọ̄-lin′i-ạn). [In part, < ML. *Carolinus* (see *Caroline*); in part, < *Carolina* (North and South), named from Charles (ML. *Carolus*) II. of England.] **I.** *a.* Of or pertaining to some person named Charles, as Charles the Great (Charlemagne); also, of or pertaining to the two States of North and South Carolina or either one of them. **II.** *n.* A native or inhabitant of either North or South Carolina.

car-o-lus (kar′ọ̄-lus), *n.*; pl. *-luses*, L. *-li* (-lī). [ML. *Carolus*, Charles.] Any of various coins issued under monarchs named Charles, esp. an English gold coin struck in the reign of Charles I., orig. worth 20 shillings, but later 23 shillings.

Obverse. Reverse.
Carolus of Charles I., in the British Museum.

car-om (kar′ọm), *n.* [Earlier *carambole*, < F. *carambole*, < Sp. *carambola*; origin uncertain.] In *billiards*, a shot in which the ball struck with the cue is made to hit two balls in succession.—**car′om,** *v. i.* To make a carom; also, to strike and rebound.

ca-rot-id (ka-rot′id). [Gr. καρωτίδες, pl., < κάρος, stupor (thought to be caused by compression of these arteries).] In *anat.*: **I.** *n.* Either of the two great arteries, one on each side of the neck, which carry blood to the head. **II.** *a.* Pertaining to the carotids.—**ca-rot′i-dal,** *a.*

ca-rotte (ka-rot′), *n.* [F., 'carrot.'] A cylindrical roll of tobacco, esp. of perique.

ca-rou-sal (kạ-rou′zạl), *n.* Carousing; a carouse.

ca-rouse (kạ-rouz′), *n.* [F. (obs.) *carous* (now *carrousse*), < G. *gar aus*, 'quite out.'] A full draft of liquor†; also, a drinking-bout; a revel or orgy of drinking.—**ca-rouse′,** *v. i.*; *-roused, -rousing.* To engage in a carouse; drink deeply.

car-ou-sel (kar-ọ̈-zel′), *n.* See *carrousel.*

ca-rous-er (kạ-rou′zėr), *n.* One who carouses.

carp[1] (kärp), *v. i.* [Prob. < Icel. *karpa*, boast, but affected in sense by L. *carpere*, pick, carp at.] To talk†; also, to find fault; cavil ill-naturedly (*at*).

carp[2] (kärp), *n.*; pl. *carps* or (esp. collectively) *carp.* [OF. F. *carpe*, < LL. *carpa*; origin unknown.] A fresh-water fish, *Cyprinus carpio* (family *Cyprinidæ*), with a compressed body, commonly bred in ponds; also, any of various other fishes of the same family, or of certain fishes of other families.

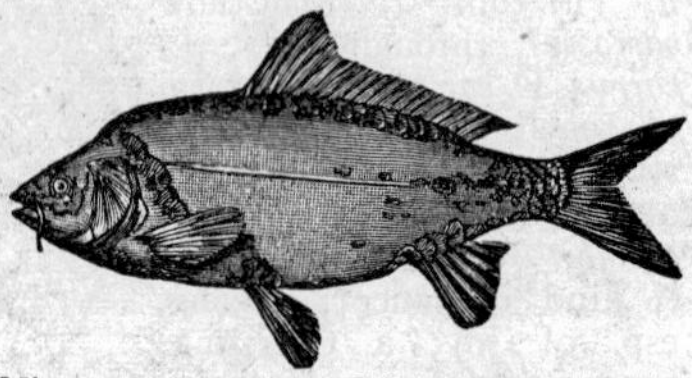

Mirror-carp, a variety of *Cyprinus carpio* with only a few large scales.

-carp. Noun termination from Gr. καρπός, fruit, used in botanical terms, as *cremocarp, endocarp, pericarp.*

car-pal (kär′pạl), *a.* [NL. *carpalis.*] Pertaining to the carpus.—**carpal joint,** in *anat.*, a joint of the carpus; specif., in man, the joint between the radius and the carpus; also, a corresponding joint in other vertebrates.

car-pa-le (kär-pā′lē), *n.*; pl. *-lia* (-li-ạ̈). [NL., neut. of *carpalis*, E. *carpal.*] In *anat.*, any bone of the carpus, esp. one of the distal row articulating directly with the metacarpal bones.

car-pel (kär′pel), *n.* [NL. *carpellum*, < Gr. καρπός, fruit.] In *bot.*, a simple pistil, or a single member of a compound pistil: regarded as a modified leaf.—**car′pel-la-ry** (-pe-lạ̄-ri), *a.* Pertaining to or of the nature of a carpel.—**car′pel-late** (-pe-lāt), *a.* Having carpels.

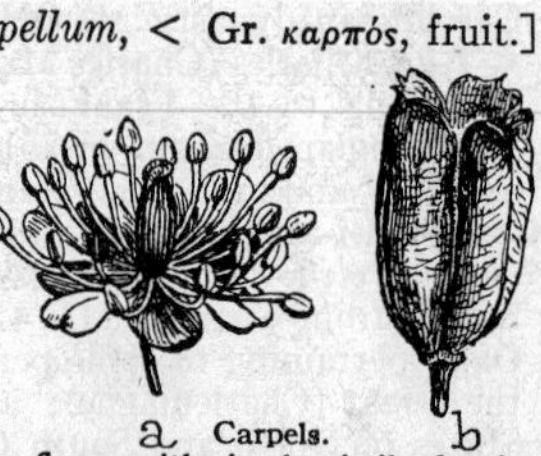

Carpels.
a, flower with simple pistil; *b*, tricarpellary fruit.

car-pen-ter (kär′pẹn-tėr), *n.* [OF. *carpentier* (F. *charpentier*), < LL. *carpentarius*, wagon-maker, < L. *carpentum*, wagon.] An artificer who works in wood; one who executes the woodwork of houses, ships, etc.; also, an officer whose duty it is to keep a ship's woodwork in repair.—**car′pen-ter,** *v. i.* or *t.* To do carpenter's work, or make by carpentry.—**car′penter=bee,** *n.* Any of various solitary bees of the genus *Xylocopa* and allied genera that make their nests in wood, boring tunnels divided by partitions into small compartments in which to deposit their eggs.—**car′pen-try,** *n.* The art or the work of a carpenter.

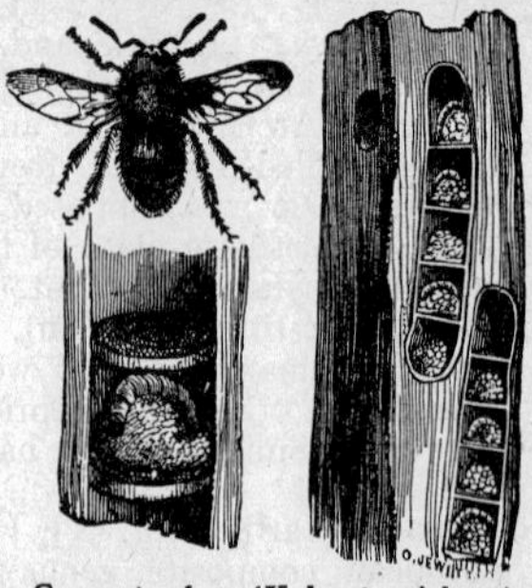

Carpenter-bee (*Xylocopa violacea*), with a piece of wood bored by the bee, showing grubs and food deposited in the cells, and with cells on a larger scale.

carp-er (kär′pėr), *n.* One who carps.

car-pet (kär′pet), *n.* [OF. *carpite*, < ML. *carpita*, kind of thick woolen cloth, < L. *carpere*, pick, card (wool).] A heavy woolen fabric used for covering tables, etc.†; also, a heavy fabric, commonly of wool, for covering floors, stairs, etc.; a covering of this material; fig., any covering resembling or suggesting a carpet (as, a *carpet* of turf or flowers).—**on the carpet,** on the table-cloth or table, as for consideration or investigation; under discussion.—**car′pet,** *v. t.*; *-peted, -peting.* To cover or furnish with or as with a carpet.—**car′pet=bag,** *n.* A traveling-bag, properly one made of carpeting.—**car′pet=bag″ger,** *n.* One who travels with (only) a carpet-bag: applied in contempt, after the American Civil War, to Northerners who went to the South to seek political or other advantages made possible by the disorganized condition of political affairs.—**car′pet=bee″tle,** *n.* A small beetle, *Anthrenus scrophulariæ*, whose larvæ are destructive to carpets and other woolen fabrics. Also **car′pet=bug.**—**car′pet-ing,** *n.* Material for carpets; carpets in general.—**car′pet=knight,** *n.* [Orig., prob., a knight dubbed while kneeling on the carpet before the sovereign's chair, rather than on the battle-field.] A knight or soldier accustomed to carpeted abodes and peaceful ease rather than to the hardships of the field: as, "His square-turn'd joints, and strength of limb, Show'd him no *carpet knight* so trim, But in close fight a champion grim" (Scott's "Marmion," i. 5).—**car′pet-less,** *a.* Without a carpet.—**car′pet=weed,** *n.* A North American prostrate weed, *Mollugo verticillata*, which forms mats over the ground.

carp-ing (kär′ping), *p. a.* That carps; faultfinding.—**carp′ing-ly,** *adv.*

car-pin-te-ro (kär-pin-tā′rō), *n.*; pl. *-ros* (-rōz). [Sp., 'carpenter.'] Any of various woodpeckers of the western United States.

carpo-. Form of Gr. καρπός, fruit, used in combination.—**car-pọ-gen-ic** (kär-pọ̄-jen′ik), *a.* [+ *-genic.*] Fruit-producing.—**car′po-lite** (-līt), *n.* [+ *-lite.*] A fossil fruit.—**car-pol′o-gy** (-pol′ọ̄-ji), *n.* [+ *-logy.*] The part of botany that relates to fruits.—**car-po-log′i-cal** (-loj′i-kạl), *a.*—**car-pol′o-gist,** *n.*—**car-poph′a-gous** (-pof′ạ-gus), *a.* [+ *-phagous.*] Fruit-eating.—**car′po-phore** (-fōr), *n.* [+ *-phore.*] In *bot.*, a slender prolongation of the floral axis, bearing the carpels of some compound fruits, as in the geranium and in many umbelliferous plants; also, less properly, any stipe supporting an ovary.

Carpophore (with carpels) of an umbelliferous plant.

-carpous. Adjective termination from Gr. καρπός, fruit, used in botanical terms, as *apocarpous, caulocarpous, trichocarpous.*

carp=suck-er (kärp′suk″-ėr), *n.* Any of several North American carp-like fresh-water fishes of the genus *Carpiodes* (subfamily *Ictiobinæ*). Also called *buffalo-fish.*

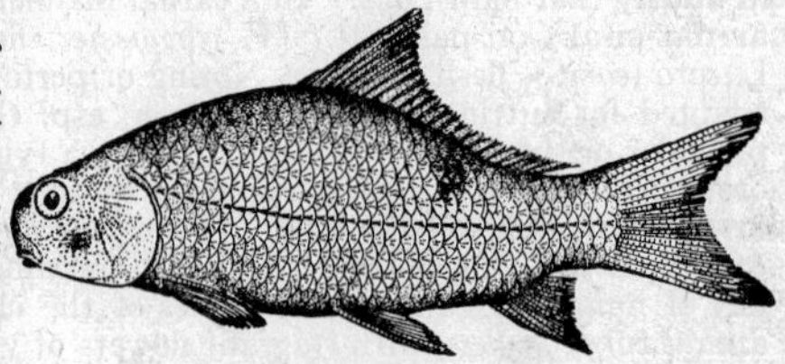

Carp-sucker.

car-pus (kär′pus), *n.*; pl. *-pi* (-pī). [NL., < Gr. καρπός, wrist.] In *anat.*, the proximal portion or segment of the hand; the wrist; the wrist-bones collectively; the collection of bones between the radius and the metacarpus.
car-rack (kar′ak), *n.* See *carack.*
car-ra-geen, car-ra-gheen (kar′a-gēn), *n.* [From *Carragheen*, or *Carrigeen*, in southern Ireland.] A seaweed, *Chondrus crispus*, of the Atlantic coasts of Europe and North America, abounding in a nutritious mucilage and hence used (by boiling) in making blancmange, soups, etc.; Irish moss.
car-riage (kar′āj), *n.* [OF. *cariage*, < *carier*: see *carry.*] The act of carrying; conveyance; commercial transportation, or its cost; also, a means of carrying; a wheeled vehicle for conveying persons; a wheeled passenger-vehicle drawn by horses, esp. one designed with a view to comfort and elegance; a wheeled support, as for a cannon; a part, as of a machine, designed for carrying something; also, that which is carried†; also, execution or management; also, a carrying by assault; capture; also, manner of carrying or holding; bearing or mien; behavior (archaic).—**car′riage-a-ble,** *a.* Portable; also, passable by carriages, as a road.—**car′riage-way,** *n.* A way or road for the passage of carriages.
car-rick=bend (kar′ik-bend′), *n.* [Cf. *carack.*] *Naut.*, a kind of knot for joining cables or hawsers.—**car′rick=bitt′,** *n.* *Naut.*, one of the bitts which support the windlass.
car-ried (kar′id), *p. a.* Carried away in mind, as by some feeling or thought; transported with emotion; rapt in thought; abstracted. [Chiefly Sc.]
car-ri-er (kar′i-ėr), *n.* One who or that which carries; a person or an association of persons that undertakes to convey goods or persons for hire (as, a common *carrier*, one that undertakes to convey goods or persons for hire as a public calling, inviting the employment of the public generally); a carrier-pigeon; in *mach.*, a mechanism by which something is carried or moved; in *chem.*, a catalytic agent which brings about a transfer of an element or group of atoms from one compound to another.—**car′ri-er=pi″geon,** *n.* A pigeon trained to fly home from great distances and thus transport written messages; a homing pigeon; also, one of a breed of pigeons characterized by a huge wattle at the base of the beak.
car-ri-ole (kar′i-ōl), *n.* See *cariole.*
car-ri-on (kar′i-on), *n.* [OF. *caroine* (also *charoigne*, F. *charogne*), < L. *caro*, flesh.] A dead body†; a living body or person (in contempt: obs. or archaic); dead and putrefying flesh.—**car′ri-on=crow,** *n.* Any of various crows, as the common European crow, *Corvus corone*; also, the black vulture, *Catharista atrata*, of the southern U. S., etc.

Carrion-crow (*Corvus corone*).

car-roc-cio (kär-rot′chō), *n.*; pl. *carrocci* (-chē). [It., < L. *carrus*, E. *car.*] The car of war, on which the standard was borne into battle, peculiar to the Italian republics of the middle ages.
car-rom (kar′om), *n.* and *v.* See *carom.*
car-ro-ma-ta (kär-rō-mä′tä), *n.* [Philippine Sp.] In the Philippines, a light, two-wheeled covered vehicle, usually drawn by a single horse.
car-ro-nade (kar-o-nād′), *n.* [From *Carron*, in Stirlingshire, Scotland, where it was first cast.] A short piece of ordnance of large caliber, formerly in use, esp. in ships.

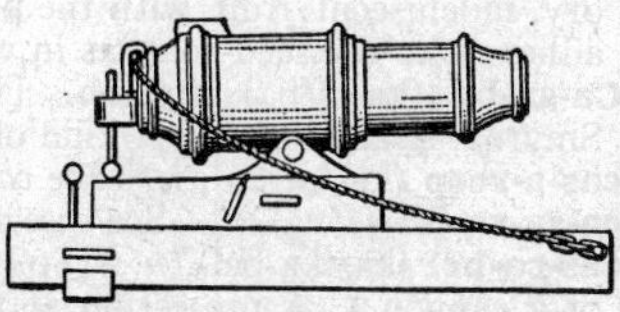
Carronade.

car-ron=oil (kar′on-oil′), *n.* [From its use at the *Carron* iron-works in Scotland: see *carronade.*] A liniment composed of equal parts of lime-water and linseed-oil, used as an application for burns and scalds.
car-rot (kar′ot), *n.* [F. *carotte*, < L. *carota.*] A plant of the apiaceous genus *Daucus*, esp. *D. carota*, in its wild form a widespread, familiar weed, and in cultivation valued for its yellowish-red edible root; also, the root, much used as a vegetable.—**car′rot-y,** *a.* Carrot-like; yellowish-red; having yellowish-red hair.

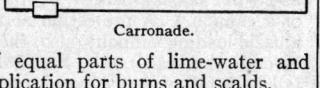

Carrot (*Daucus carota*).—Flowering branch, with fruit (*a*).

car-rou-sel (kar-ö-zel′), *n.* [F., < It. *carosello*; origin uncertain.] A merry-go-round.
car′ru-cate, *n.* See *carucate.*
car-ry (kar′i), *v.*; *-ried, -rying.* [OF. *carier* (also *charier*, F. *charrier*), < ML. *carricare*, convey by wagon, < L. *carrus*: see *car.*] **I.** *tr.* To convey from one place to another, as in a car or cart; transport (a thing) while bearing it up; transfer in any manner; take or bring; conduct or lead; conduct, prosecute, or maintain (with *on*); put into operation or effect, as a plan or scheme (with *through* or *out*); impel or drive; lead or impel mentally; influence greatly or affect beyond reason (with *away*); extend or continue in a given direction or to a certain point; take by force, as from an enemy; capture; gain possession or control of; win; secure the election of (a candidate) or the adoption of (a motion or bill); also, to bear up or support (something) while moving it; bear the weight, burden, etc., of; sustain; keep on hand or in stock; have as an attribute, property, etc.; have as a consequence, or involve; hold or contain; hold (the body, head, etc.) in a certain manner; behave or comport (one's self); *milit.*, to hold (a rifle, etc.) in a vertical position against the right shoulder with the arm hanging to its full length near the body. **II.** *intr.* To act as a bearer or conductor; have or exert propelling force; bear the head in a particular manner, as a horse; behave†; be transmitted, propelled, or sustained.—**to carry on,** to continue or persevere in a course, as of conduct; prosecute a purpose to the desired end; also, to conduct one's self in a frolicsome, wild, or improper manner (colloq.).—**car′ry,** *n.*; pl. *carries* (-iz). A carrying; also, land separating navigable waters, over which a canoe or boat must be carried; a portage; range, as of a gun; the distance traversed by a golf-ball before it alights; *milit.*, the position assumed at the command to carry arms.
car-ry-all (kar′i-âl), *n.* [In part, an altered form of *cariole*; in part, < *carry* + *all.*] A light, covered, four-wheeled one-horse carriage, with two seats; also, a large, long omnibus-like vehicle used for picnic-parties, etc.
car-ry=o-ver (kar′i-ō′vėr), *n.* Something carried over to a new period, account, or the like, as a stock of grain.
carse (kärs), *n.* [Origin uncertain.] Low, fertile land, usually along the side of a stream. [Sc.]
cart (kärt), *n.* [Prob. < Icel. *kartr*, cart, = AS. *cræt*, chariot.] A chariot† or car†; a heavy two-wheeled vehicle, commonly without springs, for the conveyance of heavy goods; a light two-wheeled vehicle with springs, used for pleasure or business; also, any small vehicle moved by hand.—**cart,** *v. t.* To convey in or as in a cart.—**cart′age** (-āj), *n.* The act or the cost of carting.
carte[1] (kärt), *n.* In *fencing*, same as *quarte.*
carte[2] (kärt), *n.* [F.: see *card*[1].] A card; a bill of fare; a map or chart.—**à la carte.** See entry *à la carte.*—**carte blanche** (blänsh). [F., 'blank card.'] A signed paper left blank for the person to whom it is given to fill in his own conditions; hence, unqualified authority in a particular matter; full discretionary power.—**carte=de=vi-site** (-dė-vē-zēt), *n.*; pl. *cartes-* (F. kärt-). [F. *carte de visite*, visiting-card.] A photographic portrait mounted on a small card.
car-tel (kär′tel), *n.* [F., < It. *cartello*, dim. < L. *charta*, paper: see *chart.*] A written agreement between nations, esp. when at war, for the exchange of prisoners or for some other purpose; a letter of defiance or challenge; a written or printed paper or card; also, in continental European use, a combination or combine; a syndicate or trust.
cart-er (kär′tėr), *n.* One who drives a cart.
Car-te-sian (kär-tē′zian), *a.* Pertaining to the French philosopher and mathematician René Descartes (1596–1650), or to his doctrines.—**Cartesian devil,** a philosophical toy consisting of a hollow figure filled with air in the upper part

and water in the lower, and often fashioned in the form of a devil, which is made to fall and rise in a vessel or cylinder of water because of changes in pressure produced by manipulating a sheet of rubber or the like stretched over the top of the vessel, pressure on the rubber causing more water to enter the lower part of the figure and to compress the air within, thereby causing the figure to sink.—**Car-te′sian-ism,** *n.*

cart-ful (kärt′fu̇l), *n.*; pl. *-fuls.* As much as a cart will hold.

Car-tha-gin-i-an (kär-thạ-jin′i-ạn). [L. *Carthaginiensis*, < *Carthago*, Carthage.] **I.** *a.* Of or pertaining to ancient Carthage, a city and state on the northern coast of Africa. **II.** *n.* A native or inhabitant of Carthage.

cart=horse (kärt′hôrs), *n.* A horse used to draw a cart, esp. for heavy work.

Car-thu-sian (kär-thū′ziạn). [Said to be from the name of a place near which the first monastery of the order was built.] **I.** *a.* Belonging to an austere monastic order founded by St. Bruno in 1086 near Grenoble, France. **II.** *n.* A member of the Carthusian order.

car-ti-lage (kär′ti-lạ̄j), *n.* [F. *cartilage*, < L. *cartilago* (*cartilagin-*), gristle.] A firm, elastic, flexible substance of a translucent whitish color, consisting of connective tissue, and forming parts of the skeleton of vertebrates (in embryos and the very young, the greater part); gristle; also, a part or structure composed of cartilage.—**car′ti-lage=bone,** *n.* A bone that is developed or preformed in cartilage: distinguished from *membrane-bone.*—**car-ti-lag′i-nous** (-laj′i-nus), *a.* [L. *cartilaginosus.*] Of, containing, or resembling cartilage; gristly; in *zoöl.*, having the skeleton composed mostly of cartilage, as certain fishes.

Car-tist (kär′tist), *n.* [Sp. and Pg. *cartista*, < *carta*, charter, < L. *charta*: see *chart.*] A supporter of the constitution, as in Spain.

car-tog-ra-phy (kär-tog′rạ-fi), *n.* [ML. *carta*, map, chart: see *chart* and *-graphy.*] The drawing or making of charts or maps.—**car-tog′ra-pher,** *n.*—**car-to-graph-ic, car-to-graph-i-cal** (kär-tọ̄-graf′ik, -i-kạl), *a.*

car-to-man-cy (kär′tọ̄-man-si), *n.* [ML. *carta*, card: see *chart* and *-mancy.*] Divination by means of playing-cards.

car-ton (kär′tọn), *n.* [F.: see *cartoon.*] A kind of thin pasteboard; a box made of it; also, a white disk within the bull's-eye of a target; a shot which strikes this.

car-toon (kär-tön′), *n.* [F. *carton*, < It. *cartone*, pasteboard, cartoon, aug. of *carta*, < L. *charta*, paper: see *chart.*] A drawing, commonly on strong paper, of the same size as a proposed decoration or pattern in fresco, mosaic, tapestry, etc., for which it is intended to serve as a model to be transferred or copied; also, a more or less sketchy picture, as in a newspaper or periodical, illustrating symbolically or in caricature some subject of current interest, often in a partizan spirit.—**car-toon′,** *v. t.* To make a cartoon or preliminary sketch of; also, to represent by a cartoon, as in approbation or ridicule.—**car-toon′ist,** *n.* One who draws cartoons.

car-touche, car-touch (kär-tösh′), *n.* [F. *cartouche*, < It. *cartoccio*, < *carta*, < L. *charta*, paper: see *chart.*] A cartridge; a box for cartridges; the case containing the inflammable materials in certain fireworks; a scroll-shaped ornament; an ornamental tablet; an oval or oblong figure, as on ancient Egyptian monuments, inclosing characters expressing royal names, etc.

Cartouche of Cleopatra.

Cartouche of Rameses II.

car-tridge (kär′trij), *n.* [Corruption of *cartouche.*] A case of pasteboard, metal, or the like, for holding a complete charge of powder, and often also the bullet or the shot, for a firearm; a case containing any explosive charge, as for blasting; also, a roll of unexposed films for a camera.—**blank cartridge,** a cartridge containing powder only, without ball or shot.—**car′tridge=pa″per,** *n.* A thick, strong paper used orig. for making cartridges, and later as drawing-paper; also, a kind of wall-paper.

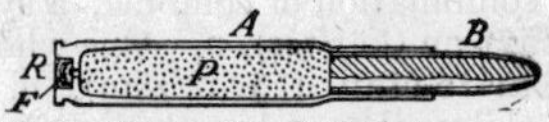

Center-fire Cartridge.

A, metallic case of copper or brass; *B*, bullet; *R*, primer; *F*, fulminate; *P*, powder.

car-tu-la-ry (kär′tụ̄-lạ̄-ri), *n.* See *chartulary.*

cart-way (kärt′wā), *n.* A way along which carts, etc., may pass.

cart-wright (kärt′rīt), *n.* A cart-maker.

car-u-cate, car-ru-cate (kar′ọ̄-kāt), *n.* [ML. *carucata*, *carrucata*, < *carruca*, plow, L. coach, < L. *carrus*, E. *car.*] Formerly, in England, a measure of land and a unit for assessment, often about 100 acres, but varying according to the nature of the soil, etc. Cf. *hide*[2] and *plowland.*

car-un-cle (kar′ung-kl), *n.* [L. *caruncula*, dim. of *caro*, flesh.] A fleshy excrescence, as on the head of a bird; a fowl's comb; in *bot.*, a protuberance at or surrounding the hilum of a seed.—**ca-run-cu-lar** (ka-rung′kụ̄-lạr), *a.* Of or like a caruncle.—**ca-run′cu-late, ca-run′cu-lat-ed** (-lāt, -lā-ted), *a.* Having a caruncle.

Caruncle. — Carunculate seed, entire and cut longitudinally.

carve (kärv), *v.*; *carved* (archaic pp. also *carven*), *carving.* [AS. *ceorfan*, cut, = G. *kerben*, notch; prob. akin to Gr. γράφειν, mark, write.] **I.** *tr.* To cut; fashion (stone, wood, etc.) or produce (an image, etc.) by cutting; adorn by or as by cutting figures, etc., in or on; cut into slices or pieces, as meat. **II.** *intr.* To cut; cut figures in stone, wood, etc.; cut up meat at table.

car-vel (kär′vel), *n.* Same as *caravel.*—**car′vel=built,** *a.* Of a ship or boat, built with the planks flush, not overlapping. Cf. *clincher-built.*

carv-en (kär′vn), *p. a.* Carved; fashioned or ornamented by carving: as, "the *carven* cedarn doors" (Tennyson's "Recollections of the Arabian Nights," 115). [Archaic.]

carv-er (kär′vėr), *n.* One who or that which carves; a carving-knife.

carv-ing (kär′ving), *n.* The act or art of one who carves; also, carved work; a carved design.—**carv′ing=knife,** *n.* A knife for carving meat, as at table.

car-y-at-id (kar-i-at′id), *n.* [L. *Caryatides*, pl., < Gr. Καρυάτιδες, lit. 'women of Caryæ (town in Greece).'] In *arch.*, a figure of a woman used like a supporting column. Cf. *atlantes.*—**car-y-at′i-dal** (-i-dạl), *a.*—**car-y-at′i-des** (-dēz), *n. pl.* [L.] Caryatids.

Caryatids. — Porch of the Erechtheum, Athens.

caryo-, etc. See *karyo-*, etc.

car-y-o-phyl-la-ceous (kar″i-ọ̄-fi-lā′shius), *a.* [NL. *caryophyllus* (as in *Dianthus caryophyllus*, the clove-pink), < Gr. καρυόφυλλον, clove-tree, < κάρυον, nut, + φύλλον, leaf.] Belonging to the *Caryophyllaceæ* (better *Silenaceæ*: see *silenaceous*), or pink family of plants; pink-like; having five petals with long claws in a tubular calyx, as in the pink.

Caryophyllaceous Flower (*Dianthus*).

car-y-op-sis (kar-i-op′sis), *n.*; pl. *-opses* (-op′sēz) or *-opsides* (-op′si-dēz). [Gr. κάρυον, nut, + ὄψις, appearance.] In *bot.*, a small, one-celled, one-seeded, dry, indehiscent fruit with the pericarp adherent to the seed-coat, as in wheat.

Ca-sa-ba (ka-sä′bạ̈) **mel′on.** [From *Kassaba*, town near Smyrna, Asia Minor.] A kind of winter muskmelon.

cas-a-reep (kas′ạ-rēp), *n.* See *cassareep.*

ca-sa-va (ka-sä′vạ̈), *n.* See *cassava.*

cas-ca-bel (kas′kạ-bel), *n.* [Sp., little bell, knob at the end of a cannon.] A projection at the rear of the breech of a muzzle-loading cannon; also, the rear part of the breech.

cas-cade (kas-kād′), *n.* [F. *cascade*, < It. *cascata*, < *cascare*, fall.] A fall of water over a precipice or other declivity; a waterfall smaller than a cataract; also, an arrangement of lace, etc., in folds falling one over another in a zigzag fashion.

—**cas-cade′**, *v. i.*; *-caded*, *-cading*. To fall in or like a cascade.

cas-ca-ra (kas′kạ-rä, commonly kas-kar′ạ̈), *n.* Shortened form of *cuscara sagrada*.—**cas′ca-ra buck′thorn.** A buckthorn, *Rhamnus purshiana*, of the Pacific coast of the U. S., yielding cascara sagrada.

cas-ca-ra sa-gra-da (kas′kạ-rạ sạ-grä′dạ). [Sp. *cáscara sagrada*, 'sacred bark.'] The bark of a buckthorn, *Rhamnus purshiana*, of the Pacific coast of the U. S., used as a cathartic or laxative.

cas-ca-ril-la (kas-kạ-ril′ạ̈), *n.* [Sp., dim. of *cáscara*, bark.] The bitter aromatic bark of a West Indian euphorbiaceous shrub, *Croton eluteria*, used as a tonic; also, the shrub itself.

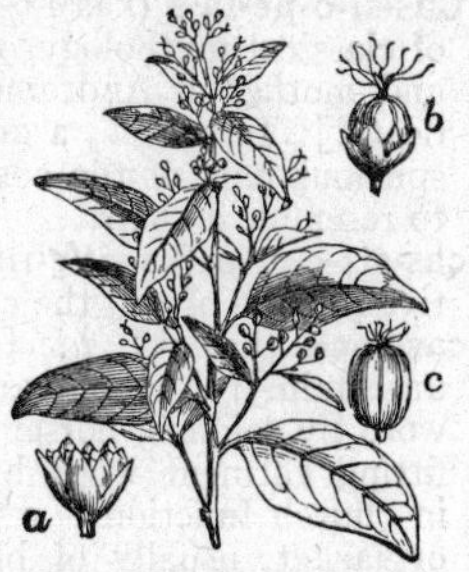

Cascarilla-plant. — *a*, male flower; *b*, female flower; *c*, fruit.

case[1] (kās), *n.* [OF. F. *cas*, < L. *casus*, < *cadere*, fall.] That which befalls or happens†; an instance of the occurrence or existence of something; an instance of disease or other condition requiring medical or surgical treatment, or the patient exhibiting it; a person viewed as an instance of some peculiarity (colloq.: as, a hard *case*; he's a *case*); also, the actual state of things (as, that is not the *case*); situation, condition, or plight (as, in good *case*, well off); also, a state of things involving a question for discussion or decision; a suit or action at law; a cause; the presentation of facts or evidence on which a party to litigation relies for success (also fig.); also, a question of moral conduct concerning which conscience is in doubt ('case of conscience'); in *gram.*, one of the set of forms of a noun, pronoun, or adjective, in inflected languages, that express the various relations in which it may stand to other words in a sentence; a particular relation of this kind, whether expressed by a distinct form or not; the distinction of such relations as a grammatical principle.—**case law,** law established by judicial decision in particular cases.—**case system,** an inductive method of teaching law based upon the study of reported cases rather than of textbooks and commentaries.—**in any case,** in any event; at all events; anyhow.

case[2] (kās), *n.* [OF. *casse*, < L. *capsa*, box, receptacle, < *capere*, hold.] A thing for containing or inclosing something; a receptacle; a box, sheath, or outer covering; a book-cover made separately from the book it is to inclose; an inclosing frame or framework, as of a door; the skin† or hide†; a box with its contents; a quantity contained in a box; a set (as, a *case* of teeth); in *printing*, a tray, as of wood, divided into compartments for holding types for the use of the compositor (usually arranged in a set of two, the 'upper case' for capitals, etc., and the 'lower case' for small letters, etc.).—**case**[2], *v. t.*; *cased*, *casing*. To put or inclose in a case; incase.

ca-se-ate (kā′sẹ-āt), *v. i.*; *-ated*, *-ating*. [L. *caseus*, cheese.] To become like cheese: said esp. of animal tissue.—**ca-se-a′tion** (-ā′shọn), *n.*

case=bay (kās′bā), *n.* In *carp.*, any division of a roof (except that adjoining the end-wall or gable) comprising two principal rafters with the purlins, etc., between them; a corresponding division of a floor, comprising two girders and the intervening joists, etc.

case=bot-tle (kās′bot″l), *n.* A bottle, often square in form, fitting into a case with others; also, a bottle inclosed in a protecting case.

case=hard-en (kās′här″dn), *v. t.* To harden (iron or steel) on the surface by converting the exterior portions into steel or a harder form of steel; fig., to render insensible to external impressions or influences.

ca-se-in (kā′sẹ-in), *n.* [L. *caseus*, cheese.] A proteid precipitated from milk, as by rennet, and forming the basis of cheese.—**ca-se-in′o-gen** (-ọ-jen), *n.* [See *-gen*.] The principal proteid of milk, which in the presence of rennet is converted into casein.

case=knife (kās′nīf), *n.* A knife carried in a case; also, a table-knife.

case-mate (kās′māt), *n.* [F. *casemate*, < It. *casamatta*; origin uncertain.] A vault or chamber, esp. in the thickness of a rampart, with embrasures for artillery; a shell-proof vault; an armored inclosure surrounding guns in a war-ship.—**case′mat-ed** (-mā-ted), *a.* Furnished with a casemate or casemates; strongly fortified.

case-ment (kās′mẹnt), *n.* [Prob. < *case*[2].] A window-sash opening by swinging on hinges, which are generally attached to the upright side of its frame; a window with such sashes; any window (poetic: as, "A *casement* high and triple-arch'd . . . And diamonded with panes of quaint device," Keats's "Eve of St. Agnes," xxiv.); also, a casing or covering.—**case′ment-ed,** *a.* Having casements.

ca-se-ose (kā′sẹ-ōs), *n.* [From *casein*.] In *physiol. chem.*, any of various soluble products formed in the gastric and pancreatic digestion of casein and caseinogen.

ca-se-ous (kā′sẹ-us), *a.* [L. *caseus*, cheese.] Of or like cheese; cheesy: as, *caseous* degeneration (in *pathol.*, a morbid process in which tissues are converted into a thick, cheese-like mass).

ca-sern, ca-serne (kạ-zėrn′), *n.* [F. *caserne*; origin uncertain.] A lodging for soldiers in a garrison town; a barrack.

case=shot (kās′shot), *n.* A collection of small projectiles in a case, to be fired from a cannon; also, a shrapnel.

case=worm (kās′wėrm), *n.* A caddis-worm: so called from the case which it constructs to protect its body.

cash[1] (kash), *n.*; pl. *cash*. [E. Ind. (Dravidian).] Any of various coins of small value of India, China, etc.; esp., a Chinese alloyed copper coin worth about one fifteenth of a U. S. cent.

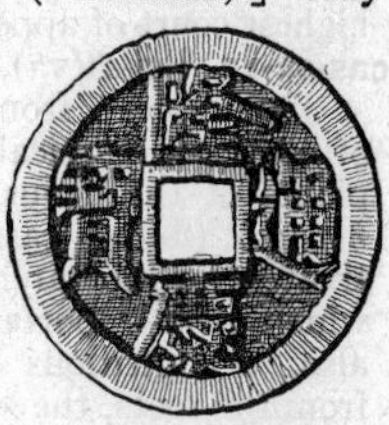
Chinese Cash, 16th century.

cash[2] (kash), *n.* [F. *casse*, < It. *cassa*, < L. *capsa*, box: see *case*[2].] A money-box†; money, esp. ready money; money, or an equivalent, as a check, paid at the time of making a purchase.—**cash**[2], *v. t.* To give or obtain cash for (a check, etc.).—**cash′=book,** *n.* A book in which to record money received and paid out.—**cash′=box,** *n.* A box for holding cash.

ca-shew (kạ-shö′), *n.* [For *acajou*.] A tree, *Anacardium occidentale*, native in tropical America, which bears a small, edible, kidney-shaped nut ('cashew-nut') on an edible, fleshy receptacle of the shape and size of a pear ('cashew-apple'), and which has a medicinal bark that yields the gum acajou ('cashew-gum').

Cashew. — 1, Cashew-nut.

cash-ier[1] (kash-ēr′), *v. t.* [D. *casseren*, < F. *casser*, break, discharge, annul, < L. *quassare*, shake, break, and LL. *cassare*, annul.] To discharge or disband, as troops†; dismiss from a position of command or trust, esp. with ignominy; discard or reject.

cash-ier[2] (kash-ēr′), *n.* [F. *caissier*, < *caisse*, cash-box, = *casse*, E. *cash*[2].] One who has charge of cash or money; one who superintends monetary transactions, as in a bank.—**cashier's check,** a check drawn by a bank upon its own funds and signed by its cashier.

cash-mere (kash′mēr), *n.* [From *Cashmere* (*Kashmir*), native state in northern India.] The fine, soft under-wool of a breed of goats of Kashmir and Tibet; a costly kind of shawl woven in characteristic patterns and colors, made of this wool (usually called 'Cashmere shawl,' or 'India shawl'); a fine, soft woolen dress-fabric with a twilled face; a knitted woolen fabric for underwear and hosiery.

ca-shoo (kạ-shö′), *n.* [Cf. *cachou*.] Same as *catechu*.

cash=reg-is-ter (kash′rej″is-tėr), *n.* A cash-box with a mechanism for recording sums deposited, indicating amounts of purchases, etc.

cas-ing (kā′sing), *n.* The act of covering or fitting with a case; also, a case or covering; also, material for incasing.

ca-si-no (kạ-sē′nō), *n.*; pl. *-nos* (-nōz). [It., dim. of *casa*, house, < L. *casa*, cottage.] A small country-house or lodge; a building or apartment for meetings, amusements, etc.; a club-house; also, a kind of card-game in which the ten of diamonds ('big casino') and the two of spades ('little casino') have special counting value (also spelled *cassino*).

cask (kȧsk), *n.* [Appar. < Sp. *casco*, skull, helmet, cask (for wine, etc.), = F. *casque*, helmet.] A barrel-shaped vessel made of staves, and of varying size, for holding liquids, etc., often one larger and stronger than an ordinary barrel; the quantity such a vessel holds; also, a casket†; also, a casque†.

cas-ket (kȧs'ket), *n.* [Origin uncertain.] A small chest or box, as for jewels; also, a coffin (U. S.).—**cas'ket,** *v. t.*; *-keted, -keting.* To put or inclose in a casket.

Cas-lon (kaz'lọn), *n.* In *printing*, an old-style type modeled after the types of the English type-founder William Caslon (1692–1766). See *type.*

casque (kȧsk), *n.* [F.: see *cask.*] A helmet.—**casqued,** *a.* Wearing a casque.

Cas-sa'ba mel'on. See *Casaba melon.*

Cas-san-dra (ka-san'drạ̈), *n.* [From the prophetess *Cassandra*, of ancient Troy, who was fated never to be believed.] One who prophesies or warns in vain of coming evil.

cas-sa-reep (kas'ạ-rēp), *n.* [Carib.] The inspissated juice of the root of the bitter cassava, the chief ingredient in the West Indian dish pepper-pot.

cas-sa-tion (ka-sā'shọn), *n.* [F., < *casser*, annul: see *cashier*[1].] Annulment; reversal.—**Court of Cassation,** in France, the highest court of appeal.

cas-sa-va (ka-sä'vạ̈), *n.* [F. *cassave*, < Sp. *casabe*; from Haitian.] Any of several tropical euphorbiaceous plants of the genus *Manihot*, as *M. manihot* ('bitter cassava'), much cultivated for its starchy tuberous roots, which yield important food-products; also, a nutritious starch obtained from the roots, the source of tapioca.

Branch of Bitter Cassava.

cas-se-role (kas'ẹ-rōl), *n.* [F., < *casse*, pan.] A stew-pan; a dish in which food is cooked and served; a dish-like mold of rice, mashed potatoes, or the like, served with a filling of meat, vegetables, etc.; a small dish with a handle, used in chemical laboratories.

Laboratory Casserole.

cas-sette (ka-set'), *n.* [F., < It. *cassetta*, dim. of *cassa*, box: see *cash*[2].] A casket; in *photog.*, a plate-holder of a camera.

cas-sia (kash'iạ), *n.* [L. *cassia, casia*, < Gr. κασία; from Semitic.] A variety of cinnamon from the tree *Cinnamomum cassia*, of southern China ('cassia-bark'); the tree itself; also, any of the cæsalpiniaceous herbs, shrubs, and trees constituting the genus *Cassia*, as *C. fistula*, an ornamental tropical tree with long cylindrical pods ('cassia-pods') whose pulp ('cassia-pulp') is a mild laxative, and *C. acutifolia* and *C. angustifolia*, the two officinal species which yield the drug senna; also, cassia-pods or cassia-pulp.—**cas'sia=buds,** *n. pl.* The buds of the cassia *Cinnamomum cassia*: used as a spice.

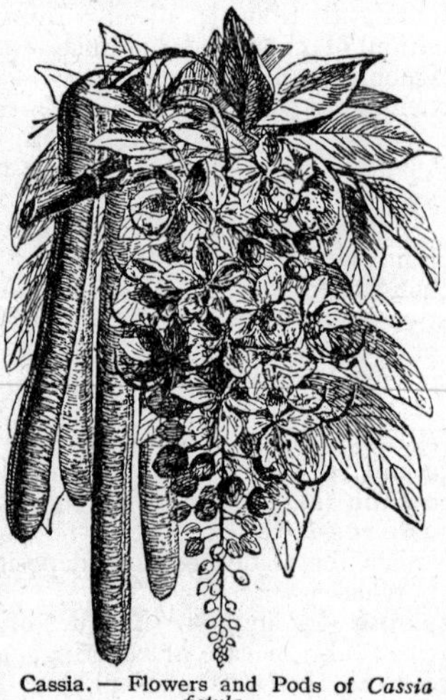

Cassia.—Flowers and Pods of *Cassia fistula.*

cas-si-mere (kas'i-mēr), *n.* [= *cashmere.*] A plain or twilled woolen cloth, used esp. for men's wear.

cas-si'no, *n.* See *casino.*

cas-si-o-ber-ry (kas'-i-ọ̄-ber''i), *n.*; pl. *-berries* (-iz). [From N. Amer. Indian name.] The fruit of any of certain plants, as the caprifoliaceous shrub *Viburnum obovatum* and the aquifoliaceous shrub or small tree *Ilex vomitoria* (the yapon), both of the southern U. S.; also, any of these plants.

Cas-si-o-pe-ia's (kas''i-ọ̄-pē'yạ̈z) **Chair.** [From *Cassiopeia*, of classical mythology, wife of the Ethiopian king Cepheus and mother of Andromeda: placed among the stars after death.] In *astron.*, a group of stars forming the most conspicuous part of the constellation Cassiopeia and supposed to resemble a chair.

cas-sit-e-rite (ka-sit'ẹ-rīt), *n.* [Gr. κασσίτερος, tin.] Native dioxide of tin, the chief source of the metal.

cas-sock (kas'ọk), *n.* [F. *casaque*, < It. *casacca*; origin uncertain.] Any of various long outer garments formerly worn by soldiers, horsemen, and others; also, a long, close-fitting garment worn by ecclesiastics and others engaged in church functions; a shorter, light, double-breasted coat or jacket, usually of black silk, worn under the Geneva gown; also, the clerical office, esp. in the Church of England; also, a clergyman.—**cas'socked,** *a.* Wearing a cassock.

cas-so-wa-ry (kas'ọ̄-wạ̄-ri), *n.*; pl. *-ries* (-riz). [Malay *kasuwāri.*] Any of several large, three-toed, flightless ratite birds constituting the genus *Casuarius*, of Australasian regions, resembling the ostrich but smaller.

Cassowary (*Casuarius galeatus*).

cast (kȧst), *v.*; *cast, casting.* [ME. *casten*, from Scand.: cf. Icel. and Sw. *kasta*, Dan. *kaste*, cast.] **I.** *tr.* To throw; fling or hurl (often with *away, off, out*, etc.); direct, as the eye or glance; cause (light, etc.) to fall upon something or in a certain direction; cover by throwing on mortar, etc.†; throw out, as a fishing-line, anchor, etc.; also, to throw down; throw (a beast) on its back or side; throw to the ground, as in wrestling; defeat in a lawsuit; convict†; condemn†; also, to throw off or away; part with, or lose; shed or drop, as hair, fruit, etc., esp. prematurely; bring forth (young), esp. abortively; send off (a swarm), as bees do; throw or set aside; discard or reject; dismiss or disband; throw forth, as from within; emit or eject; vomit; throw up (earth, etc.), as with a shovel; also, to put or place, esp. hastily or forcibly; deposit, as a vote; bestow or confer; also, to dispose or arrange; allot (the parts), or the parts of (a play), to the actors; assign a part to (an actor); also, to form (molten metal, etc.) into a particular shape by pouring into a mold, or produce (an object or article) by such a process; stereotype or electrotype; also, to compute or calculate; add, as a column of figures; calculate astrologically, as a horoscope; forecast; also, to ponder or consider; contrive, devise, or plan; also, to turn or twist; warp; bring (a boat) round; tip (a scale or balance: archaic); also, to let go or let loose, as a vessel from a mooring (with *loose, off*, etc.). **II.** *intr.* To throw; receive form in a mold; calculate or add; conjecture or forecast; consider; plan or scheme; look about one mentally, as for an excuse (usually with *about*); search this way and that, as for a lost scent in hunting (often with *about*); warp, as timber; *naut.*, to turn, esp. so as to get the head of the boat away from the wind; tack; also, to loosen a vessel from a mooring (with *off*).—**cast,** *n.* The act of casting; that which is cast; the distance to which a thing may be cast or thrown; a throw of dice; a stroke of fortune; fortune or lot; a lift on one's way in a conveyance; also, disposition or arrangement; the assignment of the parts of a play to the actors; the actors to whom the parts in a play are assigned; also, the act of casting or founding; the quantity of metal cast at one time; something shaped in a mold while in a fluid or plastic state; a casting; a reproduction or copy, as of a statue, made in a mold; an impression or mold made from a thing; hence, mold or stamp; form or appearance; sort, kind, or style; also, bent or tendency; also, a permanent twist or turn (as, to have a *cast* in one's eye); a warp; also, a slight tinge of some color; hue; shade; also, a dash or trace; a small amount; also, computation or calculation; addition; also, a conjecture or forecast.

Cas-ta-lia (kas-tā′lią), *n.* [L., < Gr. Κασταλία.] A spring on Mount Parnassus, Greece, sacred to Apollo and the Muses and regarded as a source of inspiration.—**Cas-ta′-lian,** *a.*

cas-ta-net (kas′tą-net or kas-tą-net′), *n.* [Sp. *castañeta,* dim. of *castaña,* < L. *castanea,* chestnut.] A pair, or one of a pair, of shells of ivory or hard wood held in the palm of the hand and struck together as an accompaniment to music and dancing.

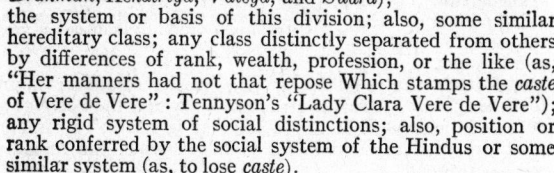

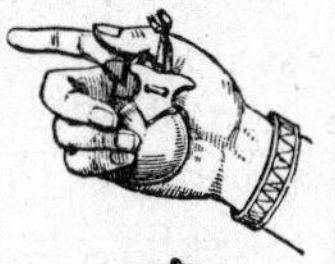

Castanets.

cast-a-way (kȧst′ą-wā″). **I.** *a.* Thrown away; rejected; cast adrift. **II.** *n.* One who or that which has been cast away; a shipwrecked person; an outcast.

caste (kȧst), *n.* [Sp. and Pg. *casta,* breed, race, < L. *castus,* pure, E. *chaste.*] Any of the several hereditary social classes into which the Hindus are divided (see *Brahman, Kshatriya, Vaisya,* and *Sudra*); the system or basis of this division; also, some similar hereditary class; any class distinctly separated from others by differences of rank, wealth, profession, or the like (as, "Her manners had not that repose Which stamps the *caste* of Vere de Vere": Tennyson's "Lady Clara Vere de Vere"); any rigid system of social distinctions; also, position or rank conferred by the social system of the Hindus or some similar system (as, to lose *caste*).

cas-tel-lan (kas′tę-lạn), *n.* [OF. *castelain* (also *chastelain,* F. *châtelain*), < ML. *castellanus,* < L. *castellum*: see *castle.*] The governor of a castle.—**cas′tel-la-ny** (-lą-ni), *n.*; pl. *-nies* (-niz). The office or jurisdiction of a castellan; the territory belonging to a castle.

cas-tel-lat-ed (kas′tę-lā-ted), *a.* [ML. *castellatus,* < L. *castellum*: see *castle.*] Built like a castle, as with turrets and battlements; also, furnished with castles, as a region. —**cas-tel-la′tion** (-lā′shọn), *n.*

cast-er (kȧs′tėr), *n.* One who or that which casts; a bottle or cruet for holding a condiment, or a stand containing a set of such bottles for table use (commonly spelled *castor*); a small wheel on a swivel, set under a piece of furniture, etc., to facilitate moving it (commonly *castor*).

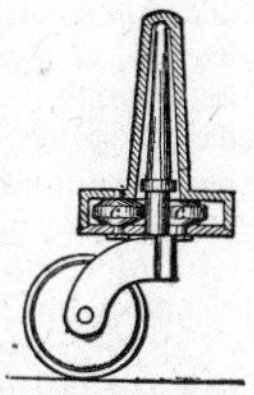

Table-leg Caster, having antifriction rollers, *c, c.*

cas-ti-gate (kas′ti-gāt), *v. t.*; *-gated, -gating.* [L. *castigatus,* pp. of *castigare,* < *castus,* pure, + *agere,* drive, do.] To censure, chasten, or punish in order to correct; criticize severely; emend (a text).—**cas-ti-ga′tion** (-gā′shọn), *n.* The act of castigating.—**cas′-ti-ga-tor,** *n.*—**cas′ti-ga-to-ry** (-gą-tō-ri), *a.* Serving to castigate; corrective; punitive.

Cas-tile (kas-tēl′) **soap.** [From *Castile,* in Spain.] A hard soap made with olive-oil and soda.

Cas-til-ian (kas-til′iạn). **I.** *a.* Of or pertaining to Castile, a former kingdom in central Spain: as, *Castilian* Spanish (the accepted standard form of the Spanish language in literature and in cultivated use). **II.** *n.* A native or inhabitant of Castile; also, Castilian Spanish.

cast-ing (kȧs′ting), *n.* The act or process of one who or that which casts; also, that which is cast; any article which has been cast in a mold.—**cast′ing,** *p. a.* That casts; esp., that tips or turns the scale, or decides (as, the *casting* vote, the vote cast by the presiding officer to decide a question when the votes of an assembly or council are equally divided).

cast=i-ron (kȧst′ī′ėrn). **I.** *n.* A hard, brittle, impure form of iron obtained by remelting pig-iron with limestone, etc., and running it into molds; also, pig-iron. **II.** *a.* Made of cast-iron; fig., resembling cast-iron; inflexible or unyielding.

cas-tle (kȧs′l), *n.* [OF. *castel* (also *chastel,* F. *château*), < L. *castellum,* fortress, castle, dim. of *castrum,* fortified place, *castra,* pl., camp.] A building, or series of connected buildings, fortified for defense against an enemy; a fortified residence, as of a prince in feudal times; hence, a large and stately residence, as of a great noble or a person of great wealth; also, a tower, esp. one for defense; also, a chessman (the rook) fashioned like a castle or tower.—**castle in Spain,** or **castle in the air,** a visionary project; an impracticable scheme; a day-dream. — **cas′tle,** *v.*; *-tled, -tling.* **I.** *tr.* To place or inclose in or as in a castle; in *chess,* to move (the king) in castling (see *castle, v. i.*). **II.** *intr.* In *chess,* to move the king two squares and bring the castle to the square the king has passed over; of the king, to be moved in this manner.—**cas′tled,** *a.* Having a castle or castles; also, built like a castle (as, "the *castled* house": M. Arnold's "Youth of Man"); castellated.

Castle of Coucy, near Laon, Aisne, France; 13th century. (This castle, a famous historic relic, but useless in modern warfare, was blown up by the Germans in March, 1917, during their retreat.)

a, fosse; *b,* gate; *c,* guard-rooms with sleeping-apartments; *d,* inner courtyard; *e,* covered buildings for defenders; *f,* apartments for family; *g,* grand staircase leading to them; *h,* great hall; *i,* donjon or keep; *k,* postern leading from donjon; *l, m, n, o,* chief towers flanking outer walls.

cast=off (kȧst′ôf). **I.** *a.* Rejected; discarded. **II.** *n.* The act of casting off; also, a person or thing that has been cast off.

cas-tor[1] (kas′tọr), *n.* [L., < Gr. κάστωρ.] A beaver; also, a beaver hat, or some similar hat; also, a heavy woolen cloth for overcoats, etc.; also, a soft-finished glove-leather, usually gray in color.

cas-tor[2] (kas′tọr), *n.* [L. *castoreum,* < *castor,* beaver, E. *castor*[1].] A brownish unctuous substance with a strong, penetrating odor, secreted by certain glands in the groin of the beaver, formerly of high repute in medicine, but now used chiefly in perfumery.

cas-tor[3] (kas′tọr), *n.* See *caster.*

cas-tor=bean (kas′tọr-bēn′), *n.* The seed of the castor-oil plant, *Ricinus communis.*

Castor-bean. — *a,* fruit of castor-oil plant; *b,* seed (castor-bean); *c,* section of same.

cas-to-re-um (kas-tō′rę-um), *n.* [L.] Same as *castor*[2].

cas-tor=oil (kas′tọr-oil′), *n.* [Cf. *castor*[2].] A viscid oil obtained from the castor-bean, used as a cathartic, etc.—**castor=oil plant,** a tall euphorbiaceous plant, *Ricinus communis,* native in India but widely naturalized, yielding the castor-bean and castor-oil: sometimes cultivated as a foliage-plant.

cas-tra-me-ta-tion (kas″trą-mę-tā′shọn), *n.* [F. *castramétation,* < L. *castra,* camp, + *metari,* measure, lay out.] The laying out of camps.

cas-trate (kas′trāt), *v. t.*; *-trated, -trating.* [L. *castratus,* pp. of *castrare.*] To deprive of the testicles; emasculate; also, to mutilate (a book or the like) by removing a leaf or leaves; expurgate. — **cas-tra′tion** (-trā′shọn), *n.*

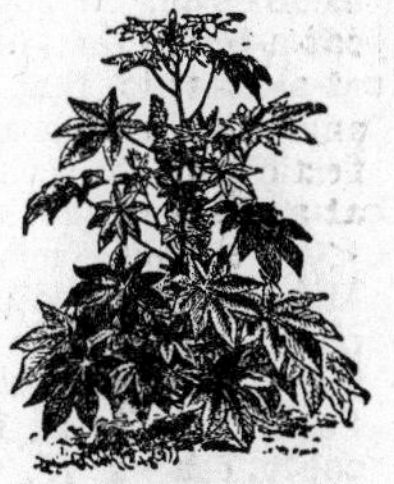

Castor-oil Plant (*Ricinus communis*).

cas-u-al (kazh′ū̦-ạl). [OF. F. *casuel,* < LL. *casualis,* < L. *casus,* chance, E. *case*[1].] **I.** *a.* Happening by chance; accidental; fortuitous; also, occurring or coming irregularly; occasional; incidental; uncertain; indefinite; also, precarious†; also, without design or premeditation; unpremeditated; offhand; also, without plan or method; careless; also, concerned with what is occasional and not regular (as, a *casual* laborer, one who does odd jobs; a *casual* ward in a hospital). **II.** *n.* Something casual; a soldier who for the time being is separated from his regiment or other body, as one who has been wounded or is absent on furlough; a casual laborer; one who receives occasional relief at a workhouse or the like.—**cas′u-al-ism,** *n.* A state of things in which chance prevails; also, the doctrine that all things exist or are governed by chance or accident.—**cas′u-al-ist,** *n.* One who believes in the doctrine of casualism. —**cas′u-al-ly,** *adv.*—**cas′u-al-ness,** *n.*—**cas′u-al-ty** (-ti), *n.*; pl. *-ties* (-tiz). Chance or accident; contingency; also, a mishap; an unfortunate chance or accident, esp. one involving bodily injury or death; *milit.*, the loss of a man through any cause, as death, wounds, capture, or desertion.

cas-u-a-ri-na (kas″ū̦-a̦-rī′nä̦), *n.* [NL., < *casuarius*, cassowary; from a fancied resemblance to the feathers of the bird.] Any tree or shrub of the genus *Casuarina*, native chiefly in Australia, with characteristic long, jointed, whiplike green branches bearing whorls of small scales at the nodes.

cas-u-ist (kazh′ū̦-ist), *n.* [F. *casuiste*, < L. *casus*, E. *case*[1].] One who studies and resolves cases of conscience or conduct; hence, an oversubtle or disingenuous reasoner upon such matters.—**cas-u-is′tic, cas-u-is′ti-cal,** *a.* Pertaining to casuists or casuistry; hence, sophistical.—**cas-u-is′ti-cal-ly,** *adv.*—**cas-u-is′tics,** *n.* Casuistry.—**cas′u-ist-ry** (-ri), *n.*; pl. *-ries* (-riz). The science or art of the casuist; the application of general ethical principles to particular cases of conscience or conduct; hence, oversubtle or quibbling reasoning or teaching upon such matters.

ca-sus bel-li (kā′sus bel′ī). [L.] Occasion of war; a ground or reason for declaring war.

cat (kat), *n.* [AS. *catt, catte*, akin to G. *katze*, F. *chat*, LL. *cattus*.] A common domesticated carnivorous quadruped, *Felis domestica*; any animal of the family *Felidæ*, including also the lion, tiger, leopard, etc.; also, any of various similar animals, as the polecat; also, a spiteful woman (colloq.); a catfish; a double tripod, with six feet; a tackle for hoisting an anchor to the cat-head; a cat-o'-nine-tails; the tapering piece of wood used in the game of tip-cat, or the game itself; a boys' game of ball; a first rough coat of plaster.—**cats and dogs,** worthless stocks or other securities. [Colloq.]—**cat,** *v.*; *catted, catting.* **I.** *tr.* To hoist (an anchor) to the cat-head; also, to flog with a cat-o'-nine-tails. **II.** *intr.* To fish for catfish. [Colloq., U. S.]

cata-, cat-. [Gr. κατα-, also (before a vowel) κατ-, (before an aspirate) καθ-, repr. κατά, prep., down, through, against, according to.] A prefix meaning 'down,' 'against,' 'back,' occurring orig. in words from the Greek, but used also in modern words (English and other) formed after the Greek type.

ca-tab-a-sis (ka-tab′a̦-sis), *n.*; pl. *-ases* (-a̦-sēz). [LL., < Gr. κατάβασις, < καταβαίνειν, go down, < κατά, down, + βαίνειν, go.] A going down. Cf. *anabasis.*

ca-tab-o-lism (ka-tab′ǫ-lizm), *n.* [Gr. καταβολή, a throwing down, < καταβάλλειν, throw down, < κατά, down, + βάλλειν, throw.] In *biol.*, descending or destructive metabolism: opposed to *anabolism.* See *metabolism.*—**cat-a-bol-ic** (kat-a̦-bol′ik), *a.*

cat-a-caus-tic (kat-a̦-kâs′tik), *a.* [See *cata-*.] In *math.* and *optics*, noting a caustic surface or curve formed by reflection of light. Cf. *diacaustic.*

cat-a-chre-sis (kat-a̦-krē′sis), *n.* [L., < Gr. κατάχρησις, < καταχρῆσθαι, misuse, < κατά, against, + χρῆσθαι, use.] Misuse or strained use of words, as in an inconsistent metaphor; misuse of word-elements, as in a perverted word-form.—**cat-a-chres′tic** (-kres′tik), *a.* [Gr. καταχρηστικός.] Pertaining to or involving catachresis.—**cat-a-chres′ti-cal-ly,** *adv.*

cat-a-cli-nal (kat-a̦-klī′na̦l), *a.* [Gr. κατά, down, + κλίνειν, incline.] In *geol.*, descending with the dip, as a valley.

cat-a-clysm (kat′a̦-klizm), *n.* [L. *cataclysmos*, < Gr. κατακλυσμός, < κατακλύζειν, inundate, < κατά, down, + κλύζειν, wash.] An extensive overflowing of water; a deluge; a flood; also, a sudden and violent physical action producing changes in the earth's surface; fig., any violent upheaval, esp. one of a social or political nature.—**cat-a-clys′mal** (-kliz′ma̦l), *a.* Cataclysmic.—**cat-a-clys′mic,** *a.* Of, pertaining to, or resulting from a cataclysm; of the nature of, or having the effect of, a cataclysm.—**cat-a-clys′mi-cal-ly,** *adv.*

cat-a-comb (kat′a̦-kōm), *n.* [It. *catacomba*, < LL. *catacumbas*; origin uncertain.] A subterranean burial-place, esp. one consisting of galleries with excavated recesses for tombs: usually in *pl.*

Catacomb. — Tomb of St. Cornelius, Catacombs of St. Calixtus, Rome; 3d century.

cat-a-cous-tics (kat-a̦-kös′tiks or -kous′tiks), *n.* [See *cata-*.] The science of reflected sound. Cf. *acoustics.*

cat-a-di-op-tric (kat″a̦-dī-op′trik), *a.* [See *cata-*.] Involving both reflection and refraction of light. Cf. *dioptric.* —**cat″a-di-op′trics,** *n.* A branch of optics embracing catadioptric phenomena.

ca-tad-ro-mous (ka-tad′rǫ-mus), *a.* [Gr. κατά, down, + -δρομος, < δραμεῖν, run.] Of fishes, going down a river to the sea to spawn. Cf. *anadromous.*

cat-a-falque (kat′a̦-falk), *n.* [F., < It. *catafalco*; akin to E. *scaffold.*] A raised structure on which the body of a deceased personage lies or is carried in state; a similar structure used at services for the dead when the remains are not present.

Ca-tai-an† (ka-tā′a̦n), *n.* A native of Cathay (China): used as a vague term of reproach (see Shakspere's "Merry Wives of Windsor," ii. 1. 148).

Cat-a-lan (kat′a̦-la̦n). **I.** *a.* Pertaining to Catalonia, formerly a province, now a division comprising several provinces, in northeastern Spain, or to its inhabitants or language. **II.** *n.* A native or inhabitant of Catalonia; also, the (Romance) dialect spoken in Catalonia, etc., closely related to Provençal.

cat-a-lec-tic (kat-a̦-lek′tik), *a.* [LL. *catalecticus*, < Gr. καταληκτικός, < καταλήγειν, leave off, < κατά, down, + λήγειν, stop, cease.] In *pros.*, lacking part of the last foot, as a verse.

cat-a-lep-sy (kat′a̦-lep-si), *n.* [Gr. κατάληψις, seizure, < καταλαμβάνειν, seize, < κατά, down, + λαμβάνειν, take.] In *pathol.*, a morbid bodily condition marked by suspension of sensation and consciousness, with muscular rigidity. —**cat-a-lep′tic.** [Gr. καταληπτικός.] **I.** *a.* Pertaining to, of the nature of, or affected with catalepsy. **II.** *n.* A person subject to catalepsy.—**cat-a-lep′ti-form** (-ti-fôrm), *a.* Resembling catalepsy.

cat-a-lo (kat′a̦-lō), *n.*; pl. *-loes* (-lōz). [From *cat(tle)* + *(buff)alo.*] A hybrid between domesticated cattle and the American buffalo.

cat′a-log, cat′a-log-er, etc. See *catalogue*, etc.

cat-a-logue (kat′a̦-log), *n.* [F., < LL. *catalogus*, < Gr. κατάλογος, < καταλέγειν, reckon, enroll, < κατά, down, + λέγειν, pick, reckon, tell.] A list or register; esp., a list arranged in alphabetical or other methodical order, with brief particulars concerning the names, articles, etc., listed. —**ca-ta-logue rai-son-né** (kä-tä-log rā-zo-nā). [F., 'reasoned catalogue.'] A catalogue of books, paintings, or the like, classified according to subject, usually with notes or comments.—**cat′a-logue,** *v. t.*; *-logued, -loguing.* To make a catalogue of; enter in a catalogue.—**cat′a-lo-guer** (-log-ėr), **cat′a-lo-guist** (-log-ist), *n.*

ca-tal-pa (ka̦-tal′pä̦), *n.* [NL.; from N. Amer. Ind.] Any tree of the bignoniaceous genus *Catalpa*, of America and Asia, as *C. speciosa*, of the U. S., having large cordate leaves and terminal panicles of bell-shaped flowers: much cultivated for ornament and shade.

ca-tal-y-sis (ka-tal′i-sis), *n.*; pl. *-yses* (-i-sēz). [NL., < Gr. κατάλυσις, < καταλύειν, dissolve, < κατά, down, + λύειν, loose.] Dissolution; also, in *chem.*, the causing or accelerating of a chemical change by the addition of a substance (catalytic agent) which is not permanently affected by the reaction.—**cat-a-lyt-ic** (kat-a̦-lit′ik), *a.* [Gr. καταλυτικός.] Pertaining to or causing catalysis.—**cat′a-ly-za″tor** (-li-zā″tọr), *n.* In catalysis, the substance which causes the chemical change; a catalytic agent.—**cat′a-lyze** (-līz), *v. t.*; *-lyzed, -lyzing.* To act upon by catalysis.—**cat′a-lyz-er,** *n.* A catalyzator.

cat-a-ma-ran (kat″ạ-mạ-ran′), *n.* [E. Ind. (Dravidian).] A float or raft, usually of several logs or pieces of wood lashed together; also, any craft with twin parallel hulls; also, a quarrelsome woman (colloq.).

cat-a-me-ni-a (kat-ạ-mē′ni-ặ), *n. pl.* [NL., < Gr. καταμήνια, neut. pl. of καταμήνιος, monthly, < κατά, according to, + μήν, month.] Same as *menses.*—**cat-a-me′ni-al,** *a.*

cat-a-mount (kat′ạ-mount), *n.* [Short for *catamountain.*] A wild animal of the cat family; esp., in America, the cougar, also the lynx.

cat-a-moun-tain (kat-ạ-moun′tặn), *n.* [Orig. *cat of the mountain.*] A wild animal of the cat family, as the European wildcat, or the leopard or panther.

cat-a-phon-ic (kat-ạ-fon′ik), *a.* [Gr. κατά, against, + φωνή, sound.] Pertaining to reflected sound.—**cat-a-phon′ics,** *n.* Catacoustics.

cat-a-pho-re-sis (kat″ạ-fọ-rē′sis), *n.* [NL., < Gr. καταφορεῖν, carry down, < κατά, down, + φορεῖν, freq. of φέρειν, bear.] In *med.*, the causing of medicinal substances to pass through or into living tissues in the direction of flow of a positive electric current.—**cat″a-pho-ret′ic** (-ret′ik), *a.*

cat-a-phract (kat′ạ-frakt), *n.* [L. *cataphractes*, coat of mail, *cataphractus*, mailed, < Gr. καταφράκτης, n., κατάφρακτος, a., < καταφράσσειν, cover with mail, < κατά, down, + φράσσειν, fence in.] An ancient defensive armor composed of scales of metal, etc., attached to a garment of leather or other material, often covering the whole body; also, a soldier wearing this (as, "Before him and behind, Archers and slingers, *cataphracts* and spears": Milton's "Samson Agonistes," 1619).

cat-a-plasm (kat′ạ-plazm), *n.* [L. *cataplasma*, < Gr. κατάπλασμα, < καταπλάσσειν, plaster over, < κατά, down, + πλάσσειν, form.] In *med.*, a poultice.

cat-a-pult (kat′ạ-pult), *n.* [L. *catapulta*, < Gr. καταπέλτης, prob. < κατά, down, + πάλλειν, swing, throw.] An ancient military engine for throwing darts, stones, etc.; also, a small forked stick to each prong of which is attached an elastic band, usually with a piece of leather in the middle, used by boys for throwing stones, peas, etc.—**cat′a-pult,** *v. t.* To hurl as from a catapult.

cat-a-ract (kat′ạ-rakt), *n.* [L. *cataracta*, < Gr. καταράκτης, < καταράσσειν, dash down, < κατά, down, + ἀράσσειν, dash.] A descent of water over a steeply sloping surface; a waterfall, esp. one of considerable size; hence, any furious rush or downpour of water; also, a flood-gate† (as, the *cataracts* of heaven); also, a waterspout†; in *pathol.*, an opacity of the crystalline lens of the eye, or of its capsule, or of both, producing more or less impairment of vision.

ca-tarrh (kạ-tär′), *n.* [L. *catarrhus*, < Gr. κατάρροος, < καταρρεῖν, flow down, < κατά, down, + ῥεῖν, flow.] In *pathol.*, inflammation of a mucous membrane, esp. of the respiratory tract, accompanied by exaggerated secretions.—**ca-tar′rhal** (-tär′ạl), *a.*

ca-tas-ta-sis (ka-tas′tạ-sis), *n.*; pl. *-tases* (-tạ-sēz). [NL., < Gr. κατάστασις, appointment, settlement, condition, < καθιστάναι, set down, < κατά, down, + ἱστάναι, cause to stand.] The part of a drama, preceding the catastrophe, in which the action is at its height; also, in *rhet.*, that part of a speech, usually the exordium, in which the orator sets forth the subject to be discussed.

ca-tas-tro-phe (kạ-tas′trọ-fẹ), *n.* [LL., < Gr. καταστροφή, < καταστρέφειν, overturn, < κατά, down, + στρέφειν, turn.] A turn or change introducing the close or conclusion of a drama; the group of actions constituting such a conclusion; the dénouement; also, a final event or conclusion, usually an unfortunate one; a disastrous end; any great calamity; also, a sudden, violent disturbance, esp. of the earth's surface; a cataclysm.—**cat-as-troph-ic** (kat-ạs-trof′ik), *a.*—**ca-tas′tro-phism,** *n.* The doctrine that certain vast geological changes in the earth's history were caused by catastrophes rather than gradual evolutionary processes.—**ca-tas′tro-phist,** *n.*

Ca-taw-ba (kạ-tâ′bặ), *n.* [From the *Catawba* River, in N. and S. Carolina.] A reddish grape of the U. S., or a light wine made from it.

cat-bird (kat′bėrd), *n.* A North American song-bird, *Galeoscoptes carolinensis*, allied to the mocking-bird, having a call resembling the mewing of a cat; in Australia, any of several bower-birds which produce cat-like cries.

Catbird (*Galeoscoptes carolinensis*).

cat=block (kat′blok), *n.* *Naut.*, a heavy block with a large hook, used in hoisting an anchor to the cat-head.

Cat-block.

cat-boat (kat′bōt), *n.* A boat with one mast, which is set well forward, and a sail extended by gaff and boom.

Catboat.

cat=bri-er (kat′brī″ėr), *n.* Any of various species of smilax, as the greenbrier, *Smilax rotundifolia.*

cat-call (kat′kâl), *n.* A cry like that of a cat, or an instrument for producing a similar sound, used to express disapproval, as of a theatrical performance: as, "The *cat-call* has struck a damp into generals, and frighted heroes off the stage" (Addison, in "Spectator," 361).—**cat′call,** *v. i.* or *t.* To sound catcalls, or assail with catcalls.

catch (kach), *v.*; *caught, catching.* [OF. *cachier* (also *chacier*, F. *chasser*), < L. *captare*, strive to take, freq. of *capere*, take.] **I.** *tr.* To chase† or drive†; capture, esp. after pursuit; take captive; insnare, entrap, or deceive; gain possession of†; overtake, as something in motion; be in time to reach (a train, boat, etc.); come upon suddenly; surprise or detect, as in some action; reach (a person) with a blow; hit (as, the missile *caught* him on the head); intercept and seize (something approaching or passing, as a ball); take advantage of (an opportunity, etc.); check, as one's breath; get, receive, incur, or contract (as, to *catch* a cold); lay hold of; grasp, seize, or snatch; grip or entangle (as, "a ram *caught* in a thicket by his horns": Gen. xxii. 13); fasten with or as with a catch; seize upon by attraction or impression (as, to *catch* the eye or the attention); captivate or charm; seize or apprehend by the senses or intellect (as, to *catch* a speaker's words; to *catch* a person's meaning). **II.** *intr.* To overtake something moving (with *up*); act as catcher in a baseball game; take hold; become entangled or fastened; grasp or snatch (*at*); spread or be communicated.—**catch,** *n.* The act of catching; also, one who catches; anything that catches, as a device for fastening something or for checking motion; also, that which is caught, as a quantity of fish; anything worth catching; an acquisition; a matrimonial prize; a fragment, as of a song; in *music*, a round, esp. one in which the words are so arranged as to produce ludicrous effects.—**catch′a-ble,** *a.* That may be caught.—**catch′=all,** *n.* A bag, basket, or other receptacle for odds and ends.—**catch′=ba″sin,** *n.* A receptacle at an opening into a sewer to retain matter that would not pass readily through the sewer.—**catch′=crop,** *n.* A minor crop occupying the soil between the times of two principal crops, or growing between the rows of another crop.—**catch′=crop″ping,** *n.*—**catch′er,** *n.* One who or that which catches; in *baseball*, the player who stands behind the bat or home base to catch the pitched ball.—**catch′fly,** *n.*; pl. *-flies* (-flīz). Any of various plants, esp. of the genus *Silene*, having a viscid secretion on stem and calyx in which small insects are sometimes caught.—**catch′ing,** *p. a.* Infectious; also, attractive; captivating.—**catch′ment,** *n.* The act of catching; drainage.—**catch′pen″ny. I.** *n.*;

pl. *-pennies* (-iz). Anything of little value or use, made merely for quick sale. **II.** *a.* Made merely to sell, regardless of permanent value or use.

catch-poll (kach′pōl), *n.* [= OF. *chacepol* (ML. *chacipollus*), 'chase-fowl.'] A petty officer of justice, esp. one who makes arrests for debt; a bumbailiff.

catch-up, ketch-up (kach′up, kech′up), *n.* [Malay *kĕchap.*] Any of several sauces or condiments used with meat, fish, etc.: as, mushroom *catchup*; tomato *catchup*; walnut *catchup* (made with the unripe nuts).

catch-weight (kach′wāt), *n.* In sports, the chance or optional weight of a contestant, as contrasted with a weight fixed by agreement, etc.

catch-word (kach′wėrd), *n.* A word formerly inserted at the lower right-hand corner of a page, below the last line, being the same as the first word of the following page; an actor's cue; any word so placed or used as to attract attention; a word or phrase caught up and repeated for effect, as by a political or other party.

catch-y (kach′i), *a.* That catches; deceptive; attractive or taking; also, readily caught up, as a tune; also, occurring in snatches; fitful.

cate (kāt), *n.* [Earlier *acate*, < OF. *acat*, < *acater* (F. *acheter*), buy, < ML. *accaptare*, acquire, < L. *ad*, to, + *captare*: see *catch.*] An article of food, orig. one that was bought rather than of home production; a choice viand; a delicacy; a dainty: usually in *pl.*: as, "All *cates* and dainties shall be stored there Quickly on this feast-night" (Keats's "Eve of St. Agnes," xx.). [Archaic.]

cat-e-chet-ic (kat-ē-ket′ik), *a.* [Gr. κατηχητικός, < κατηχεῖν: see *catechize.*] Pertaining to teaching by question and answer, as by a catechism; pertaining to or in accordance with the catechism of a church. Also **cat-e-chet′i-cal.**—**cat-e-chet′ics,** *n.* The art of catechetic instruction.

cat-e-chin (kat′ẹ-chin), *n.* [From *catechu.*] In *chem.*, a white crystalline principle contained in catechu.

cat-e-chise (kat′ē-kīz), etc. See *catechize*, etc.

cat-e-chism (kat′ē-kizm), *n.* [LL. *catechismus*, < Gr. κατηχίζειν: see *catechize.*] Catechetic instruction†; also, an elementary book containing a summary of the principles of the Christian religion, esp. as maintained by a particular church, in the form of questions and answers; hence, a similar book of instruction in other subjects; also, a series of formal questions put to candidates, etc.—**cat-e-chis′mal** (-kiz′mạl), *a.*

cat-e-chist (kat′ē-kist), *n.* One who catechizes.—**cat-e-chis′tic, cat-e-chis′ti-cal,** *a.*—**cat-e-chis′ti-cal-ly,** *adv.*

cat-e-chize (kat′ē-kīz), *v. t.*; *-chized, -chizing.* [LL. *catechizare*, < Gr. κατηχίζειν, for κατηχεῖν, resound, teach orally, < κατά, down, + ἠχεῖν, sound.] To instruct orally by means of questions and answers, esp. in Christian doctrine; instruct by means of a catechism; also, to question with reference to belief; also, to question closely; call to account.—**cat″e-chi-za′tion** (-ki-zā′shọn), *n.*—**cat′e-chiz-er** (-kī-zėr), *n.*

cat-e-chu (kat′ẹ-chö), *n.* [NL., < Malay *kāchu.*] Any of several astringent substances obtained from various tropical plants, esp. from the wood of two East Indian species of acacia, *Acacia catechu* and *A. suma*, used in medicine, dyeing, tanning, etc.; cutch.—**cat-e-chu′ic,** *a.*

cat-e-chu-men (kat-ē-kū′men), *n.* [LL. *catechumenus*, < Gr. κατηχούμενος, ppr. pass. of κατηχεῖν: see *catechize.*] One under instruction in the rudiments of Christianity, as in the early church; a neophyte.—**cat-e-chu′me-nal** (-mẹ-nạl), *a.*

cat-e-gor-e-mat-ic (kat″ē-gor-ē-mat′ik), *a.* [Gr. κατηγόρημα, a predicate, < κατηγορεῖν: see *category.*] In *logic*, of a word, capable of being used by itself as a complete term, as a noun or an adjective.

cat-e-gor-i-cal (kat-ē-gor′i-kạl), *a.* [Gr. κατηγορικός, accusatory, affirmative, categorical, < κατηγορεῖν: see *category.*] Positive, as a proposition or statement; unqualified or unconditional; explicit; also, of or pertaining to a category.—**categorical syllogism,** in *logic*, a syllogism consisting only of categorical propositions, or such as do not involve a condition or hypothesis.—**cat-e-gor′i-cal-ly,** *adv.* —**cat-e-gor′i-cal-ness,** *n.*

cat-e-go-ry (kat′ē-gọ-ri), *n.*; pl. *-ries* (-riz). [LL. *categoria*, < Gr. κατηγορία, < κατηγορεῖν, accuse, assert, predicate, < κατά, against, + ἀγορεύειν, speak, < ἀγορά, assembly.] In *logic* and *metaph.*, one of the highest notions or forms involved in thought; hence, in general, any general or comprehensive division in classification; a class.

cat-e-lec-trode (kat-ẹ-lek′trōd), *n.* [See *cata-.*] In *elect.*, the cathode.

ca-te-na (ka-tē′nạ), *n.*; pl. *-næ* (-nē). [L., chain.] A chain or connected series, esp. of extracts from the writings of the fathers of the church.—**cat-e-na-ri-an** (kat-ẹ-nā′ri-ạn), *a.* Catenary.—**cat′e-na-ry** (-nạ-ri). [L. *catenarius.*] **I.** *a.* Pertaining to or resembling a chain. **II.** *n.*; pl. *-ries* (-riz). In *math.*, the curve of a perfectly flexible, inextensible, infinitely fine cord when at rest under the action of forces; esp., the curve ('common catenary') assumed approximately by a heavy cord or chain hanging freely from two points not in the same vertical line.

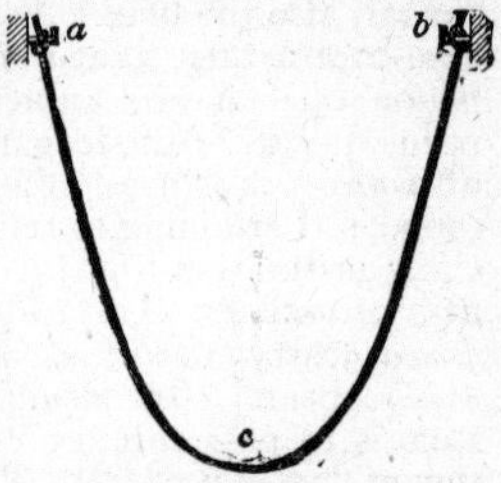

Catenary.
The cord, *a, c, b,* hangs in a portion of the common catenary.

cat-e-nate (kat′ē-nāt), *v. t.*; *-nated, -nating.* [L. *catenatus*, pp. of *catenare*, < *catena*, chain.] To link together; form into a connected series. — **cat-e-na′tion** (-nā′shọn), *n.*

ca-ten-u-late (ka-ten′ū-lāt), *a.* [L. *catenula*, dim. of *catena*, chain.] Chain-like in form or appearance.

ca-ter[1] (kā′tėr), *v. i.* [From obs. *cater*, earlier *acatour*, buyer of provisions, < OF. *acateor*, buyer: see *cate.*] To purvey food (*for*); also, to provide requisites (*for*); supply means of gratification (*to*).

ca-ter[2] (kā′tėr or kat′ėr), *n.* [F. *quatre*, four: see *quatre.*] Four†; the four at cards or dice (obs. or archaic).

cat-er-an (kat′ẹ-rạn), *n.* [Gael.: cf. *kern*[3].] An irregular soldier or marauder of the Scottish Highlands; a freebooter.

ca-ter=cor-nered (kā′tėr-kôr″nėrd or kat′ėr-), *a.* [Cf. *cater*[2].] Diagonal; placed or running diagonally. [Colloq.]

ca-ter=cous-in (kā′tėr-kuz″n), *n.* [Cf. *cater*[2].] One related by or as by cousinship; an intimate friend. See Shakspere's "Merchant of Venice," ii. 2. 139.

ca-ter-er (kā′tėr-ėr), *n.* One who caters; esp., a purveyor of food or provisions, as for entertainments, etc.—**ca′ter-ess,** *n.* A female caterer.

cat-er-pil-lar (kat′ėr-pil-ạr). [Cf. OF. *chatepelose*, caterpillar, lit. 'hairy cat.'] **I.** *n.* The worm-like larva of a butterfly or a moth; also, the similar larva of certain other insects, as the saw-flies; fig., one who preys on others; an extortioner; also, specif., a kind of self-propelled tractor used esp. for drawing heavy loads over rough or soft ground, being provided at each side with a device consisting of a series of broad, flat plates or specially shaped pieces joined side by side in an endless chain or belt about a combination of wheels, the chain or belt, which rests on the ground, being driven by one of the wheels and forming a sort of endless track, laid down in front and taken up behind, on which the machine runs (called in full *caterpillar tractor*: a proprietary name, registered in the U. S. Patent Office) (see *tank*, and cf. *pedrail*). **II.** *a.* Pertaining to or resembling a caterpillar; also, specif., of the nature of or pertaining to the kind of tractor called a caterpillar (see above); drawn by or mounted on such a tractor or tractors (as, a *caterpillar* plow; *caterpillar* artillery).

cat-er-waul (kat′ėr-wâl), *v. i.* [Cf. *waul.*] To cry as cats in rutting time; hence, to utter a similar sound; howl or screech.—**cat′er-waul,** *n.*

cat=fall (kat′fâl), *n.* *Naut.*, the rope or tackle for hoisting an anchor to the cat-head.

cat-fish (kat′fish), *n.* Any of numerous fishes having some fancied resemblance to a cat; esp., one of the

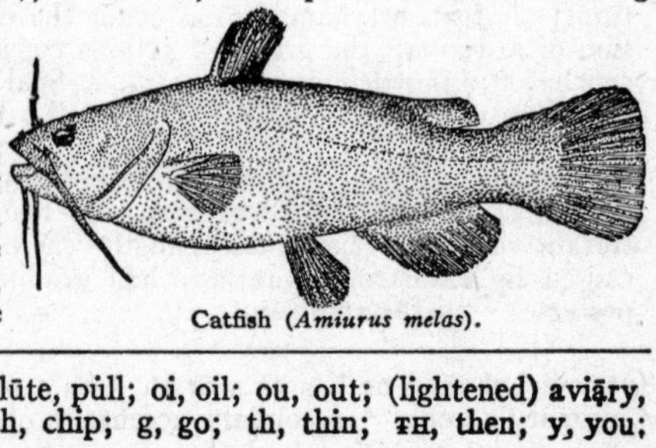
Catfish (*Amiurus melas*).

fishes, chiefly of fresh waters, and characterized by long barbels, which constitute the large family *Siluridæ*, many of which are used for food.

cat=foot-ed (kat′fůt″ed), *a.* Having feet like those of a cat; digitigrade, with sharp, retractile claws; also, soft-footed; noiseless, quiet, or stealthy.

cat-gut (kat′gut), *n.* The intestines of sheep or other animals, dried and twisted, used as strings for musical instruments, etc.; hence, a violin, or stringed instruments collectively; also, the goat's-rue, *Cracca virginiana*, which has long, slender, tough roots.

cath-. Form of *cata-* by combination with following *h*.

cat=hammed (kat′hamd), *a.* Having hams or thighs like those of a cat: said of certain horses and cattle.

cath-a-rine=wheel (kath′a̤-rin-hwēl), *n.* [From St. *Catharine* of Alexandria, who was condemned to torture on the wheel.] A figure of a wheel with projecting spikes (see etym.); also, a firework which revolves like a wheel while burning; a pinwheel; also, a circular window with radiating divisions; also, in *embroidery*, a wheel-like combination of stitches radiating from a central point, serving to fill a round space or hole.

Cath-a-rist (kath′a̤-rist), *n.* [ML. *Catharistæ*, pl., < Gr. καθαρός, pure.] A member of any of various sects aiming at or professing a superior purity; a puritan.—**Cath′a-rism,** *n.*—**Cath-a-ris′tic,** *a.*

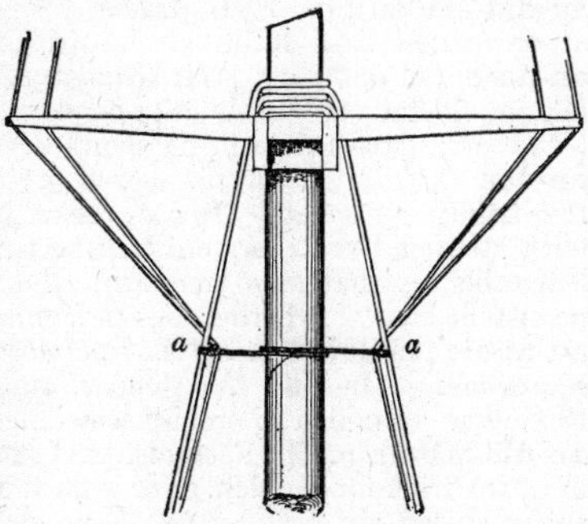

Cat-harpings, *a, a.*

cat=harp-ings, cat=harp-ins (kat′här″pingz, -pinz), *n. pl.* [Cf. *harpings.*] *Naut.*, the short ropes or iron cramps used to bind in the shrouds at the masthead, so as to facilitate the horizontal movements of the yards.

ca-thar-sis (ka-thär′sis), *n.* [NL., < Gr. κάθαρσις, < καθαίρειν, cleanse, < καθαρός, pure.] In *med.*, purgation.—**ca-thar′tic.** [Gr. καθαρτικός.] In *med.*: **I.** *a.* Evacuating the bowels; purgative: as, *cathartic* acid (the active purgative principle of senna). **II.** *n.* A purgative.

A, Cat-head; *B*, Cat-block; *C*, Cat-fall.

Ca-thay (ka-thā′), *n.* [From Tatar.] An old name for China.

cat=head (kat′hed), *n.* *Naut.*, a projecting timber or beam near the bow of a ship, to which the anchor is hoisted after having been raised to the water's edge.—**cat′head,** *v. t.* To hoist (an anchor) to the cat-head.

Ancient Cathedra in the Cathedral of Augsburg, Germany.

ca-the-dra (ka̤-thē′dra̤ or kath′ḗ-), *n.*; pl. *-dræ* (-drē). [L., < Gr. καθέδρα, < κατά, down, + ἕζεσθαι, sit: see *sit*, and cf. *chair*.] The seat or throne of a bishop in the principal church of his diocese; also, an official chair, as of a professor in a university.

ca-the-dral (ka̤-thē′dra̤l). [ML. *cathedralis*, < L. *cathedra*: see *cathedra*.] **I.** *a.* Of, pertaining to, or containing a bishop's seat or throne; also, pertaining to or emanating from a chair of office or authority; authoritative. **II.** *n.* The principal church of a diocese, containing the bishop's throne; sometimes, in non-episcopal denominations, any of various important churches.—**ca-the′draled,** *a.* Having a cathedral; also, cathedral-like.

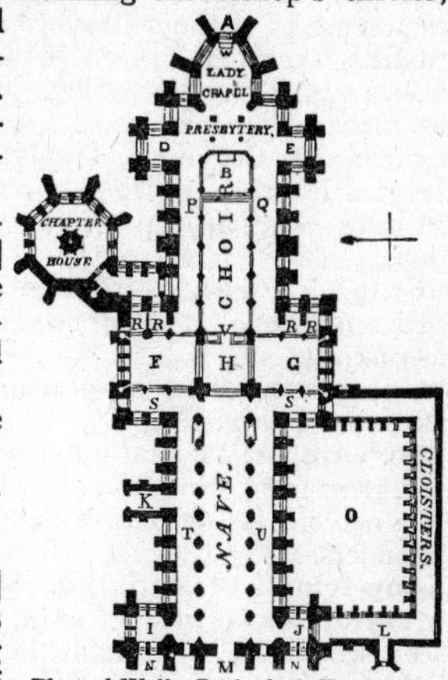

Plan of Wells Cathedral, England.
A, apse; *B*, altar, altar-platform, and altar-steps; *D*, *E*, eastern or lesser transept; *F*, *G*, western or greater transept; *H*, central tower; *I*, *J*, western towers; *K*, north porch; *L*, library; *M*, principal or western doorway; *N*, *N*, western side-doors; *O*, cloister-yard; *P*, *Q*, north and south aisles of choir; *R*, *R*, chapels; *S*, *S*, aisles of transept; *T*, *U*, north and south aisles of nave; *V*, rood-screen or organ-loft; *W*, altar of Lady chapel.

cath-e-drat-ic (kath-ḗ-drat′ik), *a.* [ML. *cathedraticus.*] Of or pertaining to the bishop's cathedra or the episcopal see; also, pronounced ex cathedra; authoritative.

cath′e-rine=wheel, *n.* See *catharine-wheel.*

cath-e-ter (kath′e-tėr), *n.* [LL., < Gr. καθετήρ, < καθιέναι, send down, < κατά, down, + ἱέναι, send.] In *med.*, any of various instruments for introducing into canals or passages of the body, esp. a tubular instrument for passing into the bladder through the urethra to draw off urine.—**cath′e-ter-ize,** *v. t.*; *-ized*, *-izing.* To introduce a catheter into.

cath-e-tom-e-ter (kath-e-tom′e-tėr), *n.* [Gr. κάθετος, perpendicular: see *-meter.*] An instrument for measuring vertical distances, esp. small differences of level.

cath-ode (kath′ōd), *n.* [Gr. κάθοδος, way down, < κατά, down, + ὁδός, way.] The negative pole of a battery or other electric source; that terminal at which the current leaves an electrolytic cell or the like: opposed to *anode.*—**cathode rays.** See under *ray*[3], *n.*—**ca-thod-ic** (ka-thod′ik), *a.*—**ca-thod′o-graph** (-ō̤-gråf), *n.* [See *-graph.*] A photograph taken with Röntgen rays.—**cath-o-dog′ra-phy** (-ō̤-dog′ra̤-fi), *n.*

cat=hole (kat′hōl), *n.* *Naut.*, either of two holes at the stern of a ship, through which hawsers may be passed.

cath-o-lic (kath′o̤-lik). [L. *catholicus*, < Gr. καθολικός, universal, < κατά, according to, + ὅλος, whole.] **I.** *a.* Universal in extent; embracing all; also, touching the interests or sympathies of all; also, having sympathies with all; broad-minded; liberal; *eccles.*, of or pertaining to the whole Christian body or church; [*cap.*] noting or pertaining to the Western Church; also, noting or pertaining to the Church of Rome (often 'Roman Catholic'); also, among Anglicans, noting or pertaining to the Christian body held to represent the ancient undivided Christian church, comprising the Anglican Church, along with the Roman Catholic Church and the Greek Church (cf. *Anglo-Catholic*). **II.** *n.* [*cap.*] A member of a Catholic church, esp. of the Church of Rome.—**Old Catholics.** See under *old*, *a.*—**ca-thol-i-cal-ly** (ka̤-thol′i-ka̤l-i), *adv.*—**ca-thol′i-cism** (-sizm), *n.* [Usually *cap.*] The faith, system, and practice of a Catholic church, esp. of the Church of Rome.—**cath-o-li′ci-ty** (-lis′i-ti), *n.* The quality of being catholic; universality; broad-mindedness; also [usually *cap.*], catholicism.—**ca-thol′i-cize** (-sīz), *v. t.* or *i.*; *-cized*, *-cizing.* To make or become catholic or [*cap.*] Catholic.—**cath′o-lic-ly,** *adv.*

ca-thol-i-con (ka̤-thol′i-ko̤n), *n.* [ML., < Gr. καθολικόν, neut. of καθολικός: see *catholic.*] A universal remedy; a panacea. Also fig.

cath-o-scope (kath′ō̤-skōp), *n.* [See *cathode* and *-scope.*] An instrument for exhibiting the optical effects of the Röntgen rays.

Cat-i-line (kat′i-līn), *n.* [From the Roman conspirator *Catiline* (died 62 B.C.), who was publicly assailed by Cicero in a series of famous orations, and driven from Rome.] A thoroughly base political conspirator.

cat-i-on (kat′ī-o̤n or kat′i-o̤n), *n.* [Gr. κατιόν, ppr. neut. of κατιέναι, go down, < κατά, down, + ἱέναι, go.] The product liberated at the cathode during electrolysis; an electropositive ion.

cat-kin (kat′kin), *n.* [MD. *katteken,* 'little cat.'] In *bot.,* an ament, as of the willow or birch.

Catkins of Birch. — *a,* male; *b, b,* female.

cat-ling (kat′ling), *n.* A little cat; a kitten; also, catgut; a catgut string.

cat-mint (kat′mint), *n.* A plant, *Nepeta cataria,* of the mint family, with strongly scented leaves of which cats are fond.

cat=nap (kat′nap), *n.* A short, light nap or doze.

cat-nip (kat′nip), *n.* [From *cat* + obs. or prov. *nep, nip,* < L. *nepeta,* catmint.] Same as *catmint.* [U. S.]

cat=o'=moun-tain (kat-ǫ-moun′tạn), *n.* Same as *catamountain.*

cat=o'=nine=tails (kat-ǫ-nīn′tālz), *n.* An instrument consisting of nine pieces of knotted line or cord fastened to a handle, used to flog offenders.

ca-top-tric (ka-top′trik), *a.* [Gr. κατοπτρικός, < κάτοπτρον, mirror, < κατά, against, + ὀπ-, see: see *optic.*] Pertaining to the reflection of light, as from mirrors. Also **ca-top′tri-cal.**—**ca-top′tri-cal-ly,** *adv.*—**ca-top′trics,** *n.* That branch of optics which deals with the reflection of light. Cf. *dioptrics.*

ca-tos-to-mid (ka-tos′tō-mid). [NL. *Catostomidæ,* pl., < Gr. κάτω, down, + στόμα, mouth.] **I.** *n.* Any of the *Catostomidæ,* a family of fresh-water cyprinoid fishes comprising the true suckers. **II.** *a.* Pertaining to the catostomids; belonging to the *Catostomidæ.*—**ca-tos′to-moid. I.** *a.* Resembling a catostomid; belonging to the *Catostomidæ* (see *catostomid*). **II.** *n.* A catostomid.

cat=rig (kat′rig), *n.* *Naut.,* the rig of a catboat; a rig like that of a catboat.—**cat′=rigged,** *a.* Rigged like a catboat.

cat's=claw (kats′klâ), *n.* Any of various plants, as, in the U. S., any of certain mimosaceous shrubs, or, in England, the kidney-vetch.

cat's=cra-dle (kats′krā/dl), *n.* A child's game played with a string looped over the fingers of both hands.

cat's=eye (kats′ī), *n.* Any of certain gems exhibiting a chatoyant luster, as a variety of chrysoberyl (the oriental or precious cat's-eye) or of chalcedony.

cat-skin (kat′skin), *n.* The skin or furry pelt of the cat.

cat's=paw, cats-paw (kats′pâ), *n.* The paw of a cat; also, a person used by another to serve his purposes (in allusion to the story of the monkey which used the paw of a cat to draw roasted chestnuts out of the fire); a tool; *naut.,* a light breeze which ruffles the surface of the water over a comparatively small area; also, a kind of hitch in the bight of a rope, made to hook a tackle on.

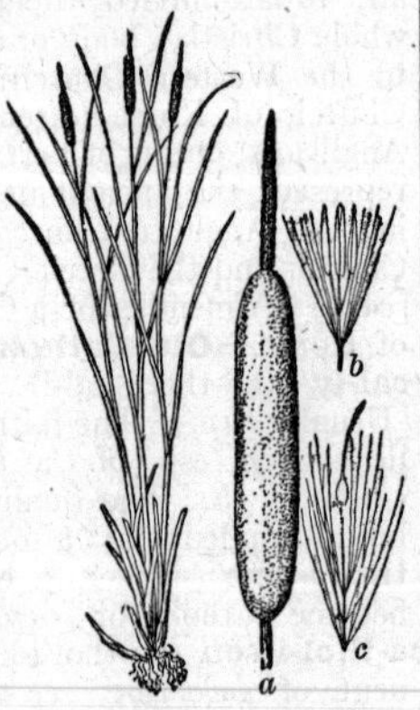

Cat-tail (*Typha latifolia*). *a,* the spike, with male flowers above and female ones below; *b,* a male flower; *c,* a female flower.

cat's=tail (kats′tāl), *n.* Any of several plants with parts suggesting the tail of a cat, as the cat-tail or certain species of horsetail; also, timothy-grass (Eng.).

cat=stick (kat′stik), *n.* A stick or bat used in certain games, as tip-cat.

cat-sup (kat′sup), *n.* Same as *catchup.*

cat=tail (kat′tāl), *n.* A tall, reed-like marsh-plant, *Typha latifolia,* with flowers in long, dense cylindrical spikes; reed-mace; also, any of several other plants of the same genus; also, an ament or catkin.

cat′ta-lo, *n.* See *catalo.*

cat-tish (kat′ish), *a.* Cat-like; feline; catty.

cat-tle (kat′l), *n.* [OF. *catel,* < ML. *captale,* for *capitale,* wealth, stock: see *capital*[2].] Property† or goods†; also, a chattel†; also, live stock, now usually of the bovine kind; also, an opprobrious term for human beings.—**cat′tle-man** (-mạn), *n.*; pl. *-men.* One engaged in rearing or tending cattle.

cat-ty[1] (kat′i), *a.* Cat-like; quietly or slyly malicious; spiteful.

cat-ty[2] (kat′i), *n.*; pl. *catties* (-iz). [Malay *kātī.*] In China and elsewhere in the East, a weight equal to about $1\frac{1}{3}$ pounds avoirdupois.

cat-ty=cor-nered (kat′i-kôr″nėrd), *a.* Same as *cater-cornered.*

cat=whisk-er (kat′hwis″kėr), *n.* See *crystal detector.*

Cau-ca-sian (kâ-kash′ạn, -kā′shạn, or -kā′zhạn). **I.** *a.* Of or pertaining to the Caucasus, a range of mountains between Europe and Asia, extending from the Black Sea to the Caspian Sea; also, noting or pertaining to the so-called 'white' race, embracing the chief peoples of Europe, southwestern Asia, and northern Africa, so named because the native peoples of the Caucasus were considered typical. **II.** *n.* A native of the Caucasus; also, a member of the Caucasian race.—**Cau-cas′ic** (-kas′ik or -kā′sik), *a.*

cau-cus (kâ′kus), *n.*; pl. *-cuses.* [Prob. from N. Amer. Ind.] In the U. S., a meeting of the local members of a political party to nominate candidates, elect delegates to a convention, etc., or of the members of a legislative body who belong to the same party to determine upon action in that body; any preliminary meeting of similar character; in England, a committee or organization within a political party exercising a certain control over its affairs or action.—**cau′cus,** *v. i.*; *-cused, -cusing.* To hold a caucus.

cau-dad (kâ′dad), *adv.* [L. *cauda,* tail: see *-ad.*] In *anat.,* toward the tail: opposed to *cephalad.*

cau-dal (kâ′dạl), *a.* [NL. *caudalis,* < L. *cauda,* tail.] Of, at, or near the tail; tail-like.—**cau′dal-ly,** *adv.*

cau-date (kâ′dāt), *a.* [NL. *caudatus,* < L. *cauda,* tail.] Having a tail or tail-like appendage. Also **cau′dat-ed** (-dā-ted).—**cau-da′tion** (-dā′shọn), *n.* Caudate condition.

cau-dex (kâ′deks), *n.*; pl. *-dexes* or *-dices* (-di-sēz). [L., tree-trunk: see *codex.*] In *bot.,* the axis of a plant, including both stem and root; a stem bearing the remains or scars of leafstalks, as that of a tree-fern; the woody or thickened persistent base of a herbaceous perennial.

cau-di-cle (kâ′di-kl), *n.* [NL. *caudicula,* dim. < L. *caudex:* see *caudex.*] In *bot.,* the slender, stalk-like appendage of the masses of pollen in orchidaceous plants.

cau-dle (kâ′dl), *n.* [OF. *caudel,* < L. *calidus,* hot.] A kind of warm drink for the sick, as of wine or ale mixed with bread, sugar, spices, etc.

caught (kât). Preterit and past participle of *catch.*

caul (kâl), *n.* [OF. F. *cale,* kind of cap.] A woman's netted head-dress†; the back of a woman's cap; also, any investing membrane†; now, the great omentum; also, the amnion; esp., a part of the amnion sometimes covering the head of a child at birth, superstitiously supposed to bring good luck and to be an infallible preservative against drowning.

cauld (kâld), *a.* and *n.* Scotch form of *cold.*

caul-dron (kâl′drọn), *n.* See *caldron.*

cau-les-cent (kâ-les′ẹnt), *a.* [L. *caulis,* stalk.] In *bot.,* having an obvious stem rising above the ground.

cau-li-cle (kâ′li-kl), *n.* [L. *cauliculus,* dim. of *caulis,* stalk.] In *bot.,* a small or rudimentary stem.

cau-li-flow-er (kâ′li-flou″ėr), *n.* [Earlier *cole-flory:* modified form (after E. *cole* or L. *caulis* and E. *flower*) < F. *chou fleuri* (now *chou-fleur*), 'flowered cabbage': see *chou.*] A plant of the cabbage family, a cultivated variety of *Brassica oleracea* whose inflorescence forms a compact, fleshy head; also, the head, much esteemed as a vegetable.—**cauliflower ear,** an (external) ear which has become misshapen from injury, as from battering blows.

cau-li-form (kâ′li-fôrm), *a.* [L. *caulis,* stalk, stem: see *-form.*] In *bot.,* having the form of a stem; stem-like.

cau-line (kâ′lin), *a.* [L. *caulis,* stalk.] In *bot.,* of or pertaining to a stem; esp., pertaining to or arising from the upper part of a stem.

cau-lis (kâ′lis), *n.*; pl. *caules* (-lēz). [L., stalk, stem.] In *bot.,* the stalk or stem of a plant, esp. of a herbaceous plant.

caulk (kâk), etc. See *calk*[1], etc.

cau-lo-car-pous (kâ-lǫ-kär′pus), *a.* [Gr. καυλός, stalk, + καρπός, fruit.] In *bot.,* bearing fruit repeatedly upon the same stem.

cau-lome (kâ′lōm), *n.* [Gr. καυλός, stalk, + *-ome* as in *rhizome.*] In *bot.,* the axis or stem of a plant, or a structure morphologically corresponding to it.—**cau-lo′mic** (-lō′mik), *a.*

caus-a-ble (kâ′zạ-bl), *a.* Capable of being caused.

cau-sal (kâ′zạl), *a.* [LL. *causalis.*] Of, constituting, or implying a cause; in *gram.*, expressing a cause, as a conjunction.—**cau-sal′i-ty** (-zal′i-ti), *n.*; pl. *-ties* (-tiz). Causal quality or agency; also, the relation of cause and effect; in *phren.*, the faculty of tracing effects to their causes.—**cau′sal-ly,** *adv.*

cau-sa-tion (kâ-zā′shọn), *n.* [ML. *causatio(n-)*, < *causare*, to cause, < L. *causa*, E. *cause.*] The action of causing; the operation of a cause.—**cau′sa-tive** (-zạ-tiv). **I.** *a.* Acting as a cause; productive (*of*); in *gram.*, expressing causation, as certain verbs (as *fell*, 'cause to fall'). **II.** *n.* In *gram.*, a causative word or form.—**cau′sa-tive-ly,** *adv.* —**cau′sa-tive-ness, cau-sa-tiv′i-ty** (-tiv′i-ti), *n.*

cause (kâz), *n.* [OF. F. *cause*, < L. *causa.*] That which produces an effect; the group of circumstances which must precede and which invariably result in an effect; also, the end or purpose for which a thing is done or produced (now only in 'final cause'); also, the ground of any action or result; an occasion, reason, or motive; sake† or interest†; good or sufficient reason (as, to complain without *cause*); also, a ground of legal action; the matter over which a person goes to law (also fig.); also, a case for judicial decision; hence, any subject of discussion or debate; also, that side of a question which a person or party supports; an object as pursued by a body of persons advocating it; a public movement.—**cause,** *v. t.*; *caused, causing.* To be the cause of; produce; effect; occasion; impel or induce.—**cause′less,** *a.* Having no cause; not due to any cause; without just cause; groundless.—**cause′less-ly,** *adv.*—**caus′er,** *n.*

cause-rie (kōz-rē), *n.* [F., < *causer*, talk, < L. *causari*, plead, < *causa*, E. *cause.*] A talk or chat; an informal discourse or written article.

cau-seuse (kō-zėz), *n.* [F., fem. of *causeur*, talkative, a talker, < *causer*, talk.] A small sofa for two persons.

cause-way (kâz′wā), *n.* [For *causey way*: see *causey.*] A raised road or path, as across low or wet ground; also, a highway or paved way.—**cause′way,** *v. t.* To provide with a causeway; also, to pave, as a road or street, with cobbles or pebbles.

cau-sey (kâ′zi), *n.* [OF. *caucie* (also *chaucie*, F. *chaussée*), < ML. *calciata*, paved road, appar. < L. *calx*, small stone, lime.] A causeway.

caus-tic (kâs′tik). [L. *causticus*, < Gr. καυστικός, < καίειν, burn.] **I.** *a.* Capable of burning, corroding, or destroying animal tissue (as, *caustic* soda, sodium hydroxide; *caustic* potash, potassium hydroxide); fig., severely critical or sarcastic; in *math.* and *optics*, noting a surface to which all the light-rays emanating from a single point and reflected by a curved surface (as a concave mirror) are tangent; noting a curve formed by a plane section of such a surface; noting an analogous surface or curve resulting from refraction. **II.** *n.* A caustic substance (as, lunar *caustic*, silver nitrate); in *math.* and *optics*, a caustic surface or curve. —**caus′ti-cal-ly,** *adv.*—**caus-ti′ci-ty** (-tis′i-ti), *n.* Caustic quality; corrosiveness; pungent taste; severe sarcasm.

cau-tel (kâ′tel), *n.* [OF. *cautele* (F. *cautèle*), < L. *cautela*, < *cavere*: see *caution.*] Caution or wariness; a precaution; also, a warning or direction; also, subtlety, craftiness, or wiliness. [Obs. or archaic.]—**cau′te-lous,** *a.* Cautious or wary; also, crafty or wily. [Obs. or archaic.]

cau-ter (kâ′tėr), *n.* [LL. *cauter*, < Gr. καυτήρ, branding-iron, < καίειν, burn.] A surgical instrument for burning or cauterizing.—**cau′ter-ize** (-īz), *v. t.*; *-ized, -izing.* To burn with a hot instrument, or with fire or a caustic, esp. for curative purposes; treat with a cautery.—**cau″ter-i-za′tion** (-i-zā′shọn), *n.*—**cau′ter-y,** *n.*; pl. *-ies* (-iz). [L. *cauterium*, < Gr. καυτήριον, dim. of καυτήρ.] An instrument or a caustic substance used to burn or cauterize; also, the process of searing with a hot iron ('actual cautery') or with a caustic ('potential cautery').

cau-tion (kâ′shọn), *n.* [OF. F. *caution*, < L. *cautio(n-)*, < *cavere* (pp. *cautus*), be on one's guard, take heed: see *show.*] A warning, as against danger or evil; anything serving as a warning; something exciting alarm or astonishment (colloq.); also, prudence in regard to danger or evil; wariness; circumspectness; also, a precaution†; also, security or bail, or the person who becomes security (now chiefly Sc.).—**cau′tion,** *v. t.* To give a caution or warning to; warn; urge to take heed.—**cau′tion-a-ry** (-ā-ri), *a.* Of the nature of or containing a caution or warning; also, pertaining to or of the nature of a pledge or security (now chiefly Sc.).—**cau′tion-er,** *n.*

cau-tious (kâ′shus), *a.* [From *caution.*] Having or showing caution or prudence in regard to danger or evil; wary; circumspect.—**cau′tious-ly,** *adv.*—**cau′tious-ness,** *n.*

cav-al-cade (kav-ạl-kād′), *n.* [F., < It. *cavalcata*, < L. *caballus*, horse.] A procession of persons on horseback or in horse-drawn carriages.—**cav-al-cade′,** *v. i.*; *-caded, -cading.* To ride in a cavalcade.

cav-a-lier (kav-ạ-lēr′). [F., < It. *cavaliere*, < ML. *caballarius*, < L. *caballus*, horse.] **I.** *n.* A horseman, esp. a mounted soldier; a knight; one having the spirit or bearing of a knight; a courtly gentleman; a gallant; a gay or swaggering fellow; a man attending on or escorting a woman, or acting as her partner in dancing; [*cap.*] an adherent of Charles I. of England in his contest with Parliament. **II.** *a.* Knightly† or gallant†; also, offhand or unceremonious; also, haughty, disdainful, or supercilious; also [*cap.*], of or pertaining to the Cavaliers.—**cav-a-lier′,** *v. i.* To play the cavalier; be haughty or domineering.

ca-va-lie-re ser-ven-te (kä-vä-lyā′rā ser-ven′tā). [It., 'serving cavalier.'] A man who devotes himself to attending upon a lady, esp. a married lady, as her professed cavalier or gallant.

cav-a-lier-ism (kav-ạ-lēr′izm), *n.* The practice or principles of cavaliers, esp. of the adherents of Charles I.; also, an expression characteristic of the Cavalier party.

cav-a-lier-ly (kav-ạ-lēr′li), *adv.* In a cavalier manner.—**cav-a-lier′ness,** *n.*

ca-val-la (kạ-val′ä), *n.* Same as *cavally.*

ca-val-ly (kạ-val′i), *n.*; pl. *cavallies* (-iz). [Sp. *caballa*, < L. *caballus*, horse.] Any of various carangoid fishes of the genus *Carangus*, esp. *C. hippos*, a food-fish of both coasts of tropical America, on the Atlantic coast found north to Cape Cod; also, the cero (fish).

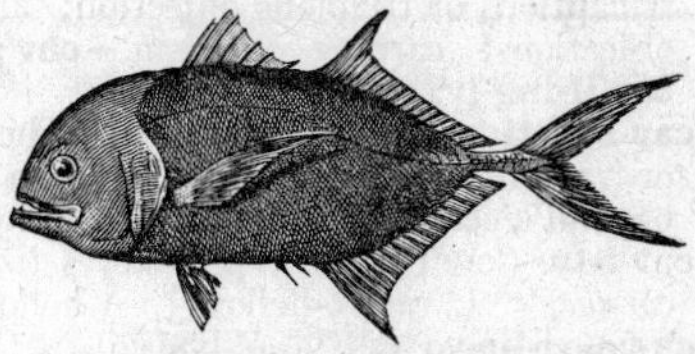

Cavally (*Carangus hippos*).

cav-al-ry (kav′ạl-ri), *n.*; pl. *-ries* (-riz). [F. *cavalerie*, < It. *cavalleria*, < *cavaliere*: see *cavalier.*] Horsemanship, esp. of a knight†; mounted soldiers collectively; that part of a military force composed of troops that serve on horseback; horsemen, horses, etc., collectively.—**cav′al-ry-man** (-mạn), *n.*; pl. *-men.*

ca-vate (kā′vāt), *a.* [L. *cavatus*, pp. of *cavare*, hollow out, < *cavus*, hollow.] Hollowed out, as a class of prehistoric dwellings.

ca-va-ti-na (kä-vạ-tē′nạ), *n.*; pl. *-ne* (-nā). [It.] In *music*, a simple song or melody, properly one without a second part and a repeat; an air.

cave (kāv), *n.* [OF. F. *cave*, < L. *cavus*, hollow.] A hollow in the earth, esp. one opening more or less horizontally into a hill, mountain, etc.; a cavern; a den; also, any cavity†; also, in *Eng. politics*, a secession, or a group of seceders, from a political party on some special question (applied orig., in the phrase 'cave of Adullam,' to a body of seceders from the Liberal party in 1866: see *Adullamite*).—**cave,** *v.*; *caved, caving.* **I.** *tr.* To hollow out; also, to cause to fall (*in*). **II.** *intr.* To dwell in a cave; also, to fall or sink (*in*), as ground; fig., to give (*in*), yield, or submit (colloq.).

ca-ve-at (kā′vẹ-at), *n.* [L., 'let him beware.'] A legal notice to some officer to suspend a certain proceeding until the notifier is given a hearing; in U. S. patent laws, a description of an invention filed to prevent the issuance of a patent for the same invention to another without notice; in general, a warning or caution.—**ca′ve-a-tor** (-ā-tọr), *n.* One who enters a caveat.

cave=dwell-er (kāv′dwel″ėr), *n.* One of a prehistoric race dwelling in caves.

cav-el, kev-el (kav′ẹl, kev′ẹl), *n.* [OF. *keville* (also *cheville*, F. *cheville*), pin, peg, < L. *clavicula*, dim. of *clavis*, key.] *Naut.*, a wooden cleat or the like to which sheets or other ropes are belayed.

cave=man (kāv′man), *n.*; pl. *-men.* A cave-dweller: often taken as the type of the primitive or natural man unaffected in character or habits by civilization.

cav-en-dish (kav′ẹn-dish), *n.* [From *Cavendish*, proper name.] Tobacco softened, sweetened, and pressed into cakes.

cav-ern (kav′ėrn), *n.* [OF. F. *caverne*, < L. *caverna*, < *cavus*, hollow.] A cave, esp. a large cave; also, any cavity†. —**cav′ern,** *v. t.* To put or inclose in or as in a cavern; also, to hollow out in the form of a cavern.—**cav′er-nous,** *a.* [L. *cavernosus.*] Containing caverns; of or like a cavern; also, full of or containing small cavities or interstices; having a porous texture.—**cav′er-nous-ly,** *adv.*

cav-es-son (kav′ẹ-sọn), *n.* [F. *caveçon*, < It. *cavezzone*, < L. *caput*, head.] A kind of stiff nose-band, as of iron or leather, put upon the nose of a horse to wring it, in order to aid in breaking him; also, a halter with such a nose-band.

ca-vet-to (kä-vet′tō), *n.*; pl. *cavettos* (-tōz), It. *cavetti* (-tē). [It., dim. < *cavo*, < L. *cavus*, hollow.] In *arch.*, a concave molding, as in a cornice, with the curve usually a quarter-circle.

cav-i-ar, cav-i-are (kav-i-är′ or kav′i-är), *n.* [F. *caviar*, < It. *caviaro*, now *caviale*; perhaps from Tatar.] The roe of sturgeon and other large fish, salted and prepared for use as a relish; fig., something beyond the popular taste (as, "For the play, I remember, pleased not the million; 'twas *caviare* to the general: but it was . . . an excellent play": Shakspere's "Hamlet," ii. 2. 457).

cav-i-corn (kav′i-kôrn). [L. *cavus*, hollow, + *cornu*, horn.] **I.** *a.* Hollow-horned, as one group of ruminants. **II.** *n.* A hollow-horned ruminant.

cav-il (kav′il), *v.*; *-iled* or *-illed*, *-iling* or *-illing.* [L. *cavillari*, < *cavilla*, a jeering.] **I.** *intr.* To raise captious and frivolous objections; carp. **II.** *tr.* To cavil at.—**cav′il,** *n.* A captious or frivolous objection; also, the raising of such objections; carping criticism.—**cav′il-er, cav′il-ler,** *n.*—**cav′il-ing-ly, cav′il-ling-ly,** *adv.*

cav-i-ta-tion (kav-i-tā′shọn), *n.* The formation of a cavity or vacuum around a propeller or a fan when it revolves beyond a certain speed, resulting in loss of efficiency.

cav-i-ty (kav′i-ti), *n.*; pl. *-ties* (-tiz). [F. *cavité*, < LL. *cavitas*, < L. *cavus*, hollow.] A hollow place; a hollow.

ca-vo=ri-lie-vo (kä″vō-rē-lyā′vō), *n.*; pl. *-vos* (-vōz). [It., 'hollow relief.'] In *sculp.*, relief in which the highest portions are level with the general surface.

ca-vort (kạ-vôrt′), *v. i.* [Cf. *curvet.*] To prance or caper about. [Colloq., U. S.]

ca-vy (kā′vi), *n.*; pl. *-vies* (-viz). [S. Amer.] Any of various short-tailed South American rodents constituting the genus *Cavia* (including the domesticated guinea-pig) or the family *Caviidæ*; any of several allied rodents.

caw (kâ), *v. i.* [Imit.] Of a crow, raven, etc., to utter its characteristic cry; hence, to utter a similar sound.—**caw,** *n.*

Cax-ton (kak′stọn), *n.* Any of the books printed by William Caxton (about 1422–91), the first English printer, all of which are printed in black-letter; also, a kind of printing-type in imitation of the black-letter used by Caxton.

A Device of William Caxton.

cay (kā), *n.* [Sp. *cayo*, shoal, islet: see *key*[2] and *quay.*] A reef or low island; a key.

cay-enne (kī-en′ or kā-), *n.* [From *Cayenne*, in French Guiana.] A hot, biting condiment composed of the ground pods and seeds of species of capsicum; red pepper.

cay-man (kā′mạn), *n.*; pl. *-mans.* [Prob. from Carib.] Any of several tropical American alligators constituting the genus *Caiman.*

cay-use (kī-ūs′), *n.* [From the *Cayuse* Indians of Oregon.] An Indian pony. [Western U. S.]

ca-zique (kạ-zēk′), *n.* See *cacique.*

cease (sēs), *v.*; *ceased, ceasing.* [OF. F. *cesser*, < L. *cessare*, freq. of *cedere*, go, yield: see *cede.*] **I.** *intr.* To leave off; desist (*from*); also, to come to an end. **II.** *tr.* To leave off; desist from; also, to put an end or stop to (something other than one's own action)†.—**cease,** *n.* Cessation.—**cease′less,** *a.* Without stop or pause; unending; incessant.—**cease′less-ly,** *adv.*—**cease′less-ness,** *n.*

ce-cal (sē′kạl), etc. See *cæcal*, etc.

ce-ci-ty (sē′si-ti), *n.* [L. *cæcitas*, < *cæcus*, blind.] Blindness. [Now rare.]

ce-cro-pi-a (sẹ-krō′pi-ạ̈), *n.* [NL.; from *Cecrops*, legendary king of Attica.] A large silkworm-moth, *Samia cecropia*, of the eastern U. S., whose larva feeds on many trees.

ce-cum (sē′kum), *n.* See *cæcum.*

ce-dar (sē′dạ̈r), *n.* [OF. *cedre* (F. *cèdre*), < L. *cedrus*, < Gr. κέδρος.] Any of the old-world pinaceous trees constituting the genus *Cedrus*, as *C. libani* ('cedar of Lebanon'), a stately tree native in Asia Minor, etc.; any of various junipers, as *Juniperus virginiana* ('red cedar'), an American tree with a fragrant reddish wood used for making lead pencils, etc.; any of various other pinaceous trees, as *Chamæcyparis thyoides*, a species of the swamps of the eastern U. S., and *Thuja occidentalis*, the arbor-vitæ (both called 'white cedar'); any of various non-pinaceous tropical trees, as *Cedrela odorata* ('Spanish cedar'), a timber-tree whose wood is used for cigar-boxes; also, the wood of any such tree.—**ce′dar=bird,** *n.* A waxwing, *Ampelis cedrorum*, of North America.—**ce′dared,** *a.* Furnished with cedars.—**ce′darn** (-dạ̈rn), *a.* Of or pertaining to cedars (as, "*cedarn* alleys": Milton's "Comus," 990); also, made of cedar-wood (as, "a *cedarn* cabinet": Tennyson's "Marriage of Geraint," 136). [Poetic.]

Atlas Cedar (*Cedrus atlantica*).

cede (sēd), *v. t.*; *ceded, ceding.* [L. *cedere* (pp. *cessus*), go, withdraw, yield, grant.] To yield or formally resign and surrender to another; make over, as by treaty.

ce-dil-la (sẹ-dil′ạ̈), *n.* [Sp. *cedilla*, now *zedilla*, the mark (orig. a *z* written after *c*), < L. *zeta*, < Gr. ζῆτα, the letter *z.*] A mark placed under *c* before *a*, *o*, or *u*, as in *façade*, to show that it has the sound of *s.*

ce-drine (sē′drin), *a.* [L. *cedrinus.*] Of or like cedar.

ced-u-la (sed′ū-lạ̈, Sp. thā′dö-lä), *n.* [Sp. *cédula*, = E. *schedule.*] In Spanish countries, any of various orders, certificates, or the like; any of certain securities issued by South and Central American governments; in the Philippine Islands, a personal registration tax certificate, or the tax itself.

ceil (sēl), *v. t.* [Prob. < OF. F. *ciel*, sky, heaven, canopy, < L. *cælum*, sky, heaven.] To overlay (the interior upper surface or side walls of a building or room) with wood, plaster, etc.†; esp., to cover the inner side of the roof of (a building or room), as with plaster; provide with a ceiling; *naut.*, to line (the inside of a ship's frame), as with planks. —**ceil′er,** *n.*—**ceil′ing,** *n.* The act of one who ceils; also, the overhead interior lining of a room; the surface of a room opposite the floor; *naut.*, the lining of planks on the inside of a ship's frame; in *aëronautics*, the maximum altitude to which a particular aircraft can rise.

cel-a-don (sel′ạ-don), *n.* [From *Céladon*, the sentimental hero of Honoré d'Urfé's romance, "Astrée" (1610).] A pale-green color, much used in porcelain: as, "Porcelain leaves . . . with spots and stains Of violet and of crimson dye . . . And beautiful with *celadon*" (Longfellow's "Kéramos," 324).

cel-an-dine (sel′ạn-dīn), *n.* [OF. *celidoine*, < L. *chelidonia*, < Gr. χελιδών, swallow.] A papaveraceous plant, *Chelidonium majus* ('greater celandine'), with yellow flowers; also, a ranunculaceous plant, *Ficaria ficaria* ('lesser celandine'), also bearing yellow flowers.

cel-as-tra-ceous (sel-as-trā′shius), *a.* [NL. *Celastrus*, the staff-tree genus, < Gr. κήλαστρος, kind of evergreen.] Belonging to the *Celastraceæ*, a family of plants including the staff-trees, climbing bittersweet, spindle-tree, strawberry-bush, etc.

-cele. Noun termination from Gr. κήλη, tumor, used in pathological terms, as *bubonocele, cystocele, laparocele.*
cel-e-brant (sel′ẹ-brạnt), *n.* One who celebrates, as the officiating priest in the celebration of the eucharist.
cel-e-brate (sel′ẹ-brāt), *v.*; *-brated, -brating.* [L. *celebratus,* pp. of *celebrare,* < *celeber,* frequented, famous.] **I.** *tr.* To perform with appropriate rites and ceremonies; solemnize; also, to observe (a day, etc.) or commemorate (an event) with ceremonies or festivities; also, to sound the praises of; extol; also, to make known publicly; proclaim. **II.** *intr.* To perform a religious ceremony; also, to observe a festival or commemorate an event with ceremonies or festivities. —**cel′e-brat-ed,** *p. a.* Famous; renowned; well-known. —**cel-e-bra′tion** (-brā′shọn), *n.* [L. *celebratio(n-).*] The act of celebrating; that which is done to celebrate anything. —**cel′e-bra-tor,** *n.*
ce-leb-ri-ty (sẹ-leb′ri-ti), *n.*; pl. *-ties* (-tiz). [L. *celebritas,* < *celeber*: see *celebrate.*] The state of being celebrated, extolled, or talked about; fame; renown; also, a celebrated person.
ce-ler-i-ac (sẹ-ler′i-ak), *n.* [See *celery.*] A variety of celery producing an edible turnip-like root.
ce-ler-i-ty (sẹ-ler′i-ti), *n.* [L. *celeritas,* < *celer,* swift.] Swiftness; speed.
cel-e-ry (sel′ẹ-ri), *n.* [F. *céleri,* < LL. *selinon,* < Gr. σέλινον, parsley.] A plant, *Apium graveolens,* of the parsley family, whose blanched leafstalks are extensively used raw for salad, and cooked as a vegetable, in soups, etc.
ce-les-ta (sẹ-les′tạ), *n.* [F. *célesta,* < L. *cælestis,* heavenly: see *celestial.*] A musical instrument with a keyboard, the tones of which are produced by blows of hammers upon steel plates.
ce-les-tial (sẹ-les′tịal). [OF. *celestial,* < L. *cælestis,* < *cælum,* sky, heaven.] **I.** *a.* Of or pertaining to the sky or visible heaven (as, the *celestial* equator, see *equator*; the *celestial* sphere, see *sphere, n.*); also, of or pertaining to the spiritual or invisible heaven; heavenly; divine; also [*cap.*], noting or pertaining to the former Chinese Empire (considered as ruled by a divinely appointed dynasty) or the Chinese. **II.** *n.* An inhabitant of heaven; [*cap.*] a native of China; a Chinese. —**ce-les-ti-al′i-ty** (-tị-al′i-ti), *n.* —**ce-les′tial-ly,** *adv.*
Cel-es-tine[1] (sel′es-tin), *n.* A monk of a branch of the Benedictine order, named from the founder, who became Pope under the title of Celestine V.
cel-es-tine[2] (sel′es-tin), *n.* Same as *celestite.*
cel-es-tite (sel′es-tīt), *n.* [L. *cælestis,* heavenly (in allusion to the delicate blue color of some specimens): see *celestial.*] A mineral consisting of strontium sulphate, crystallizing in the orthorhombic system, usually white in color, but sometimes delicate blue.
ce-li-ac, cœ-li-ac (sē′li-ak), *a.* [L. *cœliacus,* < Gr. κοιλιακός, < κοιλία, belly, < κοῖλος, hollow.] Pertaining to the cavity of the abdomen.
cel-i-bate (sel′i-bāt). [L. *cælibatus,* < *cælebs,* unmarried.] **I.** *n.* Single life (archaic); one who remains single or unmarried, esp. for religious reasons. **II.** *a.* Unmarried. —**cel′i-ba-cy** (-bạ-si), *n.*
cell (sel), *n.* [L. *cella,* room, chamber, hut, store-room.] A small apartment, as in a convent or a prison; a small or mean place of abode, as a hermitage; a monastery or nunnery, usually of small size, dependent on a larger religious house; any small compartment, bounded area, receptacle, case, or the like; a minute cavity or interstice, as in animal or plant tissue; in *elect.,* a device which generates electricity and which forms the whole or a part of a voltaic battery, consisting in one of its simplest forms of two plates, each of a different metal, placed in a jar containing a dilute acid ('voltaic cell'); a device for producing electrolysis, consisting essentially of the electrolyte, its container, and the electrodes ('electrolytic cell'); in *biol.,* a small mass of protoplasm, usually having a nucleus and often a bounding wall ('cell-wall'), constituting in itself an entire organism, or entering or capable of entering into the structure of one.

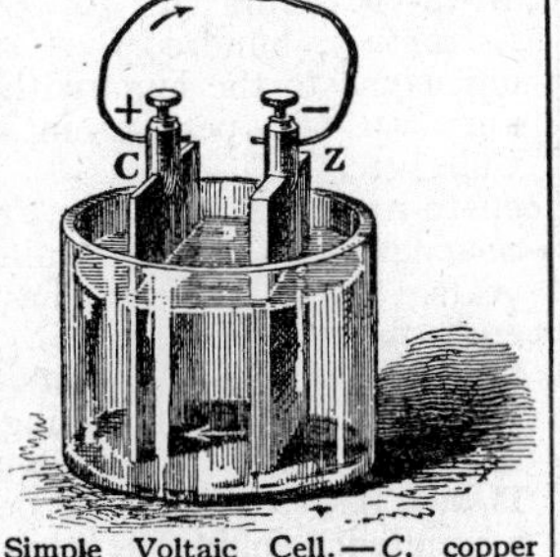

Simple Voltaic Cell.—*C,* copper plate; *Z,* zinc plate.

cel-la (sel′ạ), *n.*; pl. *cellæ* (-ē). [L.: see *cell.*] In *arch.,* the inclosed part of an ancient Greek or Roman temple, as distinct from the porticoes and other external structures.
cel-lar (sel′ạr), *n.* [OF. *celier* (F. *cellier*), < L. *cellarium,* pantry, < *cella*: see *cell.*] A room or set of rooms for the storage of provisions, etc., now always either wholly or partly underground, and usually beneath a building; hence, an underground room or story; often, a wine-cellar, or a store or stock of wines. —**cel′lar,** *v. t.* To place or store in a cellar. —**cel′lar-age** (-ạj), *n.* Cellar space; cellars collectively; also, charges for storage in a cellar. —**cel′lar-er,** *n.* One in charge of a cellar and provisions, as the steward of a monastery; a cellarman. —**cel-lar-et′,** *n.* A cabinet for wine-bottles, etc. Also **cel-lar-ette′** (-et′). —**cel′lar-man** (-mạn), *n.*; pl. *-men.* A man in charge of or employed in a cellar, esp. a wine-cellar; also, a wine-merchant.
cel-late, cel-lat-ed (sel′āt, -ā-ted), *a.* Celled.
cell=di-vi-sion (sel′di-vizh″ọn), *n.* In *biol.,* the division of a cell in the process of reproduction or growth. Cf. *mitosis, amitosis,* and *segmentation.*
celled (seld), *a.* Having a cell or cells.
cel-lo, 'cel-lo (chel′ō), *n.*; pl. *cellos, 'cellos* (-ōz). Shortened form of *violoncello.* —**cel′list, 'cel′list,** *n.*
cel-lo-phane (sel′ọ-fān), *n.* [From *cell(ulose)*[1] + Gr. φαίνειν, show.] A transparent, paper-like product of viscose, impervious to moisture, germs, etc., used as a wrapping for candy, tobacco, drugs, etc. [Proprietary name.]
cel-lu-lar (sel′ụ̄-lạr), *a.* Pertaining to or characterized by cellules or cells, esp. minute compartments or cavities, as in animal or plant tissue. —**cel-lu-lar′i-ty** (-lar′i-ti), *n.*
cel-lu-late, cel-lu-lat-ed (sel′ụ̄-lāt, -lā-ted), *a.* Having cellular structure. —**cel-lu-la′tion** (-lā′shọn), *n.* Cell-formation.
cel-lule (sel′ūl), *n.* [L. *cellula,* dim. of *cella.*] A little cell.
cel-lu-li-tis (sel-ụ̄-lī′tis), *n.* [NL.] In *pathol.,* inflammation of cellular tissue.
cel-lu-loid (sel′ụ̄-loid), *n.* [From *cellulose*[1].] A substance consisting essentially of soluble guncotton and camphor, usually highly inflammable, variously used as a substitute for ivory, vulcanite, etc. [Proprietary name.]
cel-lu-lose[1] (sel′ụ̄-lōs), *n.* [F., < L. *cellula*: see *cellule.*] An inert substance, a carbohydrate, the chief constituent of the cell-walls of plants, and forming an essential part of wood, cotton, hemp, paper, etc.; also, a light material, as of cornstalk pith, which swells rapidly in water, and has been used at the back of the armor of war-ships to prevent water from entering shot-holes. —**cellulose nitrate,** any of various nitrates produced when cellulose is treated with nitric acid or a mixture of nitric and sulphuric acids. Cf. *guncotton.*
cel-lu-lose[2], **cel-lu-lous** (sel′ụ̄-lōs, -lus), *a.* [L. *cellula*: see *cellule.*] Abounding in or consisting of cellules or cells.
ce-lom (sē′lọm), *n.* See *cœlom.*
Cel-si-us (sel′sẹ-ụs) **ther-mom′e-ter.** [From Anders *Celsius* (1701–44), Swedish astronomer, who introduced it.] The centigrade thermometer. See *centigrade.*
celt[1] (selt), *n.* [LL. *celtis,* chisel.] In *archæol.,* an implement resembling a chisel or ax-blade.

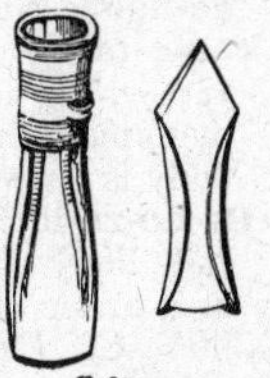
Celts.

Celt[2] (selt), *n.* [L. *Celtæ,* pl., < Gr. Κελτοί.] A member of an Indo-European people now represented chiefly by the Irish, Gaels, Welsh, and Bretons. —**Cel′tic.** **I.** *a.* Of or pertaining to the Celts or their language. **II.** *n.* The group of dialects spoken by the Celts, including Irish, Gaelic, Welsh, and Breton. —**Cel′ti-cism** (-ti-sizm), *n.* Celtic spirit or practice; a Celtic idiom or mode of expression. —**Cel′ti-cize,** *v. t.*; *-cized, -cizing.* To render Celtic.
cel-ti-um (sel′shi-um), *n.* [NL., < L. *Celtæ,* the Celts.] In *chem.,* a supposed new rare element.
Cel-to- (sel′tọ-). Form of *Celt* used in combination, as in *Celto-Roman* (both Celtic and Roman), *Celto-Slavic, Celto-Teutonic.*
ce-ment (sẹ-ment′ or sem′ẹnt), *n.* [OF. F. *ciment,* < L. *cæmentum,* rough stone, < *cædere,* cut.] Any of various

substances which are soft when first prepared but after a time become hard or stone-like, used for joining stones, making floors, etc.; esp., a material of this kind (the ordinary variety, often called 'hydraulic cement') commonly made by burning a mixture of clay and limestone, used for making concrete for foundations or the like, covering floors, etc. (see *Portland cement*); hence, any of various substances, as glue, used for making other substances cohere; fig., anything that binds or unites; in *anat.*, the substance which forms the outer crust of a tooth from where the enamel terminates to the apex of the root.—**ce-ment** (sẹ-ment′), *v.* **I.** *tr.* To unite by or as by cement; also, to coat or cover with cement. **II.** *intr.* To become cemented; stick or cohere.—**cem-en-ta-tion** (sem-ẹn-tā′shọn), *n.* The act, process, or result of cementing; in *metal.*, etc., the heating of two substances in contact in order to effect some change in one of them; esp., the formation of steel by heating iron in powdered charcoal.—**ce-ment′er,** *n.*—**ce-ment′=gun,** *n.* A machine by which a mixture of cement and sand, or other cementitious materials, is forced through a hose to a nozzle, where water, brought through a separate hose, is added, the combined materials being driven forcibly from the nozzle: used in constructing buildings, piling, etc., repairing and rebuilding masonry structures, lining irrigation-ditches and reservoirs, protecting the roofs of mines and tunnels, lining steel ladles, and for other purposes. [Proprietary name.]—**cem-en-ti′tious** (-tish′us), *a.* Of the nature of cement.

cem-e-ter-y (sem′ẹ̄-ter-i), *n.*; pl. *-ies* (-iz). [LL. *cœmeterium*, < Gr. κοιμητήριον, < κοιμᾶν, put to sleep.] A burial-ground, esp. one not attached to a church.—**cem-e-te′ri-al** (-tē′ri-ạl), *a.*

cen-a-cle (sen′ạ-kl), *n.* [L. *cenaculum*, < *cena*, dinner, supper.] A dining-room; esp., the "upper room" in which the Last Supper was eaten (Mark, xiv. 15; Luke, xxii. 12).

cen-dré (soṅ-drā), *a.* [F. (fem. *cendrée*), < *cendre*, ash, cinder.] Ash-colored; having a grayish tinge, as certain shades of blond hair.

ce-nes-the-sia (sē-nes-thē′ziạ), etc. See *cœnæsthesia*, etc.

cen-o-bite, cœn-o-bite (sen′ọ-bīt or sē′nọ-), *n.* [LL. *cœnobita*, < *cœnobium*, < Gr. κοινόβιον, convent, neut. of κοινόβιος, living in community, < κοινός, common, + βίος, life.] One of a religious order living in a convent or community.—**cen-o-bit′ic, cœn-o-bit′ic** (-bit′ik), *a.*—**cen′o-bit-ism, cœn′o-bit-ism** (-bī-tizm), *n.* The state, system, or practices of cenobites.—**cen′o-by, cœn′o-by** (-bi), *n.*; pl. *-bies* (-biz). [LL. *cœnobium.*] A conventual establishment; a religious community.

ce-nog-a-my, cœ-nog-a-my (sẹ-nog′ạ-mi), *n.* [Gr. κοινός, common, + γάμος, marriage.] The practice of having husbands or wives in common, as among some primitive tribes.

ce-no-gen-e-sis (sē-nọ-jen′e-sis or sen-ọ-), *n.* [Gr. καινός, new, + γένεσις, genesis.] In *biol.*, that development of an individual which does not repeat the phylogeny of its race, stock, or group: opposed to *palingenesis.*—**ce″no-ge-net′ic** (-jẹ-net′ik), *a.*

cen-o-taph (sen′ọ-tȧf), *n.* [L. *cenotaphium*, < Gr. κενοτάφιον, < κενός, empty, + τάφος, tomb.] A sepulchral monument erected in memory of a deceased person whose body is elsewhere.—**cen-o-taph′ic** (-taf′ik), *a.*

Ce-no-zo-ic (sē-nọ-zō′ik or sen-ọ-). [Gr. καινός, new, + ζωή, life.] **I.** *a.* Noting or pertaining to a geological era or a group of rocks whose fossils represent recent forms of life. Cf. *Paleozoic, Mesozoic.* **II.** *n.* The Cenozoic era or group.

cense (sens), *v. t.*; *censed, censing.* [For *incense*[1], *v.*] To burn incense before or about; perfume with incense.—**cen′ser,** *n.* [Cf. OF. *censier*, for *encensier.*] A vessel in which incense is burned.

cen-sor (sen′sọr), *n.* [L., < *censere*, tax, rate, judge, think.] Either of two ancient Roman officials who kept the register or census of the citizens, and also supervised manners and morals; hence, any one who exercises supervision of manners and morals; esp., an official charged with examining books, plays, news accounts, etc., and empowered to prohibit them or suppress parts if deemed objectionable on moral, political, military, or other grounds; also, one who censures; an adverse critic; one given to faultfinding.—**cen′sor,** *v. t.* To examine, pass upon, or revise as a censor does; esp., to suppress parts of (letters, press despatches, etc.) before permitting them to be transmitted to their destination, as for military reasons in time of war.—**cen-so′ri-al** (-sō′ri-ạl), *a.* Pertaining to a censor.—**cen-so′ri-ous,** *a.* [L. *censorius.*] Addicted to censure; severely critical; faultfinding; carping.—**cen-so′ri-ous-ly,** *adv.*—**cen-so′ri-ous-ness,** *n.*—**cen′sor-ship,** *n.*

cen-sur-a-ble (sen′shụr-ạ-bl), *a.* Worthy of censure.—**cen′sur-a-ble-ness,** *n.*—**cen′sur-a-bly,** *adv.*

cen-sure (sen′shụr), *n.* [L. *censura*, < *censere*: see *censor.*] Judgment†; judicial sentence†; a criticizing, esp. adversely; expression of disapproval; condemnation; a hostile criticism; *eccles.*, a penalty, imposed upon an offender, as a public rebuke or a suspension from office.—**cen′sure,** *v.*; *-sured, -suring.* **I.** *tr.* To judge†; sentence judicially†; criticize, esp. adversely; pass adverse judgment on; express disapprobation of; find fault with; condemn; *eccles.*, to discipline by public rebuke, etc. **II.** *intr.* To give censure, adverse criticism, or blame.—**cen′sur-er,** *n.*

cen-sus (sen′sus), *n.*; pl. *-suses.* [L., < *censere*: see *censor.*] In ancient Rome, the registration of citizens and their property, for purposes of taxation; in modern times, an official enumeration of inhabitants, with details as to age, sex, pursuits, etc.—**cen′sus,** *v. t.*; *-sused, -susing.* To take a census of; enumerate in a census.

cent (sent), *n.* [F. *cent*, < L. *centum*, hundred.] The hundredth part of the U. S. dollar, or a copper coin of this value; also, the hundredth part of monetary units elsewhere.

cen-tal (sen′tạl), *n.* [L. *centum*, hundred.] A weight of 100 pounds avoirdupois.

cen-tare (sen′tãr), *n.* Same as *centiare.*

cen-taur (sen′târ), *n.* [L. *Centaurus*, < Gr. Κένταυρος, one of a savage race in Thessaly; origin uncertain.] In *Gr. myth.*, one of a race of monsters having the head, trunk, and arms of a man, and the body and legs of a horse; [*cap.*] in *astron.*, the southern constellation Centaurus. — **cen′taur-ess,** *n.* A female centaur.—**cen-tau-rom′a-chy** (-tâ-rom′ạ-ki), *n.*; pl. *-chies* (-kiz). [L. *Centauromachia*, < Gr. Κενταυρομαχία: see *-machy.*] A combat or battle with centaurs.

Centaur. — Capitoline Museum, Rome.

cen-tau-ry (sen′tâ-ri), *n.* [ML. *centauria*, L. *centaureum*, < Gr. κενταύρειον, < Κένταυρος, centaur (here the centaur Chiron, reputed discoverer of the plant's medicinal virtues).] Either of two gentianaceous herbs, *Chlora perfoliata* and *Erythræa centaurium*, with medicinal properties; any plant of the genus *Erythræa*; also, any of certain other plants, as those of the gentianaceous genus *Sabbatia* ('American centaury').

cen-ta-vo (sen-tä′vō), *n.*; pl. *-vos* (-vōz). [Amer. Sp., < L. *centum*, hundred.] A small coin or minor monetary unit equal to the hundredth part of a particular monetary unit, esp. of a peso, as in Mexico, the Philippine Islands, Cuba, etc.

cen-te-na-ri-an (sen-te-nā′ri-ạn). [L. *centenarius*: see *centenary.*] **I.** *a.* Pertaining to or having lived a hundred years. **II.** *n.* One who has reached the age of a hundred.

cen-te-na-ry (sen′te-nạ-ri). [L. *centenarius*, of or containing a hundred, < *centeni*, a hundred each, < *centum*, hundred.] **I.** *a.* Pertaining to a hundred or a period of a hundred years; recurring once in every hundred years. **II.** *n.*; pl. *-ries* (-riz). A period of a hundred years; also, a hundredth anniversary; a centennial celebration.

cen-ten-ni-al (sen-ten′i-ạl). [ML. *centennis*, < L. *centum*, hundred, + *annus*, year.] **I.** *a.* Pertaining to, or marking the completion of, a hundred years; pertaining to a hundredth anniversary; also, lasting a hundred years; a hundred years old. **II.** *n.* A hundredth anniversary, or its celebration.—**cen-ten′ni-al-ly,** *adv.*—**cen-ten′ni-um** (-um), *n.*; pl. *-niums* or *-nia* (-ạ̈). [NL.] A period of a hundred years; a century.

cen-ter^1, cen-tre^1 (sen′tėr), *n.* [F. *cintre,* ult. < L. *cinctura,* girdle.] Same as *centering.*

cen-ter^2, cen-tre^2 (sen′tėr), *n.* [OF. F. *centre,* < L. *centrum,* < Gr. *κέντρον,* sharp point, center, < *κεντεῖν,* prick.] A point within a circle or sphere equally distant from all points of the circumference or surface; the middle point, place, or part of anything; the middle point of the earth†; the earth as the supposed middle point of the universe†; a person or thing, or a group, as of troops, occupying the middle position; [usually *cap.*] in continental Europe, that part of a legislative assembly which sits in the center of the chamber, a position customarily assigned to representatives holding views intermediate between those of the conservatives or Right and the liberals or Left; a party holding such views; [*l. c.*] a point, pivot, axis, etc., round which anything rotates or revolves; a point toward which concentration, or from which diffusion, takes place; a principal point, place, or object; in *football,* etc., the middle player in the forward line; in *mech.,* the point on either spindle of a lathe, upon which the work to be turned is placed (as, the live *center,* on the live spindle; the dead *center,* on the dead spindle: see *spindle*).—**center of buoyancy,** a point in a ship or other floating body, corresponding to the center of gravity of the water it displaces.—**center of gravity,** that point of a body (or system of bodies) from which it could be suspended or on which it could be supported and be in equilibrium in any position.—**cen′ter^2, cen′tre^2,** *v.*; *-tered* or *-tred, -tering* or *-tring.* **I.** *tr.* To place in or on a center; collect at a center, or concentrate; determine or mark the center of; adjust, shape, or modify (an object, part, etc.) so that its axis or the like is in a central or normal position. **II.** *intr.* To be at or come to a center; concentrate.—**cen′ter=bit,** *n.* A carpenter's bit with a sharp, projecting central point and two cutting wings, used for boring holes.—**cen′ter=board,** *n.* *Naut.,* a wooden or metal slab pivoted or arranged so that it can be lowered through a fore-and-aft slot (having above it a vertical water-tight casing) in the bottom of a sail-boat, in order to increase the draft and so prevent a drifting to leeward.

cen-ter-ing, cen-tring (sen′tėr-ing, -tring), *n.* [See *center^1.*] A temporary timber framing for supporting an arch or vault during its erection.

cen-ter-piece (sen′tėr-pēs), *n.* A piece in or for the center of something; esp., an ornamental piece of silver, glass, or the like, or of embroidery, lace, or like material, for the center of a dining-table.

cen-tes-i-mal (sen-tes′i-mạl). [L. *centesimus,* < *centum,* hundred.] **I.** *a.* Hundredth; pertaining to division into hundredths. **II.** *n.* A hundredth.—**cen-tes′i-mal-ly,** *adv.*

cen-tes-i-mate (sen-tes′i-māt), *v. t.*; *-mated, -mating.* [L. *centesimatus,* pp. of *centesimare,* < *centesimus,* hundredth: see *centesimal,* and cf. *decimate.*] To take one in every hundred of (soldiers, etc.) for punishment, as for mutiny.—**cen-tes-i-ma′tion** (-mā′shọn), *n.*

cen-tes-i-mo (chen-tez′ē-mō), *n.*; pl. *-mi* (-mē). [It., < L. *centesimus,* hundredth: see *centesimal.*] An Italian copper coin and monetary unit, the hundredth part of a lira.

cent-ge-ner (sent′jẹ-nėr), *n.* [L. *centum,* hundred, + *genus* (*gener-*), kind.] One hundred or any considerable number of representatives of a race, variety, or strain of domesticated animals or cultivated plants, considered as a type or true sample of the whole.

centi-. Form of L. *centum,* hundred, used in combination, sometimes in the sense of 'one hundredth,' as in terms of the metric system.

cen-ti-are (sen′ti-ãr), *n.* [F.: see *centi-.*] In the *metric system,* a surface measure equal to one hundredth of an are, or one square meter.

cen-ti-grade (sen′ti-grād), *a.* [F., < L. *centum,* hundred, + *gradus,* step, degree.] Divided into 100 degrees, as a scale; specif., noting or pertaining to a thermometer which reckons 100 degrees from the melting-point of ice, or zero, to the boiling-point of water, or 100° (abbreviated *C.*).

cen-ti-gram, cen-ti-gramme (sen′ti-gram), *n.* [F. *centigramme*: see *centi-.*] In the *metric system,* a unit of weight equal to one hundredth of a gram, or 0.1543 grain.

cen-ti-li-ter, cen-ti-li-tre (sen′ti-lē-tėr), *n.* [F. *centilitre*: see *centi-.*] In the *metric system,* a unit of capacity equal to one hundredth of a liter, 0.6102 cubic inch, or 0.338 U. S. fluid ounce.

cen-time (soṅ-tēm), *n.* [F., < L. *centesimus,* hundredth: see *centesimal.*] In the French coinage system, the hundredth part of a franc.

Obverse. Reverse.
Centime of Napoleon III., in the British Museum.

cen-ti-me-ter, cen-ti-me-tre (sen′ti-mē-tėr), *n.* [F. *centimètre*: see *centi-.*] In the *metric system,* a measure of length equal to one hundredth of a meter, or 0.3937 inch.—**centimeter=gram=second system,** a system of units employed in physical science, in which the centimeter, gram, and second are taken as the fundamental units of length, mass, and time: commonly abbreviated *c. g. s. system.*

cen-ti-pede, cen-ti-ped (sen′ti-pēd, -ped), *n.* [L. *centipeda,* < *centum,* hundred, + *pes* (*ped-*), foot.] Any myriapod of the order or group *Chilopoda,* containing both harmless and poisonous species, characterized by a single pair of legs for each segment of the body. Cf. *millepede.*

Centipede.

cen-ti-stere (sen′ti-stēr), *n.* [F. *centistère*: see *centi-.*] In the *metric system,* a unit of volume equal to one hundredth of a stere.

cent-ner (sent′nėr), *n.* [G., < L. *centenarius*: see *centenary.*] A weight in various European countries corresponding to the hundredweight, in several cases fixed at 50 kilograms, or 110.23 pounds avoirdupois.

cen-to (sen′tō), *n.*; pl. *-tos* (-tōz). [L., patchwork.] A literary or musical composition made up of bits from various sources.

cen-trad (sen′trad), *adv.* [L. *centrum,* center: see *-ad.*] In *anat.,* toward the center.

cen-tral (sen′trạl), *a.* [L. *centralis,* < *centrum,* center.] Of, pertaining to, or forming the center; in, at, or near the center; also, constituting that from which other related things proceed or upon which they depend; hence, principal; chief; dominant.—**central nervous system.** See *nervous system.*—**Central Powers,** in the World War, Germany and Austria-Hungary, often with their allies Turkey and Bulgaria, as opposed to the Allies (Great Britain, France, etc.). Cf. *ally, n.,* and see *World War,* under *world.*—**central time.** See *standard time,* under *standard, a.*—**cen′tral,** *n.* The central office of a telephone system, in which connections are made between different lines.—**cen′tral-ism,** *n.* Centralization, or a centralizing system; the principle of centralization, esp. in government.—**cen′tral-ist,** *n.*—**cen-tral-is′tic,** *a.*—**cen-tral′i-ty** (-tral′i-ti), *n.* Central position or character.—**cen″tral-i-za′tion** (-i-zā′shọn), *n.* The act of centralizing, or the fact of being centralized; in *politics,* the concentration of administrative power in a central government.—**cen′tral-ize** (-īz), *v.*; *-ized, -izing.* **I.** *tr.* To draw to or toward a center; bring under one control, esp. in government. **II.** *intr.* To come together at a center.—**cen′tral-iz-er,** *n.*—**cen′tral-ly,** *adv.*—**cen′tral-ness,** *n.*

cen-tre^1, cen-tre^2 (sen′tėr). British preferred form of *center^1, center^2.*

cen-tric (sen′trik), *a.* [Gr. *κεντρικός,* < *κέντρον,* center.] Pertaining to or situated at the center; central; in *physiol.,* pertaining to or originating at a nerve-center. Also **cen′tri-cal.**—**cen′tri-cal-ly,** *adv.*—**cen-tri′ci-ty** (-tris′i-ti), *n.* Centric state.

cen-trif-u-gal (sen-trif′ụ̄-gạl). [NL. *centrifugus,* < L. *centrum,* center, + *fugere,* flee.] **I.** *a.* Proceeding or directed outward from the center (as, *centrifugal* force, the supposed force tending to cause a body moving around a center to fly away from that center, being really the inertia

(variable) ḍ as d or j, ṣ as s or sh, ṭ as t or ch, ẓ as z or zh; ọ, F. cloche; ü, F. menu; ḉh, Sc. loch; ṅ, F. bonbon; **′**, primary accent; **″**, secondary accent; †, obsolete; <, from; +, and; =, equals. **See also lists at beginning of book.**

of the body; the supposed force equal and opposite to centripetal force; *centrifugal* action, action which causes substances, objects, etc., to fly away from a central part or structure, as when a substance is placed in a revolving drum); pertaining to or operating by centrifugal action (as, a *centrifugal* machine, any of various devices for separating substances of different specific gravity, drying cloth, or the like, consisting essentially of a revolving structure, as a perforated drum); in *bot.*, tending outward or developing from the center outward (as, a *centrifugal* inflorescence, a determinate inflorescence: so called because the flowers expand or develop successively from the center or apex of the cluster to the circumference or base): opposed to *centripetal*. **II.** *n.* A centrifugal machine; the drum-like part of such a machine; also, sugar freed from liquids by a centrifugal machine.—**cen-trif′u-gal-ize** (-īz), *v. t.*; *-ized*, *-izing*. To subject to centrifugal action, esp. in a centrifugal machine.—**cen-trif″u-gal-i-za′tion** (-i-zā′shọn), *n.*—**cen-trif′u-gal-ly,** *adv.*

cen-trip-e-tal (sen-trip′e-tạl), *a.* [NL. *centripetus*, < L. *centrum*, center, + *petere*, seek.] Proceeding or directed toward the center (as, *centripetal* force, a force directed toward the center of a circle or curve, acting on a body which is moving in the circle or curve; *centripetal* action); operating by centripetal action; in *bot.*, tending inward or developing from without toward the center (as, a *centripetal* inflorescence, an indeterminate inflorescence: so called because the flowers expand or develop successively from the circumference or base of the cluster to the center or apex): opposed to *centrifugal*.—**cen-trip′e-tal-ly,** *adv.* —**cen-trip′e-tence,** *n.* Centripetal action or movement.

Cen-trist (sen′trist), *n.* In continental Europe, a member of a political party of the Center.

centro-. Form of Gr. κέντρον, or L. *centrum*, center, used in combination.—**cen-tro-bar-ic** (sen-trọ̄-bar′ik), *a.* [+ Gr. βάρος, weight.] Pertaining to the center of gravity. —**cen′tro-some** (-sōm), *n.* [+ *-some*³.] In *biol.*, a minute protoplasmic body regarded by some as the active center of cell-division in mitosis. Cf. *centrosphere*.—**cen′tro-sphere** (-sfēr), *n.* In *biol.*, the mass of protoplasm surrounding a centrosome; the central portion of an aster, containing the centrosome.

cen-trum (sen′trum), *n.*; pl. *-trums* or *-tra* (-trạ̈). [L.: see *center*².] A center; in *anat.*, the body of a vertebra.

cen-tum-vir (sen-tum′vėr), *n.*; pl. *-viri* (-vi-rī) or *-virs*. [L. *centumviri*, pl., < *centum*, hundred, + *viri*, pl. of *vir*, man.] In ancient Rome, one of a body of one hundred judges (actually 105, 3 from each of the 35 tribes) appointed to decide common causes among the people.—**cen-tum′vi-ral** (-vi-rạl), *a.*—**cen-tum′vi-rate** (-rāt), *n.* The office of centumvir; the body of centumvirs.

cen-tu-ple (sen′tụ̄-pl), *a.* [LL. *centuplus*, < L. *centum*, hundred, + *-plus*: see *double*.] A hundred times as great; hundredfold.—**cen′tu-ple,** *v. t.*; *-pled*, *-pling*. To make a hundred times as great.

cen-tu-pli-cate (sen-tū′pli-kāt), *v. t.*; *-cated*, *-cating*. [L. *centuplicatus*, pp. of *centuplicare*, < *centuplex*, hundredfold, < *centum*, hundred, + *-plex*: see *duplex*.] To make a hundred times as great; centuple.—**cen-tu′pli-cate** (-kạ̄t). **I.** *a.* Hundredfold; centuple. **II.** *n.* A hundred-fold number or quantity.—**cen-tu-pli-ca′tion** (-kā′shọn), *n.*

cen-tu-ply (sen′tụ̄-pli), *adv.* In centuple measure or quantity.

cen-tu-ri-al (sen-tū′ri-ạl), *a.* Pertaining to a century.

cen-tu-ried (sen′ṭụ̄-rid), *a.* That has lasted for a century or for centuries; centuries old.

cen-tu-ri-on (sen-tū′ri-ọn), *n.* [L. *centurio(n-)*, < *centuria*: see *century*.] The commander of a Roman military century.

cen-tu-ry (sen′ṭụ̄-ri), *n.*; pl. *-ries* (-riz). [L. *centuria*, < *centum*, hundred.] A hundred of something; a period of one hundred years; one of the successive periods of one hundred years reckoned forward or backward from a recognized chronological epoch, esp. from the assumed date of the birth of Christ (as, the 1st *century* of the Christian era, up to the close of the year 100; the 19th *century*, beginning with 1801 and ending with 1900; the 4th *century* before Christ, extending from 301 B.C. backward through 400 B.C., both included); a subdivision, probably orig. consisting of one hundred men, in the ancient Roman army; one of the divisions of the ancient Roman people formed with reference to voting, each division having one vote.—**cen′tu-ry=plant,** *n.* A Mexican species of agave, *Agave americana*, cultivated for ornament: popularly supposed not to blossom until a century old.

Century-plant.

ceorl (keọrl), *n.* [AS.: see *churl*.] In old English times, a freeman of the lowest rank; a churl.

ceph-a-lad (sef′ạ-lad), *adv.* [Gr. κεφαλή, head: see *-ad*.] In *anat.*, toward the head: opposed to *caudad*.

ceph-a-lal-gia (sef-ạ-lal′jiạ̈), *n.* [L., < Gr. κεφαλή, head, + ἄλγος, pain.] Headache.—**ceph-a-lal′gic. I.** *a.* Pertaining to or affected with headache. **II.** *n.* A remedy for headache.

ceph-a-late (sef′ạ-lāt), *a.* [Gr. κεφαλή, head.] Having a head, as a mollusk.

ce-phal-ic (se-fal′ik), *a.* [L. *cephalicus*, < Gr. κεφαλικός, < κεφαλή, head.] Of or pertaining to the head; situated or directed toward the head; of the nature of a head.—**cephalic index,** in *craniom.*, the ratio of the greatest breadth of skull to the greatest length from front to back, multiplied by 100.

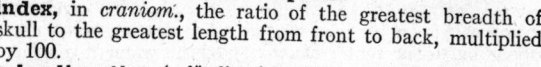

ceph-a-li-za-tion (sef″ạ-li-zā′shọn), *n.* [Gr. κεφαλή, head.] In *biol.*, a tendency in the development of animals to localization of important organs or parts in or near the head, indicating progress toward higher development.

cephalo-. Form of Gr. κεφαλή, head, used in combination. —**ceph-a-lo-gen-e-sis** (sef″ạ-lọ̄-jen′e-sis), *n.* The genesis or development of the head or brain.—**ceph″a-lo-ge-net′ic** (-jẹ̄-net′ik), *a.*—**ceph-a-lom′e-ter** (-lom′e-tėr), *n.* [+ *-meter*.] An instrument for measuring the head or skull; a craniometer.—**ceph-a-lom′e-try,** *n.*

ceph-a-lo-pod (sef′ạ-lọ̄-pod). [NL. *Cephalopoda*, pl., < Gr. κεφαλή, head, + πούς (ποδ-), foot.] **I.** *n.* Any of the *Cephalopoda*, the most highly organized class of mollusks, including the cuttlefish, squid, octopus, etc., the members of which have tentacles attached to the head. **II.** *a.* Pertaining to the cephalopods; belonging to the *Cephalopoda*. —**ceph-a-lop′o-dous** (-lop′ọ̄-dus), *a.*

ceph-a-lo-tho-rax (sef″ạ-lọ̄-thō′raks), *n.* [See *cephalo-*.] In *zoöl.*, the anterior part of the body in certain arachnids and crustaceans, consisting of the coalesced head and thorax.

ceph-a-lous (sef′ạ-lus), *a.* [Gr. κεφαλή, head.] Having a head; cephalate.

ce-ra-ceous (sẹ̄-rā′shius), *a.* [L. *cera*, wax.] Of the nature of wax; waxy.

ce-ram-ic (se-ram′ik), *a.* [Gr. κεραμικός, < κέραμος, potters' clay, pottery.] Pertaining to pottery, or earthenware, porcelain, etc., or to their manufacture.—**ce-ram′ics,** *n.* The art of making pottery, or earthenware, porcelain, etc.; also (as *pl.*), pieces or specimens of earthenware, porcelain, etc. —**cer-a-mist** (ser′ạ-mist), *n.* One versed in ceramics.

ce-rar-gy-rite (se-rär′ji-rīt), *n.* [Gr. κέρας, horn, + ἄργυρος, silver.] Native chloride of silver, a white, yellowish, or grayish mineral, darkening on exposure to light, presenting somewhat the appearance of horn, and forming an important ore of silver; horn-silver.

ce-ras-tes (se-ras′tēz), *n.* [L., < Gr. κεράστης, < κέρας, horn.] Any of the venomous serpents of the genus *Cerastes*, of northern Africa and parts of Asia, as *C. cornutus*, which has a horny process over each eye; the horned viper.

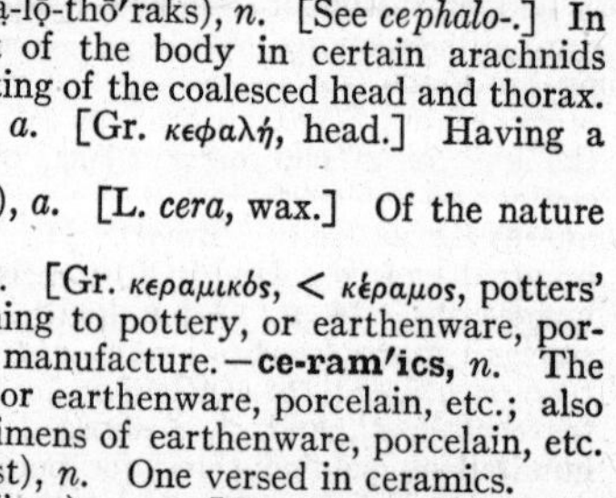
Cerastes (*C. cornutus*).

ce-rate (sē′rāt), *n.* [L. *ceratum*, prop. neut. of *ceratus*, pp. of *cerare*, cover with wax, < *cera*, wax.] An unctuous (often medicated) preparation for external application, consisting of lard or oil mixed with wax, rosin, or the like, esp. one which has a firmer consistence than a typical ointment and does not melt when in contact with the skin.—**ce′rat-ed** (-rā-ted), *a.* [L. *ceratus*, pp.] Covered with wax; waxed.

cer-a-tin (ser′ą-tin), *n.* [Gr. κέρας (κερατ-), horn.] An albuminous substance forming the chief constituent of horn, hair, feathers, etc.

cer-a-ti-tis (ser-ą-tī′tis), *n.* [NL., < Gr. κέρας (κερατ-), horn.] In *pathol.*, inflammation of the cornea.

cerato-, cerat-. Forms of Gr. κέρας (κερατ-), horn, used in combination.

ce-rat-o-dus (se-rat′ǫ-dus), *n.* [NL., < Gr. κέρας (κερατ-), horn, + ὀδούς, tooth.] A fish of the extinct dipnoous genus *Ceratodus*, or of the closely related existent genus *Neoceratodus*, as *N. forsteri*, the barramunda of Australia: so called from the horn-like ridges of the teeth.

cer-a-to-fi-brous (ser″ą-tǫ-fī′brus), *a.* [See *cerato-*.] Consisting of horny fibers.

cer-a-toid (ser′ą-toid), *a.* [Gr. κερατοειδής, < κέρας (κερατ-), horn, + εἶδος, form.] Resembling horn; horny; also, shaped like a horn.

ce-rau-no-graph (se-râ′nǫ-gråf), *n.* [Gr. κεραυνός, thunderbolt: see *-graph*.] An instrument for recording electrical disturbances in the atmosphere due to thunderstorms or lightning.

Cer-be-rus (sėr′bę-rus), *n.* [L., < Gr. Κέρβερος.] In *class. myth.*, a dog, usually represented as having three heads, which guarded the entrance of the infernal regions; hence, a watchful and formidable or surly keeper or guard.—**Cer-be′re-an** (-bē′rę-ąn), *a.*

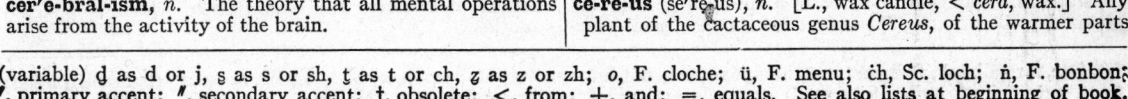

Cerberus. — Antique bronze.

cer-ca-ri-a (sėr-kā′ri-ą̈), *n.*; pl. *-riæ* (-ri-ē). [NL., < Gr. κέρκος, tail.] In *zoöl.*, a larval stage of trematode worms, characterized by an oval or discoidal body terminated by a tail-like appendage.—**cer-ca′ri-an,** *a.* and *n.*

cere (sēr), *n.* [L. *cera* = Gr. κηρός, wax.] A membrane of waxy appearance at the base of the upper mandible of certain birds, esp. birds of prey and parrots, in which the nostrils open.—**cere,** *v. t.*; *cered, cering.* [L. *cerare*, < *cera*.] To cover or coat with wax†; also, to wrap in or as in a cerecloth; also, to wrap or spread like a cerecloth (poetic: as, "Let the silent years Be closed and *cered* over their memory," Shelley's "Julian and Maddalo," 614).

ce-re-al (sē′rę-ąl). [L. *Cerealis*, pertaining to Ceres, goddess of agriculture, and hence to grain.] **I.** *a.* Of or pertaining to grain or the plants producing it. **II.** *n.* Any gramineous plant yielding an edible farinaceous grain, as wheat, rye, oats, rice, maize, etc.; also, the grain itself, or some preparation of it.

Ce-re-a-li-a (sē-rę-ā′li-ą̈), *n. pl.* [L., prop. neut. pl. of *Cerealis*: see *cereal*.] An ancient Roman festival in honor of Ceres.

ce-re-al-ist (sē′rę-ąl-ist), *n.* One versed in the subject of cereals.

cer-e-bel-lum (ser-ę-bel′um), *n.*; pl. *-bellums*, L. *-bella* (-ą̈). [L., dim. of *cerebrum*, brain.] A dorsal portion of the brain, concerned with the coördination of movements, in man lying at the back of and below the cerebrum and consisting of two lateral lobes and a central lobe.—**cer-e-bel′lar** (-bel′ą̈r), *a.*

cer-e-bral (ser′ę-brąl). [NL. *cerebralis*.] **I.** *a.* Of or pertaining to the cerebrum or the brain; also, especially given to thinking; also, in *phonetics*, noting certain consonants, as in Sanskrit, pronounced by bringing the tip of the tongue backward and placing its under surface against the roof of the mouth. **II.** *n.* In *phonetics*, a cerebral consonant.—**cer′e-bral-ism,** *n.* The theory that all mental operations arise from the activity of the brain.

cer-e-brate (ser′ę-brāt), *v.*; *-brated, -brating.* [L. *cerebrum*, brain.] **I.** *intr.* To use the cerebrum or brain; experience brain-action. **II.** *tr.* To perform by brain-action.—**cer-e-bra′tion** (-brā′shǫn), *n.* The action (conscious or unconscious) of the cerebrum or brain.

cer-e-bric (ser′ę-brik), *a.* [L. *cerebrum*, brain.] Pertaining to or derived from the brain.

cer-e-bri-tis (ser-ę-brī′tis), *n.* [NL.] In *pathol.*, inflammation of the cerebrum.

cerebro-. Form of L. *cerebrum*, brain, used in combination.

cer-e-bro-spi-nal (ser″ę-brō-spī′nąl), *a.* [See *cerebro-*.] Pertaining to or affecting both the brain and the spinal cord.—**cerebrospinal fever,** or **epidemic cerebrospinal meningitis,** in *pathol.*, a dangerous, infectious, but non-contagious febrile disease characterized by inflammation of the meninges of the brain and spinal cord, and often by small red or purplish spots on the skin.—**cerebrospinal nervous system.** See *nervous system.*

cer-e-brum (ser′ę-brum), *n.*; pl. *-brums*, L. *-bra* (-brą̈). [L., brain.] The anterior and upper part of the brain, consisting of two hemispheres separated by a deep fissure and connected below by a broad band of fibers, and concerned with voluntary and conscious processes; also, more broadly, these two hemispheres together with other adjacent parts; the prosencephalon; the prosencephalon, thalamencephalon, and mesencephalon together.

cere-cloth (sēr′klôth), *n.* [Earlier *cered cloth*: see *cere, v.*] Waxed cloth, or a waxed cloth, used esp. for wrapping the dead.

cered (sērd), *a.* Of birds, having a cere.

cere-less (sēr′les), *a.* Of birds, having no cere.

cere-ment (sēr′mēnt), *n.* [See *cere, v.*] A cerecloth; any cloth for wrapping the dead: usually in *pl.*: as, "Tell Why thy canonized bones . . . Have burst their *cerements*" (Shakspere's "Hamlet," i. 4. 48).

cer-e-mo-ni-al (ser-ę-mō′ni-ąl). [LL. *cærimonialis*.] **I.** *a.* Pertaining to, marked by, or of the nature of ceremonies or ceremony; ritual; formal. **II.** *n.* A system of ceremonies, rites, or formalities prescribed for or observed on any particular occasion; a rite or ceremony; a formality, as of etiquette; the observance of ceremony; in the *Rom. Cath. Ch.*, the order for rites and ceremonies, or a book containing it.—**cer-e-mo′ni-al-ism,** *n.* Ceremonies collectively; adherence to or fondness for ceremonies, as in religion.—**cer-e-mo′ni-al-ist,** *n.* One adhering to or fond of ceremonies.—**cer-e-mo′ni-al-ly,** *adv.*—**cer-e-mo′ni-al-ness,** *n.*

cer-e-mo-ni-ous (ser-ę-mō′ni-us), *a.* [LL. *cærimoniosus*.] Pertaining to, marked by, or consisting of ceremony; formal (as, "The Puritans . . . rejected with contempt the *ceremonious* homage which other sects substituted for the pure worship of the soul": Macaulay's "Essays," Milton); carefully observant of ceremony, as persons; formally or elaborately polite.—**cer-e-mo′ni-ous-ly,** *adv.*—**cer-e-mo′ni-ous-ness,** *n.*

cer-e-mo-ny (ser′ę-mǫ-ni), *n.*; pl. *-nies* (-niz). [L. *cærimonia*, sacredness, reverence, sacred rite.] A formal religious or sacred observance; a solemn rite; also, any formal act or observance; an empty form (in disparagement); a usage of politeness or civility; also, formal observances or usages collectively; ceremonial observance; strict adherence to conventional forms; formality; also, a ceremonial symbol†; also, an omen†.

Ceres. — Wall-painting from Pompeii, in Museo Nazionale, Naples.

Ce-res (sē′rēz), *n.* [L.] An ancient Italian goddess of agriculture, under whose name the Romans adopted the worship of the Greek goddess Demeter. See *Demeter.*

ce-re-us (sē′rę-us), *n.* [L., wax candle, < *cera*, wax.] Any plant of the cactaceous genus *Cereus*, of the warmer parts of America, as *C. giganteus*, sometimes growing to a height of 50 or 60 feet, or *C. grandiflorus* ('night-blooming cereus'), bearing fragrant flowers opening at night.

ce-ri-a (sē'ri-ą), *n.* In *chem.*, cerium oxide: used in small percentages in incandescent mantles for gas-burners.

Ce-ri-a-li-a (sē-ri-ā'li-ą), *n. pl.* See *Cerealia.*

ce-ric (sē'rik), *a.* Of or containing cerium. See *cerous.*

ce-rif-er-ous (sē-rif'ẹ-rus), *a.* [L. *cera*, wax, + *ferre*, bear.] Producing wax.

cer-iph (ser'if), *n.* See *serif.*

ce-rise (sẹ-rēz'), *n.* [F.: see *cherry.*] A clear, bright red color with a pinkish tinge.

ce-rite (sē'rīt), *n.* A native hydrous silicate of cerium and other metals.

ce-ri-um (sē'ri-um), *n.* [NL.; from the asteroid *Ceres.*] Chem. sym., Ce; at. wt., 140.25; sp. gr., 6.7. A steel-gray, ductile metallic element, found only in combination.

Cereus (*C. giganteus*), the Giant Cactus.

cer-nu-ous (sėr'nū-us), *a.* [L. *cernuus*, stooping.] Drooping or bowing downward, as a flower or bud.

ce-ro (sē'rō), *n.*; pl. *-ros* (-rōz). [Sp. *sierra*, saw.] Either of two large fishes of the mackerel family, *Scomberomorus cavalla* and *S. regalis.*

cero-. Form of Gr. κηρός, wax, used in combination.—**ce-rog-ra-phy** (sẹ-rog'rą-fi), *n.* [Gr. κηρογραφία: see *-graphy.*] The art of writing or engraving on wax; also, encaustic painting.—**ce-ro-graph-ic** (sē-rọ-graf'ik), *a.*—**ce-rog'ra-phist,** *n.*—**ce-ro-plas'tic** (-plas'tik), *a.* [Gr. κηροπλαστικός (πλάσσειν, form).] Of or pertaining to modeling in wax; also, modeled in wax.—**ce'ro-type** (-tīp), *n.* [+ *-type.*] A process of engraving in which the design or the like is cut on a wax-coated metal plate, from which a printing surface is subsequently produced by stereotyping or by electrotyping.

ce-rous (sē'rus), *a.* Containing cerium (in larger proportion than a corresponding ceric compound).

-cerous. Adjective termination from Gr. κέρας, horn, as in *decacerous.*

cer-tain (sėr'tąn), *a.* [OF. F. *certain*, < L. *certus*, fixed, certain, pp. of *cernere*, separate, distinguish, decide, akin to Gr. κρίνειν: see *crisis, critic.*] Fixed, settled, or determined (as, a day *certain*); exact or precise (archaic); definite or particular, but not named or specified (as, a *certain* person; *certain* persons: sometimes used pronominally, as, *certain* of them); also, that may be depended on; trustworthy; unfailing; unerring; inevitable; also, established as true or sure; unquestionable; indisputable; also, having no doubt; confident; assured; also, sure (with an infinitive: as, *certain* to happen).—**cer'tain-ly,** *adv.* With certainty; without doubt; without fail.—**cer'tain-ness,** *n.*—**cer'tain-ty** (-ti), *n.*; pl. *-ties* (-tiz). The state of being certain; also, something certain; an assured fact.

cer-tes (sėr'tez), *adv.* [OF. F. *certes*, < L. *certus*: see *certain.*] Certainly; verily; in truth: as, "*Certes*, Madame, ye have great cause of plaint" (Spenser's "Faerie Queene," i. 7. 52). [Archaic.]

cer-ti-fi-a-ble (sėr'ti-fī-ą-bl), *a.* Capable of being certified.

cer-tif-i-cate (sėr-tif'i-kąt), *n.* [ML. *certificatum*, neut. of *certificatus*, pp. of *certificare*: see *certify.*] A writing or paper certifying to the truth of something, or to status, qualifications, privileges, etc.; a document making formal certification; hence, anything that certifies, attests, or warrants.—**certificate of deposit,** a written acknowledgment of a bank that it has received from the person named a specified sum of money as a deposit: it is a negotiable instrument.—**gold** or **silver certificate,** a certificate, issued by the U. S. government and circulating as money, bearing a statement that gold or silver to a specified amount has been deposited in the Treasury for its redemption.—**cer-tif'i-cate** (-kāt), *v. t.*; *-cated, -cating.* To attest by a certificate; also, to furnish with or authorize by a certificate.

cer-ti-fi-ca-tion (sėr"ti-fi-kā'shọn), *n.* [ML. *certificatio(n-)*, < *certificare*: see *certify.*] The act of certifying, or the state of being certified; attestation; assurance; formal notice; also, that which certifies.—**cer-tif'i-ca-to-ry** (-tif'i-ką-tọ-ri), *a.* Giving certification.

cer-ti-fy (sėr'ti-fī), *v.*; *-fied, -fying.* [OF. F. *certifier*, < ML. *certificare*, < L. *certus*, certain, + *facere*, make.] **I.** *tr.* To guarantee as certain; give certain or reliable information of; vouch for; also, to testify to or vouch for in writing; specif., of a bank (or one of its officials), to mark (a check drawn upon it) as guaranteed to be good; also, to assure or inform (a person) with certainty. **II.** *intr.* To give warrant or assurance; testify (*to*); vouch (*for*).—**cer'ti-fi-er** (-fī-ėr), *n.*

cer-ti-o-ra-ri (sėr"shi-ọ-rā'rī), *n.* [L., 'to be informed' (lit. 'made more certain').] In *law*, a writ issuing from a superior court to call up the record of a proceeding in an inferior court for trial or review in the superior one.

cer-ti-tude (sėr'ti-tūd), *n.* [LL. *certitudo.*] Certainty.

ce-ru-le-an (sẹ-rö'lẹ-ąn), *a.* [L. *cæruleus.*] Blue; sky-blue; azure.

ce-ru-men (sẹ-rö'mẹn), *n.* [NL., < L. *cera*, wax.] Ear-wax.—**ce-ru'mi-nous** (-mi-nus), *a.*

ce-ruse (sē'rös or sẹ-rös'), *n.* [OF. *ceruze* (F. *céruse*), < L. *cerussa.*] White lead, or a cosmetic containing it.

ce-rus-site (sē'rọ-sīt), *n.* [L. *cerussa*, white lead: cf. *ceruse.*] A mineral consisting of carbonate of lead, in orthorhombic crystals or massive or fibrous, with an adamantine luster, and forming an important ore of lead.

cer-ve-lat (ser-vė-lä), *n.* [F. *cervelat* (now *cervelas*), < It. *cervellata*, kind of sausage containing hogs' brains, < *cervello*, brain, < L. *cerebellum*: see *cerebellum.*] A kind of highly seasoned, dry sausage, orig. made of brains but now usually of young pork salted; saveloy.

cer-vi-cal (sėr'vi-kąl), *a.* Pertaining to the cervix or neck.

cer-vine (sėr'vin), *a.* [L. *cervinus*, < *cervus*, deer.] Pertaining to deer; deer-like; also, of a deep tawny color.

cer-vix (sėr'viks), *n.*; pl. *-vixes* or *-vices* (-vi-sēz). [L.] The neck, esp. the back of the neck; also, any neck-like part.

cer-void (sėr'void), *a.* [L. *cervus*, deer: see *-oid.*] Deer-like.

ces-pi-tose (ses'pi-tōs), *a.* [L. *cæspes* (*cæspit-*), turf.] Matted like turf; growing in dense tufts. Also **ces'pi-tous.**—**ces'pi-tose-ly,** *adv.*

cess (ses), *v. t.* [Prop. *sess*, for *assess.*] To assess.—**cess,** *n.* A tax or rate; also, estimation†.

ces-sa-tion (se-sā'shọn), *n.* [L. *cessatio(n-)*, < *cessare*: see *cease.*] A ceasing; discontinuance; pause; stop.

ces-sion (sesh'ọn), *n.* [L. *cessio(n-)*, < *cedere*: see *cede.*] The act of ceding; a making over, as by treaty; also, something, as a tract of territory, ceded.—**ces'sion-a-ry** (-ą-ri), *a.* and *n.*

cess=pipe (ses'pīp), *n.* A pipe for carrying off drainage from a cesspool, sink, or the like.

cess-pool (ses'pöl), *n.* [Origin uncertain.] A cistern, well, or pit for retaining the sediment of a drain or for receiving the filth of a water-closet, etc.; fig., any receptacle of filth.

cest (sest), *n.* Same as *cestus*[1]. [Obs. or archaic.]

ces-tode (ses'tōd). [NL. *Cestoda*, pl., < Gr. κεστός, girdle: see *cestus*[1].] **I.** *a.* Belonging to the *Cestoda*, a class or group of internally parasitic platyhelminths or flatworms, including the tapeworms, etc. **II.** *n.* A cestode platyhelminth.

ces-toid (ses'toid). [Gr. κεστός, girdle: see *-oid.*] **I.** *a.* Of worms, girdle-shaped or tapeworm-like; cestode; sometimes, noting or pertaining to the adult as distinguished from the larval state of a tapeworm. **II.** *n.* A cestoid worm; a cestode.

ces-tui (ses'twẹ or set'i), *pron.* [OF.] In *law*, he; the person.—**cestui que trust** (kẹ trust), the beneficiary of a trust.—**cestui que use** (ūs), one entitled to a use, or the benefit of property the legal title to which is vested in another.

ces-tus[1] (ses′tus̜), *n.* [L., < Gr. κεστός, girdle, lit. 'stitched,' < κεντεῖν, prick, stitch.] In *Gr.* and *Rom. antiq.*, a belt or girdle; esp., the girdle of Aphrodite or Venus, which was said to be decorated with everything that could awaken love.

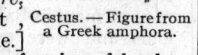

Forms of Cestus.

Cestus.—Figure from a Greek amphora.

ces-tus[2] (ses′-tus), *n.* [L. *cæstus*, < *cædere*, cut, strike.] In *Rom. antiq.*, a hand-covering made of strips of leather, sometimes loaded with metal, worn by boxers.

ce-su-ra (sẹ̄-ẕū′rạ̈), etc. See *cæsura*, etc.

ce-ta-cean (sẹ̄-tā′shiạn). [NL. *Cetacea*, pl., < L. *cetus*, < Gr. κῆτος, whale.] **I.** *a.* Belonging to the *Cetacea*, an order of aquatic, chiefly marine, mammals including the whales, dolphins, porpoises, etc. **II.** *n.* A cetacean animal.—**ce-ta′ceous** (-shius), *a.* Of the whale kind.

ce-tol-o-gy (sẹ̄-tol′ọ̄-ji), *n.* [Gr. κῆτος, whale: see *-logy*.] The science that treats of whales.

Cey-lon-ese (sē-lon-ēs′ or -ēz′). **I.** *a.* Of or pertaining to Ceylon, a large island lying to the south of India. **II.** *n.*; pl. *-ese*. A native or inhabitant of Ceylon, esp. a member of its principal native race; a Singhalese.

c. g. s. sys′tem. See *centimeter-gram-second system*, under *centimeter*.

chab-a-zite, chab-a-site (kab′ạ-zīt, -sīt), *n.* [From an erroneous form of Gr. χαλάζιος, kind of stone, < χάλαζα, hail.] A mineral, a hydrous silicate, essentially of aluminium and calcium, occurring in transparent to translucent crystals varying in color from white to yellow and red.

Cha-blis (shȧ-blē), *n.* [From *Chablis*, town in north-central France.] A French white wine of the Burgundy class.

cha-bouk, cha-buk (chä′bu̇k), *n.* [Pers. and Hind. *chābuk*: cf. *sjambok*.] A horsewhip: often used in the East for inflicting corporal punishment.

chac-ma (chak′mạ̈), *n.* [Hottentot.] A large South African baboon, *Papio* (or *Cynocephalus*) *porcarius*, about the size of a mastiff.

cha-conne (shȧ-kon), *n.* [F., < Sp. *chacona*.] An old-time dance, probably of Spanish origin, or music for it.

chæ-ta (kē′tạ̈), *n.*; pl. *-tæ* (-tē). [NL., < Gr. χαίτη, hair.] In *zoöl.*, a bristle or seta, esp. of a chætopod.

chæto-. Form of Gr. χαίτη, hair, used in combination.

chæ-to-dont (kē′tọ̄-dont), *n.* [NL. *Chætodon*, < Gr. χαίτη, hair, + ὀδούς (ὀδοντ-), tooth.] Any of the small or moderate-sized tropical acanthopterygian marine fishes constituting the family *Chætodontidæ*, and esp. the genus *Chætodon*, generally remarkable for their brilliant coloring: so called on account of their bristle-like teeth.

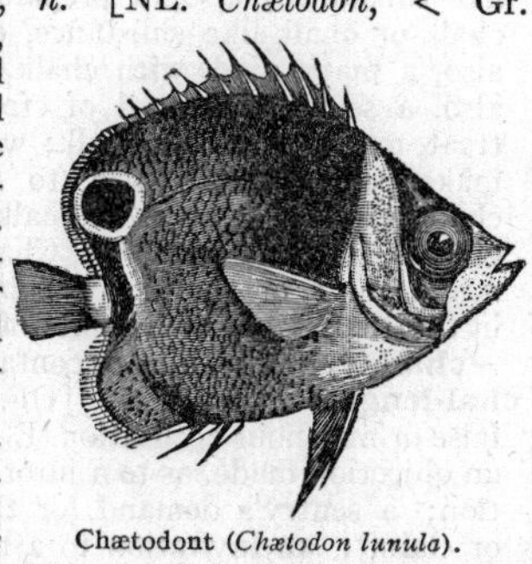

Chætodont (*Chætodon lunula*).

chæ-tog-nath (kē′tog-nath), *n.* [NL. *Chætognatha*, pl., < Gr. χαίτη, hair, + γνάθος, jaw.] Any of the *Chætognatha*, a class or group of small, transparent, arrow-shaped, (chiefly) marine worms.—**chæ-tog-na-thous** (kẹ̄-tog′nạ-thus), *a.*

chæ-to-pod (kē′tọ̄-pod), *n.* [NL. *Chætopoda*, pl., < Gr. χαίτη, hair, + πούς (ποδ-), foot.] Any of the *Chætopoda*, a class or group of annelids having the body made up of more or less similar segments provided with muscular processes bearing setæ.—**chæ-top-o-dous** (kẹ̄-top′ọ̄-dus), *a.*

chafe (chāf), *v.*; *chafed, chafing.* [OF. *chaufer* (F. *chauffer*), < L. *calefacere*, make hot: see *calefacient*.] **I.** *tr.* To heat† or warm†; now, to warm by rubbing; also, to wear or abrade by friction; also, to irritate or annoy. **II.** *intr.* To rub; press with friction; also, to become worn or injured by friction; also, to fret or fume with irritation.—**chafe,** *n.* Heat or wear, as from friction; also, fret; irritation.—

chaf-er[1] (chā′fėr), *n.* A chafing-dish†; a small portable furnace.

cha-fer[2] (chā′fėr), *n.* [AS. *ceafor* = G. *käfer*.] Any of various beetles of the family *Scarabæidæ*, as a cockchafer.

Melancholy Sap-chafer (*Euphoria melancholica*).

chaff[1] (chȧf), *n.* [AS. *ceaf* = D. *kaf* = G. *kaff*.] The husks of grains and grasses separated from the seed; also, straw cut small for fodder; fig., worthless matter; refuse; in *bot.*, the scales or bracts which subtend the florets in the heads of many composite plants.

chaff[2] (chȧf), *v.* [Prob. var. of *chafe*.] **I.** *tr.* To banter; rally; tease. **II.** *intr.* To use bantering language.—**chaff**[2], *n.* Banter; raillery.—**chaff′er**[1], *n.*

chaf-fer[2] (chaf′ėr), *n.* [ME. *chaffare*, < AS. *cēap*, trade, + *faru*, a going.] Bargaining; haggling; also, merchandise†. —**chaf′fer**[2], *v.* **I.** *intr.* To bargain; haggle; also, to bandy words. **II.** *tr.* To traffic in; barter; also, to bandy (words).—**chaf′fer-er,** *n.*

chaf-finch (chaf′inch), *n.* [See *chaff*[1].] A common European finch, *Fringilla cœlebs*, with a pleasant short song: often kept as a cage-bird.

Chaffinch.

chaff-weed (chȧf′-wēd), *n.* A low primulaceous herb, *Centunculus minimus*.

chaff-y (chȧf′i), *a.* Of, like, or containing chaff; fig., worthless.

chaf-ing=dish (chā′fing-dish), *n.* A vessel to hold charcoal, etc., for heating anything placed over it; also, an apparatus consisting of a metal dish with a lamp or heating appliance beneath it, for cooking food or keeping it hot.

chaft (chȧft), *n.* [Cf. Icel. *kjaptr*, mouth, jaw, and E. *jowl*[1].] The jaw; *pl.*, the chaps. [North. Eng. and Sc.]

cha-grin (shạ-grin′), *n.* [F., < OF. *chagrin*, troubled, vexed; origin unknown. F. *chagrin*, shagreen, is appar. a later and different word.] Trouble† or worry†; also, a feeling of vexation and disappointment or humiliation; mortification. —**cha-grin′,** *v. t.*; *-grined, -grining.* To affect with chagrin; mortify.

chain (chān), *n.* [OF. *chaeine* (F. *chaîne*), < L. *catena*, chain: cf. *catena*.] A connected series of metal or other links for various uses, as for connecting, supporting, drawing, confining, restraining, etc., or for ornament; fig., something that binds or restrains; *pl.*, bonds or fetters; imprisonment or bondage; *sing.*, a series of things connected or following in succession; a range of mountains; in *weaving*, the warp; in *surv.*, a measuring instrument consisting of 100 wire rods or links, each 7.92 inches long ('Gunter's chain'), or one foot long; the length of such an instrument, 66 feet or 100 feet; in *mech.*, a combination of two or more kinematic links ('kinematic chain'); *naut.*, one of the plates or bars of iron bolted to a ship's side in order to hold the deadeyes which secure the shrouds; *pl.*, the channels, which spread the shrouds.—**chain,** *v. t.* To fasten or secure with or as with a chain; fetter; confine or restrain; enslave. —**chain′=bridge,** *n.* A suspension-bridge supported by chains.—**chain′=gang,** *n.* A gang, as of convicts, chained

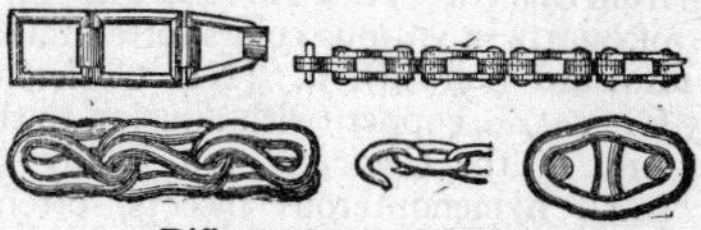

Different forms of Chains.

together while in transit, during outdoor labor, etc.—**chain′less,** *a.* Without a chain; unfettered.—**chain′let,** *n.* A little chain.—**chain′=light′ning,** *n.* Lightning visible in wavy, zigzag, or broken lines.—**chain′=mail,** *n.* A kind of flexible armor composed of rings of metal interlinked as in a chain but extended in width as well as in length.—**chain′man** (-mạn), *n.*; pl. *-men.* A man who carries the chain in surveying.—**chain′=pump,** *n.* A pump in which the water is raised by an endless chain fitted with disks, buckets, or the like.—**chain′=shot,** *n.* A shot consisting of two balls or half-balls connected by a short chain.—**chain′=stitch,** *n.* A kind of stitching (by hand or by sewing-machine) in which each stitch forms a loop through the forward end of which the next (new) stitch is taken.—**chain′=wale,** *n. Naut.*, same as *channel*[1].—**chain′=work,** *n.* Work linked or looped together in the manner of a chain; decorative work resembling chains.

Suit of Chain-mail (about 1200). — *A*, hood of leather under conical helmet; *B*, camail of chain-mail secured to hood.

Chain-shot.

chair (chãr), *n.* [OF. *chaiere* (F. *chaire*), < L. *cathedra*: see *cathedra*.] A seat with a back, and often arms, usually for one person; a seat of office or authority, or the office itself; the person occupying the seat or office, esp. the chairman of a meeting; a sedan-chair; a chaise†; a metal block or clutch to support and secure a rail in a railroad.—**chair,** *v. t.* To place or seat in a chair; install in a chair of office; also, to place in a chair and carry aloft, as in triumph; also, to furnish with a chair or chairs.—**chair′=car,** *n.* A railroad passenger-car fitted with chairs (instead of double seats).—**chair′man** (-mạn), *n.*; pl. *-men.* The presiding officer of a meeting, committee, etc.; also, one employed to carry or wheel a person in a chair.—**chair′man-ship,** *n.*—**chair′wom″an,** *n.*; pl. *-women* (-wim″en). A female presiding officer, as of a meeting or committee.

chaise (shāz), *n.* [F. *chaise*, chair, chaise, var. of *chaire*: see *chair*.] A light open carriage, usually with a hood, esp. a one-horse, two-wheeled carriage for two persons; also, a post-chaise.

chaise longue (shāz lôṅg). [F., 'long chair.'] A kind of reclining-chair with the seat prolonged forward.

cha-la-za (ka-lā′zạ̈), *n.*; pl. *-zæ* (-zē). [NL., < Gr. χάλαζα, hail, lump.] In *bot.*, the point of an ovule or seed where the integuments are united to the central mass of tissue; in *zoöl.*, either of the two spiral albuminous cords passing through the white of a bird's egg, holding the yolk in place by binding it to the lining membrane at the ends of the shell.—**cha-la′zal,** *a.*

chal-ced-o-ny (kal-sed′ọ-ni or kal′sē-dọ-ni), *n.*; pl. *-nies* (-niz). [L. *chalcedonius*, < Gr. χαλκηδών; appar. named from *Chalcedon*, town in Asia Minor.] A translucent variety of quartz in various colors, often milky or grayish.

chal-cid (kal′sid), *n.* [NL. *Chalcidæ* (also *Chalcididæ*), < Gr. χαλκός, copper (with allusion to the metallic coloration).] Any of the *Chalcididæ*, a family or group of small hymenopterous insects, often of bright metallic colors, whose larvæ are mostly parasitic on the larvæ and pupæ of other insects.—**chal-cid′i-an,** *a.* and *n.*

Chalcid. (Line shows natural size.)

chalco-. Form of Gr. χαλκός, copper, brass, used in combination.

chal-co-cite (kal′kọ-sīt), *n.* [Gr. χαλκός, copper.] Native sulphide of copper, a mineral of a dark-gray to black color with a metallic luster, occurring massive or in crystals, and forming an important ore of copper.

chal-cog-ra-phy (kal-kog′rạ-fi), *n.* [See *chalco-* and *-graphy*.] The art of engraving on copper or brass, esp. for printing.—**chal-cog′ra-pher,** *n.*—**chal-co-graph′ic, chal-co-graph′i-cal** (-kọ-graf′ik, -i-kạl), *a.*

chal-co-py-rite (kal-kọ-pī′rīt), *n.* [See *chalco-* and *pyrites*.] Native sulphide of copper and iron, a yellow mineral with a metallic luster, occurring massive and in crystals, and forming an important ore of copper.

chal-co-stib-ite (kal-kọ-stib′īt), *n.* [See *chalco-* and *stibium*.] A native sulphide of copper and antimony.

Chal-da-ic (kal-dā′ik). [L. *Chaldaicus*.] **I.** *a.* Pertaining to ancient Chaldea (southern Babylonia). **II.** *n.* The (Semitic) language of Chaldea.

Chal-de-an (kal-dē′ạn). [L. *Chaldæus*.] **I.** *a.* Of or belonging to ancient Chaldea (southern Babylonia); also, pertaining to astrology, occult learning, etc. **II.** *n.* An inhabitant of Chaldea; one of an ancient Semitic people that formed the dominant element in Babylonia and were celebrated as warriors, astrologers, magicians, etc.; hence, one versed in astrology, occult learning, etc.; an astrologer, soothsayer, or seer. See Dan. ii. 2.—**Chal′dee** (-dē). **I.** *a.* Chaldean. **II.** *n.* A Chaldean; also, Chaldaic.

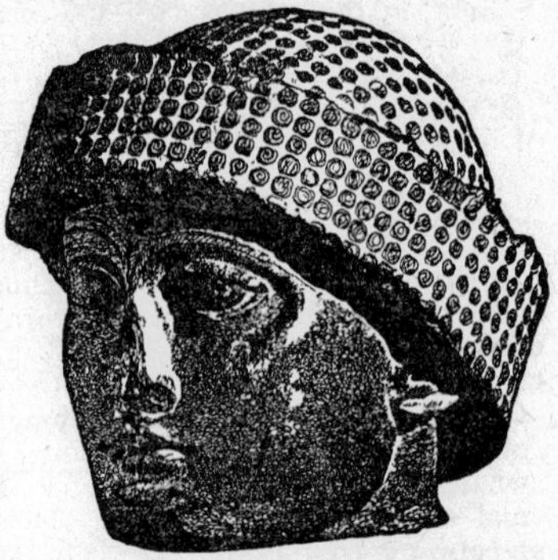
Chaldean Art. — Sculptured head from Tello (Lagash), in the Louvre.

chal-dron (châl′drọn), *n.* [OF. *chauderon*, kettle, = E. *caldron*.] An old English dry measure for coal, coke, lime, etc., commonly equal to 32 bushels or 36 bushels, but varying with commodity and locality.

chal-et (shal′ā, F. shȧ-lā), *n.* [F. (Swiss).] A herdsman's hut in the Swiss mountains; also, a kind of cottage, low and with wide eaves, common in Alpine regions, esp. in Switzerland; hence, any cottage or villa built in this style.

chal-ice (chal′is), *n.* [OF. *chalice* (F. *calice*), < L. *calix*, cup.] A drinking-cup (poetic); specif., a cup for the wine of the eucharist or mass; also, a cup-like blossom (as, "Saffron crocus in whose *chalice* bright A cool libation hoarded for the noon Is kept": Hood's "Midsummer Fairies," xxxvii.).—**chal′iced,** *a.* Contained in a chalice or cup; of flowers, having a cup-like blossom.

Chalice, from Treasury in Mainz Cathedral.

chalk (châk), *n.* [AS. *cealc*, < L. *calx*, lime.] A soft limestone, usually white or yellowish, consisting chiefly of the shells of foraminifers; also, some chalk-like substance; also, a preparation or a prepared piece of chalk or chalk-like substance, esp. for marking; a crayon; also, a mark made with chalk, as in keeping an account; also, a score, or record of credit given.—**chalk,** *v. t.* To treat, mix, or rub with chalk; whiten with chalk; hence, to make pale; blanch; also, to mark, write, or draw with chalk; record in or as in chalk (esp. an account of credit given).—**chalk′i-ness,** *n.* Chalky quality.—**chalk′stone,** *n.* A mass of chalk; in *pathol.*, a chalk-like concretion in the tissues or small joints of persons affected with gout.—**chalk′y,** *a.* Of, like, or containing chalk.

chal-lenge (chal′enj), *n.* [OF. *chalenge*, < L. *calumnia*, false or malicious accusation, E. *calumny*.] An accusation†; an objection made, as to a juror or a vote; a calling in question; a sentry's demand for the countersign; a demand† or claim†; an invitation to a trial or contest of any kind; a summons to fight, esp. in a duel.—**chal′lenge,** *v. t.*; *-lenged, -lenging.* [OF. *chalengier*, < L. *calumniari*, E. *calumniate*.] To accuse†; also, to take formal exception to (a juror, vote, etc.); call in question (as, to *challenge* the wisdom of a measure); also, to call on (a person) to account for himself; demand the countersign from, as a sentinel does; also, to lay claim to (archaic); have a claim to in virtue of qualities or character (as, a matter which *challenges* attention); also, to invite or summon to a trial or contest of any kind; dare; defy; hence, to invite (competition, criticism, etc.); specif., to summon to fight, esp. to a duel (as, "Whosoe'er gainsays King Edward's right . . . I *challenge* him to single fight": Shakspere's "3 Henry VI.," iv. 7. 75).—**chal′lenge-a-ble,** *a.* That may be challenged.—**chal′len-ger,** *n.*

chal-lie (shal′i), *n.* See *challis.*

chal-lis (shal′i), *n.* [F.; origin uncertain.] A light-weight dress-fabric, orig. of silk and wool, but now commonly of wool, plain-woven, and either plain or printed.

cha-lu-meau (shȧ-lü-mō), *n.*; pl. *-meaux* (-mōz, F. -mō). [F., < LL. *calamellus,* dim. of L. *calamus,* reed.] An obsolete musical instrument of the clarinet type; also, the shawm; also, the lowest register of the clarinet.

Chal-y-be-an (kal-i-bē′ạn), *a.* [L. *Chalybes,* < Gr. Χάλυβες, pl. of Χάλυψ, one of the people called Chalybes, the same word as χάλυψ, steel: cf. *chalybeate.*] Of or pertaining to the Chalybes, an ancient people of Pontus in Asia Minor famed as workers in iron and steel: as, "*Chalybean* temper'd steel, and frock of mail Adamantean proof" (Milton's "Samson Agonistes," 133).

cha-lyb-e-ate (kạ-lib′ẹ-āt). [L. *chalybs,* < Gr. χάλυψ, steel: cf. *Chalybean.*] **I.** *a.* Containing or impregnated with salts of iron, as a mineral spring; pertaining to water, medicine, etc., containing iron. **II.** *n.* A chalybeate water, medicine, or the like.

chal-y-bite (kal′i-bīt), *n.* [L. *chalybs*: see *chalybeate.*] A mineral consisting of a carbonate of iron; siderite.

cham (kam), *n.* An old form of *khan*²: as, the great *Cham* of Tartary, or of Cathay. See Shakspere's "Much Ado about Nothing," ii. 1. 277.

cha-made (shạ-mäd′), *n.* [F., < It. *chiamata,* < L. *clamare,* cry out.] *Milit.,* a signal by drum or trumpet, inviting to a parley.

cha-mæ-le-on (kạ-mē′lẹ-ọn), *n.* See *chameleon.*

cham-ber (chām′bėr), *n.* [OF. F. *chambre,* < L. *camera*: see *camera.*] A room or apartment, usually a private room, and esp. a bedroom; a reception-room in a palace, etc.; *pl.,* rooms for residence in the house or building of another; apartments; rooms for offices, etc., as of lawyers; any place out of court where a judge settles minor or urgent questions of procedure; *sing.,* the hall of meeting of a legislative or other assembly; a legislative, judicial, or other like body (as, the upper or the lower *chamber* of a legislature; a *chamber* of commerce, a board or association organized to protect and promote the commercial interests of a city, etc.; the Imperial *Chamber* of the old German Empire, see under *imperial*); also, the place where the moneys due a government, etc., are received and kept; a treasury or chamberlain's office; also, a compartment or inclosed space; a cavity; that part of the barrel of a gun which receives the charge; any of the receptacles for cartridges in the cylinder of a revolver, etc.; also, a chamber vessel.—**cham′ber,** *v.* **I.** *tr.* To put or inclose in or as in a chamber; furnish with a chamber, as a gun; form into a chamber or hollow. **II.** *intr.* To reside in or occupy a chamber.—**cham′ber=con″cert,** *n.* A concert of chamber-music.—**cham′bered,** *a.* Having a chamber or chambers (as, a many-*chambered* mansion); divided into compartments (as, "The *Chambered* Nautilus," the title of a poem by Oliver Wendell Holmes).—**cham′ber-er,** *n.* A chambermaid†; also, a chamberlain† or valet†; also, one who frequents ladies' chambers or society (archaic: as, "You bid me turn a *chamberer,* To pick up gloves, and fans, and knitting-needles," Byron's "Werner," iv. 1).

cham-ber-lain (chām′bėr-lạn), *n.* [OF. *chamberlenc* (F. *chambellan*), < OHG. *chamarlinc,* < L. *camera,* E. *chamber.*] One who attends on a king or nobleman in his bedchamber (archaic), or in his private apartments (sometimes a title conferred as an honor, as to indicate close relationship); also, an important officer charged, among other duties, with the direction and management of a sovereign's private apartments; also, a person having charge of a treasure-chamber; an officer who receives rents and revenues, as of a municipal corporation; a treasurer; also, the factor or high steward of a nobleman; also, an attendant at an inn, in charge of the bedchambers (obs. or archaic: as, "But Guilt was my grim *Chamberlain* That lighted me to bed," Hood's "Dream of Eugene Aram," 141).—**cham′ber-lain-ship,** *n.* The office or dignity of a chamberlain.

cham-ber-maid (chām′bėr-mād), *n.* A female servant who takes care of bedchambers; also, a lady's-maid†.

Chambranle. — North door of the Erechtheum, Athens.

cham-ber=mu-sic (chām′bėr-mū″zik), *n.* Music suited for performance in a small room: commonly applied to concerted music for solo instruments.

Cham-ber-tin (shäṅ-ber-taṅ), *n.* A choice French red wine of the Burgundy class.

cham-branle (shäṅ-bräṅl), *n.* [F.; origin uncertain.] In *arch.,* a frame-like decoration around the sides and top of a door, window, fireplace, or the like.

cham-bray (sham′brā), *n.* [Cf. *cambric.*] A fine variety of gingham, commonly plain but with the warp and weft of different colors.

cha-me-le-on (kạ-mē′lẹ-ọn), *n.* [L. *chamæleon,* < Gr. χαμαιλέων, < χαμαί, on the ground, + λέων, lion.] Any of a group of old-world lizards, esp. of the genus *Chamæleon,* characterized by a laterally compressed body, a prehensile tail, and esp. by the power of changing the color of the skin; any of various small American lizards having the power of changing color; fig., something likened to a chameleon, as an inconstant person.—**cha-me-le-on′ic** (-on′ik), *a.* Like a chameleon; changeable; inconstant; fickle.

Chameleon (*Chamæleon vulgaris*).

cham-fer (cham′fėr), *v. t.* [OF. F. *chanfraindre,* < OF. *chant,* side, + *fraindre,* < L. *frangere,* break.] To groove or channel (wood, stone, etc.); also, to cut obliquely at the edge or corner; bevel.—**cham′fer,** *n.* A groove or furrow, as in wood, etc.; also, an oblique surface produced by cutting away an edge or corner.

cham-fron (cham′frọn), *n.* [OF. *chanfrain* (F. *chanfrein*); origin unknown.] Armor for the front of a horse's head.

cham-ois (sham′i, F. shȧ-mwo), *n.*; pl. *chamois* (sham′iz or, esp. collectively, of the animals, sham′i, F. shȧ-mwo). [F.; prob. from Teut. (cf. G. *gemse*).] An agile goat-like antelope, *Rupicapra tragus,* of high mountains of Europe and southwestern Asia; also, a soft, pliable leather made from various skins dressed with oil (esp. fish-oil), orig. prepared from the skin of the chamois.—**cham-ois** (sham′i), *v. t.* To prepare or dress in the manner of chamois leather.

Chamois.

cham-o-mile (kam′ọ-mīl), *n.* See *camomile.*

Cha-mor-ro (chạ-mor′ō). **I.** *n.*; pl. *Chamorros* (-ōz). A member of the native race of Guam and the Mariana (or Ladrone) Islands (in the Pacific Ocean east of the Philippines), of Micronesian (Malayo-Polynesian) stock with strong Filipino and Spanish admixture; also, the language of this race. **II.** *a.* Of or pertaining to the Chamorros or their language.

champ (champ), *v.* [Origin uncertain; perhaps from Scand.] **I.** *tr.* To crush with the teeth and chew vigorously or noisily; munch; also, to bite upon, esp. impatiently, as a horse its bit; also, to crush, mash, or trample (Sc. and north. Eng.). **II.** *intr.* To make vigorous chewing or biting movements with the jaws and teeth.—**champ,** *n.* An act of champing.

cham'pac, *n.* See *champak.*

cham-pagne (sham-pān'), *n.* [From *Champagne*, a former province in northeastern France.] An effervescent wine, usually white, made in Champagne, France, or elsewhere; also, a pale brownish-yellow color.

cham-paign (sham-pān' or cham'pān). [OF. *champaigne*, < ML. *campania*: see *campaign.*] **I.** *n.* Level, open country; a plain. **II.** *a.* Level and open.

cham-pak (cham'pak), *n.* [Hind.] An East Indian tree, *Michelia champaca*, of the magnolia family, with fragrant golden flowers and a handsome wood used for making images, furniture, etc.

cham-per-ty (cham'pėr-ti), *n.* [OF. *champart*, share of the produce of land, < L. *campus*, field, + *pars* (*part-*), part.] In *law*, an illegal proceeding whereby a party not otherwise interested in a suit aids a plaintiff or defendant in consideration of a share of the matter in suit in case of success.—**cham'per-tor,** *n.*—**cham'per-tous,** *a.*

cham-pi-gnon (shäṅ-pē-nyôṅ), *n.* [F., ult. < L. *campus*, field.] A mushroom.

cham-pi-on (cham'pi-ọn), *n.* [OF. F. *champion*, < ML. *campio(n-)*, < L. *campus*, field.] A fighter or warrior, esp. one who fought in single combat in behalf of another; one who fights for or defends any person or cause; one who holds first place in any sport, etc., having defeated all opponents; anything that takes first place in competition.—**seven champions of Christendom.** See under *seven, a.*—**cham'pi-on,** *a.* First among all contestants or competitors; unexcelled or first-rate (colloq.).—**cham'pi-on,** *v. t.* To challenge† or defy†; defend as a champion.—**cham'pi-on-ess,** *n.* A female champion.—**cham'pi-on-less,** *a.* Without a champion.—**cham'pi-on-ship,** *n.* The position of a champion; advocacy or defense; the honor of being champion, or holding the first place for success in competition.

champ-le-vé (shamp-lẹ-vā', F. shäṅ-lė-vā). [F., pp. of *champlever*, < *champ*, field, ground, + *lever*, raise, remove.] **I.** *a.* Of enameled work, having the ground cut out or depressed in places to receive the enamel. **II.** *n.* Champlevé work, or the process of producing it.

chance (chȧns), *n.* [OF. *cheance* (F. *chance*), < ML. *cadentia*, a falling: see *cadence.*] The befalling or happening of events; a happening of things in a particular way; a fortuitous event; a mishap (archaic); one's lot or fortune† (as, "if it be thy *chance* to kill me": Shakspere's "Twelfth Night," iii. 4. 177); an opportunity (as, now is your *chance*); a possibility or probability of anything happening (as, the *chances* are against his success); a risk or hazard; absence of design or cause in the occurrence of events, often viewed as a real agency (as, "the slaves of *chance*": Shakspere's "Winter's Tale," iv. 4. 551); in the game of hazard, a throw of the dice which neither wins nor loses when first thrown (see *hazard*).—**the main chance.** See under *main*², *a.*—**chance,** *a.* Due to chance; casual.—**chance,** *v.*; *chanced, chancing.* **I.** *intr.* To happen or occur by chance; also, to come by chance (*on* or *upon*). **II.** *tr.* To take the chances or risks of; risk. [Colloq.]—**chance'-ful,** *a.* Marked by chance; uncertain; perilous; eventful.

chan-cel (chȧn'sẹl), *n.* [OF. *chancel*, < ML. *cancellus*, chancel, < L. *cancelli*, pl., bars, lattice.] The space about the altar of a church, usually inclosed, reserved for the clergy and other officials.

chan-cel-le-ry (chȧn'sẹ-lẹ-ri), *n.*; pl. *-ries* (-riz). [OF. *chancelerie* (F. *chancellerie*), < *chancelier*: see *chancellor.*] The position of a chancellor; the office or department of a chancellor; the office attached to an embassy, etc.; the building or room occupied by a chancellor's department.

chan-cel-lor (chȧn'sẹ-lọr), *n.* [OF. F. *chancelier*, < LL. *cancellarius*, orig. an officer stationed at the bars inclosing a tribunal, < L. *cancelli*, bars, lattice.] A secretary, as of a king, nobleman, or embassy; the title of various high officials, as in Great Britain the highest judicial officer of the crown ('lord high chancellor') and the highest finance minister ('chancellor of the Exchequer'), and in certain other European countries the chief minister of state; the head of certain universities; a judge, esp. the presiding judge, of a court of chancery (U. S.).—**chan'cel-lor-ship,** *n.*—**chan'cel-lor-y,** *n.* Same as *chancellery.*

chance-med-ley (chȧns'med'li), *n.* [AF. *chance medlee*, 'mixed chance.'] In *law*, accident or casualty not purely accidental, as in case of unpremeditated manslaughter. Also fig.

chan-ce-ry (chȧn'sẹ-ri), *n.*; pl. *-ries* (-riz). [Contr. of *chancellery.*] The office or department of a chancellor; the building or room occupied by a chancellor's department; a chancellery; esp., the court of the lord high chancellor of England, now a division of the High Court of Justice; also, a court of equity in the U. S., etc.; also, equity; litigation in a court of chancery or equity; fig., a position of helplessness or embarrassment (in the phrase 'in chancery,' as, in pugilism, of a contestant's head when held under his opponent's arm: slang); also, a court of record; an office of public records.

chan-cre (shang'kėr), *n.* [F., < L. *cancer*, crab, cancer.] In *pathol.*, the initial lesion of syphilis, commonly a more or less distinct ulcer or sore with a hard base.—**chan-croid** (shang'kroid), *n.* In *pathol.*, a soft, local venereal sore, not leading to systemic infection.—**chan'crous,** *a.* Of or like a chancre.

chan-cy (chȧn'si), *a.* Dependent on chance, or uncertain (colloq. or prov.: as, "Human life is *chancy* at any kind of trade," Kipling's "Mulholland's Contract"); also, lucky (Sc.); also, safe to deal with (Sc.).

chan-de-lier (shan-dẹ-lēr'), *n.* [F.: see *chandler.*] A branched support for a number of lights, esp. one suspended from a ceiling.

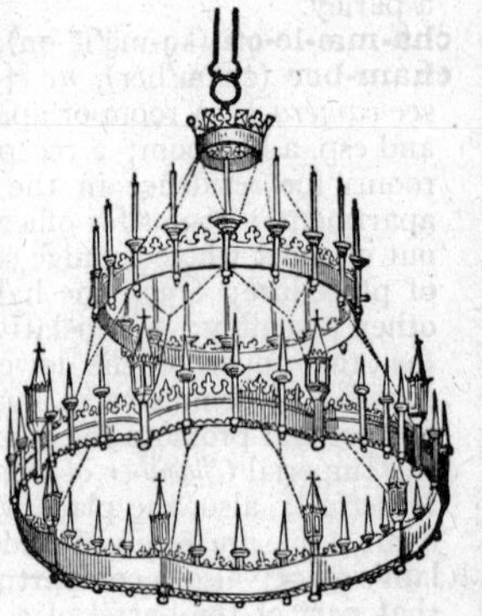

Chandelier.

chan-dler (chan'dlėr), *n.* [OF. F. *chandelier*, candle-seller, also candlestick, < ML. *candelarius*, < L. *candela*, candle.] One who makes or sells candles; also, a retailer of groceries, etc.; also, a dealer or trader (in compounds: as, a corn-*chandler*). See *ship-chandler.*—**chan'dler-y,** *n.*; pl. *-ies* (-iz). A store-room for candles; also, the warehouse, wares, or business of a chandler.

chan-doo (chan-dö'), *n.* [Hind.] Opium for smoking.

change (chānj), *v. t.*; *changed, changing.* [OF. *changier* (F. *changer*), < ML. *cambiare*, for L. *cambire*, exchange.] To substitute another or others for; replace by another; exchange for something else; also, to give or procure money of another kind, as of another country or of a smaller denomination, for; also, to substitute one for the other of (two things); give and take reciprocally; interchange; also, to make different; alter in appearance, condition, etc.; turn (*into*).—**to change hands,** to pass from one hand or possessor to another; also, to substitute the left hand for the right, or vice versa.—**change,** *v. i.* To make a change or an exchange; change one's clothes; change vehicles; also, to become different; turn (*into*); pass from one phase to another, as the moon.—**change,** *n.* [OF. F. *change.*] The act of changing, or the fact of being changed; the substitution of one thing for another; the supplanting of one thing by another in succession; a passing from one place or one state to another; any alteration, mutation, or variation; a modulation, or change of key, in music; any of the various sequences in which a peal of bells may be rung, the name properly denoting a variation from the diatonic sequence from the highest bell to the lowest, but sometimes including this sequence also (as, to ring the *changes*, to go through all the changes in ringing a peal of bells; fig., to go through all the variations of any process; repeat something in every possible order or form); variety or novelty; changefulness† or caprice†; also, that which is or may be substituted for another; money given in exchange for an equivalent of higher denomination; coins of low denomination; a balance of money that remains over and is returned when the sum tendered in payment is larger than the sum due; also, a giving and receiving reciprocally†; exchange†; sometimes, commerce†; also, an exchange, or place where merchants, etc., meet to transact business (commonly written *'change*).—**change of life,** in *physiol.*, the menopause.—**change'a-ble,** *a.* Liable to change or to be changed; variable, inconstant, or fickle; alterable; of changing color or appearance (as, *changeable* silk).—**change-a-bil'i-ty** (-bil'i-ti), **change'a-ble-ness,** *n.*—**change'a-bly,** *adv.*—**change'ful,** *a.* Full of change; changing; variable; inconstant.—**change'ful-ness,** *n.*—**change'=house,** *n.* A tavern. [Sc.]—**change'less,** *a.* Unchanging.—**change'less-ness,** *n.*

change-ling (chānj'ling), *n.* [From *change* + *-ling*[1].] A child secretly substituted for another, esp. a strange, stupid, or ugly child supposed to have been left by fairies in place of one carried off by them; an idiot (archaic or prov.); any person or thing substituted secretly†; a person given to change, an inconstant person, or a turncoat (archaic).

chan-ger (chān'jėr), *n.* One who or that which changes; a money-changer†.

change=ring-ing (chānj'ring''ing), *n.* The act of ringing the changes on a peal of bells; the art of ringing a peal of bells in a regularly varying order so that all the possible sequences may be produced. See *change*, *n.*

chan-nel[1] (chan'ęl), *n.* [Corruption of *chain-wale.*] *Naut.*, one of the horizontal planks or ledges attached to the outside of a ship, nearly abreast of a mast, to give more spread to the lower shrouds.

Shrouds extended on the Channel.

chan-nel[2] (chan'ęl), *n.* [OF. *chanel*, < L. *canalis*, E. *canal.*] The bed of a stream or waterway; the deeper part of a waterway; a wide strait, as between a continent and an island; a wide arm of the sea extending inland a considerable distance; an artificial course for water or liquid; a tubular passage, as for liquids or fluids; also, a groove or furrow; also, a course or line of procedure (as, to divert conversation to a new *channel*); a means of passing, conveying, or transmitting (as, *channels* of trade).—**chan'nel**[2], *v. t.*; *-neled* or *-nelled*, *-neling* or *-nelling.* To form a channel in; groove; also, to excavate as a channel; also, to convey through a channel.—**chan'nel=i''ron,** *n.* A rolled iron bar whose section is channel-shaped, like three sides of a rectangle.

chan-son (shäṅ-sôṅ), *n.* [F., < L. *cantio(n-)*, < *canere*, sing.] A song.—**chanson de geste** (dė zhest). [F., 'song of deed.'] One of a class of old French epic poems (as the "Chanson de Roland") narrating heroic exploits.

chan-son-nette (shäṅ-so-net), *n.* [F., dim. of *chanson.*] A little song.

chant (chȧnt), *v.* [OF. F. *chanter*, < L. *cantare*, freq. of *canere*, sing.] **I.** *tr.* To sing; also, to celebrate in song; also, to sing to a chant, or in the manner of a chant, esp. in the church service; intone; also, to describe (a horse) falsely, or sell through such description (slang). **II.** *intr.* To sing; also, to sing a chant.—**chant,** *n.* A song; singing; esp., a short, simple melody, specif. one characterized by single notes to which an indefinite number of syllables are intoned, used in singing the psalms, canticles, etc., in the church service; a psalm, canticle, or the like chanted or for chanting; hence, any monotonous song; a monotonous or singing intonation of the voice in speaking.

chan-tage (shäṅ-täzh), *n.* [F.: cf. F. *faire chanter*, 'to make (one) sing,' to extort a confession, payment, etc.] Blackmailing.

chant-er (chȧn'tėr), *n.* One who chants; a singer; a chorister; a precentor; also, the finger-pipe of a bagpipe, on which the melody is played; also, the hedge-sparrow, *Accentor modularis.*

chan-te-relle[1] (shȧn-tę-rel'), *n.* [F., < *chanter*, sing: see *chant.*] The highest string of some stringed musical instruments, as the violin or guitar.

chan-te-relle[2] (shȧn-tę-rel'), *n.* [F., < L. *cantharus*, drinking-vessel.] An edible mushroom, *Cantharellus cibarius*, of a yellow color.

Chanterelle.

chan-tey, chan-ty (shan'ti), *n.*; pl. *-teys*, *-ties* (-tiz). [Prob. < F. *chanter*, sing: see *chant.*] A sailors' song, esp. one sung in rhythm with their work by sailors hauling or heaving together.—**chan'tey=man, chan'ty=man** (-man), *n.*; pl. *-men.* The leader of a chantey.

Chan-ti-cleer (chan'ti-klēr), *n.* [OF. *Chantecler*, < *chanter*, sing, + *cler*, clear.] A name for the cock, orig. in the medieval epic "Reynard the Fox" (as, "But now bold *Chanticleer*, from farm to farm, Challeng'd the dawn creeping o'er eastern land": Hood's "Midsummer Fairies," cxxv.); also [*l. c.*], a cock.

chan-tress (chȧn'tres), *n.* A female chanter or singer.

chan-try (chȧn'tri), *n.*; pl. *-tries* (-triz). [OF. *chanterie*, < *chanter*, sing: see *chant.*] An endowment for the singing or saying of mass for the souls of the founders or of persons named by them; also, the priests, or the chapel or the like, so endowed; also, a chapel attached to a church, used for minor services.

chan'ty, etc. See *chantey*, etc.

cha-os (kā'os), *n.* [L., < Gr. χάος, empty space, abyss, akin to χαίνειν, yawn.] A chasm† or abyss†; the infinity of space or formless matter supposed to precede the existence of the ordered universe; any assemblage of elements wholly without organization or order; utter confusion or disorder.—**cha-ot-ic** (kā-ot'ik), *a.* Of or like chaos; in utter confusion or disorder: as, "Opinions were still in a state of *chaotic* anarchy" (Macaulay's "Essays," Lord Bacon).—**cha-ot'i-cal-ly,** *adv.*

chap[1] (chap), *v.*; *chapped, chapping.* [ME., var. of *chop*[1].] **I.** *tr.* To split; crack; make rough: used esp. of the action of cold on the skin. **II.** *intr.* To become chapped, as the skin.—**chap**[1], *n.* A fissure or crack, esp. in the skin from chapping.

chap[2], **chop**[3] (chap, chop), *n.* [Cf. *chaft.*] Either of the jaws; *pl.*, the jaw; also, *sing.*, a cheek.

chap[3] (chap), *n.* [Short for *chapman.*] A customer (now prov.); a fellow (applied familiarly to a man or boy: colloq.).

cha-pa-re-jos (chä-pä-rā'hōs), *n. pl.* [Mex. Sp.] Strong leather breeches or overalls worn by horsemen, esp. by cowboys.

chap-ar-ral (chap-ą-ral'), *n.* [Sp., < *chaparro*, evergreen oak.] A close growth of low evergreen oaks; any dense thicket. [Western U. S.]—**chap-ar-ral'=cock,** *n.* A terrestrial bird of the cuckoo family, *Geococcyx californianus*, of the southwestern U. S.—**chap-ar-ral'=hen,** *n.* The female of the chaparral-cock.

chap=book (chap'bůk), *n.* [Cf. *chapman.*] One of a class of small books or pamphlets of popular tales, ballads, etc., such as were formerly hawked about by chapmen.

chape (chāp), *n.* [OF. F. *chape*, cape, cope, covering, < ML. *capa*, *cappa*, E. *cape*[2], *cap.*] The metal mounting or trimming of a scabbard, esp. at the point; also, a part of an object by which it is attached to something else, esp. the piece at the back of a buckle by which it is fastened to a strap.

cha-peau (shȧ-pō), *n.*; pl. *-peaux* (-pōz, F. -pō). [F. *chapeau*, OF. *chapel*, < ML. *capellus*, dim. of *capa*, *cappa*, E. *cap.*] A hat.—**chapeau bras** (brä). [F. *bras*, arm.] A kind of small three-cornered hat formerly in use, which could be carried under the arm.

chap-el (chap'ęl), *n.* [OF. *chapele* (F. *chapelle*), < ML. *capella*, sanctuary for relics, orig. cloak (as that of St. Martin, preserved as a relic), dim. of *capa*, *cappa*, E. *cape*[2], *cap.*] A private or subordinate place of prayer or worship; an oratory; a part of or addition to a church, separately dedicated, devoted to special services; a room or building for worship, in or connected with a royal palace, a castle, a college, etc.; a separate place of public worship dependent on the church of a parish; an independent place of worship, usually small, specially authorized or devoted to special services; a place of worship of a religious body outside of an established church, as in England; also, religious service in a chapel; also, a choir or orchestra of a chapel, court, etc.; also, a printing-house, or the body of printers belonging to it.—**chapel of ease,** a subordinate church for the convenience of distant parishioners.—**chap′el=mas″ter,** *n.* [Cf. *kapellmeister.*] The director of a choir or orchestra, as of a royal chapel.—**chap′el-ry** (-ri), *n.*; pl. *-ries* (-riz). The district assigned to, or the jurisdiction of, a chapel.

Chapel, 14th century. — Church of Notre Dame, Mantes, France.

chap-e-ron (shap′ę-rōn), *n.* [OF. F. *chaperon,* hood, < *chape*: see *chape.*] A hood† or cap†; also, an older woman, usually a matron, who, for conventional propriety, attends a young unmarried woman in public or accompanies a party of young unmarried persons of both sexes.—**chap′e-ron,** *v. t.* To attend or accompany as chaperon.—**chap′e-ron-age** (-ąj), *n.* The attendance of a chaperon.

chap-fall-en, chop-fall-en (chap′fâ″ln, chop′-), *a.* Having the lower chap or jaw depressed, as from exhaustion, humiliation, or dejection; chagrined; dispirited.

chap-i-ter (chap′i-tėr), *n.* [OF. *chapitre, chapitle,* capital, chapter: see *chapter.*] The capital of a column or pillar. See 1 Kings, vii. 19. [Archaic.]

chap-lain (chap′lạn), *n.* [OF. F. *chapelain,* < ML. *capellanus,* < *capella,* E. *chapel.*] An ecclesiastic attached to a chapel, as of a great personage; a clergyman officially attached to a court, institution, legislative body, society, etc., or to the army or navy, to perform religious functions.—**chap′lain-cy** (-si), *n.* The office or post of a chaplain. Also **chap′lain-ship.**

chap-let (chap′let), *n.* [OF. F. *chapelet,* dim. of OF. *chapel,* head-dress: see *chapeau.*] A wreath or garland for the head; a string of beads; a string of beads for counting prayers, one third of the length of a rosary; the prayers so counted; anything resembling a string of beads; in *arch.,* a small molding carved into beads or the like; in *foundry-work,* a metal form to hold the core in place in a mold.—**chap′let-ed,** *a.* Adorned with a chaplet or garland.

chap-man (chap′mạn), *n.*; pl. *-men.* [AS. *cēapman,* < *cēap,* trade, + *man,* man.] A merchant (archaic); a hawker or peddler; a customer (obs. or prov.).

cha-po-te (chä-pō′tä), *n.* [Mex. Sp.] A persimmon, *Diospyros texana,* of Texas and northern Mexico, bearing a black fruit.

chap-py (chap′i), *a.* Full of chaps or cracks; cleft.

chaps (chaps), *n. pl.* Chaparejos. [Western U. S.]

chap-ter (chap′tėr), *n.* [OF. *chapitre, chapitle* (F. *chapitre*), < L. *capitulum,* small head, capital of column, chapter: see *capitulum.*] A main division, usually numbered, of a book, treatise, or the like, or of one of its parts; also, a general assembly of the canons of a church, or of the members of any of various organizations; the body of such canons or members collectively; also, a branch of a society or fraternity.—**chap′ter,** *v. t.* To divide into or arrange in chapters.—**chap′ter=house,** *n.* A building attached to a cathedral, etc., in which the chapter meets; also, the building of a chapter of a society, etc.

cha-que-ta (chä-kā′tä), *n.* [Sp.] A jacket; esp., a heavy leather or other jacket worn by cowboys.

char[1]**, chare** (chär, chãr), *n.* [AS. *cerr, cyrr,* turn, time, occasion, affair.] A turn or single piece of work, esp. household work; an odd job; a chore.—**char**[1]**, chare,** *v.*; *charred, chared, charring, charing.* **I.** *tr.* To do (chars or odd jobs). **II.** *intr.* To do small jobs; do housework by the day.

char[2] (chär), *v.*; *charred, charring.* [Appar. detached from *charcoal.*] **I.** *tr.* To burn or reduce to charcoal; also, to burn slightly; scorch. **II.** *intr.* To become charred.—**char**[2], *n.* Charcoal; a charred substance.

char[3] (chär), *n.*; pl. *chars* or (esp. collectively) *char.* [Cf. Gael. *ceara,* red.] Any trout of the genus *Salvelinus,* esp. *S. alpinus* (the common char of Europe). See *trout.*

char=à=banc (shär-ä-bäṅ), *n.* See *char-à-bancs.*

char=à=bancs (shär-ä-bäṅ), *n.* [F. *char à bancs,* 'car with benches.'] A kind of long, light vehicle with transverse seats; in later use, a large motor-bus with transverse seats, for carrying a number of persons.

char-act (kar′akt), *n.* [OF. *characte.*] A character, mark, or symbol. See Shakspere's "Measure for Measure," v. 1. 56. [Archaic.]

char-ac-ter (kar′ąk-tėr), *n.* [L., < Gr. χαρακτήρ, < χαράσσειν, make sharp, engrave.] A significant mark made by cutting, stamping, drawing, etc.; a symbol as used in writing or printing, esp. one employed in recording speech, as a letter of the alphabet; writing or printing, or a style of writing or printing; the system of symbols employed in writing a particular language (as, the Greek *character*); also, a distinguishing mark or feature; a characteristic; also, the aggregate of characteristics or distinguishing features of a thing; peculiar quality; also, moral constitution, as of a person or a people; often, strongly developed moral quality; also, reputation; often, good repute; also, an account of the qualities or peculiarities of a person or thing; esp., a formal statement from an employer concerning the qualities and habits of a former servant or employee; also, status or capacity; also, a person considered as exhibiting certain qualities; also, one of the persons represented in a drama, novel, etc.; hence, a part or rôle; also, a person of marked peculiarities (colloq.).—**char′ac-ter,** *v. t.* To engrave or inscribe; also, to portray; describe; also, to distinguish by a mark, etc.; be a characteristic of; also, to impart a character to.—**char″ac-ter-is′tic.** [Gr. χαρακτηριστικός.] **I.** *a.* Pertaining to, constituting, or indicating the character or peculiar quality; typical; distinctive. **II.** *n.* A distinguishing feature or quality; in *math.,* the integral part of a logarithm.—**char″ac-ter-is′ti-cal-ly,** *adv.*—**char″ac-ter-i-za′tion** (-i-zā′shọn), *n.* The act of characterizing; portrayal; description; often, the creation of fictitious characters.—**char′ac-ter-ize** (-īz), *v. t.*; *-ized, -izing.* [Gr. χαρακτηρίζειν.] To engrave† or inscribe†; also, to portray; describe the character or peculiar quality of; also, to mark or distinguish as a characteristic; be a characteristic of; also, to give character to.—**char′ac-ter-iz-er,** *n.*—**char′ac-ter-less,** *a.* Without a character; without distinctive character.—**char′ac-ter-y,** *n.*; pl. *-ies* (-iz). The conveying of ideas by characters or symbols; characters or symbols collectively. See Shakspere's "Merry Wives of Windsor," v. 5. 77.

cha-rade (shą-rād′ or -räd′), *n.* [F.; origin uncertain.] An enigma whose solution is a word of two or more separately significant syllables, which must be discovered from description or dramatic representation.

char-bon (shär′bon, F. shär-bôṅ), *n.* [F., < L. *carbo(n-),* coal, charcoal.] In *pathol.,* the disease anthrax.

char-coal (chär′kōl), *n.* [Origin uncertain; appar. a much older word than *char*[2].] The carbonaceous material obtained by the imperfect combustion of wood or other organic substances; also, a pencil of charcoal for drawing, or a drawing made with such a pencil.—**char′coal,** *v. t.* To blacken, write, or draw with charcoal; also, to suffocate with the fumes of charcoal.—**char′coal=burn″er,** *n.* A person employed in the manufacture of charcoal by burning wood, etc.

chard (chärd), *n.* [L. *carduus,* thistle, artichoke.] The crisp leafstalks of the cardoon or the artichoke, blanched for table use; also, a variety of beet having large leafstalks and midribs which are used as a vegetable ('Swiss chard').

chare, chare′wom″an. See *char*[1], *charwoman.*

charge (chärj), *v.*; *charged, charging.* [OF. *chargier, charger* (F. *charger*), < ML. *carricare,* < L. *carrus,* E. *car.*] **I.** *tr.* To put a load or burden on or in; fill or furnish (a thing) with the quantity, as of powder, fuel, or electricity, that it is fitted to receive; fill (air, water, etc.) with other matter in a state of diffusion or solution; load or burden (the mind, heart, etc.); also, to impose a task or responsibility upon; intrust or commission (*with*); also, to lay a command or injunction upon; command; exhort; instruct authoritatively, as a judge does a jury; also, to lay blame upon; blame; accuse (usually with *with*); also, to impute as a fault; bring as an accusation; also, to make or hold liable for payment; register as a debt or liability; impose or ask as a price; also, to put (a weapon, as a bayonet) in the position for attack; also, to rush against in hostility; attack by a violent rush; in *her.*, to place a bearing on (a shield, etc.). **II.** *intr.* To demand a price; ask payment; also, to make a debit, as in an account; also, to make an onset; rush, as to an attack; also, of dogs, to lie down at command.—**charge,** *n.* [OF. F. *charge.*] A load or burden; the quantity of anything which an apparatus is fitted to hold, or holds, at one time, as of powder, etc., for one discharge of a firearm, or as of electricity, etc.; a quantity of powder, etc., exploded at one time, as in blasting; also, a duty or responsibility laid upon or intrusted to one; care, custody, or superintendence (as, to have *charge* of a thing); anything committed to one's care or management; a parish or congregation committed to the spiritual care of a pastor; also, a command or injunction; an exhortation; an official instruction (as, a judge's *charge* to the jury); also, an imputation of something culpable; an accusation; also, expense or cost (as, improvements made at a tenant's own *charge*); a sum or price charged (as, a *charge* of 50 cents for admission); a liability to pay; the imposition of such a liability (as, to make a *charge* for expenses); an entry of something due, as in an account; also, an impetuous onset or attack, as of soldiers, or the signal for this; in *her.*, a bearing.

char-gé (shär-zhā), *n.* Same as *chargé d'affaires.*

charge-a-ble (chär'ja̤-bl), *a.* That may be charged; also, liable to become a charge on the public; also, burdensome†; expensive†.

char-gé d'af-faires (shär-zhā dá-fãr); pl. *chargés d'affaires* (shär-zhā dá-fãr). [F., lit. 'charged with affairs.'] An official left in charge of diplomatic business at a foreign court during the temporary absence of the ambassador or minister; also, a diplomatic representative accredited to the department for foreign affairs of a state to which a diplomatist of higher grade is not appointed.

charge-less (chärj'les), *a.* Without a charge, as a clergyman having no parish or congregation.

char-ger (chär'jėr), *n.* One who or that which charges; esp., a war-horse ridden in charging the enemy; the horse of a military officer; also, a platter (dish).

char-i-ly (chãr'i-li), *adv.* In a chary manner; carefully; warily; sparingly.—**char'i-ness,** *n.* Chary quality; also, scrupulous integrity†.

char-i-ot (char'i-o̤t), *n.* [OF. F. *chariot,* < *char*: see *car.*] A two-wheeled vehicle used by the ancients in war, racing, processions, etc.; any more or less stately car or carriage; a kind of light four-wheeled pleasure-carriage formerly in use.—**char'-i-ot,** *v.* **I.** *tr.* To convey in a chariot. **II.** *intr.* To drive a chariot; ride in a chariot.—**char"i-ot-eer'** (-ēr'), *n.* One who drives a chariot; [*cap.*] in *astron.*, the northern constellation Auriga.—**char"i-ot-eer',** *v.* **I.** *intr.* To drive as a charioteer. **II.** *tr.* To drive (a chariot), or (a person) in a chariot.

Greek Chariot. — From a vase.

char-ism (kar'izm), *n.* [Gr. χάρισμα, < χαρίζεσθαι, show favor, < χάρις, grace.] In *theol.*, a special gift or power divinely conferred, as the gift of prophecy. Also **cha-ris-ma** (ka-riz'mạ̈); pl. *-mata* (-ma̤-tạ̈).—**char-is-mat'ic,** *a.*

char-i-ta-ble (char'i-ta̤-bl), *a.* [OF. F. *charitable.*] Exhibiting charity; kindly; lenient in judging others; disposed to relieve the needs of others; liberal in almsgiving; also, pertaining to or concerned with charity; relating to almsgiving.—**char'i-ta-ble-ness,** *n.*—**char'i-ta-bly,** *adv.*

char-i-ty (char'i-ti), *n.*; pl. *-ties* (-tiz). [OF. *charite* (F. *charité*), < L. *caritas*, dearness, love, < *carus*, dear, loving.] Christian love; love for one's fellow-men; good-will to others; leniency in judging others or their actions; benevolent feeling or action toward those in need; almsgiving; the private or public relief of the poor; a charitable act or work; something given to a person or persons in need; a charitable bequest, foundation, or institution.

cha-ri-va-ri (shä-ri-vä'ri, also sha̤-riv-a̤-rē'), *n.* [F.; origin obscure.] A mock serenade or concert of discordant noises made with kettles, pans, horns, etc.: as, "We . . . played a *charivari* with the ruler and desk, the fender and fire-irons" (C. Brontë's "Jane Eyre," xvii.).

chark (chärk), *v. t.* [Appar. < *charcoal.*] To reduce to charcoal; char; convert (coal) into coke.—**chark,** *n.* Charcoal: as, "I contrived to burn some wood . . . under turf, till it became *chark,* or dry coal" (Defoe's "Robinson Crusoe," i. 12).

char-la-tan (shär'la̤-ta̤n), *n.* [F. *charlatan,* < It. *ciarlatano,* < *ciarlare,* chatter.] One who pretends to more knowledge or skill than he possesses, esp. in medicine; a quack; a pretentious impostor.—**char-la-tan'ic** (-tan'ik), *a.*—**char'-la-tan-ism,** *n.* The practices of a charlatan. Also **char'la-tan-ry.**

Charles's Wain (chärl'zez wān). [AS. *Carles wǣn*; with reference to Charlemagne.] In *astron.*, the seven brightest stars in the constellation Ursa Major, regarded as resembling a wain or wagon in their outline; the Dipper.

char-ley=horse, char-lie=horse (chär'li-hôrs), *n.* [From *Charley, Charlie,* for *Charles,* man's name.] Stiffness of the leg or arm, as of a baseball player. [Slang, U. S.]

char-lock (chär'lo̤k), *n.* [AS. *cerlic.*] The wild mustard, *Brassica arvensis,* often troublesome as a weed in grain-fields; also, any of various other brassicaceous plants, as the herb *Raphanus raphanistrum* ('jointed charlock').

char-lotte (shär'lo̤t), *n.* [F., < *Charlotte,* woman's name.] A sweet dish (hot or cold) of many varieties, commonly made by lining a mold with cake or bread and filling with fruit or a cream, custard, or gelatin preparation.—**charlotte russe** (rös). [F., 'Russian charlotte.'] A mold of sponge-cake filled with whipped cream.

charm (chärm), *n.* [OF. F. *charme,* < L. *carmen,* song, incantation.] The chanting or recitation of a verse believed to possess magic power; hence, any action or thing supposed to have such power; a talisman; an amulet; also, a trinket worn on a watch-chain, etc.; also, some quality or feature exerting a fascinating influence (as, feminine *charms*); also, fascinating quality; attractiveness.—**charm,** *v.* [OF. F. *charmer.*] **I.** *tr.* To act upon with or as with a charm; enchant; allay; soothe; also, to endow with or protect by supernatural powers; also, to attract powerfully by beauty, etc.; please greatly; delight; also, to entreat†. **II.** *intr.* To use charms; act as a charm; be fascinating or pleasing; also, to give forth musical sounds†.—**charm'er,** *n.* One who or that which charms: often used of a woman.

char-meuse (shär-mė̄z), *n.* [F., fem. of *charmeur,* one who charms.] A soft, flexible variety of satin.

charm-ing (chär'ming), *p. a.* That charms; exercising magic power; fascinating, highly pleasing, or delightful.—**charm'ing-ly,** *adv.*—**charm'ing-ness,** *n.*

charm-less (chärm'les), *a.* Destitute of charms.

char-nel (chär'ne̤l). [OF. *charnel,* < ML. *carnale,* prop. neut. of LL. *carnalis,* E. *carnal.*] **I.** *n.* A common repository for dead bodies; a charnel-house. **II.** *a.* Of, like, or used for a charnel.—**char'nel=house,** *n.* A house or place in which the bodies or bones of the dead are deposited.

Cha-ron (kā'ro̤n), *n.* [L., < Gr. Χάρων.] In *class. myth.*, the ferryman who conveyed the souls of the dead across the river Styx; hence, any ferryman (humorous).

char-pie (shär'pi, F. shär-pē), *n.* [F., pp. fem. of (OF.) *charpir,* pick to pieces, < L. *carpere,* pick.] Lint for dressing wounds, etc.

char-poy (chär'poi), *n.* [Hind. *chārpāī,* lit. 'four-footed'; from Pers.] The common light bedstead of India.

char-qui (chär'kẹ̄), *n.* [Peruvian.] Jerked meat, esp. beef.

char-ry (chär'i), *a.* Of or like charcoal; charred.

chart (chärt), *n.* [OF. *charte* (also *carte*), < L. *charta*, later *carta*, paper, writing, ML. card, map, chart, charter, < Gr. χάρτης, leaf of paper, thin sheet.] A map, esp. a hydrographic or marine map; an outline map showing special conditions or facts (as, a weather *chart*); a graphic representation, as by curves, of fluctuations in temperature, prices, etc.; a sheet exhibiting information in a tabulated or methodical form.—**chart,** *v. t.* To make a chart of; map.

char-ta-ceous (kär-tā′shius), *a.* [LL. *chartaceus*, < L. *charta*, paper: see *chart.*] Of or like paper.

char-ter (chär′tėr), *n.* [OF. *chartre*, < L. *chartula*, dim. of *charta*: see *chart.*] A formal written document, given by a sovereign, legislature, or other authority, bestowing certain rights and privileges; also, a written evidence, as of a conveyance or a contract, esp. of a contract for the letting or hiring of a ship; the contract made; hiring or hire; also, special privilege or immunity.—**char′ter,** *v. t.* To grant a charter to or for; license; also, to let or hire by charter or charter-party; hire (a car, etc.).—**char′ter-a-ble,** *a.* That may be chartered.—**char′ter-er,** *n.*—**char′ter-less,** *a.* Without a charter.

char-ter=par-ty (chär′tėr-pär″ti), *n.* [F. *charte-partie*, 'charter divided' (one half being given to each contractor).] In *com.*, a written agreement for the letting or hiring of a ship.

Chart-ism (chär′tizm), *n.* [Cf. *charter.*] The principles or movement of a party of political reformers, chiefly working-men, active in England from 1838 to 1848: so called from the "People's Charter," the document which contained their principles and demands.—**Chart′ist,** *n.* An adherent of Chartism.

chart-less (chärt′les), *a.* Without a chart.

char-tog-ra-phy (kär-tog′rạ-fi), etc. See *cartography*, etc.

Char-treuse (shär-trėz), *n.* [F.] A Carthusian monastery; [*l. c.*] an aromatic liqueur (green, yellow, or white) made by the Carthusian monks, orig. at the monastery of La Grande Chartreuse, near Grenoble, France; also, a clear, light green with a yellowish tinge.

char-tu-la-ry (kär′ṭū-lạ-ri), *n.*; pl. *-ries* (-riz). [ML. *chartularium*, also *cartularium*, < L. *chartula*: see *charter.*] A collection or book of charters, title-deeds, etc., as of a monastery.

char-wom-an (chär′wům″ạn), *n.*; pl. *-women* (-wim″en). [See *char*[1].] A woman hired to do chars, or odd jobs of household work, or to do such work by the day.

char-y (chãr′i), *a.*; compar. *charier*, superl. *chariest.* [AS. *cearig*, < *cearu*, *caru*, E. *care.*] Careful; wary; shy; fastidious; sparing: often with *of*: as, "Miss Matty Jenkyns was *chary* of candles. We had many devices to use as few as possible" (Mrs. Gaskell's "Cranford," v.).

Cha-ryb-dis (kạ-rib′dis), *n.* [L., < Gr. Χάρυβδις.] See *Scylla.*

chase[1] (chās), *v.*; *chased, chasing.* [OF. *chacier* (F. *chasser*), chase, = *cachier*, E. *catch.*] **I.** *tr.* To pursue with intent to capture or kill, as game; hunt; also, to pursue in order to seize, overtake, etc.; follow persistently; also, to drive by pursuing; put to flight. **II.** *intr.* To hunt†; follow in pursuit; run or hasten (now colloq.).—**chase**[1], *n.* [OF. *chace* (F. *chasse*).] The act of chasing; pursuit; esp., the occupation or sport of hunting wild animals ('the chase'); also, an object of pursuit, as a hunted animal; also, a body of persons pursuing game; also, an uninclosed tract of privately owned land reserved for animals to be hunted as game (Eng.).

chase[2] (chās), *n.* [F. *châsse*, OF. *chasse*, also *casse*: see *case*[2].] A rectangular iron frame in which composed type to print from or make plates from is secured; also, a lengthened hollow; a groove, furrow, or trench; the bore of a gun, or the part containing the bore.

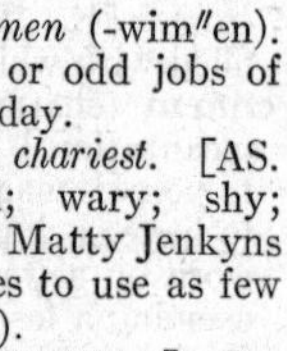
Printers' Chase.
a, frame; *b*, *b*, *b*, furniture of wood or metal; *c*, *c*, *c*, quoins.

chase[3] (chās), *v. t.*; *chased, chasing.* [Appar. < *enchase.*] To ornament (metal) by engraving or embossing; also, to cut in making a screw.

chas-er[1] (chā′sėr), *n.* One who or that which chases or pursues; a small, swift, armed aëroplane for pursuing enemy aircraft; a ship's gun at the bow or the stern for use when pursuing or being pursued; also, a draft of mild drink, as of water, taken after a draft of liquor (colloq.).

chas-er[2] (chā′sėr), *n.* One who or that which chases metal; also, a tool used in cutting screw-threads.—**chas′ing,** *n.* The act or work of one who chases metal; also, the design executed.

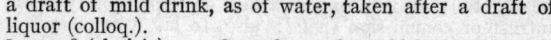

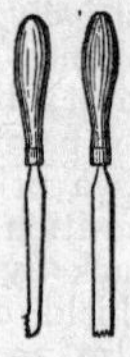
Chasers for cutting screws.

chasm (kazm), *n.* [L. *chasma*, < Gr. χάσμα, akin to χαίνειν, yawn, and χάος, E. *chaos.*] A yawning fissure, as in the earth's surface; a wide, deep cleft; fig., a sundering breach, as in relations; a gap or hiatus, as in a narrative.—**chas-mal** (kaz′mạl), *a.* Of or like a chasm.—**chasmed,** *a.* Having a chasm or chasms.—**chas′my** (-mi), *a.* Having chasms; also, chasm-like (as, "the *chasmy* torrent's foam-lit bed": Wordsworth's "Descriptive Sketches," 464).

chasse (shȧs), *n.* [Short for F. *chasse-café*, 'chase-coffee.'] A small glass or draft of spirituous liquor taken to remove the taste or odor of coffee, tobacco, etc., or to aid digestion.

chas-sé (shȧ-sā′), *n.* [F., < *chasser*: see *chase*[1].] In *dancing*, a kind of gliding step or movement in which one foot is kept in advance of the other.—**chas-sé′,** *v. i.*; *-séd, -séing.* In *dancing*, to execute a chassé.

chasse-pot (shȧs-pō), *n.* [From A. A. *Chassepot* (1833–1905), the (French) inventor.] A type of breech-loading rifle used in the French army from 1866 to 1874.

chas-seur (shȧ-sėr), *n.* [F., < *chasser*: see *chase*[1].] A huntsman; one of a body of troops (cavalry or infantry) equipped and trained for rapid movements; an attendant or servitor dressed in semi-military style.

chas-sis (shȧs′ẹ̄, F. shȧ-sē), *n.*; pl. *chassis* (shȧs′ẹ̄z, F. shȧ-sē). [F. *châssis*, < *châsse*: see *chase*[2].] A window-sash; the frame or railway on which a gun-carriage moves backward and forward; the lower part of an automobile, including the frame, motor, gearing, wheels, etc., but not the body, seats, etc.; the rigid framework which supports the body of an aëroplane, and to which the wheels or floats are attached.

chaste (chāst), *a.* [OF. F. *chaste*, < L. *castus.*] Pure with respect to unlawful sexual intercourse; virtuous; fig., undefiled or stainless; also, unmarried†; also, free from obscenity; decent; also, restrained; pure in style; without meretricious ornament; simple.—**chaste′ly,** *adv.*

chas-ten (chā′sn), *v. t.* [Earlier *chaste*, ME. *chasten*, *chastien*, < OF. *chastier* (F. *châtier*), < L. *castigare*: see *castigate.*] To inflict suffering upon for purposes of moral improvement; discipline or subdue, as by adversity; also, to restrain, moderate, or temper; make chaste in style.—**chas′ten-er,** *n.*

chaste-ness (chāst′nes), *n.* The quality of being chaste.

chaste=tree (chāst′trē), *n.* The shrub or small tree agnus castus.

chas-tise (chas-tīz′), *v. t.*; *-tised, -tising.* [ME. *chastisen*, for *chastien*: see *chasten.*] To inflict punishment upon for the purpose of moral improvement; now, esp., to inflict corporal punishment upon; beat or thrash; also, to correct the faults of†; also, to restrain, refine, or purify (archaic).—**chas-tis′a-ble** (-tī′zạ-bl), *a.*—**chas-tise-ment** (chas′tiz-mẹnt), *n.* The act of chastising; punishment.—**chas-tis′er,** *n.*

chas-ti-ty (chas′ti-ti), *n.* The quality of being chaste.

chas-u-ble (chaz̧′ū-bl), *n.* [OF. F. *chasuble*, < ML. *casubula*, for *casula*, cloak, dim. of L. *casa*, house.] *Eccles.*, a sleeveless outer vestment worn by the celebrant at mass or the eucharist.

chat (chat), *v. i.*; *chatted, chatting.* [Appar. < *chatter.*] To chatter†; also, to converse in a familiar or informal manner.—**chat,** *n.* Chatter†; also, familiar conversation; also, any of several birds, as *Icteria virens* ('yellow-breasted chat') of the U. S., so called from their chattering cries.

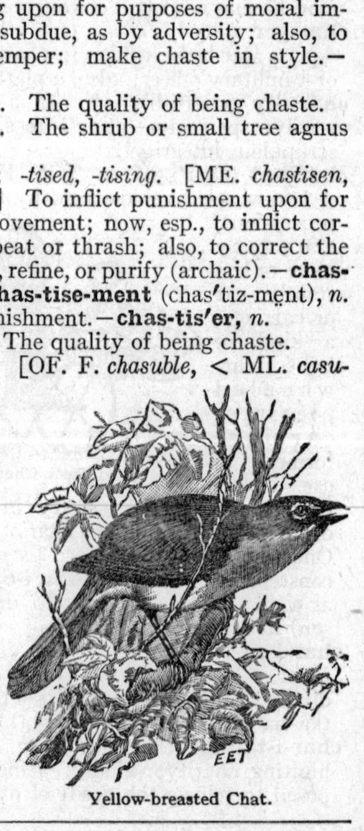
Yellow-breasted Chat.

châ-teau (shä-tō), *n.*; pl. *-teaux* (-tōz, F. -tō). [F.: see *castle.*] In French use, a castle; a seigniorial residence; a country-seat.—**château d'eau** (dō). [F., 'castle of water.'] A fountain with an elaborate architectural setting.

Château d'Eau, Rome.

chat-e-laine (shat′ẹ-lān). [F. *châtelaine*, fem. of *châtelain*: see *castellan.*] **I.** *n.* The mistress of a castle; also, a device for suspending keys, sewing implements, trinkets, etc., worn at the waist by women. **II.** *a.* Worn suspended, as from a chatelaine or pin.

cha-toy-ant (shạ-toi′ạnt, F. shȧ-two-yäṅ). [F., ppr. of *chatoyer*, change luster like a cat's eye, < *chat*, cat.] **I.** *a.* Changing in luster or color, like a cat's eye in the dark. **II.** *n.* A hard stone, as the cat's-eye, having a chatoyant luster.

chat-tel (chat′ẹl), *n.* [OF. *chatel*, also *catel*: see *cattle.*] Property† or goods†; also, a movable possession; any article of property other than real estate or a freehold; sometimes, a slave.—**chat′tel-hood** (-hùd), **chat′tel-ship,** *n.*

chat-ter (chat′ėr), *v.* [ME.; imit.] **I.** *intr.* To utter a succession of quick, inarticulate speech-like sounds, as a magpie or a monkey; also, to talk rapidly and to little purpose; prate; also, to make a rapid clicking noise by striking together, as the teeth from cold; also, to rattle; vibrate in cutting, as a tool, so as to form a series of nicks or notches. **II.** *tr.* To utter rapidly or idly; also, to cause to chatter.—**chat′ter,** *n.* The act or sound of chattering. —**chat′ter-box,** *n.* One who chatters or talks incessantly. —**chat′ter-er,** *n.*—**chat′ter=mark,** *n.* A mark left by a tool that chatters (see *chatter*, *v. i.*); also, in *geol.*, one of a series of irregular gouges made on surfaces over which a glacier passes, by the slipping of rock fragments held in the lower portion of the ice.

chat-ty (chat′i), *a.*; compar. *chattier*, superl. *chattiest.* Given to or full of chat or familiar talk; conversational: as, "I was quite ready to be as sociable and *chatty* as I could be" (Kinglake's "Eothen," xvii.).—**chat′ti-ness,** *n.*

Chau-ce-ri-an (châ-sē′ri-ạn), *a.* Of, pertaining to, or characteristic of the English poet Geoffrey Chaucer (about 1340–1400) or his writings.

chaud=froid (shō-frwo), *n.* [F., 'hot-cold.'] A dish of chicken, game, or the like, prepared hot in a sauce and served cold.

chau-dron (châ′drọn), *n.* [OF. *chaudun.*] The entrails of an animal, esp. as used for food. See Shakspere's "Macbeth," iv. i. 33. [Obs. or prov. Eng.]

chauf-feur (shō-fėr′), *n.* [F., stoker, < *chauffer*, heat: see *chafe.*] One who drives, esp. one who is hired to drive, an automobile.—**chauf-feuse** (shō-fėz′), *n.* [F.] A female chauffeur.

chaul-mu-gra, chaul-moo-gra (châl-mö′grạ), *n.* [E. Ind.] An East Indian tree, *Gynocardia odorata*, bearing a large fruit whose seeds yield a medicinal oil used in leprosy and other cutaneous diseases, rheumatism, etc.

chaunt (chânt), *v.* and *n.* An old form of *chant.*

chaus-ses (shō′sez, F. shōs), *n. pl.* [F., < L. *calceus*, shoe.] Tight coverings for the legs and feet and the body below the waist, formerly worn by men; also, medieval armor for the legs and feet.

chaus-sure (shō-sür), *n.* [F., < *chausser*, to shoe, < L. *calceare*: see *calceate.*] A foot-covering, as a shoe, boot, slipper, or the like.

Chau-tau-qua (shạ-tâ′kwạ). **I.** *a.* Noting or pertaining to an institution, or a system of popular education, employing summer schools assembling annually at Chautauqua, N. Y., with courses of home reading and study; [often *l. c.*] modeled on or resembling this institution or system; pertaining to a chautauqua. **II.** *n.* The annual Chautauqua assembly; [often *l. c.*] any assembly of similar character or aims; an assembly for education and entertainment through lectures, concerts, etc., meeting in a permanent structure or a tent, at sessions extending over a period of a few days, a week, or longer (often being one of a number of such assemblies meeting in a circuit of communities, each provided with the same program).—**Chau-tau′quan. I.** *a.* Pertaining to the Chautauqua institution, system, or assembly, or [often *l. c.*] to a chautauqua. **II.** *n.* [Often *l. c.*] A person connected with a chautauqua; a chautauqua lecturer or entertainer.

chau-vin (shō-vaṅ), *n.* [F.; from Nicholas *Chauvin*, an old soldier and enthusiastic admirer of Napoleon I.] [Also *cap.*] A name applied to any old soldier of the first French empire who professed an idolatrous admiration for Napoleon and his achievements; hence, any person who has a blind and extravagant admiration or enthusiasm for his country's military glory.—**chau-vin-ism** (shō′vin-ism), *n.* Blind enthusiasm for one's country's military glory; jealous and belligerent patriotism or devotion to any cause.—**chau′-vin-ist,** *n.* One imbued with chauvinism.—**chau-vin-is′tic,** *a.*

chaw (châ), *v.* and *n.* Same as *chew.* [Now vulgar.]

chaw-dron (châ′drọn), *n.* See *chaudron.*

chay[1] (shā), *n.* See *shay.*

chay[2], **chay-a** (chā or chī, chā′ạ or chī′ạ), *n.* [E. Ind.] The root of an East Indian rubiaceous plant, *Oldenlandia umbellata*, yielding a red dye resembling madder; also, the plant itself. Also **chay′=root, chay′a=root.**

cha-yo-te (chä-yō′tā), *n.* [Sp.; from Mex.] A tropical American vegetable, the fruit of a cucurbitaceous climbing vine, *Chayota edulis* (or *Sechium edule*), being pear-like in form, pale-green or white in color, and in texture and flavor (when cooked) resembling squash; also, the plant, which has been introduced into cultivation in southern Europe, the southern U. S., and elsewhere.

cheap† (chēp), *n.* [AS. *cēap* = G. *kauf*, trade, bargain, purchase.] Trade; a market-place; price; a bargain; abundance of supply; cheapness.—**good cheap**†, a good bargain from the buyer's point of view; a good market or an abundant supply; lowness of price: sometimes used as an adjective or an adverb.—**cheap.** [From *good cheap.*] **I.** *a.* At a low price or a bargain; inexpensive; obtainable at a low rate of interest, as money; charging low prices, as a dealer; also, costing little labor or trouble; also, of small value; poor; mean; of little account. **II.** *adv.* At a low price; at small cost.—**cheap′en,** *v.* **I.** *tr.* To ask the price of, or bargain for (archaic); also, to make cheap; lower the price of; lower the value or estimation of; belittle. **II.** *intr.* To become cheap.—**cheap′en-er,** *n.*—**cheap′ly,** *adv.*—**cheap′ness,** *n.*

cheat[1] (chēt), *n.* [Orig. for *escheat.* Some senses are from *cheat*[1], *v.*] An escheat†; booty†; a fraud or swindle; something fraudulent or deceptive; a swindler; a deceiver or impostor; also, the grass or weed *Bromus secalinus*; chess. —**cheat**[1], *v.* **I.** *tr.* To defraud (*of*); swindle; also, to deceive; impose upon; also, to beguile; elude. **II.** *intr.* To practise fraud.

cheat[2]† (chēt), *n.* [Origin uncertain.] A kind of wheaten bread, inferior to manchet.

cheat[3]† (chēt), *n.* [Origin uncertain.] A thing; esp., the gallows. [Thieves' cant.]

cheat-a-ble (chē′tạ-bl), *a.* That may be cheated.

cheat-er (chē′tėr), *n.* An escheator†; also, one who cheats.

che-bec (chẹ-bek′), *n.* [Prob. imit. of its note.] A North American flycatcher (bird), *Empidonax minimus*, of the family *Tyrannidæ.*

che-cha-co (chẹ-chä′kō), *n.*; pl. *-cos* (-kōz). [Prob. of native origin.] In Alaska, Yukon, etc., an inexperienced new-comer. Cf. *sour-dough.*

check (chek). [OF. *eschec* (F. *échec*), interj. and n. (pl. *eschecs*, F. *échecs*, the game of chess), through Ar. < Pers. *shāh*, king.] **I.** *interj.* In *chess*, a call to warn one's opponent that his king is exposed to direct attack. **II.** *n.* The exposure of the king in the game of chess to direct attack; an attack†; a reprimand or rebuke (archaic); a rebuff, repulse, or reverse; also, a sudden arrest or stoppage; also, restriction of movement or action; a person or thing that checks or restrains; a device for limiting or controlling action; a check-rein; also, control with a view to preventing error; a means to insure against error, fraud, etc.; a mark put against an item or the like, to indicate that it has been examined or verified; a token given as a means of identification, as for baggage, a theater-seat, etc.; a counter representing a certain money value, used in card-games (U. S.: as, to cash, hand, or pass in one's *checks*, as when retiring from the game; fig., to die); a written order directing a bank to pay money; also, a pattern formed of squares, as on a checker-board; one of the squares; a fabric with such a pattern; also, a crack or chink, as in timber; in *phonetics*, same as *stop*; in *carp.*, etc., a joint having two parts (as a tongue and a groove) which fit one into the other; in *masonry*, a rabbet-shaped cutting on the edge of a stone, by which it is fitted to another stone. **III.** *a.* Serving to check, control, verify, or the like; also, ornamented with a checkered pattern; checkered.—**check,** *v.* **I.** *tr.* To place (an opponent's king) in immediate danger, in the game of chess; reprimand or rebuke (archaic); stop suddenly or forcibly; also, to restrain; hold in restraint or control; also, to control or verify as to correctness; note (an item, etc.) with a mark, as to indicate examination or correctness; attach a check of identification to, or obtain such a check for (one's hat, a trunk in transit, etc.); also, to mark in a pattern of checks or squares; checker; also, to make cracks or chinks in (timber, etc.). **II.** *intr.* To place an opponent's king at chess in immediate danger; also, to come into hostile contact†; clash†; also, to make a stop; pause; also, to draw a check, or draw money by a check (U. S.); also, to crack or split, as timber; in *hunting*, of dogs, to stop, as on losing the scent; in *falconry*, of a hawk, to forsake the proper prey and follow baser game (with *at*).—**check'age** (-ạ̄j), *n.* A checking, as of items in a list; also, items, etc., checked.—**check'=book,** *n.* A book containing items by which others are checked or verified; also, a book containing blank checks or orders on a bank.—**checked,** *p. a.* Marked with a pattern of squares; checkered.—**check'er**[1], *n.*

check-er[2] (chek'ėr), *n.* [OF. *eschequier* (F. *échiquier*), chess-board, < *eschec*: see *check*.] A chess-board†; chess†; *pl.* (now construed as *sing.*), a game played by two persons, each with twelve pieces, on a checker-board (also, esp. in England, called *draughts*); *sing.*, one of the pieces used in this game; also, one of the squares of a checkered pattern; the pattern itself; also, *pl.*, the checkered or spotted fruits or berries of either of the European service-trees, *Sorbus domestica* and *S. torminalis*; *sing.*, either of these trees.—**check'er**[2], *v. t.* To mark like a checker-board, with a pattern of squares, esp. squares of alternating colors; hence, to diversify in color; variegate; also, to diversify in character; subject to alternations, as of prosperity and adversity.—**check'er-ber"ry,** *n.* The red fruit of the American wintergreen, *Gaultheria procumbens*; the plant itself; also, the partridge-berry, *Mitchella repens.*—**check'er=board,** *n.* A board marked off into sixty-four squares of two alternating colors, on which checkers and chess are played.—**check'ered,** *p. a.* Marked with squares like a checker-board; hence, diversified in color; also, diversified in character; marked by frequent alternations, as of good and bad fortune.—**check'er=tree,** *n.* Either of the service-trees, *Sorbus domestica* and *S. torminalis.*—**check'er-work,** *n.* Work resembling a checker-board in pattern; fig., a diversified combination or whole (as, "How strange a *chequer-work* of Providence is the life of man!" Defoe's "Robinson Crusoe," i. 11).

check-less (chek'les), *a.* Without check or restraint.

check=line (chek'līn), *n.* A check-rein.

check=list (chek'list), *n.* An alphabetical or systematic list of names of persons or things, intended for purposes of reference, registration, comparison, or verification: as, a *check-list* of the birds of a region; a *check-list* of voters.

check-mate (chek'māt). [OF. *eschec et mat*, < Pers. *shāh māt*, 'the king is helpless': cf. *mate*[2].] **I.** *interj.* In *chess*, an exclamation by a player when he puts his opponent's king into inextricable check. **II.** *n.* The act of putting, or the move that puts, the opponent's king at chess into inextricable check, thus bringing the game to a close; also, the position of a checkmated king; fig., complete check; defeat; overthrow.—**check'mate,** *v. t.*; *-mated, -mating.* To put (an opponent's king at chess) into inextricable check; fig., to check completely; defeat; frustrate.

check=rein (chek'rān), *n.* A short rein attached to the saddle of a harness to prevent a horse from lowering its head; also, a short rein joining the bit of one of a span of horses to the driving-rein of the other.

check=row (chek'rō), *n.* One of a number of rows of trees or plants, esp. corn, in which adjacent trees or plants (or hills of plants) are placed at a distance apart equal to the distance between adjacent rows, the result being two series of rows intersecting at right angles, the trees or plants occurring at the intersections and marking the land off into checks or squares.—**check'=row,** *v. t.* To plant in check-rows; plant (corn) with a check-rower.—**check'=row"er,** *n.* An attachment fitted to a corn-planter to cause the seed to drop at the regular intervals requisite to form check-rows.

check=up (chek'up), *n.* A checking up or verifying, as of a list or number of items, individuals, etc.

Ched-dar (ched'ạ̈r) **cheese.** [From *Cheddar*, town in southwestern England.] A common white or yellow hard cheese made from unskimmed or skimmed milk.

cheek (chēk), *n.* [AS. *cēace* = D. *kaak.*] A jaw† or jawbone†; either side of the face below the eye; something resembling the human cheek in form or position, as either of two parts forming corresponding sides of a thing; also, impudence or effrontery (slang or colloq.).—**cheek by jowl,** side by side; in close intimacy.—**cheek,** *v. t.* To form a cheek or side to; also, to address or confront with impudence or effrontery (slang).—**cheek'=bone,** *n.* The jaw-bone†; the bone or bony prominence below the outer angle of the eye.—**cheeked,** *a.* Having a cheek or cheeks: as, red-*cheeked.*—**cheek'y,** *a.* Impudently bold; impudent; insolent. [Slang or colloq.]—**cheek'i-ly,** *adv.*—**cheek'i-ness,** *n.*

cheep (chēp), *v.* [Imit.] **I.** *intr.* To chirp; peep; squeak. **II.** *tr.* To utter or express by cheeps.—**cheep,** *n.* A chirp; a squeak.—**cheep'er,** *n.*

cheer (chēr), *n.* [OF. *chere* (F. *chère*), < LL. *cara*, face: cf. Gr. κάρα, head.] The face†; expression of countenance (archaic); also, state of feeling or spirits (as, what *cheer?* how are you?); gladness, gaiety, or animation (as, to make *cheer*); also, hospitable entertainment†; fare or viands provided; also, that which gives joy or gladness; comfort; encouragement; also, a shout of encouragement, approval, congratulation, etc.—**cheer,** *v.* **I.** *tr.* To inspire with cheer; gladden; enliven; comfort; solace; also, to inspirit or incite, as by words of encouragement; also, to salute with shouts of approval, congratulation, etc. **II.** *intr.* To be in a particular state of spirits†; also, to become cheerful (often with *up*); also, to utter cheers of approval, etc.—**cheer'er,** *n.*—**cheer'ful,** *a.* Full of cheer; in good spirits; joyous; hearty or ungrudging (as, "God loveth a *cheerful* giver": 2 Cor. ix. 7); also, promoting cheer; gladdening.—**cheer'ful-ly,** *adv.*—**cheer'ful-ness,** *n.*—**cheer'i-ly,** *adv.* In a cheery manner.—**cheer'i-ness,** *n.*—**cheer'ing-ly,** *adv.*—**cheer'less,** *a.* Without cheer; joyless; gloomy.—**cheer'less-ly,** *adv.*—**cheer'less-ness,** *n.*—**cheer'ly,** *adv.* Cheerfully; cheerily. [Archaic.]—**cheer'y,** *a.*; compar. *cheerier*, superl. *cheeriest.* In good spirits; blithe; gay; also, promoting cheer; enlivening.

cheese[1] (chēz), *n.* [Cf. Hind. *chīz*, thing.] The correct or proper thing. [Slang.]

cheese[2] (chēz), *v. t.*; *cheesed, cheesing.* [Cf. *cease.*] To stop; leave off: often followed by indefinite *it.* [Slang.]

cheese[3] (chēz), *n.* [AS. *cēse*, < L. *caseus.*] The curd of milk (with or without cream) separated from the whey and prepared in many varieties as food; a mass or cake of this substance of definite shape or size; also, something of similar shape or consistence, as a mass of pomace in cider-making, or the fruit of the dwarf mallow, or a kind of thick marmalade; an inflated effect of a woman's skirt produced by whirling about and then suddenly sinking down; hence, a low curtsy.—**cheese'=cake,** *n.* A kind of open pie filled with a custard-like preparation containing cheese, esp. cottage cheese.—**cheese′=cloth,** *n.* A coarse cotton fabric of open texture, orig. used for wrapping cheeses.—**cheese′-mong″er** (-mung″gėr), *n.* One who sells or deals in cheese. —**cheese′=par″ing.** **I.** *n.* The paring of cheese; niggardly economy; also, a pared bit of the rind of cheese; something of little or no value. **II.** *a.* Meanly economical; parsimonious.—**chees′y,** *a.* Of or like cheese.—**chees′-i-ness,** *n.*

chee-ta, chee-tah (chē′tạ̈), *n.* See *chetah.*

chef (shef), *n.* [F.: see *chief.*] A head or chief; esp., a head cook.

chef=d'œuvre (she-dėvr), *n.*; pl. *chefs-d'œuvre* (she-dėvr). [F., 'chief of work.'] A masterpiece.

chef-fo-nier (shef-ọ-nēr′), *n.* Same as *chiffonier.*

cheilo-, etc., **cheiro-,** etc. See *chilo-*, etc., *chiro-*, etc.

che=la[1] (chā′lạ̈), *n.* [Hind.] In India, a disciple of a religious teacher.

che-la[2] (kē′lạ̈), *n.*; pl. *chelæ* (-lē). [NL., < Gr. χηλή, claw.] The nipper-like organ or claw terminating certain limbs of crustaceans and arachnids. —**che′late** (-lāt), *a.* Having a chela. —**che-lif-er-ous** (kẹ-lif′ẹ-rus), *a.* [See *-ferous.*] Bearing chelæ.—**che-li-form** (kē′li-fôrm or kel′i-), *a.* [See *-form.*] Having the form of a chela; nipper-like.—**che′loid,** *n.* [See *-oid.*] In *pathol.*, a kind of fibrous tumor forming hard, irregular, claw-like excrescences upon the skin. Also spelled *keloid.*

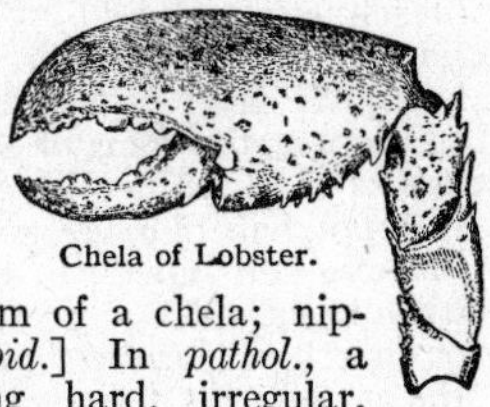

Chela of Lobster.

che-lo-ni-an (kẹ-lō′ni-ạn). [NL. *Chelonia*, pl., < Gr. χελώνη, tortoise.] **I.** *a.* Belonging to the *Chelonia*, an order or group of reptiles comprising the tortoises and turtles. **II.** *n.* A chelonian reptile.

chem-ic (kem′ik), *a.* [For *alchemic.*] Alchemic; also, chemical.—**chem′i-cal,** *a.* Alchemical†; also, of, pertaining to, or concerned with the science or the operations or processes of chemistry.—**chemical warfare,** warfare with asphyxiating, poisonous, and corrosive gases, oil flames, etc. —**chem′i-cal,** *n.* A substance produced by or used in a chemical process.—**chem′i-cal-ly,** *adv.*

Chem-i-gum (kem′i-gum), *n.* [*chemi(cal)* + *gum.*] The trade-mark name for a synthetic rubber used for tires, etc.

che-mise (shẹ-mēz′), *n.* [F., < LL. *camisia*, shirt.] A woman's loose-fitting shirt-like undergarment.

chem-i-sette (shem-i-zet′), *n.* [F., dim. of *chemise.*] A garment of linen, lace, or the like, worn with a low-cut or open bodice by women to cover the neck and breast.

chem-ism (kem′izm), *n.* Chemical action.

chem-ist (kem′ist), *n.* [For *alchemist.*] An alchemist†; also, one versed in chemistry or professionally engaged in chemical operations; also, a druggist (Eng.).—**chem′is-try,** *n.* The science that treats of or investigates the composition of substances and the various elementary forms of matter ('chemical elements').

chemo-. Form of *chemic* or *chemical* used in combination. —**che-mol-y-sis** (ke-mol′i-sis), *n.* [+ *-lysis.*] Chemical decomposition or analysis.—**chem-o-lyt-ic** (kem-ọ̄-lit′ik), *a.*—**chem-o-tax′is** (-tak′sis), *n.* [+ *-taxis.*] In *biol.*, the property in a cell or organism of exhibiting attraction or repulsion in relation to chemical substances.—**chem″o-ther-a-peu′tic** (-ther-ạ-pū′tik), *a.* Pertaining to treatment by chemotherapy.—**chem-o-ther′a-py** (-ther′ạ-pi), *n.* In *med.*, the treatment of disease by means of chemicals which have a specific toxic effect upon the disease-producing micro-organisms.—**che-mot′ro-pism** (-mot′rọ̄-pizm), *n.* [+ *-tropism.*] In *biol.*, the property in plant and other organisms of turning or bending (toward or away), as in growth, under the influence of chemical substances.

chem-ur-gy (kem′ėr-ji), *n.* [From *chemistry* and -εργός, working.] The chemistry of the utilization of farm products.

che-nar (chẹ̄-när′), *n.* Same as *chinar.*

che-nille (shẹ-nēl′), *n.* [F., caterpillar.] A velvety cord of silk or worsted, used in embroidery, fringe, etc.

che-no-pod (kē′nọ̄-pod or ken′ọ̄-), *n.* [NL. *Chenopodium*, < Gr. χήν, goose, + πούς (ποδ-), foot.] Any plant of the genus *Chenopodium* or the family *Chenopodiaceæ*; a goosefoot.—**che″no-po-di-a′ceous** (-pō-di-ā′shius), *a.* Belonging to the *Chenopodiaceæ*, or goosefoot family of plants, which includes the beet and mangel-wurzel, spinach, and orach, also many species peculiar to saline, alkaline, or desert regions.

cheque (chek), *n.* British preferred form of *check* in the sense of a written order directing a bank to pay money.

che-quer (chek′ėr), etc. British preferred form of *checker*[2], etc.

cher-ish (cher′ish), *v. t.* [OF. *cherir* (*cheriss-*) (F. *chérir*), < *cher*, < L. *carus*, dear.] To hold or treat as dear; care for tenderly; nurture or foster; also, to entertain in the mind (as, "Each *cherished* a secret, which she did not confide to the other": Longfellow's "Kavanagh," xxiii.); cling fondly to (ideas, etc.); also, to entertain hospitably†.—**cher′ish-er,** *n.*—**cher′ish-ing-ly,** *adv.*

che-root (shẹ-röt′ or chẹ-), *n.* [E. Ind. (Dravidian).] A cigar having both ends truncated, not pointed, and often thicker at one end than the other.

cher-ry (cher′i). [OF. *cherise* (prob. adapted as an E. pl.), for *cerise* (F. *cerise*), < L. *cerasus*, < Gr. κερασός, cherry-tree.] **I.** *n.*; pl. *cherries* (-iz). The fruit of any of various trees of the amygdalaceous genus *Prunus*, consisting of a pulpy, globular drupe inclosing a one-seeded smooth stone; a tree bearing such fruit; the wood of such a tree; also, cherry-color; also, any of various fruits or plants resembling the cherry. **II.** *a.* Like the common red cherry in color; of a bright red; also, made of the wood of the cherry-tree. —**cher′ry=bounce′,** *n.* A popular cordial made of brandy or whisky, cherries, and sugar.—**cher′ry=bran′dy,** *n.* Brandy in which cherries have been steeped.—**cher′ry=col″or,** *n.* A clear, bright-red color.—**cher′ry=col″ored,** *a.*—**cher′ry=stone,** *n.* The stone of a cherry: as, "Milton . . . could cut a Colossus from a rock, but could not carve heads upon *cherry-stones*" (Johnson, in Boswell's "Johnson," June 13, 1784).

cher-so-nese (kėr′sọ̄-nēs or -nēz), *n.* [L. *chersonesus*, < Gr. χερσόνησος, < χέρσος, land, + νῆσος, island.] A peninsula: as, the Golden *Chersonese* (L. *Chersonesus Aurea*, ancient name for the Malay Peninsula: see Milton's "Paradise Lost," xi. 392).

chert (chėrt), *n.* [Origin uncertain.] A compact rock consisting essentially of a mixture of cryptocrystalline quartz and hydrated silica; also, any of certain similar rocks.—**chert′y,** *a.*

cher-ub (cher′ub), *n.*; pl. *-ubs* or *-ubim* (-ọ̈-bim) (also erron. *-ubims*). [LL., < Heb. *k'rūb*, pl. *k'rūbīm.*] A kind of celestial being (see Gen. iii. 24, Ezek. i. and x.); also, a member of the second order of angels, distinguished by knowledge, often represented as a beautiful winged child or simply as a winged head of a child; also (pl. *cherubs*), a cherubic person, esp. a child; a person with a chubby, innocent face. Cf. *seraph.* —**che-ru-bic** (chẹ-rö′bik), *a.* Of, like, or befitting a cherub.—**che-ru′-bi-cal-ly,** *adv.*

Cherub by Donatello. — Basilica of St. Anthony, Padua.

cher′u-bim, *n. pl.* See *cherub.*

cher-vil (chėr′vil), *n.* [AS. *cerfille*, < L. *cærefolium*, < Gr. χαιρέφυλλον, < χαίρειν, rejoice, + φύλλον, leaf.] An apiaceous plant, *Anthriscus cerefolium*, with aromatic leaves which are used to flavor soups, salads, etc.; also, any of various plants of the same genus or allied genera.

Chesh-ire (chesh′ėr) **cheese.** [From *Cheshire*, county in western England.] A hard, deep-colored cheese made from unskimmed milk.

chess[1] (ches), *n.* [Origin uncertain.] Any of various grasses of the genus *Bromus*, esp. *B. secalinus*, or cheat, which often occurs as a weed in wheat-fields.

chess[2] (ches), *n.* [Origin uncertain.] A row, esp. one of a series of parallel rows (now prov.); *pl.*, the transverse parallel planks which form the roadway of a pontoon-bridge.

chess[3] (ches), *n.* [OF. *esches, eschecs,* pl.: see *check.*] A game played by two persons, each with sixteen pieces, on a board marked into sixty-four squares of two alternating colors.—**chess'=board,** *n.*—**chess'man** (-man), *n.*; pl. *-men.* One of the pieces used in the game of chess.

Chess-board, with pieces in position.

ches-sy-lite (ches'i-līt), *n.* [From *Chessy,* town near Lyons, France.] A crystallized variety of azurite.

chest (chest), *n.* [AS. *cest,* < L. *cista,* < Gr. κίστη, box.] A box, esp. one of large size and strong construction, as for the safe-keeping of articles of value; the place where the funds of a public institution, etc., are kept, or the funds themselves; a box in which certain goods, as tea, are packed for transit; the quantity contained in such a box; a close receptacle for steam, liquids, etc.; a coffin†; also, the trunk of the body from the neck to the belly; the thorax.—**chest of drawers,** a piece of furniture consisting of a set of drawers fitted into a frame: now used chiefly to contain clothing, linen, etc.—**chest,** *v. t.* To put into a chest.—**chest'ed,** *a.* Having a chest: as, broad-*chested.*

ches-ter-field (ches'tėr-fēld), *n.* [Named from the fourth Earl of Chesterfield: see *Chesterfieldian.*] A single-breasted overcoat of medium length, with the buttons concealed.

Ches-ter-field-i-an (ches-tėr-fēl'di-ạn), *a.* Of, pertaining to, or suggestive of the fourth Earl of Chesterfield (1694–1773), whose letters to his son contain directions as to manners and etiquette.

chest-nut (ches'nut). [For earlier *chesten nut*: OF. *chastaigne* (F. *châtaigne*), < L. *castanea,* < Gr. καστανέα, chestnut-tree, chestnut.] **I.** *n.* The edible nut of trees of the genus *Castanea,* of the beech family; a tree bearing this nut, as *C. sativa* ('European chestnut'), *C. dentata* ('American chestnut'), or *C. crenata* ('Japanese chestnut'); the wood of such a tree; also, a reddish-brown color; also, any of various fruits or trees resembling the chestnut, as the horse-chestnut; also, the callosity on the inner side of a horse's leg; also, an old or stale joke, anecdote, etc. (slang). **II.** *a.* Of a reddish-brown color.—**chest'nut=blight,** *n.* A fungus, *Diaporthe parasitica,* very destructive to the chestnut-tree.

Flowering Branch and Bur of Chestnut (*Castanea sativa*).

chest=tone (chest'tōn), *n.* In *singing,* a tone so produced as to bring the cavity of the chest or thorax into sympathetic vibration.

chest=voice (chest'vois), *n.* In *singing,* that method of using the voice, or that portion of the singer's compass or register, which tends to produce chest-tones.

che-tah (chē'tą̈), *n.* [Hind. *chītā.*] An animal of the cat family, *Cynælurus jubatus,* of southern Asia and Africa, resembling the leopard and having certain dog-like characteristics: often trained for hunting deer, etc.

Chetah.

che-val=de=frise (shė-vȧl'dė-frēz'), *n.* Occasional singular of *chevaux-de-frise.*

che-val=glass (shẹ-vȧl'glȧs), *n.* [F. *cheval,* horse.] A tall mirror mounted so as to swing in a frame.

chev-a-lier (shev-ạ-lēr', F. shė-vȧ-lyā), *n.* [OF. F. *chevalier,* < ML. *caballarius*: see *cavalier.*] A horseman or mounted soldier (archaic); a knight; in French use, esp., a cadet of the old nobility; also, a member of certain orders of honor or merit, esp. a member of the lowest grade (as, a *chevalier* of the Legion of Honor).

che-vaux=de=frise (shė-vō'dė-frēz'), *n. pl.* [F. *chevaux de frise,* lit. 'horses of Friesland' (where they were first used).] Pieces of timber traversed crosswise by spikes of iron or iron-pointed wood projecting at different angles, used to check an advance of cavalry, stop a breach, etc.

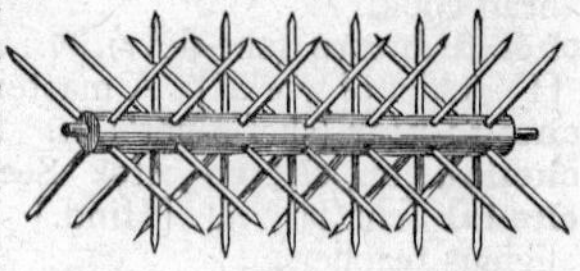

Example of one form of Chevaux-de-frise.

cheve-lure (shėv-lür), *n.* [F., < L. *capillatura,* < *capillus,* hair.] A head of hair; a wig†; in *astron.,* a nebulous envelop, as the coma of a comet.

chev-er-el† (chev'ẹ-rel), *n.* [OF. *chevrel,* kid, < *chevre,* < L. *capra,* fem. of *caper,* goat.] Kid leather. See Shakspere's "Romeo and Juliet," ii. 4. 87.

che-vet (shė-vā), *n.* [F., < ML. *capitium,* head (upper end) of church, L. head-covering, < L. *caput,* head.] In *arch.,* the apse, or the termination of the apse, of a church; esp., the apsidal end of a church when consisting of a main apse and several (usually five) secondary apses or chapels radiating from it.

Chev-i-ot (chev'i-ọt or chē'vi-ọt), *n.* A sheep of a breed valued for their thick wool, so called from the Cheviot Hills between England and Scotland; [*l. c.*] (pron. shev'-i-ọt) a rough-finished twilled woolen cloth; also, a soft-finished cotton shirting woven of fairly large threads.

chev-ron (shev'rọn), *n.* [OF. F. *chevron,* ult. < L. *caper,* goat.] A heraldic device consisting of two broad bands meeting like an inverted V; a similar decoration, as in an architectural molding; a badge consisting of stripes meeting at an angle, worn on the sleeve as an indication of rank (by non-commissioned officers, policemen, etc.), of service or wounds in war (as in the U. S. army and navy), etc.—**chev'ron=bone,** *n.* A V-shaped bone articulating with, and forming an inverted arch beneath, the spinal column of many vertebrates, esp. in the caudal region, the series of such bones forming a canal through which blood-vessels may run.—**chev'roned,** *a.* Decorated with chevrons.—**chev'ron-wise,** *adv.* In the manner of a chevron.

Heraldic Chevron, accompanied by three crosses.

Chevron-molding. — Cathedral of Durham, England.

chev-ro-tain (shev'rọ-tān), *n.* [F., < OF. *chevrot,* kid, < *chevre*: see *cheverel.*] Any of the very small ungulates (family *Tragulidæ*) of the genera *Tragulus,* of Asia, and *Dorcatherium,* of Africa, having deer-like characteristics.

Pygmy Chevrotain (*Tragulus kanchil*).

chev-y (chev′i), *n.*; pl. *-ies* (-iz). [Perhaps < *Chevy Chase*, title of an old English ballad describing the battle of Otterburn (1388): cf. OF. *chevauchie*, a riding, raid.] A hunting-cry; also, a hunt, chase, or pursuit; also, the game of prisoners' base.—**chev′y,** *v.*; *chevied, chevying.* **I.** *tr.* To chase. [Eng.] **II.** *intr.* To race; scamper. [Eng.]

chew (chö), *v.* [AS. *cēowan*, akin to G. *kauen.*] **I.** *tr.* To crush or grind with the teeth; masticate; fig., to meditate on; consider deliberately. **II.** *intr.* To perform the act of crushing or grinding with the teeth; use tobacco for chewing (colloq.); fig., to meditate.—**chew,** *n.* The act of chewing; also, that which is chewed; a portion, as of tobacco, for chewing.—**chew′er,** *n.*—**chew′ing=gum,** *n.* A preparation of spruce-gum, chicle, or some similar substance, usually sweetened and flavored, for use as a masticatory.

che-wink (chē-wingk′), *n.* [Imit. of its note.] A bird, *Pipilo erythrophthalmus*, of the finch family, common in eastern North America.

Chewink.

chi (kī or kē), *n.* [Gr. χῖ.] The twenty-second letter (X, χ, = English ch or kh) of the Greek alphabet. Cf. *X*².

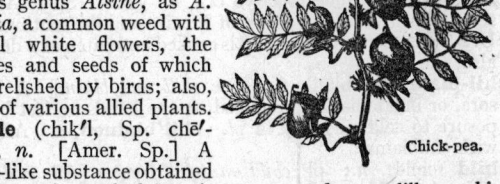

chi-a (chē′ạ), *n.* [Mex. Sp.] Any of several species of salvia, of Mexico and the southwestern U. S., the seeds of which are used as food and in the preparation of a mucilaginous beverage; also, the seeds, or the beverage.

Chi-an (kī′ạn). **I.** *a.* Of or pertaining to Chios (the modern Scio), an island in the Ægean Sea. **II.** *n.* A native or inhabitant of Chios; also, Chian wine.

Chi-an-ti (kē-än′tē), *n.* [From the *Chianti* Mountains, in Tuscany.] A dry red Italian wine.

chia-ro-scu-ro (kyä-rọ-skö′rō), *n.* [It., 'clear-obscure.'] The treatment or general distribution of light and shade in a picture; also, pictorial art employing only light and shade; also, a sketch in black and white.—**chia-ro-scu′rist,** *n.*

chi-asm (kī′azm), *n.* [NL. *chiasma*, < Gr. χίασμα, < χιάζειν, arrange in the form of the Greek letter X, χ.] In *anat.*, a crossing or decussation, esp. that of the optic nerves at the base of the brain. Also **chi-as′ma** (-az′mạ); pl. *-mata* (-mạ-tạ).—**chi-as′mal,** *a.*

chi-as-to-lite (kī-as′tọ-līt), *n.* [Gr. χιαστός, arranged crosswise, < χιάζειν: see *chiasm.*] A kind of andalusite whose crystals have a tessellated appearance in cross-section.

Sections of a Crystal of Chiastolite.

chi-bouk, chi-bouque, chi-buk (chi-bök′), *n.* [= F. *chibouque*, < Turk. *chibūq.*] A Turkish tobacco-pipe with a long, stiff stem (sometimes four or five feet long): as, "the long *chibouque's* dissolving cloud" (Byron's "Corsair," ii. 2).

chic (shēk). [F., perhaps < *chicane*, chicane.] **I.** *n.* Artistic cleverness and facility, as in painting; cleverly effective style, as in dress. **II.** *a.* Cleverly effective in style.

chi-ca-lo-te (chē-kä-lō′tā), *n.* [Mex. Sp.] A prickly, (usually) white-flowered, papaveraceous plant, *Argemone platyceras*, of Mexico and the southwestern U. S.

chi-cane (shi-kān′), *v.*; *-caned, -caning.* [F. *chicaner*; origin unknown.] **I.** *intr.* To use quibbling, caviling, or petty shifts to impede the settlement of a question, as at law; quibble; cavil. **II.** *tr.* To quibble over; cavil at; also, to overreach or trick by chicanery.—**chi-cane′,** *n.* The use of petty shifts or subterfuges, as at law; quibbling; sophistry; trickery; a quibble or subterfuge; in the game of bridge, a hand without trumps.—**chi-can′er** (-kā′nėr), *n.*—**chi-can′er-y,** *n.*; pl. *-ies* (-iz). Chicane; quibbling, sophistry, or trickery; a quibble or subterfuge.

chich (chich), *n.* [OF. F. *chiche*, < L. *cicer.*] The chick-pea.—**chich′ling,** *n.* Same as *chickling.*

chick (chik), *n.* [For *chicken.*] A young chicken (or other bird); also, a child.

chick-a-dee (chik′ạ-dē), *n.* [Imit. of its note.] Any of various titmice (birds), esp. the black-capped titmouse.

chick-a-ree (chik′ạ-rē), *n.* [Imit. of its cry.] The red squirrel, *Sciurus hudsonius*, of North America.

Chickaree.

chick-en (chik′en). [AS. *cīcen* = D. *kieken.*] **I.** *n.* The young of the domestic fowl (or of certain other birds); a domestic fowl of any age, or its flesh; any of certain other birds (as, Mother Carey's *chicken*, the stormy petrel; the prairie-*chicken*, the prairie-hen); also, a young person, esp. a young girl (now colloq. or slang). **II.** *a.* Young; small: as, a *chicken* lobster; a *chicken* halibut.—**chick′en=breast,** *n.* A malformation of the chest in which there is abnormal projection of the sternum and the sternal region: often associated with rickets.—**chick′en=breast″ed,** *a.*—**chick′en=feed,** *n.* Food for chickens; also, small change, as one-cent pieces and nickels (slang or colloq.).—**chick′en=heart″ed,** *a.* Timid; cowardly.—**chick′en=pox,** *n.* In *pathol.*, a mild, contagious eruptive disease, commonly of children; varicella.

chick-ling (chik′ling), *n.* [For *chichling.*] A European vetch, *Lathyrus sativus*, cultivated for its edible seeds, and also used as a forage-plant. Also **chick′ling=vetch.**

chick=pea (chik′pē), *n.* [Earlier *chich pea*: see *chich.*] A fabaceous plant, *Cicer arietinum*, bearing edible pea-like seeds, much used for food in southern Europe; also, the seed of this plant.

Chick-pea.

chick-weed (chik′wēd), *n.* [See *chick.*] Any of various plants of the silenaceous genus *Alsine*, as *A. media*, a common weed with small white flowers, the leaves and seeds of which are relished by birds; also, any of various allied plants.

chic-le (chik′l, Sp. chē′klā), *n.* [Amer. Sp.] A gum-like substance obtained from certain tropical American trees, as the sapodilla, used in the manufacture of chewing-gum, etc. Also **chic′le=gum.**

chic-o-ry (chik′ọ-ri), *n.* [F. *chicorée*, < L. *cichorium*, < Gr. κίχορα.] A perennial cichoriaceous plant, *Cichorium intybus*, with bright-blue flowers, cultivated for its root, which is used roasted and ground as a substitute for or adulterant of coffee, and for use as salad; also, the root.

Chicory.

chide (chīd), *v.*; pret. *chid* or *chided*, pp. *chidden, chided* or *chid*, ppr. *chiding.* [AS. *cīdan.*] **I.** *intr.* To wrangle noisily†; also, to scold; utter rebukes; also, to make a clamorous noise (as, "the *chiding* flood": Shakspere's "Henry VIII.," iii. 2. 197). **II.** *tr.* To reprove or rebuke; find fault with; reproach; also, to drive, impel, etc., by chiding.—**chid-er** (chī′dėr), *n.*—**chid′ing-ly,** *adv.*

chief (chēf), *n.* [OF. *chief, chef* (F. *chef*), < L. *caput*, head.] The head or leader of a body of men; the person highest in authority; the head or ruler of a clan or a tribe; the most important, best, or main part of anything (archaic); in *her.*, the upper third of an escutcheon.—**in chief,** in the highest position; at the head: as, a commander-*in-chief*.—**chief. I.** *a.* Standing at the head; highest in rank or authority; most important; principal; leading; also, intimate, as friends (Sc.). **II.** *adv.* Chiefly; principally. [Archaic.]—**chief′dom** (-dọm), *n.* The position or authority of a chief.—**chief′ess,** *n.* A female chief.—**chief′less,** *a.* Without a chief.—**chief′ly,** *a.* Pertaining or proper to a chief.—**chief′ly,** *adv.* Principally; above all; also, mainly; mostly.—**chief′ship,** *n.*

Heraldic Chief (at top).

chief-tain (chēf′tạn), *n.* [OF. *chevetaine*, < ML. *capitaneus*: see *captain*.] A captain or leader; the chief of a clan or a tribe.—**chief′tain-cy** (-si), *n.* The position or rank of chieftain.—**chief′tain-ess,** *n.* A female chieftain.—**chief′tain-ship,** *n.*

chiel, chield (chēl, chēld), *n.* [Cf. *child, childe*.] A young man; a fellow. [Sc.]

chif-fon (shif′on, F. shē-fôṅ), *n.* [F., < *chiffe*, rag.] Any bit of feminine finery, as of ribbon or lace; also, a soft, plain-woven, very thin, transparent fabric made of silk.—**chif′fon,** *a.* Of fabrics, as velvet or broadcloth, of light weight and fine quality.

chif-fo-nier (shif-ọ-nēr′), *n.* [F. *chiffonnier*, < *chiffon*: see *chiffon*.] A cabinet with drawers; a case of drawers, high in proportion to its width.

chig-ger (chig′ėr), *n.* Same as *chigo*.

chi-gnon (shē-nyôṅ), *n.* [F., < OF. *chaaignon*, nape of the neck, < L. *catena*, chain.] A large rolled arrangement of the hair, often drawn over a cushion, worn at the back of the head by women.

chig-o (chig′ō), *n.*; pl. *-os* or *-oes* (-ōz). [W. Ind.] A minute flea, *Sarcopsylla penetrans*, of the West Indies, South America, etc., the impregnated female of which burrows beneath the skin of men and animals, esp. of the human foot, where it becomes distended with eggs and causes severe irritation and often serious sores. Also **chig-re** (chig′ėr).

Chigo.
1, Anterior part of female before development of eggs (magnified); *a, a*, rudimentary wings; 2, male (natural size); 3, female, full of eggs (natural size), as taken from a human toe; 4, male (magnified).

chi-la-ca-yo-te (chē″lä-kä-yō′tā), *n.* [Mex. Sp.] Any of several cucurbitaceous plants of Mexico and the southwestern U. S., with a fruit whose pulp is cooked and eaten as a dessert; also, the fruit.

chil-blain (chil′blān), *n.* [See *chill* and *blain*.] A blain, sore, or inflammation produced on the hands or feet by exposure to cold: usually in *pl.*—**chil′blained,** *a.* Affected with chilblains.

child (chīld), *n.*; pl. *children* (chil′drẹn). [AS. *cild*; pl. *cild*, also *cildru, cildra*, whence E. *childer* (now prov.), *children*.] A baby or infant; a female infant (prov. Eng.); a boy or girl; a childish person; a youth of gentle birth (archaic, and now usually spelled *childe*); a son or daughter; any descendant; a person related as if by the ties uniting offspring to parent; any person or thing looked upon as the product or result of particular agencies, forces, influences, etc. (as, *children* of light).—**with child,** pregnant.—**child,** *v. i.* or *t.* To give birth to (a child): as, "Many a *childing* mother then, And new-born baby died" (Southey's "Battle of Blenheim," viii.). [Obs. or archaic.]—**child′=bear″ing,** *n.* and *a.*—**child′bed,** *n.* The situation of a woman giving birth to a child; parturition.—**child′birth,** *n.* Parturition.

childe (chīld), *n.* Archaic spelling of *child* (youth of gentle birth): as, "*Childe* Harold's Pilgrimage" (title of a poem by Byron).

chil-der (chil′dėr), *n.* Obs. or prov. plural of *child*.

Chil-der-mas (chil′dėr-mạs), *n.* [ME. *chyldermasse*, < AS. *cildra*, children, + *mæsse*, mass: see *child* and *-mas*.] Holy Innocents' Day, Dec. 28.

child-hood (chīld′hụd), *n.* The state or time of being a child.—**second childhood,** the childishness often incident to old age; dotage.

child-ish (chīl′dish), *a.* Of, like, or befitting a child; in disparaging use, puerile, weak, or silly.—**child′ish-ly,** *adv.*—**child′ish-ness,** *n.*

child-less (chīld′les), *a.* Having no child.—**child′less-ness,** *n.*

child-like (chīld′līk), *a.* Like or befitting a child, as in innocence or artlessness.—**child′like-ness,** *n.*

child-ly (chīld′li), *a.* Childlike; childish.

child-ness (chīld′nes), *n.* The state of being a child; also, childish humor† (see Shakspere's "Winter's Tale," i. 2. 170).

chil-dren (chil′drẹn), *n.* Plural of *child*.

Chil-e-an (chil′ẹ-ạn). **I.** *a.* Of, pertaining to, or characteristic of Chile or its inhabitants. **II.** *n.* A native or inhabitant of Chile.

chil-i (chil′i), *n.* See *chilli*.

chil-i-ad (kil′i-ad), *n.* [Gr. χιλιάς (χιλιαδ-), < χίλιοι, thousand.] A thousand; also, a period of a thousand years.

chil-i-arch (kil′i-ärk), *n.* [Gr. χιλιάρχης, < χίλιοι, thousand, + ἄρχειν, lead, rule.] The commander of a thousand men.

chil-i-asm (kil′i-azm), *n.* [Gr. χιλιασμός, < χιλιάς: see *chiliad*.] The doctrine of the millennium.—**chil′i-ast** (-ast), *n.* A millenarian.—**chil-i-as′tic,** *a.*

chill (chil). [AS. *ciele*, coldness; akin to E. *cool, cold*.] **I.** *n.* Coldness, esp. a moderate but penetrating coldness, as in the air; also, a sensation of cold, usually with shivering; the cold stage of ague, etc.; fig., a depressing influence or sensation; also, a metal mold for making chilled castings. **II.** *a.* Cold; tending to cause shivering; also, depressingly affected by cold; shivering with cold; fig., depressing or discouraging (as, "*chill* penury": Gray's "Elegy," xiii.); not warm or hearty (as, a *chill* reception); repressed or deadened.—**chill,** *v.* **I.** *intr.* To become cold; be seized with a chill; in *metal.*, to harden, esp. on the surface, by sudden cooling. **II.** *tr.* To affect with cold; make chilly; fig., to depress or dispirit; in *metal.*, to cool suddenly, so as to harden; esp., to harden (cast-iron or steel) on the surface by casting in a metal mold.—**chill′er,** *n.*

chil-li (chil′i), *n.*; pl. *chillies* (-iz). [Mex.] The pod of species of capsicum, esp. *Capsicum annuum*. See *capsicum*.—**chilli sauce,** a condiment made of tomatoes cooked with chillies, spices, and other seasoning ingredients.

chill-i-ly (chil′i-li), *adv.* In a chilly manner.—**chill′i-ness,** *n.* Chilly quality or state.

chill-ing (chil′ing), *p. a.* That chills; chill; cold; depressing; discouraging.—**chill′ing-ly,** *adv.*

chill-ness (chil′nes), *n.* Chill quality or state.

chill-y[1] (chil′i), *a.*; compar. *chillier*, superl. *chilliest*. Producing a sensation of cold; so cold as to cause shivering; also, feeling a sensation of cold; sensitive to cold; fig., without warmth of feeling.

chil-ly[2] (chil′li), *adv.* In a chill manner.

chilo-. Form of Gr. χεῖλος, lip, used in combination.

chi-log-nath (kī′lọg-nath), *n.* [NL. *Chilognatha*, pl., < Gr. χεῖλος, lip, + γνάθος, jaw.] A myriapod of the order or group *Chilognatha*; a millepede.—**chi-log′na-thous** (-log′nạ-thus), *a.*

chi-lo-plas-ty (kī′lō-plas-ti), *n.* [See *chilo-* and *-plasty*.] Plastic surgery as concerned with the lip.

chi-lo-pod (kī′lọ-pod), *n.* [NL. *Chilopoda*, pl., < Gr. χεῖλος, lip, + πούς (ποδ-), foot.] A myriapod of the order or group *Chilopoda*; a centipede.—**chi-lop′o-dous** (-lop′ọ-dus), *a.*

chi-mæ-ra (ki-mē′rạ̈ or kī-), *n.* See *chimera*.

chim-ar (chim′ạ̈r), *n.* Same as *chimere*.

chimb (chīm), *n.* See *chime*[2].

chime[1] (chīm), *n.* [ME. *chimbe*, ult. < L. *cymbalum*, E. *cymbal*.] A cymbal†; an arrangement for striking a bell or bells so as to produce a musical sound; a set of bells, as in a tower or an organ, which are musically attuned; also, the sounds or music produced by such a set of bells (often in *pl.*); hence, harmonious sound in general; music; melody; fig., harmonious correspondence or relation; accord.—**chime**[1], *v.*; *chimed, chiming*. **I.** *intr.* To emit a sound like that of a bell; ring; tinkle; sound harmoniously or in chimes, as a set of bells; also, to produce a musical sound by striking a bell, etc.; ring chimes; also, to speak in cadence or singsong; also, to sound in consonance; fig., to harmonize or agree; join harmoniously (*in*). **II.** *tr.* To give forth (music, etc.), as a bell or bells; also, to strike (a bell, a set of chimes, etc.) so as to produce musical sound; also, to utter or repeat in cadence or singsong; also, to put, bring, etc., by chiming.

chime[2], **chimb** (chīm), *n.* [ME. *chymbe*; akin to D. *kim*, G. *kimme.*] The edge or brim of a cask or the like, formed by the ends of the staves projecting beyond the head or bottom.

chim-er[1] (chī′mėr), *n.* One who plays chimes, as of bells.

chim-er[2] (chim′ėr), *n.* Same as *chimere.*

chi-me-ra, chi-mæ-ra (ki-mē′rạ̈ or kī-), *n.*; pl. *-ras.* [L. *Chimæra*, < Gr. Χί-μαιρα, lit. 'she-goat.'] [*cap.* or *l. c.*] A mythological fire-breathing monster, commonly represented with a lion's head, a goat's body, and a serpent's tail; [*l. c.*] a grotesque monster, as in decorative art; fig., a horrible or unreal creature of the imagination; a bogy; a vain or idle fancy (as, "I now see how fatally I betrayed my quiet, by suffering *chimeras* to prey upon me in secret": Johnson's "Rasselas," xlvii.).

Chimera. — Lycian terra-cotta, British Museum.

chi-mere (chi-mēr′, shi-mēr′), *n.* [AL. *chimera* = OF. *chamarre*: see *simar.*] A loose upper robe; esp., one worn by a bishop, to which the lawn sleeves are usually attached.

chi-mer-ic (ki-mer′ik or kī-), *a.* Chimerical.—**chi-mer′i-cal,** *a.* Pertaining to or of the nature of a chimera; unreal; imaginary; visionary; also, given to entertaining chimeras; wildly fanciful.—**chi-mer′i-cal-ly,** *adv.*

chim-ney (chim′ni), *n.*; pl. *-neys* (-niz). [OF. *chiminee* (F. *cheminée*), < ML. *caminata*, < L. *caminus*, < Gr. κάμινος, furnace.] A fireplace; a structure, usually vertical, containing a passage or flue by which the smoke, gases, etc., of a fire or furnace are carried off and a draft is created; that part of such a structure which rises above a roof; the smoke-stack or funnel of a locomotive, steamship, etc.; a tube, commonly of glass, surrounding the flame of a lamp to promote combustion and keep the flame steady; anything resembling a chimney, as the vent of a volcano.—**chim′ney=cor″ner,** *n.* The corner or side of a fireplace; the fireside; a place near the fire.—**chim′neyed,** *a.* Having a chimney or chimneys.—**chim′ney-less,** *a.* Without a chimney.—**chim′ney-piece,** *n.* A picture or other decorative piece placed over a fireplace†; also, a mantelpiece; also, a mantelshelf.—**chim′ney=pot,** *n.* A cylindrical or other pipe, as of earthenware or sheet-metal, fitted on the top of a chimney to increase the draft and prevent smoking.—**chim′ney=swal″low,** *n.* The common European swallow, *Hirundo rustica*; in the U. S., the chimney-swift.—**chim′ney=sweep, chim′ney=sweep″er,** *n.* One whose business it is to clean out chimneys.—**chim′ney=swift,** *n.* An American swift, *Chætura pelagica*, which often builds its nest in a disused chimney.

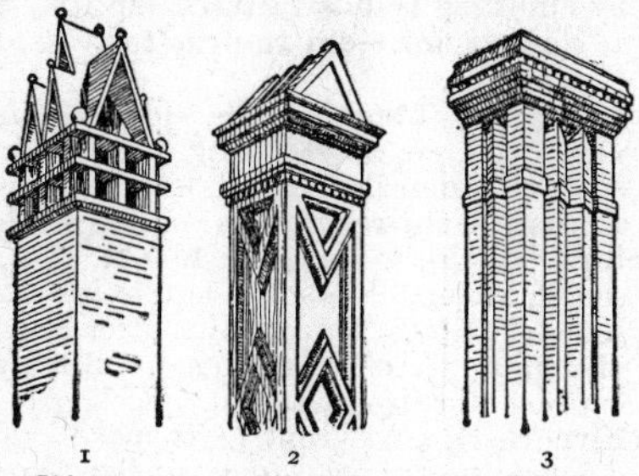

1 2 3

Chimneys. — 1. Fifteenth century, Strasburg. 2. Sixteenth century, Château de Chambord, France. 3. Modern, New York.

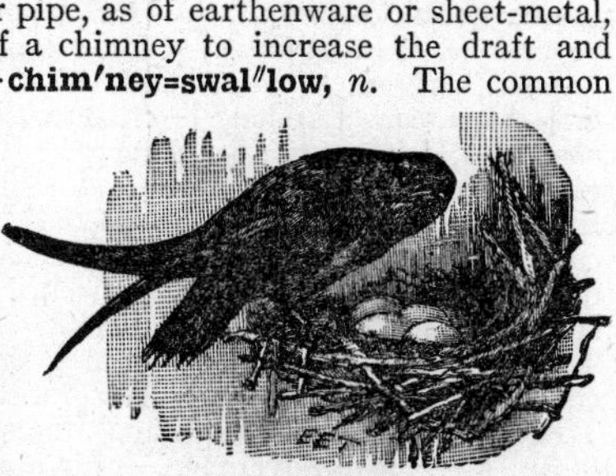

Chimney-swift.

chim-pan-zee (chim-pan′zē̦ or -pan-zē′), *n.* [W. Afr.] An anthropoid ape, *Anthropopithecus troglodytes*, of equatorial Africa, smaller and less ferocious than the gorilla.

Chimpanzee.

chin (chin), *n.* [AS. *cin* = G. *kinn*; akin to L. *gena*, cheek, Gr. γένυς, jaw.] The lower extremity of the face, below the mouth; the point of the under jaw.—**chin,** *v.*; *chinned, chinning.* **I.** *tr.* To bring up to the chin, as a violin; also, to bring one's chin up to (a horizontal bar on which one is hanging by the hands) by lifting the body by the arms; also, to talk to (slang). **II.** *intr.* To talk. [Slang.]

chi-na[1] (chī′nạ̈), *n.* [From *China*, country in Asia.] A fine kind of ceramic material or ware orig. produced in China; porcelain: now often applied also to the coarser varieties.

chi-na[2] (kē′nạ̈ or kī′nạ̈), *n.* [Peruvian *kina*, bark: cf. *quina.*] Cinchona (bark); also, any of various similar barks.

chi-na-ber-ry (chī′nạ̈-ber″i), *n.*; pl. *-berries* (-iz). The china-tree or its fruit; also, a soapberry, *Sapindus marginatus*, of Mexico, the West Indies, and the southern U. S.

Chi-na-man (chī′nạ̈-mạn), *n.*; pl. *-men.* A man belonging to the Chinese race.—**Chinaman's chance,** a very slight or poor chance: as, he hasn't a *Chinaman's chance.* [Colloq.]

chi-nar (chi-när′), *n.* [Pers.] The plane-tree *Platanus orientalis.*

Chi-na-town (chī′nạ̈-toun), *n.* The Chinese quarter in a city.

chi-na=tree (chī′nạ̈-trē), *n.* The azedarach.

chi-na-ware (chī′nạ̈-wãr), *n.* Ware or vessels made of china or porcelain.

chin-ca-pin (ching′kạ-pin), *n.* See *chinkapin.*

chinch (chinch), *n.* [Sp. *chinche*, < L. *cimex*, bug.] The bedbug; also, a fetid American hemipterous insect of the genus *Blissus*, destructive to wheat, etc., esp. *B. leucopterus.* Also **chinch′=bug.**

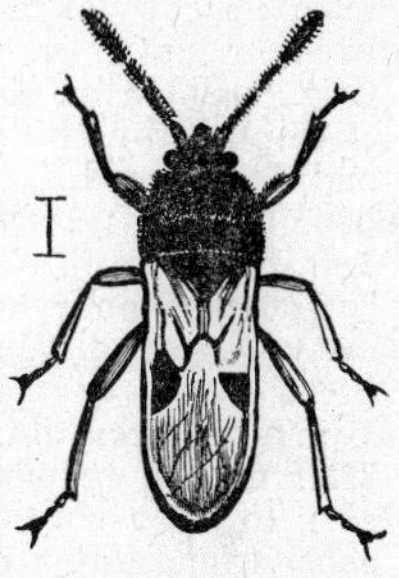

Chinch (*Blissus leucopterus*). (Vertical line shows natural size.)

chin-chil-la (chin-chil′ạ̈), *n.* [Sp.] A small South American rodent of the genus *Chinchilla*, whose skin is dressed as a fur; also, the fur, fine, soft, and whitish-gray; also, a thick woolen fabric with a long nap forming small, closely set tufts, used for warm outer garments.

Chinchilla (*C. lanigera*).

chine[1] (chīn), *n.* [AS. *cinu*, fissure.] A fissure†; a ravine formed in rock by the action of running water (local, Eng.).

chine[2] (chīn), *n.* [OF. *eschine* (F. *échine*); from Teut.] The backbone or spine; the whole or a piece of the backbone of an animal with adjoining parts, cut for cooking; also, a ridge or crest, as of land.

chine[3] (chīn), *n.* Same as *chime*[2].

chi-né (shē-nā), *a.* [F., pp. of *chiner*, color in a particular manner derived from the Chinese, < *Chine*, China.] Of fabrics, esp. silk, having the warp-threads so printed in colors as to produce, when woven, a pattern of which the outlines are more or less indistinct.

Chi-nee (chī-nē′), *n.* [From *Chinese.*] A Chinaman: as, "For ways that are dark, And for tricks that are vain, The heathen *Chinee* is peculiar" (Bret Harte's "Plain Language from Truthful James"). [Colloq.]

Chi-nese (chī-nēs′ or -nēz′), *a.* Of or pertaining to China, its inhabitants, or their language.—**Chinese lantern,** a collapsible lantern of thin, usually variously colored paper arranged in folds like the sides of an accordion, used (esp.

by the Chinese and Japanese) for illuminations.—**Chi-nese′,** *n.*; pl. *-nese.* A member of the native race of China; also, the language of China, a monosyllabic tongue.

chink[1] (chingk), *n.* [Origin uncertain: cf. *chine*[1].] A crack, cleft, or fissure; a narrow opening.—**chink**[1], *v.* **I.**† *intr.* To crack. **II.** *tr.* To crack; also, to fill up chinks in.

chink[2] (chingk), *v. i.* or *t.* [Imit.] To make, or cause to make, a short, sharp, ringing sound, as of coins or glasses striking together.—**chink**[2], *n.* A chinking sound; also, coin or ready cash (colloq.).

Chink[3] (chingk), *n.* A Chinaman. [Slang, U. S.]

chin-ka-pin (ching′ka-pin), *n.* [N. Amer. Ind.] The dwarf chestnut, *Castanea pumila*, a shrub or small tree of the U. S., bearing a small, edible nut, solitary in the bur; the nut itself; also, a related shrub or tree, *Castanopsis chrysophylla*, of Oregon and California, or its nut.

chink-y (ching′ki), *a.* Full of chinks or fissures.

chinned (chind), *a.* Having a chin: as, long-*chinned.*

Chi-nook (chi-nök′), *n.* A member of any of various Indian tribes of the Columbia River region of western North America; also, a jargon of Indian, French, and English, used in the northwestern part of America; [*l. c.*] a warm, moist southwest wind on the coast of Washington and Oregon ('wet chinook'); also, a warm, dry wind which blows at intervals down the slopes of the Rocky Mountains.

chin-qua-pin (ching′ka-pin), *n.* See *chinkapin.*

chinse (chins), *v. t.*; *chinsed, chinsing.* [Cf. *chink*[1].] *Naut.*, to calk slightly or temporarily.

chintz (chints), *n.* [Earlier *chints*, pl., < Hind. *chīnt.*] Orig., painted or stained calico from India; now, cotton cloth printed with floral or other patterns in various colors, and often glazed.

chip[1] (chip), *v.*; *chipped, chipping.* [ME.; akin to *chop*[1].] **I.** *tr.* To pare (bread) by cutting away the crust†; hew or cut, as with an ax or chisel; shape or produce by cutting away pieces; disfigure by breaking off fragments; cut or break off (bits or fragments); also, to bet by means of chips, as in poker; contribute, as to a fund (often with *in*: colloq.). **II.** *intr.* To become chipped; break off in small pieces; also, to bet a chip or chips, as in poker; contribute to a general fund (often with *in*: colloq.); interpolate a remark into the conversation of others (with *in*: colloq.).—**chip**[1], *n.* A small piece, as of wood, separated by chopping, cutting, or breaking; a small (cut) piece of diamond, etc.; a very thin slice of potato fried crisp; wood or woody fiber in thin strips, for weaving into hats; a counter, as of ivory or bone, used in certain card-games; anything trivial or worthless, or dried up or without flavor; a piece of dried dung, as of the American bison; also, a mark made by chipping.

chip[2] (chip), *v. i.*; *chipped, chipping.* [Imit.: cf. *cheep.*] To utter a short chirping or squeaking sound.—**chip**[2], *n.* A short chirping or squeaking cry.—**chip′=bird,** *n.* The chipping sparrow *Spizella socialis.*

Chipmunk (*Tamias striatus*).

chip-munk (chip′mungk), *n.* [N. Amer. Ind.] Any of various small striped American squirrels of the genus *Tamias*, esp. *T. striatus* of eastern North America.

Chip-pen-dale (chip′en-dāl), *a.* Pertaining to, or in the style of, Thomas Chippendale, an English furniture-designer of the 18th century.

Chippendale Chair.

chip-per[1] (chip′ėr), *v. i.* [Cf. *chip*[2].] To chirp or twitter; chatter or babble.—**chip′per**[1], *n.* Chirping; chatter.

chip-per[2] (chip′ėr), *a.* [Origin uncertain.] Lively; cheerful: as, "She's the *chipperest*, light-heartedest . . . little creetur" (Mrs. Stowe's "Oldtown Folks," xlvi.). [Colloq., U. S.]—**chip′per**[2], *v. t.* To cheer (*up*). [Colloq., U. S.]

chip-ping[1] (chip′ing), *n.* A small piece or bit chipped off; a fragment: usually in *pl.*

chip-ping[2] (chip′ing), *p. a.* Making a short chirping or squeaking sound.—**chipping sparrow,** any of several small North American sparrows of the genus *Spizella*, as *S. socialis*, which is common about houses.—**chipping squirrel,** the chipmunk.

chip-py (chip′i), *n.*; pl. *chippies* (-iz). The chipping sparrow *Spizella socialis.*

chirk (chėrk), *a.* [Origin uncertain.] Lively; cheerful: as, "She was jest as *chirk* and chipper as a wren" (Mrs. Stowe's "Oldtown Fireside Stories," ii.). [Colloq., U. S.]—**chirk,** *v. i.* or *t.* To cheer (*up*). [Colloq., U. S.]

chirm (chėrm), *v. i.* [AS. *cirman*, cry out.] To chirp, as a bird; sing or warble; croon; babble or chatter. [Archaic or prov.]—**chirm,** *n.* The chirping of birds; confused noise, as of the notes of birds, human voices, etc.; din. [Archaic or prov.]

chiro-. Form of Gr. χείρ, hand, used in combination.

chi-rog-no-my (kī-rog′nọ-mi), *n.* [From *chiro-* + *-gnomy* as in *physiognomy.*] The branch of palmistry concerned with judging of character from the hand.

chi-ro-graph (kī′rọ-gråf), *n.* [L. *chirographum*, < Gr. χειρόγραφον, neut. of χειρόγραφος, written with the hand: see *chiro-* and *-graph.*] Any of various formally written or signed legal or other documents; a writing executed in duplicate on a single sheet, and then divided through letters, etc., or along an indented line, between the copies; a document in one's own handwriting.—**chi-rog′ra-phy** (-rog′-ra-fi), *n.* [See *-graphy.*] Handwriting.—**chi-rog′ra-pher,** *n.*—**chi-ro-graph′ic** (-graf′ik), *a.*

chi-ro-man-cy (kī′rọ-man-si), *n.* [See *chiro-* and *-mancy.*] Divination of the future from the hand: a branch of palmistry.—**chi′ro-man-cer, chi′ro-mant** (-mant), *n.*

chi-rop-o-dist (kī-rop′ọ-dist), *n.* [Gr. χείρ, hand, + πούς (ποδ-), foot.] One who treats diseases of the hands and feet; also, one who removes corns, etc.—**chi-rop′o-dy,** *n.*

chi-ro-prac-tic (kī-rọ-prak′tik), *n.* [Gr. χείρ, hand, + πρακτική, practical science.] A system of therapeutics based upon the theory that disease is caused by interference with nerve function, the method being to restore normal condition by adjusting body structures, esp. the spinal column; also, a chiropractor.—**chi-ro-prac′tor,** *n.* One who practises chiropractic.

chi-rop-ter (kī-rop′tėr), *n.* [NL. *Chiroptera*, pl., < Gr. χείρ, hand, + πτερόν, wing.] One of the *Chiroptera*, an order of mammals (the bats) having the fore limbs modified as wings.—**chi-rop′ter-an,** *a.* and *n.*—**chi-rop′ter-ous,** *a.*

chirp (chėrp), *v.* [Imit.] **I.** *intr.* To make a short, sharp sound, as small birds and certain insects; make any similar sound. **II.** *tr.* To sound or utter in a chirping manner.—**chirp,** *n.* A chirping sound.—**chirp′er,** *n.*—**chirp′y,** *a.* Inclined to chirp; cheerful. [Colloq.]

chirr (chėr), *v. i.* [Imit.] To make a shrill trilling sound, as a grasshopper; make some similar sound.—**chirr,** *n.* The sound of chirring.

chir-rup (chir′up), *v.*; *-ruped, -ruping.* [Var. of *chirp.*] **I.** *intr.* To chirp; also, to make a chirping sound, as to a cage-bird or a horse. **II.** *tr.* To utter with chirps; also, to make a chirping sound to; also, to cheer or applaud (a public performer) for pay (slang, Eng.).—**chir′rup,** *n.* The act or sound of chirruping.—**chir′rup-y,** *a.* Chirpy; cheerful. [Colloq.]

chi-rur-geon (kī-rėr′jọn), *n.* [OF. *cirurgien* (F. *chirurgien*), < *cirurgie*, < L. *chirurgia*, < Gr. χειρουργία, surgery, < χειρουργός, surgeon, < χείρ, hand, + -εργός, working, worker.] A surgeon. [Archaic.]—**chi-rur′ger-y** (-jėr-i), *n.* [OF. *cirurgerie*, for *cirurgie.*] Surgery. [Archaic.]—**chi-rur′gic, chi-rur′gi-cal** (-jik, -ji-kal), *a.* Surgical. [Archaic.]

chis-el (chiz′el), *n.* [OF. *chisel, cisel* (F. *ciseau*), < L. *cædere*, cut.] A tool, as of steel, with a cutting edge at the extremity, usually transverse to the axis, for cutting or shaping wood, stone, etc.—**chis′el,** *v.*; *-eled* or *-elled, -eling* or *-elling.* **I.** *tr.* To cut, shape, etc., with a chisel; also (slang), to cheat; get by cheating or trickery; get by unfair or mean methods. **II.** *intr.* To work with a chisel; also (slang), to use trickery; cut in unfairly; take mean advantage.—**chis′eled, chis′elled,** *p. a.* Cut, shaped, etc., with a chisel; hence, clear-cut.—**chis′el-er, chis′el-ler,** *n.* One who chisels; esp. (slang), a cheater; one who cuts in unfairly; a mean or petty profit-seeker.

chit[1] (chit), *n.* [Cf. AS. *cīth*, sprout.] A sprout of a seed; a shoot, as of a potato.—**chit**[1], *v. i.*; *chitted, chitting.* To sprout.

chit[2] (chit), *n.* [Cf. *kit*[2], *kitten.*] A young animal†; a kitten (now prov.); a young person, esp. a girl (used in contempt).

chit[3] (chit), *n.* [Hind.] In India, etc., a note; a short writing.

chit=chat (chit′chat), *n.* [Varied redupl. of *chat.*] Chat or familiar conversation on one subject or another; also, current gossip (as, "the common *chit-chat* of the town": Steele, in "Tatler," 197).

chi-tin (kī′tin), *n.* [F. *chitine*, < Gr. χιτών, tunic.] The organic substance forming the chief constituent of the elytra and integuments of insects and the shells of crustaceans.—**chi′ti-nous,** *a.* Of or like chitin.

chi-ton (kī′ton), *n.* [Gr. χιτών.] In *Gr. antiq.*, a garment for both sexes, usually worn next to the skin; in *zoöl.*, any of a group of sluggish, limpet-like mollusks (genus *Chiton*, etc.) which adhere to rocks.

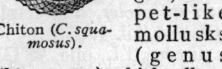

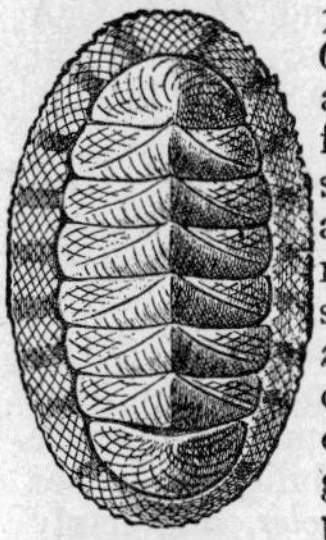
Chiton (*C. squamosus*).

Ionian Chiton. — Tanagra figurine, Berlin Museum.

chit-ter-ling (chit′ėr-ling), *n.* [Origin uncertain.] A part of the small intestine of swine, etc., esp. as cooked for food (usually in *pl.*); also, a frill† or ruff†.

chit-ty (chit′i), *n.* Same as *chit*[3].

chiv-al-resque (shiv-ạl-resk′), *a.* [F. *chevaleresque*, < *chevalier*, E. *chevalier.*] Proper or suited to the age of chivalry.

chiv-al-ric (shiv′ạl-rik or shi-val′rik), *a.* Pertaining to chivalry; knightly; chivalrous.

chiv-al-rous (shiv′ạl-rus), *a.* [OF. *chevalereus*, < *chevalier*, E. *chevalier.*] Knightly; of knightly spirit or virtues; nobly gallant, courteous, considerate, or helpful; proper to or worthy of the age of chivalry.—**chiv′al-rous-ly,** *adv.*—**chiv′al-rous-ness,** *n.*

chiv-al-ry (shiv′ạl-ri), *n.* [OF. F. *chevalerie*, < *chevalier*, E. *chevalier.*] Knights collectively; hence, gallant warriors or gentlemen; also, the position or character of a knight; knightly practice or skill; a knightly deed†; also, the medieval institution of knighthood as bound by a special code of honor and duty; also, the spirit or virtues proper to a knight; knightly valor, magnanimity, courtesy, or helpfulness; noble gallantry.

chive, cive (chīv, sīv), *n.* [OF. *chive, cive* (F. *cive*), < L. *cæpa*, onion.] A small bulbous plant, *Allium schœnoprasum*, related to the leek and onion, with long, slender leaves which are used as a seasoning in cookery: chiefly in *pl.*

chiv-y (chiv′i), *n.*; pl. *-ies* (-iz). [= *chevy.*] Same as *chevy, n.*—**chiv′y,** *v.*; *chivied, chivying.* **I.** *tr.* To chase; also, to torment; tease; chaff. [Eng.] **II.** *intr.* To race; scamper. [Eng.]

chlam-y-date (klam′i-dāt), *a.* [L. *chlamys* (*chlamyd-*), < Gr. χλαμύς (χλαμυδ-), mantle.] In *zoöl.*, having a mantle or pallium, as a mollusk.—**chla-myd-e-ous** (klạ-mid′ẹ̄-us), *a.* In *bot.*, pertaining to or having a floral envelop.

chla-mys (klā′mis or klam′is), *n.*; pl. *chlamydes* (klam′i-dēz). [L., < Gr. χλαμύς.] In *Gr. antiq.*, a kind of short mantle or cloak worn by men.

chlo-an-thite (klọ̄-an′thīt), *n.* [Gr. χλοανθής, budding (with allusion to a coating of green often seen on the mineral), < χλόη, green shoot, + ἄνθος, flower.] A native arsenide of nickel, a mineral of white to grayish or black color with a metallic luster, usually occurring massive.

Chlo-e (klō′ẹ̄), *n.* [L., < Gr. Χλόη, 'green shoot.'] In pastoral and other literature, a name for a maiden, esp. one beloved.

chlo-ral (klō′rạl), *n.* [From *chlor*(*ine*) + *al*(*cohol*).] A colorless mobile liquid first prepared from chlorine and alcohol; also, a white crystalline substance ('chloral hydrate') formed by combining liquid chloral with water, and used as a hypnotic and anesthetic.—**chlo′ral-ism,** *n.* The habitual use of chloral; a morbid condition due to the use of chloral.—**chlo′ral-ize,** *v. t.*; *-ized, -izing.* To bring under the influence of chloral.

chlor-al-um (klōr-al′um), *n.* [From *chlor*(*ine*) + *alum*(*inium*).] An antiseptic and disinfectant preparation consisting of an aqueous solution of chloride of aluminium.

chlo-rate (klō′rāt), *n.* In *chem.*, a salt of chloric acid.

chlor-hy-dric (klōr-hī′drik), *a.* Same as *hydrochloric.*

chlo-ric (klō′rik), *a.* Pertaining to or containing chlorine (see *chlorous*): as, *chloric* acid ($HClO_3$).

chlo-ri-date (klō′ri-dāt), *v. t.*; *-dated, -dating.* To treat with a chloride; also, to combine with chlorine; form into a chloride.

chlo-ride, chlo-rid (klō′rīd or -rid, -rid), *n.* In *chem.*, a compound of chlorine with an element or radical; a salt of hydrochloric acid.—**chloride of lime,** a white powder used in bleaching and disinfecting, made by treating slaked lime with chlorine, and regarded (when dry) as calcium oxychloride, $CaOCl_2$.—**chlo-rid-ic** (klọ̄-rid′ik), *a.*—**chlo′rid-ize** (-ri-dīz), *v. t.*; *-ized, -izing.* To convert into a chloride; esp., to roast (a silver ore) with salt in order to convert the silver into chloride; also, to treat with a chloride.

chlo-ri-nate (klō′ri-nāt), *v. t.*; *-nated, -nating.* To combine or treat with chlorine; treat (a gold ore) with chlorine gas in order that the gold may be removed as a soluble chloride; disinfect (water) by means of chlorine.—**chlo-ri-na′tion** (-nā′shọn), *n.*

chlo-rine, chlo-rin (klō′rin), *n.* [Gr. χλωρός, greenish-yellow, green.] Chem. sym., Cl; at. wt., 35.46. A greenish-yellow gaseous element, incombustible, highly irritating to the organs of respiration, being a powerful bleaching agent and used in various industrial processes, and occurring combined in common salt, etc.

chlo-rite[1] (klō′rīt), *n.* In *chem.*, a salt of chlorous acid.

chlo-rite[2] (klō′rīt), *n.* [Gr. χλωρῖτις, kind of green stone, < χλωρός, green.] A name for a group of minerals, hydrous silicates of aluminium, ferrous iron, and magnesium, most of which are green.—**chlo-rit-ic** (klọ̄-rit′ik), *a.* Pertaining to or containing chlorite.—**chlo′ri-toid** (-ri-toid), *n.* A mineral, a native silicate of aluminium, ferrous iron, and magnesium, having a dark-green color and occurring usually in brittle laminæ.

chlo-ro-dyne (klō′rọ̄-dīn), *n.* [From *chloro*(*form*) + (*ano*)*dyne.*] A powerful anodyne of varying composition, containing morphine, chloroform, hydrocyanic acid, extract of Indian hemp, etc.

chlo-ro-form (klō′rọ̄-fôrm), *n.* [From *chlor*(*ine*) + *form*(*yl*).] A colorless volatile liquid, $CHCl_3$, used as an anesthetic and a solvent.—**chlo′ro-form,** *v. t.* To administer chloroform to, as to cause insensibility or death; put chloroform on (a cloth, etc.).—**chlo′ro-form-ist,** *n.* One who administers chloroform professionally, as to patients: as, "He was dentist and *chloroformist*, besides being chemist and druggist" (Ian Maclaren's "Beside the Bonnie Brier Bush," vii. 1).

chlo-rom-e-ter (klọ̄-rom′e-tėr), *n.* [See *chlorine* and *-meter.*] An instrument or device for estimating the amount of chlorine available for bleaching in chloride of lime, etc.

chlo-ro-phane (klō′rọ̄-fān), *n.* [Gr. χλωρός, green, + φαίνεσθαι, appear.] A variety of fluor-spar, which exhibits a bright-green glow when heated.

chlo-ro-phyl, chlo-ro-phyll (klō′rọ̄-fil), *n.* [Gr. χλωρός, green, + φύλλον, leaf.] The green coloring matter of plants, a product associated with the production of carbohydrates by photosynthesis.—**chlo″ro-phyl-la′ceous** (-fi-lā′shius), *a.* Of the nature of chlorophyl; chlorophyllous.—**chlo-ro-phyl′lous, chlo-ro-phyl′lose** (-fil′ōs), *a.* Pertaining to or containing chlorophyl.

chlo-ro-plast (klō′rọ̄-plast), *n.* [Gr. χλωρός, green, + πλαστός, formed.] In *bot.*, a plastid containing chlorophyl.

chlo-ro-prene (klō′rọ̄-prēn), *n.* [*chloro-* + (*iso*)*prene.*] In *chem.*, an organic compound used in making neoprene.

(variable) ḍ as d or j, ṣ as s or sh, ṭ as t or ch, ẓ as z or zh; ȯ, F. cloche; ü, F. menu; ḣ, Sc. loch; ṅ, F. bonbon; ′, primary accent; ″, secondary accent; †, obsolete; <, from; +, and; =, equals. See also lists at beginning of book.

chlo-ro-sis (klǫ-rō′sis), *n.* [NL., < Gr. χλωρός, green.] A form of anemia affecting young women, characterized by a pale or greenish complexion, disordered nutrition, etc.; greensickness; in *bot.*, loss of the normal green color in a plant, as from lack of iron in the soil; also, transformation of the ordinarily colored parts of a flower into green leaf-like organs.—**chlo-rot′ic** (-rot′ik), *a.*

chlo-ro-spin-el (klō-rǫ-spin′el), *n.* [Gr. χλωρός, green, + E. *spinel.*] A variety of spinel having a grass-green color, which is due to the presence of copper.

chlo-rous (klō′rus), *a.* Pertaining to chlorine; containing chlorine (esp. in a larger proportion than a corresponding chloric compound): as, *chlorous* acid ($HClO_2$).

chock (chok), *n.* [Cf. OF. *chouque, chocque* (F. *souche*), stump, stock.] A block, as of wood; a block or wedge of wood, etc., for filling in a space, esp. for preventing movement, as of a wheel or a cask; *naut.*, one of the pieces of wood placed under a boat when stowed on a vessel's deck; also, a metal casting or block of wood, attached to a deck, with a recess, commonly between two short horn-like arms which curve together but do not meet, through which a hawser or cable passes.—**chock,** *v. t.* To furnish with or secure by a chock or chocks; place (a boat) upon chocks.—**chock,** *adv.* As close or tight as possible; quite.—**chock′=a=block** (-ą-blok), *adv.* *Naut.*, with the blocks drawn close together, as when a tackle is hauled to the utmost; fig., in a jammed or crowded condition.

chock=full (chok′fu̇l′), *a.* [ME. *chokkefulle*: origin uncertain; commonly associated with *choke.*] Full to the utmost; crammed.

choc-o-late (chok′ǫ-lạt), *n.* [Sp., < Mex. *chocolatl.*] A preparation of the seeds of cacao, roasted, husked, and ground (without removing any of the fat), often sweetened and flavored, as with vanilla; a beverage or a confection made from this; also, a dark-brown color, like that of chocolate.

chog-set (chog′set), *n.* [N. Amer. Ind.] The cunner (fish), *Tautogolabrus adspersus.*

choice (chois), *n.* [OF. *chois* (F. *choix*), < *choisir*, choose; from Teut., and akin to E. *choose.*] The act of choosing; selection; election; also, the power of choosing; option; also, an alternative; also, care in selecting; discrimination; also, the person or thing chosen; also, that which is preferred or preferable to others; the best part of anything; also, an abundance and variety from which to choose; a well-chosen supply.—**Hobson's choice.** See entry in alphabetical place.—**choice,** *a.*; compar. *choicer*, superl. *choicest.* Worthy of being chosen; excellent; superior; also, carefully selected; fit; also, careful, as from caution, fastidiousness, or high regard (often with *of*: now colloq. or prov.: as, "The old woman is just as *choice* of her boys as ef she hadn't got just es many es she has," Mrs. Stowe's "Oldtown Folks," xxxvii.).—**choice′ly,** *adv.*—**choice′-ness,** *n.*

choir (kwīr), *n.* [OF. *cuer* (F. *chœur*), < L. *chorus*: see *chorus.*] A company of singers, esp. an organized body employed in church service; any company or band, as of dancers; any of the nine orders of the celestial hierarchy (see *order, n.*, and *angel*); also, that part of a church appropriated to the singers; in cathedrals, etc., that part between the nave and the main altar reserved for the choristers, etc.—**choir,** *v. i.* or *t.* To sing in chorus.—**choir′=boy,** *n.* A boy who sings in a choir.

choke (chōk), *v.*; *choked, choking.* [ME. *choken, cheken*: cf. AS. *āceocian*, choke.] **I.** *tr.* To stop the breath of, by stricture of or obstruction in the windpipe; strangle; stifle; suffocate; also, to stop, as the breath or utterance, by or as by strangling or stifling; also, to check the growth, progress, or action of; suppress, as a feeling or emotion; also, to stop by filling; obstruct; clog; congest; also, to fill chock-full. **II.** *intr.* To suffer strangling or suffocation; also, to be obstructed or clogged.—**choke,** *n.* The act or sound of choking; a constriction, as of the bore of a gun.—**choke′-ber″ry,** *n.* The astringent berry-like fruit of shrubs of the North American malaceous genus *Aronia*, esp. *A. arbutifolia*; also, a plant bearing this fruit.—**choke′=bore,** *n.* In a gun, a bore which narrows toward the muzzle, to keep the shot from scattering; also, a gun with such a bore.—**choke′=cher″ry,** *n.* Any of several species of cherry, esp. *Prunus virginiana* of North America, which bear an astringent fruit; also, the fruit itself.—**choke′=coil,** *n.* A choking-coil, esp. one used in radio apparatus.—**choke′=damp,** *n.* In *coal-mining*, a heavy gas consisting essentially of carbon dioxide, which accumulates at the bottom of undisturbed workings, etc.; black-damp.

choke=full (chōk′fu̇l′), *a.* Same as *chock-full.*

choke=pear (chōk′pãr), *n.* A kind of pear with a harsh, astringent taste.

chok-er (chō′kėr), *n.* One who or that which chokes; a neck-cloth or a high collar (colloq.); in *elect.*, a choking-coil.

chok-ing=coil (chō′king-koil), *n.* In *elect.*, a coil of large inductance, which, when interposed in an electric circuit, allows steady currents to pass freely, but chokes off or greatly weakens all rapid fluctuations.

chok-y[1] (chō′ki), *a.* Tending to choke or suffocate one; also, inclined to choke.

cho-ky[2] (chō′ki), *n.*; pl. *-kies* (-kiz). [Hind. *chaukī.*] A station, as for the collection of customs or tolls, or for palanquin-bearers, police, or the like; also, a jail or lockup. [India.]

chol-a-gogue (kol′ą-gog), *n.* [F., < Gr. χολαγωγός, carrying off bile, < χολή, bile, + ἀγωγός, leading, < ἄγειν, lead.] A substance that promotes the flow of bile.—**chol-a-gog′ic** (-goj′ik), *a.* and *n.*

chol-er (kol′ėr), *n.* [OF. *colere*, bile, F. *colère*, anger, < LL. *cholera*, bile: see *cholera.*] Bile (in the old physiology, that one of the four humors supposed when predominant to cause irascibility and anger); biliousness†; irascibility, anger, or wrath (as, "He is . . . very sudden in *choler*, and haply may strike at you": Shakspere's "Othello," ii. 1. 279).

chol-e-ra (kol′ę-rạ), *n.* [L., bilious disease, LL. bile, < Gr. χολέρα, cholera, appar. < χολή, gall, bile.] Choler† or bile†; in *pathol.*, an acute, non-epidemic disorder of the digestive tract, marked by purging, vomiting, cramps, etc. ('sporadic cholera,' 'bilious cholera,' or 'cholera morbus'); also, an acute, infectious disease, due to a specific micro-organism, endemic in India, etc., and epidemic generally, marked by profuse purging, vomiting, cramps, etc., and often fatal ('Asiatic cholera').—**chol′e-ra in-fan-tum** (in-fan′-tum). [L., 'cholera of infants.'] Sporadic cholera in infants.—**chol′e-ra mor-bus** (môr′bus). [L., 'cholera disease.'] Sporadic cholera.—**chol-e-ra′ic** (-rā′ik), *a.*

chol-er-ic (kol′ę-rik), *a.* [OF. *colerique* (F. *colérique*), < L. *cholericus*, bilious: cf. *choler.*] Bilious†; also, disposed to choler; irascible; angry.—**chol′er-ic-ly,** *adv.*

chol-e-rine (kol′ę-rin, -rēn, or -rīn), *n.* [= F. *cholérine.*] In *pathol.*, the early stage, or a mild form, of Asiatic cholera; also, sporadic cholera.

chol-e-roid (kol′ę-roid), *a.* Resembling cholera.

cho-les-te-rin (kǫ-les′tę-rin), *n.* [Gr. χολή, bile, + στερεός, solid.] A fat-like substance found in bile and biliary calculi, also in the blood and brain, the yolk of eggs, etc. Also **cho-les′te-rol** (-rol or -rōl).

chol-ic (kol′ik), *a.* [Gr. χολικός, < χολή, bile.] Pertaining to or obtained from bile.

chol-la (chōl′yä), *n.* [Mex.] Any of several spiny, tree-like cactuses of the genus *Opuntia*, esp. *O. fulgida*, of the southwestern U. S. and Mexico.

Cholla (*Opuntia fulgida*).

chon-dri-fy (kon′dri-fī), *v. t.* or *i.*; *-fied, -fying.* [Gr. χόνδρος, cartilage: see *-fy.*] To convert or be converted into cartilage.—**chon″dri-fi-ca′tion** (-fi-kā′-shǫn), *n.*

chon-drite (kon′drīt), *n.* [See *chondrus.*] Meteoric stone containing crystalline spherules (*chondri*).—**chon-drit′ic** (-drit′-ik), *a.*

chon-dro-dite (kon′drǫ-dīt), *n.* [Gr. χονδρώδης, granular, < χόνδρος, E. *chondrus.*] A yellow to red mineral, a fluosilicate of magnesium, often occurring in granular form in crystalline limestones.

chon-droid (kon′droid), *a.* [Gr. χόνδρος, cartilage: see *-oid.*] Resembling cartilage; cartilaginous.

chon-dro-ma (kon-drō′mạ̈), *n.*; pl. *-mas* or *-mata* (-mạ-tạ̈). [NL., < Gr. χόνδρος, cartilage: see *-oma.*] In *pathol.*, a cartilaginous tumor or growth.

chon-drot-o-my (kon-drot′ọ̄-mi), *n.* [Gr. χόνδρος, cartilage, + -τομία, < τέμνειν, cut.] The cutting or dissection of cartilage.

chon-drule (kon′dröl), *n.* Same as *chondrus.*

chon-drus (kon′drus), *n.*; pl. *-dri* (-drī). [Gr. χόνδρος, grit, grain, cartilage.] One of the spherules of crystalline matter found in certain meteorites.

choose (chöz), *v.*; pret. *chose*, pp. *chosen*, ppr. *choosing.* [AS. *cēosan* = G. *kiesen* = Goth. *kiusan*; akin to L. *gustus*, a tasting, *gustare*, Gr. γεύεσθαι, taste, Skt. *jush-*, relish.] **I.** *tr.* To select from a number, or in preference to another or others, or to something else; also, to prefer and decide, or think fit (with an infinitive: as, he did not *choose* to accept). **II.** *intr.* To make a choice.—**cannot choose but,** cannot do otherwise than.—**choos′er,** *n.*

chop[1] (chop), *v.*; *chopped, chopping.* [ME.: cf. D. and LG. *kappen*, Dan. *kappe*, Sw. *kappa*, cut.] **I.** *tr.* To cut with a quick, heavy blow, as of an ax, or with a succession of such blows; also, to make by so cutting; also, to cut in pieces by repeated strokes; mince. **II.** *intr.* To make a quick, heavy stroke, or a succession of such strokes, as with an ax; also, to go, come, or move suddenly or violently; interrupt, as during a conversation (with *in*).—**chop**[1], *n.* An act of chopping; a cutting blow; also, a piece chopped off; a slice of mutton, veal, pork, etc., usually one containing a rib; also, material that has been chopped; also, a short, irregular, broken motion of waves; also, a chap†, crack†, or cleft†.

chop[2] (chop), *v.*; *chopped, chopping.* [Akin to *cheap* and *chapman.*] **I.** *intr.* To barter†; turn, shift, or change suddenly, as the wind; bandy words†. **II.** *tr.* To barter; exchange. [Now prov. Eng.]—**to chop logic,** to reason or dispute argumentatively; argue: as, "A man must not presume to use his reason unless he has studied the categories, and can *chop logic* by mode and figure" (Smollett's "Humphry Clinker," April 20).—**chop**[2], *n.* An exchange (now prov. Eng.); a change (in the phrase 'chops and changes').

chop[3] (chop), *n.* See *chap*[2].

chop[4] (chop), *n.* [Hind. *chhāp*, impression, stamp.] In India, China, etc., an official stamp or seal, or a permit or clearance; in China, a mark or brand on goods; also, a kind or brand of goods; hence, in general, grade or quality (colloq.).

chop-fall-en (chop′fâ″ln), *a.* See *chapfallen.*

chop=house (chop′hous), *n.* An eating-house making a specialty of chops, steaks, etc.

chop-in (chop′in), *n.* [OF. F. *chopine*, akin to G. *schoppen.*] Any of several liquid measures, chiefly obsolete, equal to about a pint or a quart.

cho-pine (chọ̄-pēn′), *n.* [Sp. *chapin.*] A kind of shoe with a very thick sole of cork or the like, sometimes suggesting a short stilt, formerly worn, esp. by women.

Chopines.

chop-per (chop′ėr), *n.* One who or that which chops.

chop-ping (chop′ing), *p. a.* Making quick, sharp movements; jerky; of the sea, etc., forming short, irregular, broken waves. Also **chop′py**[1], *a.*

chop-py[2] (chop′i), *a.* Shifting or changing suddenly or irregularly, as the wind.

chop-py[3] (chop′i), *a.* Same as *chappy.*

chop=stick (chop′stik), *n.* [Pidgin-English *chop*, quick.] One of the small tapering sticks, as of wood or ivory, used in pairs by the Chinese, etc., to raise food to the mouth.

Chop-sticks.

chop=su-ey (chop-sö′i), *n.* [Chinese.] A mixed dish served in Chinese restaurants, consisting of fowl or other meat cut into bits with onions, bean sprouts, green peppers, mushrooms, or other vegetables and seasoning, in a gravy or sauce: eaten commonly with rice. [U. S.]

cho-ra-gus (kọ̄-rā′gus), *n.*; pl. *-gi* (-jī). [L., < Gr. χοραγός, χορηγός, < χορός, chorus, + ἄγειν, lead.] The leader of an ancient Greek chorus. Also fig.—**cho-rag′ic** (-raj′ik), *a.*

cho-ral (kō′rạl), *a.* [ML. *choralis*, < L. *chorus*: see *chorus.*] Of or pertaining to a chorus or a choir; sung by or adapted for a chorus or a choir.—**cho-ral** (kọ̄-räl′ or kō′rạl), *n.* [G.] A choral composition; a hymn tune; esp., a simple sacred tune having a plain melody, a strong harmony, and a stately rhythm. Also **cho-rale** (kọ̄-räl′).—**cho′ral-ist,** *n.* One who sings in a chorus or a choir; also, a composer of choral music.—**cho′ral-ly,** *adv.*

chord[1] (kôrd), *n.* [L. *chorda*, cord, string, < Gr. χορδή, gut, string of a musical instrument: cf. *cord.*] A cord† or string†; a string of a musical instrument; fig., a feeling or emotion; in *geom.*, that part of a straight line between two of its intersections with a curve; a straight line joining the extremities of an arc of a circle; in *engin.*, a main horizontal member of a bridge-truss; in *anat.*, a cord.

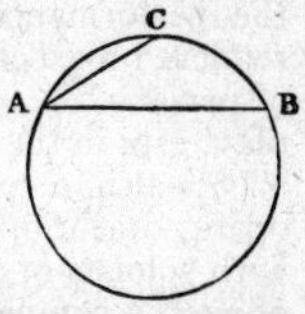

Geometrical Chords. *AB, AC*, are chords of the arcs they subtend.

chord[2] (kôrd), *n.* [Earlier *cord*, for *accord.*] Accord†; in *music*, a combination of three or more tones in harmonic relation, sounded simultaneously (as, the common *chord*, the combination of any tone with its third and fifth, with or without the octave); often, the common chord.—**chord**[2], *v. i.* or *t.* To sound or combine in harmony.—**chord′al,** *a.*

chord-ed (kôr′ded), *a.* Having chords or strings, as a musical instrument.

chore (chōr), *n.* [Var. of *char*[1].] A small or odd job; a piece of minor domestic work: as, "We did our nightly *chores*,—Brought in the wood . . . Littered the stalls" (Whittier's "Snow-Bound"). [Chiefly prov.]

cho-re-a (kọ̄-rē′ạ̈), *n.* [NL., < Gr. χορεία, dance, < χορός: see *chorus.*] In *pathol.*, a nervous disease, occurring chiefly in children, marked by irregular and involuntary contractions of the muscles, esp. of the face and limbs; St. Vitus's dance.—**cho-re′al,** *a.*

cho-ree (kō′rē or kọ̄-rē′), *n.* [L. *choreus*, < Gr. χορεῖος, < χορός: see *chorus.*] In *pros.*, a trochee.

cho-reg-ra-phy (kọ̄-reg′rạ-fi), *n.* [F. *chorégraphie*, < Gr. χορεία, dance, + γράφειν, write.] The art of representing the various movements in dancing by a system of notation; the art of arranging ballets, etc.; the art of dancing.—**cho-re-graph-ic** (kō-rẹ̄-graf′ik), *a.*

cho-re-ic (kọ̄-rē′ik), *a.* Pertaining to or affected with chorea.

cho-re-og-ra-phy (kō-rẹ̄-og′rạ-fi), etc. Same as *choregraphy*, etc.

cho-ri-amb (kō′ri-amb), *n.* Same as *choriambus.*

cho-ri-am-bus (kō-ri-am′bus), *n.*; pl. *-bi* (-bī) or *-buses.* [L., < Gr. χορίαμβος, < χορεῖος, choree, + ἴαμβος, iambus.] In *pros.*, a foot of four syllables, two short between two long, like a choree with an iambus added.—**cho-ri-am′bic,** *a.*

cho-ric (kō′rik or kor′ik), *a.* Of or for a chorus.

cho-ri-on (kō′ri-on), *n.* [NL., < Gr. χόριον, chorion, membrane.] In *anat.*, the outer membrane enveloping a fetus, inclosing the amnion.

cho-ri-pet-a-lous (kō-ri-pet′ạ-lus), *a.* [Gr. χωρίς, asunder: see *petal.*] In *bot.*, having the petals separate.—**cho-ri-phyl′lous** (-fil′us), *a.* [See *-phyllous.*] In *bot.*, composed of separate leaves or parts, as a perianth.—**cho-ri-sep′a-lous** (-sep′ạ-lus), *a.* [See *sepal.*] In *bot.*, having the sepals separate.

cho-rist (kō′rist or kor′ist), *n.* A member of a chorus or a choir.—**chor-is-ter** (kor′is-tėr), *n.* A singer in a choir; esp., a male singer in a church choir; a choir-boy; also, a choir-leader; also, fig., one of a flock of birds that sing (as, feathered *choristers*).

cho-rog-ra-phy[1] (kọ̄-rog′rạ-fi), *n.* [L. *chorographia*, < Gr. χωρογραφία, < χῶρος, place, country, + γράφειν, write.] The systematic description or mapping of particular countries or districts; a description or delineation of a particular country or district; also, the natural configuration and features of a region.—**cho-rog′ra-pher,** *n.*—**cho-ro-graph-ic, cho-ro-graph-i-cal** (kō-rō-graf′ik, -i-kạl), *a.*

cho-rog-ra-phy[2] (kọ-rog′rạ-fi), etc. Same as *choregraphy,* etc.

cho-roid (kō′roid). [Gr. χοροειδής, prop. χοριοειδής, < χόριον, chorion, + εἶδος, form.] In *anat.*: **I.** *a.* Like the chorion; membranous: applied esp. to a delicate, highly vascular membrane or coat of the eyeball, between the sclerotic coat and the retina. **II.** *n.* The choroid coat of the eye.—**cho-roi-di-tis** (kō-roi-dī′tis), *n.* [NL.] In *pathol.*, inflammation of the choroid coat of the eye.

chor-tle (chôr′tl), *v. i.* or *t.*; *-tled, -tling.* [Coined by C. L. Dodgson ("Lewis Carroll"), in "Through the Looking-Glass" (1871).] To chuckle or utter with glee.

cho-rus (kō′rus), *n.*; pl. *-ruses.* [L., < Gr. χορός, dance, band of dancers, chorus: see def.] In ancient Greek use, a dance performed by a company of persons and accompanied with song, orig. as a religious rite; a company of singers and dancers in the ancient Greek drama, supplementing the performance of the main actors; a part of a drama rendered by such a company; hence, in later use, a company of persons, or a single person, having a similar function in a play, esp. in the Elizabethan drama (see Shakspere's "Henry V."); also, a company of persons singing in concert; in an opera, oratorio, etc., such a company singing in connection with soloists or individual singers; also, the singing or song of such a company; a piece of music for singing in concert; a part of a song in which others join the principal singer or singers; any recurring refrain; also, simultaneous utterance in singing, speaking, etc., or the sounds uttered.—**cho′rus,** *v.*; *-rused, -rusing.* **I.** *intr.* To sing or speak in chorus. **II.** *tr.* To sing or utter in chorus; furnish with a chorus or refrain; sing the chorus of; assent to or echo (another's utterances).—**cho′rus=girl,** *n.* A female member of the chorus of a musical comedy or the like.

chose[1] (chōz). Preterit of *choose.*

chose[2] (shōz), *n.* [F., thing, < L. *causa*, E. *cause.*] In *law*, a thing; a piece of personal property.—**chose in action,** an incorporeal right enforceable by legal action.

chos-en (chō′zn), *p. a.* [See *choose.*] Selected from a number; preferred; in *theol.*, elect.—**chosen freeholder,** in New Jersey, one of a board of county officers having charge of the finances of the county.—**the chosen people,** the Israelites; the Jews. See 1 Chron. xvi. 13.

chou (shö), *n.*; pl. *choux* (shö). [F., lit. 'cabbage,' < L. *caulis*, stalk, cabbage.] An ornamental knot or rosette of ribbon, lace, or the like.

chough (chuf), *n.* [Cf. AS. *cēo*, chough.] A bird of the old-world genus *Pyrrhocorax*, of the crow family; esp., the red-legged or Cornish crow, *P. graculus*, of a black color, with red feet and beak.

chouse (chous), *n.* [Said to be < Turk. *chāush*, messenger, interpreter, orig. with reference to one who in 1609 perpetrated a swindle.] A swindler†; also, a dupe† (as, "sillier than a sottish *chouse*": Butler's "Hudibras," iii. 3); also, a swindle (colloq.).—**chouse,** *v. t.*; *choused, chousing.* To swindle; cheat; dupe: often with *of* or *out of.* [Colloq.]—**chous′er,** *n.*

chow[1] (chou), *n.* [For *chow-chow.*] Food (China, the Philippines, etc., and hence U. S. army slang); a Chinaman (Australia); one of a Chinese breed of dogs of medium size, with a thick, even coat of brown or black hair and a black tongue.

chow[2] (chou), *n.* [Chinese.] In China, a prefecture or district of the second rank; also, the chief city of such a district.

chow=chow (chou′chou), *n.* [Pidgin-English.] A Chinese mixed preserve; any mixed food, or food in general, or a meal (China, India, etc.); a mixed pickle in mustard (orig. East Indian); a chow dog.

chow-der (chou′dėr), *n.* [Prob. < F. *chaudière*, caldron.] A kind of soup or stew made of clams or fish with potatoes, onions, and various other ingredients or seasoning.

chow-ry (chou′ri), *n.*; pl. *-ries* (-riz). [Hind. *chaunrī.*] In the East Indies, a whisk for driving off flies: usually made of a yak's tail, and being in this form an ancient ensign of royalty.

choy, choy-a (choi, choi′ạ), etc. Same as *chay*[2], *chaya*, etc.

chre-ma-tis-tic (krē-mạ-tis′tik), *a.* [Gr. χρηματιστικός, < χρηματίζειν, transact business, < χρήματα, pl., goods, money, < χρῆσθαι, use.] Pertaining to money-making or the acquisition of wealth.—**chre-ma-tis′tics,** *n.* The science of wealth; political economy as concerned with the accumulation and management of wealth.

chres-tom-a-thy (kres-tom′ạ-thi), *n.*; pl. *-thies* (-thiz). [Gr. χρηστομάθεια, < χρηστός, useful, + μανθάνειν, learn.] A collection of choice extracts, esp. from a foreign language.

chrism (krizm), *n.* [AS. *crisma*, < LL. *chrisma*, < Gr. χρῖσμα, unguent, unction, < χρίειν, rub, anoint.] *Eccles.*, a consecrated oil used by certain churches in the rites of baptism, confirmation, etc.; also, a sacramental anointing; the rite of confirmation, esp. as administered in the Greek Church; extreme unction (see under *unction*).—**chris-mal** (kriz′mạl), *a.*—**chris-ma′tion** (-mā′shọn), *n.* [ML. *chrismatio(n-).*] The application of chrism.—**chris′ma-to-ry** (-mạ-tọ-ri), *n.*; pl. *-ries* (-riz). [ML. *chrismatorium.*] A receptacle for the chrism.

Chrismatory.

chris-om (kriz′ọm), *n.* [Var. of *chrism.*] A white cloth or robe formerly put on a child at baptism, and also at burial if the child died soon after baptism.—**chris′om=child†,** *n.* A child at about the age for baptism. See Shakspere's "Henry V.," ii. 3. 12.

Christ (krīst), *n.* [AS. *Crist*, < L. *Christus*, < Gr. Χριστός, < χρίειν, rub, anoint.] 'The Anointed'; the Messiah expected by the Jews; Jesus of Nazareth, as fulfilling this expectation.

Chris-ta-del-phi-an (kris-tạ-del′fi-ạn), *n.* [LGr. Χριστάδελφος, in brotherhood with Christ, < Gr. Χριστός, Christ, + ἀδελφός, brother.] A member of a religious sect founded in the U. S. by Dr. John Thomas about 1850, which rejects the doctrine of the Trinity and holds that only the righteous attain immortality.

Christ=child (krīst′chīld), *n.* Christ as a child (used only with the definite article); also, a picture or image of Christ in his childhood.

christ=cross (kris′krôs), *n.* The figure or mark of a cross.—**christ′cross=row′** (-rō′), *n.* The alphabet: so called from the figure of a cross set before it in hornbooks: as, "infant-conning of the *Christ-cross-row*" (Wordsworth's "Excursion, viii. 413). [Archaic or prov.]

chris-ten (kris′n), *v. t.* [AS. *cristnian*, < *cristen*, < L. *Christianus*, Christian.] To make Christian (archaic); also, to receive into the Christian church by baptism; baptize; also, to give a name to at baptism; hence, to name and dedicate; give a name to; name.

Chris-ten-dom (kris′n-dọm), *n.* [AS. *cristendōm*, < *cristen*, Christian: see *-dom.*] The condition or faith of a Christian†; Christianity†; the Christian world; Christians collectively.

Christ-hood (krīst′hůd), *n.* The condition of being the Christ.

Chris-tian (kris′chạn), *a.* [L. *Christianus*, < *Christus*: see *Christ.*] Of, pertaining to, or derived from Jesus Christ or his teachings; believing in or belonging to the religion of Jesus Christ; of or pertaining to Christianity or Christians; also, exhibiting a spirit proper to a follower of Jesus Christ; Christlike; also, human, or not brutal (colloq.); decent or respectable (colloq.).—**Christian era,** the era reckoned from the assumed date of Christ's birth, adopted in Christian countries.—**Christian name,** the name given one at baptism, as distinguished from the family name; the given name.—**Christian Science,** a system of religious teaching, based on the Scriptures, the most notable application of which is the treatment of disease by mental and spiritual means: founded about 1866 by Mrs. Mary Baker Glover Eddy, of Concord, New Hampshire.—**Christian Scientist,** one who believes in Christian Science, or who practises its teachings.—**Christian socialism.** See under *socialism.*—**Chris′tian,** *n.* One who believes in Jesus Christ; an adherent of Christianity; also, one who exemplifies in his life the teachings of Christ; also, a human being as distinguished from a brute (colloq.); a decent or presentable person (colloq.).—**Chris′tian-ism,** *n.* The Christian religion; Christianity: often in disparaging use.—**Chris-ti-an-i-ty** (kris-ti-an′i-ti), *n.*; pl. *-ties* (-tiz). [LL. *Christianitas.*]

Christendom†; the Christian religion; Christian principles, practice, or character; also, a particular Christian religious system.—**Chris′tian-ize** (-īz), *v.*; *-ized, -izing.* **I.** *tr.* To make Christian; convert to Christianity; imbue with Christian principles. **II.** *intr.* To become Christian; profess Christianity.—**Chris″tian-i-za′tion** (-i-zā′shọn), *n.*—**Chris′tian-ly,** *a.* Like or befitting a Christian.—**Chris′tian-ly,** *adv.*

Christ-less (krīst′les), *a.* Without Christ or the spirit of Christ; unchristian: as, "The *Christless* code That must have life for a blow" (Tennyson's "Maud," ii. 1. 1).—**Christ′less-ness,** *n.*

Christ-like (krīst′līk), *a.* Like Christ; Christly.—**Christ′-like-ness,** *n.*

Christ-ly (krīst′li), *a.* Of or like Christ; showing the spirit of Christ.—**Christ′li-ness,** *n.*

Christ-mas (kris′mạs), *n.* [ME. *cristmasse*: see *-mas.*] The annual festival of the Christian church commemorating the birth of Christ, celebrated on Dec. 25; hence, Dec. 25 ('Christmas Day'), now generally observed as an occasion for gifts, greetings, etc.—**Christmas box,** orig., a box used at Christmas for the reception of presents of money to apprentices, servants, porters, etc.; hence, a gratuity given at Christmas to a servant or employee, letter-carrier, policeman, etc. (Eng.); in general, a Christmas present (Eng.); also, a box of presents at Christmas.—**Christmas tree,** an evergreen tree set up in a room or other place of assembly, hung with decorations and often gifts, as a feature of Christmas festivities.—**Christ′mas-tide** (-tīd), *n.* The season of Christmas.—**Christ′mas-y, Christ′mas-sy,** *a.* Christmas-like; proper to or suggestive of Christmas.

Christo-. Form of Gr. Χριστός, Christ, used in combination.—**Chris-tol-a-try** (kris-tol′ạ-tri), *n.* [+ *-latry.*] Worship of Christ.—**Chris-tol′o-gy** (-ọ-ji), *n.* [+ *-logy.*] The branch of theology which treats of Christ; a doctrine concerning Christ.—**Chris-to-log′i-cal** (-tọ-loj′i-kạl), *a.*—**Chris-toph′a-ny** (-tof′ạ-ni), *n.*; pl. *-nies* (-niz). [+ *-phany.*] An appearance of Christ to men after his death.

Christ's=thorn (krīsts′thôrn), *n.* Any of certain old-world thorny shrubs or small trees supposed to have been used for Christ's crown of thorns, as either of the rhamnaceous plants *Zizyphus spina-Christi* and *Paliurus aculeatus.*

-chroic, -chroous. [Gr. -χροος, < χρόα, skin, complexion, color.] Terminations of adjectives indicating color, sometimes the color of the skin, as in *amphichroic, dichroic, melanochroic, xanthochroic, allochroous, isochroous.*

chro-ma (krō′mạ̈), *n.* [Gr. χρῶμα, color.] The purity of a color, or the degree of its freedom from white or gray; the intensity of distinctive hue.

chro-mate (krō′māt), *n.* In *chem.*, a salt of chromic acid.

chro-mat-ic (krọ-mat′ik), *a.* [Gr. χρωματικός, < χρῶμα, color.] Of or pertaining to color or colors; in *music*, involving a modification of the normal scale by the use of semitones; progressing by semitones, and not by the regular intervals of the diatonic scale.—**chromatic aberration.** See *aberration.*—**chro-mat′i-cal-ly,** *adv.*—**chro-mat′ics,** *n.* The science of colors.

chro-ma-tin (krō′mạ-tin), *n.* [Gr. χρῶμα (χρωματ-), color.] In *biol.*, that portion of the animal or plant cell-nucleus which readily takes on stains. Cf. *mitosis.*—**chromatin granule,** one of the minute bodies of which a chromosome is made up; an id.

chro-ma-tism (krō′mạ-tizm), *n.* [Gr. χρωματισμός, coloring, < χρωματίζειν, to color, < χρῶμα, color.] Abnormal coloration, as of the normally green parts of plants; also, chromatic aberration (see *aberration*).

chromato-, chromat-. Forms of Gr. χρῶμα (χρωματ-), color, used in combination. Cf. *chromo-.*—**chro-ma-to-phore** (krō′mạ-tọ-fōr), *n.* [+ *-phore.*] In *zoöl.*, a colored mass of protoplasm; a pigmented body or cell, as one of those which through contraction and expansion produce a temporary color in cuttlefishes, etc.; in *bot.*, one of the plastids in plant-cells.—**chro″ma-to-phor′ic** (-for′ik), *a.*—**chro-ma-top′si-a** (-top′si-ạ̈), *n.* [NL. (Gr. ὄψις, sight).] In *pathol.*, colored vision; an abnormal state in which sensations of color arise independently of external causes, or things are seen unnaturally colored.—**chro′ma-to-scope** (-skōp), *n.* [+ *-scope.*] A device for compounding colors by combining light-rays of different colors.

chro-ma-trope (krō′mạ-trōp), *n.* [Gr. χρῶμα, color: see *-trope.*] An arrangement in a magic lantern or stereopticon for producing effects similar to those of a kaleidoscope; also, a device consisting of a disk on which are painted circular arcs of bright colors, so placed that when the disk is revolved rapidly streams of color seem to flow to or from the center.

chro-ma-type (krō′mạ-tīp), *n.* [From *chromium* + *-type.*] In *photog.*, a picture made upon paper sensitized with bichromate of potassium or some other salt of chromium; also, the process of making such pictures.

chrome (krōm), *n.* [F., < Gr. χρῶμα, color.] Chromium, esp. as the source of various pigments (chrome-green, chrome-orange, chrome-yellow, etc.).—**chrome,** *v. t.*; *chromed, chroming.* In *dyeing*, to subject to a bath of bichromate of potassium.—**chrome′=al′um,** *n.* In *chem.*, a dark-violet double sulphate of chromium and potassium, crystallizing like common alum, and used in dyeing and calico-printing.—**chro-mic** (krō′mik), *a.* Of or containing chromium: as, *chromic* acid (H_2CrO_4). See *chromous.*—**chro′mite** (-mīt), *n.* A mineral containing iron and chromium, and forming an important source of chromium; in *chem.*, a salt of the so-called chromous acid, $HCrO_2$.

chro-mi-um (krō′mi-um), *n.* [NL., for F. and E. *chrome.*] Chem. sym., Cr; at. wt., 52.0; sp. gr., 6.9. A lustrous, hard, brittle metallic element occurring in compounds, which are used for making dyes and pigments and in photography, etc.

chromo-. Form of Gr. χρῶμα, color, used in combination. Cf. *chromato-.*

chro-mo (krō′mō), *n.*; pl. *-mos* (-mōz). Shortened form of *chromolithograph.*

chro-mo-gen (krō′mọ-jen), *n.* [See *chromo-* and *-gen.*] The coloring matter of a plant; in *chem.*, a compound which, although not itself a dye, is capable of being converted into one, owing to its color-forming atomic groups; also, a naphthalene derivative which colors wool brown when applied to it and oxidized.—**chro-mo-gen′ic,** *a.* Pertaining to chromogen or a chromogen; also, producing color; of bacteria, forming some characteristic color or pigment.

chro-mo-gram (krō′mọ-gram), *n.* [See *chromo-* and *-gram.*] Any of the three negatives taken through differently colored screens, produced in the process of photographing objects in their natural colors.

chro-mo-lith-o-graph (krō-mọ-lith′ọ-gråf), *n.* [See *chromo-.*] A picture produced by chromolithography.—**chro″mo-li-thog′ra-phy** (-li-thog′rạ-fi), *n.* The process of lithographing in colors.—**chro″mo-lith-o-graph′ic** (-graf′ik), *a.*

chro-mo-pho-to-graph (krō-mọ-fō′tọ-gråf), *n.* [See *chromo-.*] A picture produced by chromophotography.—**chro″mo-pho-tog′ra-phy** (-fọ-tog′rạ-fi), *n.* Photography in colors.—**chro″mo-pho-to-graph′ic** (-graf′ik), *a.*

chro-mo-plast (krō′mọ-plast), *n.* [See *chromo-* and *-plast.*] In *bot.*, a plastid, or specialized mass of protoplasm, containing other coloring matter than chlorophyl.

chro-mo-some (krō′mọ-sōm), *n.* [See *chromo-* and *-some*[3].] In *biol.*, one of the definite segments or pieces of chromatin of the cell-nucleus, formed during the process of mitosis.

chro-mo-sphere (krō′mọ-sfēr), *n.* [See *chromo-* and *sphere.*] A scarlet, gaseous envelop surrounding the sun outside the photosphere; also, a gaseous envelop surrounding a star.—**chro-mo-spher′ic** (-sfer′ik), *a.*

chro-mo-type (krō′mọ-tīp), *n.* [See *chromo-* and *-type.*] A print in colors, produced by any process, as chromolithography; a photograph in colors.

chro-mous (krō′mus), *a.* Containing chromium (in larger proportion than a corresponding chromic compound): as, *chromous* acid ($HCrO_2$, a compound acting as a weak acid).

chron-ic (kron′ik), *a.* [L. *chronicus*, < Gr. χρονικός, < χρόνος, time.] Pertaining to time; also, continuing a long time; inveterate; constant; of disease, long-continued and slow or mild (opposed to *acute*); also, having long had a disease, habit, or the like (as, a *chronic* invalid).—**chron′-i-cal-ly,** *adv.*—**chro-ni-ci-ty** (krọ-nis′i-ti), *n.* Chronic character; long continuance.

chron-i-cle (kron′i-kl), *n.* [ME. *cronicle,* < OF. *cronique* (F. *chronique*), < L. *chronica,* < Gr. χρονικά, annals, neut. pl. of χρονικός: see *chronic.*] A record of events in the order of time; a history; *pl.* [*cap.*], two historical books of the Old Testament, following Kings.—**chron′i-cle,** *v. t.*; *-cled, -cling.* To record in or as in a chronicle: as, "This deed is *chronicled* in hell" (Shakspere's "Richard II.," v. 5. 117).—**chron′i-cler,** *n.*

chrono-. Form of Gr. χρόνος, time, used in combination. —**chron-o-gram** (kron′ǫ-gram), *n.* [+ *-gram.*] An inscription or the like in which certain of the letters, usually distinguished from the others, express by their values as Roman numerals a date or epoch; also, a record made by a chronograph.—**chron′o-graph** (-gräf), *n.* [+ *-graph.*] An astronomical or other instrument for recording the exact instant of occurrences, or for measuring small intervals of time.—**chron-o-graph′ic** (-graf′ik), *a.*

chro-nol-o-ger (krǫ-nol′ǫ-jėr), *n.* [See *chronology.*] A chronologist.—**chron-o-log-ic, chron-o-log-i-cal** (kron-ǫ-loj′ik, -i-kạl), *a.* Of, pertaining to, or in accordance with chronology; arranged in the order of time.—**chron-o-log′i-cal-ly,** *adv.*—**chro-nol′o-gist,** *n.* One versed in chronology.—**chro-nol′o-gize** (-jīz), *v. t.*; *-gized, -gizing.* To arrange chronologically.

chro-nol-o-gy (krǫ-nol′ǫ-ji), *n.*; pl. *-gies* (-jiz). [See *chrono-* and *-logy.*] The science of time; the science or art of arranging time in periods and ascertaining the exact dates and true historical order of past events; also, a particular statement of the supposed or accepted order of past events.

chro-nom-e-ter (krǫ-nom′e-tėr), *n.* [See *chrono-* and *-meter.*] Any instrument for measuring time; esp., a timekeeper with special mechanism for ensuring accuracy, for use in determining longitude at sea or for any other purpose where very exact measurement of time is required.—**chron-o-met-ric, chron-o-met-ri-cal** (kron-ǫ-met′rik, -ri-kạl), *a.* Pertaining to chronometry or chronometers.—**chro-nom′e-try,** *n.* [See *-metry.*] The art of accurately measuring time.

chron-o-pho-to-graph (kron-ǫ-fō′tǫ-gräf), *n.* [See *chrono-.*] One of a series of photographs of a moving object, taken at equal intervals to record the stages of the motion; also, the series.—**chron″o-pho-tog′ra-phy** (-fǫ-tog′rạ-fi), *n.*

chron-o-scope (kron′ǫ-skōp), *n.* [See *chrono-* and *-scope.*] An instrument for measuring accurately very small intervals of time, as in determining the velocity of projectiles.

-chroous. See *-chroic.*

chrys-a-lid (kris′ạ-lid). **I.** *n.* A chrysalis. **II.** *a.* Pertaining to a chrysalis.

chrys-a-lis (kris′ạ-lis), *n.*; pl. *chrysalises* or *chrysalides* (kri-sal′i-dēz). [L. *chrysallis,* < Gr. χρυσαλλίς (-λιδ-), gold-colored sheath of butterflies, < χρυσός, gold.] The quiescent pupa stage of most insects when passing from the larval to the winged or perfect state: often fig.: as, "Courage, Saint Simeon! This dull *chrysalis* Cracks into shining wings" (Tennyson's "St. Simeon Stylites," 153).

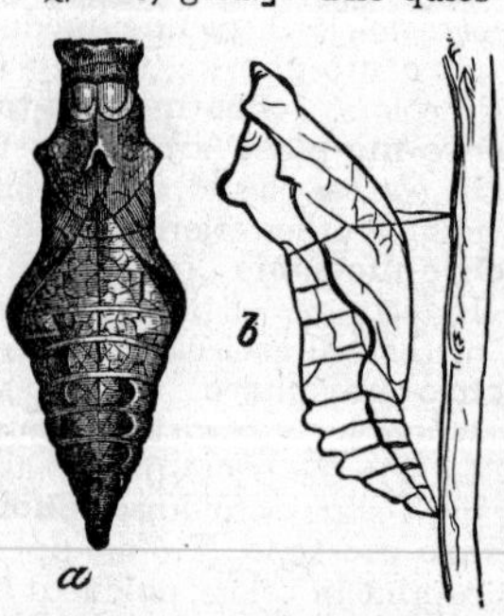

Chrysalis of a Swallowtail Butterfly.
a, dorsal view; *b,* lateral view, illustrating characteristic mode of hanging by a girdle.

chrys-an-i-line (kris-an′i-lin), *n.* [Gr. χρυσός, gold, + E. *aniline.*] A yellow crystalline powder obtained as a by-product in the manufacture of rosaniline and used chiefly in dyeing leather and silk.

chry-san-the-mum (kri-san′thę-mum), *n.* [L., < Gr. χρυσάνθεμον, < χρυσός, gold, + ἄνθεμον, flower.] Any of the perennial asteraceous plants constituting the genus *Chrysanthemum,* as *C. leucanthemum,* the oxeye daisy; more commonly, any of many cultivated varieties of *C. sinense,* a native of China, and of other species of *Chrysanthemum,* notable for the diversity of color, shape, and size of their autumnal flowers; also, the flower of such a plant.

chrys-a-ro-bin (kris-ạ-rō′bin), *n.* [Gr. χρυσός, gold, + E. *ar(ar)oba.*] A yellow microcrystalline powder forming the essential constituent of Goa powder, used chiefly in the treatment of certain skin-diseases.

chrys-el-e-phan-tine (kris″el-ę-fan′tin), *a.* [Gr. χρυσελεφάντινος, < χρυσός, gold, + ἐλέφας, elephant, ivory.] Made of or overlaid with gold and ivory.

chryso-. Form of Gr. χρυσός, gold, used in combination. —**chrys-o=ar-is-toc-ra-cy** (kris″ǫ-ar-is-tok′rạ-si), *n.* An aristocracy of gold or wealth.

chrys-o-ber-yl (kris′ǫ-ber-il), *n.* [L. *chrysoberyllus,* < Gr. χρυσοβήρυλλος, < χρυσός, gold, + βήρυλλος, beryl.] A native aluminate of glucinum, commonly of a yellow or greenish color, sometimes used as a gem.

chrys-o-chlore (kris′ǫ-klōr), *n.* [NL. *Chrysochloris,* < Gr. χρυσός, gold, + χλωρός, green.] Any of the South African moles of the genus *Chrysochloris* or family *Chrysochloridæ,* noted for the brilliant metallic luster of their fur.

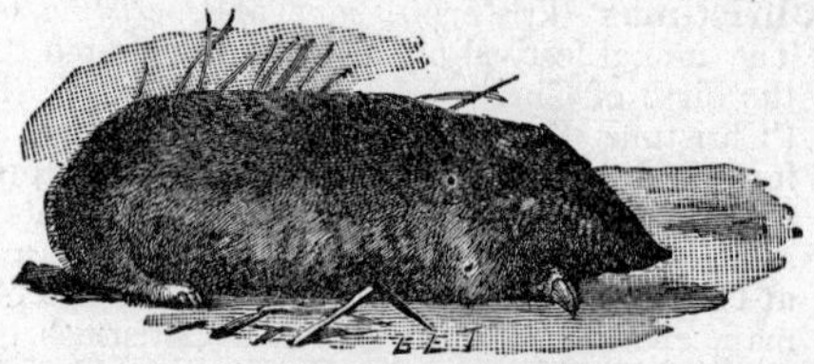
Chrysochlore.

chrys-o-col-la (kris-ǫ-kol′ä), *n.* [L., < Gr. χρυσόκολλα, solder for gold, < χρυσός, gold, + κόλλα, glue.] A mineral consisting of a hydrous silicate of copper, varying in color from green to blue.

chrys-oc-ra-cy (kris-ok′rạ-si), *n.* [See *chryso-* and *-cracy.*] The rule of gold or wealth; plutocracy.

chrys-o-lite (kris′ǫ-līt), *n.* [OF. *crisolite* (F. *chrysolithe*), < L. *chrysolithos,* < Gr. χρυσόλιθος, < χρυσός, gold, + λίθος, stone.] A native silicate of magnesium and iron, varying from yellow to green, in some forms used as a gem.

chrys-o-prase (kris′ǫ-prāz), *n.* [OF. *crisopase* (F. *chrysoprase*), < L. *chrysoprasus,* < Gr. χρυσόπρασος, < χρυσός, gold, + πράσον, leek.] A kind of chalcedony, commonly apple-green, much used in jewelry.

chrys-o-tile (kris′ǫ-til), *n.* [Gr. χρυσός, gold, + τίλος, fiber.] A fibrous variety of serpentine.

chtho-ni-an (thō′ni-ạn), *a.* [Gr. χθόνιος, < χθών, earth.] Dwelling in or beneath the surface of the earth; noting or pertaining to the deities or spirits of the underworld. Also **chthon-ic** (thon′ik).

chthon-o-pha-gi-a (thon-ǫ-fā′ji-ä), *n.* [NL., < Gr. χθών, earth, + φαγεῖν, eat.] In *pathol.,* a morbid propensity for eating earth or dirt.

chub (chub), *n.*; pl. *chubs* or (esp. collectively) *chub.* [ME. *chubbe*; origin unknown.] A common cyprinoid fish, *Leuciscus cephalus,* of Europe, with a thick fusiform body; also, any of various other fishes, as the allied *Semotilus atromaculatus* of America.

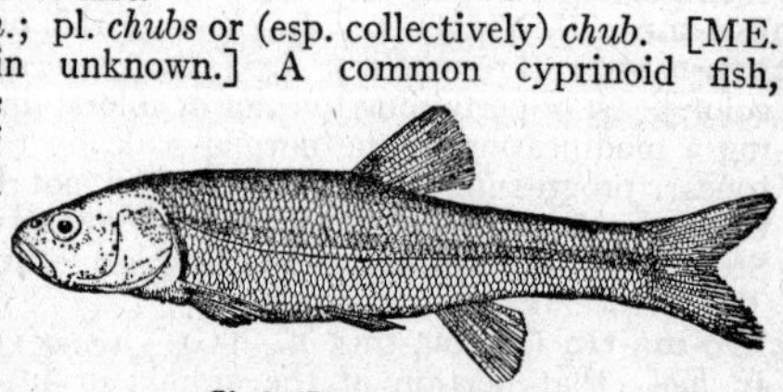
Chub (*Leuciscus cephalus*).

chub-by (chub′i), *a.*; compar. *chubbier,* superl. *chubbiest.* [Appar. < *chub.*] Round and plump.—**chub′bi-ness,** *n.*

chuck[1] (chuk), *v. i.* or *t.* [Imit.] To cluck.—**chuck**[1], *n.* A clucking sound.

chuck[2] (chuk), *n.* [Prob. var. of *chick.*] A chicken (now prov.); also, a term of endearment for a person (archaic: as, "Pray, *chuck,* come hither," Shakspere's "Othello," iv. 2. 24).

chuck[3] (chuk), *v. t.* [Cf. F. *choquer,* strike against, shock.] To strike lightly, as under the chin; also, to throw lightly or with careless ease (colloq.: as, "England now Is but a ball *chuck'd* between France and Spain," Tennyson's "Queen Mary," iii. 1. 62).—**chuck**[3], *n.* A light or playful tap, as under the chin; also, a toss or jerk (colloq.).

chuck[4] (chuk), *n.* [Prob. var. of *chock.*] A block, log, or lump (prov. Eng.); the cut of beef between the neck and the shoulder-blade; food (slang); in *mech.*, a clamp or the like, as on a drill or lathe, for holding a boring tool, or work while being shaped, etc.—**chuck[4]**, *v. t.* To fix in a chuck.

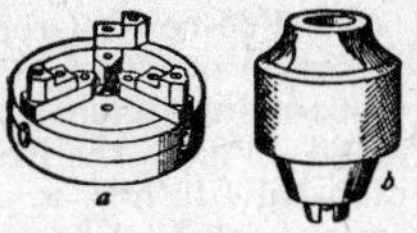
a, Lathe-chuck; b, Drill-chuck.

chuck-er (chuk′ėr), *n.* See *chukker*.

chuck=full (chuk′fůl′), *a.* Same as *chock-full*.

chuck-le (chuk′l), *v. i.*; *-led, -ling.* [Imit.: cf. *chuck[1]*.] To laugh in an easy, amused manner, with a degree of satisfaction; laugh to one's self; also, to cluck, as a fowl.—**chuck′le,** *n.* The act or sound of chuckling.

chuck-le=head (chuk′l-hed), *n.* [Cf. *chuck[4]*.] A blockhead; a numskull. [Colloq.]—**chuck′le=head″ed,** *a.* Thick-headed; stupid. [Colloq.]

chuck-wal-la (chuk′wol″ä), *n.* [N. Amer. Ind.] A large, dark-colored lizard, *Sauromalus ater*, of the southwestern U. S.

chuck=will's=wid-ow (chuk′wilz-wid′ō), *n.* [Imit. of its note.] A goat-sucker, *Antrostomus carolinensis*, of the southern U. S., resembling the whip-poorwill but larger.

Chuck-will's-widow.

chud-dah (chud′ä), *n.* Same as *chudder*.

chud-der, chud-dar (chud′ėr, -är), *n.* [Hind. *chadar*.] A kind of fine, plain-colored woolen shawl made in India.

chu-fa (chö′fä), *n.* [Sp.] A sedge, *Cyperus esculentus*, a native of southern Europe, but widely cultivated elsewhere, bearing small edible tubers.

chuff[1] (chuf), *n.* [ME. *chuffe*; origin unknown.] A rustic; a boor; a churl; a miserly fellow.

chuff[2] (chuf), *n.* [= *chaft*.] The jaw or chap. [Now prov. Eng.]—**chuff′y,** *a.* Fat-cheeked; chubby. [Now prov. Eng.]

chuk-ker (chuk′ėr), *n.* [Hind. *chakar*.] One of the periods of play in the game of polo.

chum[1] (chum), *n.* [Origin unknown.] A fish-bait, consisting usually of pieces of some oily fish, as the menhaden, used for baiting the hooks and also thrown into the water in large quantities to attract the fish.—**chum[1],** *v. i.*; *chummed, chumming.* To fish with chum.

chum[2] (chum), *n.* [Origin uncertain.] One who lodges or resides in the same chamber or rooms with another; a room-mate, as at college; also, an intimate companion (as, "Then seek good-humour'd tavern *chums*, And play at cards": M. Green's "The Spleen"). [Now colloq.]—**chum[2],** *v.*; *chummed, chumming.* **I.** *intr.* To share the same chamber or rooms; associate intimately. [Colloq.] **II.** *tr.* To assign to the same room or rooms with another. [Colloq.]—**chum′my,** *a.* Like a chum or chums; intimate; sociable. [Colloq.]

chump (chump), *n.* [Cf. *chunk*.] A short, thick lump of wood; the thick, blunt end of anything; the head (slang); a blockhead or dolt (slang).

chu-nam (chö-nam′), *n.* [E. Ind.] In the East Indies, prepared lime, esp. a fine kind made from calcined shells and chewed with the areca-nut and the betel-leaf; also, a fine plaster for building, susceptible of high polish.

chunk (chungk), *n.* [Prob. var. of *chuck[4]*.] A thick mass or lump of anything, as wood, bread, or meat; also, a thick-set and strong person or beast. [Colloq.]—**chunk′y,** *a.* In or like a chunk; thick-set. [Colloq.]

church (chėrch), *n.* [AS. *circe, cirice*, = G. *kirche*, prob. < LGr. κυριακόν, 'Lord's house,' < Gr. κύριος, lord.] An edifice for public Christian worship; also, the whole body of believers in Christ; any division of this body professing the same creed and acknowledging the same ecclesiastical authority; a Christian denomination; that part of the whole Christian body, or of a particular denomination, belonging to the same city, country, nation, etc.; a body of Christians worshiping in a particular edifice or constituting one congregation; also, the ecclesiastical organization as distinguished from the state; the clerical order or profession; also, public worship of God in a church; church service; also, by extension, a place of public worship of a non-Christian religion; any non-Christian religious society, organization, or congregation (as, the Jewish *Church*); loosely, a society, school, or the like, holding a set of opinions in common.—**church text,** a style of letters or type much used in ecclesiastical work, being a tall, slender form of black-letter. See *type*.—**church,** *v. t.* To conduct or bring to church, as for special services; perform a church service of thanksgiving for (a woman after childbirth).—**church′=go″er,** *n.* One who goes to church, esp. habitually.—**church′=go″ing,** *n.* and *a.*—**church′=house,** *n.* A building belonging to a church, used for various purposes of business, entertainment, etc.—**church′less,** *a.* Without a church; not belonging to or attending any church; not sanctioned by the church.—**church′ly,** *a.* Of, pertaining to, or appropriate for the church or a church; ecclesiastical.—**church′man** (-man), *n.*; pl. *-men.* A man of the church; an ecclesiastic; a clergyman; also, an adherent of the church; often, a member of an established or national church; in the U. S., among Episcopalians, a member of the Protestant Episcopal Church.—**church′man-ly,** *a.* Of or befitting a churchman.—**church′man-ship,** *n.*—**church′war″den,** *n.* A lay officer in an Anglican church whose duties include esp. the oversight and management of the church property; also, a clay tobacco-pipe with a very long stem (colloq.).—**church′wom″an,** *n.*; pl. *-women* (-wim″en). A female member of a church, esp. of an Anglican church.—**church′y,** *a.* Pertaining to or suggestive of a church or the church; also, excessively devoted to a church or to church forms. [Colloq.]—**church′yard,** *n.* The yard or ground adjoining a church, often used as a graveyard.

churl (chėrl), *n.* [AS. *ceorl* = G. *kerl*: cf. *carl*.] In old English times, a freeman of the lowest rank; hence, in general, a peasant; a rustic; a rude or boorish fellow; a surly person; a niggard or miser.—**churl′ish,** *a.* Of, pertaining to, or like a churl; boorish; rude; surly; niggardly; sordid; also, difficult to work or deal with, as soil.—**churl′ish-ly,** *adv.*—**churl′ish-ness,** *n.*

churn (chėrn), *n.* [AS. *cyrin*.] A vessel or machine in which cream or milk is agitated to make butter; any of various similar vessels or machines.—**churn,** *v.* **I.** *tr.* To agitate (cream or milk) in a churn, to make butter; make (butter) by doing this; also, to agitate as in a churn; produce, as foam, by such agitation. **II.** *intr.* To operate a churn; also, to move in agitation, as a liquid or any loose matter (as, "I could hear the boughs tossing and the leaves *churning* through half a mile of forest": Stevenson's "Travels with a Donkey," ii. 1).—**churn′ing,** *n.* The act of one that churns; also, the butter made at one time.

churr (chėr), *v.* and *n.* Same as *chirr*.

chut (chut), *interj.* [F.] An exclamation expressing impatience.

chute (shöt), *n.* [F., a fall, ult. < L. *cadere*, fall.] A waterfall; a steep descent, as in a river; a rapid; also, a channel, trough, tube, shaft, or the like, for conveying water, floating objects, grain, coal, etc., to a lower level; a shoot; a steep slope, as for tobogganing.—**chute,** *v. t.*; *chuted, chuting.* To send down a chute.

chut-ney (chut′ni), *n.* [Hind. *chatnī*.] A sauce or relish of East Indian origin compounded of both sweet and sour ingredients (fruits, herbs, etc.), with spices and other seasoning.

chyle (kīl), *n.* [NL. *chylus*, < Gr. χυλός, juice, chyle, < χεῖν, pour.] A milky fluid containing emulsified fat and other products of digestion, formed from the chyme in the small intestine and conveyed by the lacteals and the thoracic duct to the veins.—**chy-lif-er-ous** (kī-lif′e-rus), *a.* [See *-ferous*.] Conveying chyle.—**chy-lif′ic,** *a.* [See *-fic*.] Forming chyle.—**chy-li-fi-ca-tion** (kī″li-fi-kā′shon), *n.* The forming of chyle.—**chy′li-fy** (-fī), *v. t.* or *i.*; *-fied, -fying.* [See *-fy*.] To convert or be converted into chyle.—**chy′lous,** *a.* Of or like chyle.

chyme (kīm), *n.* [LL. *chymus*, < Gr. χυμός, juice, < χεῖν, pour.] The pulpy matter into which food is converted by gastric digestion.

chym-ic, chym-ist (kim′ik, -ist), etc. Old forms of *chemic, chemist*, etc.

chy-mif-er-ous (kī-mif′ẹ-rus), *a.* [See *-ferous.*] Conveying chyme.

chy-mi-fy (kī′mi-fī), *v. t.* or *i.*; *-fied, -fying.* [See *-fy.*] To convert or be converted into chyme.—**chy″mi-fi-ca′tion** (-fi-kā′shọn), *n.*

chy-mous (kī′mus), *a.* Of or like chyme.

cib-ol (sib′ọl), *n.* [F. *ciboule*, ult. < L. *cæpa*, onion.] An onion-like plant, *Allium fistulosum*, cultivated in various parts of Europe; also, the shallot, *A. ascalonicum.*

ci-bo-ri-um (si-bō′ri-um), *n.*; pl. *-ria* (-ri-ạ̈). [ML. *ciborium*, canopy, L. drinking-cup, < Gr. κιβώριον, cup, seed-vessel of the Egyptian bean.] A permanent canopy, resembling an inverted cup, placed over an altar; a baldachin; also, a vessel or receptacle for containing the consecrated bread of the eucharist, esp. one having the form of a chalice with a dome-shaped cover.

Ciborium (for the eucharist), 13th century. — Treasury of Sens Cathedral, France.

ci-ca-da (si-kā′dạ̈), *n.*; pl. *-das*, L. *-dæ* (-dē). [L.] Any insect of the family *Cicadidæ*, which comprises large homopterous insects having a heavy body, blunt head, and large, transparent wings, and noted for the shrill sound produced by the male by means of vibrating membranes or drums on the under side of the abdomen; esp., one belonging to the genus *Cicada*, as *C. septendecim* (commonly called 'seventeen-year locust'), a species remarkable for its length of life in the larval state underground; loosely, some other insect that makes a shrill or chirring sound, as a grasshopper or a cricket.

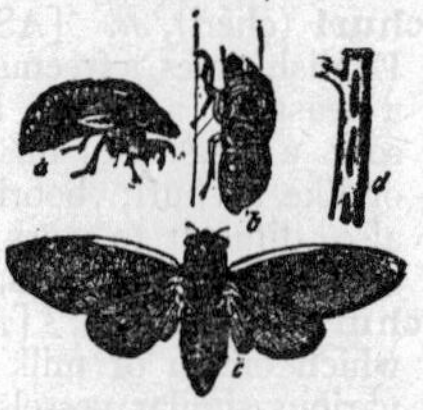

Cicada (*C. septendecim*). — *a*, pupa; *b*, cast pupa-shell; *c*, imago; *d*, punctured twig in which eggs are deposited.

ci-ca-la (si-kä′lạ̈), *n.*; pl. *-las*, It. *-le* (-lā). [It.] A cicada: as, "At eve a dry *cicala* sung" (Tennyson's "Mariana in the South," 85).

cic-a-trice (sik′ạ-tris), *n.* [F., < L. *cicatrix.*] A cicatrix; a scar.—**cic-a-tri′cial** (-trish′ạl), *a.* Pertaining to or of the nature of a cicatrix.

cic-a-tric-u-la (sik-ạ-trik′ụ̄-lạ̈), *n.*; pl. *-læ* (-lē). [L., dim. of *cicatrix.*] A small cicatrix; also, the germinating point in the yolk of an egg. Also **cic′a-tri-cle** (-tri-kl).—**cic-a-tric′u-lar** (-lạ̈r), *a.*

ci-ca-trix (si-kā′triks or sik′ạ-), *n.*; pl. *cicatrices* (sik-ạ-trī′sēz). [L.] The new tissue which forms over a wound or the like, and later contracts into the scar; a scar; in *bot.*, the scar left by a fallen leaf, etc.

cic-a-trize (sik′ạ-trīz), *v.*; *-trized, -trizing.* [F. *cicatriser*, < L. *cicatrix.*] **I.** *tr.* To heal by inducing the formation of a cicatrix. **II.** *intr.* To become healed by the formation of a cicatrix.—**cic″a-tri-za′tion** (-tri-zā′shọn), *n.*—**cic′a-triz-er** (-trī-zėr), *n.*

ci-ce-ly (sis′ẹ-li), *n.* [L. *seselis*, < Gr. σέσελις, kind of plant.] Any of several apiaceous plants nearly allied to chervil, as *Myrrhis odorata* (the 'sweet cicely' of England), sometimes used as a pot-herb, or some species of *Washingtonia* (the 'sweet cicely' of North America).

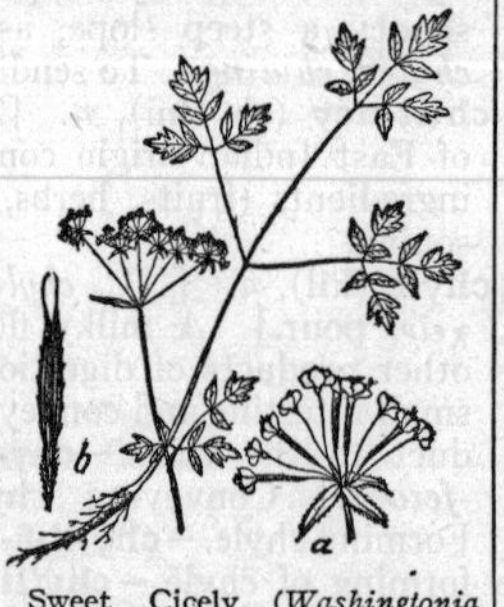

Sweet Cicely (*Washingtonia longistylis*).—*a*, an umbellet with the involucre; *b*, the fruit.

ci-ce-ro-ne (sis-ẹ-rō′nē, It. chē-chā-rō′nā), *n.*; pl. *-nes* (-nēz), It. *-ni* (-nē). [It., < L. *Cicero*, the Roman orator Cicero.] One who shows and explains the antiquities, curiosities, etc., of a place to strangers; a guide.—**ci′ce-ro-nage** (-rō-nạ̄j), *n.*—**ci′ce-rone** (-rōn), *v. t.*; *-roned, -roning.* To act as cicerone or guide to.

Ci-ce-ro-ni-an (sis-ẹ-rō′ni-ạn), *a.* Of, like, or befitting Cicero (106–43 B.C.), the Roman orator.

cich-lid (sik′lid), *n.* [NL. *Cichlidæ*, pl., < Gr. κίχλη, kind of sea-fish.] Any of the *Cichlidæ*, a family of fresh-water acanthopterygian fishes of Africa, South and Central America, etc., superficially resembling the American sunfishes.

ci-cho-ri-a-ceous (si-kō-ri-ā′shius), *a.* [L. *cichorium*, chicory.] Belonging to the *Cichoriaceæ*, or chicory family of plants, as the dandelion, endive, lettuce, salsify, etc.

ci-cis-be-o (chē-chēz-bā′ō), *n.*; pl. *-bei* (-bā′ē). [It.] In Italy, a professed gallant and attendant of a married woman.

Cid (sid, Sp. thēᴛʜ), *n.* [Sp., < Ar. *sayyid.*] Lord; chief: a title applied in Spanish literature to Ruy Díaz de Bivar (about 1040–99), famed as the champion (*el Campeador*) of Christian Spain against the Moors.

-cide. [L. *-cida*, killer, or *-cidium*, a killing, < *cædere*, kill.] A noun suffix meaning 'killer,' 'slayer,' as in *germicide*, or 'a killing,' 'a slaying,' as in *avicide*: both senses occurring in many words, as in *fratricide, homicide, parricide, regicide, suicide.*

ci-der (sī′dėr), *n.* [OF. *sidre* (F. *cidre*), < LL. *sicera*, < Gr. σίκερα, < Heb. *shēkār*, strong drink.] A strong liquor†; also, the expressed juice of apples (or formerly of some other fruit), used for drinking, either before fermentation ('sweet cider') or after fermentation ('hard cider'), or for making apple-jack, vinegar, etc.

ci=de-vant (sē-dė-väṅ), *a.* [F., heretofore.] Former; late; ex-: as, a *ci-devant* official; "More than a just proportion of the renowned names of the mother-country are . . . to be found in her *ci-devant* colonies" (Cooper's "Prairie," vi.).

ci-gar (si-gär′), *n.* [= F. *cigare*, < Sp. *cigarro.*] A small, shaped roll of tobacco leaves prepared for smoking.

cig-a-rette (sig-ạ-ret′), *n.* [F., dim. of *cigare*: see *cigar.*] A roll of finely cut tobacco for smoking, usually inclosed in thin paper; also, a similar roll of some other material, as cubebs.—**cig-a-rette′=bee″tle**, *n.* A widely distributed beetle, *Lasioderma serricorne*, destructive to dried tobacco, cigars, cigarettes, etc.

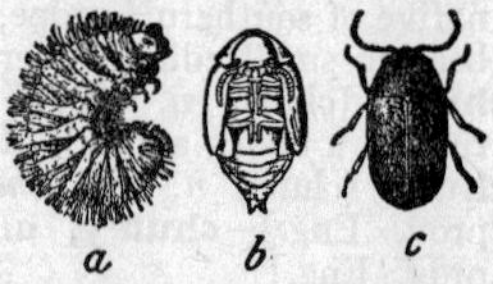

Cigarette-beetle.—*a*, larva; *b*, pupa; *c*, adult. (Enlarged.)

cil-i-a (sil′i-ạ̈), *n. pl.* [NL., pl. of *cilium*, eyelash, L. eyelid.] In *anat.*, the eyelashes; in *zoöl.* and *bot.*, minute, hair-like processes; esp., in cells, animalcules, etc., such processes capable of active vibration and serving to cause motion.—**cil′i-a-ry** (-ạ̄-ri), *a.* Pertaining to or resembling cilia; also, noting or pertaining to certain delicate structures of the eyeball.—**cil′i-ate, cil′i-at-ed** (-āt, -ā-ted), *a.* Furnished with cilia.—**cil-i-a′tion** (-ā′shọn), *n.* Ciliate state; also, cilia.

Flower with Cilia.

cil-ice (sil′is), *n.* [F., < L. *cilicium*, < Gr. κιλίκιον, coarse cloth made of (orig. Cilician) goat's hair.] Haircloth; also, an undergarment or shirt of haircloth; a hair shirt.

Ci-li-cian (si-lish′ạn). **I.** *a.* Of or pertaining to Cilicia, an ancient country on the southeastern coast of Asia Minor. **II.** *n.* A native or inhabitant of Cilicia.

cil-i-i-form (sil′i-i-fôrm), *a.* Having the form of cilia; fine and hair-like.

cil-i-o-late (sil′i-ọ-lāt), *a.* [NL. *ciliolum*, dim. of *cilium*: see *cilia.*] Furnished with minute cilia.

cil-i-um (sil′i-um), *n.* Infrequently used singular of *cilia*.

cim-e-ter (sim′e-tėr), *n.* See *simitar.*

ci-mex (sī′meks), *n.*; pl. *cimices* (sim′i-sēz). [L., bug.] The bedbug (of the genus *Cimex*).

Cim-me-ri-an (si-mē′ri-ạn), *a.* [L. *Cimmerius*, < Gr. Κιμμέριος.] Pertaining to or suggestive of the Cimmerii, a people said by Homer to dwell in perpetual darkness: as, "There, under ebon shades . . . In dark *Cimmerian* desert ever dwell" (Milton's "L'Allegro," 10).

cinch (sinch), *n.* [Sp. *cincha*, < ML. *cincta*, girdle, < L. *cingere*, gird.] A strong girth for a saddle or pack, made of leather, canvas, or woven horsehair (western U. S.); also, a firm hold or grip on anything (slang, U. S.); also, something sure or easy (slang, U. S.); also, a variety of the card-game of seven-up, in which the players seek to 'cinch' certain tricks.—**cinch,** *v. t.* To gird with a cinch; gird or bind firmly; hence, to seize on or make sure of (slang, U. S.); in the game of cinch, to protect (a trick) by playing a trump higher than the five.

cin-cho-na (sin-kō′nä), *n.* [NL.; from the Countess of *Chinchón* (1576–1639), wife of a Spanish viceroy of Peru.] Any of the rubiaceous trees or shrubs constituting the genus *Cinchona*, as *C. calisaya*, native in the Andes, and cultivated there and elsewhere for their bark, which yields quinine and other alkaloids; also, the medicinal bark of such trees or shrubs; Peruvian bark; also, a drug prepared from this bark.—**cin-chon′ic** (-kon′ik), *a.* Pertaining to or derived from cinchona.—**cin-cho-nid′i-a** (-kō-nid′-i-ä), *n.* Cinchonidine.—**cin-chon′i-dine** (-i-din), *n.* An alkaloid obtained from several species of cinchona, resembling quinine in action, but less powerful.—**cin′cho-nine** (-nin), *n.* An alkaloid obtained from species of *Cinchona* or allied plants, resembling quinine in action, but weaker.—**cin′cho-nism,** *n.* An abnormal condition due to the excessive use of cinchona or quinine, characterized by buzzing in the ears, giddiness, etc.—**cin′cho-nize** (-nīz), *v. t.*; *-nized, -nizing.* To impregnate or treat with cinchona or quinine; also, to cause cinchonism in.—**cin″cho-ni-za′tion** (-ni-zā′shọn), *n.*

Cinchona (*C. calisaya*).

cinct (singkt), *a.* [L. *cinctus*, pp. of *cingere*, gird.] Girt or girdled; encircled; surrounded.

cinc-ture (singk′tūr), *n.* [L. *cinctura*, < *cingere*, gird.] A belt or girdle (as, "Such of late Columbus found the American, so girt With feather'd *cincture*": Milton's "Paradise Lost," ix. 1117); also, something surrounding or encompassing like a girdle; a surrounding border; also, a girding or encompassing.—**cinc′ture,** *v. t.*; *-tured, -turing.* To gird with or as with a cincture; encircle; encompass.

cin-der (sin′dėr), *n.* [AS. *sinder* = G. *sinter*, dross of iron, E. *sinter*.] The dross of iron, etc.; slag; scoria; also, a burned-out or partially burned piece of coal, wood, or other substance (often in *pl.*); *pl.*, any residue of combustion; ashes.—**cin′der,** *v. t.* To reduce to cinders.

Cin-der-el-la (sin-dėr-el′ä), *n.* [From *Cinderella* (dim. < *cinder*), heroine of a well-known fairy-tale.] A young girl, esp. one of unrecognized beauty, who is forced to labor as a household drudge, or who, for the time being, is despised and oppressed.

cin-der-ous (sin′dėr-us), *a.* Of or like cinders.

cin-der-y (sin′dėr-i), *a.* Of the nature of, containing, or resembling cinders; begrimed with cinders.

cin-e-ma (sin′ē-mä), *n.*; pl. *-mas* (-mäz). [Short for *cinematograph*.] The cinematograph; also, the continuous picture projected by a cinematograph; *pl.*, moving pictures; also, *sing.*, a motion-picture theater. [Chiefly Eng.]—**cin-e-mat′ic**[1] (-mat′ik), *a.*

cin-e-mat-ic[2] (sin-ē-mat′ik), etc. Same as *kinematic*, etc.

cin-e-mat-o-graph (sin-ē-mat′ō-gráf), *n.* [F. *cinématographe*, < Gr. κίνημα, motion, + γράφειν, draw, write.] An apparatus for projecting on a screen in rapid succession a series of photographs of moving objects so as to give the impression of continuous motion; also, the apparatus for taking the photographs.—**cin-e-mat′o-graph,** *v. t.* To reproduce by a cinematograph.—**cin″e-ma-tog′ra-pher** (-mạ-tog′rạ-fėr), *n.*—**cin″e-mat-o-graph′ic** (-graf′ik), *a.* Of or pertaining to the cinematograph.—**cin″e-mat-o-graph′i-cal-ly,** *adv.*—**cin″e-ma-tog′ra-phy,** *n.*

cin-e-ol (sin′ē-ol or -ōl), *n.* [NL. *cina*, wormseed, + L. *oleum*, oil.] Eucalyptol.

cin-e-ra-ri-a (sin-ẹ-rā′ri-ä), *n.* [NL., prop. fem. of L. *cinerarius*, pertaining to ashes (with reference to the soft white down on the leaves): see *cinerary*.] Any of various horticultural varieties of the asteraceous plant *Senecio cruentus* (or *Cineraria cruenta*), a native of the Canary Islands, with heart-shaped leaves and clusters of flowers with white, blue, purple, red, or variegated rays.

Cineraria.

cin-e-ra-ri-um (sin-ẹ-rā′ri-um), *n.*; pl. *-ria* (-ri-ä). [L., neut. of *cinerarius*: see *cinerary*.] A place for depositing the ashes of the dead after cremation.

cin-e-ra-ry (sin′ẹ-rạ-ri), *a.* [L. *cinerarius*, < *cinis*, ashes.] Pertaining to ashes; used to hold the ashes of the dead, as sepulchral urns.

cin-e-ra-tion (sin-ẹ-rā′shọn), *n.* [Cf. ML. *cineratus*, reduced to ashes, also E. *incinerate*.] The reduction of anything to ashes, as by burning.—**cin′e-ra-tor,** *n.* A furnace for cineration; an incinerator.

ci-ne-re-ous (si-nē′rē-us), *a.* [L. *cinereus*, < *cinis*, ashes.] In the state of ashes (as, "a dead *cinereous* heap": Carlyle's "Sartor Resartus," iii. 7); also, resembling ashes, esp. in color; ashen; ashy; ash-colored; grayish. Also **cin-e-ri-tious** (sin-ẹ-rish′us).

Cin-ga-lese (sing-gạ-lēs′ or -lēz′), *a.* and *n.* See *Singhalese*.

cin-gu-lum (sing′gū-lum), *n.*; pl. *-la* (-lä). [L., girdle, < *cingere*, gird.] In *anat.* and *zoöl.*, a belt, zone, or girdle-like part; also, a part constricted as if by a girdle.

cin-na-bar (sin′ạ-bär), *n.* [L. *cinnabaris*, < Gr. κιννάβαρι.] Native mercuric sulphide, a reddish or brownish mineral constituting the chief source of mercury; also, artificial mercuric sulphide, used as a red pigment.—**cin-na-bar′ic** (-bar′ik), *a.*

cin-na-mon (sin′ạ-mọn). [L. *cinnamomum*, < Gr. κιννάμωμον.] **I.** *n.* The aromatic inner bark of any of several lauraceous trees of the genus *Cinnamomum* of the East Indies, etc., esp. *C. zeylanicum*, much used as a spice, and in medicine as a cordial and carminative; also, a tree yielding cinnamon; also, any of various allied or similar trees. **II.** *a.* Of the color of cinnamon, a light reddish brown.—**cin-nam-ic** (si-nam′ik), *a.*—**cin′na-mon=stone,** *n.* A certain variety of garnet, esp. when of a cinnamon color.

Cinnamon (*Cinnamomum zeylanicum*).

cinque (singk), *n.* [OF. *cinq, cinc* (F. *cinq*), < L. *quinque*, five.] Five; the five at dice, etc.

cin-que-cen-to (chēng-kwā-chen′tō), *n.* [It., five hundred, short for *mille cinquecento*, one thousand five hundred.] The 16th century, with reference to Italy, and esp. to the Italian art or literature of that period.—**cin-que-cen′tist,** *n.*

cinque-foil (singk′foil), *n.* [OF. *cinq*, five, + *foil*, leaf: see *cinque* and *foil*[1].] A European potentilla, *Potentilla reptans*, with a compound leaf composed of five leaflets;

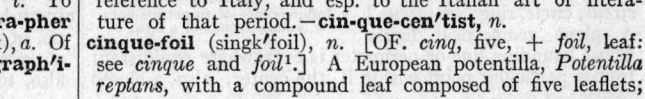

any species of *Potentilla*; also, a decorative design or feature resembling the leaf of cinquefoil, as an architectural ornament or opening of a generally circular or rounded form divided into five lobes by cusps.

Cinquefoil. — Lincoln Cathedral, England.

cin-que-pace† (singʹkę-pās), *n.* [See *cinque* and *pace*².] An old dance of lively character, apparently characterized by a movement of five steps. See Shakspere's "Much Ado about Nothing," ii. 1. 77.

Cinque Ports (singk pōrts). [AF., 'five ports.'] A group of seaports (orig. five) in southeastern England, constituting a corporation which formerly supplied a certain number of ships and men in case of war, receiving in return important privileges and franchises.

ci-pher (sīʹfėr), *n.* [OF. *cifre* (F. *chiffre*), < Ar. *çifr*, lit. 'empty': cf. *zero.*] An arithmetical symbol (0) which denotes naught, or no quantity or magnitude; hence, something of no value or importance, esp. a person of no influence; a nonentity; also, any of the Arabic numerals or figures; also, a combination of letters, as the initials of a name, in one complex device; a monogram; also, a secret method of writing, as by a specially formed code of symbols; writing executed by such a method; the key to this. —**ciʹpher,** *v.* **I.** *intr.* To use figures or numerals arithmetically; also, of an organ-pipe or an organ, to sound independently of the action of the player, in consequence of some derangement. **II.** *tr.* To calculate numerically; figure; also, to write in or as in cipher; also, to decipher†; in *ship-building*, to bevel or chamfer.—**ciʹpher-er,** *n.*

cip-o-lin (sipʹǫ-lin), *n.* [F., < It. *cipollino* (so called from its layered structure), < *cipolla*, < L. *cæpa*, onion.] A variety of marble with alternate white and greenish zones and a laminated structure. Also (It.) **ci-pol-li-no** (chē-pǫl-lēʹnō).

cir-ca (sėrʹkạ), *adv.* and *prep.* [L.] About: used esp. in giving approximate dates, and often abbreviated *c.* or *c* (as, *c.* 1550).

Cir-cas-sian (sėr-kashʹiạn), *a.* Of or pertaining to Circassia, a region on the northern slope of the Caucasus Mountains, and bordering on the Black Sea.—**Circassian walnut,** a kind of walnut, a variety of *Juglans regia*, native in the Old World, whose wood is used in making furniture.—**Cir-casʹsian,** *n.* A native or inhabitant of Circassia; one of the native Caucasian race of Circassia, noted for physical beauty and courage; also, their language.

Cir-ce (sėrʹsē), *n.* [From the enchantress *Circe*, represented by Homer as having turned the companions of Odysseus into swine by a magic drink.] A dangerously or irresistibly fascinating woman.—**Cir-ceʹan,** *a.* Of, like, or befitting the enchantress Circe; tempting but harmful: as, "With caution taste the sweet *Circean* cup" (Cowper's "Progress of Error," 580).

cir-cen-sian (sėr-senʹshiạn), *a.* [L. *circensis*, < *circus*, circus.] Of or pertaining to the (Roman) circus.

cir-ci-nal (sėrʹsi-nạl), *a.* Circinate.

cir-ci-nate (sėrʹsi-nāt), *a.* [L. *circinatus*, pp. of *circinare*, make round, < *circinus*, compasses.] Made round; ring-shaped; rolled up on the axis at the apex, as a frond, leaf, etc.—**cirʹci-nate-ly,** *adv.*

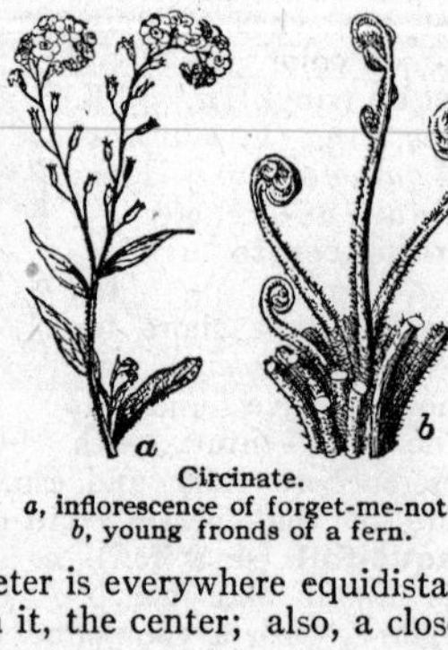

Circinate.
a, inflorescence of forget-me-not; *b*, young fronds of a fern.

cir-cle (sėrʹkl), *n.* [OF. F. *cercle*, < L. *circulus*, dim. of *circus*, circle, ring: see *circus.*] A plane geometrical figure whose bounding line or perimeter is everywhere equidistant from a particular point within it, the center; also, a closed plane curve representing the bounding line (or circumference) of such a figure; also, any circular object, formation, or arrangement; a ring; a circlet or crown; the orbit of a heavenly body, or the period of revolution of the body; an astronomical or other instrument of which a graduated circle is an essential part; a sphere or orb; also, a number of persons bound by a common tie; a coterie; also, a series ending where it begins, and perpetually repeated (as, the *circle* of the year); a complete series forming a connected whole (as, the *circle* of the sciences); in *logic*, an inconclusive form of reasoning in which unproved statements, or their equivalents, are used to prove each other ('vicious circle').—**circle of latitude,** in *geog.*, a meridian of the terrestrial globe; also, a parallel of latitude; in *astron.*, any great circle of the celestial sphere that is perpendicular to the plane of the ecliptic.—**great circle,** a circle on the surface of a sphere, the plane of which passes through the center of the sphere: opposed to a *small circle*, a similar circle whose plane does not pass through the center of the sphere.—**cirʹcle,** *v.*; *-cled, -cling.* **I.** *tr.* To inclose in a circle; surround; also, to move in a circle or circuit round. **II.** *intr.* To move in a circle; also, to form a circle.—**cirʹcler,** *n.*—**cirʹclet** (-klet), *n.* A small circle; a ring; a ring-shaped ornament, esp. for the head (as, "On her head A diamond *circlet*": Tennyson's "Lover's Tale," iv. 286).—**cirʹcle-wise,** *adv.* In the manner of a circle.

cir-cuit (sėrʹkit), *n.* [OF. F. *circuit*, < L. *circuitus*, < *circuire*, *circumire*, go around, < *circum*, around, + *ire*, go.] The act of going or moving around; a circular journey; a round; also, a roundabout journey or course; also, a periodical journey from place to place, to perform certain duties, as of judges to hold court or of ministers to preach; the persons making such a journey; the route followed, places visited, or district covered by such a journey; also, the line going around or bounding any area or object; the distance about an area or object; also, a ring† or circlet†; also, the space within a bounding line; in *elect.*, the complete path of an electric current, usually including the generating apparatus; sometimes, a distinct portion of such a path.—**cirʹcuit,** *v.* **I.** *tr.* To go or move around; make the circuit of. **II.** *intr.* To go or move in a circuit.—**cir-cuʹi-tous** (-kūʹi-tus), *a.* [ML. *circuitosus.*] Of the nature of a circuit; roundabout; not direct.—**cir-cuʹi-tous-ly,** *adv.*—**cir-cuʹi-tous-ness,** *n.*—**cirʹcuit=ridʺer,** *n.* An itinerant Methodist minister who rides from place to place to preach along a circuit.—**cir-cuʹi-ty** (-ti), *n.*; pl. *-ties* (-tiz). Circuitous quality; roundabout character; also, a circuitous course or proceeding.

cir-cu-la-ble (sėrʹkū-lạ-bl), *a.* That may be circulated.

cir-cu-lar (sėrʹkū-lạr), *a.* [LL. *circularis*, < L. *circulus*: see *circle.*] Of or pertaining to a circle; having the form of a circle; round like a disk; disk-shaped; round like a ring; ring-shaped; also, moving in or describing a circle or a circuit; fig., moving or occurring in a round or cycle; also, noting or pertaining to that form of reasoning called the circle; also, circuitous, roundabout, or indirect; also, pertaining to a circle or set of persons; of a letter, etc., addressed to a number of persons (whether in the form of a single copy to be passed from hand to hand, or of individual copies for various recipients), or intended for general circulation.—**circular number,** in *math.*, a number whose powers are expressed by numbers the last figure in which is the number itself, as 5 and 6.—**circular saw,** a saw consisting of a circular plate or disk with a toothed edge, which is rotated at high speed in machines for sawing logs, cutting lumber, etc.—**cirʹcu-lar,** *n.* A circular letter or notice; a notice or statement separately printed in quantities for circulation among the general public, for business or other purposes; also, a kind of long cape or sleeveless cloak worn by women.—**cir-cu-larʹi-ty** (-larʹi-ti), *n.* Circular form.—**cirʹcu-lar-ize** (-lạr-īz), *v. t.*; *-ized, -izing.* To make circular; also, to send circulars to; ply with circulars.—**cirʺcu-lar-i-zaʹtion** (-i-zāʹshǫn), *n.*—**cirʹcu-lar-iz-er** (-ī-zėr), *n.*—**cirʹcu-lar-ly,** *adv.*

cir-cu-late (sėrʹkū-lāt), *v.*; *-lated, -lating.* [L. *circulatus*, pp. of *circulare*, make circular, encircle, *circulari*, go about, < *circulus*: see *circle.*] **I.** *tr.* To make a circuit of†; also, to cause to pass from place to place, from person to person, etc., as rumors or money; give currency to; disseminate; distribute. **II.** *intr.* To move in a circle or circuit; move or pass through a circuit back to the starting-point, as the blood in the body; also, to pass from place to place, from person to person, etc.; be disseminated or distributed.—**circulating decimal.** See under *decimal*, *n.* —**circulating library,** a library the books of which circulate among the members or subscribers.—**cir-cu-la′tion** (-lā′shọn), *n.* [L. *circulatio(n-)*.] The act of circulating, or moving in a circle or circuit; esp., the movement of the blood through the various vessels of the body; any similar circuit or passage, as of the sap in plants; also, the transmission or passage of anything from place to place, person to person, etc.; esp., the distribution of copies of a publication among readers; the extent of such distribution; the number of copies of a newspaper, magazine, etc., distributed at each issue; also, coin, notes, bills, etc., in use as currency; currency.—**cir′cu-la-tive** (-lạ-tiv), *a.* Circulating; causing circulation.—**cir′cu-la-tor** (-lā-tọr), *n.*—**cir′cu-la-to-ry** (-lạ-tọ̄-ri), *a.* Pertaining to or of the nature of circulation, as of the blood.

circum-. [L., repr. *circum*, adv. and prep., orig. acc. of *circus*, circle, ring: see *circus*.] A prefix of Latin origin, meaning 'around,' 'about,' sometimes used as an English formative, as in *circumcentral* (around the center), *circum-Mediterranean.*

cir-cum-am-bi-ent (sėr-kum-am′bi-ẹnt), *a.* [LL. *circumambiens (-ent-)*, ppr. of *circumambire*, < L. *circum*, around, + *ambire*: see *ambient*.] Surrounding; encompassing: as, "the immeasurable *circumambient* realm of Nothingness and Night" (Carlyle's "Sartor Resartus," i. 1).—**cir-cum-am′bi-en-cy,** *n.*

cir-cum-am-bu-late (sėr-kum-am′bụ̄-lāt), *v. t.* or *i.*; *-lated, -lating.* [LL. *circumambulatus*, pp. of *circumambulare*, < L. *circum*, around, + *ambulare*, walk.] To walk or go about.—**cir″cum-am-bu-la′tion** (-lā′shọn), *n.*—**cir-cum-am′bu-la-tor,** *n.*

cir-cum-ben-di-bus (sėr-kum-ben′di-bus), *n.* [L. *circum*, around, + E. *bend*[2].] A roundabout way; a circumlocution. [Humorous.]

cir-cum-cise (sėr′kum-sīz), *v. t.*; *-cised, -cising.* [L. *circumcisus*, pp. of *circumcidere*, cut around, < *circum*, around, + *cædere*, cut.] To cut off the foreskin of (males), esp. as a religious rite; perform an analogous operation on (females); fig., to purify spiritually.—**cir′cum-cis-er** (-sī-zėr), *n.*—**cir-cum-ci′sion** (-sizh′ọn), *n.* [LL. *circumcisio(n-)*.] The act or the rite of circumcising; fig., spiritual purification; also, the Jews, as the circumcised people of the Bible; those spiritually purified; [*cap.*] a church festival in honor of the circumcision of Christ, observed on Jan. 1.

cir-cum-fer-ence (sėr-kum′fẹ-rẹns), *n.* [L. *circumferentia*, < *circumferre*, carry around, < *circum*, around, + *ferre*, bear.] The line that bounds a circle; the bounding line or perimeter of any regular plane curvilinear figure; the encompassing boundary of any figure; also, distance around; also, the space within a bounding line.—**cir-cum-fer-en′tial** (-fẹ-ren′shạl), *a.* Of or pertaining to the circumference. —**cir-cum-fer-en′tial-ly,** *adv.*

cir-cum-flect (sėr-kum-flekt′), *v. t.* [L. *circumflectere* (pp. *circumflexus*), < *circum*, around, + *flectere*, bend.] To bend around; also, to place a circumflex accent on.—**cir-cum-flec′tion, cir-cum-flex′ion** (-flek′shọn), *n.* [LL. *circumflexio(n-)*.] A bending around; a circuitous course; also, a marking with the circumflex.

cir-cum-flex (sėr′kum-fleks). [L. *circumflexus*, pp.: see *circumflect*.] **I.** *a.* Bending or winding around; specif., noting or having a particular accent (^ , ⌒ , ~) indicating orig. a combination of raised and lowered pitch (as in ancient Greek), later a long vowel (as in the French *bête*, earlier *beste*), quality of sound (as in phonetic notation), etc. **II.** *n.* The circumflex accent.—**cir′cum-flex,** *v. t.* To bend around; also, to mark with the circumflex; pronounce as so marked.

cir-cum-flex′ion, *n.* See *circumflection.*

cir-cum-flu-ent (sėr-kum′flọ̈-ẹnt), *a.* [L. *circumfluens (-ent-)*, ppr. of *circumfluere*, < *circum*, around, + *fluere*, flow.] Flowing around; encompassing. Also **cir-cum′-flu-ous.**

cir-cum-fo-ra-ne-ous (sėr″kum-fọ̄-rā′nẹ̄-us), *a.* [L. *circumforaneus*, < *circum*, around, + *forum*, market-place.] Wandering from market-place to market-place; vagrant; vagabond; quack.

cir-cum-fuse (sėr-kum-fūz′), *v. t.*; *-fused, -fusing.* [L. *circumfusus*, pp. of *circumfundere*, < *circum*, around, + *fundere*, pour.] To pour around; diffuse; also, to surround as with a fluid; suffuse.—**cir-cum-fu′sion** (-fū′zhọn), *n.*

cir-cum-gy-rate (sėr-kum-jī′rāt), *v. t.* or *i.*; *-rated, -rating.* [LL. *circumgyratus*, pp. of *circumgyrare*, < L. *circum*, around, + *gyrare*, turn.] To turn, wheel, or go round.—**cir″cum-gy-ra′tion** (-rā′shọn), *n.*—**cir-cum-gy′ra-to-ry** (-rạ-tọ̄-ri), *a.*

cir-cum-ja-cent (sėr-kum-jā′sẹnt), *a.* [L. *circumjacens (-ent-)*, ppr. of *circumjacere*, < *circum*, around, + *jacere*, lie.] Lying around; surrounding: as, "A paper to get folk to take shares . . . was carried through the *circumjacent* parishes" (Galt's "Annals of the Parish," vi.).—**cir-cum-ja′cence, cir-cum-ja′cen-cy,** *n.*

cir-cum-lo-cu-tion (sėr″kum-lọ̄-kū′shọn), *n.* [L. *circumlocutio(n-)*, < *circum*, around, + *loqui*, speak.] A speaking in a roundabout way; the use of several words for one or of many for few; a roundabout expression.—**cir-cum-loc′u-to-ry** (-lok′ụ̄-tọ̄-ri), *a.*

cir-cum-mure (sėr-kum-mūr′), *v. t.*; *-mured, -muring.* [L. *circum*, around, + LL. *murare*, wall.] To wall about: as, "a garden *circummured* with brick" (Shakspere's "Measure for Measure," iv. 1. 28).

cir-cum-nav-i-gate (sėr-kum-nav′i-gāt), *v. t.*; *-gated, -gating.* [L. *circumnavigatus*, pp. of *circumnavigare*, < *circum*, around, + *navigare*, sail.] To sail around; make the circuit of by navigation.—**cir-cum-nav′i-ga-ble,** *a.*—**cir″cum-nav-i-ga′tion** (-gā′shọn), *n.*—**cir-cum-nav′i-ga-tor,** *n.*

cir-cum-nu-tate (sėr-kum-nū′tāt), *v. i.*; *-tated, -tating.* [L. *circum*, about, + *nutatus*, pp. of *nutare*, nod.] In *bot.*, of the apex of a stem or other growing part of a plant, to bend or move around in an irregular circular or elliptical path.—**cir″cum-nu-ta′tion** (-nụ̄-tā′shọn), *n.*

cir-cum-po-lar (sėr-kum-pō′lạ̈r), *a.* [See *circum-*.] Around one of the poles of the earth or of the heavens.

cir-cum-po-lar-ize (sėr-kum-pō′lạ̈r-īz), *v. t.*; *-ized, -izing.* [See *circum-*.] In *optics*, to rotate the plane of polarization of (light).—**cir″cum-po″lar-i-za′tion** (-i-zā′shọn), *n.*

cir-cum-po-si-tion (sėr″kum-pọ̄-zish′ọn), *n.* [LL. *circumpositio(n-)*, < L. *circumponere*, < *circum*, around, + *ponere*, place.] The act of placing, or the state of being placed, round about.

cir-cum-ro-tate (sėr-kum-rō′tāt), *v. i.*; *-tated, -tating.* [L. *circumrotatus*, pp. of *circumrotare*, < *circum*, around, + *rotare*: see *rotate*.] To rotate like a wheel.—**cir″cum-ro-ta′tion** (-rọ̄-tā′shọn), *n.*—**cir-cum-ro′ta-to-ry** (-tạ-tọ̄-ri), *a.*

cir-cum-scis-sile (sėr-kum-sis′il), *a.* [L. *circum*, about, + *scissilis*, easily split.] In *bot.*, opening along a transverse circular line, as the seed-vessel of certain plants.

Circumscissile Pod of Pimpernel.

cir-cum-scribe (sėr-kum-skrīb′), *v. t.*; *-scribed, -scribing.* [L. *circumscribere* (pp. *circumscriptus*), < *circum*, around, + *scribere*, write, draw.] To draw a line around; encircle or surround; inclose within bounds; limit or confine, esp. narrowly; mark off or define; in *geom.*, to draw (a figure) around another figure so as to touch as many points as possible; of a figure, to inclose (another figure) in this manner.—**cir-cum-scrib′a-ble** (-skrī′bạ-bl), *a.*—**cir-cum-scrib′er,** *n.*—**cir′cum-script** (-skript), *a.* [L. *circumscriptus*, pp.] Circumscribed; limited.—**cir-cum-scrip′tion** (-skrip′shọn), *n.* [L. *circumscriptio(n-)*.] The act of circumscribing; circumscribed state; limitation; also, periphery or outline; also, anything that circumscribes or incloses; also, a circumscribed space; also, a circular inscription, as on a coin or seal.—**cir-cum-scrip′tive,** *a.* Circumscribing; also, circumscribed or limited.

cir-cum-so-lar (sėr-kum-sō′lạ̈r), *a.* [See *circum-*.] Around the sun.

cir-cum-spect (sėr′kum-spekt), *a.* [L. *circumspectus*, pp. of *circumspicere*, look about, < *circum*, around, + *specere*, look at.] Watchful on all sides; cautious; prudent; also, marked by circumspection; well-considered.—**cir-cum-spec′tion** (-spek′shǫn), *n.* [L. *circumspectio(n-).*] Circumspect observation or action; caution; heedfulness.—**cir-cum-spec′tive,** *a.* Given to or marked by circumspection; watchful; cautious.—**cir′cum-spect-ly,** *adv.*—**cir′cum-spect-ness,** *n.*

cir-cum-stance (sėr′kum-stans or, esp. Brit., -stąns), *n.* [L. *circumstantia*, < *circumstare*, stand around, < *circum*, around, + *stare*, stand.] That which stands around or surrounds†; surroundings†; also, a condition, with respect to time, place, manner, agent, etc., which accompanies, determines, or modifies a fact or event; the existing condition or state of affairs surrounding and affecting an agent (usually in *pl.*: as, to be forced by *circumstances* to do a thing); the condition or state of a person with respect to material welfare (now always in *pl.*: as, a family in reduced *circumstances*); also, an unessential accompaniment of any fact or event; a matter of secondary importance; an accessory matter; a particular or detail; also, an incident or occurrence (as, his arrival was a fortunate *circumstance*); also, detailed or circuitous narration; specification of particulars; also, ceremonious accompaniment or display (archaic: as, "pride, pomp and *circumstance* of glorious war," Shakspere's "Othello," iii. 3. 354).—**cir′cum-stance,** *v. t.*; *-stanced, -stancing.* To place in particular circumstances or relations; also, to furnish with details†.

cir-cum-stan-tial (sėr-kum-stan′shąl). [L. *circumstantia*: see *circumstance.*] **I.** *a.* Of, pertaining to, or derived from circumstances (as, *circumstantial* evidence, the evidence bearing on a case, afforded by various more or less relevant circumstances, as distinguished from direct testimony); pertaining to conditions of material welfare (as, *circumstantial* prosperity); also, of the nature of a circumstance or unessential accompaniment; secondary; incidental; also, dealing with or giving circumstances or details; detailed; particular; also, marked by circumstance, ceremony, or pomp (archaic). **II.** *n.* Something circumstantial; an attendant circumstance; a detail; an incidental feature.—**cir-cum-stan-ti-al′i-ty** (-shi-al′i-ti), **cir-cum-stan′tial-ness,** *n.*—**cir-cum-stan′tial-ly,** *adv.*

cir-cum-stan-ti-ate (sėr-kum-stan′shi-āt), *v. t.*; *-ated, -ating.* [L. *circumstantia*: see *circumstance.*] To place in particular circumstances†; also, to set forth or support with circumstances or particulars.—**cir-cum-stan-ti-a′tion** (-ā′shǫn), *n.*

cir-cum-ter-res-tri-al (sėr″kum-te-res′tri-ąl), *a.* [See *circum-.*] Around the earth.

cir-cum-val-late (sėr-kum-val′āt), *v. t.*; *-lated, -lating.* [L. *circumvallatus*, pp. of *circumvallare*, < *circum*, around, + *vallare*: see *vallate.*] To surround with or as with a rampart.—**cir-cum-val′late,** *a.* Surrounded as with a rampart.—**cir″cum-val-la′tion** (-va-lā′shǫn), *n.* In *fort.*, the act or art of constructing a rampart or intrenchment about a place, esp. in besieging; also, the line of works so constructed.

cir-cum-vent (sėr-kum-vent′), *v. t.* [L. *circumventus*, pp. of *circumvenire*, < *circum*, around, + *venire*, come.] To surround or encompass as by stratagem; entrap; also, to gain advantage over by artfulness or deception; outwit; overreach; also, to go around, or circuit (as, "By making a détour to the right, he could completely *circumvent* the bridge": Motley's "Dutch Republic," iv. 2).—**cir-cum-ven′tion** (-ven′shǫn), *n.* [LL. *circumventio(n-).*] The act of circumventing.—**cir-cum-ven′tive,** *a.*—**cir-cum-vent′or, cir-cum-vent′er,** *n.*

cir-cum-vo-lant (sėr-kum′vǫ-ląnt), *a.* [L. *circumvolans* (*-ant-*), ppr. of *circumvolare*, < *circum*, around, + *volare*, fly.] Flying around.

cir-cum-vo-lu-tion (sėr″kum-vǫ-lū′shǫn), *n.* [See *circumvolve.*] The act of rolling or turning around; a single complete turn; also, a winding or folding about something; one of the folds of anything so wound; also, a winding in a sinuous course; a sinuosity; fig., roundabout course or procedure (as, "He had neither time nor temper for sentimental *circumvolutions*": Disraeli's "Coningsby," vi. 2).

cir-cum-volve (sėr-kum-volv′), *v.*; *-volved, -volving.* [L. *circumvolvere* (pp. *circumvolutus*), roll around, < *circum*, around, + *volvere*, roll.] **I.** *tr.* To revolve; also, to wind, fold, or wrap about something†; also, to encompass†. **II.** *intr.* To revolve.

cir-cus (sėr′kus), *n.*; pl. *-cuses.* [L., circle, ring, circus, = Gr. κίρκος, κρίκος, ring.] In ancient Rome, a large, usually oblong or oval, roofless inclosure, surrounded by tiers of seats rising one above another, for chariot-races, public games, etc.; in modern times, a circular arena surrounded by tiers of seats, for the exhibition of equestrian and acrobatic feats, etc.; the company of performers and their equipage, esp. a traveling company of such performers; the performance itself; also, a squadron of aëroplanes that operate together ('flying circus'); also, something suggestive of the Roman circus, as a natural amphitheater, or a circular range of houses or circular open space in a city (as, Oxford *Circus*, London); also, a circle† or ring†.

cirl=bunt-ing (sėrl′bun″ting), *n.* [NL. *cirlus*, < It. *cirlo*: cf. It. *zirlo*, whistling (of thrushes, etc.).] A common European bunting, *Emberiza cirlus.*

Cirl-bunting.

cirque (sėrk), *n.* [F., < L. *circus*: see *circus.*] A circus; also, a circular space, esp. a natural amphitheater, as in mountains; also, a circle or ring of any kind (poetic: as, "Like a dismal *cirque* Of Druid stones, upon a forlorn moor," Keats's "Hyperion," ii.).

cir-rate (sir′āt), *a.* Having cirri; cirriferous.

cir-rhose (sir′ōs), *a.* See *cirrose.*

cir-rho-sis (si-rō′sis), *n.* [NL., < Gr. κιρρός, tawny.] In *pathol.*, a morbid condition of the substance of the liver, kidneys, etc., consisting in induration and contraction due to excessive formation of interstitial connective tissue.—**cir-rhot-ic** (si-rot′ik), *a.*

cir-ri (sir′ī), *n.* Plural of *cirrus.*

cirri-. Form of *cirrus* used in combination.—**cir-rif-er-ous** (si-rif′ẹ-rus), *a.* [+ *-ferous.*] Bearing cirri, tendrils, or filaments.—**cir-ri-grade** (sir′i-grād), *a.* [+ *-grade.*] Moving by means of cirri.

cir-ri-ped (sir′i-ped), *n.* [NL. *Cirripedia*, pl., < L. *cirrus* (see *cirrus*) + *pes* (*ped-*), foot.] Any of the *Cirripedia*, an order or group of crustaceans typically having feet in the form of cirri or filaments. See *barnacle*[1].

cir-ro=cu-mu-lus (sir-ǫ-kū′mų-lus), *n.* [See *cirrus* and *cumulus.*] A cloud of high altitude, consisting of small fleecy balls or wisps, which are often arranged in rows.

cir-rose (sir′ōs), *a.* Having a cirrus or cirri; resembling cirri; also, of the nature of cirrus clouds.

cir-ro=stra-tus (sir-ǫ-strā′tus), *n.* [See *cirrus* and *stratus.*] A high veil-like cloud or haze, often giving rise to halos around the sun and moon.

cir-rous (sir′us), *a.* Same as *cirrose.*

cir-rus (sir′us), *n.*; pl. *cirri* (-ī). [L., curl, tuft, fringe.] In *bot.*, a tendril; in *zoöl.*, a filament or slender appendage serving as a barbel, tentacle, foot, arm, etc.; in *meteor.*, a variety of cloud having a thin fleecy or filamentous appearance, normally occurring at great altitudes and consisting of minute ice-crystals.

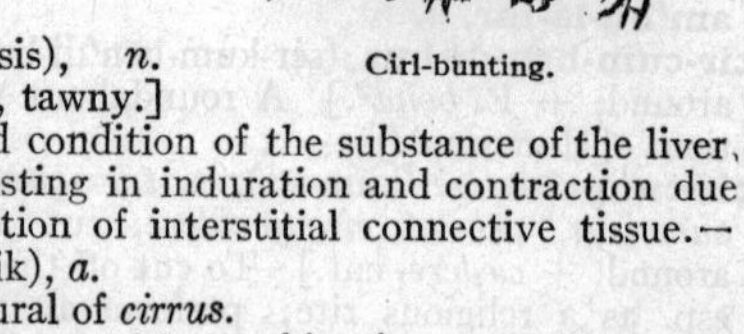

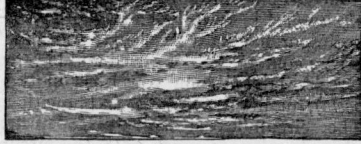

Cirrus.

cir-soid (sėr′soid), *a.* [Gr. κιρσοειδής, < κιρσός, enlargement of a vein, + εἶδος, form.] Varix-like; varicose.

cis-. [L., repr. *cis*, prep.: cf. *citra-*.] A prefix of Latin origin, meaning 'on this side of,' sometimes used as an English formative: opposed to *trans-* or *ultra-*.

cis-al-pine (sis-al'pin or -pīn), *a.* [L. *cisalpinus*: see *cis-*.] On this (the Roman or south) side of the Alps.

cis-at-lan-tic (sis-at-lan'tik), *a.* [See *cis-*.] On this (the speaker's or writer's) side of the Atlantic.

cis-cau-ca-sian (sis-kâ-kash'ạn), *a.* [See *cis-*.] On this (the European) side of the Caucasus Mountains.

cis-co (sis'kō), *n.*; pl. *-coes* (-kōz). [N. Amer. Ind.] Any of several species of whitefish of the genus *Argyrosomus*, as *A. artedi*, the lake-herring, of the Great Lakes, or *A. hoyi*, of Lake Michigan.

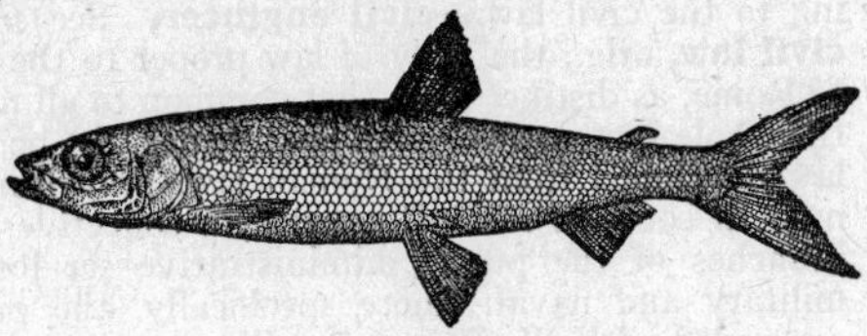

Cisco (*Argyrosomus hoyi*).

Cis-lei-than (sis-lī'thạn), *a.* [See *cis-*.] On this side of the river Leitha (between Austria and Hungary): applied to the division of the former Austro-Hungarian Empire with its seat in Vienna.

cis-mon-tane (sis-mon'tān), *a.* [L. *cismontanus*, < *cis* (see *cis-*) + *mons* (*mont-*), mountain.] On this (the nearer) side of the mountains; esp., on the northern side of the Alps.

cis-pa-dane (sis-pā'dān or sis'pạ-dān), *a.* [L. *cis* (see *cis-*) + *Padus*, the Po.] On this (the Roman or south) side of the river Po.

cis-pon-tine (sis-pon'tin), *a.* [L. *cis* (see *cis-*) + *pons* (*pont-*), bridge.] On this (the nearer) side of a bridge; esp., on the northern side of the Thames in London.

cis-rhe-nane (sis-rē'nān or sis'rẹ-nān), *a.* [L. *cisrhenanus*, < *cis* (see *cis-*) + *Rhenus*, the Rhine.] On this (the western) side of the river Rhine.

cis-soid (sis'oid), *n.* [Gr. κισσοειδής, ivy-like, < κισσός, ivy, + εἶδος, form.] In *math.*, a kind of curve with a cusp at the origin, invented by Diocles, a geometer of the 2d century B.C.

cist[1] (sist), *n.* [L. *cista*, < Gr. κίστη, box, E. *chest*.] In *class. antiq.*, a box or chest, esp. one for holding sacred utensils.

Cist (toilet casket), 3d century B.C., found near Palestrina, Italy. — Kircherian Museum, Rome.

cist[2] (sist, W. kist), *n.* [W. *cist*, < L. *cista*: see *cist*[1].] A prehistoric sepulchral chest or chamber; a cistvaen.

cis-ta-ceous (sis-tā'shius), *a.* [See *cistus*.] Belonging to the *Cistaceæ*, or rock-rose family of plants.

Cis-ter-cian (sis-tėr'shiạn). [ML. *Cistercium*, Cîteaux.] **I.** *a.* Belonging to an order of monks and nuns founded in 1098 at Cîteaux, near Dijon, France, under the rule of St. Benedict. **II.** *n.* A member of the Cistercian order.

cis-tern (sis'tėrn), *n.* [OF. *cisterne* (F. *citerne*), < L. *cisterna*, < *cista*: see *cist*[1].] A reservoir, tank, or vessel for holding water or other liquid: as, "A *cistern* containing a hundred and twenty gallons of punch was emptied to his Majesty's health" (Macaulay's "Hist. of Eng.," xxi.).

cis-tus (sis'tus), *n.* [NL., < Gr. κίστος, κίσθος.] Any plant of the genus *Cistus*, native in Mediterranean regions, some species of which yield ladanum, while others are cultivated for their flowers; a rock-rose.

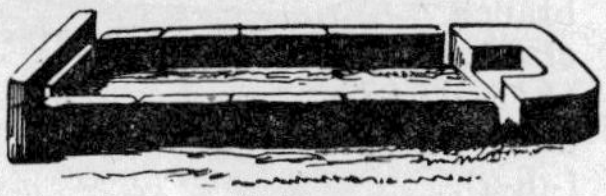

Cistvaen.

cist-vaen, kist-vaen (kist'-vīn), *n.* [W. *cistfaen*, 'stone chest': see *cist*[2].] A prehistoric stone coffin or burial chamber; a tomb made of slabs of stone.

cit (sit), *n.* [Short for *citizen*.] An inhabitant of a city, or a city person (used in disparagement); also, *pl.*, citizen's or civilian clothes as opposed to military uniform (slang).

cit-a-ble (sī'tạ-bl), *a.* That may be cited.

cit-a-del (sit'ạ-dẹl), *n.* [F. *citadelle*, < It. *cittadella*, dim. of *città*, < L. *civitas*, E. *city*.] A fortress commanding a city, serving as a protection and final point of defense, and also to keep the inhabitants in subjection; hence, any strongly fortified place; a stronghold; also, a heavily armored structure on a war-ship.

ci-ta-tion (sī-tā'shọn), *n.* [OF. F. *citation*, < L. *citatio(n-)*.] The act of citing; a call or summons, esp. to appear in court; a document containing such a summons; also, the quoting of a passage, book, author, etc.; a reference to an authority or a precedent; a passage cited; a quotation; also, mention or enumeration; *milit.*, mention of a soldier, corps, etc., in orders, as for gallantry.—**ci'ta-to-ry** (-tạ-tọ-ri), *a.*

cite (sīt), *v. t.*; *cited, citing.* [OF. F. *citer*, < L. *citare*, freq. of *ciere, cire*, move, excite, call.] To summon officially or authoritatively to appear in court; in general, to summon or call; rouse to action; also, to quote (a passage, book, author, etc.), esp. as an authority; refer to as an instance; adduce in support, proof, or confirmation; also, to call to mind; mention; also, to indicate†; *milit.*, to mention (a soldier, corps, etc.) in orders, as for gallantry.—**cit-er** (sī'tėr), *n.*

cith-a-ra (sith'ạ-rạ), *n.* [L., < Gr. κιθάρα.] An ancient stringed musical instrument of the lyre class.—**cith'a-rist,** *n.* A player on the cithara.

cith-er (sith'ėr), *n.* [= *cithara*.] The cithara; also, the cithern.

cith-ern, cit-tern (sith'ėrn, sit'ėrn), *n.* [Ult. < L. *cithara*: see *cithara*.] An old stringed musical instrument, shaped like a lute but having a flat back, and played with a plectrum.

Cithern.

cit-ied (sit'id), *a.* Formed into a city; like a city; occupied by a city or cities.

cit-i-fied (sit'i-fīd), *a.* Conformed to city ways or fashions: as, "This boy was well dressed . . . He had a *citified* air about him" (Mark Twain's "Tom Sawyer," i.).

cit-i-zen (sit'i-zẹn), *n.* [AF. *citezein*, OF. *citeain* (F. *citoyen*), < L. *civitas*, E. *city*.] An inhabitant of a city or town, esp. one entitled to its privileges or franchises (as, "a *citizen* of no mean city": Acts, xxi. 39); a townsman, as distinguished from a countryman; a civilian, as distinguished from a soldier, policeman, etc.; formerly, a person engaged in trade, as distinguished from the landed nobility or gentry; also, a member, native or naturalized, of a state or nation, as distinguished from an alien; a person owing allegiance to a government and entitled to its protection; also, an inhabitant or denizen.—**cit'i-zen-ess,** *n.* A female citizen.—**cit'i-zen-ry,** *n.* Citizens collectively.—**cit'i-zen-ship,** *n.* The status of a citizen.

cit-ole (sit'ōl or si-tōl'), *n.* [OF. *citole*, < L. *cithara*: see *cithara*.] An old stringed musical instrument, probably a form of cithara.

cit-ra- (sit'rạ-). [L. *citra*, adv. and prep., akin to *cis*: see *cis-*.] A prefix of Latin origin, meaning 'on this side of,' occasionally used as an English formative, as in *citracaucasian* (equivalent to *ciscaucasian*).

cit-ral (sit'ral), *n.* [From *citr(us)* + *al(dehyde)*.] In *chem.*, a liquid aldehyde with a strong lemon-like odor, obtained from the oils of lemon, orange, etc.: used in perfumery.

cit-ra-mon-tane (sit-rạ-mon'tān), *a.* [L. *citra* (see *citra-*) + *mons* (*mont-*), mountain.] On this (the nearer) side of the mountains; cismontane.

cit-range (sit'rạnj), *n.* [From *citr(us)* + *(or)ange*.] A hybrid fruit produced by crossing the trifoliate orange and the common sweet orange.

cit-rate (sit'rāt), *n.* In *chem.*, a salt of citric acid.

cit-re-ous (sit'rẹ-us), *a.* [L. *citreus*.] Citrine.

cit-ric (sit'rik), *a.* [See *citrus*.] Pertaining to or derived from lemons and similar fruits: as, *citric* acid (a white crystalline compound).

cit-rine (sit'rin). [See *citrus*.] **I.** *a.* Of the pale-yellow color of the citron or lemon; lemon-colored. **II.** *n.* Citrine color; lemon-color; also, a pellucid yellow variety of quartz.

cit-ron (sit′rọn), *n.* [F. *citron*, < L. *citrus*: see *citrus*.] A pale-yellow fruit resembling the lemon but larger, less acid, and with thicker rind, borne by a tree, a variety of *Citrus medica*, allied to the lemon and lime; the tree itself; the rind of the fruit, candied or preserved; also, a round, hard-fleshed variety of watermelon, used for preserving (also called *citron melon*).

cit-ro-nel-la (sit-rọ-nel′ạ̈), *n.* [Named from its citron-like odor.] A fragrant grass, *Andropogon nardus*, of southern Asia, cultivated as the source of an oil used in making liniment, perfume, and soap.

cit-ron=wood (sit′rọn-wụ̇d), *n.* The wood of the citron, a variety of *Citrus medica*; also, the wood of the sandarac, *Callitris quadrivalvis*.

cit-rous (sit′rus), *a.* [See *citrus*.] Of or pertaining to the genus *Citrus*, of rutaceous trees and shrubs. See *citrus*.

cit-rus (sit′rus), *n.* [L., citron-tree: cf. Gr. κιτρέα, the tree, κίτριον, κίτρον, the fruit.] Any tree or shrub of the rutaceous genus *Citrus*, which includes the citron, lemon, lime, orange, etc.

cit′tern, *n.* See *cithern*.

cit-y (sit′i), *n.*; pl. *cities* (-iz). [OF. *cite* (F. *cité*), < L. *civitas*, citizenship, the state, a city, < *civis*, citizen.] A town† or village†; a large or important town; in the U. S., an incorporated municipality, usually governed by a mayor and a board of aldermen or councilmen; also, the inhabitants of a city collectively; [*cap.*] with *the*, the part of London, England, situated within the ancient boundaries, governed by a lord mayor, aldermen, and common councilmen having no jurisdiction over the rest of the metropolis, and being the part of London in which the commercial and financial interests are chiefly centered (in full, *the City of London*).—**city editor,** in Great Britain, the editor in charge of the financial and commercial news in a London or other newspaper (written *City editor*); in the U. S., the editor who superintends the collection and classification of local news for a newspaper.—**city of God,** heaven, as the dwelling-place of God and the blessed.—**city of refuge,** in the Mosaic dispensation, any one of six cities to which a person who had accidentally slain a human being might flee for refuge.—**cit′y-fied** (-fīd), *a.* See *citified*.—**cit′y=state,** *n.* A sovereign state consisting of an autonomous city with its dependencies.

cive (sīv), *n.* See *chive*.

civ-et (siv′et), *n.* [F. *civette*, < Ar. *zabād*.] A yellowish unctuous substance with a strong musk-like odor, obtained from a pouch in the genital region of civet-cats, and used in perfumery; also, a civet-cat.—**civ′et=cat,** *n.* Any animal of the genus *Viverra*, which comprises small carnivorous quadrupeds having glands in the genital region that secrete civet, esp. *V. civetta* of Africa; also, any of certain allied or similar animals.

Civet-cat (*Viverra civetta*).

civ-ic (siv′ik), *a.* [L. *civicus*, < *civis*, citizen.] Of or pertaining to citizens, a city, or citizenship; municipal; civil.—**civ′i-cal-ly,** *adv.*—**civ′i-cism** (-i-sizm), *n.* Civic spirit or condition; the principle of civic rights and duties.—**civ′ics,** *n.* The science of civic affairs.

civ-ies, civ-vies (siv′iz), *n. pl.* [From *civilian* (*clothes* or *dress*).] Civilian clothes or dress as opposed to military uniform. [Slang.]

civ-il (siv′il), *a.* [OF. F. *civil*, < L. *civilis*, < *civis*, citizen.] Of, pertaining to, or consisting of citizens (as, *civil* life; *civil* society); of or pertaining to the commonwealth or state (as, *civil* affairs); of or pertaining to citizens in their ordinary capacity, or the ordinary life and affairs of citizens (distinguished from *military*, *ecclesiastical*, etc.); of or pertaining to the citizen as an individual (as, *civil* liberty); becoming or befitting a citizen (as, a *civil* duty); also, in a condition of, or pertaining to a state of, social order or organized government; civilized; educated† or refined†; seemly or sober, as apparel†; humane† or kind†; polite or courteous; often, merely, not rude or discourteous; also, pertaining to the private rights of individuals and to legal proceedings connected with these (distinguished from *criminal* or *political*); with reference to legal rights (as, *civil* death); of divisions of time, legally recognized in the ordinary affairs of life (as, the *civil* year; the *civil* day); also, of or pertaining to the civil law.—**civil engineer.** See *engineer*, *n.*—**civil law,** orig., the body of law proper to the city or state of Rome, as distinct from that common to all nations; also, the whole system of Roman law; hence, the body of private law developed from the Roman law, prevailing in various modern countries.—**civil service,** a collective name for all branches of the public administrative service except the military and naval; more specifically, the public service concerned with all affairs not military, naval, legislative, or judicial.—**civil war,** a war between parties within their own country: as, the English *civil wars* (between the parties of Charles I. and Parliament); the American *Civil War* (between the North and the South, 1861–65).

ci-vil-ian (si-vil′yạn). [OF. *civilien*, civil (with reference to law), < *civil*, E. *civil*.] **I.** *n.* One versed in or studying the Roman or civil law; also, one engaged in civil pursuits, as distinguished from a soldier, ecclesiastic, etc. **II.** *a.* Of or pertaining to civilians.

ci-vil-i-ty (si-vil′i-ti), *n.*; pl. *-ties* (-tiz). [OF. *civilite* (F. *civilité*), < L. *civilitas*, < *civilis*, E. *civil*.] Citizenship†; civil government or order†; civilization, culture, or good breeding (archaic); courtesy or politeness; a polite attention or expression (as, "The Emperor . . . returned an answer consisting of many *civilities* and excuses": Swift's "Gulliver's Travels," i. 8).

civ-il-iz-a-ble (siv′i-lī-zạ-bl), *a.* Capable of being civilized.

civ-il-i-za-tion (siv″i-li-zā′shọn), *n.* The act of civilizing; civilized condition; an advanced state of human society; a form or instance of advancement in social culture.

civ-il-ize (siv′i-līz), *v. t.*; *-ized*, *-izing*. [F. *civiliser*, < *civil*, E. *civil*.] To make civil, or bring out of a savage state; elevate in social and individual life; enlighten; refine.—**civ′il-iz-er,** *n.*

civ-il-ly (siv′i-li), *adv.* In a civil manner or respect.

civ-ism (siv′izm), *n.* [F. *civisme*, < L. *civis*, citizen.] Good citizenship.

civ-vies (siv′iz), *n. pl.* See *civies*.

clab-ber (klab′ėr), *n.* [See *bonnyclabber*.] Bonnyclabber.—**clab′ber,** *v. i.* Of milk, to become thick in souring.

clach-an (klåċh′ạn), *n.* [Gael.] A small village or hamlet: as, "I often wondered what brought Mrs. Malcolm to our *clachan*, instead of going to a populous town" (Galt's "Annals of the Parish," i.). [Chiefly Sc.]

clack (klak), *v.* [Imit.: cf. D. *klakken*, F. *claquer*.] **I.** *intr.* To make a quick, sharp sound, or a succession of such sounds, as by striking or cracking; also, to talk rapidly and continually, or with sharpness and abruptness; chatter; also, to cluck or cackle, as a hen. **II.** *tr.* To cause to clack; clap together; also, to utter by clacking.—**clack,** *n.* A clacking sound; also, something that clacks, as a rattle, a device worked by the wind for scaring away birds, or a clack-valve; also, rapid and continual talk; chatter.—**clack′=dish,** *n.* A wooden dish with a lid capable of being clacked, formerly used by beggars in soliciting alms.—**clack′er,** *n.*—**clack′=valve,** *n.* In pumps, etc., a valve consisting of a lid-like disk hinged at one edge.

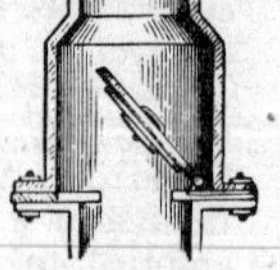
Clack-valve.

clad (klad). Preterit and past participle of *clothe*.

clad-ode (klad′ōd), *n.* [Gr. κλάδος, branch: see *-ode*[2].] In *bot.*, a leaf-like flattened branch. Also **cla-do-di-um** (kla-dō′di-um); pl. *-dia* (-di-ạ̈).

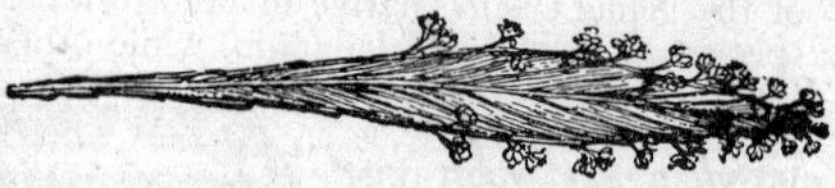
Cladode.

clad-o-phyl, clad-o-phyll (klad′ọ̄-fil), *n.* [Gr. κλάδος, branch, + φύλλον, leaf.] Same as *cladode*.

claes (klāz), *n. pl.* Scotch form of *clothes.*
claim (klām), *v.* [OF. *claimer, clamer,* < L. *clamare,* cry out, shout, call.] **I.** *intr.* To cry out†; call†; also, to put forward a claim; assert a right. **II.** *tr.* To proclaim†; call† or name†; also, to cry or call for†; also, to demand by or as by virtue of a right; demand as a right or as due; also, to assert, and demand the recognition of (a right, title, possession, etc.); assert one's right to; also, to assert or maintain as a fact; also, of things, to require as due or fitting. —**claim,** *n.* A cry† or call†; a demand for something as due; an assertion of a right or alleged right; an assertion of something as a fact; also, a right to claim or demand; a just title to something; also, that which is claimed; a piece of public land to which formal claim is made for mining or other purposes.—**claim'a-ble,** *a.* That may be claimed.—**claim'ant,** *n.* One who makes a claim.—**claim'er,** *n.*
clair-au-di-ent (klãr-â'di-ẹnt). [F. *clair,* clear, + L. *audiens* (*-ent-*), ppr. of *audire,* hear.] **I.** *a.* Having the power of hearing, esp. in a state of trance, sounds beyond the natural range of hearing. **II.** *n.* A clairaudient person.—**clair-au'di-ence,** *n.*
claire-cole, clear-cole (klãr'kōl, klēr'-), *n.* [F. *claire colle,* 'clear glue.'] In *painting,* a preparation of size put on an absorbent surface to prevent the sinking in of subsequent coats of paint; in *gilding,* a coating of size over which gold-leaf is to be applied.
clair=ob-scure (klãr'ọb-skūr'), *n.* [F. *clair-obscur.*] Same as *chiaroscuro.*
clair-schach (klär'shăċh), *n.* [Gael. and Ir. *clairseach.*] The old Celtic harp, strung with wire.
clair-voy-ant (klãr-voi'ạnt). [F., < *clair,* clear, + *voyant,* ppr. of *voir,* < L. *videre,* see.] **I.** *a.* Having the power of seeing, at times or in certain states, things beyond the natural range of vision. **II.** *n.* A clairvoyant person.—**clair-voy'ance,** *n.*
clam[1] (klam), *n.* [AS. *clam,* band, bond.] A clamp; a vise; *pl.,* pincers or tongs for various uses.
clam[2] (klam), *v.*; *clammed, clamming.* [Cf. AS. *clǣman,* smear, also ME. *clam,* sticky.] **I.** *tr.* To smear; daub; clog. [Now prov.] **II.** *intr.* To stick fast; be moist or clammy. [Now prov.]—**clam**[2], *n.* Clamminess. [Chiefly prov.]
clam[3] (klam), *n.* [= *clam*[1]; prob. orig. in *clam-shell.*] Any of various bivalve mollusks, esp. certain edible species, as *Venus mercenaria* (the 'hard clam' or 'round clam') or *Mya arenaria* (the 'soft clam' or 'long clam') of the Atlantic coast of North America; also, a taciturn or stupidly silent person (colloq., U. S.).—**clam**[3], *v. i.*; *clammed, clamming.* To gather or dig clams.
clam[4] (klam), *v.* See *clem.*
clam-ant (klam'ạnt or klā'mạnt), *a.* [L. *clamans* (*-ant-*), ppr. of *clamare*: see *claim.*] Crying out, or clamorous (as, "*clamant* children": Thomson's "Seasons," Autumn, 350); fig., crying, or demanding attention; urgent.
clam-a-to-ri-al (klam-ạ-tō'ri-ạl), *a.* [NL. *Clamatores,* pl. of L. *clamator,* one who cries out, < *clamare*: see *claim.*] Of or pertaining to the *Clamatores,* a large group of passerine birds, containing those with relatively simple vocal organs and little power of song, as the flycatchers.
clam=bake (klam'bāk), *n.* An entertainment or picnic at the seashore at which the baking of clams, usually on hot stones under seaweed, is a main feature. [U. S.]
clam-ber (klam'bėr), *v. i.* or *t.* [ME. *clambren*; origin uncertain: cf. *climb* and *clamp*[1].] To climb, using both feet and hands; climb with effort or difficulty.—**clam'ber,** *n.* A clambering.—**clam'ber-er,** *n.*
clam-jam-fry (klam-jam'fri), *n.* See *clanjamfry.*
clam-mer (klam'ėr), *n.* One who gathers or digs clams.
clam-my (klam'i), *a.*; compar. *clammier,* superl. *clammiest.* [Cf. *clam*[2].] Sticky; covered with a sticky moisture; cold and damp.—**clam'mi-ly,** *adv.*—**clam'mi-ness,** *n.*
clam-or (klam'ọr), *n.* [OF. *clamor* (F. *clameur*), < L. *clamor,* < *clamare*: see *claim.*] A loud outcry; vociferation; hence, a vehement expression of desire or dissatisfaction; popular outcry; also, any loud and continued noise.—**clam'or,** *v.* **I.** *intr.* To make a clamor; raise an outcry. **II.** *tr.* To disturb with clamor†; drive, force, put, etc., by clamoring; also, to utter noisily.—**clam'or-er,** *n.*—**clam'or-ous,** *a.* [ML. *clamorosus.*] Full of, marked by, or of the nature of clamor; vociferous; noisy; urgent or importunate in demands or complaints (as, "a time when nature was most impetuous and most *clamorous*": J. H. Newman's "Callista," ix.).—**clam'or-ous-ly,** *adv.*—**clam'or-ous-ness,** *n.*
clam'our, clam'our-er. British preferred forms of *clamor, clamorer.*
clamp[1] (klamp), *n.* [Akin to the earlier *clam*[1]: cf. D. *klamp,* clamp, cleat.] A device, usually of some rigid material, for strengthening or supporting objects or fastening them together; specif., an appliance with opposite sides or parts that may be screwed or otherwise brought together to hold or compress something; also, one of a pair of movable pieces, made of lead or other soft material, for covering the jaws of a vise and enabling it to grasp without bruising.—**clamp**[1], *v. t.* To fasten with or fix in a clamp.
clamp[2] (klamp), *n.* [Cf. D. *klamp,* heap.] A heap or pile of any of various materials; esp., a pile or stack of bricks built up into a kind of hollow chamber for burning.
clamp[3] (klamp), *v. i.* [Appar. imit.] To tread heavily; clump.—**clamp**[3], *n.* A heavy tread or footstep.

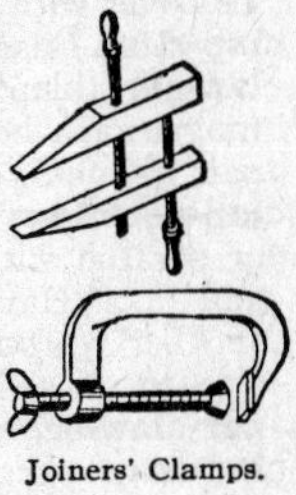
Joiners' Clamps.

clamp-er (klam'pėr), *n.* A clamp; also, an iron frame with sharp prongs, fastened to the sole of the shoe to prevent slipping on ice.
clam=shell (klam'shel), *n.* The shell of a clam.
clan (klan), *n.* [Gael. *clann.*] A group of families or households, as among the Scottish Highlanders, the heads of which claim descent from a common ancestor; a group of people of common descent; in general, a clique, set, society, or party.
clan-des-tine (klan-des'tin), *a.* [L. *clandestinus,* < *clam,* secretly.] Secret; private; concealed: generally implying craft or deception.—**clan-des'tine-ly,** *adv.*—**clan-des'tine-ness, clan-des-tin'i-ty,** *n.*
clang (klang), *v.* [Imit.: cf. L. *clangere,* clang.] **I.** *intr.* To give out a loud, resonant sound, as metal when struck; ring loudly or harshly. **II.** *tr.* To cause to resound or ring loudly.—**clang,** *n.* A clanging sound.
clan-gor (klang'gọr or klang'ọr), *n.* [L., < *clangere,* clang.] Loud, resonant sound, as of pieces of metal struck together or of a trumpet; a clang; clamorous noise.—**clan'gor,** *v. i.* To make a clangor; clang.—**clan'gor-ous,** *a.* [ML. *clangorosus.*] Full of, marked by, or of the nature of clangor.—**clan'gor-ous-ly,** *adv.*
clan'gour, *n.* and *v.* British alternative form of *clangor.*
clan-jam-fry (klan-jam'fri), *n.* [Origin obscure.] A set of worthless persons: as, "A gang of playactors came . . . They were the first of that *clanjamfrey* who had ever been in the parish" (Galt's "Annals of the Parish," xxxvi.). [Chiefly Sc.]
clank (klangk), *v.* [Imit.: cf. *clink*[1] and *clang.*] **I.** *intr.* To make a short, sharp, harsh, metallic sound; move with such sounds. **II.** *tr.* To cause to resound sharply, as metal in collision.—**clank,** *n.* A clanking sound.
clan-nish (klan'ish), *a.* [See *clan.*] Of, pertaining to, or characteristic of a clan; disposed to adhere closely, as the members of a clan; imbued with or influenced by the sentiments, prejudices, etc., peculiar to clans.—**clan'nish-ly,** *adv.*—**clan'nish-ness,** *n.*—**clan'ship,** *n.* Association in or as in clans; attachment to one's clan.—**clans-man** (klanz'mạn), *n.*; pl. *-men.* A member of a clan.—**clans'wom″an,** *n.*; pl. *-women* (-wim″en).
clap (klap), *v.*; *clapped, clapping.* [ME. *clappen*: cf. D. and LG. *klappen,* Icel. and Sw. *klappa.*] **I.** *tr.* To strike with a quick, smart blow, producing an abrupt, sharp sound; slap; pat; also, to strike together resoundingly, as the hands to express applause; applaud in this manner; also, to clasp (hands) in token of an agreement†; flap (the wings); also, to push, shut, or open forcibly and with a sharp noise; slam; put, place, apply, etc., promptly and effectively; with *up,* etc., to make or arrange hastily (now colloq.). **II.** *intr.* To make an abrupt, sharp sound as of bodies in collision; move or strike with such a sound; also, to clap the hands, as in applause; also, to come, go, etc., suddenly or energeti-

cally.—**clap,** *n.* The act or sound of clapping; a resounding blow; a slap; a sudden stroke, blow, or act; a sudden mishap†; a loud and abrupt or explosive noise, as of thunder; an applauding; applause; also, a clapper.

clap-board (klap′bōrd, commonly klab′ọrd), *n.* [For obs. *clapholt,* < LG. *klappholt* = G. *klappholz,* clapboards.] Orig., a size of oak board used for making barrel-staves and for wainscoting; in the U. S., a long, thin board, thicker along one edge than along the other, used in covering the outer walls of buildings, being laid horizontally, the thick edge of each board overlapping the thin edge of the board below it; also, a similar roofing-board.—**clap′board,** *v. t.* To cover with clapboards.

clap=dish (klap′dish), *n.* Same as *clack-dish.*

clap-per (klap′ėr), *n.* One who or that which claps; the tongue of a bell; any clapping contrivance, as either of a pair of bones.

clap-per-claw (klap′ėr-klâ), *v. t.* [Cf. *clapper.*] To claw or scratch with the hand and nails; fight with tooth and nail (as, "Have always been at daggers-drawing, And one another *clapper-clawing*": Butler's "Hudibras," ii. 2); also, to abuse in speech; revile. [Archaic or prov.]—**clap′-per-claw-er,** *n.*

clap-trap (klap′trap), *n.* Any artifice or expedient for winning applause or impressing the public; pretentious but insincere or empty language.

claque (klȧk), *n.* [F., < *claquer,* clap.] A set of hired applauders in a theater; any body of persons ready to applaud from interested motives.—**cla-queur** (klȧ-kėr), *n.* [F.] A member of a claque.

clar-a-bel-la (klar-ạ-bel′ä̤), *n.* [L. *clara,* fem. of *clarus,* clear, + *bella,* fem. of *bellus,* beautiful.] An organ-stop which gives soft, sweet tones.

clar-ence (klar′ẹns), *n.* [From the Duke of *Clarence* (afterward William IV. of England).] A close four-wheeled carriage, with a curved glass front and inside seats for four persons.

Clar-en-cieux, Clar-en-ceux (klar′ẹn-sū), *n.* [AF.; named from *Clarence* (< *Clare,* in Suffolk), dukedom created for a son of Edward III.] In England, the title of the second king-of-arms, ranking after Garter king-of-arms.

clar-en-don (klar′ẹn-dọn), *n.* [From *Clarendon,* proper name.] A condensed form of printing-type, like roman in outline but with thicker lines. See *type.*

clar-et (klar′et), *n.* [OF. *claret* (F. *clairet*), somewhat clear, light-colored, dim. of *cler,* < L. *clarus,* E. *clear.*] A general name in English for the red (orig. the light-red or yellowish) wines of France, except those of Burgundy, and for similar wines made elsewhere; also, a dark purplish-red color.—**clar′et=col″ored,** *a.*—**clar′et=cup,** *n.* An iced beverage made of claret and carbonated water with lemon-juice, brandy (or other spirits), sugar, etc.

clar-i-bel-la (klar-i-bel′ä̤), *n.* See *clarabella.*

clar-i-fy (klar′i-fī), *v.;* *-fied, -fying.* [OF. F. *clarifier,* < LL. *clarificare,* < L. *clarus,* clear, bright, + *facere,* make.] **I.** *tr.* To make clear; make clear and pure; free from defects; rid of obscurities; render intelligible. **II.** *intr.* To become clear.—**clar″i-fi-ca′tion** (-fi-kā′shọn), *n.*—**clar′i-fi-er** (-fī-ėr), *n.*

clar-i-net (klar′i-net or klar-i-net′), *n.* [F. *clarinette,* < It. *clarinetto,* dim. of *clarino,* clarion.] A wooden wind-instrument in the form of a cylindrical tube with a flaring mouth, and having a single reed.—**clar-i-net′tist,** *n.* A clarinet-player.

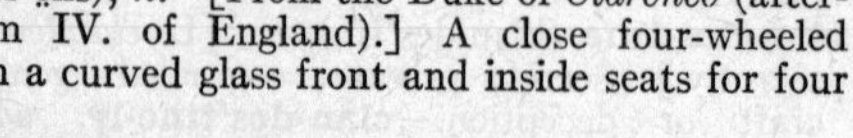

Clarinet.

clar-i-on (klar′i-ọn), *n.* [OF. *claron* (F. *clairon*), < ML. *claro(n-), clario(n-),* < L. *clarus,* E. *clear.*] A narrow-tubed trumpet with clear, shrill tones (now chiefly poetic); the sound of this instrument, or any similar sound (poetic: as, "the cock's shrill *clarion,*" Gray's "Elegy," v.).—**clar-i-o-net** (klar′i-ọ-net or klar″i-ọ-net′), *n.* Same as *clarinet.*

clar-i-ty (klar′i-ti), *n.* [L. *claritas,* < *clarus,* E. *clear.*] Clearness; also, brightness† or luster†.

cla-ro (klä′rō), *a.* [Sp., < L. *clarus,* E. *clear.*] Of cigars, light-colored and, usually, mild.

clart (klärt), *v. t.* [Origin unknown.] To smear or spot with something sticky or dirty; befoul with dirt. [Sc. and north. Eng.]—**clart,** *n.* A smear or clot of something sticky, dirty, or moist; *pl.,* mud or dirt. [Sc. and north. Eng.]—**clart′y,** *a.*

cla-ry (klā′ri), *n.;* pl. *-ries* (-riz). [ML. *sclarea;* origin unknown.] Any of several species of salvia or sage, esp. *Salvia sclarea,* which is cultivated as a pot-herb.

clash (klash), *v.* [Appar. imit.] **I.** *intr.* To make a loud, harsh noise, as by the collision of weapons; collide, esp. noisily; also, to come into conflict; disagree. **II.** *tr.* To strike with a resounding collision, as weapons; strike violently together; also, to produce (sound, etc.) by or as by collision.—**clash,** *n.* The noise of or as of a collision, as of weapons; a collision, esp. a noisy one; also, a conflict; opposition, as of views or interests.—**clash′er,** *n.*—**clash′-ing-ly,** *adv.*

clasp (klȧsp), *n.* [ME. *claspe, clapse:* origin uncertain.] A device, usually of metal, for fastening things or parts together; any fastening or connection; anything that clasps; a military decoration consisting of a narrow bar of metal fixed transversely on the ribbon by which a medal is hung, and representing some operation in which the bearer took part; also, the act of clasping or embracing; a grasp; an embrace.—**clasp,** *v. t.* To fasten with or as with a clasp; furnish with a clasp; also, to take hold of with an infolding grasp; embrace closely; inclose or infold; also, to fold (the arms, tentacles, etc.) around or over something.—**clasp′er,** *n.*—**clasp′=knife,** *n.* A knife with a blade or blades folding into the handle, esp. a large knife with a single blade which when open may be secured in place by a catch.

class (klȧs), *n.* [F. *classe,* < L. *classis,* class (of people, etc.), army, fleet.] Each of six divisions of the ancient Roman people made according to their wealth, for purposes of taxation; hence, any division of society according to status; also, the system of dividing society in this manner; caste; also, social rank, esp. high rank; also, a number of pupils in a school, or of students in a college, pursuing the same studies, ranked together, or graduated in the same year; the assembly of such a body; also, any division of persons or things according to rank or grade; also, excellence or merit (slang); also, a number of persons or things regarded as forming one body through the possession of common attributes; a kind or sort; a zoölogical or botanical group or category ranking below a subkingdom or phylum, and above an order; *eccles.,* a classis; in the *Methodist Ch.,* one of several small companies, each composed of about twelve members under a leader, into which each society or congregation is divided.—**the classes,** the higher classes of society, as distinguished from the masses.—**class,** *v.* **I.** *tr.* To arrange in classes; also, to place or rate as to class. **II.** *intr.* To be classed; take or have a place in a particular class.—**class′a-ble,** *a.* That may be classed.—**class′=day,** *n.* In American colleges and schools, a day during the commencement season on which the members of the graduating class celebrate the completion of their course with literary and other exercises.—**class′er,** *n.*

clas-sic (klas′ik). [= F. *classique,* < L. *classicus,* pertaining to a class, of the first or highest class, < *classis:* see *class.*] **I.** *a.* Of the first or highest class or rank; serving as a standard, model, or guide; also, of, pertaining to, or characteristic of Greek and Roman antiquity, esp. with reference to literature and art; in the style of the ancient Greek and Roman literature or art; classical; hence, of literary or historical renown. **II.** *n.* An author or a literary production of the first rank, esp. in Greek or Latin; *pl.,* the literature of ancient Greece and Rome; *sing.,* an artist or an artistic production of the highest class; also, one versed in the classics; one who adheres to classical rules and models.—**clas′si-cal,** *a.* Classic; esp., in accordance with ancient Greek and Roman models in literature or art, or with later systems of principles modeled upon them; marked by classicism; pertaining to or versed in the ancient classics; *eccles.,* pertaining to a classis.—**clas′si-cal-ism,** *n.* Classicism.—**clas-si-cal′i-ty** (-kal′i-ti), *n.* Classical quality.—**clas′si-cal-ly,** *adv.*—**clas′si-cal-ness,** *n.*—**clas′si-cism** (-sizm), *n.* The principles of classic literature or art, or adherence to them; the classical style in literature or art, characterized esp. by attention to form with the general effect of regularity, simplicity, and restraint (cf. *romanticism*); also, a classical idiom or form; also, classical scholarship or learning.—**clas'si-cist** (-sist), *n.* A classical scholar; also, one who advocates the study of the ancient classics; also, an adherent of classicism in literature or art. —**clas-si-cis'tic**, *a.*—**clas'si-cize** (-sīz), *v. t.* or *i.*; *-cized, -cizing.* To conform to the classic style.

clas-si-fi-a-ble (klas'i-fī-ạ-bl), *a.* That may be classified.

clas-sif-ic (klạ-sif'ik), *a.* [L. *classis*, class: see *-fic.*] Distinguishing a class; pertaining to classification.—**clas-sif'i-cal-ly**, *adv.*

clas-si-fi-ca-tion (klas″i-fi-kā'shọn), *n.* The act or the result of classifying.—**clas'si-fi-ca-to-ry** (-kā-tọ-ri), *a.*

clas-si-fy (klas'i-fī), *v. t.*; *-fied, -fying.* [L. *classis*, class: see *-fy.*] To arrange or distribute in classes; place according to class.—**clas'si-fi-er** (-fī-ėr), *n.*

clas-sis (klas'is), *n.*; pl. *classes* (-ēz). [L.] A class†; *eccles.*, in certain Reformed churches, a judicatory corresponding to a presbytery in Presbyterian churches; formerly, a presbytery.

class-mate (klȧs'māt), *n.* A member of the same class, as at school or college.

class-y (klas'i), *a.* Of high class, rank, or grade; stylish; fine. [Slang.]

clas-tic (klas'tik), *a.* [Gr. κλαστός, broken, < κλᾶν, break.] Breaking up or dividing into fragments or parts; pertaining to such division; noting or pertaining to an anatomical model made up of detachable pieces; in *geol.*, fragmental.

clath-rate (klath'rāt), *a.* [L. *clathratus*, < *clathri*, lattice, < Gr. κλεῖθρον, a bar: see *cleithral.*] Resembling a lattice; divided or marked like latticework.

clat-ter (klat'ėr), *v.* [Cf. AS. *clatrunge*, a clattering, D. *klateren*, clatter.] **I.** *intr.* To make a rattling sound, as of hard bodies striking rapidly together; move rapidly with such a sound; also, to talk fast and noisily; talk idly. **II.** *tr.* To cause to clatter.—**clat'ter**, *n.* A clattering noise; also, noisy talk; confused din of voices (as, "He heard a *clatter* of voices speaking quickly in the passage": Trollope's "Warden," xvii.); also, idle talk; gossip.—**clat'ter-er**, *n.* —**clat'ter-ing-ly**, *adv.*

Claude Lor-rain (klȧd lọ-rān') **glass** or **mir'ror.** [From *Claude Lorrain* (1600–82), French landscape-painter.] A dark or colored, slightly convex mirror for bringing into small compass the features of a landscape: so called from the fancied similarity of its effects to the pictures of Claude Lorrain.

Clau-di-an (klȧ'di-ạn), *a.* Pertaining to any of several distinguished Romans of the name of Claudius, or to either of two gentes, one patrician and the other plebeian, of which they were members; esp., pertaining to the emperors Tiberius, Caligula, Claudius, and Nero, who were members of the patrician gens, or to their period (A.D. 14–68).

clau-di-ca-tion (klȧ-di-kā'shọn), *n.* [L. *claudicatio(n-)*, < *claudicare*, limp, < *claudus*, lame.] A halting or limping; a limp.

clause (klȧz), *n.* [OF. F. *clause*, < ML. *clausa*, < L. *claudere*, shut, close.] A distinct portion of a discourse or writing, as a sentence or paragraph; a distinct article, stipulation, proviso, etc., in a formal or legal document; in *gram.*, a group of words, containing a subject and a predicate, forming part of a compound or complex sentence.

claus-tral (klȧs'trạl), *a.* [ML. *claustralis*, < *claustrum*, E. *cloister.*] Cloistral; cloister-like.

cla-vate, cla-vat-ed (klā'vāt, -vā-ted), *a.* [L. *clava*, club.] Club-shaped.—**cla'vate-ly**, *adv.*

clave[1], **clave**[2] (klāv). Archaic preterit of *cleave*[1], *cleave*[2].

clav-e-cin (klav'ẹ-sin), *n.* [F., < ML. *clavicymbalum*, < L. *clavis*, key, + *cymbalum*, cymbal.] A harpsichord.—**clav'e-cin-ist**, *n.* A player on the clavecin.

cla-ver (klā'vėr), *v. i.* [Origin uncertain.] To talk idly; prate; gossip. [Chiefly Sc.]—**cla'ver**, *n.* Idle talk; a piece of gossip. [Chiefly Sc.]

clav-i-chord (klav'i-kȯrd), *n.* [ML. *clavicordium*, < L. *clavis*, key, + *chorda*, string.] A stringed musical instrument with a keyboard, whose tones were produced by the action of brass pins raised and held against the strings: now superseded by the pianoforte.

clav-i-cle (klav'i-kl), *n.* [L. *clavicula*, dim. of *clavis*, key.] In *anat.* and *zoöl.*, a bone of the pectoral arch; in man, either of two slender bones each articulating with the sternum and a scapula and forming the anterior part of a shoulder; the collar-bone.

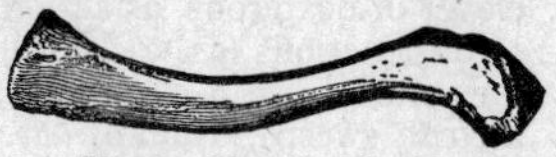

Human Clavicle, left side.

clav-i-corn (klav'i-kȯrn). [NL. *clavicornis*, < L. *clava*, club, + *cornu*, horn.] **I.** *a.* Having club-shaped antennæ, as many beetles of the group *Clavicornia*; belonging to this group. **II.** *n.* A clavicorn beetle.

cla-vic-u-lar (kla-vik'ū-lạr), *a.* Pertaining to the clavicle or collar-bone.

clav-i-er (klav'i-ėr or klạ-vēr'), *n.* [F. *clavier*, keyboard, also G. *klavier*, keyboard instrument (from F.), < L. *clavis*, key.] The keyboard of a musical instrument; also (pron. klạ-vēr'), any musical instrument with a keyboard, as a harpsichord, clavichord, or pianoforte; also, a kind of dumb keyboard for use in finger-gymnastics.

clav-i-form (klav'i-fȯrm), *a.* [L. *clava*, club: see *-form.*] Club-shaped; clavate.

claw (klȧ), *n.* [AS. *clawu*, *clēa*, akin to D. *klauw*, G. *klaue.*] A sharp, usually curved nail on the foot of an animal; the foot of an animal armed with such nails; also, any similar process; the nipper-like organ, or chela, terminating certain limbs in some crustaceans and arachnids; also, any part or thing resembling a claw, as the cleft end of the head of a hammer.—**claw**, *v.* **I.** *tr.* To tear, scratch, seize, pull, etc., with or as with claws or nails; also, to scratch gently, as to relieve itching; also, to make, bring, etc., by clawing. **II.** *intr.* To use the claws or nails; scratch, clutch, etc. (*at*).—**clawed**, *a.* Having claws.—**claw'=ham″mer**, *n.* A hammer having a head with one end curved and cleft for drawing nails; also, a dress-coat (colloq.).

clay (clā), *n.* [AS. *clǣg* = D. and G. *klei.*] A natural earthy material resulting from the decomposition of certain rocks, consisting essentially of a hydrated silicate of aluminium, and used for making bricks, pottery, etc.; loosely, earth or mud; also, earth as the material from which the human body was orig. formed (see Gen. ii. 7; Job, xxxiii. 6); hence, the human body.—**clay pigeon**, a saucer of baked clay or other material to be thrown into the air as a target in trap-shooting.—**clay**, *v. t.* To treat with clay; cover or daub with clay.—**clay'=bank**, *n.* A bank of clay; also, a dun-yellowish color; also, a horse of this color.—**clay'=eat″er**, *n.* One of a class of persons, as in parts of South America and of the southern U. S., who make a practice of eating clay or other earthy matter.—**clay'ey** (-i), *a.* Consisting of, resembling, or containing clay (as, "The high *clayey* bank was wet and slimy": Wiseman's "Fabiola," ii. 19); also, covered or daubed with clay.

clay-more (klā'mōr), *n.* [Gael. *claidheamh mor*, 'great sword.'] A heavy two-edged sword formerly used by the Scottish Highlanders; less exactly, a basket-hilted broadsword, often single-edged, used by Highlanders.

True Claymore.

clay-to-ni-a (klạ-tō'ni-ạ̈), *n.* [NL.; from Dr. J. *Clayton* (1693–1773), American botanist.] Any of the low, succulent portulacaceous herbs constituting the genus *Claytonia*, as the spring-beauty *C. virginica.*

clead-ing (klē'ding), *n.* [= *clothing.*] Clothing (Sc. and north. Eng.); in *engin.*, *arch.*, etc., a covering, casing, or lining, as the felting put around steam-pipes to prevent radiation.

clean (klēn), *a.* [AS. *clǣne*, clean, clear, = D. and G. *klein*, small.] Free from foreign or extraneous matter; unadulterated; pure; also, free from dirt or filth; unsoiled or unstained; hence, free from any form of defilement; morally pure; innocent; upright; honorable; often, free from or not causing ceremonial defilement; sometimes, free from dirty habits, as an animal; cleanly; also, free from defect or blemish; neatly made or proportioned, shapely, or trim; clever or dexterous, as action; also, free from encumbrances or obstructions (as, a *clean* harbor); without irregularity or unevenness (as, a *clean* cut); also, complete or perfect (as, a *clean* sweep).—**clean,** *adv.* In a clean manner; cleanly; wholly, completely, or quite.—**clean,** *v.* **I.** *tr.* To make clean; with *off*, etc., to remove in the process of cleaning. **II.** *intr.* To perform or to undergo a process of cleaning.—**clean,** *n.* A cleaning.—**clean′a-ble,** *a.* That may be cleaned.—**clean′=cut′,** *a.* Clear-cut; distinctly outlined or defined; well-cut; shapely; also, of a well-defined or well-constituted character or personality, as a person.—**clean′er,** *n.* One who or that which cleans; an apparatus or preparation for cleaning.—**clean′=limbed′,** *a.* Having well-shaped limbs; shapely; well-proportioned.

clean-ly[1] (klen′li), *a.*; compar. *cleanlier*, superl. *cleanliest.* [AS. *clǣnlīc*: see *clean*, *a.*, and *-ly*[1].] Clean; habitually clean; conducive to cleanness.—**clean′li-ly,** *adv.*—**clean′li-ness,** *n.*

clean-ly[2] (klēn′li), *adv.* [AS. *clǣnlīce*: see *clean*, *a.*, and *-ly*[2].] In a clean manner; neatly; purely; chastely; completely or clean.—**clean′ness,** *n.*

cleanse (klenz), *v. t.*; *cleansed, cleansing.* [AS. *clǣnsian*, < *clǣne*, E. *clean.*] To make clean; also, to remove by or as by cleaning (as, "And immediately his leprosy was *cleansed*": Mat. viii. 3).—**cleans′a-ble,** *a.*—**cleans′er,** *n.*

clear (klēr). [OF. *cler* (F. *clair*), < L. *clarus*, clear, bright.] **I.** *a.* Bright† or shining†; free from darkness, obscurity, or cloudiness; transparent or pellucid; of a pure, even color, as the complexion; also, distinctly perceptible to the eye, ear, or mind; easily seen, heard, or understood; distinct; evident; plain; free from confusion, uncertainty, or doubt, as a person; perceiving or discerning distinctly; convinced or certain; also, serene or untroubled (as, "with calm aspect and *clear*": Milton's "Paradise Lost," v. 733); also, free from guilt or blame; innocent; also, free from obstructions or obstacles; open (as, a *clear* space); also, unentangled or disengaged; free; quit or rid (*of*); also, without obligation or liability; free from debt; also, without deduction or diminution (as, a *clear* thousand); hence, without limitation or qualification (as, the *clear* contrary); absolute; sheer. **II.** *n.* A clear or unobstructed space: as, to measure so much in the *clear* (that is, in the interior or between bounding parts).—**clear,** *adv.* In a clear manner; clearly; distinctly; entirely or quite.—**clear,** *v.* **I.** *tr.* To make clear; free from darkness, cloudiness, muddiness, indistinctness, confusion, uncertainty, obstruction, contents, entanglement, obligation, liability, etc.; free from imputation, as of guilt; prove or declare to be innocent; pass without entanglement or collision (as, to *clear* a rock at sea by a few yards); leap over without touching; get past or over; free (a ship, cargo, etc.) from legal detention at a port by satisfying the customs and other required conditions; gain as clear profit (as, to *clear* $1,000 in a transaction); pass (checks, etc.) through a clearing-house; remove so as to leave something clear (with *away*, etc.). **II.** *intr.* To become clear; pass away or disappear, as clouds or mist (with *away*, etc.); exchange checks and bills, and settle balances, as in a clearing-house; specif., of a ship, to comply with the customs and other conditions legally imposed upon leaving or entering a port; leave port after having complied with such conditions.—**clear′ance,** *n.* The act of clearing; also, a clear space; a clearing; in *mech.*, etc., an intervening space, as between machine parts for free play; *naut.*, the clearing of a ship at a port, or the official certificate or papers ('clearance papers') indicating this.

clear-cole (klēr′kōl), *n.* See *clairecole.*

clear=cut (klēr′kut′), *a.* Cut or formed with clearly defined outlines; distinctly defined.

clear-er (klēr′ėr), *n.* One who or that which clears.

clear=head-ed (klēr′hed′ed), *a.* Having or showing a clear head or understanding.—**clear′=head′ed-ness,** *n.*

clear-ing (klēr′ing), *n.* The act of one who or that which clears; a tract of cleared land, as in a forest; *pl.*, the total of claims settled at a clearing-house.—**clear′ing=house,** *n.* A place or institution where mutual claims are settled and accounts adjusted, as between banks.

clear-ly (klēr′li), *adv.* In a clear manner; without obscurity; distinctly; plainly.—**clear′ness,** *n.*

clear=ob-scure (klēr′ọb-skūr′), *n.* Same as *chiaroscuro.*

clear=sight-ed (klēr′sī′ted), *a.* Having clear sight; having keen mental perception; discerning; perspicacious.—**clear′=sight′ed-ness,** *n.*

clear-starch (klēr′stärch), *v. t.* or *i.* To stiffen and dress (linen, etc.) with clear or transparent (boiled) starch.—**clear′starch″er,** *n.*

clear-sto-ry, clere-sto-ry (klēr′stō″ri), *n.*; pl. *-ries* (-riz). The upper part of the nave, transepts, and choir of a church, perforated by a series of windows above the aisle-roofs or triforium, and forming the chief source of light for the central parts of the building; also, any similar raised construction, as that for ventilating a railroad-car.

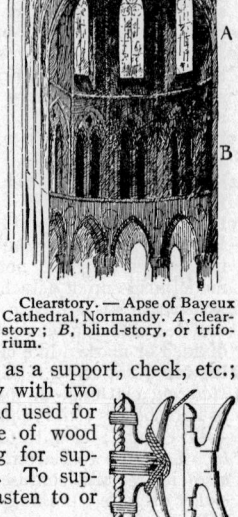

Clearstory. — Apse of Bayeux Cathedral, Normandy. *A*, clearstory; *B*, blind-story, or triforium.

clear-wing (klēr′wing), *n.* A moth with wings for the most part destitute of scales and transparent; esp., any of those constituting the family *Sesiidæ*, many species of which are, in the larval stage, injurious to fruit-trees and other plants, or any of certain sphinx-moths.

cleat (klēt), *n.* [ME. *clete, clote*, wedge; akin to E. *clot.*] A small wedge-shaped block, as one fastened to a spar or the like as a support, check, etc.; a piece of wood or iron, usually with two arms, for fastening to a part, and used for securing ropes or lines; a piece of wood or iron fastened across anything for support, security, etc.—**cleat,** *v. t.* To supply or strengthen with cleats; fasten to or with a cleat.

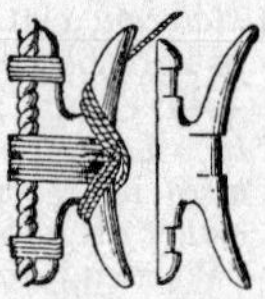
Cleats, one of which is lashed to a stay.

cleav-a-ble (klē′vạ-bl), *a.* That may be cleft or split.

cleav-age (klē′vāj), *n.* The act of cleaving, or the state of being cleft or split; division; specif., the property possessed by many crystallized minerals or other substances of breaking readily in one or more directions, and by certain rocks of being easily split into thin layers; in *biol.*, segmentation, esp. of the egg or ovum; in *chem.*, the breaking down of a molecule or compound into simpler molecules or compounds.

cleave[1] (klēv), *v. i.*; *cleaved* (archaic pret. *clave*), *cleaving.* [AS. *cleofian, clifian*, = G. *kleben.*] To stick or adhere; cling or hold fast (*to*); be attached or faithful (*to*: as, "Therefore shall a man leave his father and mother, and shall *cleave* unto his wife," Gen. ii. 24).

cleave[2] (klēv), *v.*; pret. *cleft, cleaved,* or *clove* (archaic *clave*), pp. *cleft, cleaved,* or *cloven* (archaic *clove*), ppr. *cleaving.* [AS. *clēofan* = G. *klieben*: cf. Gr. γλύφειν, carve.] **I.** *tr.* To part by or as by a cutting blow, esp. along a natural line of division, as the grain of wood; split; rend apart; rive; also, to penetrate or pass through (air, water, etc.); also, to make by or as by cutting (as, to *cleave* a path through the wilderness); also, to separate or sever by or as by splitting. **II.** *intr.* To part or split, esp. along a natural line of division; also, to penetrate or pass (*through*).—**cleav′er,** *n.* One who or that which cleaves; a heavy knife or long-bladed hatchet used by butchers for cutting up carcasses.

cleav-ers (klē′vėrz), *n.* [Appar. < *cleave*[1].] A rubiaceous plant, *Galium aparine*, with short hooked bristles by means of which it adheres to clothing, etc.; any of certain related species.

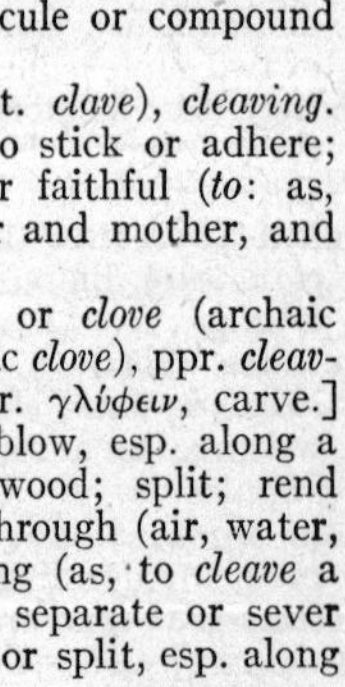
Cleavers (*Galium aparine*).

cleek, cleik (klēk), *n.* [Cf. *clutch.*] An iron hook, as for suspending a pot over a fire (chiefly Sc.); in *golf*, a club having an iron head with a long, narrow face.

clef (klef), *n.* [F., < L. *clavis*, key.] In *music*, a character placed upon a staff to indicate the name and pitch of the notes corresponding to its lines and spaces: as, the G *clef* and the F *clef* (the familiar treble and bass clefs, the first indicating that the second line of the staff corresponds to the G next above middle C, the second that the fourth line of the staff corresponds to the F next below middle C).

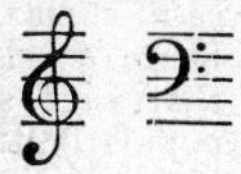

G Clef. F Clef.

cleft[1] (kleft), *n.* [ME. *clift*; akin to *cleave*[2].] A space or opening made by cleavage; a fissure; a crevice; a split or crack; also, a division formed by cleaving.

cleft[2] (kleft). Preterit and past participle of *cleave*[2]. —**cleft**[2], *p. a.* Cloven, split, or divided (as, *cleft* palate, a congenital defect of the palate in which a longitudinal fissure exists in the roof of the mouth); in *bot.*, of a leaf, having divisions formed by incisions or narrow sinuses which extend half-way or more than half-way to the midrib or the base.

cleik (klēk), *n.* See *cleek.*

cleis-tog-a-my, clis-tog-a-my (klīs-tog′ạ-mi), *n.* [Gr. κλειστός, closed, + γάμος, marriage.] In *bot.*, the condition of having (usually in addition to the ordinary, fully developed flowers) small, inconspicuous flowers which do not open, but are pollinated from their own anthers, as in the case of the pansy.—**cleis-to-gam′ic, clis-to-gam′ic** (-tọ-gam′ik), *a.*—**cleis-tog′a-mous, clis-tog′a-mous,** *a.*

cleith-ral, clith-ral (klīth′rạl), *a.* [Gr. κλεῖθρον, a bar, < κλείειν, shut.] Of a temple, having a roof; roofed over: opposed to *hypethral.*

clem, clam[4] (klem, klam), *v.*; *clemmed, clammed, clemming, clamming.* [= D. and G. *klemmen*, pinch; akin to *clam*[1].] **I.** *tr.* To pinch with hunger; starve; parch with thirst; nip or benumb with cold. [Now prov. Eng.] **II.** *intr.* To suffer from hunger, thirst, or cold. [Now prov. Eng.]

clem-a-tis (klem′ạ-tis), *n.* [L., < Gr. κληματίς, dim. of κλῆμα, vine-branch, < κλᾶν, break.] Any of the flowering vines or erect shrubs constituting the ranunculaceous genus *Clematis*, as *C. virginiana*, the virgin's-bower of the U. S., or *C. vitalba*, the traveler's-joy of Europe, or *C. paniculata*, a species native in Japan and common in cultivation; also, any plant of the allied genus *Atragene*, often included in the genus *Clematis.*

clem-ent (klem′ẹnt), *a.* [L. *clemens* (*clement-*).] Mild in temper or disposition; lenient; compassionate; also, of the weather, etc., mild or pleasant (rare). Cf. *inclement.* —**clem′en-cy,** *n.*—**clem′ent-ly,** *adv.*

Clem-ent-ine (klem′ẹn-tin or -tīn), *a.* Of or pertaining to some person named Clement, as St. Clement I. of Rome, Clement of Alexandria, or Pope Clement V.

clench (klench), *v. t.* [ME. *clenchen*; akin to D. *klinken*, clench, rivet.] To clinch, as a nail, or work nailed together (see *clinch*); close (the hands, teeth, etc.) tightly; grasp firmly, or grip; settle decisively (see *clinch*); *naut.*, to clinch.—**clench,** *n.* The act of clenching; tight hold; grip; *naut.*, a clinch.—**clench′er,** *n.*

cle-o-me (klẹ̄-ō′mē), *n.* [NL.; origin uncertain.] Any of the numerous herbaceous or shrubby plants constituting the capparidaceous genus *Cleome*, mostly natives of tropical regions, and often bearing showy flowers.

clepe (klēp), *v. t.*; *cleped* or *clept* (also *ycleped* or *yclept*), *cleping.* [AS. *cleopian, clipian.*] To call; name: now chiefly or only in the past participle, esp. as *ycleped* or *yclept.* [Archaic.]

clep-sy-dra (klep′si-drä̤), *n.*; pl. *-dras* or *-dræ* (-drē). [L., < Gr. κλεψύδρα, < κλέπτειν, steal, + ὕδωρ, water.] A device for measuring time by the regulated flow of water or mercury through a small aperture: as, "She . . . turns her glance towards a *clepsydra* or water-clock, on a bracket near her" (Wiseman's "Fabiola," i. 1).

clep-to-ma-ni-a (klep-tọ-mā′ni-ä̤), etc. See *kleptomania*, etc.

clere-sto-ry (klēr′stō″ri), *n.* See *clearstory.*

cler-gy (klėr′ji), *n.* [OF. *clergie*, < LL. *clericus*: see *cleric.*] The estate or office of a cleric or clergyman†; now, the body of men ordained for ministration in the Christian church, in distinction from the laity; also, learning† or scholarship†; also, benefit of clergy.—**benefit of clergy.** See under *benefit, n.*—**cler′gy=house,** *n.* The residence of the clergymen or clergyman in charge of a church. —**cler′gy-man** (-mạn), *n.*; pl. *-men.* A member of the clergy; an ordained Christian minister.—**cler′gy-wom″an,** *n.*; pl. *-women* (-wim″en). A woman dedicated to religion, as a nun†; a female Christian minister.

cler-ic (kler′ik). [LL. *clericus*, < Gr. κληρικός, < κλῆρος, clergy, orig. lot, allotment.] **I.** *a.* Pertaining to the clergy; clerical. **II.** *n.* A member of the clergy.—**cler′i-cal. I.** *a.* Of, pertaining to, or characteristic of the clergy or a clergyman; upholding the power or influence of the clergy, esp. in politics (as, a *clerical* party); also, pertaining to a clerk or copyist, or to clerks (as, a *clerical* error, one inadvertently made in copying or writing). **II.** *n.* A cleric; a member of a clerical party; *pl.*, clerical garments (colloq.).—**cler′i-cal-ism,** *n.* Clerical principles; clerical power or influence, esp. in politics; support of such power or influence; clerical partizanship.—**cler′i-cal-ist,** *n.*—**cler-i-cal′i-ty** (-kal′i-ti), *n.* Clerical character or condition.—**cler′i-cal-ly,** *adv.*

cler-i-sy (kler′i-si), *n.* [ML. *clericia*, < LL. *clericus*: see *cleric.*] Learned men as a class; the literati: as, "There is a certain ridicule, among superficial people, thrown on the scholars or *clerisy*" (Emerson's "Representative Men," vii.).

clerk (klėrk, Brit. commonly klärk), *n.* [AS. *clerc, cleric*, and OF. F. *clerc*, < LL. *clericus*: see *cleric.*] A clergyman or ecclesiastic (now chiefly legal); a layman charged with various minor ecclesiastical duties; a person able to read, or to read and write (archaic); a scholar (archaic); a writer† or scribe†; one who keeps the records and performs the routine business of a court, legislature, board, etc.; one employed in an office, shop, etc., to keep records or accounts, attend to correspondence, etc.; an assistant in business, esp. a retail salesman or saleswoman (U. S.). —**clerk,** *v. i.* To act or serve as a clerk.—**clerk′ly,** *a.* Of or pertaining to a clerk or clerks; clerical; scholarly (archaic).—**clerk′li-ness,** *n.*—**clerk′ly,** *adv.*—**clerk′ship,** *n.* The position or business of a clerk; scholarship (archaic).

cle-ruch (klē′rök), *n.* [Gr. κληροῦχος, < κλῆρος, lot, + ἔχειν, have.] In ancient Athens, a citizen who received an allotment of land in conquered foreign territory, but retained his Athenian citizenship.—**cle′ru-chy** (-rö-ki), *n.*; pl. *-chies* (-kiz). [Gr. κληρουχία.] In ancient Athens, allotment of land in conquered foreign territory among cleruchs; also, a body of cleruchs.—**cle-ru-chi-al** (klẹ̄-rö′ki-ạl), *a.*

cleugh, cleuch (klüch), *n.* [= *clough.*] A ravine. [Sc.]

cleve-ite (klēv′īt), *n.* [From P. T. *Cleve* (born 1840), Swedish chemist.] A crystallized variety of uraninite with radioactive properties, found in Norway.

clev-er (klev′ėr), *a.* [Origin uncertain.] Dexterous or nimble with the hands or body; also, adroit mentally; possessing quick intelligence with capability; smart; able; skilful; ingenious; showing adroitness or ingenuity (as, a *clever* remark; a *clever* device); also, well-shaped or handsome (chiefly prov. Eng.); suitable, convenient, agreeable, or pleasant (now colloq. or prov.); good-natured or obliging (colloq., U. S.).—**clev′er-ly,** *adv.*—**clev′er-ness,** *n.*

clev-is, clev-y (klev′is, -i), *n.*; pl. *-ises, -ies* (-iz). [Cf. *cleave*[2].] A piece of metal, usually U-shaped, with a pin or bolt passing through holes at the two ends, as for attaching a draft-chain, etc., to a plow or the like.

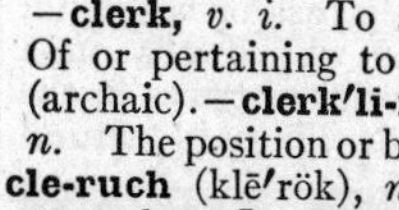

Clevis.

clew (klö), etc. Var. spelling of *clue*, etc. (now esp. *naut.*).

cli-an-thus (klī-an′thus), *n.* [NL., < Gr. κλέος, fame, glory, + ἄνθος, flower.] Any plant of the fabaceous genus *Clianthus*, native in Australia and New Zealand, and comprising two species, shrubs or vines with handsome flowers, which are cultivated in hothouses and gardens; the glory-pea.

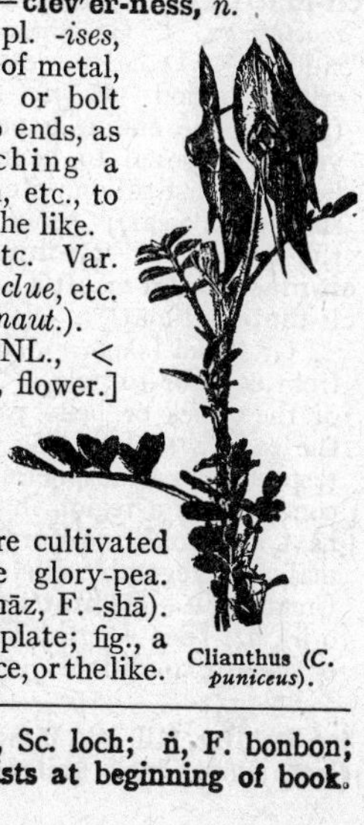

Clianthus (*C. puniceus*).

cli-ché (klē-shā), *n.*; pl. *clichés* (-shāz, F. -shā). [F.] A stereotype or electrotype plate; fig., a stereotyped expression, idea, practice, or the like.

click (klik), *v.* [Imit.: cf. *clack.*] **I.** *intr.* To emit or make a slight, sharp sound, as of the cocking of a pistol; produce a succession of such sounds. **II.** *tr.* To cause to click; strike with a click.—**click,** *n.* A slight, sharp sound, as of the cocking of a pistol; also, any of a class of sounds in South African languages, produced by withdrawing the tongue by a sucking action from a part of the mouth with which it has been in contact; also, some clicking mechanism, as a detent or a pawl.—**click′=bee″tle,** *n.* An elaterid: so called from the clicking sound made in springing up, as after having been laid on its back.—**click′er,** *n.*

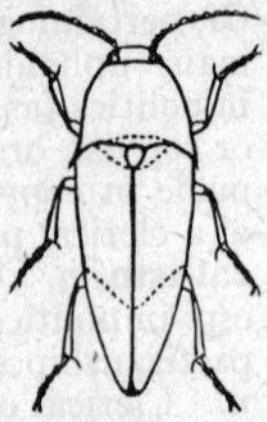
Click-beetle, natural size.

cli-do-man-cy (klī′dọ-man-si), *n.* [Gr. κλείς (κλειδ-), key, + μαντεία, divination.] Divination by means of a key.

cli-ent (klī′ẹnt), *n.* [L. *cliens* (*client-*), for *cluens,* prop. ppr. of *cluere,* hear: see *loud.*] An ancient Roman plebeian who lived under the patronage of a patrician; hence, any one under the patronage or protection of another; a dependent; a vassal; a follower; also, one who applies to a lawyer for advice or commits his cause or legal interests to a lawyer's management; hence, in general, one who resorts to another for professional or business services; a customer.—**cli′en-tage** (-ẹn-tạj), *n.* Clientship; also, clients collectively.—**cli′en-tal,** *a.* Of or pertaining to a client.—**cli-en-tele** (klī-ẹn-tēl′ or -tel′), *n.* [L. *clientela.*] Clientship†; also, clients collectively; a body of clients, or followers, customers, etc. Also (F.) **cli-en-tèle** (klē-oṅ-tel).—**cli′ent-less,** *a.* Having no clients.—**cli′ent-ship,** *n.* The condition or relation of a client.

cliff (klif), *n.* [AS. *clif* = D., LG., and Icel. *klif.*] The high, steep face of a rocky mass; a steep rock or headland; a precipice.—**cliff′=dwell″er,** *n.* One who dwells on a cliff; esp., a member of one of the aboriginal tribes in the southwestern U. S. who built their dwellings in natural recesses in cliffs.—**cliff′=dwell″ing,** *n.* A dwelling of cliff-dwellers.—**cliff′y,** *a.* Having cliffs, or formed by cliffs; craggy: as, "The hills . . . were still tall and bare, with *cliffy* battlements" (Stevenson's "Travels with a Donkey," v. 3).

Cliff-dwellings.

clift (klift), *n.* Var. of *cliff.* [Archaic or prov.]

cli-maç-ter-ic (klī-mak-ter′ik or klī-mak′tẹ-rik). [L. *climactericus,* < Gr. κλιμακτηρικός, < κλιμακτήρ, step of a ladder, < κλῖμαξ: see *climax.*] **I.** *a.* Pertaining to a critical period. **II.** *n.* A critical period in life; a year (usually one ending a period or an odd multiple of seven years) supposed to be marked by important changes in health, constitution, etc. (as, the grand *climacteric,* the sixty-third year); hence, any critical period; in *physiol.,* the menopause.—**cli-mac-ter′i-cal,** *a.*

cli-mac-tic (klī-mak′tik), *a.* Pertaining to a climax.

cli-mate (klī′māt), *n.* [OF. F. *climat,* < LL. *clima* (*climat-*), < Gr. κλίμα (κλιματ-), clime, zone, lit. 'slope' (of the earth from equator to pole), < κλίνειν, incline: see *lean*[1].] Any of the zones or belts parallel to the equator into which the earth's surface was formerly divided†; a region with respect to its atmospheric conditions; also, the characteristic condition of a region in respect to amount or variation of heat and cold, moisture, wind, etc., esp. as affecting animal and vegetable life.—**cli′ma-tal** (-mā-tạl), **cli-mat′ic** (-mat′ik), *a.*—**cli-mat′i-cal-ly,** *adv.*—**cli-ma-tol′o-gy** (-tol′ọ-ji), *n.* [See *-logy.*] The science that deals with climate or climatic conditions.—**cli″ma-to-log′i-cal** (-tọ-loj′i-kạl), *a.*—**cli-ma-tol′o-gist,** *n.*—**cli′ma-ture†** (-tūr), *n.* Climate; also, a clime or region (see Shakspere's "Hamlet," i. 1. 125).

cli-max (klī′maks), *n.* [LL., < Gr. κλῖμαξ, ladder, staircase, climax, < κλίνειν, incline: see *lean*[1].] A rhetorical figure consisting in a series of related ideas so arranged that each surpasses the preceding in force or intensity; popularly, the last term or member of this figure; hence, the highest point of anything; the culmination.

climb (klīm), *v.* [AS. *climban* = D. and G. *klimmen.*] **I.** *intr.* To mount or ascend, esp. by using both hands and feet; rise slowly by or as by continued effort; ascend by twining or by means of tendrils, adhesive fibers, etc., as a plant; slope upward; also (with *down*), to descend, esp. by using both hands and feet, or (colloq.) to withdraw from some untenable position taken. **II.** *tr.* To ascend, go up, or get to the top of, as by the use of hands and feet.—**climb,** *n.* A climbing; an ascent by climbing; also, a place to be climbed.—**climb′a-ble,** *a.* That may be climbed.—**climb′er,** *n.* One who or that which climbs; a climbing plant; a device to assist in climbing, as a spiked arrangement attached to a shoe, etc., to assist in climbing poles.—**climb′ing=fish′,** *n.* A small East Indian acanthopterygian fish, *Anabas scandens,* which is able to live for a considerable time out of water and to travel for some distance on land, and is reputed to climb trees. Also **climb′ing=perch′.**

Climbing-fish.

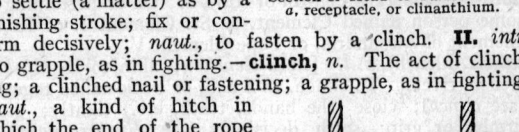

clime (klīm), *n.* [LL. *clima:* see *climate.*] A tract or region of the earth (now chiefly poetic); sometimes, climate (poetic: see Cowper's "Task," ii. 209).

cli-nan-dri-um (kli-nan′dri-um), *n.*; pl. *-dria* (-dri-ạ). [NL., < Gr. κλίνη, bed, + ἀνήρ (ἀνδρ-), man.] In *bot.,* a cavity in the apex of the column in orchids, in which the anthers rest; the androclinium.

cli-nan-thi-um (kli-nan′thi-um), *n.*; pl. *-thia* (-thi-ạ). [NL., < Gr. κλίνη, bed, + ἄνθος, flower.] In *bot.,* the receptacle of the florets in a composite plant; the anthoclinium.

Section of Head of Sunflower.—*a,* receptacle, or clinanthium.

clinch (klinch), *v.* [Later form of *clench:* now more common in some senses.] **I.** *tr.* To secure (a driven nail, etc.) by beating down the point; fasten (work) together thus; rivet; also, to settle (a matter) as by a finishing stroke; fix or confirm decisively; *naut.,* to fasten by a clinch. **II.** *intr.* To grapple, as in fighting.—**clinch,** *n.* The act of clinching; a clinched nail or fastening; a grapple, as in fighting; *naut.,* a kind of hitch in which the end of the rope is fastened back by seizing.—**clinch′er,** *n.* A person or thing that clinches; something decisive (colloq.).—**clinch′er=built, clink′er=built,** *a.* Having the outside planks or metal plates overlapping one another, as a boat or a boiler. Cf. *carvel built.*

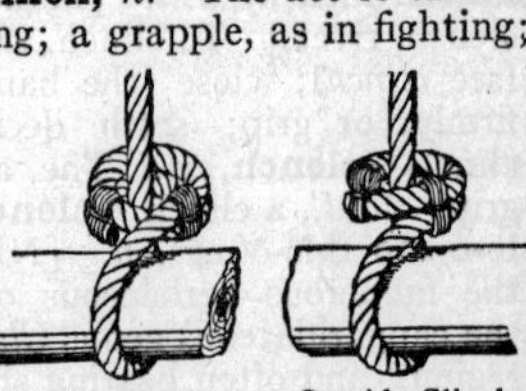
Inside Clinch. Outside Clinch.

cling (kling), *v.*; *clung, clinging.* [AS. *clingan,* stick or draw together, shrivel.] **I.** *intr.* To cohere†; shrivel or wither (now prov.); also, to adhere closely; stick (*to*); also, to hold fast, as by grasping or embracing, cleave (*to*); hence, to be or remain close. **II.** *tr.* To shrivel or wither (archaic); cause to adhere (now prov.); apply closely and firmly†.—**cling,** *n.* The act of clinging.—**cling′er,** *n.*—**cling′ing-ly,** *adv.*—**cling′-**

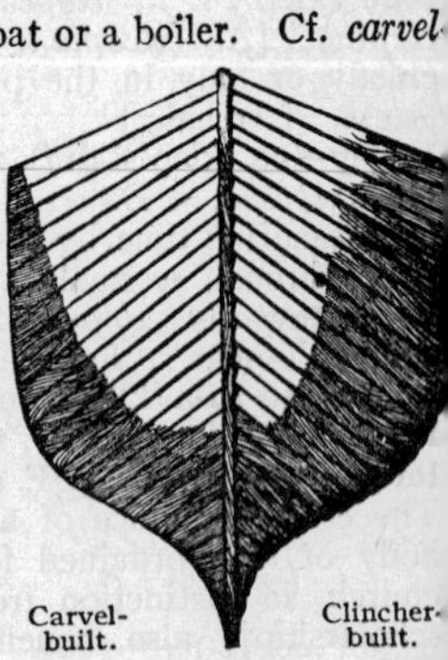
Carvel-built. Clincher-built.

stone. **I.** *a.* Having a stone to which the pulp adheres closely, as certain peaches. **II.** *n.* A clingstone peach.—**cling′y,** *a.* Apt to cling; adhesive.

clin-ic (klin′ik). [LL. *clinicus*, < Gr. κλινικός, < κλίνη, bed, < κλίνειν, incline.] **I.** *a.* Pertaining to a sick-bed or to a clinic. **II.** *n.* One confined to bed by sickness (rare); the instruction of medical students by examining or treating patients in their presence; a class of students assembled for such instruction; a place, as in connection with a medical school or a hospital, for such treatment or for the free treatment of patients.—**clin′i-cal,** *a.* Pertaining to a clinic; clinic.—**clin′i-cal-ly,** *adv.*—**cli-ni-cian** (kli-nish′ạn), *n.* A physician who studies diseases at the bedside, or is skilled in clinical methods.

clink¹ (klingk), *v. i.* or *t.* [Imit.] To make, or cause to make, a light, sharp, ringing sound.—**clink**¹, *n.* A clinking sound.

clink² (klingk), *v.* Var. of *clinch.* [Now prov.]

clink³ (klingk), *n.* [From the *Clink*, a prison in Southwark, London.] A prison, jail, or lockup: as, "I'm here in the *Clink* for a thundering drink and blacking the Corporal's eye" (Kipling's "Cells"). [Eng.]

clink-er¹ (kling′kėr), *n.* One who or that which clinks.

clink-er² (kling′kėr), *n.* [D. *klinker*, kind of brick, < *klinken* = E. *clink*¹, *v.*] A kind of hard Dutch brick used for paving; also, a partially vitrified mass of brick; also, a mass of incombustible matter fused together, as in the burning of coal; slag; volcanic material; the scale of oxide formed on iron during forging.—**clink′er**², *v. i.* To form clinkers in burning, as coal.

clink-er=built (kling′kėr-bilt), *a.* See *clincher-built.*

clink-stone (klingk′stōn), *n.* [See *clink*¹.] Any of several varieties of phonolite which give out a ringing sound when struck.

clino-. Form of Gr. κλίνειν, incline, used in combination. —**cli-no=ax-is** (klī″nọ-ak′sis), *n.* Same as *clinodiagonal.* —**cli′no-chlore** (-klōr), *n.* [+ Gr. χλωρός, green.] A mineral, a variety of chlorite, occurring usually in scaly or granular aggregates, but also in monoclinic crystals. —**cli″no-di-ag′o-nal** (-dī-ag′ọ-nạl), *n.* In *crystal.*, the diagonal or lateral axis in monoclinic crystals which forms an oblique angle with the vertical axis.—**cli′no-graph** (-gråf), *n.* [+ *-graph.*] An apparatus used in mining, etc., for determining the deviation of a boring from the vertical; also, a device for drawing angles, consisting of two straight-edges pivoted together.—**cli-nom′e-ter** (-nom′e-tėr), *n.* [+ *-meter.*] An instrument for measuring inclination, as the dip of strata or the heeling of a ship.—**cli-no-met′ric** (-met′rik), *a.* Pertaining to or determined by a clinometer; also, pertaining to oblique crystalline forms, or to solids which have oblique angles between the axes.—**cli-nom′e-try,** *n.*

clin-quant (kling′kạnt). [F., ppr. of obs. *clinquer*, clink, tinkle, glitter.] **I.** *a.* Glittering, as with tinsel; tinseled; decked with garish finery. See Shakspere's "Henry VIII.," i. 1. 19. **II.** *n.* Imitation gold-leaf; tinsel.

clin-to-ni-a (klin-tō′ni-ạ̈), *n.* [NL.; from De Witt *Clinton* (1769–1828), American statesman.] Any plant of the convallariaceous genus *Clintonia*, comprising stemless perennial herbs with a few broad, ribbed, basal leaves, and white or greenish-yellow flowers on a short peduncle.

Cli-o (klī′ō), *n.* [L., < Gr. Κλειώ, < κλέιειν, celebrate.] The Muse of history.

Clio.—Statue in the Vatican, Rome.

clip¹ (klip), *v. t.*; *clipped, clipping.* [AS. *clyppan*, embrace.] To embrace or hug (archaic or prov.); encircle or encompass; grip tightly, as by a spring.—**clip**¹, *n.* An embrace (archaic or prov.); also, a device for gripping and holding tightly; a metal clasp; a flange on the upper surface of a horseshoe.

clip² (klip), *v.*; *clipped, clipping.* [Cf. Icel. *klippa*, clip.] **I.** *tr.* To cut, or cut off or out, as with shears; trim by cutting; also, to cut or trim the hair or fleece of; shear; also, to pare the edge of (coin) fraudulently; also, to cut short; curtail; esp., to omit syllables of (words) in pronouncing. **II.** *intr.* To clip or cut something; also, to move swiftly.—**clip**², *n.* An act of clipping; anything clipped off, esp. the wool shorn at a single shearing of sheep; a smart blow or stroke, as with the hand (colloq.); a rapid gait or motion (colloq.); *pl.*, shears.—**clip′per,** *n.* One who or that which clips or cuts; also, one that clips, or moves swiftly, as a horse; a sailing-vessel built and rigged for speed; also, a first-rate person or thing (slang).—**clip′ping,** *n.* The act of one who or that which clips; also, a piece clipped off or out, as from a newspaper.—**clip′ping,** *p. a.* That clips; also, first-rate or excellent (slang). —**clip′ping-ly,** *adv.*

clique (klēk), *n.* [F., < OF. *cliquer*, make a sharp sound: cf. *claque.*] A small set or coterie, esp. one associated for some exclusive or intriguing purpose; also, cliquism. —**clique,** *v. i.*; *cliqued, cliquing.* To form, or associate in, a clique.—**cli-quey, cli-quy** (klē′ki), *a.* Forming, or inclined to form, a clique or cliques.—**cli-quish** (klē′kish), *a.* Of, pertaining to, or savoring of a clique; disposed to form cliques; actuated by a petty party spirit.—**cli′quish-ness,** *n.*—**cli′quism,** *n.* Cliquish principles or spirit.

clis-tog-a-my (klīs-tog′ạ-mi), etc. See *cleistogamy*, etc.

clith-ral (klīth′rạl), *a.* See *cleithral.*

cli-to-ris (klī′tọ-ris or klit′ọ-ris), *n.* [NL., < Gr. κλειτορίς, < κλείειν, shut.] In *anat.*, an organ of the female of most mammals, homologous to the penis of the male.

clo-a-ca (klọ-ā′kạ̈), *n.*; pl. *cloacæ* (-sē). [L., prob. < *cluere*, cleanse.] A sewer; a privy; in *zoöl.*, the common cavity into which the intestinal, urinary, and generative canals open in birds, reptiles, amphibians, many fishes, and certain mammals (monotremes); a similar cavity in invertebrates; in fig. use, a receptacle of moral filth.—**clo-a′cal,** *a.*

cloak (klōk), *n.* [OF. *cloke, cloque*, < ML. *cloca*, cloak, orig. bell: see *clock*¹.] A loose outer garment; fig., that which covers or conceals; a disguise; a pretext.—**cloak,** *v. t.* To cover with or as with a cloak; hide; conceal. —**cloak′ing,** *n.* Material for making cloaks.—**cloak′=room,** *n.* A room, as in a school or a theater, where cloaks, overcoats, etc., may be left temporarily.

cloche (klosh), *n.* [F., lit. bell: see *clock*¹.] A bell-glass under which plants are grown.

clock¹ (klok), *n.* [Appar. < OF. *cloque*, also *cloche* (F. *cloche*), < ML. *cloca, clocca*, bell; prob. from Celtic: cf. D. *klok*, G. *glocke*, bell, clock.] An instrument for measuring and indicating time, commonly one whose mechanism consists of a train of wheels set in motion by a weight or a spring, and having hands or pointers which move round on a dial to mark the hours, etc., and orig. and properly one giving notice of the hours by the stroke of a hammer on a gong or the like; esp., such a timepiece not carried on the person (as distinguished from a *watch*).—**clock**¹, *v. t.* To time, test, or ascertain by the clock.

clock² (klok), *n.* [Origin uncertain.] An embroidered or woven ornament on each side of a stocking, extending from the ankle upward.—**clocked,** *a.* Ornamented with clocks.

clock-wise (klok′wīz), *adv.* and *a.* In the direction of rotation of the hands of a clock.

clock-work (klok′wėrk), *n.* The work or working of a clock (as, to go like *clockwork*; regular as *clockwork*); also, the mechanism of a clock; any mechanism similar to that of a clock (as, "The King . . . conceived I might be a piece of *clock-work* . . . contrived by some ingenious artist": Swift's "Gulliver's Travels," ii. 3).

clod (klod), *n.* [Var. of *clot.*] A lump or coherent mass, esp. of earth or clay; earth or soil; fig., anything earthy or base, as the body of a man in comparison with his soul (as, "this corporeal *clod*": Milton's "Paradise Lost," x. 786); also, a blockhead or dolt; also, a part of the shoulder of beef.—**clod,** *v. t.*; *clodded, clodding.* To form into clods; pelt with clods; throw with violence (Sc. and north. Eng.).—**clod′dish,** *a.* Clod-like; base; stupid; boorish; uncouth.—**clod′dish-ness,** *n.*—**clod′dy,** *a.* Abounding in clods; clod-like.—**clod′hop″per,** *n.* A countryman;

a clumsy boor; *pl.*, coarse, heavy shoes.—**clod′hop″ping,** *a.*—**clod′pate,** *n.* A clodpoll.—**clod′pat″ed** (-pā″ted), *a.* —**clod′poll** (-pōl), *n.* A blockhead; a dolt.

cloff (klof), *n.* [Origin unknown.] In *com.*, a small allowance in weight, as to cover losses in retailing.

clog (klog), *n.* [ME. *clog, clogge*; origin uncertain: cf. *log*[1].] A thick piece of wood (now chiefly north. Eng.); a heavy block, as of wood, fastened to a man or beast to impede movement; hence, anything that impedes motion or action; an encumbrance; a hindrance; also, a kind of shoe with a thick sole, usually of wood; a similar but lighter shoe worn in the clog-dance; also, a clog-dance. —**clog,** *v.*; *clogged, clogging.* **I.** *tr.* To fasten a clog or block to; impede or restrain with or as with a clog; encumber; hamper; hinder; also, to encumber or impede by the adhesion of sticky matter; also, to fill up with something that hinders proper action or function; choke up. **II.** *intr.* To become clogged; become encumbered or choked up; stick, or stick together.—**clog′=al″ma-nac,** *n.* An early form of almanac or calendar, made by cutting notches and characters on a clog or block, usually of wood. —**clog′=dance,** *n.* A dance performed with clogs, or shoes having wooden soles or heels, in which the feet perform a noisy accompaniment to music.—**clog′=dan″cer,** *n.*—**clog′gy,** *a.* Clog-like; clogging, or apt to clog; adhesive; sticky; full of clogging matter.

cloi-son-né (kloi-zọ-nā′, F. klwo-zo-nā), *a.* [F., < *cloison*, partition, < L. *claudere*, shut, close.] Partitioned: applied to enamel in which thin metal bands, fixed on edge to a ground, outline the design and form partitions between the colors.

clois-ter (klois′tėr), *n.* [OF. *cloistre* (F. *cloître*), < ML. *claustrum*, cloister, L. lock, bar, < *claudere*, shut, close.] An inclosure†; also, a place of religious seclusion; a monastery or nunnery; a convent; also, a covered walk in connection with a monastic or other ecclesiastical building, commonly running round an open court and having a plain wall on one side and an open arcade or colonnade on the other; a similar walk in connection with some other building.—**clois′ter,** *v. t.* To shut up or confine in a cloister or convent; hence, to shut up in retirement; confine; also, to convert into a cloister or convent; also, to furnish with a cloister or covered walk.—**clois′tral,** *a.* Of, pertaining to, or living in a cloister; cloister-like.—**clois′tress**†, *n.* A nun. See Shakspere's "Twelfth Night," i. 1. 28.

Cloister of Las Huelgas, Burgos, Spain.

cloke (klōk), *n.* and *v.* Old spelling of *cloak.*

clomb (klōm). Archaic preterit and past participle of *climb.*

clon (klon), *n.* [Gr. κλών, twig, slip, < κλᾶν, break.] A group of cultivated plants consisting of individuals derived from a single original seedling or stock, the propagation having been by the use of vegetative parts such as buds, grafts, tubers, etc.

clo-nus (klō′nus), *n.* [NL., < Gr. κλόνος, commotion, turmoil.] In *pathol.*, a series of convulsive alternating muscular contractions and relaxations.—**clon-ic** (klon′ik), *a.*

cloop (klöp), *n.* [Imit.] The sound made when a cork is drawn from a bottle; any similar sound.—**cloop,** *v. i.* To make such a sound.

cloot (klöt), *n.* [Cf. *cleave*[2].] One of the divisions of a cloven hoof; a cloven hoof as a whole; [*cap.*] usually *pl.*, the devil. [Chiefly Sc.]—**Cloot′ie,** *n.* The devil: as, "O thou ! whatever title suit thee . . . Satan, Nick, or *Clootie*" (Burns's "Address to the Deil," 2). [Chiefly Sc.]

clos-a-ble (klō′zạ-bl), *a.* That may be closed.

close[1] (klōz), *v. t.*; *closed, closing.* [ME. *closen* (after OF. *clos*: see *close*[2]), for earlier *clusen*, < L. *clusus, clausus*, pp. of *cludere, claudere*, shut, close.] To shut in or surround on all sides; inclose; cover in; stop or obstruct (a gap, entrance, aperture, etc.); put (a door or other barrier) in position to obstruct an entrance, aperture, or the like; stop or obstruct the entrances, apertures, or gaps in; prevent ingress to or egress from; also, to bring together the parts of, join, or unite (as, to *close* the ranks of troops); also, to bring to an end (as, to *close* a debate); conclude or complete (as, to *close* a bargain); *naut.*, to come close to.—**closed shop.** See under *shop, n.*—**close**[1], *v. i.* To become closed; shut; also, to come together or unite; also, to come close; grapple, or engage in close-encounter (*with*); also, to come to terms (*with*); agree; also, to come to an end; terminate.—**close**[1], *n.* The act of closing; a junction or union; a close encounter; a grapple; the end or conclusion.

close[2] (klōs), *a.*; compar. *closer*, superl. *closest.* [OF. F. *clos*, pp. of *clore*, < L. *claudere*, shut, E. *close*[1].] Closed; shut in or inclosed; without opening, or with all openings covered or closed; confined or narrow (as, *close* quarters); lacking fresh or freely circulating air (as, a *close* room); heavy or oppressive, as the air; narrowly confined, as a prisoner; strictly guarded; secluded or retired; hidden or secret; practising secrecy, as a person; reserved or reticent; parsimonious, stingy, or niggardly; scarce, as money; not open to public or general admission or competition (as, a *close* corporation, a corporation which fills its own vacancies); under prohibition as to hunting or fishing, as a season; also, having the parts near together (as, a *close* texture); compact or condensed; near, or near together, in space, time, or relation; in immediate proximity (as, *close* contact); intimate or confidential (as, *close* friendship); fitting tightly, as a cap; not deviating from the subject under consideration (as, *close* attention); strict, searching, or minute (as, *close* investigation); not deviating from a model or original (as, a *close* translation; a *close* copy); nearly even or equal, as a contest; in *phonetics*, uttered with a relatively contracted opening of the oral cavity (cf. *open, a.*).—**close reef,** *naut.*, the last ordinary reef in a sail, producing the greatest reduction in size. Cf. *close-reefed.*—**close**[2], *adv.* In a close manner; closely.—**close to the wind,** *naut.*, with the head of the vessel directed as nearly as possible to the point from which the wind blows, so as just to fill the sails without shaking them. See also *to sail close to the wind*, under *wind*[2], *n.*—**close**[2] (klōs), *n.* [OF. *clos*, orig. pp.] An inclosed place; an inclosure; any piece of land held as private property; an inclosure about or beside a building; a precinct, as of a cathedral; a narrow entry or alley, or a court to which it leads (Sc. and local Eng.). —**close′=fist′ed,** *a.* Miserly; penurious.—**close′=fit′ting,** *a.* Of garments, fitting closely to the body.—**close′=grained′,** *a.* Having the grain close or fine in texture, as wood.—**close′=hauled′,** *a.* *Naut.*, having the sails set for sailing as nearly in the direction from which the wind blows as possible.—**close′ly,** *adv.*—**close′=mouthed′** (-mouᴛʜd′), *a.* Reticent; uncommunicative.—**close′ness,** *n.*

clos-er (klō′zėr), *n.* One who or that which closes.

close=reefed (klōs′rēft′), *a.* *Naut.*, of a sail, having the last reef taken in; of a vessel, having the sail or sails so reefed.

close=stool (klōs′stöl), *n.* A box with a seat and a lid, containing a chamber vessel, as for use in a sick-room.

clos-et (kloz′et). [OF. *closet*, dim. of *clos*, E. *close*[2], *n.*] **I.** *n.* A private room, esp. one of comparatively small size, as for retirement, counsel, or devotions; also, a small room, inclosed recess, or cabinet for clothing, provisions, utensils, etc.; also, a water-closet. **II.** *a.* Pertaining to a closet; private; secluded; also, suited for use or enjoyment in privacy (as, a *closet* drama, one to be read rather than acted); also, engaged in private study or speculation; speculative; unpractical.—**clos′et,** *v. t.*; *-eted, -eting.* To shut up in a closet or private apartment, as for a conference or interview: chiefly in *pp.*: as, "He was *closeted* for an hour with my father" (Bulwer-Lytton's "Caxtons," iv. 2).

close=tongued (klōs′tungd′), *a.* Close-mouthed.

close=up (klōs′up), *n.* In moving pictures, a picture taken at close range, being on a relatively large scale, with increased clearness of detail; fig., an intimate view or presentation of anything.

clo-sure (klō′zhụ̈r), *n.* [OF. *closure*, < LL. *clausura*, < L. *claudere*: see *close*¹.] The act of closing, or the state of being closed; a bringing to an end; conclusion; that which incloses or shuts in; an inclosure; that which closes or shuts; in parliamentary procedure, a method of closing a debate and causing an immediate vote to be taken on the question under discussion, as by moving the previous question (see *previous question*, under *previous*, *a.*).—**clo′-sure,** *v. t.*; *-sured, -suring.* In parliamentary procedure, to end by closure, as a debate.

clot (klot), *n.* [AS. *clott*, mass, = G. *klotz*, block.] A mass or lump; a semisolid mass, as of coagulated blood; a clod (now prov. Eng.).—**clot,** *v.*; *clotted, clotting.* **I.** *intr.* To form into clots; coagulate. **II.** *tr.* To cause to clot; mat together by clots; cover with clots.

cloth (klôth), *n.*; pl. *cloths* (klôᴛʜz). [AS. *clāth*, cloth (pl. *clāthas*, clothes), = D. *kleed*, G. *kleid*, garment.] A pliable fabric formed by weaving, felting, etc., from wool or hair, or silk, flax, cotton, or other fiber, used for garments, upholstery, and many other purposes; esp., a woolen fabric of some thickness or body; also, a piece of such a fabric used for a particular purpose, as a table-cloth; a sail†; sails collectively; also, a garment†; clothing†; a livery or customary garb, as of a trade or profession†; a particular profession, esp. that of a clergyman; with *the*, the clergy.

clothe (klōᴛʜ), *v. t.*; *clothed* or *clad, clothing.* [AS. *clāthian*, also *clǣthan* (pret. *clǣdde*, whence E. *clad*), < *clāth*, E. *cloth.*] To cover with or as with clothing; dress; attire; invest; also, to provide with clothing.

clothes (klōᴛʜz), *n. pl.* [AS. *clāthas*, pl.: see *cloth.*] Garments or coverings for the body; articles of dress or raiment; wearing apparel; also, bedclothes.—**clothes′=horse,** *n.* A frame on which to hang clothes, household linen, etc., esp. for drying.—**clothes′=line,** *n.* A rope on which to hang clothes, etc., to dry after being washed.—**clothes′=pin,** *n.* A forked piece of wood or other device for fastening articles on a clothes-line.—**clothes′=press,** *n.* A receptacle for clothes, as a chest, wardrobe, or closet.—**clothes′=tree,** *n.* An article of furniture consisting of an upright pole with branches near the top for hanging coats, hats, etc., on.

cloth-ier (klōᴛʜ′yėr), *n.* [ME. *clothyer*, *clother*, < *cloth*, E. *cloth.*] A maker or seller of woolen cloth or of clothes; a dealer in ready-made clothing.

cloth-ing (klō′ᴛʜing), *n.* Garments collectively; clothes; raiment; apparel.

clot-ty (klot′i), *a.* Full of clots; clotted.

clô-ture (klō-tür), *n.* [F.] In parliamentary procedure, closure of a debate.

cloud (kloud), *n.* [Prob. < AS. *clūd*, mass of rock, hill.] A visible collection of particles of water or ice suspended in the air, usually at a considerable elevation above the earth's surface; any similar mass, as of smoke or flying dust; a dim or obscure area in something otherwise clear or transparent; an ill-defined patch or spot differing in color from the surrounding surface; a great number of insects, birds, etc., flying together (as, "A pitchy *cloud* Of locusts": Milton's "Paradise Lost," i. 340); a throng or multitude (as, "so great a *cloud* of witnesses": Heb. xii. 1); a loosely knit woolen scarf worn by women; in fig. use, anything that obscures or darkens, or overspreads with gloom, trouble, suspicion, disgrace, etc. (as, "the *clouds* that lour'd upon our house": Shakspere's "Richard III.," i. 1. 3).—**cloud,** *v.* **I.** *tr.* To overspread or cover with or as with a cloud or clouds; overshadow; obscure or darken; render gloomy; place under a cloud, as of suspicion, disgrace, etc.; also, to variegate with ill-defined patches of another color. **II.** *intr.* To grow cloudy; become clouded.—**cloud′ber″ry,** *n.* The orange-yellow edible fruit of *Rubus chamæmorus*, a small raspberry of the northern hemisphere; also, the plant.—

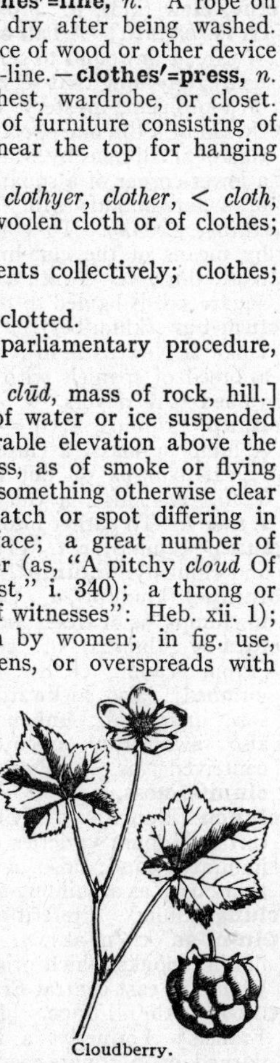

Cloudberry.

cloud′=burst, *n.* A violent downpour of rain.—**cloud′i-ly,** *adv.* In a cloudy manner.—**cloud′i-ness,** *n.*—**cloud′land** (-land), *n.* The region of the clouds; also, a region of obscurity or unreality.—**cloud′less,** *a.* Without clouds; clear.—**cloud′less-ly,** *adv.*—**cloud′less-ness,** *n.*—**cloud′let,** *n.* A little cloud.—**cloud′scape** (-skāp), *n.* [With *-scape* as in *landscape.*] A picture or a view of the clouds.—**cloud′ward, cloud′wards** (-wạ̈rd, -wạ̈rdz), *adv.* Toward the clouds.—**cloud′y,** *a.*; compar. *cloudier*, superl. *cloudiest.* Of the nature of cloud; resembling a cloud or clouds; pertaining to clouds; also, characterized by or overcast with clouds (as, a *cloudy* sky); also, not clear or transparent (as, a *cloudy* liquid); having cloud-like markings, or clouded (as, *cloudy* marble); also, fig., obscure or indistinct (as, *cloudy* notions); darkened by gloom, trouble, etc. (as, "when *cloudy* looks are cleared": Spenser's "Amoretti," xl.); under a cloud of suspicion, disgrace, etc. (as, a *cloudy* reputation).

clough (kluf or klou), *n.* [ME.; origin uncertain.] A narrow valley; a ravine; a glen. [Prov. Eng. and Sc.]

clour (klör), *n.* [Cf. Icel. *klōr*, scratch.] A lump or a dent due to a blow; also, a blow (as, "My head can stand a gey *clour*": Scott's "Guy Mannering," xxiii.). [Sc.]—**clour,** *v. t.* To strike with a blow that produces a lump or dent; batter: as, "Twa or three chields wad needs fight . . . and they got their crouns weel *cloured*" (Scott's "Old Mortality," xiv.). [Sc.]

clout¹ (klout), *n.* [AS. *clūt*, piece of cloth or metal: cf. *clot.*] A patch, or piece of cloth or other material used to mend something (archaic or prov.); an iron plate, as on an axletree, to prevent wear; any piece of cloth, esp. one which is worthless or used for a mean purpose (archaic or prov.); also, the mark shot at in archery, or a shot that hits the mark.—**clout**¹, *v. t.* To put a clout on; patch or mend; bandage; also, to stud with clout-nails, as the sole of a shoe. [Archaic or prov.]

clout² (klout), *n.* [ME. *clowte*; origin uncertain.] A blow, esp. with the hand; a cuff. [Colloq. or prov.]—**clout**², *v. t.* To strike, esp. with the hand; cuff. [Colloq. or prov.]

clout=nail (klout′nāl), *n.* A nail with a large, flat head, used for fastening clouts, as on axletrees, studding the soles of heavy shoes, etc.

clove¹ (klōv). Pret. and archaic pp. of *cleave*².

clove² (klōv), *n.* [AS. *clufe*; akin to E. *cleave*².] One of the small bulbs formed in the axils of the scales of a mother bulb, as in garlic.

clove³ (klōv), *n.* [D. *klove*, *kloof*, cleft.] A rocky cleft; a ravine; a gorge: in place-names. [New York.]

clove⁴ (klōv), *n.* [OF. *clou* (< L. *clavus*, nail), in *clou de gilofre*, 'nail of clove' (see *gillyflower*), so called from the shape.] The dried flower-bud of a tropical myrtaceous tree, *Caryophyllus aromaticus*, used as a spice; also, the tree.—**clove′=gil′ly-flow″er,** *n.* [Corruption of ME. *clow gilofre*, clove, < OF. *clou de gilofre*: see *clove*⁴.] The clove-pink or carnation.

clove=hitch (klōv′hich), *n.* [See *clove*¹.] *Naut.*, a form of hitch for fastening a rope about a spar, etc., in which two rounds of rope are formed about the spar, crossing at one point, with the ends of the rope issuing in opposite directions between the crossed parts.

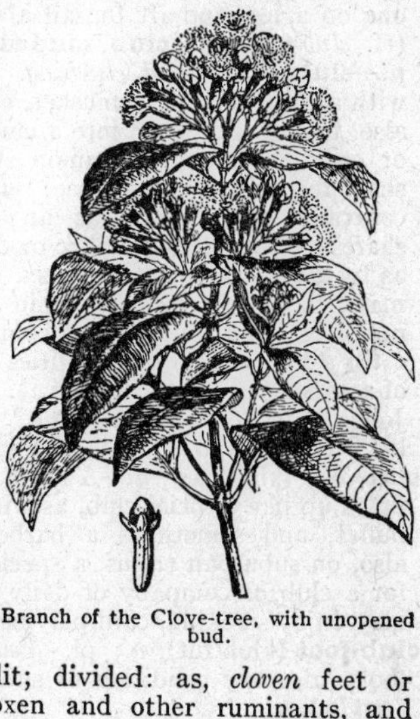

Branch of the Clove-tree, with unopened bud.

clov-en (klō′vn), *p. a.* [See *cleave*².] Cleft; split; divided: as, *cloven* feet or hoofs (characteristic of oxen and other ruminants, and also attributed to the devil: see *hoof*, *n.*).—**clov′en=foot″ed, clov′en=hoofed,** *a.*

clove=pink (klōv′pingk′), *n.* A pink, *Dianthus caryophyllus,* with a spicy scent like that of cloves; a carnation.

Clove-pink.

clo-ver (klō′vėr), *n.* [AS. *clāfre, clǣfre,* = D. *klaver,* akin to G. *klee.*] Any of various herbs of the fabaceous genus *Trifolium,* with trifoliolate leaves and dense flower-heads, many species of which, as *T. pratense* (the common 'red clover'), are cultivated as forage-plants; trefoil; also, any of various plants of allied genera, as melilot ('sweet clover').—**to be in clover,** to be like a cow in a clover-field; be in comfortable or luxurious circumstances.—**clo′vered,** *a.* Covered with a growth of clover.—**clo′ver=worm,** *n.* A green caterpillar, the larva of *Plathypena scabra,* an American noctuid moth.—**clo′ver-y,** *a.* Abounding in clover; clover-like.

clown (kloun), *n.* [Cf. Icel. *klunni,* a clumsy, boorish fellow, Sw. *kluns,* a lump, clod (also fig. of persons).] A peasant or rustic; a coarse, ill-bred fellow; a boor; also, a professional jester; a buffoon; [*cap.* or *l. c.*] a male character in English pantomime, typically having a whitened face and wearing a baggy white costume; [*l. c.*] a similar character in a circus, etc.—**clown′er-y,** *n.*; pl. *-ies* (-iz). The character or behavior of a clown; a clownish act or practice.—**clown′ish,** *a.* Of or pertaining to a clown or clowns; clown-like.—**clown′ish-ly,** *adv.*—**clown′ish-ness,** *n.*

cloy (kloi), *v. t.* [OF. *cloer* (F. *clouer*), nail (*encloer,* drive a nail or spike into), < *clou,* < L. *clavus,* nail.] To spike (a gun)†; also, to stop up†; also, to surfeit; satiate, as with food, sweetness, pleasure, etc., to the point of causing disgust.—**cloy′ing-ly,** *adv.*—**cloy′ing-ness,** *n.*—**cloy′less,** *a.* That does not cloy.

club (klub), *n.* [Cf. Icel. *klubba, klumba,* club, and E. *clump*[1].] A heavy stick, usually thicker at one end than at the other, suitable for a weapon; a cudgel; a stick or bat used to drive a ball, etc., in various games, esp. a stick with a crooked head used in golf, hockey, etc.; an Indian club; also, a rounded solid mass; a knob or bunch; a black trefoil-shaped figure on a playing-card, or a card of the suit bearing such figures; also, a company of persons organized for social intercourse, or for the promotion of some common object (literary, athletic, political, etc.); the building or rooms occupied by such a company; a meeting or assembly for social intercourse, etc., as at a tavern†; a combination of contributions toward a common expense†; an individual share of a joint expense†; *naut.,* a small spar to which the foot of certain sails is bent, esp. one on a fore-and-aft topsail above a mainsail or the like (cf. *club-topsail*).—**club sandwich.** See under *sandwich,* *n.*—**club,** *v.*; *clubbed, clubbing.* **I.** *tr.* To beat with or as with a club; invert (a musket, etc.) so as to use as a club; also, to gather or form into a club-like mass; also, to unite or combine, as in a common stock; contribute as one's share toward a joint expense; make up, as a sum, by joint contributions; defray, as an expense, by proportional shares; *milit.,* to demoralize or confuse (a body of troops), as by a blunder in maneuvers. **II.** *intr.* To gather into a mass; also, to combine or join together as for a common purpose; contribute to a common fund.—**club′ba-ble, club′a-ble,** *a.* Having qualities that fit one to be a member of a social club (as, "Boswell . . . is a very *clubable* man": Johnson, in Boswell's "Johnson," Dec. 4, 1783, note); sociable.—**clubbed,** *a.* Club-shaped; thick at the end.

club=car (klub′kär), *n.* A railroad passenger-car (for men) fitted up like a social club, as with easy-chairs, card-tables, buffet, and sometimes a barber-shop and a bathroom; also, on suburban trains, a specially equipped car reserved for a club or company of daily passengers, in which they may enjoy smoking, card-playing, etc.

club-foot (klub′fůt), *n.*; pl. *-feet.* A deformed or distorted foot; also, the condition of such a foot; talipes.—**club′-foot″ed,** *a.*

club-haul (klub′hâl), *v. t.* *Naut.,* to cause (a ship), in an emergency, to go on the other tack by letting go the lee anchor and pulling on a hawser leading from the anchor to the lee quarter, the hawser then being cut.

club=house (klub′hous), *n.* A house or building occupied by a club.

club-man (klub′mąn), *n.*; pl. *-men.* A man armed with a club; also (pron. -man), a member of a club or clubs, esp. of fashionable social clubs.

club=moss (klub′môs), *n.* Any plant of the family *Lycopodiaceæ,* esp. of the genus *Lycopodium,* as *L. clavatum* (see *lycopodium*).

club-root (klub′röt), *n.* A disease of cabbages and allied plants, due to a myxomycetous organism, *Plasmodiophora brassicæ,* which causes swellings to develop on the roots.

club=rush (klub′rush), *n.* Any of the cyperaceous plants constituting the genus *Scirpus*; a bulrush (genus *Scirpus*); also, the cat-tail, *Typha latifolia.*

club=shaped (klub′shāpt), *a.* Having the shape of a club; thicker at one end than at the other.

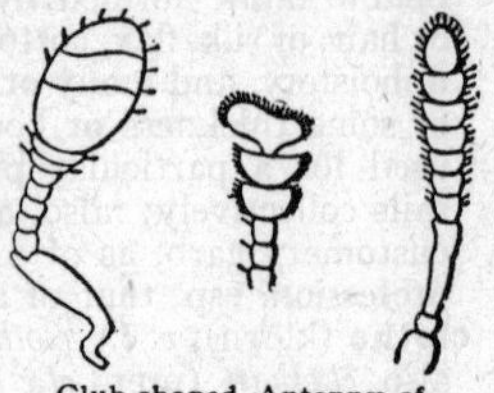
Club-shaped Antennæ of Insects.

club=top-sail (klub′top″sāl, naut. -sl), *n.* *Naut.,* a large fore-and-aft topsail set above a mainsail or the like, with its head extended by a light spar and its foot bent to a club.

club-wom-an (klub′wům″ąn), *n.*; pl. *-women* (-wim″en). A woman belonging to a club or clubs.

cluck (kluk), *v.* [Imit.: cf. G. *glucken,* Dan. *klukke,* Sw. *klucka,* also AS. *cloccian,* cluck.] **I.** *intr.* To utter the cry or call of a hen brooding or with young chicks; make a similar sound. **II.** *tr.* To call by clucking.—**cluck,** *n.* A clucking sound.

clue, clew (klö), *n.* [AS. *cliwen* = D. *kluwen,* clue, ball: cf. G. *knäuel.*] A ball of yarn or thread; in legend, a ball of thread unwound to serve as a guide through a labyrinth; hence, anything that serves to guide or direct in the solution of a problem, mystery, etc.; also, a thread or cord; the thread of a discourse, etc.; *naut., pl.* or *sing.,* the combination of small lines by which a hammock is suspended; *sing.,* a lower corner of a square sail; also, the after lower corner of a fore-and-aft sail.—**clue, clew,** *v. t.*; *clued, clewed, cluing, clewing.* To coil into a ball; *naut.,* to haul (*up*) by means of the clue-lines.—**clue′=line, clew′=line** (-līn, naut. -lin), *n.* *Naut.,* a rope by which a clue of an upper square sail is hauled to the yard.

clum-ber (klum′bėr), *n.* [From *Clumber,* estate of the Duke of Newcastle in Nottinghamshire, England.] One of a breed of spaniels with short legs and long, heavy body, valued as retrievers.

clump[1] (klump), *n.* [= D. *klomp* = LG. and G. *klump.*] A lump or mass; a cluster, as of trees or other plants (as, "great *clumps* of tall rank grass": Parkman's "Oregon Trail," iv.); also, a thick extra sole on a shoe.—**clump**[1], *v. t.* or *i.* To gather into or form a clump; mass.

clump[2] (klump), *v. i.* [Prob. < *clump*[1].] To walk heavily and clumsily.—**clump**[2], *n.* A clumping tread.

clump-y (klum′pi), *a.* Of the nature of a clump; abounding in clumps, as of trees; heavy and clumsy.

clum-sy (klum′zi), *a.*; compar. *clumsier,* superl. *clumsiest.* [From Scand.: cf. Sw. dial. *klummsen,* benumbed.] Benumbed†; also, awkward in movement or action, as a person; ungraceful; unhandy; wanting in dexterity or grace; also, awkwardly executed; inelegant or unwieldy; ill-contrived (as, a *clumsy* apology).—**clum′si-ly,** *adv.*—**clum′si-ness,** *n.*

clunch (klunch), *n.* [Cf. D. *klont,* lump, clod.] Any of certain impure varieties of clay found in England, esp. an indurated kind; also, a soft limestone of England, sometimes used as a building-stone.

clung (klung). Preterit and past participle of *cling.*

Clu-ni-ac (klö′ni-ak), *n.* One of a reformed order of Benedictine monks which originated about 910 in the abbey of Cluny, in east-central France.

Clu-ny (klö′ni) **lace.** [From *Cluny,* town in east-central France.] Formerly, a kind of lace having the pattern darned on a square-meshed net ground; now, usually, a lace of the guipure class, often made of heavy linen thread.

clu-pe-id (klö′pē̦-id). [NL. *Clupeidæ*, pl., < *Clupea*, the herring genus, L. *clupea*, kind of small river-fish.] **I.** *n.* Any of the *Clupeidæ*, a family of (chiefly) marine, teleostean fishes, including the herrings, sardines, menhaden, etc. **II.** *a.* Pertaining to the clupeids; belonging to the *Clupeidæ*.—**clu′pe-i-form** (-i-fôrm), *a.* [NL. *Clupea*: see *-form*.] Having the form or appearance of a herring.—**clu′pe-oid.** [NL. *Clupea*: see *-oid*.] **I.** *a.* Herring-like; of the herring family (*Clupeidæ*). **II.** *n.* A clupeoid fish.

clu-si-a-ceous (klö-si-ā′shius), *a.* [NL. *Clusia*, the typical genus; named from C. de *Lescluse*, French botanist.] Belonging to the *Clusiaceæ*, a family of tropical trees and shrubs yielding resins (as gamboge and tacamahac), fruits (as the mammee and mangosteen), and woods.

clus-ter (klus′tėr), *n.* [AS. *clyster*.] A number of things of the same kind, as fruits or flowers, growing or held together; a bunch; also, a number of things or persons collected or situated near together; a group; a crowd.—**clus′ter,** *v.* **I.** *tr.* To gather into a cluster; also, to furnish with clusters. **II.** *intr.* To form a cluster or clusters: as, "His sunny hair *Cluster'd* about his temples like a God's" (Tennyson's "Œnone," 59).—**clus′tered,** *p.a.* Gathered into or forming a cluster (as, a *clustered* column or pillar, one which consists, or appears to consist, of several columns or shafts clustered together); also, furnished or covered with clusters.—**clus′ter-y,** *a.* Having or forming clusters.

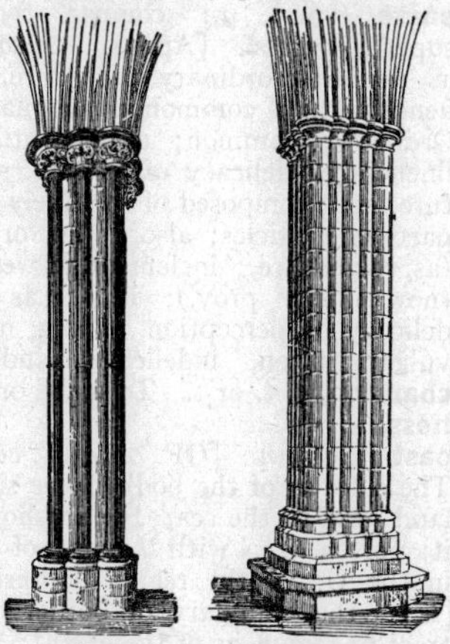

1 2
Clustered Columns, 13th century. 1, from Worcester Cathedral; 2, from Exeter Cathedral.

clutch[1] (kluch), *v.* [ME. *clucchen*, *clycchen*, < AS. *clyccean*, bend, clench.] **I.** *tr.* To clench (the hand or fingers)†; also, to seize with or as with the hands or claws; snatch; also, to grip or hold tightly or firmly. **II.** *intr.* To try to seize or grasp; snatch: with *at*.—**clutch**[1], *n.* A claw, talon, or paw (chiefly in *pl.*); the hand, esp. as representing rapacity or power (chiefly in *pl.*); also, the act of clutching; a snatch or grasp; a tight grip or hold; also, a device for gripping something; a coupling or appliance by which working parts of machinery (as a pulley and a shaft) may be made to engage or disengage at will.

clutch[2] (kluch), *n.* [Earlier *cletch*; akin to Icel. *klekja*, hatch.] A hatch of eggs; the number of eggs incubated at one time; a brood of chickens.

clut-ter (klut′ėr), *v.* [Var. of obs. *clotter*, freq. of *clot*, *v.*; in later use associated with *clatter*.] **I.** *intr.* To form clots†; collect together; run in disorder; move with bustle and confusion; make a clatter; speak hurriedly and confusedly. **II.** *tr.* To heap together or strew about in a disorderly manner; litter with things in confusion.—**clut′ter,** *n.* A disorderly heap or assemblage; litter; hence, confusion or disorder; also, confused noise; clatter.

Clydes-dale (klīdz′dāl), *n.* One of a breed of draft-horses combining activity, strength, and endurance, orig. raised in the valley of the upper Clyde (Clydesdale), Lanarkshire, Scotland.

clyp-e-ate (klip′ē̦-āt), *a.* [L. *clypeatus*, < *clypeus*, *clipeus*, shield.] Shaped like a round shield or buckler. Also **clyp′e-i-form** (-i-fôrm).

clys-ter (klis′tėr), *n.* [L., < Gr. κλυστήρ, < κλύζειν, wash.] In *med.*, an enema.

cne-mis (nē′mis), *n.* [NL., < Gr. κνημίς, greave, legging, < κνήμη, lower leg.] In *anat.*, the leg from knee to ankle; the shin-bone or tibia.—**cne-mi-al** (nē′mi-ạl), *a.*

co-. [L. *co-*, a form of *com-* used before a vowel or *h*: see *com-*.] A prefix of Latin origin, meaning 'with,' 'together,' 'jointly,' 'reciprocally,' 'mutually,' freely used as an English formative, as in *coadaptation*, *coadventurer*, *codefendant*, *cofounder*, *cotrustee*, and many other (mostly self-explanatory) words. In certain mathematical and astronomical terms *co-* represents NL. *complementi*, 'of the complement,' or E. *complement*, as in *cosine*, *cotangent*, *co-altitude*, *co-declination*.

coach (kōch), *n.* [F. *coche*, < Hung. *kocsi*; named from a village in Hungary.] A large, close, four-wheeled carriage, often a public passenger-vehicle; a railroad passenger-car, esp. one of the ordinary kind as distinguished from a parlor-car, a sleeping-car, etc.; also, a private tutor who prepares a candidate for an examination; one who instructs others in preparation for an athletic contest, etc.; a member of a baseball club stationed near first or third base to advise the players of his team while they run the bases.—**coach,** *v.* **I.** *tr.* To convey in a coach; also, to give instruction or advice to in the capacity of a coach. **II.** *intr.* To ride or drive in a coach; also, to act as a coach; study with or be instructed by a coach.—**coach′=dog,** *n.* One of a breed of dogs trained to accompany a vehicle, resembling the pointer in form and stature, and of a white color profusely marked with small black or liver-colored spots. Also called *Dalmatian dog*.—**coach-ee** (kō′chē̦), *n.* A coach-driver. [Colloq.]—**coach′er,** *n.*—**coach′=fel″low,** *n.* Either of a pair of coach-horses; hence, a close companion; a comrade.—**coach′ful** (-fůl), *n.*; pl. *-fuls*.—**coach′=horse,** *n.* A horse used or fitted to draw a coach.—**coach′man** (-mạn), *n.*; pl. *-men*. A man employed to drive a coach or carriage; also, a certain kind of artificial fly for angling.—**coach′man-ship,** *n.* The work of a coachman; skill in driving a coach.

co-act (kō̦-akt′), *v. t.* [L. *coactus*, pp. of *cogere*: see *cogent*.] To compel or coerce; control. [Obs. or archaic.]—**co-ac′tion** (-ak′shọn), *n.*—**co-ac′tive,** *a.* Compulsory; coercive.

co=act (kō-akt′), *v. i.* [See *co-*.] To act together. See Shakspere's "Troilus and Cressida," v. 2. 118.—**co=ac′tion** (-ak′shọn), *n.* Action in concert.—**co=ac′tive,** *a.*—**co=ac′tor,** *n.*

co-ad-just (kō-ạ-just′), *v. t.* [See *co-*.] To adjust mutually, or each to the other.—**co-ad-just′ment,** *n.*

co-ad-ju-tor (kō-ạ-jö′tọr), *n.* [L., < *co-*, with, + *adjutor*, helper, < *adjuvare*: see *aid*.] One who helps another; an assistant; *eccles.*, an assistant to a bishop or other ecclesiastic; also, a bishop appointed as assistant to another bishop, with the right of succession.—**co-ad-ju′tor-ship,** *n.*—**co-ad-ju′tress,** *n.* A female assistant. Also **co-ad-ju′trix.**

co-ad-ju-vant (kō-aj′ọ̈-vạnt). [See *co-* and *adjuvant*.] **I.** *a.* Assisting; coöperating. **II.** *n.* A coöperating agent; an ingredient serving to increase the effect of another ingredient in a medical prescription.—**co-ad′ju-van-cy,** *n.*

co-ad-u-nate (kō̦-ạd′ụ̄-nāt), *v. t.*; *-nated*, *-nating*. [LL. *coadunatus*, pp. of *coadunare*, < *co-*, with, + *adunare*, make one, < L. *ad*, to, + *unus*, one.] To make one; unite; combine.—**co-ad′u-nate** (-nạ̄t), *a.* United; combined.—**co-ad-u-na′tion** (-nā′shọn), *n.*

co-a-gen-cy (kō-ā′jẹn-si), *n.* [See *co-*.] Joint agency.—**co-a′gent,** *n.* A joint agent; an assistant.

co-ag-u-la-ble (kō̦-ag′ụ̄-lạ-bl), *a.* Capable of being coagulated.—**co-ag″u-la-bil′i-ty** (-bil′i-ti), *n.*

co-ag-u-late (kō̦-ag′ụ̄-lāt), *v. t.* or *i.*; *-lated*, *-lating*. [L. *coagulatus*, pp. of *coagulare*, < *coagulum*: see *coagulum*.] To change from a fluid into a thickened mass; curdle; clot; congeal.—**co-ag-u-la′tion** (-lā′shọn), *n.* The act of coagulating; also, a coagulated mass.—**co-ag′u-la-tive** (-lạ̄-tiv), *a.* Tending to coagulate.—**co-ag′u-la-tor** (-lā-tọr), *n.* A coagulating agent.

co-ag-u-len (kō̦-ag′ụ̄-len), *n.* [L. *coagulum*: see *coagulum*.] A concentrated preparation of thrombin or allied substances which causes the clotting of blood and is used to stop hemorrhage.

co-ag-u-lin (kō̦-ag′ụ̄-lin), *n.* [L. *coagulum*: see *coagulum*.] Any of various coagulators (substances) produced in animal organisms by the injection of certain proteid solutions.

co-ag-u-lum (kō̦-ag′ụ̄-lum), *n.*; pl. *-la* (-lạ̈). [L., < *cogere*, collect, curdle: see *cogent*.] A coagulating agent†; also, a coagulated mass; a clot, as of blood.

coak (kōk), *n.* [Origin uncertain.] In *ship-carp.*, a projection from a piece of wood or timber fitting into a hole in another piece at their joint, or a cylinder or pin of hard wood or the like let into both pieces.—**coak,** *v. t.* To unite, as the ends of two pieces of wood, by means of a coak or coaks.

coal (kōl), *n.* [AS. *col* = D. *kool* = G. *kohle* = Icel. *kol.*] A piece of wood or other combustible substance either glowing ('live coal') or charred or burned out; also, charcoal; also, a black or dark-brown combustible mineral substance consisting of carbonized vegetable matter, used as a fuel (as, hard *coal,* anthracite; soft *coal,* bituminous coal; brown *coal,* lignite); a piece of this substance.—**white coal.** See under *white, a.*—**coal,** *v.* **I.** *tr.* To burn to coal or charcoal; also, to provide with coal. **II.** *intr.* To take in coal for fuel, as a vessel.—**coal′=black′,** *a.* Black as coal; very black.—**coal′=box,** *n.* Same as *black Maria* (explosive shell): see under *black, a.* [Soldiers' slang.]—**coal′er,** *n.*

co-a-lesce (kō-ạ-les′), *v. i.*; *-lesced, -lescing.* [L. *coalescere* (pp. *coalitus*), < *co-,* with, + *alescere,* grow up, < *alere,* nourish.] To grow together or into one body; unite so as to form one mass, party, community, etc.: as, "The wide earth . . . has converged and *coalesced* in all its various parts into one Rome" (J. H. Newman's "Callista," xxviii.).—**co-a-les′cence** (-les′ẹns), *n.* The act of coalescing; growth into one body; union into one mass, party, etc.—**co-a-les′cent,** *a.* Coalescing; growing together.

coal=field (kōl′fēld), *n.* An area containing coal deposits.

coal-fish (kōl′fish), *n.* An Atlantic food-fish, *Pollachius carbonarius,* a species of pollack; also, the beshow, *Anoplopoma fimbria*; also, the sergeant-fish, *Rachycentron canadus.*

coal=gas (kōl′gas), *n.* The gas formed by burning coal; also, a gas used for illuminating and heating, produced by distilling bituminous coal.

coal=goose (kōl′gös), *n.* A cormorant. [Eng.]

coal=heav-er (kōl′hē″vėr), *n.* One who carries or shovels coal.

coal-ing=sta-tion (kō′ling-stā″shọn), *n.* A station or place at which coal is stored for supplying vessels, as of a navy, or locomotives.

co-a-li-tion (kō-ạ-lish′ọn), *n.* [ML. *coalitio(n-),* < L. *coalescere*: see *coalesce.*] Growth into one body; union in a body or mass; combination, as of interests; esp., a temporary political alliance between persons, parties, or states (as, "Carteret . . . aimed at a German *coalition,* for the purpose of wresting Alsace and Lorraine from France": Lecky's "Hist. of Eng. in the 18th Century," iii.).—**co-a-li′tion-ist,** *n.* An adherent of a coalition.

co-a-lize (kō′ạ-līz), *v. t.*; *-lized, -lizing.* [F. *coaliser,* < L. *coalescere*: see *coalesce.*] To join in a coalition.—**co′a-liz-er** (-lī-zėr), *n.*

coal-less (kōl′les), *a.* Having or containing no coal.

coal=meas-ures (kōl′mezh″ụrz), *n. pl.* In *geol.,* coal-bearing strata; specif., a portion of the Carboniferous system, characterized by coal deposits.

coal=mine (kōl′mīn), *n.* A mine or pit from which coal is obtained.—**coal′=min″er,** *n.*—**coal′=min″ing,** *n.*

coal=oil (kōl′oil), *n.* Orig., an oil obtained by distilling coal, etc., formerly much used for illuminating purposes; hence, petroleum or, esp., kerosene.

coal=pit (kōl′pit), *n.* A place where charcoal is made (now only in U. S.); also, a pit where coal is dug.

coal=plant (kōl′plant), *n.* A fossil plant found in association with or entering into the composition of coal.

coal=pock-et (kōl′pok″et), *n.* A structure with bunkers and appliances for receiving, storing, and loading coal.

coal=sack (kōl′sak), *n.* A sack made of strong, coarse material, for containing or carrying coal; in *astron.,* any of the dark spaces, almost completely devoid of stars, in the Milky Way, esp. [*cap.*] a large one near the constellation Crux.

coal=tar (kōl′tär), *n.* A thick, black, viscid liquid which is formed during the distillation of coal (as in the manufacture of illuminating gas), and which upon further distillation yields various important products, as benzene, anthracene, phenol, etc. (from which are derived a large number of dyes and synthetic compounds), and a final residuum ('coal-tar pitch') which is used in making pavements, etc.

coal=tit (kōl′tit), *n.* A European titmouse (bird), *Parus ater,* with black markings on the head and throat.

co=al-ti-tude (kō-al′ti-tūd), *n.* [See *co-.*] In *astron., surv.,* etc., the complement of the altitude.

coal=whip-per (kōl′whip″ėr), *n.* One who or a machine that raises coal from the hold of a ship to unload it. [Eng.]

coal-y (kō′li), *a.* Of, like, or containing coal.

coam-ing (kō′ming), *n.* [Origin uncertain.] *Naut.,* a raised border around a hatchway or other opening in a deck, designed to prevent water from running below; also, one of the pieces, esp. of the fore-and-aft pieces, of such a border.

co-ap-tate (kọ-ap′tāt), *v. t.*; *-tated, -tating.* [LL. *coaptatus,* pp. of *coaptare,* < L. *co-,* with, + *aptare,* fit, < *aptus*: see *apt.*] To fit together, as in surgical adjustment of broken bones.—**co-ap-ta-tion** (kō-ap-tā′shọn), *n.*

co-arb (kō′ärb), *n.* [Ir. *comharba.*] In the Celtic church, a successor in an ecclesiastical office.

co-arc-tate (kọ-ärk′tāt), *a.* [L. *coarctatus,* pp. of *coarctare, coartare,* < *co-,* with, + *artare,* press together.] Pressed together; compressed; contracted; in *entom.,* of a pupa, inclosed in an oval corneous case, and having no external indication of the organs.—**co-arc-ta-tion** (kō-ärk-tā′shọn), *n.*

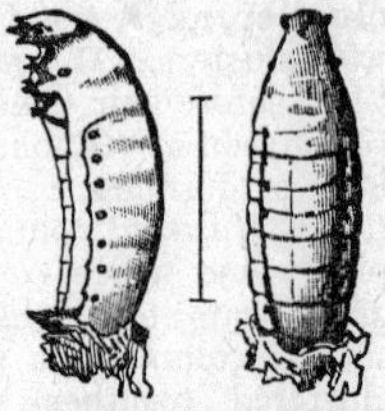

Coarctate Pupa, lateral and dorsal views. (Vertical line shows natural size.)

coarse (kōrs), *a.*; compar. *coarser,* superl. *coarsest.* [Appar. < *course,* as denoting ordinary procedure, and hence perhaps common use or quality.] Ordinary; common; also, wanting in fineness or delicacy of texture, structure, etc.; composed of relatively large parts or particles; also, rough or rude (as, *coarse* fare); inclement, as weather (now chiefly prov.); harsh, as sound; also, wanting in delicacy of perception, feeling, manner, etc.; not refined; vulgar; often, indelicate; indecent.—**coarse′ly,** *adv.*—**coars′en,** *v. t.* or *i.* To make or become coarse.—**coarse′ness,** *n.*

coast (kōst), *n.* [OF. *coste* (F. *côte*), < L. *costa,* rib, side.] The side, as of the body†; the side, edge, or margin of the land next to the sea; the seashore, or the region adjoining it; [often *cap.*] with *the,* any of certain littoral regions, as, in the U. S., the region bordering on the Pacific Ocean; [*l. c.*] the boundary or border of a country (archaic); a tract or region, as of the earth†; also, a snowy or icy hillside or incline down which one may slide on a sled; also, a slide down such an incline; a ride down a hill, etc., as on a bicycle, without using pedals or propelling power.—**coast,** *v.* **I.** *tr.* To keep alongside of (a person moving)†; go or pass by the side or border of†; proceed along the coast of; go along or near to (a coast). **II.** *intr.* To approach†; go or pass (*along,* etc.)†; proceed in a roundabout way†; border†; proceed or sail along, or sail from port to port of, a coast; also, to slide on a sled down a snowy or icy hillside or incline; descend a hill, etc., as on a bicycle, without using pedals or propelling power.—**coast′al,** *a.* Of or pertaining to a coast.—**coast′er,** *n.* One who or that which coasts; a vessel engaged in coastwise trade; also, one who lives near a coast; also, one who coasts on a sled or a bicycle; a sled or the like for use in coasting; also, an amusement railway with dips and curves, on which cars run by gravity; also, a tray, sometimes on wheels, for holding a decanter to be passed around a dining-table (as, "a pair of silver *coasters* . . . one holding a cut-glass decanter of Madeira, the other awaiting its customary bottle of claret": F. H. Smith's "Colonel Carter of Cartersville," i.).—**coast′er=brake,** *n.* A form of brake in bicycles which are fitted with a free-wheel, operated by back pressure on the pedals: so called because a person may coast with such a bicycle when the pedals are held stationary.—**coast′=guard,** *n.* A guard stationed on or along the coast; esp., in Great Britain, orig. a guard for the prevention of smuggling, now a general police force for the coast; in the U. S., the body of men employed in the coastal life-saving service.—**coast′ward, coast′wards** (-wạrd, -wạrdz), *adv.* Toward the coast.—**coast′wise,** *adv.* and *a.* Along the coast.

coat (kōt), *n.* [OF. *cote* (F. *cotte*), < ML. *cota, cotta*; perhaps from Teut.] An outer garment with sleeves, covering the upper part of the body; a tunic† or chiton†; a petticoat or skirt (obs. or prov.); a coat of arms; vesture as indicating profession, class, etc.†, or profession, class, etc., so indicated†; a natural integument or covering, as the hair, fur, or wool of an animal, the bark of a tree, or the skin of a fruit; one of a number of concentric layers, as of an onion; a thin layer of something, as paint or varnish, covering a surface; fig., anything that covers or conceals. —**coat of arms,** in *her.*, a surcoat or tabard embroidered with heraldic devices, worn by medieval knights over their armor; also, the complete heraldic bearings of a person; a hatchment; an escutcheon. —**coat of mail,** a defensive garment made of interlinked metal rings, overlapping metal plates, etc. See *mail*[1], *n.*—**coat,** *v. t.* To cover or provide with a coat; also, to cover with a layer or coating; cover as a layer or coating does.—**coat′=card,** *n.* See *court-card.*—**coat-ee** (kō-tē′), *n.* A short coat.

Coat of Mail, western Europe; 13th century.

co-a-ti (kọ-ä′tē), *n.*; pl. *-tis* (-tēz). [Brazilian.] Either of two tropical American animals constituting the genus *Nasua*, nearly related to the racoon, and having an elongated body, a long tail, and an attenuated, flexible snout. Also **co-a″-ti-mon′di, co-a″ti-mun′di** (-mon′dē, -mun′dē).

Red Coati (*Nasua rufa*).

coat-ing (kō′ting), *n.* A layer of any substance spread over a surface; also, material for making coats.

co=au-thor (kō-â′thọr), *n.* [See *co-*.] A joint author.

coax (kōks), *v.* [From obs. *cokes*, a fool; origin uncertain.] **I.** *tr.* To befool†; also, to fondle†; also, to influence by blandishments or gentle persuasions (as, "a froward child, that must be humour'd and *coax'd* a little till it falls asleep": Goldsmith's "Good-Natured Man," i.); wheedle; cajole. **II.** *intr.* To use blandishing persuasions. — **coax′er,** *n.* — **coax′-ing-ly,** *adv.*

co-ax-i-al (kō-ak′si-ạl), *a.* [See *co-*.] Having a common axis.—**co-ax′i-al-ly,** *adv.*

cob[1] (kob), *n.* [Origin obscure.] A roundish mass, lump, or heap (now chiefly prov. Eng.); a cobnut; a building material of clay, straw, etc.; a seeding head of wheat, clover, etc. (prov. Eng.); the cylindrical shoot on which the grains of maize grow; a corn-cob; a man of importance, or a leader (now prov. Eng.); a short-legged, thick-set horse; a male swan; the old Spanish dollar, or peso.

cob[2] (kob), *n.* [= East Fries. *kobbe.*] A gull; esp., the great black-backed gull, *Larus marinus*.

cob[3] (kob), *v. t.*; *cobbed, cobbing.* [Cf. ME. *cobben*, fight.] To strike; beat; esp., to beat on the buttocks with something flat.

co-bæ-a (kọ-bē′ạ), *n.* [NL.; from B. *Cobo* (1582–1657), Spanish missionary and naturalist.] Any plant of the polemoniaceous genus *Rosenbergia* (or *Cobæa*), of tropical America, esp. *R. scandens*, a vine with pinnate leaves and large bell-shaped purple or white flowers, familiar in cultivation.

Flower of Cobæa (*Rosenbergia scandens*).

co-balt (kō′bâlt), *n.* [G. *kobalt*, prob. = *kobold*, goblin.] Chem. sym., Co; at. wt., 58.97; sp. gr., 8.52 to 8.95. A metallic element of a silver-white color with a faint pinkish tinge, occurring in compounds some of which afford important blue coloring substances.—**cobalt blue, cobalt green,** etc., pigments consisting of cobalt compounds.—**co-bal-tic** (kọ-bâl′tik), *a.* Of or containing cobalt. See *cobaltous.*—**co-bal-tif-er-ous** (kō-bâl-tif′ẹ-rus), *a.* [See *-ferous.*] Containing or yielding cobalt.—**co′bal-tite** (-tīt), *n.* A mineral containing cobalt, arsenic, and sulphur.—**co-bal′tous,** *a.* Containing cobalt (in larger proportion than a corresponding cobaltic compound).

co-bang (kō′bang), *n.* See *kobang*.

cob-ble[1] (kob′l), *n.* [Cf. *cob*[1].] A cobblestone.—**cob′ble**[1], *v. t.*; *-bled, -bling.* To pave with cobblestones.

cob-ble[2] (kob′l), *v. t.*; *-bled, -bling.* [Appar. < *cobbler.*] To mend (shoes, etc.); patch; also, to put together roughly or clumsily.

cob-ble[3] (kob′l), *n.* See *coble*.

cob-bler (kob′lėr), *n.* [Origin uncertain: cf. *cobble*[2], appar. a later word.] One who mends shoes; also, a clumsy workman; also, an iced drink made of wine, fruit-juice, etc.; also, a fruit pie baked in a deep dish lined with thick paste (U. S.).

cob-ble-stone (kob′l-stōn), *n.* A naturally rounded stone, of a size suitable for use in paving.

co-ble (kō′bl or kob′l), *n.* [ME. *coble*: cf. AS. (Northumbrian) *cuopel* and W. *ceubal.*] A kind of flat-bottomed rowboat (Sc.) or fishing-boat (north. Eng. and Sc.).

cob-nut (kob′nut), *n.* The nut of certain cultivated varieties of hazel; a tree bearing such nuts; also, a children's game played with nuts.

co-bold (kō′bold), *n.* See *kobold*.

co-bra (kō′brạ), *n.*; pl. *-bras.* [Pg., < L. *colubra*, serpent.] The cobra-de-capello; also, some related snake, as an asp, *Naja haje*, of Africa.—**co′bra=de=ca-pel′lo** (-dē-kạ-pel′ō), *n.* [Pg. *cobra de capello*, 'serpent of (the) hood.'] A very venomous snake, *Naja tripudians*, of the warmer parts of Asia, esp. India, having the power of dilating the head and neck so that they assume a hood-like form.

Cobra-de-capello.

cob-web (kob′web), *n.* [ME. *coppeweb* (*coppe*, spider).] The web or net spun by a spider to catch its prey; a single thread spun by a spider; fig., a network of plot or intrigue; an insidious snare; also, anything fine-spun, flimsy, or unsubstantial (as, "I cannot but lament thy splendid wit Entangled in the *cobwebs* of the schools": Cowper's "Task," iv. 726); also, any musty accumulation, accretion, etc.—**cob′webbed,** *a.* Covered or hung with cobwebs.—**cob′web″by,** *a.* Of or like a cobweb; cobwebbed.

cob-work (kob′wėrk), *n.* Work consisting of logs laid horizontally with the ends joined so as to form a rectangular or other inclosure, as in a log house.

co-ca (kō′kạ), *n.* [Sp.; from Peruvian.] A shrub, *Erythroxylum coca*, native in the Andes and cultivated elsewhere, or its dried leaves, which are chewed for their stimulant properties and which yield cocaine and other alkaloids.

co-ca-ine (kō′kạ-in, commonly kọ-kān′), *n.* [From *coca.*] A bitter crystalline alkaloid, obtained from coca leaves, used as a local anesthetic and as a stimulant. — **co′ca-in-ism,** *n.* The morbid condition due to excessive or habitual use of cocaine.—**co′ca-in-ize** (-īz), *v. t.*; *-ized, -izing.* To treat with or affect by cocaine.—**co″ca-in-i-za′tion** (-i-zā′shọn), *n.*

Flowering Branch of Coca.

cocco-, cocc-. Forms of Gr. κόκκος, grain, seed, or of NL. *coccus* (see *coccus*), used in combination.—**coc-coid** (kok′oid). [See *-oid.*] **I.** *a.* Resembling or pertaining to a coccus; berry-like; globose, as certain micro-organisms. **II.** *n.* A coccoid micro-organism.—**coc-co-lith** (kok′ǫ-lith), *n.* [+ *-lith.*] A minute calcareous body found in the ooze of sea-beds, and supposed to be formed by a unicellular plant.—**coc′co-sphere** (-sfēr), *n.* A spheroidal mass of coccoliths.

coc-cu-lus in-di-cus (kok′ū-lus in′di-kus). [NL., 'little berry of India.'] The dried, berry-like fruit of a menispermaceous climbing shrub, *Anamirta cocculus* (or *paniculata*), of the East Indies, containing the bitter poisonous principle called *picrotoxin.*

coc-cus (kok′us), *n.*; pl. *cocci* (kok′sī). [NL., < Gr. κόκκος, grain, seed.] In *bot.*, one of the carpels of a schizocarp; in *bact.*, a spherical bacterium, as a micrococcus; in *zoöl.*, any of the homopterous insects constituting the genus *Coccus*, as *C. cacti*, the insect yielding cochineal, or *C.* (or *Kermes*) *ilicis*, the insect yielding kermes; in *phar.*, cochineal.

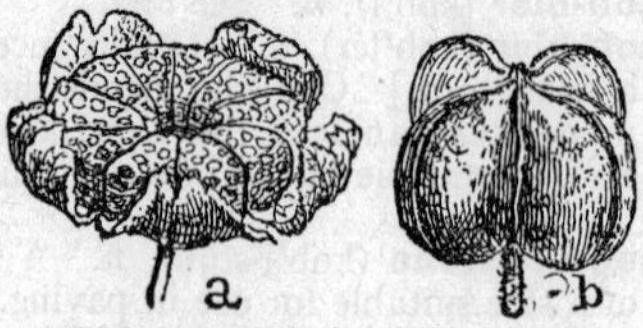

a, Fruit composed of ten Cocci; *b*, Fruit composed of four Cocci.

coc-cyx (kok′siks), *n.*; pl. *coccyges* (kok-sī′jēz). [NL., < Gr. κόκκυξ, coccyx, orig. cuckoo.] In *anat.*, a small triangular bone forming the lower extremity of the spinal column in man, consisting of four ankylosed rudimentary vertebræ; also, a corresponding part in certain other animals.—**coc-cyg-e-al** (kok-sij′ę-ąl), *a.*

co-chin (kō′chin), *n.* [From *Cochin China*, in southeastern Asia.] One of a breed of large domestic fowls, of Asiatic origin, resembling the brahma but slightly smaller.

coch-i-neal (koch′i-nēl or koch-i-nēl′), *n.* [F. *cochenille*, < Sp. *cochinilla*, < L. *coccinus*, scarlet, < *coccum*, < Gr. κόκκος, grain, seed, kermes.] A red dyestuff consisting of the dried bodies of the females of a scale-insect, *Coccus cacti*, which lives on various cactuses, as the nopal, of Mexico, Central America, and other warm regions; also, the insect itself. Cf. *kermes.*

Female Cochineal; dried specimen of commerce. (Line shows natural size.)

coch-le-a (kok′lę-ą), *n.*; pl. *-leæ* (-lę-ē). [L., < Gr. κοχλίας, snail, something spiral.] In *anat.*, a division of the internal ear, in man and most other mammals spiral in form.—**coch′le-ar** (-ąr), *a.* Of or pertaining to the cochlea.—**coch′le-ate, coch′le-at-ed** (-āt, -ā-ted), *a.* [L. *cochleatus.*] Shaped like a snail-shell; spiral.

cock[1] (kok), *n.* [AS. *coc* = OF. *coc*, F. *coq*, = ML. *coccus*; prob. ult. imit.] The male of the domestic fowl; the male of any of various birds, esp. of the gallinaceous kind; the crowing of the cock, or the time of its crowing, in the early morning (archaic); a figure or representation of a cock (one of the national emblems of France: from a word-play on the Latin *gallus*, a cock, and *Gallus*, a Gaul); a weather-vane in the shape of a cock; a weathercock; a leader or ruling spirit, often one who makes a vainglorious show of leadership or victory (as, *cock* of the walk); a chap or fellow (colloq.); a device for permitting or arresting the flow of a liquid or gas from a receptacle or through a pipe; a faucet, tap, or valve; in a firearm, that part of the lock which by its fall or action causes the discharge; the hammer; the position into which the cock or hammer of a firearm is brought by being drawn partly or completely back, preparatory to firing; the gnomon of a sun-dial; the mark aimed at in the game of curling; a cock-and-bull story (slang, Eng.).—**cock=and=bull story,** an idle, improbable story given out as true (as, "They told some *cock and bull stories* about their being kings and princes at home": Irving's "Knickerbocker's New York," ii. 3); a canard.—**cock**[1], *a.* Of birds and, sometimes, other animals, male.—**cock**[1], *v. t.* To pull back and set the cock or hammer of (a firearm), preparatory to firing.

Head of Domestic Cock.

cock[2] (kok), *v.* [Prob. < *cock*[1].] **I.** *intr.* To strut, swagger, or put on airs of importance (now prov.); also, to stand or stick up conspicuously. **II.** *tr.* To set or turn up or to one side, often in an assertive, jaunty, or significant manner; put (one's hat) jauntily on one side of the head; turn up the brim of (a hat).—**cock**[2], *n.* An act of cocking; cocked position; an upward turn; something cocked, as part of the brim of a hat (as, "One of the *cocks* of his hat having fallen down, he let it hang from that day forth": Stevenson's "Treasure Island," i.).

cock[3] (kok), *n.* [ME. *cocke*: cf. Icel. *kökkr*, lump.] A conical pile, as of hay.—**cock**[3], *v. t.* To pile (hay, etc.) in cocks: as, "I hope Barnes has got my hay made and safe *cocked* by this time" (Smollett's "Humphry Clinker," June 14).

cock[4]† (kok), *n.* [OF. *coque*, *coque*, boat, ship; origin uncertain.] A small boat; a cockboat. See Shakspere's "King Lear," iv. 6. 19.

cock[5] (kok), *n.* A perverted form substituted for *God* in oaths. [Obs. or archaic.]

cock=a=bon-dy (kok-ą-bon′di), *n.*; pl. *-dies* (-diz). [W. *coch a bon ddu*, 'red with black trunk or stem.'] A certain kind of artificial fly for angling.

cock-ade (ko-kād′), *n.* [F. *cocarde*, < *coq*, cock: see *cock*[1].] A knot of ribbon, a rosette, or the like, worn on the hat as a badge or a part of a livery.—**cock-ad-ed** (ko-kā′ded), *a.*

cock=a=doo-dle=doo (kok″ą-dö-dl-dö′), *interj.* and *n.* [Imit.] An imitation of the crow of the cock.

cock=a=hoop (kok-ą-höp′), *adv.* and *a.* [Orig. in phrase *to set cock a* (or *on*) *hoop*, to set liquor flowing freely, cast off restraint.] In a state of unrestrained joy or exultation: as, "Yes, it makes you *cock-a-hoop* to be 'Rider' to your troop" (Kipling's "Gentlemen-Rankers").

Cock-aigne (ko-kān′), *n.* [OF. *cokaigne* (F. *cocagne*); origin uncertain.] An imaginary land of luxury and idleness.

cock-a-leek-ie (kok-ą-lē′ki), *n.* See *cockie-leekie.*

cock-a-lo-rum (kok-ą-lō′rum), *n.* [A humorous formation < *cock*[1], appar. simulating Latin.] A person of consequence; a self-important person; also, boastful talk. [Colloq.]

cock-a-teel (kok-ą-tēl′), *n.* [D. *kaketielje*: cf. *cockatoo.*] A small, long-tailed Australian parrot, *Calopsitta novæ-hollandiæ*, common as a cage-bird.

cock-a-too (kok-ą-tö′), *n.*; pl. *-toos* (-töz′). [Malay *kakatūa.*] Any of the crested parrots constituting the genus *Cacatua* or subfamily *Cacatuinæ*, of the East Indies, Australia, etc., often white, or white and yellow, pink, or red.

Cockatoo.

cock-a-trice (kok′ą-tris or -trīs), *n.* [OF. *cocatris*, from a ML. form from L. *calcare*, tread, used to render Gr. ἰχνεύμων, 'tracker,' E. *ichneumon.* In later use associated with the cock.] A fabulous serpent with deadly glance, reputed to be hatched by a serpent from a cock's egg, and commonly represented with the head, legs, and wings of a cock and the body and tail of a serpent; in the Bible, some species of venomous serpent.

Cockatrice as a heraldic bearing.

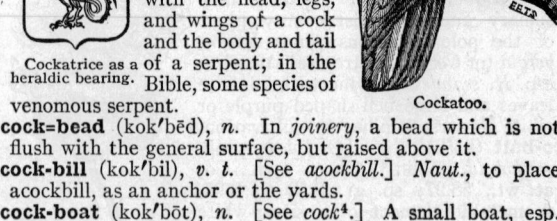

cock=bead (kok′bēd), *n.* In *joinery*, a bead which is not flush with the general surface, but raised above it.

cock-bill (kok′bil), *v. t.* [See *acockbill.*] *Naut.*, to place acockbill, as an anchor or the yards.

cock-boat (kok′bōt), *n.* [See *cock*[4].] A small boat, esp. one used as a tender.

cock-cha-fer (kok′chā″fėr), *n.* A large scarabæid beetle, *Melolontha vulgaris*, of Europe, in both the larval and perfect forms destructive to vegetation; also, any of various allied beetles.

cock-crow (kok′krō), *n.* The crowing of a cock; also, the time at which cocks crow, esp. at dawn; hence, dawn. Also **cock′crow″ing.**

cocked (kokt), *p. a.* Turned up or to one side.—**cocked hat,** any of various styles of hat having the brim turned up, esp. on two opposite sides or triangularly on three sides; also, a hat pointed before and behind and in lateral view of a triangular form, worn as part of certain naval, military, and other official costumes; also, a game similar to ninepins, but employing only three pins, which are set up in triangular position.

cock-er[1] (kok′ėr), *n.* One who promotes or patronizes cock-fighting; also, one of a breed of small spaniels trained for use in hunting or kept as pets (also called 'cocker spaniel').

cock-er[2] (kok′ėr), *v. t.* [Origin uncertain.] To indulge; pamper: as, "I have not been *cockered* in wantonness or indulgence" (Scott's "Quentin Durward," xiii.).

cock-er-el (kok′e̦-rel), *n.* [Dim. of *cock*[1].] A young domestic cock.

cock′er span′iel. See *cocker*[1].

cock-et (kok′et), *n.* [Origin uncertain.] A seal of the custom-house; also, a document sealed and delivered by custom-house officers as a warrant that goods have been duly entered and have paid duty. [Eng.]

cock-eye (kok′ī), *n.* An eye that squints, or is affected with strabismus.—**cock′eyed,** *a.*

cock=fight (kok′fīt), *n.* A fight between cocks; a match between game-cocks, usually armed with steel spurs.—**cock′=fight″ing,** *n.* The fighting of cocks, esp. as a sport.

cock-horse (kok′hôrs′), *n.* A child's rocking-horse or hobby-horse.

cock-ie=leek-ie (kok-i-lē′ki), *n.* Soup made of a cock or other fowl boiled with leeks. [Sc.]

cock-i-ly (kok′i-li), *adv.* In a cocky manner; smartly; pertly. [Colloq.]—**cock′i-ness,** *n.*

cock-ing (kok′ing), *n.* Cock-fighting; also, the shooting of woodcocks.

cock-ish (kok′ish), *a.* Cock-like; cocky. [Colloq.]

cock=laird (kok′lãrd), *n.* The owner and cultivator of a small landed property. [Humorous, Sc.]

cock-le[1] (kok′l), *n.* [OF. F. *coquille*, < L. *conchylium*, < Gr. κογχύλιον, < κόγχη, mussel or cockle, E. *conch.*] Any of the bivalve mollusks, with somewhat heart-shaped, radially ribbed valves, which constitute the genus *Cardium*, esp. *C. edule*, the common edible species of Europe; any of various allied or similar mollusks; also, a cockle-shell; also, a small shallow or light boat; a small crisp confection of sugar and flour, bearing a motto (U. S.); a wrinkle or pucker; *pl.*, the cockles of the heart.—**cockles of the heart,** the inmost recesses or depths of the heart.—**cock′le**[1], *v.*; *-led, -ling.* **I.** *intr.* To contract into wrinkles; pucker; of the sea, to rise into short, irregular waves. **II.** *tr.* To cause to wrinkle or pucker.

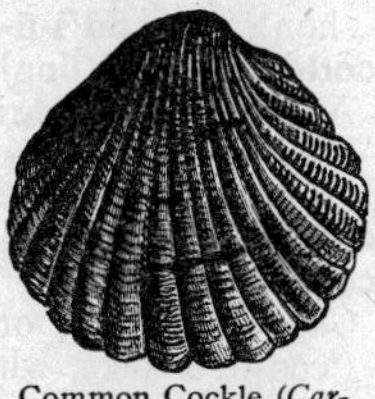
Common Cockle (*Cardium edule*).

cock-le[2] (kok′l), *n.* [AS. *coccel.*] The corn-cockle; also, darnel.

cock-le[3] (kok′l), *n.* [Origin uncertain.] Any of various forms of stove; also, any of certain parts of a stove, as the fire-chamber of an air-stove.

cock-le=bur (kok′l-bėr), *n.* Any plant of the ambrosiaceous genus *Xanthium*, comprising coarse weeds with spiny burs; also, the burdock, *Arctium lappa.*

cock-le=hat (kok′l-hat), *n.* A hat adorned with a cockle-shell, the badge of a pilgrim. See Shakspere's "Hamlet," iv. 5. 25.

cock-ler (kok′lėr), *n.* One who gathers or sells cockles or mollusks.

cock-le=shell (kok′l-shel), *n.* The shell of the cockle, or one of its valves; also, a small, light boat.

cock-loft (kok′lôft), *n.* A small upper loft; a small garret.

cock-ney (kok′ni). [ME. *cokeney*, appar. 'cock's egg,' an imperfect egg (ME. *ey*, egg).] **I.** *n.*; pl. *-neys* (-niz). An egg† (see etym.); a pampered child†; a squeamish, affected, or effeminate person†; a native or a permanent resident of London (usually with disparaging force, and often with reference to certain classes of the population characterized by marked peculiarities of pronunciation and dialect). **II.** *a.* Of or pertaining to cockneys or their dialect.—**cock′ney-dom** (-do̦m), *n.* The region of cockneys; also, cockneys collectively.—**cock′ney-fy** (-fī), *v. t.*; *-fied, -fying.* [See *-fy.*] To give a cockney character to.—**cock″ney-fi-ca′-tion** (-fi-kā′sho̦n), *n.*—**cock′ney-ish,** *a.* Cockney-like.—**cock′ney-ism,** *n.* Cockney quality or usage; also, a cockney peculiarity, as of speech.

cock-pit (kok′pit), *n.* A pit or inclosed place for cock-fights; a place where a contest is fought, or which has been the scene of many contests or battles (as, Belgium, the *cockpit* of Europe); the pit of a theater†; in some aëroplanes, an inclosed space containing a seat, as for a pilot or passenger; *naut.*, in the old type of war-ship, an apartment below the water-line, used as quarters for certain officers and as a place for the wounded; hence, a depression in the deck of a boat; esp., in yachts, the pit (abaft the cabin) occupied by the helmsman, etc.

cock-roach (kok′rōch), *n.* [Sp. *cucaracha.*] Any of various orthopterous insects of the family *Blattidæ*, usually of nocturnal habits and having a flattened body, as *Stylopyga* (or *Periplaneta*) *orientalis*, a common large black species (often called 'black beetle'), *Periplaneta americana*, a large reddish-brown tropical American species which has been introduced into many seaports, and *Blattella* (or *Phyllodromia*) *germanica*, the croton-bug, a small brownish or yellowish species introduced into America from Europe and now commonly found in kitchens, around water-pipes, etc.

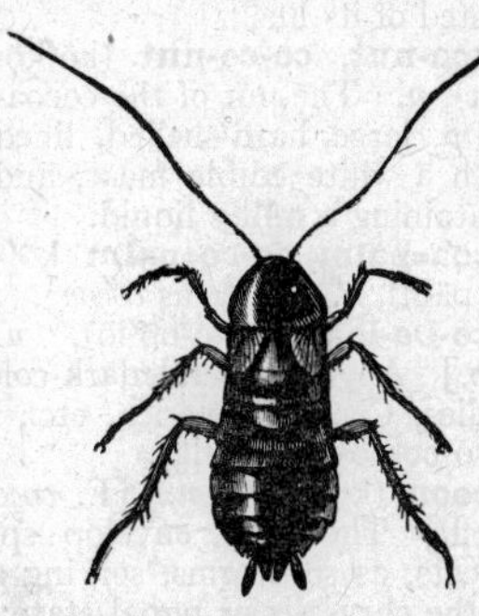
Female Cockroach (*Stylopyga orientalis*).

cock=rob-in (kok′rob′in), *n.* The male of the robin.

cocks-comb (koks′kōm), *n.* The comb or caruncle of a cock; the cap of a professional fool, resembling a cock's comb; the head†; a silly fellow†, fop†, or coxcomb†; also, an amarantaceous garden plant, *Celosia cristata*, with flowers, commonly crimson or purple, in a dense spike somewhat resembling the comb or crest of a cock; also, some other species of *Celosia.*

cocks-foot (koks′fu̇t), *n.* A tall, coarse perennial grass, *Dactylis glomerata*, valuable for hay and pasture: so called from the appearance of its branched panicle.

cock-shut (kok′shut), *n.* The close of the day; evening twilight. See Shakspere's "Richard III.," v. 3. 70. [Obs. or prov. Eng.]

cock-shy (kok′shī), *n.* The act or sport of shying or throwing missiles at a target, orig. a cock; also, the object thrown at; hence, an object of attack; also, a booth or the like where objects are thrown at targets, as for a prize.

Cockscomb (*Celosia cristata*).

cock-spur (kok′spėr), *n.* A spur of a cock; also, any of several plants with spur-like thorns or branches, esp. *Cratægus crus-galli*, a North American species of hawthorn.

cock=sure (kok′shör′), *a.* [Appar. < *cock*[1].] Perfectly secure or safe†; also, perfectly sure or certain; perfectly certain in one's own mind; also, too certain; overconfident.—**cock′=sure′,** *adv.*—**cock′=sure′ness,** *n.*

cock-swain (kok′swān, naut. kok′sn), *n.* See *coxswain.*

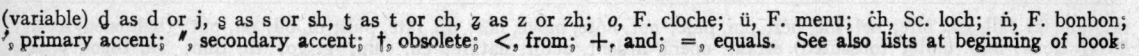

cock-tail (kok′tāl), *n.* A horse with a docked tail; a horse which is not thoroughbred; an underbred person; any of various alcoholic mixed drinks, containing spirits, bitters, etc. (orig. U. S.); a portion of raw oysters or clams, or of crab-meat or the like, served in a small glass with a sauce of tomato catchup and various other ingredients; a preparation of fruits served in a glass.

cock-y (kok'i), *a.* Arrogantly smart; pertly self-assertive; conceited. [Colloq.]

cock-y=leek'y, *n.* See *cockie-leekie.*

cock-y-ol-ly (kok-i-ol'i) **bird.** A pet name for any small bird.

co-coa[1], **co-co** (kō'kō), *n.* [Sp. and Pg. *coco.* The spelling *cocoa* is due to confusion with *cocoa*[2], *cacao.*] A tall tropical palm, *Cocos nucifera,* which produces the cocoanut; also, the cocoanut.

Cocoa-palm (*Cocos nucifera*).

co-coa[2] (kō'kō), *n.* [Corruption of *cacao.*] The roasted, husked, and ground seeds of the cacao, *Theobroma cacao,* from which much of the fat has been removed; also, a beverage made from this powder. —**co'coa=but'ter,** *n.* Same as *cacao-butter.*—**co'coa=nib,** *n.* A roasted cacao-seed divested of its husk.

co-coa-nut, co-co-nut (kō'kọ-nut), *n.* The nut of the cocoa-palm, large, hard-shelled, lined with a white edible meat, and containing a milky liquid.

co-coa=palm, co-co=palm (kō'-kọ-päm), *n.* Same as *cocoa*[1].

co-co-bo-lo (kō-kọ-bō'lō), *n.* [Sp.] Any of several dark-colored hard woods of the West Indies, Central America, etc., used in cabinet-making, etc. Also **co-co-bo'la** (-lạ̈).

co-coon (kọ-kön'), *n.* [F. *cocon,* < Pr. *coucoun,* < *coco,* shell.] The silky envelop spun by the larvæ of many insects, as silkworms, serving as a covering while they are in the chrysalis or pupal state; any of various similar protective coverings, as the silky case in which certain spiders inclose their eggs.—**co-coon',** *v.* **I.** *intr.* To form a cocoon. **II.** *tr.* To wrap as in a cocoon.—**co-coon'er-y,** *n.*; pl. *-ies* (-iz). A place for the care of silkworms.

co-cotte (ko-kot), *n.* [F., 'hen.'] In French use, a courtezan.

coc-tile (kok'til), *a.* [L. *coctilis,* < *coquere,* cook.] Made by baking, as bricks.

coc-tion (kok'shọn), *n.* [L. *coctio(n-),* < *coquere,* cook.] The process of cooking; also, digestion†.

cod[1] (kod), *n.* [AS. *codd.*] A bag†; also, a pod or shell, as of peas and beans; also, the scrotum.

cod[2] (kod), *n.*; pl. *cods* or (esp. collectively) *cod.* [ME. *cod;* origin uncertain.] An important food-fish, *Gadus callarias,* of the northern Atlantic, when fully grown measuring usually about 3 feet in length; any of various other fishes of this genus or allied genera; also, any of various similar but unrelated fishes.

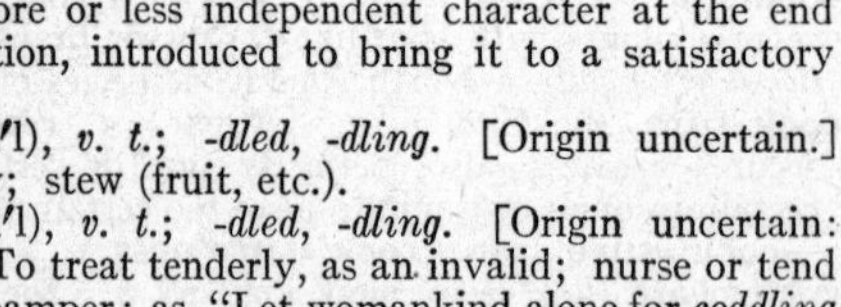

Cod (*Gadus callarias*).

co-da (kō'dạ̈), *n.* [It., < L. *cauda,* tail.] In *music,* a passage of more or less independent character at the end of a composition, introduced to bring it to a satisfactory close.

cod-dle[1] (kod'l), *v. t.*; *-dled, -dling.* [Origin uncertain.] To boil gently; stew (fruit, etc.).

cod-dle[2] (kod'l), *v. t.*; *-dled, -dling.* [Origin uncertain: cf. *caudle.*] To treat tenderly, as an invalid; nurse or tend indulgently; pamper: as, "Let womankind alone for *coddling* each other" (Scott's "Antiquary," ix.).

code (kōd), *n.* [F., < L. *codex:* see *codex.*] One of the systematic collections of Roman law made under later Roman emperors (as, the Justinian *Code,* the body of Roman law compiled and annotated at the command of Justinian in the 6th century); any systematic collection or digest of the existing laws of a country, or of those relating to a particular subject (as, the *Code* of Hammurabi, a collection of laws published by Hammurabi, an early king of Babylonia; the Civil *Code* of France, F. *Code civil,* the first of the five divisions of the Code of Napoleon, dealing with civil or private law; the *Code* of Napoleon, F. *Code Napoléon,* the body of French law contained in five codes promulgated between 1804 and 1810, commonly the first of these codes, the Civil Code); any system or collection of rules and regulations; also, a system of signals for communication by telegraph, heliograph, etc.; also, a system of arbitrarily chosen words, etc., used for brevity or secrecy, as in telegraphing; a cipher.—**code,** *v. t.*; *coded, coding.* To arrange in a code; enter in a code; also, to translate into a code or cipher.

co-dec-li-na-tion (kō"dek-li-nā'shọn), *n.* [See *co-.*] In *astron.,* the complement of the declination.

co-de-fend-ant (kō-dẹ-fen'dạnt), *n.* [See *co-.*] A joint defendant.

co-de-ine (kọ-dē'in or kō'dẹ-in), *n.* [Gr. κώδεια, head, poppy-head.] A white, crystalline, slightly bitter alkaloid obtained from opium, used in medicine as an analgesic, sedative, and hypnotic.

co-det-ta (kọ-det'ạ̈), *n.* [It.] In *music,* a short coda.

co-dex (kō'deks), *n.*; pl. *codices* (kō'di-sēz or kod'i-). [L., earlier *caudex,* tree-trunk, block, block of writing-tablets, book, code.] A code†; also, a manuscript volume, as of an ancient classic or of the Scriptures (as, the Sinaitic and Vatican *codices,* 4th century uncial manuscripts of the Greek Bible, the former now in Petrograd and the latter in Rome).

cod-fish (kod'fish), *n.* Same as *cod*[2].

codg-er (koj'ėr), *n.* [Cf. *cadger.*] A mean, miserly person (prov. Eng.); an odd or peculiar (old) person (colloq.); a fellow or chap (colloq.: as, "I haven't been drinking your health, my *codger,*" Dickens's "Nicholas Nickleby," lx.).

co-di-ces (kō'di-sēz or kod'i-), *n.* Plural of *codex.*

cod-i-cil (kod'i-sil), *n.* [L. *codicillus,* dim. of *codex:* see *codex.*] A supplement to a will containing an explanation, modification, or revocation of something contained in the will; hence, some similar supplement.—**cod-i-cil'la-ry** (-sil'ạ-ri), *a.*

cod-i-fy (kod'i-fī or kō'di-), *v. t.*; *-fied, -fying.* [See *code* and *-fy.*] To reduce (laws, etc.) to a code; digest; arrange in a systematic collection.—**cod"i-fi-ca'tion** (-fi-kā'-shọn), *n.*—**cod'i-fi-er** (-fī-ėr), *n.*

cod-ling[1] (kod'ling), *n.* [ME. *querdlyng;* origin unknown.] Any of several varieties of small, half-wild, inferior apples, used for cooking purposes (Eng.); an unripe, half-grown apple.

cod-ling[2] (kod'ling), *n.* The young of the cod.

cod=liv-er (kod'liv"ėr), *n.* The liver of the common cod, *Gadus callarias,* or of allied species, yielding a fixed oil ('cod-liver oil'), which is extensively used in medicine as a nutrient and tonic.

cod=piece (kod'pēs), *n.* [See *cod*[1].] A bagged appendage to the front of a style of tight-fitting hose or breeches formerly worn by men.

co-ed (kō'ed'), *n.* A female student in a coeducational institution. [Colloq.]

co-ed-u-ca-tion (kō"ed-ū-kā'shọn), *n.* [See *co-.*] Joint education, esp. of both sexes in the same institution and classes.—**co"ed-u-ca'tion-al,** *a.*

co-ef-fi-cient (kō-e-fish'ẹnt). [See *co-.*] **I.** *a.* Coöperating. **II.** *n.* That which unites in action with something else to produce an effect; in *math.,* a number or quantity placed (generally) before and multiplying another quantity (as, 3 is the *coefficient* of x in $3x$); in *physics,* a numerical quantity, constant for a given substance, used to measure some one of its properties.

coe-horn (kō'hôrn), *n.* [From Baron M. van *Coehoorn* (1641–1704), Dutch military engineer, who invented it.] A small mortar for throwing grenades.

cœ-len-ter-ate (sẹ-len'tẹ-rạt). [NL. *Cœlenterata,* pl., < Gr. κοῖλος, hollow, + ἔντερον, intestine.] **I.** *a.* Belonging to the *Cœlenterata* or *Cœlentera,* a group or phylum of invertebrate animals including the hydras, jellyfishes, sea-anemones, corals, etc., and characterized by an internal cavity serving for digestion, excretion, and other functions. **II.** *n.* A cœlenterate animal.

cœ-len-te-ron (sę-len′tę-ron), *n.*; pl. *-ra* (-rą). [NL., < Gr. κοῖλος, hollow, + ἔντερον, intestine.] In *zoöl.*, the body-cavity of a cœlenterate, combining the functions of a digestive tract with those of the cœlom of the higher animals; also, the archenteron.

cœ-li-ac (sē′li-ak), *a.* See *celiac.*

cœ-lom (sē′lom), *n.* [NL. *cœloma*, < Gr. κοίλωμα, a hollow, < κοῖλος, hollow.] In *zoöl.*, *anat.*, etc., the body-cavity of a metazoan, as distinguished from the intestinal cavity. Also **cœ-lo-ma** (sę-lō′mą), **cœ-lome** (sē′lōm).

cœ-lo-stat (sē′lǫ-stat), *n.* [L. *cœlum*, *cælum*, sky, + Gr. στατός, standing.] An instrument in which a reflected image of the sky is made to appear stationary by means of a mirror which revolves slowly by clockwork.

co-emp-tion (kǫ-emp′shǫn), *n.* [L. *coemptio(n-)*, < *coemere*, buy together, < *co-*, with, + *emere*, buy.] The purchase of all of a given commodity in the market, in order to control its price; in *Rom. law*, a kind of fictitious purchase, used esp. as a mode of civil marriage.

cœ-næs-the-sia (sē-nes-thē′zią), *n.* [NL., < Gr. κοινός, common, + αἴσθησις, perception, sensation.] In *psychol.*, the general sense of life, the bodily consciousness, or the total impression from all contemporaneous organic sensations, as distinct from special and well-defined sensations, such as those of touch or sight. Also **cœ-næs-the′sis** (-sis).

cœ-nen-chy-ma (sę-neng′ki-mą), *n.* [NL., < Gr. κοινός, common, + *-enchyma* as in *parenchyma.*] In *zoöl.*, the common calcareous tissue uniting the individual polyps or zoöids of a compound actinozoan.—**cœ-nen′chy-mal,** *a.*

cœn-o-bite (sen′ǭ-bīt or sē′nǭ-), etc. See *cenobite*, etc.

cœ-nog-a-my (sę-nog′ą-mi), *n.* See *cenogamy.*

cœ-no-sarc (sē′nǭ-särk), *n.* [Gr. κοινός, common, + σάρξ (σαρκ-), flesh.] In *zoöl.*, the common soft tissue which unites the individual polyps or zoöids of a compound zoöphyte, as coral, and serves to circulate and distribute nutriment through the colony.—**cœ-no-sar′cal, cœ-no-sar′cous,** *a.*

cœ-nu-rus (sę-nū′rus), *n.* [NL., < Gr. κοινός, common, + οὐρά, tail.] The larva of a tapeworm, *Tænia cœnurus*, infesting the brain of sheep, etc., and causing the disease called *gid*: in the adult form parasitic in the dog and wolf. Also **cœ-nure** (sē′nūr).

co-e-qual (kō-ē′kwąl). [See *co-*.] **I.** *a.* Equal, as one with another: as, "If once he come to be a cardinal, He'll make his cap *co-equal* with the crown" (Shakspere's "1 Henry VI.," v. 1. 33). **II.** *n.* One coequal with another.—**co-e-qual′i-ty** (-ę-kwol′i-ti), *n.*—**co-e′qual-ly,** *adv.*

co-erce (kǫ-ėrs′), *v. t.*; *coerced, coercing.* [L. *coercere*, hold together, hold in, < *co-*, with, + *arcere*, keep.] To restrain or constrain by force or authority; constrain to obedience or submission by forcible means; force or compel, as to do something; also, to effect by compulsion (as, to *coerce* obedience).—**co-er′cer,** *n.*—**co-er′ci-ble,** *a.* That may be coerced; also, compressible or condensable, as gases.—**co-er′cion** (-ėr′shǫn), *n.* [L. *coertio(n-)*, for *coercitio(n-)*.] The act or power of coercing; forcible constraint; compulsion; government by force; also, physical pressure or compression.—**co-er′cive** (-siv), *a.* Serving or tending to coerce, convince, or compress.—**co-er′cive-ly,** *adv.*—**co-er′cive-ness,** *n.*

co-es-sen-tial (kō-e-sen′shąl), *a.* [See *co-*.] United in essence; having the same essence or nature.—**co″es-sen-ti-al′i-ty** (-shi-al′i-ti), *n.*—**co-es-sen′tial-ly,** *adv.*

co-es-tab-lish-ment (kō-es-tab′lish-męnt), *n.* [See *co-*.] Joint establishment.

co-e-ta-ne-ous (kō-ę-tā′nę-us), *a.* [LL. *coætaneus*, < L. *co-*, with, + *ætas*, age.] Of the same age or duration; coeval; contemporary.

co-e-ter-nal (kō-ę-tėr′nąl), *a.* [LL. *coæternus*, < L. *co-*, with, + *æternus*, eternal.] Equally eternal; existing with another eternally.—**co-e-ter′nal-ly,** *adv.*—**co-e-ter′ni-ty,** *n.*

co-e-val (kǫ-ē′vąl). [LL. *coævus*, < L. *co-*, with, + *ævum*, age.] **I.** *a.* Of the same age, date, or duration; equally old; contemporary; coincident. **II.** *n.* One who is of the same age (as, "A schoolmaster . . . is forlorn among his *coevals*; his juniors cannot be his friends": Lamb's "The Old and the New Schoolmaster"); a contemporary.—**co-e′val-ly,** *adv.*

co-ex-ec-u-tor (kō-eg-zek′ū-tǫr), *n.* [See *co-*.] A joint executor.—**co-ex-ec′u-trix,** *n.*

co-ex-ist (kō-eg-zist′), *v. i.* [See *co-*.] To exist together or at the same time.—**co-ex-ist′ence,** *n.* Existence together.—**co-ex-ist′ent. I.** *a.* Coexisting. **II.** *n.* Something that coexists.

co-ex-tend (kō-eks-tend′), *v. t.* or *i.* [See *co-*.] To extend equally or coincidently.—**co-ex-ten′sion** (-ten′shǫn), *n.* Equal or coincident extension.—**co-ex-ten′sive** (-siv), *a.* Having equal or coincident extension.

cof-fee (kof′ę or kôf′ę), *n.* [Turk. *qahveh*, < Ar. *qahwah.*] A beverage consisting of a decoction or infusion of the roasted and ground or crushed seeds ('coffee-beans') of the two-seeded fruit ('coffee-berry') of *Coffea arabica* and other species of *Coffea*, rubiaceous trees and shrubs of tropical regions (as, black *coffee*, coffee served without cream or milk); the berries or the seeds themselves; a tree or shrub yielding such berries or seeds; also, any of various substances used as imitations of or substitutes for coffee.—**cof′fee=col″or,** *n.* The color of coffee (the beverage), esp. with cream added; café au lait.—**cof′fee=col″ored,** *a.*—**cof′fee=cup,** *n.* A cup for drinking coffee from: usually larger than a tea-cup.—**cof′fee=house,** *n.* A house of entertainment where coffee and other refreshments are supplied.—**cof′fee=nut,** *n.* The fruit of the Kentucky coffee-tree, *Gymnocladus dioica*; also, the tree.—**cof′fee=pot,** *n.* A pot or vessel for making or serving coffee in.—**cof′fee=room,** *n.* A public room, as in a hotel, where coffee and other refreshments are served. [Eng.]—**cof′fee=tree,** *n.* Any tree, as *Coffea arabica*, yielding coffee; also, a tall cæsalpiniaceous tree, *Gymnocladus dioica*, of the U. S. ('Kentucky coffee-tree'), whose seeds have been used as a substitute for coffee; also, the cascara buckthorn ('California coffee-tree').

Fruiting Branch of Coffee-plant (*Coffea arabica*).

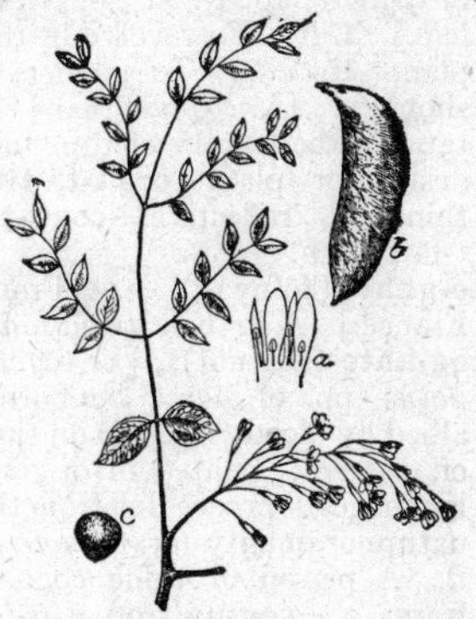

Kentucky Coffee-tree. — *a*, part of male flower, showing stamens; *b*, fruit; *c*, seed.

cof-fer (kof′ėr or kôf′ėr), *n.* [OF. *cofre* (F. *coffre*), chest, < L. *cophinus*, basket: see *coffin.*] A box or chest, esp. one for valuables; *pl.*, a treasury; funds or pecuniary resources; *sing.*, an ornamental sunken panel in a ceiling or soffit; also, any of various box-like inclosures, as a coffer-dam.—**cof′fer,** *v. t.* To deposit or lay up in or as in a coffer or chest; also, to ornament with coffers or sunken panels.—**cof′fer=dam,** *n.* A water-tight inclosure (as one constructed of piles and clay) built in rivers, etc., and used, after pumping the water out, for laying foundations of bridges, etc., or doing other work below the surface of the water.

Coffers of a Ceiling. — Palace of Fontainebleau, France.

cof-fin (kof′in or kôf′in), *n.* [OF. *cofin*, small basket, coffin, < L. *cophinus*, < Gr. κόφινος, basket.] A basket†; a mold of paste for a pie†; the crust of a pie†; a box† or case†; the case in which a corpse is placed for burial; the part of a horse's foot (hoof) containing the coffin-bone. —**cof′fin,** *v. t.* To put or inclose in or as in a coffin.—

cof′fin=bone, *n.* The terminal phalanx in the foot of the horse and allied animals, inclosed in the hoof.—**cof′fin=joint,** *n.* The joint next above the coffin-bone, at the top of the hoof in the horse and allied animals.

cof-fle (kof′l), *n.* [Ar. *qāfilah,* caravan.] A train of men or beasts, esp. of slaves, fastened together: as, "From the black slave-ship's foul and loathsome hell, And *coffle's* weary chain" (Whittier's "Christian Slave").

cog[1]† (kog), *n.* [= *cock*[4].] A small boat; also, a kind of ship.

cog[2] (kog), *n.* [ME. *cogge* = Sw. *kugge.*] A tooth or projection (usually one of a series) on a wheel, etc., for transmitting motion to or receiving motion from a corresponding tooth or part on another wheel or the like with which it engages; also, a cog-wheel; also, a projection or tenon on a beam, fitting into a notch in another beam.—**cog**[2], *v. t.*; *cogged, cogging.* To furnish with cogs; also, to stop motion in or make steady as by a wedge (prov.); also, to connect (beams) by a cog.

cog[3], **cogue** (kōg), *n.* [Origin uncertain.] A wooden pail, bowl, or cup. [Chiefly Sc.]

cog[4] (kog), *v.*; *cogged, cogging.* [Origin uncertain.] **I.** *tr.* To manipulate (dice) so as to control the fall; later, to load (dice); also, to beguile†; cajole†; also, to foist†. **II.** *intr.* To cheat at dice; also, to use guile†; also, to employ flattery† (as, "I cannot *cog* and say thou art this and that": Shakspere's "Merry Wives of Windsor," iii. 3. 76).

co-gent (kō′jent), *a.* [L. *cogens* (*-ent-*), ppr. of *cogere,* drive together, collect, constrain, < *co-,* with, + *agere,* drive.] Constraining, esp. to assent or believe; forcible; convincing. —**co′gen-cy,** *n.*—**co′gent-ly,** *adv.*

cog-ger (kog′ėr), *n.* One who or that which cogs.

cog-i-ta-ble (koj′i-tạ-bl), *a.* [L. *cogitabilis.*] Capable of being thought.

cog-i-tate (koj′i-tāt), *v.*; *-tated, -tating.* [L. *cogitatus,* pp. of *cogitare,* appar. < *co-,* with, + *agitare,* consider, E. *agitate.*] **I.** *tr.* To revolve in the mind; consider; meditate; plan. **II.** *intr.* To ponder; think.—**cog-i-ta′tion** (-tā′-shọn), *n.* [L. *cogitatio(n-).*] The act of cogitating; meditation; the faculty of thinking; a thought or reflection; a design or plan.—**cog′i-ta-tive** (-tạ-tiv), *a.* Cogitating; thinking; reflective.—**cog′i-ta-tive-ly,** *adv.*—**cog′i-ta-tor** (-tā-tọr), *n.*

co-gnac (kō′nyak), *n.* [From *Cognac,* town in western France.] A French brandy of superior quality.

cog-nate (kog′nāt). [L. *cognatus,* < *co-,* with, + *gnatus, natus,* pp. of *nasci,* be born.] **I.** *a.* Related by birth; allied by blood (whether on the father's or the mother's side: cf. *agnate*); related in origin (as, *cognate* words; *cognate* languages); proceeding from the same stock or root; allied in nature or quality (as, *cognate* sounds); having affinity. **II.** *n.* A person or thing cognate with another.—**cog′nate-ness,** *n.*—**cog-na′tion** (-nā′shọn), *n.* [L. *cognatio(n-).*] Cognate relationship or relation; kinship; affinity.

cog-ni-tion (kog-nish′ọn), *n.* [L. *cognitio(n-),* < *cognoscere,* come to know, recognize, acknowledge, < *co-,* with, + *gnoscere, noscere,* know.] The act or fact of coming to know or of knowing; perception; cognizance; knowledge.—**cog′ni-tive** (-ni-tiv), *a.* Pertaining to cognition; cognizing.

cog-ni-za-ble (kog′ni-zạ-bl or kon′i-), *a.* Within cognizance; capable of being perceived or known; within the jurisdiction of a court.—**cog′ni-za-bly,** *adv.*

cog-ni-zance (kog′ni-zạns or kon′i-), *n.* [OF. *conoissance* (F. *connaissance*), < *conoistre,* < L. *cognoscere:* see *cognition.*] Perception; notice; knowledge; specif., in legal use, judicial notice as taken by a court in dealing with a cause; exercise of jurisdiction; the right of taking judicial notice, as possessed by a court; also, a distinguishing badge, esp. as formerly worn by retainers of a noble house; a device.—**cog′ni-zant,** *a.* Having cognizance; aware (*of*); competent to take judicial notice, as of causes.

cog-nize (kog′nīz), *v. t.*; *-nized, -nizing.* [L. *cognoscere* (see *cognition*), with ending as in E. *recognize.*] To perceive; become conscious of; know.

cog-no-men (kog-nō′men), *n.*; pl. *-nomens,* L. *-nomina* (-nom′i-nạ̈). [L., < *co-,* with, + *nomen,* name, akin to *noscere, gnoscere,* know.] The third and commonly the last name (in order) of a Roman citizen, indicating his house or family, as in 'Caius Julius Cæsar' (cf. *prænomen, nomen, agnomen*); in general, a surname; any name or appellative (as, "Priscilla! . . . this quaint and prim *cognomen*": Hawthorne's "Blithedale Romance," iv.); a nickname.—**cog-nom′i-nal** (-nom′i-nạl), *a.*

cog-nosce (kog-nos′), *v. t.*; *-nosced, -noscing.* [L. *cognoscere:* see *cognition.*] In *Sc. law,* to inquire into or investigate judicially; examine into and declare the legal status of; esp., to pronounce insane.

co-gno-scen-te (kō-nyō-shen′tā), *n.*; pl. *-ti* (-tē). [It., usually *conoscente,* ppr. of *conoscere,* < L. *cognoscere:* see *cognition.*] A connoisseur.

cog-nos-ci-ble (kog-nos′i-bl), *a.* [LL. *cognoscibilis,* < L. *cognoscere:* see *cognition.*] Capable of being known.—**cog-nos-ci-bil′i-ty** (-bil′i-ti), *n.*

cog-no-vit (kog-nō′vit), *n.* [L., 'he has acknowledged.'] In *law,* an acknowledgment or confession by a defendant that the plaintiff's cause, or a part of it, is just, wherefore the defendant, to save expense, suffers judgment to be entered without trial.

co-gon (kọ-gōn′), *n.* [Philippine Sp.] A tall, coarse grass, *Imperata arundinacea,* of the Philippine Islands, etc., furnishing an excellent material for thatching.

cogue (kōg), *n.* See *cog*[3].

cog=wheel (kog′hwēl), *n.* A wheel with cogs, for transmitting or receiving motion.

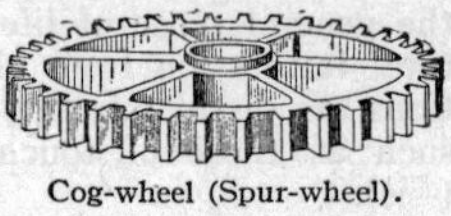

Cog-wheel (Spur-wheel).

co-hab-it (kọ-hab′it), *v. i.* [LL. *cohabitare,* < L. *co-,* with, + *habitare,* dwell.] To dwell or reside in company or in the same place (archaic); specif., to live together as husband and wife (often with reference to persons not legally married).—**co-hab′it-ant,** *n.*—**co-hab-i-ta′tion** (-i-tā′shọn), *n.*

co-heir (kō-âr′), *n.* [See *co-.*] A joint heir.—**co-heir′ess,** *n.* A joint heiress.—**co-heir′ship,** *n.*

co-here (kọ-hēr′), *v. i.*; *-hered, -hering.* [L. *cohærere* (pp. *cohæsus*), < *co-,* with, + *hærere,* stick.] To stick together; be united; hold fast, as parts of the same mass; also, to be naturally or logically connected; also, to agree; be congruous.—**co-her′ence, co-her′en-cy** (-hēr′ẹns, -ẹn-si), *n.* The act or state of cohering; cohesion; natural or logical connection; congruity or consistency.—**co-her′ent,** *a.* Cohering; sticking together; also, having a natural or due agreement of parts; connected; consistent; logical; also, suited† or accordant†.—**co-her′ent-ly,** *adv.*—**co-her′er,** *n.* In *elect.,* a device, usually consisting of a tube filled with a conducting substance in granular form, whose electrical resistance decreases when struck by Hertzian waves: used in detecting the waves sent out by a wireless telegraph apparatus.—**co-he′si-ble** (-hē′zi-bl), *a.* Capable of cohesion.—**co-he′sion** (-zhọn), *n.* The act or state of cohering; in *physics,* the attraction by which the molecules of a body or substance are bound together; in *bot.,* the congenital union of one part with another.—**co-he′sive** (-siv), *a.* Cohering, or tending to cohere; characterized by or causing cohesion.—**co-he′sive-ly,** *adv.*—**co-he′sive-ness,** *n.*

co-ho-bate (kō′họ-bāt), *v. t.*; *-bated, -bating.* [ML. *cohobatus,* pp. of *cohobare*; prob. from Ar.] In *phar.,* to distil again from the same or a similar substance, as a distilled liquid poured back upon the matter remaining in the vessel, or upon another mass of similar matter.

co-hort (kō′hôrt), *n.* [L. *cohors* (*cohort-*), division of troops, company, multitude, orig. inclosure: see *court.*] One of the ten infantry divisions in an ancient Roman legion, numbering from 300 to 600 men; a similar body of auxiliary troops, or later of cavalry, in the Roman army; hence, any body of warriors; fig., a band or company; in certain botanical and zoölogical classifications, a large group, usually ranking above an order in botany and below an order in zoölogy.

co-hosh (kọ-hosh′ or kō′hosh), *n.* [N. Amer. Ind.] Any of several North American plants used medicinally, as *Cimicifuga racemosa* ('black cohosh'), *Caulophyllum thalictroides* ('blue cohosh'), etc.

co-hune (kọ-hön′), *n.* [Native name.] A pinnate-leaved palm, *Attalea cohune,* a native of Central America, bearing large nuts whose hard shell is made into ornaments and whose meat yields an oil resembling that of the cocoanut.

coif (koif), *n.* [OF. *coife* (F. *coiffe*), < LL. *cofia*, head-covering, cap; appar. from Teut. (cf. G. *kopf*, head).] A close-fitting cap of various kinds, as one worn by European peasant women, or one formerly worn by lawyers; also, the calling or rank of a serjeant at law.—**coif,** *v. t.* To cover or dress with or as with a coif.

coif-feur (kwo-fėr), *n.* [F., < *coiffer*: see *coiffure.*] A hair-dresser.

coif-fure (koif′ūr, F. kwo-für), *n.* [F., < *coiffer*, furnish with a coif or head-covering, dress the hair of, < *coiffe*, E. *coif.*] A head-covering or head-dress; also, a mode of arranging or dressing the hair.

coign (koin), *n.* [Old form of *coin.*] A wedge; also, a projecting corner.—**coign of vantage,** a position (properly a projecting corner) affording advantage for observation or action. See Shakspere's "Macbeth," i. 6. 7.

coil[1] (koil), *v.* [OF. *coillir* (F. *cueillir*), gather, < L. *colligere*: see *collect.*] **I.** *tr.* To wind into concentric rings; twist or wind spirally; also, to infold or inwrap in or as in a coil or coils. **II.** *intr.* To assume a coiled or spiral form; wind; also, to move in a winding course.—**coil**[1], *n.* A connected series of concentric rings or spirals into which a rope or the like is wound; a single such ring; also, an electrical conductor, as a copper wire, wound up in a spiral or other form; a device composed essentially of such a conductor; also, an arrangement of pipes, coiled or in a connected series, as in a radiator.

coil[2] (koil), *n.* [Origin uncertain.] Stir; bustle; turmoil; ado: as, "when we have shuffled off this mortal *coil*" (Shakspere's "Hamlet," iii. 1. 67). [Archaic or prov.]

coin (koin), *n.* [OF. F. *coin*, wedge, corner, die, < L. *cuneus*, wedge.] A wedge†; a corner†; a corner-stone; a wedge-shaped stone of an arch; also, a die for stamping money†; a piece of metal stamped and issued by the authority of the government for use as money; such pieces collectively; fig., anything serving for payment or recompense; by transfer, any coin-like token.—**coin,** *v. t.* To make (money) by stamping metal; make or gain (money) rapidly (colloq.); convert (metal) into money; represent on a coin†; fig., to make, invent, or fabricate (as, to *coin* words).—**coin′a-ble,** *a.* That may be coined.—**coin′age** (-āj), *n.* The act of coining; the process or right of making coins; also, that which is coined; coins collectively; the currency; fig., anything made, invented, or fabricated (as, "This is the very *coinage* of your brain": Shakspere's "Hamlet," iii. 4. 137).

co-in-cide (kō-in-sīd′), *v. i.*; *-cided, -ciding.* [ML. *coincidere*, < L. *co-*, with, + *incidere*, fall on: see *incident.*] To occupy the same place in space, the same point or period in time, or the same relative position; also, to correspond exactly, as in nature or character; also, to agree or concur, as in opinion.—**co-in-ci-dence** (kọ-in′si-dẹns), *n.* The condition or fact of being coincident; occurrence or existence at the same place in space, the same point or period in time, or the same relative position; exact correspondence, as in nature or character; an agreement in circumstances, character, etc.; a concurrence in opinion or sentiment; esp., a striking occurrence of two or more events at one time apparently by mere chance.—**co-in′ci-dent,** *a.* Coinciding; occupying the same place or position; happening at the same time; exactly corresponding; in exact agreement.—**co-in-ci-den′tal** (-den′tạl), *a.* Involving coincidence.—**co-in-ci-den′tal-ly,** *adv.*—**co-in′ci-dent-ly,** *adv.*

co-in-di-ca-tion (kō″in-di-kā′shọn), *n.* [See *co-.*] One of two or more concurrent indications, signs, or symptoms.

coin-er (koi′nėr), *n.* One who coins money; esp., a maker of counterfeit coin; fig., an inventor, as of words.

co-in-here (kō-in-hēr′), *v. i.*; *-hered, -hering.* [See *co-.*] To inhere together; be included or exist together in the same thing.—**co-in-her′ence,** *n.*—**co-in-her′ent,** *a.*

co-in-her-it-ance (kō-in-her′i-tạns), *n.* [See *co-.*] Joint inheritance.—**co-in-her′i-tor,** *n.*

co-in-stan-ta-ne-ous (kō″in-stạn-tā′nę-us), *a.* [See *co-.*] Happening at the same instant.—**co″in-stan-ta′ne-ous-ly,** *adv.*

co-in-sur-ance (kō-in-shör′ạns), *n.* [See *co-.*] Insurance jointly with another or others; esp., a form of fire insurance in which a person taking out insurance on property for less than its full value is regarded as a joint insurer and becomes jointly responsible for losses.—**co-in-sure′,** *v. t.* or *i.*; *-sured, -suring.* To insure jointly with another or others; esp., to insure on a basis of coinsurance.

coir (koir), *n.* [E. Ind. (Dravidian).] The prepared fiber of the husk of the cocoanut, used in making rope, matting, etc.

cois-trel (kois′trel), *n.* [Cf. OF. *coustillier*, a soldier armed with a dagger, < *coustille*, dagger.] An inferior groom employed to care for a knight's horses; hence, a mean, paltry fellow, or a knave (see Shakspere's "Twelfth Night," i. 3. 43). [Archaic.]

co-i-tion (kọ-ish′ọn), *n.* [L. *coitio(n-)*, < *coire*, go together, < *co-*, with, + *ire*, go.] Sexual intercourse. Also **co-i-tus** (kō′i-tus).

coke[1] (kōk), *n.* [Origin uncertain.] The solid product from the distillation of coal in an oven or closed chamber (analogous to charcoal as made from wood): used as a fuel in metallurgy, etc.—**coke**[1], *v. t.* or *i.*; *coked, coking.* To convert into or become coke.

coke[2] (kōk), *n.* Shortened form of *cocaine.* [Slang.]

col (kol, F. kol), *n.* [F., < L. *collum*, neck.] A marked depression in a ridge or mountain-chain, usually forming a pass from one slope to the other.

co-la[1], **co-la**[2] (kō′lạ̈), *n.* Plural of *colon*[1], *colon*[2].

co-la[3] (kō′lạ̈), **co′la=nut,** *n.* See *kola, kola-nut.*

co-la-bor-er (kō-lā′bọr-ėr), *n.* [See *co-.*] A fellow-laborer.

col-an-der (kul′ạn-dėr), *n.* [Prob. ult. < L. *colare*, strain, < *colum*, strainer.] A perforated vessel for draining off liquids, as in cookery.

co-lat-i-tude (kō-lat′i-tūd), *n.* [See *co-.*] The complement of the latitude; the difference between a given latitude, expressed in degrees, and 90°.

col-can-non (kol-kan′ọn), *n.* [From *cole* + *-cannon* (of uncertain origin and meaning).] An Irish dish made of cabbage (or greens) and potatoes boiled and mashed together and seasoned.

col-chi-cum (kol′ki-kum, often kol′chi-), *n.* [L., < Gr. κολχικόν; appar. named from Colchis in Asia, the country of the sorceress Medea.] Any plant of the old-world melanthiaceous genus *Colchicum*, esp. *C. autumnale*, a crocus-like plant whose corm and seeds are used in medicine, chiefly for gout; also, the medicine or drug prepared from them.

Colchicum (*C. autumnale*) and section of flower.

col-co-thar (kol′kọ-thạ̈r), *n.* [ML.; from Ar.] The brownish-red oxide of iron which remains after the heating of ferrous sulphate: used as a polishing agent, etc.

cold (kōld), *a.* [AS. *cald, ceald*, = D. *koud* = G. *kalt* = Icel. *kaldr* = Goth. *kalds*, cold; all orig. pp. from a Teut. verb-stem (cf. AS. *calan*, be cold) akin to L. *gelidus*, icy cold.] Producing or feeling, esp. in a high degree, the peculiar sensation resulting when heat is withdrawn from the body; chilly; frigid; having a temperature sensibly lower than the normal temperature of the body; having a relatively low temperature; having no warmth, or having lost warmth; fig., deficient in passion, emotion, enthusiasm, ardor, etc.; apathetic; indifferent; imperturbable; void of sensual desire; chaste; not affectionate, cordial, or friendly; unresponsive; failing to excite feeling or interest; depressing or dispiriting; faint or weak, as a scent; of coloring, inclining to blue or gray (rather than red or yellow).—**cold cream,** a kind of cooling unguent for the skin.—**cold feet,** loss of courage or confidence for carrying out some undertaking proposed or begun. [Slang.]—**cold light,** light lacking the heat of the light due to ordinary combustion or incandescence: applied to the light of phosphorescence, fluorescence, etc. (including that of fireflies and certain other organisms), and to certain other kinds of light produced artificially.—**cold shoulder,** an open show of coldness, indifference, or neglect in one's treatment of another: as, to give one the *cold shoulder.*—**cold storage,** the storage of provisions, etc., in a place artificially cooled.—**in cold blood,** in a calm state of mind; coolly and deliberately.—**cold,** *n.* [AS. *cald, ceald.*] The relative absence of heat; coldness; a temperature below the freezing-point of water (as, 10° of *cold*, that is, 22° F. or

10° below zero C.); the sensation produced by loss of heat from the body, as by contact with anything having a sensibly lower temperature than that of the body; also, an indisposition caused by exposure to cold, characterized by catarrh, hoarseness, coughing, etc.—**cold′=blood′ed,** *a.* Having cold blood; noting or pertaining to animals, as fishes and reptiles, whose blood temperature ranges from the freezing-point upward, in accordance with the temperature of the surrounding medium; fig., lacking in emotion; unimpassioned; unsympathetic; cruel.—**cold′=blood′ed-ly,** *adv.*—**cold′=blood′ed-ness,** *n.*—**cold′=chis″el,** *n.* A strong chisel of tempered steel for cutting cold metal.—**cold′=heart′ed,** *a.* Wanting sympathy or feeling; indifferent; unkind.—**cold′=heart′ed-ly,** *adv.*—**cold′=heart′ed-ness,** *n.*—**cold′ish,** *a.* Rather cold.—**cold′ly,** *adv.*—**cold′ness,** *n.*—**cold′=saw,** *n.* A saw for cutting cold metal.—**cold′=short,** *a.* Of iron, brittle when cold.—**cold′=short″ness,** *n.*—**cold′=shoul′der,** *v. t.* To give the cold shoulder to; treat with coldness, indifference, or neglect.

cold=slaw (kōld′slâ), *n.* Erroneous form of *cole-slaw.*

cold=sore (kōld′sōr), *n.* A vesicular eruption about the mouth often accompanying a cold or a febrile condition.

cole (kōl), *n.* [AS. *cāwel,* < L. *caulis,* stalk, cabbage.] Any of various plants of the cabbage kind; esp., rape, *Brassica napus.*

-cole. [F. *-cole,* < L. *colere,* inhabit.] An adjective termination meaning 'inhabiting,' 'living in or on,' as in *arboricole, corticole.* Cf. *-colous.*

cole-man-ite (kōl′mạn-īt), *n.* [From W. T. *Coleman,* of San Francisco.] A mineral consisting of a hydrous borate of calcium, occurring in California in colorless to white monoclinic crystals with a brilliant luster.

col-e-op-ter (kol-ẹ̄-op′tėr or kō-lẹ̄-), *n.* [NL. *Coleoptera,* pl., < Gr. κολεόπτερος, sheath-winged, < κολεός, sheath, + πτερόν, wing.] Any of the *Coleoptera,* an order of insects (the beetles) having a pair of membranous posterior wings sheathed by a pair of hard, horny, modified anterior wings or wing-covers.—**col-e-op′ter-an,** *a.* and *n.*—**col-e-op′ter-ist,** *n.* One versed in the study of coleopters.—**col-e-op′ter-ous,** *a.* Having the wings sheathed, as the coleopters; belonging to the *Coleoptera* (see *coleopter*).

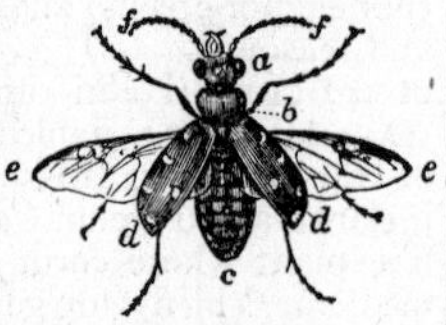

Coleopter (*Cicindela campestris*).—*a,* head; *b,* prothorax; *c,* abdomen; *d, d,* elytra, or wing-covers; *e, e,* wings; *f, f,* antennæ.

col-e-o-rhi-za (kol″ẹ̄-ọ̄-rī′zạ̈ or kō″lẹ̄-), *n.*; pl. *-zæ* (-zē). [NL., < Gr. κολεός, sheath, + ῥίζα, root.] In *bot.,* the sheath which envelops the radicle in certain plants, and which is penetrated by the root in germination.

cole=seed (kōl′sēd), *n.* Rape-seed; also, rape.

cole=slaw (kōl′slâ), *n.* [D. *kool,* cabbage, + *sla,* for *salade,* salad.] A salad of finely sliced cabbage. [U. S.]

co=les-see (kō-le-sē′), *n.* [See *co-.*] A partner in holding a lease; a joint tenant.—**co=les′sor,** *n.* A partner in granting a lease.

co-le-us (kō′lẹ̄-us), *n.*; pl. *coleuses,* L. *colei* (-lẹ̄-ī). [NL. (so called from the union of the filaments about the style), < Gr. κολεός, sheath.] Any plant of the menthaceous genus *Coleus,* of tropical Asia and Africa, species of which are cultivated for their showy colored foliage.

cole-wort (kōl′wėrt), *n.* Any plant of the cabbage kind; esp., a variety of cabbage which does not form compact heads, as kale; also, a young cabbage.

col-i-bri (kol′i-bri), *n.* [F. *colibri* or Sp. *colibrí*; from Carib.] Any humming-bird.

col-ic (kol′ik). [LL. *colicus,* < Gr. κωλικός, < κῶλον, for κόλον, E. *colon*[2].] **I.** *a.* Pertaining to or affecting the colon or the bowels. **II.** *n.* Paroxysmal pain in the abdomen or bowels.—**col′ick-y,** *a.*—**col′ic=root,** *n.* Either of two North American liliaceous herbs, *Aletris farinosa* and *A. aurea,* having small yellow or white flowers in a spike-like raceme, and a root which is reputed to relieve colic; also, any of certain other plants reputed to cure colic, as the asteraceous herb *Laciniaria squarrosa.*

co-lie, co-ly (kō′li), *n.*; pl. *-lies* (-liz). [NL. *Colius,* < Gr. κολιός, woodpecker.] Any bird of the African genus *Colius,* of small, non-passerine, fruit-eating birds having a long tail.

col-in (kol′in), *n.* [For Mex. *çolin, zolin.*] The common quail or partridge, or bob-white, *Colinus virginianus,* of the U. S.; also, any of various related species.

Col-i-se-um (kol-i-sē′um), *n.* See *Colosseum.*

co-li-tis (kọ̄-lī′tis), *n.* [NL.] In *pathol.,* inflammation of the mucous membrane of the colon.

col-lab-o-rate (kọ-lab′ọ̄-rāt), *v. i.*; *-rated, -rating.* [LL. *collaboratus,* pp. of *collaborare,* < L. *com-,* with, + *laborare,* E. *labor, v.*] To work, one with another; coöperate, as in literary work.—**col-lab-o-ra′tion** (-rā′shọn), *n.*—**col-lab′o-ra-tor,** *n.*

col-laps-a-ble (kọ-lap′sạ-bl), *a.* See *collapsible.*

col-lapse (kọ-laps′), *v. i.*; *-lapsed, -lapsing.* [L. *collapsus,* pp. of *collabi,* < *com-,* with, together, + *labi,* fall.] To fall together, as a building through the falling in of its sides; fall into an irregular mass or a flattened form, through loss of rigidity or support; fall or cave in; fig., to break down or fail; come to nothing; also, to lose strength, courage, etc., suddenly.—**col-lapse′,** *n.* A collapsing, or the resulting state; a complete failure; a breakdown; sudden failure of the vital powers, as from exhaustion.—**col-laps′i-ble,** *a.* Capable of collapsing; made to collapse, or fold together.

col-lar (kol′ạ̈r), *n.* [OF. *colier* (F. *collier*), < L. *collum,* neck.] Anything worn or placed about the neck for dress, ornament, restraint, etc.; also, an encircling band, ring, etc., resembling or suggesting this, as a flange or ring on a shaft for holding a pulley or the like in position; in *zoöl.,* any of various markings or structures about the neck, suggesting a collar; a torques.—**collar of S's** or **SS** or **esses,** an ornamental collar comprising a number of S's, sometimes combined with other figures, long in use in England, having been worn as a badge by adherents of the royal house of Lancaster, and still forming a part of the ceremonial dress of certain officials.—**col′lar,** *v. t.* To put a collar on; furnish with a collar; also, to seize by the collar or neck; hence, to lay hold of, seize, or take (slang: as, "S'pose people left money laying around . . . He *collared* it," Mark Twain's "Huckleberry Finn," xxiii.); also, to roll up and bind (meat, fish, etc.) for cooking.—**col′lar=beam,** *n.* A horizontal beam extending between two opposite rafters at some height above their base.—**col′lar=bone,** *n.* The clavicle.

col-lard (kol′ạ̈rd), *n.* [Corruption of *colewort.*] A kind of kale, eaten as a green vegetable.

col-lared (kol′ạ̈rd), *p. a.* Wearing or having a collar; also, rolled up and bound with a string, as a piece of meat.

col-lar-ette (kol-ạ̈r-et′), *n.* A woman's collar or neck-piece of lace, embroidery, chiffon, fur, or other material.

col-lar-less (kol′ạ̈r-les), *a.* Without a collar.

col-lar=work (kol′ạ̈r-wėrk), *n.* Heavy or uphill work, such as compels a horse to press against the collar; fig., difficult work of any kind.

col-late (kọ-lāt′), *v. t.*; *-lated, -lating.* [L. *collatus,* pp. of *conferre,* bring together: see *confer.*] To compare (texts, statements, etc.), in order to note points of agreement or disagreement; examine and verify the arrangement of (the sheets of a book) before binding; also, to confer† or bestow†; *eccles.,* to present by collation, as to a benefice.

col-lat-er-al (kọ-lat′ẹ-rạl). [ML. *collateralis,* < L. *com-,* with, + *latus,* side.] **I.** *a.* Situated at the side; running side by side; fig., accompanying or attendant; corresponding; also, aside from the main subject, course, etc.; secondary; indirect; also, additional or confirming (as, *collateral* security, such as is given to insure the fulfilment of a contract or other obligation); secured by collateral (as, a *collateral* loan); also, descended from the same stock, but in a different line, or pertaining to those so descended (cf. *lineal*). **II.** *n.* Collateral security; also, a collateral kinsman.—**col-lat′er-al-ly,** *adv.*

col-la-tion (kọ-lā′shọn), *n.* [OF. F. *collation,* < L. *collatio(n-),* < *collatus*: see *collate.*] The act of collating; critical comparison, as of texts; also, conference† or consultation†; a repast (orig. of monks in a monastery); an entertainment of food and drink; also, the act of conferring or bestowing†; *eccles.,* the presentation of a clergyman to a benefice, esp. by a bishop who is himself the patron or has acquired the patron's rights.—**col-la′tive,** *a.* [L. *collativus.*] Collating; *eccles.,* presented by collation.—**col-la′tor,** *n.* [L.] One who collates.

col-league[1] (kọ-lēg′), *v.*; *-leagued, -leaguing.* [Obs. F. *colleguer, colliguer,* < L. *colligare:* see *colligate.*] **I.**† *tr.* To join in alliance. **II.** *intr.* To enter into an alliance; combine; also, to conspire.

col-league[2] (kol′ēg), *n.* [F. *collègue,* < L. *collega,* < *com-,* with, + *legare,* depute.] An associate in office or in special work.—**col′league-ship,** *n.*

col-lect (kọ-lekt′), *v.* [L. *collectus,* pp. of *colligere,* < *com-,* with, together, + *legere,* gather.] **I.** *tr.* To gather together; assemble; accumulate; make a collection of; also, to receive or compel payment of; also, to regain control of (one's thoughts, faculties, etc., or one's self); also, to gather or infer (now rare: as, "By all best conjectures, I *collect* Thou art to be my fatal enemy," Milton's "Paradise Regained," iv. 524). **II.** *intr.* To gather together; assemble; accumulate.—**col-lect** (kol′ekt), *n.* [ML. *collecta.*] Any of certain brief prayers used in Western churches, as before the epistle in the eucharistic service, and, in Anglican churches, in morning and evening prayer.—**col-lect′a-ble, col-lect′i-ble,** *a.* That may be collected.

col-lec-ta-ne-a (kol-ek-tā′nẹ-ạ̈), *n. pl.* [L., neut. pl. of *collectaneus,* collected, < *colligere:* see *collect, v.*] Collected passages; a miscellany.

col-lect-ed (kọ-lek′ted), *p. a.* [See *collect, v.*] Having control of one's faculties; self-possessed.—**col-lect′ed-ly,** *adv.* —**col-lect′ed-ness,** *n.*

col-lec-tion (kọ-lek′shọn), *n.* [L. *collectio(n-).*] The act of collecting; also, that which is collected; a set of objects, specimens, writings, etc., gathered together; a sum of money collected, as for church use or for charity.

col-lec-tive (kọ-lek′tiv), *a.* [L. *collectivus.*] Formed by collection; forming a collection or aggregate; aggregate; combined; also, pertaining to a group of individuals taken together; in *bot.,* of a fruit, formed by the coalescence of the pistils of several flowers, as the mulberry or the pineapple (cf. *aggregate*); in *gram.,* of nouns, expressing under the singular form a plurality of individual objects or persons, as *herd, jury, clergy* (which as subjects may take their verbs in either the singular or the plural, according as they are used to express more prominently the idea of unity or of plurality).—**collective bargaining,** the practice or principle of bargaining by employees collectively with their employers, as with reference to wages, hours of work, etc., or by representatives of bodies of employees with employers or their representatives.—**col-lec′tive,** *n.* A collective body; an aggregate; in *gram.,* a collective noun.—**col-lec′tive-ly,** *adv.* —**col-lec′tive-ness,** *n.*—**col-lec′tiv-ism,** *n.* The socialistic principle of control by the people collectively, or the state, of all means of production or economic activities. Cf. *individualism.*—**col-lec′tiv-ist,** *n.*—**col-lec-tiv-i-ty** (kol-ek-tiv′i-ti), *n.* Collective character; a collective whole; the people collectively; collectivism.—**col-lec′tiv-ize** (-īz), *v. t.*; *-ized, -izing.* To make collective; gather into one; combine.—**col-lec″tiv-i-za′tion** (-i-zā′shọn), *n.*

col-lec-tor (kọ-lek′tọr), *n.* [LL.] One who or that which collects; an official appointed to collect taxes or customs; any arrangement for collecting electricity.—**col-lec′tor-ate** (-ạ̄t), *n.* The district of a collector, as of taxes.—**col-lec′tor-ship,** *n.* The office or jurisdiction of a collector, as of taxes or customs.—**col-lec′tress,** *n.* A female collector.

col-leen (kol′ēn or ko-lēn′), *n.* [Ir. *cailín.*] A girl. [Ir.]

col-lege (kol′ej), *n.* [OF. *college* (F. *collège*), < L. *collegium,* association, a society, < *collega:* see *colleague*[2].] An organized association of persons invested with certain powers and rights, and performing certain duties or engaged in a particular pursuit (as, an electoral *college,* a body of electors; the Sacred *College,* the body of cardinals in the Roman Catholic Church); a company or assemblage; a body of clergy living together on a foundation for religious service, etc.; an endowed, self-governing association of scholars incorporated within a university for purposes of instruction, as at the universities of Oxford and Cambridge in England; a similar corporation outside a university; an institution of learning of the highest grade, esp. one not divided (like a university) into distinct schools and faculties, and affording a general or liberal education rather than technical or professional training; the academic department of a university, furnishing courses of instruction in the liberal arts and sciences, leading to the degree of bachelor (as distinguished from the professional and graduate schools); an institution for special or professional instruction, as in medicine, pharmacy, agriculture, or music; sometimes (as in French use), an institution for secondary education; also, the building or buildings occupied by any such association or institution.—**college ice.** Same as *sundae.*—**college widow,** an unmarried woman living in a college town, who has received the attentions of students of several successive classes. [Colloq.]—**col-leg-er** (kol′e-jẻr), *n.* A member of a college; at Eton College, England, a student who is supported on the foundation.

col-le-gi-al (kọ-lē′ji-ạl), *a.* [L. *collegialis.*] Of, pertaining to, or constituting a college; also, pertaining to collegialism.—**col-le′gi-al-ism,** *n.* The theory of church polity maintaining that the church is a voluntary association in which the highest ecclesiastical authority is vested in the whole society, and not in a clerical order or in the state.

col-le-gi-an (kọ-lē′ji-ạn), *n.* A member of a college; a student in, or one who has been educated at, a college.

col-le-gi-ate (kọ-lē′ji-ạ̄t), *a.* [ML. *collegiatus.*] Of or pertaining to a college; of the nature of or constituted as a college.—**collegiate church,** a church which has a college or chapter but not a bishop's see; in the U. S., a church or association of churches administered by several pastors jointly; a consolidation of formerly distinct churches under one or more pastors.

col-leg-ing (kol′e-jing), *n.* Training or education at college: as, "I am glad That here what *colleging* was mine I had" (Lowell's "Indian-Summer Reverie," 265).

col-len-chy-ma (ko-leng′ki-mạ̈), *n.* [NL., < Gr. κόλλα, glue, + *-enchyma* as in *parenchyma.*] In *bot.,* a layer of modified parenchyma immediately beneath the epidermis, consisting of cells which are thickened at the angles and commonly elongated.

col-let (kol′et), *n.* [F. *collet,* dim. of *col,* < L. *collum,* neck.] A collar or inclosing band; the inclosing rim within which a jewel is set.—**col′let,** *v. t.*; *-leted, -leting.* To set in a collet.

col-lide (kọ-līd′), *v. i.*; *-lided, -liding.* [L. *collidere* (pp. *collisus*), < *com-,* with, + *lædere,* hurt by striking.] To come violently into contact; encounter with a shock; fig., to clash or conflict.

col-lie (kol′i), *n.* [Origin uncertain.] A dog of any of certain intelligent varieties much used for tending sheep, esp. one of a Scotch breed with a heavy coat of long hair and a bushy tail.

Collie.

col-lied (kol′id). Pret. and pp. of *colly*[1].

col-lier (kol′yẻr), *n.* [ME. *colyer,* < *col,* E. *coal.*] One who carries or sells coal†; a coal-miner; a ship for carrying coal.—**col′lier-y,** *n.*; pl. *-ies* (-iz). A coal-mining establishment.

col-li-gate (kol′i-gāt), *v. t.*; *-gated, -gating.* [L. *colligatus,* pp. of *colligare,* < *com-,* with, together, + *ligare,* bind.] To bind together; connect.—**col-li-ga′tion** (-gā′shọn), *n.*

col-li-mate (kol′i-māt), *v. t.*; *-mated, -mating.* [From a false reading of L. *collineatus* (taken as *collimatus*), pp. of *collineare,* < *com-,* with, + *lineare,* reduce to a straight line.] To bring into line; make parallel; adjust accurately the line of sight of (a telescope).—**col-li-ma′tion** (-mā′shọn), *n.*—**col′li-ma-tor,** *n.* A fixed telescope for use in collimating other instruments; also, the receiving telescope of a spectroscope.

col-lin-e-ar (ko-lin′ẹ̄-ạ̈r), *a.* [L. *com-,* with, + *linea,* line.] Lying in the same straight line.—**col-lin-e-ar′i-ty** (-ar′i-ti), *n.*—**col-lin′e-ar-ly,** *adv.*

col-lin-gual (ko-ling′gwạl), *a.* [L. *com-,* with, + *lingua,* tongue.] Speaking the same language.

col-lin-si-a (ko-lin′si-ạ̈), *n.* [NL.; from Z. *Collins* (1764–1831), American botanist.] Any of the scrophulariaceous herbs constituting the genus *Collinsia,* bearing whorled, (usually) party-colored flowers.

col-li-quate† (kol′i-kwāt), *v. t.*; *-quated*, *-quating*. [L. *com-*, with, + *liquare* (pp. *liquatus*), melt.] To melt together; also, to melt; liquefy.—**col-li-qua-tive** (kǫ-lik′wą-tiv), *a.* Melting; in *pathol.*, profuse or excessive in flow, so as to cause exhaustion (as, a *colliquative* sweat).

col-li-sion (kǫ-lizh′ǫn), *n.* [LL. *collisio(n-)*, < L. *collidere*, E. *collide*.] The act of colliding; a coming violently into contact, as of one body with another or of two bodies suddenly meeting; fig., a clash or conflict (as, "The houses . . . had already been the scene of *collisions* between the domestic slaves and the multitude": J. H. Newman's "Callista," xvii.).

col-lo-cate (kol′ǭ-kāt), *v. t.*; *-cated*, *-cating*. [L. *collocatus*, pp. of *collocare*, < *com-*, with, + *locare*, place, E. *locate*.] To place together; arrange; put in place.—**col-lo-ca′tion** (-kā′shǫn), *n.* [L. *collocatio(n-)*.] The act of collocating, or the state or manner of being collocated; disposition with, or in relation to, others; arrangement, as of words in a sentence.—**col′lo-ca-tive** (-ką-tiv), *a.*

col-lo-cu-tion (kol-ǭ-kū′shǫn), *n.* [L. *collocutio(n-)*, < *colloqui*: see *colloquy*.] A speaking together; colloquy.—**col-loc-u-tor** (kǫ-lok′ū-tǫr), *n.* [LL.] A speaker in a colloquy.

col-lo-di-on (kǫ-lō′di-ǫn), *n.* [Gr. κολλώδης, glue-like, < κόλλα, glue, + εἶδος, form.] Soluble guncotton dissolved in ether or in a mixture of ether and alcohol: used to form a coating or film on wounds, photographic plates, etc.—**col-lo′di-on-ize**, *v. t.*; *-ized*, *-izing*. To treat with collodion.—**col-lo′di-um** (-um), *n.* Collodion.

col-logue (kǫ-lōg′), *v. i.*; *-logued*, *-loguing*. [Origin uncertain; perhaps akin to *colloquy*.] To use flattery†; also, to confer secretly; plot mischief; conspire (as, "How long have you been so thick with Dunsey that you must *collogue* with him to embezzle my money?" George Eliot's "Silas Marner," ix.). [Now colloq. or prov.]

col-loid (kol′oid). [Gr. κόλλα, glue: see *-oid*.] **I.** *a.* Glue-like; gelatinous; colloidal. **II.** *n.* A gelatinous or other substance which when dissolved in a liquid will not diffuse readily through vegetable or animal membranes. Cf. *crystalloid*.—**col′loid**, *v. t.* To reduce to the form of a colloid.—**col-loi-dal** (ko-loi′dąl), *a.* Pertaining to, of the nature of, or resembling a colloid: as, *colloidal* gold, silver, etc. (gold, silver, etc., in a condition of extreme subdivision, in which it remains suspended or dissolved in water).—**colloidal fuel**, a fuel consisting of an oil (as petroleum) containing a finely powdered carbonaceous substance (as coal) in suspension, recommended as more economical than ordinary fuels and less dangerous to store than petroleum: invented by Lindon W. Bates. [Proprietary name.]—**colloidal particles**, the fine particles which the ultramicroscope shows to be present in a solution containing a colloid.

col-lop (kol′ǫp), *n.* [ME. *colope*, *colloppe*; origin uncertain.] A small slice of bacon or other meat; hence, a small slice or piece of anything; also, a fold or roll of flesh on the body. [Now chiefly prov.]

col-lo-qui-al (kǫ-lō′kwi-ąl), *a.* [L. *colloquium*: see *colloquy*.] Of or pertaining to colloquy or conversation; conversational; of words, phrases, etc., peculiar or appropriate to the language of ordinary or familiar conversation, but not admissible in formal speech or writing.—**col-lo′qui-al-ism**, *n.* Colloquial style, quality, or usage; a colloquial expression.—**col-lo′qui-al-ly**, *adv.*

col-lo-quist (kol′ǭ-kwist), *n.* A speaker in a colloquy; an interlocutor.

col-lo-quize (kol′ǭ-kwīz), *v. i.*; *-quized*, *-quizing*. To take part in a colloquy; converse: as, "All I had now to do was to obey him in silence; no need for me to *colloquize* further" (C. Brontë's "Jane Eyre," xxii.).

col-lo-quy (kol′ǭ-kwi), *n.*; pl. *-quies* (-kwiz). [L. *colloquium*, < *colloqui*, speak together, < *com-*, with, + *loqui*, speak.] A speaking together; a dialogue or conversation; a conference; *eccles.*, in Reformed Presbyterian churches, a judicatory corresponding to a presbytery.

col-lo-type (kol′ǭ-tīp), *n.* [Gr. κόλλα, glue: see *-type*.] A photomechanical process of printing in ink from a gelatin plate; also, the plate, or a print made from it.

col-low (kol′ō), *v. t.* Same as *colly*[1]. [Now prov.]

col-lude (kǫ-lūd′), *v. i.*; *-luded*, *-luding*. [L. *colludere* (pp. *collusus*), < *com-*, with, + *ludere*, play.] To act in concert through a secret understanding; conspire in a fraud.—**col-lud′er**, *n.*

col-lu-sion (kǫ-lū′zhǫn), *n.* [L. *collusio(n-)*, < *colludere*, E. *collude*.] Secret agreement for an unworthy or fraudulent purpose.—**col-lu′sive** (-siv), *a.* Involving collusion; fraudulently concerted.—**col-lu′sive-ly**, *adv.*—**col-lu′sive-ness**, *n.*

col-ly[1] (kol′i), *v. t.*; *-lied*, *-lying*. [Akin to *coal*.] To blacken as with coal-dust; begrime. [Archaic or prov.]

col-ly[2] (kol′i), *n.* See *collie*.

col-lyr-i-um (ko-lir′i-um), *n.*; pl. *-ia* (-i-ä). [L., < Gr. κολλύριον, poultice, eye-salve.] An eye-salve or eye-wash.

col-o-cynth (kol′ǭ-sinth), *n.* [L. *colocynthis*, < Gr. κολοκυνθίς.] A cucurbitaceous plant, *Citrullus colocynthis*, of the warmer parts of Asia, the Mediterranean region, etc., bearing a fruit with a very bitter pulp which yields a purgative drug; also, the fruit, or the drug.

Colocynth. — Flowering branch and fruit.

co-logne (kǫ-lōn′), *n.* [For *Cologne water* (made at Cologne, Germany, since 1709).] A perfumed spirit or toilet-water.

Co-lom-bi-an (kǫ-lom′bi-ąn). **I.** *a.* Of or pertaining to the South American republic of Colombia. **II.** *n.* A native or inhabitant of Colombia.

co-lon[1] (kō′lǫn), *n.*; pl. (1st sense) *colons*, (2d sense) *cola* (-lä). [L., < Gr. κῶλον, limb, member, clause.] A point of punctuation (:) marking off a main portion of a sentence (intermediate in force between the semicolon and the period); in *anc. pros.*, one of the members or sections of a rhythmical period, consisting of a sequence of from two to six feet united under a principal ictus or beat.

co-lon[2] (kō′lǫn), *n.*; pl. *cola* (-lä). [L., < Gr. κόλον, food, colon.] In *anat.*, that portion of the large intestine which extends from the cæcum to the rectum.

colo-nel (kėr′nęl), *n.* [Earlier *coronel* (whence the modern pronunciation), < F. *coronel*, now *colonel*, < It. *colonnello*, dim. of *colonna*, (army) column, < L. *columna*, E. *column*.] An officer in command of a regiment, or holding an equivalent position, and ranking in the U. S. next below a brigadier-general.—**Colonel Bogey.** See under *bogey*[1].—**colo′nel-cy** (-si), *n.*; pl. *-cies* (-siz). The office, rank, or commission of a colonel. Also **colo′nel-ship.**

co-lo-ni-al (kǭ-lō′ni-ąl). **I.** *a.* Of or pertaining to a colony or colonies; esp., pertaining to the thirteen British colonies which became the United States of America, or to their period. **II.** *n.* An inhabitant of a colony.—**co-lo′ni-al-ism**, *n.* Colonial character or usage; a colonial practice or idiom; the colonial system.—**co-lo′ni-al-ly**, *adv.*

col-o-nist (kol′ǭ-nist), *n.* An inhabitant of a colony; a member of a colonizing expedition.

col-o-ni-tis (kol-ǭ-nī′tis), *n.* Same as *colitis*.

col-o-nize (kol′ǭ-nīz), *v.*; *-nized*, *-nizing*. **I.** *tr.* To establish a colony in (a place); settle; also, to establish (persons) in a colony. **II.** *intr.* To form a colony; settle in a colony.—**col″o-ni-za′tion** (-ni-zā′shǫn), *n.*—**col′o-niz-er** (-nī-zėr), *n.*

col-on-nade (kol-ǫ-nād′), *n.* [F., < It. *colonnata*, < *colonna*, < L. *columna*, E. *column*.] In *arch.*, a series of columns set at regular intervals, and usually supporting an entablature.—**col-on-nad′ed** (-nā′ded), *a.*

col-o-ny (kol′ǭ-ni), *n.*; pl. *-nies* (-niz). [L. *colonia*, < *colonus*, husbandman, colonist, < *colere*, cultivate.] A body of people who leave their native country to form in a new land a settlement subject to or connected with the parent state; such people and their descendants, so long as the connection with the parent state is retained; the country or district settled or colonized; any people or territory distant from but subject to a ruling power; also, a number of foreigners from a particular country living in a city or country, esp. in one locality (as, the American *colony* in Paris); any group of individuals of like nature or character settled among others or living by themselves (as, a *colony* of artists; a *colony* of lepers); the district or quarter inhabited by any such number or group; in *biol.*, a group of animals or plants of the same kind living or growing together in close association; a number of individual animals united in a connected structure, as polyzoans, etc.; an aggregation of bacteria in a culture.

col-o-phon (kol′ǭ-fǫn), *n.* [LL., < Gr. κολοφών, summit, finishing touch.] An inscription or device commonly used in former times to terminate a manuscript or book, and often giving the subject, the scribe's or printer's name, the date and place of production, etc.; in modern use, an inscription, a printer's device, or the like, at the end of a book; hence, a publisher's device as used on a title-page, etc.

col-o-pho-ny (kol′ǭ-fǭ-ni or kǭ-lof′ǭ-ni), *n.* [L. *Colophonia* (*resina*), (resin) of Colophon (Ionian city in Asia Minor).] Common rosin, the hard amorphous substance derived from the oleoresin of the pine.

col-o-quin-ti-da (kol-ǭ-kwin′ti-dạ̈), *n.* [ML.] Colocynth. See Shakspere's "Othello," i. 3. 355.

col-or (kul′ǫr), *n.* [OF. *color* (F. *couleur*), < L. *color*, color, hue.] A quality of a thing or appearance, distinct from form, which is perceived by the eye alone, and is associated with the effect of particular light-vibrations on the optic nerve; hue; a particular hue or tint, esp. one other than black or white; also, racial hue or complexion other than that of white peoples, esp. that of the negro race; also, the natural hue of the face; complexion; a ruddy complexion; the flush caused by blushing; also, coloring, as in a painting; an effect of coloration produced by chiaroscuro, as in an engraving; also, vivid or distinctive quality, as of literary work; timbre of sound; also, that which is used for coloring; a pigment, paint, or dye; also, any hue adopted for distinction, as for a badge; usually *pl.*, a flag, ensign, etc., as of a military body or a ship; *pl.*, in the U. S. navy, the ceremony of hoisting the national flag at 8 A.M., and of lowering it at sunset; also, *sing.*, valuable mineral, esp. gold as shown by washing auriferous gravel, etc.; a trace or particle of such mineral; also, outward appearance or aspect; guise or show; a pretext; an apparent or prima facie right or ground (esp. in legal use: as, to hold possession under *color* of title); also, general character; kind or sort.—**complementary colors,** pairs of colors that when mixed produce white or gray light.—**primary colors,** the seven colors of the spectrum, red, orange, yellow, green, blue, indigo, and violet; sometimes, the red, green, and violet of the spectrum, or the red, yellow, and blue of pigments.—**col′or,** *v.* [OF. F. *colorer*, < L. *colorare* (pp. *coloratus*), < *color*.] **I.** *tr.* To give or apply color to; tinge; paint; dye; fig., to cause to appear different from the reality; also, to give a special character or distinguishing quality to (as, an account *colored* by personal feelings). **II.** *intr.* To take on or change color; flush; blush.—**col′or-a-ble,** *a.* Capable of being colored; also, specious or plausible; also, pretended; deceptive.—**col′or-a-bly,** *adv.*

col-o-ra-do (kol-ǭ-rä′dō), *a.* [Sp., colored, red.] Of cigars, of medium color and strength.

Col-o-ra-do (kol-ǭ-rä′dō) **bee′tle.** Same as *potato-beetle.*

col-or-ant (kul′ǫr-ạnt), *n.* [F. *colorant*, prop. ppr.] A coloring matter.

col-or-a-tion (kul-ǫ-rā′shǫn), *n.* [F. *coloration.*] Coloring; appearance as to color.

co-lo-ra-tu-ra (kō-lō-rä-tö′rä), *n.* [= G. *coloratur*, < It. *coloratura*, < LL. *coloratura*, coloring, < L. *colorare*, E. *color*, *v.*] Runs, trills, and other florid decorations in vocal music. Also **col-or-a-ture** (kul′ǫr-ạ-ṯūr).

col-or=bear-er (kul′ǫr-bãr″ėr), *n.* One who carries the colors or standard, as of a military body.

col-or=blind (kul′ǫr-blīnd), *a.* Incapable of perceiving certain colors; unable to discriminate between particular colors.—**col′or=blind″ness,** *n.*

col-ored (kul′ǫrd), *a.* Having color; of a hue other than black or white: also, belonging wholly or in part to some other race than the white, esp. to the negro race; pertaining to the negro race; in *bot.*, of some hue other than green.

col-or-er (kul′ǫr-ėr), *n.* One who or that which colors.

col-or-ful (kul′ǫr-fu̇l), *a.* Abounding in color; fig., richly picturesque (as, a *colorful* historical period); presenting or suggesting vivid or striking scenes (as, a *colorful* narrative).—**col′or-ful-ly,** *adv.*—**col′or-ful-ness,** *n.*

col-or=guard (kul′ǫr-gärd), *n.* A guard having charge of the colors, as of a regiment.

col-or-if-ic (kul-ǫ-rif′ik), *a.* [See *-fic.*] Producing or imparting color.

col-or-im-e-ter (kul-ǫ-rim′e-tėr), *n.* [See *-meter.*] An instrument for determining the strength of colors, esp. of dyes.—**col″or-i-met′ric, col″or-i-met′ri-cal** (-ǫ-ri-met′rik, -ri-kạl), *a.*—**col-or-im′e-try,** *n.*

col-or-ing (kul′ǫr-ing), *n.* The act or the mode of applying color; appearance as to color; fig., characteristic aspect or tone; also, specious appearance; show; also, a substance used to color something.

col-or-ist (kul′ǫr-ist), *n.* A user of color, as in painting; a painter who devotes himself specially to effects of color.—**col-or-is′tic,** *a.*

col-or-less (kul′ǫr-les), *a.* Without color; pallid; dull in color; fig., without vividness or distinctive character (as, a *colorless* narrative; a *colorless* person); sometimes, unbiased; neutral.—**col′or-less-ly,** *adv.*—**col′or-less-ness,** *n.*

color=line (kul′ǫr-līn), *n.* The line of social or political distinction between the white and colored races. [Chiefly U. S.]

col-or=ser-geant (kul′ǫr-sär″jẹnt), *n.* A sergeant who has charge of battalion or regimental colors.

co-los-sal (kǭ-los′ạl), *a.* Like a colossus; gigantic; huge; vast.—**co-los′sal-ly,** *adv.*

Col-os-se-um, Col-i-se-um (kol-ǫ-sē′um, kol-i-), *n.* [ML. *Colosseum*, also *Coliseum*, prop. neut. of L. *colosseus*, colossal, < *colossus*: see *colossus.*] An amphitheater in Rome, the greatest ancient amphitheater, begun by the emperor Vespasian and finished (A.D. 80) by Titus (as, "While stands the Coliseum, Rome shall stand; When falls the Coliseum, Rome shall fall; And when Rome falls—the World": Byron's "Childe Harold," iv. 145); hence, a name applied to various other amphitheaters and large theaters and halls.

Remains of the Colosseum in Rome.

Co-los-sian (kǭ-los̱′iạn). **I.** *a.* Belonging to Colossæ, an ancient city of Phrygia, in Asia Minor. **II.** *n.* An inhabitant of Colossæ; *pl.*, the book of the New Testament called "The Epistle of Paul the Apostle to the Colossians."

co-los-sus (kǭ-los′us), *n.*; pl. *colossi* (-ī) or *colossuses.* [L., < Gr. κολοσσός.] A statue of gigantic size, as the bronze statue of Apollo at Rhodes ('Colossus of Rhodes': overthrown by earthquake in 224 B.C.); hence, anything colossal or gigantic.

co-los-trum (kǭ-los′trum), *n.* [L.] The milk secreted before and for a few days after parturition.—**co-los′tric,** *a.*

co-lot-o-my (kǭ-lot′ǭ-mi), *n.* [Gr. κόλον, colon, + -τομία, < τέμνειν, cut.] In *surg.*, the operation of making an incision into the colon.

col-our (kul′ǫr), **col′our-a-ble,** etc. (including most derivatives formed in English from these words). British preferred forms of *color*, *colorable*, etc.

-colous. [L. *colere*, inhabit.] An adjective termination meaning 'inhabiting,' 'living in or on,' as in *aquicolous*, *arenicolous*, *lignicolous*.

col-por-tage (kol′pôr-tạ̄j, F. kol-por-täzh), *n.* [F., < *colporter*, hawk, lit. 'carry on the neck,' < *col*, neck, + *porter*, carry.] The work of a colporteur.—**col-por-teur** (kol′pôr-tėr, F. kol-por-tėr), *n.* [F.] A hawker of books, etc.; esp., one employed to travel about distributing Bibles, religious tracts, etc., gratuitously or at a low price.

colt (kōlt), *n.* [AS. *colt*, young ass or camel.] A young horse or animal of the horse kind, esp. a young male; fig., a young or inexperienced person; *naut.*, a rope's end used in chastising (as, "He always carried in his pocket a *colt* . . . for the benefit of the youngsters": Marryat's "King's Own," viii.).

col-ter, coul-ter (kōl′tėr), *n.* [AS. *culter*, < L. *culter*, colter, knife.] A sharp blade or wheel attached to a plowbeam, used to cut the ground in advance of the plowshare.

Knife-colter.

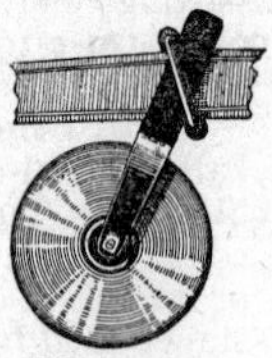
Wheel-colter.

colt-ish (kōl′tish), *a.* Colt-like; frisky; wanton.—**colt′ish-ness,** *n.*

colts-foot (kōlts′fu̇t), *n.* An asteraceous plant, *Tussilago farfara*, with large cordate leaves which were formerly much used in medicine.

Coltsfoot.

col-u-brine (kol′ū̦-brin), *a.* [L. *colubrinus*, < *coluber*, serpent.] Pertaining to a serpent or snake; snake-like; in *zoöl.*, of or pertaining to a group of snakes (suborder *Colubrina* or family *Colubridæ*) which is sometimes regarded as containing only non-venomous species and sometimes both non-venomous and venomous, and which includes many common non-venomous snakes of Europe and North America.

co-lu-go (kǫ-lö′gō), *n.*; pl. *-gos* (-gōz). [E. Ind.] The flying-lemur.

col-um-ba-ri-um (kol-um-bā′ri-um), *n.*; pl. *-riums* or *-ria* (-ri-ä̤). [L., < *columba*, dove.] A dove-cote; also, a sepulchral vault or other structure with recesses in the walls to receive the ashes of the dead; also, one of the recesses.—**col′um-ba-ry** (-bä̤-ri), *n.*; pl. *-ries* (-riz). A dove-cote.

Columbarium, near gate of St. Sebastian, Rome.

Co-lum-bi-a (kǫ-lum′bi-ä̤), *n.* [From Christopher *Columbus*, discoverer of America.] America, or the United States, esp. as a feminine personification.—**Co-lum′bi-ad** (-ad), *n.* An epic of America (as, "The *Columbiad*," the title of an epic poem by Joel Barlow, published in 1807); also [*l. c.*], a kind of heavy smooth-bore cannon formerly used in the U. S.—**Co-lum′bi-an. I.** *a.* Pertaining to America or the United States, or to Columbus. **II.** *n.* [Also *l. c.*] A printing-type (16 point) of a size between English and great primer. See *type*.

co-lum-bic (kǫ-lum′bik), *a.* Of or pertaining to columbium; niobic.

col-um-bine¹ (kol′um-bin), *a.* [L. *columbinus*, < *columba*, dove.] Of or pertaining to a dove; dove-like; dove-colored.

col-um-bine² (kol′um-bīn), *n.* [LL. *columbina*, prop. fem. of L. *columbinus*, dove-like; from the resemblance of the inverted flower to a group of doves.] Any plant of the ranunculaceous genus *Aquilegia*, comprising erect branching herbs with handsome flowers having five colored sepals alternating with as many petals produced backward between the sepals to form hollow spurs, as *A. canadensis* (the common wild columbine of North America), commonly having red flowers, and various other species, with blue, purple, white, pink, or yellow flowers, some of which are familiar in cultivation.

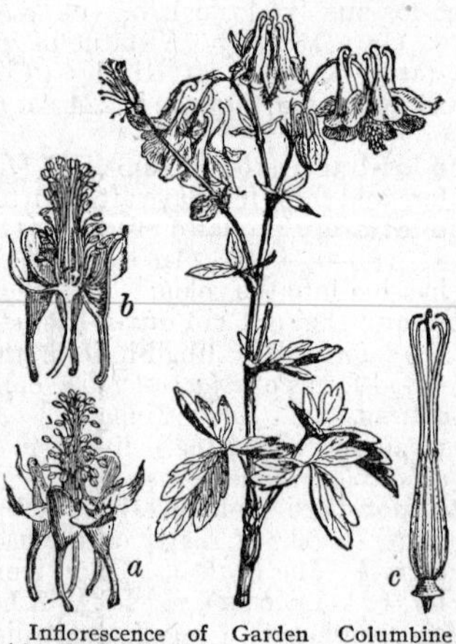

Inflorescence of Garden Columbine (*Aquilegia vulgaris*). — *a*, flower; *b*, same, cut vertically; *c*, pistils.

Col-um-bine³ (kol′um-bīn), *n.* [It. *Colombina.*] [Also *l. c.*] A female character in comedy (orig. the early Italian) and pantomime, the sweetheart of Harlequin.

co-lum-bite (kǫ-lum′bīt), *n.* A black crystalline mineral consisting of a compound of iron and columbium, containing often manganese and tantalum.

co-lum-bi-um (kǫ-lum′bi-um), *n.* [NL.; from *Columbia*, the United States.] Chem. sym., Cb (or Nb); at. wt., 93.5; sp. gr., 7.06. A steel-gray metallic element resembling tantalum in its chemical properties. Also called *niobium.*

co-lum-bo (kǫ-lum′bō), *n.* Same as *calumba.*

Co-lum-bus (kǫ-lum′bus), *n.* [From Christopher *Columbus* (about 1446–1506).] The maker of some momentous discovery; a discoverer: as, a *Columbus* of the obvious.—**Co-lum′bus Day.** A day, Oct. 12, publicly appointed or observed as a holiday in various individual States of the U. S., in honor of the discovery of America by Columbus on Oct. 12, 1492.

col-u-mel-la (kol-ū̦-mel′ä̤), *n.*; pl. *-mellæ* (-ē). [L., dim. of *columna*, E. *column.*] In *anat.*, *zoöl.*, and *bot.*, a column-like part; an axis.—**col-u-mel′lar,** *a.*

col-umn (kol′um), *n.* [L. *columna*, akin to *columen*, *culmen*, top (see *culminate*), *celsus*, high, *excellere*, raise, rise, E. *excel*, also to E. *hill.*] An upright shaft or body of greater length than thickness, usually serving as a support; a pillar; esp., a vertical architectural member consisting typically of an approximately cylindrical shaft with a base and a capital; also, one of the supporting uprights in iron and steel construction work; hence, any column-like object, mass, or formation; esp., one of the two or more vertical rows of lines of type or printed matter of a page, etc.; in journalistic use, such a row of lines, constituting a special department of a newspaper, furnished regularly by a particular editor or writer; often, such a department devoted to short articles, jottings, poems, etc., of a humorous, entertaining, or especially readable kind, furnished by a particular editor or writer without or with the aid of contributors; also, a formation of troops narrow laterally and extended from front to rear; a line of ships following one after another; in *bot.*, a body formed by the union of filaments, as in mallows, or by the union of stamens and styles, as in orchids.—**co-lum-nar** (kǫ-lum′nä̤r), *a.* [LL. *columnaris.*] Of, pertaining to, or of the nature of a column or columns; column-like.—**col′umned,** *a.* Having columns; formed into columns.—**co-lum-ni-a′tion** (-ni-ā′shǫn), *n.* The use of columns, or the columns used, in a structure.—**co-lum′ni-form,** *a.* Column-shaped.—**col′umn-ist,** *n.* The editor or conductor of a special column in a newspaper. See *column.*

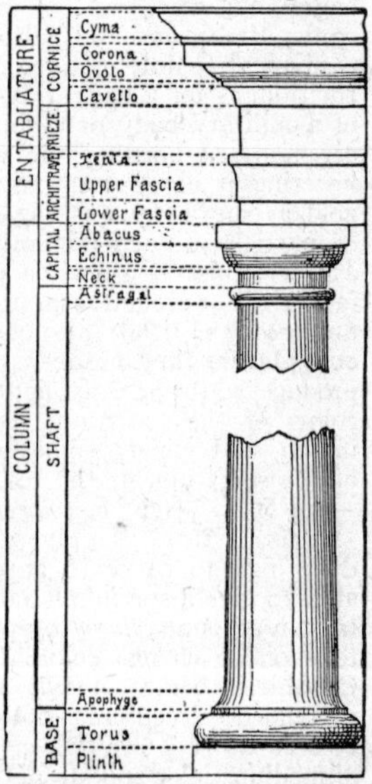

Architectural Column (Tuscan order), illustrating the terms applied to the several parts.

co-lure (kǫ-lūr′ or kō′lū̦r), *n.* [LL. *colurus*, < Gr. κόλουρος, < κόλος, docked, + οὐρά, tail (the colures being cut off by the horizon).] Either of two great circles of the celestial sphere intersecting each other at the poles, one passing through the equinoctial and the other through the solstitial points of the ecliptic.

co-ly (kō′li), *n.* See *colie.*

col-za (kol′zä̤), *n.* [F., < D. *koolzaad* = E. *cole-seed.*] Cole-seed; rape.

com-. [L. *com-* (also *co-*, *col-*, *con-*, *cor-*), repr. *cum*, prep., with.] A prefix of Latin origin, meaning 'with,' 'together,' 'altogether,' occasionally used as an English formative, as in *commingle, commutual.* Cf. *co-*.

co-ma[1] (kō′mạ̈), *n.* [NL., < Gr. κῶμα, < κεῖσθαι, lie.] A state of prolonged unconsciousness from which it is difficult or impossible to rouse a person, due to disease, injury, poison, etc.; stupor.

co-ma[2] (kō′mạ̈), *n.*; pl. *comæ* (-mē). [L., < Gr. κόμη, hair.] In *bot.*, a tuft of silky hairs at the end of a seed; in *astron.*, the nebulous envelop around the nucleus of a comet; in *optics*, the blurred appearance or hazy border surrounding an object viewed through a lens which is not free from spherical aberration.—**co′mal,** *a.*

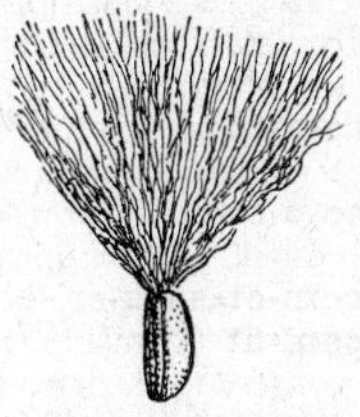

Seed of Willow-herb (*Chamænerion*), with Coma.

Co-man-che-an (kọ-man′chẹ-ạn). [From *Comanche*, town and county in north-central Texas.] In *geol.*: **I.** *a.* Noting or pertaining to a geological period or a system of rocks in North America equivalent to the earlier portion of the Cretaceous period or system. **II.** *n.* The Comanchean period or system.

co-marb (kō′märb), *n.* Same as *coarb.*

co-mate (kō′māt), *a.* [L. *comatus*, < *coma*, hair, E. *coma*[2].] Hairy; tufted; in *bot.*, having a coma.

co=mate (kō′māt or kō-māt′), *n.* [See *co-*.] A mate or companion: as, "my *co-mates* and brothers in exile" (Shakspere's "As You Like It," ii. 1. 1).

co-ma-tose (kō′mạ-tōs), *a.* Of, pertaining to, or of the nature of coma; affected with coma; lethargic.—**co′ma-tose-ly,** *adv.*

co-mat-u-la (kọ-mat′ụ̄-lạ̈), *n.*; pl. *-læ* (-lē). [NL., prop. fem. of L. *comatulus*, dim. of *comatus*, E. *comate.*] Any of certain crinoids of the genus *Antedon*, etc., having a feathery appearance and radiate form, and free-swimming in the adult stage; a feather-star.

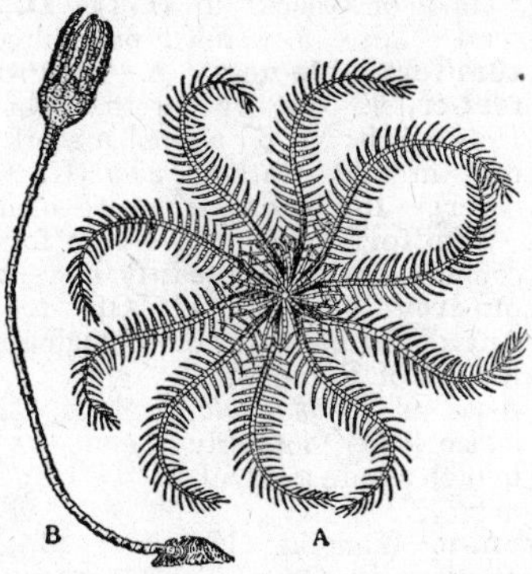

A, Comatula (*Antedon rosacea*), adult free form; *B*, Comatula (*Antedon dentata*), young stalked and fixed form (slightly enlarged).

comb[1] (kōm), *n.* [AS. *camb* = D. *kam* = G. *kamm.*] A toothed instrument, as of bone, metal, etc., for arranging or cleansing the hair, or for keeping it in place; a curry-comb; a card for dressing wool, etc.; any comb-like instrument, object, or formation; also, the fleshy, more or less serrated excrescence or growth on the head of the domestic fowl; something resembling or suggesting this, as the top or crest of a wave; also, a honeycomb, or any similar mass of cells.—**comb**[1], *v.* **I.** *tr.* To dress (the hair, etc.) with or as with a comb; card, as wool; scrape as with a comb. **II.** *intr.* To roll over or break at the crest, as a wave: as, "All round me were little ripples, *combing* over with a sharp, bristling sound" (Stevenson's "Treasure Island," xxiii.).

comb[2], **combe, coomb** (köm or kōm, köm), *n.* [AS. *cumb.*] A narrow valley or deep hollow, esp. one inclosed on all sides but one: as, "From those heights We dropped, at pleasure, into sylvan *combs*" (Wordsworth's "Excursion," iii. 545); "The Forest above and the *Combe* below, On a bright September morn!" (H. Newbolt's "Song of Exmoor"). [Eng.]

com-bat (kom′bat or kum′-), *v.*; *-bated, -bating.* [F. *combattre*, < L. *com-*, with, + *battere*, for *batuere*, beat.] **I.** *intr.* To fight (*with* or *against*); battle; contend. **II.** *tr.* To fight or contend against; oppose vigorously.—**com′bat,** *n.* [F.] A fight, esp. between two ('single combat'); in general, a struggle; a conflict.—**com′bat-a-ble** (-bat-ạ-bl), *a.* Capable of being combated.—**com′bat-ant** (-bạ-tạnt). **I.** *a.* Combating; fighting; also, disposed to combat or contend; in *her.*, rampant as if in combat, as two lions, etc., facing each other. **II.** *n.* One who takes part in combat or fighting, or in any conflict.—**com′bat-er** (-bat-ėr), *n.*—**com′ba-tive** (-bạ-tiv), *a.* Disposed to combat; pugnacious.—**com′ba-tive-ly,** *adv.*—**com′ba-tive-ness,** *n.* Propensity to combat: in *phren.*, a special faculty.

Two Lions Combatant.

combe, *n.* See *comb*[2].

comb-er (kō′mėr), *n.* One who or that which combs; esp., a long, curling wave (as, "Out of the mist into the mirk The glimmering *combers* roll": Kipling's "Song in Storm").

com-bin-a-ble (kọm-bī′nạ-bl), *a.* That may be combined; admitting of combination.

com-bi-na-tion (kom-bi-nā′shọn), *n.* [LL. *combinatio(n-).*] The act of combining, or the resulting state; also, a number of things combined, or something formed by combining; an alliance of persons or parties; the set or series of numbers or letters used in setting the mechanism of a certain type of lock used on safes, etc. ('combination lock'), or the parts of the mechanism operated by this; a suit of underwear in one piece; also, chemical union; also, in *math.*, the arrangement of a number of individuals into various groups, each group containing a given number of the individuals (as *a*, *b*, and *c* into *ab*, *ac*, and *bc*); also, one of the groups formed.—**com-bi-na′tion-al,** *a.*—**com′bi-na-tive** (-nạ̄-tiv), **com-bi-na-to-ry** (kọm-bī′nạ-tọ̄-ri), *a.* Tending or serving to combine; also, pertaining to combination.

com-bine (kọm-bīn′), *v.*; *-bined, -bining.* [LL. *combinare*, < L. *com-*, with, + *bini*, two at a time.] **I.** *tr.* To bring or join into a close union or whole; unite; associate; also, to cause to coalesce, as in one body or substance; also, to possess or exhibit in union (as, a plan which *combines* the best features of several other plans). **II.** *intr.* To come together, as into one body; unite; coalesce; specif., to enter into chemical union; also, often, to unite for a common purpose or end; join forces; league together; form a combination.—**combining weight,** in *chem.*, the relative quantity in which an element unites with another element to form a compound.—**com-bine** (kọm-bīn′ or kom′bīn), *n.* A combination; esp., a combination of persons for the furtherance of their political or commercial interests; also, a composite machine formed by combining several simpler machines, as a combined harvester and thresher.—**com-bin′ed-ly** (-bī′ned-li), *adv.*—**com-bin′er,** *n.*

comb-ing (kō′ming), *n.* The act of a person or thing that combs; *pl.*, hairs removed with a comb.

com-bin-ing=form (kọm-bī′ning-fôrm), *n.* A form of a word (English or other) used for combining with other words or word-elements, as *Anglo-* (for L. *Anglus*) in *Anglo-French, Anglophil, aëro-* (for Gr. ἀήρ) in *aëroboat, aërophyte, magneto-* (for *magnetic*) in *magnetometer.*

comb-less (kōm′les), *a.* Without a comb.

comb=rat (kōm′rat), *n.* Same as *ctenodactyl.*

com-bre-ta-ceous (kom-brẹ̄-tā′shius), *a.* [NL. *Combretum*, the typical genus, L. *combretum*, kind of rush.] Belonging to the *Combretaceæ*, a family of shrubs and plants, mostly tropical, yielding tanning and dyeing materials, as the myrobalan.

com-bust (kọm-bust′), *a.* [L. *combustus*, pp. of *comburere*, burn up (cf. *urere*, burn).] Burnt†; in *astrol.*, so near the sun as to be obscured by it.

com-bus-ti-ble (kọm-bus′ti-bl). [F. *combustible*, < L. *comburere* (pp. *combustus*): see *combust.*] **I.** *a.* Capable of taking fire and burning; inflammable; fig., easily excited. **II.** *n.* A combustible substance.—**com-bus-ti-bil′i-ty** (-bil′i-ti), **com-bus′ti-ble-ness,** *n.*

com-bus-tion (kọm-bus′chọn), *n.* [LL. *combustio(n-)*, < L. *comburere* (pp. *combustus*): see *combust.*] The act or process of burning; the action of fire on inflammable material; fig., violent excitement; tumult; in *chem.*, rapid oxidation accompanied with heat and usually light; chemical combination attended by heat and light; also, slow oxidation not accompanied by high temperature and light.—**com-bus′tive,** *a.* Pertaining to or characterized by combustion.

comb-y (kō′mi), *a.* Comb-like; honeycombed.

come (kum), *v.*; pret. *came*, pp. *come*, ppr. *coming.* [AS. *cuman* = G. *kommen.*] **I.** *intr.* To move toward the speaker or toward a place in mind; approach; arrive by movement or in course of progress; approach or arrive in time, succession, etc.; approach in character; occur at a certain point or in a certain position; extend or reach (as, the dress *comes* to her knees); move into sight, or appear; fall to a person, or befall; occur to the mind; take place, occur, or happen; issue, emanate, or be derived; arrive or appear as a result (as, this *comes* of carelessness); enter or be brought into a specified state or condition (as, to *come* into use); enter into being or existence; germinate, as grain; reach the desired state; become (as, to *come* loose or untied); turn out to be (as, his dream *came* true): also used in the imperative to call attention, express remonstrance, etc. (as, *come*, that will do!). Used in many phrases: as, *to come about* (to arrive in due course; come to pass); *to come across* (to meet with, esp. by chance); *to come back* (to return, as in space or time; esp., in colloq. use, to return to a former position or state of advancement, favor, prosperity, predominance, or the like); *to come by* (to obtain; acquire); *to come down* (to descend; be transmitted); *to come in for* (to receive; get); *to come round* (to relent; also, to recover, as after illness); *to come to* (to amount to; also, to recover, as from a swoon). **II.** *tr.* To do or perform (colloq. or slang); play the part of (colloq. or slang).—**come,** *n.* A coming; approach; arrival: esp. in the phrase *come and go.*—**come=at′=a-ble,** *a.* Accessible. [Colloq.]—**come′=back,** *n.* A coming back; esp., a return to a former position of favor, prosperity, or the like, or one who or that which so returns (colloq.); also, a coming back in complaint, as at treatment received, or a ground for such complaint (slang); a retort or repartee (slang); something unfortunate coming to a person as a consequence of his own action (slang).

co-me-di-an (kǫ-mē′di-ạn), *n.* [F. *comédien*, < *comédie*, comedy.] An actor in comedy; also, a writer of comedy.

co-mé-dienne (ko-mā-dyen), *n.* [F., fem. of *comédien*, E. *comedian.*] An actress in comedy.

co-me-di-et-ta (kǫ-mē-di-et′ä), *n.* [It. *commedietta.*] A short comedy; a comedy of slight character.

com-e-dist (kom′ę-dist), *n.* A writer of comedies.

com-e-do (kom′ę̄-dō), *n.*; pl. *comedones* (kom-ę̄-dō′nēz). [L., glutton, < *comedere*: see *comestible.*] A small, wormlike, black-tipped, fatty mass in a follicle of the face, etc.

come=down (kum′doun), *n.* An unexpected or humiliating descent from dignity, importance, or prosperity. [Colloq.]

com-e-dy (kom′ę-di), *n.*; pl. *-dies* (-diz). [OF. *comedie* (F. *comédie*), < L. *comœdia*, < Gr. κωμῳδία, < κῶμος, revel (or perhaps κώμη, village), + ἀείδειν, sing.] A dramatic composition of light and humorous character, typically with a happy or cheerful ending; that branch of the drama which concerns itself with this form of composition; the comic element of drama, of literature generally, or of life; any literary composition dealing with a theme suitable for comedy, or employing the methods of comedy; any comic or humorous incident or series of incidents.—**high comedy.** See under *high, a.*—**low comedy.** See under *low*[4], *a.*

come-ly (kum′li), *a.*; compar. *comelier*, superl. *comeliest.* [AS. *cȳmlīc*, < *cȳme*, fine, beautiful.] Pleasing in appearance; fair; handsome; also, proper; seemly; becoming.—**come′li-ness,** *n.*

com-er (kum′ėr), *n.* One who or that which comes, or has lately come (as, all *comers*, every one that comes, or that chooses to come); sometimes (colloq.), one who or something that is coming on or promising well; a person who is on the way to note or distinction.

co-mes-ti-ble (kǫ-mes′ti-bl). [OF. F. *comestible*, < LL. *comestibilis*, < L. *comedere* (pp. *comestus*), eat up, < *com-*, altogether, + *edere*, eat.] **I.** *a.* Edible; eatable. **II.** *n.* Something edible; an article of food.

com-et (kom′et), *n.* [L. *cometa*, < Gr. κομήτης, lit. 'long-haired,' < κομᾶν, wear long hair, < κόμη, hair.] A celestial body which moves about the sun in an elongated orbit, usually elliptical or parabolic, and which usually consists of a star-like mass (the *nucleus*) surrounded by a misty luminous envelop (the *coma*) extended into a stream of light (the *tail*).—**com′e-ta-ry** (-e-tā-ri), *a.* Of, pertaining to, or resembling a comet.—**com′et=find″er,** *n.* In *astron.*, a telescope of low power but with a wide field, used to search for comets.

co-meth-er (kǫ-meᴛʜ′ėr), *n.* [For *come hither.*] An inviting, persuasive, or controlling influence: usually in the phrase 'to put one's, or the, comether on (a person)': as, "He . . . looks pistols at any one who attempts putting his *comether* on the widow" (Lover's "Handy Andy," ii.). [Ir. or colloq.]

co-met-ic (ko-met′ik), *a.* Of, pertaining to, or resembling a comet; cometary.

com-et-oid (kom′e-toid), *a.* [See *-oid.*] Resembling a comet, as in appearance or in orbital character.

com-et=seek-er (kom′et-sē″kėr), *n.* A comet-finder.

com-fit (kum′fit), *n.* [OF. *confit*, < L. *confectus*, pp.: see *confect.*] A dry sweetmeat; a sugar-plum; a bonbon.

com-fort (kum′fǫrt), *v. t.* [OF. *conforter*, < LL. *confortare*, < L. *con-*, altogether, + *fortis*, strong.] To strengthen†; aid or encourage (now archaic or legal); soothe when in grief; console; cheer; also, to make physically comfortable.—**com′fort,** *n.* [OF. *confort.*] Strengthening aid, or assistance (now archaic or legal); also, relief in affliction; consolation; solace; the feeling of relief or consolation; a person or thing that affords consolation (as, "my fellow-workers . . . which have been a *comfort* unto me": Col. iv. 11); a cause or matter of relief or satisfaction; also, a state of ease, with freedom from pain and anxiety, and satisfaction of bodily wants; that which promotes such a state; also (U. S.), a comfortable (bed-cover).—**com′fort-a-ble. I.** *a.* Giving comfort or support (archaic); also, affording consolation; producing or attended with comfort or ease of mind or body; also, being in a state of comfort or ease; easy and undisturbed; also, cheerful† (as, "His *comfortable* temper has forsook him": Shakspere's "Timon of Athens," iii. 4. 71). **II.** *n.* A comforter (woolen scarf); also, a wadded or quilted bed-cover (U. S.).—**com′fort-a-ble-ness,** *n.*—**com′fort-a-bly,** *adv.*—**com′fort-er,** *n.* One who or that which comforts; [*cap.*] the Holy Spirit; [*l. c.*] a woolen scarf for wrapping round the neck in cold weather; also (U. S.), a comfortable (bed-cover).—**Job's comforter.** See entry in vocabulary place.—**com′fort-ing-ly,** *adv.*—**com′fort-less,** *a.* Destitute of comfort.—**com′fort-less-ly,** *adv.*—**com′fort-less-ness,** *n.*

com-frey (kum′fri), *n.* [OF. *cunfirie*: cf. L. *conferva.*] Any of the plants of the boraginaceous genus *Symphytum*, natives of Europe and Asia, as *S. officinale*, which was formerly in high repute as a vulnerary.

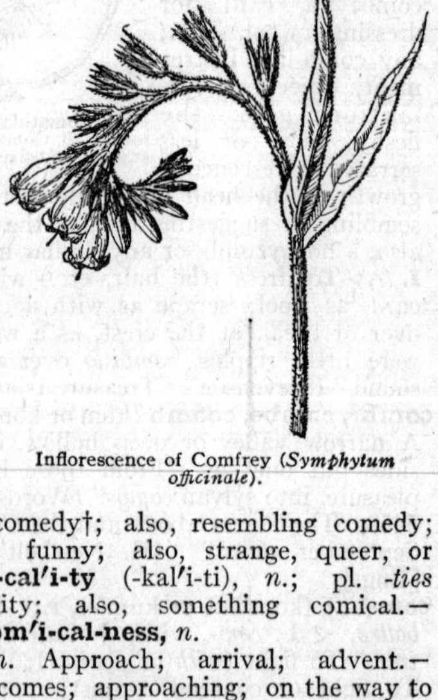
Inflorescence of Comfrey (*Symphytum officinale*).

com-ic (kom′ik). [L. *comicus*, < Gr. κωμικός, < κῶμος, revel.] **I.** *a.* Of, pertaining to, or of the nature of comedy, as distinct from tragedy; acting in or composing comedy; also, exciting mirth; humorous; funny; laughable. **II.** *n.* A comic actor† or comic writer†; a comic paper or periodical (colloq.).—**com′i-cal,** *a.* Pertaining to or of the nature of comedy†; also, resembling comedy; exciting mirth; droll; funny; also, strange, queer, or odd (colloq.).—**com-i-cal′i-ty** (-kal′i-ti), *n.*; pl. *-ties* (-tiz). Comical quality; also, something comical.—**com′i-cal-ly,** *adv.*—**com′i-cal-ness,** *n.*

com-ing (kum′ing), *n.* Approach; arrival; advent.—**com′ing,** *p. a.* That comes; approaching; on the way to note or distinction (colloq.); also, ready to make or meet advances, complaisant, or forward (obs. or rare).—**com′ing=in′,** *n.*, pl. *comings-in.* Entrance; introduction; also, income†; *pl.*, revenues†.

co-mi-tia (kọ-mish′iạ), *n. pl.* [L., pl. of *comitium*, place of assembly, < *com-*, with, + *ire*, go.] In *Rom. antiq.*, an assembly of the people convened to pass on laws, nominate magistrates, etc.—**co-mi′tial,** *a.*

co-mi-ti-va (kō-mē-tē′vä), *n.*; pl. *-ve* (-vā). [It.] An organized band of brigands or lawless persons in southern Italy.

com-i-trag-e-dy (kom-i-traj′ẹ-di), *n.*; pl. *-dies* (-diz). [Formed to parallel *tragicomedy.*] A tragedy containing an element of comedy.

com-i-ty (kom′i-ti), *n.*; pl. *-ties* (-tiz). [L. *comitas*, < *comis*, courteous, friendly.] Courtesy or civility (as, "It is the rule of mere *comity* and courtesy to agree where you can": Emerson's "Representative Men," iv.); esp., courtesy between nations, as in respect shown by one country for the laws and institutions of another.

com-ma (kom′ä), *n.*; pl. *commas*, also (in pros.) *commata* (kom′ạ-tạ). [L., < Gr. κόμμα, short clause, < κόπτειν, strike, cut.] A mark of punctuation (,) used to indicate the smallest interruptions in continuity of thought or grammatical construction; in *anc. pros.*, a fragment or smaller section of a colon; also, the part of a dactylic hexameter ending with, or that beginning with, the cæsura; also, the cæsura itself.—**comma bacillus,** a bacterial micro-organism, *Microspira comma*, the cause of Asiatic cholera, often occurring in the form of a slightly curved rod: formerly supposed to be a bacillus but later found to be a spirillum.

com-mand (kọ-månd′), *v.* [OF. *comander* (F. *commander*), < ML. *commandare*, < L. *com-*, with, + *mandare*, commit, enjoin: cf. *commend.*] **I.** *tr.* To order or direct with authority; enjoin; charge; also, to have or exercise power or authority over; be in command over; be master of; have at one's bidding or disposal (as, "Such aid as I can spare you shall *command*": Shakspere's "2 Henry VI.," iv. 5. 7); exact, compel, or secure (respect, sympathy, etc.) by just claim; also, to dominate by reason of location; overlook (as, "The house of the farmer Stood on the side of a hill *commanding* the sea": Longfellow's "Evangeline," i. 1). **II.** *intr.* To issue commands; also, to have or exercise power or authority; be commander; also, to occupy a dominating position; look down upon or over a region, etc.—**com-mand′,** *n.* The act of commanding or ordering; bidding; an authoritative order; a commandment; the possession or exercise of controlling authority; control; mastery; disposal; a position or post in which one has the right to command; a body of troops, etc., or a district, under a commander; also, power of dominating a region by reason of location; extent of view or outlook (as, "The Stygian Fury . . . takes a steepy stand, Which overlooks the vale with wide *command*": Dryden's tr. Virgil's "Æneid," vii. 663).—**com-mand′a-ble,** *a.* Capable of being commanded.

com-man-dant (kom-ạn-dånt′), *n.* [F., orig. ppr. of *commander*, E. *command.*] A commander; the commanding or chief officer (irrespective of rank) of a place, military body, etc. (as, the *commandant* of a navy-yard, with the rank of captain).—**com-man-dant′ship,** *n.*

com-man-deer (kom-ạn-dēr′), *v. t.* [D. *commandeeren*, < F. *commander*, E. *command.*] To order or force into active military service; seize (private property) for military or other public use; hence, to seize arbitrarily (colloq.).

com-mand-er (kọ-mån′dėr), *n.* One who commands; one who exercises authority; a leader; a chief officer; a member of a higher class in a modern order of knighthood; the chief officer (irrespective of rank) of a military organization or a part of it (as, the *commander* of a department, with the rank of major-general); specif., in the navy, an officer ranking below a captain and above a lieutenant-commander, and sometimes having command of a war-ship.—**com-mand′er=in=chief′,** *n.*; pl. *commanders-in-chief.* One who has supreme command of the armed forces of a nation or state (as, the President of the United States is the *commander-in-chief* of the army and navy); an officer in command of a particular portion of an army or navy (as, an admiral or rear-admiral acting as *commander-in-chief* of a fleet).—**com-mand′er-ship,** *n.*—**com-mand′er-y,** *n.*; pl. *-ies* (-iz). [F. *commanderie.*] The office or district of a commander; esp., among certain medieval orders of knights, a district controlled by a commander; hence, a local branch or lodge in certain secret orders.

com-mand-ing (kọ-mån′ding), *p. a.* That commands; possessing or exercising command; controlling; powerful; impressive; dominating by virtue of position.—**com-mand′ing-ly,** *adv.*

com-mand-ment (kọ-månd′mẹnt), *n.* [OF. F. *commandement.*] The act, fact, or power of commanding; a command or mandate; a divine command; any one of the precepts ('the ten commandments') delivered to Moses on Mount Sinai (see Ex. xx. 2–17).

com-man-do (kọ-mån′dō), *n.*; pl. *-dos* or *-does* (-dōz). [D., < Pg. *commando*, < *commandar*, v., = E. *command.*] In South Africa, an armed force raised for service against marauders, etc.; an expedition thus undertaken; a unit in the army of the former Dutch republics of South Africa; [*cap.*] a member of a modern military raiding unit.

com-mand-ress (kọ-mån′dres), *n.* A female commander.

com-meas-ur-a-ble (kọ-mezh′ūr-ạ-bl), *a.* [See *com-.*] Having the same measure; commensurate.

com-meas-ure (kọ-mezh′ūr), *v. t.*; *-ured, -uring.* [See *com-.*] To equal in measure; be coextensive with: as, "To push thee forward . . . until endurance grow Sinew'd with action, and the full-grown will . . . *Commeasure* perfect freedom" (Tennyson's "Œnone," 164).

com-mel-i-na-ceous (kọ-mel-i-nā′shius), *a.* [NL. *Commelina*, the typical genus; named from J. and K. *Commelin*, Dutch botanists.] Belonging to the *Commelinaceæ*, or spiderwort family of plants.

com-mem-o-ra-ble (kọ-mem′ọ̄-rạ-bl), *a.* [L. *commemorabilis.*] Worthy to be commemorated; memorable; noteworthy.

com-mem-o-rate (kọ-mem′ọ̄-rāt), *v. t.*; *-rated, -rating.* [L. *commemoratus*, pp. of *commemorare*, < *com-*, with, + *memorare*, bring to remembrance, < *memor*, mindful: see *memory.*] To call to remembrance; make honorable mention of; also, to honor the memory of by some solemnity or celebration; also, to serve as a memento of.—**com-mem-o-ra′tion** (-rā′shọn), *n.* [L. *commemoratio(n-).*] The act of commemorating; a service, celebration, etc., in memory of some person or event; a memorial.—**com-mem′o-ra-tive** (-rạ-tiv), *a.* Serving to commemorate.—**com-mem′o-ra-tor** (-rā-tọr), *n.*—**com-mem′o-ra-to-ry** (-rạ-tọ̄-ri), *a.* Commemorative.

com-mence (kọ-mens′), *v.*; *-menced, -mencing.* [OF. *comencer* (F. *commencer*), < L. *com-*, with, + *initiare*: see *initiate.*] **I.** *tr.* To begin; start. **II.** *intr.* To begin to exist; enter upon an act; make or have a start; also, to start or set up as (archaic: as, to *commence* author); also, to take a degree at a university or college (usually with a complement: as, to *commence* M. A.).—**com-mence′ment,** *n.* The act or fact of commencing; beginning; in universities, colleges, etc., the ceremony of conferring degrees or granting diplomas at the end of the academic year, or the day on which this takes place.—**com-men′cer,** *n.*

com-mend (kọ-mend′), *v. t.* [L. *commendare*, < *com-*, with, + *mandare*, commit: cf. *command.*] To intrust or give in charge (as, "Father, into thy hands I *commend* my spirit": Luke, xxiii. 46); deliver with confidence; commit; also, to present as worthy of confidence, notice, kindness, etc.; recommend; also, to mention with approbation; praise; also, to recommend (a person) to the kindly remembrance of another (archaic).—**com-mend′**†, *n.* Commendation; recommendation; greeting.—**com-mend′a-ble,** *a.* Worthy of commendation; laudable.—**com-mend′a-ble-ness,** *n.*—**com-mend′a-bly,** *adv.*—**com-men-dam** (kọ-men′dam), *n.* [ML. (*in*) *commendam*, (in) trust.] *Eccles.*, the tenure of a benefice to be held until the appointment of a regular incumbent (the benefice being said to be held *in commendam*); also, a benefice so held.—**com-men-da-tion** (kom-en-dā′shọn), *n.* [L. *commendatio(n-).*] The act of commending; recommendation; praise; something that commends; *pl.*, complimentary greetings (archaic).—**com-men-da-to-ry** (kọ-men′dạ-tọ̄-ri), *a.* Serving to commend; also, holding a benefice in commendam; also, held in commendam.—**com-mend′er,** *n.*—**com-mend′ing-ly,** *adv.*

com-men-sal (ko-men′sạl). [ML. *commensalis*, < L. *com-*, with, + *mensa*, table.] **I.** *a.* Eating together at the same table; in *zoöl.* and *bot.*, of an animal or plant, living with, on, or in another, but neither one at the expense of the other as in the case of a parasite. **II.** *n.* A companion at table; in *zoöl.* and *bot.*, a commensal animal or plant.—**com-men′sal-ism,** *n.*—**com-men′-sal-ly,** *adv.*

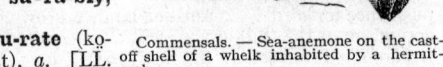

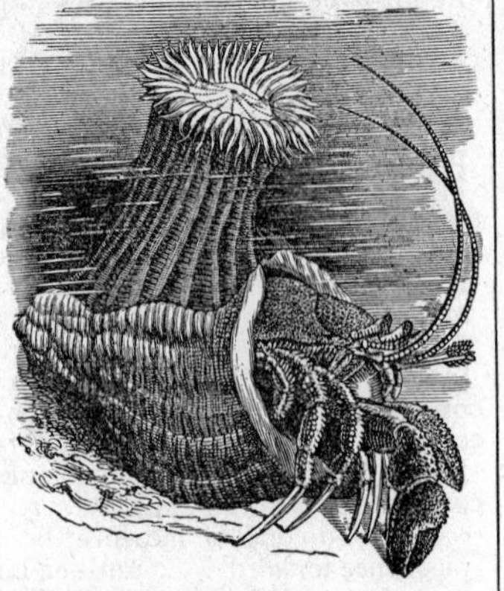
Commensals. — Sea-anemone on the cast-off shell of a whelk inhabited by a hermit-crab.

com-men-su-ra-ble (kọ-men′shū-rạ-bl), *a.* [LL. *commensurabilis*, < *commensurare*: see *commensurate*.] Having a common measure or divisor; also, suitable in measure; proportionate.—**com-men″su-ra-bil′i-ty** (-bil′i-ti), **com-men′-su-ra-ble-ness,** *n.*—**com-men′su-ra-bly,** *adv.*

com-men-su-rate (kọ-men′shū-rạt), *a.* [LL. *commensuratus*, pp. of *commensurare*, make commensurate, < L. *com-*, with, + *mensurare*, E. *measure*, *v.*] Having the same measure; of equal extent or duration; also, corresponding in amount, magnitude, or degree; proportionate; adequate; also, having a common measure; commensurable.—**com-men′su-rate-ly,** *adv.*—**com-men′su-rate-ness,** *n.*—**com-men-su-ra′tion** (-rā′shọn), *n.* [LL. *commensuratio(n-)*.] The act of making or the state of being commensurate; proportion; also, a measuring together; comparison.

com-ment (kom′ent), *n.* [OF. *comment*, < LL. *commentum*, exposition, L. contrivance, invention, prop. pp. neut. of *comminisci*, devise by careful thought, akin to *reminisci*, remember, and *mens*, mind.] An expository treatise†; also, a note in explanation, expansion, or criticism of a passage in a writing, book, etc.; an annotation; a remark, observation, or criticism; also, explanatory or critical matter added to a text; also, the act of commenting; animadversion.—**com-ment** (kom′ent or kọ-ment′), *v.* **I.** *intr.* To write explanatory or critical notes upon a text; make comments or remarks. **II.** *tr.* To furnish with comments; make comments or remarks on.—**com-men-ta-ry** (kom′en-tā-ri), *n.*; pl. *-ries* (-riz). [L. *commentarius*, < *commentum*.] A series of comments or annotations; an explanatory essay or treatise; also, anything serving to illustrate a point; a comment or remark; also, a record of facts or events (usually in *pl.*: as, the *Commentaries* of Cæsar).—**com-men-ta′ri-al** (-tā′ri-ạl), *a.*—**com′men-tate** (-tāt), *v. i.* or *t.*; *-tated*, *-tating*. [Appar. < *commentator*.] To write, make, or furnish with, comments.—**com-men-ta′-tion** (-tā′shọn), *n.* [L. *commentatio(n-)*, < *commentari*, freq. of *comminisci*: see *comment*, *n.*] The making of comments; also, a commentary†.—**com′men-ta-tor** (-tā-tọr), *n.* [L.] One who writes comments or annotations; an annotator.—**com-men-ta-to-ri-al** (kọ-men-tạ-tō′ri-ạl), *a.*—**com′ment-er,** *n.*

com-merce (kom′ėrs), *n.* [F. *commerce*, < L. *commercium*, < *com-*, with, + *merx* (*merc-*), goods, wares: cf. *merchant*.] Interchange of goods or commodities, esp. on a large scale between different countries ('foreign commerce') or between different parts of the same country ('internal commerce'); business intercourse; also, social intercourse; also, sexual intercourse; also, a kind of card-game, played by from three to twelve persons, in which each player in succession may exchange one of his cards for another until some one refuses to exchange, whereupon the cards are shown and the best hand wins.—**com-merce** (kọ-mėrs′), *v. i.*; *-merced*, *-mercing*. To traffic†; hold intercourse or converse (archaic).—**com′merce=de-stroy″er,** *n.* A fast armed vessel, as a cruiser, designed to capture or destroy an enemy's merchant vessels.—**com-mer-cial** (kọ-mėr′shạl), *a.* Of, pertaining to, or of the nature of commerce; engaged in commerce.—**commercial agency.** Same as *mercantile agency*, under *mercantile*.—**commercial paper,** negotiable paper, such as promissory notes, drafts, etc., given in the due course of business.—**commercial traveler,** a traveling agent, as for a wholesale business house, who solicits orders for goods.—**com-mer′cial-ism,** *n.* The principles and practices of commerce; the commercial spirit; also, a commercial custom or expression.—**com-mer-ci-al′i-ty** (-shi-al′i-ti), *n.* Commercial character or spirit.—**com-mer′cial-ize** (-īz), *v. t.*; *-ized*, *-izing*. To render commercial in character, methods, or spirit; make a matter of trade: as, "Agriculture . . . has been, in America, *commercialized*, and become really a branch of trade" (Bryce's "American Commonwealth," ci.).—**com-mer″cial-i-za′tion** (-i-zā′shọn), *n.*—**com-mer′cial-ly,** *adv.*

com-mers (ko-mers′), *n.* See *kommers*.

com-mi-nate (kom′i-nāt), *v.*; *-nated*, *-nating*. [L. *comminatus*, pp. of *comminari*, < *com-*, with, + *minari*, threaten: see *menace*.] **I.** *tr.* To threaten; anathematize; denounce. **II.** *intr.* To utter threats or anathemas.—**com-mi-na′tion** (-nā′shọn), *n.* [L. *comminatio(n-)*.] A threatening; a threat of punishment or vengeance; a denunciation; in the liturgy of the Church of England, a penitential office proclaiming God's anger and judgments against sinners.—**com′mi-na-tor,** *n.*—**com-min-a-to-ry** (kọ-min′ạ-tō-ri), *a.* Threatening; denunciatory.

com-min-gle (kọ-ming′gl), *v. t.* or *i.*; *-gled*, *-gling*. [See *com-*.] To mingle together; commix; blend.—**com-min′-gle-ment,** *n.*

com-mi-nute (kom′i-nūt), *v. t.*; *-nuted*, *-nuting*. [L. *comminutus*, pp. of *comminuere*, < *com-*, with, + *minuere*, make smaller: see *minute*[1].] To reduce to minute particles or to a fine powder, as by braying; pulverize; triturate.—**com-mi-nu′tion** (-nū′shọn), *n.* The act of comminuting, or the state of being comminuted; pulverization; in *surg.*, fracture of a bone into several pieces.

com-mis-er-ate (kọ-miz′ẹ-rāt), *v. t.*; *-ated*, *-ating*. [L. *commiseratus*, pp. of *commiserari*, < *com-*, with, + *miserari*, pity: see *miserable*.] To feel or express sorrow or compassion for; pity; condole with.—**com-mis′er-at-ing-ly,** *adv.*—**com-mis-er-a′tion** (-ẹ-rā′shọn), *n.* [L. *commiseratio(n-)*.] The act of commiserating; compassion; condolence.—**com-mis′er-a-tive** (-ẹ-rā-tiv), *a.* Compassionate.—**com-mis′er-a-tor** (-ẹ-rā-tọr), *n.*

com-mis-sa-ri-al (kom-i-sā′ri-ạl), *a.* Of or pertaining to a commissary.

com-mis-sa-ri-at (kom-i-sā′ri-at), *n.* [F., < ML. *commissarius*: see *commissary*.] The department of an army charged with supplying provisions, etc.; in general, a food or subsistence department; also, a food supply.

com-mis-sa-ry (kom′i-sā-ri), *n.*; pl. *-ries* (-riz). [ML. *commissarius*, < L. *committere*: see *commit*.] One to whom some charge is committed by a superior power; a deputy; also, an officer of the commissariat.—**com′mis-sa-ry=gen′er-al,** *n.*; pl. *-als*. A chief commissary; the head of the commissariat department of an army.—**com′-mis-sa-ry-ship,** *n.*

com-mis-sion (kọ-mish′ọn), *n.* [OF. F. *commission*, < L. *commissio(n-)*, < *committere*: see *commit*.] The act of committing or giving in charge; authoritative charge or direction; authority committed, as for particular action or functions; the position or rank of an officer in the army or navy (as, to hold or resign a *commission*); an instrument or warrant granting authority to act in a given capacity or conferring a particular rank; a body of persons authoritatively charged with particular functions; also, the condition of being placed under special authoritative charge; in naval use, the condition of a ship assigned to the charge of an officer for active service; hence, the condition of anything in active service or use (as, to be in or out of *commission*); also, a task or matter committed to one's charge; authority to act as agent for another or others in commercial transactions; a sum or percentage allowed to the agent for his services; also, the committing or perpetrating of a crime, error, or the like.—**com-mis′sion,** *v. t.* To give a commission to; authorize; delegate; send on a mission: also, to put in commission, as a war-ship; also, to give a commission or order for.—**com-mis-sion-aire′** (-ãr′), *n.*

[F. *commissionnaire.*] In European cities, a person whose business it is to execute miscellaneous small commissions for the public; a messenger or porter.—**com-mis'sion-al,** *a.* Pertaining to a commission.—**com-mis'sioned,** *p. a.* Furnished with a commission: as, *commissioned* officers (army and navy officers holding rank by commission, including in the U. S. the second lieutenants, ensigns, and all those above them).—**com-mis'sion-er,** *n.* One commissioned to act officially; a member of a commission; also, one who commissions.—**com-mis'sion-er-ship,** *n.*—**com-mis'sion=mer''chant,** *n.* A merchant engaged in buying or selling goods for others on commission.

com-mis-sure (kom'i-şūr), *n.* [L. *commissura,* < *committere*: see *commit.*] A joint, seam, or suture; specif., in *bot.*, the joint or face by which one carpel coheres with another; also, in *anat.* and *zoöl.*, a connecting band of nerve-tissue, etc.—**com-mis-su-ral** (kǫ-miş'ū-rạl or kom-i-şū'rạl), *a.*

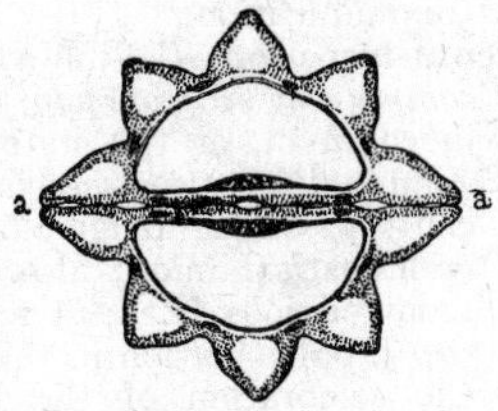

Botanical Commissure. — Section of fruit of fool's parsley, enlarged; *a, a,* line of the commissural faces of the two carpels.

com-mit (kǫ-mit'), *v. t.*; *-mitted, -mitting.* [L. *committere* (pp. *commissus*), bring together, join, intrust, do, < *com-*, with, + *mittere*, send.] To give in trust or charge; intrust; consign; consign for preservation (as, to *commit* to writing; to *commit* to memory); memorize; consign (a criminal, etc.) to custody; refer (a bill, etc.) to a committee for consideration; also, to do (something wrong); perpetrate (a crime, error, folly, etc.); also, to involve or compromise; bind by pledge or assurance, actual or implied.—**com-mit'ment,** *n.* The act of committing, or the state of being committed; consignment, as to prison; a warrant committing a person to prison; perpetration or commission, as of a crime; the act of committing, pledging, or engaging one's self.—**com-mit'ta-ble,** *a.* That may be committed.—**com-mit'tal,** *n.* Commitment.—**com-mit-tee** (kǫ-mit'ẹ), *n.* A person or a body of persons appointed to investigate, report, or act in special cases; in *law* (also pron. kom-i-tē'), one to whom the care of a person or an estate is committed.—**committee of the whole,** a committee of a legislative body consisting of all the members present, sitting in a deliberative rather than a legislative character, for formal consultation and preliminary consideration of matters awaiting legislative action.—**com-mit'tee-man** (-mạn), *n.*; pl. *-men.* A member of a committee.—**com-mit'ter,** (in *law*) **com-mit'tor,** *n.*

com-mix (kǫ-miks'), *v. t.* or *i.* [L. *commixtus*, pp. of *commiscere*, < *com-*, with, + *miscere*, mix.] To mix together; commingle.—**com-mix'ture** (-ţūr), *n.* Mixture together; also, the product of mixing; a mixture.

com-mode (kǫ-mōd'). [F. *commode*, < L. *commodus*, fit, convenient, useful, < *com-*, with, + *modus*, measure, E. *mode.*] **I.**† *a.* Suitable; convenient; accommodating. **II.** *n.* A large, high head-dress worn by women about 1700 (as, "When we say of a woman, she has a fine, a long or a good head, we speak only in relation to her *commode*": Addison, in "Spectator," 265); also, a piece of furniture containing drawers or shelves; also, a stand or a stool containing a chamber vessel.

com-mo-di-ous (kǫ-mō'di-us), *a.* [ML. *commodiosus*, < L. *commodum*, convenience, prop. neut. of *commodus*: see *commode.*] Useful†; advantageous†; convenient or satisfactory for the purpose; now, usually, conveniently roomy or spacious.—**com-mo'di-ous-ly,** *adv.*—**com-mo'di-ous-ness,** *n.*

com-mod-i-ty (kǫ-mod'i-ti), *n.*; pl. *-ties* (-tiz). [OF. *commodite* (F. *commodité*), < L. *commoditas*, < *commodus*: see *commode.*] Usefulness†; convenience†; advantage†; also, a thing that is of use or advantage; an article of trade or commerce; also, a quantity of goods†.

com-mo-dore (kom'ǫ-dōr), *n.* [Appar. = *commander*; relations uncertain.] In the U. S. navy, an officer of a rank (now abolished on the active list) next below that of rear-admiral; in the British navy, an officer in temporary command of a squadron, sometimes having a captain under him on the same ship; by extension, the senior captain of a line of merchant vessels; also, the president or head of a yacht-club or boat-club.

com-mon (kom'ǫn), *a.* [OF. *comun* (F. *commun*), < L. *communis*, appar. < *com-*, with, + *-munis*, bound, as in *immunis*, not bound, exempt.] Belonging equally to or shared alike by two or more or all in question; general; joint or united (as, to make *common* cause against an enemy of all); also, pertaining or belonging to the whole community; public; also, generally or publicly known; notorious; also, of frequent occurrence; usual; hence, hackneyed or trite; also, not distinguished by special characteristics; ordinary; often, belonging to or constituting the general mass of the people (as, the *common* man; the *common* people); not distinguished by rank or position; hence, of mediocre or inferior quality; mean; low or vulgar; also, ceremonially unclean (as, "I have never eaten any thing that is *common* or unclean": Acts, x. 14); in *gram.*, of a name or noun, designating any individual of a class, as *boy, city, day* (cf. *proper*); also, optionally masculine or feminine; in *pros.*, either long or short.—**common carrier.** See under *carrier.*—**common chord.** See *chord*[2], *n.*—**common council,** the local legislative body of a city, or its lower branch.—**common fraction.** See *fraction, n.*—**common law,** the English system of law, in force among English-speaking peoples, as distinct from the civil or Roman law and the canon or ecclesiastical law; also, the unwritten law, esp. of England, based on usage and custom, as distinct from statute law; also, the ordinary law of a community, as distinct from equity, local law, etc.—**common pleas.** See under *plea.*—**common school,** in the U. S., a public school below the grade of a high school.—**common sense,** the intelligence proper to all mankind; also, sound practical sense.—**common time** (in *music*). See *time, n.*—**com'mon,** *n.* The community† or public†; the common people†; the commons† (see *commons*); a tract of land possessed or used in common, esp. by all the members of a community; in *law*, the right to take a profit from the land or waters of another, as by pasturing cattle, catching fish, etc. See also *commons.*—**in common,** in joint possession, use, action, relation, etc.; jointly.—**com'mon-a-ble,** *a.* Held in common, or subject to general use, as lands; of beasts, that may be pastured on common land.—**com'mon-age** (-āj), *n.* The use of anything in common, esp. of a pasture; the right to such use; the state of being held in common; that which is so held, as land; also, the commonalty.

com-mon-al-ty (kom'ǫn-ạl-ti), *n.* [OF. *communalte* (F. *communauté*), < OF. F. *communal*: see *communal.*] The common or general body of the people of a community†; the members of an incorporated body; the common people as distinguished from the nobility, from those in authority, etc.; hence, the general body or mass, as of mankind.

com-mon-er (kom'ǫn-ėr), *n.* One of the common people; a member of the commonalty; also, a member of the House of Commons; also, at Oxford University, etc., a student who pays for his commons, etc., and is not supported by any foundation; also, one who has a joint right in common land.

com-mon-ly (kom'ǫn-li), *adv.* In a common manner; usually or generally; in an ordinary degree; meanly.—**com'mon-ness,** *n.*

com-mon-place (kom'ǫn-plās). **I.** *n.* A place or passage in a book or writing, noted as important for reference or quotation; also, a common or customary subject of remark; a stock remark; a trite saying; a platitude; also, anything common, ordinary, or uninteresting; that which is commonplace; commonplace quality. **II.** *a.* Not novel or striking; trite; common or ordinary.—**com'mon-place=book,** *n.* A book in which commonplaces, or notable or striking passages, are noted; a book in which things especially to be remembered or referred to are recorded.—**com'mon-place-ness,** *n.*

com-mons (kom'ǫnz), *n. pl.* The common people as distinguished from their rulers or a ruling class; the commonalty; the body of people not ennobled, as represented in England by the lower house of Parliament ('House of Commons'); [*cap.*] the representatives of this body; the lower house of the British Parliament, or of the Canadian

Parliament; also [*l. c.*], food provided at a common table, as in colleges; hence, food or provisions in general.

com-mon-weal (kom′ǫn-wēl′), *n.* [See *weal*[1].] The common welfare; the public good; also, the body politic; a commonwealth (as, "Solon . . . who built his *commonweal* On equity's wide base": Thomson's "Seasons," Winter, 446). [Archaic.]

com-mon-wealth (kom′ǫn-welth), *n.* The public welfare†; also, the whole body of people of a nation or state; the body politic; also, a state in which the supreme power is held by the people; a republican or democratic state; [*cap.*] the government existing in England from the abolition of the monarchy in 1649 until the Restoration in 1660 (or until the establishment of the Protectorate in 1653); also [*l. c.*], any body of persons united by some common interest.

com-mo-rant (kom′ǭ-rạnt), *a.* [L. *commorans* (*-ant-*), ppr. of *commorari*, < *com-*, with, + *morari*, delay.] Dwelling; ordinarily residing: now only in legal phraseology. —**com′mo-ran-cy,** *n.*

com-mo-tion (kǫ-mō′shǫn), *n.* [OF. F. *commotion*, < L. *commotio*(*n-*), < *commovere*: see *commove*.] Violent or tumultuous motion; agitation; disturbance; tumult.—**com-mo′tion-al,** *a.*

com-move (kǫ-möv′), *v. t.*; *-moved, -moving.* [OF. F. *commouvoir*, < L. *commovere*, < *com-*, altogether, + *movere*, E. *move*.] To move violently; agitate; excite.

com-mu-nal (kom′ū̦-nạl or kǫ-mū′nạl), *a.* [F. *communal*, < ML. *communalis*, < *communa*, E. *commune*[2].] Pertaining to a commune or a community.—**com′mu-nal-ism,** *n.* A theory or system of government according to which each commune is virtually an independent state, and the nation merely a federation of such states.—**com′mu-nal-ist,** *n.* An advocate of communalism.—**com″mu-nal-is′tic,** *a.* —**com′mu-nal-ize** (-īz), *v. t.*; *-ized, -izing.* To render communal; convert into municipal property.—**com″mu-nal-i-za′tion** (-i-zā′shǫn), *n.*—**com′mu-nal-ly,** *adv.*

com-mu-nard (kom′ū̦-närd), *n.* [F.] A communalist; esp. [usually *cap.*], a member or supporter of the Paris Commune of 1871.

com-mune[1] (kǫ-mūn′), *v. i.*; *-muned, -muning.* [OF. *comuner*, make common, share (< *comun*, common), also *communier*, give or receive the communion, < L. *communicare*, E. *communicate*.] To hold converse (*with*); interchange thoughts or feelings; also, to partake of the eucharist.—**com-mune**[1] (kom′ūn), *n.* Communion or intercourse; converse.

com-mune[2] (kom′ūn), *n.* [F. *commune*, < ML. *communa*, < L. *communis*: see *common*.] A community; the smallest administrative division in France, governed by a mayor assisted by a municipal council; a similar division in some other country; [usually *cap.*] with *the*, during the French Revolution of 1789–95, the municipal government of Paris, which for a time exercised a dominating power in the state, being responsible for much of the bloodshed of the period; also, a communalistic government which ruled over Paris from March 18 to May 28, 1871.

com-mu-ni-ca-ble (kǫ-mū′ni-kạ-bl), *a.* [ML. *communicabilis*.] Capable of being communicated or imparted; also, communicative; ready to converse or to impart information.—**com-mu″ni-ca-bil′i-ty** (-bil′i-ti), **com-mu′ni-ca-ble-ness,** *n.*—**com-mu′ni-ca-bly,** *adv.*

com-mu-ni-cant (kǫ-mū′ni-kạnt). **I.** *a.* Communicating; esp., partaking of the eucharist; being a communicant. **II.** *n.* One who communicates; esp., one who partakes, or is entitled to partake, of the eucharist; a member of a church.

com-mu-ni-cate (kǫ-mū′ni-kāt), *v.*; *-cated, -cating.* [L. *communicatus*, pp. of *communicare*, < *communis*: see *common*.] **I.** *tr.* To give to another as a partaker; impart; transmit; also, to impart knowledge of; make known; also, to share in or partake of (archaic); also, to administer the eucharist to (as, "Baptized he was, confirmed, *communicated*": J. H. Newman's "Callista," ii.). **II.** *intr.* To take part† or participate†; also, to partake of the eucharist; also, to have interchange of thoughts; hold communication; also, to have or form a connecting passage.—**com-mu-ni-ca′tion** (-kā′shǫn), *n.* [L. *communicatio*(*n-*).] The act or fact of communicating; transmission; esp., the imparting or interchange of thoughts, opinions, or information by speech, writing, or signs; intercourse by speech, writing, etc.; also, that which is communicated or imparted; a document or message imparting views, information, etc.; also, intercourse in general; also, passage, opportunity of passage, or a means of passage, between places, etc.—**com-mu′ni-ca-tive** (-kā̦-tiv), *a.* Inclined to communicate or impart; generous†; sociable†; diffusive†; esp., disposed to impart or disclose information, opinions, etc.; not reserved; talkative; also, adapted or intended for communicating information, etc.; also, communicable†; also, of or pertaining to communication.—**com-mu′ni-ca-tive-ly,** *adv.*—**com-mu′ni-ca-tive-ness,** *n.*—**com-mu′ni-ca-tor** (-kā-tǫr), *n.* One who or that which communicates. —**com-mu′ni-ca-to-ry** (-kā̦-tǭ-ri), *a.* Of or pertaining to communication.

com-mu-nion (kǫ-mū′nyǫn), *n.* [L. *communio*(*n-*), < *communis*: see *common*.] The act of sharing, or holding in common, or the state of things so held; participation; community; also, association or fellowship; mutual intercourse; often, religious fellowship or intercourse; also, ecclesiastical union; also, a body of persons having one common religious faith; a religious denomination; also [often *cap.*], participation in the sacrament of the Lord's Supper; the celebration of the Lord's Supper; the eucharist.—**com-mu′nion-ist,** *n.*

com-mu-ni-qué (ko-mü-nē-kā), *n.* [F.] An official communication, as from the government to the press or the public.

com-mu-nism (kom′ū̦-nizm), *n.* [= F. *communisme*, < L. *communis* (or F. *commun*): see *common*.] A theory or system of social organization based on the holding of property in common, actual ownership being ascribed to the community as a whole or to the state; a theory or system by which the state controls the means of production and the distribution and consumption of industrial products; also, communalism.—**com′mu-nist.** [= F. *communiste*.] **I.** *n.* An advocate of communism; also [usually *cap.*], a Communard. **II.** *a.* Pertaining to communists or communism. —**com-mu-nis′tic,** *a.*—**com-mu-nis′ti-cal-ly,** *adv.*

com-mu-ni-ta-ri-an (kǫ-mū-ni-tā′ri-ạn), *n.* A member of a communistic community; also, an advocate of such communities.

com-mu-ni-ty (kǫ-mū′ni-ti), *n.*; pl. *-ties* (-tiz). [L. *communitas*, < *communis*: see *common*.] The state of being held in common; common possession, enjoyment, liability, etc.; also, common character; agreement; identity; also, social intercourse; association; life in association with others; the social state; also, a number of individuals associated together by the fact of residence in the same locality, or of subjection to the same laws and regulations; a number of persons having common ties or interests and living in the same locality; hence, any body or group living together; esp., a monastic body; a communistic society; also, the body of people of a place; the public; also, commonness† or frequency†.

com-mu-nize (kom′ū̦-nīz), *v. t.*; *-nized, -nizing.* [L. *communis*: see *common*.] To make the property of the community.—**com″mu-ni-za′tion** (-ni-zā′shǫn), *n.*

com-mu-ta-ble (kǫ-mū′tạ-bl), *a.* [L. *commutabilis*.] That may be commuted; exchangeable.—**com-mu-ta-bil′i-ty** (-bil′i-ti), **com-mu′ta-ble-ness,** *n.*

com-mu-tate (kom′ū̦-tāt), *v. t.*; *-tated, -tating.* [Back-formation from *commutator*.] In *elect.*, to reverse the direction of (a current or currents), as by a commutator.

com-mu-ta-tion (kom-ū̦-tā′shǫn), *n.* [L. *commutatio*(*n-*).] The act or process of commuting; exchange; substitution; the substitution of one kind of payment for another; the changing of a penalty, etc., for another less severe.—**com-mu-ta′tion=tick″et,** *n.* A ticket issued at a reduced rate, as by a railroad company, entitling the holder to be carried over a given route a certain number of times or during a certain period; any ticket issued on a similar plan of collective payment.

com-mu-ta-tive (kǫ-mū′tạ-tiv or kom′ū̦-tā̦-tiv), *a.* [ML. *commutativus*.] Of or pertaining to commutation, exchange, substitution, or interchange; also, pertaining to mutual dealings.—**com-mu′ta-tive-ly,** *adv.*

com-mu-ta-tor (kom'ū-tā-tọr), *n.* [NL., < L. *commutare*, E. *commute*.] In *elect.*, a device for reversing the direction of a current; also, in a dynamo or motor, a segmented revolving part through which currents are conveyed to or from the brushes.

com-mute (kọ-mūt'), *v.*; *-muted, -muting.* [L. *commutare* (pp. *commutatus*), < *com-*, with, + *mutare*, change.] **I.** *tr.* To exchange for another or something else; give and take reciprocally; interchange; change (one kind of payment) into or for another as by substitution; change (an obligation, penalty, etc.) for one less burdensome or severe; in *elect.*, to alter or direct (a current or currents) by a commutator. **II.** *intr.* To make substitution; compensate; serve as a substitute; make a collective payment, esp. of a reduced amount, as an equivalent for a number of payments; use a commutation-ticket.—**com-mut-er** (kọ-mū'tėr), *n.*

com-mu-tu-al (kọ-mū'ṭū-ạl), *a.* [See *com-*.] Mutual; reciprocal: as, "long *commutual* friendship" (Pope's tr. Homer's "Odyssey," xix.). [Chiefly poetic.]

co-mose (kō'mōs), *a.* [L. *comosus*, < *coma*, hair, E. *coma*².] Hairy; comate.

com-pact¹ (kom'pakt), *n.* [L. *compactum*, prop. pp. neut. of *compacisci*, agree with, < *com-*, with, + *pacisci*, agree.] An agreement between parties; a covenant; a contract.

com-pact² (kọm-pakt'), *a.* [L. *compactus*, pp. of *compingere*, join together, < *com-*, with, + *pangere*, fasten, fix.] Joined or packed together; closely and firmly united; dense; solid; arranged within a relatively small compass; also, expressed concisely; pithy; terse; not diffuse; also, composed or made (*of*).—**com-pact'**², *v. t.* To join or pack closely together; consolidate; condense; hence, to make firm or stable; also, to form or make by close union or conjunction; make up or compose.—**com-pact'ly,** *adv.*—**com-pact'ness,** *n.*

com-pa-ges (kom-pā'jēz), *n.* [L., akin to *compingere*: see *compact*².] A complex structure or system; also, solid or firm structure; consistence.

com-pan-ion¹ (kọm-pan'yọn), *n.* [Cf. D. *kampanje*, quarter-deck.] *Naut.*, a kind of skylight on an upper deck (obs. or rare); also, a covering or hood over the top of a companionway; sometimes, a companionway.

com-pan-ion² (kọm-pan'yọn), *n.* [OF. *compaignon* (F. *compagnon*), also *compain, compaing, compainz*, < L. *com-*, with, + *panis*, bread.] One who accompanies another; a mate; a comrade; an associate; a member, now esp. of the lowest rank, in an order of knighthood; specif., a person, usually a woman, employed to afford company or assistance to another; also, a mate or match for a thing; also, a fellow† (used in contempt).—**com-pan'ion**², *v.* **I.** *tr.* To be a companion to; accompany; also, to make (one) a companion or fellow†. **II.** *intr.* To associate or keep company (*with*).—**com-pan'ion-a-ble,** *a.* Fitted to be a companion; sociable. — **com-pan'ion-a-ble-ness,** *n.* — **com-pan'ion-a-bly,** *adv.*—**com-pan'ion-age** (-āj), *n.* Companionship; also, the body of (knight) companions, or a list of them.

com-pan-ion=hatch (kọm-pan'yọn-hach), *n.* *Naut.*, the covering or hood over a cabin stairway; a companion.

com-pan-ion=lad-der (kọm-pan'yọn-lad"ėr), *n.* *Naut.*, the steps or ladder by which officers ascend to or descend from the quarter-deck or poop; the steps or ladder leading down from the deck to a cabin.

com-pan-ion-less (kọm-pan'yọn-les), *a.* Without a companion; unaccompanied; solitary.

com-pan-ion-ship (kọm-pan'yọn-ship), *n.* The state or relation of a companion; the presence of a companion; association as companions; fellowship; also, a body of companions.

com-pan-ion-way (kọm-pan'yọn-wā), *n.* *Naut.*, the space or shaft occupied by the steps leading down from the deck to a cabin; also, the steps themselves.

com-pa-ny (kum'pạ-ni), *n.*; pl. *-nies* (-niz). [OF. *compaignie* (F. *compagnie*), < *compain*: see *companion*².] Companionship; fellowship; association; also, a number of individuals assembled or associated together; a party; a band; a companion or companions; an assemblage of persons for social purposes; a guest or guests; society collectively; esp., a number of persons united or incorporated for joint action; a medieval trade gild, or a corporation historically representing such a gild (as, the *Company* of Stationers of the City of London); an association for carrying on a commercial enterprise; the member or members of a firm not specifically named in the firm's title; *milit.*, a subdivision of an infantry regiment or battalion, commanded by a captain; *naut.*, a ship's crew, including the officers.—**com'pa-ny,** *v.*; *-nied, -nying.* [OF. *compaignier*.] **I.** *tr.* To accompany. [Archaic.] **II.** *intr.* To associate; consort: as, "these men which have *companied* with us all the time" (Acts, i. 21).

com-pa-ra-ble (kom'pạ-rạ-bl), *a.* [L. *comparabilis*.] Capable of being compared; worthy of comparison.—**com"pa-ra-bil'i-ty** (-bil'i-ti), **com'pa-ra-ble-ness,** *n.*—**com'pa-ra-bly,** *adv.*

com-par-a-scope (kọm-par'ạ-skōp), *n.* [L. *comparare*, compare: see *-scope*.] A device attached to a microscope to permit the simultaneous comparison of two slides.

com-par-a-tive (kọm-par'ạ-tiv). [L. *comparativus*.] **I.** *a.* Of or pertaining to comparison; proceeding by or founded on comparison (as, *comparative* philology); also, estimated by comparison; not positive or absolute; relative; in *gram.*, expressing a greater degree of the quality or manner denoted by a positive adjective or adverb (cf. *positive, a.*). **II.** *n.* In *gram.*, the comparative degree, or that form of an adjective or adverb expressing it.—**com-par-a-ti'val** (-tī'vạl), *a.* —**com-par'a-tive-ly,** *adv.*

com-pa-ra-tor (kom'pạ-rā-tọr), *n.* [L., a comparer.] Any of various instruments for making comparisons, as of lengths or distances, tints of color, etc.

com-pare (kọm-pãr'), *v.*; *-pared, -paring.* [L. *comparare*, < *compar*, equal, like, < *com-*, with, + *par*, equal.] **I.** *tr.* To represent as similar or analogous (*to*); liken; also, to note the similarities and differences of; bring together, one with another, for the purpose of noting the points of likeness and difference; in *gram.*, to modify (an adjective or adverb), as by inflection, so as to express different degrees of the quality or manner denoted by the simple form; form or name the positive, comparative, and superlative degrees of. **II.** *intr.* To bear comparison; be held equal; vie.—**com-pare',** *n.* Comparison: as, "bliss beyond *compare*" (Burns's "Cotter's Saturday Night," 74).—**com-par'er** (-pãr'ėr), *n.*

com-par-i-son (kọm-par'i-sọn), *n.* [OF. F. *comparaison*, < L. *comparatio(n-)*, < *comparare*, E. *compare*.] The act of comparing, or the state of being compared; a likening; an illustration by similitude; a comparative estimate or statement; also, capability of being compared or likened; in *gram.*, the modification of an adjective or adverb to express degrees of quality or manner.

com-part (kọm-pärt'), *v. t.* [LL. *compartiri*, divide, share, < L. *com-*, with, + *partire*, divide: see *part, v.*] To divide into parts or distinct spaces.

com-part-ment (kọm-pärt'mẹnt), *n.* [F. *compartiment*, < It. *compartimento*, < LL. *compartiri*, E. *compart*.] A part or space marked or partitioned off.—**com-part'ment,** *v. t.* To divide into compartments.—**com-part-men-tal** (kom-pärt-men'tạl), *a.* Divided into or characterized by compartments.

com-pass (kum'pạs), *n.* [OF. F. *compas*, appar. < ML. *compassus*, circle, compasses, < L. *com-*, with, + *passus*, step, pace.] A circle†; the inclosing line or limits of any area; measurement round; also, due or proper limits; moderate bounds; also, space within limits; area; extent; range; scope; also, a passing round; a circuit; a detour; also, usually *pl.*, an instrument for describing circles, measuring distances, etc., consisting generally of two movable legs hinged at one end; *sing.*, an instrument for determining directions, consisting essentially of a freely moving magnetized needle or bar which points to the magnetic north and south, esp. ('mariners' compass') a form of this instrument used for the guidance of vessels at sea; in *music*, the total range of tones of a voice or of a musical instrument. —**com'pass,** *v.* [OF. F. *compasser*.] **I.** *tr.* To go or move round; make the circuit of; also, to extend or stretch round; hem in; encircle; also, to grasp, as with the mind; also, to attain or achieve; accomplish; obtain; also, to contrive or scheme; also, to make curved or circular. **II.** *intr.* To curve, as timber.—**com'pass-a-ble,** *a.* Capable of being compassed.—**com′pass=card,** *n.* A circular card attached to the needle of a mariners' compass, on which the points indicating direction are marked.—**com′pass-er,** *n.*—**com′-pass=flow″er,** *n.* The compass-plant.

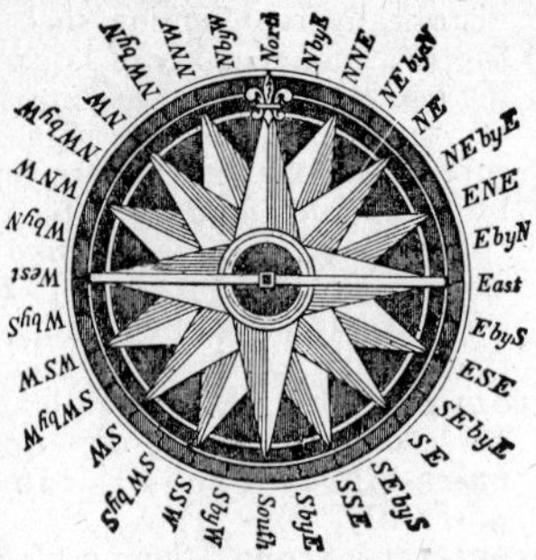

Compass-card.

com-pas-sion (kọm-pash′ọn), *n.* [OF. F. *compassion,* < LL. *compassio(n-),* < *compati,* suffer with, < L. *com-,* with, + *pati,* suffer.] A sympathetic emotion excited by the misfortunes of another; pitying sorrow or mercy.—**com-pas′sion,** *v. t.* To compassionate.—**com-pas′sion-ate** (-ạt), *a.* Having or showing compassion; pitying; also, pitiable†.—**com-pas′sion-ate** (-āt), *v. t.*; *-ated, -ating.* To feel compassion for; take pity on.—**com-pas′sion-ate-ly** (-ạt-li), *adv.*—**com-pas′sion-ate-ness,** *n.*

com-pass=plane (kum′pạs-plān), *n.* A carpenters' plane with a convex under surface, used for smoothing concave surfaces.

com-pass=plant (kum′pạs-plant), *n.* Any of various plants whose leaf-edges or branches tend to point north and south; esp., *Silphium laciniatum,* a composite plant of the American prairies, whose leaf-edges do this, or *Lotus americanus,* a fabaceous plant of the western U. S., whose branches do it.

com-pass=saw (kum′pạs-sâ), *n.* A narrow-bladed saw for cutting in curves.

Compass-plant (*Lotus americanus*).

com-pat-i-ble (kọm-pat′i-bl), *a.* [OF. F. *compatible,* < ML. *compatibilis,* < LL. *compati,* suffer with: see *compassion.*] Capable of existing together in harmony; such as to agree; consistent; congruous.—**com-pat-i-bil′i-ty** (-bil′i-ti), **com-pat′i-ble-ness,** *n.*—**com-pat′i-bly,** *adv.*

com-pa-tri-ot (kọm-pā′tri-ọt), *n.* [F. *compatriote,* < LL. *compatriota,* < L. *com-,* with, + LL. *patriota,* countryman.] A fellow-countryman or fellow-countrywoman.—**com-pa-tri-ot′ic** (-ot′ik), *a.*—**com-pa′tri-ot-ism** (-ọt-izm), *n.*

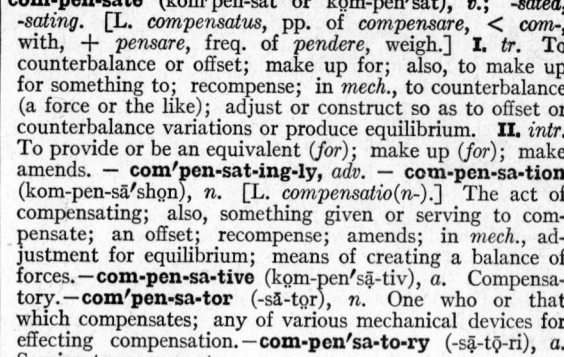

com-peer (kọm-pēr′), *n.* [ME. *comper* = F. *compair,* < L. *compar,* orig. adj., equal, like: see *compare.*] An equal or peer; a comrade; an associate.—**com-peer′,** *v. t.* To be the compeer of; equal. [Archaic.]

com-pel (kọm-pel′), *v. t.*; *-pelled, -pelling.* [L. *compellere* (pp. *compulsus*), drive together, compel, < *com-,* with, + *pellere,* drive.] To drive, as to a course of action; constrain; force; also, to secure or bring about by force; also, to drive forcibly (now rare); also, to overpower†.—**com-pel′la-ble,** *a.*

com-pel-la-tion (kom-pe-lā′shọn), *n.* [L. *compellatio(n-),* < *compellare,* address: cf. *appellation, appeal, v.*] The act or the mode of addressing a person; form of address or designation; an appellation.—**com-pel-la-tive** (kọm-pel′-ạ-tiv), *n.* A term of address; an appellation.

com-pel-ler (kọm-pel′ėr), *n.* One who compels.

com-pend (kom′pend), *n.* Same as *compendium.*

com-pen-di-ous (kọm-pen′di-us), *a.* [L. *compendiosus,* < *compendium*: see *compendium.*] Containing the substance of a subject in a brief form; concise.—**com-pen′di-ous-ly,** *adv.*—**com-pen′di-ous-ness,** *n.*

com-pen-di-um (kọm-pen′di-um), *n.*; pl. *-diums* or *-dia* (-di-ạ̈). [L., a saving, a short way, < *compendere,* weigh together, < *com-,* with, + *pendere,* weigh.] A comprehensive summary of a subject; a concise treatise; an epitome.

com-pen-sa-ble (kọm-pen′sạ-bl), *a.* [F.] That can be compensated†; also, entitled or entitling to compensation.

com-pen-sate (kom′pen-sāt or kọm-pen′sāt), *v.*; *-sated, -sating.* [L. *compensatus,* pp. of *compensare,* < *com-,* with, + *pensare,* freq. of *pendere,* weigh.] **I.** *tr.* To counterbalance or offset; make up for; also, to make up for something to; recompense; in *mech.,* to counterbalance (a force or the like); adjust or construct so as to offset or counterbalance variations or produce equilibrium. **II.** *intr.* To provide or be an equivalent (*for*); make up (*for*); make amends. — **com′pen-sat-ing-ly,** *adv.* — **com-pen-sa-tion** (kom-pen-sā′shọn), *n.* [L. *compensatio(n-).*] The act of compensating; also, something given or serving to compensate; an offset; recompense; amends; in *mech.,* adjustment for equilibrium; means of creating a balance of forces.—**com-pen-sa-tive** (kọm-pen′sạ-tiv), *a.* Compensatory.—**com′pen-sa-tor** (-sā-tọr), *n.* One who or that which compensates; any of various mechanical devices for effecting compensation.—**com-pen′sa-to-ry** (-sạ-tō-ri), *a.* Serving to compensate.

com-pete (kọm-pēt′), *v. i.*; *-peted, -peting.* [L. *competere* (pp. *competitus*), contend for, earlier come together, agree, be fit, < *com-,* with, + *petere,* fall on, aim at, seek.] To contend with another for some prize or advantage; engage in a contest; vie.

com-pe-tence, com-pe-ten-cy (kom′pē-tẹns, -tẹn-si), *n.* The quality of being competent; adequacy; due qualification or capacity; esp., sufficiency of means of subsistence (as, "Subsistence scant, Not *competence* and yet not want": Whittier's "Snow-Bound"); an income sufficient for ordinary wants.

com-pe-tent (kom′pē-tẹnt), *a.* [L. *competens (-ent-),* ppr. of *competere,* be fit: see *compete.*] Fitting, suitable, or sufficient for the purpose; adequate; properly qualified; having legal capacity or qualification; also, rightfully belonging (*to*); permissible.—**com′pe-tent-ly,** *adv.*

com-pe-ti-tion (kom-pē-tish′ọn), *n.* [LL. *competitio(n-),* < L. *competere*: see *compete.*] The act of competing; a contest for some prize or advantage.—**com-pet-i-tive** (kọm-pet′i-tiv), *a.* Of, pertaining to, or involving competition.—**com-pet′i-tive-ly,** *adv.*

com-pet-i-tor (kọm-pet′i-tọr), *n.* [L.] One who competes; a rival; also, an associate†.—**com-pet′i-tor-ship,** *n.*—**com-pet′i-to-ry** (-tō-ri), *a.* Competitive.—**com-pet′i-tress,** *n.* A female competitor.

com-pi-la-tion (kom-pi-lā′shọn), *n.* [L. *compilatio(n-).*] The act of compiling; also, something compiled, as a book.—**com-pi-la-to-ry** (kọm-pī′lạ-tō-ri), *a.* Pertaining to a compiler or to compilation.

com-pile (kọm-pīl′), *v. t.*; *-piled, -piling.* [OF. F. *compiler,* < L. *compilare,* snatch together and carry off, plunder, < *com-,* with, + *pilare,* pillage.] To put together (literary materials) in one book or work; make (a book, etc.) of materials from various sources; also, to write† or compose†.—**com-pil′er** (-pī′lėr), *n.*

com-pla-cence, com-pla-cen-cy (kọm-plā′sẹns, -sẹn-si), *n.* The state of being complacent; self-satisfaction; also, complaisance.

com-pla-cent (kọm-plā′sẹnt), *a.* [LL. *complacens (-ent-),* ppr. of *complacere,* take pleasure, L. please at the same time, be pleasing, < L. *com-,* with, + *placere,* please.] Pleased, esp. with one's self or one's own merits, advantages, etc.; self-satisfied; also, pleasant; complaisant.—**com-pla′cent-ly,** *adv.*

com-plain (kọm-plān′), *v. i.* [OF. F. *complaindre,* < ML. *complangere,* < L. *com-,* with, + *plangere,* beat (the breast, etc.), lament.] To lament; also, to express discontent or resentment; murmur; also, to state a grievance; make a formal accusation; also, to tell of one's pains, ailments, etc.; be ailing (Sc.).—**com-plain′ant,** *n.* One who makes a complaint, as in a legal action.—**com-plain′er,** *n.*—**com-plain′ing-ly,** *adv.*

com-plaint (kọm-plānt′), *n.* [OF. F. *complainte,* < *complaindre*: see *complain.*] The act, utterance, or statement of one who complains; a lament; an expression of discontent; a declaration of a grievance; a formal accusation; the first pleading of the plaintiff in a civil action (U. S.); also, a cause of complaining; a bodily ill or ailment (as, "His *complaints* had been aggravated by a severe attack of smallpox": Macaulay's "Hist. of Eng.," vii.).

com-plai-sance (kom′plā̤-zạns or -zȧns, kom-plā̤-zȧns′, or kọm-plā̤′zạns), *n.* The quality of being complaisant; complaisant behavior.
com-plai-sant (kom′plā̤-zạnt or -zȧnt, kom-plā̤-zȧnt′, or kọm-plā̤′zạnt), *a.* [F., ppr. of *complaire*, please, humor, < L. *complacere*: see *complacent.*] Disposed to please; obliging; agreeable; gracious; compliant.—**com′plai-sant-ly,** *adv.*—**com′plai-sant-ness,** *n.*
com-pla-nate (kom′plā̤-nāt), *a.* [L. *complanatus*, pp. of *complanare*, make level, < *com-*, with, + *planus*, E. *plane*².] Made level; flattened.—**com-pla-na′tion** (-nā′shọn), *n.*
com-plect-ed (kọm-plek′ted), *a.* Complexioned: as, dark-*complected.* [Prov. or colloq., U. S.]
com-ple-ment (kom′plẹ̄-mẹnt), *n.* [L. *complementum*, that which fills up, later fulfilment, accomplishment, < *complere*: see *complete.* Cf. *compliment.*] That which completes or makes perfect; specif., a word or words used to complete a grammatical predication; also, the quantity or amount that completes anything; full quantity or amount; complete allowance (as, "He had the usual *complement* of eyes and ears": Parkman's "Oregon Trail," v.); specif., the full number of officers and crew required to man a ship; also, the quantity or amount which when added completes a whole; either of two parts or things needed to complete each other; specif., the angular amount needed to bring a given arc or angle to 90° (as, in the figure, the arc BD is the *complement* of the arc AB, and the angle BCD is the *complement* of the angle ACB); also, the interval which added to a given interval completes a musical octave; also, compliment†.

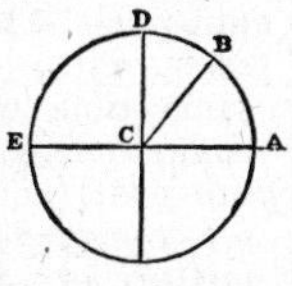

—**com′ple-ment** (-ment), *v. t.* To complete; form a complement to; also, to compliment†.—**com-ple-men′tal** (-men′tạl), *a.* Complementary. — **com-ple-men′ta-ry** (-tạ-ri), *a.* Forming a complement; completing; also, complementing each other.—**complementary colors.** See under *color, n.*
com-plete (kọm-plēt′), *a.* [L. *completus*, pp. of *complere*, fill up, complete, < *com-*, altogether, + *plere*, fill.] Having all its parts or elements; whole, entire, or full; also, finished, ended, or concluded; also, entire or thorough; also, perfect in kind or quality; of persons, accomplished or consummate (archaic: as, a *complete* gentleman).—**complete′,** *v. t.*; *-pleted, -pleting.* To make complete; make whole or entire; make up the full number or amount of; bring to an end, or finish; make perfect; fulfil or accomplish. — **com-plete′ly,** *adv.* — **com-plete′ness,** *n.* — **com-plet′er** (-plē′tėr), *n.*—**com-ple′tion** (-plē′shọn), *n.* [LL. *completio(n-).*] The act of completing, or the state of being completed; conclusion; fulfilment.—**com-ple′tive,** *a.* [LL. *completivus.*] Serving to complete.
com-plex (kom′pleks), *a.* [L. *complexus*, pp. of *complecti*, entwine, embrace, < *com-*, with, + *plectere*, plait.] Composed of interconnected parts; compound; composite; esp., characterized by an involved combination of parts; complicated; intricate.—**complex fraction.** See *fraction, n.* —**complex sentence,** a sentence containing one or more dependent clauses in addition to the principal clause.—**com′plex,** *n.* [L. *complexus*, n., < *complecti.*] A complex whole or system; a complicated assemblage of particulars; in *psychoanalysis*, a group of ideas or mental processes which for some reason has been inhibited or restrained, or has not been assimilated by or brought into harmony with the main body of the mental processes, and which is regarded as the causative agent in the production of certain abnormal mental states; an emotional experience which has been repressed because of its painful or disagreeable content; in colloq. use, a fixed idea; an obsessing or predominating notion.—**com-plex′,** *v. t.* To combine intricately; complicate: as, "Mere murder got *complexed* with wile" (Browning's "Ring and the Book," viii.). [Rare.]
com-plex-ion (kọm-plek′shọn), *n.* [OF. F. *complexion*, < LL. *complexio(n-)*, constitution, L. combination, < L. *complecti*: see *complex.*] Constitution or habit of body and mind, regarded as the result of combined qualities (orig. a term of the old physiology); nature†, disposition†, or temperament†; also, the natural color and appearance of the skin, esp. of the face; hence, appearance; aspect; character. —**com-plex′ion-al,** *a.*—**com-plex′ioned,** *a.* Having a complexion: as, dark-*complexioned.*
com-plex-i-ty (kọm-plek′si-ti), *n.*; pl. *-ties* (-tiz). The state or quality of being complex; intricacy; also, something complex.—**com-plex-ly** (kom′pleks-li), *adv.* In a complex manner.—**com′plex-ness,** *n.*
com-plex-us (kọm-plek′sus), *n.* [L.] A complex.
com-pli-ance (kọm-plī′ạns), *n.* The act of complying; an acquiescing or yielding; also, a disposition to yield to others. Also **com-pli′an-cy.**
com-pli-ant (kọm-plī′ạnt), *a.* Complying; yielding; obliging.—**com-pli′ant-ly,** *adv.*
com-pli-ca-cy (kom′pli-kā̤-si), *n.*; pl. *-cies* (-siz). Complicated state; also, a complication.
com-pli-cate (kom′pli-kāt), *v. t.*; *-cated, -cating.* [L. *complicatus*, pp. of *complicare*, < *com-*, with, + *plicare*, fold.] To fold or twine together; combine intricately (*with*); render complex, intricate, or involved.—**com′pli-cate** (-kā̤t), *a.* Complex or involved; in *bot.*, folded upon itself; in *zoöl.*, of insects' wings, folded longitudinally one or more times.—**com′pli-cat-ed** (-kā-ted), *p. a.* Involved; intricate.—**com′pli-cat-ed-ly,** *adv.*—**com′pli-cat-ed-ness,** *n.* —**com-pli-ca′tion** (-kā′shọn), *n.* [LL. *complicatio(n-).*] The act of complicating; a complicated or involved state or condition; also, a complex combination of elements or things; also, a complicating element.
com-plice (kom′plis), *n.* [OF. F. *complice*, < LL. *complex* (*complic-*), closely connected, confederate, akin to L. *complicare*: see *complicate.*] An accomplice. [Archaic.]—**com-pli-ci-ty** (kọm-plis′i-ti), *n.* [F. *complicité.*] The state of being an accomplice; partnership in wrong-doing; also, complexity.
com-pli-er (kọm-plī′ėr), *n.* [See *comply.*] One who complies.
com-pli-ment (kom′pli-mẹnt), *n.* [F. *compliment*, < It. *complimento*, < L. *complementum*: see *complement.*] Ceremonious courtesy; complaisant civility or politeness; politely flattering language; also, an act or expression of civility or flattering esteem; a politely commendatory or flattering remark; *pl.*, polite remembrances or greetings. —**com′pli-ment** (-ment), *v.* **I.** *tr.* To pay a compliment to; felicitate; also, to present (a person) with something by way of compliment. **II.** *intr.* To employ compliment; pay compliments.—**com-pli-men′ta-ry** (-men′tạ-ri), *a.* Of the nature of, conveying, or addressing a compliment; politely flattering.—**com-pli-men′ta-ri-ly,** *adv.*—**com-pli-men′ta-ri-ness,** *n.*—**com′pli-ment-er,** *n.*
com-plin, com-pline (kom′plin), *n.* [ME. *complin, compli*, < OF. *complie* (F. *complies*, pl.), < ML. *completa*, prop. fem. of L. *completus*: see *complete.*] *Eccles.*, the last of the seven canonical hours, or the service for it, orig. occurring after the evening meal, but now usually following immediately upon vespers.
com-plot (kom′plot), *n.* [F. *complot*, plot, OF. concerted plan, also crowd, struggle; origin uncertain.] A joint plot; a conspiracy: as, "*complots* of mischief" (Shakspere's "Titus Andronicus," v. l. 65).—**com-plot** (kọm-plot′), *v. t.* or *i.*; *-plotted, -plotting.* To plot together.—**com-plot′ter,** *n.*
Com-plu-ten-sian (kom-plö-ten′shiạn), *a.* [L. *Complutensis.*] Of Complutum, now Alcalá de Henares, a town near Madrid, Spain: as, the *Complutensian* Polyglot (the earliest complete polyglot Bible, published there in 1522).
com-plu-vi-um (kom-plö′vi-um), *n.*; pl. *-via* (-vi-ạ̈). [L., < *compluere*, flow together in raining, < *com-*, together, + *pluere*, rain.] In ancient Roman houses, a quadrangular opening in the roof of the atrium, toward which the roof sloped and through which the rain-water fell into the impluvium.
com-ply (kọm-plī′), *v.*; *-plied, -plying.* [Appar. < It. *complire*, fulfil, complete, < L. *complere*: see *complete.* In part appar. affected by E. *ply.*] **I.**† *tr.* To fulfil; execute. **II.** *intr.* To use compliment†; also, to be complaisant or accommodating†; also, to act in accordance with wishes, requests, commands, requirements, conditions, etc.; acquiesce; yield; conform.
com-po (kom′pō), *n.*; pl. *-pos* (-pōz). Shortened form of *composition*, esp. as the name of various composite substances in industrial use.

com-po-né, com-po-ny (kom-pō′nā, -ni), *a.* [F. *componé.*] In *her.*, of a bend, etc., composed of small squares of two alternate tinctures in one row.

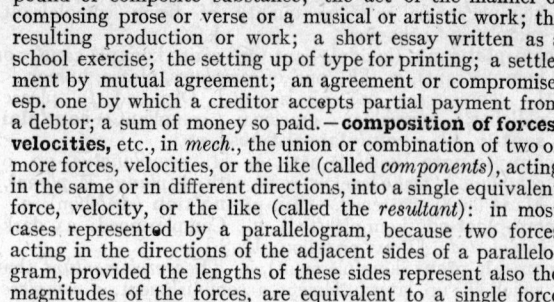

Bordure Componé.

com-po-nent (kọm-pō′nẹnt). [L. *componens* (*-ent-*), ppr. of *componere*: see *composite.*] **I.** *a.* Composing; constituent. **II.** *n.* A constituent part; in *mech.*, one of the parts of a force, velocity, or the like, out of which the whole may be compounded or into which it may be resolved (see *composition of forces, velocities*, etc.).

com-port[1] (kom′pōrt), *n.* [Appar. a corruption of *compote.*] A dish, usually having a supporting stem, for holding compotes, fruit, etc.; a compotier.

com-port[2] (kọm-pōrt′), *v.* [F. *comporter*, bear, behave, < L. *comportare*, carry together, < *com-*, with, + *portare*, carry.] **I.** *tr.* To bear or conduct (one's self); behave; also, to endure†. **II.** *intr.* To bear (*with*)†; also, to agree or accord (*with*); suit.—**com-port′ment,** *n.* Bearing; demeanor; behavior.

com-pose (kọm-pōz′), *v.*; *-posed, -posing.* [OF. F. *composer*, < *com-* (< L. *com-*), with, + *poser*, put (see *pose*[1]), but associated with derivatives of L. *componere*: see *composite, composition*, and *compositor.*] **I.** *tr.* To make or form by uniting parts or elements; be the parts or elements of; make up or constitute (as, a currency *composed* of silver); devise and make (a literary or musical production); arrange the parts or elements of (a picture, etc.); put or dispose in proper form or order; arrange or settle, as a quarrel, etc.; bring (the body or mind) to a particular adjustment or condition, as of repose or calmness; calm, quiet, or tranquilize, as one's thoughts or emotions; in *printing*, to set (type); set the types for (an article, etc.). **II.** *intr.* To practise composition; also, to enter into composition; also, to come to an agreement†.—**com-posed′.** *p. a.* Calm; tranquil.—**com-pos′ed-ly** (-pō′zed-li), *adv.*—**com-pos′ed-ness,** *n.*—**com-pos′er,** *n.* One who or that which composes; esp., a writer of music.—**com-pos′ing-room,** *n.* The room in which compositors work in a printing establishment.—**com-pos′ing-stick,** *n.* A small (usually) metal tray of adjustable width, in which type is set.

Composing-stick.

com-pos-ite (kọm-poz′it or, Brit. now usually, kom′pọ-zit), *a.* [L. *compositus*, pp. of *componere*, put together, compound, compose, < *com-*, with, + *ponere*, place, put: cf. *compose.*] Made up of various parts or elements; compound; [*cap.*] in *arch.*, noting or pertaining to a classical (Roman) order in which the capital contains features of other orders; [*l. c.*] in *bot.*, belonging to the *Compositæ*, a group or order of plants, including the daisy, dandelion, aster, etc., in which the florets are borne in a close head surrounded by a common involucre of bracts.—**composite number,** in *math.*, a number exactly divisible by some number other than itself and unity.—**composite photograph,** a single photographic portrait obtained by combining the photographs of two or more persons.—**com-pos′ite,** *n.* Something composite; a compound; in *bot.*, a composite plant.—**com-pos′ite-ly,** *adv.*—**com-pos′ite-ness,** *n.*

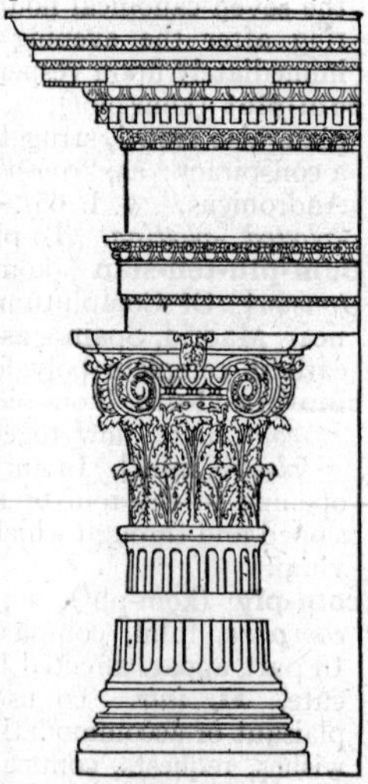

Composite Order.

com-po-si-tion (kom-pọ-zish′ọn), *n.* [OF. F. *composition*, < L. *compositio*(*n-*), < *componere*: see *composite.*] The act of combining parts or elements to form a whole, or the manner in which such parts are combined; the resulting state or product; make-up or constitution; a compound or composite substance; the act or the manner of composing prose or verse or a musical or artistic work; the resulting production or work; a short essay written as a school exercise; the setting up of type for printing; a settlement by mutual agreement; an agreement or compromise, esp. one by which a creditor accepts partial payment from a debtor; a sum of money so paid.—**composition of forces, velocities,** etc., in *mech.*, the union or combination of two or more forces, velocities, or the like (called *components*), acting in the same or in different directions, into a single equivalent force, velocity, or the like (called the *resultant*): in most cases represented by a parallelogram, because two forces acting in the directions of the adjacent sides of a parallelogram, provided the lengths of these sides represent also the magnitudes of the forces, are equivalent to a single force having the direction and magnitude of the intervening diagonal of the parallelogram.—**com-pos-i-tive** (kọm-poz′i-tiv), *a.* Involving composition.

com-pos-i-tor (kọm-poz′i-tọr), *n.* [L., a composer, arranger, < *componere*: see *composite.*] In *printing*, one who sets type; a type-setter.—**com-pos-i-to′ri-al** (-tō′ri-ạl), *a.*

com-pos men-tis (kom′pos men′tis). [L., having control of one's mind.] Of sound mind. Cf. *non compos mentis.*

com-pos-si-ble (kọm-pos′i-bl), *a.* [ML. *compossibilis*, < L. *com-*, with, + *possibilis*, E. *possible.*] Possible at the same time with something else; capable of coexisting; compatible.—**com-pos-si-bil′i-ty** (-bil′i-ti), *n.*

com-post (kom′pōst), *n.* [OF. *compost*, < L. *compositus*: see *composite.*] A composition or compound; esp., a mixture of various substances, as dung, dead leaves, etc., for fertilizing land.—**com′post,** *v. t.* To treat with or make into compost.

com-po-sure (kọm-pō′zhụr), *n.* The act of composing†; composition†; make-up† or constitution†; temperament†; composed state, as of the mind; calmness; tranquillity; also, that which is composed†; a composition†; a combination† (as, "My body was all covered with an artificial *composure* of the skins and hairs of other animals": Swift's "Gulliver's Travels," iv. 9).

com-po-ta-tion (kom-pọ-tā′shọn), *n.* [L. *compotatio*(*n-*), < *com-*, with, + *potare*, drink.] A drinking or tippling together.—**com′po-ta-tor,** *n.* [LL.] A fellow-drinker: as, "Charles Dennison . . . would be rejoiced to see his old *compotator*" (Smollett's "Humphry Clinker," Oct. 11).

com-pote (kom′pōt), *n.* [F. *compote*, OF. *composte*, < L. *composita*, fem. of *compositus*: see *composite.*] A preparation or dish of fruit stewed in a syrup; also, a compotier.—**com-po-tier** (kôṅ-po-tyā), *n.* [F.] A dish, usually of glass or china and having a supporting stem, used for holding compotes, fruit, etc.

com-pound[1] (kom′pound), *n.* [Cf. Malay *kampong*, inclosure.] In the East Indies, etc., an inclosure containing a residence or other establishment of Europeans.

com-pound[2] (kọm-pound′), *v.* [ME. *compounen*, < OF. *compondre*, < L. *componere*: see *composite.*] **I.** *tr.* To put together into a whole; combine; also, to make or form by combining parts, elements, etc.; construct; also, to make up† or constitute†; also, to settle or adjust by agreement, esp. for a reduced amount, as a debt; specif., to agree, for a consideration, not to prosecute (a crime, etc.); also, in *elect.*, to wind (a dynamo or a motor) so that part of the field-magnet coils are in series with the armature circuit and part are shunted from it. **II.** *intr.* To make a bargain (as, "They would have *compounded* to give us everything we desired to be rid of us": Defoe's "Captain Singleton," iii.); come to terms; compromise; settle a debt, etc., by compromise.—**com-pound**[2] (kom′pound), *a.* Composed of two or more parts, elements, or ingredients, or involving two or more actions, functions, etc.; composite; in *zoöl.*, of an animal, composed of a number of distinct individuals which are connected to form a united whole or colony.—**compound dynamo,** in *elect.*, a compound-wound dynamo.—**compound engine,** one in which the steam or other working fluid after doing work in a high-pressure cylinder is further utilized in a low-pressure cylinder.—**compound flower,** the flower-head of a composite plant.—**compound fraction.** See *fraction*, *n.*—**compound interest.** See under *interest, n.*—**compound leaf,** one composed of a number of leaflets on a common stalk. It may be either digitately or pinnately compound, and the leaflets may be themselves compound.—**compound motor,** in *elect.*, a compound-wound motor.—**compound number,** a quantity expressed in more than one denomination or unit, as the length 1 foot 6 inches.—**compound sentence,** one containing two or more subjects, predicates, or clauses, esp. one consisting of coördinate independent clauses.—**compound word,** one made up of two or more words which retain their separate form and signification.—**com′pound²,** *n.* Something formed by compounding or combining parts, elements, etc., as a substance or a word.—**com-pound′a-ble,** *a.* Capable of being compounded.—**com-pound′er,** *n.*—**com′pound=wound,** *a.* In *elect.*, noting a dynamo or a motor of which part of the field-magnet coils are in series with the armature circuit and part are shunted from it. Cf. *series-wound* and *shunt-wound.*

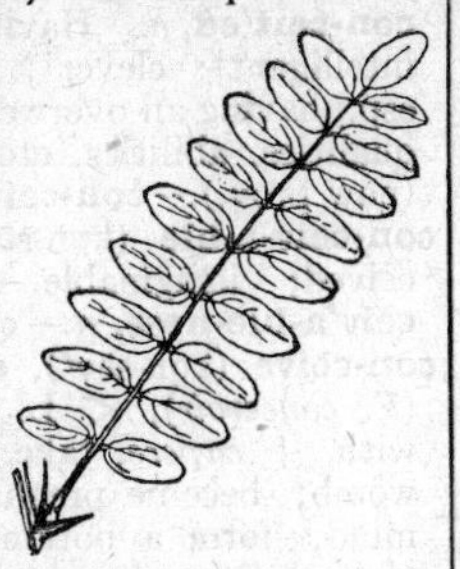
Pinnately Compound Leaf.

com-pra-dor (kom-prạ-dôr′ or kom′prạ-dôr), *n.* [Pg., a buyer, purveyor.] In China, etc., a native agent or factotum, as of a foreign business house.

com-pre-hend (kom-prẹ-hend′), *v. t.* [L. *comprehendere* (pp. *comprehensus*), < *com-*, together, + *prehendere*, seize.] To take in or embrace; include; comprise; esp., to take into the mind; conceive; understand.—**com-pre-hend′er,** *n.*—**com-pre-hend′ing-ly,** *adv.*—**com-pre-hen′si-ble** (-hen′si-bl), *a.* [L. *comprehensibilis.*] Capable of being comprehended; intelligible.—**com-pre-hen-si-bil′i-ty** (-bil′i-ti), **com-pre-hen′si-ble-ness,** *n.*—**com-pre-hen′si-bly,** *adv.*—**com-pre-hen′sion** (-shọn), *n.* [L. *comprehensio(n-)*.] The act or fact of comprehending; inclusion; comprehensiveness; perception or understanding; an adequate notion; capacity of the mind to understand; in *logic*, intension.—**com-pre-hen′sive** (-siv), *a.* Comprehending or inclusive; comprehending much; of large scope; esp., comprehending mentally; characterized by wide mental grasp.—**com-pre-hen′sive-ly,** *adv.*—**com-pre-hen′sive-ness,** *n.*

com-press (kọm-pres′), *v. t.* [L. *compressus*, pp. of *comprimere*, < *com-*, together, + *premere*, press.] To press together; force into smaller compass; condense.—**com-press** (kom′pres), *n.* An apparatus or establishment for compressing cotton-bales, etc.; in *med.*, a soft pad of lint, linen, or the like, held in place by a bandage, used as a means of pressure or for other purposes; a wet cloth applied to relieve inflammation, etc.—**com-pressed′,** *p. a.* Pressed into narrow compass; condensed; in *bot.*, flattened laterally or along the length; in *zoöl.*, narrow from side to side, and therefore of greater height than width.—**compressed air,** air which has been mechanically compressed, and which on account of its expansive force is used to operate drills, brakes, etc.—**com-press′i-ble,** *a.* Capable of being compressed.—**com-press-i-bil′i-ty** (-bil′i-ti), **com-press′i-ble-ness,** *n.*—**com-pres′sion** (-presh′ọn), *n.* [L. *compressio(n-)*.] The act of compressing; compressed state.—**com-pres′sion-al,** *a.*—**com-pres′sive** (-pres′iv), *a.* Compressing; tending to compress.—**com-pres′sive-ly,** *adv.*—**com-pres′sor,** *n.* [L.] One who or that which compresses; in *anat.*, a muscle that compresses some part of the body; in *surg.*, an instrument for compressing a part of the body.—**com-pres′sure** (-presh′ụr), *n.* Compression.

com-pris-a-ble (kọm-prī′zạ-bl), *a.* That may be comprised.

com-prise (kọm-prīz′), *v. t.*; *-prised, -prising.* [OF. F. *compris*, pp. of *comprendre*, < L. *comprendere*, for *comprehendere*: see *comprehend.*] To comprehend; embrace; include; contain.

com-pro-mise (kom′prọ-mīz), *n.* [OF. F. *compromis*, < L. *compromissum*, prop. pp. neut. of *compromittere*: see *compromit.*] An agreement to abide by the decision of an arbiter†; arbitration; a settlement of differences by mutual concessions; an adjustment of conflicting claims, principles, etc., by the sacrifice or surrender of a part of each; anything resulting from compromise; also, something intermediate between different things (colloq.); also, a compromising or endangering, as of reputation.—**com′pro-mise,** *v.*; *-mised, -mising.* **I.** *tr.* To settle by a compromise; also, to bring to terms†; also, to render liable to suspicion by lax conduct; endanger as to reputation; involve unfavorably; commit. **II.** *intr.* To make a compromise.—**com′pro-mis-er** (-mī-zėr), *n.*—**com′pro-mis-ing-ly,** *adv.*

com-pro-mit (kom-prọ-mit′), *v. t.*; *-mitted, -mitting.* [L. *compromittere* (pp. *compromissus*), < *com-*, with, + *promittere*: see *promise.*] To pledge (one's self) to abide by arbitration†; settle by arbitration†; endanger (archaic).

compt-er (koun′tėr), *n.* Old form of *counter²* (prison).

Comp-tom-e-ter (komp-tom′e-tėr), *n.* A certain high-speed adding and calculating machine. [Registered trade-mark.]—**Comp-tom′e-try,** *n.* The method or science of operating a Comptometer. [Proprietary term.]

comp-trol-ler (kọn-trō′lėr), *n.* Erroneous spelling of *controller*, still used in titles.—**comp-trol′ler-ship,** *n.*

com-pul-sa-tive (kọm-pul′sạ-tiv), *a.* Compulsory. Also **com-pul′sa-to-ry** (-tọ-ri). [Obs. or rare.]

com-pul-sion (kọm-pul′shọn), *n.* [LL. *compulsio(n-)*, < L. *compellere* (pp. *compulsus*): see *compel.*] The act of compelling, or the state of being compelled; constraint; coercion.—**com-pul′sive** (-siv), *a.* [L. *compulsus*, pp.] Compulsory.—**com-pul′sive-ly,** *adv.*—**com-pul′sive-ness,** *n.*—**com-pul′so-ry** (-sọ-ri), *a.* Exercising compulsion; constraining; coercive; also, compelled; forced; obligatory.—**com-pul′so-ri-ly,** *adv.*—**com-pul′so-ri-ness,** *n.*

com-punc-tion (kọm-pungk′shọn), *n.* [LL. *compunctio(n-)*, < L. *compungere*, prick severely, < *com-*, altogether, + *pungere*, prick.] The pricking of conscience; pangs of remorse or regret, as for wrong-doing.—**com-punc′tious** (-shus), *a.* Of or having compunction; remorseful.—**com-punc′tious-ly,** *adv.*

com-pur-ga-tion (kom-pėr-gā′shọn), *n.* [LL. *compurgatio(n-)*, < L. *compurgare*, purify completely, < *com-*, altogether, + *purgare*, E. *purge.*] The legal clearing of one accused, by the oaths of persons testifying to his innocence or veracity; in general, a vindication of one accused.—**com′pur-ga-tor,** *n.* [ML.] One who testifies to another's innocence or veracity.—**com-pur-ga-to-ry** (kọm-pėr′gạ-tọ-ri), *a.*

com-pu-ta-ble (kọm-pū′tạ-bl), *a.* [L. *computabilis.*] Capable of being computed.—**com-pu-ta-bil′i-ty** (-bil′i-ti), *n.*

com-pu-ta-tion (kom-pụ-tā′shọn), *n.* [L. *computatio(n-)*.] The act or process of computing; calculation; a reckoning.—**com-pu-ta-tive** (kọm-pū′tạ-tiv), *a.*

com-pute (kọm-pūt′), *v.*; *-puted, -puting.* [L. *computare*, < *com-*, with, + *putare*, reckon: see *putative.*] **I.** *tr.* To determine by reckoning or calculation; calculate; estimate. **II.** *intr.* To reckon; calculate.—**com-pute′,** *n.* Computation; reckoning.—**com-put′er** (-pū′tėr), *n.*—**com-pu-tist** (kom′pụ-tist), *n.* One who computes; one skilled in computing; esp., one skilled in the computus (set of tables).—**com′pu-tus** (-tus), *n.*; pl. *-tuses*, L. *-ti* (-tī). [LL., < L. *computare.*] A computation; an account; also, a set of tables for calculating movable dates of the calendar and astronomical occurrences; a calendar. [Chiefly hist.]

com-rade (kom′rad or -rạd), *n.* [F. *camarade*, < Sp. *camarada*, lit. 'chamber-mate,' < L. *camera*, E. *chamber.*] A familiar associate; a close companion; a mate.—**com′rade-ly,** *a.* Of, like, or befitting a comrade.—**com′rade-ry, com′rade-ship,** *n.* The state of being a comrade; the relation of comrades; friendly fellowship.

com-rogue (kom′rōg), *n.* [See *com-.*] A fellow-rogue. [Obs. or archaic.]

comte (kônt), *n.* [F., = E. *count¹.*] In French use, a count. See *count¹.*—**com-tesse** (kôn-tes), *n.* [F.] In French use, a countess.

Comt-i-an (kom′ti-ạn or kôn′-), *a.* Of or pertaining to the French philosopher Auguste Comte (1798–1857), or his system of philosophy. See *positivism.*—**Comt′ism,** *n.* The philosophical system founded by Auguste Comte; positivism.—**Comt′ist,** *n.*

con¹ (kon), *v. t.*; *conned, conning.* [AS. *cunnan*: see *can¹.*] To know†; also, to learn; study; commit to memory; peruse or examine carefully.

con², **conn** (kon), *v. t.*; *conned, conning.* [Origin uncertain; perhaps ult. < L. *conducere*, E. *conduct.*] To direct the steering of (a ship): as, "Over the turret, shut in his iron-clad tower, Craven was *conning* his ship through smoke and flame" (H. Newbolt's "Craven").

con³ (kon), *adv.* [Abbr. of L. *contra*, adv., in opposition, as prep., against.] Against a proposition, opinion, etc.: opposed to *pro*, and often used as a noun. See *pro.*

con⁴ (kon), *n.* Abbreviation of *confidence*, as in *con game*, *con man*. See under *confidence*. [Slang.]

con-. A form of the prefix *com-*, 'with,' 'together,' 'altogether,' occasionally used as an English formative, as in *confocal*.

co-na-tion (kō-nā'shọn), *n.* [L. *conatio(n-)*, < *conari* (pp. *conatus*), endeavor, try.] In *psychol.*, voluntary agency, embracing desire and volition.—**co-na-tive** (kō'nạ-tiv or kon'ạ-), *a.* [L. *conatus*, pp.] In *psychol.*, pertaining to or of the nature of conation; in *gram.*, expressing endeavor or effort (as, a *conative* verb).—**co-na'tus** (-tus), *n.*; pl. *-tus.* [L., < *conari.*] An effort or striving; also, a force or tendency simulating a human effort.

con-cam-er-at-ed (kon-kam'ẹ-rā-ted), *a.* [L. *concameratus*, pp. of *concamerare*, < *con-*, with, + *camerare*, arch over, vault, < *camera*: see *camera.*] Arched† or vaulted†; also, divided into chambers, as a shell.—**con-cam-er-a'tion** (-ẹ-rā'shọn), *n.* Concamerated or chambered formation; also, a chamber or cell.

con-cat-e-nate (kon-kat'ẹ-nāt), *v. t.*; *-nated, -nating.* [LL. *concatenatus*, pp. of *concatenare*, < L. *con-*, with, + *catenare*, chain: see *catenate.*] To link together; unite in a series or chain.—**con-cat'e-nate,** *a.* Concatenated.—**con-cat-e-na'tion** (-nā'shọn), *n.* [LL. *concatenatio(n-).*] The act of concatenating, or the state of being concatenated; connection as in a chain; also, a series of concatenated or interdependent things or events.

con-cave (kon'kāv). [L. *concavus*, < *con-*, altogether, + *cavus*, hollow.] **I.** *a.* Hollow†; also, curved like the interior of a circle or of a hollow sphere; hollow and curved. **II.** *n.* A hollow†; a concave surface, part, or thing. —**con'cave,** *v. t.*; *-caved, -caving.* To make concave.—**con'cave-ly,** *adv.*—**con'cave-ness,** *n.* —**con-cav-i-ty** (kọn-kav'i-ti), *n.*; pl. *-ties* (-tiz). The state of being concave; a concave surface or thing; a hollow or cavity.—**con-ca-vo=con-cave** (kon-kā'vō-kon'kāv), *a.* Concave on both sides, as a lens.—**con-ca'vo=con'vex,** *a.* Concave on one side and convex on the other, as a lens; specif., noting or pertaining to a lens in which the concave face has a greater degree of curvature than the convex face, the lens being thinnest in the middle.

Concave (or Plano-concave) Lens (cross-section).

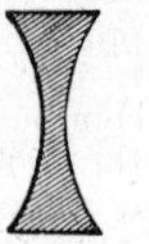

Concavo-concave Lens.

Concavo-convex Lens.

con-ceal (kọn-sēl'), *v. t.* [OF. *conceler*, < L. *concelare*, < *con-*, altogether, + *celare*, hide: see *hall.*] To withdraw or keep from sight; shield from observation; hide; also, to keep secret.—**con-ceal'a-ble,** *a.* That may be concealed. —**con-ceal'er,** *n.*—**con-ceal'ment,** *n.* The act of concealing, or the state of being concealed; also, a means or place of hiding; also, a secret†.

con-cede (kọn-sēd'), *v. t.*; *-ceded, -ceding.* [L. *concedere* (pp. *concessus*), < *con-*, with, + *cedere*, go, yield.] To grant as a right or privilege; also, to admit as just or true; allow.—**con-ced'ed-ly** (-sē'ded-li), *adv.*—**con-ced'er,** *n.*

con-ceit (kọn-sēt'), *n.* [ME. *conceyte*; related to *conceive* as *deceit* to *deceive.*] That which is conceived in the mind†; a thought†; an idea†; also, the faculty of conceiving†; apprehension†; also, personal opinion or estimation; hence, favorable opinion; esteem; often, overweening self-esteem; also, imagination or fancy; a fancy or whim; a fanciful practice; an ingenious or witty thought or expression; a fanciful thought, idea, or turn of words, esp. of strained or far-fetched nature; the use of such thoughts, ideas, etc., as a literary characteristic; also, a fancy article†.—**con-ceit',** *v.* **I.** *tr.* To conceive mentally; apprehend; imagine; also, to flatter (one's self); have a good opinion of; also, to take a fancy to. [Chiefly archaic or prov.] **II.** *intr.* To form a notion or opinion. [Archaic or prov.]—**con-ceit'ed,** *a.* Having conception or apprehension†; also, intelligent†; clever†; also, having an opinion (now prov.); esp., having an overweening opinion of one's self, or of one's qualities, abilities, etc.; vain; also, fanciful or whimsical (now prov.).—**con-ceit'ed-ly,** *adv.*—**con-ceit'ed-ness,** *n.*

con-ceiv-a-ble (kọn-sē'vạ-bl), *a.* Capable of being conceived; imaginable.—**con-ceiv-a-bil'i-ty** (-bil'i-ti), **con-ceiv'a-ble-ness,** *n.*—**con-ceiv'a-bly,** *adv.*

con-ceive (kọn-sēv'), *v.*; *-ceived, -ceiving.* [OF. *conceveir* (F. *concevoir*), < L. *concipere* (pp. *conceptus*), < *con-*, with, + *capere*, take.] **I.** *tr.* To receive (seed) into the womb; become pregnant with; also, to apprehend in the mind; form a notion or idea of; imagine; understand; also, to form (a notion, opinion, purpose, etc.); also, to experience or entertain (a feeling); also, to express, as in words. **II.** *intr.* To become pregnant; also, to form an idea (*of*); think.—**con-ceiv'er,** *n.*

con-cent (kọn-sent'), *n.* [L. *concentus*, < *concinere*, sing together, < *con-*, with, + *canere*, sing.] Concord of sounds; concert of voices; harmony; accord: as, "that undisturbed song of pure *concent*" (Milton's "At a Solemn Musick," 6). [Now rare.]

con-cen-ter, con-cen-tre (kọn-sen'tėr), *v. t.* or *i.*; *-tered, -tred, -tering, -tring.* [F. *concentrer*, < L. *con-*, with, + *centrum*, center.] To bring or converge to a common center; concentrate.

con-cen-trate (kon'sẹn-trāt or kọn-sen'-), *v.*; *-trated, -trating.* [L. *con-*, with, + *centrum*, center.] **I.** *tr.* To bring to a common center; bring to bear on one point or object; focus; also, to condense; make stronger, purer, or more intense; in *mining*, to separate (metal or ore) from rock, sand, etc. **II.** *intr.* To converge to a center; also, to become stronger or purer.—**con-cen-trate** (kon'sẹn-trāt or kọn-sen'-). **I.** *a.* Concentrated. **II.** *n.* A concentrated form of something; a product of concentration.—**con-cen-tra-tion** (kon-sẹn-trā'shọn), *n.* The act of concentrating; concentrated state; exclusive attention to one object; close mental application; also, something concentrated.—**concentration camp,** a camp in which hostile non-combatants in a country are collected to prevent them from giving aid or information to the enemy.—**con-cen-tra-tive** (kọn-sen'trạ-tiv), *a.* Tending to concentrate.—**con-cen'tra-tive-ness,** *n.* Concentrative tendency; in *phren.*, the faculty of mental concentration.—**con'cen-tra-tor** (-trā-tọr), *n.* One who or that which concentrates; any apparatus for concentrating ores, etc.

con-cen'tre, *v.* See *concenter*.

con-cen-tric (kọn-sen'trik), *a.* [ML. *concentricus*, < L. *con-*, with, + *centrum*, center.] Having a common center, as circles or spheres; specif., in *mineral.*, occurring in or having parallel layers arranged about a common center. Also **con-cen'tri-cal.**—**con-cen'tri-cal-ly,** *adv.*—**con-cen-tri-ci-ty** (kon-sen-tris'i-ti), *n.*

Concentric Structure, in polished agate.

con-cept (kon'sept), *n.* [L. *conceptus*, a conceiving, a thought, < *concipere*: see *conceive.*] That which is conceived in the mind; a general notion or idea; a conception.

con-cep-ta-cle (kọn-sep'tạ-kl), *n.* [L. *conceptaculum*, < *concipere*: see *conceive.*] A receptacle; in *biol.*, an organ or cavity inclosing reproductive bodies.

con-cep-tion (kọn-sep'shọn), *n.* [OF. F. *conception*, < L. *conceptio(n-)*, < *concipere*: see *conceive.*] The act of conceiving, or the state of being conceived; a becoming pregnant; the inception of life; fig., beginning; also, that which is conceived; the embryo or fetus; also, the act or power of forming notions, ideas, or concepts; also, a notion or idea; a concept; also, a design or plan.—**con-cep'tion-al,** *a.*—**con-cep'tive,** *a.* Conceiving; forming conceptions.

con-cep-tu-al (kọn-sep'ṭū-ạl), *a.* [L. *conceptus*: see *concept.*] Pertaining to the forming of concepts or to concepts.

—**con-cep′tu-al-ism,** *n.* The philosophical doctrine, midway between nominalism and realism, that universals have existence, in that they exist in the mind; also, the doctrine that general and abstract terms, as *horse, red,* can be fully represented in thought.—**con-cep′tu-al-ist,** *n.*—**con-cep″-tu-al-is′tic,** *a.*—**con-cep′tu-al-ly,** *adv.*

con-cern (kọn-sėrn′), *v. t.* [ML. *concernere,* relate to, LL. mix, < L. *con-,* with, + *cernere,* separate, sift, distinguish, perceive, have respect to: see *certain.*] To relate to; be connected with; be of interest or importance to; affect; also, to interest, engage, or involve (used reflexively or in the passive, often with *with* or *in*: as, to *concern* one's self with a matter; to be *concerned* in a transaction, or in a plot); also, to disquiet or trouble (now in the passive: as, to be much *concerned* about a person's health).—**con-cern′,** *n.* Relation; important relation or bearing; also, interest; also, participation; also, solicitude or anxiety; also, a matter or affair; a matter that engages one's attention, interest, or care; a commercial or manufacturing firm or establishment; any material object or contrivance (colloq.).—**con-cerned′,** *p. a.* Interested; troubled or anxious.—**con-cern′ed-ly,** *adv.*—**con-cern′ing,** *prep.* [Orig. ppr.] Relating to; regarding; about.—**con-cern′ment,** *n.* Relation or bearing; importance or moment; interest; participation; anxiety or solicitude; also, a concern or affair.

con-cert (kọn-sėrt′), *v.* [F. *concerter,* < It. *concertare*: cf. L. *concertare,* contend, also *conserere* (pp. *consertus*), join together.] **I.** *tr.* To contrive or arrange by agreement; plan; devise; in *music,* to arrange in parts for several voices or instruments. **II.** *intr.* To plan or act together.—**con-cert** (kon′sėrt), *n.* [F. *concert,* < It. *concerto,* < *concertare.*] Agreement of two or more in a design or plan; combined action; accord or harmony; also, a musical performance in which several singers or players, or both, participate.—**con-cert′ed,** *p. a.* Contrived or arranged by agreement; prearranged; planned or devised; done in concert; in *music,* arranged in parts for several voices or instruments.

con-cer-ti-na (kon-sėr-tē′nạ̈), *n.* [From *concert, n.*] A small, portable bellows-like musical instrument, commonly with polygonal ends, similar in principle to the accordion but with greater musical possibilities.—**con-cer-ti′-nist,** *n.* One who plays on the concertina.

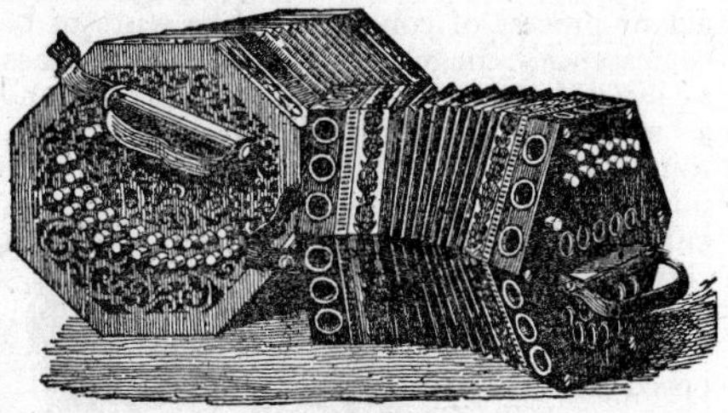

Concertinas.

con-cer-ti-no (kon-cher-tē′nō), *n.*; pl. *-ni* (-nē). [It., dim. of *concerto.*] In *music,* a short concerto.

con-cert-meis-ter (kon-tsert′mīs″tėr), *n.* [G.] The leader, usually the first violinist, of an orchestra, ranking next to the conductor.

con-cer-to (kọn-sėr′tō, It. kon-cher′tō), *n.*; pl. *-tos* (-tōz), It. *-ti* (-tē). [It.] In *music,* a composition for one or more principal instruments, with orchestral accompaniment: now usually in symphonic form.

con-cert=pitch (kon′sėrt-pich), *n.* In *music,* a pitch slightly higher than the ordinary pitch, used in tuning instruments for concert use.

con-ces-sion (kọn-sesh′ọn), *n.* [L. *concessio(n-),* < *concedere*: see *concede.*] The act of conceding or yielding, as a right or privilege, or as a point or fact in an argument; also, that which is conceded; esp., something conceded by a government or a controlling authority, as a grant of land or a privilege.—**con-ces-sion-aire′** (-ãr′), *n.* [F. *concessionnaire.*] One to whom a concession has been granted, as by a government.—**con-ces′sion-a-ry** (-ạ̄-ri). **I.** *a.* Pertaining to concession; of the nature of a concession. **II.** *n.*; pl. *-ries* (-riz). A concessionaire.—**con-ces-sion-naire** (kôṅ-ses-yo-nãr), *n.* [F.] A concessionaire.—**con-ces′sive.** [LL. *concessivus.*] **I.** *a.* Tending or serving to concede; in *gram.,* expressing concession, as the conjunction *though.* **II.** *n.* In *gram.,* a concessive word, clause, or sentence.—**con-ces′sive-ly,** *adv.*

conch (kongk), *n.* [L. *concha,* < Gr. κόγχη, mussel or cockle, shell, shell-like part or thing, external ear.] A shellfish, or its shell; any of several marine gastropods, esp. *Strombus gigas* (see *stromb*); the spiral shell of a gastropod, often used as a trumpet; the fabled shell trumpet of the Tritons; one of the lower-class whites of the Bahamas and the Florida Keys, who live largely on shell-fish; in *anat.,* the external ear; in *arch.,* the concave surface of a dome.

con-cha (kong′kạ̈), *n.*; pl. *conchæ* (-kē). [L. and NL.: see *conch.*] In *anat.,* the external ear, or the central hollow part of it; also, a turbinate bone (of the nose); in *arch.,* a conch.

con-chif-er-ous (kong-kif′ẹ-rus), *a.* [L. *concha,* shell: see *-ferous.*] Shell-bearing; in *zoöl.,* belonging or pertaining to the *Conchifera* (now equivalent to the *Lamellibranchiata*: see *lamellibranch*), a group or class of mollusks including the oyster, clam, etc.

con-chi-form (kong′ki-fôrm), *a.* [L. *concha,* shell: see *-form.*] Shell-shaped.

con-choid, con-choi-dal (kong′koid, kong-koi′dạl), *a.* [Gr. κογχοειδής, < κόγχη, shell, + εἶδος, form.] In *mineral.,* noting or pertaining to a fracture characterized by convex shell-like elevations and concave shell-like depressions.

Conchoidal Fracture, in obsidian.

con-chol-o-gy (kong-kol′ọ̄-ji), *n.* [Gr. κόγχη, shell: see *-logy.*] The science of shells and shell-fish.—**con-cho-log′i-cal** (-kọ̄-loj′i-kạl), *a.*—**con-chol′o-gist,** *n.*

con-cho-scope (kong′-kọ̄-skōp), *n.* [NL. *concha,* turbinate bone: see *-scope.*] An instrument for examining the nasal cavity.

con-chy (kon′shi), *n.*; pl. *-chies* (-shiz). Short for *conscientious objector* (see under *conscientious*). [British slang.]

con-cierge (kôṅ-syerzh), *n.* [F.; origin uncertain.] In France, etc., one who has charge of the entrance of a building; a janitor or doorkeeper.—**con-cierge-rie** (-rē), *n.* [F.] The office, room, or lodge of a concierge.

con-cil-i-a-bule (kọn-sil′i-ạ-būl), *n.* [L. *conciliabulum,* < *concilium*: see *council.*] A small, secret, or unauthorized council or assembly, esp. one occupied with ecclesiastical matters.

con-cil-i-ar (kọn-sil′i-ạ̈r), *a.* [L. *concilium*: see *council.*] Pertaining to a council.

con-cil-i-ate (kọn-sil′i-āt), *v. t.*; *-ated, -ating.* [L. *conciliatus,* pp. of *conciliare,* bring together, < *concilium,* assembly, union: see *council.*] To overcome the distrust or hostility of, by soothing or pacifying means; placate; win over; also, to win or gain (regard or favor); also, to render accordant or compatible; reconcile.—**con-cil′i-at-ing-ly,** *adv.*—**con-cil-i-a′tion** (-ā′shọn), *n.* [L. *conciliatio(n-).*] The act of conciliating, or the fact of being conciliated.—**con-cil′i-a-tive** (-ạ̄-tiv), *a.* Conciliatory.—**con-cil′i-a-tor** (-ā-tọr), *n.*—**con-cil′i-a-to-ry** (-ạ̄-tọ̄-ri), *a.* Tending to conciliate.—**con-cil′i-a-to-ri-ness,** *n.*

con-cin-ni-ty (kọn-sin′i-ti), *n.*; pl. *-ties* (-tiz). [L. *concinnitas,* < *concinnus,* well put together.] Harmonious adaptation of parts; esp., fine adjustment of words and clauses in discourse or writing; elegance of structure or style; an example of rhetorical elegance (as, "A discourse in which the fundamental topic was . . . omitted, was not likely, with all its *concinnities,* to make much impression": Motley's "Dutch Republic," ii. 3).

con-cise (kọn-sīs′), *a.* [L. *concisus,* pp. of *concidere,* cut up or off, < *con-,* altogether, + *cædere,* cut.] Comprehending much in few words; brief and comprehensive; succinct; terse.—**con-cise′ly,** *adv.*—**con-cise′ness,** *n.*

con-ci-sion (kọn-sizh′ọn), *n.* [L. *concisio(n-),* < *concidere*: see *concise.*] A cutting up or off; mutilation; also, concise quality; brevity; terseness.

con-clave (kon′klāv), *n.* [OF. F. *conclave*, < L. *conclave*, place that may be locked, < *con-*, with, + *clavis*, key.] A private room†; the place in which the cardinals of the Roman Catholic Church meet in private for the election of a pope; the assembly or meeting of the cardinals for the election of a pope; the body of cardinals; any private meeting, esp. one of an ecclesiastical nature.—**con′clav-ist** (-klā-vist), *n.* Either of two persons who attend upon a cardinal in conclave, one a secretary (usually an ecclesiastic) and the other a servant.

con-clude (kǫn-klöd′), *v.*; *-cluded, -cluding.* [L. *concludere* (pp. *conclusus*), < *con-*, altogether, + *cludere, claudere*, shut, close.] **I.** *tr.* To shut up or inclose (obs. or archaic); include† or comprise†; restrict† or confine†; restrain or stop (now only legal); bind or oblige (now only legal); also, to bring to an end; finish; terminate; sometimes, to say in conclusion (as, "'I spare you any farther allusions and illustrations,' *concluded* Dr. X—": Maria Edgeworth's "Belinda," vii.); also, to determine by reasoning; deduce; infer; also, to decide, determine, or resolve; also, to bring to a decision or settlement; settle or arrange finally. **II.** *intr.* To come to an end; finish; also, to arrive at an opinion or judgment; come to a decision; decide.—**con-clud′er** (-klö′dėr), *n.*—**con-clu′sion** (-klö′zhǫn), *n.* [L. *conclusio(n-)*.] The end or close; the final part; the last main division of a discourse, containing a summing up of the points; a result, issue, or outcome; a deduction or inference; a proposition concluded or inferred from premises; a proposition† or problem†; final decision; final settlement or arrangement, as of a treaty; in *law*, an estoppel; in *gram.*, the apodosis of a conditional sentence.—**con-clu′sive** (-siv), *a.* Concluding or closing (now rare); also, serving to settle or decide a question; decisive; convincing.—**con-clu′sive-ly,** *adv.*—**con-clu′sive-ness,** *n.*

con-coct (kǫn-kokt′), *v. t.* [L. *concoctus*, pp. of *concoquere*, cook together, digest, < *con-*, with, + *coquere*, cook.] To prepare with heat†; digest†; mature†; also, to make by combining ingredients, as in cookery; hence, to prepare with art; make up; contrive.—**con-coct′er,** *n.*—**con-coc′tion** (-kok′shǫn), *n.* [L. *concoctio(n-)*.] The process of concocting; also, something concocted; a fictitious statement.—**con-coc′tive** (-tiv), *a.* Pertaining to concoction; digestive†.—**con-coc′tor,** *n.*

con-col-or (kon′kul-ǫr), *a.* [L. *concolor*, < *con-*, with, + *color*, color.] Of the same color; of one color. Also **con-col′or-ate** (-āt), **con-col′or-ous.**

con-com-i-tant (kǫn-kom′i-tąnt). [LL. *concomitans* (*-ant-*), ppr. of *concomitari*, < L. *con-*, with, + *comitari*, accompany, < *comes*, companion.] **I.** *a.* Accompanying; concurrent; attending. **II.** *n.* A concomitant quality, circumstance, or thing; an accompaniment.—**con-com′i-tance, con-com′i-tan-cy,** *n.*—**con-com′i-tant-ly,** *adv.*

con-cord (kong′kôrd or kon′-), *n.* [OF. F. *concorde*, < L. *concordia*, < *concors*, of the same mind, < *con-*, with, + *cor* (*cord-*), heart.] Agreement between persons; concurrence in opinions, sentiments, etc.; unanimity; accord; hence, peace; sometimes, a compact or treaty; also, agreement between things; harmony; in *music*, a harmonious combination of tones sounded together; in *gram.*, agreement of words grammatically connected, as in gender, number, case, or person.—**con-cord** (kǫn-kôrd′), *v. i.* [OF. F. *concorder*, < L. *concordare*, < *concors*.] To agree; harmonize. [Now rare.]—**con-cord′ance,** *n.* The state of being concordant; agreement; harmony; also, an alphabetical index of the principal words of a book, as of the Bible, with a reference to the passage in which each occurs and usually some part of the context; also, an alphabetical index of subjects or topics.—**con-cord′ant,** *a.* Agreeing; harmonious; correspondent; consistent.—**con-cord′ant-ly,** *adv.*

con-cor-dat (kǫn-kôr′dat), *n.* [F., < ML. *concordatum*, prop. pp. neut. of L. *concordare*, agree, E. *concord*, *v.*] An agreement; a compact; esp., an agreement between the Pope and a secular government regarding the regulation of ecclesiastical matters.

con-cor-po-rate (kon-kôr′pǭ-rāt), *v. t.*; *-rated, -rating.* [L. *concorporatus*, pp. of *concorporare*, < *con-*, with, + *corporare*, embody: see *corporate*.] To unite in one body or substance; incorporate. [Now rare.]

con-course (kong′kōrs or kon′-), *n.* [OF. F. *concours*, < L. *concursus*, < *concurrere*, run together: see *concur*.] A running or coming together, as of things or people; confluence; also, an assemblage, esp. of people (as, "A mighty *concourse* of people appeared upon my arrival": Swift's "Gulliver's Travels," i. 8); a throng; also, a place to which throngs resort, as a driveway or promenade in a park, an open space in a railroad station, or grounds for racing, athletic sports, etc.

con-cre-ment (kon′krę-męnt), *n.* [L. *concrementum*, < *concrescere*: see *concrete*.] Concretion; a concreted mass.

con-cres-cence (kǫn-kres′ęns), *n.* [L. *concrescentia*, < *concrescere*: see *concrete*.] A growing together, as of parts, cells, etc.; coalescence.—**con-cres′cent,** *a.*

con-crete (kon′krēt or kon-krēt′). [L. *concretus*, pp. of *concrescere*, grow together, harden, < *con-*, with, + *crescere*, grow.] **I.** *a.* Formed by coalescence of separate particles into a mass; united in a coagulated, condensed, or solid state; also, made of concrete; also, of an idea, term, or name, representing or applied to an actual substance or thing as opposed to an abstract quality; hence, in general, constituting an actual thing or instance; particular as opposed to general; pertaining to or concerned with realities or actual instances rather than abstractions; in *arith.*, noting a number which relates to a particular object or thing (see *abstract*, *a.*). **II.** *n.* A mass formed by coalescence or concretion of particles of matter; an artificial stone-like material used for foundations, etc., made by mixing cement, sand, and broken stones, etc., with water, and allowing the mixture to harden; this material strengthened by a system of embedded iron or steel bars, netting, or the like, used for building ('reinforced concrete'); any of various other artificial building or paving materials, as those containing tar; also, a concrete idea or term; a concrete object or thing.—**con-crete** (kǫn-krēt′), *v.*; *-creted, -creting.* **I.** *tr.* To form into a mass by coalescence of particles; render solid; also, to unite or combine, as qualities or attributes; also, to make concrete, as an idea; also (pron. kon′krēt), to treat or lay with concrete. **II.** *intr.* To coalesce into a mass; become solid; harden; also (pron. kon′krēt), to use or apply concrete.—**con′crete-ly,** *adv.*—**con′crete-ness,** *n.*—**con-cre-tion** (kǫn-krē′shǫn), *n.* [L. *concretio(n-)*.] The act or process of concreting; the state of being concreted; coalescence; congelation; also, a solid mass formed by or as by coalescence or cohesion; a lump; a nodule; in *geol.*, a more or less rounded mass of mineral matter occurring in sandstone, clay, etc., usually calcareous or siliceous and often composed of concentric layers deposited about a fossil, grain of sand, or other nucleus.—**con-cre′tion-al,** *a.* Concretionary.—**con-cre′tion-a-ry** (-ā-ri), *a.* Formed by concretion; consisting of concreted matter or masses.—**con-cre′tive** (-tiv), *a.* Tending to concrete.—**con-cre′tive-ly,** *adv.*

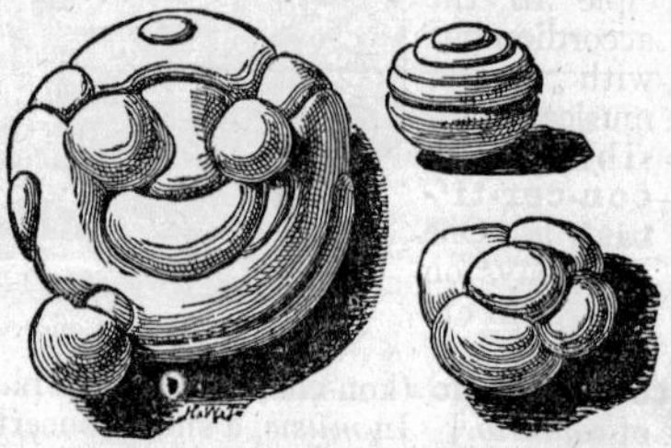

Calcareous Concretions from Clay-beds.

con-cu-bi-nage (kǫn-kū′bi-nāj), *n.* [See *concubine*.] Cohabitation without legal marriage; the condition of a concubine.—**con-cu′bi-nal** (-nąl), *a.* Concubinary.—**con-cu′bi-na-ry** (-nā-ri), *a.* Pertaining to a concubine; living in concubinage.

con-cu-bine (kong′kū-bīn), *n.* [F. *concubine*, < L. *concubina*, < *con-*, with, + *cubare*, lie.] A woman who cohabits with a man without being married to him; a kept mistress; among some peoples, a wife of inferior condition.

con-cu-pis-cence (kǫn-kū′pi-sęns), *n.* [LL. *concupiscentia*, < L. *concupiscens*, ppr. of *concupiscere*, desire greatly, < *con-*, altogether, + *cupere*, desire.] Eager or illicit desire; sensual appetite; lust.—**con-cu′pis-cent,** *a.* [L. *concupiscens* (*-ent-*), ppr.] Eagerly desirous; lustful; sensual. Also **con-cu′pis-ci-ble** (-pi-si-bl).

con-cur (kǫn-kėr′), *v. i.*; *-curred, -curring.* [L. *concurrere* (pp. *concursus*), < *con-*, with, + *currere*, run.] To run together†; also, to come together, as lines; unite; coincide; also, to coöperate; also, to accord in opinion; agree.—**con-cur'rence** (-kur'ęns), *n.* The act of concurring; a meeting of lines, etc.; simultaneous occurrence; coincidence; coöperation, as of agents or causes; accordance in opinion; agreement.—**con-cur'rent. I.** *a.* Concurring; tending to or meeting in the same point; occurring or existing together or side by side; having equal authority or jurisdiction; coördinate; acting in conjunction; coöperating; accordant or agreeing. **II.** *n.* One who or that which concurs; something joint or contributory; also, a rival or competitor.—**con-cur'rent-ly,** *adv.*—**con-cur'rent-ness,** *n.*

con-cuss (kǫn-kus'), *v. t.* [L. *concussus*, pp. of *concutere*, < *con-*, with, + *quatere*, shake, strike.] To shake or shock as by a blow; also, to coerce.—**con-cus'sion** (-kush'ǫn), *n.* [L. *concussio(n-)*.] The act of shaking or shocking, as by a blow; shock occasioned by a blow or collision; injury to the brain, spine, etc., from a blow, fall, etc.—**con-cus'sive,** *a.* Attended with concussion.

con-cu-tient (kǫn-kū'shięnt), *a.* [L. *concutiens* (*-ent-*), ppr. of *concutere*: see *concuss*.] Meeting with concussion; colliding with a shock: as, "The negroes . . . would meet in combat like two *concutient* cannon-balls" (Thackeray's "Virginians," xl.).

con-demn (kǫn-dem'), *v. t.* [L. *condemnare*, < *con-*, altogether, + *damnare*, E. *damn*.] To pronounce adverse judgment on; express strong disapproval of; censure; also, to afford occasion for convicting (as, his very looks *condemn* him); also, to pronounce to be guilty; sentence to punishment; doom; also, to adjudge to be unfit for use or service, as a ship; pronounce to be forfeited, as a prize of war; pronounce subject to use for a public purpose, under the right of eminent domain; also, to block or close up, as a door or a window (a French use).—**con-dem'na-ble** (-dem'nạ-bl), *a.* [LL. *condemnabilis*.] Deserving to be condemned.—**con-dem-na-tion** (kon-dem-nā'shǫn), *n.* [L. *condemnatio(n-)*.] The act of condemning, or the state of being condemned; also, cause or reason for condemning.—**con-dem-na-to-ry** (kǫn-dem'nạ-tǭ-ri), *a.* Serving to condemn.—**con-demn'er** (-dem'ėr), *n.*—**con-demn'ing-ly,** *adv.*

con-dens-a-ble (kǫn-den'sạ-bl), *a.* Capable of being condensed.—**con-dens-a-bil'i-ty** (-bil'i-ti), *n.*

con-den-sate (kǫn-den'sāt), *v. t.* or *i.*; *-sated, -sating.* [L. *condensatus*, pp. of *condensare*: see *condense*.] To make or become more dense; condense. [Obs. or rare.]—**con-den'sate. I.** *a.* Condensed. [Obs. or rare.] **II.** *n.* Something formed by condensation.

con-den-sa-tion (kon-den-sā'shǫn), *n.* [LL. *condensatio(n-)*.] The act of condensing; a condensed state or form; a condensed mass.—**con-den-sa'tion-al,** *a.*—**con-den-sa-tive** (kǫn-den'sạ-tiv), *a.* Tending to condense.

con-den-sa-tor (kon'den-sā-tǫr), *n.* [NL.] A condenser.

con-dense (kǫn-dens'), *v.*; *-densed, -densing.* [L. *condensare* (pp. *condensatus*), < *con-*, altogether, + *densus*, E. *dense*.] **I.** *tr.* To make more dense or compact; reduce the volume or compass of; compress; concentrate; also, to reduce to another and denser form, as a gas or vapor to a liquid or solid state. **II.** *intr.* To become more dense; become liquid or solid, as a gas or vapor.—**con-densed',** *p. a.* That has undergone condensing; compressed; concentrated; compact.—**condensed milk,** milk reduced by evaporation to a thick, viscid consistence, or sometimes to dryness, for preservation.—**condensed type,** a kind of type narrow in proportion to its height. See *type*.—**con-dens'er,** *n.* One who or that which condenses; an apparatus for condensing; in *elect.*, a device for accumulating and holding a charge of electricity, in a simple form consisting of two conducting surfaces separated by a non-conductor or dielectric (used for various purposes, esp. in radio apparatus, as for modifying the electrical capacity in a circuit, for blocking the flow of a direct current, etc., and called a *fixed condenser* when its capacity cannot be changed, and a *variable condenser* when its capacity can be changed).—**con-dens'i-ble,** etc. See *condensable*, etc.

con-den-si-ty (kǫn-den'si-ti), *n.* [Obs. F. *condensité*, < L. *condensus*, very dense, < *con-*, altogether, + *densus*, E. *dense*.] Density†; also, condensed form or character; conciseness.

con-de-scend (kon-dę̄-send'), *v. i.* [OF. F. *condescendre*, < LL. *condescendere*, < L. *con-*, with, + *descendere*, E. *descend*.] To descend as to the level of another; stoop (*to*); also, to yield†; also, to assent†.—**con-de-scend'er,** *n.*—**con-de-scend'ing,** *p. a.* Showing or implying a gracious descent from dignity; patronizing.—**con-de-scend'ing-ly,** *adv.*—**con-de-scen'sion** (-sen'shǫn), *n.* [LL. *condescensio(n-)*.] The act of condescending; gracious or patronizing complaisance.

con-dign (kǫn-dīn'), *a.* [OF. F. *condigne*, < L. *condignus*, < *con-*, altogether, + *dignus*, worthy.] Wholly worthy†; deserving†; also (now chiefly of punishment, etc.), well-deserved; fitting; adequate.—**con-dign'ly,** *adv.*—**con-dign'ness,** *n.*

con-di-ment (kon'di-męnt), *n.* [L. *condimentum*, < *condire*, preserve, season, < *condere*, put together, lay up, < *con-*, with, + *-dere*, put: see *do*[1].] Something used to give flavor and relish to food, as a sauce or seasoning: as, "He proceeded to spread the board . . . with salt, spices, and other *condiments*" (Scott's "Fair Maid of Perth," ii.).—**con-di-men'tal** (-men'tąl), *a.*

con-dis-ci-ple (kon-di-sī'pl), *n.* [L. *condiscipulus*, < *con-*, with, + *discipulus*, E. *disciple*.] A fellow-disciple; a fellow-student.

con-di-tion (kǫn-dish'ǫn), *n.* [OF. *condicion* (F. *condition*), < L. *condicio(n-)*, erron. *conditio(n-)*, agreement, stipulation, circumstances, < *con-*, with, + *dic-* as in *dicere*, say.] Something demanded as an essential part of an agreement; a stipulation; also, a circumstance indispensable to some result; a prerequisite; that on which something else is contingent; specif., a requirement imposed on a college student who fails to reach a prescribed standard in a study as at examination, or the study or subject to which the requirement is attached (U. S.); also, a restricting, limiting, or modifying circumstance; also, situation with respect to circumstances; state of health; social position (as, "I am in my *condition* A prince": Shakspere's "Tempest," iii. 1. 59); disposition†; often, fit or requisite state; also, quality† or character†; a characteristic†; in *logic*, the antecedent (expressing the condition) of a hypothetical proposition; in *gram.*, the protasis of a conditional sentence.—**con-di'tion,** *v.* [OF. *condicioner* (F. *conditionner*).] **I.** *tr.* To subject to something as a condition; make conditional (*on*); also, to form or be a condition of; determine, limit, or restrict as a condition; also, to make it a condition; stipulate; also, to impose a condition on (a student: U. S.); also, to subject to particular conditions or circumstances; also, to test (a commodity) to ascertain its condition; also, to put in fit or proper state. **II.** *intr.* To make conditions.—**con-di'tion-al,** *a.* Subject to a condition; dependent or contingent, as on conditions; in *logic* and *gram.*, involving or expressing a condition (as, the *conditional* mood).—**con-di-tion-al'i-ty** (-al'i-ti), *n.* The quality of being conditional.—**con-di'tion-al-ly,** *adv.*—**con-di'tioned,** *a.* Being in a certain condition; circumstanced; also, having a nature or disposition as specified (as, ill-*conditioned*).—**con-di'tion-er,** *n.* One who or that which conditions; in *milling*, a machine for drying damp or musty grains.

con-do-la-to-ry (kǫn-dō'lạ-tǭ-ri), *a.* Condoling.

con-dole (kǫn-dōl'), *v.*; *-doled, -doling.* [LL. *condolere*, < L. *con-*, with, + *dolere*, suffer, grieve.] **I.** *intr.* To grieve (*with*); express sympathy with one in affliction. **II.**† *tr.* To grieve with (another) or over (another's misfortune).—**con-dole'ment,** *n.* Condolence; also, sorrowing† or lamentation† (see Shakspere's "Hamlet," i. 2. 93).—**con-dol'ence** (-dō'lęns), *n.* Expression of sympathy with a person in affliction.—**con-dol'er,** *n.*—**con-dol'ing-ly,** *adv.*

con-do-min-i-um (kon-dǫ-min'i-um), *n.* [NL., < L. *con-*, with, + *dominium*, lordship.] Joint or concurrent dominion.

con-don-ance (kǫn-dō'nąns), *n.* Condonation.

con-do-na-tion (kon-dǫ-nā'shǫn), *n.* The act of condoning; the overlooking or implied forgiving of an offense.

con-done (kǫn-dōn'), *v. t.*; *-doned, -doning.* [L. *condonare*, < *con-*, with, + *donare*, give: see *donate*.] To pardon or overlook (an offense); of actions, etc., to cause the condonation of; in *law*, to forgive, or act so as to imply forgiveness of (a violation of the marriage vow).—**con-don'er** (-dō'nėr), *n.*

con-dor (kon′dọr), *n.* [Sp., < Peruvian *cuntur.*] A large American vulture, *Sarcorhamphus gryphus,* inhabiting the higher regions of the Andes, having the head and upper part of the neck bare, and with blackish plumage varied round the neck and on the wings with white; also, a large vulture of California, *Pseudogryphus californianus;* also, a gold coin of South American countries, bearing the figure of a condor, that of Chile being worth about $7.30 and that of Ecuador about $4.86.

California Condor (*Pseudogryphus californianus*).

con-dot-tie-re (kon-dot-tyā′rā), *n.;* pl. *-ri* (-rē). [It., ult. < L. *conducere,* lead together, also hire: see *conduce, conduct.*] In Italy and elsewhere, esp. in the 14th and 15th centuries, a professional military captain or leader of mercenaries, in the service of princes or states at war: as, "War was not merely the trade of the *condottiere,* but also his monopoly, and he was thus able to obtain whatever terms he asked, whether money payments or political concessions" (Encyc. Brit., 11th ed., VI. 854).

con-duce (kọn-dūs′), *v. i.;* *-duced, -ducing.* [L. *conducere* (pp. *conductus*), lead together, hire, conduce, < *con-,* with, + *ducere,* lead: cf. *conduct.*] To lead or contribute to a result: with *to* or an infinitive.—**con-du′cive** (-dū′siv), *a.* Conducing (*to*); contributive; helpful: as, "Nothing is more *conducive* to happiness than the free exercise of the mind in pursuits congenial to it" (Macaulay's "Essays," Mitford's Hist. of Greece).—**con-du′cive-ness,** *n.*

con-duct (kọn-dukt′), *v.* [L. *conductus,* pp. of *conducere:* see *conduce.*] **I.** *tr.* To lead or guide; escort; also, to direct in action or course; manage; carry on; specif., to direct (an orchestra, etc.) as leader; also, to behave (one's self); also, to serve as a channel or medium for; in *physics,* to serve as a medium for transmitting (heat, electricity, etc.). **II.** *intr.* To lead; also, to act as conductor; in *physics,* to transmit heat, electricity, etc.—**con-duct** (kon′dukt), *n.* [ML. *conductus,* n., < L. *conducere.*] The act of conducting; guidance; escort; also, a guide†; an escort†; a document securing safe-conduct†; also, direction or management; execution; also, behavior or deportment; also, a conduit†.—**con-duct-ance** (kọn-duk′tạns), *n.* In *elect.,* conducting power as affected by the shape, length, etc., of the conductor.—**con-duct′i-ble,** *a.* Capable of conducting or of being conducted.—**con-duct-i-bil′i-ty** (-bil′i-ti), *n.*—**con-duc′tion** (-duk′shọn), *n.* [L. *conductio(n-).*] A conducting, as of water through a pipe; in *physics,* transmission through a conductor, as the conveyance of heat through a body by the raising of the temperature of its particles but without the visible transfer of matter, or the conveyance of electricity through a body without any sensible transfer of its particles (cf. *convection* and *radiation*).—**con-duc-ti-tious** (kon-duk-tish′us), *a.* [L. *conducticius.*] Hired; serving for hire; open to hire.—**con-duc-tive** (kọn-duk′tiv), *a.* Having the property of conducting; pertaining to conduction.—**con-duc′tive-ly,** *adv.*—**con-duc-tiv-i-ty** (kon-duk-tiv′i-ti), *n.* Power of conducting heat, electricity, sound, etc.—**con-duc-tor** (kọn-duk′tọr), *n.* [L.] One who conducts; a leader; a guide; a director or manager; the director of an orchestra or chorus, who indicates to the performers the rhythm and expression of the music as by motions of a baton; the official in charge of a railroad-train, street-car, etc.; also, that which conducts, esp. a substance which conducts heat, electricity, etc.; hence, a lightning-rod.—**con-duc′tor-ship,** *n.*—**con-duc′tress,** *n.* A female conductor.

con-duit (kon′dit or kun′-), *n.* [OF. *conduit,* < ML. *conductus:* see *conduct, n.*] Conduct†; also, a pipe, tube, or the like, for conveying water or other fluid; some similar natural passage; a fountain†; a tube or series of tubes or the like, to receive and protect electric wires, etc.; fig., anything serving as a channel for conveyance or passage (as, "These republics . . . became the *conduits* through which the produce of the East flowed in": Hallam's "Europe during the Middle Ages," iii. 2).

con-du-pli-cate, con-du-pli-cat-ed (kon-dū′pli-kạt, -kā-ted), *a.* [L. *conduplicatus,* pp. of *conduplicare,* < *con-,* together, + *duplicare,* double, E. *duplicate.*] Doubled or folded over or together; in *bot.,* noting or pertaining to a leaf in the bud when it is folded lengthwise down the middle with the upper face of the blade within.—**con-du-pli-ca′tion** (-kā′shọn), *n.*

con-dyle (kon′dil), *n.* [L. *condylus,* < Gr. κόνδυλος, knuckle, bony knob.] In *anat.,* a rounded protuberance on a bone, serving to form an articulation with another bone.—**con′dy-lar** (-di-lạr), *a.*—**con′dy-loid,** *a.* [See *-oid.*] Resembling, or pertaining to, a condyle.

con-dy-lo-ma (kon-di-lō′mạ), *n.;* pl. *-mas* or *-mata* (-mạ-tạ). [L., < Gr. κονδύλωμα, < κόνδυλος, E. *condyle.*] In *pathol.,* a wart-like excrescence on the skin, usually in the region of the anus or genitals.—**con-dy-lom′a-tous** (-lom′ạ-tus), *a.*

con-dyl-o-pod (kon-dil′ọ-pod), *n.* [NL. *Condylopoda,* pl., < Gr. κόνδυλος, condyle, + πούς (ποδ-), foot.] An arthropod.

cone (kōn), *n.* [L. *conus,* < Gr. κῶνος.] A geometrical solid generated by the revolution of a right-angled triangle upon one of its legs as an axis ('right circular cone'); a similar solid with an axis oblique to the base ('oblique circular cone'); a similar solid having an ellipse or the like for a base; also, a surface generated by a moving straight line, one point of which is fixed, which constantly touches a fixed curve; a conical surface; also, anything cone-shaped, as a volcanic peak; in *bot.,* the more or less conical multiple fruit of the pine, fir, etc., consisting of imbricated or valvate scales bearing naked ovules or seeds; a strobile; also, a similar fruit, as in most cycads.—**cone,** *v.;* *coned, coning.* **I.** *tr.* To shape like a cone or the segment of a cone. **II.** *intr.* To bear cones.—**cone′=flow″er,** *n.* Any plant of the asteraceous genus *Rudbeckia,* having flowers with a cone-shaped disk, as *R. hirta,* the yellow daisy; also, any of various allied plants.—**cone′=nose,** *n.* A large blood-sucking hemipterous insect, *Conorhinus sanguisuga,* a species of kissing-bug often infesting houses, esp. in the southern and western U. S.

Cone of Larch.

Cone of Pine.

co-ne-pa-tl (kō-nạ-pä′tl), *n.* [Mex.] A large white-backed skunk, *Conepatus mapurito,* of Texas, Mexico, and Central and South America.

Conepatl.

cones (kōnz), *n.* [Origin uncertain.] A fine white flour used by bakers for dusting or sprinkling their dough, vessels, etc.

Con-es-to-ga (kon-es-tō′gạ) **wag′on.** [From *Conestoga,* town in southeastern Pennsylvania.] A kind of large broad-wheeled wagon, usually covered, used esp. for transporting goods over deep soil, which became the common vehicle of emigrants crossing the prairies and plains of North America before the construction of railroads.

cone=wheel (kōn′hwēl), *n.* A cone-shaped pulley, used to transmit and vary mechanical motion.

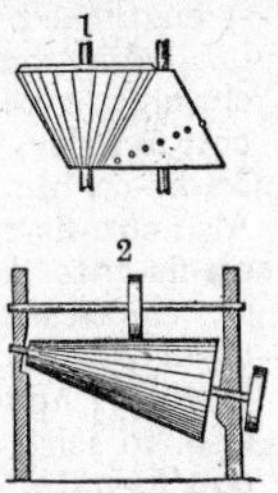

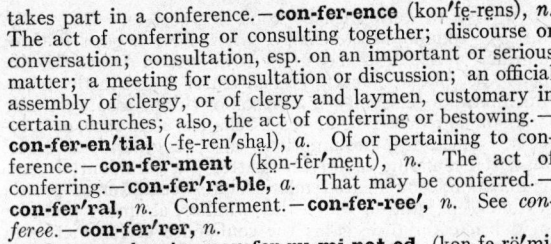

Cone-wheels.
In fig. 1 two frustums are in apposition, one having teeth on its face and the other a spirally arranged row of studs. The frustum in fig. 2 when driven by the motor communicates motion to the wheel above it.

co-ney (kō′ni or kun′i), *n.* See *cony.*

con-fab (kon′fab), *n.* A confabulation. [Colloq.]

con-fab-u-late (kǫn-fab′ū-lāt), *v. i.*; *-lated, -lating.* [L. *confabulatus*, pp. of *confabulari*, < *con-*, with, + *fabulari*, talk.] To talk together; converse; chat: as, "I shall not ask Jean Jacques Rousseau If birds *confabulate* or no" (Cowper's "Pairing Time Anticipated," 2).—**con-fab-u-la′tion** (-lā′shǫn), *n.* [LL. *confabulatio(n-).*] A talking together; a familiar talk; a chat.—**con-fab′u-la-tor**, *n.*—**con-fab′u-la-to-ry** (-lạ-tọ-ri), *a.*

con-far-re-a-tion (kǫn-far-ẹ-ā′shǫn), *n.* [L. *confarreatio(n-)*, < *confarreare*, join by this form of marriage, < *con-*, with, + *farreum*, cake made of spelt, < *far*, spelt.] The highest form of marriage among the ancient Romans, marked by the offering of a cake made of spelt.

con-fect (kǫn-fekt′), *v. t.* [L. *confectus*, pp. of *conficere*, < *con-*, together, + *facere*, make.] To make up, compound, or prepare from ingredients or materials; also, to make into a preserve or sweetmeat; in general, to construct, form, or make; also, to mix (ingredients)†.—**con-fect** (kon′fekt), *n.* A preserved, candied, or other sweet confection.

con-fec-tion (kǫn-fek′shǫn), *n.* [OF. F. *confection*, < L. *confectio(n-)*, < *conficere*: see *confect.*] The process of compounding, preparing, or making, or that which is made; a medicinal preparation, now one made with the aid of sugar, honey, or syrup; a sweet preparation (liquid or dry) of fruit or the like, as a preserve or any sweetmeat; a candy or bonbon; a ready-made garment, esp. a women's cloak or wrap (a French use); any more or less elaborate and elegant article of feminine dress (often used humorously in default of a more definite term).—**con-fec′tion**, *v. t.* To prepare as a confection; compound; make.—**con-fec′tion-a-ry** (-ạ-ri). **I.** *a.* Of the nature of a confection or sweetmeat; of or pertaining to confections or their making. **II.** *n.*; pl. *-ries* (-riz). A confectioner†; a place where confections are kept or made; a confection or sweetmeat.—**con-fec′tion-er**, *n.* A compounder of preparations, as drugs†; one who makes or sells candies or bonbons, and sometimes ice-cream, cakes, etc.—**con-fec′tion-er-y** (-er-i), *n.*; pl. *-ies* (-iz). Confections or sweetmeats collectively; the work or business of a confectioner; a confectioner's shop.

con-fed-er-a-cy (kǫn-fed′ėr-ạ-si), *n.*; pl. *-cies* (-siz). A union of confederated persons, parties, etc.; a league or alliance; also, a combination for unlawful purposes; a conspiracy; also, a body of confederated persons, parties, or states (as, "merely a *confederacy* of sovereignties, not a representative republic": Motley's "Dutch Republic," vi. 1); a confederation; [*cap.*] with *the*, in *U. S. hist.*, the Confederate States of America.

con-fed-er-ate (kǫn-fed′ėr-āt), *v. t.* or *i.*; *-ated, -ating.* [LL. *confœderatus*, pp. of *confœderare*, < L. *con-*, with, + *fœderare*, E. *federate.*] To unite in a league or alliance, or a conspiracy.—**con-fed′er-ate** (-ạt). **I.** *a.* Confederated; united in a league or alliance, or a conspiracy; [*cap.*] in *U. S. hist.*, noting or pertaining to the southern States which seceded from the Union in 1860–61 and formed a separate government ('Confederate States of America'). **II.** *n.* One united with others in a confederacy; an ally; an accomplice; [*cap.*] an adherent of the Confederate States of America.—**con-fed-er-a′tion** (-ẹ-rā′shǫn), *n.* [LL. *confœderatio(n-).*] The act of confederating, or the state of being confederated; a league or alliance; also, a body of confederates, esp. of states more or less permanently united for common purposes.—**con-fed′er-a-tive** (-ạ-tiv), *a.* Pertaining to a confederation.

con-fer (kǫn-fėr′), *v.*; *-ferred, -ferring.* [L. *conferre*, < *con-*, with, + *ferre*, bear.] **I.** *tr.* To bring or put together†; also, to compare†; also, to bestow as a gift, favor, honor, etc. (*on* or *upon*). **II.** *intr.* To consult together; take counsel.—**con-fer-ee** (kon-fėr-ē′), *n.* One on whom something is conferred; also, one who is conferred with or who takes part in a conference.—**con-fer-ence** (kon′fẹ-rẹns), *n.* The act of conferring or consulting together; discourse or conversation; consultation, esp. on an important or serious matter; a meeting for consultation or discussion; an official assembly of clergy, or of clergy and laymen, customary in certain churches; also, the act of conferring or bestowing.—**con-fer-en′tial** (-fẹ-ren′shạl), *a.* Of or pertaining to conference.—**con-fer-ment** (kǫn-fėr′mẹnt), *n.* The act of conferring.—**con-fer′ra-ble**, *a.* That may be conferred.—**con-fer′ral**, *n.* Conferment.—**con-fer-ree′**, *n.* See *conferee.*—**con-fer′rer**, *n.*

con-fer-ru-mi-nate, con-fer-ru-mi-nat-ed (kon-fe-rö′mi-nāt, -nā-ted), *a.* [L. *conferruminatus*, pp. of *conferruminare*, solder together.] In *bot.*, closely adherent, as the cotyledons of the horse-chestnut.

con-fer-va (kon-fėr′vạ), *n.*; pl. *-væ* (-vē). [L., kind of water-plant.] Any plant of the genus *Conferva*, formerly held to comprise various heterogeneous species of filamentous cryptogams, but now limited to non-gelatinous green fresh-water algæ composed of simple many-celled filaments; any simple filamentous green alga.—**con-fer′void**, *a.* and *n.*

con-fess (kǫn-fes′), *v.* [OF. F. *confesser*, < L. *confessus*, pp. of *confiteri*, confess, < *con-*, with, + *fateri*, acknowledge.] **I.** *tr.* To acknowledge or avow (a secret, fault, crime, debt, etc.); own or admit; admit the truth or validity of; also, to acknowledge one's belief in; declare adhesion to; also, to reveal by circumstances (poetic); also, to declare (one's sins) or declare the sins of (one's self), esp. to a priest, for the obtaining of absolution; of a priest, to hear the confession of. **II.** *intr.* To make confession; plead guilty; own (*to*); make confession of sins, esp. to a priest.—**con-fess′ed-ly**, *adv.* By confession or acknowledgment; admittedly.—**con-fes′sion** (-fesh′ǫn), *n.* [L. *confessio(n-).*] The act of confessing; acknowledgment or avowal; admission or concession; acknowledgment of belief; profession of faith; acknowledgment of sin or sinfulness; a disclosing of sins to a priest; also, that which is confessed; specif., a formulary containing articles of religious faith; a creed; also, a formulary containing an acknowledgment of sinfulness.—**con-fes′sion-al. I.** *a.* Pertaining to or of the nature of confession; also, pertaining to a confession or creed. **II.** *n.* A small cabinet, stall, or box in which a priest sits to hear confessions; hence, the practice of confessing sins to a priest.—**con-fes′sion-a-ry** (-ạ-ri), *a.* Of or pertaining to confession, esp. auricular confession of sins.—**con-fes′sor**, *n.* [L.] One who confesses; specif., one who confesses and adheres to the Christian religion, esp. in spite of persecution and torture (as, Edward the *Confessor*); also, a priest authorized to hear confessions; the private spiritual director of a king, etc.—**con-fes′sor-ship**, *n.*

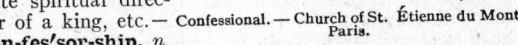

Confessional.—Church of St. Étienne du Mont, Paris.

con-fet-to (kon-fet′tō), *n.*; pl. *-ti* (-tē). [It., < L. *confectus*: see *confect.*] A confection; a bonbon; also, a plaster imitation of a bonbon, or a small bit of colored paper, thrown at carnivals, weddings, etc. (usually in *pl.*).

con-fi-dant (kon-fi-dant′), *n.* [Appar. < F. *confidant*, obs. form of *confident*, < It. *confidente*, prop. adj., confided in, trusted, orig. confiding, = E. *confident.*] One to whom secrets are confided; a confidential friend.—**con-fi-dante′** (-dant′), *n.* [= F. *confidente*, fem.] A female confidant: as, "Susan . . . persuaded our hero to make her a *confidante* of his doubts and fears" (Marryat's "King's Own," lviii.).

con-fide (kǫn-fīd′), *v.*; *-fided, -fiding.* [L. *confidere*, < *con-*, altogether, + *fidere*, trust.] **I.** *intr.* To have full trust (*in*); also, to show trust by imparting secrets. **II.** *tr.* To intrust; commit to the charge, knowledge, or good faith of another; tell in assurance of secrecy.—**con-fi-dence** (kon′fi-dẹns), *n.* [L. *confidentia.*] Full trust; belief in the trustworthiness or reliability of a person or thing; also, certitude or assured expectation; also, self-reliance, assurance, or boldness; sometimes, presumption; also, a ground of trust; also, the confiding of private matters; a confidential communication; confidential relationship.—**confidence game,** a kind of swindle in which the swindler, as under pretense of old acquaintance, gains the confidence of his victim in order to fleece him at cards, betting, etc.—**confidence man,** one who swindles by a confidence game.—**con′fi-dent.** [L. *confidens* (*-ent-*), ppr.] **I.** *a.* Trustful† or confiding†; also, having strong belief or full assurance; sure; also, sure of one's self; bold; sometimes, overbold. **II.** *n.* A confidant.—**con-fi-den′tial** (-den′shạl), *a.* Of the nature of confidence; spoken or written in confidence; also, betokening confidence or intimacy; imparting private matters; also, enjoying the confidence of another; intrusted with secrets or with private affairs.—**con-fi-den-ti-al′i-ty** (-shi-al′i-ti), **con-fi-den′tial-ness,** *n.*—**con-fi-den′tial-ly,** *adv.*—**con′fi-dent-ly,** *adv.*—**con-fid-er** (kọn-fī′dėr), *n.*—**con-fid′ing,** *p. a.* That confides; reposing confidence; trustful; credulous or unsuspicious.—**con-fid′ing-ly,** *adv.*—**con-fid′ing-ness,** *n.*

con-fig-u-rate (kọn-fig′ū-rāt), *v. t.*; *-rated, -rating.* [L. *configuratus,* pp. of *configurare*: see *configure.*] To arrange as to form; configure. [Now rare.]

con-fig-u-ra-tion (kọn-fig-ū-rā′shọn), *n.* [LL. *configuratio(n-),* < L. *configurare*: see *configure.*] The relative disposition of the parts or elements of a thing; external form, as resulting from this; conformation; esp., relative position or aspect of the planets or other heavenly bodies (esp. in *astrol.*); also, a group of stars.

con-fig-ure (kọn-fig′ūr), *v. t.*; *-ured, -uring.* [L. *configurare* (pp. *configuratus*), < *con-,* with, + *figurare,* form, E. *figure, v.*] To make or arrange in a certain form; conform.

con-fin-a-ble (kọn-fī′nạ-bl), *a.* That may be confined.

con-fine (kon′fīn), *n.* [OF. F. *confins,* pl., < L. *confine,* prop. neut. of *confinis,* bordering, contiguous, < *con-,* with, + *finis,* boundary, border, end.] A boundary or bound (now in *pl.*); a border or frontier (usually in *pl.*); a region† (usually in *pl.*); also (pron. kọn-fīn′), confinement (poetic); a place of confinement†.—**con-fine** (kọn-fīn′), *v.*; *-fined, -fining.* [OF. F. *confiner.*] **I.** *intr.* To have a common boundary (*with*); border (*on*). [Now rare.] **II.** *tr.* To inclose within bounds; limit or restrict; shut or keep in; imprison; in the passive, to be in childbed, or be delivered of a child.—**con-fine′less,** *a.* Boundless.—**con-fine′ment,** *n.* The act of confining, or the state of being confined; a keeping or being kept indoors; imprisonment; the lying-in of a woman in childbed.—**con-fin′er** (-fī′nėr), *n.* One who or that which confines; also, one who dwells on the confines, border, or frontier†; also, an inhabitant†.—**con-fin′ing,** *p. a.* That confines; limiting; restricting; of occupations, etc., keeping one closely housed or steadily engaged, without opportunity for change, exercise, relaxation, etc.—**con-fin′ing-ly,** *adv.*

con-firm (kọn-fėrm′), *v. t.* [OF. *confermer* (F. *confirmer*), < L. *confirmare,* < *con-,* altogether, + *firmare,* make firm, < *firmus,* E. *firm.*] To make firm or more firm; add strength to; settle or establish firmly; also, to make valid or binding by some formal or legal act; sanction; ratify; also, to strengthen in habit, resolution, opinion, etc.; also, to make certain or sure; corroborate; verify; *eccles.,* to administer the rite of confirmation to.—**con-firm′a-ble,** *a.* Capable of being confirmed.—**con-fir-ma-tion** (kon-fėr-mā′shọn), *n.* [L. *confirmatio(n-).*] The act of confirming; also, that which confirms, as a corroborative statement; *eccles.,* a rite administered to baptized persons, in some churches as a sacrament for confirming and strengthening the recipient in the Christian faith, in others as a rite without sacramental character by which the recipient is admitted to full communion with the church; among the Jews, a solemn form of initiation of the Jewish youth into their ancestral faith.—**con-fir-ma-tive, con-fir-ma-to-ry** (kọn-fėr′mạ-tiv, -tọ-ri), *a.* Serving to confirm; corroborative.—**con-fir′ma-tive-ly,** *adv.*—**con-firmed′,** *p. a.* Made firm, strengthened, settled, ratified, etc.; also, firmly established in a habit, condition, etc.; habitual; inveterate; of a disease, chronic; *eccles.,* that has received the rite of confirmation.—**con-firm′er,** *n.*

con-fis-ca-ble (kọn-fis′kạ-bl), *a.* Liable to be confiscated. Also **con-fis-cat-a-ble** (kon′fis-kā-tạ-bl).

con-fis-cate (kon′fis-kāt or kọn-fis′kāt), *v. t.*; *-cated, -cating.* [L. *confiscatus,* pp. of *confiscare,* < *con-,* with, + *fiscus,* basket, chest, treasury.] To seize as forfeited to the public treasury; appropriate, by way of penalty, to public use; also, to seize as if by authority; appropriate summarily.—**con′fis-cate,** *a.* Confiscated; forfeited. See Shakspere's "Merchant of Venice," iv. 1. 311.—**con-fis-ca′tion** (-kā′-shọn), *n.* [L. *confiscatio(n-).*] The act of confiscating, or the state of being confiscated.—**con′fis-ca-tor,** *n.*—**con-fis-ca-to-ry** (kọn-fis′kạ-tọ-ri), *a.* Characterized by or effecting confiscation.

Con-fit-e-or (kon-fit′ẹ-ôr), *n.* [L., 'I confess.'] In the *Rom. Cath. Ch.,* a form of prayer beginning with "Confiteor" (see etym.), in which confession of sins is made, used at the beginning of the mass and on other occasions.

con-fi-ture (kôṅ-fē-tür), *n.* [F., < L. *confectura,* < *conficere*: see *confect.*] A confection; a preserve, as of fruit.

con-fla-grant (kọn-flā′grạnt), *a.* [L. *conflagrans* (*-ant-*), ppr. of *conflagrare*: see *conflagrate.*] Burning up, as in a conflagration: as, "Then raise From the *conflagrant* mass, purged and refined, New heavens, new earth" (Milton's "Paradise Lost," xii. 548). [Now rare.]

con-fla-grate (kon′flạ-grāt), *v.*; *-grated, -grating.* [L. *conflagratus,* pp. of *conflagrare,* < *con-,* altogether, + *flagrare,* blaze, burn.] **I.** *intr.* To burn up; burn; burst into flame. **II.** *tr.* To consume with fire; set ablaze.—**con-fla-gra′tion** (-grā′shọn), *n.* [L. *conflagratio(n-).*] A burning up; a fire; esp., a large and destructive fire.

con-flate (kọn-flāt′), *v. t.*; *-flated, -flating.* [L. *conflatus,* pp. of *conflare,* blow together, fuse, < *con-,* with, + *flare,* blow.] To bring or put together; compose of various elements; specif., to form (a text, etc.) by inadvertent combination of two readings.—**con-flate** (kon′flāt), *a.* Conflated; of a text, passage, etc., formed by inadvertent combination of two readings.—**con-fla-tion** (kọn-flā′shọn), *n.* [LL. *conflatio(n-).*] The act or result of conflating.

con-flict (kọn-flikt′), *v. i.* [L. *conflictus,* pp. of *confligere,* strike together, < *con-,* with, + *fligere,* strike.] To come into collision; clash, or be in opposition or at variance; contend; fight, or do battle.—**con-flict** (kon′flikt), *n.* [L. *conflictus,* n., < *confligere.*] A striking together; collision; clashing; direct opposition; a struggle for mastery, esp. a prolonged struggle; a battle; strife.—**con-flict-ing** (kọn-flik′ting), *p. a.* That conflicts; being in conflict; clashing; contradictory; at variance.—**con-flic′tion** (-flik′shọn), *n.* [L. *conflictio(n-).*] The act or fact of conflicting; conflict.—**con-flic′tive** (-tiv), *a.* Tending to conflict.

con-flu-ence (kon′flọ-ẹns), *n.* [LL. *confluentia,* < L. *confluens*: see *confluent.*] A flowing together; the junction of confluent streams; also, a coming together of people or things; a throng; an assemblage.

con-flu-ent (kon′flọ-ẹnt). [L. *confluens* (*-ent-*), ppr. of *confluere,* flow together, < *con-,* with, + *fluere,* flow.] **I.** *a.* Flowing or running together; blending into one. **II.** *n.* One of two or more confluent streams; loosely, a tributary stream.—**con′flu-ent-ly,** *adv.*

con-flux (kon′fluks), *n.* [LL. *confluxus,* < L. *confluere*: see *confluent.*] A flowing together; a confluence.

con-fo-cal (kon-fō′kạl), *a.* [See *con-.*] In *math.,* having the same focus or foci.

con-form[1] (kọn-fôrm′), *a.* [LL. *conformis,* < L. *con-,* with, + *forma,* E. *form, n.*] Of the same form or character; similar; also, in agreement or harmony; consistent; accordant.

con-form[2] (kọn-fôrm′), *v.* [OF. F. *conformer,* < L. *conformare,* < *con-,* with, + *formare,* E. *form, v.*] **I.** *tr.* To make of the same form or character; make like; also, to bring into correspondence or harmony; make agreeable; adapt. **II.** *intr.* To become the same in form; correspond in form or character; also, to act in accord or harmony; show compliance; in *Eng. hist.,* to comply with the usages of the Established Church.—**con-form'a-ble,** *a.* Corresponding in form or character; similar; also, exhibiting agreement or harmony; agreeable; consistent; adapted; adjusted; also, compliant, acquiescent, or submissive; in *geol.*, of strata or beds, having the same dip and direction, as a result of successive depositions under the same conditions.—**con-form-a-bil'i-ty** (-bil'i-ti), **con-form'a-ble-ness,** *n.*

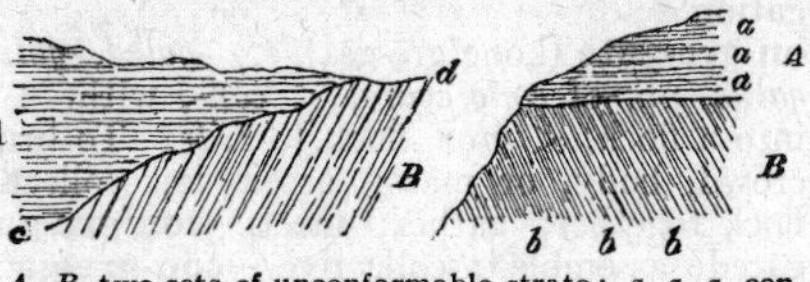

A, B, two sets of unconformable strata; *a, a, a,* conformable with one another; *b, b, b,* the same; *c, d,* line of junction of *A* and *B.*

—**con-form'a-bly,** *adv.*—**con-form'ance,** *n.* The act of conforming; conformity.—**con-for-ma-tion** (kon-fôr-mā'shọn), *n.* [L. *conformatio(n-)*.] The act of conforming, or the state of being conformed; adaptation; adjustment; also, symmetrical disposition or arrangement of the parts of a thing; also, manner of formation; structure; form.—**con'for-ma-tor,** *n.* An apparatus for ascertaining the conformation of anything, as of the head in order to make a pattern for a hat.—**con-form-er** (kọn-fôr'mėr), *n.*—**con-form'ist,** *n.* One who conforms to a usage or practice; esp., in England, one who conforms to the usages of the Established Church.

con-for-mi-ty (kọn-fôr'mi-ti), *n.*; pl. *-ties* (-tiz). [F. *conformité,* < LL. *conformitas,* < *conformis*: see *conform*¹.] Correspondence in form or character; agreement, congruity, or accordance; compliance or acquiescence; in *Eng. hist.*, compliance with the usages of the Established Church.

con-found (kọn-found'), *v. t.* [OF. F. *confondre,* < L. *confundere* (pp. *confusus*), pour together, mix, confuse, < *con-*, with, + *fundere,* pour.] To mingle so that the elements cannot be distinguished or separated; also, to treat or regard erroneously as identical; mix or associate by mistake; also, to throw into confusion or disorder; also, to perplex, as with sudden disturbance or surprise; also, to put to shame; abash; also, to defeat or overthrow; bring to ruin or naught (sometimes used in mild imprecations); also, to spend uselessly† or waste†.—**con-found'ed,** *p. a.* Execrable; odious; detestable: as, "'Tis a *confounded* lie!" (Sheridan's "Rivals," ii. 1). [Colloq.]—**con-found'ed-ly,** *adv.*—**con-found'er,** *n.*

con-fra-ter-ni-ty (kon-frạ-tėr'ni-ti), *n.*; pl. *-ties* (-tiz). [ML. *confraternitas,* < *confrater*: see *confrère.*] A brotherhood; a society or body of men united for some purpose or in some profession; esp., a brotherhood devoted to some particular religious or charitable service.

con-frère (kon'frãr, F. kôṅ-frãr), *n.* [F., < ML. *confrater,* < L. *con-*, with, + *frater,* brother.] A fellow-member of a fraternity, profession, etc.; a colleague.

con-front (kọn-frunt'), *v. t.* [F. *confronter,* < ML. *confrontari,* < L. *con-*, with, + *frons,* forehead, E. *front.*] To stand or come in front of; stand or meet facing; esp., to face in hostility or defiance; oppose; also, to set face to face; also, to bring together for examination or comparison.—**con-fron-ta-tion** (kon-frun-tā'shọn), *n.* The act of confronting; a bringing together, as of persons for interrogation or of objects for comparison.—**con-front-er** (kọn-frun'tėr), *n.*—**con-front'ment,** *n.* Confrontation.

Con-fu-cian (kọn-fū'shiạn). **I.** *a.* Of or pertaining to the Chinese philosopher Confucius (about 550–478 B.C.) or his teachings or followers. **II.** *n.* A follower of Confucius.—**Con-fu'cian-ism,** *n.* The principles or system of morality taught by Confucius and his disciples.—**Con-fu'cian-ist,** *n.*

con-fuse (kọn-fūz'), *v. t.*; *-fused, -fusing.* [First in *confused,* pp., < OF. F. *confus,* < L. *confusus,* pp. of *confundere*: see *confound.*] To combine without order or clearness; jumble; render indistinct; also, to fail to distinguish between; associate by mistake; confound; also, to throw into disorder; also, to perplex or bewilder; also, to disconcert or abash; also, to bring to ruin or naught†.—**con-fus'a-ble** (-fū'zạ-bl), *a.*—**con-fused',** *p. a.* Involved or disordered; lacking clearness, as an idea or an utterance; also, perplexed, embarrassed, or disconcerted.—**con-fus'ed-ly,** *adv.*—**con-fus'ed-ness,** *n.*—**con-fu'sion** (-fū'zhọn), *n.* [OF. F. *confusion,* < L. *confusio(n-)*.] The act of confusing, or the state of being confused; disorder; lack of clearness or distinctness; embarrassment or abashment; also, overthrow or ruin.—**con-fu'sion-al,** *a.*

con-fut-a-ble (kọn-fū'tạ-bl), *a.* Capable of being confuted.

con-fu-ta-tion (kon-fụ-tā'shọn), *n.* [L. *confutatio(n-)*.] The act of confuting; also, that which confutes.—**con-fu-ta-tive** (kọn-fū'tạ-tiv), *a.* Serving to confute.—**con-fu-ta-tor** (kon'fụ-tā-tọr), *n.* [LL.] One who confutes.

con-fute (kọn-fūt'), *v. t.*; *-futed, -futing.* [L. *confutare* (pp. *confutatus*), check, put down, confute, < *con-*, with, + *-futare,* prob. akin to *fundere,* pour: cf. L. *confundere,* E. *confound,* also *refute.*] To prove (a person) to be wrong; convict of error by argument or proof; silence; also, to prove (an argument, etc.) to be false or defective; disprove; also, to confound or bring to naught.—**con-fut'er** (-fū'tėr), *n.*

con-gé (kôṅ-zhā), *n.* [F.: see *congee*¹.] Leave to depart; dismissal; also, permission.

con-geal (kọn-jēl'), *v. t.* or *i.* [OF. F. *congeler,* < L. *congelare,* < *con-*, with, + *gelare,* freeze.] To change from a fluid or soft to a solid or rigid state, as by freezing or cooling; freeze; stiffen; coagulate.—**con-geal'a-ble,** *a.* Capable of being congealed.—**con-geal'er,** *n.*—**con-geal'ment,** *n.* Congelation.

con-gee¹ (kon'jē), *n.* [OF. *congiet* (F. *congé*), < L. *commeatus,* a going to and fro, leave of absence, < *commeare,* go and come, < *con-*, with, + *meare,* go.] Leave to depart, or dismissal; leave or permission; congé; also, a bow or obeisance. [Archaic.]—**con'gee**¹, *v. i.*; *-geed, -geeing.* To take one's leave; also, to bow. [Archaic.]

con-gee², **con-jee** (kon'jē), *n.* [E. Ind.] In India, water in which rice has been boiled: used in the diet of invalids and as starch.

con-ge-la-tion (kon-jẹ-lā'shọn), *n.* [L. *congelatio(n-)*.] The act or process of congealing, or the state of being congealed; also, the product of congealing; a concretion; a coagulation.

con-ge-ner (kon'jẹ-nėr), *n.* [L., of the same kind, < *con-*, with, + *genus* (*gener-*), race, kind, genus.] One of the same kind or class; a fellow-member of a genus or family, as of plants or animals.—**con-ge-ner'ic** (-ner'ik), *a.* Of the same kind or genus. Also **con-gen'er-ous** (-jen'ẹ-rus).

con-ge-net-ic (kon-jẹ-net'ik), *a.* [See *con-* and *genetic.*] Of like origin.

con-ge-nial (kọn-jē'niạl), *a.* [L. *con-*, with, + *genius,* spirit, E. *genius.*] Suited or adapted in spirit, feeling, temper, etc.; sympathetic; also, agreeable or pleasing; agreeing or suited in nature or character.—**con-ge-ni-al'i-ty** (-ni-al'i-ti), **con-ge'nial-ness,** *n.*—**con-ge'nial-ly,** *adv.*

con-gen-i-tal (kọn-jen'i-tạl), *a.* [L. *congenitus,* < *con-*, with, + *genitus,* pp. of *gignere,* beget, bear.] Born with one; existing at or from one's birth, as a physical defect; connate.—**con-gen'i-tal-ly,** *adv.*

con-ger (kong'gėr), *n.* [L. *conger, congrus,* < Gr. γόγγρος.] A large marine eel, *Leptocephalus conger,* sometimes growing to the length of 10 feet, which is caught for food, esp. along the coasts of Europe; also, any of certain other eels or eel-like fishes, as the American eel-pout, *Zoarces anguillaris.* Also **con'ger=eel'.**

Conger (*Leptocephalus conger*).

con-ge-ri-es (kọn-jē'ri-ēz), *n.* [L., < *congerere*: see *congest.*] A collection of particles or bodies in one mass; a mass or heap; an aggregation or assemblage: as, "a *congeries* of houses and huts" (Carlyle's "Sartor Resartus," ii. 6).

con-gest (kọn-jest'), *v.* [L. *congestus,* pp. of *congerere,* bring together, < *con-*, with, + *gerere,* bear.] **I.** *tr.* To heap together†; also, to collect in undue quantity; also, to fill to excess; overcrowd; in *pathol.*, to cause an unnatural accumulation of blood in the vessels of (an organ or part). **II.** *intr.* To gather or collect together, esp. in undue quantity; also, to become congested.—**con-ges'tion** (-jes'chọn), *n.* [L. *congestio(n-)*.] A heaping together†; a congested condition; in *pathol.*, an abnormal accumulation of blood in the vessels of an organ or part.—**con-ges′tive** (-tiv), *a.* Pertaining to or characterized by congestion.

con-gi-us (kon′ji-us), *n.*; pl. *-gii* (-ji-ī). [L.] A liquid measure of capacity among the ancient Romans, equal to about nine tenths of the old English wine-gallon; in *phar.*, a gallon.

con-glo-bate (kọn-glō′bāt or kon′glọ-bāt), *v. t.* or *i.*; *-bated, -bating.* [L. *conglobatus*, pp. of *conglobare*, < *con-*, with, + *globare*, form into a ball, < *globus*, ball.] To collect or form into a ball or rounded mass.—**con-glo′bate,** *a.* Formed into a ball.—**con-glo-ba-tion** (kon-glọ-bā′shọn), *n.* [L. *conglobatio(n-)*.] Formation into a ball; also, a rounded formation.

con-globe (kọn-glōb′), *v. t.* or *i.*; *-globed, -globing.* [L. *conglobare*: see *conglobate.*] To conglobate.

con-glom-er-ate (kọn-glom′ẹ-rāt), *v.*; *-ated, -ating.* [L. *conglomeratus*, pp. of *conglomerare*, < *con-*, with, + *glomerare*, form into a ball, < *glomus*, ball.] **I.** *tr.* To gather into a ball or rounded mass†; bring together into a cohering mass; form into a whole, without regard to homogeneity or congruity of the parts. **II.** *intr.* To collect or cluster together.—**con-glom′er-ate** (-ẹ-rạt). **I.** *a.* Gathered into a rounded mass; consisting of parts so gathered; clustered; in *bot.*, densely clustered; in *geol.*, of the nature of a conglomerate. **II.** *n.* Anything composed of heterogeneous materials or elements; in *geol.*, a rock consisting of rounded and water-worn pebbles, etc., embedded in a finer cementing material; consolidated gravel.—**con-glom-er-at′ic** (-ẹ-rat′ik), *a.* In *geol.*, pertaining to or of the nature of a conglomerate.—**con-glom-er-a′tion** (-ẹ-rā′shọn), *n.* [LL. *conglomeratio(n-)*.] The act of conglomerating, or the state of being conglomerated; also, that which is conglomerated; a cohering mass; a cluster; a heterogeneous combination (as, "What is any public question but a *conglomeration* of private interests?" Trollope's "Warden," xv.).—**con-glom-er-it′ic** (-ẹ-rit′ik), *a.* Same as *conglomeratic.*

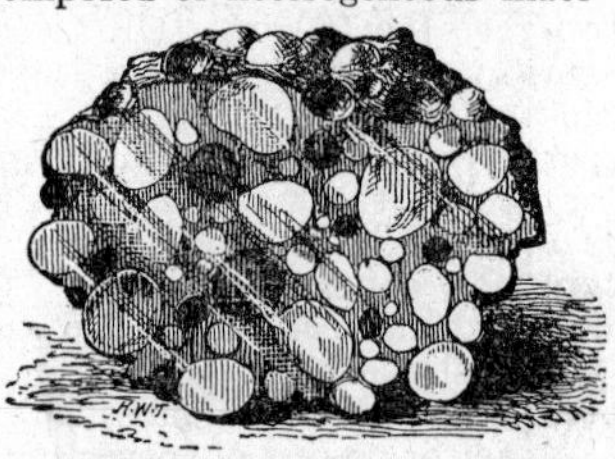

Conglomerate, polished surface.

con-glu-ti-nant (kọn-glö′ti-nạnt), *a.* Conglutinating; in *med.*, promoting the union of severed parts, as of a wound.

con-glu-ti-nate (kọn-glö′ti-nāt), *v. t.* or *i.*; *-nated, -nating.* [L. *conglutinatus*, pp. of *conglutinare*, < *con-*, with, + *glutinare*, glue fast, < *gluten*, glue.] To join or become joined as with glue.—**con-glu′ti-nate** (-nạt), *a.* Conglutinated; cohering.—**con-glu-ti-na′tion** (-nā′shọn), *n.* [L. *conglutinatio(n-)*.] The act of conglutinating; cohesive union; coalescence.—**con-glu′ti-na-tive** (-nạ-tiv), *a.* Tending to conglutinate.—**con-glu′ti-na-tor** (-nā-tọr), *n.*

Con-go (kong′gō) **col′ors.** [With reference to the *Congo* (*Kongo*) regions in Africa.] A group of coal-tar colors or dyes (red, violet, yellow, etc.) possessing the property of dyeing cotton and other vegetable fibers without the presence of a mordant, the typical member of the group being 'Congo red,' a derivative of benzidine.

con-go=eel (kong′gō-ēl′), *n.* [Cf. *conger-eel.*] An eel-shaped amphibian, *Siren lacertina*, of the southern U. S., having small fore limbs but no hind ones; a siren; also, an eel-pout.

Con-go (kong′gō) **snake.** [Cf. *congo-eel.*] A snake-like amphibian, *Amphiuma means*, of the southeastern U. S., sometimes attaining a length of 3 feet.

con-gou (kong′gö), *n.* [Chinese *kung-fu*, labor.] A kind of black tea from China.

con-grat-u-lant (kọn-grat′ū-lạnt). **I.** *a.* Congratulating. **II.** *n.* One who congratulates.

con-grat-u-late (kọn-grat′ū-lāt), *v. t.*; *-lated, -lating.* [L. *congratulatus*, pp. of *congratulari*, < *con-*, with, + *gratulari*, express joy, E. *gratulate.*] To express sympathetic joy or satisfaction at (an event or circumstance)†; also, to express sympathetic joy to (a person), as on a happy occasion; compliment or command with expressions of sympathetic pleasure; felicitate; also, to salute†.—**con-grat-u-la′tion** (-lā′shọn), *n.* [L. *congratulatio(n-)*.] The act of congratulating; also, a congratulatory expression.—**con-grat′u-la-tor,** *n.*—**con-grat′u-la-to-ry** (-lạ-tọ-ri), *a.* Conveying congratulation; inclined to congratulate.

con-gre-gant (kong′grẹ-gạnt), *n.* [L. *congregans* (*-ant-*), ppr. of *congregare*: see *congregate.*] A member of a congregation.

con-gre-gate (kong′grẹ-gāt), *v.*; *-gated, -gating.* [L. *congregatus*, pp. of *congregare*, < *con-*, with, + *gregare*, collect into a flock, < *grex*, flock.] **I.** *tr.* To bring together in a crowd, body, or mass; assemble; collect. **II.** *intr.* To flock together; gather; meet.—**con′gre-gate,** *a.* Congregated; assembled; collective.—**con-gre-ga′tion** (-gā′shọn), *n.* [L. *congregatio(n-)*.] The act of congregating; also, a congregated body; an assemblage; esp., a body of persons assembled for religious worship and instruction; also, a body of persons associated together for the purpose of holding religious services in common (see *congregationalism*); in the Old Testament, the whole body of the Hebrews; in the New Testament, the Christian church in general, or a particular assemblage of worshipers; in the *Rom. Cath. Ch.*, a committee of cardinals or other ecclesiastics; a religious community or order with a common rule but not under solemn vows; an associated group of monasteries.—**con-gre-ga′tion-al,** *a.* Pertaining to a congregation; recognizing the governing power of the congregation; [*cap.*] pertaining or adhering to a form of church government in which each congregation or church acts as an independent, self-governing body, while maintaining fellowship with other like congregations.—**con-gre-ga′tion-al-ism,** *n.* The principle of church government by individual congregations; [*cap.*] the system of government and doctrine of the Congregational churches.—**con-gre-ga′tion-al-ist,** *n.* One who holds to the congregational principle of church government; [*cap.*] a member of the Congregational denomination.—**con-gre-ga′tion-al-ly,** *adv.*—**con′gre-ga-tive,** *a.* Tending to congregate.—**con′gre-ga-tive-ness,** *n.*—**con′gre-ga-tor,** *n.*

con-gress (kong′gres), *n.* [L. *congressus*, < *congredi*, come together, < *con-*, with, + *gradi*, walk, go, < *gradus*, step.] The act of coming together; an encounter; an interview; sexual intercourse; social intercourse; converse; esp., a formal meeting or assembly of representatives, as envoys of sovereign states, for the discussion, arrangement, or promotion of some matter of common interest; the national legislative body of a nation, esp. of a republic; [*cap.*] the national legislative body of the U. S., consisting of the Senate (upper house) and the House of Representatives (lower house), as a continuous institution; this body as it exists for the two years during which the representatives hold their seats (as, the 69th *Congress*, March 4, 1925–March 4, 1927); the session of this body; also, the lower house of the Spanish Cortes.—**congress boot** or **gaiter,** a high shoe with elastic sides, by the stretching of which it is drawn on to the foot.—**con′gress,** *v. i.* To meet in congress.—**con-gres-sion** (kọn-gresh′ọn), *n.* [L. *congressio(n-)*.] A coming together; congress. [Obs. or rare.]—**con-gres′sion-al,** *a.* Of or pertaining to a congress, esp. [*cap.*] the Congress of the U. S.—**con-gres′sion-al-ist,** *n.* An adherent or supporter of a congress; a member of a congressional party.—**con-gres′sion-al-ly,** *adv.*—**con′gress-ist,** *n.* A member of a congress.—**Con′gress-man** (-mạn), *n.*; pl. *-men.* A member of the U. S. Congress, esp. of the House of Representatives.—**Con′gress-wom″an,** *n.*; pl. *women* (-wim″en).

con-greve (kong′grēv), *n.* [From Sir W. *Congreve* (1772–1828), English inventor.] A kind of lucifer match (short for *Congreve match*); also, a kind of rocket formerly used as a weapon of attack in warfare (short for *Congreve rocket*).

con-grue† (kọn-grö′ or kong′grö), *v. i.*; *-grued, -gruing.* [L. *congruere*, come together, agree.] To agree; be in accord. See Shakspere's "Hamlet," iv. 3. 66.

con-gru-ent (kong′grọ-ẹnt), *a.* [L. *congruens* (*-ent-*), ppr. of *congruere*: see *congrue.*] Agreeing; accordant; congruous.—**con′gru-ence, con′gru-en-cy,** *n.*—**con′gru-ent-ly,** *adv.*

con-gru-i-ty (kọn-grö′i-ti), *n.*; pl. *-ties* (-tiz). The quality of being congruous; also, a point of agreement; in *geom.*, equality; capacity of being superposed.

con-gru-ous (kong′grǫ-us), *a.* [L. *congruus*, < *congruere*: see *congrue.*] Agreeing or harmonious in character; accordant (*with* or *to*); consonant; consistent; appropriate or fitting; also, exhibiting harmony of parts; in *geom.*, having congruity.—**con′gru-ous-ly,** *adv.*—**con′gru-ous-ness,** *n.*

con-ic (kon′ik). [Gr. κωνικός.] **I.** *a.* Having the form of or resembling a cone; round, and tapering to a point; also, pertaining to a cone (as, a *conic* section, a curve formed by the intersection of a plane with a right circular cone, as an ellipse, a parabola, or a hyperbola; *conic* sections, the branch of mathematics dealing with the ellipse, the parabola, and the hyperbola). **II.** *n.* A conic section.—**con′i-cal,** *a.* Conic; cone-shaped.—**con′i-cal-ly,** *adv.*—**con′i-cal-ness,** *n.*—**con′ics,** *n.* The branch of mathematics dealing with conic sections.

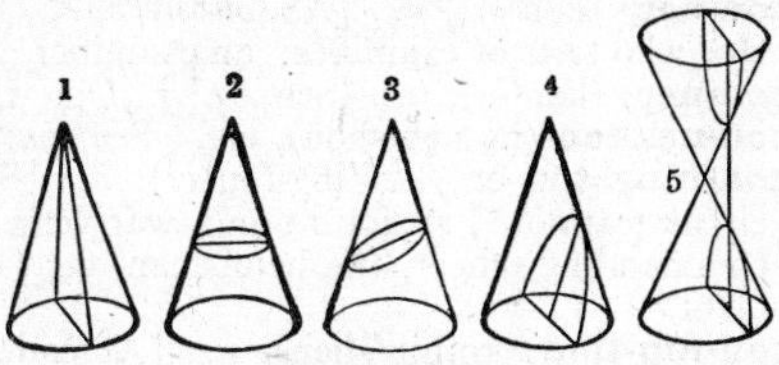

Conic Sections.

The two principal forms are fig. 5, giving the hyperbola, and fig. 3, giving the ellipse. Fig. 4 is the intermediate case, giving the parabola. The degenerate form of the hyperbola is a pair of straight lines, as shown in fig. 1. Fig. 2 shows the circle as a special case of the ellipse, in which the plane becomes perpendicular to the axis of the cone.

co-nid-i-a (kǭ-nid′i-ą̈), *n.* Plural of *conidium.*

co-nid-i-al (kǭ-nid′i-ąl), *a.* Pertaining to, of the nature of, or producing conidia. Also **co-nid′i-an.**

co-nid-i-o-phore (kǭ-nid′i-ǭ-fōr), *n.* [See *-phore.*] In certain fungi, a special stalk or branch of the mycelium, bearing conidia.

co-nid-i-um (kǭ-nid′i-um), *n.*; pl. *-ia* (-i-ą̈). [NL., dim. < Gr. κόνις, dust.] In fungi, a propagative body or cell which is asexual in its origin and functions.

co-ni-fer (kō′ni-fėr), *n.* [L. *conifer*, cone-bearing, < *conus*, cone, + *ferre*, bear.] Any of the (mostly evergreen) trees and shrubs constituting the gymnospermous order or group *Coniferæ* or *Pinales*, including the pine, fir, spruce, and other cone-bearing trees and shrubs, and also the yews and their allies, which bear drupaceous fruit.—**co-nif-er-ous** (kǭ-nif′ę-rus), *a.* In *bot.*, bearing cones; belonging or pertaining to the *Coniferæ* or *Pinales* (see *conifer*).

co-nine, co-ni-ine (kō′nin, kǭ-nī′in), *n.* [See *conium.*] A highly poisonous volatile alkaloid constituting the active principle of *Conium maculatum*, the poison-hemlock.

co-ni-ros-ter (kō-ni-ros′tėr), *n.* [NL. *Conirostres*, pl., < L. *conus*, cone, + *rostrum*, beak.] Any of the *Conirostres*, a group of birds with cone-shaped bills, including the finches, etc.—**co-ni-ros′tral,** *a.* Having a conical bill; belonging or pertaining to the conirosters.

co-ni-um (kǭ-nī′um), *n.* [LL., < Gr. κώνειον, hemlock.] The poison-hemlock, *Conium maculatum*; also, a preparation of this plant, used in medicine as a sedative, anodyne, etc.

Conirostral Bird (Hawfinch).

con-jec-tur-a-ble (kǫn-jek′tų̄-rą-bl), *a.* That may be conjectured.—**con-jec′tur-a-bly,** *adv.*

con-jec-tur-al (kǫn-jek′tų̄-rąl), *a.* Of, pertaining to, or of the nature of conjecture; involving conjecture; problematical; also, given to making conjectures.—**con-jec′tur-al-ly,** *adv.*

con-jec-ture (kǫn-jek′tų̄r), *n.* [L. *conjectura*, < *conjicere* (pp. *conjectus*), throw together, infer, guess, < *con-*, with, + *jacere*, throw.] The interpretation of signs or omens†; also, the formation or expression of an opinion without sufficient evidence for proof; also, an opinion so formed or expressed; a surmise; a guess.—**con-jec′ture,** *v.*; *-tured, -turing.* **I.** *tr.* To conclude or suppose from grounds or evidence insufficient to ensure the reliability of the opinion; surmise; guess. **II.** *intr.* To form conjectures.—**con-jec′tur-er,** *n.*

con-jee (kon′jē), *n.* See *congee*[2].

con-join (kǫn-join′), *v.* [OF. F. *conjoindre*, < L. *conjungere* (pp. *conjunctus*), < *con-*, with, + *jungere*, join.] **I.** *tr.* To join together; unite; combine; associate. **II.** *intr.* To become joined together; unite.—**con-join′er,** *n.*

con-joint (kǫn-joint′), *a.* [OF. F. *conjoint*, pp. of *conjoindre*: see *conjoin.*] Joined together; united; combined; associated; also, pertaining to or formed by two or more in combination; joint.—**con-joint′ly,** *adv.*

con-ju-bi-lant (kǫn-jö′bi-ląnt), *a.* [ML. *conjubilans* (*-ant-*), < L. *con-*, with, + *jubilare*, E. *jubilate.*] Rejoicing together: as, "They stand, those halls of Zion, *Conjubilant* with song" (J. M. Neale's tr. Bernard of Cluny, "Jerusalem the Golden"). [Poetic.]

con-ju-gal (kon′jǫ-gąl), *a.* [L. *conjugalis*, < *conjux*, *conjunx*, husband or wife, < *conjungere*: see *conjoin.*] Of, pertaining to, or of the nature of marriage; matrimonial; pertaining to the relation of husband and wife; connubial.—**con-ju-gal′i-ty** (-gal′i-ti), *n.*—**con′ju-gal-ly,** *adv.*

con-ju-gate (kon′jǫ-gāt), *v.*; *-gated, -gating.* [L. *conjugatus*, pp. of *conjugare*, < *con-*, with, + *jugare*, yoke, join, < *jugum*, a yoke.] **I.** *tr.* To yoke or join together†; in *gram.*, to inflect (a verb) through all its various forms of voice, mode, tense, number, and person. **II.** *intr.* In *biol.*, to unite in conjugation.—**con′ju-gate** (-gąt). **I.** *a.* Joined together, esp. in a pair or pairs; coupled; in *gram.* and *rhet.*, of words, having a common derivation, and thus usually kindred in meaning; in *bot.*, of a pinnate leaf, having only one pair of leaflets; in *math.*, of two points, lines, etc., so related as to be interchangeable in the enunciation of certain properties. **II.** *n.* In *gram.* and *rhet.*, one of a group of conjugate words.—**con-ju-ga′tion** (-gā′shǫn), *n.* [L. *conjugatio*(*n-*).] The act of joining, or the state of being joined, together; union; conjunction; in *gram.*, the inflection of a verb in its different forms according to voice, mode, tense, number, and person; a systematic arrangement of these forms; a class of verbs similarly conjugated (as, a Latin verb of the third *conjugation*); in *biol.*, the union or fusion, for reproduction, of two cells or individuals, as in certain plants and lower animals.—**con-ju-ga′tion-al,** *a.*—**con-ju-ga′tion-al-ly,** *adv.*—**con′ju-ga-tive** (-gā-tiv), *a.* Pertaining to or characterized by conjugation.

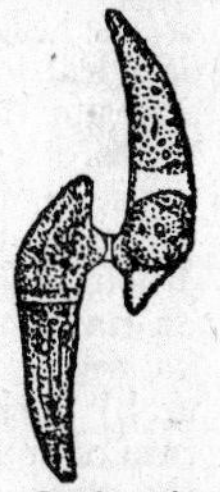

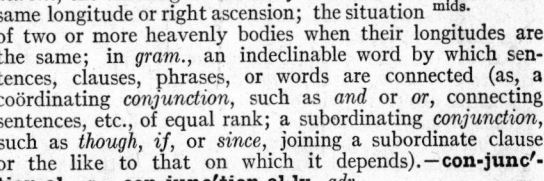

Conjugation of two Desmids.

con-junct (kǫn-jungkt′). [L. *conjunctus*, pp. of *conjungere*: see *conjoin.*] **I.** *a.* Conjoined; associate; also, formed by conjunction. **II.** *n.* A person or thing conjoined with another.

con-junc-tion (kǫn-jungk′shǫn), *n.* [L. *conjunctio*(*n-*), < *conjungere*: see *conjoin.*] The act of conjoining, or the state of being conjoined; union; combination; association; in *astron.*, the meeting of heavenly bodies in the same longitude or right ascension; the situation of two or more heavenly bodies when their longitudes are the same; in *gram.*, an indeclinable word by which sentences, clauses, phrases, or words are connected (as, a coördinating *conjunction*, such as *and* or *or*, connecting sentences, etc., of equal rank; a subordinating *conjunction*, such as *though*, *if*, or *since*, joining a subordinate clause or the like to that on which it depends).—**con-junc′tion-al,** *a.*—**con-junc′tion-al-ly,** *adv.*

con-junc-ti-va (kon-jungk-tī′vą̈), *n.*; pl. *-væ* (-vē). [NL., prop. fem. of LL. *conjunctivus*: see *conjunctive.*] In *anat.*, the mucous membrane which lines the inner surface of the eyelids and is reflected over the fore part of the sclerotic and the cornea.—**con-junc-ti′val,** *a.*

con-junc-tive (kǫn-jungk′tiv). [LL. *conjunctivus*, < L. *conjungere*: see *conjoin.*] **I.** *a.* Serving to conjoin; connective; also, conjoined; joint; in *gram.*, of the nature of a conjunction; also, connecting in meaning as well as grammatically (as, a *conjunctive* or copulative conjunction); also, of a mode, subjunctive. **II.** *n.* In *gram.*, a conjunctive word; a conjunction; also, the conjunctive mode, or a verb-form belonging to it.—**con-junc′tive-ly,** *adv.*

con-junc-ti-vi-tis (kǫn-jungk-ti-vī′tis), *n.* [NL.] In *pathol.*, inflammation of the conjunctiva.

con-junct-ly (kǫn-jungkt′li), *adv.* In a conjunct manner; in conjunction.

con-junc-ture (kǫn-jungk′tų̄r), *n.* [ML. *conjunctura*, < L. *conjungere*: see *conjoin.*] Conjunction†; meeting† or a place of meeting†; also, a combination of circumstances or affairs; a particular state of affairs; esp., a critical state of affairs, or crisis (as, "one of those critical *conjunctures* that will periodically occur in all states": Disraeli's "Coningsby," ii. 5).

con-ju-ra-tion (kon-jọ̈-rā′shọn), *n.* [OF. F. *conjuration*, < L. *conjuratio(n-)*.] A conjuring† or swearing together†; a conspiracy†; also, the act of calling on or invoking by a sacred name; adjuration; also, supernatural accomplishment by invocation or spell; also, an incantation; a spell or charm; also, the practice of legerdemain.

con-jure (kọn-jör′ or kun′jėr), *v.*; *-jured*, *-juring*. [OF. F. *conjurer*, < L. *conjurare*, < *con-*, with, + *jurare*, swear.] **I.** *intr.* (pron. kọn-jör′) To swear together†; conspire†; also (pron. kun′jėr), to call upon or command a devil or spirit by invocation or spell; practise magic; hence, to practise legerdemain. **II.** *tr.* (pron. kọn-jör′) To constrain by putting under oath†; also, to charge solemnly; also, to appeal to solemnly or earnestly; implore; entreat; also (pron. kun′jėr), to call upon or command (a devil or spirit) by invocation or spell; affect or influence by or as by invocation or spell; effect, produce, bring, convey, etc., by or as by magic or jugglery.—**con-jur-er, con-jur-or** (kọn-jö′rėr, -rọr), *n.* One bound with others by an oath; also, one who solemnly charges or entreats; also (pron. kun′jėr-ėr, -ọr), one who conjures spirits, or who pretends to perform miracles by their aid; a magician; also, one who practises legerdemain; a juggler.—**con-jur-y** (kun′jėr-i), *n.* Magic; legerdemain; jugglery.

conn (kon), *v. t.* See *con*².

con-nate (kon′āt or ko-nāt′), *a.* [LL. *connatus*, pp. of *connasci*, be born at the same time, < L. *con-*, with, + *nasci*, be born.] Existing in a person or thing from birth or origin; inborn; congenital; also, associated in birth or origin; also, allied or agreeing in nature; cognate; congenial; in *bot.* and *zoöl.*, congenitally or firmly united into one body (as, a *connate* leaf, a leaf of which the lower lobes or basal edges are united about the stem or above the petiole, or a leaf formed by the union about the stem of a pair of opposite leaves).—**con′nate-ly,** *adv.*—**con′nate=per-fo′-li-ate,** *a.* In *bot.*, formed by the union about the stem of a pair of opposite leaves, as a leaf.—**con-na-tion** (ko-nā′shọn), *n.* Connate condition.

Connate-perfoliate Leaves.

con-nat-u-ral (ko-nat′ū-rạl), *a.* [ML. *connaturalis*, < L. *con-*, with, + *naturalis*, natural.] Belonging to a person or thing by nature or from birth or origin; connate; also, of the same or like nature (as, "How we may come To death, and mix with our *connatural* dust": Milton's "Paradise Lost," xi. 529); cognate.—**con-nat′u-ral-ly,** *adv.*

con-nect (kọ-nekt′), *v.* [L. *connectere* (pp. *connexus*), *conectere*, < *con-*, with, + *nectere*, bind.] **I.** *tr.* To bind or fasten together; join or unite; link, as two things together or one with another; also, to establish communication between; put in communication (*with*); also, to bring into association or relation; associate, as with something. **II.** *intr.* To become connected; join or unite; be in communication; of railroad-trains, etc., to run in connection.—**con-nect′ed,** *p. a.* Bound or fastened together; joined in order or sequence, as words or ideas; associated; related (as, well *connected* socially).—**con-nect′ed-ly,** *adv.*—**con-nect′ed-ness,** *n.*—**con-nect′er, con-nect′or,** *n.*—**con-nect′i-ble, con-nect′a-ble,** *a.* Capable of being connected.—**con-nect′ing=rod,** *n.* A rod or bar connecting (movable) parts, esp. one on a steam-engine or gas-engine connecting the piston-rod, cross-head, or the like with the crank.—**con-nec-tion, con-nex-ion** (kọ-nek′shọn), *n.* [L. *connexio(n-)*.] The act of connecting, or the state of being connected; junction; union; union in due order or sequence of words or ideas; contextual relation; communication; association; relationship; sexual relation; also, anything that connects; a bond or tie; a connecting part; also, a person related to another or others, esp. by marriage or distant consanguinity; also, a body of persons connected, as by political or religious ties; a religious denomination; also, the meeting of means of conveyance for transfer of passengers without delay.—**con-nec′tion-al, con-nex′-ion-al,** *a.*—**con-nec-ti-val** (kon-ek-tī′vạl), *a.* Of or pertaining to a connective.—**con-nec-tive** (kọ-nek′tiv). **I.** *a.* Serving or tending to connect: as, *connective* tissue (a tissue of mesoblastic origin, which connects, supports, or surrounds other tissues, organs, etc., and occurs in various forms throughout the body). **II.** *n.* Anything that serves to connect; in *gram.*, a word used to connect words, phrases, clauses, and sentences, as a conjunction.—**con-nec′tive-ly,** *adv.*—**con-nec-tiv-i-ty** (kon-ek-tiv′i-ti), *n.*

con-ner¹ (kon′ėr), *n.* [AS. *cunnere*, < *cunnian*, try, test.] One who tests or examines; an examiner.

con-ner² (kon′ėr), *n.* [See *con*¹.] One who cons or studies.

con-nex-ion (kọ-nek′shọn), etc. See *connection*, etc.

con-ning=tow-er (kon′ing-tou″ėr), *n.* [See *con*².] A low, circular armored structure on a war-vessel, occupied by the commanding officer, the helmsman, etc., during an engagement.

con-nip-tion (kọ-nip′shọn), *n.* [A made word.] A fit of hysterics or hysterical excitement. Also called *conniption fit.* [Colloq.]

con-niv-ance (kọ-nī′vạns), *n.* [Earlier *connivence*, < LL. *conniventia*.] The act of conniving; feigned ignorance or tacit encouragement of wrong-doing, etc. Also **con-niv′-an-cy.**

con-nive (kọ-nīv′), *v. i.*; *-nived*, *-niving*. [L. *connivere*, < *con-*, with, + *-nivere*, akin to *nictare*, wink.] To shut one's eyes to or avoid noticing something that one cannot well prevent (with *at*: archaic); also, to avoid noticing that which one should oppose or condemn but secretly approves; give aid to wrong-doing, etc., by forbearing to act or speak; be secretly accessory; also, to coöperate secretly (*with*); also, to wink†.—**con-niv-ence** (kọ-nī′vẹns), *n.* See *connivance*.—**con-niv′ent,** *a.* Conniving†; in *bot.* and *zoöl.*, converging, as petals.—**con-niv′er,** *n.*

con-nois-seur (kon-i-sėr′ or -sūr′), *n.* [F. (now *connaisseur*), OF. *conoissere*, < *conoistre*, < L. *cognoscere*, come to know: see *cognition*.] One competent to pass critical judgments in an art, esp. one of the fine arts, or in matters of taste: as, "I have no great confidence in the taste and judgment of coffee-house *connoisseurs*" (Smollett's "Humphry Clinker," May 19).—**con-nois-seur′ship,** *n.*

con-no-tate (kon′ọ̄-tāt), *v. t.*; *-tated*, *-tating*. [ML. *connotatus*, pp. of *connotare*: see *connote*.] To connote.

con-no-ta-tion (kon-ọ̄-tā′shọn), *n.* [ML. *connotatio(n-)*.] The act or fact of connoting; also, that which is connoted.—**con-no-ta-tive** (kọ-nō′tạ-tiv or kon′ọ̄-tạ-tiv), *a.* Having the quality of connoting; also, pertaining to connotation.—**con-no′ta-tive-ly,** *adv.*

con-note (kọ-nōt′), *v. t.*; *-noted*, *-noting*. [ML. *connotare* (pp. *connotatus*), < L. *con-*, with, + *notare*, mark, E. *note*, *v.*] To denote secondarily; signify in addition to the primary meaning; imply; also, to involve as a condition or accompaniment. Cf. *denote*.—**con-no′tive** (-nō′tiv), *a.* Connotative.—**con-no′tive-ly,** *adv.*

con-nu-bi-al (kọ-nū′bi-ạl), *a.* [L. *connubialis*, < *connubium*, marriage, < *con-*, with, + *nubere*, veil, marry.] Of or pertaining to marriage or wedlock; matrimonial; conjugal.—**con-nu-bi-al′i-ty** (-al′i-ti), *n.*—**con-nu′bi-al-ly,** *adv.*

co-no-dont (kō′nọ̄-dont), *n.* [Gr. κῶνος, cone, + ὀδούς (ὀδοντ-), tooth.] Any of certain minute fossils of a conical, tooth-like form, found in Silurian and other rocks: supposed to be the jaws of annelids.

co-noid (kō′noid). [Gr. κωνοειδής, < κῶνος, cone, + εἶδος, form.] **I.** *a.* Resembling or approaching a cone in shape; conoidal. **II.** *n.* A geometrical solid formed by the revolution of a conic section about one of its axes; a geometrical surface generated by a straight line moving so as to touch a fixed straight line and a fixed curve, and continue parallel to a given plane; any object, as a bullet, approaching a cone in shape.—**co-noi-dal** (kọ̄-noi′dạl), *a.* Pertaining to or of the nature of a conoid; approaching a cone in shape.

co-no-scen-te (kō-nō-shen′tā), *n.* [It.] See *cognoscente*.

con-quer (kong′kėr), *v.* [OF. *conquerre* (also *conquerir*, F. *conquérir*), < L. *conquærere*, *conquirere* (pp. *conquisitus*), < *con-*, altogether, + *quærere*, seek.] **I.** *tr.* To acquire by force of arms; win in war; gain or obtain by effort; also, to overcome by force; subdue; vanquish; gain the victory over; surmount (obstacles, etc.). **II.** *intr.* To make conquests; gain the victory.—**con′quer-a-ble,** *a.* That may be conquered.—**con′quer-ess,** *n.* A female conqueror.—**con′quer-ing-ly,** *adv.*—**con′quer-or,** *n.* One who conquers.—**the Conqueror,** William I., King of England and Duke of Normandy: so called on account of his conquest of England in 1066.

con-quest (kong′kwest), *n.* [OF. *conqueste, conquest* (F. *conquête, conquêt*), from ML. fem. and neut. forms < L. *conquirere* (pp. *conquisitus*): see *conquer.*] The act of conquering; acquisition by force; captivation, as of favor or affections; vanquishment; also, that which is conquered or won.—**the Conquest,** the conquering of England by William, Duke of Normandy (William the Conqueror), in 1066.

con-qui-an (kong′ki-an), *n.* [Sp. *con quién,* 'with whom?'] A card-game for two players, the object of each being to form sets of three or four cards of the same denomination or sequences of three or more cards of the same suit.

con-quis-ta-dor (kon-kwis′tạ-dôr, Sp. kōn-kēs-tä-ᴛʜōr′), *n.*; pl. *-dors* (-dôrz), Sp. *-dores* (-ᴛʜō′räs). [Sp.] A conqueror: used esp. of the Spanish conquerors of Mexico and Peru in the 16th century.

con-san-guine (kon-sang′gwin). [L. *consanguineus,* < *con-,* with, + *sanguis,* blood.] **I.** *a.* Of the same blood; consanguineous. **II.** *n.* One of the same blood as, or related by birth to, another.—**con-san-guin′e-ous** (-gwin′ẹ-us), *a.* Of the same blood; related by birth; akin; pertaining to consanguinity; also, related as having had the same father (cf. *uterine*).—**con-san-guin′e-ous-ly,** *adv.*—**con-san-guin′i-ty,** *n.* The condition of being of the same blood; relationship by blood; kinship; fig., relationship or affinity.

con-science (kon′shẹns), *n.* [OF. F. *conscience,* < L. *conscientia,* < *consciens* (*-ent-*), ppr. of *conscire,* be conscious of, < *con-,* with, + *scire,* know.] Consciousness†; also, inmost thought†; also, the internal recognition of right and wrong as regards one's actions and motives; the faculty which decides upon the moral quality of one's actions and motives, enjoining one to conformity with the moral law; also, conscientiousness.—**conscience clause,** a clause or article inserted in an act or law, which specially relieves persons whose conscientious or religious scruples forbid their compliance with it.—**conscience money,** money paid to relieve the conscience, as for obligations previously evaded.—**in (all) conscience,** in (all) reason and fairness; in truth; also, most certainly; assuredly.—**con′science-less,** *a.* Without conscience; unscrupulous.

con-sci-en-tious (kon-ṣi-en′shus), *a.* [ML. *conscientiosus.*] Controlled by or done according to conscience; scrupulous.—**conscientious objector,** one who objects, from conscientious scruples, to some course of action or procedure; esp., one who, when called upon in time of war to fight for his country, refuses to do so because of conscientious objections.—**con-sci-en′tious-ly,** *adv.*—**con-sci-en′tious-ness,** *n.*

con-scion-a-ble (kon′shọn-ạ-bl), *a.* [Irreg. < *conscience.*] Having a conscience†, or governed by conscience† (as, "a knave . . . no further *conscionable* than in putting on the mere form of civil and humane seeming": Shakspere's "Othello," ii. 1. 242); also, conformable to conscience; just. Cf. *unconscionable.*

con-scious (kon′shus), *a.* [L. *conscius,* < *con-,* with, + *scire,* know.] Knowing something together with another (obs. or archaic); inwardly sensible or aware of something (as, *conscious* of one's own faults); inwardly sensible of wrong-doing†; also, aware of one's own existence, sensations, cognitions, etc.; endowed with consciousness; also, having the mental faculties awake; also, aware of what one is doing (as, a *conscious* liar); also, present to consciousness; known to one's self; felt; sometimes, deliberate or intentional; also, directing one's thoughts and attention unduly toward one's self; self-conscious; betraying self-consciousness.—**con′scious-ly,** *adv.*—**con′scious-ness,** *n.* The state of being conscious; inward sensibility of something; knowledge of one's own existence, sensations, cognitions, etc.; the thoughts and feelings, collectively, of an individual, or of an aggregate of people (as, the moral *consciousness* of a nation); activity of mental faculties (as, to regain *consciousness* after a swoon).

con-scribe (kọn-skrīb′), *v. t.*; *-scribed, -scribing.* [L. *conscribere* (pp. *conscriptus*), < *con-,* with, + *scribere,* write.] To enroll†; enlist†; also, to enlist for military or naval service by conscription; enlist compulsorily.

con-script (kon′skript). [L. *conscriptus,* pp. of *conscribere*: see *conscribe.*] **I.** *a.* Enrolled or elected (as, the *conscript* fathers, the senators of ancient Rome); also, enrolled or formed by conscription; drafted. **II.** *n.* A recruit obtained by conscription.—**con-script** (kọn-skript′), *v. t.* To enroll by conscription; draft.—**con-scrip′tion** (-skrip′shọn), *n.* [L. *conscriptio(n-).*] The act of conscribing; compulsory enrolment of men for military or naval service; a draft.

con-se-crate (kon′sẹ-krāt), *v. t.*; *-crated, -crating.* [L. *consecratus,* pp. of *consecrare,* < *con-,* with, + *sacrare,* consecrate: see *sacre.*] To make or declare sacred; set apart or dedicate to the service of the Deity; ordain to a sacred office; also, to devote or dedicate to some purpose (as, a life *consecrated* to science); also, to make an object of veneration (as, a custom *consecrated* by time).—**con′se-crate,** *a.* Consecrated; sacred. [Archaic.]—**con-se-cra′tion** (-krā′shọn), *n.* [L. *consecratio(n-).*] The act of consecrating; dedication to the service and worship of God; the act of giving the sacramental character to the eucharistic elements of bread and wine; ordination to a sacred office, esp. to the episcopate.—**con′se-cra-tor,** *n.*—**con′se-cra-to-ry** (-krạ-tọ-ri), *a.* Serving to consecrate.

con-se-cu-tion (kon-sẹ-kū′shọn), *n.* [L. *consecutio(n-),* < *consequi,* follow after: see *consequent.*] Succession; sequence; also, logical sequence; inference.

con-sec-u-tive (kọn-sek′ụ-tiv), *a.* [F. *consécutif,* < L. *consequi*: see *consecution.*] Following one another in uninterrupted succession; uninterrupted in course or succession; successive; also, marked by logical sequence; in *gram.,* expressing consequence or result (as, a *consecutive* clause).—**consecutive points,** in *math.,* two or more points infinitely close one to another on the same branch of a curve.—**con-sec′u-tive-ly,** *adv.*—**con-sec′u-tive-ness,** *n.*

con-sen-su-al (kọn-sen′shụ-ạl), *a.* [L. *consensus*: see *consensus.*] Formed or existing by mere consent (as, a *consensual* marriage); in *physiol.,* noting or pertaining to involuntary movement accompanying or correlative with voluntary movement, as the contraction of the iris when the eye is opened to receive the light; in *psychol.,* noting or pertaining to reflex action initiated by a distinctly conscious sensation.—**con-sen′su-al-ly,** *adv*

con-sen-sus (kọn-sen′sus), *n.* [L., < *consentire*: see *consent.*] A general agreement or concord, as in opinion.

con-sent (kọn-sent′), *v. i.* [OF. F. *consentir,* < L. *consentire,* < *con-,* with, + *sentire,* feel.] To agree in sentiment, opinion, etc.†; be in harmony†; also, to give assent, as to a proposal; agree; comply or yield.—**con-sent′,** *n.* [OF.] Agreement in sentiment, opinion, a course of action, etc.; accord; concord; harmony; also, assent, as to a proposal (as, "You see she says nothing. Silence gives *consent*": Goldsmith's "Good-Natured Man," ii.); acquiescence; permission; compliance.

con-sen-ta-ne-ous (kon-sen-tā′nẹ-us), *a.* [L. *consentaneus,* < *consentire*: see *consent.*] Agreeing or accordant; also, done by common consent; unanimous; simultaneous.—**con-sen-ta-ne-i-ty** (kọn-sen-tạ-nē′i-ti), **con-sen-ta′ne-ous-ness,** *n.*—**con-sen-ta′ne-ous-ly,** *adv.*

con-sent-er (kọn-sen′tėr), *n.* One who consents.

con-sen-tience (kọn-sen′shiẹns), *n.* [See *consentient.*] Agreement or accordance; also, sensuous impressions collectively, either of a person or of an animal; the union or synthesis of sensations which takes place, apart from consciousness, in a sentient being.

con-sen-tient (kọn-sen′shiẹnt), *a.* [L. *consentiens* (*-ent-*), ppr. of *consentire*: see *consent.*] Agreeing or accordant; agreeing with each other; unanimous, as an opinion; acting in agreement or harmony; giving consent; also, endowed with consentience; of the nature of consentience.

con-sent-ing (kọn-sen′ting), *p. a.* That consents; giving consent.—**con-sent′ing-ly,** *adv.*

con-se-quence (kon′sẹ-kwens), *n.* [L. *consequentia,* < *consequens,* ppr.: see *consequent.*] The act or fact of following as an effect or result upon something antecedent; that which so follows; an effect or result; also, logical sequence; a logical result; a deduction or inference; also, importance or significance; importance in rank or position; distinction; sometimes, assumed importance; in *astron.*, motion from west to east; position to the east.—**in consequence,** as a result; consequently.—**in consequence of,** as the result of; by reason of.

con-se-quent (kon′sē̦-kwent). [L. *consequens* (*-ent-*), ppr. of *consequi*, follow after, < *con-*, with, + *sequi*, follow.] **I.** *a.* Following as an effect or result; resulting; also, following as a logical conclusion; also, logically consistent. **II.** *n.* An effect† or result†; anything that follows upon something else (without implication of causal relation); in *logic*, a conclusion or inference; also, that member of a hypothetical proposition which contains the conclusion; in *math.*, the second term of a ratio. See *antecedent, n.*

con-se-quen-tial (kon-sē̦-kwen′shạl), *a.* [L. *consequentia*: see *consequence.*] Of the nature of a consequence; following as an effect or result, or as a logical conclusion or inference; consequent; resultant; also, logically consistent; also, of consequence or importance; also, self-important; pompous.—**con-se-quen-ti-al′i-ty** (-shi-al′i-ti), **con-se-quen′tial-ness,** *n.*—**con-se-quen′tial-ly,** *adv.*

con-se-quent-ly (kon′sē̦-kwent-li), *adv.* By way of consequence; in consequence of something antecedent; therefore; also, subsequently.

con-serv-a-ble (kọn-sėr′vạ-bl), *a.* Capable of being conserved; preservable.

con-ser-van-cy (kọn-sėr′vạn-si), *n.* [For earlier *conservacy*, < ML. *conservatia.*] Conservation, as of rivers or forests; in England, a commission or court regulating fisheries, navigation, etc.

con-ser-va-tion (kon-sėr-vā′shọn), *n.* [L. *conservatio*(*n-*).] The act of conserving; preservation; also, official supervision of rivers, forests, etc.; a district under such supervision.—**law of the conservation of energy,** the principle that the total energy of the universe is constant, no energy being created or destroyed in any of the processes of nature.—**con-ser-va′tion-al,** *a.* Pertaining to conservation.—**con-ser-va′tion-ist,** *n.* One who advocates or promotes conservation, esp. of the natural resources of a country; one engaged in protecting game and fish, preserving forests, conserving the food and fuel supply, or the like, in the public interest.

con-ser-va-tism (kọn-sėr′vạ-tizm), *n.* [From *conservative.*] The disposition to preserve what is established; opposition to innovation or change; [sometimes *cap.*] the principles and practices of political conservatives.—**con-ser′va-tist,** *n.* A conservative.

con-ser-va-tive (kọn-sėr′vạ-tiv). [ML. *conservativus.*] **I.** *a.* Having the power or tendency to conserve; preservative; esp., disposed to preserve existing conditions, institutions, etc.; [often *cap.*] noting or pertaining to a political party whose characteristic principle is opposition to change in the institutions of a country (as, the *Conservative* party in British politics). Cf. *liberal.* **II.** *n.* A preservative; also, a person of conservative principles; [often *cap.*] a member of a conservative party in politics, esp. that in England.—**con-ser′va-tive-ly,** *adv.*—**con-ser′va-tive-ness,** *n.*

con-ser-va-toire (kôṅ-ser-vȧ-twor), *n.* [F.] A conservatory (of music, etc.).

con-ser-va-tor (kon′sėr-vā-tọr), *n.* [L.] One who conserves or preserves; a preserver; a guardian; a custodian.—**con′ser-va-tor-ship,** *n.*

con-ser-va-to-ry (kọn-sėr′vạ-tō̦-ri). [ML. *conservatorius* (as n., *conservatorium*).] **I.** *a.* Serving or adapted to conserve; preservative. **II.** *n.*; pl. *-ries* (-riz). A preservative†; also, a place where things are preserved; a greenhouse, now usually a glass-covered house or apartment for the display of plants in bloom, exotics, etc.; also, a place for instruction in music and declamation; a school of music.

con-serve (kọn-sėrv′), *v. t.*; *-served, -serving.* [OF. F. *conserver*, < L. *conservare* (pp. *conservatus*), < *con-*, with, + *servare*, keep.] To keep in a safe or sound state; preserve from loss, decay, waste, or injury; keep unimpaired; also, to preserve, as fruit, with sugar, etc.—**con-serve** (kọn-sėrv′ or kon′sėrv), *n.* [OF. F. *conserve.*] That which is conserved; a confection; a preserve.—**con-serv′er,** *n.*

con-sid-er (kọn-sid′ėr), *v.* [OF. *considerer* (F. *considérer*), < L. *considerare* (pp. *consideratus*), perhaps orig. 'observe the stars,' < *con-*, with, + *sidus*, constellation, star: cf. L. *desiderare*, E. *desiderate.*] **I.** *tr.* To view attentively, or scrutinize (archaic); also, to contemplate mentally; meditate or reflect on; also, to pay attention to; regard; hence, to make allowance for; also, to recompense† or remunerate†; also, to think (*highly*, etc.) of; esteem; also, to regard as or deem to be (often with *as* or an infinitive expressed). **II.** *intr.* To look attentively (obs. or archaic); also, to think deliberately or carefully; reflect.—**con-sid′er-a-ble,** *a.* [ML. *considerabilis.*] Worthy of consideration; important; of distinction; also, being of an amount, extent, etc., worthy of consideration; fairly large or great; much (sometimes used substantively).—**con-sid′er-a-bly,** *adv.* To a degree or extent deserving notice; much.—**con-sid′er-ate** (-ạt), *a.* [L. *consideratus*, pp.] Marked by consideration or reflection; deliberate; also, given to consideration or reflection; thoughtful; prudent; also, showing consideration or regard for another's circumstances, feelings, etc.—**con-sid′er-ate-ly,** *adv.*—**con-sid′er-ate-ness,** *n.*—**con-sid-er-a′tion** (-ẹ-rā′shọn), *n.* [L. *consideratio*(*n-*).] The act of considering; reflection, meditation, or deliberation; a thought or reflection; also, regard or account; something taken, or to be taken, into account; also, a recompense for service rendered, etc.; a compensation; also, thoughtful or sympathetic regard or respect; thoughtfulness for others; also, estimation; esteem; importance or consequence; in *law*, that which a contracting party accepts as an equivalent for a service; the price of a promise.—**con-sid′er-er,** *n.*—**con-sid′er-ing,** *prep.* [Orig. ppr.] Taking into account; in view of.—**con-sid′er-ing-ly,** *adv.*

con-sign (kọn-sīn′), *v.* [OF. F. *consigner*, < L. *consignare*, < *con-*, with, + *signare*, mark, E. *sign, v.*] **I.** *tr.* To mark with a sign or seal†; attest† or confirm†; also, to hand over or deliver formally (*to*); commit (*to*); also, to transfer to another's custody or charge; intrust; also, to set apart, as to a purpose or use; in *com.*, to transmit, as by public carrier, esp. for sale or custody; address for such transmission. **II.**† *intr.* To yield or submit; also, to agree or assent.—**con-sign′a-ble,** *a.* That may be consigned.—**con-sig-na-tion** (kon-sig-nā′shọn), *n.* [L. *consignatio*(*n-*).] The act of consigning; consignment.—**con-sign-ee** (kon-sī-nē′ or -si-nē′), *n.* One to whom goods, etc., are consigned.—**con-sign′er,** *n.* One who consigns.—**con-sign′ment,** *n.* The act of consigning; that which is consigned; the writing by which anything is consigned.—**con-sign-or** (kọn-sī′nọr or kon-si-nôr′), *n.* One who consigns goods, etc.

con-sil-i-ent (kọn-sil′i-ẹnt), *a.* [L. *con-*, with, + *salire*, leap.] Coming together or agreeing; coinciding; concurring.—**con-sil′i-ence,** *n.*

con-sist (kọn-sist′), *v. i.* [L. *consistere*, < *con-*, with, + *sistere*, stand.] To stand still or firm†; exist (obs. or archaic); exist together† or be capable of existing together†; harmonize or agree, or be consistent (*with*); insist (*on*)†; esp., to be comprised or contained (*in*); also, to be made up or composed (*of*).—**con-sist′ence,** *n.* A standing still†; quiescence†; also, material coherence with retention of form; solidity or firmness; degree of firmness, as of a viscous liquid; also, consistency.—**con-sist′en-cy,** *n.*; pl. *-cies* (-siz). Consistence; also, agreement, harmony, or compatibility; agreement among themselves of the parts of a complex thing; constant adherence to the same principles, course, etc. (as, "A foolish *consistency* is the hobgoblin of little minds . . . With *consistency* a great soul has simply nothing to do": Emerson's "Essays," Self-Reliance).—**con-sist′ent,** *a.* Standing still or firm†; also, holding firmly together; cohering; also, agreeing or accordant; compatible; not self-opposed or self-contradictory; constantly adhering to the same principles, course, etc.—**con-sist′ent-ly,** *adv.*

con-sis-to-ry (kọn-sis′tō̦-ri or kon′sis-tō̦-ri), *n.*; pl. *-ries* (-riz). [LL. *consistorium*, place of assembly, < L. *consistere*: see *consist.*] A council-chamber†; also, an assembly or council; esp., any of various ecclesiastical councils or tribunals, as, in certain Reformed churches, a court corresponding to a session in Presbyterian churches, or, in the Roman Catholic Church, a senate, consisting of the whole body of the cardinals, usually presided over by the Pope, which deliberates upon the affairs of the church; also, the meeting of any such body; also, the place where it meets.—**con-sis-to-ri-al** (kon-sis-tō′ri-ạl), *a.*

con-so-ci-ate (kọn-sō′shi-āt), *v. t.* or *i.*; *-ated, -ating.* [L. *consociatus*, pp. of *consociare*, < *con-*, with, + *sociare*, join: see *sociable.*] To associate together; join in a consociation. —**con-so′ci-ate** (-ạt). **I.** *a.* Associated together; joined in a consociation. **II.** *n.* One associated with another or others; an associate; a companion.—**con-so-ci-a′tion** (-ṣi-ā′shọn), *n.* [L. *consociatio(n-).*] Intimate association of persons or things; fellowship; also, a confederation or union of churches, esp. Congregational churches.—**con-so-ci-a′tion-al,** *a.*—**con-so-ci-a′tion-ism,** *n.*

Architectural Console.

con-sol-a-ble (kọn-sō′lạ-bl), *a.* [L. *consolabilis.*] That may be consoled.

con-so-la-tion (kon-sọ-lā′shọn), *n.* [L. *consolatio(n-).*] The act of consoling, or the state of being consoled; also, one who or that which consoles.—**con-sol-a-to-ry** (kọn-sol′ạ-tọ-ri). **I.** *a.* Affording consolation; consoling. **II.**† *n.*; pl. *-ries* (-riz). A consoling speech or writing. See Milton's "Samson Agonistes," 657.

con-sole[1] (kon′sōl), *n.* [F.; origin uncertain.] An ornamental bracket-like architectural member, as for supporting a cornice, bust, or the like; any bracket or bracket-like support; also, a console-table; also, a desk-like structure containing the keyboards, etc., of an organ, esp. when separate from the body of the instrument.

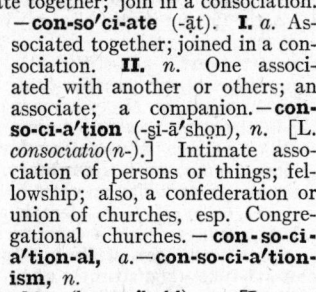

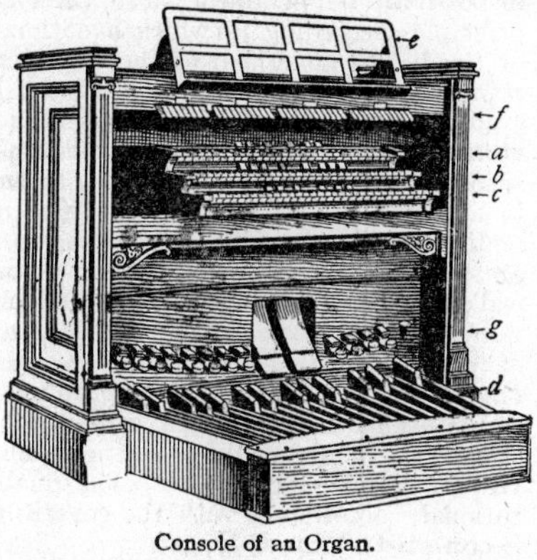

Console of an Organ.

a, b, c, manual keyboards; *d,* pedal keyboard; *e,* music-rack; *f,* tablets (in place of the older knobs) controlling stops and couplers; *g,* combination pedals, with two swell-pedals in the center.

con-sole[2] (kọn-sōl′), *v. t.*; *-soled, -soling.* [L. *consolari* (pp. *consolatus*), < *con-*, altogether, + *solari*, comfort.] To alleviate the grief or sorrow of; comfort; solace; cheer.—**con-sol′er** (-sō′lėr), *n.*

con-sole=ta-ble (kon′sōl-tā′bl), *n.* A table supported by consoles or brackets fixed to a wall; also, a table with curved console-like legs.

con-sol-i-date (kọn-sol′i-dāt), *v.*; *-dated, -dating.* [L. *consolidatus*, pp. of *consolidare*, < *con-*, with, + *solidare*, make solid, < *solidus*, E. *solid.*] **I.** *tr.* To make solid or firm; solidify; strengthen; also, to bring together compactly in one mass or connected whole; unite; combine. **II.** *intr.* To become solid or firm; also, to unite or combine.—**con-sol′i-date,** *a.* Consolidated. [Archaic.]—**con-sol-i-da′tion** (-dā′shọn), *n.* [LL. *consolidatio(n-).*] The act of consolidating, or the state of being consolidated; solidification; strengthening; unification; combination; also, a consolidated whole.—**con-sol′i-da-tor,** *n.*

con-sols (kọn-solz′ or kon′solz), *n. pl.* [Short for *consolidated annuities.*] The funded government securities of Great Britain, which originated in the consolidation in 1751 of various public securities, chiefly in the form of annuities, into a single stock.

con-som-mé (kon-sọ-mā′, F. kôṅ-so-mā), *n.* [F., prop. pp. of *consommer*, < L. *consummare*: see *consummate.*] A strong, clear soup made by boiling meat long and slowly, until all the nutritive properties are extracted.

con-so-nance (kon′sọ-nạns), *n.* The state of being consonant; correspondence of sounds; harmony of sounds; fig., accord or agreement; in *music*, a simultaneous combination of tones, as of a note and its fifth, that is agreeable to the ear; in *physics*, sympathetic vibration; resonance. Also **con′so-nan-cy.**

con-so-nant (kon′sọ-nạnt). [L. *consonans* (*-ant-*), ppr. of *consonare*, sound together, < *con-*, with, + *sonare*, sound.] **I.** *a.* Corresponding in sound, as words; harmonious, as sounds; fig., in agreement; agreeable or accordant (*to*); consistent (*with*); also, consonantal; in *music*, constituting a consonance; in *physics*, characterized by or pertaining to consonance. **II.** *n.* One of the closer speech-sounds which are combined with more open sounds, called *vowels*, to form syllables; an element of speech other than a vowel; also, a letter or character representing such a sound or element. Cf. *vowel.*—**con-so-nan′tal** (-nan′tạl), *a.* Of, pertaining to, or of the nature of a consonant; marked by consonant sounds.—**con′so-nant-ly,** *adv.*

con-sort (kon′sôrt), *n.* [L. *consors* (*consort-*), sharer, partner, orig. adj., sharing, < *con-*, with, + *sors*, lot. Some senses are appar. from *consort, v.*, and others due to confusion with *concert.*] A companion† or partner†; a husband or wife; a spouse; the mate of an animal; one vessel or ship accompanying another; also, a company† or assembly†; also, company or association (obs. or archaic: as, "He was cut off for ever from *consort* with the living," Wiseman's "Fabiola," ii. 18); also, accord† or agreement†; also, harmony of sounds†; a concert†; a number of musicians playing or singing together†.—**con-sort** (kọn-sôrt′), *v.* [Appar. < *consort, n.*] **I.** *tr.* To accompany†; espouse†; associate: sound in harmony†. **II.** *intr.* To associate; have intercourse; also, to agree or harmonize.

con-sor-ti-um (kọn-sôr′shi-um), *n.* [L., < *consors* (*consort-*), partner: see *consort.*] An association or union; specif., a combination of financial institutions, capitalists, etc., for the purpose of carrying into effect some financial operation requiring large resources of capital, as that formed in 1920 between groups of banks and bankers of the U. S., Great Britain, France, and Japan, with the approval of the four governments, to make loans to China for public purposes.

con-spe-cies (kon-spē′shēz), *n.*; pl. *-species.* [See *con-*.] A species of the same genus with other species; also, a subspecies or variety.—**con-spe-cif′ic** (-spẹ-sif′ik), *a.* Of the same species.

con-spec-tus (kọn-spek′tus), *n.* [L., < *conspicere*, view, survey, < *con-*, together, + *specere*, look at.] A general or comprehensive view; also, a digest; a résumé.

con-spic-u-ous (kọn-spik′ụ̄-us), *a.* [L. *conspicuus*, < *conspicere*: see *conspectus.*] Easy to be seen; clearly visible; catching the eye; also, readily attracting the attention; striking; noteworthy.—**con-spic′u-ous-ly,** *adv.*—**con-spic′u-ous-ness,** *n.*

con-spir-a-cy (kọn-spir′ạ-si), *n.*; pl. *-cies* (-siz). The act of conspiring; a combination of persons for an evil or unlawful purpose; a plot; also, any concurrence in action (archaic).

con-spir-ant (kọn-spīr′ạnt), *a.* Conspiring.

con-spi-ra-tion (kon-spi-rā′shọn), *n.* [L. *conspiratio(n-).*] The act of conspiring†; a conspiracy†; also, joint action or effort.

con-spir-a-tor (kọn-spir′ạ-tọr), *n.* [ML.] One who conspires; a joint plotter; esp., one who conspires with others to commit treason.—**con-spir-a-to′ri-al** (-tō′ri-ạl), *a.*—**con-spir′a-tress,** *n.* A female conspirator.

con-spire (kọn-spīr′), *v.*; *-spired, -spiring.* [OF. F. *conspirer*, < L. *conspirare* (pp. *conspiratus*), < *con-*, with, + *spirare*, breathe.] **I.** *intr.* To agree together, esp. secretly, to do something reprehensible or illegal; combine for an evil or unlawful purpose; plot; also, to act in combination; contribute jointly to a result. **II.** *tr.* To plot (something evil or unlawful).—**con-spir′er,** *n.*—**con-spir′ing-ly,** *adv.*

con-spue (kọn-spū′), *v. t.*; *-spued, -spuing.* [F. *conspuer*, < L. *conspuere*, < *con-*, with, + *spuere*, spit.] To spit upon in contempt; assail publicly with demonstrations of contempt. [A French use.]

con-sta-ble (kun′stạ-bl or kon′-), *n.* [OF. *conestable* (F. *connétable*), < LL. *comes stabuli*, 'count of the stable,' master of the horse.] An officer of high rank in medieval monarchies, orig. the head groom of the stable, later the chief officer of the household, court, army, or the like; the keeper or governor of a royal fortress or castle; a military officer†; now, esp., any of various officers of the peace, as one who executes the processes of a justice of the peace; in England, a policeman.—**con′sta-ble-ship,** *n.* The office of constable.—**con-stab-u-la-ry** (kọn-stab′ū-lā-ri). [ML. *constabularius* (as n., *constabularia*).] **I.** *a.* Of or pertaining to constables. **II.** *n.*; pl. *-ries* (-riz). A district under a constable; also, the body of constables of a district or locality; a body of officers of the peace organized on a military basis.

con-stan-cy (kon′stạn-si), *n.*; pl. *-cies* (-siz). The quality of being constant; firmness or fortitude; faithfulness to a person or cause; certainty†; invariableness, uniformity, or regularity; also, something permanent.

con-stant (kon′stạnt). [OF. F. *constant*, < L. *constans* (*constant-*), ppr. of *constare*, stand together, stand firm, < *con-*, with, + *stare*, stand.] **I.** *a.* Standing firm in mind or purpose; resolute; also, steadfast, as in attachment; faithful; also, certain† or confident†; also, invariable or unchanging; uniform; always present; also, continuing without intermission; regularly recurrent; continual; persistent; also, settled† or steady† (as, "Prithee, do not turn me about; my stomach is not *constant*": Shakspere's "Tempest," ii. 2. 119). **II.** *n.* Something constant, invariable, or unchanging; in *math.*, a quantity assumed to be invariable throughout a given discussion; in *physics*, a numerical quantity expressing a relation or value (as of a physical property of a substance) which remains unchanged under certain conditions.—**con′stant-ly,** *adv.*

con-state (kọn-stāt′), *v. t.*; *-stated, -stating.* [F. *constater*, < L. *constare*, stand firm (*constat*, it is established or certain): see *constant.*] To establish; authenticate; ascertain; prove.

con-stel-late (kon′ste-lāt), *v. t.* or *i.*; *-lated, -lating.* [See *constellation*, and cf. LL. *constellatus*, studded with stars.] To cluster together as stars in a constellation.

con-stel-la-tion (kon-ste-lā′shọn), *n.* [OF. *constellacion* (F. *constellation*), < LL. *constellatio(n-)*, < L. *con-*, together, + *stella*, star.] The grouping or relative position of the stars as supposed to influence events, esp. at the time of a person's birth; hence, character as supposed to be determined by the stars†; also, any of various groups of fixed stars to which definite names have been given, as Ursa Major, Ursa Minor, Boötes, Cancer, Orion, Canis Major, Canis Minor, etc.; a division of the heavens occupied by such a group; fig., any brilliant assemblage.—**con-stel-la-to-ry** (kọn-stel′ạ-tō-ri), *a.*

The Constellation Orion, pictured according to ancient descriptions. See *Orion.*

con-ster (kon′stėr), *v.* An old form of *construe.*

con-ster-na-tion (kon-stėr-nā′shọn), *n.* [L. *consternatio(n-)*, < *consternare*, prostrate, overcome, < *con-*, altogether, + *sternere*, spread out: see *stratum.*] Amazement and dread tending to confound the faculties and incapacitate for deliberate thought and action; paralyzing dismay.

con-sti-pate (kon′sti-pāt), *v. t.*; *-pated, -pating.* [L. *constipatus*, pp. of *constipare*, < *con-*, together, + *stipare*, crowd, pack.] To crowd or pack closely together†; thicken (liquids)†; constrict†; in *med.*, to cause constipation in; make costive.—**con-sti-pa′tion** (-pā′shọn), *n.* [LL. *constipatio(n-)*.] The act of constipating, or the state of being constipated; a condition of the bowels marked by defective or difficult evacuation.

con-stit-u-en-cy (kọn-stit′ū-ẹn-si), *n.*; pl. *-cies* (-siz). A body of constituents; the body of voters, or, loosely, of residents, in a district represented by an elective officer; also, the district itself; also, any body of supporters, customers, etc.; a clientele.

con-stit-u-ent (kọn-stit′ū-ẹnt). [L. *constituens* (*-ent-*), ppr. of *constituere*: see *constitute.*] **I.** *a.* That constitutes; that appoints or elects a representative (as, a *constituent* body); having power to frame or alter a political constitution (as, a *constituent* assembly); serving to make up a thing; component; elementary. **II.** *n.* One who constitutes or appoints another his agent or representative; a voter, or, loosely, a resident, in a district represented by an elective officer; also, a constituent element, material, etc.; a component.—**con-stit′u-ent-ly,** *adv.*

con-sti-tute (kon′sti-tūt), *v. t.*; *-tuted, -tuting.* [L. *constitutus*, pp. of *constituere*, < *con-*, together, + *statuere*, set up, set, establish: see *statute.*] To set† or place†; also, to appoint to an office or function; make or create (as, he was *constituted* captain); also, to set up or establish; found; give legal form to; also, to make up or form of elements, material, etc.; frame; of elements, etc., to compose; form.

con-sti-tu-tion (kon-sti-tū′shọn), *n.* [L. *constitutio(n-)*.] The act of constituting, or the state of being constituted; establishment; formation; also, a decree, law, or regulation, as one made by a superior civil or ecclesiastical authority; hence, any established arrangement or custom; also, the way in which anything is constituted; make-up or composition; esp., the physical character of the body as to strength, health, etc.; also, character or condition of mind; disposition; temperament; also, the system of fundamental principles according to which a nation, state, corporation, or the like is governed, or the document embodying these principles (as, the *Constitution* of the U. S.); hence, any system of fundamental principles of action.—**con-sti-tu′tion-al. I.** *a.* Pertaining to the constitution or composition of a thing; essential; also, belonging to or inherent in a person's constitution of body or mind; affecting the bodily constitution; also, pertaining to, in accordance with, or subject to the constitution of a state, etc. **II.** *n.* A walk or other exercise taken for the benefit of the constitution or health.—**con-sti-tu′tion-al-ism,** *n.* The principles of constitutional government, or adherence to them.—**con-sti-tu′tion-al-ist,** *n.* An adherent or advocate of constitutionalism, or of an existing constitution; also, a student of or writer on a political constitution.—**con-sti-tu-tion-al′i-ty** (-al′i-ti), *n.* The quality of being constitutional; accordance with the constitution of a state, etc.—**con-sti-tu′tion-al-ly,** *adv.*

con-sti-tu-tive (kon′sti-tū-tiv), *a.* Constituting, or capable of constituting; having power to establish or enact; instituting; making up or forming a thing; constituent; making a thing what it is; essential.—**con′sti-tu-tive-ly,** *adv.*

con-sti-tu-tor (kon′sti-tū-tọr), *n.* [L.] One who or that which constitutes.

con-strain (kọn-strān′), *v. t.* [OF. *constreindre, constraindre* (F. *contraindre*), < L. *constringere* (pp. *constrictus*), draw together, constrict, constrain, < *con-*, together, + *stringere*, draw tight.] To force, compel, or oblige; bring about by compulsion (as, to *constrain* obedience); also, to confine forcibly, as by bonds; hence, to repress or restrain; in *mech.*, to prevent the occurrence of (motion), or of motion in (a body), except in a particular manner or direction.—**con-strain′a-ble,** *a.* That may be constrained.—**con-strained′,** *p. a.* Forced; cramped; restrained; stiff or unnatural.—**con-strain′ed-ly,** *adv.*—**con-strain′er,** *n.*

con-straint (kọn-strānt′), *n.* [OF. *constrainte* (F. *contrainte*).] The act of constraining, or the condition of being constrained; compulsion; confinement or restriction; repression of natural feelings and impulses; unnatural restraint in manner, etc.; embarrassment; also, something that constrains (as, "Commands are no *constraints.* If I obey them, I do it freely": Milton's "Samson Agonistes," 1372).

con-strict (kon-strikt′), *v. t.* [L. *constrictus*, pp. of *constringere*: see *constrain*.] To draw together as by an encircling pressure; compress; cramp; also, to cause to contract or shrink.—**con-stric′tion** (-strik′shon), *n.* [L. *constrictio(n-)*.] The act of constricting, or the state of being constricted; compression; contraction; also, a constricted part; also, something that constricts.—**con-stric′tive,** *a.* Constricting, or tending to constrict; of or pertaining to constriction.—**con-stric′tor,** *n.* [NL.] One who or that which constricts; a serpent that crushes its prey in its coils; in *anat.*, a muscle that constricts or draws together a part or parts.

con-stringe (kon-strinj′), *v. t.*; *-stringed, -stringing.* [L. *constringere*: see *constrain*.] To constrict; compress; cause to contract.—**con-strin′gent** (-strin′jent), *a.* Constringing; causing constriction.—**con-strin′gen-cy,** *n.*

con-stru-a-ble (kon-strö′a-bl), *a.* That may be construed.

con-struct (kon-strukt′), *v. t.* [L. *constructus*, pp. of *construere*, pile or put together, construct, < *con-*, together, + *struere*, pile up, build, make: cf. *construe*.] To form by putting together parts; build; frame; devise; also, to construe†; in *geom.*, etc., to draw, as a figure, so as to fulfil given conditions.—**con-struct′i-ble,** *a.* That may be constructed.

con-struc-tion (kon-struk′shon), *n.* [L. *constructio(n-)*, < *construere*: see *construct* and *construe*.] The act or art of constructing; the way in which a thing is constructed; structure; that which is constructed; a structure; also, the act or manner of construing; the arrangement and connection of words in a sentence according to established usages; syntactical connection; also, explanation or interpretation, as of a law or a text, or of conduct or the like; a particular explanation or interpretation (as, "Religion . . . produces good-will towards men, and puts the mildest *construction* upon every accident that befalls them": Addison, in "Spectator," 483).—**con-struc′tion-al,** *a.* Of or pertaining to construction.—**con-struc′tion-al-ly,** *adv.*—**con-struc′tion-ist,** *n.* One who construes or interprets, esp. laws or the like.

con-struc-tive (kon-struk′tiv), *a.* [ML. *constructivus*.] Constructing, or tending to construct; also, of, pertaining to, or of the nature of construction; structural; also, deduced by construction or interpretation; inferential; virtual.—**con-struc′tive-ly,** *adv.*—**con-struc′tive-ness,** *n.*

con-struc-tor (kon-struk′tor), *n.* [ML.] One who constructs; a builder: as, a naval *constructor* (one of a corps of naval officers charged with the construction and repair of war-ships).—**con-struc′tor-ship,** *n.*

con-strue (kon′strö or kon-strö′), *v.*; *-strued, -struing.* [L. *construere*: see *construct*.] **I.** *tr.* To construct†; also, to arrange or combine (words, etc.) syntactically; also, to analyze the grammatical construction of (a sentence, passage, etc.), esp. in the study of a foreign language; hence, to translate, esp. orally; also, to show the meaning or intention of; explain; interpret; put a particular interpretation on; also, to deduce by construction or interpretation; infer. **II.** *intr.* To admit of grammatical analysis or interpretation.—**con′strue,** *n.* A construing of a sentence, passage, etc., esp. in the study of a foreign language; the resulting analysis, translation, or the like.—**con′stru-er,** *n.*

con-sub-stan-tial (kon-sub-stan′shal), *a.* [LL. *consubstantialis*, < L. *con-*, with, + *substantia*, substance.] Of one and the same substance, essence, or nature.—**con-sub-stan-ti-al′i-ty** (-shi-al′i-ti), *n.*—**con-sub-stan′tial-ly,** *adv.*

con-sub-stan-ti-ate (kon-sub-stan′shi-āt), *v.*; *-ated, -ating.* [NL. *consubstantiatus*, pp. of *consubstantiare*, < L. *con-*, with, + *substantia*, substance.] **I.** *tr.* To unite in one common substance or nature, or regard as so united. **II.** *intr.* To become united in one common substance or nature; also, to profess the doctrine of consubstantiation.—**con-sub-stan-ti-a′tion** (-ā′shon), *n.* [NL. *consubstantiatio(n-)*.] A consubstantiating; in *theol.*, the substantial union of the body and blood of Christ with the eucharistic elements after consecration. Cf. *impanation* and *transubstantiation.*

con-sue-tude (kon′swē-tūd), *n.* [L. *consuetudo (consuetudin-)*, < *consuescere* (pp. *consuetus*), accustom, < *con-*, with, + *suescere*, become used, accustom: cf. *custom*.] Custom, esp. as having legal force; usage; also, familiarity; social intercourse.—**con-sue-tu′di-na-ry** (-tū′di-nā-ri), *a.* Customary.

con-sul (kon′sul), *n.* [L., prob. < *consulere*, deliberate: see *consult*.] Either of the two chief magistrates of the ancient Roman republic; one of the three supreme magistrates of the French republic from 1799 to 1804; also, a councilor†; also, an agent appointed by a sovereign state to reside in a foreign city or town and care for the commercial and other interests there of citizens of that state.—**con′sul,** *v. t.*; *-suled, -suling.* In *com.*, to submit to a consul for examination and certification, as an invoice.—**con′su-lar** (-sū-lär), *a.* [L. *consularis*.] Of, pertaining to, or serving as a consul.—**consular agent,** an officer performing the duties of a consul at a place of small commercial importance.—**con′su-late** (-lāt), *n.* [L. *consulatus*.] A government by consuls, as in ancient Rome, or in France from 1799 to 1804; also, the office or position of a consul; also, the premises officially occupied by a (commercial) consul.—**con′sul=gen′er-al,** *n.*; pl. *consuls-*. A consular officer of the highest rank, as one stationed at a place of commercial importance.—**con′sul-ship,** *n.* The office or term of office of a consul.

con-sult (kon-sult′), *v.* [L. *consultare*, freq. of *consulere*, deliberate, take counsel: cf. L. *consilium*, E. *counsel*, *n.*] **I.** *tr.* To consider (a matter)†; also, to meditate†, plan†, or contrive†; also, to have regard for (a person's interest, convenience, etc.) in making plans; also, to seek counsel from; ask advice of; refer to (a book, etc.) for information. **II.** *intr.* To consider or deliberate; take counsel; confer (*with*).—**con-sult** (kon-sult′ or kon′sult), *n.* The act of consulting; a consultation; a council; a cabal. [Now rare.]—**con-sult′a-ble,** *a.* That may be consulted.—**con-sult′ant,** *n.* One who consults; also, one who gives professional advice, as a consulting physician.—**con-sul-ta-tion** (kon-sul-tā′shon), *n.* [L. *consultatio(n-)*.] The act of consulting; conference; a meeting for deliberation or conference.—**con-sul-ta-tive** (kon-sul′ta-tiv), *a.* Of or pertaining to consultation; advisory. Also **con-sul′ta-to-ry** (-tō-ri).—**con-sult′er,** *n.*—**con-sult′ing,** *p. a.* That consults, or asks advice; also, employed in giving professional advice, either to the public or to those practising the profession.

con-sum-a-ble (kon-sū′ma-bl), *a.* Capable of being consumed.

con-sume (kon-sūm′), *v.*; *-sumed, -suming.* [L. *consumere* (pp. *consumptus*), < *con-*, altogether, + *sumere*, take, use, spend.] **I.** *tr.* To destroy, as by decomposition or burning; also, to destroy or expend by use; use up; often, to spend (money, time, etc.) wastefully; waste; squander; also, to make away with (food, etc.); eat or drink up; devour. **II.** *intr.* To be consumed; suffer destruction; waste away.—**con-sum′ed-ly** (-sū′med-li), *adv.* Excessively; extremely; greatly; heartily: as, "I believe they talk'd of me, for they laugh'd *consumedly*" (Farquhar's "Beaux' Stratagem," iii. 1).—**con-sum′er,** *n.* One who or that which consumes; in *polit. econ.*, one who uses up a commodity and thus destroys its exchangeable value (opposed to *producer*).—**con-sum′ing-ly,** *adv.*

con-sum-mate (kon′su-māt or kon-sum′āt), *v. t.*; *-mated, -mating.* [L. *consummatus*, pp. of *consummare*, < *con-*, altogether, + *summa*, top, culmination, completion, E. *sum*.] To bring to completion; complete; perfect; fulfil; specif., to complete (a marriage) by sexual intercourse.—**con-sum-mate** (kon-sum′āt or kon′su-māt), *a.* Complete or perfect; supremely qualified; of the highest quality.—**con-sum′mate-ly,** *adv.*—**con-sum-ma-tion** (kon-su-mā′shon), *n.* [L. *consummatio(n-)*.] The act of consummating, or the state of being consummated; completion; perfection; fulfilment.—**con′sum-ma-tive** (-mā-tiv), *a.* Serving to consummate.—**con′sum-ma-tor** (-mā-tor), *n.*

con-sump-tion (kon-sump′shon), *n.* [L. *consumptio(n-)*, < *consumere*: see *consume*.] The act of consuming, or the state of being consumed; destruction; decay; destruction by use; in *pathol.*, progressive wasting of the body, esp. from tuberculosis of the lungs; a wasting disease, esp. tuberculosis of the lungs; in *polit. econ.*, the using up of articles having an exchangeable value.—**con-sump′tive.**

I. *a.* Tending to consume; destructive; wasteful; also, pertaining to consumption by use; in *pathol.*, pertaining to or of the nature of consumption; disposed to or affected with consumption. **II.** *n.* One who suffers from consumption.—**con-sump'tive-ly,** *adv.*—**con-sump'tive-ness,** *n.*

con-tact (kon'takt), *n.* [L. *contactus*, < *contingere*, touch: see *contingent*.] The state or fact of touching; a touching or meeting of bodies; immediate proximity or association; in *elect.*, a connection or junction between two conductors which allows the flow of a current; a device or part for producing such a connection; in *med.*, one who has lately been in close proximity to a person found to be infected with a contagious disease.—**con'tact,** *v.* **I.** *tr.* To put or bring into contact. **II.** *intr.* To enter into or be in contact.—**con'tact=break"er,** *n.* A contrivance for automatically breaking, or breaking and making, an electrical circuit.—**con-tac-tu-al** (kọn-tak'ṭū-ạl), *a.* Pertaining to or involving contact.—**con-tac'tu-al-ly,** *adv.*

con-ta-di-na (kon-tä-dē'nä), *n.*; pl. *-nas* (-näz), It. *-ne* (-nā). [It., fem. of *contadino*.] In Italian use, a peasant woman or girl.—**con-ta-di'no** (-nō), *n.*; pl. *-nos* (-nōz), It. *-ni* (-nē). [It., < *contado*, country, county, = E. *county*².] In Italian use, a peasant or countryman.

con-ta-gion (kọn-tā'jọn), *n.* [L. *contagio(n-)*, < *contingere*, touch: see *contingent*.] The communication of disease by direct or indirect contact (cf. *infection*); a disease so communicated; the medium by which a contagious disease is transmitted; fig., pestilential influence; hurtful contact or influence; moral corruption; also, the communication of any influence, as enthusiasm, from one to another.—**con-ta'gious** (-jus), *a.* [LL. *contagiosus*.] Causing or involving contagion; noxious; also, communicable by contagion, as a disease; fig., tending to spread from one to another; communicable.—**con-ta'gious-ly,** *adv.*—**con-ta'gious-ness,** *n.*—**con-ta'gi-um** (-ji-um), *n.*; pl. *-gia* (-ji-ạ̈). [L.] The medium, or morbific matter, by which a contagious disease is communicated.

con-tain (kọn-tān'), *v.* [OF. F. *contenir*, < L. *continere* (pp. *contentus*), hold together, hold, hold back, restrain, < *con-*, together, + *tenere*, hold.] **I.** *tr.* To have within itself; hold within fixed limits; also, to be capable of holding; have capacity for; also, to be equal to (as, a quart *contains* two pints); also, to have as contents or constituent parts; comprise; include; also, to keep within proper bounds; restrain, as one's self or one's feelings or passions; also, to retain†; in *math.*, to be divisible by, esp. without a remainder. **II.** *intr.* To restrain one's self or one's feelings, passions, etc.—**con-tain'a-ble,** *a.* That may be contained. —**con-tain'er,** *n.* One who or that which contains; often a vessel, receptacle, or other containing or inclosing structure.

con-tam-i-nate (kọn-tam'i-nāt), *v. t.*; *-nated, -nating.* [L. *contaminatus*, pp. of *contaminare*, ult. < *con-*, with, + *tangere*, touch.] To render impure by contact or mixture; defile; pollute; taint; corrupt.—**con-tam'i-nate,** *a.* Contaminated. [Archaic.]—**con-tam-i-na'tion** (-nā'shọn), *n.* [LL. *contaminatio(n-)*.] The act of contaminating, or the state of being contaminated; also, something that contaminates.—**con-tam'i-na-tive** (-nạ̄-tiv), *a.* Causing or involving contamination.—**con-tam'i-na-tor** (-nā-tọr), *n.*

con-tan-go (kọn-tang'gō), *n.*; pl. *-goes* (-gōz). [Origin obscure.] A premium paid by a buyer of stock to the seller to postpone its delivery. Cf. *backwardation*. [Eng.]

con-te¹ (kōn'tā), *n.*; pl. *-ti* (-tē). [It., = E. *count*¹.] In Italian use, a count.

conte² (kônt), *n.*; pl. *contes* (kônt). [F., = E. *count*², *n.*] A tale or short story, esp. of extraordinary and usually imaginary events.

con-temn (kọn-tem'), *v. t.* [L. *contemnere* (pp. *contemptus*), < *con-*, altogether, + *temnere*, despise.] To treat disdainfully or scornfully; view with contempt; despise; scorn; slight; disregard contemptuously (as, "They . . . *contemned* the counsel of the most High": Ps. cvii. 11).—**con-tem'ner** (-tem'nėr or -tem'ėr), *n.*

con-tem-per (kọn-tem'pėr), *v. t.* [L. *contemperare*, < *con-*, with, + *temperare*, E. *temper*.] To temper; blend; modify; adjust. [Now rare.]

con-tem-plate (kon'tem-plāt or kọn-tem'plāt), *v.*; *-plated, -plating.* [L. *contemplatus*, pp. of *contemplari*, < *con-*, with, + *templum*, open space for augurial observations, E. *temple*³.] **I.** *tr.* To look at or view with continued attention; observe thoughtfully; hence, to consider attentively; reflect upon; also, to consider in a certain aspect; regard; also, to have in view as a future event; also, to have in view as a purpose; intend; also, to have reference to. **II.** *intr.* To think studiously; meditate; consider deliberately.—**con-tem-pla-tion** (kon-tem-plā'shọn), *n.* [L. *contemplatio(n-)*.] The act of contemplating; thoughtful observation; attentive consideration; musing; reflection; religious meditation; matter for reflection or meditation; regard or view (as, an artificial person existing only in *contemplation* of law); prospect or expectation (as, to act in *contemplation* of probable changes); purpose or intention (as, projects in *contemplation*).—**con-tem-pla-tive** (kọn-tem'plạ̄-tiv). [L. *contemplativus*.] **I.** *a.* Given to or characterized by contemplation; thoughtful; reflective; meditative; often, given to contemplation as opposed to action. **II.** *n.* One given to contemplation.—**con-tem'pla-tive-ly,** *adv.*—**con-tem'pla-tive-ness,** *n.*—**con'tem-pla-tor** (-plā-tọr), *n.*

con-tem-po-ra-ne-ous (kọn-tem-pọ̄-rā'nẹ̄-us), *a.* [L. *contemporaneus*, < *con-*, with, + *tempus* (*tempor-*), time.] Belonging to the same time or period; contemporary.—**con-tem"po-ra-ne'i-ty** (-rạ̄-nē'i-ti), **con-tem-po-ra'ne-ous-ness,** *n.*—**con-tem-po-ra'ne-ous-ly,** *adv.*

con-tem-po-ra-ry (kọn-tem'pọ̄-rạ̄-ri). [L. *con-*, with, + *tempus* (*tempor-*), time.] **I.** *a.* Belonging to the same time; existing or occurring at the same time; also, of the same age or date. **II.** *n.*; pl. *-ries* (-riz). One belonging to the same time or period with another or others; also, a person of the same age as another.—**con-tem'po-ra-ri-ness,** *n.*

con-tem-po-rize (kọn-tem'pọ̄-rīz), *v. t.*; *-rized, -rizing.* [L. *con-*, with, + *tempus* (*tempor-*), time.] To make contemporary; place in, or regard as belonging to, the same age or time.

con-tempt (kọn-tempt'), *n.* [L. *contemptus*, < *contemnere*: see *contemn*.] The act of contemning or despising; the feeling with which one regards anything considered mean, vile, or worthless; disdain; scorn; also, the state of being despised; dishonor; disgrace; in *law*, disobedience to, or open disrespect of, the rules or orders of a court, legislature, or the like.—**con-temp'ti-ble.** [LL. *contemptibilis*, < L. *contemnere*.] **I.** *a.* Deserving of or held in contempt; despicable; mean; paltry or worthless; also, contemptuous†. **II.** *n.* A contemptible person or thing; [*cap.*] a soldier of the "contemptible little army" (as it is said to have been called by Kaiser William II. of Germany in demanding its destruction) sent by Great Britain to France and Belgium in 1914 to aid in opposing the German advance (usually in *pl.*: humorous).—**con-temp'ti-ble-ness,** *n.*—**con-temp'ti-bly,** *adv.*—**con-temp'tu-ous** (-ṭū-us), *a.* Manifesting or expressing contempt; disdainful; scornful; insolent; also, contemptible†.—**con-temp'tu-ous-ly,** *adv.*—**con-temp'tu-ous-ness,** *n.*

con-tend (kọn-tend'), *v.* [L. *contendere* (pp. *contentus*), < *con-*, with, + *tendere*, stretch, strive, E. *tend*¹.] **I.** *intr.* To make vigorous efforts†; also, to struggle in opposition; also, to strive in rivalry; compete; vie; also, to strive in debate; dispute earnestly; argue. **II.** *tr.* To contend for†; also, to assert or maintain earnestly.—**con-tend'er,** *n.*

con-tent¹ (kon'tent or kọn-tent'), *n.* [L. *contentus*, pp. of *continere*: see *contain*.] That which is contained, as in a cask, room, or book (usually in *pl.*); also, substance or purport, as of a document; also, the sum of the attributes or notions composing a given conception; the substance or matter of cognition, etc.; also, power of containing; capacity; volume; area; extent; size.

con-tent² (kọn-tent'), *a.* [OF. F. *content*, < L. *contentus*, satisfied, prop. pp. of *continere*: see *contain*.] Having the desires limited by what one has; satisfied, as with something specified; easy in mind; also, willing or resigned; assenting. —**con-tent'**², *v. t.* [OF. F. *contenter*, < ML. *contentare*, < L. *contentus*.] To make content; satisfy; also, to remunerate†.—**con-tent'**², *n.* The state or feeling of being contented; contentment; also, in the British House of

Lords, an affirmative vote or voter.—**con-tent'ed,** *a.* Satisfied, as with what one has or with something mentioned; content; resigned; marked by contentment.—**con-tent'ed-ly,** *adv.*—**con-tent'ed-ness,** *n.*

con-ten-tion (kọn-ten'shọn), *n.* [L. *contentio(n-)*, < *contendere*: see *contend.*] The act of contending; vigorous effort (obs. or archaic); a struggling together in opposition; strife; a quarrel; a striving in rivalry; competition; a contest; strife in debate; a dispute; a controversy; a point contended for or affirmed in controversy.—**con-ten'tious** (-shus), *a.* [L. *contentiosus.*] Given to or characterized by contention (as, "As coals are to burning coals . . . so is a *contentious* man to kindle strife": Prov. xxvi. 21); dissentious; in *law*, pertaining to causes between contending parties.—**con-ten'tious-ly,** *adv.*—**con-ten'tious-ness,** *n.*

con-tent-ment (kọn-tent'mẹnt), *n.* The act of contenting, or the state of being contented; satisfaction, as with actual conditions; ease of mind due to freedom from ambitious or harassing desires.

con-tents (kon'tents or kọn-tents'), *n. pl.* See *content*[1].

con-ter-mi-nal (kon-tėr'mi-nạl), *a.* Conterminous; in *entom.*, attached end to end, as parts of a jointed organ.

con-ter-mi-nous (kon-tėr'mi-nus), *a.* [L. *conterminus*, < *con-*, with, + *terminus*, boundary.] Having a common boundary; bordering; contiguous; meeting at their ends; also, having the same boundaries or limits; coextensive.—**con-ter'mi-nous-ly,** *adv.*—**con-ter'mi-nous-ness,** *n.*

con-tes-sa (kōn-tes'sä), *n.*; pl. *-se* (-sā). [It., fem. of *conte*: see *conte*[1].] In Italian use, a countess.

con-test (kọn-test'), *v.* [OF. F. *contester*, < L. *contestari*, call to witness, bring a legal action, < *con-*, with, + *testari*, bear witness, < *testis*, a witness.] **I.** *tr.* To call to witness†; also, to call in question; argue against; dispute; also, to struggle or fight for, as in battle; contend for in rivalry. **II.** *intr.* To bear witness†; also, to dispute; contend; compete.—**con-test** (kon'test), *n.* Strife in argument; dispute; controversy; also, struggle for victory; a conflict; also, conflict between competitors; a competition.—**con-test'a-ble,** *a.* That may be contested.—**con-test'ant,** *n.* One who contests.—**con-tes-ta-tion** (kon-tes-tā'shọn), *n.* [L. *contestatio(n-)*.] The act of contesting; disputation or controversy; conflict; competition; also, an assertion contended for; a contention.—**con-test'er,** *n.*

con-text (kon'tekst), *n.* [L. *contextus*, < *contexere*, weave together, < *con-*, with, + *texere*, weave.] The entire connected structure of a discourse or writing†; the parts of a discourse or writing which precede or follow, and are directly connected with, a given passage or word.—**con-tex-tu-al** (kọn-teks'ṭū-ạl), *a.* Of or pertaining to the context; depending on the context.—**con-tex'tu-al-ly,** *adv.*

con-tex-ture (kọn-teks'ṭūr), *n.* [F. *contexture*, < L. *contexere*: see *context.*] The act of weaving together; the fact or manner of being woven together; hence, the disposition and union of the constituent parts of anything; constitution; structure; also, an interwoven structure; a fabric; also, context.

con-tig-na-tion (kon-tig-nā'shọn), *n.* [L. *contignatio(n-)*, < *contignare*, join with beams, < *con-*, with, + *tignum*, beam.] The act of joining together beams. boards, etc.; the manner of their being joined; also, a frame, as of boards; a framework; a floor or stage. [Archaic.]

con-ti-gu-i-ty (kon-ti-gū'i-ti), *n.* The state of being contiguous; also, a series of things in continuous connection; a continuous mass or extent (as, "some boundless *contiguity* of shade": Cowper's "Task," ii. 2).

con-tig-u-ous (kọn-tig'ū-us), *a.* [L. *contiguus*, < *contingere*, touch, border on: see *contingent.*] Touching; being in contact; adjoining; immediately successive; also, being in close proximity without actually touching; near.—**con-tig'u-ous-ly,** *adv.*—**con-tig'u-ous-ness,** *n.*

con-ti-nence (kon'ti-nẹns), *n.* [L. *continentia*, < *continens*, ppr.: see *continent*[1].] Self-restraint, esp. in regard to the sexual passion. Also **con'ti-nen-cy.**

con-ti-nent[1] (kon'ti-nẹnt), *a.* [L. *continens* (*-ent-*), ppr. of *continere*, hold back, restrain: see *contain*, and cf. *continent*[2], from the same L. word in other senses.] Exercising restraint in relation to the desires or passions; temperate; esp., characterized by self-restraint in regard to the sexual passion; also, restraining† or restrictive†.

con-ti-nent[2] (kon'ti-nẹnt). [L. *continens* (*-ent-*), holding together, continuous, also holding or containing, ppr. of *continere*: see *contain*, also *continent*[1].] **I.** *a.* Continuous†; forming a continuous tract, as land†; also, containing; being a container; capacious. **II.** *n.* A continuous tract or extent, as of land; land as opposed to water, etc.†; the mainland, as distinguished from islands or peninsulas; [*cap.*] with *the*, the mainland of Europe, as distinguished from the British Isles; [*l. c.*] one of the main land-masses of the globe, sometimes reckoned as two in number (the Old World and the New World), but usually as five or six (Europe, Asia, Africa, North America, and South America, and sometimes Australia); [*cap.*] with *the*, the American colonies collectively during and immediately after the Revolutionary War†; also [*l. c.*], that which contains, holds, or comprises (archaic).—**con-ti-nen'tal** (-nen'tạl). **I.** *a.* Of, pertaining to, or of the nature of a continent; [usually *cap.*] of or pertaining to the mainland of Europe; [*cap.*] in *Amer. hist.*, of or pertaining to the colonies during and immediately after the Revolutionary War (as, the *Continental* Congress). **II.** *n.* An inhabitant of a continent, esp. [usually *cap.*] of the mainland of Europe; in *Amer. hist.*, [*cap.*] a soldier of the Continental army in the Revolutionary War; [usually *l. c.*] a piece of paper money issued by the Continental Congress during the war (as, not worth a *continental*); *pl.*, the uniform of the Continental army.—**con-ti-nen'tal-ly,** *adv.*

con-ti-nent-ly (kon'ti-nẹnt-li), *adv.* In a continent manner; temperately.

con-tin-gence (kọn-tin'jẹns), *n.* The state of being contingent; touching, contact, or tangency; chance or contingency.—**con-tin'gen-cy** (-jẹn-si), *n.*; pl. *-cies* (-siz). The state or character of being contingent; fortuitousness; uncertainty; dependence on chance, on the will of a free agent, or on the fulfilment of some condition; also, a contingent event; a chance or accident; a possibility; a thing contingent or conditional on something uncertain; also, a matter of uncertainty on which something is contingent; also, something incidental to a thing.

con-tin-gent (kọn-tin'jẹnt). [L. *contingens* (*-ent-*), ppr. of *contingere*, touch, border on, reach, befall, happen, < *con-*, with, + *tangere*, touch.] **I.** *a.* Touching or meeting, as tangent or intersecting lines; also, happening by chance or without known cause; fortuitous; accidental; also, liable to happen or not; uncertain; possible; sometimes, dependent on the will of a free agent; hence, dependent for existence, occurrence, character, etc., on something not yet certain (often with *on* or *upon*); provisionally liable to exist, occur, take effect, etc.; conditional. **II.** *n.* Something contingent; a contingency; also, the proportion that falls to one in a division, as a share to be contributed or furnished; esp., a quota of troops furnished (as, "It was necessary that Oubacha should contribute his usual *contingent* of martial aid": De Quincey's "Revolt of the Tartars"); hence, any one of the representative groups composing an assemblage (as, the New York *contingent* at a national convention).—**con-tin'gent-ly,** *adv.*—**con-tin'gent-ness,** *n.*

con-tin-u-a-ble (kọn-tin'ū-ạ-bl), *a.* Capable of being continued.

con-tin-u-al (kọn-tin'ū-ạl), *a.* [OF. F. *continuel*, < L. *continuus*: see *continuous.*] Proceeding without interruption or cessation; continuous in time; unceasing; also, of regular or frequent recurrence; often repeated; very frequent.—**con-tin'u-al-ly,** *adv.*—**con-tin'u-al-ness,** *n.*

con-tin-u-ance (kọn-tin'ū-ạns), *n.* [OF. *continuance*, < *continuer*, E. *continue.*] The act or fact of continuing; continuation; duration; also, a continuation or sequel; in *law*, adjournment, as of a trial or suit, to a future day.

con-tin-u-ant (kọn-tin'ū-ạnt), *n.* [L. *continuans* (*-ant-*), ppr.] In *phonetics*, a consonant, such as *f*, *v*, etc., which may be prolonged in utterance, as distinguished from a 'stop,' as *p*, *b*, etc., which involves a complete closure of the vocal organs.

con-tin-u-ate† (kọn-tin'ū-ạt), *a.* [L. *continuatus*, pp.] Continued; continuous; uninterrupted; lasting.

con-tin-u-a-tion (kǫn-tin-ū̦-ā'shǫn), *n.* [L. *continuatio(n-).*] The act or fact of continuing; the state of being continued; also, that by which anything is continued; a sequel, as to a story; *pl.*, gaiters or trousers (slang).—**continuation school,** a school in which instruction (special or general) is given in continuation or extension of that given in the lower schools, for the benefit of those who have left school while in the lower grades in order to engage in some occupation.

con-tin-u-a-tive (kǫn-tin'ū̦-ā̦-tiv). [LL. *continuativus.*] **I.** *a.* Tending or serving to continue, or to cause continuation or prolongation; in *gram.*, expressing continuance of thought. **II.** *n.* Something continuative; in *gram.*, a continuative word or expression.—**con-tin'u-a-tive-ly,** *adv.* —**con-tin'u-a-tive-ness,** *n.*

con-tin-u-a-tor (kǫn-tin'ū̦-ā-tǫr), *n.* [NL.] One who or that which continues something; esp., one who carries forward a literary work begun by another.

con-tin-ue (kǫn-tin'ū̦), *v.*; *-ued, -uing.* [OF. F. *continuer,* < L. *continuare* (pp. *continuatus*), < *continuus*: see *continuous.*] **I.** *tr.* To make continuous†, connect†, or unite†; also, to extend from one point to another in space; prolong; also, to cause to last or endure; maintain or retain, as in a position; go on with or persist in (an action, etc.); also, to carry on from the point of suspension or interruption, as a narrative; say in continuation (as, "When she made no answer . . . he *continued*: 'But you must not misunderstand us' ": Wister's "Virginian," xxxiii.); also, to carry on by means of a successor or successors; also, to carry over, postpone, or adjourn, as a legal proceeding. **II.** *intr.* To go forward or onward in any course or action; keep on; also, to go on after suspension or interruption; also, to last or endure; also, to remain in a place; abide; stay; also, to remain in a particular state or capacity.—**con-tin'u-er** (-ū̦-ėr), *n.*

con-ti-nu-i-ty (kon-ti-nū'i-ti), *n.*; pl. *-ties* (-tiz). The state or quality of being continuous; also, a continuous or connected whole; specif., a moving-picture scenario written in such a form as to give the complete action, scenes, etc., in detail and in the order in which they are to be shown on the screen.

con-tin-u-ous (kǫn-tin'ū̦-us), *a.* [L. *continuus,* < *continere,* hold together: see *contain.*] Holding together without break or interruption; uninterrupted in substance; having the parts in immediate connection; also, uninterrupted in time, sequence, existence, or action; without cessation.—**continuous waves,** in *wireless teleg.* and *teleph.*, electric waves which are not intermittent or broken up into damped wave-trains, but (unless intentionally interrupted) follow one another without any interval of time between: characterized by being of constant amplitude or intensity when not modified by telephonic means or the like, and distinguished from *damped waves,* which are transmitted in damped wave-trains (groups of waves) with intervals of time between.—**con-tin'u-ous-ly,** *adv.*—**con-tin'u-ous-ness,** *n.*

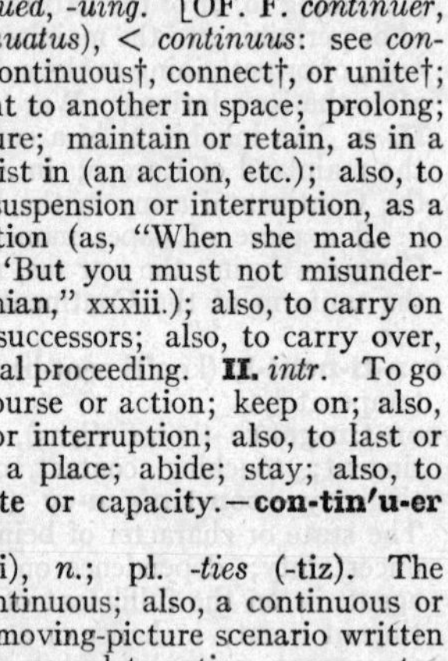

Obverse.

Reverse.
Contorniate with head of Trajan.—British Museum.

con-tin-u-um (kǫn-tin'ū̦-um), *n.*; pl. *-ua* (-ū̦-ā̦). [L., neut. of *continuus,* E. *continuous.*] A continuous extent, series, or whole.

con-tor-ni-ate (kǫn-tôr'ni-āt). [= F. *contorniate,* < It. *contorniato,* < *contorno,* contour, outline.] In *numis.*: **I.** *a.* Having a bordering furrow within the edge, as a class of Roman medals or coin-like pieces. **II.** *n.* One of a class of Roman medals or circular coin-like pieces of copper or bronze having a furrow on each side within the edge, and bearing on one side a head and on the other devices relating to the public games or spectacles, in connection with which these pieces are supposed to have been issued, probably first in the 4th century.

con-tort (kǫn-tôrt'), *v. t.* [L. *contortus,* pp. of *contorquere,* < *con-*, together, + *torquere,* twist.] To twist; twist, bend, or draw out of shape; distort.—**con-tor'tion** (-tôr'shǫn), *n.* [L. *contortio(n-).*] The act of contorting, or the state of being contorted; a writhing, esp. spasmodically; distortion; also, a distorted form.—**con-tor'tion-ist,** *n.* One who practises contortion; esp., one who performs gymnastic feats involving contorted postures.—**con-tor'tive,** *a.* Tending to or characterized by contortion.

con-tour (kon'tör or kon-tör'), *n.* [F. *contour,* < *contourner,* fix or mark the contour of, < L. *con-*, altogether, + *tornare,* turn, round off.] The outline of a figure or body; the line that defines or bounds anything; also, a contour-line.—**con-tour',** *v. t.* To make or form the contour or outline of; also, to mark with contour-lines; also, to build (a road, etc.) in conformity to a contour.—**con'tour=feath"er,** *n.* Any of the feathers which form the surface-plumage of a bird and determine the contour of the body. —**con'tour=line,** *n.* In *surv.*, a line carried along the surface of a region at a uniform height above sea-level; the representation of such a line on a map.

contra-. [L., repr. *contra,* adv. and prep.: cf. *counter-.*] A prefix of Latin origin, meaning 'in opposition,' 'against,' sometimes used as an English formative, as in *contradistinction, contraindicant, contranatural, contra-Scriptural.*

con-tra-band (kon'trā̦-band). [It. *contrabbando* or Sp. *contrabando,* < L. *contra,* against, + ML. *bandum, bannum,* proclamation, E. *ban*[1], *n.*] **I.** *n.* Illegal or prohibited traffic; smuggling; also, anything prohibited by law to be imported or exported; goods imported or exported contrary to law or proclamation; specif., goods which, by international law, subjects of neutral states cannot supply to one belligerent in time of war except at the risk of seizure and confiscation by the other ('contraband of war'); also, in the U. S., during the Civil War, a negro slave who escaped to or was brought within the Union lines. **II.** *a.* Prohibited by law, proclamation, or treaty, to be imported or exported; fig., forbidden; unauthorized.—**con'tra-band-age** (-bandā̦j), **con'tra-band-ism,** *n.* Trafficking in contraband goods; smuggling.—**con'tra-band-ist,** *n.*

con-tra-bass (kon'trā̦-bās), *n.* [It. *contrabbasso,* < *contra,* against, counter to, + *basso,* bass.] The lowest bass voice or instrument; esp., the instrument of the viol kind known as the double-bass. Also **con-tra-bas'so** (-bȧs'ō).—**con'tra-bass-ist,** *n.* A player on the contrabass or double-bass.

con-tra-cep-tion (kon-trā̦-sep'shǫn), *n.* [From *contra-* + *(con)ception.*] The prevention of conception or impregnation, by deliberate measures, in order to prevent childbirth. Cf. *birth-control.*—**con-tra-cep'tive** (-tiv). **I.** *a.* Tending or serving to prevent conception or impregnation; pertaining to contraception. **II.** *n.* A contraceptive agent or device.

con-tra=clock-wise (kon'trā̦-klok"wīz), *adv.* and *a.* Same as *counter-clockwise.*

con-tract (kǫn-trakt'), *v.* [L. *contractus,* pp. of *contrahere,* < *con-*, together, + *trahere,* draw.] **I.** *tr.* To draw together or into smaller compass; draw the parts of together; wrinkle; also, to shorten or narrow as by drawing together; lessen; condense; abridge; specif., to shorten (a word, etc.) by combining or omitting some of its elements; also, to settle or establish (an alliance, etc.) by agreement; hence, to betroth or affiance; also, to enter into (a relation, as of friendship); acquire, as by habit or contagion; incur, as a liability or obligation. **II.** *intr.* To be drawn together or reduced in compass; become smaller; shrink; also, to enter into an agreement.—**con-tract** (kon'trakt), *n.* [L. *contractus,* n., < *contrahere.*] An agreement between two or more parties for the doing or not doing of some definite thing; the writing containing such an agreement; esp., an agreement enforceable by law; specif., the formal agreement of marriage;

betrothal; also, contract bridge (see under *bridge*²).—**con-tract-a-ble** (kǫn-trak′tą-bl), *a.* Contractible.—**con-tract′-ant,** *n.* A contracting party.—**con-tract′ed,** *p. a.* Drawn together; shrunken; hence, condensed; abridged; fig., narrow or illiberal; restricted in opportunities or means (as, *contracted* circumstances); also, arranged for by contract; betrothed or affianced; also, acquired or incurred. —**con-tract′ed-ly,** *adv.*—**con-tract′ed-ness,** *n.*—**con-tract′i-ble,** *a.* Capable of being contracted.—**con-tract-i-bil′i-ty** (-bil′i-ti), **con-tract′i-ble-ness,** *n.*—**con-trac′-tile** (-trak′til), *a.* Capable of undergoing or of producing contraction.—**con-trac-til-i-ty** (kon-trak-til′i-ti), *n.* The quality or property of being contractile.—**con-trac-tion** (kǫn-trak′shǫn), *n.* [L. *contractio(n-).*] The act of contracting, or the state of being contracted; also, something contracted; a shortened form of a word, etc., as *e'er* for *ever*, *can't* for *cannot*.—**con-trac′tion-al,** *a.*—**con-trac′-tive,** *a.* Serving or tending to contract.—**con-trac′tor,** *n.* [LL.] One who or that which contracts; esp., one who contracts to furnish supplies or perform work at a certain price or rate; in *anat.*, a muscle that contracts or draws together some part of the body.—**con-trac′tu-al** (-tū-ąl), *a.* Of, pertaining to, or of the nature of a contract.—**con-trac′ture** (-tūr), *n.* [L. *contractura.*] Contraction; esp., a permanent shortening of a muscle.

con-tra=dance (kon′trą̈-dȧns), *n.* Same as *contredanse.*

con-tra-dict (kon-trą̈-dikt′), *v.* [L. *contradictus*, pp. of *contradicere*, < *contra*, against, + *dicere*, say.] **I.** *tr.* To speak or declare against†; oppose†; also, to assert the contrary or opposite of; deny directly and categorically; deny the words or assertion of (a person); of a statement, action, etc., to be directly contrary to. **II.** *intr.* To speak in opposition†; also, to utter a contrary statement.—**con-tra-dict′a-ble,** *a.* That may be contradicted.—**con-tra-dic′tion** (-dik′shǫn), *n.* [L. *contradictio(n-).*] The act of contradicting; gainsaying or opposition; assertion of the contrary or opposite; denial; direct opposition or repugnance between things compared; inconsistency; absolute logical inconsistency; also, a statement or proposition that contradicts or denies another; a self-contradictory statement or phrase ('contradiction in terms'); a contradictory act, fact, etc.; a person characterized by contradictory qualities.—**con-tra-dic′tious** (-shus), *a.* Inclined to contradict or cavil; disputatious; also, self-contradictory (archaic). —**con-tra-dic′tious-ly,** *adv.*—**con-tra-dic′tious-ness,** *n.*—**con-tra-dic′tive,** *a.* Tending to contradict; involving contradiction.—**con-tra-dic′tor,** *n.*—**con-tra-dic′to-ry** (-tǭ-ri). [LL. *contradictorius.*] **I.** *a.* Of the nature of a contradiction; asserting the contrary or opposite; contradicting each other; inconsistent in one's self or itself; of an opposite nature or character; also, given to contradiction; contradictious. **II.** *n.*; pl. *-ries* (-riz). A contradictory assertion, proposition, etc.; also, the contrary.—**con-tra-dic′to-ri-ly,** *adv.*—**con-tra-dic′to-ri-ness,** *n.*

con-tra-dis-tinc-tion (kon″trą̈-dis-tingk′shǫn), *n.* [See *contra-.*] Distinction by opposition or contrast.—**con″tra-dis-tinc′tive,** *a.* Serving to contradistinguish.—**con″tra-dis-tin′guish** (-ting′gwish), *v. t.* To distinguish by contrasting opposite qualities; discriminate by direct contrast.

con-tra-fa-got-to (kon″trä-fä-got′tō), *n.*; pl. *-ti* (-tē). [It., < *contra*, against, counter to, + *fagotto*, bassoon.] A double bassoon.

con-tra-in-di-cant (kon-trą̈-in′di-kąnt). [See *contra-.*] In *med.*: **I.** *a.* Indicating a particular or usual remedy or treatment to be inadvisable. **II.** *n.* A contraindicant symptom or condition.—**con-tra-in′di-cate** (-kāt), *v. t.*; *-cated, -cating.* In *med.*, of a symptom or condition, to give indication against the advisability of (a particular or usual remedy or treatment).—**con″tra-in-di-ca′tion** (-kā′shǫn), *n.* In *med.*, a symptom or condition which indicates a particular or usual remedy or treatment to be inadvisable.

con-tral-to (kǫn-tral′tō). [It., < *contra*, against, counter to, + *alto*, alto.] In *music*: **I.** *n.*; pl. *-tos* (-tōz), It. *-ti* (-tē). The lowest female voice or voice-part, intermediate between soprano and tenor; sometimes, the alto, or highest male voice or voice-part; also, a singer with a contralto voice. **II.** *a.* Of or pertaining to the contralto; having the compass of the contralto.

con-tra-nat-u-ral (kon-trą̈-naṭ′ū-rąl), *a.* [See *contra-.*] Contrary to what is natural.

con-tra-plex (kon′trą̈-pleks), *a.* [From *contra-* + *-plex* as in *duplex.*] Noting or pertaining to a system of telegraphy for sending two messages simultaneously over the same wire in opposite directions.

con-tra-po-si-tion (kon″trą̈-pǭ-zish′ǫn), *n.* [LL. *contrapositio(n-)*, < L. *contraponere*, place opposite, < *contra*, against, + *ponere*, place.] A placing over against; opposite position; antithesis; contrast.—**con-tra-pos′i-tive** (-poz′i-tiv), *a.*

con-trap-tion (kǫn-trap′shǫn), *n.* [A made word.] A contrivance; a device. [Colloq.]

con-tra-pun-tal (kon-trą̈-pun′tąl), *a.* [It. *contrappunto*, counterpoint.] In *music*, of or pertaining to counterpoint; in accordance with the rules of counterpoint.—**con-tra-pun′tal-ly,** *adv.*—**con-tra-pun′tist,** *n.* One skilled in the rules and practice of counterpoint.

con-tra-ri-e-ty (kon-trą-rī′ę-ti), *n.*; pl. *-ties* (-tiz). [LL. *contrarietas.*] The state or quality of being contrary; also, something contrary or of opposite character; a contrary fact or statement (as, "He will be here, and yet he is not here: How can these *contrarieties* agree?" Shakspere's "1 Henry VI," ii. 3. 59); an adverse or untoward circumstance.

con-tra-ri-ly (kon′trą̈-ri-li), *adv.* In a contrary manner.—**con′tra-ri-ness,** *n.*

con-tra-ri-ous (kǫn-trā′ri-us), *a.* [ML. *contrariosus.*] Contrary; perverse; adverse or unfavorable. [Now rare.]

con-tra-ri-wise (kon′trą̈-ri-wīz), *adv.* In a contrary manner; on the contrary; in the opposite way; perversely.

con-tra-ry (kon′trą̈-ri). [L. *contrarius*, < *contra*, in opposition.] **I.** *a.* Opposite in nature or character; diametrically opposed; mutually opposed; also, being the opposite one of two; also, antagonistic† or hostile†; hence, perverse (sometimes with colloq. pron. kǫn-trā′ri); also, opposite in direction or position; also, untoward or unfavorable; in *bot.*, at right angles. **II.** *n.*; pl. *-ries* (-riz). That which is contrary or opposite (as, to prove the *contrary* of a statement); also, either of two contrary things; also, hostility†; also, a denial†.—**by contraries,** by way of opposition; also, contrary to expectation.—**on the contrary,** in extreme opposition to what has been stated.—**to the contrary,** to the opposite or a different effect; in opposition to or reversal of something stated.—**con′tra-ry,** *adv.* Contrarily; contrariwise.—**con′tra-ry,** *v. t.*; *-ried, -rying.* To act contrary to; oppose; contradict. [Obs. or prov.]

con-trast (kǫn-trȧst′), *v.* [F. *contraster*, < It. *contrastare*, < ML. *contrastare*, withstand, oppose, < L. *contra*, against, + *stare*, stand.] **I.** *tr.* To set in opposition in order to show unlikeness; compare by observing differences; place in immediate relation in order to heighten an effect by emphasizing differences; also, to afford or form a contrast to; set off. **II.** *intr.* To exhibit unlikeness on comparison; form a contrast.—**con-trast** (kon′trȧst), *n.* [F. *contraste*, < It. *contrasto*, < *contrastare.*] The act of contrasting, or the state of being contrasted; a striking exhibition of unlikeness; also, something strikingly unlike (as, "She was a *contrast* to her father in temper and in character": Wiseman's "Fabiola," i. 4).—**con-trast-a-ble** (kǫn-trȧs′tą-bl), *a.* That may be contrasted.—**con-trast′ing-ly,** *adv.*—**con-tras′tive,** *a.* Affording a contrast.

con-tra-val-la-tion (kon″trą̈-va-lā′shǫn), *n.* [F. *contrevallation*, < L. *contra*, against, + *vallare*: see *vallate*, and cf. *circumvallate.*] In *fort.*, a chain of redoubts and breastworks raised by besiegers about the place invested.

con-tra-vene (kon-trą̈-vēn′), *v. t.*; *-vened, -vening.* [LL. *contravenire*, < L. *contra*, against, + *venire*, come.] To come or be in conflict with; oppose; go or act counter to; violate, infringe, or transgress, as a law.—**con-tra-ven′er** (-vē′nėr), *n.*—**con-tra-ven′tion** (-ven′shǫn), *n.* The act of contravening; action counter to something; violation.

con-tra-yer-va (kon-trą̈-yėr′vą̈), *n.* [Sp. *contrayerba*, 'counter-herb,' antidote.] The root of certain plants of the tropical American moraceous genus *Dorstenia*, esp. *D. contrayerva*, used as a stimulant, tonic, and diaphoretic; also, the root of certain West Indian plants of the genus *Aristolochia*, similarly used.

(variable) ḑ as d or j, ş as s or sh, ţ as t or ch, z̧ as z or zh; ǫ, F. cloche; ü, F. menu; ċh, Sc. loch; ṅ, F. bonbon; ′, primary accent; ″, secondary accent; †, obsolete; <, from; +, and; =, equals. **See also lists at beginning of book.**

con-tre-danse (kôṅ-trė-däṅs), *n.* [F., a corruption of E. *country-dance.*] A graceful dance, based on the country-dance, in which the partners stand opposite one another; also, a piece of music suitable for such a dance.

con-tre-temps (kôṅ-trė-toṅ), *n.*; pl. *-temps* (-toṅ). [F., < L. *contra*, against, + *tempus*, time.] An inopportune occurrence; an embarrassing mischance: as, "The blunder of Champfort . . . it was rather unlucky; so awkward, such a *contretemps!*" (Maria Edgeworth's "Belinda," xv.).

con-trib-ut-a-ble (kọn-trib′ū̦-tạ-bl), *a.* Capable of being contributed; payable as a contribution; also, of persons, subject to contribution.

con-trib-ute (kọn-trib′ū̦t), *v.*; *-uted*, *-uting.* [L. *contributus*, pp. of *contribuere*, < *con-*, with, + *tribuere*, give, pay.] **I.** *tr.* To give in common with others; give to a common stock or for a common purpose; furnish as a share or constituent part of anything. **II.** *intr.* To make contribution; furnish a contribution.—**con-tri-bu-tion** (kon-tri-bū′shọn), *n.* [LL. *contributio(n-).*] The act of contributing; also, something contributed; specif., an article contributed to a magazine or the like; also, an impost or levy.—**con-trib-u-tive** (kọn-trib′ū̦-tiv), *a.* Tending to contribute; contributing.—**con-trib′u-tor,** *n.* One that contributes; esp., one who contributes articles to a newspaper, magazine, or other joint literary work.—**con-trib′u-tor-ship,** *n.*—**con-trib′u-to-ry** (-tọ-ri). **I.** *a.* Contributing; furnishing something toward a result (as, *contributory* negligence, in *law*, negligence on the part of a person injured which has contributed to bring about the injury); also, subject to contribution or levy; also, pertaining to or of the nature of contribution. **II.** *n.*; pl. *-ries* (-riz). One who or that which contributes.

con-trite (kon′trīt), *a.* [L. *contritus*, pp. of *conterere*, grind, wear down, < *con-*, together, + *terere*, rub.] Bruised†; also, broken in spirit by a sense of guilt; penitent; also, proceeding from contrition.—**con′trite-ly,** *adv.*—**con′trite-ness,** *n.*—**con-tri-tion** (kọn-trish′ọn), *n.* [LL. *contritio(n-).*] The act of grinding, pounding, or bruising†; also, the condition of being contrite; sincere penitence; in *theol.*, sorrow for and detestation of sin with a true purpose of amendment, arising from a love of God for his own perfections ('perfect contrition'), or from some inferior motive, as fear of divine punishment ('imperfect contrition').

con-triv-a-ble (kọn-trī′vạ-bl), *a.* That may be contrived.

con-triv-ance (kọn-trī′vạns), *n.* The act or manner of contriving; the faculty or power of contriving; also, something contrived; a plan or scheme; an expedient (as, "For every difficulty he had a *contrivance* ready": Macaulay's "Essays," Warren Hastings); a device, esp. a mechanical one.

con-trive (kọn-trīv′), *v.*; *-trived*, *-triving.* [Earlier *contreve*, *controve*, < OF. *controver* (F. *controuver*), < *con-*, with, + *trover*, find: see *trover.*] **I.** *tr.* To plan with ingenuity; devise; invent; sometimes, to plot (evil); also, to bring about or effect by or as by devising; manage (to do something). **II.** *intr.* To form schemes or designs; plan; sometimes, to plot.—**con-triv′er** (-trī′vėr), *n.*

con-trol (kọn-trōl′), *v. t.*; *-trolled*, *-trolling.* [OF. *contreroller* (F. *contrôler*), < *contrerolle*, 'counter-roll,' < L. *contra*, against, + ML. *rotulus*, E. *roll.*] To check or regulate (payments, etc.), orig. by means of a duplicate register; also, to exercise restraint or direction over; dominate; command; also, to hold in check; curb; also, to overpower†.—**con-trol′,** *n.* The act or power of controlling; regulation; domination or command; check or restraint; also, something that serves to control; a check; a standard of comparison in scientific experimentation; also, a person who acts as a check; a controller; in *mach.*, a controlling device or mechanism, as for operating the rudders, etc., on an aëroplane.—**con-trol′la-ble,** *a.* That may be controlled.—**con-trol′ler,** *n.* [OF. *contrerolleur* (F. *contrôleur*).] One employed to check expenditures, etc.; a comptroller; also, one who regulates, directs, or restrains; also, a regulating mechanism.—**con-trol′ler-ship,** *n.*—**con-trol′less,** *a.* Free from control; uncontrolled.—**con-trol′ling-ly,** *adv.*—**con-trol′ment,** *n.* Control; restraint.

con-tro-ver-sial (kon-trọ-vėr′shạl), *a.* Of, pertaining to, or of the nature of controversy; polemical; also, given to controversy; disputatious; also, subject to controversy; debatable.—**con-tro-ver′sial-ist,** *n.* One who engages or is skilled in controversy; a disputant.—**con-tro-ver′sial-ly,** *adv.*

con-tro-ver-sy (kon′trọ-vėr-si), *n.*; pl. *-sies* (-siz). [L. *controversia*, < *controversus*, turned against, < *contro-* (= *contra-*), against, + *versus*, pp. of *vertere*, turn.] Dispute, debate, or contention; disputation concerning a matter of opinion; also, a dispute or contention.

con-tro-vert (kon-trọ-vėrt′ or kon′trọ-vėrt), *v.* [L. *contro-*, against, + *vertere*, turn: cf. *controversy.*] **I.** *tr.* To contend against in discussion; dispute; deny; oppose; also, to contend about in discussion; debate; discuss. **II.** *intr.* To engage in controversy.—**con-tro-vert′er,** *n.*—**con-tro-vert′i-ble,** *a.* That may be controverted.—**con-tro-vert′i-bly,** *adv.*—**con-tro-vert′ist,** *n.* One given to controverting; a controversialist: as, "disputations . . . often continued till neither *controvertist* remembered upon what question they began" (Johnson's "Rasselas," xxii.).

con-tu-ma-cious (kon-tū̦-mā′shus), *a.* [Obs. F. *contumacieux*, < *contumace*, < L. *contumacia*, E. *contumacy.*] Exhibiting contumacy; stubbornly perverse or rebellious; wilfully and obstinately disobedient.—**con-tu-ma′cious-ly,** *adv.*—**con-tu-ma′cious-ness, con-tu-ma′ci-ty** (-mas′-i-ti), *n.*

con-tu-ma-cy (kon′tū̦-mạ-si), *n.*; pl. *-cies* (-siz). [L. *contumacia*, < *contumax*, stubborn, contumacious.] Stubborn perverseness or rebelliousness; wilful and obstinate resistance or disobedience to authority; in *law*, wilful disobedience to an order or summons of a court.

con-tu-me-li-ous (kon-tū̦-mē′li-us), *a.* [L. *contumeliosus.*] Exhibiting or involving contumely; humiliatingly insolent.—**con-tu-me′li-ous-ly,** *adv.*—**con-tu-me′li-ous-ness,** *n.*

con-tu-me-ly (kon′tū̦-mẹ-li), *n.*; pl. *-lies* (-liz). [L. *contumelia.*] Insulting manifestation of contempt in words or actions; contemptuous or humiliating treatment; also, a humiliating insult.

con-tuse (kọn-tūz′), *v. t.*; *-tused*, *-tusing.* [L. *contusus*, pp. of *contundere*, < *con-*, together, + *tundere*, beat.] To pound† or bray†; also, to injure as by a blow with a blunt instrument, without breaking the skin; bruise.—**con-tu′sion** (-tū′zhọn), *n.* [L. *contusio(n-).*] The act of contusing, or the state of being contused; also, an injury as from a blow with a blunt instrument, without breaking of the skin; a bruise.

co-nun-drum (kọ-nun′drum), *n.* [Origin obscure.] A whim† or conceit†; also, a pun†; also, a riddle the answer to which involves a pun or play on words; hence, anything that puzzles.

con-va-lesce (kon-vạ-les′), *v. i.*; *-lesced*, *-lescing.* [L. *convalescere*, < *con-*, altogether, + *valescere*, grow strong, < *valere*, be strong.] To grow stronger after illness; make progress toward recovery of health.—**con-va-les′cence** (-les′ẹns), *n.* The gradual recovery of health and strength after illness.—**con-va-les′cent.** **I.** *a.* Convalescing; also, of or pertaining to convalescence or convalescents. **II.** *n.* A convalescent person.

con-val-la-ri-a-ceous (kon-vạ-lā-ri-ā′shius), *a.* [NL. *Convallaria*, the lily-of-the-valley genus, < L. *convallis*, valley inclosed on all sides, < *con-*, altogether, + *vallis*, valley.] Belonging to the *Convallariaceæ*, a family of plants including the lily-of-the-valley, asparagus, trillium, etc.

con-vec-tion (kọn-vek′shọn), *n.* [LL. *convectio(n-)*, < L. *convehere*, carry together, < *con-*, together, + *vehere*, carry.] Conveyance; in *physics*, the transference of heat or electricity by the circulation or movement of the heated or electrified parts of a liquid or gas.—**con-vec′tion-al,** *a.*—**con-vec′tive,** *a.* Capable of conveying; transporting; also, pertaining to or resulting from convection.—**con-vec′tive-ly,** *adv.*

con-ven-a-ble (kọn-vē′nạ-bl), *a.* That may be convened or assembled.

conve-nance (kôṅv-näṅs), *n.*; pl. *-nances* (-näṅs). [F.] Suitability; expediency; propriety; *pl.*, the proprieties or conventionalities.

con-vene (kọn-vēn′), *v.*; *-vened*, *-vening.* [L. *convenire* (pp. *conventus*), come together, also agree, accord, suit, be proper, < *con-*, together, + *venire*, come.] **I.** *intr.* To come together; assemble, as persons, usually for some public purpose. **II.** *tr.* To cause to assemble; convoke;

also, to summon to appear, as before a judicial officer.—**con-ven'er** (-vē'nėr), *n.*

con-ve-nience (kǫn-vē'niẹns), *n.* [L. *convenientia.*] The quality of being convenient; agreement†; appropriateness†; special suitability for the needs or purpose; adaptedness for easy use; also, advantage as from something convenient (as, a shelter for the *convenience* of travelers); a situation of affairs or a time convenient for one (as, to consider or to await one's *convenience;* to do a thing at one's *convenience*); hence, anything convenient; an advantage; an accommodation; a convenient appliance, utensil, or the like.—**con-ve'nience,** *v. t.*; *-nienced, -niencing.* To afford convenience to; accommodate.—**con-ve'nien-cy** (-niẹn-si), *n.*; pl. *-cies* (-siz). Convenience; esp., a convenient arrangement, appliance, etc.

con-ve-nient (kǫn-vē'niẹnt), *a.* [L. *conveniens* (*-ent-*), ppr. of *convenire,* agree, accord, suit, be proper: see *convene.*] Agreeing, as in opinion†; also, fitting† or appropriate†; also, agreeable to the needs or purpose; well suited with respect to facility or ease in use; favorable, easy, or comfortable for use; commodious; sometimes, in satisfactory nearness (colloq.).—**con-ve'nient-ly,** *adv.*

con-vent[1]† (kǫn-vent'), *v. i.* or *t.* Same as *convene.* See Shakspere's "Henry VIII.," v. 1. 52.

con-vent[2] (kon'vent), *n.* [L. *conventus,* meeting, assembly, company, ML. convent, < L. *convenire:* see *convene.*] A meeting† or assembly†; also, a community of persons devoted to religious life under a superior; a society of monks, friars, or nuns, in popular usage only of nuns; also, the building or buildings occupied by such a society; a monastery or nunnery; in popular usage, a nunnery.

con-ven-ti-cle (kǫn-ven'ti-kl), *n.* [L. *conventiculum,* dim. of *conventus,* meeting: see *convent*[2].] A meeting† or assembly†; a small or private assembly†; a secret or unauthorized meeting, esp. for religious worship, as those held by Protestant dissenters from the Church of England during the period when they were prohibited by law; also, a place of meeting or assembly, esp. a nonconformist meeting-house.—**con-ven'ti-cler,** *n.* An attendant or supporter of conventicles.—**con-ven-tic-u-lar** (kon-ven-tik'ū-lạ̈r), *a.* Of or pertaining to a conventicle.

con-ven-tion (kǫn-ven'shǫn), *n.* [L. *conventio*(*n-*), meeting, agreement, < *convenire:* see *convene.*] A coming together†; a meeting or assembly; esp., a formal assembly, as of representatives or delegates, for action on particular matters; also, the calling together of an assembly; also, an agreement, compact, or contract; specif., an international agreement, esp. one other than a treaty and dealing with a specific matter, as postal service, copyright, patents, etc.; also, general agreement or consent; accepted usage, esp. as a standard of procedure; sometimes, conventionalism; also, a rule, method, or practice established by general consent or accepted usage.—**con-ven'tion-al,** *a.* [LL. *conventionalis.*] Of or pertaining to a convention or assembly; also, of or pertaining to a convention, agreement, or compact; also, pertaining to convention or general agreement; established by general consent or accepted usage; arbitrarily determined; also, conforming or adhering to accepted standards, as of conduct or taste; formal, rather than spontaneous or original; in the *fine arts,* in accordance with accepted models or traditions, rather than in precise imitation of nature.—**con-ven'tion-al-ism,** *n.* Adherence or the tendency to adhere to that which is conventional; also, something conventional.—**con-ven'tion-al-ist,** *n.*—**con-ven-tion-al'i-ty** (-al'i-ti), *n.*; pl. *-ties* (-tiz). Conventional quality or character; adherence to convention; also, a conventional practice, principle, form, etc.; *pl.,* with *the,* the conventional rules of propriety.—**con-ven'tion-al-ize** (-īz), *v. t.*; *-ized, -izing.* To render conventional; in the *fine arts,* to represent in a conventional manner.—**con-ven"tion-al-i-za'tion** (-i-zā'shǫn), *n.*—**con-ven'tion-al-ly,** *adv.*

con-ven-tu-al (kǫn-ven'tụ̄-ạl). **I.** *a.* Of, belonging to, or characteristic of a convent. **II.** *n.* An inmate of a convent; [*cap.*] one of an order of Franciscan friars which in the 15th century was separated from the Observants, and which follows a mitigated rule.—**con-ven'tu-al-ly,** *adv.*

con-verge (kǫn-vėrj'), *v.*; *-verged, -verging.* [LL. *convergere,* < L. *con-,* together, + *vergere,* incline, E. *verge*[2].] **I.** *intr.* To tend to meet in a point or line; incline toward each other, as lines which are not parallel; fig., to tend to a common result, conclusion, etc. **II.** *tr.* To cause to converge.—**con-ver'gence** (-vėr'jẹns), *n.* The act or fact of converging; convergent state or quality. Also **con-ver'gen-cy.**—**con-ver'gent,** *a.* Converging; formed by convergence, as of lines.—**con-ver'ging-ly,** *adv.*

con-vers-a-ble (kǫn-vėr'sạ-bl), *a.* [F. *conversable,* < ML. *conversabilis,* < L. *conversari:* see *converse*[1].] That may be conversed with, esp. easily and agreeably; also, able or disposed to converse; also, pertaining to or proper for social intercourse.—**con-vers'a-ble-ness,** *n.*—**con-vers'a-bly,** *adv.*

con-ver-sant (kon'vėr-sạnt), *a.* [OF. *conversant,* < L. *conversans* (*-ant-*), ppr. of *conversari:* see *converse*[1].] Accustomed to dwell or abide in a particular place†; also, having regular or frequent intercourse; intimately associating; acquainted; also, familiar by use or study; having a thorough or intimate knowledge or proficiency; also, having concern or connection; concerned or occupied; also, disposed to converse.—**con'ver-sance,** *n.*—**con'ver-sant-ly,** *adv.*

con-ver-sa-tion (kon-vėr-sā'shǫn), *n.* [OF. F. *conversation,* < L. *conversatio*(*n-*), < *conversari:* see *converse*[1].] An abiding† or dwelling†; behavior, or manner of living (archaic); association or intercourse; sexual intercourse; intimate acquaintance; esp., informal interchange of thoughts by spoken words; a talk or colloquy; also, a gathering of persons for conversation or discussion†; a conversazione†.—**con-ver-sa'tion-al,** *a.* Of, pertaining to, or characteristic of conversation; also, able or ready to converse; given to conversation.—**con-ver-sa'tion-al-ist,** *n.* One given to or excelling in conversation.—**con-ver-sa'tion-al-ly,** *adv.*—**con-ver-sa'tion-ist,** *n.* A conversationalist.

con-ver-sa-zi-o-ne (kon-ver-sä-tsē-ō'nā), *n.*; pl. *-nes* (-nāz), It. *-ni* (-nē). [It.] In Italy and elsewhere, a social gathering for conversation, etc. (as, "By means of frequenting the Duchess of B—'s *conversazione* . . . at Rome, Mrs. Baynard became acquainted with all the fashionable people of that city": Smollett's "Humphry Clinker," Sept. 30); also, an assembly for conversation or speaking on literary or scholarly subjects.

con-verse[1] (kǫn-vėrs'), *v. i.*; *-versed, -versing.* [OF. F. *converser,* < L. *conversari,* dwell or associate with, < *con-,* with, + *versari,* dwell, occupy or busy one's self: see *versed*[2].] To dwell†; hold intercourse, or have to do (obs. or archaic); hold inward communion (*with*); esp., to talk informally with another; interchange thoughts by speech.—**con-verse**[1] (kon'vėrs), *n.* Intercourse; inward communion; familiar discourse or talk; conversation.

con-verse[2] (kon'vėrs). [L. *conversus,* pp. of *convertere,* turn about: see *convert.*] **I.** *a.* Turned about; opposite or contrary in direction or action. **II.** *n.* A thing which is the opposite or contrary of another; esp., one form of words that corresponds to another form of words but with a significant pair of terms interchanged in place (as, 'warm in winter but cold in summer' is the *converse* of 'cold in winter but warm in summer'); in *logic,* a proposition obtained by conversion.—**con-verse-ly** (kon'vėrs-li or kǫn-vėrs'li), *adv.*

con-vers-er (kǫn-vėr'sėr), *n.* One who converses.

con-vers-i-ble (kǫn-vėr'si-bl), *a.* See *conversable.*

con-ver-sion (kǫn-vėr'shǫn), *n.* [L. *conversio*(*n-*), < *convertere:* see *convert.*] The act of converting, or the state of being converted; transposition; diversion of a thing from the proper or intended use; unauthorized appropriation of another's property; change in character, form, or function; spiritual change from sinfulness to righteousness; change from one religion, party, etc., to another; exchange for an equivalent; in *logic,* the transposition of the subject and the predicate of a proposition, in accordance with certain rules, so as to form a new proposition by immediate inference (as, 'no good man is unhappy' becomes by *conversion* 'no unhappy man is good').

con-vert (kǫn-vėrt'), *v.* [L. *convertere* (pp. *conversus*), turn about, turn, change, < *con-,* altogether, + *vertere,* turn.] **I.** *tr.* To turn about in position or direction†; also, to invert or transpose; transpose the subject and predicate of (a proposition) by logical conversion; also, to turn to another or a particular use or purpose; divert from the proper or intended use; appropriate wrongfully to one's own use; also, to change in character; cause to turn from an evil life to a righteous one; cause to adopt a different religion, party, opinion, etc., esp. one regarded as better; also, to change into something of different form or properties (as, to *convert* grain into spirits); transmute; transform; also, to exchange for an equivalent (as, to *convert* bank-notes into gold). **II.** *intr.* To turn†; also, to turn aside†; also, to be converted.—**con-vert** (kon′vėrt), *n.* One who has been converted, as to a religion or an opinion.—**con-vert-er** (kọn-vėr′tėr), *n.* One who or that which converts; specif., one engaged in converting textile fabrics, esp. cotton cloths, from the raw state, as they come from the loom, into the finished product ready for the market, as by bleaching, dyeing, glossing, etc.; also, an oval vessel in which pig-iron is converted into steel by the Bessemer process; also, in *elect.*, a device for changing the form of an electric current.—**con-vert′i-ble,** *a.* [LL. *convertibilis.*] Capable of being converted; interchangeable or equivalent; transformable; exchangeable for an equivalent; esp., of paper money, capable of being converted into specie.—**con-vert-i-bil′i-ty** (-bil′i-ti), **con-vert′i-ble-ness,** *n.*—**con-vert′i-bly,** *adv.*—**con-ver-tite** (kon′vėr-tīt), *n.* A convert. See Shakspere's "King John," v. 1. 19. [Archaic.]

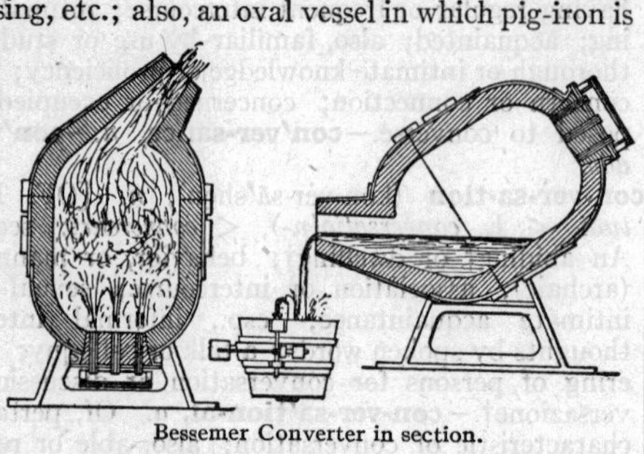
Bessemer Converter in section.

con-vex (kon′veks). [L. *convexus*, < *convehere*, carry together: see *convection.*] **I.** *a.* Curved like a circle or sphere when viewed from without; bulging and curved. **II.** *n.* A convex surface, part, or thing.—**con-vex** (kon′veks or kọn-veks′), *v. i.* or *t.* To bend or curve in a convex form.—**con-vex-i-ty** (kọn-vek′si-ti), *n.*; pl. *-ties* (-tiz). The state of being convex; also, a convex surface or thing.—**con′vex-ly,** *adv.*—**con′vex-ness,** *n.*—**con-vex-o=con-cave** (kon-vek′sō-kon′kāv), *a.* Convex on one side and concave on the other, as a lens; specif., noting or pertaining to a lens in which the convex face has a greater degree of curvature than the concave face, the lens being thickest in the middle.—**con-vex′o=con′vex,** *a.* Convex on both sides, as a lens.

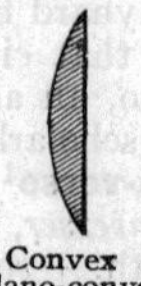
Convex (or Plano-convex) Lens (cross-section).

con-vey (kọn-vā′), *v. t.* [OF. *conveier* (also *convoier*, F. *convoyer*, E. *convoy*), < ML. *conviare*, < L. *con-*, with, + *viare*, travel, < *via*, way.] To escort†; guide†; carry or transport from one place to another; also, to take away secretly†; hence, to steal†; also, to lead or conduct as a channel or medium; transmit; also, to communicate or impart; also, to transfer or make over (property); also, to carry on† or manage† (as, "I will . . . *convey* the business as I shall find means": Shakspere's "King Lear," i. 2. 109).—**con-vey′a-ble,** *a.* That may be conveyed.—**con-vey′ance,** *n.* The act of conveying; transmission; communication; management†; also, an artifice† or trick†; also, a means of conveyance; a vehicle; a carriage; in *law*, the transfer of property from one person to another, or the deed by which this is effected.—**con-vey′an-cer,** *n.* One that brings about the conveyance of anything; esp., a person engaged in conveyancing.—**con-vey′an-cing,** *n.* The drawing of deeds, etc., for the conveyance of property from one person to another.—**con-vey′er,** *n.* One who or that which conveys; a mechanical contrivance for transporting material, as from one part of a building to another. Also **con-vey′or.**

Convexo-concave Lens.

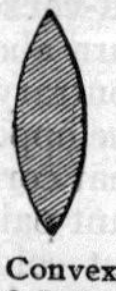
Convexo-convex Lens.

con-vict (kọn-vikt′), *v. t.* [L. *convictus*, pp. of *convincere*: see *convince.*] To prove or find guilty of an offense, esp. after trial before a legal tribunal; prove or declare guilty of wrong-doing, error, etc.; also, to impress with the sense of guilt; also, to confute (archaic); also, to convince† or persuade†.—**con-vict′,** *a.* Convicted; proved guilty. [Archaic.]—**con-vict** (kon′vikt), *n.* One who has been convicted, as before a legal tribunal; now, a convicted person undergoing penal servitude.

con-vic-tion (kọn-vik′shọn), *n.* [LL. *convictio(n-)*, < L. *convincere*: see *convict* and *convince.*] The act of convicting, as before a legal tribunal, or the fact or state of being convicted; also, the act of convincing, or bringing to a recognition of the truth of a thing, or the state of being convinced; settled persuasion; a fixed or firm belief; also, the fact of being convicted or convinced of wrong-doing or sin; religious compunction.—**con-vic′tion-al,** *a.*

con-vict-ism (kon′vikt-izm), *n.* The convict system; the system of transporting convicts to penal settlements; also, the class or body of convicts.

con-vic-tive (kọn-vik′tiv), *a.* Producing conviction; tending to convince.

con-vince (kọn-vins′), *v. t.*; *-vinced, -vincing.* [L. *convincere* (pp. *convictus*), overcome by argument or proof, convict of error or crime, prove, < *con-*, altogether, + *vincere*, conquer: cf. *convict.*] To bring to a recognition of the truth of a thing by argument or proof; confute†; refute†; prove or find guilty†; demonstrate† or prove†; overcome† or vanquish†.—**con-vin′ced-ly** (-vin′sed-li), *adv.*—**con-vin′ced-ness,** *n.*—**con-vince′ment,** *n.* The act or fact of convincing, or the state of being convinced; specif., conviction of sin.—**con-vin′cer,** *n.*—**con-vin′ci-ble,** *a.* That may be convinced.—**con-vin′cing-ly,** *adv.*—**con-vin′cing-ness,** *n.*

con-vive (kon′vīv, F. kôṅ-vēv), *n.* [F., < L. *conviva*, < *con-*, with, + *vivere*, live.] A companion at table, or at a feast or convivial entertainment.

con-viv-i-al (kọn-viv′i-ạl), *a.* [L. *convivialis*, < *convivium*, a feast, < *con-*, with, + *vivere*, live.] Of or pertaining to eating and drinking together as a form of pleasure or social entertainment; also, given or disposed to festivities of the table, or, more particularly, to social drinking.—**con-viv-i-al′i-ty** (-al′i-ti), *n.*; pl. *-ties* (-tiz). The quality of being convivial; convivial pleasure; *pl.*, convivial festivities.—**con-viv′i-al-ly,** *adv.*

con-vo-ca-tion (kon-vọ-kā′shọn), *n.* [L. *convocatio(n-).*] The act of convoking, or the fact or state of being convoked; also, a number of persons met in answer to a summons; an assembly; a provincial synod or assembly of the clergy of the Church of England; an assembly of the clergy of a division of a diocese in the American Protestant Episcopal Church.—**con-vo-ca′tion-al,** *a.*

con-vo-ca-tor (kon′vọ-kā-tọr), *n.* [ML.] One who convokes an assembly; also, a member of a convocation.

con-voke (kọn-vōk′), *v. t.*; *-voked, -voking.* [L. *convocare* (pp. *convocatus*), < *con-*, together, + *vocare*, call.] To call together; assemble by summons.—**con-vok′er** (-vō′kėr), *n.*

con-vo-lute (kon′vọ-lūt), *v. t.*; *-luted, -luting.* [L. *convolutus*, pp. of *convolvere*: see *convolve.*] To coil up; form into a twisted shape.—**con′vo-lute,** *a.* Rolled up together, or one part over another; in *bot.*, coiled up longitudinally, so that one margin is within the coil and the other without, as a leaf in the bud.—**con′vo-lute-ly,** *adv.*—**con-vo-lu′tion** (-lū′shọn), *n.* A rolling or coiling together; rolled up or coiled condition; also, a turn or winding of anything coiled; a whorl; a sinuosity; esp., one of the sinuous folds or ridges of the surface of the brain.—**con-vo-lu′tion-al,** **con-vo-lu′tion-a-ry** (-ā-ri), *a.*

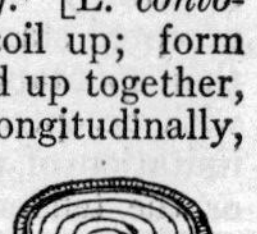
Convolute Cotyledons (cross-section).

con-volve (kọn-volv′), *v.*; *-volved, -volving.* [L. *convolvere* (pp. *convolutus*), < *con-*, together, + *volvere*, roll.] **I.** *tr.* To roll or wind together; coil; twist. **II.** *intr.* To form convolutions; roll or wind involvedly.—**con-volve′ment,** *n.*

con-vol-vu-la-ceous (kọn-vol-vụ-lā′shius), *a.* [See *convolvulus.*] Belonging to the *Convolvulaceæ*, or morning-glory family of plants, which includes the convolvuluses, ipomœas, etc.

con-vol-vu-lus (kọn-vol′vụ̄-lus), *n.*; pl. *-luses*, L. *-li* (-lī). [L., bindweed, < *convolvere*: see *convolve*.] Any plant of the genus *Convolvulus*, which comprises erect, twining, or prostrate herbs with trumpet-shaped flowers, certain of which are cultivated for ornament. Cf. *morning-glory* and *bindweed*.

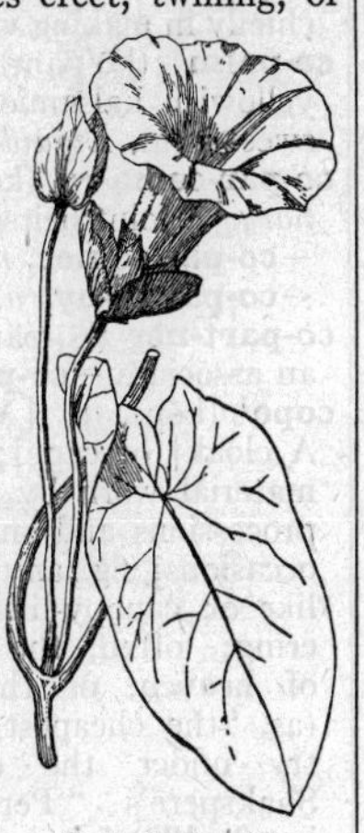

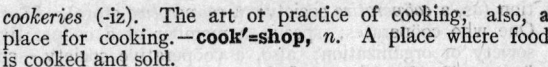

Convolvulus (*C. sepium*).

con-voy (kọn-voi′), *v. t.* [OF. *convoier* (F. *convoyer*): see *convey*.] To accompany or escort, now usually for protection: as, baggage-wagons *convoyed* by troops; a merchantman *convoyed* by a war-ship.—**con-voy** (kon′-voi), *n.* [OF. F. *convoi*.] The act of convoying; the protection afforded by an escort; an escort, esp. for protection, as an armed force, a war-ship, etc. (as, "For those who must journey Henceforward alone Have need of stout *convoy* Now Great-Heart is gone": Kipling's "Great-Heart: Theodore Roosevelt in 1919"); a party, supply of stores, ship, etc., convoyed (as, "As golden *convoys* sunk at sea Whose wealth might root out penury": Rossetti's "Dante at Verona"); also, a conducting medium†; a channel† or way†; also, a friction-brake, as for a wagon.

con-vulse (kọn-vuls′), *v. t.*; *-vulsed*, *-vulsing*. [L. *convulsus*, pp. of *convellere*, < *con-*, altogether, + *vellere*, pluck.] To shake violently; cause violent agitation or disturbance in; specif., to affect with successive violent and involuntary contractions of the muscles; affect with irregular spasms; hence, to cause to laugh violently.—**con-vul′sion** (-vul′-shọn), *n.* [L. *convulsio(n-)*.] A convulsing or being convulsed; violent agitation or disturbance; commotion; specif., a violent and involuntary spasmodic contraction of the muscles, or, in *pl.*, an affection marked by such contractions; hence, a violent fit of laughter.—**con-vul′sion-a-ry** (-ạ̄-ri), *a.* Pertaining to, of the nature of, or affected with convulsion.—**con-vul′sive** (-siv), *a.* Tending to convulse; of the nature of or characterized by convulsion; affected with convulsion.—**con-vul′sive-ly**, *adv.*—**con-vul′sive-ness**, *n.*

co-ny, co-ney (kō′ni or kun′i), *n.*; pl. *conies*, *coneys* (kō′niz or kun′iz). [OF. *conil*, *connil*, < L. *cuniculus*, rabbit.] A rabbit; the skin or fur of the rabbit (obs. or prov. Eng.); the daman, some other animal of the same genus, or a pika; also, a simpleton†.—**co′ny=catch**†, *v. t.* or *i.* To gull or cheat. See Shakspere's "Taming of the Shrew," v. 1. 102.—**co′ny=catch″er**†, *n.* A swindler; a cheat.

coo (kö), *v.*; *cooed*, *cooing*. [Imit.] **I.** *intr.* To utter the soft, murmuring sound characteristic of pigeons or doves, or a similar sound; hence, to murmur or talk fondly or amorously. **II.** *tr.* To utter by cooing.—**coo**, *n.* A cooing sound.—**coo′er**, *n.*—**coo′ing-ly**, *adv.*

coo-ee, coo-ey (kö′ē, kö′i), *interj.* and *n.* [Of native origin.] A prolonged, shrill, clear call or cry used as a signal by the Australian aborigines and adopted by the settlers in the country.—**coo′ee, coo′ey**, *v. i.*; *cooeed*, *cooeyed*, *cooeeing*, *cooeying*. To utter the call 'cooee': as, "They all began *co'eeing* again, and they heard the others in reply" (H. Kingsley's "Geoffry Hamlyn," xxxviii.).

cook (kůk), *n.* [AS. *cōc*, < L. *coquus*, a cook, < *coquere*, cook.] One whose occupation is the preparation of food by heat or otherwise for the table; one who cooks.—**cook**, *v.* **I.** *intr.* To act as cook; prepare food by the action of heat; of food, to undergo cooking. **II.** *tr.* To prepare (food) by the action of heat, as by boiling, baking, roasting, etc.; subject (anything) to the action of heat; also (often with *up*), to concoct; invent falsely; alter surreptitiously or falsify (colloq.); also, to ruin or spoil (slang).—**cook′=book**, *n.* A book containing recipes and instructions for cooking.—**cook′er**, *n.* One who or that which cooks; an apparatus or vessel for cooking (as, a steam *cooker*; a fireless *cooker*, a close box-like device into which food, after a preliminary heating, is placed in order to retain the heat and so complete the process of cooking).—**cook′er-y**, *n.*; pl. *cookeries* (-iz). The art or practice of cooking; also, a place for cooking.—**cook′=shop**, *n.* A place where food is cooked and sold.

cook-y, cook-ie (kůk′i), *n.*; pl. *-ies* (-iz). [D. *koekje*, dim. of *koek*, cake.] A small cake; esp., in the U. S., a small, flat, sweet cake.

cool (köl), *a.* [AS. *cōl*; akin to E. *cold*, *chill*.] Moderately cold; neither warm nor very cold; imparting or permitting a sensation of moderate coldness (as, a *cool* dress); fig., not excited by passion; calm; unmoved; not hasty; deliberate; also, deficient in ardor or enthusiasm (as, "'Twill make them *cool* in zeal unto your grace": Shakspere's "2 Henry VI.," iii. 1. 177); lacking in cordiality (as, a *cool* reception); also, calmly audacious or impudent; also, of a number or sum, without exaggeration or qualification (colloq.: as, a *cool* thousand dollars).—**cool**, *n.* That which is cool; the cool part, place, time, etc.; also, coolness.—**cool**, *v.* [AS. *cōlian*.] **I.** *intr.* To become cool; fig., to lose the heat of passion or emotion; become less ardent, cordial, etc.; become more moderate. **II.** *tr.* To make cool; impart a sensation of coolness to; fig., to abate the ardor or intensity of; allay, as passion or emotion; moderate, as zeal or strong feeling.—**cool′er**, *n.* One that cools or makes cool; a vessel or apparatus for cooling liquids, etc.; a jail (slang); a cell, as in a jail, for violent or refractory prisoners (slang).—**cool′=head′ed**, *a.* Having a cool head; free from excitement, passion, etc.; not easily excited.—**cool′=head′ed-ness**, *n.*

Coo-lidge (kö′lij) **tube.** [From the inventor, W. D. *Coolidge* (born 1873), American physical chemist.] A tube for the generation of Röntgen rays by means of a cathode consisting of a spiral of tungsten heated to incandescence.

coo-lie, coo-ly (kö′li), *n.*; pl. *-lies* (-liz). [E. Ind.] Among Europeans in India, China, etc., an unskilled native laborer; also, such a laborer employed for cheap service elsewhere.

cool-ish (kö′lish), *a.* Somewhat cool.

cool-ly (köl′li), *adv.* In a cool manner.—**cool′ness**, *n.*

coolth (költh), *n.* [Cf. *warmth*.] The state of being cool; coolness. [Now chiefly prov.]

coo′ly, *n.* See *coolie*.

coom (köm), *n.* [= *culm*¹.] Soot; dust or refuse, as coal-dust, sawdust, grease from axle-boxes, etc. [Prov.]

coomb (köm), *n.* See *comb*².

coon (kön), *n.* [For *racoon*.] The racoon; also, a negro (slang, U. S.).

coon-can (kön′kan), *n.* Same as *conquian*.

coop (köp), *n.* [ME. *cupe*: cf. AS. *cȳpe*, basket, D. *kuip*, tub, G. *kufe*, coop, tub, vat, L. *cupa*, tub, cask.] A basket†; a kind of basket for catching fish (Eng.); a box or the like, as with bars or wires on one side or more, in which fowls are confined for fattening, transportation, etc.; an inclosure, cage, or pen for poultry, etc.; any narrow confining thing or place, as a room or cell; a prison (slang).—**coop**, *v. t.* To place in or as in a coop; confine narrowly: often with *up*: as, "I had often . . . thought it hard to remain during my youth *cooped* up in one place" (Mrs. Shelley's "Frankenstein," iii.).

coop-er (kö′pėr), *n.* [ME. *couper* = D. *kuiper* = G. *küfer*: cf. *coop*.] One who makes or repairs vessels formed of staves and hoops, as casks, barrels, tubs, etc.—**coop′er**, *v.* **I.** *tr.* To make or repair (casks, barrels, etc.); also, to furbish or fix (*up*: colloq.: as, "I'll get the hut *coopered* up a bit for you," H. Kingsley's "Geoffry Hamlyn," xxvii.). **II.** *intr.* To work as a cooper.—**coop′er-age** (-ạ̄j), *n.* The work or business, of a cooper, or the place where it is carried on; the price paid for coopers' work.

co-öp-er-ant (kọ̄-op′ẹ-rạnt). **I.** *a.* Coöperating; operating together. **II.** *n.* A coöperating agent.—**co-öp′er-an-cy**, *n.*

co-öp-er-ate (kọ̄-op′ẹ-rāt), *v. i.*; *-ated*, *-ating*. [LL. *cooperatus*, pp. of *cooperari*, < L. *co-*, with, + *operari*: see *operate*.] To work or act together or jointly; unite in producing an effect; specif., to practise economic coöperation.—**co-öp-er-a′tion** (-ẹ-rā′shọn), *n.* [LL. *cooperatio(n-)*.] The act or fact of coöperating; joint operation or action; in *polit. econ.*, the combination of persons for purposes of production, purchase, or distribution for their joint benefit.—**co-öp′er-a-tive** (-ẹ-rạ̄-tiv). **I.** *a.* Coöperating; of or pertaining to coöperation; pertaining to economic coöperation (as, a *coöperative* society; a *coöperative* store). **II.** *n.* One who coöperates; specif., a member of a coöperative society or organization; also, a coöperative society.—**co-öp′er-a-tive-ly,** *adv.*—**co-öp′er-a-tor** (-ẹ-rā-tọr), *n.* [LL.] One who coöperates; specif., a member of a coöperative society.

coop-er-y (kö′pėr-i), *n.*; pl. *-ies* (-iz). The work of a cooper; a cooper's shop; articles made by a cooper.

co-öpt (kọ-opt′), *v. t.* [L. *cooptare* (pp. *cooptatus*), < *co-*, with, + *optare*, choose.] To elect into a body by the votes of the existing members. Also **co-öp′tate** (-op′tāt).—**co-öp-ta-tion** (kō-op-tā′shọn), *n.* Election to membership in a body by the votes of the existing members.—**co-öp-ta-tive** (kọ-op′tạ-tiv), *a.* Pertaining to or chosen by coöptation.—**co-öp′tion** (-shọn), *n.* Same as *coöptation.*

co-ör-di-nal (kọ-ôr′di-nạl), *a.* [L. *co-*, with, + *ordo* (*ordin-*), order.] In *bot.*, belonging to the same order.

co-ör-di-nate (kọ-ôr′di-nạt). [L. *co-*, with, + *ordinatus*, ordered, arranged: see *ordinate.*] **I.** *a.* Of the same order or degree; equal in rank or importance; also, involving coördination; in *math.*, pertaining to coördinates. **II.** *n.* One who or that which is equal in rank or importance; an equal; in *math.*, any of two or more magnitudes which define the position of a point, line, or the like, by reference to a fixed figure, system of lines, etc.; esp., either of two lines ('Cartesian coördinates'), defining the position of a point in a plane, with reference to two intersecting fixed lines or axes, each defining line being drawn from the point to one axis, parallel to the other axis (either defining line properly being an *ordinate*, with the distance along the axis from the point where it intersects the axis to the point of intersection of the axes themselves as its *abscissa*, although *ordinate* is commonly applied to the defining line drawn to the horizontal axis or to a corresponding length along the other axis, and *abscissa* to the defining line parallel to the horizontal axis or to a corresponding length along the horizontal axis).—**co-ör′di-nate** (-nāt), *v.*; *-nated, -nating.* **I.** *tr.* To place or class in the same order, rank, division, etc.; also, to place or arrange in due order or proper relative position; combine in harmonious relation or action. **II.** *intr.* To become coördinate; also, to assume proper order or relation; act in harmonious combination.—**co-ör′di-nate-ly** (-nạt-li), *adv.*—**co-ör-di-na′tion** (-nā′shọn), *n.* The act of coördinating, or the state of being coördinated; a making or being coördinate; due ordering or proper relation; harmonious combination.—**co-ör′di-na-tive** (-nạ-tiv), *a.* Coördinating; expressing or indicating coördination.—**co-ör′di-na-tor** (-nā-tọr), *n.*

coot (köt), *n.* [ME. *coote, cote,* = D. *koet.*] Any of the aquatic birds constituting the genus *Fulica*, characterized by lobate toes and short wings and tail, as *F. atra* ('bald coot') of Europe; also, any of various other swimming or diving birds, as the scoter; also, a fool or simpleton (colloq.).

European Coot (*Fulica atra*).

coot-ie (kö′ti), *n.* [Origin uncertain.] A louse. [Soldiers' slang.]

cop[1] (kop), *n.* [AS. *cop, copp,* top, summit: cf. D. *kop*, G. *kopf*, head.] The top or crest of anything, esp. of a hill (obs. or prov.); a conical heap (prov. Eng.); in *spinning*, a conical mass of thread, etc., wound on a spindle in a spinning-machine.

cop[2] (kop), *v. t.*; *copped, copping.* [Origin uncertain.] To catch; lay hold of; also, to steal. [Slang.]—**cop**[2], *n.* A policeman. [Slang.]

co-pai-ba (kọ-pī′bạ̈ or -pā′bạ̈), *n.* [Sp. and Pg. *copaiba*; from Brazilian name.] An oleoresin with aromatic odor and acrid taste, obtained from various tropical (chiefly South American) trees of the cæsalpiniaceous genus *Copaiva* (or *Copaiba* or *Copaifera*), used in medicine (as a stimulant and diuretic) and in the arts. Also **co-pai′va** (-pī′vạ̈ or -pā′vạ̈).

co-pal (kō′pạl), *n.* [Sp. *copal*, < Mex. *copalli*, resin.] A hard, lustrous resin yielded by various tropical trees, used chiefly in making varnishes.

co-palm (kō′päm), *n.* [Origin unknown.] A fragrant yellowish balsamic liquid exuded in warm regions by the sweet-gum, *Liquidambar styraciflua*; also, the tree.

co-par-ce-na-ry (kō-pär′sẹ-nạ-ri), *n.* [See *co-* and *parcenary.*] Joint heirship; also, copartnership; joint ownership.—**co-par′ce-ner,** *n.* [See *parcener.*] A coheir or coheiress.—**co-par′ce-ny,** *n.* Coparcenary.

co-part-ner (kō-pärt′nėr), *n.* [See *co-*.] A fellow-partner; an associate.—**co-part′ner-ship,** *n.*

cope[1] (kōp), *n.* [ME. *cope, cape,* < ML. *capa*, E. *cape*[2].] A cloak† or cape†; specif., a long mantle of silk or other material worn by ecclesiastics over the alb or surplice in processions and on other occasions; fig., any cloak-like or canopy-like covering; often, the vault of heaven, or the sky (as, "the cheapest country under the *cope*": Shakspere's "Pericles," iv. 6. 132); in *arch.*, a coping.—**cope**[1], *v.*; *coped, coping.* **I.** *tr.* To furnish with or as with a cope; provide with or as with a coping. **II.** *intr.* To slope downward like a coping.

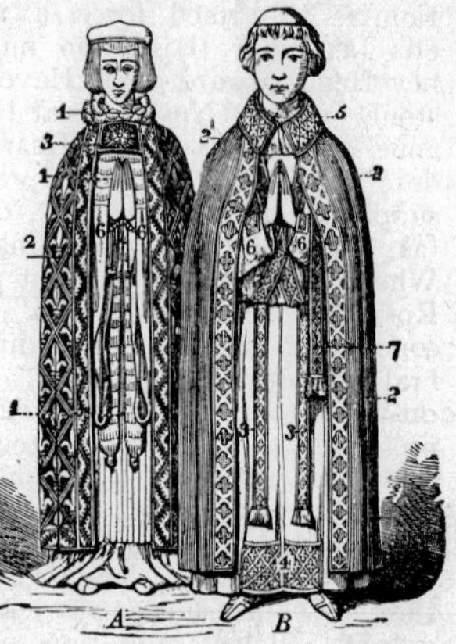

Copes.

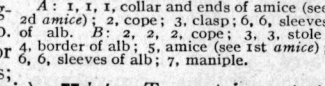

A: 1, 1, 1, collar and ends of amice (see 2d *amice*); 2, cope; 3, clasp; 6, 6, sleeves of alb. *B*: 2, 2, 2, cope; 3, 3, stole; 4, border of alb; 5, amice (see 1st *amice*); 6, 6, sleeves of alb; 7, maniple.

cope[2] (kōp), *v.*; *coped, coping.* [OF. *couper*, strike (F. *couper*, cut), < *coup*, stroke, blow: see *coup*[1].] **I.** *intr.* To come to blows†; struggle or contend (*with*), esp. on fairly even terms or with a degree of success; have to do (*with*: archaic). **II.**† *tr.* To meet in contest.

cope[3] (kōp), *v. t.*; *coped, coping.* [= D. *koopen*, buy.] To buy†; bargain for; barter; exchange. [Prov. Eng.]

co-peck (kō′pek), *n.* See *kopeck.*

co-pe-pod (kō′pẹ-pod). [NL. *Copepoda*, pl., < Gr. κώπη, handle, oar, + πούς (ποδ-), foot.] **I.** *n.* Any of the *Copepoda*, a large order of (mostly) minute fresh-water and marine crustaceans, many of which have 4 or 5 pairs of oar-like appendages for swimming, etc. **II.** *a.* Pertaining to the *Copepoda.*—**co-pep-o-dous** (kọ-pep′ọ-dus), *a.*

cop-er (kō′pėr), *n.* [See *cope*[3].] A dealer; esp., a horse-dealer. [Eng.]

Co-per-ni-can (kọ-pėr′ni-kạn), *a.* Of or pertaining to the astronomer Copernicus (1473–1543), who promulgated the now accepted astronomical theory that the earth and the planets move about the sun.

copes-mate† (kōps′māt), *n.* [Earlier *copemate*: see *cope*[2].] A person with whom one copes or contends; an antagonist; also, a companion (see Shakspere's "Lucrece," 925).

cope-stone (kōp′stōn), *n.* The top stone of a building or the like; a stone used for or in a coping; fig., the crown.

cop-i-a-ble (kop′i-ạ-bl), *a.* That may be copied.

cop-i-er (kop′i-ėr), *n.* One who copies; a copyist.

cop-ing (kō′ping), *n.* The uppermost course of a wall or the like, usually made sloping so as to carry off water.

co-pi-ous (kō′pi-us), *a.* [L. *copiosus*, < *copia*, plenty: see *copy.*] Having or yielding an abundant supply; often, exhibiting abundance or fullness, as of thoughts or words; also, large in quantity or number; abundant; plentiful; ample.—**co′pi-ous-ly,** *adv.*—**co′pi-ous-ness,** *n.*

co-pol-y-mer (kọ-pol′i-mėr), *n.* In *chem.*, a compound made by copolymerizing one or more hydrocarbons.—**co-pol-y-mer-ize** (kọ-pol′i-mėr-īz), *v. t.* or *i.* [*co-* + *polymerize.*] To subject to or undergo a change analogous to polymerization but with a union of unlike molecules.—**co-pol″y-mer-i-za′tion** (kọ-pol″i-mėr-i-zā′shọn), *n.*

copped (kopt), *a.* [See *cop*[1].] Rising to a point; conical.

cop-per[1] (kop′ėr). [AS. *coper, copor,* < LL. *cuprum,* for L. *Cyprium,* 'Cyprian metal,' < *Cyprus,* the island of Cyprus in the eastern Mediterranean.] **I.** *n.* Chem. sym., Cu (see *cuprum*); at. wt., 63.57; sp. gr., 8.84. A malleable, ductile metallic element having a characteristic reddish-brown color; also, a copper coin, as the English penny or halfpenny or the U. S. cent; a vessel made of copper, esp. a large boiler, as for cooking on shipboard; a copper plate with an engraved or etched design, prepared for printing. **II.** *a.* Made of copper; pertaining to copper; copper-colored.—**copper pyrites,** chalcopyrite.—**cop′per**[1], *v. t.* To cover, coat, or sheathe with copper; also, in the game of faro, to place a copper cent or other token upon (a card) to indicate that the player wishes to bet against that card; hence (slang), to bet against (a tip, etc.); act in opposition to (a scheme, etc.).

cop-per[2] (kop′ėr), *n.* [See *cop*[2].] A policeman. [Slang.]

cop-per-as (kop′e̤-ra̤s), *n.* [OF. *copperose, couperose* (F. *couperose*), < ML. *cuprosa,* < LL. *cuprum*: see *copper*[1].] Vitriol†; in present use, green vitriol, or ferrous sulphate, used in dyeing, ink-making, medicine, photography, etc.

cop-per=col-or (kop′ėr-kul″o̤r), *n.* A lustrous reddish-brown color.—**cop′per=col″ored,** *a.*

cop-per=glance (kop′ėr-gläns), *n.* Same as *chalcocite.*

cop-per-head (kop′ėr-hed), *n.* A venomous snake, *Ancistrodon contortrix,* of the U. S., having a copper-colored head, and reaching a length of about 3 feet; also [often *cap.*], a Northern sympathizer with the South during the American Civil War; hence, any one who opposes the government of his own country in the interest of another country.—**cop′per-head-ism,** *n.* The principles or practices of copperheads.

Copperhead.

cop-per-ish (kop′ėr-ish), *a.* Copper-like; coppery.

cop-per=nick-el (kop′ėr-nik″e̤l), *n.* Same as *niccolite.*

cop-per-plate (kop′ėr-plāt). **I.** *n.* A plate of copper on which something is engraved or etched for printing; also, a print from such a plate; also, engraving or printing of this kind. **II.** *a.* Engraved or etched on copper, or printed from a copperplate.

cop-per=smith (kop′ėr-smith), *n.* A worker in copper; one who manufactures copper utensils; also, the crimson-breasted barbet, *Megalæma hæmacephala,* a common bird in India, etc., remarkable for its ringing metallic notes.

cop-per-worm (kop′ėr-wėrm), *n.* A ship-worm.

cop-per-y (kop′ėr-i), *a.* Of, like, or containing copper.

cop-pice (kop′is), *n.* [OF. *copeiz,* < *coper, couper,* cut: see *coupé.*] A wood or thicket of small trees or bushes, esp. one grown for periodical cutting (as, "When first the liquid note . . . in April suddenly Breaks from a *coppice* gemm'd with green and red": Tennyson's "Marriage of Geraint," 339); also, small trees or bushes collectively; brushwood or underwood.—**cop′pice,** *v. t.*; *-piced, -picing.* To treat as a coppice; cut so as to produce coppice; also, to cover or inclose with or as with a coppice.

cop-ple (kop′l), *n.* [Dim. of *cop*[1].] A crest on a bird's head. [Now prov.]—**cop′ple=crown,** *n.* A tuft of feathers on a bird's head; hence, a crested fowl. [Now prov.]—**cop′ple=crowned,** *a.*

cop-ra (kop′ra̤), *n.* [E. Ind.] The dried kernel or meat of the cocoanut, from which cocoanut-oil is expressed.

co-pre-mi-a, co-præ-mi-a (ko-prē′mi-a̤), *n.* [NL., < Gr. κόπρος, dung, + αἷμα, blood.] In *pathol.,* blood-poisoning due to absorption of fecal matter.—**co-pre′mic, co-præ′mic,** *a.*

copro-. Form of Gr. κόπρος, dung, used in combination.—**cop-ro-lite** (kop′rọ-līt), *n.* [+ *-lite.*] A roundish, stony mass consisting of petrified fecal matter of animals.—**co-prol-o-gy** (ko-prol′ọ-ji), *n.* [+ Gr. -λογία, < λέγειν, pick, gather.] A gathering of ordure or filth; filth in literature or art.—**co-proph′a-gous** (-prof′a̤-gus), *a.* [Gr. κοπροφάγος: see *-phagous.*] Feeding on dung, as certain beetles.

copse (kops), *n.* [= *coppice.*] A coppice: as, "We arrived at a *copse* of trees, close to the road-side" (Marryat's "Peter Simple," xxiii.).—**copse′wood,** *n.* A coppice; the wood of a coppice.

Copt (kopt), *n.* [Cf. Ar. *Qibtī,* Copt, Gr. Αἰγύπτιος, Egyptian.] One of the natives of Egypt descended from the ancient Egyptians; an Egyptian Christian of the sect of the Monophysites.—**Cop′tic. I.** *a.* Of or pertaining to the Copts. **II.** *n.* The language of the Copts, still used in the Coptic Church.

cop-u-la (kop′ū-la̤), *n.*; pl. *-las,* L. *-læ* (-lē). [L., a band, bond, < *co-,* together, + *apere,* fasten, join.] Something that connects or links together; in *gram.* and *logic,* that word or part of a proposition, esp. a form of the verb *be,* which expresses the relation between the subject and the predicate; in *anat.,* a connecting bone, cartilage, etc.—**cop′u-lar** (-la̤r), *a.* Pertaining to or of the nature of a copula.

cop-u-late (kop′ū-lāt), *v.*; *-lated, -lating.* [L. *copulatus,* pp. of *copulare,* < *copula*: see *copula.*] **I.**† *tr.* To join together; couple. **II.** *intr.* To join together†; specif., to unite in sexual intercourse.—**cop-u-la′tion** (-lā′sho̤n), *n.* [L. *copulatio(n-).*] A joining together or coupling, or the resulting state; specif., sexual union or intercourse.—**cop′u-la-tive** (-la̤-tiv). [LL. *copulativus.*] **I.** *a.* Serving to unite or couple (as, a *copulative* conjunction, one, like *and,* that connects the meaning as well as the construction: cf. *disjunctive*); involving connected words or clauses (as, a *copulative* sentence); of the nature of a copula (as, a *copulative* verb, such as *became* in 'he became captain'); also, of or pertaining to copulation. **II.** *n.* A copulative word; a copulative conjunction; also, a person about to be married† (see Shakspere's "As You Like It," v. 4. 58).—**cop′u-la-tive-ly,** *adv.*—**cop′u-la-to-ry** (-tọ-ri), *a.* Pertaining to or serving for copulation; copulative.

cop-y (kop′i), *n.*; pl. *copies* (-iz). [OF. F. *copie,* < L. *copia,* plenty, abundance, facilities, ML. a copy or transcript, < L. *co-,* together, + *ops,* power, means, wealth.] Plenty†; fullness† or richness†; also, a transcript, reproduction, or imitation of an original; hence, copyhold; also, one of the various examples or specimens of the same book, engraving, or the like; also, that which is to be transcribed, reproduced, or imitated; an example of penmanship to be copied by a pupil; written or printed matter to be reproduced in type; also, copyright†.—**cop′y,** *v.*; *copied, copying.* [OF. F. *copier,* < ML. *copiare,* < *copia.*] **I.** *tr.* To make a copy of; transcribe; reproduce; also, to follow as a pattern or model; imitate; also, to produce as a copy of something else. **II.** *intr.* To make a copy or copies; make or do something in imitation of something else.

cop-y=book (kop′i-bụk), *n.* A book for or containing copies, as of documents; also, a book in which copies are written or printed for learners to imitate.

cop-y-hold (kop′i-hōld), *n.* In England, a tenure of lands of a manor by transcript of the roll or record of the manorial court; also, an estate held by this tenure.—**cop′y-hold″er,** *n.* One who holds an estate in copyhold.

cop-y=hold-er (kop′i-hōl″dėr), *n.* One who or that which holds copy; a proof-reader's assistant who reads the copy aloud, or follows it while the proof is read, for the detection of deviations from it in the proof.

cop-y-ing (kop′i-ing), *n.* The act of one who or that which copies: often in composition, as in *copying-ink* (ink suitable for making originals from which copies are to be taken in a copying-press), *copying-paper* (thin unsized paper used in making copies in a copying-press), *copying-press* (a machine for taking by pressure copies of originals made with copying-ink), *copying-ribbon* (a ribbon prepared with copying-ink, for use in typewriting matter to be copied in a copying-press).

cop-y-ist (kop′i-ist), *n.* A copier; esp., a transcriber of documents.

cop-y-right (kop′i-rīt). **I.** *n.* The exclusive right, granted by law for a certain term of years, to make and dispose of copies of, and otherwise to control, a literary, musical, or artistic work. **II.** *a.* Protected by copyright.—**cop′y-right,** *v. t.* To secure a copyright on; protect by copyright.—**cop′y-right″er,** *n.*

coque (kok, F. kok), *n.* [F., 'shell.'] A loop, knot, or bow of ribbon for trimming.

coque-li-cot (kōk′li-kō, F. kok-lē-kō), *n.* [F., poppy, orig. an imitative word for the crow of the cock, whose red crest the flower was thought to resemble.] The common red poppy, *Papaver rhœas*; also, the bright-red color of its corolla.

co-quet (kǫ-ket′). [F., dim. of *coq*, cock.] **I.** *n.* A male flirt; also, a coquette. [Obs. or archaic.] **II.** *a.* Coquettish.—**co-quet′,** *v. i.*; *-quetted, -quetting.* [F. *coqueter.*] To trifle in love; flirt; play the coquette; in general, to act without seriousness or decision; trifle or dally (*with*).—**co-quet-ry** (kō′ket-ri), *n.*; pl. *-ries* (-riz). [F. *coquetterie.*] The behavior or arts of a coquette; flirtation; trifling.—**co-quette** (kǫ-ket′), *n.* [F., fem. of *coquet.*] A woman who endeavors to gain the admiration and affections of men for mere self-gratification; a flirt: as, "Ichabod . . . had to win his way to the heart of a country *coquette*, beset with a labyrinth of whims and caprices" (Irving's "Sketch-Book," Sleepy Hollow).—**co-quet′tish,** *a.* Resembling a coquette; pertaining to or characterized by coquetry.—**co-quet′-tish-ly,** *adv.*

co-quil-la=nut (kǫ-kēl′yą-nut), *n.* [Pg. *coquilho*, dim. of *coco*, cocoanut.] The elongated oval fruit or nut of a South American palm, *Attalea funifera*, having a very hard brown shell, which is extensively used in turnery.

co-qui-na (kǫ-kē′ną), *n.* [Sp., shell-fish, cockle.] A soft, whitish rock composed of fragments of marine shells.

co-qui-to (kǫ-kē′tō), *n.*; pl. *-tos* (-tōz). [Sp., dim. of *coco*, cocoanut.] A palm, *Jubæa spectabilis*, of Chile, bearing small edible nuts, and yielding a sap which is boiled to a sweet syrup.

cor-a-cle (kor′ą-kl), *n.* [W. *corwgl.*] A small boat of a type used in Wales and elsewhere, made by covering a wicker frame with leather, oilcloth, or the like: as, "In his hand The stripling held an oar, and on his back, Like a broad shield, the *coracle* was hung" (Southey's "Madoc," i. 13. 172).—**cor′a-cler** (-klėr), *n.* One who uses a coracle.

Fisherman with Coracle.

cor-a-coid (kor′ą-koid). [Gr. κορακοειδής, < κόραξ, raven, crow, + εἶδος, form.] **I.** *a.* Resembling a crow's beak; noting or pertaining to a bony process extending from the scapula toward the sternum of most mammals, or a homologous part forming a distinct bone in the pectoral arch of monotremes, birds, reptiles, etc. **II.** *n.* The coracoid process or bone.

cor-al (kor′ąl). [OF. *coral* (F. *corail*), < LL. *corallum*, L. *corallium*, < Gr. κοράλλιον.] **I.** *n.* The hard, calcareous (red, white, black, etc.) skeleton of any of various mostly compound, marine cœlenterate animals, the individual polyps of which come forth by budding; such skeletons collectively, as forming reefs, islands, etc.; an animal of this kind; something made of coral, as an ornament, child's toy, etc.; also, the unimpregnated roe or eggs of the lobster, which when boiled assume the color of red coral. **II.** *a.* Composed of or containing coral; pertaining to or resembling coral, esp. red coral.—**cor′al=ber″ry,** *n.* A North American caprifoliaceous shrub, *Symphoricarpos symphoricarpos*, bearing clusters of coral-red berries in the axils of the leaves.—**cor′aled, cor′alled,** *a.* Abounding in coral.—**cor-al-lif-er-ous** (kor-ą-lif′ẹ-rus), *a.* [See *-ferous.*] Bearing or producing coral.—**cor′al-line** (-lin). [LL. *corallinus.*] **I.** *a.* Consisting of or containing coral; coral-like; coral-red. **II.** *n.* Any alga or seaweed of the genus *Corallina* or related genera, having a red color and calcareous fronds; also, any of various coral-like animals.—**cor′al-lite** (-līt), *n.* In *paleon.*, a fossil coral; in *zoöl.*, the coral skeleton of an individual polyp.—**cor′al-loid,** *a.* [See *-oid.*] Having the form or appearance of coral. Also **cor-al-loi′dal.**—**co-ral-lum** (ko-ral′um), *n.*; pl. *coralla* (-ä). [LL.] The calcareous skeleton of a compound coral, consisting of individual corallites.—**cor′al-root,** *n.* Any species of the orchidaceous genus *Corallorhiza*, comprising brownish or yellowish plants destitute of green foliage and parasitic on the roots of other plants: so called from the coral-like rootstock.—**cor′al=snake,** *n.* Any of various snakes with red markings, esp. of the venomous genus *Elaps*, as *E. fulvius* of the southern United States.

Fan-coral (*Rhipidogorgia flabellum*).

co-ran-to (ko-ran′tō), *n.* Same as *courante.*

cor-ban (kôr′ban), *n.* [Heb. *qorbān.*] Among the ancient Jews, an offering of any kind made to God, esp. in fulfilment of a vow.

cor-beil (kôr′bel), *n.* [F. *corbeille*, < LL. *corbicula*, dim. of L. *corbis*, basket.] In *arch.*, a sculptured ornament in the form of a basket of flowers, fruit, etc.

cor-bel (kôr′bel), *n.* [OF. *corbel* (F. *corbeau*), dim. of *corb, corf*, < L. *corvus*, raven.] In *arch.*, a supporting projection of stone, wood, etc., on the face of a wall.—**cor′bel,** *v.*; *-beled* or *-belled, -beling* or *-belling.* **I.** *tr.* To furnish with or support by a corbel or corbels. **II.** *intr.* To project on or as on corbels.—**cor′bel-ing, cor′bel-ling,** *n.* In *arch.*, the construction of corbels; work consisting of corbels; specif., an overlapping arrangement of stones, etc., each course projecting beyond the one below.

Corbel.

cor-bie (kôr-bi), *n.* [OF. *corb*, raven: see *corbel.*] A raven; a crow. [Sc.]—**cor′bie=steps,** *n. pl.* A series of step-like projections on the sloping sides of a gable.

cord (kôrd), *n.* [OF. F. *corde*, < L. *chorda*, cord, string: see *chord*[1].] A string or small rope composed of several strands twisted or woven together; sometimes, a hangman's rope; also, something resembling a cord or rope; a cord-like rib on the surface of cloth; hence, a ribbed fabric, esp. corduroy; *pl.*, corduroy breeches or trousers; *sing.*, in fig. use, any influence which binds, restrains, etc.; also, a measure of cut wood (orig. measured with a cord), equal to 128 cubic feet, or a pile 8 feet long, 4 feet high, and 4 feet broad; in *anat.*, a cord-like structure (as, the spinal *cord* or the vocal *cords*: see under *spinal* and *vocal*).—**cord foot,** a measure of cut wood equal to one eighth of a cord, or 16 cubic feet.—**cord,** *v. t.* To furnish with a cord; bind or fasten with cords; also, to pile or stack up (wood) in cords.—**cord-age** (kôr′dāj), *n.* Cords or ropes collectively, esp. in a ship's rigging (as, "He . . . Heard . . . the rattle of *cordage* Thrown on the deck": Longfellow's "Courtship of Miles Standish," iv.); also, quantity of wood measured in cords.

Corbie-steps.—Schaffhausen, Switzerland.

cor-date (kôr′dāt), *a.* [NL. *cordatus*, < L. *cor* (*cord-*), heart.] Heart-shaped, as a shell; esp., of leaves, heart-shaped with the attachment at the notched end. Cf. *obcordate.*—**cor′date-ly,** *adv.*

cord-ed (kôr′ded), *p. a.* Furnished with, made of, or in the form of cords; ribbed, as a fabric; bound with cords; also, of wood, stacked up in cords.

Cordate Leaf.

Cor-de-lier (kôr-dẹ-lēr′, F. kôr-dė-lyā), *n.* [F.] A Franciscan friar (so called from his girdle of knotted cord); *pl.*, a certain Parisian political club in the time of the French Revolution, which met in an old convent of the Cordeliers or Franciscans.

cor-delle (kôr′del or kôr-del′), *n.* [F., dim. of *corde*, E. *cord.*] A tow-line. [Canada and local, U. S.]—**cor-delle** (kôr′del or kôr-del′), *v. t.* or *i.*; *-delled, -delling.* To tow (a boat) with a cordelle. [Canada and local, U. S.]

cord-er (kôr′dėr), *n.* One who or that which furnishes with or applies a cord.

cor-dial (kôr′ḍịal). [OF. F. *cordial*, < ML. *cordialis*, < L. *cor* (*cord-*), heart.] **I.** *a.* Of or pertaining to the heart†; also, invigorating the heart; stimulating; fig., hearty; warmly friendly. **II.** *n.* Anything that invigorates or exhilarates; esp., a cordial or stimulating medicine; also, a strong, sweet, aromatic alcoholic liquor; a liqueur.—**cor-dial′i-ty** (-ḍial′i-ti), *n.*; pl. *-ties* (-tiz). Cordial quality or feeling; heartiness; warm friendliness; an instance or expression of cordial feeling.—**cor′dial-ly,** *adv.*—**cor′dial-ness,** *n.*

cor-di-form (kôr′di-fôrm), *a.* [L. *cor* (*cord-*), heart: see *-form.*] Heart-shaped.

cor-dil-le-ra (kôr-dil-yā′rạ), *n.* [Sp., ult. < L. *chorda*, cord, a string.] A chain of mountains: often in *pl.*, as, the *Cordilleras* of the Andes or of western North America.—**cor-dil-le′ran,** *a.*

cord-ing (kôr′ding), *n.* The act or work of one who or that which cords; also, an arrangement of cord on or about something, as for ornament or for fastening; also, the cords or ribs of a corded fabric.

cord-ite (kôr′dīt), *n.* [So named from its cord-like or cylindrical form.] A smokeless powder composed chiefly of nitroglycerin and guncotton.

cor-don (kôr′dọn), *n.* [F. *cordon*, < *corde*, E. *cord.*] A cord or braid worn for ornament or as a fastening; a ribbon worn, usually diagonally across the breast, as a badge of a knightly or honorary order; a line of sentinels, military posts, or the like, inclosing or guarding a particular place; a line beyond which passage is prohibited, as about an infected district; in *fort.*, a projecting course of stones at the base of a parapet; also, the coping of an escarp; in *arch.*, a string-course.—**sanitary cordon.** See under *sanitary, a.*—**cor-don bleu** (kôr-dôṅ blė). [F., blue ribbon.] The sky-blue ribbon worn as a badge by knights of the old French order of the Holy Ghost, the highest order of knighthood under the Bourbons; hence, some similar high distinction; also, one entitled to wear the cordon bleu; hence, any person of great distinction in his field.—**cor-don sa-ni-taire** (kôr-dôṅ sȧ-nē-tãr). [F.] Same as *sanitary cordon*, under *sanitary, a.*

Cor-do-van (kôr′dọ-vạn). **I.** *a.* Of or pertaining to Cordova, Spain; [*l. c.*] designating a kind of leather made orig. at Cordova, at first of goatskin tanned and dressed, but later also of split horsehide, etc.; also, made of this leather. **II.** *n.* A native or inhabitant of Cordova; [*l. c.*] cordovan leather.

cor-du-roy (kôr′dụ-roi). [Appar. < F. *corde du roi*, 'king's cord' (not found, however, in F. as a name for the fabric).] **I.** *n.* A thick cotton stuff corded or ribbed on the surface; *pl.*, trousers or breeches made of this; *sing.*, a corduroy road. **II.** *a.* Made of corduroy; also, resembling corduroy; specif., constructed of logs laid together transversely, as a road across swampy ground.—**cor′du-roy,** *v. t.* To form, as a road, by laying logs together transversely; also, to make a corduroy road over.

cord-wain (kôrd′wān), *n.* [OF. *cordoan*, < Sp. *cordovan* (now *cordobán*), leather of Cordova.] Cordovan leather: as, "Buskins he wore of costliest *cordwayne*" (Spenser's "Faerie Queene," vi. 2. 6). [Archaic.]—**cord′wain-er,** *n.* A worker in cordwain or cordovan leather, or in leather of any kind; a shoemaker. [Archaic.]—**cord′wain-er-y,** *n.* The craft or occupation of a cordwainer; working in leather; shoemaking. [Archaic.]

cord-y (kôr′di), *a.* Of or like cord.

core (kōr), *n.* [ME. *core*: cf. L. *cor*, heart.] The central part of a fleshy fruit, containing the seeds; hence, the central part of anything, as the unburnt part in the center of a piece of coal, or the fibrous innermost part of a boil; also, a central portion cut out and removed; a central part left after the surrounding parts have been cut away; also, a central part different from what surrounds it; also, the heart, or innermost or most essential part, of anything; in *founding*, an inner mold placed within an outer mold to fill a space intended to be left hollow in a casting; in *elect.*, the piece of iron, bundle of iron wires, or the like, forming the central or inner portion of an electromagnet, induction-coil, or the like; in *teleg.*, the central conducting wires in a submarine or subterranean cable.—**core,** *v. t.*; *cored, coring.* To remove the core of (fruit); also, to cut from the central part of something (as, "From one vast mount of marble stone The mighty temple had been *cored*": Joaquin Miller's "Walker in Nicaragua," i. 33); also, to inclose in the center of something; in *founding*, to make or mold on a core.

co-re-li-gion-ist (kō-rẹ-lij′ọn-ist), *n.* [See *co-.*] An adherent of the same religion as another.

co-re-op-sis (kō-rẹ-op′sis), *n.* [NL., < Gr. κόρις, bug, + ὄψις, appearance; so called from the form of the seed.] Any plant of the asteraceous genus *Coreopsis*, including familiar garden species with yellow, brownish-red, or party-colored (yellow and red) flowers.

cor-e-plas-ty (kor′ẹ-plas-ti), *n.* [Gr. κόρη, pupil: see *-plasty.*] In *surg.*, a plastic operation on the pupil of the eye, esp. one for forming an artificial pupil.—**cor-e-plas′-tic,** *a.*

cor-er (kōr′ėr), *n.* An instrument for cutting the core out of apples, etc.

co=re-spond-ent (kō-rẹ-spon′dẹnt), *n.* [See *co-.*] In *law*, a joint respondent, esp. in a divorce proceeding.—**co=re-spond′en-cy,** *n.*

corf (kôrf), *n.*; pl. *corves* (kôrvz). [Cf. D. *korf*, basket.] A basket (obs. or prov. Eng.); formerly, a large, strong basket used for carrying ore, coal, etc., in mining; now, a wooden or iron box or tub so used.

Cor-fi-ote (kôr′fi-ōt), *n.* [See *-ote.*] A native or inhabitant of the island of Corfu, the most northerly of the Ionian Islands (to the west of Greece). Also **Cor′fute** (-fūt).

co-ri-a-ceous (kō-ri-ā′shius), *a.* [LL. *coriaceus*, < L. *corium*, leather.] Resembling leather; also, consisting of leather.

co-ri-an-der (kō-ri-an′dėr), *n.* [OF. F. *coriandre*, < L. *coriandrum*, < Gr. κορίαννον.] An apiaceous plant, *Coriandrum sativum*, bearing aromatic seedlike fruit ('coriander-seeds') used in cookery and medicine; also, the fruit or seeds.

Coriander.

Co-rin-thi-an (kọ-rin′thi-ạn). **I.** *a.* Pertaining to Corinth, a city of ancient Greece noted for its artistic adornment, luxury, and licentiousness; hence, ornate, as literary style; luxurious; licentious; also, amateur; in *arch.*, noting or pertaining to one of the three Greek orders, distinguished by a capital adorned with rows of acanthus-leaves. **II.** *n.* A native or inhabitant of Corinth; also, a gay, licentious, or shameless fellow†; a man of fashion; a wealthy amateur sportsman; an amateur, esp. an amateur yachtsman; *pl.*, the two books or epistles of the New Testament addressed by St. Paul to the Corinthians.

Corinthian Order (Roman example).

co-ri-um (kō′ri-um), *n.*; pl. *coria* (-ạ). [L., skin, hide, leather.] In *anat.*, the sensitive vascular layer of the skin, beneath the epidermis; the derma; also, the corresponding layer of the mucous membrane.

cork (kôrk), *n.* [ME. *cork* = D. *kurk* = G. *kork*; perhaps through Sp. < L. *cortex*, bark, or possibly L. *quercus*, oak.] The outer bark of a species of oak, *Quercus suber*, of Mediterranean countries, used for making stoppers of bottles, floats, etc.; also, the tree itself; also, something made of cork; a piece of cork, or of other material (as rubber), used as a stopper for a bottle, etc.; in *bot.*, an outer tissue of bark (much developed in the oak *Quercus suber*) produced by and exterior to the phellogen.—**cork cambium.** See *cambium.*—**cork,** *v. t.* To provide or fit with cork or a cork; stop with or as with a cork (often with *up*); also, to blacken with burnt cork.

cork-age (kôr′kāj), *n.* The corking or uncorking of bottles, or a charge made for this; specif., a charge made by hotel-keepers, etc., for uncorking and serving bottles of wine or other liquor not supplied by the house.

corked (kôrkt), *p. a.* Provided or stopped with a cork; also, blackened with burnt cork; also, of wine, tasting of the cork, or having the flavor spoiled by poor corking.

cork-er (kôr′kėr), *n.* One who or that which corks; also (slang), something that closes a discussion or settles a question; something striking or astonishing; something very good of its kind.

cork-i-ness (kôr′ki-nes), *n.* Corky quality.

cork-ing (kôr′king), *p. a.* That corks; also, excellent or fine (slang).

cork-screw (kôrk′skrö). **I.** *n.* An instrument consisting of a metal screw or helix with a sharp point and a transverse handle, used to draw corks from bottles. **II.** *a.* Resembling a corkscrew; helical or spiral.—**cork′screw,** *v.* **I.** *tr.* To cause to advance in a spiral or zigzag course; also, to draw with or as with a corkscrew. **II.** *intr.* To move in a spiral course.

cork=tree (kôrk′trē), *n.* The tree *Quercus suber*, a species of oak, from which cork is obtained; also, any of certain trees with a wood resembling cork.

cork-wood (kôrk′wůd), *n.* Cork†; also, the light and porous wood of any of certain trees and shrubs, as the balsa, *Ochroma lagopus*, or a widely distributed tropical malvaceous tree, *Pariti tiliaceum* (or *Hibiscus tiliaceus*), or, esp. in the U. S., a stout shrub or small tree, *Leitneria floridana*, with shining deciduous leaves, densely pubescent aments, and a drupaceous fruit; also, any of these trees or shrubs.

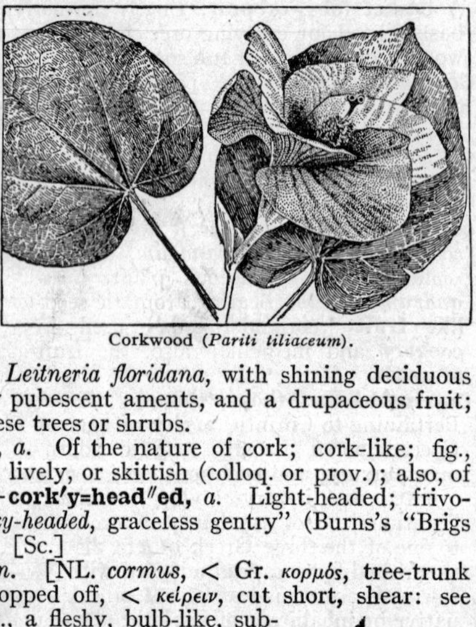
Corkwood (*Pariti tiliaceum*).

cork-y (kôr′ki), *a.* Of the nature of cork; cork-like; fig., light, buoyant, lively, or skittish (colloq. or prov.); also, of wine, corked.—**cork′y=head″ed,** *a.* Light-headed; frivolous: as, "*corky-headed*, graceless gentry" (Burns's "Brigs of Ayr," 170). [Sc.]

corm (kôrm), *n.* [NL. *cormus*, < Gr. κορμός, tree-trunk with boughs lopped off, < κείρειν, cut short, shear: see *shear.*] In *bot.*, a fleshy, bulb-like, subterranean stem, producing leaves and buds on the upper surface and roots usually on the lower, and sometimes covered by a few membranous scales (as in the crocus) or sometimes naked. Cf. *bulb.*

cor-mo-phyte (kôr′mǫ-fīt), *n.* [NL. *Cormophyta*, pl., < Gr. κορμός (see *corm*) + φυτόν, plant.] Any of the *Cormophyta*, an old primary division or group of plants having an axis differentiated into stem and root, and including all phanerogams and the higher cryptogams.—**cor-mo-phyt′ic** (-fit′ik), *a.*

Corm of Crocus.

cor-mo-rant (kôr′mǫ-rant), *n.* [OF. *cormaran* (F. *cormoran*), < ML. *corvus marinus*, sea-raven.] Any bird of the genus *Phalacrocorax*, comprising large, voracious, totipalmate water-birds with a long neck and a pouch under the beak in which they hold captured fish, as *P. carbo*, a common species of America, Europe, and Asia; fig., a greedy or rapacious person (as, "His treasured stores these *cormorants* consume": Pope's tr. Homer's "Odyssey," i.).

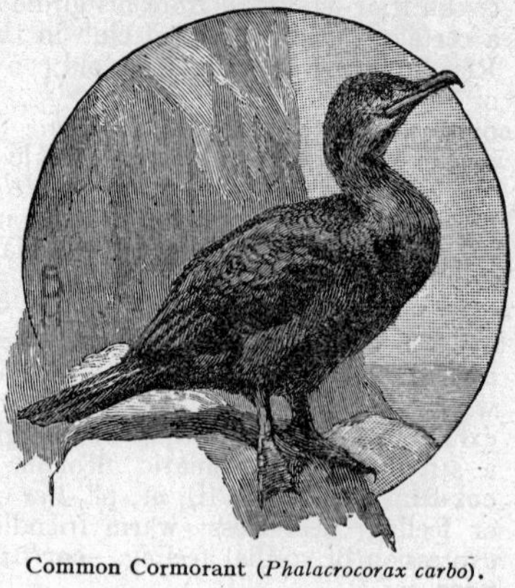
Common Cormorant (*Phalacrocorax carbo*).

corn[1] (kôrn), *n.* [AS. *corn* = D. *koren* = G. *korn* = Icel. *korn* = Goth. *kaurn*; akin to L. *granum*, grain.] A grain, as of sand (now chiefly prov.); also, a small, hard seed or fruit, esp. of a cereal plant; collectively, the seeds of cereal plants, or the plants themselves (used in Great Britain of grain generally, in England esp. of wheat, and in Scotland esp. of oats; in the U. S., commonly restricted to maize or Indian corn).—**corn**[1], *v.* **I.** *tr.* To granulate, as gunpowder; also, to preserve and season with salt in grains; lay down in brine, as meat; also, to plant (land) with corn; also, to feed with corn; also, to make drunk (slang). **II.** *intr.* Of plants, to form corns or seeds.

corn[2] (kôrn), *n.* [OF. *corn*, horn (F. *cor*, horn, corn on the foot), < L. *cornu*, horn.] A horny induration or callosity of the epidermis, usually with a central core, caused by undue pressure or friction, esp. on the toes or feet.

-corn. Termination from L. *cornu*, horn, in adjectives and nouns, as *bicorn*, *cavicorn*, *longicorn*, *plumicorn*, *unicorn*.

cor-na-ceous (kôr-nā′shius), *a.* [L. *cornus*, cornel, < *cornu*, horn.] Belonging to the *Cornaceæ*, a family of plants, mostly shrubs and trees, including the cornel or dogwood, tupelo, etc.

corn=bread (kôrn′bred′), *n.* A kind of bread made of corn-meal.

corn=cob (kôrn′kob), *n.* The elongated woody receptacle in which the grains of an ear of maize are embedded; also, a tobacco-pipe with a bowl made of this.

corn=cock-le (kôrn′kok″l), *n.* A silenaceous annual, *Agrostemma githago*, bearing red or white flowers, common as a weed among crops of grain.

corn=col-or (kôrn′kul″ǫr), *n.* A light, soft yellow.—**corn′=col″ored,** *a.*

corn=crack-er (kôrn′krak″ėr), *n.* One of a low class of whites in the southeastern U. S.; a cracker; also, the corn-crake.

corn=crake (kôrn′krāk), *n.* A European rail, *Crex pratensis*, a bird common in grain-fields.

corn=crib (kôrn′krib), *n.* A ventilated structure used for the storage of unshelled Indian corn.

corn=dodg-er (kôrn′doj″ėr), *n.* A kind of cake made of Indian meal, fried or baked hard. [Southern U. S.]

cor-ne-a (kôr′nę-ą), *n.* [NL., fem. of L. *corneus*, horny: see *corneous.*] In *anat.*, the transparent anterior part of the external coat of the eye, covering the iris and the pupil. Cf. *sclerotica.*—**cor′ne-al,** *a.*

corned (kôrnd), *p. a.* Granulated; also, preserved or cured with salt, as beef; also, intoxicated (slang).

cor-nel (kôr′nel), *n.* [OF. *cornille*, *corneille*, also *cornolle* (F. *cornouille*), < L. *cornus*, cornel-tree.] Any of the trees or shrubs, or rarely herbs, constituting the genus *Cornus*, as *C. sanguinea*, the European dogwood, or *C. florida*, the flowering dogwood of America.—**cor-ne′lian**[1] (-nē′lyąn), *a.* Pertaining to or resembling the cornel.

cor-ne-lian[2] (kôr-nē′lyąn), *n.* See *carnelian.*

cor-ne-ous (kôr′nę-us), *a.* [L. *corneus*, < *cornu*, horn.] Consisting of a horny substance; horny; horn-like.

cor-ner (kôr′nėr), *n.* [OF. *cornere*, *corniere*, < *corne*, horn, horn-like projection, < L. *cornu*, horn.] The meeting-place of two converging lines or surfaces; an angle; also, a projecting angle, esp. the place where two streets meet; sometimes, an end or margin; also, the space between two converging lines or surfaces near their intersection; hence, any narrow, secluded, or secret place; any part, even the least or the most remote; a region or quarter (as, all the *corners* of the earth); also, a piece to protect the corner of anything; also, a monopolizing or a monopoly of the available supply of a stock or commodity, for the purpose of raising the price.—**cor′ner,** *v.* **I.** *tr.* To furnish with corners; also, to place in or drive into a corner; fig., to force into an awkward or difficult position, or one from which escape is impossible; also, to form a corner in (a stock, etc.). **II.** *intr.* To meet in, or be situated on or at, a corner; also, to form a corner in a stock or commodity.—**cor′nered,** *a.* Having a corner or corners: as, four-*cornered*.—**cor′ner-er,** *n.*—**cor′ner=stone,** *n.* A stone which lies at the corner of two walls, and serves to unite them; specif., a stone built into a corner of the foundation of an important edifice as the actual or nominal starting-point in building, usually laid with formal ceremonies, and often hollowed out and made the repository of documents, etc.; fig., something of fundamental importance (see Eph. ii. 20).—**cor′ner-wise,** *adv.* In the manner of a corner; so as to form a corner; also, from corner to corner; diagonally.

cor-net (kôr′net or kôr-net′), *n.* [OF. F. *cornet,* horn, also F. *cornette,* head-dress, standard, cavalry cornet, < OF. *corne,* < L. *cornu,* horn.] Orig., a musical wind-instrument made of or resembling a horn†; later, a rude musical instrument of the oboe class†; now, a brass wind-instrument of the trumpet class, with valves and pistons ('cornet-à-pistons'); also, a little cone of paper twisted at the end, used for inclosing small wares; also, a head-dress formerly worn by women; the great white cap worn by Sisters of Charity; also, the standard or flag of a troop of cavalry†; the troop itself†; formerly, an officer in a troop of cavalry, who carried the colors.—**cor′net=à=pis′tons** (-ạ-pis′tọnz), *n.*; pl. *cornets-à-pistons.* [F., 'cornet with pistons.'] A musical instrument of the trumpet class, with valves and pistons; a cornet.—**cor′net-cy** (-si), *n.* The commission or rank of a cornet in a troop of cavalry.—**cor′net-ist, cor-net′tist,** *n.* A player upon the cornet.

Cornets-à-pistons.
1. Ordinary shape. 2. Circular shape.

corn=field (kôrn′fēld), *n.* A field in which corn (in the U. S., maize or Indian corn) is grown.

corn-flow-er (kôrn′flou″ėr), *n.* Any of several plants growing in grain-fields, as *Centaurea cyanus,* an asteraceous plant with blue (varying to white) flowers, growing wild in Europe and often cultivated for ornament.

cor-nice (kôr′nis), *n.* [F. *cornice,* now *corniche,* < It. *cornice,* possibly < L. *cornix,* crow: cf. *corbel,* ult. < L. *corvus,* raven.] A horizontal molded projection which crowns or finishes a wall, building, etc.; specif., the uppermost member of an entablature, resting on the frieze; also, any of various other ornamental moldings or bands, as for concealing hooks or rods from which curtains are hung or for supporting picture-hooks.—**cor′nice,** *v. t.*; *-niced, -nicing.* To furnish or finish with or as with a cornice.

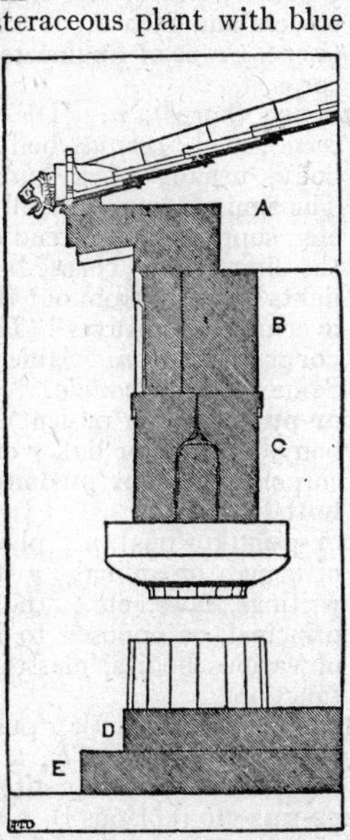

Doric Cornice Construction.
A, cornice; *B,* frieze; *C,* architrave; *D,* stylobate; *E,* stereobate.

cor-nic-u-late (kôr-nik′ū-lāt), *a.* [L. *corniculatus,* < *corniculum,* dim. of *cornu,* horn.] Horned; having small horn-like processes.

Cor-nif-er-ous (kôr-nif′ẹ-rus), *a.* [L. *cornu,* horn: see *-ferous.*] In *geol.,* noting or pertaining to a portion of the Devonian system containing hornstone.

Cor-nish (kôr′nish). **I.** *a.* Of or pertaining to Cornwall in southwestern England, its inhabitants, or the Celtic language formerly spoken by them. **II.** *n.* The ancient Celtic language of Cornwall.—**Cor′nish-man** (-mạn), *n.*; pl. *-men.*

corn=law (kôrn′lâ), *n.* A law relating to trade in grain, esp. to its exportation or importation; in *Eng. hist.,* one of a series of laws regulating the home and foreign grain-trade, repealed in 1846.

corn=meal (kôrn′mēl′), *n.* Meal made of corn or grain; oatmeal (Sc.); Indian meal (U. S.).

corn=oys-ter (kôrn′ois″tėr), *n.* A fritter containing Indian corn cut from the cob: in appearance somewhat like a fried oyster.

corn=pith (kôrn′pith), *n.* The pith of the stalk of maize, which is used in the manufacture of paper and has been used at the back of the armor of war-ships to prevent water from entering shot-holes.

corn=pone (kôrn′pōn), *n.* Corn-bread, esp. of a plain or simple kind; a cake or loaf of this. [Southern U. S.]

corn=pop-per (kôrn′pop″ėr), *n.* A utensil, as a long-handled covered pan of woven wire, in which pop-corn is popped.

corn=rose (kôrn′rōz), *n.* The common red poppy, *Papaver rhœas*; also, the corn-cockle.

corn=sal-ad (kôrn′sal′ạd), *n.* Any of several plants of the genus *Valerianella,* sometimes found wild in grain-fields, and used for salad.

corn=stalk (kôrn′stâk), *n.* The stalk or stem of corn, esp. Indian corn.

corn=starch (kôrn′stärch), *n.* A starch, or a starchy flour used for making puddings, etc., made from Indian corn.

corn=sug-ar (kôrn′shůg′ạr), *n.* A sugar made from Indian corn, being the common form of glucose.

cor-nu (kôr′nū), *n.*; pl. *cornua* (-nụ̄-ạ). [L.: see *horn.*] A horn, or horn-like part or process.

cor-nu-co-pi-a (kôr-nụ̄-kō′pi-ạ), *n.* [LL., for L. *cornu copiæ,* 'horn of plenty.'] The fabulous horn of the goat Amalthea, which suckled Zeus, represented as overflowing with flowers, fruit, etc., and symbolizing plenty; hence, an overflowing supply; also, a horn-shaped or conical receptacle or ornament.—**cor-nu-co′pi-ate** (-āt), *a.* Having the shape of a cornucopia, as certain shells.

cor-nute (kôr-nūt′), *a.* [L. *cornutus,* < *cornu,* horn.] Having horns; horn-shaped; in *bot.* and *zoöl.,* furnished with a horn-like appendage or process. Also **cor-nut′ed** (-nū′-ted).

corn-y (kôr′ni), *a.* Of, pertaining to, or abounding in corn; also, unpleasantly sentimental or unsophisticated, as certain music (slang); hence, of poor quality (slang).

cor-o-dy, cor-ro-dy (kor′ọ-di), *n.*; pl. *-dies* (-diz). [ML. *corrodium, corredium*; akin to E. *curry*².] An allowance, as of food, etc., for one's maintenance; also, the right to this. [Now chiefly hist.]

co-rol-la (kọ-rol′ạ), *n.*; pl. *-las.* [L., garland, dim. of *corona*: see *corona.*] In *bot.,* the internal envelop or floral leaves of a flower, usually of delicate texture and of some color other than green; the petals.—**cor-ol′lar,** *a.*

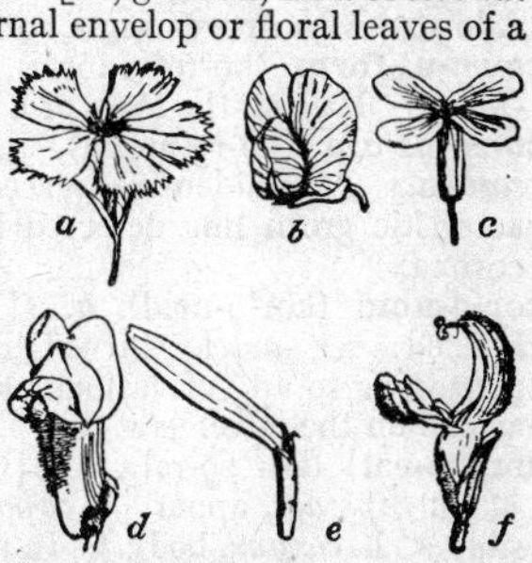

Corollas.
Polypetalous Corollas: *a,* unguiculate; *b,* papilionaceous; *c,* cruciate. Gamopetalous Corollas: *d,* personate; *e,* ligulate; *f,* labiate.

cor-ol-la-ry (kor′ọ-lā-ri, Brit. also kọ-rol′ạ-ri), *n.*; pl. *-ries* (-riz). [LL. *corollarium,* corollary, L. gift, gratuity, orig. garland, < L. *corolla*: see *corolla.*] A mathematical proposition incidentally proved in proving another; hence, an immediate or easily drawn inference; also, a natural consequence or result; also, an appendix†; also, something in excess†, or a surplus† (see Shakspere's "Tempest," iv. 1. 57).

cor-ol-late (kor′ọ-lāt), *a.* In *bot.,* having or resembling a corolla. Also **cor′ol-lat-ed** (-lā-ted).

co-ro-na (kọ-rō′nạ), *n.*; pl. *-nas,* L. *-næ* (-nē). [L., garland, wreath, E. *crown.*] A crown or garland, esp. that bestowed among the ancient Romans as a reward for distinguished services; a circular chandelier suspended from the roof or vaulting of a church; a white or colored circle of light seen round a luminous body, esp. the sun or moon (in meteorology, restricted to those circles due to the diffraction produced by thin clouds or mist: cf. *halo*); in *astron.*, a luminous envelop outside of the sun's chromosphere, observable during eclipses and remarkable for its radiating streamers; in *arch.*, that part of a cornice supported by and projecting beyond the bed-molding, and surmounted by the cymatium; in *anat.*, the upper portion or crown of a part, as of the head or a tooth; in *bot.*, a crown-like appendage, esp. one on the inner side of a corolla, as in the narcissus.

cor-o-nach (kor′ǫ-naċh), *n.* [Gael. *coranach*, outcry, dirge.] In Scotland and Ireland, a song or lamentation for the dead; a dirge: as, "The village maids and matrons round The dismal *coronach* resound" (Scott's "Lady of the Lake," iii. 15).

cor-o-nal (kor′ǫ-nạl or kǫ-rō′-), *a.* [L. *coronalis*, < *corona*: see *corona*.] Pertaining to or resembling a crown or corona; in *anat.*, noting or pertaining to a suture extending across the skull between the frontal bone and the parietal bones.—**cor′o-nal,** *n.* A crown or coronet; a garland; in *anat.*, the coronal suture.—**cor′o-nal-ly,** *adv.*

cor-o-na-ry (kor′ǫ-nạ̄-ri), *a.* [L. *coronarius*, < *corona*: see *corona*.] Pertaining to or resembling a crown; in *anat.*, encircling like a crown, as certain blood-vessels.—**coronary cushion,** a thickened ring of tissue encircling the upper part of the hoof in horses and allied animals, which secretes the horny material constituting the wall of the hoof.

cor-o-nate, cor-o-nat-ed (kor′ǫ-nāt, -nā-ted), *a.* [L. *coronatus*, pp. of *coronare*, to crown, < *corona*: see *corona*.] In *bot.*, etc., having a corona or a crown-like part.

cor-o-na-tion (kor-ǫ-nā′shǫn), *n.* [OF. *coronacion*, < L. *coronare*, to crown: see *coronate*.] The act or ceremony of investing a king, etc., with a crown; fig., the crowning of a work; completion.

cor-o-ner (kor′ǫ-nėr), *n.* [AF. *corouner*, 'officer of the crown,' < *coroune*: see *crown*.] An officer, as of a county or municipality, orig. (in England) charged with the interests of the crown, but whose chief function in modern times is to investigate, by inquest before a jury, any death not clearly due to natural causes.—**cor′o-ner-ship,** *n.*

cor-o-net (kor′ǫ-net), *n.* [OF. *coronnette*, dim. of *corone*: see *crown*.] A small or inferior crown; specif., a crown representing a dignity inferior to that of the sovereign; also, a crown-like ornament for the head, as of gold or jewels; also, some crown-like part; the lowest part of the pastern of a horse, just above the hoof.—**cor′o-net-ed,** *a.* Adorned with or wearing a coronet.

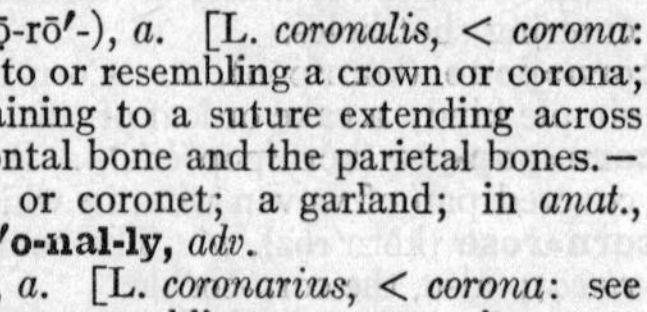

1 2
British Coronets.
1, of Prince of Wales; 2, of younger princes.

co-ro-ni-form (kǫ-rō′ni-fôrm), *a.* [L. *corona*, crown: see *-form*.] Having the form of a crown; crown-shaped.

co-ro-ni-um (kǫ-rō′ni-um), *n.* [NL., < L. *corona*: see *corona*.] An unidentified gaseous substance having a characteristic green line detected in the spectrum of the sun's corona.

cor-o-noid (kor′ǫ-noid), *a.* [Gr. κορώνη, crow, something hooked: see *-oid*.] Curved like a crow's beak; noting or pertaining to any of various processes of bone of this shape, as one on the lower jaw.

cor-po-ral[1] (kôr′pǫ-rạl), *n.* [Obs. F. *corporal*, for *caporal*, < It. *caporale*, appar. < *capo* (< L. *caput*), head, or possibly < L. *corpus*, body.] In the army, a non-commissioned officer ranking next below a sergeant and having charge of a squad.—**corporal's guard,** a small detachment under arms, such as is usually placed under the command of a corporal; in general, a very small body of persons.—**Little Corporal.** See under *little, a.*

cor-po-ral[2] (kôr′pǫ-rạl). [L. *corporalis* (as n., ML. *corporale*), < *corpus*, body.] **I.** *a.* Of or pertaining to the human body (as, *corporal* punishment, punishment inflicted on the body); bodily; physical; also, personal (as, *corporal* possession); also, corporeal† or material†; in *zoöl.*, of or pertaining to the body proper, as distinguished from the head and limbs. **II.** *n. Eccles.*, a fine cloth, usually of linen, on which the consecrated elements are placed during the celebration of the eucharist.—**cor-po-ral′i-ty** (-ral′i-ti), *n.*—**cor′po-ral-ly,** *adv.*

cor-po-rate (kôr′pǫ-rāt), *v.*; *-rated, -rating.* [L. *corporatus*, pp. of *corporare*, < *corpus*, body.] **I.** *tr.* To incorporate; unite in one body; embody. [Archaic.] **II.** *intr.* To join or unite in one body. [Archaic.]—**cor′po-rate** (-rạ̄t), *a.* United in one body; also, pertaining to a united body, as of persons; also, forming a corporation; also, of or pertaining to a corporation.—**cor′po-rate-ly,** *adv.*—**cor-po-ra′tion** (-rā′shǫn), *n.* [LL. *corporatio(n-)*.] A number of persons united or regarded as united in one body; specif., an artificial person, created by law, or under authority of law, from a group or succession of natural persons, and having a continuous existence irrespective of that of its members, and powers and liabilities distinct from those of its members (as, a *corporation* aggregate, one consisting of a number of members at the same time, as the mayor and aldermen of a city or the governing body of a college; a *corporation* sole, one consisting of but one person at a time, as a king and his successors; a joint-stock *corporation*, one whose ownership is divided into transferable shares, the object usually being the division of profits among the members in proportion to the number of shares held by each); also, the abdomen, esp. when large and prominent (colloq.).—**cor′po-ra-tive** (-rạ̄-tiv), *a.* Corporate.—**cor′po-ra-tor** (-rā-tǫr), *n.* A member of a corporation, esp. one of the original members.

cor-po-re-al (kôr-pō′rẹ̄-ạl), *a.* [L. *corporeus*, < *corpus*, body.] Of the nature of the physical body; bodily; of the nature of matter; material; tangible; pertaining to material things.—**cor-po-re-al′i-ty** (-al′i-ti), **cor-po′re-al-ness,** *n.*—**cor-po′re-al-ly,** *adv.*

cor-po-re-i-ty (kôr-pǫ-rē′i-ti), *n.* [ML. *corporeitas*, < L. *corporeus*: see *corporeal*.] Corporeal nature or quality; materiality.

cor-po-sant (kôr′pǫ-zant), *n.* [Pg. *corpo santo*, 'holy body.'] A light, due to atmospheric electricity, sometimes seen on the mastheads, yard-arms, etc., of ships and on church-towers, tree-tops, etc.: as, "Sailors have a notion that if the *corposant* rises in the rigging, it is a sign of fair weather, but if it comes lower down, there will be a storm" (Dana's "Two Years before the Mast," xxxiv.).

corps (kōr, F. kôr), *n.*; pl. *corps* (kōrz, F. kôr). [F.: see *corpse*.] A body or number of persons associated or acting together; *milit.*, an organized military body consisting of officers and men or of officers alone (as, the U. S. Marine *Corps*, *Corps* of Engineers, or Signal *Corps*); also, an army-corps.

corpse (kôrps), *n.* [OF. (also F.) *corps*, earlier *cors* (see *corse*), < L. *corpus*, body.] A living body†; also, a dead body, usually of a human being.—**corpse′=can″dle,** *n.* The ignis fatuus, or will-o'-the-wisp, seen in churchyards etc., supposed to portend death and to indicate by its course the direction the corpse-bearers will take: as, "And dreadful lights crept up from out the marsh — *Corpse-candles* gliding over nameless graves" (Tennyson's "Harold," iii. 1. 214).—**corpse′=gate,** *n.* Same as *lich-gate.*—**corpse′=light,** *n.* Same as *corpse-candle.*

cor-pu-lent (kôr′pū-lẹnt), *a.* [L. *corpulentus*, < *corpus*, body.] Large or bulky of body; portly; stout; fat; also, corporeal†. — **cor′pu-lence, cor′pu-len-cy,** *n.* — **cor′pu-lent-ly,** *adv.*

cor-pus (kôr′pus), *n.*; pl. *corpora* (-pǫ-rạ̈). [L.] The body of a man or animal; a body or complete collection, as of writings, laws, etc.; the material substance of anything; principal, as opposed to interest or income; in *anat.*, any of various bodies, masses, or parts of special character or function.

Cor-pus Chris-ti (kôr′pus kris′ti). [L., 'body of Christ.'] In the *Rom. Cath. Ch.*, a festival in honor of the eucharist, kept on the Thursday after Trinity Sunday.

cor-pus-cle (kôr′pus-l), *n.* [L. *corpusculum*, dim. of *corpus*, body.] A minute particle; a minute body forming a more or less distinct part of an organism; in *physics* and *chem.*, a minute or elementary particle of matter; specif., an electron;

in *physiol.*, one of the minute bodies which form a constituent of the blood ('blood-corpuscles,' both red and white), the lymph ('lymph-corpuscles,' white only), etc.—**cor-pus'cu-lar** (-kū-lạr), *a.* Pertaining to or of the nature of a corpuscle or corpuscles; consisting of corpuscles.—**cor-pus'cule** (-kūl), *n.* A corpuscle.

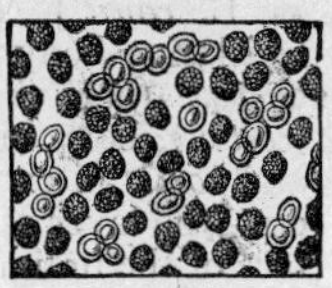

Human Blood-corpuscles (magnified).

cor-rade (kǫ-rād'), *v. t.*; *-raded, -rading.* [L. *corradere* (pp. *corrasus*), < *com-*, together, + *radere*, scrape.] To scrape or rub together; wear by scraping; in *geol.*, to cause (rock fragments, etc., transported by streams, etc.) to rub together and become worn down into finer material; also, to erode.

cor-ral (kǫ-ral'), *n.* [Sp.: cf. *kraal.*] A pen or inclosure for horses, cattle, etc. (as, "the *corral*, a narrow place, encompassed by the high clay walls, where . . . the horses and mules of the fort are crowded for safe-keeping": Parkman's "Oregon Trail," ix.); also, an inclosure formed of wagons during an encampment, for defense against attack.—**cor-ral'**, *v. t.*; *-ralled, -ralling.* To confine in or as in a corral; hence, to seize or capture (colloq., U. S.); also, to form (wagons) into a corral.

cor-ra-sion (kǫ-rā'zhọn), *n.* [See *corrade.*] The act of corrading: specif. in *geol.*

cor-rect (kǫ-rekt'), *v. t.* [L. *correctus*, pp. of *corrigere*, < *com-*, together, + *regere*, keep straight, direct.] To set right; remove the errors or faults of; rectify; also, to point out or mark the errors in; also, to admonish or rebuke in order to cause amendment; discipline; punish; also, to counteract the operation or effect of (something hurtful); in *math.*, *physics*, etc., to alter or adjust so as to bring into accordance with a standard or the like.—**cor-rect'**, *a.* In accordance with an acknowledged or accepted standard; proper; also, conforming to fact or truth; free from error; accurate.—**cor-rect'a-ble, cor-rect'i-ble,** *a.* That may be corrected.—**cor-rect'ing-ly,** *adv.*—**cor-rec'tion** (-rek'shọn), *n.* [L. *correctio(n-)*.] The act of correcting, or the state of being corrected; also, that which is substituted or proposed for what is wrong; an emendation.—**cor-rec'tion-al,** *a.*—**cor-rec'tion-al-ly,** *adv.*—**cor-rec'tive. I.** *a.* Tending to correct; having the quality of correcting. **II.** *n.* A corrective agent.—**cor-rec'tive-ly,** *adv.*—**cor-rect'ly,** *adv.*—**cor-rect'ness,** *n.*—**cor-rec'tor,** *n.*

cor-re-late (kor'ẹ-lāt or kor-ẹ-lāt'), *v.*; *-lated, -lating.* [L. *com-*, with, + *relatus*, pp.: see *relate.*] **I.** *intr.* To have a mutual relation; stand in correlation. **II.** *tr.* To place in or bring into mutual relation or orderly connection.—**cor-re-late** (kor'ẹ-lāt). **I.** *a.* Mutually related; correlated. **II.** *n.* Either of two related things, esp. when one implies the other.—**cor-re-la'tion** (-lā'shọn), *n.* The act of correlating, or the state of being correlated; mutual relation of two or more things, parts, etc.—**cor-rel-a-tive** (kǫ-rel'ạ-tiv). **I.** *a.* Being in correlation; mutually related; esp., so related that each implies or complements the other. **II.** *n.* Either of two things, as two terms, which are correlative.—**cor-rel'a-tive-ly,** *adv.*—**cor-rel'a-tive-ness, cor-rel-a-tiv'i-ty** (-tiv'i-ti), *n.*

cor-rep-tion (kǫ-rep'shọn), *n.* [L. *correptio(n-)*, < *corripere*, seize on, shorten, < *com-*, with, + *rapere*, seize.] A shortening in pronunciation; in *anc. pros.*, the treating as metrically short of a syllable usually taken as long.

cor-re-spond (kor-ẹ-spond'), *v. i.* [L. *com-*, together, + *respondere*: see *respond.*] To be similar or analogous, as one thing to another; answer in function, position, amount, etc.; be in agreement or conformity; agree (*with*); be conformable (*to*); also, to have intercourse†; esp., to communicate by exchange of letters.—**cor-re-spond'ence,** *n.* The act or fact of corresponding; relation of similarity or analogy; agreement; conformity; also, intercourse†; esp., communication by exchange of letters; also, letters that pass between correspondents; letters contributed to a newspaper, etc.—**correspondence school,** a school which gives instruction by correspondence.—**cor-re-spond'ent. I.** *a.* Corresponding; having a relation of correspondence; also, responsive† or submissive† (as, "I will be *correspondent* to command": Shakspere's "Tempest," i. 2. 297). **II.** *n.* A thing that corresponds to something else; also, one who has regular business relations with another, esp. at a distance; also, one who communicates by letters; one who contributes letters to a newspaper, etc., esp. one employed to contribute news, etc., regularly from a distant place.—**cor-re-spond'ent-ly,** *adv.*—**cor-re-spond'ing,** *p. a.* That corresponds; correspondent; corresponding by letters.—**cor-re-spond'ing-ly,** *adv.*—**cor-re-spon'sive** (-spon'siv), *a.* Corresponding; correspondent.

cor-ri-dor (kor'i-dôr or -dọr), *n.* [F. *corridor*, < It. *corridore*, < *correre*, < L. *currere*, run.] A covered walk or passage (now rare); also, a gallery or passage connecting parts of a building; a passage into which several apartments open; specif., a narrow passage along the side of a railroad-car, into which a number of separate compartments open (hence, *corridor-car*, a car having such a passage; *corridor-train*, a train of corridor-cars); also, a narrow tract of land forming a passageway, as one belonging to an inland country and affording an outlet to the sea.

cor-rie (kor'i), *n.* [Gael. *coire*, caldron.] A circular hollow in the side of a hill or mountain. [Sc.]

cor-ri-gen-dum (kor-i-jen'dum), *n.*; pl. *-da* (-dạ). [L., neut. gerundive of *corrigere*: see *correct.*] An error to be corrected; esp., an error in print indicated as such (chiefly in *pl.*).

cor-ri-gi-ble (kor'i-ji-bl), *a.* [ML. *corrigibilis*, < L. *corrigere*: see *correct.*] Capable of being corrected; submissive to correction; also, corrective† (see Shakspere's "Othello," i. 3. 329).—**cor″ri-gi-bil'i-ty** (-bil'i-ti), *n.*—**cor'ri-gi-bly,** *adv.*

cor-ri-val (kǫ-rī'vạl). [L. *corrivalis*, < *com-*, with, + *rivalis*, rival.] **I.** *n.* A rival; a competitor; also, a partner† (see Shakspere's "1 Henry IV," iv. 4. 31). **II.** *a.* Being in rivalry or competition.

cor-rob-o-rant (kǫ-rob'ọ-rạnt). [See *corroborate.*] **I.** *a.* Strengthening; invigorating. **II.** *n.* Something that strengthens; a strengthening medicine; a corroboratory fact, statement, etc.

cor-rob-o-rate (kǫ-rob'ọ-rāt), *v. t.*; *-rated, -rating.* [L. *corroboratus*, pp. of *corroborare*, < *com-*, altogether, + *roborare*, strengthen: see *roborant.*] To strengthen†; also, to make more certain; confirm.—**cor-rob-o-ra'tion** (-rā'shọn), *n.* The act of corroborating; confirmation, as of a statement; also, that which corroborates; a corroboratory fact, statement, etc. (as, "If my testimony were without *corroborations* you would reject it as incredible": C. B. Brown's "Wieland," i.).—**cor-rob'o-ra-tive** (-rạ-tiv), *a.* Having the quality of corroborating; verifying; confirmatory.—**cor-rob'o-ra-tive-ly,** *adv.*—**cor-rob'o-ra-tor** (-rā-tọr), *n.*—**cor-rob'o-ra-to-ry** (-rạ-tọ-ri), *a.* Corroborative.

cor-rob-o-ree (kǫ-rob'ǫ-rẹ), *n.* [Native Australian.] A native Australian dance of sacred, festive, or warlike character; hence (chiefly Australian), any large or noisy gathering; a disturbance; an uproar.

cor-rode (kǫ-rōd'), *v.*; *-roded, -roding.* [L. *corrodere* (pp. *corrosus*), < *com-*, altogether, + *rodere*, gnaw.] **I.** *tr.* To eat away gradually as if by gnawing, esp. by chemical action. **II.** *intr.* To penetrate by corrosion; also, to become corroded; undergo corrosion.—**cor-rod'er** (-rō'dėr), *n.*—**cor-rod'i-ble,** *a.* That may be corroded.

cor'ro-dy, *n.* See *corody.*

cor-ro-sion (kǫ-rō'zhọn), *n.* [LL. *corrosio(n-)*.] The act or process of corroding; corroded condition; also, a product of corroding, as rust.

cor-ro-sive (kǫ-rō'siv), *a.* Having the quality of corroding, eating away, or consuming.—**corrosive sublimate,** bichloride of mercury, $HgCl_2$, a strongly acrid, highly poisonous, white crystalline salt, prepared by sublimation, much used as an antiseptic and sometimes internally in minute doses as medicine.—**cor-ro'sive,** *n.* Something corrosive, as an acid, drug, etc.—**cor-ro'sive-ly,** *adv.*—**cor-ro'sive-ness,** *n.*

cor-ru-gate (kor'ǫ-gāt), *v.*; *-gated, -gating.* [L. *corrugatus*, pp. of *corrugare*, < *com-*, altogether, + *rugare*, wrinkle, < *ruga*, a wrinkle.] **I.** *tr.* To wrinkle (the skin, etc.); in general, to draw or bend into folds or alternate furrows and ridges. **II.** *intr.* To become corrugated.—**cor'ru-gate,** *a.* Corrugated; wrinkled; furrowed.—**cor-ru-ga'tion** (-gā'shọn), *n.* The act of corrugating, or the state of being corrugated; also, a wrinkle, fold, furrow, or ridge.

cor-rupt (kọ-rupt′), *v.* [L. *corruptus*, pp. of *corrumpere*, < *com-*, altogether, + *rumpere*, break.] **I.** *tr.* To mar, spoil, or destroy (archaic); also, to change from a sound to a putrid or putrescent state; infect or taint; contaminate; also, to vitiate morally; pervert; deprave; also, to vitiate the integrity of; make venal; bribe; also, to alter (a language, text, etc.) for the worse; debase. **II.** *intr.* To become corrupted or corrupt.—**cor-rupt′,** *a.* Corrupted; putrid; infected or tainted; depraved or debased; dishonest or venal; influenced by bribery; vitiated by errors or alterations, as a text.—**cor-rupt′er,** *n.*—**cor-rup′ti-ble** (-rup′ti-bl), *a.* [LL. *corruptibilis.*] That may be corrupted.—**cor-rup-ti-bil′i-ty** (-bil′i-ti), **cor-rup′ti-ble-ness,** *n.*—**cor-rup′ti-bly,** *adv.*—**cor-rup′tion** (-shọn), *n.* [L. *corruptio(n-)*.] The act of corrupting, or the state of being corrupt; putrefactive decomposition; putrid matter; moral perversion; depravity; perversion of integrity; corrupt or dishonest proceedings; bribery; perversion from a state of purity; debasement, as of a language; a debased form of a word; also, any corrupting influence or agency; in *law*, formerly, a taint or defect ('corruption of blood') in consequence of attainder of treason or felony, by which the person attainted was disabled from inheriting, holding, or transmitting lands, etc.—**cor-rup′tion-ist,** *n.* One who advocates or uses corruption, esp. in public affairs.—**cor-rup′tive,** *a.* Tending to corrupt.—**cor-rupt′ly,** *adv.*—**cor-rupt′ness,** *n.*

cor-sage (kôr′sạj, F. kor-säzh), *n.* [OF. F. *corsage*, < *cors*: see *corse*.] The body†; the bust†; also, the body or waist of a woman's dress; a bodice.

cor-sair (kôr′sãr), *n.* [F. *corsaire*, < ML. *cursarius*, < *cursus*, hostile excursion, booty, L. a running, E. *course*.] One engaged in privateering, esp. one of the privateersmen of the Barbary coast; also, the vessel employed; a privateer; sometimes, a pirate or a piratical vessel; also, a rockfish, *Sebastodes rosaceus*, of the California coast.

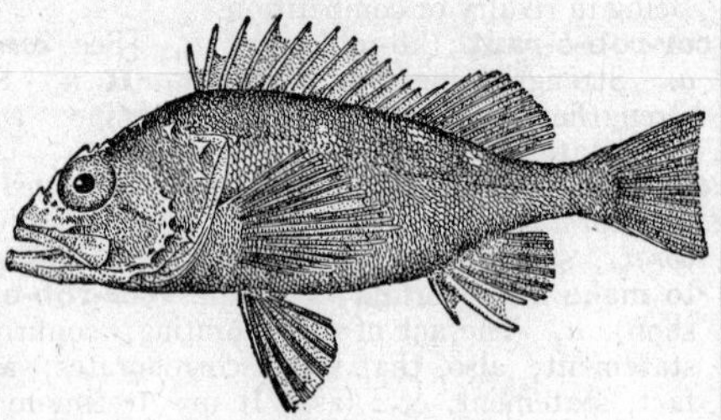

Corsair (*Sebastodes rosaceus*).

Corsair. A U. S. Navy fighter plane (Chance Vought).

corse (kôrs), *n.* [OF. *cors*, body: see *corpse*.] A living body†; also, a corpse, or dead body (archaic: as, "A mantle o'er the *corse* he laid . . .": Scott's "Rokeby," vi. 33).

corse-let, cors-let (kôrs′let), *n.* [OF. F. *corselet*, dim. of *cors*: see *corse*.] Armor for the body, esp. the breastplate and the piece for the back taken together; in *zoöl.*, the thorax of an insect.

cor-set (kôr′set), *n.* [OF. F. *corset*, dim. of *cors*: see *corse*.] A close-fitting outer body-garment†; *sing.* or *pl.*, a shaped, close-fitting inner garment stiffened with whalebone or the like and capable of being tightened by lacing, inclosing the trunk and extending for a distance above and below the waist-line, worn, chiefly by women, to give shape and support to the body; stays.—**cor′set=cov″er,** *n.* A woman's under-garment, a kind of bodice, usually sleeveless, for wearing over the corset.—**cor′set-ed,** *a.* Wearing a corset.—**cor-se-tière** (kor-sė-tyãr), *n.* [F. (masc. *corsetier*).] A woman who makes or sells corsets.

Corselet of German or Flemish Pikeman (about 1600), with tasses (*t*) and morion (*m*).

Cor-si-can (kôr′si-kạn). **I.** *a.* Of or pertaining to the island of Corsica, its inhabitants, or their dialect. **II.** *n.* A native or inhabitant of the island of Corsica; also, the Corsican dialect of Italian.

cors-let (kôrs′let), *n.* See *corselet*.

cor-tège (kôr-tāzh′, F. kor-tāzh), *n.* [F. *cortège*, < It. *corteggio*, < *corte*, = E. *court*.] A train of attendants; a procession.

Cor-tes (kôr′tes), *n. pl.* or *sing.* [Sp. and Pg., pl. of *corte*, = E. *court*.] The two houses constituting the national legislative body of Spain, or those of Portugal.

cor-tex (kôr′teks), *n.*; pl. *cortices* (-ti-sēz). [L. *cortex* (*cortic-*), bark, rind, shell.] In *bot.*, bark or rind; in *anat.* and *zoöl.*, an external or superficial layer, as of the kidney; esp., the layer of gray matter which invests most of the surface of the brain.—**cor′ti-cal** (-ti-kạl), *a.* Of, pertaining to, or of the nature of cortex.—**cor′ti-cate, cor′ti-cat-ed** (-kāt, -kā-ted), *a.* [L. *corticatus.*] Having a cortex.—**cor′ti-cole** (-kōl), **cor-tic′o-lous** (-tik′ọ-lus), *a.* [See *-cole*, *-colous*.] Living or growing on bark, as certain lichens.—**cor′ti-cose** (-kōs), **cor′ti-cous,** *a.* [L. *corticosus.*] Consisting of or resembling cortex; also, having a cortex.

co-run-dum (kọ-run′dum), *n.* [Tamil *kurundam*, < Skt. *kuruvinda*, ruby.] A native oxide of aluminium, occurring in many varieties, including the sapphire, ruby, etc.; specif., any of certain opaque forms of this mineral used as abrasives.

co-rus-cant (kọ-rus′kạnt), *a.* Coruscating; flashing.

cor-us-cate (kor′us-kāt or kọ-rus′kāt), *v. i.*; *-cated*, *-cating.* [L. *coruscatus*, pp. of *coruscare*, move quickly, flash.] To emit vivid flashes of light; shine with a quivering light; flash or sparkle; sometimes fig.: as, "the blaze of Apollonia's *coruscating* conversation" (Disraeli's "Lothair," viii.).—**cor-us-ca-tion** (kor-us-kā′shọn), *n.* The act of coruscating; flashing or a flash of light. Also fig.

cor-vée (kôr-vā′), *n.* [F. *corvée*, < ML. *corrogata*, required work, < L. *corrogare*, < *com-*, together, + *rogare*, ask.] Labor, as on the repair of roads, exacted by a feudal lord.

cor-vette (kôr-vet′), *n.* [F. *corvette*, < L. *corbita*, ship of burden, < *corbis*, basket.] A war-ship of the old sailing class, having a flush deck and usually only one tier of guns.

cor-vine (kôr′vin), *a.* [L. *corvinus*, < *corvus*, raven.] Pertaining to or resembling a crow; belonging or pertaining to the *Corvidæ*, a family of birds including the crows, ravens, jays, etc.

Cor-y-bant (kor′i-bant), *n.* [L. *Corybas* (pl. *Corybantes*), < Gr. Κορύβας (pl. Κορύβαντες).] One of the spirits or secondary divinities fabled to form the train of the Asiatic goddess Cybele, following her over the mountains by torch-light with wild music and dancing; also, one of the priests of Cybele, who conducted her worship with similar frenzied rites.—**Cor-y-ban′tic,** *a.*

co-ryd-a-lis (kọ-rid′ạ-lis), *n.* [NL., < Gr. κορυδαλλίς, crested lark, < κόρυς, helmet.] Any plant of the papaveraceous genus *Capnoides*, comprising erect or climbing herbs with divided leaves, tuberous or fibrous roots, and very irregular spurred flowers.

Corydalis. — Inflorescence.

Cor-y-don (kor′i-dọn), *n.* [L., < Gr. Κορυδών.] In pastoral literature, a name for a shepherd or rustic.

cor-ymb (kor′imb), *n.* [L. *corymbus*, < Gr. κόρυμβος, head, top, cluster of fruit or flowers.] In *bot.*, a form of inflorescence resembling a raceme but having a relatively shorter rachis and longer lower pedicels, so that the flowers form a flat-topped or convex cluster, the outermost flowers being the first to expand.—**cor-ym-bif′er-ous** (-im-bif′ẹ-rus), *a.* [See *-ferous*.] Bearing corymbs.—**co-rym-bose** (kọ-rim′bōs or kor-im-bōs′), *a.* Characterized by or growing in corymbs; corymb-like.—**co-rym′bose-ly,** *adv.*

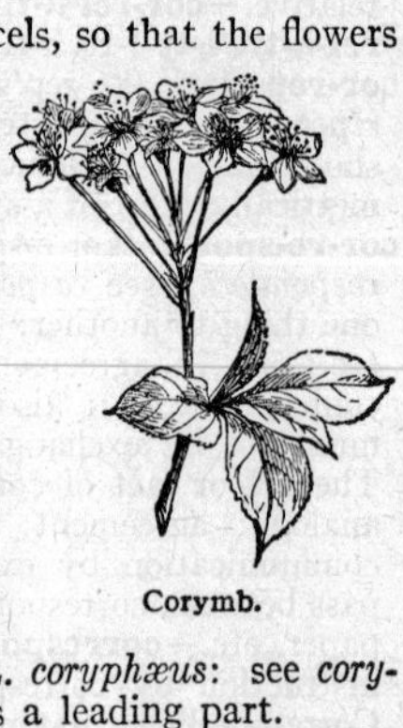

Corymb.

cor-y-phæ-us (kor-i-fē′us), *n.*; pl. *-phæi* (-fē′ī). [L., < Gr. κορυφαῖος, < κορυφή, head.] The leader of the chorus in the ancient Greek drama; the leader of any chorus; in general, a leader.

co-ry-phée (ko-rē-fā), *n.* [F., < L. *coryphæus*: see *coryphæus*.] A ballet-dancer who takes a leading part.

co-ry-za (kọ-rī′zạ), *n.* [LL., < Gr. κόρυζα.] In *pathol.*, acute inflammation of the mucous membrane of the nasal cavities; cold in the head.

co-se-cant (kō-sē′kant or -kạnt), *n.* [NL. *cosecans* (*-ant-*): see *co-* and *secant.*] In *trigon.*, the secant of the complement of a given angle or arc.

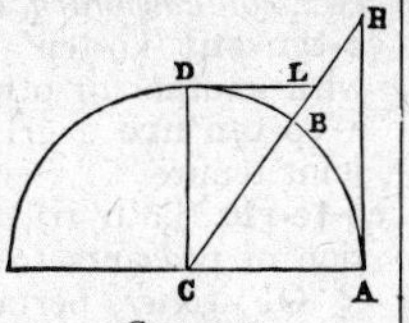

Cosecant.

ACB being the angle, the ratio of LC to DC or AC is the cosecant; or, DC being equal to unity, it is the line LC.

co-seis-mal (kō-sīs′mạl or -sīz′mạl). [See *co-.*] **I.** *a.* Noting or pertaining to a line, curve, etc., connecting or comprising points on the earth's surface where an earthquake wave arrives simultaneously. **II.** *n.* A coseismal line or the like.—**co-seis′mic,** *a.* Coseismal.

co-sey (kō′zi), etc. See *cozy*, etc.

cosh-er[1] (kosh′ėr), *v. t.* [Origin uncertain.] To pamper; cocker; coddle.

cosh-er[2] (kosh′ėr), *v. i.* [Ir. *coisir*, a feast.] To feast or lodge at the expense of dependents or kinsmen; live at the expense of others: as, "Sometimes he contrived . . . to live by *coshering,* that is to say, by quartering himself on the old tenants of his family" (Macaulay's "Hist. of Eng.," vi.). [Ireland.]—**cosh′er-er,** *n.* —**cosh′er-y,** *n.* In Ireland, the custom whereby a feudal chief could quarter himself and his followers upon a dependent or tenant.

co-sig-na-to-ry (kō-sig′nạ-tō̦-ri). [See *co-.*] **I.** *a.* Signing jointly with another or others. **II,** *n.*; pl. *-ries* (-riz). One who signs a document jointly with another or others.

co-sine (kō′sīn), *n.* [NL. *cosinus*: see *co-* and *sine*[1].] In *trigon.*, the sine of the complement of a given angle or arc.

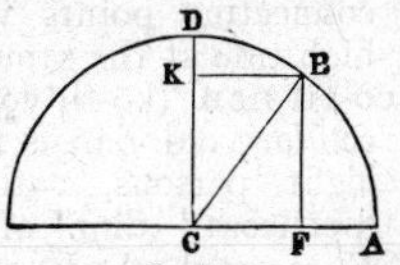

Cosine.

ACB being the angle, the ratio of FC to BC, or that of BK to CD, is the cosine; or, CD being equal to unity, it is the line BK.

Cos (kos) **let′tuce.** [From *Cos* (*Kos*), island off the coast of Asia Minor.] A kind of lettuce, including the romaine and other varieties, with erect oblong heads and generally crisp leaves.

cos-met-ic (koz-met′ik). [Gr. *κοσμητικός*, < *κοσμεῖν*, arrange, adorn, < *κόσμος*: see *cosmos.*] **I.** *a.* Serving to beautify; imparting or improving beauty, esp. of the complexion. **II.** *n.* A preparation for beautifying the complexion, skin, etc.—**cos-met′i-cal-ly,** *adv.*

cos-mic (koz′mik), *a.* [Gr. *κοσμικός.*] Of or pertaining to the cosmos (as, *cosmic* philosophy, cosmism); also, characteristic of the cosmos or its phenomena; immeasurably extended in space or time; vast; also, forming a part of the material universe, esp. outside of the earth; also, orderly or harmonious.—**cosmic dust,** matter in fine particles falling from space, like meteorites, upon the earth.—**cos′mi-cal,** *a.* Cosmic; also, of or pertaining to cosmism; in *astron.*, occurring at sunrise, as the rising or setting of a star.—**cos′mi-cal-ly,** *adv.*

cos-mism (koz′mizm), *n.* [See *cosmos.*] The philosophy of cosmic evolution.—**cos′mist,** *n.*

cosmo-. Form of Gr. *κόσμος*, world, universe (see *cosmos*), used in combination.

cos-mo-crat (koz′mō̦-krat), *n.* [See *cosmo-* and *-crat.*] Ruler of the world.—**cos-mo-crat′ic,** *a.*

cos-mog-e-ny (koz-moj′e-ni), *n.* [Gr. *κοσμογένεια*: see *cosmo-* and *-geny.*] The genesis or evolution of the universe; cosmogony.

cos-mog-o-ny (koz-mog′ō̦-ni), *n.*; pl. *-nies* (-niz). [Gr. *κοσμογονία*: see *cosmo-* and *-gony.*] The genesis or origination of the universe, esp. as a subject of study or speculation; also, a theory or account of the origin of the universe.—**cos-mo-gon′ic, cos-mo-gon′i-cal** (-mō̦-gon′ik, -i-kạl), *a.*—**cos-mog′o-nist,** *n.*

cos-mog-ra-phy (koz-mog′rạ-fi), *n.*; pl. *-phies* (-fiz). [LL. *cosmographia*, < Gr. *κοσμογραφία*: see *cosmo-* and *-graphy.*] The science which describes and maps the main features of the heavens and the earth, embracing astronomy, geography, and sometimes geology; also, a description or representation of the universe in its main features.—**cos-mog′ra-pher,** *n.* —**cos-mo-graph′ic, cos-mo-graph′i-cal** (-mō̦-graf′ik, -i-kạl), *a.*

cos-mol-o-gy (koz-mol′ō̦-ji), *n.* [See *cosmo-* and *-logy.*] The general science or theory of the cosmos or material universe, its parts, elements, and laws.—**cos-mo-log′i-cal** (-mō̦-loj′i-kạl), *a.*—**cos-mol′o-gist,** *n.*

cos-mo-plas-tic (koz-mō̦-plas′tik), *a.* [See *cosmo-* and *plastic.*] Pertaining to or concerned with the formation of the universe; cosmogonic.

cos-mo-pol-i-tan (koz-mō̦-pol′i-tạn). [See *cosmopolite.*] **I.** *a.* Pertaining to or characteristic of a cosmopolite, or citizen of the world; being a citizen of the world; free from national or local attachments or prejudices; also, belonging to all parts of the world; not restricted to any one country or its inhabitants; in *bot.* and *zoöl.*, widely distributed over the globe. **II.** *n.* A cosmopolite.—**cos-mo-pol′i-tan-ism,** *n.* Cosmopolitan character.—**cos-mo-pol′i-tan-ize,** *v. t.*; *-ized, -izing.* To render cosmopolitan.

cos-mop-o-lite (koz-mop′ō̦-līt), *n.* [Gr. *κοσμοπολίτης*, < *κόσμος*, world, + *πολίτης*, citizen, < *πόλις*, city, state.] A citizen of the world, or one at home in all parts of the world (as, "He is a polished gentleman,—a citizen of the world,—yes, a true *cosmopolite*": Hawthorne's "Twice-Told Tales," The Prophetic Pictures); a person free from national or local attachments or prejudices; also, an animal or plant of world-wide distribution.—**cos-mop′o-lit-ism** (-lī-tizm), *n.*

cos-mo-ra-ma (koz-mō̦-rä′mạ̈), *n.* [Gr. *κόσμος*, world, + *ὅραμα*, view.] A view or series of views of the world; a peep-show exhibiting characteristic views of all the world. —**cos-mo-ram′ic** (-ram′ik), *a.*

cos-mos (koz′mos), *n.* [NL., < Gr. *κόσμος*, order, form, the world or universe as an ordered whole, ornament, embellishment.] Order or harmony; also, the world or universe as an embodiment of order and harmony; hence, any complete and harmonious system; also, any plant of the asteraceous genus *Cosmos*, of tropical America, some species of which, as *C. bipinnatus* and *C. sulphureus*, are cultivated for their showy flowers.

Cos-sack (kos′ak), *n.* [Turki *quzzāq*, adventurer, freebooter.] One of a people of southern European Russia and adjoining parts of Asia, noted as horsemen or light cavalry. —**Cossack post,** *milit.*, a group of four men on outguard duty, usually consisting of a non-commissioned officer and three privates.

cos-set (kos′et), *n.* [Origin uncertain.] A lamb brought up by hand; a pet lamb; hence, a pet of any kind.—**cos′set,** *v. t.*; *-seted, -seting.* To treat as a cosset; pet; pamper; coddle: as, "Miss Matilda looked miserably ill; and I prepared to comfort and *cosset* her" (Mrs. Gaskell's "Cranford," iv.).

cost (kôst), *v.*; *cost, costing.* [OF. *coster* (F. *coûter*), < L. *constare*, stand together, stand at, cost, < *con-*, with, + *stare*, stand.] **I.** *intr.* To be acquired at a specified price; require the expenditure of money, time, labor, etc., as stated; entail a particular sacrifice, loss, or penalty: orig. and properly intransitive, with an adverbial (often phrasal) adjunct expressing the price and often also with an indirect personal object, but in many cases simulating a transitive (as, it *cost* me little or nothing; it may *cost* him his life). Also, to estimate or determine the cost, as of production (orig. British). **II.** *tr.* To estimate or determine the cost of (manufactured articles, etc.). [Orig. British.]—**cost,** *n.* [OF. *cost* (F. *coût*).] That which must be given to acquire, produce, accomplish, or maintain anything; the price paid, or a sacrifice, loss, or penalty endured, for a thing; outlay or expenditure, as of money, time, labor, trouble, etc.; *pl.*, in *law*, expenses in litigation or other legal transaction.

cos-ta (kos′tạ̈), *n.*; pl. *costæ* (-tē). [L., rib, side.] A rib or rib-like part; a ridge.—**cos′tal,** *a.*

cos-tard (kos′tạ̈rd), *n.* [ME., perhaps < OF. *coste*, < L. *costa*, rib.] A kind of large English apple with prominent ribs; humorously, the head (archaic).

cos-tate (kos′tāt), *a.* [L. *costatus*, < *costa*, rib.] Having a rib or ribs; ribbed; ridged.

cos-ter (kos′tėr), *n.* Same as *costermonger.*

cos-ter-mong-er (kos′tėr-mung″gėr), *n.* [Earlier *costardmonger*: see *costard.*] A hawker of fruit, vegetables, fish, etc. [Chiefly Eng.]

cos-tive (kos′tiv), *a.* [OF. *costeve*, < L. *constipatus*, pp.: see *constipate.*] Suffering from constipation; constipated; fig., slow in action; uncommunicative; stingy.—**cos′tive-ly,** *adv.*—**cos′tive-ness,** *n.*

cost-less (kôst′les), *a.* Free of cost; costing nothing.

cost-ly (kôst′li), *a.*; compar. *costlier*, superl. *costliest*. Costing much; of great price or value; sumptuous; also, occasioning great expenditure (as, a *costly* experiment); expensive; dear; also, lavish or extravagant (archaic).—**cost′li-ness,** *n.*

cost-ma-ry (kost′mā̤-ri), *n.* [ME. *cost* (< L. *costum*, kind of aromatic plant) + *Mary*.] A perennial asteraceous plant, *Chrysanthemum balsamita*, with fragrant leaves, used as a pot-herb and in salads, etc.

cos-trel (kos′trel), *n.* [OF. *costerel*, appar. orig. a flask hung at the side, < *coste*, < L. *costa*, rib, side.] A bottle or vessel of leather, earthenware, or wood, often of flattened form and commonly having an ear or ears to suspend it by, as from the waist, formerly in general use, and still used in rural England for carrying drink to the field: as, "A youth that, following with a *costrel*, bore The means of goodly welcome, flesh and wine" (Tennyson's "Marriage of Geraint," 386). Sometimes called *pilgrim-bottle*.

Costrels.
1, old form, of leather; 2, old form, of earthenware; 3, modern form (West of England), of earthenware.

cos-tume (kos′tūm or kos-tūm′), *n.* [F. *costume*, < It. *costume*, < L. *consuetudo*, custom: see *consuetude*.] The custom or usage, with respect to manner, dress, furniture, etc., of the place or period of something represented in art or literature; the manner, dress, etc., thus represented; also, the style of dress, including ornaments and the way of wearing the hair, peculiar to a nation, class, or period; also, fashion of dress appropriate to a particular occasion or season (as, court *costume*; winter *costume*); hence, dress with reference to its fashion or style; garb; also, dress or garb belonging to another period, place, etc., as worn on the stage, at balls, etc. (also attrib.: as, a *costume* drama, one in which such dress is worn, esp. one laid in another period than the present); also, a set of outer garments, esp. for a woman.—**cos-tume** (kos′tūm or kos-tūm′), *v. t.*; *-tumed*, *-tuming*. To furnish with a costume or dress; provide appropriate dress for.—**cos-tum-er** (kos′tū-mėr or kos-tū′mėr), *n.* One who makes or deals in costumes. Also (F.) **cos-tu-mier** (kos-tü-myā).

co-sy (kō′zi), etc. See *cozy*, etc.

cot[1] (kot), *n.* [AS. *cot*, neut. (also *cote*, fem.), = D., LG., and Icel. *kot* = G. *koth*.] A small or humble dwelling-house; a cottage; also, a small erection for shelter or protection; also, a sheath or covering, as a finger-stall.

cot[2] (kot), *n.* [Anglo-Ind.; from Hind.] A light bedstead; a light portable bed, as one of canvas or the like stretched on a frame; a small bed or crib for a child; *naut.*, a swinging bed made of canvas.

co-tan-gent (kō-tan′jent), *n.* [NL. *cotangens* (*-ent-*): see *co-* and *tangent*.] In *trigon.*, the tangent of the complement of a given angle or arc.—**co-tan-gen′tial** (-jen′shạl), *a.*

cot-bet-ty (kot′bet″i), *n.*; pl. *-betties* (-iz). [See *cot*[1] and *betty*.] A man who meddles with household affairs proper to women. [U. S.]

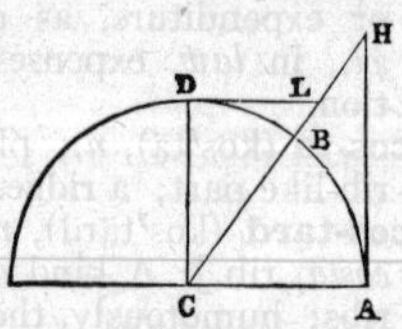

Cotangent.
ACB being the angle, the ratio of DL to DC, or that of AC to AH, is the cotangent; or, DC being taken as unity, it is the line DL.

cote[1] (kōt), *n.* [AS. *cote*: see *cot*[1].] A cot or small house (now only north. Eng.); also, a shelter for sheep, pigs, pigeons, etc.

cote[2] (kōt), *v. t.*; *coted*, *coting*. [Cf. F. *côtoyer*, go by the side of, ult. < L. *costa*, rib, side.] To pass by and get before; outstrip; surpass. [Obs. or archaic.]

co-teau (kō-tō′), *n.*; pl. *-teaux* (-tōz′, F. -tō). [F., dim. of *côte*, hillside, < L. *costa*, rib, side.] An upland; a broad, flat-topped ridge of moderate elevation. [Northwestern U. S.]

côte-lette (kōt-let), *n.* [F.] A cutlet.

co-tem-po-ra-ne-ous (kō-tem-pọ-rā′nẹ-us), etc., **co-tem-po-ra-ry** (kō-tem′pọ-rā-ri), etc. Same as *contemporaneous*, etc., *contemporary*, etc.

co-ten-ant (kō-ten′ạnt), *n.* [See *co-*.] A tenant in common with another or others; a joint tenant.—**co-ten′an-cy,** *n.* —**co-ten′ure** (-ūr), *n.* Tenure with another or others; joint tenure.

co-te-rie (kō′tẹ-ri), *n.* [F., set, coterie, earlier an association of peasants to hold land from a lord, cotters' tenure, < OF. *cotier*, pertaining to or holding by cotters' tenure: cf. *cotter*[1].] A set or circle of persons who are in the habit of associating together, esp. for social purposes; sometimes, a clique.

co-ter-mi-nous (kō-tėr′mi-nus), etc. Same as *conterminous*, etc.

co-thurn (kọ-thėrn′), *n.* Same as *cothurnus*.

co-thur-nus (kọ-thėr′nus), *n.*; pl. *-ni* (-nī). [L., < Gr. κόθορνος.] The buskin or high shoe of the Greeks and Romans; specif., the high, thick-soled shoe worn by ancient Greek and Roman tragic actors, often taken as symbolic of tragedy.

Cothurnus. — Figure of Artemis, from a Greek vase.

co-ti-dal (kō-tī′dạl), *a.* [See *co-*.] Pertaining to a coincidence of tides; noting a line connecting points where it is high tide at the same time.

co-til-lion (kọ-til′yọn), *n.* [F. *cotillon*, old dance for four or eight persons, cotillion, orig. 'petticoat,' dim. of OF. *cote*, E. *coat*.] Any of various dances of the quadrille kind; in the U. S., a complex dance, or entertainment of dancing, consisting of picturesque or elaborate 'figures,' with changing of partners and giving of 'favors'; a german.

co-til-lon (ko-tē-yôṅ), *n.* [F.] A cotillion.

cot-quean† (kot′kwēn), *n.* [Appar. < *cot*[1] + *quean*.] A common or vulgar housewife; a coarse hussy; also, a man who busies himself with women's household affairs (cf. *cotbetty*).

co-trust-ee (kō-trus-tē′), *n.* [See *co-*.] A joint trustee.

Cots-wold (kots′wọld), *n.* One of a breed of large sheep with long wool: so called from the Cotswold Hills, in Gloucestershire, England.

cot-ta (kot′ạ), *n.*; pl. *cottas*. [ML.: see *coat*.] *Eccles.*, a surplice; esp., a short surplice, with short sleeves or sleeveless, worn esp. by choristers.

cot-ta-bus (kot′ạ-bus), *n.* [L., < Gr. κότταβος.] An ancient Greek game which consisted in throwing wine from a drinking-cup into a vessel or upon a specified object, as a plate of bronze, so as to produce a clear sound and without scattering the liquid.

cot-tage (kot′āj), *n.* [ML. *cotagium*, < *cota*, cot, = E. *cote*[1].] A small dwelling-house of humble character; a small country residence or detached suburban house; one of several detached houses forming an institution, as an asylum or a hospital; a temporary residence, as at a pleasure-resort, often large and costly (U. S.).—**cottage cheese,** a kind of soft white cheese made of skim-milk curds.—**cot′taged,** *a.* Studded with cottages.—**cot-tag-er** (kot′ā-jėr), *n.* One who lives in a cottage.

cot-ter[1], **cot-tar** (kot′ėr, -ạr), *n.* [ML. *cotarius*, < *cota*, cot, = E. *cote*[1].] One occupying a cot, or a cot and land, by tenure of labor; also, a Scottish peasant occupying a cot and holding a plot of land under a system similar to cottier tenure; also, an Irish cottier.

cot-ter[2] (kot′ėr), *n.* [Origin obscure.] A pin, wedge, key, or the like, fitted or driven into an opening in order to secure something or hold parts together. Also **cot′ter-el.**

cot-ti-er (kot′i-ėr), *n.* [Cf. OF. *cotier*, adj.: see *coterie*.] A peasant occupying a cot; a cotter; specif., an Irish peasant holding a portion of land directly from the owner, the amount of rent being fixed not by custom or private agreement but by public competition ('cottier tenure').

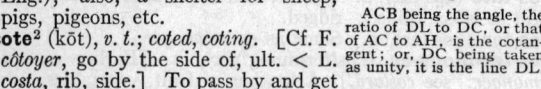

cot-to-lene (kot′ǫ-lēn), *n.* [From *cotton* + L. *oleum*, oil.] A preparation of cotton-seed oil, used like lard in cookery.

cot-ton (kot′n), *n.* [OF. F. *coton*, < Ar. *qutun.*] A soft, white, downy substance consisting of the hairs or fibers attached to the seeds of plants of the malvaceous genus *Gossypium*, used in making fabrics, thread, wadding, gun-cotton, etc.; also, a plant yielding cotton, as *G. hirsutum* ('upland cotton') or *G. barbadense* ('sea-island cotton'): such plants collectively, as a cultivated crop; also, cloth, thread, etc., made of cotton; also, any soft, downy substance resembling cotton, growing on some other plant.

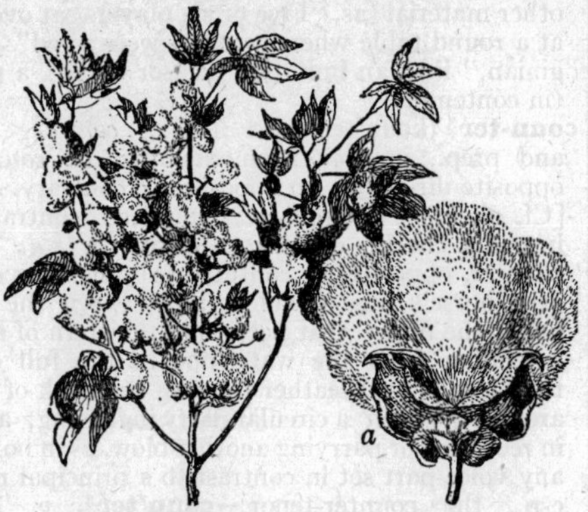

Branch of Cotton-plant (*Gossypium herbaceum*). *a*, opened boll or capsule.

—**cotton batting,** cotton-wool in bats or sheets.—**cot′-ton,** *v.* **I.** *tr.* To form a nap on†; also, to furnish with or envelop in cotton. **II.** *intr.* To form a nap, as cloth†; also, to prosper† or succeed†; also (colloq.), to get on together, or agree; make friends (as, "He and I *cottoned* together": H. Kingsley's "Geoffry Hamlyn," xxxi.); become attached (*to*).—**cot′ton=cake,** *n.* A mass of compressed cotton-seeds after the oil has been expressed, used for feeding cattle, etc.—**cot′ton=gin,** *n.* A machine for separating the fibers of cotton from the seeds: invented by Eli Whitney in 1792 or 1793.—**cot′ton=grass,** *n.* Any of the rush-like cyperaceous plants constituting the genus *Eriophorum*, common in swampy places and bearing spikes resembling tufts of cotton.—**cot′ton=seed,** *n.* The seed of the cotton-plant, yielding an oil ('cotton-seed oil') which is used as a substitute for olive-oil, etc.—**cot′ton-tail,** *n.* The common rabbit, *Lepus sylvaticus*, of the U. S.: so named from its fluffy white tail.—**cot′ton=waste′,** *n.* Refuse cotton yarn used to wipe oil and dust from machinery and as packing for axle-boxes, etc.—**cot′-ton-weed,** *n.* Any of certain plants with stems and leaves covered with a soft, hoary pubescence, as any plant of the asteraceous genus *Gnaphalium* or any of various plants of allied genera.

Cottontail.

—**cot′ton-wood,** *n.* Any of several American species of poplar (as *Populus deltoides*) with cotton-like tufts on the seeds.—**cot′ton=wool′,** *n.* Cotton in its raw state, as on the boll or gathered for use.—**cot′ton=worm,** *n.* The destructive larva of a noctuid moth, *Aletia argillacea*, which attacks the leaves of the cotton-plant.—**cot′ton-y,** *a.* Of the nature of or resembling cotton; also, covered with a down or nap resembling cotton.

cot-y-le (kot′i-lē), *n.*; pl. *-læ* (-lē). [NL., < Gr. κοτύλη, something hollow, cup, socket.] In *anat.* and *zoöl.*, a cup-like cavity; an acetabulum.

cot-y-le-don (kot-i-lē′dǫn), *n.* [NL., < Gr. κοτυληδών, any cup-shaped hollow, < κοτύλη: see *cotyle.*] In *bot.*, the primary or rudimentary leaf, or one of the first pair or whorl of leaves, of the embryo of plants.—**cot-y-le′don-a-ry** (-ā-ri), **cot-y-le′don-ous,** *a.*

cot-y-loid (kot′i-loid), *a.* [Gr. κοτυλοειδής, < κοτύλη, cup, + εἶδος, form.] Shaped like a cup, as the acetabulum or socket of the thigh-bone.

couch¹ (kouch), *n.* [Var. of *quitch.*] Couch-grass.

couch² (kouch), *v.* [OF. F. *coucher*, < L. *collocare*, lay in place: see *collocate.*] **I.** *tr.* To lay or put down; cause to lie down; lay or spread flat; also, to overlay; embroider with thread laid flat on a surface and caught down at intervals; also, to lower or bend down, as the head; lower (a spear, etc.) to a horizontal position, as for attack; also, to place or lodge; conceal; also, to arrange or frame (words, a sentence, etc.); put into words; express; sometimes, to express indirectly; in *surg.*, to remove (a cataract) by inserting a needle and pushing the opaque crystalline lens downward in the vitreous humor below the axis of vision; remove a cataract from (a person) in this manner. **II.** *intr.* To lie at rest; repose; recline; also, to crouch or cower; bend or stoop; also, to lie in ambush; lurk; also, to lie in a heap for decomposition or fermentation, as leaves.—**couch²,** *n.* [OF. F. *couche.*] A bed or other place of rest; a lounge; any place used for repose, as the lair of a wild beast; also, the frame on which barley is spread to be malted; also, a bed or stratum; a coat of paint, etc.—**couch-ant** (kou′-chąnt), *a.* [OF. F., ppr. of *coucher.*] Lying down; in *her.*, of an animal, lying down with the body resting on the legs and the head raised.—**cou-chee** (kö′shā), *n.* [F. *couché*, usually *coucher.*] A reception held about bedtime, as by a king; hence, an evening reception.—**couch′er,** *n.*

Lion Couchant.

couch=grass (kouch′grȧs), *n.* [See *couch¹.*] Any of various grasses, esp. *Agropyron repens*, known chiefly as troublesome weeds, and characterized by creeping rootstocks which spread rapidly.

couch-ing (kou′ching), *n.* The act of one who or that which couches; esp., a method of embroidering in which a thread, often heavy, laid upon the surface of the material is caught down at intervals by stitches taken with another thread through the material; also, work so made.

cou-gar (kö′gär), *n.* [F. *couguar*; from Brazilian name.] A large, tawny feline quadruped, *Felis concolor*, of North and South America; the puma or mountain-lion.

cough (kôf), *v.* [ME.; akin to D. *kuchen*, cough, G. *keuchen*, gasp, pant.] **I.** *intr.* To expel the air from the lungs suddenly and with a characteristic noise; force out obstructing or irritating matter from the air-passages in this manner. **II.** *tr.* To expel by coughing (with *up* or *out*); with *down*, to silence (a speaker) by coughing.—**cough,** *n.* The act or sound of coughing; an affection characterized by frequent coughing.—**cough′er,** *n.*

could (kůd). Preterit of *can¹*.

cou-lée (kö′lę̄, F. kö-lā), *n.* [F., < *couler*, flow, slide, < L. *colare*, strain: see *colander.*] A stream of lava; also, a deep ravine or gulch, usually dry, which has been worn by running water (western North America).

cou-lisse (kö-lēs′), *n.* [F., < *couler*: see *coulée.*] A grooved piece or groove in which something slides; also, one of the side scenes of a stage in a theater; *pl.*, the part of a theater behind the scenes.

cou-loir (kö-lwor), *n.* [F., < *couler*: see *coulée.*] A steep gorge or gully on the side of a mountain.

cou-lomb (kö-lom′), *n.* [From C. A. de *Coulomb* (1736–1806), French physicist.] In *elect.*, the unit of quantity, the quantity of electricity furnished by a current of one ampere in one second.

coul-ter (kōl′tėr), *n.* See *colter.*

cou-ma-rin (kö′mą-rin), *n.* [F. *coumarine*, < *coumarou.*] A white crystalline substance with a vanilla-like odor, obtained from the tonka-bean and certain other plants, or prepared synthetically, and used for flavoring and in perfumery.—**cou-ma-ric** (kö′mą-rik or kö-mar′ik), *a.*

cou-ma-rou (kö-mą-rö′), *n.* [F.; from native name in Guiana.] The tonka-bean tree, *Coumarouna odorata*; also, its seeds.

coun-cil (koun′sil), *n.* [Prop. < OF. F. *concile*, < L. *concilium*, assembly, union (< *con-*, together, + *calare*, call), but with sense affected by L. *consilium*, E. *counsel.*] An assembly of persons summoned or convened for consultation, deliberation, or advice; specif., an ecclesiastical assembly for deciding matters of doctrine or discipline; also, a body of persons specially designated or selected to act in an advisory, administrative, or legislative capacity.—**coun′cil-man** (-mạn), *n.*; pl. *-men.* A member of a council, esp. the local legislative council of a city.—**coun′cil-or, coun′cil-lor,** *n.* A member of a council.—**coun′cil-or-ship, coun′cil-lor-ship,** *n.*

coun-sel (koun′sel), *n.* [OF. F. *conseil,* < L. *consilium,* consultation, plan, advice, good judgment, council, counselor, akin to *consulere,* deliberate: see *consult,* and cf. *council.*] Interchange of opinions as to future procedure; consultation; deliberation; also, aid or instruction for directing the judgment; advice; also, wisdom or prudence (archaic: as, "With him is wisdom and strength, he hath *counsel* and understanding," Job, xii. 13); also, deliberate purpose; plan; design; also, a secret† (as, "That they of Rome are enter'd in our *counsels* And know how we proceed": Shakspere's "Coriolanus," i. 2. 2); also, a body of advisers†; esp., the advocates or advocate engaged in the direction of a cause in court; a legal adviser, or counselor; in *theol.,* one of the advisory declarations of Christ, considered as not universally binding but as given for aid in attaining greater moral perfection.—**coun′sel,** *v.*; *-seled* or *-selled, -seling* or *-selling.* [OF. F. *conseiller,* < L. *consiliari,* < *consilium.*] **I.** *tr.* To give counsel or advice to; advise; also, to urge the doing or adoption of; recommend (a plan, etc.). **II.** *intr.* To give counsel or advice; also, to take counsel.—**coun′sel-or, coun′sel-lor,** *n.* One who counsels or advises; an adviser; esp., one whose profession it is to give legal advice and conduct his clients' cases in court; in some courts of the U. S., an advocate who pleads a cause at the trial, as distinguished from an *attorney,* who is employed in the management of the formal part of the suit.—**coun′sel-or-ship, coun′sel-lor-ship,** *n.*

count[1] (kount), *n.* [OF. *conte* (F. *comte*), < L. *comes* (*comit-*), companion, later a title of office or honor, < *com-,* with, + *ire,* go.] Any of various officials of high rank in former times, as one set by a sovereign over a district and charged with the preservation therein of the royal authority; later, a feudal proprietor who was the hereditary ruler of lands and territories; now, in some European countries, a nobleman corresponding in rank to the English earl.—**count palatine,** formerly, in Germany, a count having supreme jurisdiction in his fief or province, or in England, an earl, or other county proprietor, who exercised royal prerogatives within his county.

count[2] (kount), *v.* [OF. *conter* (F. *compter, conter*), < L. *computare*: see *compute.*] **I.** *tr.* To tell over one by one (the individuals of a collection) in order to ascertain their total number; enumerate; repeat the numerals up to (as, to *count* ten); reckon up or calculate; compute; also, to include in a reckoning; take into account; also, to esteem or consider; also, to ascribe† or impute†. **II.** *intr.* To count the individuals of a collection; repeat numerals in order; reckon numerically; also, to take account (*of*)†; also, to depend or rely (*on*); also, to have a numerical value (as specified); be accounted (as, a book which *counts* as a masterpiece); enter into consideration (as, every effort *counts*).—**count**[2], *n.* [OF. *conte* (F. *compte, conte*), < LL. *computus,* < L. *computare.*] The act of counting; enumeration; reckoning; calculation; also, the number representing the result of a process of counting; the total number; also, an accounting; also, regard, notice, or consideration (archaic); in *law,* a distinct charge or allegation in a declaration or indictment.—**count′a-ble,** *a.* Capable of being counted.

coun-te-nance (koun′tẹ-nạns), *n.* [OF. F. *contenance,* < ML. *continentia,* demeanor, L. restraint: see *continence.*] Bearing† or behavior†; also, aspect or appearance; esp., the look or expression of the face; hence, the face or visage; also, composed expression of face (as, out of *countenance,* visibly disconcerted, or abashed); also, appearance of favor; encouragement; moral support.—**coun′te-nance,** *v. t.*; *-nanced, -nancing.* To give countenance or show favor to; encourage; support; also, to be in keeping with† (see Shakspere's "Macbeth," ii. 3. 85).—**coun′te-nan-cer,** *n.*

count-er[1] (koun′tėr), *n.* One who counts; also, an apparatus for keeping count of revolutions or other movements.

coun-ter[2] (koun′tėr), *n.* [OF. *comptoer, comptoir* (F. *comptoir*), < ML. *computatorium,* counting-house, counting-table, < L. *computare,* E. *count*[2], *compute.*] A counting-room† or counting-house†; a table or board on which money is counted, business is transacted, or goods are laid for examination; formerly, in England, a prison, esp. for debtors; also, anything used in keeping account, as in games, esp. a round or otherwise shaped piece of metal, ivory, wood, or other material (as, "Five or six players sat over in the corner at a round table where *counters* were piled": Wister's "Virginian," ii.); an imitation coin or token; a piece of money (in contempt).

coun-ter[3] (koun′tėr), *adv.* [OF. F. *contre,* < L. *contra,* adv. and prep., in opposition, against: cf. *counter-.*] In the opposite direction; in opposition; contrary.—**coun′ter**[3], *a.* [Cf. *counter-.*] Opposite; opposed; contrary; also, serving as a check; duplicate.—**coun′ter**[3], *n.* That which is counter, opposite, or contrary to something else; that part of a horse's breast which lies between the shoulders and under the neck; that portion of the stern of a boat or vessel extending from the water-line to the full outward swell; the piece of stiff leather forming the back of a shoe or boot around the heel; a circular parry in fencing; a blow delivered in receiving or parrying another blow, as in boxing; in *music,* any voice-part set in contrast to a principal melody or part; esp., the counter-tenor.—**coun′ter**[3], *v.* **I.** *tr.* To go counter to; oppose; controvert; also, to meet or answer (a move, blow, etc.) by another in return; also, to put a counter upon (a shoe). **II.** *intr.* To make a counter or opposing move, etc.; also, to give a blow while receiving or parrying one, as in boxing.

counter-. [OF. F. *contre-,* prefixal use of *contre,* < L. *contra*: see *counter*[3], *adv.,* and cf. *contra-.*] A prefix of Latin origin, meaning 'in opposition,' 'against,' 'so as to correspond, offset, or reverse,' 'in reciprocation or return,' orig. occurring in words derived from the French, as *counterfeit, counterfort, countermand,* but now freely used as an English formative, as in *counter-accusation, counter-appeal, counter-influence, counter-proof, counter-revolution,* and many other words, mostly self-explanatory.

coun-ter-act (koun-tėr-akt′), *v. t.* To act in opposition to; frustrate by contrary action.—**coun-ter-ac′tion** (-ak′shọn), *n.* Action in opposition.—**coun-ter-ac′tive. I.** *a.* Tending to counteract. **II.** *n.* A counteracting agent.

coun-ter=at-tack (koun′tėr-ạ-tak″), *n.* An attack designed to counteract another attack; a responsive attack.—**coun″ter=at-tack′,** *v. t.* or *i.* To attack as an offsetting or responsive measure.

coun-ter=at-trac-tion (koun′tėr-ạ-trak″shọn), *n.* Attraction of an opposite character; an attraction counter to another attraction.

coun-ter-bal-ance (koun′tėr-bal″ạns), *n.* A weight balancing another weight; an equal weight, power, or influence acting in opposition; a counterpoise.—**coun″ter-bal′ance,** *v. t.*; *-anced, -ancing.* To weight or act against with an equal weight or force; offset.—**coun″ter-bal′an-cer,** *n.*

coun-ter-blast (koun′tėr-blȧst), *n.* An opposing blast; a blast in opposition to another blast.

coun-ter-bore (koun-tėr-bōr′), *v. t.*; *-bored, -boring.* To bore out (a cylindrical hole) for a certain distance so as to form a flat-bottomed enlargement for receiving the head of a screw or the like; form a counterbore or counterbores in.—**coun′ter-bore,** *n.* An enlargement of a hole made by counterboring; also, a tool for counterboring a hole.

coun-ter-brace (koun′tėr-brās), *n.* A brace which transmits a strain in an opposite direction from a main brace.—**coun-ter-brace′,** *v. t.*; *-braced, -bracing.* To brace in opposite directions.

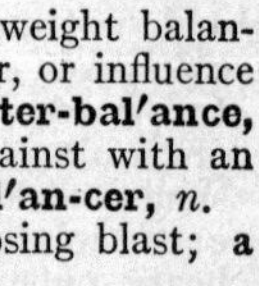
Boar Counter-changed, as a heraldic charge.

coun-ter-change (koun-tėr-chānj′), *v. t.*; *-changed, -changing.* To change to the opposite; cause to change places, qualities, etc.; also, to alternate; diversify; specif., in *her.,* to give (a charge on a field of two tinctures) the tinctures of the field reversed.—**coun′ter-change,** *n.* Transposition; interchange; exchange; reciprocation.

coun-ter-charge (koun-tėr-chärj′), *v. t.*; *-charged, -charging.* To charge in return; make an accusation against (one's

accuser).—**coun′ter-charge,** *n.* An opposing charge; a charge made by an accused person against his accuser.
coun-ter-charm (koun′tėr-chärm), *n.* That which counteracts the effect of a charm; an opposing charm.—**coun-ter-charm′,** *v. t.* To counteract the effect of (a charm, spell, etc.); affect by an opposing charm.
coun-ter-check (koun′tėr-chek), *n.* A check; also, a check controlling another check.—**coun-ter-check′,** *v. t.* To check by contrary action or some obstacle; also, to check by a second check.
coun-ter=claim (koun′tėr-klām), *n.* A claim set up against another claim.—**coun-ter=claim′,** *v. i.* To set up a counter-claim.—**coun′ter=claim″ant,** *n.*
coun-ter=clock-wise (koun′tėr-klok″wīz), *adv.* and *a.* In a direction counter or opposite to that of the rotation of the hands of a clock.
coun-ter=cur-rent (koun′tėr-kur″ent), *n.* A current in an opposite direction.
coun-ter=dem-on-stra-tion (koun′tėr-dem-on-strā″shon), *n.* A demonstration intended to offset the effect of a preceding demonstration.
coun-ter=drive (koun′tėr-drīv), *n.* A drive, onset, or military offensive designed to counteract another drive.
coun-ter-feit (koun′tėr-fit). [OF. F. *contrefait,* pp. of *contrefaire,* < ML. *contrafacere,* imitate, counterfeit, < L. *contra,* against, + *facere,* make.] **I.** *a.* Made to imitate, and pass for, something else; not genuine; spurious; forged; feigned; sham; pretended; also, pretending† or deceitful† (as, "an arrant *counterfeit* rascal": Shakspere's "Henry V.," iii. 6. 64); also, pictured† or portrayed† (as, "Look here, upon this picture, and on this, The *counterfeit* presentment of two brothers": Shakspere's "Hamlet," iii. 4. 54). **II.** *n.* An imitation designed to pass as an original; a forgery; also, an impostor†; also, a likeness†; a copy or double (archaic).—**coun′ter-feit,** *v.* **I.** *tr.* To make a counterfeit of; imitate fraudulently; also, to make as a counterfeit; forge; also, to make a pretense of; simulate; also, to assume the appearance of; resemble. **II.** *intr.* To make counterfeits, as of money; also, to feign or dissemble.—**coun′ter-feit-er,** *n.*
coun-ter-foil (koun′tėr-foil), *n.* [See *foil*[1].] A complementary part of a bank-check, etc., which is retained by the issuer, and on which particulars are noted; a stub.
coun-ter-fort (koun′tėr-fōrt), *n.* [F. *contrefort,* < *contre* (see *counter*[3], *adv.*) + *fort,* < L. *fortis,* strong.] A buttress or projecting piece of masonry strengthening a wall or the like; also, a spur of a mountain or mountain-chain.
coun-ter=glow (koun′tėr-glō), *n.* In *astron.,* a patch of extremely faint luminosity seen in the heavens near the ecliptic at a point exactly opposite to the sun.
coun-ter=guard (koun′tėr-gärd), *n.* [F. *contre-garde.*] In *fort.,* a small detached rampart in front of a bastion, ravelin, or the like, to protect it from being breached.
coun-ter=ir-ri-tant (koun″tėr-ir′i-tant), *n.* In *med.,* an agent for producing irritation in one part to counteract irritation or relieve pain or inflammation elsewhere.—**coun″ter=ir-ri-ta′tion** (-tā′shon), *n.*
coun-ter=jump-er (koun′tėr-jum″pėr), *n.* [See *counter*[2].] A salesman at a counter, as in a dry-goods store. [Colloq.]
coun-ter-mand (koun-tėr-mand′ or koun′tėr-mand), *v. t.* [OF. F. *contremander,* < ML. *contramandare,* < L. *contra,* against, + *mandare,* enjoin.] To revoke (a command, order, etc.); also, to recall or stop by a contrary order.—**coun′ter-mand,** *n.* A command, order, etc., revoking a previous one.
coun-ter-march (koun-tėr-märch′ or koun′tėr-märch), *v.* **I.** *intr.* To march in a contrary direction; march back; execute a countermarch. **II.** *tr.* To cause to countermarch.—**coun′ter-march,** *n.* A march in a contrary direction or back again; a military evolution by which a body of men changes direction; fig., a complete reversal of conduct or measures.
coun-ter-mark (koun′tėr-märk), *n.* An additional mark placed on something previously marked, as for greater security; also, an artificial cavity made in the teeth of horses to disguise their age.—**coun-ter-mark′,** *v. t.* To add a countermark to.
coun-ter-mine (koun′tėr-mīn), *n.* A mine intended to intercept or destroy an enemy's mine; hence, a counterplot.—**coun-ter-mine′,** *v.*; *-mined, -mining.* **I.** *intr.* To make or place countermines. **II.** *tr.* To make or place countermines against; oppose or defeat by a countermine; hence, to counterplot.
coun-ter-move (koun′tėr-möv), *n.* A contrary move; a move in opposition to another move.
coun-ter-pane (koun′tėr-pān), *n.* [Corruption of *counterpoint*[1].] A quilt or coverlet for a bed.
coun-ter-part (koun′tėr-pärt), *n.* A part that answers to another, as each part of a document executed in duplicate; a copy or duplicate; fig., a person or thing closely resembling another (as, "He, that seem'd our *counterpart* at first, Soon shows the strong similitude revers'd": Cowper's "Tirocinium," 442); also, one of two parts which fit each other; a thing that complements something else; in *music,* a part to accompany another.
coun-ter=plea (koun′tėr-plē), *n.* In *law,* a replication to a plea.
coun-ter-plot (koun′tėr-plot), *n.* A plot directed against another plot.—**coun-ter-plot** (koun-tėr-plot′ or koun′tėr-plot), *v.*; *-plotted, -plotting.* **I.** *intr.* To devise a counterplot; plot in opposition. **II.** *tr.* To plot against (a plot or plotter); frustrate by a counterplot.
coun-ter-point[1]† (koun′tėr-point), *n.* [OF. *contrepointe,* for *coutepointe* (F. *courtepointe*), < ML. *culcita puncta,* 'stitched quilt.'] A coverlet for a bed; a counterpane.
coun-ter-point[2] (koun′tėr-point), *n.* [OF. F. *contrepoint,* < ML. *contrapunctum,* < L. *contra,* against, + *punctus,* pp. of *pungere,* prick.] In *music,* a melody or voice-part added to another as accompaniment; also, the art of adding one or more melodies to a given melody according to fixed rules; the art of polyphonic or concerted composition.
coun-ter-poise (koun′tėr-poiz), *n.* [OF. *contrepois* (F. *contrepoids*).] A counterbalancing weight; any equal and opposing power or force; also, the state of being in equilibrium; also, in *wireless teleg.* and *teleph.,* a wire, system of wires, wire netting, or the like, placed below an aërial, usually near the ground, to serve as a substitute for a ground-connection.—**coun-ter-poise′,** *v. t.*; *-poised, -poising.* To balance by an opposing weight; counteract by an opposing force; also, to bring into equilibrium; also, to weigh (one thing) against another.
coun-ter-poi-son (koun′tėr-poi″zn), *n.* [F. *contrepoison.*] An agent for counteracting a poison; an antidote; also, an opposite poison.
coun-ter=ref-or-ma-tion (koun′tėr-ref-ôr-mā″shon), *n.* A reformation opposed to or counteracting a previous reformation; esp. (written *Counter-Reformation*), the movement within the Roman Catholic Church which followed the Protestant Reformation of the 16th century.
coun-ter-scarp (koun′tėr-skärp), *n.* [F. *contrescarpe.*] In *fort.,* the exterior slope or wall of the ditch, which supports the covered way; sometimes, this slope with the covered way and glacis.
coun-ter=shaft (koun′tėr-shaft), *n.* An intermediate shaft driven by a belt or gearing from a main shaft.
coun-ter-sign (koun-tėr-sīn′ or koun′tėr-sīn), *v. t.* To sign (a document) opposite to or in addition to another signature; add one's signature to (something already signed by another) by way of authentication, etc.; fig., to confirm; ratify.—**coun′ter-sign,** *n.* A sign used in reply to another sign; a private signal, as a word, phrase, or number, which must be given to pass a sentry; a watchword; also, a sign or mark put on something to authenticate or identify it; also, a signature added to another signature, as for authentication.—**coun-ter-sig′na-ture** (-sig′na-tūr), *n.* A signature added by way of countersigning.
coun-ter-sink (koun-tėr-singk′ or koun′tėr-singk), *v. t.*; *-sunk, -sinking.* To enlarge the upper part of (a hole or cavity), esp. by chamfering, to receive the head of a screw, bolt, etc.; also, to cause (the head of a screw, bolt, etc.) to sink into a depression made for it, so as to be flush with or below the surface.—**coun′ter-sink,** *n.* A tool for countersinking a hole; also, a countersunk hole.
coun-ter-stroke (koun′tėr-strōk), *n.* A stroke or blow given in return.

coun-ter=ten-or (koun′tėr-ten″ǫr), *n.* In *music*, an adult male voice or voice-part higher than the tenor; also, a singer with such a voice; a high tenor.

coun-ter-thrust (koun′tėr-thrust), *n.* A thrust made in opposition or return.

coun-ter-vail (koun-tėr-vāl′), *v.* [OF. *contrevaloir*, < L. *contra*, against, + *valere*, be strong, avail: see *avail*.] **I.** *tr.* To act or avail against with equal power, force, or effect; counteract; also, to furnish an equivalent of or a compensation for; offset; also, to equal (archaic). **II.** *intr.* To be of equal force in opposition; avail.—**coun′ter-vail,** *n.*

coun-ter-weight (koun′tėr-wāt), *n.* A counterbalancing weight; a counterpoise.—**coun′ter-weight-ed,** *a.*

coun-ter-work (koun′tėr-wėrk), *n.* Opposing work or action; a work in opposition to another work.—**coun-ter-work′,** *v.* **I.** *intr.* To work in opposition. **II.** *tr.* To work in opposition to; hinder or frustrate by contrary operations: as, "I made use of no means to prevent or *counterwork* their machinations" (C. B. Brown's "Wieland," vi.).—**coun-ter-work′er,** *n.*

coun-tess (koun′tes), *n.* [OF. *contesse* (F. *comtesse*), < ML. *comitissa*, fem. of L. *comes*: see *count*[1].] The wife or widow of a count in the nobility of continental Europe, or of an earl in the British peerage; also, a woman having the rank of a count or earl in her own right.

count-ing=house (koun′ting-hous), *n.* A building or office appropriated to bookkeeping, etc., as in a mercantile or manufacturing establishment.—**count′ing=room,** *n.* A room used as a counting-house.

count-less (kount′les), *a.* Incapable of being counted; innumerable.

coun-tri-fy (kun′tri-fī), *v. t.*; *-fied*, *-fying*. [See *-fy*.] To impart the characteristics of the country or of rural life; to make rustic: usually in *countrified*, *p. a.*—**coun′tri-fied-ness,** *n.*

coun-try (kun′tri). [OF. *contree* (F. *contrée*), < ML. *contrata*, lit. 'that which lies opposite or before one,' < L. *contra*, against.] **I.** *n.*; pl. *-tries* (-triz). A tract of land of undefined extent, or considered apart from geographical or political limits; a region; a district; also, land, with reference to character, features, etc. (as, wild *country*; mountainous *country*); also, the territory of a nation; a state distinct in name, race, language, etc.; also, the land of one's birth or citizenship; also, rural districts, as opposed to cities or towns; also, the people of a district, state, or nation; the public; the body of voters; in *law*, the public at large, as represented by a jury. **II.** *a.* Of or pertaining to a country or one's own country; also, pertaining to the country, or rural districts; rural; rustic.—**country club,** a club in the country, often in the vicinity of a city, with a house, grounds, and facilities for outdoor sports, etc.—**coun′try=dance,** *n.* [So named as being of rural origin.] A dance of rural (or native) English origin; esp., a dance in which the partners stand facing each other in two lines.—**coun′try-man** (-mạn), *n.*; pl. *-men.* A native or inhabitant of a particular region (as, "I'm not this *countryman*, you may tell by my tongue, sir": George Eliot's "Adam Bede," ii.); also, a man of one's own country; a compatriot; also, a man who lives in the country; a rustic.—**coun′try=seat,** *n.* A country estate, esp. a fine one, often one used for only part of the year.—**coun′try=side,** *n.* A particular section of a country (as, "Smaller or greater adventurers seized a castle or a *countryside* and ruled an uncertain area": H. G. Wells's "Outline of History," xxxiii. § 1); also, its inhabitants.—**coun′try-wom″an,** *n.*; pl. *-women* (-wim″en). A female native or inhabitant of a particular region; also, a woman of one's own country; also, a woman who lives in a rural district.

coun-ty[1] (koun′ti), *n.* Same as *count*[1]. [Obs. or archaic.]

coun-ty[2] (koun′ti), *n.*; pl. *-ties* (-tiz). [AF. *counte*, OF. *contey* (F. *comté*), < L. *comitatus*, < *comes*: see *count*[1].] The domain of a count or an earl (obs. or hist.); one of the chief administrative divisions of a country or state, as in Great Britain and Ireland; the political unit next below the State in the U. S.; one of the larger divisions for purposes of local administration, etc., in Canada, New Zealand, etc.; also, the inhabitants of a county.—**coun′ty=seat,** *n.* The seat of government of a county.

coup[1] (kö), *n.* [F. *coup*, OF. *coup*, *colp*, < L. *colaphus*, < Gr. κόλαφος, blow, < κολάπτειν, strike.] A stroke or blow; a sudden move or proceeding; an unexpected and successful stroke.—**coup de grâce** (dė gräs). [F., 'stroke of grace.'] A stroke that mercifully ends life, as for a condemned person under torture or one mortally wounded; in general, a finishing stroke; a quietus.—**coup de main** (maṅ). [F., 'stroke of hand.'] A sudden military attack by main force; hence, any sudden, energetic action intended to effect a purpose by surprise.—**coup de maître** (mãtr). [F.] A master-stroke.—**coup de soleil** (so-lā-y′). [F.] A sunstroke.—**coup d'état** (dā-tä). [F., 'stroke of state.'] A sudden and decisive measure in politics, esp. one effecting a change of government illegally or by force.—**coup de théâtre** (tā-ätr). [F., 'stroke of theater.'] A sudden, exciting turn or striking effect in a play; hence, any sudden, sensational action or occurrence.—**coup d'œil** (dė-y′). [F., 'stroke of eye.'] A glance of the eye; a view as it strikes the eye at a glance (as, "There you saw, all in one *coup-d'œil*, the real good blood of Rome, the young blood of the new generation, and promise of the future": J. H. Newman's "Callista," v.); *milit.*, the act or faculty of estimating rapidly the advantages and disadvantages of a military position, arrangement of troops, etc.—**coup manqué** (mäṅ-kā). [F.] A stroke that failed; an abortive attempt.

coup[2] (koup or köp), *v.* [= *cope*[2].] **I.** *intr.* To strike†; come to blows†; also, to upset, overturn, or tilt (Sc.). **II.** *tr.* To upset; tilt; also, to empty out. [Sc.]

cou-pé (kö-pā′), *n.* [F., prop. pp. of *couper*, cut, OF. *couper*, cut, strike, < *coup*, stroke, blow: see *coup*[1].] An end compartment in a European diligence or railway-carriage; also, a short four-wheeled close carriage with (usually) a single cross-seat for two persons and with an outside seat for the driver; also, an inclosed automobile seating two or three persons, with the driver's seat inside.

coup-le (kup′l), *n.* [OF. *cople* (F. *couple*), < L. *copula*, band, bond: see *copula*.] A leash for holding two hounds together; also, a combination of two; a brace or pair; a man and a woman united by marriage or betrothal, or associated as partners in a dance or the like; two of the same sort connected or considered together; in *elect.*, a voltaic couple or a thermo-electric couple (see *voltaic* and *thermo-electric*); in *mech.*, a pair of equal, parallel forces acting in opposite directions and tending to produce rotation.—**coup′le,** *v.*; *-led*, *-ling*. [OF. *copler* (F. *coupler*), < L. *copulare*: see *copulate*.] **I.** *tr.* To fasten, link, or associate together in a pair or pairs; in general, to join or connect; also, to unite in matrimony (now colloq.); specif., in *wireless teleg.* and *teleph.*, to join or associate by means of a coupler. **II.** *intr.* To join in a pair; pair; also, to copulate.—**coup′led,** *p. a.* Fastened or associated together in a pair or pairs; joined: as, *coupled* columns (columns disposed in pairs close together, the capitals and bases of each pair often being united); *coupled* windows (windows disposed in pairs side by side, each pair forming an architectural whole).—**coup′le-ment,** *n.* The act of coupling, or the fact of being coupled; also, a couple or pair; also, a coupling, or connecting device.—**coup′ler,** *n.* One who or that which couples, or links together; specif., a device in an organ for connecting keys, manuals, or a manual and pedals, so that they are played together when one is played;

Coupled Columns, 12th century. — Cathedral of Monreale, Sicily.

also, in *wireless teleg.* and *teleph.*, a device for transferring electrical energy from one circuit to another, as a transformer which joins parts of a radio apparatus together by means of induction.—**coup'let,** *n.* [F., dim. of *couple.*] A pair of successive lines of verse, esp. such as rime together and are of the same length; in general, a pair or couple; in *music*, two equal notes occupying the time of three notes of the same kind in a passage in triple time.—**coup'ling,** *n.* The act of one who or that which couples; also, anything that couples; any of various mechanical devices for uniting or connecting parts or things; the part of the body between the tops of the shoulder-blades and the tops of the hip-joints in a dog, etc.—**coup'ling=pin,** *n.* A pin used in coupling or joining railroad-cars, parts of machines, etc.

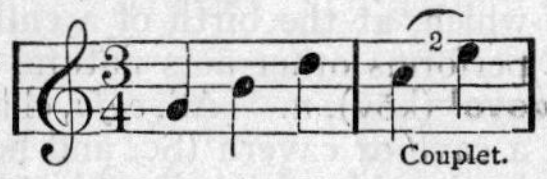

Couplet.

cou-pon (kö'pon), *n.* [F., < *couper*, cut: see *coupé.*] A separable part of a certificate, ticket, etc., entitling the holder to something; esp., one of a number of such parts calling for periodical payments on a bond; also, sometimes, a separate ticket or the like, for some similar purpose.

cour-age (kur'āj), *n.* [OF. *corage* (F. *courage*), < L. *cor*, heart.] Heart†; mind†; disposition†; also, the quality of mind that enables one to encounter difficulties and danger with firmness or without fear; valor; bravery.—**cou-ra-geous** (ku-rā'jus), *a.* [OF. *corageus* (F. *courageux*).] Possessing or characterized by courage; brave; valiant.—**cou-ra'geous-ly,** *adv.*—**cou-ra'geous-ness,** *n.*

cou-rant (kö-rånt' or kö'rant), *n.* [F. *courant*, prop. ppr. of *courir*, < L. *currere*, run.] A news-letter or newspaper: now only as the name of particular newspapers.

cou-rante (kö-rånt', F. kö-räṅt), *n.* [F. *courante*, prop. fem. of *courant*, ppr.: see *courant.*] An old-fashioned dance characterized by a running or gliding step; also, a piece of music for or suited to this dance; a movement in the suite, following the allemande.

cou-reur de bois (kö-rėr dė bwo); pl. *coureurs de bois* (kö-rėr dė bwo). [F., 'runner of woods.'] One of a class of hunters and trappers of French blood or descent in Canada and adjoining parts of North America.

cou-ri-er (kö'ri-ėr), *n.* [F. *courier*, now *courrier*, < It. *corriere*, < *correre*, < L. *currere*, run.] A messenger sent in haste; also, an attendant engaged by travelers to take charge of the arrangements of a journey.

cour-lan (kör'lan, F. kör-läṅ), *n.* [F.; from S. Amer. name.] A bird of the tropical American genus *Aramus*, comprising two species, *A. giganteus* (or *pictus*) and *A. scolopaceus*, large, long-billed, rail-like birds notable for their peculiar cry.

course (kōrs), *n.* [OF. F. *cours* (also *course*, fem.), < L. *cursus*, a running, course, < *currere*, run.] The action of running†; advance in a particular direction; a race (archaic); a charge, as in tilting; a bout or round; the pursuit of game with hounds; a race of dogs after a hare, etc.; also, the path or route along which anything moves; a way or channel in which water, etc., flows; the ground, water, etc., on which a race is run, sailed, etc.; a race-course; also, the direction in which anything moves or runs; the point of the compass toward which a ship sails; also, the continuous passage of time; progress onward or through a succession of stages; also, customary manner of procedure; regular or natural order of events; also, a particular manner of proceeding; *pl.*, personal behavior or conduct (archaic: as, to mend one's *courses*); also, *sing.*, succession, turn, or rotation, or one of a number of shifts or sets appointed to serve in turn (obs. or archaic); also, a number of things in regular sequence; a systematized or prescribed series, as of studies, lectures, medical treatments, etc.; also, a part of a meal served at one time; also, a continuous horizontal (or inclined) range of stones, bricks, or the like, in a wall, the face of a building, etc.; also, the lowest square sail on any mast of a square-rigged ship; *pl.*, the menses.—**of course,** in the common manner of proceeding; hence, naturally; as would be expected in the circumstances; obviously; certainly.—**course,** *v.*; *coursed, coursing.* **I.** *tr.* To pursue or hunt (game) with hounds, esp. by sight and not by scent; in general, to chase or pursue; also, to run through or over; also, to cause to run; cause (dogs) to pursue game. **II.** *intr.* To practise coursing; also, to run; move swiftly; also, to follow a course; direct one's course.—**cours'er,** *n.* One who or that which courses; a dog used for coursing; also, a swift horse (now chiefly poetic); also, any of certain swift-footed, plover-like birds constituting the genus *Cursorius*, of the desert regions of Africa and Asia, as *C. gallicus*, which is occasionally found also in Europe.—**cours'ing,** *n.* The act of one who or that which courses; esp., the sport of pursuing hares, etc., with hounds, when the game is started in sight of the hounds.

Double-collared Courser (*Cursorius bicinctus*).

court (kōrt), *n.* [OF. *court*, *cort* (F. *cour*), < ML. *cortis*, < L. *cors* (*cort-*), for *cohors* (*cohort-*), inclosure, yard, pen, also division of troops (see *cohort*); akin to E. *yard*[1].] A clear space wholly or partly inclosed by a wall or the like, or by buildings, as about or before a castle or large house, or in the center of a building; also, a large building standing within such a space; a stately dwelling; also, a short arm of a street, built around with houses; also, a smooth, level area on which to play tennis, rackets, handball, lawn-tennis, or some similar game; one of the divisions of such an area; also, the residence of a sovereign or other high dignitary; the place where a sovereign holds state, surrounded by his tokens of dignity; the establishment and surroundings of a sovereign or other high dignitary with his retinue; the collective body of persons forming the retinue; a sovereign and his councilors as the representatives of a state; also, a formal assembly held by a sovereign; also, homage paid, as to a sovereign; assiduous attention directed to gain favor; also, a place where justice is administered; a judicial tribunal duly constituted for the hearing and determination of causes; a session of a judicial assembly; also, the body of qualified members of a corporation, council, board, or the like; an assembly of such members.—**court,** *v.* **I.** *tr.* To pay court to; endeavor to win the favor of; also, to seek the affections of; woo; also, to attempt to gain (applause, favor, etc.); solicit or seek (as, "He had *courted* a decision, when, perhaps, his safety lay in patience and time": Reade's "Peg Woffington," i.); also, to hold out inducements to; invite. **II.** *intr.* To pay court; woo.—**court'=bar'on,** *n.* [AF. *court de baroun*, 'baron's court.'] An English manorial court, now nearly extinct, presided over by the lord or his steward and concerned with the redressing of misdemeanors in the manor, the settling of tenants' disputes, etc.

court=card (kōrt'kärd), *n.* [For the earlier *coat-card* (having reference to the dress of the characters represented).] A playing-card bearing the figure of a king, queen, or knave.

court=cup-board (kōrt'kub'ord), *n.* A kind of cabinet or sideboard with shelves, formerly used for the display of plate, etc. See Shakspere's "Romeo and Juliet," i. 5. 8.

cour-te-ous (kėr'tē-us or, chiefly Brit., kōr'tyus), *a.* [OF. *corteis* (F. *courtois*), < *cort*, E. *court.*] Having courtly manners; polite in behavior toward others; characterized by politeness.—**cour'te-ous-ly,** *adv.*—**cour'te-ous-ness,** *n.*

cour'te-san, etc. See *courtezan*, etc.

cour-te-sy (kėr'tē-si, Brit. kōr'tē-si), *n.*; pl. *-sies* (-siz). [OF. *cortesie* (F. *courtoisie*), < *corteis*, E. *courteous.*] Courtliness of manners or behavior; courteous behavior; politeness; also, favor or indulgence; conventional as distinguished from legal right; also, a courteous act or expression; also, the expression of respect by a gesture or bow†; hence, a curtsy.—**courtesy title,** a title to which one has no valid claim, but which is given by courtesy or social custom, as the title *Lord* prefixed to the Christian name and surname of the younger sons of British dukes and marquises (as in 'Lord Randolph Churchill').—**cour-te-sy** (kėr'tẹ̄-si or kėrt'si), *v. i.*; *-sied, -sying.* To curtsy.

cour-te-zan, cour-te-san (kōr'tẹ̄-zan or kėr'-), *n.* [F. *courtisane*, < It. *cortigiana*, court lady, courtezan, < *corte*, = E. *court.*] A prostitute, orig. and still usually one of relatively high pretensions.—**cour'te-zan-ship, cour'te-san-ship,** *n.*

court=hand (kōrt'hand), *n.* A style of handwriting formerly used in the English law-courts.

court=house (kōrt'hous), *n.* A building in which courts of law are held; also, a county-seat (U. S.).

cour-tier (kōr'tịėr), *n.* [Cf. OF. *cortoier*, be at court.] One in attendance at the court of a sovereign; also, one who courts favor.—**cour'tier-ly,** *a.* Courtier-like.—**cour'tier-ship,** *n.*

court=leet (kōrt'lēt), *n.* [See *leet.*] An English court, now nearly extinct, held before a lord or his steward, and having jurisdiction over petty offenses and the civil affairs of its district.

court-ly (kōrt'li), *a.*; compar. *courtlier*, superl. *courtliest.* Of or pertaining to the court of a sovereign; having manners befitting the court; polished; polite; elegant or refined (as, "You have too *courtly* a wit for me": Shakspere's "As You Like It," iii. 2. 72); also, flattering; sometimes, obsequious to the court or sovereign.—**court'li-ness,** *n.*—**court'ly,** *adv.*

court=mar-tial (kōrt'mär'shal), *n.*; pl. *courts-martial.* [Orig. *martial court.*] A court consisting of military or naval officers summoned to try charges of offense against military or naval law.—**court'=mar'tial,** *v. t.*; *-tialed* or *-tialled*, *-tialing* or *-tialling.* To arraign or try by court-martial.

court=plas-ter (kōrt'plȧs''tėr), *n.* [Named from its use by *court* ladies for patches for the face.] Silk or other fabric coated on one side with an adhesive preparation, as of isinglass and glycerin, used for covering slight cuts, etc., on the skin.

court-ship (kōrt'ship), *n.* Courtly manners or behavior†; flattery†; the paying of court, as to a dignitary†; the action or process of courting or wooing a woman; fig., solicitation, as of favors.

court=ten-nis (kōrt'ten'is), *n.* The older form of tennis, played in an inclosed court. See *tennis.*

court-yard (kōrt'yärd), *n.* A court, or space inclosed by walls, adjacent to, or within the limits of, a castle, large house, etc.

cous-cous (kůs'kůs), *n.* [F., < Ar. *kuskus*, < *kaskasa*, pound small.] A North African dish consisting of granulated flour cooked in the steam of meat or broth.

cous-in (kuz'n), *n.* [OF. *cosin* (F. *cousin*), < L. *consobrinus*, < *con-*, with, + *sobrinus*, mother's sister's child, < *soror*, sister.] A collateral relative more remote than a brother or sister; a kinsman or kinswoman; esp., a child of one's uncle or aunt; also, a term of address from one sovereign to another or to a great noble.—**first cousins,** or **cousins german,** children of brothers or sisters: *second cousins* being children of first cousins, and so on, and a *first cousin once removed* (sometimes loosely called a *second cousin*) being a child of one's first cousin.—**cous'in-hood** (-hůd), *n.* The relationship of a cousin or cousins; also, cousins or kinsfolk collectively.—**cous'in-ly,** *a.* Like or befitting a cousin.—**cous'in-ly,** *adv.*—**cous'in-ry,** *n.* Cousins collectively; kinsfolk.—**cous'in-ship,** *n.* Cousinhood.

cou-teau (kö-tō), *n.*; pl. *-teaux* (-tōz, F. -tō). [F. *couteau*, OF. *coutel*, < L. *cultellus*, dim. of *culter*, knife.] A knife; esp., a large knife formerly carried as a weapon.

couth (köth), *a.* [AS. *cūth*, known, pp. of *cunnan*, E. *can*[1]: cf. *uncouth.*] Known†, well-known†, or familiar†; friendly, kind, or pleasant; comfortable, cozy, or snug. [Now Sc. and north. Eng.]

couth-ie, couth-y (kö'thi), *a.* [From *couth.*] Friendly or sociable; kind or pleasant (as, "Gie her a *couthy* welcome": Ian Maclaren's "Beside the Bonnie Brier Bush," iv. 3); also, comfortable or cozy; also, well-to-do. [Sc. and north. Eng.]—**couth'i-ly,** *adv.*—**couth'i-ness,** *n.*

cou-til (kö-tēl'), *n.* [F.] A closely woven cotton fabric with a plain or a herring-bone weave, used esp. for making corsets. Also **cou-tille'** (-tēl').

cou-tu-rier (kö-tü-ryā), *n.* [F., < *couture*, sewing, < L. *consuere*, sew together, < *con-*, together, + *suere*, sew.] A (man) dressmaker.—**cou-tu-rière** (-ryãr), *n.* [F.] Fem. of *couturier.*

cou-vade (kö-väd'), *n.* [F., < *couver*, brood, incubate: see *covey.*] A practice among some primitive peoples by which, at the birth of a child, the father takes to bed and performs other acts natural rather to the mother.

cove[1] (kōv), *n.* [AS. *cofa*, chamber.] A closet† or chamber†; a cave or cavern (Sc. and north. Eng.); a hollow or recess in the side of a mountain; a sheltered nook; a small sheltered bay, inlet, or creek; in *arch.*, a concavity; a concave molding or member.—**cove**[1], *v. t.* or *i.*; *coved, coving.* To form into a cove; arch: as, a *coved* ceiling (one which is curved or arched at its junction with the side walls).

Coved Ceiling. — Louvre Palace, Paris.

cove[2] (kōv), *n.* [Origin obscure; first in rogues' slang.] A person; a fellow: as, "Do you see that old *cove* at the book-stall?" (Dickens's "Oliver Twist," x.). [Slang.]

co-vel-line, co-vel-lite (kọ-vel'in, -īt), *n.* [From N. *Covelli*, who in 1839 found it in lava from Vesuvius.] A mineral, a native sulphide of copper, CuS, usually occurring in masses of an indigo-blue color.

cov-e-nant (kuv'ẹ-nant), *n.* [OF. *covenant, convenant*, orig. ppr. of *convenir*, < L. *convenire*, agree: see *convene.*] An agreement between two or more persons to do or refrain from doing some act; a compact; a contract; in Biblical usage, the agreement or engagement of God with man as set forth in the Old and the New Testament; in *law*, a formal agreement of legal validity, esp. one under seal; an incidental clause of agreement in such an agreement; [*cap.*] in *Scottish hist.*, one of certain bonds of agreement signed by the Scottish Presbyterians for the defense or promotion of their religion, esp. the 'National Covenant' of 1638, or the 'Solemn League and Covenant' of 1643 (entered into with England).—**cov'e-nant,** *v.* **I.** *intr.* To enter into a covenant. **II.** *tr.* To agree to by covenant; stipulate.—**cov''e-nant-ee'** (-nan-tē'), *n.* The one to whom a promise by covenant is made.—**cov'e-nant-er,** *n.* One who enters into a covenant; [*cap.*] in *Scottish hist.*, a subscriber or adherent of the National Covenant or of the Solemn League and Covenant.—**cov'e-nant-or,** *n.* The one by whom a promise by covenant is made.

cov-ent (kov'ẹnt or kuv'-), *n.* Old form of *convent*: seen in the name of *Covent Garden* in London (a district, now occupied in part by a famous market, orig. a garden belonging to the abbey of St. Peter, Westminster).

Cov-en-try (kuv'ẹn-tri, Brit. kov'- or kuv'-), *n.* [From *Coventry*, town in Warwickshire, England.] A place to which persons are said to be sent when excluded from social relations; the situation of one socially ostracized or ignored, as for objectionable conduct.

cov-er (kuv'ėr), *v.* [OF. *covrir* (F. *couvrir*), < L. *cooperire*, < *co-*, altogether, + *operire*, cover.] **I.** *tr.* To put something over or upon, as for protection or concealment; overlay or overspread; put a cover or covering on; clothe; invest; put one's hat on (one's head); also, to deposit the equivalent of (money deposited), as in wagering; accept the conditions of (a bet, etc.); also, to serve as a covering for; extend over; occupy the surface of; of a male animal, to copulate with (the female); of a bird, to brood or sit on (eggs or chicks); also, to shelter or protect; serve as a defense to; also, to hide from view; screen; also, to aim directly at, as with a pistol; also, to have within range, as a fortress does certain territory; also, to include, comprise, or provide for; also, to act as reporter or photographer of or at (occurrences, performances, etc.), as for a newspaper; also, to pass or travel over; also, to suffice to defray or meet (a charge, expense, etc.); offset (an outlay, loss, liability, etc.); *milit.*, to be in line with by occupying a position directly before or behind (as, one soldier, or one body of troops, *covers* another). **II.** *intr.* To provide or serve as a covering; also, to become covered; also, to put one's hat on.—**cov′er,** *n.* That which covers, as the lid of a vessel, the binding of a book, the wrapper of a letter, etc.; protection, shelter, or concealment; a screen or cloak; woods, underbrush, etc., serving to shelter and conceal wild animals or game; a covert; funds to cover liability or secure against risk of loss; a set of articles (plate, knife, fork, etc.) laid at table for one person.—**cov′er-age** (-ā̤j), *n.* A covering, or providing for, something by agreement or contract, or that which is so covered.—**cov′ered,** *p. a.* Provided with a covering; having a cover; clothed with some growth (as, moss-*covered*); wearing one's hat.—**covered way,** in *fort.*, an open corridor running along the top of the counterscarp round the outworks, covered from the enemy's fire by a parapet or embankment.—**cov′er-er,** *n.*—**cov′er=glass,** *n.* A piece of thin glass used to cover a microscopical preparation.—**cov′er-ing,** *n.* The act of one who or that which covers; also, that which covers; something laid over or wrapped about a thing.—**cov′er-less,** *a.* Without a cover. —**cov′er-let,** *n.* [ME. *coverlite*, appar. < OF. *covrir*, cover, + *lit*, bed.] The outer covering of a bed; a bedspread; a counterpane; in general, a covering or cover.—**cov′er-lid,** *n.* Same as *coverlet.* See Tennyson's "Lancelot and Elaine," 1150.—**cov′er=point,** *n.* In *cricket*, *lacrosse*, etc., a player who supports the player called *point*.

co=versed (kō-vėrst′), *a.* [See *co-* and *versed*[1].] In the phrase *co-versed sine*, in *trigon.*, the versed sine of the complement of an angle or arc.

cov-ert (kuv′ėrt). [OF. *covert* (F. *couvert*), pp., *covert*, *coverte* (F. *couvert*, *couverte*), n., < *covrir*, cover: see *cover.*] **I.** *a.* Covered; sheltered; fig., concealed; secret; disguised; in *law*, under cover or protection of a husband. **II.** *n.* A covering or cover; shelter; concealment; disguise; a hiding-place; a thicket giving shelter to wild animals or game; *pl.*, in *ornith.*, the smaller and weaker feathers that cover the bases of the large feathers of the wing and tail.—**covert cloth,** a well-fulled, twilled woolen cloth woven with warp-yarn combining two colors, often with a light-brown or tan effect, used for outer coats.—**covert coat,** a short, light overcoat, properly of covert cloth.—**cov′ert=bar′on,** *a.* In *law*, covert.—**cov′ert-ly,** *adv.* In a covert manner; secretly; indirectly; by implication.—**cov′ert-ness,** *n.*—**cov′er-ture** (-ėr-t̤ṳ̄r), *n.* [OF. *coverture* (F. *couverture*).] A cover or covering; shelter; concealment; in *law,* the status of a married woman considered as under the protection and authority of her husband.

cov-et (kuv′et), *v.* [OF. *coveiter* (F. *convoiter*), ult. < L. *cupere*, desire.] **I.** *tr.* To wish for, esp. eagerly; usually, to desire inordinately, or without due regard to the rights of others; desire wrongfully. **II.** *intr.* To have an inordinate or wrongful desire.—**cov′et-a-ble,** *a.* That may be coveted.—**cov′et-er,** *n.*—**cov′et-ous,** *a.* [OF. *coveitos* (F. *convoiteux*).] Eagerly desirous; esp., inordinately desirous of possessions or wealth; grasping; avaricious; often, eager to possess that to which one has no right.—**cov′et-ous-ly,** *adv.*—**cov′et-ous-ness,** *n.*

cov-ey (kuv′i), *n.*; pl. *-eys* (-iz). [OF. *covee* (F. *couvée*), orig. pp. fem. of *cover* (F. *couver*), brood, incubate, < L. *cubare*, lie.] A brood or small flock of partridges or similar birds; fig., a company; a group.

cov-in (kuv′in), *n.* [OF. *covin*, < ML. *convenium*, < L. *convenire*, agree: see *convene.*] A secret or collusive agreement between two or more to the prejudice of another (obs. or legal); also, fraud (obs. or archaic).

cov-ing (kō′ving), *n.* [See *cove*[1].] An arched or coved part of a building projecting beyond the parts below; a cove or series of coves; coved work; *pl.*, the curved or splayed sides of a fireplace which narrows toward the back.

cov-in-ous (kuv′i-nus), *a.* In *law*, of the nature of or involving covin; collusive; fraudulent.

cow[1] (kou), *n.*; pl. *cows*, archaic *kine* (kīn). [AS. *cū* = D. *koe* = G. *kuh* = Icel. *kȳr*, cow: see *beef.*] The female of a bovine animal, esp. of the domestic species *Bos taurus*; also, the female of various other large animals, as the elephant, whale, etc.

cow[2] (kou), *v. t.* [Cf. Icel. *kūga*, cow, force, tyrannize over.] To depress with fear; dispirit; intimidate; overawe.

cow[3] (kou), *n.* [For *cowl*[2].] A cowl for a chimney.

cow-age (kou′ā̤j), *n.* See *cowhage.*

co=walk-er (kō-wâ′kėr), *n.* [See *co-*, and cf. *doppelgänger.*] An apparitional double or counterpart of a living person.

cow-an (kou′a̤n or kō′a̤n), *n.* [Origin unknown.] One who builds stone walls without mortar (used contemptuously of one who does the work of a mason without having served the regular apprenticeship: Sc.); hence, one who is not a freemason.

cow-ard (kou′ä̤rd). [OF. *couart* (F. *couard*), < *coue*, *coe*, < L. *cauda*, tail; variously explained, from its use as an epithet of the timid hare, as applied to an animal with its tail between its legs, and otherwise.] **I.** *n.* One who lacks courage to meet danger or difficulty; one who is basely timid; a craven. **II.** *a.* Destitute of courage; cowardly.—**cow′ar-dice** (-ä̤r-dis), *n.* [OF. *coardise* (F. *couardise*).] Want of courage; ignoble fear; pusillanimity.—**cow′ard-ly,** *a.* Lacking courage; basely timid; characteristic of or befitting a coward.—**cow′ard-li-ness,** *n.*—**cow′ard-ly,** *adv.*

cow-bane (kou′bān), *n.* Any of several apiaceous plants supposed to be poisonous to cattle, as the water-hemlock, *Cicuta virosa*, or an American swamp-plant, *Oxypolis rigidior*.

cow=bell (kou′bel), *n.* A bell hung round a cow's neck, to indicate her whereabouts.

cow-ber-ry (kou′ber″i), *n.*; pl. *-berries* (-iz). The berry or fruit of any of various shrubs, as *Vaccinium vitis-idæa*, that grow in pastures; also, any of these shrubs.

cow-bird (kou′bėrd), *n.* Any of the American blackbirds constituting the genus *Molothrus*, esp. *M. ater* of North America: so called because they accompany cattle. Also **cow′=black′bird.**

Cowbird (*Molothrus ater*).

cow-boy (kou′boi), *n.* A boy who tends cows; also, in the western U. S., a man employed in the care of the cattle of a ranch, doing his work largely on horseback (as, "We emerged . . . suddenly upon five hundred cattle and some *cow-boys* branding calves": Wister's "Virginian," iv.).

cow=catch-er (kou′kach″-ėr), *n.* A frame fixed to the front of a locomotive, for throwing aside from the track straying cattle or other obstructions; a similar contrivance on an electric car, etc.

cow-er (kou′ėr), *v. i.* [ME. *couren*: cf. Icel. *kūra*, sleep, doze, G. *kauern*, cower, squat.] To bend with the knees and back; stand or squat in a bent position; esp., to crouch in fear or shame.—**cow′er-ing-ly,** *adv.*

cow=fish (kou′fish), *n.* A sirenian, as the manatee; also, any of various small cetaceans, as a porpoise or dolphin or the grampus (*Grampus griseus*); also, any of various marine fishes with horn-like projections over the eyes, as *Lactophrys tricornis*, a fish that is found along the southern Atlantic coast of the U. S.

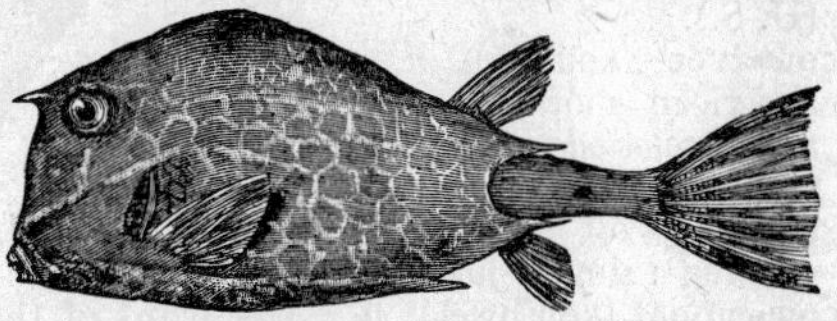
Cow-fish (*Lactophrys tricornis*).

cow-hage (kou′ā̤j), *n.* [Hind. *kawānch.*] The hairs of the pods of a tropical fabaceous plant, *Stizolobium* (or *Mucuna*) *pruriens*, which cause intense itching and are sometimes used as a vermifuge; also, the pods, or the plant.

cow-herd (kou′hėrd), *n.* One whose occupation is the tending of cows.

cow-hide (kou′hīd), *n.* The hide of a cow, or the leather made from it; also, a strong, flexible whip made of rawhide or of braided leather.—**cow′hide,** *v. t.*; *-hided, -hiding.* To whip with a cowhide.

cow-ish (kou′ish), *n.* [N. Amer. Ind.] An apiaceous plant, *Lomatium cous*, of Oregon, having edible tuberous roots used as food by the Indians; also, the root.

cowl[1] (koul), *n.* [OF. *cuvele*, < LL. *cupella*, dim. of L. *cupa*, tub, cask.] A large tub or the like for water, etc., esp. one with two ears through which a cowlstaff can be passed.

cowl[2] (koul), *n.* [AS. *cūle, cūgele*, < LL. *cuculla*, L. *cucullus*, hood.] A hooded garment worn by monks; the hood of this garment; hence, a monk; also, a hood-shaped covering for a chimney or ventilating shaft, to increase the draft; a wire cage for the top of the funnel of a locomotive.—**cowl**[2], *v. t.* To put a monk's cowl on; make a monk of; also, to cover with or as with a cowl.—**cowled,** *a.* Wearing a cowl; also, shaped like a cowl; cucullate.

cow-lick (kou′lik), *n.* A tuft of hair turned up, usually over the forehead, so that it appears as if licked by a cow.

cowl-staff (koul′stȧf), *n.* [See *cowl*[1].] A staff or pole on which a cowl or other vessel or weight is carried between two persons.

cow=man (kou′man), *n.*; pl. *-men.* An owner of cattle; a ranchman. [Western U. S.]

co=work-er (kō-wėr′kėr), *n.* [See *co-*.] One who works with another; a coöperator.

cow=pars-ley (kou′pärs″li), *n.* [See *cow*[1].] An apiaceous plant, *Anthriscus sylvestris*, of Europe.

cow=pars-nip (kou′pärs″nip), *n.* Any plant of the apiaceous genus *Heracleum*, as *H. sphondylium*, of Europe, or *H. lanatum*, of North America.

cow=pea (kou′pē), *n.* An annual fabaceous plant, *Vigna sinensis*, extensively cultivated in the southern U. S. for forage, manure, etc., and having seeds sometimes used for human food; also, the seed.

cow=pi-lot (kou′pī″lọt), *n.* A small fish, *Abudefduf saxatilis*, marked with deep indigo stripes, common in the West Indies and along both coasts of tropical America.

cow=po-ny (kou′pō″ni), *n.*; pl. *-nies* (-niz). A pony used in herding cattle. [Western U. S.]

cow-pox (kou′poks), *n.* An eruptive disease of a cow's udder, marked by vesicles which contain a virus used in vaccination; vaccinia.

cow=punch-er (kou′pun″chėr), *n.* A cattle-driver in the western U. S.; a cowboy: as, "It is only the somewhat green and unseasoned *cow-puncher* who struts before the public in spurs and deadly weapons" (Wister's "Virginian," xxxv.). [Colloq.]

cow-ry, cow-rie (kou′ri), *n.*; pl. *-ries* (-riz). [Hind. *kaurī.*] The shell of any of the marine gastropods constituting the genus *Cypræa*, as that of *C. moneta*, used as money in certain parts of Asia and Africa (see *money-cowry*), or that of *C. tigris*, a large, handsome shell often used as a mantel ornament; also, the animal itself.

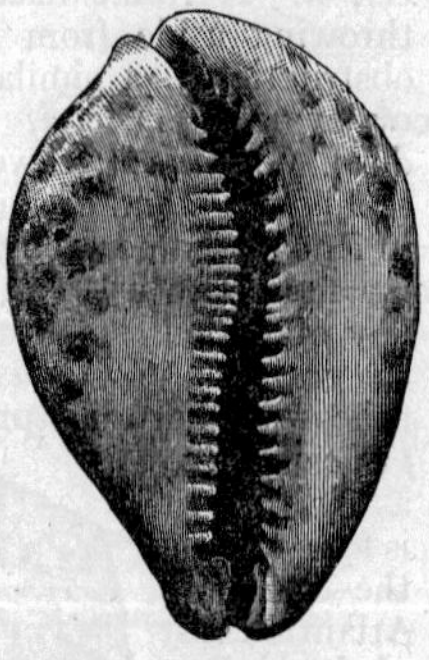

Cowry (*Cypræa tigris*).

cow-slip (kou′slip), *n.* [AS. *cūslyppe*: cf. *oxlip*.] An English primrose, *Primula officinalis* (or *veris*), bearing yellow flowers; also, the marsh-marigold, *Caltha palustris* (U. S.).

cow=tree (kou′trē), *n.* A South American moraceous tree, *Brosimum galactodendron*, whose trunk yields a nutritious milky juice; also, any of various other trees yielding a similar juice.

cow=wheat (kou′hwēt), *n.* Any plant of the scrophulariaceous genus *Melampyrum*; esp., a weed, *M. arvense*, found in the wheat-fields of Europe.

cox (koks), *n.* Colloquial abbreviation of *coxswain.*—**cox,** *v. t.* or *i.* To act as cox or coxswain to (a boat).

cox-a (kok′sạ̈), *n.*; pl. *coxæ* (-sē). [L., hip.] In *anat.*, the innominate bone; also, the joint of the hip; in *zoöl.*, the first or proximal segment or joint of the leg in insects and other arthropods.—**cox′al,** *a.*—**cox-al-gia** (kok-sal′jiạ̈), *n.* [NL.: see *-algia.*] In *pathol.*, pain in the hip.—**cox-al′gic,** *a.*

Leg of Beetle, enlarged.
a, coxa; *b*, trochanter; *c*, femur; *d*, tibia; *e*, tarsus.

cox-comb (koks′kōm), *n.* [For *cockscomb.*] The cap, resembling a cock's comb, formerly worn by professional fools†; also, the head†; also, a fool† or simpleton†; hence, a vain, showy fellow; a conceited dandy; a fop.—**cox-comb′i-cal,** *a.*—**cox′comb-ry,** *n.*; pl. *-ries* (-riz). The manners or behavior of a coxcomb; also, a foppish trait or thing; also, coxcombs collectively.

cox-swain (kok′swān, naut. kok′sn), *n.* [Earlier *cockswain*: see *cock*[4] and *swain.*] The steersman of a boat; on a ship, one who has charge of a boat and its crew.

coy (koi), *a.* [OF. *coi, quoi, queit* (F. *coi*), < L. *quietus*, E. *quiet*[2], *a.*] Quiet†; also, manifesting or affecting shyness or modesty (now usually of girls and young women); affectedly shy or reserved; also, disdainful† (as, "I find you passing gentle. 'Twas told me you were rough and *coy* and sullen": Shakspere's "Taming of the Shrew," ii. 1. 245).—**coy,** *v.* **I.**† *tr.* To render quiet; pat or caress; blandish or coax. **II.** *intr.* To act in a coy manner; affect reserve. [Archaic.]—**coy′ly,** *adv.*—**coy′ness,** *n.*

Coyote.

coy-o-te (kī-ō′tę̄ or kī′ōt, Sp. kō-yō′tā), *n.* [Mex. Sp.] A wild animal of the wolf kind, *Canis latrans*, of western North America, noted for loud and prolonged howling at night; the prairie-wolf.

coy-pu (koi′pö), *n.*; pl. *coypus* (-pöz) or (esp. collectively) *coypu.* [S. Amer.] A large South American aquatic rodent, *Myocastor* (or *Myopotamus*) *coypus*, yielding the fur nutria.

Coypu.

coz (kuz), *n.* Shortened form of *cousin*, used in familiar address.

coze (kōz), *v. i.*; *cozed, cozing.* [Cf. F. *causer*, talk, chat.] To converse in a familiar or friendly way; chat.—**coze,** *n.* A friendly talk; a chat.

coz-en (kuz′n), *v.* [Origin obscure.] **I.** *tr.* To cheat; deceive; beguile. **II.** *intr.* To practise cheating.—**coz′en-age** (-āj), *n.* The practice of cozening; the fact of being cozened; also, a fraud; a deception.—**coz′en-er,** *n.*

co-zier (kō′zhėr), *n.* [OF. *cousere*, < *cosdre* (F. *coudre*), sew, < L. *consuere*: see *couturier.*] A cobbler. See Shakspere's "Twelfth Night," ii. 3. 97. [Obs. or prov. Eng.]

co-zy, co-sy (kō′zi). [Origin obscure.] **I.** *a.*; compar. *cozier, cosier*, superl. *coziest, cosiest.* Snug; comfortable. **II.** *n.* A padded covering for a tea-pot, etc., to retain the heat.—**co′zi-ly, co′si-ly,** *adv.*—**co′zi-ness, co′si-ness,** *n.*

C Q D (sē kū dē). The letters represented by the radiotelegraphic code-signal formerly used, as by ships in distress, to summon assistance. Cf. *S O S.*

crab[1] (krab), *n.* [AS. *crabba* = D. *krab* = G. *krabbe* = Icel. *krabbi.*] Any of the stalk-eyed decapod crustaceans constituting the suborder *Brachyura* ('true crabs'), having a short, broad, more or

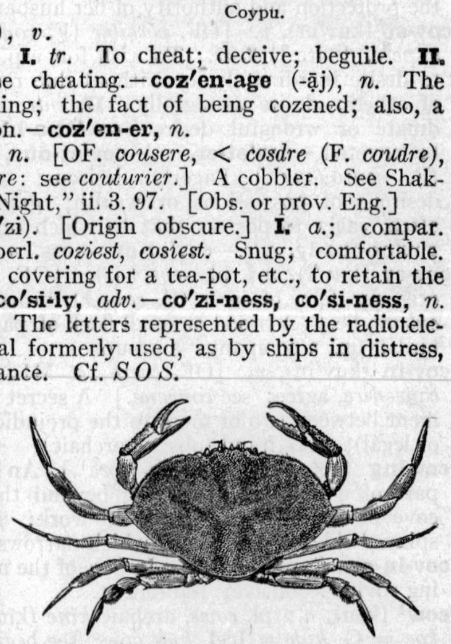

Common Crab of the Pacific Coast of America (*Cancer magister*).

less flattened body, the abdomen or so-called tail being small and folded under the thorax; hence, any of various other crustaceans (see *hermit-crab*) or other animals (see *king-crab*) resembling the true crabs; also, any of various mechanical contrivances for hoisting or drawing; also, an ill-tempered or crabbed person; also, *pl.*, a losing throw, as two aces, in the game of hazard; also, *sing.* [*cap.*], the zodiacal constellation or sign Cancer.—**to catch a crab,** to make a faulty stroke in rowing, so that the oar becomes blocked by the water.—**crab[1],** *v.*; *crabbed, crabbing.* **I.** *intr.* To catch crabs; also, to act like a crab in crawling backward, or back out (colloq.); also, of hawks, to claw each other. **II.** *tr.* To claw, as a hawk; hence, to find fault with (colloq.); also, to mar or spoil (colloq.).

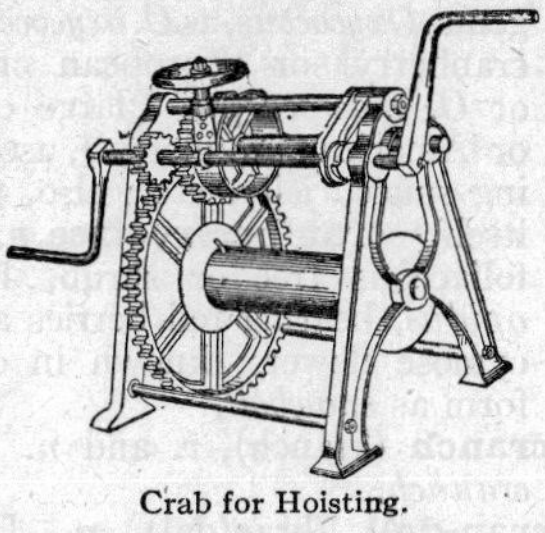
Crab for Hoisting.

crab[2] (krab), *n.* [ME. *crabbe*; perhaps the same word as *crab[1]*: cf. *crabbed.*] A small, sour wild apple; any of various cultivated varieties of apple, small, sour, and astringent or slightly bitter, used for making jelly and preserves; also, any tree bearing such fruit; also, a stick or cudgel of the wood of such a tree.—**crab′=ap″ple,** *n.* A crab (fruit or tree).

crab-bed (krab′ed), *a.* [ME.; from *crab[1]*.] Perverse or contrary; ill-conditioned; ill-natured or churlish; irritable; also, perplexing or intricate, as an author or his writings; also, difficult to decipher, as handwriting; also (with allusion to *crab[2]*), sour-tempered.—**crab′bed-ly,** *adv.*—**crab′bed-ness,** *n.*

crab-ber (krab′ėr), *n.* One who catches crabs; also, a boat used in catching crabs.—**crab′bing,** *n.*

crab-stick (krab′stik), *n.* A stick, cane, or club made of the wood of the crab-tree, or, by extension, of other wood; fig., an ill-tempered or crabbed person.

crab=tree (krab′trē), *n.* A tree which bears crab-apples.

crack (krak), *v.* [AS. *cracian* = D. *kraken* = G. *krachen*, crack; imit.] **I.** *intr.* To make a sudden, sharp sound in or as in breaking; snap, as a whip; brag or boast (now chiefly prov.); chat or gossip (chiefly Sc.); break with a sudden, sharp sound; break without complete separation of parts; become fissured; fail or give way (now slang); of the voice, to break abruptly and discordantly, esp. into an upper register. **II.** *tr.* To cause to make a sudden, sharp sound; make a snapping sound with (a whip, etc.); strike with a sharp noise (colloq.); utter or tell, as a joke; boast†; break (a nut, etc.) with a sudden, sharp sound; open and drink (a bottle of wine, etc.); break into (thieves' slang: chiefly in the phrase 'to crack a crib,' to break into a house, shop, etc.); subject to the process of cracking in the distillation of petroleum, etc. (see *cracking*); break without complete separation of parts; break into fissures; render unsound mentally; damage (credit, etc.); render (the voice) harsh or unmanageable; with *up*, to praise or extol (colloq.).—**crack. I.** *n.* A cracking sound; a sudden, sharp noise, as of something breaking; the snap of a whip, etc.; a shot, as with a rifle (colloq.); a try (colloq.); an opportunity or chance (colloq.); a resounding blow (colloq.); a moment or instant (colloq.: as, "He was on his feet again in a *crack*," Stevenson's "Treasure Island," xxi.); a boast or a lie (now chiefly prov.); conversation, or a tale or joke (Sc. or prov.); a break without complete separation of parts; a fissure; a flaw; a mental flaw; a crazy fellow†; a broken or changing tone of the voice; a lively boy†; one who or that which excels in some respect (colloq.). **II.** *a.* Of superior excellence; first-rate. [Colloq.]—**crack′a-ble,** *a.* That may be cracked.

crack-a-jack (krak′ạ-jak), *n.* and *a.* Same as *crackerjack.*

crack-brain (krak′brān), *n.* A crack-brained person.—**crack′=brained,** *a.* Having a cracked brain; impaired in intellect; crazy.

cracked (krakt), *p. a.* Broken; broken without separation of parts; fissured; damaged; mentally unsound (colloq.); broken in tone, as the voice.

crack-er (krak′ėr), *n.* One who or that which cracks; a boaster or a liar (obs. or prov.); a fire-cracker; a small paper roll containing an explosive, and usually a sweetmeat, motto, etc., which explodes when pulled sharply at both ends (in full, *cracker bonbon*); one of a class of poor whites in parts of the southeastern U. S.; a thin, crisp biscuit.

crack-er-jack (krak′ėr-jak). [Also *crackajack*: cf. *crack*, *a.*, and *jack[3]*.] **I.** *n.* A person of marked ability in some respect; something exceptionally fine of its kind; a trade-mark name (*Cracker Jack*) for a pop-corn confection. [Slang.] **II.** *a.* Of marked ability; exceptionally fine: as, a *crackerjack* ball-player; a *crackerjack* idea. [Slang.]

crack-ing (krak′ing), *n.* The act of one who or that which cracks; specif., in the distillation of petroleum or the like, the process of breaking down certain hydrocarbons into simpler ones of lower boiling-points, by means of excess heat, distillation under pressure, etc., in order to give a greater yield of low-boiling fractions than could be obtained by simple distillation.

crack-le (krak′l), *v.*; *-led, -ling.* [Dim. of *crack.*] **I.** *intr.* To make slight cracks, or sudden, sharp noises, rapidly repeated; crepitate. **II.** *tr.* To cause to crackle; break with a crackling noise; also, to cover with a network of minute cracks, as porcelain and glass.—**crack′le,** *n.* The act of crackling; a crackling noise; also, a network of fine cracks, as in the surface-glaze of some kinds of porcelain; porcelain or other ware with such a glaze.—**crack′led,** *p. a.* Covered with a network of minute cracks, as porcelain or glass; also, covered with crackling, as roast pork.—**crack′ling,** *n.* The making of slight cracking sounds rapidly repeated; also, the crisp browned skin or rind of roast pork; usually *pl.*, the crisp residue of hogs' fat after the lard has been tried out; also, the residue of tallow-melting.—**crack′ly,** *a.* Apt to crackle.

crack-nel (krak′nẹl), *n.* [Cf. F. *craquelin*, D. *krakeling*, and E. *crackling.*] A hard, brittle cake or biscuit; *pl.*, small bits of fat pork fried crisp.

crack-pot (krak′pot), *n.* A crack-brained person. [Slang.]

cracks-man (kraks′mạn), *n.*; pl. *-men.* A housebreaker; a burglar. [Slang.]

-cracy. [OF. *-cracie, -cratie*, F. *-cratie* (with *t* pronounced as *s*), < Gr. *-κρατία, -κράτεια,* < *κρατεῖν*, rule.] A noun termination meaning 'rule,' 'government,' 'governing body,' as in *aristocracy, autocracy, bureaucracy, democracy, plutocracy.* Cf. *-crat.*

cra-dle (krā′dl), *n.* [AS. *cradol.*] A little bed or cot for an infant, usually one constructed to admit of a rocking or swinging motion; fig., the place where anything is nurtured during its early existence; also, any of various contrivances likened to a child's cradle, as the framework on which a ship rests during construction or repair, or a frame or case for protecting a broken limb; a kind of box on rockers used by miners for washing auriferous gravel or sand to separate the gold; a frame of wood attached to a scythe, for laying grain evenly as it is cut; an engravers' tool for laying mezzotint grounds.—**cra′dle,** *v.*; *-dled, -dling.* **I.** *tr.* To place or rock in or as in a cradle; receive or hold as a cradle; hence, to nurture during infancy; also, to place in a ship's cradle; wash in a miner's cradle; cut (grain) with a cradle-scythe. **II.** *intr.* To lie in or as in a cradle.—**cra′dler,** *n.*—**cra′dle=scythe,** *n.* A scythe fitted with a cradle.—**cra′dle=song,** *n.* A song for singing to a child in the cradle; a lullaby.

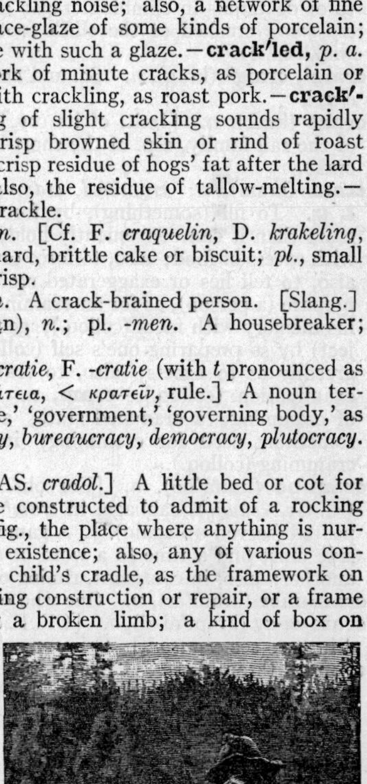
Miner's Cradle.

(variable) ḍ as d or j, ṣ as s or sh, ṭ as t or ch, ẓ as z or zh; *o*, F. cloche; ü, F. menu; ċh, Sc. loch; ṅ, F. bonbon; **′, primary accent; ″, secondary accent; †, obsolete; <, from; +, and; =, equals. See also lists at beginning of book.**

craft (kråft), *n.* [AS. *cræft* = D. *kracht* = G. *kraft* = Icel. *kraptr.*] Strength†; also, skill; ingenuity; dexterity; specif., skill or art applied to bad purposes; cunning; deceit; guile; also, an art, trade, or occupation requiring special skill, esp. manual skill; a handicraft; also, the members of a trade or profession collectively; a gild; also, vessels or boats collectively (construed as *pl.*); a vessel or boat; also, fishing-gear, esp. as used in whale-fishing.—**craft'i-ly,** *adv.* In a crafty manner; cunningly; with artful guile.—**craft'i-ness,** *n.*—**crafts'man** (-mạn), *n.*; pl. *-men.* One who practises a craft; an artisan; sometimes, an artist.—**crafts'man-ship,** *n.* The performance or skill of a craftsman.—**craft'y,** *a.*; compar. *craftier,* superl. *craftiest.* [AS. *cræftig.*] Possessing or displaying craft; skilful, ingenious, or dexterous (archaic); skilful in devising and executing underhand or evil schemes; cunning; artful; characterized by craft or deceit.

crag[1] (krag), *n.* [Cf. D. *kraag,* G. *kragen,* collar.] The neck; the throat; the craw. [Sc. and north. Eng.]

crag[2] (krag), *n.* [ME.; from Celtic.] A steep, rugged rock; a rough, broken projecting part of a rock.—**crag'ged,** *a.* Craggy.—**crag'gy,** *a.* Abounding in crags; of the nature of a crag; steep and rugged; rough.—**crag'gi-ness,** *n.*—**crags'man** (-mạn), *n.*; pl. *-men.* One accustomed to or dexterous in climbing crags: as, "I had fallen . . . A *cragsman* crushed at the cliff's foot" (Swinburne's "Bothwell," iii. 1).

craig[1], **craig**[2] (krāg), *n.* Sc. and north. Eng. form of *crag*[1], *crag*[2].

crake (krāk), *n.* [Imit. of its cry.] Any of various birds of the rail family, esp. of the short-billed kind, as the corncrake.

cram (kram), *v.*; *crammed, cramming.* [AS. *crammian.*] **I.** *tr.* To fill (something), by force or compression, with more than it can conveniently hold; esp., to fill with or as with excess of food; also, to force or stuff (*into, down,* etc.); also, to tell lies or exaggerated stories to (slang); also, to prepare (a person), as for an examination, by hastily storing his memory with facts (colloq.); get a knowledge of (a subject) by so preparing one's self (colloq.). **II.** *intr.* To eat greedily or to excess; also, to cram a subject, as for an examination (colloq.).—**cram,** *n.* The act or the result of cramming; a crammed state; a dense crowd (colloq.); something used for cramming; information acquired by cramming (colloq.).

cram-bo (kram'bō), *n.* [For obs. *crambe,* < L. *crambe* (< Gr. κράμβη), cabbage, in *crambe repetita,* 'cabbage repeated (served up again).'] A game in which one person or side must find a rime to a word or a line of verse given by another; also, in contempt, riming or rime.

cram-mer (kram'ėr), *n.* One who or that which crams.

cram-oi-sy (kram'oi-zi), *a.* [OF. F. *cramoisi,* < Ar. *qirmizī,* crimson: see *crimson.*] Crimson. [Archaic.]

cramp[1] (kramp), *n.* [Cf. MD. and MLG. *krampe,* OHG. *chramph,* hook, also E. *cramp*[2].] A grappling-iron†; also, a small metal bar with bent ends, for holding together timbers, masonry, etc.; a clamp; also, a portable frame or tool with a movable part which can be screwed up to hold things together; hence, anything that confines or restrains; also, a cramped state or part.—**cramp**[1], *v. t.* To fasten or hold with a cramp; also, to confine narrowly; also, to restrict; restrain; hamper.—**cramp**[1], *a.* Cramped; also, hard to decipher or understand; difficult; knotty.

cramp[2] (kramp), *n.* [OF. F. *crampe*; from Teut., and akin to E. *cramp*[1].] An involuntary, spasmodic, painful contraction of a muscle or muscles, as from a slight strain, a sudden chill, etc.; also, a paralytic affection of particular muscles, as of the hand, due to excessive use.—**cramp**[2], *v. t.* To affect with or as with a cramp.—**cramp'=fish,** *n.* The electric ray (fish).

cramp=i-ron (kramp'ī''ėrn), *n.* A grappling-iron†; also, a cramp, or piece of iron with bent ends, for holding together pieces of stone, etc.

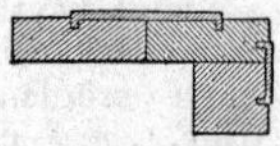

Cramp-irons.

cram-pon (kram'pọn), *n.* [F.; from Teut., and akin to E. *cramp*[1], *cramp*[2].] A grappling-iron, esp. one of a pair used together for raising heavy weights; also, a spiked iron plate worn on the shoe to prevent slipping.

cran-age (krā'nāj), *n.* The use of a crane to move goods; also, the charge made for this.

cran-ber-ry (kran'ber''i), *n.*; pl. *-berries* (-iz). [= G. *kranbeere, kranichbeere,* 'crane berry': see *crane.*] The red, acid fruit or berry of any plant of the vacciniaceous genus *Oxycoccus,* as *O. oxycoccus* ('small cranberry' or 'European cranberry') or *O. macrocarpus* ('large cranberry' or 'American cranberry'), used in making sauce, jelly, etc.; also, the plant itself.—**cran'ber''ry=tree,** *n.* A caprifoliaceous tree or shrub, *Viburnum opulus,* bearing red berries and white cymose flowers: known in cultivated form as *snowball.*

Cranberry (*Oxycoccus macrocarpus*).

cranch (krȧnch), *v.* and *n.* Same as *craunch.*

cran-dall (kran'dạl), *n.* [Prob. from *Crandall,* proper name.] A hammer-like masons' tool for dressing soft stone.—**cran'dall,** *v. t.* To treat or dress with a crandall.

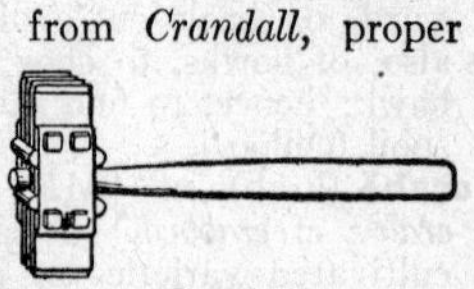

Crandall.

crane (krān), *n.* [AS. *cran,* akin to G. *kranich.*] Any of a group of large wading birds (family *Gruidæ*) with very long legs and neck; popularly, any of various similar birds, as the great blue heron, *Ardea herodias* (family *Ardeidæ*); also, a device for moving heavy weights, having two motions, one a direct lift and the other a horizontal movement, and consisting in one of its simplest forms of an upright post turning on its vertical axis and bearing a projecting arm on which the hoisting tackle is fitted; any of various similar devices, as a horizontally swinging arm by a fireplace, used for suspending pots, etc., over the fire; also, a siphon or bent pipe for drawing off a liquid; [*cap.*] in *astron.,* the southern constellation Grus.—**crane,** *v.*; *craned, craning.* **I.** *tr.* To stretch (the neck) as a crane does; also, to hoist, lower, or move by or as by a crane. **II.** *intr.* To stretch out one's neck; also, to stop and look before a dangerous leap in hunting; hence, to hesitate at danger, difficulty, etc. (colloq.).—**crane'=fly,** *n.* Any of the dipterous insects constituting the family *Tipulidæ,* characterized by very long legs; the daddy-long-legs of Great Britain.—**crane's'=bill, cranes'bill,** *n.* Any plant of the genus *Geranium* (see *geranium*): so called from the long, slender beak of the fruit.

Whooping Crane (*Grus americana*).

cra-ni-al (krā'ni-ạl), *a.* Of or pertaining to the cranium or skull.—**cra'ni-al-ly,** *adv.*

cra-ni-ate (krā'ni-āt). **I.** *a.* Having a cranium or skull; belonging to the *Craniata,* a primary division of vertebrates, comprising those which possess a skull and brain, and including the mammals, birds, reptiles, amphibians, and fishes. **II.** *n.* A craniate animal.

cranio-. Form of Gr. κρανίον, skull, used in combination.—**cra-ni-og-no-my** (krā-ni-og'nǫ-mi), *n.* [+ *-gnomy* as in *physiognomy.*] The art of judging mental or personal qualities from the form and other characteristics of the skull.—**cra'ni-o-graph** (-ǫ-grȧf), *n.* [+ *-graph.*] An instrument for making outline drawings of the skull.—**cra-ni-og'ra-phy** (-rạ-fi), *n.* [+ *-graphy.*] The description of skulls.—**cra-ni-ol'o-gy** (-ol'ǫ-ji), *n.* [+ *-logy.*] The science that deals with the size, shape, and other characteristics of skulls.—**cra''ni-o-log'i-cal** (-loj'i-kạl), *a.*—**cra-ni-ol'o-gist,** *n.*—**cra-ni-om'e-ter** (-om'e-tėr), *n.* [+ *-meter.*] An instrument for measuring skulls.—**cra-ni-**

om'e-try, *n.* [+ *-metry.*] The science of the measurement of skulls.—**cra″ni-o-met'ric, cra″ni-o-met'ri-cal** (-met'-rik, -ri-kạl), *a.*—**cra-ni-om'e-trist,** *n.*—**cra'ni-o-plas″ty** (-plas″ti), *n.* [+ *-plasty.*] Plastic surgery as concerned with the cranium.—**cra-ni-os'co-py** (-os'kọ̄-pi), *n.* [+ *-scopy.*] Observation of the shape and other characteristics of the skull; formerly, phrenology.—**cra-ni-os'co-pist,** *n.*

cra-ni-um (krā'ni-um), *n.*; pl. *-niums* or *-nia* (-ni-ạ̈). [ML., < Gr. *κρανίον.*] The skull of a vertebrate; esp., that part of the skull which incloses the brain.

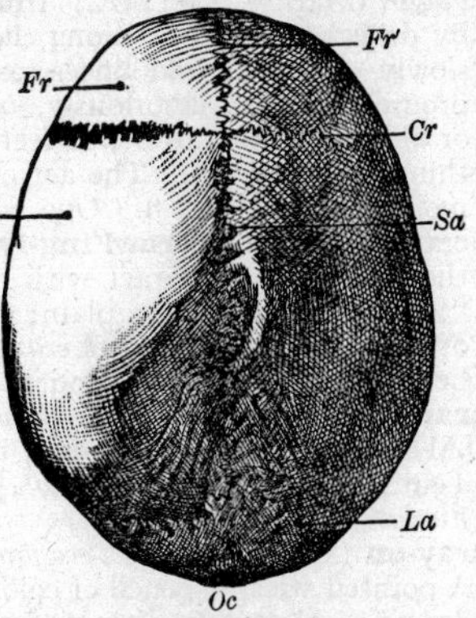

Human Cranium, from above.
Fr, Pa, Oc, frontal, parietal, and occipital bones; *Fr', Cr, Sa, La,* frontal, coronal, sagittal, and lambdoid sutures.

crank[1] (krangk), *n.* [ME. *cranke*: cf. AS. *cranc-stæf*, weaver's implement; akin to E. *cringe, crinkle.*] A device for communicating motion, or for changing rotary motion into reciprocating motion, or vice versa, consisting in its simplest form of an arm projecting at an angle from, or secured at right angles at the end of, the axis or shaft which receives or imparts the motion, and in the steam-engine, etc., forming the member between the connecting-rod and the shaft; also, a bend† or winding†; a turn of speech; a verbal conceit; an eccentric notion; a person subject to eccentric or impracticable notions, often a person possessed by a particular notion and disposed to urge it in season and out of season (colloq.).—**crank**[1], *v.* **I.** *tr.* To bend into or make in the shape of a crank; furnish with a crank; turn with a crank; turn (an automobile engine, etc.) by means of a hand-crank in order to set it in operation; start the engine of (an automobile, etc.) by doing this; move by means of a crank. **II.** *intr.* To turn a crank, as in starting an automobile engine; also, to twist† or wind†.

crank[2] (krangk), *a.* [ME. *cranke*; origin obscure.] Lively; in high spirits; complacently cheerful; disposed to exult: as, "David . . . was *crank* as could be when he thought Nathan was a talkin' about other people's sins" (Mrs. Stowe's "Oldtown Folks," xxviii.). [Obs. or prov.]

crank[3] (krangk), *a.* [Cf. D. *krengen*, careen, D. and G. *krank*, sick, feeble, crazy (as a ship).] Liable to lurch or capsize, as a ship; in an unstable or shaky condition, as machinery; infirm in health (prov.).

crank=case (krangk'kās), *n.* In an internal-combustion engine, the case which incloses the crank-shaft, connecting-rods, and allied parts, and which, in two-cycle engines, is constructed tightly enough to contain a quantity of fuel mixture while being compressed.

crank-i-ly (krang'ki-li), *adv.* In a cranky manner.—**crank'-i-ness,** *n.*

cran-kle (krang'kl), *v.*; *-kled, -kling.* [Freq. of *crank*[1].] **I.** *intr.* To bend in and out; wind. **II.** *tr.* To bend sinuously.—**cran'kle,** *n.* A bend or turn; a crinkle.

crank=pin (krangk'pin), *n.* A pin or cylinder at the outer end or part of a crank, as for holding a connecting-rod.

crank=shaft (krangk'shȧft), *n.* A shaft receiving motion from or imparting motion to a crank.

crank-y (krang'ki), *a.*; compar. *crankier*, superl. *crankiest.* [Partly < *crank*[1], partly < *crank*[3].] Full of bends or windings; crooked; also, subject to eccentric notions; eccentric; queer; also, ill-tempered or cross; also, liable to lurch or capsize, as a boat; shaky or out of order, as machinery; sickly or infirm (prov. Eng.).

cran-nied (kran'id), *a.* Having crannies; like a cranny.

cran-nog (kran'og), *n.* [Ir.] An ancient lake-dwelling or artificial island in a lake in Ireland or Scotland.

cran-ny (kran'i), *n.*; pl. *crannies* (-iz). [ME. *crany*: cf. F. *cran*, notch, fissure (see *crenel*).] A small, narrow opening, as in a wall, rock, etc.; a chink; a crevice; a fissure.

cran-reuch (krȧn'ruch), *n.* [Appar. from Gaelic.] Hoar-frost. [Sc.]

crants† (krants), *n.* [Cf. D. *krans*, G. *kranz*, wreath, crown.] A garland; a wreath. See Shakspere's "Hamlet," v. 1. 255.

crap (krap), *n.* [Appar. < *crabs*, as used in the game of hazard: see *crab*[1].] A losing throw, in which the total of pips shown on the two dice is 2, 3, or 12, in a modern and simplified form of the old game of hazard called 'craps'; also, the game of craps.

crape (krāp), *n.* [For *crêpe.*] A thin, light fabric of silk, cotton, or other fiber, with a finely crinkled or ridged surface; esp., a black (or white) silk fabric of this kind, used for mourning veils, trimmings, etc.; also, a band or piece of this material, as for a token of mourning.—**crape,** *v. t.*; *craped, craping.* To cover, clothe, or drape with crape; put crape on.

crap-pie (krap'i), *n.* [Origin obscure.] A small fish, *Pomoxys annularis*, of the central parts of the U. S.; also, the related calico-bass, *P. sparoides.*

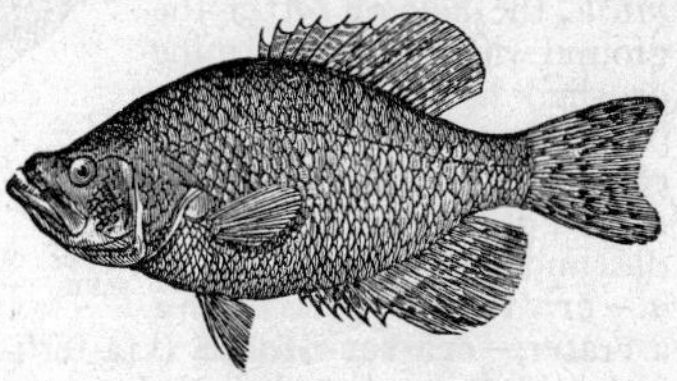
Crappie (*Pomoxys annularis*).

craps (kraps), *n. pl.* See *crap.*

crap-u-lent (krap'ụ̄-lẹnt), *a.* [LL. *crapulentus*, < L. *crapula*, < Gr. *κραιπάλη*, headache or nausea from drunkenness.] Sick from gross excess in drinking or eating; crapulous.—**crap'u-lence,** *n.*

crap-u-lous (krap'ụ̄-lus), *a.* [LL. *crapulosus*, < L. *crapula*: see *crapulent.*] Given to or characterized by gross excess in drinking or eating; suffering from or due to such excess.—**crap'u-lous-ness,** *n.*

crash[1] (krash), *v.* [ME.; imit.] **I.** *tr.* To break in pieces violently and noisily; shatter; also, to force or drive (*in, through, out,* etc.) with violence and noise; in *aëronautics*, to cause (an aircraft) to make a landing in an abnormal manner, usually damaging or wrecking the apparatus. **II.** *intr.* To break or fall to pieces with noise; also, to make a loud, clattering noise, as of something dashed to pieces; also, to move or go with a crash; strike with a crash; in *aëronautics*, to land in an abnormal manner, usually damaging or wrecking the apparatus.—**crash**[1], *n.* A breaking or falling to pieces with loud noise; the shock of collision and breaking; fig., a sudden and violent falling to ruin; specif., a sudden collapse of a financial undertaking or the like; also, a sudden, loud noise, as of something dashed to pieces; the sound of thunder, loud music, etc.; in *aëronautics*, an act of crashing.

crash[2] (krash), *n.* [Prob. from Russ.] A coarse linen fabric used for towels, carpet-coverings, clothing, etc.

cra-sis (krā'sis), *n.* [ML., < Gr. *κρᾶσις*, < *κεραννύναι*, mix.] A combination or blending of elements, as in the animal body†; bodily constitution†; temperament†; in *gram.*, a combination of the vowels of two syllables, esp. at the end of one word and the beginning of the next, into one long vowel or a diphthong.

crass (kras), *a.* [L. *crassus*, solid, thick, dense, fat.] Thick or coarse; also, gross, stupid, or dense (as, *crass* ignorance; a *crass* mind).

cras-sa-men-tum (kras-ạ-men'tum), *n.* [L., < *crassare*, thicken, < *crassus*: see *crass.*] The thick, jelly-like part of coagulated blood; the clot.

cras-si-tude (kras'i-tūd), *n.* [L. *crassitudo.*] The state or quality of being crass; thickness or grossness; gross ignorance, stupidity, or dullness.

crass-ly (kras'li), *adv.* In a crass manner; densely.—**crass'ness,** *n.*

cras-su-la-ceous (kras-ụ̄-lā'shius), *a.* [NL. *Crassula*, the typical genus, < L. *crassus*, thick.] Belonging to the *Crassulaceæ*, a family of plants, mostly fleshy or succulent herbs, including the houseleek, stonecrop, etc.

-crat. [F. *-crate*, < Gr. *-κρατής*, ruling, < *κρατεῖν*, rule.] A noun termination meaning 'ruler,' 'member of a ruling body,' 'advocate of a particular form of rule,' as in *aristocrat, autocrat, democrat, mobocrat, plutocrat.* Cf. *-cracy.*

(variable) ḑ as d or j, ş as s or sh, ţ as t or ch, z̧ as z or zh; *o*, F. cloche; ü, F. menu; ċh, Sc. loch; ṅ, F. bonbon; **'**, primary accent; **″**, secondary accent; †, obsolete; <, from; +, and; =, equals. **See also lists at beginning of book.**

cratch (krach), *n.* [OF. *cresche:* see *crèche.*] A crib to hold fodder for horses, etc.; a manger. [Archaic or prov.]
crate (krāt), *n.* [L. *cratis*, wickerwork.] A basket or hamper of wickerwork, for the transportation of crockery, etc.; any openwork casing, as a box made of slats for packing and transporting commodities.—**crate,** *v. t.*; *crated, crating.* To put or pack in a crate.
cra-ter (krā'tėr), *n.* [L., < Gr. κρατήρ, orig. bowl for mixing wine and water in, < κεραννύναι, mix.] A large vessel or bowl used by the ancient Greeks and Romans, orig. for mixing wine with water; also, the cup-shaped depression or cavity marking the orifice of a volcano; in *elect.*, a cavity formed in the positive carbon of an arc-lamp using a continuous current; *milit.*, the hole or pit in the ground where a military mine or shell has exploded; also [*cap.*], in *astron.*, a southern constellation represented as a bowl or vase with two handles and a base.—**cra'ter-al,** *a.*—**cra'tered,** *a.* Having a crater.—**cra-ter-i-form** (krạ-ter'i-fôrm), *a.* Having the form of a crater; bowl-shaped.

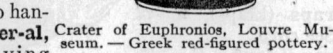

Crater of Euphronios, Louvre Museum.—Greek red-figured pottery.

craunch (krânch or kränch), *v.* [Appar. imit.] **I.** *tr.* To crush with or as with the teeth; crunch: as, "She would *craunch* the wing of a lark, bones and all, between her teeth" (Swift's "Gulliver's Travels," ii. 3). **II.** *intr.* To crunch.—**craunch,** *n.* A craunching or crunch.
cra-vat (krạ-vat'), *n.* [F. *cravate*; so called because adopted from the Croats (F. *Cravates*).] A neck-cloth, esp. for men; a necktie.—**cra-vat',** *v. t.* or *i.*; *-vatted, -vatting.* To equip with or put on a cravat.
crave (krāv), *v.*; *craved, craving.* [AS. *crafian*, akin to Icel. *krefja.*] **I.** *tr.* To ask earnestly for (something); beg for; also, to long for or desire eagerly; also, to need greatly; require; also, to ask (a person) earnestly for something or to do something. **II.** *intr.* To beg or plead (*for*); also, to long (*for* or *after*).
cra-ven (krā'vn). [ME. *cravant*, vanquished: cf. OF. *cravanter*, crush, overthrow, < L. *crepare*, rattle, crack.] **I.** *a.* Vanquished or defeated (now only in the archaic phrase 'to cry craven,' to acknowledge one's self beaten, or surrender); also, cowardly, pusillanimous, or mean-spirited. **II.** *n.* An acknowledged coward; a pusillanimous fellow; a dastard.—**cra'ven,** *v. t.* To make craven.
cra-ven-ette (krā-vn-et'), *n.* [From *Craven*, proper name.] A textile fabric subjected to a special waterproofing process, used for outer garments. [Proprietary name.]—**cra-ven-ette',** *v. t.*; *-etted, -etting.* To subject to the waterproofing process employed on cravenette.
cra-ven-ly (krā'vn-li), *adv.* In a craven manner.—**cra'ven-ness,** *n.*
crav-er (krā'vėr), *n.* One who craves; a beggar.
crav-ing (krā'ving), *n.* Earnest asking or entreating; begging; also, eager or urgent desire; longing; yearning.—**crav'ing-ly,** *adv.*
craw (krâ), *n.* [ME. *crawe*; prob. from Scand.] The crop of a bird or insect; hence, the stomach of any animal.
craw-fish (krâ'fish), *n.*; pl. *-fishes* or (esp. collectively) *-fish.* [= *crayfish.*] Any of numerous fresh-water decapod crustaceans of the suborder *Macrura*, closely related to the lobsters but smaller, as *Astacus fluviatilis*, of Europe, and various American species of the genus *Cambarus*; any of certain similar marine crustaceans; also, one who backs out or retreats from a position or undertaking (colloq.).—**craw'fish,** *v. i.* To back out or retreat from a position or undertaking. [Colloq.]

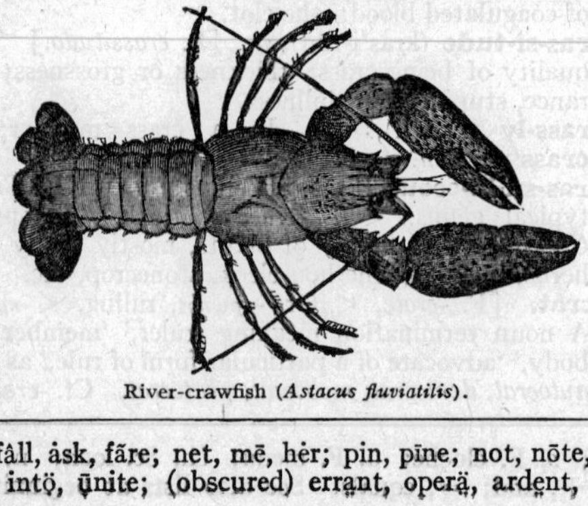
River-crawfish (*Astacus fluviatilis*).

crawl[1] (krâl), *n.* [= *kraal.*] An inclosure of stakes and hurdles in shallow water on the seacoast, for containing fish, turtles, etc.
crawl[2] (krâl), *v. i.* [ME.; from Scand.] To move slowly by dragging the body along the ground, as a worm; move slowly on hands and knees, as a child; creep; hence, to progress slowly, laboriously, or timorously; go stealthily or abjectly; also, to be, or feel as if, overrun with crawling things.—**crawl**[2], *n.* The act of crawling; a slow, crawling motion.—**crawl'er,** *n.* One who or that which crawls; a crawling animal.—**crawl'ing-ly,** *adv.*—**crawl'y,** *a.* Having the sensation of contact with crawling things; creepy: as, "We . . . heard them plain; but we couldn't see no sign of them; it made you feel *crawly*" (Mark Twain's "Huckleberry Finn," xix.). [Colloq.]
cray-fish (krā'fish), *n.*; pl. *-fishes* or (esp. collectively) *-fish.* [ME. *crevise*, < OF. *crevice, crevisse* (F. *écrevisse*); from Teut., and akin to E. *crab*[1].] A crawfish, esp. *Astacus fluviatilis* of Europe.
cray-on (krā'ọn), *n.* [F. *crayon*, < *craie*, < L. *creta*, chalk.] A pointed stick or pencil of colored clay, chalk, etc., used for drawing; also, a drawing in crayons.—**cray'on,** *v. t.*; *-oned, -oning.* To draw with a crayon or crayons; fig., to sketch out, as a plan; also, to cover with crayon drawings.—**cray'on-ist,** *n.* One who draws with crayons.
craze (krāz), *v.*; *crazed, crazing.* [ME. *crasen*, break, akin to F. *écraser*, crush; from Scand.] **I.** *tr.* To break† or shatter†; also, to crack (obs. or prov.); specif., to make small cracks on the surface of (pottery, etc.); crackle; also, to weaken or impair (health, etc.: archaic or prov.); also, to impair in intellect; make insane. **II.** *intr.* To break†; also, to become minutely cracked, as the glaze on the surface of pottery; also, to become insane.—**craze,** *n.* A crack (obs. or prov.); a minute crack in the glaze of pottery, etc.; also, insanity; an insane condition; also, a mania; an unreasoning liking or fancy for some object of interest, esp. as current among a number of people or the public generally; a rage.—**crazed,** *p. a.* Broken, cracked, or impaired (obs. or prov.); having small cracks in the glaze, as pottery; also, rendered insane; demented.—**cra'zy,** *a.*; compar. *crazier*, superl. *craziest.* Impaired or dilapidated; shaky; frail; also, broken in mind; demented; insane; mad.—**cra'zi-ly,** *adv.*—**cra'zi-ness,** *n.*—**cra'zy=bone,** *n.* The funny-bone.—**cra'zy=quilt,** *n.* A patchwork quilt made of patches of irregular shape combined with little or no regard to pattern.—**cra'zy=weed,** *n.* The loco-weed.
creak (krēk), *v.* [ME. *creken*; imit.] **I.** *intr.* To make a sharp, harsh, grating or squeaking sound; move with creaking. **II.** *tr.* To cause to creak.—**creak,** *n.* A creaking sound.—**creak'ing-ly,** *adv.*—**creak'y,** *a.*; compar. *creakier*, superl. *creakiest.* Creaking; apt to creak.
cream (krēm), *n.* [OF. *cresme* (F. *crème*), < LL. *chrisma*: see *chrism.*] The fatty part of milk, which rises to the surface when the liquid is allowed to stand; also, something containing or resembling this substance, as a table delicacy, a confection, a cosmetic, etc.; fig., the best part of anything; also, cream-color.—**cream of tartar,** purified and crystallized potassium bitartrate: used as a baking-powder ingredient, etc. Cf. *tartar*[1].—**cream sauce,** a sauce made of cream or milk, flour, butter, etc.—**cream,** *v.* **I.** *intr.* To form cream; hence, to froth; foam. **II.** *tr.* To allow (milk) to form cream; skim (milk); separate as cream; take the cream or best part of; add cream to (tea, coffee, etc.); in *cookery*, to work (butter, butter and sugar, etc.) to a smooth, creamy mass; prepare (chicken, oysters, vegetables, etc.) with cream, milk, or a cream sauce.—**cream'=cheese',** *n.* Any of various soft, rich cheeses made of cream, or with an extra proportion of cream.—**cream'=col"or,** *n.* White, or a whitish color, with a tinge of yellow or buff.—**cream'=col"ored,** *a.*—**cream'=cups,** *n.* A papaveraceous plant, *Platystemon californicus*, of California, bearing small pale-yellow or cream-colored flowers.—**cream'er,** *n.* One who or that which creams; a refriger-

ator in which milk is placed to facilitate the formation of cream; a vessel or apparatus for separating cream from milk; also, a small jug, pitcher, etc., for holding cream.—**cream'er-y,** *n.*; pl. *-ies* (-iz). A place where milk is set to form cream; an establishment engaged in the production of butter and cheese; a place for the sale of milk and its products.—**cream'i-ness,** *n.* Creamy quality.—**cream'=nut,** *n.* The Brazil-nut.—**cream-om-e-ter** (krē-mom'e-tėr), *n.* [See *-meter.*] An instrument for determining the percentage of cream in a sample of milk.—**cream'y,** *a.*; compar. *creamier,* superl. *creamiest.* Containing cream; resembling cream, as in appearance or consistence; soft and rich; cream-colored.

crease[1] (krēs), *n.* See *creese.*

crease[2] (krēs), *n.* [Formerly also *creast:* cf. *crest.*] A line or mark produced in anything by folding; a fold; a ridge; a furrow; in *cricket,* one of certain lines marked on the ground to define the positions of the bowler and the batsman.—**crease**[2], *v.*; *creased, creasing.* **I.** *tr.* To make a crease or creases in or on; wrinkle; also, to wound or stun by a furrowing or superficial shot (U. S.). **II.** *intr.* To become creased.—**creas'er,** *n.*—**creas'y,** *a.* Full of creases.

cre-a-sote (krē'a̤-sōt), *n.* and *v.* See *creosote.*

cre-at-a-ble (krẹ-ā'ta̤-bl), *a.* That may be created.

cre-ate (krẹ-āt'), *v.*; *-ated, -ating.* [L. *creatus,* pp. of *creare,* bring into being.] **I.** *tr.* To bring into being; cause to exist; produce; specif., to evolve from one's own thought or imagination; also, to be the first to represent (a part or rôle); also, to make by investing with new character or functions (as, to *create* a peer); constitute; appoint; also, to be the cause or occasion of; give rise to. **II.** *intr.* To create something.—**cre-ate',** *a.* Created. [Archaic.]—**cre-a'tion** (-ā'sho̤n), *n.* [L. *creatio(n-).*] The act of creating, or the fact of being created; [often *cap.*] with *the,* the original bringing into existence of the universe by the Deity; [*l. c.*] that which is created; the world or universe; creatures collectively; specif., a product of inventive ingenuity; an original work, esp. of the imaginative faculty.—**cre-a'tion-al,** *a.*—**cre-a'tion-ism,** *n.* The doctrine that matter and all things were created, substantially as they now exist, by the fiat of an omnipotent Creator, and not gradually evolved or developed (cf. *evolutionism*); also, the doctrine that God immediately creates out of nothing a new human soul for each individual born (cf. *infusionism* and *traducianism*).—**cre-a'tion-ist,** *n.*—**cre-a'tive,** *a.* Having the quality or power of creating; originative; productive (*of*).—**cre-a'tive-ly,** *adv.*—**cre-a'tive-ness,** *n.*—**cre-a'tor,** *n.* [L.] One who or that which creates; esp. [*cap.*], with *the,* God.—**cre-a'tor-ship,** *n.*—**cre-a'tress,** *n.* A female creator.—**cre-a'trix,** *n.* [L.] A creatress.

crea-tur-al (krē'ṯūr-a̤l), *a.* Of, pertaining to, or of the nature of a creature or creatures.

crea-ture (krē'ṯūr), *n.* [OF. *creature* (F. *créature*), < LL. *creatura,* < L. *creare:* see *create.*] Anything created, animate or inanimate; an animate being; an animal, as distinct from man (applied in the U. S. esp. to cattle, horses, etc.); a human being or person (often used in contempt, commiseration, or endearment); something produced by or springing from something else; a result or product; a person owing his rise and fortune to another, or subject to the will or influence of another; intoxicating liquor, esp. whisky (humorous: as, "when he chanced to have taken an overdose of the *creature,*" Scott's "Guy Mannering," xliv.).—**creature comforts,** things, as food, which minister to bodily comfort.—**crea'ture-hood** (-hu̇d), **crea'ture-ship,** *n.* The condition of a creature.—**crea'ture-ly,** *a.* Of or pertaining to a creature or creatures; creatural.

crèche (krāsh or kresh), *n.* [F. *crèche,* OF. *cresche,* crib, manger; from Teut., and akin to E. *crib.*] A public nursery where the children of the poor are cared for while their mothers are away from home at work, etc.; also, an asylum for foundlings.

cre-dence (krē'de̤ns), *n.* [ML. *credentia,* belief, credit, also sideboard, < L. *credens,* ppr.: see *credent.*] Belief or credit (as, to give *credence* to a person or a statement); also, that which is believed; also, something giving a claim to credit or confidence (now only in 'letter of credence,' a letter commending the bearer to confidence); also, the tasting of food before serving, as a precaution against poisoning†; a side-table at which this was done†; any side-table or sideboard†; *eccles.,* a small side-table, shelf, or niche for holding articles used in the eucharistic service (also called *credence-table*).

Ecclesiastical Credence; 16th century.

cre-den-dum (krẹ-den'dum), *n.*; pl. *-da* (-dä). [L., neut. gerundive of *credere:* see *credit.*] That which is to be believed; an article of faith: distinguished from *agendum.*

cre-dent (krē'de̤nt), *a.* [L. *credens* (*credent-*), ppr. of *credere:* see *credit.*] Believing; also, having credit or repute† (see Shakspere's "Measure for Measure," iv. 4. 29); credible† (see Shakspere's "Winter's Tale," i. 2. 142).

cre-den-tial (krẹ-den'sha̤l). [ML. *credentia:* see *credence.*] **I.** *a.* Giving a title to credit or confidence. **II.** *n.* That which gives a title to credit or confidence; a letter or other testimonial attesting the bearer's right to confidence or authority (usually in *pl.*).

cred-i-ble (kred'i-bl), *a.* [L. *credibilis,* < *credere:* see *credit.*] Capable of being believed; believable; also, worthy of belief or confidence; trustworthy.—**cred-i-bil'i-ty** (-bil'i-ti), *n.*—**cred'i-bly,** *adv.*

cred-it (kred'it), *v. t.* [L. *creditus,* pp. of *credere,* trust, believe.] To believe; put confidence in; also, to intrust†; trust with goods, etc.†; also, to give reputation or honor to (archaic); also, to enter upon the credit side of an account; give the benefit of such an entry to (a person, etc.); hence, to ascribe (something) to a person, etc.; make ascription of something to (a person, etc.: with *with*).—**cred'it,** *n.* [OF. *credit* (F. *crédit*), < It. *credito,* < L. *creditus,* pp.] Belief or trust; also, trustworthiness or credibility; also, something credited or believed† (as, "There I found this *credit,* That he did range the town to seek me out": Shakspere's "Twelfth Night," iv. 3. 6); also, repute or reputation; esp., favorable estimation; also, influence or authority resulting from the confidence of others or from one's reputation; also, commendation or honor given for some action, quality, etc.; a source of commendation or honor; also, confidence in a purchaser's ability and intention to pay, displayed by intrusting him with goods, etc., without immediate payment; time allowed for payment for goods, etc., obtained on trust; reputation of solvency and probity, entitling a person to be trusted in buying or borrowing; power to buy or borrow on trust; also, the acknowledgment or an entry of payment or value received, in an account; the side (right-hand) of an account on which such entries are made (opposed to *debit*); the balance in one's favor in an account; also, any sum on deposit or against which one may draw; a bill, note, etc., on the security of which one may obtain funds; also, the ascription or acknowledgment of something as due or properly attributable to a person, etc.—**credit man,** in a business establishment, an employee who fixes the amount of credit to be allowed to customers.—**letter of credit.** See under *letter*[2], *n.*—**cred'it-a-ble,** *a.* Worthy of credit or belief†; also, bringing credit or honor (as, "Clive made a *creditable* use of his riches": Macaulay's "Essays," Lord Clive); reputable; respectable.—**cred'it-a-ble-ness,** *n.*—**cred'it-a-bly,** *adv.*

cré-dit fon-cier (krā-dē fôn-syā). [F., 'credit on lands' (*foncier,* < *fonds,* land: see *fund*).] Credit based on security consisting of landed property.

cred-it-less (kred'it-les), *a.* Without credit.

cré-dit mo-bi-lier (krā-dē mo-bē-lyā). [F., 'credit on movables' (*mobilier,* < *mobile,* E. *mobile*).] Credit based on security consisting of movable or personal property.

cred-i-tor (kred'i-to̤r), *n.* [L.] One who gives credit in business transactions, or, generally, one to whom money

(variable) ḍ as d or j, ṣ as s or sh, ṯ as t or ch, ẓ as z or zh; *o,* F. cloche; ü, F. menu; ch, Sc. loch; ṅ, F. bonbon; ', primary accent; '', secondary accent; †, obsolete; <, from; +, and; =, equals. See also lists at beginning of book.

is due (opposed to *debtor*); in *bookkeeping*, the credit side of an account.—**cred'i-tor-ship,** *n.*

cre-do (krē'dō), *n.*; pl. *-dos* (-dōz). [L., 'I believe': the first word of the Apostles' and the Nicene Creed in Latin.] The Apostles' or the Nicene Creed; a musical setting of the creed, usually of the Nicene Creed; in general, any creed or formula of belief.

cred-u-lous (kred'ū-lus), *a.* [L. *credulus*, < *credere*: see *credit.*] Ready or disposed to believe, esp. on weak or insufficient evidence; also, marked by or arising from credulity.—**cre-du-li-ty** (krę-dū'li-ti), **cred'u-lous-ness,** *n.*—**cred'u-lous-ly,** *adv.*

creed (krēd), *n.* [AS. *crēda*, < L. *credo*: see *credo.*] An authoritative formulated statement of the chief articles of Christian belief, as the Apostles', the Nicene, or the Athanasian Creed (see under *apostle*, *Nicene*, and *Athanasian*); usually, the Apostles' Creed; in general, any formula of religious belief, as of a particular denomination; also, an accepted system of religious belief; hence, any system of belief or of opinion.—**creed'al,** *a.* Of or pertaining to a creed or creeds.—**creed'less,** *a.* Without a creed.

creek (krēk, in U. S. commonly krik), *n.* [ME. *creke*, *crike*: cf. D. *kreek*, F. *crique*, creek, Icel. *kriki*, crack, nook.] A narrow recess in the shore of the sea, a river, etc.; a small inlet or bay; a small port or harbor (Eng.); also, a small stream, as a branch of a river; a rivulet; also, a narrow or winding passage†; a nook†; a turn† or winding†.

creel (krēl), *n.* [Perhaps through F. < L. *craticula*, dim. of *cratis*, wickerwork: cf. *grille.*] A wickerwork basket, esp. one used by anglers for holding fish; a wickerwork trap to catch fish, lobsters, etc.; a framework, esp. one for holding bobbins in a spinning-machine.—**creel,** *v. t.* To put into a creel in angling; succeed in catching.

creep (krēp), *v.*; *crept*, *creeping.* [AS. *crēopan* = D. *kruipen* = Icel. *krjūpa.*] **I.** *intr.* To move with the body close to the ground, as a reptile or an insect, or a child on hands and knees; hence, to move slowly, imperceptibly, or stealthily; move or behave timidly or servilely; also, to grow along the ground, a wall, etc., as a plant, esp. one that roots at intervals; also, to slip or move along gradually, as a railroad-track under traffic; also, to have a sensation as of something creeping over the skin. **II.** *tr.* To creep along or over.—**creep,** *n.* The act of creeping; the slow bulging up of the floor of a gallery in a coal-mine; any slow movement of the earth's crust, mining ground, or the like; a sensation as of something creeping over the skin (usually in *pl.*).—**creep'er,** *n.* One who or that which creeps; one of a breed of domestic fowls with short legs; any of various birds that creep about on trees, bushes, etc. (as, the black-and-white *creeper*, a warbler, *Mniotilta varia*, of the U. S., having plumage streaked and spotted with black and white); a creeping plant (as, the Virginia *creeper*: see entry in alphabetical place); a grappling device for dragging the bottom of a river, etc.; a spiked piece of iron worn on the heel of the shoe to prevent slipping on ice, etc.; *pl.*, a loose garment, usually bifurcated, worn by creeping children.—**creep'=hole,** *n.* A hole by which one may creep in or out; a hole into which an animal creeps to escape notice or danger; fig., a subterfuge or excuse.—**creep'ing,** *p. a.* That creeps; in *bot.*, growing along or just beneath the surface of the ground, or on any other surface, and (usually) sending out rootlets at intervals.—**creep'ing-ly,** *adv.*—**creep'y,** *a.*; compar. *creepier*, superl. *creepiest.* That creeps, as an insect; also, having or causing a creeping sensation of the skin, as from horror or dread (as, "The stillness was awful *creepy* and uncomfortable": Mark Twain's "Huckleberry Finn," xxii.).

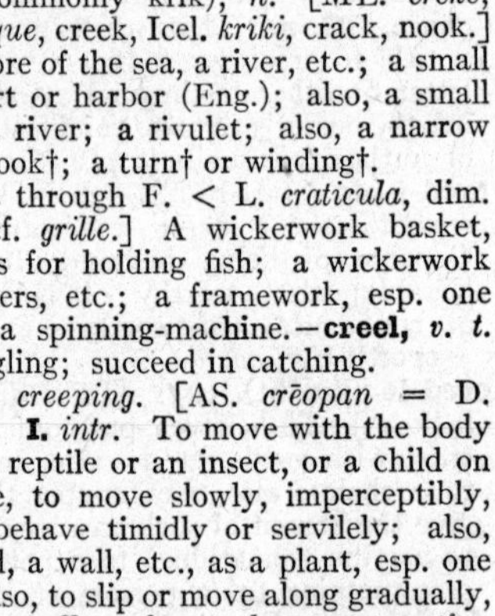

Black-and-white Creeper (*Mniotilta varia*).

creese, kris (krēs, krēs or kris), *n.* [Malay *krīs.*] A short sword or heavy dagger with a waved blade, used by the Malays.

cre-mate (krę-māt' or krē'māt), *v. t.*; *-mated*, *-mating.* [L. *crematus*, pp. of *cremare*, consume by fire.] To consume by fire; burn; esp., to reduce (a corpse) to ashes.—**cre-ma'tion** (-mā'shon), *n.* [L. *crematio(n-).*] The act or custom of cremating.—**cre-ma'tion-ist,** *n.* One who advocates cremation instead of burial of the bodies of the dead.—**cre-ma'tor,** *n.* [LL.] One who cremates; a furnace for cremating dead bodies or other matter.—**cre-ma-to-ri-um** (krē-mą-tō'ri-um or krem-ą-), *n.*; pl. *-riums* or *-ria* (-ri-ą). [NL.] A crematory.—**cre-ma-to-ry** (krē'mą-tǭ-ri or krem'ą-). **I.** *a.* Of or pertaining to cremation. **II.** *n.*; pl. *-ries* (-riz). A furnace or an establishment for cremating dead bodies or other matter.

crème (krām, F. krām), *n.* [F.: see *cream.*] Cream; a cream-like preparation or liquid; one of a class of liqueurs of thick, oily or syrupy consistence.—**crème de menthe** (dė moṅt). [F., 'cream of mint.'] A liqueur flavored with mint.

crem-o-carp (krem'ǭ-kärp), *n.* [Gr. κρεμαννύναι, hang, + καρπός, fruit.] In *bot.*, the characteristic dry fruit of apiaceous plants, consisting of two indehiscent one-seeded carpels which separate from each other at maturity and remain hanging at the end of the axis.

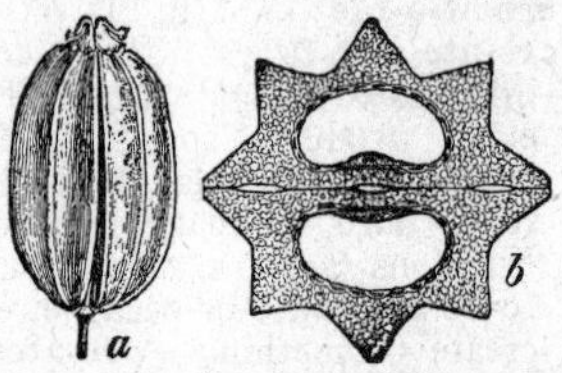

Cremocarp.

a, fruit of samphire (*Crithmum maritimum*); *b*, section of same, showing the two distinct one-seeded carpels.

Cre-mo-na (krę-mō'ną), *n.* One of a class of violins of superior quality made at Cremona, Italy, during the 16th, 17th, and 18th centuries.

cre-na (krē'ną), *n.*; pl. *-næ* (-nē). [NL.: cf. OF. *cren*, *crenne*, notch, *crenel*, E. *crenel.*] A notch or indentation; also, a tooth or scallop.—**cre'nate** (-nāt), *a.* [NL. *crenatus.*] Having the margin notched so as to form a series of rounded teeth, as a leaf. Also **cre'nat-ed** (-nā-ted).—**cre'nate-ly,** *adv.*—**cre-na-tion** (krę-nā'shon), *n.* Crenate state; also, a rounded projection or tooth, as on the margin of a leaf.—**cren-a-ture** (kren'ą-tūr or krē'ną-), *n.* A rounded tooth, as of a crenate leaf; also, a notch between teeth.

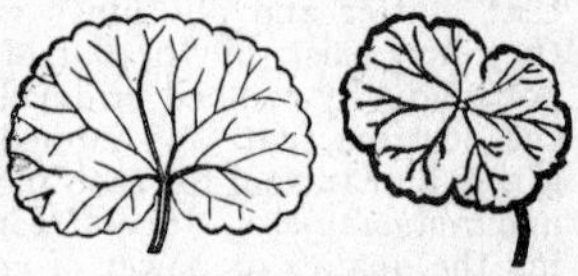

Crenate and Doubly Crenate Leaves.

cren-el (kren'el), *n.* [OF. *crenel* (F. *créneau*), dim. of *cren* (F. *cran*), notch, of uncertain origin: cf. *crena*, *cranny.*] One of the open spaces between the merlons of a battlement; also, a crenature.—**cren'el,** *v. t.*; *-eled* or *-elled*, *-eling* or *-elling.* To crenelate.—**cren-e-late, cren-el-late** (kren'e-lāt), *v. t.*; *-lated*, *-lating.* [Cf. F. *créneler.*] To furnish with crenels or battlements; specif., in *arch.*, to form with square indentations, as a molding.—**cren-e-la'tion, cren-el-la'tion** (-lā'shon), *n.* The act of crenelating, or the state of being crenelated; also, a battlement; also, a notch or indentation.

cre-nelle (kre-nel'), *n.* Same as *crenel.*

cren-u-late (kren'ū-lāt), *a.* [NL. *crenulatus*, < *crenula*, dim. of *crena*, notch.] Minutely crenate, as a leaf. Also **cren'u-lat-ed** (-lā-ted).—**cren-u-la'tion** (-lā'shon), *n.* Crenulate state; also, a minute crenation.

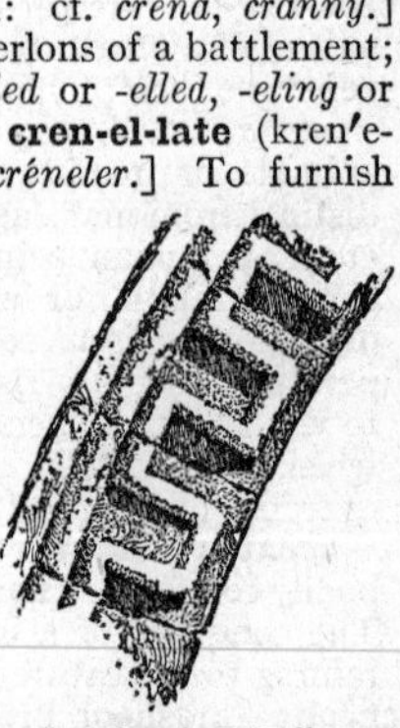

Crenelated Molding.—Norman doorway, Kenilworth church, Warwickshire, England.

cre-o-dont (krē'ǭ-dont), *n.* [NL. *Creodonta*, pl., < Gr. κρέας, flesh, + ὀδούς (ὀδοντ-), tooth.] Any of the *Creodonta*, a group of primitive carnivorous mammals, characterized by small brains, regarded as the ancestors of the modern carnivores.

cre-ole (krē'ōl). [F. *créole*, < Sp. *criollo.*] **I.** *n.* Orig., in the West Indies and Spanish America, one born in the region but of European (usually Spanish) ancestry; similarly, in Louisiana and elsewhere, a person born in the region but of French ancestry; in general, a person born in a place but of foreign ancestry, as distinguished from the aborigines and half-breeds (sometimes applied to negroes born in America). **II.** *a.* Of, belonging to, or characteristic of the creoles (as, a *creole* dialect; *creole* French); also, bred or growing in a country, but of foreign origin, as an animal or plant; in *cookery*, noting a sauce made of stewed tomatoes, peppers, etc.

cre-oph-a-gous (krḗ-of′ạ-gus), *a.* [Gr. κρεοφάγος, < κρέας, flesh, + φαγεῖν, eat.] Flesh-eating; carnivorous.—**cre-oph′a-gy** (-ji), *n.*

cre-o-sol (krē′ọ-sol or -sōl), *n.* [From *creosote.*] In *chem.*, a colorless oily liquid with an agreeable odor and burning taste, resembling carbolic acid, obtained from wood-tar and guaiacum resin.

cre-o-sote (krē′ọ-sōt), *n.* [Gr. κρέας, flesh, + σώζειν, save.] An oily liquid with a burning taste and a penetrating odor, obtained by the distillation of wood-tar, and used as a preservative and antiseptic.—**cre′o-sote,** *v. t.*; *-soted, -soting.* To treat with creosote.—**cre′o-sote=bush,** *n.* A zygophyllaceous evergreen shrub, *Covillea tridentata* (or *Larrea mexicana*), of northern Mexico and adjacent regions, bearing resinous foliage with a strong odor of creosote.

crêpe (krāp, F. krãp), *n.* [F. *crêpe*, earlier *crespe*, < L. *crispus*, curled, crimped, E. *crisp.*] Crape.—**crêpe de Chine** (dė shēn). [F., 'crape of China.'] A light, soft, thin silk fabric with minute irregularities of surface.—**crêpe lisse** (lēs). [F., 'smooth crape.'] A very thin, fine variety of crape in which the irregularity of surface is almost imperceptible: used esp. for making ruching.

crep-i-tant (krep′i-tạnt), *a.* Crepitating; crackling.

crep-i-tate (krep′i-tāt), *v. i.*; *-tated, -tating.* [L. *crepitatus*, pp. of *crepitare*, freq. of *crepare*, rattle, crack.] To make a crackling sound; crackle; rattle.—**crep-i-ta′tion** (-tā′-shọn), *n.* The act or sound of crepitating; a crackling sound.

cré-pon (krā′pon, F. krā-pôṅ), *n.* [F.] A dress-fabric of wool, silk, or cotton, crinkled or ridged like crape but heavier.

crept (krept). Preterit and past participle of *creep.*

cre-pus-cu-lar (krḗ-pus′kụ̄-lạ̈r), *a.* [L. *crepusculum*, twilight: see *crepuscule.*] Of, pertaining to, or resembling twilight; dim; indistinct; in *zoöl.*, appearing or flying in the twilight.

cre-pus-cule (krḗ-pus′kūl or krep′us-kūl), *n.* [OF. *crepuscule* (F. *crépuscule*), < L. *crepusculum*, twilight, < *creper*, dark, obscure.] Twilight; dusk; crepusculum.—**cre-pus′cu-line** (-kụ̄-lin), *a.* Pertaining to twilight; dusky; dim.

cre-pus-cu-lum (krḗ-pus′kụ̄-lum), *n.* [L.: see *crepuscule.*] Twilight.

cres-cen-do (kre-sen′dō, It. kre-shen′dō). [It., gerund of *crescere*, < L. *crescere*: see *crescent.*] In *music*: **I.** *a.* Gradually increasing in force or loudness: opposed to *decrescendo* or *diminuendo.* **II.** *n.*; pl. *-dos* (-dōz). An increase in force or loudness; also, a crescendo passage.

cres-cent (kres′ẹnt). [L. *crescens* (*crescent-*), ppr. of *crescere*, grow, increase; as n., through OF. *cressant* (F. *croissant*).] **I.** *a.* Increasing or growing, as the new moon or the moon during its first quarter; also, shaped like the moon in its first quarter. **II.** *n.* The crescent moon; the convexo-concave figure of the moon in its first quarter, or the similar figure of the moon in its last quarter, resembling a bow terminating in points; also, a representation of this; specif., such a representation as the Turkish emblem (as, "the fanatical zeal which animated the followers of the Cross and of the *Crescent* against each other": Scott's "Talisman," ii.); hence, the Turkish or Mohammedan power; also, any crescent-shaped object.—**cres-cen-tade** (kres-ẹn-tād′), *n.* [Cf. *crusade.*] A war or a military expedition under the flag of Turkey, for the defense or extension of Mohammedanism.—**cres′cent-ed,** *a.* Formed as a crescent; also, decorated with crescents.—**cres-cen-tic** (kre-sen′tik), *a.* Crescent-shaped.—**cres′cent=shaped,** *a.* Having the shape of a crescent, or new moon.

Heraldic Crescent.

cres-cive (kres′iv), *a.* [L. *crescere*: see *crescent.*] Increasing; growing.

cres-co-graph (kres′kọ-gråf), *n.* [L. *crescere*, grow, increase: see *-graph.*] A device invented by Sir Jagadis Chandra Bose (born 1858), of India, for observing and recording small movements of growth, etc., in plants, by greatly magnifying the actual movements.—**cres-co-graph′ic** (-graf′ik), *a.*

cre-sol (krē′sol or -sōl), *n.* [From *creosote.*] In *chem.*, any one of three isomeric phenols occurring in coal-tar and wood-tar.

cress (kres), *n.* [AS. *cresse, cerse*, = D. *kers* = G. *kresse.*] Any of various brassicaceous plants whose leaves have a slightly pungent taste and are often used for salad and as a garnish (as, the water-*cress*: see *water-cress*); also, any of various similar plants.

cres-set (kres′et), *n.* [OF. *craisset, grasset*, appar. < *craisse, graisse*, E. *grease.*] A vessel of iron or the like, often mounted on a pole or suspended from above, containing combustible material which is burned for light or as a beacon.

Cressets.

cress-y (kres′i), *a.* Abounding in cresses.

crest (krest), *n.* [OF. *creste* (F. *crête*), < L. *crista.*] A tuft or other natural growth on the top of an animal's head, as the comb of a cock; hence, anything resembling or suggesting such a tuft; a plume or other ornament on the top of a helmet; a figure borne above the escutcheon in a coat of arms, and also used separately as a cognizance; the apex of a helmet; a helmet; also, the head or top of anything; the summit of a hill, etc.; fig., the highest or best of the kind (as, "One feast, of holy days the *crest*, I, though no Churchman, love to keep": Lowell's "All-Saints"); also, the ornamental part which surmounts a roof-ridge, wall, etc.; also, a ridge or ridge-like formation; the ridge of the neck of a horse, dog, etc.; the foamy top of a wave.—**crest,** *v.* **I.** *tr.* To furnish with a crest; also, to serve as a crest for; crown or top; also, to reach the crest or summit of (a hill, etc.). **II.** *intr.* To form or rise into a crest, as a wave.—**crest′ed,** *a.* Having or bearing a crest.—**crest′fall″en,** *a.* With drooping crest; chagrined or mortified; dejected or dispirited.—**crest′fall″en-ly,** *adv.*—**crest′fall″en-ness,** *n.*—**crest′ing,** *n.* In *arch.*, an ornamental finish of stone, metal, or the like, surmounting a wall, roof-ridge, etc.—**crest′less,** *a.* Without a crest.

Helmet and Crest.—From the frieze of the Parthenon (Athens).

Heraldic Crest.—Royal crest of Scotland.

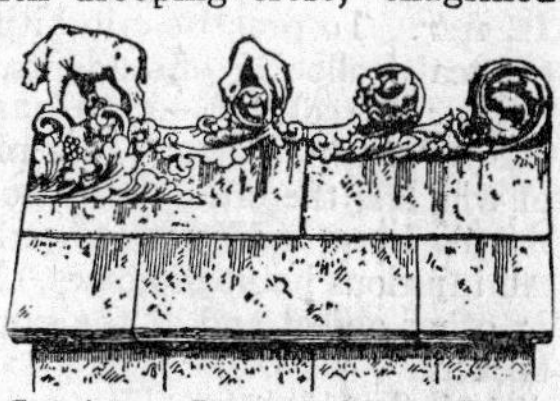
Cresting.—Buttress of Notre Dame, Dijon, France; 13th century.

cre-syl (krē′sil), *n.* [From *cresol*: see *-yl.*] In *chem.*, the univalent radical tolyl, of which cresol is the hydroxide.—**cre-syl′ic,** *a.*

cre-ta-ceous (krḗ-tā′shius). [L. *cretaceus*, < *creta*, chalk.] **I.** *a.* Of the nature of, resembling, or containing chalk; [*cap.*] noting or pertaining to a geological period or a system of rocks preceding the Tertiary and succeeding the Jurassic, and constituting the latest principal division of the Mesozoic. **II.** *n.* [*cap.*] The Cretaceous period or system.

Cre-tan (krē′tạn). **I.** *a.* Of or pertaining to the island of Crete (southeast of Greece) or its inhabitants. **II.** *n.* A native or inhabitant of Crete; esp., one of the indigenous Grecian population of Crete.

cre-tic (krē′tik). [L. *Creticus*, < Gr. Κρητικός, Cretan, < Κρήτη, Crete.] In *anc. pros.*: **I.** *a.* Noting a foot of three syllables, the first and third being long, the second being short; of verse, characterized by such feet. **II.** *n.* A cretic foot or verse.

cre-tin (krē′tin), *n.* [F. (orig. Swiss) *crétin*, by some connected with *chrétien*, Christian.] A person afflicted with cretinism.—**cre′tin-ism,** *n.* In *pathol.*, a chronic disease, due to absence or deficiency of the normal thyroid secretion, characterized by physical deformity (often with goiter), stunted growth, idiocy, etc., and occurring esp. in certain valleys in Switzerland and elsewhere.—**cre′tin-ous,** *a.*

cre-tonne (krẹ-ton′ or krē′ton), *n.* [F., < *Creton*, village in Normandy.] A strong cotton fabric printed in colors in large floral and other designs, used for curtains, furniture-coverings, etc.

cre-vasse (krẹ-vas′), *n.* [F.: see *crevice*.] A fissure or deep cleft in the ice of a glacier; also, a breach in the embankment or levee of a river (U. S.).—**cre-vasse′,** *v. t.*; *-vassed, -vassing.* To fissure with crevasses.

crev-ice (krev′is), *n.* [OF. *crevace* (F. *crevasse*), < *crever*, split, burst, < L. *crepare*, rattle, crack.] A crack forming an opening; a cleft; a rift; a fissure.—**crev′iced,** *a.* Having a crevice or crevices; fissured.

crew[1] (krö), *n.* [OF. *creue* (F. *crue*), increase, augmentation, orig. pp. fem. of *creistre* (F. *croître*), < L. *crescere*, grow, increase.] A reinforcement of soldiers†; any force or band of armed men; a company, assemblage, or crowd (often derogatory); a body of persons engaged upon a particular work (as, a train *crew*); *naut.*, the company of men who man a ship or boat; specif., the common sailors of a ship's company; also, a particular gang of a ship's company.

crew[2] (krö). Archaic preterit of *crow*[1].

crew-el (krö′ẹl), *n.* [ME. *crule*; origin uncertain.] A kind of worsted yarn or thread used for embroidery, etc. —**crew′el=work,** *n.*

crib (krib), *n.* [AS. *crib* = D. *krib* = G. *krippe*.] A rack or manger for fodder, as in a stable or house for cattle; specif., the manger in which the infant Christ was laid; a representation of this, as in a church at Christmas; also, a child's bed with inclosed sides; also, a stall or pen for cattle; also, a small habitation; a narrow room; any confined space; a house, shop, etc. (thieves' slang); also, a bin for storing grain, salt, etc.; any of various frameworks, as of logs or timbers, used in construction work; the wooden lining on the inside of a shaft; also, a petty theft, or something purloined, as a passage from an author (colloq.); a translation or other illicit aid used by students (colloq.); in *cribbage*, a set of cards made up by equal contributions from each player's hand, and belonging to the dealer.—**crib,** *v.*; *cribbed, cribbing.* **I.** *tr.* To shut up or confine in or as in a crib; also, to provide with cribs, racks, or stalls; furnish with a crib or wooden framework; line with timber or planking; also, to pilfer or steal, as a passage from an author (colloq.); translate by means of a crib (colloq.). **II.** *intr.* To practise crib-biting, as a horse; also, to pilfer or steal (colloq.); of students, to use a translation or other illicit aid (colloq.).—**crib-bage** (krib′ạj), *n.* A game at cards, for two, three, or four players, a characteristic feature of which is the crib.—**crib′ber,** *n.*—**crib′=bit″er** (-bī″tėr), *n.* A horse addicted to crib-biting.—**crib′=bit″ing,** *n.* An injurious habit of horses, consisting in biting the manger or other object and at the same time noisily drawing in the breath.

cri-blé (krē-blā), *a.* [F., pp. of *cribler*, riddle with holes, < *crible*, < L. *cribrum*, sieve.] Engraved by a method in which light and shade are indicated by numerous small round holes sun in the wooden block; also, decorated with minute punctures or depressions, as a surface of metal or wood.

crib-ri-form (krib′ri-fôrm), *a.* [L. *cribrum*, sieve: see *-form*.] Having the form of a sieve; perforated with many small openings.

crib-rose (krib′rōs), *a.* [L. *cribrum*, sieve.] Cribriform.

crib-work (krib′wėrk), *n.* Structural work consisting of layers of logs or beams arranged one above another, the logs of each layer being at right angles to those below.

crick[1] (krik), *n.* [ME. *crykke*; origin uncertain.] A painful spasmodic affection of the muscles, as of the neck or back, making it difficult to move the part.—**crick**[1], *v. t.* To give a crick or wrench to (the neck, etc.).

crick[2] (krik), *n.* Same as *creek*. [Colloq.]

crick-et[1] (krik′et), *n.* [OF. F. *criquet*; ult. imit.] Any of the saltatorial orthopterous insects comprising the family *Gryllidæ*, which mostly have long antennæ and are noted for the shrill sound produced by the male by friction of the fore wings; esp., one belonging to the genus *Gryllus*; loosely, any of various similar insects.

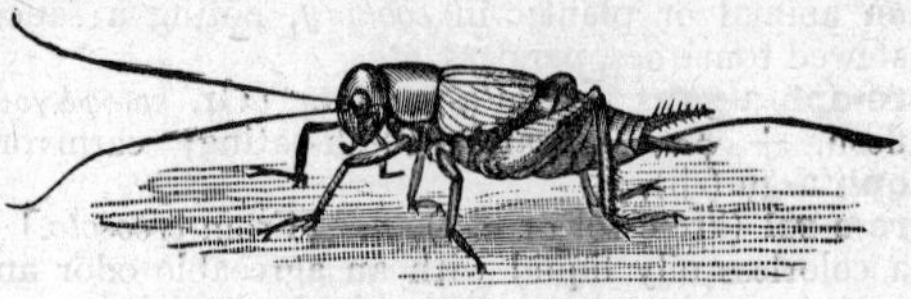

House-cricket (*Gryllus domesticus*).

crick-et[2] (krik′et), *n.* [Origin obscure.] A small, low stool.

crick-et[3] (krik′et), *n.* [Cf. OF. *criquet*, stick.] An open-air game played with ball, bats, and wickets, by two sides of eleven players each.—**crick′et**[3], *v. i.* To play cricket: as, "They boated and they *cricketed*" (Tennyson's "Princess," Prologue, 159).—**crick′et-er,** *n.*

cri-coid (krī′koid). [Gr. κρικοειδής, < κρίκος, κίρκος, ring, + εἶδος, form.] In *anat.*: **I.** *a.* Ring-shaped: applied to a cartilage at the lower part of the larynx. **II.** *n.* The cricoid cartilage.

cried (krīd). Preterit and past participle of *cry*.

cri-er (krī′ėr), *n.* [See *cry*, *v.*] One who cries; specif., an official, as of a court or a town, who makes public announcements; also, one who cries goods for sale; a hawker.

crime (krīm), *n.* [OF. F. *crime*, < L. *crimen*, accusation, fault, offense, crime.] An act or omission, esp. one of a grave nature, punishable by law as forbidden by statute or injurious to the public welfare; hence, serious violation of human law (as, steeped in *crime*); also, more generally, any offense, esp. one of a grave character; hence, serious wrong-doing; sin.

Cri-me-an (kri-mē′ạn or krī-), *a.* Of or pertaining to the Crimea, a large peninsula extending into the Black Sea from the north: as, the *Crimean* War (a war between Great Britain, France, Turkey, and Sardinia on the one hand, and Russia on the other, carried on chiefly in the Crimea, from 1854 until 1856).

crime-ful (krīm′fụl), *a.* Full of crime; criminal. See Shakspere's "Hamlet," iv. 7. 7.

crime-less (krīm′les), *a.* Free from crime; innocent.

crim-i-nal (krim′i-nạl), *a.* [LL. *criminalis*, < L. *crimen*, E. *crime*.] Of or pertaining to crime or its punishment (as, *criminal* law); also, of the nature of or involving crime; also, guilty of crime.—**criminal conversation,** in *law*, adultery; specif., illicit intercourse with a married woman: often abbreviated *crim. con.*—**crim′i-nal,** *n.* One guilty, or, commonly, one convicted, of a crime.—**crim′i-nal-ist,** *n.* One versed in criminal law; also, one versed in criminology.—**crim″i-nal-is′tic,** *a.* Of or pertaining to criminalists or criminology.—**crim″i-nal-is′tics,** *n.* Criminology.—**crim-i-nal′i-ty** (-nal′i-ti), *n.*; pl. *-ties* (-tiz). The quality of being criminal; also, a criminal act or practice.—**crim′i-nal-ly,** *adv.*—**crim′i-nal-oid,** *n.* [See *-oid*.] A person of a type believed to be predisposed to criminal acts.

crim-i-nate (krim′i-nāt), *v. t.*; *-nated, -nating.* [L. *criminatus*, pp. of *criminari*, *criminare*, < *crimen*, E. *crime*.] To charge with a crime; also, to furnish evidence of the criminal guilt of; incriminate; also, to censure (an act, etc.) as criminal; condemn.—**crim-i-na′tion** (-nā′shọn), *n.* [L. *criminatio(n-)*.] The act of criminating; severe accusation or censure.—**crim′i-na-tive** (-nạ-tiv), **crim′i-na-to-ry** (-tọ-ri), *a.* Tending to or involving crimination; accusatory.—**crim′i-na-tor** (-nā-tọr), *n.*

crim-i-nol-o-gy (krim-i-nol′ọ-ji), *n.* [L. *crimen* (*crimin-*), crime: see *-logy*.] The science dealing with crimes and criminals.—**crim″i-no-log′i-cal** (-nọ-loj′i-kạl), *a.*—**crim-i-nol′o-gist,** *n.*

crim-mer (krim′ėr), *n.* See *krimmer*.

crimp¹ (krimp), *v. t.* [Cf. D. *krimpen*, shrink, contract, Sw. *krympa*, Dan. *krympe*, shrink (cloth), and E. *cramp²*.] To press or form into small regular folds or undulations; wrinkle; make wavy, as the hair; corrugate; also, to turn over the edge of (a cartridge-case), in order to confine the charge; also, to cause (the flesh of fish) to contract and become firmer by gashing it; also, to bend (leather) into shape.—**crimp¹**, *n.* The act of crimping; crimped condition or form; something crimped, as a lock of hair (usually in *pl.*).

crimp² (krimp), *n.* [Origin uncertain.] An agent who procures seamen, soldiers, etc., by decoying or impressing them: as, "The same night we . . . went on shore to a *crimp's* house . . . and took out of it twenty-three fine able seamen" (Marryat's "Peter Simple," xli.).—**crimp²**, *v. t.* To procure (seamen, soldiers, etc.) by decoying or impressing them; in general, to decoy or entrap.

crimp-er (krim′pėr), *n.* One who or that which crimps; an apparatus for crimping.

crim-ple (krim′pl), *v. t.* or *i.*; *-pled, -pling.* [Freq. of *crimp¹*.] To wrinkle, crinkle, or curl; wrinkle finely.

crimp-y (krim′pi), *a.* Of a crimped form or appearance.

crim-son (krim′zn). [ME. *cremesyn*, through It. or Sp. < Ar. *qirmizī*, crimson, < *qirmiz*, E. *kermes*.] **I.** *a.* Of a deep-red color with a purplish tinge; fig., sanguinary. **II.** *n.* A crimson color, pigment, or dye.—**crim′son,** *v. t.* or *i.* To make or become crimson: as, "A gorgeous sunset was *crimsoning* the palms and pigeon-towers" (Amelia B. Edwards's "Thousand Miles up the Nile," iv.).

cringe (krinj), *v. i.*; *cringed, cringing.* [ME. *crenge*, < AS. *cringan, crincan*, yield, fall in battle, prob. orig. 'bend, contract, shrink': cf. *crank¹*.] To shrink, bend, or crouch, esp. from fear or servility; cower; fawn.—**cringe,** *n.* A cringing; a servile or fawning obeisance.—**crin-ger** (krin′jėr), *n.*—**crin′ging-ly,** *adv.*

crin-gle (kring′gl), *n.* [Prob. from LG.: cf. MLG. *kringel*, ring, circle.] *Naut.*, a ring or eye of rope or the like, esp. on the edge of a sail.

Cringle.

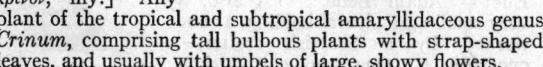

cri-nite¹ (krī′nīt), *a.* [L. *crinitus*, < *crinis*, hair.] Hairy; having tufts of hairy growth.

cri-nite² (krī′nīt or krin′īt), *n.* [Gr. κρίνον, lily.] A fossil crinoid.

crin-kle (kring′kl), *v. i.* or *t.*; *-kled, -kling.* [= D. *krinkelen*; akin to E. *cringe* and *crank¹*.] To wind or turn in and out; wrinkle or crimple; ripple; also, to make slight, sharp sounds; rustle.—**crin′kle,** *n.* A turn or twist; a wrinkle; a ripple; also, a crinkling sound.—**crin′kle-root,** *n.* A North American brassicaceous plant, *Dentaria diphylla*, with a fleshy, pungent rootstock.—**crin′kly,** *a.* Full of crinkles.

crin-kum=cran-kum (kring′kum-krang′kum), *n.* [A made word, simulating Latin: cf. *crinkle* and *crankle*.] Something full of twists and turns. [Colloq.]

cri-noid (krī′noid or krin′oid). [Gr. κρινοειδής, < κρίνον, lily, + εἶδος, form.] **I.** *a.* Lily-like; of or pertaining to the *Crinoidea*, a class or group of echinoderms usually having the body rayed and borne on a stalk. **II.** *n.* A crinoid echinoderm.—**cri-noi′dal,** *a.*

crin-o-line (krin′ǫ-lin or -lēn), *n.* [F., < *crin*, < L. *crinis*, hair.] A kind of haircloth used for stiffening or distending garments; a stiffened cotton fabric similarly used; also, a petticoat of the haircloth or some other stiff material, formerly worn by women under a full dress-skirt; hence, a hoop-skirt.

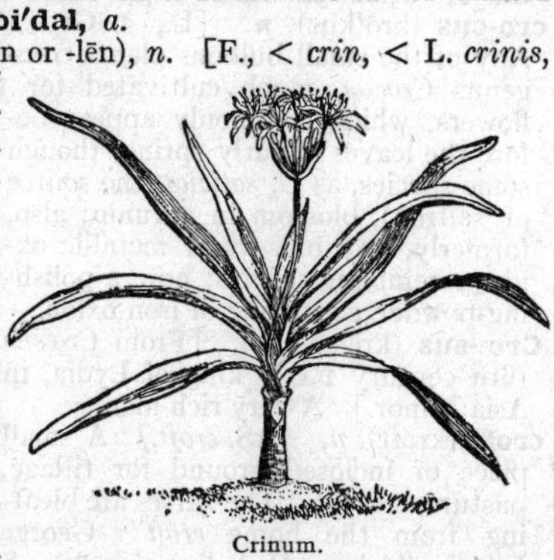

Crinum.

cri-num (krī′num), *n.* [NL., < Gr. κρίνον, lily.] Any plant of the tropical and subtropical amaryllidaceous genus *Crinum*, comprising tall bulbous plants with strap-shaped leaves, and usually with umbels of large, showy flowers.

cri-o-sphinx (krī′ǫ-sfingks), *n.* [Gr. κριός, ram, + σφίγξ, sphinx.] A sphinx with the head of a ram.

Criosphinx.

crip-ple (krip′l), *n.* [AS. (Northumbrian) *crypel*; akin to AS. *crēopan*, E. *creep*.] One who is partially or wholly deprived of the use of one or more of his limbs; a lame person; also, a dense thicket in swampy or low land (local, U. S.); also, a rocky shallow in a stream (local, U. S.).—**crip′ple,** *v. t.*; *-pled, -pling.* To make a cripple of; lame; hence, to disable; impair.—**crip′pler,** *n.*

cri-sis (krī′sis), *n.*; pl. *crises* (-sēz). [L., < Gr. κρίσις, < κρίνειν, separate, distinguish, decide, judge, akin to L. *cernere*: see *certain*.] The point in the course of a disease at which a decisive change occurs, leading either to recovery or to death; the change itself; hence, a decisive or vitally important stage in the course of anything; a turning-point; a critical time or occasion.

crisp (krisp), *a.* [AS. *crisp*, < L. *crispus*, curled, crimped.] In small, stiff or firm curls, as hair; curly; crinkled, wrinkled, or rippled, as skin or water; also, brittle, as cakes; firm and fresh, as grass or vegetables; brisk, sharp, or decided, as manner, speech, etc.; bracing, as air.—**crisp,** *v.* **I.** *tr.* To make crisp or curly; crinkle, wrinkle, or ripple (as, "as swiftly as a reach of still water is *crisped* by the wind": Kipling's "Light That Failed," ii.); also, to make crisp or brittle. **II.** *intr.* To curl; also, to become crisp or brittle.

cris-pate (kris′pāt), *a.* [L. *crispatus*, pp. of *crispare*, curl, wave, < *crispus*, E. *crisp*.] Crisped or curled. Also **cris′-pat-ed** (-pā-ted).—**cris-pa′tion** (-pā′shǫn), *n.* The act of crisping or curling, or the state of being crisped; also, a slight contraction; a minute undulation.

crisp-er (kris′pėr), *n.* One who or that which crisps.

Cris-pin (kris′pin), *n.* [From St. *Crispin*, patron of the craft.] A shoemaker.

crisp-ly (krisp′li), *adv.* In a crisp manner.—**crisp′ness,** *n.*

crisp-y (kris′pi), *a.* Crisp; curly or wavy; brittle; brisk.

criss-cross (kris′krôs). [For *christ-cross*.] **I.** *n.* A christ-cross; also, a crossing or intersection; also, a children's game in which two players set down alternately, in the nine compartments of a figure made of crossed lines, the one a cross, and the other a cipher, the object of the game being to get three crosses or three ciphers in a row. **II.** *a.* In crossing lines; crossed; crossing; marked by crossings. **III.** *adv.* In a crisscross manner; crosswise.—**criss′cross,** *v. t.* or *i.* To mark with or form crossing lines.—**criss′-cross=row′** (-rō′), *n.* Same as *christcross-row.*

cris-sum (kris′um), *n.*; pl. *crissa* (-ạ̈). [NL., < L. *crissare*, move the haunches.] In *ornith.*, the region surrounding the cloacal opening of a bird; the feathers of this region collectively.

cris-tate (kris′tāt), *a.* [L. *cristatus*, < *crista*, E. *crest*.] Having a crest; crested; also, forming a crest. Also **cris′tat-ed** (-tā-ted).

cri-te-ri-on (krī-tē′ri-ǫn), *n.*; pl. *-rions* or *-ria* (-ri-ạ̈). [Gr. κριτήριον, < κριτής, a judge, < κρίνειν: see *crisis*.] A standard of judgment or criticism; an established rule or principle for testing anything: as, "If discipline and subordination be the *criterion* of merit, these soldiers were worthless indeed" (Parkman's "Oregon Trail," xxvi.).

crith (krith), *n.* [Gr. κριθή, barleycorn.] In *physics*, the weight of one liter of hydrogen at standard pressure and temperature: used as a unit of weight for gases.

crit-ic (krit′ik). [L. *criticus*, < Gr. κριτικός, skilled in judging, decisive, critical (as n., a critic), < κρίνειν: see *crisis*.] **I.** *a.* Skilful in judging, esp. in literary or artistic matters; of or pertaining to criticism; also, censorious or faultfinding; also, pertaining to or of the nature of a crisis†. **II.** *n.* A person skilled in judging of the qualities or merits of some class of things, esp. of literary or artistic work; one who writes criticisms or critiques; one who passes judgment on anything; esp., one who passes severe judgment; a censurer; a carper; also, criticism†; also, a critique.—**crit′i-cal,** *a.* Of or pertaining to critics or criticism; involving criticism or skilful judgment; also, occupied with or skilled in criticism; nicely judicial; also, inclined to criticize; captious; censorious; carping; also, pertaining to or of the nature of a crisis; of decisive importance with respect to the outcome; involving suspense; attended with risk or peril; hazardous; also, tending to determine or decide; decisive; crucial; in *math.* and *physics*, limiting, or indicative of a coalescence or change (as, the *critical* point of a gas, the temperature above which it cannot be liquefied by increasing the pressure); in *zoöl.* and *bot.*, distinguished by minute differences (as, *critical* species).—**crit'i-cal-ly,** *adv.* —**crit'i-cal-ness,** *n.*

crit-ic-as-ter (krit'i-kas-tėr), *n.* [See *-aster.*] An inferior or incompetent critic.

crit'i-cise, etc. See *criticize*, etc.

crit-i-cism (krit'i-sizm), *n.* [From *critic.*] The act or art of criticizing, esp. of criticizing literary or artistic work; investigation of the text, origin, etc., of literary, esp. Biblical, documents (as, lower or textual *criticism*, dealing with text alone; higher *criticism*, dealing with authorship, dates, etc.); the act of passing judgment as to the merits of anything; esp., the act of passing severe judgment; censure; faultfinding; also, a critical comment, article, or essay; a critique.

crit-i-ciz-a-ble, crit-i-cis-a-ble (krit'i-sī-zạ-bl), *a.* That may be criticized; open to criticism.

crit-i-cize, crit-i-cise (krit'i-sīz), *v.*; *-cized, -cised, -cizing, -cising.* [From *critic.*] **I.** *intr.* To act as a critic; pass judgment as to merits and faults; esp., to find fault. **II.** *tr.* To judge as a critic; discuss the merits and faults of; esp., to censure; find fault with.—**crit'i-ciz-er, crit'i-cis-er** (-sī-zėr), *n.*

cri-tique (kri-tēk'), *n.* [F., < Gr. κριτική, the critical art, prop. fem. of κριτικός: see *critic.*] The act or art of criticizing; also, an article or essay criticizing a literary or other work; a review.

crit-ter (krit'ėr), *n.* Prov. or vulgar form of *creature.*

croak (krōk), *v.* [Prob. imit.] **I.** *intr.* To utter a low, hoarse, dismal cry, as a frog or a raven; hence, to speak with a low, hollow voice; fig., to talk despondingly; forebode evil; grumble; also, to die (slang). **II.** *tr.* To utter or announce by croaking; also, to kill (slang).—**croak,** *n.* The act or sound of croaking.—**croak'er,** *n.* One who or that which croaks; specif., any of various fishes that make a croaking or grunting noise, as *Micropogon undulatus*, a small food-fish common on the Atlantic coast of the southern U. S.—**croak'y,** *a.* Making a croaking sound; given to croaking.

Croaker (*Micropogon undulatus*).

Cro-at (krō'at), *n.* A native or inhabitant of Croatia, a district to the east of the northern Adriatic Sea, esp. one belonging to the Slavic race inhabiting it. —**Cro-a'tian** (-ā'shiạn). **I.** *a.* Of or pertaining to Croatia or the Croats. **II.** *n.* A Croat; also, the Slavic dialect of the Croats, closely allied to Serbian.

cro-ce-in (krō'sẹ-in), *n.* [L. *croceus*, saffron-colored, < *crocus*, saffron.] Any of several coal-tar dyestuffs producing orange or scarlet colors.

cro-chet (krō-shā', Brit. krō'shā), *n.* [F. *crochet*, OF. *crochet, croquet*, hook, hooked implement, dim. of *croc*, hook.] A kind of knitting done with a needle having at one end a small hook for drawing the thread or yarn into place; the work or fabric made.—**cro-chet',** *v. t.* or *i.*; *-cheted* (-shād'), *-cheting* (-shā'ing). To knit by crochet.—**cro-chet'-work,** *n.*

cro-cid-o-lite (krọ-sid'ọ-līt), *n.* [Gr. κροκίς (κροκιδ-), for κροκύς, nap, wool, + λίθος, stone.] A mineral consisting principally of a silicate of iron and sodium, often occurring in fibers of a delicate blue color, and appearing in an altered form as the (golden-brown) tiger's-eye.

crock[1] (krok), *n.* [Origin obscure.] Soot; smut; soil or marking from imperfectly dyed cloth.—**crock**[1], *v.* **I.** *tr.* To soil with crock. **II.** *intr.* To give off crock.

crock[2] (krok), *n.* [Cf. LG. *krakke*, Sw. *krake*, worn-out horse.] An old ewe; an old worn-out horse; a broken-down, feeble, worthless, or inefficient person. [Chiefly prov. or colloq.]

Crockets on a Pinnacle — Cathedral of Châlons-sur-Marne, France; 13th century.

crock[3] (krok), *n.* [AS. *crocca*, akin to Icel. *krukka*, pot, also G. *krug* and F. *cruche*, pitcher.] An earthen pot, jar, or other vessel; sometimes, a vessel of metal; also, a potsherd.—**crock'er**†, *n.* A potter.—**crock'er-y,** *n.* Crocks or earthen vessels collectively; earthenware; often, earthenware finished to imitate porcelain.

crock-et (krok'et), *n.* [OF. *croquet*: see *crochet.*] A roll of hair formerly worn†; a terminal snag on a stag's horn; in *arch.*, an ornament, usually in the form of recurved foliage, placed on the angles of the inclined sides of pinnacles, etc.—**crock'et-ed,** *a.* Having crockets, as a stag's horn; in *arch.*, decorated with crockets.

croc-o-dile (krok'ọ-dīl), *n.* [L. *crocodilus*, < Gr. κροκόδειλος.] Any of the large, thick-skinned, lizard-like reptiles which constitute the genus *Crocodilus* (order *Crocodilia*), inhabiting the waters of tropical Africa, Asia, Australia, and America, esp. *C. niloticus* of the Nile; in a wider sense, any animal of the order *Crocodilia*, including the alligators of America and the gavial of India; fig., one who sheds crocodile tears or makes a hypocritical show of sorrow.—**crocodile tears,** false or insincere tears, as the tears fabled to be shed by crocodiles over those they devour; hypocritical show of sorrow.—**croc'o-dile-bird,** *n.* An African plover, *Pluvianus ægyptius*, which often sits upon basking crocodiles and feeds on its insect parasites, etc.—**croc-o-dil'i-an** (-dil'i-ạn). **I.** *a.* Of or pertaining to the crocodile; specif., pertaining to the crocodilians (order *Crocodilia*); also, hypocritical. **II.** *n.* Any of the *Crocodilia*, an order of reptiles including the crocodiles, alligators, etc.

Crocodile (*Crocodilus niloticus*).

cro-co-ite (krō'kọ-īt), *n.* [Earlier *crocoisite*, < Gr. κροκόεις, saffron-colored, < κρόκος, crocus, saffron.] A mineral consisting of native lead chromate, occurring in monoclinic crystals of various shades of bright red.

cro-cus (krō'kus), *n.* [L., < Gr. κρόκος, crocus, saffron.] Any of the small bulbous plants constituting the iridaceous genus *Crocus*, much cultivated for their showy, solitary flowers, which commonly appear before the leaves in early spring, though some species, as *C. sativus* (the source of saffron), blossom in autumn; also, formerly, any of several metallic oxides resembling saffron; now, a polishing-powder consisting of iron oxide.

Crœ-sus (krē'sus), *n.* [From *Crœsus* (6th century B.C.), king of Lydia, in Asia Minor.] A very rich man.

croft (krôft), *n.* [AS. *croft.*] A small piece of inclosed ground for tillage, pasture, etc. (as, "The calves are bleating from the home *croft*": George Eliot's "Adam Bede," vi.); also, a very small agricultural holding, as one worked by a Scottish crofter.—**croft'er,** *n.* One who cultivates a

Crocus (*C. sativus*).

croft; one who rents and tills a croft in parts of Scotland.—**croft′ing,** *n.* The tenancy of crofts; also, the holding of a crofter.

crom-lech (krom′lek), *n.* [W. *cromlech* (= Bret. *kroumlech*), < *crom*, bent, bowed, + *llech*, flat stone.] In *archæol.*, a circle of upright stones or monoliths; also, a dolmen.

cro-mor-na (krǫ-môr′nạ), *n.* [F. *cromorne*, < G. *krummhorn*, lit. 'crooked horn.'] An organ-stop which gives a tone like that of a clarinet.

crone (krōn), *n.* [Cf. OF. *caroingne* (F. *carogne*), term of abuse for a woman, = *caroine*, E. *carrion*.] An old woman; sometimes, an old man: applied in disparagement or contempt.

cro-ny (krō′ni), *n.*; pl. *-nies* (-niz). [Origin obscure.] An intimate friend or companion; a chum: as, "And at his elbow, Souter Johnny, His ancient, trusty, drouthy *crony*" (Burns's "Tam o' Shanter," 42).

crook (krůk), *n.* [ME.: cf. Icel. *krōkr*, crook, hook.] A bent or curved implement, piece, appendage, etc.; a hook; the hooked part of anything; an instrument or implement having a bent or curved part, as a shepherd's staff hooked at one end or as the crozier of a bishop or abbot; also, the act of crooking or bending; a bending, turn, or curve; fig., an artifice†; also, a dishonest person, esp. a sharper, swindler, or thief (colloq.).—**crook,** *v.* **I.** *tr.* To cause to assume an angular or curved form; bend; curve; make a crook in; fig., to pervert†. **II.** *intr.* To bend; curve.—**crook′-back,** *n.* A humpback.—**crook′ed,** *p. a.* Bent; not straight; curved; deformed; also, not straightforward or honest; dishonest; fraudulent.—**crook′ed-ly,** *adv.*—**crook′-ed-ness,** *n.*

Crookes (krůks) **tube.** [From Sir W. *Crookes* (1832–1919), English scientist.] A form of vacuum-tube.

crook-neck (krůk′nek), *n.* A variety of squash with a long, recurved neck.

croon (krön), *v.* [Cf. MLG. *kronen*, murmur, grumble, MD. *kronen*, D. *kreunen*, groan.] **I.** *intr.* To bellow or roar (Sc. and north. Eng.); also, to utter a low murmuring sound; sing softly and monotonously. **II.** *tr.* To sing in a low murmuring tone.—**croon,** *n.* The act or sound of crooning.

crop (krop), *n.* [AS. *crop*, *cropp*, = D. *krop* = G. *kropf*: cf. *croup*² and *group*. Some E. senses are from *crop*, *v.*] A special pouch-like enlargement of the gullet of many birds, in which the food undergoes partial preparation for digestion, or a similar organ in other animals; the craw; also, the rounded head or other top part of anything, as of an herb, tree, etc. (now chiefly prov.); also, the stock or handle of a whip; a short riding-whip with a loop instead of a lash; also, the cultivated produce of the ground, as grain or fruit, while growing or when gathered; the yield of such produce for a particular season; hence, the yield of some other product in a season (as, the ice-*crop*); fig., a supply produced; also, an entire tanned hide of an animal; also, the act of cropping; a cutting off, as of the hair; a style of wearing the hair cut short, or a head of hair so cut; a mark produced by clipping the ears, as of an animal; also, an outcrop of a vein or seam.—**crop,** *v.*; *cropped*, *cropping*. **I.** *tr.* To cut off or remove the head or top of (a plant, etc.); cut off the ends or a part of; cut short; clip the ears, hair, etc., of; cut closely the margins of (a book); also, to remove by or as by cutting; also, to cause to bear a crop or crops. **II.** *intr.* To bear or yield a crop or crops; also, to come to the surface of the ground, as a vein of ore (usually with *up* or *out*); fig., to appear incidentally or unexpectedly (usually with *up* or *out*).—**crop′=eared,** *a.* Having the ears cropped, as an animal for identification or a person for punishment; also, having the hair cropped short, so that the ears are conspicuous (applied in disparagement to English Puritans or Roundheads).—**crop′per,** *n.* One who or that which crops; a cloth-shearing machine; also, one who raises a crop, esp. on shares; a plant which furnishes a crop; also, a heavy fall, as from a horse, or, fig., a failure or collapse (colloq.).

cro-quet (krō-kā′, Brit. krō′kạ), *n.* [Appar. a var. of F. *crochet*, hook, hooked implement: cf. OF. *croquet* (see *crochet*).] An outdoor game played by knocking wooden balls through a series of iron arches by means of mallets; also, in this game, the act of driving away an opponent's ball by striking one's own when the two are in contact.—**cro-quet′,** *v. t.*; *-queted* (-kād′), *-queting* (-kā′ing). To drive away (a ball) by a croquet.

cro-quette (krō-ket′), *n.* [F., < *croquer*, crunch.] A small mass of minced meat or fish, or of rice, potato, or other material, often of cylindrical or conical form, coated with bread-crumbs and fried.

crore (krōr), *n.* [Hind.] Ten millions; one hundred lacs: as, a *crore* of rupees. [India.]

cro-sier (krō′zhėr), *n.* See *crozier*.

Monumental Cross, Eyam, Derbyshire, England.

cross (krôs), *n.* [AS. *cros*, < OIr. *cros* = Icel. *kross*, < L. *crux* (*cruc-*), cross.] A structure consisting essentially of an upright and a transverse piece, upon which persons were formerly nailed or otherwise fastened in putting them to death, esp. [often *cap.*], with *the*, the one upon which Christ died; [*l. c.*] a figure of the cross as a Christian emblem, badge, etc.; a crucifix, or a representation of one; the sign of the cross made with the right hand as an act of devotion; a structure or monument in the form of a cross, or with a cross upon it, set up by the wayside, in a market-place, or elsewhere, for devotional purposes, as a memorial, etc.; also, any of various conventional representations or modifications of the Christian emblem as used symbolically or for ornament, as in heraldry, art, etc. (as, a Latin, Greek, St. Anthony's, St. Andrew's, St. George's, or Maltese *cross*: see under *Latin*, *Greek*, *saint*, and *Maltese*); a decoration in the form of such a figure, as of an order of knighthood or honor (as, the Victoria *Cross*: see under *Victoria*); a person entitled to wear such a decoration; a coin bearing a representation of a cross†; also, the cross as the symbol of Christianity; the Christian religion; the crucifixion of Christ as the culmination of his redemptive mission; hence, any suffering borne for Christ's sake; in general, any misfortune or trial; also, any object, figure, or mark resembling a cross, as two intersecting lines; such a mark made instead of a signature by a person unable to write; also, a crossing, or a place of crossing; the accidental contact of two electrical conductors; fig., an opposing or thwarting; also, a crossing of animals or plants; a mixing of breeds; an animal, plant, breed, or the like, produced by crossing; a cross-breed; fig., something intermediate in character between two things; also, a contest the result of which is dishonestly arranged beforehand (slang).—**cross,** *v.* **I.** *tr.* To make the sign of the cross upon or over, as in devotion; mark with a cross; also, to cancel by marking with a cross or with a line or lines; also, to place in the form of a cross or crosswise; set (a yard, etc.) in position across a mast; also, to lie or pass across (something); intersect; also, to put or draw something, as a line, across (a thing); also, to move or pass, or extend, from one side to the other side of (a street, river, etc.); also, to transport across something; also, to meet and pass, as one person or letter does another going in the opposite direction; also, to encounter (archaic); fig., to oppose or thwart; also, to cause (members of different genera, species, varieties, or the like) to produce offspring

Forms of Crosses.

1. Cross of Calvary. 2. Latin cross. 3. Tau-cross (so called from being formed like the Greek letter *tau*), or cross of St. Anthony. 4. Cross of Lorraine. 5. Patriarchal cross. 6. St. Andrew's cross. 7. Greek cross, or cross of St. George, the national saint of England. 8. Papal cross. 9. Cross nowy quadrant. 10. Maltese cross, the badge of the Knights of Malta. 11. Cross fourché. 12. Cross patté. 13. Jerusalem cross. 14. Cross fleury.

or propagate; mix the breed of; cross-fertilize; also, to arrange the result of (a contest) dishonestly beforehand (slang). **II.** *intr.* To lie or be athwart or crosswise, as two lines; intersect; also, to move or pass, or extend, from one side or place to another; also, to meet and pass, as two letters going in opposite directions; also, to breed together, being of different species, varieties, etc.; interbreed.—**cross.** [= *across.*] **I.** *adv.* Crosswise, transversely, or across; in opposition; adversely. [Now rare.] **II.** *prep.* Across. [Now chiefly colloq.]—**cross,** *a.* Lying or passing crosswise or across each other; also, lying or passing across, or transversely to, a main direction; transverse; hence, passing from side to side; passing or referring from one of two objects, parts, etc., to the other (cf. *cross-reference*); also, involving interchange; reciprocal; also, contrary or opposite; also, adverse or unfavorable; also, perverse† or contrary†; ill-humored or peevish, or expressing ill humor (colloq.: as, "I have never had a *cross* word from him in my life," Jane Austen's "Pride and Prejudice," xliii.); also, cross-bred or hybrid; also, dishonest (slang).—**cross′a-ble,** *a.* That may be crossed.

cross=bar (krôs′bär), *n.* A transverse bar, line, or stripe; a bar laid or fixed across another bar.—**cross′=barred,** *a.* Furnished or marked with cross-bars.

cross=beam (krôs′bēm), *n.* A transverse beam, as one crossing another beam or extending between two walls, etc.

cross-bill (krôs′bil), *n.* Any bird of the fringilline genus *Loxia*, characterized by mandibles curved so that the tips cross each other when the bill is closed.

Red Crossbill (*Loxia curvirostra*).

cross=bones (krôs′bōnz), *n. pl.* Two bones placed crosswise, usually below a skull, symbolizing death.

cross-bow (krôs′bō), *n.* An old weapon for shooting missiles, consisting of a bow fixed transversely on a stock having a groove or barrel to direct the missile.—**cross′bow″man** (-man), *n.*; pl. *-men.*

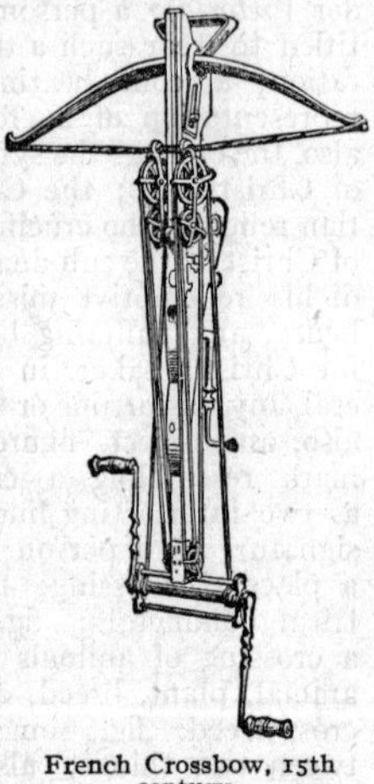

French Crossbow, 15th century.

cross=bred (krôs′bred). **I.** *a.* Produced by cross-breeding. **II.** *n.* An animal or a plant produced by cross-breeding.—**cross′=breed** (-brēd), *n.* A breed, strain, or the like, or an individual, produced by cross-breeding (sometimes restricted, in horticulture, to those produced by varieties or modifications of the same species).—**cross′=breed″ing,** *n.* The act of breeding from individuals of different breeds, varieties, species, or the like.

cross=bun (krôs′bun′), *n.* A bun indented with a cross, eaten esp. on Good Friday.

cross=coun-try (krôs′kun″tri), *a.* Directed across fields or open country; not following the roads or the great highways.

cross=cut (krôs-kut′), *v. t.*; *-cut, -cutting.* To cut across. —**cross′=cut. I.** *n.* A transverse cut or course; a direct course between two points, as one diagonal to a main way. **II.** *a.* Adapted for transverse cutting, as a saw; also, cut crosswise or transversely.

crosse (krôs), *n.* [F. *crosse*, OF. *croce*, stick with curved end, crozier, akin to *croc*, hook: cf. *crochet.*] A kind of long-handled racket used in the game of lacrosse.

cross-er (krôs′ėr), *n.* One who or that which crosses.

cross=ex-am-ine (krôs-eg-zam′in), *v. t.* To examine by questions intended to check a previous examination; examine closely or minutely; specif., to examine (a witness called by the opposing side), as for the purpose of disproving his testimony.—**cross″=ex-am-i-na′tion** (-i-nā′shọn), *n.*—**cross=ex-am′in-er,** *n.*

cross=eye (krôs′ī), *n.* Strabismus, esp. the form in which both eyes turn toward the nose.—**cross′=eyed,** *a.*

cross=fer-ti-li-za-tion (krôs″fėr-ti-li-zā′shọn), *n.* In *bot.*, fertilization of one flower or plant by pollen from another: opposed to *self-fertilization.*—**cross=fer′ti-lize** (-līz), *v. t.* To cause the cross-fertilization of.

cross=fire (krôs′fīr′), *n.* *Milit.*, lines of fire from two or more positions, crossing one another, or a single one of such lines. Also fig.

cross=grained (krôs′grānd), *a.* Having the grain running transversely or diagonally, or having an irregular or gnarled grain, as timber; fig., perverse or intractable (as, "a *cross-grained*, old-fashioned, whimsical fellow with an ugly face": Goldsmith's "She Stoops to Conquer," i. 2).

cross=hair (krôs′hãr), *n.* A very fine strand of quartz fiber or other material, or a line ruled on glass, forming a cross with another strand or line, and employed in a telescope, microscope, or the like, to define a line of sight; also, such a strand or line not necessarily forming a cross, as either of the two horizontal parallel lines used in a transit for stadia measurements.

cross=hatch (krôs′hach), *v. t.* To hatch or shade with two series of parallel lines crossing each other.—**cross′=hatch″-ing,** *n.* The act of one that cross-hatches, or the marking or shading produced.

cross=head (krôs′hed), *n.* A bar across the top or end of something; specif., the sliding piece or structure of a steam-engine or gas-engine, between the piston-rod and the connecting-rod.

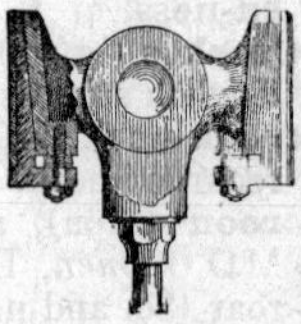

Cross-head of Steam-engine.

cross-ing (krôs′ing), *n.* The act of one who or that which crosses; also, a place where lines, tracks, etc., cross each other; also, a place at which a road, river, etc., may be crossed.

cross=jack (krôs′jak, naut. krô′jek), *n.* *Naut.*, a square sail carried on the lower yard of a mizzenmast.

cross=legged (krôs′legd or -leg″ed), *a.* Having the legs crossed; having one leg laid across the other.

cross-let (krôs′let), *n.* A small cross: chiefly in heraldry.

cross-ly (krôs′li), *adv.* In a cross manner.—**cross′ness,** *n.*

cross-patch (krôs′pach), *n.* [See *patch*[1].] An ill-humored person. [Colloq.]

cross-piece (krôs′pēs), *n.* A piece of any material placed across something; a transverse piece.

cross=pol-li-na-tion (krôs″pol-i-nā′shọn), *n.* In *bot.*, pollination in which the stigma of one flower receives the pollen of another.

cross=pur-pose (krôs′pėr′pọs), *n.* An opposing or counter purpose; *pl.*, a kind of conversational game in which words are taken in different senses.—**to be at cross=purposes,** to misunderstand another's, or each other's, purpose, or act under such a misunderstanding.

cross=ques-tion (krôs′kwes′chọn), *n.* A question asked by way of cross-examination.—**cross=ques′tion,** *v. t.* To put cross-questions to; cross-examine; question closely or minutely.

cross=re-fer (krôs-rẹ-fėr′), *v. t.* or *i.*; *-ferred, -ferring.* To refer by a cross-reference.—**cross′=ref′er-ence** (-ref′ẹ-rẹns), *n.* A reference from one part of a book, etc., to a word, item, etc., in another part.

cross=road (krôs′rōd), *n.* A road that crosses another road, or one that runs transversely to main roads; a by-road; also, the place where roads intersect (often in *pl.*, construed as *sing.*).

cross=ruff (krôs′ruf′), *n.* [See *ruff*[4].] In *whist*, a seesaw.

cross=seat (krôs′sēt), *n.* A seat extending across a carriage, etc.

cross=sec-tion (krôs′sek′shọn), *n.* The act of cutting anything across; a section made by a plane cutting anything transversely, esp. at right angles to the longest axis; a piece so cut off.

cross=shaped (krôs′shāpt), *a.* Having the shape of a cross; in the form of a cross.

cross=staff (krôs′stàf), *n.* In *surv.*, an instrument for measuring offsets.

cross=stitch (krôs′stich), *n.* A kind of stitching employing pairs of diagonal stitches of the same length crossing each other in the middle at right angles.
cross=street (krôs′strēt), *n.* A street crossing another street, or one running transversely to main streets.
cross=tie (krôs′tī), *n.* A tie placed transversely to form a foundation or support, as a sleeper under a railroad-track.
cross=town (krôs′toun), *a.* That runs across the town: as, a *cross-town* car.
cross-tree (krôs′trē), *n.* *Naut.*, one of the horizontal transverse pieces of timber or metal placed at the head of a lower mast or topmast in order to support the top, spread the shrouds, etc. Cf. *trestletree.*
cross-way (krôs′wā), *n.* A cross-road.
cross-ways (krôs′wāz), *adv.* Same as *crosswise.*
cross=wire (krôs′wīr), *n.* A wire that crosses; a cross-hair.
cross-wise (krôs′wīz), *adv.* In the form of a cross; across or transversely; contrarily.
cross=word (krôs′wėrd) **puz′zle.** A puzzle in which words corresponding to given meanings are to be supplied and fitted into a particular figure divided into spaces, the letters of the words being arranged across the figure, or vertically, or sometimes otherwise.
cro-ta-line (krō′tạ-lin or krot′ạ-), *a.* [NL. *Crotalus*, genus of rattlesnakes, < Gr. *κρόταλον*, clapper.] Of or belonging to the rattlesnakes (family *Crotalidæ*).
crotch (kroch), *n.* [Origin uncertain: cf. *crutch.*] A forked piece or part; a forked support for something; a forking or place of forking, as of the human body between the legs.—**crotched,** *a.* Having a crotch; forked.
crotch-et (kroch′et), *n.* [OF. *crochet*: see *crochet.*] A small hook; a hook-like device or part; also, a quarter-note in music; also, an odd fancy or whimsical notion (as, "an honest fellow . . . without *crotchets* or hobbies of any kind": J. H. Newman's "Callista," ix.); in *arch.*, a crocket. —**crotch-et-eer′** (-ēr′), *n.* A person devoted to a crotchet, whim, or hobby.—**crotch′et-y,** *a.* Given to crotchets or odd fancies: full of crotchets; of the nature of a crotchet.—**crotch′et-i-ness,** *n.*

Croton (*C. tiglium*).

cro-ton (krō′tọn), *n.* [NL., < Gr. *κροτών*, a tick, also a plant having tick-like seeds.] Any of the chiefly tropical euphorbiaceous plants constituting the genus *Croton*, many species of which, as *C. tiglium* (see *croton-oil*), have important medicinal properties; also, among florists, any plant of the related genus *Phyllaurea* (or *Codiæum*), cultivated for the ornamental foliage.
cro-ton=bug (krō′tọn-bug), *n.* [From the *Croton* Aqueduct water, introduced into New York City in 1842.] The small cockroach *Blattella* (or *Phyllodromia*) *germanica.* See *cockroach.*
cro-ton=oil (krō′tọn-oil′), *n.* A powerful purgative oil from *Croton tiglium* ('croton-oil plant'), a euphorbiaceous shrub or tree of the East Indies.

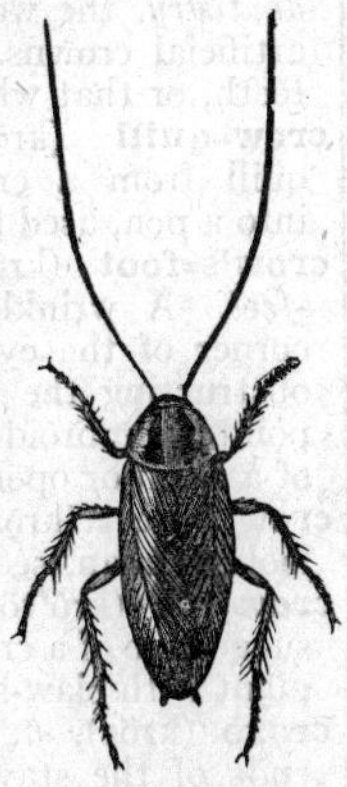
Croton-bug (*Blattella germanica*).

crouch (krouch), *v.* [ME.; origin uncertain.] **I.** *intr.* To stoop or bend low; bend close to the ground, as an animal preparing to spring or shrinking with fear; also, to bow or stoop servilely; cringe. **II.** *tr.* To bend low.—**crouch,** *n.* An act of crouching; a stooping or bending low.—**crouch′ing-ly,** *adv.*
croup^1 (kröp), *v. i.* [Prob. imit.] To cry hoarsely; speak hoarsely; cough in a hoarse manner. [Now chiefly Sc.]—**croup^1,** *n.* [Orig. Sc.] In *pathol.*, any affection of the larynx or trachea characterized by a hoarse cough and difficult breathing; esp., such a disease when accompanied by the formation of a false membrane in the air-passages ('true croup' or 'membranous croup').
croup^2 (kröp), *n.* [OF. *crupe* (F. *croupe*); from Teut., and akin to E. *crop.*] The rump or buttocks of certain animals, esp. of a horse.
crou-pi-er (krö′pi-ėr, F. krö-pyā), *n.* [F., orig. one who rides behind on the croup of another's horse, < *croupe*: see *croup^2*.] An attendant who rakes in the money at a gaming-table; also, one who at a public dinner sits at the lower end of the table as assistant chairman.
croup-ous (krö′pus), *a.* [See *croup^1*.] Of the nature of, pertaining to, or affected with croup. Also **croup′y.**
crouse (krös), *a.* [ME. *crus*; prob. from LG.] Bold; self-satisfied; brisk; lively; cheerful. [Sc. and north. Eng.]—**crouse′ly,** *adv.*
crous-tade (krös-täd), *n.* [F.: see *custard.*] A cup-like form of bread, rice, hominy, or the like, made crisp by frying or otherwise, for filling with a meat, fish, or other preparation.
croû-ton (krö-tôṅ), *n.* [F., < *croûte*: see *crust.*] A small piece of fried or toasted bread, used in soups, etc.
crow^1 (krō), *v. i.*; pret. *crowed* (archaic *crew*), pp. *crowed*, ppr. *crowing.* [AS. *crāwan* = D. *kraaien* = G. *krähen*; imit.] To utter the characteristic cry of a cock; also, to utter an inarticulate cry of pleasure, as an infant does; also, to exult loudly; boast.—**crow^1,** *n.* The act or sound of crowing.
crow^2 (krō), *n.* [AS. *crāwe* = D. *kraai* = G. *krähe*; from the Teut. verb represented by E. *crow^1*.] Any of the oscine birds constituting the genus *Corvus* (family *Corvidæ*), with lustrous black plumage and a characteristic harsh cry or caw, as *C. corone* of Europe ('carrion-crow') and *C. americanus* of North America; any bird of the family *Corvidæ*, as the chough, *Pyrrhocorax graculus* ('Cornish crow'); any of various similar birds of other families; also, an iron bar, as with a slightly bent or beaked end, used as a lever, etc.; a crowbar; also [*cap.*], in *astron.*, the southern constellation Corvus.—**crow′bar,** *n.* A bar of iron, often with a wedge-shaped end, for use as a lever, etc.—**crow′ber″ry,** *n.* The insipid black berry or fruit of an evergreen heath-like shrub, *Empetrum nigrum*, of northern regions; the plant itself; also, any of certain other fruits or the plants bearing them, as the bearberry, *Arctostaphylos uva-ursi.*—**crow′=black′bird,** *n.* Any of several American birds of the genus *Quiscalus* (family *Icteridæ*), as *Q. purpureus*, the purple grackle, noted for their dark plumage.

Crow-blackbird (*Quiscalus purpureus*).

crowd^1 (kroud), *n.* [W. *crwth.*] An ancient Celtic musical instrument of the viol type; hence, a fiddle or a fiddler (chiefly prov.).
crowd^2 (kroud), *v.* [AS. *crūdan* = MD. *kruyden* (D. *kruien*).] **I.** *intr.* To press forward; advance by pushing; also, to congregate in numbers; throng; swarm. **II.** *tr.* To push or shove; press closely together; compress; force into a confined space; also, to fill full or to excess; fill by crowding or pressing into; also, to beset, encumber, or incommode, as with excess of numbers (now colloq.); also, to urge, press by solicitation, or annoy by urging (colloq.).—**to crowd sail,** *naut.*, to set all the sail a ship can possibly stand, in order to accelerate the speed, as in escaping from an enemy.—**crowd^2,** *n.* A large number of persons gathered closely together; a throng; hence, any

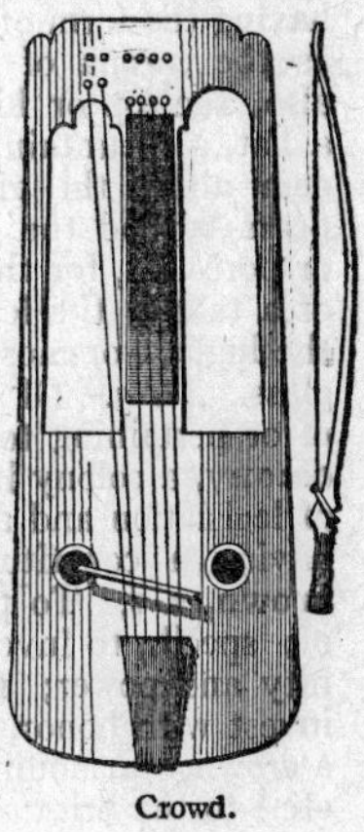
Crowd.

large number of persons; people in general, or the multitude (as, "far from the madding *crowd's* ignoble strife": Gray's "Elegy," xix.); a company of persons (colloq.); also, a large number of things gathered or considered together.—**crowd'ed-ly,** *adv.*—**crowd'ed-ness,** *n.*

crowd-er[1] (krou'dėr), *n.* A player on a crowd; hence, a fiddler (chiefly prov.).

crowd-er[2] (krou'dėr), *n.* One who or that which crowds.

crow-die, crow-dy (krou'di), *n.* [Origin obscure.] A thick gruel made of oatmeal with water, etc.; porridge. [Sc. and north. Eng.]

crow-er (krō'ėr), *n.* A cock or a person that crows.

crow=flow-er (krō'flou"ėr), *n.* Any of certain species of crowfoot (genus *Ranunculus*); also, any of various other plants, as the ragged-robin, *Lychnis flos-cuculi,* and the marsh-marigold, *Caltha palustris.*

crow-foot (krō'fu̇t), *n.*; pl. *-feet,* in bot. *-foots.* A kind of wrinkle, a crow's-foot; also, a caltrop for obstructing the passage of cavalry, etc.; *naut.,* a device consisting of small diverging lines or cords rove through a block of wood, used for suspending awnings, etc.; in *bot.,* any plant of the genus *Ranunculus,* esp. one with divided leaves suggestive of a crow's foot; a buttercup; also, any of various other plants with leaves or other parts suggestive of a bird's foot, as certain species of the genus *Geranium*; in *elect.,* a piece of zinc shaped somewhat like a crow's foot, used as an element in certain voltaic cells.

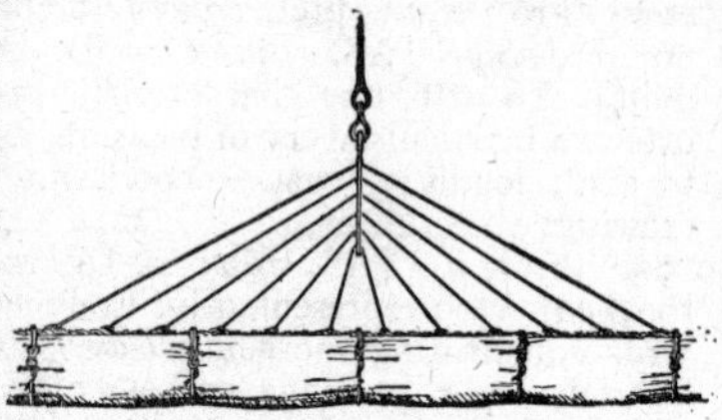
Awning Furled and Suspended by Crowfoot.

crow=keep-er (krō'kē"pėr), *n.* One employed to keep the crows from crops; also, a scarecrow. [Now prov.]

crown (kroun). [AF. *coroune,* OF. *curune, corone* (F. *couronne*), < L. *corona,* garland, wreath, crown: cf. *corona.*] **I.** *n.* An ornamental fillet for the head, as the wreath or garland conferred by the ancients as a mark of victory or distinction; hence, honorary distinction or reward; specif., a decorative fillet or covering for the head, worn as a symbol of sovereignty; the power or dominion of a sovereign; [often *cap.*] with *the,* the sovereign as head of the state, or the supreme governing power of a state under a monarchical government; fig. [*l. c.*], an exalting or chief attribute; also, any of various coins, orig. one bearing the representation of a crown or a crowned head; a British silver coin of the value of 5 shillings; sometimes, a krone or a krona; also, something having the form of a crown, as the corona of a flower; also, the top or highest part of anything, as of the head, a hat, a mountain, etc.; the head itself; the part of a cut gem above the girdle; that part of a tooth which appears beyond the gum; an artificial substitute, as of gold or porcelain, for the crown of a tooth; the grinding surface of a tooth; the leaves and living branches of a tree; fig., the highest or most perfect state of anything; also, crown-glass. **II.** *a.* Of or pertaining to a crown or the crown; of or pertaining to the sovereign or his authority.—**crown colony,** a colony in which the crown has the entire control of legislation and administration, as distinguished from one having a constitution and representative government.—**crown,** *v. t.* To place a crown or garland upon the head of; specif., to invest with a regal crown, or with regal dignity and power; fig., to honor as with a crown; reward; invest with honor, dignity, etc.; also, to surmount as with a crown; surmount as a crown does; also, to fill up (a cup, etc.) to the brim; also, to complete worthily, or bring to a successful or effective conclusion (as, "Sudden death is here made to *crown* the climax in a grand ascent of calamities": De Quincey's "English Mail-Coach," ii.); *milit.,* to effect a lodgment and establish works upon.

1. Imperial Crown (Charlemagne's). 2. Austrian Crown. 3. Russian Crown. 4. French Crown.

crown-al (krou'nal), *n.* [Var. of *coronal.*] A coronet; a garland. [Archaic.]

crown=ant-ler (kroun'ant"lėr), *n.* A topmost branch or antler of a stag's horn.

crowned (kround), *a.* Having a crown (in various senses): as, the *crowned* heads (sovereigns) of Europe; the *crowned* (crested) pigeon, *Goura coronata,* of New Guinea; a high-*crowned* hat.

crown-er[1] (krou'nėr), *n.* One who or that which crowns.

crown-er[2] (krou'nėr), *n.* Same as *coroner.* [Now prov. Eng.]

crown-et† (krou'net), *n.* Same as *coronet.*

crown=glass (kroun'glȧs'), *n.* A glass containing silicon, potassium or sodium, and calcium (but no lead), blown and whirled into sheets, formerly much used for windows; hence, any glass of such composition, no matter how prepared.

crown=im-pe-ri-al (kroun'im-pē'ri-al), *n.* A liliaceous plant, *Fritillaria imperialis,* bearing pendent flowers collected into a whorl round a terminal leafy tuft.

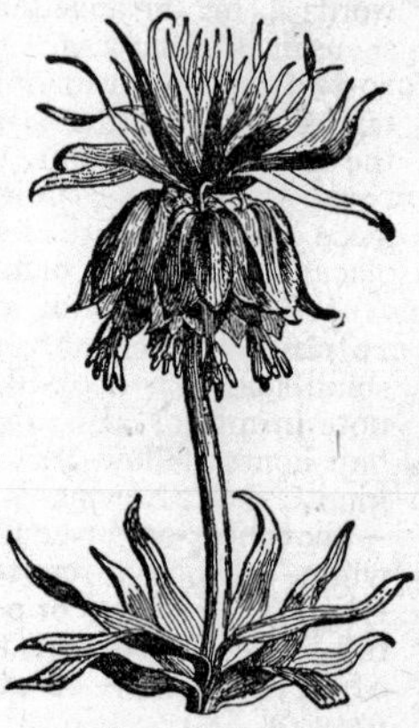
Crown-imperial.

crown-land (kroun'land), *n.* [= G. *kronland.*] Land belonging to the crown, the revenue of which goes to the reigning sovereign; also, one of the provinces, or great administrative divisions, of the former empire of Austria-Hungary.

crown=piece (kroun'pēs), *n.* A piece of money, a crown; also, a piece or part forming or fitting the crown or top of anything.

crown=post (kroun'pōst), *n.* A king-post.

crown=prince (kroun'prins'), *n.* [= G. *kronprinz.*] The heir apparent of a monarch.—**crown'=prin'cess,** *n.* [= G. *kronprinzessin.*] The wife of a crown-prince.

crown=saw (kroun'sâ), *n.* A rotary saw consisting of a hollow cylinder with teeth on its end or edge.

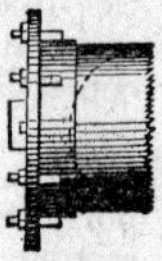
Crown-saw.

crown=wheel (kroun'hwēl), *n.* A wheel having cogs at right angles to its plane.

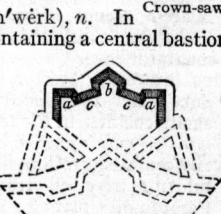

Crown-wheel of Watch.

crown=work (kroun'wėrk), *n.* In *fort.,* an outwork containing a central bastion with a curtain and demi-bastion on each side; in *dentistry,* the work of attaching artificial crowns to the roots of teeth, or that which is attached.

Crown-work.—*a, a,* demi-bastions; *b,* entire bastion; *c, c,* curtains.

crow=quill (krō'kwil), *n.* A quill from a crow's wing, cut into a pen, used for fine writing.

crow's=foot (krōz'fu̇t), *n.*; pl. *-feet.* A wrinkle at the outer corner of the eye (usually in *pl.*); also, a caltrop, as for obstructing the passage of cavalry; in *tailoring,* a three-pointed embroidered figure used as a finish, as at the end of a seam or opening.

crow's=nest (krōz'nest), *n.* *Naut.,* a box or shelter for the lookout man, secured near the top of a mast.

crow=toe (krō'tō), *n.* Any of various plants with parts suggestive of a crow's foot, as *Lotus corniculatus,* a fabaceous plant with claw-shaped pods.

croze (krōz), *n.* [Origin uncertain.] The groove at the ends of the staves of a barrel, cask, etc., into which the edge of the head fits; also, a tool for cutting such a groove.—**croze,** *v. t.*; *crozed, crozing.* To cut a croze in.

cro-zier, cro-sier (krō'zhėr), *n.* [Cf. OF. *crosser* (ML. *crociarius*), bearer of a crozier or pastoral staff, < *croce*

(ML. *crocia*), crozier: see *crosse*.] The bearer of a bishop's pastoral staff†; the pastoral staff of a bishop or an abbot, hooked at one end like a shepherd's staff; in *bot.*, the circinate young frond of a fern.

cru-cial (krö'shạl), *a.* [F. *crucial*, < L. *crux* (*cruc-*), E. *cross*.] Of the form of a cross; cross-shaped; also, decisive, as between two hypotheses; critical; sometimes, trying or severe.—**cru'cial-ly**, *adv.*

cru-ci-ate (krö'shi-āt), *a.* [NL. *cruciatus*, < L. *crux* (*cruc-*), E. *cross*.] Of the form of a cross; cross-shaped; also, marked with a cross.

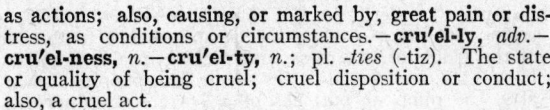

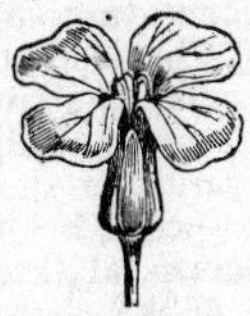
Cruciate Flower.

cru-ci-ble (krö'si-bl), *n.* [ML. *crucibulum*, night-lamp, melting-pot; origin uncertain.] A vessel of clay, porcelain, graphite, platinum, or the like, in which metals, etc., can be melted or heated; in a metallurgical furnace, the hollow part at the bottom, in which molten metal collects; fig., a severe test.—**crucible steel**, steel made in a crucible, esp. a high-grade steel prepared by melting together selected materials.

cru-ci-fer (krö'si-fėr), *n.* [LL. *crucifer*, < L. *crux* (*cruc-*), cross, + *ferre*, bear.] A cross-bearer, as in ecclesiastical processions; in *bot.*, a cruciferous plant.—**cru-cif'er-ous** (-sif'ẹ-rus), *a.* Bearing a cross; in *bot.*, belonging or pertaining to the family *Cruciferæ* or *Brassicaceæ*, whose members bear flowers having a cross-like, four-petaled corolla; brassicaceous.

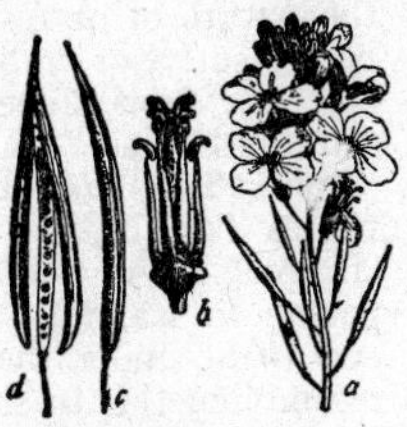

Cruciferous Plant. — *a*, flower-cluster of cabbage; *b*, flower with sepals and petals removed; *c*, pod; *d*, same, dehiscing.

cru-ci-fi-er (krö'si-fī-ėr), *n.* One who crucifies.

cru-ci-fix (krö'si-fiks), *n.* [L. *crucifixus*, pp. of *crucifigere*, earlier *cruci figere*, 'fix to a cross.'] One crucified†; Christ on the cross†; a cross, or a representation of a cross, with the figure of Christ crucified upon it.

cru-ci-fix-ion (krö-si-fik'shọn), *n.* [LL. *crucifixio*(*n-*), < L. *crucifigere*: see *crucifix*.] The act of crucifying; specif. [*cap.*], the putting to death of Christ upon the cross ('the Crucifixion'); also, a picture or other representation of this.

cru-ci-form (krö'si-fôrm), *a.* [L. *crux* (*cruc-*), cross: see *-form*.] Cross-shaped: as, "A circular vestibule . . . led into one of the shorter arms of a *cruciform* hall" (Wiseman's "Fabiola," ii. 20).

Bronze Crucifix. — Romanesque style, decorated with enamels.

cru-ci-fy (krö'si-fī), *v. t.*; *-fied*, *-fying*. [OF. F. *crucifier*, < LL. *crucificare*, for L. *crucifigere*: see *crucifix*.] To put to death by nailing or otherwise affixing to a cross; fig., to mortify or subdue (passion, sin, etc.); excruciate or torment; treat with grievous severity.

crud (krud), **crud-dle** (krud'l). Obs. or prov. forms of *curd*, *curdle*.

crude (kröd), *a.*; compar. *cruder*, superl. *crudest*. [L. *crudus*, raw, crude, rough: cf. *cruel*.] Being in a raw or unprepared state, as manufacturing materials; unripe, as fruit; not matured, as disease; undeveloped or imperfect, as ideas or opinions; lacking finish or polish, as literary or artistic work; lacking in culture, refinement, tact, or the like, as persons or their behavior or speech (as, "He [Gibbon] idealized the *crude* and gross plutocracy of Rome into a world of fine gentlemen": H. G. Wells's "Outline of History," xxxvi. § 11).—**crude'ly**, *adv.*—**crude'ness**, *n.*—**cru-di-ty** (krö'di-ti), *n.*; pl. *-ties* (-tiz). The state or quality of being crude; also, an instance of this; anything crude.

cru-el (krö'ẹl), *a.* [OF. F. *cruel*, < L. *crudelis*, hard, cruel, akin to *crudus*, E. *crude*.] Disposed to inflict suffering; indifferent to or taking pleasure in the pain or distress of others; destitute of compassion; pitiless; also, proceeding from, or exhibiting, indifference to the suffering of others, as actions; also, causing, or marked by, great pain or distress, as conditions or circumstances.—**cru'el-ly**, *adv.*—**cru'el-ness**, *n.*—**cru'el-ty**, *n.*; pl. *-ties* (-tiz). The state or quality of being cruel; cruel disposition or conduct; also, a cruel act.

cru-et (krö'et), *n.* [ME. *cruette*, appar. dim. < OF. *crue*, *cruie*, pitcher, pot, from Teut., and akin to F. *cruche*, pitcher, and E. *crock*³.] A glass bottle, esp. one for holding vinegar, oil, etc., for the table.

cruise (kröz), *v.*; *cruised*, *cruising*. [D. *kruisen*, cross, cruise, < *kruis*, = E. *cross*, *n.*] **I.** *intr.* To sail to and fro, or from place to place, as in search of hostile ships, or for pleasure; move hither and thither on land (colloq.); in *forestry*, to survey, and estimate the amount and value of, standing timber. **II.** *tr.* To cruise over; in *forestry*, to survey (wooded land, etc.) in order to estimate the amount and value of the timber.—**cruise**, *n.* An act of cruising; a voyage made by cruising.—**cruis'er**, *n.* One who or that which cruises, as a person or a ship; esp., an armed vessel or war-ship of fair or superior speed, used to protect a nation's commerce, give battle to an enemy's ships, or perform other duties; specif., one of a class of war-ships just below the armored cruiser class.—**armored cruiser**, one of a class of war-ships below the battle-ship class, having less armor and armament and greater speed than a battle-ship.—**battle cruiser**, a fast armored war-ship of a class between battle-ships and armored cruisers.—**protected cruiser**, a cruiser having an armored deck but no vertical side armor.—**unprotected cruiser**, an unarmored cruiser.

crul-ler (krul'ėr), *n.* [Prob. of Dutch origin: cf. D. *krullen*, curl.] A light, sweet cake cut from a rolled dough and fried in boiling lard: often having a curled or twisted form when cooked.

crumb (krum), *n.* [AS. *cruma* = D. *kruim* = G. *krume*.] A small particle of bread, cake, etc., such as breaks or falls off; hence, a small particle or portion of anything; also, the soft inner portion of a loaf, as of bread (distinguished from *crust*).—**crumb**, *v. t.* To break into crumbs or small fragments; in *cookery*, to dress or prepare with bread-crumbs.—**crumb'=cloth**, *n.* A cloth, commonly of stout linen damask, spread over a dining-room floor under the table to protect the carpet from falling crumbs, etc.

crum-ble (krum'bl), *v.*; *-bled*, *-bling*. [For earlier *crimble*, freq. < AS. *cruma*, E. *crumb*.] **I.** *tr.* To break into crumbs; reduce to small fragments. **II.** *intr.* To fall into small particles; become disintegrated; fall to decay.—**crum'ble**, *n.* A small or tiny crumb or fragment (now prov.); also, something crumbling or crumbled.—**crum'bly**, *a.* Apt to crumble; friable.

crumb-y (krum'i), *a.* Of the nature of the crumb or soft inner part of bread, etc.; also, full of crumbs.

crump (krump), *v.* [Imit.] **I.** *tr.* To crunch with the teeth; also, to strike heavily. **II.** *intr.* To make a crunching sound, as in walking over snow, or as snow when trodden on; also, to make a loud, crashing sound, as a cannon or a bursting shell.—**crump**, *n.* A crunching sound; also, a heavy blow; also, a loud, crashing sound, as of a bursting shell; also, a soldiers' term for a large explosive shell.

crum-pet (krum'pet), *n.* [Origin uncertain.] A kind of light, soft cake resembling a muffin, cooked on a griddle or the like, and often toasted for eating.

crum-ple (krum'pl), *v.*; *-pled*, *-pling*. [ME. (first in *crumpled*, pp.), freq. < AS. *crump*, *crumb*, crooked.] **I.** *tr.* To make crooked; bend together; contort; bend spirally; also, to crush into irregular creases or folds; rumple; also, to ripple. **II.** *intr.* To become crumpled; contract into folds or wrinkles; shrivel.—**crum'ple**, *n.* An irregular fold or wrinkle produced by crumpling.—**crum'pler**, *n.*—**crum'ply**, *a.* Full of crumples or wrinkles.

crunch (krunch), *v.* [Var. of *craunch*.] **I.** *tr.* To crush with the teeth; chew with a crushing noise; also, to crush or grind noisily. **II.** *intr.* To chew with a crushing sound; also, to produce, or proceed with, a crushing noise.—**crunch**, *n.* The act or sound of crunching.

cru-node (krö'nōd), *n.* [Irreg. < L. *crux*, cross, + *nodus*, E. *node*.] In *geom.*, a point at which a curve crosses itself.

cru-or (krö'ôr), *n.* [L., blood, gore.] Coagulated blood, or that portion of the blood which forms the clot.

crup-per (krup′ėr), *n.* [OF. *crupiere* (F. *croupière*), < *crupe*: see *croup*².] A leather strap attached to the back of the saddle of a harness, and passing in a loop under a horse's tail, for preventing the saddle from slipping forward; also, the rump or buttocks of a horse.—**crup′per,** *v. t.* To put a crupper on.

cru-ral (krö′ral), *a.* [L. *cruralis*, < *crus*, leg.] Of or pertaining to the leg or the hind limb; of or pertaining to the leg proper, or crus.

crus (krus), *n.*; pl. *crura* (krö′rä). [L., leg.] In *anat.* and *zoöl.*, that part of the leg or hind limb between the femur or thigh and the ankle or tarsus; the shank; also, any of various parts likened to a leg, as one of a pair of supporting parts.

cru-sade (krö-sād′), *n.* [F. *croisade* (also Sp. *cruzada*), < *croiser* (Sp. *cruzar*), mark with a cross, < L. *crux*, cross.] [Often *cap.*] Any of the military expeditions undertaken by the Christians of Europe in the 11th, 12th, and 13th centuries for the recovery of the Holy Land from the Mohammedans; [*l. c.*] any war carried on under papal sanction; in general, any aggressive movement for the defense or advancement of an idea or cause, or against a public evil.—**cru-sade′,** *v. i.*; *-saded, -sading.* To go on or engage in a crusade: as, "and cease *crusading* against sense" (M. Green's "Grotto").—**cru-sad′er** (-sā′dėr), *n.* One who engages in a crusade; esp. [often *cap.*], one of those who took part in the Crusades of the middle ages.

cru-sa-do, cru-za-do (krö-zā′dō), *n.*; pl. *-does* or *-dos* (-dōz). [Pg. *cruzado*, prop. pp. of *cruzar*, mark with a

Obverse. Reverse.
Silver Crusado of John V.—British Museum.

cross: cf. *crusade*.] An old Portuguese coin of gold or silver, bearing the figure of a cross.

cruse (krös or kröz), *n.* [ME. *cruse, cruce*: cf. Icel. *krūs*, pot, tankard, D. *kroes*, cup, pot.] An earthen pot or bottle, or any small vessel for liquids (see 1 Kings, xvii. 12–16); also, a drinking-vessel. [Archaic.]

crush (krush), *v. t.* [Appar. < OF. *croissir*, crash, gnash, break, crush, prob. from Teut.] To press and bruise, as between two hard bodies; squeeze or batter out of shape or normal condition; crumple, as by rough handling; also, to press or squeeze forcibly or violently; also, to put down, overpower, or subdue completely; overwhelm; also, to oppress grievously; also, to break into small fragments or particles, as ore, stone, etc.; also, to force (*out*) by pressing or squeezing; also, to drink (wine, etc.).—**crushed strawberry,** a deep, dull purplish-pink color.—**crush,** *v. i.* To become crushed; also, to advance with crushing; press or crowd forcibly.—**crush,** *n.* The act of crushing, or the state of being crushed; esp., the crowding together of persons or things, or the mass crowded together; a great crowd; a crowded social gathering (colloq.).—**crush′er,** *n.* One who or that which crushes; a machine for crushing ore, stone, etc.—**crush′=hat′,** *n.* A hat which can be crushed or folded without injury; a soft felt hat; an opera-hat.—**crush′ing,** *p. a.* That crushes; bruising; overwhelming.—**crush′ing-ly,** *adv.*

crust (krust), *n.* [OF. *crouste* (F. *croûte*), < L. *crusta*, hard surface, rind, shell, crust.] The hard outer portion of a loaf, as of bread (distinguished from *crumb*); a piece of this; the outside covering of a pie; also, any more or less hard external covering or coating; a scab or eschar; the exterior portion of the earth, accessible to examination; the hard outer shell or covering of an animal or plant.—**crust,** *v.* **I.** *tr.* To cover with or as with a crust; incrust; also, to form into a crust; also, to crust-hunt for (deer, etc.). **II.** *intr.* To form or contract a crust; also, to form into a crust; also, to crust-hunt.

crus-ta-cean (krus-tā′shian). [NL. *Crustacea*, neut. pl. of *crustaceus*, E. *crustaceous*.] **I.** *a.* Belonging to the *Crustacea*, a class of (chiefly aquatic) arthropods, including the lobsters, shrimps, crabs, barnacles, wood-lice, etc., commonly having the body covered with a hard shell or crust. **II.** *n.* A crustacean animal.

crus-ta-ce-ol-o-gy (krus-tā-shē-ol′ō-ji), *n.* [See *-logy*.] The science or study of crustaceans.

crus-ta-ceous (krus-tā′shius), *a.* [NL. *crustaceus*, < L. *crusta*, shell, E. *crust*.] Of the nature of or pertaining to a crust or shell; also, having a hard covering, as an animal; specif., belonging to the *Crustacea*; crustacean.

crus-tal (krus′tal), *a.* Of or pertaining to a crust, as that of the earth.

crust=hunt (krust′hunt), *v. i.* To hunt deer, etc., on the crust of snow when it is strong enough to support the hunter but not the game.—**crust′=hunt″er,** *n.*

crust-y (krus′ti), *a.*; compar. *crustier*, superl. *crustiest.* Of the nature of or resembling a crust; having a crust; fig., harsh, surly, or crabbed, as persons or the manner, speech, etc. (as, "Aunt Chloe set a chair for her in a manner decidedly gruff and *crusty*": Mrs. Stowe's "Uncle Tom's Cabin," x.).—**crust′i-ly,** *adv.*—**crust′i-ness,** *n.*

crutch (kruch), *n.* [AS. *crycc* = D. *kruk* = G. *krücke*: cf. *crook*.] A staff or support to assist a lame or infirm person in walking, now usually with a crosspiece at one end to fit under the armpit; also, any of various devices resembling this in shape or use; a forked support or part.—**crutch,** *v. t.* To support with or as with a crutch; prop or sustain.

crutch-ed (kruch′ed), *a.* [Earlier *crouched*, < ME. *crouche*, < L. *crux* (*cruc-*), cross.] Having or bearing a cross: as, a *crutched* friar (one of a former order of friars that bore or wore a cross).

crux (kruks), *n.*; pl. *cruxes*, L. *cruces* (krö′sēz). [L., cross, torment, trouble.] A cross; fig. (from the use of the cross as an instrument of torture), something that torments by its puzzling nature; a perplexing difficulty; [*cap.*] in *astron.*, the Southern Cross, a southern constellation having its four chief stars arranged in the form of a cross.—**crux ansata** (an-sā′tä). [L., 'cross with a handle.'] A tau-cross, or St. Anthony's cross, with a loop at the top.

cru-za′do, *n.* See *crusado*.

cry (krī), *v.*; *cried, crying.* [OF. F. *crier*, < L. *quiritare*, cry, shriek, lament.] **I.** *intr.* To call loudly; shout; also, to utter inarticulate sounds, esp. of lamentation, grief, or suffering, usually with tears; wail and weep; hence, simply, to shed tears; also, to give forth vocal sounds or characteristic calls, as animals; yelp, as hounds in the chase. **II.** *tr.* To utter or pronounce loudly; call out; also, to beg for or implore in a loud voice (archaic); also, to announce orally in public; sell by outcry; sometimes, to proclaim the marriage banns of; also, to call for† or demand† (as, "The affair *cries* haste": Shakspere's "Othello," i. 3. 277); also, to bring by weeping (as, to *cry* one's self to sleep).—**to cry down,** to condemn by proclamation; also, to disparage; belittle.—**to cry up,** to praise; extol.—**to cry wolf.** See under *wolf*, *n.*—**cry,** *n.*; pl. *cries* (krīz). [OF. F. *cri*.] The act or sound of crying; any loud utterance or exclamation; a shout; a scream; a wail; an entreaty or appeal; an oral proclamation or announcement; a call of wares for sale, etc., as by a street-vender; also, public report; an opinion generally expressed; also, a battle-cry; a political or party catchword; also, a fit of weeping; also, the vocal utterance or characteristic call of an animal; the yelping of hounds in the chase; hence, a pack of hounds; fig., the peculiar noise made by a metal, as tin, when bent.—**cry′=ba″by,** *n.* One given to crying like a baby, or to weak display of injured feeling.—**cry′ing,** *p. a.* That cries; clamorous; wailing; weeping; demanding attention or remedy, or notorious (as, a *crying* evil).—**cry′ing-ly,** *adv.*

cry-mo-ther-a-py (krī-mō-ther′a-pi), *n.* [Gr. κρυμός, icy cold: see *therapy*.] Treatment of disease by means of cold.

cryo-. Form of Gr. κρύος, icy cold, frost, used in combination.—**cry-o-gen** (krī′ō-jen), *n.* [+ *-gen*.] A substance for producing low temperatures; a freezing-mixture.—**cry-o-gen'ic,** *a.* Of or pertaining to cryogens or the production of low temperatures.—**cry-o-hy'drate** (-hī'drāt), *n.* In *chem.*, a definite mixture of ice and a crystallized salt, obtained by freezing a saturated aqueous solution of the salt.—**cry'o-lite** (-līt), *n.* [+ *-lite.*] A native fluoride of sodium and aluminium, used as a source of aluminium and in making glass, etc.—**cry-om'e-ter** (-om'e-tėr), *n.* [+ *-meter.*] A thermometer for the measurement of low temperatures, as one containing alcohol instead of mercury.—**cry-oph'o-rus** (-of'ọ̄-rus), *n.* [NL. (Gr. -φόρος, bearing: see *-phorous*).] An instrument for showing the fall of temperature or the freezing of water by evaporation.—**cry'o-scope** (-skōp), *n.* [+ *-scope.*] An instrument for determining the freezing-points of liquids or solutions, as in testing milk to learn whether, or to what extent, it has been watered.—**cry-os'co-py** (-os'kọ̄-pi), *n.* [+ *-scopy.*] The determination of the freezing-points of liquids or solutions, or of the lowering of the freezing-points of liquids by dissolved substances; in *med.*, the determination of the freezing-points of certain bodily fluids, as urine, for diagnosis.—**cry-o-scop'ic** (-skop'ik), *a.*

crypt (kript), *n.* [L. *crypta*, < Gr. κρυπτή, prop. fem. of κρυπτός, hidden, < κρύπτειν, hide.] A subterranean chamber or vault; esp., one beneath the main floor of a church, used as a burial-place, etc.; in *anat.*, a follicle; a small glandular cavity.—**cryp-tal** (krip'tạl), *a.*

Crypt. — Cathedral of Bourges, France.

cryp-tic (krip'tik), *a.* [LL. *crypticus*, < Gr. κρυπτικός, < κρύπτειν, hide.] Hidden; secret; occult; in *zoöl.*, fitted for concealing.—**cryp'ti-cal-ly,** *adv.*

crypto-. Form of Gr. κρυπτός, hidden, secret, used in combination.—**cryp-to-clas-tic** (krip-tọ̄-klas'tik), *a.* [See *clastic.*] In *petrog.*, composed of fragments too small to be seen by the unaided eye.—**cryp-to-crys'tal-line** (-kris'tạ-lin), *a.* Indistinctly crystalline; noting or pertaining to rocks whose crystals are so small as to be indistinguishable, even with the microscope.

cryp-to-gam (krip'tọ̄-gam), *n.* [F. *cryptogame* = NL. *cryptogamus*, cryptogamous, < Gr. κρυπτός, hidden, + γάμος, marriage.] In *bot.*, any of the *Cryptogamia*, an old primary division of plants comprising those without stamens and pistils, and therefore without flowers and seeds, as the ferns, mosses, and thallophytes; a plant without a true seed: opposed to *phanerogam.*—**cryp-to-gam'ic,** *a.* Of or pertaining to the cryptogams.—**cryp-tog'a-mous** (-tog'ạ-mus), *a.* Having the characters of the cryptogams.

cryp-to-gen-ic (krip-tọ̄-jen'ik), *a.* [See *crypto-* and *-genic.*] Of obscure or unknown origin, as a disease. Also **cryptog'e-nous** (-toj'e-nus).

cryp-to-gram (krip'tọ̄-gram), *n.* [See *crypto-* and *-gram.*] A piece of writing in secret characters; something written in cipher.—**cryp''to-gram-mat'ic** (-grạ-mat'ik), *a.*

cryp-to-graph (krip'tọ̄-gråf), *n.* [See *crypto-* and *-graph.*] A cryptogram (as, "We see it [a character] doubled no less than five times, although the *cryptograph* is brief": Poe's "Gold-Bug"); also, a system of secret writing; a cipher; also, the form or method of writing employing secret characters.—**cryp-tog'ra-phy** (-tog'rạ-fi), *n.* [See *-graphy.*] The process or art of writing in secret characters, or in cipher; also, anything so written.—**cryp-to-graph'ic** (-graf'ik), *a.*—**cryp-tog'ra-phist,** *n.*

cryp-tol-o-gy (krip-tol'ọ̄-ji), *n.* [See *crypto-* and *-logy.*] Occult or enigmatical language.

cryp-to-nym (krip'tọ̄-nim), *n.* [See *crypto-* and *-onym.*] A secret name.—**cryp-ton'y-mous** (-ton'i-mus), *a.* Having the name concealed; anonymous.

crys-tal (kris'tạl). [OF. F. *cristal*, < L. *crystallum*, < Gr. κρύσταλλος, ice, crystal, < κρύος, icy cold, frost.] **I.** *n.* A clear, transparent mineral resembling ice, esp. the transparent or nearly transparent form of pure quartz; anything made of or resembling such a substance; also, glass of a high degree of brilliance; sometimes, cut glass; also, the glass cover over the face of a watch; in *chem.* and *mineral.*, a body having a specific internal structure and inclosed by symmetrically arranged plane surfaces, formed by the solidification of a substance, and consisting of a single element or a compound; in *wireless teleg.* and *teleph.*, the piece of galena, carborundum, or the like forming the essential part of a crystal detector, or the detector itself. **II.** *a.* Composed of crystal; also, resembling crystal; clear; transparent; also, in *wireless teleg.* and *teleph.*, pertaining to or employing a crystal detector.—**crystal detector,** in *wireless teleg.* and *teleph.*, a device for rectifying the alternating currents in a radio receiving apparatus, consisting essentially of a crystal, as of galena or carborundum, which permits a current to pass freely in one direction only: commonly constructed by embedding the lower part of the crystal in a mass of soft metal, which serves as one electrical contact, and allowing the free surface of the crystal to be touched by a fine, adjustable wire (called a *cat-whisker*), which serves as the other electrical contact.—**crys'tal,** *v. t.*; *-taled* or *-talled*, *-taling* or *-talling*. To make into crystal; crystallize.—**crys'tal=gaz''ing** (-gā''zing), *n.* A steady staring at a crystal or glass ball or other clear object in order to arouse visual perceptions, as of distant happenings, the future, etc.—**crys'tal=gaz''er,** *n.*

crys-tal-lif-er-ous, crys-tal-lig-er-ous (kris-tạ-lif'ẹ-rus, -lij'ẹ-rus), *a.* [L. *crystallum*, crystal: see *-ferous* and *-gerous.*] Bearing, containing, or yielding crystals.

crys-tal-line (kris'tạ-lin or -līn), *a.* [OF. F. *cristallin*, < L. *crystallinus*, < Gr. κρυστάλλινος.] Of or like crystal; clear; transparent; also, formed by crystallization; also, composed of crystals, as rocks; also, pertaining to crystals or their formation.—**crystalline heaven** or **sphere,** in the Ptolemaic system of astronomy, a sphere, or one of two spheres, supposed to exist between the primum mobile outside and the firmament of the fixed stars inside, and to communicate motion to all within.—**crystalline lens,** in *anat.*, a doubly convex, transparent, lens-like body in the eye, situated behind the iris and serving to focus the rays of light on the retina.—**crys-tal-lin'i-ty** (-lin'i-ti), *n.*

crys-tal-li-tis (kris-tạ-lī'tis), *n.* [NL.] In *pathol.*, inflammation of the crystalline lens of the eye.

crys-tal-liz-a-ble (kris'tạ-lī-zạ-bl), *a.* Capable of being crystallized.

crys-tal-li-za-tion (kris''tạ-li-zā'shọn), *n.* The act of crystallizing; the process of forming crystals; also, a crystallized body or formation.

crys-tal-lize (kris'tạ-līz), *v.*; *-lized*, *-lizing.* [= F. *cristalliser.*] **I.** *tr.* To form into crystals; cause to assume crystalline form; fig., to give definite or concrete form to. **II.** *intr.* To form crystals; become crystalline in form; fig., to assume definite or concrete form.—**crys'tal-lized,** *p. a.* Formed into crystals; crystalline; also, candied, as ginger.—**crys'tal-liz-er,** *n.*

crys-tal-lo-. Form of Gr. κρύσταλλος, crystal, used in combination.—**crys-tal-lo-gen-e-sis** (kris''tạ-lọ̄-jen'e-sis), *n.* The genesis or formation of crystals, esp. as a subject of scientific study. Also **crys-tal-log'e-ny** (-loj'e-ni).—**crys''-tal-lo-gen'ic,** *a.*—**crys-tal-log'ra-phy** (-log'rạ-fi), *n.* [See *-graphy.*] The science dealing with crystallization and the forms and structure of crystals.—**crys-tal-log'ra-pher,** *n.*—**crys''tal-lo-graph'ic** (-graf'ik), *a.*

crys-tal-loid (kris'tạ-loid). [Gr. κρυσταλλοειδής: see *crystal* and *-oid.*] **I.** *a.* Resembling a crystal; of the nature of a crystalloid. **II.** *n.* A substance (usually crystallizable) which when dissolved in a liquid will diffuse readily through vegetable or animal membranes (cf. *colloid*); in *bot.*, one of certain minute crystal-like granules of protein, found in the tissues of various seeds.—**crys-tal-loi′dal,** *a.*

crys-tal-lo-man-cy (kris′tạ-lō-man″si), *n.* [See *crystallo-* and *-mancy.*] Divination by means of a crystal ball or other transparent body. Cf. *crystal-gazing.*

crys-tal=vi-sion (kris′tạl-vizh″ọn), *n.* Visual perception, as of distant happenings, the future, etc., supposed to be aroused by crystal-gazing; also, the image or images which seem to be perceived.

csar-das (chär′däsh), *n.* [Hung.] A Hungarian national dance in two movements, one slow and the other fast.

cten-o-dac-tyl (ten-ọ-dak′til), *n.* [NL. *Ctenodactylus*, < Gr. κτείς (κτεν-), comb, + δάκτυλος, finger or toe.] A hystricomorphic rodent, *Ctenodactylus massoni* (or *gundi*), of northern Africa, with small ears, a stumpy tail, and hind limbs having a fringe of bristles on the inner toes; the comb-rat or gundi.

Ctenodactyl.

cten-oid (ten′oid or tē′noid). [Gr. κτενοειδής, < κτείς (κτεν-), comb, + εἶδος, form.] **I.** *a.* Comb-like or pectinate, as the scales or the dentition of certain fishes; having such scales, as a fish. **II.** *n.* A fish with ctenoid scales.—**cte-noi-de-an** (te-noi′dē-ạn), *a.* and *n.*

cte-noph-o-ran (te-nof′ọ-rạn). [NL. *Ctenophora*, pl., < Gr. κτείς (κτεν-), comb, + -φόρος, bearing: see *-phorous.*] **I.** *a.* Belonging or pertaining to the *Ctenophora*, a small group of cœlenterates, now regarded as a class, comprising certain free-swimming jellyfishes which move chiefly by means of eight meridional rows of transverse comb-like plates. **II.** *n.* A ctenophoran animal.—**cten-o-phore** (ten′ọ-fōr or tē′nọ-), *n.* One of the rows of comb-like plates which form the chief locomotive organs of the *Ctenophora*; also, a ctenophoran animal.

cuar-ta (kwär′tạ), *n.* [Amer. Sp.] A long rawhide whip. [Southwestern U. S.]

cub[1] (kub), *n.* [Origin obscure.] The young of certain animals, as the fox, bear, etc.; hence, an awkward or uncouth youth (humorous or contemptuous); also, an inexperienced newspaper reporter (journalistic slang).—**cub**[1], *v. t.* or *i.*; *cubbed, cubbing.* To bring forth (a cub or cubs).

cub[2] (kub), *n.* [Prob. from LG.] A stall or pen for cattle; a coop; a crib for fodder; a bin or chest. [Chiefly prov. Eng.]

cu-bage (kū′bạj), *n.* The determination of the cubic contents of a thing; also, the cubic contents determined.

Cu-ban (kū′bạn). **I.** *a.* Of or pertaining to Cuba, in the West Indies. **II.** *n.* A native or inhabitant of Cuba.

cu-ba-ture (kū′bạ-ṭūr), *n.* The determination of the cubic contents of a thing; also, cubic contents.

cub-by (kub′i), *n.*; pl. *cubbies* (-iz). [Cf. *cub*[2].] A snug, confined place; a cubby-hole: as, "Up garret was a little *cubby*, with a pallet in it" (Mark Twain's "Huckleberry Finn," xxvi.).—**cub′by=hole,** *n.* A small inclosed space; a small apartment; a closet; a very small house.—**cub′by=house,** *n.* A little house, as one built by children in play.

cube (kūb), *n.* [F. *cube*, < L. *cubus*, < Gr. κύβος, die, cube.] A solid bounded by six equal squares, the angle between any two adjacent faces being a right angle; a piece of anything of this form; in *arith.* and *alg.*, the third power of a quantity (as, the *cube* of 4 is 4 × 4 × 4, or 64).—**cube root,** the quantity of which a given quantity is the cube: as, 4 is the *cube root* of 64.—**cube,** *v. t.*; *cubed, cubing.* To measure the cubic contents of; also, to raise to the third power; find the cube of.

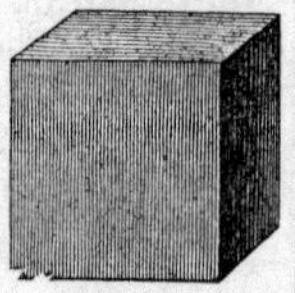
Cube.

cu-beb (kū′beb), *n.* [F. *cubèbe*, < Ar. *kabābah.*] The spicy fruit or berry of an East Indian piperaceous climbing shrub, *Piper cubeba*: dried in an unripe but fully grown state, and much used in medicine in the treatment of urinary and bronchial disorders.

Cubeb-plant and Cubebs.

cu-bic (kū′bik), *a.* [L. *cubicus*, < Gr. κυβικός.] Having the form of a cube; also, of three dimensions, solid, or pertaining to solid content (as, a *cubic* foot, the volume of a cube whose edges are each a foot long; *cubic* measure, see below); in *arith.*, *alg.*, etc., being of the third power or degree; in *crystal.*, belonging or pertaining to the isometric system of crystallization.—**cubic measure,** the measurement of volume in cubic units; a system of such units, esp. that in which 1,728 cubic inches = 1 cubic foot, 27 cubic feet = 1 cubic yard.—**cu′bi-cal,** *a.* Cubic.—**cu′bi-cal-ly,** *adv.*—**cu′bi-cal-ness,** *n.*

cu-bi-cle (kū′bi-kl), *n.* [L. *cubiculum*, < *cubare*, lie.] A bedchamber, esp. one of a number of small ones in a divided dormitory; hence, any small space or compartment partitioned off. Also **cu′bi-cule** (-kūl).

cu-bic-u-lum (kū-bik′ụ-lum), *n.*; pl. *-la* (-lạ). [L.: see *cubicle.*] A cubicle; in *archæol.*, a burial-chamber, as in catacombs.

cu-bi-form (kū′bi-fôrm), *a.* Having the form of a cube.

cu-bism (kū′bizm), *n.* A recent movement in pictorial art characteristically involving representation by cube-like and other geometrical figures.—**cu′bist,** *n.*

cu-bit (kū′bit), *n.* [L. *cubitum*, also *cubitus*, elbow, cubit.] The forearm†; also, the ulna†; also, an ancient linear unit based on the length of the forearm, varying in extent, but usually from 17 to 21 inches.—**cu′bi-tal,** *a.* [L. *cubitalis.*] Of or pertaining to the forearm or the ulna; also, of the length of a cubit.—**cu′bi-tus** (-tus), *n.* [L.] In *anat.*, the forearm; also, the ulna.

cu-boid (kū′boid). [Gr. κυβοειδής: see *-oid.*] **I.** *a.* Resembling a cube in form; in *anat.*, noting or pertaining to the outermost bone of the distal row of tarsal bones. **II.** *n.* Something resembling a cube in form; in *anat.*, the cuboid bone; in *math.*, a rectangular parallelepiped.—**cu-boi-dal** (kū-boi′dạl), *a.*

cuck-ing=stool (kuk′ing-stöl), *n.* [Cf. obs. *cuck*, void excrement.] A former instrument of punishment consisting of a chair, sometimes in the form of a close-stool, in which an offender, esp. a common scold, was strapped, to be jeered at and pelted by the crowd, or, sometimes, to be ducked. Cf. *ducking-stool.*

cuck-old (kuk′ọld), *n.* [OF. *cucuault*, < *cucu*, cuckoo; in allusion to the female cuckoo's laying her eggs in the nests of other birds.] The husband of an unfaithful wife.—**cuck′old,** *v. t.* To make a cuckold of (a husband).—**cuck′old-ly,** *a.*—**cuck′old-ry,** *n.*

cuck-oo (kůk′ö), *n.*; pl. *-oos* (-öz). [OF. *cucu* (F. *coucou*), cuckoo; imit. of the bird's call: cf. D. *koekoek*, LG. *kukuk*, G. *kuckuk*, L. *cuculus*, Gr. κόκκυξ, cuckoo.] Any bird of the genus *Cuculus* (family *Cuculidæ*), esp. *C. canorus*, a common European migratory bird noted for its characteristic call, and for the female's habit of laying her eggs in the nests of other birds, for the young to be reared by foster-parents; any bird of the family *Cuculidæ*, as a member of the American genus *Coccyzus* or the chaparral-cock, *Geococcyx californianus*; also, the call of the cuckoo, or an imitation of it; also, a fool or simpleton.—**cuck'oo,** *v.* **I.** *intr.* To utter the call of the cuckoo, or an imitation of it. **II.** *tr.* To repeat monotonously.—**cuck'oo=clock,** *n.* A clock which announces the hours by a sound like the call of the cuckoo.—**cuck'oo=flow″er,** *n.* Any of various plants, as the lady's-smock, *Cardamine pratensis,* or the ragged-robin, *Lychnis flos-cuculi.*—**cuck'oo=pint** (-pint), *n.* [Earlier *cuckoo-pintle.*] A common European species of arum, *Arum maculatum.* Also called *wake-robin.*—**cuck'oo=spit,** *n.* A frothy secretion found on plants, exuded as a protective covering by the young of certain insects as the froghoppers; also, an insect secreting this. Also **cuck'oo=spit″tle.**

Cuckoo (*Cuculus canorus*).

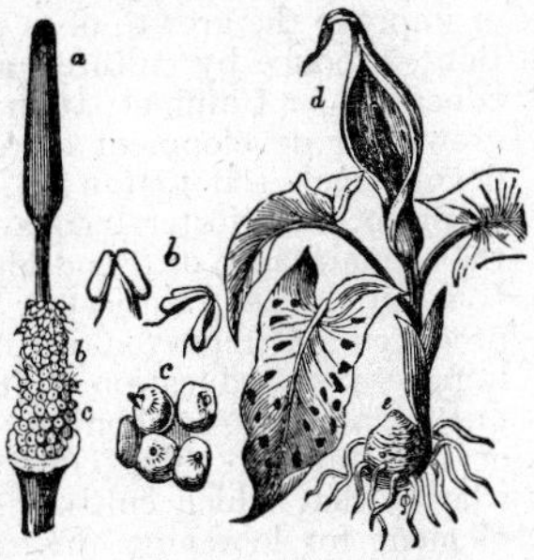

Cuckoo-pint, or Wake-robin.
a, spadix; *b, b,* stamens, or male flowers; *c, c,* ovaries, or female flowers; *d,* spathe; *e,* corm.

cu-cul-late (kū'ku-lāt or kū̧-kul'āt), *a.* [LL. *cucullatus,* hooded, < L. *cucullus,* hood.] Cowled; hooded; also, resembling a cowl or hood. Also **cu'cul-lat-ed.**—**cu'cul-late-ly,** *adv.*

cu-cul-li-form (kū̧-kul'i-fôrm), *a.* [L. *cucullus,* hood: see *-form.*] Hood-shaped.

cu-cum-ber (kū'kum-bėr), *n.* [OF. *coucombre* (F. *concombre*), < L. *cucumis* (*cucumer-*).] A cucurbitaceous creeping plant, *Cucumis sativus,* occurring in many cultivated forms, yielding a long fleshy fruit which is commonly eaten green as a salad and when young used for pickling; the fruit of this plant; also, any of various allied or similar plants, or its fruit.—**cu'cum-ber=tree,** *n.* Any of several American magnolias, esp. *Magnolia acuminata;* also, any of certain other trees, as the bilimbi.

cu-cu-mi-form (kū̧-kū'mi-fôrm), *a.* [L. *cucumis,* cucumber: see *-form.*] Shaped like a cucumber; approximately cylindrical, with rounded or tapering ends.

cu-cur-bit (kū̧-kėr'bit), *n.* [L. *cucurbita,* gourd.] A gourd; any cucurbitaceous plant; also, a roundish vessel formerly used as the lower part of a distilling apparatus.—**cu-cur-bi-ta'ceous** (-bi-tā'shius), *a.* Belonging to the *Cucurbitaceæ,* or gourd family of plants, which includes the pumpkin, squash, cucumber, muskmelon, watermelon, colocynth, etc.

cud (kud), *n.* [AS. *cudu, cwidu:* cf. *quid*[1].] The portion of food which a ruminating animal returns from the first stomach to the mouth to chew a second time.

cud-bear (kud'bãr), *n.* [From Dr. *Cuthbert* Gordon (18th century), who patented it.] A violet coloring matter obtained from various lichens, esp. *Lecanora tartarea;* also, a lichen yielding this.

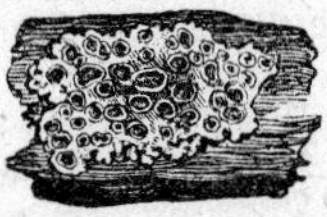

Cudbear-plant (*Lecanora tartarea*).

cud-dle (kud'l), *v.;* *-dled, -dling.* [Origin uncertain.] **I.** *tr.* To draw or hold close in an affectionate manner; hug tenderly; fondle. **II.** *intr.* To lie close and snug; nestle; curl up in going to sleep.—**cud'dle,** *n.* An act of cuddling; a hug or embrace.

cud-dy[1] (kud'i), *n.;* pl. *cuddies* (-iz). [Origin uncertain.] A donkey; fig., a stupid fellow. [Chiefly Sc.]

cud-dy[2] (kud'i), *n.;* pl. *cuddies* (-iz). [Origin uncertain.] A small cabin on a ship or boat, esp. one under the poop; also, a small room; a cupboard.

cudg-el (kuj'ẹl), *n.* [AS. *cycgel.*] A short, thick stick used as a weapon; a club.—**cudg'el,** *v. t.;* *-eled* or *-elled, -eling* or *-elling.* To strike with a cudgel; beat (sometimes fig.: as, "*Cudgel* thy brains no more about it, for your dull ass will not mend his pace with beating," Shakspere's "Hamlet," v. 1. 63).—**cudg'el-er, cudg'el-ler,** *n.*

cud-weed (kud'wēd), *n.* Any of the woolly herbs constituting the asteraceous genus *Gnaphalium;* also, any of various plants of allied genera.

cue[1] (kū), *n.* [Formerly *q, qu,* as if an abbreviation, possibly for L. *qualis,* of what kind, or *quando,* when.] The concluding word or words of an actor's speech, serving as the signal for an answering speech, the entrance of another actor, etc; fig., any indication or direction when or how to speak or act; a guiding hint or suggestion; also, the part one is to play at a particular juncture; the course of action one ought to pursue; also, humor or disposition.

cue[2] (kū), *n.* [F. *queue:* see *queue.*] A queue of hair; a queue or file, as of persons awaiting their turn; a long, straight tapering rod tipped with a soft pad, used to strike the ball in billiards, pool, etc.—**cue'=ball,** *n.* In *billiards,* etc., the ball struck by the cue as distinguished from the other balls on the table.—**cue'ist,** *n.* One who uses a cue, as in billiards; esp., an expert in the use of the cue.

cuff[1] (kuf), *v. t.* [Origin uncertain.] To strike with the fist or the open hand; beat; buffet: as, "Tom *cuffed* Sid's ears" (Mark Twain's "Tom Sawyer," xxxiv.).—**cuff**[1], *n.* A blow with the fist or the open hand; a buffet.

cuff[2] (kuf), *n.* [ME. *cuffe, coffe,* glove, mitten; origin uncertain.] A glove† or mitten†; a fold, band, or variously shaped piece serving as a trimming or finish for a sleeve at the wrist; a turned-up fold at the bottom of trouser-legs, etc.; a separate or detachable band or piece of linen or other material worn about the wrist, inside or outside of the sleeve; the part of a gauntlet or long glove that extends over the wrist; a handcuff.

Cu-fic, Ku-fic (kū'fik). **I.** *a.* Of or pertaining to Cufa, or Kufa, an old city south of Babylon: applied esp. to a form of Arabic characters employed by the copyists of Cufa in transcribing the Koran. **II.** *n.* The Cufic characters collectively.

cui bo-no? (kī bō'nō). [L., 'to whom (is it) for a benefit?'] For whose benefit? also, loosely, for what use? of what good?—a phrase sometimes used adjectively (as, *cui bono* considerations) and as a noun (as, "Will you allow me . . . to inquire into the *cui bono* of all the pains and expense you have incurred?" Peacock's "Nightmare Abbey," vii.).

cui-rass (kwē-ras'), *n.* [OF. *cuirace* (F. *cuirasse*), < LL. *coriacea,* fem. of *coriaceus,* made of leather, E. *coriaceous.*] A piece of defensive armor for the body, combining a breastplate and a piece for the back; sometimes, the breastplate alone; also, any similar covering, as the protective armor of a ship.—**cui-rass',** *v. t.* To equip or cover with a cuirass.—**cui-ras-sier** (kwē-rạ-sēr'), *n.* [F.] A cavalry soldier wearing a cuirass; a soldier of a class of heavy cavalry in France, etc.

Ancient Greek Cuirasses. — From a cup, 5th century B. C., in Berlin Museum.

cuir=bou-illi (kwēr-bö-yē), *n.* [F. *cuir bouilli,* 'leather boiled.'] Leather boiled or soaked in hot water and pressed into any required shape, which it is capable of retaining on becoming dry: owing to its extreme hardness it offers considerable resistance to cuts, blows, etc.

cuish (kwish), *n.* Same as *cuisse.*

cui-sine (kwi-zēn', F. kwē-zēn), *n.* [F., < ML. *cocina,* L. *coquina,* kitchen: see *kitchen.*] The kitchen; the culinary department of a house, hotel, etc.; also, style of cooking; cookery.

cuisse (kwis), *n.* [OF. *cuissaux*, pl. of *cuissel*, < *cuisse*, thigh, < L. *coxa*, hip.] A piece of armor to protect the thigh.

cui-tle (kü′tl), *v. t.*; *-tled*, *-tling*. [Prob. = *kittle*.] To wheedle, cajole, or coax. [Sc.]

culch (kulch), *n.* [Origin uncertain.] Rubbish or refuse (chiefly prov. Eng.); the stones, old shells, etc., forming an oyster-bed and furnishing points of attachment for the spawn of the oyster; also, the spawn.—**culch,** *v. t.* To prepare (an oyster-bed) with culch.

Cul-dee (kul′dē), *n.* [NL. *Culdei*, pl., earlier *Keldei*, < OIr. *cēle dē*, companion (or servant) of God.] One of a class of anchorites or hermits existing in Ireland, Scotland, and Wales from the 8th to the 16th century.—**Cul-de′an,** *a.*

cul=de=sac (kü-dė-sȧk, often kül-), *n.*; pl. *culs-* (kü-, often kül-). [F., 'bottom of sack.'] A sac-like cavity, tube, or the like, open only at one end, as the cæcum; also, a street, lane, or other passage closed at one end; *milit.*, the situation of a military force hemmed in on all sides except behind.

-cule. [F. *-cule*, < L. *-culus*, *-cula*, *-culum*.] A diminutive suffix of nouns, as in *animalcule*, *molecule*, *poeticule*. Cf. *-ule*.

cu-let (kū′let), *n.* [Dim. of F. *cul*, bottom: cf. F. *culasse*, culet.] The flat face forming the bottom of a brilliant; also, the part of medieval armor protecting the back of the body below the waist.

cu-li-cid (kụ-lis′id). [NL. *Culicidæ*, pl., < L. *culex*, gnat.] **I.** *n.* Any of the *Culicidæ*, a family of dipterous insects including the mosquitoes, etc. **II.** *a.* Pertaining to the culicids; belonging to the *Culicidæ*.

cu-li-na-ry (kū′li-nạ̄-ri), *a.* [L. *culinarius*, < *culina*, kitchen.] Pertaining to the kitchen or to cookery; used in cooking.

cull (kul), *v. t.* [OF. *cuillir*, *coillir* (F. *cueillir*), < L. *colligere*, E. *collect*: cf. *coil*[1].] To choose or select; pick; also, to collect or gather; pluck; also, to gather the choice things or parts from.—**cull,** *n.* The act of culling; also, something culled; esp., something picked out and put aside as inferior.

cul-len-der (kul′ẹn-dėr), *n.* See *colander*.

cull-er (kul′ėr), *n.* One who culls, selects, or gathers; also, an inspector, as of timber.—**cull′ing,** *n.* The act of one that culls; also, something culled; esp., something picked out as inferior.

cul-lion (kul′yọn), *n.* [OF. *coillon* (F. *couillon*), < L. *coleus*, testicle.] A testicle†; also, a base or vile fellow (obs. or archaic: as, "Away, base *cullions!*" Shakspere's "2 Henry VI.," i. 3. 43).—**cul′lion-ly,** *a.*

cul-lis (kul′is), *n.* [OF. *coleis* (F. *coulis*), < L. *colare*, strain.] Broth of boiled meat strained.

cul-ly (kul′i), *n.*; pl. *cullies* (-iz). [Origin uncertain.] A man or fellow; also, one who is easily imposed upon or cheated; a dupe; a gull. [Slang or colloq.]

culm[1] (kulm), *n.* [ME. *culme*; perhaps akin to *coal*.] Soot (obs. or prov.); also, coal-dust or refuse coal; also, anthracite, esp. of inferior grade.

culm[2] (kulm), *n.* [L. *culmus*: cf. *halm*.] In *bot.*, a stem or stalk, esp. the jointed and usually hollow stem of grasses. —**cul-mif-er-ous** (kul-mif′ẹ-rus), *a.* [See *-ferous*.] Bearing culms.

cul-mi-nant (kul′mi-nạnt), *a.* Culminating; reaching the greatest altitude; topmost.

cul-mi-nate (kul′mi-nāt), *v.*; *-nated*, *-nating*. [LL. *culminatus*, pp. of *culminare*, crown, < L. *culmen*, *columen*, top, summit: see *column*.] **I.**† *tr.* To top, cap, or crown; bring to the highest point. **II.** *intr.* To reach the highest point, the summit, or the highest development; specif., to be on the meridian, or reach the highest or the lowest altitude, as a star.—**cul-mi-na′tion** (-nā′shọn), *n.* The act or fact of culminating; also, that in which anything culminates; the highest point; the acme.

cul-pa-ble (kul′pạ-bl), *a.* [OF. F. *coupable*, < L. *culpabilis*, < *culpare*, blame, censure, < *culpa*, fault.] Guilty†; also, deserving blame or censure; blameworthy.—**cul-pa-bil′i-ty** (-bil′i-ti), **cul′pa-ble-ness,** *n.*—**cul′pa-bly,** *adv.*

cul-prit (kul′prit), *n.* [First recorded as addressed to a prisoner who had pleaded not guilty, by a crown officer who apparently thus announced his readiness to prove the prisoner's guilt; said to come from an old legal formula abbreviated *cul. prit*, for AF. *culpable* (or L. *culpabilis*), guilty, and *prit* or *prist* (OF. *prest*), ready.] A person arraigned for an offense; hence, one guilty of an offense or fault; an offender.

cult (kult), *n.* [L. *cultus*, < *colere*, cultivate, till, care for, worship, inhabit.] Worship†; now, a particular system of religious worship, esp. with reference to its rites and ceremonies; hence, an instance of a fixed, almost religious veneration for a person or thing, esp. as manifested by a body of admirers (as, "A *cult* of him [Napoleon] as of something mystically heroic grew up after his death": H. G. Wells's "Outline of History," xxxviii. § 5); also, the object of such devotion.

cultch, *n.* and *v.* See *culch*.

cul-ti-va-ble (kul′ti-vạ-bl), *a.* Capable of being cultivated. Also **cul′ti-vat-a-ble** (-vā-tạ-bl).

cul-ti-vate (kul′ti-vāt), *v. t.*; *-vated*, *-vating*. [ML. *cultivatus*, pp. of *cultivare*, < *cultivus*, tilled, < L. *colere*: see *cult*.] To bestow labor upon (land) in raising crops; till; improve by husbandry; use a cultivator on; also, to promote or improve the growth of (a plant, etc.) by labor and attention; produce by culture; also, to develop or improve by education or training; train; refine; also, to promote the growth or development of (an art, science, etc.); also, to devote one's self to (an art, pursuit, practice, etc.); seek to promote or foster (acquaintance, friendship, etc.); seek the acquaintance or friendship of (a person).—**cul′ti-vat-ed** (-vā-ted), *p. a.* Subjected to cultivation, as land; also, produced or improved by cultivation, as a plant; also, improved by education or training; refined; cultured.—**cul-ti-va′tion** (-vā′shọn), *n.* The act or art of cultivating, or the state of being cultivated.—**cul′ti-va-tor,** *n.* One who or that which cultivates; specif., an agricultural implement for loosening the earth and destroying weeds when drawn between rows of growing plants.

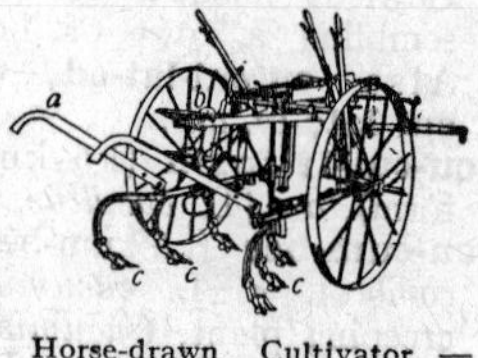

Horse-drawn Cultivator. — *a*, handles for operator when walking; *b*, seat for operator when riding; *c, c, c*, cultivator-teeth.

cul-trate (kul′trāt), *a.* [L. *cultratus*, knife-shaped, < *culter*, knife.] Sharp-edged and pointed, as a leaf. Also **cul′trat-ed** (-trā-ted).

cul-tur-a-ble (kul′ṭūr-ạ-bl), *a.* Susceptible of culture or cultivation; cultivable.

cul-tur-al (kul′ṭūr-ạl), *a.* Of or pertaining to culture or cultivation.—**cul′tur-al-ly,** *adv.*

cul-ture (kul′ṭūr), *n.* [L. *cultura*, < *colere*: see *cult*.] The action or practice of cultivating the soil; tillage; also, the raising of plants or animals, esp. with a view to their improvement; also, the cultivation of micro-organisms, as bacteria, for scientific study, medicinal use, etc.; the product or growth resulting from such cultivation; also, development or improvement by education or training; enlightenment or refinement resulting from such development; a particular state or stage of this, as in the case of a certain nation or period; also, in a map, all those features represented which are artificial or of human origin, such as meridians, parallels, and symbols for roads, bridges, etc.—**cul′ture,** *v. t.*; *-tured*, *-turing*. To subject to culture; cultivate. —**cul′tured,** *p. a.* Cultivated; enlightened or refined. —**cul′tur-ist,** *n.* A cultivator; also, an advocate or devotee of culture.—**cul′ture-less,** *a.* Without culture.

cul-tus (kul′tus), *n.* [L.: see *cult*.] A cult.

cul-tus=cod (kul′tus-kod), *n.* [Chinook *cultus*, worthless.] A common marine food-fish, *Ophiodon elongatus*, of the Pacific coast of the U. S.

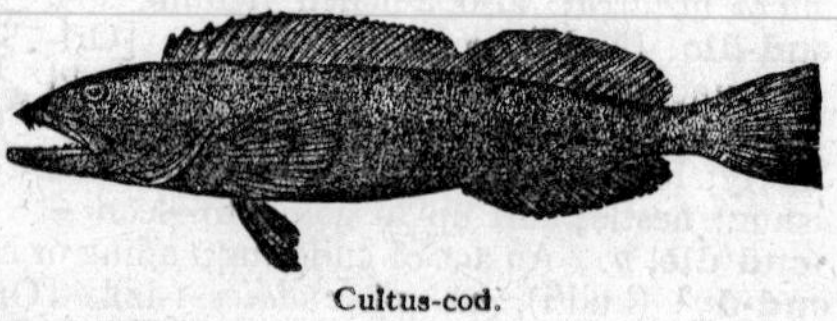
Cultus-cod.

cul-ver[1] (kul′vėr), *n.* [AS. *culfre*.] A dove; a pigeon.

cul-ver[2]† (kul′vėr), *n.* Same as *culverin*.

cul-ver-in (kul′vẹ-rin), *n.* [OF. F. *coulevrine*, < *couleuvre*, < L. *colubra*, serpent: cf. *cobra*.] A rude form of musket, also a kind of heavy cannon, formerly in use.—**cul″ver-**

in-eer′ (-ēr′), *n.* A soldier armed with or in charge of a culverin.

Cul-ver's=root (kul′vėrz-röt), *n.* [From a Dr. *Culver.*] The root of a tall scrophulariaceous herb, *Veronica virginica*, used in medicine as a cathartic and emetic; also, the plant.

cul-vert (kul′vėrt), *n.* [Origin uncertain.] A drain crossing under a road, etc., for the passage of water; a sewer; a conduit.

cum (kum), *prep.* [L.] With; together with; including: used sometimes in financial phrases, as *cum dividend*, etc., which are often abbreviated simply *cum.* Cf. *ex.*

Cu-mæ-an (kū̦-mē′a̦n), *a.* Of or pertaining to the ancient city of Cumæ, in Italy: as, the *Cumæan* sibyl (one of the legendary women of antiquity whose authority in matters of divination was acknowledged by the Romans).

cum-ber (kum′bėr), *v. t.* [Appar. a shortened form of *encumber.*] To hinder or hamper; overload or burden; incommode or trouble.—**cum′ber,** *n.* The act of cumbering, or the state of being cumbered; hindrance; embarrassment or trouble (archaic); also, that which cumbers; a hindrance; a burden.—**cum′ber-er,** *n.*—**cum′ber-some** (-sum), *a.* Hindering† or obstructing†; burdensome or troublesome; unwieldy or clumsy.—**cum′ber-some-ly,** *adv.*—**cum′ber-some-ness,** *n.*—**cum′brous,** *a.* Cumbersome.—**cum′brous-ly,** *adv.*—**cum′brous-ness,** *n.*

cum-in, cum-min (kum′in), *n.* [L. *cuminum, cyminum,* < Gr. κύμινον.] A small apiaceous plant, *Cuminum cyminum*, bearing aromatic seed-like fruit ('cumin-seeds') used in cookery and medicine; the fruit or seeds; also, any of various similar plants of other genera.

cum-mer (kum′ėr), *n.* [OF. *coumere* (F. *commère*), < ML. *commater*, < L. *com-*, with, + *mater*, mother.] A godmother; a female companion; a woman; a girl or lass; also, a witch. [Sc.]

cum-mer-bund (kum′ėr-bund), *n.* [Hind. *kamarband*, 'loin band.'] In India, a shawl or sash worn as a belt round the waist.

cum-quat, kum-quat (kum′kwot), *n.* [From Chinese name meaning 'golden orange.'] A small, round or oblong orange with a sweet rind and acid pulp, used chiefly for preserves, being the fruit of *Citrus japonica*, a low rutaceous tree native in China and cultivated in Japan, California, etc.; also, the tree itself.

cum-shaw (kum′shâ), *n.* [Prob. from Chinese.] In Chinese ports, a present or gratuity.

cu-mu-late (kū′mū̦-lāt), *v. t.*; *-lated, -lating.* [L. *cumulatus*, pp. of *cumulare*, heap up, < *cumulus*, a heap.] To heap up; amass; accumulate.—**cu′mu-late,** *a.* Cumulated; heaped up.—**cu-mu-la′tion** (-lā′sho̦n), *n.* The act of cumulating; accumulation; also, a heap or mass.—**cu′mu-la-tive** (-lā̦-tiv), *a.* Increasing or growing by accumulation or successive additions; formed by or resulting from accumulation or the addition of successive parts or elements; also, increasing the amount, force, etc., of something else by forming an addition, or one of a number of successive additions, to it; also, pertaining to or characterized by accumulation.—**cumulative dividend,** a dividend which if not paid in full when due must be added to the following dividend.—**cumulative stock,** stock bearing cumulative dividends.—**cumulative system of voting,** a system which gives each voter as many votes as there are persons to be elected as a group to some representative office, allowing him to accumulate them on one candidate or to distribute them.—**cu′mu-la-tive-ly,** *adv.*—**cu′mu-la-tive-ness,** *n.*

cu-mu-lo=nim-bus (kū″mū̦-lō̦-nim′bus), *n.* [See *cumulus* and *nimbus.*] A cloud with a cumulus-like summit and a nimbus-like base, characteristic of thunder-storms.

cu-mu-lous (kū′mū̦-lus), *a.* Of the form of a cumulus cloud; composed of cumuli.

cu-mu-lus (kū′mū̦-lus), *n.*; pl. *-li* (-lī). [L., a heap.] A heap or pile; also, a cloud with summit dome-like or made up of rounded heaps, and with flat base, seen in fair weather.

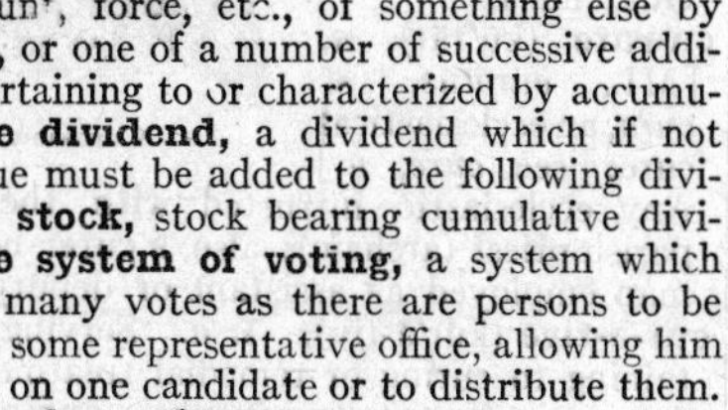

Cumulus.

cu-nab-u-la (kū̦-nab′ū̦-lā̦), *n.* [L., pl., dim. of *cunæ*, cradle.] A cradle; fig., the earliest abode.

cunc-ta-tion (kungk-tā′sho̦n), *n.* [L. *cunctatio(n-)*, < *cunctari*, delay.] Tardy action; delay.—**cunc′ta-tive** (-tā̦-tiv), **cunc′ta-to-ry** (-tō̦-ri), *a.* Given to cunctation or delay.—**cunc-ta′tor,** *n.* [L.] One who acts tardily; a delayer.

cunc-tip-o-tent (kungk-tip′ō̦-te̦nt), *a.* [LL. *cunctipotens* (*-ent-*), < L. *cunctus*, all, + *potens*, E. *potent.*] All-powerful; omnipotent. [Archaic.]

cu-ne-al (kū′nē̦-a̦l), *a.* [L. *cuneus*, wedge.] Wedge-like; wedge-shaped.

cu-ne-ate (kū′nē̦-āt), *a.* [L. *cuneatus*, pp. of *cuneare*, make wedge-shaped, < *cuneus*, wedge.] Wedge-shaped; of leaves, triangular, and tapering to a point at the base. Also **cu′ne-at-ed** (-ā-ted).—**cu′ne-ate-ly,** *adv.*—**cu-ne-at′ic** (-at′ik), *a.* Cuneiform.

Cuneate Leaf.

cu-ne-i-form (kū′nē̦-i-fôrm or kū̦-nē′-). [L. *cuneus*, wedge: see *-form.*] **I.** *a.* Having the form of a wedge; wedge-shaped, as the characters anciently used in writing in Persia, Assyria, etc.; noting or pertaining to this kind of writing; in *anat.*, noting or pertaining to any of various wedge-shaped bones, as of the tarsus. **II.** *n.* Cuneiform characters or writing; in *anat.*, a cuneiform bone.—**cu′ne-i-form-ist,** *n.* One versed in the subject of cuneiform writing.

Assyrian Cuneiform Characters.

cu-nic-u-lus (kū̦-nik′ū̦-lus), *n.*; pl. *-li* (-lī). [L., underground passage, burrow, orig. rabbit: cf. *cony.*] An underground passage, as a burrow or a drain.

cun-ner (kun′ėr), *n.* [Origin obscure.] Either of two small marine food-fishes, *Crenilabrus melops*, of the British coasts, and *Tautogolabrus adspersus*, of the Atlantic coast of North America.

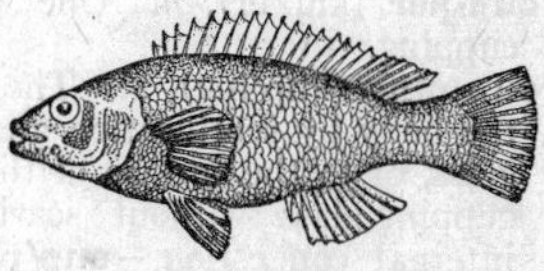

Cunner (*Tautogolabrus adspersus*).

cun-ning (kun′ing), *n.* [ME., verbal noun of *cunnen*, < AS. *cunnan*, know, be able: see *can*[1].] Knowledge†; also, ability, skill, or expertness; also, an art† or craft†; also, skill employed in a crafty manner; skilful deceit; skilfulness in deceiving; craftiness; guile.—**cun′ning,** *a.* [ME., ppr. of *cunnen.*] Having knowledge†; learned†; also, skilful, expert, or clever (archaic); also, exhibiting or wrought with ingenuity; also, artfully subtle or shrewd; crafty; sly; guileful; also, quaintly pleasing or attractive, as a child or something little (colloq., U. S.).—**cun′ning-ly,** *adv.*—**cun′ning-ness,** *n.*

cup (kup), *n.* [AS. *cuppe*, < ML. *cuppa, cupa*, cup, L. *cupa*, tub, cask.] A small, open vessel, as of porcelain or metal, used esp. to drink from, made either with or without a handle, and sometimes with but commonly without a stem and foot; the chalice used in the eucharist; a loving-cup; an ornamental cup or other vessel or article, as of precious metal, offered as a prize for a contest; the containing part of a goblet or the like; also, any cup-like utensil, organ, part, cavity, etc.; a cupping-glass; also, a cup with its contents; the quantity contained in a cup; the wine of the eucharist; any of various beverages, as a mixture of wine and various ingredients (as, claret-*cup*); fig., something to be partaken of or endured, as suffering; *pl.*, the drinking of intoxicating liquors; also, a state of intoxication; *sing.* [*cap.*], in *astron.*, the southern constellation Crater.—**cup,** *v.*; *cupped, cupping.* **I.** *tr.* To take or place in or as in a cup; also, to use a cupping-glass on; also, to supply with cups, as of liquor†. **II.** *intr.* To become cup-shaped; also, to use a cupping-glass.—**cup′=bear″er,** *n.* One who carries a cup; an attendant who fills and hands the cups in which drink is served.—**cup-board** (kub′o̦rd), *n.* A board or table for holding cups, etc.†; a closet with shelves for dishes, etc.; any small closet or cabinet.—**cupboard love,** love inspired by considerations of good feeding; interested affection.

cu-pel (kū′pel), *n.* [F. *coupelle*, < ML. *cupella*, dim. of *cupa*, *cuppa*, E. *cup*.] A small, cup-like porous vessel, usually made of bone-ash, used in assaying, as for separating gold and silver from lead; also, a receptacle or furnace-bottom in which silver is refined.—**cu-pel** (kū′pel or kū̦-pel′), *v. t.*; *-peled* or *-pelled*, *-peling* or *-pelling*. To heat or refine in a cupel.—**cu-pel-la′tion** (-pe-lā′shọn), *n.*

cup-ful (kup′fůl), *n.*; pl. *-fuls*. A quantity sufficient to fill a cup.

Cu-pid (kū′pid), *n.* [L. *Cupido*, lit. 'desire, passion,' < *cupere*, desire.] The Roman god of love, son of Venus, commonly represented as a winged boy with bow and arrows; also [*l. c.*], a similar winged being, or a representation of one, esp. as symbolical of love.

Cupid.—Vatican Museum, Rome.

cu-pid-i-ty (kū̦-pid′i-ti), *n.* [F. *cupidité*, < L. *cupiditas*, < *cupidus*, desirous, < *cupere*, desire.] Eager or inordinate desire, esp. to possess something (as, "They gazed with envy and *cupidity* at the noble mansions": J. H. Newman's "Callista," xvii.); covetous greed; passion for gain.

cu-po-la (kū′pō̤-lạ̈), *n.*; pl. *-las*. [It., dome, < LL. *cupula*, dim. of L. *cupa*, tub, cask.] A rounded vault or dome constituting, or built upon, a roof; a small dome-like or tower-like structure on a roof; any of various dome-like structures, organs, etc.; a furnace for melting cast-iron, etc.—**cu′po-laed** (-lạ̈d), *a.* Having a cupola.

cupped (kupt), *a.* Hollowed out like a cup; cup-shaped.

cup-per (kup′ėr), *n.* One who performs the operation of cupping.

cup-ping (kup′ing), *n.* The process of drawing blood from the body by scarification and the application of a cupping-glass, or to the surface of the body by the application of a cupping-glass without scarification, as for the relief of internal congestion.—**cup′ping=glass,** *n.* A glass vessel in which a partial vacuum is created, as by heat, used in the process of cupping.

cup=plant (kup′plant), *n.* A tall yellow-flowered asteraceous plant, *Silphium perfoliatum*, of the U. S., with large opposite leaves, the upper pairs being connate at their base and forming a cup-like cavity.

cup-py (kup′i), *a.* Cup-shaped; also, full of cup-like cavities; also, characterized by cup-shakes.

cu-pre-ous (kū′prē̦-us), *a.* [LL. *cupreus*, < *cuprum*, copper: see *copper*[1].] Consisting of or containing copper; also, copper-colored.

cu-pres-sin-e-ous (kū-pre-sin′ē̦-us), *a.* [NL. *Cupressineæ*, pl., < L. *cupressus*, cypress.] Of or pertaining to the *Cupressineæ*, or cypress tribe of trees and shrubs.

cu-pric (kū′prik), *a.* [LL. *cuprum*, copper: see *copper*[1].] Of or containing copper. See *cuprous*.—**cu-prif-er-ous** (kū̦-prif′ẹ-rus), *a.* [See *-ferous*.] Yielding copper.—**cu′-prite** (-prīt), *n.* A mineral consisting of native cuprous oxide, occurring in crystals and granular masses, and forming an important ore of copper.—**cu′prous,** *a.* Containing copper (in larger proportion than a corresponding cupric compound).

cu-prum (kū′prum), *n.* [LL.: see *copper*[1].] Copper: in *chem.*, abbreviated *Cu* (without period).

cup-seed (kup′sēd), *n.* A tall, climbing menispermaceous vine, *Calycocarpum lyoni*, of the southern U. S., bearing a large drupe which contains a bony seed hollowed out like a cup on one side.

cup=shake (kup′shāk), *n.* A crack or fissure sometimes occurring between the annual rings of a tree or timber.

cu-pule (kū′pūl), *n.* [NL. *cupula*, dim. of ML. *cupa*, *cuppa*, E. *cup*.] In *bot.*, a cup-shaped involucre consisting of indurated, cohering bracts, as in the acorn; also, an ascocarp shaped like the cup of an acorn, occurring in fungi of the genus *Peziza*, etc.; in *zoöl.*, a small cup-shaped sucker or similar organ or part.—**cu′pu-lar** (-pū̦-lạ̈r), *a.*

Cupules.—*a*, acorn-cupules; *b*, fungus-cupules (*Peziza*).

cur (kėr), *n.* [ME. *curre*, earlier *kur dogge*: cf. MD. *korre*, Sw. dial. *kurre*, dog, Icel. *kurra*, murmur, grumble, Sw. *kurra*, coo, croak, rumble.] A dog (now only in disparagement); a snarling, worthless, or outcast dog; hence, a low, despicable fellow (as, "What would you have, you *curs*, That like nor peace nor war?" Shakspere's "Coriolanus," i. 1. 172).

cur-a-ble (kūr′ạ-bl), *a.* [LL. *curabilis*.] That may be cured.—**cur-a-bil′i-ty** (-bil′i-ti), **cur′a-ble-ness,** *n.*—**cur′a-bly,** *adv.*

cu-ra-çao (kū-rạ-sō′), *n.* [From the island of *Curaçao*, north of Venezuela.] A cordial or liqueur flavored with the peel of the (bitter) Curaçao orange. Also (erroneously) **cu-ra-çoa′** (-sō′).

cu-ra-cy (kū′rạ̄-si), *n.*; pl. *-cies* (-siz). The office or position of a curate.

cu-ra-re, cu-ra-ri (kö-rä′rē̦), *n.* [S. Amer.] A blackish resin-like substance from *Strychnos toxifera* and other tropical plants of the genus *Strychnos*, used by South American Indians for poisoning arrows, and employed in physiological experiments, etc., for arresting the action of the motor nerves; also, a plant yielding it.—**cu-ra′rize** (-rīz), *v. t.*; *-rized*, *-rizing*. To administer curare to, as in vivisection.—**cu-ra-ri-za′tion** (-ri-zā′shọn), *n.*

cu-ras-sow (kū′rạ-sō or kū̦-ras′ō), *n.* [From the island of *Curaçao*: cf. *curaçao*.] Any of various large, arboreal, gallinaceous South and Central American birds constituting the subfamily *Cracinæ* (family *Cracidæ*), somewhat resembling the turkey and sometimes domesticated; also, an allied bird, *Oreophasis derbianus* ('mountain curassow'), the single species of the subfamily *Oreophasinæ* (family *Cracidæ*), inhabiting the high wooded parts of Guatemala.

Curassow (*Crax globicera*).

cu-rate (kū′rạ̄t), *n.* [ML. *curatus*, < *cura*, an ecclesiastical cure: see *cure*, *n.*] Any ecclesiastic intrusted with the cure of souls, as a parish priest (archaic); also, a curé; now, usually, a clergyman employed as assistant or deputy of a rector or vicar.

cur-a-tive (kūr′ạ̄-tiv). **I.** *a.* Serving to cure or heal; pertaining to curing or remedial treatment; remedial. **II.** *n.* A curative agent; a remedy.—**cur′a-tive-ly,** *adv.*—**cur′a-tive-ness,** *n.*

cu-ra-tor (kū̦-rā′tọr), *n.* [L., < *curare*: see *cure*, *v.*] A guardian, as of a minor, lunatic, etc.; also, a manager, overseer, or superintendent; also, the person in charge of a museum, art collection, etc.; a custodian.—**cu-ra-to-ri-al** (kū-rạ̄-tō′ri-ạl), *a.*—**cu-ra′tor-ship,** *n.* The office of a curator.—**cu′ra-to-ry** (-rạ̄-tọ̄-ri), *n.* The office of a curator; also, a body of curators.

curb[1]† (kėrb), *v. t.* or *i.* [OF. F. *courber*, < L. *curvare*, < *curvus*, bent, curved.] To curve, bend, or bow.

curb[2] (kėrb), *n.* [Appar. < *curb*[1], with some senses < F. *courbe*, curved piece in construction.] A chain or strap attached to the upper ends of the branches of a bit and passing under the horse's lower jaw, used in restraining the horse; hence, anything that restrains or controls; a restraint; a check; also, an inclosing framework or border; the framework round the top of a well; the border, as of stone, at the outer edge of a sidewalk, etc.; the sidewalk or street as a market for the sale of securities, as those not dealt in on the stock-exchange; in *vet. science*, a swelling on the lower part of the back of the hock of a horse, often causing lameness. —**curb**[2], *v. t.* To put a curb on (a horse); hence, to control as with a curb; restrain; check; also, to furnish with or protect by a curb or curbstone.—**curb′a-ble,** *a.* That may be curbed.—**curb′=bit′,** *n.* A bit having a curb.—**curb′er,** *n.*—**curb′ing,** *n.* The material, as stones, forming a curb.—**curb′-less,** *a.* Without curb; unrestrained.—**curb′=roof′,** *n.* A roof with two slopes to each face, the lower being the steeper. Cf. *mansard.* —**curb′stone,** *n.* One of the stones, or a range of stones, forming a curb, as along the outer edge of a sidewalk, etc.

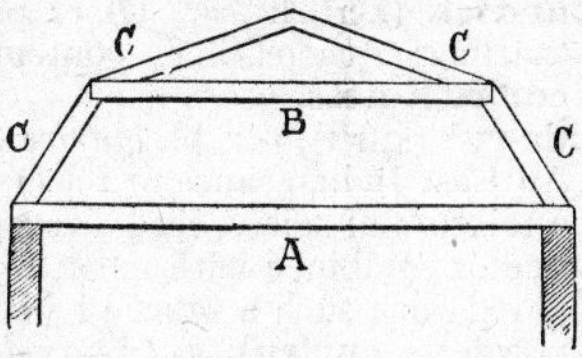

Diagram of Curb-roof. — *A, B,* tie-beams; *C, C,* rafters.

:ur-cu-li-o (kėr-kū′li-ō), *n.*; pl. *-os* (-ōz). [L., weevil.] Any snout-beetle or weevil; esp., one of various forms injurious to fruit, as *Conotrachelus nenuphar* ('plum-curculio').

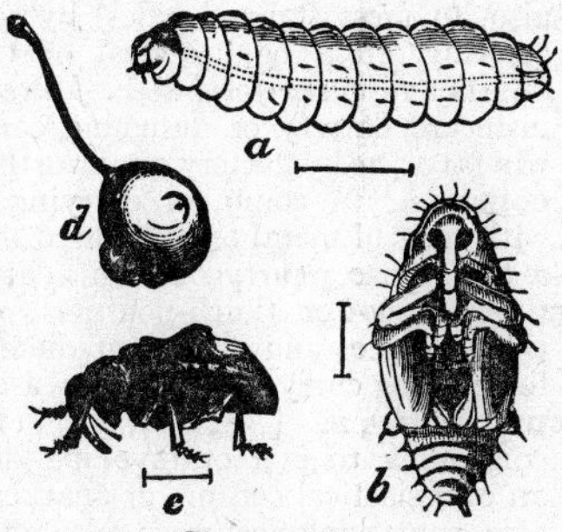

Plum-curculio.
a, larva; *b*, pupa; *c*, imago; *d*, plum and curculio, the plum bearing one of the punctures. (Lines show natural sizes.)

:ur-cu-ma (kėr′kụ̄-mạ̈), *n.* [NL., < Ar. *kurkum,* saffron, turmeric.] Any plant of the zingiberaceous genus *Curcuma,* of the East Indies, etc., as *C. longa* or *C. zedoaria,* the former yielding turmeric and the latter zedoary.—**cur′cu-min,** *n.* A yellow crystalline substance, the coloring matter of turmeric; also, an artificial yellow dye.

urd (kėrd), *n.* [ME. *crud*; origin uncertain.] A substance consisting of casein, etc., obtained from milk by coagulation, used for making into cheese or eaten as food (often in *pl.*); also, any substance resembling this.—**curd,** *v. t.* or *i.* To turn into curd; coagulate; congeal.

ur-dle (kėr′dl), *v. t.* or *i.*; *-dled, -dling.* [Freq. of *curd.*] To change into curd; coagulate; congeal.

urd-y (kėr′di), *a.* Like curd; full of or containing curd; coagulated.

ure (kūr), *n.* [OF. F. *cure,* < L. *cura,* care, charge, medical treatment, concern, anxiety, ML. an ecclesiastical cure.] Care† or concern†; charge†; spiritual charge or oversight of the people in a certain district, as a parish ('cure of souls'); the office or district of one exercising such care or oversight; also, a method or course of remedial treatment, as for disease; hence, successful remedial treatment; restoration to health; also, a means of healing or curing; a remedy; also, the act or a method of curing meat, fish, etc.—**cure,** *v.*; *cured, curing.* [OF. *curer* (F. *curer,* cleanse), < L. *curare* (pp. *curatus*), care for, have charge of, treat medically, cure.] **I.** *tr.* To care for†; restore to health; relieve or rid of something troublesome or detrimental, as a bad habit, etc.; also, to remove by remedial means, as a disease; remedy or eradicate (an evil); also, to prepare (meat, fish, etc.) for preservation, by salting, drying, etc.; vulcanize (caoutchouc, etc.). **II.** *intr.* To effect a cure; also, to become cured.

u-ré (kü-rā), *n.* [F., < ML. *curatus*: see *curate.*] In French use, a parish priest.

ure=all (kūr′âl), *n.* A cure for all ills; a panacea: as, "Men . . . expect . . . A wondrous *cure-all* in equality" (Lowell's "Cathedral," 755).

ure-less (kūr′les), *a.* Without cure; incurable.—**cure′-less-ly,** *adv.*

ur-er (kūr′ėr), *n.* One who or that which cures.

cu-ret-tage (kụ̄-ret′ạ̄j, F. kü-re-täzh), *n.* [F.] The process of curetting.

cu-rette (kụ̄-ret′), *n.* [F., < *curer,* cleanse: see *cure, v.*] A scoop-shaped surgical instrument for removing or scraping away foreign matter, granulations, etc., as from the walls of a cavity.—**cu-rette′,** *v. t.*; *-retted, -retting.* To scrape with a curette.—**cu-rette′ment,** *n.*

cur-few (kėr′fū), *n.* [OF. *cuevrefu* (F. *couvre-feu*), 'cover-fire.'] The ringing of a bell at a fixed hour in the evening as a signal for covering or extinguishing fires, as practised in medieval Europe; the ringing of an evening bell as later practised; the giving of a signal, esp. by a bell, at a certain hour in the evening, as for children to retire from the streets; also, the time of ringing, the bell itself, or its sound.

cu-ri-a (kū′ri-ạ̈), *n.*; pl. *curiæ* (-ē). [L. and ML.] One of the political subdivisions of each of the three tribes of ancient Roman citizens; the building in which such a division or group met, as for worship or public deliberation; the senate-house in ancient Rome; the senate of ancient Italian towns; in legal use, a court, as of justice or administration, esp. of medieval times; [*cap.*] the papal court; the Pope and those about him at Rome engaged in the administration of the papal authority.—**cu′ri-al,** *a.* Of or pertaining to a curia. —**cu′ri-al-ism,** *n.* A curial system; esp., the policy or system of the papal Curia; Vaticanism.—**cu′ri-al-ist,** *n.* —**cu″ri-al-is′tic,** *a.*

cu-rie (kū′rẹ̄, F. kü-rē), *n.* [From Mme. *Curie* (1867–1934), discoverer (with her husband, Pierre Curie, 1859–1906) of radium.] In *chem.,* a unit of radioactivity equal to the amount of emanation in equilibrium with one gram of radium.

Cu-rie (kū′rẹ̄, F. kü-rē) **point.** [From Pierre *Curie*: see *curie.*] In *physics,* the temperature at which a body, as iron, loses its magnetic susceptibility.—**Cu-rie's law.** In *physics,* the law that the magnetic susceptibility of gases is inversely proportional to the absolute temperature.

cu-ri-o (kū′ri-ō), *n.*; pl. *-os* (-ōz). [Short for *curiosity.*] Any article, object of art, piece of bric-à-brac, etc., valued as a curiosity.

cu-ri-o-log-ic (kū″ri-ọ̄-loj′ik), etc. See *cyriologic,* etc.

cu-ri-os-i-ty (kū-ri-os′i-ti), *n.*; pl. *-ties* (-tiz). [OF. *curiosete* (F. *curiosité*), < L. *curiositas,* < *curiosus*: see *curious.*] Carefulness†, or the exercise of care or pains†; accuracy†; skill†; fastidiousness†; the desire to learn or know about anything; inquisitiveness; also, delicacy, nicety, or elaborateness of construction (archaic); curious or interesting quality, as from strangeness; also, a subtlety†; a curious, rare, or novel thing (as, "I desired leave of this prince to see the *curiosities* of the island": Swift's "Gulliver's Travels," iii. 3).

cu-ri-ous (kū′ri-us), *a.* [OF. *curios* (F. *curieux*), < L. *curiosus,* careful, inquiring, inquisitive, < *cura*: see *cure, n.*] Exercising care or pains†; accurate†; expert†; fastidious†; cautious†; desirous of learning or knowing; often, inquisitive or prying; having the interest or knowledge of a connoisseur†; also, made or prepared with skill or art (archaic); marked by special care or pains, as an inquiry or investigation; marked by intricacy or subtlety†; excellent† or fine†; exciting attention or interest because of strangeness or novelty; odd; in booksellers' and collectors' catalogues, of books, indelicate, indecent, or obscene.—**cu′ri-ous-ly,** *adv.*—**cu′ri-ous-ness,** *n.*

curl (kėrl), *v.* [ME. *curlyd, crulled,* pp.; akin to D. *krullen,* G. *krollen,* Sw. *krulla,* curl.] **I.** *tr.* To form into ringlets, as the hair; also, to adorn with or as with curls or ringlets† (as, "The snaky locks That *curl'd* Megæra": Milton's "Paradise Lost," x. 560); also, to form into a spiral or curved shape; coil; make undulations in. **II.** *intr.* To form curls or ringlets, as the hair; also, to coil; become curved or undulated; also, to play at curling (Sc.).—**curl,** *n.* A ringlet of hair; also, anything of a spiral or curved shape; a coil; a convolution; an undulation; also, any of various diseases of plants in which the leaves, etc., curl up; also, the act of curling, or the state of being curled.—**curl′er,** *n.* One who or that which curls; also, a player at curling.

cur-lew (kėr′lū), *n.* [OF. F. *courlieu*; perhaps imit.] Any of the limicoline birds, with a long, slender, downwardly curved bill, which constitute the genus *Numenius,* of the snipe family, as *N. arquatus*, the common curlew of Europe, or *N. longirostris*, the 'long-billed curlew' of America; also, any of various similar birds.

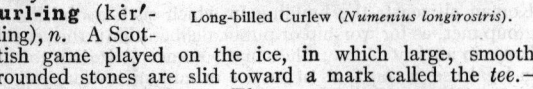

Long-billed Curlew (*Numenius longirostris*).

curl-i-cue (kėr'li-kū), *n.* [Appar. < *curly* + *cue*[2].] A fantastic curl or twist.

curl-i-ness (kėr'-li-nes), *n.* The state of being curly.

curl-ing (kėr'-ling), *n.* A Scottish game played on the ice, in which large, smooth, rounded stones are slid toward a mark called the *tee.*—**curl'ing=stone,** *n.* The stone used in the game of curling.

Curling-stone.

curl=pa-per (kėrl'pā"pėr), *n.* A piece of paper with which a lock of hair is rolled up tightly, to remain until it has become fixed in curl.

curl-y (kėr'li), *a.*; compar. *curlier*, superl. *curliest.* Curling or tending to curl; having curls.

curl'y-cue, *n.* See *curlicue.*

cur-mudg-eon (kėr-muj'ọn), *n.* [Origin unknown.] An avaricious, churlish fellow; a miser: as, "Let all be done liberally, for . . . I would be no *curmudgeon* in these matters" (Disraeli's "Lothair," xxii.).—**cur-mudg'eon-ly,** *a.*

cur-mur-ring (kėr-mėr'ing), *n.* [Imit.] A low, rumbling sound. [Sc.]

curn (kėrn), *n.* [= *corn*[1].] A grain; also, a small quantity or number. [Sc.]

curr (kėr), *v. i.* [Imit.] To make a low, murmuring sound, like the purring of a cat.

cur-rach, cur-ragh (kur'ạch or kur'ạ̈), *n.* [ME. *currok*: cf. Gael. *curach*, Ir. *corrach.*] A coracle. [Sc. and Ir.]

cur-ra-jong (kur'ạ-jông), *n.* See *kurrajong.*

cur-rant (kur'ạnt), *n.* [AF. (*raisins de*) *Corauntz*, (raisins of) Corinth: so called as coming from Corinth in Greece.] A small seedless raisin, produced chiefly in the Levant, used in cookery, etc.; also, the small, edible, acid round fruit or berry of certain wild or cultivated shrubs of the grossulariaceous genus, *Ribes*, as *R. rubrum* ('red currant'), *R. nigrum* ('black currant'), or *R. americanum* (also 'black currant'); the shrub itself; any of various similar fruits or shrubs.—**cur'rant=worm,** *n.* Any of several insect larvæ destructive to currants.

cur-ren-cy (kur'ẹn-si), *n.*; pl. *-cies* (-siz). [See *current.*] A running or flowing (obs. or rare); the fact or state of passing in time; also, the fact or quality of being passed on, as from person to person; circulation, as of coin; also, that which is current as a medium of exchange; the money in actual use; also, general acceptance; prevalence; vogue.

cur-rent (kur'ẹnt). [OF. *curant* (F. *courant*), < L. *currens* (*current-*), ppr. of *currere*, run.] **I.** *a.* Running or flowing (now rare); passing in time, or belonging to the time actually passing; also, passing from one to another; circulating, as coin; hence, genuine† or authentic†; also, publicly reported or known; prevalent; also, generally accepted; in vogue. **II** *n.* A flowing; flow, as of a river; also, that which flows, as a stream; a portion of a large body of water, or of air, etc., moving in a certain direction; fig., course, as of time or events; the main course; the general tendency; in *elect.*, a movement or flow of electricity.—**cur'rent-ly,** *adv.*

cur-ri-cle (kur'i-kl), *n.* [L. *curriculum*, a running, course, race, race-chariot, < *currere*, run.] A light two-wheeled carriage drawn by two horses abreast: as, "That *curricle*, with the greys and the outriders, is quite superb" (Marryat's "King's Own," xlvii.).

cur-ric-u-lum (ku-rik'ụ̄-lum), *n.*; pl. *-lums*, L. *-la* (-lạ̈). [L.: see *curricle.*] A course; esp., the regular or a particular course of study in a college, etc.

cur-ried (kur'id), *p. a.* Of food, prepared with curry or curry-powder.

cur-ri-er (kur'i-ėr), *n.* [OF. *corier*, < L. *coriarius*, tanner, currier, < *corium*, skin, hide, leather; now associated with *curry*[2].] One who dresses and colors leather after it is tanned; also, one who curries (a horse, etc.).—**cur'ri-er-y,** *n.* The occupation or business of a currier, or the place where it is carried on.

cur-rish (kėr'ish), *a.* Of or pertaining to a cur; cur-like; snarling; quarrelsome; contemptible.—**cur'rish-ly,** *adv.*—**cur'rish-ness,** *n.*

cur-ry[1] (kur'i), *n.*; pl. *curries* (-iz). [E. Ind. (Dravidian).] An East Indian sauce or relish in many varieties, containing a mixture of spices, seeds, vegetables, fruits, etc., eaten with rice or combined with meat, fish, or other food; a dish prepared with such a sauce or with curry-powder; also, curry-powder.—**cur'ry**[1], *v. t.*; *-ried, -rying.* To prepare (food) with a curry sauce or with curry-powder.

cur-ry[2] (kur'i), *v. t.*; *-ried, -rying.* [OF. *coreer, conreer*, put in order, dress, curry (F. *corroyer*), < *con-*, together, + *-reer* as in *areer*, E. *array, v.*] To rub and clean (a horse, etc.) with a comb; currycomb; also, to blandish† or flatter†; also, to dress (tanned hides) by soaking, scraping, beating, coloring, etc.; fig., to beat or thrash.—**to curry favor.** [Earlier *to curry favel* (OF. *fauvel*, a fallow horse), to use insincere flattery or designing complaisance.] To seek to win favor, as by flattery or unworthy complaisance.—**cur'ry-comb,** *n.* A comb for currying horses, etc., usually one with rows of metal teeth secured to a plate.—**cur'ry-comb,** *v. t.* To use a currycomb on; curry.

cur-ry=pow-der (kur'i-pou"dėr), *n.* A powdered preparation of spices and other ingredients, notably turmeric, used for making curry sauce or for seasoning food.

curse (kėrs), *n.* [AS. *curs*; origin uncertain.] An utterance consigning to evil or invoking divine vengeance; specif., an ecclesiastical censure or anathema; also, a profane oath; also, something accursed; also, evil inflicted as in response to an imprecation; a great evil; a bane.—**curse,** *v.*; *cursed* (sometimes *curst*), *cursing.* [AS. *cursian.*] **I.** *tr.* To pronounce a curse or utter an imprecation against; damn; specif., to anathematize or excommunicate; also, to utter maledictions against; swear at; also, to speak impiously against (the Deity, etc.); blaspheme; also, to afflict with great evil. **II.** *intr.* To utter curses; swear profanely.—**curs'ed,** *p. a.* Laid under a curse; damned; anathematized; afflicted; also, deserving a curse; damnable; execrable; abominable.—**curs'ed-ly,** *adv.*—**curs'ed-ness,** *n.*—**curs'er,** *n.*

cur-sive (kėr'siv). [ML. *cursivus*, < L. *currere*, run.] **I.** *a.* Of writing, written in a running or flowing hand, with the letters joined one to another. **II.** *n.* A cursive character; also, a manuscript written in cursive characters.—**cur'sive-ly,** *adv.*

cur-sor (kėr'sọr), *n.* [L., runner, < *currere*, run.] A runner†; a sliding part of a mathematical instrument.

cur-so-ri-al (kėr-sō'ri-ạl), *a.* [L. *cursorius*, < *cursor*, runner see *cursor.*] In *zoöl.*, fitted for running, as the limbs of an animal; having limbs adapted for running, as certain birds insects, etc.

cur-so-ry (kėr'sọ-ri), *a.* [L. *cursorius*: see *cursorial.*] Running about†; also, going rapidly over something, as a subject, without noticing details; hasty; superficial; also cursorial, as the limbs of an animal.—**cur'so-ri-ly,** *adv.*—**cur'so-ri-ness,** *n.*

curst (kėrst), *p. a.* Cursed; also, perverse, ill-tempered, or vicious (obs. or prov. Eng.: as, "It is said, 'God sends a *curst* cow short horns,'" Shakspere's "Much Ado about Nothing," ii. 1. 25).

curt (kėrt), *a.* [L. *curtus*, cut short, clipped, mutilated: cf. *short.*] Short or shortened; brief or terse, as speech, style etc.; unduly or rudely short, as speech, manner, etc., or a person.

cur-tail (kėr-tāl'), *v. t.* [Earlier *curtal*, < *curtal, a.*] To cut short; cut off the end or any part of; abridge; reduce; diminish; also, to deprive (*of*).—**cur-tail'er,** *n.*—**cur-tail'ment,** *n.*

cur-tail=step (kėr′tāl-step), *n.* [Origin uncertain.] The first or bottom step of a stair, when it is finished in a curved line at its outer end.

cur-tain (kėr′tạn), *n.* [OF. *curtine* (F. *courtine*), < LL. *cortina*, curtain.] A movable hanging piece of material used to screen, conceal, adorn, etc.; hence, anything serving to shut off, cover, or conceal (as, a *curtain* of artillery fire, a barrage); in *fort.*, the part of a wall or rampart connecting two bastions, towers, or the like; in *arch.*, a flat portion of a wall, connecting two towers, projecting structures, or the like.—**cur′tain,** *v. t.* To provide, shut off, conceal, or adorn with or as with a curtain or curtains.—**cur′tain=lec″ture,** *n.* A scolding given privately, orig. behind the bed-curtains at night, by a wife to her husband.—**cur′tain=rais″er,** *n.* A short play acted before a principal play.

cur-tal (kėr′tạl). [OF. *courtaut* (F. *courtaud*), < *court*, short, < L. *curtus*: see *curt*.] **I.** *a.* Short; shortened; abridged; brief; curt; also, having the tail docked, as a horse; having the tail cut short or cut off, as a dog; also, of a friar, wearing a short gown. [Obs. or archaic.] **II.** *n.* A curtal animal, as a horse or a dog; anything docked or cut short; a kind of short cannon formerly in use; an old musical instrument, a kind of bassoon. [Obs. or archaic.]

cur-tal=ax, cur-tle=ax (kėr′tạl-aks, kėr′tl-), *n.* A perverted form of *cutlass*. [Obs. or archaic.]

cur-tate (kėr′tāt), *a.* [L. *curtatus*, pp. of *curtare*, shorten, < *curtus*: see *curt*.] Shortened or reduced.

cur-ti-lage (kėr′ti-lāj), *n.* [OF. *cortillage*, < *cortil*, < ML. *cortile*, court, yard, < *cortis*, E. *court*.] In *law*, the area of land occupied by a dwelling and its yard and outbuildings, actually inclosed or considered as inclosed.

curt-ly (kėrt′li), *adv.* In a curt manner.—**curt′ness,** *n.*

curt-sy (kėrt′si), *n.* [= *courtesy*.] An obeisance made by women, consisting of a bending of the knees and a sinking of the body.—**curt′sy,** *v. i.*; *-sied*, *-sying*. To make a curtsy.

cu-rule (kū′röl), *a.* [L. *curulis*: cf. *currulis*, *curulis*, pertaining to a chariot, < *currus*, chariot.] Noting a special form of chair or seat used by the highest magistrates of ancient Rome; also, privileged to sit in such a chair; hence, in general, of the highest rank.

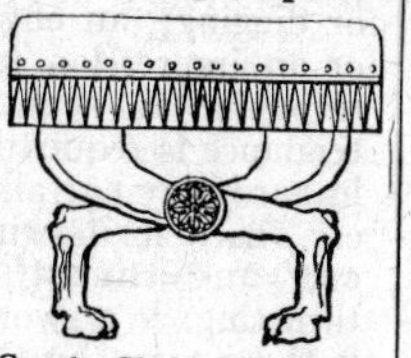
Curule Chair, from drawing found in Pompeii.

cur-vate, cur-vat-ed (kėr′vāt, -vā-ted), *a.* [L. *curvatus*, pp.: see *curve*, *v.*] Curved; bent in a regular form.—**cur-va′tion** (-vā′shọn), *n.* [L. *curvatio*(*n*-).] A curving or being curved.

cur-va-ture (kėr′vạ-t̩ūr), *n.* [L. *curvatura*.] The act of curving; curved condition; degree of curving; a curve or bend.

curve (kėrv). [L. *curvus*, bent, curved.] **I.** *a.* Bending or bent into rounded form; curved. [Now rare.] **II.** *n.* A continuously bending line, without angles; in mathematical usage, a line no part of which is straight; a line or lines capable of being defined by an equation or equations; the path of a moving point; in general, a curved outline, form, thing, or part; a curved ruler used by draftsmen; also, a curving; in *baseball*, the curved course (other than the ordinary one due to the force of gravity) given to a ball by the pitcher; a curved ball.—**curve,** *v. t.* or *i.*; *curved*, *curving*. [L. *curvare* (pp. *curvatus*), bend, curve, < *curvus*.] To bend in a curve; cause to take, or take, the course of a curve.—**curv′ed-ness,** *n.*

cur-vet (kėr′vet or kėr-vet′), *n.* [It. *corvetta*, < L. *curvus*, bent, curved.] A leap of a horse in which the fore legs are raised together and equally advanced, and then, as they are falling, the hind legs are raised with a spring, so that all the legs are off the ground at once; fig., a prank or frolic.—**cur-vet** (kėr-vet′ or kėr′vet), *v.*; *-vetted* or *-veted*, *-vetting* or *-veting*. **I.** *intr.* To leap in a curvet, as a horse; cause one's horse to do this; fig., to leap and frisk. **II.** *tr.* To cause to make a curvet.

curvi-. Form of L. *curvus*, curved, used in combination.—**cur-vi-fo-li-ate** (kėr-vi-fō′li-ạt), *a.* [+ L. *folium*, leaf.] In *bot.*, having curved leaves.—**cur′vi-form,** *a.* [+ *-form*.] Having a curved form.—**cur-vi-lin′e-al** (-lin′ẹ-ạl), *a.* Curvilinear.—**cur-vi-lin′e-ar** (-ạr), *a.* [+ L. *linea*, line.] Forming, or moving in, a curved line; formed or characterized by curved lines.—**cur-vi-lin′e-ar-ly,** *adv.*—**cur-vi-ros′tral** (-ros′trạl), *a.* [+ L. *rostrum*, beak.] Having a curved bill, as certain birds.

cus-cus (kus′kus), *n.* [Pers. and Hind. *khaskhas*.] The long, fibrous, aromatic roots of an East Indian grass, *Andropogon squarrosus*, used for making hangings, screens, etc.

cush-at (kush′ạt or kůsh′ạt), *n.* [AS. *cūscote*.] The ring-dove, *Columba palumbus*.

cu-shaw (ků-shâ′), *n.* [N. Amer. Ind.] Any of various long-necked squashes, esp. varieties of *Cucurbita moschata*.

cush-ion (kůsh′ọn), *n.* [OF. *cussin*, *coissin* (F. *coussin*), < ML. *coxinus*, < L. *coxa*, hip.] A bag-like case of cloth, leather, or rubber, filled with feathers, wool, air, etc., used to support or ease the body in reclining, sitting, or kneeling; also, anything that serves the same purposes, or that resembles this in appearance, properties, or use; a pillow used in lace-making; a pincushion; a pad, as one worn under the hair by women; the elastic raised rim of the top of a billiard-table; something to counteract sudden shock, jar, or jolt, as in machinery; a body of air or steam serving as an elastic check or buffer.—**cush′ion,** *v. t.* To place on or support by a cushion; furnish with a cushion or cushions; check the motion of (a piston, etc.) by a cushion, as of steam; form (steam, etc.) into a cushion; also, fig., to suppress quietly, as by ignoring (as, "There my courage failed: I preferred to *cushion* the matter": C. Brontë's "Shirley," xxviii.).—**cush′ion-y,** *a.* Cushion-like; soft and elastic.

cush-y (kůsh′i), *a.* [Cf. *cushion*.] Soft; comfortable; easy: as, a *cushy* job. [Slang.]

cusk (kusk), *n.* [Origin unknown.] An edible marine fish, *Brosme brosme*, of both coasts of the northern Atlantic; also, the American burbot, *Lota maculosa*.

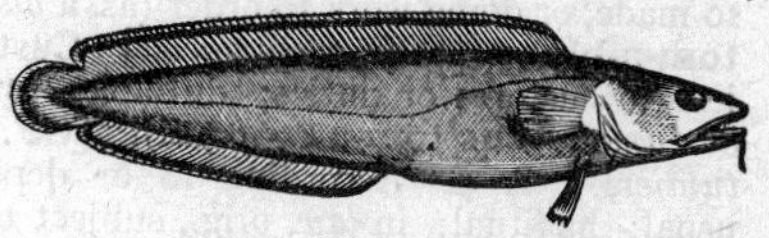
Cusk (*Brosme brosme*).

cusp (kusp), *n.* [L. *cuspis* (*cuspid-*), point.] A point or pointed end; in *astron.*, a point of a crescent, esp. of the moon; in *astrol.*, the entrance of a house in the calculation of nativities; in *geom.*, a point where two branches of a curve meet, end, and are tangent; in *arch.*, etc., a point or figure formed by the intersection of two small arcs or curved members, as one of the pointed projections sometimes decorating the internal curve of an arch; in *anat.*, *zoöl.*, and *bot.*, a point, projection, or protuberance, as on the crown of a tooth.—**cus-pate, cus-pat-ed** (kus′pāt, -pā-ted), *a.* Cusped.—**cusped,** *a.* Having a cusp or cusps; cusp-like.

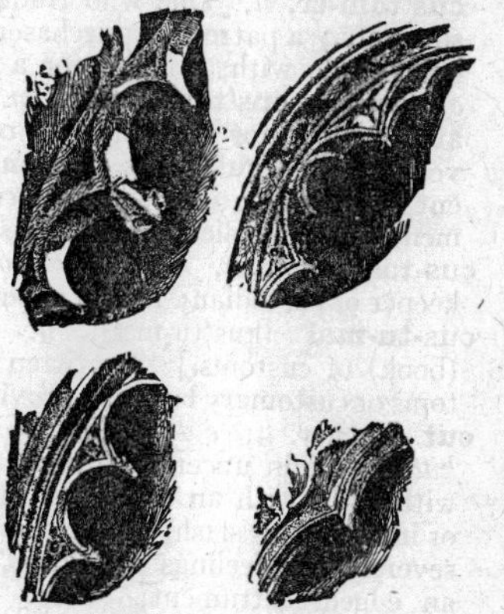
Architectural Cusps.

cus-pid (kus′pid), *n.* [L. *cuspis* (*cuspid-*): see *cusp*.] A cuspidate tooth; a canine tooth.—**cus′pi-dal** (-pi-dạl), *a.* Pertaining to, of the nature of, or having a cusp; cuspidate.—**cus′pi-date** (-dāt), *a.* Having a cusp or cusps; ending in a cusp or sharp point, as a canine tooth. Also **cus′pi-dat-ed** (-dā-ted).—**cus-pi-da′tion** (-dā′shọn), *n.* Decoration with cusps, as in architecture.

cus-pi-dor (kus′pi-dôr), *n.* [Pg., spitter, spittoon, < *cuspir*, < L. *conspuere*, spit upon: see *conspue*.] A spittoon.

cuss (kus), *n.* [Vulgar form of *curse*; in second sense associated by some with *customer*.] A curse; also, a fellow. [Colloq., U. S.]—**cuss,** *v. t.* or *i.* To curse. [Colloq., U. S.]—**cuss′ed-ly,** *adv.*—**cuss′ed-ness,** *n.* Viciousness; perversity. [Colloq., U. S.]

cus-so (kůs′ō), *n.* [Native name.] The dried pistillate inflorescence of an Abyssinian rosaceous tree, *Hagenia abyssinica*, used as a vermifuge, esp. to expel the tapeworm.

cus-tard (kus′tąrd), *n.* [For earlier *crustade* = F. *croustade*, kind of patty, = It. *crostata*, pie, tart; all < L. *crustata*, pp. fem. of *crustare*, cover with a crust, < *crusta*, E. *crust*.] A kind of pie or pasty†; a dish made of eggs and milk sweetened and baked or boiled.—**cus′tard=ap″ple,** *n.* The fruit of a small West Indian tree, *Anona reticulata*, having an edible yellowish pulp; the tree itself; also, some related tree or its fruit, as *Asimina triloba*, the North American papaw.

cus-to-di-al (kus-tō′di-ąl), *a.* Pertaining to custody.

cus-to-di-an (kus-tō′di-ąn), *n.* One who has the custody of something; a keeper or guardian.—**cus-to′di-an-ship,** *n.*

cus-to-dy (kus′tǫ-di), *n.* [L. *custodia*, < *custos* (*custod-*), keeper, guard.] Keeping or guardianship; charge; specif., the keeping or charge of officers of the law; detention by such officers, as of a person charged with an offense against the law; confinement.

cus-tom (kus′tǫm). [OF. *costume* (F. *coutume*), < L. *consuetudo* (*consuetudin-*), custom: see *consuetude*, and cf. *costume*.] **I.** *n.* A habitual practice, either of an individual or of a number of persons; a habit or usage; the usual way of acting in given circumstances; habits or usages collectively; also, a long continued usage which has become established and has acquired the force of law; such usages collectively; also, a customary tax, tribute, or service due by feudal tenants to their lord; toll or duty; *pl.*, duties imposed by law on imported or, rarely, exported goods; the governmental department employed in collecting such duties; *sing.*, habitual patronage of a particular shop, etc.; business patronage. **II.** *a.* Made specially for individual customers, or to order (as, *custom* shoes); dealing in things so made, or doing work to order (as, a *custom* tailor).—**cus′tom-a-ble,** *a.* [OF. *costumable*.] Customary†; also, subject to customs or duties; dutiable.—**cus′tom-al,** *n.* See *custumal*.—**cus′tom-a-ry** (-ą-ri). [OF. *costumier* (F. *coutumier*).] **I.** *a.* According to or depending on custom; usual; habitual; in *law*, orig., subject to customs or feudal dues; later, holding or held by custom, as of a manor; also, pertaining to or established by custom as distinguished from law. **II.** *n.*; pl. *-ries* (-riz). A book or document containing a collection of the legal customs or customary laws of a province, city, etc.; also, any body of such customs or laws.—**cus′tom-a-ri-ly,** *adv.*—**cus′tom-a-ri-ness,** *n.*—**cus′tom-er,** *n.* One who trades regularly at a particular shop, etc.; a patron; a purchaser or buyer; also, a person to have to do with, a fellow, or a chap (colloq.: as, a queer *customer*).—**cus′tom=house,** *n.* A government office, as at a seaport, for the collection of customs, the clearance of vessels, etc.—**cus′toms=u″nion,** *n.* A union of independent states or nations to effect common or similar arrangements for the collection of duties on imports, etc.

cus-tos (kus′tos), *n.*; pl. *custodes* (kus-tō′dēz). [L.] A keeper or custodian; also, a superior in the Franciscan order.

cus-tu-mal (kus′tū-mąl), *n.* [ML. (*liber*) *custumalis*, (book) of customs.] A written collection of the legal customs or customary laws of a province, city, etc.; a customary.

cut (kut), *v. t.*; *cut, cutting.* [ME. *cutten, kutten, kytten, kitten*; origin uncertain; prob. from Teut.] To penetrate with or as with an edged instrument; make an incision in or into; gash; slash; strike sharply, as with a whip; wound severely the feelings of; also, to divide with or as with an edged instrument; sever; carve (meat); dissolve or make miscible (as, to *cut* phlegm); also, to detach with or as with an edged instrument; separate from the main body; lop off; also, to pass through or across; cross; intersect; cleave (air, water, etc.); also, to shorten or reduce by cutting; trim; abridge; diminish, as a price; also, to make or fashion by cutting, as a statue, jewel, garment, etc.; hollow out, as a hole; perform or execute (as, to *cut* a caper or a dash); also, to refuse to recognize socially (colloq.); renounce or give up (colloq.); absent one's self from (colloq.); in *surg.*, etc., to castrate; also, to perform lithotomy on; in *card-playing*, to divide (a pack of cards) at random into two or more parts, by removing cards from the top.—**to cut off,** to separate; shut out; disinherit; intercept; interrupt; bring to a sudden end.—**to cut out,** to excise; hence, to omit; also, to supplant (a rival).—**to cut teeth,** to have the teeth grow through the gums.—**cut,** *v. i.* To penetrate or divide something as with an edged instrument; make an incision or division, as an edged instrument does; also, to admit of being cut, or turn out upon being cut; also, to strike sharply, as with a whip; also, to pass, go, or come (*across, through, in*, etc.); run away or make off (slang); also, of a horse, to interfere; in *card-playing*, to cut the cards.—**to cut up,** to turn out (well or badly) when cut up, as a carcass (used fig. of a deceased person, with reference to the estate left by him: as, "Our ancient friend, when dying, was declared, in whatever slang then prevailed, to *cut up* exceeding well," Trollope's "Warden," xv.); also, to behave (in a specified manner: colloq.); behave badly (colloq.); play pranks (colloq.).—**cut,** *p. a.* That has been subjected to cutting; divided into pieces by cutting; detached by cutting (as, *cut* flowers); reduced by or as by cutting (as, *cut* rates); fashioned by cutting; having the surface shaped or ornamented by grinding and polishing (as, *cut* glass); drunk (slang); in *bot.*, incised.—**cut and dried,** fig., fixed or settled in advance; lacking freshness or spontaneity.—**cut,** *n.* The act of cutting; a stroke or a blow, as with a knife, whip, etc.; an act, speech, etc., which wounds the feelings; an excision or omission of a part; a part excised or omitted; a piece cut off, esp. of meat; the quantity, as of lumber, cut; a reduction in price; also, a passage or course straight across (as, a short *cut*); also, the manner or fashion in which anything is cut; fig., style; manner; kind; also, the result of cutting, as an incision, wound, etc.; a passage, channel, etc., made by cutting or digging; an engraved block or plate for printing from or an impression from it (cf. *woodcut*); also, a refusal to recognize an acquaintance (colloq.); an absence when attendance is required (colloq.); also, a cutting of the cards in card-playing; also, one of several pieces of straw, paper, etc., used in drawing lots (as, to draw *cuts* for a thing).—**cut′=and=thrust′,** *a.* Designed for both cutting and thrusting, as a sword.

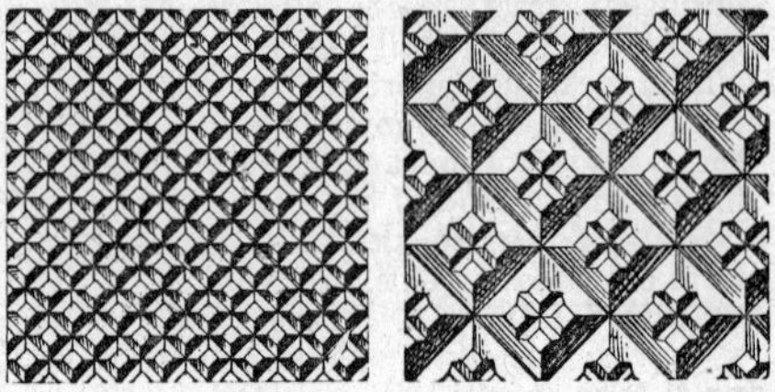

1 2

Two Standard Patterns of Cut Glass. — 1, table diamond cut; 2, strawberry diamond cut.

cu-ta-ne-ous (kū-tā′nẹ-us), *a.* [L. *cutis*, skin.] Of, pertaining to, or affecting the cutis or skin.—**cu-ta′ne-ous-ly,** *adv.*

cut-a-way (kut′ą-wā″). **I** *a.* Of a coat, having the skirt cut away from the waist in front in a curve or slope. **II.** *n.* A cutaway coat.

cut=back (kut′bak), *n.* A going back in the course of presenting a story, esp. by moving pictures, in order to bring up some event or period of the past.

cutch (kuch), *n.* [Malay *kāchu*.] Same as *catechu*.

cutch-er-ry, cutch-e-ry (ku-cher′i, kuch′ẹ-ri), *n.* [Hind. *kachahri*.] In India, a public administrative or judicial office; also, any administrative office.

cute (kūt), *a.*; compar. *cuter*, superl. *cutest*. [For *acute*.] Acute mentally; clever; shrewd; also, quaintly pleasing or attractive; 'cunning.' [Colloq.]—**cute′ly,** *adv.*—**cute′ness,** *n.*

cut=grass (kut′gràs), *n.* Any of various grasses with blades whose rough edges cut the flesh when drawn against it, esp. grasses of the genus *Homalocenchrus*, as *H. oryzoides* ('rice cut-grass').

cu-ti-cle (kū′ti-kl), *n.* [L. *cuticula*, dim. of *cutis*, skin.] The epidermis; also, any superficial integument, membrane, or the like; in *bot.*, a very thin hyaline film covering the surface of plants, and derived from the outer surfaces of the epidermal cells.—**cu-tic-u-lar** (kū-tik′ū-lär), *a.*

cu-tin (kū′tin), *n.* [L. *cutis*, skin.] A transparent waxy substance constituting together with cellulose the cuticle of plants.

cu-tis (kū′tis), *n.* [L., skin.] The corium or true skin, beneath the epidermis.—**cutis vera** (vē′rą). [L., 'true skin.'] The cutis.

cut-lass (kut′lạs), *n.* [F. *coutelas*, < OF. *coutel*, < L. *cultellus*: see *cutler*.] A short, heavy, slightly curved sword, used esp. at sea.

cut-ler (kut′lėr), *n.* [OF. F. *coutelier*, < ML. *cultellarius*, < L. *cultellus*, dim. of *culter*, knife.] One who makes, sells, or repairs knives and other cutting instruments.—**cut′ler-y,** *n.* [OF. *coutelerie* (F. *coutellerie*).] The art or business of a cutler; also, cutting instruments collectively.

cut-let (kut′let), *n.* [F. *côtelette*, dim. of *côte*, < L. *costa*, rib.] A slice of meat for broiling or frying, orig. one, as of mutton, containing a rib, but now commonly one cut from the leg, esp. of veal or mutton; also, a kind of croquette in a flattened form, made of minced chicken, lobster, or the like.

cut=off (kut′ôf), *n.* A cutting off, or something that cuts off; a shorter passage or way, as one across a bend; specif., the arresting of the passage of steam or working fluid to the cylinder of an engine, or the mechanism effecting it.

cut=out (kut′out), *n.* A cutting out; also, something that cuts out; a device for breaking an electric circuit or for eliminating part of it; a device in the exhaust-pipe of an internal-combustion engine exhausting through a muffler, which when open permits the engine to exhaust directly into the air; also, something cut out from something else.

cut-purse (kut′pėrs), *n.* One who stole by cutting purses (a practice common when men wore purses at their girdles); hence, a pickpocket.

cut-ter (kut′ėr), *n.* One who or that which cuts; also, a medium-sized boat for rowing or sailing, or a launch, belonging to a ship of war; a one-masted boat or vessel with a comparatively narrow and deep hull, rigged more or less like a sloop; a light-armed government vessel or steamship ('revenue cutter'), used to prevent smuggling and enforce the customs regulations; also, a small, light, commonly single-seated sleigh, usually for one horse.

cut-throat (kut′thrōt). **I.** *n.* One who cuts throats; a murderer. **II.** *a.* Murderous; hence, relentless (as, *cutthroat* competition).

cut-ting (kut′ing), *n.* The act of one who or that which cuts; also, something cut off; a small shoot cut from a plant to grow a new plant; a clipping from a newspaper, etc.; also, something produced by cutting; an excavation made through rising ground, as in constructing a road, etc. —**cut′ting,** *p. a.* That cuts; penetrating or dividing by or as by a cut; piercing, as a wind; wounding the feelings severely, as a remark.—**cut′ting-ly,** *adv.*

cut-tle (kut′l), *n.* [AS. *cudele.*] A cuttlefish.—**cut′tle-bone,** *n.* The calcareous internal shell or plate of true cuttlefishes, used to make powder for polishing, and fed to canaries to supply the necessary lime, etc.—**cut′tle-fish,** *n.*; pl. *-fishes* or (esp. collectively) *-fish.* Any of various decapod dibranchiate cephalopods, esp. of the genus *Sepia*, having sucker-bearing arms and the power of ejecting a black ink-like fluid when pursued; hence, any dibranchiate cephalopod, as the squid or the octopus.

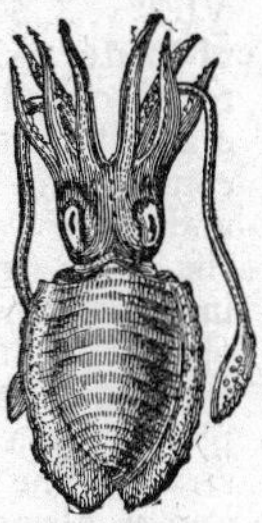

Cuttlefish of the Decapod Type (*Sepia officinalis*).

cut-ty (kut′i). [From *cut.*] **I.** *a.* Cut short; short; also, testy. [Chiefly Sc.] **II.** *n.*; pl. *cutties* (-iz). A short spoon; a short-stemmed tobacco-pipe; also, a term of reproach for a girl or a woman (as, "The great Babylonian madam is now, indeed, but a very little *cutty*": Galt's "Ayrshire Legatees," iv.). [Chiefly Sc.]—**cut′ty=stool,** *n.* A low stool; also, a seat in old churches in Scotland, where offenders against chastity, or other delinquents, had to sit and receive a public rebuke. [Sc.]

cut=up (kut′up), *n.* One who cuts up, or plays pranks. [Colloq.]

cut-wa-ter (kut′wâ″tėr), *n.* The fore part of a ship's stem or prow, which cuts the water; also, the sharp edge of a pier of a bridge, which resists the action of water or ice; also, the black skimmer (bird), *Rhynchops nigra* (see *skimmer*).

cut=work (kut′wėrk), *n.* A kind of openwork embroidery in which the ground is cut out about the pattern; also, appliqué work.

cut-worm (kut′wėrm), *n.* Any of various caterpillars of certain noctuid moths, which feed at night on the young plants of corn, cabbage, etc., cutting them off at or near the ground.

cy-an-am-ide (sī-ạn-am′īd or -id), *n.* [From *cyan(ogen)* + *amide.*] In *chem.*, a white crystalline compound prepared by the action of ammonia on cyanogen chloride.

cy-a-nate (sī′ạ-nāt), *n.* In *chem.*, a salt of cyanic acid.

cy-an-ic (sī-an′ik), *a.* [Gr. κύανος, dark-blue; in part with reference to *cyanogen.*] Blue (applied esp. to a series of colors in flowers, including the blues and all colors which tend toward blue); also, pertaining to or containing cyanogen (as, *cyanic* acid, HOCN).

cy-a-nide (sī′ạ-nīd or -nid), *n.* [From *cyan(ogen)* + *-ide.*] In *chem.*, a combination of cyanogen with an element or a radical: as, potassium *cyanide* (a powerful poison).—**cy′a-nide,** *v. t.*; *-nided, -niding.* To treat with a cyanide, as an ore in the process of extracting gold.

cy-a-nite (sī′ạ-nīt), *n.* [Gr. κύανος, dark-blue.] A mineral consisting of silicate of aluminium, occurring commonly in sky-blue, blade-shaped, triclinic crystals.

Cyanite, showing blade-like structure.

cyano-. Form of Gr. κύανος, a dark-blue substance, dark-blue, used in combination.

cy-an-o-gen (sī-an′ọ-jen), *n.* [F. *cyanogène*, < Gr. κύανος, dark-blue, + γεν-, bear, produce.] In *chem.*, a univalent radical, CN, consisting of one atom of carbon and one of nitrogen, and occurring in various compounds, some of which are blue; also, a poisonous, inflammable gas, C_2N_2.

cy-a-nom-e-ter (sī-ạ-nom′e-tėr), *n.* [See *cyano-* and *-meter.*] An instrument for measuring degrees of blueness, as of the sky.—**cy-a-nom′e-try,** *n.*

cy-a-nop-a-thy (sī-ạ-nop′ạ-thi), *n.* [See *cyano-* and *-pathy.*] Same as *cyanosis.*

cy-a-no-sis (sī-ạ-nō′sis), *n.* [NL., < Gr. κυάνωσις, dark-blue color, < κύανος: see *cyano-*.] In *pathol.*, blueness or lividness of the skin, as from imperfectly oxygenated blood. —**cy-a-not′ic** (-not′ik), *a.*

cy-an-o-type (sī-an′ọ-tīp), *n.* [See *cyano-* and *-type.*] A process of photographic printing in which a cyanide is employed, yielding prints which are usually blue in color; also, a print made by such a process.

cy-a-nu-ric (sī-ạ-nū′rik), *a.* [See *cyano-* and *uric.*] In *chem.*, noting or pertaining to a white crystalline acid, $C_3N_3O_3H_3$, obtained by heating urea and in other ways.

cy-cad (sī′kad), *n.* [NL. *Cycas* (*Cycad-*), the typical genus, < Gr. κύκας, erron. for κόϊκας, acc. pl. of κόϊξ, kind of palm.] Any of the *Cycadaceæ*, a family, order, or group of gymnospermous plants intermediate in appearance between the tree-ferns and the palms, the species commonly having a thick, unbranched columnar trunk which bears a crown of large pinnate

Cycad (*Cycas circinalis*).

leaves.—**cyc-a-da-ceous** (sik-ạ-dā'shius), *a.* Belonging to the *Cycadaceæ*, or cycad family or group of plants.

cyc-la-men (sik'lạ-men), *n.* [NL., < Gr. κυκλάμινος.] Any plant of the primulaceous genus *Cyclamen*, comprising low-growing herbs with tuberous rootstocks and nodding white, purple, pink, or crimson flowers with reflexed petals.

cy-cle (sī'kl), *n.* [LL. *cyclus*, < Gr. κύκλος, ring, circle, wheel, round, revolution, cycle: see *wheel*.] An orbit in the heavens; also, a round of years or a recurring period of time, esp. one in which certain events or phenomena repeat themselves in the same order and at the same intervals; hence, any long period of years; an age; also, any round of operations or events; a series which returns upon itself; any complete course or series; specif., one of the complete series of changes in the working fluid in the cylinder of an internal-combustion engine; also, a complete or double alternation or reversal of an alternating electric current; also, a series of poetic or prose narratives gathering round some mythical or heroic theme (as, the Arthurian *cycle*; the Charlemagne *cycle*); also, a bicycle, tricycle, or the like.—**cy'cle**, *v. i.*; *-cled, -cling.* To move or revolve in cycles; pass through cycles; also, to ride a bicycle, tricycle, or the like; travel by cycle.—**cy'cle=car**, *n.* A light automobile built somewhat on the order of a motor-cycle but having four wheels.—**cy'cler**, *n.*

cyc-lic (sik'lik), *a.* [F. *cyclique*, < L. *cyclicus*, < Gr. κυκλικός.] Of or pertaining to a cycle or cycles; revolving or recurring in cycles; characterized by recurrence in cycles; in *bot.*, arranged in whorls, as the parts of a flower; of a flower, having the parts so arranged; in *chem.*, noting or pertaining to a compound whose structural formula contains a closed chain or ring of atoms. Also **cyc'li-cal.**—**cyc'li-cal-ly**, *adv.*

cy-clist (sī'klist), *n.* One who reckons by cycles; one who recognizes the cyclic recurrence of certain phenomena; also, one who rides a bicycle, tricycle, etc.

cyclo-. Form of Gr. κύκλος, ring, circle, wheel, used in combination.

cy-clo-graph (sī'klọ-grȧf), *n.* [See *cyclo-* and *-graph*.] An arcograph; in *photog.*, a form of camera for obtaining a panoramic view of the periphery of an object, as a vase.

cy-cloid (sī'kloid). [Gr. κυκλοειδής, < κύκλος, circle, + εἶδος, form.] **I.** *a.* Resembling a circle; in *ichth.*, more or less circular in form, with concentric striations, as the scales of certain fishes; having such scales, as a fish. **II.** *n.* In *geom.*, a curve generated by a point in the circumference or on a radius or prolonged radius of a circle when the circle is rolled along a straight line and kept always in the same plane; in *ichth.*, a cycloid fish.—**cy-cloi'dal**, *a.*—**cy-cloi'dal-ly**, *adv.*

cy-clom-e-ter (sī-klom'e-tėr), *n.* [See *cyclo-* and *-meter*.] A device for recording the revolutions of a wheel and hence the distance traversed by a wheeled vehicle.

cy-clo-nal (sī'klō-nạl), *a.* Of, pertaining to, or of the nature of a cyclone; cyclonic.

cy-clone (sī'klōn), *n.* [Gr. κυκλῶν, ppr. of κυκλοῦν, move in a circle, < κύκλος: see *cycle*.] Orig., any of certain storms in which the wind was supposed to have a circular motion; now, an extensive horizontal movement of the atmosphere spirally around and toward a gradually progressing central region of low barometric pressure (cf. *anticyclone*), sometimes moderate in character, and sometimes violent, as a hurricane, tropical storm, etc. (distinguished from a *tornado*, which is less extensive and has its origin in a vertical disturbance of the atmosphere); popularly, a tornado.—**cy'clone=cel''lar**, *n.* A cellar or underground room or excavation made for refuge from tornadoes (cyclones).—**cy-clon'ic** (-klon'ik), *a.* Of, pertaining to, or resembling a cyclone. Also **cy-clon'i-cal.**—**cy-clon'i-cal-ly**, *adv.*—**cy-clo-nol'o-gy** (-klọ-nol'ọ-ji), *n.* [See *-logy*.] The science dealing with cyclones.—**cy-clo'no-scope** (-klō'nọ-skōp), *n.* [See *-scope*.] A device for determining the center of a cyclone.

cy-clo-pæ'di-a, etc. See *cyclopedia*, etc.

Cy-clo-pe-an (sī-klọ-pē'ạn), *a.* Of, pertaining to, or characteristic of the Cyclops; hence [sometimes *l. c.*], gigantic; vast; in *arch.*, noting, pertaining to, or resembling an early style of masonry employing massive stones more or less irregular in shape.

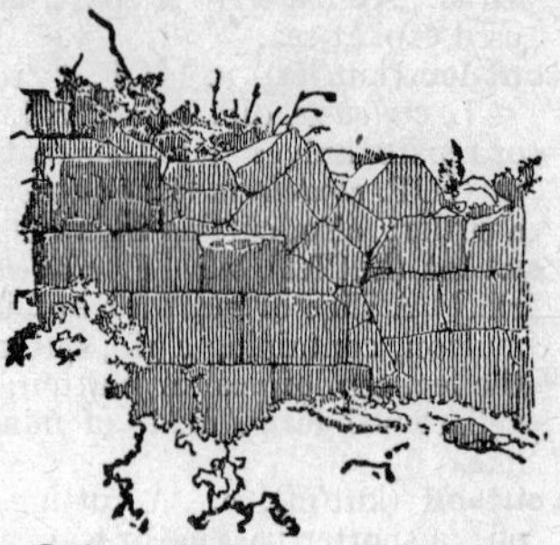

Cyclopean Masonry. — Walls of Assos, in the Troad (in northwestern Asia Minor).

cy-clo-pe-di-a, cy-clo-pæ-di-a (sī-klọ-pē'di-ạ), *n.* [NL., < Gr. κύκλος, circle, + παιδεία, education.] A work comprising articles on subjects from all branches of knowledge; an encyclopedia; sometimes, a work comprising articles on all the principal subjects of a particular branch of knowledge (as, a *cyclopedia* of botany).—**cy-clo-pe'dic, cy-clo-pæ'dic**, *a.*—**cy-clo-pe'dist, cy-clo-pæ'dist**, *n.*

Cy-clops (sī'klops), *n.*; pl. *Cyclops* or *Cyclopses*, L. *Cyclopes* (sī-klō'pēz). [L., < Gr. Κύκλωψ, lit. 'round-eyed,' < κύκλος, circle, + ὤψ, eye.] In *Gr. myth.*, one of a race of giants with but one eye, which was circular and in the middle of the forehead, fabled to have forged thunderbolts for Zeus and to have built the great prehistoric walls of Greece.—**Cy-clop'ic** (-klop'ik), *a.*

cy-clo-ra-ma (sī-klọ-rä'mạ), *n.* [Gr. κύκλος, circle, + ὅραμα, view.] A pictorial representation, in natural perspective, of a landscape, a battle, etc., on the inner wall of a cylindrical room or hall, the spectators occupying a position in the center.—**cy-clo-ram'ic** (-ram'ik), *a.*

cy-clo-stom-a-tous (sī-klọ-stom'ạ-tus), *a.* [See *cyclostome*.] Having a circular mouth; specif., belonging or pertaining to the *Cyclostomata* (see *cyclostome*). Also **cy-clos'to-mate** (-klos'tọ-māt).

cy-clo-stome (sī'klọ-stōm). [Gr. κύκλος, circle, + στόμα (στοματ-), mouth.] **I.** *a.* Having a circular mouth; specif., belonging or pertaining to the *Cyclostomata*, a group or class of eel-like aquatic vertebrates (the lampreys and hags) characterized by pouch-like gills and a circular suctorial mouth without hinged jaws. **II.** *n.* A cyclostome vertebrate; a lamprey or a hag.—**cy-clos'to-mous** (-klos'tọ-mus), *a.* Cyclostomatous.

cy-clo-style (sī'klọ-stīl), *n.* [See *cyclo-* and *style*.] A manifolding device consisting of a kind of pen with a small toothed wheel at the end which cuts minute holes in a specially prepared paper stretched over a smooth surface, thus forming a stencil from which copies are printed.

cyg-net (sig'net), *n.* [Dim. of F. *cygne*, < L. *cygnus*, *cycnus*, < Gr. κύκνος, swan.] A young swan: as, "So doth the swan her downy *cygnets* save" (Shakspere's "1 Henry VI.," v. 3. 56).

cyl-in-der (sil'in-dėr), *n.* [L. *cylindrus*, < Gr. κύλινδρος, roller, cylinder, < κυλίνδειν, roll.] A geometrical solid generated by the revolution of a rectangle about one of its sides, constituting a figure inclosed by two parallel circular bases and a curved surface whose elements are perpendicular to the bases ('right circular cylinder'); a similar solid in which the elements of the curved surface are oblique to the circular bases ('oblique circular cylinder'); any solid bounded by two parallel planes and a curved surface generated by a moving straight line which constantly touches a fixed curve and is always parallel to its original position; a curved surface generated in this manner; also, any cylinder-like object or part, whether solid or hollow; the rotating part of a revolver, which contains the chambers for the cartridges; the chamber in an engine in which the working fluid acts upon the piston; in certain printing-presses, a rotating cylinder which produces the impression under which a flat form to be printed from passes, or either of two cylinders, one carrying a curved form or plate to be printed from, which rotate against each other in opposite directions.—**cyl'in-der**, *v. t.* To furnish with a cylinder or cylinders; also, to subject to the action of a cylinder or cylinders.—**cy-lin-dric, cy-lin-dri-cal** (si-lin'drik, -dri-kạl), *a.* [Gr. κυλινδρικός.] Of, pertaining to, or of the form of a cylinder.—**cy-lin'dri-cal-ly**, *adv.*—**cyl'in-droid.** [Gr.

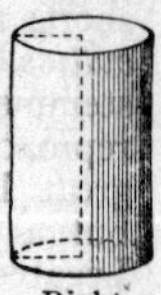

Right Circular Cylinder.

κυλινδροειδής: see *-oid*.] **I.** *a.* Resembling a cylinder; pertaining to or of the nature of a cylindroid. **II.** *n.* A solid having the form of a cylinder with equal and parallel elliptical bases.

cy-lix (sī'liks or sil'iks), *n.*; pl. *cylices* (sil'i-sēz). [Gr. κύλιξ.] In *Gr. antiq.*, a drinking-cup, usually broad and shallow, with or without a stem and foot, and provided with two handles not extending above the rim.

Cylix. — Museum of Fine Arts, Boston.

Cyl-le-ni-an (si-lē'ni-an), *a.* [L. *Cyllenius.*] Pertaining to Mount Cyllene, in northern Peloponnesus, Greece, or to the god Hermes, reputed to have been born there.

cy-ma (sī'mạ̈), *n.*; pl. *-mæ* (-mē). [NL., < Gr. κῦμα, something swollen, wave, waved molding, sprout, < κυεῖν, be pregnant.] In *arch.*, a molding whose profile is an ogee (called a *cyma recta* when concave at the top, and a *cyma reversa* when convex at the top); in *bot.*, a cyme.—**cy'ma-graph** (-mạ-gráf), *n.* [See *-graph.*] An instrument for tracing the outline or contour of moldings, profiles, etc.

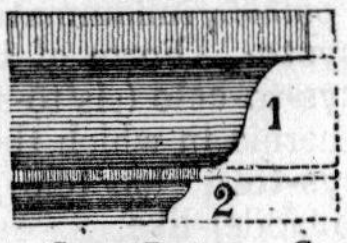

1, Cyma Recta; 2, Cyma Reversa.

cy-mar (si-mär'), *n.* See *simar.*

cy-ma-ti-um (sī-mā'shi-um or si-), *n.*; pl. *-tia* (-shi-ạ̈). [L., < Gr. κυμάτιον, dim. of κῦμα, E. *cyma.*] In *arch.*, a cyma; esp., the capping or crowning molding of a cornice, placed above the corona, and commonly having the form of a cyma recta.

cym-bal (sim'bạl), *n.* [L. *cymbalum*, < Gr. κύμβαλον, < κύμβη, cup, bowl.] One of a pair of concave plates of brass or bronze which are struck together to produce a sharp, ringing sound: as, "I am become as sounding brass, or a tinkling *cymbal*" (1 Cor. xiii. 1).—**cym'baled,** *a.* Furnished with cymbals.—**cym'bal-ist,** *n.* One who plays the cymbals.

cyme (sīm), *n.* [L. *cyma*, sprout, < Gr. κῦμα: see *cyma.*] In *bot.*, an inflorescence in which the primary axis bears a single terminal flower which develops first, the inflorescence being continued by secondary, tertiary, and other axes; esp., a flat or convex inflorescence of this type.

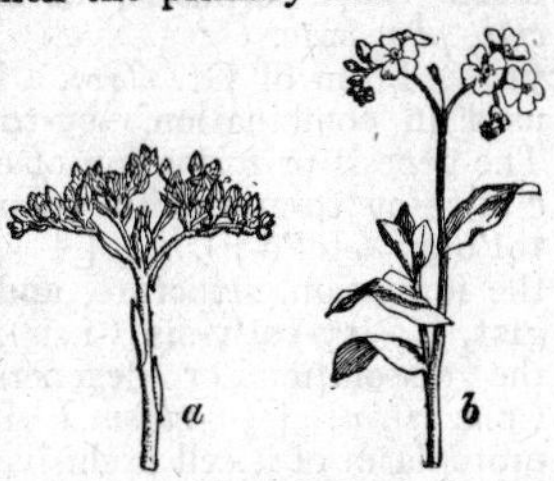

a, Cyme of houseleek; *b*, Cyme of forget-me-not.

cy-mene (sī'mēn), *n.* [L. *cyminum*: see *cumin.*] In *chem.*, a liquid hydrocarbon with a pleasant smell, occurring in the volatile oil of the common cumin, *Cuminum cyminum.*

cy-mo-gene (sī'mọ-jēn), *n.* [From *cymene* + Gr. -γενής, produced.] In *chem.*, a mixture of very volatile inflammable hydrocarbons obtained at the beginning of the distillation of crude petroleum: used for producing low temperatures by evaporation.

cy-mo-graph (sī'mọ-gráf), etc. Same as *kymograph*, etc.

cy-mom-e-ter (sī-mom'e-tėr), *n.* [Gr. κῦμα, wave: see *-meter.*] In *elect.*, an instrument for measuring Hertzian or electric waves.

cy-mo-phane (sī'mọ-fān), *n.* [Gr. κῦμα, wave, + φαίνεσθαι, appear.] Chrysoberyl.

cy-mo-scope (sī'mọ-skōp), *n.* [Gr. κῦμα, wave: see *-scope.*] A device for detecting the presence of electric waves.

cy-mose (sī'mōs or sī-mōs'), *a.* [L. *cymosus.*] In *bot.*, bearing a cyme or cymes; of the nature of or pertaining to a cyme.—**cy'mose-ly,** *adv.*

Cym-ric (kim'rik). **I.** *a.* Pertaining to the Cymry or Welsh, or to the branch of the Celtic race to which they belong, comprising also the Cornish people and the Bretons: distinguished from *Gadhelic.* **II.** *n.* The Welsh language; the group of dialects or languages spoken by the Cymric Celts.

Cym-ry (kim'ri), *n. pl.* [W., pl. of *Cymro*, Welshman: cf. W. *Cymru*, Wales.] The Welsh; the branch of the Celtic race to which the Welsh belong, comprising also the Cornish people and the Bretons.

cyn-e-get-ic (sin-ẹ̄-jet'ik), *a.* [Gr. κυνηγετικός, < κυνηγέτης, hunter, < κύων (κυν-), dog, + ἡγεῖσθαι, lead.] Of or pertaining to hunting or the chase.—**cyn-e-get'ics,** *n.* Hunting; the chase.

cyn-ic (sin'ik). [L. *cynicus*, < Gr. κυνικός, dog-like, churlish, Cynic, < κύων (κυν-), dog.] **I.** *a.* [*cap.*] Belonging or pertaining to a sect of ancient Greek philosophers who taught that virtue is the only good, that the essence of virtue is self-control, and that pleasure is an evil if sought for its own sake, and who made an ostentatious show of contempt for riches, ease, and enjoyment; also [*l. c.*], cynical. **II.** *n.* [*cap.*] A Cynic philosopher; also [*l. c.*], a sneering faultfinder; one who disbelieves in the goodness of human motives, and who is given to displaying his disbelief by sneers, sarcasm, etc.—**cyn'i-cal,** *a.* Resembling or suggestive of the Cynics or their doctrines; like or characteristic of a cynic; sneering; having or showing a disposition to disbelieve in the goodness of human motives.—**cyn'i-cal-ly,** *adv.*—**cyn'i-cal-ness,** *n.*—**cyn'i-cism** (-sizm), *n.* [*cap.*] The doctrines or practices of the Cynics; [*l. c.*] cynical disposition or character; also, a cynical remark.

cy-no-ceph-a-lous (sī-nọ-sef'ạ-lus or sin-ọ-), *a.* [Gr. κυνοκέφαλος, < κύων (κυν-), dog, + κεφαλή, head.] Having a head like that of a dog.

cy-no-sure (sī'nọ-shụ̈r or sin'ọ-), *n.* [L. *Cynosura*, < Gr. Κυνόσουρα, lit. 'dog's tail,' < κύων (κυν-), dog, + οὐρά, tail.] [*cap.*] The constellation Ursa Minor, which contains the pole-star at the tip of the so-called tail, and which was formerly used by mariners as a guide; also, the pole-star; [*l. c.*] something serving for guidance or direction; also, something that strongly attracts attention, as by its brilliance, etc.; a center of attraction, interest, or attention (as, "All the critics of the Court at once recognised her as the *cynosure* of the Empyrean": Disraeli's "Lothair," xxi.).—**cy-no-su-ral** (sī-nọ-shụ̈'rạl or sin-ọ-), *a.*

Cyn-thi-a (sin'thi-ạ̈), *n.* [L., < Gr. Κυνθία, < Κύνθος, Mount Cynthus in Delos, birthplace of Artemis and Apollo.] Artemis (Diana); hence, in poetry, the moon, the emblem of Artemis.

cy-pe-ra-ceous (sī-pẹ-rā'shius or sip-ẹ-), *a.* [NL. *Cyperus*, the typical genus, < Gr. κύπειρος, kind of marsh-plant.] Belonging to the *Cyperaceæ*, or sedge family of plants.

cy-pher (sī'fėr), *n.* and *v.* See *cipher.*

cy-press[1] (sī'pres), *n.* [OF. *cipres* (F. *cyprès*), < LL. *cypressus*, < Gr. κυπάρισσος.] Any of the evergreen trees constituting the pinaceous genus *Cupressus*, distinguished by dark-green, scale-like, overlapping leaves, a hard, durable wood, and symmetrical growth, as *C. sempervirens* of southern Europe (in one form with upright appressed branches, like the Lombardy poplar) or *C. macrocarpa* of California; any of various other pinaceous trees allied to the true cypress, as *Taxodium distichum* ('swamp,' 'bald,' or 'red cypress') of the southern U. S.; the wood of any such tree; also, any of various other plants in some way resembling the true cypress, as *Gilia coronopifolia* ('standing cypress'), a tall, slender, polemoniaceous herb of the U. S.; also, the branches of the true cypress (*Cupressus sempervirens*) as an emblem of mourning, from their ancient use at funerals (as, "But that remorseless iron hour Made *cypress* of her orange flower": Tennyson's "In Memoriam," lxxxiv.).

Cypress (*Cupressus sempervirens*, appressed form).

cy-press[2]† (sī'pres), *n.* [ME. *cipres*; appar. named from the island of Cyprus.] Any of several rich fabrics brought from Cyprus; also, a fine, thin fabric resembling lawn or crape, which was formerly much used in black for mourning garments, etc.

cy-pressed (sī'prest), *a.* Abounding in or planted with trees of the cypress kind.
cy-press=vine (sī'pres-vīn), *n.* A convolvulaceous garden-plant, *Quamoclit quamoclit*, with finely parted leaves and scarlet or white tubular flowers.
Cyp-ri-an (sip'ri-ạn). **I.** *a.* Pertaining to Cyprus, an island in the eastern Mediterranean, early famous for its worship of Aphrodite (Venus); hence, lewd; licentious. **II.** *n.* A native or inhabitant of Cyprus; a Cypriote; also, a lewd or licentious person; a prostitute.
cyp-ri-nid (sip'ri-nid or si-prī'nid). [NL. *Cyprinidæ*, pl., < *Cyprinus*, the carp genus, < L. *cyprinus*: see *cyprinoid.*] **I.** *n.* Any fish belonging to the *Cyprinidæ*, or carp family. **II.** *a.* Belonging or pertaining to the carp family of fishes.
cy-prin-i-form (si-prin'i-fôrm), *a.* [L. *cyprinus*, carp: see *-form.*] Carp-like in form or structure.
cy-prin-o-dont (si-prin'ọ-dont), *n.* [NL. *Cyprinodon*, the typical genus, < Gr. κυπρῖνος, carp, + ὀδούς (ὀδοντ-), tooth.] Any of the *Cyprinodontidæ*, a family of small soft-finned fishes, mostly inhabiting the fresh and brackish waters of America, and including the killifishes, certain minnows, etc.
cyp-ri-noid (sip'ri-noid). [L. *cyprinus*, < Gr. κυπρῖνος, carp: see *-oid.*] **I.** *a.* Resembling a carp; belonging to the *Cyprinoidea*, a group of fishes including the carps, suckers, loaches, etc. **II.** *n.* A cyprinoid fish.

Typical Cyprinodont (*Cyprinodon variegatus*).

Cyp-ri-ot (sip'ri-ot), *n.* and *a.* See *Cypriote.*
Cyp-ri-ote (sip'ri-ōt). [See *-ote.*] **I.** *n.* A native or inhabitant of Cyprus, in the eastern Mediterranean; also, the Greek dialect of Cyprus. **II.** *a.* Of or pertaining to Cyprus; Cyprian.
cyp-ri-pe-di-um (sip-ri-pē'di-um), *n.* [NL., < L. *Cypris*, Venus, + *pes* (*ped-*), foot.] Any plant of the genus *Cypripedium*, comprising orchids having large drooping flowers with a protruding sac-like labellum; a lady's-slipper.
cy-prus† (sī'prus), *n.* See *cypress²*.
cyp-se-la (sip'sẹ-lạ̈), *n.*; pl. *-læ* (-lē). [NL., < Gr. κυψέλη, hollow vessel.] In *bot.*, an achene with an adherent calyx, as in the composite plants.
cyp-se-line (sip'sẹ-lin), *a.* [L. *cypselus*, < Gr. κύψελος, the swift.] Pertaining to or resembling a swift; belonging to the swift family of birds.

Cypripedium (*C. reginæ*).

Cy-re-na-ic (sī-rẹ-nā'ik or sir-ẹ̄-). [L. *Cyrenaicus*, < Gr. Κυρηναϊκός, < Κυρήνη, Cyrene.] **I.** *a.* Of or pertaining to Cyrenaica, an ancient country of northern Africa, or its chief city, Cyrene; also, noting or pertaining to a school of philosophy founded by Aristippus of Cyrene, who taught that pleasure is the only rational aim of life. **II.** *n.* A native or inhabitant of Cyrenaica; also, a disciple of the Cyrenaic school of philosophy.
Cy-ril-lic (si-ril'ik), *a.* Of or pertaining to St. Cyril, missionary to the Slavs in the 9th century; esp., noting or pertaining to an old Slavic alphabet, of which the Russian is a slight modification, reputed to have been invented by St. Cyril.
cyr-i-o-log-ic, cyr-i-o-log-i-cal (sir"i-ọ-loj'ik, -i-kạl), *a.* [Gr. κυριολογικός, speaking literally, < κύριος, authoritative, proper, literal, + λόγος, speech.] Noting or pertaining to a form of hieroglyphic writing in which objects are represented by pictures, not by symbols.
cyr-to-graph (sėr'tọ-grȧf), *n.* Same as *cyrtometer.*
cyr-tom-e-ter (sėr-tom'e-tėr), *n.* [Gr. κυρτός, curved: see *-meter.*] An instrument for measuring and recording the curves, etc., of the chest and other parts of the body.
cyr-to-sis (sėr-tō'sis), *n.* [NL., < Gr. κύρτωσις, < κυρτός, curved.] In *pathol.*, curvature of the spine.
cyr-to-style (sėr'tọ-stīl). [Gr. κυρτός, curved, + στῦλος, pillar, column.] In *arch.*: **I.** *a.* Having columns arranged in a projecting curve, as a portico. **II.** *n.* A cyrtostyle portico.
cyst (sist), *n.* [NL. *cystis*, < Gr. κύστις, bladder, bag, pouch.] A bladder, sac, or vesicle; in *pathol.*, a closed bladder-like sac formed in animal tissues, containing fluid or semifluid morbid matter; in *zoöl.*, a capsule or resistant covering; esp., the sac developed by larval tapeworms which live in the tissues of certain animals, or a larval tapeworm with such a sac; a hydatid; in *bot.*, a cell or cavity inclosing reproductive bodies, etc.—**cys-tec-to-my** (sis-tek'tọ-mi), *n.* [Gr. κύστις + ἐκ, out of, + -τομία, E. *-tomy.*] In *surg.*, excision of a cyst or bladder.—**cys-tic** (sis'tik), *a.* Pertaining to, of the nature of, or having a cyst or cysts; encysted.
cys-ti-cer-cus (sis-ti-sėr'kus), *n.*; pl. *-cerci* (-sėr'sī). [NL., < *cystis*, E. *cyst*, + Gr. κέρκος, tail.] In *zoöl.*, the encysted larva of certain tapeworms; a hydatid.
cys-ti-form (sis'ti-fôrm), *a.* Having the form of a cyst or bladder.
cys-ti-tis (sis-tī'tis), *n.* [NL., < *cystis*: see *cyst.*] In *pathol.*, inflammation of the urinary bladder.
cysto-. Form of Gr. κύστις, bladder, used in combination.
cys-to-cele (sis'tọ-sēl), *n.* [See *cysto-* and *-cele.*] In *pathol.*, hernia in which the urinary bladder protrudes.
cys-toid (sis'toid), *a.* [See *-oid.*] Resembling a cyst; bladder-like.
cys-to-scope (sis'tọ-skōp), *n.* [See *cysto-* and *-scope.*] In *med.*, an instrument for examining the interior of the urinary bladder.—**cys-to-scop'ic** (-skop'ik), *a.*
cys-tot-o-my (sis-tot'ọ-mi), *n.* [See *cysto-* and *-tomy.*] In *surg.*, the operation of cutting into the urinary bladder, esp. in lithotomy.

Cystoscope, with bulb attachment for inflating the bladder.

-cyte. Noun termination from Gr. κύτος, a hollow, used to mean 'cell,' 'corpuscle,' as in *erythrocyte, leucocyte, microcyte, phagocyte.*
cyto-. Form of Gr. κύτος, a hollow (hence taken as 'cell'), used in combination.—**cy-to-gen-e-sis** (sī-tọ-jen'e-sis), *n.* The genesis or formation of cells. Also **cy-tog'e-ny** (-toj'e-ni).—**cy"to-ge-net'ic** (-jẹ̄-net'ik), **cy-to-gen'ic**, *a.*—**cy-tol'o-gy** (-tol'ọ-ji), *n.* [+ *-logy.*] The scientific study of the formation, structure, and functions of cells.—**cy-tol'o-gist**, *n.*—**cy-tol'y-sis** (-i-sis), *n.* [+ *-lysis.*] In *physiol.*, the dissolution or degeneration of cells.—**cy'to-plasm** (-plazm), *n.* [+ *-plasm.*] In *biol.*, the living substance or protoplasm of a cell exclusive of the nucleus.—**cy-to-plas'mic** (-plaz'mik), *a.*
czar, tsar (zär, tsär), *n.* [Russ. *tsar*, < L. *Cæsar*, Cæsar.] An emperor or king; esp. [usually *cap.*], the emperor of Russia; hence [*l. c.* or *cap.*], an autocratic master or leader.
czar-das (chär'däsh), *n.* See *csardas.*
czar-e-vitch, tsar-e-vitch (zär'ẹ-vich, tsär'-), *n.* [Russ. *tsarevich.*] A son of a czar; in earlier use, any son of the emperor of Russia; later, the eldest son.
cza-rev-na, tsa-rev-na (zä-rev'nạ̈, tsä-), *n.* [Russ. *tsarevna.*] A daughter of a czar; in later use, in Russia, the wife of the czarevitch.
cza-ri-na, tsa-ri-na (zä-rē'nạ̈, tsä-), *n.* [= F. *czarine, tsarine*, = Sp. *zarina* = Pg. and It. *czarina* = G. *czarin*: cf. *czaritza.*] The wife of a czar; a Russian empress.
cza-rit-za, tsa-rit-sa (zä-rit'zạ̈, tsä-), *n.* [Russ. *tsaritsa.*] Same as *czarina.*
Czech (chek), *n.* A member of the most westerly branch of the Slavs, comprising the Bohemians (or Czechs proper), the Moravians, and the Slovaks; also, the language of the Czechs; Bohemian.—**Czech'ic, Czech'ish**, *a.*—**Czech'o=Slo-vak', Czech'o-slo-vak'** (-ọ-slọ-vak' or -slō'vak). **I.** *n.* A member of the branch of the Slavic race comprising the Czechs proper, the Slovaks, etc. **II.** *a.* Of or pertaining to the Czecho-Slovaks.

D

D, d (dē); pl. *D's, d's* (dēz). A consonant, the 4th letter of the English alphabet.

dab[1] (dab), *v.*; *dabbed, dabbing.* [ME. *dabben*: cf. MD. *dabben*, pinch, knead, fumble, dabble, G. *tappen*, fumble.] **I.** *tr.* To strike, esp. lightly, as with the hand; strike with light blows from something soft; also, to cause to strike lightly against something; also, to apply (a substance) by light strokes; also, to pick holes in (the surface of stone) with a pointed tool. **II.** *intr.* To strike lightly; peck; use a dabber.—**dab**[1], *n.* A quick or light blow; a pat, as with the hand or something soft; a stroke with a dabber; also, a small mass dabbed on anything; hence, a small or trifling quantity or thing; also, a dabber.

dab[2] (dab), *n.* [Origin uncertain: cf. *dab*[1], *n.*] Any of several flat-fishes allied to the flounder, esp. *Limanda limanda*, of Europe, or *L. ferruginea* ('rusty dab'), of America.

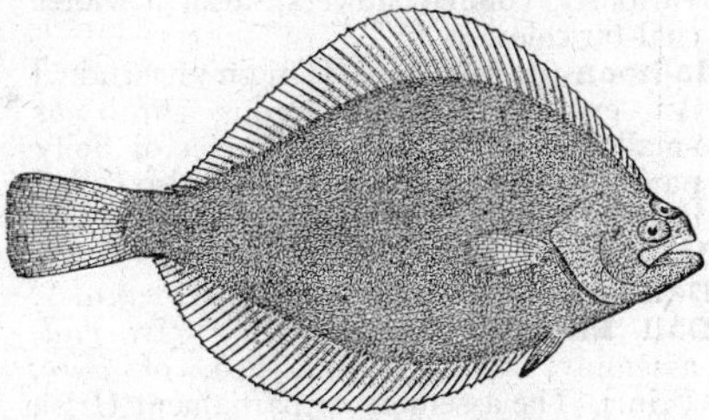
Dab (*Limanda limanda*).

dab[3] (dab), *n.* [Perhaps < *dab*[1], *v.*] An expert; a dabster: as, "he being, in his own phrase, 'something of a *dab*' . . . at the shoemaking business" (Hawthorne's "Blithedale Romance," v.). [Colloq.]

dab-ber (dab′ėr), *n.* One who or that which dabs; esp., a cushion-like article used for applying ink, etc., as by printers and engravers.

Etchers' Dabber.

dab-ble (dab′l), *v.*; *-bled, -bling.* [Freq. of *dab*[1].] **I.** *tr.* To wet slightly or repeatedly in or with a liquid; splash; spatter. **II.** *intr.* To move about in water, etc., with splashing; play in water, as with the hands; also, to employ one's self in a superficial manner (*in*, etc.), as for pastime; also, to meddle†.—**dab′bler,** *n.*

dab-chick (dab′chik), *n.* [Cf. *dab*[1].] A small grebe (bird), esp. the little grebe, *Podiceps fluviatilis* (or *minor*), of Europe, or the pied-billed grebe, *Podilymbus podiceps*, of America.

dab-ster (dab′stėr), *n.* [See *dab*[3].] An expert at something; a proficient; a dab; also, a dabbler; a superficial worker. [Colloq.]

da ca-po (dä kä′pō). [It., 'from (the) head.'] In *music*, from the beginning: a direction to repeat.

dace (dās), *n.*; pl. *daces* or (esp. collectively) *dace.* [OF. *dars*, dace, = *dart*, E. *dart.*] A small fresh-water cyprinoid fish, *Leuciscus leuciscus*, of Europe, with a stout, fusiform body; also, any of several similar or related fishes of the U. S.

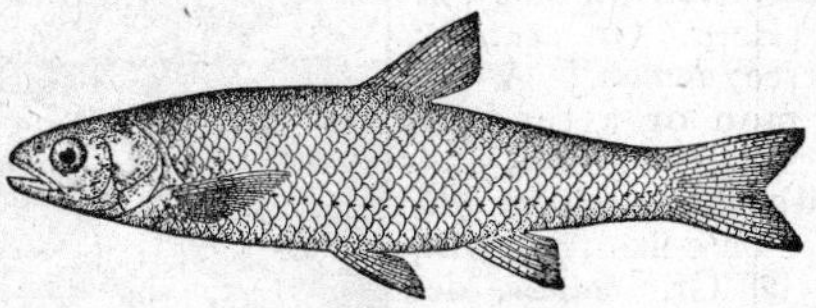
Dace (*Leuciscus leuciscus*).

dachs-hund (däks′hůnt), *n.* [G., < *dachs*, badger, + *hund*, dog.] One of a German breed of small hounds with a long body and very short legs.

Da-cian (dā′shiạn), *a.* Pertaining or belonging to Dacia, an ancient region north of the Danube (corresponding to Rumania and adjoining regions), or to its people.

da-cite (dā′sīt), *n.* [From *Dacia*: cf. *Dacian.*] An igneous rock, generally of a porphyritic structure, consisting essentially of plagioclase and quartz, with biotite, hornblende, and pyroxene.

dack-er, dai-ker (dak′ėr, dā′kėr), *v. i.* [Cf. MD. *dakeren.*] To totter; toddle; saunter; potter; vacillate. [Sc. and north Eng.]

da-coit (dạ-koit′), *n.* [Hind. *dakait.*] One of a class of robbers in India and Burma, who plunder in bands.—**da-coit′y,** *n.* [Hind. *dakaitī.*] The system of robbing practised by the dacoits; also, a robbery of this kind.

dac-tyl (dak′til), *n.* [L. *dactylus*, < Gr. δάκτυλος, finger or toe, date (see *date*[1]), metrical foot.] In *zoöl.*, a finger or toe; in *pros.*, a foot of three syllables, one long followed by two short, or, in modern verse, one accented followed by two unaccented.—**dac-tyl′ic.** In *pros.*: **I.** *a.* Pertaining to or of the nature of a dactyl; consisting of or characterized by dactyls. **II.** *n.* A dactylic verse.

dactylio-. Form of Gr. δακτύλιος, finger-ring, used in combination.—**dac-tyl-i-og-ly-phy** (dak-til-i-og′li-fi), *n.* [Gr. δακτυλιογλυφία (γλύφειν, carve).] The art of engraving gems for rings, etc.—**dac-tyl-i-og′ra-phy** (-rạ-fi), *n.* [+ *-graphy.*] The description or study of finger-rings.—**dac-tyl′i-o-man″cy** (-ǭ-man″si), *n.* [+ *-mancy.*] Divination by means of a finger-ring.

dactylo-. Form of Gr. δάκτυλος, finger or toe, used in combination.—**dac-ty-log-ra-phy** (dak-ti-log′rạ-fi), *n.* [+ *-graphy.*] Dactylology; also, the study of fingerprints, as for purposes of identification.—**dac-ty-lol′o-gy** (-lol′ǭ-ji), *n.* [+ *-logy.*] The art of communicating ideas by signs made with the fingers, as in a manual alphabet used by the deaf and dumb.—**dac-ty-los′co-py** (-los′kǭ-pi), *n.* [+ *-scopy.*] The identification of criminals, etc., by means of fingerprints.

dad (dad), *n.* [Appar. orig. in childish speech.] Father; papa. [Childish or familiar.]—**dad′dy,** *n.*; pl. *daddies* (-iz). Diminutive form of *dad.*—**dad″dy=long′=legs,** *n.*; pl. *-legs.* In Great Britain, any of the dipterous insects constituting the family *Tipulidæ*; a crane-fly; in the U. S., any of the arachnids constituting the order *Phalangidea*; a harvestman.

da-do (dā′dō), *n.*; pl. *-dos* (-dōz). [It., die, cube, pedestal, = E. *die*[2].] The part of a pedestal between the base and the cornice or cap; a similar part in other structures, as at the bottom of an exterior wall; a broad finish of wood on the lower part of an interior wall, esp. a flat portion of this between bottom and top moldings; a similar broad finish of wall-paper, a fabric, paint, etc., on the lower part of an interior wall.

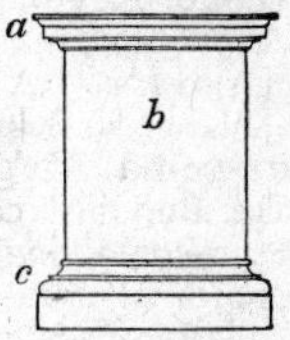

Pedestal.

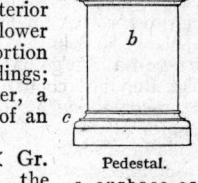

a, surbase or cornice; *b*, dado or die; *c*, base.

dæ-dal (dē′dạl), *a.* [L. *dædalus*, < Gr. δαίδαλος.] Skilful or ingenious (as, the sculptor's *dædal* hand; "the *dædal* imagination of the author of 'Faust,' " Disraeli's "Lothair," lxxvii.); also, devised with or displaying artistic skill or cunning; hence, intricate or maze-like; diversified or variously adorned. [Chiefly poetic.]

Dæ-da-lus (dē′dạ-lus or ded′ạ-), *n.* [From *Dædalus*, the 'cunning worker' (cf. *dædal*), who devised the Cretan labyrinth and made wings for flying.] A cunning worker or artificer; an ingenious inventor.—**Dæ-da-lian** (dẹ-dā′liạn), *a.*

daem-mer-schlaf (dem′ėr-shläf), *n.* See *dämmerschlaf.*

dæ-mon (dē′mọn), etc. See *demon*, etc.

daff[1] (dȧf), *n.* [ME. *daffe*: cf. *daft.*] A simpleton or fool; also, a coward. [Now only north. Eng.]—**daff**[1], *v. i.* To act the fool; make sport; play; jest: as, "Let us have no more of such unbecoming *daffing*" (Scott's "Quentin Durward," xxxi.). [Chiefly Sc.]

daff[2] (dȧf), *v. t.* [Var. of *doff.*] To doff† (as, "There my white stole of chastity I *daff'd*": Shakspere's "Lover's Complaint," 297); also, to put or turn aside (as, "The nimble-footed madcap Prince of Wales, And his comrades, that *daff'd* the world aside, And bid it pass": Shakspere's "1 Henry IV.," iv. 1. 96).

daf-fo-dil (daf′ǫ-dil), *n.* [For ME. *affodylle*, < L. *asphodelus*: see *asphodel*.] Formerly, any plant of the genus *Narcissus* (see *narcissus*); now, a species, *N. pseudo-narcissus*, with single or double yellow nodding flowers, blooming in the spring. Also **daf′fo-dil″ly, daf″fo-down-dil′ly**; pl. *-dillies* (-iz).

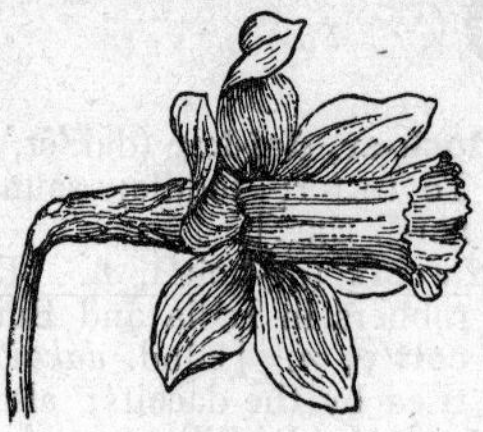

Flower of Daffodil (*Narcissus pseudo-narcissus*).

daff-y (daf′i), *a.* [See *daff*[1].] Silly; weak-minded; crazy. [Prov. or colloq.]

daft (daft), *a.* [= *deft*.] Gentle† or meek†; also (prov. or colloq.), simple or foolish; mad or crazy (as, to go *daft*); madly gay (as, "in a frolic *daft*": Burns's "Twa Dogs," 155).—**daft′ly,** *adv.*—**daft′ness,** *n.*

dag[1] (dag), *n.* [F. *dague*, dagger: cf. *dagger*.] A pointed piece of metal; a pin; a bolt; also, the pointed unbranched horn of a young stag.

dag[2] (dag), *n.* [Origin unknown.] A heavy pistol formerly in use.

dag-ger (dag′ėr), *n.* [ME. *dagger*, akin to OF. F. *dague*, Sp. and It. *daga*.] A short edged and pointed weapon, like a small sword, used for thrusting and stabbing; in *printing*, a mark (†) used for references, etc.; the obelisk.—**at daggers drawn,** with daggers ready to strike; hence, in a state of open hostility.—**dagger of lath.** See *lath*, *n.*—**double dagger,** in *printing*, a mark (‡) used for references, etc.; the double obelisk.—**dag′ger,** *v. t.* To stab with a dagger; in *printing*, to mark with a dagger.

Daggers.

dag-gle (dag′l), *v. t.* or *i.*; *-gled*, *-gling*. [Cf. ME. *dagged*, clogged with dirt.] To drag or trail through mud, water, etc.; make wet and dirty or limp; draggle: as, "The warrior's very plume, I say, Was *daggled* by the dashing spray" (Scott's "Lay of the Last Minstrel," i. 29).

Da-go (dā′gō), *n.*; pl. *-gos* or *-goes* (-gōz). [Said to be < Sp. *Diego*, man's name, < LL. *Jacobus*, E. *Jacob*, *James*.] [Also *l. c.*] A Spaniard, a Portuguese, or, esp., an Italian. [Slang, U. S.]

da-go-ba (dä′gǫ-bą), *n.*; pl. *-bas*. [Singhalese *dāgaba*.] In Buddhist countries, a dome-shaped monumental structure containing relics of Buddha or of some Buddhist saint.

Ceylonese Dagoba.

da-guerre-o-type (dą-ger′ǫ-tīp), *n.* [From L. J. M. *Daguerre* (1789–1851), (French) inventor.] An early photographic process in which the impression was made on a silver surface sensitized to the action of light by iodine, and then developed by mercury vapor; also, a picture made by this process.—**da-guerre′o-type,** *v. t.*; *-typed*, *-typing*. To photograph by the daguerreotype process; fig., to picture or impress as if by this process (obs. or rare: as, "That camp is *daguerreotyped* on my memory," Parkman's "Oregon Trail," x.).—**da-guerre′o-typ-er** (-tī-pėr), **da-guerre′o-typ-ist,** *n.*—**da-guerre′o-ty-py** (-tī-pi), *n.* The daguerreotype process.

da-ha-be′ah, da-ha-bee′yah, *n.* See *dahabiya*.

da-ha-bi-ya, da-ha-bi-yeh (dä-hą-bē′yą), *n.* [Ar. *dhahabīyah*.] A kind of house-boat or passenger-boat used on the Nile, typically with one or more lateen sails and provided with oars, but now often propelled by steam.

Dahabiya.

dahl-ia (däl′yą, also dal′yą, or dāl′yą), *n.* [NL.; from A. *Dahl*, Swedish botanist.] Any plant of the asteraceous genus *Dahlia*, native in Mexico and Central America, widely cultivated for its showy, variously colored flowers; also, a violet coal-tar color.

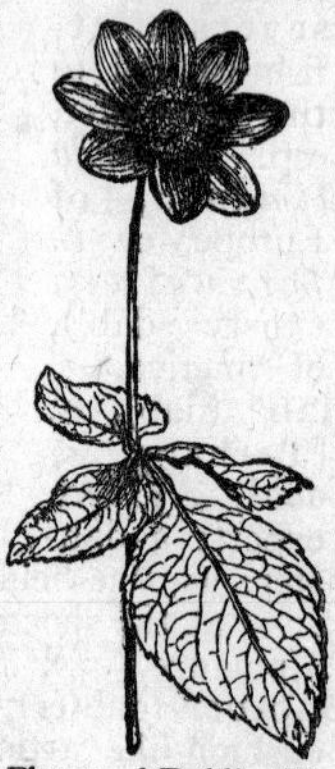

Flower of Dahlia (*D. variabilis*).

da-hoon (dą-hön′), *n.* [Origin uncertain.] An evergreen aquifoliaceous shrub or small tree, *Ilex cassine*, a species of holly native in the southern U. S. Also called *dahoon holly*.

dai-ker (dā′kėr), *v. i.* See *dacker*.

Dail (ᴛʜâil), *n.* Same as *Dail Eireann*.

Dail Eir-eann (ᴛʜâil ãr′ąn). [Ir. *dáil*, assembly, and *Éireann*, gen. of *Éire*, Erin.] The assembly or parliament (Irish Republican Parliament) which was established at Dublin on Jan. 21, 1919, by elected representatives of the Sinn Fein organization, and which ratified the establishment of the Irish Republic as proclaimed at Dublin in the rebellion of Easter Monday, April 24, 1916; later (after the establishment of the Irish Free State, through an agreement reached on Dec. 6, 1921, and ratified by the British Parliament in the same month and by the aforesaid Irish assembly on Jan. 7, 1922), the representative assembly, subsequently the lower house of parliament, of the Irish Free State; since 1937, the House of Representatives of the State of Ireland (see *Oireachtas*).

dai-ly (dā′li). [AS. *dæglīc*.] **I.** *a.* Of, pertaining to, occurring, or issued each successive day or, sometimes, each successive week-day. **II.** *n.*; pl. *-lies* (-liz). A newspaper or other periodical appearing each day or each week-day. **III.** *adv.* Every day; day by day.

dai-mio (dī′myō), *n.*; pl. *-mios* (-myōz). [Jap., lit. 'great name'; from Chinese.] One of a former class of great feudal nobles of Japan, vassals of the emperor.—**dai′mi-ate** (-mi-āt), *n.*

dai-mon (dī′mōn), *n.* [Repr. Gr. δαίμων: see *demon*.] A demon or attendant spirit; a genius.

dai-mon-e-lix (dī-mon′e-liks), *n.* [NL., < Gr. δαίμων, demon, + ἕλιξ, spiral.] A gigantic spiral fossil, probably of vegetable origin, found in parts of Nebraska, Wyoming, and South Dakota. Also called *devil's corkscrew*.

Daimonelix in position, Sioux County, Nebraska. Average height six to seven feet.

dain-ty (dān′ti). [OF. *daintie*, *deintie*, < L.

dignitas: see *dignity*.] **I.** *n.*; pl. *-ties* (-tiz). Estimation†; also, joy† or pleasure†; also, fastidiousness†; also, something esteemed or choice†; esp., something especially delicious to the palate; a choice viand; a delicacy. **II.** *a.*; compar. *daintier*, superl. *daintiest.* Excellent†; choice†; also, rare†; also, delicately pleasing to the palate; toothsome; delicious; also, of delicate beauty or charm; exquisite; also, nice in discrimination or taste; fastidious; sometimes, overnice, or too particular (as, "When men were starving they could not afford to be *dainty*": Motley's "Dutch Republic," vi. 5).—**dain′ti-ly,** *adv.*—**dain′ti-ness,** *n.*

dair-y (dãr′i), *n.*; pl. *-ies* (-iz). [ME. *deierie*, < *deie*, *daie*, maid, dairymaid, < AS. *dǣge* (= Icel. *deigja*), lit. 'kneader,' 'bread-maker,' akin to *dāh*, E. *dough*.] A place, as a room or building, where milk and cream are kept and made into butter and cheese; a shop where milk, butter, etc., are sold; also, the business of producing milk and manufacturing butter and cheese; also, a dairy-farm; the cows on a farm.—**dair′y=farm,** *n.* A farm devoted chiefly to the production of milk and the manufacture of butter and cheese.—**dair′y=farm″er,** *n.*—**dair′y=farm″ing,** *n.*—**dair′y-ing,** *n.* The business of a dairy.—**dair′y-maid,** *n.* A female servant employed in a dairy.—**dair′y-man** (-mạn), *n.*; pl. *-men.* An owner or manager of, or an employee in, a dairy.—**dair′y-wom″an,** *n.*; pl. *-women* (-wim″en).

da-is (dā′is), *n.* [OF. *deis* (F. *dais*), < ML. *discus*, table, L. discus, disk, dish: see *discus*.] A high or principal table in a hall, as for distinguished persons at a feast†; also, a raised platform, as at the end of a room, for a throne, seats of honor, a lecturer's desk, etc.; also, a canopy; also, a bench, settle, or church pew (Sc.).

Dais. — Throne-room, Windsor Castle, England.

dai-sy (dā′zi), *n.*; pl. *-sies* (-ziz). [AS. *dæges ēage*, 'day's eye.'] An asteraceous plant, *Bellis perennis*, common in Europe, and often cultivated, bearing flowers with yellow disk and white rays often tipped with pink ('English daisy'); any of various other asteraceous plants, esp. *Chrysanthemum leucanthemum*, the common 'white daisy' of the U. S., whose flower-heads have a yellow disk and white rays; also, something fine or first-rate (slang).—**Michaelmas daisy,** any of various species of aster blooming about Michaelmas. [Eng.]—**oxeye daisy,** the white daisy, *Chrysanthemum leucanthemum*; also, the yellow daisy.—**Paris daisy,** the marguerite.—**yellow daisy,** the common rudbeckia, *Rudbeckia hirta*.—**dai′sied,** *a.*—**dai′sy=cut″ter,** *n.* A horse that in trotting lifts its feet only a little way from the ground; in *baseball*, etc., a ball so batted or propelled that it skims along the ground.

1. Branch with heads of White or Oxeye Daisy (*Chrysanthemum leucanthemum*). 2. The lower part of the plant. *a*, a ray-flower; *b*, a disk-flower.

dak (däk or dâk), *n.* [Hind. *dāk*.] In the East Indies, transportation, as of letters, etc., or of travelers, by relays of men or horses; hence, the post or mail; also, any arrangement for transportation or travel by relays.

Da-kin's (dā′kinz) **so-lu′tion.** [From H. D. *Dakin* (born 1880), chemist, the originator.] A liquid antiseptic, an approximately neutral solution containing about 0.5 per cent of sodium hypochlorite, used in treating infected wounds (in which, besides acting as an antiseptic, it dissolves necrotic or dead tissue), and extensively employed in military hospitals during the World War.

da-koit (dạ-koit′), etc. See *dacoit*, etc.

dal (däl), *n.* [Hind. *dāl*.] In the East Indies, split pulse used for porridge, etc.; also, a plant yielding pulse so used.

Da-lai=la-ma (dä-lī′lä′mä), *n.* [Mongol. *dalai*, ocean.] 'Ocean lama': the title of the Grand Lama of Tibet.

dale (dāl), *n.* [AS. *dæl* = D. *dal* = G. *thal* = Icel. *dalr* = Goth. *dal*.] A vale or valley.—**dales′man** (-mạn), *n.*; pl. *-men.* One living in a dale or valley, esp. in the northern counties of England.

dalles (dalz), *n. pl.* [Canadian F., < F. *dalle*, gutter, trough.] In western North America, rapids flowing over a flat rock-bottom in a narrowed portion of a river.

dal-li-ance (dal′i-ạns), *n.* The act of dallying; familiar and easy conversation†; sport or play; amorous toying; wantonness; idle or frivolous action; trifling; idle delay.

dal-ly (dal′i), *v.*; *-lied*, *-lying*. [OF. *dalier*, talk, chat; perhaps from Teut.] **I.** *intr.* To talk lightly or idly†; also, to sport or play, esp. amorously; wanton; also, to coquet, as with danger or temptation; also, to trifle; play mockingly; also, to loiter or idle. **II.** *tr.* With *away*, to spend (time) in dallying.—**dal′li-er,** *n.*—**dal′ly-ing-ly,** *adv.*

Dal-ma-tian (dal-mā′shiạn). **I.** *a.* Of, pertaining to, or named from Dalmatia, along the east coast of the Adriatic Sea: as, a *Dalmatian* dog (the coach-dog). **II.** *n.* An inhabitant of Dalmatia, esp. a member of the native Slavic-speaking race; also, a Dalmatian dog.

dal-mat-ic (dal-mat′ik), *n.* [LL. *dalmatica*, prop. fem. of L. *Dalmaticus*, Dalmatian.] An ecclesiastical vestment worn over the alb by the deacon, as at the celebration of the mass, and worn by bishops on certain occasions; also, a similar robe worn by monarchs at coronation, etc.; also, a garment formerly worn by noblemen and gentlemen, as in France.

Gentleman's Dalmatic (about 1400).

dal-ton-ism (dâl′tọn-izm), *n.* [From J. *Dalton* (1766–1844), English chemist, who suffered from and described this defect.] Color-blindness; esp., inability to distinguish red from green.

dam[1] (dam), *n.* [ME. *dam* = D. *dam* = G. *damm* = Icel. *dammr*.] A barrier to obstruct the flow of a liquid, esp. one of earth, masonry, etc., built across a stream; a body of water confined by a dam; also, any dam-like barrier, as one to keep out water, gas, etc., from a mine.—**dam**[1], *v. t.*; *dammed*, *damming*. To furnish with a dam; obstruct or confine with a dam; in general, to stop up or shut up.

dam[2] (dam), *n.* [= *dame*.] A female parent: used esp. of quadrupeds: as, "I laid down the *dam*, and took the kid in my arms" (Defoe's "Robinson Crusoe," i. 4).

dam-age (dam′ạj), *n.* [OF. *damage* (F. *dommage*), < L. *damnum*, harm, loss.] Loss or detriment (archaic); injury or harm, esp. physical injury impairing value or usefulness; cost or expense (colloq.); *pl.*, in *law*, the estimated money equivalent for detriment or injury sustained.—**dam′age,** *v. t.*; *-aged*, *-aging*. [OF. *damagier*.] To cause damage to; injure; harm; impair.—**dam′age-a-ble,** *a.* Susceptible of damage or injury.—**dam′ag-ing-ly,** *adv.*

Daman (*Procavia syriaca*).

dam-an (dam′ạn), *n.* [Ar.] A small, rabbit-like, ungulate mammal, *Procavia syriaca* (or

Hyrax syriacus), inhabiting Syria, Palestine, etc. (the cony of the English Bible: see Lev. xi. 5, etc.); also, any of various other animals of the same genus. Cf. *hyrax*.

Dam-as-cene (dam-ạ-sēn′ or dam′ạ-sēn). [L. *Damascenus*.] **I.** *a*. Of or pertaining to the city of Damascus, in Syria, once celebrated for its work in steel; [*l. c.*] of or pertaining to the art of damascening. **II.** *n*. An inhabitant of Damascus; [*l. c.*] work or patterns produced by damascening; also, a damson.—**dam-as-cene′**, *v. t.*; *-cened, -cening*. To ornament, or form designs on (metal, as steel), as by inlaying with gold, etc., or by etching; also, to produce a wavy or variegated pattern on (steel, etc.), like that of the sword-blades of Damascus steel.—**dam-as-cen′er** (-sē′nėr), *n*.—**dam-as-cen′ing**, *n*. The act or art of producing damascened metal or articles; also, the design, pattern, or wavy appearance on damascened metal.

Da-mas-cus (dạ-mas′kus) **steel.** [From *Damascus*, city in Syria, famous for metalwork, fabrics, etc.] A kind of steel originally made in the East, chiefly at Damascus, and used for making sword-blades, the surfaces of which exhibit a wavy or variegated pattern; also, a product of similar appearance, as that produced by welding iron and steel together, or by etching a wavy pattern on ordinary steel. Also called *damascus*.

dam-ask (dam′ạsk). [ME. *Damaske*, < L. *Damascus*, < Gr. Δαμασκός, Damascus.] **I.** *a*. Of, from, or named from the city of Damascus in Syria (as, *damask* or Damascus steel; *damask* silk or linen; the *damask* rose, a fragrant pink rose, *Rosa damascena*); also, pink (like the damask rose). **II.** *n*. Damascus steel, or the peculiar pattern or wavy appearance on its surface; also, a fabric of silk, linen, cotton, or wool, with a woven, often elaborate pattern; also, the pink color of the damask rose.—**dam′ask**, *v. t.* To damascene by inlaying, etc.; also, to weave or adorn with elaborate designs; hence, to variegate; also, to make of the pink color of the damask rose; also, to deface or destroy by stamping or marking.

dam-as-keen (dam-ạs-kēn′), *v. t.* [F. *damasquiner*.] Same as *damascene*.

dam-as-sé (dam-ạ-sā′), *a*. [F., pp. of *damasser*, weave in the manner of damask, < *damas*, damask.] Having a woven pattern, as silks.

dam-bon-ite (dam′bọn-īt), *n*. [From native African name.] In *chem.*, a crystalline derivative of inosite, occurring in a certain kind of caoutchouc from western Africa.

dame (dām), *n*. [OF. F. *dame*, < L. *domina*, mistress, lady, fem. of *dominus*, master, lord.] A woman of authority, as a female ruler, the mistress of a household, or the mistress of a school (now chiefly archaic); a woman of rank or position (now chiefly archaic or poetic); in general, a woman (recent slang); also, a form of address used to, or [*cap.*] a title prefixed to the name of, a woman of rank or position, or, in later use, other women, as housewives or elderly matrons (now chiefly archaic or prov.); specif. [*cap.*], in British use, the legal title prefixed to the Christian name and surname of the wife of a knight or baronet (cf. *lady*); also, in later use (since 1917), the distinctive title employed before the name of a woman upon whom a dignity corresponding to that of a knight (see *knight, n.*) has been conferred (as, *Dame* Nellie Melba); also, a mother, or female parent, whether of a human being or an animal† (cf. *dam*²).—**dame′=school**, *n*. An elementary school for children, kept by a woman.

dam-i-an-a (dam-i-an′ä̤ or -ā′nä̤), *n*. [Said to be from *Damia*, an ancient Greek goddess identified with the Roman Bona Dea, goddess of fruitfulness.] A drug consisting of the leaves of certain Mexican plants, supposed to have tonic, stimulant, and aphrodisiac properties.

dam-mar (dam′ä̤r), *n*. [Malay *damar*, resin.] A copal-like resin from various coniferous trees of the genus *Dammara*, of India and the islands of the southwestern Pacific, which is much used for making colorless varnish; also, any of various similar resins from trees of other genera. Also **dam′mer.**

däm-mer-schlaf (dem′ėr-shläf), *n*. [G.] Twilight sleep. See under *twilight*.

damn (dam), *v*. [OF. F. *damner*, < L. *damnare* (pp. *damnatus*), condemn, doom, < *damnum*, harm, loss, penalty.] **I.** *tr*. To pronounce guilty†; sentence† or doom†; also, to pronounce (something) to be bad; condemn (a literary or dramatic work) as a failure; also, to bring condemnation upon (as, "Hence, vile instrument! Thou shalt not *damn* my hand": Shakspere's "Cymbeline," iii. 4. 76); also, to doom to eternal punishment, or condemn to hell (hence used in profane imprecations and emphatic expressions); also, to address with the imprecation 'damn.' **II.** *intr*. To use the imprecation 'damn'; swear.—**damn**, *n*. The utterance of the word 'damn' by way of imprecation or emphasis; a curse; an oath.—**dam-na-ble** (dam′nạ-bl), *a*. [OF. F., < LL. *damnabilis*.] Worthy of damnation; detestable, abominable, or outrageous.—**dam′na-ble-ness**, *n*. —**dam′na-bly**, *adv*.—**dam-na′tion** (-nā′shọn), *n*. [OF. F., < L. *damnatio(n-)*.] The act of damning, or the fact of being damned; also, a cause or occasion of being damned; sin as incurring or deserving eternal punishment: also sometimes used as a term of imprecation, objurgation, etc. —**dam′na-to-ry** (-nạ-tō̤-ri), *a*. [L. *damnatorius*.] Conveying or occasioning condemnation; damning.—**damned** (damd), *p. a*. Condemned, esp. to eternal punishment; accursed: much used profanely, or as an emphatic expletive or intensive (sometimes used adverbially).—**damn-er** (dam′ėr), *n*.—**damn-ing** (dam′ing or dam′ning), *p. a*. That damns or condemns; occasioning condemnation.—**damn′ing-ly**, *adv*.

Dam-o-cle-an (dam-ō̤-klē′ạn), *a*. Of or pertaining to Damocles, a flatterer, who, having extolled the happiness of Dionysius, tyrant of Syracuse, was placed by the latter at a magnificent banquet, with a sword suspended over his head by a single hair, to show him the perilous nature of that happiness.

dam-o-sel, dam-o-zel (dam′ō̤-zel), *n*. [= *damsel*.] A young unmarried lady; a maiden: as, "The blessed *damozel* leaned out From the gold bar of Heaven" (Rossetti's "Blessed Damozel"). [Archaic.]

damp (damp). [= D. and LG. *damp* = G. *dampf*, vapor, steam.] **I.** *n*. Moisture; humidity; moist air; fog; also, a noxious or stifling vapor or gas, esp. in a mine; also, a state of dejection; a check or discouragement. **II.** *a*. Moist; humid; moderately wet; clammy; also, dejected (archaic: as, "With looks Downcast and *damp*," Milton's "Paradise Lost," i. 523).—**damp**, *v*. **I.** *tr*. To make damp; dampen; moisten; also, to stifle or suffocate; extinguish; dull or deaden; check or retard the action of (a vibrating string, etc.); bank (a fire); hence, to deaden the energy or ardor of; depress; discourage; specif., in *elect.*, etc., to cause the members of (a group or series of consecutive oscillations or waves) to fall off in amplitude as the end of the group or series is approached. **II.** *intr*. In *hort.*, to rot (*off*).—**damped**, *p. a*. Dampened; deadened; retarded in action; in *elect.*, etc., reduced gradually in amplitude (see *damp, v. t.*: as, *damped* electric oscillations, which when occurring in the antenna of a wireless apparatus give rise to damped wave-trains in the ether; *damped* waves, see phrase following, and cf. *continuous waves*, under *continuous*). —**damped wave=train**, in *wireless teleg.*, a wave-train composed of electric waves which are large in amplitude at or near the beginning of the group or series, and which gradually decrease in amplitude as the end is approached: a form of wave-train characteristic of certain wireless telegraph systems, each wave-train being separated from the one ahead and the one behind by an interval of time.—**damp′en**, *v*. **I.** *tr*. To make damp; moisten; also, to dull or deaden; depress; damp. **II.** *intr*. To become damp.—**damp′en-er**, *n*.—**damp′er**, *n*. One who or that which damps; a movable plate for regulating the draft in a stove, furnace, etc.; a device for checking vibration, as of a piano-string or a magnetic needle; also, a kind of unleavened bread made of flour and water and baked in hot ashes (Australia: as, "to feed you on *damper*, or some other nameless abomination," H. Kingsley's "Geoffry Hamlyn," xxxiv.).—**damp′ly**, *adv*.—**damp′ness**, *n*.

dam-sel (dam′zẹl), *n*. [OF. *dameisele*, *damoisele* (F. *demoiselle*), < ML. *domnicella*, dim. < L. *domina*, mistress, lady: see *dame*.] A young unmarried lady; in general, a young woman; a girl; also, a maid or female attendant (obs. or archaic).

dam-son (dam′zn), *n.* [ME. *damascene*, 'plum of Damascus,' < L. *Damascenus*, E. *Damascene.*] The small dark-blue or purple fruit of a variety, *Prunus domestica damascena*, of the common plum, introduced into Europe from Asia Minor; also, the tree bearing this fruit.

dan[1] (dan), *n.* [OF. *dan* (F. *dom*), < L. *dominus*, master, lord.] A title of honor formerly in use, equivalent to *master* or *sir*: as, *Dan* Chaucer; *Dan* Cupid. [Archaic.]

dan[2] (dan), *n.* [Origin uncertain.] A small buoy with a pole on which is displayed a flag by day and a lantern by night, as for indicating the position of deep-sea fish-lines or a center about which a trawler is worked.

Dan.

Dan-a-i-de-an (dan″ā-i-dē′ạn), *a.* Pertaining to or suggestive of the mythical Danaides, or daughters of Danaus, who for killing their husbands were condemned in Hades to pour water forever into a perforated or bottomless vessel; hence, laborious, useless, and endless, as a task; futile.

dance (dȧns), *v.*; *danced, dancing.* [OF. *dancer* (F. *danser*); prob. from Teut.] **I.** *intr.* To leap, spring, or take steps in a more or less regular or rhythmical manner; move with the feet or body rhythmically, esp. to music; engage, or take part, in a dance; also, to leap, skip, etc., as from excitement or emotion; move nimbly or quickly; also, to bob up and down. **II.** *tr.* To cause to dance; dandle; also, to perform, or take part in (a dance); also, to bring about or cause to be by dancing.—**to dance attendance,** to attend assiduously or obsequiously, as on a person.—**dance,** *n.* [OF. *dance* (F. *danse*).] A succession of more or less regularly ordered steps and movements of the body, usually performed to musical accompaniment; an act or round of dancing; also, any of the many regulated successions of steps, etc., which constitute particular forms of dancing; also, any recurring leaping, springing, or similar movement; also, a piece of music suited in rhythm to a particular form of dancing; also, a social gathering for dancing; a ball.—**dance of death.** See *macabre.*—**dan-cer** (dȧn′sėr), *n.* One who dances; one who dances professionally, as on the stage; *pl.*, the aurora borealis (also called *merry dancers*).—**dan′cing=girl,** *n.* A female professional dancer.—**dan′cing-ly,** *adv.*

dan-de-li-on (dan′dẹ̄-lī-ọn), *n.* [F. *dent de lion*, 'lion's tooth' (with allusion to the toothed leaves).] A common cichoriaceous plant, *Taraxacum taraxacum*, abundant as a weed, characterized by deeply toothed or notched leaves and golden-yellow flowers; any other plant of the genus *Taraxacum*; also, any of various similar plants of other genera, as *Leontodon autumnale*, a cichoriaceous herb with yellow flowers ('fall dandelion').

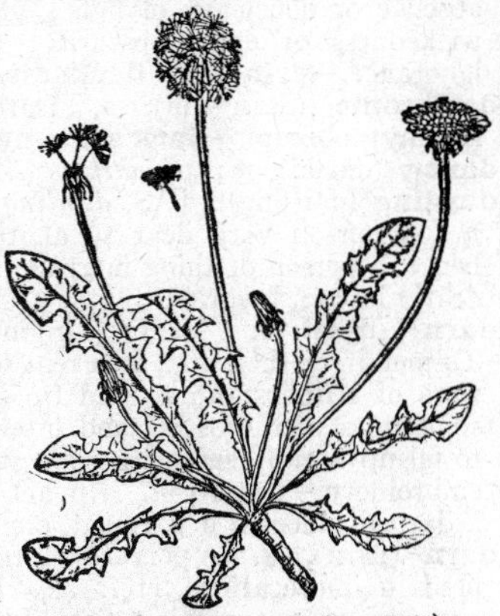

Dandelion (*Taraxacum taraxacum*).

dan-der[1] (dan′dėr), *n.* [Origin obscure.] Anger or temper: as, "He 'pears to know just how long he can torment me before I get my *dander* up" (Mark Twain's "Tom Sawyer," i.). [Colloq.]

dan-der[2] (dan′dėr), *v. i.* [Cf. *dandle.*] To wander about aimlessly, stroll, or saunter; talk incoherently; shake or tremble; make a loud reverberating sound. [Prov.]

dan-di (dan′di), *n.* See *dandy*[1].

Dan-die Din-mont (dan′di din′mont). [From *Dandie* (Andrew) *Dinmont*, in Scott's "Guy Mannering," said to own the progenitors of the breed.] One of a breed of small terriers with a long body, short legs, and long pendulous ears.

dan-di-fy (dan′di-fī), *v. t.*; *-fied, -fying.* [See *-fy.*] To make dandy-like or foppish.—**dan″di-fi-ca′tion** (-fi-kā′shọn), *n.*

dan-di-prat (dan′di-prat), *n.* [Origin unknown.] A small 16th century English coin, worth three halfpence; hence (obs. or archaic), a dwarf or pygmy; a child or urchin; an insignificant fellow, or whipper-snapper.

dan-dle (dan′dl), *v. t.*; *-dled, -dling.* [Origin uncertain: cf. It. *dandolare* (now *dondolare*), dandle, swing, dally, loiter.] To move lightly up and down, as a child on the knees or in the arms; also, to pet; fondle; also, to trifle or play with†.—**dan′dler,** *n.*

dan-druff (dan′druf), *n.* [Origin unknown.] A scurf which forms on the scalp and comes off in small scales.

dan-dy[1] (dan′di), *n.*; pl. *-dies* (-diz). [Hind. *dāndi*, < *dānd*, staff, oar.] A boatman of the Ganges; also, a kind of ascetic who carries a staff; also, a kind of litter consisting of a strong cloth strung like a hammock to a bamboo staff. [India.]

dan-dy[2] (dan′di), *n.* Corruption of *dengue.*

dan-dy[3] (dan′di). [Perhaps a use of *Dandy*, var. of *Andy*, for *Andrew*, man's name.] **I.** *n.*; pl. *-dies* (-diz). A man conspicuous for careful elegance of dress and appearance; an exquisite; a fop; a coxcomb; also, something very fine or first-rate (slang); also, any of various pieces of mechanism, accessories or attachments to machines, etc.; in *paper-making*, a dandy-roller; *naut.*, a vessel rigged as a sloop and having also a jigger-mast on which usually a lug-sail is set. **II.** *a.* Foppish; affectedly neat or fine; also, fine or first-rate (slang).—**dan′dy-ish,** *a.* Like or characteristic of a dandy; foppish.—**dan′dy-ism,** *n.* The style or manners of a dandy; foppishness.

dan′dy-prat, *n.* See *dandiprat.*

dan-dy=roll-er (dan′di-rō″lėr), *n.* In *paper-making*, a roller for compacting the web of paper-pulp and impressing the watermark. Also **dan′dy=roll.**

Dane (dān), *n.* [LL. *Dani*, pl.] A native or inhabitant of Denmark; a person of Danish descent; also, one of a breed of large, powerful, short-haired dogs, somewhat resembling the mastiff but slighter in build (usually called *great Dane*).—**Dane′-law,** *n.* [For AS. *Dena lagu*, Danes' law.] The Danish law anciently in force in the districts of northern and northeastern England which were occupied or held by the Danes; also, that part of England under this law. Also **Dane′lagh** (-lâ).—**Danes″=blood,** *n.* Any of several plants reputed to have sprung orig. from the blood of Danes slain in battle, as the danewort, *Sambucus ebulus*, or a bell-flower, *Campanula glomerata*, or the pasque-flower, *Pulsatilla pulsatilla.* [Local, Eng.]—**dane′wort** (-wėrt), *n.* A small European herbaceous elder, *Sambucus ebulus*, bearing purplish flowers and a dark fruit. Also called *Danes'-blood* and *dwarf elder.*

Great Dane.

dan-ger (dān′jėr), *n.* [OF. *dangier* (F. *danger*), < L. *dominium*, lordship, < *dominus*, master, lord.] The power of a lord or master†; power to dispose of or to harm†; also, liability, as to loss or punishment†; also, hesitation† or reluctance†; also, ungraciousness†; also, liability or exposure to harm or injury; risk; peril; an instance or cause of peril; also, harm† or injury† (as, "We put a sting in him, That at his will he may do *danger* with": Shakspere's "Julius Cæsar," ii. 1. 17).—**dan′ger-less,** *a.* Without danger.—**dan′ger-ous,** *a.* [OF. *dangerous* (F. *dangereux*).] Haughty†; reluctant†; fastidious†; also, fraught with danger or risk; causing danger; perilous; hazardous; unsafe; also, in danger from illness (colloq.).—**dan′ger-ous-ly,** *adv.*—**dan′ger-ous-ness,** *n.*—**dan′ger-some** (-sum), *a.* Fraught with danger. [Prov.]

dan-gle (dang′gl), *v.*; *-gled, -gling.* [Cf. Dan. *dangle*, Sw. *dangla*, Icel. *dingla*, dangle.] **I.** *intr.* To hang loosely and swaying; also, to hang about or follow after a person, as if seeking favor; dance attendance. **II.** *tr.* To make to dangle; hold or carry swaying loosely.—**dan′gle,** *n.* The act of dangling; also, something that dangles.—**dan′gler,** *n.*

Dan-ish (dā′nish). **I.** *a.* Of or pertaining to the Danes, their country, or their language. **II.** *n.* The language of the Danes, a Scandinavian tongue.

Dan-ite (dan′īt), *n.* [From *Dan*, son of Jacob, who was to be "a serpent by the way": see Gen. xlix. 17.] A member of an alleged secret order of Mormons supposed to have been formed about 1837 and to have been guilty of various atrocious crimes.

dank (dangk). [ME. *danke*; perhaps from Scand.] **I.** *a.* Wet; oozy; unpleasantly moist or humid; damp. **II.†** *n.* Wetness; humidity; also, a wet place.—**dank′ish,** *a.* Somewhat dank; damp.—**dank′ly,** *adv.*—**dank′ness,** *n.*

Dan-ne-brog (dan′ẹ-brog), *n.* [Dan.] The Danish national flag; also, a Danish order of knighthood.

dan-seuse (däṅ-sėz), *n.*; pl. *-seuses* (F. -sėz). [F., fem. of *danseur*, dancer, < *danser*, E. *dance*.] A female dancer; a professional female dancer, esp. a ballet-dancer.

Dan-tesque (dan-tesk′), *a.* [See *-esque*.] In the style of the poet Dante (1265–1321); characterized by impressive elevation of style with deep solemnity or somberness of feeling.

dap (dap), *v. i.*; *dapped, dapping.* [Prob. var. of *dab*[1].] To fish by letting the bait fall lightly on the water; also, to dip lightly or suddenly into water.

daph-ne (daf′nē), *n.* [L., < Gr. δάφνη, laurel.] The laurel, *Laurus nobilis*; also, any plant of the thymelæaceous genus *Daphne*, of Europe and Asia, comprising small shrubs of which some species, as *D. mezereum* (see *mezereon*), are cultivated for their fragrant flowers.

dap-per (dap′ėr), *a.* [ME. *dapyr*, pretty, neat: cf. D. *dapper*, G. *tapfer*, brave, stout, gallant.] Neat; trim; smart; also, small and active (as, "And, on the tawny sands and shelves, Trip the pert faeries and the *dapper* elves": Milton's "Comus," 118).—**dap′per-ling,** *n.* A little dapper fellow.—**dap′per-ly,** *adv.*—**dap′per-ness,** *n.*

dap-ple (dap′l). [Origin uncertain: cf. Icel. *depill*, spot, dot.] **I.** *n.* A spot† or small blotch of coloring†; mottled marking, as of an animal's skin or coat; an animal with a mottled skin or coat. **II.** *a.* Dappled; spotted.—**dap′ple,** *v. t.* or *i.*; *-pled, -pling.* To mark or become marked with spots of color.—**dap′ple=gray′,** *a.* Gray with spots or patches of a darker shade.

dar-by (där′bi), *n.*; pl. *-bies* (-biz). [From *Darby* or *Derby*, proper name.] A plasterer's tool for leveling a surface of plaster; *pl.*, handcuffs or fetters (slang).

Dar-by and Joan (där′bi ạnd jōn). [Perhaps from an 18th century poem.] The typical 'old married couple' contentedly leading a life of placid, uneventful domesticity.

Dar-dan, Dar-da-ni-an (där′dạn, där-dā′ni-ạn). [L. *Dardanus, Dardanius*, < Gr. Δάρδανος, Δαρδάνιος.] **I.** *a.* Pertaining to or descended or named from Dardanus, mythical ancestor of the Trojan race; Trojan. **II.** *n.* A Trojan.

dare (dãr), *v.*; 3d pers. sing. pres. ind. *dare* or *dares*, pret. *dared* or *durst*, pp. *dared*, ppr. *daring.* [AS. *dear, dearr*, 1st and 3d pers. sing. pres. ind. of *durran*, akin to OHG. *giturran*, Goth. *gadaursan*, dare, Gr. θρασύς, bold, Skt. *dharsh-*, dare.] **I.** *intr.* To have the necessary courage or boldness for something; be bold enough: followed by an infinitive expressed (with or without *to*) or understood. **II.** *tr.* To have the necessary courage for; venture on; also, to venture to expose one's self to; meet defiantly; also, to defy or challenge; seek to provoke (one) to action, as by asserting his lack of courage.—**dare,** *n.* Daring† or boldness†; also, an act of daring or defying; a defiance; a challenge.—**dare′dev″il. I.** *n.* One ready to dare the devil, or fearing nothing; one who is recklessly daring. **II.** *a.* Recklessly daring.—**dare′dev″il-try, dare′dev″il-ry,** *n.*—**dare′ful,** *a.* Full of daring.—**dar′er,** *n.*

darg (därg), *n.* [ME. *dawerk*, 'day work.'] A day's work; also, a certain quantity of work; a set task. [Sc. and north. Eng.]

Obverse. Reverse.
Daric, in the British Museum.

dar-ic (dar′ik), *n.* [Gr. δαρεικός; from Pers.] A gold coin, also a silver one, of ancient Persia.

dar-ing (dãr′ing), *n.* The act of one that dares; adventurous courage; boldness; intrepidity.—**dar′ing,** *p. a.* That dares; bold; intrepid; adventurous; audacious.—**dar′ing-ly,** *adv.*—**dar′ing-ness,** *n.*

dark (därk), *a.* [AS. *deorc*, dark: cf. OHG. *tarchanjan*, conceal.] Devoid of or deficient in light; unilluminated; also, radiating or reflecting little light; dim; also, approaching black in hue (as, a *dark* brown); not fair (as, a *dark* complexion); also, devoid of moral or spiritual light; evil; wicked; iniquitous; also, characterized by or producing gloom; cheerless; dismal; sad; also, sullen; frowning; also, obscure to the understanding; difficult to interpret or explain; also, hidden or secret; also, silent or reticent; also, about whom or which little or nothing is known; also, unable to see; hence, mentally or spiritually blind; unenlightened; destitute of knowledge or culture.—**dark ages.** See *ages in history.*—**dark horse,** a race-horse whose performances or capabilities are not generally known; any competitor concerning whom nothing certain is known or who unexpectedly comes to the front; one unexpectedly brought forward for or receiving a nomination, as in a political convention, as in case of inability to agree upon any of the leading candidates.—**dark lantern,** a partially inclosed hand-lantern whose light can be obscured by an opaque slide or cover at the opening.—**dark room,** in *photog.*, a room from which the actinic rays of light have been excluded by using only a ruby or orange-red illumination: used for the manufacturing, handling, and developing of photographic plates, etc.—**dark,** *n.* Darkness; also, the dark time; night; nightfall; also, a dark place; also, a dark color; also, obscurity; also, secrecy; also, ignorance.—**dark,** *v. i.* or *t.* To darken. [Obs. or archaic.]—**dark′en,** *v.* **I.** *intr.* To become dark or darker; become obscure; grow clouded, as with gloom or anger; become blind. **II.** *tr.* To make dark or darker; deprive of light; shut out the light of; obscure; dim; cloud; render gloomy; sully; make blind; deprive of mental or spiritual light.—**dark′en-er,** *n.*—**dark′ey,** *n.* See *darky.*—**dark′ish,** *a.* Somewhat dark.

dar-kle (där′kl), *v.*; *-kled, -kling.* [From *darkling, adv.*, taken as ppr.] **I.** *intr.* To appear dark; show indistinctly; also, to grow dark; become dark with anger, etc. **II.** *tr.* To render dark or obscure.

dark-ling (därk′ling). [See *-ling*[2].] **I.** *adv.* In the dark; in darkness. See Shakspere's "Midsummer Night's Dream," ii. 2. 86. **II.** *a.* Being or occurring in the dark; dark; darksome; obscure.

dark-ly (därk′li), *adv.* In a dark manner.

dark-ness (därk′nes), *n.* The state or quality of being dark; absence or deficiency of light; gloom; sorrow or trouble; wickedness or evil; obscurity; concealment; blindness; ignorance.—**prince of darkness.** See under *prince.*

dark-some (därk′sum), *a.* Dark or darkish; somber; gloomy; obscure.—**dark′some-ness,** *n.*

dark-y (där′ki), *n.*; pl. *darkies* (-kiz). A negro. [Colloq.]

dar-ling (där′ling). [AS. *dēorling*, < *dēore*, E. *dear*[2].] **I.** *n.* A person very dear to another; one much beloved; hence, a person or thing in great favor. **II.** *a.* Very dear; dearly loved; favorite.

darn[1] (därn), *v. t.* or *i.* [Origin uncertain.] To mend (clothes, etc., or a rent or hole) with rows of stitches run to and fro side by side, sometimes with crossing and interwoven rows to fill up a gap; sew with such stitches, as in embroidery.—**darn**[1], *n.* An act of darning; a darned place in a garment, etc.

darn[2] (därn), *v. t.* A perverted form of *damn* as used in imprecations, etc.: as, "Under great pressure of provocation Sam Lawson freely said, '*Darn* it!'" (Mrs. Stowe's "Oldtown Folks," xxx.).

Darnel (*Lolium temulentum*).

dar-nel (där′nẹl), *n.* [ME. *darnel*: cf. F. dial. *darnelle.*] An annual grass, *Lolium temulentum*, found as a weed in grain-fields, with seed reputed to have narcotic and poisonous properties; also, any grass of the genus *Lolium*.

darn-er (där′nėr), *n.* One who darns; also, a darning-needle (implement).

darn-ing (där′ning), *n.* The act of one who darns; the result produced; articles darned, or to be darned.—**darn′-**

Canvasback
Ruffed Grouse, or Partridge, or Pheasant
Blue-winged Teal
Prairie-hen, or Pinnated Grouse
California Partridge, or Helmet-quail
Woodcock
Golden Plover, or Field-plover
Bob-white, or Quail
Redhead, or American Pochard
Mallard, or Wild Duck
Canada Goose
Wild Turkey

GAME-BIRDS OF NORTH AMERICA

ing=nee″dle, *n.* A long needle with a long eye, used in darning; also, a dragon-fly ('devil's darning-needle').

dar-rein (dar′ạn or dạ-rān′), *a.* [OF. *derrain*, ult. < L. *de*, from, + *retro*, back, behind: cf. *dernier*.] In *old law*, last; dernier: as, *darrein* presentment (the last or previous presentation to an ecclesiastical benefice regarded as proof of the right to make presentation).

dart (därt), *n.* [OF. *dart* (F. *dard*); prob. from Teut.] A long, slender, pointed missile weapon thrown by the hand or otherwise; also, something resembling such a weapon, as the sting of an insect; a seam uniting two edges of cloth, etc., where a piece has been cut out to adjust the fit of a garment; also, the act of darting; a sudden, swift movement. —**dart,** *v.* **I.** *tr.* To throw with a sudden thrust, as a dart; throw or thrust suddenly and rapidly; shoot; emit; also, to pierce with or as with a dart†. **II.** *intr.* To throw a dart or other missile weapon; also, to move swiftly, like a dart; spring or start suddenly and run swiftly.—**dart′er,** *n.* One who throws or shoots darts; a soldier armed with a dart; also, one who or that which darts or moves swiftly; specif., any fish of the American subfamily *Etheostominæ*, comprising small fresh-water fishes which dart quickly when disturbed; also, a snake-bird.—**dart′ing-ly,** *adv.*

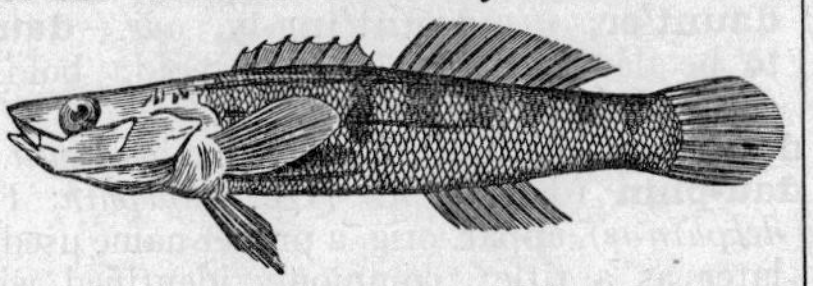

Darter (*Etheostoma flabellare*).

dar-tle (där′tl), *v. t.* or *i.* [Freq. of *dart*.] To dart or shoot forth repeatedly: as, "They would fain see, too, My star that *dartles* the red and the blue" (Browning's "My Star").

dartre (därtr), *n.* [F.] In *pathol.*, any of various cutaneous diseases, esp. herpes.—**dar-trous** (där′trus), *a.*

dart=snake (därt′snāk), *n.* Any of the serpent-like lizards of the genus *Acontias*: so called from the manner in which they dart on their prey.

Dart-snake (*Acontias meleagris*).

Dar-win-i-an (där-win′i-ạn). **I.** *a.* Of or pertaining to the English naturalist Charles Robert Darwin (1809–82) or his doctrines. **II.** *n.* A follower of Charles Robert Darwin; one who accepts Darwinism. — **Dar′win-ism,** *n.* The body of biological doctrine maintained by Charles Robert Darwin respecting the origin of species as derived by descent, with variation, from parent forms, with the perpetuation, as by a process of natural selection, of those best adapted to survive in the struggle for existence.—**Dar′win-ist, Dar′win-ite** (-īt), *n.*

dash (dash), *v.* [ME. *daschen*; prob. from Scand.] **I.** *tr.* To strike violently, esp. so as to break to pieces; smash; also, to throw or thrust violently or suddenly; impel violently; also, to splash violently against something; apply roughly as by splashing; also, to splash with water, etc.; mark with or as with splashes; extinguish (a fire) by throwing water on it; also, to throw something into so as to produce a mixture; qualify or adulterate by admixture; also, to ruin or frustrate (hopes, plans, etc.); also, to depress or dispirit; confound or abash; also, to write or sketch (*down* or *off*) hastily; cancel (writing); mark with a dash; underline; also, a euphemism for *damn* as used in imprecations, etc. **II.** *intr.* To strike with violence; also, to move with violence; rush; also, to make an ostentatious display (colloq.).—**dash,** *n.* A violent blow or stroke; fig., a check or discouragement; also, the throwing or splashing of water, etc., against a thing; the sound of the splashing; the water, etc., splashed; also, a small spot or patch, as of color; a small quantity of anything thrown into or mingled with something else; a touch or tinge; also, a hasty stroke, as of a pen; hence, a line produced by or as by such a stroke; a horizontal line of varying length, used in writing and printing as a mark of punctuation (as to note an abrupt break or pause in a sentence, or to begin and to end a parenthetic clause), as an indication of omission of letters or words or of intermediate terms of a series, as a dividing line between distinct portions of matter, and for other purposes; a short line used in musical notation, as a vertical one placed over or under a note to indicate a staccato effect; also, an impetuous movement; a rush; a sudden onset; a sprint or short race (as, a hundred-yard *dash*); hence, spirited action; vigor in action or style; also, an ostentatious display (colloq.: as, to cut a *dash*).—**dash′board,** *n.* A board or leather apron on the fore part of a vehicle, to protect the occupants from mud, etc.; a similar protection against spray, as at the bow of a launch; also, a paddle of a paddle-wheel.

da-sheen (da-shēn′), *n.* [Appar. a corruption of F. *de Chine*, of China, whence the plant is supposed to have been derived.] A variety of the taro, *Caladium colocasia*, introduced into the southern U. S. from the West Indies, and cultivated for its edible corms and tubers, which are used like potatoes; also, a corm or a tuber of this plant. Cf. *taro* and *caladium*.

dash-er (dash′ėr), *n.* One who or that which dashes; the plunger of a churn; a dashboard; a dashing or ostentatious person (colloq.).

dash-ing (dash′ing), *p. a.* That dashes; splashing; impetuous; spirited or lively; brilliant or showy; stylish.—**dash′ing-ly,** *adv.*

dash=pot (dash′pot), *n.* A device for checking motion in a mechanism, consisting of a cylinder or chamber in which the movement of a piston is retarded by a cushion of air or liquid.

dash-y (dash′i), *a.* Dashing; brilliant or showy; stylish.

das-tard (das′tạrd). [ME. *dastard*; prob. connected with *daze*.] **I.** *n.* A dullard†; also, a base or sneaking coward. **II.** *a.* Characterized by base cowardice.—**das′tard-ly,** *a.* Like or characteristic of a dastard; characterized by base cowardice.—**das′tard-li-ness,** *n.*—**das′tard-y,** *n.* Base cowardice. [Archaic.]

das-y-ure (das′i-ūr), *n.* [NL. *Dasyurus*, < Gr. δασύς, hairy, shaggy, thick, + οὐρά, tail.] Any of the small carnivorous marsupials constituting the genus *Dasyurus*, native in Australia, Tasmania, etc.; also, some related animal, as the Tasmanian devil, *Sarcophilus ursinus* ('ursine dasyure') (see phrase under *Tasmanian*). — **das-y-u′rine** (-ū′rin), *a.*

Spotted Dasyure (*Dasyurus maculatus*).

da-ta (dā′tạ), *n.* Plural of *datum*.

dat-a-ble (dā′tạ-bl), *a.* That may be dated.

da-ta-ry (dā′tạ-ri), *n.*; pl. *-ries* (-riz). [ML. *datarius* (the officer), *dataria* (the office), < *data*, E. *date*².] An officer, now a cardinal, at the head of a certain office or department of the papal Curia whose chief function now is to investigate the fitness of candidates for benefices in the gift of the papal see; also, this office or department.

date¹ (dāt), *n.* [OF. *date* (F. *datte*), < L. *dactylus*, < Gr. δάκτυλος: see *dactyl*.] The oblong, fleshy, one-seeded fruit of a species of palm, *Phœnix dactylifera*, forming a staple food in northern Africa, Arabia, etc., and largely exported to other countries; also, the tree bearing this fruit (see *date-palm*).

date² (dāt), *n.* [OF. F. *date*, < ML. *data*, prop. pp. fem. of L. *dare*, give.] An inscription on a writing, coin, etc., specifying the time, or time and place, of execution; also, the time or period of an event or to which anything belongs; a particular point or period of time; also, the time during which anything lasts; duration; also, the end of a period of time (archaic: as, "What Time would spare, from steel receives its *date*," Pope's "Rape of the Lock," iii. 171); also, an appointment made for a particular time (colloq.).—**down**

to date, down to the present time.—**out of date,** out of season; no longer in vogue or style; old-fashioned; obsolete.—**up to date,** up to the present time; also, in accordance with the prevailing standard or style: also used (written *up-to-date*) as an adjective.—**date²,** *v.*; *dated, dating.* **I.** *tr.* To mark or furnish with a date; also, to ascertain or fix the date or time of; assign a date or time to; also, to reckon by dates. **II.** *intr.* To bear a date; also, to be assigned to a particular time or period; have its origin; take its rise; also, to reckon from some point in time.—**date′less,** *a.* Without a date; undated; endless; of indefinitely long duration.—**date′=line,** *n.* A line, theoretically coinciding with the meridian of 180° from Greenwich, the regions on either side of which are counted as differing by one day in their calendar dates (occasioned by the difference in time between different points on the earth, due to the (apparent) movement of the sun); also, a line in a letter, newspaper article, or the like, giving the date (and often the place) of origin.

date=palm (dāt′päm′), *n.* The species of palm *Phœnix dactylifera,* which bears dates, having a stem usually from 60 to 80 feet in height, terminating in a crown of pinnate leaves.

Date-palm.

date=plum (dāt′plum′), *n.* The fruit of any of several trees of the genus *Diospyros,* as the persimmon, *D. virginiana*; also, any of these trees.

dat-er (dā′tėr), *n.* One who dates; also, an apparatus for stamping dates.

da-tive (dā′tiv). [L. *dativus,* of or belonging to giving, < *dare,* give.] In *gram.*: **I.** *a.* Indicating one to whom something is given, said, or done; noting a case in declension, in Latin and other languages, used most commonly to indicate the indirect object of a verb, and corresponding to the objective case in English as preceded by *to* or *for*; being in or pertaining to this case. **II.** *n.* The dative case, or a word in that case.—**da-ti-val** (dạ-tī′vạl), *a.*—**da′tive-ly,** *adv.*

da-to (dä′tō), *n.*; pl. *-tos* (-tōz). [Philippine Sp.] In the Philippines, a native chief or governor; also, the head-man of a barrio.

dat-o-lite (dat′ọ-līt), *n.* [Gr. δατεῖσθαι, divide, + λίθος, stone.] A native complex silicate containing boron and calcium, occurring commonly in glassy, variously colored crystals.

dat-to (dät′ō), *n.* See *dato.*

da-tum (dā′tum), *n.*; pl. *data* (-tạ). [L., pp. neut. of *dare,* give.] A fact given, afforded, or taken for use, as for a basis of reasoning; any fact from which conclusions may be drawn; a fact in connection with a subject: commonly in *pl.*—**datum level, plane,** or **line,** in *engin.* and *surv.*, a level, etc., from which heights and depths are measured or calculated.

da-tu-ra (dạ-tū′rạ), *n.* [NL.; from Hind.] Any plant of the solanaceous genus *Datura,* the species of which have funnel-shaped flowers, prickly pods, and narcotic properties. See *jimson-weed.*

daub (dâb), *v.* [OF. *dauber,* < L. *dealbare,* whiten, plaster, < *de-,* completely, + *albus,* white.] **I.** *tr.* To cover or coat with soft, adhesive matter, as plaster; also, to smear; soil or defile; also, to paint unskilfully; deck ostentatiously†; give a specious appearance to†; also, to spread (plaster, mud, etc.) on or over something; lay on (paint) unskilfully. **II.** *intr.* To daub something; paint unskilfully; also, to put on a false show†; use flattery (now only prov. Eng.).—**daub,** *n.* Material, esp. of an inferior kind, for daubing walls, etc.; anything daubed on; fig., flattery (prov. Eng.); also, an act of daubing; also, a smear; a crude, inartistic painting.—**daub′er,** *n.* One who or that which daubs; an unskilful painter; anything to daub with, as a brush to spread blacking upon shoes.—**daub′er-y,** *n.* A daubing; the work of a dauber.—**daub′y,** *a.* Of the nature of or resembling a daub; also, given to daubing.

daugh-ter (dâ′tėr), *n.* [AS. *dohtor* = D. *dochter* = G. *tochter* = Icel. *dōttir* = Goth. *dauhtar*; akin to Gr. θυγάτηρ, Skt. *duhitar,* daughter.] A female child or person in relation to her parents; a daughter-in-law; a familiar term of address to a woman or girl from an older person, an ecclesiastic, etc.; any female descendant; one related as if by the ties binding daughter to parent; a female person looked upon as the product or result of particular agencies, forces, influences, etc.; anything (personified as female) considered with respect to its origin.—**daugh′ter=in=law″,** *n.*; pl. *daughters-in-law.* The wife of one's son.—**daugh′ter-ly,** *a.* Pertaining to, befitting, or like a daughter.—**daugh′ter-li-ness,** *n.*

daunt (dânt or dänt), *v. t.* [OF. *danter, donter* (F. *dompter*), < L. *domitare,* freq. of *domare,* tame, subdue.] To tame†; also, to subdue†; also, to overcome with fear; intimidate; hence, to abate the courage of; discourage; dispirit.—**daunt′er,** *n.*—**daunt′ing-ly,** *adv.*—**daunt′less,** *a.* Not to be daunted; fearless; intrepid; bold.—**daunt′less-ly,** *adv.*—**daunt′less-ness,** *n.*

daun-ton (dân′tọn), *v. t.* Same as *daunt.* [Sc.]

dau-phin (dâ′fin), *n.* [OF. *daulphin,* F. *dauphin* (ML. *delphinus*), appar. orig. a proper name used as a surname and later as a title; commonly identified with L. *delphinus,* dolphin.] The distinctive title of the eldest son of the king of France, from 1349 to 1830.—**dau′phine** (-fēn), *n.* [F.] The wife of the dauphin. Also **dau′phin-ess.**

dauw (dou or dâ), *n.* [S. Afr. D.; from native name.] Burchell's zebra, *Equus burchelli.* See *zebra.*

Dauw.

dav-en-port (dav′n-pōrt), *n.* [From *Davenport,* proper name.] A kind of small writing-table; also, a kind of large sofa or divan, often one convertible into a bed.

dav-it (dav′it), *n.* [Appar. < *David,* man's name.] *Naut.*, one of a pair of projecting pieces of wood or iron on the side or stern of a vessel, fitted with a tackle, etc., for raising, lowering, or suspending a small boat; also, any of various similar hoisting devices.

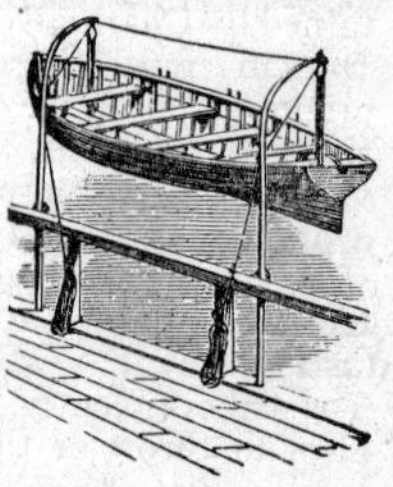

Davits.

Da-vy Jones (dā′vi jōnz). *Naut.*, the spirit of the sea; the sailors' devil.—**Davy Jones's locker,** the ocean, esp. as the grave of all who perish at sea: as, "One boat's crew of 'em is gone to *Davy Jones's locker*" (H. Melville's "Omoo," lxxvi.).

daw¹ (dâ), *n.* [ME. *dawe*; akin to G. *dohle.*] A jackdaw; also, in fig. use, a simpleton; a sluggard (Sc.); a slattern (Sc.).

daw² (dâ), *v. i.* [AS. *dagian,* < *dæg,* E. *day.*] To dawn. [Now Sc. and north Eng.]

daw-dle (dâ′dl), *v.*; *-dled, -dling.* [Origin uncertain.] **I.** *intr.* To idle; waste time; trifle; loiter. **II.** *tr.* To waste (time) by trifling: usually with *away.*—**daw′dle,** *n.* One who dawdles; also, the act of dawdling.—**daw′dler,** *n.*—**daw′dling-ly,** *adv.*

dawk (dâk), *n.* See *dak.*

dawn (dân), *v. i.* [First as in ME. *dawninge,* n., for earlier *dawunge,* < AS. *dagung,* daybreak, dawn, < *dagian,* E. *daw².*] To begin to grow light in the morning (as, the day *dawns*); begin to shine, as the sun; fig., to begin to open or develop; also, to begin to brighten with or as with the light of morning (as, "the *dawning* hills": Tennyson's

"Œnone," 46); hence, to begin to appear; become visible; begin to be perceived.—**dawn,** *n.* The first appearance of daylight in the morning; hence, the beginning or rise of anything.

day (dā), *n.* [AS. *dæg* = D. *dag* = G. *tag* = Icel. *dagr* = Sw. and Dan. *dag* = Goth. *dags*, day.] The interval of light between two successive nights; the time between sunrise and sunset; also, the light of day; daylight; also, the period during which the earth (or a heavenly body) makes one revolution on its axis; the interval of time which elapses between two consecutive returns of the same terrestrial meridian to the sun ('solar day'); the average length of this interval, twenty-four hours ('mean solar day'); a period reckoned from midnight to midnight and equivalent in length to the mean solar day ('civil day'), as contrasted with a similar period reckoned from noon to noon ('astronomical day'); also, a day's journey; also, the portion of a day allotted to labor (as, an eight-hour *day*); also, a day as a point or unit of time, or on which something occurs (as, "The third *day* he shall rise again": Mat. xx. 19); also, a day assigned to a particular purpose or observance (as, settling-*day*; New Year's *Day*); a day of settlement or payment; a day fixed for receiving callers, as when a hostess is 'at home'; a day of contest, or the combat or conflict of such a day (as, to win the *day*); also, a space of time, esp. as allowed for payment, etc.†; a particular time or period (often in *pl.*: as, at the present *day*; in *days* of old); period of life or activity (often in *pl.*: as, a man honored in his *day*; to end one's *days* in peace); period of power or influence (as, a man who has had his *day*).—**day letter.** See *letter*², *n.* —**Day of Atonement,** a Jewish fast-day: see *Yom Kippur.* —**day of doom,** the day of judgment.—**day of judgment,** the day of the Last Judgment, at the end of the world. Also (with capitals) *Day of Judgment.*—**days of grace,** days (commonly three) allowed by law or custom for payment after a bill or note falls due.—**days of obligation.** See under *obligation.*—**sidereal day.** See *sidereal.*

da-yal (dä-yäl′), *n.* [Hind. *dahiyāl.*] Any of certain song-birds of the East Indies, esp. *Copsichus saularis.*

Dayal (*Copsichus saularis*).

day=blind-ness (dā′blīnd″nes), *n.* Hemeralopia.

day=book (dā′bůk), *n.* In *book-keeping*, a book in which the transactions of the day are entered in the order of their occurrence.

day-break (dā′brāk), *n.* The first appearance of light in the morning; dawn.

day=coach (dā′kōch), *n.* A railroad passenger-car of the ordinary kind, as distinguished from a sleeping-car, a parlor-car, etc.

day=dream (dā′drēm), *n.* A visionary fancy indulged in while awake; a reverie.—**day′=dream,** *v. i.* To indulge in day-dreams.—**day′=dream″-er,** *n.*

day=flow-er (dā′flou″ėr), *n.* Any plant of the genus *Commelina*, of the spiderwort family, mostly bearing cymes of small blue ephemeral flowers.

day=fly (dā′flī), *n.*; pl. *-flies* (-flīz). Any insect of the family *Ephemeridæ*; an ephemerid.

day=la-bor (dā′lā′bọr), *n.* Labor performed or hired by the day.—**day′=la′bor-er,** *n.*

day-less (dā′les), *a.* Devoid of the light of day; dark; also, not divided into days.

day-light (dā′līt), *n.* The light of day; fig., openness or publicity; also, daytime; also, daybreak.—**daylight saving,** the saving of daylight hours, for more advantageous use, by changes in the reckoning of time to conform to the seasonal changes in the sun's hours of rising and setting, as by the moving forward of the hands of the clock one hour, by a country or community, at a designated time during the spring, with a corresponding moving backward of the hands one hour at a designated time during the autumn. Cf. *summer time*, under *summer*³, *a.*

day=lil-y (dā′lil″i), *n.* Any plant of the liliaceous genus *Hemerocallis*, with yellow or orange flowers which commonly last only for a day; also, any plant of the liliaceous genus *Niobe* (or *Funkia*), with white or blue flowers.

day=long (dā′lông), *a.* Lasting all day.

day=nurs-er-y (dā′nėr″sėr-i), *n.* A nursery for the care of small children during the day, while the mothers are at work.

day=school (dā′sköl), *n.* A school held in the daytime (distinguished from *night-school*); a school held on week-days (distinguished from *Sunday-school*); a school at which board and lodging are not furnished for the pupils (distinguished from *boarding-school*).

days-man (dāz′mạn), *n.*; pl. *-men.* An umpire or mediator (archaic: see Job, ix. 33); also, one who works by the day; a day-laborer.

day-spring (dā′spring), *n.* The dawn; daybreak. [Chiefly poetic.]

day=star (dā′stär), *n.* The morning star (see under *morning*); also, the sun (poetic: as, "So sinks the *day-star* in the ocean bed," Milton's "Lycidas," 168).

day-time (dā′tīm), *n.* The time during which there is daylight; the time between sunrise and sunset.

daze (dāz), *v. t.*; *dazed, dazing.* [ME. *dasen*; from Scand.] To stun or stupefy, as by a blow, a shock, strong drink, etc.; confuse or bewilder; dazzle.—**daze,** *n.* The state of being dazed.—**daz-ed-ly** (dā′zed-li), *adv.*

daz-zle (daz′l), *v.*; *-zled, -zling.* [Freq. of *daze.*] **I.** *tr.* To overpower or dim (the vision) by intense light; hence, to bewilder by brilliancy or display of any kind; also, to treat by dazzle-painting, as a vessel. **II.** *intr.* To be overpowered by light; also, to be overpoweringly bright; fig., to excite admiration by brilliancy.—**daz′zle,** *n.* The act or fact of dazzling; bewildering brightness; also, dazzle-painting.—**daz′zle-ment,** *n.* The act of dazzling, or the state of being dazzled; also, that which dazzles.—**daz′zle=paint′ing,** *n.* The act or method of painting vessels in specially designed dazzling patterns of various colors, or the patterns used, employed during the World War to render it difficult for attacking submarines to estimate the course of the vessels accurately. Sometimes called *naval camouflage.*—**daz′zler,** *n.*—**daz′zling-ly,** *adv.*

de (dė), *prep.* [F., < L. *de*, from: see *de-*.] From; of: much used in French personal names, orig. before place-names to indicate place of origin, esp. territorial estate, and hence accepted as evidence of noble or gentle descent, although of no value as evidence, because often assumed without right. Cf. *von.*

de-. [Partly < L. *de-* (OF. *de-*, F. *de-*, usually *dé-*), off, away, down, out, utterly, completely, much, sometimes also with privative or negative force, repr. *de*, prep., from, away or down from, out of; partly < OF. *de-*, *des-*, F. *dé-*, < L. *dis-*, apart, asunder, away, utterly, also with privative, negative, or reversing force: see *dis-*.] A prefix of Latin origin, denoting primarily separation or removal, and hence deprivation, negation, or reversal (cf. *dis-* and *un-*²), used freely, esp. with these latter significations, as an English formative, as in *debloom, decivilize, deforest, dehorn, demeritorious, deodorant, desulphurize, dethrone, detrain.* In a few cases *de-* has an intensive force, or denotes repetition, as in *decomplex, decompound.*

dea-con (dē′kọn), *n.* [AS. *dēacon, diacon*, < LL. *diaconus*, < Gr. διάκονος, servant, minister, deacon.] A subordinate officer in the early Christian church; in hierarchical churches, a member of the clerical order next below that of priest; in other churches, an appointed or elected officer having variously defined duties.—**dea′con,** *v. t.* To make or ordain deacon; also, to read out (a hymn, etc.), a line or two at a time, for repetition in singing as soon as read (colloq., U. S.); also, to pack (fruit, etc.) with the best specimens on top (slang, U. S.); falsify, adulterate, or doctor (slang, U. S.).—**dea′con-ess,** *n.* A female deacon; in certain Protestant churches, one of an order of women who care for the sick and poor.—**dea′con-ry** (-ri), *n.*; pl. *-ries* (-riz). The office of a deacon; also, deacons collectively.—**dea′con-ship,** *n.*

dead (ded), *a.* [AS. *dēad* = D. *dood* = G. *tot* = Icel. *daudhr* = Goth. *dauths*, dead; all orig. pp. from the Teut. verb-stem represented by E. *die*¹.] Having ceased to live; deprived of life; also, bereft of sensation; benumbed; insensible; death-like (as, a *dead* faint); also, having ceased to exist in a particular capacity; deprived of civil rights; without spiritual life or vigor; also, no longer in existence or use; extinct (as, *dead* languages); also, not endowed with life; inanimate; also, infertile or barren; also, deprived of or lacking some animating force or characteristic quality; extinguished, as a fire; tasteless or flat, as liquor; lacking brightness, as a color; without resonance, as sound; also, without vigor or animation; ineffectual or inoperative; inactive or dull (as, the *dead* season); unproductive (as, *dead* capital); out of play (as, a *dead* ball); having been used, or rejected, as type set up or copy for printing; bearing no current, or unconnected with a source of electricity, as a wire or a circuit; also, motionless, or not communicating motion or power (as, the *dead* center on a lathe); characterized by abrupt stoppage of motion, etc. (as, a *dead* stop); also, unvarying or uniform (as, a *dead* wall); complete, absolute, or utter (as, a *dead* loss); unerring (as, a *dead* shot); direct or straight (as, a *dead* line); also, of or pertaining to one who or that which is dead.—**dead angle,** or **dead space,** in *fort.*, an angle or space outside a fortification which cannot be reached by the fire of its defenders.—**dead beat,** one who avoids paying for what he gets, living by evasions; an utterly dishonest, worthless fellow. Cf. *beat, n.* [Slang.]—**dead heat,** a heat or race in which two or more competitors reach the goal simultaneously.—**dead letter,** a law, ordinance, etc., which has lost its force, though not formally repealed or abolished; also, a letter which lies unclaimed for a certain time at a post-office, or which, because of faulty address, etc., cannot be delivered, such letters being sent to and handled in a special division or department ('dead-letter office') of the general post-office.—**dead load.** See *load, n.*—**dead men's shoes,** a situation or possession formerly held by a person who has died.—**Dead Sea apple.** See under *apple.*—**dead space.** See *dead angle,* above.—**dead steam,** exhaust-steam.—**dead,** *n.* One who is dead, or dead persons collectively (usually with *the*); also, the period of greatest darkness, coldness, etc. (as, the *dead* of night; the *dead* of winter).—**dead,** *adv.* In a dead manner; to a degree suggesting death; with abrupt stoppage of motion, etc.; absolutely or utterly; directly (as, *dead* against; "a gale *dead* from the eastward," Dana's "Two Years before the Mast," xxxi.).

dead=beat (ded'bēt'), *a.* In *physics, clock-making,* etc., beating without recoil; free from oscillation.

dead=born (ded'bôrn), *a.* Still-born.

dead=cen-ter (ded'sen"tėr), *n.* In a steam-engine, etc., either of two positions of the crank in which the connecting-rod has no power to turn it, occurring when the crank and connecting-rod are in the same straight line, at each end of a stroke.

dead-en (ded'n), *v.* **I.** *tr.* To deprive of life; kill (trees) by girdling; benumb; dull; deprive of vitality or animation; reduce the motion of; deprive of characteristic quality; reduce in brilliance, resonance, etc.; make impervious to sound, as a floor. **II.** *intr.* To become dead.—**dead'en-er,** *n.*—**dead'en-ing,** *n.* The act of one who or that which deadens; that which deadens color, sound, etc.; a clearing made by deadening trees (U. S.).

dead-er (ded'ėr), *n.* A dead person; a corpse. [Slang.]

dead-eye (ded'ī), *n.* *Naut.*, a round, laterally flattened wooden block encircled by a rope or an iron band and pierced with three holes; esp., either of a pair of such blocks, one fastened to a shroud and the other to a corresponding chain, the two blocks being connected together by a rope (the lanyard) rove through the holes.

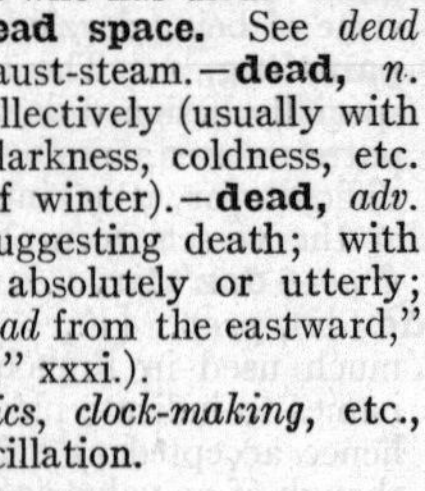

Front and side views of a Deadeye.

dead-fall (ded'fâl), *n.* A trap, esp. for large game, in which a weight falls upon and crushes the prey; also, a mass of fallen trees and underbrush.

dead=hand (ded'hand), *n.* [Tr. OF. *mortemain:* see *mortmain.*] Same as *mortmain.*

dead-head (ded'hed), *n.* One admitted to a theater, allowed to ride in a public conveyance, or granted some similar privilege having its public price, without payment. [Colloq.]

dead=house (ded'hous), *n.* A building or place where dead bodies are kept for a time; a morgue.

dead=light (ded'līt), *n.* *Naut.*, a strong wooden or iron shutter for a cabin-window or port-hole, to prevent water from entering.

dead-li-ly (ded'li-li), *adv.* In a deadly manner.

dead=line (ded'līn), *n.* A line around a military prison, which no prisoner can cross without the liability or penalty of being shot; fig., any line or limit beyond which it is impossible to go with impunity.

dead-li-ness (ded'li-nes), *n.* Deadly quality or character.

dead-lock (ded'lok), *n.* A state of affairs in which procedure or decision is for the time impossible, as from mutual opposition or conflict between the persons or parties involved: as, "I have them all at a *dead lock!*—for every one of them is afraid to let go first" (Sheridan's "Critic," iii. 1).—**dead'-lock,** *v. t.* To bring to a deadlock.

dead-ly (ded'li), *a.*; compar. *deadlier,* superl. *deadliest.* [AS. *dēadlīc.*] Subject to death†; also, causing death; fatal; poisonous; involving spiritual death (as, a *deadly* sin; the seven *deadly* sins, pride, covetousness, lust, anger, gluttony, envy, and sloth); also, aiming to kill or destroy, or involving such an aim (as, a *deadly* foe; *deadly* enmity); implacable; also, resembling or suggestive of death; deathlike; also, excessive (colloq.: as, *deadly* haste).—**dead'ly,** *adv.* [AS. *dēadlīce.*] Mortally† or fatally†; implacably†; in a manner resembling or suggesting death (as, *deadly* pale); excessively (colloq.: as, *deadly* dull).

dead=march (ded'märch), *n.* A piece of solemn music suited to accompany a funeral procession, esp. one played at a military funeral.

dead-ness (ded'nes), *n.* The state or quality of being dead.

dead=point (ded'point), *n.* Same as *dead-center.*

dead=reck-on-ing (ded'rek'n-ing), *n.* *Naut.*, the calculation of a ship's position without astronomical observations, by means of the distances sailed on the various courses as shown by the log and compass, with corrections for currents, etc.

dead=wa-ter (ded'wâ"tėr), *n.* *Naut.*, the water which eddies about a ship's stern during progress.

dead=weight (ded'wāt'), *n.* The heavy, unrelieved weight of anything inert; also, a heavy or oppressive burden; specif., the lading of a vessel; also, the weight of a railroad-car, etc., as distinct from its load.

dead=wood (ded'wůd), *n.* The dead limbs upon a tree; dead branches or trees; fig., anything useless; in *ship-building,* a reinforcing built-up body of timber above the keel at either end of a ship.

deaf (def), *a.* [AS. *dēaf* = D. *doof* = G. *taub* = Icel. *daufr* = Goth. *daubs,* deaf.] Lacking, or deprived of, the sense of hearing, wholly or partially; unable to hear; sometimes, insensible to certain kinds of sounds; also, refusing to listen or to give heed; inattentive; also, dull or muffled, as sound†; also, hollow, empty, barren, or blasted (chiefly prov. Eng.).—**deaf,** *v. t.* To deafen. [Archaic or prov. Eng.]—**deaf'en,** *v. t.* To make deaf; stun with noise; also, to render (a sound) inaudible, as by a louder sound; in *arch.*, to render impervious to sound.—**deaf'en-ing-ly,** *adv.*—**deaf'ly,** *adv.*—**deaf'=mute',** *n.* A person who is deaf and dumb, esp. one in whom dumbness is due to congenital or early deafness. Communication with and between deaf-mutes is effected in various ways, as by means of a manual alphabet formed by positions of the fingers of one or both hands, or through lip-reading.—**deaf'ness,** *n.*

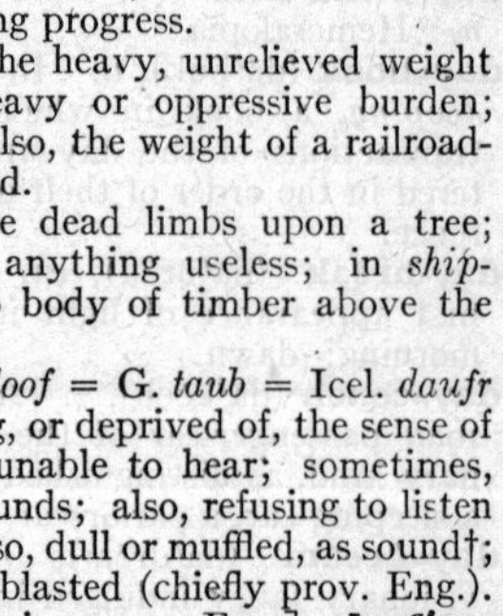

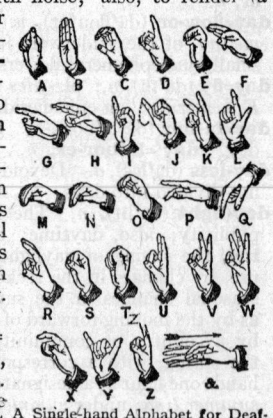

A Single-hand Alphabet for Deaf-mutes.

deal[1] (dēl), *n.* [MLG. *dele* = D. *deel* = G. *diele,* board, plank.] A board or plank, esp. of fir or pine, and usually more than 7 inches wide and 6 feet long, and less than 3 inches thick; such boards collectively; also, wood of fir or pine, such as deals are made from.

deal² (dēl), *n.* [AS. *dǣl* = D. *deel* = G. *teil* = Goth. *dails*, part, portion, share. Later E. senses are from *deal*², *v.*] A part†, portion†, or share†; a quantity, amount, extent, or degree (as, a good *deal*; a great *deal*); an undefined but considerable or large amount or extent (as, a *deal* of money); also, the act of dealing or distributing; the distribution to the players of the cards used in a game; also, a business transaction (colloq.); a bargain or arrangement for mutual advantage, as in commerce or politics, often a secret or underhand one (colloq.).—**deal**², *v.*; *dealt* (delt), *dealing*. [AS. *dǣlan* = D. *deelen* = G. *teilen* = Icel. *deila* = Goth. *dailjan*; from the noun (AS. *dǣl*, etc.).] **I.** *tr.* To divide in portions†; also, to distribute among a number of recipients, as the cards required in a game; apportion; also, to give to one as his share or portion; also, to deliver (blows, etc.). **II.** *intr.* To distribute the cards required in a game; also, to have intercourse (*with*); treat or negotiate (*with*); trade or do business (as, to *deal* with a firm; to *deal* in an article); occupy one's self or itself (*with* or *in*); take action with respect to a thing or person (usually with *with*); take effective or successful action (*with*); conduct one's self toward persons in a specified way (as, "Let us *deal* justly": Shakspere's "King Lear," iii. 6. 42).—**deal'er**, *n.* One who deals or distributes; the player who distributes the cards in a game; also, one who deals with a person, in an article, etc.; a trader, esp. one who buys articles and sells them without altering their condition.

deal=fish (dēl'fish), *n.* [See *deal*¹.] Any of the deep-sea fishes constituting the genus *Trachypterus*, characterized by a long, compressed, tape-like body.

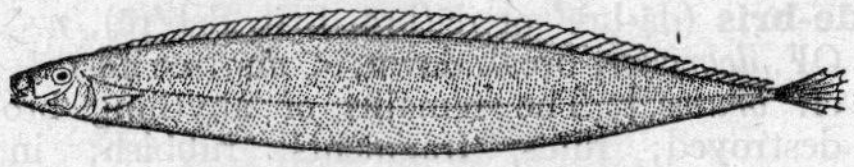

Deal-fish (*Trachypterus arcticus*).

deal-ing (dē'ling), *n.* The act of one that deals; distribution; intercourse, as of friendship or business; trading; action with respect to matters or persons; conduct toward others.

dean¹, **dene** (dēn), *n.* [AS. *denu*, valley, akin to *denn*, E. *den*.] A valley; a deep, narrow, wooded valley or dell, esp. one through which a stream flows. [Now chiefly local, Eng., except in place-names.]

dean² (dēn), *n.* [OF. *deien* (F. *doyen*), < LL. *decanus*, one set over ten (soldiers, monks, etc.), < L. *decem*, ten.] A chief of a division of ten†; the chief over ten monks in a monastery†; the head of the chapter of a cathedral or a collegiate church; any of various other ecclesiastical dignitaries, as the head of a division of an archdeaconry ('rural dean'); the head of a faculty, or sometimes its registrar or secretary, in a university or college; the head of certain other bodies; the senior member, in length of service, of any body.—**dean'er-y**, *n.*; pl. *-ies* (-iz). The office, jurisdiction, district, or residence of a dean.—**dean'ship**, *n.*

de-an-thro-po-mor-phize (dē-an"thrō-pō-môr'fīz), *v. t.*; *-phized*, *-phizing*. [See *de-*.] To divest of anthropomorphic attributes or character.

dear¹ (dēr), *a.* [AS. *dēor*.] Hard; severe; grievous; dire: as, "in our *dear* peril" (Shakspere's "Timon of Athens," v. 1. 231). [Archaic.]

dear² (dēr). [AS. *dēore* = D. *dier* = G. *teuer* = Icel. *dȳrr*.] **I.** *a.* Honorable† or worthy†; regarded with esteem or affection (often, when used in address, as in the introduction of a letter, a mere conventional expression of regard); beloved or loved (as, the *dear* ones at home); precious in one's regard (as, our *dearest* possessions; to run for *dear* life); also, of great value or importance†; high-priced, costly, or expensive, as commodities; charging, or marked by, high prices, as a dealer or a season; also, heartfelt†; earnest†. **II.** *n.* One who is dear; a beloved one: often used in direct address (as, my *dear*).—**dear**², *adv.* Dearly; fondly; also, at a high price, or at great cost.—**dear**², *interj.* An exclamation indicating surprise, distress, or other emotion.

dear-born (dēr'bọrn), *n.* [From *Dearborn*, personal name.] A kind of four-wheeled country carriage used in the U. S.

dear-ly (dēr'li), *adv.* In a dear manner; fondly or affectionately; also, at a high price, or at great cost.—**dear'-ness**, *n.*

dearth (dėrth), *n.* [ME. *derthe*, < *dere*, E. *dear*².] Costliness†; also, scarcity and dearness of food; famine; hence, scarcity or scanty supply of anything; want or lack.

dear-y, **dear-ie** (dēr'i), *n.*; pl. *-ies* (-iz). A little dear; a darling.

death (deth), *n.* [AS. *dēath* = D. *dood* = G. *tod* = Icel. *daudhr* = Goth. *dauthus*, death; akin to E. *dead* and *die*¹.] The act or fact of dying; the total and permanent cessation of all the vital functions of an animal or plant; [often *cap.*] the annihilating power personified, usually represented as a skeleton; [*l. c.*] the state of being dead; fig., loss or absence of spiritual life; loss or deprivation of civil life; extinction or destruction; also, bloodshed or murder; also, a cause or occasion of death (as, "The clamorous lapwings feel the leaden *death*": Pope's "Windsor Forest," 132); also, a pestilence (as, the black *death*: see under *black*, *a.*).—**dance of death.** See *macabre*.

death=bed (deth'bed), *n.* [Cf. AS. *dēathbedd*, the grave.] The bed on which a person dies.

death=blow (deth'blō), *n.* A blow causing death. Also fig.

death=cup (deth'kup), *n.* A common, extremely poisonous mushroom (toadstool), *Amanita phalloides*, having a cup-like enlargement which receives the base of the stem; also, the enlargement itself.

death=damp (deth'damp), *n.* The cold sweat which sometimes precedes death.

death-ful (deth'fůl), *a.* Full of or fraught with death; deadly; fatal; destructive; also, liable to death; mortal; also, resembling death; death-like.—**death'ful-ly**, *adv.*—**death'ful-ness**, *n.*

death=house (deth'hous), *n.* A building or part of a prison in which persons condemned to death are kept awaiting execution.

death-less (deth'les), *a.* Not subject to death; immortal.—**death'less-ly**, *adv.*—**death'less-ness**, *n.*

death-ly (deth'li), *a.* [AS. *dēathlīc*.] Causing death; deadly; also, death-like.—**death'li-ness**, *n.*—**death'ly**, *adv.* In the manner of death.

death=mask (deth'mȧsk), *n.* A cast of a person's face taken after death.

death=rate (deth'rāt), *n.* The proportion of the number of deaths in a place in a given time to the total population.

death=rat-tle (deth'rat"l), *n.* A rattling sound often heard in the throat of a dying person.

death's=head (deths'hed), *n.* A human skull, esp. as a symbol of mortality.—**death's=head moth**, the large old-world hawk-moth *Acherontia atropos*, with markings on the back of the thorax resembling the figure of a skull.

Death's-head Moth.

deaths-man (deths'mạn), *n.*; pl. *-men*. One who puts another to death; an executioner. [Archaic.]

death=trap (deth'trap), *n.* A structure or situation involving imminent risk of death.

death-ward (deth'wạrd), *adv.* Toward death.

death=war-rant (deth'wor"ạnt), *n.* An official order for the execution of the sentence of death. Also fig.

death=watch (deth'woch), *n.* A watch or vigil beside any one dying or dead; a guard set over a condemned person before execution; also, any of various small insects, as the beetle *Anobium tessellatum*, which make a sound like the ticking of a watch, supposed to presage death.

death=wound (deth'wönd), *n.* A wound that causes death.

death-y (deth'i). **I.** *a.* Death-like; deathly. **II.** *adv.* Deathly.

deave (dēv), *v. t.*; *deaved, deaving.* [= *deaf, v.*] To make deaf; deafen. [Now prov.]

de-ba-cle (dẹ-bä'kl or -bak'l), *n.* [F. *débâcle*, < *débâcler*, unbar, clear, break up as ice, < *dé-* (see *dis-*) + *bâcler*, bar, < L. *baculum*, stick, rod.] A breaking up of ice in a river; a violent rush of waters, carrying along debris; hence, a general break-up, rout, or overthrow.

de-bar (dẹ-bär'), *v. t.*; *-barred, -barring.* [OF. *debarrer*, *desbarrer* (F. *débarrer*), < *des-* (see *dis-*) + *barrer*, E. *bar, v.*] To bar out or exclude from a place or condition; hinder from approach, entry, use, etc.; also, to prevent or prohibit (an action, etc.).—**de-bar'ment,** *n.*

de-bark (dẹ-bärk'), *v. t.* or *i.* [F. *débarquer*, < *dé-* (see *dis-*) + *barque*, E. *bark*[3].] To disembark.—**de-bar-ka-tion** (dē-bär-kā'shọn), *n.*

de-bar-rass (dẹ-bar'ạs), *v. t.* [F. *débarrasser*: cf. *embarrass.*] To disembarrass; disencumber: as, "Mrs. Vane . . . wore a thick mantle and a hood . . . Of these Triplet *debarrassed* her" (Reade's "Peg Woffington," xiii.).

de-base (dẹ-bās'), *v. t.*; *-based, -basing.* [See *de-* and *base*[1].] To lower in rank or dignity†; also, to decry† or depreciate†; also, to reduce in quality or value; make base; adulterate; specif., to depreciate (coin), as by admixture of an alloy. —**de-base'ment,** *n.* The act of debasing, or the state of being debased; also, something debasing.—**de-bas'er** (-bā'sėr), *n.*—**de-bas'ing-ly,** *adv.*

de-bat-a-ble (dẹ-bā'tạ-bl), *a.* Capable of being debated; subject to controversy or contention.—**debatable land,** land in dispute, as a border district between two countries that is claimed by both. Also fig.

de-bate (dẹ-bāt'), *v.*; *-bated, -bating.* [OF. *debatre* (F. *débattre*), < *de-* (see *de-*) + *batre*, beat, E. *bate*[1].] **I.** *intr.* To fight†, contend†, or quarrel†; also, to engage in discussion, esp. in a legislative or other public assembly; also, to deliberate or consider. **II.** *tr.* To contend for or over (archaic: as, "We two had turn'd the battle's tide, In many a well-*debated* field," Scott's "Rokeby," i. 16); also, to dispute about; discuss or argue (a question), as in a public assembly; also, to deliberate upon or consider.—**de-bate',** *n.* [OF. *debat* (F. *débat*).] Strife or contention (archaic); also, contention by argument; discussion; a discussion, esp. of a public question in an assembly; also, deliberation or consideration.—**de-bat'er** (-bā'tėr), *n.*—**de-bat'ing-ly,** *adv.*

de-bauch (dẹ-bâch'), *v.* [F. *débaucher*, OF. *desbaucher*, < *des-* (see *dis-*) + *-baucher*, of uncertain origin and meaning.] **I.** *tr.* To lead away, as from allegiance or duty; also, to seduce from virtue or morality; esp., to corrupt by sensuality, intemperance, etc.; in general, to corrupt or pervert; deprave; vitiate; also, to vilify† or depreciate†. **II.** *intr.* To indulge in a debauch.—**de-bauch',** *n.* [F. *débauche.*] A period of excessive indulgence in sensual pleasures, esp. in drinking; also, the practice of such indulgence; debauchery.—**deb-au-chee** (deb-â-shē'), *n.* [F. *débauché*, pp.] One addicted to excessive indulgence in sensual pleasures; one given to debauchery.—**de-bauch'er,** *n.*—**de-bauch'er-y,** *n.*; pl. *-ies* (-iz). Seduction from allegiance or duty; also, seduction from virtue or morality; esp., excessive indulgence in sensual pleasures; intemperance.—**de-bauch'ment,** *n.*

de-ben-ture (dẹ-ben'ṭụr), *n.* [L. *debentur*, 'there are owing.'] A certificate of indebtedness signed by an officer, esp. of a government; a certificate of drawback issued at a custom-house; an instrument in which a corporation or company acknowledges indebtedness for a specified sum on which interest is due until the principal is paid.—**de-ben'-tured,** *a.* Furnished with or secured by a debenture.

deb-ile (deb'il), *a.* [L. *debilis*, < *de-* priv. + *habilis*, E. *able.*] Weak; feeble. [Archaic.]

de-bil-i-tate (dẹ-bil'i-tāt), *v. t.*; *-tated, -tating.* [L. *debilitatus*, pp. of *debilitare*, < *debilis*: see *debile.*] To make weak or feeble; weaken; enfeeble.—**de-bil-i-ta'tion** (-tā'shọn), *n.* [L. *debilitatio(n-).*] The act of debilitating; debilitated condition.—**de-bil'i-ta-tive,** *a.* Tending to debilitate.

de-bil-i-ty (dẹ-bil'i-ti), *n.* [L. *debilitas*, < *debilis*: see *debile.*] The state of being weak or feeble; weakness; esp., a condition of the body in which the vital functions are feebly discharged.

deb-it (deb'it), *n.* [L. *debitum*, something owed: see *debt.*] A debt†; the recording or an entry of debt in an account; the side (left-hand) of an account on which such entries are made (opposed to *credit*); a balance against one in an account.—**deb'it,** *v. t.*; *-ited, -iting.* To charge with a debt; also, to charge as a debt; enter upon the debit side of an account.

de-blat-e-rate (dẹ-blat'ẹ-rāt), *v. i.*; *-rated, -rating.* [L. *deblateratus*, pp. of *deblaterare*, < *de-*, away, + *blaterare*, talk foolishly, babble: cf. F. *déblatérer.*] To babble; prate; rail against something.—**de-blat-e-ra'tion** (-rā'shọn), *n.*

de-bloom (dē-blöm'), *v. t.* [See *de-.*] To remove the bloom or fluorescence from (an oil).

deb-o-nair (deb-ọ-nãr'), *a.* [OF. *debonaire* (F. *débonnaire*), orig. phrase, *de bon aire*, 'of good disposition.'] Of gentle disposition†; also, of pleasant manners; courteous; affable; gay.—**deb-o-nair'ly,** *adv.*—**deb-o-nair'ness,** *n.*

de-bosh (dẹ-bosh'), *v.* Archaic form of *debauch.*

de-bouch (dẹ-bösh'), *v. i.* [F. *déboucher*, < *dé-* (see *dis-*) + *bouche*, mouth, < L. *bucca*, cheek, mouth.] To march out from a narrow or confined place into open country, as a body of troops; hence, in general, to issue or emerge.—**dé-bou-ché** (dā-bö-shā), *n.* [F.] A place where troops may debouch; any place of exit; an opening; an outlet.—**de-bouch'ment,** *n.* The act or fact of debouching; also, a debouchure.—**de-bou-chure** (F. dā-bö-shür), *n.* [Appar. a pseudo-French formation, on the analogy of (F.) *embouchure.*] A mouth or outlet, as of a river or a pass: as, "The next morning I reached the *debouchure* of the Jordan" (Kinglake's "Eothen," xiii.).

de-bris (dạ-brē' or dā'brē, Brit. deb'rē), *n.* [F. *débris*, < OF. *debrisier*, break down, < *de-* (see *de-*) + *brisier*, break: cf. *bruise.*] The remains of anything broken down or destroyed; ruins; fragments; rubbish; in *geol.*, an accumulation of loose fragments of rock, etc.

debt (det), *n.* [OF. *dete* (F. *dette*), < ML. *debita*, for L. *debitum*, something owed, prop. pp. neut. of *debere*, owe, lit. 'have or keep from (one),' < *de*, from, + *habere*, have, hold, keep.] That which is owed; that which one person is bound to pay to or perform for another; also, a liability or obligation to pay or render something; the condition of being under such obligation; also, an offense requiring reparation; a sin; a trespass.—**debt'or,** *n.* [OF. *detor* (F. *detteur*), < L. *debitor*, < *debere.*] One who is in debt or under obligations to another; one who receives credit in business transactions (opposed to *creditor*); in *bookkeeping*, the debit side of an account.—**debt'or-ship,** *n.*

dé-but (dā-bü' or dā'bü, F. dā-bü), *n.* [F., < *débuter*, make the first stroke in a game, make one's first appearance, begin, < *dé-* (see *de-*) + *but*, goal, mark.] A first appearance in society or before the public.—**dé-bu-tant** (dā-bụ-tänt' or deb-ụ-, F. dā-bü-täṅ), *n.* [F., masc., prop. ppr. of *débuter.*] A man making a début, as an actor or speaker appearing for the first time before the public.—**dé-bu-tante'** (-tänt', F. -täṅt), *n.* [F., fem. of *débutant.*] A woman making a début; esp., a young woman during her first season in society.

deca-. Form of Gr. δέκα, ten, used in combination.

de-ca-cer-ous (de-kas'ẹ-rus), *a.* [See *deca-* and *-cerous.*] Having ten horns or horn-like processes (arms, tentacles, etc.).

dec-ad (dek'ad or -ạd), *n.* [L. *decas* (*decad-*), < Gr. δεκάς (δεκαδ-), < δέκα, ten.] The number ten; also, a group of ten; a decade.—**dec'a-dal** (-ạ-dạl), *a.* Of or pertaining to a decad or decade.—**dec'ade** (-ād or -ạd), *n.* [F. *décade*, < L. *decas* (*decad-*).] A group, set, or series of ten; esp., a period of ten years; also, a period of ten days substituted for the week in the calendar of the first French republic; also, a division of a literary work, containing ten parts or books.—**decade ring,** a ring used like a rosary in counting prayers, usually having on the circumference ten knobs or bosses of one form for aves, with an additional knob for the pater, and sometimes also a twelfth for the credo.

Decade Ring, with ten knobs for aves, one for the pater, and the seal for the credo.

dec-a-dence (dek'ạ-dẹns or dẹ-kā'dẹns), *n.* [F. *décadence*, < ML.

decadentia, < L. *de*, from, + *cadere*, fall: cf. *decay*.] A falling off or away from a state of excellence, prosperity, etc.; decline; decay; deteriorated condition: as, "Judged by these tests the period . . . exhibited . . . a great *decadence* and deficiency" (Lecky's "Hist. of Eng. in the 18th Century," iii.). Also **dec′a-den-cy.**—**dec-a-dent** (dek′ạ-dẹnt or dē-kā′dẹnt). [F. *décadent*, < *décadence*.] **I.** *a.* Falling off or deteriorating; being in a state of decline or decay; also, pertaining to or suggestive of the decadents. **II.** *n.* One who is decadent; esp., one of a group of French (and other) writers and artists toward the end of the 19th century whose work was characterized by great refinement or subtlety of style with a marked tendency toward the artificial and abnormal, and was thus held to exemplify a general decadence.—**dec′a-dent-ly,** *adv.*

dec-a-gon (dek′ạ-gon), *n.* [See *deca-* and *-gon.*] A plane figure having ten angles and ten sides.—**de-cag-o-nal** (de-kag′ọ-nạl), *a.*

dec-a-gram, dec-a-gramme (dek′ạ-gram), *n.* [F. *décagramme*: = E. *deca-* + *gram.*] In the *metric system*, a unit of weight equal to 10 grams, or 0.3527 ounce avoirdupois.

dec-a-he-dron (dek-ạ-hē′drọn), *n.*; pl. *-drons* or *-dra* (-drạ). [See *deca-* and *-hedron.*] A solid figure having ten faces.—**dec-a-he′dral,** *a.*

de-cal-ci-fy (dē-kal′si-fī), *v. t.*; *-fied, -fying.* [See *de-*.] To deprive, as a bone, of lime or calcareous matter.—**de-cal″ci-fi-ca′tion** (-fi-kā′shọn), *n.*

de-cal-co-ma-ni-a (dẹ-kal-kọ-mā′ni-ạ), *n.* [F. *décalcomanie*, < *décalquer*, transfer a tracing of (cf. *calk*[2]), + *manie*, E. *mania.*] The art or process of transferring pictures or designs from specially prepared paper to china, glass, etc.; the piece of paper bearing such a picture or design, or the picture or design as transferred.

de-ca-les-cence (dē-kạ-les′ẹns), *n.* [See *de-* and *calescent.*] In the heating of iron, the sudden absorption of heat observed as it passes a certain temperature.—**de-ca-les′cent,** *a.*

dec-a-li-ter, dec-a-li-tre (dek′ạ-lē-tėr), *n.* [F. *décalitre*: = E. *deca-* + *liter.*] In the *metric system*, a unit of capacity equal to 10 liters, 9.08 quarts U. S. dry measure, or 2.64 gallons U. S. liquid measure.

dec-a-logue (dek′ạ-log), *n.* [F. *décalogue*, < LL. *decalogus*, < Gr. δεκάλογος, < δέκα, ten, + λόγος, word, speech.] [Also *cap.*] The ten commandments. See *commandment.*

dec-a-me-ter, dec-a-me-tre (dek′ạ-mē-tėr), *n.* [F. *décamètre*: = E. *deca-* + *meter*[2].] In the *metric system*, a measure of length equal to 10 meters, or 32.8 feet.

de-camp (dẹ-kamp′), *v. i.* [F. *décamper*, < *dé-* (see *dis-*) + *camper*, encamp.] To depart from a camp or camping-ground; break camp; also, to depart quickly, secretly, or unceremoniously (as, "My uncle Toby and Trim had privately *decamped* from my father's house in town": Sterne's "Tristram Shandy," vi. 6); take one's self off.—**de-camp′ment,** *n.*

dec-a-nal (dek′ạ-nạl or dē-kā′nạl), *a.* [LL. *decanus*: see *dean*[2].] Of or pertaining to a dean or deanery.

dec-ane (dek′ān), *n.* [Gr. δέκα, ten (with reference to the atoms of carbon).] In *chem.*, a hydrocarbon, $C_{10}H_{22}$, of the methane series, occurring in several isomeric forms.

de-cant (dẹ-kant′), *v. t.* [F. *décanter*, < ML. *decanthare*, < L. *de*, from, + ML. *canthus, cantus*, corner, side, E. *cant*[1].] To pour off gently, as liquor, without disturbing the sediment; also, to pour from one vessel into another; pour, as from or into a decanter.—**de-can-ta-tion** (dē-kan-tā′shọn), *n.* The act or process of decanting.—**de-cant′er,** *n.* One who decants; also, a vessel used for decanting, or for receiving decanted liquors; a vessel, usually an ornamental bottle, from which wine, water, etc., are served at table.

de-cap-i-tate (dẹ-kap′i-tāt), *v. t.*; *-tated, -tating.* [ML. *decapitatus*, pp. of *decapitare*, < L. *de-* priv. + *caput*, head.] To cut off the head of; behead; kill by beheading; fig., to remove summarily from office (slang, U. S.).—**de-cap-i-ta′tion** (-tā′shọn), *n.*—**de-cap′i-ta-tor,** *n.*

dec-a-pod (dek′ạ-pod). [NL. *Decapoda*, pl., < Gr. δέκα, ten, + πούς (ποδ-), foot.] **I.** *n.* Any of the *Decapoda*, an order of ten-footed crustaceans, which includes the lobsters, crabs, etc.; also, any of the *Decapoda*, an order of ten-armed dibranchiate cephalopods, which includes the cuttlefishes, squids, etc. **II.** *a.* Belonging to the *Decapoda*; having ten feet or legs.—**de-cap-o-dous** (de-kap′ọ-dus), *a.*

de-car-bo-nate (dē-kär′bọ-nāt), *v. t.*; *-nated, -nating.* [See *de-*.] To deprive of carbon or carbonic acid.

de-car-bon-ize (dē-kär′bọ-nīz), *v. t.*; *-ized, -izing.* Same as *decarburize*.—**de-car″bon-i-za′tion** (-bọ-ni-zā′shọn), *n.*

de-car-bu-rize (dē-kär′bụ̄-rīz), *v. t.*; *-rized, -rizing.* [See *de-*.] To deprive of carbon, wholly or in part, as cast-iron in making steel.—**de-car″bu-ri-za′tion** (-ri-zā′shọn), *n.*

dec-a-stere (dek′ạ-stēr), *n.* [F. *décastère*: = E. *deca-* + *stere.*] In the *metric system*, a unit of volume equal to 10 steres.

dec-a-stich (dek′ạ-stik), *n.* [Gr. δέκα, ten, + στίχος, row, line.] A poem of ten lines.

dec-a-style (dek′ạ-stīl), *a.* [Gr. δεκάστυλος, < δέκα, ten, + στῦλος, pillar, column.] Having ten columns in front, as a temple or a portico.

de-cas-u-al-ize (dē-kazh′ụ̄-ạl-īz), *v. t.*; *-ized, -izing.* [See *de-*.] To render no longer casual; change from a casual, irregular, or uncertain condition by giving a regular or permanent character: as, to *decasualize* labor by providing steady employment.—**de-cas″u-al-i-za′tion** (-i-zā′shọn), *n.*

dec-a-syl-la-ble (dek-ạ-sil′ạ-bl), *n.* [See *deca-*.] A line of ten syllables.—**dec″a-syl-lab′ic** (-si-lab′ik), *a.*

de-cath-lon (de-kath′lon), *n.* [Gr. δέκα, ten, + ἆθλον, ἆθλος, contest.] An athletic contest comprising ten different exercises or events, and won by the contestant having the highest total score.

de-cay (dẹ-kā′), *v.* [OF. *decair* (also *dechaeir*, F. *déchoir*), < L. *de*, from, + *cadere*, fall: cf. *decadence.*] **I.** *intr.* To fall away from a state of excellence, prosperity, etc.; deteriorate; become impaired; decline; also, to fall into ruin; waste or wear away; specif., to become decomposed; rot. **II.** *tr.* To cause to decay.—**de-cay′,** *n.* The process of decaying, or the resulting state; a gradual falling into an inferior condition; progressive decline; impairment; loss of strength, health, intellect, etc.; a wasting disease, esp. consumption†; a falling into ruin; a wasting or wearing away; dilapidation; decomposition or rotting; also, a cause of decaying or deterioration†.—**de-cay′a-ble,** *a.* Liable to decay.—**de-cayed′,** *p. a.* Having fallen away or declined from the former state of excellence, well-being, etc.; reduced in fortune (as, "an ancient asylum for superannuated tradesmen and *decayed* householders": Irving's "Sketch-Book," London Antiques); affected with physical decay, as buildings, teeth, fruit, etc.—**de-cay′er,** *n.*—**de-cay′less,** *a.* Not subject to decay.

de-cease (dẹ-sēs′), *n.* [OF. *deces* (F. *décès*), < L. *decessus*, departure, death, < *decedere*: see *decedent.*] Departure from life; death.—**de-cease′,** *v. i.*; *-ceased, -ceasing.* To depart from life; die.—**de-ceased′,** *p. a.* Departed from life; dead; esp., lately dead.

de-ce-dent (dẹ-sē′dẹnt), *n.* [L. *decedens* (-*ent*-), ppr. of *decedere*, depart, withdraw, die, < *de*, from, + *cedere*, go.] A deceased person.

de-ceit (dẹ-sēt′), *n.* [OF. *deceite*, < L. *decepta*, pp. fem. of *decipere*: see *deceive.*] The act or practice of deceiving; concealment or perversion of the truth for the purpose of misleading; deception; fraud; cheating; also, an act or device intended to deceive; a trick or stratagem; also, deceiving quality; deceitfulness.—**de-ceit′ful,** *a.* Full of deceit; given to deceiving; misleading; fraudulent; deceptive.—**de-ceit′ful-ly,** *adv.*—**de-ceit′ful-ness,** *n.*

de-ceiv-a-ble (dẹ-sē′vạ-bl), *a.* Deceitful or deceptive (archaic); also, that may be deceived.—**de-ceiv′a-ble-ness,** *n.*—**de-ceiv′a-bly,** *adv.*

de-ceive (dẹ-sēv′), *v.*; *-ceived, -ceiving.* [OF. *deceveir* (F. *décevoir*), < L. *decipere* (pp. *deceptus*), catch, insnare, deceive, < *de*, from, + *capere*, take.] **I.** *tr.* To insnare†; also, to cause to believe what is false or to disbelieve what is true; mislead; delude; also, to disappoint (hopes, expectations, etc.); also, to cheat† or defraud†; also, to beguile or while away (time, etc.)†. **II.** *intr.* To practise deceit; act deceitfully.—**de-ceiv′er,** *n.*—**de-ceiv′ing-ly,** *adv.*

de-cel-er-ate (dē-sel′ẹ-rāt), *v.*; *-ated, -ating.* [L. *de-* priv. + *celerare*, quicken, < *celer*, quick: cf. *accelerate.*] **I.** *tr.* To decrease the velocity of. **II.** *intr.* To decrease in velocity.—**de-cel-er-a′tion** (-ẹ-rā′shọn), *n.* The act of decelerating; decrease in velocity; negative acceleration.

De-cem-ber (dẹ̄-sem′bėr), *n.* [L. *December*, the tenth month of the Roman year, < *decem*, ten.] The twelfth month of the year, containing 31 days.

de-cem-vir (dẹ̄-sem′vėr), *n.*; pl. *-viri* (-vi-rī) or *-virs.* [L., orig. pl., *decemviri*, < *decem*, ten, + *viri*, pl. of *vir*, man.] One of a commission or council of ten men in ancient Rome, esp. a member of either of two bodies of magistrates appointed respectively in 451 and 450 B.C. to prepare a system of laws and exercising absolute powers of government; hence, a member of any council or ruling body of ten.—**decem′vi-ral** (-vi-rạl), *a.*—**de-cem′vi-rate** (-rāt), *n.* [L. *decemviratus.*] The office or government of decemvirs; a body of decemvirs.

de-cen-cy (dē′sẹn-si), *n.*; pl. *-cies* (-siz). [L. *decentia.*] The state or quality of being decent; fitness†; conformity to the recognized standard of propriety or good taste; proper regard for modesty or delicacy; respectability; also, something decent or proper; *pl.*, the requirements or observances of decent life or conduct (as, "He became careless of the *decencies* which were expected from a man so highly distinguished in the literary and political world": Macaulay's "Essays," Machiavelli).

de-cen-na-ry (dẹ̄-sen′ạ-ri), *n.*; pl. *-ries* (-riz). [L. *decennis*: see *decennial.*] A period of ten years; a decennium.

de-cen-ni-ad (dẹ̄-sen′i-ad), *n.* A decennium.

de-cen-ni-al (dẹ̄-sen′i-ạl). [L. *decennis*, of ten years, < *decem*, ten, + *annus*, year.] **I.** *a.* Of or for ten years; occurring every ten years. **II.** *n.* A decennial anniversary, or its celebration.—**de-cen′ni-al-ly,** *adv.*—**de-cen′ni-um** (-um), *n.*; pl. *-niums* or *-nia* (-ạ̈). [L., < *decennis.*] A period of ten years; a decade.

de-cent (dē′sẹnt), *a.* [L. *decens* (*decent-*), ppr. of *decere*, be fitting.] Fitting or appropriate; also, comely† or handsome†; also, conforming to the recognized standard of propriety or good taste, as in behavior or speech; proper with regard to modesty or delicacy; free from indelicacy; also, respectable or worthy (as, a *decent* family; a very *decent* fellow); of seemly appearance (as, quite *decent* clothes; a very *decent* house); fair, tolerable, or passable (as, a *decent* fortune).

de-cen-ter (dē-sen′tėr), *v. t.* [See *de-.*] To put out of center; render eccentric.

de-cent-ly (dē′sẹnt-li), *adv.* In a decent manner; properly; respectably; fairly.—**de′cent-ness,** *n.*

de-cen-tral-ize (dē-sen′trạl-īz), *v. t.*; *-ized*, *-izing.* [See *de-.*] To remove from a center; undo the centralization of (administrative power, etc.).—**de-cen″tral-i-za′tion** (-i-zā′shọn), *n.*

de-cen-tre (dē-sen′tėr), *v. t.* See *decenter.*

de-cep-tion (dẹ̄-sep′shọn), *n.* [OF. *deception* (F. *déception*), < LL. *deceptio(n-)*, < L. *decipere*: see *deceive.*] The act of deceiving, or the state of being deceived; also, something that deceives or is intended to deceive; an artifice; a sham or cheat.—**de-cep′tious** (-shus), *a.* Deceitful; deceptive. See Shakspere's "Troilus and Cressida," v. 2. 123. [Obs. or rare.]

de-cep-tive (dẹ̄-sep′tiv), *a.* [F. *déceptif*, < L. *decipere*: see *deceive.*] Apt or tending to deceive.—**de-cep′tive-ly,** *adv.*—**de-cep′tive-ness,** *n.*

de-cern (dẹ̄-sėrn′), *v. t.* [L. *decernere* (pp. *decretus*), decide, decree, < *de*, from, + *cernere*, separate, decide: see *certain.*] To decide† or determine†; decree by judicial sentence (now only in *Sc. law*); also, to discern.

de-chris-tian-ize (dē-kris′chạn-īz), *v. t.*; *-ized*, *-izing.* [See *de-.*] To divest of Christian character.—**de-chris″tian-i-za′tion** (-i-zā′shọn), *n.*

de-cid-a-ble (dẹ̄-sī′dạ-bl), *a.* That may be decided.

de-cide (dẹ̄-sīd′), *v.*; *-cided*, *-ciding.* [L. *decidere* (pp. *decisus*), < *de*, from, + *cædere*, cut.] **I.** *tr.* To determine or settle (a question, controversy, struggle, etc.) by giving victory to one side or the other; adjust or settle (anything in dispute or doubt); also, to bring (a person) to a decision or resolve. **II.** *intr.* To settle something in dispute or doubt; pronounce a judgment; also, to come to a conclusion; resolve.—**de-cid′ed** (-sī′ded), *p. a.* Settled; free from ambiguity; unquestionable; unmistakable; also, free from hesitation or wavering; resolute; determined.—**de-cid′ed-ly,** *adv.*—**de-cid′ed-ness,** *n.*—**de-cid′er,** *n.*

de-cid-u-a (dẹ̄-sid′ụ̄-ạ̈), *n.* [NL., prop. fem. of L. *deciduus*: see *deciduous.*] In *physiol.*, a membrane which arises from the alteration of the upper layer of the mucous membrane of the uterus, after the reception into the latter of the fertilized ovum, and which is cast off at parturition.—**de-cid′u-al,** *a.* Of or pertaining to the decidua.—**de-cid′u-ate** (-āt), *a.* Characterized by or having a decidua (as, a *deciduate* mammal); pertaining to a decidua (as, a *deciduate* placenta, a placenta which is composed in part of a decidua).

de-cid-u-ous (dẹ̄-sid′ụ̄-us), *a.* [L. *deciduus*, < *decidere*, fall off, < *de*, from, + *cadere*, fall.] Falling off or shed at a particular season, stage of growth, etc., as leaves, horns, teeth, etc.; shedding the leaves annually, as trees, shrubs, etc.; fig., not permanent; transitory (as, "They discover that all which at first drew them together . . . was *deciduous*, had a prospective end": Emerson's "Essays," Love).—**de-cid′u-ous-ly,** *adv.*—**de-cid′u-ous-ness,** *n.*

de-ci-gram, de-ci-gramme (des′i-gram), *n.* [F. *décigramme*, < L. *decimus*, tenth, + F. *gramme*: see *gram*².] In the *metric system*, a unit of weight equal to one tenth of a gram, or 1.543 grains.

de-ci-li-ter, de-ci-li-tre (des′i-lē-tėr), *n.* [F. *décilitre*, < L. *decimus*, tenth, + F. *litre*: see *liter.*] In the *metric system*, a unit of capacity equal to one tenth of a liter, 6.102 cubic inches, or 0.845 U. S. gill.

de-cil-lion (dẹ̄-sil′yọn), *n.* [L. *decem*, ten, + E. (*m*)*illion.*] In Great Britain, the tenth power of a million, represented by 1 followed by 60 ciphers; in France and the U. S., a thousand nonillions, represented by 1 followed by 33 ciphers.—**de-cil′lionth,** *a.* and *n.*

de-ci-mal (des′i-mạl). [L. *decimus*, tenth, < *decem*, ten.] **I.** *a.* Pertaining to tenths, or to the number ten; proceeding by tens: as, a *decimal* fraction (a fraction whose denominator is ten or some power of ten, usually indicated by figures written to the right of the whole number, if any, after a dot or point, the 'decimal point,' and denoting so many tenths, hundredths, thousandths, etc., 3.1, .02, and .126, for example, denoting respectively three and one tenth, two hundredths, and one hundred and twenty-six thousandths); a *decimal* system (any system of counting or measurement whose units are powers of ten). **II.** *n.* A decimal fraction.—**circulating, recurring,** or **repeating decimal,** a decimal in which, after a certain point, there is an indefinite repetition of the same digit (specif. called *repeating decimal*) or series of digits (specif. called *circulating decimal*).—**de′ci-mal-ize** (-īz), *v. t.*; *-ized*, *-izing.* To render decimal; reduce to a decimal system.—**de″ci-mal-i-za′tion** (-i-zā′shọn), *n.*—**de′ci-mal-ly,** *adv.*

de-ci-mate (des′i-māt), *v. t.*; *-mated*, *-mating.* [L. *decimatus*, pp. of *decimare*, < *decimus*, tenth: see *decimal.*] To take a tenth or tithe of or from†; specif., to select by lot and execute every tenth man of (as, to *decimate* a captured army or a body of mutineers); hence, to destroy a tenth or any considerable proportion of.—**de-ci-ma′tion** (-mā′shọn), *n.*—**de′ci-ma-tor,** *n.*

dé-cime (dā-sēm), *n.* [F., < L. *decima*, fem. of *decimus*, tenth: see *decimal.*] A French copper coin equal to 10 centimes or about 2 U. S. cents.

de-ci-me-ter, de-ci-me-tre (des′i-mē-tėr), *n.* [F. *décimètre*, < L. *decimus*, tenth, + F. *mètre*: see *meter*².] In the *metric system*, a measure of length equal to one tenth of a meter, or 3.937 inches.

de-ci-pher (dẹ̄-sī′fėr), *v. t.* [See *de-.*] To convert (something in cipher) into ordinary writing; interpret by the use of a key; also, to make out the meaning of (hieroglyphics, poor or partially obliterated writing, etc.); discover the meaning of (anything obscure or difficult to trace or understand); also, to find out† or detect†; also, to reveal†; also, to depict†.—**de-ci′pher,** *n.* The interpretation or translation of a cipher or of something in cipher.—**de-ci′pher-a-ble,** *a.* That may be deciphered.—**de-ci′pher-er,** *n.*—**de-ci′pher-ment,** *n.* The act of deciphering; interpretation, as of something written in cipher.

de-ci-sion (dẹ̄-sizh′ọn), *n.* [L. *decisio(n-)*, < *decidere*: see *decide.*] The act of deciding; determination, as of a question or controversy; a judgment, as one formally pronounced by a court; a making up of one's mind; a resolution; also, the quality of being decided; firmness, as of character.

de-ci-sive (dē-sī'siv), *a.* [ML. *decisivus*, < L. *decidere*: see *decide*.] Serving to decide; determinative; conclusive; beyond question or doubt; unquestionable; also, characterized by or displaying decision (as, "So his lordship decreed . . . *Decisive* and clear, without one if or but": Cowper's "Report of an Adjudged Case," 30); resolute; determined.—**de-ci'sive-ly,** *adv.*—**de-ci'sive-ness,** *n.*

de-ci-stere (des'i-stēr), *n.* [F. *décistère*, < L. *decimus*, tenth, + F. *stère*: see *stere*.] In the *metric system*, a unit of volume equal to one tenth of a stere.

de-civ-il-ize (dē-siv'i-līz), *v. t.*; *-ized, -izing.* [See *de-*.] To reduce or degrade from a civilized condition.—**de-civ"il-i-za'tion** (-i-li-zā'shọn), *n.*

deck (dek), *v. t.* [MD. *decken* (D. *dekken*) = G. *decken*, cover; akin to E. *thatch*.] To cover†; also, to clothe or attire in something ornamental; array; adorn; also, to cover or furnish with or as with a deck.—**deck,** *n.* [= D. *dek*.] A covering†; also, a platform extending from side to side of a ship or of a part of a ship, forming a covering for the space below and itself serving as a floor; hence, a platform or part resembling this; a horizontal, platform-like main surface on an aëroplane; also, a pack of playing-cards; that part of a pack which contains the cards required in a particular game; the portion of the pack remaining after the hands have been dealt; also, a small package, as of cocaine or heroin, for illicit sale (colloq.).—**decked,** *a.* Having a deck or decks: as, a three-*decked* ship.—**deck'er,** *n.* One who or that which decks; also, a vessel, vehicle, etc., having a deck or decks (in composition: as, a three-*decker*).—**deck'=hand,** *n.* A sailor or workman employed on the deck of a vessel.

deck-le (dek'l), *n.* [G. *deckel*, dim. of *decke*, cover.] In *paper-making*, any contrivance to keep the paper-pulp from spreading beyond desired limits, thus determining the size or the width of the sheet; also, a deckle-edge.—**deck'le=edge,** *n.* The rough edge of untrimmed paper, formed by the deckle; the ragged edge of hand-made paper.—**deck'le=edged,** *a.* Of paper, having a deckle-edge.

de-claim (dē-klām'), *v.* [L. *declamare* (pp. *declamatus*), < *de-*, away, + *clamare*, cry out, shout.] **I.** *intr.* To speak aloud rhetorically; make a formal speech or oration; inveigh (*against*); also, to recite in public to exhibit elocutionary skill; also, to speak or write for oratorical effect, without sincerity or sound argument. **II.** *tr.* To utter aloud in a rhetorical manner; also, to recite as an exercise in elocution.—**de-claim'er,** *n.*—**dec-la-ma-tion** (dek-lạ-mā'shọn), *n.* [L. *declamatio(n-)*.] The act or art of declaiming; also, that which is declaimed; a set speech; an exercise in oratory or elocution; impassioned oratory; speech or writing for oratorical effect; in *music*, the proper rhetorical enunciation of the words, esp. in recitative and in dramatic music.—**de-clam-a-to-ry** (dē-klam'ạ-tọ̄-ri), *a.* [L. *declamatorius*.] Pertaining to, of the nature of, or characterized by declamation; esp., merely rhetorical; stilted.

de-clar-ant (dē-klār'ạnt), *n.* [L. *declarans* (*-ant-*), ppr. of *declarare*: see *declare*.] One who makes a declaration: chiefly in legal use.

dec-la-ra-tion (dek-lạ-rā'shọn), *n.* [L. *declaratio(n-)*, < *declarare*: see *declare*.] The act of declaring; a positive, explicit, or formal statement, announcement, etc.; an assertion; an affirmation; a proclamation (as, a *declaration* of war); also, that which is proclaimed, or the document embodying the proclamation (as, the *Declaration* of Independence, in *U. S. hist.*, the public act by which the Continental Congress, on July 4, 1776, declared the colonies to be free and independent of Great Britain); a statement of goods, etc., liable to duty; in *law*, the formal statement in which a plaintiff presents his claim in an action; a complaint. — **de-clar-a-tive, de-clar-a-to-ry** (dē-klar'ạ-tiv, -tọ̄-ri), *a.* Serving to declare, make known, or explain; of the nature of a declaration or formal assertion.

de-clare (dē-klãr'), *v.*; *-clared, -claring.* [OF. *declarer* (F. *déclarer*), < L. *declarare* (pp. *declaratus*), < *de-*, completely, + *clarare*, make clear, < *clarus*, E. *clear*.] **I.** *tr.* To make clear or plain†; also, to make known, esp. in explicit or formal terms; proclaim; announce officially; also, to state emphatically; affirm; also, to manifest or reveal (as, "The heavens *declare* the glory of God": Ps. xix. 1); also, to make due statement of (dutiable goods, etc.). **II.** *intr.* To make a declaration; proclaim one's self.—**de-clared',** *p. a.* Openly or formally made known; avowed; professed.—**de-clar'ed-ly,** *adv.*—**de-clar'er,** *n.*

de-class (dē-klȧs'), *v. t.* [F. *déclasser*, < *dé-* (see *dis-*) + *classe*, E. *class*.] To remove or degrade from one's class (social or other); cause to lose caste or standing.

dé-clas-sé (dā-klȧ-sā). [F., pp.] **I.** *a.* Declassed. **II.** *n.* A declassed person.—**dé-clas-sée** (dā-klȧ-sā), *a.* and *n.* Fem. of *déclassé*.

de-clen-sion (dē-klen'shọn), *n.* [Irreg. (prob. through F. *déclinaison*) < L. *declinatio(n-)*: see *declination*.] The act or fact of declining, or bending or sloping downward; a sinking down, as of the sun toward setting; also, a sinking or falling into a lower or inferior state; deterioration; decline; sunken or fallen condition; also, deviation, as from a standard; also, non-acceptance or courteous refusal (rare); in *gram.*, the formation of the cases of a noun, pronoun, or adjective by the addition of inflectional endings to the stem; the setting forth in order of the cases of such a word; a class of such words of a language, grouped according to their inflectional endings.—**de-clen'sion-al,** *a.*

de-clin-a-ble (dē-klī'nạ-bl), *a.* [LL. *declinabilis*.] That may be declined; in *gram.*, subject to declension, as a noun.

dec-li-nate (dek'li-nāt), *a.* [L. *declinatus*, pp. of *declinare*: see *decline*.] In *bot.* and *zoöl.*, bent or bending downward or aside.

dec-li-na-tion (dek-li-nā'shọn), *n.* [L. *declinatio(n-)*, < *declinare*: see *decline*, and cf. *declension*.] The act or fact of declining, or bending or sloping downward; descent, as of the sun†; also, deterioration or decline; also, a swerving or deviating, as from a standard; also, a withholding of consent or acceptance; polite refusal; in *astron.*, the angular distance of a heavenly body from the celestial equator, measured on a great circle passing through the celestial pole and the body; in *magnetism*, etc., the deviation of the magnetic needle or compass from the true north and south line of a place; the angular measure of this deviation; in *gram.*, declension†.—**de-cli-na-to-ry** (dē-klī'nạ-tọ̄-ri), *a.* [ML. *declinatorius*.] Expressing or implying declination or refusal.

de-cli-na-ture (dē-klī'nạ-ṭūr), *n.* The act of declining or refusing.

de-cline (dē-klīn'), *v.*; *-clined, -clining.* [OF. *decliner* (F. *décliner*), < L. *declinare* (pp. *declinatus*), bend from, turn aside, avoid, inflect, < *de*, from, + *-clinare* (= Gr. κλίνειν), bend, incline: see *lean*[1].] **I.** *tr.* To turn aside†; avert†; divert†; deflect†; also, to turn away from (danger, etc.)†; also, to withhold consent to do, enter upon, or accept (as, to *decline* a contest or an offer); refuse; also, to give up† or abandon†; also, to bend or bow down; cause to slope or incline downward; also, to lower† or bring down†; debase†; in *gram.*, to inflect (a noun, pronoun, or adjective) through its cases. **II.** *intr.* To turn aside†; turn away†; deviate†; diverge†; also, to incline† or tend† (see Shakspere's "Comedy of Errors," iii. 2. 44); also, to express courteous refusal; refuse; also, to bend or bow down; slope or incline downward; descend toward setting, as the sun; hence, to draw toward the close, as the day; also, to fall† or come down†; fall or sink morally; fail in strength, vigor, character, value, etc.; deteriorate.—**de-cline',** *n.* [OF. *declin* (F. *déclin*).] A downward incline or slope; also, progress downward or toward a close, as of the sun or the day; also, a failing or gradual loss, as in strength, vigor, character, etc.; deterioration; diminution; esp., gradual fall in price or value; also, a gradual decay of the physical powers, as in later life; specif., a wasting disease, esp. tuberculosis of the lungs (as, "We must give up mining, or die of *decline*": Kingsley's "Yeast," xiii.).—**de-clin'er** (-klī'nėr), *n.*

dec-li-nom-e-ter (dek-li-nom'e-tėr), *n.* [L. *declinare*, bend from: see *-meter*.] An instrument for measuring the declination of the magnetic needle.

de-cliv-i-ty (dē-kliv'i-ti), *n.*; pl. *-ties* (-tiz). [L. *declivitas*, < *declivis*, sloping downward, < *de*, down from, + *clivus*, slope.] A downward slope, as of ground: opposed to *acclivity*.—**de-cliv'i-tous,** *a.*—**de-cli'vous** (-klī'vus), *a.* [L. *declivus*, for *declivis*.] Sloping downward.

de-coct (dę̄-kokt′), *v. t.* [L. *decoctus*, pp. of *decoquere*, boil down, < *de*, down from, + *coquere*, cook.] To boil down†, or concentrate by boiling†; boil† or cook†; digest in the stomach†; boil (a medicinal substance, etc.) in water, etc., to extract the essence or principles; also, to concoct†.—**de-coc′tion** (-kok′shọn), *n.* [L. *decoctio(n-)*.] The act of decocting; also, an extract obtained by decocting; a liquor in which a substance, usually animal or vegetable, has been boiled, and which thus contains the soluble constituents or principles of the substance.

de-code (dē-kōd′), *v. t.*; *-coded, -coding.* [See *de-*.] To translate (a message or the like in a code or cipher) into the original language or form.

de-co-here (dē-kō̤-hēr′), *v. i.*; *-hered, -hering.* [See *de-*.] In *elect.*, to become less united, as the contents of a coherer when it is tapped; of a coherer, to return to normal condition through such tapping or the like.—**de-co-her′ence** (-hēr′ęns), *n.* In *elect.*, decohering action.—**de-co-her′er,** *n.* In *elect.*, a device for restoring a coherer to normal condition after it has been affected by an electric wave.—**de-co-he′sion** (-hē′zhọn), *n.* In *elect.*, the act of decohering; the effect of decoherence.

de-col-late (dę̄-kol′āt), *v. t.*; *-lated, -lating.* [L. *decollatus*, pp. of *decollare*, < *de*, from, + *collum*, neck.] To behead; decapitate; in *conch.*, to remove the apex of (a shell).—**de-col-la-tion** (dē-ko-lā′shọn), *n.*—**de′col-la-tor,** *n.*

dé-colle-té (dā-kol-tā), *a.* [F. *décolleté*, masc., *décolletée*, fem., pp. of *décolleter*, bare the neck of, < *dé-* (see *dis-*) + *collet*, collar.] Having the neck and shoulders exposed, as when wearing a low-necked garment (of a woman, properly *décolletée*: as, "a stout countess of sixty, *décolletée*, painted," Thackeray's "Vanity Fair," xlviii.); of a garment, low-necked.

de-col-or (dē-kul′ọr), *v. t.* [L. *decolorare*, < *de-* (see *de-*) + *colorare*, E. *color*, *v.*] To deprive of color; bleach.—**de-col′or-ant.** **I.** *a.* Having the property of removing color; bleaching. **II.** *n.* A decolorant substance or agent.—**de-col-or-a′tion** (-ọ-rā′shọn), *n.*

de-col-or-ize (dē-kul′ọr-īz), *v. t.*; *-ized, -izing.* [See *de-*.] To decolor.—**de-col″or-i-za′tion** (-i-zā′shọn), *n.*—**de-col′or-iz-er** (-ī-zėr), *n.*

de-com-plex (dē′kom-pleks), *a.* [See *de-*.] Compounded of parts which are themselves complex; repeatedly complex.

de-com-pos-a-ble (dē-kọm-pō′zạ-bl), *a.* Capable of being decomposed.—**de-com-pos-a-bil′i-ty** (-bil′i-ti), *n.*

de-com-pose (dē-kọm-pōz′), *v. t.* or *i.*; *-posed, -posing.* [F. *décomposer*, < *dé-* (see *dis-*) + *composer*, compose.] To separate or resolve into constituent parts or elements; disintegrate; specif., to rot or putrefy.—**de-com-pos′er** (-pō′zėr), *n.*

de-com-pos-ite (dē-kọm-poz′it or dę̄-kom′pō̤-zit). [LL. *decompositus*, formed from a compound, < L. *de-* (see *de-*) + *compositus*, E. *composite*.] **I.** *a.* Compounded more than once; compounded of things already composite: as, a *decomposite* leaf (a decompound leaf). **II.** *n.* Anything compounded of composite things.

de-com-po-si-tion (dē-kom-pō̤-zish′ọn), *n.* [F. *décomposition*, associated with *décomposer*, E. *decompose*, as E. *composition* with *compose*.] The act or process of decomposing, or the state of being decomposed; dissolution; disintegration; decay or putrescence.

de-com-pound (dē-kọm-pound′), *v. t.* [See *de-*.] To compound a second time or further, or of things already compound; also, to decompose.—**de′com-pound** (-kom-pound). **I.** *a.* Composed of things which are themselves compound; further or repeatedly compound: as, a *decompound* leaf (in *bot.*, one which is more than once compounded, as when the primary petiole gives off subsidiary petioles, each supporting a compound leaf). **II.** *n.* Something further compounded, or composed of parts which are themselves compound.

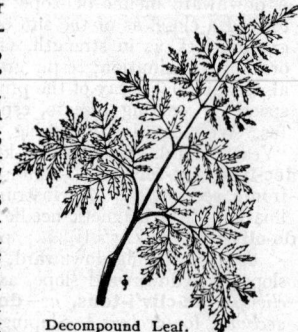

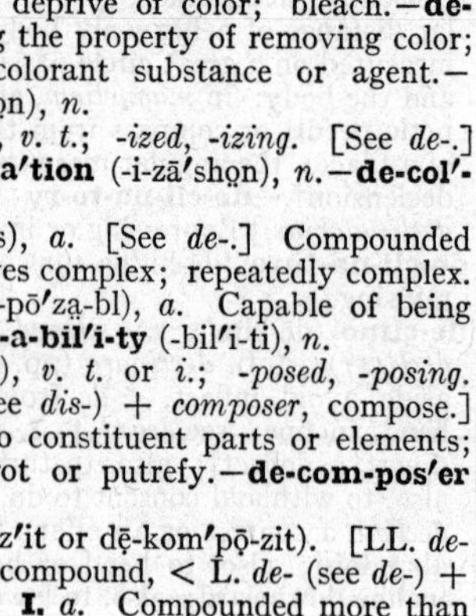
Decompound Leaf.

de-con-cen-trate (dē-kon′sęn-trāt), *v. t.*; *-trated, -trating.* [See *de-*.] To change from a concentrated state; break up the concentration of.—**de-con-cen-tra′tion** (-trā′shọn), *n.*

de-con-se-crate (dē-kon′sę̄-krāt), *v. t.*; *-crated, -crating.* [See *de-*.] To undo the consecration of; deprive of sacred character.—**de-con-se-cra′tion** (-krā′shọn), *n.*

de-con-sid-er (dē-kọn-sid′ėr), *v. t.* [F. *déconsidérer*, < *dé-* (see *dis-*) + *considérer*, consider.] To deprive of consideration; discredit; disconsider.—**de-con-sid-er-a′tion** (-ę-rā′shọn), *n.*

de-con-trol (dē-kọn-trōl′), *v. t.*; *-trolled, -trolling.* [See *de-*.] To bring out of a controlled state; release or remove from control: as, to *decontrol* industries subjected to governmental control.—**de-con-trol′,** *n.* The act of decontrolling, or the state of being decontrolled.

dé-cor (dā-kôr), *n.* [F., < *décorer*, decorate, < L. *decorare*: see *decorate*.] Decoration, or a decoration, esp. on the stage; scenic decoration or effect; theatrical scenery.

dec-o-rate (dek′ō̤-rāt), *v. t.*; *-rated, -rating.* [L. *decoratus*, pp. of *decorare*, < *decus*, ornament, akin to *decor*, what is becoming: see *decorous*.] To grace or honor (archaic); also, to furnish or deck with something becoming or ornamental; embellish; also, to confer distinction upon by the badge of an order, a medal of honor, etc.—**dec′o-rat-ed** (-rā-ted), *p. a.* Ornamented; adorned; embellished; in *arch.*, noting or pertaining to the Gothic style prevalent in England throughout the greater part of the 14th century, characterized by more or less elaborate decoration.—**dec-o-ra′tion** (-rā′shọn), *n.* [ML. *decoratio(n-)*.] The act of decorating; adornment; embellishment; also, that which decorates; an embellishment or ornament; also, a badge of an order, medal, etc., conferred and worn as a mark of honor.—**Decoration Day.** See *Memorial Day*.—**dec′o-ra-tive** (-rạ-tiv), *a.* Serving or tending to decorate; pertaining to decoration.—**dec′o-ra-tive-ly,** *adv.*—**dec′o-ra-tive-ness,** *n.*—**dec′o-ra-tor** (-rā-tọr), *n.* One who decorates; esp., one who professionally decorates houses or buildings, particularly in their interior.

Decorated Architecture. — Tomb of Bishop Bridport, Salisbury Cathedral, England.

de-co-rous (dę̄-kō′rus or dek′ō̤-), *a.* [L. *decorus*, becoming, seemly, < *decor*, what is becoming, comeliness, beauty, akin to *decere*, be fitting: see *decent*, and cf. *decorate*.] Characterized by seemliness in conduct, manners, appearance, character, etc.; conforming to the recognized standards of propriety.—**de-co′rous-ly,** *adv.*—**de-co′rous-ness,** *n.*

de-cor-ti-cate (dę̄-kôr′ti-kāt), *v. t.*; *-cated, -cating.* [L. *decorticatus*, pp. of *decorticare*, < *de-* (see *de-*) + *cortex*, bark.] To remove the bark, husk, or outer covering from; fig., to expose; criticize severely.—**de-cor-ti-ca′tion** (-kā′shọn), *n.*—**de-cor′ti-ca-tor,** *n.* One who or that which decorticates; a machine or instrument for removing bark.

de-co-rum (dę̄-kō′rum), *n.* [L., prop. neut. of *decorus*: see *decorous*.] That which is proper or seemly; fitness; congruity; propriety; esp., propriety of behavior, speech, dress, etc.; also, an observance or requirement of polite society (as, "A man in distressed circumstances has not time for all those elegant *decorums* which other people may observe": Jane Austen's "Pride and Prejudice," xxvii.).

de-coy (dę̄-koi′), *n.* [D. *kooi*, cage, pen (cf. D. *de kooi*, 'the cage'), < L. *cavea*, inclosure, E. *cage*.] A pond into which wild ducks or other fowl are lured to permit their capture;

fig., a place into which persons are enticed; also, a trained bird or other animal used to entice game into a trap or within gunshot; an image of a bird used for the same purpose; hence, a swindler†; one who entices or allures, as into a trap, danger, etc.; also, anything employed to do this; a lure.—**de-coy′**, *v.* **I.** *tr.* To lure (wild-fowl, etc.) into a snare or within gunshot; also, to entice (persons) by cunning or deception; allure. **II.** *intr.* To be decoyed.—**de-coy′=duck**, *n.* A duck, or an imitation of one, used as a decoy; a person who entices another, as into a trap or danger.—**de-coy′er**, *n.*

de-crease (dē-krēs′), *v.*; *-creased, -creasing.* [OF. *decreistre*, < L. *decrescere*, < *de*, down from, + *crescere*, grow.] **I.** *intr.* To grow less; diminish gradually; lessen. **II.** *tr.* To make less; cause to diminish.—**de-crease** (dē-krēs′ or dē′krēs), *n.* [OF. *decreis.*] The process of growing less, or the resulting condition; gradual diminution; also, the amount by which a thing is lessened.—**de-creas′ing-ly**, *adv.*

de-cree (dē-krē′), *n.* [OF. *decre* (F. *décret*), < L. *decretum*, prop. pp. neut. of *decernere*, decide, decree: see *decern.*] An ordinance or edict promulgated by civil or other authority; an authoritative decision; in *law*, a judicial decision; in *theol.*, one of the eternal purposes of God, by which events are foreordained.—**de-cree′**, *v.*; *-creed, -creeing.* **I.** *tr.* To ordain or pronounce by decree; decide authoritatively; also, to determine or resolve (archaic). **II.** *intr.* To ordain or decide.—**de-cree′a-ble**, *a.* That may be decreed.—**de-cre′er**, *n.*

dec-re-ment (dek′rē-mẹnt), *n.* [L. *decrementum*, < *decrescere*: see *decrease.*] The process or fact of decreasing; gradual diminution; lessening; also, the amount lost by diminution.

de-crep-id (dē-krep′id), *a.* Erroneous form of *decrepit.*

de-crep-it (dē-krep′it), *a.* [L. *decrepitus*, < *de-*, down, + *crepare*, rattle, crack, break.] Broken down or weakened by old age; old and feeble; weakened; infirm.

de-crep-i-tate (dē-krep′i-tāt), *v.*; *-tated, -tating.* [L. *de-*, down, away, + *crepitare* (pp. *crepitatus*), crackle: see *crepitate.*] **I.** *tr.* To roast or calcine (salt, etc.) so as to cause crackling or until crackling ceases. **II.** *intr.* To make a crackling noise, as salt in roasting.—**de-crep-i-ta′tion** (-tā′shọn), *n.*

de-crep-it-ly (dē-krep′it-li), *adv.* In a decrepit manner.

de-crep-i-tude (dē-krep′i-tūd), *n.* [F. *décrépitude.*] Decrepit condition; feebleness, as from old age.

de-cres-cen-do (dē-kre-sen′dō, It. dā-kre-shen′dō). [It., gerund of *decrescere*, < L. *decrescere*: see *decrease.*] In *music*: **I.** *a.* Gradually decreasing in force or loudness; diminuendo: opposed to *crescendo.* **II.** *n.*; pl. *-dos* (-dōz). A gradual decrease in force or loudness; a decrescendo passage.

de-cres-cent (dē-kres′ẹnt), *a.* [L. *decrescens* (*-ent-*), ppr. of *decrescere*: see *decrease.*] Decreasing; esp., waning, as the moon (see Tennyson's "Gareth and Lynette," 519).

de-cre-tal (dē-krē′tạl). [LL. *decretalis* (as n., ML. *decretale*), < L. *decretum*: see *decree.*] **I.** *a.* Pertaining to, of the nature of, or containing a decree or decrees. **II.** *n.* A papal decree or epistle authoritatively determining some point of doctrine or ecclesiastical law; *pl.* [*cap.*], the body or collection of such decrees as a part of the canon law.—**de-cre′tal-ist, de-cre′tist**, *n.* One versed in the Decretals.

dec-re-to-ry (dek′rē-tō-ri or dē-krē′-), *a.* [L. *decretorius*, < *decernere*, decide, decree: see *decern.*] Pertaining to or of the nature of an authoritative decision or decree; definitive; decisive.

de-cri-al (dē-krī′ạl), *n.* The act of decrying.

de-cry (dē-krī′), *v. t.*; *-cried, -crying.* [F. *décrier*, OF. *descrier*, decry, proclaim, < *des-* (see *dis-*) + *crier*, E. *cry.*] To cry down; condemn or depreciate by proclamation, as foreign or obsolete coins; also, to reduce the value of by disparaging statements; also, to condemn or disparage openly; attack the reputation of.—**de-cri′er** (-krī′ėr), *n.*

dec-u-man (dek′ū-mạn), *a.* [L. *decumanus, decimanus*, of the tenth, large (from the notion that every tenth wave, or egg, is a large one), < *decimus*, tenth.] Large or immense, as a wave; in *Rom. antiq.*, pertaining to the tenth cohort (applied to the principal gate of a camp, being that farthest from the enemy).

de-cum-bent (dē-kum′bẹnt), *a.* [L. *decumbens* (*-ent-*), ppr. of *decumbere*, lie down, < *de-*, down, + *-cumbere*, lie: cf. *accumbent.*] Lying down; in *bot.*, of stems, branches, etc., lying or trailing on the ground with the extremity tending to ascend.—**de-cum′bence, de-cum′ben-cy**, *n.*—**de-cum′bent-ly**, *adv.*

dec-u-ple (dek′ū-pl). [L. *decuplus*, < *decem*, ten, + *-plus*: see *double.*] **I.** *a.* Tenfold; ten times as great. **II.** *n.* A tenfold quantity or multiple.—**dec′u-ple**, *v. t.*; *-pled, -pling.* To make ten times as great.

de-cu-ri-on (dē-kū′ri-ọn), *n.* [L. *decurio(n-)*, < *decuria*: see *decury.*] An officer in the ancient Roman army, commanding a company of ten horsemen; the head of a decury; any commander or overseer of ten; also, a member of the senate of an ancient Roman colony or municipality.

de-cur-rent (dē-kur′ẹnt), *a.* [L. *decurrens* (*-ent-*), ppr. of *decurrere*, run down, < *de-*, down, + *currere*, run.] In *bot.*, extending down the stem below the place of insertion, as certain leaves.

Decurrent Leaf (Thistle).

de-curve (dē-kėrv′), *v. t.*; *-curved, -curving.* [L. *de-*, down, + *curvare*, bend, curve.] To curve downward.—**de-cur-va-tion** (dē-kėr-vā′shọn), *n.*

dec-u-ry (dek′ū-ri), *n.*; pl. *-ries* (-riz). [L. *decuria*, < *decem*, ten.] In *Rom. hist.*, a division or company of ten men, or of any number; in general, a division, group, or class.

de-cus-sate (dē-kus′āt or dek′u-sāt), *v. t.* or *i.*; *-sated, -sating.* [L. *decussatus*, pp. of *decussare*, divide in the form of an X, < *decussis*, the number ten (represented by X), < *decem*, ten, + *as*, a unit.] To cross in the form of the letter X; intersect.—**de-cus′sate**, *a.* In the form of the letter X; crossed; having intersections; in *bot.*, of leaves, etc., arranged along the stem in pairs, each pair at right angles to the pair next above or below.—**de-cus-sa-tion** (dē-ku-sā′shọn or dek-u-), *n.*

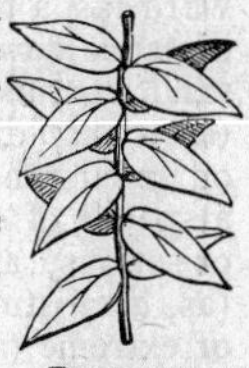
Decussate Leaves.

de-dal (dē′dạl), *a.* See *dædal.*

de-dans (dė-däṅ), *n.* [F., interior, noun use of *dedans*, adv., within.] In *court-tennis*, an open gallery for spectators, at the service end of the court; hence, the spectators.

ded-i-cant (ded′i-kạnt), *n.* One who dedicates.

ded-i-cate (ded′i-kāt), *v. t.*; *-cated, -cating.* [L. *dedicatus*, pp. of *dedicare*, proclaim, devote, consecrate, < *de*, from, + *dicare*, declare.] To set apart and consecrate to a deity or to a sacred purpose; hence, to devote formally to a particular use; give up wholly or earnestly, as to some person or end; set apart or appropriate; also, to inscribe or address (a book, piece of music, etc.) to a patron, friend, etc., as in testimony of respect or affection.—**ded′i-cate**, *a.* Dedicated. [Archaic.]—**ded″i-ca-tee′** (-kạ-tē′), *n.* One to whom something is dedicated.—**ded-i-ca′tion** (-kā′shọn), *n.* [L. *dedicatio(n-).*] The act of dedicating, or the fact of being dedicated; the form of words used in dedicating anything; the inscription prefixed or attached to a book, etc., dedicating it to some person.—**ded′i-ca-tor**, *n.*—**ded′i-ca-to-ry** (-kạ-tō-ri), *a.* Pertaining to or of the nature of dedication; serving as a dedication.

de-duce (dē-dūs′), *v. t.*; *-duced, -ducing.* [L. *deducere* (pp. *deductus*), < *de*, from, + *ducere*, lead: cf. *deduct.*] To lead forth, bring, or convey (archaic); also, to draw or obtain from some source; also, to trace the course of; trace the derivation of; esp., to derive as a conclusion from something known or assumed; infer; also, to deduct†; also, to reduce†.—**de-du′ci-ble** (-dū′si-bl), *a.* That may be deduced.

de-duct (dē-dukt′), *v. t.* [L. *deductus*, pp. of *deducere*: see *deduce.*] To take away, as from a sum or amount; subtract; also, to deduce†.—**de-duct′i-ble**, *a.* That may be deducted.—**de-duc′tion** (-duk′shọn), *n.* [L. *deductio(n-).*] The act of deducting; subtraction; abatement; that which is deducted; also, the act of deducing; the process of drawing a conclusion from something known or assumed; that which is deduced; a conclusion; in *logic*, inference by reasoning from generals to particulars (opposed to *induction*).—**de-duc′tive,** *a.* [L. *deductivus.*] Of the nature of or characterized by deduction, esp. in logic; reasoning deductively.—**de-duc′tive-ly,** *adv.*

de-du-pli-ca-tion (dē-dū-pli-kā′shọn), *n.* [See *de-*.] In *bot.*, the congenital separation of one organ into two or more.

deed (dēd), *n.* [AS. *dǣd* = D. *daad* = G. *that*, deed; from the Teut. verb represented by E. *do*[1].] That which is done, performed, or accomplished; an act; often, an exploit or achievement; also, action or performance, often as contrasted with words; in *law*, a writing or document executed under seal and delivered in token of agreement or conveyance, esp. one conveying real estate.—**in deed,** in action; hence, in fact or reality: as, "Let us not love in word, neither in tongue; but *in deed* and in truth" (1 John, iii. 18). See *indeed*.—**deed,** *v. t.* To convey or transfer by deed.—**deed′ful,** *a.* Full of deeds; active; effective.—**deed′less,** *a.* Without deeds or action; inactive.

deem (dēm), *v.* [AS. *dēman* = Icel. *dæma* = Goth. *dōmjan*, deem; from the Teut. noun represented by E. *doom.*] **I.** *intr.* To pronounce judgment†; also, to form or have an opinion; judge; think. **II.** *tr.* To sit in judgment on†; also, to sentence†; also, to administer (law: archaic); also, to estimate†; also, to decree† or ordain†; also, to hold as an opinion; judge; think; believe; regard; consider.—**deem**†, *n.* Judgment; opinion. See Shakspere's "Troilus and Cressida," iv. 4. 61.—**deem′er,** *n.*—**deem′ster** (-stėr), *n.* [See *-ster.*] A judge (archaic); esp., either of the two justices of the Isle of Man, one having jurisdiction over the northern division, the other over the southern.

deep (dēp). [AS. *dēop* = D. *diep* = G. *tief* = Icel. *djūpr* = Goth. *diups*, deep; akin to E. *dip.*] **I.** *a.* Having great or considerable extension downward from the surface, inward from without, or backward from the front; also, having a specified dimension downward, inward, or backward (as, a tank 8 feet *deep*); also, situated far or a certain distance down, in, or back; covered with a depth of mud, sand, etc., as a road†; extending to or coming from a depth (as, a *deep* dive; a *deep* breath); also, difficult to penetrate or understand; abstruse; also, lying below the surface (as, a speech of *deep* significance); not superficial; also, grave or serious; also, heartfelt (as, *deep* sorrow); also, absorbing (as, *deep* study); also, great in measure or degree; intense or extreme (as, *deep* sleep, silence, color, etc.); also, low in pitch, as sound; also, having penetrating intellectual powers; characterized by profound insight or learning; profound; sometimes, profoundly cunning or artful; also, much involved (as, *deep* in debt); absorbed (as, *deep* in thought). **II.** *n.* The deep part of the sea, a river, etc.; the sea or ocean (poetic); also, any deep space or place; a deep pit or cavity in the earth; also, the part of greatest intensity, as of winter; also, something profound or incomprehensible (as, "Thy judgments are a great *deep*": Ps. xxxvi. 6); *naut.*, one of the points on a hand lead-line, at 1, 4, 6, 8, etc., fathoms, distinguished from the *marks* by being unmarked.—**deep,** *adv.* [AS. *dēope.*] In a deep manner; to or at a considerable or specified depth; far on (in time); profoundly; intensely.—**deep′en,** *v. t.* or *i.* To make or become deep or deeper.—**deep′en-er,** *n.*—**deep′=laid′,** *a.* Deeply laid; planned with profound cunning: as, a *deep-laid* plot.—**deep′ly,** *adv.*—**deep′most,** *a. superl.* Deepest.—**deep′=mouthed′** (-mouᴛʜd′), *a.* Having a deep, sonorous voice (as, "the *deep-mouth'd* bloodhound's heavy bay": Scott's "Lady of the Lake," i. 1); also, deep and sonorous, as the baying of a hound.—**deep′ness,** *n.*—**deep′=root′ed,** *a.* Deeply rooted; firmly implanted.—**deep′=sea,** *a.* Of or pertaining to the deeper parts of the sea: as, *deep-sea* soundings.—**deep′=seat′ed,** *a.* Situated far beneath the surface; deeply rooted or lodged; firmly implanted.

deer (dēr), *n.*; pl. *deer*, occasionally (esp. with reference to different species) *deers.* [AS. *dēor* = D. *dier* = G. *tier* = Icel. *dȳr.*] A beast, esp. a quadruped†; now, any animal of the family *Cervidæ*, comprising ruminants most of which have solid deciduous horns or antlers (usually in the male only), as *Cervus elaphus* (common red deer of Europe), *Cariacus virginianus* (common deer of North America), *Dama platyceros* (or *Cervus dama*) (fallow-deer of Europe), *Alces americanus* (common moose), *Alces machlis* (old-world elk), etc.; popularly and commonly, any of the smaller species of this family, as distinguished from the moose, elk, etc.—**deer′ber″ry,** *n.* The fruit of a vacciniaceous shrub, *Vaccinium stamineum*, related to the blueberry, but having a tart, inedible fruit; also, the plant; also, the partridge-berry, *Mitchella repens*, or the winter-green, *Gaultheria procumbens.*—**deer′=grass,** *n.* Any plant of the genus *Rhexia*, esp. the common meadow-beauty, *R. virginica.*—**deer′hound,** *n.* A hound used for hunting deer, esp. one of a Scottish breed allied to and resembling the greyhound but larger and having a shaggy coat.—**deer′let,** *n.* A little deer; also, a chevrotain.—**deer′=mouse,** *n.* A yellowish-brown mouse, *Zapus hudsonius* (family *Zapodidæ*), of North America, having strongly developed hind legs which enable it to leap several feet at a bound; also, any of several species of true mice (family *Muridæ*), esp. the widely distributed white-footed mouse, *Peromyscus leucopus*, of North America.—**deer′skin,** *n.* The skin of a deer; leather made from this; a garment made of such leather.—**deer′=stalk″er,** *n.* One who stalks deer; one who hunts deer by stealing upon them unawares; also, a kind of close-fitting cap, worn esp. in stalking deer (Eng.).—**deer′=stalk″ing,** *n.*—**deer′=weed,** *n.* A fabaceous plant, *Lotus glaber*, of California, with yellow flowers and trifoliate leaves.

Skeleton of the extinct Irish Deer (*Cervus giganteus*), remarkable for its large size and great spread of antlers.

Deer-mouse, or White-footed Mouse (*Peromyscus leucopus*).

de-face (dẹ-fās′), *v. t.*; *-faced, -facing.* [OF. *defacier*, *desfacier*, < *des-* (see *dis-*) + *face*, E. *face.*] To mar the face or appearance of; disfigure; also, to render useless by disfiguring; cancel; blot out, obliterate, or efface (as, "He . . . *defaced* the very appearance of the savages being there; so that . . . I could scarce know where it was": Defoe's "Robinson Crusoe," i. 16); extinguish.—**de-face′a-ble,** *a.* Capable of being defaced.—**de-face′ment,** *n.* The act of defacing, or the state of being defaced; also, that which defaces; a disfigurement.—**de-fa′cer** (-fā′sėr), *n.*

de fac-to (dē fak′tō). [L., 'from fact.'] In fact; in reality: a phrase sometimes used adjectively (as, a *de facto* government, one actually existing, whether with or without right). Cf. *de jure.*

de-fal-cate (dẹ-fal′kāt), *v.*; *-cated, -cating.* [ML. *defalcatus*, pp. of *defalcare*, < L. *de*, from, + ML. *falcare*, cut with a sickle, < L. *falx*, sickle.] **I.**† *tr.* To lop off; deduct or subtract; also, to cut off or deduct a part from; curtail; reduce. **II.** *intr.* To be guilty of defalcation; misappropriate money, etc., in one's charge.—**de-fal-ca-tion** (dē-fal-kā′shọn or def-ạl-), *n.* [ML. *defalcatio(n-).*] The act of defalcating; deduction or reduction, or a deduction or abatement (archaic); reduction of the amount of a claim, etc., by the amount of a counter-claim; falling off or deficit (archaic); falling away or defection; a shortcoming; a misappropriation of money, etc., held in trust, or a sum misappropriated.—**def-al-ca-tor** (def′ạl-kā-tọr or dē′fal-), *n.*

def-a-ma-tion (def-ạ-mā′shọn), *n.* The act of defaming, or the fact of being defamed; slander; libel; calumny.—**de-fam-a-to-ry** (dẹ-fam′ạ-tō-ri), *a.* Of the nature of, characterized by, or employing defamation.

de-fame (dẹ-fām′), *v. t.*; *-famed, -faming.* [OF. *deffamer*, *diffamer* (F. *diffamer*), < L. *diffamare*, < *dis-* (see *dis-*) +

fama, report, reputation, fame.] To disgrace, or bring ill fame upon (archaic); also, to attack the good fame or reputation of, as by uttering or publishing maliciously anything injurious; slander; libel; calumniate; also, to accuse†.—**de-fam'er** (-fā'mėr), *n.*

de-fault (dẹ-fâlt'), *n.* [OF. *defaute* (also *defaut*, F. *défaut*), < *defaillir*, < *de-* (see *de-*) + *faillir*, E. *fail.*] Want, lack, or absence (now chiefly in 'in default of'); also, an imperfection or defect (archaic); also, failure in duty†; a fault†, misdeed†, or mistake†; also, failure to act; neglect; specif., failure to meet financial obligations; in *law*, failure to perform an act or obligation legally required, esp. to appear in court or to plead at a time assigned.—**de-fault'**, *v.* **I.** *intr.* To be wanting (now rare); also, to fail in fulfilling an obligation, esp. a legal or financial one; fail to appear in court; fail to meet financial engagements, or to account properly for money, etc., in one's care. **II.** *tr.* To declare to be in default, esp. legally; also, to fail to perform or pay.—**de-fault'er**, *n.* One who defaults, or fails to fulfil an obligation, esp. a legal or financial one; specif., one who fails to account properly for money, etc., intrusted to his care, esp. through having misappropriated it to his own use.

de-fea-sance (dẹ-fē'zạns), *n.* [OF. *defesance*, < *defaire*, *desfaire*, undo: see *defeat.*] An undoing, defeat, or overthrow; also, a rendering null and void: in *law*, a condition on the performance of which a deed or other instrument is defeated or rendered void; a collateral deed or other writing embodying such a condition.—**de-fea'si-ble** (-zi-bl), *a.* That may be abrogated or annulled.

de-feat (dẹ-fēt'), *v. t.* [OF. *defait*, *desfait*. pp. of *defaire*, *desfaire* (F. *défaire*), undo, destroy, defeat, < L. *dis-* (see *dis-*) + *facere*, do, make.] To undo†, destroy†, or ruin† (as, "His unkindness may *defeat* my life": Shakspere's "Othello," iv. 2. 160): also, to frustrate or thwart; also, to deprive of something expected (as, "Death . . . *Defeated* of his seizure": Milton's "Paradise Lost," xi. 254); also, to overcome in a contest; vanquish; gain the victory over; in *law*, to annul.—**de-feat'**, *n.* [= F. *défaite.*] Undoing†, destruction†, or ruin†; also, a bringing to naught; frustration; also, the act of overcoming in a contest, or the fact of being so overcome; an overthrow or vanquishment; in *law*, annulment.—**de-feat'er**, *n.*—**de-feat'ism**, *n.* [= F. *défaitisme.*] The spirit, policy, or procedure of those who desire or seek their country's defeat in war, as for the purpose of realizing their own theories or schemes.—**de-feat'ist.** [=F. *défaitiste.*] **I.** *n.* One who is imbued with the spirit or adheres to the policy of defeatism. **II.** *a.* Pertaining to or characterized by defeatism.—**de-fea'ture** (-fē'tụ̈r), *n.* [OF. *deffaiture.*] Defeat†, ruin†, or overthrow†; also, disfigurement (archaic: as, "And careful hours with time's deformed hand Have written strange *defeatures* in my face," Shakspere's "Comedy of Errors," v. 1. 299).

def-e-cate (def'ẹ-kāt), *v.*; *-cated*, *-cating.* [L. *defæcatus*, pp. of *defæcare*, < *de*, from, + *fæx*, pl. *fæces*, dregs.] **I.** *tr.* To clear of dregs; purify; refine; also, to remove (dregs, impurities, etc.). **II.** *intr.* To become clear of dregs or impurities; also, to void excrement.—**def-e-ca'tion** (-kā'shọn), *n.* [LL. *defæcatio(n-).*] The act of defecating; purification; also, the voiding of excrement.—**def'e-ca-tor**, *n.* One who or that which defecates; in *sugar-manuf.*, an apparatus for purifying the raw syrup.

de-fect (dẹ-fekt'), *n.* [L. *defectus*, n., < *deficere*, be wanting: see *defection.*] Want or lack, esp. of something essential to perfection or completeness; deficiency; also, a falling short; a fault or imperfection; also, the amount by which anything falls short.

de-fec-ti-ble (dẹ-fek'ti-bl), *a.* [L. *defectus*, pp. of *deficere*: see *defection.*] Liable to fall short; subject to defect. [Obs. or rare.]—**de-fec-ti-bil'i-ty** (-bil'i-ti), *n.*

de-fec-tion (dẹ-fek'shọn), *n.* [L. *defectio(n-)*, < *deficere*, leave, desert, be wanting, fail, < *de*, from, + *facere*, do, make.] The act or fact of failing, falling short, or becoming defective; failure; also, a falling away from allegiance, duty, virtue, etc.; desertion; backsliding; apostasy.

de-fec-tive (dẹ-fek'tiv). [LL. *defectivus*, < L. *deficere*, be wanting: see *defection*, *defect.*] **I.** *a.* Having a defect or defects; faulty; imperfect; incomplete; also, wanting or lacking; in *gram.*, lacking one or more of the usual forms of inflection. **II.** *n.* One who or that which is defective; a person characterized by some mental, moral, or physical defect; in *gram.*, a defective word.—**de-fec'tive-ly**, *adv.*—**de-fec'tive-ness**, *n.*

de-fec-tor (dẹ-fek'tọr), *n.* [L., < *deficere*, leave, desert: see *defection.*] One who abandons a leader, party, cause, etc.

de-fence', etc. See *defense*, etc.

de-fend (dẹ-fend'), *v.* [OF. *defendre* (F. *défendre*), < L. *defendere*, < *de*, from, + *-fendere*, strike.] **I.** *tr.* To ward off or repel (obs. or Sc.); also, to forbid† or prohibit† (as, "No interdict *Defends* the touching of these viands pure": Milton's "Paradise Regained," ii. 370); also, to ward off attack from; guard against assault or injury; protect; also, to uphold or support by speech, argument, etc., or by legal measures; also, to contest (a legal charge, claim, etc.). **II.** *intr.* In *law*, to enter or make a defense.—**de-fend'a-ble**, *a.* Capable of being defended.—**de-fend'ant**, *n.* [OF. *defendant* (F. *défendant*), ppr. of *defendre.*] A defender†; in *law*, the party contesting the claim or charge of the plaintiff; the person against whom an action is brought.—**de-fend'er**, *n.* One who defends; a protector; a champion; an upholder.—**Defender of the Faith** [tr. L. *Fidei Defensor*], a title borne by the sovereigns of England since the time of Henry VIII., on whom it was conferred in 1521 by Pope Leo X.—**de-fend'ress**, *n.* A female defender.

de-fen-es-tra-tion (dẹ-fen-es-trā'shọn), *n.* [L. *de*, from, + *fenestra*, window.] The act of throwing out of a window: as, the *defenestration* of Prague (the throwing of certain imperial commissioners out of the window of the palace of the Hradschin at Prague in 1618, which was the immediate occasion of the Thirty Years' War).

de-fense, de-fence (dẹ-fens'), *n.* [OF. *defense* (F. *défense*), < LL. *defensa*, < L. *defendere*: see *defend.*] The act of defending; prohibition†; legal prohibition to take game or fish (Eng.); resistance against attack; protection; the practice or art of defending one's self against attack, as in fencing or boxing; something that defends, esp. a fortification; the defending or maintaining of a cause or the like by speech, argument, etc.; a speech, argument, etc., in vindication; in *law*, the denial or pleading of the defendant in answer to the claim or charge against him; the proceedings adopted by a defendant, or his legal agents, for defending himself; also, a defendant and his legal agents collectively.—**de-fense'less, de-fence'less**, *a.* Without defense; unprotected.—**de-fense'less-ly, de-fence'less-ly**, *adv.*—**de-fense'less-ness, de-fence'less-ness**, *n.*

de-fen-si-ble (dẹ-fen'si-bl), *a.* [LL. *defensibilis.*] Capable of being defended against assault or injury; also, capable of being defended in argument; justifiable; also, capable of affording or making defense†.—**de-fen-si-bil'i-ty** (-bil'i-ti), **de-fen'si-ble-ness**, *n.*—**de-fen'si-bly**, *adv.*

de-fen-sive (dẹ-fen'siv). [ML. *defensivus.*] **I.** *a.* Serving to defend; protective; also, made or carried on for the purpose of defense (as, a *defensive* war); also, of or pertaining to defense (as, a *defensive* attitude). **II.** *n.* Something that serves to defend; also, defensive position or attitude.—**de-fen'sive-ly**, *adv.*—**de-fen'sive-ness**, *n.*

de-fer[1] (dẹ-fėr'), *v.*; *-ferred*, *-ferring.* [OF. *differer* (F. *différer*), < L. *differre*, carry apart, put off, delay: see *differ.*] **I.** *tr.* To put off (action, etc.) to a future time; postpone; also, to put off (a person) to a future time†; delay (a matter, etc.); relegate (something) to a place later in order. **II.** *intr.* To put off action; delay.

de-fer[2] (dẹ-fėr'), *v.*; *-ferred*, *-ferring.* [OF. *deferer* (F. *déférer*), < L. *deferre*, carry from or down, bring, deliver, report, accuse, < *de*, from, + *ferre*, bear: cf. *delate.*] **I.**† *tr.* To carry down or away; also, to offer; also, to refer. **II.** *intr.* To yield in judgment or opinion (*to*); pay deference (*to*).—**def-er-ence** (def'ẹ-rẹns), *n.* [F. *déférence.*] The act of deferring; submission or yielding to the judgment, opinion, will, etc., of another; hence, respectful or courteous regard.—**def'er-ent**, *a.* [L. *deferens* (*-ent-*), ppr.] Carrying down or away; efferent, as a duct; also, showing deference.—**def-er-en'tial** (-ẹ-ren'shạl), *a.* Characterized by or showing deference; respectful.—**def-er-en'tial-ly**, *adv.*

de-fer-ment (dē̦-fėr′mẹnt), *n.* The act of deferring or putting off; postponement.

de-fer-rer (dē̦-fėr′ėr), *n.* One who defers.

de-feu-dal-ize (dē-fū′dạl-īz), *v. t.*; *-ized, -izing.* [See *de-*.] To deprive of feudal character.

de-fi (dē̦-fī′), *n.* [Cf. F. *défi*, defiance, challenge.] A defiance; a challenge. [Colloq.]

de-fi-ance (dē̦-fī′ạns), *n.* [OF. *defiance*, *deffiance*, < *defier*: see *defy*.] The act of defying; renunciation of faith, fealty, or amity†; a challenge to meet in combat or contest; a daring or bold resistance to authority or to any opposing force; open disregard (as, in *defiance* of criticism).—**de-fi′ant,** *a.* Characterized by or showing defiance.—**de-fi′ant-ly,** *adv.*—**de-fi′ant-ness,** *n.*

de-fi-cien-cy (dē̦-fish′ẹn-si), *n.*; pl. *-cies* (-siz). The state or fact of being deficient; incompleteness, imperfection, or defect; insufficiency; absence or want; that in which anything is deficient; esp., insufficiency or lack of funds for meeting demands; the amount lacked; a deficit.

de-fi-cient (dē̦-fish′ẹnt), *a.* [L. *deficiens* (*-ent-*), ppr. of *deficere*, be wanting: see *defection*.] Wanting some element or characteristic necessary to completeness, or having an insufficient measure of it; falling short of completeness or a standard; also, present in less than the proper amount; not present; wanting or lacking.—**de-fi′cient-ly,** *adv.*

def-i-cit (def′i-sit), *n.* [L., 'there is wanting,' 3d pers. sing. pres. ind. of *deficere*: see *defection*.] A falling short; the amount by which a sum of money falls short of the required amount.

de-fi-er (dē̦-fī′ėr), *n.* [See *defy*.] One who defies.

def-i-lade (def-i-lād′), *v. t.*; *-laded, -lading.* [F. *défiler*, defilade, orig. unthread, < *dé-* (see *dis-*) + *-filer* as in *enfiler*: see *enfilade*.] In *fort.*, to arrange the plan and profile of (a fortification) so as to protect its lines from enfilading fire and its interior from plunging or reverse fire.—**def-i-lade′,** *n.* In *fort.*, the act or operation of defilading; the determination of the directions and heights of the lines of ramparts, etc., needed to defilade a fortification.

de-file[1] (dē̦-fīl′), *v. i.*; *-filed, -filing.* [F. *défiler*, < *dé-* (see *de-*) + *file*, E. *file*[3].] To march in a line, or by files; file off.—**de-file**[1] (dē̦-fīl′ or dē′fīl), *n.* [Earlier *defilé*, < F. *défilé*, orig. pp. of *défiler*.] A narrow passage through which troops can pass only in narrow columns; any narrow passage, as between mountains (as, "a narrow pass or *defile*, between steep and closely-hanging hills": Motley's "Dutch Republic," i. 2); also, the act of defiling.

de-file[2] (dē̦-fīl′), *v. t.*; *-filed, -filing.* [Altered form (simulating *file*[2]) of obs. *defoul*, < OF. *defouler*, trample down, oppress, outrage, < *de-* (see *de-*) + *fouler*, trample: see *foil*[2].] To make foul, dirty, or unclean, either physically or morally; pollute; taint; violate; desecrate or profane; make ceremonially unclean.—**de-file′ment,** *n.* The act of defiling, or the state of being defiled; also, a thing that defiles.—**de-fil′er** (-fī′lėr), *n.*—**de-fil′ing-ly,** *adv.*

de-fin-a-ble (dē̦-fī′nạ-bl), *a.* That may be defined.—**de-fin-a-bil′i-ty** (-bil′i-ti), *n.*—**de-fin′a-bly,** *adv.*

de-fine (dē̦-fīn′), *v. t.*; *-fined, -fining.* [OF. *definer*, for *definir* (F. *définir*), < L. *definire* (pp. *definitus*), limit, determine, explain, terminate, < *de-*, completely, + *finire*, bound, limit, terminate, E. *finish*.] To bring to an end†; decide or settle (a controversy, etc.)†; also, to determine or fix the boundaries or extent of; make clear the outline or form of; also, to fix or lay down definitely; specify distinctly; also, to explain the nature or essential qualities of; describe; state or set forth the meaning or signification of (a word, phrase, etc.); also, to be a distinguishing feature of; characterize.—**de-fine′ment,** *n.* The act of defining; description; definition.—**de-fin′er** (-fī′nėr), *n.*

def-i-nite (def′i-nit), *a.* [L. *definitus*, pp.: see *define*.] Having fixed limits; clearly defined or determined; not vague or general; precisely prescribed or established; fixed; precise; exact; of persons, clear or specific in thought, statement, etc.; in *gram.*, specifying precisely or with limitation (as, the *definite* article 'the'); in *bot.*, of stamens, etc., of a constant number not exceeding twenty; of an inflorescence, determinate.—**def′i-nite-ly,** *adv.*—**def′i-nite-ness,** *n.*

def-i-ni-tion (def-i-nish′ọn), *n.* [L. *definitio*(*n-*), < *definire*: see *define*.] The act of defining, or making definite or clear; the capacity of a lens, etc., to give a clear, distinct image of an object; the condition of being definite; distinctness, as of an optical image; also, the explanation or description of the nature or properties of a thing; a statement of the essential nature of anything; a formal statement of the meaning or signification of a word, phrase, etc.—**def-i-ni′tion-al,** *a.*

de-fin-i-tive (dē̦-fin′i-tiv), *a.* [L. *definitivus*, < *definire*: see *define*.] Having the function of deciding or settling; determinative; conclusive; final; hence, settled in a conclusive or final manner; having its fixed and final form (esp. in *biol.*: as, a *definitive* organ); also, serving to fix or specify definitely; specific or precise in force or application; definitely fixed or specified; precisely expressed; definite.—**de-fin′i-tive-ly,** *adv.*—**de-fin′i-tive-ness,** *n.*

de-fin-i-tude (dē̦-fin′i-tūd), *n.* The quality of being definite.

def-la-grate (def′lạ-grāt), *v. i.* or *t.*; *-grated, -grating.* [L. *deflagratus*, pp. of *deflagrare*, < *de-*, away, + *flagrare*, blaze, burn.] To burn, esp. suddenly and violently.—**def-la-gra′tion** (-grā′shọn), *n.* [L. *deflagratio*(*n-*).] The act of deflagrating; combustion, esp. when violent.—**def′la-gra-tor,** *n.* A device for producing deflagration.

de-flate (dē̦-flāt′), *v. t.*; *-flated, -flating.* [L. *de*, from, + *flare* (pp. *flatus*), blow.] To release the air or gas from (something inflated, as a balloon); also, to reduce (currency, prices, etc.) from an inflated condition.—**de-fla′tion** (-flā′shọn), *n.*

de-flect (dē̦-flekt′), *v. t.* or *i.* [L. *deflectere* (pp. *deflexus*), < *de*, from, + *flectere*, bend.] To bend or turn aside; turn from a true course or right line; swerve.—**de-flec′tion, de-flex′ion** (-flek′shọn), *n.* [LL. *deflexio*(*n-*).] The act of deflecting, or the state of being deflected; a turning from a true course or right line; a bending, esp. downward; deviation; amount of deviation; in *optics*, the bending of rays of light from a straight line; in *elect.*, etc., the deviation or swing of the needle or indicator of a scientific instrument from the position regarded as zero.—**de-flec′tive,** *a.* Causing deflection.—**de-flec′tor,** *n.* Anything that deflects, as a device for deflecting a current of air, gas, etc.—**de-flex′** (-fleks′), *v. t.* [L. *deflexus*, pp.] To deflect, esp. downward.

de-floc-cu-late (dē-flok′ụ̄-lāt), *v.*; *-lated, -lating.* [See *de-*.] **I.** *tr.* To change from a flocculated state; separate into non-flocculated masses or particles; reduce to what is supposed to be a molecular state of subdivision, as graphite. **II.** *intr.* To become deflocculated.—**de-floc-cu-la′tion** (-lā′shọn), *n.*

def-lo-ra-tion (def-lọ̄-rā′shọn), *n.* [LL. *defloratio*(*n-*), < *deflorare*: see *deflower*.] The act of deflowering; a selection of the flower or finest parts of anything, as of a book; the act of depriving a woman of virginity.

de-flow-er (dē̦-flou′ėr), *v. t.* [OF. *deflorer* (F. *déflorer*), < LL. *deflorare*, < L. *de-* (see *de-*) + *flos* (*flor-*), flower.] To deprive or strip of flowers (as, "Garlands . . . From vales *deflower'd*": Keats's "Lamia," ii.); also, to deprive (a woman) of virginity; ravish; also, to despoil of beauty, freshness, sanctity, etc.; spoil; desecrate.—**de-flow′er-er,** *n.*

de-flux-ion (dē̦-fluk′shọn), *n.* [LL. *defluxio*(*n-*), < L. *defluere*, flow down, < *de*, down from, + *fluere*, flow.] In *pathol.*, a copious discharge of fluid matter, as in catarrh.

de-fo-li-ate (dē̦-fō′li-āt), *v. t.*; *-ated, -ating.* [ML. *defoliatus*, pp. of *defoliare*, < L. *de-* (see *de-*) + *folium*, leaf.] To strip or deprive (a tree, etc.) of leaves.—**de-fo-li-a′tion** (-ā′shọn), *n.*—**de-fo′li-a-tor,** *n.*

de-force (dē̦-fōrs′), *v. t.*; *-forced, -forcing.* [OF. *deforcer*, < *de-* (see *de-*) + *forcer*, E. *force*[3], *v.*] In *law*, to withhold (something) by force or violence, as from the rightful owner; also, to deprive (a person) forcibly or wrongfully of property, etc.; in *Sc. law*, to prevent (an officer of the law) from executing his official duty.—**de-force′ment,** *n.*—**de-for′ciant** (-fōr′shiạnt), *n.* One who deforces.

de-for-est (dē-for′est), *v. t.* [See *de-*.] To reduce from the status of a forest; disafforest; also, to divest of forests or trees.—**de-for-es-ta′tion** (-es-tā′shọn), *n.*—**de-for′est-er,** *n.*

de-form[1] (dē̦-fôrm′), *a.* [L. *deformis*, < *de-* (see *de-*) + *forma*, E. *form*, *n.*] Deformed; misshapen; ugly or hideous. [Archaic.]

de-form[2] (dē̦-fôrm′), *v. t.* [OF. *deformer* (F. *déformer*), < L. *deformare*, < *de-* (see *de-*) + *formare*, E. *form*, *v.*] To put out of the proper form or shape; misshape; distort; also, to mar the appearance of; disfigure; spoil; also, to change the form of; transform; in *mech.*, to subject to deformation.—**de-form′a-ble,** *a.* Capable of being deformed; susceptible of change of form.—**de-form-a-bil′i-ty** (-bil′i-ti), *n.*—**de-for-ma-tion** (dē-fôr-mā′shọn), *n.* [L. *deformatio(n-).*] The act or result of deforming; distortion; disfigurement; change of form; also, an altered form; in *mech.*, a change in the shape or dimensions of a body, resulting from stress; strain.—**de-formed′,** *p. a.* Misshapen, distorted, or malformed; also, disfigured, unsightly, or ugly; also, without regular form†.—**de-form′er,** *n.*

de-for-mi-ty (dę̄-fôr′mi-ti), *n.*; pl. *-ties* (-tiz). [L. *deformitas*, < *deformis*: see *deform*[1], *a.*] The quality of being deformed; unshapeliness or malformation; a distortion or malformation, esp. of the body; disfigurement, unsightliness, or ugliness; also, a deformed person or thing; also, something disfiguring.

de-fraud (dę̄-frâd′), *v. t.* [L. *defraudare*, < *de-* (see *de-*) + *fraudare*, cheat, < *fraus*, E. *fraud.*] To deprive of some right or property by fraud; cheat.—**de-frau-da-tion** (dē-frâ-dā′shọn), *n.*—**de-fraud′er,** *n.*

de-fray (dę̄-frā′), *v. t.* [F. *défrayer*, OF. *deffrayer*, < *de-* (see *dis-*) + *frait, fret* (F. *frais*, pl.), expense, cost.] To pay the charges or expenses of (a person)†; also, to pay the charges for or of (a thing: now rare); also, to discharge (costs or expenses) by payment; pay or meet; also, to pay out or expend (money)†.—**de-fray′a-ble,** *a.* That may be or is to be defrayed.—**de-fray′al,** *n.* Defrayment.—**de-fray′er,** *n.*—**de-fray′ment,** *n.* The act of defraying; payment of charges or expenses.

deft (deft), *a.* [ME. *defte*, < AS. *gedæfte*, gentle, meek, akin to *gedafen*, becoming, fit, and Goth. *gadaban*, befit.] Neat, spruce, or pretty (now only prov. Eng.); also, dexterous; nimble; skilful; clever; also, quiet or silent (prov. Eng.).—**deft′ly,** *adv.*—**deft′ness,** *n.*

de-funct (dę̄-fungkt′). [L. *defunctus*, pp. of *defungi*, discharge, finish, die, < *de-*, completely, + *fungi*, perform.] **I.** *a.* Deceased; dead; extinct. **II.** *n.* A dead person, esp. one recently deceased: usually with *the.*—**de-funct′ness,** *n.*

de-fy (dę̄-fī′), *v. t.*; *-fied, -fying.* [OF. *defier, deffier, desfier* (F. *défier*), < ML. *diffidare, disfidare*, < L. *dis-* (see *dis-*) + *fides*, faith.] To renounce faith or fealty to†; declare war against†; also, to challenge to a combat or contest (archaic); also, to challenge (one) to do something deemed impossible (as, "Betty . . . *defied* me to deny it": Blackmore's "Lorna Doone," xxxii.); also, to challenge the power of; resist boldly or openly; express or show contemptuous disregard of; of things, to offer effective resistance to (as, a fort which *defies* attacks); also, to reject†; repudiate†; disdain†; revolt at†.—**de-fy′ing-ly,** *adv.*

dé-ga-gé (dā-gȧ-zhā), *a.* [F. (fem. *dégagée*), pp. of *dégager*, disengage, put at ease.] Unconstrained; unembarrassed; easy, as in manner.

de-gas (dē-gas′), *v. t.*; *-gassed, -gassing.* [See *de-.*] *Milit.*, to treat or relieve (one who has been gassed).—**de-gas′ser,** *n.*

de-gen-er-a-cy (dę̄-jen′ẹ-rā-si), *n.* Degenerate state or character.

de-gen-er-ate (dę̄-jen′ẹ-rāt), *v. i.*; *-ated, -ating.* [L. *degeneratus*, pp. of *degenerare*, < *degener*, that departs from its race or kind, base, < *de*, from, + *genus*, race, kind.] To fall away from the normal state or condition; decline in physical, mental, or moral qualities; deteriorate.—**de-gen′er-ate** (-ẹ-rāt). **I.** *a.* Having degenerated; deteriorated; degraded; exhibiting degeneration. **II.** *n.* One who has retrograded from a normal type or standard, as in morals or character; one exhibiting certain morbid physical and mental traits and tendencies, esp. from birth.—**de-gen′er-ate-ly,** *adv.*—**de-gen′er-ate-ness,** *n.*—**de-gen-er-a′tion** (-ẹ-rā′shọn), *n.* The process of degenerating, or the state of being degenerate; deterioration; degradation; degeneracy; in *biol.*, progressive deterioration or simplification; reversion to a less highly organized or a simpler type; in *pathol.*, a process by which normal tissue becomes converted into or replaced by tissue of an inferior quality (as, fatty *degeneration*, characterized by the formation of fat); the morbid condition produced by such a process.—**de-gen′er-a-tive** (-ẹ-rā-tiv), *a.* Tending to degenerate; characterized by degeneration.

deg-lu-ti-tion (deg-lọ̈-tish′ọn or dē-glọ̈-), *n.* [F. *déglutition*, < L. *deglutire*, swallow down, < *de-*, down, + *glutire*, swallow.] The act or process of swallowing.—**de-glu-ti-to-ry** (dę̄-glö′ti-tọ̄-ri), *a.* Of or pertaining to deglutition.

deg-ra-da-tion (deg-rā̜-dā′shọn), *n.* [ML. *degradatio(n-).*] The act of degrading, or the state of being degraded.—**deg-ra-da′tion-al,** *a.*

de-grade (dę̄-grād′), *v.*; *-graded, -grading.* [OF. *degrader* (F. *dégrader*), < ML. *degradare*, reduce in rank, < L. *de*, down from, + *gradus*, E. *grade.*] **I.** *tr.* To reduce from a higher to a lower rank, degree, etc.; deprive of office, rank, degree, or title as a punishment; also, to lower in dignity or estimation; bring into contempt; also, to lower in character or quality; debase; deprave; also, to reduce in amount, strength, intensity, etc.; tone down in color; in *biol.*, to lower in the scale of classification; also, to reduce in complexity of structure or function; in *geol.*, to wear down by erosion, as hills (opposed to *aggrade*). **II.** *intr.* To become lower in grade, type, or character; deteriorate; degenerate.—**de-grad′ed** (-grā′ded), *p. a.* Reduced or lowered in rank, estimation, character, etc.; debased; degenerate; reduced in intensity.—**de-grad′ed-ness,** *n.*—**de-grad′er,** *n.*—**de-grad′ing,** *p. a.* That degrades; debasing.—**de-grad′ing-ly,** *adv.*

dé-gras (dā-grä), *n.* [F.] The fat or grease recovered after treating certain skins with fish-oil, forming a valuable dressing for hides.

de-gree (dę̄-grē′), *n.* [OF. *degre, degret* (F. *degré*), < L. *de*, down from, + *gradus*, step, degree, E. *grade.*] A step, as of a stair†; a step or stage in an ascending or descending scale, or in a course or process (as, by *degrees*, gradually); also, one step or remove in direct line of descent; measure of relationship in the direct line reckoned by such steps; measure of relationship between two collateral descendants, reckoned in the canon law by the number of generations between the common ancestor and the descendant farther from him, and in the civil law by the number of generations upward from one descendant to the common ancestor and from him downward to the other; also, a stage in a scale of rank or dignity; relative rank, station, etc. (as, "High was his *degree* in heaven": Milton's "Paradise Lost," v. 707); also, relative condition; manner, way, or respect; also, an academic rank or grade conferred by a diploma in universities and colleges as an indication of proficiency in learning or as an honorary recognition of achievement; also, a stage in a scale of intensity or amount (as, to the last *degree*; to a *degree*, to an undefined but considerable extent); relative extent or measure; also, one of a number of equal divisions of a graduated scale, as on a thermometer, taken as a unit of measure (often indicated by the sign °: as, 32° Fahrenheit); in *law*, a relative measure of criminality (as, murder in the first *degree*); in *gram.*, one of the three stages (positive, comparative, and superlative) in the comparison of an adjective or adverb; in *geom.*, etc., the 360th part of the circumference of a circle, as used to measure arcs and angles (often indicated by the sign °: as, 45°); in *music*, the interval between successive notes of a scale, or between any line or space of the staff and its adjoining space or line; each of the successive notes of the scale, or each of the successive lines and spaces of the staff; in *alg.*, rank as determined by an exponent or sum of exponents (as, a^3 and a^2b are terms of the third *degree*; $2x^2y + ax = 4$ is an equation of the third *degree*, three being the sum of the exponents of the unknown quantities in that term in which such sum is the greatest).

de-gres-sion (dę̄-gresh′ọn), *n.* [L. *degredi* (pp. *degressus*), go down, < *de*, down from, + *gradi*, walk, go: see *gradient.*] A going down; descent; also, the decrease in rate for sums below a certain amount, in degressive taxation.—**de-gres′sive** (-gres′iv), *a.* Noting or pertaining to a form of taxation in which the rate is constant on sums of and above a certain fixed amount, but diminishes gradually on sums below that amount.

dé-grin-go-lade (dā-grañ-go-läd), *n.* [F., < *dégringoler*, fall or roll precipitately downward.] A swift, involuntary descent; a precipitate downward course.

deg-u (deg′ö), *n.* [S. Amer.] Any of several small hystricomorphic rodents of western South America, constituting the genus *Octodon.*

Degu.

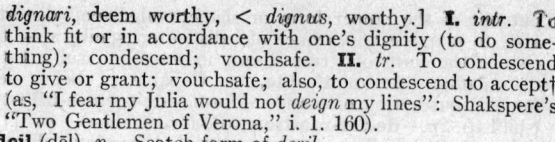

de-gum (dē-gum′), *v. t.*; *-gummed, -gumming.* [See *de-.*] To free from gum.

de-gust (dẹ̄-gust′), *v. t.* or *i.* [L. *degustare,* < *de,* from, + *gustare,* taste.] To taste.—**de-gus-ta-tion** (dē-gus-tā′shọn), *n.*

de-hair (dē-hãr′), *v. t.* [See *de-.*] To remove the hair from (hides or skins); unhair.

de-hisce (dẹ̄-his′), *v. i.*; *-hisced, -hiscing.* [L. *dehiscere,* gape, split open, < *de,* from, + *hiscere,* inceptive of *hiare,* gape: cf. *hiatus.*] To gape; burst open, as the capsules of plants.—**de-his′cence** (-his′ẹns), *n.* A gaping or bursting open; in *bot.*, the natural bursting open of capsules, fruits, anthers, etc., for the discharge of their contents.—**de-his′cent,** *a.* Gaping open; characterized by dehiscence.

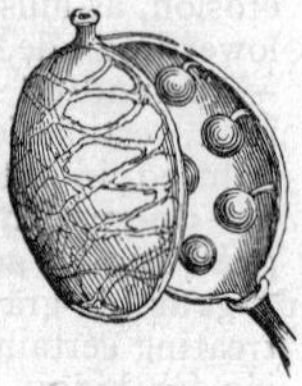
Dehiscent Seed-vessel.

de-horn (dē-hôrn′), *v. t.* [See *de-.*] To deprive (cattle) of horns; prevent the growth of the horns of.—**de-horn′er,** *n.* One who or that which dehorns; an instrument for dehorning cattle.

de-hort (dē-hôrt′), *v. t.* [L. *dehortari,* < *de,* from, + *hortari,* urge.] To seek to dissuade; also, to counsel against†.—**de-hor-ta-tion** (dē-hôr-tā′shọn), *n.*—**de-hort′er,** *n.*

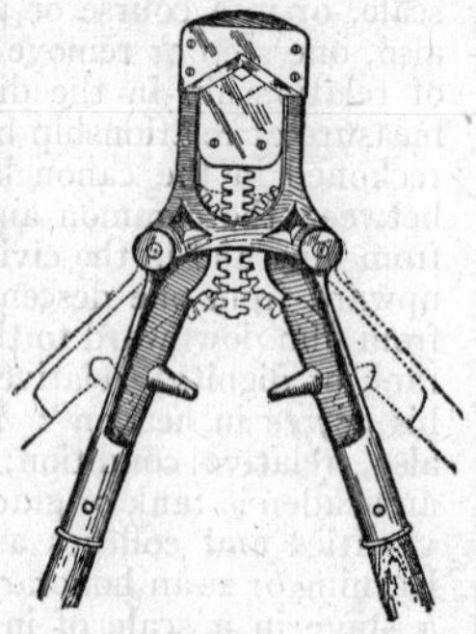
Dehorner.

de-hu-man-ize (dē-hū′mạn-īz), *v. t.*; *-ized, -izing.* [See *de-.*] To deprive of human character or attributes.—**de-hu″man-i-za′tion** (-i-zā′shọn), *n.*

de-hy-drate (dē-hī′drāt), *v.*; *-drated, -drating.* [See *de-.*] **I.** *tr.* To deprive (a chemical compound) of water or the elements of water; also, to free (vegetables, etc.) from moisture, for preservation; desiccate; dry. **II.** *intr.* To lose water or moisture.—**de-hy-dra′tion** (-drā′shọn), *n.*

de-hy-dro-gen-ize (dē-hī′drọ̄-jen-īz), *v. t.*; *-ized, -izing.* [See *de-.*] In *chem.*, to deprive of hydrogen; remove hydrogen from (a compound).

de-hyp-no-tize (dē-hip′nọ̄-tīz), *v. t.*; *-tized, -tizing.* [See *de-.*] To bring out of the hypnotic state.

de-i-cide (dē′i-sīd), *n.* [LL. *deicida,* < L. *deus,* god: see *-cide.*] One who kills a god; also, the killing of a god.—**de′i-ci-dal** (-sī-dạl), *a.*

deic-tic (dīk′tik), *a.* [Gr. δεικτικός, serving to show, < δεικνύναι, show.] Pointing out directly; demonstrative; proving directly, as reasoning.

de-if-ic (dẹ̄-if′ik), *a.* [LL. *deificus,* < L. *deus,* god, + *facere,* make.] Deifying; making divine.

de-i-fi-ca-tion (dē″i-fi-kā′shọn), *n.* The act of deifying, or the state of being deified; a deified embodiment.

de-i-fi-er (dē′i-fī-ėr), *n.* One who or that which deifies.

de-i-form (dē′i-fôrm), *a.* [ML. *deiformis,* < L. *deus,* god, + *forma,* form.] Godlike; divine; conformable to what is divine.—**de-i-for′mi-ty** (-fôr′mi-ti), *n.*

de-i-fy (dē′i-fī), *v. t.*; *-fied, -fying.* [OF. *deifier* (F. *déifier*), < LL. *deificare,* < *deificus*: see *deific.*] To make a god of; exalt to the rank of a deity; also, to adore or regard as a deity (as, "The old man *deifies* prudence: the youth commits himself to magnanimity and chance": Johnson's "Rasselas," xxvi.); also, to render godlike; exalt spiritually.

deign (dān), *v.* [OF. *deignier* (F. *daigner*), < L. *dignare,* *dignari,* deem worthy, < *dignus,* worthy.] **I.** *intr.* To think fit or in accordance with one's dignity (to do something); condescend; vouchsafe. **II.** *tr.* To condescend to give or grant; vouchsafe; also, to condescend to accept† (as, "I fear my Julia would not *deign* my lines": Shakspere's "Two Gentlemen of Verona," i. 1. 160).

deil (dēl), *n.* Scotch form of *devil.*

deip-nos-o-phist (dīp-nos′ọ̄-fist), *n.* [Gr. δειπνοσοφιστής, < δεῖπνον, dinner, + σοφιστής, wise man.] One who converses learnedly at dinner: from the title of a celebrated work of the Greek writer Athenæus (flourished about A.D. 200), in which a number of learned men are represented as at dinner, discoursing on literature, matters of the table, and other topics.—**deip-nos-o-phis′tic** (-fis′tik), *a.*

de-ism (dē′izm), *n.* [F. *déisme,* < L. *deus,* god.] Belief in the existence of a God on the evidence of reason and nature only, with rejection of supernatural revelation (distinguished from *theism*); sometimes, belief in a God separate and remote from the world and man (distinguished from *atheism, pantheism,* and *theism*).—**de′ist,** *n.* [F. *déiste.*] One who believes in deism.—**de-is-tic, de-is-ti-cal** (dẹ̄-is′tik, -ti-kạl), *a.*—**de-is′ti-cal-ly,** *adv.*

de-i-ty (dē′i-ti), *n.*; pl. *-ties* (-tiz). [OF. *deite* (F. *déité*), < LL. *deitas,* < L. *deus,* god; akin to L. *divus,* divine, *Jovis,* Jove, Gr. Ζεύς (gen. Διός), Zeus, Skt. *deva,* god, *dyāus,* heaven, and AS. *Tīw,* the Teutonic god of war (see *Tuesday*).] The estate or rank of a god; divine character or nature; godhood; esp., the character or nature of the Supreme Being; also, a god or goddess; a person or thing deified; [*cap.*] usually with *the,* the Supreme Being; God.

de-ject (dẹ̄-jekt′), *v. t.* [L. *dejectus,* pp. of *dejicere,* < *de,* down from, + *jacere,* throw.] To throw or cast down (archaic); depose†; abase† or humble†; now, to depress the spirits of; dispirit; dishearten.—**de-ject′,** *a.* Dejected; downcast. [Obs. or archaic.]—**de-jec′ta** (-jek′tạ̈), *n. pl.* [NL., prop. neut. pl. of L. *dejectus,* pp.] Excrements.—**de-ject′ed,** *p. a.* Thrown or cast down (archaic); humbled†; now, depressed in spirits; disheartened; low-spirited.—**de-ject′ed-ly,** *adv.*—**de-ject′ed-ness,** *n.*—**de-jec′tile** (-til), *n. Milit.*, a missile hurled down upon an enemy.—**de-jec′tion** (-shọn), *n.* [L. *dejectio(n-).*] The act of dejecting, or the fact of being dejected; depression of spirits; in *med.*, evacuation of the bowels; fecal discharge; also, excrement.

dé-jeu-ner (dā-zhė-nā), *n.* [F., orig. inf., OF. *desjeuner,* break one's fast, < *des-* (see *dis-*) + *jeun,* fasting, < L. *jejunus,* E. *jejune*: cf. *dine.*] Breakfast: in French use applied both to the morning meal, usually light, and to a more substantial midday meal (luncheon).

de ju-re (dē jö′rē). [L., 'from right or law.'] By right; according to law: a phrase sometimes used adjectively (as, a *de jure* ruler, one who has a legal right to rule, whether actually exercising it or not). Cf. *de facto.*

deka-, etc. See *deca-,* etc.

de-knight (dē-nīt′), *v. t.* [See *de-.*] To deprive of knighthood; degrade from the rank of knight.

de-laine (dẹ̄-lān′), *n.* Same as *mousseline de laine.* See under *mousseline.*

de-lam-i-nate (dē-lam′i-nāt), *v. i.*; *-nated, -nating.* [See *de-.*] To split into laminæ or thin layers.—**de-lam-i-na′tion** (-nā′shọn), *n.* A splitting apart into layers; esp., in *embryol.*, the splitting of a primitive blastoderm into two layers of cells.

de-late (dẹ̄-lāt′), *v. t.*; *-lated, -lating.* [L. *delatus,* pp. of *deferre,* carry from or down, bring, report, accuse: see *defer*[2].] To carry down or away†; also, to transmit†; also, to relate or report; report (an offense, etc.); also, to inform against, denounce, or accuse (as, "Yes, go and be a Christian . . . And then be *delated* and taken up, and torn to shreds on the rack": J. H. Newman's "Callista," vi.).—**de-la′tion** (-lā′shọn), *n.* [L. *delatio(n-).*] The act of delating; transmission†; an informing against or accusing; denouncement; accusation.—**de-la′tor,** *n.* [L.] An informer or accuser; a secret or professional informer.

de-lay (dẹ̄-lā′), *v.* [OF. *delaier, deslaier* (F. *dilayer*), perhaps < ML. *dilatare,* freq. of L. *differre,* E. *defer*[1].] **I.** *tr.* To put off to a later time; defer; postpone; also, to impede the progress of; retard; hinder. **II.** *intr.* To put off action; tarry; linger; loiter.—**de-lay′**, *n.* [OF. *delai* (F. *délai*).] The act of delaying, or the fact of being delayed; procrastination; lingering; loitering; hindrance to progress. —**de-lay′er**, *n.*—**de-lay′ing-ly**, *adv.*

de-le (dē′lē). [L., impv. of *delere*, do away with, E. *delete*.] Take out; omit: a direction (usually represented by the symbol ϑ) on a printer's proof, with express indication of the matter to be omitted.—**de′le**, *v. t.*; *-led* (-lēd), *-leing* (-lę̄-ing). To indicate for omission; delete.

del-e-ble (del′ę̄-bl), *a.* See *delible.*

de-lec-ta-ble (dę̄-lek′tą-bl), *a.* [L. *delectabilis*, < *delectare*: see *delight*.] Delightful; highly pleasing; enjoyable.—**de-lec-ta-bil′i-ty** (-bil′i-ti), **de-lec′ta-ble-ness**, *n.*—**de-lec′ta-bly**, *adv.*

de-lec-ta-tion (dē-lek-tā′shǫn), *n.* [L. *delectatio(n-)*, < *delectare*: see *delight*.] The act of delighting; delight.

de-lec-tus (dę̄-lek′tus), *n.*; pl. *-tuses*, L. *-tus.* [L., selection, < *deligere*, select, < *de*, from, + *legere*, gather.] A selection of passages, esp. from Latin or Greek authors, for translation.

del-e-ga-cy (del′ę̄-gā-si), *n.*; pl. *-cies* (-siz). The position or commission of a delegate; the sending or appointing of a delegate; a body of delegates.

del-e-gate (del′ę̄-gāt), *v. t.*; *-gated*, *-gating.* [L. *delegatus*, pp. of *delegare*, < *de*, from, + *legare*, send, depute.] To send or appoint (a person) as deputy; also, to commit (powers, functions, etc.) to another as agent or deputy.—**del′e-gate. I.** *a.* Delegated. **II.** *n.* One delegated to act for or represent another or others; a deputy; a commissioner; a representative, as in a convention or other assembly; the representative of a Territory in the House of Representatives of the U. S.—**del′e-gate-ship**, *n.*—**del-e-ga′tion** (-gā′shǫn), *n.* [L. *delegatio(n-)*.] The act of delegating, or the fact of being delegated; the commission or authority of a delegate; a body of persons delegated; the appointed representatives of an association or body of persons, as in a convention or other assembly.—**del′e-ga-tor**, *n.*

de-lete (dę̄-lēt′), *v. t.*; *-leted*, *-leting.* [L. *deletus*, pp. of *delere*, do away with, destroy, blot out.] To do away with† or destroy†; also, to strike out or take out (anything written or printed); cancel; erase; expunge.

del-e-te-ri-ous (del-ę̄-tē′ri-us), *a.* [Gr. δηλητήριος, < δηλεῖσθαι, hurt.] Injurious to health (as, "'Tis pity wine should be so *deleterious*": Bryon's "Don Juan," iv. 52); noxious; poisonous; hence, in general, hurtful; harmful; injurious.—**del-e-te′ri-ous-ly**, *adv.*—**del-e-te′ri-ous-ness**, *n.*

de-le-tion (dę̄-lē′shǫn), *n.* [L. *deletio(n-)*.] The act of deleting, or the fact of being deleted; an erasure; a deleted passage.

delf (delf), *n.* Same as *delft.*

delft (delft), *n.* [For *Delft ware*.] A kind of glazed earthenware decorated in colors, esp. in blue, made at Delft, in Holland; any pottery resembling this; any glazed earthenware for table use, etc. (Eng.).

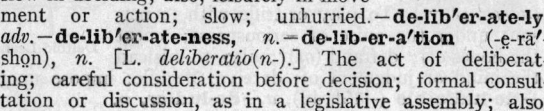

Delft Ware, 17th century.

De-li-an (dē′li-ąn), *a.* Of or pertaining to Delos, a small island in the Ægean Sea, the reputed birthplace of Apollo and Artemis.

de-lib-er-ate (dę̄-lib′ę-rāt), *v.*; *-ated*, *-ating.* [L. *deliberatus*, pp. of *deliberare*, < *de-*, completely, + *librare*, balance, weigh: see *librate*.] **I.** *tr.* To weigh in the mind; consider. **II.** *intr.* To think carefully or attentively; reflect about a decision or choice to be made; also, to consult or confer formally; hold formal discussion, as with reference to proposed measures.—**de-lib′er-ate** (-ę-rąt), *a.* Carefully weighed or considered; studied; intentional; also, characterized by deliberation; careful or slow in deciding; also, leisurely in movement or action; slow; unhurried.—**de-lib′er-ate-ly**, *adv.*—**de-lib′er-ate-ness**, *n.*—**de-lib-er-a′tion** (-ę-rā′shǫn), *n.* [L. *deliberatio(n-)*.] The act of deliberating; careful consideration before decision; formal consultation or discussion, as in a legislative assembly; also, deliberate quality; leisureliness of movement or action; slowness.—**de-lib′er-a-tive** (-ę-rą-tiv), *a.* [L. *deliberativus*.] Pertaining to or characterized by deliberation; having the function of deliberating, as a legislative assembly. —**de-lib′er-a-tive-ly**, *adv.*—**de-lib′er-a-tive-ness**, *n.*—**de-lib′er-a-tor** (-ę-rā-tǫr), *n.*

del-i-ble (del′i-bl), *a.* [Earlier *deleble*, < L. *delebilis*, < *delere*: see *delete*.] That may be taken out or effaced.

del-i-ca-cy (del′i-kā-si), *n.*; pl. *-cies* (-siz). Delicate quality or character; pleasantness†; pleasure† or gratification†; luxury†; tenderness, as of constitution; bodily weakness; liability to sickness; fastidiousness†; fineness of perception or feeling; sensitiveness; nicety of action or operation; minute accuracy; fineness of texture, quality, etc.; softness; subtle quality; the quality of requiring or involving great care or tact (as, negotiations of great *delicacy*); fineness of feeling with regard to what is fitting, proper, etc.; consideration for the feelings of others; also, something delightful or pleasing, esp. to the palate; a dainty; a nicety or refinement; a delicate trait, observance, etc.

del-i-cate (del′i-kąt). [L. *delicatus*, delightful, luxurious, soft, tender, dainty; usually associated with L. *deliciæ*, delight: see *delicious*.] **I.** *a.* Delightful or pleasing, esp. to the senses†; also, luxurious† or voluptuous† (as, "soft and *delicate* desires": Shakspere's "Much Ado about Nothing," i. 1. 305); tender† or effeminate†; susceptible to sickness or bodily harm; weakly; easily damaged, or fragile; also, fastidious† or nice†; exquisite or refined in perception or feeling; finely sensitive; fine or exquisite in action or execution, as an instrument; distinguishing subtle differences; also, fine in texture, quality, construction, etc.; dainty or choice, as food; soft or faint, as color; sometimes, so fine or slight as to be scarcely perceptible; subtle; also, requiring great care or tact (as, a *delicate* mission); ticklish; also, regardful of what is becoming, proper, etc., or of the feelings of others. **II.** *n.* A luxurious or fastidious person†; also, a luxury†; a choice viand (archaic).—**del′i-cate-ly**, *adv.*—**del′i-cate-ness**, *n.*

del-i-ca-tes-sen (del″i-ką-tes′ęn), *n. pl.* [G., < F. *délicatesse*, delicacy, < *délicat*, < L. *delicatus*, E. *delicate*.] Table delicacies as sold in a shop, esp. such as are ready or require little preparation for serving, as cooked meats, smoked fish, sausages, cheese, salads, pickles, canned goods, etc.

de-li-cious (dę̄-lish′us), *a.* [OF. *delicious* (F. *délicieux*), < LL. *deliciosus*, < L. *deliciæ*, delight, < *delicere*, allure: see *delight*.] Pleasing in the highest degree; delightful; sometimes, delightfully amusing; also, highly pleasing to the senses, esp. to taste or smell; also, voluptuous†; luxurious†.—**de-li′cious-ly**, *adv.*—**de-li′cious-ness**, *n.*

de-lict (dę̄-likt′), *n.* [L. *delictum*, orig. pp. neut. of *delinquere*: see *delinquent*.] A transgression; an offense; a misdemeanor.

de-light (dę̄-līt′), *v.* [OF. *delitier*, < L. *delectare*, freq. of *delicere*, allure, < *de*, from, + *lacere*, entice.] **I.** *tr.* To affect with lively pleasure; please highly; charm. **II.** *intr.* To have great pleasure; take pleasure: with *in* or an infinitive.—**de-light′**, *n.* [OF. *delit*.] A high degree of pleasure or enjoyment; joy; rapture; also, something that gives great pleasure; also, delightfulness (chiefly poetic: as, "Sweets grown common lose their dear *delight*," Shakspere's "Sonnets," cii.).—**de-light′ed**, *p. a.* Highly pleased; filled with delight; also, delightful†.—**de-light′ed-ly**, *adv.* —**de-light′er**, *n.*—**de-light′ful**, *a.* Affording delight; highly pleasing.—**de-light′ful-ly**, *adv.*—**de-light′ful-ness**, *n.*—**de-light′less**, *a.* Destitute of delight; cheerless.—**de-light′some** (-sum), *a.* Delightful.—**de-light′some-ly**, *adv.*—**de-light′some-ness**, *n.*

De-li-lah (dę̄-lī′lą), *n.* [From *Delilah*, Samson's mistress, who betrayed him to the Philistines: see Judges, xvi.] A beguiling and treacherous woman; a seductive temptress.

de-lim-it (dę̄-lim′it), *v. t.* [F. *délimiter*, < L. *delimitare* (pp. *delimitatus*), < *de*, from, + *limitare*, E. *limit*, *v.*] To fix or mark the limits of; demarcate; also, to mark or determine as a limit or boundary. Also **de-lim′i-tate** (-i-tāt). —**de-lim-i-ta′tion** (-tā′shǫn), *n.*—**de-lim′i-ta-tive** (-tą-tiv), *a.*

de-lin-e-ate (dę̄-lin′ę̄-āt), *v. t.*; *-ated*, *-ating.* [L. *delineatus*, pp. of *delineare*, < *de*, from, + *lineare*, mark with lines, <

linea, E. *line*[2].] To trace the outline of; sketch or trace in outline; represent pictorially; fig., to portray in words; describe.—**de-lin-e-a′tion** (-ā′shọn), *n.* [LL. *delineatio(n-)*.] The act of delineating; a chart or diagram; a sketch; a rough draft; a portrait; a description.—**de-lin′e-a-tive** (-ạ-tiv), *a.* Serving to delineate or depict.—**de-lin′e-a-tor** (-ā-tọr), *n.* One who or that which delineates; a surveying instrument on wheels, which records the distance traversed and delineates the profile of the country; a tailors' pattern which can be adjusted for cutting garments of different sizes.

de-lin-quen-cy (dẹ̄-ling′kwẹn-si), *n.*; pl. *-cies* (-siz). Delinquent state or quality; failure in or neglect of duty or obligation; fault; guilt; also, a shortcoming; a misdeed or offense.

de-lin-quent (dẹ̄-ling′kwẹnt). [L. *delinquens* (*-ent-*), ppr. of *delinquere*, fail, commit a fault, < *de*, from, + *linquere*, leave.] **I.** *a.* Failing in or neglectful of a duty or obligation; guilty of a misdeed or offense; also, of or pertaining to delinquents. **II.** *n.* One who is delinquent.—**de-lin′quent-ly**, *adv.*

del-i-quesce (del-i-kwes′), *v. i.*; *-quesced*, *-quescing*. [L. *deliquescere*, < *de-*, away, + *liquescere*, become liquid: see *liquescent*.] To become liquid by absorbing moisture from the air, as certain salts; liquefy or melt away, as certain parts of some fungi in the process of growth.—**del-i-ques′cence** (-kwes′ẹns), *n.* The act or process of deliquescing; also, the liquid produced when something deliquesces.—**del-i-ques′cent**, *a.* Having the property of deliquescing; liquefying by the absorption of moisture from the air, as certain salts; melting away; hence, in *bot.*, branching in such a way that the main stem is lost in the branches.

de-li-qui-um (dẹ̄-lik′wi-um), *n.* [L., failure, eclipse (< *delinquere*: see *delinquent*); in part confused with obs. *deliquium*, deliquescence, < LL. *deliquium*, a flowing down.] A failure of vital force; syncope; specif., mental failing or weakness; also, deliquescence.

del-i-ra-tion (del-i-rā′shọn), *n.* [L. *deliratio(n-)*, < *delirare*, be deranged, rave, lit. 'go out of the furrow,' < *de*, from, + *lira*, ridge or furrow in plowing.] Mental derangement; raving; delirium: as, "in this universal dotage and *deliration*" (Carlyle's "Sartor Resartus," ii. 10).

de-lir-i-ant (dẹ̄-lir′i-ạnt). **I.** *a.* Causing delirium, as certain drugs. **II.** *n.* A deliriant substance or agent.

de-lir-i-ous (dẹ̄-lir′i-us), *a.* Affected with delirium; wandering in mind; raving; pertaining to or characteristic of delirium; fig., affected as if by delirium; wild with excitement, enthusiasm, etc.; frantic.—**de-lir′i-ous-ly**, *adv.*—**de-lir′i-ous-ness**, *n.*

de-lir-i-um (dẹ̄-lir′i-um), *n.* [L., < *delirare*: see *deliration*.] A more or less temporary disorder of the mental faculties, as in fevers, insanity, and intoxication, characterized by restlessness, excitement, delusions, hallucinations, etc.; fig., a state of violent excitement or emotion; mad rapture or enthusiasm; also, a wild fancy.—**delirium tremens** (trē′menz). [NL., 'trembling delirium.'] A violent delirium due to excessive indulgence in alcoholic liquors, etc., characterized by trembling, by terrifying visual hallucinations, etc.

del-i-tes-cent (del-i-tes′ẹnt), *a.* [L. *delitescens* (*-ent-*), ppr. of *delitescere*, hide away, < *de*, from, + *latescere*, hide one's self: see *latescent*.] Lying hid; concealed.—**del-i-tes′cence**, *n.*

de-liv-er (dẹ̄-liv′ėr), *v.* [OF. *delivrer* (F. *délivrer*), < ML. *deliberare*, < L. *de*, from, + *liberare*: see *liberate*.] **I.** *tr.* To set free; liberate; release or save, as from evil or trouble; also, to rid or clear (as, to *deliver* a jail, to clear it of prisoners by bringing them to trial); disburden (a woman) of a child in childbirth; relieve of contents, or unload; disburden (one's self) of thoughts, opinions, etc.; also, to give up or surrender; give into another's possession or keeping; hand over, as to a recipient; carry and turn over (letters, goods, etc.) to the intended recipients; also, to give forth or emit; discharge, launch, or direct; cast, throw, or project; give forth in words, utter, or pronounce (as, to *deliver* a course of lectures; to *deliver* a verdict); make known† or assert† (as, "I . . . heard the old shepherd *deliver* the manner how he found it": Shakspere's "Winter's Tale," v. 2. 4); in *molding*, to set free from the mold. **II.** *intr.* To make delivery; pronounce an opinion, verdict, etc.; in *molding*, to leave the mold easily.—**de-liv′er**, *a.* [OF. *delivre*, < *delivrer*.] Free in movement; nimble; deft; quick. [Obs. or archaic.]—**de-liv′er-a-ble**, *a.* That may be or is to be delivered.—**de-liv′er-ance**, *n.* [OF. *delivrance* (F. *délivrance*).] The act of delivering, or the fact of being delivered; liberation; release; rescue; delivery in childbirth†; a giving or handing over to another; the act or manner of uttering words†; the expression of a thought, opinion, etc.; a thought or judgment expressed; a formal or authoritative pronouncement; a verdict.—**de-liv′er-er**, *n.*—**de-liv′er-ly**, *adv.* [See *deliver*, *a.*] Nimbly; deftly. [Obs. or archaic.]—**de-liv′er-y**, *n.*; pl. *-ies* (-iz). The act of delivering, or the fact of being delivered; release or rescue (archaic); the clearing of a jail of prisoners by bringing them to trial; the being delivered of, or giving birth to, a child; parturition; the assisting of a woman in childbirth; a giving up or surrender; a handing or turning over into another's possession; the delivering of letters, goods, etc.; the act or manner of giving or sending forth; discharge; the throwing of a ball, as by the pitcher in baseball; the utterance or enunciation of words; manner of utterance; oratorical style.

dell (del), *n.* [ME. *delle*; akin to E. *dale*.] A deep natural hollow in land, often with wooded slopes; a small valley; a vale.

Del-la=Crus-can (del-ạ-krus′kạn). [From the (It.) *Accademia della Crusca*, 'Academy of the Bran,' founded in 1582 at Florence, mainly for promoting the purity of the Italian language, and having a sieve as its emblem.] **I.** *a.* Of, pertaining to, or after the manner of the Accademia della Crusca (see etym.); also, noting or pertaining to a school of English poetry affecting an artificial style, started by certain Englishmen at Florence toward the end of the 18th century. **II.** *n.* A member of the Accademia della Crusca, or of the English school named after it.

de-lo-cal-ize (dē-lō′kạl-īz), *v. t.*; *-ized*, *-izing*. [See *de-*.] To remove from the proper or usual locality; free from local limitations.—**de-lo″cal-i-za′tion** (-i-zā′shọn), *n.*

Del-phi-an (del′fi-ạn), *a.* Pertaining to the ancient Greek town of Delphi, to the temple and oracle of Apollo there, or to Apollo himself; hence, oracular; obscure or ambiguous. Also **Del′phic.**

Del-phin (del′fin), *a.* [ML. *delphinus*, dauphin: see *dauphin*.] Of or pertaining to the dauphin of France: applied to an edition of Latin classics prepared for the use of the dauphin, son of Louis XIV.

del-phi-nine (del′fi-nin), *n.* [NL. *Delphinium*, < Gr. δελφίνιον, larkspur.] In *chem.*, a bitter, poisonous, crystalline alkaloid obtained from various species of larkspur, genus *Delphinium*, esp. *D. staphisagria.*

Del-sar-ti-an (del-sär′ti-ạn), *a.* Pertaining to François Delsarte (1811–71), a French musician and teacher of musical and dramatic expression, or to a system of esthetic gymnastics, for developing bodily grace and improving physical expression, based on his theories.

del-ta (del′tạ), *n.* [L., < Gr. δέλτα.] The fourth letter (Δ, δ, = English D, d) of the Greek alphabet; hence, the fourth of any series (esp. in scientific classification); also, anything triangular, like the Greek capital Δ; esp., a triangular tract of alluvial land between diverging branches of the mouth of a river, often intersected by other branches (as, the *delta* of the Nile).—**del-ta′ic** (-tā′ik), *a.* Of, pertaining to, or forming a river delta; having a delta. Also **del′tic.**—**del′toid**, *a.* [Gr. δελτοειδής: see *-oid*.] Shaped like the Greek capital delta (Δ); triangular: as, a *deltoid* leaf; the *deltoid* muscle (a large triangular muscle covering the joint of the shoulder and serving to raise the arm away from the side of the body).

Deltoid Leaf.

de-lude (dẹ̄-lūd′), *v. t.*; *-luded*, *-luding*. [L. *deludere* (pp. *delusus*), < *de-* (see *de-*) + *ludere*, play.] To play or trifle with (a person) under the guise of seriousness†; cheat the hopes of†; defraud (*of*)†; also, to mislead the mind or judgment of; deceive; beguile; impose upon.—**de-lud′a-ble** (-lū′dạ-bl), *a.*—**de-lud′er**, *n.*

del-uge (del'ūj), *n.* [OF. *deluge* (F. *déluge*), < L. *diluvium*, flood: see *diluvium.*] A great overflowing of water; an inundation; [often *cap.*] with *the*, the great flood in the days of Noah (Gen. vii.); fig. [*l. c.*], anything that overwhelms like a flood.—**del'uge,** *v. t.*; *-uged, -uging.* To overflow in a deluge; flood; inundate; cover or drench with a deluge; fig., to overrun like a flood, or overwhelm (as, "At length corruption, like a general flood . . . Shall *deluge* all": Pope's "Moral Essays," iii. 137).

del-un-dung (del'un-dung), *n.* [Javanese.] A strikingly marked viverrine quadruped, *Prionodon* (or *Linsang*) *gracilis*, of Java, etc., one of the linsangs.

Delundung.

de-lu-sion (dẹ-lū'zhọn), *n.* [LL. *delusio(n-)*.] The act of deluding, or the fact of being deluded; also, something that deludes; a deception; a false belief or opinion; a fixed or persistent false mental conception with regard to actual things or matters of fact.—**de-lu'sion-al,** *a.* Pertaining to or characterized by delusions: as, *delusional* insanity.—**de-lu'sive** (-siv), *a.* Tending to delude; deceptive; of the nature of a delusion; false; unreal.—**de-lu'sive-ly,** *adv.*—**de-lu'sive-ness,** *n.*—**de-lu'so-ry** (-sọ-ri), *a.* Delusive.

de luxe (dė lüks). [F., 'of luxury.'] Of especial elegance, sumptuousness, or fineness: as, a *de luxe* edition (F. *édition de luxe*); a *de luxe* binding.

delve (delv), *v.*; *delved, delving.* [AS. *delfan* = D. *delven*, dig.] **I.** *tr.* To dig; turn up with a spade or other tool, as ground in preparation for a crop; make or obtain by digging. [Now chiefly prov. or archaic.] **II.** *intr.* To dig, or labor with a spade (now chiefly prov. or archaic); hence, to carry on laborious research for information, etc.; also, to take a sudden downward inclination, as a road.—**delve,** *n.* An excavation; a pit; a cave; a hollow or depression; also, an act of delving. [Now rare.]—**delv'er,** *n.*

de-mag-net-ize (dē-mag'net-īz), *v. t.*; *-ized, -izing.* [See *de-*.] To deprive of magnetic properties; also, to demesmerize.—**de-mag"net-i-za'tion** (-i-zā'shọn), *n.*—**de-mag'net-iz-er** (-ī-zėr), *n.*

dem-a-gog-ic, dem-a-gog-i-cal (dem-ạ-goj'ik, -i-kạl), *a.* [Gr. δημαγωγικός.] Pertaining to, of the nature of, or characteristic of a demagogue.

dem'a-gog-ism, *n.* See *demagoguism.*

dem-a-gogue (dem'ạ-gog), *n.* [Gr. δημαγωγός, < δῆμος, people, + ἀγωγός, leading, < ἄγειν, lead.] Historically, a leader of the people; a leader or orator upholding the cause of a popular faction; now, a popular leader who plays on the passions or prejudices of the populace to further his own interests; an unprincipled popular orator or agitator.—**dem'a-gogue-ry** (-gog-ẹ-ri), *n.* The methods or practices of a demagogue.—**dem'a-go-guism, dem'a-gog-ism** (-gog-izm), *n.* Demagoguery.—**dem'a-gog-y** (-goj-i or -gog-i), *n.* [Gr. δημαγωγία.] The character of a demagogue; demagogic practices; a body of demagogues.

de-mand (dẹ-månd'), *v.* [OF. F. *demander*, < ML. *demandare*, demand, L. give in charge, intrust, < L. *de*, from, + *mandare*, commit, enjoin.] **I.** *tr.* To ask for with authority, or as that to which one has valid claim; ask for peremptorily or urgently; lay formal legal claim to; also, to summon, as to court; also, to call for or require as just, proper, or necessary (as, a task which *demands* patience); also, to ask authoritatively or peremptorily to know, or request to be told (as, to *demand* a person's name); interrogate (a person)†. **II.** *intr.* To make a demand; inquire or ask.—**de-mand',** *n.* [OF. F. *demande.*] The act of demanding; an authoritative or peremptory request or claim (as, a note payable on *demand*); a requisition; a legal claim; call or desire, as for a commodity; the state of being in request for purchase or use (as, an article in great *demand*); an urgent or pressing requirement (as, *demands* upon one's time or one's resources); an inquiry or question; also, that which is demanded; in *polit. econ.*, the desire to purchase a commodity, etc., coupled with the power to purchase it, or the quantity of it demanded at a particular price (cf. *supply, n.*).—**de-mand'a-ble,** *a.* That may be demanded.—**de-mand'ant,** *n.* One who demands; in *law*, the plaintiff in a real action; any plaintiff.—**de-mand'er,** *n.*

de-man-toid (dẹ-man'toid), *n.* [G. *demant*, diamond: see *-oid.*] A transparent green garnet, of brilliant luster, found in the Ural Mountains and used as a gem.

de-mar-cate (dẹ-mär'kāt or dē'mär-), *v. t.*; *-cated, -cating.* [From *demarcation.*] To mark off the boundaries of; separate by distinct boundaries; also, to mark or determine as a boundary.

de-mar-ca-tion (dē-mär-kā'shọn), *n.* [Sp. *demarcación*, < *demarcar*, mark off, < *de-* (< L. *de*, from), + *marcar*, mark.] The marking off of the boundaries of something; separation by distinct boundaries; the defining of boundaries.

de-march (dē'märk), *n.* [Gr. δήμαρχος, < δῆμος, deme, + ἄρχειν, lead, rule.] The chief magistrate of a deme.

dé-marche (dā-märsh), *n.* [F., < *démarcher*, march.] Walk; step; proceeding.

de-mar-ka'tion, *n.* See *demarcation.*

de-ma-te-ri-al-ize (dē-mạ-tē'ri-ạl-īz), *v. t.* or *i.*; *-ized, -izing.* [See *de-*.] To deprive of or lose material character.—**de-ma-te"ri-al-i-za'tion** (-i-zā'shọn), *n.*

deme (dēm), *n.* [Gr. δῆμος, district, country, people, commons.] One of the administrative divisions of ancient Attica and of modern Greece; a township; a commune.

de-mean[1] (dẹ-mēn'), *v. t.* [See *de-* and *mean*[2], and cf. *debase.*] To lower in dignity or standing; debase; esp., to lower or humiliate (one's self: as, "It puts him where he can make the advances without *demeaning* himself," Howells's "Rise of Silas Lapham," ix.).

de-mean[2] (dẹ-mēn'), *v. t.* [OF. *demener* (F. *démener*), < *de-* (see *de-*) + *mener*, bring. lead, < L. *minare*, drive.] To carry on (a business, etc.)†; manage†; also, to treat, esp. badly (obs. or Sc.); also, to conduct or behave (one's self) in a specified manner.—**de-mean'or** (-mē'nọr), *n.* Way of acting; conduct; behavior; bearing.—**de-mean'our,** *n.* British preferred form of *demeanor.*

de-ment (dẹ-ment'). [L. *demens* (*dement-*), out of one's mind, < *de*, from, + *mens*, mind.] **I.** *a.* Out of one's mind; insane: as, "Are you dumb as well as *dement?*" (J. H. Newman's "Callista," xxii.). [Archaic.] **II.** *n.* One who is out of his mind.—**de-ment',** *v. t.* [L. *dementare*, < *demens.*] To put out of one's mind; make mad or insane.—**de-men-ta-tion** (dē-men-tā'shọn), *n.* The act of dementing, or the state of being demented; madness.—**de-ment'ed,** *p. a.* Out of one's mind; crazed; insane; affected with dementia.—**de-ment'ed-ly,** *adv.*—**de-ment'ed-ness,** *n.*

dé-men-ti (dā-moṅ-tē), *n.* [F., < *démentir*, give the lie to, contradict, < *dé-* (see *dis-*) + *mentir*, < L. *mentiri*, lie.] The act of giving the lie; formal or official denial, as of a report.

de-men-tia (dẹ-men'shiạ), *n.* [L., < *demens*: see *dement.*] In *pathol.*, a form of insanity consisting in impairment or loss of the mental powers, usually characterized by apathy, and commonly consequent upon mental or other disease.—**dementia præcox** (prē'koks). [L., precocious insanity.] In *pathol.*, a form of insanity occurring or beginning at puberty.

de-mer-it (dẹ-mer'it), *n.* [OF. *demerite* (F. *démérite*), < L. *demeritum*, pp. neut. of *demerere*, deserve (esp. well), < *de-* (see *de-*) + *merere*, deserve: see *merit.*] Merit† or desert†; now, desert in a bad sense; censurable or punishable quality; ill desert; also, a fault; lack of merit; defect; also, in schools, a mark against a pupil for misconduct or deficiency.

de-mer-i-to-ri-ous (dē"mer-i-tō'ri-us), *a.* [See *de-*.] The opposite of meritorious; blameworthy.

de-mes-mer-ize (dē-mez'mėr-īz), *v. t.*; *-ized, -izing.* [See *de-*.] To bring out of mesmeric influence.

de-mesne (dẹ-mān' or -mēn'), *n.* [AF. *demesne*, OF. *demeine, domeine* (F. *domaine*): see *domain.*] Possession (of land) as one's own; possession and actual use of land; in general, possession† or dominion†; also, an estate possessed, or in the actual possession or use of the owner; in modern use, the land adjacent to a manor-house, reserved for the owner's use; also, the dominion or territory of a sovereign or state; a domain; a district or region.

De-me-ter (dę̄-mē′tėr), *n.* [Gr. Δημήτηρ.] A Greek deity, goddess of the fruitful earth and protectress of social order and of marriage, identified by the Romans with Ceres.

Demeter of Cnidus (in Asia Minor). British Museum.

demi-. [F. *demi-*, repr. *demi*, adj. (also n. and adv.), < L. *dimidius*, half, < *di-*, for *dis-*, apart, + *medius*, middle.] A prefix meaning 'half,' orig. occurring in terms from the French, and hence used also as an English formative. Cf. *semi-*.

dem-i=bas-tion (dem′i-bas′-chọn), *n.* [F., 'half-bastion.'] In *fort.*, a work consisting of half a bastion, and hence having one face and one flank.

dem-i-god (dem′i-god), *n.* [See *demi-*.] One partly divine and partly human; an inferior or minor deity; a deified mortal. Also fig.—**dem′i-god″dess,** *n.* A female demigod.

dem-i-john (dem′i-jon), *n.* [F. *dame-jeanne*, earlier *dame-jane*, appar. a popular name, 'Dame Jane.'] A large glass bottle with a small neck, usually cased in wickerwork.

dem-i=lance (dem′i-lȧns), *n.* [See *demi-*.] A short, light lance formerly in use; a horseman armed with such a lance.

de-mil-i-ta-rize (dē-mil′i-tą-rīz), *v. t.*; *-rized, -rizing.* [See *de-*.] To deprive of military character; free from militarism; remove the military organization from; place under civil instead of military control.—**de-mil″i-ta-ri-za′tion** (-ri-zā′shọn), *n.*

dem-i-lune (dem′i-lūn), *n.* [F. *demi-lune*, 'half-moon.'] A half-moon or a crescent; in *fort.*, a kind of outwork, usually triangular; a ravelin.

dem-i=mon-daine (dem′i-mon′dān, F. dė-mē-môṅ-dān), *n.* [F.] A woman of the demi-monde.

dem-i=monde (dem′i-mond′, F. dė-mē-môṅd), *n.* [F., 'half-world'; a term introduced by A. Dumas the younger.] The world or class of women who have become socially declassed, or of doubtful reputation and standing, as intermediate between those of unquestioned respectability and the courtezan class; commonly, but less correctly, the world or class of courtezans.

dem-i-qua-ver (dem′i-kwā″vėr), *n.* [See *demi-*.] In *music*, a semiquaver or sixteenth-note.

dem-i=re-lief (dem′i-rę̄-lēf″), *n.* [See *demi-*.] Same as *mezzo-rilievo*.

dem-i-rep (dem′i-rep), *n.* [Short for *demi-reputation*: see *demi-*.] A woman of doubtful or compromised reputation.

de-mis-a-ble (dę̄-mī′zą-bl), *a.* That may be demised.

de-mise (dę̄-mīz′), *n.* [OF. *demise*, pp. of *demetre*, send or put away: see *demit*.] The conveyance or transfer of an estate, esp. by will or lease; transfer of sovereignty, as by the death or deposition of the sovereign; also, a death or decease occasioning the transfer of an estate, etc.; hence, any death or decease.—**de-mise′**, *v.*; *-mised, -mising.* **I.** *tr.* To convey or transfer (an estate, etc.), as by will or lease; transfer (sovereignty), as by the death or abdication of the sovereign. **II.** *intr.* To transfer sovereignty to a successor, as at death; hence, to die; also, to pass by bequest or inheritance.

dem-i-sem-i-qua-ver (dem′i-sem′i-kwā″vėr), *n.* [See *demi-*.] In *music*, a note having half the time-value of a semiquaver; a thirty-second-note. See note under *note*, *n.*

de-mis-sion (dę̄-mish′ọn), *n.* [F. *démission*, < *démettre*: see *demit*.] A sending away or dismissal (rare); also, a putting away or letting go, as of a dignity or office; relinquishment; resignation; abdication.

de-mit (dę̄-mit′), *v.*; *-mitted, -mitting.* [OF. *demetre, desmetre* (F. *démettre*), send or put away, < L. *de-* or *dis-* (see *de-*) + *mittere*, send.] **I.** *tr.* To let go or dismiss (archaic); also, to give up, as a dignity or office; resign. **II.** *intr.* To resign.—**de-mit′**, *n.* A demitting or resigning; also, a letter or paper certifying to this, as used in transferring membership from one masonic lodge to another.

dem-i=tasse (dem′i-tas′, F. dė-mē-täs), *n.* [F., 'half-cup.'] A small cup such as is used for serving black coffee after dinner; the contents of such a cup.

dem-i=tint (dem′i-tint), *n.* [See *demi-*.] Same as *half-tint*.

dem-i=toi-let (dem′i-toi″let), *n.* [See *demi-*.] Dress intermediate in elegance or elaborateness between ordinary and full dress.

dem-i-urge (dem′i-ėrj), *n.* [Gr. δημιουργός, worker for the people, artificer, maker, < δήμιος, of the people (< δῆμος: see *deme*), + -εργός, working, worker.] In the Platonic philosophy, the Creator of the world; in the Gnostic and certain other systems, a supernatural being imagined as creating or fashioning the world in subordination to the Supreme Being, and sometimes regarded as the originator of evil. Also (L.) **de-mi-ur-gus** (dē-mi-ėr′gus).—**dem-i-ur′gic** (-ėr′jik), *a.*

dem-i=volt (dem′i-vōlt), *n.* [See *demi-* and *volt*[1].] In the *manège*, a half-turn made by a horse with the fore legs raised.

dem-i=wolf (dem′i-wu̇lf), *n.*; pl. *-wolves* (-wu̇lvz). [See *demi-*.] A cross between a wolf and a dog; a wolf-like dog. See Shakspere's "Macbeth," iii. 1. 94.

de-mo-bi-lize (dē-mō′bi-līz), *v. t.* or *i.*; *-lized, -lizing.* [See *de-*.] To change from a condition of mobilization; disband.—**de-mo″bi-li-za′tion** (-li-zā′shọn), *n.*

de-moc-ra-cy (dę̄-mok′rą-si), *n.*; pl. *-cies* (-siz). [F. *démocratie*, < Gr. δημοκρατία, < δῆμος, people (see *deme*), + κρατεῖν, rule.] Government by the people; a form of government in which the supreme power is vested in the people and exercised by them or their elected agents; also, a state having such a form of government; in a restricted sense, a state in which the supreme power is vested in the people and exercised directly by them rather than by elected representatives (cf. *republic*); also, a state of society characterized by nominal equality of rights and privileges; political or social equality; democratic spirit; also, the common people of a community as distinguished from any privileged class; the common people with respect to their political power; [*cap.*] in *U. S. politics*, the principles of the Democratic party; the members of the Democratic party collectively.—**dem-o-crat** (dem′ọ-krat), *n.* [F. *démocrate*.] An advocate of democracy; one who maintains the political or social equality of men; also, a light four-wheeled wagon without a top, having two or more seats, one behind another (local, U. S.); [*cap.*] in *U. S. politics*, a member of the Democratic party.—**dem-o-crat′ic,** *a.* [Gr. δημοκρατικός.] Pertaining to or of the nature of democracy or a democracy; advocating or upholding democracy; pertaining to or characterized by the principle of political or social equality for all; disregarding distinctions of privilege or position; [*cap.*] in *U. S. politics*, noting or pertaining to a party whose distinctive principles include a strict interpretation of the Constitution with respect to the powers delegated to the general government and those reserved by the individual States. Also **dem-o-crat′i-cal.**—**dem-o-crat′i-cal-ly,** *adv.*—**de-moc′ra-tize** (-tīz), *v. t.*; *-tized, -tizing.* To render democratic; give democratic character to; bring to a common level.—**de-moc″ra-ti-za′tion** (-ti-zā′shọn), *n.*

de-mod-ed (dē-mō′ded), *a.* [F. *démodé*, pp. of *démoder*, put out of fashion, < *dé-* (see *dis-*) + *mode*, E. *mode*.] No longer in fashion.

De-mo-gor-gon (dē-mọ-gôr′gọn or dem-ọ-), *n.* [ML.; origin uncertain.] A vague, mysterious power or divinity of medieval mythology, variously represented, but always as an object of awe or fear: as, "By them stood Orcus and Ades, and the dreaded name Of *Demogorgon*" (Milton's "Paradise Lost," ii. 965).

de-mog-ra-phy (dę̄-mog′rą-fi), *n.* [Gr. δῆμος, district, country, people: see *-graphy*.] The science of vital and social statistics, or of the facts respecting the births, deaths, diseases, marriages, etc., of communities of people.—**de-mog′ra-pher, de-mog′ra-phist,** *n.*—**dem-o-graph-ic** (dem-ọ-graf′ik), *a.*—**dem-o-graph′i-cal-ly,** *adv.*

dem-oi-selle (dem-wo-zel′), *n.* [F.: see *damsel.*] A young lady; a damsel; also, the Numidian crane, *Anthropoides virgo*, of northern Africa, Asia, and Europe, having long white plumes behind the eyes; also, any of various slender-bodied dragonflies which hold their wings vertically when at rest.

Demoiselle (*Anthropoides virgo*).

de-mol-ish (dę̄-mol′ish), *v. t.* [F. *démolir* (*démoliss-*), < L. *demoliri* (pp. *demolitus*), < *de-* (see *de-*) + *moliri*, build, construct, < *moles*, mass, massive structure, E. *mole*³.] To throw or pull down (a building, etc.); reduce to ruins; fig., to destroy; put an end to.—**de-mol′ish-er,** *n.*—**de-mol′ish-ment,** *n.*—**dem-o-li-tion** (dem-ǫ-lish′ǫn or dē-mǫ-), *n.* [L. *demolitio*(*n*-).] The act of demolishing, or the state of being demolished; destruction; overthrow.

de-mon (dē′mǫn), *n.* [L. *dæmon*, spirit, evil spirit, < Gr. δαίμων, deity, tutelary divinity, genius, later evil spirit.] A supernatural being of Greek mythology, holding a place between gods and men; an inferior deity; often, an attendant or indwelling spirit, or genius (as, "I know . . . what of life and what of death The *demon* taught to Socrates": Whittier's "Questions of Life"); an animating influence of irresistible power; hence, a person of great energy, etc.; also, an evil spirit; a devil; hence, an atrociously wicked or cruel person; an evil passion or influence.—**de′mon-ess,** *n.* A female demon.

de-mon-e-tize (dē-mon′e-tīz or dē-mun′-), *v. t.*; *-tized, -tizing.* [F. *démonétiser*, < *dé-* (see *dis-*) + L. *moneta*, money.] To divest of standard monetary value; withdraw from use as money.—**de-mon″e-ti-za′tion** (-ti-zā′shǫn), *n.*

de-mo-ni-ac (dę̄-mō′ni-ak). [LL. *dæmoniacus.*] **I.** *a.* Of, pertaining to, or of the nature of a demon or demons; also, inspired as if by a demon; demonic; also, characteristic of a demon or evil spirit; fiendish; also, possessed by an evil spirit, or pertaining to such possession; raging; frantic. **II.** *n.* One seemingly possessed by a demon or evil spirit; a lunatic.—**de-mo-ni-a-cal** (dē-mǫ-nī′ą-kąl), *a.* Demoniac.—**de-mo-ni′a-cal-ly,** *adv.*

de-mo-ni-an (dę̄-mō′ni-ąn), *a.* Pertaining to or of the nature of a demon.

de-mon-ic (dę̄-mon′ik), *a.* [Gr. δαιμονικός.] Of, pertaining to, or of the nature of a demon; also, inspired as if by a demon, indwelling spirit, or genius.

de-mon-ism (dē′mǫn-izm), *n.* Belief in demons; worship of demons.—**de′mon-ist,** *n.*

de-mon-ize (dē′mǫn-īz), *v. t.*; *-ized, -izing.* To turn into or make like a demon; render demoniac; subject to the influence of demons.

demono-. Form of Gr. δαίμων, demon, used in combination.—**de-mon-og-ra-phy** (dē-mǫn-og′rą-fi), *n.* [+ *-graphy.*] Descriptive demonology.—**de-mon-og′ra-pher,** *n.*—**de-mon-ol′a-try** (-ol′ą-tri), *n.* [+ *-latry.*] The worship of demons.—**de-mon-ol′a-ter,** *n.*—**de-mon-ol′o-gy** (-ǫ-ji), *n.* [+ *-logy.*] The doctrine of demons; the study of demons or of beliefs about demons.—**de-mon-ol′o-gist,** *n.*

de-mon-stra-ble (dę̄-mon′strą-bl or dem′ǫn-), *a.* [L. *demonstrabilis.*] Capable of being demonstrated.—**de-mon-stra-bil′i-ty** (-bil′i-ti), *n.*—**de-mon′stra-bly,** *adv.*

dem-on-strate (dem′ǫn-strāt or dę̄-mon′-), *v.*; *-strated, -strating.* [L. *demonstratus*, pp. of *demonstrare*, < *de-* (see *de-*) + *monstrare*, show.] **I.** *tr.* To point out† or indicate†; also, to manifest or exhibit (as, "every thing about you *demonstrating* a careless desolation": Shakspere's "As You Like It," iii. 2. 400); also, to describe and explain with the help of specimens or by experiment; also, to make evident by arguments or reasoning; in general, to establish the truth of; prove. **II.** *intr.* To make, give, or take part in, a demonstration.—**dem-on-stra′tion** (-strā′shǫn), *n.* [L. *demonstratio*(*n*-).] The act of demonstrating; exhibition, as of feeling; a display or manifestation; a public exhibition of sympathy, opposition, etc., as in the form of a parade or mass-meeting; a show of military force or of offensive operations, esp. for a strategic purpose; a description or explanation, as of a process, given with the help of specimens or by experiment; the proving of anything conclusively, as by arguments or reasoning, or by evidence; proof; anything serving as proof.—**dem-on-stra′tion-al,** *a.*—**dem-on-stra′tion-ist,** *n.* One who makes, or takes part in, a demonstration.—**de-mon-stra-tive** (dę̄-mon′strą-tiv). [L. *demonstrativus.*] **I.** *a.* Serving to demonstrate; indicating or exhibiting clearly; explanatory or illustrative; also, characterized by or given to open exhibition or expression of the feelings, etc.; also, serving to demonstrate logically; pertaining to logical demonstration; in general, serving to prove the truth of anything; indubitably conclusive; also, evident by demonstration; demonstrable; in *gram.*, pointing out or indicating the thing referred to (as, a *demonstrative* pronoun or adjective, as *this* or *that*). **II.** *n.* In *gram.*, a demonstrative pronoun or adjective.—**de-mon′stra-tive-ly,** *adv.*—**de-mon′stra-tive-ness,** *n.*—**dem′on-stra-tor** (-strā-tǫr), *n.* [L.] One who or that which demonstrates; one who takes part in a public demonstration; one who explains or teaches by practical demonstrations, esp. a demonstrating instructor in a medical or dental school; one who exhibits some article for sale, explaining and illustrating its use.

dem-o-phil, dem-o-phile (dem′ǫ-fil), *n.* [Gr. δῆμος, people, + φίλος, loving.] A friend of the people.—**de-moph-i-lism** (dę̄-mof′i-lizm), *n.*

de-mor-al-ize (dę̄-mor′ąl-īz), *v. t.*; *-ized, -izing.* [F. *démoraliser*, < *dé-* (see *dis-*) + *moraliser*, E. *moralize.*] To corrupt or undermine the morals of; pervert morally; also, to weaken or destroy the moral influence of; also, to deprive (troops, etc.) of spirit, courage, discipline, or the like; reduce to a state of weakness or disorder.—**de-mor″al-i-za′tion** (-i-zā′shǫn), *n.*—**de-mor′al-iz-er** (-ī-zėr), *n.*

de-mos (dē′mos), *n.* [Gr. δῆμος: see *deme.*] The people or commons of an ancient Greek state; hence, the common people; the populace; the mob.

de-mote (dę̄-mōt′), *v. t.*; *-moted, -moting.* [From *de-* + *-mote* as in *promote.*] To reduce to a lower grade or class: opposed to *promote.*

de-mot-ic (dę̄-mot′ik), *a.* [Gr. δημοτικός, < δῆμος, E. *demos, deme.*] Of or pertaining to the common people; popular; vulgar; specif., noting or pertaining to the ancient Egyptian handwriting of ordinary life, a simplified form of the hieratic character.—**de-mot′ics,** *n.* The scientific study of the people; sociology.

de-mo-tion (dę̄-mō′shǫn), *n.* The act of demoting, or the fact of being demoted.

de-mot-ist (dę̄-mot′ist), *n.* One versed in the ancient Egyptian demotic writing.

de-mount (dē-mount′), *v. t.* [See *de-.*] To remove from its mounting, setting, or place of support, as a gun; take apart (an aëroplane, etc.), as for transportation.—**de-mount′a-ble,** *a.* That may be demounted: as, a *demountable* rim (a form of wheel-rim used on automobiles, which, in case of damage to the tire it bears, can be quickly removed and replaced by a similar rim fitted with a fully inflated tire).—**de-mount-a-bil′i-ty** (-bil′i-ti), *n.*

de-mul-cent (dę̄-mul′sęnt). [L. *demulcens* (*-ent-*), ppr. of *demulcere*, stroke down, soften, < *de-*, down, + *mulcere*, stroke.] **I.** *a.* Soothing or mollifying, as a medicinal substance. **II.** *n.* A demulcent (often mucilaginous) substance or agent, as for soothing or protecting an irritated mucous membrane.

de-mur (dę̄-mėr′), *v.*; *-murred, -murring.* [OF. *demurer*, *demourer* (F. *demeurer*), < L. *demorari*, linger, delay, < *de-* (see *de-*) + *morari*, delay.] **I.** *intr.* To linger†; tarry†, delay†; also, to hesitate†; also, to make objection; take exception; object; in *law*, to interpose a demurrer. **II.** *tr.* To put off†; delay†; also, to make objection to.—**de-mur′,** *n.* [OF. F. *demeure.*] Delay†; also, hesitation†; also, a making objection; demurral; an objection raised.

de-mure (dē-mūr′), *a.*; compar. *demurer*, superl. *demurest*. [ME. *demure*, appar. for *mure*, grave, discreet, < OF. *meur*, < L. *maturus*, ripe, E. *mature*.] Sober; serious; sedate; decorous; esp., affectedly or unnaturally sedate, decorous, or prim.—**de-mure′ly,** *adv.*—**de-mure′ness,** *n.*

de-mur-rage (dē-mur′āj), *n.* [OF. *demourage*, < *demourer*, E. *demur*.] Delaying† or delay†; in *com.*, the detention of a vessel by a freighter, as in loading or unloading, beyond the time agreed upon; similar detention of a railroad-car, etc.; a charge for such detention; in *finance*, a deduction from the market-price of gold bullion, made by the Bank of England in furnishing coin or notes for it.

de-mur-ral (dē-mėr′al), *n.* The act of demurring; demur.

de-mur-rant (dē-mur′ant), *n.* In *law*, a party to an action who puts in a demurrer.

de-mur-rer[1] (dē-mėr′ėr), *n.* One who demurs.

de-mur-rer[2] (dē-mur′ėr), *n.* [OF. *demurer*, inf., used as noun: see *demur*.] In legal use, a pleading in effect that even if the facts are as alleged by the opposite party, they do not sustain the contention based on them; hence, in general, an objection or demur.

de-my (dē-mī′), *n.*; pl. *-mies* (-mīz′). [F. *demi*, half: see *demi-*.] A foundation scholar at Magdalen College, Oxford (so called because orig. receiving half the allowance of a fellow); also, a size of paper (in America, applied to writing-paper 16 × 21 inches; in Great Britain, to writing-paper 15½ × 20 inches and to printing-paper 17½ × 22½ inches).

den (den), *n.* [AS. *denn*: cf. *dean*[1].] A retired place, as a cave, serving as the habitation of a beast; a cave, recess, or the like, as a place of shelter, concealment, etc.; a secret lurking-place, as of thieves; a low place of resort; a squalid or vile abode or place; any small, confined room or quarters; a cozy or retired room for personal use; also, a dell or glen (chiefly Sc.: as, "Here and there the progress of rills . . . has formed dells, glens, or, as they are provincially termed, *dens*, on whose high and rocky banks trees and shrubs . . . grow with a luxuriant profusion," Scott's "Antiquary," xvii.).—**den,** *v. i.*; *denned, denning.* To live in or as in a den; escape or retire into a den.

de-na-ri-us (dē-nā′ri-us), *n.*; pl. *-rii* (-ri-ī). [L., orig. adj., 'containing ten (asses)': see *denary*.] An ancient Roman silver coin of varying value, long equivalent to about 17 U. S. cents; also, an ancient Roman gold coin; in English monetary reckoning, a penny (abbreviated *d.*).

Obverse. Reverse.
Roman Silver Denarius (the penny of the New Testament).—British Museum.

den-a-ry (den′a-ri or dē′na-ri), *a.* [L. *denarius*, < *deni*, ten at a time, < *decem*, ten.] Of or pertaining to the number ten; proceeding by tens; decimal.

de-na-tion-al-ize (dē-nash′on-al-īz), *v. t.*; *-ized, -izing.* [See *de-*.] To deprive of national status, national attachments or characteristics, or the status of a national institution.—**de-na″tion-al-i-za′tion** (-i-zā′shon), *n.*

de-nat-u-ral-ize (dē-nat′ū-ral-īz), *v. t.*; *-ized, -izing.* [See *de-*.] To deprive of the original nature; render unnatural; also, to deprive of the rights and privileges of citizenship or of naturalization.—**de-nat″u-ral-i-za′tion** (-i-zā′shon), *n.*

de-na-ture (dē-nā′tūr), *v. t.*; *-tured, -turing.* [F. *dénaturer*, < *dé-* (see *dis-*) + *nature*, nature.] To deprive of its peculiar nature; render (alcohol, etc.) unfit for drinking or eating, as by the addition of an unwholesome substance, without altering the usefulness for other purposes.—**de-na-tu-ra′tion** (-tū-rā′shon), *n.*

de-na-tur-ize (dē-nā′tūr-īz), *v. t.*; *-ized, -izing.* [See *de-*.] To denature.—**de-na″tur-i-za′tion** (-i-zā′shon), *n.*

den-dri-form (den′dri-fôrm), *a.* [Gr. δένδρον, tree: see *-form*.] Tree-like in form.

den-drite (den′drīt), *n.* [Gr. δενδρίτης, of a tree, < δένδρον, tree.] A branching figure or marking, resembling a tree or shrub in form, found on or in certain stones or minerals, and due to the presence of a foreign mineral; a stone or mineral so marked; also, any arborescent crystalline growth.—**den-drit′ic** (-drit′ik), *a.* Formed or marked like a dendrite; of a branching form; arborescent.—**den-drit′i-cal-ly,** *adv.*

Dendrite.

dendro-. Form of Gr. δένδρον, tree, used in combination.—**den-dro-graph** (den′drō-grȧf), *n.* [+ *-graph*.] A device for recording the growth of a tree by measuring the trunk's changes in volume.—**den′droid** (-droid), *a.* [Gr. δενδροειδής: see *-oid*.] Tree-like; branching like a tree; arborescent. Also **den-droi′dal.**—**den-drol′a-try** (-drol′a-tri), *n.* [+ *-latry*.] The worship of trees; arborolatry.—**den′dro-lite** (-līt), *n.* [+ *-lite*.] A petrified or fossil tree or part of a tree.—**den-drol′o-gy** (-ō-ji), *n.* [+ *-logy*.] The part of botany that treats of trees.—**den-dro-log′i-cal** (-loj′i-kal), *a.*—**den-drol′o-gist,** *n.*—**den-drom′e-ter** (-drom′e-tėr), *n.* [+ *-meter*.] An instrument for measuring trees.—**den-droph′i-lous** (-drof′i-lus), *a.* [+ *-philous*.] Tree-loving; of plants, growing on or twining about trees.

dene (dēn), *n.* See *dean*[1].

den-e-ga-tion (den-ē-gā′shon), *n.* [F. *dénégation*, < L. *denegare*: see *deny*.] Denial; contradiction: as, "I sought to interrupt him with some not very truthful *denegation*" (Stevenson's "Master of Ballantrae," viii.).

dene=hole (dēn′hōl), *n.* [Variously explained, as < *dene* (*dean*[1]), *den*, or *Dane*.] Any of a class of ancient excavations, found chiefly in Essex and Kent in England and in the valley of the Somme in France, consisting of a vertical shaft about 3 feet in diameter sunk to the chalk formation, on an average to a depth of 60 feet, and there widened out into a chamber or chambers.

den-gue (deng′gā), *n.* [W. Ind. Sp.; of African origin.] In *pathol.*, an infectious, eruptive, usually epidemic fever of warm climates, characterized esp. by severe pains in the joints and muscles; breakbone fever.

de-ni-a-ble (dē-nī′a-bl), *a.* That may be denied.

de-ni-al (dē-nī′al), *n.* The act of denying; contradiction of a statement, etc.; refusal to believe a doctrine, etc.; disbelief in the existence or reality of a thing; refusal to recognize or acknowledge; a disowning or disavowal; the refusal of a claim, request, etc., or of a person making a request.

de-nier[1] (de-nēr′), *n.* [OF. F. *denier*, < L. *denarius*: see *denarius*.] Any of certain old French coins, orig. one of silver, ultimately a copper coin of little value; hence, a very small sum.

Obverse. Reverse.
Silver Denier struck by Edward III. of England for his French dominions.—British Museum.

de-ni-er[2] (dē-nī′ėr), *n.* [See *deny*.] One who denies.

den-i-grate (den′i-grāt), *v. t.*; *-grated, -grating.* [L. *denigratus*, pp. of *denigrare*, < *de-*, completely, + *nigrare*, blacken, < *niger*, black.] To blacken; sully; defame.—**den-i-gra′tion** (-grā′shon), *n.*—**den′i-gra-tor,** *n.*

den-im (den′im), *n.* [F. *serge de Nîmes*, serge of Nîmes (city in southern France).] A heavy cotton fabric woven with a twilled face and commonly dyed in plain colors, used for overalls, upholstery, etc.

de-ni-trate (dē-nī′trāt), *v. t.*; *-trated, -trating.* [See *de-*.] To free from nitric acid or nitrates; remove oxides of nitrogen from.—**de-ni-tra′tion** (-trā′shon), *n.*

de-ni-tri-fy (dē-nī′tri-fī), *v. t.*; *-fied, -fying.* [See *de-*.] To reduce from a nitrified state: as, to *denitrify* soil by bacterial action (by breaking down nitrates into lower nitrogen compounds).—**de-ni″tri-fi-ca′tion** (-fi-kā′shon), *n.*

den-i-za-tion (den-i-zā′shon), *n.* [AF.] The act of making one a denizen; the fact of being made a denizen.

den-i-zen (den′i-zen), *n.* [OF. *deinzein*, < *deinz*, *denz* (F. *dans*), within, in, < L. *de*, from, + *intus*, within.] An inhabitant or citizen; a dweller in a particular place; esp., an alien admitted to residence and certain rights of citizenship in a country; also, anything adapted to a new place, condition, etc., as a naturalized foreign word, or an animal or plant not indigenous to a place but successfully naturalized.—**den′i-zen,** *v. t.* To make (one) a denizen; naturalize.—**den′i-zen-ship,** *n.*

de-nom-i-na-ble (dẹ-nom′i-nạ-bl), *a.* That may be denominated or named.

de-nom-i-nate (dẹ-nom′i-nāt), *v. t.*; *-nated, -nating.* [L. *denominatus*, pp. of *denominare*, < *de*, from, + *nominare*, name, E. *nominate.*] To give a name to; name; esp., to call by a specified name; entitle.—**de-nom′i-nate,** *a.* Named or called (archaic); in *arith.*, of a number, concrete, or used with the name of a particular kind of object (opposed to *abstract*: thus, *seven* alone is an abstract number, but in the expression *seven pounds* a *denominate* number).—**de-nom-i-na′tion** (-nā′shọn), *n.* [L. *denominatio(n-).*] The act of denominating; also, a name or designation, esp. one for a class of things; hence, a class or kind of persons or things distinguished by a specific name; one of the grades or degrees in a series of designations of quantity, value, measure, weight, etc. (as, money of small *denominations*); a collection or society of individuals called by the same name, esp. a religious sect.—**de-nom-i-na′tion-al,** *a.* Of or pertaining to a denomination, esp. a religious denomination; sectarian.—**de-nom-i-na′tion-al-ism,** *n.* Denominational or sectarian spirit or policy; the tendency to divide into denominations or sects.—**de-nom-i-na′tion-al-ize** (-īz), *v. t.*; *-ized, - izing.* To render denominational.—**de-nom-i-na′tion-al-ly,** *adv.*—**de-nom′i-na-tive** (-nạ-tiv). [LL. *denominativus.*] **I.** *a.* Conferring or constituting a distinctive denomination or name; appellative; in *gram.*, formed from a substantive or an adjective (as, a *denominative* verb). **II.** *n.* In *gram.*, a denominative word, esp. a verb.—**de-nom′i-na-tor** (-nā-tọr), *n.* [ML.] One who or that which denominates; in *math.*, that term (usually written under the line) of a fraction which indicates its denomination, or shows the number of equal parts into which the unit is divided (cf. *numerator*); a divisor placed under a dividend.

de-not-a-ble (dẹ-nō′tạ-bl), *a.* That may be denoted.

de-no-ta-tion (dē-nọ-tā′shọn), *n.* [L. *denotatio(n-).*] The act or fact of denoting, marking out, or indicating; indication; also, something that denotes; a mark, sign, or symbol; a name or designation; also, that which a term denotes; signification or meaning; esp., the primary meaning of a word, as distinguished from its connotation.—**de-no-ta-tive** (dẹ-nō′tạ-tiv or dē′nọ-tā-tiv), *a.* Having the quality of denoting.—**de-no′ta-tive-ly,** *adv.*

de-note (dẹ-nōt′), *v. t.*; *-noted, -noting.* [L. *denotāre* (pp. *denotatus*), < *de*, from, + *notare*, mark, write, E. *note, v.*] To mark out from others; distinguish by a sign; be a mark or sign of; also, to represent by a symbol; stand as a symbol for; in general, to indicate or make known; specif., to be a name or designation for; designate; esp., to designate merely, without implication or connotation (cf. *connote*); also, to note down†.—**de-note′ment,** *n.* The act or fact of denoting; indication; also, a means of denoting; a sign; a token.—**de-no′tive** (-nō′tiv), *a.* Serving to denote; indicative; denotative.

dé-noue-ment (dā-nö-moṅ), *n.* [F., also *dénoûment*, < *dénouer*, untie, < *dé-* (see *dis-*) + *nouer*, < L. *nodare*, knot, tie, < *nodus*, a knot.] The final disentangling of the intricacies of a plot, as of a drama or novel; the catastrophe; hence, the solution of a difficulty, mystery, etc.; the outcome, as of an affair (as, "The particulars of the *dénouement* you shall know in due season": Smollett's "Humphry Clinker," June 10).

de-nounce (dẹ-nouns′), *v. t.*; *-nounced, -nouncing.* [OF. *denoncier* (F. *dénoncer*), < L. *denuntiare*, < *de-* (see *de-*) + *nuntiare*, announce, declare, < *nuntius*, messenger.] To make formal or public announcement of (obs. or archaic); announce or proclaim (something evil, as a curse, threatened punishment, etc.); serve to announce†, or portend†; also, to proclaim (a person) to be something specified, as a rebel, coward, swindler, etc.; hence, to condemn openly; assail with censure; also, to make formal accusation against (an offender) to the authorities; inform against; also, to give formal notice of the termination of (a treaty, etc.); also, in Mexico, etc., to announce formally to the authorities the discovery of (a new mine) or the abandonment or forfeiture of (an old mine), thus laying claim to work it.—**de-nounce′ment,** *n.* The act of denouncing; denunciation.—**de-noun′cer,** *n.*

dense (dens), *a.*; compar. *denser*, superl. *densest.* [L. *densus*, thick, thickly set; akin to Gr. δασύς, hairy, shaggy, thick.] Having the component parts closely compacted together; compact; closely set, as parts or objects; crowded with closely set objects; also, profound or intense, as ignorance; thick-headed, obtuse, or stupid, as persons; also, deep or dark, as color; in *photog.*, of a developed negative, relatively opaque, and yielding prints with strong contrasts of light and shade.—**dense′ly,** *adv.*—**dense′ness,** *n.*—**den-sim-e-ter** (den-sim′e-tėr), *n.* [See *-meter.*] An apparatus for ascertaining the relative density or specific gravity of a substance.—**den-si-met′ric** (-si-met′rik), *a.*—**den′si-ty** (-ti), *n.*; pl. *-ties* (-tiz). [L. *densitas.*] The state or quality of being dense; compactness; closely set or crowded condition; specif., the mass or amount of matter per unit of bulk or volume; the ratio of the mass of a given volume of a substance to that of an equal volume of a standard substance, water being the standard for solids and liquids, and hydrogen or air for gases (often called *relative density* or *specific gravity*); in *elect.*, the quantity of electricity per unit of area on a charged surface; in *photog.*, relative opacity of a developed negative.

dent[1] (dent), *n.* [Var. of *dint.*] A stroke† or blow†; also, a hollow or depression in a surface, as from a blow.—**dent**[1], *v.* **I.** *tr.* To make a dent in or on; indent; also, to impress as a dent. **II.** *intr.* To sink in, making a dent; also, to become indented.

dent[2] (dent), *n.* [F. *dent*, < L. *dens* (*dent-*), tooth.] A tooth-like projection, as a tooth of a gear-wheel; also, a notch or indentation (as, "High was his comb . . . In *dents* embattled like a castle wall": Dryden's "Cock and the Fox," 50).

den-tal (den′tạl). [L. *dens* (*dent-*), tooth.] **I.** *a.* Of or pertaining to the teeth; also, of or pertaining to dentistry; in *phonetics*, of speech-sounds, formed by placing the tip of the tongue against or near the upper front teeth, as *d, t, n.* **II.** *n.* In *phonetics*, a dental sound.—**den′tal-ize** (-īz), *v. t.*; *-ized, -izing.* In *phonetics*, to convert into a dental sound.—**den″tal-i-za′tion** (-i-zā′shọn), *n.*

den-tate (den′tāt), *a.* [L. *dentatus*, < *dens* (*dent-*), tooth.] Toothed; notched; in *bot.* and *zoöl.*, having a toothed margin, or tooth-like projections or processes; specif., of a leaf, having sharp marginal teeth directed outward (cf. *serrate*). Also **den′tat-ed** (-tā-ted).—**den′tate-ly,** *adv.*—**den-ta′tion** (-tā′shọn), *n.* Dentate state or form.

Dentate Leaf.

den-tel (den′tel), *n.* Same as *dentil.*

den-te-lat-ed (den′te-lā-ted), *a.* [F. *dentelé*, < OF. *dentele*, dim. of *dent*, < L. *dens* (*dent-*), tooth.] Having small teeth or tooth-like markings; finely notched.

den-ti-cle (den′ti-kl), *n* [L. *denticulus*, dim. of *dens* (*dent-*), tooth.] A small tooth or tooth-like part; in *arch.*, a dentil.—**den-tic′u-lar** (-tik′ū-lạr), *a.* Having the form of a small tooth; in *arch.*, having dentils.—**den-tic′u-late, den-tic′u-la-ted** (-lạt, -lā-ted), *a.* [L. *denticulatus.*] Finely dentate or toothed, as a leaf; in *arch.*, having dentils.—**den-tic′u-late-ly,** *adv.*—**den-tic-u-la′tion** (-lā′shọn), *n.* Denticulate state or form; a denticle, or a series of denticles.

den-ti-form (den′ti-fôrm), *a.* [L. *dens* (*dent-*), tooth: see *-form.*] Of the form of a tooth; tooth-shaped.

den-ti-frice (den′ti-fris), *n.* [F. *dentifrice*, < L. *dentifricium*, < *dens* (*dent-*), tooth, + *fricare*, rub.] A powder, paste, or other preparation for rubbing or cleaning the teeth.

den-tig-er-ous (den-tij′ẹ-rus), *a.* [L. *dens* (*dent-*), tooth: see *-gerous.*] Bearing, or supplied with, teeth.

den-til (den′til), *n.* [Obs. F. *dentille*, dim. < L. *dens* (*dent-*), tooth.] In *arch.*, one of a series of small rectangular blocks arranged like a row of teeth, as in the lower part of a cornice.

den-ti-la-bi-al (den-ti-lā′bi-ạl), *a.* Same as *labiodental.*

den-ti-lin-gual (den-ti-ling′gwạl), *a.* [L. *dens* (*dent-*), tooth, + *lingua*, tongue.] In *phonetics*, of

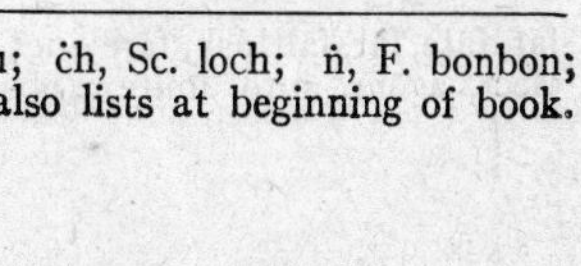

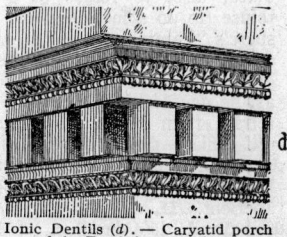

Ionic Dentils (*d*). — Caryatid porch of the Erechtheum, Athens.

speech-sounds, uttered with the coöperation of the teeth and the tongue: said esp. of the sounds of *th* in *thin* and *this*.

den-tin, den-tine (den′tin), *n.* [L. *dens* (*dent-*), tooth.] In *anat.*, the hard calcareous tissue beneath the enamel and the cement of a tooth, inclosing the pulp, and composing the greater part of the tooth.—**den′ti-nal,** *a.*

den-ti-phone (den′ti-fōn), *n.* [L. *dens* (*dent-*), tooth: see *-phone*.] An instrument held against the teeth to assist hearing by transmitting sound-vibrations to the auditory nerve.

den-ti-ros-tral (den-ti-ros′trạl), *a.* [L. *dens* (*dent-*), tooth, + *rostrum*, beak.] Having a toothed or notched bill; specif., belonging or pertaining to the *Dentirostres*, a group of passerine birds in old classifications, including the shrikes, typically with a tooth or notch on each side of the upper mandible near the tip.

Dentirostral Bird (Shrike).

den-tist (den′tist), *n.* [F. *dentiste*, < *dent*, < L. *dens* (*dent-*), tooth.] One whose profession is dentistry.—**den-tis′tic, den-tis′ti-cal,** *a.*—**den′tist-ry,** *n.* The science or art dealing with the prevention and treatment of oral disease, esp. in relation to the health of the body as a whole and including such operations as the filling and crowning of teeth, the construction of artificial dentures, etc.; also, dental work, as fillings; also, the dental profession.

den-ti-tion (den-tish′ọn), *n.* [L. *dentitio*(*n-*), < *dentire*, cut teeth, < *dens* (*dent-*), tooth.] The process or period of cutting the teeth; also, the kind, number, and arrangement of teeth, as of a particular animal.

den-ture (den′ṭūr), *n.* [F. *denture*, < *dent*, < L. *dens* (*dent-*), tooth.] A set of teeth, esp. artificial teeth.

den-u-date (den′ụ-dāt or dẹ-nū′-), *v. t.*; *-dated, -dating.* [L. *denudatus*, pp. of *denudare*: see *denude*.] To denude.—**de-nu-date** (dẹ-nū′dāt or den′ụ-), *a.* Denuded; bare.

den-u-da-tion (den-ụ-dā′shọn or dē-nụ-), *n.* [LL. *denudatio*(*n-*).] The act of denuding; denuded or bare condition; divestiture; in *geol.*, the laying bare of rock by erosive processes.—**de-nu-da-tive** (dẹ-nū′dạ-tiv), *a.*

de-nude (dẹ-nūd′), *v. t.*; *-nuded, -nuding.* [L. *denudare*, < *de-*, completely, + *nudare*, lay bare, < *nudus*, E. *nude*.] To make naked or bare; strip of clothing or of covering; fig., to deprive; in *geol.*, to subject to denudation.

de-nun-ci-ate (dẹ-nun′ṣi-āt), *v. t.*; *-ated, -ating.* [L. *denuntiatus*, pp. of *denuntiare*: see *denounce*.] To denounce; condemn openly.—**de-nun-ci-a′tion** (-ā′shọn), *n.* [L. *denuntiatio*(*n-*).] The act of denouncing; formal or public announcement† (see Shakspere's "Measure for Measure," i. 2. 152); announcement of impending evil, as in the way of a threat or warning; a denouncing as evil; open and vehement condemnation; an invective; an accusing before a public prosecutor; formal notice of the termination of a treaty. — **de-nun′ci-a-tive** (-ạ-tiv), **de-nun′ci-a-to-ry** (-ạ-tọ-ri), *a.* Characterized by or given to denunciation. —**de-nun′ci-a-tor** (-ā-tọr), *n.*

de-nu-tri-tion (dē-nụ-trish′ọn), *n.* [See *de-*.] Want or deprivation of nutrition.

de-ny (dẹ-nī′), *v. t.*; *-nied, -nying.* [OF. *denier* (F. *dénier*), < L. *denegare*, < *de-* (see *de-*) + *negare*, say no.] To assert the negative of (a statement, an alleged fact, etc.); declare not to be true; also, to refuse to believe (a doctrine, etc.); reject as false or erroneous; also, to refuse to believe in the existence or reality of; also, to refuse to recognize or acknowledge (a person or thing); disown; disavow; repudiate; also, to refuse to grant (a claim, request, etc.); refuse (to do something: as, "if she *deny* to wed," Shakspere's "Taming of the Shrew," ii. 1. 180)†; refuse to accept†; also, to refuse (a person who asks); forbid (a person, etc.) to do something†; also, to refuse access to (one visited: as, he *denied* himself to callers).—**to deny one's self,** to refrain from the gratification of one's desires; exercise self-denial.—**de-ny′ing-ly,** *adv.*

de-ob-stru-ent (dē-ob′strọ-ẹnt). [See *de-* and *obstruent*.] In *med.*: **I.** *a.* Removing obstructions, as certain drugs; aperient. **II.** *n.* A deobstruent medicine.

de-o-dand (dē′ọ-dand), *n.* [ML. *deodandum*, 'a thing to be given to God,' < L. *deus*, god, + *dare*, give.] A thing to be given or forfeited to God; formerly, in *Eng. law*, a personal chattel which, having been the immediate occasion of the death of a human being, was forfeited to the crown to be applied to pious uses.

de-o-dar (dē′ọ-där), *n.* [Hind., < Skt. *devadāru*, 'wood of the gods.'] A species of cedar, *Cedrus deodara*, a large tree valued for its durable wood, native in the Himalayas, but also grown elsewhere for ornament.

de-o-dor-ant (dē-ō′dọr-ạnt), *n.* [See *de-*.] An agent for destroying odors.

de-o-dor-ize (dē-ō′dọr-īz), *v. t.*; *-ized, -izing.* [See *de-*.] To deprive of odor, esp. of the fetid odor arising from impurities.—**de-o″dor-i-za′tion** (-i-zā′shọn), *n.*—**de-o′dor-iz-er** (-ī-zėr), *n.*

de-on-tol-o-gy (dē-on-tol′ọ-ji), *n.* [Gr. δέον, that which is binding or needful, prop. ppr. neut. of δεῖν, bind: see *-logy*.] The science of duty or moral obligation; ethics.—**de-on-to-log-i-cal** (dẹ-on-tọ-loj′i-kạl), *a.*—**de-on-tol′o-gist,** *n.*

de-ox-i-date (dē-ok′si-dāt), *v. t.*; *-dated, -dating.* [See *de-*.] To deoxidize.—**de-ox-i-da′tion** (-dā′shọn), *n.*

de-ox-id-ize (dē-ok′si-dīz), *v. t.*; *-ized, -izing.* [See *de-*.] To remove oxygen from; reduce from the state of an oxide. —**de-ox″id-i-za′tion** (-ok″si-di-zā′shọn), *n.*—**de-ox′id-i-zer** (-ok′si-dī-zėr), *n.*

de-ox-y-gen-ate (dē-ok′si-jen-āt), *v. t.*; *-ated, -ating.* [See *de-*.] To remove oxygen from.—Also **de-ox′y-gen-ize** (-īz).

de-part (dẹ-pärt′), *v.* [OF. *departir* (F. *départir*), < L. *de*, from, + *partire*, divide: see *part*, *v.*] **I.** *tr.* To divide into parts†; distribute† or deal out†; divide with others† or share†; also, to separate† or sunder†; also, to go away from or leave (as, to *depart* this life). **II.** *intr.* To become divided†; part†; part company†; also, to go away, as from a place; take one's leave; start; also, to pass away, as from life or existence (archaic); also, to turn aside or away in course or procedure (as, "*Depart* from evil, and do good": Ps. xxxiv. 14); diverge; deviate.—**de-part′**†, *n.* [OF. *depart* (F. *départ*).] The act of departing; division; parting; departure; death.—**de-part′ed,** *p. a.* Gone; past; esp., deceased; dead.—**de-part′er,** *n.*

de-part-ment (dẹ-pärt′mẹnt), *n.* [OF. *departement* (F. *département*), < *departir*: see *depart*.] The act of departing†; also, a distinct part of anything arranged in divisions; a division of a complex whole or organized system; a division of business or official duties or functions; one of the separate branches of a governmental organization; one of the (large) districts into which a country, as France, is divided for administrative purposes; one of the large geographical divisions of the U. S. as divided for military purposes.—**department store,** a large store in which many different lines of retail business are carried on in separate departments under one general management.—**de-part-men-tal** (dē-pärt-men′tạl), *a.*—**de-part-men′tal-ly,** *adv.*

de-par-ture (dẹ-pär′ṭūr), *n.* [OF. *departeure*, < *departir*: see *depart*.] The act of departing; separation†; a going away; a setting out or starting; decease or death (archaic); divergence or deviation; *naut.*, the distance due east or west made by a ship when sailing on any course not due north or south; also, the bearing or position of an object from which a vessel commences her dead-reckoning; in *surv.*, distance due east or west.

de-pas-ture (dẹ-pȧs′ṭūr), *v.*; *-tured, -turing.* [See *de-*.] **I.** *tr.* To consume the produce of (land) as pasture; use for pasturage; also, to pasture (cattle); also, of land, to supply pasturage for (cattle). **II.** *intr.* To graze.—**de-pas′tur-age** (-ṭūr-ạj), *n.*

de-pau-per-ate (dẹ-pâ′pėr-āt), *v. t.*; *-ated, -ating.* [ML. *depauperatus*, pp. of *depauperare*, < L. *de-* (see *de-*) + *pauperare*, make poor, < *pauper*, poor.] To make poor; impoverish; reduce in quality, vigor, etc.—**de-pau′per-ate,** *a.* Depauperated; impoverished; reduced in quality, etc. —**de-pau-per-a′tion** (-ā′shọn), *n.*

de-pau-per-ize (dē-pâ′pėr-īz), *v. t.*; *-ized, -izing.* [See *de-*.] To free from pauperism or poverty.—**de-pau″per-i-za′tion** (-i-zā′shọn), *n.*

de-pend (dẹ-pend′), *v. i.* [OF. *dependre* (F. *dépendre*), < L. *dependere*, < *de*, down from, + *pendere*, hang.] To hang down, or be suspended; fig., to be conditioned or contingent (as, a decision on which many matters *depend*); rest in a subordinate relation; rest for support, maintenance, supply, etc. (as, children *depend* on their parents); rest in confidence, or rely (as, you may *depend* on the accuracy of the report); wait in suspense†; be undetermined, waiting for settlement, or pending (as, a suit *depending* in court); impend† or be imminent†.—**de-pend'a-ble,** *a.* That may be depended on; reliable.—**de-pend'a-ble-ness,** *n.*—**de-pend'a-bly,** *adv.*—**de-pend'ance, de-pend'an-cy, de-pend'ant.** Var. of *dependence, dependency, dependent,* after the French.—**de-pend'ence,** *n.* [= F. *dépendance,* < ML. *dependentia.*] A depending or hanging down (obs. or rare); also, the state of being conditional or contingent on something; natural or logical sequence; also, subordination or subjection (as, the *dependence* of the church upon the state); a being dependent for aid, support, etc.; also, something subordinate or dependent; a separate building forming an addition to a hotel (a French use); also, reliance, confidence, or trust; an object of reliance or trust; reliability† or trustworthiness†; also, the condition, as of a lawsuit, of awaiting settlement.—**de-pend'en-cy,** *n.*; pl. *-cies* (-siz). The state of being dependent; dependence; contingent relation; subordination or subjection; also, something dependent or subordinate; an appurtenance; an outbuilding or annex to a main building; a subject territory which is not an integral part of the ruling country.—**de-pend'ent.** [= F. *dépendant,* < L. *dependens* (*-ent-*), ppr.] **I.** *a.* Depending, hanging down, or pendent; conditioned or contingent; subordinate or subject; depending on something else for aid, support, etc. **II.** *n.* (Often spelled *dependant.*) Something dependent or subordinate†; an appurtenance†; also, one who depends on or looks to another for support, favor, etc.; a retainer.—**de-pend'ent-ly,** *adv.*—**de-pend'er,** *n.*

de-per-son-al-ize (dē-pėr'sọn-ạl-īz), *v. t.*; *-ized, -izing.* [See *de-.*] To deprive of personality or personal quality.—**de-per"son-al-i-za'tion** (-i-zā'shọn), *n.*

de-phase (dē-fāz'), *v. t.*; *-phased, -phasing.* [See *de-.*] In *physics,* to put out of phase.

de-phlo-gis-ti-cate (dē-flọ-jis'ti-kāt), *v. t.*; *-cated, -cating.* [See *de-* and *phlogiston.*] To deprive of phlogiston†; in *med.,* to reduce inflammation in.—**de-phlo-gis-ti-ca'tion** (-kā'shọn), *n.*

de-phos-pho-rize (dē-fos'fọ-rīz), *v. t.*; *-rized, -rizing.* [See *de-.*] To remove phosphorus from.—**de-phos"pho-ri-za'tion** (-ri-zā'shọn), *n.*

de-pict (dẹ-pikt'), *v. t.* [L. *depictus,* pp. of *depingere,* < *de,* from, + *pingere,* paint.] To represent by or as by painting; portray; delineate; hence, to represent in words; describe.—**de-pict'er,** *n.*—**de-pic'tion** (-pik'shọn), **de-pic'ture**[1] (-ṭūr), *n.*

de-pic-ture[2] (dẹ-pik'ṭūr), *v. t.*; *-tured, -turing.* [From *de-* + *picture,* after *depict.*] To represent by or as by a picture; depict: as, "Language fails, — Shrinks from *depicturing* his turpitude!" (Browning's "Ring and the Book," viii.).

de-pig-ment (dē-pig'mẹnt), *v. t.* [See *de-.*] To deprive of pigment.—**de-pig-men-ta'tion** (-mẹn-tā'shọn), *n.*

dep-i-late (dep'i-lāt), *v. t.*; *-lated, -lating.* [L. *depilatus,* pp. of *depilare,* < *de,* from, + *pilare,* deprive of hair, < *pilus,* hair.] To remove the hair from.—**dep-i-la'tion** (-lā'shọn), *n.*—**de-pil-a-to-ry** (dẹ-pil'ạ-tọ-ri). **I.** *a.* Having the property of removing hair. **II.** *n.*; pl. *-ries* (-riz). A depilatory agent.

de-plen-ish (dē-plen'ish), *v. t.* [See *de-* and *plenish.*] To empty; deplete; remove the furnishings or equipments of.

de-plete (dẹ-plēt'), *v. t.*; *-pleted, -pleting.* [L. *depletus,* pp. of *deplere,* < *de-* (see *de-*) + *plere,* fill.] To deprive of that which fills; decrease the fullness of; reduce the stock or amount of; in *med.,* to empty or relieve (overcharged vessels, etc.), as by bloodletting or purging.—**de-ple'tion** (-plē'shọn), *n.*—**de-ple'tive, de-ple'to-ry** (-tọ-ri), *a.* Tending to deplete.

de-plor-a-ble (dẹ-plōr'ạ-bl), *a.* That is to be deplored; lamentable.—**de-plor'a-ble-ness,** *n.*—**de-plor'a-bly,** *adv.*

de-plore (dẹ-plōr'), *v. t.*; *-plored, -ploring.* [L. *deplorare,* < *de-* (see *de-*) + *plorare,* cry out, wail.] To weep or mourn for; lament; regret deeply; also, to narrate with grief† (as, "Never more Will I my master's tears to you *deplore*": Shakspere's "Twelfth Night," iii. 1. 174); also, to despair of†.—**de-plor'er,** *n.*—**de-plor'ing-ly,** *adv.*

de-ploy (dẹ-ploi'), *v.* [F. *déployer,* OF. *desploier, despleier*: see *display.*] *Milit.*: **I.** *tr.* To spread out (troops) so as to form an extended front of small depth. **II.** *intr.* Of troops, to spread out so as to form an extended front.—**de-ploy',** *n. Milit.,* an act of deploying.—**de-ploy'ment,** *n.*

de-plu-mate (dẹ-plö'māt), *a.* [ML. *deplumatus,* pp. of *deplumare*: see *deplume.*] Stripped of feathers.

de-plume (dẹ-plöm'), *v. t.*; *-plumed, -pluming.* [ML. *deplumare,* < L. *de-* (see *de-*) + *pluma,* feather.] To deprive of plumage or feathers; pluck; fig., to strip of honor, wealth, etc.—**de-plu-ma-tion** (dē-plö-mā'shọn), *n.*

de-po-lar-ize (dē-pō'lạr-īz), *v. t.*; *-ized, -izing.* [See *de-.*] To deprive of polarity or polarization.—**de-po"lar-i-za'tion** (-i-zā'shọn), *n.*—**de-po'lar-iz-er** (-ī-zėr), *n.*

de-pol-ish (dē-pol'ish), *v. t.* [See *de-.*] To destroy the polish of; dull.

de-pone (dẹ-pōn'), *v.*; *-poned, -poning.* [L. *deponere* (pp. *depositus*), put away or down, deposit, ML. testify: see *deposit.*] **I.** *tr.* To put aside or down†; deposit†; also, to testify under oath; depose. **II.** *intr.* To give testimony under oath; depose.—**de-po'nent** (-pō'nẹnt). **I.** *a.* In *gram.,* having put aside the regular meaning; passive (or middle) in form but active in meaning: applied to a class of Latin verbs, orig. reflexive, and to similar verbs in Greek, etc. **II.** *n.* A deponent verb; also, one who testifies under oath, esp. in writing.

de-pop-u-lar-ize (dē-pop'ụ̄-lạr-īz), *v. t.*; *-ized, -izing.* [See *de-.*] To deprive of popularity.

de-pop-u-late (dẹ-pop'ụ̄-lāt), *v. t.*; *-lated, -lating.* [ML. *depopulatus,* pp. of *depopulare,* < L. *de-* (see *de-*) + ML. *populare,* E. *populate.*] To deprive of inhabitants, wholly or in part, as by destruction or expulsion; reduce the population of.—**de-pop'u-late** (-lạt), *a.* Depopulated. [Archaic.]—**de-pop-u-la'tion** (-lā'shọn), *n.*—**de-pop'u-la-tor,** *n.*

de-port (dẹ-pōrt'), *v. t.* [Partly < L. *deportare,* carry away, transport, banish, < *de,* from, + *portare,* carry; partly < F. *déporter,* conduct (one's self), from the same L. elements.] To carry off; remove; esp., to transport from a country by way of banishment or expulsion; also, to bear, conduct, or behave (one's self) in a particular manner.—**de-por-ta-tion** (dē-pọr-tā'shọn), *n.* [L. *deportatio(n-).*] The act of deporting; a carrying off; esp., transportation from a country by way of banishment or expulsion.—**de-port-ee'** (-pọr-tē'), *n.* One who is deported, as from a country.—**de-port'er,** *n.*—**de-port'ment,** *n.* [F. *déportement.*] Manner of deporting one's self; bodily carriage; demeanor; conduct; behavior; fig., manner of acting, as of a substance, under particular conditions.

de-pos-a-ble (dẹ-pō'zạ-bl), *a.* That may be deposed.

de-po-sal (dẹ-pō'zạl), *n.* Deposition, as from office.

de-pose (dẹ-pōz'), *v.*; *-posed, -posing.* [OF. *deposer* (F. *déposer*), put down, < *de-* (see *de-*) + *poser,* put (see *pose*[1]), but associated with derivatives of L. *deponere*: see *deposit.*] **I.** *tr.* To put down or deposit (archaic); lay aside†; also, to remove from office or position, esp. high office; dethrone; also, to take away† (as, "You may my glories and my state *depose*": Shakspere's "Richard II.," iv. 1. 192); divest or deprive (a person) of something†; also, to declare or testify; esp., to declare on oath, usually in writing; also, to examine on oath† (as, "*Depose* him in the justice of his cause": Shakspere's "Richard II.," i. 3. 30). **II.** *intr.* To bear witness; give sworn testimony, esp. in writing.—**de-pos'er** (-pō'zėr), *n.*

de-pos-it (dẹ-poz'it), *v.* [L. *depositus,* pp. of *deponere,* put away or down, deposit, ML. testify (see *depone*), < L. *de,* away or down from, + *ponere,* place, put.] **I.** *tr.* To put or lay down; place; put; also, to throw down or precipitate; also, to lay aside†; also, to place for safe-keeping or in trust; give as security or in part payment. **II.** *intr.* To settle, or be precipitated.—**de-pos'it,** *n.* [L. *depositum,* prop. neut. of *depositus,* pp.] Anything laid or thrown down, as matter precipitated from a fluid; sediment; a coating of metal deposited by an electric current; also, anything laid away or intrusted to another for safe-keeping, as money placed in a bank; anything given as security or in part payment; also, the act of depositing, or the fact of being deposited; also, a place for depositing or storing things; a depository.—**de-pos'i-ta-ry** (-i-tā-ri), *n.*; pl. *-ries* (-riz). [LL. *depositarius.*] One to whom anything is given in trust; a trustee; also, a depository.—**dep-o-si-tion** (dep-ō-zish'on or dē-pō-), *n.* [L. *depositio(n-)*, < *deponere.*] A deposing or putting down; [sometimes *cap.*] the taking down of Christ's body from the cross; a representation of this in art; also [*l. c.*], removal from an office or position; degradation; dethronement; also, statement, testimony, or allegation; the giving of testimony under oath; the testimony so given; esp., a statement under oath, taken down in writing, to be used in court in place of the production of the witness; also, a depositing, or putting in place or position; precipitation; matter precipitated; a deposit; also, a depositing for safe-keeping or in trust; that which is so deposited.—**de-pos'i-tor,** *n.* [LL.] One who or that which deposits; esp., one who deposits money in a bank.—**de-pos'i-to-ry** (-tō-ri), *n.*; pl. *-ries* (-riz). A place where anything is deposited or stored for safe-keeping; a repository; a storehouse; also, a depositary.

de-pot (dē'pō, dā'pō, or, chiefly Brit., dep'ō), *n.* [F. *dépôt*, < L. *depositum*, E. *deposit, n.*] A depository or storehouse; a railroad-station (U. S.); *milit.*, a place where military supplies and materials are collected for distribution; a place where recruits are received and trained.

de-prave (dē-prāv'), *v. t.*; *-praved, -praving.* [L. *depravare*, < *de-* (see *de-*) + *pravus*, crooked, perverse, wrong, bad.] To make bad or worse; impair; vitiate; corrupt; esp., to corrupt or pervert morally (as, "Devoted to his pleasures, he *depraved* those under his command": Motley's "Dutch Republic," vi. 4); also, to defame†.—**dep-ra-va-tion** (dep-ra-vā'shon or dē-pra-), *n.*—**de-praved',** *p. a.* Made bad or worse; vitiated; corrupt or perverted, esp. morally; wicked.—**de-prav'ed-ness** (-prā'ved-nes), *n.*—**de-prav'er,** *n.*—**de-prav'i-ty** (-prav'i-ti), *n.*; pl. *-ties* (-tiz). The state of being depraved or corrupt; viciousness; wickedness; also, a depraved act or practice; in *theol.*, the inherent tendency of mankind to commit sin.

dep-re-cate (dep'rē-kāt), *v. t.*; *-cated, -cating.* [L. *deprecatus*, pp. of *deprecari*, < *de*, from, + *precari*, pray.] To pray for deliverance from (archaic); also, to plead or protest against; express earnest disapproval of; also, to make supplication to (obs. or rare); also, to invoke (evil)†.—**dep're-cat-ing-ly,** *adv.*—**dep-re-ca'tion** (-kā'shon), *n.* [L. *deprecatio(n-)*.] The act of deprecating; prayer for deliverance from evil; a pleading or protesting against something; earnest expression of disapproval.—**dep're-ca-tive** (-kā-tiv), *a.* Deprecatory.—**dep're-ca-tor** (-kā-tor), *n.*—**dep're-ca-to-ry** (-ka-tō-ri), *a.* Of the nature of deprecation; expressing deprecation.

de-pre-ci-ate (dē-prē'shi-āt), *v.*; *-ated, -ating.* [LL. *depretiatus*, pp. of *depretiare*, < L. *de*, down from, + *pretium*, price.] **I.** *tr.* To lessen the value of; reduce the purchasing value of (money); also, to undervalue; disparage; belittle. **II.** *intr.* To decline in value.—**de-pre'ci-at-ing-ly,** *adv.*—**de-pre-ci-a'tion** (-si-ā'shon), *n.* The act or fact of depreciating, or the state of being depreciated; lowering in value; lowering in estimation; disparagement.—**de-pre'ci-a-tive** (-shi-ā-tiv), *a.* Depreciatory.—**de-pre'ci-a-tor** (-ā-tor), *n.*—**de-pre'ci-a-to-ry** (-a-tō-ri), *a.* Tending to depreciate.

dep-re-date (dep'rē-dāt), *v.*; *-dated, -dating.* [L. *deprædatus*, pp. of *deprædari*, < *de-* (see *de-*) + *prædari*, take booty, E. *prey, v.*] **I.** *tr.* To prey upon; plunder; lay waste. **II.** *intr.* To prey; make depredations.—**dep-re-da'tion** (-dā'shon), *n.* [LL. *deprædatio(n-)*.] A preying upon or plundering; robbery; ravage; waste.—**dep're-da-tor,** *n.*—**dep're-da-to-ry** (-dā-tō-ri), *a.* Characterized by depredation; preying; ravaging.

de-press (dē-pres'), *v. t.* [L. *depressus*, pp. of *deprimere*, < *de*, down from, + *premere*, press.] To press down; put into a lower position, as by pressure; lower; also, to bring down in station, influence, etc. (now rare); subjugate†; oppress†; suppress†; depreciate†; also, to lower in force, vigor, etc.; weaken; make dull; also, to lower in spirits; deject; dispirit; also, to lower in amount or value; in *music*, to lower in pitch.—**de-press'ant.** In *med.*: **I.** *a.* Having the quality of depressing or lowering the vital activities; sedative. **II.** *n.* A depressant substance or agent; a sedative.—**de-pressed',** *p. a.* Pressed down; lowered; lower than the general surface; also, lowered in force, amount, etc.; also, dejected or downcast; in *bot.* and *zoöl.*, flattened down, or with respect to the vertical axis; broader than high.—**de-press'i-ble,** *a.* Capable of being depressed. — **de-press'ing-ly,** *adv.* — **de-pres'sion** (-presh'on), *n.* [L. *depressio(n-)*.] The act of depressing, or the state of being depressed; a low state of vital powers or functional activity; dullness or inactivity, as of trade; dejection of spirits; also, a depressed or sunken place or part; a hollow; in *astron.*, etc., angular distance below the horizon; in *music*, a lowering in pitch; the flatting of a tone.—**de-pres'sive** (-pres'iv), *a.* Tending to depress.—**de-pres"so-mo'tor** (-pres"ō-mō'tor). In *med.*: **I.** *a.* Causing a retardation of motor activity: as, *depressomotor* nerves. **II.** *n.* A depressomotor agent, as bromine.—**de-pres'sor.** [NL.] **I.** *n.* One who or that which depresses; in *anat.*, a muscle that draws down a part; in *surg.*, an instrument for pressing down a protruding part. **II.** *a.* In *physiol.*, that depresses; reducing activity: as, a *depressor* nerve (a nerve whose stimulation causes a decrease of blood-pressure).

de-print (dē-print'), *v. t.* [See *de-*.] To reprint (an article) from the original types, but separately from the whole of which it forms a part.—**de'print,** *n.* A deprinted article.

de-priv-a-ble (dē-prī'va-bl), *a.* Liable to be deprived.

de-pri-val (dē-prī'val), *n.* Deprivation.

dep-ri-va-tion (dep-ri-vā'shon), *n.* [ML. *deprivatio(n-)*.] The act of depriving, or the fact of being deprived; dispossession; loss; specif., a depriving of an office or dignity, esp. in the church.—**de-priv-a-tive** (dē-priv'a-tiv), *a.* Tending to deprive; characterized by deprivation.

de-prive (dē-prīv'), *v. t.*; *-prived, -priving.* [OF. *depriver*, < ML. *deprivare*, < L. *de-* (see *de-*) + *privare*, deprive.] To divest of something possessed or enjoyed; dispossess; strip; bereave; specif., to divest of an office or dignity, esp. in the church; also, to keep (a person, etc.) from possessing or enjoying something withheld (as, "I am *deprived* of the residue of my years": Isa. xxxviii. 10); debar; also, to take away†.—**de-priv'er** (-prī'vėr), *n.*

depth (depth), *n.* [ME.; < *deep.*] The quality of being deep; deepness; measure or distance downward, inward, or backward; deepness, as of water, suited to or safe for a person or thing (as, beyond one's *depth*, fig., beyond one's capacity or ability); abstruseness, as of a subject; intellectual penetration, sagacity, or profundity, as of persons; gravity or seriousness; emotional profundity (as, *depth* of woe); intensity, as of silence, color, etc.; lowness of pitch; also, a deep part or place, as of the sea; an unfathomable space, or abyss; a deep or underlying region, as of feeling; the remotest or extreme part, as of space; the inmost part (as, "in *depth* of woods embraced": Pope's "Essay on Man," i. 105); the part of greatest intensity, as of night or winter.—**depth bomb,** a bomb which is dropped or thrown into the water from a ship or an aëroplane and explodes at a certain depth: used to destroy submarines, etc., results being obtained even at some distance from the point of explosion.—**depth'less,** *a.* Without depth; shallow; superficial; also, of immeasurable depth; fathomless.

dep-u-rate (dep'ū-rāt or dē-pū'-), *v. t.*; *-rated, -rating.* [ML. *depuratus*, pp. of *depurare*, < L. *de-* (see *de-*) + *purare*, purify, < *purus*, E. *pure.*] To free from impurities; purify; cleanse.—**dep-u-ra'tion** (-rā'shon), *n.*—**dep'u-ra-tive** (-rā-tiv). **I.** *a.* Serving to depurate; purifying. **II.** *n.* A depurative agent or substance.—**dep'u-ra-tor** (-rā-tor), *n.*

de-pu-ta-ble (dē-pū'ta-bl), *a.* That may be deputed.

dep-u-ta-tion (dep-ū-tā'shon), *n.* The act of deputing, or the state of being deputed; appointment or assignment, as to an office or function†; appointment to represent or act for another or others; also, the person or (usually) body of persons so appointed or authorized.

de-pute (dē-pūt'), *v. t.*; *-puted, -puting.* [OF. *deputer* (F. *députer*), < LL. *deputare*, destine, allot, L. count as, consider, < L. *de-* (see *de-*) + *putare*, reckon: see *putative.*] To ordain or set apart for a particular purpose†; also, to assign (a charge, etc.) to a substitute or deputy; also, to appoint (a person) as one's substitute or agent.

dep-u-tize (dep'ū-tīz), *v.*; *-tized, -tizing.* [From *deputy.*] **I.** *tr.* To appoint as deputy; depute. **II.** *intr.* To act as a deputy or substitute. [Colloq.]

dep-u-ty (dep'ū-ti). [OF. *depute* (F. *député*), prop. pp. of *deputer*, E. *depute.*] **I.** *n.*; pl. *-ties* (-tiz). A person appointed or authorized to act for another or others; a substitute; an authorized representative or agent; a person representing a constituency in any of certain legislative bodies (as, the French Chamber of *Deputies*, the second or lower house of the national assembly); in *law*, one authorized to exercise another's office, or some function of it, but having no interest in the office. **II.** *a.* Acting as deputy for another.—**dep'u-ty-ship,** *n.*

de-ra-ci-nate (dē-ras'i-nāt), *v. t.*; *-nated, -nating.* [F. *déraciner*, < *dé-* (see *dis-*) + *racine*, < L. *radix*, root.] To pluck up by the roots; uproot; extirpate; eradicate.—**de-ra-ci-na'tion** (-nā'shọn), *n.*

de-raign (dē-rān'), *v. t.* [OF. *deraisnier, desraisnier*, < ML. *deratıonare, disrationare*, < L. *de-, dis-* (see *de-*), + ML. *rationare*, reason, discourse: cf. *arraign.*] To prove or vindicate (a right, claim, etc.), esp. by wager of battle; dispute or contest (a claim, etc., of another); also, to maintain or vindicate a claim to (something); also, to settle or decide, as by wager of battle; also, to maintain or engage in, or dispose troops for (battle); set (troops) in battle array. [Now only hist.]—**de-raign'ment,** *n.*

de-rail (dē-rāl'), *v.* [F. *dérailler*, < *dé-* (see *dis-*) + *rail*, rail.] **I.** *intr.* Of a train, etc., to run off the rails or track. **II.** *tr.* To cause (a train, etc.) to run off the rails.—**de-rail** (dē'rāl), *n.* In *railroading*, a switch designed to divert or throw a train or car from the track, as to stop its progress.—**de-rail'er,** *n.* A derail.—**de-rail'ment,** *n.*

de-range (dē-rānj'), *v. t.*; *-ranged, -ranging.* [F. *déranger*, OF. *desrengier*, < *des-* (see *dis-*) + *rengier*, E. *range, v.*] To disturb the arrangement or order of; throw into confusion; disarrange; also, to disturb the condition, action, or functions of; put out of proper condition; disorder; specif., to unsettle the reason of; make insane.—**de-ranged',** *p. a.* Disarranged; disordered; insane (as, "The few persons whom he met . . . thought him furious or *deranged*": J. H. Newman's "Callista," xii.).—**de-range'ment,** *n.* The act of deranging, or the state of being deranged; disarrangement; disorder; esp., mental disorder; insanity.

de-ray (dē-rā'), *n.* [OF. *desrei*, < *desreer*, put out of order, < *des-* (see *dis-*) + *-reer* as in *areer*, E. *array, v.*] Disorder; uproar; disorderly merrymaking. [Archaic or prov.]

Der-by (dėr'bi, Eng. där'bi), *n.*; pl. *-bies* (-biz). A celebrated horse-race in England, founded in 1780 by the twelfth Earl of Derby, and run annually at Epsom, near London; hence, some other important race, whether of horses or of automobiles or aëroplanes; also [*l. c.*], a stiff felt hat with rounded crown and narrow brim, worn chiefly by men.

der-e-lict (der'ẹ-likt). [L. *derelictus*, pp. of *derelinquere*, forsake utterly, < *de-* (see *de-*) + *relinquere*, leave, E. *relinquish.*] **I.** *a.* Left or abandoned, as by the owner or guardian (said esp. of a ship abandoned at sea); also, neglectful of duty; delinquent; unfaithful. **II.** *n.* Something left or abandoned, as by the owner or guardian, esp. a ship abandoned at sea; land left dry by a change of the water-line; a person forsaken or abandoned; also, one guilty of neglect of duty.

der-e-lic-tion (der-ẹ-lik'shọn), *n.* [L. *derelictio(n-)*, < *derelinquere*: see *derelict.*] The act of abandoning, or the state of being abandoned; a leaving dry of land by change of the water-line; the land thus left dry; also, culpable abandonment or neglect, as of duty; delinquency; a delinquency or fault.

de-ride (dē-rīd'), *v. t.*; *-rided, -riding.* [L. *deridere* (pp. *derisus*), < *de-* (see *de-*) + *ridere*, laugh.] To laugh at in contempt; scoff or jeer at; make sport of; mock.—**de-rid'er** (-rī'dėr), *n.*—**de-rid'ing-ly,** *adv.*

de-ris-i-ble (dē-riz'i-bl), *a.* Subject to or worthy of derision.

de-ri-sion (dē-rizh'ọn), *n.* [LL. *derisio(n-)*, < L. *deridere*: see *deride.*] The act of deriding, or the state of being derided; ridicule; mockery; also, an object of ridicule.—**de-ri'sive** (-rī'siv), *a.* [L. *derisus*, pp.] Characterized by derision; ridiculing; mocking.—**de-ri'sive-ly,** *adv.*—**de-ri'sive-ness,** *n.*—**de-ri'so-ry** (-sọ-ri), *a.* Derisive.

de-riv-a-ble (dē-rī'vạ-bl), *a.* Capable of being derived.

de-ri-val (dē-rī'vạl), *n.* Derivation.

der-i-vate (der'i-vāt). [L. *derivatus*, pp.] **I.** *a.* Derived [Obs. or archaic.] **II.** *n.* Something derived; a derivative, as a word or a chemical product.

der-i-va-tion (der-i-vā'shọn), *n.* [L. *derivatio(n-).*] The act of deriving, or the fact of being derived; a drawing or obtaining, as from a source; extraction; origination; the formation of a word from a root, stem, or the like; the tracing of the origin of a word; a statement or theory of such origin or formation; also, something derived; a derivative; in *med.*, the drawing away of the fluids of an inflamed part, as by blistering.—**der-i-va'tion-al,** *a.*

de-riv-a-tive (dē-riv'ạ-tiv). [LL. *derivativus.*] **I.** *a.* Derived; drawn or having proceeded from a source or from something else; not original or primitive; secondary; also, pertaining to derivation; in *med.*, producing derivation. **II.** *n.* Something derived or derivative; specif., a word derived from another word or from a root, stem, or the like; in *med.*, a derivative agent or method; in *chem.*, a substance or compound obtained from, or so constituted as to be regarded as derived from, another substance or compound.—**de-riv'a-tive-ly,** *adv.*

de-rive (dē-rīv'), *v.*; *-rived, -riving.* [L. *derivare* (pp. *derivatus*), lead off (water, etc.), divert, derive, < *de*, from, + *rivus*, a stream.] **I.** *tr.* To conduct (a stream of water, etc.) from one place to another, as by a channel (archaic); draw off† or divert†; lead† or extend†; transmit or pass on, as by descent (archaic); bring or direct (*to, on, upon*, etc.)†; now, to draw or obtain from a source or origin; specif., to take (a word) from a particular source; form from a root, stem, or the like; also, to trace from a source or origin, as a custom or word; declare to come from a particular source; also, to obtain by reasoning; deduce. **II.** *intr.* To be transmitted; come from a source; originate.—**de-rived',** *p. a.* Drawn, obtained, or descended from a source.—**derived unit,** in *physics*, any of the units (as of area, velocity, etc.) which are derived from fundamental units.—**de-riv'er** (-rī'vėr), *n.*

-derm. Noun termination from Gr. δέρμα, skin, as in *blastoderm, endoderm, phelloderm.*

der-ma (dėr'mạ), *n.* [NL., < Gr. δέρμα (δερματ-), skin.] The corium or true skin, beneath the epidermis; also, the skin in general.—**der'mal,** *a.* Of or pertaining to the derma or the skin; cutaneous.—**der-ma-ti'tis** (-mạ-tī'tis), *n.* [NL.] In *pathol.*, inflammation of the derma.

dermato-. Form of Gr. δέρμα (δερματ-), skin, used in combination. — **der-ma-to-gen** (dėr'mạ-tọ-jen), *n.* [+ *-gen.*] In *bot.*, a thin layer of meristem in plant-embryos and the growing ends of stems and roots, which gives rise to the epidermis.—**der'ma-toid,** *a.* [See *-oid.*] Resembling skin; skin-like.—**der-ma-tol'o-gy** (-tol'ọ-ji), *n.* [+ *-logy.*] The science of the skin and its diseases.—**der''ma-to-log'i-cal** (-loj'i-kạl), *a.*—**der-ma-tol'o-gist,** *n.*—**der'ma-to-phyte** (-fīt), *n.* [+ *-phyte.*] Any fungus parasitic on the skin and causing disease.—**der'ma-to-plas''ty** (-plas''ti), *n.* [+ *-plasty.*] Plastic surgery of the skin. Cf. *skin-grafting.*

der-ma-to-sis (dėr-mạ-tō'sis), *n.*; pl. *-toses* (-tō'sēz). [NL., < Gr. δέρμα (δερματ-), skin: see *-osis.*] In *pathol.*, any disease of the skin.

der-mic (dėr'mik), *a.* Dermal.

der-mis (dėr'mis), *n.* [NL.: cf. *epidermis.*] Same as *derma.*

dermo-. Same as *dermato-.*—**der-moid** (dėr'moid), *a.* [See *-oid.*] Skin-like; dermatoid; also, dermal.—**der-mo-skel'e-ton** (-mọ-skel'ẹ-tọn), *n.* The exoskeleton.

dern (dėrn), *a.* [AS. *derne, dierne.*] Hidden or secret (as, "There's not a *dern* nook, or cove . . . in the whole country, that he's not acquainted with": Scott's "Waverley," xviii.); hence, dark; somber; dreary. [Archaic or Sc.]

der-ni-er (dėr'ni-ėr, F. der-nyā), *a.* [F., ult. < L. *de*, from, + *retro*, back, behind.] Last; final; ultimate: now only as French.—**dernier ressort** (der-nyā rė-sôr). [F.] Last resort; final resource.

der-o-gate (der'ọ-gāt), *v.*; *-gated, -gating.* [L. *derogatus*, pp. of *derogare*, repeal part of a law, take or detract from, < *de*, from, + *rogare*, ask, propose a law.] **I.** *tr.* To abrogate (a law, etc.) in part†; detract from† or depreciate†; take away (something) from a thing so as to impair it. **II.** *intr.* To detract, as from authority, estimation, etc.; also, to fall away in character or conduct; degenerate.—**der′o-gate,** *a.* Abrogated in part†; deteriorated or debased (obs. or archaic).—**der-o-ga′tion** (-gā′shọn), *n.* [L. *derogatio(n-).*] The act of derogating; partial abrogation of a law, legal right, etc.; lessening of authority, estimation, etc.; detraction, disparagement, or depreciation; deterioration or debasement.—**de-rog-a-tive** (dẹ-rog′ạ-tiv), *a.* Derogatory.—**de-rog′a-tive-ly,** *adv.*—**de-rog′a-to-ry** (-tọ-ri), *a.* Tending to derogate or detract, as from authority or estimation; disparaging; depreciatory.—**de-rog′a-to-ri-ly,** *adv.* —**de-rog′a-to-ri-ness,** *n.*

der-rick (der′ik), *n.* [From *Derrick,* a hangman at Tyburn, London, about 1600.] A hangman†; a gallows†; any of various devices for lifting and moving heavy weights, as an oblique tackle-bearing spar secured to the deck of a ship and steadied by guys, or an upright revolving post to the lower end of which is pivoted a movable tackle-bearing spar or boom; a horizontal projecting beam fitted with a tackle for hoisting, placed near the top of a building, etc.; the tower-like framework over an oil-well or the like.

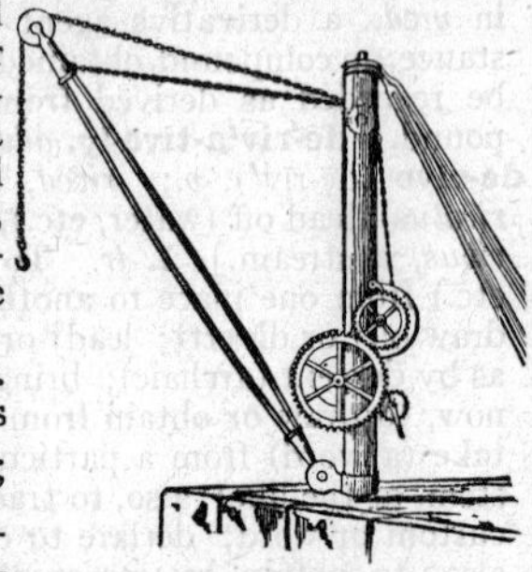

One Form of Derrick.

der-ring=do (der′ing-dö′), *n.* [Orig. a phrase in Chaucer's "Troilus and Cressida," ME. *dorryng don,* 'daring (to) do,' adopted by Spenser and erroneously used as a noun.] Daring deeds; heroic daring: as, "A man of mickle name, Renowmed much in armes and *derring doe*" (Spenser's "Faerie Queene," vi. 5. 37). [Pseudo-archaic.]

der-rin-ger (der′in-jėr), *n.* [Named from the inventor, an American.] A short-barreled pistol of large caliber.

der-vish (dėr′vish), *n.* [Turk. *dervīsh* = Ar. *darwīsh,* < Pers. *darwīsh.*] A member of any of various ascetic orders of Mohammedan religious enthusiasts, some of which are distinguished by characteristic ecstatic observances, such as violent dancing, and pirouetting ('dancing dervishes,' 'spinning dervishes,' or 'whirling dervishes') or vociferous chanting or shouting ('howling dervishes').

des-cant (des′kant), *n.* [OF. *descant, deschant* (F. *déchant*), < ML. *discantus,* < L. *dis-,* apart, + *canere,* sing.] A melody or counterpoint accompanying a simple musical theme and usually written above it; also, in part-music, the soprano; also, the art of singing or composing music in parts; a harmonized composition; also, an instrumental prelude consisting of variations on a theme; in general, a song or melody; also, a variation upon anything; comment on a subject; esp., an extended and varied comment; a disquisition or discourse.—**des-cant′,** *v. i.* To sing or play a melody in harmony with the chief melody; in general, to sing; also, to make comments on a subject; discourse at length and with variety.—**des-cant′er,** *n.*

de-scend (dẹ-send′), *v.* [OF. F. *descendre,* < L. *descendere* (pp. *descensus*), < *de,* down from, + *scandere,* climb.] **I.** *intr.* To move or pass from a higher to a lower place (opposed to *ascend*); go or come down; fall; sink; also, to slope or tend downward; also, to come down in a hostile manner, as an army; also, to pass from higher to lower in any scale; go from generals to particulars; proceed to something later in time or order; also, to come down from a certain intellectual, moral, or social standard; stoop; condescend; also, to be derived by birth or extraction; also, to come down by transmission, as from ancestors; in *astron.,* to move toward the horizon, or toward the south, as a star. **II.** *tr.* To move downward upon or along; go down (a hill, stairs, etc.).—**de-scend′a-ble,** *a.* Descendible.—**de-scend′ant.** [F. *descendant,* ppr.] **I.** *a.* Descendent. **II.** *n.* One descended from an ancestor; an offspring, near or remote.—**de-scend′ent,** *a.* [L. *descendens* (*-ent-*), ppr.] Descending; going or coming down; descending from an ancestor; in *her.,* descending toward the base of the shield, as a bird used as a bearing.—**de-scend′er,** *n.* —**de-scend′i-ble,** *a.* That may be descended, as a hill; also, that may descend or pass, as to an heir; capable of being transmitted by inheritance.

An Eagle Descendent.

de-scen-sion (dẹ-sen′shọn), *n.* [L. *descensio(n-).*] The act or fact of descending; descent. [Now rare.]—**de-scen′sion-al,** *a.*

de-scen-sive (dẹ-sen′siv), *a.* Tending to descend; characterized by downward tendency; descending.

de-scent (dẹ-sent′), *n.* [OF. F. *descente,* < *descendre:* see *descend.*] The act or fact of descending; a going or coming down; a falling or sinking; also, a downward inclination or slope; the lowest part†; also, a sudden incursion or attack; also, any passing from higher to lower in degree or state; also, the state of being descended from an ancestor; extraction; lineage; specif., evolution (as, Darwin's "*Descent* of Man"); also, a descendant†; descendants collectively†; also, a single stage in the line of descent from an ancestor; a generation; also, transmission by inheritance or succession, as of property, title, etc.

de-scribe (dẹ-skrīb′), *v. t.*; *-scribed, -scribing.* [L. *describere* (pp. *descriptus*), copy off, sketch off, describe, < *de,* from, + *scribere,* write, draw.] To write down†; also, to enroll†; also, to set forth in written or spoken words; give an account of; also, to delineate as in a picture†; draw (a geometrical or other figure); form (a particular figure), as an object does by its path of motion; also, to descry† (see Milton's "Paradise Lost," iv. 567).—**de-scrib′a-ble** (-skrī′bạ-bl), *a.*—**de-scrib′er,** *n.*

des-cri-er (des-krī′ėr), *n.* [See *descry.*] One who descries.

de-scrip-tion (dẹ-skrip′shọn), *n.* [L. *descriptio(n-).*] The act of describing; representation by written or spoken words; a statement that describes; also, the combination of qualities characterizing an individual or class; hence, a sort, kind, or variety (as, "tinkers, gipsies, and persons of that *description*": Scott's "Guy Mannering," lvi.).

de-scrip-tive (dẹ-skrip′tiv), *a.* [LL. *descriptivus.*] Having the quality of describing; characterized by description.—**descriptive geometry.** See under *geometry.*—**de-scrip′tive-ly,** *adv.*—**de-scrip′tive-ness,** *n.*

des-cry (des-krī′), *v. t.*; *-cried, -crying.* [Appar. < OF. *descrier,* proclaim: see *decry.*] To proclaim† or announce†; also, to reveal† or betray†; also, to make out by looking; espy; in general, to discover by observation; see; perceive; detect; also, to spy out†.

des-e-crate (des′ẹ-krāt), *v. t.*; *-crated, -crating.* [L. *de-* (see *de-*) + *sacrare* (pp. *sacratus*), consecrate: cf. *consecrate.*] To divest of sacred or hallowed character or office; divert from a sacred to a profane purpose; treat with sacrilege; profane.—**des-e-cra′tion** (-krā′shọn), *n.*—**des′e-cra-tor,** *n.*

de-seg-men-ta-tion (dē-seg-mẹn-tā′shọn), *n.* [See *de-.*] Change from a segmented condition; reduction of the number of segments by the coalescence of two or more, as in the carapace of a lobster.—**de-seg′ment-ed,** *a.*

de-sen-si-tize (dē-sen′si-tīz), *v. t.*; *-tized, -tizing.* [See *de-.*] To lessen the sensitiveness of; deprive of sensitiveness; in *photog.,* to render less sensitive or wholly insensitive to light, as a photographic plate.—**de-sen″si-ti-za′tion** (-ti-zā′shọn), *n.*—**de-sen′si-tiz-er** (-tī-zėr), *n.*

de-sert[1] (dẹ-zėrt′), *n.* [OF. *deserte,* < *deservir:* see *deserve.*] The fact of deserving; worthiness of reward or punishment; merit or demerit; a ground for reward or punishment; sometimes, the fact of deserving well; merit; a virtue; also, that which is deserved; a due reward or punishment.

des-ert[2] (dez′ėrt). [OF. *desert* (F. *désert*), < L. *desertus* (as n., *desertum,* neut.), pp. of *deserere,* abandon, forsake, desert, lit. 'undo one's connection with,' < *de-* (see *de-*) + *serere,* join: cf. *series.*] **I.** *a.* Abandoned or deserted (archaic: sometimes pron. dẹ-zėrt′); also, uninhabited or desolate; uncultivated, waste, or barren; of, pertaining to, or of the nature of a desert. **II.** *n.* An uninhabited and uncultivated region; esp., an arid, uninhabitable region of considerable extent, with scanty vegetation (as, the *desert* of Sahara).

de-sert[3] (dẹ-zėrt′), *v.* [F. *déserter*, < ML. *desertare*, freq. of L. *deserere*, abandon, forsake: see *desert*[2].] **I.** *tr.* To abandon or forsake; relinquish; depart from; esp., to forsake or leave in violation of duty; of a soldier or sailor, to run away from (the service, a post of duty, etc.). **II.** *intr.* To forsake one's duty, etc.; of a soldier or sailor, to quit the service without permission; run away.—**de-sert′er,** *n.* One who deserts; esp., a soldier or sailor who deserts from the service.—**de-ser′tion** (-zėr′shọn), *n.* [LL. *desertio(n-)*, < L. *deserere.*] The act of deserting, esp. in violation of duty or obligation; abandonment; also, the state of being deserted; desolation; in *law*, wilful abandonment, esp. of one's wife or husband, in violation of legal or moral obligation.

de-sert-less (dẹ-zėrt′les), *a.* Without desert or merit; undeserving: as, "O miserable and *desertless* that I am" (Swinburne's "Bothwell," i. 5).

de-serve (dẹ-zėrv′), *v.*; *-served, -serving.* [OF. *deservir*, *desservir*, < ML. *deservire*, deserve, L. serve zealously, < L. *de-* (see *de-*) + *servire*, E. *serve.*] **I.** *tr.* To acquire or earn by serving or by good or bad actions or qualities (archaic); now, to have a just claim or right to (reward, esteem, etc.) through having served, or in return for good actions or qualities; merit (punishment, disesteem, etc.) in return for bad actions or qualities; also, to serve†, or serve well†. **II.** *intr.* To be worthy of recompense.—**de-serv′ed-ly,** *adv.*—**de-serv′er,** *n.*—**de-serv′ing,** *p. a.* That deserves; esp., worthy of reward or praise; meritorious.—**de-serv′ing-ly,** *adv.*—**de-serv′ing-ness,** *n.*

des-ha-bille (dez-ạ-bēl′), *n.* See *dishabille.*

des-ic-cant (des′i-kạnt). **I.** *a.* Desiccating or drying, as a medicinal substance. **II.** *n.* A desiccant substance or agent.

des-ic-cate (des′i-kāt), *v.*; *-cated, -cating.* [L. *desiccatus*, pp. of *desiccare*, < *de-* (see *de-*) + *siccare*, make dry, < *siccus*, dry.] **I.** *tr.* To dry thoroughly; dry up; specif., to deprive (food, etc.) of moisture, as for preservation. **II.** *intr.* To become dried up; dry.—**des-ic-ca′tion** (-kā′shọn), *n.*—**des′ic-ca-tive** (-kạ-tiv), **des′ic-ca-to-ry** (-kạ-tọ-ri), *a.* Tending to desiccate or dry; desiccant.—**des′ic-ca-tor** (-kā-tọr), *n.* One who or that which desiccates; an apparatus for drying fruit, milk, etc., or for absorbing the moisture present in a chemical substance, etc.

de-sid-er-a-ta (dẹ-sid-ẹ-rā′tạ or dẹ-zid-), *n.* Plural of *desideratum.*

de-sid-er-ate (dẹ-sid′ẹ-rāt or dẹ-zid′-), *v. t.*; *-ated, -ating.* [L. *desideratus*, pp. of *desiderare*, long for, desire, appar. < *de-* (see *de-*) + *-siderare* as in *considerare*, E. *consider.*] To feel a desire for; long for; feel the want of; want: as, "For an oracle . . . he would have looked in another direction; but he *desiderated* something more on a level with himself" (J. H. Newman's "Callista," ix.).—**de-sid-er-a′tion** (-ẹ-rā′shọn), *n.* [L. *desideratio(n-)*.] The act of desiderating; longing; desire; also, a thing desired; a desideratum.—**de-sid′er-a-tive** (-ẹ-rạ-tiv). [LL. *desiderativus.*] **I.** *a.* Having or expressing desire; of or pertaining to desire; in *gram.*, of a secondary verb, expressing desire to do the action implied in the primitive. **II.** *n.* In *gram.*, a desiderative verb.

de-sid-er-a-tum (dẹ-sid-ẹ-rā′tum or dẹ-zid-), *n.*; pl. *-erata* (-ẹ-rā′tạ). [L., neut. of *desideratus*, pp.: see *desiderate.*] Something desired; a thing wanted or needed.

de-sign (dẹ-zīn′), *v.* [F. *désigner*, designate, indicate, also obs. *dessigner*, *desseigner* (It. *disegnare*), design, plan (F. *dessiner*, draw), < L. *designare*, mark out, designate, represent, contrive, arrange, < *de*, from, + *signare*, mark, E. *sign, v.*] **I.** *tr.* To mark out, as by a sign†; indicate†; designate by a name, etc. (archaic); appoint† or nominate†; devote† or destine†; assign† or bestow†; assign in thought or intention (as, "Their mounting shot is on our sails *designed*": Dryden's "Annus Mirabilis," lx.); also, to intend, purpose, or mean (as, to *design* to do a thing; a gesture *designed* to express contempt); also, to form or conceive in the mind; contrive; plan; also, to have in view; contemplate; also, to draw the outline or figure of; prepare the preliminary sketch or the plans for (a work to be executed); plan and fashion artistically or skilfully; furnish or decorate with a design or designs. **II.** *intr.* To have intentions or purposes; also, to intend to go to, or be bound for, a place (archaic); also, to make drawings, preliminary sketches, or plans; plan and fashion a work of art, etc.; devise artistic or decorative patterns, figures, etc.—**de-sign′,** *n.* [= F. *dessein*, plan, purpose, *dessin*, drawing, sketch, pattern, design.] Intention, purpose, or aim; also, a plan conceived in the mind; a project; a scheme; sometimes, a hostile plan, or evil, crafty, or selfish intention; also, the object of a plan or purpose; the end in view; also, adaptation of means to a preconceived end; contrivance; sometimes, crafty scheming (archaic); also, an outline, sketch, or plan, as of a work of art, an edifice, or a machine to be executed or constructed; also, the combination of details or features of a picture, building, etc.; the pattern or device of artistic work; also, a thing artistically designed; a piece of artistic work; also, the art of designing (as, a school of *design*).

des-ig-nate (dez′ig-nāt or des′-), *v. t.*; *-nated, -nating.* [L. *designatus*, pp. of *designare*, mark out, indicate, appoint: see *design.*] To mark or point out; indicate; show; specify; also, to name, entitle, or style; also, to serve as an indication or name of; also, to nominate or select for a duty, office, etc.; appoint; assign; set apart.—**des′ig-nate,** *a.* Designated, as to an office; nominated or appointed to an office, but not yet installed.—**des-ig-na′tion** (-nā′shọn), *n.* [L. *designatio(n-)*.] The act of designating, or the fact of being designated; also, that which designates; an indication; a descriptive name or appellation; a statement of profession, trade, etc., added to a person's name for purposes of identification.—**des′ig-na-tive** (-nạ-tiv), **des′ig-na-to-ry** (-nạ-tọ-ri), *a.* Serving to designate.—**des′ig-na-tor** (-nā-tọr), *n.*

de-sign-ed-ly (dẹ-zī′ned-li), *adv.* By design; purposely.

de-sign-er (dẹ-zī′nėr), *n.* One who designs; a contriver; a schemer or intriguer; one who makes designs, as for works of art, machines, etc.; one who devises artistic or decorative patterns, etc.

de-sign-ing (dẹ-zī′ning), *p. a.* Scheming; artful.—**de-sign′ing-ly,** *adv.*

de-sign-less (dẹ-zīn′les), *a.* Without design, plan, or purpose.

de-sign-ment† (dẹ-zīn′mẹnt), *n.* Designation; design.

de-sil-ver-ize (dē-sil′vėr-īz), *v. t.*; *-ized, -izing.* [See *de-*.] To remove the silver from.—**de-sil″ver-i-za′tion** (-i-zā′shọn), *n.*

des-i-nence (des′i-nẹns), *n.* [F. *désinence*, < L. *desinere* (pp. *desitus*), < *de*, from, + *sinere*, let.] Termination or ending, as of a line of verse; in *gram.*, a termination, ending, or suffix of a word.

de-sip-i-ent (dẹ-sip′i-ẹnt), *a.* [L. *desipiens* (*-ent-*), ppr. of *desipere*, be foolish, < *de-* (see *de-*) + *sapere*, be wise.] Fooling; indulging in playful trifling.—**de-sip′i-ence,** *n.*

de-sir-a-ble (dẹ-zīr′ạ-bl). **I.** *a.* Worthy to be desired; pleasing, excellent, or fine. **II.** *n.* One who or that which is desirable.—**de-sir-a-bil′i-ty** (-bil′i-ti), **de-sir′a-ble-ness,** *n.*—**de-sir′a-bly,** *adv.*

de-sire (dẹ-zīr′), *v.*; *-sired, -siring.* [OF. *desirer* (F. *désirer*), < L. *desiderare*: see *desiderate.*] **I.** *tr.* To wish or long for; crave; want; also, to need† or require†; also, to feel the loss of, miss, or regret (archaic); also, to express a wish to obtain, ask for, or request; make a request to (a person); invite† or summon† (as, "I would *desire* My famous cousin to our Grecian tents": Shakspere's "Troilus and Cressida," iv. 5. 150). **II.** *intr.* To have or feel a desire.—**de-sire′,** *n.* [OF. *desir* (F. *désir*).] The fact or state of desiring; a longing or craving; a wish; specif., sensual appetite; lust; also, an expressed wish; a request; also, something desired.—**de-sir′er,** *n.*—**de-sir′ous,** *a.* [OF. *desiros* (F. *désireux*).] Having or characterized by desire; desiring; also, desirable†.—**de-sir′ous-ly,** *adv.*—**de-sir′ous-ness,** *n.*

de-sist (dẹ-zist′ or -sist′), *v. i.* [L. *desistere*, < *de*, from, + *sistere*, stand.] To cease, as from some action or proceeding; stop.—**de-sist′ance, de-sist′ence,** *n.*

de-si-tion (dẹ-sish′ọn), *n.* [L. *desinere* (pp. *desitus*): see *desinence.*] Cessation of being; ending.

desk (desk), *n.* [ME. *deske* = It. *desco*, < ML. *discus*, table (see *dais*), L. discus, disk, dish: see *discus.*] A table, stand, or case in various forms, for supporting paper in writing or a book, etc., in reading, in some forms provided with drawers, pigeonholes, etc.; specif., a frame for supporting a book from which the service is read in a church; sometimes, a pulpit.

des-man (des′mạn), *n.*; pl. *-mans.* [Sw. *desman*, musk.] Either of two aquatic, insectivorous, rat-like mammals, *Myogale moschata*, of southeastern Russia, and *M. pyrenaica*, of the Pyrenees.

Desman (*Myogale moschata*).

des-mid (des′mid), *n.* [NL. *Desmidium*, the typical genus, < Gr. δεσμός, band, chain: see *desmoid.*] Any of the microscopic fresh-water algæ constituting the family *Desmidiaceæ.*

des-moid (des′moid), *a.* [Gr. δεσμός, band, chain, ligament, also δέσμη, bundle, both < δεῖν, bind: see *-oid.*] In *anat.*, resembling a ligament; ligamentous; in *pathol.*, resembling a bundle (applied to certain fibrous tumors).

des-o-late (des′ọ-lāt), *v. t.*; *-lated, -lating.* [L. *desolatus*, pp. of *desolare*, leave alone, forsake, < *de-* (see *de-*) + *solus*, alone.] To forsake or abandon; hence, to render disconsolate; also, to deprive of inhabitants; depopulate; also, to make unfit for habitation; lay waste; devastate. —**des′o-late** (-lạt), *a.* Left alone; forsaken; lonely; hence, miserable or disconsolate; also, deprived or destitute of inhabitants; deserted; hence, dreary or dismal; also, barren or waste; devastated; also, deprived, destitute, or devoid (*of*).—**des′o-late-ly,** *adv.*—**des′o-late-ness,** *n.*—**des-o-la′tion** (-lā′shọn), *n.* [LL. *desolatio*(*n*-).] The act of desolating, or the state of being desolated; deprivation of companionship or comfort; loneliness; disconsolateness; depopulation or devastation; dreariness; barrenness; ruin; also, a desolate place.—**des′o-la-tor,** *n.*

de-spair (dẹ-spãr′), *v.* [OF. *desperer*, < L. *desperare*, < *de-* (see *de-*) + *sperare*, hope.] **I.** *intr.* To lose or give up hope; be without hope. **II.** *tr.* To deprive of hope†; give up hope of (archaic).—**de-spair′,** *n.* Loss of hope; a state of mind in which one is without hope; hopelessness; also, something causing loss of hope, esp. as being without remedy or unattainable.—**de-spair′er,** *n.*—**de-spair′ful,** *a.* Full of despair; despairing.—**de-spair′ful-ly,** *adv.*—**de-spair′ing-ly,** *adv.*

des-patch, dis-patch (des-pach′, dis-pach′), *v.* [Appar. < Sp. *despachar* or It. *dispacciare*, despatch, prob. < L. *dis-* (see *dis-*) + *pactus*, pp. of *pangere*, fasten, fix.] **I.** *tr.* To send (a messenger, letter, etc.) to a destination with haste or expedition; in general, to send off, or put under way; also, to dismiss (a person), as after an audience or conference; also, to get rid of by putting to death; kill; also, to transact or dispose of (business, etc.) promptly or speedily; execute quickly; settle; also, to eat up or consume (food: colloq.); also, to rid or free (a person, etc.) of an encumbrance, etc.†; deprive† (as, "Thus was I, sleeping, by a brother's hand Of life . . . *dispatch'd*": Shakspere's "Hamlet," i. 5. 75). **II.** *intr.* To hasten away†; make haste (archaic); conclude or dispose of an affair†.—**des-patch′, dis-patch′,** *n.* The act of despatching; the sending off of a messenger, letter, etc., to a destination; dismissal of a person after the transaction of his business; a getting rid of by putting to death; prompt or speedy transaction, as of business; expeditious performance, promptitude, or speed (as, "Our orders were to proceed with all possible *despatch*": Marryat's "Peter Simple," lii.); also, a written message sent with expedition, esp. an official communication sent by special messenger; a telegram; also, a conveyance or organization for the expeditious transmission of merchandise, etc.—**des-patch′er, dis-patch′er,** *n.*

des-pe-ra-do (des-pẹ-rā′dō), *n.*; pl. *-does* or *-dos* (-dōz). [Cf. OSp. *desperado*, desperate, < L. *desperatus*: see *desperate.*] A person in despair, or in a desperate condition†; also, a desperate or reckless man; one ready for any desperate deed.

des-pe-rate (des′pẹ-rạt), *a.* [L. *desperatus*, pp. of *desperare*: see *despair.*] Having no hope (archaic); indicating hopelessness or despair (archaic); also, leaving little or no hope (as, a *desperate* case); very serious or dangerous; hopeless; also, reckless from despair; heedless of safety; ready to run any risk; also, characterized by the recklessness of despair, as actions, etc.; violent; also, extremely bad; extreme or excessive.—**des′pe-rate-ly,** *adv.*—**des′pe-rate-ness,** *n.*—**des-pe-ra′tion** (-rā′shọn), *n.* [L. *desperatio*(*n*-).] The act or fact of despairing; despair; hopelessness; also, the state of being desperate; the recklessness of despair.

des-pi-ca-ble (des′pi-kạ-bl), *a.* [LL. *despicabilis*, < L. *despicari*, despise, < *despicere*: see *despise.*] That is to be despised; contemptible.—**des″pi-ca-bil′i-ty** (-bil′i-ti), **des′pi-ca-ble-ness,** *n.*—**des′pi-ca-bly,** *adv.*

de-spise (dẹ-spīz′), *v. t.*; *-spised, -spising.* [OF. *despire* (*despis-*), < L. *despicere*, look down upon, despise, < *de*, down from, + *specere*, look at.] To look down upon, as in contempt; scorn; disdain; also, to show contempt for†. —**de-spis′a-ble** (-spī′zạ-bl), *a.*—**de-spis′er,** *n.*

de-spite (dẹ-spīt′), *n.* [OF. *despit* (F. *dépit*), < L. *despectus*, a looking down upon, < *despicere*: see *despise*, and cf. *spite.*] Contempt or scorn (archaic); indignation or resentment (archaic); malice, hatred, or spite; also, contemptuous treatment; insult; outrage; an insult or injury; also, disregard of opposition; defiance.—**in despite of,** in contempt or defiance of; in spite of; notwithstanding. —**de-spite′,** *prep.* [Short for *in despite of.*] In spite of; notwithstanding: as, "I love him still, *despite* my wrongs" (Scott's "Lady of the Lake," ii. 32).—**de-spite′,** *v. t.*; *-spited, -spiting.* [OF. *despiter* (F. *dépiter*), < *despit.*] To regard or treat with contempt (archaic); also, to offend†; vex†; spite†.—**de-spite′ful,** *a.* Full of despite; contemptuous; malicious or spiteful. [Archaic.]—**de-spite′ful-ly,** *adv.*—**de-spite′ful-ness,** *n.*

des-pit-e-ous (des-pit′ẹ-us), *a.* [For earlier *despitous*, < OF. *despitous*, < *despit*, E. *despite, n.*] Contemptuous; also, malicious; spiteful. [Archaic.]—**des-pit′e-ous-ly,** *adv.*

de-spoil (dẹ-spoil′), *v. t.* [OF. *despoillier* (F. *dépouiller*), < L. *despoliare* (pp. *despoliatus*), < *de-* (see *de-*) + *spoliare*, E. *spoil, v.*] To strip of possessions; rob; plunder; pillage; also, to undress†.—**de-spoil′er,** *n.*—**de-spoil′ment,** *n.* Despoliation.

de-spo-li-a-tion (dẹ-spō-li-ā′shọn), *n.* [LL. *despoliatio*(*n*-), < L. *despoliare*: see *despoil.*] The act of despoiling, or the fact of being despoiled.

de-spond (dẹ-spond′), *v. i.* [L. *despondere*, promise, give up, lose (heart), < *de*, from, + *spondere*, promise.] To lose heart, courage, or hope; become or be depressed or dejected from loss of courage or hope.—**de-spond′,** *n.* Despondency. [Archaic.]—**Slough of Despond.** See under *slough*[1].—**de-spond′ence,** *n.* Despondency.—**de-spond′en-cy,** *n.* A being despondent; depression of spirits from loss of courage or hope; dejection.—**de-spond′ent,** *a.* Desponding; depressed or dejected.—**de-spond′ent-ly,** *adv.* —**de-spond′er,** *n.*—**de-spond′ing-ly,** *adv.*

des-pot (des′pot or -pọt), *n.* [Gr. δεσπότης, master, lord: see *potent.*] Master or lord (used in Byzantine times as a title of the emperor and also, as in later times, of certain other persons of rank or office); also, an absolute ruler; an autocrat; hence, a tyrannical ruler; a tyrant or oppressor. —**des-pot′ic** (-pot′ik), *a.* [Gr. δεσποτικός.] Of, pertaining to, or of the nature of a despot or despotism; autocratic; arbitrary; tyrannical.—**des-pot′i-cal-ly,** *adv.*—**des′pot-ism** (-pọt-izm), *n.* The rule of a despot; the exercise of absolute authority; hence, absolute power or control; tyranny; also, an absolute or autocratic government; a country ruled by a despot.—**des′pot-ize,** *v. i.*; *-ized, -izing.* To rule or act as a despot.

de-spu-mate (dẹ-spū′māt or des′pụ-), *v.*; *-mated, -mating.* [L. *despumatus*, pp. of *despumare*, < *de-* (see *de-*) + *spuma* foam.] **I.** *tr.* To free from froth or scum; skim; clarify by removing the froth or scum; also, to throw off in or as froth. **II.** *intr.* To throw off froth, scum, or impurities. —**des-pu-ma-tion** (des-pụ-mā′shọn), *n.*

des-qua-mate (des′kwạ-māt), *v. i.*; *-mated, -mating.* [L. *desquamatus*, pp. of *desquamare*, < *de-* (see *de-*) + *squama*, scale.] To come off in scales, as the epidermis in certain diseases; scale or peel off.—**des-qua-ma′tion** (-mā′shọn), *n.* The process of desquamating; that which comes off in scales.—**des-quam′a-tive** (-kwam′ạ-tiv), **des-quam′a-to-ry** (-tọ̄-ri), *a.* Pertaining to or characterized by desquamation.

des-sert (de-zėrt′), *n.* [F. *dessert*, < *desservir*, clear the table, < *des-* (see *dis-*) + *servir*, < L. *servire*, serve.] A course of fruits, sweetmeats, etc., at the close of a repast: in the U. S. often used to include pies, puddings, etc.—**des-sert′=spoon,** *n.* A spoon intermediate in size between a tablespoon and a teaspoon.—**des-sert′=spoon″ful** (-fụl), *n.*; pl. *-fuls.*

des-ti-na-tion (des-ti-nā′shọn), *n.* [L. *destinatio(n-).*] The act of destining, or the fact of being destined; also, the purpose for which anything is destined; ultimate end or design; also, the place for which a person or thing is destined; the predetermined end of a journey or voyage; the goal.

des-tine (des′tin), *v. t.*; *-tined, -tining.* [OF. F. *destiner*, < L. *destinare* (pp. *destinatus*), make fast, establish, appoint, < *de-* (see *de-*) + *-stinare*, akin to *stare*, stand: cf. *obstinate.*] To appoint or ordain beforehand, as by divine decree; foreordain; predetermine; also, to set apart for a particular use, purpose, etc.; design; intend; also, in the passive, to be bound for a certain place.—**des′tined,** *p. a.* Foreordained or predetermined; designed or intended; bound for a certain destination.

des-ti-ny (des′ti-ni), *n.*; pl. *-nies* (-niz). [OF. *destinee* (F. *destinée*), < L. *destinata*, fem. of *destinatus*, pp. of *destinare*: see *destine.*] That which is destined or predetermined to happen; the predetermined course of events; fate; also, that which is to happen to a particular person or thing; one's lot or fortune; what will become, or has become, of a person or thing; also, the power or agency which determines the course of events; overruling necessity; [*cap.*] this power personified or represented as a goddess; *pl.*, the Fates.

des-ti-tute (des′ti-tūt), *a.* [L. *destitutus*, pp. of *destituere*, put away, abandon, forsake, < *de*, from, + *statuere*, set up, set: see *statute.*] Abandoned† or deserted†; left friendless†; also, deprived or devoid of something specified; often, bereft of means or resources; lacking the means of subsistence.—**des′ti-tute-ness,** *n.*

des-ti-tu-tion (des-ti-tū′shọn), *n.* [L. *destitutio(n-)*, < *destituere*: see *destitute.*] Abandonment† or desertion†; also, deprivation of or dismissal from office; deprivation, want, or absence of anything specified; now, usually, want of the means of subsistence; utter poverty; destitute condition.

des-tri-er (des′tri-ėr or des-trēr′), *n.* [ME. *destrier, destrer*, < OF. *destrier*, < ML. *dextrarius*, lit. '(horse) led at the right hand,' < L. *dexter*, right.] A war-horse; a charger: as, "I would crave of thee the use of some palfrey whose pace may be softer than that of my *destrier*" (Scott's "Ivanhoe," xl.). [Archaic.]

de-stroy (dē̦-stroi′), *v. t.* [OF. *destruire* (F. *détruire*), < L. *destruere* (pp. *destructus*), pull down, destroy, < *de-* (see *de-*) + *struere*, pile up, build.] To pull down (a structure); raze; demolish; also, to lay waste† or ravage†; also, to reduce to pieces or to a useless form; ruin or spoil; consume; also, to put an end to; annihilate; extinguish; often, to deprive of life; kill; slay; also, to render ineffective; nullify; invalidate.—**de-stroy′a-ble,** *a.* That may be destroyed.—**de-stroy′er,** *n.* One who or that which destroys; specif., a torpedo-boat destroyer (see under *torpedo-boat*).—**de-stroy′ing-ly,** *adv.*

de-struc-ti-ble (dē̦-struk′ti-bl), *a.* [LL. *destructibilis.*] That may be destroyed; liable to destruction.—**de-struc-ti-bil′i-ty** (-bil′i-ti), **de-struc′ti-ble-ness,** *n.*

de-struc-tion (dē̦-struk′shọn), *n.* [L. *destructio(n-).*] The act of destroying, or the fact or condition of being destroyed; demolition; ruin; annihilation; slaughter; also, a cause or means of destroying.—**de-struc′tion-ist,** *n.* One who engages in or favors destruction; esp., an advocate of the destruction of an existing political institution or the like.

de-struc-tive (dē̦-struk′tiv), *a.* [LL. *destructivus.*] Tending to destroy; causing destruction; demolishing; ruinous; annihilating; refuting or disproving: as, *destructive* criticism (criticism that tends to overthrow, disprove, or discredit).—**destructive distillation.** See *distillation.*—**de-struc′tive-ly,** *adv.*—**de-struc′tive-ness,** *n.*

de-struc-tor (dē̦-struk′tọr), *n.* [LL.] A destroyer; a furnace for the burning of refuse.

des-u-da-tion (des-ụ̄-dā′shọn), *n.* [LL. *desudatio(n-)*, < L. *desudare*, sweat greatly, < *de-* (see *de-*) + *sudare*, sweat.] In *med.*, a profuse or morbid sweating.

des-ue-tude (des′wē̦-tūd), *n.* [L. *desuetudo*, < *desuescere* (pp. *desuetus*), disuse, < *de-* (see *de-*) + *suescere*, become used, accustom.] Discontinuance of the use or practice of anything†; also, the state of being no longer used or practised; the state of disuse.

de-sul-phu-rize (dē-sul′fụ̄-rīz), *v. t.*; *-rized, -rizing.* [See *de-.*] To free from sulphur, as an ore.—**de-sul″phu-ri-za′tion** (-ri-zā′shọn), *n.*

des-ul-to-ry (des′ul-tọ̄-ri), *a.* [L. *desultorius*, < *desultor*, leaper, vaulter, < *desilire*, leap down, < *de*, down from, + *salire*, leap.] Leaping or skipping about (obs. or archaic); shifting irregularly in course (often fig.); veering about from one thing to another; disconnected, unmethodical, or fitful, as reading, study, or conversation; random, as a thought.—**des′ul-to-ri-ly,** *adv.*—**des′ul-to-ri-ness,** *n.*

de-sy-non-y-mize (dē-si-non′i-mīz), *v. t.*; *-mized, -mizing.* [See *de-.*] To deprive (words) of synonymous character; differentiate in meaning.—**de-sy-non″y-mi-za′tion** (-mi-zā′shọn), *n.*

de-tach (dē̦-tach′), *v.* [F. *détacher*, OF. *destachier*, < *des-* (see *dis-*) + *-tachier* as in *atachier*, E. *attach.*] **I.** *tr.* To unfasten and separate; disengage; disunite; specif., to separate, as a number of troops from a main body, for a special purpose; send away (a regiment, ship, etc.) on a special mission. **II.** *intr.* To become detached or separated.—**de-tach′a-ble,** *a.* Capable of being detached.—**de-tach-a-bil′i-ty** (-bil′i-ti), *n.*—**de-tached′,** *p. a.* Separated or disengaged; separate; unattached; standing apart.—**de-tach′er,** *n.*—**de-tach′ment,** *n.* The act of detaching, or the condition of being detached; separation; disengagement; a state of aloofness, as from worldly affairs, or from the concerns of others; also, something detached, as a number of troops separated from a main body for special service.

de-tail (dē̦-tāl′), *v. t.* [F. *détailler*, cut in pieces, retail, detail, < *dé-* (see *de-*) + *tailler*, cut: see *tail*[1].] To deal with or treat part by part; set forth fully and circumstantially; enumerate or mention separately; also, to tell off or appoint for a special service, as a troop, an officer, etc.—**de-tail** (dē̦-tāl′ or dē′tāl), *n.* [F. *détail.*] A dealing with or treating part by part or item by item; full and circumstantial treatment, as in narration; also, a minute or circumstantial account (as, "I entreated him to be explicit, and to give me a *detail* of what he had heard and what he had seen": C. B. Brown's "Wieland," xiii.); a narrative or report of particulars; also, an individual part, as of a complex whole; an item or particular; a minute part or circumstance; often, particulars collectively; minutiæ; specif., one of the smaller or subordinate parts of a work of art, building, machine, etc., or such parts collectively; a drawing of a part of a building, machine, etc., with dimensions or other information for use in construction, or such drawings collectively; also, the distribution of duties, as of the members of a military force; a list showing such distribution; a particular assignment of duty; also, a detailing or telling off, as of a small force or an officer, for a special service; the party or person so detailed.—**de-tailed′,** *p. a.* Treated in or with detail; full of details; particularized; minute.—**de-tailed′ness,** *n.*—**de-tail′er,** *n.*

de-tain (dē̦-tān′), *v. t.* [OF. *detenir* (F. *détenir*), < L. *detinere* (pp. *detentus*), hold off, keep back, detain, < *de*, from, + *tenere*, hold.] To keep back or withhold, as from a person; also, to keep from proceeding; keep waiting; delay; often, to keep under restraint or in custody.—**de-tain′er**[1], *n.* One who or that which detains.—**de-tain′er**[2], *n.* [AF. *detener*, inf., OF. *detenir.*] In *law*, the detaining or keeping possession of what belongs to another; also, the detaining of a person in custody; a writ for the further detention of a person already in custody.—**de-tain'ing-ly,** *adv.*—**de-tain'ment,** *n.* Detention.

de-tect (dę-tekt'), *v. t.* [L. *detectus*, pp. of *detegere*, uncover, discover, < *de-* (see *de-*) + *tegere*, cover.] To uncover†; also, to expose†; inform against†; accuse†; also, to discover or catch (a person) in the performance of some act; find out the action or character of (as, to *detect* a hypocrite); also, to bring to light; discover the presence, existence, or fact of; specif., in *wireless teleg.* and *teleph.*, to subject to the action of a detector (see *detector*).—**de-tect'a-ble, de-tect'i-ble,** *a.* That may be detected.

de-tec-ta-phone (dę-tek'tą-fōn), *n.* [See *detect* and *-phone.*] A sensitive telephonic device used to transmit conversations, as of persons under suspicion, so that they may be heard in another room or place. [Proprietary name, registered as *detecta phone.*]

de-tect-er (dę-tek'tėr), *n.* One who or that which detects.

de-tec-tion (dę-tek'shǫn), *n.* [LL. *detectio(n-).*] The act of detecting, or the fact of being detected; discovery, as of error or crime.

de-tec-tive (dę-tek'tiv). **I.** *a.* Serving to detect; having the function of detecting; also, pertaining to detection or detectives (as, a *detective* story). **II.** *n.* A member of the police force whose function it is secretly to obtain information and evidence, as of offenses against the law; also, a person employed unofficially by individuals for secret investigations, protection, etc.

de-tec-tor (dę-tek'tǫr), *n.* [LL.] One who or that which detects; any of various instruments or devices for indicating the presence or the state of a thing; in *wireless teleg.* and *teleph.*, a device for detecting electric oscillations or waves; specif., a device (as a crystal detector or a vacuum-tube) which rectifies the alternating currents in a radio receiver.

det-en-ee (det-e-nē'), *n.* [Made word.] A person confined in a detention camp.

de-tent (dę-tent'), *n.* [F. *détente*, < *détendre*, relax, < *dé-* (see *dis-*) + *tendre*, < L. *tendere*, stretch, E. *tend*[1].] A piece of a mechanism which when disengaged releases the operating power, or by which the action is prevented or checked; a catch, as in a lock; a pawl.

de-ten-tion (dę-ten'shǫn), *n.* [LL. *detentio(n-)*, < *detinere*: see *detain.*] The act of detaining, or the state of being detained; the withholding of what belongs to or is claimed by another; a keeping from proceeding; forced stoppage; a keeping in custody; confinement.

dé-tenu (dāt-nü), *n.* [F. (fem. *détenue*), prop. pp. of *détenir*: see *detain.*] One detained in custody; a prisoner.

de-ter (dę-tėr'), *v. t.*; *-terred, -terring.* [L. *deterrere*, < *de*, from, + *terrere*, frighten.] To discourage and stop by fear; restrain from acting or proceeding by any discouraging or countervailing means: as, "Do not seek to *deter* me from my purpose" (Johnson's "Rasselas," xii.).

de-terge (dę-tėrj'), *v. t.*; *-terged, -terging.* [L. *detergere* (pp. *detersus*), < *de*, from, + *tergere*, wipe.] To wipe away; also, to cleanse by removing foul or morbid matter, as a wound.—**de-ter'gent** (-tėr'jęnt). **I.** *a.* Cleansing; clearing away foul matter, as a medicinal substance. **II.** *n.* A detergent substance or agent.—**de-ter'gen-cy,** *n.*

de-te-ri-o-rate (dę-tē'ri-ǫ-rāt), *v. t.* or *i.*; *-rated, -rating.* [LL. *deterioratus*, pp. of *deteriorare*, < L. *deterior*, worse, compar. adj. < *de-*, down: see *de-.*] To make or become worse; make or become lower in character or quality.—**de-te''ri-o-ra'tion** (-rā'shǫn), *n.* The act or process of deteriorating, or the state of having deteriorated.—**de-te'ri-o-ra-tive** (-rą-tiv), *a.* Tending to deteriorate.—**de-te'ri-o-ra-tor** (-rā-tǫr), *n.*

de-ter-ment (dę-tėr'męnt), *n.* The act of deterring; also, something that deters; a deterrent.

de-ter-mi-na-ble (dę-tėr'mi-ną-bl), *a.* [LL. *determinabilis.*] Capable of being determined.

de-ter-mi-nant (dę-tėr'mi-nąnt). [L. *determinans* (*-ant-*), ppr.] **I.** *a.* Determining. **II.** *n.* Something that determines; a determining agent or factor; in *math.*, the sum of all the products which can be formed according to special laws from a certain number of quantities arranged in a square block; in *biol.*, a hypothetical unit of germ-plasm, regarded as an aggregation of biophores, concerned in the transmission of hereditary qualities.

de-ter-mi-nate (dę-tėr'mi-nąt), *a.* [L. *determinatus*, pp.] Having defined limits; fixed; definite; also, settled or positive; also, determined upon; conclusive; final; also, determined or resolute; in *bot.*, of an inflorescence, having the primary and each secondary axis ending in a flower or bud, thus preventing further elongation.—**de-ter'mi-nate-ly,** *adv.*—**de-ter'mi-nate-ness,** *n.*

de-ter-mi-na-tion (dę-tėr-mi-nā'shǫn), *n.* [L. *determinatio(n-).*] The act of determining, or the state of being determined; the setting of bounds or limits; conclusion or termination (archaic except in legal use); the settlement of a dispute, etc., by authoritative decision; the decision arrived at or pronounced; a fixing or settling definitely of the amount, character, etc., of anything; ascertainment, as after observation or investigation; a result ascertained; a solution; also, fixed direction or tendency, as of the blood toward a particular part, or of the intellect or will toward some object or end; also, the mental act of coming to a decision; the fixing or settling of a purpose; a fixed purpose or intention; also, the quality of being determined or resolute; firmness of purpose; in *logic*, the rendering of a notion more definite by the addition of differentiating characters; also, a differentiating character added.

de-ter-mi-na-tive (dę-tėr'mi-ną-tiv). **I.** *a.* Serving to determine; determining, fixing, or deciding. **II.** *n.* Something that determines.—**de-ter'mi-na-tive-ly,** *adv.*—**de-ter'mi-na-tive-ness,** *n.*

de-ter-mine (dę-tėr'min), *v.*; *-mined, -mining.* [L. *determinare* (pp. *determinatus*), bound, limit, prescribe, fix, < *de-* (see *de-*) + *terminare*, bound, limit, E. *terminate.*] **I.** *tr.* To set limits to† or bound†; limit, as an idea, by adding differentiating characters; also, to put an end to, conclude, or terminate (now chiefly legal); also, to settle or decide (a dispute, question, etc.) by an authoritative decision; in general, to fix or settle definitely; also, to decide upon; also, to conclude from reasoning or investigation; ascertain definitely, as after observation, investigation, etc.; also, to direct to an end; give direction or tendency to; impel; also, to lead or bring (a person) to a decision; in *geom.*, to fix the position of. **II.** *intr.* To come to an end (now chiefly legal); also, to come to a decision or resolution; decide; also, to take a course to a definite point or end (archaic).—**de-ter'mined,** *p. a.* Characterized by determination or firmness of purpose (as, "She is a lady of very *determined* character": G. B. Shaw's "Fanny's First Play," iii.); resolute; unflinching.—**de-ter'mined-ly,** *adv.*—**de-ter'mined-ness,** *n.*—**de-ter'min-er,** *n.*—**de-ter'min-ism,** *n.* The doctrine that human actions are not free, but the necessary result of antecedent psychological and other conditions; also, the doctrine that whatever is or happens is determined by antecedent causes.—**de-ter'min-ist,** *n.*—**de-ter-min-is'tic,** *a.*

de-ter-rent (dę-tėr'ęnt or dę-ter'-). **I.** *a.* Deterring; restraining. **II.** *n.* Something that deters.—**de-ter'rence,** *n.*—**de-ter'rent-ly,** *adv.*

de-ter-sion (dę-tėr'shǫn), *n.* [LL. *detersio(n-)*, < L. *detergere*: see *deterge.*] Detergent action; a cleansing, as of a sore.—**de-ter'sive** (-siv). **I.** *a.* Detergent; cleansing. **II.** *n.* A detersive agent or medicine.

de-test (dę-test'), *v. t.* [L. *detestari*, curse while calling a deity to witness, execrate, < *de-* (see *de-*) + *testari*, bear witness, call to witness, < *testis*, a witness.] To curse or denounce solemnly†; also, to feel abhorrence of; hate; dislike intensely.—**de-test'a-ble,** *a.* To be detested; abominable; execrable; hateful; odious.—**de-test-a-bil'i-ty** (-bil'i-ti), **de-test'a-ble-ness,** *n.*—**de-test'a-bly,** *adv.*—**de-tes-ta-tion** (dē-tes-tā'shǫn), *n.* [L. *detestatio(n-).*] The act or feeling of detesting; abhorrence; hatred; also, the object of such feeling.—**de-test'er,** *n.*

de-throne (dę-thrōn'), *v. t.*; *-throned, -throning.* [See *de-.*] To remove from the throne; depose.—**de-throne'ment,** *n.* Removal, as of a sovereign, from the throne; deposition.—**de-thron'er** (-thrō'nėr), *n.*

de-tin (dē-tin'), *v. t.*; *-tinned, -tinning.* [See *de-.*] To remove the tin from (articles plated with tin).

det-i-nue (det′i-nū), *n.* [OF. *detenue*, detention, orig. pp. fem. of *detenir*, E. *detain.*] In *law*, the unlawful detention of personal property, or an action to recover the property so detained.

det-o-nate (det′ọ-nāt or dē′tọ-), *v.*; *-nated*, *-nating.* [L. *detonatus*, pp. of *detonare*, thunder forth, < *de*, from, + *tonare*, thunder.] **I.** *intr.* To explode, esp. with great noise; specif., to explode suddenly and violently because of extremely rapid decomposition or change. **II.** *tr.* To cause to explode, esp. with great noise or with suddenness and violence; cause (an explosive, as gunpowder) to explode by exploding a small amount of another explosive, as a fulminate, in contact with it.—**det′o-na-ble** (-nạ-bl), *a.*—**det-o-na′tion** (-nā′shọn), *n.* The act of detonating; an explosion, esp. one which produces a great noise, or which involves a very rapid change and is accompanied by a shattering effect; in general, a loud noise or report.—**det′o-na-tive** (-nạ-tiv), *a.* Tending to detonate; explosive; of the nature of a detonation.—**det′o-na-tor** (-nā-tọr), *n.* Something that detonates, as an explosive which produces a great noise or which acts suddenly and violently; a device, as a percussion-cap, or an explosive, used for causing another substance to explode.

de-tour (dẹ-tör′), *n.* [F. *détour*, < *détourner*, turn aside, < *dé-* (see *dis-*) + *tourner*, turn.] A turning aside from the direct road; a roundabout or circuitous way or course. Also (F.) **dé-tour** (dā-tör).

de-tox-i-cate (dē-tok′si-kāt), *v. t.*; *-cated*, *-cating.* [See *de-*.] To deprive of toxic or poisonous properties.—**de-tox-i-ca′-tion** (-kā′shọn), *n.*

de-tract (dẹ-trakt′), *v.* [L. *detractus*, pp. of *detrahere*, draw away or down, detract, < *de*, from, + *trahere*, draw.] **I.** *tr.* To draw away† or divert†; also, to take away (a part); abate; also, to disparage, belittle, or defame (now rare). **II.** *intr.* To take away a part, as from quality, value, or reputation; take away merit or reputation; speak disparagingly.—**de-tract′ing-ly,** *adv.*—**de-trac′tion** (-trak′shọn), *n.* [L. *detractio(n-)*.] The act of detracting; a taking away, as from merit or reputation; a detracting from a person's credit or reputation, as by disparaging language (as, "The first sentence . . . was, that all females addicted to censoriousness and *detraction* should lose the use of speech": Addison, in "Tatler," 102).—**de-trac′tive,** *a.* Tending or seeking to detract; depreciative.—**de-trac′tor,** *n.*—**de-trac′to-ry** (-tọ-ri), *a.* Detractive.

de-train (dē-trān′), *v. t.* or *i.* [See *de-*.] To discharge or alight from a railroad-train.

det-ri-ment (det′ri-mẹnt), *n.* [L. *detrimentum*, loss, damage, < *deterere*, rub away: see *detritus.*] Loss, damage, or injury; a cause of loss or damage.—**det-ri-men′tal** (-men′-tạl). **I.** *a.* Causing detriment; injurious; prejudicial. **II.** *n.* A person or thing prejudicial to anything; a suitor, esp. the younger brother of an heir, whose attentions are considered as injuring a young woman's chances of making a good match (Eng.).—**det-ri-men′tal-ly,** *adv.*

de-tri-tal (dẹ-trī′tạl), *a.* Pertaining to or composed of detritus.

de-trit-ed (dẹ-trī′ted), *a.* Reduced to detritus.

de-tri-tion (dẹ-trish′ọn), *n.* [L. *deterere* (pp. *detritus*): see *detritus.*] The act of wearing away by rubbing.

de-tri-tus (dẹ-trī′tus), *n.* [L. *detritus*, n., a rubbing away, < *deterere* (pp. *detritus*), rub away, < *de*, from, + *terere*, rub.] A rubbing or wearing away†; also, particles of rock or other material worn away from a mass, as by the action of water; hence, any disintegrated material; debris; also, an aggregate of fragmental material or debris.

de trop (dė trō). [F.] Too much; too many; in the way, as one whose presence is unwelcome.

de-trude (dẹ-tröd′), *v. t.*; *-truded*, *-truding.* [L. *detrudere* (pp. *detrusus*), < *de-*, away, down, + *trudere*, thrust.] To thrust out or away; expel; also, to thrust or force down.

de-trun-cate (dẹ-trung′kāt), *v. t.*; *-cated*, *-cating.* [L. *detruncatus*, pp. of *detruncare*, < *de*, from, + *truncare*: see *truncate.*] To reduce by cutting off a part; cut down.—**de-trun-ca-tion** (dē-trung-kā′shọn), *n.*

de-tru-sion (dẹ-trö′zhọn), *n.* [LL. *detrusio(n-)*.] The act of detruding.

de-tur (dē′tėr), *n.* [L., 'let there be given.'] A prize awarded annually to undergraduates in Harvard College who have attained a certain grade in the work of the preceding year and have not previously received the honor: it is in the form of a specially bound book, as on some subject in the recipient's field of study.

deuce[1] (dūs), *n.* [OF. *deus* (F. *deux*), < L. *duos*, acc. of *duo*, two.] In *cards* or *dice*, two; a card, or the side of a die, having two pips; in *lawn-tennis*, a stage of the score when each side has gained three points (or the score 40) in a game, or five games in a set, and either side must gain two more points or games in succession to win.

deuce[2] (dūs), *n.* [Prob. from LG., and ult. identical with E. *deuce*[1] (the two at dice being the lowest and worst throw).] Bad luck; the mischief; the devil: used in imprecations and exclamations, and (esp. as a substitute for *devil*) in various phrases. [Slang.]

deuce=ace (dūs′ās), *n.* [See *deuce*[1].] A low throw with two dice, of deuce and ace; hence, bad luck.

deu-ced (dū′sed or dūst), *a.* [See *deuce*[2].] Confounded; devilish; excessive. [Slang.]—**deu′ced, deu′ced-ly,** *adv.*

deu-ter-ag-o-nist (dū-tẹ-rag′ọ-nist), *n.* [Gr. δευτεραγωνιστής, < δεύτερος, second, + ἀγωνιστής, contender, actor, E. *agonist.*] In the ancient Greek drama, the character of second importance (after the *protagonist*).

deutero-. Form of Gr. δεύτερος, second, used in combination.

deu-ter-o-ca-non-i-cal (dū″tẹ-rō-kạ-non′i-kạl), *a.* [See *deutero-*.] Of or forming a second canon: as, *deuterocanonical* books (the books of the Bible other than those designated *protocanonical*: applied specif. to those books as received by the Roman Catholic Church which are regarded by it as canonical but were not universally acknowledged as such in the early church, including, in the Old Testament, most of the Protestant Apocrypha, and, in the New Testament, the antilegomena). Cf. *protocanonical.*

deu-ter-og-a-my (dū-tẹ-rog′ạ-mi), *n.* [Gr. δευτερογαμία, < δεύτερος, second, + γάμος, marriage.] A second marriage, after the death or divorce of a first husband or wife; the custom of contracting such marriages.—**deu-ter-og′a-mist,** *n.*

Deu-ter-on-o-my (dū-tẹ-ron′ọ-mi), *n.* [LL. *Deuteronomium*, < Gr. Δευτερονόμιον, < δεύτερος, second, + νόμος, law.] The fifth book of the Pentateuch: so named as containing a second statement of the law of Moses.

deu-ter-op-a-thy (dū-tẹ-rop′ạ-thi), *n.* [See *deutero-* and *-pathy.*] In *pathol.*, a secondary affection, sympathetic with or consequent upon another.

deu-ter-o-plasm (dū′tẹ-rọ-plazm), *n.* Same as *deutoplasm.*

deuto-. Shortened form of *deutero-*, second: in *chem.*, sometimes used to denote the second in a series, as in *deutoxide* (cf. *protoxide*).

deu-to-plasm (dū′tọ-plazm), *n.* [See *deuto-* and *-plasm.*] In *biol.*, that part of the yolk of an egg or ovum which furnishes food for the nourishment of the embryo.—**deu-to-plas′mic** (-plaz′mik), *a.*

deut-zi-a (dūt′si-ạ̈ or doit′si-ạ̈), *n.* [NL.; from J. *Deutz*, of Amsterdam.] Any of the shrubs constituting the saxifragaceous genus *Deutzia*, bearing panicles or corymbs of white bell-shaped flowers, much cultivated for ornament.

dev (dāv), *n.* Same as *div.*

de-va (dā′vạ̈), *n.* [Skt.] In *Hindu myth.*, a god or divinity; one of an order of good spirits.

de-val-u-ate (dē-val′ụ̄-āt), *v. t.*; *-ated*, *-ating.* To deprive of value; reduce the value of; specif., to fix a lower legal value on (a currency which has depreciated).—**de-val-u-a′-tion** (-ā′shọn), *n.*

de-val-ue (dē-val′ụ̄), *v. t.*; *-ued*, *-uing.* To devaluate.

dev-as-tate (dev′ạs-tāt), *v. t.*; *-tated*, *-tating.* [L. *devastatus*, pp. of *devastare*, < *de-* (see *de-*) + *vastare*, lay waste, < *vastus*, waste.] To lay waste; ravage; make desolate.—**dev-as-ta′tion** (-tā′shọn), *n.* The act of devastating, or the state of being devastated; ravage; desolation.—**dev′as-ta-tive,** *a.* Devastating; ravaging.—**dev′as-ta-tor,** *n.*

de-vel-op (dẹ-vel′ọp), *v.*; *-oped*, *-oping.* [Also *develope*; F. *développer*, OF. *desvoluper*, < *des-* (see *dis-*) + *voluper*, *voloper*, wrap: cf. *envelop.*] **I.** *tr.* To unwrap†; unfold† or unroll†; disclose, reveal, or make known (obs. or rare); also, to bring out the capabilities or possibilities of; bring to a more advanced or effective state; cause to grow or expand; work up in detail, or elaborate; also, to bring into being or activity; generate; evolve; hence, to exhibit or display (as, to *develop* a tendency to disregard instructions); in *geom.*, to bend (a surface) into another form; unroll or flatten out (a curved surface) into a plane; in *math.*, to express in an extended form, as in a series; in *photog.*, to render visible (the latent image in the exposed sensitized film of a photographic plate, etc.); treat (a photographic plate, etc.) with chemical agents so as to bring out the latent image. **II.** *intr.* To come out or be disclosed; also, to grow into a more mature or advanced state; advance; expand; also, to come gradually into existence or operation; be evolved; in *photog.*, to become apparent, as a photographic image; undergo developing, as a photographic plate.—**de-vel′op-a-ble,** *a.* That may be developed.—**de-vel′op-er,** *n.* One who or that which develops; esp., a chemical agent used in developing a latent photographic image.—**de-vel′op-ment,** *n.* The act of developing; an unfolding or disclosing; a bringing out of the latent capabilities of anything; a bringing or coming to a more mature, advanced, or effective state; expansion or growth; elaboration; a bringing or coming gradually into existence or activity; evolution; also, a developed state, form, or product.—**de-vel-op-men′tal** (-men′tal), *a.*

de-vest (dẹ-vest′), *v. t.* [Obs. F. *devestir* (F. *dévêtir*), OF. *desvestir*, < *des-* (see *dis-*) + *vestir*, < L. *vestire*, clothe: cf. *divest.*] To undress†; hence, to divest†; in *law*, to deprive of a right, title, etc.; also, to take away (a right, etc.).

de-vi-ate (dē′vi-āt), *v.*; *-ated*, *-ating*. [LL. *deviatus*, pp. of *deviare*, < L. *de*, from, + *via*, way.] **I.** *intr.* To turn aside from the way or course; diverge, as from a line of direction; depart or swerve, as from a course of action or procedure; digress, as from a line of thought or reasoning. **II.** *tr.* To cause to swerve; turn aside; change the direction of.—**de-vi-a′tion** (-ā′shọn), *n.* The act of deviating, as from the way or course, or from a line, method, standard, etc.; divergence; variation; amount of divergence.—**de′vi-a-tor,** *n.*

de-vice (dẹ-vīs′), *n.* [OF. F. *devis*, masc., *devise*, fem., < L. *divisus*, masc., *divisa*, fem., pp. of *dividere*: see *divide*, and cf. *devise*, *n.*] Command† or order†; will, desire, or inclination (as, left to his own *devices*); purpose† or intention†; opinion† or judgment†; also, the act or faculty of planning, contriving, or inventing; manner of being contrived or designed (as, "plate of rare *device*": Shakspere's "Cymbeline," i. 6. 189); also, a plan or scheme for effecting a purpose; a clever expedient; often, a crafty scheme; a trick; a stratagem; also, an invention or contrivance; a mechanical contrivance for a particular purpose; also, something artistically designed; a decorative figure or design; an artistic figure or design used as a heraldic bearing (often accompanied by a motto), or as an emblem, badge, trademark, or the like; hence, a motto (as, "A banner with the strange *device*, Excelsior": Longfellow's "Excelsior"); also, a fanciful or ingenious writing or expression (archaic); a fanciful dramatic or spectacular production (archaic).

Device of Francis I. of France.

dev-il (dev′l), *n.* [AS. *dēofol*, < LL. *diabolus*, < Gr. διάβολος, devil, orig. slanderer, < διαβάλλειν, slander, traduce, < διά, across, + βάλλειν, throw.] The supreme spirit of evil, Satan (usually preceded by *the*: sometimes *cap.*); hence, any evil spirit; a demon; a fiend; an evil spirit supposed to possess a demoniac; an evil passion or influence; a false god, or idol; also, an emphatic expletive used in disgust, vexation, wonder, strong negation, etc. (usually preceded by *the*); also, something diabolically or supremely evil, bad, unpleasant, etc.; an atrociously wicked, cruel, or ill-tempered person; also, a person of great cleverness, energy, or recklessness; cleverness, spirit, energy, etc., suggestive of a devil; a fellow, esp. an unfortunate one (as, a poor *devil*); the errand-boy or the youngest apprentice in a printing-office ('printer's devil'); one who does work under another, for which the latter receives the credit or the remuneration, as a literary hack; also, any of various animals characterized by fierceness, ugliness, or the like (as, the Tasmanian *devil*: see under *Tasmanian*); any of various mechanical devices, as a machine for tearing rags, etc.; any of various highly seasoned dishes.—**devil dog,** or **devil hound,** a nickname for a member of the U. S. Marine Corps: a rendering of G. *teufelshund*, a name said to have been applied by the Germans to the marines during the World War, on account of their fierceness in attack.—**devil on two sticks,** the piece of wood used in the game of diabolo, or the game itself.—**devil's advocate,** a person appointed to present the arguments against a proposed canonization as a saint; hence, an adverse critic, esp. of what is deemed good; an advocate of an opposing or bad cause.—**devil's bones,** dice.—**devil's books,** playing-cards.—**devil's corkscrew.** Same as *daimonelix*.—**devil's darning-needle,** a dragon-fly.—**devil's tattoo,** a meaningless beating or drumming with the hands or feet.—**dev′il,** *v.*, *-iled* or *-illed*, *-iling* or *-illing*. **I.** *tr.* To harass, torment, or plague; do (work) as a devil or hack, or give out (work) to a devil; tear (rags, etc.) to pieces with a machine called a devil; prepare (food) with hot or savory seasoning. **II.** *intr.* To act as devil for another, as in literary work.—**dev′il-dom** (-dọm), *n.* The rule of a devil; the realm of devils; devils collectively.—**dev′il-fish,** *n.* Any of various marine animals, as certain large rays, esp. *Manta birostris*, which is sometimes twenty feet wide, or various large cephalopods, as the octopus.—**dev′il-hood** (-hůd), *n.* The condition or character of a devil.—**dev′il-ish.** **I.** *a.* Of, like, or befitting a devil; diabolical; fiendish; also, terrible, excessive, or very great (colloq.). **II.** *adv.* Excessively; extremely: as, "It is *devilish* fine wine" (Thackeray's "Vanity Fair," xiii.). [Colloq.]—**dev′il-ish-ly,** *adv.*—**dev′il-ish-ness,** *n.*—**dev′il-kin,** *n.* A little devil; an imp.—**dev′il-may-care′,** *a.* Cheerfully careless of consequences or responsibility; gaily or wildly reckless.—**dev′il-ment,** *n.* Devilish action or conduct; mischief; also, a devilish device.—**dev′il-ship,** *n.* The condition or character of a devil.—**dev′il-try, dev′il-ry** (-tri, -ri), *n.*; pl. *-tries* (-triz), *-ries* (-riz). Diabolic magic or art; also, devilish action or conduct; extreme wickedness; wicked or reckless mischief; also, devils collectively; a company of devils; also, demonology.—**dev′il-wood,** *n.* A small oleaceous tree, *Osmanthus americanus*, of the U. S., with a hard, strong, close-grained wood.

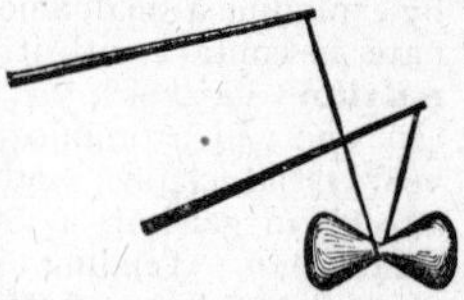
Devil on Two Sticks, showing the manner of rotating it.

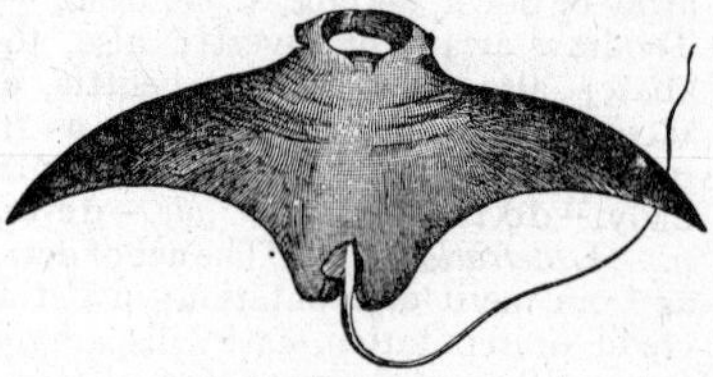
Devil-fish (*Manta birostris*).

de-vi-ous (dē′vi-us), *a.* [L. *devius*, < *de*, from, + *via*, way.] Out of the direct or common way; remote; also, departing from the direct way; circuitous, as a course; also, turning aside from the way; swerving; straying; fig., erring.—**de′vi-ous-ly,** *adv.*—**de′vi-ous-ness,** *n.*

de-vis-a-ble (dẹ-vī′zạ-bl), *a.* That may be devised.

de-vi-sal (dẹ-vī′zạl), *n.* The act of devising; contrivance; invention.

de-vise (dẹ-vīz′), *n.* [Var. of *device* (OF. *devis*, *devise*, < L. *divisus*, *divisa*), differentiated in legal use by association with the related *devise*, *v.*] In *law*, the act of assigning or disposing of property by will; a will, or a clause in a will, disposing of property; the property disposed of: now used specif. with reference to real property.—**de-vise′,** *v.*; *-vised*, *-vising*. [OF. *deviser* = It. *divisare*, freq. < L. *dividere* (pp. *divisus*): see *divide*.] **I.** *tr.* To divide†; distribute†; assign† or appoint†; assign or transmit (property, now specif real property) by will; also, to order or arrange the plan of elaborate in the mind; think out; plan, contrive, or invent, also, to plot or scheme (archaic); feign (archaic); also, to conceive† or imagine† (as, "I . . . love thee better than thou canst *devise*": Shakspere's "Romeo and Juliet," iii. 1. 72). **II.** *intr.* To form a plan; contrive.—**dev-i-see** (dev-i-zē′ or dẹ-vī-), *n.* In *law*, one to whom a devise is made.—**de-vis′er** (-vī′zėr), *n.* One who devises; esp., one who plans, contrives, or invents; a contriver; an inventor.—**de-vi′sor** (-zọr or -zôr), *n.* In *law*, one who makes a devise of property.

de-vi-tal-ize (dē-vī′tạl-īz), *v. t.*; *-ized, -izing.* [See *de-*.] To deprive of vitality or vital properties; render lifeless.—**de-vi″tal-i-za′tion** (-i-zā′shọn), *n.*

de-vit-ri-fy (dē-vit′ri-fī), *v. t.*; *-fied, -fying.* [See *de-*.] To deprive, wholly or partly, of vitreous character or properties. —**de-vit″ri-fi-ca′tion** (-fi-kā′shọn), *n.*

de-vo-cal-ize (dē-vō′kạl-īz), *v. t.*; *-ized, -izing.* [See *de-*.] In *phonetics*, to deprive of vocal or sonant quality.—**de-vo″cal-i-za′tion** (-i-zā′shọn), *n.*

de-void (dẹ-void′), *a.* [Orig. pp. of obs. *devoid, v.*, < OF. *desvuidier*, empty out, < *des-* (see *dis-*) + *vuidier*, empty, E. *void, v.*] Empty, void, or destitute (*of*).

dev-oir (dev′wor or dev-wor′, F. dė-vwor), *n.* [F., orig. inf., < L. *debere*, owe: see *debt.*] Duty, or action or service due (archaic); also, an act of civility or respect; *pl.*, respects or compliments; also, *sing.*, an endeavor† or effort†.

dev-o-lu-tion (dev-ọ-lū′shọn), *n.* [ML. *devolutio(n-)*, < L. *devolvere*: see *devolve.*] The act or fact of devolving; passage onward from stage to stage; the transmitting or passing of property, etc., as by inheritance or succession; the passing on to a successor of an unexercised right; the delegating or passing of duty, responsibility, etc., to another; in *biol.*, degeneration (opposed to *evolution*).

de-volve (dẹ-volv′), *v.*; *-volved, -volving.* [L. *devolvere* (pp. *devolutus*), < *de*, down from, + *volvere*, roll.] **I.** *tr.* To roll downward, unroll, or roll (archaic); also, to cause to pass on, as from one stage or condition into another; also, to cause to pass to or fall upon a person; transmit, as by inheritance or succession; transfer or delegate (a duty, responsibility, etc.) to or upon another. **II.** *intr.* To roll down (archaic); also, to pass from one stage or condition into another; also, to pass to or fall upon a person; descend, as by inheritance; pass in succession, as authority or an unexercised right; fall as a duty or responsibility on a person; also, to sink or degenerate.—**de-volve′ment,** *n.*

Dev-on (dev′ọn), *n.* One of a noted breed of cattle, usually of a red color, originating in Devonshire, England.

De-vo-ni-an (de-vō′ni-ạn). **I.** *a.* Of or pertaining to Devonshire, England; specif., noting or pertaining to a geological period or a system of rocks preceding the Carboniferous. **II.** *n.* A native or inhabitant of Devonshire; in *geol.*, the Devonian period or system.—**De-von′ic** (-von′ik), *a.* Devonian.

de-vote (dẹ-vōt′), *v. t.*; *-voted, -voting.* [L. *devotus*, pp. of *devovere*, < *de*, from, + *vovere*, vow.] To appropriate by or as by a vow; set apart or dedicate by a solemn or formal act; consecrate; also, to give up or appropriate to a particular pursuit, occupation, purpose, cause, person, etc.; also, to consign to evil, as by a curse; curse; doom.—**de-vote′,** *a.* Devoted; also, devout. [Archaic.]—**de-vot′ed** (-vō′ted), *p. a.* Set apart by or as by a vow; dedicated; consecrated; also, zealous or ardent in attachment; also, accursed or doomed (as, "He . . . vowed revenge on her *devoted* head": Dryden's "Theodore and Honoria," 124).—**de-vot′ed-ly,** *adv.*—**de-vot′ed-ness,** *n.*—**dev-o-tee** (dev-ọ-tē′), *n.* One zealously devoted to religion, or to a particular form or object of religious worship; sometimes, an extravagantly or fanatically devout person; also, one ardently devoted to anything.—**de-vote′ment,** *n.* The act of devoting, or the state of being devoted; devotion; dedication.—**de-vot′er,** *n.*

de-vo-tion (dẹ-vō′shọn), *n.* [OF. *devocion* (F. *dévotion*), < L. *devotio(n-)*, < *devovere*: see *devote.*] The act of devoting, or the state of being devoted; dedication; consecration; also, religious observance or worship; a religious observance; an exercise of prayer and praise; a form of prayer or worship for special use; also, religious zeal; devoutness; also, a giving over or appropriating to any purpose, cause, etc.; also, earnest attachment to a cause, person, etc.; hence, command† or disposal†; also, object† or purpose†.—**de-vo′tion-al,** *a.* Of, pertaining to, of the nature of, or characterized by devotion, esp. religious devotion.—**de-vo′tion-al-ism,** *n.* Devotional spirit or character.—**de-vo′tion-al-ist,** *n.* A person given to devotion; a religious devotee.—**de-vo′tion-al-ly,** *adv.*

de-vour (dẹ-vour′), *v. t.* [OF. *devorer* (F. *dévorer*), < L. *devorare*, < *de-*, down, + *vorare*, swallow, devour.] To swallow or eat up voraciously; eat ravenously or like a beast; consume by eating; also, to consume destructively, recklessly, or wantonly; make away with; destroy; waste; also, to swallow up or engulf (as, "The jaws of darkness do *devour* it up": Shakspere's "Midsummer Night's Dream," i. 1. 148); take in greedily with the senses or intellect; gaze upon with avidity; seize greedily or selfishly; suppress (grief, chagrin, etc.); of things, to absorb or engross wholly (as, "in sorrow all *devour'd*": Shakspere's "Pericles," iv. 4. 25).—**de-vour′er,** *n.*—**de-vour′ing-ly,** *adv.*—**de-vour′ment,** *n.*

de-vout (dẹ-vout′), *a.* [OF. *devot* (F. *dévot*), < L. *devotus*, pp.: see *devote.*] Devoted to divine worship or service; pious; religious; also, expressing devotion or piety (as, "With uplifted hands, and eyes *devout*, Grateful to Heaven": Milton's "Paradise Lost," xi. 863); reverential; also, zealous in attachment; earnest or sincere; hearty.—**de-vout′ly,** *adv.*—**de-vout′ness,** *n.*

dew (dū), *n.* [AS. *dēaw* = D. *dauw* = G. *tau* = Icel. *dögg*, dew.] Moisture condensed from the atmosphere, esp. during the night, and deposited in the form of small drops upon any cool surface; fig., something likened to dew, as serving to refresh (as, "the timely *dew* of sleep": Milton's "Paradise Lost," iv. 614), or as suggestive of morning and hence of youth (as, "in the morn and liquid *dew* of youth": Shakspere's "Hamlet," i. 3. 41); also, moisture in small drops on a surface, as tears, perspiration, etc.; sometimes, liquor (as, "That's Billy Crow's own whisky . . . there isn't such *dew* in the county": Lever's "Harry Lorrequer," xix.).—**dew,** *v. t.* To wet with or as with dew; moisten; bedew.

de-wan (dẹ-wän′), *n.* See *diwan.*

dew-ber-ry (dū′ber″i), *n.*; pl. *-berries* (-iz). In England, the fruit of *Rubus cæsius*, a procumbent species of bramble or blackberry; in North America, the fruit of other species of *Rubus*, as *R. villosus*, *R. trivialis*, etc., with low, running stems; also, a plant bearing such a fruit.

dew=claw (dū′klâ), *n.* A functionless inner claw or digit in the foot of some dogs, not reaching the ground in walking; an analogous false hoof of deer, hogs, etc.

Left Fore Foot of a Terrier. — X, dew-claw.

dew-drop (dū′drop), *n.* A drop of dew.

dew-fall (dū′fâl), *n.* The formation or deposition of dew; the time when this begins, in the evening.

dew-i-ly (dū′i-li), *adv.* In a dewy manner; like dew.—**dew′i-ness,** *n.* Dewy state.

dew-lap (dū′lap), *n.* [Appar. < *dew* + *lap*².] but with orig. notion unexplained.] The pendulous fold of skin under the throat of cattle; any similar part, as the loose skin under the throat of some dogs, the wattle of fowls, etc.—**dew′lapped,** *a.*

dew-less (dū′les), *a.* Without dew.

dew=plant (dū′plant), *n.* The sundew; also, the ice-plant.

dew=point (dū′point), *n.* The temperature of the air at which dew begins to be deposited.

dew=pond (dū′pond), *n.* A small and shallow pond, usually artificial, located on a hill or the like, and supplied by mist, dew, etc.

dew-y (dū′i), *a.*; compar. *dewier*, superl. *dewiest.* [AS. *dēawig.*] Of, pertaining to, or like dew; resembling dew in refreshing effect (as, "*dewy* sleep": Milton's "Paradise Lost," ix. 1044); abounding in dew (as, "from noon to *dewy* eve": Milton's "Paradise Lost," i. 743); moist with or as with dew.

dex-i-o-car-di-a (dek″si-ọ-kär′di-ạ̈), *n.* [NL., < Gr. δεξιός, right, + καρδία, heart.] In *anat.*, an abnormal condition in which the heart is on the right side.

dex-ter (deks′tėr), *a.* [L. *dexter*, right, on the right, dexterous, favorable.] Pertaining to or situated on the right side; right; right-hand; also, favorable, as an omen†; also, dexterous†; in *her.*, situated to the right of the bearer, and hence to the left of the spectator (opposed to *sinister*).

dex-ter-i-ty (deks-ter′i-ti), *n.* [L. *dexteritas.*] The quality of being dexterous; manual adroitness or skill; adroitness in the use of the body generally; also, mental adroitness or skill; cleverness; also, right-handedness, or the use of the right hand in preference to the left.

dex-ter-ous, dex-trous (deks′tẹ-rus, -trus), *a.* [L. *dexter*: see *dexter.*] Having skill with the hands; adroit or skilful in bodily movements generally; deft; nimble; also, having mental adroitness or skill; clever; also, done with or exhibiting dexterity; also, right-handed, or using the right hand in preference to the left.—**dex′ter-ous-ly, dex′trous-ly,** *adv.*—**dex′ter-ous-ness, dex′trous-ness,** *n.*

dex-trad (deks′trad), *adv.* [L. *dexter*, right: see *-ad.*] To the right: opposed to *sinistrad*.

dex-tral (deks′trạl), *a.* [L. *dexter*, right.] Of or pertaining to the right side; right; right-handed; of a spiral shell, having the whorl rising from left to right, as viewed from the outside.—**dex′tral-ly,** *adv.*

dex-tri-er (deks′tri-ėr), *n.* Same as *destrier*. [Archaic.]

dex-trin, dex-trine (deks′trin), *n.* [L. *dexter*, right.] A soluble gummy substance formed from starch by the action of heat, ferments, etc., occurring in various forms and having dextrorotatory properties: used as a substitute for gum arabic, etc.

dextro-. Form of L. *dexter*, right, on the right, used in combination.—**dex-tro-car-di-a** (deks-trō-kär′di-ạ), *n.* Same as *dexiocardia*.—**dex-tro-glu′cose** (-glö′kōs), *n.* Common dextrorotatory glucose.—**dex″tro-ro-ta′tion** (-rọ-tā′shọn), *n.* Rotation toward the right or in a clockwise direction; in *optics*, *chem.*, etc., a turning of the plane of polarization of light to the right.—**dex-tro-ro′ta-to-ry** (-rō′tạ-tọ-ri), *a.* Turning or causing to turn toward the right or in a clockwise direction; in *optics*, *chem.*, etc., turning the plane of polarization of light to the right, as certain crystals and compounds.

dex-trorse (deks-trôrs′), *a.* [L. *dextrorsum*, toward the right, < *dexter*, right, + *versum*, toward.] Rising spirally from left to right (from a point of view at the center of the spiral), as a stem: by some authorities taken in the opposite sense (from a point of view on the outside of the spiral). Cf. *sinistrorse*. Also **dex-tror′sal.**

dex-trose (deks′trōs), *n.* Same as *dextroglucose*.

dex′trous, etc. See *dexterous*, etc.

dey (dā), *n.* [F. *dey*, < Turk. *dāi*, orig. 'maternal uncle.'] The title of the governor of Algiers before the French conquest in 1830; also, a title formerly sometimes borne by the rulers of Tunis and Tripoli.—**dey′ship,** *n.* The position or dignity of a dey.

de-zy-mo-tize (dē-zī′mọ-tīz), *v. t.*; *-tized*, *-tizing*. [From *de-* + *zymotic.*] To free from disease-germs.

dhak (däk or dâk), *n.* [Hind. *dhāk.*] An East Indian fabaceous tree, *Butea frondosa*, bearing orange-colored flowers and yielding an astringent gum.

dhar-ma (där′mạ or dur′-), *n.* [Skt. *dharma.*] In Hinduism and Buddhism, law, or conformity to law; religion; virtue.

dhar-na (dur′nä), *n.* [Hind. *dharnā.*] The practice, formerly common in India, etc., of sitting without tasting food at a person's door until he complies with some demand, esp. for payment of a debt: chiefly in the phrase 'to sit dharna,' or 'to sit in dharna.'

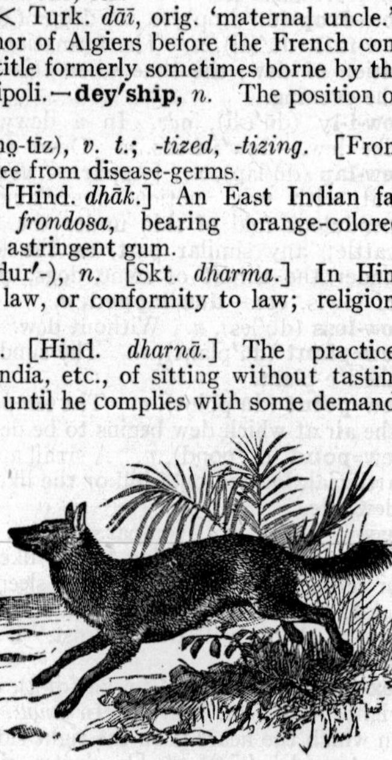

Dhole.

dho-bi (dō′bi), *n.* [Hind. *dhōbī.*] In India, a native washerman.

dhole (dōl), *n.* [E. Ind.] A fierce species of wild dog, *Canis* (or *Cyon*) *dukkunensis*, of India, hunting in packs, and capable of running down large game.

dholl (dol), *n.* Same as *dal*.

dhow (dou), *n.* [Origin uncertain.] An Arab coasting vessel, usually lateen-rigged, used in the Arabian Sea, etc.

Dhow.—From model in Victoria and Albert Museum, London.

dhur-rie (dur′i), *n.* [Hind. *darī.*] A kind of coarse, durable cotton carpeting made in India, usually in fringed squares.

di-[1]. [Gr. δι-, repr. δίς, twice, doubly; akin to δύο, two: see *bi-.*] A prefix of Greek origin, meaning 'twice,' 'doubly,' 'two,' freely used (like *bi-*) as an English formative, as in *dicotyledon*, *dipetalous*, *dipolar*, and in many chemical terms, as *diatomic*, *disulphide*. See *mono-*.

dia-, di-[2]. [Gr. δια-, repr. διά, prep., through, between, across, by, of; akin to δύο, two, and δι-, E. *di-*[1].] A prefix of Greek origin, meaning 'through,' 'between,' 'asunder,' 'thoroughly,' sometimes used as an English formative in scientific terms, as *diacaustic*, *diamagnetic*, *diactinic*, *dielectric*.

di-a-base (dī′ạ-bās), *n.* [F., < *dia-* (erron. for *di-*, two, = E. *di-*[1]) + *base*, E. *base*[2].] Diorite†; also, a dark-colored igneous rock consisting essentially of augite and feldspar.—**di-a-ba′sic** (-bā′sik), *a.*

di-a-be-tes (dī-ạ-bē′tēz), *n.* [NL., < Gr. διαβήτης, < διαβαίνειν, go through, < διά, through, + βαίνειν, go.] In *pathol.*, a disease characterized by a persistent, abnormally large discharge of urine ('diabetes insipidus'), often with an excessive amount of sugar in the urine ('diabetes mellitus').—**di-a-bet′ic** (-bet′ik or -bē′tik). **I.** *a.* Of, pertaining to, or affected with diabetes. **II.** *n.* A person suffering from diabetes.

di-a-ble-rie (di-ä′blẹ-ri, F. dyä-blė-rē), *n.* [F., < *diable*, < LL. *diabolus*, E. *devil.*] Diabolic magic or art; dealings with the devil; sorcery; also, deviltry, reckless mischief, or wildness (as, "Her talent for every species of drollery . . . seemed inexhaustible . . . Miss Eva . . . appeared to be fascinated by her wild *diablerie*": Mrs. Stowe's "Uncle Tom's Cabin," xx.); also, the domain or realm of devils; also, the lore of devils; demonology.

di-a-bol-ic, di-a-bol-i-cal (dī-ạ-bol′ik, -i-kạl), *a.* [LL. *diabolicus*, < Gr. διαβολικός, < διάβολος, E. *devil.*] Of, pertaining to, actuated by, or of the nature of the devil or a devil; also, characteristic of or befitting the devil; devilish; fiendish; atrocious.—**di-a-bol′i-cal-ly,** *adv.*—**di-a-bol′i-cal-ness,** *n.*

di-ab-o-lism (dī-ab′ọ-lizm), *n.* [Gr. διάβολος, E. *devil.*] Action aided by the devil; sorcery; witchcraft; also, action befitting the devil; deviltry; also, doctrine concerning devils; belief in or worship of devils; also, the character or condition of a devil.—**di-ab′o-list,** *n.* One who believes in or writes of diabolism.—**di-ab′o-lize** (-līz), *v. t.*; *-lized*, *-lizing*. To render diabolical or devilish; represent as diabolical; subject to diabolical influence.

di-ab-o-lo (di-ab′ọ-lō), *n.* [It., < LL. *diabolus*, E. *devil.*] A sport consisting of rotating, tossing, and catching a piece of wood shaped like an hour-glass, by means of a cord fastened at the ends of two sticks held in the hands; also, the piece of wood.

di-a-bo-lol-o-gy (dī″ạ-bọ-lol′ọ-ji), *n.* [Gr. διάβολος, devil: see *-logy.*] Doctrine concerning the devil or devils; diabolical lore. Also **di-a-bol′o-gy** (-bol′ọ-ji).

di-a-caus-tic (dī-ạ-kâs′tik), *a.* [See *dia-.*] In *math.* and *optics*, noting a caustic surface or curve formed by refraction of light. Cf. *catacaustic*.

di-ach-y-lon, di-ach-y-lum (dī-ak′i-lon, -lum), *n.*; pl. *-la* (-lạ). [ML. *diachylum*, L. *diachylon*, < Gr. διὰ χυλῶν, 'of juices.'] Orig., an ointment made from vegetable juices; now, an adhesive plaster consisting essentially of lead oxide and oil, much used as the basis for other plasters.

di-a-cid (dī-as′id), *a.* [See *di-*¹.] In *chem.*, capable of combining with two molecules of a monobasic acid.

di-ac-o-nal (dī-ak′ǭ-nąl), *a.* [LL. *diaconalis*, < *diaconus*, E. *deacon.*] Of or pertaining to a deacon.

di-ac-o-nate (dī-ak′ǭ-nāt), *n.* [LL. *diaconatus.*] The office or dignity of a deacon; also, a body of deacons.

di-a-cous-tics (dī-ą-kös′tiks or -kous′tiks), *n.* [See *di-*² and *acoustics.*] The science of refracted sound.—**di-a-cous′tic,** *a.*

di-a-crit-ic (dī-ą-krit′ik). [Gr. διακριτικός, < διακρίνειν, separate one from another, < διά, between, + κρίνειν, separate, distinguish.] **I.** *a.* Diacritical. **II.** *n.* A diacritical mark, point, or sign.—**di-a-crit′i-cal,** *a.* Serving to distinguish; distinctive; also, capable of distinguishing or discerning.—**diacritical mark, point,** or **sign,** one added or put adjacent to a letter or character to distinguish it from another of similar form, to give it a particular phonetic value, to indicate stress, etc.—**di-a-crit′i-cal-ly,** *adv.*

di-ac-tin-ic (dī-ak-tin′ik), *a.* [See *di-*².] Capable of transmitting the actinic rays of light.

di-a-del-phous (dī-ą-del′fus), *a.* [Gr. δι-, two, + ἀδελφός, brother.] In *bot.*, of stamens, united into two bundles or sets by their filaments; of plants, having the stamens so united.

Diadelphous Stamens.

di-a-dem (dī′ą-dem), *n.* [L. *diadema*, < Gr. διάδημα, < διαδεῖν, bind round, < διά, across, + δεῖν, bind.] A band, wreath, or the like for the head, worn as a mark of rank or honor, or for ornament; esp., such a band or the like worn as a symbol of royal dignity; a crown; specif., a distinctive cloth head-band, sometimes adorned with jewels, formerly worn by kings; hence, the dignity or authority denoted by a crown or the like; sovereignty; in *her.*, any of the arches that rise from the rim of a crown and support the globe or other symbol at the top.—**di′a-dem,** *v. t.*; *-demed, -deming.* To adorn with or as with a diadem; crown: as, "*diadem'd* with rays divine" (Pope's "Epilogue to the Satires," ii. 232).

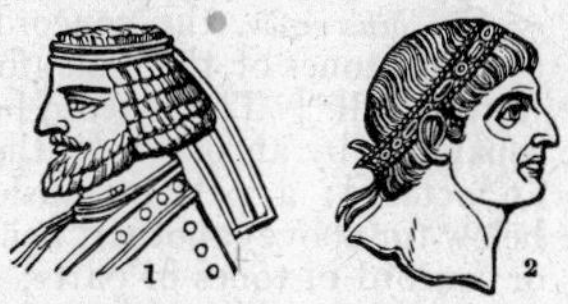

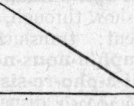

1. Parthian Diadem. 2. Jeweled Diadem of Constantine. (From ancient coins.)

di-ær-e-sis (dī-er′e-sis), *n.* See *dieresis.*

di-ag-nose (dī-ag-nōs′ or -nōz′), *v. t.* or *i.*; *-nosed, -nosing.* [From *diagnosis.*] To make a diagnosis of (a case, disease, etc.).

di-ag-no-sis (dī-ag-nō′sis), *n.*; pl. *-noses* (-nō′sēz). [NL., < Gr. διάγνωσις, < διαγιγνώσκειν, know one from another, < διά, between, + γιγνώσκειν, know.] The process of determining by examination the nature and circumstances of a diseased condition; the decision reached from such an examination; hence, any analogous examination or analysis; in *biol.*, etc., scientific determination; a description which classifies precisely.—**di-ag-nos′tic** (-nos′tik). [Gr. διαγνωστικός.] **I.** *a.* Of or pertaining to diagnosis; serving to indicate the nature or character of anything, as of disease. **II.** *n.* Diagnosis; also, a symptom or characteristic of value in diagnosis.—**di-ag-nos′ti-cal-ly,** *adv.*—**di-ag-nos′ti-cate** (-kāt), *v. t.* or *i.*; *-cated, -cating.* To diagnose.—**di″ag-nos-ti′cian** (-tish′ąn), *n.* One skilled in diagnosis.—**di-ag-nos′tics,** *n.* The art or science of diagnosis.

di-ag-o-nal (dī-ag′ǭ-nąl). [L. *diagonalis*, < Gr. διαγώνιος, < διά, across, + γωνία, angle.] **I.** *a.* Connecting, as a straight line, two non-adjacent angles or vertices of a quadrilateral, polygon, or polyhedron; extending, as a plane, from one edge of a solid figure to an opposite edge; in general, having an oblique direction; also, characterized by oblique lines, ridges, etc. (as, *diagonal* cloth); also, situated obliquely opposite. **II.** *n.* A diagonal line; also, anything extending in the manner of such a line, or lying obliquely to other things; also, diagonal cloth.—**di-ag′o-nal-ly,** *adv.*

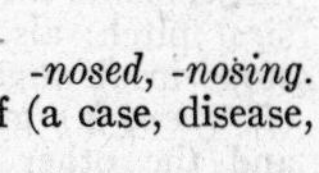
Diagonal of a Rectangle.

di-a-gram (dī′ą-gram), *n.* [Gr. διάγραμμα, < διαγράφειν, mark out by lines, < διά, through, + γράφειν, mark, draw, write.] A figure, or set of lines, marks, etc., to accompany a geometrical demonstration, give the outlines or general features of an object, show the course or results of a process, etc.; a chart, plan, or scheme.—**di′a-gram,** *v. t.*; *-grammed* or *-gramed, -gramming* or *-graming.* To represent by a diagram; make a diagram of.—**di″a-gram-mat′ic** (-grą-mat′ik), *a.* Of, pertaining to, or of the nature of a diagram; represented by a diagram; schematic. — **di″a-gram-mat′i-cal-ly,** *adv.* — **di-a-gram′ma-tize** (-gram′ą-tīz), *v. t.*; *-tized, -tizing.* To make a diagram of; diagram.

di-a-graph (dī′ą-gräf), *n.* [Gr. διαγράφειν, mark out by lines: see *diagram.*] A device for drawing, used in reproducing mechanically, on any desired scale, outlines, plans, etc.; also, a combined protractor and scale.

di-al (dī′ąl), *n.* [ME. *dial*, < ML. *dialis*, daily, < L. *dies*, day.] An instrument for indicating the time of day by means of a shadow cast by the sun (sometimes by the moon) upon a graduated plate; hence, a timepiece of any kind†; also, the face of a clock or watch; also, a plate or disk with graduations or figures, as for the indication of pressure, number of revolutions, etc., as by the movements of a pointer; a kind of plate or disk with letters and numbers, used in connection with a telephone in making telephone calls without the service of a central operator; also, an instrument having such a plate or disk; in *mining*, a kind of compass used for underground surveying.—**di′al,** *v.*; *-aled* or *-alled, -aling* or *-alling.* **I.** *tr.* To measure with or as with a dial; indicate as on a dial; also, to indicate on a telephone dial; call by means of a telephone dial, as another telephone or a person; also, to inscribe or mark as a dial; in *mining*, to survey with the aid of a dial or compass. **II.** *intr.* To use a telephone dial.

di-al=bird (dī′ąl-bėrd), *n.* Same as *dayal.*

di-a-lect (dī′ą-lekt), *n.* [L. *dialectus*, < Gr. διάλεκτος, discourse, language, dialect, < διαλέγεσθαι, converse, discuss, argue, < διά, between, + λέγειν, speak.] Manner of speaking; phraseology; idiom; also, a form of a language prevailing in a particular district, and marked by peculiarities of vocabulary, pronunciation, etc., esp. such a form as distinguished from the accepted or literary form of the language; also, a special variety or branch of a language, or one of a number of languages regarded as a family (as, the Romance *dialects*).—**di-a-lec′tal** (-lek′tąl), *a.* Of, pertaining to, or characteristic of a dialect; of the nature of a dialect.—**di-a-lec′tal-ly,** *adv.*

di-a-lec-tic (dī-ą-lek′tik). [L. *dialecticus*, < Gr. διαλεκτικός (as n., L. *dialectica*, < Gr. διαλεκτική), < διαλέγεσθαι: see *dialect.*] **I.** *a.* Of, pertaining to, or of the nature of logical argumentation; given to logical disputation; also, of or pertaining to a dialect; dialectal. **II.** *n.* The art or practice of logical discussion as employed in investigating the truth of a theory or opinion; logical argumentation; logic.—**di-a-lec′ti-cal,** *a.* Dialectic.—**di-a-lec′ti-cal-ly,** *adv.*—**di″a-lec-ti′cian** (-tish′ąn), *n.* One skilled in dialectic; a logician.—**di-a-lec′ti-cism** (-ti-sizm), *n.* Dialectal speech or usage.—**di-a-lec′tics,** *n.* Dialectic.

di-a-lec-tol-o-gy (dī″ą-lek-tol′ǭ-ji), *n.* [See *-logy.*] The study of dialects; that branch of philology which treats of dialects.—**di″a-lec-tol′o-gist,** *n.*

di-al-ing, di-al-ling (dī′ąl-ing), *n.* The art of constructing dials; in *mining*, surveying with a dial.

di-al-lage (dī′ą-lāj), *n.* [F., < Gr. διαλλαγή, interchange, difference; with allusion to its dissimilar cleavages.] A laminated or foliated variety of pyroxene, usually of a green color.

di-a-log-ic, di-a-log-i-cal (dī-ą-loj′ik, -i-kąl), *a.* [Gr. διαλογικός, < διάλογος: see *dialogue.*] Of, pertaining to, or of the nature of dialogue; taking part in a dialogue.—**di-a-log′i-cal-ly,** *adv.*

di-al-o-gism (dī-al′ǭ-jizm), *n.* [Gr. διαλογισμός, < διαλογίζεσθαι, converse, debate, < διάλογος: see *dialogue.*] The discussion of a subject by a speaker or writer under the form of an imaginary dialogue; also, an actual dialogue.—**di-al′o-gist** (-jist), *n.* A speaker in dialogue; also, a writer of dialogue.—**di-a-lo-gis-tic** (dī″ą-lǭ-jis′tik), *a.*—**di-al′o-gize** (-jīz), *v. i.*; *-gized, -gizing.* [Gr. διαλογίζεσθαι.] To carry on a dialogue; dialogue.

di-a-logue (dī′ạ-log), *n.* [F. *dialogue*, < L. *dialogus*, < Gr. διάλογος, conversation, dialogue, < διαλέγεσθαι, converse: see *dialect.*] A conversation between two or more persons; a colloquy; also, conversation; also, a literary work in the form of a conversation; also, literary composition of this kind; the conversation between characters in a novel, drama, etc.—**di′a-logue,** *v.*; *-logued, -loguing.* **I.** *intr.* To carry on a dialogue: as, "*Var. Serv.* How dost, fool? *Apem.* Dost *dialogue* with thy shadow?" (Shakspere's "Timon of Athens," ii. 2. 52). **II.** *tr.* To put into the form of a dialogue; furnish with dialogue.—**di′a-lo-guer** (-log-ėr), *n.*

di-a-lyse (dī′ạ-līz), etc. See *dialyze*, etc.

di-al-y-sis (dī-al′i-sis), *n.*; pl. *-yses* (-i-sēz). [L. *dialysis*, < Gr. διάλυσις, < διαλύειν, separate, dissolve, < διά, between, + λύειν, loose.] Dieresis†; in *anat.* and *bot.*, the separation of parts normally united; in *chem.*, the separation of crystalloids from colloids in a solution by diffusion through a membrane.—**di-a-lyt′ic** (-ạ-lit′ik), *a.* [Gr. διαλυτικός.] Of, pertaining to, or of the nature of dialysis; characterized by separation.—**di-a-lyt′i-cal-ly,** *adv.*—**di′a-lyze, di′a-lyse** (-līz), *v. t.*; *-lyzed, -lysed, -lyzing, -lysing.* [From *dialysis*: cf. *analyze* and *analysis.*] In *chem.*, to subject to dialysis; separate or procure by dialysis.—**di′a-lyz-er, di′a-lys-er** (-lī-zėr), *n.*

di-a-mag-net-ic (dī″ạ-mag-net′ik), *a.* [See *dia-*.] Noting or pertaining to a class of substances (as copper, silver, water, etc.) which, when placed in a magnetic field, tend to take a position with the longer axis at right angles to the lines of force: opposed to *paramagnetic* and *ferromagnetic*.—**di-a-mag′net-ism,** *n.* The quality of being diamagnetic; diamagnetic phenomena, or the science dealing with them.

di-a-man-tif-er-ous (dī″ạ-man-tif′ẹ-rus), *a.* [F. *diamantifère*, < *diamant*, diamond, + L. *ferre*, bear.] Yielding or producing diamonds.

di-am-e-ter (dī-am′e-tėr), *n.* [OF. *dyametre* (F. *diamètre*), < L. *diametros*, < Gr. διάμετρος, a diagonal, diameter, < διά, through, across, + μέτρον, measure.] A straight line passing through the center of a circle or sphere and terminated at each end by the circumference or surface; a straight line passing from side to side of any figure or body, through its center; also, the length of a diameter; thickness; width.—**di-am′e-tral** (-trạl), *a.* Of, pertaining to, or forming a diameter.—**di-am′e-tral-ly,** *adv.*—**di-a-met-ric, di-a-met-ri-cal** (dī-ạ-met′rik, -ri-kạl), *a.* [Gr. διαμετρικός.] Of, pertaining to, or forming a diameter; diametral; also, of opposition, opposites, etc., direct or extreme (as with reference to the opposite ends of a diameter); directly opposed.—**di-a-met′ri-cal-ly,** *adv.*

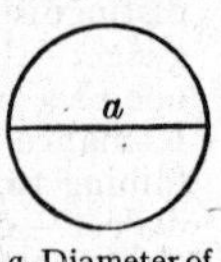

a, Diameter of a Circle.

di-a-mond (dī′ạ-mọnd), *n.* [OF. F. *diamant*, < L. *adamas* (*adamant-*), adamant, diamond: see *adamant.*] Adamant†; also, a precious stone, colorless or colored, a pure or nearly pure form of carbon, of extreme hardness and great brilliancy; a piece of this stone; a tool provided with an uncut diamond, used for cutting glass; also, a plane figure bounded by four equal straight lines forming two acute and two obtuse angles (sometimes four right angles), esp. as placed with its diagonals vertical and horizontal; a lozenge or rhomb; a red lozenge-shaped figure on a playing-card, or a card of the suit bearing such figures; the space inclosed within the four bases of a baseball ground; also, a printing-type (4½ point) of a size between brilliant and pearl (see *type*).—**black diamond.** See under *black*, *a.*—**diamond hitch,** a hitch used esp. in fastening a pack on an animal, in which a diamond-shaped arrangement of rope is formed on the top of the pack.—**di′a-mond,** *v. t.* To adorn with or as with diamonds; also, to shape like a diamond; divide into diamond-shaped parts.—**di′a-mond=back,** *n.* Any of several terrapins or edible turtles of the genus *Malaclemmys*, living in the salt-water marshes of the eastern and southern U. S., and characterized by diamond-shaped markings on the back.—**di′a-mond=backed,** *a.* Having the back marked with diamond-shaped figures.—**di′a-mond=bee″tle,** *n.* A large South American beetle (weevil), *Entimus imperialis*, remarkable for its coloration of black studded with points of brilliant golden green.—**di″a-mon-dif′er-ous** (-mọn-dif′ẹ-rus), *a.* Yielding diamonds; diamantiferous.—**di′a-mond=shaped,** *a.* Having the shape of a diamond or lozenge.

Diamond.

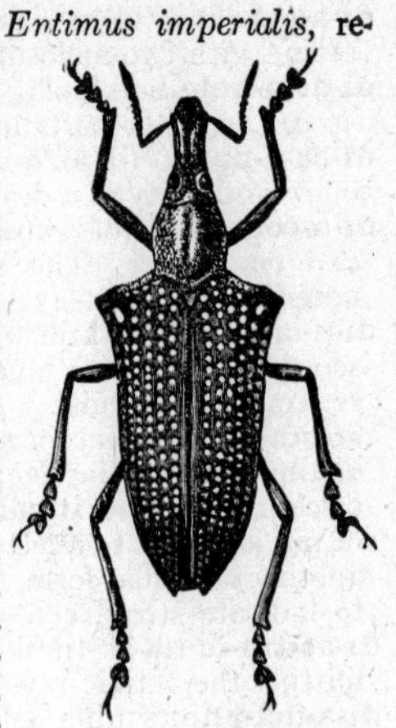
Diamond-beetle.

Di-an-a (dī-an′ạ̈), *n.* [L.] An ancient Italian deity, goddess of the moon and of hunting, and protectress of women; hence, a young woman of fine physique and easy, graceful carriage. Cf. *Artemis.*

di-an-drous (dī-an′drus), *a.* [Gr. δι-, two, + ἀνήρ (ἀνδρ-), man.] In *bot.*, of a flower, having two stamens; of a plant, having flowers with two stamens.

Diandrous Flower.

di-a-no-ët-ic (dī″ạ-nọ-et′ik). [Gr. διανοητικός, < διανοεῖσθαι, think over, < διά, through, + νοεῖν, think, < νόος, νοῦς, mind.] **I.** *a.* Of or pertaining to thought or reasoning, esp. discursive reasoning. **II.** *n.* That part of logic which treats of discursive reasoning.

di-an-thus (dī-an′thus), *n.* [NL., < Gr. Διός, of Zeus, + ἄνθος, flower.] Any plant of the silenaceous genus *Dianthus*, as the carnation or the sweet-william.

di-a-pa-son (dī-ạ-pā′zọn), *n.* [L. *diapason*, < Gr. διαπασῶν, the concord of the first and last tones of the scale, for διὰ πασῶν, 'through all.'] The concord between tones separated by an octave†; the interval of an octave†; a part in music an octave below (or above) another; hence, harmony or concord of tones or parts; a melody or strain; a swelling musical sound; the whole range of tones in a scale, or the compass of a voice or instrument; also, a rule or scale employed in tuning musical instruments; also, a fixed standard of musical pitch; also, either of two principal stops in an organ, one ('open diapason': cf. *open*, *a.*) giving full majestic tones, and the other ('stopped diapason': cf. *stopped*, *p. a.*) powerful flute-like tones; any of several other organ-stops.—**di″a-pa-son′ic** (-pā-zon′ik), *a.*

Dianthus (China Pink) (*D. chinensis*).

di-a-per (dī′ạ-pėr), *n.* [OF. *diapre*, *diaspre*, a figured silk fabric (often white), < ML. *diasprum*, < MGr. δίασπρος, (appar.) pure white, < Gr. δια-, thoroughly, + MGr. ἄσπρος, white.] A rich figured silk fabric†; also, a linen or cotton fabric with a woven pattern of small, constantly repeated figures; a towel or napkin of this material or some substitute, esp. a napkin for wrapping about a baby's breech; also, any decorative pattern composed of small, closely set, constantly repeated figures.—**di′a-per,** *v. t.* To diversify or adorn with a diaper-like pattern: as, "Down-droop'd, in many a floating fold . . . *diaper'd* With inwrought flowers, a cloth of gold" (Tennyson's "Recollections of the Arabian Nights," 148).

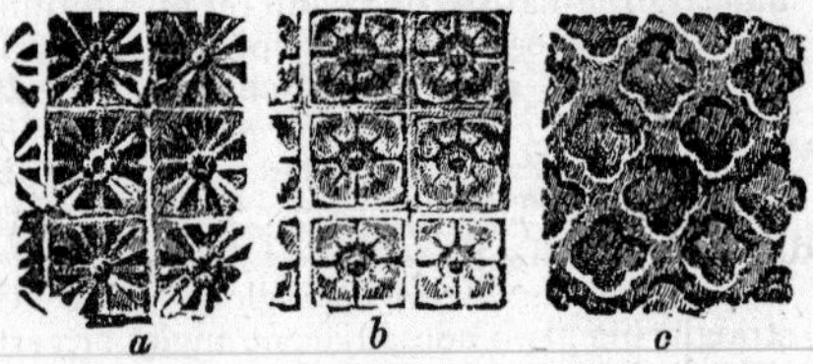

Diapers.—*a*, from Westminster Abbey, and *b*, *c*, from Lincoln Cathedral, England.

di-aph-a-nous (dī-af′ạ-nus), *a.* [Gr. διαφανής, < διαφαίνειν, show through, < διά, through, + φαίνειν, show.] Transparent; translucent.—**di-a-pha-ne-i-ty** (dī″ạ-fạ-nē′i-ti), **di-aph′a-nous-ness,** *n.*—**di-aph′a-nous-ly,** *adv.*

di-a-pho-re-sis (dī″ạ-fọ-rē′sis), *n.* [LL., < Gr. διαφόρησις, < διαφορεῖν, disperse, throw off by perspiration, < δια-, asunder, + φορεῖν, freq. of φέρειν, bear.] In *med.*, perspiration, esp.

when artificially produced.—**di″a-pho-ret′ic** (-ret′ik). In *med.*: **I.** *a.* Producing perspiration. **II.** *n.* A diaphoretic medicine.

di-a-phragm (dī′ą-fram), *n.* [LL. *diaphragma*, < Gr. διάφραγμα, < διαφράσσειν, fence asunder, < διά, between, + φράσσειν, fence in.] A partition or septum; a plate with a circular hole, used in cameras and optical instruments to cut off marginal beams of light; a vibrating membrane or disk, as in a telephone or a phonograph; in *anat.*, the partly muscular, partly tendinous partition separating the thoracic cavity from the abdominal cavity in mammals; in *physical chem.*, etc., a semipermeable membrane or the like (see *semipermeable*).—**di′a-phragm,** *v.*; *-phragmed*, *-phragming.* **I.** *tr.* To furnish or act upon with a diaphragm; in *photog.*, etc., to reduce the aperture of (a lens or objective) by means of a diaphragm (usually with *down*). **II.** *intr.* To employ a diaphragm.—**di″a-phrag-mat′ic** (-frag-mat′ik), *a.* Of, pertaining to, or of the nature of a diaphragm.—**di″a-phrag-mat′i-cal-ly,** *adv.*

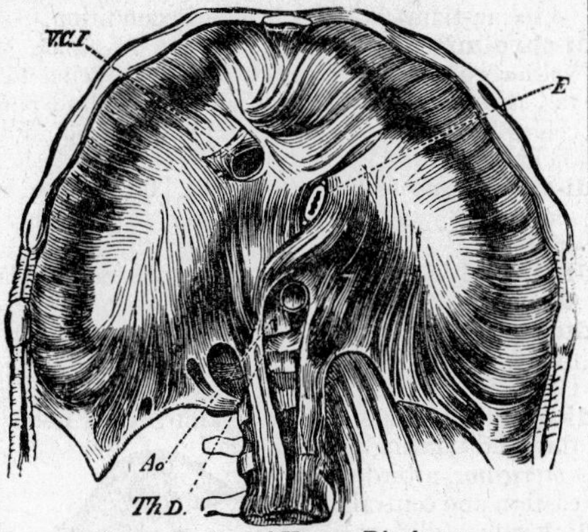

Lower Surface of Human Diaphragm.
E, esophagus; *VCI*, inferior vena cava; *ThD*, thoracic duct; *Ao*, aorta.

di-aph-y-sis (dī-af′i-sis), *n.*; pl. *-yses* (-i-sēz). [NL., < Gr. διάφυσις, a growing through, < διαφύεσθαι, grow through, < διά, through, + φύειν, produce.] In *bot.*, an abnormal elongation of the axis of an inflorescence; in *anat.*, the shaft of a long bone.

di-a-poph-y-sis (dī-ą-pof′i-sis), *n.*; pl. *-yses* (-i-sēz). [NL.: see *di-*[2] and *apophysis*.] In *anat.* and *zoöl.*, the transverse process proper of a vertebra.—**di″a-po-phys′i-al** (-pǫ-fiz′i-ąl), *a.*

di-ar-chy (dī′är-ki), *n.*; pl. *-chies* (-kiz). [See *di-*[1] and *-archy*.] Government or a government in which the executive power is vested in two rulers or ruling authorities.—**di-ar′chi-al** (-ki-ąl), *a.*

di-a-ri-al (dī-ā′ri-ąl), *a.* Of or pertaining to a diary.

di-a-rist (dī′ą-rist), *n.* One who keeps a diary.

di-a-rize (dī′ą-rīz), *v. i.*; *-rized, -rizing.* To make records in a diary.

di-ar-rhe-a, di-ar-rhœ-a (dī-ą-rē′ä), *n.* [LL. *diarrhœa*, < Gr. διάρροια, < διαρρεῖν, flow through, < διά, through, + ῥεῖν, flow.] In *pathol.*, an intestinal disorder characterized by morbid frequency and fluidity of fecal evacuations.—**di-ar-rhe′al, di-ar-rhœ′al,** *a.* Of or pertaining to diarrhea.—**di-ar-rhe′ic, di-ar-rhœ′ic,** *a.*

di-ar-thro-sis (dī-är-thrō′sis), *n.*; pl. *-throses* (-thrō′sēz). [NL., < Gr. διάρθρωσις: see *dia-* and *arthrosis*.] In *anat.*, a form of articulation which permits considerable motion, as the hip-joint.

di-a-ry (dī′ą-ri), *n.*; pl. *-ries* (-riz). [L. *diarium*, < *dies*, day.] A daily record, esp. of the writer's own experiences or observations; also, a book prepared for keeping such a record; sometimes, a printed book giving memoranda with reference to each day of the year.

Di-as-po-ra (dī-as′pǫ-rä), *n.* [Gr. διασπορά, a scattering, < διασπείρειν, scatter about, < διά, through, + σπείρειν, sow, scatter.] Among the Hellenistic Jews, the whole body of Jews living scattered among the Gentiles after the Babylonian captivity; the Dispersion; among the early Jewish Christians, the body of Jewish Christians outside Palestine.

di-a-spore (dī′ą-spōr), *n.* [Gr. διασπορά, a scattering (see *Diaspora*); from its action before the blowpipe.] A native hydroxide of aluminium, occurring in crystals, or more usually in lamellar or scaly masses.

di-a-stase (dī′ą-stās), *n.* [F., < Gr. διάστασις, separation, < διιστάναι, separate, < διά, between, + ἱστάναι, set up, stand.] An enzyme present in germinated barley, potatoes, etc., possessing the property of converting starch into dextrin and maltose.—**di-a-sta′sic** (-stā′sik), **di-a-stat′ic** (-stat′ik), *a.*

di-as-to-le (dī-as′tǫ-lē), *n.* [LL., < Gr. διαστολή, a putting asunder, dilatation, lengthening, < διαστέλλειν, put asunder, < δια-, asunder, + στέλλειν, set, place, send.] In *physiol.*, etc., the normal rhythmical dilatation of the heart, esp. that of the ventricles (cf. *systole*); any of various other rhythmical dilatations; in *Gr. gram.*, a mark, similar to a comma, used to separate words; in *anc. pros.*, the lengthening of a syllable regularly short, esp. before a pause or at the ictus.—**di-as-tol′ic** (-ąs-tol′ik), *a.*

di-as-tro-phism (dī-as′trǫ-fizm), *n.* [Gr. διαστροφή, < διαστρέφειν, distort, < δια-, asunder, + στρέφειν, turn.] In *geol.*, the action of the forces which have caused the deformation of the earth's crust, producing continents, mountains, etc.—**di-as-troph′ic** (-ąs-trof′ik), *a.*

di-a-style (dī′ą-stīl). [L. *diastylos*, < Gr. διάστυλος, < διά, through, + στῦλος, pillar, column.] In *arch.*: **I.** *a.* Noting or pertaining to an arrangement of columns in which the intercolumniation measures three diameters. **II.** *n.* A diastyle colonnade.

di-a-tes-sa-ron (dī-ą-tes′ą-ron), *n.* [Gr. διὰ τεσσάρων, 'of four.'] A harmony of the four Gospels.

di-a-ther-ma-nous (dī-ą-thėr′mą-nus), *a.* [F. *diathermane*, < Gr. διά, through, + θερμαίνειν, heat, < θερμός, hot.] In *physics*, permeable by radiant heat. Cf. *athermanous*.—**di-a-ther′mance, di-a-ther′man-cy** (-mąns, -mąn-si), *n.*

di-a-ther-mi-a, di-a-ther-my (dī-ą-thėr′mi-ä, -mi), *n.* [NL. *diathermia*, < Gr. διά, through, + θερμός, hot.] In *med.*, a method of therapeutic treatment which consists in raising parts of the body to a comparatively high temperature by means of electric currents.

di-a-ther-mic (dī-ą-thėr′mik), *a.* Same as *diathermanous.*

di-ath-e-sis (dī-ath′e-sis), *n.*; pl. *-eses* (-e-sēz). [NL., < Gr. διάθεσις, arrangement, disposition, < διατιθέναι, place separately, arrange, < δια-, asunder, + τιθέναι, set.] In *med.*, a constitutional predisposition or tendency, as to a particular disease or affection.—**di-a-thet′ic** (-ą-thet′ik), *a.*

di-a-tom (dī′ą-tom), *n.* [NL. *Diatoma*, a genus of diatoms, < LGr. διάτομος, verbal adj. of Gr. διατέμνειν, cut through, < διά, through, + τέμνειν, cut.] Any of numerous microscopic, unicellular, marine or fresh-water algæ, characterized by siliceous cell-walls or shells consisting of two valves, which form extensive fossil deposits in many localities. Cf. *bergmehl* and *kieselguhr*.—**di″a-to-ma′ceous** (-tǫ-mā′shius), *a.* Of or pertaining to diatoms; consisting of or containing diatoms or their fossil remains.

Diatoms (magnified).

di-a-tom-ic (dī-ą-tom′ik), *a.* [See *di-*[1].] In *chem.*, having two atoms in the molecule; also, containing two replaceable atoms or groups.

di-at-o-mite (dī-at′ǫ-mīt), *n.* [See *diatom*.] Diatomaceous or infusorial earth. See *infusorial.*

di-a-ton-ic (dī-ą-ton′ik), *a.* [LL. *diatonicus*, < Gr. διατονικός, for διάτονος, diatonic, < διατείνειν, stretch out, extend, continue, < διά, through, + τείνειν, stretch.] In *music*, consisting of, using, or involving only the tones of a standard major or minor scale without chromatic alteration.—**di-a-ton′i-cal-ly,** *adv.*

di-a-tribe (dī′ą-trīb), *n.* [ML. *diatriba*, < Gr. διατριβή, pastime, employment, study, discourse, < διατρίβειν, rub away, < διά, through, + τρίβειν, rub.] A discourse or dissertation, now esp. one vehemently denouncing some person or thing; a strain of invective: as, "breaking out into fierce *diatribes* against that . . . outrageous swindle" (Thackeray's "Newcomes," lxx.).—**di′a-trib-ist** (-trī-bist), *n.*

di-az-o- (dī-az′ǫ-). [See *di-*[1] and *azo-*.] In *chem.*, a combining-form signifying that a compound contains a group of two nitrogen atoms, N_2, united with one hydrocarbon radical or with one hydrocarbon radical and another atom or group of atoms. Also **di-az′o,** *a.*—**di-az′o-tize** (-ǫ-tīz), *v. t.*; *-tized, -tizing.* In *chem.*, to treat so as to convert into a diazo compound.

dib (dib), *v. i.*; *dibbed, dibbing.* [Cf. *dab*[1].] To fish by letting the bait bob lightly on the water; also, to dibble.

di-ba-sic (dī-bā′sik), *a.* [See *di-*[1].] Same as *bibasic.*

dib-ber (dib′ėr), *n.* A dibble.

dib-ble (dib′l), *n.* [ME. *debylle*: cf. *dib* and *dab*[1].] An implement with one or more tapering points for making holes in the ground for planting seeds, bulbs, etc.—**dib′ble,** *v.*; *-bled, -bling.* **I.** *tr.* To make a hole in (the ground) with or as with a dibble; also, to sow or plant with a dibble. **II.** *intr.* To use a dibble.—**dib′bler,** *n.*

di-bran-chi-ate (dī-brang′ki-āt). [NL. *Dibranchiata*, pl., < Gr. δι-, two, + βράγχια, gills.] **I.** *a.* Belonging to the *Dibranchiata*, a subclass of cephalopods with two gills, including the decapods and octopods. **II.** *n.* A dibranchiate cephalopod.

di-cast (dī′kast), *n.* [Gr. δικαστής, < δικάζειν, judge, < δίκη, right, justice.] In ancient Athens, one of 6,000 citizens chosen annually to try cases in the courts of law in a capacity that combined the functions of the modern judge and juryman.—**di-cas′te-ry** (-kas′tẹ-ri), *n.*; pl. *-ries* (-riz). [Gr. δικαστήριον.] One of the courts in which the dicasts sat; a body of dicasts.—**di-cas′tic,** *a.* Of or pertaining to the dicasts.

dice (dīs), *n. pl.* [Pl. of *die*[2].] Small cubes whose sides are marked with different numbers of spots, thrown from a box or the hand in gaming; the game played; also, any small cubes or square blocks.—**dice,** *v.*; *diced, dicing.* **I.** *intr.* To play at dice. **II.** *tr.* To cut into dice or cubes, as vegetables in cookery; also, to decorate with cube-like figures; checker.—**dice′-box,** *n.* The box from which dice are thrown, usually in the form of a hollow cylinder open at one end and sometimes contracted in the middle.

di-cen-tra (dī-sen′trạ̈), *n.* [NL., < Gr. δι-, two, + κέντρον, sharp point, spur.] Any of the plants constituting the papaveraceous genus *Dicentra* (or *Bikukulla*), with racemes of drooping flowers having a two-spurred or heart-shaped corolla, as the Dutchman's-breeches or the bleeding-heart.

di-ceph-a-lous (dī-sef′ạ-lus), *a.* [Gr. δικέφαλος, < δι-, two, + κεφαλή, head.] Having two heads.

di-cer (dī′sėr), *n.* One who plays at dice; also, a hat, esp. a stiff hat (slang).

di-cha-si-um (dī-kā′zi-um), *n.*; pl. *-sia* (-zi-ạ̈). [NL., < Gr. δι-, two, + χάσις, separation: cf. *monochasium.*] In *bot.*, a form of cymose inflorescence in which each axis produces a pair of lateral axes.—**di-cha′si-al,** *a.*

di-chla-myd-e-ous (dī-klạ-mid′ẹ̄-us), *a.* [Gr. δι-, two, + χλαμύς (χλαμυδ-), mantle.] In *bot.*, having both a calyx and a corolla.

di-chlo-ride (dī-klō′rīd or -rid), *n.* [See *di-*[1].] Same as *bichloride.*

di-chog-a-mous (dī-kog′ạ-mus), *a.* [Gr. δίχα, in two, + γάμος, marriage.] In *bot.*, having the stamens and pistils maturing at different times (thus preventing self-fertilization), as a monoclinous flower: opposed to *homogamous.*—**di-chog′a-my,** *n.* Dichogamous condition.

di-cho-tom-ic (dī-kọ̄-tom′ik), *a.* Dichotomous.

di-chot-o-mize (dī-kot′ọ̄-mīz), *v.*; *-mized, -mizing.* [See *dichotomous.*] **I.** *tr.* To divide into two parts; divide into pairs. **II.** *intr.* To separate into two parts; become dichotomous.—**di-chot″o-mi-za′tion** (-mi-zā′shọn), *n.*

di-chot-o-mous (dī-kot′ọ̄-mus), *a.* [Gr. διχότομος, cut in two, < δίχα, in two, + τέμνειν, cut.] Divided or dividing into two parts; characterized by or involving successive division or branching into two parts; pertaining to dichotomy.—**di-chot′o-mous-ly,** *adv.*—**di-chot′o-my,** *n.*; pl. *-mies* (-miz). [Gr. διχοτομία.] Division into two parts; dichotomous division; in *logic*, classification by division, or by successive subdivision, into two groups or sections; in *bot.*, a mode of branching by constant bifurcation; in *astron.*, the phase of the moon, or of an inferior planet, when half of its disk is visible.

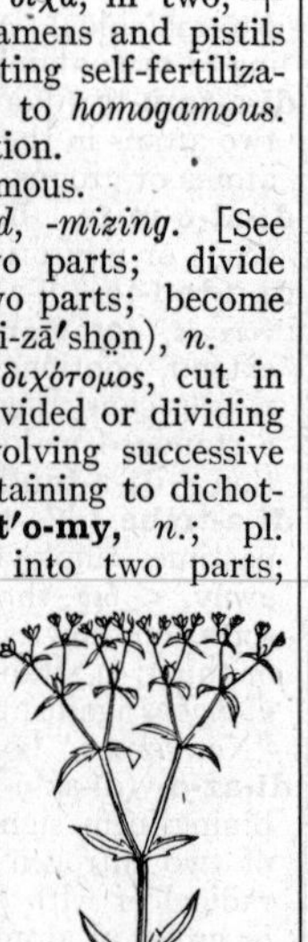

Dichotomy.

di-chro-ic (dī-krō′ik), *a.* [Gr. δίχροος, of two colors, < δι-, two, + χρόα, color.] Having or exhibiting two colors; of a crystal, exhibiting different colors in two different directions when viewed by transmitted light.—**di′chro-ism** (-krọ̄-izm), *n.* The property of being dichroic.—**di′chro-ite** (-īt), *n.* Iolite, whose crystals are often dichroic.—**di-chro-it′ic** (-it′ik), *a.* Dichroic.

di-chro-mate (dī-krō′māt), *n.* [See *di-*[1].] Same as *bichromate.*

di-chro-mat-ic (dī-krọ̄-mat′ik), *a.* [Gr. δι-, two, + χρῶμα (χρωματ-), color.] Having or showing two colors; dichromic; in *zoöl.*, exhibiting regularly or frequently a coloration different from the normal.—**di-chro′ma-tism** (-krō′mạ-tizm), *n.* Dichromatic condition.

di-chro-mic (dī-krō′mik), *a.* [Gr. δίχρωμος, < δι-, two, + χρῶμα, color.] Pertaining to or embracing two colors only (as, *dichromic* vision, that of a color-blind person who perceives only two of the three primary colors); of a crystal, dichroic.

di-chro-scope (dī′krọ̄-skōp), *n.* [Gr. δίχροος, of two colors: see *-scope.*] An instrument for testing the dichroism of crystals.

di-cing (dī′sing), *n.* The act or practice of playing at dice; also, decoration with cube-like figures.

dick (dik), *n.* [From *Dick*, for *Richard*, man's name.] A man or fellow (colloq.: as, a queer *dick*; "He's a gone *dick*," Galt's "Ayrshire Legatees," v.); also, a detective (slang).

dick-cis-sel (dik-sis′ẹl), *n.* [Imit. of its note.] The black-throated bunting, *Spiza americana*, a bird of the eastern and central U. S.

Dickcissel.

dick-ens (dik′ẹnz), *n.* [Appar. < *Dickon*, dim. of *Dick*, for *Richard*, man's name: cf. the surname *Dickens.*] The devil; the deuce: used in colloquial exclamations and phrases, usually preceded by *the*: as, "What the *dickens* do you want to be educating yourself for, pray?" (Kingsley's "Alton Locke," iv.).

dick-er[1] (dik′ėr), *n.* [ME. *dyker* = Icel. *dekr* = G. *decher*, < L. *decuria*, company of ten: see *decury.*] The number or quantity ten; esp., a lot of ten hides or skins.

dick-er[2] (dik′ėr), *v.* [Perhaps < *dicker*[1], orig. with reference to the frontier trade in skins.] **I.** *intr.* To trade by barter or by petty bargaining; barter; haggle. [Chiefly U. S.] **II.** *tr.* To barter. [Chiefly U. S.]—**dick′er**[2], *n.* The act or practice of dickering; barter; also, a transaction by barter; a petty bargain. [Chiefly U. S.]

dick-y[1], **dick-ey**[1] (dik′i), *n.*; pl. *-ies, -eys* (-iz). [Cf. *dick.*] A male donkey; any donkey; a small bird, as a sparrow or a canary-bird; a detached shirt-front; a linen shirt-collar; the driver's seat on the outside of a carriage, or a seat behind for servants, etc.

dick-y[2], **dick-ey**[2] (dik′i), *a.* [Perhaps < *dicky*[1].] Poor in quality or condition; unsound; shaky. [Slang or colloq., Eng.]

di-cli-nous (dī-klī′nus), *a.* [Gr. δι-, two, + κλίνη, bed.] In *bot.*, of a plant species, etc., having the andrœcium and the gynœcium in separate flowers, either on the same plant or on different plants; either monœcious or diœcious; of a flower, having only stamens or only pistils; unisexual. Cf. *monoclinous.*

di-cot-y-le-don (dī″kot-i-lē′dọn), *n.* [See *di-*[1].] In *bot.*, a plant with two cotyledons; a member of the group *Dicotyledones*, one of the two subclasses of angiospermous plants, characterized by producing seeds with two cotyledons or seed-leaves, and by an exogenous mode of growth. Cf. *exogen*, also *monocotyledon.*—**di″cot-y-le′don-ous,** *a.* In *bot.*, having two cotyledons; belonging or pertaining to the *Dicotyledones* (see *dicotyledon*).

di-crot-ic (dī-krot′ik), *a.* [Gr. δίκροτος, double-beating, < δι-, two, + κρότος, beat.] Having two arterial beats for one heart-beat, as certain pulses; pertaining to such a pulse.—**di′cro-tism** (-krọ-tizm), *n.* Dicrotic condition.

dic-ta (dik′tạ̈), *n.* Plural of *dictum.*

dic-ta-graph (dik′tạ-gråf), *n.* See *dictograph.*

dic-ta-phone (dik′tạ-fōn), *n.* [See *dictate* and *-phone.*] A phonographic instrument that records and reproduces dictation. [Proprietary name.]

dic-tate (dik′tāt or dik-tāt′), *v.*; *-tated, -tating.* [L. *dictatus,* pp. of *dictare,* pronounce, dictate, compose, prescribe, freq. of *dicere,* say: see *diction.*] **I.** *tr.* To utter (something) to be taken down in writing or otherwise; also, to prescribe positively or with authority (sometimes with a thing as subject: as, necessity *dictated* the abandonment of the ship). **II.** *intr.* To utter something to be taken down in writing, etc.; also, to prescribe what is to be done; give orders.—**dic′tate,** *n.* [L. *dictatum,* prop. pp. neut.] Something dictated in order to be written down†; also, a dictum†; also, a positive or authoritative prescription as to conduct, etc.; a command; an injunction.—**dic-ta′tion** (-tā′shọn), *n.* [LL. *dictatio(n-).*] The act of dictating for reproduction in writing, etc.; words dictated, or taken down as dictated; also, the act of prescribing positively or authoritatively; sometimes, dictatorial or imperious direction; also, something dictated or prescribed.—**dic-ta′tor,** *n.* [L.] One who dictates; one who authoritatively prescribes conduct, usage, etc.; a person exercising absolute authority, esp. in government, as a chief magistrate appointed in ancient Rome in times of emergency, or a similar magistrate in some other state.—**dic-ta-to′ri-al** (-tạ-tō′ri-ạl), *a.* [L. *dictatorius.*] Of or pertaining to a dictator; also, characteristic of a dictator; also, inclined to dictate or command; imperious; overbearing.—**dic-ta-to′ri-al-ly,** *adv.*—**dic-ta-to′ri-al-ness,** *n.*—**dic-ta′tor-ship,** *n.* The office or dignity of a dictator; absolute authority.—**dic′ta-to-ry** (-tạ-tọ-ri), *a.* Dictatorial.—**dic-ta′tress,** *n.* A female dictator.—**dic-ta′ture** (-tụr), *n.* [L. *dictatura.*] Dictatorship.

dic-tion (dik′shọn), *n.* [L. *dictio(n-),* saying, style of speaking, mode of expression, LL. a word, < L. *dicere,* say, akin to *dicare,* declare, Gr. δεικνύναι, G. *zeigen,* AS. *tǣcan,* show, E. *teach.*] Manner of expressing ideas in words; style of speaking or writing as dependent upon choice of words; also, manner of using the voice in speaking; delivery.

dic-tion-a-ry (dik′shọn-ā-ri), *n.*; pl. *-ries* (-riz). [ML. *dictionarium,* < LL. *dictio(n-),* word: see *diction.*] A book containing a more or less extensive selection of the words of a language, or of a particular class of words, usually arranged alphabetically, with explanations of their meanings and other information concerning them, expressed either in the same or in another language (as, a *dictionary* of the English language; the English Dialect *Dictionary*; a French-English *dictionary*); a lexicon; a glossary; also, a book giving information on a particular subject, under head-words or headings which are usually arranged alphabetically (as, a biographical *dictionary*).

dic-to-graph (dik′tọ-gråf), *n.* [L. *dictum,* something said: see *-graph.*] A telephonic device with a highly sensitive transmitter obviating the necessity of a mouthpiece, much used for secretly listening to or obtaining a record of the conversation of persons under suspicion. [Proprietary name.]

dic-tum (dik′tum), *n.*; pl. *dicta* (-tạ). [L., something said, a saying, a command, prop. pp. neut. of *dicere,* say: see *diction.*] A saying; an authoritative utterance or pronouncement; in *law,* an expression of opinion by a judge on the trial of a case, which is not part of the formal resolution or determination of the court.

did (did). Preterit of *do*[1].

Did-a-che (did′ạ-kē), *n.* [Gr. διδαχή, teaching, < διδάσκειν, teach.] A Christian treatise of the first or second century, called more fully "The Teaching of the Twelve Apostles." —**Did′a-chist** (-kist), **Did-a-chog′ra-pher** (-kog′rạ-fėr), *n.* The writer or compiler of the Didache.

di-dac-tic (di-dak′tik or dī-), *a.* [Gr. διδακτικός, < διδάσκειν, teach.] Serving or aiming to give instruction; instructive.—**di-dac′ti-cal-ly,** *adv.*—**di-dac′ti-cism** (-sizm), *n.* The quality or practice of conveying or aiming to convey instruction.—**di-dac′tics,** *n.* The art or science of teaching.

di-dac-tyl (dī-dak′til), *a.* [Gr. δι-, two, + δάκτυλος, finger or toe.] In *zoöl.,* having only two fingers, claws, or toes to each limb. Also **di-dac′ty-lous** (-ti-lus).

di-dap-per (dī′dap″ėr), *n.* [Cf. AS. *dūfedoppa,* diving bird.] A dabchick.

did-der (did′ėr), *v. i.* [ME. *diddir:* cf. *dodder*[2].] To tremble; shiver; quiver; dither. [Now prov. Eng.]

did-dle[1] (did′l), *v. i.*; *-dled, -dling.* [Cf. *didder.*] To move rapidly up and down or backward and forward. [Colloq. or prov.]

did-dle[2] (did′l), *v. t.*; *-dled, -dling.* [Origin uncertain.] To cheat or swindle; victimize; also, to undo or ruin; also, to waste (time). [Colloq.]—**did′dler,** *n.*

di-do (dī′dō), *n.*; pl. *-does* or *-dos* (-dōz). [Origin uncertain.] A prank; an antic; a disorderly performance: often in *pl.* [Colloq.]

didst (didst). Second person sing. pret. of *do*[1]: now only in poetic or solemn use.

di-dym-i-um (dī-dim′i-um or di-), *n.* [NL., < Gr. δίδυμος, twin: see *didymous.*] In *chem.,* a substance containing neodymium and praseodymium: formerly supposed to be an element, and called the 'twin brother of lanthanum.'

did-y-mous (did′i-mus), *a.* [Gr. δίδυμος, double, twofold, twin, redupl. of δύο, two.] In *bot.* and *zoöl.,* occurring in pairs; paired; twin.

die[1] (dī), *v. i.*; *died, dying.* [ME. *dien, deien,* = Icel. *deyja* = OHG. *touwan,* die: cf. *dead* and *death.*] To suffer the total and permanent cessation of all the vital functions, as an animal or a plant; cease to live; suffer death; cease to perform the functions of life; also, to cease to live in a particular respect; in theological use, to lose spiritual life; also, to lose force, strength, or active qualities; come to an end, or pass out of existence (as, "And so *dies* my revenge": Shakspere's "Much Ado about Nothing," v. 1. 301); pass gradually away, or fade away (as, "I hear soft music *die* along the grove": Pope's "Windsor Forest," 268); pass gradually (*into:* as, "The twilight *died* into the dark," Tennyson's "Day-Dream," 188); also, to suffer as if dying; pine with desire, or have great desire.

die[2] (dī), *n.*; pl. *dice* (in first two senses: see *dice*) or *dies* (in other senses). [ME. *de,* < OF. *de,* F. *dé,* = It. *dado* (see *dado*), < L. *datum,* pp. neut. of *dare,* give.] A small cube or block whose sides are marked with different numbers of spots, thrown from a box or the hand in gaming; any small cube or square block; also, the dado of a pedestal, esp. when cubical; also, an engraved stamp for impressing a design, etc., upon some softer material, as in coining money; one of a pair of stamps or the like formed as counterparts, for impressing, shaping, or forming something; also, any of various other devices for shaping material; a hollow device of steel, often composed of several pieces to be fitted into a stock, for cutting the threads of bolts, etc., or one of the separate pieces of such a device; in a punching-machine, a perforated block upon which the object to be punched is rested.—**die**[2], *v. t.*; *died, dieing.* To impress or shape with a die.

Roman Die, found in the south of France.

die=a-way (dī′ạ-wā″), *a.* Languishing; languid.

di-e-cious (dī-ē′shus), *a.* See *diœcious.*

die=hard (dī′härd). **I.** *a.* That dies hard or with a struggle; fig., resisting vigorously to the last; yielding only at the last extremity. **II.** *n.* One who dies hard; fig., one who resists vigorously to the last.

di-e-lec-tric (dī-ẹ-lek′trik). [See *di-*[2].] **I.** *a.* Conveying electric effects otherwise than by conduction, as a medium through which electricity acts in the process of induction; non-conducting; also, pertaining to such transmission. **II.** *n.* A dielectric substance.—**di-e-lec′tri-cal-ly,** *adv.*

di-er (dī′ėr), *n.* One who dies.

di-er-e-sis, di-ær-e-sis (dī-er′e-sis), *n.*; pl. *-eses* (-e-sēz). [LL. *diæresis,* < Gr. διαίρεσις, < διαιρεῖν, divide, < δια-, asunder, + αἱρεῖν, take.] The separate pronunciation of two adjacent vowels, esp. two usually united as a diphthong, a sign (¨) placed over the second of two adjacent vowels to indicate separate pronunciation; in *pros.,* the division made in a line or verse by coincidence of the end of a foot and the end of a word.

di-es (dī′ēz), *n.*; pl. *dies.* [L.] Day.—**Dies Iræ** (ī′rē). [ML., 'day of wrath' (the first words of the hymn).] A famous medieval Latin hymn on the Day of Judgment (commonly ascribed to Thomas of Celano, a Franciscan of the first half of the 13th century), sung esp. in masses for the dead.—**dies non** (non). [For L. *dies non juridicus*, 'a day not juridical.'] In *law*, a day on which no courts can be held or no legal business transacted.

Die-sel (dē′zẹl) **en′gine.** [From Dr. Rudolf *Diesel*, of Munich, the inventor.] A type of internal-combustion engine in which a heavy oil is sprayed into the cylinder after the air in it has been compressed to incandescence, thus causing the ignition of the oil, which undergoes a form of combustion slower than an explosion. Also **Die′sel mo′tor.**

die=sink-er (dī′sing″kėr), *n.* An engraver of dies for coins, etc.—**die′=sink″ing,** *n.*

die=stock (dī′stok), *n.* A stock for holding the dies used in cutting screws.

Die-stock.

di-et[1] (dī′et), *n.* [ML. *dieta, diæta*, appar. the same word as L. *diæta* (see *diet*[2]), with sense affected by L. *dies*, day.] A day set for a meeting or assembly (Sc.); also, a session, as of a court (Sc.); also, a formal assembly for discussing or acting upon public or state affairs, as the general assembly of the estates of the former Holy Roman Empire or as the German Reichstag; the members, collectively, of such an assembly.

di-et[2] (dī′et), *n.* [OF. *diete* (F. *diète*), < L. *diæta*, < Gr. *δίαιτα*, way of living, diet.] Way of living†; esp., manner of living as regards food; also, a particular course of food, as one prescribed to improve the physical condition or cure a disease; also, food, esp. as considered in relation to its quality and effects.—**di′et**[2], *v.*; *-eted, -eting.* **I.** *tr.* To feed, esp. with a particular kind of food; also, to regulate the food of, as to improve the physical condition. **II.** *intr.* To eat; feed; also, to adhere to a particular diet.—**di-e-ta-ri-an** (dī-e-tā′ri-ạn), *n.* One who adheres to a dietary or diet.—**di′e-ta-ry** (-tạ-ri). **I.** *a.* Pertaining to diet. **II.** *n.*; pl. *-ries* (-riz). A system or course of diet: also, a regulated allowance of food, as for inmates of a hospital or prison.—**di′et-er,** *n.*

di-e-tet-ic (dī-e-tet′ik), *a.* [L. *diæteticus*, < Gr. *διαιτητικός*, < *δίαιτα*, E. *diet*[2].] Pertaining to diet or to regulation of the use of food. Also **di-e-tet′i-cal.**—**di-e-tet′i-cal-ly,** *adv.*—**di-e-tet′ics,** *n.* The department of medicine concerned with the regulation of diet.—**di-e-tet′ist,** *n.* One versed in dietetics; a physician who gives the first place to dietetics in the treatment of disease.

di-e-ti-cian, di-e-ti-tian (dī-e-tish′an), *n.* [From *diet*[2].] One versed in the regulation of diet; a dietetist.

di-et=kitch-en (dī′et-kich″ẹn), *n.* An establishment, usually connected with a dispensary or with the outdoor department of a hospital, for preparing and dispensing suitable diet for invalids, esp. among the poor.

di-et-o-ther-a-py (dī″e-tọ̄-ther′ạ-pi), *n.* [See *diet*[2] and *therapy*.] The treatment of disease by the regulation of diet.

dif-fer (dif′ėr), *v. i.* [OF. *differer* (F. *différer*), < L. *differre*, carry apart, put off, delay (see *defer*[1]), be different, < *dis-*, apart, + *ferre*, bear.] To be unlike, dissimilar, or distinct, as in nature or qualities; also, to be at variance in opinion, belief, etc.; disagree; also, to give expression to disagreement†; dispute†.—**dif′fer,** *n.* Difference: as, "I'll pay you the *differ* out o' my wages" (Lover's "Handy Andy," ix.). [Sc., Ir., and prov. Eng.]

dif-fer-ence (dif′ẹ-rẹns), *n.* [OF. *difference* (F. *différence*), < L. *differentia*.] The state or relation of being different; dissimilarity; also, an instance of unlikeness or dissimilarity; a point in which things differ; also, a character which one thing has and another has not; a distinguishing characteristic; specif., an alteration or addition employed to differentiate the coats of arms of two persons, which would otherwise be identical; also, distinction or discrimination, or a distinction or discrimination made (as, "to make a *difference* between the unclean and the clean": Lev. xi. 47); also, a disagreement in opinion; a dispute or quarrel; also, the degree in which one thing differs from another; the amount by which one quantity is greater or less than another; the remainder in subtraction.—**to make a difference,** to alter or affect the case; matter: as, the way you say it *makes a difference*, or *a* great *difference*; whether you go or not *makes* little *difference* (that is, matters little); what you say *makes* no *difference* (that is, does not matter). Also, to make a distinction (see def. with quotation above).—**dif′fer-ence,** *v. t.*; *-enced, -encing.* To cause or constitute a difference in or between; make different; also, to perceive the difference in or between; discriminate.

dif-fer-ent (dif′ẹ-rẹnt), *a.* [OF. *different* (F. *différent*), < L. *differens* (*-ent-*), ppr. of *differre*, E. *differ*.] Differing in character (when followed by a preposition, usually taking *from*, in England often *to* or sometimes *than*, although the constructions with *to* and *than* are by many considered improper); having unlike qualities; dissimilar; altered or changed; also, not the same, or not identical; distinct; various or several.

dif-fer-en-ti-a (dif-ẹ-ren′shi-ạ̈), *n.*; pl. *-tiæ* (-shi-ē). [L., difference.] In *logic*, the character or attribute by which one species is distinguished from all others of the same genus.

dif-fer-en-ti-a-ble (dif-ẹ-ren′shi-ạ-bl), *a.* Capable of being differentiated.

dif-fer-en-tial (dif-ẹ-ren′shạl). [L. *differentia*, E. *difference*.] **I.** *a.* Of or pertaining to difference or diversity; also, exhibiting or depending upon a difference or distinction (as, a *differential* duty, an import duty imposed unequally on merchandise according to various circumstances, such as place of production, manner of importation, etc.; a *differential* rate, a special lower rate, as one charged by one of two or more competing transportation lines, or one to one of two or more places competing for the same traffic); discriminative; also, constituting a difference or differentia; distinguishing; distinctive; also, pertaining to distinguishing characteristics (as, *differential* diagnosis, the distinguishing between two more or less similar diseases or objects of natural history); in *math.*, pertaining to or involving differentials (as, *differential* calculus, see *calculus*; a *differential* coefficient, the measure of the rate of change of a function relatively to its variable); in *physics, mach.*, etc., pertaining to or involving the difference of two or more motions, forces, etc. (as, a *differential* windlass, a windlass with a barrel composed of two parts of different diameter, one upon which the rope winds and the other upon which it unwinds, the amount of lift and of power exerted being determined by the difference in the two diameters; a *differential* gear, an arrangement of gears in the transmission system of an automobile, which allows for the difference in speed of the two driving-wheels, as in going around corners, or any of various analogous arrangements of gears). **II.** *n.* A differential duty or rate; the difference involved in a differential rate; also, a differentiating characteristic; in *math.*, an infinitesimal difference between consecutive values of a variable quantity; in *elect.*, a coil of wire in which the polar action produced is opposite to that of another coil; in *mach.*, a differential gear.—**dif-fer-en′tial-ly,** *adv.* In a differential manner; with reference to a difference, as between quantities or forces; distinctively, or by way of difference.

dif-fer-en-ti-ate (dif-ẹ-ren′shi-āt), *v.*; *-ated, -ating.* [L. *differentia*, E. *difference*.] **I.** *tr.* To mark off by differences; distinguish; alter or change; make different by modification, as a biological species; also, to perceive the difference in or between; discriminate; in *math.*, to obtain the differential or the differential coefficient of. **II.** *intr.* To become unlike or dissimilar; change in character; also, to make a distinction; discriminate.—**dif-fer-en-ti-a′tion** (-ā′shọn), *n.* The act or process of differentiating, or the resulting state; a making or becoming different; alteration; modification during development; a differentiated or altered form; also, discrimination or distinction; in *math.*, the finding of a differential or a differential coefficient.—**dif-fer-en′ti-a-tor,** *n.*

dif-fer-ent-ly (dif′ẹ-rẹnt-li), *adv.* In a different manner; dissimilarly; otherwise.—**dif′fer-ent-ness,** *n.*

dif-fi-cile (dē-fē-sēl), *a.* [F., < L. *difficilis*, < *dis-* (see *dis-*) + *facilis*, easy.] Difficult; hard to deal with, get on with, please, or satisfy.

dif-fi-cult (dif′i-kult), *a.* [From *difficulty.*] Hard to do, perform, or accomplish; not easy; requiring effort; arduous; laborious; attended with or occasioning trouble; troublesome; sometimes, hard to understand; perplexing; also, of a person, hard to deal with or get on with (as, "A *difficult* child was Frederick II for Mother Church": H. G. Wells's "Outline of History," xxxiii. § 12); hard to please or satisfy; hard to induce or persuade.—**dif′fi-cult-ly,** *adv.*—**dif′fi-cult-ness,** *n.*

dif-fi-cul-ty (dif′i-kul-ti), *n.*; pl. *-ties* (-tiz). [OF. *difficulte* (F. *difficulté*), < L. *difficultas*, < *difficul*, old form of *difficilis*, difficult: see *difficile.*] The fact or condition of being difficult; arduousness; troublesomeness; perplexing character; embarrassing situation, as of affairs; a trouble; a financial embarrassment; also, a cause of trouble or embarrassment; also, reluctance or unwillingness; a demur or objection; also, a disagreement or quarrel.

dif-fi-dence (dif′i-dẹns), *n.* [L. *diffidentia*, < *diffidens*, ppr. of *diffidere*, feel distrust, < *dis-* (see *dis-*) + *fidere*, trust.] Distrust or doubt (now rare); esp., distrust of one's self; want of self-confidence; shyness.—**dif′fi-dent,** *a.* [L. *diffidens* (*-ent-*), ppr.] Distrustful (now rare); esp., distrustful of one's self; lacking self-confidence; shy; timid.—**dif′fi-dent-ly,** *adv.*

dif-flu-ent (dif′lö-ẹnt), *a.* [L. *diffluens* (*-ent-*), ppr. of *diffluere*, flow apart or away, < *dis-*, apart, + *fluere*, flow.] Tending to flow apart; readily dissolving.—**dif′flu-ence,** *n.*

dif-form (di-fôrm′), *a.* [ML. *difformis*, < L. *dis-*, apart, + *forma*, E. *form, n.*] Differing in form; dissimilar; of diverse forms; also, irregular in form; not uniform.—**dif-for′mi-ty** (-fôr′mi-ti), *n.* Difference or diversity in form; lack of uniformity.

dif-fract (di-frakt′), *v. t.* [L. *diffractus*, pp. of *diffringere*, < *dis-*, apart, + *frangere*, break.] To break up by diffraction.—**dif-frac′tion** (-frak′shọn), *n.* A modification that light undergoes when it passes by the edge of an opaque body or through a small aperture, or is reflected from a glass or metal surface ruled with fine parallel lines, resulting in the formation of a series of light and dark bands, prismatic colors, or spectra; also, an analogous modification produced upon sound-waves.—**diffraction grating.** See *grating*[1], *n.*—**dif-frac′tive,** *a.* Causing or pertaining to diffraction.

Diffraction Bands.

dif-fran-gi-ble (di-fran′ji-bl), *a.* [L. *dis-*, apart, + *frangere*, break: cf. *diffract.*] Capable of being diffracted.—**dif-fran-gi-bil′i-ty** (-bil′i-ti), *n.*

dif-fuse (di-fūz′), *v.*; *-fused, -fusing.* [L. *diffusus*, pp. of *diffundere*, < *dis-*, apart, + *fundere*, pour.] **I.** *tr.* To pour out and spread, as a fluid; spread or scatter widely; disseminate; in *physics*, to spread by diffusion. **II.** *intr.* To spread; in *physics*, to intermingle or pass by diffusion.—**dif-fuse′** (-fūs′), *a.* Widely spread or scattered; dispersed; characterized by scattering; also, characterized by great length or discursiveness in speech or writing; not concise; verbose.—**dif-fus′ed-ly** (-fū′zed-li), *adv.*—**dif-fuse′ly** (-fūs′li), *adv.*—**dif-fuse′ness,** *n.*—**dif-fus′er** (-fū′zėr), *n.* One who or that which diffuses; a device for diffusing light, air, etc.—**dif-fus′i-ble,** *a.* Capable of being diffused.—**dif-fus-i-bil′i-ty** (-bil′i-ti), *n.*—**dif-fu′sion** (-fū′zhọn), *n.* [L. *diffusio*(*n-*).] The act of diffusing, or the state of being diffused; distribution; dissemination; also, diffuseness or prolixity of speech or writing; in *physics*, the spontaneous intermingling of the particles or molecules of two fluids brought into contact; the permeation of one fluid by another.—**dif-fu′sive** (-siv), *a.* Tending to diffuse; characterized by diffusion; also, diffuse or prolix.—**dif-fu′sive-ly,** *adv.*—**dif-fu′sive-ness,** *n.*

dig (dig), *v. i.*; *dug* or *digged, digging.* [ME. *diggen*; prob. from OF., and ult. akin to E. *dike* and *ditch.*] To break up, turn over, or remove earth, etc., as with a spade; make an excavation; fig., to work hard, as at lessons (colloq., U. S.); also, to make a thrust or stab; also, to make one's way by or as by digging.—**to dig in,** in soldiers' use, to dig a hole or trench for occupancy in a zone subject to the enemy's fire.—**to dig out,** to depart suddenly; decamp. [Slang, U. S.]—**dig,** *v. t.* To break up and turn over, or penetrate and loosen (the ground), with a spade, etc. (often with *up*); make (a hole, etc.) by removing material, as with a spade; obtain or remove by or as by excavation (often with *out* or *up*); also, to make a thrust or stab into; prod; also, to thrust or plunge (an implement, etc.) into something.—**to dig up the hatchet.** See under *hatchet.*—**dig,** *n.* The act or an act of digging; a thrust or poke; also, a diligent or plodding student (students' slang, U. S.).

di-gam-ma (dī-gam′ạ), *n.* [L., < Gr. δίγαμμα, < δι-, two, + γάμμα, gamma; from its likeness to two gammas (Γ), one above the other.] A symbol once forming the sixth letter of the Greek alphabet, but early in disuse, corresponding in form to, and preserved in, the Latin and English F, and itself having the value of the English w.—**di-gam′mat-ed** (-gam′ā-ted), *a.* Spelled with or having the digamma.

dig-a-mous (dig′ạ-mus), *a.* [LL. *digamus*, < Gr. δίγαμος, < δι-, two, + γάμος, marriage.] Practising or advocating digamy; pertaining to digamy.—**dig′a-my,** *n.* [LL. *digamia*, < Gr. διγαμία.] Second marriage; the practice of marrying again after the death of the first spouse.

di-gas-tric (dī-gas′trik), *a.* [Gr. δι-, two, + γαστήρ, belly.] In *anat.*, having two fleshy bellies with an intervening tendinous part, as certain muscles.

di-gen-e-sis (dī-jen′e-sis), *n.* [See *di-*[1] and *genesis.*] In *biol.*, successive generation by two different processes, as sexual and asexual.—**di-ge-net′ic** (-jẹ-net′ik), *a.*

di-gest (di-jest′ or dī-), *v.* [L. *digestus*, pp. of *digerere*, separate, distribute, arrange, dissolve, digest, < *di-*, for *dis-*, apart, + *gerere*, bear.] **I.** *tr.* To divide†; distribute†; also, to dispose methodically; reduce to a systematic form, usually with condensation; also, to arrange methodically in the mind; think over; also, to prepare (food) in the alimentary canal for assimilation into the system; prepare or convert similarly, as insectivorous plants do their prey; promote the digestion of (food); fig., to bear with patience; endure; also, to assimilate mentally; derive mental nourishment from; also, to bring to a perfected state, as by means of heat†; reduce or prepare (substances) by the application of moisture and heat, chemicals, etc. **II.** *intr.* To digest food; also, to undergo digestion, as food.—**di-gest** (dī′jest), *n.* [L. *digestum* (usually pl., *digesta*), prop. pp. neut.] A collection or summary, as of literary, historical, legal, or scientific matter, arranged in some convenient order; esp., in *law*, [*cap.*] a body of Roman laws compiled by order of the emperor Justinian in the 6th century; the Pandects; [*l. c.*] a systematic abstract of some body of law.—**di-gest′ant,** *n.* In *med.*, an agent that promotes digestion.—**di-gest′er,** *n.* One who or that which digests; an apparatus in which substances are reduced or prepared by moisture and heat, chemical action, etc.—**di-gest′i-ble,** *a.* [LL. *digestibilis.*] Capable of being digested; easily digested.—**di-gest-i-bil′i-ty** (-bil′i-ti), **di-gest′i-ble-ness,** *n.*—**di-gest′i-bly,** *adv.*—**di-ges′tion** (-jes′chọn), *n.* [L. *digestio*(*n-*).] The act of digesting, or the resulting state; the process by which food is digested; the function or power of digesting food.—**di-ges′tive.** **I.** *a.* Serving for or pertaining to digestion; having the function of digesting food; promoting digestion; also, digestible. **II.** *n.* A substance or agent which promotes digestion.—**di-ges′tive-ly,** *adv.*

dig-ger (dig′ėr), *n.* One who or that which digs; a miner; a soldiers' term for a soldier from Australia or New Zealand (cf. *to dig in*, under *dig, v. i.*); [*cap.*] one of a group of Indians of western North America, who subsist largely on roots dug from the ground; [*l. c.*] an instrument for digging.—**dig′ger=wasp,** *n.* Any of a large group of solitary, fossorial hymenopterous insects (families *Scoliidæ*, *Pompilidæ*, *Sphegidæ*, etc.), most of which build their nests in burrows in the ground and provision them with the bodies of spiders, caterpillars, etc., for their young; also, any wasp that burrows.

Digger-wasp (*Bembex fasciata*).

dig-ging (dig′ing), *n.* The act of one who or that which digs; also, that which is dug out; also, a place where digging is carried on; *pl.*, a mining locality; any locality or place (colloq.); quarters or abode (colloq.).

dight (dīt), *v. t.*; *dight, dighting.* [AS. *dihtan*, compose, ordain, order, arrange, < L. *dictare*: see *dictate.*] To prescribe† or ordain†; consign or put (to death, etc.)†; also, to frame†, construct†, or make†; also (archaic or prov.), to set in order; arrange; make ready; prepare; repair; clean; equip or furnish; dress or clothe; deck or adorn (as, "Slowly, in all his splendors *dight*, The great sun rises": Longfellow's "Building of the Ship," 264).

dig-it (dij'it), *n.* [L. *digitus*, finger, toe.] A finger or toe; the breadth of a finger used as a linear measure, usually equal to three-fourths of an inch; any of the Arabic figures from 1 to 9, sometimes also including the cipher (0); in *astron.*, the twelfth part of the diameter of the sun or the moon.—**dig'i-tal** (-i-tal). **I.** *a.* Of or pertaining to a digit or digits, esp. the digits or fingers; resembling a digit or finger; having digits or digit-like parts. **II.** *n.* A finger or toe (rare); also, a key played with the finger, as in a piano or organ.

dig-i-ta-lin (dij-i-tā'lin or dij'i-tạ-), *n.* [See *digitalis.*] Any of several extracts obtained from digitalis.

dig-i-ta-lis (dij-i-tā'lis), *n.* [NL. *Digitalis*, the genus-name (after the G. name *fingerhut*, 'thimble'; from the shape of the corolla), < L. *digitalis*, pertaining to the finger, < *digitus*, E. *digit.*] Any plant of the scrophulariaceous genus *Digitalis*, esp. the common foxglove, *D. purpurea*; the dried leaves of the common foxglove, used in medicine, esp. as a heart-stimulant.

dig-i-tate (dij'i-tāt), *a.* [L. *digitatus.*] In *zoöl.*, having digits or digit-like processes; in *bot.*, having radiating divisions or leaflets resembling the fingers of a hand. Also **dig'i-tat-ed** (-tā-ted).—**dig'i-tate-ly**, *adv.*—**dig-i-ta'tion** (-tā'shọn), *n.* Digitate formation; a digit-like process or division.

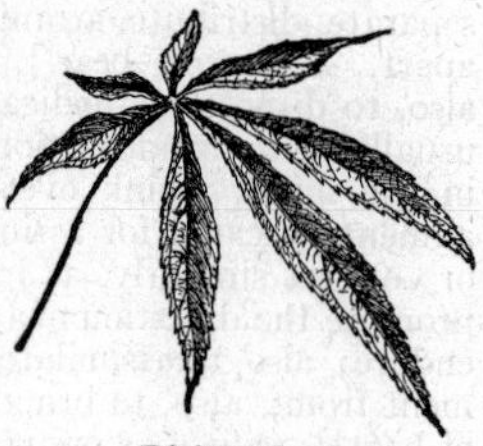

Digitate Leaf.

digiti-. Form of L. *digitus*, finger, toe, used in combination.

—**dig-i-ti-form** (dij'i-ti-fôrm), *a.* [+ *-form.*] Finger-like.—**dig'i-ti-grade** (-grād). [+ *-grade.*] **I.** *a.* Walking on the toes, as most quadrupeds. **II.** *n.* A digitigrade animal.

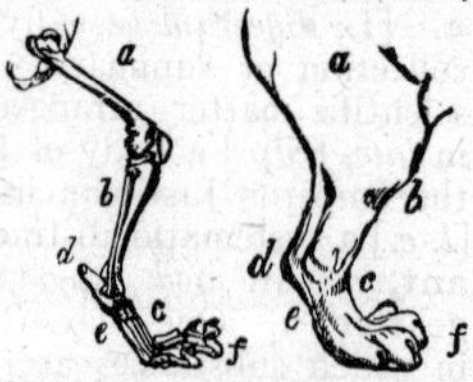

Digitigrade.—Hind Leg of Lion. *a*, femur or thigh; *b*, tibia; *c*, tarsus and metatarsus, or foot exclusive of toes; *d*, heel; *e*, sole of foot; *f*, digits or toes.

di-glad-i-a-tion (dī-glad-i-ā'shọn), *n.* [L. *digladiari* (pp. *digladiatus*), contend fiercely, < *di-*, for *dis-* (see *dis-*), + *gladius*, sword.] Combat with swords; hence, a contest of any kind; a quarrel; a dispute. [Archaic.]

di-glot (dī'glot). [Gr. δίγλωττος, < δι-, two, + γλῶττα, γλῶσσα, tongue.] **I.** *a.* Using or containing two languages; bilingual. **II.** *n.* A diglot book or edition.—**di-glot'tic**, *a.*

dig-ni-fied (dig'ni-fīd), *p. a.* Invested with dignity; exalted; also, marked by dignity of aspect or manner; stately; decorously grave.—**dig'ni-fied-ly**, *adv.*

dig-ni-fy (dig'ni-fī), *v. t.*; *-fied, -fying.* [OF. *dignifier*, < ML. *dignificare*, < L. *dignus*, worthy, + *facere*, make.] To invest with honor or dignity; honor; ennoble; also, to render stately, as literary style; sometimes, to confer unmerited dignity upon; invest with a pretentious title or name.

dig-ni-ta-ry (dig'ni-tạ-ri), *n.*; pl. *-ries* (-riz). [L. *dignitas*: see *dignity.*] One who holds an exalted office, esp. in the church.—**dig-ni-ta'ri-al** (-tā'ri-ạl), *a.*

dig-ni-ty (dig'ni-ti), *n.*; pl. *-ties* (-tiz). [OF. *dignite* (F. *dignité*), < L. *dignitas*, worthiness, dignity, rank, office, < *dignus*, worthy.] Worthiness or worth; nobleness; also, honorable or elevated position or standing; honor; eminence; hence, relative standing; rank; also, an exalted office or title; the person holding it (as, "These filthy dreamers . . . speak evil of *dignities*": Jude, 8); persons of high rank or standing collectively; also, nobility of manner or style; stateliness; gravity.

di-graph (dī'grȧf), *n.* [Gr. δι-, two, + γραφή, writing.] A group of two letters representing a single speech-sound, as *ea* in *head*, or *th* in *path.*—**di-graph'ic** (-graf'ik), *a.* Pertaining to or of the nature of a digraph; also, written in two different characters or alphabets.

di-gress (di-gres' or dī-), *v. i.* [L. *digressus*, pp. of *digredi*, < *di-*, for *dis-*, apart, + *gradi*, walk, go: see *gradient.*] To turn aside, as from a direct course; diverge; also, to transgress† (as, "this deadly blot in thy *digressing* son": Shakspere's "Richard II.," v. 3. 66); also, to deviate from the main subject, theme, etc., as in a discourse.—**di-gress'er**, *n.* —**di-gres'sion** (-gresh'ọn), *n.* [L. *digressio(n-)*.] The act of digressing; a portion of a discourse, etc., deviating from the main theme.—**di-gres'sion-al**, *a.*—**di-gres'sive** (-gres'iv), *a.* [LL. *digressivus.*] Tending to digress; involving digression.—**di-gres'sive-ly**, *adv.*—**di-gres'sive-ness**, *n.*

di-he-dral (dī-hē'drạl), *a.* [Gr. δι-, two, + ἕδρα, seat, base.] Having, or formed by, two planes (as, a *dihedral* angle); pertaining to or having a dihedral angle or angles; specif., of two (right and left) planes or wings on an aëroplane or the like, inclined upward or downward with reference to a horizontal transverse line; pertaining to such planes or wings or their inclination.

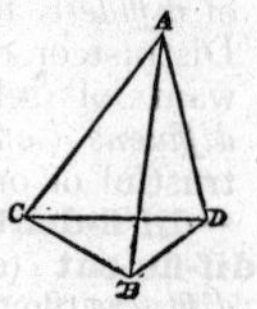

Dihedral Angle, included between the planes *ABD* and *ABC*.

dike (dīk), *n.* [AS. *dīc* = D. *dijk* = F. *digue*: cf. *ditch* and *dig.*] A long, narrow excavation, esp. for holding or conducting water; a ditch; also, a ridge or bank of earth as thrown up in excavating; a causeway; a low wall or fence, as of earth or stone, for dividing or inclosing land; an embankment for resisting the encroachments of the waters of the sea or a stream; fig., an obstacle or barrier; in *geol.*, a long, usually narrow mass of igneous or eruptive rock intruded into a fissure in older rock; loosely, a similar mass of rock composed of material, as sandstone, which is not igneous or eruptive.—**dike**, *v. t.*; *diked, diking.* To furnish with a dike or dikes; protect by a dike or embankment.—**dik-er** (dī'kėr), *n.*

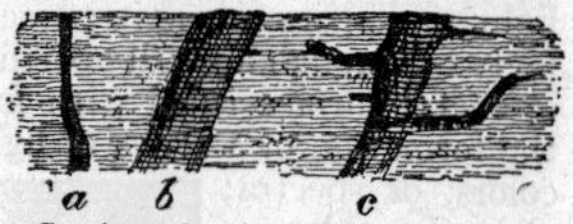

Section showing Dikes traversing Stratified Rocks.—*a, b*, simple dikes; *c*, branching dike.

di-la-cer-ate (di-las'ẹ-rāt or dī-), *v. t.*; *-ated, -ating.* [L. *dilaceratus*, pp. of *dilacerare*, < *di-*, for *dis-*, apart, + *lacerare*, tear: see *lacerate.*] To rend asunder; tear in pieces.—**di-la-cer-a'tion** (-las-ẹ-rā'shọn), *n.*

di-lap-i-date (di-lap'i-dāt), *v.*; *-dated, -dating.* [L. *dilapidatus*, pp. of *dilapidare*, < *di-*, for *dis-*, apart, + *lapidare*, throw stones, < *lapis*, stone.] **I.** *tr.* To bring (a building, etc.) into a ruinous condition, as by misuse or neglect; cause or allow (anything) to fall into ruin or decay; squander or waste, as an estate. **II.** *intr.* To fall into ruin or decay. —**di-lap'i-dat-ed** (-dā-ted), *p. a.* Reduced to or fallen into ruin or decay.—**di-lap-i-da'tion** (-dā'shọn), *n.* [LL. *dilapidatio(n-)*.] The act or fact of dilapidating; dilapidated condition.—**di-lap'i-da-tor**, *n.*

di-lat-a-ble (di-lā'tạ-bl or dī-), *a.* Capable of being dilated. —**di-lat-a-bil'i-ty** (-bil'i-ti), *n.*

di-lat-an-cy (di-lā'tạn-si or dī-), *n.* The property of dilating; in *physics*, the property of granular masses of expanding in bulk with change of shape, due to the increase of space between the rigid particles as they change their relative positions.—**di-lat'ant.** **I.** *a.* Dilating or expanding; pertaining to or characterized by dilatancy. **II.** *n.* An agent or instrument that dilates something; a surgeon's dilator; also, a substance having the property of dilating or expanding; a substance having the property of dilatancy.

dil-a-ta-tion (dil-ạ-tā'shọn or dī-lạ-), *n.* [L. *dilatatio(n-)*.] The act of dilating, or the state of being dilated; also, a dilated formation or part.

dil-a-ta-tor (dil'ạ-tā-tọr or dī'lạ-), *n.* A dilator.

di-late (di-lāt' or dī-), *v.*; *-lated, -lating.* [OF. F. *dilater*, < L. *dilatare*, spread out, extend, < *di-*, for *dis-*, apart, + *latus*, broad.] **I.** *tr.* To make wider or larger; expand; distend; enlarge; also, to spread abroad†; also, to set forth at length†, or expatiate upon† (as, "A prayer . . .

That I would all my pilgrimage *dilate*": Shakspere's "Othello," i. 3. 153). **II.** *intr.* To expand or enlarge; also, to expatiate.—**di-la'tion** (-lā'shǫn), *n.* The act of dilating; dilated condition; dilatation.—**di-la'tive,** *a.* Serving to dilate.—**dil-a-tom-e-ter** (dil-ą-tom'e-tėr or dī-lą-), *n.* [See *-meter.*] An instrument for determining the expansion of substances.—**di-la'tor,** *n.* One who or that which dilates; in *anat.*, a muscle that dilates some part of the body; in *surg.*, an instrument for dilating wounds, canals, etc.

dil-a-to-ry (dil'ą-tō-ri), *a.* [L. *dilatorius,* < *dilator,* delayer, < *differre* (pp. *dilatus*), E. *defer*[1].] Such as to cause delay; also, marked by or given to delay or procrastination; not prompt.—**dil'a-to-ri-ly,** *adv.*—**dil'a-to-ri-ness,** *n.*

dil-do† (dil'dō). [Origin unknown.] A word used without definite meaning in the refrains of old songs. See Shakspere's "Winter's Tale," iv. 4. 195.

di-lem-ma (di-lem'ą or dī-), *n.* [LL., < Gr. δίλημμα, < δι-, two, + λῆμμα, assumption, E. *lemma.*] A form of argument in which one must choose between two (or more) equally unfavorable alternatives; hence, a situation requiring a choice between such alternatives; an embarrassing situation.—**dil-em-mat-ic** (dil-e-mat'ik or dī-le-), *a.*

dil-et-tant (dil-ę-tânt'), *n.* and *a.* Same as *dilettante.*

dil-et-tan-te (dil-ę-tan'tę, It. dē-let-tän'tā). [It., prop. ppr. of *dilettare,* < L. *delectare,* E. *delight, v.*] **I.** *n.*; pl. *-tes* (-tęz), It. *-ti* (-tē). A lover or amateur of an art or science, esp. of a fine art; now, esp., one who pursues an art or science desultorily or merely for amusement; a dabbler. **II.** *a.* Being a dilettante; of or pertaining to dilettantes. —**dil-et-tan'tish, dil-et-tan'te-ish,** *a.* Like or suggestive of a dilettante.—**dil-et-tan'tism, dil-et-tan'te-ism,** *n.* The practice or characteristics of a dilettante.

dil-i-gence[1] (dil'i-jęns), *n.* [OF. F. *diligence,* < L. *diligentia.*] The quality of being diligent; industry; assiduity; care; also, speed†.

dil-i-gence[2] (dil'i-jęns, F. dē-lē-zhoṅs), *n.* [F., for *carrosse de diligence,* 'coach of speed,' post-coach.] A public stagecoach: orig. with reference to France and hence to other countries, esp. of continental Europe.

dil-i-gent (dil'i-jęnt), *a.* [OF. F. *diligent,* < L. *diligens* (*-ent-*), prop. ppr. of *diligere,* choose, like, love, < *di-,* for *dis-,* apart, + *legere,* gather, choose.] Constant in effort to accomplish something; industrious; assiduous; also, pursued with persevering attention; painstaking.—**dil'i-gent-ly,** *adv.*

dill (dil), *n.* [AS. *dile.*] An apiaceous plant, *Anethum graveolens,* bearing aromatic seed-like fruit used in medicine and for flavoring pickles, etc.

dil-ly (dil'i), *n.* [For *sapodilla.*] A small sapotaceous tree, *Mimusops sieberi,* of southern Florida and the West Indies, having a heavy, hard, dark-brown wood susceptible of a beautiful polish, and bearing a small globose fruit.

dil-ly=dal-ly (dil'i-dal'i), *v. i.*; *-lied, -lying.* [Varied redupl. of *dally.*] To dally; trifle; loiter; hesitate: as, "There is no time to *dilly-dally* in our work" (Stevenson's "Treasure Island," xvi.).

dil-u-ent (dil'ū-ęnt). [L. *diluens* (*-ent-*), ppr.] **I.** *a.* Diluting. **II.** *n.* A diluting substance, esp. one that dilutes the blood.

di-lute (di-lūt' or dī-), *v.*; *-luted, -luting.* [L. *dilutus,* pp. of *diluere,* wash to pieces, dissolve, dilute, < *di-,* for *dis-,* apart, + *luere,* wash.] **I.** *tr.* To make thinner or weaker by the addition of water or the like, as a liquid; reduce the strength of (a fluid) by admixture; make fainter, as color; fig., to reduce the strength, force, or efficiency of as by admixture; specif., to place a certain proportion of unskilled workers, whether women or others, at work among (a body of skilled workers), as in order to increase output or to release some of the skilled workers for service in war (orig. Eng.). **II.** *intr.* To become diluted.—**di-lute',** *a.* Diluted; reduced in strength, as a chemical by admixture; weak.—**di-lut-ee'** (-lū-tē'), *n.* A worker employed in diluting skilled labor. See *dilute, v. t.* [Eng.]—**di-lut'er** (-lū'tėr), *n.*—**di-lu'tion** (-lū'shǫn), *n.* The act of diluting, or the state of being diluted; specif., the diluting of labor (see *dilute, v. t.*); also, something diluted; a diluted form of anything.

di-lu-vi-al (di-lū'vi-ąl or dī-), *a.* [See *diluvium.*] Pertaining to a deluge or flood; in *geol.*, pertaining to or consisting of diluvium.—**di-lu'vi-an,** *a.* Pertaining to a deluge.—**di-lu'vi-an-ism,** *n.* The theory which attributes certain geological phenomena to a former universal deluge.

di-lu-vi-um (di-lū'vi-um or dī-), *n.*; pl. *-via* (-vi-ą). [L., flood, < *diluere,* wash to pieces, wash away: see *dilute.*] In *geol.*, coarse superficial deposits formerly attributed to a general deluge but now regarded as glacial drift.

dim (dim), *a.*; compar. *dimmer,* superl. *dimmest.* [AS. *dim* = Icel. *dimmr.*] Faintly luminous, as light; somewhat dark; also, not clearly seen, as an object; indistinct; fig., not clear to the mind; also, not bright, as a color; faint, as a sound; also, not seeing clearly (as, "eyes . . . *dim* with glorious tears": Tennyson's "Two Voices," 151); fig., dull of apprehension.—**dim,** *v. t.* or *i.*; *dimmed, dimming.* To make or become dim.

dime (dīm), *n.* [OF. *disme* (F. *dîme*), < L. *decima,* tenth part, tithe, prop. fem. of *decimus,* tenth, < *decem,* ten.] A silver coin of the U. S., of the value of 10 cents.

Obverse. Reverse.
Dime of 1875.

di-men-sion (di-men'shǫn), *n.* [L. *dimensio(n-),* < *dimetiri,* measure off, < *di-,* for *dis-,* apart, + *metiri,* measure.] The act of measuring†; also, measure, extent, size, or magnitude (now usually in *pl.*); magnitude measured in a particular direction, or along a diameter or principal axis; length, breadth, or thickness; in *math.*, a mode of spatial extension (as, the fourth *dimension,* an assumed dimension in addition to length, breadth, and thickness); in *alg.*, a literal factor of a product (as, a^3 and a^2b and $2abc$ are terms of three *dimensions,* or of the third degree: cf. *degree*); in *physics,* the degree with which a fundamental unit (as of mass, length, or time) enters, alone or in combination with other units, into a derived unit (as of force, velocity, etc.).—**di-men'sion,** *v. t.* To measure; bring to the required size; mark with dimensions.—**di-men'sion-al,** *a.*—**dimensional sound,** sound, as music, etc., resulting from a multiplicity of reproducers each supplied from a pick-up by an independent channel and arranged to produce certain effects, as stereophonic illusion, artistic enhancement, etc.—**di-men'sioned,** *a.*—**di-men'sion-less,** *a.* Without dimension; immeasurable.

dim-er-ous (dim'ę-rus), *a.* [Gr. διμερής, < δι-, two, + μέρος, part.] Consisting of or divided into two parts; in *bot.*, of flowers, having two members in each whorl.

Dimerous Flower, and diagram of same.
b, bract; *s,* sepals; *p,* petals; *st, st,* stamens; *o,* two-celled ovary.

dim-e-ter (dim'e-tėr). [LL., < Gr. δίμετρος, < δι-, two, + μέτρον, measure.] In *pros.*: **I.** *a.* Consisting of two measures; divisible into two feet or two dipodies. **II.** *n.* A verse or period of two measures.

di-met-ric (dī-met'rik), *a.* [Gr. δι-, two, + μέτρον, measure.] In *crystal.*, tetragonal.

di-mid-i-ate (di-mid'i-āt or dī-), *v. t.*; *-ated, -ating.* [L. *dimidiatus,* pp. of *dimidiare,* halve, < *dimidius,* half: see *demi-.*] To divide into halves; reduce to the half.—**di-mid'i-ate,** *a.* Divided into halves; half; in *biol.*, of an organ, having one half wanting or appearing to be wanting; also, having sides structurally different.—**di-mid-i-a'tion** (-ā'shǫn), *n.*

di-min-ish (di-min'ish), *v.* [An altered form (after *minish*) of the earlier *diminue,* < OF. F. *diminuer,* < ML. *diminuere,* for L. *deminuere,* < *de,* from, + *minuere,* make smaller: see *minute*[1].] **I.** *tr.* To make, or cause to seem, smaller; lessen; reduce; also, to detract from or disparage (archaic); also, to subtract†; in *arch.*, etc., to cause to taper. **II.** *intr.* To lessen; decrease.—**di-min'ish-a-ble,** *a.* Capable of being diminished.—**di-min'ished,** *p. a.* Made smaller; lessened; caused to taper, as a column; in *music,* of an interval, smaller by a half-step than the corresponding perfect or minor interval.—**di-min′ish-er,** *n.* —**di-min′ish-ing-ly,** *adv.*—**di-min′ish-ment,** *n.* Diminution.

di-min-u-en-do (di-min-ū-en′dō, It. dē-mē-nö-en′dō). [It., gerund of *diminuire*, < ML. *diminuere*: see *diminish.*] In *music*: **I.** *a.* Gradually diminishing in force or loudness; decrescendo: opposed to *crescendo.* **II.** *n.*; pl. *-dos* (-dōz). A gradual decrease in force or loudness; a diminuendo passage.

dim-i-nu-tion (dim-i-nū′shon), *n.* [L. *diminutio(n-)*, for *deminutio(n-)*, < *deminuere*: see *diminish.*] The act, fact, or process of diminishing; lessening; reduction; in *law*, an omission in the record of a case sent up to a court of review.

di-min-u-ti-val (di-min-ū-tī′val), *a.* Of, pertaining to, or of the nature of a diminutive.

di-min-u-tive (di-min′ū-tiv). [ML. *diminutivus*, for LL. *deminutivus.*] **I.** *a.* Tending to diminish†; also, characterized by diminution; small; little; tiny; in *gram.*, expressing diminution or smallness, as a derivative word (as *droplet*) or a suffix (as *-let*). **II.** *n.* A diminutive specimen or form of anything; a small thing or person; in *gram.*, a diminutive word or suffix.—**di-min′u-tive-ly,** *adv.*—**di-min′u-tive-ness,** *n.*

dim-is-so-ri-al (dim-i-sō′ri-al), *a.* Same as *dimissory.*

dim-is-so-ry (dim′i-sō-ri), *a.* [LL. *dimissorius*, < L. *dimittere*, send away, < *di-*, for *dis-*, apart, + *mittere*, send.] Pertaining to dismissal or leave-taking.—**dimissory letter,** a letter dismissing a clergyman from one diocese and recommending him to another; also, a letter issued by a pope, bishop, abbot, etc., authorizing the bearer as a candidate for ordination: often, as plural, *letters dimissory.*

dim-i-ty (dim′i-ti), *n.*; pl. *-ties* (-tiz). [It. *dimito*, < Gr. δίμιτος, of double thread, < δι-, two, + μίτος, thread: cf. *samite.*] A stout cotton fabric woven with raised stripes or figures, and sometimes having a printed pattern, used for upholstery, etc.; also, a thin cotton fabric, with or without printed figures, woven with cords or heavy threads at intervals in striped or cross-barred arrangement, used for women's dresses, etc.

dim-ly (dim′li), *adv.* In a dim manner; obscurely; indistinctly.

dim-mer (dim′ėr), *n.* One who or that which dims; a device for reducing the candle-power of electric lamps; specif., an arrangement for reducing the intensity of an automobile headlight.

dim-mish (dim′ish), *a.* Somewhat dim.

dim-ness (dim′nes), *n.* The state or quality of being dim.

di-morph (dī′môrf), *n.* [Gr. δίμορφος, having two forms, < δι-, two, + μορφή, form.] In *crystal.*, either of the two forms assumed by a dimorphous substance.—**di-mor′phic** (-môr′fik), *a.* Dimorphous.—**di-mor′phism,** *n.* Dimorphous property or condition; in *crystal.*, the property of some substances of crystallizing in two distinct forms; in *bot.*, the occurrence of two different forms of flowers, leaves, etc., on the same plant or on distinct plants of the same species; in *zoöl.*, the occurrence of two forms distinct in structure, coloration, etc., among animals of the same species.—**di-mor′phous,** *a.* [Gr. δίμορφος.] Existing in or assuming two distinct forms; exhibiting dimorphism.

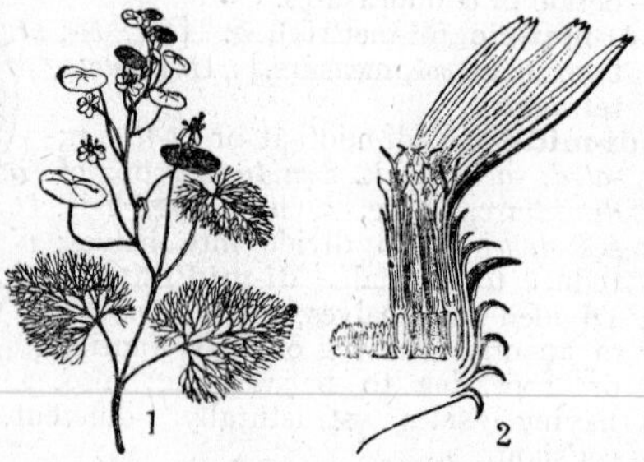

Dimorphism in Plants.

1. Submerged and floating leaves of water-shield (*Cabomba*). 2. Disk-florets and ray-florets of aster.

dim-ple (dim′pl), *n.* [Origin uncertain.] A small natural hollow, permanent or transient, in some soft part of the human body, esp. one produced in the cheek in smiling; hence, any slight depression resembling or suggesting this; also, the act of dimpling.—**dim′ple,** *v.*; *-pled, -pling.* **I.** *tr.* To mark with or as with dimples; produce dimples in. **II.** *intr.* To form dimples; sink into slight depressions or inequalities; ripple.—**dim′ply,** *a.* Full of dimples; dimpled.

din (din), *n.* [AS. *dyne* = Icel. *dynr.*] A loud, confused noise; a continued loud or tumultuous sound; noisy clamor. —**din,** *v.*; *dinned, dinning.* **I.** *tr.* To assail with din; also, to sound or utter with clamor or persistent repetition (as, "Her brother had ever been *dinning* into her ears that maxim . . . 'Enjoy the present' ": J. H. Newman's "Callista," xxix.). **II.** *intr.* To make a din.

di-nar (dē-när′), *n.* [Ar. and Pers., < Gr. δηνάριον, < L. *denarius*: see *denarius.*] Any of certain Oriental coins, esp. gold coins of ancient Arab governments; a small monetary unit of Persia, equal to one thousandth part of a kran; a silver coin of Serbia, worth about 19.3 U. S. cents.

Obverse. Reverse.
Dinar of Harun al-Rashid (A.D. 788). British Museum.

dine (dīn), *v.*; *dined, dining.* [OF. *disner* (F. *dîner*), < L. *dis-* (see *dis-*) + LL. *jejunare*, fast, < L. *jejunus*, fasting, E. *jejune*: cf. *déjeuner.*] **I.** *intr.* To eat the principal meal of the day; take dinner; take a meal. **II.** *tr.* To provide with dinner; entertain at dinner.—**din-er** (dī′nėr), *n.* One who dines; also, a railroad dining-car (U. S.).

ding[1] (ding), *v.* [ME.: cf. Icel. *dengja*, hammer.] **I.** *tr.* To strike; beat; knock; dash; also, to overcome; surpass; also, a substitute for *damn.* [Now chiefly prov.] **II.** *intr.* To strike; beat; dash; fall heavily, as rain; also, to fling one's self about; bluster; also, to yield, as to blows or force. [Now chiefly prov.]—**ding**[1], *n.* The act of dinging; a blow; a knock; a thrust. [Prov.]

ding[2] (ding), *v.* [Imit.] **I.** *intr.* To sound as a bell when struck; ring, esp. continuously; also, to keep talking importunately or harassingly. **II.** *tr.* To force by repetition. —**ding**[2], *adv.* and *n.* A word imitative of the sound of a stroke of a bell or the like.—**ding′=dong** (-dông or -dong), *adv.* and *n.* [Varied redupl. of *ding*[2].] A word imitative of the sound of repeated strokes of a bell or the like.

dinge (dinj), *v. t.*; *dinged, dingeing.* [Cf. *ding*[1].] To make a depression or hollow on the surface of, as by a knock or blow; dent.—**dinge,** *n.* A depression or hollow on a surface, resulting from a blow or pressure; a dent.

din-ghy, din-gey (ding′gi), *n.*; pl. *-ghies, -geys* (-giz). [Hind.] Any of various boats for rowing or sailing used in the East Indies; hence, any of various small boats used elsewhere, as one serving as a tender to a yacht.

din-gi-ly (din′ji-li), *adv.* In a dingy manner.—**din′gi-ness,** *n.*

din-gle[1] (ding′gl), *n.* [Origin uncertain.] A deep, narrow cleft between hills; a shady dell: as, "The long and level sunbeams . . . Searched each thicket, *dingle*, hollow" (Longfellow's "Hiawatha," xxii. 170).

din-gle[2] (ding′gl), *v. i.*; *-gled, -gling.* [Cf. *ding*[2] and *tingle.*] To tinkle or jingle; also, to tingle, as from cold; also, to vibrate.

din-go (ding′gō), *n.*; pl. *-goes* (-gōz). [Native Australian.] A wolf-like wild dog, *Canis dingo*, of Australia.

Dingo.

din-gy[1] (din′ji), *a.*; compar. *dingier*, superl. *dingiest.* [Origin uncertain.] Of a dark, dull, or dirty color or aspect; discolored as if with dirt; lacking brightness or freshness.

din-gy[2] (ding′gi), *n.* See *dinghy.*

din-ing (dī′ning), *n.* The act of taking dinner.—**din′ing=car,** *n.* A railroad-car fitted up as a dining-room or restaurant, and supplied with a kitchen, pantry, etc.—**din′ing=room,** *n.* A room in which dinner and other meals are taken.

dink (dingk), *a.* [Origin unknown.] Neatly dressed; trim; fine: as, "The mechanic, in his leathern apron, elbowed the *dink* and dainty dame" (Scott's "Kenilworth," xxv.). [Sc.]—**dink,** *v. t.* To deck; array: as, "I am now too old to *dink* myself as a gallant to grace the bower of dames" (Scott's "Abbot," xx.). [Sc.]—**dink-y** (ding′ki). **I.** *a.* Neat, fine, or nice (esp. of small or trifling things); small or trifling but pretentious; of small size. [Colloq. or prov.] **II.** *n.*; pl. *dinkies* (-kiz). Something small of its kind; a small locomotive; a small boat, esp. when used as a tender to a larger one. [Colloq.]

din-ner (din′ėr), *n.* [OF. *disner* (F. *dîner*), orig. inf.: see *dine.*] The principal meal of the day, esp. as taken about noon or (now) in the evening; also, a formal repast in honor of some person or occasion.—**din′ner-less,** *a.* Without dinner.—**din′ner=ring,** *n.* A banquet-ring.

dino-. Form of Gr. δεινός, terrible, used in combination.

di-no-ce-ras (dī-nos′ẹ-rạs), *n.* [NL., < Gr. δεινός, terrible, + κέρας, horn.] Any animal of the extinct genus *Dinoceras,* comprising huge horned ungulate mammals of the Eocene of North America.—**di-no-cer′a-tan** (-nọ-ser′ạ-tạn), *a.*

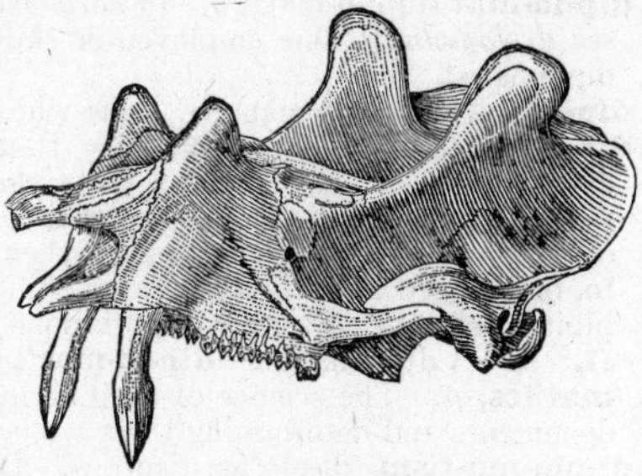

Skull of Dinoceras.

di-nor-nis (dī-nôr′nis), *n.* [NL., < Gr. δεινός, terrible, + ὄρνις, bird.] Any of the huge flightless birds constituting the extinct genus *Dinornis,* and comprising the typical moas.

di-no-saur (dī′nọ-sâr), *n.* [NL. *dinosaurus:* see *dino-* and *-saur.*] Any member of the extinct group *Dinosauria,* comprising Mesozoic reptiles, mostly of gigantic size.—**di-no-sau′ri-an,** *a.* and *n.*

Duck-billed Dinosaur (restored).

di-no-there (dī′nọ-thēr), *n.* [NL. *dinotherium:* see *dino-* and *-there.*] Any animal of the extinct genus *Dinotherium,* comprising elephant-like mammals of the later Tertiary of Europe and Asia. Also **di-no-the′ri-um** (-thē′ri-um); pl. *-ria* (-ri-ạ̈).

Dinothere (restored).

dint (dint), *n.* [AS. *dynt* = Icel. *dyntr.*] A blow† or stroke†; violence, force, or effective action (now chiefly in the phrase 'by dint of,' by force or means of: as, "He . . . would, in all human probability, be lord chancellor by sheer *dint* of his own industry and his own talent," Trollope's "Warden," xvii.); also, a hollow or depression made by a blow or by pressure; a dent.—**dint,** *v. t.* To strike† or beat†; also, to make a dint or dints in; also, to impress or drive in with force.—**dint′less,** *a.* Without dints or depressions; making no dint.

di-o-ce-san (dī-os′ẹ̄-sạn or dī′ọ-sē-). [OF. *diocezain* (F. *diocésain*).] **I.** *a.* Of or pertaining to a diocese. **II.** *n.* The bishop in charge of a diocese; also, one of the clergy or people of a diocese.

di-o-cese (dī′ọ-sēs or -ses), *n.* [OF. *diocese* (F. *diocèse*), < L. *diœcesis,* < Gr. διοίκησις, housekeeping, administration, province, diocese, < διοικεῖν, keep house, govern, < διά, through, + οἰκεῖν, inhabit, manage, < οἶκος, house.] An administrative district of a country, esp. one of those into which the four prefectures of the Roman Empire were divided after the time of Diocletian and Constantine; also, the district under the pastoral care of a bishop.

di-œ-cious, di-e-cious (dī-ē′shus), *a.* [Gr. δι-, two, + οἶκος, house.] In *biol.,* having the male and female organs in separate and distinct individuals; specif., in *bot.,* of a plant species, etc., having the andrœcium and the gynœcium in separate flowers on different plants (cf. *monœcious*).

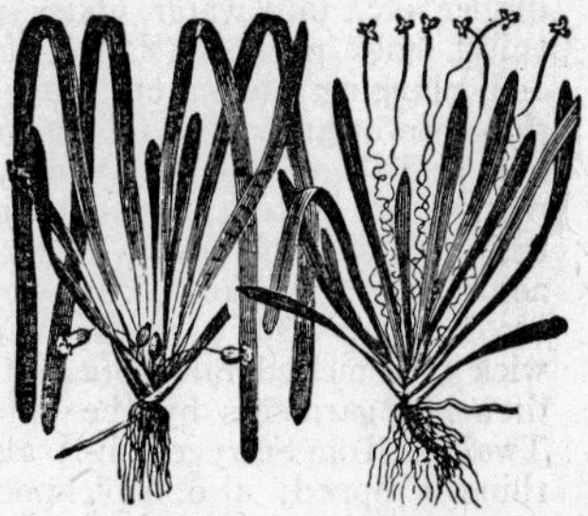

Diœcious Plants (Male and Female) of *Vallisneria spiralis.*

Di-og-e-nes (dī-oj′e-nēz), *n.* [From *Diogenes,* the Greek Cynic philosopher.] A churlish, cynical person.

di-o-næ-a (dī-ọ-nē′ạ̈), *n.* [NL., < Gr. Διώνη, Dione, or Aphrodite (Venus).] A plant, the Venus's fly-trap.

Di-o-nys-i-a (dī-ọ̄-nis′i-ạ̈), *n. pl.* [L., < Gr. Διονύσια.] In *class. antiq.,* festivals in honor of Dionysus, celebrated periodically in various parts of Greece.—**Di-o-nys′i-ac** (-ak), *a.* [Gr. Διονυσιακός.] Pertaining to the Dionysia or to Dionysus; Bacchic.—**Di″o-ny-si′a-cal-ly** (-ni-sī′ạ-kạl-i), *adv.*

Di-o-nys-i-an (dī-ọ-nis′i-ạn), *a.* Pertaining to Dionysus or Bacchus; also, pertaining to the monk Dionysius Exiguus (6th century), who is reputed to have introduced the method of reckoning events from the birth of Christ.

Di-o-ny-sus (dī-ọ-nī′sus), *n.* [L., < Gr. Διόνυσος.] The Greek god of the vine and of wine; Bacchus.

di-op-side (dī-op′sīd or -sid), *n.* [F., < Gr. δι-, two, + ὄψις, appearance.] A variety of pyroxene, occurring in various colors, sometimes used for making jewelry.

di-op-tase (dī-op′tās), *n.* [F., < Gr. διά, through, + ὀπ-, see: cf. *diopter.*] A mineral consisting of a hydrous silicate of copper, occurring in emerald-green rhombohedral crystals.

di-op-ter (dī-op′tėr), *n.* [L. *dioptra,* < Gr. διόπτρα, kind of leveling instrument, < διά, through, + ὀπ-, see: see *optic.*] An ancient form of theodolite; in *optics,* a unit of refractive power, equal to that of a lens whose focal length is one meter.—**di-op′tric.** [Gr. διοπτρικός.] **I.** *a.* Of or pertaining to a diopter; also, affording a medium for the sight; assisting vision; also, pertaining to the refraction of light, as by lenses. **II.** *n.* In *optics,* a diopter.—**di-op′tri-cal-ly,** *adv.*—**di-op′trics,** *n.* That branch of optics which deals with the refraction of light. Cf. *catoptrics.*—**di-op′try** (-tri), *n.*; pl. *-tries* (-triz). In *optics,* a diopter.

di-o-ra-ma (dī-ọ-rä′mạ̈), *n.* [F., < Gr. διά, through, + ὅραμα, view.] A spectacular picture, partly translucent, for exhibition through an aperture, made more realistic by various illuminating devices; a place where such pictures are exhibited.—**di-o-ram′ic** (-ram′ik), *a.*

di-o-rite (dī′ọ-rīt), *n.* [F., < Gr. διορίζειν, distinguish, < διά, through, + ὁρίζειν, bound: see *horizon.*] An igneous rock commonly consisting essentially of feldspar (plagioclase) and hornblende.—**di-o-rit′ic** (-rit′ik), *a.*

di-os-co-re-a-ceous (dī-os-kō-rẹ̄-ā′shius), *a.* [NL. *Dioscorea,* the typical genus; named from *Dioscorides,* Greek physician.] Belonging to the *Dioscoreaceæ,* or yam family of plants.

di-os-mo-sis (dī-os-mō′sis or dī-oz-), *n.* [See *di-*[2] and *osmosis.*] Osmosis.—**di-os-mot′ic** (-mot′ik), *a.*

di-os-py-ra-ceous (dī-os-pi-rā′shius), *a.* [NL. *Diospyros,* the typical genus, < Gr. διόσπυρος, kind of plant.] Same as *ebenaceous.*

di-ox-ide (dī-ok′sīd or -sid), *n.* [See *di-*[1].] In *chem.,* an oxide with two atoms of oxygen and one of a metal or other element.

dip (dip), *v.*; *dipped, dipping.* [AS. *dyppan,* dip, akin to D. *doopen,* G. *taufen,* Goth. *daupjan,* baptize, and E. *deep.*] **I.** *tr.* To plunge temporarily into a liquid, as to wet or to take up some of the liquid; immerse; plunge lightly; baptize by immersion; color by immersion, or dye; immerse (a sheep, etc.) in a germicidal or antiseptic solution to destroy germs, parasites, or the like; also, to lower and raise as if immersing temporarily in a liquid (as, to *dip* a flag in salutation); cause to sink, or depress; also, to involve or implicate in some affair; involve in debt; also, to obtain or take by dipping; also, to make (a candle) by repeatedly dipping a wick into melted tallow. **II.** *intr.* To plunge into water or other liquid and emerge quickly; plunge the hand, a dipper, etc., into water, etc., esp. in order to remove something; pick pockets (slang); also, to sink or drop down, as if plunging into water; make a curtsy; also, to incline or slope downward; also, to engage slightly in a subject; read here and there in a book.—**dip,** *n.* The act of dipping; a plunge into water, etc.; a bath; also, a lowering momentarily; a sinking down; a short downward plunge of an aëroplane or the like; a curtsy; also, that which is taken up by dipping; also, a candle made by repeatedly dipping a wick into melted tallow (as "Tom . . . was surveying his drenched garments by the light of a tallow *dip*": Mark Twain's "Tom Sawyer," iii.); also, a liquid into which something is dipped; also, a pickpocket (slang); also, extension downward from a particular level, or the amount of such extension; the angular amount by which the horizon lies below the level of the eye; also, downward inclination or slope; also, a hollow or depression in the land; in *magnetism*, the angle which a freely poised magnetic needle makes with the plane of the horizon; in *geol.* and *mining*, the downward inclination of a stratum or vein.

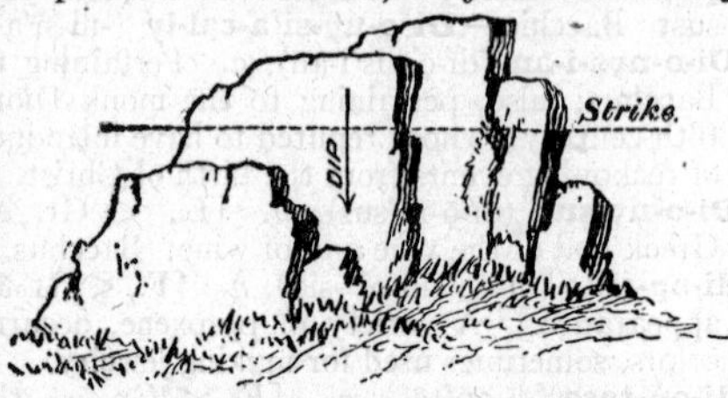

Outcrop of Rock, showing Dip and Strike.

di-pet-a-lous (dī-pet′ạ-lus), *a.* [See *di-*[1].] In *bot.*, having two petals; bipetalous.

di-phase (dī′fāz), *a.* [See *di-*[1].] Having two phases; noting or pertaining to a system combining two alternating electric currents that differ from each other in phase. Also **di-pha′sic** (-fā′zik).

di-phe-nyl-am-ine (dī-fē-nil-am′in), *n.* [From *di-*[1] + *phenyl* + *amine.*] In *chem.*, an aromatic crystalline benzene derivative used in the preparation of various dyes.

diph-the-ri-a (dif-thē′ri-ạ̈), *n.* [NL., < Gr. διφθέρα, skin, leather.] In *pathol.*, a febrile infectious disease caused by a specific bacillus, and characterized by the formation of a false membrane in the air-passages, esp. the throat.—**diph-the-rit′ic** (-thē-rit′ik), *a.*—**diph′the-roid,** *a.* Resembling diphtheria.

diph-thong (dif′thông), *n.* [LL. *diphthongus*, < Gr. δίφθογγος, prop. adj., having two sounds, < δι-, two, + φθόγγος, sound.] A union of two vowels pronounced in one syllable, as in *noise, out;* less properly, a digraph; also, either of the ligatures *æ, œ,* used in printing.—**diph-thon′gal** (-thông′gạl), *a.*—**diph′thong-ize** (-īz), *v. t.* or *i.*; *-ized, -izing.* To change into or unite in a diphthong.—**diph″thong-i-za′tion** (-i-zā′shọn), *n.*

di-phyl-lous (dī-fil′us), *a.* [Gr. δι-, two, + φύλλον, leaf.] In *bot.*, having two leaves.

diph-y-o-dont (dif′i-ọ-dont). [Gr. διφυής, double (< δι-, two, + φύειν, produce), + ὀδούς (ὀδοντ-), tooth.] **I.** *a.* Having two successive sets of teeth, as most mammals. **II.** *n.* A diphyodont mammal.

di-plex (dī′pleks), *a.* [From *di-*[1] + *-plex* as in *duplex.*] Noting or pertaining to a system of telegraphy for sending two messages simultaneously over the same wire in the same direction.

dip-lo-coc-cus (dip-lọ-kok′us), *n.*; pl. *-cocci* (-kok′sī). [NL., < Gr. διπλόος, double, + NL. *coccus*: see *coccus.*] Any of certain bacteria occurring characteristically as paired cells.

di-plod-o-cus (di-plod′ọ-kus), *n.* [NL., < Gr. διπλόος, double, + δοκός, beam.] Any animal of the extinct genus *Diplodocus*, comprising gigantic dinosaurs of the upper Jurassic of western North America.

dip-lo-ë (dip′lọ-ē), *n.* [NL., < Gr. διπλόν, fold, doubling, < διπλόος, double.] In *anat.*, the cancellated bony tissue between the hard inner and outer walls of the bones of the cranium.—**di-plo-ic** (di-plō′ik), *a.*

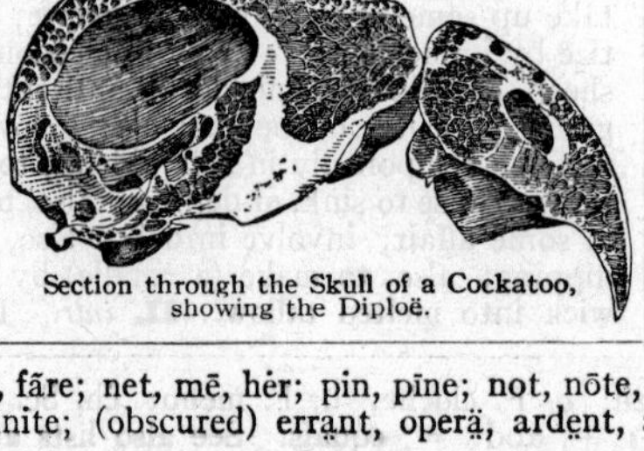
Section through the Skull of a Cockatoo, showing the Diploë.

di-plo-ma (di-plō′mạ̈), *n.*; pl. *-mas*, L., *-mata* (-mạ-tạ̈). [L., < Gr. δίπλωμα (διπλωματ-), paper folded double, letter of recommendation, license, etc., < διπλοῦν, fold double, < διπλόος, double.] A public or official document; esp., an original document as an object of historical or other study; also, a document conferring some honor, privilege, or power, esp. one given by a university, etc., conferring a degree on a person or certifying to his qualifications.—**di-plo′ma,** *v. t.*; *-maed* (mạ̈d), *-maing* (-mạ̈-ing). To furnish with a diploma.

di-plo-ma-cy (di-plō′mạ-si), *n.*; pl. *-cies* (-siz). [F. *diplomatie* (with *t* pron. as *s*), < *diplomatique*: see *diplomatic.*] The conduct of intercourse and negotiations between nations; the science of conducting such negotiations; skill in managing such negotiations; hence, skill in managing any negotiations; artful management in dealing with others; astute tact; also, a diplomatic proceeding.

dip-lo-mat (dip′lọ-mat), *n.* [F. *diplomate*, < *diplomatique*: see *diplomatic.*] One employed or skilled in diplomacy; a diplomatist.

dip-lo-mate (dip′lọ-māt), *n.* One who holds a diploma.

dip-lo-mat-ic (dip-lọ-mat′ik). [= F. *diplomatique*, < NL. *diplomaticus*, < L. *diploma*: see *diploma.*] **I.** *a.* Of or pertaining to public or official documents; pertaining to original documents, or the study of them; also, of, pertaining to, or engaged in diplomacy; also, skilled in diplomacy; exhibiting skill or address in negotiations of any kind; tactful. **II.** *n.* A diplomatist.—**dip-lo-mat′i-cal-ly,** *adv.*—**dip-lo-mat′ics,** *n.* The science of deciphering original or ancient documents and determining their age, authenticity, etc.

di-plo-ma-tism (di-plō′mạ-tizm), *n.* Diplomacy.

di-plo-ma-tist (di-plō′mạ-tist), *n.* [Cf. *diplomat.*] One employed or versed in international diplomacy (as, "As a negotiator he [Marlborough] ranks with the most skilful *diplomatists* of his age": Lecky's "Hist. of Eng. in the 18th Century," i.); also, one who is astute and tactful in any negotiations.

di-plo-ma-tize (di-plō′mạ-tīz), *v. i.*; *-tized, -tizing.* To use diplomacy or astute tact.

di-plo-pi-a (di-plō′pi-ạ̈), *n.* [NL., < Gr. διπλόος, double, + ὤψ, eye.] In *pathol.*, a morbid condition of vision in which a single object appears double.—**di-plop′ic** (-plop′ik), *a.*

dip-lo-ste-mo-nous (dip-lọ-stē′mọ-nus or -stem′ọ-nus), *a.* [Gr. διπλόος, double, + στήμων, warp, thread.] In *bot.*, having two series of stamens, or twice as many stamens as petals.

dip-no-an (dip′nọ-ạn). [NL. *Dipnoi*, pl., < Gr. δίπνοος, having two breathing apertures, < δι-, twice, + πνεῖν, blow, breathe.] **I.** *a.* Belonging or pertaining to the *Dipnoi*, a subclass or group of fishes having both gills and lungs, by some considered to be intermediate between fishes and batrachians. **II.** *n.* A dipnoan fish.—**dip′no-ous,** *a.* [Gr. δίπνοος.] Having both gills and lungs, as the dipnoans; of the nature of a dipnoan.

dip-o-dy (dip′ọ-di), *n.*; pl. *-dies* (-diz). [LL. *dipodia*, < Gr. διποδία, < δίπους, two-footed, < δι-, two, + πούς, foot.] In *pros.*, a group of two feet; a pair of feet constituting a single measure.

di-po-lar (dī-pō′lạ̈r), *a.* [See *di-*[1].] Pertaining to or having two poles.

dip-per (dip′ėr), *n.* One who or that which dips; any of various diving birds, esp. of the genus *Cinclus*, as *C. aquaticus*, the common European water-ouzel; a vessel provided with a

Dipper (*Cinclus aquaticus*).

handle and used to dip liquids; [*cap.*] in *astron.*, the group of seven bright stars in Ursa Major resembling such a vessel in outline; also, a similar group in Ursa Minor ('Little Dipper'). — **dip′per-ful** (-fu̇l), *n.*; pl. *-fuls.*

dip-ping=com-pass (dip′ing-kum″pạs), *n.* An instrument consisting essentially of a vertical graduated circle in which a dipping-needle is mounted; an inclinometer.

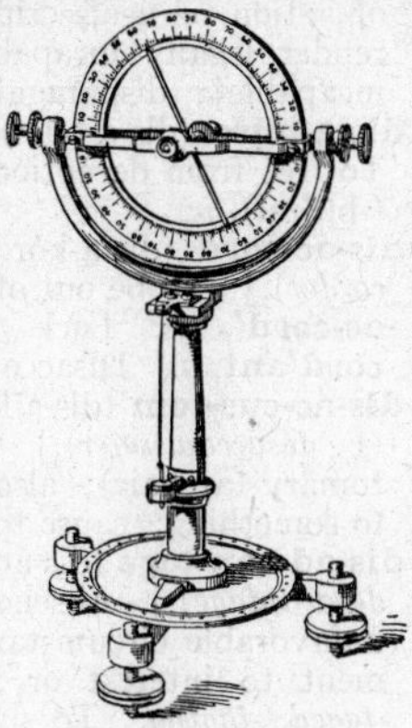

Dipping-compass.

dip-ping=nee-dle (dip′ing-nē″dl), *n.* A magnetic needle mounted so as to be capable of moving freely about its center of gravity in a vertical plane, and indicating by its dip the direction of the earth's magnetism.

dip-sa-ca-ceous (dip-sạ-kā′shius), *a.* [NL. *Dipsacus*, the typical genus, < Gr. δίψακος, teazel.] Belonging to the *Dipsacaceæ*, or teazel family of plants.

dip-sas (dip′sas), *n.*; pl. *dipsades* (dip′sạ-dēz). [L., < Gr. διψάς, < δίψα, thirst.] A fabulous serpent whose bite was said to produce a mortal thirst.

dip-sey, dip-sy (dip′si), *a.* A nautical corruption of *deep-sea.*

dip-so-ma-ni-a (dip-sọ-mā′ni-ạ̈), *n.* [NL., < Gr. δίψα, thirst, + μανία, E. *mania.*] In *pathol.*, an irresistible, generally periodic, craving for intoxicating drink. — **dip-so-ma′ni-ac** (-ak), *n.*

dip-ter (dip′tėr), *n.* [NL. *diptera*, pl., < Gr. δίπτερος, two-winged, < δι-, two, + πτερόν, wing.] One of the *Diptera*, an order of insects, including the common house-flies, gnats, mosquitoes, etc., characterized typically by a single pair of membranous wings. — **dip′ter-an,** *a.* and *n.*

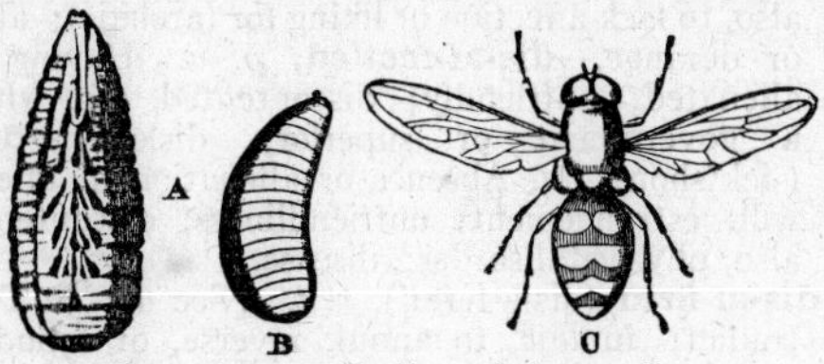

A Dipter (*Syrphus ribesii*). — *A*, larva; *B*, pupa; *C*, imago. (Enlarged.)

dip-ter-al (dip′tẹ-rạl), *a.* [L. *dipteros*, < Gr. δίπτερος, two-winged: see *dipter.*] In *arch.*, having two rows of columns on all sides, as a temple.

dip-ter-o-car-pa-ceous (dip″tẹ-rō-kär-pā′shius), *a.* [NL. *Dipterocarpus*, the typical genus, < Gr. δίπτερος, two-winged, + καρπός, fruit.] Belonging to the *Dipterocarpaceæ*, a family of trees, chiefly natives of tropical Asia, characterized by a two-winged fruit, and noted for their aromatic oils and resins.

dip-ter-ous (dip′tẹ-rus), *a.* [Gr. δίπτερος: see *dipter.*] In *entom.*, two-winged; belonging to or resembling the dipters; in *bot.*, having two wing-like appendages, as seeds, stems, etc.

dip-tych (dip′tik), *n.* [LL. *diptycha*, pl., < Gr. δίπτυχα, neut. pl. of δίπτυχος, double-folded, < δι-, two, + πτυχή, a fold.] A hinged two-leaved tablet used by the ancients for writing on with the stylus; a pair of pictures or carvings on two panels hinged together; *pl.*, in the early church, the tablets containing the names of those to be especially commemorated at the celebration of the eucharist; also, the intercessions for such persons.

Fruit of Dipterocarpaceous Tree.

Dir-cæ-an (dėr-sē′ạn), *a.* [L. *Dircæus.*] Of or pertaining to the fountain Dirce, near Thebes, in Bœotia (as, the *Dircæan* Swan, a name applied by Horace to Pindar, who lived in Thebes); hence, Pindaric; poetic.

dir-dum (dir′dum or dėr′-), *n.* [Origin unknown.] Tumult or din; outcry; a scolding; blame; a blow; ill humor; *pl.*, low spirits. [Sc. and north. Eng.]

dire (dīr), *a.*; compar. *direr*, superl. *direst.* [L. *dirus.*] Causing or attended with great fear or suffering; dreadful; awful: as, *dire* portents; a *dire* calamity; "*dire* necessity" (Milton's "Samson Agonistes," 1666).

di-rect (di-rekt′), *v.* [L. *directus*, pp. of *dirigere*, set or send in a straight line, arrange, guide, direct, < *di-*, for *dis-*, apart, + *regere*, keep straight, direct, rule.] **I.** *tr.* To point or aim toward a particular place or thing; cause to move or act toward a certain object or end; also, to tell or show (a person) the way to a place, etc.; also, to guide with advice; regulate the course of; conduct; manage; control; also, to give authoritative instructions to; command; order or ordain (something); also, to address (words, etc.) to a person (as, "In the morning will I *direct* my prayer unto thee": Ps. v. 3); mark (a letter, etc.) as intended for or sent to a particular person; dedicate (a book, etc.) to a person†. **II.** *intr.* To act as a guide or conductor; also, to give commands or orders. — **di-rect′,** *a.* [L. *directus*, straight, direct, prop. pp.: see *direct, v.*] Proceeding in a straight line or by the shortest course; straight; undeviating; also, proceeding or lying at right angles or perpendicularly; not oblique or inclined; also, proceeding in uninterrupted succession; proceeding in an unbroken line of descent; lineal, not collateral; also, following the natural order, as in mathematics; not inverse; also, without intervening agency; immediate; immediate in time; also, going straight to the point, without circumlocution or ambiguity; straightforward; downright; also, absolute or exact (as, the *direct* contrary); in *elect.*, of a current, flowing in one direction (cf. *alternating*); in *astron.*, noting an apparent or actual motion in a direction corresponding to the order of the signs, or from west to east; having such a motion, as a planet. — **direct action.** (*a*) Action which takes effect without any intervening agency or intermediate instrumentality, as that in a steam-engine in which the piston-rod or cross-head is directly connected by a rod with the crank. (*b*) Any method of action employed to enforce demands directly rather than by indirect or ordinary (political or other) means, esp. some such method employed by workers in order to coerce their employers; specif., some practice such as the general strike or as terrorism, sabotage, or any violent or criminal procedure, employed by workers against employers or against the capitalist class in general, and regarded by the workers as a justifiable method of ultimately bringing possession of the means of production and distribution, and control of society and government, into the hands of federated bodies of workers. Cf. *syndicalism.* Hence **di-rect′=ac′tion-ist,** *n.* — **direct discourse.** See under *discourse, n.* — **direct object.** See *object, n.* — **direct tax.** See under *tax, n.* — **di-rect′,** *adv.* Directly. — **di-rect′,** *n.* In *music*, a sign placed at the end of a staff or page to indicate the position of the first note of the next staff or page. — **di-rect′a-ble,** *a.* That may be directed; dirigible. — **di-rect′er,** *n.* See *director.*

di-rec-tion (di-rek′shọn), *n.* [L. *directio(n-).*] The act of directing, pointing, aiming, etc.; also, the line along which anything lies, faces, moves, etc., with reference to the point or region toward which it is directed; the line toward some point or region, or the point or region itself, as indicating position or course; fig., a line of action, tendency, etc.; also, guidance; instruction; an instruction how to go to a place, etc., or how to proceed or act; order or command; an order to be carried out; management or control; also, the office of a director; a body of directors; a directorate; also, administrative faculty† (as, "men of sound *direction*": Shakspere's "Richard III.," v. 3. 16); also, the directing or addressing of a letter, etc.; the superscription on a letter, etc., giving the name and address of the intended recipient; in *law*, that part of a bill in equity containing the address to the court (U. S.). — **di-rec′tion-al,** *a.* Of, pertaining to, or characterized by direction in space. — **directional wireless,** wireless employed to discover position through the direction of messages received or intercepted, as by the navigator of an aircraft in flight at sea or the navigator of a vessel at sea; also, wireless in which the waves are sent out in only one direction, as from one station to another, as in order to maintain secrecy.

di-rec-tive (di-rek′tiv), *a.* Serving to direct; directing. — **di-rec′tive-ly,** *adv.*

di-rect-ly (di-rekt′li), *adv.* In a direct line, way, or manner; straight; perpendicularly; immediately, or without the intervention of any medium; straightway, or at once; sometimes, presently; without circumlocution, or straightforwardly; absolutely, exactly, or precisely.—**di-rect′ness,** *n.*
Di-rec-toire (dē-rek-twor). [F., = E. *directory.*] **I.** *n.* The French Directory. **II.** *a.* In the style of the period of the French Directory: applied to costume.
di-rec-tor (di-rek′tọr), *n.* [= F. *directeur.*] One who or that which directs; esp., a chief administrative official; also, one of a body of persons chosen to manage the affairs of a company or corporation.—**di-rec′tor-ate** (-ạt), *n.* The office of a director or body of directors; also, a body of directors.—**dir-ec-to-ri-al** (dir-ek-tō′ri-ạl), *a.* Pertaining to a director or directorate.—**di-rec′tor-ship,** *n.*
di-rec-to-ry (di-rek′tọ-ri). [= F. *directoire* (now as n.), < LL. *directorius,* that directs, < L. *dirigere*: see *direct, v.*] **I.** *a.* Serving to direct; directing. **II.** *n.*; pl. *-ries* (-riz). Something serving to direct; a book of directions, esp. for saying church offices; a book containing an alphabetical list of the inhabitants of a city or district, of a particular class of persons, etc., with addresses and the like; also, a body of directors; [*cap.*] the body of five directors forming the executive of France from 1795 to 1799.
di-rec-tress (di-rek′tres), *n.* A female director.
di-rec-trix (di-rek′triks), *n.*; pl. *-trixes,* L. *-trices* (-tri-sēz). [NL.] A directress; in *math.*, a fixed line required for the description of a curve or surface.
dire-ful (dīr′fu̇l), *a.* Dire; dreadful; awful; terrible.—**dire′ful-ly,** *adv.*—**dire′ful-ness,** *n.*
dire-ly (dīr′li), *adv.* In a dire manner.—**dire′ness,** *n.*
dirge (dėrj), *n.* [Orig. *dirige,* the first word of the L. antiphon "Dirige, Domine, Deus meus, in conspectu tuo viam meam" (Direct, Lord, my God, in thy sight my way), sung in the office of the dead.] The office of the dead, or the funeral service as sung; hence, a funeral song or tune, or one expressing mourning.—**dirge′ful,** *a.* Sounding a dirge; mournful.
dir-i-gi-ble (dir′i-ji-bl). [L. *dirigere*: see *direct, v.*] **I.** *a.* That may be directed or steered. **II.** *n.* A dirigible balloon.
dir-i-ment (dir′i-mẹnt), *a.* [L. *dirimens* (*-ent-*), ppr. of *dirimere,* separate, break off, dissolve, < *dis-,* apart, + *emere,* take.] That renders absolutely void; nullifying.
dirk (dėrk), *n.* [Origin unknown.] A stabbing weapon; a dagger.—**dirk,** *v. t.* To stab with a dirk.
dirn-dl (dėrn′dl), *n.* [G., < *dirne,* girl, maid.] A type of woman's dress with full skirt and close-fitting bodice, commonly of colorful and strikingly patterned material, derived from German peasant use.
dirt (dėrt), *n.* [ME. *drit*: cf. Icel. *drit,* excrement.] Any foul or filthy substance; excrement; filth; mud; mire; dust; whatever adhering to anything renders it foul or unclean; also, earth or soil, esp. when loose; earth, etc., dug or worked in mining, esp. the material from which the gold is separated by washing in placer-mining; also, something vile, mean, or worthless; moral filth; also, uncleanness, vileness, or meanness.—**dirt,** *v. t.* To dirty.—**dirt′y,** *a.*; compar. *dirtier,* superl. *dirtiest.* Characterized by the presence of dirt; soiled with dirt; foul; unclean; also, imparting dirt; soiling; also, vile, mean, or contemptible; morally unclean; indecent; also, inclement, stormy, or squally, as the weather (as, "It begins to look very *dirty* to windward": Marryat's "Mr. Midshipman Easy," xviii.); also, appearing as if soiled; dark-colored; dingy.—**dirt′i-ly,** *adv.* —**dirt′i-ness,** *n.*—**dirt′y,** *v. t.*; *dirtied, dirtying.* To make dirty; soil; befoul.

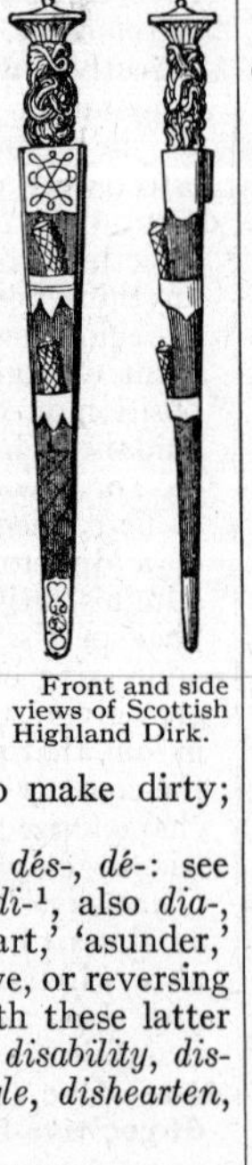
Front and side views of Scottish Highland Dirk.

dis-. [L. *dis-* (OF. *dis-, des-, de-,* F. *dis-, des-, dés-, dé-*: see *de-*); akin to L. *bis,* Gr. δίς, twice: see *bi-, di-*[1], also *dia-, di-*[2].] A prefix of Latin origin, meaning 'apart,' 'asunder,' 'away,' 'utterly,' or having a privative, negative, or reversing force (cf. *de-* and *un-*[2]), used freely, esp. with these latter significations, as an English formative, as in *disability, disaffirm, disbar, disbelief, discontent, disentangle, dishearten, disinfect, dislike, disown, disrelish, disunion.*
dis-a-bil-i-ty (dis-ạ-bil′i-ti), *n.*; pl. *-ties* (-tiz). [See *dis-.*] Lack of ability or power; incapacity; also, lack of competent means or instruments; also, legal incapacity; a legal disqualification.—**dis-a′ble** (-ā′bl), *v. t.*; *-bled, -bling.* To deprive of ability or power; incapacitate; render incapable of action or use; cripple; injure† or impair†; specif., to render legally incapable; disqualify; also, to pronounce incapable†; disparage† or belittle†.—**dis-a′ble-ment,** *n.*
dis-a-buse (dis-ạ-būz′), *v. t.*; *-bused, -busing.* [See *dis-.*] To free from deception or error; undeceive.—**dis-a-bu′sal** (-bū′zạl), *n.*
dis-ac-cord (dis-ạ-kôrd′), *v. i.* [OF. *desacorder* (F. *désaccorder*).] To be out of accord or harmony; disagree.—**dis-ac-cord′,** *n.* Lack of accord; disagreement.—**dis-ac-cord′ant,** *a.* Disaccording; not in accord.
dis-ac-cus-tom (dis-ạ-kus′tọm), *v. t.* [OF. *desacoustumer* (F. *désaccoutumer*).] To make (something) no longer customary (archaic); also, to render (a person) unaccustomed to something; cause to lose a habit.
dis-ad-van-tage (dis-ạd-vȧn′tạj), *n.* [OF. *desavantage* (F. *désavantage*).] Absence or deprivation of advantage; an unfavorable circumstance or condition; also, loss or detriment to interest or reputation.—**dis-ad-van′tage,** *v. t.*; *-taged, -taging.* To subject to disadvantage.—**dis-ad-van-ta′geous** (-ad-vạn-tā′jus), *a.* Attended with disadvantage; unfavorable; detrimental; prejudicial.—**dis-ad-van-ta′geous-ly,** *adv.*—**dis-ad-van-ta′geous-ness,** *n.*
dis-ad-vise (dis-ạd-vīz′), *v. t.*; *-vised, -vising.* [See *dis-.*] To advise against (a course, etc.); also, to advise (a person) against a course, etc.
dis-af-fect (dis-ạ-fekt′), *v. t.* [See *dis-.*] To alienate the affection of; make ill-affected, discontented, or disloyal; also, to lack affection or liking for (archaic); also, to disorder or derange.—**dis-af-fect′ed,** *p. a.* Having the affection alienated; unfriendly; discontented, esp. with the acts of a government or superior; disloyal.—**dis-af-fec′tion** (-fek′shọn), *n.* Absence or alienation of affection or good will; estrangement; unfriendliness; discontent; disloyalty; also, physical disorder; disease.
dis-af-firm (dis-ạ-fėrm′), *v. t.* [See *dis-.*] To deny; contradict; in *law,* to annul, reverse, or repudiate.—**dis-af-firm′ance, dis-af-fir-ma′tion** (-af-ėr-mā′shọn), *n.*
dis-af-for-est (dis-ạ-for′est), *v. t.* [ML. *disafforestare.*] To reduce from the legal status of a forest to that of common land; also, to strip of forests.—**dis-af-for-es-ta′tion** (-es-tā′shọn), **dis-af-for′est-ment,** *n.*
dis-ag-gre-gate (dis-ag′rē-gāt), *v. t.*; *-gated, -gating.* [See *dis-.*] To separate (an aggregate) into its component parts.—**dis-ag-gre-ga′tion** (-gā′shọn), *n.*
dis-a-gree (dis-ạ-grē′), *v. i.*; *-greed, -greeing.* [OF. *desagreer* (F. *désagréer*).] To fail to agree; differ; be unlike; also, to differ in opinion; dissent; hence, to be at variance; quarrel; also, to conflict in action or effect (as, food that *disagrees* with one).—**dis-a-gree′a-ble.** [OF. *desagreable* (F. *désagréable*).] **I.** *a.* Not in agreement†; not conformable†; also, contrary to one's taste or liking; unpleasant; offensive; repugnant; of a person, unpleasant in temper or humor; unamiable. **II.** *n.* A disagreeable thing: usually in *pl.*: as, "the noise, dust, and damp *disagreeables* of a country inn" (Lever's "Harry Lorrequer," xix.); "always . . . seeing difficulties and *disagreeables* in everything" (Mrs. Gaskell's "Cranford," xi.).—**dis-a-gree′a-ble-ness,** *n.* —**dis-a-gree′a-bly,** *adv.*—**dis-a-gree′ment,** *n.* The state or fact of disagreeing; want of agreement; diversity; unlikeness; difference of opinion; dissent; variance, dissension, or strife; a quarrel; unwholesome action or effect, as of food.
dis-al-low (dis-ạ-lou′), *v.* [OF. *desalouer.*] **I.** *tr.* To refuse to allow; refuse to admit the truth or validity of (a statement, claim, etc.); reject (a request, etc.); refuse to permit; withhold approval or sanction of, or disapprove. **II.** *intr.* To refuse allowance; withhold sanction. See Shakspere's "King John," i. 1. 16.—**dis-al-low′ance,** *n.*
dis-an-i-mate (dis-an′i-māt), *v. t.*; *-mated, -mating.* [See *dis-.*] To deprive of life; also, to dispirit or discourage.—**dis-an-i-ma′tion** (-mā′shọn), *n.*
dis-an-nex (dis-ạ-neks′), *v. t.* [OF. *desannexer.*] To separate (something annexed); disjoin; detach.—**dis-an-nex-a′tion** (-an-ek-sā′shọn), *n.*

dis-an-nul (dis-ạ-nul′), *v. t.*; *-nulled, -nulling.* [See *dis-.*] To annul utterly; make void.—**dis-an-nul′ment,** *n.*

dis-a-noint (dis-ạ-noint′), *v. t.* [See *dis-.*] To render invalid the anointing or consecration of.

dis-ap-pear (dis-ạ-pēr′), *v. i.* [See *dis-.*] To cease to appear or be seen; vanish from sight; also, to cease to exist or be known; pass away; end gradually or without abrupt termination.—**dis-ap-pear′ance,** *n.* The act of disappearing; a vanishing; cessation.—**dis-ap-pear′er,** *n.*—**dis-ap-pear′ing,** *p. a.* That disappears: as, a *disappearing* gun (a gun which after being fired descends to the loading position behind the protection of a parapet).

dis-ap-point (dis-ạ-point′), *v. t.* [OF. *desapointier* (F. *désappointer*).] To undo the appointment of†; also, to break an appointment or engagement with; also, to frustrate or fall short of the expectations or wishes of (a person); deceive the hopes of; also, to defeat the realization or fulfilment of (hopes, plans, etc.); thwart.—**dis-ap-point′ed,** *p. a.* Deceived in expectations or hopes; frustrated; thwarted; also, improperly appointed, equipped, or prepared† (see Shakspere's "Hamlet," i. 5. 77).—**dis-ap-point′er,** *n.*—**dis-ap-point′ing-ly,** *adv.*—**dis-ap-point′ment,** *n.* The act or fact of disappointing; the state or feeling of being disappointed; also, something that disappoints.

dis-ap-pro-ba-tion (dis-ap-rọ-bā′shọn), *n.* [See *dis-.*] The reverse of approbation; condemnatory sentiment; disapproval.—**dis-ap′pro-ba-tive** (-bā-tiv), **dis-ap′pro-ba-to-ry** (-bạ-tọ-ri), *a.*

dis-ap-prove (dis-ạ-pröv′), *v.*; *-proved, -proving.* [See *dis-.*] **I.** *tr.* To regard with the reverse of approval; feel or express disapprobation of; also, to decline to sanction. **II.** *intr.* To feel or express disapprobation.—**dis-ap-prov′al** (-prö′vạl), *n.*—**dis-ap-prov′ing-ly,** *adv.*

dis-arm (dis-ärm′), *v.* [OF. *desarmer* (F. *désarmer*).] **I.** *tr.* To deprive of arms or weapons; divest of armor; reduce to a peace footing, as an army or navy; also, to deprive of means of attack or defense (as, "their jaws disabled and their claws *disarmed*": Dryden's "Hind and the Panther," i. 300); render harmless or defenseless; hence, to deprive of power of opposing or harming; divest of hostility, suspicion, etc. **II.** *intr.* To lay down arms; divest one's self of armor; reduce a national armament to a peace footing.—**dis-ar′ma-ment** (-är′mạ-mẹnt), *n.* The act of disarming; the reduction of a national armament to a peace footing.—**dis-arm′er,** *n.*

dis-ar-range (dis-ạ-rānj′), *v. t.*; *-ranged, -ranging.* [See *dis-.*] To disturb the arrangement of; disorder; unsettle.—**dis-ar-range′ment,** *n.*—**dis-ar-ran′ger** (-rān′jėr), *n.*

dis-ar-ray (dis-ạ-rā′), *v. t.* [OF. *desarreier.*] To put out of array or order; throw into disorder; rout, as troops; also, to divest of personal array; disrobe; undress; strip.—**dis-ar-ray′,** *n.* [Cf. OF. *desarroy.*] Absence or deprivation of array or order; disorder; confusion; also, disorder of apparel, or disorderly dress (as, "A wicked Hag . . . In ragged robes and filthy *disaray*": Spenser's "Faerie Queene," ii. 4. 4).

dis-ar-tic-u-late (dis-är-tik′ū-lāt), *v. t.* or *i.*; *-lated, -lating.* [See *dis-.*] To take or come apart at the joints.—**dis-ar-tic-u-la′tion** (-lā′shọn), *n.*—**dis-ar-tic′u-la-tor,** *n.*

dis-as-sim-i-late (dis-ạ-sim′i-lāt), *v. t.*; *-lated, -lating.* [See *dis-.*] To cause the reverse of assimilation in; transform by catabolism.—**dis-as-sim-i-la′tion** (-lā′shọn), *n.*

dis-as-so-ci-ate (dis-ạ-sō′shi-āt), *v. t.*; *-ated, -ating.* [See *dis-.*] To dissociate.—**dis-as-so-ci-a′tion** (-ṣi-ā′shọn), *n.*

dis-as-ter (di-zas′tėr), *n.* [F. *désastre,* < L. *dis-* (see *dis-*) + *astrum,* star.] Mischance or misfortune; fatal or ruinous misfortune; also, a mishap; a sudden or great misfortune; a calamity.—**dis-as′trous,** *a.* Unfortunate or unlucky (now rare); also, fraught with disaster; entailing disaster; ruinous; calamitous; also, foreboding disaster (archaic: as, "As when the sun . . . In dim eclipse, *disastrous* twilight sheds," Milton's "Paradise Lost," i. 597).—**dis-as′trous-ly,** *adv.*—**dis-as′trous-ness,** *n.*

dis-a-vow (dis-ạ-vou′), *v. t.* [OF. *desavouer* (F. *désavouer*).] To refuse to avow; disclaim knowledge of, connection with, or responsibility for; disown; repudiate; also, to deny†.—**dis-a-vow′al,** *n.*—**dis-a-vow′er,** *n.*

dis-band (dis-band′), *v.* [F. *desbander* (now *débander*).] **I.** *tr.* To break up or disorganize (a band or company); dissolve (a military force) by dismissing from service; also, to dismiss or discharge from a band†; send away†. **II.** *intr.* To break up as a band or company.—**dis-band′ment,** *n.*

dis-bar (dis-bär′), *v. t.*; *-barred, -barring.* [See *dis-.*] To expel from the bar or the legal profession; deprive (an attorney, etc.) of legal status.—**dis-bar′ment,** *n.*

dis-be-lief (dis-bẹ-lēf′), *n.* [See *dis-.*] The reverse of belief; conviction of the untrustworthiness or falseness of a thing.—**dis-be-lieve′** (-lēv′), *v.*; *-lieved, -lieving.* **I.** *tr.* To have no belief in; refuse to credit; regard as untrustworthy or false. **II.** *intr.* To be without belief; esp., to refuse belief in a divine revelation.—**dis-be-liev′er,** *n.*—**dis-be-liev′ing-ly,** *adv.*

dis-bench (dis-bench′), *v. t.* [See *dis-.*] To remove from or deprive of a bench or seat; in *Eng. law,* to deprive of the status of a bencher.—**dis-bench′ment,** *n.*

dis-bod-y (dis-bod′i), *v. t.*; *-bodied, -bodying.* [See *dis-.*] To disembody.—**dis-bos′om** (-bůz′ọm), *v. t.* To unbosom.—**dis-bow′el** (-bou′ẹl), *v. t.*; *-eled* or *-elled, -eling* or *-elling.* To disembowel.—**dis-brain′** (-brān′), *v. t.* To deprive of the brain.

dis-branch (dis-brȧnch′), *v. t.* [Cf. OF. *desbrancher.*] To deprive of branches, as a tree; also, to cut or break off, as a branch from a tree.

dis-bud (dis-bud′), *v. t.*; *-budded, -budding.* [See *dis-.*] To deprive of buds; remove unnecessary buds from.

dis-bur-den (dis-bėr′dn), *v. t.* [See *dis-.*] To rid or relieve of a burden; also, to get rid of (a burden); discharge.—**dis-bur′den-ment,** *n.*

dis-burse (dis-bėrs′), *v. t.*; *-bursed, -bursing.* [OF. *desbourser* (F. *débourser*), < *des-* (see *dis-*) + *bourse,* purse, < ML. *bursa*: see *bursa.*] To pay out (money); expend; also, to defray (charges)†.—**dis-burs′a-ble,** *a.*—**dis-burse′ment,** *n.* The act of disbursing; also, that which is disbursed; money expended.—**dis-burs′er,** *n.*

dis-bur-then (dis-bėr′ᴛʜn), etc. Same as *disburden,* etc. [Archaic.]

disc (disk), *n.* See *disk.*

dis-cage (dis-kāj′), *v. t.*; *-caged, -caging.* [See *dis-.*] To release from or as from a cage; uncage: as, "Until she let me fly *discaged* to sweep In ever-highering eagle-circles" (Tennyson's "Gareth and Lynette," 20).

dis-cal (dis′kạl), *a.* [L. *discus,* E. *disk.*] Of, pertaining to, or having the form of a disk.

dis-cal-ce-ate (dis-kal′sẹ-āt), *a.* [L. *discalceatus*: see *dis-* and *calceate.*] Unshod; barefooted, as certain religious congregations of men and women. Also **dis-calced′** (-kalst′).

dis-cant (dis′kant), etc. See *descant,* etc.

dis-card (dis-kärd′), *v.* [See *dis-.*] **I.** *tr.* To throw out (a card or cards) from one's hand in a game; also, to play (a card, not a trump, of a different suit from that of the card led); hence, to cast aside; reject; dismiss, as from employment. **II.** *intr.* To discard a card or cards.—**dis-card** (dis-kärd′ or dis′kärd), *n.* The act of discarding; also, the card or cards discarded.—**dis-card′er,** *n.*—**dis-card′ment,** *n.*

dis-case (dis-kās′), *v. t.*; *-cased, -casing.* [See *dis-.*] To uncase; strip.

dis-cern (di-zėrn′), *v.* [OF. F. *discerner,* < L. *discernere* (pp. *discretus*), separate, distinguish between, discern, < *dis-,* apart, + *cernere,* separate: see *certain.*] **I.** *tr.* To separate as distinct (obs. or rare); also, to distinguish mentally; recognize as distinct or different; discriminate; also, to perceive by the sight or some other sense or by the intellect; see, recognize, or apprehend clearly. **II.** *intr.* To distinguish or discriminate; also, to have distinct perception.—**dis-cern′er,** *n.*—**dis-cern′i-ble,** *a.* [LL. *discernibilis.*] Capable of being discerned; distinguishable.—**dis-cern′i-ble-ness,** *n.*—**dis-cern′i-bly,** *adv.*—**dis-cern′ing,** *p. a.* Showing discernment; discriminating; penetrating; acute.—**dis-cern′ing-ly,** *adv.*—**dis-cern′ment,** *n.* The act or faculty of discerning; discrimination; acuteness of judgment; penetration.

dis-cerp (di-sėrp′), *v. t.* [L. *discerpere* (pp. *discerptus*), < *dis-,* apart, + *carpere,* pick.] To tear to pieces; dismember; divide into parts; also, to tear off; separate. [Archaic.]

—**dis-cerp′ti-ble,** *a.* Capable of being torn apart; divisible.—**dis-cerp′tion** (-shọn), *n.*

dis-charge (dis-chärj′), *v.*; *-charged, -charging.* [OF. *deschargier* (F. *décharger*).] **I.** *tr.* To relieve of a charge or load; unload (a ship, etc.); send forth a missile from (a gun, bow, etc.); rid (something) of a charge of electricity; rid, relieve, or free of anything, as a fabric of dye; fig., to relieve of obligation, responsibility, etc.; also, to relieve or deprive of office, employment, etc.; dismiss from service; also, to clear of a charge, accusation, etc.†; set free from custody or legal restraint; send away or allow to go; also, to remove, send forth, or get rid of (a charge, load, etc.); unload, as a cargo; let drive, as a missile; pour forth, as water; emit, as an oath; relieve one's self of (an obligation, etc.); pay (a debt); pay off (a creditor)†; fulfil, perform, or execute (a duty, function, etc.); in *law,* to set aside or annul, as an order of a court. **II.** *intr.* To discharge a burden or load; also, to throw off a burden; deliver a charge or load; emit contents; also, to be discharged; come or pour forth.—**dis-charge′,** *n.* The act of discharging a ship, a gun, etc., or its load; also, a sending or coming forth, as of water from a pipe; ejection; emission; rate or amount of issue; a place where a flow of water, etc., is discharged; something discharged or emitted; also, a relieving or ridding, or a getting rid, of something of the nature of a charge; a relieving or being relieved of obligation or liability; the fulfilling of an obligation; the payment of a debt; performance or execution, as of a duty; also, release or dismissal from office, employment, etc.; also, acquittal or exoneration; also, release from custody; a sending away or allowing to go; also, a certificate of release, as from obligation or liability; in *elect.,* the withdrawing or transference of an electric charge; the equalization of the difference of potential between two terminals or the like; in *law,* annulment, as of a court order.—**discharge′a-ble,** *a.* That may be or is to be discharged.—**dis-char′ger,** *n.*

disci-. Form of L. *discus,* discus, disk, used in combination. —**dis-cif-er-ous** (di-sif′ẹ-rus), *a.* [+ *-ferous.*] Disk-bearing; having a disk.—**dis-ci-flo-ral** (dis-i-flō′rạl), *a.* [+ L. *flos* (*flor-*), flower.] In *bot.,* having flowers in which the receptacle is expanded into a conspicuous disk.—**dis′ci-form,** *a.* [+ *-form.*] Disk-shaped; discoid.—**dis-ciger-ous** (di-sij′ẹ-rus), *a.* [+ *-gerous.*] Disk-bearing.

dis-ci-ple (di-sī′pl), *n.* [OF. F. *disciple,* < L. *discipulus,* < *discere,* learn.] A pupil or scholar (archaic); a follower of a particular teacher; an adherent of the principles of some leader of thought; esp., one of the twelve personal followers of Jesus Christ; sometimes, any follower of Christ. —**Disciples of Christ,** a denomination of Christians, founded in the U. S. in the early part of the 19th century by Alexander Campbell (1788–1866), which rejects all formulas or creeds, accepts the Bible alone as a sufficient and infallible rule of faith and practice, and administers baptism by immersion only.—**dis-ci′ple,** *v. t.*; *-pled, -pling.* To teach† or train† (see Shakspere's "All's Well," i. 2. 28); also, to make a disciple or disciples of.—**dis-ci′ple-ship,** *n.*

dis-ci-plin-a-ble (dis′i-plin-ạ-bl), *a.* Capable of being disciplined or instructed; also, subject to or meriting discipline or correction.

dis-ci-plin-al (dis′i-plin-ạl or dis-i-plī′nạl), *a.* Of, pertaining to, or of the nature of discipline.

dis-ci-plin-ant (dis′i-plin-ạnt), *n.* [Sp. and It. *disciplinante,* < ML. *disciplinans* (*-ant-*), ppr. of *disciplinare,* E. *discipline, v.*] One who subjects himself to discipline; specif. [also *cap.*], a member of a former Spanish religious order who scourged themselves publicly and inflicted upon themselves other severe tortures.

dis-ci-pli-na-ri-an (dis″i-pli-nā′ri-ạn). **I.** *a.* Disciplinary. **II.** *n.* One who enforces or advocates discipline.

dis-ci-pli-na-ry (dis′i-pli-nā-ri), *a.* [ML. *disciplinarius.*] Of or for discipline; promoting discipline. Also **dis′ci-plin″a-to-ry** (-plin″ạ-tọ-ri).

dis-ci-pline (dis′i-plin), *n.* [OF. F. *discipline,* < L. *disciplina,* < *discipulus,* E. *disciple.*] Instruction†, teaching†, or education†; a branch of instruction or learning (archaic); instruction and exercise designed to train to proper conduct or action; systematic training under direction and control; drill; fig., the training effect of experience, adversity, etc.; also, the state of being trained; also, subjection to rules of conduct or behavior; a state of order maintained by training and control; also, a particular system of regulations for conduct; specif., the methods or rules employed in regulating the conduct of the members of a church; hence, the system of government regulating the practice of a church as distinguished from its doctrine; also, punishment inflicted by way of correction and training; religious mortification or penance; also, an instrument of punishment, esp. a scourge for religious penance.—**dis′ci-pline,** *v. t.*; *-plined, -plining.* [OF. F. *discipliner,* < ML. *disciplinare,* < L. *disciplina.*] To instruct†; train by instruction and exercise; drill; esp., to bring to a state of order and obedience by training and control; also, to subject to discipline or punishment; correct; chastise; subject to mortification or penance.—**dis′ci-plin-er,** *n.*

dis-cip-u-lar (di-sip′ū-lạr), *a.* [L. *discipulus,* E. *disciple.*] Of, befitting, or being a disciple.

dis-claim (dis-klām′), *v.* [AF. *disclaimer, desclamer.*] **I.** *intr.* To renounce or repudiate a legal claim; also, to disavow interest (*in*)†; proclaim one's withdrawal or dissent (*from*)†. **II.** *tr.* To renounce claim to; also, to repudiate or deny interest in or connection with, disavow, or disown (as, "They earnestly *disclaimed* all participation in so horrid a custom [cannibalism]": H. Melville's "Typee," xii.); also, to reject the claims or authority of; refuse to admit.—**dis-claim′er¹,** *n.* One who disclaims.—**disclaim′er²,** *n.* [AF., prop. inf.] The act of disclaiming; the renouncing, repudiating, or denying of a claim; disavowal.—**dis-cla-ma′tion** (-klạ-mā′shọn), *n.* The act of disclaiming; renunciation; disavowal.—**dis-clam′a-to-ry** (-klam′ạ-tọ-ri), *a.*

dis-close (dis-klōz′), *v. t.*; *-closed, -closing.* [ME. *disclosen, desclosen,* < OF. *desclore* (pp. *desclos*) (F. *déclore*), < *des-* (see *dis-*) + *clore,* shut: see *close², a.*] To unclose† or unfold†; also, to remove a cover from and expose to view; uncover; also, to make known; reveal; divulge.—**disclose′**†, *n.* Disclosure.—**dis-clos′er** (-klō′zėr), *n.*—**disclo′sure** (-klō′zhụr), *n.* The act of disclosing; exposure; revelation; also, that which is disclosed; a revelation.

dis-cob-o-lus (dis-kob′ọ-lus), *n.*; pl. *-li* (-lī). [L., < Gr. δισκοβόλος, < δίσκος, discus, + βάλλειν, throw.] In *class. antiq.,* a thrower of the discus; esp. [*cap.*], a famous statue of a discus thrower by the Greek sculptor Myron (5th century B.C.).

Discobolus (after Myron). — Vatican Museum, Rome.

dis-coid (dis′koid), *a.* [LL. *discoides,* < Gr. δισκοειδής, < δίσκος, discus, disk, + εἶδος, form.] Having the form of a discus or disk; disk-like; flat and circular; in *bot.,* of a composite flower-head, consisting of a disk only, without rays. Also **dis-coi′dal.**

dis-col-or (dis-kul′ọr), *v.* [OF. *descolorer.*] **I.** *tr.* To alter the color of; deprive of color; spoil the color of; stain. **II.** *intr.* To change color; become faded or stained.—**dis-col-or-a′tion** (-ọ-rā′shọn), *n.* The act or fact of discoloring, or the state of being discolored; also, a discolored marking; a stain.—**dis-col′our,** *v.* British preferred form of *discolor.*

dis-com-fit (dis-kum′fit), *v. t.* [OF. *desconfit,* pp. of *desconfire* (F. *déconfire*), < ML. *disconficere,* < L. *dis-* (see *dis-*) + *conficere,* make, accomplish: see *confect.*] To overcome completely in battle; defeat utterly; rout; also, to frustrate the plans of; thwart; foil; also, to throw into perplexity and dejection; disconcert.—**dis-com′fit**†, *n.* Discomfiture. See Shakspere's "2 Henry VI," v. 2. 86.—**dis-com′fit-er,** *n.*—**dis-com′fi-ture** (-fi-ṭūr), *n.* The act of discomfiting, or the state of being discomfited; utter defeat; overthrow; frustration of hopes or plans; disconcertment or confusion.

dis-com-fort (dis-kum′fọrt), *v. t.* [OF. *desconforter* (F. *déconforter*).] To disturb the comfort of; distress; sadden; esp., to make uncomfortable or uneasy.—**dis-com′fort,** *n.* [OF. *desconfort* (F. *déconfort*).] The reverse of comfort; uncomfortable state or feeling; also, anything that disturbs the comfort.—**dis-com'fort-a-ble,** *a.* Such as to discomfort; discomforting; lacking in comfort or convenience; also, experiencing discomfort, uncomfortable, or uneasy (as, "I never saw . . . such a *discomfortable* collection of human beings": Kinglake's "Eothen," xvi.).

dis-com-mend (dis-ko-mend'), *v. t.* [See *dis-*.] To express disapprobation of; represent as undesirable; also, to bring into disfavor.—**dis-com-mend'a-ble,** *a.* That is to be discommended.—**dis-com-men-da'tion** (-kom-en-dā'shon), *n.* The act of discommending; expression of disapprobation; dispraise.—**dis-com-mend'er,** *n.*

dis-com-mode (dis-ko-mōd'), *v. t.*; *-moded, -moding.* [L. *dis-* (see *dis-*) + *commodare,* make fit, < *commodus,* fit, convenient, useful: see *commode.*] To incommode; inconvenience.

dis-com-mod-i-ty (dis-ko-mod'i-ti), *n.*; pl. *-ties* (-tiz). [See *dis-* and *commodity.*] Inconvenience or disadvantageousness; also, a disadvantage; a source of inconvenience or trouble.

dis-com-mon (dis-kom'on), *v. t.* [See *dis-*.] To deprive of the character of a common, as a piece of land; also, to deprive of the right of common, as cattle; also, to deprive of the privileges of a place.

dis-com-pose (dis-kom-pōz'), *v. t.*; *-posed, -posing.* [See *dis-*.] To bring into disorder; disarrange; unsettle; also, to disturb the composure of; agitate; perturb.—**dis-com-pos'ed-ly** (-pō'zed-li), *adv.*—**dis-com-pos'ing-ly,** *adv.*—**dis-com-po'sure** (-pō'zhūr), *n.* The state of being discomposed; disorder; agitation or perturbation.

dis-con-cert (dis-kon-sėrt'), *v. t.* [Obs. F. *disconcerter* (now *déconcerter*).] To throw out of concert or agreement; throw into confusion; frustrate; also, to disturb the self-possession of; confuse; abash.—**dis-con-cert'ed-ly,** *adv.*—**dis-con-cert'ed-ness,** *n.*—**dis-con-cert'ing-ly,** *adv.*—**dis-con-cert'ment, dis-con-cer'tion** (-sėr'shon), *n.* The act of disconcerting; disconcerted state.

dis-con-for-mi-ty (dis-kon-fôr'mi-ti), *n.* [See *dis-*.] The reverse of conformity; refusal or failure to conform.

dis-con-nect (dis-ko-nekt'), *v. t.* [See *dis-*.] To sever or interrupt the connection of or between; disunite; disjoin.—**dis-con-nect'ed,** *p. a.* Disjoined; broken; incoherent.—**dis-con-nect'ed-ly,** *adv.*—**dis-con-nect'ed-ness,** *n.*—**dis-con-nec'tion, dis-con-nex'ion** (-nek'shon), *n.* The act of disconnecting, or the state of being disconnected; separation; lack of union.

dis-con-sid-er (dis-kon-sid'ėr), *v. t.* [See *dis-*, and cf. *deconsider.*] To deprive of consideration or esteem; discredit: as, "The man was now *disconsidered* and as good as deposed" (Stevenson's "Master of Ballantrae," iii.).—**dis-con-sid-er-a'tion** (-e-rā'shon), *n.*

dis-con-so-late (dis-kon'sō-lāt), *a.* [ML. *disconsolatus,* < L. *dis-* (see *dis-*) + *consolatus,* pp. of *consolari,* E. *console*².] Destitute of consolation or solace; unhappy; inconsolable; also, characterized by or causing discomfort; cheerless; gloomy.—**dis-con'so-late-ly,** *adv.*—**dis-con'so-late-ness, dis-con-so-la'tion** (-lā'shon), *n.*

dis-con-tent (dis-kon-tent'), *a.* [See *dis-*.] Not content; dissatisfied; discontented.—**dis-con-tent',** *n.* The reverse of content (as, "the winter of our *discontent*": Shakspere's "Richard III.," i. 1. 1); dissatisfaction; also, a malcontent (see Shakspere's "1 Henry IV.," v. 1. 76).—**dis-con-tent',** *v. t.* To deprive of content; dissatisfy; displease: now usually in *discontented,* pp.—**dis-con-tent'ed-ly,** *adv.*—**dis-con-tent'ed-ness,** *n.*—**dis-con-tent'ment,** *n.* Discontented state or feeling; discontent.

dis-con-tin-ue (dis-kon-tin'ū), *v.*; *-ued, -uing.* [OF. F. *discontinuer.*] **I.** *tr.* To stop the continuance of; cause to cease; put an end or stop to; cease from; leave off; cease to take, use, etc. (as, to *discontinue* a newspaper); in *law,* to terminate or abandon (a suit, etc.). **II.** *intr.* To come to an end or stop; cease; desist; also, to be severed or separated†; absent one's self†.—**dis-con-tin'u-ance** (-ū-ans), **dis-con-tin-u-a'tion** (-ā'shon), *n.*—**dis-con-tin'u-er,** *n.*

dis-con-tin-u-ous (dis-kon-tin'ū-us), *a.* [ML. *discontinuus.*] Not continuous; broken; interrupted; intermittent.—**dis-con-ti-nu'i-ty** (-kon-ti-nū'i-ti), **dis-con-tin'u-ous-ness,** *n.*—**dis-con-tin'u-ous-ly,** *adv.*

dis-cord (dis-kôrd'), *v. i.* [OF. F. *discorder,* < L. *discordare,* < *discors* (*discord-*), disagreeing, < *dis-* (see *dis-*) + *cor* (*cord-*), heart.] To disagree; be at variance; be out of concord or harmony.—**dis'cord,** *n.* [OF. F. *discord.*] The state of discording; disagreement; variance or dissension; the opposite of concord or harmony; in *music,* an inharmonious combination of musical tones sounded together; a dissonance; hence, in general, any confused or harsh noise (as, "Arms on armour clashing bray'd Horrible *discord*": Milton's "Paradise Lost," vi. 210).—**dis-cord'ance,** *n.* Discordant character; disagreement; discord or dissonance. Also **dis-cord'an-cy.**—**dis-cord'ant,** *a.* Discording; disagreeing; clashing; inharmonious; dissonant.—**dis-cord'ant-ly,** *adv.*

dis-count (dis'kount or dis-kount'), *v. t.* [OF. *desconter* (F. *décompter*), < ML. *discomputare,* < L. *dis-* (see *dis-*) + *computare,* E. *compute, count*².] To reckon off or deduct, as a certain amount in settling a bill; make a reduction of; hence, to leave out of account; disregard; also, to purchase or sell (a bill or note) before maturity at a reduction equivalent to the interest at a certain percentage for the time it still has to run; hence, to make a deduction from; allow for exaggeration in (a statement, etc.); also, to exchange an interest in (something future) for a present consideration; take (an event, etc.) into account in advance, esp. with loss of value, effectiveness, etc.; in *billiards,* to allow a discount to (an inferior player).—**dis'count,** *n.* An allowance or deduction from an amount due, made for payment before it is due, for prompt settlement, etc.; any deduction from the nominal value; a deduction, or the rate of percentage of deduction, from the face value of a bill or note when purchased or sold before maturity (being usually, under the name of *bank discount,* simple interest reckoned, not on the sum advanced, but on the amount of the bill or note, as distinguished from *true discount,* or the sum which would, if added to the actual present worth of the bill or note, calculated with reference to the time it still has to run and the rate of interest involved, make a sum equal to the face value); also, the act of discounting; in *billiards,* a deduction from the score of a superior player in favor of his opponent.—**at a discount,** below par; hence, in low esteem or regard.—**dis-count'a-ble,** *a.* That may be discounted.

dis-coun-te-nance (dis-koun'te-nans), *v. t.*; *-nanced, -nancing.* [F. *descontenancer* (now *décontenancer*).] To put out of countenance; disconcert; abash; also, to show disapproval of; treat with disfavor; bring into discredit.—**dis-coun'te-nance,** *n.* The act of discountenancing, or treating with disfavor; a show of disapproval.—**dis-coun'te-nan-cer,** *n.*

dis-count-er (dis'koun-tėr), *n.* One who discounts.

dis-cour-age (dis-kur'āj), *v. t.*; *-aged, -aging.* [OF. *descoragier* (F. *décourager*).] To deprive of courage; dishearten; dispirit; dissuade (*from*); also, to lessen or repress courage for; discountenance; express disapproval of.—**dis-cour'age-ment,** *n.* The act of discouraging, or the state of being discouraged; depression of spirit; also, something that discourages; a disheartening act, circumstance, etc.; a deterrent.—**dis-cour'ag-er,** *n.*—**dis-cour'ag-ing-ly,** *adv.*

dis-course (dis-kōrs' or dis'kōrs), *n.* [F. *discours,* < L. *discursus,* < *discurrere,* run to and fro, run through, discourse, < *dis-*, apart, + *currere,* run.] Course, as of time or events†; also, the process or the faculty of reasoning (archaic); also, communication of thought by words; talk; conversation; also, the faculty of conversing†; also, a formal discussion of a subject in speech or writing, as a dissertation, treatise, sermon, etc.—**direct discourse,** a form of discourse, or a grammatical construction, in which a statement is quoted in the exact words of the original speaker or writer, as distinguished from *indirect discourse,* in which the substance of such a statement is reported, but in words conforming to the point of view of the reporter: thus, "he said, 'I shall soon arrive'" is in *direct discourse,* while "he said that he would soon arrive" is in *indirect discourse.*—**dis-course',** *v.*; *-coursed, -coursing.* **I.** *intr.* To reason†; also, to communicate thoughts orally; talk; converse; also, to treat of a subject formally in speech or writing. **II.** *tr.* To discuss (archaic); narrate (archaic); utter or give forth (musical sounds: as, "Give it [pipe] breath with your mouth, and it will *discourse* most eloquent music," Shakspere's "Hamlet," iii. 2. 374); also, to talk to (archaic).—**dis-cours'er,** *n.*

dis-cour-te-ous (dis-kėr'tę-us or, chiefly Brit., -kōr'tyus), *a.* [See *dis-*.] Wanting in courtesy; impolite; uncivil; rude.—**dis-cour'te-ous-ly,** *adv.*—**dis-cour'te-ous-ness,** *n.*—**dis-cour'te-sy** (-kėr'tę-si, Brit. -kōr'tę-si), *n.*; pl. *-sies* (-siz). Lack or breach of courtesy; incivility; rudeness; also, a discourteous or uncivil act.

dis-cov-er (dis-kuv'ėr), *v. t.* [OF. *descovrir* (F. *découvrir*).] To uncover†; remove (a covering)†; also, to disclose, exhibit, make known, or reveal (archaic); also, to catch sight of; get knowledge of, learn of, or find out; gain sight or knowledge of (something previously unseen or unknown); make discovery of.—**dis-cov'er-a-ble,** *a.* Capable of being discovered.—**dis-cov'er-er,** *n.*

dis-cov-ert (dis-kuv'ėrt), *a.* [See *dis-* and *covert*.] In *law*, not covert; not under the protection of a husband: applied to an unmarried woman or a widow.—**dis-cov'er-ture** (-ėr-tūr), *n.*

dis-cov-er-y (dis-kuv'ėr-i), *n.*; pl. *-ies* (-iz). The act of discovering; disclosure or revelation (archaic); a viewing† or investigation†; a getting knowledge of or finding out something; the getting sight or knowledge of something previously unseen or unknown; also, something discovered; in *law*, compulsory disclosure, as of facts or documents.—**Discovery Day.** Same as *Columbus Day*.

dis-cred-it (dis-kred'it), *v. t.* [See *dis-*.] To refuse to credit; disbelieve; also, to show to be undeserving of credit or belief; destroy confidence in; also, to injure the credit or reputation of.—**dis-cred'it,** *n.* Loss or want of credit, belief, or confidence; disbelief; distrust; specif., lack of commercial credit; also, loss or want of repute or esteem; disrepute.—**dis-cred'it-a-ble,** *a.* Such as to bring discredit; disgraceful.—**dis-cred'it-a-bly,** *adv.*

dis-creet (dis-krēt'), *a.* [OF. F. *discret*, < L. *discretus*, pp. of *discernere*, separate, distinguish between, discern: see *discern*.] Characterized by discernment as to what is expedient; exercising or showing a wise control over one's actions or speech; circumspect; also, civil or polite (Sc.).—**dis-creet'ly,** *adv.*—**dis-creet'ness,** *n.*

dis-crep-ance (dis-krep'ạns or dis'krę-pạns), *n.* [OF. *discrepance*, < L. *discrepantia*.] Discrepancy.

dis-crep-an-cy (dis-krep'ạn-si or dis'krę-pạn-si), *n.*; pl. *-cies* (-siz). [See *discrepance*.] The state or quality of being discrepant; difference; disagreement; also, a difference or inconsistency.

dis-crep-ant (dis-krep'ạnt or dis'krę-pạnt), *a.* [L. *discrepans (-ant-)*, ppr. of *discrepare*, be discordant, disagree, < *dis-*, apart, + *crepare*, rattle, crack.] Differing or disagreeing; different; discordant; inconsistent.—**dis-crep'-ant-ly,** *adv.*

dis-crete (dis-krēt'), *a.* [L. *discretus*: see *discreet*.] Separate; detached from others; distinct; also, consisting of or characterized by distinct or individual parts; discontinuous.—**dis-crete'ly,** *adv.*—**dis-crete'ness,** *n.*

dis-cre-tion (dis-kresh'ọn), *n.* [OF. *discretion* (F. *discrétion*), < L. *discretio(n-)*, separation, distinction, LL. discernment, < L. *discernere*: see *discern, discreet*.] Separation or distinction (now rare); also, the faculty of discerning†; judgment† or decision†; esp., power or right of deciding, or of acting according to one's own judgment; freedom of judgment or choice; also, the quality of being discreet; discernment of what is judicious or expedient, esp. with reference to one's own actions or speech; circumspectness; prudence; sound judgment.—**dis-cre'tion-al,** *a.* Discretionary.—**dis-cre'tion-al-ly,** *adv.*—**dis-cre'tion-a-ry** (-ā-ri), *a.* Of or pertaining to discretion, or the power of acting according to one's own judgment; subject or left to one's discretion.—**dis-cre'tion-a-ri-ly,** *adv.*

dis-cre-tive (dis-krē'tiv), *a.* [LL. *discretivus*, < L. *discernere*: see *discern*.] Serving to separate or divide; noting or pertaining to disjunction; disjunctive; also, serving to distinguish†; discriminating†.—**dis-cre'tive-ly,** *adv.*

dis-crim-i-nate (dis-krim'i-nāt), *v.*; *-nated, -nating.* [L. *discriminatus*, pp. of *discriminare*, < *discrimen*, a space between, distinction, difference, < *discernere*: see *discern*.] **I.** *tr.* To make or constitute a distinction in or between; differentiate; also, to note or distinguish as different. **II.** *intr.* To make a distinction, as in favor of or against a person or thing; also, to note or observe a difference; distinguish accurately.—**dis-crim'i-nate** (-nạt), *a.* Discriminated or distinct (archaic); also, marked by discrimination; making nice distinctions.—**dis-crim'i-nate-ly,** *adv.*—**dis-crim'i-nat-ing** (-nā-ting), *p. a.* That discriminates; differentiating; distinctive; specif., differential, as a duty, etc.; also, noting differences or distinctions with nicety; possessing discrimination.—**dis-crim'i-nat-ing-ly,** *adv.*—**dis-crim-i-na'tion** (-nā'shọn), *n.* [LL. *discriminatio(n-)*.] The act of discriminating or differentiating, or the resulting state; differentiation; something that serves to differentiate†; the making of a difference in particular cases, as in favor of or against a person or thing; also, the recognizing of differences; the power of making nice distinctions; discriminating judgment.—**dis-crim'i-na-tive** (-nā-tiv), *a.* Discriminating; of a duty, etc., differential.—**dis-crim'i-na-tive-ly,** *adv.*—**dis-crim'i-na-tor** (-nā-tọr), *n.*—**dis-crim'i-na-to-ry** (-nạ-tō-ri), *a.* Discriminative.

dis-crown (dis-kroun'), *v. t.* [See *dis-*.] To deprive of a crown.

dis-cul-pate (dis-kul'pāt), *v. t.*; *-pated, -pating.* [ML. *disculpatus*, pp. of *disculpare*, < L. *dis-* (see *dis-*) + *culpare*, blame: see *culpable*.] To free from blame; exculpate: as, "If . . . she should be obliged to succumb, she chose to *disculpate* herself in advance before God and Christian princes" (Motley's "Dutch Republic," iii. 1).—**dis-cul-pa'tion** (-pā'shọn), *n.*

dis-cum-ber (dis-kum'bėr), *v. t.* [See *dis-*.] To disencumber.

dis-cur-sive (dis-kėr'siv), *a.* [L. *discurrere* (pp. *discursus*), run to and fro, run through: see *discourse*.] Running to and fro†; fig., passing rapidly or irregularly from one subject to another; rambling; digressive; covering a wide range of subjects; also, proceeding by reasoning or argument (opposed to *intuitive*).—**dis-cur'sive-ly,** *adv.*—**dis-cur'sive-ness,** *n.*

dis-cus (dis'kus), *n.*; pl. *discuses*, L. *disci* (dis'ī). [L., < Gr. δίσκος, discus, disk, dish, < δικεῖν, throw: cf. *disk, dish*, also *dais, desk*.] A circular plate of stone or metal for throwing to a distance as a gymnastic exercise, as among the ancient Greeks and Romans; the exercise or game of throwing this; also, any round plate; a disk.

dis-cuss (dis-kus'), *v. t.* [L. *discussus*, pp. of *discutere*, lit. 'strike asunder,' < *dis-*, apart, + *quatere*, shake, strike.] To dispel† or disperse†; examine† or investigate†; settle† or decide†; also, to examine by argument; sift the considerations for and against; debate; talk over; hence, to try the quality of (food or drink) by consuming (humorous); also, to make known† or reveal† (as, "*Discuss* the same in French unto him": Shakspere's "Henry V.," iv. 4. 30); also, in *civil law*, to exhaust legal proceedings against for debt, as the actual debtor or his property, before proceeding against the property of a person secondarily liable for the debt.—**dis-cuss'er,** *n.*—**dis-cuss'i-ble,** *a.* That may be discussed.—**dis-cus'sion** (-kush'ọn), *n.* [L. *discussio(n-)*.] The act of discussing; examination by argument; a debate.

dis-cu-tient (dis-kū'shiẹnt). [L. *discutiens (-ent-)*, ppr. of *discutere*: see *discuss*.] **I.** *a.* Serving to disperse morbid matter, as a medicinal substance. **II.** *n.* A discutient medicine or agent.

dis-dain (dis-dān'), *v. t.* [OF. *desdeignier* (F. *dédaigner*), < *des-* (see *dis-*) + *deignier*, E. *deign*.] To think unworthy of one's notice; look upon or treat with contempt; despise; scorn; also, to be indignant at†.—**dis-dain',** *n.* [OF. *desdeign* (F. *dédain*).] A feeling of contempt for anything regarded as unworthy; haughty contempt; scorn; also, indignation†.—**dis-dain'ful,** *a.* Full of or showing disdain; scornful.—**dis-dain'ful-ly,** *adv.*—**dis-dain'ful-ness,** *n.*

dis-ease (di-zēz'), *n.* [AF. *disease*, OF. *desaise*, < *des-* (see *dis-*) + *aise*, ease.] Deprivation or lack of ease†; discomfort†; an annoyance†; also, a morbid condition of the body, or of some organ or part; illness; sickness; an ailment or malady; a malady or disorder exhibiting characteristic symptoms or affecting a particular organ or part (as, Bright's *disease* of the kidneys); a similar disorder in plants; fig., any deranged or depraved condition, as of the mind, public affairs, etc.—**dis-ease′**, *v. t.*; *-eased, -easing.* To deprive of ease†; trouble†; disturb†; also, to affect with disease; make ill; fig., to disorder: now chiefly in *diseased, pp.*—**dis-ease′ful,** *a.* Affected with disease; diseased; also, producing disease; unwholesome.

dis-edge (dis-ej′), *v. t.*; *-edged, -edging.* [See *dis-*.] To take the edge off; blunt; dull.

dis-ed-i-fy (dis-ed′i-fī), *v. t.*; *-fied, -fying.* [See *dis-*.] To affect in a manner the reverse of edifying; impair the moral progress of; scandalize.—**dis-ed″i-fi-ca′tion** (-fi-kā′shọn), *n.*

dis-e-lec-tri-fy (dis-ę̄-lek′tri-fī), *v. t.*; *-fied, -fying.* [See *dis-*.] To free from electricity; make non-electric.—**dis-e-lec″tri-fi-ca′tion** (-fi-kā′shọn), *n.*

dis-em-bark (dis-em-bärk′), *v. t.* or *i.* [F. *désembarquer.*] To put or go on shore from a ship; land.—**dis-em-bar-ka′tion** (-bär-kā′shọn), *n.*

dis-em-bar-rass (dis-em-bar′ạs), *v. t.* [See *dis-*.] To free from embarrassment; relieve; rid.—**dis-em-bar′rass-ment,** *n.*

dis-em-bed (dis-em-bed′), *v. t.*; *-bedded, -bedding.* [See *dis-*.] To remove from the place of embedment.

dis-em-bel-lish (dis-em-bel′ish), *v. t.* [See *dis-*.] To deprive of embellishment.

dis-em-bod-y (dis-em-bod′i), *v. t.*; *-bodied, -bodying.* [See *dis-*.] To divest (a soul, etc.) of the body; also, to disband (troops).—**dis-em-bod′i-ment,** *n.*

dis-em-bogue (dis-em-bōg′), *v.*; *-bogued, -boguing.* [Sp. *desembocar*, < *des-* (< L. *dis-*: see *dis-*) + *embocar*, enter by the mouth, < L. *in*, in, + *bucca*, cheek, mouth.] **I.** *intr.* To pass out of the mouth of a river, etc., into the open sea†; also, to flow out at the mouth into another body of water, as a river; empty; fig., to emerge or issue. **II.** *tr.* To pour out (itself, or its waters) at the mouth, as a river; empty; fig., to discharge; cast forth.—**dis-em-bogue′ment,** *n.*

dis-em-bos-om (dis-em-bůz′ọm), *v. t.* [See *dis-*.] To cast out from the bosom; unbosom.

dis-em-bow-el (dis-em-bou′ẹl), *v. t.*; *-eled* or *-elled, -eling* or *-elling.* [See *dis-*.] To remove the bowels or entrails from; eviscerate; also, to produce from the bowels, as the web of a spider.—**dis-em-bow′el-ment,** *n.*

dis-em-broil (dis-em-broil′), *v. t.* [See *dis-*.] To free from embroilment, entanglement, or confusion.

dis-em-ploy (dis-em-ploi′), *v. t.* [See *dis-*.] To dismiss or release from employment.—**dis-em-ploy′ment,** *n.*

dis-en-a-ble (dis-e-nā′bl), *v. t.*; *-bled, -bling.* [See *dis-*.] To deprive of ability; make unable; prevent: as, "He thought . . . that the absurdly strong colouring of the picture would *disenable* the work from doing either good or harm" (Trollope's "Warden," xv.).—**dis-en-a′ble-ment,** *n.*

dis-en-chant (dis-en-chȧnt′), *v. t.* [F. *désenchanter.*] To free from enchantment; disillusion.—**dis-en-chant′er,** *n.*—**dis-en-chant′ment,** *n.*

dis-en-cum-ber (dis-en-kum′bėr), *v. t.* [F. *désencombrer.*] To free from encumbrance; disburden.—**dis-en-cum′ber-ment,** *n.*

dis-en-dow (dis-en-dou′), *v. t.* [See *dis-*.] To deprive of endowment, as a church.—**dis-en-dow′er,** *n.*—**dis-en-dow′ment,** *n.*

dis-en-fran-chise (dis-en-fran′chīz or -chiz), *v. t.*; *-chised, -chising.* [See *dis-*.] To disfranchise.

dis-en-gage (dis-en-gāj′), *v.*; *-gaged, -gaging.* [See *dis-*.] **I.** *tr.* To free from engagement, pledge, obligation, etc.; also, to free or release from anything that holds; liberate; detach; also, to loosen (a bond, etc.). **II.** *intr.* To become disengaged; free one's self.—**dis-en-gaged′,** *p. a.* Freed from engagement; not engaged; at liberty or unoccupied; unconstrained or easy; released or detached.—**dis-en-ga′ged-ness** (-gā′jed-nes), *n.*—**dis-en-gage′ment,** *n.* The act of disengaging, or the state of being disengaged; freedom from obligation or occupation; freedom from constraint; ease of manner; liberation or detachment.

dis-en-no-ble (dis-e-nō′bl), *v. t.*; *-bled, -bling.* [See *dis-*.] To deprive of nobility; render ignoble.

dis-en-tail (dis-en-tāl′), *v. t.* [See *dis-*.] To free (an estate) from entail.—**dis-en-tail′, dis-en-tail′ment,** *n.*

dis-en-tan-gle (dis-en-tang′gl), *v. t.*; *-gled, -gling.* [See *dis-*.] To free from entanglement or tangles; untangle; extricate (*from*).—**dis-en-tan′gle-ment,** *n.*—**dis-en-tan′gler,** *n.*

dis-en-thrall (dis-en-thrâl′), *v. t.* [See *dis-*.] To free from thraldom.—**dis-en-thral′ment,** *n.*

dis-en-throne (dis-en-thrōn′), *v. t.*; *-throned, -throning.* [See *dis-*.] To dethrone.—**dis-en-throne′ment,** *n.*

dis-en-ti-tle (dis-en-tī′tl), *v. t.*; *-tled, -tling.* [See *dis-*.] To deprive of title or right.

dis-en-tomb (dis-en-töm′), *v. t.* [See *dis-*.] To take from the tomb; disinter.—**dis-en-tomb′ment,** *n.*

dis-en-trance (dis-en-trȧns′), *v. t.*; *-tranced, -trancing.* [See *dis-*.] To bring out of an entranced condition.—**dis-en-trance′ment,** *n.*

dis-en-twine (dis-en-twīn′), *v. t.* or *i.*; *-twined, -twining.* [See *dis-*.] To bring or come out of an entwined or intertwined state; untwine.

di-sep-a-lous (dī-sep′ạ-lus), *a.* [See *di-*[1].] In *bot.*, having two sepals.

dis-es-tab-lish (dis-es-tab′lish), *v. t.* [See *dis-*.] To deprive of the character of being established; esp., to withdraw exclusive state recognition or support from (a church).—**dis-es-tab′lish-ment,** *n.*

dis-es-teem (dis-es-tēm′), *v. t.* [See *dis-*.] To hold in low esteem; think slightingly of; despise.—**dis-es-teem′,** *n.* Low esteem or regard; disfavor.

di-seur (dē-zėr), *n.* [F., one who says or tells, < *dire*, < L. *dicere*, say.] A professional public entertainer by talking, recitation, etc.—**di-seuse** (-zėz), *n.* [F.] Fem. of *diseur.*

dis-fa-vor (dis-fā′vọr), *n.* [See *dis-*.] The reverse of favor; unfavorable regard; disesteem; also, the state of being regarded unfavorably.—**dis-fa′vor,** *v. t.* To regard or treat with disfavor.

dis-fa′vour, *n.* and *v.* British preferred form of *disfavor.*

dis-fea-ture (dis-fē′ţūr), *v. t.*; *-tured, -turing.* [See *dis-*.] To mar the features of; disfigure.—**dis-fea′ture-ment,** *n.*

dis-fig-ure (dis-fig′ūr), *v. t.*; *-ured, -uring.* [OF. *desfigurer* (F. *défigurer*), < L. *dis-* (see *dis-*) + *figurare*, form, E. *figure, v.*] To mar the figure, appearance, or beauty of; deform; deface; fig., to mar the effect or excellence of (as, "His merits were *disfigured* by a most unpleasant affectation": Macaulay's "Essays," Petrarch); also, to disguise†.—**dis-fig-u-ra′tion** (-ū-rā′shọn), *n.*—**dis-fig′ure-ment,** *n.* The act of disfiguring; disfigured condition; something that disfigures.—**dis-fig′ur-er,** *n.*

dis-for-est (dis-for′est), *v. t.* [OF. *desforester.*] To disafforest.—**dis-for-es-ta′tion** (-es-tā′shọn), *n.*

dis-fran-chise (dis-fran′chīz or -chiz), *v. t.*; *-chised, -chising.* [See *dis-*.] To deprive of a franchise, privilege, or right; esp., to deprive (persons) of rights of citizenship, as of the right to vote.—**dis-fran′chise-ment** (-chiz-mẹnt), *n.*

dis-fur-nish (dis-fėr′nish), *v. t.* [See *dis-*.] To deprive of something with which a person or thing is furnished; strip.—**dis-fur′nish-ment,** *n.*

dis-gav-el (dis-gav′ẹl), *v. t.*; *-elled, -elling.* [See *dis-* and *gavelkind.*] In *Eng. law*, to relieve from the tenure of gavelkind.

dis-gorge (dis-gôrj′), *v.*; *-gorged, -gorging.* [OF. *desgorger* (F. *dégorger*), < *des-* (see *dis-*) + *gorge*, throat, E. *gorge.*] **I.** *tr.* To eject or throw out from or as from the gorge or throat; vomit forth; discharge; fig., to give up unwillingly (something wrongfully appropriated); also, to empty (the stomach, etc.) of contents. **II.** *intr.* To disgorge something; fig., to restore something wrongfully appropriated.—**dis-gorge′ment,** *n.*—**dis-gor′ger** (-gôr′jėr), *n.*

dis-grace (dis-grās′), *n.* [F. *disgrâce*, < It. *disgrazia*, < L. *dis-* (see *dis-*) + *gratia*: see *grace.*] Want of grace of person or mind (rare); also, the state of being out of favor; exclusion from favor, confidence, or trust; also, the state of being in dishonor; ignominy; shame; also, that which dishonors; a cause or occasion of shame or reproach.—**dis-grace′,** *v. t.*; *-graced, -gracing.* [F. *disgracier*, < It. *disgraziare.*] To deprive of grace or pleasing quality†; also to put out of grace or favor; treat with disfavor; dismiss with discredit; also, to bring or reflect shame or reproach upon; put to shame; also, to revile†.—**dis-grace′ful,** *a.* Void of grace or pleasing quality†; also, fraught with disgrace; dishonorable; shameful; also, inflicting disgrace; degrading.—**dis-grace′ful-ly,** *adv.*—**dis-grace′-ful-ness,** *n.*—**dis-gra′cer** (-grā′sėr), *n.*

dis-grun-tle (dis-grun′tl), *v. t.*; *-tled, -tling.* [See *dis-* and *gruntle.*] To put into a state of sulky dissatisfaction; chagrin; disgust: usually in *disgruntled, pp.*: as, "Every *disgruntled* Polish patriot flew off to some foreign enemy to wreak his indignation upon his ungrateful country" (H. G. Wells's "Outline of History," xxxvi. § 7).—**dis-grun′tle-ment,** *n.*

dis-guise (dis-gīz′), *v. t.*; *-guised, -guising.* [OF. *desguiser* (F. *déguiser*), < *des-* (see *dis-*) + *guise*, E. *guise.*] To change the guise or appearance of†; also, to change the guise or appearance of so as to conceal identity or to mislead; conceal the identity of by means of a misleading garb, etc.; also, to exhibit in a false light; misrepresent; also, to conceal the real state or character of; also, to intoxicate (archaic or colloq.).—**dis-guise′,** *n.* The state of being disguised; altered fashion of garb, etc., as for concealing identity; also, that which disguises; clothing, etc., assumed in order to conceal identity or mislead; any false appearance or show; also, the act of disguising; concealment; also, a masque†; also, intoxication (obs. or rare).—**dis-guised′,** *p. a.* Having the appearance altered by a disguise; also, intoxicated (archaic or colloq.).—**dis-guise′ment,** *n.* A disguising, or a being disguised; also, something that disguises; a disguise.—**dis-guis′er** (-gī′zėr), *n.*

dis-gust (dis-gust′), *v. t.* [F. *desgouster* (now *dégoûter*), < *des-* (see *dis-*) + *goust* (now *goût*), taste, relish, < L. *gustus*, E. *gust*².] To feel a strong distaste for or aversion to†; also, to excite nausea or loathing in; hence, to offend the sensibilities of; excite aversion or impatient dissatisfaction in; also, to dissuade by exciting aversion.—**dis-gust′,** *n.* [F. *desgoust* (now *dégoût*).] Strong distaste; nausea; loathing; hence, repugnance excited by something offensive; strong aversion; impatient dissatisfaction.—**dis-gust′ed-ly,** *adv.*—**dis-gust′ful,** *a.* Causing disgust; nauseous; offensive; also, characterized by disgust.—**dis-gust′ing-ly,** *adv.*

dish (dish), *n.* [AS. *disc*, dish, plate, bowl, < L. *discus*, discus, disk, dish: see *discus.*] An open, more or less shallow vessel of pottery, glass, metal, wood, etc., used for various purposes, esp. for holding or serving food; in general, any vessel such as is used at table; also, that which is served or contained in a dish; a particular article or preparation of food; also, as much as a dish will hold; a dishful; also, any of various dish-like vessels or articles; a concavity like that of a dish; concave state, or the degree of concavity, as of a wheel.—**dish,** *v.* **I.** *tr.* To put into or serve in a dish, as food; also, to fashion like a dish; make concave; also, to defeat, frustrate, or cheat (slang). **II.** *intr.* To be or become concave.

dis-ha-bille (dis-ạ-bēl′ or -bil′), *n.* [Also *deshabille*, < F. *déshabillé*, prop. pp. of *déshabiller*, undress, < *dés-* (see *dis-*) + *habiller*, dress: see *habiliment.*] Undress or négligé (as, "At eight in the morning we go in *dishabille* to the pump-room": Smollett's "Humphry Clinker," April 26); also, a garment or costume worn in undress.

dis-ha-bit-u-ate (dis-hạ-bit′ū-āt), *v. t.*; *-ated, -ating.* [See *dis-.*] To cause to be no longer habituated or accustomed; disaccustom.

dis-hal-low (dis-hal′ō), *v. t.* [See *dis-.*] To profane.

dis-har-mo-ni-ous (dis-här-mō′ni-us), *a.* [See *dis-.*] Inharmonious; discordant.—**dis-har′mo-nize** (-mọ-nīz), *v. t.* or *i.*; *-nized, -nizing.* To make or be inharmonious.—**dis-har′mo-ny,** *n.*; pl. *-nies* (-niz). Discord; also, something discordant.

dish=cloth (dish′klôth), *n.* A cloth for use in washing dishes. Also **dish′=clout** (-klout).

dis-heart-en (dis-här′tn), *v. t.* [See *dis-.*] To discourage; make despondent.—**dis-heart′en-ing-ly,** *adv.*—**dis-heart′-en-ment,** *n.*

dis-helm (dis-helm′), *v. t.* or *i.* [See *dis-.*] To divest of or take off the helm or helmet. [Archaic.]

dis-her-i-son (dis-her′i-zọn), *n.* [OF. *desheriteison*, < *desheriter*: see *disherit.*] The act of disinheriting; disinheritance.

dis-her-it (dis-her′it), *v. t.* [OF. *desheriter* (F. *déshériter*), < L. *dis-* (see *dis-*) + LL. *hereditare*, inherit, < L. *heres*, E. *heir.*] To disinherit. [Obs. or rare.]—**dis-her′it-ment,** *n.*

di-shev-el (di-shev′ẹl), *v. t.*; *-eled* or *-elled, -eling* or *-elling.* [OF. *descheveler* (F. *décheveler*), < *des-* (see *dis-*) + *chevel*, < L. *capillus*, hair.] To let down (the hair); let hang in loose disorder: now only as in *disheveled, p. a.*—**di-shev′-eled, di-shev′elled,** *p. a.* Hanging loosely or in disorder, as the hair; disordered as to hair, dress, etc.—**di-shev′el-ment,** *n.*

dish=faced (dish′fāst), *a.* Having a flattened or somewhat hollow face.

dish-ful (dish′fůl), *n.*; pl. *-fuls.* As much as a dish will hold.

dish-ing (dish′ing), *p. a.* That dishes; esp., taking or having the form of a dish; concave.

dis-hon-est (dis-on′est), *a.* [OF. *deshoneste* (F. *déshonnête*).] Not honest; lacking in probity or integrity; disposed to lie, cheat, or steal; also, proceeding from or exhibiting lack of honesty; fraudulent; also, unchaste†; also, dishonorable† or discreditable† (as, "inglorious triumphs and *dishonest* scars": Pope's "Windsor Forest," 326).—**dis-hon′est-ly,** *adv.*—**dis-hon′es-ty,** *n.*; pl. *-ties* (-tiz). The reverse of honesty; lack of probity or integrity; disposition to lie, cheat, or steal; fraud or theft; a dishonest act; also, unchastity†; also, dishonor†.

dis-hon-or (dis-on′ọr), *n.* [OF. *deshonor* (F. *déshonneur*).] The reverse of honor; disgrace; ignominy; shame; an indignity or insult; also, a cause of shame; a disgrace; in *com.*, failure or refusal to honor a draft, etc., by payment.—**dis-hon′or,** *v. t.* To deprive of honor; treat with indignity; also, to violate the chastity of; also, to bring reproach or shame on; disgrace; in *com.*, to fail or refuse to honor (a draft, etc.) by payment.—**dis-hon′or-a-ble,** *a.* Characterized by or involving lack of honor; ignoble or base; discreditable, disgraceful, or shameful.—**dis-hon′or-a-ble-ness,** *n.*—**dis-hon′or-a-bly,** *adv.*—**dis-hon′or-er,** *n.*

dis-hon′our, dis-hon′our-a-ble, etc. British preferred forms of *dishonor, dishonorable*, etc.

dis-horn (dis-hôrn′), *v. t.* [See *dis-.*] To deprive of horns; dehorn.

dis-house (dis-houz′), *v. t.*; *-housed, -housing.* [See *dis-.*] To expel or evict from a house; also, to clear (ground) of houses.

dish=wa-ter (dish′wâ″tėr), *n.* Water in which dishes have been washed.

dis-il-lu-sion (dis-i-lū′zhọn), *n.* [See *dis-.*] A freeing or a being freed from illusion; disenchantment.—**dis-il-lu′sion,** *v. t.* To free from illusion; disenchant. Also **dis-il-lu′-sion-ize**; *-ized, -izing.*—**dis-il-lu′sion-ment,** *n.*

dis-im-mure (dis-i-mūr′), *v. t.*; *-mured, -muring.* [See *dis-.*] To free from immurement, or confinement within walls.

dis-im-pas-sioned (dis-im-pash′ọnd), *a.* [See *dis-.*] Dispassionate; passionless; calm.

dis-im-pris-on (dis-im-priz′n), *v. t.* [See *dis-.*] To release from imprisonment.—**dis-im-pris′on-ment,** *n.*

dis-in-cli-na-tion (dis-in-kli-nā′shọn), *n.* [See *dis-.*] The reverse of inclination; averseness; distaste; unwillingness.—**dis-in-cline′** (-klīn′), *v. t.* or *i.*; *-clined, -clining.* To render or be averse or indisposed: as, "The overthrow of these men *disinclined* me to pursue my accustomed studies" (Mrs. Shelley's "Frankenstein," ii.).

dis-in-cor-po-rate (dis-in-kôr′pọ-rāt), *v. t.*; *-rated, -rating.* [See *dis-.*] To deprive of the character or powers of a corporation.—**dis-in-cor-po-ra′tion** (-rā′shọn), *n.*

dis-in-fect (dis-in-fekt′), *v. t.* [See *dis-.*] To cleanse (rooms, clothing, etc.) from infection; destroy the disease-germs in.—**dis-in-fect′ant.** **I.** *a.* Disinfecting. **II.** *n.* A disinfecting agent.—**dis-in-fec′tion** (-fek′shọn), *n.* The process of disinfecting.—**dis-in-fec′tor,** *n.*

dis-in-gen-u-ous (dis-in-jen′ū-us), *a.* [See *dis-.*] Not ingenuous; lacking in frankness, candor, or sincerity; insincere: as, "persons entirely *disingenuous*, who really do not believe the opinion they defend" (Hume's "Principles of Morals," i.).—**dis-in-gen′u-ous-ly,** *adv.*—**dis-in-gen′u-ous-ness,** *n.*

dis-in-her-it (dis-in-her′it), *v. t.* [See *dis-.*] To deprive of an inheritance, or of the right to inherit; esp., of the owner of property, to prevent (an heir) from inheriting, as by an adverse will.—**dis-in-her′i-son** (-i-zọn), **dis-in-her′it-ance,** *n.*

dis-in-te-grate (dis-in′tẹ-grāt), *v. t.* or *i.*; *-grated, -grating.* [See *dis-.*] To reduce or become reduced to particles or fragments; break up.—**dis-in′te-gra-ble** (-gra̤-bl), *a.*—**dis-in-te-gra′tion** (-grā′shọn), *n.* The process of disintegrating, or a disintegrated condition; reduction to the component particles; in *geol.*, the wearing down of rocks by rain, frost, and other atmospheric influences.—**disintegration product,** in *chem.*, a substance formed by the chemical disintegration of another substance; esp., a substance produced by the breaking down of a radioactive substance.—**dis-in′te-gra-tive** (-grā-tiv), *a.* Serving or tending to disintegrate.—**dis-in′te-gra-tor** (-grā-tọr), *n.* One who or that which disintegrates; a machine for breaking up or pulverizing some kind of material.

dis-in-ter (dis-in-tėr′), *v. t.*; *-terred, -terring.* [F. *désenterrer.*] To take out of the place of interment; exhume; unearth.

dis-in-ter-est (dis-in′tėr-est), *n.* [See *dis-.*] The reverse of interest or advantage; disadvantage; also, absence of interest; indifference; also, freedom from self-interest†.—**dis-in′ter-est,** *v. t.* To divest of interest or concern.—**dis-in′ter-est-ed,** *a.* Not interested; free from considerations of personal interest or advantage; not influenced by selfish motives.—**dis-in′ter-est-ed-ly,** *adv.*—**dis-in′ter-est-ed-ness,** *n.*

dis-in-ter-ment (dis-in-tėr′mẹnt), *n.* The act of disinterring; exhumation; also, something disinterred.

dis-in-trench (dis-in-trench′), *v. t.* [See *dis-.*] To eject or drive from intrenchments.

dis-ject (dis-jekt′), *v. t.* [L. *disjectus*, pp. of *disjicere*, < *dis-*, apart, + *jacere*, throw.] To cast asunder; scatter; disperse.—**dis-jec′tion** (-jek′shọn), *n.*

dis-join (dis-join′), *v.* [OF. *desjoindre* (F. *déjoindre*), < L. *disjungere*, < *dis-* (see *dis-*) + *jungere*, join.] **I.** *tr.* To undo or dissolve the junction or union of; disunite; separate; also, to prevent from being joined; also, to dissolve (a union, etc.). **II.** *intr.* To become disunited; separate.

dis-joint (dis-joint′), *v.* [See *dis-.*] **I.** *tr.* To take apart at the joints; disarticulate; break up; disjoin; also, to put out of joint; dislocate; put out of order. **II.** *intr.* To come apart; be put out of joint: as, "Let the frame of things *disjoint*" (Shakspere's "Macbeth," iii. 2. 16).—**dis-joint′**†, *a.* Disjointed; out of joint. See Shakspere's "Hamlet," i. 2. 20.—**dis-joint′ed,** *p. a.* Disarticulated; disconnected; broken; incoherent.—**dis-joint′ed-ly,** *adv.*—**dis-joint′ed-ness,** *n.*

dis-junct (dis-jungkt′), *a.* [L. *disjunctus*, pp. of *disjungere*: see *disjoin.*] Disjoined; separated; in *entom.*, having the head, thorax, and abdomen separated by deep constrictions.—**dis-junc′tion** (-jungk′shọn), *n.* [L. *disjunctio(n-)*, < *disjungere.*] The act of disjoining, or the state of being disjoined; disunion; separation; in *logic*, the relation between the terms of a disjunctive proposition; also, the proposition itself.—**dis-junc′tive.** [L. *disjunctivus.*] **I.** *a.* Serving to disjoin; characterized by or involving disjunction; in *gram.*, connecting grammatically words, etc., disjoined in meaning, as the conjunctions *but* and *yet, or* and *nor* (cf. *copulative*); adversative; alternative; in *logic*, alternative (as, a *disjunctive* proposition, one which asserts that one or the other of two things is true). **II.** *n.* In *gram.*, a disjunctive conjunction; in *logic*, a disjunctive proposition; hence, in general, a statement, etc., involving alternatives.—**dis-junc′tive-ly,** *adv.*

disk, disc (disk), *n.* [L. *discus*, discus, disk, dish: see *discus.*] A discus; hence, any thin, flat, circular plate or object; also, a round, flat area; specif., the apparently flat surface of the sun, etc.; in *bot.*, *zoöl.*, etc., any of various roundish, flat structures or parts; in the daisy and other composite plants, the central portion of the flower-head, composed of tubular florets; the flat surface of a leaf, etc., in distinction from the margin; an enlargement of the torus of a flower, about the pistil; the area around an owl's eye.

Flower of Common Daisy (*Bellis perennis*).—*r, r,* rays, *d,* disk.

dis-leave (dis-lēv′), *v. t.*; *-leaved, -leaving.* [See *dis-.*] To deprive of leaves: as, "bare trunk and *disleaved* bough" (Lowell's "The Nest"). Also **dis-leaf′**

dis-like (dis-līk′), *v. t.*; *-liked, -liking.* [See *dis-.*] To displease† (as, "I'll do 't; but it *dislikes* me": Shakspere's "Othello," ii. 3. 49); also, to regard with the reverse of liking; regard with displeasure or aversion; disrelish.—**dis-lik′a-ble** (-lī′ka̤-bl), *a.*—**dis-like′,** *n.* Displeasure† or disapproval†; also, the feeling of disliking; distaste; repugnance; aversion; also, disagreement†.

dis-lik-en† (dis-lī′kn), *v. t.* [See *dis-.*] To make unlike; disguise. See Shakspere's "Winter's Tale," iv. 4. 666.

dis-limn (dis-lim′), *v. t.* [See *dis-.*] To obliterate (a picture); efface. [Archaic or poetic.]

dis-link (dis-lingk′), *v. t.* [See *dis-.*] To unlink.

dis-lo-cate (dis′lọ-kāt), *v. t.*; *-cated, -cating.* [ML. *dislocatus*, pp. of *dislocare*, < L. *dis-* (see *dis-*) + *locare*, place, E. *locate.*] To put out of place; displace; put out of proper relative position; put (a bone) out of joint; fig., to throw out of order; derange; upset; disorder.—**dis-lo-ca′tion** (-kā′shọn), *n.* The act of dislocating, or the state of being dislocated; displacement, as of a bone, a geological stratum, etc.; derangement.—**dis′lo-ca-to-ry** (-ka̤-tọ-ri), *a.*

dis-lodge (dis-loj′), *v.*; *-lodged, -lodging.* [OF. *deslogier* (F. *déloger*).] **I.** *tr.* To remove or drive from a place of lodgment; drive from a position occupied. **II.** *intr.* To go from a place of lodgment.—**dis-lodg′ment, dis-lodge′ment,** *n.*

dis-loy-al (dis-loi′a̤l), *a.* [OF. *desloial* (F. *déloyal*).] Not loyal; false to one's obligations or allegiance; faithless; treacherous.—**dis-loy′al-ist,** *n.* A disloyal person.—**dis-loy′al-ly,** *adv.*—**dis-loy′al-ty,** *n.*; pl. *-ties* (-tiz). The quality of being disloyal; unfaithfulness; esp., violation of allegiance or duty, as to a government; also, a disloyal act.

dis-mal (diz′ma̤l). [Prob. < OF. *dis mal*, < L. *dies mali*, evil days.] **I.** *a.* Evil† or unlucky†; also, disastrous or calamitous (now rare); also, terrible or dreadful; hence, causing gloom or dejection; gloomy, dreary, or cheerless; melancholy. **II.** *n.* Something dismal; specif., any of certain tracts of swampy land along or near the southern Atlantic coast of the U. S.; *pl.*, mourning garments; also, low spirits (as, "I was simply trying to joke away the *dismals!*" G. W. Cable's "John March, Southerner," xliv.).—**dis′mal-ly,** *adv.*—**dis′mal-ness,** *n.*

dis-man-tle (dis-man′tl), *v. t.*; *-tled, -tling.* [F. *desmanteler* (now *démanteler*), < *des-* (see *dis-*) + *manteau*, cloak, mantle.] To uncloak†; also, to divest of dress, covering, etc.; strip (a house, fortress, vessel, etc.), as of furniture, defenses, equipment, etc.; also, to pull down; take apart; take to pieces.—**dis-man′tle-ment,** *n.*

dis-mask† (dis-mȧsk′), *v. t.* [See *dis-.*] To unmask.

dis-mast (dis-mȧst′), *v. t.* [See *dis-.*] To deprive of masts; break off the masts of.—**dis-mast′ment,** *n.*

dis-may (dis-mā′), *v. t.* [ME. *desmaien*, prob. < OF. *des-* (see *dis-*) + *-maier*, be able (cf. *esmaier*, dismay), from Teut., and akin to E. *may*[1].] To break down the courage of utterly, as by sudden danger or trouble; dishearten utterly; daunt; also, to put to rout†.—**dis-may′,** *n.* Sudden or complete loss of courage; utter disheartenment; consternation.

dis-mem-ber (dis-mem′bėr), *v. t.* [OF. *desmembrer* (F. *démembrer*), < ML. *dismembrare*, < L. *dis-* (see *dis-*) + *membrum*, E. *member.*] To deprive of members or limbs; divide limb from limb; fig., to separate into parts; divide, and distribute the parts of (a kingdom, etc.); also, to cut off (a limb, part, etc.: obs. or rare); also, to exclude from membership.—**dis-mem′ber-er,** *n.*—**dis-mem′ber-ment,** *n.*

dis-miss (dis-mis′), *v. t.* [L. *dis-*, apart, + *missus*, pp. of *mittere*, send: cf. OF. *desmis*, pp. of *desmetre*, send or put away (see *demit*), from the same L. elements.] To direct or allow (an assembly of persons, etc.) to disperse; also, to bid or allow (a person) to go; give permission to depart; hence, to send forth (a thing); let go; also, to discharge or remove, as from office or service; also, to discard or reject; also, to put off or away; lay aside; esp., to put aside from consideration; also, to have done with (a subject) after summary treatment; in *law*, to put out of court, as a complaint or appeal.—**dis-mis′sal,** *n.* The act of dismissing, or the state of being dismissed; a spoken or written order of discharge.—**dis-miss′i-ble,** *a.* That may be dismissed.—

dis-mis′sion (-mish′ọn), *n.* Dismissal.—**dis-mis′sive** (-mis′iv), **dis-mis′so-ry** (-mis′ọ-ri), *a.*

dis-mount (dis-mount′), *v.* [See *dis-*.] **I.** *intr.* To descend from a height (obs. or rare); also, to get off or alight, as from a horse, bicycle, etc. **II.** *tr.* To come down from (a height: obs. or rare); descend (stairs); get off or alight from (a horse, etc.); also, to bring or throw down, as from a horse; unhorse; also, to deprive (troops, etc.) of horses or mounts; also, to remove (a thing) from its mounting, support, setting, etc.; take (a piece of mechanism) to pieces. —**dis-mount′**, *n.* The act or manner of dismounting.—**dis-mount′a-ble,** *a.* That may be dismounted.

dis-na-ture (dis-nā′tūr), *v. t.*; *-tured, -turing.* [OF. *desnaturer* (F. *dénaturer*): cf. *denature.*] To deprive of the proper nature; render unnatural.

dis-o-be-di-ent (dis-ọ-bē′di-ẹnt), *a.* [OF. *desobedient.*] Neglecting or refusing to obey; refractory.—**dis-o-be′di-ence,** *n.*—**dis-o-be′di-ent-ly,** *adv.*

dis-o-bey (dis-ọ-bā′), *v. t.* or *i.* [OF. *desobeir* (F. *désobéir*).] To neglect or refuse to obey.—**dis-o-bey′al,** *n.* The act of disobeying.—**dis-o-bey′er,** *n.*

dis-o-blige (dis-ọ-blīj′), *v. t.*; *-bliged, -bliging.* [F. *désobliger.*] To release from obligation†; also, to neglect or refuse to oblige; fail to accommodate; hence, to give offense to; affront.—**dis-o-bli′ger** (-blī′jėr), *n.*—**dis-o-bli′ging,** *p. a.* That disobliges; disinclined to accommodate others; unaccommodating; churlish.—**dis-o-bli′ging-ly,** *adv.*—**dis-o-bli′ging-ness,** *n.*

dis-orb (dis-ôrb′), *v. t.* [See *dis-*.] To throw out of the orb or orbit; also, to deprive of the orb or mound of sovereignty.

dis-or-der (dis-ôr′dėr), *n.* [See *dis-*.] Lack of order or regular arrangement; disarrangement; confusion; also, an irregularity; specif., an irregularity in conduct†; a misdemeanor†; also, breach of order; disorderly conduct; a public disturbance; also, agitation of mind†; also, a derangement of physical or mental health or functions; an ailment; a disease.—**dis-or′der,** *v. t.* To destroy the order or regular arrangement of; disarrange; throw into confusion or disorder; also, to perturb† or disconcert†; also, to derange the physical or mental health or functions of.—**dis-or′der-er,** *n.*—**dis-or′der-ly,** *a.* Characterized by disorder; irregular; untidy; confused; also, unruly, turbulent, or tumultuous; specif., in *law*, violating, or opposed to, constituted order; contrary to public order or morality.—**dis-or′der-li-ness,** *n.*—**dis-or′der-ly,** *adv.*

dis-or-gan-ize (dis-ôr′gạn-īz), *v. t.*; *-ized, -izing.* [F. *désorganiser.*] To bring out of an organized state; throw into confusion or disorder.—**dis-or″gan-i-za′tion** (-i-zā′shọn), *n.*—**dis-or′gan-iz-er** (-ī-zėr), *n.*

dis-o-ri-ent (dis-ō′ri-ent), *v. t.* [See *dis-*.] To turn from the east; hence, to cause to lose one's bearings; disconcert. Also **dis-o′ri-en-tate** (-en-tāt).—**dis-o″ri-en-ta′tion** (-tā′shọn), *n.*

dis-own (dis-ōn′), *v. t.* [See *dis-*.] To refuse to acknowledge as one's own or as pertaining to one's self (as, to *disown* a person as one's son; "Never did he *disown* his debts," G. B. Shaw's "Dark Lady of the Sonnets"); repudiate; renounce; also, to refuse to own or acknowledge as true or valid (obs. or rare).—**dis-own′ment,** *n.*

dis-par-age (dis-par′āj), *v. t.*; *-aged, -aging.* [OF. *desparagier*, < *des-* (see *dis-*) + *parage*, rank, prob. < L. *par*, equal.] To marry to a person of inferior rank or condition†; dishonor by such a marriage†; also, to degrade†; also, to bring reproach or discredit upon; lower the estimation of; also, to speak of or treat slightingly; depreciate; belittle.—**dis-par′age-ment,** *n.* The act of disparaging; also, something that causes loss of dignity or reputation.—**dis-par′ag-er,** *n.*—**dis-par′ag-ing-ly,** *adv.*

dis-pa-rate (dis′pạ-rāt), *a.* [L. *disparatus*, pp. of *disparare*, separate, < *dis-*, apart, + *parare*, make ready.] Distinct in kind; essentially different; dissimilar; unlike; having no common genus.—**dis′pa-rate-ly,** *adv.*—**dis′pa-rate-ness,** *n.*

dis-par-i-ty (dis-par′i-ti), *n.*; pl. *-ties* (-tiz). [F. *disparité.*] Want of parity or equality; inequality; also, dissimilarity or difference; also, a point of inequality or difference.

dis-park (dis-pärk′), *v. t.* [See *dis-*.] To divest of the character of a park; throw open (a private park) to common use. See Shakspere's "Richard II.," iii. 1. 23.

dis-part (dis-pärt′), *v.* [Cf. It. *dispartire*, part, separate, divide, < L. *dispartire*, distribute, divide, < *dis-*, apart, + *partire*: see *part, v.*] **I.** *tr.* To part asunder; separate; divide into parts; in *gun.*, to estimate, or allow for, the dispart of; also, to provide with a dispart-sight. **II.** *intr.* To separate; break up.—**dis-part′,** *n.* In *gun.*, the difference between the maximum semidiameter at the breech of a gun and that at the swell of the muzzle; also, a sight ('dispart-sight') which allows for this difference.—**dis-part′ment,** *n.*

dis-pas-sion (dis-pash′ọn), *n.* [See *dis-*.] Freedom from passion; dispassionate state or quality.—**dis-pas′sion-ate** (-āt), *a.* Free from or unaffected by passion; devoid of personal feeling or bias; impartial; calm.—**dis-pas′sion-ate-ly,** *adv.*—**dis-pas′sion-ate-ness,** *n.*

dis-patch (dis-pach′), etc. See *despatch*, etc.

dis-pau-per (dis-pâ′pėr), *v. t.* [See *dis-*.] In *law*, to decide (a person) to be no longer a pauper; disqualify from suing as a pauper (without payment of fees).—**dis-pau′per-ize** (-īz), *v. t.*; *-ized, -izing.* To free from a condition of pauperism; also, to free from paupers.—**dis-pau″per-i-za′tion** (-i-zā′shọn), *n.*

dis-peace (dis-pēs′), *n.* [See *dis-*.] The reverse of peace; discord; dissension; strife.

dis-pel (dis-pel′), *v.*; *-pelled, -pelling.* [L. *dispellere*, drive asunder, < *dis-*, apart, + *pellere*, drive.] **I.** *tr.* To drive off in various directions; scatter; disperse; dissipate. **II.** *intr.* To become dispersed or dissipated: as, "The clouds *dispel*" (Dryden's tr. Virgil's "Æneid," x. 157).—**dis-pel′ler,** *n.*

dis-pend (dis-pend′), *v. t.* [OF. *despendre* (F. *dépendre*), < L. *dispendere*, weigh out, < *dis-*, apart, + *pendere*, weigh.] To pay out; expend; spend. [Obs. or archaic.]

dis-pens-a-ble (dis-pen′sạ-bl), *a.* Capable of being dispensed or administered; also, admitting of dispensation; that may be condoned, as an offense or a sin; that may be declared not binding in a particular case, as a law or rule; also, that may be dispensed with or done without; unimportant.—**dis-pens-a-bil′i-ty** (-bil′i-ti), *n.*

dis-pen-sa-ry (dis-pen′sạ-ri), *n.*; pl. *-ries* (-riz). [= F. *dispensaire.*] A place where something is dispensed, esp. medicines; specif., a charitable or public institution where medicines are furnished and medical advice is given gratuitously or for a small fee; also, formerly, in parts of the U. S., a place for the sale by a legally authorized agent, under certain restrictions, of intoxicating liquors, not to be drunk on the premises, all other sale being prohibited.

dis-pen-sa-tion (dis-pen-sā′shọn), *n.* [L. *dispensatio(n-).*] The act of dispensing; distribution; administration; management; the divine ordering of the affairs of the world; an appointment or arrangement, as by God; an appointed order or system; a divinely appointed order or system (as, the old, Mosaic, or Jewish *dispensation*; the new, gospel, or Christian *dispensation*); also, the relaxation or suspension of a law or requirement in a special case, or an exemption from the penalty for its violation; official permission, as from the Pope, to do something forbidden or omit something required; release, as from an obligation, vow, etc.; a license granting such relaxation, permission, exemption, or release; also, a dispensing with, doing away with, or doing without something.—**dis-pen-sa′tion-al,** *a.*

dis-pen-sa-tor (dis′pen-sā-tọr), *n.* [L.] One who dispenses; a distributor; an administrator.

dis-pen-sa-to-ry (dis-pen′sạ-tō-ri), *n.*; pl. *-ries* (-riz). [NL. *dispensatorium.*] A book in which the composition, preparation, and uses of medicinal substances are described; a non-official pharmacopœia; also, a dispensary.

dis-pense (dis-pens′), *v.*; *-pensed, -pensing.* [OF. F. *dispenser*, < L. *dispensare* (pp. *dispensatus*), weigh out, disburse, distribute, administer, ML. grant dispensation, freq. of L. *dispendere*, weigh out: see *dispend.*] **I.** *tr.* To deal out or distribute; put up and distribute (medicine), esp. on prescription; administer (laws, etc.); also, to grant a dispensation to, for, or from; exempt or release; excuse; suspend or annul; also, to do without†. **II.** *intr.* To grant dispensation.—**to dispense with,** to grant dispensation, exemption, or pardon to (a person) or for (an offense, fault, etc.)†; sometimes, to compound with for an offense†; also, to put up with patiently†; also, to grant exemption or relief from (a law, rule, promise, etc.); sometimes, to disregard (an obligation)†; also, to do away with (a requirement, need, etc.); also, to do without; forgo.—**dis-pens′er,** *n.*

dis-peo-ple (dis-pē′pl), *v. t.*; *-pled, -pling.* [See *dis-*.] To deprive of people or inhabitants; depopulate: as, "The whole earth . . . was still and lifeless as some *dispeopled* and forgotten world" (Kinglake's "Eothen," xvii.).

di-sper-mous (dī-spėr′mus), *a.* [See *di-*¹ and *-spermous.*] In *bot.*, two-seeded.

dis-per-sal (dis-pėr′sạl), *n.* Dispersion.

dis-perse (dis-pėrs′), *v.*; *-persed, -persing.* [L. *dispersus*, pp. of *dispergere*, < *dis-*, apart, + *spargere*, scatter.] **I.** *tr.* To scatter abroad; send or drive off in various directions; also, to distribute, diffuse, or disseminate; also, to dissipate or dispel; in *physics*, to subject to dispersion. **II.** *intr.* To separate or move apart in various directions; become dissipated or dispelled.—**dis-pers′ed-ly,** *adv.*—**dis-pers′er,** *n.* —**dis-per′sion** (-pėr′shọn), *n.* [L. *dispersio(n-)*.] The act of dispersing, or the state of being dispersed; [also *cap.*] the Jews dispersed among the Gentiles after the Babylonian captivity; the scattered communities of the Jews, or the communities or community in a particular region; [*l. c.*] in *physics*, the separation of white or complex light into its constituent colors, as by a prism, owing to the varying amounts of refractions for rays of different color; also, an analogous phenomenon in the case of other kinds of radiant energy (see *spectrum*).—**dis-per′sive** (-siv), *a.* Serving or tending to disperse.

di-spir-it (di-spir′it), *v. t.* [For *disspirit*: see *dis-*.] To deprive of spirit; depress the spirits of; discourage; dishearten; depress.—**di-spir′it-ed,** *p. a.* Deprived of spirit; spiritless; discouraged; depressed.—**di-spir′it-ed-ly,** *adv.* —**di-spir′it-ed-ness,** *n.*—**di-spir′it-ing,** *p. a.* That dispirits; disheartening; depressing.—**di-spir′it-ing-ly,** *adv.*—**di-spir′it-ment,** *n.*

dis-pit-e-ous (dis-pit′ẹ-us), *a.* [Var. of *despiteous.*] Malicious; cruel; pitiless. See Shakspere's "King John," iv. 1. 34. [Chiefly poetic.]

dis-place (dis-plās′), *v. t.*; *-placed, -placing.* [F. *desplacer* (now *déplacer*).] To put out of place; dislodge; also, to remove from a position, office, or dignity; also, to put something else in the place of; also, to take the place of; replace. —**dis-place′a-ble,** *a.* That may be displaced.—**dis-place′-ment,** *n.* The act of displacing, or the state of being displaced; dislocation, or the amount of dislocation; removal from an office, etc.; the displacing or replacing of one thing by another, as of water by something immersed or floating in it; the amount so displaced; esp., the weight of the volume of water displaced by a floating body (as a ship), which is a weight equivalent to that of the floating body.—**dis-pla′cer** (-plā′sėr), *n.*

dis-plant (dis-plant′), *v. t.* [F. *desplanter* (now *déplanter*).] To pluck up (a plant); hence, to dislodge†; also, to break up (a plantation, etc.)†; also, to supplant†.

dis-play (dis-plā′), *v.* [OF. *despleier* (also *desploier*, F. *déployer*: see *deploy*), < ML. *displicare*, unfold, < L. *dis-* (see *dis-*) + *plicare*, fold.] **I.** *tr.* To unfold, open out, or spread out, as a banner or a sail; spread out with limbs extended, as a bird used as a heraldic bearing; also, to show forth to the view or the mind; exhibit, reveal, or betray (as, "Few 'letters home' of successful men or women *display* the graces of modesty and self-forgetfulness": H. G. Wells's "Outline of History," xxxviii. § 3); also, to declare† or relate† (as, "He . . . did his tale *display*": Scott's "Marmion," iv. 2); also, to show ostentatiously; make a show of; in *printing*, to give special prominence to (words, etc.) by choice and arrangement of type. **II.** *intr.* To make a show or display.—**dis-play′,** *n.* The act of displaying; exhibition; show; an exhibit or exhibition; ostentatious show; in *printing*, the giving of prominence to particular words, etc., by the choice and arrangement of types used, as in an advertisement; also, printed matter thus displayed.—**dis-play′er,** *n.*

Eagle Displayed.

dis-please (dis-plēz′), *v.*; *-pleased, -pleasing.* [OF. *desplaisir.*] **I.** *intr.* To be the reverse of pleasing; be unpleasant; cause dissatisfaction or dislike. **II.** *tr.* To be displeasing to; offend; annoy; make angry.—**dis-pleas′ed-ly,** *adv.*—**dis-pleas′ing-ly,** *adv.*

dis-pleas-ure (dis-plezh′ụr), *n.* [OF. *desplaisir* (F. *déplaisir*), n., orig. inf.: cf. *displease.*] The state of being displeased; dissatisfaction; annoyance; anger; also, discomfort, uneasiness, or pain (archaic); also, a cause of offense, annoyance, or injury (archaic: as, "Now shall I be more blameless than the Philistines, though I do them a *displeasure*," Judges, xv. 3).—**dis-pleas′ure,** *v. t.*; *-ured, -uring.* To displease. [Archaic.]—**dis-pleas′ure-ment,** *n.*

dis-plode† (dis-plōd′), *v. t.* or *i.* [L. *displodere* (pp. *displosus*), burst asunder, < *dis-*, apart, + *plodere, plaudere*, clap.] To explode.—**dis-plo′sion†** (-plō′zhọn), *n.*

dis-plume (dis-plöm′), *v. t.*; *-plumed, -pluming.* [See *dis-*.] To strip of plumes; deplume.

dis-pone (dis-pōn′), *v. t.*; *-poned, -poning.* [L. *disponere* (pp. *dispositus*), place here and there, arrange, dispose: see *disposition.*] To arrange† or dispose†; in *Sc. law*, to make over or convey by legal process.—**dis-pon′er** (-pō′nėr), *n.*

dis-ponge (dis-punj′), *v. t.* See *dispunge.*

dis-pope (dis-pōp′), *v. t.*; *-poped, -poping.* [See *dis-*.] To deprive of the dignity of pope.

dis-port (dis-pōrt′), *v.* [OF. *desporter, deporter*, < *des-, de-* (see *dis-, de-*), + *porter*, < L. *portare*, carry.] **I.** *tr.* To divert or amuse (now only reflexively); now, esp., to exercise or display (one's self) in a sportive manner. **II.** *intr.* To divert one's self; sport.—**dis-port′,** *n.* [OF. *desport, deport.*] Diversion; amusement; also, a pastime; a game. [Archaic.]—**dis-port′ment,** *n.*

dis-pos-a-ble (dis-pō′zạ-bl), *a.* Capable of being disposed or inclined; also, capable of being disposed of; subject to disposal; available.

dis-po-sal (dis-pō′zạl), *n.* The act of disposing, or of disposing of, something; arrangement; regulation†; a dealing with something definitely; bestowal or assignment; a disposing of as by gift or sale; also, power or right to dispose of a thing; control.

dis-pose (dis-pōz′), *v.*; *-posed, -posing.* [OF. F. *disposer*, < *dis-* (see *dis-*) + *poser*, put (see *pose*¹), but associated with derivatives of L. *disponere*: see *disposition.*] **I.** *tr.* To put in a particular or the proper order or arrangement; adjust by the arrangement of parts; put in a particular or suitable place; also, to regulate† or order†; also, to bestow†; distribute†; also, to make fit or ready; prepare; also, to give a tendency or inclination to; incline; specif., to make physically liable or subject. **II.** *intr.* To arrange or decide matters; also, to make terms† (as, "You did suspect She had *disposed* with Cæsar": Shakspere's "Antony and Cleopatra," iv. 14. 123).—**to dispose of,** to regulate† or order†; also, to deal with definitely; get rid of; also, to make over or part with, as by gift or sale.—**dis-pose′,** *n.* Arrangement†; regulation†; disposal†; disposition or habit (archaic).—**dis-posed′,** *p. a.* Arranged; prepared; also, conditioned, esp. as to health (obs. or rare); also, inclined or minded; esp., favorably inclined; also, physically liable or subject.—**dis-pos′ed-ness** (-pō′zed-nes), *n.* —**dis-pos′er,** *n.*

dis-po-si-tion (dis-pọ-zish′ọn), *n.* [OF. F. *disposition*, < L. *dispositio(n-)*, < *disponere*, place here and there, arrange, dispose, < *dis-*, apart, + *ponere*, place, put: cf. *dispone* and *dispose.*] The act of disposing, or the resulting state; arrangement, as of troops or buildings; also, regulation, appointment, or dispensation; also, final settlement of a matter; also, bestowal, as by gift or sale; also, power to dispose of a thing; control; also, mental or moral constitution; turn of mind; also, mental inclination; willingness; also, physical constitution or state†; also, physical inclination or tendency.—**dis-po-si′tioned,** *a.* Having a disposition: as, good-*dispositioned.*—**dis-pos′i-tive** (-poz′i-tiv), *a.* Pertaining to or effecting a disposition of something; disposing.

dis-pos-sess (dis-pọ-zes′), *v. t.* [OF. *despossesser.*] To put (a person) out of possession, esp. of real property; oust; also, to deprive of something (as, "Why does my blood thus muster to my heart . . . *dispossessing* all my other parts Of necessary fitness?" Shakspere's "Measure for Measure," ii. 4. 22); also, to rid (a person) of an evil spirit.—**dis-**

pos-ses′sion (-zesh′ọn), *n.* The act of dispossessing, or the state of being dispossessed.—**dis-pos-ses′sor** (-zes′ọr), *n.*—**dis-pos-ses′so-ry** (-zes′ọ-ri), *a.*

dis-po-sure (dis-pō′zhụr), *n.* Disposal; disposition.

dis-praise (dis-prāz′), *v. t.*; *-praised, -praising.* [OF. *despreisier, despriser* (F. *dépriser*), < *des-* (see *dis-*) + *preisier*, E. *praise.*] To do the reverse of praising; speak of as undeserving; censure.—**dis-praise′**, *n.* The act of dispraising; censure: as, "In praise and in *dispraise* the same, A man of well-attemper'd frame" (Tennyson's "Ode on the Death of the Duke of Wellington," v.).—**dis-prais′er**, *n.*—**dis-prais′ing-ly**, *adv.*

di-spread (di-spred′), *v. t.* or *i.*; *-spread, -spreading.* [For *disspread*: see *dis-*.] To spread out; extend. [Archaic.]

dis-prize (dis-prīz′), *v. t.*; *-prized, -prizing.* [OF. *despriser*: see *dispraise.*] To hold in small esteem; despise; disdain. [Archaic.]

dis-prof-it (dis-prof′it), *v. t.* [See *dis-*.] To be disadvantageous to. [Archaic.]—**dis-prof′it**, *n.*

dis-proof (dis-pröf′), *n.* The act of disproving; proof to the contrary; confutation; refutation.

dis-pro-por-tion (dis-prọ-pôr′shọn), *n.* [See *dis-*.] Lack of proportion; want of due relation, as in size, number, etc.; also, something out of proportion.—**dis-pro-por′tion**, *v. t.* To render disproportionate.—**dis-pro-por′tion-a-ble**, *a.* Disproportionate.—**dis-pro-por′tion-a-ble-ness**, *n.*—**dis-pro-por′tion-a-bly**, *adv.*—**dis-pro-por′tion-al**, *a.* Disproportionate.—**dis-pro-por′tion-al-ly**, *adv.*—**dis-pro-por′tion-ate** (-ạt), *a.* Not proportionate; out of proportion, as in size, number, etc.—**dis-pro-por′tion-ate-ly**, *adv.*—**dis-pro-por′tion-ate-ness**, *n.*

dis-prove (dis-pröv′), *v. t.*; *-proved, -proving.* [OF. *desprover.*] To prove (an assertion, claim, etc.) to be false or wrong; refute; invalidate; also, to prove (a person) to be in the wrong†; also, to disapprove†.—**dis-prov′a-ble** (-prö′vạ-bl), *a.*—**dis-prov′al**, *n.*

dis-punge (dis-punj′), *v. t.*; *-punged, -punging.* [Appar. < *dis-* + *sponge.*] To let drip or fall as from a sponge (archaic); also, to wipe out† or expunge†.

dis-pu-ta-ble (dis′pụ-tạ-bl or dis-pū′-), *a.* [L. *disputabilis.*] That may be disputed; liable to be called in question; questionable; also, disputatious† (as, "He is too *disputable* for my company": Shakspere's "As You Like It," ii. 5. 36).—**dis″pu-ta-bil′i-ty** (-bil′i-ti), *n.*—**dis′pu-ta-bly**, *adv.*

dis-pu-tant (dis′pụ-tạnt). [L. *disputans (-ant-)*, ppr.] **I.** *a.* Disputing. **II.** *n.* One who disputes or debates; a debater.

dis-pu-ta-tion (dis-pụ-tā′shọn), *n.* [L. *disputatio(n-).*] The act of disputing or debating; verbal controversy; a discussion or debate; an academic exercise consisting of the arguing of a thesis between its maintainer and his opponents; also, conversation†.—**dis-pu-ta′tious** (-shus), *a.* Given to disputation; argumentative; contentious.—**dis-pu-ta′tious-ly**, *adv.*—**dis-pu-ta′tious-ness**, *n.*—**dis-pu′ta-tive** (-pū′tạ-tiv), *a.* Disputatious.

dis-pute (dis-pūt′), *v.*; *-puted, -puting.* [OF. *desputer* (F. *disputer*), < L. *disputare* (pp. *disputatus*), compute, examine, discuss, dispute, < *dis-*, apart, + *putare*, reckon: see *putative.*] **I.** *intr.* To engage in argument or discussion; often, to argue vehemently; wrangle or quarrel; hence, to contend. **II.** *tr.* To argue or debate about; discuss; also, to argue against; call in question; also, to contend with in argument; also, to quarrel or fight about; contest; also, to strive against; oppose.—**dis-pute′**, *n.* The act of disputing; argumentation; debate; verbal contention; a debate or controversy; a quarrel; also, strife or contest; a struggle.—**dis-put′er** (-pū′tėr), *n.*

dis-qual-i-fi-ca-tion (dis-kwol″i-fi-kā′shọn), *n.* The act of disqualifying, or the state of being disqualified; also, something that disqualifies (as, "It is recorded as a sufficient *disqualification* of a certain wife, that speaking of her husband, she said, God forgive him": Addison, in "Spectator," 608).

dis-qual-i-fy (dis-kwol′i-fī), *v. t.*; *-fied, -fying.* [See *dis-*.] To deprive of qualification or fitness; render unfit; incapacitate; specif., to deprive of legal or other rights or privileges; pronounce unqualified.

dis-quan-ti-ty (dis-kwon′ti-ti), *v. t.*; *-tied, -tying.* [See *dis-*.] To diminish in quantity (obs. or rare: as, "Be then desired . . . A little to *disquantity* your train," Shakspere's "King Lear," i. 4. 270); also, to deprive of metrical quantity, as syllables.

dis-qui-et (dis-kwī′et), *v. t.* [See *dis-*.] To deprive of quiet, rest, or peace; disturb; make uneasy.—**dis-qui′et**, *n.* The reverse of quiet; disturbance; unrest; uneasiness.—**dis-qui′et**, *a.* Unquiet; uneasy. See Shakspere's "Taming of the Shrew," iv. 1. 171. [Now rare.]—**dis-qui′et-ly**, *adv.*—**dis-qui′e-tude** (-e-tūd), *n.* A state of disquiet; uneasiness; also, a disquieting feeling or circumstance.

dis-qui-si-tion (dis-kwi-zish′ọn), *n.* [L. *disquisitio(n-)*, < *disquirere*, inquire diligently, < *dis-*, apart, + *quærere*, seek.] Investigation or research; an examination; also, a formal discourse or treatise in which a subject is examined and discussed; a dissertation.—**dis-quis′i-tive** (-kwiz′i-tiv), *a.* Pertaining or given to disquisition.—**dis-quis′i-tor**, *n.* The author of a disquisition.

dis-rate (dis-rāt′), *v. t.*; *-rated, -rating.* [See *dis-*.] To reduce to a lower rank.

dis-re-gard (dis-rẹ-gärd′), *v. t.* [See *dis-*.] To pay no regard to; leave out of consideration; also, to treat without due regard, respect, or attention.—**dis-re-gard′**, *n.* Lack of regard or attention; neglect; also, lack of due or respectful regard.—**dis-re-gard′er**, *n.*—**dis-re-gard′ful**, *a.* Lacking in regard; neglectful; careless.

dis-rel-ish (dis-rel′ish), *v. t.* [See *dis-*.] To destroy the relish or flavor of†; also, to have a distaste for; dislike.—**dis-rel′ish**, *n.* Distaste; dislike: as, "taking his punishment with characteristic *disrelish*" (Amelia B. Edwards's "Thousand Miles up the Nile," xvi.).

dis-re-mem-ber (dis-rẹ-mem′bėr), *v. t.* or *i.* [See *dis-*.] To fail to remember; forget: as, "I *disremember* her name" (Mark Twain's "Huckleberry Finn," xiii.). [Colloq.]

dis-re-pair (dis-rẹ-pãr′), *n.* [See *dis-*.] The state of being out of repair; impaired condition.

dis-rep-u-ta-ble (dis-rep′ụ-tạ-bl), *a.* [See *dis-*.] Not reputable; having a bad reputation; discreditable; dishonorable.—**dis-rep″u-ta-bil′i-ty** (-bil′i-ti), **dis-rep′u-ta-ble-ness**, *n.*—**dis-rep′u-ta-bly**, *adv.*—**dis-rep-u-ta′tion** (-tā′shọn), *n.* Loss of or damage to reputation; disrepute. [Archaic.]—**dis-re-pute′** (-rẹ-pūt′), *n.* Ill repute; discredit.

dis-re-spect (dis-rẹ-spekt′), *v. t.* [See *dis-*.] To regard or treat with the reverse of respect; regard or treat with contempt or rudeness.—**dis-re-spect′**, *n.* The reverse of respect; disesteem; rudeness.—**dis-re-spect′a-ble**, *a.* Not respectable.—**dis-re-spect-a-bil′i-ty** (-bil′i-ti), *n.*—**dis-re-spect′ful**, *a.* Characterized by disrespect; having or showing disrespect.—**dis-re-spect′ful-ly**, *adv.*—**dis-re-spect′ful-ness**, *n.*

dis-robe (dis-rōb′), *v. t.* or *i.*; *-robed, -robing.* [See *dis-*.] To divest of or put off a robe; undress; strip.—**dis-robe′ment**, *n.*—**dis-rob′er** (-rō′bėr), *n.*

dis-roof (dis-röf′), *v. t.* [See *dis-*.] To unroof.

dis-root (dis-röt′), *v. t.* [See *dis-*.] To uproot; dislodge.

dis-rupt (dis-rupt′), *v. t.* [L. *disruptus*, pp. of *disrumpere*, < *dis-*, apart, + *rumpere*, break.] To break or rend asunder; break up.—**dis-rupt′**, *a.* Disrupted; rent asunder.—**dis-rup′tion** (-rup′shọn), *n.* The act of disrupting; disrupted state.—**dis-rup′tive**, *a.* Disrupting; pertaining to disruption.—**dis-rup′tor**, *n.* One who or that which disrupts; esp., a high explosive.—**dis-rup′ture** (-tụr), *n.* Disruption.—**dis-rup′ture**, *v. t.*; *-tured, -turing.* To disrupt.

dis-sat-is-fac-tion (dis-sat-is-fak′shọn), *n.* [See *dis-*.] The reverse of satisfaction; discontent or displeasure over something that comes short of one's wishes or expectations.—**dis-sat-is-fac′to-ry** (-tọ-ri), *a.* Causing dissatisfaction.—**dis-sat′is-fy** (-fī), *v. t.*; *-fied, -fying.* To render ill-satisfied, ill-pleased, or discontented.—**dis-sat′is-fied-ly**, *adv.*

dis-seat (dis-sēt′), *v. t.* [See *dis-*.] To unseat.

dis-sect (di-sekt′), *v. t.* [L. *dissectus*, pp. of *dissecare*, < *dis-*, apart, + *secare*, cut.] To cut in pieces; cut apart (an animal body, plant, etc.) to examine the structure, relation of parts, or the like; also, to remove (an organ, etc.) by cutting; fig., to take apart; examine minutely part by part; analyze;

divide or separate as if by cutting.—**dis-sect′ed,** *p. a.* In *bot.*, deeply cut into numerous segments, as a leaf; in *geol.*, cut up by irregular valleys, as a plateau.—**dis-sect′i-ble,** *a.* Capable of being dissected.—**dis-sec′tion** (-sek′shọn), *n.* The act of dissecting; also, something that has been dissected.—**dis-sec′tor,** *n.*

A Dissected Mountain-range, Utah.

dis-seize, dis-seise (dis-sēz′), *v. t.*; *-seized, -seised, -seizing, -seising.* [OF. F. *dessaisir.*] In *law*, to deprive (a person) of seizin or possession, esp. wrongfully or by force; oust; in general, to dispossess; rob.—**dis-sei-zee′, dis-sei-see′** (-sē-zē′), *n.* One who is disseized.—**dis-sei′zin, dis-sei′sin** (-zin), *n.* [OF. *dessaisine.*] In *law*, the act of disseizing, or the state of being disseized.—**dis-sei′zor, dis-sei′sor,** *n.* One who disseizes another.

dis-sem-blance[1] (di-sem′blạns), *n.* [OF. *dessemblance* (F. *dissemblance*).] Want of resemblance; dissimilarity; unlikeness. [Archaic.]

dis-sem-blance[2] (di-sem′blạns), *n.* Dissembling; dissimulation. [Archaic.]

dis-sem-ble (di-sem′bl), *v.*; *-bled, -bling.* [Appar. for earlier *dissimule*, < OF. *dissimuler*, < L. *dissimulare*: see *dissimulate.*] **I.** *tr.* To disguise, as by a misleading garb†; give a false semblance to; conceal the real nature of; also, to let pass unnoticed; ignore; also, to put on the appearance of, or feign (as, "All this concern was *dissembled*": Smollett's "Humphry Clinker," May 6). **II.** *intr.* To give a false impression; conceal one's motives, etc., under some pretense; speak or act hypocritically.—**dis-sem′bler,** *n.* —**dis-sem′bling-ly,** *adv.*

dis-sem-i-nate (di-sem′i-nāt), *v. t.*; *-nated, -nating.* [L. *disseminatus*, pp. of *disseminare*, < *dis-*, apart, + *seminare*, sow, E. *seminate.*] To scatter, as seed in sowing; spread abroad; diffuse; promulgate.—**dis-sem-i-na′tion** (-nā′shọn), *n.*—**dis-sem′i-na-tor,** *n.*

dis-sen-sion (di-sen′shọn), *n.* [OF. F. *dissension*, < L. *dissensio(n-)*, < *dissentire*: see *dissent.*] Difference in sentiment or opinion; disagreement, esp. violent disagreement; discord; a contention or quarrel.

dis-sent (di-sent′), *v. i.* [OF. F. *dissentir*, < L. *dissentire*, < *dis-*, apart, + *sentire*, feel.] To differ in sentiment or opinion; disagree; withhold assent; specif., to differ in religious opinion; reject the doctrines or authority of an established church; also, to differ in sense, nature, etc.†.—**dis-sent′,** *n.* Difference in sentiment or opinion; a declaration of disagreement; specif., separation from an established church, esp. that of England; nonconformity; also, difference in sense, nature, etc.†.—**dis-sent′er,** *n.* One who dissents, as from an established church; esp. [sometimes *cap.*], a person, now esp. a Protestant, who dissents from the Church of England.

dis-sen-tient (di-sen′shiẹnt). [L. *dissentiens* (*-ent-*), ppr. of *dissentire*: see *dissent.*] **I.** *a.* Dissenting, esp. from the opinion of the majority. **II.** *n.* One who dissents.—**dis-sen′tience,** *n.*

dis-sent-ing (di-sen′ting), *p. a.* That dissents; dissentient; specif., disagreeing with the doctrines of an established church.—**dis-sent′ing-ly,** *adv.*

dis-sen-tious (di-sen′shus), *a.* [For *dissensious.*] Full of or given to dissension; contentious; quarrelsome.

dis-sep-i-ment (di-sep′i-mẹnt), *n.* [L. *dissæpimentum*, < *dissæpire*, separate, < *dis-*, apart, + *sæpire*, hedge in: see *septum.*] A partition or septum; esp., in *bot.*, one of the partitions within ovaries and fruits, formed by the coherence of the sides of the constituent carpels.—**dis-sep-i-men′tal** (-men′tạl), *a.*

a, a, Dissepiments.

dis-sert (di-sėrt′), *v. i.* [L. *dissertus*, pp. of *disserere*, examine, discuss, discourse, < *dis-*, apart, + *serere*, join.] To discourse on a subject. [Obs. or rare.]

dis-ser-tate (dis′ėr-tāt), *v. i.*; *-tated, -tating.* [L. *dissertatus*, pp. of *dissertare*, freq. of *disserere*: see *dissert.*] To treat of a subject in a discourse; make a dissertation.—**dis-ser-ta′tion** (-tā′shọn), *n.* [L. *dissertatio(n-)*.] A formal discourse on a subject; a disquisition.—**dis′ser-ta-tor,** *n.*

dis-serve (dis-sėrv′), *v. t.*; *-served, -serving.* [See *dis-*.] To serve ill; do an ill turn to.—**dis-ser′vice** (-sėr′vis), *n.* The reverse of service; harm; injury; an ill turn.—**dis-ser′vice-a-ble,** *a.* Harmful; detrimental.

dis-sev-er (di-sev′ėr), *v.* [OF. *dessevrer.*] **I.** *tr.* To sever; separate; also, to divide into parts. **II.** *intr.* To part; separate.—**dis-sev′er-ance, dis-sev-er-a′tion** (-ā′shọn), **dis-sev′er-ment,** *n.*

dis-si-dent (dis′i-dẹnt). [L. *dissidens* (*-ent-*), ppr. of *dissidere*, sit apart, differ, < *dis-*, apart, + *sedere*, sit.] **I.** *a.* Differing; disagreeing; dissenting. **II.** *n.* One who differs, esp. in opinion or doctrine; a dissenter.—**dis′si-dence,** *n.*

dis-sight (dis-sīt′ or dis′sīt), *n.* [See *dis-*.] An unsightly object; an eyesore. [Chiefly prov. Eng.]

dis-sil-i-ent (di-sil′i-ẹnt), *a.* [L. *dissiliens* (*-ent-*), ppr. of *dissilire*, fly apart, < *dis-*, apart, + *salire*, leap.] Flying or bursting asunder; in *bot.*, bursting open forcibly, as the ripe seed-vessels of some plants.—**dis-sil′i-ence, dis-sil′i-en-cy,** *n.*

Dissilient Capsule at the moment of bursting.

dis-sim-i-lar (di-sim′i-lạ̈r), *a.* [See *dis-*.] Not similar; unlike; different.—**dis-sim-i-lar′i-ty** (-lar′i-ti), *n.*; pl. *-ties* (-tiz). Unlikeness; difference; also, a point of difference.—**dis-sim′i-lar-ly,** *adv.*

dis-sim-i-late (di-sim′i-lāt), *v. t.* or *i.*; *-lated, -lating.* [L. *dis-* (see *dis-*) + *similis*, like.] To make or become unlike.—**dis-sim-i-la′tion** (-lā′shọn), *n.* A making or becoming unlike; in *biol.*, catabolism; in *phonetics*, change of one of two similar sounds which would otherwise occur near together in a word (cf. *assimilation*). —**dis-sim′i-la-tive** (-lạ-tiv), *a.*

dis-si-mil-i-tude (dis-i-mil′i-tūd), *n.* [L. *dissimilitudo*, < *dissimilis*, unlike, < *dis-* (see *dis-*) + *similis*, like.] Unlikeness; difference; also, a point of difference.

dis-sim-u-late (di-sim′ụ-lāt), *v.*; *-lated, -lating.* [L. *dissimulatus*, pp. of *dissimulare*, disguise, conceal, < *dis-* (see *dis-*) + *simulare*, E. *simulate.*] **I.** *tr.* To disguise or conceal under a false semblance; dissemble. **II.** *intr.* To use dissimulation; dissemble: as, "He could neither simulate nor *dissimulate*" (H. James's "Europeans," x.).—**dis-sim-u-la′tion** (-lā′shọn), *n.* [L. *dissimulatio(n-)*.] The act of dissimulating; feigning; hypocrisy.—**dis-sim′u-la-tive** (-lạ-tiv), *a.* Characterized by or pertaining to dissimulation.—**dis-sim′u-la-tor** (-lā-tọr), *n.*

dis-si-pate (dis′i-pāt), *v.*; *-pated, -pating.* [L. *dissipatus*, pp. of *dissipare*, scatter abroad, disperse, demolish, squander, < *dis-*, apart, + *sipare*, *supare*, throw, scatter.] **I.** *tr.* To scatter in various directions; disperse; dispel; disintegrate; also, to squander; waste. **II.** *intr.* To become scattered or dispersed; be dispelled; disintegrate; also, to indulge in extravagant, intemperate, or dissolute pleasures; practise dissipation.—**dis′si-pat-ed** (-pā-ted), *p. a.* Indulging in or characterized by excessive devotion to pleasure; intemperate; dissolute.—**dis′si-pat-ed-ly,** *adv.*—**dis′si-pat-ed-ness,** *n.*—**dis-si-pa′tion** (-pā′shọn), *n.* [L. *dissipatio(n-)*.] The act of dissipating, or the state of being dissipated; dispersion; disintegration; a wasting by misuse; also, mental distraction; a diversion; also, undue or vicious indulgence in pleasure; intemperance; dissolute mode of living.—**dis′si-pa-tive** (-pạ-tiv), *a.* Tending to dissipate.—**dis′si-pa-tor** (-pā-tọr), *n.*

dis-so-cia-ble (di-sō′shạ-bl), *a.* Capable of being dissociated; separable; also, unsociable.

dis-so-cial (di-sō′shạl), *a.* [See *dis-*.] Unsocial; disinclined to or unsuitable for society.

dis-so-ci-ate (di-sō′shi-āt), *v.*; *-ated, -ating.* [L. *dissociatus*, pp. of *dissociare*, < *dis-* (see *dis-*) + *sociare*, join: see *sociable.*] **I.** *tr.* To sever the association of; disunite; separate; in *chem.*, to subject to dissociation. **II.** *intr.* To withdraw from association; in *chem.*, to undergo dissociation.—**dis-so-ci-a′tion** (-si-ā′shọn), *n.* [L. *dissociatio(n-).*] The act of dissociating, or the state of being dissociated; disunion; in *chem.*, the reversible resolution or decomposition of a complex substance into simpler constituents, due to variation in the physical conditions, as when water heated to a very high temperature gradually decomposes into hydrogen and oxygen in such a way that upon a subsequent lowering of the temperature the liberated elements recombine and again form water; the separation of the molecule of an electrolyte into its constituent ions ('electrolytic dissociation'). —**dis-so′ci-a-tive** (-shi-ạ-tiv), *a.* Tending to dissociate; causing dissociation.

dis-so-lu-ble (dis′ọ-lụ-bl or di-sol′ụ-bl), *a.* [L. *dissolubilis,* < *dissolvere*: see *dissolve.*] Capable of being dissolved, decomposed, broken up, or undone.

dis-so-lute (dis′ọ-lūt), *a.* [L. *dissolutus*, pp.: see *dissolve.*] Disunited† or disconnected†; relaxed† or weakened†; lax†, slack†, or negligent†; unrestrained (obs. or rare); now, indifferent to moral restraints; given over to dissipation or vicious courses; profligate; licentious.—**dis′so-lute-ly,** *adv.* —**dis′so-lute-ness,** *n.*

dis-so-lu-tion (dis-ọ-lū′shọn), *n.* [L. *dissolutio(n-),* < *dissolvere*: see *dissolve.*] The act of resolving into parts or elements, or the resulting state; disintegration; decomposition; also, reduction from a solid to a liquid form; liquefaction; solution in a liquid substance; a solution†; also, relaxation† or enfeeblement†; also, looseness in morals or conduct (obs. or rare); also, the undoing or breaking up of a tie, bond, union, etc.; also, the breaking up of an assembly or organization; dismissal; dispersal; also, a bringing or coming to an end; destruction; also, death or decease.—**dis′so-lu-tive,** *a.* Pertaining to or involving dissolution.

dis-solve (di-zolv′), *v.*; *-solved, -solving.* [L. *dissolvere* (pp. *dissolutus*), < *dis-*, apart, + *solvere*, loosen.] **I.** *tr.* To resolve into parts or elements, disintegrate, or decompose (now rare); also, to reduce to a liquid form; liquefy; melt; esp., to make a solution of in a liquid; also, to weaken† or enfeeble†; also, to loosen or set free (archaic); also, to undo (a tie or bond); break up (a connection, union, etc.); destroy the binding power of (as, "to frustrate and *dissolve* these magic spells": Milton's "Samson Agonistes," 1149); also, to solve or resolve (a question, etc.: archaic); also, to break up (an assembly or organization); dismiss; disperse; also, to bring to an end; destroy; dispel; also, to cause to die†. **II.** *intr.* To become dissolved; melt; become liquefied, esp. on immersion in a liquid; also, to lose binding force; also, to break up or disperse; also, to disappear gradually; fade from sight or apprehension.—**dis-solv′a-ble,** *a.*—**dis-sol′vent** (-zol′vẹnt). [L. *dissolvens* (*-ent-*), ppr.] **I.** *a.* Dissolving; solvent. **II.** *n.* A solvent.—**dis-solv′er,** *n.* —**dis-solv′ing,** *p. a.* That dissolves.—**dissolving views,** pictures thrown on a screen by a magic lantern in such a way that they seem to dissolve one into another, without any interval between them.—**dis-solv′ing-ly,** *adv.*

dis-so-nance (dis′ọ-nạns), *n.* The quality of being dissonant; discord; a combination of dissonant or inharmonious sounds; an inharmonious or harsh sound; also, disagreement or incongruity.

dis-so-nant (dis′ọ-nạnt), *a.* [L. *dissonans* (*-ant-*), ppr. of *dissonare,* disagree in sound, < *dis-*, apart, + *sonare*, sound.] Disagreeing or harsh in sound; discordant; also, out of harmony; incongruous; at variance.—**dis′so-nant-ly,** *adv.*

dis-spread (di-spred′), *v.* See *dispread.*

dis-suade (di-swād′), *v. t.*; *-suaded, -suading.* [L. *dissuadere* (pp. *dissuasus*), < *dis-*, apart, + *suadere*, advise, urge.] To advise or urge against (an action, etc.: archaic); seek to deter (a person) from an action, etc., by advice (archaic); deter by advice or persuasion.—**dis-suad′er** (-swā′dėr), *n.*—**dis-sua′sion** (-swā′zhọn), *n.* [L. *dissuasio(n-).*] The act of dissuading; advice or exhortation against something.—**dis-sua′sive** (-siv). **I.** *a.* Tending to dissuade. **II.** *n.* A dissuasive speech or argument (as, "No *dissuasives* could alter her resolve": Mrs. Gaskell's "Cranford," ii.); anything dissuasive or intended to dissuade.—**dis-sua′sive-ly,** *adv.*

dis-syl-la-ble (di-sil′ạ-bl), *n.* [F. *dissyllabe,* < L. *disyllabus,* < Gr. δισύλλαβος, of two syllables, < δι-, two, + συλλαβή: see *syllable.*] A word of two syllables, as *virtue.*—**dis-syl-lab-ic** (dis-i-lab′ik), *a.*

dis-sym-met-ric, dis-sym-met-ri-cal (dis-si-met′rik, -ri-kạl), *a.* [See *dis-.*] Not symmetric; also, having the same form but not superposable, as the right and left hands; reversely symmetric.—**dis-sym′me-try** (-sim′e-tri), *n.* Absence of symmetry; also, dissymmetric, or reversely symmetric, form or character.

dis-tad (dis′tad), *adv.* [See *distal* and *-ad.*] In *anat.*, toward the end or distal part.

dis-taff (dis′tåf), *n.* [AS. *distæf,* appar. < *dis-*, akin to LG. *diesse*, bunch of flax on a distaff (cf. *dizen*), + *stæf*, E. *staff*[2].] A staff with a cleft end, formerly used for holding the wool, flax, etc., from which the thread was drawn in spinning by hand; an analogous part of a spinning-wheel, for holding flax to be spun; hence (with reference to the distaff as a woman's implement), the female sex; the female side of a family (also called *distaff side*, or *spindle side*, as opposed to *spear side*); a female heir; a woman.

dis-tain (dis-tān′), *v. t.* [OF. *desteindre* (F. *déteindre*), < *des-* (see *dis*) + *teindre*, < L. *tingere*, wet, dye, E. *tinge.*] To discolor; stain; sully. [Archaic.]

dis-tal (dis′tạl), *a.* [= F. *distal,* < L. *distans,* E. *distant.*] Situated away from the point of origin or attachment, as of a limb or bone; terminal: opposed to *proximal.*—**dis′tal-ly,** *adv.*

dis-tance (dis′tạns), *n.* [OF. F. *distance,* < L. *distantia.*] The state or fact of being distant, as of one thing from another; remoteness; also, the extent of space intervening between things or points; a specified interval of space, as between two soldiers in a rank, two ranks of soldiers, or the combatants in a duel; a space measured back from the winning-post on a race-track, which a horse must have reached when the winning horse has finished the heat, in order to qualify for subsequent heats; also, the interval between two points of time; also, remoteness in any respect; remoteness in intercourse; reserve or aloofness; deferential aloofness; one's proper degree of aloofness (as, to keep one's *distance*); also, a distant point or place; the distant region; the distant part of a landscape, etc.; also, difference† or diversity†; disagreement† or dissension†; a quarrel†.—**dis′tance,** *v. t.*; *-tanced, -tancing.* To place at a distance; also, to cause to appear distant; also, to leave behind at a distance, as in a race; surpass; in *horse-racing*, to beat by at least a distance.

dis-tant (dis′tạnt), *a.* [OF. F. *distant,* < L. *distans* (*distant-*), ppr. of *distare*, stand apart, be distant, differ, < *di-*, for *dis-*, apart, + *stare*, stand.] Separate or apart in space (as, a place an inch, or a mile, *distant*); also, far off or apart in space; not near at hand; remote; also, apart or far off in time; also, far apart in any respect, as in resemblance, kinship, etc.; also, reserved in intercourse; not familiar or cordial; also, different† or diverse†.—**dis′tant-ly,** *adv.*—**dis′tant-ness,** *n.*

dis-taste (dis-tāst′), *v.*; *-tasted, -tasting.* [See *dis-.*] **I.** *tr.* To dislike the taste of†; dislike (archaic); also, to offend the taste of†; displease or offend; also, to render distasteful†. **II.** *intr.* To offend the taste†; cause offense.—**dis-taste′,** *n.* Disrelish for food or drink (now rare); dislike or disinclination; also, annoyance† or offense†; a cause of annoyance†; also, dissension†.—**dis-taste′ful,** *a.* Full of dislike†; also, unpleasant to the taste; also, causing dislike, displeasing, or offensive (as, "The idea of limited monarchy was *distasteful* to the crowned heads of Europe at that time": H. G. Wells's "Outline of History," xxxvi. § 3).—**dis-taste′ful-ly,** *adv.*—**dis-taste′ful-ness,** *n.*

dis-tem-per[1] (dis-tem′pėr), *v. t.* [ML. *distemperare,* < L. *dis-* (see *dis-*) + *temperare*, E. *temper.*] To disturb the temper or due proportions of†; also, to derange physically or mentally; vex, trouble, or disquiet (archaic); also, to put out of proper condition (as, "Sin, that first *Distemper'd* all things": Milton's "Paradise Lost," xi. 56); also, to intoxicate†.—**dis-tem′per**[1], *n.* Want of due proportion, as of parts or qualities†; also, deranged condition of body or mind; a disorder or disease; any of various diseases of animals, as a catarrhal disease of dogs or the disease called strangles of horses, etc.; vexation or disquiet (archaic); also, disorder or disturbance; also, intoxication†.

dis-tem-per^{2} (dis-tem′pėr), *v. t.* [OF. *destemprer* (F. *détremper*), < ML. *distemperare*, dilute, soak, another use of *distemperare*, E. *distemper*^{1}.] To dilute, dissolve, or soak (obs. or archaic); also, to paint in distemper.—**dis-tem′per**^{2}, *n.* A method of painting in which the colors are mixed with some binding medium, as yolk of egg mixed with water, usually executed upon a ground of chalk or plaster mixed with gum, and chiefly employed for scene-painting, mural decoration, or the like; the pigment, or the ground, so prepared; a painting executed by this method.

dis-tem-per-a-ture (dis-tem′pėr-ạ-ţūr), *n.* [See *distemper*^{1}.] Distempered or disordered condition; disturbance of health, mind, or temper; disorder; also, intemperateness; excess. [Archaic.]

dis-tend (dis-tend′), *v.* [L. *distendere* (pp. *distentus*, LL. *distensus*), < *dis-*, apart, + *tendere*, stretch, E. *tend*^{1}.] **I.** *tr.* To stretch apart or asunder; stretch out; also, to expand by stretching; dilate; swell out (something hollow and elastic). **II.** *intr.* To become distended; expand; swell out.—**dis-tend′er,** *n.*

dis-ten-si-ble (dis-ten′si-bl), *a.* [LL. *distensus*, pp.: see *distend.*] Capable of being distended.—**dis-ten-si-bil′i-ty** (-bil′i-ti), *n.*

dis-ten′sion, *n.* See *distention.*

dis-tent (dis-tent′), *a.* [L. *distentus*, pp.: see *distend.*] Distended. [Now rare.]

dis-ten-tion, dis-ten-sion (dis-ten′shọn), *n.* [L. *distentio(n-)*, < *distendere*: see *distend.*] The act of distending, or the state of being distended.

dis-tich (dis′tik), *n.* [L. *distichon*, < Gr. δίστιχον, neut. of δίστιχος, of two rows or lines, < δι-, two, + στίχος, row, line.] In *pros.*, a group of two lines of verse, usually making complete sense; a couplet; often, a riming couplet.

dis-ti-chous (dis′ti-kus), *a.* [L. *distichus*, < Gr. δίστιχος: see *distich.*] Disposed in two opposite rows; in *bot.*, arranged alternately in two vertical rows on opposite sides of an axis, as leaves.—**dis′ti-chous-ly,** *adv.*

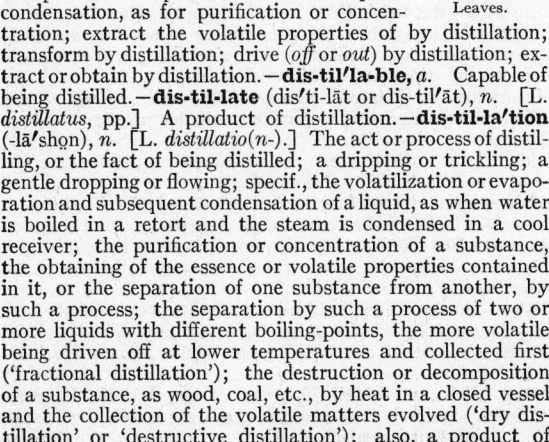

Distichous Leaves.

dis-til, dis-till (dis-til′), *v.*; *-tilled, -tilling.* [L. *distillare* (pp. *distillatus*), for *destillare*, < *de*, down from, + *stillare*, drop, drip, < *stilla*, a drop.] **I.** *intr.* To fall in drops; trickle; exude; hence, to flow gently; also, to let fall drops; also, specif., to drop, pass, or condense as a distillate; become vaporized and then condensed in distillation; undergo distillation; also, to practise distillation. **II.** *tr.* To let fall in drops; give forth in or as in drops; infuse; specif., to subject to a process of vaporization and subsequent condensation, as for purification or concentration; extract the volatile properties of by distillation; transform by distillation; drive (*off* or *out*) by distillation; extract or obtain by distillation.—**dis-til′la-ble,** *a.* Capable of being distilled.—**dis-til-late** (dis′ti-lāt or dis-til′āt), *n.* [L. *distillatus*, pp.] A product of distillation.—**dis-til-la′tion** (-lā′shọn), *n.* [L. *distillatio(n-)*.] The act or process of distilling, or the fact of being distilled; a dripping or trickling; a gentle dropping or flowing; specif., the volatilization or evaporation and subsequent condensation of a liquid, as when water is boiled in a retort and the steam is condensed in a cool receiver; the purification or concentration of a substance, the obtaining of the essence or volatile properties contained in it, or the separation of one substance from another, by such a process; the separation by such a process of two or more liquids with different boiling-points, the more volatile being driven off at lower temperatures and collected first ('fractional distillation'); the destruction or decomposition of a substance, as wood, coal, etc., by heat in a closed vessel and the collection of the volatile matters evolved ('dry distillation' or 'destructive distillation'); also, a product of distilling; a distillate.—**dis-til′la-to-ry** (-til′ạ-tō-ri), *a.* Pertaining to distillation.—**dis-tilled′,** *p. a.* Subjected to distillation, as for purification or concentration; obtained or produced by distillation.—**dis-til′ler,** *n.* One who or that which distils; one whose business it is to extract spirituous liquors by distillation; an apparatus for distilling, esp. one for the distillation of salt water at sea.—**dis-til′ler-y,** *n.*; pl. *-ies* (-iz). The act or art of distilling†; also, a place or establishment where distilling, esp. the distilling of spirituous liquors, is carried on.—**dis-til′ment, dis-till′ment,** *n.* The act or process of distilling; also, the product of distilling.

dis-tinct (dis-tingkt′), *a.* [L. *distinctus*, pp. of *distinguere*: see *distinguish.*] Distinguished as not being the same; not identical; separate; also, different in nature or qualities; dissimilar; also, clear to the senses or intellect; plain; definite; unmistakable; also, distinguishing clearly, as the vision; also, decorated or adorned (poetic: as, "Dark-blue the deep sphere overhead, *Distinct* with vivid stars inlaid," Tennyson's "Recollections of the Arabian Nights," 90).—**dis-tinc′tion** (-tingk′shọn), *n.* [L. *distinctio(n-)*, < *distinguere.*] Division† or separation†; also, a division† or section†; a class†; also, a marking off or distinguishing as different; a distinguishing characteristic; also, the recognizing or noting of differences; discrimination; a discrimination made between things as different; the faculty of observing differences†; also, the condition of being different; a difference; also, clearness† or distinctness†; also, a distinguishing or treating with special attention or favor; a mark of special favor; also, note or eminence; marked superiority; sometimes, distinguished appearance.—**dis-tinc′tive,** *a.* Distinguishing; serving to distinguish; characteristic.—**dis-tinc′tive-ly,** *adv.*—**dis-tinc′tive-ness,** *n.*—**dis-tinct′ly,** *adv.*—**dis-tinct′ness,** *n.*

dis-tin-gué (dēs-taṅ-gā), *a.* [F. (fem. *distinguée*).] Distinguished; having an air of distinction: said esp. of persons or their appearance, manners, etc.

dis-tin-guish (dis-ting′gwish), *v.* [L. *distinguere* (pp. *distinctus*), separate, distinguish, set off, adorn, < *di-*, for *dis-*, apart, + *-stinguere* (= Gr. στίζειν), prick: see *stick*^{2}, and cf. *instinct, extinguish.*] **I.** *tr.* To divide into separate parts†; divide one from another†; also, to divide into classes; classify; also, to mark off as different; also, to serve to separate as different; be a distinctive characteristic of; characterize; also, to recognize as distinct or different; discriminate; also, to perceive clearly by sight or other sense; discern; recognize; also, to single out for or honor with special attention (archaic); also, to make prominent, conspicuous, or eminent; sometimes, to adorn†. **II.** *intr.* To indicate or show a difference; also, to recognize or note differences; discriminate.—**dis-tin′guish-a-ble,** *a.* Capable of being distinguished.—**dis-tin′guish-a-ble-ness,** *n.*—**dis-tin′guish-a-bly,** *adv.*—**dis-tin′guished,** *p. a.* Conspicuous, marked, or signal; noted; eminent; famous; also, having an air of distinction; distingué.—**Distinguished Service Cross,** a cross (instituted in 1918, and ranking below the Medal of Honor) awarded by the President of the U. S., or in his name, to any man or woman who while serving in any capacity with the army distinguishes himself or herself by extraordinary heroism in connection with military operations against an armed enemy or under circumstances which do not justify the award of the Medal of Honor.—**Distinguished Service Medal,** a medal (instituted in 1918, and ranking below the Distinguished Service Cross) awarded by the President of the U. S. to any person who while serving in any capacity in the army distinguishes himself or herself by exceptionally meritorious service to the government in a duty of great responsibility in time of war or in connection with military operations against an armed enemy.—**dis-tin′guish-er,** *n.*—**dis-tin′guish-ing-ly,** *adv.*—**dis-tin′guish-ment,** *n.* The act of distinguishing, or the resulting state; also, something that distinguishes.

dis-tort (dis-tôrt′), *v. t.* [L. *distortus*, pp. of *distorquere*, < *dis-*, apart, + *torquere*, twist.] To twist awry or out of shape; make crooked or deformed; fig., to pervert; misrepresent.—**dis-tort′ed-ly,** *adv.*—**dis-tort′ed-ness,** *n.*—**dis-tort′er,** *n.*—**dis-tor′tion** (-tôr′shọn), *n.* [L. *distortio(n-)*.] The act of distorting, or the state of being distorted; also, anything distorted.—**dis-tor′tion-al,** *a.*

dis-tract (dis-trakt′), *v. t.* [L. *distractus*, pp. of *distrahere*, < *dis-*, apart, + *trahere*, draw.] To draw apart†; also, to rend by dissension or strife; also, to divide (the mind, attention, etc.) between different objects; perplex or bewilder; disturb or trouble greatly in mind; also, to derange mentally; craze; also, to draw away or divert, as the mind or attention.—**dis-tract′**, *a.* [L. *distractus*, pp.: cf. *distraught.*] Distracted. [Archaic.]—**dis-tract′ed**, *p. a.* Rent by dissension or strife; also, divided by conflicting interests, as the mind; perplexed or bewildered; much disturbed or troubled mentally; also, mentally deranged; crazed; mad.—**dis-tract′ed-ly**, *adv.*—**dis-tract′er**, *n.*—**dis-tract′ing-ly**, *adv.*—**dis-trac′tion** (-trak′shọn), *n.* [L. *distractio(n-).*] The act of distracting, or the state of being distracted; division or disorder due to dissension; tumult; division, as of mind, between conflicting interests; perplexity or bewilderment; violent disturbance of mind; mental derangement, or madness; also, diversion of the mind or attention; also, something that distracts or diverts the mind.—**dis-trac′tive**, *a.* Tending to distract.

dis-train (dis-trān′), *v.* [OF. *destreindre*, press, oppress, constrain, < L. *distringere* (pp. *districtus*), draw asunder, detain, hinder, ML. constrain, coerce, < L. *di-*, for *dis-*, apart, + *stringere*, draw tight.] **I.** *tr.* To pull apart or off†; press† or squeeze†; distress† or oppress†; constrain† or compel†; in *law*, to constrain by seizing and holding goods, etc., to pay a debt, discharge an obligation, etc.; levy a distress upon, as for unpaid rent. **II.** *intr.* In *law*, to levy a distress.—**dis-train′a-ble**, *a.* Liable to be distrained.—**dis-train′er**, **dis-train′or**, *n.*—**dis-train′ment**, *n.*—**dis-traint′** (-trānt′), *n.* In *law*, the act of distraining; a distress.

dis-trait (dēs-trā), *a.* [F., pp. of *distraire*, < L. *distrahere*: see *distract.*] Abstracted in thought; absent-minded: as, "So much *distrait* he was, that all could see That something was the matter" (Byron's "Don Juan," xvi. 30).—**dis-traite** (-trāt), *a.* [F.] Fem. of *distrait*.

dis-traught (dis-trât′), *a.* [Var. of *distract, a.*] Distracted; bewildered; deeply agitated mentally; crazed.

dis-tress (dis-tres′), *n.* [OF. *destrece* (F. *détresse*), < L. *districtus*, pp.: see *distrain.*] Pressure†; stress†; constraint†; also, great pain, anxiety, or sorrow; acute suffering; affliction; trouble; a state of extreme necessity; the state of a ship requiring immediate assistance, as because of accident; in *law*, the act of distraining; the legal seizure of the goods of another as security or satisfaction for debt, etc.; also, the thing seized.—**dis-tress′**, *v. t.* [OF. *destresser, destrecier.*] To subject to pressure, stress, or strain; embarrass or exhaust by strain; also, to constrain; also, to afflict with pain, anxiety, or sorrow; trouble sorely; make miserable; worry or bother; in *law*, to levy a distress upon.—**dis-tress′ed-ly**, *adv.*—**dis-tress′ful**, *a.* Full of distress; feeling or indicating distress; also, causing or involving distress.—**dis-tress′ful-ly**, *adv.*—**dis-tress′ful-ness**, *n.*—**dis-tress′ing-ly**, *adv.*

dis-trib-ute (dis-trib′ūt), *v. t.*; *-uted, -uting.* [L. *distributus*, pp. of *distribuere*, < *dis-*, apart, + *tribuere*, grant, give, pay.] To divide and bestow in shares; deal out; allot; also, to disperse through a space or over an area; spread; scatter; also, to divide into parts of distinct character; also, to divide into classes; classify; also, to sort out according to kind, as printing-types; in *logic*, to employ (a term) in its full extension.—**dis-trib′ut-a-ble**, *a.*—**dis-trib′ut-er**, *n.* Same as *distributor*.—**dis-tri-bu′tion** (-tri-bū′shọn), *n.* [L. *distributio(n-).*] The act of distributing, or the state or manner of being distributed; dealing out; allotment; dispersion; scattering; diffusion; division and arrangement; classification; sorting, as of type; also, that which is distributed; in *polit. econ.*, the division of the aggregate produce of the industry of any society among its members or among the factors of production; also, the dispersion of commodities among consumers; in *logic*, the use of a term in its full extension; in *arch.*, the arrangement of the parts of a building.—**dis-tri-bu′tion-al**, *a.*—**dis-trib′u-tive** (-ū-tiv). [LL. *distributivus.*] **I.** *a.* That distributes; characterized by or pertaining to distribution; in *gram.* and *logic*, having reference to each individual of a group or class considered separately. **II.** *n.* In *gram.*, a distributive word, as *each, every, either, neither*.—**dis-trib′u-tive-ly**, *adv.*—**dis-trib′u-tive-ness**, *n.*—**dis-trib′u-tor**, *n.* [L.] One who or that which distributes; one engaged in and controlling the general distribution or marketing of some manufactured article or other commodity; a device or apparatus for distributing.

dis-trict (dis′trikt), *n.* [F. *district*, < ML. *districtus*, territory under jurisdiction, < *distringere*, constrain, coerce: see *distrain.*] A division of territory, as of a country, state, county, etc., marked off for administrative, electoral, or other purposes; in general, a region or locality.—**dis′trict**, *v. t.* To divide into districts.

dis-trust (dis-trust′), *n.* [See *dis-*.] The reverse of trust; doubt; suspicion.—**dis-trust′**, *v. t.* To feel distrust of; regard with doubt or suspicion.—**dis-trust′er**, *n.*—**dis-trust′ful**, *a.* Full of distrust; doubtful; suspicious.—**dis-trust′ful-ly**, *adv.*—**dis-trust′ful-ness**, *n.*

dis-tune (dis-tūn′), *v. t.*; *-tuned, -tuning.* [See *dis-*.] To put out of tune: as, "This frets my faith, *Distunes* me into discord with myself" (Swinburne's "Bothwell," i. 1).

dis-turb (dis-tėrb′), *v. t.* [OF. *desturber*, < L. *disturbare*, < *dis-*, apart, + *turbare*, throw into disorder, disturb, < *turba*, disorder, tumult.] To throw into commotion or disorder; agitate; disorder; disarrange; unsettle; also, to interrupt the quiet, rest, or peace of; disquiet; also, to agitate the mind of; perplex; trouble; also, to interfere with, interrupt; hinder; throw out of course.—**dis-turb′ance**, *n.* [OF. *desturbance.*] The act of disturbing, or the state of being disturbed; also, an instance of this; a commotion; specif., an outbreak of disorder; a breach of public peace; in *law*, interference with the peaceful exercise of a right or privilege.—**dis-turb′er**, *n.*—**dis-turb′ing-ly**, *adv.*

dis-tyle (dis′tīl or dī′stīl). [Gr. δι-, two, + στῦλος, pillar, column.] In *arch.*: **I.** *a.* Having two columns, as a portico. **II.** *n.* A distyle portico.

di-sul-phate (dī-sul′fāt), *n.* [See *di-*¹.] In *chem.*, a salt of disulphuric acid; also, a bisulphate.—**di-sul′phide** (-fīd or -fid), *n.* In *chem.*, a bisulphide.—**di-sul-phu′ric** (-fū′rik), *a.* In *chem.*, noting or pertaining to a crystalline acid, $H_2S_2O_7$, obtained when sulphur trioxide is dissolved in sulphuric acid.

dis-u-nion (dis-ū′nyọn), *n.* [See *dis-*.] Severance of union; separation; disjunction; also, want of union; dissension.—**dis-u′nion-ism**, *n.* The doctrine of disunionists.—**dis-u′nion-ist**, *n.* An advocate of disunion; in U. S. politics during the Civil War period, an advocate of the disruption of the U. S.; in English politics, an advocate of the repeal or modification of the Act of Union with Ireland.—**dis-u-nite′** (-ū-nīt′), *v.*; *-nited, -niting.* **I.** *tr.* To sever the union of; separate; disjoin; set at variance, or alienate. **II.** *intr.* To part; fall asunder.—**dis-u′ni-ty** (-ū′ni-ti), *n* Lack of unity; disunion.

dis-use (dis-ūz′), *v. t.*; *-used, -using.* [OF. *desuser.*] To cease to use; discontinue the use or practice of; also, to disaccustom to or wean from some use or practice†; also, to misuse†.—**dis-use′** (-ūs′), *n.* Discontinuance of use or practice; the state of being no longer in use; desuetude.

dis-u-til-i-ty (dis-ū-til′i-ti), *n.* [See *dis-*.] The opposite of utility; the quality of causing inconvenience or harm; injuriousness.—**dis-u′ti-lize** (-ū′ti-līz), *v. t.*; *-lized, -lizing.* To divert from a useful purpose; render useless.

dis-val-ue (dis-val′ū), *v. t.*; *-ued, -uing.* [See *dis-*.] To depreciate; disparage. See Shakspere's "Measure for Measure," v. 1. 221. [Now rare.]

dis-war-ren (dis-wor′en), *v. t.* [See *dis-*.] In *Eng. law*, to deprive (land) of the character of a warren; make common.

di-syl-la-ble (dī-sil′ạ-bl or di-), etc. Same as *dissyllable*, etc.

dis-yoke (dis-yōk′), *v. t.*; *-yoked, -yoking.* [See *dis-*.] To free from or as from a yoke.

di-ta (dē′tạ), *n.* [Philippine.] An apocynaceous tree, *Alstonia scholaris*, of tropical Asia and elsewhere, the bark of which is used medicinally as a tonic and antiperiodic; also, the bark.

ditch (dich), *n.* [ME. *dich*, var. of *dic*, AS. *dīc*, E. *dike.*] A long, narrow hollow made in the earth by digging, as one for draining or irrigating land or one dug round the rampart or wall of a fortification; a trench; hence, any similar hollow or open passage, as a natural channel or waterway; also, a bank or ridge of earth, such as is thrown up in digging a trench (now prov.).—**ditch**, *v.* **I.** *tr.* To dig a ditch or ditches in; drain by or surround with a ditch; also, to throw into or as into a ditch, as a railroad-train. **II.** *intr.* To dig or repair ditches.—**ditch′er,** *n.*—**ditch′=wa″ter,** *n.* Foul water, as found in ditches.

di-the-ism (dī′thē̜-izm), *n.* [Gr. δι-, two, + θεός, god.] Belief in two supreme gods; esp., belief in the existence of two independent antagonistic principles, one good and the other evil.—**di′the-ist,** *n.*—**di-the-is′tic,** *a.*

dith-er (diᴛʜ′ėr), *v. i.* [Var. of *didder.*] To tremble; shiver; quiver; vibrate. [Chiefly prov. Eng.]—**dith′er,** *n.*

di-thi-on-ic (dī-thī-on′ik or dith-i-), *a.* [See *di-*[1] and *thionic.*] In *chem.*, noting or pertaining to an acid, $H_2S_2O_6$, not known in the pure state, but forming recognized salts.

dith-y-ramb (dith′i-ramb or -ram), *n.* [L. *dithyrambus,* < Gr. διθύραμβος; origin unknown.] A Greek choral song of vehement or wild character and usually irregular in form, orig. in honor of Dionysus or Bacchus; hence, any poem or other composition having similar characteristics.—**dith-y-ram′bic** (-ram′bik), *a.* Of, pertaining to, or of the nature of a dithyramb; wildly enthusiastic; wildly irregular in form.

dit-ta-ny (dit′a̜-ni), *n.*; pl. *-nies* (-niz). [OF. *ditan* (F. *dictame*), < L. *dictamnus,* < Gr. δίκταμνος, said to be so called from Mount Dicte in Crete, where it abounded.] A menthaceous plant, *Origanum dictamnus* ('dittany of Crete'), formerly in high repute for its alleged medicinal virtues; also, a rutaceous plant, *Dictamnus albus,* cultivated for its showy flowers; also, a menthaceous plant, *Cunila origanoides,* of North America, bearing clusters of purplish flowers.

dit-tied (dit′id), *p. a.* Composed or sung as a ditty.

dit-to (dit′ō). [It. *ditto* (now *detto*), said, aforesaid, < L. *dictus,* pp. of *dicere,* say.] **I.** *n.*; pl. *dittos* (-ōz). The aforesaid; the same: a term used in accounts, lists, etc., to avoid repetition, often abbreviated *do.,* or expressed by two marks ("). Also (colloq.), a duplicate or copy (as, "Rip's son and heir, who was the *ditto* of himself": Irving's "Sketch-Book," Rip Van Winkle); also, cloth of the same color and material throughout; *pl.,* a suit made of such cloth. **II.** *adv.* As already stated; likewise.—**dit′to,** *v. t.*; *-toed, -toing.* To duplicate; copy.

dit-tog-ra-phy (di-tog′ra̜-fi), *n.* [Gr. διττός, twofold, double: see *-graphy.*] The unintentional repetition of a letter or word, or of a series of letters or words, in writing; also, the resulting passage or reading: opposed to *haplography.*—**dit-to-graph-ic** (dit-ō̜-graf′ik), *a.*

dit-ty (dit′i), *n.*; pl. *ditties* (-iz). [OF. *dite, ditie,* < L. *dictatus,* pp. of *dictare,* pronounce, dictate, compose: see *dictate, v.*] A poem intended to be sung; a song; a short, simple song; also, the words of a song, as distinguished from the music†; hence, theme† or subject†.—**dit′ty,** *v.*; *-tied, -tying.* **I.** *intr.* To sing a ditty. **II.** *tr.* To compose or sing as a ditty.

dit-ty=bag (dit′i-bag), *n.* [Origin obscure.] A bag used by sailors to hold sewing implements and other necessaries.—**dit′ty=box,** *n.* A small box used like a ditty-bag.

di-u-re-sis (dī-ū̜-rē′sis), *n.* [NL., < Gr. διουρεῖν, pass urine, < διά, through, + οὐρεῖν, urinate, < οὖρον, urine.] In *pathol.,* excessive discharge of urine.—**di-u-ret′ic** (-ret′ik). [LL. *diureticus,* < Gr. διουρητικός.] In *med.*: **I.** *a.* Exciting the secretion or discharge of urine, as a medicinal substance. **II.** *n.* A diuretic medicine or agent.

di-ur-nal (dī-ėr′na̜l). [LL. *diurnalis,* < L. *diurnus,* of the day, daily, < *dies,* day: cf. *journal.*] **I.** *a.* Of or pertaining to each day; daily; also, lasting but a day; ephemeral; also, of or belonging to the daytime; active by day, as certain birds and insects; opening by day and closing by night, as certain flowers. **II.** *n.* A diary (archaic); a daily or other newspaper (archaic); a service-book containing the offices for the day hours of prayer; a diurnal bird or insect.—**di-ur′nal-ly,** *adv.*

di-u-tur-nal (dī-ū̜-tėr′na̜l), *a.* [L. *diuturnus,* < *diu,* for a long time, akin to *dies,* day.] Of long duration.—**di-u-tur′ni-ty** (-ni-ti), *n.*

div (d̜ēv), *n.* [Pers. *dīv.*] In *Persian myth.,* an evil spirit; a demon; an evil genius.

di-va (dē′vä), *n.*; pl. *divas,* It. *dive* (-vā). [It., < L. *diva,* goddess: see *divine.*] A distinguished female singer; a prima donna.

di-va-gate (dī′va̜-gāt), *v. i.*; *-gated, -gating.* [LL. *divagatus,* pp. of *divagari,* < L. *di-,* for *dis-,* apart, + *vagari,* wander, < *vagus,* wandering, E. *vague.*] To wander; stray.—**di-va-ga′tion** (-gā′sho̜n), *n.* A wandering or straying; a digression.

di-va-lent (dī-vā′le̜nt or div′a̜-), *a.* [See *di-*[1] and *-valent.*] Same as *bivalent.*

di-van (di-van′), *n.* [Turk. *divān* = Ar. *dīwān,* < Pers. *dīwān.*] A council of state in Turkey and other Oriental countries; any council; also, an Oriental council-chamber, judgment-hall, audience-chamber, or bureau of state; also, a long cushioned seat against a wall, as in Oriental countries; a sofa or couch (commonly pron. dī′van or dī-van′); also, a smoking-room, as in connection with a tobacco-shop (as, "She . . . directed him to the cigar *divan* on the other side of the street": Trollope's "Warden," xvi.); also, a collection of Persian or other Oriental poems, esp. a series by a single author.

di-var-i-cate (dī-var′i-kāt), *v.*; *-cated, -cating.* [L. *divaricatus,* pp. of *divaricare,* < *di-,* for *dis-,* apart, + *varicare,* straddle, < *varus,* bent.] **I.** *tr.* To stretch (the legs, etc.) widely apart; also, to divide into branches. **II.** *intr.* To spread apart; branch; diverge; in *bot.* and *zoöl.,* to branch at a wide angle.—**di-var′i-cate,** *a.* Spread apart; widely divergent; in *bot.* and *zoöl.,* branching at a wide angle.—**di-var′i-cate-ly,** *adv.*—**di-var-i-ca′tion** (-kā′sho̜n), *n.*

dive (dīv), *v.*; pret. *dived* (sometimes *dove*), pp. *dived,* ppr. *diving.* [In form < AS. *dȳfan,* tr., dip, < *dūfan,* intr., dive, sink, but with sense due rather to *dūfan*; ult. akin to E. *dip* and *deep.*] **I.** *intr.* To plunge head first, as into water; plunge deeply; also, to penetrate suddenly into anything, as with the hand; fig., to enter deeply into anything; also, to dart; in *aëronautics,* of an aëroplane, to plunge downward at a greater angle than when gliding. **II.** *tr.* To plunge; also, to plunge into or through (something: rare).—**dive,** *n.* An act of diving; a downward plunge of an aëroplane (see *dive, v. i.*); a sudden dart; also, a low place of resort, as for drinking, gambling, etc.(colloq.).—**dive′=bomb″er,** *n.* A war plane that aims its bombs while on a steep dive.—**div-er** (dī′vėr), *n.* One who or that which dives; one who does work under water in a special dress or armor; any of various birds that habitually dive, as loons, grebes, etc. (see *loon*[2]).

di-verge (di-vėrj′ or dī-), *v.*; *-verged, -verging.* [L. *di-,* for *dis-,* apart, + *vergere,* incline, E. *verge*[2].] **I.** *intr.* To move or lie in different directions from a common point; branch off; hence, to take different courses or a different course; deviate; differ in opinion or character. **II.** *tr.* To cause to diverge.—**di-ver′gence** (-vėr′je̜ns), *n.* The act, fact, or amount of diverging. Also **di-ver′gen-cy.**—**di-ver′gent,** *a.* Diverging; deviating; also, pertaining to divergence.—**di-ver′gent-ly, di-ver′ging-ly,** *adv.*

di-vers (dī′vėrz), *a.* [ME. *divers* (also *diverse*), < OF. F. *divers,* < L. *diversus,* lit. 'turned different ways,' pp. of *divertere*: see *divert.*] Diverse†; also, several or sundry (sometimes used pronominally: as, *divers* of them).

di-verse (di-vėrs′, dī-vėrs′, or dī′vėrs), *a.* [Var. of *divers,* but now associated more directly with L. *diversus.*] Different in kind, form, character, etc.; unlike; also, of various kinds or forms; multiform; also, divers†.—**di-verse′ly,** *adv.*—**di-verse′ness,** *n.*

di-ver-si-fi-ca-tion (di-vėr″si-fi-kā′sho̜n or dī-), *n.* The act of diversifying; diversified state or form.

di-ver-si-form (di-vėr′si-fôrm or dī-), *a.* Diverse or differing in form; of various forms.

di-ver-si-fy (di-vėr′si-fī or dī-), *v. t.*; *-fied, -fying.* [OF. F. *diversifier,* < ML. *diversificare,* < L. *diversus,* diverse, + *facere,* make.] To make diverse, as in form or character; give variety or diversity to; variegate.

di-ver-sion (di-vėr′sho̜n or dī-), *n.* [ML. *diversio(n-),* < L. *divertere*: see *divert.*] The act of diverting or turning aside, as from a course; also, a feint intended to draw off attention from a point aimed at, as in a military attack; also, distraction from business, care, etc.; recreation; entertainment; amusement; a pastime.

di-ver-si-ty (di-vėr′si-ti or dī-), *n.*; pl. *-ties* (-tiz). [OF. *diversite* (F. *diversité*), < L. *diversus*: see *divers, diverse.*] The state or fact of being diverse; difference or unlikeness;

variety or multiformity; also, a point of difference; also, a particular variety.
di-vers-ly (dī′vėrz-li), *adv.* In divers or various ways.
di-vert (di-vėrt′ or dī-), *v.* [OF. F. *divertir*, < L. *divertere*, turn or go different ways, turn aside, separate, < *di-*, for *dis-*, apart, + *vertere*, turn.] **I.** *tr.* To turn aside, or from a path or course; deflect; also, to draw off to a different object, purpose, etc.; also, to distract from serious occupation; entertain or amuse (as, "I *diverted* myself with talking to my parrot": Defoe's "Robinson Crusoe," i. 8). **II.** *intr.* To turn aside; deviate.—**di-vert′er,** *n.*—**di-vert′i-ble,** *a.* Capable of being diverted.
di-ver-tic-u-lum (dī-vėr-tik′ū-lum), *n.*; pl. *-la* (-lä). [L. *diverticulum*, for *deverticulum*, < *devertere*, turn aside, < *de*, from, + *vertere*, turn.] In *anat.*, a blind tubular sac or process, branching off from a canal or cavity.—**di-ver-tic′u-lar** (-lär), *a.*
di-ver-ti-men-to (dē-ver-tē-men′tō), *n.*; pl. *-ti* (-tē). [It.] Any of various pieces of music, as a potpourri or fantasia or an episode in a fugue.
di-vert-ing (di-vėr′ting or dī-), *p. a.* That diverts; entertaining; amusing.—**di-vert′ing-ly,** *adv.*
di-ver-tise-ment (di-vėr′tiz-ment), *n.* [F. *divertissement.*] Diversion; amusement; also, an entertainment; a divertissement (ballet, etc.). [Archaic.]
di-ver-tisse-ment (dē-ver-tēs-mon), *n.* [F., < *divertir*: see *divert.*] A diversion or entertainment; esp., a short ballet or other performance given between or in the course of acts or longer pieces; also, a divertimento.
di-ver-tive (di-vėr′tiv or dī-), *a.* Serving to divert; amusing.
Di-ves (dī′vēz), *n.* [L. *dives*, rich (as applied in the Vulgate).] The rich man of the parable in Luke, xvi. 19–31: hence used of any rich man.
di-vest (di-vest′ or dī-), *v. t.* [Var. of *devest*, conformed to the equivalent ML. *divestire.*] To strip of clothing, etc.; disrobe; fig., to strip or deprive of anything; dispossess; rid; also, to put off or lay aside (clothing, etc.); in *law*, to take away or alienate (property, etc.).—**di-vest′i-ble,** *a.* Capable of being divested.—**di-ves′ti-ture** (-ves′ti-tūr), *n.* The act of divesting, or the state of being divested. Also **di-vest′ment.**
di-vette (dē-vet), *n.* [F.] A lesser diva; a female singer of the music-halls, the musical comedy stage, or the like.
di-vid-a-ble (di-vī′da-bl), *a.* Capable of being divided.
di-vide (di-vīd′), *v.*; *-vided, -viding.* [L. *dividere* (pp. *divisus*), force asunder, cleave, part, distribute, < *di-*, for *dis-*, apart, + *-videre*, perhaps akin to Skt. *vidh-*, bore through, pierce.] **I.** *tr.* To separate into parts; also, to pass through or across; also, to mark off or arrange in parts; graduate (a rule, etc.); also, to separate (a legislature, etc.) into two groups in ascertaining the vote on a question; also, to separate or part from each other or from something else; sunder; cut off; also, to distinguish or discriminate; also, to distinguish the kinds of; classify; also, to separate in opinion or feeling; cause to disagree; perplex, as by conflicting opinions; also, to deal out in parts; apportion; distribute; share; in *math.*, to separate into equal parts by the process of division; also, to be a divisor of, without a remainder. **II.** *intr.* To make separation; also, to become divided or separated; undergo division; part; become disunited; differ in opinion or feeling; also, to vote by separating into two groups.—**di-vide′,** *n.* The act of dividing; also, a ridge of land dividing two drainage-areas (as, the Great *Divide*, the Rocky Mountain range); a watershed.—**di-vid′ed** (-vī′ded), *p. a.* Separated into or marked off in parts (as, a *divided* skirt, one divided into two parts, so as to resemble a pair of exceedingly loose trousers); also, separated or sundered; separate; also, disunited in opinion or feeling; also, distributed among a number of things or persons; in *bot.*, of a leaf, cut into distinct portions by incisions which extend to the midrib or the base.—**di-vid′ed-ly,** *adv.*—**di-vid′ed-ness,** *n.*
div-i-dend (div′i-dend), *n.* [L. *dividendum*, a thing to be divided, neut. gerundive of *dividere*: see *divide.*] A sum to be divided; a sum to be divided as profit among shareholders, etc.; a sum out of an insolvent estate to be divided among the creditors; also, a share of anything divided, esp. an individual share of divided profits; in *math.*, a number or quantity to be divided by another number or quantity (the divisor).
di-vid-er (di-vī′dėr), *n.* One who or that which divides; *pl.*, a pair of compasses as used for dividing lines, measuring, etc.
div-i=div-i (div′i-div′i), *n.* [Carib.] A shrub or small tree, *Cæsalpinia coriaria*, of tropical America, the astringent pods of which are much used in tanning and dyeing; also, the pods; also, the related species *C. tinctoria*, or its pods.

Pods of Divi-divi (*Cæsalpinia coriaria*).

di-vid-u-al (di-vid′ū-al), *a.* [L. *dividuus*, < *dividere*: see *divide.*] Divisible or divided; also, separate or distinct; also, distributed or shared (as, "The moon . . . her reign With thousand lesser lights *dividual* holds": Milton's "Paradise Lost," vii. 382).—**di-vid′u-al-ly,** *adv.*
di-vin-a-ble (di-vī′na-bl), *a.* Capable of being divined.
div-i-na-tion (div-i-nā′shon), *n.* [L. *divinatio(n-).*] The act of divining; the discovering of what is obscure or the foretelling of future events, as by supernatural means; augury; a prophecy; also, instinctive prevision; conjecture.
div-i-na-tor (div′i-nā-tor), *n.* [LL.] One who divines, or practises divination.—**di-vin-a-to-ry** (di-vin′a-tō-ri), *a.* Pertaining to a diviner or to divination.
di-vine (di-vīn′). [OF. *devin, divin*, F. *divin* (as n., OF. F. *devin*, soothsayer), < L. *divinus*, divine, divinely inspired, prophetic (as n., soothsayer, ML. theologian), < *dīvus*, divine (as n., *divus*, god, fem. *diva*, goddess); akin to *deus*, god: see *deity.*] **I.** *a.*; compar. *diviner*, superl. *divinest.* Of or pertaining to a god, esp. the Supreme Being; also, addressed or appropriated to God; religious; sacred; also, proceeding from God (as, the *divine* right of kings, the right to rule derived directly from God, not from the consent of the people, claimed for legitimate kings according to a doctrine now exploded); also, being a god, or God; godlike; characteristic of or befitting deity; heavenly; celestial; hence, of superhuman or surpassing excellence; also, pertaining to divinity or theology. **II.** *n.* A soothsayer†; also, one versed in divinity; a theologian; a priest or clergyman (as, "It is a good *divine* that follows his own instructions": Shakspere's "Merchant of Venice," i. 2. 16).—**di-vine′,** *v.*; *-vined, -vining.* [OF. F. *deviner*, < L. *divinare*, < *divinus.*] **I.** *tr.* To discover or declare (something obscure or future), as by supernatural means; prophesy; also, to perceive by intuition or insight; conjecture; also, to portend (obs. or archaic); also, to make divine† (as, "She . . . seem'd of Angels race, Living on earth like Angell new *divinde*": Spenser's "Daphnaïda," 214). **II.** *intr.* To use or practise divination; prophesy; also, to have perception by intuition or insight; conjecture.—**di-vine′ly,** *adv.*—**di-vine′ness,** *n.*—**di-vin′er** (-vī′nėr), *n.* One who divines; a soothsayer; a prophet; a conjecturer.—**di-vin′er-ess,** *n.* [OF. F. *devineresse.*] A female diviner or soothsayer.
div-ing=bee-tle (dī′ving-bē″tl), *n.* Any of various predaceous coleopterous beetles of the family *Dytiscidæ*, that live habitually in water, and frequently dive to the bottom.
div-ing=bell (dī′ving-bel), *n.* A heavy vessel, orig. bell-shaped, having the bottom open, and filled with air, in which persons may descend and work below the surface of the water.

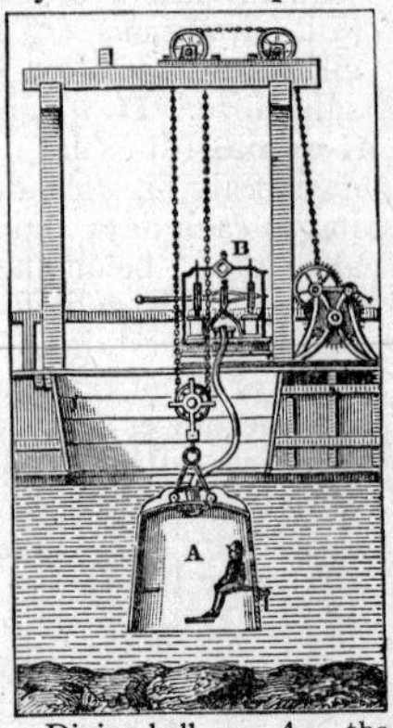

Diving-bell. — *A*, the bell; *B*, pump for introducing fresh air.

di-vin-ing=rod (di-vī′ning-rod), *n.* A rod used in divining; esp., a forked stick, commonly of hazel, supposed to be useful in locating spots where water, metal, etc., may be found underground; a dowsing-rod.
di-vin-i-ty (di-vin′i-ti), *n.*; pl. *-ties* (-tiz). [OF. *devinite* (F. *divinité*), < L. *divinitas.*] The quality of being divine; divine nature; deity;

godhood; also, a divine being, or god (as, "There's a *divinity* that shapes our ends, Rough-hew them how we will": Shakspere's "Hamlet," v. 2. 10); [*cap.*] the Deity; fig. [*l. c.*], an object of adoration; also, godlike character; supreme excellence; also, the science of divine things; theology.—**divinity circuit,** a flexible leather bookbinding with projecting flaps which inclose the edges of the book: much used for binding Bibles, etc.

div-i-nize (div′i-nīz), *v. t.*; *-nized, -nizing.* [F. *diviniser,* < *divin:* see *divine, a.*] To make divine; deify.—**div″i-ni-za′tion** (-ni-zā′shọn), *n.*

di-vis-i-ble (di-viz′i-bl), *a.* [LL. *divisibilis.*] Capable of being divided.—**di-vis-i-bil′i-ty** (-bil′i-ti), **di-vis′i-ble-ness,** *n.*—**di-vis′i-bly,** *adv.*

di-vi-sion (di-vizh′ọn), *n.* [L. *divisio(n-).*] The act of dividing, or the state of being divided; partition; a marking off or arranging in parts; the separation of a legislature, etc., into two groups, in taking a vote; the execution of a rapid and florid melodic passage (conceived as the elaboration of a series of long tones by the division of each tone into several short ones)†, or such a passage itself† (see Shakspere's "1 Henry IV.," iii. 1. 211); a separation from each other or from something else; analysis or classification; separation by difference of opinion or feeling; apportionment, distribution, or sharing; disposition† or arrangement† (see Shakspere's "Othello," i. 1. 23); also, something that divides; a dividing line or mark; a partition; also, one of the parts into which a thing is divided; a section; one of the parts into which a country or the like is divided for political, administrative, judicial, military, or other purposes; a unit of organization in an army or fleet; one of the main subdivisions of an army, next in importance below an army-corps, as one comprising two or three brigades of infantry and a certain amount of cavalry, artillery, etc.; in *math.*, the act or process of dividing a number or quantity into equal parts; the process or method of finding how many times one number or quantity (the divisor) is contained in another (the dividend).—**di-vi′sion-al, di-vi′sion-a-ry** (-ạ-ri), *a.*

di-vi-sive (di-vī′siv), *a.* Serving or tending to divide.—**di-vi′sive-ly,** *adv.*—**di-vi′sive-ness,** *n.*

di-vi-sor (di-vī′zọr), *n.* [L., a divider.] In *math.*, a number or quantity by which another number or quantity (the dividend) is divided; also, a number or quantity contained in another number or quantity a certain number of times, without a remainder.

di-vorce (di-vôrs′), *n.* [OF. F. *divorce,* < L. *divortium,* < *divortere, divertere,* separate: see *divert.*] A legal dissolution of the marriage relation; in the strictest sense, an absolute legal dissolution of the marriage bond ('absolute divorce'), but in a broader sense including also a judicial separation of man and wife, or termination of cohabitation, without dissolution of the marriage bond ('limited divorce' or 'divorce from bed and board'); any formal separation of man and wife according to established custom, as among uncivilized tribes; a judicial declaration of the nullity of a supposed marriage; hence, a complete separation of any kind (as, the *divorce* of church and state).—**di-vorce′,** *v. t.*; *-vorced, -vorcing.* [OF. F. *divorcer.*] To separate by divorce; put away (one's husband or wife) by divorce; fig., to separate; cut off (as, "a priest and a soldier, two classes of men circumstantially *divorced* from the kind and homely ties of life": Stevenson's "Travels with a Donkey," iii. 3); put away; repudiate.—**di-vor-cé** (dē-vôr-sā), *n.* [F., prop. pp. of *divorcer.*] A divorced man.—**di-vorce′a-ble,** *a.* That may be divorced.—**di-vor-cee** (di-vôr-sē′), *n.* [See *-ee.*] A divorced person.—**di-vor-cée** (dē-vôr-sā), *n.* [F., fem. of *divorcé.*] A divorced woman.—**di-vorce′ment,** *n.* The act of divorcing; divorce. See Deut. xxiv. 1.—**di-vor′cer,** *n.*

div-ot (div′ọt), *n.* [Origin obscure.] A piece of turf, or a sod, as for covering a cottage (chiefly Sc.); in *golf,* a piece of turf cut out with a club in making a stroke.

di-vul-gate (di-vul′gāt or dī-), *v. t.*; *-gated, -gating.* [L. *divulgatus,* pp. of *divulgare:* see *divulge.*] To make publicly known; publish abroad.—**div-ul-ga-tion** (div-ul-gā′shọn), *n.* [LL. *divulgatio(n-).*] The act of divulgating, or the state of being divulgated.—**di-vul′ga-to-ry** (-gạ-tō-ri), *a.*

di-vulge (di-vulj′ or dī-), *v.*; *-vulged, -vulging.* [L. *divulgare,* < *di-,* for *dis-,* apart, + *vulgare,* spread among the multitude: see *vulgate.*] **I.** *tr.* To make publicly known†; publish†; also, to disclose or reveal (something private, secret, or previously unknown: as, "I *divulged* the news of our misfortune," Goldsmith's "Vicar of Wakefield," ii.). **II.** *intr.* To become known.—**di-vulge′ment, di-vul′gence** (-vul′jẹns), *n.*—**di-vul′ger,** *n.*

di-vul-sion (dī-vul′shọn), *n.* [L. *divulsio(n-),* < *divellere,* tear asunder, < *di-,* for *dis-,* apart, + *vellere,* pluck.] A tearing asunder; violent separation.—**di-vul′sive,** *a.*

di-wan, de-wan (dẹ-wän′), *n.* [Ar. and Pers. *dīwān:* see *divan.*] A divan; also, in India, any of certain officials or servants, as a minister of finance formerly appointed under Mohammedan governments, a chief minister of a native state, a native steward of a business house, etc.

Dix-ie[1] (dik′si), *n.* [Origin uncertain.] A popular name for the Southern States of the U. S. (also called *Dixie's Land*); also, any of several songs with this name, esp. one by D. D. Emmett (1859) which became a popular Confederate war-song.

dix-ie[2] (dik′si), *n.* [Of East Indian origin.] In British army use, a pot or kettle used in field service.

dix-it (dik′sit), *n.* [L., 'he has said.'] An utterance or statement.

diz-en (diz′n or dī′zn), *v. t.* [Prob. akin to *dis-* in *distaff.*] To put flax, etc., on (a distaff) for spinning†; also, to deck with clothes or finery; bedizen.—**diz′en-ment,** *n.*

diz-zy (diz′i), *a.*; compar. *dizzier,* superl. *dizziest.* [AS. *dysig,* foolish, = MLG. *dusich,* stupefied, dizzy.] Foolish or stupid (now prov. Eng.); also, affected with or causing a sensation of whirling, with tendency to fall; giddy; vertiginous; fig., unsteady; thoughtless.—**diz′zi-ly,** *adv.*—**diz′zi-ness,** *n.*—**diz′zy,** *v. t.*; *-zied, -zying.* To make dizzy.

do[1] (dö), *v.*; pres. 1 *do,* 2 *doest* or *dost,* 3 *does, doeth,* or *doth,* pl. *do*; pret. *did*; pp. *done*; ppr. *doing.* [AS. *dōn* (pret. *dyde*) = D. *doen* = G. *thun,* do; akin to L. *-dere,* Gr. τιθέναι, Skt. *dhā-,* put.] **I.** *tr.* To put (archaic: as, to *do* one to death); make† or have† (some one do something); be the cause of (good, harm, credit, etc.); bring about; effect; perform (acts, duty, penance, a problem, a part, one's best, etc.); render (homage, justice, etc.); execute (a piece or amount of work, etc.); accomplish; finish; in a very general and often very vague sense, to deal with (anything) as the case may require (as, to *do* (dress) the hair, *do* (cook) meat, *do* (wash) the dishes; to *do* a book, as author, reviser, translator, student, etc.; to *do* a town in sight-seeing; please *do* my things next); in slang use, to cheat or swindle (often with *out of*). Used in various phrases: as, to *do* away (now, intransitively, followed by *with*) (to put an end to; abolish); to *do* over (to do again; renovate); to *do* up (to wrap and tie up; comb out and pin up; renovate; launder); to have nothing to *do* (no connection or concern) with a person or thing; what to *do* with a thing (how to deal with or use it). **II.** *intr.* To act, esp. effectively; behave or proceed (*wisely,* etc.); deal (as, to *do* well by a man); also, to get along, or fare; manage (*with, without,* etc.); be as to health (as, how do you *do?*); also, to finish (only in the perfect tenses, with *have* or *be* as auxiliary, and often in the expression 'have done' ('cease!') with the effect of a present imperative); also, to accomplish defeat, ruin, death, etc. (*for*); also, to serve or be satisfactory, as for the purpose; suffice, or be enough. **III.** *auxiliary.* Used without special meaning in interrogative, negative, and inverted constructions, in imperatives with *thou* or *you* expressed, and occasionally as a metrical expedient in verse; also used to lend emphasis to a principal verb. **IV.** *substitute.* Used to avoid repetition of a verb or full verb-expression: as, I think as you *do*; make your application when we *do.*—**do**[1], *n.* Doing, action, or work (now prov. Eng.); ado or to-do (now prov. Eng.); a performance, affair, or festivity (prov. Eng.); a swindle (slang).

do[2] (dō), *n.* In *music,* the syllable used for the first tone or key-note of the scale (C, in the major scale of C), and sometimes for the tone C. Cf. *ut,* and see *sol-fa.*

do-a-ble (dö′ạ-bl), *a.* That may be done.

doat (dōt), etc. See *dote,* etc.

dob-bie (dob′i), *n.* See *dobby.*
Dob-bin (dob′in), *n.* [Var. of *Robin*, for *Robert*, man's name.] A name for a horse, esp. a quiet, plodding horse for farm work, family use, etc.; [*l. c.*] a horse of this kind.
dob-by, dob-bie (dob′i), *n.*; pl. *dobbies* (-iz). [Cf. *Dobbin.*] A simpleton or dunce; also, a sprite or goblin (as, "He . . . in the phrase of his brother Wilfred, needed not to care 'for ghaist or . . . devil or *dobbie*'": Scott's "Rob Roy," xiv.). [Prov.]
do-blon (dō-blōn′), *n.* [Sp. *doblón.*] A doubloon.
do-bra (dō′brạ), *n.* [Pg.] Any of several former Portu-

Obverse. Reverse.
Dobra of John V., King of Portugal, 1732. — British Museum.

guese coins, esp. a gold coin first issued by King John V. and having twice the value of the Johannes.
dob-son (dob′sọn), *n.* [Origin obscure.] A hellgrammite; also, the larva of any of various other insects of the same family (*Sialidæ*).
do-by (dō′bi), *n.*; pl. *-bies* (-biz). Corruption of *adobe.*
do-cent (dō′sent, G. dō-tsent′), *n.* Same as *privatdocent.* —**do′cent-ship,** *n.*
doch-mi-us (dok′mi-us), *n.*; pl. *-mii* (-mi-ī). [L., < Gr. δόχμιος.] In *anc. pros.*, a foot of five syllables, typically having the first and fourth short and the rest long.—**doch′-mi-ac** (-ak), *a.* and *n.*
do-cile (dos′il, Brit. also dō′sīl), *a.* [L. *docilis*, < *docere*, teach.] Apt to learn; teachable; hence, amenable to training or discipline; also, of things, easily managed or handled; tractable.—**do′cile-ly,** *adv.*—**do-cil-i-ty** (dọ-sil′i-ti), *n.* The quality of being docile; teachableness; amenableness to training or discipline; tractableness.
do-ci-ma-sy (dos′i-mạ-si), *n.* [Gr. δοκιμασία, < δοκιμάζειν, assay, test, < δόκιμος, assayed, tested, approved, < δέχεσθαι, take, receive.] A judicial inquiry into the character, etc., of candidates for office, citizenship, etc., among the ancient Greeks; also, the process or art of ascertaining something by test, as the nature or quality of metals or drugs, or whether a child was born alive.—**do-ci-mas-tic** (dos-i-mas′tik), *a.*
dock[1] (dok), *n.* [AS. *docce.*] Any of various plants of the polygonaceous genus *Rumex*, as *R. obtusifolius* ('bitter dock') or *R. acetosa* ('sour dock'), mostly troublesome weeds with long tap-roots; also, any of various other plants, mostly coarse weeds.
dock[2] (dok), *n.* [ME. *dok*: cf. Icel. *dockr.*] The solid or fleshy part of an animal's tail, as distinguished from the hair; the part of a tail left after cutting or clipping; also, the act of docking; a cutting off or reduction.—**dock**[2], *v. t.* To cut short the tail of; cut short in any part; also, to deduct from the wages of; also, to cut off the end of, as a tail; cut off or deduct a part from (as, "Came, with a month's leave . . . to the sea; For which his gains were *dock'd*": Tennyson's "Sea Dreams," 7); deprive (*of*); also, to cut off or remove.
dock[3] (dok), *n.* [= D. *dok*; origin uncertain.] An inclosed water-space communicating by means of gates with a stream or harbor, used for keeping a vessel afloat at the level of high tide to facilitate loading or unloading ('wet dock'), or for the reception of a vessel while being repaired (cf. *dry-dock*); a floating structure ('floating dock') which may be partially submerged to permit a vessel to enter, and then raised to lift the vessel out of the water for repairs, etc., as in a dry-dock; also, any artificial basin or inlet for a vessel, esp. the space or waterway between two piers or wharves, as for receiving a ship while in port; such a waterway, inclosed or open, together with the surrounding piers, wharves, etc.; also, a wharf.—**dock**[3], *v.* **I.** *tr.* To bring into a dock; lay up in a dock; also, to provide with docks. **II.** *intr.* To come or go into a dock.

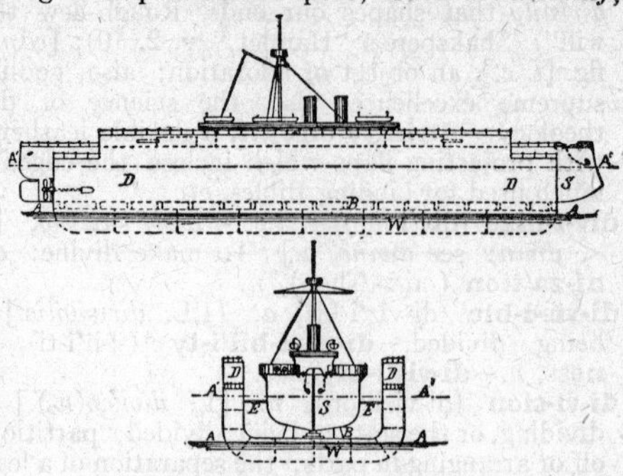

Side and End Elevations of Floating Dock.
A, A, water-line; *A′, A′*, immersed water-line for taking in ships; *B*, blocks for supporting ships; *D, D*, dock; *E, E*, shores for side support; *S*, ship raised on dock; *W*, water-tight compartments.

dock[4] (dok), *n.* [Cf. Flem. *dok*, cage.] The place in a court-room where a prisoner is placed during trial.
dock-age[1] (dok′āj), *n.* [See *dock*[2], *v.*] Curtailment; deduction, as from wages.
dock-age[2] (dok′āj), *n.* [See *dock*[3], *n.* and *v.*] Docking accommodations; a charge for the use of a dock; the act of docking a vessel.
dock-er[1] (dok′ėr), *n.* [See *dock*[2], *v.*] One who or that which docks, cuts short, or cuts off.
dock-er[2] (dok′ėr), *n.* [See *dock*[3], *n.*] A dock laborer.
dock-et (dok′et), *n.* [Appar. < *dock*[2], *v.*] An abridgment, abstract, or digest; an official memorandum or entry of proceedings in a legal cause, or a register of such entries; a list of causes in court for trial, or of the names of the parties who have causes pending; any similar list; also, a writing on a letter or document, stating its contents; any statement of particulars attached to a package, etc.; a label; a ticket.—**dock′et,** *v. t.*; *-eted, -eting.* To make an abstract or entry of in a docket; also, indorse (a letter, etc.) with a memorandum, as of contents; mark with a ticket.
dock-mack-ie (dok′mak-i), *n.* [N. Amer. Ind.] A caprifoliaceous shrub, *Viburnum acerifolium*, of North America, with cymes of yellowish-white flowers, and ovoid, almost black berries.
dock=wal-lop-er (dok′wol″ọp-ėr), *n.* A casual laborer about docks or wharves. [Slang.]—**dock′=wal″lop-ing,** *n.*
dock-yard (dok′yärd), *n.* An inclosure containing docks, shops, warehouses, etc., where ships are repaired, fitted out, and built; in England, a navy-yard.
doc-tor (dok′tọr), *n.* [OF. *doctor* (F. *docteur*), < L. *doctor*, teacher, < *docere*, teach.] A teacher (archaic); also, a man of great learning (as, "Who shall decide, when *doctors* disagree?" Pope's "Moral Essays," iii. 1); a sage; also, a person who has received the highest degree conferred by a faculty of a university; the academic title possessed by such a person, orig. implying qualification to teach; also, a person licensed to practise medicine, or some branch of medicine; a physician; a surgeon; also, a cook, as on shipboard (colloq.); also, any of various mechanical contrivances for particular purposes; a donkey-engine; a kind of artificial fly for angling; a false or loaded die (old slang). —**doc′tor,** *v.*; *-tored, -toring.* **I.** *tr.* To confer the degree of doctor upon; also, to treat medicinally; repair or mend (colloq.); also, to tamper with; falsify; adulterate. **II.** *intr.* To practise medicine; also, to take medicine; receive medical treatment.—**doc′tor-al,** *a.*—**doc′tor-ate** (-āt), *n.* The degree of doctor.—**doc′tor-ess, doc′tress,** *n.* A female doctor.—**doc′tor-ship,** *n.*
doc-tri-naire (dok-tri-nãr′), *n.* [F.] One of a political party that arose in France soon after 1815, opposed to absolutism and to revolutionary ideas, and regarded as devoted more to abstract doctrines and theories than to practical politics; hence, one who tries to apply some doctrine or theory without a sufficient regard to practical considerations; an impractical theorist.—**doc-tri-nair′ism,** *n.*
doc-tri-nal (dok′tri-nạl), *a.* Of, pertaining to, or concerned with doctrine.—**doc′tri-nal-ly,** *adv.*

doc-trine (dok′trin), *n.* [OF. F. *doctrine*, < L. *doctrina*, teaching, learning, < *doctor*: see *doctor*.] The act of teaching†; a lesson†; also, that which is taught; teachings collectively; a body or system of teachings relating to a particular subject; a system of beliefs advocated; a particular principle taught or advocated (as, the Monroe *doctrine*: see *Monroe doctrine*); a tenet or dogma.

doc-u-ment (dok′ū-mȩnt), *n.* [OF. F. *document*, < L. *documentum*, lesson, example, ML. official paper, < L. *docere*, teach.] A lesson†; teaching†; also, evidence† or proof†; also, a written or printed paper furnishing information or evidence; a legal or official paper; hence, any object, as a monument or a coin, furnishing information or evidence.—**doc′u-ment** (-ment), *v. t.* To instruct†; also, to support by documentary evidence; also, to furnish with documents, evidence, or the like.—**doc-u-men′tal** (-men′tạl), *a.* Documentary.—**doc-u-men′ta-ry** (-tạ-ri), *a.* Pertaining to, consisting of, or derived from documents.—**doc″u-men-ta′tion** (-tā′shọn), *n.* Instruction†; also, the use of documentary evidence; also, a furnishing with documents.

dod-der[1] (dod′ėr), *n.* [ME. *doder* = MLG. *doder* = G. *dotter*.] Any of the leafless parasitic plants comprising the genus *Cuscuta*, with yellowish, reddish, or white thread-like stems that twine about clover, flax, etc.

Lesser Dodder (*Cuscuta epithymum*).

dod-der[2] (dod′ėr), *v. i.* [Cf. ME. *dadir*, shiver, and E. *didder*, *dither*.] To shake; tremble; totter.

dod-dered (dod′ėrd), *a.* [Cf. ME. *doddyd*, polled, as trees.] Having lost the branches through age or decay, as an oak; also, infirm; feeble.

dod-der-ing (dod′ėr-ing), *p. a.* That dodders; shaking; tottering; senile.

dodeca-. Form of Gr. δώδεκα, twelve, used in combination.—**do-dec-a-gon** (dō-dek′ạ-gon), *n.* [Gr. δωδεκάγωνον: see *-gon*.] A plane figure having twelve angles and twelve sides.—**do-de-cag′o-nal** (-de-kag′ō-nạl), *a.*—**do″dec-a-he′dron** (-hē′drọn), *n.*; pl. *-drons* or *-dra* (-drạ̈). [Gr. δωδεκάεδρον: see *-hedron*.] A solid figure having twelve faces.—**do″dec-a-he′dral,** *a.*—**do′dec-a-style** (-stīl). [+ *-style*.] In *arch.*: **I.** *a.* Having twelve columns in front, as a temple or portico. **II.** *n.* A dodecastyle structure.—**do″dec-a-syl′la-ble** (-sil′ạ-bl), *n.* A verse or a word of twelve syllables.—**do″dec-a-syl-lab′ic** (-si-lab′ik), *a.*

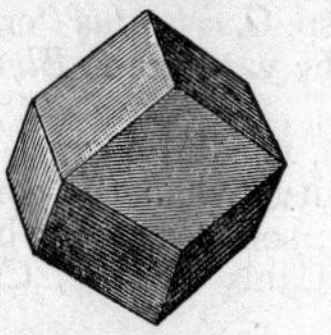
Rhombic Dodecahedron.

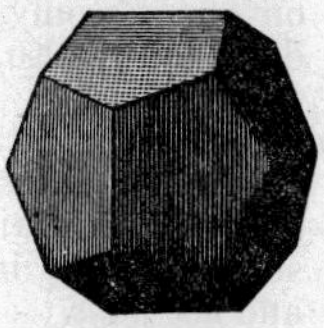
Pentagonal Dodecahedron.

dodge (doj), *v.*; *dodged*, *dodging*. [Origin uncertain.] **I.** *intr.* To move back and forth or to and fro; move aside or change position suddenly, as to avoid a blow or to get behind something; hence, to use evasive methods; prevaricate. **II.** *tr.* To elude by a sudden shift of position or by strategy; hence, to deal indirectly or evasively with; trifle with; also, to follow stealthily; dog; also, to move or drive about.—**dodge,** *n.* An act of dodging; a spring aside; a shifty trick; an ingenious expedient or contrivance (colloq.).—**dodg′er,** *n.* One who dodges; a shifty person; a small handbill (U. S.); a corn-dodger (southern U. S.: as, "corn-cake, in all its varieties of hoe-cake, *dodgers*, muffins, and other species," Mrs. Stowe's "Uncle Tom's Cabin," iv.).

Dodo. — From a painting in the Belvedere, Vienna.

do-do (dō′dō), *n.*; pl. *-dos* or *-does* (-dōz). [Pg. *doudo*, *doido*, foolish, silly.] A clumsy flightless bird, *Didus ineptus*, about the size of a swan, formerly inhabiting the island of Mauritius but extinct since the advent of European settlers; also (colloq.), one hopelessly behind the times; an old fogy.

Do-do-næ-an, Do-do-ne-an (dō-dọ-nē′ạn), *a.* [L. *Dodonæus*, < Gr. Δωδωναῖος.] Of or pertaining to Dodona, an ancient town of Epirus, famed for a sanctuary and oracle of Zeus located there in a grove of oaks.

doe (dō), *n.* [AS. *dā*.] The female of the deer, esp. of the fallow-deer; also, the female of the antelope, the rabbit, and other animals.

Doe of the Virginia Deer (*Cariacus virginianus*).

do-er (dö′ėr), *n.* One who or that which does something; a performer; an actor; one who acts for another (chiefly Sc.).

does (duz). Third person sing. pres. ind. of *do*[1].

doe-skin (dō′skin), *n.* The skin of a doe; leather made from this; also, a smoothly finished, closely woven, finely twilled woolen cloth, used esp. for men's clothes.

do-est, do-eth (dö′est, -eth). Second and third persons sing. pres. ind., respectively, of *do*[1]: now only in poetic or solemn use.

doff (dof), *v. t.* [For *do off*: cf. *don*[1].] To put or take off, as dress; remove (the hat) in salutation; hence, to throw off; lay aside; get rid of.—**doff′er,** *n.*

dog (dog or dôg), *n.* [AS. *docga*; origin unknown.] A domesticated carnivorous quadruped of many varieties, the so-called *Canis familiaris*; any animal belonging to the same family (*Canidæ*), which includes the wolves, jackals, foxes, etc.; the male of such an animal (cf. *bitch*); also, any of various animals allied to or suggesting the dog; a prairie-dog; also, a dogfish; also, a despicable fellow; a fellow in general (as, a gay *dog*); [*cap.*] either of two constellations, Canis Major ('Great Dog') and Canis Minor ('Little Dog'), situated near Orion; also, either of the dog-stars; [*l. c.*] an andiron; also, any of various mechanical devices, as for gripping or holding something.—**dog in the manger,** a person who, like the dog in the fable, churlishly keeps possession of something which is of no particular use to himself and which thus cannot be used by others.—**to go to the dogs,** to go to ruin.—**dog,** *v. t.*; *dogged*, *dogging*. To follow or track like a dog, esp. with hostile intent (as, "The avenger would *dog* their footsteps everywhere": Parkman's "Oregon Trail," xi.); hound; also, to drive or chase with a dog or dogs; also, to fasten with a mechanical dog.

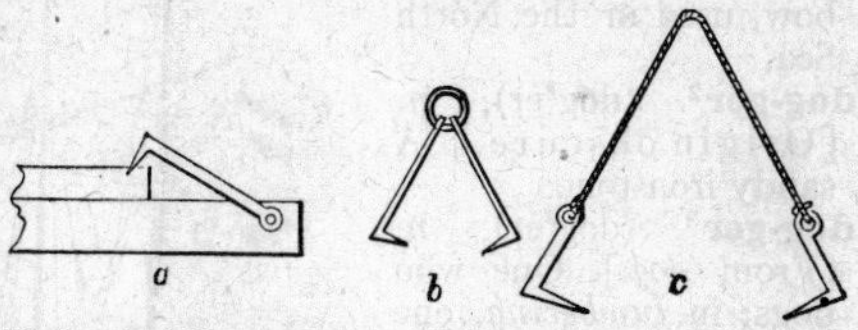

Mechanical Dogs. — *a*, bench-dog; *b*, ring-dogs or span-dogs; *c*, sling-dogs.

do-ga-na (dō-gä′nä), *n.* [It., = F. *douane*: see *douane*.] In Italian use, a custom-house.

dog=ape (dog′āp), *n.* A baboon, or some similar monkey.

do-gate (dō′gāt), *n.* The office or dignity of a doge.

dog-bane (dog′bān), *n.* Any plant of the genus *Apocynum*, esp. *A. androsæmifolium*, a perennial herb abounding in an acrid milky juice and having an intensely bitter root that has been used in medicine.

dog-ber-ry (dog′ber″i), *n.*; pl. *-berries* (-iz). The berry or fruit of any of various plants, as the European dogwood (*Cornus sanguinea*), the chokeberry (*Aronia arbutifolia*), or the mountain-ash (*Sorbus americana*); also, the plant itself.

dog=cart (dog′kärt), *n.* A cart drawn by dogs; a light carriage with a box for sportsmen's dogs; a light vehicle for ordinary driving, with two transverse seats back to back.

dog=catch-er (dog′kach″ėr), *n.* An official, as of a town, charged with seizing stray or unlicensed dogs.

dog=col-lar (dog′kol″är), *n.* A collar for a dog; also, a close-fitting band-like collar worn by persons; a close-fitting ornamental band made of beads, jewels, velvet, or other material, worn about the neck by women.

dog=days (dog′dāz), *n. pl.* A sultry part of the summer supposed to occur about the time of the heliacal rising of one or the other of the dog-stars: now often reckoned from July 3 to Aug. 11.

doge (dōj), *n.* [It. (Venetian) *doge*, < L. *dux* (*duc-*), leader, E. *duke*.] The chief magistrate of the old republics of Venice and Genoa.

Doge of Venice.

dog=ear (dog′ēr), *n.* and *v.* Same as *dog's-ear*.

doge-ship (dōj′ship), *n.* The office or magistracy of a doge.

dog=faced (dog′fāst), *a.* Having a face like that of a dog.

dog=fen-nel (dog′fen″ẹl), *n.* The mayweed; also, the eupatorium, *E. capillifolium*.

dog=fight (dog′fīt), *n.* A violent engagement of war planes at close quarters.

dog-fish (dog′fish), *n.* Any of various small sharks, as *Squalus acanthias*, which is common on both coasts of the northern Atlantic and destructive to food-fishes; any of various other fishes.

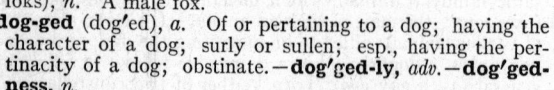

Dogfish (*Squalus acanthias*).

dog=fox (dog′foks), *n.* A male fox.

dog-ged (dog′ed), *a.* Of or pertaining to a dog; having the character of a dog; surly or sullen; esp., having the pertinacity of a dog; obstinate.—**dog′ged-ly,** *adv.*—**dog′ged-ness,** *n.*

dog-ger[1] (dog′ėr), *n.* [ME.: cf. D. *dogger*, Icel. *dugga*.] A two-masted Dutch fishing-vessel with a blunt bow, used in the North Sea.

Dutch Dogger.

dog-ger[2] (dog′ėr), *n.* [Origin obscure.] A sandy ironstone.

dog-ger[3] (dog′ėr), *n.* [From *dog*.] One who dogs; in *lumbering*, one who attaches dogs or hooks to a log when it is to be drawn by means of a cable.

dog-ger-el (dog′ẹ-rel). [ME. *dogerel*; perhaps < *dog*.] **I.** *a.* Of verse, comic or burlesque, and usually loose or irregular in measure; hence, more generally, rude, crude, or poor: as, "singing . . . a *doggerel* ballad—half Flemish, half German—in which their wrongs were expressed with uncouth vigor" (Motley's "Dutch Republic," vi. 1). **II.** *n.* Doggerel verse; a doggerel poem.—**dog′ger-el-ist,** *n.* A writer of doggerel.—**dog′ger-el-ize,** *v. i.* or *t.*; *-ized*, *-izing*. To write, or turn into, doggerel.

dog-ger-y (dog′ėr-i), *n.*; pl. *-ies* (-iz). Doggish behavior or conduct; mean or mischievous action; also, dogs collectively; hence, canaille; rabble.

dog-gish (dog′ish), *a.* Dog-like; surly; cynical.

dog-go (dog′ō), *a.* or *adv.* [Origin obscure.] In hiding: as, to lie *doggo*. [Slang.]

dog=gone (dôg′gôn′), *v. t.* [Appar. from the Scotch imprecation *dog on it!*] A word used in vague malediction or as a substitute for profanity. [Slang.]—**dog′=goned′,** *p. a.* Cursed; confounded. [Slang.]

dog-gy, dog-gie (dog′i), *n.*; pl. *doggies* (-iz). A little dog; hence, a pet term for any dog.

dog=head-ed (dog′hed″ed), *a.* Having a head like that of a dog; cynocephalous.

dog=hole (dog′hōl), *n.* A hole or kennel for a dog; hence, a place fit only for dogs; a mean or vile habitation.

dog=Lat-in (dog′lat′in), *n.* Mongrel or spurious Latin.

dog-ma (dog′mạ̈ or dôg′-), *n.*; pl. *-mas*, L. *-mata* (-mạ-tạ̈). [L. *dogma*, < Gr. δόγμα, < δοκεῖν, think, seem, seem good.] A settled opinion; a belief; a principle; esp., a tenet or doctrine authoritatively laid down, as by a church; sometimes, an arrogant declaration of opinion; also, a system of principles or tenets, as of a church; prescribed doctrine.—**dog-mat′ic** (-mat′ik), *a.* [LL. *dogmaticus*, < Gr. δογματικός.] Of, pertaining to, or of the nature of a dogma or dogmas; doctrinal; also, asserting opinions in an authoritative, positive, or arrogant manner, or without presenting evidence; positive; opinionated. Also **dog-mat′i-cal.**—**dog-mat′i-cal-ly,** *adv.*—**dog-ma-ti′cian** (-mạ-tish′ạn), *n.* A student of dogmatics; also, a dogmatist.—**dog-mat′ics,** *n.* Dogmatic or doctrinal theology.—**dog′ma-tism,** *n.* Dogmatic character; authoritative, positive, or arrogant assertion of opinions.—**dog′ma-tist,** *n.* One who lays down dogmas; esp., one who asserts positively his own opinions; a dogmatic person.—**dog′ma-tize** (-tīz), *v.*; *-tized*, *-tizing*. [LL. *dogmatizare*, < Gr. δογματίζειν.] **I.** *intr.* To make dogmatic assertions; speak or write dogmatically. **II.** *tr.* To assert or deliver as a dogma.—**dog″ma-ti-za′tion** (-ti-zā′shọn), *n.*—**dog′ma-tiz-er** (-tī-zėr), *n.*

dog-rose (dog′rōz), *n.* A species of wild rose, *Rosa canina*, having pale red flowers: a common British plant.

dog's=bane (dogz′bān), *n.* Same as *dogbane*.

dog's=ear (dogz′ēr), *n.* The corner of a leaf in a book folded over like a dog's ear, as by careless use or to mark a place.—**dog's′=ear,** *v. t.* To disfigure with dog's-ears.

dog's=fen-nel (dogz′fen″ẹl), *n.* Same as *dog-fennel*.

dog=sick (dog′sik′), *a.* Wretchedly sick; nauseated.

dog-skin (dog′skin), *n.* The skin of a dog; leather made from this skin or some substitute, as sheepskin.

dog=sleep (dog′slēp), *n.* A light sleep, easily disturbed.

dog's=tail (dogz′tāl), *n.* Any grass of the old-world genus *Cynosurus*, the species of which have the spikes fringed on one side only, esp. *C. cristatus* ('crested dog's-tail'); also, the yard-grass, *Eleusine indica*.

Dog-tooth Molding.

dog=star (dog′stär), *n.* [Also *cap.*] The bright star Sirius, situated in the constellation Canis Major; sometimes, the bright star Procyon, in Canis Minor. Cf. *dog* and *dog-days*.

dog's=tongue (dogz′tung), *n.* Hound's-tongue.

dog=tired (dog′tīrd′), *a.* Tired as a dog after a long chase; very tired.

dog=tooth (dog′töth), *n.*; pl. *-teeth* (-tēth). A canine tooth; in *arch.*, a tooth-like ornament, or a molding cut in projecting teeth.—**dog=tooth spar,** a variety of calcite occurring in acute crystals resembling canine teeth.—**dog=tooth violet,** a bulbous liliaceous plant, *Erythronium dens-canis*, of Europe, bearing purple flowers; any of several American plants of the same genus, as *E. americanum*, bearing yellow flowers, or *E. albidum*, bearing white flowers.

Dog-tooth Spar.

dog=trot (dog′trot), *n.* A gentle trot, like that of a dog.

dog=vane (dog′vān), *n.* *Naut.*, a small vane, composed of bunting or the like, set on the weather gunwale of a vessel to show the direction of the wind.

dog=watch (dog′woch), *n.* *Naut.*, either of two short watches on shipboard, from 4 to 6 P.M. and from 6 to 8 P.M.

dog=wear-y (dog′wēr′i), *a.* Dog-tired. See Shakspere's "Taming of the Shrew," iv. 2. 60.

dog-wood (dôg′wůd), *n.* Any tree or shrub of the genus *Cornus*, esp. *C. sanguinea*, of Europe, or *C. florida* ('flowering dogwood'), an American ornamental tree with large white or pinkish flowers; the wood of any such tree; also, any of various other trees and shrubs.

Dogwood (*Cornus florida*).

doi-ly (doi′li), *n.*; pl. *-lies* (-liz). [From the name of a 17th century maker or dealer, of London.] A woolen fabric for summer clothing†; a small ornamental napkin used at table at dessert, etc.; any small ornamental mat, as of embroidery or lace, used on the table or elsewhere.

do-ing (dö′ing), *n.* Action; performance; execution; *pl.*, deeds; proceedings.

doit (doit), *n.* [D. *duit.*] A small copper coin formerly current among the Dutch; hence, any small coin or sum; fig., a bit or jot.

Obverse. Reverse.
Doit struck for Java by the Dutch, 1765. — British Museum.

doit-ed (doi′ted), *a.* [Cf. *dote.*] Enfeebled in mind, esp. by age; childish. [Sc.]

do-lab-ri-form (dō-lab′ri-fôrm), *a.* [L. *dolabra*, pickax, ax: see *-form.*] In *bot.* and *zoöl.*, shaped like an ax or a cleaver.

Dolabriform Leaf.

dol-ce (dōl′chā), *a.* [It., < L. *dulcis*, sweet.] In *music*, sweet; soft.

dol-drum (dol′drum), *n.* [Perhaps connected with *dull.*] A dullard†; *pl.*, dullness; low spirits; *naut.*, certain parts of the ocean near the equator that abound in calms, squalls, and light baffling winds; also, the calms or weather variations characteristic of such parts; a becalmed state.

dole[1] (dōl), *n.* [AS. *dāl*, part, portion, = *dǣl*, E. *deal*[2], *n.*] A part or share allotted or belonging to one (archaic); one's fate or destiny (archaic); also, a portion of money, food, etc., given, esp. in charity or for maintenance (as, "a full measure of bread, wine, and olives being his *dole* [in prison]": J. H. Newman's "Callista," xxii.); hence, a portion sparingly doled out; also, a dealing out or distributing, esp. in charity. —**dole**[1], *v. t.*; *doled, doling.* To deal out in portions, as alms to the poor; distribute in charity; also, to give out in small quantities, or in a sparing or niggardly manner.

dole[2] (dōl), *n.* [OF. *dol, doel* (F. *deuil*), < LL. *dolium*, grief, < L. *dolere*: see *dolent.*] Grief or sorrow; lamentation: as, "She died. So that day there was *dole* in Astolat" (Tennyson's "Lancelot and Elaine," 1129). [Archaic or prov.]—**dole′ful,** *a.* Full of dole or grief; sorrowful; gloomy.—**dole′ful-ly,** *adv.*—**dole′ful-ness,** *n.*

do-lent (dō′lęnt), *a.* [OF. F. *dolent*, < L. *dolens* (*dolent-*), ppr. of *dolere*, suffer, grieve.] Grieving; sorrowful; mournful. [Archaic.]

dol-e-rite (dol′ę-rīt), *n.* [F. *dolérite*, < Gr. δολερός, deceptive.] A coarse-grained variety of basalt; sometimes, any of various other igneous rocks, as diabase.—**dol-er-it′ic** (-ę-rit′ik), *a.*

dole-some (dōl′sum), *a.* Doleful. [Archaic or prov.]

dol-i-cho-ce-phal-ic (dol″i-kō-se-fal′ik), *a.* [Gr. δολιχός, long, + κεφαλή, head.] Long-headed; having a breadth of skull small in proportion to the length from front to back: opposed to *brachycephalic.* Also **dol″i-cho-ceph′a-lous** (-sef′ą-lus).—**dol″i-cho-ceph′a-ly,** *n.*

doll (dol), *n.* [From *Doll, Dolly*, for *Dorothy*, woman's name.] A toy puppet representing a child or other human being; a child's toy baby; hence, a pretty but expressionless or unintelligent woman.—**doll,** *v. t.* To dress (*up* or *out*) in a smart or showy manner. [Slang.]

dol-lar (dol′är), *n.* [LG. *daler* = D. *daalder*, < G. *thaler*, for *Joachimsthaler*, 'coin of Joachimsthal' (place of silver-mines in Bohemia).] The English name for the German thaler, a large silver coin of varying value, current in various German states from the 16th century (see *thaler*); any of various similar or other coins, as the Spanish peso or the Mexican peso; esp., the monetary unit of the U. S., equivalent to 100 cents; a gold coin (no longer issued) of this value, or a silver coin or a paper note having a corresponding legal value; also, a corresponding unit, coin, or note elsewhere, as in Canada.—**trade dollar,** a former silver coin of the U. S., intended for the uses of the trade with China, etc.—**dol′lar=bird,** *n.* A roller of the genus *Eurystomus*, of Africa, India, etc., as *E. pacificus* (or *australis*) of Australasia: so called from a round white spot on the wing, shown when the wing is spread.—**dol′lar=fish,** *n.* The butterfish, *Poronotus triacanthus.*—**dol′lar=mark,** *n.* The character $, meaning dollar or dollars, placed before a number: as, $1 (one dollar); $5 (five dollars).

Dollar-bird (*Eurystomus pacificus*).

doll-ish (dol′ish), *a.* Somewhat doll-like; pretty but unintelligent.—**doll′ish-ly,** *adv.*—**doll′ish-ness,** *n.*

dol-lop (dol′ǫp), *n.* [Origin obscure.] A lump; a mass; a large quantity. [Colloq.]

dol-ly (dol′i), *n.*; pl. *dollies* (-iz). [From *Dolly*, for *Dorothy*, proper name.] A child's name for a doll; also, any of various mechanical devices, as an extension-piece placed on the head of a pile while being driven, or a tool for receiving and holding the head of a rivet while the other end is being headed.

Dol-ly Var-den (dol′i vär′dęn). [From *Dolly Varden*, a character in Dickens's "Barnaby Rudge."] A style of gay-flowered print gown, also a broad-brimmed flower-trimmed hat, formerly worn by women.

dol-man (dol′mạn), *n.*; pl. *-mans.* [F., through G. or Hung. < Turk. *dōlāmān.*] A long outer robe worn by Turks; the jacket of a hussar, worn like a cloak with sleeves hanging loose; a woman's mantle with cape-like arm-pieces instead of sleeves.

dol-men (dol′men), *n.* [F.; from Breton.] In *archæol.*, a structure, usually regarded as a tomb, consisting of two or more large upright stones set with a space between and capped by a horizontal stone. Cf. *cromlech.*

Dolmen.

dol-o-mite (dol′ǭ-mīt), *n.* [From D. G. de *Dolomieu* (1750–1801), French geologist.] A native carbonate of calcium and magnesium (when in granular crystalline rock-masses called *dolomite marble*); *pl.* [*cap.*], with *the*, the lofty mountains of dolomite in southern Tyrol.—**dol-o-mit′ic** (-mit′ik), *a.*

do-lor (dō′lǫr), *n.* [OF. *dolor* (F. *douleur*), < L. *dolor*, pain, grief, < *dolere*, suffer, grieve.] Pain†; also, sorrow or grief (now chiefly poetic).—**do-lo-ro-so** (dō-lō-rō′sō), *a.* [It.] In *music*, soft and pathetic; plaintive.—**dol-o-rous** (dol′ǫ-rus), *a.* [LL. *dolorosus.*] Full of, expressing, or causing pain or sorrow; distressed; grievous; mournful: as, "Still with a voice of *dolorous* pitch She sang the 'Song of the Shirt!'" (Hood's "Song of the Shirt," 7).—**dol'o-rous-ly,** *adv.*—**dol'o-rous-ness,** *n.*

do'lour, *n.* British preferred form of *dolor*.

dol-phin (dol'fin), *n.* [OF. *daufin, delfin* (F. *dauphin*), < L. *delphinus*, < Gr. δελφίς, dolphin: cf. *dauphin*.] Any of various cetaceans of the family *Delphinidæ*, some of which are commonly called porpoises, esp. *Delphinus delphis*, which has a long, sharp nose and abounds in the Mediterranean and the temperate Atlantic; also, either of two large pelagic fishes constituting the genus *Coryphæna*, esp. *C. hippurus*, remarkable for its changes of color when removed from the water; also, a post or buoy to which to moor a vessel; [*cap.*] in *astron.*, the northe n constellation Delphinus.—**dol'phin=strik"er,** *n.* *Naut.*, a martingale (spar under the end of a bowsprit).

Dolphin (*Delphinus delphis*).

dolt (dōlt), *n.* [Cf. AS. *dol*, foolish, stupid, and E. *dull*.] A dull, stupid fellow; a blockhead.—**dolt'ish,** *a.*

Dom (dom), *n.* [Pg. and F. *dom* = Sp. *don*, < L. *dominus*, master, lord.] A title prefixed to the name of certain Portuguese and Brazilian dignitaries; also, a title given to certain Roman Catholic ecclesiastics, esp. Benedictine and Carthusian monks.

-dom. [AS. *-dōm*, suffix, = *dōm*, n., judgment, authority: see *doom*.] A noun suffix denoting position, dignity, authority, jurisdiction, domain or realm, world, state or condition, inhabitants or members collectively, etc., as in *Christendom, earldom, freedom, heathendom, kingdom, officialdom*.

do-main (dō-mān'), *n.* [F. *domaine*, OF. *domeine* (also *demeine*: see *demesne*), orig. adj., < L. *dominicus*, belonging to a lord: see *dominical*.] Possession or dominion (as, eminent *domain*, the dominion of the sovereign power over all the property within the state, by which it can appropriate private property, compensation being given for it); also, an estate in land; a demesne; also, a territory under rule or influence; a realm; fig., a field of action, thought, etc. (as, the *domain* of commerce, of science, or of letters).—**do-ma'ni-al** (-mā'ni-al), *a.*

dome (dōm), *n.* [L. *domus*, house; in part through F. *dôme*, < It. *duomo*, cathedral, cupola, dome.] A house, mansion, or stately building (poetic); also, a large hemispherical or approximately hemispherical roof; a cupola, esp. a large one; also, anything shaped like a cupola; in *crystal.*, a form whose planes intersect the vertical axis, but are parallel to one of the lateral axes (so called because it has above or below a horizontal edge like the roof of a house).—**dome,** *v.*; *domed, doming.* **I.** *tr.* To cover with or as with a dome; also, to shape like a dome. **II.** *intr.* To rise or swell as a dome.

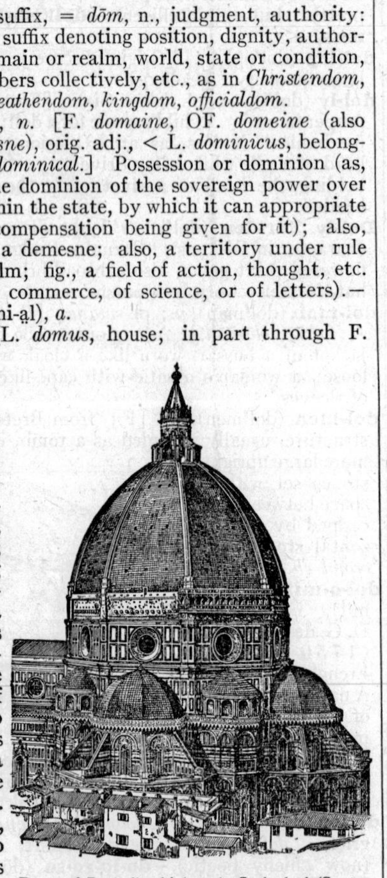
Dome of Brunelleschi (1420), Cathedral (Santa Maria del Fiore), Florence, Italy.

domes-day (dōmz'dā or dömz'-), *n.* Old form of *doomsday*.—**Domesday Book,** a record of a survey of the lands of England made by order of William the Conqueror about 1086, giving the ownership, extent, value, etc., of the properties.

do-mes-tic (dō-mes'tik). [L. *domesticus*, < *domus*, house.] **I.** *a.* Of or pertaining to the home, the household, or household affairs; also, devoted to home life or affairs; also, of or pertaining to one's own or a particular country as apart from other countries; belonging, existing, or produced within a country (as, *domestic* trade; *domestic* manufactures); not foreign; also, of an animal, living with man; tame. **II.** *n.* A member of a household†; also, a hired household attendant; *pl.*, home manufactures or goods, esp. common cotton cloths.—**do-mes'ti-ca-ble,** *a.* Capable of being domesticated.—**do-mes'ti-cal-ly,** *adv.*—**do-mes'ti-cate** (-kāt), *v. t.*; *-cated, -cating.* [ML. *domesticatus*, pp. of *domesticare*, < L. *domesticus*.] To make (one) a member of a household (as, "I am *domesticated* with the Trevanions": Bulwer-Lytton's "Caxtons," vi. 7); cause to be or feel at home; naturalize; also, to attach to home life or affairs; also, to convert to domestic uses; tame, as an animal; reclaim from a wild state.—**do-mes-ti-ca'tion** (-kā'shon), *n.*—**do-mes'ti-ca-tor,** *n.*—**do-mes-ti-ci-ty** (dō-mes-tis'i-ti), *n.*; pl. *-ties* (-tiz). The state of being domestic; domestic or home life; *pl.*, domestic affairs.—**do-mes'ti-cize** (-sīz), *v. t.*; *-cized, -cizing.* To make domestic.

do-mi-cal (dō'mi-kal), *a.* Dome-like; also, having a dome or domes.—**do'mi-cal-ly,** *adv.*

Domical Church. — Cathedral of Périgueux, France; 11th century.

dom-i-cile (dom'i-sil or, esp. Brit., -sīl), *n.* [OF. F. *domicile*, < L. *domicilium*, < *domus*, house.] A place of residence; an abode; a house or home; in *law*, the place where one has his home or permanent residence, to which, if absent, he intends to return.—**dom'i-cile,** *v.*; *-ciled, -ciling.* **I.** *tr.* To establish in a domicile. **II.** *intr.* To have one's domicile (*at, in*, etc.); dwell.—**dom-i-cil'i-a-ry** (-sil'i-ā-ri), *a.* [Cf. F. *domiciliaire*.] Of or pertaining to a domicile.—**dom-i-cil'i-ate** (-āt), *v. t.* or *i.*; *-ated, -ating.* To domicile.—**dom-i-cil-i-a'tion** (-ā'shon), *n.*

dom-i-nant (dom'i-nant), *a.* [L. *dominans* (*-ant-*), ppr. of *dominari*: see *dominate*.] Ruling, governing, or controlling; most influential; also, occupying a commanding position; in Mendelian phraseology, pertaining to or exhibiting a dominant, as opposed to a recessive, character (see *dominant character*, below); in *music*, pertaining to or based on the dominant (as, the *dominant* chord).—**dominant character,** in Mendelian phraseology, that one of any pair of antagonistic or mutually incompatible characters, as tallness and dwarfishness, occurring one in each of two parent animals or plants of pure breed, which is visibly manifested to the apparent exclusion of the other in the first generation of hybrids, and which occurs, always visibly, in a certain definite proportion of individuals in each succeeding generation.—**dominant tenement,** in *law*, a tenement in favor of which a servitude exists over a servient tenement.—**dom'i-nant,** *n.* In Mendelian phraseology, a dominant character, or an individual exhibiting it; in *music*, the fifth tone of a scale.—**dom'i-nance, dom'i-nan-cy,** *n.*—**dom'i-nant-ly,** *adv.*

dom-i-nate (dom'i-nāt), *v.*; *-nated, -nating.* [L. *dominatus*, pp. of *dominari*, bear rule, < *dominus*, master, lord.] **I.** *tr.* To bear rule over; govern; control or influence by mastery; sway; also, to tower above; overshadow. **II.** *intr.* To bear rule; exercise control; predominate; prevail; also, to occupy a commanding position.—**dom-i-na′tion** (-nā′-shọn), *n.* [L. *dominatio(n-)*.] The act of dominating; rule or sway, often of an arbitrary character; *pl.*, an order of angels (see *angel*).—**dom′i-na-tive** (-nạ-tiv), *a.* Dominating; controlling.—**dom′i-na-tor** (-nā-tọr), *n.*

dom-i-neer (dom-i-nēr′), *v.* [D. *domineeren*, < F. *dominer*, < L. *dominari*: see *dominate.*] **I.** *intr.* To rule arbitrarily or despotically; tyrannize; hence, to assert authority arrogantly; also, to tower (*over* or *above*). **II.** *tr.* To govern arbitrarily or despotically; tyrannize over; also, to tower over or above (something).—**dom-i-neer′,** *n.* Domineering action or manner.—**dom-i-neer′er,** *n.*—**dom-i-neer′ing-ly,** *adv.*

do-min-i-cal (dọ-min′i-kạl). [ML. *dominicalis*, of or pertaining to the Lord or the Lord's Day (ML. *dominica*), < L. *dominicus*, belonging to a lord or (LL.) the Lord, < *dominus*, master, lord.] **I.** *a.* Of or pertaining to Jesus Christ as Lord; also, of or pertaining to the Lord's Day, or Sunday (as, the *dominical* letter, that one of the seven letters A to G which is used in calendars to mark the Sundays throughout a particular year, and serving primarily to aid in determining the date of Easter). **II.**† *n.* A dominical letter. See Shakspere's "Love's Labour's Lost," v. 2. 44.

Do-min-i-can (dọ-min′i-kạn). **I.** *a.* Of or pertaining to St. Dominic (1170–1221), or the mendicant religious order founded by him; also, of or pertaining to the Dominican Republic, or Santo Domingo, in the West Indies. **II.** *n.* A member of the order of St. Dominic; a black friar; also, a native or inhabitant of the Dominican Republic, or Santo Domingo.

dom-i-nie (dom′i-ni), *n.* [L. *domine*, voc. of *dominus*, master, lord.] A schoolmaster (now chiefly Sc.: as, "Abel Sampson, commonly called, from his occupation as a pedagogue, *Dominie* Sampson," Scott's "Guy Mannering," ii.); also, a clergyman, pastor, or parson.

do-min-ion (dọ-min′yọn), *n.* [OF. *dominion*, < L. *dominium*, lordship, ownership, < *dominus*, master, lord.] The power or right of governing and controlling; sovereign authority; rule or sway; control or influence; also, lands or domains subject to sovereignty or control; a territory under a particular form of government (as, the *Dominion* of Canada, or, colloq., the *Dominion*, the title under which the provinces of Canada were united into one government on July 1, 1867; the Old *Dominion*, a popular name for the State of Virginia); specif., a territory constituting a self-governing commonwealth and being one of a number of such territories united in a community of nations, or empire (a term applied to self-governing divisions of the British Empire, as Canada, New Zealand, etc.); also, *pl.*, the dominations (angels: see Col. i. 16); also, *sing.*, in *law*, dominium.—**Dominion Day,** in Canada, a legal holiday, July 1, celebrating the formation of the Dominion on July 1, 1867.

Dom-i-nique (dom′i-nēk), *n.* [F. *Dominique*, the West Indian island of Dominica.] One of a breed of domestic fowls characterized by a rose-colored comb, yellow legs, and black-barred pale-gray plumage.

do-min-i-um (dọ-min′i-um), *n.* [L.: see *dominion.*] In *law*, ownership, as opposed to a mere life interest, an equitable right, etc.; property; right of possession or use.

dom-i-no (dom′i-nō), *n.*; pl. *-noes* or *-nos* (-nōz). [F. and It. *domino*, < L. *dominus*, master, lord.] A hooded cloak formerly worn by ecclesiastics in winter; also, a large, loose cloak, usually hooded, worn together with a face-mask by persons in masquerade; sometimes, the face-mask; a person wearing such dress; also, *pl.* (construed as *sing.*), any of various games played with flat, oblong pieces of ivory, bone, or wood, the face of which is divided into two parts, each left blank or marked with pips, usually from one to six; *sing.*, one of these pieces.—**dom′i-noed,** *a.* Wearing a domino.

Sir Joshua Reynolds in a Domino.

don[1] (don), *v. t.*; *donned*, *donning*. [For *do on*: cf. *doff.*] To put on (clothing, etc.).

don[2] (don), *n.* [Sp. *don* = Pg. *dom*, < L. *dominus*, master, lord.] [*cap.*] A Spanish title prefixed to a man's Christian name, formerly given only to a nobleman, but now applied in courtesy to any man; [*l. c.*] a Spanish lord or gentleman; a person of great importance; an adept (colloq.); in the English universities, a head, fellow, or tutor of a college (colloq.).—**Don Juan** (jū′ạn, Sp. hwän), a legendary Spanish nobleman of dissolute life; hence, a libertine or rake.

do-ña (dō′nyä), *n.* [Sp. *doña* = Pg. *dona* = It. *donna*, < L. *domina*, fem. of *dominus*: see *don*[2].] In Spanish use, a lady: also used as a title of respect.

do-nate (dō′nāt or dọ-nāt′), *v. t.*; *-nated*, *-nating*. [L. *donatus*, pp. of *donare*, give, present, < *donum*, gift, < *dare*, give.] To present as a gift; make a gift or donation of, as to a fund or cause; contribute.—**do-na-tion** (dọ-nā′shọn), *n.* [L. *donatio(n-)*.] The act of presenting something as a gift; also, that which is presented; a gift, as to a fund; a contribution.

Don-a-tist (don′ạ-tist), *n.* [LL. *Donatista*, < *Donatus*, Donatus (prob. Donatus Magnus, who became the Donatist bishop of Carthage in 315).] One of a Christian sect which arose in northern Africa in the year 311, and which maintained that it constituted the whole and only true church and that the baptisms and ordinations of the orthodox clergy were invalid.—**Don′a-tism,** *n.*

don-a-tive (don′ạ-tiv). **I.** *a.* Of the nature of a donation; vested or vesting by donation, as a benefice. **II.** *n.* A gift or donation; a largess; specif., a benefice bestowed by the founder or patron without presentation, institution, or induction by the ordinary.

do-na-tor (dọ-nā′tọr), *n.* One who donates; a donor.

don-cel-la (don-sel′ạ), *n.* [Sp., lit. 'damsel.'] Any of certain fishes of the West Indies, Florida, etc., as of the labroid genus *Iridio*.

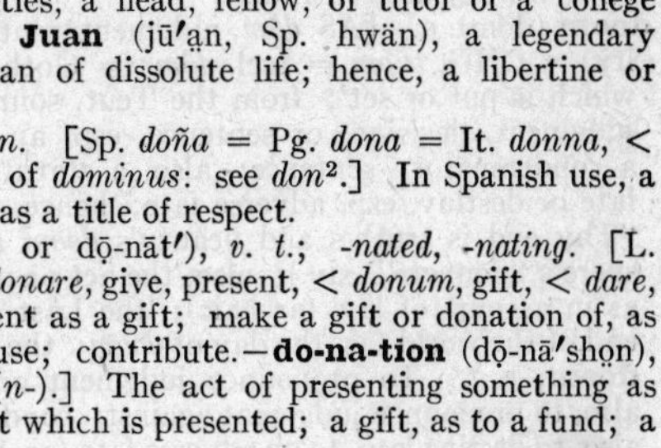

Doncella (*Iridio radiatus*).

done (dun). Past participle of *do*[1].—**done,** *p.a.* Executed; completed; finished; settled; cooked; worn (*out*); used (*up*).

do-nee (dō-nē′), *n.* [See *donor* and *-ee.*] One to whom something is given or donated; in *law*, one to whom an estate is given in fee tail, or upon whom a power is conferred.

don-ga (dong′gạ), *n.* [Zulu.] A gully or ravine. [South Africa.]

don-go-la (dong′gọ-lạ), *n.* [From *Dongola*, province of the Anglo-Egyptian Sudan.] A leather made from goatskin, sheepskin, etc., resembling kid, with a bright or a dull finish.

don-jon (dun′jọn, also don′-), *n.* [Archaic form of *dungeon.*] The inner tower, keep, or stronghold of a castle: as, "It [a tower] was the oldest part of the chateau, and had in ancient times been the *donjon* or stronghold" (Irving's "Tales of a Traveler," i. 3).

don-key (dong′ki, also dung′-), *n.*; pl. *-keys* (-kiz). [Origin uncertain: cf. *dun*[1].] The ass; also, a stupid, silly, or obstinate person.—**don′key=en″gine,** *n.* A small, usually subsidiary, steam-engine.

don-na (don′ạ, It. don′nä), *n.* [It.: see *doña.*] In Italian use, a lady: also used as a title of respect for an Italian lady, and sometimes for a Spanish or a Portuguese lady.

don-nish (don′ish), *a.* Resembling, or characteristic of, an English university don.—**don′nish-ness,** *n.*

do-nor (dō′nọr), *n.* [OF. *doneor* (F. *donneur*), < L. *donator*, < *donare*: see *donate.*] One who gives or donates; in *law*, one who grants an estate in fee tail, or who confers a power; in *med.*, a person or animal furnishing blood for transfusion.

do=noth-ing (dö′nuth″ing). **I.** *n.* One who does nothing; an idler. **II.** *a.* Doing nothing; idle; indolent.

don't (dōnt). Contraction of *do not*, also used improperly for *does not.*

don-zel (don′zel), *n.* [It. *donzello*, < ML. *domnicellus*, dim. < L. *dominus*, master, lord.] A young gentleman not yet knighted; a squire; a page. [Archaic.]

doo-dad (dö′dad), *n.* [Appar. a made word.] Any trifling ornament or bit of decorative finery. [Colloq.]

doo-dle (dö′dl), *n.* [Origin obscure.] A silly or foolish fellow; a simpleton. [Colloq.]—**doo′dle=bug,** *n.* An ant-lion. [Local, U. S.]

doo-ly, doo-lie (dö′li), *n.*; pl. *-lies* (-liz). [Hind.] A kind of litter used in India.

doom (döm), *n.* [AS. *dōm*, judgment, sentence, law, authority, = OHG. *tuom* = Icel. *dōmr* = Goth. *dōms*, orig. 'that which is put or set'; from the Teut. source of E. *do*[1].] A judgment, decision, or sentence, esp. an unfavorable one; a condemnatory sentence; also, a statute† or law†; also, fate or destiny, esp. adverse fate; hence, ruin or death (as, "Thy end is truth's and beauty's *doom* and date": Shakspere's "Sonnets," xiv.); also, the act or process of judging, as in a court of law (archaic); the Last Judgment, at the end of the world (as, the day of *doom*; the crack of *doom*).—**doom,** *v. t.* To pronounce judgment or sentence upon†; also, to pronounce judgment against; condemn to some fate; also, to destine, esp. to an adverse fate (as, "I am thy father's spirit, *Doom'd* for a certain term to walk the night": Shakspere's "Hamlet," i. 5. 10); also, to ordain or fix as a sentence or fate (as, "The emperor, in his rage, will *doom* her death": Shakspere's "Titus Andronicus," iv. 2. 114).—**doom′er,** *n.* —**doom′ful,** *a.* Fraught with doom; fateful.

doom=palm (döm′päm), *n.* [Ar. *dūm.*] A large African palm, *Hyphæne thebaica*, having a dichotomous trunk, and an edible fruit about the size of an apple which contains a fibrous pulp tasting somewhat like gingerbread; the gingerbread-tree.

Doom-palm.

dooms (dömz), *adv.* [Appar. < *doom.*] Very; extremely. [Sc. and north. Eng.]

dooms-day (dömz′dā), *n.* [AS. *dōmes dæg.*] The day of the Last Judgment, at the end of the world; also, any day of sentence or condemnation; also, a day of final dissolution, as at the end of the world.—**Dooms-day Book,** the Domesday Book. See under *domesday*.

doom-ster (döm′stėr), *n.* [Cf. *deemster.*] One who pronounces doom or sentence (archaic); in Scotland, formerly, the official, usually the executioner, who read or repeated the sentence.

door (dōr), *n.* [AS. *duru*, door, *dor*, door, gate, akin to G. *thür*, *thor*, Icel. *dyrr*, pl., Goth. *daur*, also L. *foris*, Gr. θύρα, Skt. *dvār*, door.] A movable barrier of wood or other material, commonly turning on hinges or sliding in a groove, for closing and opening a passage or opening into a building, room, etc.; also, the building, etc., to which a door belongs, with reference to other buildings, etc., in the same row; also, a doorway; fig., any means of approach or access, or of exit. —**in doors,** in or into a house or building.—**out of doors,** out of a house or building; in or into the open air.—**door′=bell,** *n.* A bell at a door or connected with a door, rung by persons outside seeking admittance; also, a bell connected with a door so as to ring when the door is opened.—**doored,** *a.* Having a door or doors.—**door′keep″er,** *n.* One who keeps or guards a door or entrance; in the *Rom. Cath. Ch.*, same as *ostiary*.—**door′less,** *a.* Having no door.—**door′=nail,** *n.* A large-headed nail formerly used for strengthening or ornamenting doors.—**door′=plate,** *n.* A plate on the door of a house or room, bearing a name, number, or the like. —**door′=post,** *n.* The jamb or upright side-piece of a doorway.—**door′=sill,** *n.* The sill or threshold of a doorway.—**door′=step,** *n.* A step at a door, raised above the level of the ground outside; one of a series of steps leading from the ground to a door.—**door′way,** *n.* The passage or opening into a building, room, etc., closed and opened by a door.—**door′yard,** *n.* A yard about the door of a house.

Medieval Doorway. — North Portal, or Door of the Virgin, of the western front of Notre Dame Cathedral, Paris.

dope (dōp), *n.* [D. *doop*, a dipping, sauce, < *doopen*, dip, baptize: see *dip.*] Any thick liquid or pasty preparation, as a sauce, lubricant, etc.; esp., the treacle-like preparation of opium used for smoking (slang); hence, any stupefying drug (slang); a stimulating drug, as one wrongfully given to a race-horse to induce greater speed (slang); also, information or data, as on the previous performances of a race-horse (slang); a calculation or forecast based on such information or data (slang); also, a person under the influence, or addicted to the use, of drugs (slang); also, an absorbent material used to absorb and hold a liquid, as in the manufacture of dynamite; in *aëronautics*, any of various varnish-like products for coating the cloth fabric of aëroplane wings or the like, in order to make it waterproof, stronger, etc.—**dope,** *v.*; *doped, doping.* **I.** *tr.* To affect with stupefying or stimulating drugs; also, to work or make (*out*) by calculation, inference, etc., as a problem, solution, or plan. [Slang.] **II.** *intr.* To use stupefying or stimulating drugs. [Slang.]—**dope′=fiend,** *n.* A person addicted to the use of dope or drugs. [Slang.]—**dop-ey** (dō′pi), *a.* See *dopy*.

dop-pel-gäng-er (dop′ẹl-geng″ėr), *n.* [G., 'double-goer.'] An apparitional double or counterpart of a living person; a double ganger.

dop-y (dō′pi), *a.* Affected by or as by a stupefying drug. [Slang.]

dor[1], **dorr** (dôr), *n.* [AS. *dora.*] A common European dung-beetle, *Geotrypes stercorarius*; also, any of various other beetles, as the cockchafer, *Melolontha vulgaris*.

dor[2] (dôr), *n.* [Cf. Icel. *dār*, scoff.] Scoff; mockery; a trick or deception; a practical joke. [Archaic.]

do-ra-do (dọ-rä′dō), *n.*; pl. *-dos* (-dōz). [Sp., lit. 'gilded': cf. *dory*[1].] Either of two large fishes of the genus *Coryphæna*. See *dolphin*.

dor=bee-tle (dôr′bē″tl), *n.* Same as *dor*[1].

dor=bug (dôr′bug), *n.* A dor or dor-beetle; also, any of several American beetles of the genus *Lachnosterna*, esp. *L. fusca*, one of the June-bugs.

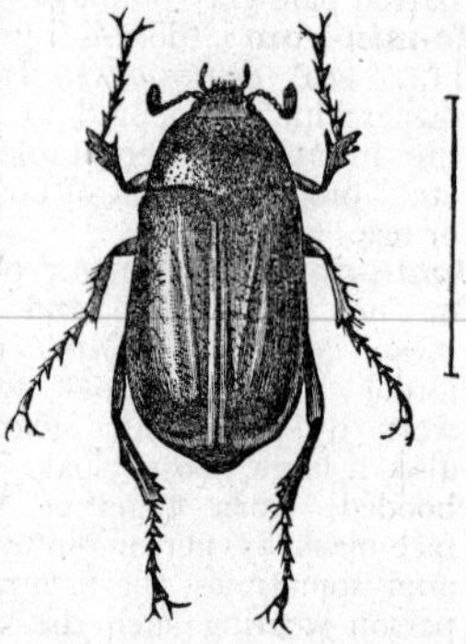
Dor-bug (*Lachnosterna fusca*). (Line shows natural size.)

Dor-cas (dôr′kạs) **so-ci′e-ty.** [From *Dorcas*, a woman Christian at Joppa who thus worked for the poor: see Acts, ix. 36.] A society of women of a church whose work it is to provide clothing for the poor.

Do-ri-an (dō′ri-ạn). **I.** *a.* Of or pertaining to Doris, a division of ancient Greece, or the race named from it, one of the principal divisions of the ancient Greeks. **II.** *n.* A Dorian Greek.

Dor-ic (dor′ik). **I.** *a.* Dorian; also, rustic, as a dialect; in *arch.*, noting or pertaining to the oldest and simplest of the three Greek orders, distinguished esp. by the absence of a base to the column. **II.** *n.* The Doric dialect of ancient Greek; also, a broad or rustic dialect of English, as the Scotch. —**Dor′i-cism** (-i-sizm), *n.* A Doric peculiarity of speech.

Doric Architecture. — The Parthenon at Athens.

Dor-king (dôr′king), *n.* [From *Dorking*, town in Surrey, southeastern England.] One of a breed of domestic fowls characterized by a long, lọw, full body and having five toes on each foot: valued esp. for the table.

dor-lach (dôr′lạch), *n.* [Gael.] A quiver†; also, a bundle or package; also, a valise or portmanteau. [Sc.]

dor-mant (dôr′mạnt), *a.* [OF. F. *dormant*, ppr. of *dormir*, < L. *dormire*, sleep, be inactive.] Sleeping; lying asleep or as if asleep; inactive as in sleep; torpid; also, in a state of rest or inactivity; quiescent; inoperative; in abeyance; in *her.*, of an animal, lying down with its head on its fore paws, as if asleep.—**dor′man-cy**, *n.*

Lion Dormant.

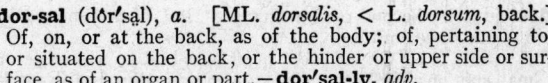

dor-mer (dôr′mėr), *n.* [OF. *dormeor*, < L. *dormitorium*: see *dormitory*.] A sleeping-apartment†; a dormer-window.—**dor′mered,** *a.* Having dormer-windows.—**dor′mer=win′dow,** *n.* A vertical window in a projection built out from a sloping roof; hence, the whole projecting structure.

Dormer-window; 15th century.

dor-mice (dôr′mīs), *n.* Plural of *dormouse*.

dor-mi-ent (dôr′mi-ẹnt), *a.* [L. *dormiens* (*dormient-*), ppr. of *dormire*, sleep.] Sleeping; dormant.

dor-mi-tion (dôr-mish′ọn), *n.* [OF. *dormicion* (F. *dormition*), < L. *dormitio(n-)*, < *dormire*, sleep.] Sleeping; a falling asleep; fig., dying or death.

dor-mi-to-ry (dôr′mi-tộ-ri), *n.*; pl. *-ries* (-riz). [L. *dormitorium*, prop. neut. of *dormitorius*, of or for sleeping, < *dormire*, sleep.] A sleeping-room (as, "a series of the queerest little *dormitories*—which . . . had once been nun's cells": C. Brontë's "Villette," viii.); specif., a sleeping-apartment containing a number of beds, or a building containing a number of sleeping-rooms.

dor-mouse (dôr′mous), *n.*; pl. *-mice* (-mīs). [ME. *dormowse*; perhaps in part < OF. *dormir*, sleep, in allusion to its hibernation.] Any of the small old-world rodents which constitute the family *Myoxidæ*, resembling small squirrels in appearance and habits.

Common Dormouse (*Muscardinus avellanarius*).

dor-my (dôr′mi), *a.* [Origin obscure.] In *golf*, of a player or side, being as many holes ahead as there remain holes to be played.

dorp (dôrp), *n.* [D., = E. *thorp*.] A village; a hamlet.

dorr, dorr′=bee″tle, dorr′=bug. See *dor*[1], etc.

dor-sad (dôr′sad), *adv.* [L. *dorsum*, back: see *-ad*.] In *anat.*, toward the back: opposed to *ventrad*.

dor-sal (dôr′sạl), *a.* [ML. *dorsalis*, < L. *dorsum*, back.] Of, on, or at the back, as of the body; of, pertaining to, or situated on the back, or the hinder or upper side or surface, as of an organ or part.—**dor′sal-ly,** *adv.*

dorsi-, dorso-. Forms of L. *dorsum*, back, used in combination.—**dor-sif-er-ous** (dôr-sif′ẹ-rus), *a.* [See *-ferous*.] In *bot.*, bearing clusters of sporangia on the back of the frond, as ferns; in *zoöl.*, hatching young upon the back, as certain toads.—**dor-sip′a-rous** (-sip′ạ-rus), *a.* [See *-parous*.] Dorsiferous.—**dor-si-ven′tral** (-si-ven′trạl), *a.* In *bot.*, having distinct dorsal and ventral sides, as most foliage leaves; in *zoöl.*, dorsoventral.—**dor-so-ven′tral** (-sộ-ven′trạl), *a.* In *zoöl.*, pertaining to the dorsal and ventral aspects of the body; extending from the dorsal to the ventral side (as, the *dorsoventral* axis); in *bot.*, dorsiventral.

dor-sum (dôr′sum), *n.*; pl. *-sa* (-sạ̈). [L.] The back, as of the body; the back or outer surface of an organ, part, etc.

Dory (*Zeus faber*).

do-ry[1] (dō′ri), *n.*; pl. *-ries* (-riz). [F. *dorée*, lit. 'gilded': cf. *dorado*.] An acanthopterygian food-fish, *Zeus faber*, of European seas (the 'John-dory'); also, the wall-eyed pike-perch of North America.

do-ry[2] (dō′ri), *n.*; pl. *-ries* (-riz). [Origin uncertain.] A small boat; esp., a boat with a narrow, flat bottom and high, flaring sides, usually propelled by oars, and used for fishing, etc.

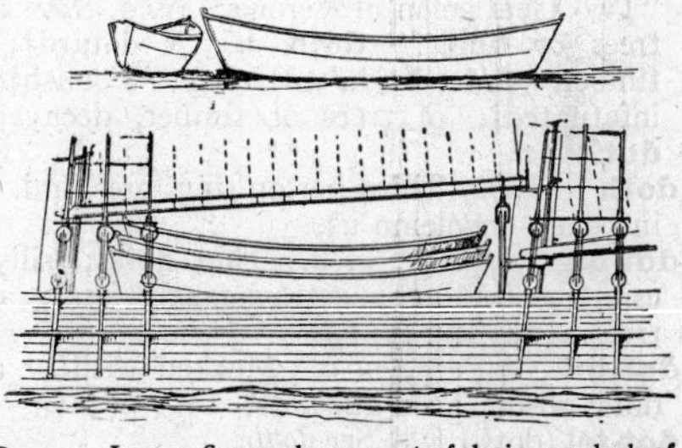
Dory. — Lower figure shows nest of dories on deck of fishing-schooner.

do-sage (dō′sạj), *n.* The administration of medicine in doses; also, the operation of dosing wine.

dose (dōs), *n.* [F. *dose*, < ML. *dosis*, < Gr. δόσις, a giving, gift, portion, dose, < διδόναι, give.] A quantity of medicine prescribed to be taken at one time; hence, a definite quantity of anything analogous to medicine; a portion or allotment of something nauseous or disagreeable; a quantity of sugar, cognac, etc., added to wine to give it its peculiar character.—**dose,** *v. t.*; *dosed*, *dosing*. To administer in or apportion for doses; also, to give doses to; specif., to add a dose to (wine).—**do-sim-e-try** (dộ-sim′e-tri), *n.*; pl. *-tries* (-triz). [See *-metry*.] The measurement of the doses of medicines.—**do-si-met-ric** (dō-si-met′rik), *a.*

doss (dos), *n.* [Origin uncertain.] A place in which to sleep; a bed, esp. in a cheap lodging-house; also, sleep. [Slang, Eng.]

dos-sal, dos-sel[1] (dos′ạl, -ẹl), *n.* [ML. *dossale*, for *dorsale*, < L. *dorsum*, back.] An ornamental covering for the back of a seat (archaic); *eccles.*, an ornamental hanging placed at the back of an altar or at the sides of the chancel.

dos-sel[2] (dos′ẹl), *n.* See *dossil*.

dos-ser (dos′ėr), *n.* [OF. F. *dossier*, < *dos*, < L. *dorsum*, back.] An ornamental covering for the back of a seat, esp. of a throne, etc.; a hanging for the walls of a hall, or the back or sides of a chancel; also, a basket for carrying objects on the back; a pannier.

doss=house (dos′hous), *n.* [See *doss*.] A cheap lodging-house. [Slang, Eng.]

dos-sier (dos′ièr, F. dō-syā), *n.* [F.: see *dosser*.] A bundle of documents all relating to the same matter or subject.

dos-sil (dos′il), *n.* [OF. *dosil* (F. *doisil*), < ML. *duciculus*, spigot, dim. of L. *dux*, leader, E. *duke*.] A spigot†; also, a plug of lint for a wound, sore, etc.; also, a roll of cloth for wiping off the excess of ink from an engraved plate before printing.

dost (dust). Second person sing. pres. ind. of *do*[1]: now only in poetic or solemn use.
dot[1] (dot), *n.* [Cf. AS. *dott*, head of a boil.] A minute or small spot on a surface; a speck; also, a small roundish mark made with or as with a pen; hence, anything relatively small or speck-like.—**dot**[1], *v.*; *dotted, dotting.* **I.** *tr.* To mark with or as with a dot or dots; also, to stud or diversify, as dots do (as, "clumps of tall bushes, *dotting* the prairie": Parkman's "Oregon Trail," vii.); also, to place like dots; also, to jot (*down*). **II.** *intr.* To make a dot or dots.
dot[2] (dot, F. dot), *n.* [F., < L. *dos* (*dot-*), dowry, endowment.] The portion brought by the wife to the husband upon marriage, the income of which is in his control; a dowry.
do-tage (dō'tāj), *n.* The condition of one who dotes; feebleness of mind, esp. resulting from old age; senility; also, a foolish thought, idea, etc.; also, excessive love or fondness; weak and foolish affection; also, something doted upon.
do-tal (dō'tal), *a.* [F. *dotal*, < L. *dotalis*, < *dos*: see *dot*[2].] Pertaining to or constituting a dot or dowry.
do-tard (dō'tärd), *n.* One who dotes, or is weak-minded, esp. from old age.
do-ta-tion (dō-tā'shon), *n.* [ML. *dotatio*(*n-*), < L. *dotare*, endow, < *dos*: see *dot*[2].] The act of endowing; endowment.
dote (dōt), *v. i.*; *doted, doting.* [ME. *doten*, akin to D. *dutten*, doze, dote, Icel. *dotta*, nod from sleep, F. *radoter*, dote.] To be silly or out of one's wits; act or talk foolishly; esp., to be weak-minded from old age; also, to bestow excessive love or extravagant fondness (*on* or *upon*: as, "You *dote* on her that cares not for your love," Shakspere's "Two Gentlemen of Verona," iv. 4. 87); also, to decay, as trees or timber.—**dote**, *n.* A dotard†; also, decay in timber.—**dot-ed** (dō'ted), *p. a.* Foolish†; weak-minded†; infatuated†; of trees or timber, decayed or unsound.—**dot'er**, *n.*
doth (duth). Third person sing. pres. ind. of *do*[1]: now only in poetic or solemn use.
dot-ing (dō'ting), *p. a.* That dotes; silly; weak-minded, esp. from old age; extravagantly fond; also, decaying, as trees.—**dot'ing-ly**, *adv.*
dot-ted (dot'ed), *p. a.* Marked with or as with a dot or dots; also, placed like dots.
dot-tel (dot'l), *n.* See *dottle.*
dot-ter (dot'ėr), *n.* One who or that which dots; an instrument for making dots.
dot-ter-el (dot'e-rel), *n.* [From *dote.*] A dotard or silly fellow (now prov.); also, a plover, *Eudromias morinellus*, of Europe and Asia, which allows itself to be approached and readily taken.

Dotterel.

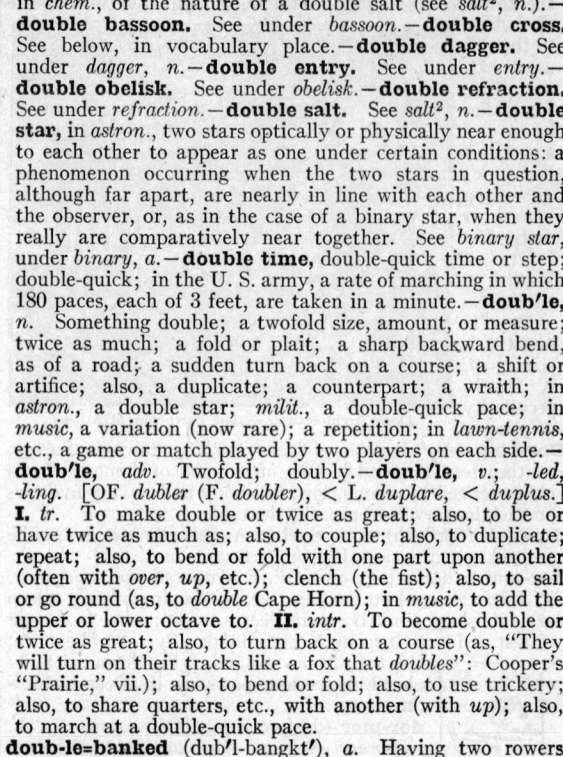

dot-tle (dot'l), *n.* [Appar. < *dot*[1].] The plug of half-smoked tobacco remaining in the bottom of a pipe after smoking.
dot-ty (dot'i), *a.* [Cf. *doty.*] Affected with mental decay or derangement; feeble-minded; crazy; also, feeble or unsteady in gait. [Colloq. or prov.]
dot-y (dō'ti), *a.* Of timber, affected with dote; decayed.
dou-ane (dö-än', F. dwän), *n.* [F., < Ar. *dīwān*, E. *divan.*] In French use, a custom-house.
Dou-ay (dö-ā') **Ver'sion** (of the Bible). See under *version.*
doub-le (dub'l), *a.* [OF. *duble, double* (F. *double*), < L. *duplus*, < *duo*, two, + *-plus*, akin to Gr. *-πλόος* (as in *διπλόος*, double) and E. *-fold.*] Twofold in form, size, amount, extent, etc.; composed of two like parts or members; paired; twice as great, heavy, strong, etc.; of extra size, weight, etc.; of flowers, having the number of petals largely increased; of musical instruments, producing a tone an octave lower; fig., twofold in character, meaning, or conduct; ambiguous; deceitful; hypocritical; insincere; in *chem.*, of the nature of a double salt (see *salt*[2], *n.*).—**double bassoon.** See under *bassoon.*—**double cross.** See below, in vocabulary place.—**double dagger.** See under *dagger*, *n.*—**double entry.** See under *entry.*—**double obelisk.** See under *obelisk.*—**double refraction.** See under *refraction.*—**double salt.** See *salt*[2], *n.*—**double star,** in *astron.*, two stars optically or physically near enough to each other to appear as one under certain conditions: a phenomenon occurring when the two stars in question, although far apart, are nearly in line with each other and the observer, or, as in the case of a binary star, when they really are comparatively near together. See *binary star*, under *binary*, *a.*—**double time,** double-quick time or step; double-quick; in the U. S. army, a rate of marching in which 180 paces, each of 3 feet, are taken in a minute.—**doub'le,** *n.* Something double; a twofold size, amount, or measure; twice as much; a fold or plait; a sharp backward bend, as of a road; a sudden turn back on a course; a shift or artifice; also, a duplicate; a counterpart; a wraith; in *astron.*, a double star; *milit.*, a double-quick pace; in *music*, a variation (now rare); a repetition; in *lawn-tennis*, etc., a game or match played by two players on each side.—**doub'le,** *adv.* Twofold; doubly.—**doub'le,** *v.*; *-led, -ling.* [OF. *dubler* (F. *doubler*), < L. *duplare*, < *duplus.*] **I.** *tr.* To make double or twice as great; also, to be or have twice as much as; also, to couple; also, to duplicate; repeat; also, to bend or fold with one part upon another (often with *over*, *up*, etc.); clench (the fist); also, to sail or go round (as, to *double* Cape Horn); in *music*, to add the upper or lower octave to. **II.** *intr.* To become double or twice as great; also, to turn back on a course (as, "They will turn on their tracks like a fox that *doubles*": Cooper's "Prairie," vii.); also, to bend or fold; also, to use trickery; also, to share quarters, etc., with another (with *up*); also, to march at a double-quick pace.
doub-le=banked (dub'l-bangkt'), *a.* Having two rowers on the same thwart, but rowing on opposite sides; also, having two rowers at the same oar; also, having two tiers of oars, one above the other, as certain galleys.
doub-le=bar-reled (dub'l-bar'eld), *a.* Having two barrels, as a gun; hence, serving a double purpose or producing a double result.
doub-le=bass (dub'l-bās'), *n.* The largest and deepest-toned instrument of the viol kind (see *viol*), now usually having four strings (sometimes three), played resting vertically on the floor; the violone. Also called *double-bass viol.*
doub-le=breast-ed (dub'l-bres'ted), *a.* Of a garment, overlapping sufficiently to form two thicknesses of considerable width on the breast, in men's clothes often with both buttonholes and buttons on each half of the front, to permit of buttoning on either side. Cf. *single-breasted.*
doub-le (dub'l) **cross.** A proving treacherous to a person with reference to some dishonest arrangement made with him, as concerning the outcome of a contest; hence, any act of treachery or perfidy; a betrayal: often in the phrase 'to give (one) the double cross.' [Slang.]—**doub'le=cross',** *v. t.* To prove treacherous to (a person) with reference to some dishonest arrangement made with him, esp. concerning the outcome of a contest, as by arranging with him to allow one's self to be beaten in the contest and then winning; hence, in general, to prove treacherous to; betray. [Slang.]
doub-le=deal-er (dub'l-dē'lėr), *n.* One guilty of duplicity or double-dealing.—**doub'le=deal'ing. I.** *n.* Duplicity; the profession of one thing and the practice of another. **II.** *a.* Using duplicity; treacherous.
doub-le=deck-er (dub'l-dek'ėr), *n.* Something with two decks, tiers, or the like, as a ship with two decks above the water-line, or a street-car having a second floor for passengers.
doub-le=dye (dub'l-dī'), *v. t.* To dye twice; fig., to imbue deeply.—**doub'le=dyed',** *p. a.* Twice dyed; fig., deeply imbued; thorough or complete.
doub-le=ea-gle (dub'l-ē'gl), *n.* A United States gold coin worth two eagles, or $20.
double en-tendre (döbl oṅ-toṅdr). [F. (obs.).] A double meaning; a word or expression with two meanings, one often indelicate.
doub-le=faced (dub'l-fāst'), *a.* Having two faces or aspects; having both surfaces finished (as, *double-faced*

cloth); also, practising duplicity; hypocritical.—**doub'le=faced'ness,** *n.*

doub-le=flow-ered (dub'l-flou'ėrd), *a.* Having double flowers, that is, flowers in which the number of petals is abnormally large.

doub-le=gang-er (dub'l-gang″ėr), *n.* Same as *doppelgänger.*

doub-le=head-ed (dub'l-hed'ed), *a.* Having or appearing to have two heads.—**doub'le=head'er,** *n.* Something with two heads; a railroad-train moved by two engines; the playing of two games, as of baseball, between the same teams on the same day in immediate succession.

doub-le=heart-ed (dub'l-här'ted), *a.* False at heart; deceitful; treacherous.—**doub'le=heart'ed-ness,** *n.*

doub-le=mind-ed (dub'l-mīn'ded), *a.* Wavering or undecided in mind: as, "A *double minded* man is unstable in all his ways" (Jas. i. 8).—**doub'le=mind'ed-ness,** *n.*

doub-le-ness (dub'l-nes), *n.* The state or quality of being double; twofold character; duplicity (as, "a hypocrite,—capable of deliberate *doubleness* for a selfish end": George Eliot's "Mill on the Floss," vi. 9).

doub-le=quick (dub'l-kwik'). **I.** *a.* Noting the quickest step or time in marching, next to the run; in general, very quick or rapid. See *double time,* under *double, a.* **II.** *n.* Double-quick step or time. **III.** *adv.* In double-quick time.—**doub'le=quick',** *v. i.* or *t.* To march in double-quick step.

doub-ler (dub'lėr), *n.* One who or that which doubles.

doub-le=rip-per (dub'l-rip'ėr), **doub-le=run-ner** (-run'ėr), *n.* A contrivance for coasting, consisting of two sleds, one behind the other, connected by a plank.

doub-let (dub'let), *n.* [OF. F. *doublet,* < *double,* E. *double, a.*] A close-fitting outer body-garment, with or without sleeves, formerly worn by men; also, one of a pair of like things; a duplicate; one of two words in the same language representing the same original, as the English *benison* and *benediction;* an unintentional repetition in printed matter; *pl.,* two dice on each of which the same number of spots turns up at a throw; also, *sing.,* a pair of like things; a couple; something formed by a union of two like things, as a combination of two simple lenses, or a counterfeit gem made of two pieces of crystal with a layer of color between them. —**doub'let-ed,** *a.* Wearing a doublet.

Doublets. — 1, time of Edward IV.; 2, 3, time of Elizabeth; 4, time of Charles I.

doub-le=tongue (dub'l-tung), *v. i.;* *-tongued, -tonguing.* In playing the flute, cornet, etc., to apply the tongue rapidly to the teeth and the hard palate alternately, so as to insure a brilliant execution of a staccato passage.

doub-le=tongued (dub'l-tungd'), *a.* Speaking inconsistently; deceitful in speech: as, "Thou art but a *double-tongued* Christian" (Defoe's "Captain Singleton," xvi.).

doub-le-tree (dub'l-trē), *n.* In a vehicle, a pivoted bar to each end of which a singletree, or swingletree, is attached: used when two horses are harnessed abreast.

doub-ling (dub'ling), *n.* The act of one who or that which doubles; the second distillation of wine; also, something doubled or folded over; a fold; also, an addition which makes double, as the lining of a mantle.

doub-loon (dub-lön'), *n.* [Sp. *doblón,* < *doble,* double, < L. *duplus:* see *double, a.*] A former Spanish gold coin, of varying value, finally worth about $5; also, a gold coin of Chile, worth about $3.65.

Obverse. Reverse.

Doubloon of Isabella II., Queen of Spain.—British Museum.

dou-blure (dö-blür), *n.* [F., < *doubler,* to double, line, E. *double, v.*] Lining, as of a garment; an ornamental lining on the inner side of a book-cover.

Doublure of Prayer-book of Edward VI.

doub-ly (dub'li), *adv.* In a double manner, measure, or degree; in two ways; with duplicity (obs. or archaic).

doubt (dout), *v.* [OF. F. *douter,* < L. *dubitare,* waver in opinion, hesitate, doubt: see *dubitable,* and cf. *dubitate.*] **I.** *intr.* To feel uncertainty as to something; be undecided **in** opinion or belief. **II.** *tr.* To be uncertain in opinion about; hold questionable; hesitate to believe; distrust; also, to fear, apprehend, or suspect (archaic or prov.).—**doubt,** *n.* [OF. F. *doute.*] Undecidedness of opinion or belief; uncertain state of mind as to the truth or reality of anything; a feeling of uncertainty; also, a state of affairs such as to occasion uncertainty; uncertainty of condition; also, a matter of uncertainty†.—**doubt'a-ble,** *a.* That may be doubted.—**doubt'er,** *n.*—**doubt'ful,** *a.* Unsettled in opinion or belief, as a person; undecided; hesitating; also, apprehensive†; also, admitting of or causing doubt, as a thing; uncertain; ambiguous; of uncertain issue (as, "the *doubtful* fray": Scott's "Rokeby," i. 19); of questionable character; in *pros.,* variable in quantity; capable of being either long or short, as a vowel.—**doubt'ful-ly,** *adv.*—**doubt'ful-ness,** *n.*—**doubt'ing,** *p. a.* That doubts: as, a *doubting* Thomas (see under *Thomas, n.*).—**doubt'ing-ly,** *adv.*—**doubt'less. I.** *a.* Free from doubt or uncertainty; indubitable; also, free from fear or suspicion† (as, "Pretty child, sleep *doubtless* and secure": Shakspere's "King John," iv. 1. 130). **II.** *adv.* Without doubt, or unquestionably (as, "And the Lord said unto David, Go up: for I will *doubtless* deliver the Philistines into thine hand": 2 Sam. v. 19); also, probably or presumably (as, "*Doubtless* the pleasure is as great Of being cheated, as to cheat": Butler's "Hudibras," ii. 3. 1).—**doubt'less-ly,** *adv.* —**doubt'less-ness,** *n.*

douce (dös), *a.* [OF. *dous,* fem. *douce* (F. *doux,* fem. *douce*), < L. *dulcis,* sweet.] Sweet† or pleasant†; also, quiet, sedate, or modest (Sc. and north. Eng.).—**douce'ly,** *adv.*—**douce'ness,** *n.*

dou-ce-peres (dö'sẹ-pārz), *n. pl.* See *douzepers.*

dou-ceur (dö-sėr), *n.* [F., < LL. *dulcor,* sweetness, < L. *dulcis,* sweet.] Sweetness, agreeableness, or amiability; also, a conciliatory gift; a gratuity, fee, or tip.

douche (dösh), *n.* [F., < It. *doccia,* conduit, shower-bath, ult. < L. *ducere,* lead.] A jet or current of water or the like applied to a particular part or organ of the body, as for medicinal purposes; the application of such a jet; an instrument for administering it.—**douche,** *v. t.;* *douched, douching.* To apply a douche to; douse.

dough (dō), *n.* [AS. *dāh* = D. *deeg* = G. *teig* = Icel. *deig* = Goth. *daigs,* dough; akin to L. *fingere,* touch, form, mold: see *feign.*] Flour or meal combined with water, milk, etc., in a mass for baking into bread, cake, etc.; paste of bread; also, any soft, pasty mass; also, money (slang).—**dough'=boy,** *n.* A flour dumpling (colloq.); also, an infantry soldier (colloq., U. S.).—**dough'face,** *n.* A face having the appearance of dough; a person with such a face; hence, a pliable or yielding person; esp., in *U. S. hist.,* in the period of controversy regarding slavery, a Northern politician disposed to show undue compliance with the wishes of the South in the matter of slavery.—**dough'nut,** *n.* A small cake of sweetened dough fried in lard.

dough-ty (dou'ti), *a.*; compar. *doughtier*, superl. *doughtiest*. [AS. *dohtig*, for *dyhtig*, < *dugan*, be good, avail: see *dow*^{1}.] Capable; strong; stout; hardy; valiant. [Now archaic, and often humorous.]—**dough'ti-ly**, *adv.*—**dough'ti-ness**, *n.*

dough-y (dō'i), *a.* Of or like dough; half-baked; soft and heavy; pallid and flabby.

Dou-kho-bors (dö'kǫ-bôrz), *n. pl.* See *Dukhobors*.

Doug-las (dug'lạs) **spruce, fir,** or **pine.** [From David *Douglas* (1798–1834), Scottish botanist and traveler.] A coniferous tree, *Pseudotsuga mucronata* (or *douglasii*), of western North America, often over 200 feet high, and yielding a strong, durable timber.

dou-ma (dö'mä), *n.* See *duma*.

doum=palm (döm'päm), *n.* See *doom-palm*.

dour (dör), *a.* [Var. of *dure*^{1}.] Hard; severe; stern; sullen; obstinate. [Chiefly Sc.]—**dour'ly,** *adv.*—**dour'-ness,** *n.*

dour-ra, dou-ra (dö'rạ̈), *n.* Same as *durra*.

douse^{1} (dous), *v. t.*; *doused, dousing*. [Cf. obs. D. *doesen*, beat, strike.] To strike (chiefly prov.); take off or doff (colloq.); put out or extinguish, as a light (slang); *naut.*, to lower in haste, as a sail; slacken suddenly; also, to close, as a port-hole.—**douse**^{1}, *n.* A stroke or blow: as, "He gave the young man a *douse* in the chops" (Smollett's "Humphry Clinker," June 3). [Chiefly prov.]

douse^{2} (dous), *v.*; *doused, dousing*. [Cf. *douse*^{1}.] **I.** *tr.* To plunge into water or the like; throw water over; drench. **II.** *intr.* To plunge or be plunged into a liquid.

douse^{3} (douz), etc. See *dowse*^{3}, etc.

dou-ze-pers, dou-ce-peres (dö'zẹ-pãrz, -sẹ-pãrz), *n. pl.* [OF. *douze pers*, twelve peers.] The twelve peers or paladins represented in old romances as in attendance on Charlemagne; historically, a group of twelve great spiritual and temporal peers of France, taken to represent those of Charlemagne.

dove^{1} (dōv). Occasional preterit of *dive*.

dove^{2} (duv), *n.* [ME. *duve* = D. *duif* = G. *taube* = Icel. *dūfa* = Goth. *dūbō*, dove; prob. from the Teut. verb-stem represented by E. *dive*.] Any bird of the pigeon family (*Columbidæ*); a pigeon; also, a person regarded as innocent, gentle, or tenderly affectionate, as a woman or child; [*cap.*] the Holy Ghost (see Luke, iii. 22); [*l. c.*] a messenger of peace and deliverance from anxiety, like the dove of Noah (see Gen. viii. 8–12); formerly, a repository for the eucharist, in the form of a dove.—**dove'=col"or,** *n.* A warm gray with a purplish or pinkish tinge.—**dove'=col"ored,** *a.*—**dove'=cote** (-kōt), **dove'=cot** (-kot), *n.* A structure, usually at a height above the ground, for the roosting and breeding of domestic pigeons. Also **dove'=house.**

Mourning-dove (*Zenaidura macrura*).

dove-kie (duv'ki), *n.* [Dim. of *dove*^{2}.] The black guillemot, *Cepphus grylle*; also, the rotche, *Alle alle*.

dove=plant (duv'plant), *n.* An orchid, *Peristeria elata*, of Central America: so called from the fancied resemblance of the central part of the flower to a white dove with expanded wings.

Do-ver's (dō'vėrz) **pow'der.** [From T. *Dover* (1660–1742), Engish physician.] In *med.*, a powder containing ipecac and opium, used as an anodyne, diaphoretic, and antispasmodic.

dove-tail (duv'tāl), *n.* In *carp.*, etc., a tenon or tongue resembling a dove's tail spread or a reversed wedge; also, the mortise or cavity into which such a tenon fits; also, a joint or fastening formed by one or more such tenons and mortises.—**dove'tail,** *v. t.* or *i.* To join or fit together by means of a dovetail or dovetails; fig., to join or fit together compactly or harmoniously.

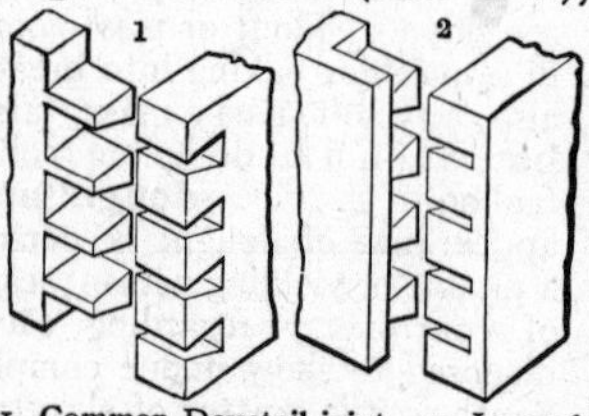

1. Common Dovetail-joint. 2. Lapped Dovetail-joint.

dow^{1} (dou), *v. i.*; pret. *dowed* or *dought* (dout). [AS. *dugan* = G. *taugen*: cf. *doughty*.] To be good or of use; be able; do well, or thrive. [Now Sc. and north. Eng.]

dow^{2} (dou), *n.* See *dhow*.

dow-a-ble (dou'ạ-bl), *a.* In *law*, entitled to dower.

dow-a-ger (dou'ạ-jėr), *n.* [OF. *douagiere*, < *douage*, dower, < *douer*, < L. *dotare*, endow: see *dotation*.] A woman who holds some title or property from her deceased husband; the widow of a king, duke, or the like, often as distinguished from the wife of her husband's heir bearing the same name; also, a dignified elderly lady (colloq.).

dow-dy (dou'di). [Earlier *dowd*, ME. *doude*; origin obscure.] **I.** *n.*; pl. *-dies* (-diz). An ill-dressed woman; a woman whose dress is noticeably lacking in pleasing effectiveness, trimness, or smartness. **II.** *a.*; compar. *dowdier*, superl. *dowdiest*. Ill-dressed; not trim, smart, or stylish.—**dow'di-ly,** *adv.*—**dow'di-ness,** *n.*—**dow'dy-ish,** *a.* Like a dowdy; somewhat dowdy.

dow-el (dou'ẹl), *n.* [Cf. G. *döbel*, peg, plug, pin.] A pin or tenon for fitting into a corresponding hole and thus serving to fasten together two pieces of wood, etc.; also, a piece of wood driven into a wall to receive nails of skirtings, etc.—**dow'el,** *v. t.*; *-eled* or *-elled*, *-eling* or *-elling*. To fasten with dowels; furnish with dowels.

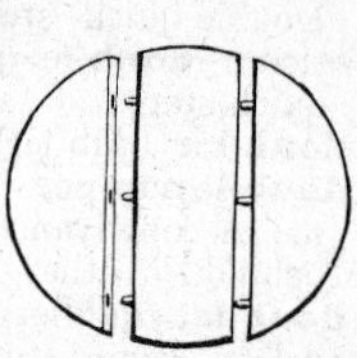

Barrel-end in three pieces joined by Dowels.

dow-er (dou'ėr), *n.* [OF. F. *douaire*, < ML. *dotarium*, < L. *dos*, dowry, E. *dot*^{2}.] Dowry, or the property which a woman brings to her husband at marriage; fig., a natural gift or endowment (as, "faith's transcendent *dower*": Wordsworth's "River Duddon," xxxiv.); also, now commonly, the portion of a deceased husband's real property allowed by the law to his widow for her life.—**dow'er,** *v. t.* To provide with a dower or dowry; endow: also, to give as a dower or dowry.—**dow'er=house,** *n.* In Great Britain, a house provided for the residence of a widow as part of her dower.—**dow'er-less,** *a.* Without a dower.

dowf (douf), *a.* [Cf. Icel. *daufr*, deaf.] Dull; flat; spiritless; stupid; melancholy; dismal. [Sc. and north. Eng.]

dow-ie (dou'i), *a.* [Akin to *dull*.] Dull; melancholy; dismal. [Sc. and north. Eng.]

dow-itch-er (dou'ich-ėr), *n.* [Prob. N. Amer. Ind.] Either of two species of snipe, *Macrorhamphus griseus* and *M. scolopaceus*, of eastern and western North America respectively.

dow-las (dou'lạs), *n.* [From *Daoulas*, near Brest, in northwestern France.] A strong, plain-woven linen fabric; also, a similar fabric of cotton.

down^{1} (doun), *n.* [Icel. *dūnn*.] The first feathering of young birds; also, the soft under plumage of birds; hence, a soft hairy growth, as the hair on the human face when first beginning to appear, or that on certain plants or fruits; the feathery coma or pappus of certain seeds; any light feathery or fluffy substance.

down^{2} (doun), *n.* [AS. *dūn* = D. *duin* = F. *dune* (see *dune*); prob. from Celtic.] A hill; a sand-hill or dune; a bare, level highland; a tract of upland pasture (in *pl.*, esp. applied to districts in southern England); *pl.* [*cap.*], with *the*, a roadstead on the coast of Kent in southeastern England, opposite Deal, Sandwich, and Ramsgate.

down^{3} (doun). [Late AS. *dūne*, for *adūne* (E. *adown*), earlier *of dūne*, 'from (the) hill': see *down*^{2}.] **I.** *adv.* From higher to lower; in a descending direction or order, as from the top, head, or beginning; into or in a lower position or condition; to or at a low point, degree, rate, pitch, etc.; below the horizon (as, the sun is going *down*); in a prostrate, depressed, or degraded condition; in due place, position, form, or state (as, to settle *down* to work; to pay cash *down*; to jot *down* an address); in *golf*, behind an opponent a specified number of holes (opposed to *up*). Sometimes (by ellipsis of a verb) used as if an imperative: as, *down*, Towser! *down* with you! *down* with tyranny! **II.** *prep.*

In a descending direction on, over, or along; adown.—**down**[3]. **I.** *a.* Downward; going or directed downward; also, downcast; dejected. **II.** *n.* A downward movement; a descent; fig., a reverse (cf. *up, n.*); in *football*, the declaring of the ball as down or out of play, or the play immediately preceding this.—**down**[3], *v.* **I.** *tr.* To put or throw down; subdue. **II.** *intr.* To go down; fall.

down-cast (doun′kȧst). **I.** *a.* Cast down; ruined; fig., dejected in spirit; depressed; also, directed downward, as the eyes. **II.** *n.* The act of casting down; overthrow or ruin; a downward look or glance.

down-come (doun′kum), *n.* Descent; downfall; also, a downcomer.—**down′com″er** (-kum″ėr), *n.* A pipe, tube, or passage for conducting solid, liquid, or gaseous material in a downward direction.

down-fall (doun′fâl), *n.* The act of falling down; sudden descent; a fall, as of rain or snow; also, descent to a lower position or standing; overthrow; ruin; also, a kind of trap or deadfall, in which a weight or missile falls upon the prey.—**down′fall″en,** *a.*

down-flow (doun′flō), *n.* A flowing down; also, that which flows down.

down-haul (doun′hâl), *n.* *Naut.*, a rope for hauling down a sail.

down-heart-ed (doun′här′ted), *a.* Dejected; depressed; discouraged.—**down′heart′ed-ness,** *n.*

down-hill (doun′hil′), *adv.* Down the slope of a hill; downward.—**down′hill,** *a.* Going or tending downward on or as on a hill.

down-i-ly (dou′ni-li), *adv.* In a downy manner; like down.—**down′i-ness,** *n.* Downy state; a downy growth.

down-land (doun′land), *n.* Land forming downs or upland tracts.

down-less (doun′les), *a.* Without down or a downy growth.

down-most (doun′mōst), *adv.* and *a.* *superl.* Furthest down.

down-pour (doun′pōr), *n.* A pouring down; a heavy, continuous fall of water, rain, etc.

down-right (doun′rīt). **I.** *adv.* Straight down; hence, in plain terms; also, completely or thoroughly (as, he is *downright* angry). **II.** *a.* Directed straight downward (as, "I cleft his beaver with a *downright* blow": Shakspere's "3 Henry VI.," i. 1. 12); hence, direct, straightforward, or plain; direct and plain in speech or behavior; also, thorough, absolute, or positive; out-and-out.—**down′right-ly,** *adv.*—**down′right-ness,** *n.*

down-rush (doun′rush), *n.* A downward rush.

down-stairs (doun′stãrz′), *adv.* Down the stairs; to or on a lower floor.—**down′stairs,** *a.* Pertaining to or situated on a lower floor.

down-take (doun′tāk), *n.* A pipe or passage leading downward, as for conducting coal, ore, gaseous products, or the like.

down-throw (doun′thrō), *n.* A throwing down or being thrown down; an overthrow; in *geol.*, a downward displacement of rock on one side of a fault (opposed to *upthrow*).

down-town (doun′toun′), *adv.* To or in the lower part of a town.—**down′town,** *a.* Moving toward, situated in, or pertaining to the lower part of a town.

down-trod-den (doun′trod″n), *a.* Trodden down; fig., tyrannized over; oppressed.

down-ward (doun′wạrd), *adv.* From a higher to a lower place or condition; down from a head, source, or beginning; also, below, or in the lower part (as, "Dagon his name; sea monster, upward man And *downward* fish": Milton's "Paradise Lost," i. 463).—**down′ward,** *a.* Moving or tending to a lower place or condition; descending from a head or beginning.—**down′ward-ly,** *adv.*—**down′wards,** *adv.* Downward.

down-y (dou′ni), *a.*; compar. *downier*, superl. *downiest.* Of the nature of or resembling down; fluffy; soft; made of down; covered with down; also, knowing or cunning (slang).

dow-ry (dou′ri), *n.*; pl. *-ries* (-riz). [See *dower.*] The money, goods, or estate which a woman brings to her husband at marriage; dot; also, any gift or reward in view of marriage†; also, a natural gift or endowment (as, "Adorn'd with wisedome and with chastitie, And all the *dowries* of a noble mind": Spenser's "Daphnaïda," 216); also, a widow's dower†.

dowse[1], **dowse**[2] (dous). See *douse*[1], *douse*[2].

dowse[3] (douz), *v. i.*; *dowsed, dowsing.* [Origin unknown.] To search for subterranean supplies of water, ore, etc., by the aid of a divining-rod.—**dows′er,** *n.*—**dows′ing=rod,** *n.* A divining-rod.

dox-ol-o-gy (dok-sol′ǫ-ji), *n.*; pl. *-gies* (-jiz). [ML. *doxologia*, < Gr. δοξολογία, a praising, < δόξα, opinion, repute, glory (< δοκεῖν, think: cf. *dogma*), + λέγειν, speak.] A hymn or form of words containing an ascription of praise to God, as the Gloria in Excelsis ('great doxology' or 'greater doxology'), the Gloria Patri ('lesser doxology'), or the metrical formula beginning "Praise God, from whom all blessings flow." See *Gloria.*—**dox-o-log-i-cal** (dok-sǭ-loj′i-kạl), *a.*

dox-y[1] (dok′si), *n.*; pl. *doxies* (-siz). [Origin unknown.] A mistress or paramour; a prostitute. [Orig. beggars' and thieves' slang.]

dox-y[2] (dok′si), *n.*; pl. *doxies* (-siz). [Detached from *orthodoxy, heterodoxy*, etc.] An opinion or doctrine: esp. with reference to controversy. [Colloq.]

do-yen (dwo-yaṅ), *n.* [F.: see *dean*[2].] A dean; the senior member of a body, class, profession, etc.

doy-ley, doy-ly (doi′li), *n.* See *doily.*

doze (dōz), *v.*; *dozed, dozing.* [Prob. from Scand.] **I.** *tr.* To stupefy†; also, to make drowsy; also, to pass or spend (time) in drowsiness. **II.** *intr.* To sleep lightly or fitfully; fall into a light sleep unintentionally; be in a state of drowsiness; be dull or half asleep.—**doze,** *n.* A fit of dozing; a light or fitful sleep.

doz-en (duz′n), *n.*; pl. *dozens* or (as after a numeral) *dozen.* [OF. F. *douzaine*, < *douze*, < L. *duodecim*, twelve: see *duodecimal.*] A group of twelve units or things.—**baker's dozen,** thirteen reckoned as a dozen.—**doz′enth,** *a.* Twelfth.

doz-er (dō′zėr), *n.* One who dozes.

doz-y (dō′zi), *a.* Inclined to doze; drowsy.—**doz′i-ness,** *n.*

drab[1] (drab), *n.* [Cf. Ir. *drabog*, Gael. *drabag*, slattern.] A dirty, untidy woman; a slattern; also, a prostitute.—**drab**[1], *v. i.*; *drabbed, drabbing.* To associate with drabs. See Shakspere's "Hamlet," ii. 1. 26.

drab[2] (drab). [F. *drap*, cloth: see *drape.*] **I.** *n.* Orig., a kind of cloth of the natural or undyed color; hence, a dull brownish or yellowish gray color. **II.** *a.* Of the color drab; brownish-gray; fig., dull; cheerless.

drab-bet (drab′et), *n.* [Dim. of *drab*[2].] A coarse drab linen fabric used for making men's smock-frocks, etc.

drab-ble (drab′l), *v.*; *-bled, -bling.* [ME. *drabelen* = LG. *drabbeln.*] **I.** *intr.* To become wet and dirty as by trailing over wet ground; draggle; also, to fish with a rod and a long line passed through a piece of lead so that the hook may be dragged along the bottom. **II.** *tr.* To draggle; make wet and dirty.—**drab′bler,** *n.* *Naut.*, a piece of canvas laced to the bottom of the bonnet of a sail, to increase its depth.

drachm (dram), *n.* Same as *drachma* and *dram.*

drach-ma (drak′mạ̈), *n.*; pl. *-mas* or *-mæ* (-mē). [L., < Gr. δραχμή, lit. 'handful,' < δράσσεσθαι, grasp.] The principal silver coin of the ancient Greeks, varying in value; the monetary unit, or a silver coin, of modern Greece, equivalent to about 19.3 U. S. cents; also, a small ancient Greek weight; any of various modern weights, esp. a dram.

Obverse. Reverse.
Drachma of Phæstus in Crete, about 400 B. C. — British Museum.

Dra-co-ni-an, Dra-con-ic (drạ-kō′ni-ạn, -kon′ik), *a.* Of, like, or befitting Draco, an Athenian legislator noted for the severity of his code of laws (about 621 B.C.); hence, rigorous; severe.—**Dra-con′i-cal-ly,** *adv.*

draff (drȧf), *n.* [ME. *draf* = D. and Icel. *draf.*] Refuse, lees, or dregs; esp., the refuse of malt after brewing or distilling.—**draff′y,** *a.* Full of draff; also, like draff; worthless.

(variable) ḓ as d or j, ș as s or sh, ț as t or ch, ẓ as z or zh; *o*, F. cloche; ü, F. menu; ċh, Sc. loch; ṅ, F. bonbon; ′, primary accent; ″, secondary accent; †, obsolete; <, from; +, and; =, equals. **See also lists at beginning of book.**

draft, draught (dråft), *n.* [ME. *draht,* later *draught, draft,* < AS. *dragan,* E. *draw.* For certain uses, as noted, one spelling or the other is now the more usual. See *draught.*] The act of drawing, or that which is drawn; a pull or haul; a take of fish, etc.; (*draught*) the drawing of a liquid from its receptacle, as of ale from a cask (hence, ale on *draught*); drinking, or a drink or potion; a current of air, esp. in a room, chimney, stove, or any inclosed space; a device for regulating such a current, as a damper in a stove; (*draft*) the taking of supplies, forces, money, etc., from a given source, or that which is taken, as a military levy or conscription, or a detachment; (*draft*) a drain or demand made on anything; (*draft*) a written order drawn by one person on another for the payment of money; the depth a vessel sinks in water; a drawing, sketch, or design; (*draft*) a first or preliminary form of any writing, subject to revision and copying; in *founding,* the slight taper given to a pattern in order that it may be drawn from the sand without injury to the mold; in *masonry,* a line or border chiseled at the edge of a stone, to serve as a guide in leveling the surfaces. See also *draughts.*—**draft, draught,** *v. t.* To draw or pull; (*draft*) take by draft, as for military service; draw the outlines or plan of, or sketch; (*draft*) draw up in written form, as a first draft; in *masonry,* to cut a draft on.—**draft-ee** (dråf-tē′), *n.* One who is drafted, as for military service. —**draft′er, draught′er,** *n.*—**draft′=horse, draught′=horse,** *n.* A horse for drawing heavy loads.—**draft′i-ness, draught′i-ness,** *n.* Drafty condition.—**draft′ing, draught′ing,** *n.* The act or work of one who drafts; esp., mechanical drawing.—**drafts′man, draughts′man** (-mạn), *n.*; pl. *-men.* One who draws sketches, plans, or designs; one employed in making mechanical drawings, as of machines, structures, etc.; (*draftsman*) one who draws up documents. Cf. *draughtsman.*—**draft′y, draught′y,** *a.* Characterized by or causing drafts (of air).

drag (drag), *v.*; *dragged, dragging.* [ME. *draggen*: cf. Icel. *draga,* also AS. *dragan,* E. *draw.*] **I.** *tr.* To draw with force, effort, or difficulty; pull heavily or slowly along; haul; trail; fig., to bring (*in*) as by main force, as an irrelevant matter; also, to protract or pass tediously (often with *out* or *on*); also, to search with a drag, grapnel, or the like; also, to break (land) with a drag or harrow. **II.** *intr.* To be drawn or hauled along; trail on the ground; also, to move heavily or with effort; proceed or pass with tedious slowness; also, to use a drag or grapnel; dredge.—**drag,** *n.* Something used by or for dragging, as a drag-net or a dredge; a grapnel, net, or other apparatus dragged through water in searching, as for dead bodies; a heavy harrow; a stout sledge or sled; a four-horse coach with seats inside and on top; sometimes, a break; a device for checking the rotation of the wheels of a vehicle; a kind of floating anchor used to keep a ship's head to the wind or to check drifting; fig., anything that retards progress; also, the act of dragging; slow, laborious movement or procedure; retardation; in *hunting,* the scent or trail of a fox, etc.; something, as anise-seed, dragged over the ground to leave an artificial scent; a hunt with such a scent.—**drag′=bar,** *n.* A drawbar (iron rod).—**drag′=bolt,** *n.* A coupling-pin.

dra-gée (drȧ-zhā), *n.* [F.: see *dredge*².] A sweetmeat in the form of a sugar-coated fruit or the like; in *phar.,* a sugar-coated medicine.

drag-gle (drag′l), *v.*; *-gled, -gling.* [Freq. of *drag.*] **I.** *tr.* To soil by dragging over damp ground or in the mud; make limp and soiled as with wet and dirt. **II.** *intr.* To hang trailing; become draggled; also, to follow slowly; straggle. —**drag′gle-tail,** *n.* A bedraggled or untidy person; a slut or slattern.—**drag′gle-tailed,** *a.* Having the skirts or garments draggled as from trailing in the wet and dirt; sluttish in dress.—**drag-gly** (drag′li), *a.*

drag=hound (drag′hound), *n.* A hound trained to follow a drag or artificial scent.

drag=hunt (drag′hunt), *n.* A hunt with a drag or artificial scent.

drag=line (drag′līn), *n.* A line or rope dragging from something; a drag-rope.

drag=link (drag′lingk), *n.* A link for connecting the cranks of two shafts; also, a rod connecting the steering device of an automobile to one of the axle stubs, transmitting the steering movements to the steering wheels; also, a drawbar (iron rod).

drag=mill (drag′mil), *n.* An arrastre.

drag=net (drag′net), *n.* A net to be drawn along the bottom of a river, pond, etc., or along the ground, to catch something. Also fig.

drag-o-man (drag′ǫ-mạn), *n.*; pl. *-mans.* [F., < Ar. *tarjumān,* interpreter.] In the Orient, a professional interpreter, as for travelers, or for an embassy or consulate: as, "The intervention of the interpreter, or *dragoman* as he is called, is fatal to the spirit of conversation" (Kinglake's "Eothen," i.).

drag-on (drag′ǫn), *n.* [OF. F. *dragon,* < L. *draco*(*n-*), < Gr. δράκων, serpent.] A huge serpent or snake (now rare); a fabulous monster variously represented, generally as a huge winged reptile with crested head and terrible claws, and often as spouting fire; in the Bible, a large serpent, a crocodile, a great marine animal, or a jackal; also, a name for Satan; also, an early form of musket†; also, a fierce, violent person; often, a severely watchful woman; a duenna; in *zoöl.,* any of the small arboreal lizards constituting the genus *Draco,* of southern Asia, having an extensile wing-like membrane on each side of the body, making possible long flying leaps; in *bot.,* any of various araceous plants, as the jack-in-the-pulpit, *Arisæma triphyllum*; [*cap.*] in *astron.,* the northern constellation Draco.—**dragon's head,** in *astron.,* the ascending node of a planet or the moon. See *node.*—**dragon's tail,** in *astron.,* the descending node of a planet or the moon. See *node.*—**drag-on-esque′** (-esk′), *a.* [See *-esque.*] Of the style or character of a dragon.—**drag′on-ess,** *n.* A female dragon.

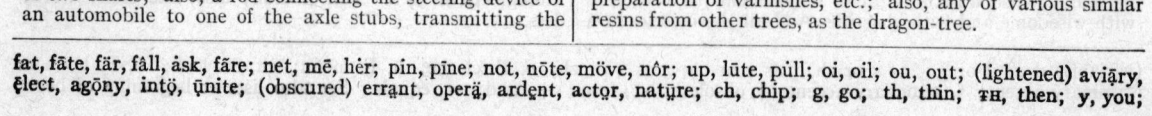

Heraldic Dragon.

Flying-dragon (*Draco volans*).

drag-on-et (drag′ǫn-et), *n.* [OF., dim. of *dragon,* E. *dragon.*] A little or young dragon; also, any fish of the genus *Callionymus,* comprising small marine fishes which mostly inhabit the temperate waters of the Old World, and which are often brightly colored.

drag-on=fish (drag′ǫn-fish), *n.* A fish, the dragonet.

drag-on=fly (drag′ǫn-flī), *n.*; pl. *-flies* (-flīz). Any of the large, harmless insects constituting the order *Odonata* (in old classifications, order *Neuroptera,* family *Libellulidæ*), which feed on mosquitoes, gnats, etc., and which are characterized by a long, slender body, large head, enormous eyes, and two pairs of large, reticulate, membranous wings.

A common Dragon-fly (*Libellula trimaculata*). (Reduced.)

drag-on-ish (drag′ǫn-ish), *a.* Dragon-like.

drag-on-nade (drag-ǫ-nād′), *n.* [F., < *dragon*: see *dragoon.*] One of a series of persecutions of French Protestants, under Louis XIV., by means of dragoons quartered upon them (as, "There was a great emigration of Protestant Huguenots from the *dragonnades* and persecution of Louis XIV.": H G. Wells's "Outline of History," xxxvi. § 8); hence, any persecution with the aid of troops.

drag-on's=blood (drag′ǫnz-blud), *n.* A red resin exuding from the fruit of *Calamus draco,* a palm of the Malay Archipelago, formerly used in medicine, but now chiefly in the preparation of varnishes, etc.; also, any of various similar resins from other trees, as the dragon-tree.

drag-on=tree (drag′on-trē), *n.* A liliaceous tree, *Dracæna draco*, of the Canary Islands, yielding a variety of dragon's-blood.

Dragon-tree.

dra-goon (dra-gön′), *n.* [F. *dragon*, dragoon, orig. dragon (referring, it is said, to the firearm carried by such troops).] A mounted infantryman armed with a short musket†; a cavalryman of a particular type, as in the British army; also, a variety of pigeon.—**dra-goon′,** *v. t.* To set dragoons or soldiers upon; persecute by armed force; hence, to oppress; harass; also, to force by rigorous and oppressive measures, or coerce (as, "Alexander . . . *dragooned* men into wisdom": Godwin's "Caleb Williams," xiii.).—**dra-goon′=bird,** *n.* An umbrella-bird.

drag=rope (drag′rōp), *n.* A rope for dragging something, as a piece of artillery; also, a rope dragging from something, as the guide-rope sometimes hung downward from a balloon.

drags-man (dragz′man), *n.*; pl. *-men.* The driver of a drag or coach; also, one employed to drag a river-bed, etc.

drain (drān), *v.* [AS. *dreahnian*, strain; prob. akin to E. *dry*.] **I.** *tr.* To draw off gradually, as a liquid; remove by degrees, as through conduits or by filtration; draw off or take away completely; also, to withdraw liquid gradually from; make empty or dry by drawing off liquid; deprive of possessions, resources, etc., by gradual withdrawal; exhaust. **II.** *intr.* To flow off gradually; also, to become empty or dry by the gradual flowing off of moisture.—**drain,** *n.* The act of draining or drawing off; gradual or continuous outflow, withdrawal, or expenditure; also, that by which anything is drained, as a pipe or conduit; also, something drained off; hence, a drink (slang: as, "If I don't have a *drain* o' rum, Jim, I'll have the horrors," Stevenson's "Treasure Island," iii.); also, *pl.*, dregs.—**drain′a-ble,** *a.* Capable of being drained.—**drain′age** (-āj), *n.* The act or process of draining; also, a system of drains, artificial or natural; also, that which is drained off, as by a system of drains; sewage.—**drain′er,** *n.* One who drains; one who constructs drains or channels for draining land; that which drains; a vessel or bag in which moist substances are put to drain.—**drain′less,** *a.* That cannot be drained or exhausted.—**drain′=pipe,** *n.* A pipe serving for draining; a waste-pipe.

drake[1] (drāk), *n.* [ME. *drake* = LG. *drake*: cf. OHG. *antrahho*, G. *enterich*, drake.] The male of any bird of the duck kind; also, a large, flat stone on which the duck is placed in the game of duck on drake.

drake[2] (drāk), *n.* [AS. *draca*, < L. *draco*: see *dragon*.] A dragon†; a small kind of cannon†; any of various ephemerids or May-flies used as bait by anglers.—**drake′=fly,** *n.* A drake or May-fly used in angling.

dram (dram), *n.* [OF. *drame*, *dragme* (F. *drachme*), < L. *drachma*: see *drachma*.] A unit of weight, the eighth part of an ounce, apothecaries' weight (60 grains), or the sixteenth part of an ounce, avoirdupois weight (27.34 grains); also, a fluid dram (see under *fluid*, *a.*); hence, a small drink of liquor; also, a small quantity of anything (as, "An inhuman wretch Uncapable of pity, void and empty From any *dram* of mercy": Shakspere's "Merchant of Venice," iv. 1. 6).—**dram,** *v.*; *drammed, dramming.* **I.** *intr.* To drink drams; tipple. **II.** *tr.* To give a dram or drams to; ply with drink.

dra-ma (drä′mä), *n.* [LL. *drama*, < Gr. δρᾶμα (δραματ-), < δρᾶν, do.] A composition in prose or verse presenting in dialogue a story of life or character, esp. one intended to be acted on the stage; a play; also, the branch of literature having such compositions as its subject; dramatic art or representation; also, any series of events having dramatic interest and leading up to a crowning issue.

dra-mat-ic (dra-mat′ik), *a.* [LL. *dramaticus*, < Gr. δραματικός.] Of or pertaining to the drama; employing the form of the drama; also, characteristic of or appropriate to the drama; forceful and animated in action or expression; theatrical.—**dra-mat′i-cal-ly,** *adv.*—**dra-mat′i-cism** (-sizm), *n.* Dramatic character.—**dra-mat′ics,** *n.* The art of producing or acting dramas.

dram-a-tis per-so-næ (dram′a-tis pėr-sō′nē). [NL.] The persons or characters in a drama.

dram-a-tist (dram′a-tist), *n.* A writer of dramas or dramatic poetry; a playwright.

dram-a-ti-za-tion (dram″a-ti-zā′shon), *n.* The act of dramatizing; construction or representation in dramatic form; also, a dramatized version.

dram-a-tize (dram′a-tīz), *v. t.*; *-tized, -tizing.* To make a drama of; put into dramatic form; also, to express or represent dramatically.—**dram′a-tiz-er** (-tī-zėr), *n.*

dram-a-turge (dram′a-tėrj), *n.* [F. *dramaturge*, < Gr. δραματουργός, < δρᾶμα (δραματ-), drama, + -εργός, working, worker.] A composer of dramas; a dramatist.—**dram-a-tur′gic, dram-a-tur′gi-cal** (-tėr′jik, -ji-kal), *a.* Of or pertaining to dramaturgy.—**dram′a-tur-gist,** *n.* A dramaturge.—**dram′a-tur-gy,** *n.* [Gr. δραματουργία.] The science of dramatic composition; the dramatic art; dramatic or theatrical representation.

dram-mock, drum-mock (dram′ok, drum′ok), *n.* [Cf. Gael. *dramaig*, foul mixture.] Meal mixed with water, without cooking. [Sc. and north. Eng.]

dram=shop (dram′shop), *n.* A liquor-saloon.

drank (drangk). Pret. and occasional pp. of *drink*.

drape (drāp), *v.*; *draped, draping.* [OF. F. *draper*, < *drap*, < ML. *drappus*, cloth; origin uncertain: cf. *trap*[3].] **I.** *tr.* To make (wool) into cloth†; weave (cloth)†; also, to cover or hang with cloth or some fabric, esp. in graceful folds; adorn with drapery; also, to adjust (hangings, clothing, etc.) in depending folds. **II.** *intr.* To fall in folds, as drapery.—**dra′per,** *n.* [OF. F. *drapier*.] A maker of cloth†; a dealer in cloths, etc. (Eng.: as, a woolen-*draper*; a linen-*draper*).—**dra′per-y,** *n.*; pl. *-ies* (-iz). [OF. F. *draperie*.] The business of a draper; also, cloths or textile fabrics collectively; also, coverings, hangings, clothing, etc., of some fabric, esp. as disposed in loose, graceful folds or with a view to decorative effect; hangings, clothing, etc., so disposed, as represented in sculpture or painting; also, the draping or disposing of hangings, clothing, etc., in graceful folds.—**dra′per-y,** *v. t.*; *-peried, -perying.* To furnish or hang with or as with drapery: as, "And then her dress—what beautiful simplicity *Draperied* her form!" (Byron's "Don Juan," xvi. 102).

Greek Relief, illustrating treatment of Drapery.

dras-tic (dras′tik). [Gr. δραστικός, < δρᾶν, do.] **I.** *a.* Acting with force or violence; violent; esp., of a medicinal substance, powerful or severe in action, as a purgative. **II.** *n.* A drastic medicine or agent.—**dras′ti-cal-ly,** *adv.*

drat (drat), *v. t.*; *dratted, dratting.* [From 'od rot (*God rot*), used in imprecation.] A word used in vague or mild malediction (prov. or vulgar); also, to use this word to or of.—**drat′ted,** *p. a.* Confounded. [Prov. or vulgar.]

draught (dråft), *n.* and *v.* Older form of *draft*, still prevalent, esp. in British use, in many (chiefly the longer existent) senses. See *draft*.—**draught′=board,** *n.* A checker-board.—**draught′=horse,** *n.* See *draft-horse*.—**draughts,** *n.* [Orig. pl., with reference to the moves.] The game of checkers.—**draughts′man** (-man), *n.*; pl. *-men.* A piece at draughts; a checker. Cf. *draftsman*.—**draught′y,** *a.* See *drafty*.

drave (drāv). Archaic preterit of *drive*.

Dra-vid-i-an (dra-vid′i-an). **I.** *a.* Of or pertaining to a race or body of peoples mostly of southern India and Ceylon; of or pertaining to the group or family of languages spoken by them, including Tamil, Telugu, Canarese, Malayalam,

Tulu, etc. **II.** *n.* A member of the Dravidian race; the Dravidian family of languages.

draw (drâ), *v.*; pret. *drew*, pp. *drawn*, ppr. *drawing*. [AS. *dragan* = Icel. *draga*, draw, = Goth. *-dragan* = D. *dragen* = G. *tragen*, carry, bear: cf. *drag*.] **I.** *tr.* To cause to come in a particular direction as by a pulling force (often with *along*, *away*, *in*, *out*, *down*, *up*, *on*, *off*, etc.); pull, haul, or drag; lead or take along; bring toward one's self or itself, as by inherent force or influence; attract; take in, as by sucking or inhaling; bring or take out, as from a receptacle or source (as, to *draw* water, ale, blood, tears, lots, teeth, money); get, derive, deduce, or elicit; make (tea) by extracting essence; leave (a contest) undecided; take contents from; drain (a pond, etc.); disembowel (a fowl, a condemned person, etc.); search (cover) for game; displace (a certain depth of water: said of a boat); pull out to full or greater length; stretch; make by attenuating, as wire by pulling a rod of metal through a succession of holes of diminishing diameter; wrinkle or shrink by contraction; mark out, trace, or delineate; write or draft (often with *up*); frame or formulate, as a contrast or a distinction. Used in many phrases: as, to *draw* rein (to check a horse); to *draw* down wrath or vengeance on one's head; to *draw* out a witness (into disclosures); to be *drawn* into a quarrel; to *draw* up an army (in due array). **II.** *intr.* To exert a pulling, moving, or attracting force; be drawn; move as under a pulling force; come, go, or pass (*on*, *off*, *out*, *near*, *toward*, etc.); take out a sword, pistol, etc., for action (often with *on*); come out of a mold, as in casting; produce or have a draft of air, etc., as a pipe or flue; effect drainage; leave a contest undecided; settle in water, as a boat; levy or call (*on*) for money, supplies, etc.; make demands; make a formal written demand, as for money due or on deposit; shrink or contract; use or practise the art of tracing or delineating figures; practise drawing.—**draw,** *n.* The act of drawing; that which is drawn, as a lot or the movable part of a drawbridge; a drawn or undecided contest; a land-basin into or through which water drains.

draw-back (drâ′bak), *n.* An amount paid back from a charge made; a portion of customs dues remitted, as on imported goods when they are subsequently exported; also, a diminution; also, a hindrance or disadvantage.

draw=bar (drâ′bär), *n.* An iron rod with an eye at each end, as for use in coupling freight-cars, or a locomotive and its tender; also, a bar in a fence, which can be removed to allow passage.

draw=bore (drâ′bōr), *n.* In *carp.*, a hole pierced through a tenon so that when a pin ('draw-bore pin') is driven in, the mortised and tenoned parts are drawn snugly together.

draw-bridge (drâ′brij), *n.* A bridge of which the whole or a part may be drawn up or aside, to prevent access or to leave a passage open for boats, etc.

Drawbridge, Château of Montargis, France.

draw-ee (drâ-ē′), *n.* One on whom an order, draft, or bill of exchange is drawn.

draw-er (drâ′ėr), *n.* One who or that which draws; a tapster; one who draws an order, draft, or bill of exchange; a sliding compartment, as in a piece of furniture, that may be drawn out in order to get access to it; *pl.*, a garment for the lower part of the body, with a separate portion for each leg.

draw=gear (drâ′gēr), *n.* A harness for draft-horses; also, a coupling for railway-carriages (Eng.).

draw-ing (drâ′ing), *n.* The act of a person or thing that draws, or the thing drawn; esp., representation by lines; delineation of form (without reference to color); a sketch, plan, or design, esp. one executed by pen, pencil, or crayon. —**draw′ing=knife,** *n.* A knife with a handle at each end of the blade, used by drawing over a surface.

draw-ing=room (drâ′ing-röm), *n.* [For *withdrawing-room*.] A room to which the company withdraws from the dining-room after dinner; a room for the reception of company; also, a formal reception, esp. at court (as, "Her only conversation was about millinery . . . and about her dress at the *Drawing-room*": Thackeray's "Newcomes," lxii.).—**drawing=room car,** a parlor-car.

drawl (drâl), *v. t.* or *i.* [Appar. a freq. form connected with *drag* and *draw*.] To drag slowly along (obs. or rare); say or speak with slow, lingering utterance.—**drawl,** *n.* The act or utterance of one who drawls.—**drawl′er,** *n.*—**drawl′ing-ly,** *adv.*

drawn (drân). Past participle of *draw*.—**drawn,** *p. a.* Undecided, as a contest in which neither side has won; disemboweled, as a fowl; melted and made into a sauce, as butter; gathered or shirred, as needlework.—**drawn′=work,** *n.* Ornamental work done by drawing threads from a fabric, the remaining portions usually being formed into lace-like patterns by needlework.

draw=plate (drâ′plāt), *n.* A plate with conical holes through which wire is drawn to regulate its size and shape.

draw=shave (drâ′shāv), *n.* A drawing-knife; also, a surgical instrument for removing thin slices of tissue, etc.

draw=tube (drâ′tūb), *n.* A tube sliding within another tube, as the tube carrying the eyepiece in a microscope.

dray (drā), *n.* [ME. *dreye*; akin to E. *draw*.] A low, strong cart without fixed sides, for carrying heavy loads; also, a sledge or sled.—**dray,** *v. t.* To convey on a dray.—**dray′age** (-āj), *n.* Carriage by dray, or a charge made for it.—**dray′=horse,** *n.*—**dray′man** (-man), *n.*; pl. *-men*. A man who drives a dray.

dread (dred), *v.* [ME. *dreden*, prob. for *adreden*, < AS. *ondrǣdan* = OHG. *intrātan*, fear.] **I.** *tr.* To fear greatly; regard with awe; look forward to with terror or apprehension; also, to frighten†. **II.** *intr.* To be in great fear. —**dread,** *n.* Great fear; deep awe or reverence; terror or apprehension as to something future; also, a person or thing dreaded (as, "Let him be your *dread*": Isa. viii. 13); also, doubt†.—**dread,** *a.* [Orig. pp.] Dreaded; dreadful; also, held in awe; revered.—**dread′er,** *n.*—**dread′ful. I.** *a.* Full of dread, fear, or reverence† (as, "*dreadfull* of daunger": Spenser's "Faerie Queene," iii. 1. 37); also, inspiring dread, fear, or reverence; terrible; awe-inspiring; also, extremely bad, unpleasant, ugly, great, etc. (colloq.). **II.** *n.* A cheap, lurid story, as of crime or adventure; a periodical given to highly sensational matter.—**dread′ful-ly,** *adv.*—**dread′ful-ness,** *n.*—**dread′ing-ly,** *adv.*—**dread′less,** *a.* Having no dread or fear; fearless; undaunted; not apprehensive.—**dread′ly,** *adv.*—**dread′ness,** *n.*

dread-naught, dread-nought (dred′nât), *n.* One who fears nothing; an outer garment of heavy cloth; a thick cloth with a long pile; (usually *dreadnought*: so called from the "Dreadnought," a British battle-ship launched in 1906) a type of battle-ship with very heavy armament.

dream (drēm), *n.* [ME. *drem* = D. *droom* = G. *traum* = Icel. *draumr*, dream.] A succession of images or ideas present in the mind during sleep; the sleeping state in which this occurs; fig., an involuntary vision occurring to one awake ('waking dream'); a visionary fancy voluntarily indulged in while awake ('day-dream'); a reverie; sometimes, a wild or vain fancy; also, an object seen in a dream (as, "Suddenly stood at my head a *dream*": Milton's "Paradise Lost," viii. 292); also, something of a beauty or charm associated with dreams rather than with reality.—**dream,** *v.*; *dreamed* or *dreamt* (dremt), *dreaming*. **I.** *intr.* To have a dream or dreams; be conscious of images and thoughts during sleep; fig., to indulge in day-dreams or reveries; give way to visionary thought or speculation; also, to think or conceive of something in a very remote way (as, "There are more things in heaven and earth, Horatio, Than are *dreamt* of in your philosophy": Shakspere's "Hamlet," i. 5. 167). **II.** *tr.* To have (a dream: as, "Your old men shall *dream* dreams," Joel, ii. 28); see or imagine in sleep or in a vision; also, to imagine as if in a dream; fancy; suppose vaguely or indefinitely; also, pass or spend (time, etc.) in dreaming (followed by *away*, etc.).—**dream′er,** *n.* One who dreams; one who indulges in day-dreams, or in visionary thought or speculation.—**dream′ful,** *a.* Abounding in dreams; dreamy: as, "into *dreamful* slumber lull'd"

(Tennyson's "Eleänore," ii.).—**dream'i-ly,** *adv.* In a dreamy manner.—**dream'i-ness,** *n.*—**dream'ing-ly,** *adv.*—**dream'land** (-land), *n.* The land or region seen in dreams; the land of imagination or fancy; the region of reverie. —**dream'less,** *a.* Free from dreams.—**dream'y,** *a.*; compar. *dreamier*, superl. *dreamiest.* Full of dreams; characterized by or causing dreams; also, given to reverie or daydreaming; also, of the nature of or characteristic of a dream; visionary; vague; indistinct; dim.

drear (drēr), *a.* Shortened form of *dreary.* [Poetic.]

drear-i-ly (drēr'i-li), *adv.* In a dreary manner; dismally.—**drear'i-ness,** *n.*

drear-i-some (drēr'i-sum), *a.* Dreary. [Chiefly prov.]

drear-y (drēr'i), *a.*; compar. *drearier*, superl. *dreariest.* [AS. *drēorig*, gory, cruel, sad, < *drēor*, gore, blood: cf. G. *traurig*, sad.] Cruel†; grievous†; also, sad or sorrowful (archaic); also, causing sadness or gloom; gloomy; dismal; dull or monotonous.

dredge[1] (drej), *n.* [Akin to *drag.*] A contrivance for gathering objects or material from the bed of a river, etc., by dragging along the bottom; a dredging-machine.—**dredge**[1], *v.*; *dredged, dredging.* **I.** *tr.* To gather and bring up (oysters, etc.), or clear out or deepen (a channel, etc.), with a dredge. **II.** *intr.* To use a dredge.

dredge[2] (drej), *n.* [OF. *dragie* (F. *dragée*), < L. *tragemata*, pl., < Gr. *τραγήματα*, pl., sweetmeats, dessert, < *τραγεῖν*, *τρώγειν*, nibble, eat (fruit, dessert, etc.).] A sweetmeat†; a mixture of powdered spices, etc.†; a mixture of various kinds of grain, esp. oats and barley, sown together (now prov.).—**dredge**[2], *v. t.*; *dredged, dredging.* In *cookery*, to sprinkle with some powdered preparation or substance, esp. flour; sprinkle (a powdered substance) over. Also fig.

dredg-er[1] (drej'ėr), *n.* One who uses a dredge; a boat used in dredging; a dredging-machine.

dredg-er[2] (drej'ėr), *n.* A box with a perforated top for sprinkling flour, etc.

dredg-ing (drej'ing), *n.* The act of one who or that which dredges; also, the material dredged up.—**dredg'ing=machine",** *n.* Any of various powerful machines for dredging up or removing earth, etc., as from the bottom of a river, by means of a scoop, a series of buckets, or the like.

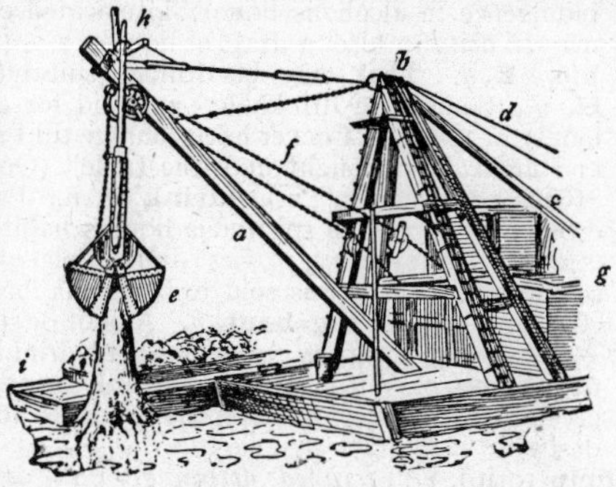

Clam-shell Dredging-machine.

a, pivoted beam; *b*, frame; *c*, stiff leg supporting frame; *d*, guy-rod; *e*, clam-shell bucket, lifting tree-stump; *f*, chains lifting bucket and controlling its operation; *g*, power-house; *h*, guide-poles; *i*, spoil-boat.

dree[1] (drē), *v. t.*; *dreed, dreeing.* [AS. *drēogan.*] To suffer or endure: as, to *dree* one's weird (to endure one's fate); "The bold adventurer . . . *dree'd* pain and dolour in that charmed apartment" (Scott's "Antiquary," ix.). [Now chiefly Sc. or archaic.]

dree[2] (drē), *a.* [Also Sc. *driech, driegh, dreigh*, < ME. *dregh*; akin to E. *dree*[1].] Long; slow; persistent; tedious; dreary; dull. [Now prov. Eng. and Sc.]

dreen (drēn), *v.* and *n.* Prov. form of *drain.*

dreep (drēp), *v.* and *n.* Prov. form of *drip.*

dreg (dreg), *n.* [Cf. Icel. *dregg.*] Usually *pl.*, the sediment of liquors; lees; grounds; any waste or worthless residue; refuse; *sing.*, a small remnant; any small quantity; a drop. —**dreg'gy,** *a.*

drei-bund (drī'bu̇nt), *n.* [G., < *drei*, three, + *bund*, alliance.] A triple alliance; esp. [*cap.*], the alliance between Germany, Austria-Hungary, and Italy, formed in 1882 and continuing until the withdrawal of Italy in May, 1915.

dreigh (drēċh), *a.* Scotch form of *dree*[2].

drench (drench), *v. t.* [AS. *drencan*, causative of *drincan*, E. *drink.*] To cause to drink; administer a draft of medicine to (an animal), esp. by force; also, to purge by physic; also, to wet thoroughly; steep; soak; also, to drown†.—**drench,** *n.* [AS. *drenc.*] A large drink or draft; a draft of medicine, esp. one administered to an animal by force; also, the act of drenching, or wetting thoroughly; also, something that drenches (as, a *drench* of rain).—**drench'er,** *n.*—**drench'ing-ly,** *adv.*

dress (dres), *v.* [OF. F. *dresser*, erect, arrange, dress, ult. < L. *directus*, straight, direct: see *direct, v.*] **I.** *tr.* To make straight; bring (troops) into line; adjust; arrange; also, to prepare (food, skins, fabrics, timber, stone, ore, etc.) by special processes; finish; trim; cultivate (land, etc.); comb out and do up (hair); treat (wounds or sores); scold or thrash (often with *down*: colloq.); also, to equip with clothing, ornaments, etc. (often with *out* or *up*); deck; clothe; attire. **II.** *intr.* To come into line, as troops; also, to clothe or attire one's self.—**dress,** *n.* Clothing; apparel; attire; garb; a woman's gown or robe; fine clothes; elaborate or ceremonious costume ('full dress'); outer covering, as the plumage of birds; external finish, as of a millstone; dressing or size, as of canvas.—**dress'=cir'cle,** *n.* A circular or curving division of seats in a theater, etc., usually the first gallery, orig. set apart for spectators in evening dress.—**dress'=coat',** *n.* A coat worn by men on occasions of ceremony; a man's close-fitting evening coat, with open front and having the skirts cut away over the hips.

dress-er[1] (dres'ėr), *n.* One who dresses; a hospital assistant who treats wounds, etc.; one employed to help at the toilet, as in a theater; also, any of several tools or devices used in various processes of dressing materials.

dress-er[2] (dres'ėr), *n.* [OF. *dreçor* (F. *dressoir*), < *dresser*, E. *dress.*] A table or sideboard on which food is dressed for serving; also, a sideboard or a set of shelves for dishes and cooking utensils (as, "The pewter plates on the *dresser* Caught and reflected the flame": Longfellow's "Evangeline," i. 2); also, a dressing-table or bureau.

dress=goods (dres'gu̇dz), *n. pl.* Fabrics for women's and children's dresses.

dress-ing (dres'ing), *n.* The act of one who or that which dresses; some process of treating or finishing materials; also, that with which something is dressed, as an application for a wound, manure or compost for land, the glaze or sizing for a fabric, a sauce for food, or stuffing for a fowl; the molding around doors, etc.; also, a scolding or thrashing (colloq.).—**dress'ing=case,** *n.* A box containing toilet articles.—**dress'ing=gown,** *n.* A loose gown or robe worn while making the toilet or when in dishabille.—**dress'ing=room,** *n.* A room for use in making the toilet.—**dress'ing=sack,** *n.* A woman's sack or jacket for wearing while making the toilet or when in dishabille.—**dress'ing=ta"ble,** *n.* A table or stand, usually surmounted by a mirror, for use in making the toilet.

dress-mak-er (dres'mā"kėr), *n.* One whose occupation is the making of women's dresses, etc.—**dress'mak"ing,** *n.*

dress=suit (dres'sūt'), *n.* A man's suit of evening clothes, with dress-coat and open-fronted waistcoat.—**dress=suit case,** an oblong case or bag for travelers, intended orig. to hold a dress-suit.

dress-y (dres'i), *a.* Fond of dress; showy in dress; stylish. [Colloq.]

drew (drö). Preterit of *draw.*

drib (drib), *v. i.* or *t.*; *dribbed, dribbing.* [Var. of *drip.*] To drip; dribble. [Obs. or prov.]—**drib,** *n.* A drop; a trifling quantity; a driblet. [Prov. or colloq.]

drib-ble (drib'l), *v.*; *-bled, -bling.* [Freq. of *drib*, in part confused with *drivel.*] **I.** *intr.* To fall or flow in drops or small quantities; trickle; also, to drivel or slaver. **II.** *tr.* To let fall in drops; give out in small portions; in sports, to move (the ball) along by a rapid succession of short kicks or pushes.—**drib'ble,** *n.* A dropping or dripping; also, a small trickling stream; a small quantity of liquid; a drop; a small quantity of anything; also, in sports, the act of dribbling.—**drib'bler,** *n.*

drib-let (drib'let), *n.* [Prob. dim. of *drib, n.*] A small portion or part; a petty or inconsiderable quantity; a small or petty sum.

driech, driegh (drēċh), *a.* Scotch forms of *dree*[2].

dried (drīd). Preterit and past participle of *dry, v.*

dri-er[1], **dry-er** (drī'ėr), *n.* [See *dry, v.*] One who or that which dries; a mechanical contrivance or apparatus for removing moisture; any substance added to paints, varnishes, etc., to make them dry quickly.

dri-er[2], **dri-est** (drī'ėr, drī'est). Compar. and superl. of *dry, a.*

drift (drift), *n.* [ME. *drift*, < AS. *drīfan*, E. *drive.*] A driving movement or force; impulse, impetus, or pressure; the thrust of an arch; movement or course under the impulse of water-currents, wind, etc.; leeway; deviation of an aircraft from a set course, due to cross winds; current or flow; direction or tendency; tenor or meaning; also, something driven, or formed by driving, as a mass of smoke or snow, or a deposit of detritus; floating matter driven by water-currents; a drove of animals (now prov.: as, "a young man with a *drift* of mountain ewes," Synge's "Shadow of the Glen"); also, an approximately horizontal excavation in mining, etc.; also, a round, tapering piece of steel for enlarging holes in metal, or for bringing holes in line to receive rivets, etc.; an implement for cleaning the vent of ordnance after discharge; also, the difference between the size of a hole and that of a piece to be inserted; also, in South Africa, a passage through a river; a ford.—**drift,** *v.* **I.** *intr.* To be carried along by currents of water or air, or, fig., by the force of circumstances; go or stray aimlessly; pass without special intention (as, "Decent and able men, after the first great period, *drifted* out of politics": H. G. Wells's "Outline of History," xxxvii. § 6); also, to be driven into masses, as snow by the wind. **II.** *tr.* To carry along as by force of tide or wind (as, "The wind *drifts* them like locusts": J. H. Newman's "Callista," vi.); form (snow, sand, etc.) into drifts; heap with drifts, as a road; also, to enlarge or shape (a hole) with a steel drift; in *mining*, etc., to excavate horizontally.—**drift'age** (-āj), *n.* The action or amount of drifting; also, drifted matter.—**drift'=an"chor,** *n.* A sea-anchor or drag.—**drift'=bolt,** *n.* A bolt used for driving out other bolts.—**drift'er,** *n.*—**drift'ing-ly,** *adv.*—**drift'=me"ter,** *n.* In *aëronautics*, an instrument for measuring the drift of aircraft.—**drift'=sail,** *n.* A sea-anchor made from a sail or the like.—**drift'way,** *n.* A road over which cattle, etc., are driven; *naut.*, leeway; in *mining*, a drift.—**drift'weed,** *n.* Seaweed drifted on shore.—**drift'wood,** *n.* Wood floating on, or cast ashore by, the water.—**drift'y,** *a.* Of the nature of, or characterized by, drifts.

drill[1] (dril), *n.* [Origin uncertain.] A small furrow made in the soil, to sow seeds in; a small ridge on top of which such a furrow is made; a row of seeds or plants thus sown; a machine for sowing seeds in rows, now usually having contrivances for making furrows and for covering the seeds when sown.—**drill**[1], *v. t.* To sow (seed) or raise (crops) in drills; plant (ground) in drills.

drill[2] (dril), *n.* [Perhaps native name: cf. *mandrill.*] A baboon, *Papio* (or *Cynocephalus*) *leucophæus*, of western Africa, smaller than the mandrill.

drill[3] (dril), *n.* Same as *drilling*[2].

drill[4] (dril), *v.* [D. *drillen*, turn round, bore, train: cf. MLG. *drillen*, roll, turn.] **I.** *tr.* To pierce or bore a hole in (anything); make (a hole) by boring; also, to twirl† or whirl†; also, to instruct and exercise in military tactics and the use of arms; train thoroughly in anything; discipline; also, to impart (knowledge) by strict training or discipline; also, to shift or shunt, as cars, engines, etc. **II.** *intr.* To bore holes; also, to go through exercises in military or other training.—**drill**[4], *n.* [D. *dril.*] A tool or machine for drilling or boring holes in metal, stone, or other hard substance; also, a gastropod, *Urosalpinx cinerea*, destructive to oysters; also, the act or method of training in military tactics and the use of arms; an exercise in such training; any strict, methodical training, instruction, or exercise; also, a drill-master.—**drill'a-ble,** *a.* Capable of being drilled.—**drill'er,** *n.*

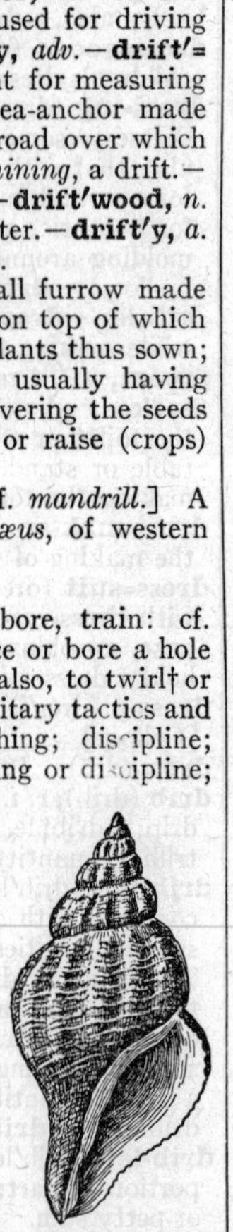

Drill (*Urosalpinx cinerea*), enlarged one half.

drill-ing[1] (dril'ing), *n.* [See *drill*[4].] The act of a person or thing that drills; also, material removed by a drill in operation.

drill-ing[2] (dril'ing), *n.* [G. *drillich*, < L. *trilix* (*trilic-*), having three threads, < *tri-*, three, + *licium*, thrum, thread.] A stout twilled cotton or linen fabric used for linings, pockets, overalls, summer clothing, etc.

drill=mas-ter (dril'mȧs"tėr), *n.* [See *drill*[4].] One who gives practical instruction in military tactics and the use of arms; hence, one who trains in anything, esp. in a mechanical manner.

drill=press (dril'pres), *n.* A machine for boring holes in metal with a drill, the revolving drill being pressed into the work by means of a screw or the like.

drill=ser-geant (dril'sär"jent), *n.* A non-commissioned officer who instructs and trains soldiers in regard to duties, military evolutions, etc.

drill=stock (dril'stok), *n.* In *mach.*, a holder for receiving the shank of a drill.

drill=yard (dril'yärd), *n.* A special railroad-yard for receiving, classifying, and forwarding freight-cars.

dri-ly (drī'li), *adv.* See *dryly.*

drink (dringk), *v. i.*; pret. *drank* (formerly *drunk*), pp. *drunk* (sometimes *drank*, formerly or as p. a. *drunken*), ppr. *drinking.* [AS. *drincan* = D. *drinken* = G. *trinken* = Icel. *drekka* = Goth. *drigkan*, drink: cf. *drench.*] To swallow water or other liquid; imbibe; partake of anything as if to satisfy thirst; specif., to imbibe spirituous liquors, esp. habitually or to excess; tipple.—**to drink to,** to salute in drinking; drink in honor of; drink with wishes for the furtherance of.—**drink,** *v. t.* To swallow (a liquid); imbibe; hence, to take in (a liquid) in any manner; absorb; also, to inhale†; also, to take in through the senses with eagerness and pleasure; gaze upon or listen to attentively or rapturously; also, to swallow the contents of (a cup, etc.); also, to consume or spend (money, etc.) in drinking; also, to make, do, or put by drinking; also, to drink in honor of, or with wishes for the success, furtherance, or accomplishment of (a toast, sentiment, etc.).—**drink,** *n.* [AS. *drinc*, *drinca.*] Any liquid which is swallowed, as to quench thirst or for nourishment; a beverage; specif., alcoholic liquor; also, excessive indulgence in alcoholic liquor; intoxicated condition (as, a man in *drink*); also, a draft of liquid; a potion.—**drink'a-ble. I.** *a.* That may be drunk; suitable for drinking. **II.** *n.* Something drinkable; a liquid for drinking: commonly in *pl.*: as, "I never have courage till I see the eatables and *drinkables* brought upo' the table" (Goldsmith's "She Stoops to Conquer," ii.).—**drink'er,** *n.* One who drinks; esp., one who drinks spirituous liquors habitually or to excess.—**drink'er-y,** *n.*; pl. *-ies* (-iz). A place where liquor or some other beverage is sold to be drunk on the premises. [Colloq.]—**drink'ing=bout,** *n.* A bout or spell of drinking.—**drink'ing=song,** *n.* A song about drinking or drink.—**drink'less,** *a.* Without drink.—**drink'=mon"ey,** *n.* Money given as a gratuity to be spent on drink (or otherwise, as desired).

drip (drip), *v.*; *dripped, dripping.* [AS. *dryppan*, akin to *dropian*, E. *drop.*] **I.** *tr.* To let fall in drops. **II.** *intr.* To let fall drops; shed drops, as from excess of moisture; also, to fall in drops, as a liquid.—**drip,** *n.* The act of dripping; a dripping condition; the liquid that drips; in *arch.*, a projecting part of a cornice or the like, so shaped as to throw off rain-water and thus protect the parts below.—**drip'=cloth,** *n.* In *aëronautics*, a strip of cloth around the equator of a balloon, which keeps the rain-drippings away from the basket.—**drip'ping,** *n.* The act of anything that drips; also, the liquid that drips (often in *pl.*); esp., the fat that exudes from meat in cooking.—**drip'ping=pan,** *n.* A pan used under roasting meat to receive the dripping.—**drip'stone,** *n.* In *arch.*, a projecting stone molding or cornice for throwing off rain-water; also, calcium carbonate occurring in the form of stalactites and stalagmites.

Gate of Close, Salisbury Cathedral, England. — *D, D*, dripstone.

fat, fāte, fär, fall, ȧsk, fãre; net, mē, hėr; pin, pīne; not, nōte, möve, nôr; up, lūte, pųll; oi, oil; ou, out; (lightened) aviąry, ẹlect, agọny, intǫ, ųnite; (obscured) errant, operą, ardent, actor, natūre; ch, chip; g, go; th, thin; ᴛʜ, then; y, you;

drive (drīv), *v.*; pret. *drove* (archaic *drave*), pp. *driven*, ppr. *driving*. [AS. *drīfan* = D. *drijven* = G. *treiben* = Icel. *drīfa* = Goth. *dreiban*, drive.] **I.** *tr.* To send along (or *away*, *off*, *in*, *out*, *back*, etc.) by compulsion; force along; chase (game); search (a district) for game; cause and guide the movement of (an animal or vehicle); convey in a vehicle; keep (machinery) going; propel; impel, constrain, or urge; compel; overwork or overtask; carry (business, a bargain, etc.) vigorously through; in *mining*, etc., to excavate horizontally (or nearly so). **II.** *intr.* To go along before an impelling force; rush or dash violently; strike or aim (*at*: often fig.); proceed or work vigorously (with *at*, *away*, etc.); act as driver; go or travel in a driven vehicle.—**drive,** *n.* The act of driving; an impelling along, as of game, cattle, or floating logs, in a particular direction; the animals, logs, etc., thus driven; a propelling or forcible stroke; a vigorous onset or onward course; a strong military offensive; a united effort to accomplish some purpose, as to raise money for a government loan or for some philanthropic object; vigorous pressure or effort, as in business; a trip in a driven vehicle; a road for driving; a driving mechanism, as of a motor-car; in *mining*, etc., a drift, or horizontal excavation or tunnel.

driv-el (driv'l), *v.*; *-eled* or *-elled*, *-eling* or *-elling*. [AS. *dreflian*.] **I.** *intr.* To let spittle flow from the mouth or mucus from the nose, as a child does; slaver; also, to issue like spittle; also, to talk childishly or idiotically; utter silly nonsense; hence, to act foolishly. **II.** *tr.* To utter childishly or idiotically (as, "*driv'ling* folly without end": Cowper's "Progress of Error," 310); with *away*, to waste childishly.—**driv'el,** *n.* Saliva flowing from the mouth, or mucus from the nose; slaver; also, childish or idiotic utterance; silly talk; twaddle.—**driv'el-er, driv'el-ler,** *n.*

driv-en (driv'n). Past participle of *drive*.

driv-er (drī'vėr), *n.* One who or that which drives; esp., one who drives an animal or animals, a vehicle, etc., as a coachman, a drover, a chauffeur, or a locomotive-engineer; an overseer of slaves or laborers; in *mach.*, a part that transmits force or motion; in *golf*, a wooden-headed club with a long shaft, used for making long shots, as from the tee.—**driv'er-less,** *a.* Without a driver.

drive-way (drīv'wā), *n.* A carriage-road or drive.

driv-ing=wheel (drī'ving-hwēl), *n.* A main wheel which communicates motion to others; one of the propelling wheels of a locomotive, etc.

driz-zle (driz'l), *v.*; *-zled*, *-zling*. [Prob. a freq. form < AS. *drēosan*, fall.] **I.** *intr.* To rain gently and steadily in fine drops; fall in fine drops. **II.** *tr.* To shed in fine drops (as, "The air doth *drizzle* dew": Shakspere's "Romeo and Juliet," iii. 5. 127); also, to sprinkle or wet with fine drops (as, "*drizzled* by the ceaseless spray": Scott's "Lady of the Lake," iv. 5).—**driz'zle,** *n.* A drizzling rain.—**driz'zly,** *a.* Characterized by drizzling.

droit (droit, F. drwo), *n.* [OF. F. *droit*, < ML. *directum*, right, prop. neut. of L. *directus*, straight, direct: see *direct*, *a.*] A legal right or claim; also, that to which one has a legal right or claim; a due; a perquisite.

droi-tu-ral (droi'ţū-ral), *a.* [F. *droiture*, < ML. *directura*, right, L. a making straight, < L. *dirigere*: see *direct*.] In *law*, relating to the right of property, as distinguished from the right of possession.

droll (drōl). [F. *drôle*; origin uncertain.] **I.** *n.* A waggish fellow; a jester; a buffoon; also, a farce†; a puppet-show†. **II.** *a.* Waggish; comical; amusing; ludicrous; funny.—**droll,** *v.* **I.** *intr.* To play the droll or buffoon; jest; joke. **II.** *tr.* To lead or influence by jesting; utter in the manner of a jester or buffoon; turn into a jest.—**droll'er-y,** *n.*; pl. *-ies* (-iz). [F. *drôlerie*.] The action or behavior of a droll; jesting; also, something amusing or funny; a jest; a facetious tale; a farce†; a puppet-show†; a comic picture†; also, droll quality, or humor (as, "the rich *drollery* of 'She Stoops to Conquer'": Macaulay's "Essays," Oliver Goldsmith).—**droll'ness,** *n.*—**drol-ly** (drōl'li), *adv.*

-drome. Noun termination from Gr. δρόμος, a running, course, race-course (cf. *dromos*), as in *aërodrome*, *hippodrome*, *motordrome*.

drom-e-da-ry (drom'ę-dā-ri or drum'-), *n.*; pl. *-ries* (-riz). [OF. F. *dromadaire*, < LL. *dromedarius*, < L. *dromas*, dromedary, < Gr. δρομάς (δρομαδ-), running, < δραμεῖν, run.] A light, swift camel bred for riding, commonly of the one-humped or Arabian species, *Camelus dromedarius*; hence, the one-humped or Arabian camel.

Arabian Camel, or Dromedary.

drom-ond (drom'ǫnd), *n.* [OF. *dromont*, *dromon*, < LL. *dromo(n-)*, < LGr. δρόμων, < Gr. δραμεῖν, run.] A large, fast-sailing vessel of the middle ages: as, "This Crusade . . . is like a large *dromond* parting asunder in the waves" (Scott's "Talisman," xiv.).

drom-os (drom'os), *n.*; Gr. pl. *dromoi* (-oi). [L., < Gr. δρόμος, a running, course, race-course, < δραμεῖν, run.] In *archæol.*, an avenue or passage of approach or entrance, often between rows of columns or statues.

drone[1] (drōn), *v.*; *droned*, *droning*. [Cf. ME. *drounen*, roar, Icel. *drynja*, roar, Dan. *dröne*, boom, G. *dröhnen*, roar, rumble, boom, drawl, Goth. *drunjus*, a sound.] **I.** *intr.* To give forth a dull, continued, monotonous sound; hum; buzz; speak in a monotonous tone. **II.** *tr.* To emit or utter in a dull, monotonous tone.—**drone**[1], *n.* A droning sound; a humming; a buzzing; a monotonous tone; also, a monotonous speaker; also, a bagpipe or similar instrument; a bass pipe of a bagpipe, or the continuous tone emitted by it.

drone[2] (drōn), *n.* [AS. *drān* = MLG. *drane*, *drone* (G. *drohne*); akin to *drone*[1].] The male of the honey-bee and other kinds of bees, stingless and making no honey; hence, an idler or sluggard.—**drone**[2], *v.*; *droned*, *droning*. **I.** *intr.* To act like a drone; live in idleness; proceed indolently. **II.** *tr.* To pass or spend (time, etc.) idly or indolently.—**drone'=fly,** *n.* A dipterous insect, *Eristalis tenax*, somewhat resembling the drone of the bee.

dron-go (drong'gō), *n.*; pl. *-gos* (-gōz). [Malagasy.] Any of various African, Asiatic, and Australian crow-like birds (family *Dicruridæ*), as *Dicrurus musicus*, a South African species, and *D. ater*, the 'black drongo,' of India and eastward.—**dron'go=shrike',** *n.* A drongo.

Black Drongo (*Dicrurus ater*).

dron-ing (drō'ning), *p. a.* [See *drone*[1].] Emitting a dull, monotonous sound; characterized by a monotonous tone or utterance.—**dron'ing-ly,** *adv.*

dron-ish (drō'nish), *a.* Like a drone; lazy; indolent; inactive.

drool (dröl), *v.* and *n.* Same as *drivel*. [Prov. or colloq.]

droop (dröp), *v.* [Icel. *drūpa*, droop, akin to AS. *dropian*, E. *drop*.] **I.** *intr.* To sink or hang down, as from weakness or exhaustion; bend or hang downward; sink, descend, or decline, as the sun (now only poetic); hence, to fall into a state of physical weakness; flag; fail; also, to lose spirit or courage; become dispirited. **II.** *tr.* To let sink or hang down; bend or cast down, as the eyes.—**droop,** *n.* A drooping.—**droop'ing,** *p. a.* That droops; hanging or bending down; flagging or failing; dejected or dispirited.—**droop'ing-ly,** *adv.*—**droop'y,** *a.* Inclined to droop; drooping; dejected.

drop (drop), *v.*; *dropped*, *dropping*. [AS. *dropian*, secondary form of *drēopan* = OS. *driopan* = OHG. *triofan* (G.

triefen) = Icel. *drjūpa*, drip, drop: cf. *drip* and *droop*.] **I.** *intr.* To fall in globules or small portions, as a liquid; also, to discharge moisture in globules; drip; also, to fall vertically like a drop or drops; have an abrupt descent; sink to the ground as if inanimate; fall wounded, dead, etc.; sometimes, to die; also, to squat or crouch, as a dog at the sight of game; also, to come to an end; cease; lapse; also, to fall lower in condition, degree, etc.; sink; also, to pass without effort into some condition (as, to *drop* asleep); also, to move down gently, as with the tide or a light wind; fall (*back, behind, to the rear*, etc.); also, to come or go casually or unexpectedly (*in, into*, etc.). **II.** *tr.* To let fall in globules or small portions; distil; shed (tears); also, to sprinkle with or as with drops (archaic: as, "coats *dropt* with gold," Milton's "Paradise Lost," vii. 406); also, to let fall like a drop; allow to sink to a lower position; give birth to (young); utter or express casually or incidentally, as a hint; send (a note, etc.) in a casual or offhand manner; lose or part with, as money (slang); bring to the ground by a blow or shot; set down, as from a ship or carriage; omit (a letter or syllable) in pronunciation or writing; let droop, or cast down, as the eyes; lower (the voice) in pitch or loudness; also, to cease to keep up or have to do with; have done with; dismiss; in *football*, to score (a goal) by a drop-kick.—**drop,** *n.* [AS. *dropa* = OS. *dropo* = OHG. *troffo* (G. *tropfen*) = Icel. *dropi.*] A small quantity of liquid which falls or is produced in a more or less spherical mass; a liquid globule; the quantity of liquid contained in such a mass; a very small quantity of liquid; a minute quantity of anything; liquid medicine given in drops (usually in *pl.*); something like or likened to a drop, as a pendant, a lozenge (confection), etc.; also, the act of dropping; a fall or descent; the distance or depth to which anything drops; a steep slope; also, that which drops or is used for dropping, as a drop-curtain, or a trap-door in the scaffold of a gallows, on which the criminal about to be executed is placed; a heavy weight or hammer that falls between guides; a drop-press; a slit or aperture into which to drop mail, as in a letter-box; in *baseball*, a ball so delivered by the pitcher that it shoots suddenly downward as it approaches the home base; in *football*, a drop-kick.—**to get, or have, the drop on one,** to get, or have, the chance to shoot before an antagonist can use his weapon; hence, to get, or have, a person at a disadvantage. [Colloq.]

drop=cake (drop′kāk), *n.* A small cake made by dropping thick batter from a spoon into boiling lard or the like, or on a greased pan for baking in the oven.

drop=cur-tain (drop′kėr″tạn), *n.* A curtain lowered, as between the acts of a play, to shut off the stage of a theater from the view of the audience.

drop=forge (drop′fōrj), *v. t.*; *-forged, -forging.* To forge by the impact of a falling mass or weight, the hot piece of metal usually being placed between dies and subjected to the blow of a drop-hammer or the like.—**drop′=for″ging,** *n.* A drop-forged forging.

drop=ham-mer (drop′ham″ėr), *n.* An apparatus for forging, etc., in which a heavy weight is made to drop on the metal to be worked, which is placed on an anvil or in dies.

drop=kick (drop′kik), *n.* In *football*, a kick given the ball as it rises from the ground after being dropped from the hands.

drop-let (drop′let), *n.* A little drop.

drop=let-ter (drop′let″ėr), *n.* A letter to be delivered from or by the same post-office in which it is posted. [U. S.]

drop=light (drop′līt), *n.* A portable gas or electric lamp connected with a fixture above by a tube or wire.

drop-per (drop′ėr), *n.* One who or that which drops; a tube with an elastic cap at one end and a small orifice at the other, for drawing in a liquid and expelling it in drops.

drop-ping (drop′ing), *n.* The act of one who or that which drops; also, that which drops or falls in drops; *pl.*, dung of animals.

drop=press (drop′pres), *n.* A drop-hammer.

drop=scene (drop′sēn), *n.* A scene that drops like a curtain; a drop-curtain; a final scene on which a curtain drops.

drop-si-cal (drop′si-kạl), *a.* Of, like, or affected with dropsy.—**drop′si-cal-ly,** *adv.*

drop-sy (drop′si), *n.* [ME. *dropesie*, for *ydropesie*, < OF. *ydropisie* (F. *hydropisie*), < L. *hydropisis*, < Gr. *ὕδρωψ*, dropsy, E. *hydrops*.] In *pathol.*, an excessive accumulation of serous fluid in a serous cavity of the body or in the subcutaneous cellular tissue; in *bot.*, a disease in succulent plants, caused by an excess of water.—**drop′sied** (-sid), *a.*

drop=worm (drop′wėrm), *n.* A larva of a geometrid moth or of certain other insects that drops from trees by means of a thread.

drop-wort (drop′wėrt), *n.* A European rosaceous herb, *Filipendula filipendula*, bearing small, scentless, white or reddish flowers; also, any plant of the apiaceous genus *Œnanthe*, as *Œ. crocata* ('water-dropwort'), an herb with small white flowers, growing in ditches and marshes.

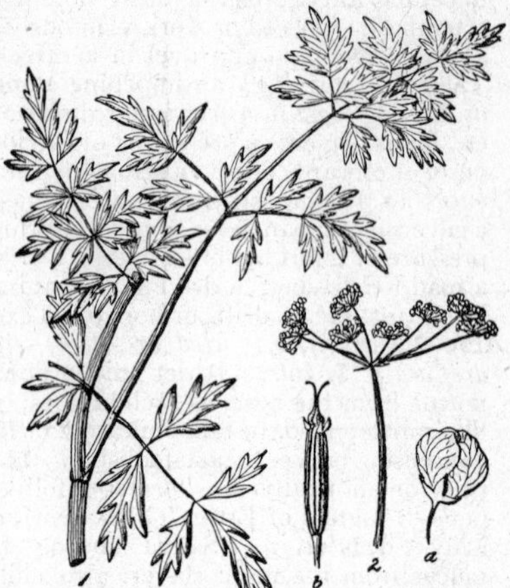

Water-dropwort. — 1. Branch with leaves. 2. The umbel: *a*, a flower; *b*, the fruit.

dros-e-ra-ceous (dros-ẹ-rā′shius), *a.* [NL. *Drosera*, the typical genus, < Gr. *δροσερός*, dewy, < *δρόσος*, dew.] Belonging to the *Droseraceæ*, or sundew family of plants.

drosh-ky, dros-ky (drosh′ki, dros′ki), *n.*; pl. *-kies* (-kiz). [Russ. *drozhki*.] A light, low, four-wheeled, open vehicle, used in Russia, in which the passengers sit astride or sideways on a long, narrow bench; any of various other vehicles, as the ordinary cab, used in Russia and elsewhere in Europe.

dross (drôs), *n.* [AS. *drōs* = MLG. *dros* = MD. *droes*, dregs: cf. G. *drusen*, dregs, husks.] The scum or foreign matter thrown off from molten metal; also, sediment, lees, or dregs; in general, waste matter; refuse.—**dross′y,** *a.* Characterized by or containing dross; of the nature of dross.—**dross′i-ness,** *n.*

drought, drouth (drout, drouth), *n.* [AS. *drūgath*, akin to *drȳge*, E. *dry*.] Dryness; specif., dry weather, or want of rain (as, "After long *drought*, when rains abundant fall, He hears the herbs and flow'rs rejoicing all": Cowper's "Needless Alarm," 59); also, thirst (archaic or prov.: as, "As one, whose *drouth* Yet scarce allay'd, still eyes the current stream," Milton's "Paradise Lost," vii. 66); fig., scarcity.—**drought′y, drouth′y,** *a.* Dry; without moisture; also, characterized by drought; wanting rain; also, thirsty.

drove[1] (drōv). Preterit of *drive*.

drove[2] (drōv), *n.* [AS. *drāf*, < *drīfan*, E. *drive*.] A number of oxen, sheep, or swine driven in a body; a herd or flock; in general, a numerous company, as of human beings, esp. in motion.—**drove**[2], *v. t.* or *i.*; *droved, droving.* To drive or deal in (cattle) as a drover.—**drov-er** (drō′vėr), *n.* One who drives droves of cattle, sheep, etc., to market; a dealer in cattle.

drow (drou), *n.* [Origin obscure.] A cold mist; a drizzle; a shower. [Sc.]

drown (droun), *v.* [ME. *drun, droun*: cf. AS. (Northumbrian) *druncnia*, sink in water, Icel. *drukna*, be drowned.] **I.** *intr.* To sink and be lost in water, as a ship†; of living creatures, to suffocate by immersion, as in water. **II.** *tr.* To suffocate (a person, etc.) by immersion in water or other liquid; also, to flood or inundate; hence, to overwhelm as by a flood.—**drown′er,** *n.*—**drown′ing-ly,** *adv.*

drowse (drouz), *v.*; *drowsed, drowsing.* [Cf. AS. *drūsian*, sink, become inactive or sluggish.] **I.** *intr.* To be heavy with sleepiness; be half asleep; fig., to be dull or sluggish. **II.** *tr.* To make heavy as with sleep; also, to pass or spend (time) in drowsing.—**drowse,** *n.* A condition of drowsing; a fit of drowsing.—**drows′i-head, drows′y-head** (-hed), *n.* Drowsy state; drowsiness. [Archaic.]—**drows′y,** *a.*; compar. *drowsier*, superl. *drowsiest.* Inclined to sleep; heavy with sleepiness; half asleep; also, marked by or resulting from sleepiness; fig., dull or sluggish; also, inducing sleepiness (as, "*Drowsy* tinklings lull the distant folds": Gray's "Elegy," ii.).—**drows'i-ly,** *adv.*—**drows'i-ness,** *n.*

drub (drub), *v. t.*; *drubbed, drubbing.* [Origin uncertain; perhaps from Ar , with reference to the bastinado.] To beat with a stick or the like; cudgel; flog; thrash; fig., to inflict abuse upon; also, to stamp (the feet).—**drub,** *n.* A blow with a stick or the like; a thump; a knock.—**drub'ber,** *n.*—**drub'bing,** *n.* A beating; a sound thrashing.

drudge (druj), *v. i.*; *drudged, drudging.* [Origin uncertain.] To perform mean, servile, or distasteful work; labor at tedious, dragging tasks; work hard or slavishly.—**drudge,** *n.* One who drudges; one who labors at servile or uninteresting tasks; a hard toiler.—**drudg'er,** *n.*—**drudg'er-y,** *n.*; pl. *-ies* (-iz). The labor of a drudge; mean, tedious, or uninteresting work; dull or wearisome toil.—**drudg'ing-ly,** *adv.*

drug (drug), *n.* [OF. F. *drogue*; origin uncertain.] Formerly, any ingredient used in chemistry, pharmacy, dyeing, or the like; now, any medicinal substance for internal or external use; often, a habit-forming medicinal substance; a narcotic; also, a commodity that is overabundant, or in excess of demand, in the market (as, "They told me poetry was a mere *drug*; everybody wrote poetry; the market was overstocked with it": Irving's "Tales of a Traveler," ii. 4). —**drug,** *v. t.*; *drugged, drugging.* To mix (food or drink) with a drug, esp. a narcotic or poisonous drug; also, to administer drugs to; esp., to stupefy or poison with a drug; also, to administer anything nauseous to; surfeit.—**drug'ger,** *n.*—**drug'ger-y,** *n.*; pl. *-ies* (-iz). Drugs collectively; medicine; also, a place where drugs are kept for sale or use.

drug-get (drug'et), *n.* [F. *droguet*; origin unknown.] A fabric woven wholly or partly of wool, used for clothing†; a thick woolen fabric either woven or felted, often with a printed design, used esp. in the form of a rug as a floor-covering.

drug-gist (drug'ist), *n.* [F. *droguiste.*] One who deals in drugs; esp., an apothecary or pharmacist.

drug=store (drug'stōr), *n.* The place of business of a druggist or pharmacist.

dru-id (drö'id), *n.* [F. *druide*, < L. *druidæ, druides*, pl.; from Celtic.] [Often *cap.*] One of an order of priests or ministers of religion among the ancient Celts of Gaul, Britain, and Ireland.—**dru'id-ess,** *n.* A female druid.—**dru-id-ic, dru-id-i-cal** (drọ̈-id'ik, -i-kạl), *a.* Of or pertaining to the druids.—**dru'id-ism,** *n.* The religion or rites of the druids.

drum[1] (drum), *n.* [Ir. and Gael. *druim*, back, ridge.] A long, narrow hill or ridge (Ir. and Sc.); in *geol.*, a drumlin.

drum[2] (drum), *n.* [= D. *trom* = LG. *trumme* = Dan. *tromme* = Sw. *trumma*, drum.] A musical instrument of the percussive class, consisting of a hollow body covered at one or both ends with a tightly stretched membrane, or head, which is struck with a stick or a pair of sticks; the sound produced by this instrument, or any noise suggestive of it; one who plays the drum; also, something resembling a drum in shape or structure, or in the noise it produces, as the tympanum or middle ear, a cylindrical part of a machine, a cylindrical box or receptacle, or a natural organ by which an animal produces a loud or bass sound; also, an assembly of fashionable people at a private house in the evening†; also, a drumfish.—**drum**[2], *v.*; *drummed, drumming.* **I.** *intr.* To beat or play on a drum; beat on anything rhythmically; also, to make a sound like that of a drum; resound; also, to solicit trade, customers, etc., as a drummer. **II.** *tr.* To beat rhythmically; perform (a tune) by drumming; also, to call or summon by or as by beating a drum; also, to solicit or obtain (trade, customers, etc.); also, to expel or dismiss in disgrace to the beat of a drum; also, to drive or force by persistent repetition.—**drum'=beat,** *n.* A beating, or the sound, of a drum.

drum-ble (drum'bl), *v. i.*; *-bled, -bling.* [Origin obscure.] To move sluggishly. See Shakspere's "Merry Wives of Windsor," iii. 3. 156. [Obs. or prov.]

drum=corps (drum'kōr), *n.* A body of drum-players under the direction of a drum-major or the like.

drum=fire (drum'fīr), *n.* [Cf. G. *trommelfeuer.*] Gunfire so heavy and continuous as to sound like the beating of drums.

drum-fish (drum'fish), *n.* Any of various American sciænoid fishes producing a drumming sound, as *Pogonias chromis* of the Atlantic coast of the United States.

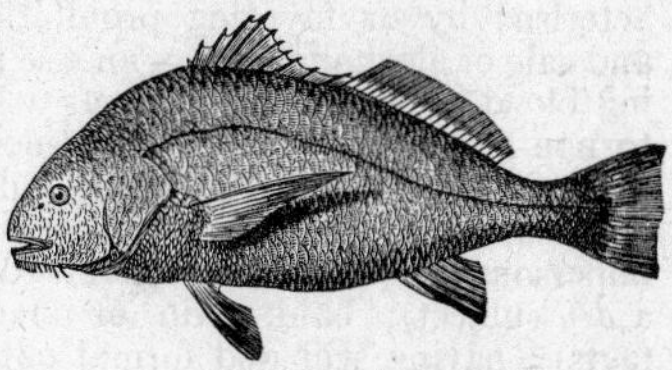

Drumfish (*Pogonias chromis*).

drum-head (drum'hed), *n.* The membrane stretched upon a drum; also, the ear-drum, or tympanic membrane; also, the top part of a capstan.—**drumhead court=martial,** a court-martial held, orig. round an upturned drum for a table, for the summary trial of charges of offenses committed during military operations.

drum-lin (drum'lin), *n.* A drum, or long, narrow hill (Ir.); in *geol.*, a long and narrow, or oval, hill of unstratified glacial drift.

drum=ma-jor (drum'mā"jọr), *n.* The director of a drum-corps or band in marching.

drum-mer (drum'ėr), *n.* One who plays a drum; also, a commercial traveler or traveling salesman (U. S.).

drum-mock (drum'ọk), *n.* See *drammock.*

Drum-mond (drum'ọnd) **light.** The calcium light: so called from its inventor, Thomas Drummond (1797–1840), a British engineer and administrator.

drum-stick (drum'stik), *n.* A stick for beating a drum; also, the lower joint of the leg of a dressed fowl.

drunk (drungk). Past participle and former preterit of *drink.*—**drunk,** *p. a.* Intoxicated with or as with strong drink; also, drenched or saturated (obs. or archaic: as, "I will make mine arrows *drunk* with blood," Deut. xxxii. 42). —**drunk,** *n.* A bout or spell of drinking to intoxication; a fit of drunkenness; also, a drunken person. [Colloq.] —**drunk-ard** (drung'kạrd), *n.* One addicted to the excessive use of strong drink; an inebriate.—**drunk'en,** *p. a.* Intoxicated; drunk; also, given to drunkenness; also, pertaining to or proceeding from intoxication; fig., acting as if drunk; unsteady; also, drenched or saturated (obs. or archaic: as, "Let the earth be *drunken* with our blood," Shakspere's "3 Henry VI.," ii. 3. 23).—**drunk'en-ly,** *adv.* —**drunk'en-ness,** *n.*

dru-pa-ceous (drọ̈-pā'shius), *a.* Drupe-like; pertaining to or producing drupes. Also **dru-pal** (drö'pạl), *a.*

drupe (dröp), *n.* [NL. *drupa*, drupe, L. *drupa, druppa*, = Gr. δρύππα, overripe olive.] A fruit, as the peach, cherry, plum, etc., consisting of an outer skin (epicarp), a (generally) pulpy and succulent layer (mesocarp), and a hard or woody inner shell or stone (endocarp) which incloses usually a single seed.—**dru-pel** (drö'pel), **drupe'let,** *n.* A little drupe, as one of the individual pericarps composing the blackberry. Also **dru'pe-ole** (-pẹ-ōl).

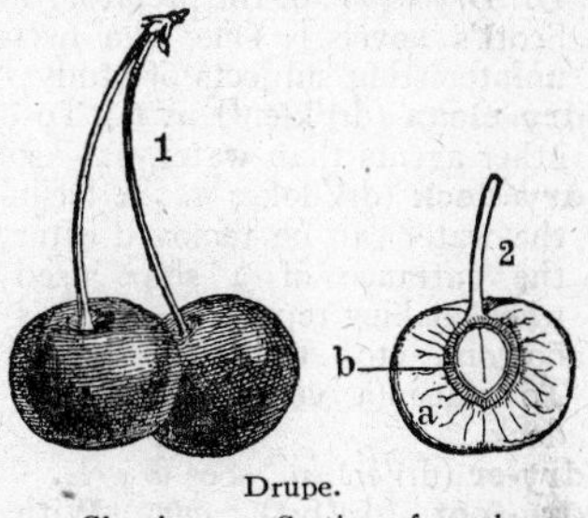

Drupe.

1. Cherries. 2. Section of a cherry: *a*, mesocarp; *b*, endocarp, inclosing the seed.

Druse[1] (dröz), *n.* One of a fanatical and warlike people and religious sect of Syria.

druse[2] (dröz), *n.* [G. *druse*, < Bohem. *druza.*] A surface or crust composed of small projecting crystals; also, a rock-cavity lined with such crystals.—**drus-y** (drö'zi), *a.* Covered or lined with small projecting crystals; also, containing crystal-lined cavities, or druses.

Druze (dröz), *n.* See *Druse*[1].

dry (drī), *a.*; compar. *drier* or *dryer*, superl. *driest* or *dryest.* [AS. *drȳge*, akin to D. *droog*, LG. *drög*, and G. *trocken*, dry.] Free from moisture, not moist, or not wet; having little or no rain, as a climate or a season; characterized by absence, deficiency, or failure of natural or ordinary moisture or liquid; not yielding milk, as a cow; free from or unaccompanied by tears; wiped or drained away, or evaporated, as a liquid; desiring drink, or thirsty; causing thirst (as, *dry* work); without butter or the like, as bread or toast; free from sweetness and fruity flavor (as, *dry* wines); characterized by or favoring prohibition of the manufacture and sale of alcoholic liquors for use as beverages; not drawing blood, or hard or severe, as a blow†; of or pertaining to non-liquid substances or commodities (as, *dry* measure: see below); fig., unemotional, indifferent, or cold (as, a *dry* answer); humorous or sarcastic in an unemotional or impersonal way (as, *dry* humor); dull or uninteresting (as, a *dry* subject); bald, plain, or unadorned (as, a list of *dry* facts); having stiff and formal outlines, as a work of art; of money, etc., paid in cash.—**dry battery,** in *elect.*, a dry cell, or a voltaic battery consisting of a number of dry cells.—**dry cell,** in *elect.*, a voltaic cell whose liquid constituents have been made more or less solid by means of absorbent material.—**dry farming,** a mode of farming practised in regions of slight or insufficient rainfall, depending largely upon tillage methods which render the soil receptive of moisture and prevent evaporation.—**dry measure,** the system of units of capacity ordinarily used in measuring dry commodities, such as grain, fruit, etc.: 2 pints = 1 quart; 4 quarts = 1 gallon; 2 gallons = 1 peck; 4 pecks = 1 bushel (approximately 2,218.192 cubic inches in the imperial, or British legal, bushel, and 2,150.42 cubic inches in the Winchester, or U. S. legal, bushel, the U. S. bushel being thus equivalent to about .97 British bushel); 8 bushels = 1 quarter. Cf. *liquid measure*, under *liquid, a.* —**dry plate,** in *photog.*, a glass plate coated with a hard and dry sensitive emulsion, upon which a negative or positive picture can be produced by exposure (as in a camera) and development.—**dry way,** in *chem.*, the method of analysis in which the reactions are produced mostly without the use of solutions and liquid reagents, as by fusing in a crucible. —**dry,** *n.*; pl. *dries* or *drys* (drīz). Dry state or condition; also, that which is dry, esp. dry land; also, a place where things are dried; a drying-house; also, a prohibitionist. —**dry,** *v.*; *dried, drying.* [AS. *drȳgan.*] **I.** *tr.* To make dry; free from moisture or liquid; desiccate; also, to remove or abstract (moisture); evaporate. **II.** *intr.* To become dry; lose moisture; of moisture, to disappear as by wiping away or evaporation.

dry-ad (drī'ad), *n.* [L. *Dryas* (pl. *Dryades*), < Gr. Δρυάς (pl. Δρυάδες), < δρῦς, tree, oak: see *tree.*] A wood-nymph; a nymph supposed to reside in a tree: as, "Knock at the rough rind of this ilex-tree, and summon forth the *Dryad!*" (Hawthorne's "Marble Faun," ix.).—**dry-ad'ic,** *a.*

dry=as=dust (drī'ạz-dust''), *a.* Very dry or uninteresting, as a writer or book.—**dry'as-dust'',** *n.* [From the fictitious Dr. *Dryasdust*, of the prefatory matter of some of Sir Walter Scott's novels.] One who occupies himself with dry or uninteresting subjects of study; a dull pedant.

dry=clean (drī'klēn'), *v. t.* To clean (garments, etc.) with other agents than water, as gasoline or the like.

dry=dock (drī'dok), *n.* A basin-like structure from which the water can be removed after the entrance of a ship: used when making repairs on a ship's bottom, etc.—**dry'=dock,** *v. t.* To place (a vessel) in a dry-dock.

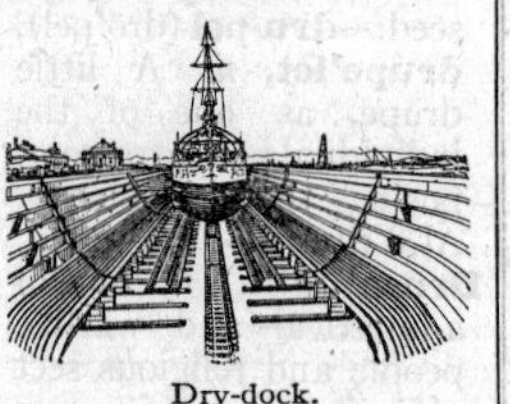
Dry-dock.

dry-er (drī'ėr), *n.* See *drier*[1].

dry-foot (drī'fu̇t), *adv.* With dry feet; in *hunting*, by the scent of the foot†.

dry=goods (drī'gu̇dz), *n. pl.* Textile fabrics and related articles of trade, in distinction from groceries, hardware, etc.

dry-ly, dri-ly (drī'li), *adv.* In a dry manner.—**dry'ness,** *n.* Dry state or character.

dry=nurse (drī'nėrs), *n.* A nurse who takes care of a child but does not suckle it: often fig., esp. of one who tutors and guides an inexperienced superior officer in the discharge of his duties.—**dry'=nurse,** *v. t.* To act as dry-nurse to.

dry=point (drī'point), *n.* A sharp-pointed needle used by engravers for cutting delicate lines on copper plates, etc. (without the use of acid, as in etching); the process of engraving in this way, or an engraving so made.

dry=rot (drī'rot'), *n.* A decay of seasoned timber causing it to become brittle and to crumble to a dry powder, due to various fungi; any of various diseases of vegetables due to fungi; also, any of these fungi; in fig. use, any concealed or unsuspected inward decay or degeneration, as of public morals.

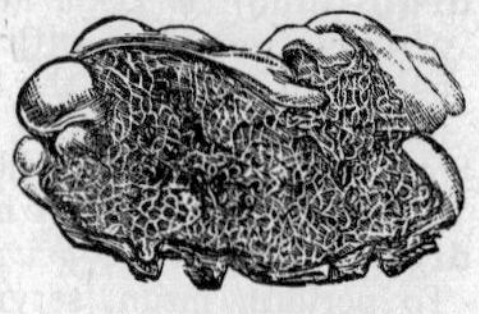
Dry-rot Fungus (*Merulius lacrymans*), the most common one affecting timber.

dry-salt-er (drī'sâl''tėr), *n.* A dealer in salted and dried meats, pickles, etc., or in drugs, dyes, gums, etc. [Eng.]—**dry'salt''-er-y,** *n.* The store or business of a drysalter; articles dealt in by a drysalter. [Eng.]

dry=shod (drī'shod'), *a.* Having the shoes or feet dry.

du-ad (dū'ad), *n.* [= *dyad.*] A group of two; a dyad.

du-al (dū'ạl), *a.* [L. *dualis*, < *duo*, two.] Of or pertaining to two; also, composed or consisting of two parts; twofold; double; in *gram.*, signifying or implying two persons or things (as, the *dual* number, as in Greek; a *dual* verb-form: cf. *singular, a.*, and *plural, a.*).—**Dual Alliance,** the alliance formed in 1891–92 between France and Russia.—**Dual Monarchy,** the united monarchy of Austria-Hungary (1867–1918).—**du'al,** *n.* In *gram.*, the dual number; a noun, verb, or other word in this number.

du-al-in (dū'ạ-lin), *n.* [From *dual*, with reference to the two substances added to the nitroglycerin.] An explosive consisting of a mixture of nitroglycerin with sawdust and saltpeter. Also called *dualin-dynamite.*

du-al-ism (dū'ạl-izm), *n.* The state of being dual or consisting of two parts; division into two; also, any system or theory based on a dual principle or involving a duality of principles; in *philos.*, the doctrine of two distinct ultimate substances or principles (cf. *monism* and *pluralism*).—**du'al-ist,** *n.* A believer in a doctrine of dualism.—**du-al-is'tic,** *a.* Of, pertaining to, or of the nature of dualism; also, dual.—**du-al-is'ti-cal-ly,** *adv.*

du-al-i-ty (dū-al'i-ti), *n.* Dual state or character.

du-al-ize (dū'ạl-īz), *v. t.*; *-ized, -izing.* To make dual; represent or regard as dual.—**du''al-i-za'tion** (-i-zā'shọn), *n.*

du-al-ly (dū'ạl-i), *adv.* In a dual manner.

dub[1] (dub), *n.* [Origin obscure.] A pool of water; a puddle; a deep, still pool in a river. [Sc. and north. Eng.]

dub[2] (dub), *v.*; *dubbed, dubbing.* [Prob. imit.] **I.** *intr.* To make a thrust; poke (*at*); also, to make the sound of a drum. **II.** *tr.* To thrust; poke; also, to beat (a drum). —**dub**[2], *n.* A thrust or blow; also, a drum-beat.

dub[3] (dub), *v. t.*; *dubbed, dubbing.* [ME. *dubben*; from OF. (cf. OF. *aduber*, later *adouber*, dub knight, equip, dress, adjust), but ult. origin uncertain.] To strike lightly with a sword in the ceremony of conferring knighthood; make, or designate as, a knight; hence, to invest with any dignity or title; style, name, or call; also, to clothe†, array†, or adorn†; dress, trim, or crop; smooth by cutting, rubbing, striking, etc. (as, "If I wanted a board, I had . . . to cut down a tree . . . hew it flat on either side . . . and then *dub* it smooth with my adze": Defoe's "Robinson Crusoe," i. 4); blunt the point or edge of (chiefly prov. Eng.).

dub[4] (dub), *n.* [Cf. *dub*[3], in the sense of 'blunt.'] A dull, stupid fellow; one who is awkward or unskilful at anything. [Slang.]

dub=a=dub (dub'ạ-dub'), *adv.* and *n.* [See *dub*[2].] A word imitative of the sound made by beating a drum.

dub-bing (dub'ing), *n.* [See *dub*[3].] The act of one that dubs; the conferring of knighthood; the accolade; also, a preparation used in dressing something, as a grease for dressing leather; the materials used for the body of an angler's fly.

du-bi-e-ty (dū-bī'ẹ-ti), *n.*; pl. *-ties* (-tiz). [LL. *dubietas*, < L. *dubius*: see *dubious.*] The state of being dubious; doubtfulness; doubt; also, a matter of doubt.

du-bi-ous (dū'bi-us), *a.* [L. *dubiosus*, < *dubius*, wavering, uncertain, doubtful, < *duo*, two.] Fraught with or involving doubt or uncertainty; open to doubt or question; doubtful; uncertain; of uncertain issue (as, "in *dubious* battel": Milton's "Paradise Lost," i. 104); of questionable character (as, a *dubious* transaction); also, feeling doubt; wavering or hesitating in opinion; inclined to doubt.—

du-bi-os′i-ty (-os′i-ti), **du′bi-ous-ness,** *n.*—**du′bi-ous-ly,** *adv.*

du-bi-ta-ble (dū′bi-tạ-bl), *a.* [L. *dubitabilis,* < *dubitare,* waver in opinion, hesitate, doubt, connected with *dubius,* wavering, uncertain: see *dubious,* also *doubt, v.*] That may be doubted; open to doubt.—**du′bi-tant** (-tạnt). [L. *dubitans* (-*ant*-), ppr. of *dubitare.*] **I.** *a.* Doubting. **II.** *n.* A doubter.—**du′bi-tate** (-tāt), *v. i.*; *-tated, -tating.* [L. *dubitatus,* pp. of *dubitare*: cf. *doubt, v.*] To doubt.—**du-bi-ta′tion** (-tā′shọn), *n.*—**du′bi-ta-tive** (-tạ-tiv), *a.* [LL. *dubitativus.*] Doubting; doubtful; expressing doubt: as, "turning his head . . . in a *dubitative* manner" (George Eliot's "Adam Bede," liii.).—**du′bi-ta-tive-ly,** *adv.*

duc (dük), *n.* [OF. F.: see *duke.*] In French use, a duke.

du-cal (dū′kạl), *a.* [OF. F. *ducal,* < LL. *ducalis,* < L. *dux*: see *duke.*] Of or pertaining to a duke.

duc-at (duk′ạt), *n.* [OF. F. *ducat,* < It. *ducato,* < ML. *ducatus,* the coin (orig. one issued in 1140 by Roger II. of Sicily as duke of Apulia), also duchy: see *duchy.*] Any of various gold coins formerly in wide use in European countries, usually worth from $2.27 to $2.32; an old silver coin of varying value; an old Venetian money of account; hence, any piece of money; *pl.,* money; cash.

Obverse. Reverse.
Ducat of Ladislaus Postumus, King of Hungary, died 1457.—British Museum.

duc-a-toon (duk-ạ-tön′), *n.* [F. *ducaton,* < It. *ducatone,* aug. of *ducato*: see *ducat.*] A former European silver coin of varying value.

duch-ess (duch′es), *n.* [OF. F. *duchesse,* < ML. *ducissa,* fem. of *dux*: see *duke.*] The wife or widow of a duke, or a woman who holds in her own right a position or rank equivalent to that of a duke. Also (F.) **du-chesse** (dü-shes).

duch-y (duch′i), *n.*; pl. *-ies* (-iz). [OF. *duche* (also *duchee,* fem.) (F. *duché*), < ML. *ducatus,* the dignity or the territory of a duke, L. leadership, command, < *dux*: see *duke.*] The territory ruled by a duke or duchess; a dukedom.

duck[1] (duk), *v.* [ME. *duken, douken,* prob. from an AS. form akin to MLG. *duken,* D. *duiken,* G. *tauchen,* dive: cf. *duck*[2].] **I.** *intr.* To plunge the whole body or the head momentarily under water; also, to stoop suddenly so as to lower the head; bob; fig., to cringe or yield. **II.** *tr.* To plunge or dip in water momentarily (as, "We . . . always '*ducked*' the boy that told On the fellow that tied the clothes": J. W. Riley's "Backward Look"); also, to lower (the head, etc.) suddenly.—**duck**[1], *n.* A ducking; a quick plunge; a sudden lowering of the body or head (as, "without *duck* or nod": Milton's "Comus," 960).

duck[2] (duk), *n.* [AS. *duce,* lit. 'ducker'; akin to E. *duck*[1].] Any of numerous wild or domesticated web-footed swimming birds of the family *Anatidæ,* esp. of the genus *Anas* and certain allied genera, characterized by a broad, flat bill, short legs and neck, and a depressed body; the female of this fowl, as distinguished from the male (or *drake*); a darling or pet (colloq.); one of the small stones used in the game of duck on drake (see below); a lame duck (colloq.: see under *lame*).—**duck and drake,** a pastime consisting in throwing shells, flat stones, etc., over the surface of water so as to strike and rebound repeatedly.—**duck on drake,** a game in which one of the players, each provided with a small stone (a *duck*), places his duck upon a large stone (the *drake*), the other players then trying to knock it off with their ducks, and to regain these and run home before the first player can replace his duck and tag them. Also called *duck on the rock, duckstone,* etc.—**lame duck.** See under *lame.*—**to make ducks and drakes of,** to handle recklessly; squander foolishly.

duck[3] (duk), *n.* [D. *doek,* cloth, linen, canvas, = G. *tuch,* cloth.] A strong, plain-woven linen or cotton fabric, similar to but lighter than canvas, used for light sails, wagon hoods, tents, bags, overalls, summer clothing, etc.; *pl.,* clothes, esp. trousers, of this material.

duck-bill (duk′bil), *n.* A small aquatic mammal (monotreme), *Ornithorhynchus anatinus* (or *paradoxus*), of Australia and Tasmania, having webbed feet and a beak like that of a duck; the duck-billed platypus.—**duck′=billed,** *a.* Having a bill like that of a duck.

Duckbill, or Duck-billed Platypus.

duck-board (duk′bōrd), *n.* A board or a section or structure of boarding laid as a floor or track over wet or muddy ground, as for military use.

duck-er[1] (duk′ėr), *n.* One who or that which ducks.

duck-er[2] (duk′ėr), *n.* One who raises ducks; also, one who hunts ducks.—**duck′er-y,** *n.*; pl. *-ies* (-iz). A place for breeding ducks.

duck=hawk (duk′hâk), *n.* In England, a harrier, *Circus æruginosus*; in the U. S., the peregrine falcon, *Falco peregrinus,* var. *anatum,* which preys upon ducks.

duck-ing[1] (duk′ing), *n.* The act of one who or that which ducks; immersion in water; sudden lowering of the head or body.

duck-ing[2] (duk′ing), *n.* The catching or shooting of wild ducks.

duck-ing=stool (duk′ing-stöl), *n.* A stool or chair, often fixed to the end of a beam pivoted on an upright post, in which common scolds, etc., were tied and plunged into water as a punishment. Cf. *cucking-stool.*

Ducking-stool.

duck-ling (duk′ling), *n.* A young duck.—**ugly duckling.** See under *ugly.*

duck=mole (duk′mōl), *n.* The duckbill.

duck=pin (duk′pin), *n.* In *bowling,* a short pin of relatively large diameter, used in a game resembling tenpins, and bowled at with small balls; also, *pl.* (construed as *sing.*), the game played with such pins.

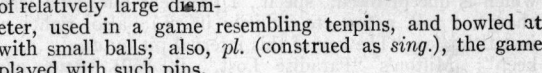

duck-stone (duk′stōn), *n.* See *duck on drake,* under *duck*[2].

duck-weed (duk′wēd), *n.* Any member of the family *Lemnaceæ,* esp. of the genus *Lemna,* comprising small aquatic plants which float free on still water.

duct (dukt), *n.* [L. *ductus,* leading, conduct, conduit, < *ducere,* lead: cf. *tow*[3].] Any tube, canal, or conduit by which fluid or other substances are conducted or conveyed; in *anat.,* a tube, canal, or vessel conveying a bodily fluid, esp. a glandular secretion.

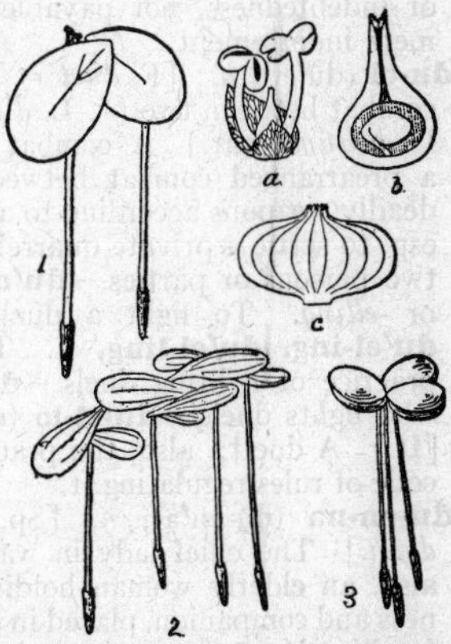

Duckweed.—1. *Lemna minor*; *a,* inflorescence; *b,* pistil cut longitudinally; *c,* fruit. 2. *Lemna trisulca.* 3. *Lemna gibba.*

duc-tile (duk′til), *a.* [L. *ductilis,* < *ducere,* lead.] Capable of being hammered out thin, as certain metals; malleable; specif., capable of being drawn out into wire or threads, as gold; also, capable of being molded or shaped; plastic; fig., susceptible of being led or drawn; compliant; tractable; also, capable of being directed through channels, as water.—**duc′tile-ly,** *adv.*—**duc-til′i-ty** (-til′i-ti), *n.* The property or quality of being ductile.

duct-less (dukt′les), *a.* Having no duct.—**ductless gland,** in *anat.*, any of certain glands which have no excretory duct, but give up their products directly to the blood or lymph, as the thyroid gland, the spleen, the thymus, etc.: a term often used as equivalent to *endocrine gland,* although inexactly, since certain endocrine glands or organs, as the pancreas, not only give up products directly to the blood or lymph, but also discharge otherwise through ducts.

dud[1] (dud), *n.* [ME. *dudde;* origin unknown.] An article of clothing; *pl.*, clothes; sometimes, old or ragged clothes; also, belongings in general (as, "Away I went to sea, with my *duds* tied up in a han'kercher": Mrs. Stowe's "Oldtown Fireside Stories," iv.). [Colloq.]

dud[2] (dud). [Cf. *dud*[1].] **I.** *n.* A shell that after being fired has failed to explode (soldiers' slang); in general, anything that proves a failure (slang). **II.** *a.* Ineffective; useless; good-for-nothing; out of order, as an engine; adverse, as weather. [Slang.]

dude (dūd), *n.* [Origin unknown.] A man of affected or excessive refinement in manners, speech, etc.; esp., a man excessively fastidious in dress; a dandy.

du-deen (dö-dēn′), *n.* [Ir.: see *-een.*] A short clay tobacco-pipe.

dudg-eon[1] (duj′on), *n.* [ME. *dogeon* (AF. *digeon*); origin unknown.] A kind of wood used esp. for the handles of knives, daggers, etc.†; a handle or hilt made of this†; a dagger having such a hilt (archaic: as, "It was a serviceable *dudgeon,* Either for fighting or for drudging," Butler's "Hudibras," i. 1. 379).

dudg-eon[2] (duj′on), *n.* [Origin unknown.] A feeling of offense or resentment; anger: as, "Calphurnius and the soldiery were still in high *dudgeon* with the populace" (J. H. Newman's "Callista," xxix.).

du-dheen (dö-dēn′), *n.* See *dudeen.*

dud-ish (dū′dish), *a.* Like or befitting a dude.

due (dū). [OF. *deu* (F. *dû*), pp. of *deveir* (F. *devoir*), < L. *debere,* owe: see *debt.*] **I.** *a.* Owed or payable as an obligation or debt; also, owing by right of circumstances or condition, or that ought to be given or rendered (often with *to*: as, the respect *due* to a magistrate; to receive the *due* reward of one's deeds); hence, rightful, proper, or fitting (as, to use *due* care; to arrive in *due* time or course); adequate or sufficient (as, to allow a *due* margin for possible delays); also, attributable, as to a cause (as, a delay *due* to an accident); also, under engagement as to time; appointed to be ready, be present, or arrive. **II.** *n.* That which is due or owed; specif., a payment due, as a legal charge, a toll, a fee, etc. (chiefly in *pl.*); also, right† or just title† (as, "The key of this infernal pit by *due* . . . I keep": Milton's "Paradise Lost," ii. 850).—**due,** *adv.* Duly (archaic); also, directly or straight (as, a *due* east course).—**due′=bill,** *n.* A brief written acknowledgment of indebtedness, not payable to order or transferable by mere indorsement.

du-el (dū′el), *n.* [F. *duel* = It. *duello,* < ML. *duellum,* a combat between two (< L. *duo,* two), orig. an early form of L. *bellum,* war.] A combat between two persons; esp., a prearranged combat between two persons, fought with deadly weapons according to an accepted code of procedure, esp. to settle a private quarrel; hence, any contest between two persons or parties.—**du′el,** *v. i.*; *-eled* or *-elled, -eling* or *-elling.* To fight a duel.—**du′el-er, du′el-ler,** *n.*—**du′el-ing, du′el-ling,** *n.* The fighting of a duel; the practice of fighting duels.—**du′el-ist, du′el-list,** *n.* One who fights duels.—**du-el-lo** (dū-el′ō), *n.*; pl. *duellos* (-ōz). [It.] A duel†; also, the practice or art of dueling, or the code of rules regulating it.

du-en-na (dū-en′ä), *n.* [Sp. *dueña,* var. of *doña*: see *doña.*] The chief lady in waiting on the queen of Spain; also, an elderly woman holding a position between governess and companion, placed in charge of the girls of a Spanish family; hence, a governess or chaperon.

du-et (dū-et′), *n.* [It. *duetto,* dim. of *duo*: see *duo.*] A musical composition for two voices or two performers.—**du-et′tist,** *n.* One who takes part in a duet.

duff[1] (duf), *n.* [Var. of *dough.*] A flour pudding boiled in a bag (as, "To enhance the value of the Sabbath to the crew, they are allowed . . . a pudding, or . . . '*duff*' . . . nothing more than flour boiled with water, and eaten with molasses," Dana's "Two Years before the Mast," iv.: cf. *plum-duff*); also, decaying vegetable matter covering forest-ground; also, fine coal; slack.

duff[2] (duf), *v. t.* [Appar. < *duffer* (recorded earlier).] To manipulate (a thing) so as to make it pass for new or for something different; specif., to alter the brand on (stolen cattle), or steal (cattle) by doing this (Australia); also, to cheat. [Slang or colloq.]

duf′fel, *n.* See *duffle.*

duf-fer (duf′ėr), *n.* [Origin obscure: cf. *duff*[2].] One who sells cheap, flashy goods as valuable, as under the pretense that they are smuggled or stolen and offered as bargains (slang, Eng.); a peddler or hawker (Eng.); one who duffs (articles for sale, cattle, etc.: colloq.); an article manipulated fraudulently or passed off as something which it is not (colloq.); anything poor of its kind or useless, as, in Australia, an unproductive mine (colloq.); one who is inefficient or incapable (colloq.); a plodding or stupid person (colloq.).

duf-fle, duf-fel (duf′l), *n.* [From *Duffel,* town near Antwerp.] A coarse woolen cloth having a thick nap; also, a sportsman's or camper's outfit.

dug[1] (dug), *n.* [Cf. Sw. *dägga,* Dan. *dægge,* suckle.] The mamma or the nipple of a female: now used with reference to the human female only in contempt.

dug[2] (dug). Preterit and past participle of *dig.*

du-gong (dö′gong), *n.* [Malay *dūyong.*] Any animal of the genus *Halicore,* comprising large herbivorous aquatic mammals of East Indian and other waters, characterized by a fish-like body, flipper-like fore limbs, no hind limbs, and a crescent-shaped tail.

Dugong (*Halicore dugong*).

dug-out (dug′out), *n.* A boat made by hollowing out a log; also, a rough shelter or dwelling formed by an excavation in the ground or in the face of a bank.

dui-ker, dui-ker-bok (dī′kėr, -bok), *n.* [D., 'diver,' 'diver buck.'] Any of the small South African antelopes constituting the genus *Cephalophus*: so called from their habit of plunging through and under bushes instead of leaping over them.

Duiker.

duke (dūk), *n.* [OF. F. *duc* = It. *duca* (also *doge*: see *doge*), < L. *dux* (*duc-*), leader, ML. duke, < L. *ducere,* lead.] A leader†; a chief† or ruler†; a sovereign prince, the ruler of a small state called a duchy; in Great Britain, a nobleman of the highest rank after that of a prince, being a member of the highest degree of the peerage and ranking next above a marquis; a nobleman of corresponding rank in certain other countries; also, the hand or fist (chiefly in *pl.*: slang).—**duke,** *v. i.*; *duked, duking.* To play the duke. See Shakspere's "Measure for Measure," iii. 2. 100.—**duke′dom** (-dom), *n.* The state or territory ruled by a duke; also, the office or rank of a duke.—**duke′ling,** *n.* A little or petty duke.—**duke′ship,** *n.* The state or dignity of a duke.

Coronet of a British Duke.

Du-kho-bors (dö'kǫ-bôrz), *n. pl.* [Russ. *Dukhobortsy*, 'spirit wrestlers,' contenders against the Holy Spirit.] A Russian Christian religious sect of peasants, dating from the 18th century, a large body of which migrated to Canada in 1899.

dul-cet (dul'set). [OF. *dolcet, doucet* (F. *doucet*), dim. of *dols, dous* (F. *doux*), < L. *dulcis*, sweet.] **I.** *a.* Sweet to the taste or smell (archaic); also, agreeable to the feelings, the eye, or, esp., the ear (as, "Not the praise the world doth give, *Dulcet* fulsome whisperer": Rossetti's "Love's Nocturn"); pleasing; soothing; melodious. **II.** *n.* An organ-stop resembling the dulciana, but an octave higher.

dul-ci-an-a (dul-si-an'ạ̈), *n.* [NL., < L. *dulcis*, sweet.] An organ-stop having metal pipes, and giving thin, incisive, somewhat string-like tones.

dul-ci-fy (dul'si-fī), *v. t.*; *-fied, -fying.* [LL. *dulcificare*, < L. *dulcis*, sweet, + *facere*, make.] To sweeten; render more agreeable; mollify; appease.—**dul"ci-fi-ca'tion** (-fi-kā'shọn), *n.*

dul-ci-mer (dul'si-mėr), *n.* [OF. *doulcemer, doulcemelle*, said to be < L. *dulcis*, sweet, + *melos*, < Gr. μέλος, song, tune, music.] A musical instrument having metallic strings, played by striking with two hammers held in the hands; also, in the Bible, a kind of bagpipe.

dul-cin-e-a (dul-sin'ẹ̄-ạ̈), *n.* [From *Dulcinea* (< Sp. *dulce*, < L. *dulcis*, sweet), name given by Don Quixote, in Cervantes's romance, to his peasant lady-love.] A lady-love; a mistress, a sweetheart.

du-li-a (dụ̄-lī'ạ̈), *n.* [ML., < Gr. δουλεία, servitude, service, < δοῦλος, slave.] In *Rom. Cath. theol.*, an inferior kind of veneration given to saints and angels as the servants and special friends of God. Cf. *hyperdulia* and *latria*.

dull (dul), *a.* [ME. *dul, dull*, akin to AS. *dol*, foolish, stupid, D. *dol*, G. *toll*, mad.] Slow of understanding; obtuse; stupid; also, lacking keenness of perception in the senses or feelings; insensible; unfeeling; hard of hearing (prov.); not intense or acute (as, a *dull* pain); also, slow in motion or action; not brisk; sluggish, as trade; drowsy or heavy; listless or spiritless; sad or melancholy; also, causing ennui or depression; tedious; uninteresting; also, not sharp, as a knife; blunt, as a point; also, not bright, intense, or clear, as color, light, sound, etc.; lusterless; dim; muffled.—**dull,** *v. t.* or *i.* To make or become dull.—**dull'ard** (-ạ̈rd), *n.* A dull or stupid person; a dolt.—**dull'ish,** *a.* Somewhat dull.—**dull'ness, dul'ness,** *n.*—**dull'=wit'ted,** *a.* Stupid.—**dul-ly** (dul'li), *adv.*

dulse (duls), *n.* [Ir. and Gael. *duileasg.*] Any of several coarse, edible seaweeds, as *Rhodymenia palmata*, which has red fronds.

du-ly (dū'li), *adv.* In a due manner; properly or fitly; in due season; punctually; adequately or sufficiently

du-ma (dö'mä), *n.* [Russ.] In Russia, a council or official assembly; esp. [*cap.*], an elective legislative assembly, constituting the lower house of parliament, which was established in 1905 by Nicholas II. See *Bolshevik, n.*

dumb (dum), *a.* [AS. *dumb* = Icel. *dumbr* = Goth. *dumbs*, dumb, mute, = D. *dom* = G. *dumm*, stupid, dull (whence in part the sense 'stupid' for E. *dumb*).] Destitute of the power of speech (as, a deaf and *dumb* person; the *dumb* brutes); bereft of the power of speech temporarily (as, to be struck *dumb* with astonishment); that does not speak, or is little addicted to speaking (as, "This spirit, *dumb* to us, will speak to him": Shakspere's "Hamlet," i. 1. 171); made, done, etc., without speech (as, "A kind Of excellent *dumb* discourse": Shakspere's "Tempest," iii. 3. 39); not giving forth or attended with sound of any kind (as, "Yet all the while his whip is *dumb!*" Wordsworth's "Waggoner," i. 39); lacking some usual property, characteristic, etc. (as, *dumb* ague: see phrase below); also, stupid or dull-witted (colloq., U. S.: as, "I used to get kep' in at recess for bein' so *dumb*," Wister's "Virginian," xii.).—**dumb ague,** an irregular form of intermittent malarial fever, lacking the usual chill.—**dumb,** *v. t.* To render dumb.—**dumb'=bell,** *n.* An instrument of wood or iron, consisting of two balls joined by a short bar, used as a weight in gymnastic exercises, esp. in pairs; also, something of similar shape.—**dumb-found',** etc. See *dumfound*, etc.—**dumb'ly,** *adv.*—**dumb'ness,** *n.*—**dumb'=show',** *n.* A part of a dramatic representation given in pantomime, common in the early English drama; also, gesture without speech.—**dumb'=wait'er,** *n.* A small stand or table placed near a dining-table to hold dishes, etc.; also, a framework with shelves drawn up and down in a shaft, for conveying food, etc., from one story to another.

dum-dum (dum'dum) **bul'let.** [From *Dum Dum*, town near Calcutta, India, where ammunition is made.] A kind of bullet that expands on impact, inflicting a severe wound.

dum-found, dumb-found (dum-found'), *v. t.* [Appar. < *dumb* + *-found* as in *confound.*] To strike dumb as with amazement and bewilderment; confound. Also **dum-foun'der, dumb-foun'der.**

dum-my (dum'i). [From *dumb.*] **I.** *n.*; pl. *dummies* (-iz). A dumb person (colloq.); one who has nothing to say or who takes no active part in affairs; one put forward to act for others while ostensibly acting for himself; also, an imitation or copy of something, as for display, to indicate appearance, etc.; a lay-figure on which to exhibit clothing, etc.; also, a kind of locomotive with a silent exhaust; also, a dolt or blockhead (colloq.); in *card-playing*, an imaginary player represented by an exposed hand which is played by and serves as partner to one of the players, or, as in bridge, the dealer's partner whose hand is exposed and played by the dealer; the cards so exposed, or a game so played. **II.** *a.* Put forward to act for others while ostensibly acting for one's self; also, counterfeit or sham; in *card-playing*, played with a dummy.—**dum'my,** *v.*; *-mied, -mying.* **I.** *tr.* To get or take while acting as a dummy for others. **II.** *intr.* To act as a dummy for others.

dump[1] (dump), *n.* [Perhaps akin to *damp.*] A reverie†; also, a dull, gloomy state of mind, or a fit of depression (now only in *pl.*: colloq.); also, a plaintive melody†; hence, a tune† (as, "O, play me some merry *dump*, to comfort me": Shakspere's "Romeo and Juliet," iv. 5. 108).

dump[2] (dump), *n.* [Origin obscure: cf. *dumpy*[2], *dumpling.*] Anything short, thick, and heavy; a clumsy leaden counter used by boys in games; a short, thick nail or bolt: any of various small coins; *pl.*, money or cash (colloq.).

dump[3] (dump), *v. t.* [ME. *dumpen*, tr. and intr., plunge down: cf. Norw. *dumpa*, Dan. *dumpe*, fall suddenly, Sw. *dumpa*, dip, *dimpa*, tumble, fall.] To throw down in a mass; fling down or drop heavily; empty out, as from a cart by tilting; also, to empty out the contents of (a cart, etc.) by tilting or overturning; in *com.*, to put (goods) on the market in large quantities and at a low price; esp., to do this in a foreign country, as at a price below that charged in the home country or below the cost of production, and so as to interfere with the ordinary trade of the foreign market.—**dump**[3], *n.* A mass of material, as rubbish, dumped or thrown down, or a place where it is deposited; a collection of ammunition, etc., deposited at some point, as near a battle front, to be distributed for use; also, the act of dumping.—**dump'age** (-ạ̄j), *n.* The act of dumping; also, that which is dumped; a pile of dumped refuse or rubbish; also, the privilege of dumping rubbish, etc., in a certain place; also, the fee paid for this privilege.—**dump'=cart,** *n.* A cart the body of which can be tilted, or the bottom opened downward, to discharge the contents.—**dump'er,** *n.*

dump-i-ness (dum'pi-nes), *n.* The state of being dumpy.

dump-ing (dum'ping), *n.* The act of one who or that which dumps. See *dump*[3], *v.*

dump-ish (dum'pish), *a.* [See *dump*[1].] Dull or stupid; also, depressed in spirits; sad; melancholy; moping.

dump-ling (dump'ling), *n.* [Cf. *dump*[2].] A rounded mass of boiled dough (often served with stewed meat, etc.); a kind of pudding consisting of a wrapping of dough inclosing an apple or other fruit, and boiled or baked; also, a short and stout person or animal (colloq.).

dump-y[1] (dum'pi), *a.* [See *dump*[1].] Dumpish; dejected; sulky.

dump-y[2] (dum'pi), *a.* [See *dump*[2].] Short and stout; squat: as, "Her stature tall—I hate a *dumpy* woman" (Byron's "Don Juan," i. 61).

dun[1] (dun). [AS. *dunn*; perhaps from Celtic.] **I.** *a.* Of a dull or grayish brown; also, dark; gloomy. **II.** *n.* Dun color; also, a dun-colored natural or artificial fly used in angling.—**dun**[1], *v. t.*; *dunned, dunning.* To make dun, or of a dull or grayish brown; also, to cure (codfish) by a process which gives them a dun color.

dun[2] (dun), *v. t.*; *dunned, dunning.* [Origin uncertain; perhaps a var. of *din.*] To make repeated and insistent demands upon, esp. for the payment of a debt.—**dun**[2], *n.* One who duns; an importunate creditor; also, a demand for payment, esp. a written one.

dun[3] (dun), *n.* [Gael. and Ir.] A hill; a fortified eminence: now chiefly in place-names, as *Dun*dee.

dunce (duns), *n.* [From *Duns* Scotus (about 1265–about 1308), the 'Subtle Doctor,' a celebrated scholastic theologian.] A disciple or follower of Duns Scotus†; hence, a hair-splitting reasoner†; a caviling sophist†; also, a dull pedant; also, a dull-witted or stupid person; a dolt.—**dun-cer-y** (dun′sėr-i), *n.* The practice or character of a follower of Duns Scotus or the schoolmen†; also, the action or character of a dunce or dolt; dullness; stupidity.

dun-der-head (dun′dėr-hed), *n.* [Origin obscure.] A dunce; a blockhead.—**dun′der-head″ed,** *a.*—**dun′der-pate,** *n.* Same as *dunderhead.*

dune (dūn), *n.* [F. *dune*: see *down*[2].] A mound, ridge, or hill of loose sand, heaped up by the wind, esp. on the seacoast.

dun-fish (dun′fish), *n.* [See *dun*[1], *v.*] Codfish cured by dunning.

dung (dung), *n.* [AS. *dung.*] Manure; also, excrement, esp. of animals; feces. Also fig.—**dung,** *v.* **I.** *tr.* To manure (ground) with or as with dung; also, to serve as dung for (the ground). **II.** *intr.* To void or eject excrement.

dun-ga-ree (dung′ga̤-rē), *n.* [Hind. *dungri.*] A coarse cotton fabric of East Indian origin, used esp. for sailors' clothing.

dung=bee-tle (dung′bē″tl), *n.* Any of various scarabæoid beetles that feed upon or breed in dung, as the dor, *Geotrypes stercorarius*, or the scarabæus, *Scarabæus sacer.*

dun-geon (dun′jo̤n), *n.* [OF. F. *donjon*, < ML. *domnio(n-)*, < L. *dominus*, master, lord.] The chief tower of a medieval castle, situated in the innermost court and often supplied with underground cells for prisoners; a donjon; also, any strong, close cell, esp. when underground.—**dun′geon,** *v. t.* To confine in or as in a dungeon.

dung-hill (dung′hil), *n.* A heap of dung; hence, a mean or vile place, abode, condition, or person.

dung-y (dung′i), *a.* Full of dung; like dung; foul or vile.

dun-ite (dun′īt), *n.* [From *Dun* Mountain, in New Zealand.] An igneous rock of granitic structure, composed chiefly of olivine with small amounts of chromite and other minerals.

du-ni-was-sal (dö′ni-wos′a̤l), *n.* [Gael. *duine*, man, + *uasal*, gentle.] Among the Highlanders of Scotland, a gentleman, esp. of secondary rank; a cadet of a family of rank.

Dun-kard (dung′kärd), *n.* Same as *Dunker.*

Dun-ker (dung′kėr), *n.* [G. *tunker*, < *tunken*, dip.] One of a sect of Baptists of German origin in America (known among themselves as 'Brethren' and 'German Baptist Brethren'), who administer baptism to adults only and by triple immersion.

dun-lin (dun′lin), *n.* [Appar. < *dun*[1].] A sandpiper, *Pelidna alpina*, about 8 inches long, widely distributed in the northern hemisphere; also, a somewhat larger American variety of this bird.

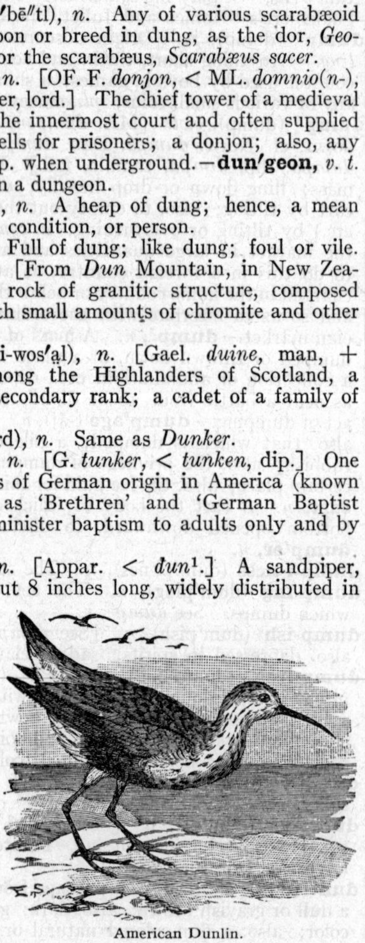

American Dunlin.

dun-nage (dun′a̤j), *n.* [Origin obscure.] *Naut.*, loose material laid beneath or wedged among cargo to prevent injury from water or chafing (as, "We covered the bottom of the hold . . . with dried brush, for *dunnage*, and . . . were ready to take in our cargo": Dana's "Two Years before the Mast," xxix.); also, baggage or personal effects.—**dun′nage,** *v. t.*; *-naged, -naging.* To stow or secure with dunnage.

dun-ner (dun′ėr), *n.* One who duns.

dunn-ite (dun′īt), *n.* [From Colonel B. W. *Dunn* (born 1860), of the U. S. army, the inventor.] An explosive (officially known as *explosive D*) used as a bursting-charge for projectiles.

dunt (dunt), *n.* [Cf. *dint, dent*[1].] A hard blow making a dull sound; a wound from such a blow; a beat of the heart. [Chiefly Sc.]—**dunt,** *v.* **I.** *tr.* To strike or knock with a dull sound. [Chiefly Sc.] **II.** *intr.* To strike with a dull sound; of the heart, to beat or throb. [Chiefly Sc.]

du-o (dū′ō, It. dö′ō), *n.*; pl. *duos* (dū′ōz), It. *dui* (dö′ē). [It., < L. *duo*, two.] In *music*, a duet.

du-o-de-ci-mal (dū-o̤-des′i-ma̤l). [L. *duodecimus*, twelfth, < *duodecim*, twelve, < *duo*, two, + *decem*, ten.] **I.** *a.* Pertaining to twelfths, or to the number twelve; proceeding by twelves. **II.** *n.* One of a system of numerals the base of which is twelve; *pl.*, a method of multiplying together quantities denoting lengths given in feet, inches, etc., in which the base is twelve instead of the ten of ordinary multiplication.—**du-o-de′ci-mal-ly,** *adv.*

du-o-de-ci-mo (dū-o̤-des′i-mō). [NL. *in duodecimo*, 'in twelfth.'] **I.** *n.*; pl. *-mos* (-mōz). The page size of a book in which each leaf is one twelfth of a whole sheet of paper; a volume of this size. Abbreviated 12*mo* or 12°. **II.** *a.* In duodecimo.

du-o-de-nal (dū-o̤-dē′na̤l), *a.* Of or pertaining to the duodenum.

du-o-den-a-ry (dū-o̤-den′a̤-ri), *a.* [L. *duodenarius*, containing twelve, < *duodeni*: see *duodenum.*] Pertaining to the number twelve; proceeding by twelves.

du-o-de-ni-tis (dū″o̤-dē-nī′tis), *n.* [NL.] In *pathol.*, inflammation of the duodenum.

du-o-de-num (dū-o̤-dē′num), *n.* [ML. (so called from its length, about twelve fingerbreadths), < L. *duodeni*, twelve each, < *duodecim*: see *duodecimal.*] In *anat.*, the first portion of the small intestine, extending from the stomach to the jejunum.

du-o-logue (dū′o̤-log), *n.* [L. *duo*, two, + E. *-logue* as in *monologue.*] A conversation between two persons; a dialogue; a dramatic performance or piece in the form of a dialogue.

duo-mo (dwō′mō, It. dwô′mō), *n.*; pl. *-mi* (-mē). [It.: see *dome.*] In Italian use, a cathedral.

dup (dup), *v. t.*; *dupped, dupping.* [For *do up.*] To raise the latch of; open (a door or gate): as, "Then up he rose, and donn'd his clothes, And *dupp'd* the chamber-door" (Shakspere's "Hamlet," iv. 5. 53). [Archaic or prov. Eng.]

dup-a-ble (dū′pa̤-bl), *a.* Capable of being duped; gullible. —**dup-a-bil′i-ty** (-bil′i-ti), *n.*

dupe (dūp), *n.* [F. *dupe*, OF. *duppe*, dupe, also the hoopoe.] A person who is imposed upon or deceived; a victim of credulity; a gull.—**dupe,** *v. t.*; *duped, duping.* To make a dupe of; deceive; delude; trick.—**dup-er** (dū′pėr), *n.*—**dup′er-y,** *n.* The act or practice of duping; deception; also, the state of one who is duped.

du-ple (dū′pl), *a.* [L. *duplus*: see *double.*] Double; twofold: as, *duple* ratio (in which the antecedent is double the consequent, as 2 to 1, 8 to 4, etc.); *duple* time or rhythm (characterized by two beats to the measure).

du-plex (dū′pleks), *a.* [L. *duplex*, < *duo*, two, + *-plex*, akin to *plicare*, fold, and prob. to *-plus*: see *double.*] Twofold; double: as, *duplex* telegraphy (a system for sending two messages simultaneously over the same wire, esp. in opposite directions); *duplex* apartment (an apartment, or suite of rooms, on two floors or stories).—**du-plex′i-ty,** *n.*

du-pli-cate (dū′pli-kāt), *v. t.*; *-cated, -cating.* [L. *duplicatus*, pp. of *duplicare*, double, < *duplex*: see *duplex.*] To double; make twofold; also, to make an exact copy of; repeat.—**du′pli-cate** (-ka̤t), *a.* Double; consisting of or existing in two corresponding parts or examples; also, consisting of twice the number or quantity; also, that is exactly like or corresponding to something else.—**duplicate whist,** a form of whist in which the hands are played over again, when each side holds the cards formerly held by its opponents.—**du′pli-cate,** *n.* One of two things exactly alike; also, a copy exactly like an original; in general, anything corresponding in all respects to something else.—**in duplicate,** in two copies, exactly alike.—**du-pli-ca′tion** (-kā′-shọn), *n.* [L. *duplicatio(n-).*] The act of duplicating, or the state of being duplicated; a duplicate; also, a folding or doubling, as of a membrane; a fold.—**du′pli-ca-tive** (-kạ-tiv), *a.* Having the quality of duplicating or doubling; producing two instead of one.—**du′pli-ca-tor** (-kā-tọr), *n.* One that duplicates anything; a machine for making duplicates.—**du′pli-ca-ture** (-kạ-ṭūr), *n.* Duplication; a fold.

du-pli-ci-den-tate (dū″pli-si-den′tāt). [L. *duplex* (*duplic-*), double, + *dens* (*dent-*), tooth.] **I.** *a.* Belonging or pertaining to the *Duplicidentata*, a suborder or division of rodents, comprising the hares, rabbits, and pikas, in which there are two pairs of upper incisor teeth, the second pair being small and placed directly behind the large first pair. **II.** *n.* A duplicidentate rodent.

du-pli-ci-ty (dụ-plis′i-ti), *n.* [OF. *duplicite* (F. *duplicité*), < LL. *duplicitas*, doubleness, < L. *duplex*: see *duplex.*] The state or quality of being twofold or double; doubleness; also, deceitful doubleness as shown in speech or conduct; the fact or practice of speaking or acting in two ways in relation to the same matter with intent to deceive; double-dealing; in *law*, the pleading of two or more distinct matters in one plea.

du-ra (dū′rạ), *n.* Same as *dura mater.*

du-ra-ble (dū′rạ-bl), *a.* [OF. F. *durable*, < L. *durabilis*, < *durare*, last: see *dure*[2].] Having the quality of lasting or enduring; holding out well against wear, decay, or any destructive change.—**du-ra-bil′i-ty** (-bil′i-ti), **du′ra-ble-ness,** *n.*—**du′ra-bly,** *adv.*

du-ral-u-min (dụ-ral′ụ-min), *n.* [G., < *Düren*, town in Rhenish Prussia where it was first made, + *alumin*, aluminium.] A strong, light alloy of aluminium, copper, and manganese, with or without magnesium: used in aircraft construction. [Proprietary name.]

du-ra ma-ter (dū′rạ mā′tėr). [ML., 'hard mother': cf. *pia mater.*] In *anat.*, the tough, fibrous membrane forming the outermost of the three coverings of the brain and spinal cord. Cf. *arachnoid* and *pia mater.*

du-ra-men (dụ-rā′men), *n.* [L., hardness, a hardened vine-branch, < *durare*, harden: see *dure*[2].] In *bot.*, the hard central wood, or heart-wood, of an exogenous tree.

du-rance (dū′rạns), *n.* [OF. *durance*, < *durer*, < L. *durare*, last: see *dure*[2].] Duration, durability, or endurance (archaic); also, forced confinement, or imprisonment (as, "In *durance* vile here must I wake and weep": Burns's "Epistle from Esopus to Maria," 57); constraint.

du-ra-tion (dụ-rā′shọn), *n.* [OF. *duration*, < ML. *duratio(n-)*, < L. *durare*, last: see *dure*[2].] Continuance in time; the length of time during which anything continues.

dur-bar (dėr′bär), *n.* [Hind. and Pers. *darbār.*] In India, the court of a native ruler; a public audience or levee held by a native prince or a British governor or viceroy; the hall or place of audience.

Düreresque Style. — Woodcut by Dürer.

dure[1] (dūr), *a.* [OF. F. *dur* (fem. *dure*), < L. *durus*, hard: cf. *dour.*] Hard; severe. [Archaic.]

dure[2] (dūr), *v. i.*; *dured*, *during.* [OF. F. *durer*, < L. *durare*, harden, be hardened, endure, last, < *durus*, hard, E. *dure*[1].] To endure; last. [Archaic.]

Dü-rer-esque (dü-rėr-esk′), *a.* [See *-esque.*] In the manner or style of Albrecht Dürer (1471–1528), the famous German painter and engraver. See cut in preceding column.

du-ress (dū′res or dụ-res′), *n.* [OF. *duresse*, *durece*, < L. *duritia*, hardness, < *durus*, hard.] Hardness†; also, affliction†; also, forcible restraint of liberty; imprisonment; also, constraint or compulsion; in *law*, constraint by which a person is illegally forced to perform or to forbear performing some act.

Dur-ham (dur′ạm), *n.* One of a breed of short-horned cattle originating in the county of Durham, England.

du-ri-an (dö′ri-ạn or dö-rē′ạn), *n.* [Malay *durīan*, < *dūrī*, thorn.] The edible fruit, with a hard, prickly rind, of a tree, *Durio zibethinus*, of the East Indies; the tree itself.

Durian.

dur-ing (dūr′ing), *prep.* [Orig. ppr. of *dure*[2], as used in absolute constructions such as 'my life *during*' (while my life dures or lasts), and hence, by inversion, '*during* my life.'] Throughout the continuance of; also, in the course of.

dur-mast (dėr′måst), *n.* [From *dur-* (of uncertain origin and meaning) + *mast*[1].] A European oak, *Quercus sessiliflora* (or *Q. pubescens*), with a heavy, elastic wood, highly valued by the builder and the cabinet-maker.

dur-ra (dụr′ä), *n.* [Ar.] A grain-sorghum (see *sorghum*), a variety of *Andropogon sorghum* with slender stalks, cultivated in Asia, etc., and introduced into the U. S. Also called *Indian millet* and *guinea-corn.*

durst (dėrst). A preterit of *dare.*

dusk (dusk). [ME. *deosc*, *dosc*: cf. AS. *dox*, dark.] **I.** *a.* Dark; tending to darkness; dusky. **II.** *n.* The state of being dusk; dusk color; moderate darkness; shade; gloom; also, the darker stage of twilight.—**dusk,** *v.* **I.** *intr.* To become dusk; grow dark; present a dusky appearance. **II.** *tr.* To make dusk; darken; dim.—**dusk′y,** *a.*; compar. *duskier*, superl. *duskiest.* Somewhat dark; dark-colored; deficient in light; dim; gloomy.—**dusk′i-ly,** *adv.*—**dusk′i-ness,** *n.*

dust (dust), *n.* [AS. *dūst* = MLG. *dust* = Icel. *dust*, dust: cf. G. *dunst*, vapor.] Earth or other matter in fine, dry particles, so small and light as to be easily raised and carried by the wind; any finely comminuted or powdered substance; fine or small particles separated in some process, as sawing; also, a single particle or grain (now rare), or a small quantity or pinch, of a finely powdered substance; a cloud of finely powdered earth or other matter in the air, as that raised by the trampling of persons or animals; fig., confusion or turmoil (as, "Great contest follows, and much learned *dust* Involves the combatants": Cowper's "Task," iii. 161); a disturbance (colloq.); also, that to which anything, as the human body, is reduced by disintegration or decay; the remains of a dead body; also, a low or mean condition, as of one prone on the ground (as, "He raiseth up the poor out of the *dust*": 1 Sam. ii. 8); also, dust, ashes, and other refuse from a house, etc. (Eng.); also, gold-dust; money or cash (slang).—**dust,** *v. t.* To soil with dust; make dusty; also, to sprinkle with dust or powder; strew or sprinkle as dust; also, to free from dust; wipe the dust from; brush, rub, or shake off as dust.—**dust′er,** *n.* One who or that which dusts; an apparatus for sprinkling a dust or powder on something; anything, as a cloth or a machine, for removing dust; a fine sieve for removing dust by sifting; a long, light overgarment to protect the clothing from dust; also, a trial well-hole which fails to reach water, or an unproductive boring for oil or gas.—**dust′i-ly,** *adv.* In a dusty manner.—**dust′i-ness,** *n.*—**dust′man** (-man), *n.*; pl. *-men.* One employed to remove dust and refuse (Eng.); also, a popular personification of sleep (cf. *sandman*).—**dust′=pan,** *n.* A utensil in which dust is collected and removed.—**dust′=storm,** *n.* A storm of wind which raises dense masses of dust into the air, as in a desert region.—**dust′y,** *a.*; compar. *dustier*, superl. *dustiest.* Filled or covered with dust; clouded with or as with dust; also, of the nature of dust; powdery.

Dutch (duch), *a.* [MD. *dutsch*, German, Dutch (D. *duitsch*, German), also G. *deutsch*, German, orig. popular, national; connected with OHG. *diota*, Icel. *thjōdh*, AS. *thēod*, Goth. *thiuda*, people, nation.] German, Germanic, or Teutonic (now only archaically, as in 'Low Dutch,' Low German, and 'High Dutch,' High German, except in colloq. or slang use); also, of, pertaining to, or characteristic of the natives or inhabitants of the Netherlands or Holland, or their country or language.—**Dutch cheese,** a small, globular, hard cheese made from skim-milk; also, cottage cheese.—**Dutch courage,** courage or boldness inspired by intoxicating drink.—**Dutch gold,** an alloy of copper and zinc in the form of thin sheets, used as a cheap imitation of gold-leaf. Also called *Dutch foil, Dutch leaf,* and *Dutch metal.*—**Dutch oven,** a tin utensil open in front, for roasting meat, etc., before an open fire or a kitchen range; also, an iron kettle for baking, having a close-fitting cover on which burning coals are placed.—**Dutch treat,** a repast or other entertainment in which each person pays for himself. [Colloq.]—**like a Dutch uncle,** with authoritativeness and unsparing candor, as in criticizing or reproving.—**Dutch,** *n.* The German language in all or any of its forms (now chiefly in 'High Dutch,' High German, and 'Low Dutch,' Low German); the language spoken by the Germans proper (now colloq. or slang); the language of the Netherlands or Holland; collectively, as a plural, the German peoples generally (archaic); the Germans proper (now colloq. or slang); the people of the Netherlands or Holland.—**Pennsylvania Dutch,** the mixed dialect, consisting of German intermingled with English, spoken by the descendants of the early German settlers in Pennsylvania; collectively, as a plural, these people themselves.—**to beat the Dutch,** to be very strange or surprising; excel anything before known or heard of. [Colloq.]

Dutch-man (duch′mạn), *n.*; pl. *-men.* A German (now only colloq.); a native or inhabitant of Holland; a Dutch ship; in *carp.*, etc., a piece or wedge inserted to hide the fault in a badly made joint, stop an opening, etc.—**Flying Dutchman.** See that entry.—**Dutch′man's=breech′es,** *n.* A delicate papaveraceous herb, *Dicentra* (or *Bikukulla*) *cucullaria*, with pale-yellow two-spurred flowers.—**Dutch′-man's=pipe′,** *n.* An aristolochiaceous climbing vine, *Aristolochia macrophylla*, with large leaves, and flowers of a curved form suggesting a tobacco-pipe.

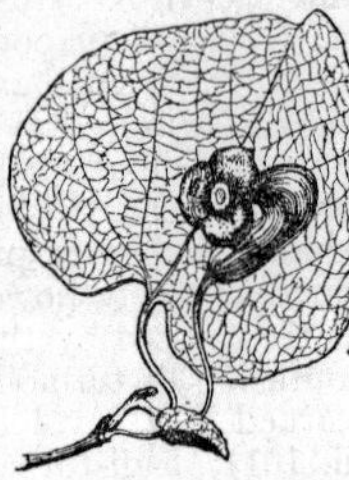
Dutchman's-pipe.

du-te-ous (dū′tẹ-us), *a.* Dutiful; obedient; submissive.—**du′te-ous-ly,** *adv.*—**du′te-ous-ness,** *n.*

du-ti-a-ble (dū′ti-ạ-bl), *a.* Subject to duty, as imported goods.

du-ti-ful (dū′ti-fu̇l), *a.* Performing the duties required of one; obedient; submissive; also, required by duty; proceeding from or expressive of a sense of duty.—**du′ti-ful-ly,** *adv.*—**du′ti-ful-ness,** *n.*

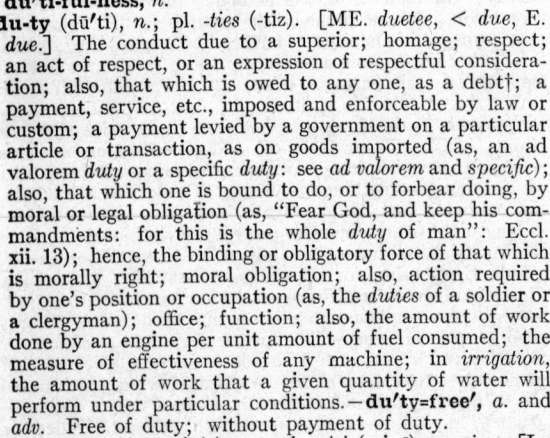

du-ty (dū′ti), *n.*; pl. *-ties* (-tiz). [ME. *duetee*, < *due*, E. *due.*] The conduct due to a superior; homage; respect; an act of respect, or an expression of respectful consideration; also, that which is owed to any one, as a debt†; a payment, service, etc., imposed and enforceable by law or custom; a payment levied by a government on a particular article or transaction, as on goods imported (as, an ad valorem *duty* or a specific *duty*: see *ad valorem* and *specific*); also, that which one is bound to do, or to forbear doing, by moral or legal obligation (as, "Fear God, and keep his commandments: for this is the whole *duty* of man": Eccl. xii. 13); hence, the binding or obligatory force of that which is morally right; moral obligation; also, action required by one's position or occupation (as, the *duties* of a soldier or a clergyman); office; function; also, the amount of work done by an engine per unit amount of fuel consumed; the measure of effectiveness of any machine; in *irrigation*, the amount of work that a given quantity of water will perform under particular conditions.—**du′ty=free′,** *a.* and *adv.* Free of duty; without payment of duty.

du-um-vir (dụ-um′vėr), *n.*; pl. *-viri* (-vi-rī) or *-virs.* [L., for *duovir*, usually pl. *duoviri*, < *duo*, two, + *viri*, pl. of *vir*, man.] In *Rom. hist.*, either of two officers or magistrates united in the same public function; in general, either of two persons associated in any office.—**du-um′vi-rate** (-vi-rāt), *n.* [L. *duumviratus.*] A union of two men in the same office, as in ancient Rome; a group of two persons associated in any office; the office or government of two such persons.

du-ve-tyn (dū-vẹ-tēn′), *n.* [Cf. F. *duvet*, down.] A soft, flexible, closely woven woolen fabric with a thick, finely matted nap.

duy-ker, duy-ker-bok (dī′kėr, -bok), *n.* See *duiker, duikerbok.*

dwarf (dwârf). [AS. *dweorg* = D. *dwerg* = G. *zwerg* = Icel. *dvergr.*] **I.** *n.* A human being much below the ordinary stature or size; a pygmy; an animal or plant much below the ordinary size of its kind or species. **II.** *a.* Of unusually small stature or size; dwarfish; diminutive.—**dwarf,** *v.* **I.** *tr.* To render dwarf or dwarfish; hinder from growing to the natural size; prevent the due development of; also, to render insignificant in extent, character, etc.; also, to cause to appear or seem small, as by comparison. **II.** *intr.* To become dwarfed or smaller.—**dwarf′-ish,** *a.* Like a dwarf; below the ordinary stature or size; diminutive.—**dwarf′ish-ly,** *adv.*—**dwarf′ish-ness,** *n.*

dwell (dwel), *v. i.*; *dwelt* (sometimes *dwelled*), *dwelling.* [ME. *dwellen*, delay, tarry, abide, earlier tr., AS. *dwellan*, *dwelian*, lead astray, hinder, delay, = Icel. *dvelja*, delay, intr. tarry, wait.] To continue for a time; linger or pause, as in thought or action; lay emphasis (as, to *dwell* upon a point in a discourse); also, to abide as a permanent resident; reside; live.—**dwell,** *n.* A stay, stoppage, or pause; the brief continuation of pressure in taking an impression, as on a hand-press; an automatic pause in the action of a part of a machine.—**dwell′er,** *n.*—**dwell′ing,** *n.* Continued or habitual residence; abode; also, a place of residence or abode; a habitation; a house.—**dwell′ing=house,** *n.*

dwin-dle (dwin′dl), *v.*; *-dled, -dling.* [Freq. of *dwine.*] **I.** *intr.* To become smaller and smaller (as, "A handful of seventy men in a barrack of mud, Foodless, waterless, *dwindling* one by one": H. Newbolt's "Guides at Cabul"); shrink; waste away; fig., to fall away, as in quality; degenerate. **II.** *tr.* To make smaller and smaller; cause to shrink.—**dwin′dle-ment,** *n.*

dwine (dwīn), *v. i.*; *dwined, dwining.* [AS. *dwīnan* = Icel. *dvīna.*] To waste away; fade. [Archaic or prov.]

dy-ad (dī′ad), *n.* [LL. *dyas* (*dyad-*), < Gr. δυάς (δυαδ-), < δύο, two.] A group of two; a couple; in *chem.*, an element, atom, or radical having a valence of two; in *biol.*, a secondary morphological unit, consisting of an aggregate of monads.—**dy-ad′ic,** *a.*

Dy-ak (dī′ak), *n.* A member of a wild people of Borneo, notorious as head-hunters, of the same stock as the Malays, who found them there on first coming to the island.

dy′ar-chy, etc. See *diarchy*, etc.

dye (dī), *n.* [AS. *dēag*, *dēah.*] Color or hue, esp. as produced by dyeing; also, a coloring material or matter; a liquid containing coloring matter, for imparting a particular hue to cloth, etc.—**dye,** *v.*; *dyed, dyeing.* [AS. *dēagian.*] **I.** *tr.* To color or stain; treat with a dye; color (cloth, etc.) by soaking in a liquid containing coloring matter; also, to impart (color) by means of a dye. **II.** *intr.* To impart color, as a dye; also, to become colored when treated with a dye.—**dye′=house,** *n.* A building in which dyeing is carried on.—**dy′er,**

Dyeweed.

n.—**dy'er's=weed,** *n.* Any of various plants yielding dyes, as the weld, *Reseda luteola*, or the dyeweed, *Genista tinctoria*, or the woad, *Isatis tinctoria*.—**dye'stuff,** *n.* A material yielding, or used as, a dye.—**dye'weed,** *n.* A fabaceous shrub, *Genista tinctoria*, a native of the Old World, bearing yellow flowers and yielding a yellow dye; woadwaxen. See cut on preceding page.—**dye'wood,** *n.* Any wood yielding a coloring matter used for dyeing.

dy-ing (dī'ing), *p. a.* [See *die*[1].] That dies; ceasing to live; expiring; mortal; drawing to a close; failing; also, pertaining to or associated with dying or death (as, "Judith and Hetty had stood by the *dying* bed of their mother": Cooper's "Deerslayer," xxi.).—**dy'ing-ly,** *adv.*

dyke (dīk), etc. See *dike*, etc.

dy-na-graph (dī'nạ-grȧf), *n.* [Gr. δύναμις, power: see *-graph.*] An apparatus used on a railroad-car to determine and record the condition of the track, speed of the train, resistance of the car, etc.

dy-nam-e-ter (dī-nam'e-tėr), *n.* [Gr. δύναμις, power: see *-meter.*] An instrument for determining the magnifying power of telescopes.

dy-nam-ic (dī-nam'ik or di-). [Gr. δυναμικός, powerful, efficacious, < δύναμις, power, < δύνασθαι, be able.] **I.** *a.* Of or pertaining to force not in equilibrium (opposed to *static*) or to force in any state; also, pertaining to dynamics; also, pertaining to or characterized by energy or effective action; active; energetic, forceful, or effective; in *med.*, functional, not organic, as a disease. **II.** *n.* Dynamics; also, motive force.—**dy-nam'i-cal,** *a.* Dynamic.—**dy-nam'i-cal-ly,** *adv.*—**dy-nam'ics,** *n.* That branch of physics or mechanics which deals with force as producing or affecting motion (thus including *kinetics* but not *statics*), or, more comprehensively, with the action of force on bodies either in motion or at rest (thus including *kinetics* and *statics*); hence, the science or principles of forces acting in any field; also, the forces, physical or moral, at work in any field.

dy-na-mism (dī'nạ-mizm), *n.* [Gr. δύναμις, power: see *dynamic.*] Any of various doctrines or philosophical systems which seek to explain the phenomena of nature by the action of some force.

dy-na-mi-tard (dī'nạ-mi-tärd''), *n.* [F.] A dynamiter.

dy-na-mite (dī'nạ-mīt, also din'ạ-), *n.* [Gr. δύναμις, power: see *dynamic.*] A high explosive consisting of nitroglycerin mixed with some absorbent substance such as kieselguhr.—**dy'na-mite,** *v. t.*; *-mited, -miting.* To mine or charge with dynamite; blow up, shatter, or destroy with dynamite.—**dy'na-mite=gun,** *n.* *Milit.*, a gun in which the projectile (a shell containing dynamite or other high explosive) is thrown by compressed air or gas.—**dy'na-mit-er** (-mī-tėr), *n.* One who dynamites; usually, one who uses dynamite and similar explosives for unlawful, esp. anarchistic, purposes.—**dy-na-mit'ic, dy-na-mit'i-cal** (-mit'ik, -i-kạl), *a.* Of or pertaining to dynamite or dynamiters.—**dy-na-mit'i-cal-ly,** *adv.*—**dy'na-mit-ism** (-mīt-izm), *n.* The use of dynamite and similar explosives for unlawful, esp. anarchistic, purposes.—**dy'na-mit-ist,** *n.* A dynamiter.

dynamo-. Form of Gr. δύναμις, power, used in combination.

dy-na-mo (dī'nạ-mō), *n.*; pl. *-mos* (-mōz). [For *dynamo-electric machine.*] A machine for converting mechanical energy into electric energy, consisting typically of a magnet (usually an electromagnet) which furnishes a field, and another portion (the armature) usually made up of insulated copper wire wound about an iron core, the current being developed in the armature when it is rotated in the field or has the field rotated about it.

dy-na-mo=e-lec-tric, dy-na-mo=e-lec-tri-cal (dī''nạ-mō-ẹ-lek'trik, -tri-kạl), *a.* Pertaining to the conversion of mechanical energy into electric energy, or vice versa: as, a *dynamo-electric* machine (a dynamo or an electric motor).

dy-nam-o-graph (dī-nam'ọ-grȧf), *n.* [See *dynamo-* and *-graph.*] An automatically registering dynamometer for measuring muscular power.

dy-na-mom-e-ter (dī-nạ-mom'e-tėr), *n.* [See *dynamo-* and *-meter.*] A device for measuring force or power.—**dy-na-mom'e-try,** *n.* [See *-metry.*] The act or art of using the dynamometer.—**dy''na-mo-met'ric, dy''na-mo-met'ri-cal** (-mọ-met'rik, -ri-kạl), *a.*

dy-na-mo-tor (dī'nạ-mō-tọr), *n.* [From *dyna(mo)* + *motor.*] A combined electrical motor and generator (dynamo), used for changing a current into one of another form.

dy-nast (dī'nast or din'ạst), *n.* [L. *dynastes*, < Gr. δυνάστης, < δύνασθαι, be able, have power.] A ruler or potentate; esp., a hereditary ruler.—**dy-nas-tic** (dī-nas'tik or di-), *a.* [Gr. δυναστικός.] Of or pertaining to a dynasty. Also **dy-nas'ti-cal.**—**dy-nas'ti-cal-ly,** *adv.*—**dy-nas'ti-cism** (-sizm), *n.* Dynastic rule.—**dy-nas-ty** (dī'nạs-ti or din'ạs-), *n.*; pl. *-ties* (-tiz). [Gr. δυναστεία.] A succession of sovereigns of the same line or family: as, "He [Walpole] succeeded . . . in establishing on an impregnable basis a *dynasty* which seemed tottering to its fall" (Lecky's "Hist. of Eng. in the 18th Century," iii.).

dyne (dīn), *n.* [Gr. δύναμις, power: see *dynamic.*] In *physics*, the unit of force in the centimeter-gram-second system, being that force which, acting on a mass of one gram for one second, gives it a velocity of one centimeter per second.

dys-. [Gr. δυσ-, akin to Skt. *dus-*, *dur-*, OHG. *zur-*, Icel. *tor-*.] A prefix of Greek origin, meaning 'hard,' 'bad,' 'ill,' sometimes used as an English formative, as in *dyslogistic*, *dysteleology*. Cf. *eu-* ('well').

dys-æs-the-sia (dis-es-thē'ziạ), *n.* [NL.: see *dys-* and *æsthesia.*] In *pathol.*, deranged or impaired sensation.

dys-cra-sia (dis-krā'ziạ), *n.* [ML., < Gr. δυσκρασία, < δύσκρατος, badly tempered, < δυσ-, ill, + κεραννύναι, mix.] In *pathol.*, a generally faulty or disordered condition of the body.—**dys-cras'ic** (-kraz'ik), *a.*

dys-cra-site (dis'krạ-sīt), *n.* [Gr. δυσ-, ill, + κρᾶσις, combination.] A mineral consisting of antimony and silver, occurring in crystals and also massive and granular.

dys-en-ter-y (dis'ẹn-ter-i), *n.* [L. *dysenteria*, < Gr. δυσεντερία, < δυσ-, ill, + ἔντερον, intestine: see *enteron.*] In *pathol.*, an infectious disease characterized by inflammation and ulceration of the lower portion of the bowels, with diarrhea that soon becomes mucous and hemorrhagic.—**dys-en-ter'ic,** *a.*

dys-gen-ic (dis-jen'ik), *a.* [Gr. δυσ-, ill, + γεν-, bear, produce.] Pertaining to or causing degeneration in the type of offspring produced: opposed to *eugenic.*—**dys-gen'ics,** *n.* The study of the operation of factors that cause degeneration in the type of offspring produced.

dys-lo-gis-tic (dis-lọ-jis'tik), *a.* [From *dys-* + *-logistic* as in *eulogistic.*] Conveying disapproval or censure; opprobrious: opposed to *eulogistic.*—**dys-lo-gis'ti-cal-ly,** *adv.*

dys-lo-gy (dis'lọ-ji), *n.* [From *dys-* + *-logy* as in *eulogy.*] Dispraise; discommendation; censure: the opposite of *eulogy*. [Rare.]

dys-men-or-rhe-a, dys-men-or-rhœ-a (dis''men-ọ-rē'ạ), *n.* [NL., < Gr. δυσ-, ill, + μήν, month, + ῥοία, a flow, < ῥεῖν, flow.] In *pathol.*, difficult or painful menstruation.—**dys''men-or-rhe'al, dys''men-or-rhœ'al,** *a.*

dys-pep-sia (dis-pep'siạ), *n.* [L., < Gr. δυσπεψία, < δύσπεπτος, hard to digest, < δυσ-, hard, + πέπτειν, cook, digest.] Deranged or impaired digestion; indigestion: opposed to *eupepsia.*—**dys-pep'tic. I.** *a.* Pertaining to, subject to, or suffering from dyspepsia; hence, morbidly gloomy or pessimistic. **II.** *n.* A person subject to or suffering from dyspepsia.—**dys-pep'ti-cal-ly,** *adv.*

dys-pha-gi-a (dis-fā'ji-ạ), *n.* [NL., < Gr. δυσ-, hard, + φαγεῖν, eat.] In *pathol.*, difficulty in swallowing.—**dys-phag'ic** (-faj'ik), *a.*

dys-pha-sia (dis-fā'ziạ), *n.* [NL., < Gr. δυσ-, hard, + φάναι, say: cf. *aphasia.*] In *pathol.*, difficulty in speaking or utterance.—**dys-pha'sic** (-fā'zik), *a.*

dys-pho-ni-a (dis-fō'ni-ạ), *n.* [NL., < Gr. δυσ-, hard, + φωνή, sound, voice.] In *pathol.*, difficulty in producing vocal sounds.—**dys-phon'ic** (-fon'ik), *a.*

dysp-nœ-a (disp-nē'ạ), *n.* [L., < Gr. δύσπνοια, < δύσπνοος, breathing with difficulty, < δυσ-, hard, + πνεῖν, blow, breathe.] In *pathol.*, difficult or labored breathing: opposed to *eupnœa.*—**dysp-nœ'al, dysp-nœ'ic,** *a.*

dys-pro-si-um (dis-prō'si-um), *n.* [NL., < Gr. δυσπρόσοδος, hard to get at, < δυσ-, hard, + πρός, to, + ὁδός, way.] Chem. sym., Dy; at. wt., 162.5. A rare element found in certain minerals.

dys-tel-e-ol-o-gy (dis″tel-ē-ol′ọ-ji or dis″tē-lē-), *n.* [See *dys-* and *teleology.*] The doctrine of purposelessness in nature, as opposed to design (teleology); the science of rudimentary or vestigial organs with reference to this doctrine.—**dys″tel-e-o-log′i-cal**(-ọ-loj′-i-kal), *a.*

dys-to-cia (dis-tō′siạ), *n.* [NL., < Gr. δυστοκία, < δύστοκος, bringing forth with pain, < δυσ-, hard, + τίκτειν, bring forth.] In *pathol.*, difficult parturition.

Dziggetai.

dys-tro-phi-a, dis-tro-phy (dis-trō′fi-ạ, dis′trọ-fi), *n.* [NL. *dystrophia*, < Gr. δυσ-, ill, + τρέφειν, nourish.] In *pathol.*, faulty nutrition.—**dys-troph′ic** (-trof′ik), *a.*

dys-u-ri-a (dis-ū′ri-ạ), *n.* [LL., < Gr. δυσουρία, < δυσ-, hard, + οὖρον, urine.] In *pathol.*, difficult or painful urination.—**dys-u′ric**, *a.*

dzig-ge-tai (dzig′gẹ-tī), *n.* [Mongol.] A wild ass, *Equus hemionus*, living in herds in central Asia. See cut in preceding column.

Dzo.

dzo (dzō), *n.* [Tibetan.] A hybrid animal, being the result of a cross between the water-buffalo and the domesticated yak.

E

E, e (ē); pl. *E's, e's* (ēz). A vowel, the 5th letter of the English alphabet.

each (ēch). [AS. *ǣlc*, < *ā*, ever, + *gelīc*, like.] **I.** *a.* Every, of two or more considered individually or one by one. **II.** *pron.* Each one.—**each other,** each the other (as, they struck *each other*, that is, they struck, *each* striking the *other*): used also (like *one another*) as a compound reciprocal pronoun in oblique cases (as, they struck at *each other*). By some grammarians *each other* is restricted to cases in which only two are concerned, *one another* being used of a greater number. See *one another*, under *one*, *pron.*

ea-ger[1], **ea-gre** (ē′gėr or ā′-), *n.* [Origin unknown.] A sudden and formidable tidal wave rushing up a narrowing estuary or tidal river; a bore.

ea-ger[2] (ē′gėr), *a.* [OF. F. *aigre*, < L. *acer* (*acr-*), sharp.] Keen or sharp to the taste or other senses†; pungent†, tart†, or acid†; acute or severe, as disease†; biting or keen (obs. or archaic: as, "It is a nipping and an *eager* air," Shakspere's "Hamlet," i. 4. 2); also, keen in action†; fierce†; also, keen or ardent in desire or feeling; impatiently longing; anxious; intense or impatient, as desire; characterized by or manifesting keenness of desire or strength of feeling, as actions, looks, etc.—**ea′ger-ly**, *adv.*—**ea′ger-ness**, *n.*

ea-gle (ē′gl), *n.* [OF. F. *aigle*, < L. *aquila*, eagle.] Any of certain large diurnal birds of prey of the falcon family, esp. of the genus *Aquila*, as *A. chrysaëtus* ('golden eagle'), or of the genus *Haliaëtus*, as *H. leucocephalus* ('bald eagle': the national bird of the U. S.), noted for their size, strength, powerful flight, and keenness of vision; a figure or representation of an eagle (much used as an emblem: as, the Roman *eagle*, surmounting a standard; the double-headed *eagle* of Austria or of Russia; the white *eagle* of Poland); a standard or the like bearing such a figure, esp. the standard of the ancient Roman army; a lectern for a church, having the upper part in the form of an eagle with outstretched wings; a gold coin of the U. S., of the value of ten dollars (having a figure of an eagle on the reverse: cf. *double-eagle*); [*cap.*] in *astron.*, the constellation Aquila; in the *U. S. navy*, one of a class of large, quickly-constructed, oil-burning boats of small draft, first launched toward the close of the World War, designed for use as submarine destroyers (also called 'Eagle boat').—**ea′gle=eyed′**, *a.* Sharp-sighted, like an eagle.—**ea′gle-stone**, *n.* A nodular mass of stone consisting of an argillaceous oxide of iron: formerly thought to be sought by the eagle to facilitate egg-laying.—**ea′glet**, *n.* A young eagle.—**ea′gle=vul″ture**, *n.* A large bird, *Gypohierax angolensis*, of western Africa.

Bald Eagle.

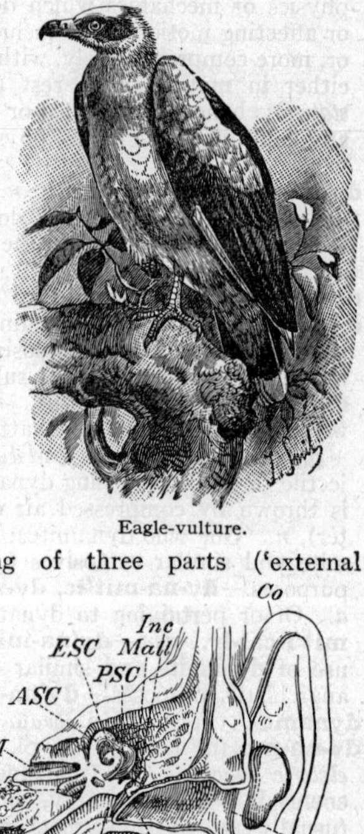

Eagle-vulture.

ea-gre (ē′gėr or ā′-), *n.* See *eager*[1].

ean (ēn), *v.* Same as *yean.* [Now prov. Eng.]—**ean′ling**†, *n.* Same as *yeanling.* See Shakspere's "Merchant of Venice," i. 3. 80.

ear[1] (ēr), *n.* [AS. *ēare* = D. *oor* = G. *ohr* = Goth. *ausō*, ear; akin to L. *auris*, Gr. οὖς, ear.] The organ of hearing, in man and mammals usually consisting of three parts ('external ear,' 'middle ear,' and 'internal ear'); often, the external part alone; also, the sense of hearing; nice perception of the differences of sound; sensitiveness to the quality and correctness of musical sounds; also, voluntary hearing; attention; heed; favorable hearing or attention (as, to have or gain a person's *ear*); also, any object resembling or suggestive of the external ear, as the handle of a pitcher, the part of a bell by which it is hung, or some other projecting part; in journalistic use, either of the small spaces or boxes in the upper corners of the front page of a newspaper, containing displayed matter, as, for example, an indication of the particular edition of the paper.—**by the ears,** in a state of discord or contention: as,

Transverse Section through Side Walls of Skull, showing the Inner Parts of the Ear.
Co, external ear; *EM*, external auditory meatus; *TyM*, tympanic membrane; *Ty*, tympanum; *Inc*, incus; *Mall*, malleus; *ASC*, *PSC*, *ESC*, anterior, posterior, and external semicircular canals; *Coc*, cochlea; *Eu*, Eustachian tube; *IM*, internal auditory meatus, through which the auditory nerve passes to the organ of hearing.

"We all sat down . . . as peaceably disposed . . . as if . . . the excellent Mr. Caxton had never set all mankind *by the ears* with an irritating invention" (Bulwer-Lytton's "Caxtons," iii. 4).—**to have** (or **keep**) **one's ear to the ground,** fig., to pay close attention to the trend of general opinion, so as to shape one's policy in accordance with it. [Colloq.]—**up to the ears,** deeply absorbed or engrossed; almost overwhelmed.

ear² (ēr), *n.* [AS. *ēar* = D. *aar* = G. *ähre* = Icel. *ax* = Goth. *ahs*, ear.] That part of a cereal plant, as corn, wheat, etc., which contains the flowers and hence the fruit, grains, or kernels.—**ear²,** *v. i.* To form or put forth ears, as corn.

ear³ (ēr), *v. t.* [AS. *erian* = OHG. *erran* = Icel. *erja* = Goth. *arjan*, akin to L. *arare*, Gr. ἀροῦν, plow.] To plow; till: as, "a rough valley, which is neither *eared* nor sown" (Deut. xxi. 4). [Archaic or prov.]

ear-ache (ēr′āk), *n.* Pain in the ear; otalgia.

ear=cock-le (ēr′kok″l), *n.* A disease of wheat due to the presence in the ear of a small nematode worm, *Tylenchus tritici.*

ear=drop (ēr′drop), *n.* An ornamental pendant to an earring; an earring with a pendant.

ear=drum (ēr′drum), *n.* The tympanum, or middle ear; also, the tympanic membrane.

eared¹ (ērd), *a.* Having ears or ear-like appendages; auriculate.

eared² (ērd), *a.* Having ears, as corn.

ear-ing (ēr′ing), *n.* [Appar. < *ear¹*.] *Naut.*, a small rope attached to a cringle of a sail: used in reefing, etc.

earl (ėrl), *n.* [AS. *eorl* = Icel. *earl*, later *jarl*: cf. *jarl*.] A man of noble rank†; an under-king† or viceroy†; a noble, the governor or proprietor of a county or shire†; a count, in the historical sense†; now, a British nobleman of a rank next below that of marquis and next above that of viscount. Cf. *count¹*.—**earl marshal,** a high officer of state in Great Britain, who is head of the Heralds' College, appointing its officers, and who directs all great ceremonies of state: the office is now hereditary in the line of the dukes of Norfolk.

Coronet of a British Earl.

ear=lap (ēr′lap), *n.* The lobe of the ear; also, the whole external ear; also, one of a pair of pieces attached to a cap, for covering the ears in cold weather.

earl-dom (ėrl′dọm), *n.* [AS. *eorldōm.*] The territory or jurisdiction of an earl†; also, the rank or title of an earl.

ear-less (ēr′les), *a.* Having no ears; deaf.

ear-li-ness (ėr′li-nes), *n.* The state of being early.

ear=lock (ēr′lok), *n.* A lock of hair near the ear.

ear-ly (ėr′li), *adv.*; compar. *earlier*, superl. *earliest*. [AS. *ǣrlīce*, < *ǣr*: see *ere*.] In or during the first part of some division of time, or of some course or series; also, far back in time; anciently; also, before the usual or appointed time; in good time; betimes.—**ear′ly,** *a.* Of, pertaining to, or occurring in the first part of some division of time, or of some course or series; occurring, appearing, etc., early in the morning, in the year, in life, etc. (as, the *early* bird catches the worm); also, belonging to a period far back in time; ancient; also, occurring before the usual or appointed time (as, to have an *early* dinner); occurring, appearing, etc., in good season; hence, occurring in the near future (as, kindly let us have an *early* reply).—**early English architecture,** the pointed (Gothic) style of medieval architecture in England, which was developed from and succeeded the Norman at the close of the 12th and in the early part of the 13th century, and which passed into the decorated style. See cut in preceding column.

Early English Architecture. — Galilee Porch and South Transept of Lincoln Cathedral.

ear-mark (ēr′märk), *n.* A mark of identification made on the ear of an animal; hence, any identifying or distinguishing mark or characteristic.—**ear′mark,** *v. t.* To mark with an earmark.

ear=muff (ēr′muf), *n.* One of a pair of adjustable coverings, commonly of velvet, for protecting the ears in cold weather.

earn¹ (ėrn), *v. t.* [AS. *earnian*, earn, akin to OHG. *arnōn*, reap, G. *ernte*, harvest.] To gain by labor or service (as, to *earn* one's living); gain as a due return or profit (as, money well invested *earns* good interest); get as one's desert or due (as, to *earn* a reputation for honesty); bring or procure as deserved (as, his fair dealing *earned* for him the confidence of all); also, to merit as compensation, as for service (as, to receive more than one has *earned*); deserve.

earn² (ėrn), *n.* See *erne.*

ear-nest¹ (ėr′nest), *n.* [ME. *ernes*, later *ernest*, appar. an altered form of *erles*, E. *arles*.] A portion of something, given or done in advance as a pledge of the remainder; a part of the price, paid down to bind a bargain; hence, anything serving as a pledge or foretaste of what is to follow (as, "His eloquence and religious fervor had already given the *earnest* of high eminence in his profession": Hawthorne's "Scarlet Letter," iii.).

ear-nest² (ėr′nest), *n.* [AS. *eornost* = D. and G. *ernst.*] Seriousness, as of intention or purpose, as opposed to jest, play, or trifling.—**in earnest,** in seriousness; seriously; having, or with, a serious purpose.—**ear′nest²,** *a.* [AS. *eorneste.*] Serious in intention, purpose, or effort; sincerely zealous; characterized by or evincing depth and sincerity of feeling (as, "On that prospect strange Their *earnest* eyes they fix'd": Milton's "Paradise Lost," x. 553); also, of serious importance, or demanding serious attention (as, "Life is real! Life is *earnest!*" Longfellow's "Psalm of Life").—**ear′nest-ly,** *adv.*—**ear′nest-ness,** *n.*

earn-ing (ėr′ning), *n.* The act of one who earns; *pl.*, money earned; wages; profits.

ear-ring (ēr′ing), *n.* A ring or other ornament worn in the lobe of the ear.

ear=shell (ēr′shel), *n.* Any gastropod of the family *Haliotidæ*: so named from the ear-shaped (oval) shell. Cf. *abalone.*

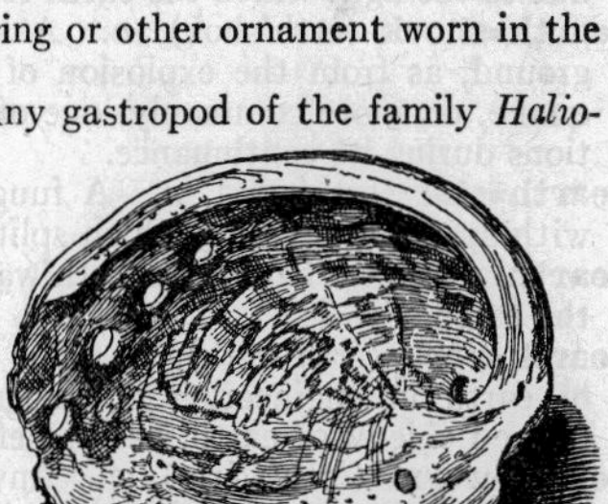

Ear-shell (Abalone).

ear-shot (ēr′shot), *n.* Reach or range of hearing.

ear=stone (ēr′stōn), *n.* An otolith.

earth (ėrth), *n.* [AS. *eorthe* = D. *aarde* = G. *erde* = Icel. *jördh* = Goth. *airtha*, earth.] The globe which we inhabit, being a major planet, the third in order from the sun (and having a diameter at the equator of about 7,926 miles and at the poles of about 7,900 miles, a mass of about six sextillions of tons, and a mean density of about 5.6 times that of water); this globe or planet as the habitation of man, often in contrast to heaven and hell; the inhabitants of the globe (as, "The whole *earth* was of one language": Gen. xi. 1); worldly matters, as distinguished from spiritual; also, a land† or country† (as, "This hand . . . That sways the *earth* this climate overlooks": Shakspere's "King John," ii. 1. 344); also, the surface of the globe; also, the solid matter of the globe; the dry land; the ground; also, the softer part of the land, as distinguished from rock; soil; dirt; also, the hole of a burrowing animal; in *chem.*, any of certain difficultly reducible metallic oxides, as alumina, zirconia, yttria, etc. (as, the alkaline *earths*, see under *alkaline*; the rare *earths*, the less common earths, as zirconia, thoria, yttria, etc.); in *elect.*, a ground.—**earth,** *v.* **I.** *tr.* To put or hide in or as in the earth; bury (now only prov.); cover with earth, as the roots and stem of a plant; drive (a fox, etc.) to his earth or burrow. **II.** *intr.* Of a fox, etc., to run to his earth or burrow; hide underground.

earth=ap-ple (ėrth′ap″l), *n.* The Jerusalem artichoke. See *artichoke.*

earth=board (ėrth′bōrd), *n.* The mold-board of a plow.

earth=born (ėrth′bôrn), *a.* Born or sprung from the earth; of earthly origin.

earth-en (ėr′thn), *a.* Composed of earth or earthy matter; made of baked clay.—**earth′en-ware** (-wãr), *n.* Earthen pottery; vessels, etc., of baked or hardened clay, esp. those of the coarser kinds; also, the material or substance of such vessels (usually restricted to the coarse, opaque varieties, the finer, translucent kinds being called *porcelain*).

earth=flea (ėrth′flē), *n.* The chigo.

earth=fly (ėrth′flī), *n.* Same as *earth-flea.*

earth=hog (ėrth′hog), *n.* The aardvark.

earth-i-ness (ėr′thi-nes), *n.* Earthy nature or properties; also, earthliness.

earth=light (ėrth′līt), *n.* Same as *earth-shine.*

earth-li-ness (ėrth′li-nes), *n.* Earthly quality or character; worldliness.

earth-ling (ėrth′ling), *n.* An inhabitant or creature of the earth; a mortal; also, one strongly attached to earthly or worldly things; a worldling.

earth-ly (ėrth′li), *a.*; compar. *earthlier*, superl. *earthliest.* [AS. *eorthlīc.*] Of or pertaining to the earth, esp. as opposed to heaven; worldly; also, possible or conceivable (as, what *earthly* purpose can it serve?); also, earthy (archaic).

earth-nut (ėrth′nut), *n.* The edible chestnut-like tuberous root of *Conopodium denudatum*, a European umbelliferous plant; any of various other roots, tubers, or subterranean growths, as the truffle and the peanut; also, any of the plants producing these.

earth=plate (ėrth′plāt), *n.* In *elect.*, a ground-plate.

earth-quake (ėrth′kwāk), *n.* A vibration or movement of a part of the earth's surface, due to the faulting of rocks, to volcanic forces, etc.

earth=shine (ėrth′shīn), *n.* In *astron.*, the faint light visible on the part of the moon not illuminated by the sun: due to the light which the earth reflects on the moon.

earth=shock (ėrth′shok), *n.* A sudden movement of the ground, as from the explosion of a mine; also, an earthquake, or, more commonly, one of the more violent oscillations during its continuance.

earth=star (ėrth′stär), *n.* A fungus of the genus *Geaster*, with an outer covering which splits into the form of a star.

earth-ward, earth-wards (ėrth′wạ̈rd, -wạ̈rdz), *adv.* Toward the earth.

earth-work (ėrth′wėrk), *n.* The removal or throwing up of earth in engineering operations; also, a construction formed chiefly of earth, as for defense.

earth-worm (ėrth′wėrm), *n.* Any worm that lives in the earth; esp., a worm of the family *Lumbricidæ*, having a long, cylindrical body tapering at each end, useful in loosening the soil, and much used as bait by anglers; fig., a mean or groveling person.

earth-y (ėr′thi), *a.*; compar. *earthier*, superl. *earthiest.* Of the nature of or consisting of earth or soil; earth-like; without luster, and rough to the touch (said of minerals); also, pertaining to or characteristic of earth, as a taste or smell; fig., gross or unrefined (as, "Thou wast a spirit too delicate To act her *earthy* and abhorr'd commands": Shakspere's "Tempest," i. 2. 273); also, earthly or worldly; in *chem.*, belonging to the class of earths.

ear=trum-pet (ēr′trum″pet), *n.* A trumpet-like device for collecting and intensifying sounds, held to the ear as an aid in defective hearing.

ear=wax (ēr′waks), *n.* A yellowish wax-like secretion from certain glands in the external auditory canal, acting as a lubricant, and arresting the entrance of dust, insects, etc.

ear-wig (ēr′wig), *n.* [AS. *ēarwicga*, 'ear insect.'] Any of numerous curiously formed beetle-like insects constituting the family *Forficulidæ*, popularly supposed to creep into and injure the human ear.—**ear′wig,** *v. t.*; *-wigged, -wigging.* To assail or ply with covert representations or insinuations; work upon by covert statements.

Earwig (*Spongophora brunneipennis*). (Line shows natural size.)

ease (ēz), *n.* [OF. F. *aise* = It. *agio*; origin uncertain.] An undisturbed state of the body or mind; freedom from labor, pain, annoyance, or obligation; leisure; comfort; tranquillity; also, facility, readiness, or dexterity; also, absence of formality, constraint, or embarrassment; also, relief or deliverance from discomfort, constraint, or obligation.—**ease,** *v.*; *eased, easing.* [OF. *aisier, aiser.*] **I.** *tr.* To give ease to; free or release from pain, annoyance, or care; relieve, as of a burden; also, to release from pressure, tension, or the like (as, to *ease* off a rope, to slacken it gradually); let sink, go, pass, etc., easily or gently (colloq.: as, to *ease* one's self into a chair; "*Ease* me through this gate, Agellius," J. H. Newman's "Callista," ix.); also, to mitigate, lighten, or lessen (as, "Is there no play, To *ease* the anguish of a torturing hour?" Shakspere's "Midsummer Night's Dream," v. 1. 37); also, to render less difficult; facilitate. **II.** *intr.* To become less painful, burdensome, etc.; also, to reduce severity, pressure, tension, etc.: often with *up.*—**ease′ful,** *a.* Attended with or affording ease; comfortable: as, "*easeful* Death" (Keats's "Ode to a Nightingale").—**ease′ful-ly,** *adv.*—**ease′ful-ness,** *n.*

ea-sel (ē′zẹl), *n.* [D. *ezel* = G. *esel*, easel, lit. 'ass': akin to E. *ass.*] A frame in the form of a tripod, for supporting an artist's canvas, a blackboard, or the like.

ease-ment (ēz′mẹnt), *n.* [OF. *aisement*, < *aiser*, E. *ease*, *v.*] An easing; relief; also, something that gives ease; a convenience; in *law*, any of certain rights held by one person in land owned by another.

eas-er (ē′zėr), *n.* One who or that which eases.

eas-i-ly (ē′zi-li), *adv.* In an easy manner; with ease; without trouble or difficulty.—**eas′i-ness,** *n.*

east (ēst), *adv.* [AS. *ēast*, akin to D. *oost*, G. *ost*, *osten*, Icel. *austr*, Sw. *ost*, Dan. *öst*, east, and ult. to L. *aurora*, Gr. ἠώς, Skt. *ushas*, dawn: cf. *Easter.*] In the direction of the sunrise; toward or in the east; also, from the east (as with reference to wind).—**east,** *n.* A cardinal point of the compass, corresponding to the point where the sun is seen to rise at the equinox; the direction in which this point lies; also [*l. c.* or *cap.*], a quarter or territory situated in this direction, as the eastern part of the U. S. in distinction from the West; [*cap.*] the countries of Asia generally, as lying east of Europe; the Orient.—**Far East,** China, Japan, and other parts of eastern Asia.—**Near East,** indefinitely, Asia Minor and neighboring parts of Asia and sometimes of Europe and Africa.—**east,** *a.* Lying toward or situated in the east; directed or proceeding toward the east; also, coming from the east, as a wind; *eccles.*, lying toward the altar as situated with respect to the nave; designating, or situated in, the end of a church containing the altar.

East-er (ēs′tėr), *n.* [AS. *ēastre*, pl. *ēastron* (= OHG. *ōstarūn*, G. *Ostern*, pl.), from the name (Northumbrian *Eostre*) of a Teutonic goddess of spring, orig. of dawn; akin to E. *east.*] An annual Christian festival in commemoration of the resurrection of Jesus Christ, observed on the first Sunday after the full moon that occurs on or next after March 21.—**Easter egg,** an egg ornamented by dyeing or the like, or an ornamental imitation of an egg or a confection in the form of an egg, used at Easter as a gift, etc.—**Easter lily.** See *lily, n.*—**Easter Monday,** the day after Easter.

east-er-ling (ēs′tėr-ling), *n.* [Cf. MLG. *osterlink*, D. *oosterling.*] A native or inhabitant of an eastern country or district (archaic); esp., formerly, a trader or native of one of the Hanse towns, or, in general, of northern Germany or the shores of the Baltic.

east-er-ly (ēs′tėr-li). **I.** *a.* Moving, directed, or situated toward the east; also, coming from the east, as a wind. **II.** *adv.* Toward the east; also, from the east.

east-ern (ēs′tėrn), *a.* [AS. *ēasterne.*] Lying toward or situated in the east; directed or proceeding toward the east; also, coming from the east, as a wind; also [*l. c.* or *cap.*], of or pertaining to the east (as, the *Eastern* Church, the *Eastern* Empire, see below; an *Eastern* Congressman, that is, of the East of the U. S.); [usually *cap.*] Oriental.—**Eastern Church,** the Greek Church (see under *Greek, a.*).—**Eastern Empire,** the eastern portion of the Roman Empire after its division in A.D. 395, which became extinct in A.D. 1453: after the fall of the Western Empire, known also as the *Byzantine Empire.*—**eastern time.** See *standard time,* under *standard, a.*—**east′ern,** *n.* One living in an eastern region or country; [*cap.*] a member of the Eastern Church.—**East′ern-er,** *n.* A person of or from the eastern U. S.—**east′ern-most,** *a. superl.* Furthest east.

East-er-tide (ēs′tėr-tīd), *n.* The Easter season.

East Indian (ēst in′di-an). **I.** *a.* Of or pertaining to the East Indies, a vague collective name for India, Indo-China, and the Malay Archipelago. **II.** *n.* A native or inhabitant of the East Indies.

east-ing (ēs′ting), *n.* The distance due east made by a ship on any course tending eastward; easterly departure; distance eastward; also, a shifting eastward; easterly direction.

East-lake (ēst′lāk), *a.* Designating or pertaining to a style of design in furniture current in England and the U. S. in the latter half of the 19th century, based on the recommendations of Charles L. Eastlake (1836–1906), English writer on matters of art.

Eastlake Chair.

east-ward (ēst′wārd). [AS. *ēasteweard.*] **I.** *adv.* Toward the east; east. **II.** *a.* Moving, bearing, facing, or situated toward the east. **III.** *n.* The eastward part, direction, or point.—**east′ward-ly. I.** *a.* Having an eastward direction or situation; also, coming from the east, as a wind. **II.** *adv.* Toward the east; also, from the east.—**east′wards,** *adv.* Eastward.

eas-y (ē′zi), *a.*; compar. *easier,* superl. *easiest.* [OF. *aisie* (F. *aisé*), pp. of *aisier,* E. *ease, v.*] Having, or characterized by, ease; free from pain or discomfort; comfortable; free from anxiety or care; tranquil; free from want, or from solicitude as to the means of living (as, *easy* circumstances); also, conducive to ease or comfort (as, an *easy* posture); also, fond of or given to ease; indolent; unconcerned; also, not difficult; requiring no great labor or effort; presenting no great obstacle; obtained with little effort (as, an *easy* victory); not burdensome or oppressive (as, on *easy* terms); also, not difficult to influence; compliant; complaisant; credulous; readily imposed upon; also, not harsh or strict (as, an *easy* master); lenient; indulgent; also, free from formality, constraint, or embarrassment; smooth or flowing, as literary style; also, not forced or hurried (as, an *easy* pace); moderate; gentle; also, not tight (as, an *easy* fit); fitting loosely; in *com.*, of a commodity, not difficult to obtain; not much in demand; of the market, not characterized by eager demand; in *whist,* of honors, equally divided between the sides (also fig.).—**easy mark,** fig., a person readily imposed upon (as if a mark or target easily or readily hit). [Slang.]—**on Easy Street,** in easy or comfortable circumstances.—**eas′y,** *adv.* In an easy manner; with ease; at one's ease; comfortably. [Now chiefly colloq.]—**eas′y-chair′,** *n.* A chair especially adapted for comfort.—**eas′y-go′ing,** *a.* Going easily, as a horse; fig., taking matters in an easy way; characterized by comfortable unconcern.

eat (ēt), *v. t.*; pret. *ate* (āt or et), also *eat* (et or ēt); pp. *eaten,* archaic or colloq. *eat* (et or ēt) or *ate* (āt or et); ppr. *eating.* The pron. et for both pret. and pp. forms, although current in Great Britain, is considered colloq. or prov. in the U. S. [AS. *etan* = D. *eten* = G. *essen* = Icel. *eta* = Goth. *itan,* eat; akin to L. *edere,* Gr. ἔδειν, Skt. *ad-*, eat.] To take into the mouth and swallow for nourishment, esp. to masticate and swallow, as solid food; devour as food, also, to consume by or as by devouring; ravage or devastate; wear or waste away; corrode; pierce or gnaw into; also, to make (a hole, passage, etc.) as by gnawing or corrosion.—**to eat crow,** to do something extremely disagreeable and humiliating, under compulsion.—**to eat one's head off,** to cost more in feeding than one is worth: said esp. of a horse, etc.—**to eat one's words,** to retract one's assertions.—**eat,** *v. i.* To consume food; take a meal; hence, to board; also, to taste or relish in a particular manner when eaten (colloq.); also, to make a way as by gnawing or corrosion.—**eat,** *n.* The act of eating†; a meal†; food (now only in *pl.*, in slang use).—**eat′a-ble. I.** *a.* That may be eaten; fit for food; edible. **II.** *n.* An article of food: commonly in *pl.*: as, "bread and other *eatables*" (Defoe's "Robinson Crusoe," ii. 2).—**eat′er,** *n.*

eath (ēᴛʜ or ēth), *a.* or *adv.* [AS. *ēathe.*] Easy or easily. [Obs. or Sc. and north. Eng.]—**eath′ly,** *adv.*

eat-ing (ē′ting), *n.* The act of one who or that which eats; the consuming of food, esp. solid food; also, food with reference to the quality perceived when eaten (as, this fish is delicious *eating*).

eau (ō), *n.*; pl. *eaux* (ōz, F. ō). [F., < L. *aqua.*] Water.—**eau de Cologne** (dė ko-lon-y′). [F.] Cologne water; cologne.—**eau de Javel** (zhȧ-vel). [F., 'water of Javel' (locality in Paris).] An aqueous solution containing potassium hypochlorite, prepared from potassium carbonate and bleaching-powder: used as a bleaching agent and a disinfectant.—**eau forte** (fôrt). [F., 'strong water.'] Aqua fortis; nitric acid.—**eau=de=vie** (-vē), *n.* [F., 'water of life.'] Brandy.

eaves (ēvz), *n. pl.* [AS. *efes* = MLG. *ovese* = OHG. *obasa* = Icel. *ups,* eaves; prob. akin to E. *over.*] The overhanging lower edge of a roof.—**eaves′drop,** *v.*; *-dropped, -dropping.* **I.** *intr.* To stand under the eaves or near the windows of a house (orig. within the dropping or dripping of water from the eaves) to listen to conversation carried on inside; hence, to listen clandestinely. **II.** *tr.* To listen to clandestinely.—**eaves′drop″per,** *n.*—**eaves′=swal″low,** *n.* A North American swallow, *Petrochelidon lunifrons,* which often builds its nest of mud under the eaves of buildings.

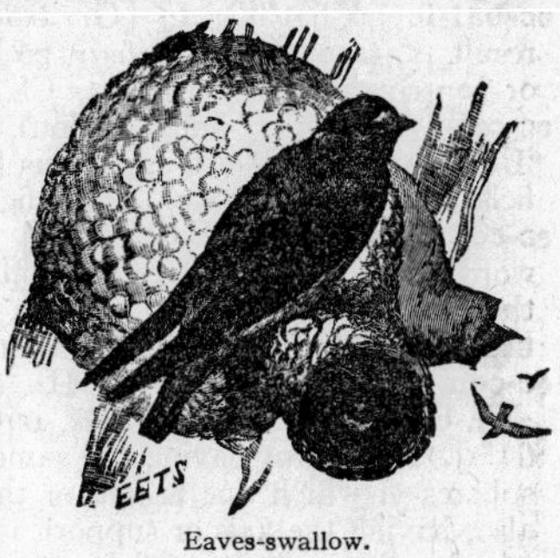

Eaves-swallow.

ebb (eb), *n.* [AS. *ebba* = D. *ebbe, eb.*] The reflux or falling of the tide (opposed to *flood* and *flow*); hence, a flowing backward or away (as, "I hate to learn the *ebb* of time, From yon dull steeple's drowsy chime": Scott's "Lady of the Lake," vi. 24); decline or decay (as, "His faintness came not from despair, But nature's *ebb*": Byron's "Island," iii. 4); a point of decline (as, his fortunes were at a low *ebb*).—**ebb,** *v. i.* [AS. *ebbian.*] To flow back or away, as the water of a tide (opposed to *flow*); hence, to recede; decline or decay; waste or fade away.—**ebb′=tide,** *n.* The reflux of the tide; the retiring tide.

eb-e-na-ceous (eb-ē-nā′shius), *a.* [L. *ebenus*: see *ebon.*] Belonging to the *Ebenaceæ,* or ebony family of trees and shrubs; diospyraceous.

eb-e-ne-zer (eb-ē-nē′zėr), *n.* [From *Eben-ezer* ('stone of help'), the name given by Samuel to the stone erected by him in recognition of divine aid in defeating the Philistines: see 1 Sam. vii. 12.] Any memorial of divine assistance; a dissenters' place of worship (Eng.).

eb-on (eb′on). [L. *ebenus,* < Gr. ἔβενος; prob. from Semitic.] **I.** *n.* Ebony. [Now poetic.] **II.** *a.* Consisting or made of ebony; also, black, dark, or somber (as, "Heaven's *ebon* vault, Studded with stars unutterably bright": Shelley's "Queen Mab," iv. 4). [Chiefly poetic.]

eb-on-ite (eb′on-īt), *n.* [From *ebony.*] Vulcanite.

eb-on-ize (eb′on-īz), *v. t.*; *-ized, -izing.* To stain or finish in imitation of ebony.

eb-on-y (eb′ǫn-i), *n.*; pl. *-ies* (-iz). [Extended form of *ebon.*] A hard, heavy, durable wood, most highly prized when black, from various tropical trees of the genus *Diospyros*, as *D. ebenum* of southern India and Ceylon, used for cabinet-work, etc.; any tree yielding such wood; also, any of various similar woods or trees.

e-brac-te-ate (ē-brak′tẹ-āt), *a.* [L. *e-*, for *ex-* (see *ex-*), + *bractea*, E. *bract.*] In *bot.*, without bracts.

e-bri-e-ty (ẹ-brī′ẹ-ti), *n.* [L. *ebrietas*, < *ebrius*, drunk.] Drunkenness.

e-bri-ose, e-bri-ous (ē′bri-ōs, -us), *a.* [L. *ebriosus*, < *ebrius*, drunk.] Drunken; drunk.—**e-bri-os′i-ty** (-os′i-ti), *n.*

e-bul-lient (ẹ-bul′yẹnt), *a.* [L. *ebulliens* (*-ent-*), ppr. of *ebullire*, boil out or up, < *e*, out of, + *bullire*, E. *boil*[2].] Boiling up; bubbling up like a boiling liquid; fig., seething or overflowing with fervor, enthusiasm, excitement, etc.—**e-bul′lience, e-bul′lien-cy,** *n.*—**e-bul′lient-ly,** *adv.*

e-bul-li-om-e-ter (ẹ-bul-i-om′e-tėr), *n.* [L. *ebullire*, boil up: see *-meter.*] An ebullioscope.

e-bul-lio-scope (ẹ-bul′yǫ-skōp), *n.* [L. *ebullire*, boil up: see *-scope.*] An instrument for indicating the boiling-points of liquids or solutions, used esp. in testing beverages to determine the amount of alcohol contained.

eb-ul-li-tion (eb-u-lish′ǫn), *n.* [LL. *ebullitio*(*n-*), < L. *ebullire*: see *ebullient.*] The act or process of boiling up; ebullient state; hence, any bubbling up; a rushing forth of water, lava, etc., in a state of agitation; fig., a seething or overflowing, as of passion or feeling (as, "This *ebullition* of feeling . . . came as a real shock to Lady and Lord Valleys": Galsworthy's "Patrician," ii. 18); an outburst.

eb-ur-na-tion (eb-ėr-nā′shǫn or ē-bėr-), *n.* [L. *eburnus*, of ivory, < *ebur*, ivory: cf. *ivory.*] In *pathol.*, a morbid change in bone or cartilage, by which it becomes hard and dense, like ivory.

e-bur-ne-an (ẹ-bėr′nẹ-ąn), *a.* [L. *eburneus*, < *ebur*, ivory.] Of or like ivory.

é-car-té (ā-kär-tā), *n.* [F., prop. pp. of *écarter*, discard.] A game at cards for two persons, in which discarding is a feature.

ec-bat-ic (ek-bat′ik), *a.* [Gr. ἐκβαίνειν, go out, come out, result, < ἐκ, out of, + βαίνειν, go.] Expressing mere result or consequence, as a clause. Cf. *telic.*

ec-cal-e-o-bi-on (e-kal″ẹ-ǫ-bī′on), *n.* [Gr. ἐκκαλέω βίον, 'I call forth life.'] An apparatus for hatching eggs by artificial heat; an incubator. Also fig.

ec-ce ho-mo (ek′sē hō′mō). [L.] "Behold the man!"—the words with which Pilate presented Christ, crowned with thorns, to the Jews (John, xix. 5); hence, in *art*, a representation of Christ crowned with thorns.

ec-cen-tric (ek-sen′trik). [ML. *eccentricus*, < Gr. ἔκκεντρος, out of the center, < ἐκ, out of, + κέντρον, E. *center*[2].] **I.** *a.* Not having the same center, as two circles or spheres of which one is within the other; not concentric; also, having the axis or support away from the center, as a wheel; also, not situated in the center, as an axis; also, deviating from a circular form, as an orbit; fig., deviating from the recognized or usual character, practice, etc.; irregular; erratic; odd; queer. **II.** *n.* A circle described about the center of an elliptical orbit, with half the major axis for radius; also, a device for converting circular into reciprocating rectilinear motion, consisting of a disk fixed somewhat out of center to a revolving shaft, and working freely in a surrounding collar ('eccentric-strap'), to which a rod ('eccentric-rod') is attached; also, something eccentric, irregular, or peculiar; an eccentric person.—**ec-cen′tri-cal-ly,** *adv.*—**ec-cen-tri′ci-ty** (-tris′i-ti), *n.*; pl. *-ties* (-tiz). The quality of being eccentric; the amount by which anything is eccentric; fig., deviation from recognized or usual methods, practice, forms, etc.; irregularity; oddity; also, an oddity or peculiarity, as of conduct (as, "a prince . . . whose *eccentricities* were such as had never before been seen out of a madhouse": Macaulay's "Essays," Frederic the Great); in *math.*, a ratio equal to the distance between any point of a conic section and a focus divided by the distance between the same point and the corresponding directrix.

ec-chy-mosed (ek′i-mōst or -mōzd), *a.* Affected with ecchymosis.

ec-chy-mo-sis (ek-i-mō′sis), *n.*; pl. *-moses* (-mō′sēz). [NL., < Gr. ἐκχύμωσις, < ἐκχυμοῦσθαι, extravasate blood, < ἐκ, out of, + χυμός, juice, E. *chyme.*] In *pathol.*, a discoloration due to extravasation of blood, as in a bruise.—**ec-chy-mot′ic** (-mot′ik), *a.*

ec-cle-si-a (e-klē′zi-ą), *n.*; pl. *-siæ* (-zi-ē). [L., < Gr. ἐκκλησία, < ἐκκαλεῖν, call out, summon, < ἐκ, out of, + καλεῖν, call.] An assembly, esp. of the freemen of ancient Athens; in Christian use, a congregation; a church.

ec-cle-si-arch (e-klē′zi-ärk), *n.* [LGr. ἐκκλησιάρχης: see *ecclesia* and *-arch.*] A ruler of the church; in the Greek Church, a sacristan.

ec-cle-si-ast (e-klē′zi-ast), *n.* [Gr. ἐκκλησιαστής, member of an ecclesia, later one who addresses an assembly, preacher (LL. *ecclesiastes*): cf. *Ecclesiastes.*] A member of the ancient Greek ecclesia; also, an ecclesiastic†; [*cap.*] with *the*, 'the Preacher' (a title of the author of the book of Ecclesiastes).

Ec-cle-si-as-tes (e-klē-zi-as′tēz), *n.* [LL., < Gr. Ἐκκλησιαστής, lit. 'preacher': see *ecclesiast.*] A book of the Old Testament ("Ecclesiastes; or, The Preacher"), the authorship of which is traditionally ascribed to Solomon.

ec-cle-si-as-tic (e-klē-zi-as′tik). [LL. *ecclesiasticus*, < Gr. ἐκκλησιαστικός, < ἐκκλησία: see *ecclesia.*] **I.** *a.* Ecclesiastical. **II.** *n.* A clergyman, or person in orders; a churchman as distinguished from a layman.—**ec-cle-si-as′ti-cal,** *a.* Of or pertaining to the church or the clergy; churchly; clerical; not secular; not lay.—**ec-cle-si-as′ti-cal-ly,** *adv.*—**ec-cle-si-as′ti-cism** (-sizm), *n.* Ecclesiastical principles, practices, or spirit; devotion to the principles or interests of the church, or the extension of its influence in its external relations.

Ec-cle-si-as-ti-cus (e-klē-zi-as′ti-kus), *n.* [LL.: see *ecclesiastic.*] The alternative name given to the book of the Apocrypha called also "The Wisdom of Jesus, the Son of Sirach."

ec-cle-si-ol-a-try (e-klē-zi-ol′ą-tri), *n.* [See *ecclesia* and *-latry.*] Worship of the church; excessive reverence for churchly forms and traditions.

ec-cle-si-ol-o-gy (e-klē-zi-ol′ǫ-ji), *n.* [See *ecclesia* and *-logy.*] The science of the church as an organized society; also, the science of church architecture and decoration.—**ec-cle″si-o-log′i-cal** (-ǫ-loj′i-kąl), *a.*—**ec-cle-si-ol′o-gist,** *n.*

ec-dy-sis (ek′di-sis), *n.*; pl. *ecdyses* (-sēz). [NL., < Gr. ἔκδυσις, < ἐκδύειν, get out of, strip off, < ἐκ, out of, + δύειν, enter, put on.] The shedding or casting off of an outer coat or integument by serpents, crustaceans, etc., or of feathers by birds.

é-chau-guette (ā-shō-get), *n.* [F.; from Teut.] A watch-turret; a bartizan.

ech-e-lon (esh′ẹ-lon), *n.* [F. *échelon*, lit. 'round of a ladder,' < *échelle*, ladder, < L. *scala*, E. *scale*[3].] A formation of troops in which groups are disposed in parallel lines, each to the right or left of the one in front, so that the whole presents the appearance of steps; one of the groups of a command so disposed; also, a similar disposition of the ships of a fleet.—**ech′e-lon,** *v. t.* or *i.*; *-loned, -loning.* To form in echelon.—**ech′e-lon=lens,** *n.* A compound lens consisting of a series of concentric annular lenses arranged round a central lens.

e-chid-na (ẹ-kid′ną), *n.*; pl. *-nas* or *-næ* (-nē). [NL., < Gr. ἔχιδνα, adder, viper.] Any animal of the genus *Echidna* (*Tachyglossus*) or family *Echidnidæ* (*Tachyglossidæ*), of Australia, etc., including spiny monotremes with a long, slender snout, somewhat resembling a large hedgehog; a porcupine ant-eater.

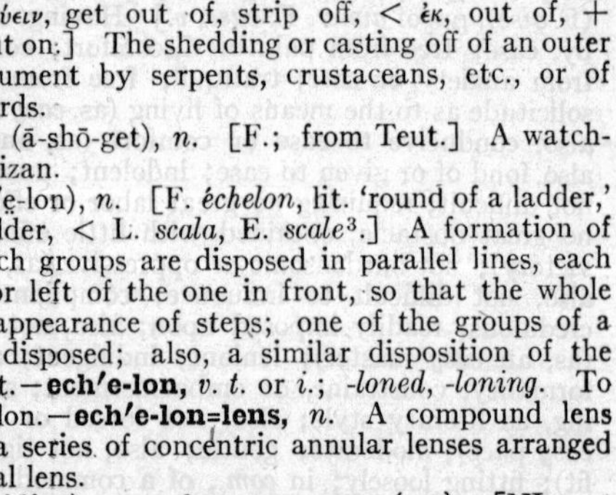

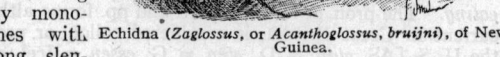

Echidna (*Zaglossus*, or *Acanthoglossus*, *bruijni*), of New Guinea.

ech-i-nate (ek′i-nāt), *a.* [L. *echinatus*, < *echinus*: see *echinus*.] Set with spines; spiny; bristly. Also **ech′i-nat-ed** (-nā-ted).

e-chi-nid (ẹ̄-kī′nid), *n.* [NL. *Echinidæ*, pl., < L. *Echinus*: see *echinus*.] Any member of the family *Echinidæ* or class *Echinoidea*; a sea-urchin. Also **e-chi′ni-dan** (-ni-dạn).

e-chi-nite (ẹ̄-kī′nīt or ek′i-), *n.* A fossil echinus or sea-urchin.

e-chi-no-derm (ẹ̄-kī′nọ̄-dėrm), *n.* [NL. *Echinodermata*, pl., < Gr. ἐχῖνος, hedgehog, sea-urchin, + δέρμα, skin.] Any of the *Echinodermata*, a phylum or subkingdom of marine animals (as the starfishes, sea-urchins, sea-cucumbers, etc.) having a radial arrangement of parts and a calcareous exoskeleton which is sometimes represented merely by scattered spicules, etc.—**e-chi-no-der′mal** (-dėr′mạl), **e-chi-no-der′ma-tous** (-mạ-tus), *a.*

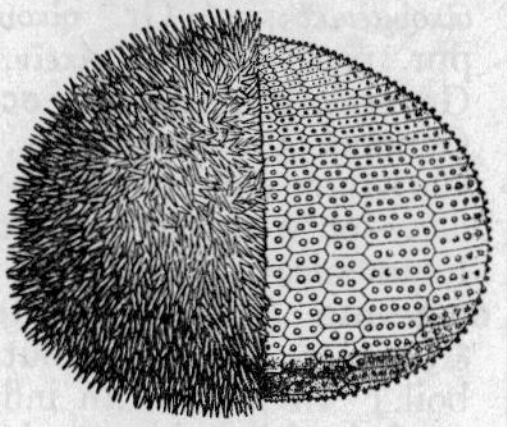

Echinus (*E. esculentus*).
Left side in natural state; right side with the spines removed, showing the bare plates.

e-chi-noid (ẹ̄-kī′noid). **I.** *a.* Resembling an echinus or sea-urchin; belonging to the *Echinoidea*, a class of echinoderms containing the sea-urchins. **II.** *n.* One of the *Echinoidea*; a sea-urchin.

e-chi-nus (ẹ̄-kī′nus), *n.*; pl. *-ni* (-nī). [L., < Gr. ἐχῖνος, hedgehog, sea-urchin, vessel, molding.] A sea-urchin of the typical genus *Echinus*, as *E. esculentus*, an edible species of the Mediterranean; in *arch.*, a rounded molding, as that supporting the abacus of a Doric capital.

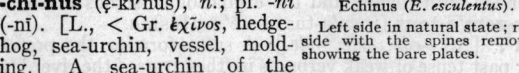

A Capital of the Parthenon. — *E*, echinus.

ech-o (ek′ō), *n.*; pl. *echoes* (-ōz). [L. *echo*, < Gr. ἠχώ, sound, echo.] A repetition of sound, produced by the reflection of sound-waves from an obstructing surface; the sound so produced; fig., any repetition or close imitation, as of the ideas or opinions of another; hence, one who imitates another; one who assents obsequiously to another's opinions; also, a sympathetic response, as to sentiments expressed; also, anything suggestive of an echo, as a response to a partner's signal in card-playing; [*cap.*] the personification of echo; in *class. myth.*, a mountain-nymph who pined away for love of the beautiful youth Narcissus until only her voice remained; [*l. c.*] in *music*, a very soft repetition of a phrase; also, a part ('echo-organ') of a large organ for the production of echo-like effects; a single stop so used ('echo-stop').—**ech′o,** *v.*; *echoed, echoing.* **I.** *intr.* To be repeated by or as by an echo; also, to emit an echo; resound with an echo. **II.** *tr.* To repeat by or as by an echo; also, to repeat or imitate the words, sentiments, etc., of (a person).—**ech′o-er,** *n.*—**e-cho-ic** (e-kō′ik), *a.* Echo-like; imitative of some sound, as the words *buzz, caw, moo*; onomatopoetic.—**ech′o-ing-ly,** *adv.*—**ech′o-ism,** *n.* The formation or use of echoic words; onomatopœia.—**ech′o-less,** *a.* Without an echo.

é-clair (ā-klãr′), *n.* [F., lit. 'lightning,' < *éclairer*, lighten.] A light, finger-shaped cake having a cream or custard filling and coated with an icing variously flavored, as with chocolate, vanilla, or coffee.

é-clair-cisse-ment (ā-klãr-sēs-moṅ), *n.* [F., < *éclaircir*, clear up.] A clearing up of something obscure; an explanation.

ec-lamp-si-a (ek-lamp′si-ạ̈), *n.* [NL., < Gr. ἐκλάμπειν, shine forth, < ἐκ, out of, + λάμπειν, shine.] In *pathol.*, a form of convulsions, esp. of a recurrent nature, as during pregnancy or parturition.—**ec-lamp′tic,** *a.*

é-clat (ā-klä), *n.* [F., fragment, also burst (of light, etc.): see *slat*[2].] Brilliance; splendor; esp., brilliance of success, reputation, etc.; glory or renown (as, "However the subalterns may furnish wisdom and skill, the principals exclusively possess the *éclat*": Godwin's "Caleb Williams," xxxv.).

ec-lec-tic (ek-lek′tik). [Gr. ἐκλεκτικός, < ἐκλέγειν, pick out, < ἐκ, out of, + λέγειν, pick, gather.] **I.** *a.* Selecting; choosing from various sources; not following any one system, as of philosophy, medicine, etc., but selecting and appropriating whatever is considered best in all systems; also, made up of what is selected from diverse sources; also, broad in acceptance of ideas, etc., from other sources. **II.** *n.* One who follows an eclectic method, as in philosophy, medicine, etc.—**ec-lec′ti-cal-ly,** *adv.*—**ec-lec′ti-cism** (-sizm), *n.* The use or advocacy of an eclectic method; an eclectic system, as of philosophy or medicine.

e-clipse (ẹ̄-klips′), *n.* [OF. *eclipse* (F. *éclipse*), < L. *eclipsis*, < Gr. ἔκλειψις, < ἐκλείπειν, leave out, leave off, be eclipsed, < ἐκ, out of, + λείπειν, leave.] The interception or obscuration of the light of the sun, moon, or other heavenly body, by the intervention of another heavenly body either between it and the eye or between it and the source of its illumination; hence, any obscuration of light; fig., any obscuration or overshadowing (as, "gaiety without *eclipse*": Tennyson's "Lilian"); loss of brilliance or splendor.—**e-clipse′,** *v. t.*; *eclipsed, eclipsing.* To cause to suffer eclipse (as, the moon *eclipses* the sun); fig., to cast a shadow upon; obscure; deprive of luster; also, to render dim by comparison; surpass; excel.

e-clip-tic (ẹ̄-klip′tik). [L. *eclipticus*, < Gr. ἐκλειπτικός, < ἐκλείπειν: see *eclipse*.] **I.** *a.* Pertaining to an eclipse; also, pertaining to the ecliptic. **II.** *n.* The great circle formed by the intersection of the plane of the earth's orbit with the celestial sphere; the apparent annual path of the sun in the heavens; also, an analogous great circle on a terrestrial globe.

ec-logue (ek′log), *n.* [L. *ecloga*, < Gr. ἐκλογή, a selection, < ἐκλέγειν, pick out: see *eclectic*.] A short poem, esp. of pastoral or idyllic character; an idyl: as, the "Eclogues," L. *Eclogæ*, of Virgil (also called "Bucolics"); "The Tea-Table: A Town *Eclogue*," by John Gay.

e-cod (ẹ̄-kod′), *interj.* Same as *egad.* [Archaic.]

e-col-o-gy (ẹ̄-kol′ọ̄-ji), *n.* [Gr. οἶκος, house: see *-logy*.] The branch of biology which treats of the relations between organisms and their environment; bionomics.—**e-co-log-i-cal** (ē-kọ̄-loj′i-kạl or ek-ọ̄-), *a.*—**e-col′o-gist,** *n.*

e-co-nom-ic (ē-kọ̄-nom′ik or ek-ọ̄-), *a.* [L. *œconomicus*, < Gr. οἰκονομικός, < οἰκονομία: see *economy*.] Pertaining to the management of a household or of private affairs, esp. with reference to pecuniary means; also, pertaining to the management of the affairs of a community, etc., with reference to income, expenditures, the development of resources, etc.; hence, of or pertaining to the material welfare, as of a community or nation; of or pertaining to the science of economics; also, pertaining to the means of living, or to the arts by which human needs and comforts are supplied (as, *economic* botany); utilitarian; also, thrifty or frugal (more commonly *economical*); also, pertaining to an economy, or system of organization or operation, esp. a method of divine administration of the world.—**e-co-nom′i-cal,** *a.* Economic; esp., characterized by economy or thrifty management; avoiding waste or extravagance; frugal; saving.—**e-co-nom′i-cal-ly,** *adv.*—**e-co-nom′ics,** *n.* The science of household or domestic management†; also, the science treating of the production, distribution, and consumption of wealth, or the material welfare of mankind; political economy; hence, economic questions or affairs.

e-con-o-mist (ẹ̄-kon′ọ̄-mist), *n.* One versed in economy or management; one who is sparing and effective in the use of means, as money, labor, or time; one who practises economy or frugality; also, one versed in the science of economics.

e-con-o-mize (ẹ̄-kon′ọ̄-mīz), *v.*; *-mized, -mizing.* **I.** *tr.* To manage economically; use sparingly; husband; use to the best advantage. **II.** *intr.* To practise economy in expenditure; avoid waste or extravagance.—**e-con″o-mi-zā′tion** (-mi-zā′shọn), *n.*—**e-con′o-miz-er** (-mī-zėr), *n.*

e-con-o-my (ẹ-kon′ọ-mi), *n.*; pl. *-mies* (-miz). [L. *œconomia*, < Gr. οἰκονομία, < οἶκος, house, + νέμειν, deal out, manage.] The management, or the science of management, of household affairs, esp. with reference to expenses; also, the management, or the science of management, of the means and resources of a community, etc., with a view to productiveness and avoidance of waste (as, political *economy*, economics); also, thrifty management; frugality in the expenditure or consumption of money, materials, etc.; an act or means of thrifty saving; a saving; also, the disposition or regulation of the parts or functions of any complex whole; arrangement; the system of organization or operation; the system in accordance with which the functions of living animals and plants are performed; the organized body of a living animal or plant; in *theol.*, the method of divine administration of the world, as at a particular time or for a particular race; a dispensation; also, a judicious or cautious presentation of doctrine.

é-cra-seur (ā-krä-zėr), *n.* [F., < *écraser*, crush.] A surgical instrument for removing tumors, etc., by the gradual tightening of a chain or wire loop.

é-croule-ment (ā-kröl-moṅ), *n.* [F., < *écrouler*, fall down.] A falling down or to pieces; a landslide.

é-cru (ā′krö or ek′rö, F. ā-krü). [F., raw, unbleached.] **I.** *a.* Of the pale yellowish or brownish color of raw silk, unbleached linen, etc. **II.** *n.* Écru color.

ec-sta-sy (ek′stạ-si), *n.*; pl. *-sies* (-siz). [OF. *extasie* (F. *extase*), < LL. *ecstasis*, < Gr. ἔκστασις, < ἐξιστάναι, put out of place or out of the normal mental state, < ἐξ, out of, + ἱστάναι, set up, stand.] The state of being beside one's self, as from some overpowering emotion; also, mental transport or rapture from the contemplation of divine things; also, the frenzy of poetic inspiration (as, "And leant upon a harp, in mood Of minstrel *ecstasy*": Scott's "Bridal of Triermain," iii. 35); also, rapturous delight (as, "He on the tender grass Would sit, and hearken ev'n to *ecstasy*": Milton's "Comus," 625); a transport of any emotion (as, an *ecstasy* of fear).—**ec-stat′ic** (-stat′ik). [Gr. ἐκστατικός.] **I.** *a.* Of, pertaining to, or characterized by ecstasy; subject to or in a state of ecstasy; transported; rapturous. **II.** *n.* One subject to fits of ecstasy; *pl.*, ecstatic transports; raptures. —**ec-stat′i-cal-ly**, *adv.*

ecto-, ect-. Forms of Gr. ἐκτός, outside, used in combination. Cf. *exo-*.—**ec-to-blast** (ek′tọ-blast), *n.* [+ *-blast.*] The outermost membrane of a cell; in *embryol.*, the ectoderm. —**ec-to-blas′tic** (-blas′tik), *a.*—**ec′to-derm** (-dėrm), *n.* [+ *-derm.*] In *embryol.*, the outer primary layer of cells in the embryo of any metazoan animal: opposed to *endoderm*.—**ec-to-der′mal** (-dėr′mạl), **ec-to-der′mic**, *a.*—**ec-to-gen′ic** (-jen′ik), *a.* Ectogenous.—**ec-tog′e-nous** (-toj′e-nus), *a.* [+ *-genous.*] Capable of developing outside of the host, as certain pathogenic bacteria.—**ec-to-par′a-site** (-par′ạ-sīt), *n.* An external parasite: opposed to *endoparasite*.—**ec′to-plasm** (-plazm), *n.* [+ *-plasm.*] In *biol.*, the outer portion of the cytoplasm in the cell of a protozoan; also, the clear outer layer of cytoplasm in a vegetable cell: opposed to *endoplasm*. Also, in *spiritualism*, a supposed emanation (described as at first vaporous, becoming pasty or putty-like) from the body of a medium while in a trance, which may take the form of a human body, face, or the like, so as to admit of being seen and photographed; that of which a materialized spirit or the like is held to be composed, or to which spiritualistic phenomena are attributed.—**ec-to-plas′mic** (-plaz′mik), *a.*—**ec′to-sarc** (-särk), *n.* [+ *-sarc.*] In *biol.*, the ectoplasm of a protozoan: opposed to *endosarc*.—**ec-tos-to′sis** (-tos-tō′sis), *n.* [NL. (with *-ostosis* as in *exostosis*).] In *anat.*, the ossification of cartilage proceeding from without inward.—**ec-to-zo′ön** (-zō′on), *n.*; pl. *-zoa* (-zō′ä). [NL.: see *-zoön.*] An external parasite, as a louse or a flea; an epizoön: opposed to *entozoön*.—**ec-to-zo′ic**, *a.*

ec-tro-pi-on, ec-tro-pi-um (ek-trō′pi-on, -um), *n.* [NL., < Gr. ἐκτρόπιον, < ἐκ, out of, + τρέπειν, turn.] In *pathol.*, an abnormal turning outward of the eyelid. Cf. *entropion*.

ec-type (ek′tīp), *n.* [Gr. ἔκτυπος, wrought in relief, formed in outline, < ἐκ, out of, + τύπτειν, strike.] A reproduction or copy: opposed to *prototype*.—**ec′ty-pal** (-ti-pạl), *a.*

é-cu (ā-kü), *n.*; pl. *écus* (F. ā-kü). [F., shield, coin bearing the figure of a shield, < L. *scutum*, shield.] Any of several gold and silver coins current in France from the 13th century onward, esp. the current silver five-franc piece.

Obverse. Reverse.
Gold Écu of Charles VI., King of France. — British Museum.

ec-u-men-ic, œc-u-men-ic (ek-ū-men′ik or ē-kū-), *a.* [LL. *œcumenicus*, < LGr. οἰκουμενικός, < Gr. οἰκουμένη, the inhabited world, prop. ppr. pass. fem. of οἰκεῖν, inhabit, < οἶκος, house, abode.] General; ecumenical.—**ec-u-men′i-cal, œc-u-men′i-cal**, *a.* General; universal; esp., *eccles.*, pertaining to the whole Christian church.—**ec-u-men′i-cal-ly, œc-u-men′i-cal-ly**, *adv.*—**ec″u-me-ni′ci-ty, œc″u-me-ni′ci-ty** (-me-nis′i-ti), *n.* Ecumenical character.

ec-ze-ma (ek′zẹ-mä, often ek-zē′mä), *n.* [NL., < Gr. ἔκζεμα, < ἐκζεῖν, boil out, break out, < ἐκ, out of, + ζεῖν, boil.] In *pathol.*, an inflammatory disease of the skin attended with itching and the exudation of serous matter.—**ec-zem′a-tous** (-zem′ạ-tus or -zē′mạ-tus), *a.*

-ed[1]. [AS. *-ede, -ode, -ade.*] A suffix forming the preterit or past tense of weak verbs, as in 'they *crossed* the river,' 'we *hurried* home,' 'he *smiled*.'

-ed[2]. [AS. *-ed, -od, -ad.*] A suffix forming the past participle of weak verbs, as in 'I had *glanced* over the book,' 'the work is *completed*,' 'he was *loved* by all,' most of such participles being usable also as adjectives ('participial adjectives'), as in 'a *completed* work,' 'a *loved* one': also serving to form adjectives from nouns, as in *bearded, moneyed, pale-faced, tender-hearted.* Cf. *-ate*[1].

e-da-cious (ẹ-dā′shus), *a.* [L. *edax* (*edac-*), < *edere*, eat: see *eat.*] Devouring; voracious; consuming.—**e-da-ci-ty** (ẹ-das′i-ti), *n.*

E-dam (ē′dam) **cheese.** [From *Edam*, town in Holland.] A hard, fine-flavored yellow cheese, made in spherical form and usually colored red on the outside.

Ed-da (ed′ä), *n.*; pl. *Eddas.* [Icel.; origin uncertain.] An old Icelandic work compiled and partly written by Snorri Sturluson (1179–1241), containing ancient myths and legends of Scandinavia, rules and theories of verse-making, poems and extracts from poems, etc. ('Younger Edda' or 'Prose Edda'); also, a collection of old Icelandic poems on mythical and religious subjects ('Elder Edda' or 'Poetic Edda'), erroneously ascribed to Sæmund Sigfusson (about 1055–1133).—**Ed-da-ic** (e-dā′ik), **Ed′dic**, *a.*

ed-dish (ed′ish), *n.* [Origin uncertain.] Grass or the like that grows after mowing; aftermath; also, stubble. [Prov. Eng.]

ed-does (ed′ōz), *n. pl.* [W. Afr.] The edible roots of the taro, or of any of several related plants.

ed-dy (ed′i), *n.*; pl. *eddies* (-iz). [Appar. from Scand.: cf. Icel. *idha*, eddy, whirlpool.] A current at variance with the main current in water, esp. one having a circular or whirling motion; hence, any similar current, as of air, dust, fog, etc.—**eddy current**, in *elect.*, a useless induced current circulating within a mass of metal (as an unlaminated core in an armature), and causing a loss by heat.—**ed′dy**, *v. i.* or *t.*; *eddied, eddying.* To move or whirl in eddies.

Ed-dy-ism (ed′i-izm), *n.* [From Mrs. Mary Baker Glover *Eddy*, founder of Christian Science.] Christian Science (see under *Christian, a.*).—**Ed′dy-ite** (-īt), *n.* A Christian Scientist.

Edelweiss.

e-del-weiss (ā′dẹl-vīs), *n.* [G., < *edel*, noble, + *weiss*, white.] A small composite herb, *Leontopodium leontopodium*, with white woolly leaves and flowers, growing in the high altitudes of the Alps. See cut on preceding page.

e-de-ma, œ-de-ma (ẹ-dē′mạ), *n.*; pl. *-mata* (-mạ-tạ). [NL., < Gr. οἴδημα, < οἰδεῖν, swell, < οἶδος, a swelling.] In *pathol.*, a swelling due to effusion of serous fluid into the interstices of the connective tissue.—**e-dem-a-tous, œ-dem-a-tous** (ẹ-dem′ạ-tus or ẹ-dē′mạ-), *a.*

E-den (ē′dn), *n.* [Heb., lit. 'pleasure' or 'delight.'] The garden which was the first home of Adam and Eve; hence, any delightful region or abode; a state of perfect happiness.—**E-den-ic** (ẹ-den′ik), *a.*

e-den-tate (ẹ-den′tāt). [L. *edentatus*, pp. of *edentare*, deprive of teeth, < *e*, out of, + *dens* (*dent-*), tooth.] **I.** *a.* Toothless; specif., belonging or pertaining to the *Edentata*, an order of mammals, including the sloths, armadillos, etc., in which the incisors and canines, or all the teeth, are lacking. **II.** *n.* An edentate mammal.

Edentate Skull of Ant-bear, or Great Ant-eater (*Myrmecophaga jubata*).

—**e-den-ta-tion** (ē-den-tā′shọn), *n.* Edentate or toothless condition.

e-den-tu-lous (ẹ-den′tū-lus), *a.* [L. *edentulus*, < *e*, out of, + *dens* (*dent-*), tooth.] Toothless.

edge (ej), *n.* [AS. *ecg* = D. *egge* = G. *ecke* = Icel. *egg*, edge; akin to L. *acies*, edge, point, Gr. ἀκίς, point, Skt. *açri*, edge, corner.] The thin, sharp side of the blade of a cutting instrument or weapon, as opposed to the back or the broad surfaces of the blade; hence, a cutting instrument or weapon (poetic); also, the sharpness proper to a blade; fig., cutting or wounding quality (as, "Slander, Whose *edge* is sharper than the sword": Shakspere's "Cymbeline," iii. 4. 36); sharpness or keenness of language, argument, appetite, desire, etc. (as, "Who can . . . cloy the hungry *edge* of appetite By bare imagination of a feast?" Shakspere's "Richard II.," i. 3. 296); fitness for action or operation; also, something resembling a cutting edge, as the crest of a ridge; the line in which two surfaces of a solid object meet; one of the narrow surfaces of a thin, flat object (as, a book with gilt *edges*); also, a border or margin (as, "From *edge* to *edge* O' the world" : Shakspere's "Antony and Cleopatra," ii. 2. 117); the brink or verge, as of a precipice; also, intoxication from drinking (slang).—**on edge,** eager or impatient; also, in a state of acute and uncomfortable sensibility (as, nerves *on edge*; to set the teeth *on edge*).—**to have the edge,** to have the advantage: usually with *on*: as, to *have the edge* on a competitor or opponent. [Slang.]—**edge,** *v.*; *edged, edging.* **I.** *tr.* To put an edge on; sharpen; also, to provide with an edge or border; border; also, to move edgeways; move or force gradually or by imperceptible degrees; also, to egg (*on*). **II.** *intr.* To move edgeways; advance gradually or by imperceptible degrees.—**edged,** *a.* Having an edge; sharp.—**edge′-tool′,** *n.* A tool with a cutting edge.—**edge′ways, edge′wise,** *adv.* With the edge directed forward; in the direction of the edge.—**edg′ing,** *n.* The act of one that edges; also, something that serves for an edge or border; trimming for edges.—**edg′y,** *a.* Sharp-edged; sharply defined, as outlines.

edh, eth (eᴛʜ), *n.* The Anglo-Saxon letter ð, capital form Đ, equivalent to the English *th* (cf. *thorn*); in modern phonetic systems, a symbol representing the sound of *th* in *then*.

ed-i-ble (ed′i-bl). [LL. *edibilis*, < L. *edere*, eat: see *eat*.] **I.** *a.* Fit to be eaten as food; eatable; esculent. **II.** *n.* Anything edible; an eatable: usually in *pl.*—**ed-i-bil′i-ty** (-bil′i-ti), **ed′i-ble-ness,** *n.*

e-dict (ē′dikt), *n.* [L. *edictum*, prop. pp. neut. of *edicere*, declare, proclaim, < *e*, out of, + *dicere*, say.] A decree issued by a sovereign or other authority; an authoritative proclamation or command.—**Edict of Nantes** (nants, F. nänt), an edict signed at Nantes in 1598 by Henry IV. of France, granting religious toleration to the Protestants (Huguenots): revoked in 1685 by Louis XIV., amid persecutions that caused the emigration, to other countries of Europe and to America, of many thousands of French Protestants, including skilled artisans, men of science and letters, and others, whose departure constituted a heavy loss to France.—**e-dic-tal** (ẹ-dik′tạl), *a.* Pertaining to or of the nature of an edict; proclaimed by edict.—**e-dic′tal-ly,** *adv.*

ed-i-fi-ca-tion (ed″i-fi-kā′shọn), *n.* The act of edifying, or the state of being edified; esp., moral improvement or benefit (as, "Never . . . was a sermon listened to with more impatience, and less *edification*": Scott's "Legend of Montrose," xiv.).

ed-i-fice (ed′i-fis), *n.* [OF. *edifice* (F. *édifice*), < L. *ædificium*, < *ædificare*: see *edify*.] A building, esp. one of large size or imposing appearance; a structure: as, "a spacious *edifice* of brick" (Hawthorne's "Scarlet Letter," The Custom House).—**ed-i-fi′cial** (-fish′ạl), *a.*

ed-i-fy (ed′i-fī), *v. t.*; *-fied, -fying.* [OF. *edifier* (F. *édifier*), < L. *ædificare*, build, < *ædes*, a building, + *facere*, make.] To build or construct (archaic); establish† or organize†; strengthen†; esp., to build up or increase the faith, morality, etc., of; instruct or benefit, esp. morally.—**ed′i-fi-er** (-fī-ėr), *n.*—**ed′i-fy-ing-ly,** *adv.*

e-dile (ē′dīl), etc. See *ædile*, etc.

ed-it (ed′it), *v. t.* [Partly < L. *editus*, pp. of *edere*, give forth, < *e*, out of, + *dare*, give; partly < E. *editor*.] To publish (a literary work, etc.)†; also, to prepare or revise (literary matter, etc.) for publication, as an editor does; also, to supervise or direct the publication of (a newspaper, magazine, etc.); act as editor of.—**e-di-tion** (ẹ-dish′ọn), *n.* [L. *editio*(*n*-).] The act of publishing†; also, the form in which a literary work is published (as, Milman's *edition* of Gibbon; a one-volume *edition* of Shakspere); also, the whole number of copies of a book, newspaper, etc., printed from one set of types and issued at one time; esp., one of a number of printings of the same book, etc., issued at different times, and differing from one another by alterations, additions, etc. (as distinguished from an *impression*, which see).—**ed′i-tor** (-i-tọr), *n.* [L.] A publisher, as of a literary work†; also, one who edits or prepares literary matter, or a particular edition of a literary work, for publication; also, the supervising director of a newspaper or other periodical, or of a special department of one.—**ed-i-to′ri-al** (-tō′ri-ạl). **I.** *a.* Of or pertaining to an editor; written by an editor, as a note or an article. **II.** *n.* An article, as in a newspaper, written by the editor or under his direction, and setting forth the position or opinion of the publication upon some subject.—**ed-i-to′ri-al-ize,** *v. i.*; *-ized, -izing.* To set forth one's position or opinion on some subject in, or as if in, an editorial.—**ed-i-to′ri-al-ly,** *adv.*—**ed′i-tor-ship,** *n.* The office or function of an editor; editorial direction.—**ed′i-tress,** *n.* A female editor.

ed-u-ca-ble (eḍ′ū-kạ-bl), *a.* That may be educated.

ed-u-cate (eḍ′ū-kāt), *v. t.*; *-cated, -cating.* [L. *educatus*, pp. of *educare*, bring up, train, educate, < *educere*, bring up: see *educe*.] To bring up† or rear†; also, to develop the faculties and powers of by teaching, instruction, or schooling; qualify by instruction or training for a particular calling, practice, etc.; train.—**ed-u-ca′tion** (-kā′shọn), *n.* [L. *educatio*(*n*-).] The act or process of educating; the imparting or acquisition of knowledge, skill, etc., as through instruction, training, or study; systematic instruction or training, as in an institution of learning; also, the result produced by instruction, training, or study; cultivation or development of the faculties and powers; also, the science or art of teaching; pedagogics.—**ed-u-ca′tion-al,** *a.* Pertaining to education.—**ed-u-ca′tion-al-ist, ed-u-ca′tion-ist,** *n.* One versed in theories and methods of education.—**ed-u-ca′tion-al-ly,** *adv.*—**ed′u-ca-tive** (-kạ-tiv), *a.* Serving to educate; pertaining to education.—**ed′u-ca-tor** (-kā-tọr), *n.* [L.] One who or that which educates; a teacher.—**ed′u-ca-to-ry** (-kạ-tō-ri), *a.* Educative.

e-duce (ẹ-dūs′), *v. t.*; *educed, educing.* [L. *educere* (pp. *eductus*), lead forth, bring out, bring up, < *e*, out of, + *ducere*, lead.] To draw forth or bring out; elicit; develop.—**e-duce′ment,** *n.* The act of educing, or the state of being educed.—**e-du-ci-ble** (ẹ-dū′si-bl), *a.* That may be educed.—**e-duct** (ē′dukt), *n.* [L. *eductus*, pp.] Something educed; in *chem.*, a substance extracted unchanged from another substance (as distinguished from a *product*).—**e-duc-tion** (ẹ-duk′shọn), *n.* [L.*eductio*(*n*-).] The act of educing; also, something educed; an educt; in *engin.*, exhaust, as of steam after having completed its work.—**e-duc′tor,** *n.*

e-dul-co-rate (ę-dul′kǭ-rāt), *v. t.*; *-rated, -rating.* [= F. *édulcorer*, < L. *e*, out of, + LL. *dulcorare*, sweeten, < *dulcor*, sweetness: see *douceur.*] To sweeten†; also, to purify; in *chem.*, to free from acids, salts, or impurities by washing.—**e-dul-co-ra′tion** (-rā′shǫn), *n.*

ee (ē), *n.* Scotch form of *eye.*

-ee. [F. *-é*, pp. ending, < L. *-atus*, E. *-ate*¹.] A suffix of nouns denoting one who is the object of some action, or undergoes or receives something (often as opposed to the person acting), as in *assignee, donee, employee* (as opposed to *assignor, donor, employer*). Cf. *-or*² and *-er*¹.

eel (ēl), *n.* [AS. *ǣl* = D. and G. *aal* = Icel. *āll*, eel.] Any of the voracious, elongated, apodal fishes of snake-like appearance constituting the genus *Anguilla* and related genera; any of various other fishes of similar appearance, as the lamprey; also, an eel-worm.—**electric eel.** See under *electric, a.*—**eel′=grass,** *n.* A marine plant, *Zostera marina*, with long, narrow, grass-like leaves, growing wholly under water.—**eel′=moth″er** (-muᴛʜ″ėr), *n.* A viviparous fish, *Zoarces viviparus*, a European eel-pout.—**eel′=pot,** *n.* A basket-like trap for catching eels.—**eel′=pout,** *n.* [AS. *ǣlepūta.*] Any of the blenny-like marine fishes constituting the family *Zoarcidæ* (or *Lycodidæ*), as *Zoarces anguillaris* of the northern Atlantic coast of America or *Z. viviparus* of Europe; also, the burbot.—**eel′=worm,** *n.* Any of various small nematode worms of the family *Anguillulidæ*, including the minute vinegar-eel, *Anguillula aceti.*—**eel′y,** *a.* Eel-like; wriggling.

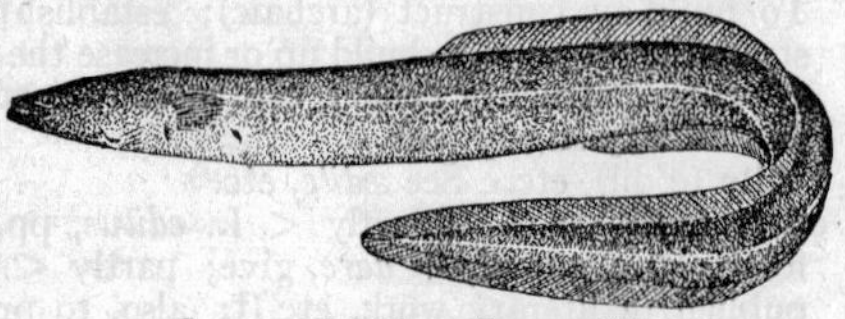

Common Eel (*Anguilla anguilla*).

Eel-grass.

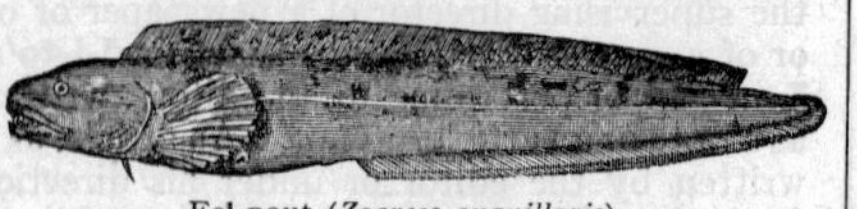

Eel-pout (*Zoarces anguillaris*).

-een. [Ir. *-ín.*] A diminutive suffix of nouns, common in words of Irish origin, as *buckeen, colleen, dudeen, poteen, squireen.*

e′en¹, **e′en**² (ēn). Contractions of *even*¹, *even*².

e′er (ãr), *adv.* Contraction of *ever.*

-eer. [F. *-ier*, < L. *-arius*: see *-ary* and *-er*².] A suffix of nouns denoting one who is concerned with, or employed in connection with, or busies himself with something, as in *auctioneer, cannoneer, engineer, pamphleteer, profiteer.*

ee-rie, ee-ry (ē′ri), *a.*; compar. *eerier*, superl. *eeriest.* [ME. *eri*: cf. AS. *earg, earh*, timid, cowardly.] Fearful; timid; affected with superstitious fear; also, inspiring fear, weird, or strange (as, "At nightfall on the marshes, the thing was *eerie* and fantastic to behold": Stevenson's "Travels with a Donkey," ii. 1).—**ee′ri-ly,** *adv.*—**ee′ri-ness,** *n.*

ef-fa-ble (ef′ą-bl), *a.* [L. *effabilis*, < *effari*, utter, < *ex*, out of, + *fari*, speak.] Utterable; expressible.

ef-face (e-fās′), *v. t.*; *-faced, -facing.* [F. *effacer*, OF. *esfacier*, < *es-* (< L. *ex*, out of) + *face*, E. *face.*] To rub out, erase, or obliterate (writing, etc.); hence, to wipe out; destroy; do away with; also, to render inconspicuous; cause to be unnoticed or not noticeable.—**ef-face′a-ble,** *a.* Capable of being effaced.—**ef-face′ment,** *n.*

ef-fect (e-fekt′), *n.* [OF. *effect* (F. *effet*), < L. *effectus*, < *efficere* (pp. *effectus*), bring about, accomplish, effect, < *ex*, out of, + *facere*, do, make.] That which is produced by some agency or cause; a result; a consequence; also, power to produce results (as, "Christ is become of no *effect* unto you": Gal. v. 4); force; validity; also, the result intended; purport or intent; tenor or significance; also, the state of being operative; operation or execution; accomplishment or fulfilment; also, the result upon the mind of what is apprehended by the faculties; a mental impression produced, as by a painting, speech, etc.; also, a combination, as of form, color, light and shade, etc., producing a particular mental impression; also, *pl.*, goods; movables; personal estate; property.—**for effect,** for the mere impression on the mind of others: as, to talk *for effect.*—**in effect,** in result or consequences (as, the two methods are the same *in effect*); in fact or reality (as, it is no other *in effect* than what it seems); also, in operation, as a law.—**ef-fect′,** *v. t.* To bring about; accomplish; fulfil; produce or make.—**ef-fect′er,** *n.*—**ef-fect′i-ble,** *a.* Capable of being effected.

ef-fec-tive (e-fek′tiv). [L. *effectivus*, < *efficere*: see *effect.*] **I.** *a.* Serving to effect the purpose; producing the intended or expected result; hence, capable of producing effect; adapted for a desired end; often, fit for action or duty, as soldiers or sailors; also, producing a striking impression, as a performance, picture, etc.; striking; picturesque; also, existing in fact; actual. **II.** *n.* One, esp. a soldier, fit for duty or active service; also, the effective total of a military force.—**ef-fec′tive-ly,** *adv.*—**ef-fec′tive-ness,** *n.*

ef-fect-less (e-fekt′les), *a.* Without effect; ineffectual.

ef-fec-tu-al (e-fek′ţū-ąl), *a.* [OF. *effectuel*, < ML. *effectualis*, < L. *effectus*, E. *effect.*] Producing, or capable of producing, an intended effect; adequately answering its purpose; valid or binding, as an agreement or document.—**ef-fec′tu-al-ly,** *adv.*—**ef-fec′tu-al-ness,** *n.*

ef-fec-tu-ate (e-fek′ţū-āt), *v. t.*; *-ated, -ating.* [F. *effectuer*, < L. *effectus*, E. *effect.*] To bring into effect; bring about; accomplish; effect.—**ef-fec-tu-a′tion** (-ā′shǫn), *n.*

ef-fem-i-nate (e-fem′i-nąt), *a.* [L. *effeminatus*, pp. of *effeminare*, make womanish, < *ex*, out of, + *femina*, woman.] Unbecomingly womanish in traits, tastes, habits, etc.; characterized by unmanly softness, delicacy, weakness, self-indulgence, etc. (as, "Shall we at last conclude *effeminate* peace?" Shakspere's "1 Henry VI.," v. 4. 107); also, in a good sense, womanly†.—**ef-fem′i-na-cy** (-ną-si), **ef-fem′i-nate-ness,** *n.*—**ef-fem′i-nate-ly,** *adv.*—**ef-fem′i-nize** (-nīz), *v. t.*; *-nized, -nizing.* To make effeminate.

ef-fen-di (e-fen′di), *n.*; pl. *-dis* (-diz). [Turk. *efendī*, < Gr. αὐθέντης, master, actual doer: see *authentic.*] A Turkish title of respect for government officials, etc.; a person bearing this title.

ef-fer-ent (ef′ę-rent), *a.* [L. *efferens* (*-ent-*), ppr. of *efferre*, bring out, raise, exalt, < *ex*, out of, + *ferre*, bear: cf. *elate.*] In *physiol.*, conveying outward from a central organ or point: opposed to *afferent.*

ef-fer-vesce (ef-ėr-ves′), *v. i.*; *-vesced, -vescing.* [L. *effervescere*, < *ex*, out of, + *fervescere*, begin to boil, < *fervere*, be boiling hot: see *fervent.*] To give off bubbles of gas, as fermenting liquors; bubble and hiss; also, to issue forth in bubbles; fig., to exhibit fervor, excitement, liveliness, etc.—**ef-fer-ves′cence** (-ves′ęns), *n.* Effervescent action or state: as, "Mr. Holbrook appeared at the door, rubbing his hands in very *effervescence* of hospitality" (Mrs. Gaskell's "Cranford," iv.).—**ef-fer-ves′cent,** *a.* Effervescing.—**ef-fer-ves′ci-ble,** *a.* Capable of effervescing.—**ef-fer-ves′cive,** *a.* Tending to effervesce.

ef-fete (e-fēt′), *a.* [L. *effetus*, < *ex*, out of, + *fetus*, breeding, having brought forth: see *fetus.*] Having lost the power of bringing forth offspring; past bearing or producing; hence, that has lost its vigor or energy; exhausted; worn out.—**ef-fete′ness,** *n.*

ef-fi-ca-cious (ef-i-kā′shus), *a.* [Obs. F. *efficacieux*, < *efficace*, < L. *efficacia*, E. *efficacy.*] Having or showing efficacy; effective as a means, measure, remedy, etc.—**ef-fi-ca′cious-ly,** *adv.*—**ef-fi-ca′cious-ness,** *n.*

ef-fi-ca-ci-ty (ef-i-kas′i-ti), *n.* [L. *efficacitas*, < *efficax*: see *efficacy.*] Efficacy.

ef-fi-ca-cy (ef′i-ką-si), *n.* [L. *efficacia*, < *efficax*, effective, efficacious, < *efficere*, accomplish: see *effect.*] Capacity for serving to produce effects; effective virtue, as of a means, measure, expedient, remedy, etc.; potency.

ef-fi-cien-cy (e-fish′ęn-si), *n.* The fact or quality of being efficient; effectual agency; competency in performance; ability to produce the best results in operation or work, as in a business establishment; in *mech.*, the ratio of the work done or energy developed by a machine, engine, etc., to the energy supplied to it.

ef-fi-cient (e-fish′ẹnt), *a.* [L. *efficiens* (*-ent-*), ppr. of *efficere*, accomplish: see *effect.*] Producing an effect, as a cause; causative; also, acting with effectiveness; adequate in operation or performance; bringing to bear the requisite knowledge, skill, and industry; competent; capable.—**ef-fi′-cient-ly,** *adv.*

ef-fig-i-es (e-fij′i-ēz), *n.* [L.: see *effigy.*] An effigy.

ef-fi-gy (ef′i-ji), *n.*; pl. *-gies* (-jiz). [L. *effigies*, < *effingere*, form, fashion, < *ex*, out of, + *fingere*, form, mold: see *feign.*] A representation or image of some object; esp., a sculptured likeness of a person, as on a sepulchral monument; also, a stuffed figure representing an obnoxious person.—**to burn,** or **hang, in effigy,** to burn, or hang, an image of (a person): formerly as a vicarious punishment when a condemned person had escaped, now only as an expression of public indignation or hatred.

Effigy.— Brass in West Lynn Church, Norfolk, England.

ef-fla-tion (e-flā′shọn), *n.* [Obs. F. *efflation*, < L. *efflare* (pp. *efflatus*), blow or breathe out, < *ex*, out of, + *flare*, blow.] A blowing or breathing forth; an emanation.

ef-flo-resce (ef-lọ-res′), *v. i.*; *-resced*, *-rescing.* [L. *efflorescere*, < *ex*, out of, + *florescere*, begin to flower: see *florescence.*] To burst into bloom; burst forth as into flower; in *chem.*, to change either throughout or on the surface to a mealy or powdery substance upon exposure to air, as a crystalline substance, through loss of water of crystallization; also, to become incrusted or covered with crystals of salt or the like through evaporation or chemical change; form such an incrustation.—**ef-flo-res′cence** (-res′ẹns), *n.* The act or process of efflorescing; the state or period of flowering; also, a mass of blossoms or flowers; also, something suggesting this (as, "a detestable human *efflorescence* upon what would otherwise have been good pasture": H. G. Wells's "Outline of History," xxxiv. § 5D); in *pathol.*, a rash or eruption; in *chem.*, an efflorescing, or the resulting powdery substance or incrustation.—**ef-flo-res′cent,** *a.* Efflorescing; subject to efflorescence; also, covered with or forming an efflorescence.

ef-flu-ence (ef′lö-ẹns), *n.* Efflux; outward flow; also, something that flows out; an emanation.

ef-flu-ent (ef′lö-ẹnt). [L. *effluens* (*-ent-*), ppr. of *effluere*, flow out, < *ex*, out of, + *fluere*, flow.] **I.** *a.* Flowing out or forth. **II.** *n.* That which flows out or forth; outflow; specif., a stream flowing out of another stream, a lake, etc.

ef-flu-vi-um (e-flö′vi-um), *n.*; pl. *-via* (-vi-ạ̈). [L., a flowing out, < *effluere*: see *effluent.*] A flowing out or forth†; also, an emanation; a subtle or invisible exhalation, esp. one that is disagreeable or noxious.—**ef-flu′vi-al,** *a.*

ef-flux (ef′luks), *n.* [L. *effluere* (pp. *effluxus*): see *effluent.*] Outward flow, as of water; hence, the lapse or passing of time; also, that which flows out; an effluence.—**ef-flux-ion** (e-fluk′shọn), *n.* A flowing out; efflux.

ef-fort (ef′ọrt), *n.* [OF. *effort*, *esfort* (F. *effort*), < *esforcier* (F. *efforcer*), < ML. *exfortiare*, force, compel, < L. *ex*, out of, + *fortis*, strong.] Exertion of power, physical or mental; a strenuous attempt; also, something done by exertion; a production or achievement, as in literature, oratory, or art.—**ef′fort-less,** *a.* Making no effort; passive; also, requiring or involving no effort; easy.

ef-fron-ter-y (e-frun′tėr-i), *n.* [F. *effronterie*, < *effronté*, shameless, < L. *effrons* (*effront-*), barefaced, shameless, < *ex*, out of, + *frons*, forehead, E. *front.*] Shameless or impudent boldness; barefaced audacity.

ef-fulge (e-fulj′), *v. i.* or *t.*; *-fulged*, *-fulging.* [L. *effulgere*, < *ex*, out of, + *fulgere*, flash, shine: see *fulgent.*] To shine or send forth brilliantly.—**ef-ful-gence** (e-ful′jẹns), *n.* Effulgent state; splendor.—**ef-ful′gent,** *a.* Shining forth brilliantly; radiant; splendid.—**ef-ful′gent-ly,** *adv.*

ef-fuse (e-fūz′), *v.*; *-fused*, *-fusing.* [L. *effusus*, pp. of *effundere*, < *ex*, out of, + *fundere*, pour.] **I.** *tr.* To pour out or forth; shed, as light; send forth, as an odor; disseminate. **II.** *intr.* To exude.—**ef-fuse** (e-fūs′), *a.* Profuse†; in *bot.*, spread out loosely; in *conch.*, having the lips separated by a gap or groove; in *entom.*, loosely joined.—**ef-fu-sion** (e-fū′zhọn), *n.* [L. *effusio*(*n-*).] The act of effusing or pouring forth; an outpour; that which is effused; fig., unrestrained expression of feelings, etc.; a speech or literary effort (as, "poets whose *effusions* entranced my soul," Mrs. Shelley's "Frankenstein," letter i.: now usually in disparagement); in *pathol.*, the escape of a fluid from its natural vessel; the fluid which escapes.—**ef-fu′sive** (-siv), *a.* Pouring out; flowing forth profusely; fig., demonstratively expressed, as emotions; also, making an extravagant or undue exhibition of feeling, as a person; unduly demonstrative; in *geol.*, noting or pertaining to rocks which have been poured out as lava on the surface of the earth.—**ef-fu′sive-ly,** *adv.*—**ef-fu′sive-ness,** *n.*

eft[1] (eft), *n.* [AS. *efete.*] Formerly, any small lizard or lizard-like animal; now, usually, a newt.

eft[2]† (eft), *adv.* [AS. *eft*: akin to E. *aft*, *after.*] Afterward; again.—**eft-soon, eft-soons** (eft-sön′, -sönz′), *adv.* Soon afterward; again; forthwith. [Archaic.]

e-gad (ẹ-gad′), *interj.* [Cf. the oath *by God.*] An expletive or mild oath: as, "*Egad*, that's true" (Sheridan's "School for Scandal," iv. 1).

e-gal† (ē′gạl), *a.* [OF. *egal* (F. *égal*), < L. *æqualis*: see *equal.*] Equal. See Shakspere's "Titus Andronicus," iv. 4. 4.—**e-gal-i-ty** (ẹ-gal′i-ti), *n.*; pl. *-ties* (-tiz). [F. *égalité.*] Equality: as, "That cursed France with her *egalities!*" (Tennyson's "Aylmer's Field," 265). [A French use.]

e-gest (ẹ-jest′), *v. t.* [L. *egestus*, pp. of *egerere*, < *e*, out of, + *gerere*, bear.] To discharge, as from the body; void; excrete: opposed to *ingest.*—**e-ges-ta** (ẹ-jes′tạ̈), *n. pl.* [L.] Matter egested from the body, as excrement.—**e-ges′tion** (-chọn), *n.* [L. *egestio*(*n-*).] The process of egesting; the voiding of the refuse of digestion.—**e-ges′tive,** *a.* Of or pertaining to egestion.

egg[1] (eg), *v. t.* [Icel. *eggja*, < *egg*, edge: see *edge.*] To incite or urge; encourage; provoke: usually with *on.*

egg[2] (eg), *n.* [Icel. *egg* = AS. *ǣg* = D. and G. *ei*: cf. L. *ovum*, Gr. ᾠόν, egg.] The roundish reproductive body inclosed in a shell or membrane, produced by the female of animals, and consisting of the ovum or female reproductive cell together with its appendages, from which the young hatches out; esp., the body of this sort produced by birds (in common usage, that of the domestic hen); in a broad biological sense, the ovum or female reproductive cell; in general, anything resembling a hen's egg; in games, zero or no score (colloq.).—**egg and dart, egg and tongue,** or **egg and anchor,** an egg-shaped ornament alternating with a dart-like, tongue-like, or anchor-like ornament, used to enrich a molding.—**egg**[2], *v.* **I.** *tr.* To prepare (food) with eggs; also, to pelt with eggs. **II.** *intr.* To gather or collect eggs.—**egg′=bird,** *n.* Any of various sea-birds whose eggs are used for food; esp., in the West Indies, the sooty tern, *Sterna fuliginosa.*—**egg′er,** *n.* One who gathers or collects eggs; also, any of various moths of the family *Lasiocampidæ.*—**egg′=nog′,** *n.* A drink made of eggs, milk, sugar, and, usually, wine or spirits.—**egg′=plant,** *n.* A plant, *Solanum melongena*, cultivated for its edible, more or less egg-shaped fruit, dark-purple (or sometimes white or

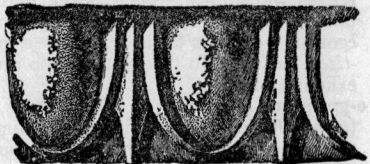

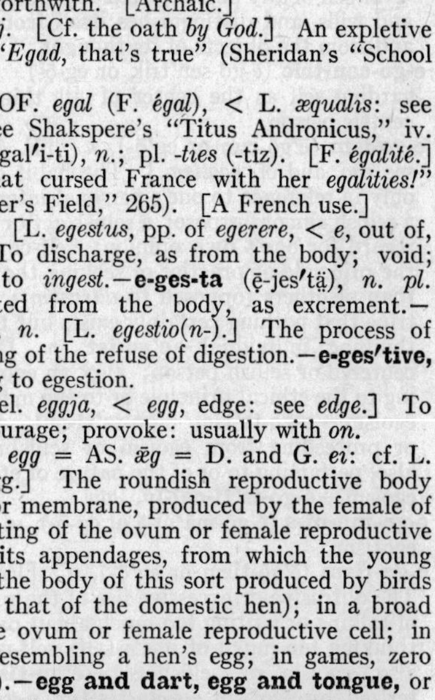
Egg-and-dart Molding.— Erechtheum, Athens.

Flowering Branch and Fruit of Egg-plant.

yellow) in color; also, the fruit, used as a table vegetable.—**egg′=shaped,** *a.* Having the general shape of an egg; of an elongated rounded (oval) form, esp. with one end broader than the other.—**egg′=shell,** *n.* The shell or calcareous covering of an egg; also, any of certain egg-like gastropods, as *Ovulum ovum.*—**egg=shell china** or **porcelain,** porcelain of extreme thinness and translucency.

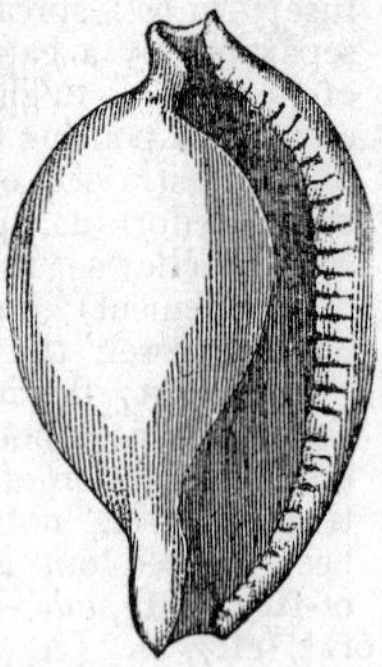
Egg-shell (*Ovulum ovum*).

e-gis (ē′jis), *n.* See *ægis.*

eg-lan-tine (eg′lạn-tīn or -tin), *n.* [F. *églantine,* < OF. *aiglent,* sweetbrier, prob. ult. < L. *acus,* needle.] The sweetbrier, *Rosa rubiginosa;* sometimes, the Austrian brier, *Rosa eglanteria;* formerly, the honeysuckle or some similar plant.

eg-la-tere (eg′lạ-tēr), *n.* [OF. *eglentier* (F. *églantier*).] Eglantine. See Tennyson's "Dirge," iv. [Obs. or poetic.]

e-go (ē′gō or eg′ō), *n.* [L. *ego* = Gr. ἐγώ, I: see *I*².] The 'I' or self of any person; that in a person which thinks, feels, and wills, and distinguishes itself from the selves of others and from the objects of its thought.

e-go-cen-tric (ē-gọ-sen′trik or eg-ọ-). **I.** *a.* Having or regarding self as the center of all things. **II.** *n.* An egocentric person.

e-go-ism (ē′gọ-izm or eg′ọ-), *n.* [F. *égoïsme,* < L. *ego,* I: see *ego,* and cf. *egotism.*] The habit of valuing everything only in reference to one's personal interest; pure selfishness; a selfish aim or purpose; a selfish act or practice; also, undue regard for one's own opinion; self-conceit; egotism; also, the principle or practice of seeking the welfare of self rather than of others (opposed to *altruism*); in *metaph.,* the doctrine that nothing certainly exists but the ego or mind of the thinking individual.—**e′go-ist,** *n.* [F. *égoïste.*] A self-centered or selfish person; also, an egotist; also, one adhering to the ethical principle or to the metaphysical doctrine of egoism.—**e-go-is′tic, e-go-is′ti-cal,** *a.* Characterized by or proceeding from egoism or selfishness; also, egotistic; also, pertaining to or of the nature of ethical or metaphysical egoism.—**e-go-is′ti-cal-ly,** *adv.*

e-go-ma-ni-a (ē-gọ-mā′ni-ạ̈ or eg-ọ-), *n.* [See *ego.*] Morbid egotism.

e-go-tism (ē′gọ-tizm or eg′ọ-), *n.* [From *ego:* cf. *egoism.*] The obtrusive or excessive use of the pronoun 'I'; the habit of talking or writing too much about one's self; the habit of thinking too much of one's self; self-conceit; boastfulness; also, egoism or selfishness.—**e′go-tist,** *n.* One characterized by egotism.—**e-go-tis′tic, e-go-tis′ti-cal,** *a.* Pertaining to or of the nature of egotism; characterized by egotism.—**e-go-tis′ti-cal-ly,** *adv.*—**e′go-tize** (-tīz), *v. i.;* *-tized, -tizing.* To talk or write too much about one's self; exhibit egotism.

e-gre-gious (ẹ-grē′jus), *a.* [L. *egregius,* < *e,* out of, + *grex* (*greg-*), flock.] Distinguished or eminent (now rare); remarkably good or great† (as, "*egregious* ransom": Shakspere's "Henry V.," iv. 4. 11); now, commonly, remarkable or extraordinary (in a bad sense); gross or flagrant (as, "In saying this, he told . . . an *egregious* falsehood": Parkman's "Oregon Trail," xii.).—**e-gre′gious-ly,** *adv.*—**e-gre′gious-ness,** *n.*

American Great White Egret.

e-gress (ē′gres), *n.* [L. *egressus,* < *egredi,* go out, < *e,* out of, + *gradi,* walk, go: see *gradient.*] The act of going or passing out, esp. from an inclosed place; also, the right of going out; also, a means or place of going out; an exit; in *astron.,* the passing of one heavenly body out from behind or before the disk of another, as at the end of an eclipse.

e-gres-sion (ẹ-gresh′ọn), *n.* [L. *egressio(n-),* < *egredi:* see *egress.*] A going out; egress.

e-gret (ē′gret), *n.* [OF. *aigrete:* see *aigrette.*] Any of various herons, as *Herodias egretta* ('great white egret' of America) or *Garzetta garzetta* ('small white egret' of Europe), bearing during the breeding season tufts of long plumes (the aigrettes of commerce) (see cut in preceding column); also, the plume of an egret; an aigrette; in *bot.,* the coma or pappus of certain seeds.

E-gyp-tian (ẹ-jip′shạn). **I.** *a.* Of or pertaining to Egypt or its people: as, *Egyptian* architecture (the architecture of ancient Egypt, which, among its monuments, exhibits its pyramids, gigantic monolithic obelisks, pillared temples, etc.); *Egyptian* bondage (bondage or servitude like that of the Israelites in Egypt: see Ex. i. 14); *Egyptian* darkness (deep or total darkness: in allusion to Ex. x. 21–23). Also, of or pertaining to the Gipsies (see Fielding's "Tom Jones," xii. 13). **II.** *n.* A native or inhabitant of Egypt; also, the language of the ancient Egyptians; also, a Gipsy.—**E-gyp′tian-ize,** *v. t.;* *-ized, -izing.* To make Egyptian, as in appearance or customs.

Egyptian Architecture.—Portico of the Temple of Edfu.

E-gyp-tol-o-gy (ē-jip-tol′ọ-ji), *n.* [See *-logy.*] The science of Egyptian antiquities.—**E-gyp-to-log-i-cal** (ẹ-jip-tọ-loj′i-kạl), *a.*—**E-gyp-tol′o-gist,** *n.*

eh (ā or e), *interj.* An interrogative utterance, sometimes expressing surprise or doubt: as, "Wasn't it lucky, *eh?*" (Goldsmith's "She Stoops to Conquer," ii. 1).

ei-dent (ī′dẹnt), *a.* [Icel. *idhinn.*] Diligent; assiduous; busy. [Sc.]

ei-der (ī′dėr), *n.* [Icel. *ædhr* (*ædhar-dūn,* eider-down).] Any of several large sea-ducks of the genus *Somateria* and allied genera, of the northern hemisphere, generally black and white, and yielding a choice kind of down; also, the down. Also called *eider-duck.*—**ei′der=down,** *n.* Down or soft feathers from the breast of the eider-duck.—**ei′der=yarn,** *n.* A soft yarn made from merino wool.

Elder (*Somateria mollissima*).

ei-do-graph (ī′dọ-gråf), *n.* [Gr. εἶδος, form: see *-graph.*] An instrument for the mechanical copying of drawings, diagrams, etc., upon the same or a reduced or enlarged scale.

ei-do-lon (ī-dō′lon), *n.;* pl. *-la* (-lạ̈). [= *idolon.*] An image; a phantom; an apparition.

eight (āt). [AS. *eahta* = D. and G. *acht* = Icel. *ātta* = Goth. *ahtau,* eight; akin to L. *octo,* Gr. ὀκτώ, Skt. *ashta,* eight.] **I.** *a.* One more than seven. **II.** *n.* A number composed of eight units, or a symbol, as 8 or viii, representing it; a set of eight persons or things, as the crew of a racing-boat; a playing-card with eight pips.

eigh-teen (ā′tēn′). [AS. *eahtatyne.*] **I.** *a.* Eight more than ten. **II.** *n.* A number composed of eighteen units, or a symbol, as 18 or xviii, representing it.—**eigh′teenth′. I.** *a.* Next after the seventeenth; also, being one of eighteen equal parts. **II.** *n.* The eighteenth member of a series; also, an eighteenth part.

eight-fold (āt′fōld). **I.** *a.* Comprising eight parts or members; eight times as great or as much. **II.** *adv.* In eightfold measure.

eighth (ātth). [AS. *eahtotha.*] **I.** *a.* Next after the seventh; also, being one of eight equal parts. **II.** *n.* The eighth member of a series; also, an eighth part; in *music*, an octave.—**eighth′ly,** *adv.*—**eighth′=note,** *n.* In *music*, a note having one eighth of the time-value of a whole-note; a quaver.

eigh-ti-eth (ā′ti-eth). **I.** *a.* Next after the seventy-ninth; also, being one of eighty equal parts. **II.** *n.* The eightieth member of a series; also, an eightieth part.

eigh-ty (ā′ti). [AS. (*hund*)*eahtatig.*] **I.** *a.* Eight times ten. **II.** *n.*; pl. *-ties* (-tiz). A number composed of eighty units, or a symbol, as 80 or lxxx, representing it.

ei-kon (ī′kon), *n.* See *icon.*

ei-kon-o-gen (ī-kon′ọ-jen), *n.* [Gr. εἰκών, image: see *-gen.*] An organic sodium salt used as a photographic developer.

Ein-stein-i-an (īn-stī′ni-ạn), *a.* Of or pertaining to Albert Einstein (born 1879), German-Swiss (Jewish) theoretical physicist, or his doctrines. See *relativity.*—**Ein-stein's** (īn′stīnz) **the′o-ry.** See *relativity.*

ei-ren-i-con (ī-ren′i-kon), *n.* See *irenicon.*

eis-tedd-fod (ās-teᴛʜ′vọd), *n.* [W., < *eistedd*, sit.] A congress of Welsh bards and minstrels.

ei-ther (ē′ᴛʜėr or ī′ᴛʜėr), *a.* and *pron.* [AS. *ǣgther*, for *ǣghwæther*, < *ā*, ever, + *ge-*, a generalizing prefix, + *hwæther*, E. *whether.*] One or the other of the two (as, "Spirits, when they please, Can *either* sex assume, or both," Milton's "Paradise Lost," i. 424; "Lepidus flatters both, Of both is flatter'd; but he neither loves, Nor *either* cares for him," Shakspere's "Antony and Cleopatra," ii. 1. 16); also, each of the two (as, "In the midst of the street of it, and on *either* side of the river, was there the tree of life," Rev. xxii. 2; "The king of Israel and Jehoshaphat king of Judah sat *either* of them on his throne," 2 Chron. xviii. 9).—**ei′ther,** *conj.* In the one case, or according to the one choice or supposition: used before the first of two or more alternative words, etc., and in correlation with *or* used to connect them (as, *either* come or write). Also used, for emphasis, in certain forms of expression, after the last of a series of contrasted ideas, which are in some instances connected by *or* or *nor*, but in others not: as, if you take that, or this *either*, you will be satisfied; I do not want this, or that, or the third one *either*; not he, nor you *either*; if you do not come, he will not come *either*; that's mine—no, it isn't, *either.*

e-jac-u-late (ẹ-jak′ū-lāt), *v.*; *-lated, -lating.* [L. *ejaculatus*, pp. of *ejaculari*, < *e*, out of, + *jaculari*, throw, hurl: see *jaculate.*] **I.** *tr.* To throw out, cast forth, or eject suddenly and swiftly (now chiefly in technical use); also, to utter in an exclamatory manner; utter suddenly and briefly. **II.** *intr.* To make ejaculation; also, to speak in an abrupt, exclamatory manner.—**e-jac-u-la′tion** (-lā′shọn), *n.* The act of ejaculating; also, that which is ejaculated; a short, earnest prayer put forth as in moments of temptation; any abrupt, exclamatory utterance.—**e-jac′u-la-tor,** *n.*—**e-jac′u-la-to-ry** (-lạ-tọ-ri), *a.* Pertaining to ejaculation; of the nature of an ejaculation or exclamatory utterance.

e-ject (ẹ-jekt′), *v. t.* [L. *ejectus*, pp. of *ejicere, eicere*, < *e*, out of, + *jacere*, throw.] To throw out or cast forth; dart forth; emit; drive out or expel, as from a place or position; dismiss, as from office, occupancy, etc.; turn out or evict, as from property.—**e-ject** (ē′jekt), *n.* Something ejected; in *psychol.*, something whose existence is inferred as a reality, but which is outside of, and from its nature inaccessible to, the consciousness of the one making the inference (thus, the consciousness of one individual is an eject to the consciousness of any other).—**e-jec-ta** (ẹ-jek′tạ), *n. pl.* [L., neut. pl. of *ejectus*, pp.] Matter ejected, as from a volcano in eruption. Also (L.) **e-jec-ta-men′ta** (-tạ-men′tạ), *n. pl.*—**e-jec′tion** (-shọn), *n.* [L. *ejectio*(*n-*).] The act of ejecting, or the state of being ejected; something ejected, as lava.—**e-jec′tive,** *a.* Serving to eject.—**e-ject′ment,** *n.* The act of ejecting; esp., the act of dispossessing or ousting.—**e-jec′tor,** *n.* One who or that which ejects.

eke[1] (ēk), *v. t.*; *eked, eking.* [ME. *eken, echen*, < AS. *ēcan, ȳcan*, akin to Icel. *auka*, Goth. *aukan*, L. *augere*, increase.] To increase; enlarge; lengthen. [Archaic or prov.]—**to eke out,** to supplement (as, "We got some cattle here to *eke out* our provisions": Defoe's "Captain Singleton," x.); supply what is lacking to; make to last by additions or by economy; prolong (a performance, etc.) or fill (a page, etc.) by various expedients; contrive to make (a living) or support (existence) by various makeshifts.

eke[2] (ēk), *adv.* and *conj.* [AS. *ēac* = G. *auch.*] Also; in addition. [Archaic.]

el (el), *n.* See *ell*[2].

e-lab-o-rate (ẹ-lab′ọ-rāt), *v. t.*; *-rated, -rating.* [L. *elaboratus*, pp. of *elaborare*, < *e-*, out, + *laborare*, E. *labor, v.*] To produce or develop by labor; make from the raw material; work out carefully or minutely; work up to perfection; of a natural agency, to produce or develop by gradual process, as from elements or sources.—**e-lab′o-rate** (-rạt), *a.* Produced by labor (archaic); also, worked out with great care and nicety of detail; highly finished; executed with great minuteness, as an operation; also, minutely careful or painstaking, as a person.—**e-lab′o-rate-ly,** *adv.*—**e-lab′o-rate-ness,** *n.*—**e-lab-o-ra′tion** (-rā′shọn), *n.* [L. *elaboratio*(*n-*).] The act of elaborating; also, the state of being elaborated; elaborateness; also, something elaborated.—**e-lab′o-ra-tive** (-rạ-tiv), *a.* Elaborating; serving to elaborate.—**e-lab′o-ra-tor** (-rā-tọr), *n.*

é-lan (ā-läṅ), *n.* [F.] Dash; impetuous ardor.—**élan vital** (vē-tȧl). [F.] In *philos.*, the vital impetus or impulse; the impelling force in living beings: a phrase used by Bergson.

e-land (ē′lạnd), *n.* [D. *eland*, < G. *elend*, elk; prob. from Lith.] A large, heavily built antelope, *Taurotragus oryx*, of southern Africa.

Eland.

el-a-phine (el′ạ-fin), *a.* [NL. *elaphus*, < Gr. ἔλαφος, deer.] Pertaining to or resembling the red deer, *Cervus elaphus.*

e-lapse (ẹ-laps′), *v. i.*; *elapsed, elapsing.* [L. *elapsus*, pp. of *elabi*, < *e*, out of, + *labi*, fall, slide.] Of time, to slip by or pass away.—**e-lapse′,** *n.* An elapsing; lapse.

e-las-mo-branch (ẹ-las′mō-brangk or ẹ-laz′-). [NL. *Elasmobranchii*, pl., < Gr. ἐλασμός, metal plate, + βράγχια, gills.] **I.** *n.* Any of the *Elasmobranchii*, a group of fishes with plate-like gills, including the sharks and rays. **II.** *a.* Belonging to the *Elasmobranchii.*—**e-las-mo-bran′chi-ate** (-brang′ki-āt), *a.* and *n.*

e-las-tic (ẹ-las′tik). [NL. *elasticus*, < Gr. ἐλαύνειν, drive.] **I.** *a.* Propulsive†; also, spontaneously expansive, as gases; also, having the property of recovering shape after deformation, as solids; resisting a change in shape; having the property of recovering original volume or bulk after being compressed into smaller volume or bulk, as solids, liquids, or gases; resisting a change in volume; pertaining to either of these properties; also, springing back or rebounding; springy (as, an *elastic* step); also, readily recovering from depression or exhaustion (as, an *elastic* temperament); buoyant; also, capable of expanding or contracting according to circumstances; flexible, yielding, or accommodating (as, *elastic* principles; an *elastic* conscience). **II.** *n.* Webbing, or material in the form of a band, made elastic with strips of india-rubber; a piece of this material; also, an india-rubber band.—**e-las′ti-cal-ly,** *adv.*—**e-las-ti-ci-ty** (ē-las-tis′i-ti), *n.* The state or quality of being elastic.

e-late (ẹ-lāt′), *v. t.*; *elated, elating.* [L. *elatus*, pp. of *efferre*, bring out, raise, exalt: see *efferent.*] To raise†; also, to uplift or exalt in spirit; put in high spirits; render exultant;

make proud.—**e-late′,** *a.* Elated: as, "The ladies returned with *elate* and animated faces" (Disraeli's "Lothair," xlvi.).—**e-lat-ed-ly** (ẹ-lā′ted-li), *adv.*—**e-lat′ed-ness,** *n.*—**e-lat′er**[1], *n.*

el-a-ter[2] (el′ạ-tėr), *n.* [NL., < Gr. ἐλατήρ, driver, < ἐλαύνειν, drive.] Elasticity†; in *bot.*, an elastic filament serving to disperse spores; in *entom.*, an elaterid of the genus *Elater;* hence, any elaterid.

Eyed Elater (*Alaus oculatus*). (Somewhat enlarged.)

e-lat-er-id (e-lat′ẹ-rid), *n.* [NL. *Elateridæ*, pl., < *elater:* see *elater*[2].] Any of the beetles constituting the family *Elateridæ*, most of which have the power of springing up when laid on their back.

e-lat-er-in (e-lat′ẹ-rin), *n.* [See *elaterium.*] In *chem.*, a white crystalline substance obtained from and constituting the active principle of elaterium: used as a cathartic.

e-lat-er-ite (e-lat′ẹ-rīt), *n.* [See *elater*[2], in sense of 'elasticity.'] A brownish, elastic, rubber-like natural bitumen found in England.

el-a-te-ri-um (el-ạ-tē′ri-um), *n.* [L., < Gr. ἐλατήριον, < ἐλατήρ, driver: see *elater*[2].] A powerful cathartic obtained from the juice of a cucurbitaceous plant, *Ecballium elaterium*, the squirting cucumber.

e-la-tion (ẹ-lā′shọn), *n.* [L. *elatio(n-)*, < *elatus:* see *elate.*] Exaltation of spirit, as from joy or pride; elated state or feeling; exultant gladness.

el-bow (el′bō), *n.* [AS. *elnboga* = G. *elbogen*, orig. 'arm bow': see *ell*[1] and *bow*[2].] The outer part of the bend or joint of the arm; the angle at this joint when bent; also, something bent like the elbow, as a sharp turn in a road or river, or a piece of pipe bent at an angle; also, the raised arm of a chair or end of a sofa, for supporting the elbow or arm.—**el′bow,** *v.* **I.** *tr.* To push with or as with the elbow; jostle; also, to make (one's way) by so pushing. **II.** *intr.* To elbow one's way.—**el′bow=chair,** *n.* A chair with elbows; an arm-chair.—**el′bow=grease,** *n.* Energetic labor, as in rubbing. [Humorous.]—**el′bow=room,** *n.* Room to extend the elbows; hence, ample room; free scope.

eld (eld), *n.* [AS. *ældu, yldu*, < *ald, eald*, E. *old.*] Age (as, tall for his *eld*); old age (as, "Weake *eld* hath left thee nothing wise": Spenser's "Faerie Queene," ii. 3. 16); an old person (as, "To the tottering *eld* Still as a daughter would she run": Coleridge's "Destiny of Nations"); antiquity (as, "lands that contain the monuments of *Eld*": Byron's "Childe Harold," i. 93). [Archaic or prov.]

el-der[1] (el′dėr), *n.* [AS. *ellærn, ellen*, = MLG. *ellern, elderne.*] Any plant of the caprifoliaceous genus *Sambucus*, which comprises shrubs and trees bearing clusters of small white or light-colored flowers and a blackish or red drupaceous fruit.

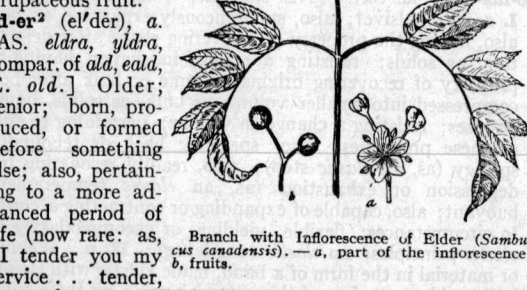

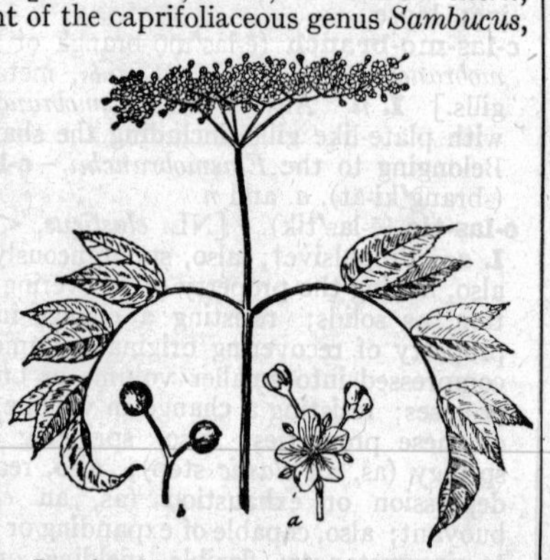
Branch with Inflorescence of Elder (*Sambucus canadensis*).—*a*, part of the inflorescence; *b*, fruits.

eld-er[2] (el′dėr), *a.* [AS. *eldra, yldra*, compar. of *ald, eald*, E. *old.*] Older; senior; born, produced, or formed before something else; also, pertaining to a more advanced period of life (now rare: as, "I tender you my service . . . tender, raw and young; Which *elder* days shall ripen," Shakspere's "Richard II.," ii. 3. 43); also, prior in appointment, validity, etc. (as, an *elder* officer; an *elder* title); also, prior in time, earlier, or former (as, in *elder* times).—**elder statesmen,** in Japan, a body of older statesmen, or men of experience and high repute in public affairs, who are consulted by the emperor on matters of state; hence, older statesmen or politicians elsewhere, or older men of experience and influence in any field, often as a class regarded as holding tenaciously to the views and policies of the past and hence as opposed to the progressive ideas of the younger generation.—**eld′er**[2], *n.* A person who is older than one's self, or who is one's senior (as, "I know my duty to my *elders*": Shakspere's "Taming of the Shrew," ii. 1. 7); also, an aged person; also, an ancestor or forefather; also, one of the older and more influential men of a tribe or community, esp. as forming a governing body; a chief or ruler; also, an officer in the early Christian church; a presbyter; in certain Protestant churches, a governing officer, either with or without teaching or pastoral functions.

el-der-ber-ry (el′dėr-ber″i), *n.*; pl. *-berries* (-iz). The drupaceous fruit of the elder, used in making a kind of wine, and employed in medicine for aperient and diuretic qualities.

eld-er-ly (el′dėr-li), *a.* Somewhat old; between middle and old age; also, of or pertaining to persons in later life.

eld-er-ship (el′dėr-ship), *n.* Seniority; also, the office of an elder; a body of elders.

eld-est (el′dest), *a. superl.* [AS. *eldest, yldest*, superl. of *ald, eald*, E. *old.*] Oldest; having been born first, or being the oldest surviving; also, earliest or first (as, "And self-defence is nature's *eldest* law": Dryden's "Absalom and Achitophel," i. 458).—**eldest hand,** in *card-playing*, the player on the dealer's left.

El Do-ra-do (el dọ-rä′dō). [Sp., 'the gilded.'] A fabled city abounding in gold or treasure, sought in northern South America by early Spanish and other explorers; hence, any place of reputed fabulous wealth.

el-dritch (el′drich), *a.* [Origin uncertain.] Weird; uncanny; unearthly; wild: as, "the *eldritch* cries of the wind among the turret-tops" (Stevenson's "Master of Ballantrae," viii.). [Sc.]

El-e-at-ic (el-ẹ-at′ik), *a.* Pertaining to Elea, an ancient Greek town in southern Italy, or to the philosophical system of Xenophanes (about 570–about 480 B.C.), Parmenides (flourished about 475 B.C.), and others who lived there.—**El-e-at′i-cism** (-i-sizm), *n.*

el-e-cam-pane (el″ẹ-kam-pān′), *n.* [L. *inula*, elecampane, + ML. *campana*, prob. 'of the fields,' < L. *campus*, field.] An asteraceous plant, *Inula helenium*, with large yellow flowers and aromatic leaves and root; also, a sweetmeat made from or flavored with its root.

Elecampane.

e-lect (ẹ-lekt′), *v. t.* [L. *electus*, pp. of *eligere*, pick out, choose, < *e*, out of, + *legere*, gather, choose.] To pick out or choose; esp., to determine in favor of (a course of action, etc.); also, to select by vote, as for an office; in *theol.*, of God, to select for divine mercy or favor, esp. for salvation or eternal life.—**e-lect′. I.** *a.* Picked out; chosen; also, select or choice; also, selected for an office, but not yet inducted (usually after the noun: as, the governor *elect*); in *theol.*, chosen by God, esp. for eternal life. **II.** *n. sing.* or *pl.* A person or the persons chosen or worthy to be chosen; in *theol.*, those chosen by God, esp. for eternal life.

e-lec-tion (ẹ-lek′shọn), *n.* [L. *electio(n-).*] The act of electing; selection; choice; also, the selection of a person or persons for office by vote; by extension, a public vote upon a proposition submitted; in *theol.*, the choice by God of particular individuals, as for a particular work, or for mercy or favor, esp. for salvation or eternal life; also, those elected by God†.—**e-lec′tion-a-ry** (-ạ-ri), *a.* Pertaining to election.—**e-lec-tion-eer′** (-ēr′), *v. i.* To work for the success of a candidate, party, ticket, etc., in an election.—**e-lec-tion-eer′er,** *n.*

e-lec-tive (ẹ-lek′tiv). [F. *électif.*] **I.** *a.* Characterized by or dependent on election; selective; optional; specif., selecting for combination or action (as, *elective* attraction, tendency to combine chemically with certain substances in preference to others); also, pertaining to the principle of electing to office, etc. (as, the *elective* franchise); having the power of electing to office, etc., as a body of persons; appointed by election, as an officer; bestowed by or derived from election, as an office. **II.** *n.* An optional study, as in a course at college; a study which a student may select from among alternatives.—**e-lec′tive-ly,** *adv.*

e-lec-tor (ē̦-lek′tọr), *n.* [L.] One who elects or may elect, esp. a qualified voter; in the Holy Roman Empire, one of the princes entitled to elect the emperor; in the U. S., one of the persons chosen by the voters of the several States to form the body which elects the President and the Vice-President.—**e-lec′tor-al,** *a.* Pertaining to electors or election; consisting of electors; specif., pertaining to or holding rank as an elector of the Holy Roman Empire.—**e-lec′tor-ate** (-ā̦t), *n.* The dignity or territory of an elector of the Holy Roman Empire; also, the body of persons entitled to vote in an election, or a particular division of them. —**e-lec′tor-ship,** *n.*—**e-lec′tress,** *n.* A female elector; also, the wife or widow of an elector of the Holy Roman Empire.

e-lec-tric (ē̦-lek′trik), *a.* [NL. *electricus,* < L. *electru* < Gr. ἤλεκτρον, amber (as a substance that develops electricity under friction): see *electrum.*] Having the property of developing electricity, as when excited by friction, as amber; pertaining to, consisting of, or containing electricity; producing, conveying, or operated or produced by electricity.—**electric catfish,** any of the large catfishes of the genus *Torpedo* (or *Malapterurus*) of Africa, which have the power of giving an electric shock, esp. *T.* (or *M.*) *electricus* of the Nile.—**electric eel,** a fish, *Electrophorus electricus,* of eel-like form, having the power of giving strong electric discharges, which serve as a means of offense and defense. It is found in the fresh waters of northern South America, and sometimes attains a length of over 6 feet.—**electric ray.** See *ray*².—**electric wave.** See under *wave, n.*—**e-lec′tric,** *n.* A substance capable of exhibiting electricity when rubbed; also, a car operated by electricity; an electric railroad. —**e-lec′tri-cal,** *a.* Electric.—**e-lec′tri-cal-ly,** *adv.*—**e-lec-tri-cian** (ē-lek-trish′ạn), *n.* One versed in the science of electricity; also, one who makes, repairs, installs, or operates electric devices.—**e-lec-tri′ci-ty** (-tris′i-ti), *n.* An agency producing various physical phenomena, as attraction and repulsion, luminous and heating effects, shock to the body, chemical decomposition, etc., which were originally thought to be caused by a kind of fluid, but are now regarded as being due to strains in the luminiferous ether or to the presence of electrons; also, the science dealing with this agency.—**e-lec′trics,** *n.* The science of electricity.

Electric Catfish (*Torpedo electricus*).

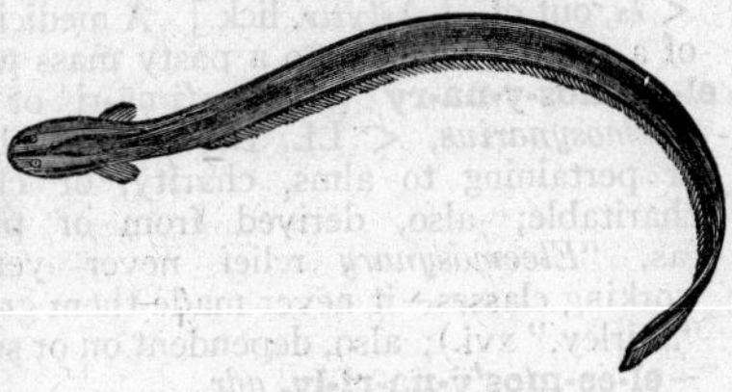

Electric Eel.

e-lec-tri-fi-a-ble (ē̦-lek′tri-fī-ạ-bl), *a.* [See *electrify.*] Capable of being electrified.—**e-lec″tri-fi-ca′tion** (-fi-kā′shọn), *n.* The act of electrifying, or the resulting state. —**e-lec′tri-fi-er** (-fī-ėr), *n.* One who or that which electrifies.

e-lec-tri-fy (ē̦-lek′tri-fī), *v. t.*; *-fied, -fying.* [See *electric* and *-fy.*] To charge with or subject to electricity; equip (a railroad, etc.) for the use of electric motive power; fig., to startle greatly, excite, or thrill (as, "The high-born Demosthenes *electrified* large assemblies by his indignant invectives against the Spanish Philip": Motley's "Dutch Republic," iii. 2).

e-lec-trize (ē̦-lek′trīz), *v. t.*; *-trized, -trizing.* To electrify. —**e-lec-tri-za′tion** (-tri-zā′shọn), *n.*—**e-lec′triz-er** (-trī-zėr), *n.*

electro-, electr-. Forms of Gr. ἤλεκτρον, amber, used to represent E. *electric, electricity,* in combination, as in *electrochronograph, electro-engraving, electrogild, electromassage, electromechanics, electrotelegraphy.*

e-lec-tro (ē̦-lek′trō), *n.*; pl. *-tros* (-trōz). Shortened form of *electrotype.*

e-lec-tro=a-nal-y-sis (ē̦-lek″trō-ạ-nal′i-sis), *n.* [See *electro-.*] Chemical analysis by electrolysis.

e-lec-tro-bi-ol-o-gy (ē̦-lek″trō-bī-ol′ō̦-ji), *n.* [See *electro-.*] The branch of biology that deals with electrical phenomena in living organisms.

e-lec-tro-cap-il-la-ry (ē̦-lek″trō-kap′i-lā̦-ri), *a.* [See *electro-.*] Capillary and electrical, as capillary phenomena produced by electricity.—**e-lec″tro-cap-il-lar′i-ty** (-lar′i-ti), *n.*

e-lec-tro-cau-ter-y (ē̦-lek″trō-kâ′tėr-i), *n.* [See *electro-.*] A cautery heated by electricity; also, cauterization with such an instrument.

e-lec-tro-chem-is-try (ē̦-lek″trō-kem′is-tri), *n.* [See *electro-.*] The branch of chemistry that deals with the chemical changes produced by electricity and the production of electricity by chemical changes.—**e-lec″tro-chem′i-cal** (-i-kạl), *a.*—**e-lec″tro-chem′i-cal-ly,** *adv.*—**e-lec″tro-chem′ist,** *n.*

e-lec-tro-cul-ture (ē̦-lek′trō̦-kul-tū̦r), *n.* [See *electro-.*] The use of electricity to stimulate the growth of plants.

e-lec-tro-cute (ē̦-lek′trō̦-kūt), *v. t.*; *-cuted, -cuting.* [From *electro-* + *-cute* in *execute.*] To execute (a criminal) by electricity; in general, to kill by electricity.—**e-lec-tro-cu′tion** (-kū′shọn), *n.*

e-lec-trode (ē̦-lek′trōd), *n.* [See *electro-* and *-ode*¹.] Either of the two poles or terminals of a battery or other electric source; either end of an open electric circuit; a conductor by which a current enters or leaves an electrolyte.

e-lec-tro-de-pos-it (ē̦-lek″trō-dē̦-poz′it), *v. t.* [See *electro-.*] To deposit (a metal, etc.) by electrolysis.—**e-lec″tro-de-pos′it,** *n.* A deposit, as of metal, produced by electrolysis. —**e-lec″tro-dep-o-si′tion** (-dep-ō̦-zish′ọn), *n.*

e-lec-tro-dy-nam-ics (ē̦-lek″trō-dī-nam′iks), *n.* [See *electro-.*] The branch of electricity that deals with the mutual action of electric currents and the interaction of currents and magnets.—**e-lec″tro-dy-nam′ic,** *a.*—**e-lec″tro-dy-na-mom′e-ter** (-nạ-mom′e-tėr), *n.* A device in which the mutual or electrodynamic action of two adjacent circuits or coils is utilized to measure electric currents.

e-lec-tro-graph (ē̦-lek′trō̦-gráf), *n.* [See *electro-* and *-graph.*] A curve, automatically traced, forming a record of the indications of an electrometer; also, an instrument for recording atmospheric electricity.—**e-lec-tro-graph′ic** (-graf′ik), *a.*

e-lec-tro-ki-net-ics (ē̦-lek″trō-ki-net′iks), *n.* [See *electro-.*] The science of electricity in motion; the branch of electricity that deals with currents.—**e-lec″tro-ki-net′ic,** *a.*

e-lec-tro-lier (ē̦-lek-trō-lēr′), *n.* [From *electro-* + *-lier* in *chandelier.*] A chandelier or support for electric lamps.

e-lec-trol-o-gy (ē-lek-trol′ō̦-ji), *n.* [See *electro-* and *-logy.*] The science of electricity.

e-lec-trol-y-sis (ē-lek-trol′i-sis), *n.* [See *electro-* and *-lysis.*] The decomposition of a chemical compound by an electric current; in *surg.,* the destruction of tumors, etc., by an electric current.—**e-lec-tro-lyte** (ē̦-lek′trō̦-līt), *n.* [See *-lyte.*] A compound that undergoes decomposition by electrolysis.—**e-lec-tro-lyt′ic, e-lec-tro-lyt′i-cal** (-lit′ik, -i-kạl), *a.* Pertaining to electrolysis or to an electrolyte. —**e-lec-tro-lyt′i-cal-ly,** *adv.*—**e-lec′tro-lyze** (-līz), *v. t.*; *-lyzed, -lyzing.* [See *-lyze.*] To decompose by electrolysis. —**e-lec″tro-ly-za′tion** (-li-zā′shọn), *n.*—**e-lec′tro-lyz-er** (-lī-zėr), *n.*

e-lec-tro-mag-net (ē̦-lek″trō-mag′net), *n.* [See *electro-.*] A core of soft iron or the like, magnetized by the passage of an electric current through a wire coiled around it.—**e-lec″tro-mag-net′ic,** *a.* Pertaining to electromagnetism. —**electromagnetic wave.** See under *wave, n.*—**e-lec″tro-mag′net-ism,** *n.* The science that deals with the relation between electric currents and magnetism; the phenomena collectively which rest upon the relation between electric currents and magnetism.

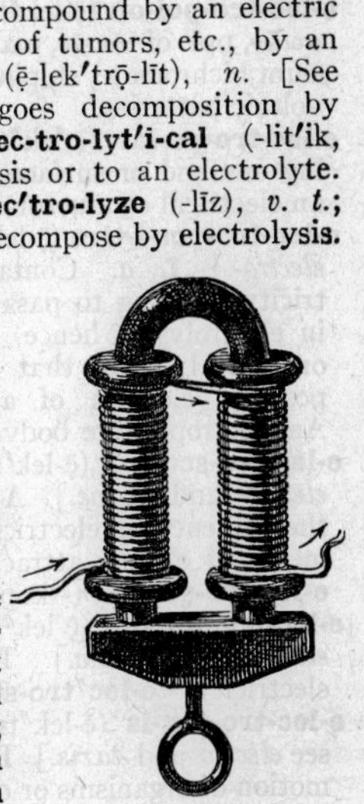

Electromagnet.

e-lec-tro-met-al-lur-gy (ę̄-lek″trǭ-met′ą-lėr-ji), *n.* [See *electro-*.] Electrical metallurgy; the art of applying electricity to metallurgical processes.—**e-lec″tro-met-al-lur′gi-cal** (-ji-kąl), *a.*—**e-lec″tro-met′al-lur-gist,** *n.*

e-lec-trom-e-ter (ē-lek-trom′e-tėr), *n.* [See *electro-* and *-meter.*] In *elect.*, an instrument for measuring differences of potential; also, an electroscope.—**e-lec-tro-met-ric, e-lec-tro-met-ri-cal** (ę̄-lek-trǭ-met′rik, -ri-kąl), *a.* Pertaining to electrometry.—**e-lec-trom′e-try,** *n.* [See *-metry.*] The measurement of electricity.

e-lec-tro-mo-tion (ę̄-lek″trǭ-mō′shǫn), *n.* [See *electro-*.] Motion of electricity; the passage of an electric current; also, mechanical motion produced by electricity.—**e-lec″tro-mo′tive** (-tiv). **I.** *a.* Pertaining to, producing, or tending to produce a flow of electricity: as, *electromotive* force (the force, due to differences of potential, that causes electric currents). **II.** *n.* An electric locomotive.—**e-lec″tro-mo-tiv′i-ty** (-mǭ-tiv′i-ti), *n.*—**e-lec″tro-mo′tor,** *n.* Anything producing an electric current, as a voltaic battery; also, an electric motor.

e-lec-tron (ę̄-lek′tron), *n.* [Gr. ἤλεκτρον: see *electrum.*] Electrum; also, in *physics* and *chem.*, an extremely small particle, having about one thousandth the mass of a hydrogen atom, supposed to be or to contain a unit of negative electricity, and regarded as the ultimate particle of which all atoms are built up.—**e-lec-tron-ic** (ē-lek-tron′ik), *a.*

e-lec-tro-neg-a-tive (ę̄-lek″trǭ-neg′ą-tiv). [See *electro-*.] **I.** *a.* Containing negative electricity; tending to pass to the positive pole in electrolysis; hence, non-metallic or acid, as an element or radical; also, that may be used as the negative element of a voltaic cell. **II.** *n.* An electronegative body.

e-lec-tron=tube (ę̄-lek′tron-tūb), *n.* In *wireless teleg.* and *teleph.*, a vacuum-tube.

e-lec-trop-a-thy (ē-lek-trop′ą-thi), *n.* [See *electro-* and *-pathy.*] Electrotherapy.—**e-lec-tro-path-ic** (ę̄-lek-trǭ-path′ik), *a.*

e-lec-tro-phone (ę̄-lek′trǭ-fōn), *n.* [See *electro-* and *-phone.*] An instrument for producing sounds, resembling trumpet-tones, by electric currents.

e-lec-troph-o-rus (ē-lek-trof′ǭ-rus), *n.*; pl. *-ri* (-rī). [NL., < *electro-* (see *electro-*) + Gr. -φόρος, bearing (see *-phorous*).] An instrument for generating static electricity by means of induction, consisting of a disk of resin or other non-conducting material easily excited by friction and a polished metal disk with an insulating handle.

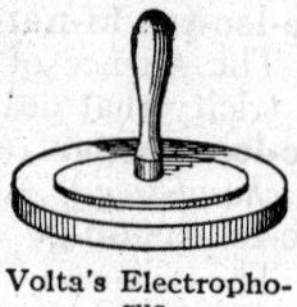

Volta's Electrophorus.

e-lec-tro-plate (ę̄-lek′trǭ-plāt), *v. t.*; *-plated, -plating.* [See *electro-*.] To plate or coat with a metal by electrolysis.—**e-lec′tro-plate,** *n.* Electroplated articles or ware.—**e-lec′tro-plat-er** (-plā-tėr), *n.*

e-lec-tro-poi-on (ę̄-lek″trǭ-poi′on), *n.* [From *electro-* + Gr. ποιῶν, ppr. of ποιεῖν, make.] A solution consisting of potassium bichromate, sulphuric acid, and water, used in certain voltaic batteries.

e-lec-tro-po-lar (ę̄-lek″trǭ-pō′lạr), *a.* [See *electro-*.] Having one end or surface positive and the other negative, as an electrical conductor.

e-lec-tro-pos-i-tive (ę̄-lek″trǭ-poz′i-tiv). [See *electro-*.] **I.** *a.* Containing positive electricity; tending to pass to the negative pole in electrolysis; hence, basic, as an element or radical; also, that may be used as the positive element of a voltaic cell. **II.** *n.* An electropositive body.

e-lec-tro-scope (ę̄-lek′trǭ-skōp), *n.* [See *electro-* and *-scope.*] A device for detecting the presence of electricity, its kind, etc., by means of electric attraction and repulsion.—**e-lec-tro-scop′ic** (-skop′ik), *a.*

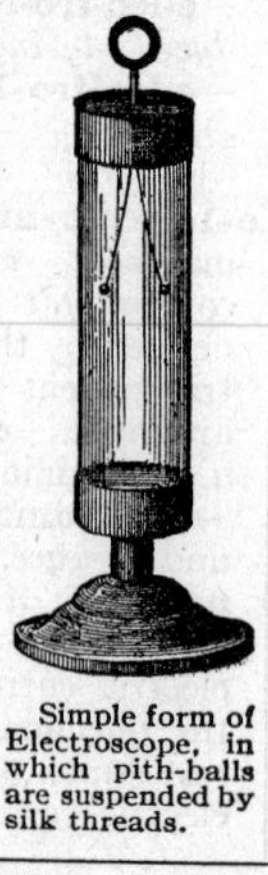

Simple form of Electroscope, in which pith-balls are suspended by silk threads.

e-lec-tro-stat-ics (ę̄-lek″trǭ-stat′iks), *n.* [See *electro-* and *static.*] The science of static electricity.—**e-lec″tro-stat′ic,** *a.*

e-lec-tro-tax-is (ę̄-lek″trǭ-tak′sis), *n.* [NL.: see *electro-* and *-taxis.*] The orientation or locomotion of organisms or cells in relation to electric currents.—**e-lec″tro-tac′tic** (-tak′tik), *a.*

e-lec-tro-tech-nics (ę̄-lek″trǭ-tek′niks), *n.* [See *electro-*.] The technics of electricity.—**e-lec″tro-tech-nol′o-gy** (-nol′ǭ-ji), *n.* The science dealing with the practical applications of electricity.

e-lec-tro-ther-a-peu-tics (ę̄-lek″trǭ-ther-ą-pū′tiks), *n.* [See *electro-*.] That branch of therapeutics which deals with the curative use of electricity.—**e-lec″tro-ther-a-peu′tic,** *a.*—**e-lec″tro-ther-a-peu′tist,** *n.* One versed in electrotherapeutics.—**e-lec″tro-ther′a-py** (-ther′ą-pi), *n.* Treatment of disease by means of electricity.

e-lec-tro-ther-mal (ę̄-lek″trǭ-thėr′mąl), *a.* [See *electro-*.] Pertaining to heat produced by electricity. Also **e-lec″tro-ther′mic.**

e-lec-trot-o-nus (ē-lek-trot′ǭ-nus), *n.* [NL., < *electro-* (see *electro-*) + Gr. τόνος, tension.] The altered state of a nerve during the passage of an electric current through it.—**e-lec-tro-ton-ic** (ę̄-lek-trǭ-ton′ik), *a.*

e-lec-tro-type (ę̄-lek′trǭ-tīp), *n.* [See *electro-* and *-type.*] A facsimile, for use in printing, of a block of type, an engraving, or the like, consisting of a thin shell of metal (usually copper), deposited by electrolytic action in a wax mold of the original, and backed with type-metal; also, a print from such a facsimile; also, electrotypy.—**e-lec′tro-type,** *v. t.*; *-typed, -typing.* To make an electrotype or electrotypes of.—**e-lec′tro-typ-er** (-tī-pėr), *n.*—**e-lec′tro-ty-py** (-tī-pi), *n.* The electrotype process.

e-lec-trum (ę̄-lek′trum), *n.* [L., < Gr. ἤλεκτρον, amber, also an alloy of gold and silver: cf. ἠλέκτωρ, the beaming sun, fire.] Amber†; also, an amber-colored alloy of gold and silver, known to the ancients.

e-lec-tu-a-ry (ę̄-lek′ţū-ā-ri), *n.*; pl. *-ries* (-riz). [LL. *electuarium*: cf. Gr. ἐκλεικτόν, electuary, < ἐκλείχειν, lick up, < ἐκ, out of, + λείχειν, lick.] A medicine composed usually of a powder mixed into a pasty mass with syrup or honey.

el-ee-mos-y-na-ry (el-ę̄-mos′i-nā-ri or el″ę̄-ę̄-), *a.* [ML. *eleemosynarius*, < LL. *eleemosyna*, alms: see *alms.*] Of or pertaining to alms, charity, or charitable donations; charitable; also, derived from or provided by charity (as, "*Eleemosynary* relief never yet tranquillized the working classes—it never made them grateful": C. Brontë's "Shirley," xvi.); also, dependent on or supported by charity.—**el-ee-mos′y-na-ri-ly,** *adv.*

el-e-gance (el′ę̄-gąns), *n.* Elegant quality; also, something elegant; an elegant characteristic; a refinement. Also **el′e-gan-cy**; pl. *-cies* (-siz).

el-e-gant (el′ę̄-gąnt), *a.* [OF. *elegant* (F. *élégant*), < L. *elegans* (*-ant-*), fastidious, nice, fine, elegant, connected with *eligere*, pick out, choose: see *elect.*] Having or showing a nice or discriminating taste; tastefully fine or luxurious in dress, manners, appointments, etc.; gracefully refined, as in tastes, habits, literary style, etc.; polite, as arts or learning; nice, choice, or pleasingly superior in quality or kind, as a contrivance, preparation, or process; characterized by a graceful distinction in form or appearance; in general, nice; choice; fine.—**é-lé-gante** (ā-lā-gäṅt), *n.* [F., fem. of *élégant.*] A woman of fashion.—**el′e-gant-ly,** *adv.*

e-le-gi-ac (e-lē′ji-ak or el-ę̄-jī′ak). [LL. *elegiacus*, < Gr. ἐλεγειακός.] **I.** *a.* Noting, pertaining to, or employing a meter consisting of a couplet ('elegiac distich') the first line of which is a dactylic hexameter and the second a (so-called) pentameter (imitated in the lines "In the hexameter rises the fountain's silvery column; In the pentameter aye falling in melody back": Coleridge's tr. Schiller's "Ovidian Elegiac Metre"), apparently used orig. in threnetic pieces, but early found in compositions of various kinds, as in the poems of Mimnermus and Callimachus among the Greeks and of Tibullus and Propertius among the Romans (as, *elegiac* verse, poetry composed in the elegiac meter; an *elegiac* pentameter or, sometimes, verse, the second line of the elegiac distich: see *pentameter*); also, of the nature of an elegy, or poem of mourning or lamentation; pertaining to or characteristic of such poems; mournful, melancholy, or plaintive; also, being a writer of elegiac poetry (as, an *elegiac* poet). **II.** *n.* An elegiac poet†; also, an elegiac pentameter; *pl.*, a succession of elegiac distichs, or a poem or poems in such distichs.—**el-e-gi-a-cal** (el-ę̄-jī′ą-kąl), *a.*

e-le-gi-ast (e-lē′ji-ast), *n.* Same as *elegist.*

el-e-gist (el′ē-jist), *n.* The author of an elegy.

el-e-gize (el′ē-jīz), *v.*; *-gized, -gizing.* **I.** *intr.* To compose an elegy. **II.** *tr.* To lament in or as in an elegy: as, "the bard who soars to *elegise* an ass" (Byron's "English Bards").

el-e-gy (el′ē-ji), *n.*; pl. *-gies* (-jiz). [F. *élégie*, < L. *elegia*, < Gr. ἐλεγεῖα, prop. neut. pl. of ἐλεγεῖος, elegiac, < ἔλεγος, song of mourning.] A mournful, melancholy, or plaintive poem, esp. a funeral song or a lament for the dead, as Milton's "Lycidas"; also, poetry or a poem written in elegiac meter.

e-lek-tron (ē-lek′tron), *n.* See *electron.*

el-e-ment (el′ē-mẹnt), *n.* [OF. *element* (F. *élément*), < L. *elementum*, a first principle, element, rudiment; origin uncertain.] One of the simple substances, usually earth, water, air, and fire, early regarded as constituting the material universe: also, one of these substances regarded as the natural habitat of something (as, "Every animal has his *element* assigned him; the birds have the air, and man and beasts the earth": Johnson's "Rasselas," vi.); hence, the sphere or environment adapted to any person or thing (as, to be in one's *element*; "When they came to make boards, and pots, and such things, they were quite out of their *element*," Defoe's "Robinson Crusoe," ii. 4); *pl.*, atmospheric agencies or forces; also, *sing.*, a component or constituent part of a whole; *pl.*, the bread and wine used in the eucharist; also, the rudimentary principles of an art, science, etc.; *sing.*, in *chem.*, one of a class of substances (of which more than eighty are now recognized) which cannot be separated into substances of other kinds, or, at least, have hitherto resisted analysis by any known chemical means; in *elect.*, either of the two dissimilar substances which constitute a voltaic couple; also, a voltaic cell; in *geom.*, one of the points, lines, planes, or other geometrical forms, by which a figure is made up; any straight line in a cylindrical or conical surface, corresponding to some position of the moving line by which the surface was generated; in *astron.*, etc., one of the data required for the solution of a problem (as, the *elements* of a planetary orbit).—**el-e-men′tal** (-men′tạl), *a.* Of, pertaining to, or of the nature of the four elements or any one of them; also, pertaining to the agencies, forces, or phenomena of physical nature; comparable to the great forces of nature, as with reference to their power; also, forming a constituent; of the nature of an ultimate constituent; simple; uncompounded; pertaining to chemical elements; sometimes, pertaining to rudiments or first principles; elementary.—**el-e-men′tal-ly,** *adv.*—**el-e-men′ta-ry** (-tạ-ri), *a.* [L. *elementarius.*] Pertaining to the four elements or to the great forces of nature; elemental; also, constituent; of the nature of an ultimate constituent; simple or uncompounded; also, pertaining to or dealing with elements, rudiments, or first principles; of the nature of elements or rudiments.—**el-e-men′ta-ri-ly,** *adv.*—**el-e-men′ta-ri-ness,** *n.*

el-e-mi (el′ē-mi), *n.* [= F. *élémi* = Sp. *elemí*; origin uncertain.] Any of various fragrant resins used in medicine, varnish-making, etc., as that yielded by *Canarium commune*, a balsameaceous tree cultivated in the Moluccas and elsewhere.

e-len-chus (ē-leng′kus), *n.*; pl. *-chi* (-kī). [L., < Gr. ἔλεγχος, < ἐλέγχειν, cross-examine, refute.] A questioning or cross-examination (as, the Socratic *elenchus*, Socrates's method of refutation by questioning an opponent); hence, a logical refutation; an argument which refutes another argument by proving the contrary of its conclusion; also, a false refutation; a sophistical argument.—**e-len′chic** (-kik), *a.*—**e-lenc-tic** (ē-lengk′tik), *a.* [Gr. ἐλεγκτικός, < ἐλέγχειν.] Of, pertaining to, or engaged in cross-examining; also, of, pertaining to, or constituting an elenchus or refutation; refutatory.

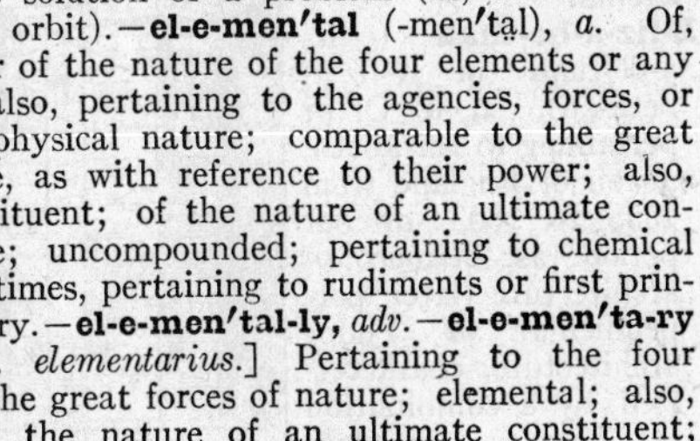
Indian Elephant (*Elephas indicus*).

el-e-phant (el′ē-fạnt), *n.*; pl. *elephants*, sometimes (esp. collectively) *elephant.* [L. *elephantus*, also *elephas* (*elephant-*), < Gr. ἐλέφας (ἐλεφαντ-), elephant, ivory.] Any of the large five-toed mammals, with long prehensile trunk or proboscis and long tusks of ivory, constituting the genus *Elephas*, comprising two existing species, *E. indicus*, of India and neighboring regions, with comparatively small ears (see cut in preceding column), and *E. africanus*, of Africa, with large, flapping ears (cf. *mammoth*, *n.*); also, fig., a burdensome or perplexing possession (as, to have an *elephant* on one's hands).—**white elephant.** See under *white*, *a.*

African Elephant (*Elephas africanus*).

el-e-phan-ti-a-sis (el″ē-fan-tī′ạ-sis), *n.* [L., < Gr. ἐλεφαντίασις, < ἐλέφας, E. *elephant.*] In *pathol.*, a chronic disease, due to lymphatic obstruction, characterized by enormous enlargement of the parts affected and hardening and fissuring of the skin, which becomes like an elephant's hide.

el-e-phan-tine (el-ē-fan′tin or -tīn), *a.* [L. *elephantinus*, < Gr. ἐλεφάντινος.] Pertaining to or resembling an elephant; hence, huge; great; ponderous; clumsy.

el-e-phant's=ear (el′ē-fạnts-ēr), *n.* A large-leaved foliage-plant. See *caladium.*

el-e-phant's=foot (el′ē-fạnts-fu̇t), *n.* A South African plant, *Testudinaria elephantipes*, having a large stem with a rough exterior and a fleshy edible interior.

el-e-phant=shrew (el′ē-fạnt-shrö), *n.* Any of the small, leaping, mouse-like insectivorous animals of the family *Macroscelididæ*, of Africa, which have a long snout suggesting the proboscis of an elephant.

Elephant-shrew (*Macroscelides typicus*).

El-eu-sin-i-a (el-ū-sin′i-ạ̈), *n. pl.* [L., < Gr. Ἐλευσίνια, < Ἐλευσίς, Eleusis.] In *Gr. antiq.*, the famous mysteries and festival celebrated at Eleusis and elsewhere in ancient Greece, in honor of Demeter (Ceres).—**El-eu-sin′i-an,** *a.* Of or pertaining to ancient Eleusis, in Attica, Greece: as, the *Eleusinian* mysteries (certain religious mysteries, in honor of Demeter (Ceres), which originated there, celebrated esp. in Attica).

El-eu-the-ri-a (el-ū-thē′ri-ạ̈), *n. pl.* [L., < Gr. ἐλευθέρια, pl., < ἐλεύθερος, free.] The feast of liberty, an ancient Greek festival celebrated at Platæa in commemoration of the great victory won there by the Greeks over the Persians in 479 B.C.

e-leu-the-ro-ma-ni-a (e-lū″thẹ-rọ-mā′ni-ạ̈), *n.* [NL., < Gr. ἐλεύθερος, free, + μανία, E. *mania.*] A mad zeal for freedom.—**e-leu″the-ro-ma′ni-ac** (-ak), *n.*

el-e-vate (el′ē-vāt), *v. t.*; *-vated, -vating.* [L. *elevatus*, pp. of *elevare*, < *e*, out of, + *levare*, lighten, lift, raise, < *levis*, light.] To lighten†; also, to move or raise from a lower to a higher place or position; hold up to view, as the host and chalice in the service of the mass; raise (the voice); direct upward, as the eyes; raise in rank or status; raise morally or intellectually; elate or exhilarate; intoxicate slightly (colloq.).—**el′e-vate,** *a.* Elevated: as, "An imperial city . . . With towers and temples proudly *elevate* On seven small hills" (Milton's "Paradise Regained," iv. 34). [Now poetic.]—**el′e-vat-ed** (-vā-ted), *p. a.* Raised up; raised above the ground or the general level; high; lofty; exalted in character or style.

el-e-va-tion (el-ē̦-vā′shọn), *n.* [L. *elevatio(n-).*] The act of elevating, or the state of being elevated; specif., the lifting up of the host and chalice in the service of the mass; also, an elevated place; an eminence; also, the height to which anything is elevated; the angle at which anything, as a gun, is raised above a horizontal direction; a particular height above a given level; also, height or loftiness; grandeur or dignity; nobleness; in *arch.*, etc., a drawing or design which represents an object or structure as being projected geometrically on a vertical plane, esp. one showing the exterior as seen from the front or the side; in *astron.*, etc., altitude.

el-e-va-tor (el′ē̦-vā-tọr), *n.* [LL.] One who or that which elevates; a mechanical device for raising articles; a building for storing grain, the grain being handled by means of mechanical elevating and conveying devices ('grain-elevator'); a moving platform or cage for conveying goods, persons, etc., from one level to another, as in a building; a hinged horizontal plane on an aëroplane, etc., used to control the longitudinal inclination; in *anat.*, a muscle that raises a part of the body; in *surg.*, an instrument for raising a depressed part.—**el′e-va-to-ry** (-vạ-tō̦-ri), *a.* Serving to elevate.

e-lev-en (ē̦-lev′n). [AS. *endleofan, endlufon,* = D. *elf* = G. *eilf* = Icel. *ellifu* = Goth. *ainlif,* eleven; from the Teut. stem represented by E. *one,* with a termination occurring also in E. *twelve.*] **I.** *a.* One more than ten. **II.** *n.* A number composed of eleven units, or a symbol, as 11 or xi, representing it; a set of eleven persons or things, as a football or cricket team.—**e-lev′enth,** *a.* [AS. *endlyfta.*] Next after the tenth; also, being one of eleven equal parts.—**the eleventh hour,** fig., the last possible hour for doing something; the time just before it is too late: in allusion to the parable of the laborers in the vineyard (Mat. xx. 1–16).—**e-lev′enth,** *n.* The eleventh member of a series; also, an eleventh part.

elf (elf), *n.*; pl. *elves* (elvz). [AS. *ælf* = Icel. *ālfr,* elf, = G. *alp,* nightmare, incubus.] One of a class of imaginary beings with magical powers, given to capricious interference in human affairs, and usually imagined to be diminutive beings in human form; a sprite; a fairy; also, a mischievous, tricksy, or spiteful person; a knave or rogue; also, a diminutive being, as a dwarf or a small child.—**elf**†, *v. t.* To tangle (the hair), as in elf-locks. See Shakspere's "King Lear," ii. 3. 10.—**elf′=child,** *n.* A changeling.—**elf′in. I.** *a.* Pertaining to elves; elf-like. **II.** *n.* An elf.—**elf′ish,** *a.* Elf-like (as, "Thou strange and *elfish* child, whence didst thou come?" Hawthorne's "Scarlet Letter," vi.); elfin; mischievous; spiteful.—**elf′ish-ly,** *adv.*—**elf′ish-ness,** *n.*—**elf′land** (-land), *n.* The land of the elves; fairyland: as, "the horns of *Elfland* faintly blowing" (Tennyson's "Princess," iv.).—**elf′=lock,** *n.* A lock of hair tangled as if by elves. See Shakspere's "Romeo and Juliet," i. 4. 90.

e-li-cit (ē̦-lis′it), *v. t.* [L. *elicitus,* pp. of *elicere,* < *e,* out of, + *lacere,* entice.] To draw or bring out or forth; educe; evoke: as, to *elicit* truth by discussion; to *elicit* information by interrogation; to *elicit* applause or approval.—**e-li-ci-ta-tion** (ē̦-lis-i-tā′shọn), *n.*—**e-li′ci-tor,** *n.*

e-lide (ē̦-līd′), *v. t.*; *elided, eliding.* [L. *elidere* (pp. *elisus*), < *e,* out of, + *lædere,* hurt by striking.] To crush† or destroy†; also, to suppress, or pass over in silence; specif., to omit, or slur over, in pronunciation (a vowel or syllable); in *law,* to annul or quash.

el-i-gi-ble (el′i-ji-bl). [F. *éligible,* < L. *eligere,* pick out, choose: see *elect.*] **I.** *a.* Fit or proper to be chosen; worthy of choice; desirable; specif., legally qualified, as for an office. **II.** *n.* A person or thing that is eligible: as, "Beautiful, accomplished, and an heiress, she had, of course, all the *eligibles* and non-eligibles of the other sex sighing at her feet" (Mrs. Stowe's "Uncle Tom's Cabin," xv.).—**el″i-gi-bil′i-ty** (-bil′i-ti), **el′i-gi-ble-ness,** *n.*—**el′i-gi-bly,** *adv.*

e-lim-i-nate (ē̦-lim′i-nāt), *v. t.*; *-nated, -nating.* [L. *eliminatus,* pp. of *eliminare,* turn out of doors, < *e,* out of, + *limen,* threshold.] To thrust out of doors (obs. or archaic); hence, to expel; remove; get rid of; sometimes, to omit as irrelevant or unimportant; ignore; in *math.,* to remove (a quantity) from an equation.—**e-lim-i-na′tion** (-nā′shọn), *n.* The act of eliminating, or the state of being eliminated; expulsion; removal.—**e-lim′i-na-tive** (-nạ-tiv), *a.* Tending or serving to eliminate.—**e-lim′i-na-tor** (-nā-tọr), *n.*

el-i-quate (el′i-kwāt), *v. t.*; *-quated, -quating.* [L. *eliquatus,* pp. of *eliquare,* < *e,* out of, + *liquare,* melt.] To separate (metal, etc.) by fusion.—**el-i-qua′tion** (-kwā′shọn), *n.*

e-li-sion (ē̦-lizh′ọn), *n.* [L. *elisio(n-),* < *elidere*: see *elide.*] A suppressing or omitting; the suppression of a vowel, syllable, or any part of a word, as for euphony or meter; often, as in poetry, the cutting off of a vowel at the end of one word when the next word begins with a vowel.

e-li-sor (ē̦-lī′zọr or el′i-zọr), *n.* [OF. *elisour,* < *elire* (F. *élire*), choose, < L. *eligere*: see *elect.*] In *law,* a person appointed in certain cases to return a panel of jurors, serve a writ, etc.

é-lite (ā-lēt′), *n.* [F., < *élire,* choose: see *elisor.*] The choice or best part, as of a body or class of persons; [*cap.*] the active army of Switzerland.

e-lix-ir (ē̦-lik′sėr), *n.* [ML. *elixir,* < Ar. *el, al,* the, + *iksīr,* philosophers' stone, prob. < Gr. ξήριον, a drying powder for wounds, < ξηρός, dry.] An alchemic preparation for transmuting base metals into gold, or for prolonging life ('elixir vitæ,' or 'elixir of life'); hence, a sovereign remedy; also, a strong extract or tincture†; fig., the quintessence or absolute embodiment of anything; in *phar.,* a tincture with more than one base, or some similar compound medicine; in modern pharmacy, an aromatic, sweetened alcoholic liquid containing medicinal agents, or for use as a vehicle for such agents.

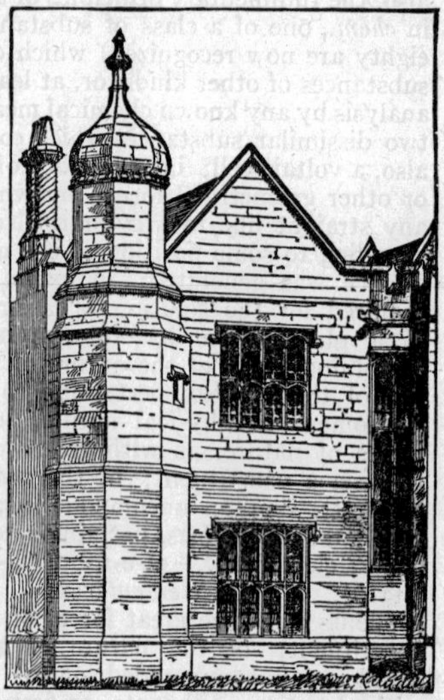
Elizabethan Architecture. — Hargrave Hall, England.

E-liz-a-be-than (ē̦-liz-ạ-bē′thạn or ē̦-liz′ạ-beth-ạn). **I.** *a.* Of or pertaining to Elizabeth, queen of England from 1558 to 1603, or her period: as, *Elizabethan* architecture (later perpendicular or Tudor architecture, characterized by a combination of features of late Gothic and degenerate Italian styles). **II.** *n.* One who lived in England during the Elizabethan period, esp. a poet or dramatist.

elk (elk), *n.*; pl. *elks* or (esp. collectively) *elk.* [ME. *elke*: cf. AS. *elch, elh,* G. *elch,* Icel. *elgr,* also L. *alces,* Gr. ἄλκη, elk.] The largest existing European and Asiatic deer, *Alces machlis,* the male of which has large palmate antlers (cf. *moose*); in America, the wapiti.

European Elk (*Alces machlis*).

ell[1] (el), *n.* [AS. *eln* = D. *el* = G. *elle* = Icel. *alin* = Goth. *aleina,* ell; orig. meaning 'arm,' 'forearm' (see *elbow*), and akin to L. *ulna,* Gr. ὠλένη.] A measure of length, now little used, varying in different countries: in England equivalent to 45 inches.

ell[2], **el** (el), *n.* The letter L, l; something shaped like an L; an extension to a building, at right angles to one end. See *L*[2].

el-lipse (e-lips′), *n.* [= F. *ellipse*, < L. *ellipsis*: see *ellipsis*.] In *gram.*, ellipsis; in *geom.*, a plane closed curve such that the sum of the distances of each point in it from two fixed points (foci) is constant.

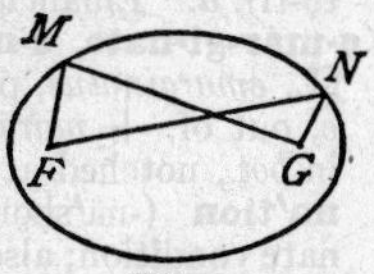

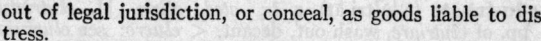

Ellipse.
F, G, foci. *FM* + *GM* equals *FN* + *GN*, *M* and *N* being any points in the curve.

el-lip-sis (e-lip′sis), *n.*; pl. *ellipses* (-sēz). [L., < Gr. ἔλλειψις, ellipsis, ellipse, < ἐλλείπειν, leave in, leave out, fall short, < ἐν, in, + λείπειν, leave: cf. *ellipse*.] In *gram.*, the omission from a sentence of a word or words needed to complete the construction or the sense; in *printing*, a mark or marks, as —, . . ., or * * *, to indicate an omission or suppression of letters or words; in *geom.*, an ellipse†.

el-lip-so-graph (e-lip′sǫ-gråf), *n.* [See *ellipse* and *-graph*.] An instrument for describing ellipses.

el-lip-soid (e-lip′soid), *n.* [See *ellipse* and *-oid*.] In *geom.*, a solid figure all plane sections of which through one axis are ellipses and all other plane sections ellipses or circles. —**el-lip-soi-dal** (el-ip-soi′dạl), *a.* Pertaining to, or having the form of, an ellipsoid.

el-lip-tic, el-lip-ti-cal (e-lip′tik, -ti-kạl), *a.* [Gr. ἐλλειπτικός, defective, elliptic, < ἐλλείπειν: see *ellipsis*.] Pertaining to or marked by grammatical ellipsis; also, pertaining to or having the form of an ellipse.—**el-lip′ti-cal-ly,** *adv.*—**el-lip-ti-ci-ty** (el-ip-tis′i-ti), *n.* The quality of being elliptic; the degree of divergence of an ellipse from the circle.

elm (elm), *n.* [AS. *elm*, akin to Icel. *ālmr* and L. *ulmus*, elm.] Any of the trees of the genus *Ulmus*, as *U. campestris* ('English elm'), *U. americana* ('white elm'), *U. fulva* ('slippery-elm'), etc., some of which are widely cultivated for shade and ornament; the wood of such a tree.—**elm-en** (el′men), *a.* Of or pertaining to the elm. [Archaic or prov. Eng.]—**elm′y,** *a.* Abounding in or consisting of elms.

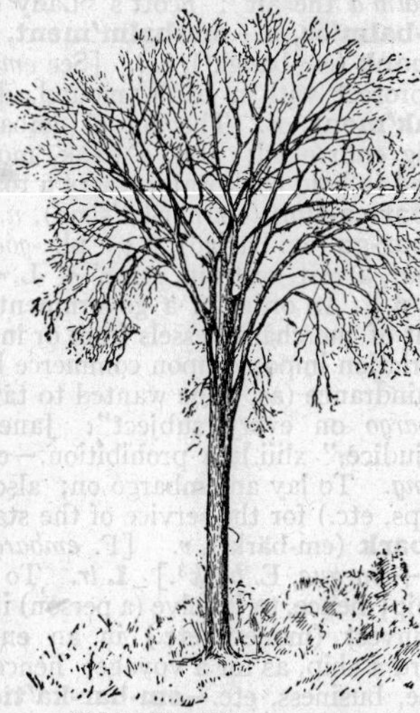
White Elm (*Ulmus americana*).

el-o-cu-tion (el-ǫ-kū′shọn), *n.* [L. *elocutio(n-)*, < *eloqui*, speak out: see *eloquent*.] Effective utterance or expression†; eloquence† or oratory†; in general, speech† (as, "Best of fruits . . . Whose taste . . . Gave *elocution* to the mute": Milton's "Paradise Lost," ix. 748); now, manner of speaking or utterance with reference to delivery, pronunciation, gesture, etc., esp. in public speaking or reading; the art of public speaking.—**el-o-cu′tion-a-ry** (-ạ-ri), *a.* Of or pertaining to elocution.—**el-o-cu′tion-ist,** *n.* One versed in the art of elocution; one who gives public recitations or readings.

é-loge (ā-lozh), *n.* [F.] A eulogy; a funeral oration.

E-lo-him (e-lō′him or -hēm, or el′ǫ-him), *n.* [Heb. *elōhīm*, pl. of *elōah*, god.] A name of God, frequent in the Hebrew text of the Old Testament.—**E-lo-hist** (e-lō′hist or el′ǫ-hist), *n.* The writer (or writers) of certain parts of the Hebrew text of the Hexateuch in which God is spoken of as *Elohim* instead of *Yahweh* (Jehovah). See *Yahwist*.—**El-o-his-tic** (el-ǫ-his′tik), *a.* Of or pertaining to the Elohist; characterized by the use of *Elohim* instead of *Yahweh* (Jehovah).

e-loin, e-loign (ẹ-loin′), *v. t.* [F. *éloigner*, OF. *esloignier*, < L. *ex*, out of, + *longe*, long, far: cf. *elongate*.] To remove to a distance; also, to carry off; specif., in *law*, to remove out of legal jurisdiction, or conceal, as goods liable to distress.

e-lon-gate (ẹ-lông′gāt or ē′lông-), *v.*; *-gated, -gating.* [LL. *elongatus*, pp. of *elongare*, remove, prolong, < L. *e*, out of, + *longe*, long, far, *longus*, long.] **I.** *tr.* To remove to a distance†; also, to draw out to greater length; lengthen; extend. **II.** *intr.* To recede, as a planet (apparently) from the sun (see *elongation*); also, to increase in length; be comparatively long.—**e-lon′gate,** *a.* Elongated; in *bot.* and *zoöl.*, comparatively or disproportionately long.—**e-lon-ga-tion** (ē-lông-gā′shọn), *n.* The act of elongating, or the state of being elongated; also, that which is elongated; an elongated part; an extension; in *astron.*, the angular distance of a planet from the sun, or of a satellite from its primary.

e-lope (ẹ-lōp′), *v. i.*; *eloped, eloping.* [AF. *aloper*: cf. D. *ontloopen* (= G. *entlaufen*), run away, elope.] To run away from one's spouse with a paramour; also, to run away from home with a lover (whether with the expectation of marrying or not); in general, to run away from one's place or duty; abscond; escape.—**e-lope′ment,** *n.*—**e-lop-er** (ẹ-lō′pėr), *n.*

el-o-quence (el′ǫ-kwẹns), *n.* The quality of being eloquent; also, the action, practice, or art of using language with fluency, power, and aptness; also, eloquent language or discourse (as, a flow of *eloquence*).

el-o-quent (el′ǫ-kwẹnt), *a.* [OF. *eloquent* (F. *éloquent*), < L. *eloquens* (*-ent-*), ppr. of *eloqui*, speak out, utter, < *e*, out of, + *loqui*, speak.] Having or exercising the power of fluent, forcible, and appropriate speech, as an orator; characterized by forcible and appropriate expression, as a speech; movingly expressive, as looks or gestures.—**el′o-quent-ly,** *adv.*

else (els), *adv.* [AS. *elles* = OHG. *elles, alles*, otherwise, else; akin to Goth. *aljis*, L. *alius*, Gr. ἄλλος, other.] In another or a different case, under other circumstances, or otherwise (often preceded by *or*: as, "Strangle her, *els* she sure will strangle thee," Spenser's "Faerie Queene," i. 1. 19; "But speak fair words, or *else* be mute," Shakspere's "Venus and Adonis," 208); also, in a different manner, respect, time, or place (as, how *else*? when *else*? anywhere *else*); also (as a quasi-adjective), other than the person or thing mentioned (following the word or words with which it is used: as, somebody *else*; no one *else*; nothing *else*; little *else*); in addition; instead. When used after *somebody, no one*, etc., in the possessive case, *else* commonly takes the *'s* (as, *somebody else's* book; *no one else's* business).—**else′where,** *adv.* Somewhere else; in or to some other place.—**else′whith″er,** *adv.* To some other place.—**else′wise,** *adv.* Otherwise.

e-lu-ci-date (ẹ-lū′si-dāt), *v. t.*; *-dated, -dating.* [LL. *elucidatus*, pp. of *elucidare*, < L. *e*, out of, + *lucidus*, light, E. *lucid*.] To make lucid or clear; throw light upon; explain: as, "Man's whole life and environment have been laid open and *elucidated*" (Carlyle's "Sartor Resartus," i. 1).—**e-lu-ci-da′tion** (-dā′shọn), *n.*—**e-lu′ci-da-tive** (-dā-tiv), *a.* Serving to elucidate; explanatory.—**e-lu′ci-da-tor** (-dā-tọr), *n.*—**e-lu′ci-da-to-ry** (-dạ-tǫ-ri), *a.* Elucidative.

e-lude (ẹ-lūd′), *v. t.*; *eluded, eluding.* [L. *eludere* (pp. *elusus*), < *e*, out of, + *ludere*, play.] To avoid or escape by dexterity or artifice (as, to *elude* a blow, attack, seizure, pursuit, or pursuer); slip away from; evade (as, to *elude* vigilance, difficulties, requirements, laws, etc.); of things, to continue to be beyond the reach of (observation, inquiry, the inquirer, etc.); baffle.—**e-lud-er** (ẹ-lū′dėr), *n.*—**e-lud′i-ble,** *a.* That may be eluded.

E-lul (e-löl′), *n.* [Heb.] In the Jewish calendar, the twelfth month (29 days) of the civil year and the sixth of the ecclesiastical year, beginning in August or in the first part of September.

e-lu-sion (ẹ-lū′zhọn), *n.* [ML. *elusio(n-)*.] The act of eluding; evasion.

e-lu-sive (ẹ-lū′siv), *a.* Tending to elude; dexterously evasive; often, eluding clear perception or complete mental grasp; hard to express or define.—**e-lu′sive-ly,** *adv.*—**e-lu′sive-ness,** *n.*

e-lu-so-ry (ẹ-lū′sǫ-ri), *a.* [ML. *elusorius*.] Elusive.

e-lu-tri-ate (ẹ-lū′tri-āt), *v. t.*; *-ated*, *-ating*. [L. *elutriatus*, pp. of *elutriare*, wash out, decant, < *eluere*: see *eluvium*.] To purify by washing and straining or decanting; separate the light and heavy particles of by washing.—**e-lu-tri-a′tion** (-ā′shọn), *n.*—**e-lu′tri-a-tor**, *n.* An elutriating apparatus used in the analysis of soils, etc.

e-lu-vi-um (ẹ-lū′vi-um), *n.*; pl. *-via* (-vi-ạ̈). [NL., < L. *eluere*, wash out or away, < *e*, out of, + *luere*, wash: cf. *alluvium*.] In *geol.*, a deposit of soil, dust, etc., originating in the place where found through decomposition of rock, or drifted by winds: distinguished from *alluvium*.—**e-lu′vi-al**, *a.*

elves (elvz), *n.* Plural of *elf*.—**elv′ish**, *a.* Elfish.

E-ly-sian (ẹ-lizh′ian), *a.* Of or pertaining to Elysium (as, *Elysian* fields, Elysium); hence, resembling Elysium or what is in Elysium; blissful; delightful.

E-ly-sium (ẹ-lizh′ium), *n.* [L., < Gr. Ἠλύσιον (πεδίον), Elysian (plain or field).] The abode of the blessed after death, according to Greek mythology, conceived of as a place of perfect delight (often called *Elysian fields*); hence, any similarly conceived abode or state of the dead; also, any place or state of perfect happiness.

el-y-trum, el-y-tron (el′i-trum, -tron), *n.*; pl. *-tra* (-trạ̈). [NL., < Gr. ἔλυτρον, cover, sheath, < ἐλύειν, roll round, wrap up.] One of the pair of hardened fore wings of certain insects, as beetles, forming a protective covering for the posterior wings.—**el′y-tral**, *a.*

El-ze-vir (el′zẹ-vėr or -vėr). **I.** *a.* Of or pertaining to the Elzevir (Elzevier, or Elsevier) family of Dutch printers and publishers, active chiefly between 1583 and 1680, and famous for their editions of classics and other works, and esp. for their small editions, which are notable for neatness and beauty; pertaining to the books or editions published by the Elzevirs. **II.** *n.* A book printed by one of the Elzevir family; also, a style of printing-type with firm hair-lines and stubby serifs (see *type*).

em[1] (em), *n.* The letter M, m; in *printing*, the square of any size of type (orig. the portion of a line occupied by the letter m), used as the unit of measurement for printed matter.

em[2], **'em** (ẹm), *pron.* [Orig. < ME. *hem*, dat. and acc. pl. of *he*, E. *he*, but now regarded as a reduced form of *them*.] Them. [Colloq.]

em-. A form of the prefix *en-*, orig. meaning 'in,' 'into,' used before *b*, *m*, and *p*, as in *embank*, *embed*, *embitter*, *embody*, *emmesh*, *empower*, *empurple*.

e-ma-ci-ate (ẹ-mā′shi-āt), *v. t.*; *-ated*, *-ating*. [L. *emaciatus*, pp. of *emaciare*, < *e-*, out, + *macies*, leanness, < *macere*, be lean.] To make lean by a gradual wasting away of flesh.—**e-ma′ci-ate**, *a.* Emaciated. [Now poetic.]—**e-ma-ci-a′tion** (-ṣi-ā′shọn), *n.*

em-a-nant (em′ạ-nạnt), *a.* Emanating; issuing as from a source.

em-a-nate (em′ạ-nāt), *v. i.*; *-nated*, *-nating*. [L. *emanatus*, pp. of *emanare*, < *e*, out of, + *manare*, flow.] To flow out, issue, or proceed as from a source or origin; come forth; originate.—**em-a-na′tion** (-nā′shọn), *n.* [LL. *emanatio(n-)*.] The act or fact of emanating; also, something that emanates, as a perfume, gaseous product (cf. *radium emanation*, under *radium*), quality, virtue, etc.; an effluence.—**em′a-na-tive** (-nạ-tiv), *a.* Emanating; characterized by emanation.—**em″a-na-to′ri-um** (-nạ-tō′ri-um), *n.*; pl. *-riums* or *-ria* (-ri-ạ̈). A room or place equipped for the therapeutic treatment of patients by means of the radium emanation.

e-man-ci-pate (ẹ-man′si-pāt), *v. t.*; *-pated*, *-pating*. [L. *emancipatus*, pp. of *emancipare*, < *e*, out of, + *mancipare*, make over as property, < *manus*, hand, + *capere*, take.] Orig., in ancient Roman legal use, to free (a child) from the paternal power; hence, in general, to set free from control, esp. from servitude or bondage; liberate; free from restraint of any kind.—**e-man′ci-pate**, *a.* Emancipated: as, "*Emancipate* From passion's dreams" (Coleridge's "Picture"). [Now chiefly poetic.]—**e-man-ci-pa′tion** (-pā′shọn), *n.* [L. *emancipatio(n-)*.] The act of emancipating, or the fact of being emancipated; liberation; [*cap.*] in *Eng. hist.*, the freeing of Roman Catholics from civil disabilities by the act of Parliament passed in 1829 ('Catholic Emancipation Act').—**Emancipation Proclamation**, in *U. S. hist.*, the proclamation by which, on Jan. 1, 1863, President Lincoln declared free all persons held as slaves within any State or part of a State then in armed rebellion.—**e-man′ci-pa-tive** (-pạ-tiv), *a.* Serving to emancipate.—**e-man′ci-pa-tor** (-pā-tọr), *n.*—**e-man′ci-pa-to-ry** (-pạ-tọ-ri), *a.* Emancipative.

e-mar-gi-nate, e-mar-gi-nat-ed (ẹ-mär′ji-nạ̄t, -nā-ted), *a.* [L. *emarginatus*, pp. of *emarginare*, deprive of the edge, < *e*, out of, + *margo*, E. *margin*.] Notched at the margin; in *bot.*, notched at the apex, as a petal or leaf.—**e-mar-gi-na′tion** (-nā′shọn), *n.* Emarginate condition; also, a notch at the margin; a notch at the apex, as of a petal or leaf.

Emarginate Leaves and Petals. *a, a*, emarginations.

e-mas-cu-late (ẹ-mas′kụ-lāt), *v. t.*; *-lated*, *-lating*. [L. *emasculatus*, pp. of *emasculare*, < *e*, out of, + *masculus*, E. *male*.] To deprive of virility or procreative power; castrate; hence, to deprive of strength or vigor; weaken; render effeminate; specif., to destroy the force of (a book, etc.), as by undue expurgation or injudicious editing.—**e-mas′cu-late** (-lạ̄t), *a.* Emasculated; unmanned; effeminate.—**e-mas-cu-la′tion** (-lā′shọn), *n.*—**e-mas′cu-la-tive** (-lạ̄-tiv), *a.* Tending to emasculate.—**e-mas′cu-la-tor** (-lā-tọr), *n.*—**e-mas′cu-la-to-ry** (-lạ̄-tọ-ri), *a.* Emasculative.

em-balm (em-bäm′), *v. t.* [OF. F. *embaumer*, < *em-* (< L. *in*, in) + *baume*, E. *balm*.] To treat (a dead body) with balsams, spices, etc., or (now usually) with drugs or chemicals, in order to preserve from decay; hence, to preserve from oblivion; keep in memory; also, to impart a balmy fragrance to, or fill with sweet scent (as, "Here eglantine *embalm'd* the air": Scott's "Lady of the Lake," i. 12).—**em-balm′er**, *n.*—**em-balm′ment**, *n.*

em-bank (em-bangk′), *v. t.* [See *em-*.] To inclose, confine, or protect with a bank, mound, dike, or the like.—**em-bank′ment**, *n.* The act of embanking, or the state of being embanked; also, a bank, mound, dike, or the like, raised to hold back water, carry a roadway, etc.

em-bar-ca-tion (em-bär-kā′shọn), *n.* See *embarkation*.

em-bar-go (em-bär′gō), *n.*; pl. *-goes* (-gōz). [Sp., < *embargar*, arrest, restrain, seize, < L. *in*, in, + ML. *barra*, E. *bar*, *n.*] An order of a government prohibiting the movement of merchant vessels from or into its ports; hence, any restriction imposed upon commerce by law; fig., a restraint or hindrance (as, "She wanted to talk, but there seemed an *embargo* on every subject": Jane Austen's "Pride and Prejudice," xliii.); a prohibition.—**em-bar′go**, *v. t.*; *-goed*, *-going*. To lay an embargo on; also, to seize or requisition (ships, etc.) for the service of the state.

em-bark (em-bärk′), *v.* [F. *embarquer*, < *em-* (< L. *in*, in) + *barque*, E. *bark*[3].] **I.** *tr.* To put or receive on board a ship; hence, to involve (a person) in an enterprise; venture or invest (money, etc.) in an enterprise. **II.** *intr.* To board a ship, as for a voyage; hence, to engage in an enterprise, business, etc.—**em-bar-ka′tion** (-bär-kā′shọn), **em-bark′ment**, *n.* The act or process of embarking.

em-bar-rass (em-bar′ạs), *v. t.* [F. *embarrasser*, < Sp. *embarazar* or It. *imbarazzare*, < L. *in*, in, + ML. *barra*, E. *bar*, *n.*] To put obstacles or difficulties in the way of; impede; hamper; also, to beset with financial difficulties; burden with debt; also, to perplex mentally; confuse; disconcert; abash; also, to render difficult or intricate, as a question or problem; complicate.—**em-bar′rassed-ly**, *adv.*—**em-bar′rass-ing-ly**, *adv.*—**em-bar′rass-ment**, *n.* The act of embarrassing; embarrassed state; also, that which embarrasses; an impediment or hindrance.

em-bas-sa-dor (em-bas′ạ-dọr), *n.* See *ambassador*.

em-bas-sage (em′bạ-sạ̄j), *n.* The mission or service of an ambassador; a message; a body of persons sent on a mission, as to a sovereign. [Archaic.]

em-bas-sy (em′bạ-si), *n.*; pl. *-sies* (-siz). [See *ambassy*.] The function or office of an ambassador; also, the sending of ambassadors; also, the message or charge intrusted to an ambassador (as, "Lastly came Ariel . . . Who bears all fairy *embassies* afar": Hood's "Midsummer Fairies," ix.); also, a body of persons intrusted with a mission to a sovereign or government; an ambassador and his retinue: also, the official residence of an ambassador.

Escutcheon with a Fesse Embattled.

em-bat-tle[1] (em-bat′l), *v. t.*; *-tled, -tling.* [OF. F. *embatailler*, < *em-* (< L. *in*, in) + *bataille*, E. *battle*[1], *n.*] To arrange in order of battle; prepare for battle; arm; also, to fortify (a town, etc.).

em-bat-tle[2] (em-bat′l), *v. t.*; *-tled, -tling.* [See *em-* and *battle*[2].] To furnish with battlements; hence, to form with square indentations: chiefly in *embattled*, *p. a.*—**em-bat′tle-ment,** *n.* A battlement.

Embattled Molding. — Cathedral of Lincoln, England.

em-bay (em-bā′), *v. t.* [See *em-*.] To put or force (a vessel) into a bay; detain within a bay; also, to inclose in or as in a bay; surround or envelop.—**em-bay′ment,** *n.* The act of embaying; the formation of a portion of water or coast into a bay; a bay or bay-like recess.

em-bed (em-bed′), *v. t.*; *-bedded, -bedding.* [See *em-*.] To fix or inclose in a surrounding mass; also, to lay in or as in a bed.—**em-bed′ment,** *n.*

em-bel-lish (em-bel′ish), *v. t.* [OF. F. *embellir* (*embelliss-*), < *em-* (< L. *in*, in) + *bel*, handsome, fine: see *beau*.] To beautify by or as by ornamentation; ornament; adorn; also, to enhance (a statement or narrative) with fictitious additions; embroider.—**em-bel′lish-er,** *n.*—**em-bel′lish-ment,** *n.* The act of embellishing, or the state of being embellished; ornamentation; also, that which embellishes; an ornament or decoration; also, a fictitious addition, as in a statement.

em-ber[1] (em′bėr), *n.* [AS. *ǣmerge* = Icel. *eimyrja*.] A small live coal, brand of wood, etc.; *pl.*, the smoldering remains of a fire (often fig.: as, "O joy! that in our *embers* Is something that doth live," Wordsworth's "Intimations of Immortality," ix.).

em-ber[2] (em′bėr), *n.* [AS. *ymbren*, appar. < *ymbryne*, circuit, course, < *ymb*, around, + *ryne*, a running.] A quarterly season of fasting and prayer (the Wednesday, Friday, and Saturday after the first Sunday in Lent, after Whitsunday, after Sept. 14, and after Dec. 13) observed in the Roman Catholic and other Western churches: only in composition, as in *ember-day, ember-eve, ember-week, embertide.*

em-ber=goose (em′bėr-gös), *n.* [From Scand.] The common loon, or great northern diver.

em-bez-zle (em-bez′l), *v. t.*; *-zled, -zling.* [AF. *embeseiller*, < *em-* (< L. *in*, in) + OF. *besillier*, maltreat, destroy, dissipate.] To make away with†; also, to squander†; dissipate†; also, to appropriate fraudulently to one's own use, as money intrusted to one's care.—**em-bez′zle-ment,** *n.*—**em-bez′zler,** *n.*

em-bi-ot-o-cid (em-bi-ot′ọ-sid), *n.* [NL. *Embiotocidæ*, pl., < Gr. ἔμβιος, in life (< ἐν, in, + βίος, life), + τίκτειν, bring forth.] Any fish of the acanthopterygian family *Embiotocidæ*, chiefly of the shallow waters of the Pacific coast of North America, notable for being viviparous.

em-bit-ter (em-bit′ėr), *v. t.* [See *em-*.] To make bitter or more bitter (often fig.); render distressful or unhappy, as one's life; make hostile, or more violent or malignant, as persons or feelings.—**em-bit′ter-ment,** *n.*

em-blaze[1] (em-blāz′), *v. t.*; *-blazed, -blazing.* [See *em-*.] To blaze or blazon heraldically; emblazon.

em-blaze[2] (em-blāz′), *v. t.*; *-blazed, -blazing.* [See *em-*.] To set ablaze; cause to blaze, glow, or shine.

em-bla-zon (em-blā′zọn), *v. t.* [See *em-*.] To portray or inscribe on or as on a heraldic shield; also, to adorn with heraldic devices; hence, to embellish or decorate; also, to proclaim; celebrate or extol.—**em-bla′zon-er,** *n.*—**em-bla′zon-ment,** *n.* The act of emblazoning; that which is emblazoned.—**em-bla′zon-ry,** *n.* The act or art of emblazoning; heraldic decoration; hence, brilliant representation or embellishment.

em-blem (em′blem), *n.* [L. *emblema*, inlaid work, ornamentation, < Gr. ἔμβλημα, an insertion, < ἐμβάλλειν, throw in, < ἐν, in, + βάλλειν, throw.] An inlaid ornament† or inlaid work† (as, "The ground, more colour'd than with stone Of costliest *emblem*": Milton's "Paradise Lost," iv. 703); also, an allegorical drawing or picture, often with explanatory writing; a fable or allegory capable of being expressed pictorially; also, an object, or a representation of it, symbolizing a quality, state, class of persons, etc.; a symbol; also, an object used symbolically as the distinctive badge of a person, family, nation, etc.—**em′blem,** *v. t.* To emblematize.—**em-blem-at′ic** (-ble-mat′ik), *a.* Pertaining to, of the nature of, or serving as an emblem; symbolic; typical. Also **em-blem-at′i-cal.**—**em-blem-at′i-cal-ly,** *adv.*—**em-blem′a-tist** (-ạ-tist), *n.* A designer, maker, or user of emblems.—**em-blem′a-tize,** *v. t.*; *-tized, -tizing.* To serve as an emblem of; represent by an emblem; symbolize.

em-ble-ments (em′blẹ-mẹnts), *n. pl.* [OF. *emblaement*, < *emblaer* (F. *emblaver*), < ML. *imbladare*, sow with grain, < L. *in*, in, + ML. *bladum*, grain.] In *law*, the products or profits of land which has been sown or planted.

em-bod-i-ment (em-bod′i-mẹnt), *n.* The act of embodying; the state or fact of being embodied; also, something embodied; that in which something is embodied; an incarnation.

em-bod-y (em-bod′i), *v.*; *-bodied, -bodying.* [See *em-*.] **I.** *tr.* To invest with a body, as a spirit; incarnate; make corporeal; also, to give a concrete form to; express or exemplify (ideas, etc.) in concrete form; also, to collect into or include in a body; organize; incorporate; also, to embrace or comprise. **II.** *intr.* To unite in a body.

em-bog (em-bog′), *v. t.*; *-bogged, -bogging.* [See *em-*.] To cause to stick in a bog.

em-bold-en (em-bōl′dn), *v. t.* [See *em-*.] To make bold or more bold; hearten or encourage.—**em-bold′en-er,** *n.*

em-bol-ic (em-bol′ik), *a.* [See *embolus*.] Inserted; intercalated; in *pathol.*, pertaining to an embolus or to embolism.

em-bo-lism (em′bọ-lizm), *n.* [LL. *embolismus*, < Gr. ἐμβάλλειν, throw in: see *emblem*.] Intercalation, as of a day in a year; a period of time intercalated; in *pathol.*, the occlusion of a blood-vessel by an embolus.—**em-bo-lis′mic** (-liz′mik), *a.*

em-bo-lus (em′bọ-lus), *n.*; pl. *-li* (-lī). [L. *embolus*, piston, < Gr. ἔμβολος, peg, stopper, < ἐμβάλλειν, throw in: see *emblem*.] Something inserted, as a piston or a wedge†; in *pathol.*, a clot of fibrin, a globule of fat, or the like, carried by the blood-current and lodged in a blood-vessel so as to obstruct the circulation.

em-bon-point (oṅ-bôṅ-pwaṅ), *n.* [F., < *en bon point*, in good condition.] Plumpness; stoutness; corpulence.

em-bor-der (em-bôr′dėr), *v. t.* [See *em-*.] To furnish with or form into a border. [Obs. or archaic.]

em-bos-om (em-bu̇z′ọm), *v. t.* [See *em-*.] To take into or hold in the bosom; embrace; cherish; foster; also, to infold, envelop, or inclose (as, "the masses of noble wood *embosoming* the villages": Kingsley's "Yeast," iii.).

em-boss[1] (em-bos′), *v. t.* [Cf. OF. *bos, bois*, wood, also E. *ambush*.] To shelter in a wood or thicket†; also, to drive (a hunted animal) to exhaustion†; cause to foam at the mouth†; cover with foam (obs. or archaic).

em-boss[2] (em-bos′ or -bôs′), *v. t.* [See *em-* and *boss*[2].] To cause to bulge out; make protuberant; cover or stud with protuberances; specif., to raise or represent in relief; also, to fashion relief work upon; also, to ornament with or as with bosses; decorate.—**em-boss′er,** *n.*—**em-boss′ment,** *n.* The act of embossing; also, a bulging or protuberance; also, an embossed ornament; embossed ornamentation.

em-bou-chure (oṅ-bö-shür), *n.* [F., < *emboucher*, put to the mouth, discharge by a mouth or outlet, < *em-* (< L. *in*, in) + *bouche*, mouth, < L. *bucca*, cheek, mouth.] The mouth of a river, etc.; hence, the opening out of a valley into a plain; also, a mouthpiece, as of a wind-instrument; the adjustment of a player's mouth to such a mouthpiece.

em-bow (em-bō′), *v. t.* [See *em-*.] To bend or curve into the form of a bow; arch or vault. [Archaic.]

em-bow-el (em-bou′ẹl), *v. t.*; *-eled* or *-elled, -eling* or *-elling.* [See *em-*.] To inclose in the bowels or innermost recesses; also, to disembowel.

em-bow-er (em-bou′ėr), *v. t.* [See *em-*.] To shelter in or as in a bower; cover or surround with foliage: as, a house *embowered* among trees.

em-brace[1] (em-brās′), *v. t.*; *-braced, -bracing.* [OF. F. *embraser*, set on fire, inflame, < *em-* (< L. *in*, in) + *brase* (F. *braise*), live coals: see *braise.*] In *law*, to attempt to influence corruptly, as a court or a jury.

em-brace[2] (em-brās′), *v.*; *-braced, -bracing.* [OF. *embracier* (F. *embrasser*), < ML. *imbrachiare*, < L. *in*, in, + *brachium*, arm.] **I.** *tr.* To take or clasp in the arms; press to the bosom; hug; hence, to take or receive gladly or eagerly; accept willingly; avail one's self of (an opportunity, etc.); also, to adopt (a profession, a religion, etc.); also, to undertake†; also, to accept with resignation; submit to (adverse fortune, etc.); also, to encircle as if with arms (as, "You'll see your Rome *embraced* with fire": Shakspere's "Coriolanus," v. 2. 7); surround; inclose; hence, to include, contain, or comprise (as, a subject *embracing* many topics); also, to take in with the eye or the mind. **II.** *intr.* To join in an embrace.—**em-brace′**[2], *n.* The act of embracing; a clasping in the arms.—**em-brace′a-ble,** *a.*—**em-brace′-ment,** *n.*

em-bra-cer[1], **em-brace-or** (em-brā′sėr, -sọr), *n.* [OF. *embraseur*, < *embraser*: see *embrace*[1].] In *law*, one who attempts to influence a jury, etc., by any corrupt means.

em-bra-cer[2] (em-brā′sėr), *n.* One who embraces, as in the arms.

em-bra-cer-y (em-brā′sėr-i), *n.* In *law*, the offense of an embracer. See *embracer*[1].

em-branch-ment (em-brȧnch′mẹnt), *n.* [See *em-*.] A branching or ramification; also, a branch.

em-bran-gle (em-brang′gl), *v. t.*; *-gled, -gling.* [See *em-* and *brangle.*] To confuse; entangle; embroil.—**em-bran′gle-ment,** *n.*

em-bra-sure (em-brā′zhụ̈r), *n.* [F. *embrasure*, < *embraser*, *ébraser*, to splay (an opening).] In *arch.*, an enlargement of the aperture of a door or window, at the inside face of the wall, by means of splayed sides; in *fort.*, an opening in a wall or parapet through which a gun may be fired, constructed with sides which flare outward; a loophole, crenel, or the like.

em-bro-cate (em′brọ-kāt), *v. t.*; *-cated, -cating.* [ML. *embrocatus*, pp. of *embrocare*, < LL. *embrocha*, < Gr. ἐμβροχή, lotion, < ἐμβρέχειν, steep, foment, < ἐν, in, + βρέχειν, wet.] To moisten and rub with a liniment or lotion.—**em-bro-ca′tion** (-kā′shọn), *n.* The act of embrocating a bruised or diseased part of the body; also, the liquid used for this; a liniment or lotion.

em-bro-glio (em-brō′lyō), *n.* Erroneous form of *imbroglio.*

em-broi-der (em-broi′dėr), *v. t.* [Appar. < *em-* + *broider*: cf. OF. *embroder.*] To decorate with ornamental needlework; execute (ornamentation) with the needle; fig., to adorn; embellish rhetorically, esp. with fictitious additions. —**em-broi′der-er,** *n.*—**em-broi′der-y,** *n.*; pl. *-ies* (-iz). The act of embroidering; also, embroidered work or ornamentation; fig., embellishment.

em-broil (em-broil′), *v. t.* [F. *embrouiller*, < *em-* (< L. *in*, in) + *brouiller*, E. *broil*[1].] To throw into a state of confusion; confuse; complicate; also, to bring into a state of discord; involve in contention or strife (as, "He has used all his efforts to render me uncomfortable, and *embroil* me with others": Marryat's "Peter Simple," lxii.).—**em-broil′er,** *n.*—**em-broil′ment,** *n.*

em-brown (em-broun′), *v. t.* or *i.* [See *em-*.] To make or become brown or dark.

em-brue (em-brö′), *v. t.* Same as *imbrue.*

em-brute (em-bröt′), etc. Same as *imbrute*, etc.

em-bry-o (em′bri-ō). [NL. *embryon*, < Gr. ἔμβρυον, embryo, < ἐν, in, + βρύειν, swell.] **I.** *n.*; pl. *-os* (-ōz). An organism in the earlier stages of its development, as before emergence from the egg; among mammals and other viviparous animals, a young animal during its earlier stages within the mother's body (cf. *fetus*); fig., the beginning or rudimentary stage of anything; in *bot.*, the rudimentary plant contained in the seed, the result of the action of pollen upon the ovule. **II.** *a.* Being in the first or rudimentary stage of development; undeveloped; immature.—**em″bry-o-gen′e-sis** (-ọ-jen′e-sis), *n.* Embryogeny.—**em″bry-o-ge-net′ic** (-jẹ-net′ik), *a.*—**em-bry-og′e-ny** (-oj′e-ni), *n.* [See *-geny.*] The formation and development of the embryo, as a subject of scientific study.—**em″bry-o-gen′ic,** *a.* —**em-bry-ol′o-gy** (-ol′ọ-ji), *n.* [See *-logy.*] The science of the embryo, its genesis, development, etc.—**em″bry-o-log′ic, em″bry-o-log′i-cal** (-loj′ik, -i-kạl), *a.*—**em-bry-ol′o-gist,** *n.*—**em′bry-o-nal** (-ọ-nạl), *a.* Of or pertaining to an embryo; embryonic.—**em-bry-on′ic** (-on′ik), *a.* Pertaining to or in the state of an embryo; rudimentary; undeveloped.—**em-bry-on′i-cal-ly,** *adv.*—**em′bry-o=sac** (-ō-sak), *n.* In *bot.*, the megaspore of a seed-bearing plant, being situated within the ovule, giving rise to the endosperm or supposed female prothallium, and forming the cell in which the embryo is developed.

e-meer (e-mēr′), *n.* See *emir.*

e-mend (ẹ-mend′), *v. t.* [L. *emendare* (pp. *emendatus*), < *e*, out of, + *mendum*, *menda*, fault, error: cf. *amend.*] To free from faults or errors; correct; now, usually, to amend (a text) by removing errors.—**e-mend′a-ble,** *a.* Capable of being emended.—**e-men-date** (ē′men-dāt), *v. t.*; *-dated, -dating.* [L. *emendatus*, pp. of *emendare.*] To emend (a text).—**e-men-da-tion** (ē-men-dā′shọn or em-en-), *n.* [L. *emendatio(n-).*] The act of emending, or the fact of being emended; a correction, as in a text.—**e′men-da-tor,** *n.* One who emends; esp., one who subjects a text to emendation.—**e-men-da-to-ry** (ẹ-men′dạ-tọ-ri), *a.* Serving to emend; also, of or pertaining to emendation.—**e-mend′er,** *n.*

em-e-rald (em′ẹ-rạld). [OF. *esmeralde* (F. *émeraude*), < L. *smaragdus*, < Gr. σμάραγδος, a green precious stone.] **I.** *n.* A green variety of beryl, used as a gem when transparent; hence, its characteristic color, a clear, deep green; also, a printing-type (6½ point) of a size between nonpareil and minion (Eng.). **II.** *a.* Of a clear, deep green color.—**Emerald Isle,** Ireland: so called from its verdure.—**em′e-rald=green′,** *a.* and *n.*

e-merge (ẹ-mėrj′), *v. i.*; *emerged, emerging.* [L. *emergere* (pp. *emersus*), < *e*, out of, + *mergere*, dip, E. *merge.*] To rise or come forth from, or as from, water or other liquid; also, to come forth into view or notice, as from concealment or obscurity; issue; also, to come up or arise, as a question or difficulty.—**e-mer-gence** (ẹ-mėr′jẹns), *n.* The act or fact of emerging; also, something that emerges; an outgrowth, as a prickle, on the surface of an organ; sometimes, an emergency.—**e-mer′gen-cy** (-jẹn-si), *n.*; pl. *-cies* (-siz). Emergence; also, an unforeseen occurrence; a sudden and urgent occasion for action; an exigency.—**e-mer′gent,** *a.* Emerging; rising from a liquid or other surrounding medium; coming into view or notice; issuing; arising casually or unexpectedly; hence, calling for immediate action; urgent. —**e-mer′gent-ly,** *adv.*

e-mer-i-tus (ẹ-mer′i-tus). [L., pp. of *emerere*, serve out one's time, < *e*, out of, + *merere*, deserve, serve.] **I.** *a.* Retired or honorably discharged from active duty because of age, infirmity, or long service, but retained on the rolls: as, a professor *emeritus.* **II.** *n.*; pl. *-ti* (-tī). One honorably discharged from active service.

em-e-rods (em′ẹ-rodz), *n. pl.* Hemorrhoids. See 1 Sam. v. 6. [Archaic.]

e-mersed (ẹ-mėrst′), *a.* [L. *emersus*, pp. of *emergere*: see *emerge.*] Having emerged; in *bot.*, risen or standing out of water, surrounding leaves, etc.—**e-mer-sion** (ẹ-mėr′shọn), *n.* The act or fact of emerging; in *astron.*, the reappearance of a heavenly body after an eclipse or occultation.

em-e-ry (em′ẹ-ri), *n.* [OF. *emmery*, *esmeril* (F. *émeri*), < It. *smeriglio*, < Gr. σμύρις, emery.] A granular mineral substance consisting typically of corundum mixed with magnetite or hematite: used in a powdered, crushed, or consolidated form for grinding and polishing.—**em′e-ry=cloth,** *n.* Cloth prepared like emery-paper.—**em′e-ry=pa″per,** *n.* Paper coated with crushed or powdered emery: used for smoothing or polishing metallic surfaces, etc.—**em′e-ry=wheel,** *n.* A wheel for grinding or polishing, consisting mostly of or faced with emery.

em-e-sis (em′e-sis), *n.* [NL., < Gr. ἔμεσις, < ἐμεῖν, vomit, akin to L. *vomere*, E. *vomit.*] In *pathol.*, vomiting.

e-met-ic (ẹ-met′ik). [L. *emeticus*, < Gr. ἐμετικός, < ἐμεῖν: see *emesis.*] **I.** *a.* Inducing vomiting, as a medicinal substance. **II.** *n.* An emetic medicine or agent.—**em-e-tine** (em′e-tin), *n.* An alkaloid with emetic and other medicinal properties, obtained from ipecacuanha.

e-meu (ē′mū), *n.* See *emu.*

é-meute (ā-mėt), *n.* [F.] A riot; a popular outbreak.
-emia, -æmia. [NL., also *-hemia, -hæmia,* < Gr. αἷμα, blood.] A noun termination occurring in pathological terms referring to the blood, as in *anemia* or *anæmia, hydremia* or *hydræmia, hyperemia, leucemia, toxemia.*
em-i-grant (em′i-grąnt). **I.** *a.* Emigrating. **II.** *n.* One who emigrates, as from his native country.
em-i-grate (em′i-grāt), *v.*; *-grated, -grating.* [L. *emigratus,* pp. of *emigrare,* < *e,* out of, + *migrare,* migrate.] **I.** *intr.* To leave one country or region for the purpose of settling in another; migrate. **II.** *tr.* To cause to emigrate.—**em-i-gra′tion** (-grā′shǫn), *n.* [LL. *emigratio(n-).*] The act of emigrating; also, a body of emigrants; emigrants collectively.—**em-i-gra′tion-al,** *a.*—**em′i-gra-tor,** *n.*
é-mi-gré (ā-mē-grā), *n.*; pl. *-grés* (F. -grā). [F., pp. of *émigrer,* < L. *emigrare:* see *emigrate.*] In French use, an emigrant; esp., one of the royalists who became refugees from France during the revolution that began in 1789.
em-i-nence (em′i-nęns), *n.* The state or quality of being eminent; height†; a high place or part; a hill or elevation; high station, rank, or repute; distinction; superiority; a superior or unusual degree†; [usually *cap.*] in the *Rom. Cath. Ch.,* the title of honor of a cardinal.—**em′i-nen-cy,** *n.* Same as *eminence.* [Now rare.]
em-i-nent (em′i-nęnt), *a.* [L. *eminens (-ent-),* ppr. of *eminere,* stand out, < *e,* out of, + *-minere,* project, akin to *minari,* jut out, threaten: see *menace.*] Lofty, or standing out above other things (now rare: as, "upon an high mountain and *eminent,*" Ezek. xvii. 22); projecting (now rare); also, high in station, rank, or repute; distinguished; also, conspicuous, signal, or noteworthy (as, *eminent* services; *eminent* fairness); also, supreme or controlling (as, *eminent* domain: see *domain*).—**em′i-nent-ly,** *adv.*
e-mir (e-mēr′), *n.* [= *amir.*] An Arabian chieftain or prince; also, a title of honor of the descendants of Mohammed; also, the title of certain Turkish officials.
em-is-sa-ry (em′i-sā-ri). [L. *emissarius,* < *emittere:* see *emit.*] **I.** *a.* Sent forth, as on a mission; pertaining to one so sent forth. **II.** *n.*; pl. *-ries* (-riz). An agent sent on a mission or errand (as, "I am your grandmother's *emissary.* She could not come herself": Hardy's "Two on a Tower," xxxv.); often, an agent sent on a mission of a secret nature (commonly used in a bad or contemptuous sense); also, an outlet; a channel; a duct.
e-mis-sion (ę-mish′ǫn), *n.* [L. *emissio(n-),* < *emittere:* see *emit.*] The act of emitting, or the state of being emitted; also, that which is emitted; a discharge; an emanation; an issue, as of bank-notes.
e-mis-sive (ę-mis′iv), *a.* Serving to emit; pertaining to emission.—**em-is-siv-i-ty** (em-i-siv′i-ti), *n.*
e-mit (ę-mit′), *v. t.*; *emitted, emitting.* [L. *emittere* (pp. *emissus*), < *e,* out of, + *mittere,* send.] To send forth or give out or forth (liquid, light, heat, sound, etc.); discharge; also, to utter, as opinions; issue, as proclamations; issue formally for circulation, as bank-notes.—**e-mit′ter,** *n.*
Em-man-u-el (e-man′ū-el), *n.* See *Immanuel.*
em-men-a-gogue (e-men′ą-gog), *n.* [Gr. ἔμμηνα, menses (< ἐν, in, + μήν, month), + ἀγωγός, leading, < ἄγειν, lead.] A medicine that promotes the menstrual discharge.
em-mer (em′ėr), *n.* [G.] Same as *amelcorn.*
em-mesh (e-mesh′), *v. t.* Same as *enmesh.*
em-met (em′et), *n.* [AS. *ǣmete:* see *ant.*] An ant: as, "The parsimonious *emmet,* provident Of future" (Milton's "Paradise Lost," vii. 485). [Archaic or prov.]
em-me-tro-pi-a (em-e-trō′pi-ą), *n.* [NL., < Gr. ἔμμετρος, in measure (< ἐν, in, + μέτρον, measure), + ὤψ, eye.] The normal refractive condition of the eye, in which the rays of light are accurately focused on the retina and there is perfect vision.—**em-me-trop′ic** (-trop′ik), *a.*
e-mol-lient (ę-mol′yęnt). [L. *emolliens (-ent-),* ppr. of *emollire,* soften, < *e-,* out, + *mollire,* make soft, < *mollis,* soft.] In *med.*: **I.** *a.* Having the power of softening or relaxing living tissues, as a medicinal substance; soothing. **II.** *n.* An emollient medicine or agent.
e-mol-u-ment (ę-mol′ū-męnt), *n.* [L. *emolumentum, emolimentum,* < *emoliri,* bring out by effort, < *e,* out of, + *moliri,* exert one's self, build: see *demolish.*] Profit arising from office or employment (as, "These men were accustomed, in addition to the large regular *emoluments* of the office, to exact heavy fees from the prisoners": Lecky's "Hist. of Eng. in the 18th Century," iii.); compensation for services, in the form of salary, fees, or perquisites; also, benefit† or advantage†.
e-mo-tion (ę-mō′shǫn), *n.* [L. *emovere* (pp. *emotus*), move out, stir up, < *e,* out of, + *movere,* E. *move.*] A moving† or agitation† (as, "The winds of Heaven mix for ever With a sweet *emotion*": Shelley's "Love's Philosophy"); also, a disturbance†; also, agitation or disturbance of mind; any agitated or intense state of mind; specif., an affective state of consciousness in which joy, sorrow, fear, hate, or the like, is experienced (distinguished from cognitive and volitional states of consciousness); any of the feelings of joy, sorrow, fear, hate, love, etc.—**e-mo′tion-al,** *a.* Pertaining to emotion or the emotions; also, appealing to the emotions; also, subject to or easily affected by emotion.—**e-mo′tion-al-ism,** *n.* Emotional character; appeal to the emotions; tendency to emotion, esp. morbid emotion; expression of emotion.—**e-mo′tion-al-ist,** *n.* One who appeals to the emotions, esp. unduly; also, one who bases theories of conduct, etc., on the emotions; also, one easily affected by emotion.—**e-mo-tion-al′i-ty** (-al′i-ti), *n.* Emotional state or quality.—**e-mo′tion-al-ize,** *v. t.*; *-ized, -izing.* To render emotional; treat as a matter of emotion.—**e-mo′tion-al-ly,** *adv.*
e-mo-tive (ę-mō′tiv), *a.* [L. *emotus,* pp.: see *emotion.*] Characterized by or pertaining to emotion; exciting emotion.—**e-mo′tive-ly,** *adv.*—**e-mo′tive-ness, e-mo-tiv-i-ty** (ē-mǫ-tiv′i-ti), *n.*
em-pale (em-pāl′), etc. Same as *impale,* etc.
em-pan-el (em-pan′ęl), etc. Same as *impanel,* etc.
em-par-a-dise (em-par′ą-dīs), *v. t.* Same as *imparadise.*
em-pa-thy (em′pą-thi), *n.* [Gr. ἐν, in, + παθεῖν, suffer, feel: formed as an equivalent of G. *einfühlung,* lit. 'in-feeling.'] In *psychol.,* mental entrance into the feeling or spirit of a person or thing; appreciative perception or understanding.—**em-path′ic** (-path′ik), *a.*
em-pen-nage (em′pę-nāj, F. oṅ-pė-näzh), *n.* [F., < *empenner,* feather (an arrow), < *em-* (< L. *in,* in) + *penne,* < L. *penna,* feather.] In *aëronautics,* an equipment of small horizontal stabilizing planes at the tail of an aëroplane or the stern of a dirigible.
em-per-or (em′pėr-ǫr), *n.* [OF. *empereor* (F. *empereur*), < L. *imperator,* < *imperare,* command: see *empire.*] A commander†; also, the sovereign or supreme ruler of an empire; in *zoöl.,* any of various moths, butterflies, birds, etc., notable for their size, color, etc.—**emperor of Japan,** a large chætodont food-fish, *Holacanthus imperator,* of the seas of southern Japan, of oblong form and brilliant coloration. Also called *emperor-fish.*—**em′per-or-ship,** *n.*

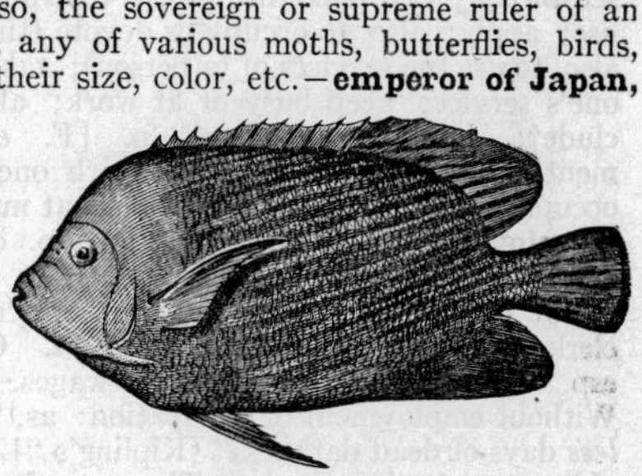
Emperor of Japan.

em-per-y (em′pėr-i), *n.* [OF. *emperie,* var. of *empire:* see *empire.*] Empire; absolute dominion; also, the territory of an emperor. [Now poetic.]
em-pha-sis (em′fą-sis), *n.*; pl. *emphases* (-sēz). [L. *emphasis,* < Gr. ἔμφασις, significance, < ἐμφαίνειν, exhibit, indicate, < ἐν, in, + φαίνειν, show.] Special and significant stress of voice laid on particular words or syllables; also, intensity or force of expression, action, etc.; also, stress laid upon, or importance or significance attached to, anything; also, prominence, as of outline.—**em′pha-size** (-sīz), *v. t.*; *-sized, -sizing.* To give emphasis to; lay stress upon; stress.
em-phat-ic (em-fat′ik), *a.* [Gr. ἐμφατικός, < ἐμφαίνειν: see *emphasis.*] Uttered, or to be uttered, with emphasis; strongly expressive; also, forcibly significant; strongly marked; striking; also, using emphasis in speech or action.—**em-phat′i-cal-ly,** *adv.*
em-phy-se-ma (em-fi-sē′mą), *n.* [NL., < Gr. ἐμφύσημα, < ἐμφυσᾶν, inflate, < ἐν, in, + φυσᾶν, blow, < φῦσα, bellows.]

In *pathol.*, abnormal distention of a part with air or other gas.—**em-phy-sem′a-tous** (-sem′ạ-tus or -sē′mạ-tus), *a.*

em-pire (em′pīr), *n.* [OF. F. *empire*, < L. *imperium*, a command, right of commanding, authority, sovereignty, realm, < *imperare*, command, < *in*, in, + *parare*, make ready, prepare, order.] Supreme command or authority; esp., supreme power in governing; sovereignty; absolute sway; also, a government under an emperor (as, the first French *empire*, 1804–15; the second French *empire*, 1852–70); also, a territory of greater extent than a kingdom ruled by a single sovereign; an aggregate of states ruled over by an emperor or other powerful sovereign or government.—**Empire Day,** May 24, the anniversary of the day of birth of Queen Victoria (1819–1901), observed throughout the British Empire.—**Empire State,** the State of New York. —**Empire style,** a style developed or in vogue under the first French empire (1804–15): applied esp. to certain characteristic styles of interior decoration, furniture, etc., and of women's dress (implying esp. a high waist-line, with undraped skirts hanging loosely).

em-pir-ic (em-pir′ik). [L. *empiricus*, < Gr. ἐμπειρικός, < ἐμπειρία, experience, < ἔμπειρος, experienced, < ἐν, in, + πεῖρα, trial, experiment.] **I.** *a.* Empirical. **II.** *n.* One of a sect of ancient Greek physicians who followed empirical methods; any one who follows an empirical method; also, a quack; a charlatan.—**em-pir′i-cal,** *a.* Pertaining to, derived from, or guided by experience or experiment; also, dependent upon experience or observation alone, without regard to science or theory, esp. in medical practice; hence, unscientific; charlatanic.—**em-pir′i-cal-ly,** *adv.*—**em-pir′i-cism** (-sizm), *n.* Empirical method or practice; esp., undue reliance upon experience; unscientific practice; quackery; in *philos.*, the doctrine that all knowledge is derived from experience.—**em-pir′i-cist** (-sist), *n.*

em-pi-rism (em′pi-rizm), *n.* [= F. *empirisme*, < Gr. ἔμπειρος: see *empiric.*] Empiricism.—**em-pi-ris′tic** (-ris′tik), *a.* Empirical.

em-place (em-plās′), *v. t.*; *-placed, -placing.* [F. *emplacer*, < *em-* (< L. *in*, in) + *place*: see *place.*] To put in place or position; fix in or on an emplacement.—**em-place′ment,** *n.* [F. *emplacement.*] A putting in place or position; location; in *fort.*, the space, platform, or the like for a gun or battery and its accessories.

em-ploy (em-ploi′), *v. t.* [OF. *emploier* (F. *employer*), apply, employ, orig. infold, for *empleier*, var. of *emplier*: see *imply.*] To make use of (an instrument, means, etc.); use; apply; also, to occupy or devote (time, energies, etc.); also, to use the services of (a person); take, have, or keep in one's service; keep busy or at work; also, to infold†; include†; imply†.—**em-ploy′,** *n.* [F. *emploi.*] Employment; service; also, that on which one is employed; an occupation.—**em-ploy′a-ble,** *a.* That may be employed.—**em-ploy-é** (oṅ-plwo-yā), *n.* [F., pp. of *employer.*] An employee.—**em-ploy-ee** (em-ploi-ē′), *n.* A person who is in the employ or regular working service of another, as a clerk, workman, etc.—**em-ploy′er,** *n.* One who employs, esp., one who employs others for wages.—**em-ploy′less,** *a.* Without employment or occupation: as, "the long, *employless* days of dead darkness" (Kipling's "Light That Failed," xi.).—**em-ploy′ment,** *n.* The act of employing, or the state of being employed; also, that on which one is employed; work; occupation; business.

em-poi-son (em-poi′zn), *v. t.* [OF. F. *empoisonner*, < *em-* (< L. *in*, in) + *poison*, E. *poison.*] To poison; taint; embitter. [Archaic.]

em-po-ri-um (em-pō′ri-um), *n.*; pl. *-ums.* [L., < Gr. ἐμπόριον, < ἔμπορος, traveler, merchant, < ἐν, in, + -πορος, akin to πόρος, passage, way, E. *pore*[2].] A place of trade; a mart; a town or city of important commerce, esp. a principal center of trade; also, a shop or bazaar.

em-pow-er (em-pou′ėr), *v. t.* [See *em-*.] To give power or authority to; authorize; license; also, to enable or permit.—**em-pow′er-ment,** *n.*

em-press (em′pres), *n.* [OF. *emperesse*, fem. of *emperere*, *empereor*, E. *emperor.*] The consort of an emperor; also, a woman ruler of an empire; fig., a supreme or sovereign mistress.

em-presse-ment (oṅ-pres-moṅ), *n.* [F., < *empresser*, refl., be eager, < *em-* (< L. *in*, in) + *presser*: see *press*[1].] Eagerness; alacrity; display of cordiality: as, "He grasped my hand with a nervous *empressement*" (Poe's "Gold-Bug").

em-prise (em-prīz′), *n.* [OF. *emprise*, < *emprendre*, undertake, < L. *in*, in, on, + *prehendere*, seize, take.] An undertaking; an adventurous enterprise; also, knightly daring or prowess (as, "giants of mighty bone and bold *emprise*": Milton's "Paradise Lost," xi. 642). [Archaic.]

emp-ti-er (emp′ti-ėr), *n.* One who or that which empties.

emp-ty (emp′ti). [AS. *æmetig*, at leisure, unoccupied, empty, < *ǣmetta*, leisure.] **I.** *a.*; compar. *emptier*, superl. *emptiest.* Containing nothing; void of the usual or appropriate contents; without money†; hungry (now only colloq.); destitute of some quality or qualities (followed by *of*); devoid (*of*); vacant, as a house; unoccupied; also, without burden or load, as a wagon; also, destitute of force, effect, or significance; unsatisfactory; meaningless; unsubstantial; also, destitute of knowledge or sense; frivolous; foolish. **II.** *n.*; pl. *-ties* (-tiz). Something empty, as a freight-car, wagon, box, sack, bottle, etc. [Colloq.]—**emp′ti-ly,** *adv.*—**emp′ti-ness,** *n.*—**emp′ty,** *v.*; *-tied, -tying.* **I.** *tr.* To make empty; deprive of contents; discharge the contents of; also, to discharge (contents). **II.** *intr.* To become empty; discharge contents, as a river.—**emp′ty=hand′ed,** *a.* Having nothing in the hands; bringing or taking nothing.—**emp′ty=head′ed,** *a.* Brainless; foolish.—**emp′ty-ing,** *n.* The act of one who or that which empties; also, something emptied out; *pl.*, yeast prepared from the lees of beer, etc. (colloq., U. S.).

emp-ty-sis (emp′ti-sis), *n.* [NL., < Gr. ἔμπτυσις, < ἐμπτύειν, spit into, < ἐν, in, + πτύειν, spit.] Expectoration, esp. of blood.

em-pur-ple (em-pėr′pl), *v. t.*; *-pled, -pling.* [See *em-*.] To tinge or color with purple.

em-py-e-ma (em-pi-ē′mạ), *n.* [NL., < Gr. ἐμπύημα, < ἐμπυεῖν, suppurate, < ἐν, in, + πύον, pus.] In *pathol.*, a collection of pus in some cavity of the body, esp. in the pleural cavity.—**em-py-em′ic** (-em′ik or -ē′mik), *a.*

em-pyr-e-al (em-pir′ẹ̄-ạl or em-pi-rē′ạl), *a.* [LL. *empyreus*, *empyrius*, < LGr. ἐμπύριος, Gr. ἔμπυρος, in fire, fiery, < ἐν, in, + πῦρ, fire.] Formed of pure fire or light; also, pertaining to the highest heaven, or empyrean (as, "Go, soar with Plato to th' *empyreal* sphere": Pope's "Essay on Man," ii. 23); hence, celestial.—**em-py-re-an** (em-pi-rē′ạn or em-pir′ẹ̄-ạn). **I.** *a.* Empyreal. **II.** *n.* The highest heaven, supposed by the ancients to contain the pure element of fire (as, "Divine interpreter . . . sent Down from the *empyrean*": Milton's "Paradise Lost," vii. 73); also, the visible heavens; the firmament.

em-py-reu-ma (em-pi-rö′mạ), *n.* [NL., < Gr. ἐμπύρευμα, live coal, < ἐμπυρεύειν, set on fire, < ἔμπυρος: see *empyreal.*] The disagreeable odor or taste of organic substances burned in close vessels.—**em″py-reu-mat′ic** (-mat′ik), *a.*

e-mu (ē′mū), *n.* [Cf. Pg. *ema*, ostrich, cassowary, orig. crane.] Either of two large, flightless, three-toed Australian birds of the ratite genus *Dromæus* (*D. novæ-hollandiæ* and *D. irroratus*), closely related to the ostrich, but smaller.—**e′mu=ap″ple,** *n.* An Australian tree, *Owenia acidula*, bearing an acid, edible fruit; also, the fruit.

Emu (*Dromæus novæ-hollandiæ*).

em-u-late (em′ū-lāt), *v. t.*; *-lated, -lating.* [L. *æmulatus*, pp. of *æmulari*, < *æmulus*, E. *emulous.*] To strive to equal or excel; imitate with effort to equal or surpass; hence, to rival with some degree of success; approach or attain equality with (as, "Thine eye would *emulate* the diamond":

Shakspere's "Merry Wives of Windsor," iii. 3. 58).—**em′u-late**†, *a.* Emulous: as, "prick'd on by a most *emulate* pride" (Shakspere's "Hamlet," i. 1. 83).—**em-u-la′tion** (-lā′shọn), *n.* [L. *æmulatio(n-)*.] Effort or desire to equal or excel others; also, jealous rivalry†; also, envy†.—**em′u-la-tive** (-lạ-tiv), *a.* Inclined to or marked by emulation.—**em′u-la-tor** (-lā-tọr), *n.*—**em′u-la-to-ry** (-lạ-tọ-ri), *a.* Pertaining to or marked by emulation.

e-mul-gent (ē̦-mul′jẹnt). [L. *emulgens* (*-ent-*), ppr. of *emulgere* (pp. *emulsus*), 'milk out,' < *e*, out of, + *mulgere*, milk.] **I.** *a.* In *anat.*, draining out, as a renal artery or vein. **II.** *n.* In *anat.*, an emulgent vessel; in *phar.*, a medicine or agent exciting the flow of bile.

em-u-lous (em′ū̦-lus), *a.* [L. *æmulus*: cf. *emulate.*] Desirous of equaling or excelling (as, "The great School of Salern . . . Where every *emulous* scholar hears . . . The rustling of another's laurels!" Longfellow's "Golden Legend," vi. 123); filled with emulation; arising from or of the nature of emulation, as actions, etc.; also, jealous†; envious†.—**em′u-lous-ly**, *adv.*—**em′u-lous-ness**, *n.*

e-mul-si-fy (ē̦-mul′si-fī), *v. t.*; *-fied*, *-fying*. [See *emulsion* and *-fy*.] To make into an emulsion.—**e-mul″si-fi-ca′tion** (-fi-kā′shọn), *n.*

e-mul-sin (ē̦-mul′sin), *n.* [L. *emulsus*, pp.: see *emulgent.*] In *chem.*, an enzyme present in almonds, etc.

e-mul-sion (ē̦-mul′shọn), *n.* [F. *émulsion*, < L. *emulgere* (pp. *emulsus*), 'milk out': see *emulgent.*] A liquid preparation of the color and consistency of milk; in *phar.*, a liquid preparation consisting of minute particles of an oily, fatty, resinous, or other substance held in suspension in an aqueous fluid by means of gum or other viscous matter; in *photog.*, a sensitive silver salt suspended in a viscous substance, as gelatin, used for coating plates, etc.—**e-mul′sion-ize**, *v. t.*; *-ized*, *-izing*. To emulsify.—**e-mul′sive** (-siv), *a.* Of the nature of an emulsion; yielding an emulsion.

e-munc-to-ry (ē̦-mungk′tọ-ri). [= F. *émonctoire*, < L. *emungere* (pp. *emunctus*), clear out the nose, < *e*, out of, + *mungere*, blow the nose: cf. *mucus.*] **I.** *a.* Excretory. **II.** *n.*; pl. *-ries* (-riz). A part or organ of the body, as the skin, a kidney, etc., carrying off waste products.

en (en), *n.* The letter N, n; in *printing*, half of the width of an em.

en-. [OF. F. *en-*, < L. *in-*, repr. *in*, prep., in, into, on, to: see *in-*[1], and cf. *em-*.] A prefix of Latin origin, meaning primarily 'in,' 'into,' first occurring in words from the French, but now used freely as an English formative, often serving to form transitive verbs from nouns or adjectives, as in *enable, enact, encage, endear, enframe, engulf, enrobe, enshrine, enslave, entangle, enthrone*, or, prefixed to verbs, to lend an intensive force (now scarcely felt) or merely to add a syllable, as for metrical purposes, as in *engild, engird, engrave, enkindle, enshield, entwine*. See *in-*[1], and cf. *em-* and *im-*[1].

-en[1]. [AS. *-an*.] A suffix forming the plural of some nouns, as in *brethren, children, oxen*, and other words, now mostly archaic, as *eyen, hosen*.

-en[2]. [AS. *-en*.] A suffix forming the past participle of strong verbs, as in *beaten, gotten, sunken*.

-en[3]. [AS. *-nian*.] A suffix forming verbs from adjectives, as in *fasten, harden, sweeten*, or from nouns, as in *heighten, lengthen, strengthen*.

-en[4]. [AS. *-en*.] A suffix of adjectives indicating material, appearance, etc., as in *ashen, earthen, golden, oaken, waxen*.

en-a-ble (e-nā′bl), *v. t.*; *-bled*, *-bling*. [See *en-*.] To make able; give power, means, or ability to; render competent; authorize; also, to make possible or easy†.—**enabling act** or **statute**, an act or statute enabling a person or a corporation to do something which would otherwise be illegal.

en-act (e-nakt′), *v. t.* [See *en-*.] To make into an act or statute; hence, to ordain; decree; also, to represent on or as on the stage; act the part of (as, "I did *enact* Julius Cæsar": Shakspere's "Hamlet," iii. 2. 108); also, to perform, as a ceremony.—**en-act′a-ble**, *a.* That may be enacted.—**en-ac-tion** (e-nak′shọn), *n.* Enactment.—**en-ac′tive**, **en-ac′to-ry** (-tọ-ri), *a.* Of or pertaining to the enactment of a law; enacting.—**en-act′ment**, *n.* The act of enacting, or the state or fact of being enacted; also, that which is enacted; a law; a statute; a single provision of a law.—**en-ac′tor**, *n.*

e-nal-la-ge (e-nal′ạ-jē), *n.* [L., < Gr. ἐναλλαγή, < ἐναλλάσσειν, interchange, < ἐν, in, + ἀλλάσσειν, change.] In *gram.*, the substitution of one form, inflection, or part of speech for another, as in "It is me" for "It is I."

e-nam-el (e-nam′ẹl), *v. t.*; *-eled* or *-elled*, *-eling* or *-elling*. [AF. *enamailler*, < OF. *en-* (see *en-*) + *esmail* (F. *émail*), enamel (from Teut., and akin to E. *smelt*[2]: cf. *smalt*).] To inlay or overlay with a vitreous composition (see *enamel, n.*); decorate or cover with enamel; also, to form an enamel-like surface upon; also, to decorate as with enamel; variegate with colors; also, to form (figures or ornaments) on a surface with or as with enamel.—**e-nam′el**, *n.* A glassy substance, usually opaque, applied by fusion to the surface of metal, pottery, etc., as for ornament or protection; hence, any of various enamel-like varnishes, paints, etc.; a coating applied to the skin to simulate a beautiful complexion; also, enameled work; an artistic work executed in enamel; ware coated with enamel; in *anat.*, the hard, glossy, calcareous outer layer of the teeth.—**e-nam′el-er**, **e-nam′el-ler**, *n.*—**e-nam′el-ing**, **e-nam′el-ling**, *n.* The act or work of one who enamels; a decoration or coating of enamel.—**e-nam′el-ist**, **e-nam′el-list**, *n.*

e-nam-or (e-nam′ọr), etc. See *enamour*, etc.

e-nam-our (e-nam′ọr), *v. t.* [OF. F. *enamourer*, < *en-* (see *en-*) + *amour*, < L. *amor*, love.] To inflame with love; charm; captivate: now usually in the passive and followed by *of*: as, "Rainscourt was reluctantly compelled to acknowledge to himself, that he was violently *enamoured* of his discarded wife" (Marryat's "King's Own," xxxvi.).—**e-nam′our-ment**, *n.*

en-ar-thro-sis (en-är-thrō′sis), *n.*; pl. *-throses* (-thrō′sēz). [NL., < Gr. ἐνάρθρωσις, < ἐν, in, + ἄρθρωσις, E. *arthrosis*.] In *anat.*, a joint, as at the shoulder, formed by the socketing of a convex end of one bone in a concavity of another; a ball-and-socket joint.

en-cæ-ni-a (en-sē′ni-ạ̈), *n. pl.* [L., < Gr ἐγκαίνια, < ἐν, in, + καινός, new.] Festive ceremonies commemorating the founding of a city or the consecration of a church; [*cap.*] ceremonies held at the University of Oxford, England, in June, in honor of founders and benefactors.

en-cage (en-kāj′), *v. t.*; *-caged*, *-caging*. [See *en-*.] To confine in or as in a cage; coop up.

en-camp (en-kamp′), *v. t.* or *i.* [See *en-*.] To settle or lodge in a camp.—**en-camp′ment**, *n.* The act of encamping; lodgment in a camp; also, the place or quarters occupied in camping; a camp.

en-car-nal-ize (en-kär′nạl-īz), *v. t.*; *-ized*, *-izing*. [See *en-*.] To invest with a carnal or fleshly form; also, to make carnal or sensual.

en-car-pus (en-kär′pus), *n.*; pl. *-pi* (-pī). [NL., < Gr. ἔγκαρπος, containing fruit, < ἐν, in, + καρπός, fruit.] In *arch.*, a sculptured ornament in imitation of a festoon of fruits, leaves, flowers, or other objects, suspended between two points.

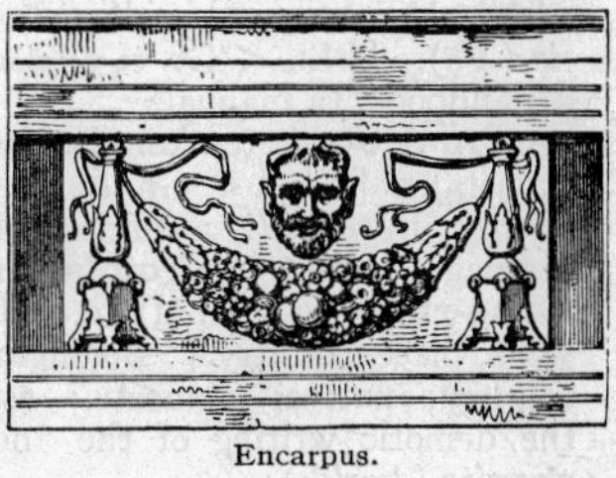
Encarpus.

en-case (en-kās′), etc. Same as *incase*, etc.

en-cash (en-kash′), *v. t.* [See *en-*.] To convert (drafts, etc.) into cash; also, to obtain (a sum, etc.) in the form of cash.—**en-cash′ment**, *n.*

en-caus-tic (en-kâs′tik). [L. *encausticus*, < Gr. καυστικός, < ἐγκαίειν, burn in, < ἐν, in, + καίειν, burn.] **I.** *a.* Noting, pertaining to, or produced by a process of painting with wax colors fixed with heat, or any process, by which colors are burned in. **II.** *n.* The art, process, or practice of encaustic painting; also, material produced by an encaustic process.

en-cave (en-kāv′), *v. t.*; *-caved*, *-caving*. [See *en-*.] To inclose or hide in or as in a cave. See Shakspere's "Othello," iv. 1. 82.

-ence. [F. *-ence*, < L. *-entia*, < *-ens*, ppr. ending (see *-ent*); or directly from L. *-entia*.] A noun suffix equivalent to *-ance*, and corresponding to *-ent* in adjectives, as in *abstinence, consistence, dependence, difference*. Cf. *-ency*.

en-ceinte[1] (oṅ-saṅt), *n.* [F., < *enceindre*, < L. *incingere*, inclose as with a girdle, < *in*, in, + *cingere*, gird.] A wall or inclosure, as of a fortified place; also, the place inclosed.

en-ceinte[2] (oṅ-saṅt), *a.* [F., < ML. *incincta*, < L. *in-*, not, + *cincta*, pp. fem. of *cingere*, gird.] Of a woman, pregnant; with child.

en-ce-phal-ic (en-se-fal′ik), *a.* Of or pertaining to the encephalon or brain; also, situated in the head or within the cranial cavity.

en-ceph-a-li-tis (en-sef-ạ-lī′tis), *n.* [NL., < *encephalon*: see *encephalon*.] In *pathol.*, inflammation of the brain.—**encephalitis lethargica** (lē-thär′ji-kạ). [NL., lethargic encephalitis.] In *pathol.*, a form of inflammation of the brain characterized by extreme drowsiness or lethargy, sometimes followed by stupor or paralysis. Also called *lethargic encephalitis* and *sleeping-sickness*.—**en-ceph-a-lit′ic** (-lit′ik), *a.*

en-ceph-a-loid (en-sef′ạ-loid), *a.* [See *encephalon* and *-oid*.] Resembling the brain-substance: applied to a soft, rapidly growing, malignant form of cancer.

en-ceph-a-lon (en-sef′ạ-lon), *n.*; pl. *-la* (-lạ). [NL., < Gr. ἐγκέφαλον, neut. of ἐγκέφαλος, within the head (as n., the brain), < ἐν, in, + κεφαλή, head.] The brain.

en-ceph-a-lop-a-thy (en-sef-ạ-lop′ạ-thi), *n.* [See *encephalon* and *-pathy*.] In *pathol.*, disease of the brain.

en-chafe (en-chāf′), *v. t.*; *-chafed, -chafing.* [See *en-*.] To heat; irritate; chafe. [Obs. or archaic.]

en-chain (en-chān′), *v. t.* [OF. *enchaeiner* (F. *enchaîner*), < *en-* (see *en-*) + *chaeine*, E. *chain*.] To fasten with or as with a chain or chains; fetter; restrain; hold fast, as the attention.—**en-chain′ment,** *n.*

en-chant (en-chȧnt′), *v. t.* [OF. F. *enchanter*, < L. *incantare*, chant a magic formula against, enchant: see *incantation*.] To subject to magical influence; cast a spell over; bewitch; also, to impart a magical quality or effect to; also, to influence as if by a charm†; delude†; also, to delight in a high degree (as, "Bid me discourse, I will *enchant* thine ear": Shakspere's "Venus and Adonis," 145); charm.—**en-chant′er,** *n.* One who enchants; a magician.—**enchanter's nightshade,** any of various low, white-flowered herbs (genus *Circæa*) found in shady woods.—**en-chant′ing-ly,** *adv.*—**en-chant′ment,** *n.* [OF. F. *enchantement*.] The act or art of enchanting; the state or fact of being enchanted; that which enchants.—**en-chan′tress,** *n.* A woman who enchants; a sorceress; also, a fascinating woman.

en-chase (en-chās′), *v. t.*; *-chased, -chasing.* [OF. *enchasser* (F. *enchâsser*), < *en-* (see *en-*) + *chasse*, shrine, case, setting, < L. *capsa*, box: see *case*[2].] To place in a setting, as a gem; serve as a setting for; also, to ornament with precious stones; decorate with inlay; adorn with figures in relief; ornament with or as with engraved figures; also, to engrave (something) on a surface; also, to inclose†.

en-chi-rid-i-on (en-ki-rid′i-on or en-kī-), *n.*; pl. *-ions* or *-ia* (-i-ạ). [LL., < Gr. ἐγχειρίδιον, < ἐν, in, + χείρ, hand.] A handbook; a manual.

en-chon-dro-ma (en-kon-drō′mạ), *n.*; pl. *-mas* or *-mata* (-mạ-tạ). [NL., < Gr. ἐν, in, + χόνδρος, cartilage: see *-oma*.] In *pathol.*, a tumor which consists essentially of cartilage.—**en-chon-drom′a-tous** (-drom′ạ-tus), *a.*

en-cho-ri-al (en-kō′ri-ạl), *a.* [Gr. ἐγχώριος, < ἐν, in, + χώρα, place, country.] Belonging to or used in a particular country; native; domestic; esp., noting or pertaining to the demotic writing of the ancient Egyptians. Also **en-chor′ic** (-kor′ik).

en-ci-na (en-sē′nạ), *n.* [Sp.] A species of live-oak, *Quercus agrifolia*, with hard, heavy wood.

en-ci-pher (en-sī′fėr), *v. t.* [See *en-*.] To put (a letter, etc.) into cipher.

en-cir-cle (en-sėr′kl), *v. t.*; *-cled, -cling.* [See *en-*.] To form a circle round; surround; encompass; also, to make a circling movement about; make the circuit of.—**en-cir′cle-ment,** *n.*

en-clasp (en-klȧsp′), *v. t.* [See *en-*.] To hold in or as in a clasp or embrace.

en-clave (en-klāv′), *v. t.*; *-claved, -claving.* [F. *enclaver*, < ML. *inclavare*, < L. *in*, in, + *clavis*, key (or perhaps *clavus*, nail).] To inclose (alien territory) within the territory of a country; surround (such territory), as a country does.—**en-clave** (en-klāv′, F. oṅ-kläv), *n.* [F.] A country, or, esp., an outlying portion of a country, entirely (or mostly) surrounded by the territory of another country. Cf. *exclave*.—**en-clave-ment** (en-klāv′mẹnt, F. oṅ-kläv-moṅ), *n.* [F.] The act or fact of enclaving; the condition of being an enclave.

en-clit-ic (en-klit′ik). [LL. *encliticus*, < Gr. ἐγκλιτικός, < ἐγκλίνειν, lean on, < ἐν, in, on, + κλίνειν, incline.] In *gram.*: **I.** *a.* Of a word, so closely connected with a preceding word as to have no independent accent. Cf. *proclitic*. **II.** *n.* An enclitic word.—**en-clit′i-cal-ly,** *adv.*

en-close (en-klōz′), etc. See *inclose*, etc.

en-cloud (en-kloud′), *v. t.* [See *en-*.] To envelop in a cloud; becloud.

en-co-mi-ast (en-kō′mi-ast), *n.* [Gr. ἐγκωμιαστής.] One who utters or writes an encomium; a eulogist.—**en-co-mi-as′tic,** *a.* Eulogistic; laudatory.—**en-co-mi-as′ti-cal-ly,** *adv.*

en-co-mi-um (en-kō′mi-um), *n.*; pl. *-ums*. [L., < Gr. ἐγκώμιον, laudatory ode, eulogy, prop. neut. of ἐγκώμιος, belonging to a Bacchic revel, < ἐν, in, + κῶμος, revel: cf. *comedy*.] A formal expression of praise; a eulogy: as, "I had often heard very extraordinary *encomiums* passed on the performances of Mr. T— . . . who paints landscapes" (Smollett's "Humphry Clinker," May 19).

en-com-pass (en-kum′pạs), *v. t.* [See *en-*]. To form a circle about; encircle; surround; inclose; also, to go round, or make the circuit of (obs. or rare); also, to outwit† (see Shakspere's "Merry Wives of Windsor," ii. 2. 159); also, to compass, bring about, or accomplish (rare).—**en-com′pass-ment,** *n.*

en-core (ong-kōr′, F. oṅ-kôr), *adv.* [F., still, yet, further, besides, = It. *ancora*; origin uncertain.] Again; once more: used in calling for a repetition of a song, etc., or for an additional number or piece.—**en-core** (ong′kōr, F. oṅ-kôr), *n.* A demand, as by applause, for a repetition of a song, etc., or for an additional number or piece; also, that which is given in response to such a demand.—**en-core** (ong-kōr′ or ong′kōr), *v. t.*; *-cored, -coring.* To call for a repetition of (a song, etc.); call for an encore from (a performer).

en-coun-ter (en-koun′tėr), *v.* [OF. *encontrer*, < L. *in*, in, + *contra*, against.] **I.** *tr.* To meet (a person, a military force, etc.) in conflict; meet with or contend against (difficulties, opposition, etc.); face resolutely; also, to fall in with or come upon (a person or thing), esp. casually or unexpectedly; also, to oppose†; contest†. **II.** *intr.* To meet, esp. in conflict: as, "We had nations of savages to *encounter* with" (Defoe's "Captain Singleton," iv.).—**en-coun′ter,** *n.* [OF. *encontre*.] A meeting in conflict or opposition; a battle; a combat; also, a meeting with a person or thing, esp. casually or unexpectedly; also, a coming together or in contact; also, manner of encountering or meeting†; behavior†.

en-cour-age (en-kur′ạj), *v. t.*; *-aged, -aging.* [OF. *encoragier* (F. *encourager*), < *en-* (see *en-*) + *corage*, E. *courage*.] To inspire with courage, spirit, or confidence; inspirit; embolden; incite or induce; recommend or advise; also, to stimulate by assistance, approval, etc.; countenance; foster; abet.—**en-cour′age-ment,** *n.* The act of encouraging, or the state of being encouraged; also, that which encourages.—**en-cour′ag-er** (-ạ-jėr), *n.*—**en-cour′ag-ing-ly,** *adv.*

en-crim-son (en-krim′zn), *v. t.* [See *en-*.] To make crimson; redden.

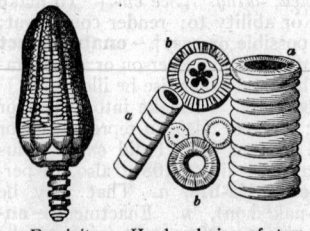

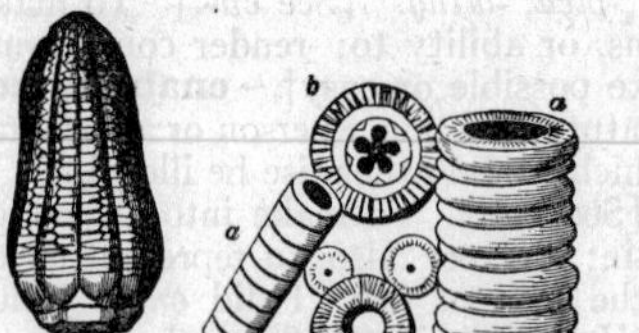

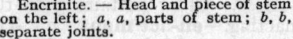

Encrinite. — Head and piece of stem on the left; *a, a,* parts of stem; *b, b,* separate joints.

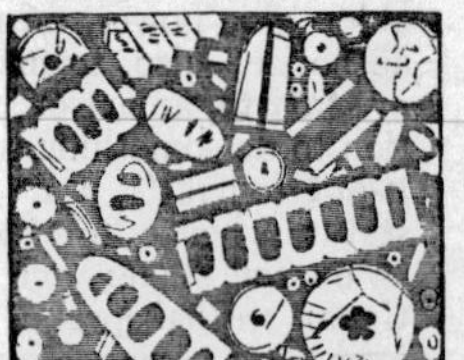

Piece of Derbyshire Marble, showing Encrinites.

en-cri-nite (en′kri-nīt), *n.* [F. *encrinite*, < Gr. ἐν, in, + κρίνον, lily.] A fossil crinoid. Vast strata of marble in many parts of the world are composed chiefly of fragments of encrinites.

en-croach (en-krōch′), *v. i.* [OF. *encrochier*, < *en-* (see *en-*) + *croc*, hook.] To trespass upon the property or rights of another, esp. stealthily or by gradual advances; make gradual inroads; advance beyond proper limits.—**en-croach′er,** *n.*—**en-croach′ing-ly,** *adv.*—**en-croach′-ment,** *n.* The act of encroaching; also, anything taken by encroaching.

en-crust (en-krust′), etc. Same as *incrust*, etc.

en-cum-ber (en-kum′bėr), *v. t.* [OF. F. *encombrer*, < ML. *incombrare*, < L. *in*, in, + ML. *combrus*, obstruction, obstacle: cf. L. *cumulus*, heap.] To impede or hamper; retard; embarrass; also, to burden with obligations, debt, etc.; charge (an estate, etc.) with a mortgage; also, to load or fill with what is obstructive or superfluous; hence, to render difficult; complicate.—**en-cum′ber-ment,** *n.*—**en-cum′brance** (-brąns), *n.* Encumbered condition†; also, that which encumbers; a burden; a hindrance; something useless or superfluous; an annoyance or trouble; a dependent person, esp. a child; in *law*, a burden or claim on property, as a mortgage.—**en-cum′bran-cer** (-brąn-sėr), *n.* In *law*, one who holds an encumbrance.

-ency. A noun suffix, an extended form of *-ence*, as in *consistency*, *dependency*, *exigency*.

en-cyc-lic (en-sik′lik or -sī′klik). [NL. *encyclicus*, for L. *encyclios*, < Gr. ἐγκύκλιος, circular, general, < ἐν, in, + κύκλος, circle.] **I.** *a.* Encyclical. **II.** *n.* An encyclical letter.—**en-cyc′li-cal. I.** *a.* Intended for wide or general circulation; circular; general: applied chiefly to ecclesiastical epistles, esp. to letters issued by the Pope to all the bishops in communion with him. **II.** *n.* An encyclical letter.

en-cy-clo-pe-di-a, en-cy-clo-pæ-di-a (en-sī-klǫ-pē′di-ä), *n.* [ML. *encyclopædia*, < Gr. ἐγκυκλοπαιδεία, for ἐγκύκλιος παιδεία, general education, complete round or course of learning: see *encyclic* and *cyclopedia*.] The entire circle or range of knowledge; also, a work treating separately various topics from all branches of knowledge, usually in alphabetical arrangement; esp. [*cap.*], the great French work edited by Diderot and D'Alembert, published during the latter half of the 18th century, distinguished by the advanced or radical character of its doctrines regarding political, social, and religious matters; also [*l. c.*], a work treating exhaustively one art or science, esp. in articles arranged alphabetically; a cyclopedia.—**en-cy-clo-pe′dic, en-cy-clo-pæ′dic,** *a.* Covering a wide range of subjects; possessing wide and varied information; pertaining to an encyclopedia. Also **en-cy-clo-pe′di-cal, en-cy-clo-pæ′di-cal.**—**en-cy-clo-pe′dism, en-cy-clo-pæ′dism,** *n.* Encyclopedic learning; also, the writing or compiling of encyclopedias, or the method of presenting information characteristic of them; also [often *cap.*], the doctrines and influence of the French Encyclopedists.—**en-cy-clo-pe′dist, en-cy-clo-pæ′dist,** *n.* A compiler of or contributor to an encyclopedia; [often *cap.*] one of the collaborators in the Encyclopedia of Diderot and D'Alembert, or an adherent of its doctrines; also [*l. c.*], one possessing encyclopedic knowledge.

en-cyst (en-sist′), *v. t.* or *i.* [See *en-*.] To inclose or become inclosed in a cyst or vesicle.—**en-cys-ta′tion** (-sis-tā′shǫn), **en-cyst′ment,** *n.*

end[1] (end), *n.* [AS. *ende* = D. *einde* = G. *ende* = Icel. *endi* = Goth. *andeis*, end: cf. Skt. *anta*, border, limit, end.] An extremity of anything that is longer than broad; an extreme or furthermost part of anything extended in space; a limit; a surface bounding an object at one of its extremities; also, termination or conclusion; the concluding part; termination of existence (as, "Of his kingdom there shall be no *end*": Luke, i. 33); death (as, he turned his thoughts to his approaching *end*); a cause of death, destruction, or ruin; also, ultimate state (as, "Mark the perfect man, and behold the upright: for the *end* of that man is peace": Ps. xxxvii. 37); also, event, issue, or result; also, a purpose or aim (as, to accomplish one's *end*; to gain one's *ends*); the object for which a thing exists (as, "I have considered the happiness of the people as the *end* of government": Gibbon's "Decline and Fall of the Roman Empire," xxiv.); also, a remnant or fragment (as, odds and *ends*: see *odd*, *n.*); in *football*, etc., either of the players at the ends of the forward line.—**end**[1], *v.* [AS. *endian*.] **I.** *tr.* To bring to an end; conclude; finish; also, to put an end to; destroy; kill; also, to form the end of; also, to set on end. **II.** *intr.* To come to an end; terminate; cease; issue or result; sometimes, to die.

end[2] (end), *v. t.* [Origin uncertain.] To put (wheat, hay, etc.) into a barn, stack, etc.: as, "His shadowy flail hath thresh'd the corn, That ten day-labourers could not *end*" (Milton's "L'Allegro," 109). [Now only prov. Eng.]

en-dam-age (en-dam′ạj), *v. t.*; *-aged*, *-aging*. [See *en-*.] To bring damage, harm, or detriment to; harm; injure.

en-dan-ger (en-dān′jėr), *v. t.* [See *en-*.] To expose to danger; imperil; also, to cause or incur the danger of†.—**en-dan′ger-ment,** *n.*

en-dear (en-dēr′), *v. t.* [See *en-*.] To make dear, esteemed, or beloved; also, to win the affection of†; attract†.—**en-dear′ing,** *p. a.* Inspiring affection; also, manifesting affection; caressing.—**en-dear′ing-ly,** *adv.*—**en-dear′-ment,** *n.* The act of endearing, or the state of being endeared; also, something that endears; an endearing attribute; also, action or utterance manifesting affection; a caress; an affectionate term.

en-deav-or (en-dev′ǫr), *v.* [OF. F. *en devoir*, 'in duty,' *se mettre en son devoir*, apply one's self to one's duty, exert one's self, endeavor: see *devoir*.] **I.** *tr.* To exert (one's self) to do a thing†; also, to try to achieve or effect (something: archaic). **II.** *intr.* To exert one's self to do or effect something; make an effort; strive; also, to direct one's efforts (*after*, *at*, or *for* something: archaic).—**en-deav′or,** *n.* The act of endeavoring; effort; a strenuous effort or attempt.—**en-deav′or-er,** *n.*

en-deav′our, etc. British preferred form of *endeavor*, etc.

endeca-, etc. Erroneous form of *hendeca-*, etc.

end-ed (en′ded), *a.* Having an end: as, blunt-*ended*; square-*ended*.

en-dem-ic (en-dem′ik). [F. *endémique*, < Gr. ἔνδημος, belonging to a people, < ἐν, in, + δῆμος, people: cf. *epidemic*.] **I.** *a.* Peculiar to a particular people or locality, as a disease. Cf. *enzoötic*. **II.** *n.* An endemic disease.—**en-dem′i-cal,** *a.* Endemic.—**en-dem′i-cal-ly,** *adv.*—**en-de-mi′ci-ty** (-de-mis′i-ti), *n.* Endemic character.

end-er (en′dėr), *n.* One who or that which ends.

en-der-mic (en-dėr′mik), *a.* [Gr. ἐν, in, + δέρμα, skin.] Acting on or through the skin, as a medicine.

end-ing (en′ding), *n.* A bringing or coming to an end; termination; close; death; also, the final or concluding part; in *gram.*, the terminating syllable or letter of a word; a termination, whether of inflection or of derivation.

en-dive (en′div or -dīv), *n.* [F. *endive*, < L. *intibus*, *intybus*.] A cichoriaceous plant, *Cichorium endivia*, of two main varieties or types, one with finely divided, much curled leaves and one with broad, fleshy leaves, both used for salads.

end-less (end′les), *a.* [AS. *endelēas*.] Having no end, limit, or conclusion (as, "the rolling flood of *endless* years": Cowper's "Conversation," 557); boundless; infinite; interminable; incessant; also, being without ends, or returning upon itself so as to exhibit neither beginning nor end (as, an *endless* chain, belt, or the like, one made continuous, as by joining the two ends of a single length).—**endless screw,** a short revolving screw whose thread engages with the teeth of a cog-wheel.—**end′less-ly,** *adv.*—**end′less-ness,** *n.*

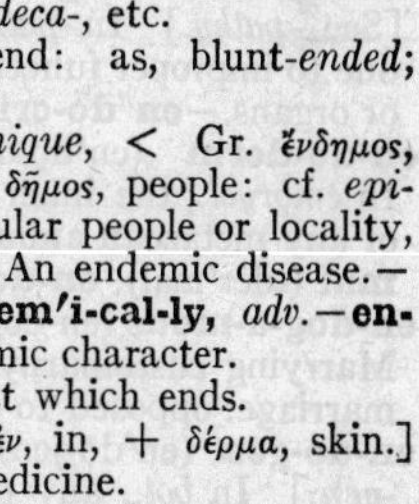

Endless Screw and Cog-wheel.

end-long (end′lông). [AS. *andlang*, along (see *along*[2]); later associated with E. *end*[1].] **I.** *prep.* Along; from end to end of. [Archaic or prov.] **II.** *adv.* At full length; lengthwise; from end to end; along; continuously. [Archaic or prov.]

end=man (end′man), *n.* A man at one end of a row or line; esp., a man at either end of the line of performers of a minstrel-troupe, who plays on the bones or the tambourine and carries on humorous dialogue with the middle-man, or interlocutor.

end-most (end′mōst), *a. superl.* Furthest.

endo-, end-. Forms of Gr. ἔνδον, within, used in combination. Cf. *ento-*.—**en-do-blast** (en′dǫ-blast), *n.* [+ *-blast.*] In *embryol.*, the endoderm.—**en-do-blas′tic** (-blas′tik), *a.*—**en-do-car′di-al** (-kär′di-ạl), *a.* [+ Gr. καρδία, heart.] Situated or occurring within the heart; also, pertaining to the endocardium.—**en″do-car-di′tis** (-dī′-tis), *n.* [NL.] In *pathol.*, inflammation of the endocardium.—**en-do-car′di-um** (-di-um), *n.* [NL. (Gr. καρδία, heart).] In *anat.*, the delicate serous membrane which lines the cavities of the heart and aids in forming the valves by its reduplications.—**en′do-carp** (-kärp), *n.* [+ *-carp.*] In *bot.*, the inner layer of a pericarp, as the stone of certain fruits.

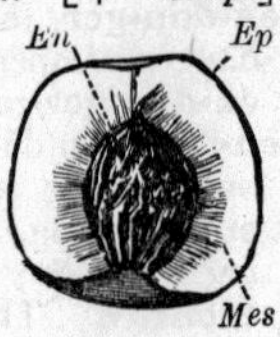

Fruit of Peach. — *En*, endocarp; *Ep*, epicarp; *Mes*, mesocarp.

en-do-crine (en′dǫ-krīn or -krin). [Gr. ἔνδον, within, + κρίνειν, separate.] In *anat.*, *physiol.*, etc.: **I.** *a.* Designating any of various glands or organs (as the thyroid gland, suprarenal bodies, pituitary body, etc.) which produce certain important internal secretions (that is, products given up directly to the blood or lymph) that act upon particular organs, and which through improper functioning may cause grave disorders or death; of or pertaining to these glands or organs (as, *endocrine* function; *endocrine* disorders). Cf. *ductless gland*, under *ductless.* **II.** *n.* An endocrine gland or organ.—**en-do-crin′ic** (-krin′ik), *a.* Of or pertaining to the endocrine glands or organs; endocrine.—**en″do-cri-nol′o-gy** (-kri-nol′ǫ-ji), *n.* [See *-logy.*] The science that deals with the endocrine glands or organs, esp. in their relation to bodily changes and disease.—**en″do-cri-no-log′i-cal** (-nǫ-loj′i-kạl), *a.*—**en″do-cri-nop′a-thy** (-nop′ạ-thi), *n.*; pl. *-thies* (-thiz). [See *-pathy.*] In *pathol.*, disease, or a diseased condition, due to improper functioning of one or more endocrine glands or organs.—**en″do-cri-no-path′ic** (-nǫ-path′ik), *a.*

en-do-derm (en′dǫ-dėrm), *n.* [See *endo-* and *-derm.*] In *embryol.*, the inner primary layer of cells in the embryo of any metazoan animal: opposed to *ectoderm.*—**en-do-der′mal** (-dėr′mạl), **en-do-der′mic,** *a.*

en-dog-a-mous (en-dog′ạ-mus), *a.* [See *endo-* and *-gamous.*] Marrying customarily within the tribe; pertaining to such marriage: opposed to *exogamous.*—**en-dog′a-my,** *n.*

en-do-gen (en′dǫ-jen), *n.* [F. *endogène*: see *endo-* and *-gen.*] In *bot.*, any plant of the obsolete class *Endogenæ*, including the monocotyledons, whose stems were erroneously supposed to grow from within: opposed to *exogen.*—**en-dog′e-nous** (-doj′e-nus), *a.* Growing or proceeding from within; originating within; in *bot.*, belonging to the endogens; of plants, as the monocotyledons, having stems which ordinarily have no distinction of pith or bark and do not show an annual ring structure; pertaining to plants having such stems.

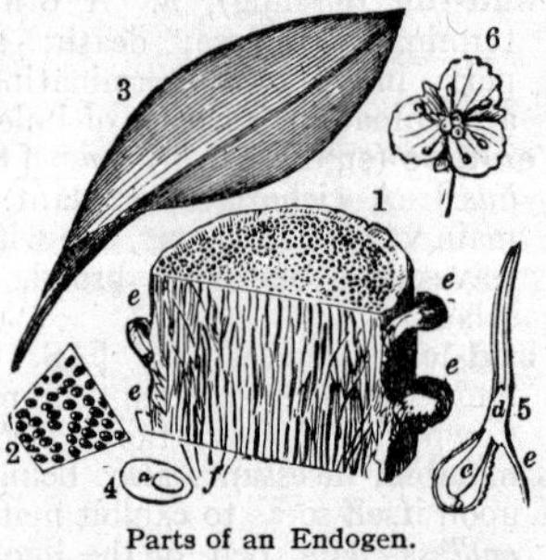

Parts of an Endogen.

1. Section of the stem of a palm: *e, e*, remains of leafstalks; *f*, bundles of woody fiber. 2. Portion of stem, showing ends of bundles of woody fiber. 3. Endogenous leaf, showing its parallel veins. 4. Monocotyledonous seed, showing (*a*) its single cotyledon. 5. Germination of palm: *b*, albumen; *c*, cotyledon; *d*, plumule; *e*, radicle issuing from a short sheath, the coleorhiza. 6. Flower of endogen.

en-do-lymph (en′dǫ-limf), *n.* [See *endo-* and *lymph.*] In *anat.*, the fluid contained within the membranous labyrinth of the ear.

en-do-morph (en′dǫ-môrf), *n.* [See *endo-* and *-morph.*] A mineral inclosed within another mineral: opposed to *perimorph.*—**en-do-mor′phic** (-môr′fik), *a.*

en-do-par-a-site (en-dǫ-par′ạ-sīt), *n.* [See *endo-.*] An internal parasite: opposed to *ectoparasite.*

en-do-phlœ-um (en-dǫ-flē′um), *n.* [NL., < Gr. ἔνδον, within, + φλοιός, bark.] In *bot.*, the liber or inner bark of plants.

en-do-phyl-lous (en-dǫ-fil′us), *a.* [See *endo-* and *-phyllous.*] In *bot.*, being or formed within a sheath, as the young leaves of monocotyledons.

en-do-phyte (en′dǫ-fīt), *n.* Same as *entophyte.*

en-do-plasm (en′dǫ-plazm), *n.* [See *endo-* and *-plasm.*] In *biol.*, the inner portion of the cytoplasm in the cell of a protozoan; also, the granular inner layer of cytoplasm in a vegetable cell: opposed to *ectoplasm.*—**en-do-plas′mic** (-plaz′mik), *a.*

en-do-plast (en′dǫ-plast), *n.* [See *endo-* and *-plast.*] In *biol.*, the nucleus of a protozoan.—**en-do-plas′tic** (-plas′-tik), *a.*

en-do-pleu-ra (en-dǫ-plö′rạ), *n.* [NL., < Gr. ἔνδον, within, + πλευρά, side: cf. *pleura.*] In *bot.*, the inner integument of a seed; the tegmen. See cut at *episperm.*

end=or-gan (end′ôr″gạn), *n.* In *physiol.*, any specialized structure which forms the terminus of a path of nervous conduction, esp. when at the periphery of the body.

en-dorse (en-dôrs′), etc. See *indorse*, etc.

en-do-sarc (en′dǫ-särk), *n.* [See *endo-* and *-sarc.*] In *biol.*, the endoplasm of a protozoan: opposed to *ectosarc.*

en-do-scope (en′dǫ-skōp), *n.* [See *endo-* and *-scope.*] In *med.*, an instrument designed to give a view of some internal part of the body.—**en-dos′co-py** (-dos′kǫ-pi), *n.*

en-do-skel-e-ton (en-dǫ-skel′ẹ-tọn), *n.* [See *endo-.*] In *anat.*, the internal skeleton or framework of the body of an animal: opposed to *exoskeleton.*

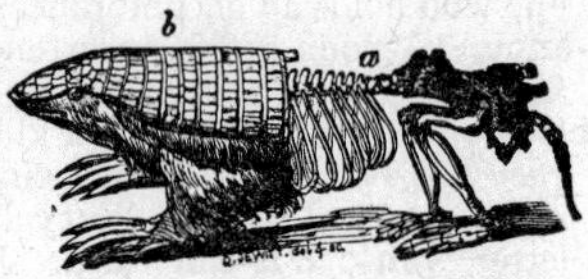

Endoskeleton (*a*) and Exoskeleton or Dermoskeleton (*b*) of Pichiciago.

en-dos-mo-sis, en-dos-mose (en-dos-mō′sis or en-doz-, en′dos-mōs or en′-doz-), *n.* [See *endo-.*] Osmosis from without inward; in the phenomena of osmosis, the action or flow of that fluid which passes with the greater rapidity into the other: opposed to *exosmosis.*—**en-dos-mot′ic** (-mot′ik), *a.*

en-do-sperm (en′dǫ-spėrm), *n.* [See *endo-* and *-sperm.*] In *bot.*, a nutritive matter in the ovule of seed-plants, derived from the embryo-sac, supposed to represent the female prothallium, and serving eventually to nourish the embryo. See cut at *episperm.*

en-do-spore (en′dǫ-spōr), *n.* [See *endo-* and *spore.*] In *bot.*, the inner coat of a spore; in *bact.*, a spore formed within a cell.—**en-do-spo′ri-um** (-spō′ri-um), *n.*; pl. *-ria* (-ri-ạ). [NL.] In *bot.*, an endospore.—**en-dos′po-rous** (-dos′pǫ-rus), *a.* In *bact.*, forming spores within a cell.

en-dos-te-um (en-dos′tẹ-um), *n.*; pl. *-tea* (-tẹ-ạ). [NL., < Gr. ἔνδον, within, + ὀστέον, bone.] In *anat.*, the vascular membrane lining the medullary cavity of a bone.

en-dos-to-sis (en-dos-tō′sis), *n.* [NL., < *endo-* + *-ostosis* as in *exostosis.*] In *anat.*, bone formation beginning in the substance of cartilage.

en-do-the-ci-um (en-dǫ-thē′shi-um), *n.*; pl. *-cia* (-shi-ạ). [NL., < Gr. ἔνδον, within, + θήκη, case.] In *bot.*, the lining of the cavity of an anther.

en-do-the-li-al (en-dǫ-thē′li-ạl), *a.* Pertaining to endothelium.—**en-do-the′li-oid,** *a.* Resembling endothelium.

en-do-the-li-o-ma (en″dǫ-thē-li-ō′mạ), *n.*; pl. *-mas* or *-mata* (-mạ-tạ). [NL., < *endothelium*: see *-oma.*] In *pathol.*, a tumor (malignant or benign) originating from the endothelium.

en-do-the-li-um (en-dǫ-thē′li-um), *n.*; pl. *-liums* or *-lia* (-li-ạ). [NL., < *endo-* + *-thelium* as in *epithelium.*] In *anat.*, the tissue which lines blood-vessels, lymphatics, serous cavities, and the like: a form of epithelium (in the broad sense).

en-do-ther-mic (en-dǫ-thėr′mik), *a.* [Gr. ἔνδον, within, + θέρμη, heat.] Noting or pertaining to a chemical change which is accompanied by an absorption of heat: opposed to *exothermic.*

en-dow (en-dou′), *v. t.* [OF. *endouer*, < *en-* (see *en-*) + *douer*, < L. *dotare*, endow: see *dotation.*] To provide with dower; also, to provide with a permanent fund or source of income; fig., to furnish, as with some gift, faculty, or quality, mental or physical; equip.—**en-dow′er,** *n.*—**en-dow′ment,** *n.* The act of endowing; also, that with which a person, institution, etc., is endowed, as property or funds; fig., an attribute of mind or body; a gift of nature.—**endowment insurance,** a form of insurance providing for the payment of a fixed sum to the insured person at a specified time, or to his heirs, or a person designated, should he die before the time named.

en-due (en-dū′), *v. t.*; *-dued, -duing.* [Var. of *indue.*] To put on; assume; also, to clothe; also, to invest or endow (as, "The jungle . . . answered as if *endued* with life, by waving its boughs": Marryat's "King's Own," xliv.).

en-dur-a-ble (en-dūr′ą-bl), *a.* That may be endured; also, likely to endure or last.—**en-dur′a-bly,** *adv.*

en-dur-ance (en-dūr′ąns), *n.* The act, fact, or power of enduring anything; something endured, as a hardship; also, duration; lasting quality.

en-dure (en-dūr′), *v.*; *-dured, -during.* [OF. F. *endurer,* < L. *indurare,* harden, ML. endure: see *indurate.*] **I.** *tr.* To harden†; also, to hold out against; sustain without impairment or yielding; undergo or suffer; also, to bear without resistance or with patience; tolerate. **II.** *intr.* To hold out; support adverse force or influence of any kind; suffer without yielding; suffer patiently; also, to continue to exist; last.—**en-dur′ing,** *p. a.* That endures; lasting; permanent.—**en-dur′ing-ly,** *adv.*—**en-dur′ing-ness,** *n.*

end-ways, end-wise (end′wāz, -wīz), *adv.* On end; with the end upward or forward; also, in the direction of the ends or end; lengthwise; also, end to end.

-ene. Noun suffix used in chemistry, in names of hydrocarbons, as *anthracene, benzene, naphthalene,* specif. those of the olefine or ethylene series, as *butylene.*

en-e-ma (en′ę-mä or e-nē′mä), *n.*; pl. *enemas,* L. *enemata* (e-nem′ą-tä). [LL., < Gr. ἔνεμα, < ἐνιέναι, send in, inject, < ἐν, in, + ἱέναι, send.] In *med.,* a fluid injected into the rectum.

en-e-my (en′ę-mi). [OF. *enemi* (F. *ennemi*), < L. *inimicus,* < *in-,* not, + *amicus,* friend: cf. *inimical.*] **I.** *n.*; pl. *-mies* (-miz). One who cherishes hatred or harmful designs against another; an adversary or opponent; something harmful or prejudicial; an armed foe; an opposing military force; a hostile nation or state, or a subject of such a state; with *the,* the hostile or opposing force (construed as either *sing.* or *pl.*); the devil; time (colloq.: as, how goes *the enemy?* what is the time?). **II.** *a.* Inimical† or opposed†; belonging to or having the status of a hostile power, as in time of war.

en-er-get-ic (en-ėr-jet′ik), *a.* [Gr. ἐνεργητικός, < ἐνεργεῖν, operate, effect, influence, < ἐνεργός, at work: see *energy.*] Operative†; also, powerful in action or effect; also, possessing or exhibiting energy; forcible; vigorous.—**en-er-get′i-cal-ly,** *adv.*—**en-er-get′ics,** *n.* The science of the laws of energy.

e-ner-gic (e-nėr′jik), *a.* Characterized by, endowed with, or exhibiting energy.

en-er-gize (en′ėr-jīz), *v.*; *-gized, -gizing.* **I.** *tr.* To impart energy to; rouse into energy or activity. **II.** *intr.* To be in operation; put forth energy: as, "The intellect of man . . . *energizes* as well as his eye or ear, and perceives in sights and sounds something beyond them" (J. H. Newman's "Idea of a University," i. 4).—**en′er-giz-er** (-jī-zėr), *n.*

en-er-gu-men (en-ėr-gū′men), *n.* [LL. *energumenos,* < Gr. ἐνεργούμενος, ppr. pass. of ἐνεργεῖν, operate, influence: see *energetic.*] One possessed by an evil spirit; a demoniac; also, a fanatical enthusiast.

en-er-gy (en′ėr-ji), *n.*; pl. *-gies* (-jiz). [LL. *energia,* < Gr. ἐνέργεια, action, agency, force, energy, < ἐνεργής, earlier ἐνεργός, at work, active, < ἐν, in, + -εργός, working.] The actual exertion of power; operation; activity; also, power as exerted; also, vigor or intensity of action; vigor or forcefulness of expression; capacity or habit of vigorous activity; also, ability to produce action or effect; in *physics,* an attribute by virtue of which one portion of matter can produce changes in another; ability to do work; sometimes, according to advanced ideas, all that we observe in the universe.

en-er-vate (en′ėr-vāt), *v. t.*; *-vated, -vating.* [L. *enervatus,* pp. of *enervare,* < *e,* out of, + *nervus,* sinew, E. *nerve.*] To deprive of nerve, force, or strength; weaken; destroy the vigor of; render ineffectual.—**e-ner-vate** (ę-nėr′vāt), *a.* Enervated: as, "I observed . . . the *enervate* slightness of his frail form" (Bulwer-Lytton's "Caxtons," xi. 5).—**en-er-va-tion** (en-ėr-vā′shǫn), *n.*—**en′er-va-tor,** *n.*

e-neuch, e-neugh (ę-nūċh′). Scotch forms of *enough.*

en-face (en-fās′), *v. t.*; *-faced, -facing.* [See *en-* and *face,* and cf. *endorse, indorse.*] To write, print, or stamp something on the face of (a note, draft, etc.); also, to write, print, or stamp (a mark or a form of words) on the face of a note, draft, etc.—**en-face′ment,** *n.*

en-fee-ble (en-fē′bl), *v. t.*; *-bled, -bling.* [OF. *enfeblir,* < *en-* (see *en-*) + *feble,* E. *feeble.*] To make feeble; weaken.—**en-fee′ble-ment,** *n.*—**en-fee′bler,** *n.*

en-feoff (en-fef′), *v. t.* [AF. *enfeoffer,* OF. *enfeffer,* < *en-* (see *en-*) + *feffer,* E. *feoff.*] To invest with a fief or fee; also, to give as a fief; hence, to surrender (as, "The skipping king . . . *Enfeoff'd* himself to popularity": Shakspere's "1 Henry IV.," iii. 2. 69).—**en-feoff′ment,** *n.*

en-fet-ter (en-fet′ėr), *v. t.* [See *en-.*] To bind with or as with fetters.

en-fi-lade (en-fi-lād′), *n.* [F., an arrangement of things as on a thread, < *enfiler,* to thread, string, go through, rake with fire, < *en-* (see *en-*) + *fil,* a thread, E. *file*[3].] *Milit.,* a situation of works, troops, etc., rendering them subject to a sweeping fire from flank to flank; also, the fire thus directed; a raking fire.—**en-fi-lade′,** *v. t.*; *-laded, -lading.* To attack, or be in position to attack, with an enfilade, or raking fire.

en-fleu-rage (oṅ-flė-räzh), *n.* [F., < *enfleurer,* impregnate with the perfume of flowers, < *en-* (see *en-*) + *fleur,* flower: see *flower.*] A process of extracting perfumes by exposing inodorous oils or fats to the exhalations from the flowers: used when the flower oils are too delicate or fugitive to undergo distillation.

en-fold (en-fōld′), etc. See *infold,* etc.

en-force (en-fōrs′), *v. t.*; *-forced, -forcing.* [OF. *enforcier* (F. *enforcir*), < ML. *infortiare,* < L. *in,* in, + *fortis,* strong.] To strengthen†; impress or urge (an argument, etc.) forcibly; lay stress upon; also, to drive by force† (as, "As swift as stones *Enforced* from the old Assyrian slings": Shakspere's "Henry V.," iv. 7. 65); use force upon† (as, "The flint . . . much *enforced,* shows a hasty spark": Shakspere's "Julius Cæsar," iv. 3. 112); compel, constrain, or oblige to do something (archaic); also, to produce or effect by force; obtain (payment, obedience, etc.) by force or compulsion; impose (a course of action) upon a person; support (a demand, etc.) by force; put or keep (laws or rules) in force; compel obedience to.—**en-force′a-ble, en-for′ci-ble,** *a.* That may be enforced.—**en-for′ced-ly,** *adv.*—**en-force′ment,** *n.* The act or process of enforcing; also, that which enforces, as a compelling influence (archaic: as, "Let gentleness my strong *enforcement* be," Shakspere's "As You Like It," ii. 7. 118).—**en-for′cer,** *n.*

en-frame (en-frām′), *v. t.*; *-framed, -framing.* [See *en-.*] To inclose in or as in a frame.

en-fran-chise (en-fran′chīz or -chiz), *v. t.*; *-chised, -chising.* [OF. *enfranchir* (*enfranchiss-*), < *en-* (see *en-*) + *franc,* free, E. *frank*[2].] To set free; liberate, as from slavery; release from obligation; also, to grant a franchise to; admit to citizenship, esp. to the right of voting; fig., to naturalize, as foreign words.—**en-fran′chise-ment** (-chiz-męnt), *n.*—**en-fran′chis-er** (-chī-zėr or -chi-zėr), *n.*

en-free-dom† (en-frē′dǫm), *v. t.* [See *en-.*] To set free. See Shakspere's "Love's Labour's Lost," iii. 1. 125.

en-gage (en-gāj′), *v.*; *-gaged, -gaging.* [F. *engager,* < *en-* (see *en-*) + *gage,* pledge, E. *gage*[1].] **I.** *tr.* To pledge, pawn, or stake (now rare: as, "This to be true, I do *engage* my life," Shakspere's "As You Like It," v. 4. 172); also, to bind as by pledge, promise, contract, or oath; make liable; specif., to betroth; also, to secure for aid, employment, use, etc. (as, to *engage* a workman; to *engage* a carriage or a room); hire; also, to urge, persuade, or induce (now rare); gain or win over (now rare); attract or please (as, "This humanity and good nature *engages* everybody to him": Addison, in "Spectator," 106); also, to attract and hold fast (the attention, interest, etc.); occupy the attention or efforts of (a person, etc.); entangle or involve (as, "O limed soul, that, struggling to be free, Art more *engaged!*" Shakspere's "Hamlet," iii. 3. 69); also, to cross (weapons); bring (troops) into conflict; enter into conflict with (as, our army *engaged* the enemy at ten o'clock); in *arch.,* to attach or secure (cf. *engaged*); in *mech.,* to cause to become interlocked; interlock with. **II.** *intr.* To pledge one's word;

enter into an agreement; take employment; also, to occupy one's self; become involved; also, to cross weapons; enter into conflict; in *mech.*, to interlock.—**en-gaged'**, *p. a.* Under engagement; pledged; betrothed; busy or occupied; involved; in *arch.*, secured to, or (actually or apparently) partly sunk into, something else, as a column with respect to a wall; in *mech.*, interlocked; of wheels, in gear with each other.—**en-gage'ment,** *n.* The act of engaging, or the state of being engaged; a pledge or promise; an obligation; an agreement; an appointment, as for a meeting; betrothal; employment, or a period or post of employment; occupation; an affair of business; partiality† or bias†; the crossing of weapons; an encounter, conflict, or battle; also, that which engages or induces to any course†; in *mech.*, the act or state of interlocking.—**en-ga'ger** (-gā'jėr), *n.*—**en-ga'ging,** *p. a.* Winning; attractive; pleasing.—**en-ga'ging-ly,** *adv.*—**en-ga'ging-ness,** *n.*

en-garb (en-gärb'), *v. t.* [See *en-*.] To put into a garb; clothe; dress; garb.

en-gar-land (en-gär'lạnd), *v. t.* [See *en-*.] To encircle with a garland.

en-gen-der (en-jen'dėr), *v.* [OF. F. *engendrer*, < L. *ingenerare*: see *ingenerate*[2].] **I.** *tr.* To beget; procreate; hence, to produce, cause, or give rise to (as, "Violence naturally *engenders* violence": Macaulay's "Hist. of Eng.," i.). **II.** *intr.* To meet in sexual embrace†; also, to be produced or caused; come into existence.—**en-gen'der-er,** *n.*—**en-gen'der-ment,** *n.*

en-gild (en-gild'), *v. t.* [See *en-*.] To gild.

en-gine (en'jin), *n.* [OF. F. *engin*, < L. *ingenium*, nature, natural capacity, cleverness, an invention, LL. a mechanical contrivance, engine, < L. *in*, in, + *gen-*, beget, produce: see *genius*.] Innate or natural ability†; ingenuity†; also, an artifice† (as, "Nor did he 'scape By all his *engines*": Milton's "Paradise Lost," i. 750); also, a means or agency; an agent†; also, any mechanical contrivance; a machine or instrument used in warfare, as a battering-ram, catapult, piece of artillery, etc.; an instrument of torture, esp. the rack†; any mechanism or machine designed to convert energy into mechanical work, as a steam-engine (which see), internal-combustion engine (which see), etc.; often, a steam-engine; in popular use, a locomotive engine, or locomotive, for moving cars on a railroad.—**en'gine,** *v. t.*; *-gined, -gining.* To contrive† or plan†; also, to furnish with an engine or engines.—**en-gi-neer'** (-ji-nēr'), *n.* [Obs. F. *enginier* (F. *ingénieur*), OF. *engignier*, < ML. *ingeniarius*, < LL. *ingenium*.] One who contrives, plans, or invents†; a constructor of military engines†; a designer and constructor of military works ('military engineer'); one versed in the design, construction, and care of roads, bridges, canals, aqueducts, harbors, etc. ('civil engineer'); one versed in the design, construction, and use of engines or machines, or in any of the various branches of engineering (as, a mechanical *engineer*; an electrical *engineer*; a mining *engineer*; a structural *engineer*); an artisan who constructs or operates machines (Eng.); one who manages a stationary or locomotive engine; a member of a division or corps of men in the army or navy, trained to engineering work; fig., one who carries through any scheme or enterprise by skill or artful management; a skilful manager.—**en-gi-neer',** *v.* **I.** *tr.* To plan, construct, or manage as an engineer; fig., to arrange, manage, or carry through by skilful or artful contrivance (as, "A conspiracy was carefully *engineered* to replace the Directory by three 'Consuls'": H. G. Wells's "Outline of History," xxxviii. § 2). **II.** *intr.* To act as, or perform the work of, an engineer.—**en-gi-neer'ing,** *n.* The action, work, or profession of an engineer; the art or science of the engineer's profession; the design and construction of military works, of roads, bridges, canals, etc., of engines or machines, or of any structures or works requiring special knowledge and application of the principles of mechanics (see *engineer*, *n.*); fig., skilful or artful contrivance; maneuvering.—**en-gi-neer'ship,** *n.*—**en'gin-er†,** *n.* Var. of *engineer*. See Shakspere's "Hamlet," iii. 4. 206.—**en'gine-ry,** *n.* The constructing of engines or machines, or the art or work of an engineer; also, engines or machines collectively; esp., engines of war; artillery; fig., skilful or artful contrivance; machinations; a system of contrivance or artifice.—**en'gine-turn''ing,** *n.* A kind of ornamental decoration, as on a watchcase, executed by means of a rose-engine.

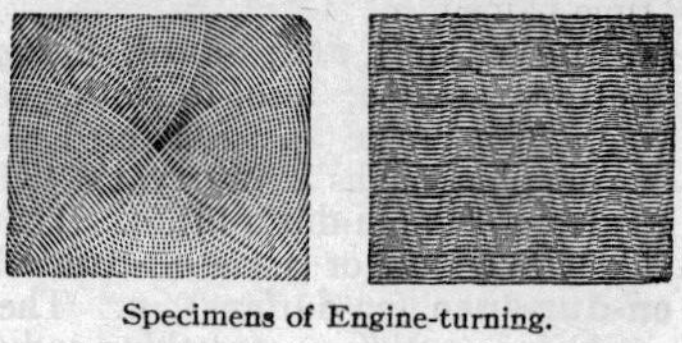
Specimens of Engine-turning.

en-gird (en-gėrd'), *v. t.*; *-girt* or *-girded, -girding.* [See *en-*.] To surround with or as with a girdle; encircle.

en-gir-dle (en-gėr'dl), *v. t.*; *-dled, -dling.* [See *en-*.] To engird; encircle.

en-gla-cial (en-glā'shiạl), *a.* [See *en-*.] In *geol.*, being within a glacier.

Eng-land-er (ing'glạn-dėr), *n.* A native of England.

Eng-lish (ing'glish), *a.* [AS. *Englisc*, < *Engle*, *Angle*, the Angles: see *Angle*[2].] Of, pertaining to, or characteristic of England or its inhabitants; also, belonging or pertaining to, or spoken or written in, the English language.—**English horn.** See under *horn*, *n.*—**Eng'lish,** *n.* The English people collectively; also, the English language (divided into Anglo-Saxon or Old English, extending to about 1150; Middle English, from about 1150 to about 1500; and modern English, from about 1500); an English translation or equivalent, as of a foreign word; the sense in plain English, as of anything obscure; also, a printing-type (14 point) of a size between pica and Columbian (see *type*); [also *l. c.*] in *billiards*, a spinning motion imparted to a ball by a quick stroke on one side of its center (U. S.).—**the king's** (or **queen's**) **English,** idiomatic or correct English.—**Eng'lish,** *v.* **I.** *tr.* To translate into English; express in plain English; adopt (a foreign word) into English; [also *l. c.*] in *billiards*, to impart English to (a ball: U. S.). **II.** *intr.* [Also *l. c.*] In *billiards*, to impart English to a ball. [U. S.]—**Eng'lish-er,** *n.* An Englishman; also, one who translates into English.—**Eng'lish-ism,** *n.* The characteristics, or a characteristic or mode (as of speech), peculiar to the English; also, attachment to what is English.—**Eng'lish-man** (-mạn), *n.*; pl. *-men.* A native, or a naturalized citizen, of England; also, an English ship.—**Eng'lish-ness,** *n.*—**Eng'lish-ry,** *n.* The state of being English; also, a population that is English or of English descent.—**Eng'lish-wom''an,** *n.*; pl. *-women* (-wim''en).

en-globe (en-glōb'), *v. t.*; *-globed, -globing.* [See *en-*.] To inclose in or form into a globe.—**en-globe'ment,** *n.*

en-glut (en-glut'), *v. t.*; *-glutted, -glutting.* [OF. *englotir* (F. *engloutir*), < ML. *inglutire*, < L. *in*, in, + *glutire*, swallow.] To swallow or gulp down; also, to glut or gorge. [Archaic.]

en-gorge (en-gôrj'), *v.*; *-gorged, -gorging.* [F. *engorger*, < *en-* (see *en-*) + *gorge*, E. *gorge*.] **I.** *tr.* To swallow greedily; also, to glut or gorge; in *pathol.*, to congest with blood. **II.** *intr.* To feed greedily.—**en-gorge'ment,** *n.* The act of engorging, or the state of being engorged; in *pathol.*, congestion with blood.

en-goue-ment, en-goû-ment (oṅ-gö-moṅ), *n.* [F., < *engouer*, choke as in gorging.] Infatuation; unreasoning fondness.

en-graft (en-gràft'), etc. Same as *ingraft*, etc.

en-grail (en-grāl'), *v. t.* [OF. *engresler* (F. *engrêler*), appar. < *en-* (see *en-*) + *gresle*, hail.] To ornament the edge of (a heraldic ordinary, etc.) with curved indentations; also, to give a serrated outline to (as, "over hills with peaky tops *engrail'd*": Tennyson's "Palace of Art," 113); also, to adorn (poetic).—**en-grail'ment,** *n.* Indentation in curved lines; also, an engrailed circle or a ring of dots round the edge of a coin, medal, etc.

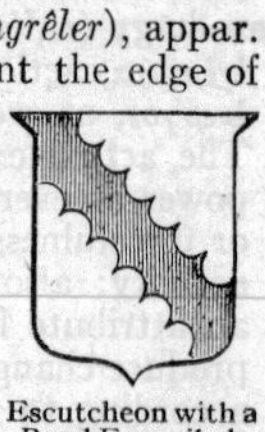
Escutcheon with a Bend Engrailed.

en-grain (en-grān'), etc. Same as *ingrain*, etc.

en-grave (en-grāv'), *v. t.*; pret. *-graved*, pp. *-graved* (archaic *-graven*), ppr. *-graving.* [See *en-* and *grave*[1].] To carve (letters, designs, etc.) on a hard surface, as of metal, stone, or wood; represent by such carving; fig., to impress deeply; infix; also, to mark or ornament with incised letters, designs, etc.—**en-grav'er** (-grā'vėr), *n.*—**en-grav'ing,** *n.* The act or art of one that engraves; the art of forming designs on a hard surface, as of metal or wood, for printing; also, the design engraved; an engraved plate or block; also, an impression from this; a print.

en-gross (en-grōs′), *v. t.* [OF. *engrossier*, make big or bigger, AF. *engrosser*, write large, also OF. *en gros*, in large quantities, by wholesale; all < L. *in*, in, + LL. *grossus*, thick, E. *gross.*] To make large, thick, or gross†; also, to acquire the whole of (a commodity), in order to control the market; get exclusive control of; monopolize; also, to occupy wholly, as the mind or attention; absorb; also, to write or copy in a fair, large hand or in a formal manner for preservation, as a public document or record.—**en-gross′er,** *n.*—**en-gross′ing,** *p. a.* That engrosses; fully occupying the mind or attention; absorbing.—**en-gross′ing-ly,** *adv.*—**en-gross′ment,** *n.*

en-gulf (en-gulf′), *v. t.* [See *en-*.] To swallow up in or as in a gulf; cast into or as into a gulf.—**en-gulf′ment,** *n.*

en-hance (en-hȧns′), *v. t.*; *-hanced, -hancing.* [AF. *enhauncer*, OF. *enhaucier*, < *en-* (see *en-*) + *haucier* (F. *hausser*), raise, < L. *altus*, high.] To raise or lift up†; also, to raise to a higher degree; intensify; make greater; increase.—**enhanced music,** reproduced music in which certain modifications have been made to create artistic effects, as by varying the relative amplification in different stereophonic channels, increasing relatively the intensity of upper harmonics, etc.—**en-hance′ment,** *n.*—**en-han′cer,** *n.*

en-har-mon-ic (en-här-mon′ik), *a.* [LL. *enharmonicus*, < Gr. ἐναρμονικός, < ἐν, in, + ἁρμονία, E. *harmony.*] In *music*, noting or pertaining to a style of music, or a scale or instrument, employing intervals smaller than a semitone; esp., pertaining to a use of notes which differ in name and in position on the staff (as G♯ and A♭), but which refer to identical tones or keys on instruments like the pianoforte.—**en-har-mon′i-cal-ly,** *adv.*

en-heart-en (en-här′tn), *v. t.* [See *en-*.] To hearten.

e-nig-ma (ē-nig′mạ), *n.*; pl. *-mas.* [L. *ænigma*, < Gr. αἴνιγμα, < αἰνίσσεσθαι, speak darkly, < αἶνος, tale, fable.] A saying, question, pictorial representation, or the like, containing a hidden meaning to be discovered; a riddle; fig., anything puzzling or inexplicable.—**e-nig-mat-ic, e-nig-mat-i-cal** (ē-nig-mat′ik, -i-kạl, or en-ig-), *a.* [LL. *ænigmaticus.*] Resembling an enigma; perplexing; mysterious.—**e-nig-mat′i-cal-ly,** *adv.*—**e-nig-ma-tize** (ẹ-nig′mạ-tīz), *v. t.*; *-tized, -tizing.* To make enigmatic.

en-isle (en-īl′), *v. t.*; *-isled, -isling.* [See *en-*.] To make an island of; place on an island; isolate. [Poetic.]

en-jamb-ment (en-jamb′mẹnt), *n.* [F. *enjambement*, < *enjamber*, stride over, project, < *en-* (see *en-*) + *jambe*, leg.] In *pros.*, the carrying over from one verse (line) or couplet to the next of an essential portion of a phrase or other closely related sequence of words.

en-join (en-join′), *v. t.* [OF. F. *enjoindre*, < L. *injungere* (pp. *injunctus*), join into or to, impose, enjoin, < *in*, in, + *jungere*, join.] To join† or unite†; also, to impose (a penalty, task, etc.); prescribe (a course of action, etc.) with authority or emphasis; order or direct (a person, etc.) to do something; also, to prohibit or forbid.—**en-join′er,** *n.*—**en-join′ment,** *n.*

en-joy (en-joi′), *v. t.* [OF. *enjoir*, < *en-* (see *en-*) + *joir*, E. *joy, v.*] To experience with joy; take pleasure in; hence, to have and use with satisfaction; have the benefit of; possess or have (usually something desirable); also, to find or experience pleasure for (one's self).—**en-joy′a-ble,** *a.* That may be enjoyed; affording enjoyment.—**en-joy′a-ble-ness,** *n.*—**en-joy′a-bly,** *adv.*—**en-joy′er,** *n.*—**en-joy′ment,** *n.* The act or experience of enjoying; pleasure; a particular form or source of pleasure.

en-kin-dle (en-kin′dl), *v. t.*; *-dled, -dling.* [See *en-*.] To kindle into flame, ardor, activity, etc.

en-lace (en-lās′), *v. t.*; *-laced, -lacing.* [OF. *enlacier* (F. *enlacer*), < *en-* (see *en-*) + *lacier*, E. *lace, v.*] To enwind or bind as with a lace or cord; also, to interlace; interweave; intertwine.—**en-lace′ment,** *n.*

en-large (en-lärj′), *v.*; *-larged, -larging.* [OF. *enlarger*, *enlargir*, < *en-* (see *en-*) + *large*, E. *large.*] **I.** *tr.* To make larger; increase in extent, bulk, or quantity; extend; add to; augment; magnify; increase the capacity or scope of; expand; also, to set at large (archaic). **II.** *intr.* To grow larger; increase; expand; also, to speak or write at large; expatiate.—**en-large′a-ble,** *a.*—**en-large′ment,** *n.* The act of enlarging; increase; expansion; amplification; release, as from confinement (as, "Then shall there *enlargement* and deliverance arise to the Jews": Esther, iv. 14); also, enlarged state or form; also, anything, as a photograph, that is an enlarged form of something else; also, anything that enlarges something else; an addition.—**en-lar′ger,** *n.*

en-light-en (en-lī′tn), *v. t.* [See *en-*.] To shed light upon (archaic); fig., to supply with intellectual or spiritual light; instruct; inform.—**en-light′ened,** *p. a.* Intellectually or morally advanced; free from ignorance, prejudice, superstition, etc.—**en-light′en-er,** *n.*—**en-light′en-ment,** *n.* The act of enlightening, or the state of being enlightened; illumination of the mind; sometimes [also *cap.*], same as *aufklärung*.

en-link (en-lingk′), *v. t.* [See *en-*.] To link or chain together.

en-list (en-list′), *v.* [See *en-*.] **I.** *tr.* To enter on a list; enroll; specif., to engage for military or naval service; hence, to secure (a person, or his services, support, sympathy, etc.) in aid of some cause, enterprise, etc.; utilize (natural forces, etc.) for a special purpose. **II.** *intr.* To engage for military or naval service; hence, to enter into some cause, enterprise, etc.—**en-list′er,** *n.*—**en-list′ment,** *n.*

en-liv-en (en-lī′vn), *v. t.* [Cf. the earlier *enlive*, *enlife*, *v.*, < *en-* + *life.*] To give life to†; hence, to make vigorous or active; invigorate; stimulate; also, to make sprightly, gay, or cheerful; brighten.—**en-liv′en-er,** *n.*—**en-liv′en-ing-ly,** *adv.*—**en-liv′en-ment,** *n.*

en-mesh (en-mesh′), *v. t.* [See *en-*.] To inclose or catch in or as in the meshes of a net; insnare; entangle.—**en-mesh′ment,** *n.*

en-mi-ty (en′mi-ti), *n.*; pl. *-ties* (-tiz). [OF. *ennemistie* (F. *inimitié*), < L. *inimicus*: see *enemy.*] A feeling or condition of hostility; hatred; ill-will; animosity; antagonism; variance.

en-ne-ad (en′ẹ-ad), *n.* [LL. *enneas* (*ennead-*), < Gr. ἐννεάς (ἐννεαδ-), < ἐννέα, nine.] The number nine; a group of nine persons or things.—**en-ne-ad′ic,** *a.*

en-ne-a-gon (en′ẹ-ạ-gon), *n.* [Gr. ἐννέα, nine, + γωνία, angle.] A plane figure having nine angles and nine sides.—**en-ne-ag′o-nal** (-ag′ọ-nạl), *a.*

en-ne-a-he-dron (en″ẹ-ạ-hē′drọn), *n.* [Gr. ἐννέα, nine, + ἕδρα, seat, base.] A solid figure having nine faces.—**en″ne-a-he′dral,** *a.*

en-no-ble (e-nō′bl), *v. t.*; *-bled, -bling.* [F. *ennoblir*, < *en-* (see *en-*) + *noble*: see *noble.*] To make noble; confer a title of nobility on; also, to impart nobility to; elevate in degree, excellence, or respect; dignify; exalt.—**en-no′ble-ment,** *n.*—**en-no′bler,** *n.*

en-nui (oṅ-nwē), *n.* [F.: see *annoy, n.*] A feeling of weariness and discontent resulting from satiety or lack of interest; boredom.—**en-nui** (oṅ′nwē), *v. t.*; *-nuied* or *-nuyed, -nuying.* To affect with ennui; bore.—**en-nuy-é** (oṅ-nwē-yā), *a.* [F. (fem. *ennuyée*), pp. of *ennuyer*: cf. *annoy, v.*] Affected with ennui; bored: as, "the constrained effort of the *ennuyé* man of the world" (Poe's "Fall of the House of Usher").

e-nol′o-gy, etc. See *œnology*, etc.

e-norm (ẹ-nôrm′), *a.* [OF. *enorme* (F. *énorme*), < L. *enormis*, < *e*, out of, + *norma*, rule, E. *norm*: cf. *enormous.*] Abnormal†; extraordinary†; abnormally large (archaic); outrageous†.

e-nor-mi-ty (ẹ-nôr′mi-ti), *n.*; pl. *-ties* (-tiz). [OF. *enormite* (F. *énormité*), < L. *enormitas*, < *enormis*, E. *enorm*, *enormous.*] Abnormal character†; also, enormous size or extent (now rare); also, outrageous or heinous character, as of an offense; atrociousness; also, something outrageous or heinous; a monstrous offense.

e-nor-mous (ẹ-nôr′mus), *a.* [L. *enormis*: see *enorm.*] Abnormal†; also, greatly exceeding the common size, extent, etc.; huge; immense; monstrous; also, outrageous or atrocious (as, *enormous* wickedness).—**e-nor′mous-ly,** *adv.*—**e-nor′mous-ness,** *n.*

e-nough (ẹ-nuf′). [AS. *genōg*, *genōh*, = D. *genoeg* = G. *genug* = Icel. *gnōgr* = Goth. *ganōhs*, enough.] **I.** *a.* Adequate for the want or need; sufficient for the purpose or to satisfy desire. **II.** *n.* An adequate quantity or number;

as much as is needed or desired; a sufficiency.—**e-nough′,** *adv.* In a quantity or degree that answers a purpose or satisfies a need or desire; sufficiently; fully or quite (as, he is ready *enough* to accept the offer); tolerably or passably (as, "Thou singest well *enough* for a shift": Shakspere's "Much Ado about Nothing," ii. 3. 80).

e-nounce (ē-nouns′), *v. t.*; *enounced, enouncing.* [F. *énoncer,* < L. *enuntiare,* < *e,* out of, + *nuntiare,* announce, declare, < *nuntius,* messenger.] To announce, declare, or proclaim; also, to state definitely, as a proposition; also, to utter or pronounce, as words.—**e-nounce′ment,** *n.*

e-now (ē-nou′). Archaic or prov. form of *enough*: as, "She has cause *enow*" (Swinburne's "Chastelard," v. 2).

en-quire (en-kwīr′), etc. Same as *inquire,* etc.

en-rage (en-rāj′), *v.*; *-raged, -raging.* [OF. F. *enrager,* intr., < *en-* (see *en-*) + *rage,* E. *rage.*] **I.**† *intr.* To go mad; be maddened; become furiously angry; rage. **II.** *tr.* To affect with madness or rabies†; put into a rage; infuriate; exasperate.—**en-raged′,** *p. a.* Maddened†; also, infuriated; furious; also, passionate†.—**en-rage′ment,** *n.*

en-rank (en-rangk′), *v. t.* [See *en-.*] To arrange in a rank or row, or in ranks.

en-rapt (en-rapt′), *a.* [See *en-* and *rapt*².] Rapt; transported; enraptured.

en-rap-ture (en-rap′tūr), *v. t.*; *-tured, -turing.* [See *en-.*] To move to rapture; delight beyond measure.

en-reg-is-ter (en-rej′is-tėr), *v. t.* [F. *enregistrer,* < *en-* (see *en-*) + *registre,* E. *register.*] To register; record.

en-rich (en-rich′), *v. t.* [OF. F. *enrichir,* < *en-* (see *en-*) + *riche,* E. *rich.*] To make rich or richer; supply with riches, wealth, abundant or valuable possessions, etc. (as, commerce *enriches* a nation; museums *enriched* by gifts); supply with abundance of anything desirable (as, to *enrich* the mind with knowledge); embellish, as with anything ornamental; make finer in quality as by supplying desirable elements or ingredients (as, to *enrich* a language with new words; to *enrich* food with cream or butter); fertilize (the soil).—**en-rich′er,** *n.*—**en-rich′ment,** *n.* The act of enriching, or the state of being enriched; also, something that enriches.

en-ridge (en-rij′), *v. t.* [See *en-.*] To form into ridges.

en-ring (en-ring′), *v. t.* [See *en-.*] To form a ring or circle about; encircle; also, to put a ring or rings on; adorn with a ring.

en-robe (en-rōb′), *v. t.*; *-robed, -robing.* [See *en-.*] To invest with or as with a robe; dress; attire.—**en-robe′-ment,** *n.*

en-roll, en-rol (en-rōl′), *v. t.*; *-rolled, -rolling.* [OF. *enroller* (F. *enrôler*), < *en-* (see *en-*) + *rolle,* E. *roll, n.*] To write (a name), or insert the name of (a person), in a roll or register; place upon a list; enlist; also, to put in a record; record; also, to engross (a document)†; also, to roll or wrap up.—**en-roll′er,** *n.*—**en-rol′ment, en-roll′ment,** *n.* The act of enrolling, or the process of being enrolled; registration, as of a deed or a judgment; also, a roll, register, or record.

en-root (en-röt′), *v. t.* [See *en-.*] To fix by the root; fig., to fix fast; implant deeply.

ens (enz), *n.*; pl. *entia* (en′shi-ạ̈). [L., ppr. of *esse,* be.] Being, considered in the abstract; also, something that is; an entity.

en-sam-ple (en-sam′pl), *n.* [OF. *ensample,* for *essample, example,* E. *example.*] An example, or instance, pattern, or warning. [Archaic.]

en-san-guine (en-sang′gwin), *v. t.*; *-guined, -guining.* [See *en-* and *sanguine.*] To stain or cover with blood; color blood-red.

en-sate (en′sāt), *a.* [NL. *ensatus,* < L. *ensis,* sword.] In *bot.* and *zoöl.,* sword-shaped; ensiform.

en-sconce (en-skons′), *v. t.*; *-sconced, -sconcing.* [See *en-* and *sconce*².] Orig., to furnish or protect with or as with a sconce or fort; also, to shelter within or as if behind a fortification (as, "Pedro de Vargas . . . alcayde of Gibraltar . . . lay *ensconced* in his old warrior rock as in a citadel": Irving's "Conquest of Granada," xi.); hence, later, to establish in any place affording concealment; settle securely or snugly (as, to *ensconce* one's self in an arm-chair).

en-seal (en-sēl′), *v. t.* [OF. *enseeler,* < *en-* (see *en-*) + *seel,* E. *seal*¹.] To put a seal or stamp on (archaic); also, to close up with a seal; seal up.

en-seam† (en-sēm′), *v. t.* [OF. *ensaimer* (F. *ensimer*), < *en-* (see *en-*) + *saim,* E. *seam*².] To make greasy; befoul with or as with grease. See Shakspere's "Hamlet," iii. 4. 92.

en-sem-ble (oṅ-soṅbl), *n.* [F., < L. *insimul,* at the same time, < *in,* in, + *simul,* at the same time, together.] All the parts of a thing taken together, so that each part is considered only in relation to the whole; the united performance of the full number of singers, musicians, etc.; the general effect, as of a work of art.

en-sep-ul-cher, en-sep-ul-chre (en-sep′ul-kėr), *v. t.*; *-chered, -chred, -chering, -chring.* [See *en-.*] To entomb.

en-sheathe (en-shēᴛʜ′), *v. t.* Same as *insheathe.*

en-shield (en-shēld′), *v. t.*; obs. pp. *enshield.* [See *en-.*] To shield.

en-shrine (en-shrīn′), *v. t.*; *-shrined, -shrining.* [See *en-.*] To inclose in or as in a shrine; cherish as sacred.—**en-shrine′ment,** *n.*

en-shroud (en-shroud′), *v. t.* [See *en-.*] To cover with or as with a shroud; shroud; conceal.

en-si-form (en′si-fôrm), *a.* [L. *ensis,* sword: see *-form.*] Sword-shaped; ensate; xiphoid.

Ensiform Leaf of Iris.

en-sign (en′sīn), *n.* [OF. F. *enseigne,* < L. *insignia*: see *insignia.*] A sign, token, emblem, or badge; esp., a badge of office or authority; also, a flag or banner, as of a nation; a body of troops serving under one banner†; a standard-bearer, formerly one in the British army; in the U. S. navy (also pron. en′sn), the lowest commissioned officer, ranking next below a lieutenant (junior grade).—**en′sign-cy** (-si), **en′sign-ship,** *n.*

en-si-lage (en′si-lāj), *n.* [F., < *ensiler*: see *ensile.*] The preservation of green fodder in a silo or pit; also, fodder thus preserved.—**en′si-lage,** *v. t.*; *-laged, -laging.* To store by ensilage; ensile.

en-sile (en-sīl′ or en′sīl), *v. t.*; *-siled, -siling.* [F. *ensiler,* < Sp. *ensilar,* < *en-* (< L. *in,* in) + *silo*: see *silo.*] To preserve (green fodder) in a silo; make into ensilage.

en-sky (en-skī′), *v. t.*; *-skied, -skying.* [See *en-.*] To place in the sky. See Shakspere's "Measure for Measure," i. 4. 34.

en-slave (en-slāv′), *v. t.*; *-slaved, -slaving.* [See *en-.*] To make a slave of; reduce to slavery.—**en-slave′ment,** *n.*—**en-slav′er** (-slā′vėr), *n.*

en-snare (en-snãr′), etc. See *insnare,* etc.

en-sor-cel, en-sor-cell (en-sôr′sẹl), *v. t.* [F. *ensorceler,* OF. *ensorcerer,* < *en-* (see *en-*) + *sorcier*: see *sorcerer.*] To use sorcery on; bewitch. [Archaic.]

en-soul (en-sōl′), *v. t.* [See *en-.*] To endow with a soul.

en-sphere (en-sfēr′), *v. t.*; *-sphered, -sphering.* [See *en-.*] To inclose in or make into a sphere.

en-steep (en-stēp′), *v. t.* Same as *insteep.*

en-sue (en-sū′), *v.*; *-sued, -suing.* [OF. F. *ensuivre,* < L. *insequi,* < *in,* in, on, + *sequi,* follow.] **I.**† *tr.* To follow; pursue: as, "Let him seek peace, and *ensue* it" (1 Pet. iii. 11). **II.** *intr.* To follow in order; come afterward, esp. in immediate succession; also, to follow as a consequence, or result (as, "That out of distance might *ensue* Desire of nearness doubly sweet": Tennyson's "In Memoriam," cxvii.).

en-sure (en-shör′), *v. t.*; *-sured, -suring.* [AF. *enseurer,* < OF. *en-* (see *en-*) + *seur,* E. *sure.*] To assure or convince (a person), as of a thing†; inform (a person) positively†; warrant (a thing) as sure or true†; engage or pledge, esp. in marriage†; guarantee against risk† (now *insure*); also, to make secure or safe, as from harm; render sure or certain to come, occur, etc. (as, measures to *ensure* the success of an undertaking); secure, or bring surely, as to a person (as, this letter will *ensure* you a hearing). See *insure.*—**en-sur′er,** *n.*

en-swathe (en-swāᴛʜ′), *v. t.*; *-swathed, -swathing.* [See *en-.*] To swathe.—**en-swathe′ment,** *n.*

-ent. [F. *-ent,* < L. *-ent-,* nom. *-ens,* ppr. ending, corresponding to E. *-ing*²; or directly from L. *-ent-.*] A suffix equivalent to *-ant,* in adjectives and nouns, as in *ardent, crescent, dependent, different, expedient, orient.* Cf. *-ence.*

en-tab-la-ture (en-tab′lạ-tūr), *n.* [Obs. F. *entablature,* < L. *in,* in, + *tabula,* board, plank, E. *table.*] That part of a classic architectural order which rests horizontally upon the columns, and consists of the architrave, frieze, and cornice; hence, a similar part in other constructions.

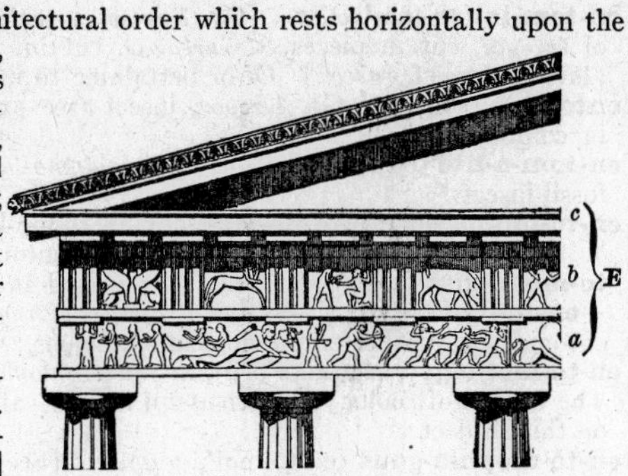

Doric Entablature.
E, entablature: *a*, architrave; *b*, frieze; *c*, cornice.

en-tail (en-tāl′), *v. t.* [See *en-* and *tail*[1].] To limit the inheritance of (a landed estate) to a specified line of heirs, so that it cannot be alienated, or bequeathed at pleasure, by any one possessor; hence, to confer as if by entail; cause to descend to a fixed series of possessors; also, to impose as a burden upon some one; hence, to bring on or involve (as, a loss *entailing* no regret).—**en-tail′**, *n.* The act of entailing, or the state of being entailed; the rule of descent settled for an estate; any predetermined order of succession, as to an office; the transmission as an inalienable inheritance of qualities, obligations, etc.; hence, necessary sequence; also, that which is entailed, as an estate.—**en-tail′er**, *n.*—**en-tail′ment**, *n.*

en-tame (en-tām′), *v. t.*; *-tamed*, *-taming*. [See *en-*.] To tame.

en-tan-gle (en-tang′gl), *v. t.*; *-gled*, *-gling*. [See *en-*.] To make tangled; complicate; also, to involve in anything tangled; insnare; involve in anything from which extrication is difficult; hence, to involve in difficulties; embarrass; perplex.—**en-tan′gle-ment**, *n.* The act of entangling, or the state of being entangled; also, that which entangles; a snare; an embarrassment; a complication.—**en-tan′gler**, *n.*—**en-tan′gling-ly**, *adv.*

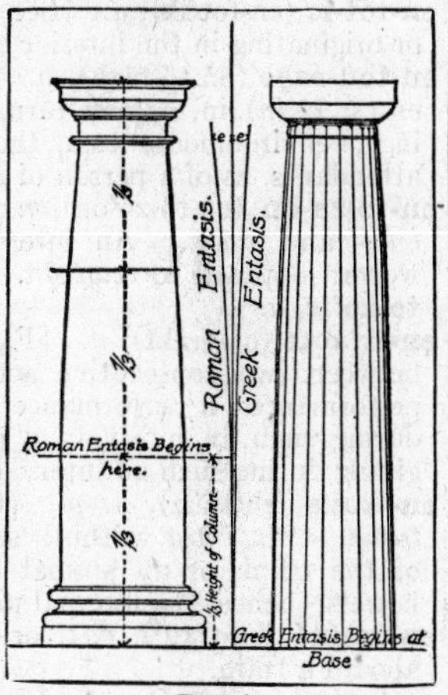

Entasis.
e, *e*, arcs of entasis. (The proportions and the amount of entasis are much exaggerated for the purpose of illustration.)

en-ta-sis (en′tą-sis), *n.* [NL., < Gr. ἔντασις, a stretching, < ἐντείνειν, < ἐν, in, + τείνειν, stretch.] In *arch.*, the swelling or outward curve of the shaft of a column.

en-tel-e-chy (en-tel′ę-ki), *n.*; pl. *-chies* (-kiz). [L. *entelechia*, < Gr. ἐντελέχεια, < ἐν τέλει ἔχειν, be in fulfilment or completion.] In *philos.*, a realization or actuality as opposed to a potentiality: an Aristotelian term.

en-tel-lus (en-tel′us), *n.* [NL.; appar. named from *Entellus*, character (elderly man) in Virgil's "Æneid."] The sacred monkey of India, *Semnopithecus entellus*, remarkable for its long tail, full beard, and cap-like growth of hair on the crown, peaked over the eyes.

Entellus.

en-tente (oṅ-toṅt), *n.* [F.] Understanding; also, the parties to an understanding.—**entente cordiale** (kôr-dyål). [F.] A cordial or friendly understanding, as between one government and another.—**Little Entente.** See under *little*, *a.*—**Triple Entente.** See under *triple*, *a.*

en-ter (en′tėr), *v.* [OF. F. *entrer*, < L. *intrare*, < *intro*, within: see *intro-*.] **I.** *tr.* To come or go into; pass within; break into; penetrate or pierce; make a beginning of or in, or begin upon; engage or become involved in; become a member of, or join; also, to put in or insert; cause to be admitted, as into a school, competition, etc.; initiate† or introduce†; make a record of, record, or register; report (a vessel, etc.) at the custom-house; place in regular form before a court, as a writ; file an application for (public lands). **II.** *intr.* To come or go in; make an entrance, as on the stage; be admitted; make a beginning.—**to enter into**, to make a beginning in; engage in; assume the obligation of; become a party to; take up the consideration of (a subject); take an interest or part in; sympathize with (a person's feelings, etc.); also, to form a constituent part or ingredient of (as, lead *enters into* the composition of pewter).—**en′ter-a-ble**, *a.* That may be entered.

en-te-ral-gia (en-tę-ral′jią̈), *n.* [NL., < Gr. ἔντερον, intestine, + ἄλγος, pain.] In *pathol.*, spasmodic pain in the intestines or abdomen; colic.

en-te-rec-to-my (en-tę-rek′tǫ-mi), *n.* [Gr. ἔντερον, intestine, + ἐκ, out of, + -τομία, E. *-tomy*.] In *surg.*, removal of a portion of the intestine.

en-ter-er (en′tėr-ėr), *n.* One who enters.

en-ter-ic (en-ter′ik), *a.* [Gr. ἐντερικός.] Pertaining to the enteron; intestinal.—**enteric fever**, typhoid fever.

en-te-ri-tis (en-tę-rī′tis), *n.* [NL., < *enteron*.] In *pathol.*, inflammation of the intestines.

en-te-ron (en′tę-ron), *n.*; pl. *-ra* (-rą̈). [NL., < Gr. ἔντερον, < ἐν, in.] In *anat.* and *zoöl.*, the alimentary canal; the digestive tract.

en-te-rot-o-my (en-tę-rot′ǫ-mi), *n.* [See *enteron* and *-tomy*.] In *surg.*, cutting or incision of the intestine.

en-ter-prise (en′tėr-prīz), *n.* [OF. F. *entreprise*, < *entreprendre*, take in hand, undertake, < L. *inter*, between, + *prehendere*, seize, take.] A project undertaken or to be undertaken, esp. one that is of some importance or that requires boldness or energy; also, engagement in such projects; also, boldness or readiness in undertaking, adventurous spirit, or energy (as, "I had ultimately mustered *enterprise* enough to visit the theatre": Hawthorne's "Blithedale Romance," xviii.).—**en′ter-prise**, *v. t.* or *i.*; *-prised*, *-prising*. To undertake; venture: now chiefly as in *enterprising*, *p. a.*—**en′ter-pris-ing**, *p. a.* That undertakes; characterized by enterprise; ready to undertake projects of importance or difficulty, or untried schemes; energetic in carrying out any undertaking.—**en′ter-pris-ing-ly**, *adv.*

en-ter-tain (en-tėr-tān′), *v.* [OF. F. *entretenir*, < L. *inter*, between, + *tenere*, hold.] **I.** *tr.* To hold mutually†; also, to maintain or keep up (archaic); take into or retain in one's service†; also, to keep engaged or occupied, as a person's time or attention†; while away (time)†; engage (an enemy's forces, etc.) in a contest or conflict†; hold the attention of agreeably, divert, or amuse; also, to give admittance or reception to; specif., to receive as a guest, esp. at one's table; show hospitality to; also, to admit into the mind; consider; also, to hold in the mind; harbor; cherish; also, to deal with† or treat†. **II.** *intr.* To exercise hospitality; entertain company; provide entertainment for guests.—**en-ter-tain′a-ble**, *a.* That may be entertained.—**en-ter-tain′er**, *n.* One who entertains; esp., a person, as a singer, reciter, or the like, who gives, or takes part in, public entertainments.—**en-ter-tain′ing**, *p. a.* Affording entertainment; amusing; diverting.—**en-ter-tain′ing-ly**, *adv.*—**en-ter-tain′ing-ness**, *n.*—**en-ter-tain′ment**, *n.* The act of entertaining, or the state of being entertained; maintenance in service†; employment†; pay†; agreeable occupation for the mind, diversion, or amusement; something affording diversion or amusement, esp. an exhibition or performance of some kind; the reception of guests; hospitable provision for the wants of guests; a feast or banquet; consideration, as of a question; a harboring or cherishing, as of a notion or design.

en-thet-ic (en-thet′ik), *a.* [Gr. ἐνθετικός, fit for implanting, < ἐντιθέναι, put in, < ἐν, in, + τιθέναι, set.] Introduced from without, as diseases propagated by inoculation.

en-thrall, en-thral (en-thrâl′), *v. t.*; *-thralled*, *-thralling*. [See *en-*.] To put or hold in thraldom; subjugate; captivate: now usually fig.—**en-thrall'er,** *n.*—**en-thral'ment, en-thrall'ment,** *n.*

en-throne (en-thrōn'), *v. t.*; *-throned, -throning.* [See *en-.*] To place on or as on a throne; invest with sovereign or episcopal authority; exalt.—**en-throne'ment,** *n.*

en-thuse (en-thūz'), *v. t.* or *i.*; *-thused, -thusing.* [From *enthusiasm.*] To move to or show enthusiasm. [Colloq.]

en-thu-si-asm (en-thū'zi-azm), *n.* [Gr. ἐνθουσιασμός, < ἐνθουσιάζειν, be divinely inspired, < ἔνθεος, possessed by a god, < ἐν, in, + θεός, god.] Possession or inspiration by a god (archaic); a belief or conceit of being divinely inspired or commissioned (archaic); hence, extravagant religious emotion (archaic); now, usually, absorbing or controlling possession of the mind by any interest or pursuit; passionate zeal; ardor; lively interest.—**en-thu'si-ast** (-ast), *n.* [Gr. ἐνθουσιαστής.] One possessed or inspired by a god (archaic); one who believes himself to be divinely instructed or commissioned; hence, one who holds extravagant and visionary religious opinions, or is characterized by excessive religious fervor; also, one who is filled with enthusiasm for some principle, pursuit, etc.; a person of ardent zeal.—**en-thu-si-as'tic,** *a.* [Gr. ἐνθουσιαστικός.] Pertaining to or of the nature of enthusiasm; also, full of or characterized by enthusiasm; ardent.—**en-thu-si-as'ti-cal-ly,** *adv.*

en-thy-meme (en'thi-mēm), *n.* [L. *enthymema*, < Gr. ἐνθύμημα, < ἐνθυμεῖσθαι, consider, infer, < ἐν, in, + θυμός, mind.] In *logic*, a syllogism in which one premise is unexpressed.

en-tice (en-tīs'), *v. t.*; *-ticed, -ticing.* [OF. *enticier*, incite, < L. *in*, in, + *titio*, firebrand.] To incite† or instigate†; also, to draw on by exciting hope or desire; allure; inveigle.—**en-tice'a-ble,** *a.* That may be enticed.—**en-tice'ment,** *n.* The act or practice of enticing, esp. to evil; the state of being enticed; also, that which entices; an allurement.—**en-ti'cer** (-tī'sėr), *n.*—**en-ti'cing-ly,** *adv.*

en-tire (en-tīr'). [OF. F. *entier*, < L. *integer*, untouched, whole: see *integer.*] **I.** *a.* Whole; complete; having all the parts or elements; also, full or thorough (as, *entire* freedom of choice); also, not broken, mutilated, or decayed; intact; not gelded (as, an *entire* horse); unimpaired or undiminished; also, being wholly of one piece; undivided; continuous; hence, having an unbroken outline; without notches or indentations, as leaves, shells, etc.; also, wholly of one kind†; unmixed† or pure†; also, unblemished† or blameless† (as, "Daughter of God and man, immortal Eve! For such thou art; from sin and blame *entire*": Milton's "Paradise Lost," ix. 292); genuine† or sincere† (as, "I have often heard Of your *entire* affection to Bianca": Shakspere's "Taming of the Shrew," iv. 2. 23); also, noting a kind of malt liquor (see *entire, n.*). **II.** *n.* The whole (as, "That one hour of misery and disgrace influenced the *entire* of a future life": Lover's "Handy Andy," xxxv.); entirety; also, an entire horse; a stallion; also (Eng.), a kind of malt liquor; porter.—**en-tire'ly,** *adv.* Wholly or fully; completely or unreservedly; solely or exclusively; heartily† or sincerely†.—**en-tire'ness,** *n.*—**en-tire'ty** (-ti), *n.*; pl. *-ties* (-tiz). [OF. *entierete*, < L. *integritas*: cf. *integrity.*] The state of being entire; completeness; also, that which is entire; the whole.

en-ti-tle (en-tī'tl), *v. t.*; *-tled, -tling.* [OF. *entituler* (F. *intituler*), < ML. *intitulare*, < L. *in*, in, + *titulus*, E. *title.*] To call (a book or other thing, or a person) by a particular title or name; name; style; often, to designate (a person) by an honorary title; also, now esp. of qualities, actions, circumstances, etc., to give (a person or thing) a title, right, or claim to something; furnish with grounds for laying claim.

en-ti-ty (en'ti-ti), *n.*; pl. *-ties* (-tiz). [ML. *entitas*, < L. *ens*: see *ens.*] Being or existence; also, essential nature; essence; also, something that has a real existence; a thing.

ento-, ent-. Forms of Gr. ἐντός, within, used in combination. Cf. *endo-.*

en-to-derm (en'tō-dėrm), etc. Same as *endoderm*, etc.

en-toil (en-toil'), *v. t.* [See *en-.*] To take in toils; insnare. [Archaic.]

en-tomb (en-töm'), *v. t.* [See *en-.*] To place in a tomb; bury; inter; also, to serve as a tomb for.—**en-tomb'ment,** *n.*

en-tom-ic (en-tom'ik), *a.* [Gr. ἔντομον, insect, prop. neut. of ἔντομος, cut in pieces, < ἐντέμνειν, cut in, < ἐν, in, + τέμνειν, cut: cf. *insect.*] Of or pertaining to insects.

entomo-. Form of Gr. ἔντομον, insect (see *entomic*), used in combination.

en-tom-o-lite (en-tom'ō-līt), *n.* [See *entomo-* and *-lite.*] A fossil insect.

en-to-mo-log-ic, en-to-mo-log-i-cal (en"tō-mō-loj'ik, -i-kal), *a.* [See *entomology.*] Of or pertaining to entomology.—**en-to-mol'o-gist** (-mol'ō-jist), *n.* One versed in entomology.—**en-to-mol'o-gize** (-jīz), *v. i.*; *-gized, -gizing.* To study entomology; gather entomological specimens.

en-to-mol-o-gy (en-tō-mol'ō-ji), *n.* [See *entomo-* and *-logy.*] The branch of zoölogy that treats of insects; also, a treatise on this subject.

en-to-moph-a-gous (en-tō-mof'a-gus), *a.* [See *entomo-* and *-phagous.*] Feeding on insects; insectivorous.

en-to-moph-i-lous (en-tō-mof'i-lus), *a.* [See *entomo-* and *-philous.*] Insect-loving: applied to plants in which fertilization is effected by insects.

en-to-mos-tra-can (en-tō-mos'tra-kan). [NL. *Entomostraca*, pl., < Gr. ἔντομος, cut in pieces, + ὄστρακον, shell.] **I.** *a.* Belonging to the *Entomostraca*, a subclass of crustaceans which have a moderately simple organization, including the cirripeds, etc. **II.** *n.* An entomostracan crustacean.

en-to-phyte (en'tō-fīt), *n.* [See *ento-* and *-phyte.*] In *bot.*, a plant living within an animal or another plant, usually as a parasite.—**en-to-phyt'ic** (-fit'ik), *a.*

en-top-tic (en-top'tik), *a.* [See *ento-* and *optic.*] Pertaining to or originating in the interior of the eye.

ent-or-gan-ism (ent-ôr'gan-izm), *n.* [See *ento-.*] An internal parasite.

en-tot-ic (en-tot'ik), *a.* [See *ento-* and *otic.*] Pertaining to or originating in the interior of the ear.

en-tou-rage (oṅ-tö-räzh), *n.* [F., < *entourer*, surround, < *en* (< L. *in*), in, + *tour*, turn, circuit: see *tour.*] Surroundings; environment; esp., those habitually about a person; attendants, as of a person of rank.

en-to-zo-ön (en-tō-zō'on), *n.*; pl. *-zoa* (-zō'ä). [NL.: see *ento-* and *-zoön.*] An internal parasite, as an intestinal worm: opposed to *ectozoön.*—**en-to-zo'an,** *a.* and *n.*—**en-to-zo'ic,** *a.*

en-tr'acte (oṅ-träkt), *n.* [F., 'between-act.'] The interval between two consecutive acts of a theatrical or operatic performance; a performance, as of music or dancing, given during such an interval; a piece of music or the like for giving during such an interval.

en-trails (en'trālz), *n. pl.* [OF. F. *entrailles*, < ML. *intralia*, < L. *intra*, within: see *intra-.*] The internal parts of the trunk of an animal body; esp., the intestines or bowels; hence, the internal parts of anything.

en-train[1] (en-trān'), *v. t.* or *i.* [See *en-.*] To put or go aboard a train.

en-train[2] (en-trān'), *v. t.* [F. *entraîner*, < *en-* (< L. *inde*, thence) + *traîner*, draw, E. *train*[2].] To draw away or on; carry along.—**en-train'ment,** *n.*

en-tram-mel (en-tram'el), *v. t.*; *-meled* or *-melled, -meling* or *-melling.* [See *en-.*] To trammel; hamper; restrain.

en-trance[1] (en'trans), *n.* [OF. *entrance*, < *entrer*: see *enter.*] The act of entering, as into a place or upon new duties; beginning† or commencement†; also, power or liberty of entering; admission; also, a point or place of entering; an opening or passage for entering; *naut.*, the bow or forepart of a vessel under the water-line.

en-trance[2] (en-trans'), *v. t.*; *-tranced, -trancing.* [See *en-.*] To put into a trance; hence, to ravish with delight or wonder, or enrapture (as, "poets whose effusions *entranced* my soul, and lifted it to heaven": Mrs. Shelley's "Frankenstein," letter i.).—**en-tran'ced-ly** (-trån'sed-li), *adv.*—**en-trance'ment,** *n.*—**en-tran'cing-ly,** *adv.*

en-trant (en'trant). [F. *entrant*, ppr. of *entrer*: see *enter.*] **I.** *a.* Entering. **II.** *n.* One who enters; a beginner; a new member.

en-trap (en-trap'), *v. t.*; *-trapped, -trapping.* [OF. *entraper*, < *en-* (see *en-*) + *trape*, trap.] To catch in or as in a trap; insnare; bring unawares into difficulty or danger; draw into contradiction or damaging admission.—**en-trap'ment,** *n.*—**en-trap'per,** *n.*

en-treas-ure (en-trezh′ụ̄r), *v. t.*; *-ured, -uring.* [See *en-*.] To lay up in or as in a treasury.
en-treat (en-trēt′), *v.* [OF. *entraitier*, < *en-* (see *en-*) + *traitier*, E. *treat.*] **I.** *tr.* To treat, or deal with (archaic); while away (time)†; also, to ask earnestly for (something); also, to make supplication to (a person); beseech; implore; also, to persuade by entreaty†. **II.** *intr.* To treat of a subject†; also, to negotiate†; also, to make an earnest request or petition.—**en-treat′ing-ly,** *adv.*—**en-treat′ment,** *n.* Treatment (archaic); also, something entreated, as a favor†.—**en-treat′y,** *n.*; pl. *-ies* (-iz). Treatment†; also, earnest request or petition; solicitation; supplication.
en-tre-chat (oṅ-trė-shä), *n.* [F.] In *dancing*, a leap during which the feet are struck together a number of times.
en-trée (on′trā, F. oṅ-trā), *n.* [F.: see *entry.*] Entry; entrance; also, a made dish such as is served at dinner before the roast or between the regular or principal courses.
en-tre-mets (oṅ-trė-mā), *n.*; pl. *-mets* (F. -mā). [F., 'between-dish.'] A dish served at dinner between the principal courses or with the roast; a side-dish.
en-trench (en-trench′), etc. Same as *intrench*, etc.
en-tre-pôt (on′trẹ-pō, F. oṅ-trė-pō), *n.* [F., < L. *interpositum*, neut. pp. of *interponere*: see *interposition.*] Temporary deposit or storage of goods; also, a building or place for such deposit; a warehouse; also, a commercial center to which goods are sent for distribution (as, "Antwerp . . . had now become the principal *entrepôt* and exchange of Europe": Motley's "Dutch Republic," Introd., xiii.).
en-tre-pre-neur (oṅ-trė-prė-nėr), *n.* [F., < *entreprendre*, undertake: see *enterprise.*] One who undertakes to carry out any enterprise; a contractor; an employer of productive labor.
en-tre-sol (en′tėr-sol, F. oṅ-trė-sol), *n.* [F., 'between-floor.'] A low story between two other stories of greater height, usually one immediately above the ground floor; a mezzanine.

House in Paris. — *E, E,* entresol.

en-tro-pi-on, en-tro-pi-um (en-trō′pi-on, -um), *n.* [NL., < Gr. ἐν, in, + -τρόπιον in ἐκτρόπιον, E. *ectropion.*] In *pathol.*, an abnormal turning or rolling inward of the eyelid, so that the lashes come in contact with the eyeball. Cf. *ectropion.*
en-trust (en-trust′), *v. t.* See *intrust.*
en-try (en′tri), *n.*; pl. *-tries* (-triz). [OF. *entree* (F. *entrée*), < *entrer*: see *enter.*] The act of entering; entrance; a formal entrance; beginning†; a place of ingress or entrance, esp. an entrance-hall or vestibule, or (in England) an alley, or passageway between houses; the act of entering or recording something in a book, register, list, etc.; the statement, etc., so entered or recorded; the giving of an account of a ship's cargo at a custom-house, to obtain permission to land the goods; in *law*, the act of taking possession of lands or tenements by entering or setting foot on them; also, the act of intrusion into a building, essential to complete the crime of burglary.—**double entry,** in *bookkeeping*, a method in which each transaction is entered twice in the ledger, once to the credit of one account, and once to the debit of another.—**single entry,** in *bookkeeping*, a method in which each transaction is entered in the ledger in but one account.—**en′try-man** (-mạn), *n.*; pl. *-men.* One who enters upon a tract of public land with intent to acquire it under the provisions of the law.—**en′try-way,** *n.* A passage for affording entrance; an entry.
en-twine (en-twīn′), *v. t.* or *i.*; *-twined, -twining.* [See *en-*.] To twine together or about.—**en-twine′ment,** *n.*
en-twist (en-twist′), *v. t.* [See *en-*.] To twist together or about.
e-nu-cle-ate (ẹ̄-nū′klẹ̄-āt), *v. t.*; *-ated, -ating.* [L. *enucleatus*, pp. of *enucleare*, < *e*, out of, + *nucleus*, kernel, E. *nucleus.*] To remove (a kernel, tumor, eyeball, etc.) from its enveloping cover; fig., to bring out; disclose; in *biol.*, to deprive of the nucleus.—**e-nu′cle-ate,** *a.* Having no nucleus.—**e-nu-cle-a′tion** (-ā′shọn), *n.*
e-nu-mer-a-ble (ẹ̄-nū′mẹ-rạ-bl), *a.* That may be enumerated.
e-nu-mer-ate (ẹ̄-nū′mẹ-rāt), *v. t.*; *-ated, -ating.* [L. *enumeratus*, pp. of *enumerare*, < *e-*, out, + *numerare*, count, E. *number, v.*] To count; ascertain the number of; more commonly, to mention separately as if in counting; name one by one; specify as in a list.—**e-nu-mer-a′tion** (-mẹ-rā′shọn), *n.* [L. *enumeratio(n-).*] The act of enumerating; a census; a specifying of things one by one, as in a list; also, a catalogue or list.—**e-nu′mer-a-tive** (-mẹ-rạ-tiv), *a.* Serving to enumerate; enumerating.—**e-nu′mer-a-tor** (-mẹ-rā-tọr), *n.*
e-nun-ci-ate (ẹ̄-nun′ṣi-āt), *v.*; *-ated, -ating.* [L. *enuntiatus*, pp. of *enuntiare*: see *enounce.*] **I.** *tr.* To announce or proclaim; also, to state or declare definitely, as a theory; enounce; also, to utter or pronounce (words, etc.), esp. in a particular manner. **II.** *intr.* To utter or pronounce words, etc., in a particular manner.—**e-nun-ci-a′tion** (-ā′shọn), *n.* [L. *enuntiatio(n-).*] The act or the manner of enunciating; announcement; statement; utterance or pronunciation.—**e-nun′ci-a-tive** (-ạ-tiv), *a.* Serving to enunciate; declaratory; also, pertaining to vocal utterance.—**e-nun′ci-a-tor** (-ā-tọr), *n.* One who or that which enunciates.—**e-nun′ci-a-to-ry** (-ạ-tọ̄-ri), *a.* Enunciative.
en-ure (en-ūr′), etc. Same as *inure*, etc.
en-veil (en-vāl′), *v. t.* [See *en-*.] To veil.
en-vel-op (en-vel′ọp), *v. t.*; *-oped, -oping.* [OF. *envoluper* (F. *envelopper*), < *en-* (see *en-*) + *voluper, voloper*, wrap: cf. *develop.*] To wrap up in or as in a covering; inwrap; also, to serve as a wrapping or covering for; also, to surround entirely.—**en-vel-op, en-ve-lope** (en-vel′ọp, en′vẹ-lōp), *n.* [F. *enveloppe.*] That which envelops; a wrapper; an integument; a surrounding cover; esp. (sometimes, when spelled *envelope*, pron. on′vẹ-lōp), a cover for a letter or the like, usually so made that it can be sealed or fastened; in *bot.*, a surrounding or inclosing part, as of leaves (see *floral envelop*, under *floral*); in *astron.*, a surrounding nebulous mass, as the coma of a comet; specif., a vaporous bow or shell (regarded as part of the coma) partly surrounding the nucleus of a comet on the side next the sun; in *geom.*, a curve or surface touching a continuous series of curves or surfaces.—**en-vel′op-er,** *n.*—**en-vel′op-ment,** *n.* The act of enveloping, or the state of being enveloped; also, a wrapping or covering.

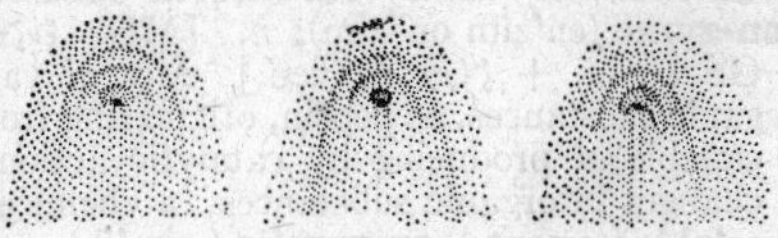
Envelops of Comets.

en-ven-om (en-ven′ọm), *v. t.* [OF. F. *envenimer*, < *en-* (see *en-*) + (OF.) *venim*, E. *venom.*] To impregnate with venom; make poisonous; hence, to embitter; also, to corrupt or vitiate.
en-vi-a-ble (en′vi-ạ-bl), *a.* That is to be envied; worthy to be envied.—**en′vi-a-ble-ness,** *n.*—**en′vi-a-bly,** *adv.*
en-vi-er (en′vi-ėr), *n.* One who envies.
en-vi-ous (en′vi-us), *a.* [OF. *envious* (F. *envieux*), < L. *invidiosus*, < *invidia*, E. *envy*: cf. *invidious.*] Spiteful† or malicious†; also, full of, feeling, or expressing envy (as, to be *envious* of a person's success; an *envious* attack); also, grudging† or sparing†; also, emulous† (as, "She saw the young Corinthian Lycius Charioting foremost in the *envious* race": Keats's "Lamia," i.); also, enviable† (as, "He to him lept, and that same *envious* gage Of victors glory from him snacht away": Spenser's "Faerie Queene," i. 4. 39).—**en′vi-ous-ly,** *adv.*—**en′vi-ous-ness,** *n.*
en-vi-ron (en-vī′rọn), *v. t.*; *-roned, -roning.* [OF. F. *environner*, < *environ*, around, about, < *en* (< L. *in*), in, + *viron*, a round, circuit, akin to *virer*, turn, E. *veer*[2].] To form a circle or ring round; surround; envelop; inclose; beset.—**en-vi′ron-ment,** *n.* The act of environing, or the state of being environed; also, that which environs; the aggregate of surrounding things, conditions, or influences.—

en-vi-ron-men'tal (-men'tal), *a.*—**en-vi-rons** (en-vī'rọnz or en'vi-rọnz), *n. pl.* [F.] Surrounding parts or districts, as of a city; outskirts; suburbs: as, "Roland . . . fixed his abode in the *environs* of Paris" (Bulwer-Lytton's "Caxtons," xvi. 4).

en-vis-age (en-viz'āj), *v. t.*; *-aged, -aging.* [F. *envisager*, < *en-* (see *en-*) + *visage*, E. *visage.*] To look in the face of; face; contemplate or regard; in *philos.*, to perceive by intuition.—**en-vis'age-ment,** *n.*

en-voy[1] (en'voi), *n.* [OF. *envoy* (F. *envoi*), < *envoier* (F. *envoyer*), earlier *enveier*, send, < L. *in*, in, on, + *via*, way.] A postscript to a poetical or prose composition, sometimes serving as a dedication; esp., a short stanza concluding a poem in certain archaic metrical forms.

en-voy[2] (en'voi), *n.* [F. *envoyé*, prop. pp. of *envoyer*, send: see *envoy*[1].] A diplomatic agent; specif., a diplomatic agent of the second rank, next in dignity after an ambassador (called, in full, 'envoy extraordinary and minister plenipotentiary'); also, any accredited messenger or representative.—**en'voy-ship,** *n.*

en-vy (en'vi), *n.*; pl. *-vies* (-viz). [OF. F. *envie*, < L. *invidia*, < *invidus*, envious, < *invidere*, look at with ill-will, envy, grudge, < *in*, in, on, + *videre*, see.] Ill-will†; also, odium† or ill repute†; also, a feeling of discontent or mortification, usually accompanied with some degree of ill-will, excited by the contemplation of another's superiority, advantages, or success; a covetous desire for some advantage possessed by another; also, an object of envious feeling.—**en'vy,** *v.*; *-vied, -vying.* **I.** *tr.* To regard with envy; be envious of; also, to begrudge†. **II.**† *intr.* To be affected with envy: as, "I *envy* at their liberty" (Shakspere's "King John," iii. 4. 73).—**en'vy-ing-ly,** *adv.*

en-wheel† (en-hwēl'), *v. t.* [See *en-*.] To encircle.

en-wind (en-wīnd'), *v. t.*; *-wound, -winding.* [See *en-*.] To wind or coil about; encircle: as, "The moony vapour rolling round the King . . . *Enwound* him fold by fold" (Tennyson's "Guinevere," 599).

en-womb (en-wöm'), *v. t.* [See *en-*.] To inclose in or as in the womb.

en-wrap (en-rap'), *v. t.* Same as *inwrap.*

en-wreathe (en-rēᴛʜ'), *v. t.* Same as *inwreathe.*

en-zo-öt-ic (en-zọ-ot'ik). [= F. *enzootique*, < Gr. ἐν, in, + ζῷον, animal: cf. *epizoötic.*] **I.** *a.* Prevailing among or afflicting animals in a particular locality: said of diseases. Cf. *endemic.* **II.** *n.* An enzoötic disease.

en-zyme (en'zīm or -zim), *n.* [MGr. ἔνζυμος, leavened, < Gr. ἐν, in, + ζύμη, leaven.] Any of various complex organic substances, as pepsin, originating from living cells, and capable of producing by catalytic action certain chemical changes in organic substances; a chemical, unorganized, or soluble ferment.—**en-zym'ic** (-zim'ik), *a.*

E-o-cene (ē'ọ-sēn). [Gr. ἠώς, dawn, + καινός, new.] In *geol.*: **I.** *a.* Noting or pertaining to the earliest principal subdivision of the Tertiary period or system. **II.** *n.* The Eocene subdivision of the Tertiary.

E-o-li-an (ē-ō'li-an), etc. See *Æolian*[1], etc.

e-o-lith (ē'ọ-lith), *n.* [Gr. ἠώς, dawn, + λίθος, stone.] A rude stone implement characteristic of the earliest stage of human culture.—**e-o-lith'ic,** *a.* Noting or pertaining to the earliest stage of human culture, characterized by the existence of the most primitive stone implements.

e-on (ē'ọn), etc. See *æon*, etc.

E-os (ē'os), *n.* [L., < Gr. Ἠώς, personification of ἠώς, dawn: see *east.*] The Greek goddess of the dawn, identified with the Roman Aurora.

e-o-sin (ē'ọ-sin), *n.* [Gr. ἠώς, dawn.] A coal-tar product, used for dyeing silk, etc., rose-red.

e-o-zo-ic (ē-ọ-zō'ik), *a.* [Gr. ἠώς, dawn, + ζωή, life.] In *geol.*, characterized by the earliest traces of life, as found in fossiliferous rocks.

ep-. See *epi-*.

e-pact (ē'pakt), *n.* [F. *épacte*, < LL. *epacta*, < Gr. ἐπακτή, prop. fem. of ἐπακτός, verbal adj. of ἐπάγειν, bring on, add, < ἐπί, on, + ἄγειν, lead.] The excess in days of a solar year over a lunar year; also, the age in days of the calendar moon at the beginning of the year (Jan. 1).

ep-arch (ep'ärk), *n.* [Gr. ἔπαρχος, < ἐπί, on, + ἄρχειν, lead, rule.] The prefect or governor of an eparchy; in the *Gr. Ch.*, a metropolitan or bishop of an eparchy.—**ep'ar-chy** (-är-ki), *n.*; pl. *-chies* (-kiz). [Gr. ἐπαρχία.] In ancient Greece, a province; in modern Greece, one of the administrative subdivisions of a province; in the *Gr. Ch.*, a diocese or archdiocese.

é-pa-tant (ā-pâ-täṅ), *a.* [F. (fem. *épatante*), pp. of *épater*, break off the foot of (a dog, a goblet, etc.), knock down, amaze.] Amazing; startling.

e-paule (e-pâl'), *n.* [F. *épaule*, shoulder, < L. *spatula*, broad piece: see *spatula.*] In *fort.*, the shoulder or angle where the face and flank of a bastion meet.

ep-au-let, ep-au-lette (ep'â-let), *n.* [F. *épaulette*, < *épaule*: see *epaule.*] An ornamental shoulder-piece worn on uniforms, chiefly by military and naval officers; also, a similar ornamental piece in women's dress; also, in *armor*, any of various pieces or coverings for protecting the shoulder.—**ep'au-let-ed, ep'au-let-ted,** *a.*

Epaulets, 15th and 16th centuries.

e-paul-ment, e-paule-ment (e-pâl'ment), *n.* [F. *épaulement*, < *épauler*, protect by an epaulment, < *épaule*: see *epaule.*] In *fort.*, an earthwork or other screen for protecting a battery, troops, or the like, as from flanking fire.

ep-ax-i-al (ep-ak'si-al), *a.* [See *epi-* and *axis*[1].] In *anat.*, above or posterior to an axis.—**ep-ax'i-al-ly,** *adv.*

ep-ei-rog-e-ny (ep-ī-roj'e-ni), etc. See *epirogeny*, etc.

ep-en-ceph-a-lon (ep-en-sef'a-lon), *n.*; pl. *-la* (-lā). [NL.: see *epi-* and *encephalon.*] In *anat.*, the part of the brain behind the mesencephalon, consisting of cerebellum and pons Varolii; the hindbrain.—**ep"en-ce-phal'ic** (-se-fal'ik), *a.*

e-pen-the-sis (e-pen'the-sis), *n.*; pl. *-theses* (-the-sēz). [LL., < Gr. ἐπένθεσις, < ἐπεντιθέναι, insert, < ἐπί, on, to, + ἐντιθέναι, put in: see *enthetic.*] In *gram.*, the insertion of a letter or syllable in the midst of a word, as to facilitate pronunciation; also, the transposition of a semivowel to the syllable preceding that in which it originally occurred.—**ep-en-thet-ic** (ep-en-thet'ik), *a.*

e-pergne (ẹ-pėrn' or e-pärn'), *n.* [Cf. F. *épargne*, saving, economy, also formerly treasury or exchequer.] An ornamental piece for the center of a dinner-table, consisting of a dish or receptacle, often elaborate in design, with several tiers, branches, or divisions, for holding fruit, flowers, etc.

ep-ex-e-ge-sis (ep-ek-sẹ-jē'sis), *n.* [NL., < Gr. ἐπεξήγησις, < ἐπεξηγεῖσθαι, explain in addition, < ἐπί, on, to, + ἐξηγεῖσθαι: see *exegesis.*] In *rhet.*, the addition of a word or words to explain a preceding word or sentence; the word or words so added.—**ep-ex-e-get'ic, ep-ex-e-get'i-cal** (-jet'ik, -i-kal), *a.*—**ep-ex-e-get'i-cal-ly,** *adv.*

e-phah (ē'fā), *n.* [Heb.] A Hebrew dry measure, equal to about a bushel. See Ezek. xlv. 11.

e-phebe (e-fēb' or ef'ēb), *n.* [L. *ephebus*, < Gr. ἔφηβος, < ἐπί, on, + ἥβη, youth, youthful prime: cf. *Hebe.*] Among the ancient Greeks, a youth just entering upon manhood or just enrolled as a citizen.—**e-phe-bic** (e-fē'bik), *a.* [Gr. ἐφηβικός.] Of or pertaining to ephebes: as, the *ephebic* oath (the oath by which ephebes bound themselves to the service and defense of their country; hence, any solemn promise made by young men to become good citizens).

eph-e-drine, eph-e-drin (ef'e-drin, also e-fed'rin), *n.* [NL. *Ephedra* (see def.; in L. the plant horsetail, < Gr. ἐφέδρα, < ἐπί, on, + ἕδρα, seat) + *-ine*[2].] In *phar.*, a crystalline alkaloid, $C_{10}H_{15}NO$, found in species of *Ephedra* (a genus of jointed, nearly leafless, equisetum-like desert shrubs): used esp. for colds, asthma, and hay-fever.

e-phem-e-ra (e-fem'ẹ-rā or ẹ-), *n.*; pl. *-ras* or *-ræ* (-rē). [ML. (the fever) and NL. (the insect), < Gr. ἐφήμερος, of or for a day, short-lived, daily, < ἐπί, on, + ἡμέρα, day.] A fever lasting but a day or a very short time; also, an ephemerid or May-fly; hence, anything short-lived or transitory.—**e-phem'e-ral,** *a.* Lasting but a day or a very short time; short-lived; transitory.—**e-phem-e-ral'i-ty** (-ral'i-ti), *n.*—**e-phem'e-ral-ly,** *adv.*

e-phem-e-rid (e-fem′ẹ-rid or ẹ̄-), *n.* [NL. *Ephemeridæ*, pl., < *ephemera*: see *ephemera*.] Any of the *Ephemeridæ*, a family of winged insects having the fore wings much larger than the hind wings and dying soon after reaching the adult stage; a May-fly.

An Ephemerid.

e-phem-e-ris (e-fem′ẹ-ris or ẹ̄-), *n.*; pl. *ephemerides* (ef-ẹ̄-mer′i-dēz). [L., < Gr. ἐφημερίς, diary, calendar, record, < ἐφήμερος: see *ephemera*.] A diary†; also, an almanac† or calendar†; also, a table showing the daily positions of a heavenly body; an astronomical almanac containing such tables.

e-phem-e-ron (e-fem′ẹ-ron or ẹ̄-), *n.*; pl. *-rons* or *-ra* (-rạ̈). [Gr. ἐφήμερον, neut. of ἐφήμερος: see *ephemera*.] An ephemerid; hence, anything short-lived or ephemeral.

e-phem-e-rous (e-fem′ẹ-rus or ẹ̄-), *a.* Ephemeral.

E-phe-sian (e-fē′zhiạn or ẹ̄-). **I.** *a.* Of or pertaining to Ephesus, an ancient city of Asia Minor, famous for its temple of Artemis (Diana). **II.** *n.* A native or inhabitant of Ephesus; a boon companion† (see Shakspere's "2 Henry IV.," ii. 2. 164); *pl.*, the book of the New Testament called in full "The Epistle of Paul the Apostle to the Ephesians."

eph-od (ef′od), *n.* [Heb.] A kind of Jewish priestly vestment, esp. that worn by the high priest.

eph-or (ef′ọr), *n.* [L. *ephorus*, < Gr. ἔφορος, < ἐφορᾶν, oversee, < ἐπί, on, + ὁρᾶν, see.] One of a body of magistrates in various ancient Dorian states, esp. at Sparta, where a body of five was annually elected by the people.—**eph′or-al,** *a.*

epi-, ep-. [Gr. ἐπι-, ἐπ-, repr. ἐπί, prep. and adv.] A prefix of Greek origin, meaning 'on,' 'upon,' 'to,' 'against,' sometimes used as an English formative, chiefly in scientific words, as *epaxial, epiblast, epicalyx, epizoön.*

ep-i-blast (ep′i-blast), *n.* [See *epi-* and *-blast*.] In *embryol.*, the ectoderm.—**ep-i-blas′tic** (-blas′tik), *a.*

ep-ic (ep′ik). [L. *epicus*, < Gr. ἐπικός, < ἔπος, word, tale: see *epos*.] **I.** *a.* Noting or pertaining to that form of poetic composition (examples of which are Homer's "Iliad" and "Odyssey" and Virgil's "Æneid") in which, in elevated style, a series of heroic achievements or events is dealt with at length as a continuous narrative and a poetic whole; hence, resembling or suggestive of such poetry; of heroic character; imposing. **II.** *n.* An epic poem; any epic-like composition; something worthy to form the subject of an epic poem (as, "That life was a noble Christian *epic*": Motley's "Dutch Republic," vi. 7).—**ep′i-cal,** *a.* Epic.—**ep′i-cal-ly,** *adv.*

ep-i-ca-lyx (ep-i-kā′liks), *n.* [See *epi-*.] In *bot.*, an involucre resembling an outer calyx, as in the mallow.

ep-i-car-di-um (ep-i-kär′di-um), *n.*; pl. *-dia* (-di-ạ̈). [NL., < Gr. ἐπί, on, + καρδία, heart.] In *anat.*, the inner serous layer of the pericardium, lying directly upon the heart.—**ep-i-car′di-al,** *a.*

ep-i-carp (ep′i-kärp), *n.* [See *epi-* and *-carp*.] In *bot.*, the outermost layer of a pericarp, as the rind or peel of certain fruits. See cut at *endocarp*.

ep-i-ce-di-um (ep-i-sē′di-um), *n.*; pl. *-diums* or *-dia* (-di-ạ̈). [L., < Gr. ἐπικήδειον, prop. neut. of ἐπικήδειος, of or for a funeral, < ἐπί, on, + κῆδος, care, funeral.] A funeral song; a dirge.

ep-i-cene (ep′i-sēn), *a.* [L. *epicœnus*, < Gr. ἐπίκοινος, < ἐπί, on, to, + κοινός, common.] Belonging to, or partaking of the characteristics of, both sexes; hence, of no definite sex or kind; in *gram.*, of nouns, having but one form of gender to denote both sexes.

ep-i-cen-ter, ep-i-cen-tre (ep′i-sen-tėr), *n.* [NL. *epicentrum*, < Gr. ἐπίκεντρος, on the center, < ἐπί, on, + κέντρον, E. *center*².] A point from which earthquake waves seem to go out, situated directly above the true center of disturbance. Also **ep-i-cen′trum** (-trum).

ep-i-cist (ep′i-sist), *n.* A writer of epic poetry.

ep-i-cot-yl (ep-i-kot′il), *n.* [From *epi-* + *cotyl(edon)*.] In *bot.*, in the embryo of a plant, that part of the stem above the cotyledons.—**ep″i-cot-y-le′don-a-ry** (-i-lē′dọn-ạ̄-ri), *a.* In *bot.*, above the cotyledons.

ep-i-cure (ep′i-kūr), *n.* [From *Epicurus*, the Greek philosopher (342?–270 B.C.).] [*cap.*] An Epicurean†; [*l. c.*] one given up to sensual enjoyment, esp. eating†; a glutton†; also, one who cultivates a refined taste in eating and drinking.

Ep-i-cu-re-an (ep″i-kụ̄-rē′ạn). **I.** *a.* Of or pertaining to the Greek philosopher Epicurus, or his system of philosophy, the chief doctrines of which were that the external world resulted from a fortuitous concourse of atoms, and that the highest good in life is pleasure, which consists in freedom from disturbance or pain; devoted to the pursuit of pleasure as the highest good in life (as, "Nothing to mar the sober majesties Of settled, sweet, *Epicurean* life": Tennyson's "Lucretius," 218); hence [*l. c.*], given or adapted to luxury, or indulgence in sensual pleasures; of luxurious tastes or habits, esp. in eating and drinking; also, fit for an epicure. **II.** *n.* A disciple of Epicurus, or a person holding similar views; [*l. c.*] one devoted to the pursuit of pleasure or luxury; an epicure.—**Ep″i-cu-re′an-ism,** *n.* The philosophical system of Epicurus, or attachment to his doctrines; [*l. c.*] epicurean indulgence or habits.

ep-i-cur-ism (ep′i-kūr-izm), *n.* The habits or tastes of an epicure; sensuality†; also [*cap.*] (pron. ep-i-kū′rizm), Epicureanism (now rare).

ep-i-cy-cle (ep′i-sī-kl), *n.* [LL. *epicyclus*, < Gr. ἐπίκυκλος, < ἐπί, on, + κύκλος, circle.] A small circle the center of which moves round in the circumference of a larger circle (used chiefly in *ancient astron.*); also, a circle which rolls (exteriorly or interiorly) around the circumference of another circle.—**ep-i-cyc′lic** (-sik′lik or -sī′klik), *a.* Of or pertaining to an epicycle.—**epicyclic train,** in *mach.*, any train of gearing the axes of the wheels of which revolve around a common center.—**ep-i-cy′cloid** (-sī′kloid), *n.* In *geom.*, a curve generated by the motion of a point on the circumference of a circle which rolls upon the convex side of a fixed circle.—**ep″i-cy-cloi′dal** (-kloi′dạl), *a.*

Epicycloid.

ep-i-deic-tic (ep-i-dīk′tik), *a.* See *epidictic*.

ep-i-dem-ic (ep-i-dem′ik). [F. *épidémique*, < Gr. ἐπίδημος, ἐπιδήμιος, prevalent, epidemic, < ἐπί, on, + δῆμος, people: cf. *endemic*.] **I.** *a.* Affecting at the same time a large or relatively large number of persons in a locality, but not permanently prevalent there, as a disease; generally diffused or prevalent. Cf. *epizoötic*. **II.** *n.* A temporary prevalence, as of a disease; an epidemic disease.—**ep-i-dem′i-cal,** *a.* Epidemic.—**ep-i-dem′i-cal-ly,** *adv.*

ep-i-de-mi-ol-o-gy (ep-i-dē-mi-ol′ọ̄-ji), *n.* [Gr. ἐπιδήμιος, epidemic: see *-logy*.] That branch of medicine which treats of epidemics.—**ep-i-de″mi-o-log′i-cal** (-ọ̄-loj′i-kạl), *a.*—**ep-i-de-mi-ol′o-gist,** *n.*

ep-i-der-mis (ep-i-dėr′mis), *n.* [LL., < Gr. ἐπιδερμίς, < ἐπί, on, + δέρμα, skin.] In *anat.*, the outer, non-vascular, non-sensitive layer of the skin, covering the true skin or cutis; in *zoöl.*, any of various outer integuments or coverings, as the chitinous covering of the shells of many mollusks; in *embryol.*, the ectoderm; in *bot.*, a thin layer of cells forming the outer integument in spermatophytes and pteridophytes.—**ep-i-der′mal, ep-i-der′mic,** *a.*—**ep-i-der-mi-za′tion** (-mi-zā′shọn), *n.* In *surg.*, skin-grafting.—**ep-i-der′moid,** *a.* Resembling epidermis.

ep-i-dic-tic, ep-i-deic-tic (ep-i-dik′tik, -dīk′tik), *a.* [L. *epidicticus*, < Gr. ἐπιδεικτικός, < ἐπιδεικνύναι, display, < ἐπί, on, to, + δεικνύναι, show.] Serving for exhibition or display, as a certain type of oratory.

ep-i-did-y-mis (ep-i-did′i-mis), *n.* [NL., < Gr. ἐπιδιδυμίς, < ἐπί, on, + δίδυμος, twin, pl. testicles.] In *anat.*, an elongated oblong body, chiefly convoluted tubes, resting upon and alongside the testicle.—**ep-i-did′y-mal,** *a.*

ep-i-dote (ep′i-dōt), *n.* [F. *épidote*, < Gr. ἐπιδιδόναι, increase, < ἐπί, on, to, + διδόναι, give.] A complex native silicate of aluminium, iron, and calcium, commonly of a yellowish-green color.

ep-i-fo-cal (ep-i-fō′kạl), *a.* [See *epi-*.] Above the focus, or true center of disturbance, of an earthquake.

ep-i-gæ-ous (ep-i-jē′us), *a.* See *epigeous*.

ep-i-gas-tri-um (ep-i-gas′tri-um), *n.* [NL., < Gr. ἐπιγάστριον, prop. neut. of ἐπιγάστριος, over the belly, < ἐπί, on, + γαστήρ, belly, stomach.] In *anat.*, the upper and median part of the abdomen, lying over the stomach.—**ep-i-gas′tric,** *a.*

ep-i-gene (ep′i-jēn), *a.* [Gr. ἐπί, on, + -γενής, produced.] In *geol.*, formed or originating on the earth's surface: opposed to *hypogene*.

ep-i-gen-e-sis (ep-i-jen′e-sis), *n.* [See *epi-*.] In *biol.*, a theoretical process of generation in which the embryo is formed by a series of new formations or successive differentiations, resulting from fertilization: opposed to *preformation*.—**ep″i-ge-net′ic** (-jẹ̄-net′ik), *a.*

e-pig-e-nous (e-pij′e-nus), *a.* [See *epigene*.] In *bot.*, growing on the surface, esp. the upper surface, as fungi on leaves. Cf. *hypogenous*.

ep-i-ge-ous (ep-i-jē′us), *a.* [Gr. ἐπίγειος, ἐπίγαιος, < ἐπί, on, + γῆ, earth.] In *bot.*, growing on or close to the ground; of cotyledons, borne above ground in germination.

ep-i-glot-tis (ep-i-glot′is), *n.* [NL., < Gr. ἐπιγλωττίς, < ἐπί, on, + γλῶττα, γλῶσσα, tongue.] In *anat.*, a thin, valve-like cartilaginous structure that covers the glottis during deglutition, preventing the entrance of food and drink into the larynx.

e-pig-na-thous (e-pig′nạ-thus), *a.* [Gr. ἐπί, on, + γνάθος, jaw.] In *ornith.*, having the end of the upper mandible decurved over and beyond that of the lower one, as a bird of prey, a parrot, etc.

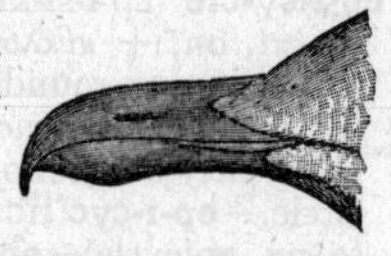

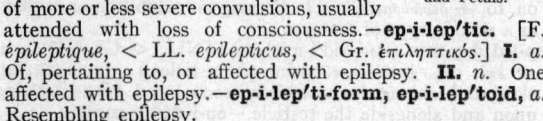

Epignathous Bill of Gull.

ep-i-gram (ep′i-gram), *n.* [F. *épigramme*, < L. *epigramma*, < Gr. ἐπίγραμμα, < ἐπιγράφειν, inscribe, < ἐπί, on, + γράφειν, write.] An inscription†; also, a short poem dealing concisely with a single subject, usually ending with a witty or ingenious turn of thought, and often satirical; hence, any witty, ingenious, or pointed saying tersely expressed; also, epigrammatic expression.—**ep″i-gram-mat′ic** (-grạ-mat′ik), *a.* [L. *epigrammaticus*.] Of or like an epigram; given to epigrams; terse and ingenious in expression.—**ep″i-gram-mat′i-cal-ly,** *adv.*—**ep-i-gram′ma-tism** (-gram′ạ-tizm), *n.* Epigrammatic character or style.—**ep-i-gram′ma-tist,** *n.* [LL. *epigrammatista*.] A maker of epigrams.—**ep-i-gram′ma-tize,** *v. t.* or *i.*; *-tized*, *-tizing*. [Gr. ἐπιγραμματίζειν.] To express by epigrams, or make epigrams.—**ep-i-gram′ma-tiz-er,** *n.*

ep-i-graph (ep′i-gráf), *n.* [Gr. ἐπιγραφή, < ἐπιγράφειν, inscribe: see *epigram*.] An inscription, esp. on a building, statue, or the like; also, a short quotation or other passage placed at the beginning of a book, chapter, or the like, as a motto.—**ep-i-graph′ic, ep-i-graph′i-cal** (-graf′ik, -i-kạl), *a.* Pertaining to epigraphs or epigraphy.—**ep-i-graph′i-cal-ly,** *adv.*—**e-pig-ra-phist** (e-pig′rạ-fist), *n.* One versed in epigraphy.—**e-pig′ra-phy,** *n.* The study or science of epigraphs or inscriptions; also, inscriptions collectively.

e-pig-y-nous (e-pij′i-nus), *a.* [Gr. ἐπί, on, + γυνή, woman, female.] In *bot.*, situated on the edge of the receptacle, immediately above the ovary, as stamens, etc.; having stamens, etc., so arranged, as a flower.—**e-pig′y-ny,** *n.*

Epigynous Stamens and Petals.

ep-i-lep-sy (ep′i-lep-si), *n.* [F. *épilepsie*, < LL. *epilepsia*, < Gr. ἐπιληψία, < ἐπιλαμβάνειν, seize on, attack, < ἐπί, on, + λαμβάνειν, take.] In *pathol.*, a nervous disease characterized by recurrent attacks of more or less severe convulsions, usually attended with loss of consciousness.—**ep-i-lep′tic.** [F. *épileptique*, < LL. *epilepticus*, < Gr. ἐπιληπτικός.] **I.** *a.* Of, pertaining to, or affected with epilepsy. **II.** *n.* One affected with epilepsy.—**ep-i-lep′ti-form, ep-i-lep′toid,** *a.* Resembling epilepsy.

e-pil-o-gist (e-pil′ọ-jist), *n.* The writer or speaker of an epilogue.

ep-i-logue (ep′i-log), *n.* [F. *épilogue*, < L. *epilogus*, < Gr. ἐπίλογος, < ἐπιλέγειν, say in addition, < ἐπί, on, to, + λέγειν, speak.] A concluding part added to a literary work; an appendix; specif., a speech, usually in verse, addressed to the audience by one of the actors after the conclusion of a play (as, "No *epilogue*, I pray you; for your play needs no excuse": Shakspere's "Midsummer Night's Dream," v. 1. 362).

ep-i-nas-ty (ep′i-nas-ti), *n.* [Gr. ἐπί, on, + ναστός, pressed close, compact, < νάσσειν, press close.] In *bot.*, increased growth along the upper surface of an organ or part, causing the part to bend downward.—**ep-i-nas′tic,** *a.*

ep-i-neu-ri-um (ep-i-nū′ri-um), *n.*; pl. *-ria* (-ri-ạ̈). [NL., < Gr. ἐπί, on, + νεῦρον, nerve.] In *anat.*, the dense sheath of connective tissue which surrounds the trunk of a nerve.

e-piph-a-ny (ẹ̄-pif′ạ-ni or e-), *n.*; pl. *-nies* (-niz). [Partly < Gr. ἐπιφάνεια, appearance, < ἐπιφαίνειν, show forth, < ἐπί, on, to, + φαίνειν, show; partly < OF. *epiphanie* (F. *Épiphanie*), < LL. *epiphania*, < LGr. ἐπιφάνια, pl., the Epiphany, < Gr. ἐπιφαίνειν.] An appearance or manifestation, esp. of a deity; [*cap.*] a Christian festival, observed on Jan. 6, commemorating the manifestation of Christ to the Gentiles in the persons of the Magi.

ep-i-phe-nom-e-non (ep″i-fẹ̄-nom′e-non), *n.*; pl. *-ena* (-e-nạ̈). [See *epi-*.] A secondary phenomenon; in *pathol.*, a secondary or additional symptom or complication arising during the course of a malady.

ep-i-phyl-lous (ep-i-fil′us), *a.* [Gr. ἐπί, on, + φύλλον, leaf.] In *bot.*, growing upon a leaf: said of certain parasitic fungi and of the floral parts of some plants.

e-piph-y-sis (e-pif′i-sis), *n.*; pl. *-yses* (-i-sēz). [NL., < Gr. ἐπίφυσις, < ἐπιφύεσθαι, grow on, < ἐπί, on, + φύειν, produce.] In *anat.*, a part or process of a bone which is separated from the main body of the bone by a layer of cartilage, and which finally becomes united with the bone through further ossification; also, the pineal body of the brain.—**ep-i-phys-i-al** (ep-i-fiz′i-ạl), *a.*

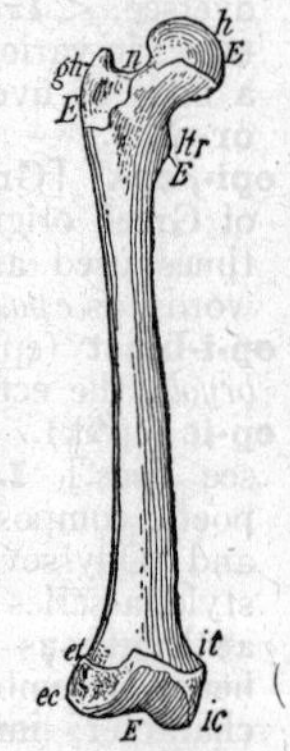

Right Femur of a Youth.
E, E, epiphyses: *gtr, ltr,* greater and lesser trochanter; *h,* head; *et, it,* external and internal tuberosity; *ec, ic,* external and internal condyle; *n,* neck.

ep-i-phyte (ep′i-fīt), *n.* [Gr. ἐπί, on, + φυτόν, plant.] In *bot.*, any of various plants, as certain mosses, lichens, orchids, etc., growing upon another plant for mechanical support, but not parasitic; an air-plant or aërophyte; in *pathol.*, a vegetable parasite living on the surface of the body.—**ep-i-phyt′ic** (-fit′ik), *a.*—**ep-i-phyt′i-cal-ly,** *adv.*

e-pip-lo-ön (e-pip′lọ-on), *n.*; pl. *-loa* (-lọ-ạ̈). [NL., < Gr. ἐπίπλοον, caul.] In *anat.*, the great omentum.

ep-i-rog-e-ny (ep-ī-roj′e-ni), *n.* [Gr. ἤπειρος, land, mainland, continent: see *-geny*.] The production of a continent; the wide changes of level which give rise to continental elevations, oceanic depressions, etc.—**e-pi-ro-gen-ic** (ẹ̄-pī-rọ-jen′ik), *a.*

e-pis-co-pa-cy (ẹ̄-pis′kọ-pạ-si), *n.* Government of the church by bishops; that form of church government in which there are three distinct orders of ministers, namely bishops, priests or presbyters, and deacons; also, the order of bishops; also, the office or incumbency of a bishop.

e-pis-co-pal (ẹ̄-pis′kọ-pạl), *a.* [LL. *episcopalis*, < *episcopus*, bishop: see *bishop*.] Pertaining to a bishop; based on or recognizing a governing order of bishops: used [*cap.*] in the titles of various churches (as, the Methodist *Episcopal* Church), and esp. to designate the Anglican Church or some branch of it (as, the Protestant *Episcopal* Church in the U. S.).—**episcopal stork,** a black stork, *Dissoura episcopus*, found in Africa, India, and elsewhere, characterized by white neck and under tail-coverts. See cut on following page.—**e-pis-co-pa′lian** (-pā′liạn). **I.** *a.* Pertaining or adhering to the episcopal form of church government, or [*cap.*] to the Episcopal Church (of the Anglican communion). **II.** *n.* An adherent of the episcopal system; [*cap.*] a member of the Episcopal Church.—**e-pis-co-pa′lian-ism,** *n.*—

e-pis′co-pal-ism, *n.* The theory of church polity according to which the supreme ecclesiastical authority is vested in the episcopal order as a whole, and not in any individual except by delegation.—**e-pis′co-pal-ly,** *adv.*

Episcopal Stork.

e-pis-co-pate (ē-pis′kō-pāt), *n.* [LL. *episcopatus*, < *episcopus*, E. *bishop*.] The office, dignity, incumbency, or see of a bishop; also, the order or body of bishops.

ep-i-sode (ep′i-sōd), *n.* [Gr. ἐπεισόδιον, a parenthetic addition, prop. neut. of ἐπεισόδιος, coming in besides, < ἐπί, on, to, + εἴσοδος, entrance, < εἰς, into, + ὁδός, way.] A part in an old Greek tragedy between two choric songs; also, an incidental narrative or digression in the course of a story, poem, or other writing; also, an incident in the course of a series of events, in a person's life or experience, etc.; in *music*, an intermediate or digressive passage, esp. in a contrapuntal composition.—**ep-i-sod′ic, ep-i-sod′i-cal** (-sod′ik, -i-kạl), *a.* Pertaining to or of the nature of an episode; incidental: as, "In an *episodical* way, he had studied and practised dentistry" (Hawthorne's "House of the Seven Gables," xii.).—**ep-i-sod′i-cal-ly,** *adv.*

ep-i-spas-tic (ep-i-spas′tik). [Gr. ἐπισπαστικός, < ἐπισπᾶν, draw on or to, < ἐπί, on, to, + σπᾶν, draw.] In *med.*: **I.** *a.* Raising a blister when applied to the skin. **II.** *n.* A blistering agent; a vesicatory.

ep-i-sperm (ep′i-spėrm), *n.* [Gr. ἐπί, on, + σπέρμα, seed.] In *bot.*, the outer integument of a seed; the testa.

Section of Seed.—*a*, episperm; *b*, endopleura; *c*, endosperm.

ep-i-stax-is (ep-i-stak′sis), *n.* [NL., < Gr. ἐπιστάζειν, drop on, < ἐπί, on, + στάζειν, drop, drip.] In *pathol.*, bleeding from the nose.

ep-i-ste-mol-o-gy (ep″i-stē-mol′ō-ji), *n.* [Gr. ἐπιστήμη, knowledge (< ἐπίστασθαι, know): see *-logy*.] The theory or science of the origin, nature, and limits of knowledge.—**ep″i-ste-mo-log′i-cal** (-stē-mō-loj′i-kạl), *a.*—**ep″i-ste-mol′o-gist,** *n.*

e-pis-tle (ē-pis′l), *n.* [OF. *epistle* (F. *épître*), < L. *epistola*, < Gr. ἐπιστολή, message, letter, < ἐπιστέλλειν, send to, < ἐπί, on, to, + στέλλειν, send.] A written communication directed or sent to a person; a letter, esp. one of formal or didactic character; often, a literary work, usually in verse, written in the form of a letter; specif. [usually *cap.*], one of the apostolic letters constituting books of the New Testament; also [often *cap.*], *eccles.*, an extract, usually from one of the Epistles of the New Testament, forming part of the eucharistic service in certain churches.—**e-pis-tler** (ē-pis′lėr), *n.* A writer of an epistle; *eccles.*, the one who reads the epistle in the eucharistic service.—**e-pis′to-la-ry** (-tō-lā-ri), *a.* [L. *epistolaris*.] Of or pertaining to epistles or correspondence; contained in or carried on by letters.—**e-pis′to-ler,** *n.* [F. *épistolier*.] Same as *epistler*.—**e-pis-to-log′ra-phy** (-log′rạ-fi), *n.* [See *-graphy*.] Letter-writing.

e-pis-tro-phe (e-pis′trō-fē), *n.* [LL., < Gr. ἐπιστροφή, < ἐπιστρέφειν, turn on or to, < ἐπί, on, to, + στρέφειν, turn.] In *rhet.*, a figure in which successive clauses or sentences end with the same word (as in 2 Cor. xi. 22).

ep-i-style (ep′i-stīl), *n.* [L. *epistylium*, < Gr. ἐπιστύλιον, < ἐπί, on, + στῦλος, pillar, column.] In *arch.*, an architrave.

ep-i-taph (ep′i-tåf), *n.* [L. *epitaphium*, < Gr. ἐπιτάφιον, neut. of ἐπιτάφιος, over or at a tomb, < ἐπί, on, + τάφος, tomb.] A commemorative inscription on a tomb or mortuary monument; any brief writing resembling such an inscription.—**ep′i-taph,** *v. t.* To commemorate in an epitaph: as, "After he is dead and buried, And *epitaphed*" (Lowell's "On Planting a Tree at Inveraray").—**ep-i-taph′ic** (-taf′ik), *a.*—**ep′i-taph-ist,** *n.* A writer of epitaphs.

e-pit-a-sis (e-pit′ạ-sis), *n.* [NL., < Gr. ἐπίτασις, < ἐπιτείνειν, intensify, < ἐπί, on, + τείνειν, stretch.] In the ancient drama, the part of the play (following the protasis) in which the action is developed, leading up to the catastrophe.

ep-i-tha-la-mi-on (ep″i-thạ-lā′mi-on), *n.* Same as *epithalamium*.

ep-i-tha-la-mi-um (ep″i-thạ-lā′mi-um), *n.*; pl. *-miums* or *-mia* (-mi-ä). [L., < Gr. ἐπιθαλάμιον, neut. of ἐπιθαλάμιος, nuptial, < ἐπί, on, + θάλαμος, bridal chamber.] A nuptial song or poem; a poem in honor of a bride and bridegroom, or of either.

ep-i-the-li-al (ep-i-thē′li-ạl), *a.* Pertaining to epithelium.—**ep-i-the′li-oid,** *a.* Resembling epithelium.

ep-i-the-li-o-ma (ep″i-thē-li-ō′mä), *n.*; pl. *-mas* or *-mata* (-mạ-tä). [NL., < *epithelium*: see *-oma*.] In *pathol.*, a malignant growth or variety of cancer consisting chiefly of epithelial cells.

ep-i-the-li-um (ep-i-thē′li-um), *n.*; pl. *-liums* or *-lia* (-li-ä). [NL., < Gr. ἐπί, on, + θηλή, nipple.] In *anat.*, the tissue forming the superficial layer of mucous membrane; hence, broadly, any tissue which covers an external or internal surface, or lines a cavity or the like, and which performs protective, secreting, or other functions, as the epidermis, the lining of blood-vessels, etc. (cf. *endothelium*); in *bot.*, a delicate layer of cells lining certain internal cavities; also, the thin epidermis of petals.

ep-i-thet (ep′i-thet), *n.* [L. *epitheton*, < Gr. ἐπίθετον, prop. neut. of ἐπίθετος, added, < ἐπιτιθέναι, put on, < ἐπί, on, + τιθέναι, set.] An adjective or other term applied to a person or thing to express an attribute (actual or ascribed); a descriptive expression applied; hence, an appellative; a name; also, a phrase† or expression† (see Shakspere's "Much Ado about Nothing," v. 2. 67).—**ep-i-thet′ic, ep-i-thet′i-cal,** *a.*

e-pit-o-me (ē-pit′ō-mē or e-), *n.* [L., < Gr. ἐπιτομή, < ἐπιτέμνειν, cut into, abridge, < ἐπί, on, + τέμνειν, cut.] A condensed account of the contents of a literary work; an abstract; an abridgment; a summary, or condensed account, of anything; a compendium; hence, a condensed representation of something (as, "A man so various that he seemed to be Not one, but all mankind's *epitome*": Dryden's "Absalom and Achitophel," i. 546).—**e-pit′o-mist,** *n.* One who makes an epitome.—**e-pit′o-mize,** *v. t.*; *-mized*, *-mizing*. To make an epitome of; abridge; summarize; also, to contain in small compass.—**e-pit′o-miz-er,** *n.*

ep-i-trite (ep′i-trīt), *n.* [L. *epitritos*, < Gr. ἐπίτριτος, containing a unit and one third, < ἐπί, on, to, + τρίτος, third.] In *pros.*, a foot consisting of three long syllables and one short one: called first, second, third, or fourth epitrite, according as the short syllable is the first, second, third, or fourth.

ep-i-zeux-is (ep-i-zūk′sis), *n.* [LL., < Gr. ἐπίζευξις, < ἐπιζευγνύναι, join to, < ἐπί, on, to, + ζευγνύναι, yoke, join.] In *rhet.*, immediate or almost immediate repetition of a word or phrase for the sake of emphasis.

ep-i-zo-ön (ep-i-zō′on), *n.*; pl. *-zoa* (-zō′ä). [NL.: see *epi-* and *-zoön*.] An external parasite; an ectozoön.—**ep-i-zo′ic,** *a.*

ep-i-zo-öt-ic (ep″i-zō-ot′ik). [= F. *épizootique*, < Gr. ἐπί, on, + ζῷον, animal: cf. *enzoötic*.] **I.** *a.* Of diseases, prevalent temporarily among animals. Cf. *epidemic*. **II.** *n.* A temporary prevalence of a disease among animals; an epizoötic disease. Also **ep-i-zo′ö-ty** (-zō′ō-ti), *n.*

ep-och (ep′ok or -ọk, or ē′pok), *n.* [ML. *epocha*, < Gr. ἐποχή, check, pause, position, epoch, < ἐπέχειν, hold on, check, < ἐπί, on, + ἔχειν, have, hold.] A point of time from which succeeding years are numbered, as at the beginning of a system of chronology; hence, the beginning of any distinctive period in the history of anything; also, a point of time distinguished by a particular event, or state of affairs, or the event itself as distinguishing the time of its occurrence; also, a particular period of time as marked by distinctive character, events, etc. (as, "We enter on an *epoch* of constitutional retrogression": Green's "Short Hist. of the Eng.

People," vi. 3); in *astron.*, an arbitrarily fixed instant of time or date (usually the beginning of a century or half-century) used as a reference in giving the elements of a planetary orbit or the like; also, the longitude of a planet as seen from the sun at such an instant or date.—**ep′o-chal** (-ǫ-kąl), *a.* Of or pertaining to an epoch or epochs; of the nature of an epoch.—**ep′och=mak″ing,** *a.* Making or fixing an epoch; opening a new era, as in human history, thought, or knowledge: as, an *epoch-making* discovery or book.

ep-ode (ep′ōd), *n.* [L. *epodos*, < Gr. ἐπῳδός, < ἐπαείδειν, sing to, < ἐπί, on, to, + ἀείδειν, sing.] In *anc. pros.*, a kind of lyric poem, invented by Archilochus (about 650 B.C.), in which a long verse is followed by a short one; also, the part of a lyric ode following the strophe and antistrophe.

ep-o-nym (ep′ǫ-nim), *n.* [Gr. ἐπώνυμος, given as a name, giving one's name to something, < ἐπί, on, to, + ὄνυμα, name.] A person, real or imaginary, from whom a tribe, place, institution, etc., takes, or is supposed to take, its name; the name of such a person; also, an Assyrian official whose name was used to designate his year of office.—**ep-o-nym′ic,** *a.*—**e-pon-y-mist** (e-pon′i-mist), *n.* An eponymous ancestor or founder.—**e-pon′y-mous,** *a.* Giving one's name to a tribe, place, etc.—**e-pon′y-my** (-mi), *n.*; pl. *-mies* (-miz). The derivation of names from eponyms; also, the year of office of an Assyrian eponym.

ep-o-pee (ep′ǫ-pē), *n.* [F. *épopée*, < NL. *epopœia*, < Gr. ἐποποιία, epic poetry, an epic, < ἔπος (see *epos*) + ποιεῖν, make.] An epic. Also (NL.) **ep-o-pœ′ia** (-pē′yä).

ep-opt (ep′opt), *n.* [Gr. ἐπόπτης, lit. 'beholder,' < ἐπί, on, + ὀπ-, see: see *optic.*] A seer or beholder; specif., one fully initiated into the Eleusinian mysteries; hence, an initiate in any secret system.—**e-pop-tic** (e-pop′tik), *a.*

ep-os (ep′os), *n.* [L., < Gr. ἔπος, word, tale, song, pl. epic poetry, akin to εἰπεῖν, speak, say: see *voice.*] An epic; also, epic poetry.

é-pris (ā-prē), *a.* [F., pp. of *éprendre*, OF. *esprendre*, seize, kindle, inflame, < L. *ex-*, out, + *prehendere*, seize.] Enamoured; in love.—**é-prise** (ā-prēz), *a.* [F.] Fem. of *épris.*

ep-si-lon (ep′si-lon), *n.* [LGr. ἒ ψιλόν, 'simple e.'] The fifth letter (Ε, ε, = English short E, e) of the Greek alphabet.

Ep-som (ep′sǫm) **salt.** [So called because first prepared from the water of the mineral springs at *Epsom*, town in Surrey, southern England.] Hydrated magnesium sulphate, used as a cathartic, etc.

ep-u-la-ry (ep′ū-lą-ri), *a.* [L. *epularis*, < *epulum*, feast.] Of or pertaining to a feast or banquet.

ep-u-lo-sis (ep-ū-lō′sis), *n.* [NL., < Gr. ἐπούλωσις, < ἐπουλοῦν, heal over, cicatrize, < ἐπί, on, + οὐλοῦν, heal, < οὖλος, whole.] In *med.*, cicatrization.—**ep-u-lot′ic** (-lot′ik), *a.*

e-qua-ble (ē′kwą-bl or ek′wą-), *a.* [L. *æquabilis*, < *æquare*: see *equate.*] Free from inequalities or variations; uniform in character, as motion or temperature; uniform in operation or effect, as laws; tranquil, even, or not easily disturbed, as the mind.—**e-qua-bil′i-ty** (-bil′i-ti), **e′qua-ble-ness,** *n.*—**e′qua-bly,** *adv.*

e-qual (ē′kwąl). [L. *æqualis*, < *æquus*, level, even, equal, equitable, just, equable, calm.] **I.** *a.* Like or alike in quantity, degree, value, etc.; of the same rank, ability, merit, etc.; as great as another (followed by *to* or *with*: as, the velocity of sound is not *equal* to that of light); also, adequate or sufficient in quantity or degree (as, the supply is *equal* to the demand); having adequate power, ability, or means (as, he was not *equal* to the task); also, evenly proportioned or balanced (as, an *equal* mixture; an *equal* contest); uniform in operation or effect (as, *equal* laws); impartial or equitable (archaic: as, an *equal* judge); even or regular, as motion; level, as a plain; tranquil or undisturbed (archaic: as, an *equal* mind). **II.** *n.* One who or that which is equal; also, a state of equality (chiefly colloq.).—**e′qual,** *v. t.*; *equaled* or *equalled, equaling* or *equalling.* To make equal; equalize; also, to compare†; also, to be or become equal to; match; also, to make or do something equal to; also, to recompense fully.

e-qual-i-ta-ri-an (ę-kwol-i-tā′ri-ąn). **I.** *a.* Pertaining or adhering to the doctrine of equality among men. **II.** *n.* One who adheres to the doctrine of equality among men.—**e-qual-i-ta′ri-an-ism,** *n.* The opinions or principles of equalitarians; the doctrine of the equality of mankind: as, "The dominant liberal ideas were freedom and a certain vague *equalitarianism*" (H. G. Wells's "Outline of History," xxxix. § 3).

e-qual-i-ty (ę-kwol′i-ti), *n.*; pl. *-ties* (-tiz). [L. *æqualitas.*] The state of being equal; correspondence in quantity, degree, value, rank, ability, etc. (as, the sign of *equality*, the sign =, read 'equals' or 'is equal to,' as used in 6 + 5 = 11, or in the etymology of the word *epizoötic* in this book); uniform character, as of motion or surface.

e-qual-ize (ē′kwąl-īz), *v. t.*; *-ized, -izing.* To make equal; also, to render uniform; also, to be or become equal to†.—**e″qual-i-za′tion** (-i-zā′shǫn), *n.*—**e′qual-iz-er** (-ī-zėr), *n.* One who or that which equalizes; any of various devices or appliances for equalizing strains, pressures, etc.

e-qual-ly (ē′kwąl-i), *adv.* In an equal manner or measure; to an equal extent or degree; in uniform manner or degree.—**e′qual-ness,** *n.*

e-qua-nim-i-ty (ē-kwą-nim′i-ti or ek-wą-), *n.* [L. *æquanimitas*, < *æquanimis*, having an even mind, < *æquus* (see *equal*) + *animus*, mind.] Evenness of mind or temper; calmness; composure; self-possession.—**e-quan-i-mous** (ę-kwan′i-mus), *a.* [L. *æquanimis.*] Of an even temper; not easily elated or depressed.

e-quate (ę-kwāt′), *v. t.*; *equated, equating.* [L. *æquatus*, pp. of *æquare*, < *æquus*: see *equal.*] To make equal; also, to reduce to an average; make such correction or allowance in as will reduce to a common standard of comparison; also, to state the equality of or between; put in the form of an equation; also, to regard, treat, or represent as equivalent; also, to be equal to (rare).—**e-qua-tion** (ę-kwā′shǫn, also -zhǫn), *n.* [L. *æquatio(n-).*] The act of making equal; equalization; equally balanced state; equilibrium; reduction to a mean or a normal value; in *astron.*, a correction or allowance in an observation or computation to compensate for a known cause of error; in *math.*, an expression of, or a proposition asserting, the equality of two quantities, employing the sign = between them; in *chem.*, a symbolic representation of a reaction.—**equation of payments,** the process of ascertaining a mean time for the equitable payment of a whole debt which is due in a number of parts payable at different times.—**equation of time,** the difference between mean solar time and apparent solar time.—**personal equation.** See under *personal, a.*—**e-qua′tion-al,** *a.* Pertaining to or involving equations.

e-qua-tor (ę-kwā′tǫr), *n.* [ML. *æquator*, lit. 'equalizer' (of day and night, as when the sun is in the equator), < L. *æquare*: see *equate.*] A great circle of the celestial sphere the plane of which is perpendicular to the axis of the earth ('celestial equator'); also, the great circle of the earth (in the plane of the celestial equator) everywhere equidistant from the two poles (as, "October 1st. Crossed the *equator* . . . I now, for the first time, felt at liberty . . . to call myself a son of Neptune": Dana's "Two Years before the Mast," iv.); hence, a similarly situated circle on any heavenly or spherical body; in *aëronautics*, the horizontal circle about a balloon at the place of its greatest width.—**magnetic equator.** See under *magnetic.*—**e-qua-to-ri-al** (ē-kwą-tō′ri-ąl). **I.** *a.* Of, pertaining to, or near an equator, esp. the equator of the earth. **II.** *n.* A telescope having two axes of motion, one parallel to the earth's axis, and the other at right angles to it.—**e-qua-to′ri-al-ly,** *adv.*

e-quer-ry (ek′wę-ri or ę-kwer′i), *n.*; pl. *-ries* (-riz). [F. *écurie*, OF. *escurie*, < ML. *scuria*, stable; from Teut. (cf. G. *scheuer*, barn).] A stable†; the stable department of a royal or other great household†; an officer of a royal or similar household, charged with the care of the horses, or with accompanying the carriage of the sovereign or other personage on certain occasions.

e-ques-tri-an (ę-kwes′tri-ąn). [L. *equester* (*equestr-*), < *eques*, horseman, < *equus*, horse.] **I.** *a.* Of or pertaining to horsemen or horsemanship; mounted on horseback; representing a person on horseback (as, an *equestrian* statue); also, of, pertaining to, or composed of knights. **II.** *n.* A rider or performer on horseback.—**e-ques′tri-an-ism,** *n.* The art or practice of an equestrian; horsemanship.—**e-ques-tri-enne′** (-en′), *n.* [Appar. spurious F.] A female rider or performer on horseback.

equi-. Form of L. *æquus*, equal, used in combination.

e-qui-an-gu-lar (ē-kwi-ang′gū-lär), *a.* [See *equi-*.] Having all the angles equal.

e-qui-dis-tant (ē-kwi-dis′tant), *a.* [LL. *æquidistans* (*-ant-*): see *equi-* and *distant.*] Equally distant.—**e-qui-dis′tance,** *n.*—**e-qui-dis′tant-ly,** *adv.*

e-qui-lat-er-al (ē-kwi-lat′ẹ-ral), *a.* [LL. *æquilateralis*: see *equi-* and *lateral.*] Having all the sides equal.—**e-qui-lat′er-al-ly,** *adv.*

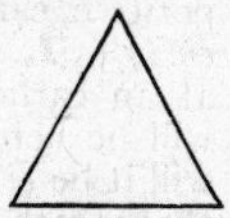

Equilateral Triangle.

e-qui-li-brate (ē-kwi-lī′brāt), *v.*; *-brated, -brating.* [LL. *æquilibratus*, in equilibrium, < L. *æquus*, equal, + *libra*, balance.] **I.** *tr.* To balance equally; keep in equipoise or equilibrium; also, to be in equilibrium with; counterpoise. **II.** *intr.* To balance.—**e″qui-li-bra′tion** (-brā′shọn), *n.* The act of balancing evenly; the state of being evenly balanced.—**e-qui-li′bra-tor,** *n.* A mechanical device for securing equilibrium, as in a balloon.—**e-qui-li′bra-to-ry** (-brạ-tō-ri), *a.*

e-quil-i-brist (ẹ-kwil′i-brist), *n.* [F. *équilibriste*, < *équilibre*, < L. *æquilibrium*, E. *equilibrium.*] One who practises balancing in unnatural positions and hazardous movements, as a rope-dancer.—**e-quil-i-bris′tic** (-bris′tik), *a.*

e-qui-lib-ri-um (ē-kwi-lib′ri-um), *n.* [L. *æquilibrium*, < *æquus*, equal, + *libra*, balance.] Equal balance between opposing forces; a state of rest due to the action of forces that counteract each other; specif., the state of a chemical system when no further change occurs in it; also, in general, equal balance between any powers, influences, etc.; equality of effect; due or just relationship; mental balance.

e-quil-i-brize (ẹ-kwil′i-brīz), *v. t.*; *-brized, -brizing.* [From *equilibrium.*] To bring into equilibrium; balance.

e-qui-mul-ti-ple (ē-kwi-mul′ti-pl). [See *equi-*.] **I.** *a.* Produced by multiplication by the same number or quantity. **II.** *n.* One of the products obtained by multiplying two or more numbers or quantities by the same number or quantity.

e-quine (ē′kwīn or ē′kwin). [L. *equinus*, < *equus*, horse.] **I.** *a.* Of, pertaining to, or resembling a horse. **II.** *n.* A horse.

e-qui-noc-tial (ē-kwi-nok′shal). [L. *æquinoctialis.*] **I.** *a.* Pertaining to an equinox or the equinoxes, or to the equality of day and night (as, the *equinoctial* line, the celestial equator, so called because when the sun is on this line night and day are of equal length all over the earth; *equinoctial* point, either of the two points in which the celestial equator and the ecliptic intersect each other, that is, the point reached by the sun's center at the vernal equinox and that reached by it at the autumnal equinox); occurring at or about the time of an equinox (as, an *equinoctial* storm); also, pertaining to the celestial equator, or to the regions or climate of the terrestrial equator; in *bot.*, of a flower, opening regularly at a certain hour. **II.** *n.* The equinoctial line; also, the terrestrial equator (now rare); also, an equinoctial gale or storm.

e-qui-nox (ē′kwi-noks), *n.* [F. *équinoxe*, < L. *æquinoctium*, < *æquus*, equal, + *nox* (*noct-*), night.] The time when the sun crosses the plane of the earth's equator, making night and day all over the earth of equal length, occurring about March 21 ('vernal equinox') and Sept. 22 ('autumnal equinox'); also, either of the equinoctial points.

e-quip (ẹ-kwip′), *v. t.*; *equipped, equipping.* [F. *équiper*, OF. *esquiper*: cf. Icel. *skipa*, put in order, arrange, man (a ship, etc.).] To fit out, as a ship; furnish or provide with whatever is needed for service or for any undertaking; fit up, dress out, or array.—**e-qui-page** (ek′wi-pāj), *n.* [F. *équipage.*] The act of equipping†, or the state of being equipped†; also, outfit, as of a ship, an army, or a soldier (sometimes denoting persons: as, "He . . . equipped three small ships . . . Eighty sailors and 100 arquebusiers formed the *equipage*": Besant's "Coligny," vii.); an equipment; accoutrements or habiliments; a set of small household articles, as of china, glass, or earthenware; a collection of small articles for personal ornament or use; also, the appurtenances of rank or position†; a retinue† or following†; a completely equipped carriage, with horses and attendant servants; sometimes, a carriage alone.—**e-quip′ment,** *n.* The act of equipping, or the state of being equipped; also, anything used in or provided for equipping; outfit.

e-qui-poise (ē′kwi-poiz), *n.* [See *equi-* and *poise.*] An equal distribution of weight; equality of weight or force; even balance; equilibrium; also, a counterpoise.

e-qui-pol-lent (ē-kwi-pol′ent). [L. *æquipollens* (*-ent-*), < *æquus*, equal, + *pollens*, ppr. of *pollere*, be strong.] **I.** *a.* Equal in power, validity, effect, etc.; equivalent. **II.** *n.* Something equal in power, effect, etc.; an equivalent.—**e-qui-pol′lence, e-qui-pol′len-cy,** *n.*

e-qui-pon-der-ant (ē-kwi-pon′dėr-ant), *a.* [See *equiponderate.*] Of equal weight or importance; evenly balanced.—**e-qui-pon′der-ance,** *n.*

e-qui-pon-der-ate (ē-kwi-pon′dėr-āt), *v.*; *-ated, -ating.* [ML. *æquiponderatus*, pp. of *æquiponderare*, < L. *æquus*, equal, + *pondus*, weight.] **I.** *tr.* To equal or offset as to weight, force, importance, etc.; counterbalance. **II.** *intr.* To be of equal weight, importance, etc.—**e-qui-pon-der-a′tion** (-ā′shọn), *n.*

e-quip-o-tent (ẹ-kwip′ọ-tent), *a.* [L. *æquus*, equal, + *potens*, E. *potent.*] Equal in power.

e-quip-per (ẹ-kwip′ėr), *n.* One who equips.

e-qui-ro-tal (ē-kwi-rō′tal), *a.* [L. *æquus*, equal, + *rota*, wheel.] Having wheels all of the same size or diameter, as a vehicle.

e-qui-se-ta-ceous (ek″wi-sẹ-tā′shius), *a.* [See *equisetum.*] Belonging to the *Equisetaceæ*, or horsetail family of plants.

e-qui-se-tum (ek-wi-sē′tum), *n.* [NL., for L. *equisætum*, < *equus*, horse, + *sæta*, bristle.] Any plant of the genus *Equisetum*; a horsetail. See *horsetail.*

e-qui-ta-ble (ek′wi-ta-bl), *a.* [F. *équitable*, < *équité*: see *equity.*] Characterized by equity or fairness; according to the principles of equity; just and right; fair; reasonable; in *law*, of, pertaining to, or valid in equity, as distinguished from the common and statute law.—**e′qui-ta-ble-ness,** *n.*—**e′qui-ta-bly,** *adv.*

e-qui-tant (ek′wi-tant), *a.* [L. *equitans* (*-ant-*), ppr. of *equitare*, ride: see *equitation.*] In *bot.*, straddling or overlapping, as certain leaves whose bases successively overlap the leaves above or within them.

e-qui-ta-tion (ek-wi-tā′shọn), *n.* [L. *equitatio(n-)*, < *equitare*, ride, < *eques*, horseman, < *equus*, horse.] The act or art of riding on horseback; horsemanship.

e-qui-ty (ek′wi-ti), *n.*; pl. *-ties* (-tiz). [OF. *equite* (F. *équité*), < L. *æquitas*, < *æquus*, equal, just: see *equal.*] The quality of being fair or impartial; fairness; impartiality; also, that which is fair and just; justice or right; in *law*, the application of the dictates of conscience or the principles of natural justice to the settlement of controversies; a system of jurisprudence or a body of doctrines and rules as to what is equitable and fair, serving to supplement, and remedy the defects of, the common and statute law; any system of jurisprudence analogous to this; also, an equitable right or claim.

e-quiv-a-lence (ẹ-kwiv′a-lens), *n.* The state or fact of being equivalent; equality in value, force, significance, etc.; in *chem.*, the quality of having equal valence; also, valence. Also **e-quiv′a-len-cy** (-len-si).

e-quiv-a-lent (ẹ-kwiv′a-lent), *a.* [LL. *æquivalens* (*-ent-*), ppr. of *æquivalere*, have equal power, < L. *æquus*, equal, + *valere*, be strong, be worth.] Equal in value, measure, force, effect, significance, etc.; tantamount; corresponding in position, function, etc.; in *geom.*, having the same extent, as a triangle and a square of equal area.—**equivalent weight,** in *chem.*, an equivalent.—**e-quiv′a-lent,** *n.* That which is equivalent; something equal, tantamount, or corresponding to something else; in *chem.*, the parts by weight in which an element will combine with or displace 8 parts of oxygen or 1.008 parts of hydrogen (also called *equivalent weight*).—**e-quiv′a-lent-ly,** *adv.*

e-quiv-o-cal (ẹ-kwiv′ọ-kal), *a.* [LL. *æquivocus*, ambiguous, < L. *æquus*, equal, + *vox* (*voc-*), voice, sound, word, speech.] Having different meanings equally possible, as a word or phrase; susceptible of double interpretation; ambiguous; hence, of uncertain significance (as, an *equivocal* proof); doubtful; also, of doubtful nature or character (as, "Unfinished things, one knows not what to call, Their generation's so *equivocal*": Pope's "Essay on Criticism," 43); questionable; dubious; suspicious.—**e-quiv′o-cal-ly,** *adv.*—**e-quiv′o-cal-ness,** *n.*

e-quiv-o-cate (ē-kwiv′ọ-kāt), *v. i.*; *-cated, -cating.* [ML. *æquivocatus*, pp. of *æquivocare*, call by the same name, < LL. *æquivocus*, ambiguous: see *equivocal.*] To use equivocal or ambiguous expressions, esp. with a view to misleading; prevaricate.—**e-quiv′o-cat-ing-ly,** *adv.*—**e-quiv-o-ca′tion** (-kā′shọn), *n.* The use of equivocal or ambiguous expressions, esp. in order to mislead; prevarication; in *logic*, a fallacy depending on the double significance of a word.—**e-quiv′o-ca-tor,** *n.*—**e-quiv′o-ca-to-ry** (-kạ-tọ-ri), *a.* Indicating, or characterized by, equivocation.

e-qui-voke (ek′wi-vōk), *n.* See *equivoque.*

e-qui-voque (ek′wi-vōk), *n.* [F. *équivoque*, < LL. *æquivocus*: see *equivocal.*] An equivocal term; an ambiguous expression; a play upon words; a pun; also, ambiguity of speech; double meaning; also, equivocation.

-er[1]. [AS. *-ere.*] A suffix (*a*) forming nouns designating persons from the object of their occupation or labor, as in *hatter, tiler, tinner, moonshiner*, or from their place of origin or abode, as in *Icelander, southerner, villager*, or designating either persons or things from some special characteristic or circumstance, as in *six-footer, three-master, teetotaler, fiver, tenner*; also (*b*) serving as the regular English formative of agent-nouns (being attached to verbs of any origin), as in *bearer, creeper, distributer* (beside *distributor*), *employer, harvester, poker, ruler, teacher, theorizer.* Cf. *-or*[2] and *-ee.*

-er[2]. [OF. *-er, -ier*, < L. *-arius*, neut. *-arium*: see *-ary.*] A suffix of nouns denoting persons or things concerned or connected with something, as in *butler, grocer, officer, garner.*

-er[3]. [AF. or OF. *-er, -re*, ending of infinitives used also as nouns.] Termination of certain nouns, mostly law-terms, denoting action or process, as in *dinner, rejoinder, remainder, trover.*

-er[4]. [In adjectives, AS. *-ra*; in adverbs, AS. *-or.*] A suffix forming the comparative degree of adjectives and adverbs, as in *better, faster, harder, sooner.*

-er[5]. [AS. *-rian.*] A suffix forming frequentative verbs, as *flicker, flutter, glimmer, patter.*

e-ra (ē′rạ), *n.* [LL. *æra*, number or epoch by which reckoning is made, era, prob. the same word as L. *æra*, counters, pl. of *æs*, copper, bronze.] A point of time from which succeeding years are numbered, as at the beginning of a system of chronology; an epoch; hence, a date or an event forming the beginning of any distinctive period; a point of time noted for some occurrence, etc.; also, a system of chronologic notation reckoned from a given date, or a period during which years are numbered and dates reckoned from a particular point of time in the past (as, the Christian *era*: see under *Christian, a.*); also, a period of time marked by distinctive character, events, etc. (as, an *era* of progress); a major division of geological time, usually regarded as of the highest rank; also, the period of time to which anything belongs or is to be assigned (as, "'Twas in November, but I'm not so sure About the day—the *era's* more obscure": Byron's "Don Juan," i. 121).

e-rad-i-ca-ble (ē-rad′i-kạ-bl), *a.* That may be eradicated.

e-rad-i-cate (ē-rad′i-kāt), *v. t.*; *-cated, -cating.* [L. *eradicatus*, pp. of *eradicare*, < *e*, out of, + *radix* (*radic-*), root.] To pull up by the roots; hence, to remove utterly; destroy utterly; extirpate.—**e-rad-i-ca′tion** (-kā′shọn), *n.*—**e-rad′i-ca-tive** (-kạ-tiv), *a.* Tending to eradicate.—**e-rad′i-ca-tor** (-kā-tọr), *n.*

e-ras-a-ble (ē-rā′sạ-bl), *a.* That may be erased.

e-rase (ē-rās′), *v. t.*; *erased, erasing.* [L. *erasus*, pp. of *eradere*, < *e*, out of, + *radere*, scrape.] To scrape or rub out, as letters or characters written, engraved, etc.; efface; expunge; obliterate.—**e-rase′ment, e-ra-sion** (ē-rā′zhọn), *n.*—**e-ras-er** (ē-rā′sėr), *n.* One who or that which erases; an instrument, as a sharp-pointed knife, or a piece of rubber or cloth, for erasing marks made with pen, pencil, chalk, etc.

E-ras-tian (e-ras′chạn). **I.** *a.* Pertaining to Thomas Erastus (1524–83), a Swiss-German theologian, a follower of Zwingli, or to his doctrines; pertaining to or advocating the doctrine of state supremacy in ecclesiastical matters, which has been attributed to Erastus. **II.** *n.* An advocate of the doctrines held by or attributed to Erastus.—**E-ras′tian-ism,** *n.*

e-ra-sure (ē-rā′zhụr), *n.* The act of erasing; a scraping or rubbing out; obliteration; also, a place from which something has been erased.

Er-a-to (er′ạ-tō), *n.* [L., < Gr. Ἐρατώ, 'lovely,' < ἐρᾶν, love.] The Muse of lyric and amatory poetry.

er-bi-um (ėr′bi-um), *n.* [NL.; named from (*Ytt*)*erby*, in Sweden: see *ytterbium.*] Chem. sym., Er; at. wt., 167.7. A rare metallic element.

ere (ãr). [AS. *ǣr*, adv. (also prep. and conj.), a compar. form (= D. *eer* = G. *eher*), earlier, sooner, before (also as positive, early), akin to Icel. *ār*, Goth. *air*, early: cf. *erst* and *early.*] **I.** *adv.* Early (now chiefly Sc.); also, formerly†; at an earlier time†. **II.** *prep.* Before (in time): as, he will be here *ere* night. **III.** *conj.* Before (as, "How long will it be *ere* they believe me?" Num. xiv. 11); also, sooner than; rather than.

Er-e-bus (er′e-bus), *n.* [L., < Gr. Ἔρεβος.] In *Gr. myth.*, a place of nether darkness through which the shades of the dead pass on their way to Hades: as, "dark as *Erebus*" (Shakspere's "Merchant of Venice," v. 1. 87).

e-rect (ē-rekt′), *v. t.* [L. *erectus*, pp. of *erigere*, set upright, raise up, build, < *e*, out of, + *regere*, direct.] To raise and set in an upright or perpendicular position; also, to raise, as a building; build; construct; hence, to set up or establish, as an institution; found; also, to form (*into*: as to *erect* territory into a state); also, to elevate or lift up, exalt, or direct upward (archaic); in *geom.*, to draw or construct (a line or figure) upon a given line, base, or the like; in *optics*, to change (an inverted image) to a normal position.—**e-rect′,** *a.* Upright in position or posture (as, to stand or sit *erect*); raised or directed upward (as, a dog with ears *erect*); fig., attentive or alert, as the mind.—**e-rect′a-ble,** *a.* That may be erected.—**e-rect′er,** *n.*—**e-rec-tile** (ē-rek′til), *a.* [F. *érectile.*] Capable of being erected or set upright; also, susceptible of being distended with blood and becoming rigid, as tissue.—**e-rec-til-i-ty** (ē-rek-til′i-ti), *n.*—**e-rec-tion** (ē-rek′shọn), *n.* [L. *erectio*(*n-*).] The act of erecting; the state of being erected; something erected, as a building or other structure; in *physiol.*, a turgid and rigid state of an organ or part into which erectile tissue enters.—**e-rec′tive,** *a.* Tending to erect.—**e-rect′ly,** *adv.*—**e-rect′ness,** *n.*—**e-rec′tor,** *n.*

ere-long (ãr′lông′), *adv.* Before long; soon.

er-e-mite (er′ē-mīt), *n.* [LL. *eremita*, < Gr. ἐρημίτης, < ἐρημία, a solitude, desert, < ἐρῆμος, desolate: cf. *hermit.*] One who has withdrawn from the world to lead a solitary life, from religious motives; a religious solitary; a hermit.—**er-e-mit′ic, er-e-mit′i-cal** (-mit′ik, -i-kạl), *a.* Pertaining to or characteristic of an eremite.—**er′e-mit-ish** (-mī-tish), *a.* Like or befitting an eremite.—**er′e-mit-ism,** *n.* The condition or mode of life of a hermit.

er-e-mu-rus (er-ē-mū′rus), *n.* [NL., < Gr. ἐρῆμος, desolate, solitary, + οὐρά, tail (with reference to the flower-stalk).] Any plant of the liliaceous genus *Eremurus*, native in Asia, and including species cultivated for their tall flower-stalks (sometimes 8 feet high) topped with a spike of white, yellow, pink, or red flowers.

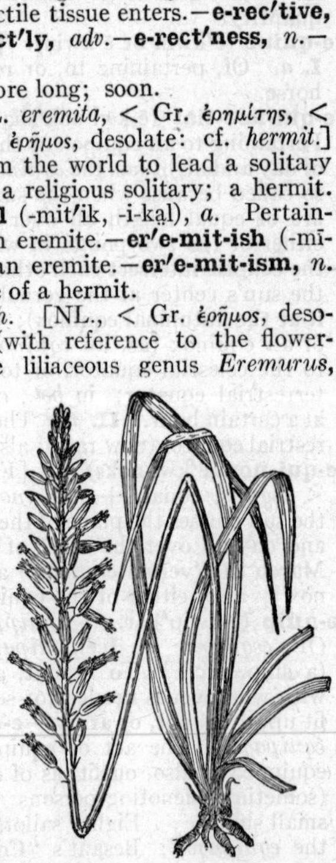

Eremurus (*E. spectabilis*).

ere-now (ãr′nou′), *adv.* Ere now; before this time.

er-e-thism (er′e-thizm), *n.* [Gr. ἐρεθισμός, < ἐρεθίζειν, excite, irritate.] In *physiol.*, an unusual or excessive degree of irritability or stimulation in an organ or tissue.

ere-while (ãr′hwīl′), *adv.* A while before: as, "all his armour stain'd, *erewhile* so bright" (Milton's "Paradise Lost," vi. 334). [Archaic.]

erg (ėrg), *n.* [Gr. ἔργον, work: see *work, n.*] In *physics*, the unit of work in the centimeter-gram-second system, being the amount of work done by one dyne acting through a distance of one centimeter.—**er-gal** (ėr′gạl), *n.* [G., < Gr. ἔργον.] In *physics*, potential energy.—**erg′me″ter** (-mē″tėr), *n.* An apparatus for measuring work or energy in ergs.

er-go (ėr′gō), *adv.* [L.] Therefore.

ergo-. Form of Gr. ἔργον, work, used in combination.—**er-go-gram** (ėr′gọ̄-gram), *n.* [+ *-gram.*] A record made by an ergograph.—**er′go-graph** (-gràf), *n.* [+ *-graph.*] An instrument for measuring and recording muscular work done, rate of fatigue, etc.—**er-gom′e-ter** (-gom′e-tėr), *n.* [+ *-meter.*] In *physics*, an instrument for measuring work done.

er-gon (ėr′gon), *n.* Same as *erg.*

er-got (ėr′gọt), *n.* [F. *ergot*, OF. *argot*, cock's spur.] A disease of rye and other cereals, due to a fungus (in rye, the fungus *Claviceps purpurea*) which develops in the ovary and replaces the grain by a hard, dark-colored body, usually resembling a cock's spur in form; also, one of the bodies so produced, esp. those of rye, used in medicine as a hemostatic, etc.—**er′got-ed,** *a.* Diseased by the attack of ergot, as rye.—**er′got-ine** (-in), *n.* An alkaloid contained in ergot; also, any of various extracts of ergot used in medicine. —**er′got-ism,** *n.* The diseased condition of rye, etc., due to ergot; also, a disease due to eating food prepared from rye, etc., affected with ergot.—**er′got-ize,** *v. t.*; *-ized, -izing.* To affect with ergot.

er-i-ca-ceous (er-i-kā′shius), *a.* [NL. *Erica*, the heath genus, < Gr. ἐρείκη, heath.] Belonging to the *Ericaceæ*, or heath family of plants, which includes the heath, arbutus, azalea, rhododendron, American laurel, etc.

e-rig-e-ron (ẹ̄-rij′ẹ-ron), *n.* [L., < Gr. ἠριγέρων, groundsel, < ἦρι, early, + γέρων, old man; with allusion to the hoary down.] Any plant of the asteraceous genus *Erigeron*, with flower-heads resembling those of the asters but having narrower and usually more numerous (white or purple) rays.

Er-in (er′in or ē′rin), *n.* [OIr. *Erinn*, dat. of *Eriu*, later *Éire*, Ireland.] An ancient name of Ireland. [Now poetic.]

er-i-na-ceous (er-i-nā′shius), *a.* [L. *erinaceus*, hedgehog.] Of the hedgehog kind or family.

e-rin-go (ẹ̄-ring′gō), *n.* See *eryngo.*

E-rin-ys (e-rin′is or e-rī′nis), *n.*; pl. *Erinyes* (e-rin′i-ēz). [L., < Gr. Ἐρινύς.] In *Gr. myth.*, an avenging female deity; a Fury. Also **E-rin-nys** (e-rin′is).

e-ris-tic (e-ris′tik). [Gr. ἐριστικός, < ἐρίζειν, wrangle, < ἔρις, strife, debate.] **I.** *a.* Pertaining to controversy or disputation; controversial. **II.** *n.* A controversialist; also, the art of disputation (see Encyc. Brit., 11th ed., XXV. 418).

erl=king (ėrl′king), *n.* [Tr. G. *erlkönig*, < Dan. *ellekonge, elverkonge*, king of the elves.] In German and Scandinavian mythology, a spirit or personified natural power which devises and works mischief, esp. to children.

er-mine (ėr′min), *n.* [OF. *ermine* (F. *hermine*); prob. from Teut.] A small, slender quadruped, *Putorius ermineus*, of the weasel kind, of northern regions, esp. when in winter pelage, which is pure white except for a black-tipped tail (also called *stoat*, esp. when in brown summer pelage); any of various allied species; also, the white fur of the ermine, esp. when having the black of the tails arranged at regular intervals, used for making garments and trimmings, and for lining and facing certain official and ceremonial garments, as the robes of English judges; hence, the office or dignity of a judge; in *her.*, one of the furs, represented with its peculiar spots black on a white ground.—**er′mine,** *v. t.*; *-mined, -mining.* To clothe, cover, or adorn with or as with ermine: chiefly in *ermined, pp.*

Ermine (*Putorius ermineus*), in winter pelage.

Heraldic Ermine.

erne (ėrn), *n.* [AS. *earn* = Icel. *örn*, eagle: cf. G. *aar*, bird of prey, eagle, also Gr. ὄρνις, bird.] An eagle, esp. a sea-eagle. [Now chiefly poetic or prov.]

e-rode (ẹ̄-rōd′), *v. t.*; *eroded, eroding.* [L. *erodere* (pp. *erosus*), < *e*, out of, + *rodere*, gnaw.] To gnaw or eat out or away; wear away as by gnawing; destroy by slow consumption; also, to form (a channel, etc.) by eating or wearing away: used esp. in geology, of the action of water, etc., on the earth's surface.—**e-rod-ent** (ẹ̄-rō′dẹnt), *a.* Eroding; erosive.—**e-rod′i-ble,** *a.* Subject to erosion.

E-ros (ē′ros), *n.* [L., < Gr. Ἔρως, personification of ἔρως, love, < ἐρᾶν, to love, be in love with.] The Greek god of love, identified by the Romans with Cupid.

e-rose (ẹ̄-rōs′), *a.* [L. *erosus*, pp. of *erodere*: see *erode.*] Uneven as if gnawed away; having the margin irregularly incised as if gnawed, as a leaf.

Erose Leaf.

e-ro-sion (ẹ̄-rō′zhọn), *n.* [L. *erosio(n-)*, < *erodere*: see *erode.*] The act of eroding, or the state of being eroded; esp., in *geol.*, the process by which the surface of the earth is worn away and sculptured by the action of water, glaciers, etc.—**e-ro′-sive** (-siv), *a.* Serving to erode; causing erosion.

Erosion. — Section showing the erosion of the summit of a mass of stratified rock bent into a low anticline.

e-rot-ic (e-rot′ik). [Gr. ἐρωτικός, < ἔρως, love: see *Eros.*] **I.** *a.* Of or pertaining to sexual love; amatory. **II.** *n.* An erotic poem or other composition.—**e-rot′i-cal-ly,** *adv.*—**e-rot′i-cism** (-sizm), *n.* Erotic character or tendency.

err (ėr), *v.* [OF. F. *errer*, < L. *errare*, wander, err.] **I.** *intr.* To wander† or roam† (as, "Around your house the greedy Grecians *err*": Dryden's tr. Virgil's "Æneid," ii. 814); also, to deviate from the true course, aim, or purpose; also, to go astray in thought or belief; be mistaken; be incorrect, as a statement; also, to go astray morally; sin. **II.**† *tr.* To miss or mistake; also, to make a mistake in.

er-rand (er′ạnd), *n.* [AS. *ǣrende* = OHG. *ārunti* = Icel. *eyrendi*, errand, message: cf. AS. *ār*, Icel. *ārr*, messenger.] A special business intrusted to a messenger; a commission; hence, the purpose of any trip or journey; also, a trip to convey a message or execute a commission; a journey for a specific purpose.

er-rant (er′ạnt), *a.* [OF. F. *errant*, prop. ppr. of OF. *errer*, journey, travel (< ML. *iterare*, < L. *iter*, way, journey), but confused with OF. F. *errant*, ppr. of *errer*, wander, E. *err.*] Journeying or traveling, as a medieval knight in quest of adventure; roving adventurously; also, wandering or straying; deviating from the regular or proper course; erring; also, arrant†.—**er′rant-ly,** *adv.*—**er′rant-ry,** *n.*; pl. *-ries* (-riz). Errant condition or deed; conduct or a performance characteristic or suggestive of a knight-errant.

er-ra-ta (e-rā′tạ̈), *n.* Plural of *erratum.*

er-rat-ic (e-rat′ik). [L. *erraticus*, < *errare*, wander, E. *err.*] **I.** *a.* Wandering; not fixed (as, an *erratic* star, a planet); also, having no certain course; also, deviating from the proper or usual course in conduct or opinion; eccentric; queer; in *med.*, irregular; changeable; moving from point to point, as rheumatic pains; in *geol.*, of boulders, etc., transported from the original site to an unusual location, as by glacial action; also, pertaining to such boulders, etc. **II.** *n.* A wanderer; also, an erratic or eccentric person; in *geol.*, an erratic boulder or block.—**er-rat′i-cal-ly,** *adv.*

er-ra-tum (e-rā′tum), *n.*; pl. *-ta* (-tạ̈). [L., prop. pp. neut. of *errare*, E. *err.*] An error in writing or printing.

er-rhine (er′īn or -in), *n.* [Gr. ἔρρινον, < ἐν, in, + ῥίς (ῥιν-), nose.] A medicine to be snuffed up the nostrils to promote sneezing and increased nasal discharges.

err-ing (ėr′ing or er′-), *p. a.* Wandering†; going astray; in error; wrong; sinning.—**err′ing-ly,** *adv.*

er-ro-ne-ous (e-rō′nẹ̄-us), *a.* [L. *erroneus*, < *erro(n-)*, wanderer, vagrant, < *errare*, wander, E. *err.*] Wandering†; also, straying from the right (obs. or archaic); also, containing error; mistaken; incorrect.—**er-ro′ne-ous-ly,** *adv.*—**er-ro′-ne-ous-ness,** *n.*

er-ror (er′ọr), *n.* [OF. *error* (F. *erreur*), < L. *error*, < *errare*, wander, E. *err.*] A wandering or roving (archaic: as, "the damsel's headlong *error* thro' the wood," Tennyson's "Gareth and Lynette," 1184); also, the belief of what is not true; false beliefs collectively, or a false belief; also, deviation from accuracy or correctness; an unintentional inaccuracy, as in speaking or writing; a mistake, as in action or procedure; also, departure from moral right; wrong-doing; a moral offense; in *math.*, etc., the difference between the observed or approximately determined value and the true value of a quantity; in *baseball*, any faulty play (except certain misplays by the pitcher or catcher, as a wild pitch or a passed ball) which prolongs a batsman's time at bat, leaves a runner safe when he should have been put out, or allows him to advance one or more bases.—**er'ror-less,** *a.* Free from error.

er-satz (er-zäts'), *n.* [G.] A substitute.

Erse (ėrs). [Var. of *Irish.*] **I.** *a.* Of or pertaining to the Celts in the Highlands of Scotland, or their language; sometimes, Irish. **II.** *n.* The Erse language; the Gaelic of the Scottish Highlanders; also, Irish.

erst (ėrst), *adv.* [AS. *ǣrest*, superl. of *ǣr*: see *ere.*] First†; at first†; also, before the present time (archaic); long ago (archaic); a little while ago (archaic).—**erst'while,** *adv.* A while before; at one time; once; formerly; heretofore. [Archaic.]

er-u-bes-cent (er-ọ̈-bes'ẹnt), *a.* [L. *erubescens* (*-ent-*), ppr. of *erubescere*, redden, < *e-*, out, + *rubescere*, become red: see *rubescent.*] Becoming red or reddish; blushing.—**er-u-bes'cence,** *n.*

e-ruct (ẹ-rukt'), *v. t.* [L. *eructare* (pp. *eructatus*), < *e*, out of, + *ructare*, belch.] To belch forth, as wind from the stomach; emit violently, as matter from a volcano. Also **e-ruc-tate** (ẹ-ruk'tāt).—**e-ruc-ta-tion** (ē-ruk-tā'shọn), *n.* [L. *eructatio*(*n-*).] The act of eructing; a belch, as of wind from the stomach or of matter from a volcano; also, that which is eructed.

er-u-dite (er'ọ̈-dīt). [L. *eruditus*, pp. of *erudire*, instruct, < *e*, out of, + *rudis*, unwrought, untaught, E. *rude.*] **I.** *a.* Learned or scholarly; characterized by erudition: as, an *erudite* professor; "an *erudite* commentary on certain points of law" (Parkman's "Oregon Trail," v.). **II.** *n.* An erudite person.—**er'u-dite-ly,** *adv.*—**er'u-dite-ness,** *n.*

er-u-di-tion (er-ọ̈-dish'ọn), *n.* [L. *eruditio*(*n-*), < *erudire*: see *erudite.*] Learning; scholarship; acquired knowledge, esp. in literature, languages, history, etc.

e-rum-pent (ẹ-rum'pẹnt), *a.* [L. *erumpens* (*-ent-*), ppr. of *erumpere*: see *erupt.*] Bursting forth; in *bot.*, prominent, as if bursting through the epidermis.

e-rupt (ẹ-rupt'), *v.* [L. *eruptus*, pp. of *erumpere*, < *e*, out of, + *rumpere*, break.] **I.** *intr.* To burst forth, as volcanic matter; of teeth, to break through the skin of the gums; of a volcano, geyser, etc., to eject matter. **II.** *tr.* To cause to burst forth; force (teeth) through the gums; of a volcano, etc., to eject (matter); belch.—**e-rup-tion** (ẹ-rup'shọn), *n.* [L. *eruptio*(*n-*).] A bursting forth; a violent emission; an issuing forth suddenly and violently; an outburst; an outbreak; also, that which bursts forth; in *geol.*, the ejection of molten rock, etc., as from a volcano; the ejection of water, etc., from a geyser; in *pathol.*, the breaking out of a rash or the like; a rash or exanthema.—**e-rup'tive. I.** *a.* Bursting forth, or tending to burst forth; pertaining to or of the nature of an eruption; in *geol.*, of rocks, formed by the eruption of molten material; in *pathol.*, causing, or attended with, an eruption or rash. **II.** *n.* In *geol.*, an eruptive rock.—**e-rup'tive-ly,** *adv.*

-ery. [OF. F. *-erie*, < *-ier* (E. *-er*^{2}) + *-ie* (E. *-y*^{3}); sometimes, also, from E. *-er*^{1} + *-y*^{3}.] A suffix of nouns denoting occupation, business, calling, or condition, place or establishment, goods or products, things collectively, qualities, actions, etc., as in *archery, bakery, cutlery, fishery, grocery, nunnery, pottery, finery, foolery, prudery, scenery, tracery, trickery, witchery.*

Er-y-man-thi-an (er-i-man'thi-ạn), *a.* Of or pertaining to Erymanthus, a mountain in ancient Greece: as, the *Erymanthian* boar (a savage beast fabled to have infested Arcadia and to have been caught by Hercules).

e-ryn-go (ẹ-ring'gō), *n.*; pl. *-goes* (-gōz). [L. *eryngion*, < Gr. ἠρύγγιον, dim. of ἤρυγγος, eryngo.] Any plant of the apiaceous genus *Eryngium*, consisting of coarse herbs with toothed or spiny leaves and heads or spikes of small white or blue flowers, esp. *E. maritimum*, the sea-holly, whose root was formerly candied as a sweetmeat.

er-y-sip-e-las (er-i-sip'ẹ-lạs), *n.* [L., < Gr. ἐρυσίπελας.] In *pathol.*, an acute, febrile, infectious disease, due to a specific streptococcus, and characterized by a diffusely spreading, deep-red inflammation of the skin or mucous membranes.—**er″y-si-pel'a-tous** (-si-pel'ạ-tus), *a.*—**er-y-sip'e-loid,** *n.* In *pathol.*, an infectious disease of the skin resembling erysipelas but not attended with fever.

er-y-the-ma (er-i-thē'mạ̈), *n.* [NL., < Gr. ἐρύθημα, < ἐρυθαίνειν, redden, < ἐρυθρός, red.] In *pathol.*, abnormal redness of the skin due to local congestion, as in inflammation.—**er″y-the-mat'ic** (-thẹ-mat'ik), **er-y-them'a-tous** (-them'ạ-tus), *a.*

er-y-thre-an, er-y-thræ-an (er-i-thrē'ạn), *a.* [L. *erythræus*, < Gr. ἐρυθραῖος, < ἐρυθρός, red.] Red: as, the *Erythrean* Sea (in *anc. geog.*, the Indian Ocean between Africa and India, with the Red Sea and the Persian Gulf; also, later, the Red Sea).

e-ryth-rin (e-rith'rin), *n.* [Gr. ἐρυθρός, red.] In *chem.*, a crystalline compound, $C_{20}H_{22}O_{10}$, obtained from certain lichens; also, a coal-tar color used to dye silk a fluorescent red.

e-ryth-rism (e-rith'rizm), *n.* [Gr. ἐρυθρός, red.] Abnormal redness, as of plumage or hair.—**er-y-thris-mal** (er-i-thriz'mạl), *a.*

e-ryth-rite (e-rith'rīt), *n.* [Gr. ἐρυθρός, red.] Cobalt bloom (see *bloom*^{1}, *n.*); in *chem.*, a crystalline compound, $C_4H_6(OH)_4$, obtained from various lichens.

e-ryth-ro-cyte (e-rith'rọ-sīt), *n.* [Gr. ἐρυθρός, red, + κύτος, a hollow.] One of the red corpuscles of the blood.

er-y-throp-si-a (er-i-throp'si-ạ̈), *n.* [NL., < Gr. ἐρυθρός, red, + ὄψις, sight.] In *pathol.*, defective vision in which all objects appear to be tinged with red.

-es^{1}. Earlier form of *-s*^{1}, plural suffix of nouns, now used chiefly after a sibilant, as in *asses, bushes, foxes, witches*, or (in some cases) after *o*, as in *mosquitoes, potatoes, tomatoes*, and regularly in the plural of nouns ending in *-y* preceded by a consonant, as in *dandies, duties, rubies* (plural of *dandy, duty, ruby*).

-es^{2}. Form of *-s*^{2}, ending of the third person singular present indicative of verbs, used after a vowel, as in *does, goes, hurries, magnifies.*

es-ca-drille (es-kạ-dril', F. es-kȧ-drē-y'), *n.* [F., dim. of *escadre*, squadron, < It. *squadra*: see *squadron.*] A small naval squadron; also, a squadron or divisional unit of aëroplanes.

es-ca-lade (es-kạ-lād'), *n.* [F., through Sp. or It. < ML. *scalare*, climb by ladder, scale, < L. *scala*, flight of steps, ladder, E. *scale*^{3}.] A scaling or mounting by means of ladders, esp. in an assault upon a fortified place.—**es-ca-lade',** *v. t.*; *-laded, -lading.* To mount, pass, or enter by means of ladders: as, "The Spaniards, by battering a breach in the wall . . . and then *escalading* the inner works . . . found themselves masters of the place" (Motley's "Dutch Republic," iii. 5).—**es-ca-lad'er** (-lā'dėr), *n.*

es-ca-la-tor (es'kạ-lā-tọr), *n.* [L. *e*, out of, from, + *scala*, flight of steps.] An apparatus consisting of a series of movable steps or corresponding parts joined together into an endless belt, which is so operated as to form a stairway or incline of which the steps or parts ascend or descend continuously. [Proprietary name.]

es-cal-lop (es-kol'ọp or es-kal'-), *n.* and *v.* Same as *scallop.*

es-cap-a-ble (es-kā'pạ-bl), *a.* That may be escaped.

es-ca-pade (es-kạ-pād'), *n.* [F., < It. *scappata*, < *scappare*: see *escape.*] An escape from confinement or restraint; a breaking loose from rules; a reckless or freakish proceeding, performance, or adventure; a wild prank.

es-cape (es-kāp'), *v.*; *-caped, -caping.* [OF. *escaper, eschaper* (F. *échapper*), = It. *scappare*, appar. orig. 'slip out of one's cloak,' < L. *ex*, out of, + ML. *capa*, cloak, E. *cape*^{2}.] **I.** *intr.* To slip or get away, as from confinement or restraint; gain or regain liberty; issue from a confining inclosure, as a fluid; also, to slip away from pursuit or peril; avoid capture, punishment, or any threatened evil. **II.** *tr.* To escape from (prison, etc.)†; slip from (a person) inadvertently, as a remark; also, to slip away from or elude (pursuit, etc.); succeed in avoiding (any threatened or possible evil); also, to elude (notice, search, etc., or one's memory); fail to be noticed or recollected by (a person).—**es-cape',** *n.* The act of escaping, or the fact of having escaped; a slipping or getting away from confinement or restraint; leakage, as of water, gas, etc.; avoidance of capture, punishment, injury, notice, etc.; preservation from harm; also, a means of escaping (as, a fire-*escape*); also, something that has escaped, esp. a plant escaped from cultivation and growing wild; also, an escapade† (as, "Rome will despise her for this foul *escape*": Shakspere's "Titus Andronicus," iv. 2. 113); an inadvertence† or blunder†.—

es-cape′ment, *n.* The act of escaping; also, a way of escape; an outlet; specif., the contrivance in a timepiece by which the pressure of the wheels and the vibratory motion of the pendulum or balance-wheel are accommodated the one to the other.—**es-cap′er** (-kā′pėr), *n.*

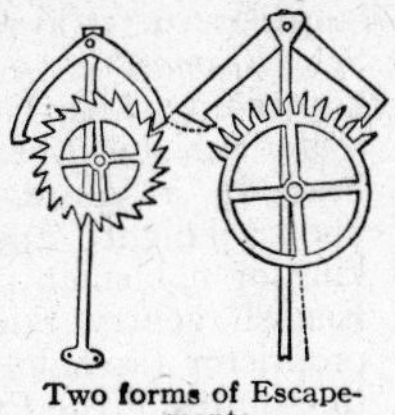

Two forms of Escapement.

es-car-got (es-kär-gō), *n.* [F.] A snail.

es-ca-role (es′ka̧-rōl), *n.* [F., < It. *scariola*.] A broad leaved kind of endive, used for salads.

es-carp (es-kärp′), *n.* [F. *escarpe*, < It. *scarpa*: cf. *scarp*.] In *fort.*, the inner slope or wall of the ditch surrounding a rampart; in general, any similar steep slope.—**es-carp′,** *v. t.* To make into an escarp; give a steep slope to; furnish with escarps.—**es-carp′ment,** *n.* Ground cut into the form of an escarp or steep slope; also, the precipitous face of a ridge of land, extent of rock, or the like; a cliff.

-esce. [L. *-escere*, with inceptive or inchoative force.] A suffix of verbs meaning 'to begin to be or do something,' 'become,' 'grow,' or 'be somewhat' (as indicated by the rest of the word), as in *convalesce*, *deliquesce*, *putresce*. Cf. *-escence* and *-escent*.

-escence. [L. *-escentia*.] Suffix of nouns denoting action or process, change, state or condition, etc., and corresponding to verbs ending in *-esce* or adjectives ending in *-escent*, as in *convalescence*, *deliquescence*, *luminescence*, *recrudescence*.

-escent. [L. *-escent-*, nom. *-escens*, ppr. ending.] A suffix of adjectives meaning 'beginning to be or do something,' 'becoming' or 'being somewhat' (as indicated), as in *convalescent*, *deliquescent*, *flavescent*, *lactescent*, *recrudescent*: often associated with verbs ending in *-esce* or nouns ending in *-escence*.

esch-a-lot (esh-a̧-lot′), *n.* Same as *shallot*.

es-char (es′kär), *n.* [LL. *eschara*, < Gr. ἐσχάρα, hearth, scar from a burn: cf. *scar*[1].] In *pathol.*, a hard crust or scab, as from a burn or caustic.—**es-cha-rot′ic** (-ka̧-rot′ik). [LL. *escharoticus*, < Gr. ἐσχαρωτικός.] **I.** *a.* Producing an eschar, as a medicinal substance; caustic. **II.** *n.* An escharotic substance or agent.

es-cha-tol-o-gy (es-ka̧-tol′o̧-ji), *n.* [Gr. ἔσχατος, uttermost, last: see *-logy*.] The doctrines of the last or final things, as death, the judgment, the future state, etc.; the branch of theology dealing with them.—**es″cha-to-log′i-cal** (-tō̧-loj′i-ka̧l), *a.*—**es-cha-tol′o-gist,** *n.*

es-cheat (es-chēt′), *n.* [OF. *eschete*, < *escheoir* (F. *échoir*), fall to one's share, < L. *ex*, out of, + *cadere*, fall.] In *law*, the reverting of land to the lord of the fee, or to the crown, as in England, or to the state, as in the U. S., through failure of persons legally qualified to inherit; in Scotland, confiscation or forfeiture of property; also, property or a possession which reverts by escheat; also, the right to take property subject to escheat.—**es-cheat′,** *v.* **I.** *intr.* To revert by escheat, as to the crown or the state: as, "The lands must *escheat*, unless the present owner made a will" (Cooper's "Two Admirals," xii). **II.** *tr.* To make an escheat of; confiscate.—**es-cheat′a-ble,** *a.*—**es-cheat′age** (-ā̧j), *n.* The right of succeeding to an escheat.—**es-cheat′or,** *n.* Formerly, in England, an officer in charge of escheats.

es-chew (es-chö′), *v. t.* [OF. *eschuer*, *eschiver*, also *eskiuwer* (see *skew*); from Teut. (cf. G. *scheuen*, shun, fear), and akin to E. *shy*[1].] To escape† (as, "What cannot be *eschew'd* must be embraced": Shakspere's "Merry Wives of Windsor," v. 5. 251); also, to abstain from; shun; avoid.—**es-chew′al,** *n.* An eschewing; avoidance.—**es-chew′er,** *n.*

esch-scholt-zi-a (e-shōlt′si-ä̧), *n.* [NL.; named from J. F. *Eschscholtz* (1793–1831), Russian naturalist.] Any plant of the papaveraceous genus *Eschscholtzia*, native in the western U. S., with finely divided glaucous leaves and showy yellow or orange-colored flowers, as *E. californica*, the California poppy.

es-clandre (es-kländ̃r), *n.* [F.: see *slander*.] Scandal; unpleasant notoriety; a scandalous occurrence; a scene.

es-cort (es′kôrt), *n.* [F. *escorte*, < It. *scorta*, < *scorgere*, guide, < L. *ex*, out of, + *corrigere*, set right, E. *correct*.] A body of persons, or a single person, accompanying another or others for protection, guidance, or compliment; specif., an armed guard; also, protection, safeguard, or guidance on a journey.—**es-cort′,** *v. t.* To attend or accompany as an escort.

es-cot† (es-kot′), *v. t.* [OF. *escoter*, < *escot*: see *scot*[1].] To pay for; support: as, "What, are they children? who maintains 'em? how are they *escoted?*" (Shakspere's "Hamlet," ii. 2. 362).

es-cri-toire (es-kri-twor′), *n.* [F. (now *écritoire*), < ML. *scriptorium*: see *scriptorium*.] A writing-desk.

es-crow (es-krō′), *n.* [AF. *escrowe*, OF. *escroe*, piece of parchment, scroll (F. *écrou*, entry in a jail register); from Teut., and akin to E. *shred*: cf. *scroll*.] In *law*, a writing fully executed by the parties, but deposited with a third person, by whom it is to be held until the fulfilment of some condition, when it is to be delivered to the grantee.

es-cu-do (es-kö′dō, Sp. -ᴛʜō), *n.*; pl. *-dos* (-dōz, Sp. -ᴛʜōs). [Sp. and Pg., < L. *scutum*, shield: cf. *écu* and *scudo*.] Any of various gold and silver coins of Spain, Chile, etc.; also, the gold monetary unit (established in 1911) of Portugal, divided into 100 equal parts called centavos, and equivalent in value to about $1.08; a Portuguese gold or silver coin of this value.

es-cu-lent (es′kū̧-lent). [L. *esculentus*, < *esca*, food, < *edere*, eat.] **I.** *a.* Suitable for use as food, esp. human food; edible. **II.** *n.* Something edible, esp. a vegetable.

es-cutch-eon (es-kuch′o̧n), *n.* [OF. *escuchon* (F. *écusson*), < *escu*, < L. *scutum*, shield.] The shield, or shield-shaped or other surface, on which armorial bearings are depicted or displayed; a hatchment; also, something resembling an escutcheon or a shield, as the panel on a ship's stern bearing her name, or the protective metal plate around a keyhole, or a marking on the rump of a deer, antelope, etc.—**es-cutch′eoned,** *a.*

-ese. [OF. *-eis* (F. *-ois*, *-ais*), < L. *-ensis*.] A suffix of adjectives and nouns having reference to locality, nationality, language, literary style, etc., as in *Bengalese*, *Chinese*, *Japanese*, *Johnsonese*, *journalese*.

es-kar, es-ker (es′kä̧r, -kėr), *n.* [Ir. *eiscir*.] In *geol.*, a serpentine ridge of gravelly and sandy drift, believed to have been formed by streams flowing under or in glacial ice.

Es-ki-mo (es′ki-mō). [Algonquian name for the people, meaning 'eaters of raw flesh': by themselves called *Innuit*.] **I.** *n.*; pl. *-mos* (-mōz) or *-mo*. One of a race or people, characterized by short or medium stature, stout build, light-brown complexion, and broad, flat face, inhabiting the arctic coasts of America from Greenland to Alaska and a small part of the adjacent Asiatic coast; also, their language. **II.** *a.* Of or pertaining to the Eskimos or their language.—**Eskimo dog,** one of a breed of strong dogs used by the Eskimos to draw sledges.—**Es-ki-mo′an,** *a.*

es-ne (ez′nȩ̄), *n.* [AS.] One of a class of domestic slaves among the Anglo-Saxons: as, "the *esne* or slave who works for hire" (Stubbs's "Constitutional Hist. of Eng.," v. § 37).

e-soph-a-gus, œ-soph-a-gus (ȩ̄-sof′a̧-gus), *n.* [NL. *œsophagus*, < Gr. οἰσοφάγος, perhaps < οἴσειν, fut. used with φέρειν, bear, + φαγεῖν, eat.] In *anat.* and *zoöl.*, the muscular tube in man and the higher animals which extends from the pharynx to the stomach; the gullet; also, an analogous tube in the lower animals, as insects.—**e-so-phag-e-al, œ-so-phag-e-al** (ē-so̧-faj′ȩ̄-a̧l), *a.*

es-o-ter-ic (es-o̧-ter′ik). [Gr. ἐσωτερικός, < ἐσωτέρω, compar. of ἔσω, within, < ἐς, εἰς, into.] **I.** *a.* Belonging or pertaining to an inner or select circle, as of disciples; communicated to or understood by the initiated only, as a doctrine; hence, private or secret; profound or recondite. Cf. *exoteric*. **II.** *n.* An esoteric doctrine (usually in *pl.*); also, one initiated or believing in esoteric doctrines.—**es-o-ter′i-cal,** *a.* Esoteric.—**es-o-ter′i-cal-ly,** *adv.*—**es-o-ter′i-cism** (-sizm), *n.* Esoteric doctrine or tendency. Also **e-sot-er-ism** (e-sot′ę-rizm).

es-pal-ier (es-pal′yėr), *n.* [F., < It. *spalliera*, lit. 'shoulder support,' < *spalla*, shoulder, < L. *spatula*, broad piece:

cf. *epaule*.] A trellis or framework on which fruit-trees or shrubs are trained to grow in flattened form, as to secure for the plant freer circulation of air or better exposure to the sun; also, a tree or plant so trained (as, "The long-tied *espaliers* . . . had grown so stout, and cramped . . . that they had pulled their stakes out of the ground": Hardy's "Mayor of Casterbridge," xii.).—**es-pal'ier,** *v. t.* To train on or furnish with an espalier.

es-par-to (es-pär'tō), *n.* [Sp., < L. *spartum*, < Gr. *σπάρτον, σπάρτος*.] Any of several grasses, esp. *Stipa tenacissima*, of southern Europe and northern Africa, used for making paper, cordage, etc. Also **es-par'to=grass.**

1 2 3 4 5

Esparto. — 1, 4, stalk and fruit of *Stipa tenacissima*; 2, 3, 5, stalk, flowering stem, and fruit of *Lygeum spartum*.

es-pe-cial (es-pesh'ạl), *a.* [OF. *especial* (F. *spécial*), < L. *specialis*: see *special*.] Special, of a particular kind, or peculiar to a particular one (archaic: as, "rend'ring general that which is *especial*," Byron's "Don Juan," xv. 25); also, having a particular function, purpose, etc.† (as, an *especial* messenger); also, distinguished from what is ordinary; exceptional; now, usually, exceptional in amount or degree (as, *especial* care; *especial* regret; of no *especial* value or importance).—**es-pe'cial-ly,** *adv.* In an especial manner or degree; particularly; principally.

es-pe-rance† (es'pẹ-rạns), *n.* [OF. *esperance* (F. *espérance*), < *esperer*, < L. *sperare*, hope.] Hope.

Es-pe-ran-to (es-pe-rän'tō), *n.* [From *Esperanto*, pseudonym of L. L. Zamenhof (1859–1917), Russian physician, who in 1887 proposed this language.] An artificial language designed as an international medium, based on words and forms common to the principal European languages.—**Es-pe-ran'tist,** *n.*

es-pi-al (es-pī'ạl), *n.* The act of espying, or the fact of being espied; discovery; also, the act of keeping watch; observation; also, a spy†.

es-piè-gle-rie (es-pye-glė-rē), *n.* [F.] Roguishness; a roguish or playful trick.

es-pi-er (es-pī'ėr), *n.* [See *espy*.] One who espies.

es-pi-o-nage (es'pi-ọ-nạj), *n.* [F. *espionnage*, < *espionner*, spy upon, < *espion*, < It. *spione*, aug. of *spia*, spy, = E. *spy, n.*] The practice of spying on others; the employment of spies.

es-pla-nade (es-plạ-nād'), *n.* [F, through Sp. or It. < L. *explanare*, flatten out: see *explain*.] The glacis of a fortification; also, the open space between the glacis of a citadel and the first houses of the town; also, any open, level space, esp. one serving for public walks or drives.

es-pou-sal (es-pou'zạl), *n.* [OF. *espousaille*, usually pl. *espousailles* (F. *épousailles*), < L. *sponsalia*, neut. pl. of *sponsalis*, pertaining to betrothal, < *sponsus*, betrothal, < *spondere*: see *espouse*.] The ceremony of betrothal or of marriage (usually in *pl.*); also, the act of espousing; adoption or advocacy, as of a cause or principle.

es-pouse (es-pouz'), *v. t.*; *-poused, -pousing.* [OF. *espouser* (F. *épouser*), < LL. *sponsare*, betroth, espouse, < L. *spondere* (pp. *sponsus*), promise, betroth: cf. *sponsor*.] To promise, engage, or bestow in marriage; betroth; also, to take in marriage; marry; hence, to make one's own, adopt, or embrace, as a cause.—**es-pous'er,** *n.*

es-prit (es-prē), *n.* [F., < L. *spiritus*, E. *spirit*.] Spirit; mind; intelligence; wit.—**esprit de corps** (dė kôr). [F., 'spirit of body.'] A sense of union and of common interests and responsibilities, as developed among a body of persons associated together.—**esprit fort** (fôr). [F., 'strong spirit.'] A strong-minded person; a freethinker.

es-py (es-pī'), *v.*; *-pied, -pying.* [OF. *espier* (F. *épier*): see *spy, v.*] **I.** *tr.* To see at a distance; catch sight of; see or discover suddenly after some effort, or unexpectedly as by chance; also, to inspect narrowly†; spy upon† (as, "Now question me no more; we are *espied*": Shakspere's "Titus Andronicus," ii. 3. 48). **II.** *intr.* To look narrowly; keep watch; spy: as, "Stand by the way, and *espy*" (Jer. xlviii. 19). [Archaic.]

-esque. [F. *-esque*, < It. *-esco*, from Teut., and akin to E. *-ish*[1].] A suffix of adjectives indicating style, manner, or distinctive character, as in *arabesque, grotesque, picturesque, Dantesque, Dürer esque, Junoesque, Romanesque.*

Es-qui-mau (es'ki-mō), *n.*; pl. *-maux* (-mōz or -mō). [F.] See *Eskimo*.

es-quire (es-kwīr'), *n.* [OF. *esquier* (F. *écuyer*), < LL. *scutarius*, shield-bearer, < L. *scutum*, shield.] A shield-bearer†; a squire, or aspirant to knighthood, attendant upon a knight; any of various officials in the service of a king or nobleman; also, a man belonging to the order of English gentry ranking next below a knight; a landed proprietor (archaic); [usually *cap.*] a title orig. belonging to esquires of the English gentry, but later applied to other persons considered to be of equivalent rank, particularly to lawyers in the U. S., and commonly to any man as a mere mark of respect, as in the addresses of letters (written after the surname preceded by the Christian name or initials and with no title, as *Mr.*, prefixed, and commonly abbreviated *Esq.* or *Esqr.*: as, John Smith, *Esq.*); also [*l. c.*], a gentleman who attends or escorts a lady in public.—**es-quire',** *v. t.*; *-quired, -quiring.* To raise to the rank of esquire; also, to address as 'Esquire'; also, to escort (a lady) as an esquire.

ess (es), *n.* The letter S, s; something shaped like an S.—**collar of esses.** See under *collar, n.*

-ess. [F. *-esse*, < L. *-issa*, < Gr. *-ισσα*.] A noun suffix forming distinctively feminine terms corresponding to nouns of masculine (or common) gender, as in *abbess, countess, governess, hostess, poetess.*

es-say (es'ā), *n.* [OF. F. *essai*, < LL. *exagium*, a weighing, < L. *ex-*, out, + *agere*, drive, do, act: cf. *assay*, also *examen, exact*.] A testing† or experiment† (as, "I hope . . . he wrote this but as an *essay* or taste of my virtue": Shakspere's "King Lear," i. 2. 47); a trial specimen†; also, an effort to perform or accomplish something; an attempt or endeavor; also, a tentative effort†; a rough copy or draft, as of a letter; also, a literary composition, usually of no great length, on a particular subject.—**es-say** (e-sā'), *v. t.* [OF. *essaier* (F. *essayer*), < *essai*.] To put to the test; make trial of; also, to try to accomplish; attempt.—**es-say'er,** *n.*—**es-say-ette** (es-ā-et'), *n.* A short essay.—**es'say-ist,** *n.* One who makes essays or trials; also, a writer of essays.

es-sence (es'ẹns), *n.* [OF. F. *essence*, < L. *essentia*, < *esse*, be.] Being† or existence†; something that is, esp. a spiritual or immaterial entity (as, "Her honour is an *essence* that's not seen": Shakspere's "Othello," iv. 1. 16); substance (as, "Spirits . . . Can either sex assume, or both; so soft And uncompounded is their *essence* pure": Milton's "Paradise Lost," i. 425); an elementary ingredient or constituent (cf. *quintessence*); also, that by which a thing is what it is; intrinsic nature; hence, the distinctive characteristic or specific difference of a thing; the important elements or features of a thing; also, a substance obtained from a plant, drug, or the like, by distillation or other process, and containing its characteristic properties in concentrated form; an alcoholic solution of an essential oil; specif., a perfume; also, gasoline, as used in operating automobiles, etc.—**es'sence,** *v. t.*; *-senced, -sencing.* To perfume; scent.

Es-sene (e-sēn'), *n.* [L. *Esseni*, pl., < Gr. Ἐσσηνοί.] One of a brotherhood or monastic order of Jews in ancient Palestine, first appearing in history in the 2d century B.C., characterized by asceticism, celibacy, and the strict observance of the non-Levitical portion of the Mosaic law.—**Es-se-ni-an** (e-sē'ni-ạn), *a.*—**Es-se'nism** (-nizm), *n.*

es-sen-tial (e-sen'shạl), *a.* [ML. *essentialis*.] Existent† or actual†; also, being such by its essence or very nature, or in the highest sense (as, *essential* happiness; *essential* poetry); also, pertaining to, constituting, or entering into the essence or nature of a thing; important, as affecting the essence of a thing; hence, absolutely necessary; indispensable; also, of the nature of an essence of a plant, etc. (as, an *essential* oil: see below); in *med.*, idiopathic.—**essential oil,** any of a class of oils obtained from plants, possessing the odor and other properties of the plant, and volatilizing completely when heated: used in making perfumes, flavors, etc.—**es-sen′tial,** *n.* Something belonging to the essence or nature of a thing; something indispensable; a chief point.—**es-sen-ti-al′i-ty** (-shi-al′i-ti), *n.*; pl. *-ties* (-tiz). The quality of being essential; essential character; also, an essential element or point.—**es-sen′tial-ly,** *adv.*—**es-sen′tial-ness,** *n.*

-est¹. [AS. *-est, -ost.*] A suffix forming the superlative degree of adjectives and adverbs, as in *eldest, fastest, hardest, soonest.*

-est², -st. [AS. *-est, -ast, -st.*] Ending of the second person singular present and preterit indicative of verbs, as in *doest* or *dost, diddest* or *didst, hast, hadst*: now occurring only in archaic forms or used in solemn or poetic language.

es-tab-lish (es-tab′lish), *v. t.* [OF. *establir* (*establiss-*) (F. *établir*), < L. *stabilire,* < *stabilis,* firm, E. *stable².*] To make stable or firm; confirm; strengthen; also, to appoint or ordain for permanence, as a law; fix unalterably; also, to set up on a firm or permanent basis, as a government or a business; institute; found; also, to fix or settle stably, as in a position; install; set up in business; settle (one's self) as if permanently; also, to set up or bring about permanently, as liberty or order; cause to be permanently accepted, as a custom; also, to show to be valid or well grounded, as a claim or an accusation; prove; also, to make (a church) a national or state institution.—**es-tab′lish-er,** *n.*—**es-tab′lish-ment,** *n.* The act of establishing, or the state or fact of being established; settlement; institution; substantiation; also, fixed or settled allowance or income; also, something established; a constituted order or system; a permanent civil, military, or other force or organization; the quota of men in an army, regiment, etc.; an organized business concern, or the building occupied by it; an institution; a household; a place of residence with everything connected with it; also, the recognition by a state of a church as the state church; the church so recognized.

es-ta-cade (es-tạ-kād′, F. es-tȧ-käd), *n.* [F., < Sp. *estacada,* < *estaca,* stake.] A dike or barrier of piles or the like set in the sea, a river, etc., to check the approach of an enemy or protect against floating objects.

es-ta-fette (es-tạ-fet′), *n.* [F., < It. *staffetta,* dim. of *staffa,* stirrup; from Teut.] A mounted courier.

es-ta-mi-net (es-tȧ-mē-nā), *n.* [F.] A café in which smoking is allowed.

es-tan-cia (es-tän′syä), *n.* [Sp., < ML. *stantia,* < L. *stare,* stand.] In Spanish America, a landed estate; a stock-farm.

es-tate (es-tāt′), *n.* [OF. *estat* (F. *état*), < L. *status*: see *state.*] State or condition of being (as, to attain to man's *estate*); condition or circumstances with reference to worldly prosperity, estimation, etc.; social status or rank; sometimes, high rank or dignity; a person of high rank†; pomp or state (archaic); also, a class or order in a community or nation (as, "We know your tenderness of heart . . . to all *estates*": Shakspere's "Richard III.," iii. 7. 213); one of the great classes or orders ('estates of the realm') constituting the body politic and participating in the government, as, now, in England, the lords spiritual, lords temporal, and commons; also, interest, ownership, or property in land or other things; hence, property or possessions; esp., property left at a person's death; the property of a deceased person, a bankrupt, etc., viewed in the aggregate as a legal person (as, to buy from the *estate* of John Smith); also, a piece of landed property, esp. one of large extent.—**fourth estate,** the public press; the newspapers, or the body of journalists.—**es-tate′,** *v. t.*; *-tated, -tating.* To establish in or as in an estate; also, to bestow as an estate† (as, "All my right of her I do *estate* unto Demetrius": Shakspere's "Midsummer Night's Dream," i. 1. 98).

es-teem (es-tēm′), *v.* [OF. F. *estimer,* < L. *æstimare*: see *estimate,* and cf. *aim.*] **I.** *tr.* To set a value on; value; rate; hold in estimation; esp., to regard as valuable; prize; regard highly or favorably; feel regard for; respect; also, to form a judgment concerning the number, extent, etc., of†; form an opinion of†; consider, think, or hold (as, "Conversation, in its better part, May be *esteem'd* a gift and not an art": Cowper's "Conversation," 4). **II.**† *intr.* To have an opinion (*of*): as, "We have always truly served you, and beseech you So to *esteem* of us" (Shakspere's "Winter's Tale," ii. 3. 149).—**es-teem′,** *n.* An estimate† or appraisal†; also, opinion or judgment of merit or demerit; estimation; esp., favorable opinion or judgment; respect or regard; also, reputation†; standing†; worth†.

es-ter (es′tėr), *n.* [Coined by L. Gmelin (1788–1853), German chemist.] In *chem.*, a compound formed by replacing the hydrogen of an acid by a hydrocarbon radical: often regarded as a salt of the hydrocarbon radical.

Esth (esth), *n.* An Esthonian.

es-the-sia (es-thē′ziạ), etc. See *æsthesia,* etc.

es-the-si-om-e-ter, æs-the-si-om-e-ter (es-thē-si-om′e-tėr), *n.* [Gr. αἴσθησις, perception, sensation: see *-meter.*] An instrument for determining the degree of tactile sensibility, esp. by finding how close two points pressed against the skin can be to each other and yet be felt as distinct points.

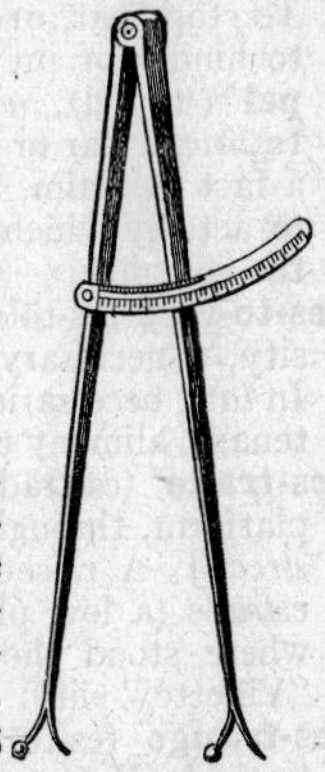

Esthesiometer.

es-thete, æs-thete (es′thēt), *n.* [Gr. αἰσθητής, one who perceives, < αἰσθάνεσθαι, perceive.] One in whom the artistic sense or faculty is highly developed; commonly, one affecting an extravagant love of the beautiful.—**es-thet′ic, æs-thet′ic** (-thet′ik). [Gr. αἰσθητικός, < αἰσθάνεσθαι.] **I.** *a.* Pertaining to the sense of the beautiful, or the science of esthetics; having an appreciation of or a love for the beautiful; conforming to the principles of the beautiful. **II.** *n.* The science of the beautiful; esthetics.—**es-thet′i-cal, æs-thet′i-cal,** *a.*—**es-thet′i-cal-ly, æs-thet′i-cal-ly,** *adv.*—**es-the-ti′cian, æs-the-ti′cian** (-thẹ-tish′ạn), *n.* One versed in esthetics.—**es-thet′i-cism, æs-thet′i-cism** (-sizm), *n.* The principles of esthetics; attachment to esthetics; appreciation of the beautiful.—**es-thet′ics, æs-thet′ics,** *n.* The doctrines or philosophy of taste; the science of the beautiful; the theory of the fine arts.

Es-tho-ni-an (es-thō′ni-ạn). **I.** *a.* Of or pertaining to Esthonia (on the eastern coast of the Baltic Sea, south of the Gulf of Finland), or the Esthonians, or their language. **II.** *n.* One of a Finnic people inhabiting Esthonia and neighboring regions; also, the language of this people.

es-ti-ma-ble (es′ti-mạ-bl), *a.* [L. *æstimabilis.*] Capable of being estimated; also, valuable† (as, "A pound of man's flesh . . . Is not so *estimable* . . . As flesh of muttons, beefs, or goats": Shakspere's "Merchant of Venice," i. 3. 167); also, worthy of esteem, regard, or good opinion.—**es′ti-ma-ble-ness,** *n.*—**es′ti-ma-bly,** *adv.*

es-ti-mate (es′ti-māt), *v.*; *-mated, -mating.* [L. *æstimatus,* pp. of *æstimare,* judge the value of, rate: cf. *esteem.*] **I.** *tr.* To set a value on† or appraise†; value† or esteem†; also, to form an approximate judgment or opinion regarding the value, amount, size, weight, etc., of; calculate approximately; also, to form an opinion of; judge. **II.** *intr.* To submit approximate figures, as of the cost of work to be done.—**es′ti-mate** (-māt), *n.* An appraisal† or valuation†; appraised value†; also, an approximate judgment or calculation, as of the value, amount, etc., of something; an approximate statement of what would be charged for certain work to be done, submitted by one ready to undertake the work; also, a judgment or opinion, as of the qualities of a person or thing; estimation or judgment.—**es-ti-ma′tion** (-mā′shọn), *n.* [L. *æstimatio(n-).*] The act of estimating or appraising†; valuation†; estimated value†; also, valuation in respect of excellence or merit; esteem; hence, account or worth in the opinion of others; repute; consequence; also, approximate calculation; also, judgment or opinion; manner of judging.—**es′ti-ma-tive** (-mạ-tiv), *a.* Pertaining to or capable of estimating.—**es′ti-ma-tor** (-mā-tọr), *n.*

e-stip-u-late (ē-stip′ū-lāt), *a.* Same as *exstipulate.*

es-ti-val, æs-ti-val (es′ti-vạl), *a.* [L. *æstivalis,* < *æstivus,* of summer, < *æstas,* summer, akin to *æstus,* heat: see *estuary.*] Pertaining or appropriate to summer.

es-ti-vate, æs-ti-vate (es′ti-vāt), *v. i.*; *-vated, -vating.* [L. *æstivatus*, pp. of *æstivare*, < *æstivus*: see *estival.*] To spend the summer; in *zoöl.*, to pass the summer in a dormant or torpid condition.—**es-ti-va′tion, æs-ti-va′tion** (-vā′shọn), *n.* The act of estivating (used esp. in *zoöl.*); in *bot.*, the disposition of the parts of a flower in the bud.—**es′ti-va-tor, æs′ti-va-tor,** *n.* An estivating animal.

es-toile (es-toil′), *n.* [OF. *estoile* (F. *étoile*), < L. *stella*, star.] In *her.*, a star-shaped figure, commonly having six points and wavy rays. Cf. *mullet*².

Estoile.

es-top (es-top′), *v. t.*; *-topped, -topping.* [OF. *estoper* (F. *étouper*), stop up, AF. *estopper* (in law), < ML. *stupare*, stop, orig. with tow, < L. *stuppa*, tow: cf. *stop.*] To stop, bar, or obstruct (archaic); in *law*, to hinder or prevent by estoppel.—**es-top′-pel** (-top′ẹl), *n.* [Cf. OF. *estoupail*, stopple, stopper.] In *law*, a bar or impediment preventing one from asserting a fact or claim, arising from a previous action, or a failure to act, by which one has admitted, implied, or established the contrary.

es-to-vers (es-tō′vėrz), *n. pl.* [OF. *estover, estovoir*, necessity, a necessary, noun use of *estovoir*, inf., be necessary.] In *law*, necessaries allowed by law, as wood and timber to a tenant, alimony to a wife, etc.

es-trade (es-träd′), *n.* [F., road, highway, later raised platform, through Pr. or It. < LL. *strata*, paved way: see *street.*] A raised platform; a dais: as, "I mounted the *estrade* (a low platform, raised a step above the flooring), where stood the teacher's chair and desk" (C. Brontë's "Villette," viii.).

es-trange (es-trānj′), *v. t.*; *-tranged, -tranging.* [OF. *estrangier* (F. *étranger*), < L. *extraneare*, < *extraneus*, that is without, foreign: see *extraneous*, and cf. *strange.*] To cause to be strange or as a stranger; remove to or keep at a distance; also, to divert from the original use or possessor (as, "They . . . have *estranged* this place, and have burned incense in it unto other gods": Jer. xix. 4); also, to turn away in feeling or affection; alienate the affections of.—**es-trange′ment,** *n.*—**es-tran′ger** (-trān′jėr), *n.*

es-tray (es-trā′), *v. i.* [OF. *estraier*: see *stray.*] To stray. [Archaic.]—**es-tray′,** *n.* A domestic animal, as a horse or a sheep, found wandering or without an owner; hence, anything strayed away.

es-treat (es-trēt′), *n.* [AF. *estrete*, OF. *estraite*, < *estraire*, < L. *extrahere*: see *extract.*] In *Eng. law*, a true copy or extract of an original writing or record, as of a fine.—**es-treat′,** *v. t.* To make an estreat of (a fine, etc.) for prosecution; also, to levy (fines) under an estreat; exact (anything) by way of fine or levy.

es-tu-a-ry (es′ṭū-ā-ri), *n.*; pl. *-ries* (-riz). [L. *æstuarium*, < *æstus*, heat, heaving motion, surge, tide, akin to Gr. αἴθειν, kindle: see *ether.*] An arm or inlet of the sea indenting the land; an arm of the sea at the mouth of a river; that part of the mouth or lower course of a river flowing into the sea which is subject to marked tidal effects.—**es′tu-a-rine** (-ạ-rin), *a.*

e-su-ri-ent (ẹ-sū′ri-ẹnt), *a.* [L. *esuriens* (*-ent-*), ppr. of *esurire*, desire to eat, < *edere*, eat.] Hungry; greedy.—**e-su′ri-ence, e-su′ri-en-cy,** *n.*

-et. [OF. *-et* (F. *-et*), masc., *-ete* (F. *-ette*), fem.] A noun suffix having properly a diminutive force (now lost in many words), as in *bullet, facet, islet, mallet, midget, owlet, plummet.* Cf. *-ette.*

e-ta (ē′tạ̈ or ā′tạ̈), *n.* [Gr. ἦτα.] The seventh letter (Η, η, = English long E, e) of the Greek alphabet.

e-tæ-ri-o (e-tē′ri-ō), *n.* Erroneous form of *hetærio.*

é-ta-gère (ā-tȧ-zhãr), *n.* [F., < *étage*, story, = E. *stage.*] An ornamental cabinet of open shelves suitable for bric-à-brac.

et-a-mine (et′ạ-min), *n.* [F. *étamine*, OF. *estamine*, < L. *stamen*, warp, thread: see *stamen.*] A dress-fabric of wool, cotton, silk, etc., with an open, canvas-like weave.

é-tape (ā-tȧp), *n.* [F.; akin to E. *staple*².] Formerly, a mart; a storehouse, as of provisions for troops; an allowance of provisions for troops on the march; in modern use, a place at which troops halt for the night; the distance marched by them during the day; in Russia, a stockaded prison-like building used to confine and shelter at night prisoners in transit.

é-tat=ma-jor (ā-tä-mȧ-zhôr), *n.* [F.] The staff of an army, regiment, etc.

et cet-e-ra (et set′ẹ-rạ̈). [L. *et cetera* (sometimes *cætera*).] And others; and the rest; and so forth: often abbreviated *etc.* or *&c.*—**et-cet′e-ra,** *n.*; pl. *-ras.* A number of other things or persons unspecified; *pl.*, extras or sundries (as, "The hall itself was strewn . . . with trunks, imperials, and . . . the hundred *etceteras* of travelling baggage": Lever's "Harry Lorrequer," vii.).

etch (ech), *v.* [D. *etsen*, < G. *ätzen*, feed, corrode, etch; akin to E. *eat.*] **I.** *tr.* To cut, bite, or corrode with an acid or the like; engrave (mẹtals, etc.) by the corrosive action of an acid or the like, esp. so as to form a design or picture in furrows which when charged with ink will give an impression on paper; also, to produce or copy by this method, as on copper. **II.** *intr.* To practise etching.—**etch′er,** *n.*—**etch′ing,** *n.* The process or art of one who etches; a process for forming a design or drawing on a metal plate from which an ink impression on paper can be taken, the method consisting of the coating of the plate with a kind of varnish, the drawing of the design on this with a sharp instrument, and the eating out of the exposed metal with acid; also, a design or plate so produced; an impression, as on paper, taken from an etched plate.

e-tern (ẹ-tėrn′), *a.* See *eterne.*

e-ter-nal (ẹ-tėr′nạl). [OF. *eternal* (F. *éternel*), < LL. *æternalis*, < L. *æternus*: see *eterne.*] **I.** *a.* Without beginning or end of duration (as, "The *eternal* God is thy refuge": Deut. xxxiii. 27); independent of time-conditions; also, of endless duration; everlasting (as, the *Eternal* City, Rome); imperishable; immutable; hence, perpetual; ceaseless; continued without cessation. **II.** *n.* That which is eternal; eternity†; [*cap.*] with *the*, God.—**e-ter′nal-ly,** *adv.*—**e-ter′nal-ness,** *n.*

e-terne (ẹ-tėrn′), *a.* [OF. *eterne*, < L. *æternus*, for *æviternus*, < *ævum*, eternity, age, akin to Gr. αἰών, E. *æon.*] Eternal; everlasting. [Archaic.]

e-ter-ni-ty (ẹ-tėr′ni-ti), *n.*; pl. *-ties* (-tiz). [OF. *eternite* (F. *éternité*), < L. *æternitas*, < *æternus*: see *eterne.*] Eternal duration or continuance; eternal existence, esp. as contrasted with mortal life (as, "All that lives must die, Passing through nature to *eternity*": Shakspere's "Hamlet," i. 2. 73); infinite time (as, "those thoughts that wander through *eternity*": Milton's "Paradise Lost," ii. 148); also, an endless or seemingly endless period or extent.

e-ter-nize (ẹ-tėr′nīz), *v. t.*; *-nized, -nizing.* [F. *éterniser*, < L. *æternus*: see *eterne.*] To make eternal; perpetuate; immortalize: as, "Men's monuments, grown old, forget their names They should *eternize*" (Lowell's "Under the Old Elm," ii. 1).

e-te-sian (ẹ-tē′zhạn), *a.* [L. *etesius*, < Gr. ἐτήσιος, < ἔτος, year.] Recurring annually: applied to certain Mediterranean winds.

eth (eᴛʜ), *n.* See *edh.*

-eth, -th³. [AS. *-eth, -ath, -th.*] Ending of the third person singular present indicative of verbs, as in *doeth* or *doth, hath, hopeth, sitteth*: now occurring only in archaic forms or used in solemn or poetic language. Cf. *-s*².

eth-ane (eth′ān), *n.* [From *ether.*] In *chem.*, an odorless, gaseous hydrocarbon present in illuminating gas and crude petroleum.

e-ther (ē′thėr), *n.* [L. *æther*, < Gr. αἰθήρ, upper air, sky, akin to αἴθειν, kindle, light up, Skt. *idh-*, kindle: cf. *estuary.*] The upper regions of space; the clear sky; the heavens; also, the medium anciently supposed to fill the upper regions; in *physics*, an extremely tenuous and elastic medium ('luminiferous ether') supposed to be diffused through all space, and to transmit light, electric waves, etc.; in *chem.*, a highly volatile and inflammable colorless liquid ('ethyl ether'), obtained by the action of sulphuric acid on alcohol, and used chiefly as an anesthetic; any of the class of compounds (oxides of hydrocarbon radicals) to which ethyl ether belongs.—**ether wave.** See under *wave, n.*

e-the-re-al (ẹ-thē′rẹ-ạl), *a.* [L. *æthereus*, for *ætherius*, < Gr. αἰθέριος, < αἰθήρ: see *ether.*] Of or pertaining to the ether or upper regions of space; hence, heavenly or celestial (as, "Go, heavenly guest, *ethereal* messenger, Sent from whose Sovran Goodness I adore!" Milton's "Paradise Lost," viii. 646); also, resembling the ether; light, airy, or tenuous; also, intangible; impalpable; extremely delicate or refined; in *physics*, pertaining to or of the nature of luminiferous ether; in *chem.*, pertaining to or resembling ethyl ether.—**e-the-re-al′i-ty** (-al′i-ti), *n.* Ethereal quality.—**e-the′re-al-ize** (-īz), *v. t.*; *-ized, -izing.* To make ethereal; refine; spiritualize; give an ethereal appearance to.—**e-the″re-al-i-za′tion** (-i-zā′shǫn), *n.*—**e-the′re-al-ly,** *adv.*—**e-the′re-al-ness,** *n.*

e-the-re-ous (ę-thē′rę-us), *a.* Ethereal.

e-the-ri-al (ę-thē′ri-ąl), etc. See *ethereal*, etc.

e-ther-ic (ę-ther′ik), *a.* Of or pertaining to the ether, or the chemical substance ether.

e-ther-i-fy (ē′thėr-i-fī or ę-ther′-), *v. t.*; *-fied, -fying.* [See *-fy.*] To convert into ether.—**e-ther-i-fi-ca-tion** (ē″thėr-i-fi-kā′shǫn or ę-ther″-), *n.*

e-ther-ize (ē′thėr-īz), *v. t.*; *-ized, -izing.* In *chem.*, to convert into ether; in *med.*, to put under the influence of ether.—**e″ther-i-za′tion** (-i-zā′shǫn), *n.*—**e′ther-iz-er** (-ī-zėr), *n.*

eth-ic (eth′ik). [L. *ethicus*, < Gr. ἠθικός, < ἦθος, custom, disposition, character.] **I.** *a.* Pertaining to morals; ethical. **II.** *n.* Ethics.—**eth′i-cal,** *a.* Pertaining to morals or the principles of morality; pertaining to right and wrong in conduct; also, in accordance with the rules for right conduct or practice.—**ethical dative,** in *gram.*, the dative of a personal pronoun introduced into a sentence to indicate a person to whom the idea expressed is of some degree of interest, as *me* in "He plucked me ope his doublet and offered them his throat to cut," or *mihi* in *Quid mihi Celsus agit?* (How does my Celsus?).—**eth′i-cal-ly,** *adv.*—**eth′i-cal-ness,** *n.*—**eth′i-cize** (-sīz), *v. t.*; *-cized, -cizing.* To make ethical; regard or treat as ethical.—**eth′ics,** *n.* The principles of morality, or the science of morals or right conduct; a treatise on this science; also, a particular ethical system; the rules of conduct recognized in respect to a particular class of human actions (as, medical *ethics*, the laws of the duties of medical men in regard to the practice of their profession); moral principles, as of an individual; also, the whole field of the moral sciences; natural jurisprudence.

E-thi-op (ē′thi-op), *n.* and *a.* [L. *Æthiops*, < Gr. Αἰθίοψ.] Same as *Ethiopian.*

E-thi-o-pi-an (ē-thi-ō′pi-ąn). **I.** *a.* Pertaining to Ethiopia, an ancient region of Africa south of Egypt; also, negro; in *zoögeog.*, belonging to Africa south of the tropic of Cancer. **II.** *n.* A native of Ethiopia; also, a negro.

E-thi-op-ic (ē-thi-op′ik). **I.** *a.* Ethiopian. **II.** *n.* The language of ancient Ethiopia, a Semitic tongue having a Christian literature.

eth-moid (eth′moid). [Gr. ἠθμοειδής, < ἠθμός, strainer, sieve, + εἶδος, form.] **I.** *a.* Sieve-like; in *anat.*, noting or pertaining to a bone of the skull situated at the root of the nose, and containing numerous perforations for the filaments of the olfactory nerve. **II.** *n.* In *anat.*, the ethmoid bone.—**eth-moi′dal,** *a.*

eth-narch (eth′närk), *n.* [Gr. ἐθνάρχης, < ἔθνος, race, nation, + ἄρχειν, lead, rule.] The governor of a nation or a province.—**eth′nar-chy** (-när-ki), *n.*; pl. *-chies* (-kiz). [Gr. ἐθναρχία.] The government or jurisdiction of an ethnarch.

eth-nic (eth′nik), *a.* [LL. *ethnicus*, < Gr. ἐθνικός, national, gentile, heathen, < ἔθνος, race, nation.] Of, pertaining to, or peculiar to a race; pertaining to races, their origin, characteristics, etc.; ethnological; also, pertaining to nations not Jewish or Christian; heathen or pagan (as, "These are ancient *ethnic* revels, Of a faith long since forsaken": Longfellow's "Drinking Song"). Also **eth′ni-cal.**—**eth′ni-cal-ly,** *adv.*

ethno-. Form of Gr. ἔθνος, race, nation, used in combination.

eth-nog-e-ny (eth-noj′e-ni), *n.* [See *ethno-* and *-geny.*] The genesis or origin of races, as a subject of scientific study.

eth-nog-ra-phy (eth-nog′rą-fi), *n.* [See *ethno-* and *-graphy.*] The scientific description and classification of the various races of mankind.—**eth-nog′ra-pher,** *n.*—**eth-no-graph′ic, eth-no-graph′i-cal** (-nǫ-graf′ik, -i-kąl), *a.*—**eth-no-graph′i-cal-ly,** *adv.*

eth-nol-o-gy (eth-nol′ǫ-ji), *n.* [See *ethno-* and *-logy.*] The science that treats of the various races of mankind, their origin, distinctive characteristics, customs, institutions, etc.—**eth-no-log′ic, eth-no-log′i-cal** (-nǫ-loj′ik, -i-kąl), *a.*—**eth-no-log′i-cal-ly,** *adv.*—**eth-nol′o-gist,** *n.*

eth-nos (eth′nos), *n.* [Gr. ἔθνος.] A race, tribe, or nation.

e-thol-o-gy (ę-thol′ǫ-ji), *n.* [Gr. ἦθος, character: see *-logy.*] The science of human character.—**eth-o-log-i-cal** (eth-ǫ-loj′i-kąl or ē-thǫ-), *a.*

e-thos (ē′thos), *n.* [Gr. ἦθος.] Character or disposition; characteristic spirit, as of a people or an institution.

eth-yl (eth′il), *n.* [From *ether.*] In *chem.*, a hydrocarbon radical, C_2H_5, occurring in ordinary alcohol ('ethyl alcohol'), ether ('ethyl ether'), etc.—**eth′yl-ate** (-i-lāt), *v. t.*; *-ated, -ating.* In *chem.*, to introduce one or more ethyl radicals into (a compound).—**eth′yl-ene** (-i-lēn), *n.* In *chem.*, a colorless, poisonous gas with an unpleasant odor, forming one of the constituents of illuminating gas: the first member of a homologous series of hydrocarbons.—**e-thyl-ic** (e-thil′ik), *a.*

e-ti-o-late (ē′ti-ǫ-lāt), *v. t.* or *i.*; *-lated, -lating.* [F. *étioler*, blanch: cf. *éteule*, stubble, < L. *stipula*, stalk, straw.] To make or become white through loss of normal color, as from lack of sunlight; blanch.—**e″ti-o-la′tion** (-lā′shǫn), *n.*

e-ti-ol-o-gy (ē-ti-ol′ǫ-ji), etc. See *ætiology*, etc.

et-i-quette (et′i-ket), *n.* [F. *étiquette*, OF. *estiquette*, label, ticket, billet, < *estiquier*, fix, stick; from Teut., and akin to E. *stick*[2].] Prescribed or accepted code of usage in matters of ceremony (as at a court), in official or other formal observances, or in polite society generally; conventional requirements as to social behavior; proprieties of conduct as established in any class or community or for any occasion.

et-na (et′nä), *n.* [From Mount *Etna*, volcano in Sicily.] A small vessel for heating water or other liquid, consisting of a cup for the liquid, with a fixed saucer surrounding it in which alcohol is burned.

E-ton (ē′tǫn) **jack′et.** A boy's short jacket reaching only to the waist-line, such as is worn by students at Eton College, England; also, a similar short jacket worn by women.

E-tru-ri-an (ę-trö′ri-ąn), *a.* and *n.* Same as *Etruscan.*

E-trus-can (ę-trus′kąn). [L. *Etruscus.*] **I.** *a.* Pertaining to Etruria, an ancient country in central Italy, or its inhabitants, or their language: as, *Etruscan* art (the art of ancient Etruria, believed to have grown up independently from the same root as the art of Greece, though in its later stages influenced by the latter, the best works of its sculpture being strongly colored terra-cotta statues and sarcophagi of terra-cotta bearing reclining figures on the lid). **II.** *n.* A native of Etruria; also, the language of Etruria.

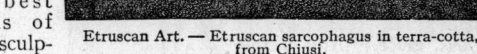

Etruscan Art. — Etruscan sarcophagus in terra-cotta, from Chiusi.

-ette. [F. *-ette*: see *-et.*] A noun suffix, the feminine form of *-et*, occurring esp. (*a*) with the original diminutive force, as in *chemisette, cigarette, pianette, statuette,* (*b*) in tradenames of imitations or substitutes, as in *leatherette*, or (*c*) as a distinctively feminine ending, as in *brunette, coquette, suffragette,* and various colloquial or humorous formations, such as *conductorette, farmerette, printerette, usherette.*

et-tle (et′l), *v.*; *-tled, -tling.* [Icel. *ætla.*] **I.** *tr.* To intend or purpose; endeavor or attempt; also, to destine or ordain; also, to direct or aim. [Sc. and north. Eng.] **II.** *intr.* To direct one's course; aim (*at*). [Sc. and north. Eng.]—**et′tle,** *n.* Intent or purpose; endeavor or attempt; aim: as, "Nannie . . . flew at Tam wi' furious *ettle*" (Burns's "Tam o' Shanter," 213). [Sc. and north. Eng.]

é-tude (ā-tüd), *n.* [F.: see *study, n.*] A study; in *music*, a composition intended mainly for the practice of some point of technique.

e-tui (e-twē′, F. ā-twē), *n.* [F. *étui*: see *stew*².] A small case, esp. one of ornamental character, for containing small objects, as needles, toilet articles, etc.

et-y-mo-log-ic, et-y-mo-log-i-cal (et″i-mō-loj′ik, -i-kạl), *a.* [L. *etymologicus*, < Gr. ἐτυμολογικός.] Of or pertaining to etymology.—**et″y-mo-log′i-cal-ly,** *adv.*

et-y-mo-log-i-con (et″i-mō-loj′i-kon), *n.* [NL., < Gr. ἐτυμολογικόν.] An etymological dictionary.

et-y-mol-o-gist (et-i-mol′ǫ-jist), *n.* One versed in etymology.

et-y-mol-o-gize (et-i-mol′ǫ-jīz), *v.*; *-gized, -gizing.* **I.** *tr.* To trace or give the origin or history of (words). **II.** *intr.* To study etymology; also, to give or suggest the etymology of words.

et-y-mol-o-gy (et-i-mol′ǫ-ji), *n.*; pl. *-gies* (-jiz). [L. *etymologia*, < Gr. ἐτυμολογία, < ἔτυμον (see *etymon*) + λέγειν, speak.] Explanation of the origin and history of words; an account of the origin of a particular word; the derivation of a word; the branch of philology concerned with the origin and history of words.

et-y-mon (et′i-mon), *n.*; pl. *-mons* or *-ma* (-mạ̈). [L. *etymon*, < Gr. ἔτυμον, the original sense, form, or element of a word, prop. neut. of ἔτυμος, true, real.] The original sense or root meaning of a word (obs. or rare); the primitive form of a word†; a primary word, from which derivatives are formed.

eu-. [Gr. εὐ-, repr. ἐύς, adj., good, brave, noble, neut. εὖ, used as adv., well.] A prefix of Greek origin, meaning 'good,' 'well,' occasionally used as an English formative, as in *eucaine.* Cf. *dys-* ('ill').

eu-ca-ine (ū′kạ̈-in or ū′kān), *n.* [From *eu-* + *(co)caine.*] A crystalline organic compound used, in the form of a salt, as a local anesthetic ('alpha-eucaine'); also, a similar but less used compound ('beta-eucaine').

eu-ca-lypt (ū′kạ-lipt), *n.* A eucalyptus.

eu-ca-lyp-tol (ū-kạ-lip′tol or -tōl), *n.* In *chem.*, a colorless liquid compound with an aromatic odor, obtained from certain essential oils, as that of eucalyptus.

eu-ca-lyp-tus (ū-kạ-lip′tus), *n.*; pl. *-tuses* or *-ti* (-tī). [NL., < Gr. εὖ, well, + καλυπτός, covered, < καλύπτειν, cover (with allusion to the cap covering the buds).] Any member of the myrtaceous genus *Eucalyptus*, including many tall trees, as *E. globulus* (the blue-gum), which yield a valuable timber and bear leaves containing an oil used in medicine in the treatment of various diseases: native in Australia and neighboring regions and cultivated elsewhere.

Flowering Branch of Blue-gum Tree (*Eucalyptus globulus*).

eu-cha-ris (ū′kạ-ris), *n.* [NL., < Gr. εὔχαρις, pleasing, < εὐ- (see *eu-*) + χάρις, grace.] Any of the amaryllidaceous plants constituting the South American genus *Eucharis*, some of which are cultivated for their large, fragrant white flowers.

eu-cha-rist (ū′kạ-rist), *n.* [LL. *eucharistia*, < Gr. εὐχαριστία, gratefulness, thanksgiving, the eucharist, < εὐχάριστος, grateful, < εὐ- (see *eu-*) + χάρις, grace, favor, gratitude.] [Also *cap.*] The sacrament of the Lord's Supper; the communion; also, the consecrated elements of the Lord's Supper, esp. the bread; [*l. c.*] the giving of thanks; thanksgiving.—**eu-cha-ris′tic,** *a.*—**eu-cha-ris′ti-cal-ly,** *adv.*

eu-chre (ū′kėr), *n.* [Origin uncertain.] A game of cards played usually by two, three, or four persons, with the 32 (or 28 or 24) highest cards in the pack; also, an instance of euchring or being euchred.—**progressive euchre.** See *progressive, a.*—**eu′chre,** *v. t.*; *-chred, -chring.* To get the better of (an opponent) in a hand at euchre by his failure to win three tricks after having made the trump; hence (colloq.), to outwit; get the better of, as by scheming.

Eu-clid (ū′klid), *n.* [From *Euclid* (about 300 B.C.), the Greek geometer.] The works of Euclid, esp. his treatise on geometry; hence, geometry.—**Eu-cli-de-an** (ū-kli-dē′ạn or ụ-klid′ẹ-ạn), *a.* Of or pertaining to Euclid or his principles: as, *Euclidean* geometry. Also **Eu-clid′i-an.**

eu-de-mon, eu-dæ-mon (ụ-dē′mọn), *n.* [Gr. εὐ-, good (see *eu-*), + δαίμων, tutelary divinity (see *demon*).] A good demon or spirit; an agathodemon.

eu-de-mon-ic, eu-dæ-mon-ic (ū-dẹ-mon′ik), *a.* [Gr. εὐδαιμονικός, < εὐδαίμων, blessed with a good genius, fortunate, happy, < εὐ- + δαίμων: see *eudemon.*] Pertaining or conducive to happiness; pertaining to eudemonics.—**eu-de-mon′ics, eu-dæ-mon′ics,** *n.* The science of happiness; also, eudemonism.—**eu-de-mon-ism, eu-dæ-mon-ism** (ụ-dē′mọn-izm), *n.* [Gr. εὐδαιμονία, happiness, < εὐδαίμων.] The system of ethics which holds that the basis of moral obligations lies in their relation to the production of happiness.—**eu-de′mon-ist, eu-dæ′mon-ist,** *n.*

eu-di-om-e-ter (ū-di-om′e-tėr), *n.* [Gr. εὔδιος, fine, clear, as weather: see *-meter.*] A device used in the analysis and volumetric measurement of gases: orig. employed for ascertaining the purity of air or the quantity of oxygen contained in it.—**eu″di-o-met′ric, eu″di-o-met′ri-cal** (-ǫ-met′rik, -ri-kạl), *a.*—**eu-di-om′e-try,** *n.* [See *-metry.*] The measurement and analysis of gases with the eudiometer.

eu-gen-ic (ụ-jen′ik), *a.* [Gr. εὖ, well, + γεν-, bear, produce.] Pertaining to or bringing about improvement in the type of offspring produced. Cf. *dysgenic.*—**eu-gen′i-cist** (-i-sist), *n.* One versed in eugenics; an advocate of eugenic measures.—**eu-gen′ics,** *n.* The science of improving the qualities of the human race; the science or art of bringing about an improved type of offspring, esp. of the human race.—**eu-ge-nist** (ū′je-nist), *n.* A eugenicist.

eu-ge-nol (ū′jẹ-nol or -nōl), *n.* [NL. *Eugenia*, genus of myrtaceous plants.] In *chem.*, a colorless, aromatic, oily compound contained in certain essential oils, as that of cloves.

eu-he-me-rism (ụ-hē′mẹ-rizm or ụ-hem′ẹ-), *n.* [From *Euhemerus* (4th century B.C.), Greek writer.] The method or system of interpretation which derives myths from traditional accounts of actual history.—**eu-he′me-rist,** *n.* One who follows the method of euhemerism.—**eu-he-me-ris′tic,** *a.*—**eu-he-me-ris′ti-cal-ly,** *adv.*—**eu-he′me-rize,** *v. t.* or *i.*; *-rized, -rizing.* To treat or explain (myths) by the method of euhemerism.

eu-la-chon (ū′lạ-kon), *n.* Same as *oolakan.*

eu-lo-gism (ū′lǫ-jizm), *n.* A eulogy; praise.—**eu′lo-gist,** *n.* One who eulogizes.—**eu-lo-gis′tic,** *a.* Eulogizing; laudatory.—**eu-lo-gis′ti-cal-ly,** *adv.*

eu-lo-gi-um (ụ-lō′ji-um), *n.*; pl. *-giums*, L. *-gia* (-ji-ạ̈). [ML.: see *eulogy.*] A eulogy; eulogistic language.

eu-lo-gize (ū′lǫ-jīz), *v. t.*; *-gized, -gizing.* To pronounce or write a eulogy upon; commend highly; laud.—**eu′lo-giz-er,** *n.*

eu-lo-gy (ū′lǫ-ji), *n.*; pl. *-gies* (-jiz). [ML. *eulogium*, for *eulogia*, < Gr. εὐλογία, good language, praise, blessing, < εὐ- (see *eu-*) + λέγειν, speak.] A speech or writing in praise of a person or thing, esp. a set oration in honor of a deceased person; also, eulogistic speech or writing (as, "A long period of unqualified depreciation has been followed by a reaction of extravagant *eulogy*": Lecky's "Hist. of Eng. in the 18th Century," i.); praise; commendation.

Eu-men-i-des (ụ-men′i-dēz), *n. pl.* [L., < Gr. Εὐμενίδες, < εὐ-, good (see *eu-*), + μένος, disposition: see *mind*².] 'The gracious ones': in *class. myth.*, a euphemistic name for the Furies or Erinyes.

eu-mi-to-sis (ū-mi-tō′sis), *n.* [NL.: see *eu-* and *mitosis.*] In *biol.*, true or typical mitosis.

eu-nuch (ū′nuk), *n.* [L. *eunuchus*, < Gr. εὐνοῦχος, chamber attendant, < εὐνή, bed, + ἔχειν, have, hold, keep.] A castrated male person, in the East often employed as a harem attendant or in affairs of state; sometimes, a chamberlain or court officer in general.

eu-pa-to-ri-um (ū-pạ-tō′ri-um), *n.* [NL., < Gr. εὐπατόριον; named from Mithridates *Eupator*, king of Pontus

120?–63 B.C.] Any plant of the large asteraceous genus *Eupatorium*, mostly native in America, with heads of white or purplish flowers, as thoroughwort and joepye-weed.

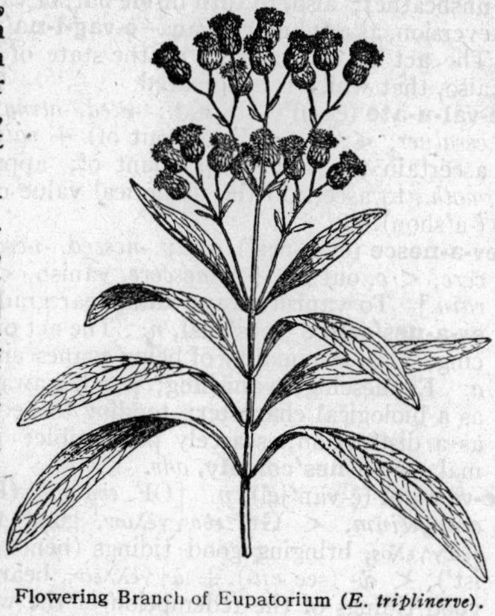
Flowering Branch of Eupatorium (*E. triplinerve*).

eu-pat-rid (ū-pat′rid), *n.* [Gr. εὐπατρίδης, < εὐ-, good (see *eu-*), + πατήρ, father.] One of the hereditary aristocrats of ancient Athens and other states of Greece, in whom exclusively, in primitive times, were vested the powers of making and administering the law; hence, in general, an aristocrat or patrician (as, "noblemen, merchants, attorneys, tradesmen, stock-jobbers—the *Eupatrids* and the commonplaces of society": Poe's "Man of the Crowd").—**eu-pat′ri-dæ** (-ri-dē), *n. pl.* [NL., < Gr. εὐπατρίδαι, pl.] The eupatrids.

eu-pep-sia (ū-pep′si̤ä), *n.* [NL., < Gr. εὐπεψία, < εὔπεπτος, having good digestion, < εὐ- (see *eu-*) + πέπτειν, cook, digest.] Good digestion: opposed to *dyspepsia*.—**eu-pep′tic,** *a.* Pertaining to or having good digestion; easy of digestion.

eu-phe-mism (ū′fē-mizm), *n.* [Gr. εὐφημισμός, < εὐφημίζειν, use fair words, < εὔφημος, fair of speech, < εὐ- (see *eu-*) + φήμη, voice, speech, < φάναι, say.] In *rhet.*, the substitution of a mild or indirect word or expression for one unpleasant or offensive though more accurate, as of 'to pass away' for 'to die'; the word or expression so substituted.—**eu′phe-mist,** *n.* One given to the use of euphemisms.—**eu-phe-mis′tic, eu-phe-mis′ti-cal,** *a.* Pertaining to, of the nature of, or characterized by euphemism.—**eu-phe-mis′ti-cal-ly,** *adv.*—**eu′phe-mize,** *v. t.* or *i.*; *-mized, -mizing.* [Gr. εὐφημίζειν.] To speak of by or speak by a euphemism.

eu-phon-ic (ū-fon′ik), *a.* Pertaining to or characterized by euphony.—**eu-phon′i-cal-ly,** *adv.*

eu-pho-ni-ous (ū-fō′ni-us), *a.* Characterized by euphony; well-sounding; agreeable to the ear.—**eu-pho′ni-ous-ly,** *adv.*—**eu-pho′ni-ous-ness,** *n.*

eu-pho-nism (ū′fō-nizm), *n.* The use of euphonious or well-sounding words or combinations of words.—**eu-pho-nis′tic,** *a.* Characterized by euphonism.

eu-pho-ni-um (ū-fō′ni-um), *n.* [NL., < Gr. εὔφωνος, well-sounding: see *euphony*.] A musical instrument consisting of a set of glass tubes, connected with graduated steel bars, to be put in vibration by the moistened finger; also, a bass instrument of the saxhorn class.

eu-pho-nize (ū′fō-nīz), *v. t.*; *-nized, -nizing.* To make euphonious.

eu-pho-ny (ū′fō-ni), *n.* [LL. *euphonia*, < Gr. εὐφωνία, < εὔφωνος, well-sounding, < εὐ- (see *eu-*) + φωνή, sound, voice.] Agreeableness of sound; pleasing effect to the ear, esp. of speech-sounds as uttered or as combined in utterance; in *philol.*, a tendency to greater ease of utterance (not, as formerly supposed, to a more pleasing effect of sound) causing modification in the pronunciation and hence in the form of words, as shown in the change of Latin *adfero* to *affero*.

eu-phor-bi-a (ū-fôr′bi-ä), *n.* [NL., for L. *euphorbea*, an African plant; named from *Euphorbus*, a Greek physician.] Any of the plants of the widespread genus *Euphorbia*, which vary greatly, but consist mostly of herbs and shrubs with an acrid milky juice having medicinal or poisonous properties; a spurge. See cut in next column.—**eu-phor-bi-a′ceous** (-ā′shius), *a.* Belonging to the *Euphorbiaceæ*, or spurge family of plants, which includes the spurges, the cascarilla, croton-oil, castor-oil, and cassava plants, several that yield caoutchouc, and many others.

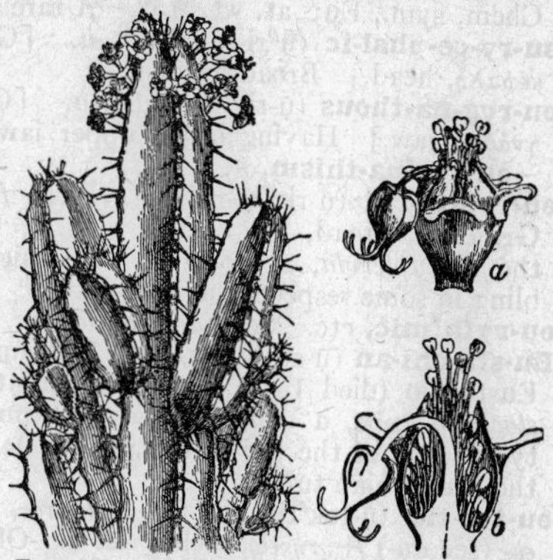
Top of Stem of Euphorbia (*E. resinifera*).—*a*, involucre with inclosed flowers; *b*, section of same.

eu-phra-sy (ū′fra̤-si), *n.* [ML. *euphrasia*, < Gr. εὐφρασία, delight, < εὐφραίνειν, gladden, < εὐ- (see *eu-*) + φρήν, heart, mind.] The plant eyebright, *Euphrasia officinalis*.

eu-phroe (ū′frō), *n.* See *uphroe*.

eu-phu-ism (ū′fū-izm), *n.* An affected style in imitation of that of John Lyly's works "Euphues, the Anatomy of Wit" (1579) and "Euphues and His England" (1580), which was fashionable in the writing and speaking of English about the end of the 16th century, and was characterized chiefly by long series of antitheses, frequent similes relating to fabulous natural history, and alliteration; any similar ornate style of writing or speaking; high-flown language; also, an instance of such style or language.—**eu′phu-ist,** *n.* One given to euphuism.—**eu-phu-is′tic,** *a.*—**eu-phu-is′ti-cal-ly,** *adv.*

eu-plas-tic (ū-plas′tik), *a.* [Gr. εὔπλαστος, easy to mold, < εὐ- (see *eu-*) + πλάσσειν, form, mold.] In *physiol.*, capable of being transformed into permanent organized tissue.

eup-nœ-a (ūp-nē′ä), *n.* [NL., < Gr. εὔπνοια, < εὔπνοος, breathing well, < εὐ- (see *eu-*) + πνεῖν, blow, breathe.] In *pathol.*, easy or normal breathing: opposed to *dyspnœa*.

Eur-af-ri-can (ū-raf′ri-ka̤n). **I.** *a.* Pertaining to Europe and Africa taken together; also, of mixed European and African descent. **II.** *n.* A person of a theoretical Eurafrican division of mankind; also, a person of mixed European and African descent.

Eur-a-sian (ū-rā′shia̤n or -zhia̤n). **I.** *a.* Of or pertaining to Europe and Asia taken together; also, of mixed European and Asiatic descent. **II.** *n.* A person of mixed European and Asiatic (esp. Indian) descent.

eu-re-ka (ū-rē′kä). [Gr. εὕρηκα.] 'I have found (it)': the reputed exclamation of Archimedes on his discovery of a method of determining (by specific gravity) the amount of base metal in King Hiero's crown, hence an exulting exclamation at any discovery.

eu-rhyth-mic (ū-riтн′mik or ū-rith′-), *a.* [Gr. εὔρυθμος, in good rhythm, < εὐ- (see *eu-*) + ῥυθμός, E. *rhythm*.] Characterized by a pleasing rhythm; harmoniously ordered or proportioned.—**eu-rhyth′mics,** *n.* The art of interpreting in graceful bodily movements the rhythm of musical compositions: applied to a method invented by Émile Jaques-Dalcroze, a Swiss composer, which aims to develop the sense of rhythm and of symmetry in general.—**eu-rhyth′my,** *n.* [Gr. εὐρυθμία, < εὔρυθμος.] Pleasing rhythm; rhythmical movement or order; harmonious proportion, as in architecture.

eu-ri-pus (ū-rī′pus), *n.*; pl. *-pi* (-pī). [L., < Gr. εὔριπος, < εὐ- (see *eu-*) + ῥιπή, impetus, rush.] A strait, esp. one in which the flow of the water in both directions is violent, as that between the island of Eubœa and Bœotia in Greece, specifically called *Euripus*.

Eu-ro-pe-an (ū-rō-pē′a̤n), *a.* Of or pertaining to Europe or its inhabitants.—**European plan,** that method of conducting a hotel according to which the fixed charge per day covers only lodging and service. Cf. *American plan*.—**Eu-ro-pe′an,** *n.* A native or inhabitant of Europe; more generally, a person of European descent or connections.—**Eu-ro-pe′an-ism,** *n.* European characteristics, ideas, methods, sympathies, etc.; a European trait or practice.—**Eu-ro-pe′an-ize** (-īz), *v. t.*; *-ized, -izing.* To make European; conform to European ways.—**Eu-ro-pe″an-i-za′tion** (-i-zā′sho̤n), *n.*

eu-ro-pi-um (ū-rō′pi-um), *n.* [NL., < L. *Europa*, Europe.] Chem. sym., Eu; at. wt., 152. A rare metallic element.
eu-ry-ce-phal-ic (ū″ri-se-fal′ik), *a.* [Gr. εὐρύς, broad, + κεφαλή, head.] Broad-headed.
eu-ryg-na-thous (ū-rig′nạ-thus), *a.* [Gr. εὐρύς, broad, + γνάθος, jaw.] Having broad upper jaws and cheek-bones.—**eu-ryg′na-thism,** *n.*
eu-ryp-te-rid (ū-rip′tẹ-rid), *n.* [NL. *Eurypterida*, pl., < Gr. εὐρύς, broad, + πτερόν, wing.] In *paleon.*, any of the *Eurypterida*, a group of Paleozoic arthropods resembling in some respects the king-crabs.
eu-ryth′mic, etc. See *eurhythmic*, etc.
Eu-sta-chi-an (ū-stā′ki-ạn), *a.* Pertaining to Bartolommeo Eustachio (died 1574), an Italian anatomist (as, the *Eustachian* tube, a canal extending from the cavity of the tympanum of the ear to the pharynx); also, pertaining to the Eustachian tube.
eu-tec-tic (ū-tek′tik). [Gr. εὔτηκτος, easily melted, < εὐ- (see *eu-*) + τήκειν, melt.] **I.** *a.* Of greatest fusibility: said of an alloy or mixture whose melting-point is lower than that of any other alloy or mixture composed of the same ingredients. **II.** *n.* A eutectic substance.—**eu-tec′toid,** *a.*
Eu-ter-pe (ū-tėr′pē), *n.* [L., < Gr. Εὐτέρπη, 'well-pleasing,' < εὐ- (see *eu-*) + τέρπειν, please, delight.] The Muse of music and lyric song.—**Eu-ter′pe-an** (-pẹ-ạn), *a.*
eu-tha-na-sia (ū-thạ-nā′ẓiạ̈), *n.* [NL., < Gr. εὐθανασία, < εὐ- (see *eu-*) + θάνατος, death.] An easy and tranquil death; the means of bringing it about; the putting of a person painlessly to death. Also **eu-than-a-sy** (ū-than′ạ-si).
eu-then-ics (ū-then′iks), *n.* [Gr. εὐθηνία, plenty, prosperity, well-being.] The science of bettering the environment or living conditions, as for improvement of the race.
eu-tro-phy (ū′trọ-fi), *n.* [Gr. εὐτροφία, < εὐ- (see *eu-*) + τρέφειν, nourish.] In *physiol.*, healthy nutrition.—**eu-troph-ic** (ū-trof′ik), *a.*
eux-e-nite (ūk′sẹ-nīt), *n.* [Gr. εὔξενος, hospitable (in allusion to its many constituents): see *Euxine.*] A brownish-black mineral found in Norway, containing the elements yttrium, columbium, titanium, uranium, etc.
Eux-ine (ūk′sin or -sīn). [L. *Euxinus*, < Gr. Εὔξεινος, Ionic form of εὔξενος, hospitable, < εὐ- (see *eu-*) + ξένος, guest.] **I.** *a.* Noting the sea between Russia and Asia Minor otherwise known as the Black Sea. **II.** *n.* The Black Sea.
e-vac-u-ant (ẹ̄-vak′ū-ạnt). **I.** *a.* Evacuating; promoting evacuation, esp. from the bowels; purgative. **II.** *n.* An evacuant medicine or agent, esp. a purgative.
e-vac-u-ate (ẹ̄-vak′ū-āt), *v. t.*; *-ated, -ating.* [L. *evacuatus*, pp. of *evacuare*, < *e*, out of, + *vacuus*, empty, E. *vacuous.*] To make empty, or expel the contents of (as, to *evacuate* the stomach by an emetic; to *evacuate* the bowels); fig., to deprive of something essential; also, to leave empty; vacate; withdraw from or quit (a town, fort, etc., occupied); also, to make void† or nullify†; also, to discharge or eject, as through the excretory passages, esp. from the bowels; remove (troops, wounded soldiers, inhabitants, etc.) from a place.—**e-vac-u-a′tion** (-ā′shọn), *n.* [LL. *evacuatio(n-).*] The act or process of evacuating, or the condition of being evacuated; a making empty of contents; expulsion, as of contents; discharge, as of waste matter through the excretory passages, esp. from the bowels; clearance by removal of troops, etc. (as, "The first scene in the withdrawal of the troops had been the *evacuation* of the citadel of Antwerp": Motley's "Dutch Republic," v. 1); the withdrawal or removal of troops, wounded soldiers, etc.; nullification†; also, that which is evacuated or discharged.—**Evacuation Day,** the anniversary of the day on which the British troops evacuated the city of New York, Nov. 25, 1783.—**e-vac′u-a-tor,** *n.*
e-vad-a-ble (ẹ̄-vā′dạ-bl), *a.* That may be evaded.
e-vade (ẹ̄-vād′), *v.*; *evaded, evading.* [L. *evadere* (pp. *evasus*), < *e*, out of, + *vadere*, go.] **I.** *intr.* To get away or escape (now rare); also, to employ elusive methods; practise evasion. **II.** *tr.* To get away from by dexterity or artifice; contrive to avoid; elude.—**e-vad-er** (ẹ̄-vā′dėr), *n.*—**e-vad′ing-ly,** *adv.*
e-vag-i-nate (ẹ̄-vaj′i-nāt), *v. t.*; *-nated, -nating.* [L. *evaginatus*, pp. of *evaginare*, < *e*, out of, + *vagina*, sheath.] To unsheathe†; also, to turn inside out, or cause to protrude by eversion, as a tubular organ.—**e-vag-i-na′tion** (-nā′shọn), *n.* The act of evaginating, or the state of being evaginated; also, that which is evaginated.
e-val-u-ate (ẹ̄-val′ū-āt), *v. t.*; *-ated, -ating.* [F. *évaluer*, OF. *esvaluer*, < *es-* (< L. *ex*, out of) + *value*, E. *value.*] To ascertain the value or amount of; appraise carefully; in *math.*, to ascertain the numerical value of.—**e-val-u-a′tion** (-ā′shọn), *n.*
ev-a-nesce (ev-ạ-nes′), *v. i.*; *-nesced, -nescing.* [L. *evanescere*, < *e*, out of, + *vanescere*, vanish, < *vanus*, empty, E. *vain.*] To vanish away; disappear gradually; fade out.—**ev-a-nes′cence** (-nes′ẹns), *n.* The act or process of evanescing; also, the quality of being evanescent.—**ev-a-nes′cent,** *a.* Evanescing; vanishing; passing away; not permanent, as a biological character; tending to become imperceptible, as a distinction; scarcely perceptible; in *math.*, infinitesimal.—**ev-a-nes′cent-ly,** *adv.*
e-van-gel (ẹ̄-van′jẹl), *n.* [OF. *evangile* (F. *évangile*), < LL. *evangelium*, < Gr. εὐαγγέλιον, good tidings, gospel, < εὐάγγελος, bringing good tidings (hence E. sense 'evangelist'), < εὐ- (see *eu-*) + ἀγγέλλειν, bear a message.] The good tidings of the redemption of the world through Jesus Christ; often, the gospel, or [usually *cap.*] any of the four Gospels; hence [*l. c.*], a principle or the like taken as a guide or regarded as of prime importance (as, "that great doctrine . . . which is our ultimate Political *Evangel*": Carlyle's "Sartor Resartus," ii. 8); also, in general, good tidings (as, "We wait for thy coming, sweet wind of the south . . . For the yearly *evangel* thou bearest from God": Whittier's "April"); also, an evangelist.
e-van-gel-ic (ē-van-jel′ik or ev-ạn-), *a.* [LL. *evangelicus*, < Gr. εὐαγγελικός.] Evangelical.—**e-van-gel′i-cal. I.** *a.* Of or pertaining to the gospel or the four Gospels; also, pertaining to or in accordance with gospel precepts or the Christian faith; specif., adhering to the doctrines of the gospel, or, esp., to an interpretation of it, held to in a section of the Protestant churches, in which distinctive prominence is given to the doctrines of the corruption of man's nature by the fall, atonement by the life, sufferings, and death of Christ, salvation by faith, etc.; pertaining to or in accordance with the school of Protestantism emphasizing these doctrines; also, spiritually minded; zealous for practical Christian living; also, seeking the conversion of sinners; evangelistic. **II.** *n.* An adherent of evangelical doctrines; a member of an evangelical church or party, as of the Low-church party of the Church of England.—**e-van-gel′i-cal-ism,** *n.* Evangelical doctrines or principles; adherence to them, or to an evangelical church or party.—**e-van-gel′i-cal-ly,** *adv.*—**e-van-gel′i-cal-ness,** *n.*—**e-van-gel′i-cism** (-sizm), *n.* Evangelicalism.
e-van-gel-ism (ẹ̄-van′jẹl-izm), *n.* The preaching or promulgation of the gospel; the work of an evangelist; also, evangelicalism.
e-van-gel-ist (ẹ̄-van′jẹl-ist), *n.* [LL. *evangelista*, < Gr. εὐαγγελιστής, < εὐαγγελίζεσθαι, E. *evangelize.*] [Often *cap.*] Any of the writers (Matthew, Mark, Luke, and John) of the four Gospels; [*l. c.*] one of a class of teachers in the early church, next in rank after apostles and prophets; also, a preacher of the gospel, as one who brings it to a heathen nation; an occasional or itinerant preacher; a revivalist.—**e-van-gel-is′tic,** *a.* Of or pertaining to the four evangelists; also, pertaining to evangelists, or preachers of the gospel; esp., seeking to evangelize; striving to convert sinners; designed or fitted to evangelize; evangelical.
e-van-gel-ize (ẹ̄-van′jẹl-īz), *v.*; *-ized, -izing.* [LL. *evangelizare*, < Gr. εὐαγγελίζεσθαι, < εὐάγγελος: see *evangel.*] **I.** *intr.* To preach the gospel; act as an evangelist. **II.** *tr.* To bring as good tidings†; also, to preach the gospel to; convert to Christianity by preaching.—**e-van″gel-i-za′tion** (-i-zā′shọn), *n.*—**e-van′gel-iz-er** (-ī-zėr), *n.*
e-van-ish (ẹ̄-van′ish), *v. i.* [OF. *esvanir* (*esvaniss-*), *esvanuir* (F. *évanouir*), formed (with *es-* < L. *ex* for *e*) after L. *evanescere*: see *evanesce.*] To vanish or disappear (as, "Or like the rainbow's lovely form *Evanishing* amid the storm": Burns's "Tam o' Shanter," 66); also, to cease to be. [Now chiefly poetic.]—**e-van′ish-ment,** *n.*

e-vap-o-ra-ble (ẹ-vap'ọ-rạ-bl), *a.* Capable of being evaporated.

e-vap-o-rate (ẹ-vap'ọ-rāt), *v.*; *-rated, -rating.* [L. *evaporatus*, pp. of *evaporare*, < *e*, out of, + *vapor*, E. *vapor*.] **I.** *tr.* To convert into vapor; convert into a gaseous state; vaporize; drive off or extract in the form of vapor; fig., to dissipate; also, to extract moisture or liquid from, as by heat, so as to make dry or to reduce to a denser state (as, to *evaporate* fruit). **II.** *intr.* To change into vapor; pass off in vapor; fig., to pass off without effect; be dissipated; also, to exhale moisture.—**e-vap-o-ra'tion** (-rā'shọn), *n.* [L. *evaporatio(n-)*.] The act or process of evaporating, or the state of being evaporated; also, matter, or the quantity of matter, evaporated or passed off in vapor.—**e-vap'o-ra-tive** (-rạ-tiv), *a.* Serving to evaporate; pertaining to evaporation.—**e-vap'o-ra-tor** (-rā-tọr), *n.* One who or that which evaporates; an apparatus for driving off superfluous moisture, as in concentrating liquids, drying fruits, etc.—**e-vap-o-rim'e-ter** (-rim'e-tėr), *n.* Same as *evaporometer*.—**e-vap-o-rom'e-ter** (-rom'e-tėr), *n.* [See *-meter*.] An atmometer.

e-va-sion (ẹ-vā'zhọn), *n.* [LL. *evasio(n-)*, < L. *evadere*: see *evade*.] The act of evading; escape (now rare); avoidance by dexterity, artifice, or stratagem; the avoiding of an argument, accusation, interrogation, or the like, as by a subterfuge or by shuffling; also, a means of evading; a subterfuge; a shift.

e-va-sive (ẹ-vā'siv), *a.* Tending or seeking to evade; characterized by evasion; shuffling; sometimes, elusive or evanescent.—**e-va'sive-ly,** *adv.*—**e-va'sive-ness,** *n.*

eve (ēv), *n.* [= *even*[1].] The evening (chiefly poetic); also, the evening, often the whole day, before a church festival, and hence before any date or event; also, the period just preceding any particular event, etc. (as, the *eve* of a revolution).

e-vec-tion (ẹ-vek'shọn), *n.* [L. *evectio(n-)*, < *evehere*, carry forth or up, < *e*, out of, + *vehere*, carry.] Elevation†; in *astron.*, a periodical disturbance by the sun of the eccentricity of the moon's orbit.—**e-vec'tion-al,** *a.*

e-ven[1] (ē'vn), *n.* [AS. *ǣfen* = D. *avond* = G. *abend*, evening.] Evening; eve. [Archaic or prov.]

e-ven[2] (ē'vn), *a.* [AS. *efen* = D. *even* = G. *eben* = Icel. *jafn* = Goth. *ibns*, even.] Level or flat, as ground; in a level or horizontal position, as a keel; free from inequalities, or smooth, as a surface; free from variations or fluctuations, as motion; uniform in character, as color; equable or unruffled, as the temper; equitable, impartial, or fair, as actions; direct† or straightforward† (as, "Be *even* and direct with me": Shakspere's "Hamlet," ii. 2. 298); also, on the same level (as, *even* with the ground); in the same plane or line; parallel, as a course, etc.; coincident or accordant, or exactly adjusted, as one thing with another; in a state of equilibrium, as a balance; leaving no balance of debt on either side, as accounts; square, as one person with another; on an equality, as persons; equal in measure or quantity (as, *even* quantities of two substances; letters of *even* date, letters of the same date); divisible into two equal integers, as a number (opposed to *odd*); denoted by such a number (as, the *even* pages of a book); exactly expressible in integers, or in tens, hundreds, etc., without fractional parts (as, an *even* mile; an *even* hundred).—**e'ven**[2], *adv.* In an even manner; evenly; also, exactly or precisely (as, it was *even* so); just (as, *even* now); fully or quite (as, *even* to death); also, used as an intensive, as for stressing the identity or truth of something (now archaic: as, "I swear to thee, *even* by thine own fair eyes," Shakspere's "Merchant of Venice," v. 1. 242), for intimating that something mentioned, or stated, or suggested as a possibility, constitutes a case of extreme character, as one that might not be expected (as, the slightest noise, *even*, disturbs him; a tree that still flourishes *even* when 300 years old; *even* if he goes, he may not take part), and for emphasizing a comparative (with the sense of 'still' or 'yet': as, this one is *even* more suitable than the other).—**e'ven**[2], *v.* **I.** *tr.* To make even; level; smooth; also, to place in an even state as to claim or obligation, as accounts; balance; also, to treat as equal; also, to compare; also, to equal, or come up to (now rare). **II.**† *intr.* To be or become even.—**e'ven=Chris'tian**†, *n.* A fellow-Christian. See Shakspere's "Hamlet," v. 1. 32.—**e'ven-er,** *n.*

e-ven-fall (ē'vn-fâl), *n.* The beginning of evening.

e-ven=hand-ed (ē'vn-han'ded), *a.* Impartial; equitable: as, "*even-handed* justice" (Shakspere's "Macbeth," i. 7. 10).—**e'ven=hand'ed-ness,** *n.*

eve-ning (ēv'ning). [AS. *ǣfnung*, < *ǣfnian*, draw toward evening, < *ǣfen*, E. *even*[1].] **I.** *n.* The latter part of the day and early part of the night; hence, any concluding or declining period, as of life. **II.** *a.* Of or pertaining to evening; occurring or seen in the evening: as, "O, thou art fairer than the *evening* air Clad in the beauty of a thousand stars" (Marlowe's "Doctor Faustus," xiv.).—**evening primrose.** See *primrose*.—**evening star,** a bright planet, as Venus (Hesperus) or Jupiter, seen in the west after sunset.—**eve'ning=snow',** *n.* A delicate polemoniaceous herb, *Linanthus dichotomus*, of California, with white flowers that open about four o'clock in the afternoon, closing in the morning, and are so abundant on open slopes as to whiten the ground.

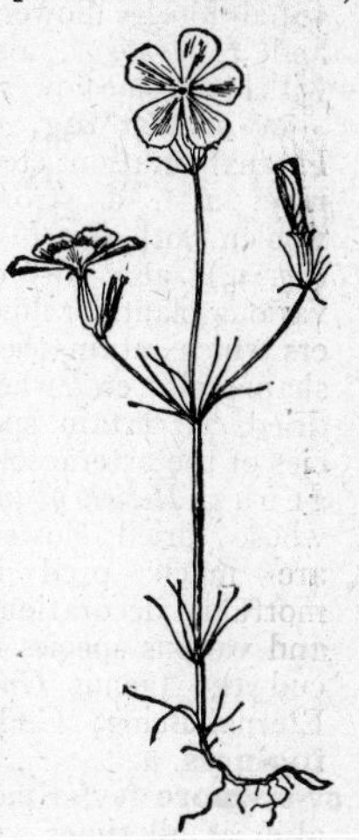
Evening-snow.

e-ven-ly (ē'vn-li), *adv.* In an even manner; smoothly; uniformly; impartially; equally.

e-ven=mind-ed (ē'vn-mīn'ded), *a.* Having an even mind; not easily ruffled, disturbed, prejudiced, etc.; calm; equable.—**e'ven=mind'ed-ness,** *n.*

e-ven-ness (ē'vn-nes), *n.* The state or quality of being even.

e-ven-song (ē'vn-sông), *n.* [AS. *ǣfensang*.] A church service said or sung at evening; vespers; also, any song sung at evening; also (archaic), the time of evensong; evening.

e-vent (ẹ-vent'), *n.* [L. *eventus*, < *evenire*, come out, happen, turn out, < *e*, out of, + *venire*, come.] The fact of happening (as, resources available in the *event* of war); also, anything that happens or is regarded as happening; an occurrence; esp., an occurrence of some importance; also, the outcome, issue, or result of anything; in *sports*, something on the outcome of which money is at stake; also, each of the items in a program of races, etc.—**at all events,** whatever happens; in any case.—**e-vent'ful,** *a.* Full of events or incidents, esp. of a striking character (as, an *eventful* period); also, having important issues or results; momentous.—**e-vent'ful-ly,** *adv.*—**e-vent'ful-ness,** *n.*

e-ven-tide (ē'vn-tīd), *n.* [AS. *ǣfentīd*.] Evening. [Now poetic.]

e-vent-less (ẹ-vent'les), *a.* Uneventful.

e-ven-tu-al (ẹ-ven'tụ-ạl), *a.* [F. *éventuel*, < L. *eventus*: see *event*.] Pertaining to the event or issue; consequent; ultimate; also, depending upon uncertain events; contingent.—**e-ven-tu-al'i-ty** (-al'i-ti), *n.*; pl. *-ties* (-tiz). The state or fact of being eventual; contingent character; also, a contingent event; a possible occurrence or circumstance; in *phren.*, the faculty of noting and remembering events.—**e-ven'tu-al-ly,** *adv.* In the event or issue; finally.

e-ven-tu-ate (ẹ-ven'tụ-āt), *v. i.*; *-ated, -ating.* [L. *eventus*: see *event*.] To have issue; result; also, to be the issue or outcome; come about.—**e-ven-tu-a'tion** (-ā'shọn), *n.*

ev-er (ev'ėr), *adv.* [AS. *ǣfre*, prob. akin to *ā*, ever: see *ay*[1].] Throughout all time (as, "Let me live here *ever*": Shakspere's "Tempest," iv. 1. 122); continuously (as, *ever* since); at all times, or on all occasions (as, you will find me *ever* at your service); constantly or incessantly (as, he was *ever* complaining); also, at any time (as, "Was there *ever* man had such luck!" Shakspere's "Cymbeline," ii. 1. 1); hence (with emphatic force, in various idiomatic constructions and phrases), in any possible case; by any chance; at all; also, in any degree.—**ever and again, ever and anon,** every now and then; continually.—**for ever,** for eternity; eternally; always; continually: commonly as one word, *forever*.

ev-er-glade (ev′ėr-glād), *n.* [Appar. < *ever* + *glade.*] A tract of low, swampy land more or less covered with tall grass.—**the Everglades,** an extensive marshy region in Florida.

ev-er-green (ev′ėr-grēn). **I.** *a.* Always green; of trees, shrubs, etc., having green leaves throughout the entire year, the leaves of the past season not being shed until after the new foliage has been completely formed; of leaves, belonging to such a tree, shrub, etc. **II.** *n.* An evergreen plant; *pl.*, evergreen twigs or branches used for decoration.

ev-er-last-ing (ev-ėr-lȧs′ting), *a.* Lasting forever; eternal; also, lasting or continuing indefinitely; also, incessant; constantly recurring; hence, wearisome.—**everlasting pea,** any of various plants of the fabaceous genus *Lathyrus*, as *L. latifolius*, a hardy species much cultivated for its flowers, and *L. venosus*, also with handsome flowers.—**ev-er-last′ing,** *n.* Eternal duration; eternity; also, a strong woolen cloth (see *lasting, n.*); also, any of various plants or flowers which retain their shape, color, etc., when dried, as certain species of the asteraceous genus *Helichrysum*, whose dried flowers are much used in mortuary decorations, and various species of cudweed (genus *Gnaphalium*); also [*cap.*], with *the*, the Eternal Being; God.—**ev-er-last′ing-ly,** *adv.*—**ev-er-last′-ing-ness,** *n.*

Flowering Branch of Everlasting Pea (*Lathyrus venosus*).— *a*, flower; *b*, fruit.

ev-er-more (ev′ėr-mōr′), *adv.* Throughout all future time; also, at all times; continually; also, at any future time; ever again: often preceded by *for* (*for evermore* or *forevermore*).

e-ver-sion (ē̜-vėr′shọn), *n.* [L. *eversio(n-)*, < *evertere*: see *evert.*] Overthrow†; also, a turning or being turned outward, or inside out.

e-vert (ē̜-vėrt′), *v. t.* [L. *evertere*, < *e-*, out, + *vertere*, turn.] To upset†; overthrow (obs. or archaic); turn outward, or inside out.

eve-ry (ev′ri). [AS. *ǣfre ǣlc*, 'ever each': see *ever* and *each.*] **I.** *a.* Each, as referring one by one to all the members of an aggregate. **II.** *pron.* Every one of a number of persons or things. [Obs. or legal.]—**eve′ry-bod″y,** *n.* Every person.—**eve′ry-day′,** *a.* Of or pertaining to every day; daily; also, of or for ordinary days as contrasted with Sundays or gala days (as, *everyday* clothes); also, such as is met with every day; ordinary; commonplace.—**eve′ry one.** Every person; everybody: often as one word, *everyone.*—**eve′ry-thing,** *n.* Every thing or particular of an aggregate or total; all; sometimes, something extremely important (as, this news means *everything* to us).—**eve′ry-way,** *adv.* In every way; in every direction, manner, or respect.—**eve′ry-when,** *adv.* At all times.—**eve′ry-where,** *adv.* In every place or part; in all places.—**eve′ry-whith″er,** *adv.* To every place; in every direction.

e-vict (ē̜-vikt′), *v. t.* [L. *evictus*, pp. of *evincere*, overcome completely, recover (property) by judicial decision, prove, < *e-*, out, + *vincere*, conquer: cf. *evince.*] To recover (property, etc.) by a judicial process or by virtue of a superior title; also, to expel (a person) from land, etc., by such means; eject (a tenant); hence, to expel by force; turn out in any compulsory way.—**e-vic-tion** (ē̜-vik′shọn), *n.* [LL. *evictio(n-)*.] The act or process of evicting, or the fact of being evicted.—**e-vic′tor,** *n.*

ev-i-dence (ev′i-dẹns), *n.* [OF. *evidence* (F. *évidence*), < L. *evidentia*, clearness, LL. a proof, < L. *evidens*: see *evident.*] The quality of being evident; clearness; also, something that makes evident or manifest; an indication; also, ground for belief; that which tends to prove or disprove something; specif., information, in the form of personal testimony, contents of documents, etc., presented in a legal investigation or trial to make clear the fact or point in question; that part of such information which is properly receivable by the court; also, one who bears testimony or witness (now chiefly in *to turn state's*, or *king's* or *queen's, evidence*, said of an accomplice in a crime who becomes a witness for the prosecution against the others involved).—**evidences of Christianity,** the proofs of the divine origin of Christianity.—**in evidence,** in a situation to be readily seen; plainly visible; conspicuous.—**ev′i-dence,** *v. t.*; *-denced, -dencing.* To make evident or clear; show clearly; manifest; also, to support by evidence.

ev-i-dent (ev′i-dẹnt), *a.* [OF. *evident* (F. *évident*), < L. *evidens* (*evident-*), clear, evident, < *e-*, out, + *videns*, ppr. of *videre*, see.] Plain or clear to the sight or the understanding; obvious; manifest; also, certain† or conclusive†.

ev-i-den-tial (ev-i-den′shạl), *a.* [L. *evidentia*: see *evidence.*] Pertaining to, based on, or of the nature of evidence.—**ev-i-den′tial-ly,** *adv.*—**ev-i-den′ti-a-ry** (-shi-ā̜-ri), *a.* Evidential.

ev-i-dent-ly (ev′i-dẹnt-li), *adv.* In an evident manner; clearly; obviously; apparently.—**ev′i-dent-ness,** *n.*

e-vil (ē′vl), *a.* [AS. *yfel* = D. *euvel* = G. *übel* = Goth. *ubils*, evil.] Effecting or apt to effect injury, mischief, trouble, or pain; bad; harmful; also, characterized or accompanied by misfortune or suffering; unfortunate; disastrous; also, violating or inconsistent with the moral law; sinful; wicked; also, due to (actual or imputed) bad character or conduct (as, *evil* repute).—**evil eye,** a faculty, superstitiously attributed to certain persons, of inflicting injury or bad luck by a look.—**the evil one,** the devil; Satan.—**e′vil,** *n.* That which is evil; evil quality, intention, or conduct; harm; mischief; misfortune; sin; also, something evil; anything causing injury or harm (as, the social *evil*, prostitution); a disease (as, king's *evil*, scrofula, sometimes called simply *the evil*: see under *king*).—**e′vil,** *adv.* In an evil manner; badly; ill.—**e′vil=do′er,** *n.* One who does evil.—**e′vil=do′ing,** *n.*—**e′vil=eyed′,** *a.* Looking with malice or envy (see Shakspere's "Cymbeline," i. 1. 72); also, supposed to possess the evil eye.—**e′vil-ly,** *adv.*—**e′vil=mind′ed,** *a.* Having an evil mind; malignant; wicked.—**e′vil-ness,** *n.*

e-vince (ē̜-vins′), *v. t.*; *evinced, evincing.* [L. *evincere*, overcome completely, prove, demonstrate: see *evict.*] To overcome† or conquer†; also, to convince†; also, to show clearly; make evident or manifest; prove; also, to reveal the possession of (a quality, trait, etc.: as, "Rip's son and heir . . . *evinced* an hereditary disposition to attend to anything else but his business," Irving's "Sketch-Book," Rip Van Winkle); exhibit.—**e-vince′ment,** *n.*—**e-vin-cive** (ē̜-vin′siv), *a.* Serving to evince; indicative.

ev-i-rate (ev′i-rāt or ē′vi-), *v. t.*; *-rated, -rating.* [L. *eviratus*, pp. of *evirare*, < *e*, out of, + *vir*, man.] To deprive of virility; castrate; emasculate.—**ev-i-ra′tion** (-rā′shọn), *n.*

e-vis-ce-rate (ē̜-vis′ẹ-rāt), *v. t.*; *-rated, -rating.* [L. *evisceratus*, pp. of *eviscerare*, < *e*, out of, + *viscera*, entrails: see *viscus.*] To remove the viscera from; disembowel; fig., to deprive of vital or essential parts.—**e-vis-ce-ra′tion** (-rā′shọn), *n.*

ev-i-ta-ble (ev′i-tạ-bl), *a.* [L. *evitabilis*, < *evitare*: see *evite.*] Avoidable. Cf. *inevitable.*

e-vite (ē̜-vīt′), *v. t.*; *evited, eviting.* [L. *evitare* (pp. *evitatus*), < *e*, out of, + *vitare*, shun.] To avoid; shun. [Archaic.] Also **ev-i-tate†** (ev′i-tāt).—**ev-i-ta′tion** (-tā′shọn), *n.*

ev-o-ca-ble (ev′ọ-kạ-bl), *a.* [L. *evocare*: see *evoke.*] That may be evoked.

ev-o-cate (ev′ọ-kāt), *v. t.*; *-cated, -cating.* [L. *evocatus*, pp. of *evocare*: see *evoke.*] To evoke. [Now rare.]—**ev-o-ca′tion** (-kā′shọn), *n.* [L. *evocatio(n-)*.] The act of evoking; a calling forth; in *law*, the evoking of a cause from an inferior to a superior tribunal.—**e-voc-a-tive** (ē̜-vok′ạ-tiv), *a.* Tending to evoke.—**e-voc′a-to-ry** (-tọ-ri), *a.* Having the function of evoking.—**ev′o-ca-tor** (-kā-tọr), *n.* [L.] One who evokes; esp., one who calls up spirits.

e-voke (ē̜-vōk′), *v. t.*; *evoked, evoking.* [L. *evocare* (pp. *evocatus*), < *e*, out of, + *vocare*, call.] To call or summon forth; in *law*, to summon or remove (a cause) from an inferior to a superior tribunal.—**e-vok-er** (ē̜-vō′kėr), *n.*

ev-o-lute (ev′ǫ-lūt). [L. *evolutus*, pp. of *evolvere*: see *evolve*.] **I.** *a.* Evolved; developed. **II.** *n.* In *geom.*, a curve which is the locus of the center of curvature of another curve (called the *involute*), or the envelop of the normals to the latter; the curve from which an involute is formed by the unwrapping of a flexible and inextensible string. Cf. *involute.*

ev-o-lu-tion (ev-ǫ-lū′shǫn), *n.* [L. *evolutio(n-)*, < *evolvere*: see *evolve.*] The act or process of evolving; an unrolling or unfolding; development; any process of formation or growth; continuous progress from unorganized simplicity to organized complexity; an evolving or giving off of gas, heat, etc.; also, something evolved; a product; also, a movement, or one of a series of movements, of troops, ships, etc., as for disposition in order of battle or in line on parade; any similar movement; in *math.*, the formation of an involute; also, the extraction of roots from powers; in *biol.*, development from a rudimentary to a mature or complete state; also, preformation (now only historical); also, in modern use, the fact or doctrine of the descent of all living things from a few simple forms of life, or from a single form. —**ev-o-lu′tion-al, ev-o-lu′tion-a-ry** (-ạ-ri), *a.*—**ev-o-lu′tion-ism,** *n.* The theory of evolution or development, as in biology, or with reference to the gradual progress of the universe from simplicity to complexity (cf. *creationism*).—**ev-o-lu′tion-ist,** *n.*

e-volv-a-ble (ẹ-vol′vạ-bl), *a.* That may be evolved.

e-volve (ẹ-volv′), *v.*; *evolved, evolving.* [L. *evolvere* (pp. *evolutus*), roll out, unroll, unfold, < *e-*, out, + *volvere*, roll.] **I.** *tr.* To unroll or unfold; open out or expand; disclose gradually to knowledge; also, to bring out gradually (something contained, involved, latent, or potential in a thing); educe, as a result or conclusion; develop, as from materials, data, etc.; produce by elaboration; sometimes, to develop or produce as a natural consequence; give off or emit, as odors, vapors, etc.; also, to develop, as by a process of growth, to a more highly organized condition. **II.** *intr.* To unfold; open out, as to view; come forth gradually into being; develop; undergo evolution.—**e-volve′ment,** *n.*—**e-volv′er,** *n.*

e-vul-sion (ẹ-vul′shǫn), *n.* [L. *evulsio(n-)*, < *evellere*, pluck out, < *e-*, out, + *vellere*, pluck.] The act of plucking or pulling out; forcible extraction.

ewe (ū), *n.* [AS. *eowu* = D. *ooi*, ewe; akin to L. *ovis*, Gr. ὄις, Skt. *avi*, sheep.] A female sheep.—**ewe′=neck,** *n.* A neck like that of a ewe, hollowed rather than arched: said with reference to horses.—**ewe′=necked,** *a.*

ew-er (ū′ėr), *n.* [OF. *esviere, aiguiere* (F. *aiguière*), < L. *aquaria*, fem. of *aquarius*, pertaining to water, < *aqua*, water.] A pitcher with a wide spout, esp. one to hold water for ablutions; in *decorative art*, a vessel having a spout and a handle, esp. a tall and slender vessel with a foot or base.

Ewer of silver-gilt in the Pitti Palace, Florence.

ex (eks), *prep.* [L.: see *ex-*.] In *commerce*, out of; free out of (used in phrases, as *ex elevator*, *ex ship*, etc., which mean 'free of charges until the time of removal out of the elevator, ship, etc.'); in *finance*, without, not including, or without the right to have (used in phrases, as *ex coupon*, *ex dividend*, *ex interest*, which are often abbreviated simply *ex* or *x*). Cf. *cum.*

ex-. [L. *ex-*, repr. *ex*, also *e*, prep., out of, from, beyond, = Gr. ἐξ, ἐκ, out of, from.] A prefix of Latin origin, meaning primarily 'out of,' 'from,' and hence 'out,' 'utterly,' 'thoroughly,' and sometimes serving to impart a privative or negative force or to indicate a former title, status, etc.: freely used as an English formative, as in *exalbuminous*, *exstipulate*, *exterritorial*, and esp. in such combinations as *ex-president* (former president), *ex-member*, *ex-pugilist*, *ex-wife.*

ex-a-cer-bate (eg-zas′ėr-bāt or ek-sas′-), *v. t.*; *-bated, -bating.* [L. *exacerbatus*, pp. of *exacerbare*, < *ex-*, utterly, + *acerbus*, sour, bitter, harsh.] To increase the bitterness or violence of (pain, disease, ill feeling, etc.: as, "if those differences are *exacerbated* by religious disputes," H. G. Wells's "Outline of History," xxxviii. § 7); aggravate; embitter; also, to embitter the feelings of (a person); irritate; exasperate. —**ex-a-cer-ba′tion** (-bā′shǫn), *n.*

ex-act (eg-zakt′), *v.* [L. *exactus*, pp. of *exigere*, drive out, force out, require, complete, measure by a standard, < *ex-*, out, + *agere*, drive, do, act.] **I.** *tr.* To force or compel the payment, yielding, or performance of; extort; also, to call for, demand, or require (as, his generosity *exacts* admiration). **II.**† *intr.* To practise exactions: with *on* or *upon*: as, "The enemy shall not *exact* upon him" (Ps. lxxxix. 22). —**ex-act′,** *a.* Conforming perfectly to the requirements or conditions of the case; strictly accurate or correct (as, an *exact* likeness, description, or translation); precise, as opposed to approximate (as, the *exact* sum due; the *exact* moment or date); also, characterized by or using strict accuracy or precision (as, the *exact* sciences; *exact* instruments; an *exact* thinker or mind); also, admitting of no deviation, as laws, discipline, etc.; strict or rigorous; also, perfect†, consummate†, or finished†.—**ex-act′a-ble,** *a.* That may be exacted.—**ex-act′er,** *n.*—**ex-act′ing,** *p. a.* Given to or characterized by exaction; extortionate; also, severe, or unduly severe, in demands or requirements, as a person; requiring close application or attention, as a task.—**ex-act′ing-ly,** *adv.*—**ex-act′ing-ness,** *n.*—**ex-ac-tion** (eg-zak′shǫn), *n.* [L. *exactio(n-)*.] The act of exacting; extortion; also, something exacted.—**ex-ac′ti-tude** (-ti-tūd), *n.* [F.] The quality of being exact; exactness.—**ex-act′ly,** *adv.*—**ex-act′ness,** *n.*—**ex-ac′tor,** *n.*

ex-ag-ger-ate (eg-zaj′ẹ-rāt), *v.*; *-ated, -ating.* [L. *exaggeratus*, pp. of *exaggerare*, < *ex-*, out, + *aggerare*, heap up, < *agger*, heap, mound.] **I.** *tr.* To heap up†; also, to magnify beyond truth or reason; overstate; represent disproportionately; also, to increase or enlarge abnormally. **II.** *intr.* To employ exaggeration, as in speech or writing.—**ex-ag′ger-at-ed,** *p. a.* Unduly magnified; abnormally increased or enlarged; in *zoöl.*, more conspicuous than is normal.—**ex-ag′ger-at-ed-ly,** *adv.*—**ex-ag′ger-at-ing-ly,** *adv.*—**ex-ag-ger-a-tion** (eg-zaj-ẹ-rā′shǫn), *n.* [L. *exaggeratio(n-)*.] The act of exaggerating, or the state of being exaggerated; an exaggerated statement or representation; an exaggerated form of something.—**ex-ag-ger-a-tive** (eg-zaj′ẹ-rā-tiv), *a.* Given to or characterized by exaggeration.—**ex-ag-ger-a-tor** (eg-zaj′ẹ-rā-tǫr), *n.*—**ex-ag-ger-a-to-ry** (eg-zaj′ẹ-rā-tǫ-ri), *a.* Characterized by exaggeration; exaggerative.

ex-al-bu-mi-nous (eks-al-bū′mi-nus), *a.* [See *ex-*.] In *bot.*, destitute of albumen, as seeds.

ex-alt (eg-zâlt′), *v. t.* [L. *exaltare*, < *ex-*, out, + *altus*, high.] To raise up or elevate (now rare in literal use); fig., to elevate in rank, honor, power, character, quality, etc.; dignify; glorify; ennoble; stimulate, as the imagination; elate, as with pride or joy; also, to attribute exaltation to; praise; extol; also, to raise in degree; intensify; heighten; in *chem.*, to purify† or refine†.—**ex-al-ta-tion** (ek-sâl-tā′shǫn), *n.* [LL. *exaltatio(n-)*.] The act of exalting, or the state of being exalted; elevation, as in rank, power, character, etc.; elation of mind or feeling, sometimes abnormal or morbid in character; abnormal intensification of the action of an organ; in *astrol.*, that situation of a planet in the zodiac where it is supposed to have the most influence.—**ex-alt′ed,** *p. a.* Elevated, as in rank or character; of high station; dignified; lofty; noble; sometimes, rapturously excited (as, "When the music was strong and bold, she looked *exalted*": Steele, in "Spectator," 503).—**ex-alt′ed-ly,** *adv.*—**ex-alt′ed-ness,** *n.*—**ex-alt′er,** *n.*

ex-a-men (eg-zā′men), *n.* [L., a weighing, consideration, < *ex-*, out, + *agere*, drive, do, act: cf. *essay* and *exact.*] An examination; an investigation or inquiry.

ex-am-in-a-ble (eg-zam′i-nạ-bl), *a.* That may be examined; subject to examination.

ex-am-i-nant (eg-zam′i-nạnt), *n.* [L. *examinans* (*-ant-*), ppr.] One who examines, or conducts an examination.

ex-am-i-nate (eg-zam′i-nāt), *n.* [L. *examinatus*, pp.] A person undergoing examination.

ex-am-i-na-tion (eg-zam-i-nā′shǫn), *n.* [L. *examinatio(n-)*.] The act of examining, or the state of being examined; inspection; inquiry; investigation; formal interrogation; a testing of pupils, candidates, etc., as by questions; also, the statements, etc., made by one examined.—**ex-am-i-na′-tion-al,** *a.*

ex-am-i-na-tor (eg-zam′i-nā-tọr), *n.* [LL.] One who examines; an examiner. [Now rare.]—**ex-am″i-na-to′ri-al** (-nạ-tō′ri-ạl), *a.*

ex-am-ine (eg-zam′in), *v. t.*; *-ined, -ining.* [OF. F. *examiner,* < L. *examinare* (pp. *examinatus*), < *examen,* a weighing, consideration: see *examen.*] To test or assay (ores, etc.)†; try by a standard or rule (obs. or rare); inspect or scrutinize carefully; inquire into or investigate; test by questioning; interrogate (a witness, etc.) as to conduct or as to knowledge of facts; test the knowledge or qualifications of (a pupil, candidate, etc.), as by questions.—**ex-am-in-ee′** (-i-nē′), *n.* One who undergoes an examination.—**ex-am′in-er,** *n.* One who examines.—**ex-am′in-ing-ly,** *adv.*

ex-am-ple (eg-zam′pl), *n.* [OF. *example* (F. *exemple*), < L. *exemplum,* < *eximere,* take out: see *exempt.*] One of a number of things, or a part of something, taken to show the character of the whole; an instance serving for illustration; a specimen; an instance illustrating a rule or method, as a mathematical problem proposed for solution; also, something to be imitated; a pattern or model; conduct inducing imitation; also, a precedent; a parallel case; also, an instance, esp. of punishment, serving for a warning; a warning.—**ex-am′ple,** *v. t.*; *-pled, -pling.* To give or be an example of; exemplify; also, to justify by an example or precedent†; also, to set an example to; instruct by example.

ex-an-i-mate (eg-zan′i-māt or ek-san′-), *a.* [L. *exanimatus,* pp. of *exanimare,* deprive of breath, life, or spirit, < *ex-* priv. (see *ex-*) + *anima,* air, breath, life.] Inanimate or lifeless; lifeless in appearance; spiritless; disheartened.

ex-an-them (ek-san′them), *n.* Same as *exanthema.*

ex-an-the-ma (ek-san-thē′mạ), *n.*; pl. *-themata* (-them′ạ-tạ). [LL., < Gr. ἐξάνθημα, < ἐξανθεῖν, blossom out, break out, < ἐξ-, out, + ἀνθεῖν, blossom, < ἄνθος, a flower.] In *pathol.,* an eruption or rash on the skin; also, an eruptive disease, esp. one attended with fever, as smallpox or measles.—**ex-an-the-mat′ic** (-thẹ-mat′ik), **ex-an-them′a-tous** (-them′ạ-tus), *a.*

ex-arch (ek′särk), *n.* [LL. *exarchus,* < Gr. ἔξαρχος, < ἐξ-, out, + ἄρχειν, lead, rule.] The ruler of a province in the Byzantine Empire; also, in the Eastern Church, orig. a patriarch, later a bishop ranking below a patriarch and above a metropolitan, now a patriarch's deputy.—**ex-ar-chate** (ek′sär-kāt or ek-sär′-), *n.* [ML. *exarchatus.*] The office, jurisdiction, or province of an exarch.

ex-as-per-ate (eg-zas′pẹ-rāt), *v. t.*; *-ated, -ating.* [L. *exasperatus,* pp. of *exasperare,* < *ex-,* utterly, + *asper,* rough.] To make rough or harsh†; increase the intensity or violence of (disease, passions, etc.: as, "tribes whose native ferocity was *exasperated* by debasing forms of superstition," De Quincey's "Revolt of the Tartars"); make (pain, etc.) more grievous; embitter (feeling, etc.); irritate to a high degree, or enrage, as a person.—**ex-as′per-at-ed-ly,** *adv.*—**ex-as′per-at-ing-ly,** *adv.*—**ex-as-per-a′tion** (-pẹ-rā′shọn), *n.* [L. *exasperatio(n-).*] The act of exasperating, or the state of being exasperated; exacerbation; great irritation; intense anger.—**ex-as′per-a-tor,** *n.*

ex ca-the-dra (eks kạ-thē′drạ or kath′ẹ-). [L., 'from the chair.'] From the seat of authority; with authority: a phrase sometimes used adjectively (as, an *ex cathedra* judgment).—**ex-ca-the′dral,** *a.*

ex-ca-vate (eks′kạ-vāt), *v. t.*; *-vated, -vating.* [L. *excavatus,* pp. of *excavare,* < *ex-,* out, + *cavare,* make hollow, < *cavus,* hollow.] To make hollow by removing the inner part; make a hole or cavity in; form into a hollow, as by digging; also, to make (a hole, tunnel, etc.) by removing material; also, to dig or scoop out (earth, etc.); also, to expose or lay bare by digging; unearth.—**ex-ca-va′tion** (-vā′shọn), *n.* [L. *excavatio(n-).*] The act of excavating; also, a hole or cavity made by excavating.—**ex′ca-va-tor,** *n.* One who or that which excavates; a machine used in excavating (see cut in preceding column).

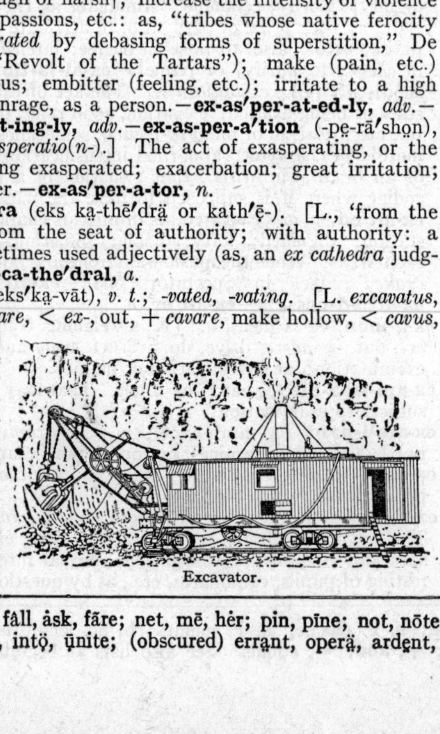
Excavator.

ex-ceed (ek-sēd′), *v.* [OF. *exceder* (F. *excéder*), < L. *excedere* (pp. *excessus*), < *ex,* out of, beyond, + *cedere,* go.] **I.** *tr.* To go beyond (a boundary, limit, or point: now usually fig.); go beyond the bounds or limits of (as, to *exceed* one's powers; to *exceed* propriety or truth); go beyond in quantity, degree, rate, etc. (as, incomes *exceeding* $5,000; to *exceed* a given age, weight, or height; to *exceed* the authorized speed); go beyond in rank, excellence, effectiveness, etc.; surpass or excel; be superior to. **II.** *intr.* To go beyond fixed or proper limits, as in conduct; exaggerate, as in statement; be greater, as in quantity or degree; surpass others, excel, or be superior.—**ex-ceed′er,** *n.*—**ex-ceed′ing. I.** *p. a.* Surpassing in quantity or degree; unusually great; extraordinary; excessive. **II.** *adv.* Exceedingly: as, "My heart is *exceeding* heavy" (Shakspere's "Much Ado about Nothing," iii. 4. 25). [Archaic.]—**ex-ceed′ing-ly,** *adv.* To an unusual degree; extremely.

ex-cel (ek-sel′), *v.*; *-celled, -celling.* [L. *excellere* (pp. *excelsus*), < *ex,* out of, beyond, + *-cellere,* rise: cf. *column.*] **I.** *intr.* To surpass others in some quality, attainment, performance, etc.; be superior in some respect. **II.** *tr.* To surpass; be superior to; outdo.

ex-cel-lence (ek′sẹ-lẹns), *n.* [OF. F. *excellence,* < L. *excellentia,* < *excellens*: see *excellent.*] The fact or state of excelling; superiority; eminence; also, an excellent quality or feature; also [often *cap.*], a title of honor (now usually *excellency,* which see).—**ex′cel-len-cy** (-lẹn-si), *n.*; pl. *-cies* (-siz). Excellence; also [often *cap.*], a title of honor given to certain high officials, as governors and ambassadors; a person so entitled.

ex-cel-lent (ek′sẹ-lẹnt), *a.* [OF. F. *excellent,* < L. *excellens* (*-ent-*), ppr. of *excellere*: see *excel.*] Excelling; possessing excellence or superior merit; remarkably good; also, extraordinary† or consummate† (as, an *excellent* hypocrite).—**ex′cel-lent-ly,** *adv.*

ex-cel-si-or (ek-sel′si-ôr), *a.* [L., compar. of *excelsus,* high, prop. pp. of *excellere*: see *excel.*] Higher: used as a motto, as by the State of New York ('the Excelsior State') and, as by Longfellow in his poem "Excelsior," as an expression of aspiration toward greater heights.—**ex-cel′si-or** (-ọr), *n.* A kind of fine wood-shavings, used for stuffing, packing, etc.; also, a printing-type (3 point) smaller than brilliant.

Seal of the Excelsior State.

ex-cept (ek-sept′), *v.* [L. *exceptus,* pp. of *excipere,* < *ex,* out of, + *capere,* take.] **I.** *tr.* To take or leave out from a number or an aggregate under consideration; leave out of account; exclude, as from the scope of a statement, rule, etc. **II.** *intr.* To make objection; object; take exception.—**ex-cept′.** [Orig. pp.] **I.** *prep.* With the exclusion of; excluding; save; but. **II.** *conj.* With the exception that (now usually with *that* expressed: as, "Parted without the least regret, *Except* that they had ever met," Cowper's "Pairing Time Anticipated"); also, if it be (or were) not that, if not, or unless (as, "*Except* the Lord build the house, they labour in vain that build it": Ps. cxxvii. 1); also, otherwise than, save, or but (as, "Nor do I know how to prevent the course of justice, *except* by paying the money myself": Goldsmith's "Vicar of Wakefield," xxiv.).—**ex-cept′er,** *n.*—**ex-cept′ing.** [Orig. ppr.] **I.** *prep.* Excluding; barring; saving; except. **II.** *conj.* Except; unless; save.

ex-cep-tion (ek-sep′shọn), *n.* [L. *exceptio(n-).*] The act of excepting, or the fact of being excepted; exclusion, as from the scope of a statement, rule, etc.; also, something excepted; an instance or case not conforming to the general rule; also, an objection, as to a ruling of the court in the course of a trial; in general, an objection or demur; an adverse criticism, esp. on a particular point; expressed opposition of opinion, or demurral (as, a statement liable to *exception*).—**to take exception,** to make objection (esp. with *to*); demur with respect to something; also, to take offense (often with *at*).—**ex-cep′tion-a-ble,** *a.* Liable to exception or objection; objectionable.—**ex-cep′tion-a-ble-ness,** *n.*—**ex-cep′tion-a-bly,** *adv.*—**ex-cep′tion-al,** *a.* Forming an exception or unusual instance; unusual; extraordinary.—**ex-cep′tion-al-ly,** *adv.*—**ex-cep′tion-al-ness,** *n.*

ex-cep-tious (ek-sep′shus), *a.* [From *exception.*] Disposed to take exception or make objection; captious.

ex-cep-tive (ek-sep′tiv), *a.* That excepts; making an exception; also, disposed to take exception; inclined to object.

ex-cep-tor (ek-sep′tọr), *n.* One who excepts.

ex-cerpt (ek-sėrpt′), *v. t.* [L. *excerptus*, pp. of *excerpere*, < *ex*, out of, + *carpere*, pick.] To cull out or take out (a passage) from a book or the like; extract.—**ex-cerpt** (ek′-sėrpt or ek-sėrpt′), *n.* [L. *excerptum* (pl. *excerpta*), prop. pp. neut.] A passage taken out of a book or the like; an extract.—**ex-cerp-tion** (ek-sėrp′shọn), *n.* [L. *excerptio(n-).*] The act of excerpting; also, an excerpt.

ex-cess (ek-ses′). [OF. *exces* (F. *excès*), < L. *excessus*, < *excedere*: see *exceed.*] **I.** *n.* A going beyond ordinary or proper limits, as of authority; an overstepping the limits of moderation; immoderate indulgence, esp. of physical appetites; intemperance; also, exuberance or superabundance; superfluity; an extreme or excessive amount or degree; also, the fact of exceeding something else in amount or degree; preponderance; also, the amount or degree by which one thing exceeds another. **II.** *a.* Being more than or above what is necessary, usual, or specified.—**ex-ces-sive** (ek-ses′iv), *a.* Exceeding the usual or proper limit or degree; characterized by excess; immoderate; extravagant; unreasonable.—**ex-ces′sive-ly,** *adv.*—**ex-ces′sive-ness,** *n.*

ex-change (eks-chānj′), *v.*; *-changed, -changing.* [OF. *eschangier* (F. *échanger*), < ML. *excambiare*, < L. *ex-*, out, + ML. *cambiare*, E. *change, v.*] **I.** *tr.* To part with for some equivalent; give up (something) for something else; sometimes, to replace by another or something else (as, please *exchange* this purchase for me; no goods will be *exchanged* during the holiday season); also, to give and receive (things) reciprocally; give to and receive from each other (things of the same kind: as, to *exchange* blows, gifts, etc.); interchange. **II.** *intr.* To make an exchange; also, to pass or be taken in exchange or as an equivalent.—**ex-change′,** *n.* [OF. *eschange* (F. *échange*).] The act of exchanging; a parting with a thing in return for some equivalent; the giving up or resigning of something for something else (as, the *exchange* of a crown for a cloister); the replacing of one thing by another or something else; return (as, to receive gold in *exchange* for silver); also, the act of giving and receiving reciprocally (as, an *exchange* of blows, gifts, etc.); interchange; specif., the mutual transference of equivalent sums of money, as in the currencies of two different countries; the business of a money-changer; the varying rate or sum, in one currency, given for a fixed sum in another currency (also called *course*, or *rate, of exchange*); the amount of the difference in value between two or more currencies, or between the values of the same currency at two or more places; also, the method or system by which debits and credits in different places are settled without the actual transference of money, by means of documents representing money-values ('bills of exchange'); the discharge of obligations in different places by the transfer of credits; sometimes, a bill of exchange; also, the amount or percentage charged for exchanging money, collecting a draft, etc.; also, that which is given or received in exchange or substitution for something else; a copy of a newspaper or periodical sent to the office of another newspaper or periodical in return for a copy of the latter; also, a place for exchanging commodities, services, etc.; a place where merchants, brokers, bankers, etc., meet to transact business; a central office, central station, or the like (as, a telephone *exchange*, where telephone lines come together and connections are made between lines).—**exchange editor,** an editor who reads the exchanges sent to his office and selects from them extracts for reproduction in his own publication.—**ex-change′a-ble,** *a.* Capable of being exchanged.—**exchangeable value,** the value of a thing measured by what may be procured in exchange.—**ex-change-a-bil′i-ty** (-bil′i-ti), *n.*—**ex-chan′ger** (-chān′-jėr), *n.*

ex-che-quer (eks-chek′ėr), *n.* [So called with reference to the table-cover marked with squares on which accounts were reckoned with counters, < OF. *eschequier*, chessboard: see *checker*[2].] [*cap.*] Formerly, in England, an office which administered the royal revenues and determined all cases affecting them; later, a court of law ('Court of Exchequer') deriving from this office, now merged in the King's Bench Division of the High Court of Justice; [*cap.* or *l. c.*] in Great Britain, the governmental department in charge of the public revenues; the national treasury; in general [*l. c.*], a treasury, as of a state or nation; also (colloq.), pecuniary resources; finances.

ex-cide (ek-sīd′), *v. t.*; *-cided, -ciding.* [L. *excidere* (pp. *excisus*), < *ex*, out of, + *cædere*, cut.] To cut out; excise.

ex-cip-i-ent (ek-sip′i-ẹnt), *n.* [L. *excipiens* (*-ent-*), ppr. of *excipere*, take out: see *except, v.*] One who or that which takes up or receives; in *phar.*, a more or less inert substance, as sugar, jelly, etc., used as the medium or vehicle for the administration of an active medicine.

ex-cis-a-ble (ek-sī′zạ-bl), *a.* Subject to excise duty.

ex-cise[1] (ek-sīz′), *v. t.*; *-cised, -cising.* [L. *excisus*, pp. of *excidere*: see *excide.*] To cut out or off, as a tumor; expunge, as a passage or sentence.

ex-cise[2] (ek-sīz′), *n.* [Prob. < MD. *excijs*, < OF. *acceis*, a tax, ult. < L. *ad*, to, + *censere*, tax.] An inland tax or duty on certain commodities, as spirits, tobacco, etc., levied on their manufacture, sale, or consumption within the country; also, a tax levied for a license to carry on certain employments, pursue certain sports, etc.; also, that branch of the civil service charged with the collection of excise duties (British).—**ex-cise′**[2], *v. t.*; *-cised, -cising.* To impose an excise on.—**ex-cise′man** (-mạn), *n.*; pl. *-men.* An officer who collects excise taxes and enforces excise laws: as, "Of all the manifold ills in the train of smuggling, surely the *excisemen* are the worst" (Galt's "Annals of the Parish," xix.). [British.]

ex-ci-sion (ek-sizh′ọn), *n.* [L. *excisio(n-)*, < *excidere*: see *excide.*] The act of excising, or cutting out or off; the state of being excised; hence, exclusion, as from a religious society; excommunication; also, extirpation or destruction.

ex-cit-a-ble (ek-sī′tạ-bl), *a.* Capable of being excited; also, easily excited.—**ex-cit-a-bil′i-ty** (-bil′i-ti), **ex-cit′a-ble-ness,** *n.*

ex-cit-ant (ek-sī′tạnt). [L. *excitans* (*-ant-*), ppr.] **I.** *a.* Exciting, or tending to excite; stimulating. **II.** *n.* Something that excites, esp. to increased vital activity; a stimulant; in *elect.*, the exciting liquid in a voltaic cell.

ex-ci-ta-tion (ek-si-tā′shọn), *n.* [LL. *excitatio(n-).*] The act of exciting, or the state of being excited; excitement.—**ex-ci-ta-tive, ex-ci-ta-to-ry** (ek-sī′tạ-tiv, -tọ-ri), *a.* Tending to excite; characterized or produced by excitement.

ex-cite (ek-sīt′), *v. t.*; *-cited, -citing.* [L. *excitare* (pp. *excitatus*), freq. of *exciere*, call forth, rouse, < *ex*, out of, + *ciere*, move, excite, call.] To call into action; stir up; incite; rouse; hence, to induce or occasion; also, to agitate or perturb mentally; also, to stimulate to activity, as the nervous organism; in *elect.*, to produce electric activity or a magnetic field in.—**ex-cit-ed-ly** (ek-sī′ted-li), *adv.*—**ex-cite′ment,** *n.* The act of exciting; excited state or condition; mental agitation; also, something that excites.—**ex-cit′er,** *n.* One who or that which excites; in *elect.*, a dynamo, battery, or other apparatus, which supplies the current for producing a magnetic field in another machine; also, a device for producing Hertzian waves.—**ex-cit′ing,** *p. a.* That excites; calling into action; stirring; producing excitement.—**ex-cit′ing-ly,** *adv.*—**ex-cit-o-mo-tor** (ek-sī″-tọ-mō′tọr), *a.* In *physiol.*, exciting muscular action; pertaining to reflex action.—**ex-ci-tor** (ek-sī′tọr), *n.* An exciter; in *physiol.*, a nerve whose stimulation excites greater action in the part supplied.—**ex-cit″o-se-cre′to-ry** (-sẹ-krē′tọ-ri), *a.* In *physiol.*, causing increased secretion.

ex-claim (eks-klām′), *v.* [L. *exclamare* (pp. *exclamatus*), < *ex-*, out, + *clamare*, cry, shout.] **I.** *intr.* To cry out or speak suddenly and vehemently, as in surprise, strong emotion, protest, etc. **II.** *tr.* To cry out; say loudly or vehemently.—**ex-claim′**, *n.* An exclamation or outcry: as, "cursing cries and deep *exclaims*" (Shakspere's "Richard III.," i. 2. 52). [Archaic.]—**ex-claim′er,** *n.*—**ex-cla-ma-tion** (eks-klạ-mā′shọn), *n.* [L. *exclamatio(n-).*] The act of exclaiming; an outcry; a sudden and vehement utterance; a loud complaint or protest; also, a punctuation-mark (!) used after an exclamation ('exclamation-mark' or 'exclamation-point'); in *gram.*, an interjection.—**ex-clam′a-tive** (-klam′ạ-tiv), **ex-clam′a-to-ry** (-tọ-ri), *a.* Using, containing, or expressing exclamation; pertaining to exclamation.

ex-clave (eks′klāv), *n.* [L. *ex*, out of, + E. *-clave* as in *enclave.*] An outlying portion of a country, entirely (or mostly) surrounded by foreign territory, considered in relation to the country to which it belongs. Cf. *enclave.*

ex-clude (eks-klöd′), *v. t.*; *-cluded, -cluding.* [L. *excludere* (pp. *exclusus*), < *ex*, out of, + *cludere, claudere*, shut, close: cf. *sluice.*] To shut or keep out (something already outside); prevent the entrance of; allow no room or part to; shut out from consideration, the scope of a privilege or grant, the application of a term or proposition, etc.; also, to expel and keep out; thrust out; eject.—**ex-clud′a-ble** (-klö′dạ-bl), *a.*—**ex-clud′er,** *n.*

ex-clu-sion (eks-klö′zhọn), *n.* [L. *exclusio(n-).*] The act of excluding, or the state of being excluded; a debarring or debarment; expulsion.—**ex-clu′sion-a-ry** (-ā-ri), *a.* Pertaining to or characterized by exclusion.—**ex-clu′sion-ism,** *n.* The principle, policy, or practice of exclusion, as from rights or privileges.—**ex-clu′sion-ist,** *n.* One who favors exclusion; one who would exclude another from some right or privilege.

ex-clu-sive (eks-klö′siv), *a.* [ML. *exclusivus.*] That excludes; not admitting of something (as, mutually *exclusive* ideas, neither of which admits of the other); excluding from consideration or account (often used adverbially: as, from 100 to 121 *exclusive*, that is, excluding 100 and 121, and including from 101 to 120); excluding all except what is specified (as, an *exclusive* proposition or particle); shutting out all others from a part or share (as, an *exclusive* grant); in which no others have a share (as, *exclusive* information); limited to the object or objects designated (as, *exclusive* attention to business); single or sole (as, the *exclusive* means of communication between two places); also, disposed to resist the admission of outsiders to association, intimacy, etc.; fastidious as to the social rank of associates.—**ex-clu′sive-ly,** *adv.*—**ex-clu′sive-ness,** *n.*

ex-cog-i-tate (eks-koj′i-tāt), *v. t.*; *-tated, -tating.* [L. *excogitatus*, pp. of *excogitare*, < *ex-*, out, + *cogitare*, think, E. *cogitate.*] To think out; contrive; devise.—**ex-cog-i-ta′tion** (-tā′shọn), *n.* The act of excogitating; reflection; mental contrivance; also, something excogitated; a plan; a contrivance.—**ex-cog′i-ta-tive** (-tạ-tiv), *a.* Of or pertaining to excogitation.—**ex-cog′i-ta-tor** (-tā-tọr), *n.*

ex-com-mu-ni-ca-ble (eks-kọ-mū′ni-kạ-bl), *a.* Liable or deserving to be excommunicated, as a person; punishable by excommunication, as an offense.

ex-com-mu-ni-cant (eks-kọ-mū′ni-kạnt), *n.* An excommunicated person; an excommunicate.

ex-com-mu-ni-cate (eks-kọ-mū′ni-kāt), *v. t.*; *-cated, -cating.* [LL. *excommunicatus*, pp. of *excommunicare*, < L. *ex-* priv. (see *ex-*) + *communicare*, E. *communicate.*] To cut off from communion or membership; esp., to exclude (a member) by ecclesiastical sentence from the sacraments and fellowship of the church.—**ex-com-mu′ni-cate. I.** *a.* Excommunicated. **II.** *n.* An excommunicated person.—**ex-com-mu-ni-ca′tion** (-kā′shọn), *n.* [LL. *excommunicatio(n-).*] The act of excommunicating, or the state of being excommunicated; the ecclesiastical sentence by which a person is excommunicated.—**ex-com-mu′ni-ca-tive** (-kạ-tiv), *a.* Disposed or serving to excommunicate.—**ex-com-mu′ni-ca-tor,** *n.*—**ex-com-mu′ni-ca-to-ry** (-kạ-tọ-ri), *a.* Pertaining to excommunication.

ex-co-ri-ate (eks-kō′ri-āt), *v. t.*; *-ated, -ating.* [L. *excoriatus*, pp. of *excoriare*, < *ex-* priv. (see *ex-*) + *corium*, skin.] To strip off or remove the skin from (as, "The corpse . . . was much bruised and *excoriated*": Poe's "Murders in the Rue Morgue"); also, to strip off (the skin); abrade.—**ex-co-ri-a′tion** (-ā′shọn), *n.* The act of excoriating, or the state of being excoriated; an excoriated place on the body.

ex-cor-ti-cate (eks-kôr′ti-kāt), *v. t.*; *-cated, -cating.* [ML. *excorticatus*, pp. of *excorticare*, < L. *ex-* priv. (see *ex-*) + *cortex*, bark.] To strip off the bark, rind, etc., from.—**ex-cor-ti-ca′tion** (-kā′shọn), *n.*

ex-cre-ment[1]† (eks′krę-mẹnt), *n.* [LL. *excrementum*, < L. *excrescere*: see *excrescent.*] A natural outgrowth or excrescence, as hair or feathers. See Shakspere's "Comedy of Errors," ii. 2. 79.

ex-cre-ment[2] (eks′krę-mẹnt), *n.* [L. *excrementum*, < *excernere*: see *excrete.*] Waste matter discharged from the body; esp., the feces.—**ex-cre-men′tal** (-men′tạl), **ex″-cre-men-ti′tious** (-tish′us), *a.* Pertaining to, consisting of, or of the nature of excrement.

ex-cres-cence (eks-kres′ẹns), *n.* [L. *excrescentia*, < *excrescens*: see *excrescent.*] A growing forth; abnormal growth or increase; also, an outgrowth; a natural appendage; esp., an abnormal or unsightly outgrowth on an animal or vegetable body; hence, any disfiguring addition.

ex-cres-cent (eks-kres′ẹnt), *a.* [L. *excrescens* (*-ent-*), ppr. of *excrescere*, grow out, < *ex*, out of, + *crescere*, grow.] Growing out from something else; esp., growing abnormally out of something else; superfluous; in *philol.*, arising, as a sound in a word, as a mere euphonic addition, as the *t* in *against.*

ex-cres-cen-tial (eks-kre-sen′shạl), *a.* Pertaining to or of the nature of an excrescence.

ex-cre-ta (eks-krē′tạ), *n. pl.* [L., neut. pl. of *excretus*: see *excrete.*] Excreted matters; the excretions of the animal body, as sweat, urine, etc.—**ex-cre′tal,** *a.*

ex-crete (eks-krēt′), *v. t.*; *-creted, -creting.* [L. *excretus*, pp. of *excernere*, sift out, discharge, < *ex*, out of, + *cernere*, separate, sift.] To separate and eliminate from an organic body; separate and expel from the blood or tissues, as waste or harmful matters.—**ex-cre′tion** (-krē′shọn), *n.* The act of excreting; also, the substance excreted, as sweat or urine, or certain plant juices.—**ex-cre′tive,** *a.* Excreting, or serving to excrete.—**ex-cre-to-ry** (eks′krę-tọ-ri or eks-krē′-), *a.* Pertaining to or concerned in excretion; having the function of excreting: as, *excretory* organs.

ex-cru-ci-ate (eks-krö′shi-āt), *v. t.*; *-ated, -ating.* [L. *excruciatus*, pp. of *excruciare*, < *ex-*, utterly, + *cruciare*, torture, crucify, < *crux* (*cruc-*), E. *cross.*] To inflict severe pain upon; torture; hence, to distress or annoy exceedingly (as, "Her presence used to *excruciate* Osborne": Thackeray's "Vanity Fair," xxix.).—**ex-cru′ci-at-ing,** *p. a.* Extremely painful; torturing; agonizing; hence, distressing in extremeness, elaborateness, etc. (as, *excruciating* politeness).—**ex-cru′ci-at-ing-ly,** *adv.*—**ex-cru-ci-a′tion** (-şi-ā′shọn), *n.*

ex-cu-bi-to-ri-um (eks-kū-bi-tō′ri-um), *n.*; pl. *-ria* (-ri-ạ). [ML. use of L. *excubitorium*, guard-house, < *excubitor*, guard, watchman, < *excubare*, keep watch.] In *arch.*, in some churches, a gallery for watchers on the eve of a festival, within view of the shrines.

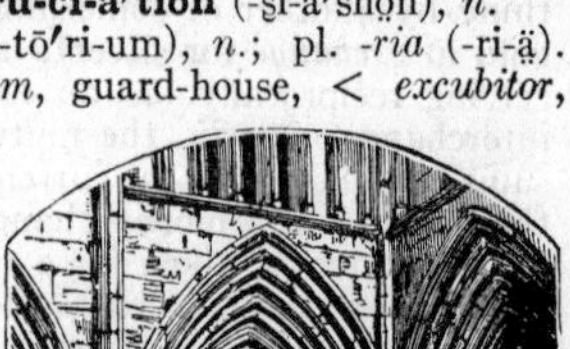

Excubitorium, St. Albans Cathedral, England.

ex-cul-pate (eks′kul-pāt or eks-kul′-), *v. t.*; *-pated, -pating.* [L. *ex-* priv. (see *ex-*) + *culpa*, fault, blame.] To clear from a charge of guilt or fault; free from blame; vindicate.—**ex-cul-pa′tion** (-pā′shọn), *n.* The act of exculpating; also, something serving to exculpate; a vindication.—**ex-cul′pa-to-ry** (-pạ-tọ-ri), *a.*

ex-cur-rent (eks-kur′ẹnt), *a.* [L. *excurrens* (*-ent-*), ppr. of *excurrere*: see *excurse.*] Running out or forth; also, admitting of or affording exit; in *bot.*, having the axis prolonged so as to form an undivided main stem or trunk, as the stem of the spruce; also, projecting beyond the apex, as the midrib in certain leaves.

ex-curse (eks-kėrs′), *v. i.*; *-cursed, -cursing.* [L. *excursus*, pp. of *excurrere*, run out, make an excursion, < *ex*, out of, + *currere*, run.] To run out or off; digress; make an excursion.

ex-cur-sion (eks-kėr′shọn), *n.* [L. *excursio(n-)*, < *excurrere*: see *excurse.*] A running out or forth†; fig., an outburst†; also, a sally or raid; also, an expedition or journey; a short journey, jaunt, or trip from a place with the intention of returning; a trip undertaken for pleasure or health; a pleasure-trip taken by a number of persons; sometimes, the persons themselves; also, deviation or digression; in *physics*, the departure of a body from its mean position or proper course; in *mach.*, the range of stroke of any moving part.—**excursion ticket,** a ticket, as for persons going on an excursion, enabling the holder to travel to a particular point and back again, usually at a reduction from the regular fare; a round-trip ticket.—**excursion train,** a train intended to carry persons making a pleasure-trip, usually at a reduced fare.—**ex-cur′sion,** *v. i.* To make an excursion.—**ex-cur′sion-al, ex-cur′sion-a-ry** (-ạ-ri), *a.* Of or pertaining to an excursion.—**ex-cur′sion-ist,** *n.* One who goes on an excursion.—**ex-cur′sion-ize,** *v.*; *-ized, -izing.* **I.** *tr.* To make excursions through. **II.** *intr.* To make excursions or an excursion.

ex-cur-sive (eks-kėr′siv), *a.* [See *excurse.*] Given to making excursions; wandering; digressive; also, of the nature of an excursion; rambling; desultory.—**ex-cur′sive-ly,** *adv.*—**ex-cur′sive-ness,** *n.*

ex-cur-sus (eks-kėr′sus), *n.*; pl. *-suses*, L. *-sus.* [L. *excursus*, n., < *excurrere*: see *excurse.*] A digression; also, a detailed discussion of some point in a book, inserted at the end of the book or of a division of it.

ex-cus-a-ble (eks-kū′zạ-bl), *a.* [L. *excusabilis.*] That may be excused; pardonable.—**ex-cus′a-ble-ness,** *n.*—**ex-cus′a-bly,** *adv.*

ex-cu-sal (eks-kū′zạl), *n.* The act of excusing.

ex-cu-sa-to-ry (eks-kū′zạ-tō-ri), *a.* Serving or intended to excuse. Also **ex-cu′sa-tive.**

ex-cuse (eks-kūz′), *v. t.*; *-cused, -cusing.* [OF. F. *excuser*, < L. *excusare*, < *ex*, out of, + *causa*, cause, judicial proceeding: cf. *accuse.*] To offer an apology for; apologize for; seek to remove the blame of; also, to serve as an apology or justification for; justify; also, to regard or judge with indulgence; pardon or forgive; overlook (a fault, etc.); also, to seek or obtain exemption or release for (as, to *excuse* one's self from duty); also, to release from an obligation or duty (as, "Your ladyship must *excuse* me; I'm called away by particular business": Sheridan's "School for Scandal," ii. 2); also, to refrain from exacting (as, to *excuse* a fine); remit; dispense with.—**ex-cuse′** (-kūs′), *n.* [OF. F. *excuse.*] The act of excusing; also, that which is offered as a reason for being excused; a plea offered in extenuation of a fault, or for release from an obligation, etc.; sometimes, a pretext or subterfuge; also, something serving to excuse (as, "My nephew's trespass may be well forgot; It hath the *excuse* of youth": Shakspere's "1 Henry IV.," v. 2. 17); a ground or reason for excusing.—**ex-cuse′less,** *a.* Having no excuse; also, admitting of no excuse; inexcusable.—**ex-cus′er** (-kū′zėr), *n.*—**ex-cus′ing-ly,** *adv.*

ex-e-cra-ble (ek′sē̜-krạ-bl), *a.* [L. *execrabilis.*] Deserving to be execrated; detestable; abominable; also, very bad, or wretched (as, an *execrable* pun).—**ex′e-cra-ble-ness,** *n.*—**ex′e-cra-bly,** *adv.*

ex-e-crate (ek′sē̜-krāt), *v.*; *-crated, -crating.* [L. *execratus*, pp. of *execrari*, for *exsecrari*, < *ex-*, out, + *sacrare*, consecrate, also declare accursed: see *sacre.*] **I.** *tr.* To curse; imprecate evil upon; hence, to detest utterly; abhor; abominate. **II.** *intr.* To utter curses.—**ex-e-cra′tion** (-krā′shọn), *n.* [L. *execratio(n-).*] The act of execrating; imprecation of evil; the utterance of curses; utter detestation or abhorrence; also, a curse or imprecation; also, a thing execrated (see Jer. xliv. 12).—**ex′e-cra-tive** (-krā-tiv), **ex′e-cra-to-ry** (-tō-ri), *a.* Pertaining to or of the nature of execration.—**ex′e-cra-tor** (-krā-tọr), *n.*

ex-e-cut-a-ble (ek′sē̜-kū-tạ-bl), *a.* That may be executed.

ex-ec-u-tant (eg-zek′ū̜-tạnt), *n.* [F. *exécutant.*] One who executes or performs; esp., a musical performer.

ex-e-cute (ek′sē̜-kūt), *v.*; *-cuted, -cuting.* [OF. *executer* (F. *exécuter*), < L. *executus*, pp. of *exequi*, for *exsequi*, < *ex-*, out, + *sequi*, follow.] **I.** *tr.* To follow out or through to the end; carry into effect, as a purpose, plan, command, or order; accomplish; give effect or force to (a law, decree, judicial sentence, etc.); carry out the terms of (a will); also, to do (something planned, commanded, or ordered, or requiring skill or care); perform (an action, maneuver, feat, etc.); also, to produce in accordance with a plan or design (as, to *execute* a statue or a picture); render (a piece of music); also, to transact or carry through (a contract, mortgage, etc.) in the manner prescribed by law; complete and give validity to (a legal instrument) by fulfilling the legal requirements, as by signing, sealing, etc.; also, to fulfil or discharge, as an office or function; also, to inflict capital punishment on; put to death by form of law; rarely, to kill. **II.** *intr.* To execute or perform something; perform a piece of music.—**ex′e-cut-er** (-kū-tėr), *n.* One who executes.—**ex-e-cu′tion** (-kū′shọn), *n.* [OF. *execucion* (F. *exécution*), < L. *executio(n-).*] The act or process of executing, or the state or fact of being executed; mode or style of performance; technical skill, as in music; effective action, esp. of weapons (as, "His brandish'd steel, Which smoked with bloody *execution*": Shakspere's "Macbeth," i. 2. 18); destructive work or effect, as of guns in warfare; the infliction of capital punishment, or, formerly, of any legal punishment; in *law*, a judicial writ ('writ of execution') directing the enforcement of a judgment.—**ex-e-cu′tion-er,** *n.* One who executes; esp., an official who inflicts capital punishment in pursuance of a legal warrant.

ex-ec-u-tive (eg-zek′ū̜-tiv), *a.* [Cf. F. *exécutif.*] Pertaining to or suited for executing or carrying into effect; charged with or pertaining to execution of laws or administration of affairs.—**Executive Mansion** [also *l. c.*], in the U. S., the official residence of the President at Washington (the 'White House'), or of the governor of one of the States.—**ex-ec′u-tive,** *n.* The executive branch of a government; esp., the person or persons in whom the supreme executive power of a government is vested; also, any person or body charged with administrative work; also, a person skilled in such work.—**ex-ec′u-tive-ly,** *adv.*

ex-ec-u-tor (eg-zek′ū̜-tọr, in first sense now ek′sē̜-kū-tọr), *n.* [OF. *executor* (F. *exécuteur*), < L. *executor*, < *exequi*: see *execute.*] One who executes, or carries out, performs, fulfils, etc.; specif., a person appointed by a testator (or by a court) to carry out the provisions of his will; also, an executioner† (see Shakspere's "Henry V.," i. 2. 203).—**ex-ec-u-to′ri-al** (-tō′ri-ạl), *a.*—**ex-ec′u-tor-ship,** *n.* The office of an executor.—**ex-ec′u-to-ry** (-tọ-ri), *a.* Executive; also, in execution or operation; operative; in *law*, intended, or of such a nature as, to take effect on a future contingency.—**ex-ec′u-trix** (-triks), *n.*; pl. *executrixes* or *executrices* (eg-zek-ū̜-trī′sēz). [ML.] A female executor.

ex-e-dra (ek′sē̜-drạ̈ or ek-sē′-), *n.*; pl. *-dræ* (-drē). [L., < Gr. ἐξέδρα, < ἐξ, out of, + ἕδρα, seat.] In *class. antiq.*, an outdoor seat or bench; any seat; a place, or a room or building, furnished with seats,

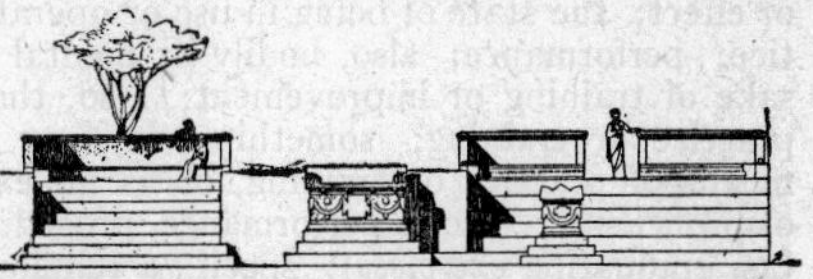

Exedra, Street of Tombs, Assos, in the Troad (in northwestern Asia Minor).

used for conversation, lectures, meetings, etc.; in *modern arch.*, an outdoor seat or bench, usually of semicircular or nearly semicircular form, esp. one of considerable size and elaborateness.

ex-e-ge-sis (ek-sē̜-jē′sis), *n.*; pl. *-geses* (-jē′sēz). [NL., < Gr. ἐξήγησις, < ἐξηγεῖσθαι, explain, < ἐξ, out of, + ἡγεῖσθαι, lead.] Critical explanation or interpretation, esp. of Scripture; also, an explanatory note; a gloss.—**ex′e-gete** (-jēt), *n.* [Gr. ἐξηγητής.] One skilled in exegesis.—**ex-e-get′ic, ex-e-get′i-cal** (-jet′ik, -i-kạl), *a.* [Gr. ἐξηγητικός.] Of or pertaining to exegesis; expository.—**ex-e-get′i-cal-ly,** *adv.*—**ex-e-get′ics,** *n.* The science of exegesis.

ex-em-plar (eg-zem′plạ̈r), *n.* [L. *exemplar*, < *exemplum*: see *example.*] A model or pattern to be copied or imitated (as, "He is indeed the perfect *exemplar* of all nobleness": Jane Porter's "Scottish Chiefs," xxxviii.); also, the model or original after which something is made; also, an instance or example; often, a typical instance; a specimen; also, a copy of a book, etc.

ex-em-pla-ry (ek'sem-plā-ri or eg-zem'plā-ri), *a.* [LL. *exemplaris*, < L. *exemplum*: see *example*.] Serving for a model or pattern; hence, worthy of imitation (as, "Her *exemplary* conduct is cried up as without a parallel": Malkin's tr. Le Sage's "Gil Blas," vii. 7); commendable; also, such as may serve for a warning, as punishment, a penalty, etc.; also, serving for an illustration or specimen; illustrative; typical.—**ex'em-pla-ri-ly,** *adv.*—**ex'em-pla-ri-ness,** *n.*

ex-em-pli-fi-ca-tion (eg-zem″pli-fi-kā'shọn), *n.* [ML. *exemplificatio(n-)*.] The act of exemplifying; also, that which exemplifies; an illustration or example; also, an attested copy of a document, under official seal.—**ex-em'pli-fi-ca-tive** (-kā-tiv), *a.* Serving to exemplify.

ex-em-pli-fy (eg-zem'pli-fī), *v. t.*; *-fied, -fying.* [ML. *exemplificare*, < L. *exemplum*, example, + *facere*, make.] To show or illustrate by example; furnish, or serve as, an example of; also, to transcribe or copy; make an attested copy of (a document) under seal.—**ex-em'pli-fi-er** (-fī-ėr), *n.*

ex-empt (eg-zempt'). [L. *exemptus*, pp. of *eximere*, take out, release, deliver, < *ex*, out of, + *emere*, take, buy.] **I.** *a.* Taken away† or removed† (as, "And this our life *exempt* from public haunt Finds tongues in trees, books in the running brooks": Shakspere's "As You Like It," ii. 1. 15); also, excepted†; also, released from, or not subject to, an obligation, liability, etc. **II.** *n.* One who is exempt from, or not subject to, an obligation, duty, etc.; also, an exon.—**ex-empt',** *v. t.* To take out or away†; remove†; also, to except†; also, to free from an obligation or liability to which others are subject; grant immunity to; dispense.—**ex-emp-tion** (eg-zemp'shọn), *n.* [L. *exemptio(n-)*, < *eximere*.] The act of exempting, or the state of being exempted; dispensation; immunity.

ex-en-te-rate (ek-sen'tẹ-rāt), *v. t.*; *-rated, -rating.* [L. *exenteratus*, pp. of *exenterare*, < Gr. ἐξ, out of, + ἔντερον, intestine.] To disembowel; eviscerate.—**ex-en-te-ra'tion** (-rā'shọn), *n.*

ex-e-qua-tur (ek-sẹ-kwā'tėr), *n.* [L., 'let him execute.'] A written recognition of a consul or commercial agent by the government to which he is accredited, authorizing him to exercise his powers; also, an authorization granted by a secular ruler for the publication of papal bulls or other ecclesiastical enactments.

ex-e-quy (ek'sẹ-kwi), *n.*; pl. *-quies* (-kwiz). [L. *exequiæ*, pl., < *exequi, exsequi*, follow out: see *execute*.] A funeral rite or ceremony; also, a funeral procession: now only in *pl.*

ex-er-cis-a-ble (ek'sėr-sī-zạ-bl), *a.* Capable of being exercised.

ex-er-cise (ek'sėr-sīz), *n.* [OF. F. *exercice*, < L. *exercitium*, < *exercere*, drive on, keep active or busy, < *ex-*, out, + *arcere*, keep.] A putting into action, use, operation, or effect; the state of being in use or operation; use; practice; performance; also, bodily or mental exertion for the sake of training or improvement; also, that which affords practice or training; something done or performed as a means of practice or training, or as an exhibition or test of proficiency; also, a performance, procedure, or ceremony (as, graduating *exercises*); specif., a religious observance or service.—**ex'er-cise,** *v.*; *-cised, -cising.* **I.** *tr.* To put (faculties, powers, rights, skill, etc.) into action, practice, or use; exert (authority, influence, etc.); use (an instrument, weapon, etc.)†; employ or busy (a person: used reflexively or in the passive); put through exercises, or forms of practice or exertion, designed to train, develop, keep in due condition, etc. (as, to *exercise* troops; to *exercise* a horse; to *exercise* the limbs, voice, or mind); also, to occupy the attention of; tax the powers of; hence, to perturb or worry (as, to be much *exercised* about one's health); also, to perform or discharge (functions, etc.); do or practice acts of (justice, severity, oppression, etc.); use or display (care, caution, forbearance, etc.) in one's action or procedure. **II.** *intr.* To go through exercises; take bodily exercise.—**ex'er-cis-er** (-sī-zėr), *n.*

ex-er-ci-ta-tion (eg-zėr-si-tā'shọn), *n.* [L. *exercitatio(n-)*, < *exercitare*, exercise diligently, practise, freq. of *exercere*: see *exercise*.] Exercise or exertion, as of faculties or powers; also, practice or training; also, an exercise or performance; also, an exercise, or display of skill; esp., a disquisition or discourse.

ex-ergue (eg-zėrg' or ek'sėrg), *n.* [F., < Gr. ἐξ, out of, + ἔργον, work.] In *numis.*, the small space below the main device on the reverse of a coin or medal; anything inscribed in this space (as, "stamped upon memory in lines as vivid, as deep, and as durable as the *exergues* of the Carthaginian medals": Poe's "William Wilson").—**ex-er-gual** (eg-zėr'gạl or ek-sėr'-), *a.*

ex-ert (eg-zėrt'), *v. t.* [L. *exertus*, pp. of *exerere*, for *exserere*, put forth, < *ex*, out of, + *serere*, join.] To thrust forth†; also, to exhibit† or reveal†; also, to put forth, as power; exercise, as ability or influence; put into vigorous action.—**to exert one's self,** to put forth one's powers; use one's efforts; strive.—**ex-er-tion** (eg-zėr'shọn), *n.* The act of exerting; exercise, as of power or faculties, or an instance of this; esp., vigorous action, or effort; an effort.—**ex-er'tive,** *a.* Having power or tendency to cause exertion.

ex-e-unt (ek'sẹ-unt). [L.] 'They (or the persons named) go out': used in the text of plays, with reference to actors. Cf. *exit*.—**exeunt omnes** (om'nēz). [L.] 'All go out.'

ex-fo-li-ate (eks-fō'li-āt), *v.*; *-ated, -ating.* [LL. *exfoliatus*, pp. of *exfoliare*, < L. *ex-* priv. (see *ex-*) + *folium*, leaf.] **I.** *intr.* To throw off scales; come off in scales; split into scales, or become scaly at the surface, as minerals. **II.** *tr.* To throw off in scales; also, to remove the surface of (a bone, etc.) in scales or laminæ.—**ex-fo-li-a'tion** (-ā'shọn), *n.* The act or process of exfoliating; the state of being exfoliated; also, that which is exfoliated, or scaled off.—**ex-fo'li-a-tive** (-ạ-tiv), *a.* Having power or tendency to cause exfoliation.

ex-hal-a-ble (eks-hā'lạ-bl), *a.* Capable of being exhaled.

ex-hal-ant (eks-hā'lạnt), *a.* Exhaling; emitting.

ex-ha-la-tion (eks-hạ-lā'shọn), *n.* [L. *exhalatio(n-)*.] The act of exhaling; also, that which is exhaled; a vapor; an emanation; an effluvium; also, a body or portion of vapor†; a meteor†.

ex-hale (eks-hāl'), *v.*; *-haled, -haling.* [L. *exhalare*, < *ex*, out of, + *halare*, breathe.] **I.** *tr.* To breathe out; emit (vapor, etc.); also, to give off as vapor; also, to draw out as a vapor or effluence; evaporate. **II.** *intr.* To emit breath or vapor; also, to pass off as vapor (as, "Thy clear fount *Exhales* in mists to heaven": Keats's "Endymion," ii.); pass off as an effluence.—**ex-hale'ment,** *n.*

ex-haust (eg-zâst'), *v.* [L. *exhaustus*, pp. of *exhaurire*, < *ex*, out of, + *haurire*, draw, drain.] **I.** *tr.* To draw out or drain off; draw or drain off completely; hence, to use up or consume completely; expend the whole of; also, to empty by drawing out the contents; specif., to create a vacuum in; also, to deprive of ingredients by the use of solvents, as a drug; also, to deprive wholly of useful or essential properties, as soil; drain of possessions, resources, etc., as a person or a country; drain of strength or energy, wear out, or fatigue greatly, as a person; also, to draw out all that is essential in (a subject, topic, etc.); treat or study thoroughly. **II.** *intr.* To pass out or escape, as spent steam from the cylinder of an engine; also, to discharge contents (as, an engine which *exhausts* directly into the air).—**ex-haust',** *n.* In *engin.*, etc., the act or process of exhausting, as the drawing off of air from a vessel, etc.; the escape of the spent steam or working fluid from the cylinder of an engine after completing its work; also, an exhausting apparatus, as a pump for removing air from a building; also, a passage through which exhausted material, as spent steam, escapes; also, exhausted material, as spent steam.—**ex-haust'ed-ly,** *adv.*—**ex-haust'er,** *n.*—**ex-haust'i-ble,** *a.* That may be exhausted.—**ex-haust'ing-ly,** *adv.*—**ex-haus-tion** (eg-zâs'chọn), *n.* The act or process of exhausting, or the state of being exhausted; esp., extreme weakness or fatigue.—**ex-haus'tive,** *a.* Tending to exhaust or drain, as of resources or strength; also, exhausting a subject, topic, etc.; comprehensive; thorough.—**ex-haus'tive-ly,** *adv.*—**ex-haus'tive-ness,** *n.*—**ex-haust'less,** *a.* Inexhaustible.—**ex-haust'=steam,** *n.* Steam which has performed its work, as that allowed to escape from the cylinder of a steam-engine after it has moved the piston.

ex-he-dra (ek'sẹ-drạ or ek-sē'-), *n.* See *exedra.*

ex-her-e-date (eks-her'ẹ-dāt), *v. t.*; *-dated, -dating.* [L. *exheredatus*, pp. of *exheredare*, < *ex-*, out, + *heres*, heir.] To disinherit.—**ex-her-e-da'tion** (-dā'shọn), *n.*

ex-hib-it (eg-zib'it), *v.* [L. *exhibitus*, pp. of *exhibere*, < *ex-*, out, + *habere*, have, hold.] **I.** *tr.* To hold forth†, offer†, or present†; provide† or furnish†; administer (a remedy, etc.); also, to offer or expose to view; present for inspection; submit (a document, etc.) in evidence in a court of law; present (a petition, charge, etc.) for consideration; set forth or represent in words, figures, etc.; manifest or display (as, to *exhibit* anger); place on show (as, to *exhibit* paintings). **II.** *intr.* To provide maintenance†; also, to make or give an exhibition; present something to public view.—**ex-hib'it,** *n.* An exhibiting or exhibition; also, that which is exhibited; a document or other object exhibited in court and referred to and identified in written evidence; an object or a collection of objects shown in an exhibition, fair, etc.—**ex-hib'it-a-ble,** *a.* That may be exhibited.—**ex-hi-bi-tion** (ek-si-bish'ọn), *n.* [L. *exhibitio(n-).*] Maintenance† or support†; an allowance of money for maintenance†; an allowance given to a student in an English college or university, usually upon the result of a competitive examination; also, administration, as of a remedy; also, an exhibiting, showing, or presenting to view; a show; a display; esp., a public display, as of works of art, manufactures, etc., or of feats of skill, etc.—**ex-hi-bi'tion-al,** *a.*—**ex-hi-bi'tion-er,** *n.* One who provides maintenance†; a student who receives an exhibition or allowance at an English college or university; also, an exhibitor.—**ex-hi-bi'tion-ism,** *n.* The making or giving of exhibitions; specif., in *pathol.*, a form of sexual perversion marked by the practice of making indecent exposure of the person.—**ex-hi-bi'tion-ist,** *n.* One who gives, or takes part in, exhibitions; one characterized by a desire to make an exhibition of himself or his powers, personality, etc.; specif., in *pathol.*, one affected with exhibitionism.—**ex-hi-bi-tion-is'tic,** *a.*—**ex-hib-i-tive** (eg-zib'i-tiv), *a.* Serving for exhibition; tending to exhibit.—**ex-hib'i-tor,** *n.*—**ex-hib'i-to-ry** (-tọ-ri), *a.* Pertaining to or intended for exhibition or display.

ex-hil-a-rant (eg-zil'ạ-rạnt). **I.** *a.* Exhilarating. **II.** *n.* Something that exhilarates.

ex-hil-a-rate (eg-zil'ạ-rāt), *v. t.*; *-rated, -rating.* [L. *exhilaratus*, pp. of *exhilarare*, < *ex-*, utterly, + *hilaris*, cheerful: see *hilarious.*] To make cheerful or merry; cheer; enliven.—**ex-hil'a-rat-ing-ly,** *adv.*—**ex-hil-a-ra'tion** (-rā'shọn), *n.* [LL. *exhilaratio(n-).*] The act of exhilarating; exhilarated condition or feeling.—**ex-hil'a-ra-tive** (-rạ-tiv), **ex-hil'a-ra-to-ry** (-tọ-ri), *a.* Tending to exhilarate.—**ex-hil'a-ra-tor** (-rā-tọr), *n.*

ex-hort (eg-zôrt'), *v.* [L. *exhortari*, < *ex-*, out, + *hortari*, urge.] **I.** *tr.* To urge, advise, or caution (a person, audience, etc.) earnestly, esp. in a formal manner, as to conduct (often with *to* or an infinitive or clause); admonish urgently; also, to recommend (something) earnestly (as, "designing or *exhorting* glorious war": Milton's "Paradise Lost," ii. 179). **II.** *intr.* To make exhortation; give admonition: as, "With many other words did he testify and *exhort*" (Acts, ii. 40).—**ex-hor-ta-tion** (ek-sôr-tā'shọn), *n.* [L. *exhortatio(n-).*] The act or process of exhorting; urgent advice or admonition as to conduct; an utterance, discourse, or formal address conveying urgent advice or recommendations.—**ex-hor-ta-tive** (eg-zôr'tạ-tiv), **ex-hor'ta-to-ry** (-tọ-ri), *a.* Serving or intended to exhort; of or pertaining to exhortation.—**ex-hort'er,** *n.* One who exhorts; specif., a person appointed to deliver religious exhortations.

ex-hume (eks-hūm'), *v. t.*; *-humed, -huming.* [ML. *exhumare*, < L. *ex*, out of, + *humus*, earth, ground.] To dig (something buried, esp. a dead body) out of the earth; disinter.—**ex-hu-ma-tion** (eks-hụ-mā'shọn), *n.*—**ex-hum'er** (-hū'mėr), *n.*

ex-i-geant (eg-zē-zhäṅ), *a.* [F., ppr. of *exiger*, < L. *exigere*: see *exact.*] Exacting.—**ex-i-geante** (-zhäṅt), *a.* Fem. of *exigeant.*

ex-i-gen-cy, ex-i-gence (ek'si-jẹn-si, -jẹns), *n.*; pl. *-gencies* (-jẹn-siz), *-gences* (-jẹn-sez). Exigent state or character; urgency; also, a case or situation which demands prompt action or remedy; an emergency; also, a circumstance or feature of a case, occasion, etc., that renders prompt action necessary; a need, demand, or requirement (now commonly in *pl.*).

ex-i-gent (ek'si-jẹnt), *a.* [L. *exigens* (*-ent-*), ppr. of *exigere*: see *exact.*] Requiring immediate action or aid; urgent; pressing; sometimes, making demand (*of*: as, "But now this body, *exigent* of rest, Will needs put in a claim," Sir H. Taylor's "Philip van Artevelde," ii. 1. 2); also, requiring a great deal, or more than is reasonable; exacting.—**ex'i-gent-ly,** *adv.*

ex-i-gi-ble (ek'si-ji-bl), *a.* [L. *exigere*: see *exact.*] That may be exacted; requirable.

ex-ig-u-ous (eg-zig'ụ-us), *a.* [L. *exiguus*, < *exigere*, measure: see *exact.*] Scanty; small; slender; diminutive.—**ex-i-gu-i-ty** (ek-si-gū'i-ti), **ex-ig'u-ous-ness,** *n.*

ex-ile[1] (ek'sil), *a.* [L. *exilis*; origin uncertain.] Thin; slender; meager; poor; also, fine-spun; overrefined. [Archaic.]

ex-ile[2] (ek'sīl), *n.* [OF. F. *exil*, < L. *exilium, exsilium*, banishment, akin to *exul, exsul*, banished person; perhaps < *ex-*, out, + *salire*, leap.] Expulsion from one's native land by authoritative decree; the fact or state of being banished; banishment; hence, prolonged separation from one's country or home, as by stress of circumstances; also, a person banished from his native land; hence, any one separated from his country or home.—**the Exile,** the Babylonian captivity of the Jews in the 6th century B.C.—**ex'ile**[2]**,** *v. t.*; *-iled, -iling.* [OF. *exilier* (F. *exiler*), < ML. *exiliare*, < L. *exilium.*] To expel or banish (a person) from his country; expatriate; hence, to separate from country, home, etc.—**ex'ile-ment,** *n.*—**ex-il-i-an** (eg-zil'i-ạn or ek-sil'-), **ex-il'ic,** *a.* Pertaining to exile, as that of the Jews in Babylon.

ex-il-i-ty (eg-zil'i-ti), *n.* [See *exile*[1].] Thinness; meagerness; tenuity; subtlety. [Archaic.]

ex-im-i-ous (eg-zim'i-us), *a.* [L. *eximius*, < *eximere*, take out: see *exempt.*] Distinguished; eminent; excellent. [Now rare.]

ex-in-an-i-tion (eg-zin-ạ-nish'on), *n.* [L. *exinanitio(n-)*, < *exinanire*, empty out, < *ex*, out of, + *inanire*: see *inanition.*] A complete emptying; exhaustion or enfeeblement as from being emptied; abasement or humiliation.

ex-ist (eg-zist'), *v. i.* [L. *existere*, for *exsistere*, stand forth, arise, be, < *ex-*, out, + *sistere*, stand.] To have actual being; be; also, to have being in a specified place or under certain conditions; be found; occur; also, to have life or animation; live; also, to continue to be or to live.—**ex-ist'ence,** *n.* The state or fact of existing; being; life; continuance in being or life (as, a struggle for *existence*); also, mode of existing (as, "Other *existences* there are, that clash with ours": M. Arnold's "Empedocles on Etna," i. 2); also, all that exists; also, something that exists, an entity, or a being (as, "all the fair *Existences* of heaven": Keats's "Hyperion," ii.).—**ex-ist'ent. I.** *a.* Existing; having existence; sometimes, esp., now existing; of the present time. **II.** *n.* Something that exists.—**ex-is-ten-tial** (ek-sis-ten'shạl), *a.* Pertaining to existence.—**ex-ist'er,** *n.*

ex-it (ek'sit). [L.] 'He (or she, or the person named) goes out': used in the text of plays, with reference to an actor. Cf. *exeunt.*—**ex'it,** *n.* The departure of a player from the stage; hence, any departure, or any passing out or away; sometimes, death; also, opportunity to pass out; also, a way or passage out; an outlet.

ex li-bris (eks lī'bris). [L., 'from the books.'] From the library (of): a phrase inscribed in or on a book, before the name of the owner.—**ex=li'bris,** *n.*; pl. *-bris.* An inscription or device in or on a book, to indicate the owner; a book-plate.—**ex=li'brism,** *n.* The collecting of book-plates.—**ex=li'brist,** *n.*

exo-, ex-. Forms of Gr. ἔξω, outside, without, used in combination.

ex-o-carp (ek'sọ-kärp), *n.* [See *exo-* and *-carp.*] In *bot.*, the epicarp.

ex-o-dus (ek'sọ-dus), *n.* [LL., < Gr. ἔξοδος, < ἐξ, out of, + ὁδός, way.] A going out; a departure or emigration, usually of a large number of people; [often *cap.*] the departure of the Israelites from Egypt under Moses; [*cap.*] the second book of the Old Testament, containing an account of this departure.

ex of-fi-ci-o (eks o̤-fish′i-ō). [L., 'from office.'] By virtue of office or official position: a phrase also used adjectively (as, *ex officio* authority).

ex-og-a-mous (ek-sog′a̤-mus), *a.* [See *exo-* and *-gamous.*] Marrying customarily outside of the tribe; pertaining to such marriage: opposed to *endogamous.*—**ex-og′a-my,** *n.*

ex-o-gen (ek′sō̤-jen), *n.* [F. *exogène*: see *exo-* and *-gen.*] In *bot.*, any plant of the obsolete class *Exogenæ*, including the dicotyledons, whose stems grow by successive concentric layers on the outside: opposed to *endogen.*—**ex-og-e-nous** (ek-soj′e-nus), *a.* Growing by additions on the outside; in *bot.*, belonging to the exogens; of plants, as the dicotyledons, having stems which grow by the addition of an annual layer of wood to the outside beneath the constantly widening bark; pertaining to plants having such stems.—**ex-og′e-nous-ly,** *adv.*

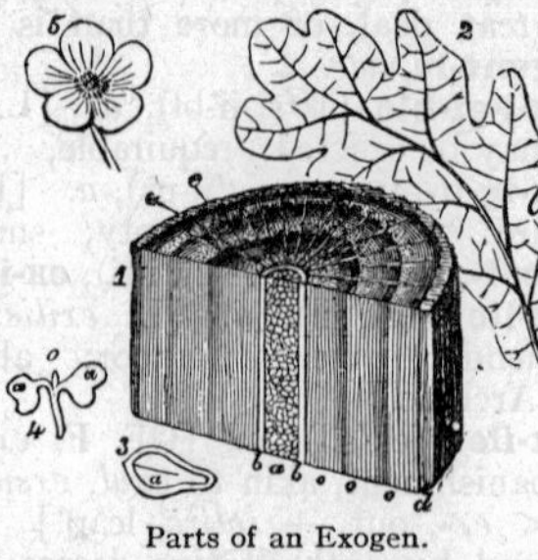

Parts of an Exogen.

1. Section of a branch of three years' growth: *a*, medulla or pith; *b*, *b*, medullary sheath; *e*, *e*, medullary rays; *c*, *c*, *c*, circles of annual growth; *d*, bark. 2. Netted veined leaf (oak). 3. Dicotyledonous seed: *a*, cotyledon. 4. Germination of dicotyledonous seed: *a*, *a*, seed-leaves or cotyledons; *o*, plumule. 5. Exogenous flower (crowfoot).

ex-on (ek′so̤n), *n.* [Earlier *exant*, for *exempt*: cf. F. *exempt*, subordinate officer (exempt from ordinary service).] In England, each of four officers (orig. corporals) of the yeomen of the royal bodyguard who in turn command in the absence of their superior officers.

ex-on-er-ate (eg-zon′e̤-rāt), *v. t.*; *-ated*, *-ating.* [L. *exoneratus*, pp. of *exonerare*, < *ex-* priv. (see *ex-*) + *onus* (*oner-*), burden.] To remove a burden from (obs. or rare); fig., to relieve, as from an obligation, duty, or task; now, usually, to clear, as of a charge; free from blame; exculpate.—**ex-on-er-a′tion** (-e̤-rā′sho̤n), *n.* [LL. *exoneratio*(*n*-).] The act of exonerating, or the state of being exonerated.—**ex-on′er-a-tive** (-e̤-ra̤-tiv), *a.*—**ex-on′er-a-tor** (-e̤-rā-to̤r), *n.*

ex-o-path-ic (ek-sō̤-path′ik), *a.* [Gr. ἔξω, outside, + παθεῖν, suffer.] In *pathol.*, pertaining to or resulting from pathogenic factors external to the organism, as a disease.

ex-oph-thal-mi-a (ek-sof-thal′mi-ä̤), *n.* [NL., < Gr. ἐξόφθαλμος, with prominent eyes, < ἐξ-, out, + ὀφθαλμός, eye.] In *pathol.*, protrusion of the eyeball from the orbit, caused by disease.—**ex-oph-thal′mic,** *a.*

ex-o-ra-ble (ek′sō̤-ra̤-bl), *a.* [L. *exorabilis*, < *exorare*, persuade by entreaty, < *ex-*, out, + *orare*, pray.] Susceptible of being persuaded or moved by entreaty. Cf. *inexorable.*—**ex″o-ra-bil′i-ty** (-bil′i-ti), *n.*

ex-or-bi-tant (eg-zôr′bi-ta̤nt), *a.* [LL. *exorbitans* (*-ant-*), ppr. of *exorbitare*, go out of the track, < L. *ex*, out of, + *orbita*, track, E. *orbit.*] Deviating from the right or usual path, course, or rule†; hence, exceeding the bounds of custom, propriety, or reason, esp. in amount or extent; in *law*, being outside of the intended scope of the law; anomalous.—**ex-or′bi-tance, ex-or′bi-tan-cy,** *n.*—**ex-or′bi-tant-ly,** *adv.*

ex-or-cise (ek′sôr-sīz), *v. t.*; *-cised*, *-cising.* [LL. *exorcizare*, < Gr. ἐξορκίζειν, < ἐξ, out of, + ὁρκίζειν, adjure, < ὅρκος, oath.] To seek to expel (an evil spirit) by adjuration or religious or solemn ceremonies; expel by or as by such means (as, "I . . . wandered up and down, like an *exorcised* spirit that had been driven from its old haunts": Hawthorne's "Blithedale Romance," xxiii.); also, to seek to deliver, or deliver, thus from evil spirits or malignant influences; also, to adjure, conjure, or conjure up (a spirit).—**ex′or-cise-ment,** *n.* The act of exorcising; exorcism.—**ex′or-cis-er** (-sī-zėr), *n.*—**ex′or-cism** (-sizm), *n.* [LL. *exorcismus*, < Gr. ἐξορκισμός.] The act or process of exorcising; the ceremony or the formula used.—**ex′or-cist,** *n.* [LL. *exorcista*, < Gr. ἐξορκιστής.] One who exorcises; in the *Rom. Cath. Ch.*, a member of the second of the minor orders, next below that of acolyte.—**ex-or-cis′tic,** *a.*

ex′or-cize, etc. See *exorcise*, etc.

ex-or-di-um (eg-zôr′di-um), *n.*; pl. *-diums* or *-dia* (-di-ä̤). [L., < *exordiri*, lay a warp, < *ex-*, out, + *ordiri*, begin to weave.] The beginning of anything; esp., the introductory part of a discourse, treatise, etc.—**ex-or′di-al,** *a.*

ex-o-skel-e-ton (ek-sō̤-skel′e̤-to̤n), *n.* [See *exo-.*] In *anat.*, an external protective covering or integument, esp. when hard, as the shell of crustaceans, the carapace of turtles, the scales and plates of fishes, etc.: opposed to *endoskeleton.* See cut at *endoskeleton.*

ex-os-mo-sis, ex-os-mose (ek-sos-mō′sis or ek-soz-, ek′sos-mōs or ek′soz-), *n.* [See *exo-.*] Osmosis from within outward; in the phenomena of osmosis, the action or flow of that fluid which passes with the lesser rapidity into the other: opposed to *endosmosis.*—**ex-os-mot′ic** (-mot′ik), *a.*

ex-os-to-sis (ek-sos-tō′sis), *n.*; pl. *-toses* (-tō′sēz). [NL., < Gr. ἐξόστωσις, < ἐξ, out of, + ὀστέον, bone.] In *pathol.*, the morbid formation of bone, or a morbid bony growth, on a bone.

ex-o-ter-ic (ek-sō̤-ter′ik). [L. *exotericus*, < Gr. ἐξωτερικός, < ἐξωτέρω, compar. of ἔξω, outside: see *exotic.*] **I.** *a.* Pertaining to the outside; external; also, not belonging or pertaining to the inner or select circle, as of disciples; communicated to or suitable for the general body of disciples or the general public, as a doctrine; hence, popular; simple; commonplace. Cf. *esoteric.* **II.** *n.* An exoteric doctrine (usually in *pl.*); also, an uninitiated person; an outsider.—**ex-o-ter′i-cal,** *a.* Exoteric.—**ex-o-ter′i-cal-ly,** *adv.*

ex-o-the-ci-um (ek-sō̤-thē′shi-um), *n.*; pl. *-cia* (-shi-ä̤). [NL., < Gr. ἔξω, outside, + θήκη, case.] In *bot.*, the outer covering of an anther.

ex-o-ther-mic (ek-sō̤-thėr′mik), *a.* [Gr. ἔξω, outside, + θέρμη, heat.] Noting or pertaining to a chemical change which is accompanied by a liberation of heat: opposed to *endothermic.*

ex-ot-ic (eg-zot′ik). [L. *exoticus*, < Gr. ἐξωτικός, < ἔξω, outside, < ἐξ, ἐκ, out of.] **I.** *a.* Of foreign origin or character; not native; introduced from abroad, but not fully naturalized or acclimatized. **II.** *n.* Anything exotic, as a plant.—**ex-ot′i-cal-ly,** *adv.*—**ex-ot′i-cism** (-sizm), *n.* Tendency to adopt what is exotic; also, exotic quality or character; anything exotic, as a foreign word or idiom.—**ex-ot′i-cist,** *n.*

ex-pand (eks-pand′), *v.* [L. *expandere* (pp. *expansus*), < *ex-*, out, + *pandere*, spread, extend.] **I.** *tr.* To spread out, or unfold (as, "*Expand* thy sails . . . and catch the nimble gales": Pope's tr. Homer's "Odyssey," xii.); spread out to view, or display (as, a great stretch of country lay *expanded* below him); also, to express in fuller form or greater detail; develop, as a statement; also, to increase in extent, size, volume, etc.; dilate; distend; enlarge; make broader in scope, or more comprehensive. **II.** *intr.* To spread out; unfold; develop; also, to increase in extent, bulk, etc.; become dilated or enlarged; increase in scope.—**ex-pand′ed,** *p. a.* Spread out; extended; also, increased in area, bulk, or volume; enlarged.—**expanded type,** a kind of type somewhat wider than is usual for its height. See *type.*—**ex-pand′er,** *n.*—**ex-pand′ing-ly,** *adv.*

ex-panse (eks-pans′), *n.* [L. *expansum*, neut. of *expansus*, pp. of *expandere*: see *expand.*] That which is expanded; an uninterrupted space or area, esp. one of considerable extent; a wide extent of anything; also, expansion or extension.

ex-pan-si-ble (eks-pan′si-bl), *a.* [Cf. F. *expansible.*] Capable of being expanded.

ex-pan-sile (eks-pan′sil), *a.* Capable of expanding; such as to expand; pertaining to expansion.

ex-pan-sion (eks-pan′sho̤n), *n.* [LL. *expansio*(*n*-).] The act of expanding, or the state of being expanded; spreading out; increase in size, volume, etc.; dilatation; distention; enlargement; also, the amount or degree of expanding; also, anything spread out; an expanse; also, an expanded, dilated, or enlarged portion or form of a thing; in *math.*, the development at length of an expression indicated in a contracted form.—**ex-pan′sion-ism,** *n.* A policy of expansion, as of territory or currency.—**ex-pan′sion-ist,** *n.*

ex-pan-sive (eks-pan′siv), *a.* Tending to cause expansion (as, the *expansive* force of heat); tending to expand, or capable of expanding (as, "No more The *expansive* atmosphere is cramped with cold": Thomson's "Seasons," Spring, 28); pertaining to or characterized by expansion; fig., effusive, as persons, feelings, or utterance; also, expanding over a large area; extensive; having a wide range; comprehensive.—**ex-pan'sive-ly,** *adv.*—**ex-pan'sive-ness,** *n.*

ex par-te (eks pär'tē). [L., 'from a part.'] From or on one side only, as in a controversy or suit; in the interest of one party: a phrase also used adjectively (as, *ex-parte* testimony).

ex-pa-ti-ate (eks-pā'shi-āt), *v.*; *-ated, -ating.* [L. *expatiatus,* pp. of *expatiari,* for *exspatiari,* < *ex-,* out, + *spatiari,* walk about, < *spatium,* E. *space.*] **I.** *intr.* To move or wander about without restraint; also, to enlarge in discourse or writing (as, "With some forbearance . . . the beauty of the prospect was not *expatiated* upon by the obsequious landlord": Marryat's "King's Own," ix.); be copious in description or discussion. **II.** *tr.* To expand; develop. [Obs. or rare.]—**ex-pa-ti-a'tion** (-ā'shọn), *n.*—**ex-pa'ti-a-tor,** *n.*

ex-pa-tri-ate (eks-pā'tri-āt), *v. t.*; *-ated, -ating.* [ML. *expatriatus,* pp. of *expatriare,* < L. *ex,* out of, + *patria,* fatherland: see *patrial.*] To banish (a person) from his native country; also, to withdraw (one's self) from residence in one's native country; esp., to withdraw (one's self) from citizenship in one country to become a citizen of another.—**ex-pa'tri-ate. I.** *a.* Expatriated. **II.** *n.* An expatriated person.—**ex-pa-tri-a'tion** (-ā'shọn), *n.*

ex-pect (eks-pekt'), *v.* [L. *expectare,* for *exspectare,* < *ex-,* out, + *spectare,* look at or to: see *spectacle.*] **I.** *tr.* To await† or wait for†; also, to look forward to in thought; regard as likely to happen; anticipate the occurrence or the coming of; sometimes, to look for with reason or justification (as, we cannot be *expected* to submit to such treatment); count upon as due or right (as, to do more than is *expected* of one); require expectantly (as, to *expect* obedience); also, to suppose or surmise (colloq.). **II.**† *intr.* To wait.—**ex-pect'ance, ex-pect'an-cy,** *n.*; pl. *-ances* (-ạn-sez), *-ancies* (-ạn-siz). The act or state of expecting, or the state of being expected; expectation; also, an object of expectation; something expected.—**ex-pect'ant. I.** *a.* Expecting; having expectations; also, characterized by expectation; also, expected or anticipated. **II.** *n.* One who expects; one who waits in expectation.—**ex-pect'ant-ly,** *adv.*—**ex-pec-ta'tion** (-pek-tā'shọn), *n.* [L. *expectatio(n-).*] The act or state of expecting, or the state of being expected (as, to wait in *expectation*; a sum of money in *expectation*); anticipation; a preconceived idea about what will take place; expectant mental attitude; also, ground for expecting something; a prospect of future good or profit (as, "I have a dev'lish rich uncle . . . from whom I have the greatest *expectations*": Sheridan's "School for Scandal," iii. 3); also, something expected; a thing looked forward to; also, the degree of probability of the occurrence of something or of the receiving of something.—**expectation of life,** the duration of life which may be expected by persons who have reached a particular age, being the average age at which persons who have lived beyond it have died, as shown by mortality tables.—**ex-pec'ta-tive** (-tạ-tiv), *a.* Of or pertaining to expectation; characterized by expectation.—**ex-pect'er,** *n.*—**ex-pect'ing-ly,** *adv.*

ex-pec-to-rant (eks-pek'tọ-rạnt). **I.** *a.* Promoting expectoration. **II.** *n.* An expectorant medicine.

ex-pec-to-rate (eks-pek'tọ-rāt), *v.*; *-rated, -rating.* [L. *expectoratus,* pp. of *expectorare,* < *ex,* out of, + *pectus* (*pector-*), breast.] **I.** *tr.* To eject or expel (phlegm, etc.) from the throat or lungs by coughing or hawking and spitting; spit. **II.** *intr.* To spit.—**ex-pec-to-ra'tion** (-rā'shọn), *n.* The act of expectorating; the ejection of phlegm or mucus from the throat or lungs by coughing, etc.—**ex-pec'to-ra-tor,** *n.*

ex-pe-di-ence (eks-pē'di-ẹns), *n.* [ML. *expedientia,* < L. *expediens*: see *expedient.*] The quality of being expedient; expediency; also, expedition† or despatch† (as, "The French . . . will with all *expedience* charge on us": Shakspere's "Henry V.," iv. 3. 70); an expedition† or enterprise† (as, "I shall break The cause of our *expedience* to the queen, And get her leave to part": Shakspere's "Antony and Cleopatra," i. 2. 185).—**ex-pe'di-en-cy** (-ẹn-si), *n.*; pl. *-cies* (-siz). The quality of being expedient; advantageousness; advisability; also, regard for what is expedient; prudential wisdom; policy; also, something expedient.

ex-pe-di-ent (eks-pē'di-ẹnt). [L. *expediens* (*-ent-*), ppr. of *expedire*: see *expedite.*] **I.** *a.* Conducive to some end or result (as, measures *expedient* for the public welfare); advantageous or advisable under the circumstances (as, "All things are lawful unto me, but all things are not *expedient*": 1 Cor. vi. 12); sometimes, conducive to advantage or interest, as opposed to *right* (as, "too fond of the right to pursue the *expedient*": Goldsmith's "Retaliation," 40); of persons, acting in accordance with expediency; also, expeditious† (as, "*Expedient* manage must be made": Shakspere's "Richard II.," i. 4. 39). **II.** *n.* A means to an end; a means devised or employed in an exigency; a resource; a shift.

ex-pe-di-en-tial (eks-pē-di-en'shạl), *a.* Pertaining to or regulated by expediency.—**ex-pe-di-en'tial-ly,** *adv.*

ex-pe-di-ent-ly (eks-pē'di-ẹnt-li), *adv.* In an expedient manner; as may be expedient.

ex-pe-dite (eks'pẹ-dīt), *v. t.*; *-dited, -diting.* [L. *expeditus,* pp. of *expedire,* extricate, help forward, send off or despatch, orig. 'free the feet of,' < *ex,* out of, + *pes* (*ped-*), foot: cf. *impede.*] To facilitate the motion or progress of; hasten; also, to accomplish promptly, as a piece of business; despatch; also, to issue officially, as a document.—**ex'pe-dit-er** (-dī-tėr), *n.*—**ex-pe-di'tion** (-dish'ọn), *n.* [L. *expeditio(n-).*] The act of expediting†; promptness or speed in accomplishing something; despatch; haste; also, an excursion, journey, or voyage made for some specific purpose, as of war or exploration; the body of persons or ships, etc., engaged in it.—**ex-pe-di'tion-a-ry** (-ā-ri), *a.* Pertaining to or composing an expedition: as, an *expeditionary* force.—**ex-pe-di'tious** (-dish'us), *a.* Characterized by expedition or prompt despatch; quick.—**ex-pe-di'tious-ly,** *adv.*—**ex-pe-di'tious-ness,** *n.*

ex-pel (eks-pel'), *v. t.*; *-pelled, -pelling.* [L. *expellere* (pp. *expulsus*), < *ex,* out of, + *pellere,* drive.] To drive or force out or away; discharge or eject (as, to *expel* air from the lungs); compel to depart from a place (as, to *expel* a traitor or an invader from a country); also, to cut off from membership or relations (as, to *expel* a member from a club; to *expel* a student from a college).—**ex-pel'la-ble,** *a.* That may be expelled.—**ex-pel'lent, ex-pel'lant. I.** *a.* Expelling; serving to expel. **II.** *n.* An expellent medicine.—**ex-pel'ler,** *n.*

ex-pend (eks-pend'), *v. t.* [L. *expendere* (pp. *expensus*), weigh out, pay out, < *ex-,* out, + *pendere,* weigh.] To pay out; disburse; spend; also, to consume by use; use up.—**ex-pend'a-ble,** *a.* That may be expended.—**ex-pend'er,** *n.*—**ex-pen'di-ture** (-pen'di-ţūr), *n.* The act of expending; disbursement; consumption; also, that which is expended; expense.

ex-pense (eks-pens'), *n.* [ML. *expensa,* prop. fem. of L. *expensus,* pp.: see *expend.*] The act of expending; expenditure; occasionally, undue expenditure; extravagance; also, that which is expended; an outlay, esp. of money; also, cost or charge; loss or injury due to any detracting cause (preceded by *at*: as, quantity at the *expense* of quality); *pl.,* charges incurred by a person in the execution of an undertaking or commission; also, money paid to a person to reimburse him for such charges (as, to receive a salary and *expenses*); *sing.,* a cause or occasion of expenditure.—**ex-pen'sive** (-pen'siv), *a.* Entailing great expense; costly.—**ex-pen'sive-ly,** *adv.*—**ex-pen'sive-ness,** *n.*

ex-pe-ri-ence (eks-pē'ri-ẹns), *n.* [OF. *experience* (F. *expérience*), < L. *experientia,* < *experiens* (*-ent-*), ppr. of *experiri* (pp. *expertus*), try, undergo, < *ex-,* out, + *per-,* occurring also in *peritus,* experienced, skilled: see *fare.*] Trial† or testing†; an experiment†; proof derived from trial†; also, the process or fact of personally observing, encountering, or undergoing something (as, to have had *experience* of a person's ways, or of the business world; long *experience* in teaching or with pupils); a particular instance of personally encountering or undergoing something (as, to have a strange *experience*); sometimes, a process of feeling forming a part of one's spiritual or religious life; also, the observing, encountering, or undergoing of things generally as they occur in the course of time (as, to learn wisdom from *experience*; things beyond the range of human *experience*); also, knowledge or practical wisdom gained from what one has observed, encountered, or undergone (as, men of ripe *experience*).—**ex-pe′ri-ence,** *v. t.*; *-enced, -encing.* To test† or try†; also, to have experience of; meet with; undergo; feel; sometimes, to learn by experience; also, to give experience to, or teach by experience (now chiefly or only in *pp.*).—**to experience religion,** to become converted to religion: as, "He promised his mother, if she would not whip him, he would *experience religion*" (Longfellow's "Kavanagh," xii.). [Colloq., U. S.]—**ex-pe′ri-enced,** *p. a.* Taught by or having experience; wise or skilful through experience. —**ex-pe′ri-ence-less,** *a.* Without experience.—**ex-pe′ri-en-cer,** *n.*—**ex-pe-ri-en′tial** (-en′shạl), *a.* Pertaining to or derived from experience.—**ex-pe-ri-en′tial-ly,** *adv.*

ex-per-i-ment (eks-per′i-mẹnt), *n.* [OF. *experiment*, < L. *experimentum*, < *experiri*, try: see *experience*.] A test or trial; a tentative procedure; an act or operation for the purpose of discovering something unknown or testing a principle, supposition, etc.; also, the conducting of such operations; experimentation; also, experience†.—**experiment station,** an establishment in which experiments in a particular line of research or activity, as agriculture or mining, are systematically carried on.—**ex-per′i-ment** (-ment), *v. i.* To make experiment or experiments.—**ex-per-i-men′tal** (-men′tạl), *a.* Pertaining to, derived from, or founded on experiment (as, *experimental* philosophy); also, of the nature of an experiment; tentative; also, based on or derived from experience (as, *experimental* religion); empirical.—**ex-per-i-men′tal-ist,** *n.* One who makes experiments.—**ex-per-i-men′tal-ize,** *v. i.*; *-ized, -izing.* To make experiments: as, "hired . . . to go into fits and be *experimentalised* upon . . . or to do something or other to promote the great science of medicine" (Dickens's "Pickwick Papers," xlviii.).—**ex-per-i-men′tal-ly,** *adv.*—**ex-per″i-men-ta′tion** (-tā′shọn), *n.* The act or practice of experimenting.—**ex-per′i-ment-er,** *n.*

ex-pert (eks-pėrt′), *a.* [OF. F. *expert*, < L. *expertus*, pp. of *experiri*, try: see *experience*.] Taught or trained by experience; practised; skilful; skilled; also, of or pertaining to an expert (as, *expert* testimony).—**ex′pert,** *n.* One who is expert; an authority; a specialist.—**ex-pert′ly,** *adv.*—**ex-pert′ness,** *n.*

ex-pi-a-ble (eks′pi-ạ-bl), *a.* That may be expiated.

ex-pi-ate (eks′pi-āt), *v. t.*; *-ated, -ating.* [L. *expiatus*, pp. of *expiare*, < *ex-*, out, + *piare*, appease, atone for, < *pius*, devout, E. *pious*.] To atone for; make amends or reparation for; also, to purge from guilt or moral stain†; also, to avert (evil)†.—**ex-pi-a′tion** (-ā′shọn), *n.* [L. *expiatio(n-)*.] The act of expiating, or the state of being expiated; also, the means by which atonement or reparation is made.—**ex′pi-a-tor,** *n.*—**ex′pi-a-to-ry** (-ạ-tō-ri), *a.* Serving to expiate.

ex-pi-ra-tion (eks-pi-rā′shọn), *n.* [L. *expiratio(n-)*.] The act of expiring, or breathing out; emission of air from the lungs; also, the last emission of breath, or death (obs. or rare); also, a coming to an end; termination; close.—**ex-pir′a-to-ry** (-pīr′ạ-tō-ri), *a.* Pertaining to the expiration of air from the lungs.

ex-pire (eks-pīr′), *v.*; *-pired, -piring.* [L. *expirare*, for *exspirare*, < *ex-*, out, + *spirare*, breathe.] **I.** *tr.* To breathe out; emit (air) from the lungs; also, to give off†, emit†, or eject†; also, to bring to an end†. **II.** *intr.* To emit the breath; also, to emit the last breath; die; hence, to die out, as a fire; also, to come to an end; terminate; also, to be breathed out†; rush forth†.—**ex-pir-ee′** (-pī-rē′), *n.* A convicted person whose term of punishment has expired. [Australia, etc.]—**ex-pir′er,** *n.*—**ex-pi-ry** (eks-pī′ri or eks′pi-), *n.* Expiration.

ex-plain (eks-plān′), *v. t.* [L. *explanare* (pp. *explanatus*), flatten out, make plain, explain, < *ex-*, out, + *planus*, flat, E. *plain*².] To spread out flat†; unfold†; also, to make plain; make clear to the mind; render intelligible; also, to assign a meaning to; interpret; also, to make clear the cause or reason of; account for.—**to explain away,** to dispel (difficulties, etc.) by explanation; nullify the significance, or the apparent significance, of (words, facts, occurrences, etc.) by explanation.—**ex-plain′,** *v. i.* To give an explanation.—**ex-plain′a-ble,** *a.* That may be explained. —**ex-plain′er,** *n.*

ex-pla-na-tion (eks-plạ-nā′shọn), *n.* [L. *explanatio(n-)*.] The act or process of explaining; elucidation; interpretation; also, that which explains, or is adduced as explaining; also, a mutual declaration of the meaning of words spoken, actions, motives, etc., with a view to adjust a misunderstanding or reconcile differences; a reconciliation.—**ex-plan′a-to-ry** (-plan′ạ-tō-ri), **ex-plan′a-tive** (-tiv), *a.* Serving to explain.—**ex-plan′a-to-ri-ly,** *adv.*

ex-ple-tive (eks′plẹ-tiv). [LL. *expletivus*, < L. *explere* (pp. *expletus*), fill out, < *ex-*, out, + *plere*, fill.] **I.** *a.* Serving to fill out; of words, etc., added merely to fill out a sentence or line, give emphasis, etc. **II.** *n.* Something that fills out; esp., an expletive syllable, word, or phrase; often, an interjectory word or expression, frequently profane, used for emphasis, etc. (as, " 'What do you mean?' asked Lancelot, with a strong *expletive*": Kingsley's "Yeast," x.); an exclamatory oath.—**ex′ple-tive-ly,** *adv.*

ex-ple-to-ry (eks′plẹ-tō-ri), *a.* Expletive.

ex-pli-ca-ble (eks′pli-kạ-bl), *a.* [L. *explicabilis*.] Capable of being explicated or explained.

ex-pli-cate (eks′pli-kāt), *v. t.*; *-cated, -cating.* [L. *explicatus*, pp. of *explicare*, unfold, display, set forth, < *ex-*, out, + *plicare*, fold.] To unfold† or unroll†; also, to develop (a principle, etc.); also, to make plain; make clear the meaning of; free of difficulties or obscurities; explain; interpret. —**ex-pli-ca′tion** (-kā′shọn), *n.* [L. *explicatio(n-)*.] The act of explicating; an explanation; an interpretation.—**ex′pli-ca-tive** (-kạ-tiv), **ex′pli-ca-to-ry** (-tō-ri), *a.* Serving to explicate; explanatory; interpretative.

ex-pli-cit (eks-plis′it), *a.* [L. *explicitus*, var. of *explicatus*, pp. of *explicare*: see *explicate*.] Free from folds or wrinkles†; smooth†; also, clearly developed or formulated, as knowledge or belief; of statements, etc., clearly expressed; leaving nothing merely implied; express; unequivocal; of persons, definite and unreserved in expression; outspoken. —**ex-pli′cit-ly,** *adv.*—**ex-pli′cit-ness,** *n.*

ex-plode (eks-plōd′), *v.*; *-ploded, -ploding.* [L. *explodere* (pp. *explosus*), < *ex*, out of, from, + *plodere*, *plaudere*, clap: cf. *applaud*.] **I.** *tr.* To drive (a player, play, etc.) from the stage by loud expressions of disapprobation†; also, to reject or discard (an opinion, custom, etc.: now only in the passive); cause to be rejected, destroy the repute of, discredit, or disprove; also, to drive forth violently†; also, to cause (gunpowder, etc., or a boiler, etc.) to explode (also fig.). **II.** *intr.* To expand with force and noise because of rapid chemical change or decomposition, as gunpowder, nitroglycerin, etc.; also, to burst, fly into pieces, or break up violently with a loud report, as a boiler from excessive pressure of steam; hence, in general, to burst forth violently, esp. with noise; often, to burst forth into laughter, violent speech, etc.—**ex-plod′ent** (-plō′dẹnt), *n.* In *phonetics*, an explosive.—**ex-plod′er,** *n.*

ex-ploit (eks′ploit or eks-ploit′), *n.* [OF. *esploit* (F. *exploit*), < L. *explicitum*, neut. of *explicitus*, pp. of *explicare*, unfold, display: see *explicit* and *explicate*.] A deed of striking or notable character; a feat; an achievement; a spirited or heroic act.—**ex-ploit′,** *v. t.* [OF. *esploitier* (F. *exploiter*).] To achieve†; perform†; also, to turn to practical account; utilize for profit; work (a mine, etc.); use (persons, etc.) selfishly for one's own ends.—**ex-ploit′a-ble,** *a.* That may be exploited.—**ex-ploit′age** (-āj), *n.* Exploitation.—**ex-ploi-ta′tion** (-ploi-tā′shọn), *n.* [F.] The act or process of exploiting; utilization for profit; selfish utilization.—**ex-ploi′ta-tive** (-tạ-tiv), *a.* Concerned with or pertaining to exploitation.—**ex-ploit′er,** *n.*

ex-plor-a-ble (eks-plōr′ạ-bl), *a.* That may be explored.

ex-plo-ra-tion (eks-plọ-rā′shọn), *n.* [L. *exploratio(n-)*.] The act of exploring; the investigation of unknown regions. —**ex-plor′a-tive** (-plōr′ạ-tiv), **ex-plor′a-to-ry** (-tō-ri), *a.* Pertaining to or concerned with exploration; inclined to make explorations.

ex-plore (eks-plōr′), *v.*; *-plored, -ploring.* [L. *explorare*, search out, seek to discover, investigate, appar. < *ex-*, out, + *plorare*, cry out, wail.] **I.** *tr.* To search for†; search out†; also, to seek to ascertain or learn (as, "Let some prophet . . . *Explore* the cause of great Apollo's rage": Pope's tr. Homer's "Iliad," i.); also, to look into closely; scrutinize; examine; esp., to traverse or range over (a region, etc.) for the purpose of discovery. **II.** *intr.* To engage in exploration.—**ex-plor′er,** *n.* One who or that which explores; esp., one who investigates unknown regions. —**ex-plor′ing-ly,** *adv.*

ex-plo-si-ble (eks-plō′zi-bl), *a.* Capable of being exploded; liable to explode.—**ex-plo-si-bil′i-ty** (-bil′i-ti), *n.*

ex-plo-sion (eks-plō′zhọn), *n.* [L. *explosio(n-)*, < *explodere*: see *explode.*] The act of exploding; a violent expansion or bursting with noise, as of gunpowder or a boiler; the noise itself; any violent bursting forth; a violent outburst of laughter, anger, etc.

ex-plo-sive (eks-plō′siv). [L. *explodere* (pp. *explosus*), E. *explode.*] **I.** *a.* Tending or serving to explode; pertaining to or of the nature of an explosion; in *phonetics*, involving a slight explosion of the breath in pronunciation, as the consonants *p*, *b*, *t*, *d*, etc. **II.** *n.* An explosive agent or substance, as gunpowder; in *phonetics*, an explosive consonant.—**explosive D.** See *dunnite.*—**ex-plo′sive-ly,** *adv.* —**ex-plo′sive-ness,** *n.*

ex-po-nent (eks-pō′nẹnt). [L. *exponens* (*-ent-*), ppr. of *exponere*: see *expound.*] **I.** *a.* Expounding; explaining. **II.** *n.* One who expounds or explains; that which serves to explain or interpret; also, one who or that which stands as a representative, type, or symbol of something; in *alg.*, a symbol placed above and at the right of another symbol to denote to what power the latter is to be raised.—**ex-po-nen′tial** (-pọ-nen′shạl), *a.* Of or pertaining to an exponent or exponents; involving unknown or variable quantities as exponents.

ex-port (eks-pōrt′), *v. t.* [L. *exportare*, < *ex*, out of, from, + *portare*, carry.] To carry or take away†; specif., to send (commodities) to other countries or places for sale or exchange.—**ex′port,** *n.* The act of exporting; exportation; also, that which is exported; an article exported.—**ex-port′a-ble,** *a.* That may be exported.—**ex-por-ta′tion** (-pọr-tā′shọn), *n.* [L. *exportatio(n-)*.] The act of exporting; the sending of commodities out of a country in trade; also, something exported.—**ex-port′er,** *n.*

ex-po-sal (eks-pō′zạl), *n.* Exposure; exposition.

ex-pose (eks-pōz′), *v. t.*; *-posed*, *-posing.* [OF. F. *exposer*, < *ex-* (< L. *ex-*), out, + *poser*, put (see *pose*[1]), but associated with derivatives of L. *exponere*: see *expound.*] To put out† or expel†; put out into an unsheltered or open place, as a child abandoned to the mercy of chance; uncover or bare to the air, cold, etc., as the neck or chest; lay open to danger, attack, harm, etc. (as, to *expose* one's self in battle); often, to lay open to something specified (as, to *expose* one's self to danger, contagion, attack, ridicule, or misunderstanding); subject, as to the action of something (as, to *expose* a sensitized photographic plate to the action of the actinic rays of light); also, to present to view, exhibit, or display (as, "the beggar who *exposes* his sores": Steele, in "Spectator," 280); show or offer publicly for sale, as goods; make known, disclose, or reveal, as intentions, secrets, etc.; unmask (crime, fraud, an impostor, etc.); hold up to public reprehension or ridicule (fault, folly, a fool, etc.).—**ex-po-sé** (eks-pọ-zā′), *n.* [F., orig. pp. of *exposer.*] A statement or recital, as of facts; an exposition; also, an exposure, as of something discreditable.—**ex-posed′,** *p. a.* Left or being without shelter or protection; also, laid open to view; unconcealed.—**ex-pos′ed-ness** (-pō′zed-nes), *n.*—**ex-pos′er,** *n.*

ex-po-si-tion (eks-pọ-zish′ọn), *n.* [OF. F. *exposition*, < L. *expositio(n-)*, < *exponere*, put out, expose, set forth, explain: see *expound.*] The act of putting out or abandoning in an unsheltered place (as, the *exposition* of children); also, the act of presenting to view; display; a public exhibition; also, the act of expounding, setting forth, or explaining; a detailed statement or explanation; an explanatory treatise; in the *Rom. Cath. Ch.*, the public exhibition of the eucharist, or consecrated bread, in a monstrance, for the adoration of the faithful.—**ex-pos′i-tive** (-poz′i-tiv), *a.* Expository.—**ex-pos′i-tor,** *n.* [LL.] One who expounds, or gives an exposition: as, "a period when the national mind . . . would seek in him a powerful *expositor* of its convictions" (Disraeli's "Coningsby," ii. 4).—**ex-pos′i-to-ry** (-tọ-ri), *a.* Serving to expound, set forth, or explain; explanatory.—**ex-pos′i-tress,** *n.* A female expositor.

ex post fac-to (eks pōst fak′tō). [For LL. *ex postfacto*, 'from what is done afterward.'] From or by subsequent action; subsequently; retrospectively: a phrase often used adjectively (as, an *ex post facto* law, one made after an offense but operative with respect to it).

ex-pos-tu-late (eks-pos′ţū-lāt), *v.*; *-lated*, *-lating.* [L. *expostulatus*, pp. of *expostulare*, demand urgently, complain, expostulate, < *ex-*, out, + *postulare*, demand, E. *postulate.*] **I.**† *tr.* To ask for or demand; also, to complain of; remonstrate about; also, to argue or debate. **II.** *intr.* To reason earnestly with a person against something he intends to do or has done; remonstrate.—**ex-pos′tu-lat-ing-ly,** *adv.* —**ex-pos-tu-la′tion** (-lā′shọn), *n.* [L. *expostulatio(n-)*.] The act of expostulating; remonstrance; an earnest and kindly protest; an expostulatory remark or address.—**ex-pos′tu-la-tive** (-lạ-tiv), *a.* Expostulating; expostulatory.—**ex-pos′tu-la-tor** (-lā-tọr), *n.*—**ex-pos′tu-la-to-ry** (-lạ-tọ-ri), *a.* Expostulating; conveying expostulation.

ex-po-sure (eks-pō′zhụr), *n.* The act of exposing, or the state of being exposed; a putting out without shelter or protection, as of an abandoned child; a laying open or subjecting to the action or influence of something (as, *exposure* to the weather, to danger, or to ridicule; the *exposure* of a sensitized photographic plate to the action of the actinic rays of light); presentation to view, esp. in an open or public manner; disclosure, as of something private or secret; unmasking, as of crime, fraud, an impostor, etc.; also, something exposed, as to view; an exposed surface; also, situation with regard to access of sunlight or wind (as, a southern *exposure*); aspect.

ex-pound (eks-pound′), *v. t.* [OF. *espondre*, < L. *exponere* (pp. *expositus*), put out, expose, set forth, explain, < *ex-*, out, + *ponere*, place, put.] To set forth or state in detail, as theories, principles, etc.; hence, to explain; interpret; also, to expose to view† (as, "First he *expounded* both his pockets, And found a watch, with rings and lockets": Butler's "Hudibras," ii. 3).—**ex-pound′er,** *n.*

ex-press (eks-pres′), *v. t.* [L. *expressus*, pp. of *exprimere*, press out, form by pressure, represent, indicate, express, < *ex-*, out, + *premere*, press.] To press or squeeze out (as, to *express* the juice of grapes); extort or elicit as by pressure†; press out the contents of (fruit, etc.); exude or emit (a liquid, odor, etc.) as if under pressure; also, to make (an image, picture, etc.) or represent (a person or other subject) by sculpture, painting, or the like (obs. or archaic); represent by a symbol, character, figure, or formula, or as a symbol or the like does; show, manifest, or reveal (as, to *express* feeling in one's countenance or tone; to *express* one's personality or one's self in one's work); set forth (thoughts, meaning, facts, etc.) in words; couch (*well*, *ill*, etc.) in words; set forth the thoughts, meaning, etc., of (one's self) in words; denote, signify, or import, as words do; sometimes, to set forth or state explicitly (opposed to *imply*); specify† (as, "these men which are *expressed* by their names": Num. i. 17); also, to send by express.—**ex-press′.** [OF. *expres* (F. *exprès*), < L. *expressus*, pp.] **I.** *a.* Duly or exactly formed or represented, as an image or likeness; also, clearly indicated, or distinctly stated or expressed (rather than implied); definite; explicit; plain; also, designed or intended for special use, service, etc.; special, or specially direct or fast, as a messenger or a railroad-train. **II.** *n.* A messenger or a message specially sent; hence, a system or company for the transmission of parcels, money, etc.; also, an express-train; also, an express-rifle. —**ex-press′,** *adv.* Specially; for a particular purpose; also, post-haste, or with speed (as, "He started off *express* for Pierre's Hole": Irving's "Captain Bonneville," vi.); now, esp., by express.—**ex-pres′sage** (-pres′ạ̄j), *n.* The business of transmitting parcels, money, etc., by express; also, the charge for such transmission.—**ex-press′er,** *n.*—**ex-press′i-ble,** *a.* Capable of being expressed.

ex-pres-sion (eks-presh′ọn), *n.* [L. *expressio(n-)*.] The act of expressing or pressing out (as, the *expression* of juices or oils from plants); also, the act of expressing or representing, as by symbols; a symbol or a combination of symbols serving to express something, as an algebraic quantity;

also, the act of showing, manifesting, or revealing; esp., indication of feeling, spirit, character, etc., as in the countenance or voice, or in artistic or musical execution; a look or intonation as expressing feeling, etc. (as, a sad, weary, or triumphant *expression*); quality or power of expressing feeling, etc. (as, a face that lacks *expression*); also, the act of expressing or setting forth in words (as, the *expression* of ideas, opinions, wishes, facts, etc.); the manner or form in which a thing is expressed or couched in words (as, "*Expression* is the dress of thought, and still Appears more decent, as more suitable": Pope's "Essay on Criticism," 318); wording, phrasing, diction, or phraseology; a particular word, phrase, or form of words, used to express something (as, colloquial, archaic. or pedantic *expressions*); power of expressing in words (as, joy beyond *expression*; ideas that baffle *expression*).—**ex-pres′sion-al,** *a.* Of or pertaining to expression.—**ex-pres′sion-ism,** *n.* [= G. *expressionismus.*] The tendencies, doctrines, and methods of certain painters, sculptors, architects, musicians, writers, etc., of Continental Europe, attracting general attention first shortly after the close of the World War, and bound together by the common desire for expression untrammeled by traditions, and holding that art should represent the artist's subjective and emotional reaction to natural objects, etc.—**ex-pres′sion-ist,** *n.*—**ex-pres-sion-is′tic,** *a.*—**ex-pres′sion-less,** *a.* Destitute of expression, as the face or voice.—**ex-pres′sion-less-ness,** *n.*

ex-pres-sive (eks-pres′iv), *a.* [F. *expressif.*] Serving to express; indicative (*of*); full of expression, as the face or voice; pertaining to or concerned with expression.—**ex-pres′sive-ly,** *adv.*—**ex-pres′sive-ness,** *n.*

ex-press-less (eks-pres′les), *a.* Inexpressible. [Archaic.]

ex-press-ly (eks-pres′li), *adv.* In an express manner; explicitly; plainly; also, for the express purpose; specially.

ex-press-man (eks-pres′mạn), *n.*; pl. *-men.* One engaged in the express business; a man in charge of an express-wagon.

ex-press-ness (eks-pres′nes), *n.* The quality of being express; definiteness; explicitness.

ex-press=ri-fle (eks-pres′rī″fl), *n.* A sporting-rifle taking a large charge of powder and a light bullet: adapted for killing large game at short range.

ex-press=train (eks-pres′trān), *n.* A railroad-train which travels at a high speed and makes few or no stops between terminal stations.

ex-press=wag-on (eks-pres′wag″ọn), *n.* A wagon used for collecting and delivering articles transmitted by express.

ex-pro-pri-ate (eks-prō′pri-āt), *v. t.*; *-ated, -ating.* [ML. *expropriatus*, pp. of *expropriare*, < L. *ex-* priv. (see *ex-*) + *proprius*, one's own, E. *proper.*] To take out of the owner's possession; esp., to take for public use by the right of eminent domain; also, to dispossess (a person) of ownership.—**ex-pro-pri-a′tion** (-ā′shọn), *n.*—**ex-pro′pri-a-tor,** *n.*

ex-pulse (eks-puls′), *v. t.*; *-pulsed, -pulsing.* [L. *expulsus*, pp. of *expellere*: see *expel.*] To drive out; expel: as, "For ever should they be *expulsed* from France" (Shakspere's "1 Henry VI.," iii. 3. 25). [Obs. or archaic.]—**ex-pul′sion** (-pul′shọn), *n.* [L. *expulsio(n-).*] The act of driving out or expelling; the state of being expelled.—**ex-pul′sive** (-siv), *a.* Tending or serving to expel; effecting expulsion: as, "a passion so potent . . . so *expulsive* of other loves" (J. H. Newman's "Callista," xix.).

ex-punc-tion (eks-pungk′shọn), *n.* [LL. *expunctio(n-).*] The act of expunging; an erasure.

ex-punge (eks-punj′), *v. t.*; *-punged, -punging.* [L. *expungere* (pp. *expunctus*), prick out, strike out, < *ex-*, out, + *pungere*, prick, pierce.] To strike or blot out; erase; obliterate; hence, to efface; wipe out or destroy.—**ex-punge′ment,** *n.*—**ex-pun′ger** (-pun′jėr), *n.*

ex-pur-gate (eks′pėr-gāt or eks-pėr′-), *v. t.*; *-gated, -gating.* [L. *expurgatus*, pp. of *expurgare*, < *ex-*, out, + *purgare*, E. *purge.*] To purge or cleanse; esp., to amend (a book, etc.) by removing offensive or objectionable matter.—**ex-pur-ga′tion** (-gā′shọn), *n.* [L. *expurgatio(n-).*] The act of expurgating; esp., the elimination of offensive or objectionable matter from a book, etc.—**ex′pur-ga-tor,** *n.* One who expurgates (esp. books, etc.).—**ex-pur-ga-to′ri-al** (-gạ-tō′ri-ạl), *a.* Pertaining to an expurgator or to expurgation.—**ex-pur′ga-to-ry** (-tọ-ri), *a.* Serving to expurgate; of or pertaining to expurgation: as, the *Expurgatory* Index (see *index*).

ex-qui-site (eks′kwi-zit). [L. *exquisitus*, pp. of *exquirere*, seek out, < *ex-*, out, + *quærere*, seek.] **I.** *a.* Carefully sought out, chosen, ascertained, devised, etc.† (as, "I have no *exquisite* reason for 't, but I have reason good enough": Shakspere's "Twelfth Night," ii. 3. 157); of exceptionally choice quality, as food, wines, laces, fabrics, etc.; of rare excellence of production or execution, as works of art, workmanship, or the artist or worker; of peculiar refinement or elegance, as taste, manners, etc., or persons; of peculiar beauty or charm, or rare and appealing excellence, as a face, a flower, coloring, music, poetry, a conception, etc.; in general, extraordinarily fine or admirable, or consummate, as skill, nicety, care, gentleness, purity, etc.; sometimes, with words of ill meaning, extraordinary, extreme, utter, or complete, as ignorance, malice, torture, or (formerly) a villain or traitor; also, intense, acute, or keen, as pleasure, pain, etc.; keenly or delicately sensitive or responsive to impressions (as, an *exquisite* ear for music; the *exquisite* sensibility of the eye to light). **II.** *n.* A person, esp. a man, who is overnice in dress, etc.; a dandy; a coxcomb.—**ex′qui-site-ly,** *adv.*—**ex′qui-site-ness,** *n.*

ex-san-gui-nate (ek-sang′gwi-nāt), *v. t.*; *-nated, -nating* [L. *exsanguinatus*, rendered bloodless, < *ex-* priv. (see *ex-*) + *sanguis* (*sanguin-*), blood.] To render bloodless.—**ex-san-gui-na′tion** (-nā′shọn), *n.*

ex-san-guine (ek-sang′gwin), *a.* [L. *ex-* priv. + *sanguis* (*sanguin-*): see *exsanguinate.*] Bloodless; deficient in blood; anemic.—**ex-san-guin′i-ty** (-gwin′i-ti), *n.*

ex-scind (ek-sind′), *v. t.* [L. *exscindere*, < *ex-*, out, + *scindere*, cut.] To cut out or off.

ex-sect (ek-sekt′), *v. t.* [L. *exsectus*, pp. of *exsecare*, < *ex-*, out, + *secare*, cut.] To cut out.—**ex-sec-tion** (ek-sek′shọn), *n.*

ex-sert (ek-sėrt′), *v. t.* [L. *exsertus*, pp. of *exserere*, put forth: see *exert.*] To thrust out.—**ex-sert′ed,** *p. a.* Projecting beyond the surrounding parts, as a stamen or a sting.—**ex-ser-tile** (ek-sėr′til), *a.* Capable of being exserted or protruded.—**ex-ser′tion** (-shọn), *n.* The act of exserting, or the state of being exserted; protrusion.

ex-sic-cant (ek-sik′ạnt). **I.** *a.* Exsiccating; having the power of drying up, as a medicine. **II.** *n.* An exsiccant medicine or agent.

ex-sic-cate (ek′si-kāt), *v. t.*; *-cated, -cating.* [L. *exsiccatus*, pp. of *exsiccare*, < *ex-*, out, utterly, + *siccare*, make dry: cf. *desiccate.*] To dry completely; remove all the moisture from, as a substance; dry up, as moisture.—**ex-sic-ca′tion** (-kā′shọn), *n.* Drying; dryness.—**ex′sic-ca-tive** (-kạ-tiv), *a.* Tending to dry.—**ex′sic-ca-tor** (-kā-tọr), *n.* A drying apparatus.

ex-stip-u-late (eks-stip′ụ̄-lāt), *a.* [See *ex-* and *stipulate*[1].] In *bot.*, without stipules.

ex-suc-cous (ek-suk′us), *a.* [L. *exsuccus*, < *ex-* priv. (see *ex-*) + *succus*, *sucus*, juice.] Without juice or sap; dry.

ex-suf-flate (ek-suf′lāt), *v. t.*; *-flated, -flating.* [LL. *exsufflatus*, pp. of *exsufflare*, < L. *ex*, out of, + *sufflare*, blow up, blow: see *sufflate.*] To blow out or away; *eccles.*, to drive off (an evil spirit) by blowing.—**ex-suf-fla-tion** (ek-su-flā′shọn), *n.*

ex-suf-fli-cate† (ek-suf′li-kāt), *a.* [Cf. *exsufflate.*] Inflated or exaggerated; windy. See Shakspere's "Othello," iii. 3. 182.

ex-tant (eks′tạnt or eks-tant′), *a.* [L. *extans* (*extant-*), for *exstans*, ppr. of *exstare*, stand out, appear, exist, < *ex-*, out, + *stare*, stand.] Standing out or protruding (archaic); also, prominent, conspicuous, or manifest (archaic); also, in existence (as, "His despatches form one of the most amusing and instructive collections *extant*": Macaulay's "Essays," Machiavelli); still existing; not destroyed or lost.

ex-tem-po-ral (eks-tem′pọ̄-rạl), *a.* [L. *extemporalis*, < *ex tempore*: see *extempore.*] Extemporaneous; extempore. [Obs. or archaic.]

ex-tem-po-ra-ne-ous (eks-tem-pọ̄-rā′nẹ-us), *a.* [L. *extemporaneus*, < *ex tempore*: see *extempore.*] Made, uttered, or performed extempore; impromptu; offhand; unpremeditated; of a person, speaking or performing extempore; also, made for the occasion, as a shelter; extemporized; of medicines, made up or prepared at the time of dispensing.—**ex-tem-po-ra′ne-ous-ly,** *adv.*—**ex-tem-po-ra′ne-ous-ness,** *n.*

ex-tem-po-ra-ry (eks-tem′pọ̄-rạ̄-ri), *a.* [L. *ex tempore*: see *extempore.*] Extemporaneous; extempore.—**ex-tem′po-ra-ri-ly,** *adv.*—**ex-tem′po-ra-ri-ness,** *n.*

ex-tem-po-re (eks-tem′pọ̄-rẹ̄). [L. *ex tempore*, 'out of the time.'] **I.** *adv.* On the spur of the moment; without premeditation or preparation; offhand; sometimes, of public speaking, without notes; of musical performance, by improvisation. **II.** *a.* Made, composed, uttered, or performed extempore; speaking or performing extempore; also, made for the occasion; extemporized; also, occasional† or casual†; sudden†.

ex-tem-po-rize (eks-tem′pọ̄-rīz), *v.*; *-rized, -rizing.* [From *extempore.*] **I.** *intr.* To speak extempore; sing, or play on an instrument, composing the music as one proceeds; improvise. **II.** *tr.* To compose offhand; improvise; also, to make or devise for the occasion (as, "The Innocent, with the aid of pine-boughs, *extemporized* a thatch for the roofless cabin": Bret Harte's "Outcasts of Poker Flat"); get up offhand.—**ex-tem″po-ri-za′tion** (-ri-zā′shọn), *n.*—**ex-tem′po-riz-er** (-rī-zėr), *n.*

ex-tend (eks-tend′), *v.* [L. *extendere* (pp. *extentus*, also *extensus*), stretch out, extend, < *ex-*, out, + *tendere*, stretch, E. *tend*[1].] **I.** *tr.* To stretch out; draw out to the full length; strain; hence, to exert (one's self); also, to place at full length, esp. horizontally, as the body, limbs, etc.; straighten out; also, to write out or transcribe at full length, as shorthand notes, etc.; also, to stretch, draw, or arrange in a given direction, or so as to reach a particular point, as a cord or a line of troops; also, to increase the length or duration of; lengthen; prolong; hence, to carry forward in development; also, to stretch out in various or all directions; expand; spread out in area; widen (boundaries); enlarge the scope of, or make more comprehensive, as operations or influence, or the meaning of a word; increase in quantity by dilution or adulteration, as liquors; also, to stretch forth or hold out, as the arm or hand; also, to hold forth as an offer or grant; offer; grant; give; in *law*, to assess or value; also, to make a seizure or levy upon, as land, by a writ of extent. **II.** *intr.* To be or become extended; stretch out; be continued in length or duration, or in various or all directions; reach, as to a particular point; increase in length, area, scope, etc. (as, his influence is gradually *extending*).—**ex-tend′ed,** *p. a.* Stretched out; continued or prolonged; spread out; widespread or extensive; having extension or spatial magnitude; also, outstretched; in *law*, valued or assessed; also, levied upon.—**extended type,** a kind of type much wider than is usual for its height. See *type.*—**ex-tend′ed-ly,** *adv.*—**ex-tend′er,** *n.*—**ex-tend′i-ble,** *a.* Capable of being extended; extensible.

ex-tense (eks-tens′), *a.* [L. *extensus*, pp.: see *extend.*] Extended; extensive. [Obs. or archaic.]

ex-ten-si-ble (eks-ten′si-bl), *a.* [F. *extensible.*] Capable of being extended; susceptible of being drawn out to greater length or breadth; extensile.—**ex-ten-si-bil′i-ty** (-bil′i-ti), *n.*

ex-ten-sile (eks-ten′sil), *a.* Capable of being extended, stretched out, or protruded.

ex-ten-sim-e-ter (eks-ten-sim′e-tėr), *n.* Same as *extensometer.*

ex-ten-sion (eks-ten′shọn), *n.* [LL. *extensio(n-)*, L. *extentio(n-)*.] The act of extending, or the state of being extended; a stretching or straining; a straightening out, or placing at full length; an extending in a particular direction or to a particular point; lengthening or prolongation; expansion or enlargement; enlargement in scope or operation; a stretching or putting forth, as of the arm or hand; also, range of extending; degree of extensiveness; extent; also, something extended; an extended object or space; also, that by which something is extended; a prolongation; an added portion or period; in *physiol.*, the straightening of a part; the action of an extensor muscle; in *physics*, etc., that property of a body by which it occupies a portion of space; spatial magnitude; in *com.*, a written engagement on the part of a creditor, allowing a debtor further time to pay a debt; in *logic*, the range of a term or concept as indicated by the number of objects which it denotes or includes (cf. *intension*).—**ex-ten′sion-al,** *a.*—**ex-ten′sion=spring,** *n.* A spiral spring designed to resist a pull or strain in line with its length.—**ex-ten′sion=ta″ble,** *n.* A table the frame of which can be drawn out in length for the insertion of additional leaves on the top.

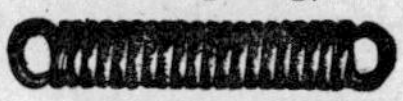

Extension-spring.

ex-ten-si-ty (eks-ten′si-ti), *n.* [L. *extensus*, pp.: see *extend*, and cf. *extense.*] The quality of having extension; in *psychol.*, that element of sensation from which the perception of extension is developed.

ex-ten-sive (eks-ten′siv), *a.* [LL. *extensivus.*] Of, pertaining to, or characterized by extension; also, of great extent; wide; broad; great; comprehensive; also, noting or pertaining to a system involving operations of wide extent carried on by less laborious or less expensive methods not calculated to result in any high degree of effectiveness, as in the cultivation of large areas of land (as where land is cheap) with a minimum of labor and expense (opposed to *intensive*).—**ex-ten′sive-ly,** *adv.*—**ex-ten′sive-ness,** *n.*

ex-ten-som-e-ter (eks-ten-som′e-tėr), *n.* [L. *extensus*, pp.: see *extend* and *-meter.*] An apparatus for measuring minute degrees of expansion, contraction, or deformation.

ex-ten-sor (eks-ten′sọr), *n.* [LL., one who extends or stretches.] A muscle which serves to extend or straighten a part of the body.

ex-tent (eks-tent′), *n.* [OF. *estente*, < *estendre*, < L. *extendere*: see *extend.*] The space or degree to which a thing extends; length, area, or size; amount; range or scope; also, something extended; an extended space; a particular length, area, or volume; something having extension; also, the act of extending†; an extending, offering, or showing, as of justice or kindness† (see Shakspere's "Titus Andronicus," iv. 4. 3; Shakspere's "Hamlet," ii. 2. 390); also, in Great Britain, assessment or valuation, as of land; also, a writ to recover debts of record due to the crown, under which land, etc., may be seized; a seizure made under such a writ; in the U. S., a writ, or a levy, by which a creditor has his debtor's lands valued and transferred to himself, absolutely or for a term of years; hence, an attack† or assault† (as, "This uncivil and unjust *extent* Against thy peace": Shakspere's "Twelfth Night," iv. 1. 57); in *logic*, extension.

ex-ten-u-ate (eks-ten′ṳ̄-āt), *v. t.*; *-ated, -ating.* [L. *extenuatus*, pp. of *extenuare*, < *ex-*, out, + *tenuare*, make thin: cf. *attenuate.*] To make thin, lean, or emaciated (archaic); reduce the consistence or density of (archaic); lessen in degree or intensity†; also, to lessen in honor† (as, "Righteous are thy decrees on all thy works: Who can *extenuate* thee?" Milton's "Paradise Lost," x. 645); underestimate, underrate, or make light of; now, esp., to represent (fault, offense, etc.) as less serious (as, "Speak of me as I am; nothing *extenuate*, Nor set down aught in malice": Shakspere's "Othello," v. 2. 342); also, to serve to make (fault, offense, etc.) seem less serious, as a mitigating circumstance does.—**ex-ten′u-at-ing-ly,** *adv.*—**ex-ten-u-a′tion** (-ā′shọn), *n.* [L. *extenuatio(n-)*.] The act of extenuating, or the state of being extenuated; also, that which extenuates; a partial excuse.—**ex-ten′u-a-tor,** *n.*—**ex-ten′u-a-to-ry** (-ạ̄-tọ̄-ri), *a.* Tending to extenuate; characterized by extenuation.

ex-te-ri-or (eks-tē′ri-ọr). [L., compar. of *exter*, *exterus*, outer, outward, compar. adj. < *ex*, out of.] **I.** *a.* Outer (as, the *exterior* side or surface of a thing); being on the outer side (as, the *exterior* decorations of a church); being outside of something (sometimes with *to*: as, points *exterior* to a curve). **II.** *n.* The outer surface or part; the outside; *pl.*, externals.—**ex-te-ri-or′i-ty** (-or′i-ti), *n.*; pl. *-ties* (-tiz). The state or fact of being exterior; also, something exterior; an outward circumstance.—**ex-te′ri-or-ize** (-ọr-īz), *v. t.*; *-ized, -izing.* To make exterior; externalize (a conception).—**ex-te′ri-or-ly,** *adv.*

ex-ter-mi-nate (eks-tėr′mi-nāt), *v. t.*; *-nated, -nating.* [L. *exterminatus*, pp. of *exterminare*, < *ex*, out of, + *terminus*, boundary.] To drive out† or expel†; also, to get rid of by destroying; destroy totally; extirpate.—**ex-ter-mi-na′tion** (-nā′shọn), *n.* [LL. *exterminatio(n-)*.] The act of exterminating; total destruction; extirpation.—**ex-ter'mi-na-tive** (-nạ-tiv), **ex-ter'mi-na-to-ry** (-tọ-ri), *a.* Serving or tending to exterminate.—**ex-ter'mi-na-tor** (-nā-tọr), *n.*

ex-tern (eks-tėrn'). [F. *externe*, < L. *externus*, < *exter*, outer, outward: see *exterior.*] **I.** *a.* Outside; outward; external. [Now chiefly poetic.] **II.** *n.* Outward form or appearance†; also (also pron. eks'tėrn), an outsider; a person connected with an institution but not residing in it, as a pupil in a boarding-school, a member of the medical staff of a hospital, etc.

ex-ter-nal (eks-tėr'nạl). [L. *externus*: see *extern.*] **I.** *a.* Of or pertaining to the outside or outer part; outer; to be applied to the outside of the body, as a remedy; also, pertaining to the outward or visible appearance or show (as, *external* acts of worship); also, situated or being outside of something; acting or coming from without; pertaining to or concerned with what is without or foreign (as, *external* commerce; the *external* relations of a country); in *metaph.*, belonging or pertaining to the world of things or phenomena, considered as outside the perceiving mind. **II.** *n.* The outside; also, that which is external; *pl.*, external or outward features, circumstances, etc. (as, the *externals* of religion).—**ex-ter'nal-ism,** *n.* Attention or devotion to externals; undue regard to externals, esp. in religion; also, phenomenalism.—**ex-ter'nal-ist,** *n.*—**ex-ter-nal'i-ty** (-nal'i-ti), *n.*; pl. *-ties* (-tiz). The state or quality of being external; also, undue regard to externals; also, something external; an outward feature or circumstance.—**ex-ter'nal-ize** (-nạl-īz), *v. t.*; *-ized, -izing.* To make external; embody in an outward form.—**ex-ter''nal-i-za'tion** (-i-zā'shọn), *n.*—**ex-ter'nal-ly,** *adv.*

ex-terne (eks-tėrn' or eks'tėrn), *n.* [F.: see *extern.*] An extern, as of a hospital.

ex-ter-ri-to-ri-al (eks''ter-i-tō'ri-ạl), *a.* [See *ex-.*] Beyond territorial limits or jurisdiction, as persons resident in a country but not subject to its laws; pertaining to such persons.—**ex''ter-ri-to-ri-al'i-ty** (-al'i-ti), *n.* Exterritorial status.—**ex''ter-ri-to'ri-al-ly,** *adv.*

ex-tinct (eks-tingkt'), *a.* [L. *extinctus*, pp. of *extinguere*: see *extinguish.*] Extinguished; quenched; having ceased eruption, as a volcano; hence, having come to an end; without a living representative, as a race, family, or species (as, "My father was dead, and my mother and all the family *extinct*": Defoe's "Robinson Crusoe," i. 19); obsolete, as an institution or office; having no qualified heritor or claimant, as a title.

ex-tinc-tion (eks-tingk'shọn), *n.* [L. *extinctio(n-)*, < *extinguere*: see *extinguish.*] The act of extinguishing, or the fact of being extinguished; a putting out or quenching; suppression; abolition; annihilation; also, a becoming extinct; a coming to an end or dying out; the condition of being extinct.—**ex-tinc'tive,** *a.* Tending or serving to extinguish.

ex-tine (eks'tin or -tīn), *n.* [L. *extimus*, outermost, superl. of *exter*: see *exterior.*] In *bot.*, the outer coat of a pollen-grain.

ex-tin-guish (eks-ting'gwish), *v. t.* [L. *extinguere* (pp. *extinctus*), for *exstinguere*, < *ex-*, out, + *stinguere*, quench, orig. prick: see *stick*², and cf. *distinguish, instinct.*] To put out (a fire, light, etc.); put out the flame of (something burning or lighted); hence, to quench (hopes, passions, etc.); obscure or eclipse, as by superior brilliancy (as, "natural graces that *extinguish* art": Shakspere's "1 Henry VI.," v. 3. 192); also, to put an end to, or wipe out of existence; suppress; abolish; annihilate; bring to an end, as a race, family, etc.; render void, as a right or claim; discharge (a debt), as by payment.—**ex-tin'guish-a-ble,** *a.* Capable of being extinguished.—**ex-tin'guish-er,** *n.* One who or that which extinguishes; a conical cap for putting over a lighted candle, etc., to extinguish it; any of various portable apparatuses for extinguishing fire (as, a chemical *extinguisher*).—**ex-tin'guish-ment,** *n.*

ex-tirp† (eks-tėrp'), *v. t.* Same as *extirpate.*

ex-tir-pate (eks'tėr-pāt or eks-tėr'-), *v. t.*; *-pated, -pating.* [L. *extirpatus*, pp. of *extirpare*, for *exstirpare*, < *ex-*, out, + *stirps*, stock, root.] To pull up by the roots; root up; hence, to remove utterly; destroy totally; exterminate; do away with.—**ex-tir-pa'tion** (-pā'shọn), *n.*—**ex'tir-pa-tor,** *n.*

ex-tol (eks-tol' or -tōl'), *v. t.*; *-tolled, -tolling.* [L. *extollere*, lift out or up, raise, exalt, praise, < *ex-*, out, + *tollere*, lift, raise.] To lift up†; also, to exalt in rank, honor, etc.†; also, to praise highly; laud; eulogize.—**ex-tol'ler,** *n.*—**ex-tol'ment,** *n.*

ex-tort (eks-tôrt'), *v. t.* [L. *extortus*, pp. of *extorquere*, twist or wrest out, < *ex-*, out, + *torquere*, twist.] To wrest or wring (something) from a person by violence, intimidation, or abuse of authority; obtain (money, information, etc.) by force, torture, threat, or the like; in *law*, to take illegally under color of office.—**ex-tort'er,** *n.*—**ex-tor'tion** (-tôr'shọn), *n.* [ML. *extortio(n-)*, LL. *extorsio(n-)*.] The act of extorting, or the fact of being extorted; oppressive or illegal exaction, as of excessive price or interest; also, something extorted; in *law*, the crime of obtaining money or other thing of value under color of office, when none is due or not so much is due, or before it is due.—**ex-tor'tion-a-ry** (-ạ-ri), *a.* Characterized by or given to extortion.—**ex-tor'tion-ate** (-ạt), *a.* Characterized by extortion, as persons; exorbitant, as demands for money; grossly excessive, as prices.—**ex-tor'tion-er,** *n.* One who practises extortion.—**ex-tor'tive,** *a.* Tending to extort; extortionary.

ex-tra (eks'trạ). [Prob. orig. short for *extraordinary*: cf. L. *extra* (see *extra-*).] **I.** *a.* Beyond or more than what is usual, expected, or necessary; additional; also, larger or better than what is usual. **II.** *n.* Something extra or additional; specif., an edition of a newspaper other than the regular edition or editions; also, something of superior quality; in *cricket*, a score or run not made from the bat, as a bye or a wide.—**ex'tra,** *adv.* In excess of the usual or specified amount (as, "I wouldn't care if I did go a little *extra* for it": Mrs. Stowe's "Uncle Tom's Cabin," xiv.); also, beyond the ordinary degree; unusually; uncommonly.

extra-. [L. *extra-*, repr. *extra*, adv. and prep., outside (of), without, < *exter*, outer, outward: see *exterior.*] A prefix of Latin origin, meaning 'outside,' 'beyond,' 'besides,' freely used as an English formative, as in *extrajudicial, extraparochial, extraterritorial*, and many other words mostly self-explanatory, as *extra-atmospheric, extra-European*, etc. Cf. *intra-*.—**ex-tra-ca-non-i-cal** (eks''trạ-kạ-non'i-kạl), *a.* Not included in the canon of Scripture.—**ex-tra-cel'lu-lar** (-sel'ū-lạr), *a.* Outside of a cell or cells.—**ex-tra-cra'ni-al** (-krā'ni-ạl), *a.* Outside of the cranium or skull.

ex-tract (eks-trakt'), *v. t.* [L. *extractus*, pp. of *extrahere*, < *ex*, out of, + *trahere*, draw.] To draw or take (a thing) out of something containing it or of which it forms a part; take or copy out (matter from a book, etc.); sometimes, to make excerpts from (the book, etc.); draw forth or get out by force (as, to *extract* a tooth); extort (money, information, etc.); separate or obtain (a juice, ingredient, principle, etc.) from a thing or substance by pressure, distillation, treatment with solvents, or the like; derive or obtain (pleasure, comfort, etc.) from a particular source; deduce (a doctrine, principle, etc.); in *math.*, to determine (the root of a quantity).—**ex'tract,** *n.* [NL. *extractum*, prop. neut. of L. *extractus*, pp.] Something extracted; esp., a passage taken from a book, etc.; an excerpt; a quotation; also, a solid or viscid substance extracted from a drug, plant, or the like; also, a solution or preparation containing the active principles of a drug, plant-juice, or the like.—**ex-tract'a-ble,** *a.* That may be extracted.—**ex-trac'tion** (-trak'shọn), *n.* [ML. *extractio(n-)*.] The act of extracting, or the state of being extracted; also, something extracted; an extract; also, descent or lineage.—**ex-trac'tive. I.** *a.* Tending or serving to extract; also, that may be extracted. **II.** *n.* Something extracted; specif., a substance present in plants which forms into a brown insoluble mass during the process of extraction.—**ex-trac'tor,** *n.*

ex-tra-dit-a-ble (eks-trạ-dī'tạ-bl), *a.* Subject to extradition (as, an *extraditable* person); also, making subject to extradition (as, an *extraditable* offense).

ex-tra-dite (eks'trạ-dīt), *v. t.*; *-dited, -diting.* [Back-formation from *extradition.*] To give up (a fugitive or prisoner) to another nation or authority; also, to obtain the extradition of.

ex-tra-di-tion (eks-trą-dish′ọn), *n.* [F., < L. *ex*, out of, from, + *traditio(n-)*, a giving over: see *tradition*.] The surrender of a fugitive or prisoner by one nation or authority to another.

ex-tra-dos (eks-trā′dos), *n.* [F., < L. *extra*, outside of, + F. *dos*, < L. *dorsum*, back.] In *arch.*, the exterior curve or surface of an arch or vault. Cf. *intrados*.

ex-tra-haz-ard-ous (eks-trą-haz′ąr-dus), *a.* [See *extra*, *adv.*] Involving more than ordinary hazard, risk, or peril: as, an *extrahazardous* occupation.

ex-tra=il-lus-trate (eks-trą-il′us-trāt), *v. t.*; *-trated*, *-trating*. To add extra illustrations to (a book) after it is printed or published, by pasting or binding them in.—**ex″tra=il-lus-tra′tion** (-trā′shọn), *n.*

ex-tra-ju-di-cial (eks″trą-jọ̈-dish′ąl), *a.* [See *extra-*.] Outside of judicial proceedings; beyond the action or authority of a court.—**ex″tra-ju-di′cial-ly,** *adv.*

ex-tra-lat-er-al (eks-trą-lat′ẹ-rąl), *a.* [See *extra-*.] Situated or extending beyond the sides; specif., noting the right of a mine-owner to a portion of his lode or vein extending beyond the side-lines of his claim but lying between vertical cross-planes through the end-lines.

ex-tra-mun-dane (eks-trą-mun′dān), *a.* [LL. *extramundanus*, < L. *extra*, outside of, + *mundus*, world.] Beyond our world or the material universe, or pertaining to a region so situated.

ex-tra-mu-ral (eks-trą-mū′rąl), *a.* [L. *extra*, outside of, + *murus*, wall.] Outside the walls or boundaries, as of a city or town or a university.

ex-tra-ne-ous (eks-trā′nẹ-us), *a.* [L. *extraneus*, that is without, foreign, < *extra*, outside, without: see *extra-*.] Introduced or coming from without; not belonging or proper to a thing (often with *to*); external; foreign; alien.—**ex-tra′ne-ous-ly,** *adv.*—**ex-tra′ne-ous-ness,** *n.*

ex-tra=of-fi-cial (eks″trą-ọ-fish′ąl), *a.* [See *extra-*.] Outside of the ordinary duties, rights, etc., of an office.

ex-traor-di-na-ry (eks-trôr′di-nā-ri or eks-trą-ôr′-), *a.* [L. *extraordinarius*, < *extra*, outside of, + *ordo* (*ordin-*), order.] Beyond what is ordinary; out of the regular or established order (as, *extraordinary* powers, measures, or expenses; *extraordinary* courses of study); exceptional in character or kind (as, an *extraordinary* fact, feat, sight, book, or man; *extraordinary* weather); unusual, uncommon, notable, or remarkable; exceptional in amount, extent, degree, etc. (as, *extraordinary* value, weight, speed, or fineness; an *extraordinary* attendance at a lecture); of officials, etc., outside of, additional to, or ranking below the ordinary or regular class (as, an envoy *extraordinary*, see below; a physician *extraordinary* to a king, cf. *in ordinary*, under *ordinary*, *n.*; an *extraordinary* professor in a German university, ranking below an ordinary one); special; additional.—**envoy extraordinary,** formerly, a diplomatic agent sent on some special mission; now, a diplomatic agent of the second class, ranking below an ambassador (see *envoy*²).—**ex-traor′di-na-ri-ly,** *adv.*—**ex-traor′di-na-ri-ness,** *n.*

ex-tra-pa-ro-chi-al (eks″trą-pą-rō′ki-ąl), *a.* [See *extra-*.] Outside of the parish, or any parish.

ex-tra-pro-fes-sion-al (eks″trą-prọ-fesh′ọn-ąl), *a.* [See *extra-*.] Outside of the ordinary limits of professional interest or duty.

ex-tra=red (eks′trą-red′), *a.* [See *extra-*.] Same as *infrared*.

ex-tra-sys-to-le (eks-trą-sis′tọ-lē), *n.* [See *extra-*.] In *pathol.*, a contraction of the heart other than the normal systole.—**ex″tra-sys-tol′ic** (-tol′ik), *a.*

ex-tra-ter-ri-to-ri-al (eks″trą-ter-i-tō′ri-ąl), *a.* [See *extra-*.] Exterritorial.—**ex″tra-ter-ri-to-ri-al′i-ty** (-al′i-ti), *n.*—**ex″-tra-ter-ri-to′ri-al-ly,** *adv.*

ex-trav-a-gance (eks-trav′ą-gąns), *n.* The quality or fact of being extravagant; unrestrained or fantastic excess, as of actions, opinions, etc.; an extravagant action, notion, etc.; also, excessive expenditure or outlay; wastefulness; prodigality; an instance of this. Also **ex-trav′a-gan-cy.**

ex-trav-a-gant (eks-trav′ą-gąnt), *a.* [OF. F. *extravagant*, < ML. *extravagans* (*-ant-*), ppr. of *extravagari*: see *extravagate*.] Wandering beyond bounds† (as, "The *extravagant* and erring spirit hies To his confine": Shakspere's "Hamlet," i. 1. 154); spreading or projecting irregularly in various directions, as roots or branches†; divergent†, different†, or irrelevant†; strange† or unusual†; now, exceeding the bounds of reason, as actions, demands, opinions, passions, etc., or, esp. formerly, persons; unrestrained by reason; unbridled; fantastically excessive; wild; esp., of persons, etc., exceeding prudence or necessity in expenditure; wasteful; prodigal; of expense, price, etc., exorbitant.—**ex-trav′a-gant-ly,** *adv.*—**ex-trav′a-gant-ness,** *n.*

ex-trav-a-gan-za (eks-trav-ą-gan′zą), *n.* [It. *estravaganza*, now *stravaganza*, extravagance.] An extravagant or fantastic composition, as in music, the drama, etc.

ex-trav-a-gate (eks-trav′ą-gāt), *v. i.*; *-gated*, *-gating*. [ML. *extravagatus*, pp. of *extravagari*, wander beyond, < L. *extra*, outside of, + *vagari*, wander: cf. *divagate* and *stray*.] To wander beyond bounds; stray; roam at will; hence, to go beyond the bounds of propriety or reason.

ex-trav-a-sate (eks-trav′ą-sāt), *v.*; *-sated*, *-sating*. [L. *extra*, outside of, + *vas*, vessel.] In *pathol.*: **I.** *tr.* To force out from the proper vessels, as blood, esp. so as to diffuse through the surrounding parts. **II.** *intr.* To be extravasated, as blood; escape from the proper vessels.—**ex-trav-a-sa′tion** (-sā′shọn), *n.* In *pathol.*, the act of extravasating; also, the matter extravasated.

ex-tra-ver-sion (eks-trą-vėr′shọn), etc. Same as *extroversion*, etc.

ex-treme (eks-trēm′). [OF. *extremę* (F. *extrême*), < L. *extremus*, superl. of *exter*, outer, outward: see *exterior*.] **I.** *a.*; compar. *extremer*, superl. *extremest*. Outermost; farthest from the center or middle; endmost; hence, farthest, utmost, or very far in any direction (as, "From th' *extremest* point Of elevation down into th' abyss": Cowper's "Task," ii. 92); also, last or final (now chiefly in 'extreme unction': see under *unction*); also, utmost or exceedingly great in degree (as, *extreme* joy; *extreme* peril); also, of a character or kind farthest removed from the ordinary or average (as, an *extreme* case; *extreme* measures); going to the utmost lengths, or exceeding the bounds of moderation (as, *extreme* fashions; *extreme* opinions); of persons, going to the utmost or very great lengths in action, habit, opinion, etc. (as, "Be not as *extreme* in submission As in offence," Shakspere's "Merry Wives of Windsor," iv. 4. 11; "In conversation frivolous, in dress *Extreme*," Cowper's "Task," ii. 380; an *extreme* socialist). **II.** *n.* The utmost point, or extremity, of something (obs. or rare); the utmost or highest degree, or a very high degree (as, showy in the *extreme*, or to an *extreme*); the furthest or utmost length, or an excessive length, beyond the ordinary or average (as, in the *extreme* of fashion; to go to *extremes* in dress); also, one of two things as remote or different from each other as possible (as, "'twixt two *extremes* of passion, joy and grief": Shakspere's "King Lear," v. 3. 198); in *math.*, the first or the last term, as of a proportion or series.—**ex-treme′ly,** *adv.* In an extreme degree; exceedingly.—**ex-treme′ness,** *n.*—**ex-trem′ism** (-trē′mizm), *n.* Tendency or disposition to go to extremes.—**ex-trem′ist. I.** *n.* One who goes to extremes; a supporter of extreme doctrines or practices. **II.** *a.* Belonging or pertaining to extremists; radical.—**ex-trem′i-ty** (-trem′i-ti), *n.*; pl. *-ties* (-tiz). [OF. *extremite* (F. *extrémité*), < L. *extremitas*, < *extremus*.] The extreme or terminal point, limit, or part of something; specif., a limb of the body, or the end part of a limb, as a hand or foot (chiefly in *pl.*); also, a person's last moments (chiefly in *pl.*); also, the utmost or an extreme degree (as, the *extremity* of joy; clear to an *extremity*; "They endured the last *extremities* of thirst and hunger," Gibbon's "Decline and Fall of the Roman Empire," xxiv.); a condition, or, in *pl.*, circumstances, of extreme need, distress, etc. (as, "Florence was reduced to the last *extremity*": Gibbon's "Decline and Fall of the Roman Empire," xxx.); an extreme measure (chiefly in *pl.*: as, to be forced to proceed to *extremities*); also, extreme character, as of views.

ex-tri-ca-ble (eks′tri-ką-bl), *a.* That may be extricated.

ex-tri-cate (eks′tri-kāt), *v. t.*; *-cated*, *-cating*. [L. *extricatus*, pp. of *extricare*, < *ex*, out of, + *tricæ*, trifles, hindrances, perplexities.] To disengage from anything that entangles; set free, as a person from an embarrassing situation, difficulties, etc.; liberate (gas, etc.) from a state of combination, as during a chemical process; also, to unravel (something tangled, literally or figuratively: now rare).—**ex-tri-ca′tion** (-kā′shọn), *n.*

ex-trin-sic (eks-trin′sik), *a.* [F. *extrinsèque*, < LL. *extrinsecus*, adj., outward, < L. *extrinsecus*, adv., from without, without, < *exter*, outer (see *exterior*), + *secus*, beside, akin to *sequi*, follow.] Being outside of a thing; outward or external; also, operating or coming from without; extraneous; adventitious; unessential.—**ex-trin′si-cal-ly,** *adv.*

ex-trorse (eks-trôrs′), *a.* [LL. *extrorsus*, in an outward direction, < L. *extra*, outside, + *versus*, toward.] In *bot.*, turned or facing outward, as anthers which open toward the perianth.—**ex-trorse′ly,** *adv.*

ex-tro-ver-sion (eks-trọ-vėr′shọn), *n.* The act of extroverting; extroverted state; in *psychol.*, interest directed outward or to things outside the self (cf. *introversion*).

ex-tro-vert (eks-trọ-vėrt′), *v. t.* [Irreg. < L. *extra*, outside, + *vertere* (pp. *versus*), turn: cf. *introvert.*] To turn outward; turn inside out; direct (the mind, etc.) toward external things.—**ex′tro-vert,** *n.* In *psychol.*, one characterized by extroversion; a person concerned chiefly with what is external or objective. Cf. *introvert.*—**ex-tro-vert′ed,** *p. a.* In *psychol.*, characterized by extroversion.

ex-trude (eks-tröd′), *v.*; *-truded, -truding.* [L. *extrudere* (pp. *extrusus*), < *ex*, out of, + *trudere*, thrust.] **I.** *tr.* To thrust out; force or press out; hence, to expel; sometimes, to protrude. **II.** *intr.* To protrude.—**ex-tru′sion** (-trö′zhọn), *n.* The act of extruding, or the fact of being extruded; expulsion; protrusion.—**ex-tru′sive** (-siv), *a.* Tending to extrude; pertaining to extrusion; in *geol.*, of rocks, having been forced out in a molten or plastic condition at the surface of the earth.

ex-u-ber-ant (eg-zū′bẹ-rạnt), *a.* [L. *exuberans* (*-ant-*), ppr. of *exuberare*: see *exuberate.*] Profuse in growth or production; richly or excessively luxuriant; superabundant; overflowing; lavish; effusive.—**ex-u′ber-ance, ex-u′ber-an-cy,** *n.*—**ex-u′ber-ant-ly,** *adv.*

ex-u-ber-ate (eg-zū′bẹ-rāt), *v. i.*; *-ated, -ating.* [L. *exuberatus*, pp. of *exuberare*, grow with great luxuriance, superabound, < *ex-*, utterly, + *uberare*, be fruitful, < *uber*, fruitful.] To be exuberant; superabound; overflow.

ex-u-date (ek′sū-dāt), *v. i.* or *t.*; *-dated, -dating.* [L. *exudatus*, pp. of *exudare*: see *exude.*] To exude. [Now rare.]—**ex′u-date,** *n.* A substance exuded; an exudation.—**ex-u-da′tion** (-dā′shọn), *n.* The act of exuding; also, that which is exuded; a sweat-like issue or discharge through pores or small openings.—**ex-u-da-tive** (ek-sū′dạ-tiv), *a.* Pertaining to or characterized by exudation.

ex-ude (ek-sūd′), *v.*; *-uded, -uding.* [L. *exudare*, for *exsudare*, < *ex*, out of, + *sudare*, sweat.] **I.** *intr.* To come out gradually in drops like sweat through pores or small openings; ooze out. **II.** *tr.* To send out like sweat; emit through pores or small openings.

ex-ul-cer-ate (eg-zul′sėr-āt), *v. t.*; *-ated, -ating.* [L. *exulceratus*, pp. of *exulcerare*, < *ex-*, utterly, + *ulcerare*: see *ulcerate.*] To ulcerate; inflame; exasperate; embitter. [Archaic.]—**ex-ul-cer-a′tion** (-ā′shọn), *n.*

ex-ult (eg-zult′), *v. i.* [L. *exultare*, for *exsultare*, freq. of *exsilire*, leap out or up, < *ex-*, out, + *salire*, leap.] To leap, esp. for joy† (as, "The sea subsiding spreads a level plain, *Exults*, and owns the monarch of the main": Pope's tr. Homer's "Iliad," xiii.); hence, to manifest or feel a lively or triumphant joy; rejoice exceedingly; be highly elated.—**ex-ult′ance, ex-ult′an-cy,** *n.* Exultation.—**ex-ult′ant,** *a.* Exulting; highly elated; triumphant.—**ex-ult′ant-ly,** *adv.*—**ex-ul-ta-tion** (ek-sul-tā′shọn), *n.* [L. *exultatio*(*n-*).] The act of exulting; lively or triumphant joy, as over success or victory.—**ex-ult′ing-ly,** *adv.*

ex-u-vi-æ (ek-sū′vi-ē), *n. pl.* [L., < *exuere*, put off, strip: cf. *induere*, put on, E. *indue.*] Cast skins, shells, or other coverings of animals.—**ex-u′vi-al,** *a.*—**ex-u′vi-ate** (-āt), *v. i.* or *t.*; *-ated, -ating.* To cast off or shed (exuviæ).—**ex-u-vi-a′tion** (-ā′shọn), *n.*

ex vo-to (eks vō′tō). [L., 'from a vow.'] In pursuance of a vow: a phrase also used as an adjective or noun, *ex-voto*, with reference to offerings made.

-ey. Form of *-y*[1], adjective suffix, used esp. after *y*, as in *clayey, skyey, wheyey.*

e-ya-let (ā-yä-let′), *n.* [Turk.] Same as *vilayet.*

ey-as (ī′ạs), *n.* [For *nyas, nias*, < OF. F. *niais*, being a nestling, < L. *nidus*, nest.] A nestling; in *falconry*, a hawk taken from the nest for training, as distinguished from one caught and trained.

eye (ī), *n.*; pl. *eyes*, archaic *eyen* (ī′ẹn) or *eyne* (īn). [AS. *ēage* = D. *oog* = G. *auge* = Icel. *auga* = Goth. *augo*, eye: cf. L. *oculus*, eye.] The organ of sight or vision; this organ with respect to the color of the iris (as, blue or brown *eyes*); the region surrounding this organ (as, the blow gave him a black *eye*); also, the action of the eyes, sight, or vision (often in *pl.*: as, a strange sight met his *eye*; to have no *eyes* for anything else); field or range of vision†; fig., mental view (as, "Methinks I see my father . . . In my mind's *eye*, Horatio": Shakspere's "Hamlet," i. 2. 185); also, look, glance, or gaze (often in *pl.*: as, to cast one's *eye* on a thing; to raise one's *eyes*); a glance (as, to make *eyes* at a person or thing, to throw amorous or covetous glances at him or it); also, attentive look, close observation, or watch (often in *pl.*: as, to keep an *eye* on a person; to be under the *eye* of some one; to be all *eyes*); regard, respect, view, aim, or intention (as, to have an *eye* to one's own advantage; to concur with an *eye* to win favor); also, power of seeing; appreciative or discriminating visual perception (as, to have an *eye* for color, or for proportion); also, manner or way of looking at a thing, estimation, or opinion (often in *pl.*: as, in the *eye* of the law; in the *eyes* of the world); also, something resembling or suggesting the eye in appearance, shape, etc., as the bud of a tuber, the central spot of a target, one of the round spots on the tail-feathers of a peacock, the hole of a needle, a hole pierced in a thing for the insertion of some object, a metal or other ring as for a rope to pass through, or the loop into which a hook is inserted (forming together with the hook a 'hook and eye'); also, in fig. use, a center of light, intelligence, influence, etc. (as, the *eye* of day, the sun; "Athens, the *eye* of Greece, mother of arts," Milton's "Paradise Regained," iv. 240); also, a tinge† or shade† (as, "*Ant.* The ground indeed is tawny. *Seb.* With an *eye* of green in 't": Shakspere's "Tempest," ii. 1. 55).—**eye of the wind,** *naut.*, the precise direction from which the wind is blowing.—**eyes right,** or **eyes left,** *milit.*, the command given to turn the head and eyes to the right or to the left.—**eye,** *v.*; *eyed, eying* or *eyeing.* **I.** *tr.* To fix the eyes upon; view; often, to observe or watch narrowly. **II.**† *intr.* To appear to the eye. See Shakspere's "Antony and Cleopatra," i. 3. 97.—**eye′a-ble,** *a.* Visible; also, pleasing to the eye.—**eye′ball,** *n.* The ball or globe of the eye.—**eye′bright,** *n.* Any of various scrophulariaceous herbs of the genus *Euphrasia*, as *E. officinalis* of Europe, which was formerly used for diseases of the eye; also, any of various other plants, as the germander speedwell, *Veronica chamædrys.*—**eye′brow,** *n.* The arch or ridge forming the upper part of the orbit of the eye, or the fringe of hair growing upon it.—**eye′=cup,** *n.* A device for applying lotions to the eye, consisting of a cup or glass with a rim shaped to fit snugly about the orbit of the eye.—**eyed** (īd), *a.* Having eyes; marked with eye-like spots.—**eye′=drop,** *n.* A tear (see Shakspere's "2

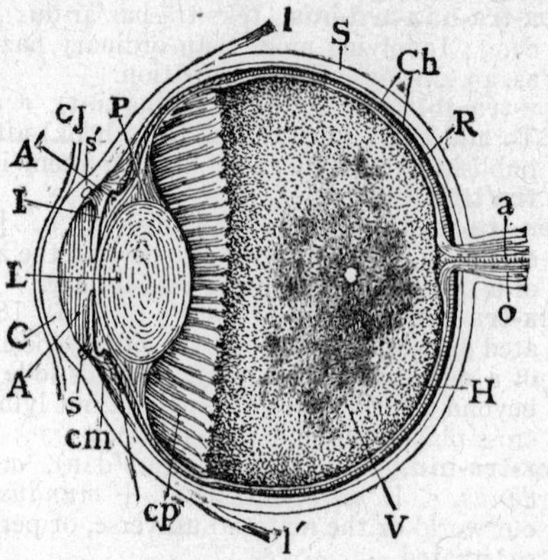

Human Eye, in median vertical anteroposterior section. (Ciliary processes shown, though not all lying in this section.)

A, anterior, and *A′*, posterior chambers of aqueous humor; *a*, central artery of retina; *C*, cornea; *Ch*, choroid; *cj*, conjunctiva; *cm*, ciliary muscle; *cp*, ciliary processes; *H*, hyaloid; *I*, iris; *L*, crystalline lens in its capsule (the reference-line passes through the pupil); *l, l′*, insertion of tendon of superior and inferior rectus muscles; *o*, optic nerve; *P*, canal of Petit; *R*, retina; *S*, sclerotic; *s, s′*, circular sinus or canal of Schlemm; *V*, vitreous body filling back part of the eye.

Henry IV.," iv. 5. 88); *pl.*, an eye-wash.—**eye′=glass,** *n.* The crystalline lens of the eye† (see Shakspere's "Winter's Tale," i. 2. 268); also, a lens to assist defective vision; *pl.*, a pair of such lenses, esp. when kept in position by a spring which compresses the nose (as distinguished from *spectacles*, which have bows for the ears); also, *sing.*, the eyepiece of a telescope, microscope, or other optical instrument; also, an eye-cup.—**eye′=glassed,** *a.* Wearing eye-glasses.—**eye′-hole,** *n.* The socket or orbit of the eye; a hole to look through, as in a mask or a curtain; a circular opening for the insertion of a pin, hook, rope, etc.—**eye′lash,** *n.* One of the short, thick, curved hairs growing as a fringe on the edge of an eyelid; also, the whole fringe of such hairs.—**eye′less,** *a.* Lacking eyes; blind.

eye-let (ī′let), *n.* [Orig. ME. *oilet*, < OF. F. *œillet*, dim. of *œil*, < L. *oculus*, eye, but later associated with E. *eye*.] A small, typically round hole, esp. one finished at the edge, as in cloth or leather, for the passage of a lace or cord, or in embroidery, for ornament; a metal ring for lining a small hole; an eyehole in a wall, mask, etc.; also, a small eye.—**eye′let,** *v. t.*; *-leted, -leting.* To make eyelets (holes) in; also, to insert metal eyelets in.—**eye-let-eer′** (-le-tēr′), *n.* A small pointed instrument for making eyelet-holes; a stiletto.—**eye′let=hole,** *n.* An eyelet, or small hole.

eye-lid (ī′lid), *n.* The movable lid of skin which serves to cover (and uncover) the eyeball.

eye=o-pen-er (ī′ō″pn-ėr), *n.* Something that causes the eyes to open, as an enlightening or startling disclosure or experience; also, a drink of liquor, esp. one taken early in the day. [Colloq.]

eye-piece (ī′pēs), *n.* In an optical instrument, the lens or combination of lenses to which the eye is applied.

ey-er (ī′ėr), *n.* One who eyes, or watches narrowly.

eye=ser-vant (ī′sėr″vạnt), *n.* A servant or other who attends to his duty only when watched by his employer. Also **eye′=serv″er.**—**eye′=ser″vice,** *n.* Service performed only under the eye or watch of the employer (see Col. iii. 22); also, homage paid with the eyes; admiring looks.

eye-shot (ī′shot), *n.* Range of vision; view; also, a glance.

eye-sight (ī′sīt), *n.* The power or faculty of seeing; also, the action or fact of seeing; also, the range of the eye.

eye-sore (ī′sōr), *n.* Something offensive to the eye; an object of dislike.

eye=spot (ī′spot), *n.* An eye-like spot, as on the tail of a peacock; one of the three round spots or scars at one end of a cocoanut; also, a rudimentary sensory organ, in many of the lower animals, supposed to have a visual function; a spot supposedly sensitive to light, on certain unicellular algæ; also, the rudiment of an eye in an embryo.

eye=stalk (ī′stâk), *n.* In *zoöl.*, the stalk or peduncle upon which the eye is borne in lobsters, shrimps, etc.

eye-stone (ī′stōn), *n.* A small calcareous body, flat on one side and convex on the other, passed between the eye and the eyelid to bring out cinders, etc.

eye=strain (ī′strān), *n.* The strained condition or weakness of the eyes caused by excessive use, uncorrected vision, reading in dim light, etc.: often giving rise to headache or other disorders.

eye=strings (ī′stringz), *n. pl.* The muscles, tendons, or nerves of the eye: formerly supposed to break at death or on loss of sight.

eye=tooth (ī′töth), *n.*; pl. *-teeth* (-tēth). A canine tooth, esp. of the upper jaw: so named from its position under the eye.

eye=wash (ī′wosh), *n.* A lotion for the eyes.

eye=wa-ter (ī′wâ″tėr), *n.* An eye-wash; also, the fluid refractive media of the eye.

eye=wink (ī′wingk), *n.* A wink of the eye; also, the time taken to wink; an instant; also, a look or glance.—**eye′=wink″er,** *n.* An eyelash.

eye=wit-ness (ī′wit′nes), *n.* One who actually beholds some act or occurrence, and hence can give testimony concerning it.

ey-ot (ī′ọt), *n.* [Var. of *ait*.] An islet; an ait. [Eng.]

ey-ra (ā′rạ), *n.* [S. Amer.] An American wildcat, *Felis eyra*, found from Paraguay to southern Texas.

Eyra.

eyre (ãr), *n.* [OF. *eire*, < *errer*, journey, travel: see *errant*.] A journey in a circuit (as, justices in *eyre*, formerly, justices who rode the circuit to hold court; "a regular system of judicial *eyres*," Stubbs's "Constitutional Hist. of Eng.," xi. § 134); also, the court held by justices in eyre.

ey-rie, ey-ry (ã′ri or ē′ri), *n.* See *aery*[2].

F

F, f (ef); pl. *F's, f's* (efs). A consonant, the 6th letter of the English alphabet.

fa (fä), *n.* In *music*, the syllable used for the fourth tone of the scale (F, in the major scale of C), and sometimes for the tone F. See *sol-fa*.

fa-ba-ceous (fạ-bā′shius), *a.* [L. *fabaceus*, < *faba*, bean.] Of the bean kind; bean-like; specif., belonging to the *Fabaceæ*, or bean family of plants, including many herbs, shrubs, and trees, as the bean, pea, lentil, furze, broom, locust, etc., which bear seeds in pods or legumes. Cf. *leguminous*.

Fa-bi-an (fā′bi-ạn). **I.** *a.* Characteristic or suggestive of Quintus Fabius Maximus Cunctator ('the Delayer'), a Roman general who sought to wear out the enemy (Hannibal) by harassing tactics without risking a decisive battle; cautiously dilatory; hence, designating or pertaining to a socialistic society founded in London about 1884, advocating a socialism of the more moderate type, to be spread gradually without attempts at revolutionary action. **II.** *n.* A member of or sympathizer with the Fabian Society.

fa-ble (fā′bl), *n.* [OF. F. *fable*, < L. *fabula*, < *fari*, speak, say.] A story or tale; esp., a short story (often with animals or inanimate things as speakers or actors) devised to convey a moral; an apologue; also, a legend or myth; legendary story; also, a mere fiction or fabrication; also, the plot of an epic or dramatic poem; also, a subject of common talk; a byword.—**fa′ble,** *v.*; *-bled, -bling.* **I.** *intr.* To tell or write fables; romance; also, to tell false stories; lie. **II.** *tr.* To invent or tell as a fable; relate, celebrate, or represent in a fable; also, to make up falsely (as, "I *fabled* nothing fair, But . . . told her all": Tennyson's "Princess," iii. 120); fabricate; feign.—**fa′bled,** *p. a.* Related or celebrated in fables; legendary; also, having no real existence; fictitious.—**fa′bler,** *n.*

fab-li-au (fab-li-ō′), *n.*; pl. *-aux* (-ōz′). [F., a dim. form < OF. *fable*, E. *fable*.] One of the short metrical tales of the medieval French trouvères.

fab-ric (fab′rik), *n.* [OF. F. *fabrique*, < L. *fabrica*, workshop, art, product of art, structure, < *faber*, artisan.] Something constructed; a structure, edifice, or frame (as, "We build with what we deem eternal rock: A distant age asks where the *fabric* stood": Cowper's "Task," v. 535); any system of combined parts; specif., a material made by weaving, felting, or otherwise combining fibers; a cloth, texture, or tissue; also, the act or process of constructing; also, mode of construction; structure, formation, or make.

fab-ri-cant (fab′ri-kạnt), *n.* [F. *fabricant*, < L. *fabricans* (*-ant-*), ppr.] One who fabricates; a manufacturer.

fab-ri-cate (fab′ri-kāt), *v. t.*; *-cated, -cating.* [L. *fabricatus*, pp. of *fabricari*, *fabricare*, make, construct, < *fabrica*: see *fabric.*] To make by art and labor; construct; frame; manufacture; specif., to construct by the putting together of standard parts or sections, as certain ships built in the U. S. during the World War from parts made, shaped, punched, etc., in different steel-mills, foundries, machine-shops, etc., and delivered to the shipyards ready for assembling; manufacture (standard parts or sections) for such construction; also, to make up or invent; concoct; devise falsely.—**fab-ri-ca′tion** (-kā′shǫn), *n.* [L. *fabricatio(n-).*] The act of fabricating; construction; manufacture; fictitious invention; also, something fabricated, as a false story. —**fab′ri-ca-tive** (-kạ-tiv), *a.* Fabricating; constructive. —**fab′ri-ca-tor** (-kā-tǫr), *n.*

fab-ri-koid (fab′ri-koid), *n.* [See *fabric* and *-oid.*] An impervious fabric, in most varieties leather-like in appearance, having a cloth foundation and a pyroxylin surface, used in upholstering furniture and automobiles, binding books, making traveling goods, and for various other purposes where it replaces leather, cloth, paper, metal, etc. [Proprietary name.]

fab-u-lar (fab′ū̦-lạr), *a.* [L. *fabularis.*] Pertaining to or of the nature of a fable; fabulous.

fab-u-list (fab′ū̦-list), *n.* [F. *fabuliste.*] One who invents or relates fables.

fab-u-lous (fab′ū̦-lus), *a.* [L. *fabulosus.*] Of the nature of a fable; characterized by fables; legendary; also, belonging to fable; mythical; imaginary; also, like a fable; incredible or amazing (as, *fabulous* wealth; a *fabulous* price); also, addicted to telling fables.—**fab′u-lous-ly,** *adv.*—**fab′u-lous-ness,** *n.*

fa-çade (fạ-säd′), *n.* [F., < It. *facciata,* < *faccia,* < L. *facies,* E. *face.*] The face or front, or a principal face, of a building.

face (fās), *n.* [OF. F. *face,* < L. *facies,* form, appearance, face.] The front of the head; the visage or countenance; an expression of countenance (as, an unhappy *face*); a grimace (as, to make *faces*); assurance or effrontery (as, to have the *face* to deny a fact); aspect, appearance, show, or semblance (as in the title of Charles Kingsley's novel, "Hypatia; or, New Foes with an Old *Face*"); front, sight, or presence (as, "Moses fled from the *face* of Pharaoh": Ex. ii. 15); in general, the front, principal, or working surface, as of a clock, a type, or a tool; any surface, as of a cube; of a document, the manifest sense or express terms; the amount specified in a bill or note, exclusive of interest; in *mining,* the front or end of a drift or excavation, where the material is being mined or was last mined; in *fort.,* either of the two outer sides which form the salient angle of a bastion or the like; sometimes, the front between two adjacent bastions; *milit.,* any side of a battalion or the like when formed in a square. Used in many fig. phrases: as, to set one's *face* against a plan; to put a good *face* on a bad matter; to hold firm in the *face* of the enemy or of danger; to save one's *face* (to save one's dignity or general credit).—**face,** *v.*; *faced, facing.* **I.** *tr.* To have or turn the face toward; look toward; hence, to confront; meet boldly; brave; also, to cause to present the face; also, to overlay with some material; also, to dress the surface of (stone, etc.). **II.** *intr.* To have or turn the face in a given direction; front (*on, to,* or *toward*).—**face′=card,** *n.* A playing-card on which a face is represented; a court-card.—**faced,** *a.* Having a face or visage (as, round-*faced*); also, having a special finish on the face or surface (as, *faced* cloth; satin-*faced* ribbon).—**face′=hard″en,** *v. t.* To harden the face or surface of (steel or other metal, or a metallic object) by chilling, case-hardening, or the like. Cf. *case-harden.*—**fa-cer** (fā′sėr), *n.* One who or that which faces; also, a blow in the face; fig., a staggering check or reverse.

Compound Eye of House-fly (side view) showing Facets. (Highly magnified.)

fa-cet (fas′et), *n.* [F. *facette,* dim. of *face,* E. *face.*] A little face, esp. one of the small polished surfaces of a cut gem; in *arch.,* the fillet between the flutings of a column; in *zoöl.,* one of the divisions of the cornea, as of an insect, forming the surface of one of the small eyes of a compound eye.—**fa′cet,** *v. t.*; *-ceted, -ceting.* To cut a facet or facets on.

fa-cete (fạ-sēt′), *a.* [L. *facetus,* fine, elegant, witty.] Elegant† or polished†; also, witty or facetious (obs. or archaic).

fa-ce-ti-æ (fạ-sē′shi-ē), *n. pl.* [L., pl. of *facetia,* a witticism, < *facetus*: see *facete.*] Witty or humorous sayings or writings (as, "The reply is . . . among the most celebrated of *facetiæ*": Motley's "Dutch Republic," i. 1); also, in booksellers' and collectors' catalogues, books of a coarsely humorous (or indecent) kind.

fa-ce-tious (fạ-sē′shus), *a.* [F. *facétieux,* < *facétie,* < L. *facetia*: see *facetiæ.*] Characterized by or given to pleasantry; jocose; jocular; waggish: as, a *facetious* remark; a *facetious* companion.—**fa-ce′tious-ly,** *adv.*—**fa-ce′tious-ness,** *n.*

fa-cial (fā′shạl), *a.* [ML. *facialis.*] Of or pertaining to the face.—**facial angle,** in *craniom.,* the angle formed by a line passing from the nostril to the center of the external auditory opening, and another line from the nostril to the most prominent part of the forehead ('facial angle of Camper').—**fa′cial-ly,** *adv.*

fa-ci-end (fā′shi-end), *n.* [L. *faciendum,* neut. gerundive of *facere,* do, make.] In *math.,* a magnitude which is operated upon, as a multiplicand.

-facient. [L. *facient-,* nom. *faciens,* ppr. of *facere,* do, make.] A termination of adjectives meaning 'making' or 'causing' (something), and of nouns denoting an agent that causes something, as in *abortifacient, absorbefacient, liquefacient, rubefacient.*

fa-cile (fas′il), *a.* [OF. F. *facile,* < L. *facilis,* easy to do, easy, < *facere,* do, make.] Easily done, performed, used, etc. (as, a *facile* task or operation; *facile* methods or means); presenting little difficulty; also, moving, acting, working, proceeding, etc., with ease (as, a *facile* hand, tongue, or pen; the gift of *facile* expression); ready; fluent; also, easy or unconstrained, as manners or persons; affable, agreeable, or complaisant; mild, indulgent, or lenient; easily influenced, pliant, or yielding (as, "Since Adam and his *facile* consort Eve Lost Paradise": Milton's "Paradise Regained," i. 51).—**fa′cile-ly,** *adv.*—**fa′cile-ness,** *n.*

fa-cil-i-tate (fạ-sil′i-tāt), *v. t.*; *-tated, -tating.* [F. *faciliter,* < L. *facilis,* easy, E. *facile.*] To make easy or less difficult; lessen the labor of; help forward (a process); also, to assist the progress of (a person).—**fa-cil-i-ta′tion** (-tā′shǫn), *n.*—**fa-cil′i-ta-tor,** *n.*

fa-cil-i-ty (fạ-sil′i-ti), *n.*; pl. *-ties* (-tiz). [F. *facilité,* < L. *facilitas,* < *facilis,* easy, E. *facile.*] The quality of being facile, or easily performed, used, etc.; also, opportunity or a means for the easy performance of something (as, to afford *facility* of movement; *facilities* for communication); also, readiness or dexterity proceeding from skill or practice; ease; aptitude; fluency, as of style; also, ease of manners; affability or complaisance; pliancy of mind or disposition.

fa-ci-ne-ri-ous† (fas-i-nē′ri-us), *a.* Same as *facinorous.* See Shakspere's "All's Well," ii. 3. 35.

fa-cing (fā′sing), *n.* The act of one who or that which faces; also, a covering in front, for ornament, protection, etc.; a superficial layer, as one of stone or other material forming the face of a wall, etc.; material applied on the face of a garment, as for trimming or protection; *pl.,* coverings of a different color applied on the collar, cuffs, or other parts of a military coat.

fa-cin-o-rous (fạ-sin′ǫ-rus), *a.* [L. *facinorosus,* < *facinus* (*facinor-*), deed, bad deed, < *facere,* do, make.] Atrociously wicked. [Archaic.]

fac-sim-i-le (fak-sim′i-lē̦). [L. *fac,* impv. of *facere,* do, make, + *simile,* neut. of *similis,* like.] **I.** *n.* An exact copy or likeness. **II.** *a.* Of the nature of a facsimile; also, producing facsimiles.—**facsimile telegraph,** a telegraphic device for transmitting facsimiles of written messages, drawings, etc.—**fac-sim′i-le,** *v. t.*; *-led* (-lē̦d), *-leing.* To make, or serve as, a facsimile of.

fact (fakt), *n.* [L. *factum,* a thing done, prop. neut. of *factus,* pp. of *facere,* do, make.] A deed or act, often an evil deed (now only in certain legal phrases, as *before the fact* and *after the fact*); also, something that has really happened, or is actually the case; a real occurrence, or state of things, as distinguished from something merely alleged or believed; hence, a truth known by actual observation or authentic testimony; loosely, something which is alleged to be, and may or may not be, the case (as, the truth of the *fact* is in question; his *facts* are not trustworthy); also, actual occurrence, or reality (as, matters of *fact*; in *fact* rather than in theory).

fac-tion (fak′shọn), *n.* [F. *faction*, < L. *factio(n-)*, a doing or making, action, party, faction, < *facere*, do, make: cf. *fashion.*] An action† or proceeding†; also, a company of persons acting or associated together or having a common end in view; now, usually, a group or body of persons with strongly and narrowly partizan aims; often, a party, or a section of a party, disposed toward unscrupulous or lawless means of advancing its purposes; also, party strife; dissension.—**fac′tion-al,** *a.*—**fac′tion-ist,** *n.* A promoter or a member of a faction.—**fac′tious** (-shus), *a.* [L. *factiosus*, < *factio(n-)*.] Given to faction or party strife; turbulent; also, pertaining to or proceeding from faction, as actions.—**fac′tious-ly,** *adv.*—**fac′tious-ness,** *n.*

fac-ti-tious (fak-tish′us), *a.* [L. *facticius*, < *facere*, do, make.] Made, manufactured, or artificial, as a product of art or labor; also, made, contrived, or worked up, rather than spontaneous or natural (as, a *factitious* demand for a commodity; a *factitious* value; *factitious* enthusiasm); made for the purpose or occasion; conventional.—**fac-ti′tious-ly,** *adv.*—**fac-ti′tious-ness,** *n.*

fac-ti-tive (fak′ti-tiv), *a.* [NL. *factitivus*, < L. *facere*, do, make.] In *gram.*, making or rendering as specified, as a verb when used with an adjunct expressing something predicated of the direct object, as in 'they *made* him their ruler' and 'to *paint* the house red'; pertaining to such a verb.—**fac′ti-tive-ly,** *adv.*

fac-tor (fak′tọr), *n.* [L., doer, maker, < *facere*, do, make.] One who does or makes something (obs. or archaic); also, one who acts, or transacts business, for another; specif., a commission-merchant; an agent intrusted with the possession of goods for sale; also, the steward or bailiff of an estate (now only Sc.); a person legally appointed to have charge of forfeited or sequestered property (Sc.); a person warned as a garnishee (local, U. S.); in *math.*, one of two or more numbers, algebraic expressions, or the like, which when multiplied together produce a given product (as, 6 and 3 are *factors* of 18); hence, in general, one of the elements that contribute to bring about any given result.—**fac′tor,** *v. t.* In *math.*, to resolve into factors.—**fac′tor-age** (-āj), *n.* The action or business of a factor; also, the allowance or commission paid to a factor.—**fac-to′ri-al** (-tō′ri-al). **I.** *a.* Of or pertaining to a factor or a factory; in *math.*, of or pertaining to factors or factorials. **II.** *n.* In *math.*, the product of an integer multiplied by all the lower integers: as, the *factorial* of 4 is $4 \times 3 \times 2 \times 1 = 24$.—**fac′tor-ize,** *v. t.*; *-ized, -izing.* In *law*, to garnish; in *math.*, to resolve into factors.—**fac′tor-ship,** *n.* The office or business of a factor.

fac-to-ry (fak′tọ-ri), *n.*; pl. *-ries* (-riz). [ML. *factoria*, < L. *factor*: see *factor.*] An establishment for factors and merchants carrying on business in a foreign country; also, a building or group of buildings, usually with equipment, where goods are manufactured (as, "Everywhere there sprang up *factories* using first water then steam power": H. G. Wells's "Outline of History," xxxvi. § 12).

fac-to-tum (fak-tō′tum), *n.* [L. *fac*, impv. of *facere*, do, make, + *totum*, neut. of *totus*, all, whole.] A busybody†; also, one employed to do all kinds of work for another (as, "Saunders was a model valet and *factotum*": Reade's "Christie Johnstone," i.).

fac-tu-al (fak′tū-al), *a.* Pertaining to facts; of the nature of fact; real.—**fac′tu-al-ly,** *adv.*

fac-tum (fak′tum), *n.*; pl. *-ta* (-tä). [L.: see *fact.*] A statement of the facts of a case or controversy; a memorial.

fac-ture (fak′tūr), *n.* [L. *factura*, < *facere*, do, make.] The act, process, or manner of making anything; construction; also, the thing made.

fac-u-la (fak′ū-lä), *n.*; pl. *-læ* (-lē). [L., dim. of *fax*, torch.] In *astron.*, one of the irregular patches on the sun's disk, brighter than the general surface.—**fac′u-lar** (-lär), *a.*

fac-ul-ta-tive (fak′ul-tā-tiv), *a.* Conferring a faculty, privilege, or permission, or the power of doing or not doing something (as, a *facultative* enactment); hence, left to one's option or choice; optional; also, that may or may not take place; that may or may not assume a specified character; in *biol.*, having the power to exist under different conditions of life (opposed to *obligate*).

fac-ul-ty (fak′ul-ti), *n.*; pl. *-ties* (-tiz). [OF. *faculte* (F. *faculté*), < L. *facultas*, ability, power, means, property, akin to *facul*, easily, *facilis*, easy: cf. *facility* and *difficulty.*] A capacity, natural or acquired, for a particular kind of action; an inherent capability of the body or of a bodily organ, as sight or hearing; one of the powers of the mind, as memory or reason; one of the aptitudes supposed in phrenology to be indicated by the natural protuberances, or bumps, of the skull; executive ability, or efficiency (colloq.); pecuniary ability, or resources (often in *pl.*: now rare); also, one of the departments of learning, as theology, medicine, or law, in a university; the teaching body, sometimes with the students, in any of these departments; the entire teaching force of a university, college, or school; also, an art or profession (archaic); the members of a learned profession, esp. the medical profession; also, a power or privilege conferred; a dispensation, license, or authorization (esp. *eccles.*).

fac-und (fak′und or fa-kund′), *a.* [OF. *facond*, < L. *facundus*, < *fari*, speak.] Eloquent. [Archaic.]

fad (fad), *n.* [Origin unknown.] A favored or popular pursuit, diversion, fashion, etc., prevailing for a time; a pet practice or notion; a hobby.—**fad′dish,** *a.* Fad-like; given to fads.—**fad′dism,** *n.* Addiction to fads.—**fad′dist,** *n.*—**fad′dy,** *a.* Faddish.

fade (fād, F. fȧd), *a.* [OF. F. *fade*, prob. < L. *vapidus*, E. *vapid.*] Having lost freshness, strength, or life; faded; colorless; dull; insipid; flat. [Archaic except as French.]—**fade,** *v.*; *faded, fading.* [OF. *fader*, < *fade.*] **I.** *intr.* To lose freshness and vigor; wither, as a plant; fail gradually in strength or health, as a person; often, to lose youthful freshness, coloring, etc., as with the passage of time; also, to lose brightness or vividness, as light or color; in general, to fail or disappear gradually; die gradually (*away* or *out*). **II.** *tr.* To cause to fade: as, "No winter could his laurels *fade*" (Dryden's "Stanzas on Oliver Cromwell," xv.).—**fade′less,** *a.* Not fading.—**fade′less-ly,** *adv.*

fadge (faj), *v. i.*; *fadged, fadging.* [Origin unknown.] To fit or suit; agree; succeed or thrive; make one's way. [Obs. or prov. Eng.]

fad-ing† (fad′ing), *n.* [Origin unknown.] The name of a kind of dance: also used in the phrase 'with a fading,' in the burden of a song (cf. Shakspere's "Winter's Tale," iv. 4. 195).

fæ-ces (fē′sēz), etc. See *feces*, etc.

fæc-u-la (fek′ū-lä), *n.* See *fecula.*

fa-er-ie, fa-er-y (fā′ėr-i). [Var. of *fairy.*] **I.** *n.* Fairyland; also, a fairy. [Archaic.] **II.** *a.* Fairy. [Archaic.]

fag[1] (fag), *v.*; *fagged, fagging.* [Origin obscure: cf. *flag*[1].] **I.** *intr.* To flag or droop (now Sc. and prov. Eng.); also, to work till wearied; work hard (as, "I *fagged* away at German": C. Brontë's "Jane Eyre," xxxiv.); labor; toil; also, to act as a fag. **II.** *tr.* To tire by labor; weary; also, to make a fag of.—**fag**[1], *n.* Drudgery; toil; also, in English schools, a boy who performs menial services for another boy in a higher form or class (as, "His lordship . . . talked much of my uncle . . . whose *fag* he had been at Eton": Lever's "Harry Lorrequer," iii.); hence, a drudge.

fag[2] (fag), *n.* [Cf. *fag*[1], *v.*] A fag-end, as of a piece of cloth or of a cigar; also, a cigarette (slang, Eng.).

fa-ga-ceous (fa-gā′shius), *a.* [L. *fagus*, beech.] Belonging to the *Fagaceæ*, or beech family of trees and shrubs, which includes the beech, chestnut, oak, etc.

fag=end (fag′end′), *n.* [See *fag*[2].] The unfinished end of a piece of cloth; the untwisted end of a rope; hence, the last and inferior part of anything; a remnant; the very end of something (as, "the *fag-end* of the eighth volume," Sterne's "Tristram Shandy," viii. 35; the *fag-end* of the evening).

fag-ger (fag′ėr), *n.* One who fags.

fag-ot, fag-got (fag′ọt), *n.* [OF. F. *fagot*; origin uncertain.] A bundle of sticks, twigs, or small branches of trees bound together, used for fuel, as a fascine, etc., and often formerly in burning heretics alive; also, a bundle of pieces of iron or steel to be welded; in fig. use, a collection (as, a *fagot* of selections).—**fag′ot, fag′got,** *v. t.* To bind or make into a fagot; also, to ornament with fagoting.—**fag′ot-ing, fag′-got-ing,** *n.* A kind of drawn-work in which threads are drawn out along a line and the remaining cross-threads are arranged in a succession of bundles, each bound together in the middle.

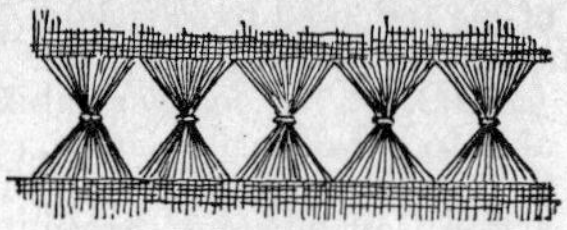

Fagoting.

fa-got-to (fä-got′tō), *n.*; pl. *-ti* (-tē). [It.] A bassoon.

fahl-band (fäl′band, G. fäl′bänt), *n.* [G., 'fallow band.'] In *mining*, a belt or zone of rock impregnated with metallic sulphides.

Fah-ren-heit (fä′ren-hīt or far′en-), *a.* Noting or pertaining to a thermometric scale introduced by G. D. Fahrenheit (1686–1736), a German physicist, in which the melting-point of ice is 32° above the zero, and the boiling-point of water 212° above the zero. Abbreviated *F.* and *Fahr.*

fa-ience (fä-yoṅs), *n.* [F. *faïence*, orig. pottery of Faenza, city in northeastern Italy.] A glazed earthenware or pottery, esp. a fine variety with highly colored designs.

Armorial Faience.

fail (fāl), *v.* [OF. F. *faillir*, < L. *fallere* (pp. *falsus*), deceive, disappoint: cf. *false* and *fault*.] **I.** *intr.* To be wanting or lacking; be inadequate or insufficient; also, to become exhausted, as supplies; fall off, dwindle, or pass away (as, "Where wealth and freedom reign, contentment *fails*": Goldsmith's "Traveller," 91); die away (as, "The sound, upon the fitful gale, In solemn wise did rise and *fail*": Scott's "Lay of the Last Minstrel," i. 31); also, to lose strength or vigor; become weaker; also, to prove deficient upon trial; break down, as under strain or pressure (as, "O let the solid ground Not *fail* beneath my feet": Tennyson's "Maud," i. 11. 1); prove wanting at need; also, to be wanting or deficient in some respect (as, the portrait *fails* in expression; an argument which *fails* of coherence); also, to come short of performing duties or functions (as, "Nature *fail'd* in me": Milton's "Paradise Lost," viii. 534); also, to prove or be unsuccessful, as in an attempt or enterprise (as, "Our envious foe hath *fail'd*," Milton's "Paradise Lost," vii. 139; "My project *fails*," Shakspere's "Tempest," Epilogue, 12); result badly, as crops; come short of obtaining something desired or accomplishing something attempted (with *of*: as, "A new translation . . . could not *fail* of a favourable reception," Johnson, in Boswell's "Johnson," 1737; "His man never *failed* of bringing in his prey," Steele, in "Guardian," 17); specif., to become insolvent or bankrupt. **II.** *tr.* To become weak or faint within (one), as the heart, courage, memory, etc.; prove of no use or avail to, as some expected or usual resource; also, to lack or want (now rare); also, to neglect to perform or observe (now chiefly with an infinitive: as, "Burst be the ear that *fails* to heed!" Scott's "Lady of the Lake," iii. 11); also, to prove unsuccessful in, or prove unable (with an infinitive: as, "You scarce can *fail* to match his masterpiece," Tennyson's "Gardener's Daughter," 31).—**fail,** *n.* [OF. *faile, faille.*] Failure: now only in the phrase following.—**without fail,** without failure as to performance, occurrence, etc.: as, I will pay you to-morrow *without fail*; come Saturday *without fail*.—**fail′er,** *n.*—**fail′ing,** *n.* The act or state of one who or that which fails; a failure; also, a defect, shortcoming, or weakness (as, "And e'en his *failings* lean'd to virtue's side": Goldsmith's "Deserted Village," 164).—**fail′ing,** *prep.* [Orig. ppr.] In default of.—**fail′ing-ly,** *adv.*

faille (fāl, F. fä-y'), *n.* [F.] A soft, transversely ribbed silk fabric.

fail-ure (fāl′ūr), *n.* [AF. *failer*, orig. inf., OF. *faillir*, E. *fail.*] The act of failing, or the state of having failed; lack or default; deficiency; a becoming exhausted; loss of strength or vigor; a giving way under trial; omission of performance of something due or required; a proving unsuccessful, or want of success; a becoming insolvent or bankrupt; also, one who or that which proves unsuccessful.

fain (fān), *a.* [AS. *fægen* = Icel. *feginn*, glad.] Glad, pleased, or rejoiced (archaic or prov.); also, content or willing (with an infinitive); hence, constrained or obliged (as, to be *fain* to acknowledge that one is in the wrong); also, desirous or eager (archaic or prov.).—**fain,** *adv.* Gladly; willingly; by preference. [Archaic.]

fai-naigue (fą-nāg′), *v.*; *-naigued, -naiguing.* [Origin uncertain: cf. *renege.*] **I.** *intr.* To revoke at cards; renege; also, to break one's word; evade duty; shirk; also, to use guile; finagle. [Prov. Eng.] **II.** *tr.* To get by guile; finagle. [Prov. Eng.]—**fai-nai′guer** (-nā′gėr), *n.*

fai-né-ant (fā-nā-äṅ). [F., < *faire*, do, + *néant*, nothing.] **I.** *a.* That does nothing; idle; indolent: an epithet applied to the later Merovingian kings. **II.** *n.* An idler.—**fai-ne-ance, fai-ne-an-cy** (fā′nā-ąns, -ąn-si), *n.*

faint (fānt), *a.* [OF. *faint, feint*, feigned, hypocritical, sluggish, spiritless, pp. of *feindre*, E. *feign.*] Feigned† or pretended†; also, wanting in courage, cowardly, or timorous (now chiefly in 'faint heart'); also, wanting in strength or vigor, as persons†; feeble or half-hearted, as actions, etc. (as, *faint* resistance; to damn with *faint* praise, see Pope's "Prologue to the Satires," 201); also, feeble in effect upon the senses or mind; deficient in brightness, vividness, loudness, strength, etc., as light, color, sound, odor, etc.; indistinct; hardly perceptible; not clear, strong, or well-defined, as a resemblance, an idea, etc.; also, having a feeling of extreme weakness or exhaustion; inclined to faint or swoon; sometimes, producing such a feeling; oppressive, as the atmosphere.—**faint,** *v. i.* To lose courage (archaic: as, "If thou *faint* in the day of adversity, thy strength is small," Prov. xxiv. 10); also, to grow weak or feeble (archaic); also, to lose brightness, vividness, etc., as color (now rare); also, to fall into a swoon.—**faint,** *n.* A swoon.—**faint′er,** *n.*—**faint′=heart′ed,** *a.* Lacking courage or energy; cowardly; timorous.—**faint′=heart′ed-ly,** *adv.*—**faint′=heart′ed-ness,** *n.*—**faint′ing-ly,** *adv.*—**faint′-ish,** *a.* Rather faint.—**faint′ly,** *adv.*—**faint′ness,** *n.*—**faints,** *n. pl.* The impure spirit which comes over first and last in the distillation of whisky, etc.

fair[1] (fãr), *a.* [AS. *fæger* = OHG. *fagar* = Icel. *fagr*, fair, = Goth. *fagrs*, fit, suitable.] Beautiful or comely; pleasing in appearance; attractive; also, specious or plausible (as, *fair* promises); also, gentle, peaceable, or civil (as, *fair* words); also, of a light hue (as, a *fair* skin); not dark; also, free from blemish or imperfection; spotless; clean; pure; clear or legible, as writing; without irregularity or unevenness, as a line or surface; also, free from bias or injustice, as statements, actions, etc.; impartial; equitable; honest; not taking undue advantage, as persons; that may be legitimately sought, pursued, etc., as game; also, passable, or moderately satisfactory; free from grave objection; average; also, marked by favoring conditions (as, to be in a *fair* way to succeed); likely; promising; also, unobstructed, as a view; also, *U. S. Weather Bureau*, fine; bright; sunny; cloudless to half cloudy; with no aspect of rain, snow, or hail; not stormy.—**fair ball** or **fair hit,** in *baseball*, a batted ball that comes to rest between home and first base or home and third base and within the foul lines, or that when bounding past first or third base is within the foul lines, or that first strikes the ground beyond first or third base and within the foul lines, or that while on or over the ground within the foul lines touches the person of the umpire or a player.—**fair catch,** in *football*, a ball so caught as to entitle the catcher's side to a free kick.—**fair copy,** a copy of a document made after final correction; also, the condition of such a copy.—**fair green,** in *golf*, that part of the links between tees and putting-greens where the grass is kept short.—**fair hit.** See *fair ball*, above.—**fair play,** fair or impartial action or treatment, as in a game; the allowance of equitable conditions or due opportunities.—**the fair sex,** the female sex; women.—**fair**[1], *n.* That which is fair; also, one of the fair sex (archaic); a woman,

esp. a beloved woman (archaic); also, fairness† or beauty†. —**fair**[1], *adv.* [AS. *fægere.*] In a fair manner; beautifully; agreeably; kindly or civilly; clearly or legibly; evenly or straight; directly or straight, as in aiming or hitting; impartially, equitably, or honestly; in a moderately satisfactory manner; favorably or auspiciously (as, to bid *fair*, to offer a good prospect, or give good promise).—**fair**[1], *v.* **I.** *intr.* To become fair; of the weather, to clear. **II.** *tr.* To make fair. See Shakspere's "Sonnets," cxxvii.

fair[2] (fãr), *n.* [OF. *feire* (F. *foire*), < L. *feria*, holiday.] A periodical gathering of buyers and sellers in an appointed place; also, a competitive exhibition of farm products, live stock, etc.; also, an exhibition and sale of fancy articles to raise money, often for some charitable purpose.

fair=faced (fãr′fāst), *a.* Having a fair or beautiful face; also, fair or light of complexion; also, fair-seeming or specious.

fair=ground (fãr′ground), *n.* An inclosure where fairs, horse-races, etc., are held: often in *pl.*

fair=haired (fãr′hãrd), *a.* Having fair or light-colored hair.

fair-i-ly (fãr′i-li), *adv.* In a fairy-like manner.

fair-ing (fãr′ing), *n.* A present given at or brought from a fair; in general, a present; a gift. [Archaic or prov.]

fair=lead, fair=lead-er (fãr′lēd, -lē″dėr), *n.* *Naut.*, a ring, thimble, or block, or a strip of board with holes in it, through which running rigging is passed to be guided and kept clear.

Fair-lead.

fair-ly (fãr′li), *adv.* In a fair manner; beautifully; courteously; clearly or distinctly; justly, impartially, or equitably; becomingly or properly; legitimately (as, to come *fairly* by a thing); moderately, passably, or tolerably (as, *fairly* good; *fairly* safe); actually, positively, or completely (as, the wheels *fairly* spun).

fair=mind-ed (fãr′mīn′ded), *a.* Fair or just in mind or judgment; impartial; unprejudiced.—**fair′=mind′ed-ness**, *n.*

fair-ness (fãr′nes), *n.* The quality of being fair.

fair=seem-ing (fãr′sē′ming), *a.* Seeming to be fair; specious; plausible.

fair=sound-ing (fãr′soun′ding), *a.* Fair or plausible in sound.

fair=spok-en (fãr′spō′kn), *a.* Fair, civil, or suave of speech; smooth-tongued.

fair-way (fãr′wā), *n.* An unobstructed passage or way; *naut.*, in a harbor, river, etc., the navigable portion or channel for vessels; the usual course taken by vessels, as in making a port; in *golf*, same as *fair green* (see under *fair*[1], *a.*).

fair=weath-er (fãr′weᴛʜ″ėr), *a.* Of or for fair weather; unfitted to endure storms; fig., weakening or failing in time of trial or adversity.

fair-y (fãr′i), *n.*; pl. *-ies* (-iz). [OF. *faerie* (F. *féerie*), < *fae*, E. *fay*[2].] Enchantment† or magic†; also, one of a class of imaginary beings, generally conceived as of diminutive human form, having magical powers capriciously exercised for good or evil in human affairs; also, such beings collectively†; also, fairyland†.—**fairy of the mine**, a kobold or gnome.—**fair′y**, *a.* Of or pertaining to fairies; also, of the nature of a fairy; fairy-like.—**fairy bluebird**, any of several East Indian passerine birds constituting the genus *Irena*, which are brilliantly blue and black in color.—**fairy ring**, a circle formed on the grass in a field by the growth of certain fungi, formerly supposed to be caused by fairies in their dances. —**fair′y-hood** (-hůd), *n.* Fairy state or nature; also, fairies collectively.—**fair′y-ism**, *n.* The state, character, or action of a fairy; fairy-like quality; also, belief in fairies.—**fair′y-land** (-land), *n.* The imaginary realm of the fairies; hence, any region such as might be the home of fairies.—**fair′y=tale**, *n.* A tale or story about fairies or other magical beings or agencies; hence, a statement or assertion of something imaginary or untrue.

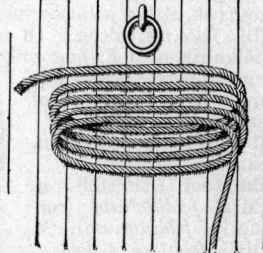

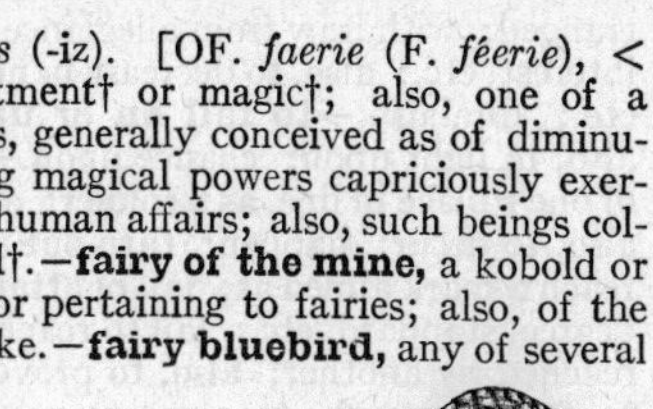
Fairy Bluebird (*Irena puella*).

faith (fāth), *n.* [OF. *feid*, *fei* (F. *foi*), < L. *fides*, faith, < *fidere*, trust.] Confidence or trust in a person or thing; belief in the truth of a statement or doctrine; often, belief due to reliance on testimony or authority; also, the doctrines which are or should be believed; esp., a system of religious belief (as, the Christian *faith*; the Jewish *faith*); often, the Christian faith ('the faith'); also, the obligation of loyalty or fidelity, as to a person or to a promise or engagement (as, to pledge one's *faith*; to keep *faith*); also, the observance of the obligations of loyalty or fidelity (as, to act in good or bad *faith*); loyalty; fidelity; faithfulness; also, truth (in asseverative phrases, as 'in faith'); in *theol.*, belief in the doctrines or teachings of religion (as, "*Faith* without works is dead": Jas. ii. 26); also, that trust in God and in his promises as made through Christ by which man is justified or saved (as, "Therefore being justified by *faith*, we have peace with God through our Lord Jesus Christ": Rom. v. 1); also, spiritual perception of truths and realities not revealed through sense or reason (as, "Now *faith* is the substance of things hoped for, the evidence of things not seen": Heb. xi. 1).—**faith**†, *v. t.* To trust; believe. See Shakspere's "King Lear," ii. 1. 72.—**faith**, *interj.* In faith; in truth; indeed. See Shakspere's "Twelfth Night," ii. 3. 11.—**faith′=cure**, *n.* A method of attempting to cure disease by prayer and religious faith alone; also, a cure effected by this method.—**faith′ful. I.** *a.* Full of faith, trusting, or believing (archaic: as, "So then they which be of faith are blessed with *faithful* Abraham," Gal. iii. 9); also, full of or showing loyalty or fidelity (as, "His *faithful* dog shall bear him company": Pope's "Essay on Man," i. 112); true to one's word, promises, vows, etc.; strict or thorough in the performance, or as the performance, of duty (as, a *faithful* servant; *faithful* services; *faithful* attendance); also, that may be relied upon, trusted, or believed; adhering or true to fact or an original (as, a *faithful* account; a *faithful* copy). **II.** *n.* With *the*, the believers; the believing members of the Christian church or of some branch of it; the adherents of the Mohammedan faith; also, the body of loyal members of any party or group.—**faith′ful-ly**, *adv.*—**faith′ful-ness**, *n.*—**faith′less**, *a.* Without trust or belief; unbelieving; esp., without religious faith; among Christians, without Christian faith; also, not adhering to allegiance, promises, vows, or duty (as, a *faithless* subject; a *faithless* wife; a *faithless* servant); disloyal; perfidious; unfaithful; also, unreliable, untrustworthy, false, or delusive (as, "Yonder *faithless* phantom flies To lure thee to thy doom": Goldsmith's "Hermit").—**faith′less-ly**, *adv.*—**faith′less-ness**, *n.*—**faith′wor″thy**, *a.* Worthy of faith, trust, or belief; trustworthy.

fai-tor, fai-tour (fā′tọr), *n.* [AF. *faitour*, impostor, OF. *faitor*, doer, maker, < L. *factor*: see *factor.*] An impostor; a rogue. [Obs. or archaic.]

fake[1] (fāk), *v. t.*; *faked*, *faking*. [Origin uncertain.] *Naut.*, to lay in a coil, as a rope or cable.—**fake**[1], *n.* *Naut.*, one of the rings or windings of a cable or hawser as it lies in a coil.

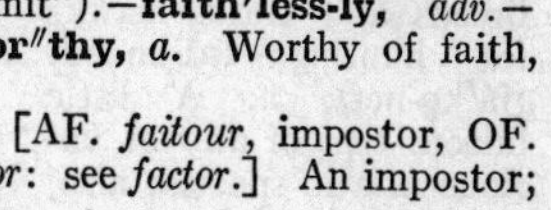
Rope in Fakes on Deck.

fake[2] (fāk), *v.*; *faked*, *faking*. [Cf. D. *vegen*, G. *fegen*, sweep, wipe, furbish.] **I.** *tr.* To get up, prepare, or make (something specious, deceptive, or fraudulent); manipulate or furbish deceptively or fraudulently (as, "He has rigged and trigged her with paint and spar, and, faith, he has *faked* her well": Kipling's "Rhyme of the Three Sealers"). [Colloq.] **II.** *intr.* To fake something; sham; pretend. [Colloq.]—**fake**[2]. **I.** *n.* Something faked up; anything made to appear otherwise than it actually is; a false report; a swindle; also, one who fakes. [Colloq.] **II.** *a.* Of the nature of a fake; designed to deceive or cheat. [Colloq.]—**fake′ment**, *n.* Something faked up; a fake. [Colloq.]

fak-er (fā′kėr), *n.* One who fakes; one who gets up fakes; a petty swindler; also, a peddler or street-vender. [Colloq.]

fa-kir (fạ-kēr′ or fā′kėr), *n.* [Ar. *faqīr*, poor.] A Mohammedan religious mendicant or ascetic; also, a Hindu devotee or ascetic of India.

fa=la (fä′lä′), *n.* [From *fa la*, used as a refrain in songs.] An old kind of part-song or madrigal.

fa-la-na-ka (fä-lạ-nä′kạ̈), *n.* [Native name.] A viverrine carnivorous quadruped, *Eupleres goudoti*, of Madagascar.

Falanaka.

fal-ba-la (fal′-bạ-lạ̈), *n.* [F.; origin uncertain.] A flounce; a furbelow.

fal-cate (fal′kāt), *a.* [L. *falcatus*, < *falx* (*falc-*), sickle.] Curved like a sickle; hooked. Also **fal′-cat-ed** (-kā-ted).—**fal-ca′tion** (-kā′shọn), *n.* Falcate condition; also, a falcate part or appendage.

fal-chion (fâl′chọn or -shọn), *n.* [OF. *fauchon*, < ML. *falcio*(*n*-), < L. *falx* (*falc-*), sickle.] A broad, short sword having a convex edge curving sharply to the point; loosely, any sword.

fal-ci-form (fal′si-fôrm), *a.* [L. *falx* (*falc-*), sickle: see *-form*.] Sickle-shaped; falcate.

fal-con (fâ′kn or fâl′kọn), *n.* [OF. F. *faucon*, < LL. *falco*(*n*-), falcon (named from its hooked talons), < L. *falx* (*falc-*), sickle.] Orig., any of various hawks used in falconry, and trained to hunt other birds and game (properly, the female only, the male being known as a *tercel*); now, any of various diurnal birds of prey of the family *Falconidæ*, esp. of the genus *Falco*, as *F. peregrinus* ('peregrine falcon'), having long wings and a notched bill, and taking their quarry as it moves; also, an old kind of cannon.—**fal-con-er** (fâ′kn-ėr), *n.* [OF. F. *fauconnier*.] One who hunts with falcons; one who follows the sport of hawking; also, one who breeds and trains hawks for hunting.—**fal-co-net** (fâ′kọ-net), *n.* A little falcon, esp. of any of various Asiatic species; also, an old kind of light cannon.—**fal-con=gen-tle** (fâ′kn-jen′tl), *n.* The female or young of the European goshawk, *Astur palumbarius*.—**fal-co-nine** (fal′kō-nin), *a.* [LL. *falco*(*n*-), falcon.] Of or like the falcons.—**fal-con-ry** (fâ′kn-ri), *n.* [F. *fauconnerie*.] The art of training falcons to pursue other birds and game; the sport of hawking.

Peregrine Falcon (Duck-hawk).

fal-de-ral (fal′dẹ-ral), *n.* Same as *folderol*.

fald-stool (fâld′stöl), *n.* [ML. *faldistolium* (corruptly *faldistorium*), < OHG. *faldstuol*, < *faldan*, fold, + *stuol*, seat: see *fold*[1] and *stool*.] A chair or seat, orig. one capable of being folded, used by a bishop or other prelate when officiating in his own church away from the throne, or in a church not his own; also, a movable folding stool or desk at which worshipers kneel during certain acts of devotion; also, a desk at which the litany is said or sung (see cut in preceding column).

Faldstool (Litany-desk).

Fa-ler-ni-an (fạ-lėr′ni-ạn). [L. *Falernus* (*Falernus ager*, the Falernian district).] **I.** *a.* Of or pertaining to a particular district in Campania, Italy, anciently famed for its wine. **II.** *n.* The wine from this district.

fall (fâl), *v. i.*; pret. *fell*, pp. *fallen*, ppr. *falling*. [AS. *feallan* = D. *vallen* = G. *fallen* = Icel. *falla*, fall.] To descend from a higher to a lower place or position through loss or lack of support; drop; lose high position, dignity, character, etc.; come as if by dropping, as stillness, night, etc.; be brought down, as the hammer of a pistol; become detached and drop off, as leaves; be dropped in birth, as an animal; issue, as speech from a person's lips; hang down, or extend downward (as, with her hair *falling* upon her shoulders); also, to sink to a lower level, as waves; decline, as in strength; slope, as land; discharge contents, as a river; subside, as water; ebb, as the tide; lose animation, as the face; be cast down, as the eyes; be reduced, as the temperature; become lowered, as the voice; decrease, as in number; be diminished in price or value; also, to come down suddenly from a standing or erect position; prostrate one's self, as in reverence or supplication; come down in fragments, as a building; succumb to attack, as a fortified place; be overthrown, as a government; succumb to temptation; esp., of a woman, to give up chastity; drop down wounded or dead; esp., to be slain; be drawn, as into danger, error, etc.; also, to be directed, as light, sight, etc., on something; have proper place or station (as, the accent *falls* on the first syllable); come as a lot, possession, burden, or duty; also, to come by chance into a particular position (as, to *fall* among thieves); also, to pass into some condition or relation (as, to *fall* asleep; to *fall* in love; to *fall* into ruin; to *fall* into arrears); become (as, to *fall* sick or lame; to *fall* vacant or due); betake or apply one's self (*to*: as, to *fall* to work, or to disputing); be naturally divisible (*into*); also, to come to pass; occur; happen.—**to fall away,** to withdraw support or allegiance; apostatize; also, to decline, decay, or perish; also, to lose flesh; become lean or emaciated.—**to fall down,** to fail. [Slang.]—**to fall for,** to be deceived by. [Slang.]—**to fall foul,** to come into collision, as ships; become entangled; also, to come into conflict; have trouble; also, to make an attack.—**to fall home,** in *ship-carp.*, to incline inward from the perpendicular: said of the topsides of a ship.—**to fall in,** to sink inward; fall to pieces inwardly; also, to take one's proper place in line, as a soldier; also, to come together; meet; agree.—**to fall off,** to drop off; also, to separate or withdraw; become estranged; withdraw from allegiance; also, to decline in vigor, interest, etc.; also, to decrease in number, amount, intensity, etc.; diminish.—**to fall on** or **upon,** to assault; attack; also, to light upon; chance upon.—**to fall out,** to drop out of one's place in line, as a soldier; also, to disagree or quarrel; also, to occur; happen; turn out.—**to fall short,** to fail to reach a mark aimed at; fail of attaining a particular amount, degree, standard, etc.; fail to reach the amount, degree, etc., reached by another; also, to prove insufficient; give out.—**to fall through,** to come to naught; fail; miscarry.—**to fall to,** to set to work; apply one's self; begin.—**to fall upon.** See *to fall on*, above.—**fall,** *v. t.* To let fall†; bring down†; chop down or fell, as a tree.—**fall. I.** *n.* The act of falling, or dropping from a higher to a lower place or position; descent, as of rain, snow, etc., or the quantity that descends; autumn, the part of the year when leaves fall from trees; the birth of animals by dropping from the parent, or the number born; descent from high estate, dignity, etc.; also, a sinking to a lower level; subsidence, as of waves; decline or decay; the discharge of the water of a river, etc.; a cataract or waterfall (usually in *pl.*: as, Niagara *Falls*); downward direction or trend; a slope or declivity; the distance through which anything falls; a decrease, as in price or value; also, a falling from an erect position, as to the ground; the fact or a method of being thrown on one's back by an opponent in wrestling; a bout at wrestling (as, to try a *fall*: also fig.); a felling of trees, or the timber cut down at one time; surrender or capture, as of a city; a succumbing to temptation, or lapse into sin; the lapse of mankind into a state of natural or innate sinfulness through the transgression of Adam and Eve ('the fall of man' or 'the fall'); death, as in battle; also, a falling, being directed, or having proper place (as, the *fall* of an accent on a syllable); also, a falling to one as a lot or share†, or that which falls†; also, the movable front of a piano, which covers the keyboard; a kind of trap for catching animals; a falling or hanging covering, or piece of material, as of lace; a loosely hanging veil; a kind of collar for the neck formerly worn, made to turn over and lie upon the shoulders; in *mech.*, etc., the part of the rope of a tackle to which the power is applied in hoisting; *pl.*, the apparatus used in lowering or hoisting a ship's boat. **II.** *a.* Of, pertaining to, characteristic of, or suitable for the season of fall or autumn (as, *fall* winds; *fall* millinery); also, suitable for sowing in the fall, as grain.—**fall wheat.** See under *wheat.*

fal-la-cious (fa-lā′shus), *a.* [L. *fallaciosus.*] Characterized by or involving fallacy; deceptive or delusive (as, "Yet how *fallacious* is all earthly bliss": Cowper's "Retirement," 457); misleading; false; of arguments, reasoning, etc., containing a fallacy; logically unsound.—**fal-la′cious-ly,** *adv.*—**fal-la′cious-ness,** *n.*

fal-la-cy (fal′ạ-si), *n.*; pl. *-cies* (-siz). [L. *fallacia*, < *fallax*, deceptive, < *fallere*, deceive.] Deception† (as, "Winning, by conquest, what the first man lost, By *fallacy* surprised": Milton's "Paradise Regained," i. 155); deceptive, delusive, misleading, or false character, as of hopes, assurances, opinions, arguments, etc.; also, something deceptive, misleading, or false, as a notion or belief; esp., a misleading or unsound argument; an unsound form of reasoning; any of various types of fault in arguments or syllogisms that render them logically unsound.

fal-lal (fal′lal′), *n.* [Appar. a made word: cf. *falbala.*] A bit of finery; a showy article of dress: as, "He found . . . his wife . . . busily engaged . . . with flounces, feathers, *fal-lals*, and finery" (Thackeray's "Newcomes," lxxi.).—**fal′lal′er-y,** *n.* Fallals collectively; finery.

fall-en (fâ′ln), *p. a.* That has dropped or come down from a higher place or level, or from an upright position; dropped; degraded; overthrown; ruined; prostrate; dead.

fall-er (fâ′lėr), *n.* One who or that which falls; any of various devices that operate by falling.

fall=fish (fâl′fish), *n.* Any of several fresh-water cyprinoid fishes of North America, as *Semotilus corporalis* of the eastern U. S.

fal-li-ble (fal′i-bl), *a.* [ML. *fallibilis*, < L. *fallere*, deceive.] Liable to be deceived or mistaken; liable to err; also, liable to be erroneous or false (as, "Do not satisfy your resolution with hopes that are *fallible*": Shakspere's "Measure for Measure," iii. 1. 170).—**fal-li-bil′i-ty** (-bil′i-ti), **fal′li-ble-ness,** *n.*—**fal′li-bly,** *adv.*

fall-ing=sick-ness (fâ′ling-sik″nes), *n.* Epilepsy.

fall-ing=star (fâ′ling-stär′), *n.* A meteor in a state of incandescence seen falling or darting through the sky; a shooting-star.

fall=line (fâl′līn), *n.* In *phys. geog.*, a line drawn through a number of rivers at points where they have falls or rapids due to a common cause.

Fal-lo-pi-an (fa-lō′pi-ạn), *a.* Pertaining to Gabriello Fallopio (1523–62), an Italian anatomist: as, the *Fallopian* tubes (a pair of slender tubes or ducts which convey the ova from the ovaries to the cavity of the uterus).

fal-low[1] (fal′ō), *a.* [AS. *fealu* = D. *vaal* = G. *fahl*, *falb*, fallow, = Icel. *fölr*, pale.] Of a pale yellowish or brownish color. Cf. *fallow-deer.*

fal-low[2] (fal′ō), *v. t.* [ME. *falewen*, appar. < AS. *fealh*, a harrow: cf. OHG. *felga*, a harrow, G. *felgen*, *falgen*, turn up ground, fallow.] To plow, harrow, and break (land) without seeding, in order to make it mellow and destroy weeds and insects.—**fal′low**[2]. [Appar. < *fallow*[2], *v.*] **I.** *n.* Land that has lain for a considerable time unseeded after plowing and harrowing; also, the state of being fallow; an interval during which land is left fallow. **II.** *a.* Of land, plowed and left unseeded for a season or more; hence, uncultivated or neglected (as, "Break up your *fallow* ground": Jer. iv. 3). Also fig.: as, "Ploughed by affliction . . . my heart lay *fallow* for every seed that fell" (Kingsley's "Alton Locke," xxxvii.).

fal-low=deer (fal′ō-dēr′), *n.* [See *fallow*[1].] A European deer, *Dama platyceros* (or *Cervus dama*), with a yellowish coat; also, a related species of western Asia.

Fallow-deer (*Dama platyceros*).

fal-low-ness (fal′ō-nes), *n.* Fallow state, as of land.

fall-way (fâl′wā), *n.* A shaft or opening through which goods are hoisted and lowered: so called from the custom of using a block and fall to do the hoisting.

false (fâls), *a.*; compar. *falser*, superl. *falsest.* [L. *falsus*, feigned, spurious, deceptive, false, pp. of *fallere*, deceive: see *fail.*] Contrary to what is true or correct; erroneous, mistaken, untrue, or incorrect, as a statement, opinion, impression, accusation, conclusion, etc.; wrong; inaccurate in pitch, as a musical note; not properly adjusted, as a balance; also, uttering or declaring what is untrue, as a witness, accuser, etc.; mendacious; lying; also, deceitful, treacherous, or faithless (as, a *false* friend; to prove *false* to one's oath or trust); deceptive, as appearances; also, not genuine; counterfeit, sham, or artificial (as, a *false* signature; *false* diamonds; *false* teeth); also, employed to deceive or mislead (as, *false* lights on a shore; *false* signals; a ship sailing under *false* colors); also, improperly so called, as from deceptive resemblance to something that properly bears the name (as, the *false* acacia, the locust-tree, *Robinia pseudacacia*); substituted for or supplementing, esp. temporarily, something properly or primarily denoted by the name (as, *false* supports for a bridge in process of construction).—**false bottom,** a horizontal partition in the lower part of a box, vessel, etc., as one fitted in a trunk to form a secret compartment.—**false face,** a counterfeit face used as a mask.—**false imprisonment,** in *law*, the imprisonment of a person contrary to law.—**false ribs.** See *rib*, *n.*—**false,** *adv.* In a false manner; incorrectly or wrongly; treacherously or faithlessly.—**false**†, *v. t.*; *falsed*, *falsing.* To make false; corrupt; falsify; also, to counterfeit; forge; also, to prove false to.—**false′=heart′ed,** *a.* Having a false or treacherous heart; deceitful; perfidious.—**false′hood** (-hůd), *n.* The quality of being false, or falsity (as, "the scandalous *falsehood* of the charges now circulated against them": J. H. Newman's "Callista," xxxi.); also, that which is false; something false; an untrue proposition, belief, etc.; also, the act of lying; a lie; false statements in general.—**false′ly,** *adv.*—**false′ness,** *n.*

fal-set-to (fâl-set′ō). [It., dim. of *falso*, < L. *falsus*, E. *false.*] **I.** *n.*; pl. *falsettos* (-ōz). An unnaturally high-pitched voice or register, esp. in a man; also, one who sings with such a voice. **II.** *a.* Having the quality of, or pertaining to, such a voice; also, unnatural, false, or assumed.—**fal-set′tist,** *n.*

fal-sid-i-cal (fâl-sid′i-kạl), *a.* [L. *falsidicus*, < *falsus*, false, + *dicere*, say.] Lying; false; illusory: opposed to *veridical.*

fal-si-fi-a-ble (fâl′si-fī-ạ-bl), *a.* Capable of being falsified.

fal-si-fi-ca-tion (fâl″si-fi-kā′shọn), *n.* [ML. *falsificatio(n-).*] The act of falsifying; fraudulent alteration; misrepresentation; disproof.

fal-si-fy (fâl′si-fī), *v.*; *-fied*, *-fying.* [OF. F. *falsifier*, < ML. *falsificare*, < L. *falsus*, false, + *facere*, make.] **I.** *tr.* To make false or incorrect, esp. so as to deceive; alter fraudulently; also, to represent falsely; misrepresent; also, to show or prove to be false; disprove; also, to prove false to (one's word, etc.)†. **II.** *intr.* To make false statements; lie.—**fal′si-fi-er** (-fī-ėr), *n.*

fal-si-ty (fâl′si-ti), *n.*; pl. *-ties* (-tiz). [LL. *falsitas.*] The quality of being false; incorrectness; untruthfulness, deceitfulness; treachery; counterfeit character; also, something false; a falsehood.

Fal-staff-i-an (fâl-staf′i-ạn), *a.* Pertaining to, characteristic of, or resembling Sir John Falstaff, a fat, jovial soldier of brazen assurance and few scruples, in certain of Shakspere's plays ("1 Henry IV.," "2 Henry IV.," and "Merry Wives of Windsor"); also, resembling the ragged band of soldiers recruited by Falstaff.

fal-ter (fâl′tėr), *v.* [ME. *falteren*; origin uncertain.] **I.** *intr.* To become unsteady in movement, as a person, an animal, or the legs, steps, etc.; stagger, stumble, or totter; move or go (*on*, etc.) with tottering steps; also, to speak hesitatingly or brokenly; stammer; come forth with unsteady or broken utterance, as the voice or speech; also, to hesitate or waver in action, purpose, etc.; begin to give way, as resolution, courage, hopes, powers, etc.; flag; fail. **II.** *tr.* To utter hesitatingly or brokenly.—**fal′ter,** *n.* The act of faltering; an unsteadiness of gait, voice, action, or the like; also, a faltering sound.—**fal′ter-ing-ly,** *adv.*

fame (fām), *n.* [OF. F. *fame*, < L. *fama* (= Gr. φήμη), < *fari* (= Gr. φάναι), speak, say.] Public report, or rumor (archaic, and sometimes personified: as, "Millions of opening mouths to *Fame* belong, And every mouth is furnished with a tongue, And round with listening ears the flying plague is hung," Dryden's tr. Virgil's "Æneid," iv. 263); the report or rumor of a particular thing (archaic: as, "The *fame* thereof was heard in Pharaoh's house, saying, Joseph's brethren are come," Gen. xlv. 16); also, reputation, as from public report or estimation (as, an attack on one's fair *fame*; a house of ill *fame*, see under *house*², *n.*); now, commonly, widespread reputation, esp. of a favorable character (as, to seek or attain *fame*; literary *fame*); celebrity; renown.—**fame,** *v. t.*; *famed, faming.* To report publicly or currently (with *as*, *for*, or an infinitive, and usually in the passive: as, to be *famed* as virtuous; to be *famed* to work wonders: archaic); also, to spread the fame of, celebrate, or make famous (now chiefly in *famed*, *pp.*: as, a place *famed* throughout the world; a far-*famed* institution).—**fame′less,** *a.* Without fame or renown.

fa-mil-iar (fa̤-mil′ya̤r). [OF. F. *familier*, < L. *familiaris*, < *familia*, E. *family*.] **I.** *a.* Of or pertaining to a family or household (now rare); personal or private (as, a *familiar* spirit, a spirit or demon supposed to attend on or serve a person, as a witch); associated in, characterized by, or proper to close personal relations (as, a *familiar* friend; *familiar* companionship or intercourse; to be on a *familiar* footing with a person); intimate; friendly; sometimes, unduly intimate, as in relations; free in behavior or manner with a person, as if assuming intimacy; taking liberties; bold, forward, or presuming; in a more favorable sense, easy, informal, or unceremonious (as, to write in a *familiar* style); also, well acquainted or thoroughly conversant, as with any matter of knowledge or experience (as, to be *familiar* with facts, a subject, book or author, process or method, tool, etc.); also, well-known, as to a person, etc. (as, a face, a book, or a subject *familiar* to one; phenomena *familiar* to the scientist, or to science); commonly or generally known or seen, common, or ordinary (as, a *familiar* sight; to take a *familiar* instance); also, of animals, accustomed to man, domesticated, or tame. **II.** *n.* A member of a family or household (obs., except as used of one who belongs to the household of the Pope or of a bishop, rendering domestic though not menial service); also, a familiar spirit; also, a familiar friend or associate; an intimate; also, an officer of the Inquisition, employed to arrest persons accused or suspected.—**fa-mil-i-ar′i-ty** (-i-ar′i-ti), *n.*; pl. *-ties* (-tiz). [OF. *familiarite* (F. *familiarité*), < L. *familiaritas*.] The state of being familiar; intimate friendly relations or intercourse; intimacy; sometimes, undue intimacy; often, freedom of behavior with a person, such as would be justified only by intimate friendly relations; an instance or manifestation of such freedom, as in action or speech (often in *pl.*); absence of formality or ceremony; familiar acquaintance or conversance, as with a thing, subject, etc.; a being well-known, as to a person or to people in general.—**fa-mil′iar-ize** (-īz), *v. t.*; *-ized, -izing.* [F. *familiariser*.] To make familiar; establish (a person) in friendly intimacy (obs. or rare); make (a person) familiarly acquainted or conversant, as with something; render (something) well-known, as to a person or to people in general; bring into common knowledge or use, as a word.—**fa-mil″iar-i-za′tion** (-i-zā′sho̤n), *n.*—**fa-mil′iar-ly,** *adv.*—**fa-mil′iar-ness,** *n.*

fa-mi-li-stère (fȧ-mē-lē-stãr), *n.* [F., < L. *familia*, family, with termination as in F. *monastère*, monastery, *phalanstère*, phalanstery.] An establishment in which a number of families live together as a community. Also **fam-i-lis-te-ry** (fam-i-lis′te̤-ri); pl. *-ries* (-riz).

fam-i-ly (fam′i-li), *n.*; pl. *-lies* (-liz). [L. *familia*, the servants of a household, a household, a family, < *famulus*, servant.] The servants of a house (now only in 'family of servants'); the retinue of an important personage†; the staff, or body of assistants, of an official; also, the collective body of persons who form a household under one head, including parents, children, servants, etc.; parents with their children, whether dwelling together or not; one's children considered collectively; all those persons descended from a common progenitor; a clan; a race; stock or lineage, esp. good or noble stock (as, young men of good *family*, or of *family*); in general, a group of related things (as, a *family* of languages); a zoölogical or botanical group or category ranking below an order and above a genus.—**family skeleton.** See *skeleton in the closet*, under *skeleton*, *n.*—**fam′i-ly=cir′cle,** *n.* A gallery in a theater, etc., esp. the topmost one.

fam-ine (fam′in), *n.* [OF. F. *famine*, < L. *fames*, hunger.] Extreme and general scarcity of food, as in a city or country; a period of extreme and general dearth, threatening or resulting in starvation; hence, an extreme and general scarcity or dearth of anything (as, "I will send a *famine* in the land, not a *famine* of bread . . . but of hearing the words of the Lord": Amos, viii. 11); also, extreme hunger; starvation; also, violent appetite, as of a starving person.

fam-ish (fam′ish), *v. t.* or *i.* [Cf. OF. *famis*, *fameis*, famished, starved, < L. *fames*, hunger.] To subject to or suffer from famine or the extremity of hunger; starve; also, to starve to death.—**fam′ish-ment,** *n.*

fa-mous (fā′mus), *a.* [L. *famosus*, < *fama*, E. *fame*.] Celebrated in fame or public report (as, "It was a *famous* victory": Southey's "Battle of Blenheim"); renowned; in an unfavorable sense, notorious†; also, first-rate or excellent (colloq.).—**fa′mous-ly,** *adv.*—**fa′mous-ness,** *n.*

fam-u-lus (fam′ṳ̄-lus), *n.*; pl. *-li* (-lī). [L.] A servant or attendant, esp., formerly, of a scholar or a magician.

fan¹ (fan), *n.* [AS. *fann*, < L. *vannus*, fan for winnowing grain.] A contrivance for winnowing grain; also, any device for agitating the air by the movement of a broad surface or a number of such surfaces; esp., a hand-implement for agitating the air and cooling the face, etc., often made up of parts which can be folded or shut up and which when spread out take the form of a sector of a circle; hence, anything resembling or spread out like such an implement, as the tail of a bird; in *mach.*, any of various devices consisting essentially of a series of radiating vanes or blades attached to and revolving with a central hub-like portion, and used to produce a current of air, regulate the velocity of light machinery, etc.; also, a small vane or sail used to keep the large sails of a windmill in the direction of the wind.—**fan**¹, *v.*; *fanned, fanning.* **I.** *tr.* To winnow (grain, etc.); also, to drive away or remove, as chaff from grain, with or as with a fan; scatter like chaff; also, to move or agitate (the air) with or as with a fan; also, to move like a fan; also, to cause air to blow upon as from a fan; cool or refresh with or as with a fan; stir to activity with or as with a fan, as a flame or, fig., passions, emotions, etc.; of a breeze, etc., to blow upon as if driven by a fan; also, to spread out like a fan; in *baseball*, of the pitcher, to strike out (a batter). **II.** *intr.* To operate a fan; move something in the manner of a fan; move as a fan does; also, to blow, or move along, as if driven by a fan; also, to assume a fan-like shape; in *baseball*, to strike out.

fan² (fan), *n.* [Cf. *fanatic*.] An enthusiastic attendant at baseball games; a devotee of any sport or amusement; in general, an enthusiastic devotee or follower (as, a Kipling *fan*). [Slang.]

fa-nat-ic (fa̤-nat′ik). [L. *fanaticus*, pertaining to a temple, inspired by a divinity, frantic, < *fanum*, temple, E. *fane*.] **I.** *a.* Possessed by a deity or other supernatural agent†, or suggestive of such possession†; frenzied†; mad†; also, fanatical, as in spirit or character. **II.** *n.* A fanatical person; an unreasoning enthusiast or zealot, in religious or other affairs.—**fa-nat′i-cal,** *a.* Possessed by a deity or the like†; frenzied†; also, actuated or characterized by an extreme, unreasoning enthusiasm or zeal, in religious or other affairs; pertaining to or characteristic of a fanatic.—**fa-nat′i-cal-ly,** *adv.*—**fa-nat′i-cal-ness,** *n.*—**fa-nat′i-cism** (-sizm), *n.* Fanatical character, spirit, or conduct.—**fa-nat′i-cize** (-sīz), *v. t.* or *i.*; *-cized, -cizing.* To infect with or exhibit fanaticism.

fan-ci-er (fan′si-ėr), *n.* One who fancies; esp., one who fancies or imagines (as, "those people who, in their speculations on politics, are not reasoners but *fanciers*": Macaulay's "Essays," Hallam); also, a person having a liking for or interested in something, as some class of animals or plants; hence, one who breeds and sells birds, dogs, etc.

fan-ci-ful (fan′si-fůl), *a.* Led by fancy rather than by reason and experience; exhibiting the influence of fancy; whimsical; also, exhibiting fancy in conception or design; quaint or odd in appearance; curious; fantastic; also, suggested by fancy; imaginary; unreal.—**fan′ci-ful-ly,** *adv.*—**fan′ci-ful-ness,** *n.*

fan-ci-less (fan′si-les), *a.* Destitute of fancy.

fan-cy (fan′si). [Contr. of *fantasy.*] **I.** *n.*; pl. *-cies* (-siz). Imagination, esp. as exercised in a capricious or desultory manner; specif., the faculty of creating illustrative or decorative imagery, as in poetical or literary composition, as distinct from the power of producing ideal creations consistent with reality (imagination); also, a mental image or conception; also, a design, invention, or contrivance; also, an idea or opinion with little foundation; a hallucination; also, caprice or capriciousness; a caprice or whim; something whimsical; also, capricious or arbitrary preference; inclination; a liking or fondness (as, to take a *fancy* to a thing); specif., love† (cf. *fancy-free*); also, critical judgment; taste; also, something that pleases or entertains without having much use or value; also, fanciers, collectively, of a particular class of things, as birds or dogs, or of a particular amusement, esp. the followers of prize-fighting ('the fancy'); the breeding of animals to develop points of beauty or excellence; sport, esp. pugilism ('the fancy'). **II.** *a.*; compar. *fancier,* superl. *fanciest.* Based on fancy or imagination; imaginative; also, depending on the exercise of fancy or caprice; capricious; whimsical; irregular; dictated by fancy or caprice, as prices; also, adapted to please the fancy or taste (as, *fancy* goods, see below; *fancy* work, see *fancywork*); not plain; fine; elegant; ornamental; varicolored, as a flower; also, dealing in, or concerned with the sale of, fancy goods (as, the *fancy* trade); also, bred to develop points of beauty or excellence, as an animal.—**fancy ball,** a ball at which fancy dress is worn.—**fancy dress,** dress chosen in accordance with the wearer's fancy, for wear at a ball or the like, as that characteristic of a particular period or place, class of persons, or historical or fictitious character.—**fancy goods,** goods or articles of trade serving for ornament or show, or merely to please the fancy, rather than for common, necessary use; miscellaneous goods, as novelties or luxurious accessories, other than the staples of trade.—**fan′cy,** *v.*; *-cied, -cying.* **I.** *tr.* To form a fancy or conception of; picture to one's self; imagine; also, to believe without being sure or certain (as, I *fancy* he will come); also, to take a fancy or liking to; like. **II.** *intr.* To imagine; also, to believe something without proof; also, to love†.—**fan′cy=free′,** *a.* Free from the influence of love (as, "in maiden meditation, *fancy-free*": Shakspere's "Midsummer Night's Dream," ii. 1. 164); hence, untrammeled.—**fan′cy-work,** *n.* Ornamental needlework, etc., such as is done for a pastime.

fan-dan-go (fan-dang′gō), *n.*; pl. *-gos* (-gōz). [Sp.; from W. Ind.] A lively Spanish or Spanish-American dance in triple time; a piece of music for such a dance or with its rhythm; sometimes, a ball or dance.

fane (fān), *n.* [L. *fanum.*] A temple; a church: as, "Beyond are the numerous chapels and *fanes* which fringe the base of the Capitoline hill" (J. H. Newman's "Callista," v.). [Archaic or poetic.]

fan-fare (fan′fãr), *n.* [F.: cf. Sp. *fanfarria,* bragging, bravado, also F. and E. *fanfaron.*] A flourish or short air played on trumpets or the like; hence, an ostentatious flourish or parade.—**fan′fa-ron** (-fa-ron), *n.* [F., = Sp. *fanfarrón*: cf. *fanfare.*] A braggart; a noisy boaster; also, a fanfare.—**fan″fa-ron-ade′** (-ron-ād′), *n.* [F. *fanfaronnade* = Sp. *fanfarronada.*] Bragging; bravado; bluster; a brag.

fang (fang), *v. t.* [ME. *fangen,* < AS. *fōn* (pret. *fēng,* pp. *fangen*) = OHG. and Goth. *fāhan.*] To seize or catch (archaic or prov.: as, "Destruction *fang* mankind!" Shakspere's "Timon of Athens," iv. 3. 23); also, to strike a fang or fangs into.—**fang,** *n.* A seizing, or that which is seized (now only Sc.); also, a long, pointed tooth of an animal; a canine tooth; a tusk; one of the long, sharp, hollow or grooved teeth of a serpent, by which venom is injected; also, the root of a tooth, or one of its prongs; in general, a pointed tapering part of a thing; the tang of a tool.—**fanged,** *a.* Having fangs.

fan-gle (fang′gl), *n.* [From *newfangle,* by misunderstanding of its elements.] A (new) fashion or invention; a novelty; also, a silly or foppish contrivance†; foppery†.—**fan′gled†,** *a.* Newfangled; foppish. See Shakspere's "Cymbeline," v. 4. 134.

fang-less (fang′les), *a.* Without fangs.

fan-ion (fan′yon), *n.* [F. *fanion,* var. of *fanon*: see *fanon.*] A small flag carried with the baggage of a military brigade, or used to mark positions, as by surveyors.

fan=light (fan′līt), *n.* A fan-shaped or other window above a door or other opening.

fan-ner (fan′ėr), *n.* One who or that which fans; a machine for winnowing grain; a fan for cooling or ventilating.

fan-on (fan′on), *n.* [F. *fanon,* < OHG. *fano,* banner, cloth: cf. *fanion, gonfalon,* and *vane.*] *Eccles.,* a maniple; also, a peculiar striped scarf-like vestment worn by the Pope over the alb when celebrating solemn pontifical mass.

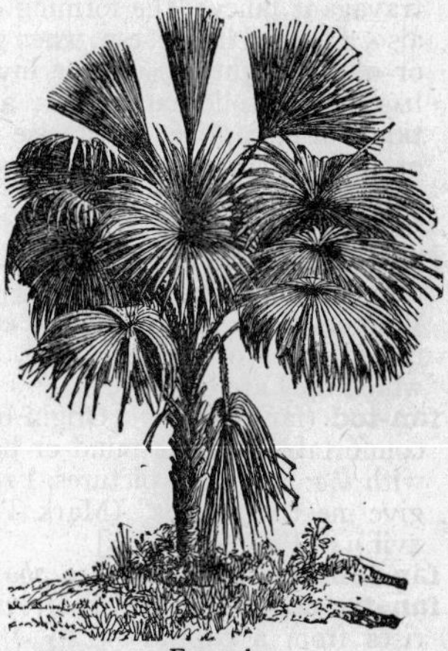
Fan-palm.

fan=palm (fan′päm), *n.* Any palm with fan-shaped leaves, as the talipot.

fan=shaped (fan′shāpt), *a.* Like a fan in shape; esp., having the form of a broad sector of a circle.

fan-tail (fan′tāl), *n.* A tail, end, or part shaped like a fan; also, any of the flycatchers of the genus *Rhipidura,* of Australian regions, having a fan-like tail; also, one of a breed of domestic pigeons with a fan-shaped tail.—**fan′=tailed,** *a.* Having a fan-shaped tail.

Fantail Pigeons.

fan=tan (fan′tan), *n.* [Chinese.] A Chinese gambling-game in which a pile of coins or counters is placed under a bowl and bets are made as to what the remainder will be after the sum of the coins or counters has been divided by four; also, a card-game in which the cards are played in sequence, the winner being the player who first gets rid of his cards.

fan-ta-si-a (fan-tạ-zē′ạ̈ or fan-tä′zi-ạ̈), *n.* [It., < L. *phantasia*: see *fantasy.*] A musical composition in fanciful or irregular rather than strict form or style; sometimes, a potpourri of well-known airs arranged with interludes and florid decorations.

fan-tasm (fan′tazm), etc. See *phantasm,* etc.

fan-tas-sin (fan′tạ-sin), *n.* [F., < It. *fantaccino,* < *fante,* boy, infantry soldier, for *infante,* < L. *infans,* E. *infant.*] An infantry soldier; a foot-soldier.

fan-tast (fan′tast), *n.* [Cf. G. *phantast.*] A fanciful person; a visionary; also, a person of fantastic ideas, mannerisms, etc.

fan-tas-tic (fan-tas′tik). [LL. *phantasticus,* < Gr. φαν-ταστικός, < φαντάζειν, present to the eye or mind: see *fantasy.*] **I.** *a.* Of or pertaining to the fantasy or imagination†; imaginative†; also, imaginary; extravagantly imagined; groundless or illusory; also, odd, quaint, eccentric, or grotesque in conception, design, character, movement, etc. (as, *fantastic* dress or ornaments; "Come, and trip it, as you go, On the light *fantastic* toe," Milton's "L'Allegro," 34); also, fanciful or capricious, as persons or their ideas, actions, etc.; often, extravagantly fanciful; irrational. **II.** *n.* One who indulges in fantastic ideas (archaic); one given to fantastic dress or manners†.—**fan-tas′ti-cal,** *a.* Fantastic.—**fan-tas-ti-cal′i-ty** (-kal′i-ti), *n.*; pl. *-ties* (-tiz). Fantastic quality; also, something fantastic; a crotchet or whim.—**fan-tas′ti-cal-ly,** *adv.*—**fan-tas′ti-cal-ness,** *n.*—**fan-tas′ti-co**† (-kō), *n.* [It.] A fantastic. See Shakspere's "Romeo and Juliet," ii. 4. 30.

fan-ta-sy, phan-ta-sy (fan′tą-si), *n.*; pl. *-sies* (-siz). [OF. *fantasie* (F. *fantaisie*), < L. *phantasia,* < Gr. φαντασία, < φαντάζειν, present to the eye or mind, < φαίνειν, show.] Imagination, esp. when unrestrained; fancy; usually, extravagant fancy; the forming of grotesque mental images; also, a mental image, esp. when grotesque; also, an ingenious or odd thought, design, or invention; also, a supposition based on no solid foundation; a visionary idea; a hallucination; also, caprice; a caprice or whim; also, inclination† or liking†; in *music,* a fantasia.—**fan′ta-sy,** *v. t.*; *-sied, -sying.* To fancy; imagine; also, to affect or sway by fancy. [Archaic.]

fan-toc-ci-ni (fan-tǫ-chē′nē), *n. pl.* [It., pl. of *fantoccino,* dim. of *fantoccio,* puppet, < *fante,* boy: see *fantassin.*] Puppets made to go through evolutions by means of concealed wires or strings; also, dramatic representations in which they are employed.

fan-tod (fan′tod), *n.* [Origin obscure.] An uneasy or uncomfortable state of mind or body; a fidget: often in *pl.,* with *the*: as, "Nice pictures, I reckon, but . . . they always give me the *fantods*" (Mark Twain's "Huckleberry Finn," xvii.). [Prov. or slang.]

fan-tom (fan′tǫm), *n.* See *phantom.*

fan=tra-cer-y (fan′trā′sėr-i), *n.* In *arch.,* tracery which rises from a capital or a corbel and diverges like the folds of a fan, spreading over the surface of a vault.

fan=win-dow (fan′-win′dō), *n.* A fan-shaped window whose sash is formed with radial bars; a fan-light.

fan-wort (fan′wėrt), *n.* A plant, *Cabomba caroliniana,* of the water-lily family, found in ponds, etc.

fap† (fap), *a.* [Origin obscure.] Intoxicated. See Shakspere's "Merry Wives of Windsor," i. 1. 183.

Fan-tracery.— Cloisters of Gloucester Cathedral, England.

fa-quir (fą-kēr′), *n.* See *fakir.*

far (fär), *adv.*; compar. *farther,* superl. *farthest* (cf. *further, furthest*). [AS. *feor* = D. *ver* = OHG. *fer* = Icel. *fjarri* = Goth. *fairra,* far; akin to Gr. πέρα, beyond, further, Skt. *paras,* beyond, far.] At or to a great distance; a long way off; to a remote point; to an advanced stage or degree (as, *far* gone); by a great interval, or widely (as, not *far* wrong); greatly, or very much (as, *far* better); also, at or to a definite distance, point of progress, or degree (preceded by *as, so, how,* etc.).—**by far,** by a great interval; very much.—**far and away,** by far; very much.—**from far,** from a distance.—**in so far,** to such an extent.—**far,** *a.*; compar. *farther,* superl. *farthest.* [AS. *feor.*] Distant or remote (as, "a *far* country": Josh. ix. 6); also, extending to a great distance (as, a *far* look ahead); long; protracted; also, more distant of the two (as, the *far* side).—**a far cry,** a great distance; a long way.—**Far East.** See under *east, n.*

far-ad (far′ad), *n.* [From Michael *Faraday* (1791–1867), English physicist.] The unit of electrical capacity: the capacity of a condenser which has a difference of potential of one volt when charged with one coulomb.—**far′a-day** (-ą-dā), *n.* In *elect.,* a unit used in electrolysis, being a quantity of electricity equal to about 96,500 coulombs.—**fa-rad-ic, far-a-da-ic** (fą-rad′ik, far-ą-dā′ik), *a.* Pertaining to or named from Faraday: applied to induced currents of electricity, as the secondary currents of induction coils, or to phenomena connected with them.—**far′a-dism** (-dizm), *n.* Induced electricity; its application for therapeutic purposes.—**far′a-dize** (-dīz), *v. t.*; *-dized, -dizing.* In *med.,* to stimulate or treat, as a muscle, with induced electric currents.—**far″a-di-za′tion** (-di-zā′shǫn), *n.*—**far′a-diz-er** (-dī-zėr), *n.*

fa-ran-dole (få-räṅ-dol), *n.* [F., < Pr. *farandolo.*] A lively dance, of Provençal origin, in which all the dancers join hands and execute various figures.

far=a-way (fär′ą-wā″), *a.* Distant; remote; also, abstracted or dreamy, as a look.

farce (färs), *v. t.*; *farced, farcing.* [OF. *farsir* (F. *farcir*), < L. *farcire,* stuff.] To stuff (a fowl, etc.) with seasoned filling†; fig., to season (a speech or composition), as with scraps of wit.—**farce,** *n.* [F.] A light dramatic composition of broadly comic character, presenting a quickly moving, laughable plot with unexpected situations, often of a highly improbable or even absurd nature; the branch or form of drama constituted by such compositions; also, foolish show; mockery; a ridiculous sham.

far-ceur (fär-sėr), *n.* [F.] An actor in farce; hence, a joker or wag.—**far-ceuse** (-sėz), *n.* [F.] Fem. of *farceur.*

far-ci (fär-sē), *a.* [F., pp. of *farcir,* E. *farce, v.*] In *cookery,* stuffed.

far-ci-cal (fär′si-kąl), *a.* Pertaining to or of the nature of farce; also, resembling farce; ludicrous; absurd.—**far-ci-cal′i-ty** (-kal′i-ti), **far′ci-cal-ness,** *n.*—**far′ci-cal-ly,** *adv.*

far-cy (fär′si), *n.* [Earlier *farcin,* < OF. F. *farcin,* < LL. *farciminum,* < L. *farcire,* stuff.] A form of the disease glanders affecting chiefly the superficial lymphatics and the skin.

fard (färd), *n.* [F.; perhaps from Teut. (cf. G. *farbe,* color).] Paint used on the face. [Obs. or archaic.]—**fard,** *v. t.* To paint (the cheeks, etc.); hence, to gloss over. [Obs. or archaic.]

far-del (fär′dęl), *n.* [OF. *fardel* (F. *fardeau*), dim. of *farde,* bundle, pack; perhaps from Ar.] A bundle; a burden. [Archaic.]

fare (fãr), *v. i.*; *fared, faring.* [AS. *faran* = D. *varen* = G. *fahren* = Icel. *fara* = Goth. *faran,* fare, go; akin to L. *peritus,* experienced, *portare,* carry, *porta,* gate, *portus,* harbor, Gr. περᾶν, pass, πόρος, passage, Skt. *par-,* bring across.] To go or travel (archaic: as, "On he *fares* . . . half on foot, Half flying," Milton's "Paradise Lost," ii. 940); conduct one's self† (as, "Thus *fares* the queen; and thus her fury blows Amidst the crowd": Dryden's tr. Virgil's "Æneid," vii. 534); seem or appear, or seem likely (prov.); impersonally, to go, turn out, or happen (as, it *fared* ill with him); of persons, etc., to get on as to circumstances (as, he *fared* well in all his undertakings); experience good or bad fortune or treatment; specif., to be entertained (*well, ill,* etc.), as with food.—**fare,** *n.* [AS. *faru.*] A going†; a journey† or voyage†; a company of persons making a journey†; the price of conveyance or passage (now only of persons); a person, or (formerly) the persons collectively, conveyed in a public vehicle; the load of a beast of burden†; a catch of fish, as of a fishing-vessel (U. S.); also, deportment† or behavior†; also, state of things, favorable or unfavorable (archaic); fortune (archaic); also, provisions for the table; food.—**far′er,** *n.*

fare-well (fãr′wel′), *interj.* [Orig. two words, *fare well*: see *fare, v.*] May you fare well; good-by.—**fare′well′.**

I. *n.* An expression of good wishes at parting; a good-by; an adieu; also, leave-taking or departure (as, "The poor exiles . . . fondly look'd their last, And took a long *farewell*": Goldsmith's "Deserted Village," 367). **II.** *a.* Pertaining to a farewell, or an occasion of leave-taking: as, a *farewell* sermon; a *farewell* performance of an actor.

far=fetched (fär′fecht′), *a.* Fetched or brought from afar (archaic); hence, remotely connected, forced, or strained (as, a *far-fetched* metaphor).

far=flung (fär′flung′), *a.* Flung or extending over a great distance: as, "our *far-flung* battle-line" (Kipling's "Recessional").

fa-ri-na (fạ-rē′nạ̈ or -rī′nạ̈), *n.* [L., < *far*, spelt.] Flour or meal made from various seeds, esp. of cereal or leguminous plants, or from certain roots, as the potato; also, a granular preparation of white maize, finer than hominy; also, starch; also, any powdery substance, as the pollen of flowers or a mealy powder found on some insects.—**far-i-na-ceous** (far-i-nā′shius), *a.* [LL. *farinaceus.*] Consisting or made of flour or meal, as food; containing or yielding starch, as seeds; pertaining to or of the nature of meal; having a mealy appearance.—**far′i-nose** (-nōs), *a.* [LL. *farinosus.*] Yielding farina; also, resembling farina or meal; in *bot.* and *zoöl.*, covered with a mealy powder.

-farious. [L. *-farius.*] An adjective suffix joined to stems that express number or quantity, and equivalent in meaning to *-fold*, or implying parts, rows, forms, kinds, etc., to the number specified, as in *bifarious*, *trifarious*, *quinquefarious*, *multifarious*, *omnifarious*.

far-kle-ber-ry (fär′kl-ber″i), *n.*; pl. *-berries* (-iz). [Origin uncertain.] A vacciniaceous shrub or small tree, *Batodendron arboreum*, of the southern U. S., bearing a small, black, many-seeded berry.

farm (färm), *n.* [OF. F. *ferme*, < ML. *firma*, < L. *firmare*, make firm, < *firmus*, E. *firm.*] A fixed yearly amount payable in the form of rent, tax, or the like†; also, a fixed annual amount accepted from a person in lieu of taxes or the like which he is authorized to collect; the letting out of the collection of public revenue; a district let out for the collection of revenue; the condition of being let out at a fixed amount (as, a district in *farm*); also, a tract of land devoted to agriculture, whether controlled by a tenant or the owner; a tract of land devoted to some allied or other industry, as the raising of domestic or other animals (as, a poultry-*farm*; an ostrich-*farm*); sometimes, a baby-farm.—**farm,** *v.* **I.** *tr.* To take or hold (land, etc.) at a certain rent†; also, to take the proceeds or profits of (a tax, undertaking, etc.) on paying a fixed sum; also, to let or lease (taxes, revenues, an enterprise, etc.) to another for a fixed sum or a percentage (often with *out*); let or lease the labor or services of (a person) for hire; also, to contract for the maintenance of (a person, institution, etc.: as, a town which *farms* its paupers); also, to cultivate (land). **II.** *intr.* To cultivate the soil; operate a farm.—**farm′er,** *n.* One who farms; one who undertakes the collection of taxes, etc., paying a fixed sum for the privilege of retaining them; one who undertakes some service, as the charge and maintenance of children, at a fixed price; one who cultivates land, or operates a farm.—**farm′er=gen′er-al,** *n.*; pl. *farmers-*. In France, under the old monarchy, a member of a company of capitalists that farmed certain taxes.—**farm′er-y,** *n.*; pl. *-ies* (-iz). The buildings, yards, etc., of a farm.—**farm′=house,** *n.* A dwelling-house on a farm.—**farm′ing,** *n.* The act or vocation of one who farms; agriculture.—**farm′stead** (-sted), *n.* A farm with its buildings; a homestead.—**farm′yard,** *n.* A yard or inclosure surrounded by or connected with farm-buildings.

far-o (fãr′ō), *n.* [From *Pharaoh*, Egyptian ruler, said to have been pictured formerly on one of the cards.] A gambling-game played with cards, in which the players bet on the cards of the dealer's or banker's pack.

far=off (fär′ôf′), *a.* Distant; remote.

far-ra-go (fạ-rā′gō), *n.* [L., mixed fodder, medley, < *far*, spelt.] A confused mixture; a hodgepodge; a medley: as, "a confounded *farrago* of doubts, fears, hopes, wishes" (Sheridan's "Rivals," ii. 1).—**far-rag′i-nous** (-raj′i-nus), *a.*

far=reach-ing (fär′rē′ching), *a.* Extending far in influence or effect.

far-ri-er (far′i-ėr), *n.* [OF. *ferrier*, < L. *ferrarius*, < *ferrum*, iron.] A blacksmith who shoes horses; also, a person who treats the diseases of horses; a veterinarian.—**far′ri-er-y,** *n.*; pl. *-ies* (-iz). The art or the establishment of a farrier.

far-row[1] (far′ō), *n.* [AS. *fearh*, akin to D. *varken*, G. *ferkel*, L. *porcus.*] A young pig; a litter of pigs.—**far′row**[1], *v.* **I.** *tr.* To bring forth (young): said of swine. **II.** *intr.* To produce a litter of pigs.

far-row[2] (far′ō), *a.* [Origin uncertain.] Not producing young in a particular season: applied only to cows.

far=see-ing (fär′sē′ing), *a.* Able to see far; far-sighted; also, having foresight, sagacious, or discerning (as, "His keen and *far-seeing* judgment perceived clearly his true interest": Lecky's "Hist. of Eng. in the 18th Century," i.).

far=sight-ed (fär′sī′ted), *a.* Seeing to a great distance; also, seeing objects at a distance more clearly than those near at hand; hypermetropic; also, foreseeing remote results; prescient; shrewd.—**far′=sight′ed-ness,** *n.*

far-ther (fär′ᴛʜėr), *adv. compar.* [Orig. var. of *further*, but now taken as an irregularly formed compar. (prop. *farrer*) of *far*, with superl. *farthest.*] At or to a greater distance; also, at or to a more advanced point; to a greater degree or extent; also, in addition, moreover, or besides.—**far′ther,** *a. compar.* More distant or remote; also, extending or tending to a greater distance; hence, further or additional.—**far′ther,** *v. t.* To help forward; advance; promote; further. [Now rare.]—**far′ther-most,** *a. superl.* Most distant or remote; farthest.—**far′thest** (-ᴛʜest), *adv.* and *a.* [Orig. var. of *furthest*: see *farther.*] Superl. of *farther*.

far-thing (fär′ᴛʜing), *n.* [AS. *fēorthung*, < *fēortha*, E. *fourth.*] An English coin, now of bronze, worth one fourth of a penny, or about half of a U. S. cent; hence, something of very small value; a bit.

Obverse. Reverse.
Copper Farthing of Charles II., 1672. British Museum.

far-thin-gale (fär′ᴛʜing-gāl), *n.* [OF. *verdugale*, < Sp. *verdugado*, < *verdugo*, young shoot, rod, < *verde*, < L. *viridis*, green.] A kind of hoop-skirt or framework for expanding a woman's skirt, worn in the 16th and 17th centuries.

fas-ces (fas′ēz), *n.* Plural of *fascis*.

fas-ci-a (fash′i-ạ̈), *n.*; pl. *fasciæ* (-ē). [L., band.] A band or fillet; in *arch.*, a long, flat member or band, esp. a horizontal division of an architrave; in *bot.* and *zoöl.*, a distinctly marked band of color; in *anat.*, a band or sheath of connective tissue investing, supporting, or binding together internal organs or parts of the body; tissue of this kind; in *surg.*, a bandage.—**fas′ci-al,** *a.*—**fas′ci-ate, fas′ci-at-ed** (-āt, -ā-ted), *a.* [L. *fasciatus*, pp. of *fasciare*, envelop with bands, < *fascia.*] Marked with a band or bands; also, bound with a band, fillet, or bandage; in *bot.*, compressed into a band or bundle; grown together, as stems.—**fas′ci-ate-ly,** *adv.*—**fas-ci-a′tion** (-ā′shọn), *n.* Fasciated condition; also, a binding up or bandaging; in *bot.*, the process of becoming fasciated, or the resulting state.

fas-ci-cle (fas′i-kl), *n.* [L. *fasciculus*, dim. of *fascis*, bundle.] A small bundle; specif., a close cluster, as of flowers or leaves; also, a single part of a printed work issued in sections.—**fas′ci-cled,** *a.*—**fas-cic-u-lar** (fa-sik′ụ-lạ̈r), *a.* Pertaining to or forming a fascicle; fasciculate.—**fas-cic′u-late, fas-cic′u-lat-ed** (-lāt, -lā-ted), *a.* Arranged in a fascicle or fascicles.—**fas′ci-cule** (-kūl), *n.* [F., < L. *fasciculus.*] A fascicle, esp. of a book.—**fas-cic′u-lus** (-lus), *n.*; pl. *-li* (-lī). [L.] A fascicle, as of nerve-fibers or muscle-fibers; also, a fascicle of a book.

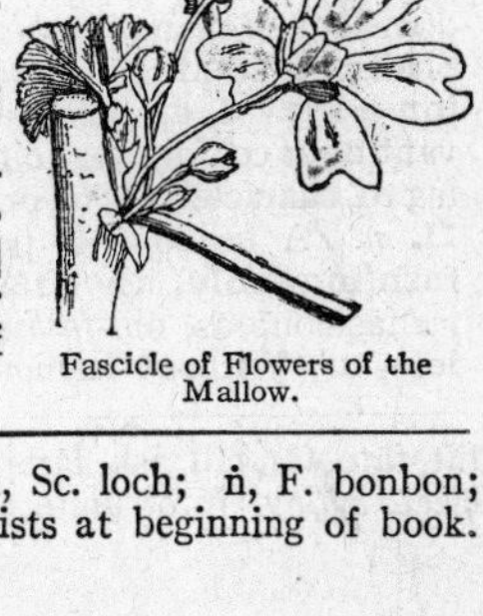

Fascicle of Flowers of the Mallow.

fas-ci-nate (fas′i-nāt), *v. t.*; *-nated, -nating.* [L. *fascinatus,* pp. of *fascinare,* < *fascinum,* spell, witchcraft.] To act on by witchcraft or magic†; bewitch†; also, to cast under a spell by a look†; hence, to deprive of the power of resistance as through terror; also, to attract powerfully or irresistibly; now, usually, to attract and hold by delightful qualities; captivate; charm; enchant.—**fas′ci-nat-ing-ly,** *adv.*—**fas-ci-na′tion** (-nā′shọn), *n.* [L. *fascinatio(n-).*] The act of fascinating; also, fascinating quality; subtle, irresistible influence; a powerful attraction; a charm; also, the state of being fascinated.—**fas′ci-na-tor,** *n.* [L.] One who or that which fascinates; also, a kind of scarf of crochet-work, lace, etc., narrowing toward the ends, worn as a head-covering by women.

fas-cine (fa-sēn′), *n.* [F., < L. *fascina,* < *fascis,* bundle.] A fagot; specif., *milit.,* a long bundle of sticks used in raising batteries, strengthening ramparts, etc.

Fascines.

fas-cis (fas′is), *n.*; pl. *fasces* (-ēz). [L., bundle.] A bundle; *pl.,* a bundle of rods containing an ax with the blade projecting, borne before Roman magistrates as an emblem of official power.

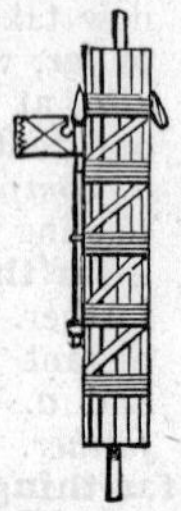
Fasces of a Roman magistrate.

Fas-cism (fas′izm or fash′izm), *n.* [It. *Fascismo.*] [Also *l. c.*] The principles or methods of the Fascisti.—**Fas′cist.** [It. *Fascista.*] [Also *l. c.*] **I.** *n.* A member of the Fascisti. **II.** *a.* Of or pertaining to the Fascisti.

Fas-cis-ti (fa-sis′ti or fa-shis′ti, It. fä-shēs′tē), *n. pl.* [It., pl. of *Fascista,* < L. *fascis,* bundle, pl. *fasces,* the fasces, or bundle of rods containing an ax, serving as an emblem of the official power of Roman magistrates.] The members of a patriotic society in Italy, animated by a strong national spirit, and organized in connection with a repressive movement directed against the socialists and communists and the disturbances excited by them during 1919 and the years following, which regarded the government as criminally negligent in failing to deal with these disturbances, and took measures on its own account, often violent ones, to combat them, and which developed into a powerful party obtaining political control of the country in Oct., 1922, under its founder and leader, Benito Mussolini, as prime minister; hence, the members of a similar society or party elsewhere.

fash (fash), *v. t.* or *i.* [OF. *fascher* (F. *fâcher*).] To annoy or be annoyed; trouble. [Sc.]—**fash,** *n.* Trouble; also, a troublesome person or thing. [Sc.]

fash-ion (fash′ọn), *n.* [OF. F. *façon,* < L. *factio(n-),* a doing or making: see *faction.*] The act or process of making†; workmanship†; also, the make or form of anything; shape; appearance; also, a particular make, shape, pattern, or style; a kind or sort; also, manner, way, or mode (as, in roundabout *fashion*; after a *fashion,* that is, in some manner or other, or to a certain extent); also, a pretense† or show† (see Shakspere's "Merchant of Venice," iv. 1. 18); also, a prevailing custom, mode, or style, as of dress; the prevailing mode of dress, etiquette, procedure, etc., esp. in polite society ('the fashion'); something fashionable ('the fashion'); conventional usage in dress, manner of life, etc., esp. of polite society, or conformity to it (as, the dictates of *fashion*; people of *fashion*; in *fashion,* or out of *fashion*); fashionable people collectively.—**fash′ion,** *v. t.* To form or shape; give a particular shape or form to; also, to accommodate or adapt (as, "Unskilful he to fawn, or seek for power, By doctrines *fashion'd* to the varying hour": Goldsmith's "Deserted Village," 146); also, to contrive† or manage† (as, "You and Douglas . . . As I will *fashion* it, shall happily meet": Shakspere's "1 Henry IV.," i. 3. 297); also, to counterfeit† (as, "It better fits my blood to be disdained of all than to *fashion* a carriage to rob love from any": Shakspere's "Much Ado about Nothing," i. 3. 30).—**fash′-ion-a-ble. I.** *a.* Capable of being fashioned†; also, observant of or conforming to the fashion; stylish; also, pertaining to, characteristic of, or patronized by the world of fashion. **II.** *n.* A fashionable person.—**fash′ion-a-ble-ness,** *n.*—**fash′ion-a-bly,** *adv.*—**fash′ioned,** *a.* Being of a particular fashion: as, old-*fashioned.*—**fash′ion-er,** *n.*—**fash′ion-less,** *a.* Without fashion; formless.—**fash′ion=mong″er** (-mung″gėr), *n.* One versed in or given over to the fashions.—**fash′ion=mong″ing,** *a.*—**fash′ion=plate,** *n.* A pictorial design showing the prevailing mode or a new mode of dress; also, a person who affects the latest style in dress (colloq.).

fash-ious (fash′us), *a.* [OF. *fascheux* (F. *fâcheux*), < *fascher*: see *fash.*] Troublesome; vexatious. [Sc.]

fast[1] (fȧst), *a.* [AS. *fæst* = D. *vast* = G. *fest* = Icel. *fastr,* fast, firm.] Firmly fixed in place, or not easily moved; securely attached to something else; that cannot escape or be extricated; firmly tied, as a knot; closed and made secure, as a door; such as to hold securely (as, to lay *fast* hold on a thing); strong against attack, or fortified, as a place (obs. or rare); firm in adherence (as, *fast* friends); deep or sound, as sleep; permanent or lasting, as a color.—**fast and loose,** now fast, now loose; sometimes, as a noun, inconstancy; also, an old cheating game in which a belt or string is so arranged that the dupe thinks he can make it fast by passing a skewer through its folds, whereas the operator can detach it at once (hence the phrase 'to play fast and loose,' to trifle deceptively or insincerely; be inconstant or unreliable).—**fast**[1]**,** *n.* That which fastens, as a mooring-rope.—**fast**[1]**,** *adv.* [AS. *fæste.*] In a fast manner; firmly; securely; soundly (as, *fast* asleep); also, close (as, *fast* by); also, immediately† or at once†.

fast[2] (fȧst), *adv.* [ME.; another use of *fast*[1], *adv.*] Quickly, swiftly, or rapidly (as, to run *fast*); in quick succession (as, "*Faster* than spring-time showers comes thought on thought": Shakspere's "2 Henry VI.," iii. 1. 337); also, in a fast mode of life.—**fast**[2]**,** *a.* [From *fast*[2], *adv.*] Quick, swift, or rapid, as motion, progress, or action, or as something that moves or acts; coming in quick succession (as, "As *fast* years flow away, The smooth brow gathers": Shelley's "Alastor," 533); also, indicating a time in advance of the correct time, as a clock; also, adapted to or productive of rapid movement (as, a *fast* track); also, pursuing pleasure at an immoderate rate or with disregard of becoming or moral restraints, as a person; characterized by such pursuit of pleasure, as a mode of life.

fast[3] (fȧst), *v. i.* [AS. *fæstan* = D. *vasten* = G. *fasten* = Icel. *fasta* = Goth. *fastan,* fast.] To abstain from all food, or eat only sparingly or of certain kinds of food, esp. as a religious observance.—**fast**[3]**,** *n.* [ME. *faste* = Icel. *fasta*: cf. AS. *fæsten.*] A fasting; an abstinence from food, or a limiting of one's food, esp. when voluntary and as a religious observance; also, a day or period of fasting.—**fast′=day,** *n.* A day on which fasting is observed, esp. such a day appointed by some ecclesiastical or civil authority.

fas-ten (fȧs′n), *v.* [AS. *fæstnian,* < *fæst,* E. *fast*[1], *a.*] **I.** *tr.* To make fast; fix firmly or securely in place or position; attach securely to something else; make secure, as an article of dress with buttons, clasps, or the like, or a door with a lock, bolt, or the like; inclose securely, as a person or an animal (with *in*); fig., to attach by any connecting agency (as, to *fasten* a nickname or a charge upon one); impose; also, to direct intently (the eyes, thoughts, etc.). **II.** *intr.* To become fast or fastened; also, to make one's self fast to something; attach one's self; lay fast hold on something.—**fas′ten-er,** *n.*—**fas′ten-ing,** *n.* Something that fastens, as a lock or clasp.

fast-er (fȧs′tėr), *n.* One who fasts.

fas-tid-i-ous (fas-tid′i-us), *a.* [L. *fastidiosus,* < *fastidium,* loathing, disgust.] Feeling disgust†; also, disdainful†; also, easily disgusted; squeamish; excessively nice or exacting in requirements of taste; also, causing disgust†.—**fas-tid′i-ous-ly,** *adv.*—**fas-tid′i-ous-ness,** *n.*

fas-tig-i-ate, fas-tig-i-at-ed (fas-tij′i-āt, -ā-ted), *a.* [L. *fastigium,* gable-top, summit, slope.] Rising to a pointed top; in *bot.,* erect and parallel, as branches; having such branches.

fast-ness[1] (fȧst′nes), *n.* [AS. *fæstnes.*] The state of being fast or firm; fixedness; also, a secure place; a stronghold.

fast-ness[2] (fȧst′nes), *n.* The state of being fast or rapid; swiftness; also, the quality of being fast, as in behavior or mode of life.

fat[1] (fat). [AS. *fǣtt,* orig. pp., fatted, fat, = D. *vet* = G. *feist,* fat.] **I.** *a.*; compar. *fatter,* superl. *fattest.* Having much flesh other than muscle; plump; corpulent; hence, thick, broad, or extended (as, *fat*-faced type); also, consisting of or containing fat; oily; unctuous; hence, abounding in a particular element, esp. a desirable one (as, *fat* pine, pine rich in resin; *fat* lime, lime comparatively pure); also, fertile, as land; profitable, as an office; affording good opportunities (as, a *fat* part in a play); prosperous or affluent, as persons (obs. or archaic); plentiful, as a supply; plentifully supplied, as a larder; also, dull or stupid, like a fat animal. **II.** *n.* An oily or greasy substance which forms the chief part of certain animal tissues (fatty or adipose tissues) and also occurs in plants; animal tissue containing this substance; specif., any of a class of organic chemical compounds of which the natural fats are usually mixtures; in fig. use, the richest or best part of anything; the best produce (as, the *fat* of the land); also, especially profitable or advantageous work.—**fat¹**, *v. t.* or *i.*; *fatted, fatting.* [AS. *fǣttian*, < *fǣtt.*] To make or become fat.

fat² (fat), *n.* [AS. *fæt* = D. *vat* = G. *fass* = Icel. *fat*, vessel.] A vessel; a tub or vat: as, "The *fats* shall overflow with wine and oil" (Joel, ii. 24). [Archaic or prov.]

fa-tal (fā′tạl), *a.* [L. *fatalis*, < *fatum*, E. *fate.*] Proceeding from or decreed by fate or overruling necessity†; fated†; also, of the nature of or resembling fate or destiny; inevitable; necessary; also, influencing or deciding fate or destiny (as, the *fatal* sisters, the three Fates); also, prophetic†; also, foreboding, or associated with, death or disaster† (as, "the black and *fatal* ravens": Marlowe's "2 Tamburlaine," iv. 3); ominous†; also, fraught with fate (as, a *fatal* day); fateful; also, causing death, destruction, or ruin (as, a *fatal* accident; a blow *fatal* to one's prospects); deadly; disastrous.—**fa′tal-ism**, *n.* The doctrine that all things are subject to fate or inevitable predetermination; also, the acceptance of all things and events as inevitable; submission to fate.—**fa′tal-ist**, *n.* A believer in fatalism; also, one whose conduct is controlled by belief in fatalism.—**fa-tal-is′tic**, *a.*—**fa-tal-i-ty** (fạ-tal′i-ti), *n.*; pl. *-ties* (-tiz). [LL. *fatalitas.*] The quality of being predetermined by or subject to fate; inevitable necessity; an unalterably predetermined course of things; the fate or destiny of a person or thing; also, a predetermined liability to disaster (as, "It seems as if a *fatality* attended the possessors of this splendid estate": Marryat's "King's Own," l.); also, the quality of causing death or disaster; deadliness; a fatal influence; also, a disaster resulting in death; a calamity or misfortune.—**fa′tal-ly**, *adv.* As decreed by fate; also, in a manner leading to death or disaster.—**fa′tal-ness**, *n.*

fa-ta Mor-ga-na (fä′tạ̈ môr-gä′nạ̈). [It., 'fairy Morgana': cf. *fay²*.] A kind of mirage seen particularly in the Strait of Messina, formerly attributed to fairy agency.

fat=bird (fat′bėrd), *n.* The guacharo; also, the pectoral sandpiper (local).

fat=brained (fat′brānd), *a.* Dull of apprehension; stupid. See Shakspere's "Henry V.," iii. 7. 143.

fate (fāt), *n.* [L. *fatum*, a prophetic declaration, oracle, fate, prop. pp. neut. of *fari*, speak.] The agency by which events are inevitably predetermined; destiny; also, that which is destined to happen; one's appointed lot or destiny; what will become, or has become, of a person or thing; hence, death, destruction, or ruin; also [*cap.*], in *class. myth.*, the goddess of fate or destiny; in *pl.*, the three goddesses, Clotho, Lachesis, and Atropos, supposed to control human destinies. —**fate**, *v. t.*; *fated, fating.* To predetermine as by the decree of fate; destine: now only in the passive.—**fat-ed** (fā′ted), *a.* Having a particular fate or destiny (as, ill-*fated*); also, subject to, guided by, or predetermined by fate; also, doomed to destruction; also, invested with the power of determining fates† (as, "The *fated* sky Gives us free scope": Shakspere's "All's Well," i. 1. 232).—**fate′ful**, *a.* Fraught with fate; involving momentous consequences; important; also, prophetic; ominous; also, fatal, deadly, or disastrous; also, controlled by irresistible destiny.—**fate′ful-ly**, *adv.*—**fate′ful-ness**, *n.*

fat-head (fat′hed), *n.* A stupid person; a dolt; also, a labroid food-fish, *Pimelometopon pulcher*, which abounds on the coast

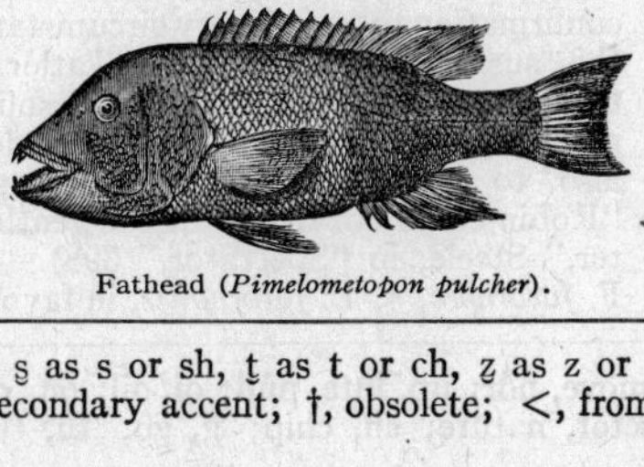

Fathead (*Pimelometopon pulcher*).

of California; also, a cyprinoid fish, *Pimephales promelas*, of the central U. S.—**fat′=head′ed**, *a.* Thick-headed; stupid.

fa-ther (fä′ᴛʜėr), *n.* [AS. *fæder* = D. *vader* = G. *vater* = Icel. *fadhir* = Goth. *fadar*, father; akin to L. *pater*, Gr. πατήρ, Skt. *pitar*, father.] He who begets a child; a male parent; the nearest male ancestor; also, any male ancestor, esp. the founder of a race, family, or line; also, a father-in-law, stepfather, or adoptive father (colloq.); also, one who exercises protecting care over others like that of a father (as, "I was a *father* to the poor": Job, xxix. 16); [*cap.*] the Supreme Being and Creator; God; with *the*, in orthodox Christian phraseology, the first person of the Trinity; [*l. c.*] a title of reverence in ecclesiastical use, as for church dignitaries, officers of monasteries, monks, confessors, and priests; a person bearing this title; also, a title of respect for an old man; the oldest member, or the one who has longest belonged to the membership, of a society, profession, etc.; also, one of the leading men of a city, etc.; a member of a city council or board of aldermen; one of the senators of ancient Rome (as, "The *Fathers* of the City Are met in high debate," Macaulay's "Battle of the Lake Regillus," viii.: cf. *conscript*, *a.*); also, one who originates or establishes something, as a founder, inventor, author, etc. (as, the *father* of lies, the devil); any of the chief early Christian writers, whose works are the main sources for the history, doctrines, and observances of the church in the early ages ('fathers of the church'); also, that which gives rise to anything (as, the wish was *father* to the thought).—**fa′ther**, *v. t.* To beget (as, "Cowards *father* cowards and base things sire base": Shakspere's "Cymbeline," iv. 2. 26); fig., to originate; be the author of; also, to act as a father toward; also, to acknowledge one's self the father of; hence, to assume as one's own; take the responsibility of; also, to provide with a father (as, "Think you I am no stronger than my sex, Being so *father'd* and so husbanded?" Shakspere's "Julius Cæsar," ii. 1. 297); also, to name the father of; charge on one the begetting of; fig., to ascribe the authorship of or responsibility for (with *on* or *upon*).—**fa′ther-hood** (-ḣud), *n.* The state of being a father; the relation or authority of a father.—**fa′ther=in=law″**, *n.*; pl. *fathers-*. The father of one's husband or wife; also, a stepfather (colloq., Eng.). —**fa′ther-land** (-land), *n.* [= D. *vaderland* = G. *vaterland.*] One's native country, or the land of one's ancestors. —**fa′ther-less**, *a.* Without a living father; also, without a known or legally responsible father.—**fa′ther-less-ness**, *n.*—**fa′ther-ly**, *a.* Of, like, or befitting a father.—**fa′ther-li-ness**, *n.*—**fa′ther-ly**, *adv.* In the manner of a father.—**fa′ther-ship**, *n.* The state or relation of a father.

fath-om (faᴛʜ′ọm), *n.*; pl. *fathoms* or (as after a numeral) *fathom.* [AS. *fæthm* = D. *vadem* = G. *faden* = Icel. *fadhmr*, fathom.] A unit of linear measurement, orig. the distance covered by the outstretched arms, now a definite measure of 6 feet, used chiefly in measuring the length of cables, etc., and the depth of water by sounding; also, intellectual capacity (obs. or archaic: as, "Another of his *fathom* they have none," Shakspere's "Othello," i. 1. 153). —**fath′om**, *v. t.* To encircle by extending the arms; also, to measure the depth of by sounding (often fig.); hence, to penetrate to the bottom of; understand thoroughly; comprehend.—**fath′om-a-ble**, *a.* Capable of being fathomed or sounded; fig., comprehensible.—**fath′om-er**, *n.*—**fath′om-less**, *a.* Incapable of being fathomed; of measureless depth; fig., incomprehensible.—**fath′om-less-ly**, *adv.*

fa-tid-ic, fa-tid-i-cal (fạ-tid′ik, -i-kạl), *a.* [L. *fatidicus*, < *fatum*, fate, + *dicere*, say.] Prophesying; prophetic.

fat-i-ga-ble (fat′i-gạ-bl), *a.* [LL. *fatigabilis.*] Easily fatigued or tired.

fat-i-gate† (fat′i-gāt), *a.* [L. *fatigatus*, pp.] Fatigued. See Shakspere's "Coriolanus," ii. 2. 121.

fa-tigue (fạ-tēg′), *v. t.*; *-tigued, -tiguing.* [F. *fatiguer*, < L. *fatigare* (pp. *fatigatus*).] To weary with bodily or mental exertion; exhaust the strength of; tire; in *mech.*, to cause the fatigue of.—**fa-tigue′**, *n.* [F.] Weariness from bodily or mental exertion; also, a cause of weariness; labor; exertion; *milit.*, fatigue-duty; in *mech.*, the weakening of metal subjected to stress, esp. a continued series of stresses. —**fa-tigue′=dress**, *n.* A soldier's uniform for fatigue-duty.—**fa-tigue′=du″ty,** *n.* Work done by soldiers other than that of a strictly military character, as repairing roads, cleaning up grounds, etc.—**fa-tigue′less,** *a.* Without fatigue; tireless.—**fa-tigue′=par″ty,** *n.* A body of soldiers engaged in fatigue-duty.—**fa-ti′guing-ly,** *adv.*

fat-less (fat′les), *a.* Without fat; lean, as meat.

fat-ling (fat′ling), *n.* [See *-ling*[1].] A young animal, as a calf or a lamb, fattened for slaughter.

fat-ly (fat′li), *adv.* In a fat manner; plumply; corpulently.

fat-ness (fat′nes), *n.* The condition of being fat; corpulence; oiliness; richness; fertility; also, fatty or oily matter; fat.

fat-ten (fat′n), *v. t.* or *i.* To make or become fat.—**fat′ten-er,** *n.*

fat-tish (fat′ish), *a.* Somewhat fat.

fat-ty (fat′i), *a.*; compar. *fattier*, superl. *fattiest.* Consisting of, containing, or resembling fat; in *pathol.*, characterized by morbid production or accumulation of fat.—**fatty acid,** in *chem.*, any of a class of organic acids certain of which (as oleic acid) are obtained from animal and vegetable fats and oils.—**fat′ti-ness,** *n.*

fa-tu-i-ty (fạ-tū′i-ti), *n.*; pl. *-ties* (-tiz). [L. *fatuitas.*] The quality of being fatuous; foolishness or silliness, or something foolish; also, idiocy or imbecility (now rare).—**fa-tu′i-tous,** *a.*

fat-u-ous (fat̤′ū̦-us), *a.* [L. *fatuus*, foolish: cf. *infatuate.*] Foolish, esp. in an unconscious, complacent manner; silly; also, idiotic or imbecile (now rare); also, unreal or illusory (as, *fatuous* fire, the ignis fatuus).—**fat′u-ous-ly,** *adv.*—**fat′u-ous-ness,** *n.*

fat=wit-ted (fat′wit′ed), *a.* Dull; stupid. See Shakspere's "1 Henry IV.," i. 2. 2.

fau-bourg (fō′börg, F. fō-bör), *n.* [F. *faubourg*, OF. *forsbourg*, < *fors* (< L. *foris*), outside, + *bourg*, town, = E. *borough.*] A part of a city outside of, or originally outside of, the walls; a suburb.

fau-ces (fâ′sēz), *n. pl.* [L.] In *anat.*, the cavity at the back of the mouth, leading into the pharynx.—**fau′cal** (-kạl), **fau′cial** (-shạl), *a.*

fau-cet (fâ′set), *n.* [OF. F. *fausset.*] A small peg or plug for stopping the vent of a cask, etc.†; also, in devices for drawing off liquids from casks, etc., the hollow wooden plug or tube whose passage is stopped by a small peg called the spigot; hence, any device for controlling the flow of liquid from a pipe or the like by opening or closing an orifice; a tap; a cock; also, the enlarged end of a pipe into which the end or spigot of another pipe enters to form a joint.

faugh (fâ), *interj.* [Cf. *foh* and *fie.*] An exclamation of disgust.

fault (fâlt), *n.* [OF. F. *faute*, < L. *fallere*, deceive, disappoint, E. *fail.*] Want† or deficiency† (as, "one it pleases me, for *fault* of a better, to call my friend": Shakspere's "2 Henry IV.," ii. 2. 45); also, a defect or imperfection; a flaw; a failing; also, an error or mistake; a misdeed or transgression; also, delinquency; culpability; cause for blame; in *geol.* and *mining*, a break in the continuity of a body of rock or of a vein, with dislocation along a plane of fracture; in *elect.*, an accidental defect in an electric circuit, as a new path opened to the current; in *tennis*, etc., a failure to serve the ball legitimately within the prescribed limits; in *hunting*, a break in the line of scent; a losing of the scent.—**at fault,** open to censure; blamable; also, having lost the scent, as in hunting; fig., puzzled; astray.—**in fault,** open to censure; blamable.—**to a fault,** to such an extent as to constitute a fault; excessively.—**to find fault.** See under *find, v. t.*—**fault,** *v.* **I.** *tr.* To find fault with, blame, or censure (now rare); in *geol.*, to cause a fault in. **II.** *intr.* To commit a fault (archaic); in *geol.*, to undergo a fault or faults.—**fault′find″er,** *n.* One who finds fault; one who complains or objects; also, a device for locating defects, as in an electric circuit.—**fault′find″ing,** *n.* and *a.*—**fault′ful,** *a.* Full of faults; faulty; culpable.—**fault′i-ly,** *adv.* In a faulty manner; defectively; culpably.—**fault′i-ness,** *n.* Faulty state or quality.—**fault′less,** *a.* Without fault or defect; perfect.—**fault′less-ly,** *adv.*—**fault′less-ness,** *n.*—**fault′y,** *a.*; compar. *faultier*, superl. *faultiest.* Containing faults or defects (as, a *faulty* design or plan); having, or marked by, imperfections or failings (as, "*faulty* friends," Browning's "La Saisiaz"; *faulty* morals); also, culpable or blamable; also, of the nature of a fault.

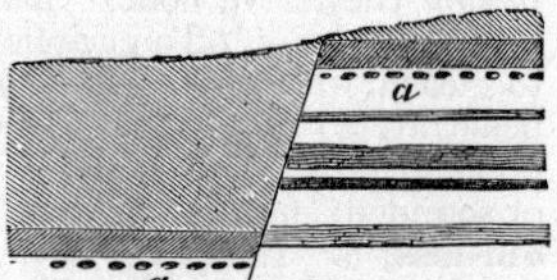

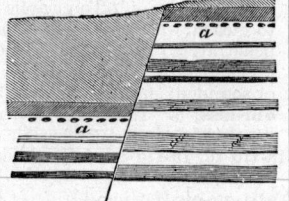

Section showing Displacement of Strata by a Fault.—*a* and *a* were once a continuous mass of rock.

faun (fân), *n.* [L. *faunus*, < *Faunus*, a Roman rural deity later identified with the Greek Pan.] In *Rom. myth.*, one of a class of rural deities represented as men with the ears, horns, and tail, and later also the hind legs, of a goat.

fau-na (fâ′nạ), *n.*; pl. *-nas* or *-næ* (-nē). [NL., < *Fauna*, a female deity, sister of Faunus: see *faun.*] The animals of a given region or period, taken collectively; also, a treatise on them.—**fau′nal,** *a.* Of or pertaining to a fauna.—**fau′nist,** *n.* A student of or writer on faunas.—**fau-nis′tic,** *a.*

fau-teuil (fō-tė-y′), *n.* [F. *fauteuil*, OF. *faudestuel*, < OHG. *faldstuol*: see *faldstool.*] An arm-chair.

faux pas (fō pä). [F.] A false step; a slip in manners or conduct; a breach of etiquette or propriety.

fa-ve-o-late (fạ-vē′ọ-lāt), *a.* [NL. *faveolus*, dim. of L. *favus*, honeycomb.] Honeycombed; cellular; alveolate; pitted.

fa-vo-ni-an (fạ-vō′ni-ạn), *a.* [L. *Favonius*, the west wind, < *favere*, be favorable.] Of or pertaining to the west wind; hence, mild; favorable; propitious.

fa-vor (fā′vọr), *n.* [OF. *favor* (F. *faveur*), < L. *favor*, < *favere*, be favorable.] Good-will or kind regard (as, "I have found *favour* in the sight of the king": Esther, v. 8); inclination or willingness to commend, support, or adopt (as, to look with *favor* on a project); the state of being approved, or held in regard (as, in *favor*; out of *favor*); also, an object of good-will or kind regard (rare: as, "Man, His chief delight and *favour*," Milton's "Paradise Lost," iii. 664); also, kindness manifested or done (as, to show *favor* to a person); gracious action proceeding from good-will; a kind act or office (as, to ask a *favor* of a person); something done or granted out of good-will, rather than from justice or for remuneration; often, a letter, esp. a commercial one (used in compliment); also, kind indulgence (as, "But, with your *favour*, I will treat it here": Dryden's "Cock and the Fox," 807); leave or permission; pardon; leniency; also, partial or biased kindness (as, a fair field and no *favor*); partiality; also, in general, aid or furtherance (as, the enemy approached under *favor* of the night); also, something bestowed as a token of good-will or kind regard; a gift, as a knot of ribbon or a glove, given usually by a woman to a man, to be worn as a token of friendship or love; a ribbon, badge, etc., worn in evidence of good-will or loyalty; any of the various small gifts given between the partners in a cotillion; also, attractiveness or beauty (archaic: as, "Thine eye desireth *favour* and beauty," Ecclus. xl. 22); an attraction or charm (archaic); also, appearance or look (archaic: as, "Folks don't use to meet for amusement with fire-arms . . . This . . . has an angry *favour*," Sheridan's "Rivals," v. 1); the face or countenance (archaic: as, "What makes thy *favour* like the bloodless head Fall'n on the block?" Tennyson's "Queen Mary," v. 2).—**in favor of,** in support of; on the side of; also, to the advantage of; of a check, etc., so as to be payable to.—**fa′vor,** *v. t.* [OF. *favorer*, < ML. *favorare*, < L. *favor.*] To regard with favor; look kindly upon; have a liking or preference for; also, to show favor to; treat kindly; encourage; patronize; indulge or oblige with something (as, "He begged to be *favoured* with a song": Goldsmith's "Vicar of Wakefield," v.); also, to deal with gently, spare, or ease (now colloq.: as, to *favor* a lame leg); also, to treat with partiality; also, to aid or support; lend support or confirmation to (as, "Every circumstance imaginable *favoured* this suspicion": Steele, in "Tatler," 209); prove advantageous to (as, "The silence and solitude of the place very much *favoured* his meditations": Addison, in "Tatler," 97); also, to resemble in features or aspect (now colloq.: as, "Robin could not deny but the gentleman *favoured* his master," Steele, in "Spectator," 398).—**fa′vor-a-ble,** *a.* [OF. F. *favorable*, < L. *favorabilis*, in favor, winning favor, pleasing.] Winning favor†; pleasing†; also, manifesting favor; well-disposed; inclined to aid or help; of a report, opinion, etc., approving or commendatory; of an answer, granting what is desired; of appearances, boding well, promising, or hopeful; also, affording aid, advantage, or convenience (as, a *favorable* position; *favorable* weather); advantageous; suitable; conducive or contributing (as, "Nothing is more *favourable* to the reputation of a writer than to be succeeded by a race inferior to himself": Macaulay's "Essays," Petrarch).—**fa′vor-a-ble-ness,** *n.*—**fa′vor-a-bly,** *adv.*—**fa′-vored,** *a.* Regarded or treated with favor; enjoying special favors or advantages; also, adorned with or wearing a favor; also, of specified appearance or looks (as, ill-*favored*).—**fa′-vor-er,** *n.*—**fa′vor-ing-ly,** *adv.*

fa-vor-ite (fā′vọr-it). [F. (obs.) *favorit* (now *favori*, fem. *favorite*), < It. *favorito*, pp. of *favorire*, favor, < L. *favor*: see *favor*.] **I.** *n.* A person or thing regarded with peculiar favor or preference; specif., a person who has gained the special favor of a superior; a person treated with special (esp. undue) favor by a prince, etc.; in *sports*, a competitor considered likely to win. **II.** *a.* Regarded with particular favor or preference: as, a *favorite* author; a *favorite* child.—**fa′vor-it-ism,** *n.* The disposition to favor, or the practice of favoring, one to the neglect of others having equal or superior claims; undue preference; partiality; also, the state of being a favorite.

fa-vose (fạ-vōs′), *a.* [L. *favus*, honeycomb.] Resembling a honeycomb.

fa′vour, fa′vour-a-ble, etc., **fa′vour-ite,** etc. British preferred forms of *favor*, *favorable*, etc., *favorite*, etc.

fa-vus (fā′vus), *n.* [L., honeycomb.] In *pathol.*, a skin disease, esp. of the scalp, characterized by dry incrustations somewhat resembling a honeycomb, due to the fungus *Achorion schönleinii*.

fawn[1] (fân), *v. i.* [AS. *fahnian*, var. of *fægnian*, rejoice, < *fægen*, glad, E. *fain*.] To show fondness by crouching, wagging the tail, licking the hand, etc. (said esp. of dogs); hence, to court notice or favor by servile demeanor; act servilely.

fawn[2] (fân), *n.* [OF. F. *faon*, < L. *fetus*, offspring, young: see *fetus*.] A young deer; a buck or doe of the first year; also, fawn-color.—**fawn**[2], *v. i.* Of deer, to bring forth young.—**fawn′=col″or,** *n.* A light yellowish-brown color. —**fawn′=col″ored,** *a.*

fawn-er (fâ′nėr), *n.* One who fawns; one who acts servilely.—**fawn′ing,** *p. a.* That fawns; showing fondness as a dog does; courting favor by servile demeanor.—**fawn′-ing-ly,** *adv.*

fay[1] (fā), *v. t.* or *i.* [AS. *fēgan* = G. *fügen*.] To fit together closely, as timbers in ship-building.

fay[2] (fā), *n.* [OF. *fae*, *fee* (F. *fée*), = It. *fata*, < L. *fatum* (pl. *fata*), E. *fate*.] A fairy: as, "Here he [Merlin] came with the *fay* Vivian" (M. Arnold's "Tristram and Iseult," iii.).

fay[3] (fā), *n.* [OF. *fei*: see *faith*.] Faith; fidelity; loyalty. [Archaic or prov.] — **by my fay,** by my faith: a phrase of asseveration. [Archaic.]

fay[4] (fā), *a.* See *fey*.

faze (fāz), *v. t.*; *fazed*, *fazing*. [= *feeze*.] To disturb; discomfit; daunt. [Colloq., U. S.]

faz-le (faz′l), *v. i.* or *t.*; *-led*, *-ling*. [ME. *faselyn* = D. *vezelen* = G. *faseln*: cf. *frazzle*.] To ravel. [Now prov. Eng.]

feal (fēl), *a.* [OF. *feal*, for *feeil*, < L. *fidelis*, faithful: see *fidelity*.] Faithful; loyal; constant. [Obs. or archaic.]

fe-al-ty (fē′ạl-ti), *n.* [OF. *feaute*, *feelte*, < L. *fidelitas*: see *fidelity*.] Fidelity to a lord (as, "They refused to dethrone the King, but they had sworn no *fealty* to his child": Green's "Short Hist. of the Eng. People," vi. 2); the obligation or the engagement to be faithful to a lord; hence, fidelity in general; faithfulness.

fear (fēr), *n.* [AS. *fǣr*, danger, calamity, akin to D. *gevaar*, G. *gefahr*, danger, Icel. *fār*, mischief, plague.] A painful emotion excited by a sense of impending danger or evil, whether for one's self or for another or for any object of solicitude; the feeling or state of being afraid; apprehensive uneasiness of mind; dread; a feeling of this kind on a particular occasion (as, to dismiss one's *fears*); such an emotion or feeling about something specified (as, *fear* of one's enemies); often, apprehension or dread of something about or liable to happen or to make trouble (as, *fear* of the consequences; *fear* of opposition); anxiety or solicitude for the safety of something (as, in *fear* of one's life); also, a feeling of reverential awe, esp. toward God (as, "The *fear* of the Lord is the beginning of knowledge": Prov. i. 7); also, ground for apprehension (as, there is no *fear* of our losing); an object of fear† (as, "Or in the night, imagining some *fear*, How easy is a bush supposed a bear!" Shakspere's "Midsummer Night's Dream," v. 1. 21); also, formidableness†, or aptness to cause fear† (as, "There is no *fear* in him; let him not die": Shakspere's "Julius Cæsar," ii. 1. 190).—**fear,** *v.* [AS. *fǣran*, frighten.] **I.** *tr.* To frighten (archaic: as, "This aspect of mine Hath *fear'd* the valiant," Shakspere's "Merchant of Venice," ii. 1. 9); drive away or keep away by fear† (as, "a scarecrow . . . to *fear* the birds of prey": Shakspere's "Measure for Measure," ii. 1. 2); also, to regard with fear, or be afraid of (as, to *fear* a person); be apprehensive of (as, "I will *fear* no evil: for thou art with me": Ps. xxiii. 4); have reverential awe of (as, "The Lord pitieth them that *fear* him": Ps. ciii. 13); also, to have fears for† (as, "He was much *fear'd* by his physicians": Shakspere's "1 Henry IV.," iv. 1. 24); also, reflexively, to be afraid (archaic: as, "A flash, I *fear me*, that will strike my blossom dead," Tennyson's "Lancelot and Elaine," 965). **II.** *intr.* To have fear; be afraid, as of something actual or present; be apprehensive, as of something about or liable to happen; have fears, as for some object of anxious solicitude (as, to *fear* for a person's safety).—**fear′er,** *n.*—**fear′-ful,** *a.* Full of fear; afraid or apprehensive of something; easily frightened, timid, or wanting courage; full of awe or reverence; also, indicative of or caused by fear (as, "Cold *fearful* drops stand on my trembling flesh": Shakspere's "Richard III.," v. 3. 181); also, causing, or apt to cause, fear; dreadful; awful; hence, extremely bad, unpleasant, ugly, etc., or very great (chiefly colloq.).—**fear′ful-ly,** *adv.* —**fear′ful-ness,** *n.*—**fear′less,** *a.* Without fear; bold; courageous.—**fear′less-ly,** *adv.*—**fear′less-ness,** *n.*—**fear′-naught, fear′nought,** *n.* A kind of stout woolen cloth.—**fear′some** (-sum), *a.* Causing fear; frightful; also, afraid; timid.—**fear′some-ly,** *adv.*—**fear′some-ness,** *n.*

fea-sance (fē′zạns), *n.* [AF. *fesance*, OF. F. *faisance*, < *faire*, do: see *feasible*.] In *law*, doing or performance, as of a condition, obligation, duty, etc.

fea-si-ble (fē′zi-bl), *a.* [OF. *faisible*, *faisable* (F. *faisable*), < *faire*, < L. *facere*, do, make.] Capable of being done, effected, or accomplished (as, a *feasible* plan); practicable; also, capable of being dealt with successfully (as, a road *feasible* for travel); also, likely or probable (as, a *feasible* theory).—**fea-si-bil′i-ty** (-bil′i-ti), **fea′si-ble-ness,** *n.*—**fea′si-bly,** *adv.*

feast (fēst), *n.* [OF. *feste* (F. *fête*) = Sp. *fiesta* = It. *festa* = G. *fest*, < L. *festa*, prop. neut. pl. of *festus*, festal (*festum*, a festival, feast).] A periodical celebration, or day or time of celebration, of religious or other character, in commemoration of some event or person or having some other special significance (as, the *feasts* of the church; the medieval *feast* of fools; the Chinese *feast* of lanterns); a festival; also, a sumptuous entertainment or repast; a banquet; also, any rich or abundant meal; fig., a rich treat.—**feast,** *v.* [OF. *fester* (F. *fêter*).] **I.** *intr.* To have, or partake of, a feast; eat sumptuously; fig., to dwell with gratification or delight, as on a picture. **II.** *tr.* To provide or entertain with a feast; fig., to gratify or delight.—**feast′er,** *n.*—**feast′ful,** *a.* Festive; joyful; also, filled with feasting.

feat[1] (fēt), *n.* [OF. F. *fait*, < L. *factum*, a thing done, prop. pp. neut. of *facere*, do, make: cf. *fact*.] An action or deed; esp., a noteworthy or extraordinary act or achievement; an action displaying strength or skill.

feat[2] (fēt), *a.* [Appar. < OF. F. *fait*, pp. of *faire*, < L. *facere*, do, make: cf. *fit*[2].] Fitting or suitable; apt; skilful or dexterous, as movements; becoming or neat, as dress; neatly attired, as a person; elegant or fine; affected, as a person. [Archaic or prov.]

feath-er (feᴛʜ′ėr), *n.* [AS. *fether* = D. *veder* = G. *feder* = Icel. *fjödhr*, feather; akin to L. *penna*, feather, Gr. πτερόν, Skt. *pattra*, feather, wing.] One of the epidermal appendages which together constitute the plumage of birds, being typically made up of a hard, tube-like portion (the quill) nearest the body of the bird, which passes into a thinner, stem-like distal portion (the rachis) bearing a series of slender processes (barbs) united in a blade-like structure (web) on each side; also, plumage; fig., attire; also, condition, as of health, spirits, etc. (as, in fine *feather*; in high *feather*); also, kind of plumage, or kind in general (as, birds of a *feather*; of every *feather*); *pl.*, wings†; *sing.*, birds collectively; also, a feather or feathers attached to the end of an arrow to direct its flight; also, something as light as a feather; hence, a trifle; also, something resembling a feather; a feather-like tuft or fringe of hair; a feather-like flaw, as in a precious stone; a projection on a board, etc., as for fitting into a groove; in *rowing*, the act of feathering.—**a feather in one's cap,** fig., a mark of distinction; an honor.—**white feather.** See under *white, a.*—**feath'er,** *v.* **I.** *tr.* To clothe or cover with or as with feathers (as, to *feather* one's nest, fig., to provide for or enrich one's self, esp. while acting in a fiduciary capacity); provide with feathers, as an arrow; furnish with a feather or tongue, or join by a tongue and a groove, as boards; in *rowing*, to turn (an oar) after a stroke so that the blade becomes nearly horizontal, and hold it thus as it is moved back into position for the next stroke. **II.** *intr.* To grow feathers; also, to be or become feathery in appearance; move like feathers (as, "the ripple *feathering* from her bows": Tennyson's "Enoch Arden," 540); in *rowing*, to feather an oar.—**feath'er-bone,** *n.* A substitute for whalebone, made from the quills of domestic fowls.—**feath'er-brain,** *n.* A light or weak brain; also, a giddy or weak-minded person.—**feath'er=brained,** *a.*—**feath'ered,** *p. a.* Clothed, covered, or provided with or as with feathers; also, winged; swift.—**feath'er=edge,** *n.* An edge as thin as a feather; the thinner edge of a wedge-shaped board, etc.—**feath'er=edged,** *a.*—**feath'er-head,** *n.* A light or empty head; also, a silly or light-headed person.—**feath'er=head''ed,** *a.*—**feath'er-i-ness,** *n.* Feathery state.—**feath'er-ing,** *n.* Plumage; the feather of an arrow; feather-like structure or marking; in *arch.*, ornamentation consisting of foils and cusps; foliation; in *violin-playing*, a very light and delicate use of the bow.—**feath'er-less,** *a.* Without feathers.—**feath'er=sedge,** *n.* A grass, *Andropogon saccharoides*, with a plume-like panicle, common in the southwestern U. S.—**feath'er=star,** *n.* Any of certain crinoids having a feathery appearance and radiate structure.—**feath'er=stitch,** *n.* An embroidery stitch producing work in which a succession of small filaments or branches extend alternately on each side of a central stem.—**feath'er=stitch,** *v.t.* To ornament by feather-stitch. —**feath'er=veined,** *a.* In *bot.*, of a leaf, having a series of veins branching from each side of the midrib toward the margin.—**feath'er=weight,** *n.* The lightest weight that may be carried by a horse in a handicap; a boxer or other contestant lighter in weight than a lightweight; a frivolous or insignificant person or thing.—**feath'er-y,** *a.* Consisting of feathers; also, resembling a feather or feathers, as in appearance or lightness; hence, light, flimsy, or unsubstantial; also, clothed or covered with feathers; feathered.

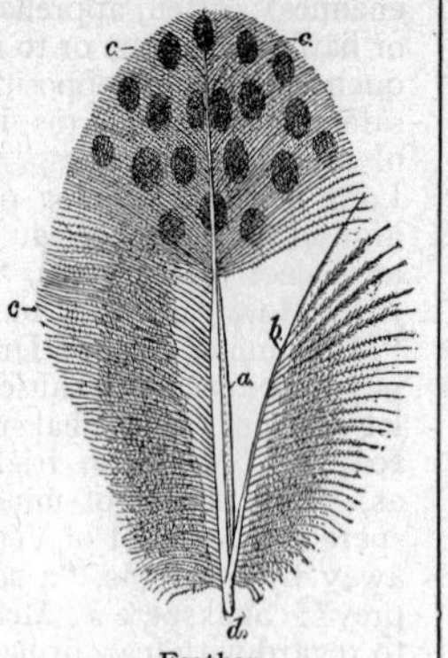

Feather.
a, d, main stem; *d*, calamus or quill; *a*, rachis; *c, c, c*, barbs, cut away on right side in order not to interfere with view of *b*, the aftershaft, the whole of the left web of which is likewise cut away.

Feather-sedge. — *a*, plant, one fourth natural size; *b*, perfect spikelet; *c*, sterile spikelet, enlarged.

feat-ly (fēt'li), *adv.* In a feat manner; fitly; skilfully; nimbly; neatly; elegantly. [Archaic or prov.]—**feat'ness,** *n.*

fea-ture (fē'ţūr), *n.* [OF. *faiture*, < L. *factura*, making, formation, < *facere*, do, make: cf. *facture*.] Make, form, or shape (obs. or archaic); also, a part of the body†; also, the form or cast of the face; any of the parts of the face, as the eye, nose, mouth, chin, etc.; *pl.*, the face or countenance; hence, *sing.*, a distinct part or characteristic of anything; a prominent or conspicuous part or characteristic.—**fea'ture,** *v. t.*; *-tured, -turing.* To resemble in features, or favor (colloq.); also, to delineate the features of; depict; outline; also, to be a feature or distinctive mark of; also, to make a feature of, or give prominence to (colloq.).—**fea'tured,** *a.* Having features, or a certain cast of features; also, formed† or fashioned†; also, made a feature of, or given prominence to (colloq.).—**fea'ture-less,** *a.* Wanting features; without distinctive features; uninteresting; uneventful.

feaze (fēz), *v.* and *n.* See *feeze.*

febri-. Form of L. *febris*, fever, used in combination.—**feb-ri-fa-cient** (feb-ri-fā'shẹnt). [+ *-facient.*] **I.** *a.* Producing fever. **II.** *n.* Something that produces fever.—**fe-brif-er-ous** (fẹ-brif'ẹ-rus), *a.* [+ *-ferous.*] Producing fever.—**fe-brif'ic,** *a.* [+ *-fic.*] Producing or marked by fever.—**fe-brif-u-gal** (fẹ-brif'ū-gạl or feb'ri-fū-gạl), *a.* Of or like a febrifuge.—**feb'ri-fuge** (-fūj). [F.: see *-fuge.*] **I.** *a.* Serving to dispel or reduce fever, as a medicine. **II.** *n.* A febrifuge medicine or agent; hence, a cooling drink.

fe-brile (fē'bril or feb'ril), *a.* [F. *fébrile*, < L. *febris*, fever.] Pertaining to or marked by fever; feverish.

Feb-ru-a-ry (feb'rö-ā-ri), *n.* [L. *Februarius*, < *februa*, pl., the Roman festival of purification, celebrated Feb. 15.] The second month of the year, containing ordinarily 28 days, in leap-years 29.

fe-ces, fæ-ces (fē'sēz), *n. pl.* [L. *fæces*, pl. of *fæx*, dregs.] Dregs; sediment; also, waste matter discharged from the intestines; excrement.—**fe'cal, fæ'cal** (-kạl), *a.*

fecht (fecht), *v.* and *n.* Scotch form of *fight.*

fe-cial (fē'shạl), *a.* and *n.* See *fetial.*

fe-cit (fē'sit). [L.] '(The person named) made it': a word often inscribed on a work of art, preceded by the name of the maker or designer.

feck (fek), *n.* [Corruption of *effect.*] Effect; efficacy; value; also, amount or quantity; the greater part. [Sc. and north. Eng.]—**feck'less,** *a.* Ineffective; weak or feeble (as, "We are now tottering with short and *feckless* steps towards the grave": Galt's "Annals of the Parish," Introd.); spiritless; helpless; worthless. [Chiefly Sc. and north. Eng.]—**feck'ly,** *adv.* For the most part; mostly; almost. [Sc. and north. Eng.]

fec-u-la (fek'ū-lạ), *n.*; pl. *-læ* (-lē). [L. *fæcula*, dim. of *fæx*, dregs: cf. *feces.*] Any form of starch obtained as a sediment by washing in water the comminuted roots, grains, or other parts of plants.

fec-u-lent (fek'ū-lẹnt), *a.* [L. *fæculentus*, < *fæx*, dregs: cf. *feces.*] Abounding in dregs or foul matter; turbid; muddy; foul.—**fec'u-lence, fec'u-len-cy,** *n.*

fec-und (fek'und or fē'kund), *a.* [L. *fecundus*, akin to *fetus*, offspring: see *fetus.*] Capable of producing offspring, or fruit, vegetation, etc., in abundance; prolific; fruitful; productive. Often fig.

fec-un-date (fek'un-dāt or fē'kun-), *v. t.*; *-dated, -dating.* [L. *fecundatus*, pp. of *fecundare*, < *fecundus*: see *fecund.*] To make prolific or fruitful; in *biol.*, to impregnate.—**fec-un-da'tion** (-dā'shọn), *n.*

fe-cun-di-ty (fẹ-kun'di-ti), *n.* [L. *fecunditas.*] The quality of being fecund; the capacity, esp. in female animals, of producing young in great numbers; fruitfulness or fertility, as of the earth; capacity of abundant production (often fig.: as, *fecundity* of imagination or invention).

fed (fed). Preterit and past participle of *feed.*

fed-er-al (fed'ėr-ạl). [= F. *fédéral*, < L. *fœdus* (*fœder-*), compact, league, akin to *fides*, faith.] **I.** *a.* Of or pertaining to a compact or a league, esp. a league between nations or states; also, pertaining to or of the nature of a union of states under a central government distinct from the individual governments of the separate states (as, a *federal* republic; the *federal* government of the U. S.); pertaining to such a central government (as, *federal* offices or officers); also, favoring a strong central government in such a union; [*cap.*] noting or pertaining to a party in early U. S. history advocating a strong central government; also, pertaining to the U. S. government during the Civil War, or to the party supporting it. **II.** *n.* An advocate of federation or federalism; [*cap.*] in the American Civil War, an adherent of the U. S. government; esp., a soldier in the Federal army.—**fed′er-al-ism,** *n.* The federal principle of government; also, the principles of the Federal party in U. S. history.—**fed′er-al-ist,** *n.* An advocate of federalism; [*cap.*] a member or supporter of the Federal party in U. S. history.—**fed′er-al-ize** (-īz), *v. t.*; *-ized, -izing.* To make federal; unite in a federal union, as different states; bring under the control of a federal union or government.—**fed″er-al-i-za′tion** (-i-zā′shọn), *n.*—**fed′er-al-ly,** *adv.*

fed-er-ate (fed′ėr-āt), *v. t.* or *i.*; *-ated, -ating.* [L. *fœderatus*, pp. of *fœderare*, < *fœdus*, compact, league: see *federal*.] To unite in a league or federation; specif., to organize on a federal basis.—**fed′er-ate** (-ạt). **I.** *a.* Federated; allied. **II.** *n.* A party to a covenant; a member of a league, confederacy, or federation.—**fed-er-a′tion** (-ẹ-rā′shọn), *n.* [ML. *fœderatio(n-)*.] The act of federating, or uniting in a league; specif., the formation of a political unity, with a central government, out of a number of separate states, etc., each of which retains control of its own internal affairs; also, a league or confederacy; esp., a federated body formed by a number of states, societies, etc., each of which retains control of its own internal affairs.—**fed-er-a′tion-ist,** *n.* An advocate of federation.—**fed′er-a-tive** (-ạ-tiv), *a.* Pertaining to or of the nature of a federation; also, inclined to federate.

fe-do-ra (fẹ-dō′rạ), *n.* [Said to take its name from *Fédora*, drama by Sardou.] A soft felt hat with a curled brim, worn with the crown creased lengthwise.

fee[1]† (fē), *n.* [AS. *feoh* = OHG. *fehu* = Icel. *fē*, cattle, property, money; akin to L. *pecu*, Skt. *paçu*, cattle: cf. *fee*[2], also *fellow*.] Cattle; live stock; property; wealth; money.

fee[2] (fē), *n.* [AF. *fee*, OF. *fe*, *fied*, *fiu*, *fieu* (F. *fief*), = ML. *feudum*, *feodum*; appar. from Teut., perhaps from the source of *fee*[1].] An estate in land held of a feudal lord on condition of the performing of certain services; a tenure of land subject to feudal obligations; also, an estate of inheritance in land, either absolute and without limitation to any particular class of heirs ('fee simple'), or limited to a particular class of heirs ('fee tail'); hence, possession or ownership (as, "Once did She hold the gorgeous east in *fee*": Wordsworth's "On the Extinction of the Venetian Republic"); also, a territory held in fee; also, service or employment, as under a feudal lord†; also, a payment for services; a charge fixed by law for the services of a public officer; a remuneration for professional service, as of a physician or a lawyer; also, a sum paid for a privilege (as, an admission *fee*); also, a gratuity or tip.—**fee**[2], *v. t.*; *feed, feeing.* To engage or employ for a fee (chiefly Sc.); also, to give a fee to; tip.

fee-ble (fē′bl), *a.*; compar. *feebler*, superl. *feeblest.* [OF. *feble*, *feible* (F. *faible*), < L. *flebilis*, lamentable, < *flere*, weep.] Physically weak, as from age, sickness, or natural disability (as, a *feeble* old man; *feeble* hands; a *feeble* condition or constitution); lacking bodily strength; infirm; more generally, of things, of little material strength (as, a *feeble* stem; a *feeble* barrier); frail; slight; of little enduring power (as, *feeble* beginnings); also, weak intellectually or morally (as, a *feeble* mind; a *feeble* will); easily shaken, as faith; also, lacking in force or effectiveness (as, *feeble* resistance; a *feeble* attempt; a *feeble* argument); also, lacking in volume, loudness, brightness, distinctness, etc. (as, a *feeble* voice or cry; a *feeble* ray of light).—**fee′ble=mind′ed,** *a.* Feeble in intellect; lacking the normal endowment of mental powers or capacity; deficient in mentality; also, lacking firmness of mind (as, "Comfort the *feeble-minded*": 1 Thes. v. 14).—**fee′ble=mind′ed-ness,** *n.*—**fee′ble-ness,** *n.*—**fee′bly,** *adv.*

feed (fēd), *v. t.*; *fed, feeding.* [AS. *fēdan*, < *fōda*, E. *food*.] To give food to; supply with nourishment; hence, to minister to; gratify; also, to provide with the requisite materials for development, maintenance, or operation; also, to yield, or serve as, food for (as, "the water snake, whom fish and paddocks *fed*": Dryden's tr. Virgil's "Georgics," iii. 812); also, to provide as food; furnish for consumption; supply for maintenance or to be operated upon, as to a machine; also, to use (land) as pasture.—**to be fed up,** to be fed to repletion; hence, to have quite enough, or more than enough, of something. [Slang.]—**feed,** *v. i.* To take food, or eat (now used of persons only colloquially or in contempt); hence, to be nourished or gratified as if by food.—**feed,** *n.* The act of feeding; a meal (colloq.); also, food, as for cattle, horses, etc.; provender; fodder; an allowance of such food; also, pasture-ground† (as, "His flocks and bounds of *feed* Are now on sale": Shakspere's "As You Like It," ii. 4. 83); also, the act or process of feeding a furnace, machine, etc.; the material, or the amount of it, so fed or supplied; a feeding mechanism.—**feed′=back,** *a.* In *wireless teleg.* and *teleph.*, noting or pertaining to a system in which some of the energy of the plate circuit of a vacuum-tube is returned (fed back) to the grid circuit, as in the process of regeneration.—**feed′er,** *n.* One who or that which supplies food or feeds something; something that ministers to the maintenance of something else, as a tributary stream or a branch railroad; a person or device that feeds a machine, etc.; also, one who or that which takes food or nourishment.—**feed′=wa″ter,** *n.* Water supplied to a boiler.

feel (fēl), *v. t.*; *felt, feeling.* [AS. *fēlan* = D. *voelen* = G. *fühlen*, feel.] To perceive by touch or by any nerves of sensation other than those of sight, hearing, taste, and smell (as, to *feel* the cold; to *feel* a pin pricking one); hence, in general, to be or become conscious of (as, to *feel* the floor sinking; to *feel* the approach of age); be sensible of; perceive; experience mentally (as, to *feel* a sensation, emotion, or inclination; "I *feel* the impulse—yet I do not plunge," Byron's "Manfred," i. 2); be emotionally affected by (as, to *feel* one's loss or disgrace keenly); be sensibly affected by, or experience the effects of (as, to *feel* the vengeance of an enemy; the whole region *felt* the storm; "Better . . . it might appear . . . That never air or ocean *felt* the wind," Pope's "Essay on Man," i. 167); also, with an adjunct or complement, to have a particular sensation, sense, or impression of (as, to *feel* one's self slighted; to *feel* a remark to be a slur upon one); have a general or thorough conviction of (as, to *feel* a thing to be true; "To *feel*, altho' no tongue can prove, That every cloud, that spreads above And veileth love, itself is love," Tennyson's "Two Voices," 445); also, to try or examine by touch, as with the hand (as, to *feel* one's pulse; *feel* this silk); test by touching or contact (as, to *feel* the ground with the foot or with a stick); find or pursue (one's way) by touching, groping, or cautious moves.—**to feel its,** or **one's, oats,** to be lively or frisky, as a horse fed on oats; hence, of persons, to have or show a lively sense of advantages enjoyed; be demonstratively complacent or self-important. [Colloq.]—**feel,** *v. i.* To have perception by touch or by any nerves of sensation other than those of sight, hearing, taste, and smell; have mental sensations or emotions (as, "From sense of grief and pain we shall be free; We shall not *feel*, because we shall not be": Dryden's tr. Lucretius, iii. 12); also, to have a sensation or sense of being (as specified: as, to *feel* warm, strong, or free); be consciously, in emotion, sentiment, opinion, etc. (as, to *feel* happy, proud, angry, or reluctant; to *feel* convinced or sure); be disposed (as, to *feel* kindly toward one); also, to have the sensibilities affected; have sympathy (*with*) or compassion (*for*); also, to produce a particular sensation; be (*cold, warm, hard,* etc.) to the touch; seem, in the impression produced (as, how does it *feel* to be rich?); also, to make examination by touch; search or seek with the hand or by touching (as, to *feel* for a coin in one's purse; to *feel* about in a dark room); grope.—**feel,** *n.* The sense of touch (as, soft to the *feel*); also, a sensation of something felt; a feeling; also, a quality of an object that is perceived by feeling or touching (as, soapstone has a soapy *feel*; liquids with an unctuous *feel*); also, the act or an act of feeling.—**feel'a-ble,** *a.* That may be felt.—**feel'er,** *n.* One who or that which feels; any special organ of touch in an animal, as an antenna or a tentacle; also, a proposal, remark, hint, or the like, designed to bring out the opinions or purposes of others.—**feel'ing,** *n.* The act of one who or that which feels; the function or the power of perceiving by touch or contact (as, a limb that has lost all *feeling*); physical sensation or sensibility not connected with sight, hearing, taste, or smell; a particular sensation of this kind (as, a *feeling* of warmth, pain, or drowsiness); also, a consciousness, sense, or impression of something (as, a *feeling* of inferiority; to have a *feeling* that something is wrong); an emotion (as, a *feeling* of joy, sorrow, hope, fear, pity, or wonder; to contemplate a thing with mingled *feelings*); a sentiment, inclination, or opinion (as, the *feeling* of the nation is against this policy); also, capacity for emotion; sensibility; *pl.*, sensibilities or susceptibilities liable to be unpleasantly affected (as, to hurt, ruffle, or soothe one's *feelings*); *sing.*, susceptibility to the higher or more refined emotions; fine emotional endowment; sympathetic perception or spirit; sympathetic appreciation of emotional meaning, as of a musical composition, as manifested in execution; also, a quality or character felt to belong to something (as, there was an uncanny *feeling* about the place); in the *fine arts*, the general impression conveyed by a work; also, emotional or sympathetic perception revealed by an artist in his work.—**feel'ing,** *p. a.* That feels; sentient; sensitive, as nerves; accessible to emotion, or sympathetic (as, a *feeling* heart); indicating emotion (as, a *feeling* response or tone); also, deeply felt, or heartfelt (as, "*feeling* sorrows": Shakspere's "King Lear," iv. 6. 226).—**feel'ing-ly,** *adv.*

feer (fēr), *n.* See *fere*[1].

feet (fēt), *n.* Plural of *foot.*

feeze, feaze (fēz), *v.*; *feezed, feazed, feezing, feazing.* [AS. *fēsian*, drive.] **I.** *tr.* To drive, beat or flog, or do for (obs. or prov.); disturb or discomfit (prov. or colloq.: see *faze*). **II.** *intr.* To fret; worry. [Prov. or colloq.]—**feeze, feaze,** *n.* A rush, or a violent impact (obs. or prov.); a fit of vexation or worry (colloq., U. S.).

feign (fān), *v.* [OF. F. *feindre* (ppr. *feignant*), < L. *fingere*, pp. *fictus* (stem *fig-*), touch, form, mold, conceive, devise, feign; akin to Gr. θιγγάνειν, touch, Skt. *dih-*, stroke, smear, and E. *dough.*] **I.** *tr.* To invent fictitiously or deceptively, as a story or an excuse; also, to represent fictitiously (as, "Things . . . worse Than fables yet have *feign'd*": Milton's "Paradise Lost," ii. 627); fable; also, to picture to one's self, or imagine (now rare); also, to maintain fictitiously, or pretend (usually with an object and infinitive, or a clause); also, to put on an appearance of (as, to *feign* death or sickness); simulate; sham; also, to imitate deceptively, or counterfeit (as, to *feign* another's voice). **II.** *intr.* To make believe; pretend.—**feigned,** *p. a.* Fictitiously invented; also, pretended, sham, or counterfeit; assumed, as a name; disguised, as a voice.—**feign-ed-ly** (fā'ned-li), *adv.*—**feign'er,** *n.*—**feign'ing-ly,** *adv.*

feint (fānt), *n.* [F. *feinte*, < *feindre*, E. *feign.*] A feigned or assumed appearance (as, to make a *feint* of deep absorption); a pretense; also, a movement made with the object of deceiving an adversary; an appearance of aiming at one part or point when another is the real object of attack.—**feint,** *v. i.* To make a feint.

feints (fānts), *n. pl.* See *faints.*

feist (fīst), *n.* Same as *fice.*

feld-spar (feld'spär), *n.* [For G. *feldspath*, 'field spar.'] Any of a group of minerals, all silicates of aluminium with potassium, sodium, calcium, or barium. Cf. *orthoclase.* Also **feld'spath** (-spath).—**feld-spath'ic, feld'spath-ose** (-ōs), *a.* Of, pertaining to, or containing feldspar.—**feld'-spath-oid,** *n.* Any of a group of minerals related to the feldspars.

Fé-libre (fā-lēbr), *n.* [F. *félibre*, < Pr. *felibre*, a word found in an old Provençal poem, perhaps meaning 'nursling,' < LL. *fellebris*, sucking.] A writer of verse or prose in the Provençal language; a member of the Félibrige.—**Fé-li-bre-an** (fā-lē'brē-ạn), *a.* [F. *félibréen.*] Of or pertaining to the Félibres.—**Fé-li-brige** (fā-lē-brēzh), *n.* [F. *félibrige*, < Pr. *felibrige*, < *felibre.*] A literary society founded in Provence in 1854 for the maintenance and purification of the Provençal language and the promotion of Provençal literature and art.

fe-li-cif-ic (fē-li-sif'ik), *a.* [L. *felix* (*felic-*), happy, + *facere*, make.] Making happy; productive of happiness.

fe-li-ci-tate (fẹ-lis'i-tāt), *v. t.*; *-tated, -tating.* [LL. *felicitatus*, pp. of *felicitare*, make happy, < L. *felix*, happy.] To make happy (now rare); also, to compliment upon a happy event; congratulate.—**fe-li'ci-tate**†, *a.* Made happy. See Shakspere's "King Lear," i. 1. 77.—**fe-li-ci-ta'tion** (-tā'-shọn), *n.* The act or an act of felicitating; a congratulatory speech or message.—**fe-li'ci-ta-tor,** *n.*

fe-li-ci-tous (fẹ-lis'i-tus), *a.* Characterized by felicity; apt or appropriate, as action, manner, or expression; apt in manner or expression, as a person.—**fe-li'ci-tous-ly,** *adv.*—**fe-li'ci-tous-ness,** *n.*

fe-li-ci-ty (fẹ-lis'i-ti), *n.*; pl. *-ties* (*-tiz*). [OF. *felicite* (F. *félicité*), < L. *felicitas*, < *felix*, happy.] The state of being happy; happiness, esp. in a high degree; an instance of this; also, a source of happiness; a blessing; also, prosperity or good fortune, or a piece of good fortune (now rare); also, a happy faculty (as, a writer's *felicity* of expression); singular grace or appropriateness, as of invention, manner, or expression; an instance or display of this; a happy turn of thought or expression.

fe-line (fē'līn or -lin). [L. *felinus*, < *feles*, cat.] **I.** *a.* Belonging or pertaining to the cat family (*Felidæ*), which includes, besides the domestic cat, the lions, tigers, leopards, etc.; cat-like in form or structure; characteristic of animals of the cat family; also, cat-like in character or quality; sly; stealthy; treacherous. **II.** *n.* An animal of the cat family.—**fe'line-ly,** *adv.*—**fe'line-ness,** *n.*

fell[1] (fel), *v. t.* [AS. *fellan*, causative of *feallan*, E. *fall.*] To cause to fall; knock or strike down, as an animal; cut down, as a tree; in *sewing*, to finish (a seam) by sewing the edge down flat.—**fell**[1], *n.* A felling; a cutting down, as of timber; the timber cut down in one season; in *sewing*, a seam finished by felling.

fell[2] (fel). Preterit of *fall.*

fell[3] (fel), *n.* [AS. *fell* = D. *vel* = G. *fell*; akin to L. *pellis*, skin.] The skin or hide of an animal; a pelt; sometimes, the skin of a human being; also, a covering of hair, wool, or the like; a fleece; a head of hair.

fell[4] (fel), *a.* [OF. *fel* (orig. nom., with acc. *felon*), < ML. *fello* (acc. *fellonem*): see *felon*[2].] Fierce or savage; cruel or ruthless; dreadful or terrible; also, intensely painful; very destructive; deadly, as poison; also, keen or eager (prov.); also, sturdy or doughty (now prov.); also, great or huge (Sc.). [Now literary or prov.]

fell[5] (fel), *n.* [Icel. *fjall* = Sw. *fjell* = Norw. *fjeld*: cf. *fjeld.*] A stretch of elevated waste land or pasture; a down. [Chiefly north. Eng. and Sc.]

fel-lah (fel'ạ̈), *n.*; pl. *fellahin* or *fellaheen* (fel-ạ-hēn'). [Ar. *fellāh.*] A native peasant or laborer in Egypt, Syria, etc.

fell-er (fel'ėr), *n.* One who or that which fells; specif., a sewing-machine attachment for felling seams.

fell-mong-er (fel'mung"gėr), *n.* A dealer in skins or hides of animals, esp. sheepskins.

fell-ness (fel'nes), *n.* The quality of being fell; fierceness; ruthlessness. [Now literary or prov.]

fel-loe (fel'ō), *n.* See *felly*[1].

fel-low (fel'ō), *n.* [ME. *felowe, felawe*, < AS. *fēolaga*, from Scand.: cf. Icel. *fēlagi*, partner, companion, < *fē*, property, money, + *leggja*, lay: see *fee*[1] and *lay*[1].] A partner†; a colleague†; an ally†; also, a companion or comrade; also, a thing that with something else makes up a pair; a mate; also, a thing that matches or resembles something else; also, one belonging to the same class; an equal or peer; also, a member, as of a company or party; a member of any of certain learned societies (as, a *fellow* of the Royal Geographical Society); an incorporated member of an English college, entitled to certain privileges; a graduate student of a university or college, to whom an allowance is granted for special study; a member of the corporation or board of trustees of a university or college; in general, a man or person (now chiefly familiar or colloq.); sometimes, in contempt, a person of small worth or no esteem (as, "Worth makes the man, and want of it the *fellow*": Pope's "Essay on Man," iv. 203). Much used in compounds to denote association, membership, or some other relation based on a common status, as in *fellow-citizen, fellow-countryman, fellow-student, fellow-worker.*—**fel′low,** *v. t.* To make, or represent as, equal with another; also, to produce a fellow or equal to; match.—**fel′low=crea′ture,** *n.* A creature produced by the same Creator: now used chiefly of human beings.—**fel′low=feel′ing,** *n.* Sympathetic feeling; sympathy; also, sense of joint interest.—**fel′low-less,** *a.* Without a fellow, companion, or mate; also, matchless or peerless.—**fel′low-ly,** *a.* Companionable; sociable; familiar. [Now prov. Eng.]—**fel′low-ship,** *n.* The condition or relation of being a fellow; community of interest, feeling, etc.; companionship; also, mutual intercourse; communion, as between members of the same church; also, friendliness (as, "The birds . . . with fearless *fellowship* Above and round him wheel and hover": Shelley's "Rosalind and Helen," 121); also, a body of fellows; a company; a gild or corporation; an association of persons having similar tastes, interests, etc.; also, the position or emoluments of a fellow of a university, etc.; a foundation for the maintenance of such a fellow; in *arith.*, the rule of proportions by which the accounts of partners in business are adjusted so that each may have a share of gain, or sustain a share of loss, in proportion to his part of the stock.—**fel′low-ship,** *v.* **I.** *tr.* To unite in fellowship†; also, to admit to fellowship, esp. religious fellowship. **II.** *intr.* To join in fellowship, esp. religious fellowship.

fel-ly[1], fel-loe (fel′i, -ō), *n.*; pl. *fellies* (-iz), *felloes* (-ōz). [AS. *felg* = D. *velg* = G. *felge.*] The circular rim, or a part of the rim, of a wheel, into which the outer ends of the spokes are inserted.

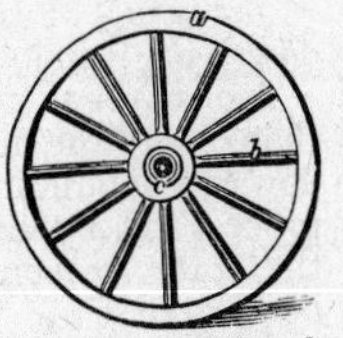

Wheel. — *a*, felly; *b*, spoke; *c*, hub.

fel-ly[2] (fel′li), *adv.* In a fell manner; fiercely; ruthlessly. [Now literary.]

fe-lo de se (fē′lō dẹ sē′); pl. *felos de se* (fē′lōz dẹ sē′). [ML., 'a felon with respect to one's self.'] One who commits suicide; also, suicide.

fel-on[1] (fel′ọn), *n.* [ME. *feloun*, appar. < ML. *fello(n-)*, an inflammatory swelling, perhaps from L. *fel*, gall, poison: cf. *felon*[2].] In *pathol.*, an acute and painful inflammation of the deeper tissues of a finger or toe, usually near the nail: a form of whitlow.

fel-on[2] (fel′ọn). [OF. *felon* (F. *félon*), n. and a., < ML. *fello(n-), felo(n-)*, traitor, felon; origin uncertain: cf. *felon*[1], also *fell*[4].] **I.** *n.* A wicked person†; in *law*, one who has committed a felony. **II.** *a.* Wicked; cruel; savage; wild. [Now poetic.]—**fe-lo-ni-ous** (fe-lō′ni-us), *a.* Wicked, base, or villainous (now chiefly poetic: as, "A bloody murderer, Or foul *felonious* thief," Shakspere's "2 Henry VI.," iii. 1. 129); in *law*, pertaining to, of the nature of, or involving a felony (as, *felonious* homicide, which comprehends murder and manslaughter; to break into a house with *felonious* intent).—**fe-lo′ni-ous-ly,** *adv.*—**fe-lo′ni-ous-ness,** *n.*—**fel′on-ry,** *n.* The whole body or class of felons; the convict population of a penal colony.—**fel′on-y,** *n.*; pl. *-ies* (-iz). [OF. *felonie* (F. *félonie*).] Wickedness†; crime†; in *law*, formerly, any crime which occasioned the forfeiture of land or goods, or both, and sometimes other penalties; now, usually, any of various offenses, as murder, burglary, etc., of graver character than those called misdemeanors.

fel-site (fel′sīt), *n.* [From *fels(par).*] A dense igneous rock or rock constituent consisting typically of minute crystals of feldspar and quartz.—**fel-sit′ic** (-sit′ik), *a.*

fel-spar, fel-spath (fel′spär, -spath), *n.* Same as *feldspar.*

felt[1] (felt). Preterit and past participle of *feel.*

felt[2] (felt), *n.* [AS. *felt* = D. *vilt* = G. *filz* = Sw. and Dan. *filt*, felt.] An unwoven fabric of wool, or of wool and fur or hair, matted together by rolling and pressure; any article of this material, esp. a hat; any matted fabric or material.—**felt[2],** *v.* **I.** *tr.* To make into felt; mat or press together; also, to cover with or as with felt. **II.** *intr.* To become matted together.—**felt′ing,** *n.* The act or process of making felt; the materials of which felt is made; felted material.—**felt′y,** *a.* Felt-like.

fe-luc-ca (fe-luk′ạ̈), *n.* [It. *felucca, feluca*; from Ar.] A long, narrow vessel propelled by oars or lateen sails, or both, used chiefly in the Mediterranean.

Felucca.

fel-wort (fel′wėrt), *n.* [AS. *feldwyrt*, 'field wort.'] Any of several plants of the gentian family, as *Gentiana amarella.*

fe-male (fē′māl). [ME. *female* (a form due to association with *male*), *femele*, < OF. F. *femelle*, < L. *femella*, dim. of *femina*, woman, female: see *fetus.*] **I.** *n.* A human being of the sex which conceives and brings forth young; a woman or girl; also, any animal of corresponding sex (as, "The *female* of the species is more deadly than the male": Kipling's "Female of the Species"); in *bot.*, a pistillate plant. **II.** *a.* Belonging to the sex which brings forth young, or any division or group corresponding to it; also, pertaining to or characteristic of this sex; feminine; also, womanish† or weakly† (as, "Boys . . . clap their *female* joints In stiff unwieldy arms": Shakspere's "Richard II.," iii. 2. 114); in *bot.*, designating or pertaining to any reproductive structure which produces or contains elements that need fertilization from the male element; of seed-plants, pistillate; in *mech.*, designating some part, etc., into which a corresponding part fits (as, a *female* screw: see *screw, n.*).—**female rime.** Same as *feminine rime*, under *feminine, a.*

feme (fem), *n.* [AF. and OF.: see *femme.*] In *law*, a woman or wife.—**feme covert,** in *law*, a married woman.—**feme sole,** in *law*, an unmarried woman, whether spinster, widow, or divorcée; also, a married woman who is independent of her husband with respect to property.—**feme sole trader,** in *law*, a married woman who is entitled to carry on business on her own account and responsibility, independently of her husband.

fem-i-ne-i-ty (fem-i-nē′i-ti), *n.* [L. *femineus*, feminine, < *femina*, woman.] Feminine nature; womanliness.

fem-i-nie (fem′i-ni), *n.* [OF. *feminie*, < L. *femina*, woman.] Women collectively; esp., the Amazons, or their country. [Archaic.]

fem-i-nine (fem′i-nin), *a.* [OF. *feminin* (F. *féminin*), < L. *femininus*, < *femina*, woman.] Belonging to the female sex (now somewhat rare); also, pertaining to or characteristic of a woman or women; womanly; sometimes, womanish; in *gram.*, noting or pertaining to the gender to which the words denoting females regularly belong.—**feminine ending,** in *gram.*, a termination or final syllable marking a feminine word; in *pros.*, an ending in which a line closes with an extra unaccented syllable instead of the normal accented syllable.—**feminine rime,** in *pros.*, a rime of two syllables of which the second is unstressed, as *motion, notion* ('double rime'), or of three syllables of which the second and third are unstressed, as *fortunate, importunate* ('triple rime'). Cf. *masculine rime*, under *masculine, a.*—**fem′i-nine,** *n.* In *gram.*, the feminine gender; a feminine word or word-form.—**fem′i-nine-ly,** *adv.*—**fem′i-nine-ness,** *n.*—**fem-i-nin′i-ty** (-nin′i-ti), *n.* The quality of being feminine; womanliness; also, women collectively.

fem-i-nism (fem′i-nizm), *n.* [L. *femina*, woman.] Feminine character; also, the doctrine advocating extension of the activities of women in social and political life.—**fem′i-nist,** *n.* A believer in or advocate of feminism.—**fem-i-nis′tic,** *a.*

fe-min-i-ty (fe-min′i-ti), *n.* Same as *femininity.*

fem-i-nize (fem′i-nīz), *v. t.* or *i.*; *-nized, -nizing.* [L. *femina*, woman.] To make or become feminine or womanish.—**fem″i-ni-za′tion** (-ni-zā′shọn), *n.*

fem-i-nol-o-gy (fem-i-nol′ọ̄-ji), *n.* [L. *femina*, woman: see *-logy.*] The science or study concerned with woman.—**fem-i-nol′o-gist,** *n.*

femme (fȧm), *n.* [F. *femme*, OF. *feme*, < L. *femina*, woman.] A woman; a wife. Cf. *feme*.—**femme de chambre** (dė shäṅbr). [F.] A lady's maid; also, a chambermaid.

fe-mur (fē′mėr), *n.*; pl. *femurs* or *femora* (fem′ō-rạ̈). [L., thigh.] In man, the single long bone in the leg which extends from the hip to the knee; the thigh-bone; also, a corresponding bone in the leg or hind limb of other animals; in *entom.*, the third segment or joint of an insect's leg (counting from the proximal end), situated between the trochanter and the tibia.—**fem-o-ral** (fem′ọ-rạl), *a.*

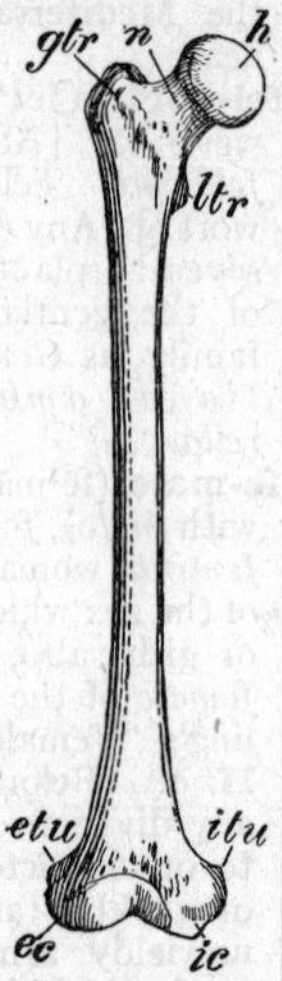

Anterior view of Human Right Femur. — *ec*, external condyle; *etu*, external tuberosity; *ic*, internal condyle; *itu*, internal tuberosity; *ltr*, lesser trochanter; *gtr*, great trochanter; *h*, head; *n*, neck.

fen (fen), *n.* [AS. *fen* = D. *veen* = G. *fenn* = Icel. *fen*, fen, = Goth. *fani*, mud.] Low land covered wholly or partially with water; boggy land; a marsh; *pl.* [often *cap.*], with *the*, certain marshy districts in Cambridgeshire, Lincolnshire, and other English counties.

fence (fens), *n.* [For *defence*, *defense*.] The act of defending†; defense†; also, a means of defense (archaic); a bulwark (archaic); also, an inclosure or barrier, as around or along a field, yard, etc.; also, the act, practice, or art of fencing; sword-play; hence, skill or adroitness in argument, etc., as in defending one's position and baffling an opponent's attacks; also, a receiver of stolen goods, or a place where such goods are received; in *mach.*, a guard or guide, as for regulating the movements of a tool or machine.—**to be on the fence,** to be undecided or neutral. [Colloq., U. S.]—**to mend one's fences.** See under *mend*, *v. t.*—**fence,** *v.*; *fenced*, *fencing*. **I.** *tr.* To defend; shield; protect; guard; also, to ward off or keep out; also, to inclose with or as with a fence; separate by or as by a fence or fences; also, to declare (a forest, river, etc.) closed against hunting or fishing. **II.** *intr.* To raise a defense or a fence; also, to leap over a fence (said of a horse); also, to use a sword, foil, etc., in defense and attack, or in exercise or exhibition of skill in that art; hence, to parry arguments; strive to evade questioning.—**fence′less,** *a.* Defenseless; also, without a fence or inclosure; open.—**fence′less-ness,** *n.*—**fence′=liz″ard,** *n.* The common small lizard, or swift, *Sceloporus undulatus*, of the U. S.—**fen′cer,** *n.* One who fences; esp., one who practises the art of fencing with a sword, foil, etc.

Fence-lizard.

fen-ci-ble (fen′si-bl). [For *defensible*.] **I.** *a.* Capable of making defense; also, capable of being defended; also, pertaining to fencibles. **II.** *n.* A soldier enlisted for defensive service in his own country only.

fen-cing (fen′sing), *n.* The act of one who fences; a raising up of a defense or of fences; also, an inclosure or railing; fences collectively; material for fences; esp., the act, practice, or art of using a sword, foil, etc., for defense and attack; hence, a parrying of arguments; an evading of questions.—**fen′cing=stick,** *n.* A stick, as of hickory with a basketwork guard for the hand, used in fencing.

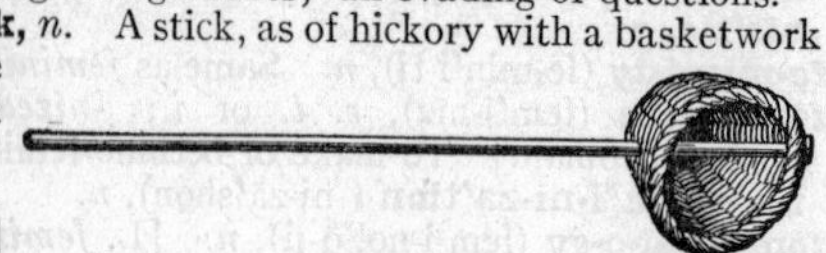
Fencing-stick.

fend (fend), *v.* [For *defend*.] **I.** *tr.* To defend (archaic); also, to ward off (often with *off*: as, to *fend* off blows); also, to support or maintain (Sc.). **II.** *intr.* To make defense; offer resistance; also, to parry or fence; also, to make shift, or provide (prov. or colloq.: as, "We may strive . . . and *fend*, but it's little we can do," George Eliot's "Silas Marner," xiv.; to *fend* for one's self).—**fend′er,** *n.* One who or that which fends; a metal guard before an open fire, to keep back falling coals; a piece of timber, bundle of rope, or the like, hung over the side of a vessel to lessen shock or prevent chafing; a device in front of a locomotive, electric car, or the like, for pushing aside or catching objects or persons in case of collision.

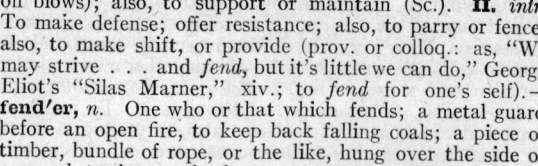

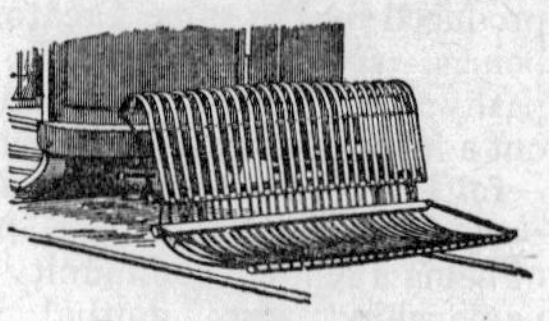
Fender for Electric Car.

fen-es-tel-la (fen-es-tel′ạ̈), *n.*; pl. *-tellæ* (-tel′ē). [L., dim. of *fenestra*, window.] A small window or window-like opening; specif., a small window-like niche in the wall on the south side of an altar, containing the piscina, and frequently also the credence.

Fenestella. — Church of Norrey, near Caen, Normandy.

fe-nes-tra (fē-nes′trạ̈), *n.*; pl. *-træ* (-trē). [L., window.] A window-like opening; in *anat.*, a small opening or perforation, as in a bone.—**fe-nes′tral,** *a.* Of, pertaining to, or of the nature of a window or fenestra.—**fe-nes′trate, fe-nes′trat-ed** (-trāt, -trā-ted), *a.* [L. *fenestratus*, pp. of *fenestrare*, furnish with windows, < *fenestra*.] Furnished with windows or window-like openings.—**fen-es-tra-tion** (fen-es-trā′shọn), *n.* The disposition of windows in a building; in *anat.*, the process of becoming perforated; the state of being fenestrate or perforated.

Fe-ni-an (fē′ni-ạn). [Ir. *Fiann*, *Feinne*, legendary band of Irish warriors.] **I.** *n.* A member of a legendary band of warriors in Ireland; also, a member of an Irish revolutionary organization ('Fenian Brotherhood'), founded in New York in 1858, which had for its aim the overthrow of English rule in Ireland. **II.** *a.* Of or pertaining to the Fenians.—**Fe′ni-an-ism,** *n.*

fen-nec, fen-nek (fen′ek), *n.* [Ar. *fenek*.] A small African fox, *Vulpes zerda*, of a pale fawn-color, and having large, pointed ears.

Fennec.

fen-nel (fen′ẹl), *n.* [AS. *fenol*, *finol*, < L. *fæniculum*, fennel, dim. of *fænum*, hay.] An apiaceous plant, *Fœniculum fœniculum*, having yellow flowers, and bearing aromatic seeds which are used in cookery and medicine; the seeds of this plant; also, any of various more or less similar plants, as *Ferula communis* ('giant fennel'), a tall, ornamental apiaceous herb.—**fen′nel=flow″er,** *n.* Any of the ranunculaceous herbs constituting the genus *Nigella*, as *N. sativa* whose seeds are used in the East as a condiment and medicine.

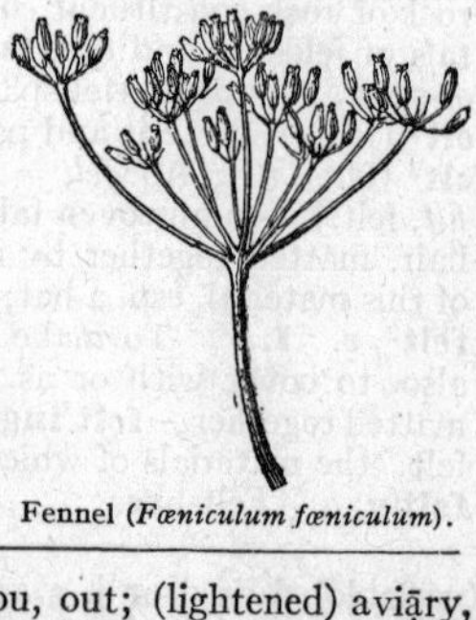
Fennel (*Fœniculum fœniculum*).

fen-ny (fen′i), *a.* Having the character of a fen; marshy; also, inhabiting, or growing in, fens (as, "a *fenny* snake," Shakspere's "Macbeth," iv. 1. 12; "through palmy fern, and rushes *fenny*," Keats's "Endymion," i.).
fent (fent), *n.* [OF. F. *fente*, < *fendre*, < L. *findere*, cleave, split.] A short slit or opening in a garment, to facilitate putting it on; a placket; a vent. [Chiefly prov.]
fen-u-greek (fen′ū-grēk), *n.* [AS. *fenogrecum*, < L. *fænum Græcum*, 'Greek hay.'] A fabaceous plant, *Trigonella fænumgræcum*, indigenous to western Asia, but extensively cultivated elsewhere, chiefly for its mucilaginous seeds, which are used as food and in veterinary medicine.

Fenugreek. — *a*, a fruit.

feod, feo-dal (fūd, fū′dąl), etc. See *feud*[2], *feudal*[2], etc.
feoff (fef), *v. t.* [AF. *feoffer*, OF. *feffer*, *fieffer* (F. *fieffer*), < *fieu*, E. *fee*[2].] To invest with a fief or fee; enfeoff.—**feoff,** *n.* A fief or fee.—**feoff-ee′** (-ē′), *n.* A person invested with a fief or fee.—**feoff′er, feoff′or,** *n.* One who grants a fief or fee.—**feoff′ment,** *n.* The act of investing with a fief or fee.
fe-ra-cious (fę-rā′shus), *a.* [L. *ferax* (*ferac-*), < *ferre*, bear.] Fruitful; productive. [Obs. or archaic.]—**fe-ra′ci-ty** (-ras′i-ti), *n.*
fe-ral[1] (fē′rąl), *a.* [L. *fera*, wild beast, prop. fem. of *ferus*, wild: see *fierce*.] Wild, or existing in a state of nature, as animals (or sometimes plants); also, having reverted to the wild state, as from domestication; also, pertaining to or characteristic of wild animals (as, the *feral* state); fig., wild; savage.
fe-ral[2] (fē′rąl), *a.* [L. *feralis*, pertaining to the dead, < *ferre*, bear (with reference to funeral processions).] Pertaining to the dead; funereal; gloomy; also, deadly; fatal.
Fe-ra-li-a (fę-rā′li-ą̈), *n. pl.* [L., prop. neut. pl. of *feralis*: see *feral*[2].] Among the ancient Romans, the general festival of the dead, held on the last day of the Parentalia.
fe-rash (fę-räsh′), *n.* [Hind., < Ar. *farrāsh*.] In the East Indies, a servant employed to spread carpets, pitch tents, etc., and in a house to do the work of a chambermaid.
fer=de=lance (fãr-dė-läṅs), *n.* [F., lit. 'iron (head) of lance.'] A large, very venomous serpent, *Lachesis lanceolatus*, of the warm parts of America.

Fer-de-lance.

fere[1] (fēr), *n.* [AS. *gefēra*, < *ge-*, together, + *-fēra*, from the root of *faran*, E. *fare*.] A companion; a mate; esp., a spouse. [Archaic.]
fere[2] (fēr), *a.* [Icel. *færr*, akin to *fara*, go, AS. *faran*, E. *fare*.] Able; strong; sound; healthy. [Now Sc.]
fer-e-to-ry (fer′ę-tō-ri), *n.*; pl. *-ries* (-riz). [ME. *feretre*, < OF. *fiertre*, < L. *feretrum*, < Gr. φέρετρον, < φέρειν, bear.] A bier (rare); also, a shrine, usually portable, designed to hold the relics of saints; also, a room or chapel in which shrines were kept.

Feretory, or Shrine. — English mediæval work in silver.

fe-ri-al (fē′ri-ąl), *a.* [ML. *ferialis*, < L. *feria*, holiday: cf. *fair*[2].] Pertaining to a holiday; *eccles.*, pertaining to week-days not set apart as festivals.
fe-rine (fē′rīn or -rin), *a.* [L. *ferinus*, < *fera*, wild beast: see *feral*[1].] Feral; wild: as, "We killed some wild *ferine* creatures at the foot of these hills" (Defoe's "Captain Singleton," viii.).
Fe-rin-ghi, Fe-rin-ghee (fę-ring′gē), *n.* [Pers. *Farangī*, Ar. *Faranjī*, lit. 'Frank': cf. *Frank*[1].] An East Indian term for a European or a person of European descent, esp. a Portuguese born in India: now usually contemptuous.
fer-i-ty (fer′i-ti), *n.* [L. *feritas*, < *ferus*, wild: see *fierce*.] Wild, untamed, or uncultivated state; hence, savagery; ferocity.
fer-ly (fėr′li). [AS. *fǣrlīc*, sudden, < *fǣr*, E. *fear*.] **I.**† *a.* Sudden or unexpected; also, dreadful or terrible; also, strange or wonderful. **II.** *n.* Something wonderful; a marvel; a sight. [Now chiefly Sc.]
fer-mail (fėr′māl), *n.* [OF. *fermail*, < ML. *firmaculum*, < L. *firmare*, E. *firm*, *v.*] A clasp, buckle, or fastening, as used in ancient costume, etc.
fer-ment (fėr′ment), *n.* [L. *fermentum*, < *fervere*, boil: see *fervent*.] Any of various agents or substances, as yeast or leaven, which produce certain changes, as effervescence or decomposition, in other substances; specif., in modern scientific use, any of various living organisms, as yeasts, certain bacteria, etc. ('organized ferments'), or any of certain complex substances derived from living cells, as pepsin, etc. (enzymes, or 'unorganized ferments,' 'chemical ferments,' or 'soluble ferments'), capable of producing certain chemical changes in organic substances; also, fermentation; fig., agitation; excitement; a tumult.—**fer-ment′,** *v.* [L. *fermentare* (pp. *fermentatus*), < *fermentum*.] **I.** *tr.* To act upon as a ferment; cause to undergo a change of the nature of or similar to that by which grape-sugar is converted into alcohol, etc., in the presence of yeast; cause to undergo fermentation; fig., to agitate; excite; also, to inflame; foment. **II.** *intr.* To be fermented; undergo fermentation; fig., to seethe with agitation or excitement.—**fer-ment′a-ble,** *a.* Capable of being fermented.—**fer-men-ta′tion** (-men-tā′shọn), *n.* The act or process of fermenting; a change brought about by a ferment, as in grape-sugar decomposed into alcohol and carbon dioxide by the action of yeast; fig., agitation; excitement.—**fer-men′ta-tive** (-tą-tiv), *a.* Tending to produce or undergo fermentation; also, pertaining to or of the nature of fermentation. Also **fer-men′tive.**
fer-me-ture (fėr′mę-ţūr), *n.* [F., < *fermer*, close: see *firm*, *v.*] A device for closing the bore or chamber of a breech-loading gun.
fern (fėrn), *n.* [AS. *fearn* = D. *varen* = G. *farn*.] Any of the pteridophytes constituting the order *Filicales*, comprising flowerless plants varying in size from small epiphytic species to herb-like and tree-like forms; also, such plants collectively. Cf. *brake*[4].—**ferned,** *a.* Abounding in ferns.—**fern′er-y,** *n.*; pl. *-ies* (-iz). A place or a glass case in which ferns are grown for ornament.—**fern′less,** *a.* Without ferns.—**fern′=seed,** *n.* The spores of ferns, formerly regarded as seeds and supposed to have the power to render persons invisible: as, "We have the receipt of *fern-seed*, we walk invisible" (Shakspere's "1 Henry IV.," ii. 1. 96).—**fern′wort** (-wėrt), *n.* Any of the pteridophytes.—**fern′y,** *a.* Of or pertaining to, consisting of, or resembling ferns; also, abounding in or overgrown with ferns (as, "a green *ferny* well": Synge's "Well of the Saints," i.).

Fern (*Dryopteris filix-mas*).

fe-ro-cious (fę-rō′shus), *a.* [L. *ferox* (*feroc-*), < *ferus*, wild, fierce: see *fierce*.] Savagely fierce, as a wild beast, a person, or disposition, action, aspect, etc.; violently cruel; savage.—**fe-ro'cious-ly,** *adv.*—**fe-ro'cious-ness, fe-ro'ci-ty** (-ros'i-ti), *n.*

-ferous. [L. *-fer*, also *-ferus*, < *ferre*, bear.] An adjective termination meaning 'bearing,' 'producing,' 'yielding,' 'containing,' 'conveying,' as in *auriferous, gypsiferous, herbiferous, lactiferous, pestiferous.*

fer-rate (fer'āt), *n.* In *chem.*, a salt of ferric acid.

fer-rel (fer'ẹl), *n.* Same as *ferrule.*

fer-re-ous (fer'ẹ̄-us), *a.* [L. *ferreus*, < *ferrum*, iron.] Of or pertaining to, consisting of, or resembling iron.

fer-ret[1] (fer'et), *n.* [It. *fioretto*, dim. of *fiore*, < L. *flos*, flower.] A narrow tape or ribbon, as of silk or cotton, used for binding, shoe-strings, etc.

fer-ret[2] (fer'et), *n.* [OF. F. *furet*, dim. < ML. *furo(n-)*, ferret, prob. < L. *fur*, thief.] A small, slender animal of the weasel kind, of whitish or pale-yellow color, bred to drive rabbits from their burrows, kill rats, etc.: usually regarded as a domesticated variety of the polecat, *Putorius fœtidus.*—**fer'ret**[2], *v.* **I.** *tr.* To hunt with ferrets; hence, to hunt after or worry, as a ferret does his prey; also, to drive out by or as by means of a ferret (as, "Measures were . . . taken . . . to *ferret* this vermin brood [buccaneers] out of the colonies": Irving's "Tales of a Traveler," iv. 2); also, to search out or bring to light (commonly with *out*: as, to *ferret* out the facts of a case). **II.** *intr.* To hunt with ferrets; hence, to search about.—**fer'ret-er,** *n.*—**fer'ret-y,** *a.* Ferret-like.

Ferret.

ferri-. Form of L. *ferrum*, iron, used in combination: in *chem.*, implying esp. combination with iron in the ferric form, as in *ferricyanic, ferricyanide.* Cf. *ferro-.*

fer-ri-age (fer'i-ạ̄j), *n.* The act or business of conveying persons and things over a stream or other water by a ferry-boat or the like; also, provision for ferrying; also, the price charged for ferrying.

fer-ric (fer'ik), *a.* [L. *ferrum*, iron.] Of or containing iron. See *ferrous.*—**ferric acid,** a hypothetical acid (H_2FeO_4) containing iron, known only through its salts.

fer-rif-er-ous (fe-rif'ẹ-rus), *a.* [See *ferri-* and *-ferous.*] Producing or yielding iron.

Fer-ris (fer'is) **wheel.** [From G. W. G. *Ferris*, the inventor.] An amusement device consisting of a large upright wheel rotating about a fixed axis, and having passenger-cars suspended at intervals around its rim.

fer-rite (fer'īt), *n.* [L. *ferrum*, iron.] Any of certain indeterminable mineral substances (probably iron compounds) frequently observed in the microscopic examination of certain igneous rocks; also, a compound formed when ferric oxide is combined with a more basic metallic oxide; also, the pure iron constituent of steel, etc., as distinguished from the iron carbides, etc.

ferro-. Form of L. *ferrum*, iron, used in combination, as in *ferro-aluminium, ferrochromium, ferromanganese, ferromolybdenum, ferrosilicon, ferrotitanium, ferrotungsten, ferrovanadium* (these being combinations of iron with aluminium, chromium, manganese, etc., respectively: all used in steel-making): in *chem.*, sometimes implying esp. combination with iron in the ferrous form, as in *ferrocyanic, ferrocyanide.* Cf. *ferri-.*—**fer-ro-bronze** (fer'ọ̄-bronz), *n.* Bronze alloyed with a small proportion of iron.—**fer-ro-con'crete** (-kon'krēt), *n.* Reinforced concrete.—**fer″ro-mag-ne'sian** (-mag-nē'shiạn or -zhiạn), *a.* Containing both iron and magnesium: applied to minerals and rocks.—**fer″ro-mag-net'ic** (-mag-net'ik), *a.* Loosely, pertaining to ordinary magnetism (opposed to *diamagnetic*); specif., noting or pertaining to a class of substances (as iron, cobalt, etc.) which are magnetic in the usual way and in a high degree, and hence tend to take a position with the longer axis parallel to the lines of force (distinguished from *paramagnetic*, and opposed to *diamagnetic*).—**fer'ro-type** (-tīp), *n.* [+ *-type.*] A photograph taken on a sensitized sheet of enameled iron or tin; a tintype; also, the process.

fer-rous (fer'us), *a.* [L. *ferrum*, iron.] Containing iron (in larger proportion than a corresponding ferric compound).

fer-ru-gi-nous, fer-ru-gin-e-ous (fe-rö'ji-nus, fer-ọ̈-jin'ẹ̄-us), *a.* [L. *ferruginus, ferrugineus*, < *ferrugo*, iron-rust, < *ferrum*, iron.] Orig., of, pertaining to, or of the nature of iron-rust; now, usually, of the nature of or containing iron; also, of the color of iron-rust; reddish-brown.

fer-rule (fer'öl or -ẹl), *n.* [F. *virole*, < ML. *virola*, < L. *viriola*, dim. < *viriæ*, bracelets.] A metal ring or cap put round the end of a post, cane, etc., for strength or protection. —**fer'rule,** *v. t.*; *-ruled, -ruling.* To furnish with a ferrule.

fer-rum (fer'um), *n.* [L.] Iron: in *chem.*, abbreviated *Fe* (without period).

fer-ry (fer'i), *v.*; *-ried, -rying.* [AS. *ferian*, akin to *faran*, E. *fare.*] **I.** *tr.* To transport†; esp., to carry or convey over a river, strait, etc., in a boat; also, to work (a boat, etc.) across a stream or other contracted body of water; also, of a vessel, to serve as a ferry-boat over (a stream, etc.). **II.** *intr.* To pass over water in a boat or by ferry.—**fer'ry,** *n.*; pl. *ferries* (-iz). A place where boats convey persons and things across a river, etc.; also, the provision, as a boat service or line, for such conveyance; a ferry-boat; also, the legal right to ferry passengers, etc., and to charge toll for the service.—**fer'ry=boat,** *n.* A boat used to convey passengers, vehicles, etc., across a river or the like.—**fer'ry-man** (-mạn), *n.*; pl. *-men.* One who keeps or plies a ferry.

fer-tile (fėr'til), *a.* [L. *fertilis*, < *ferre*, bear.] Bearing or producing vegetation, crops, etc., abundantly, as land or soil; fruitful; sometimes, bearing offspring freely, or prolific (see Milton's "Paradise Lost," vii. 454); fig., abundantly productive, or yielding abundant returns, results, etc. (as, a *fertile* mind or imagination; a *fertile* subject for investigation); producing abundance (*of*: as, "A reforming age is always *fertile* of impostors," Macaulay's "Essays," Moore's Byron); abundant or rich of production (*in*: as, a mind *fertile* in schemes or expedients); also, conducive to fruitfulness or productiveness (as, *fertile* showers); also, produced in abundance†; in *bot.*, capable of producing fruit, as a flower; capable of causing fertilization, as an anther with fully developed pollen; having spore-bearing organs, as a frond; in *biol.*, fertilized, as an egg or ovum; fecundated.—**fer'tile-ly,** *adv.*—**fer'tile-ness, fer-til'i-ty** (-til'i-ti), *n.*—**fer'ti-liz-a-ble** (-ti-lī-zạ-bl), *a.* Capable of being fertilized.—**fer″ti-li-za'tion** (-li-zā'shọn), *n.* The act or process of fertilizing, or the state of being fertilized; the enrichment of soil for the production of crops, etc.; in *biol.*, the rendering of an egg, ovum, or female cell capable of development by union with the male element; fecundation or impregnation of animals or plants; specif., in *bot.*, the process by which the pollen reaches and acts upon the ovules and assures the production of fruit; also, the analogous process in cryptogams.—**fer'ti-lize** (-līz), *v. t.*; *-lized, -lizing.* To make fertile; enrich (soil, etc.) for the production of crops, etc.; fig., to make productive (as, to *fertilize* the mind); in *biol.*, to render (an egg, ovum, or female cell) capable of development by union with the male element; fecundate or impregnate (an animal or plant); specif., in *bot.*, to render fruitful by means of pollen.—**fer'ti-liz-er** (-lī-zėr), *n.* One who or that which fertilizes; any material used to fertilize the soil; a manure, esp. a commercial manure.

fer-ule[1] (fer'öl), *n.* [L. *ferula*, the giant fennel, a rod, a cane.] A rod, cane, or flat piece of wood, used for the punishment of children, as in schools, by striking them, esp. on the hand.—**fer'ule**[1], *v. t.*; *-uled, -uling.* To punish with a ferule.

fer-ule[2] (fer'öl or -ẹl), *n.* See *ferrule.*

fer-vent (fėr'vẹnt), *a.* [OF. F. *fervent*, < L. *fervens* (*fervent-*), ppr. of *fervere*, be boiling hot, boil, glow.] Hot, burning, or glowing (as, "The elements shall melt with *fervent* heat": 2 Pet. iii. 10); fig., having, showing, or characterized by great warmth and earnestness of feeling (as, a *fervent* admirer or admiration; a *fervent* hope or prayer; *fervent* zeal); ardent; hearty.—**fer'ven-cy, fer'vent-ness,** *n.*—**fer'vent-ly,** *adv.*

fer-vid (fėr'vid), *a.* [L. *fervidus*, < *fervere*: see *fervent.*]

Hot, fiery, or burning (as, "The mounted sun Shot down direct his *fervid* rays": Milton's "Paradise Lost," v. 301); fig., heated or vehement in spirit, enthusiasm, etc. (as, a *fervid* orator or oration; *fervid* protestations); impassioned. —**fer-vid′i-ty, fer′vid-ness,** *n.*—**fer′vid-ly,** *adv.*

fer-vor (fėr′vọr), *n.* [OF. *fervor* (F. *ferveur*), < L. *fervor*, < *fervere*: see *fervent.*] Intense heat; fig., great warmth and earnestness of feeling; ardor; fervency.

fer′vour, *n.* British preferred form of *fervor.*

Fes-cen-nine (fes′ẹ-nin or -nīn), *a.* Pertaining to or associated with the ancient town of Fescennia, in Italy, as a kind of rude, jeering verses extemporized on festive occasions, and popular at Rome and elsewhere, which are said to have been introduced from Fescennia; hence, scurrilous; licentious; obscene.

fes-cue (fes′kū), *n.* [OF. *festu* (F. *fêtu*), < L. *festuca*, stalk, straw.] A straw, slender twig, or the like, used to point out the letters in teaching children to read; also, any grass of the genus *Festuca*, some species of which are cultivated as pasture grasses.

fesse, fess (fes), *n.* [OF. *fesse, faisse* (F. *fasce*), < L. *fascia*, band.] In *her.*, a wide horizontal band across the middle of an escutcheon.—**fesse′=point,** *n.* In *her.*, the central point of an escutcheon.—**fesse′wise,** *adv.* In *her.*, in the manner of a fesse.

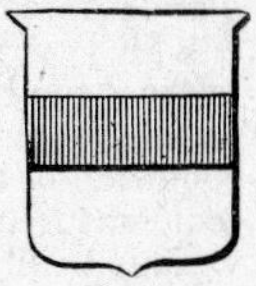
Fesse.

fest (fest), *n.* [G.: see *feast.*] A feast; a festival or festivity: much used in composition, as in *sängerfest* and in various humorous or slang formations, as *talk-fest, gab-fest, fight-fest.*

fes-ta (fes′tạ̈), *n.* [It.: see *feast.*] A feast, festival, or festivity; a festal day; a holiday.

fes-tal (fes′tạl), *a.* [OF. *festal*, < L. *festum*, a festival, feast: see *feast.*] Pertaining to or befitting a feast, festival, or gala occasion; festive; gay.—**fes′tal-ly,** *adv.*

fes-ter (fes′tėr), *n.* [OF. *festre*, < L. *fistula*: see *fistula.*] An ulcer; a rankling sore; esp., a small, purulent, superficial sore; also, a festering or rankling.—**fes′ter,** *v.* **I.** *intr.* To generate purulent matter (as, "Wounds immedicable . . . *fester*": Milton's "Samson Agonistes," 621); suppurate; also, to cause ulceration, or rankle, as something embedded in the flesh (often fig.); also, to putrefy or rot (as, "Lilies that *fester* smell far worse than weeds": Shakspere's "Sonnets," xciv.). **II.** *tr.* To cause to fester.

fes-ti-nate (fes′ti-nāt), *v. i.* or *t.*; *-nated, -nating.* [L *festinatus*, pp. of *festinare*, hasten.] To hasten.—**fes′ti-nate†,** *a.* Hasty. See Shakspere's "King Lear," iii. 7. 10. —**fes-ti-na′tion** (-nā′shọn), *n.* [L. *festinatio(n-).*] Haste†; in *pathol.*, an involuntary hurrying in walking, observed in certain nervous diseases.

fes-ti-val (fes′ti-vạl). [OF. *festival*, < ML. *festivalis*, < L. *festivus*, E. *festive.*] **I.** *a.* Of, pertaining to, or befitting a feast or holiday; festal. **II.** *n.* A festival celebration, occasion, or time; a periodical religious or other feast (as, Christian, Jewish, and Mohammedan *festivals*; the *festival* of Christmas; the Roman *festival* of the Parentalia or the Saturnalia); any course or occasion of festive or pleasurable proceedings, esp. of a public character, whether periodical or not (as, a music *festival*; a strawberry *festival*); an entertainment; also, merrymaking or revelry (archaic: as, to hold high *festival*; "The morning trumpets *festival* proclaim'd Through each high street," Milton's "Samson Agonistes," 1598).

fes-tive (fes′tiv), *a.* [L. *festivus*, < *festum*, a festival, feast: see *feast.*] Of, pertaining to, or befitting a feast or festival; characterized by gaiety, pleasurable entertainment, or good cheer; gay or merry; convivial.—**fes′tive-ly,** *adv.*—**fes′tive-ness,** *n.*—**fes-tiv′i-ty** (-tiv′i-ti), *n.*; pl. *-ties* (-tiz). [L. *festivitas.*] Festive character; festive gaiety or pleasure; also, a festive celebration or occasion; *pl.*, festive proceedings.—**fes′ti-vous,** *a.* Festive. [Now rare.]

fes-toon (fes-tön′), *n.* [F. *feston*, < It. *festone*, < *festa*, feast, festival: see *feast.*] A string or chain of flowers, foliage, ribbon, etc., suspended in a curve between two points; also, a decorative representation of this, as in architectural work or on pottery.—**fes-toon′,** *v. t.* To adorn with or as with festoons; also, to form into festoons; hang in or like festoons (as, to *festoon* draperies); also, to connect by festoons (as, "Growths of jasmine turn'd Their humid arms *festooning* tree to tree": Tennyson's "Dream of Fair Women," 70).—**fes-toon′er-y,** *n.* Festoons collectively; a decoration of festoons.

fet (fet), *v. t.* [AS. *fetian*; connections uncertain: cf. *fetch*².] To fetch. [Now prov. Eng.]

fe-tal (fē′tạl), *a.* Of, pertaining to, or having the character of a fetus.

fe-ta-tion (fẹ-tā′shọn), *n.* [L. *fetare*, bring forth, breed.] The formation or development of a fetus; pregnancy.

fetch¹ (fech), *n.* [Origin obscure.] The apparition of a living person; a wraith.

fetch² (fech), *v.* [AS. *feccan*, prob. var. of *fetian*, E. *fet.*] **I.** *tr.* To bring, or, usually, to go and bring, to the speaker or to or from a particular place (as, *fetch* me my hat; to *fetch* a child home from school); hence, to cause to come, or succeed in bringing (as, the call *fetched* him at once); draw forth (tears, blood, etc.); bring (a price, etc.); bring to terms, or to agreement or acquiescence (colloq.: as, a little flattery will *fetch* him); win the fancy of, take, or captivate (colloq.); also, to draw or derive, as from a source (now rare); also, to take (a breath); bring forth or utter (a sigh, groan, etc.); deal or deliver (a stroke, blow, etc.); perform or execute (a movement, step, leap, etc.); make (a circuit, etc.); take (a walk, etc.: archaic); also, to reach, or arrive at (chiefly *naut.* or prov.). **II.** *intr.* To go and bring things (as, to *fetch* and carry for one, like a dog or a drudge); also, to move, go, or take a course (chiefly *naut.*: as, to *fetch* about; to *fetch* to windward); also, to bring (*up*) in a specified position or place (colloq. or *naut.*).—**fetch**², *n.* The act or an act of fetching; a bringing in as from a distance; a stroke, performance, or effort (as, a *fetch* of the imagination); a trick, artifice, or dodge (as, "This excuse . . . though true in part, was principally a *fetch*": Cooper's "Deerslayer," xiv.); also, the distance of fetching or reaching; the reach or stretch of a thing (specif. with reference to the traveling of waves of the sea).—**fetch′er,** *n.*—**fetch′ing,** *p. a.* Taking; charming; captivating. [Colloq.] —**fetch′ing-ly,** *adv.*

fête (fāt, F. fāt), *n.* [F.: see *feast.*] A feast or festival; a festal day; a holiday; a festive celebration or entertainment. —**fête champêtre** (fāt shäṅ-pātr). [F.] An outdoor festival; a garden-party.—**fête** (fāt), *v. t.*; *fêted, fêting.* [F. *fêter.*] To entertain at or honor with a fête; commemorate by a fête.—**fête′=day,** *n.* A festival day; a name-day; a birthday.

fet-e-ri-ta (fet-ẹ-rē′tạ̈), *n.* [Prob. native African.] A grain-sorghum (see *sorghum*), a variety of *Andropogon sorghum* with slender stems, introduced into the U. S. from northern Africa in 1906, and cultivated for grain and forage. Also called *Sudan durra.*

fe-tial (fē′shạl). [L. *fetialis.*] **I.** *a.* Of or pertaining to the fetiales; concerned with declarations of war and treaties of peace (as, a *fetial* messenger; *fetial* law); hence, heraldic. **II.** *n.* One of the fetiales.

fe-ti-a-les (fē-shi-ā′lēz), *n. pl.* [L.] A college of priests in ancient Rome who acted as heralds and representatives of the people in disputes with foreign nations and in the declaration of war and the ratification of peace.

fe′tich, etc. See *fetish*, etc.

fe-ti-cide (fē′ti-sīd), *n.* [See *fetus* and *-cide.*] The destruction of the life of a fetus.—**fe′ti-ci-dal** (-sī-dạl), *a.*

fet-id (fet′id or fē′tid), *a.* [L. *fetidus, fœtidus*, < *fetere*, less correctly *fœtere*, stink.] Having an offensive odor; stinking.—**fe-tid-i-ty** (fe-tid′i-ti), **fet′id-ness,** *n.*—**fet′id-ly,** *adv.*

fe-tish (fē′tish or fet′ish), *n.* [F. *fétiche*, < Pg. *feitiço*, charm, fetish, orig. adj., artificial, < L. *facticius*, E. *factitious.*] A material, commonly inanimate object regarded with awe as having mysterious powers residing in it or as being the embodiment or habitation of a potent deity or spirit (first used with reference to western Africa); hence, any object of blind reverence (as, to make a *fetish* of conventional respectability).—**fe′tish-ism,** *n.* Belief in or worship

Fetishes of Dahomey, Africa.

of fetishes.—**fe'tish-ist,** *n.* A worshiper of fetishes.—**fe-tish-is'tic,** *a.*—**fe'tish=snake,** *n.* An African snake, *Hortalia natalensis* (or *Python sebæ*).

Fetish-snake.

fet-lock (fet'lok), *n.* [ME. *fetelak, fitlok,* = G. dial. *fissloch.*] A part of a horse's leg situated behind the joint between the cannon-bone and the great pastern-bone, and bearing a tuft of hair; the tuft of hair itself; the joint at this point ('fetlock-joint').

fe-tor (fē'tọr), *n.* [L. *fetor, fœtor,* < *fetere:* see *fetid.*] Any strong offensive smell; a stench.

fet-ter (fet'ėr), *n.* [AS. *feter* = OHG. *fezzera* = Icel. *fjöturr,* fetter; akin to E. *foot.*] A chain or shackle by which a person or an animal is confined by the foot; hence, any shackle; fig., anything that confines or restrains; a restraint: usually in *pl.*—**fet'ter,** *v. t.* To put fetters upon; shackle; fig., to confine or restrain.—**fet'ter=bone,** *n.* The great pastern-bone of a horse.—**fet'ter=bush,** *n.* An ericaceous evergreen shrub, *Pieris nitida,* of the southern U. S., with fragrant white flowers.—**fet'ter-er,** *n.*—**fet'ter-less,** *a.* Without fetters; unfettered.—**fet'ter-lock,** *n.* A shackle for a horse's leg or foot; also, a fetlock.

fet-tle (fet'l), *v.*; *-tled, -tling.* [ME. *fettlen,* put in order, arrange; perhaps orig. 'gird up,' < AS. *fetel,* belt.] **I.** *tr.* To make ready, put in order, or put to rights (now prov. Eng. and Sc.); specif., to line (the hearth of a puddling-furnace or the like); also, to beat (prov. Eng. and Sc.). **II.** *intr.* To prepare one's self; set to work; busy one's self. [Prov. Eng. and Sc.]—**fet'tle,** *n.* State or condition (as, to be in fine *fettle;* "getting a bit of the country into good *fettle,*" George Eliot's "Middlemarch," xl.); trim; also, the fettling for a furnace.—**fet'tling,** *n.* The material with which the hearth of a puddling-furnace or the like is lined, as a substance rich in oxides of iron.

fe-tus (fē'tus), *n.* [L. *fetus,* less correctly *fœtus,* a bringing forth, offspring, young, < *fe-,* bring forth, whence also *fetus,* breeding, having brought forth (see *effete*), *fecundus,* prolific, *femina,* woman, female; ult. akin to E. *be.*] The young of an animal in the womb or in the egg, esp. in its later stages. Cf. *embryo.*

feu (fū), *n.* [OF. *fieu:* see *fee*[2].] In *Sc. law,* a fee, or estate in land held of a feudal lord; a tenure of land subject to feudal obligations; also, a feudal tenure of land in which the holder, in place of military service, makes a return of grain or money; a grant of land under this tenure; in modern use, a perpetual lease for a fixed rent; also, a piece of land held in one of these ways.—**feu,** *v. t.* In *Sc. law,* to grant (land) upon feu.—**feu'ar** (-ạr), *n.* In *Sc. law,* one who holds land upon feu.

feud[1] (fūd), *n.* [ME. *fede,* < OF. *fede, feide, faide,* feud; from Teut. (cf. G. *fehde*), and akin to E. *foe.*] A state of bitter and continuous mutual hostility; esp., such a state existing between two families, clans, or the like, and marked by frequent or occasional sanguinary conflicts; sometimes, a quarrel or contention.—**feu-dal**[1] (fū'dạl), *a.*

feud[2] (fūd), *n.* [ML. *feudum, feodum:* see *fee*[2].] An estate in land granted by a lord to a vassal on condition of services, in default of which the land was to revert to the lord; a fee or fief; a tenure of land under, and by dependence on, a superior; also, a territory held in fee.—**feu-dal**[2] (fū'dạl), *a.* Of, pertaining to, or of the nature of a feud or fee (as, a *feudal* estate); also, of or pertaining to the holding of land in feud or fee (as, the *feudal* system, a system of political organization in Europe during the middle ages, based on the holding of lands in feud or fee, and on the resulting relations between lord and vassal); also, of or pertaining to the feudal system (as, *feudal* law; a *feudal* lord).—**feudal ages.** See *ages in history,* under *age, n.*—**feu'dal-ism,** *n.* The feudal system, or its principles and practices.—**feu'dal-ist,** *n.* A supporter of the feudal system; also, one versed in feudal law.—**feu-dal-is'tic,** *a.*—**feu-dal'i-ty** (-dal'i-ti), *n.*; pl. *-ties* (-tiz). The state or quality of being feudal; feudal principles; a feudal system; also, a feud or fee.—**feu'dal-ize** (-īz), *v. t.*; *-ized, -izing.* To make feudal; bring under or conform to the feudal system.—**feu''dal-i-za'tion** (-i-zā'shọn), *n.*—**feu'dal-ly,** *adv.*—**feu'da-ry** (-dạ-ri). **I.** *a.* Feudatory. **II.** *n.*; pl. *-ries* (-riz). A feudatory, or feudal vassal.—**feu'da-to-ry** (-tō-ri). **I.** *a.* Holding by, or held under, feudal tenure. **II.** *n.*; pl. *-ries* (-riz). One who holds his lands by feudal tenure; a feudal vassal; also, a feud or fee.—**feud'ist,** *n.* A writer or authority on feuds or fees; one versed in feudal law.

Feuil-lant (fė-yäṅ), *n.* [F.] A member of a congregation of reformed Cistercian monks, founded in 1577 by Jean de La Barrière, at Les Feuillans, near Toulouse, France, and dissolved in 1791; also, a member of a club of constitutional royalists in the French Revolution, which held its meetings in the old convent of the Feuillants in Paris.

feuille-ton (fė-y'-tôṅ), *n.* [F., < *feuillet,* dim. of *feuille,* leaf: see *foil*[1].] A part of a French newspaper (usually the bottom of one or more pages, marked off by a rule) devoted to light literature, criticism, etc.; also, an article or work printed in the feuilleton.—**feuille-to-niste** (-to-nēst), *n.* [F.] A writer for a newspaper feuilleton.—**feuille-ton-is'tic** (-tọn-is'tik), *a.*

fe-ver (fē'vėr), *n.* [AS. *fefer,* < L. *febris.*] A morbid condition of the animal body characterized by undue rise of temperature, quickening of the pulse, and disturbance of various bodily functions; also, any of a group of diseases in which high temperature is a prominent symptom (as, scarlet *fever:* see under *scarlet, a.*); fig., a state of intense nervous excitement.—**fe'ver,** *v.* **I.** *tr.* To affect with or as with fever: as, "The scorching blast . . . *fevers* the blood" (Kinglake's "Eothen," xviii.). **II.** *intr.* To become feverish; burn as with fever.

fe-ver-few (fē'vėr-fū), *n.* [AS. *feferfuge,* < LL. *febrifugia,* kind of plant, < L. *febris,* fever, + *fugare,* put to flight.] A perennial asteraceous plant, *Chrysanthemum parthenium,* bearing small white flowers: formerly used as a febrifuge.

fe-ver=heat (fē'vėr-hēt), *n.* The heat of fever; a degree of bodily heat exceeding 98.6° F.; fig., a feverish degree of excitement.

fe-ver-ish (fē'vėr-ish), *a.* Having fever, esp. a slight degree of fever; fig., excited, fitful, or restless, as if from fever; also, pertaining to, of the nature of, or resembling fever; also, infested with fever, as a region; having a tendency to produce fever, as food.—**fe'ver-ish-ly,** *adv.*—**fe'ver-ish-ness,** *n.*

fe-ver-ous (fē'vėr-us), *a.* Feverish.—**fe'ver-ous-ly,** *adv.*

fe-ver-root (fē'vėr-röt), *n.* A North American caprifoliaceous herb, *Triosteum perfoliatum,* having a purgative and emetic root: said to have been used by the Indians as a remedy for fever.

fe-ver=sore (fē'vėr-sōr), *n.* A sore connected with necrosis of a bone; also, a cold-sore.

fe-ver=tree (fē'vėr-trē), *n.* The blue-gum (tree), which is supposed to prevent malaria; also, a small rubiaceous tree, *Pinckneya pubens,* of the southeastern U. S., with a bark used as a tonic and febrifuge.

few (fū). [AS. *fēawe,* pl., = OHG. *fōhe* = Goth. *fawai;* akin to L. *paucus,* Gr. *παῦρος,* little, pl. few.] **I.** *a.* Being of some small number; not many: as, a book with *few* merits; "If *few* their wants, their pleasures are but *few*" (Goldsmith's "Traveller," 212). **II.** *n.* A small number; few individuals, as of a body or class specified; few persons; a minority: construed as *pl.*: as, "Many be called, but *few* chosen" (Mat. xx. 16); a *few,* or a *few* (of the) members, dissent.—**the few,** a small number of persons or things separated or discriminated from a larger number; the minority: as, a measure which benefits *the few* at the expense of the many.—**few'ness,** *n.* The state or fact of being few; paucity.

fey (fā), *a.* [AS. *fǣge* = D. *veeg* = Icel. *feigr.*] Fated to die; doomed to death; on the verge of a sudden death; also, dying. [Now chiefly Sc.]

fez (fez), *n.*; pl. *fezzes* (fez'ez). [F.; said to be named from the city of *Fez* in Morocco.] A felt cap, usually of a red color, having the shape of a truncated cone, and ornamented with a long black tassel: the national head-dress of the Turks.

fiacre (fyȧkr), *n.* [F.] A small four-wheeled carriage for hire; a hackney-coach.

fi-an-cé (fi-än′sā, F. fyäṅ-sā), *n.* [F., pp. of *fiancer*, betroth.] An affianced or betrothed person (male).—**fi-an-cée** (fi-än′sā, F. fyäṅ-sā), *n.* [F.] Fem. of *fiancé*.

fi-ar (fē′ạr), *n.* [Cf. *feuar*.] In *Sc. law*, the person in whom a fee simple is vested.

fi-as-co (fi-as′kō), *n.*; pl. *-cos* or *-coes* (-kōz). [It., < ML. *flascus* or *flasco*: see *flask*.] A flask or bottle; also, a failure or breakdown in a dramatic or musical performance; an ignominious failure of any kind.

fi-at (fī′at), *n.* [L., 'let it be done, or made.'] Orig., the word *fiat* (see etym.), or a formula containing it, by which a person in authority gave his sanction; hence, an authoritative sanction; also, an authoritative decree, command, or order (as, "Their fate . . . had intimated its *fiat* that their fortunes were inseparable": Scott's "Castle Dangerous," xx.).—**fiat money,** paper currency made legal tender by a fiat of the government, but not based on or convertible into coin.

fib[1] (fib), *v. t.*; *fibbed, fibbing*. [Origin obscure.] To strike or beat; deliver a rapid succession of blows upon. [Slang.]

fib[2] (fib), *n.* [Perhaps connected with *fable*.] A trivial or venial falsehood: as, "Ask me no questions, and I'll tell you no *fibs*" (Goldsmith's "She Stoops to Conquer," iii.). [Colloq.]—**fib**[2], *v. i.*; *fibbed, fibbing*. To tell a fib. [Colloq.]—**fib′ber,** *n.*

fi-ber, fi-bre (fī′bėr), *n.* [F. *fibre*, < L. *fibra*, fiber, filament.] A slender filament; a fine thread-like piece or element of a substance, as of wool, silk, cotton, jute, or asbestos; one of the thread-like elements composing the tissue of muscles, nerves, etc.; a slender, thread-like root of a plant; also, filaments collectively, or matter composed of filaments; esp., filamentous matter from the bast tissue or other parts of plants, used for industrial purposes; also, fibrous structure; fig., material, stuff, or character (as, moral *fiber*; men of stronger *fiber*).—**fiber silk.** See *silk*, *n.*—**fi′bered, fi′bred** (-bėrd), *a.* Having fibers.—**fi′ber-less, fi′bre-less,** *a.* Without fibers or fiber.—**fi′bri-form** (-bri-fôrm), *a.* [See *-form*.] Of the form of a fiber or fibers.

fi-bril (fī′bril), *n.* [NL. *fibrilla*, dim. of L. *fibra*, E. *fiber*.] A small or fine fiber. Also (NL.) **fi-bril′la** (-bril′ạ); pl. *fibrillæ* (-ē).—**fi′bril-lar, fi′bril-la-ry** (-bri-lạr, -lā-ri), *a.* Of, pertaining to, or of the nature of fibrils.—**fi′bril-late, fi′bril-lat-ed** (-lāt, -lā-ted), *a.* Having fibrils; finely fibrous.—**fi-bril-la′tion** (-lā′shọn), *n.* Fibrillate condition; also, a quivering movement of the fibrils of a muscle or nerve.—**fi-bril-lif′er-ous** (-lif′ẹ-rus), *a.* [See *-ferous*.] Bearing fibrils.—**fi-bril′li-form** (-bril′i-fôrm), *a.* [See *-form*.] Of the form of a fibril or fibrils.—**fi′bril-lose** (-bri-lōs), *a.* Composed of or furnished with fibrils.

fi-brin (fī′brin), *n.* [L. *fibra*, E. *fiber*.] A white, tough, strongly elastic, fibrous proteid, formed esp. in the coagulation of blood; also, a similar substance found in some plants.—**fi-bri-na′tion** (-bri-nā′shọn), *n.* The acquisition of an excess of fibrin in the blood, as in pleurisy.—**fi-brin′o-gen** (-ọ-jen), *n.* [See *-gen*.] A proteid found in the blood, lymph, etc., and yielding fibrin in the coagulation of blood.—**fi″bri-no-gen′ic** (-nọ-jen′ik), **fi-bri-nog′e-nous** (-noj′e-nus), *a.* Producing fibrin.—**fi′bri-nous,** *a.* Containing, composed of, or of the nature of fibrin.

fi-broid (fī′broid). **I.** *a.* Resembling fiber or fibrous tissue; composed of fibers, as a tumor. **II.** *n.* A fibroid tumor.

fi-bro-ma (fī-brō′mạ), *n.*; pl. *-mas* or *-mata* (-mạ-tạ). [NL., < L. *fibra*, fiber: see *-oma*.] In *pathol.*, a tumor consisting essentially of fibrous tissue.—**fi-brom′a-tous** (-brom′ạ-tus), *a.*

fi-brous (fī′brus), *a.* [NL. *fibrosus*, < L. *fibra*, E. *fiber*.] Containing, consisting of, or resembling fibers.—**fi′brous-ly,** *adv.*—**fi′brous-ness,** *n.*

fib-ster (fib′stėr), *n.* One who tells fibs or petty falsehoods: as, "You silly little *fibster!*" (Thackeray's "Vanity Fair," xlviii.). [Colloq.]

fib-u-la (fib′ụ-lạ), *n.*; pl. *-læ* (-lē). [L., clasp, buckle, pin, < *figere*, fix, fasten.] A clasp or buckle; in *anat.*, in man, the outer and thinner of the two bones of the lower leg, extending from the knee to the ankle; a corresponding bone (often rudimentary, or ankylosed with the tibia) of the leg or hind limb of other animals.—**fib′u-lar** (-lạr), *a.*

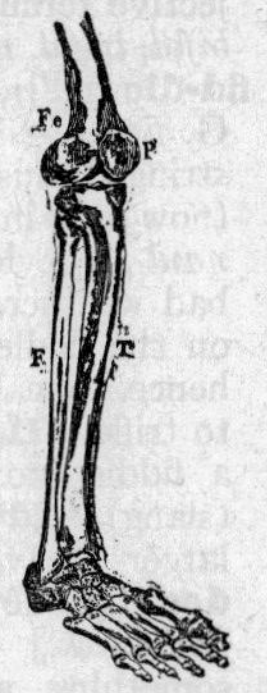

Right Human Leg, seen obliquely from the front.—*F*, fibula; *T*, tibia; *P*, patella; *Fe*, femur.

-fic. [L. *-ficus*, < *facere*, do, make.] An adjective suffix meaning 'making,' 'producing,' 'causing,' as in *colorific, frigorific, horrific, pacific, prolific, soporific*.

-fication. [L. *-ficatio(n-)*, < *-ficare*: see *-fy*.] A suffix of nouns of action or state corresponding to verbs ending in *-fy*, as in *deification, indemnification, pacification*.

fice, fist[1] (fīs, fīst), *n.* [From obs. *fist*, break wind.] A small dog; a cur. [U. S.]

fi-celle (fi-sel′, F. fē-sel), *n.* [F., string, < L. *filum*, thread.] String-colored; of a light grayish-brown.

fich-u (fish′ö, F. fē-shü), *n.* [F.; origin uncertain.] A kind of kerchief of muslin, lace, or the like, generally triangular in shape, worn about the neck by women, with the ends drawn together or crossed on the breast.

fick-le (fik′l), *a.* [AS. *ficol*, deceitful, treacherous, akin to *gefic*, deceit.] Deceitful† or treacherous†; hence, not to be relied on to continue without change; likely to change from caprice, irresolution, or instability (as, the *fickle* world; *fickle* fortune); changeable; inconstant; of weather, the sea, etc., changeful or uncertain.—**fick′le-ness,** *n.*

fi-co (fē′kō), *n.* [It., < L. *ficus*, fig.] A fig; hence, the value of a fig, or the merest trifle (as, "A *fico* for the phrase!" Shakspere's "Merry Wives of Windsor," i. 3. 33); also, a gesture of contempt made by placing the thumb between two of the fingers or in the mouth. [Obs. or archaic.]

fic-tile (fik′til), *a.* [L. *fictilis*, < *fingere*, form, mold: see *feign*.] Capable of being molded; plastic; also, molded into form by art; made of earth, clay, etc., by a potter; also, having to do with pottery.

fic-tion (fik′shọn), *n.* [OF. F. *fiction*, < L. *fictio(n-)*, < *fingere*, form, conceive, devise, feign: see *feign*.] The act of forming or fashioning†; something fashioned†; also, a pretending†; deceit†; also, the act of feigning, inventing, or imagining; something feigned, invented, or imagined; a made-up story; a false narration or statement; also, the branch of literature comprising works of imaginative narration, esp. in prose form; works of this class, as novels or tales; occasionally, a single such work; also, the intentional assuming as fact of what is not such, for the sake of convenience, decorum, or the like; something assumed in this way, esp. a legal assumption serving as a device for extending the application of the law.—**fic′tion-al,** *a.* Of, pertaining to, or of the nature of fiction.—**fic′tion-al-ly,** *adv.*—**fic′tion-ist,** *n.* A maker or writer of fiction.

fic-ti-tious (fik-tish′us), *a.* [L. *ficticius*, < *fingere*: see *fiction* and *feign*.] Made by art†, or artificial†; arbitrarily devised (as, "The notion then of a moral scheme of government is not *fictitious* but natural": J. Butler's "Analogy of Religion," i. 3); also, counterfeit or sham (as, "Two treaties were drawn up, one on white paper, the other on red, the former real, the latter *fictitious*": Macaulay's "Essays," Lord Clive); feigned or assumed, as a name or a character; also, feigned to exist, imaginary, or unreal (as, a *fictitious* claim); also, of, pertaining to, or of the nature of fiction (as, "the *fictitious* world," Macaulay's "Essays," Leigh Hunt; "the most popular writer of *fictitious* narrative then living," Macaulay's "Essays," Madame D'Arblay); also, assumed as real or genuine by a legal or conventional fiction (as, "the growing popularity of Adoption, as a method of obtaining a *fictitious* son": Maine's "Early Law and Custom," iv.).—**fic-ti′tious-ly,** *adv.*—**fic-ti′tious-ness,** *n.*

fic-tive (fik′tiv), *a.* [F. *fictif*, < L. *fingere*: see *fiction* and *feign*.] Concerned with or pertaining to the creation of fiction; also, fictitious; sham; assumed; imaginary.—**fic′tive-ly,** *adv.*

fid (fid), *n.* [Origin obscure.] A bar or pin to support or steady something; a square bar or support to hold in place a topmast, etc.; also, a conical wooden pin used to open strands of rope in splicing.

-fid. [L. *-fidus*, from *fid-*, stem of *findere*, cleave.] An adjective termination meaning 'cleft,' 'divided,' 'lobed,' as in *bifid, trifid, multifid, pinnatifid.*

fid-dle (fid'l), *n.* [ME. (and prob. AS.) *fithele* = D. *vedel* = G. *fiedel* = Icel. *fidhla*: cf. ML. *vitula, vidula*, E. *viol*.] A stringed musical instrument of the viol class, esp. a violin (now only in familiar or contemptuous use); also, a fiddler; *naut.*, a device to prevent things from rolling off the table in bad weather.—**fid'dle,** *v.*; *-dled, -dling.* **I.** *intr.* To play on the fiddle (now only in familiar or contemptuous use); hence, to make aimless movements, as with the hands; also, to trifle. **II.** *tr.* To play on (a fiddle), or play (a tune) on a fiddle (now familiar or contemptuous); also, to cheat (slang).—**fid'dle=block,** *n.* *Naut.*, a long block having a larger sheave above a smaller one.—**fid''dle=de=dee'** (-dē-dē'), *interj.* [Cf. *fiddle, v., fiddle-faddle, fiddlestick.*] An exclamation used in dismissing something as silly or trifling.—**fid'dle=fad''dle** (-fad''l). [Varied redupl. of *fiddle.*] **I.** *n.* Trifling talk or action; nonsense; something trivial; also, a trifler. [Colloq.] **II.** *a.* Trifling. [Colloq.]—**fid'dle=fad''dle,** *v. i.*; *-dled, -dling.* To busy one's self with trifles; trifle; fuss. [Colloq.]—**fid'dle=head,** *n.* An ornament at the bow of a ship, containing a scroll somewhat like that at the head of a violin; also, a head as empty as a fiddle.—**fid'dle=head''ed,** *a.* Having a fiddle-head; also, empty-headed.—**fid'dler,** *n.* One who fiddles; a violinist; in *zoöl.*, the common European sandpiper, *Tringoides hypoleucus* (so called from its habit of oscillating the body); also, the fiddler-crab.—**fid'dler=crab,** *n.* Any of the small burrowing crabs of the genus *Gelasimus*, common on the Atlantic coast of the U. S.—**fid'dle-stick,** *n.* The bow with which a fiddle is played; also, a mere nothing (used, esp. in *pl.*, as an exclamation equivalent to 'nonsense!' or 'fiddle-de-dee!').—**fid'dle=string,** *n.* One of the strings on a fiddle, which produce the sound.—**fid'dle-wood,** *n.* The heavy, hard, durable wood of any of various West Indian and other trees; also, any of the trees.

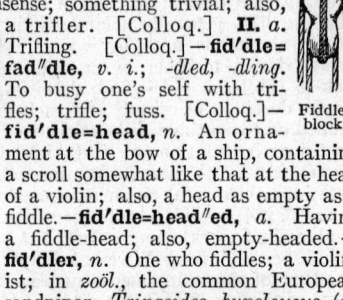

Fiddle-block.

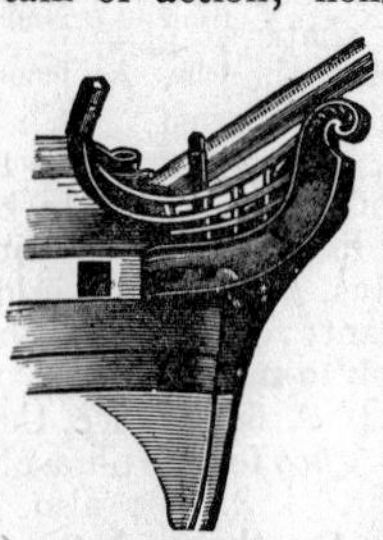
Fiddle-head.

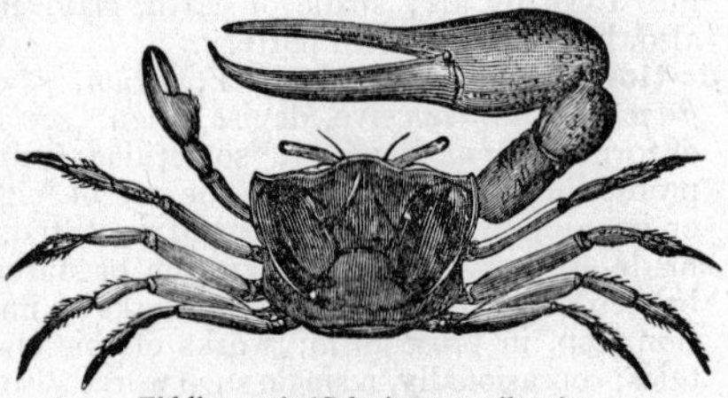
Fiddler-crab (*Gelasimus pugilator*).

fi-del-i-ty (fi-del'i-ti or fī-), *n.* [OF. *fidelite* (F. *fidélité*), < L. *fidelitas*, < *fidelis*, faithful, < *fides*, faith, < *fidere*, trust.] The quality of being faithful; loyalty, as to a person or party; strict adherence to promises, vows, etc.; conjugal faithfulness; strictness or thoroughness in the performance of duty; trustworthiness, as of a witness; adherence to fact or to an original, as of a narrative or a picture.

fidge (fij), *v. i.* or *t.*; *fidged, fidging.* [Origin uncertain.] To fidget; also, to twitch (as, "Look, Jim, how my fingers *fidges* . . . I can't keep 'em still": Stevenson's "Treasure Island," iii.). [Now prov.]

fidg-et (fij'et), *v.* [From *fidge.*] **I.** *intr.* To move about restlessly or impatiently; be uneasy. **II.** *tr.* To cause to fidget; make uneasy.—**fidg'et,** *n.* A condition of restlessness or uneasiness, expressed by irregular bodily movements (often in *pl.*: as, "But sedentary weavers of long tales Give me the *fidgets*, and my patience fails," Cowper's "Conversation," 208); also, one who fidgets.—**fidg'et-y,** *a.* Inclined to fidget; restless; uneasy.—**fidg'et-i-ness,** *n.*

fi-du-cial (fi-dū'shạl), *a.* [ML. *fiducialis*, < L. *fiducia*: see *fiduciary.*] Of, pertaining to, or of the nature of trust or reliance (as, *fiducial* dependence upon God); also, pertaining to or of the nature of a trust or trusteeship; fiduciary; in *physics, astron.*, etc., accepted as a fixed basis of reference or comparison (as, *fiducial* points, in *thermometry*, the melting-point of ice and the boiling-point of water).—**fi-du'cial-ly,** *adv.*

fi-du-ci-a-ry (fi-dū'shi-ā-ri). [L. *fiduciarius*, < *fiducia*, trust, confidence, thing held in trust, < *fidere*, trust.] **I.** *a.* Of the nature of or proceeding from trust or reliance†; depending on public confidence for value or currency, as fiat money; also, holding something in trust (as, a *fiduciary* possessor); held or given in trust (as, *fiduciary* estates); pertaining to or of the nature of a trust or trusteeship (as, in a *fiduciary* capacity). **II.** *n.* One who holds something in trust; a trustee.—**fi-du'ci-a-ri-ly,** *adv.*

fie (fī), *interj.* [ME. *fy*: cf. Icel. *fȳ*, OF. F. *fi*, L. *fi*, also E. *faugh, foh*, and *phew.*] An exclamation expressing disgust, disapprobation, etc.: as, "*Acres.* I—I—I don't feel quite so bold, somehow, as I did. *Sir Luc.* Oh *fie!*—consider your honour" (Sheridan's "Rivals," v. 3).

fief (fēf), *n.* [F. *fief*: see *fee*[2].] A fee or feud, or estate in land held of a feudal lord; a tenure of land subject to feudal obligations; also, a territory held in fee.

field (fēld), *n.* [AS. *feld* = D. *veld* = G. *feld.*] Open country†; also, a piece of open or cleared ground, esp. one suitable for pasture or tillage; also, a piece of ground devoted to sports or contests; a particular portion of it (as, left-*field* or the in*field*, in baseball); esp., the outfield in baseball; also, fielders collectively; a fielder; also, those taking part in an outdoor sport or contest, as a hunt; also, all the contestants, as in a race, not favored in the betting (as, to back a horse against the *field*); also, any region characterized by a particular feature or product (as, a gold-*field*); also, a battle-ground (as, the *field* of Waterloo), or, sometimes, a battle (as, "What though the *field* be lost? All is not lost": Milton's "Paradise Lost," i. 105); more widely, the scene of military or other operations; also, an extent or expanse of anything, as of sea or ice; the surface of a canvas, shield, etc., on which something is portrayed; also, an area, sphere, or range of operation, activity, interest, opportunity, etc.; in *physics*, a portion of space controlled or affected by a force (as, a magnetic *field*, the space through which the influence of a magnet is exerted); in *elect.*, that part of a dynamo, motor, or the like, by which the exciting magnetism is produced.—**field,** *v.* **I.** *tr.* In *baseball, cricket*, etc., to stop, or catch, and throw (the ball) as a fielder. **II.** *intr.* To take to the field; in *baseball, cricket*, etc., to act as a fielder; field the ball.—**field'=bat''ter-y,** *n.* A battery of field-guns.—**field'=book,** *n.* A book used by surveyors, naturalists, etc., in the field, for setting down measurements, observations, etc., or preserving collected specimens.—**field'=col''ors,** *n. pl.* *Milit.*, small flags for indicating the positions of squadrons, etc., and the location of headquarters.—**field'=cor''net,** *n.* A minor official having jurisdiction within a district in South Africa, charged with inquiring into and reporting crime, and with other duties.—**field'=day,** *n.* A day when troops are drawn up for exercise in field evolutions; a day devoted to outdoor sport or athletic contests, or to scientific investigations, etc. (as of a society), in the field; any day of unusual activity or display.—**field'er,** *n.* A player who fields the ball in baseball, cricket, etc.; any of the players of the infield or the outfield in baseball, esp. an outfielder.

field-fare (fēld'fãr), *n.* [ME. *feldefare*, < AS. *feldeware*, appar. repr. *feld*, field, + *faran*, E. *fare.*] A European thrush, *Turdus pilaris*, of reddish-brown color, with a blackish tail and ashy head.

Fieldfare.

field=glass (fēld'glȧs), *n.* A compact binocular telescope for use in the field; also, a small achromatic telescope.

field=gun (fēld'gun), *n.* A light cannon mounted on a carriage, for service in the field.

field=mag-net (fēld'mag''net), *n.* A magnet for producing a magnetic field; esp., a magnet (fixed or rotary) on a dynamo or electric motor, by which the exciting magnetism is produced, as distinguished from the armature.

field=mar-shal (fēld′mär′shạl), *n.* An officer of the highest military rank in the British and other armies.
field=mouse (fēld′mous), *n.* Any of various mice inhabiting fields and meadows.
field=of-fi-cer (fēld′of″i-sėr), *n.* A military officer above the rank of captain and below that of brigadier-general, as a colonel.
field=pea (fēld′pē), *n.* A plant, *Pisum arvense*, related to the cultivated pea, *P. sativum*: a valuable forage-plant.
field=piece (fēld′pēs), *n.* A field-gun.
field=span-iel (fēld′span″yẹl), *n.* See *spaniel.*
field=spar-row (fēld′spar″ō), *n.* A small fringilline bird, *Spizella pusilla* (or *agrestis*), of the U. S., frequenting fields and thickets.

Field-sparrow.

field=tri-al (fēld′trī″ạl), *n.* A trial of animals, as hunting-dogs, in actual performance in the field.
field-ward, field-wards (fēld′wạ̈rd, -wạ̈rdz), *adv.* Toward the fields: as, "Glossy bees at noon do *fieldward* pass" (Keats's "Isabella," xxxix.).
field=work (fēld′wėrk), *n.* Work done in the field, as by a surveyor, geologist, etc.; *milit.*, a temporary fortification thrown up in the field.
fiend (fēnd), *n.* [AS. *fēond* = D. *vijand* = G. *feind* = Icel. *fjāndi* = Goth. *fijands*, all orig. ppr. of a verb (AS. *fēon, fēogan*) meaning 'hate.'] An enemy†; specif., the enemy of mankind; Satan; the devil; hence, any evil spirit; a demon; also, a diabolically wicked person, esp. in the way of cruelty or malignity; also (colloq.), a person or thing that causes mischief or annoyance (as, the interviewer *fiend*); one who is hopelessly given up to some pernicious habit, as to the excessive use of a drug (as, an opium *fiend*); a student devoted to or unusually proficient in some study.—**fiend′ish,** *a.* Like or characteristic of a fiend; diabolically cruel or malignant.—**fiend′ish-ly,** *adv.*—**fiend′ish-ness,** *n.*
fierce (fērs), *a.*; compar. *fiercer*, superl. *fiercest.* [OF. *fiers, fier*, fierce (F. *fier*, proud), < L. *ferus*, wild, savage, fierce, cruel.] Vehement, without fear or restraint, in temper or action, like a wild beast (as, *fierce* animals; *fierce* savages; "Moloch . . . the strongest and the *fiercest* spirit That fought in heaven, now *fiercer* by despair," Milton's "Paradise Lost," ii. 44); boldly passionate or violent in hostile ardor, as the disposition or mood; characterized by or showing unrestrained vehemence or hostile ardor (as, a *fierce* conflict; *fierce* anger; *fierce* words or looks); also, violent in force, effects, intensity, etc. (as, *fierce* storms, winds, heat, or cold; "In that *fierce* light which beats upon a throne, And blackens every blot," Tennyson's "Idylls of the King," Dedication); severe, as grief; passionate, as desires or zeal; furiously eager or strenuous, as efforts or competition; also, high-spirited† or brave†; proud† or haughty†; also (slang), extremely bad, unpleasant, etc.; 'awful.'—**fierce′ly,** *adv.*—**fierce′ness,** *n.*
fi-e-ri fa-ci-as (fī′ẹ-rī fā′shi-as). [L., 'cause to be done.'] In *law*, a writ, issued after the award of a judgment for a sum of money, commanding the sheriff to levy upon the goods, or the goods and lands, of the judgment debtor for the collection of the amount due.
fier-y (fīr′i or fī′ėr-i), *a.*; compar. *fierier*, superl. *fieriest.* [From *fire.*] Consisting of, attended with, characterized by, or containing fire (as, a *fiery* discharge from a volcano; a *fiery* meteor; *fiery* sparks; "a burning *fiery* furnace," Dan. iii. 6); characteristic of, suggestive of, or resembling fire (as, a *fiery* glow or heat; a *fiery* red); red as fire, as the face, a blush, etc.; flashing or glowing, as the eye; burning, or intensely hot, as winds, desert sands, etc.; inflamed, as a tumor or sore; causing a burning sensation, as liquors or condiments; also, intensely ardent, impetuous, or passionate, as persons or the spirit, temper, courage, zeal, speech, etc.; high-spirited or mettlesome, as a horse; also, liable to take fire, or inflammable, as gas in a mine; containing inflammable gas, as a mine.—**fier′i-ly,** *adv.*—**fier′i-ness,** *n.*
fies-ta (fyes′tä), *n.* [Sp.: see *feast.*] A feast, festival, or festivity; a festal day; a holiday.
fife (fīf), *n.* [F. *fifre*, fife, fifer; from Teut.: cf. G. *pfeife* and E. *pipe.*] A high-pitched instrument of the flute class, much used in military music: as, "the ear-piercing *fife*" (Shakspere's "Othello," iii. 3. 352).—**fife,** *v. i.* or *t.*; *fifed, fifing.* To play on a fife.—**fif′er,** *n.*—**fife′=rail,** *n.* A rail round the lower part of a mast, for securing belaying-pins.

Fife.

fif-teen (fif′tēn′). [AS. *fīftȳne.*] **I.** *a.* Five more than ten. **II.** *n.* A number composed of fifteen units, or a symbol, as 15 or xv, representing it.—**the Fifteen,** the year 1715 as marked by the Jacobite rebellion in Scotland; the rebellion itself.—**fif′teenth′. I.** *a.* Next after the fourteenth; also, being one of fifteen equal parts. **II.** *n.* The fifteenth member of a series; also, a fifteenth part.
fifth (fifth), *a.* [AS. *fīfta.*] Next after the fourth; also, being one of five equal parts.—**fifth column,** a body of persons residing in a country who are in sympathy with its enemies, and who are serving their interests or ready to assist them in case they attack the country: applied esp. in and after 1940 to sympathizers with or agents of Nazi Germany (used orig. in allusion to a statement made in 1936 during the civil war in Spain that the insurgents under General Franco had four columns marching on Madrid and a fifth column of sympathizers in the city ready to rise and betray it). Hence **fifth columnist,** a member of a fifth column.—**fifth monarchy,** the last of the five great kingdoms referred to in the prophecy of Daniel (see Dan. ii.), the four preceding ones being taken to be those of Assyria, Persia, Greece (under Alexander the Great), and Rome.—**Fifth Monarchy Men,** an English sect of millenarians, of Oliver Cromwell's time, who identified the fifth monarchy with the millennial kingdom of Christ predicted in the Apocalypse (see Rev. xx.), and believed it was their duty to inaugurate that kingdom by force.—**fifth wheel,** a horizontal ring (or segment of a ring) consisting of two circular bands which slide on each other, placed above the forward axle of a carriage and designed to support the fore part of the body while allowing it to turn freely in a horizontal plane; also, an extra wheel for a four-wheeled vehicle; fig., any extra or superfluous thing or person.—**fifth,** *n.* The fifth member of a series; also, a fifth part; in *music*, a tone on the fifth degree from a given tone (counted as the first); the interval between such tones; the harmonic combination of such tones; in a scale, the dominant.—**fifth′ly,** *adv.*
fif-ti-eth (fif′ti-eth). [AS. *fīftigotha.*] **I.** *a.* Next after the forty-ninth; also, being one of fifty equal parts. **II.** *n.* The fiftieth member of a series; also, a fiftieth part.
fif-ty (fif′ti). [AS. *fīftig.*] **I.** *a.* Five times ten. **II.** *n.*; pl. *-ties* (-tiz). A number composed of fifty units, or a symbol, as 50 or l, representing it.—**fif′ty=fif′ty,** *adv.* and *a.* With equality of shares, as of profits: as, to go *fifty-fifty* with a person; a *fifty-fifty* arrangement. [Slang.]
fig[1] (fig), *n.* [OF. *fige* (F. *figue*), < L. *ficus*, fig-tree, fig.] Any tree or shrub of the moraceous genus *Ficus*; esp., a small tree or bush, *F. carica*, native in southwestern Asia, bearing an oblong or pear-shaped fruit which is eaten fresh or preserved or dried; also, the fruit of such a tree or shrub, esp. (in commerce) that of *F. carica*; also, the value of a fig; the merest trifle; the least bit; also, a gesture of contempt made by thrusting the thumb between two of the closed fingers or into the mouth; a fico.

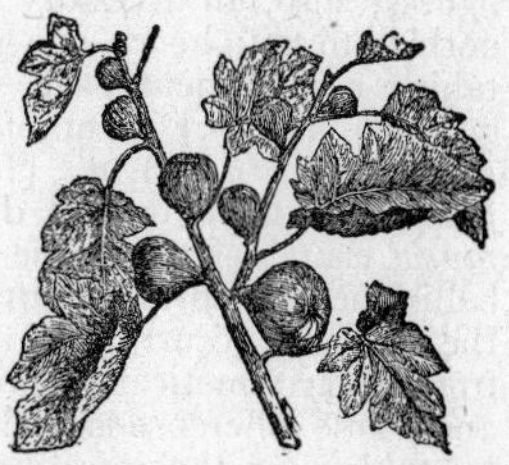
Common Fig (*Ficus carica*).

fig[2] (fig), *v. t.*; *figged, figging.* [Origin uncertain.] To dress or array (with *out*); also, to furbish (with *up*). [Colloq.] —**fig**[2], *n.* Dress or array (as, in full *fig*); also, condition (as, to be in good *fig*). [Colloq.]
fight (fīt), *v. i.*; *fought, fighting.* [AS. *feohtan* = D. *vechten* = G. *fechten*, fight.] To engage in battle or in single combat; attempt to defeat, subdue, or destroy an adversary by physical means; hence, to contend in any manner; strive

vigorously for or against something.—**to fight shy of,** to keep carefully aloof from (a person, affair, etc.).—**fight,** *v. t.* To contend with in battle or combat; war against; hence, to contend with or against in any manner; also, to carry on (a battle, duel, pugilistic match, etc.); maintain (a cause, quarrel, etc.) by fighting or contending; make (one's way) by fighting or striving; also, to cause or set (a pugilist, or a game-cock, dog, etc.) to fight; also, to manage or maneuver (troops, ships, guns, etc.) in battle.—**fight,** *n.* [AS. *feoht.*] The act of fighting (archaic: as, to fall in *fight*); a battle or combat; any contest or struggle; also, ability or inclination to fight (as, there was no *fight* left in him); also, a screen set up on a ship for protection during a battle† (see Shakspere's "Merry Wives of Windsor," ii. 2. 142).—**fight′er,** *n.*—**fight′ing=cock,** *n.* A game-cock; fig., a pugnacious fellow.—**fight′ing=top,** *n.* In a war-ship, a platform on or near the top of a mast, from which rapid-fire guns, etc., are fired.

fig=in-sect (fig′in″sekt), *n.* Any of various insects inhabiting the fig; esp., a small hymenopterous insect, *Blastophaga grossorum*, serving as an important agent in caprification. See *caprification.*

fig=leaf (fig′lēf), *n.* The leaf of a fig-tree, esp. in allusion to the first covering of Adam and Eve (see Gen. iii. 7); fig., something designed to conceal what is shameful or indecorous.

fig=mar-i-gold (fig′mar′i-gōld), *n.* Any of various herbs of the genus *Mesembryanthemum*, with showy white, yellow, or pink flowers.

fig-ment (fig′mẹnt), *n.* [L. *figmentum*, < *fingere*, form, conceive, devise: see *feign.*] Something molded or fashioned†; also, something feigned, invented, or imagined; esp., a mere product of the mind or imagination; a pure invention.—**fig′men-ta-ry** (-mẹn-tā̤-ri), *a.*

fig=paste (fig′pāst′), *n.* A confection of figs, a favorite Turkish sweetmeat; loukoum; also, a semitransparent sweetened and flavored paste cut into small blocks and dusted with fine sugar.

fig=shell (fig′shel), *n.* Any of the shells of the genus *Pyrula* (or *Ficula*), of tropical or warm seas: so called from the shape.

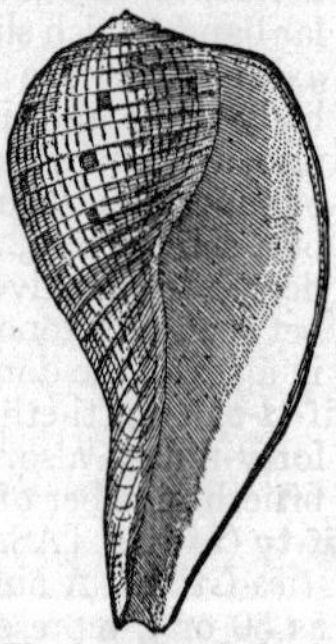
Fig-shell (*Pyrula ficus*).

fig-u-line (fig′ụ̄-lin or -līn), *n.* [F., < L. *figulina*, fem. of *figulinus*, of a potter, < *figulus*, potter, < *fingere*, form, mold: see *feign.*] A piece of pottery (as, "This Potter . . . Whose *figulines* and rustic wares Scarce find him bread": Longfellow's "Kéramos," 106); also, potters' clay.

fig-u-ra-ble (fig′ụ̄-rạ-bl), *a.* Capable of receiving or retaining a definite figure or shape.

fig-u-ral (fig′ụ̄-rạl), *a.* Pertaining to figure, or to delineation by figures; in *music*, figurate.

fig-u-rant (fig′ụ̄-rạnt, F. fē-gü-räṅ), *n.* [F., ppr. of *figurer*, < L. *figurare*, E. *figure*, *v.*] A dancer in the ballet who does not come forward alone but dances with others in groups or figures; also, an accessory character on the stage who has nothing to say; hence, one who appears in any scene without taking a prominent part.—**fig-u-rante** (fig-ụ̄-rȧnt′, F. fē-gü-räṅt), *n.* [F.] Fem. of *figurant.*

fig-u-rate (fig′ụ̄-rāt), *a.* [L. *figuratus*, pp. of *figurare*, E. *figure*, *v.*] Of a certain determinate figure or shape; in *music*, characterized by the use of passing-notes or other embellishments; florid.—**figurate number,** in *math.*, any of the numbers occurring in a series which has been derived from an arithmetical progression whose first term is unity and whose difference is a whole number, as 1, 2, 3, 4, 5, etc., by taking for the consecutive terms of the derived series the first term, the sum of the first two terms, the sum of the first three terms, and so on, of the simple progression, or any of the numbers in any series formed in like manner from such a derived series: so called because points or counters representing the units of such a number can be arranged symmetrically in the form of a figure, as a triangle, characteristic of the series to which it belongs.

fig-u-ra-tion (fig-ụ̄-rā′shọn), *n.* [L. *figuratio(n-)*, < *figurare*, E. *figure*, *v.*] The act of shaping into a particular figure; the resulting figure or shape; also, the act of representing figuratively; a figurative representation; also, the act of marking or adorning with figures or designs; in *music*, the employment of passing-notes or other embellishments; also, the figuring of a bass part.

fig-u-ra-tive (fig′ụ̄-rạ-tiv), *a.* [LL. *figurativus*, < L. *figurare*, E. *figure*, *v.*] Representing by means of a figure or likeness, as in drawing or sculpture; also, representing by a figure or emblem; emblematic; also, of the nature of or involving a figure of speech, esp. a metaphor (as, a *figurative* expression; to use a word in a *figurative* sense); metaphorical; not literal; metaphorically so called (as, this remark was a *figurative* boomerang); abounding in or addicted to figures of speech (as, *figurative* language; a *figurative* writer).—**fig′u-ra-tive-ly,** *adv.* By means of a figure or emblem; emblematically; also, by a figure of speech; in a figurative sense; metaphorically; not literally.—**fig′u-ra-tive-ness,** *n.*

fig-ure (fig′ụ̄r, Brit. usually fig′ėr), *n.* [OF. F. *figure*, < L. *figura*, < *fingere*, form, mold: see *feign.*] Form or shape, as determined by outlines or exterior surfaces (as, round, square, or cubical in *figure*); also, a line or surface or a combination of lines or surfaces disposed in a particular form or shape (as, geometrical plane *figures*, such as the circle, square, and polygon, or solid *figures*, such as the sphere, cube, and polyhedron); also, the form or appearance proper to something (as, the human *figure*; "doing, in the *figure* of a lamb, the feats of a lion," Shakspere's "Much Ado about Nothing," i. i. 15); the bodily form or frame (as, garments fitting closely to the *figure*; to have a slender or a graceful *figure*); an individual bodily form, or a person with reference to form or appearance (as, a tall *figure* stood in the doorway; he was a fine *figure* of a man; a *figure* of fun, a person of ludicrous appearance); also, a person as he appears or as presented before the eyes of the world (as, to be an interesting *figure*; minor political *figures* of the time); a character or personage, esp. one of distinction (as, to be a *figure* in society); also, the appearance or impression made by a person, or sometimes a thing, esp. a conspicuous or distinguished appearance (as, to make, or cut, a fine, dashing, or sorry *figure*; "It is my wish . . . to have my boy make some *figure* in the world," Sheridan's "Rivals," ii. 1); hence, show or display (archaic); prominence or distinction (archaic: as, persons of some *figure*); also, something perceived only as having a more or less definite shape, as in fog or darkness; a mere shape; sometimes, a phantasm† or illusion†; also, a likeness, representation, or image of something (as, "Where beams of warm imagination play, The memory's soft *figures* melt away": Pope's "Essay on Criticism," 59); an artificial representation, pictorial or sculptured, of something, specif. of the human form; a diagram, chart, or plan; an astrological diagram, or horoscope, of the heavens at a given time; an illustration or cut in a book or the like; also, an emblem or type (as, the dove is a *figure* of peace); also, an arrangement of lines, etc., forming an ornamental device; such a device as the (or a) characteristic feature of a pattern or design (as, fabrics printed or woven with a small *figure*); a pattern or design; also, a distinct movement or division of a dance; a movement or series of movements in skating; also, a written character other than a letter; specif., a numerical symbol, esp. an Arabic numeral; hence, an amount or value expressed in numbers; in *music*, a short succession of musical notes, either as melody or as a group of chords, which produces a single, complete, and distinct impression; in *rhet.*, any of various modes of expression (as metaphor, simile, personification, antithesis, etc.) in which words are used out of their literal sense, or out of ordinary locutions, to suggest a picture or image, or for other special effect (also called 'figure of speech'); in *logic*, any of the forms of the syllogism with respect to the relative position of the middle term.—**fig′ure,** *v.*; *-ured*, *-uring.* [OF. F. *figurer*, < L. *figurare* (pp. *figuratus*), < *figura.*] **I.** *tr.* To form or shape into a definite or particular figure (now only as in *figured*, *p. a.*); also, to represent by a pictorial or sculptured figure, a diagram, or the like; picture or depict; trace (an outline, etc.); fig., to picture in the mind; imagine or conceive; sometimes, to portray by speech or action: also, to represent by an emblem or symbol, or be an emblem or symbol of (as, "You, lord archbishop . . . Whose white investments *figure* innocence":

NORTH AMERICAN BUTTERFLIES

Courtesy of the American Museum of Natural History, New York City.

TWO-THIRDS NATURAL SIZE

Shakspere's "2 Henry IV.," iv. 1. 45); symbolize or typify; also, to represent or express by a figure of speech; also, to mark or adorn with figures, or with a pattern or design (as, muslin *figured* in the weaving); also, to mark with numerical figures; express in figures; compute or calculate; hence, fig., to conclude or judge, as if after calculation (with a clause: as, I *figured* that the matter was settled: colloq.); in *music*, to embellish with passing-notes or other decorations; also, to write figures above or below (a bass part) to indicate accompanying chords. **II.** *intr.* To make a figure or appearance; be seen or prominent (as, to *figure* in society; his name *figures* in all the reports of the case); be conspicuous; also, to appear (*as*: as, to *figure* as a martyr); also, to perform a figure in dancing; also, to compute or work with numerical figures; cipher; hence, fig., to count, reckon, or rely (*on*: as, we *figure* on settling the matter this week: colloq.).—**fig′ured,** *p. a.* Formed or shaped (*finely, ill,* etc.); also, represented by a pictorial or sculptured figure; also, marked or adorned with figures, or with a pattern or design (as, *figured* silk, muslin, or wall-paper); also, figurative, as language; in *music*, florid; also, of a bass part, having the accompanying chords indicated.—**fig′ure-head,** *n.* An ornamental figure, as a statue or bust, placed over the cutwater of a ship; also, a person who is nominally the head of a society, community, etc., but has no real authority or responsibility.—**fig′ure-less,** *a.* Without a figure; shapeless.—**fig′ur-er,** *n.*

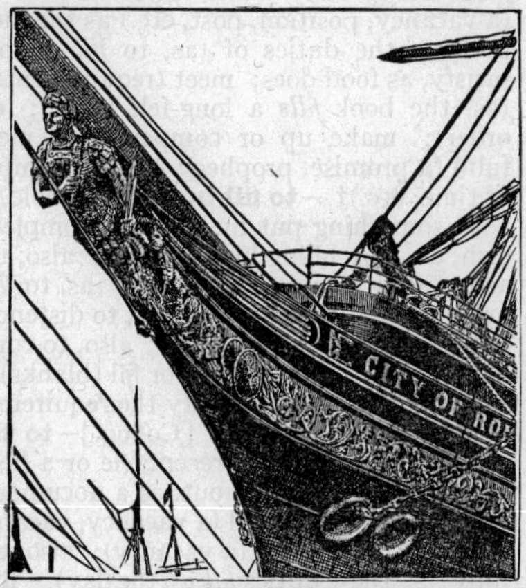

Figurehead.

fig-u-rine (fig-ṳ̄-rēn′), *n.* [F., < It. *figurina*, dim. of *figura*, < L. *figura*, E. *figure*, *n.*] A small ornamental figure of pottery, metalwork, etc.; a statuette: as, the Tanagra *figurines* (small terra-cotta figures, decorated in colors, such as have been found in ancient tombs at Tanagra in Greece).

Tanagra Figurine, 4th century B.C. — Museum of Fine Arts, Boston.

fig-wort (fig′wėrt), *n.* Any of numerous coarse herbs of the genus *Scrophularia*; also, any scrophulariaceous plant.

fike (fīk), *v.*; *fiked, fiking.* [ME. *fiken, fyken*; prob. from Scand.] **I.** *intr.* To move restlessly; fidget; fuss; trifle. [Now Sc. and north. Eng.] **II.** *tr.* To make uneasy; trouble; worry. [Sc.]—**fike,** *n.* A restless movement; bustle; stir; fuss; trouble; worry. [Sc.]

fil-a-gree (fil′ạ-grē), etc. See *filigree*, etc.

fil-a-ment (fil′ạ-mẹnt), *n.* [F. *filament*, < L. *filum*, thread.] A very fine thread or thread-like structure; a fiber or fibril; in an incandescent lamp, the thread-like, nearly infusible conductor which is placed in the bulb and raised to incandescence by the passage of the current; in *wireless teleg.* and *teleph.*, one of the interior elements of a vacuum-tube (see *vacuum-tube*); in *bot.*, the stalk-like portion of a stamen, supporting the anther.—**fil-a-men′ta-ry** (-men′tạ-ri), *a.* Pertaining to or of the nature of a filament or filaments.—**fil′a-ment-ed** (-men-ted), *a.* Provided with filaments.—**fil-a-men′tous,** *a.* Composed of or containing filaments; resembling a filament; bearing filaments; pertaining to filaments.

fi-lar (fī′lạ̈r), *a.* [L. *filum*, thread.] Of or pertaining to a thread or threads; having threads or the like; thread-like.

fi-la-ri-a (fi-lā′ri-ạ̈), *n.*; pl. *-riæ* (-ri-ē). [NL., < L. *filum*, thread.] Any of the slender, thread-like nematode worms constituting the genus *Filaria*, parasitic in the blood and tissues of vertebrates and other animals.—**fi-la′ri-al,** *a.* Belonging to the genus *Filaria* and allied genera (see *filaria*); also, caused by a filaria or filariæ, as a disease.—**fil-a-ri-a-sis** (fil-ạ-rī′ạ-sis), *n.* [NL.] In *pathol.*, the presence of filarial worms in the blood, etc.

fi-lasse (fi-làs′), *n.* [F., < *fil*, < L. *filum*, thread.] Vegetable fiber prepared for the process of manufacture.

fil-a-ture (fil′ạ-t̤ūr), *n.* [F. *filature*, < ML. *filare*, spin, < L. *filum*, thread.] The act of forming into threads; the reeling of silk from cocoons; also, a reel for drawing off silk from cocoons; also, an establishment for reeling silk.

fil-bert (fil′bėrt), *n.* [Said to be from Norman F. *noix de filbert*, 'nut of (St.) Philibert,' so called because ripe about the time of this saint's day, Aug. 22.] The thick-shelled, edible nut of certain cultivated varieties of hazel, esp. of *Corylus avellana* of Europe; also, a tree or shrub bearing such nuts.

filch (filch), *v. t.* or *i.* [Origin unknown.] To steal (esp. something of small value); pilfer: as, "He that *filches* from me my good name Robs me of that which not enriches him And makes me poor indeed" (Shakspere's "Othello," iii. 3. 159).—**filch′er,** *n.*—**filch′ing-ly,** *adv.*

file[1] (fīl), *n.* [AS. *fēol* = D. *vijl* = G. *feile*, file.] A metal (usually steel) tool of varying form and size, with numerous small cutting ridges or teeth on its surface, for abrading, smoothing, or cutting substances; fig., something serving to smooth or polish.—**file**[1], *v. t.*; *filed, filing.* To reduce, smooth, or cut with or as with a file; also, to remove with or as with a file.

file[2] (fīl), *v. t.*; *filed, filing.* [AS. *fȳlan* (recorded in compounds), < *fūl*, E. *foul*.] To defile; pollute. See Shakspere's "Macbeth," iii. 1. 65. [Archaic or prov.]

file[3] (fīl), *n.* [F. *fil*, thread, string, and *file*, file, row, < L. *filum*, thread.] A thread†; also, a string or wire on which papers are strung for preservation and reference; hence, any device, as a cabinet, by means of which papers, etc., are arranged or classified for convenient reference; also, a collection of papers so arranged or classified; any orderly collection of papers, etc.; also, a list or roll (as, "Our present musters grow upon the *file* To five and twenty thousand men of choice": Shakspere's "2 Henry IV.," i. 3. 10); also, a line of persons or things arranged one behind another; *milit.*, a number of soldiers forming a line from front to rear, esp. two soldiers forming such a line in a formation of only two ranks (distinguished from *rank*); also, a small detachment of soldiers; in *chess*, one of the lines of squares on a chess-board running directly from player to player.—**on file,** on or in a file, or in orderly arrangement for convenient reference, as papers; of a paper, etc., duly deposited among a collection of papers, etc., so arranged.—**file**[3], *v.*; *filed, filing.* **I.** *tr.* To place on or in a file, as papers; arrange (papers, etc.) methodically for preservation and convenient reference; place (a paper, etc.) on file. **II.** *intr.* To march or move in a file, one after another, as soldiers.

file[4] (fīl), *n.* [Origin unknown.] A pickpocket†; also, a cunning, shrewd, or artful person (prov. or slang, Eng.).

file=fish (fīl′fish), *n.* Any of various fishes with rough, granular skin, as *Alutera schœpfi* of the Atlantic coast of the U. S.

fil-e-mot (fil′ẹ-mot). [F. *feuille morte*, dead leaf.] **I.** *a.* Of the color of a dead leaf; yellowish-brown. [Archaic.] **II.** *n.* A yellowish-brown color. [Archaic.]

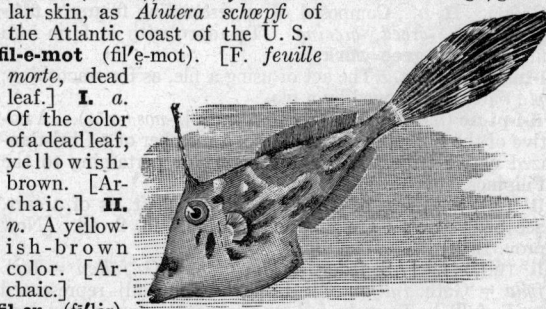

File-fish (*Alutera schœpfi*).

fil-er (fī′lėr), *n.* One who or that which files (in any of the various senses).

fi-let (fē-lā), *n.* [In part, F. *filet*, net, netting, for *filé*, < *fil*, thread, string (see *file*[3]); in part, F. *filet*, E. *fillet*.] Net, or lace with a ground of net, with a square mesh; in *cookery*, a fillet.

fil-ial (fil′yal), *a.* [LL. *filialis*, < L. *filius*, son, *filia*, daughter.] Of, pertaining to, or befitting a son or daughter (as, *filial* obedience); also, bearing the relation of a child to a parent.—**fil-ial′i-ty** (-yal′i-ti or -i-al′i-ti), **fil′ial-ness,** *n.*—**fil′ial-ly,** *adv.*

fil-i-ate (fil′i-āt), *v. t.*; *-ated*, *-ating*. [L. *filius*, son, *filia*, daughter: cf. *affiliate*.] To take or adopt as a son or daughter; join as by ties of sonship; affiliate; also, to fix the paternity of; father (*upon*).—**fil-i-a′tion** (-ā′shon), *n.* The act of filiating, or the state of being filiated; affiliation; an affiliated branch, as of a society; also, the relation of a son or daughter to a parent; sonship; the fact of being the child of a certain parent; parentage; fig., descent as if from a parent; derivation; the relation of one thing to another from which it is derived; also, the fixing of the paternity of a child upon some person (also fig.: as, "The direct *filiation* of euphuism on Spanish originals is no doubt erroneous," Saintsbury's "Hist. of Elizabethan Literature," Conclusion).

fil-i-beg (fil′i-beg), *n.* [Gael. *feileadh-beag*, 'small kilt' (as distinguished from the large one formerly worn).] The kilt or plaited skirt worn by Scottish Highlanders.

fil-i-bus-ter (fil′i-bus-tėr), *n.* [Cf. Sp. *filibustero*, F. *flibustier*, earlier *fribustier*, and obs. E. *flibutor*, all < D. *vrijbuiter*, E. *freebooter*.] A freebooter or buccaneer, esp. one of the piratical adventurers who made depredations on the Spanish colonies in the West Indies during the 17th century; also, one who engages in an unlawful military expedition into a foreign country to inaugurate or to aid a revolution, esp. one of the members of certain expeditions organized in the U. S. in the middle of the 19th century for the purpose of revolutionizing certain Spanish-American countries; more widely, an irregular military adventurer; also, a member of a minority in a legislative assembly who resorts to irregular or obstructive tactics to prevent the adoption of a measure or procedure favored by the majority (U. S.); a course of legislative filibustering (U. S.).—**fil′i-bus-ter,** *v. i.* To act as a filibuster, buccaneer, or irregular military adventurer; also, to impede legislation by irregular or obstructive tactics (U. S.).—**fil-i-bus′ter-er,** *n.*

fil-i-cide (fil′i-sīd), *n.* [L. *filius*, son, *filia*, daughter: see *-cide*.] One who kills his son or daughter; also, the act of killing one's son or daughter.—**fil′i-ci-dal** (-sī-dal), *a.*

fil-i-coid (fil′i-koid), *a.* [L. *filix* (*filic-*), fern: see *-oid*.] Resembling a fern.

fi-li-e-ty (fi-lī′e-ti), *n.* [LL. *filietas*, < L. *filius*, son.] The relation of a son to a parent.

fil-i-form (fil′i-fôrm), *a.* [L. *filum*, thread: see *-form*.] Thread-like; filamentous.

fil-i-grain, fil-i-grane (fil′i-grān), *n.* and *a.* Earlier forms of *filigree*.

fil-i-gree (fil′i-grē). [Corruption of *filigrane*, < F. *filigrane*, < It. *filigrana*, < L. *filum*, thread, + *granum*, grain.] **I.** *n.* Ornamental work of fine wire, esp. jewelers' work of gold or silver; hence, any similar ornamental openwork; fig., anything very delicate or fanciful (as, "Guarantees, he said, were mere *filigree*, pretty to look at, but too brittle to bear the slightest pressure": Macaulay's "Essays," Frederic the Great). **II.** *a.* Composed of or resembling filigree.—**fil′i-gree,** *v. t.*; *-greed*, *-greeing*. To adorn with or form into filigree.—**fil′i-gree=work,** *n.*

fil-ing (fī′ling), *n.* The act of using a file, as for smoothing; *pl.*, particles removed by a file.

Fil-i-pi-no (fil-i-pē′nō). [Sp.] **I.** *n.*; pl. *-nos* (-nōz). A native of the Philippine Islands, esp. a member of a Christianized native tribe. **II.** *a.* Belonging or pertaining to the Filipinos.

fill[1] (fil), *n.* [Var. of *thill*.] A thill or shaft, as of a cart. See Shakspere's "Troilus and Cressida," iii. 2. 48. [Now prov. Eng.]

fill[2] (fil), *v. t.* [AS. *fyllan* = D. *vullen* = G. *füllen* = Icel. *fylla* = Goth. *fulljan*, fill; from the Teut. adj. represented by E. *full*[1].] To make full, as of contents; put as much as can be held into (as, to *fill* a cup, basket, or trunk; to *fill* a room with gas, the hands with flowers, or the ears with cotton); supply to fullness or to the utmost (lit. or fig.: as, to *fill* one with food; to *fill* one's head with false notions or silly stories; to *fill* the heart with joy); complete by inserting something in blank spaces (usually with *in*, *out*, or *up*: see phrases below); supply, stock, or store plentifully (as, to *fill* a house with works of art; to *fill* a pond with fish); also, to stop up or close (a hole, crack, crevice, etc.) with something put in; supply (a blank space) with written matter, decorative work, etc.; furnish (a vacancy or vacant post) with an occupant; also, to stop up the holes, hollows, crevices, interstices, etc., of with some substance (as, to *fill* a tooth with gold; to *fill* wood or canvas by coating with varnish or size, as in preparing the surface); prepare, make up, or adulterate with some other material (see *filled*); also, to put, as contents, into a receptacle, esp. to pour (wine, tea, etc.) (obs. or archaic); put (*in*) by inserting (see *to fill in*, below); also, of contents, etc., to occupy to the full capacity (lit. or fig.: as, water *filled* the basin; the crowd *filled* the hall; matter enough to *fill* two pages; such thoughts *filled* his mind); extend throughout or pervade completely (as, the light, sound, or odor *filled* the room); be plentiful throughout (as, fish *filled* the rivers); distend, as the wind does a sail; occupy (a vacancy, position, post, etc.) as the incumbent; hold, and perform the duties of (as, to *fill* an office satisfactorily); satisfy, as food does; meet (requirements, etc.) satisfactorily (as, the book *fills* a long-felt want); execute (a business order); make up or compound (a medical prescription); fulfil (a promise, prophecy, etc.)†; complete (a work, period of time, etc.)†.—**to fill in,** to fill (a hole, hollow, blank, etc.) with something put in; also, to complete (a document, design, etc.) by filling blank spaces; also, to put in or insert so as to fill or complete something (as, to *fill in* omitted names or items of a list).—**to fill out,** to distend (sails, etc.); round out (the cheeks, figure, etc.); also, to complete (a document, list, etc.) by filling blanks, or fill (blanks) in a document, etc. —**to fill the bill,** to satisfy the requirements of the case; be or do what is wanted. [Colloq.]—**to fill up,** to fill completely, as a vessel or receptacle or a hole or hollow; fill to repletion; also, to fill out, as a document, or as blanks in a document; also, to fill (a vacancy, vacant post, etc.) with an occupant, or occupy (a vacancy); also, to take up or occupy fully (as, these duties *fill up* the day).—**fill**[2], *v. i.* To become full (as, the hall *filled* rapidly; eyes *filling* with tears); become distended, as sails with wind; become rounded (*out*), as the cheeks, figure, etc.; also, to fill a cup or other receptacle; pour out drink, as into a cup.—**fill**[2], *n.* [AS. *fyllo*.] One's full supply or desired amount (as, to take one's *fill* of food or sleep; "The stag at eve had drunk his *fill*," Scott's "Lady of the Lake," i. 1); also, a quantity sufficient to fill something (as, a *fill* of tobacco for a pipe); a single filling or charge of something; also, a mass of earth, stones, etc., used to fill a hollow, afford a road-bed, etc.—**filled,** *p. a.* Made full; charged or supplied with requisite contents; made with a filling, or an addition, of a different, usually inferior material (as, *filled* gold; *filled* cheese, cheese containing a foreign fat; *filled* milk, milk containing a substitute for the butter fat; *filled* soap; *filled* cloth). —**fill′er,** *n.* One who or that which fills; an implement used in filling, as a funnel; also, a thing or quantity of a material put in to fill something; the tobacco forming the body of a cigar, as distinguished from the wrapper; a liquid, paste, or the like used to coat wood, etc., as in preparing a surface for painting; something used to fill a vacant space (as, to use a short poem as a *filler* on a magazine page); a stop-gap.—**fill′er=vase,** *n.* In *Gr. archæol.*, a slender vase having a funnel-like bottom with a hole, apparently used to transfer liquids to narrow-necked receptacles.

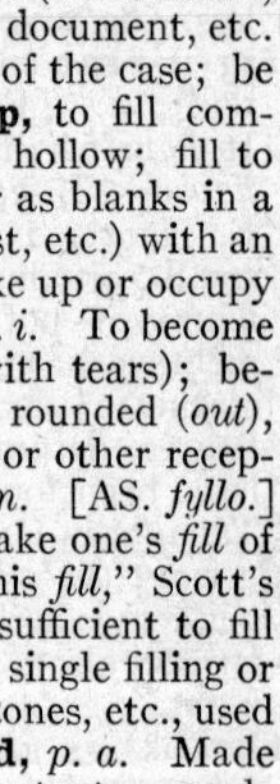
Filler-vase.

fil-let (fil′et), *n.* [OF. F. *filet*, dim. of *fil*, thread, string, < L. *filum*, thread.] A narrow band of ribbon or the like bound round the head or hair (as, "A belt her waist, a *fillet* binds her hair": Pope's "Windsor Forest," 178); a strip of any material used for binding something; also, any narrow strip of material, as wood or metal; a raised rim or ridge on a surface, as a ring on the muzzle of a gun; any band-like object or marking; specif., *pl.*, the loins, esp. of a horse; *sing.*, in *anat.*, a band of fibers, esp. of white nerve-fibers in the brain; in *cookery*, a strip or long (flat or thick) piece of meat or fish, esp. such as is easily detached from the bones or adjoining parts (as, the *fillet* of beef, the tenderloin; *fillets* of sole); a thick slice of meat, etc.; a piece of veal or other meat boned, rolled, and tied, for roasting; in *arch.*, etc., a relatively narrow molding with a plane face, as between other moldings; also, the flat surface between two flutes of a column; in *her.*, a horizontal division of an escutcheon, equal to one fourth of the depth of the chief, of which it occupies the lowest part; in *bookbinding*, a line impressed upon the cover of a book as a decoration; also, a rolling tool for impressing such lines.—**fil′let,** *v. t.*; *-leted, -leting.* To bind or adorn with or as with a fillet; in *cookery*, to cut or prepare (meat or fish) as a fillet; also, to cut fillets from.

fil-li-beg (fil′i-beg), *n.* See *filibeg.*

fil-li-bus-ter (fil′i-bus-tėr), etc. See *filibuster*, etc.

fil-li-gree (fil′i-grē), etc. See *filigree*, etc.

fill-ing (fil′ing), *n.* The act of one who or that which fills; a making or becoming full; also, that which is put in to fill something (as, a gold *filling* in a tooth; a custard *filling* for a pie; a bread *filling* for a chicken; a *filling* of earth and stones for hollow ground); carpeting of solid color used to supplement bordered carpets or rugs; in *needlework, lace*, etc., any simple stitch or work serving to fill considerable spaces; in *weaving*, material for the weft; the weft-threads of a fabric.

fil-lip (fil′ip), *v.* [Perhaps imit.: cf. *flip*[1].] **I.** *tr.* To strike with the nail of a finger snapped from the end of the thumb; hence, to tap or strike smartly; also, to drive by or as by a fillip with the fingers (as, "He *filliped* a little dust from his coat": Howells's "Foregone Conclusion," i.); toss (a coin) with a fillip. **II.** *intr.* To make a fillip with the fingers.—**fil′lip,** *n.* An act or movement of filliping; a smart tap or stroke given by filliping or otherwise; also, anything that tends to rouse, excite, or revive; a stimulus.

fil-li-peen (fil-i-pēn′), *n.* Same as *philopena.*

fil-lis-ter (fil′is-tėr), *n.* [Origin unknown.] A plane for cutting rabbets or grooves; also, a rabbet or groove, as one on a window-sash to hold the glass and putty.

fil-ly (fil′i), *n.*; pl. *fillies* (-iz). [Cf. Icel. *fylja*, fem., *foli*, masc.: see *foal.*] A female colt or foal; a young mare; also, a lively young girl (colloq.).

film (film), *n.* [AS. *filmen*, akin to *fell*, skin, E. *fell*[3].] A thin skin or membrane; a thin sheet of any material; a delicate web of filaments or fine threads, as gossamer or cobweb, or sometimes a single filament; a thin layer or coating (as, "An icy gale . . . o'er the pool Breathes a blue *film*": Thomson's "Seasons," Winter, 724); specif., the sensitive coating, as of gelatin and silver bromide, on a photographic plate; a strip or roll of celluloid coated with a sensitive emulsion, used instead of a photographic plate; such a strip of celluloid before it is coated; the celluloid strip containing the photographs exhibited in a moving-picture machine; hence, in general use, a moving picture.—**film,** *v.* **I.** *tr.* To cover with a film; also, to photograph with a moving-picture camera; reproduce in the form of moving pictures (as, to *film* a novel). **II.** *intr.* To become covered by a film.—**film′y,** *a.*; compar. *filmier*, superl. *filmiest.* Of the nature of, resembling, or covered with a film.—**film′i-ly,** *adv.*—**film′i-ness,** *n.*

fi-lo-plume (fī′lọ-plöm or fil′ọ-), *n.* [NL. *filopluma*, < L. *filum*, thread, + *pluma*, feather.] A thread-like or hair-like feather bearing a minute tuft of barbs at the tip.

Filoplume of a Goose.

fi-lose (fī′lōs), *a.* [L. *filum*, thread.] Thread-like; ending in a thread-like process.

fil-o-selle (fil-ọ-sel′ or -zel′), *n.* [F., < It. *filosello*, a dim. form (simulating It. *filo*, thread) < L. *follis*, bellows, bag: cf. ML. *follissellus, folixellus*, silkworm's cocoon.] The floss or rough, broken silk of cocoons, separated from the finer portion in reeling; an embroidery silk in untwisted strands made of it.

fils (fēs), *n.* [F., < L. *filius.*] Son: sometimes used after a name to distinguish a son from his father. See *père.*

fil-ter (fil′tėr), *n.* [F. *filtre* = It. *filtro*, < ML. *filtrum, feltrum*, felt (used as a filter); from the Teut. source of E. *felt*[2].] Any contrivance, as a piece of felt or paper, porous porcelain, a stratum of charcoal or sand, etc., through which liquid is passed to remove impurities or other matter; also, any of various analogous devices, as for removing dust from air or eliminating certain kinds of light-rays.—**fil′ter,** *v.* **I.** *tr.* To pass through or as through a filter; also, to act as a filter for; also, to remove by the action of a filter. **II.** *intr.* To pass through or as through a filter: as, "The water had . . . *filtered* through the roof" (J. H. Newman's "Callista," xxx.).—**fil′ter-a-ble,** *a.*—**fil′ter-er,** *n.*—**fil′ter=pass″er,** *n.* In *med.*, a pathogenic micro-organism, as that of influenza, which is so small that it passes through the minute interstices of a filter.—**fil′ter=pass″ing,** *a.* In *med.*, passing through a filter, as a micro-organism or virus.

filth (filth), *n.* [AS. *fȳlth*, < *fūl*, E. *foul.*] Foul condition; also, foul matter; offensive or disgusting dirt; sometimes (with plural), a particular accumulation or kind of foul matter; fig., anything morally unclean or defiling; moral impurity, or corruption; foul language, or obscenity; also, a vile person (archaic or prov. Eng.: as, "*Filth*, thou liest!" Shakspere's "Othello," v. 2. 231).—**filth′y,** *a.*; compar. *filthier*, superl. *filthiest.* Foul with, characterized by, or of the nature of filth; disgustingly dirty; fig., morally foul; vile; obscene; as a general epithet of strong condemnation, highly offensive or objectionable.—**filth′i-ly,** *adv.*—**filth′i-ness,** *n.*

fil-trate (fil′trāt), *v. t.* or *i.*; *-trated, -trating.* [NL. *filtratus*, pp. of *filtrare*, < ML. *filtrum*, felt: see *filter.*] To filter.—**fil′trate,** *n.* The liquid which has been passed through a filter.—**fil-tra′tion** (-trā′shọn), *n.*

fi-lum (fī′lum), *n.*; pl. *-la* (-lạ̈). [L., thread.] A thread-like structure or part; a filament.

fim-ble (fim′bl), *n.* [MD. *fimel.*] The male or staminate plant of hemp, which is harvested before the female or pistillate plant. Cf. *carl-hemp.*

fim-bri-a (fim′bri-ạ̈), *n.*; pl. *fimbriæ* (-ē). [LL., border, fringe: see *fringe.*] In *bot., zoöl.*, and *anat.*, a fringe or fringed border: often in *pl.*—**fim′bri-al,** *a.*—**fim′bri-ate, fim′bri-at-ed** (-āt, -ā-ted), *a.* Fringed, as the petals of certain flowers.—**fim-bri-a′tion** (-ā′shọn), *n.* Fimbriate or fringed condition; also, a fringe or fringe-like part.

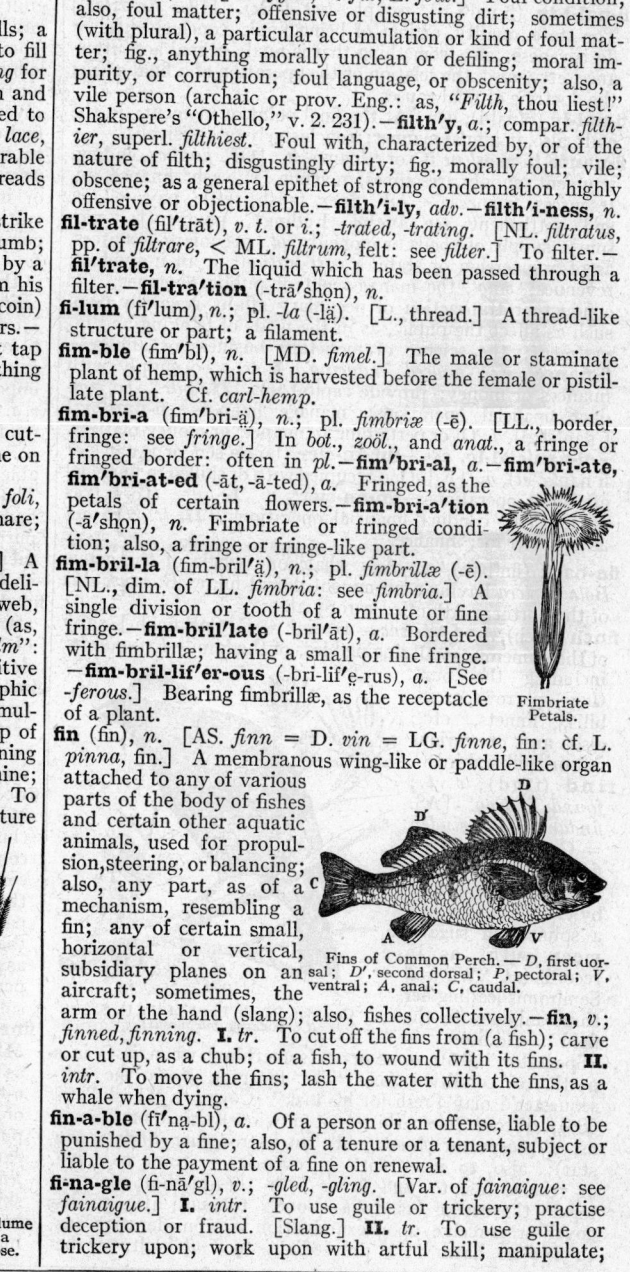

Fimbriate Petals.

fim-bril-la (fim-bril′ạ̈), *n.*; pl. *fimbrillæ* (-ē). [NL., dim. of LL. *fimbria*: see *fimbria.*] A single division or tooth of a minute or fine fringe.—**fim-bril′late** (-bril′āt), *a.* Bordered with fimbrillæ; having a small or fine fringe.—**fim-bril-lif′er-ous** (-bri-lif′ẹ-rus), *a.* [See *-ferous.*] Bearing fimbrillæ, as the receptacle of a plant.

fin (fin), *n.* [AS. *finn* = D. *vin* = LG. *finne*, fin: cf. L. *pinna*, fin.] A membranous wing-like or paddle-like organ attached to any of various parts of the body of fishes and certain other aquatic animals, used for propulsion, steering, or balancing; also, any part, as of a mechanism, resembling a fin; any of certain small, horizontal or vertical, subsidiary planes on an aircraft; sometimes, the arm or the hand (slang); also, fishes collectively.—**fin,** *v.*; *finned, finning.* **I.** *tr.* To cut off the fins from (a fish); carve or cut up, as a chub; of a fish, to wound with its fins. **II.** *intr.* To move the fins; lash the water with the fins, as a whale when dying.

Fins of Common Perch. — *D*, first dorsal; *D′*, second dorsal; *P*, pectoral; *V*, ventral; *A*, anal; *C*, caudal.

fin-a-ble (fī′nạ-bl), *a.* Of a person or an offense, liable to be punished by a fine; also, of a tenure or a tenant, subject or liable to the payment of a fine on renewal.

fi-na-gle (fi-nā′gl), *v.*; *-gled, -gling.* [Var. of *fainaigue*: see *fainaigue.*] **I.** *intr.* To use guile or trickery; practise deception or fraud. [Slang.] **II.** *tr.* To use guile or trickery upon; work upon with artful skill; manipulate;

trick or cheat (a person); get (something) by guile or trickery. [Slang.]—**fi-na'gler,** *n.*

fi-nal (fī'nạl). [OF. F. *final*, < LL. *finalis*, < L. *finis*, end, E. *fine*[1].] **I.** *a.* Pertaining to or coming at the end; last in place, order, or time (as, the *final* syllable of a word; a *final* effort; the *final* moment); also, beyond which no other may be expected, or ultimate (as, the *final* goal of all things); also, putting an end to a thing, conclusive, or decisive (as, the court's decision is *final*); also, pertaining to or expressing end or purpose (as, in *gram.*, a *final* clause); constituting the end or purpose (as, a *final* cause: see *cause*, *n.*). **II.** *n.* Something final, as a last and decisive examination or athletic contest after preliminary ones (often in *pl.*).

fi-na-le (fē-nä'lā), *n.* [It., < LL. *finalis*, E. *final.*] The final or concluding part, esp. if of impressive character, of an act of an opera, or of any musical composition; the concluding part of any performance, course of proceedings, etc.

fi-nal-ist (fī'nạl-ist), *n.* One who is entitled to take part in a final trial or round, as of an athletic contest.

fi-nal-i-ty (fī-nal'i-ti), *n.*; pl. *-ties* (-tiz). [LL. *finalitas.*] The state, quality, or fact of being final; conclusiveness or decisiveness; also, something that is final; a final act, utterance, etc.; also, the relation or the operation of a final cause; the doctrine of final causes.

fi-nal-ly (fī'nạl-i), *adv.* At the final point or moment; in the end; also, in a final manner; conclusively or decisively.

fi-nance (fi-nans' or fī-, or fī'nans), *n.* [OF. *finance*, ending, payment, supply, resources, revenue, F. cash, finance, pl. resources, finances, < OF. *finer*, finish, settle, pay, < *fin*, end, settlement: see *fine*[1].] Ending†; payment†; ransom†; supply of goods or money†; *pl.*, pecuniary resources, as of a sovereign or state, a corporation, or an individual; revenues; *sing.*, the management of public revenues; the conduct or transaction of pecuniary affairs generally, esp. such as affect the public, as in the fields of banking and investment; the science of monetary business or affairs.—**fi-nance',** *v.*; *-nanced*, *-nancing.* **I.** *tr.* To supply with finances or money; provide capital for. **II.** *intr.* To conduct financial operations; manage finances.—**fi-nan'cial** (-nan'shạl), *a.* Of or pertaining to finance, or money matters.—**fi-nan'cial-ly,** *adv.*—**fin-an-cier** (fin-an-sēr' or fī-nan-, or fi-nan'si-ėr), *n.* [F.] One occupied with or skilled in financial affairs or operations.—**fin-an-cier',** *v.* **I.** *intr.* To act as a financier; conduct financial operations. **II.** *tr.* To act as financier for; finance.

fin-back (fin'bak), *n.* Any whalebone whale of the genus *Balænoptera* having a prominent dorsal fin, as *B. musculus* of the northern Atlantic; a rorqual.

finch (finch), *n.* [AS. *finc* = D. *vink* = G. *fink*, finch.] Any of the numerous small singing birds of the family *Fringillidæ*, including the buntings, sparrows, crossbills, linnets, etc.; also, any of various non-fringilline birds.

Common Purple Finch of the U. S. (*Carpodacus purpureus*).

find (fīnd), *v. t.*; *found*, *finding.* [AS. *findan* = D. *vinden* = G. *finden* = Icel. *finna* = Goth. *finthan*, find.] To come upon by chance (as, to *find* a splinter in sugar); meet with, as in records (as, "We *find* Semiramis leading her three millions to the field": Addison, in "Spectator," 415); come upon (something) when it is in a particular condition (as, "The morning *finds* the self-sequester'd man Fresh for his task": Cowper's "Task," iii. 386); discover (something not previously seen or known: as, a prospector *finds* gold; an astronomer *finds* a new star); also, to meet with in experience, come to have, or receive (as, to *find* favor with the public); gain or regain the use of (as, to *find* one's tongue); also, to discover or perceive upon examination or consideration (as, to *find* no harm in a proceeding; to *find* fault, see below); discover (something) on examination to be as specified (as, to *find* conditions satisfactory); perceive (one's self) to be as specified (as, to *find* one's self in a dilemma; to *find* one's self weak from loss of blood); perceive (something) by experience or trial to be or do as specified (as, "He *finds* rest more agreeable than motion": Steele, in "Spectator," 6); detect (now only with *out*: see *to find out*, below); also, to discover, learn, attain, or obtain by search or effort (as, to *find* a bullet in a wound by probing; to *find* the meaning of a word by looking in a dictionary; to *find* time or money for a thing); recover (something lost); discover the right place or conditions for (one's self); hence, to attain or obtain as if by effort (as, his feelings *found* vent in words); arrive at as a destination (as, to *find* one's level); reach home to the understanding or appreciation of (as, "A verse may *find* him who a sermon flies": Herbert's "Church Porch"); also, to ascertain by study or calculation (as, to *find* some way to reduce expenses; to *find* the sum of several numbers); also, to determine after judicial inquiry (as, to *find* a person guilty); agree upon and deliver (a verdict); ascertain the validity of (an indictment, etc.); also, to provide or furnish (something) for the use of somebody (as, to *find* food and lodging for servants); also, to provide for or maintain (a person); provide food, lodging, etc., for.—**to find fault,** to discover or make known some defect, flaw, or matter of censure; find cause of blame or complaint; express dissatisfaction.—**to find one's level.** See under *level*, *n.*—**to find one's way,** to make out one's way by observation, search, or inquiry; also, to get to a place as if in spite of difficulties; come to a place by natural course or by force of circumstances (as, the river *finds its way* to the sea; the picture *found its way* to the auction-room).—**to find out,** to discover in the course of time or experience; discover by search or inquiry (as, "Canst thou by searching *find out* God?" Job, xi. 7); discover or ascertain by study, etc. (as, to *find out* a way to remedy an evil); often, to detect, as in an offense; discover the actions or character of; discover or detect (a fraud, imposture, etc.); discover the identity of (a person).—**find,** *v. i.* In *law*, to determine an issue after judicial inquiry; render a verdict: as, the jury *found* for the plaintiff.—**find,** *n.* An act of finding; a discovery, esp. of something valuable; also, something that has been found.—**find'a-ble,** *a.* That may be found.—**find'er,** *n.* One who or that which finds; in *astron.*, a small telescope attached to a larger for the purpose of finding an object more readily; in *photog.*, an attachment of a camera to indicate how the picture will appear on the sensitized plate.

fin de siècle (fañ dė syekl). [F.] 'End of century': used attributively toward the close of the 19th century in the sense of 'modern' or 'up-to-date,' and sometimes implying decadence.

find-ing (fīn'ding), *n.* The act of one who or that which finds; discovery; also, that which is found; something ascertained; a decision or verdict after judicial inquiry; *pl.*, tools, materials, etc., used by artisans (as, shoemakers' *findings*, shoemakers' supplies, excepting leather).

fine[1] (fīn), *n.* [OF. F. *fin*, < L. *finis*, boundary, border, end, ML. settlement, agreement, payment, fine.] End or conclusion (now only in 'in fine,' finally, or in short); also, a compromise of a fictitious suit, formerly in use as a mode of conveyance of land; also, a fee paid by a feudal tenant to the landlord, as on the renewal of tenure; a sum of money paid by a tenant on the commencement of his tenancy so that his rent may be small or nominal; esp., a sum exacted as a penalty for an offense or dereliction; a mulct; hence, a penalty of any kind (archaic).—**fine**[1], *v. t.*; *fined*, *fining.* To subject to a fine, or pecuniary penalty; punish by a fine.

fine[2] (fīn), *a.*; compar. *finer*, superl. *finest.* [OF. F. *fin* = ML. *finus*, appar. (as if meaning 'brought to the final point,' as of excellence) < L. *finire*, finish: see *finish.*] Of the highest or of very high grade or quality; free from imperfections or impurities; of gold, silver, etc., having a high proportion of pure metal, or having the proportion as specified (as, gold 18 carats *fine*); in general, choice, excellent, or admirable (as, a *fine* sermon; a *fine* view; to have a *fine* time); highly skilled or accomplished (as, a *fine* scholar; a *fine* musician); good-looking or handsome (as, "His wife hath . . . had much pretension to beauty, and is still a very *fine* woman":

Fielding's "Tom Jones," viii. 8); showy or smart, as dress; smartly dressed, as persons; characterized by or affecting refinement or elegance (as, a *fine* lady); polished or refined (as, *fine* manners); affectedly ornate or elegant (as, *fine* language or writing); also, delicately fashioned (as, "Heaven . . . warp those *fine* limbs To loathèd lameness!" Shelley's "Cenci," iv. 1. 133); delicate in texture (as, *fine* linen); consisting of minute particles (as, *fine* sand, meal, or shot); attenuated, rarefied, or subtle (as, "Transparent forms, too *fine* for mortal sight, Their fluid bodies half dissolved in light": Pope's "Rape of the Lock," ii. 61); very thin or slender (as, *fine* thread); keen or sharp, as a tool; trained down to the proper degree, as an athlete; sensitive to delicate impressions, as an organ or an instrument; delicate or subtle, as a distinction; also, pure†, absolute†, or sheer† (as, by *fine* force).—**fine arts.** See under *art*[2].—**fine**[2], *adv.* In a fine manner; excellently, or very well; elegantly; delicately; with nicety. [Now chiefly colloq.]—**fine**[2], *v.*; *fined*, *fining*. **I.** *tr.* To make fine; purify, clarify, or refine; make small, thin, or slender; make subtle. **II.** *intr.* To become fine; become pure, or clarify; become thin; dwindle (*away*).

fine-draw (fīn'drâ), *v. t.*; pret. *-drew*, pp. *-drawn*, ppr. *-drawing*. To sew together or up so finely or nicely that the joint is not noticed; also, to draw out to extreme fineness, tenuity, or subtlety.—**fine'drawn,** *p. a.* Drawn fine; drawn out to extreme fineness or thinness; extremely subtle.

fine-less (fīn'les), *a.* [See *fine*[1].] Endless. See Shakspere's "Othello," iii. 3. 173. [Archaic.]

fine-ly (fīn'li), *adv.* In a fine manner; excellently; elegantly; delicately; minutely; nicely; subtly.—**fine'ness,** *n.* The state or quality of being fine (in any sense); esp., the proportion of pure metal (gold or silver) in an alloy, often expressed by the number of parts in 1,000.

fin-er (fī'nėr), *n.* A refiner.

fin-er-y[1] (fī'nėr-i), *n.*; pl. *-ies* (-iz). [See *fine*[2], *a.*] Fineness, smartness, or elegance; also, fine or showy dress, ornaments, etc.

fin-er-y[2] (fī'nėr-i), *n.*; pl. *-ies* (-iz). [See *fine*[2], *v.*] In *metal.*, a hearth on which cast-iron is converted into wrought-iron.

fine=spun (fīn'spun), *a.* Spun or drawn out to a fine thread; hence, highly or excessively refined or subtle.

fi-nesse (fi-nes'), *n.* [F., < *fin*: see *fine*[2].] Fineness†; also, delicacy of execution; subtlety of discrimination; also, artful management; craft; strategy; an artifice or stratagem; in *card-playing*, an attempt to win a trick with a lower card when a higher card not in sequence with it is held, in the hope that the card or cards between may be on the right.—**fi-nesse',** *v.*; *-nessed*, *-nessing*. **I.** *intr.* To use finesse or artifice; also, to make a finesse at cards. **II.** *tr.* To bring by finesse or artifice; also, to make a finesse with (a card).

African Finfoot (*Podica senegalensis*).

fin-foot (fin'fůt), *n.*; pl. *-foots*. Any of certain pinnatiped or fin-footed aquatic birds (genus *Heliornis*, etc.) of South America and Africa, related to the rails and coots.—**fin'=foot"ed,** *a.* Web-footed; also, having feet the toes of which are separately furnished with flaps, as the finfoots, coots, etc.; pinnatiped.

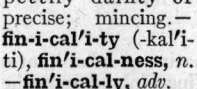

Fin-footed (Coot).

fin-ger (fing'gėr), *n.* [AS. *finger* = D. *vinger* = G. *finger* = Icel. *fingr* = Goth. *figgrs*, finger.] Any of the terminal members of the hand, esp. one other than the thumb; hence, something resembling a finger, as a ray of a starfish; something performing the office of a finger, as an index (as, "the *finger* of a clock": Cowper's "Task," iv. 118) or any of various projecting parts of machines; also, the breadth of a finger (or $\frac{3}{4}$ inch); the length of a finger (or $4\frac{1}{2}$ inches); also, a part of a glove made to receive a finger; in *music*, skill in fingering a musical instrument.—**fin'ger,** *v.* **I.** *tr.* To touch with the fingers; handle; toy or meddle with; also, to touch or take thievishly; pilfer; filch; in *music*, to play on (an instrument) with the fingers; perform or mark (a passage of music) with a certain fingering. **II.** *intr.* To touch or handle something with the fingers; in *music*, to use the fingers in playing.—**fin'ger=board,** *n.* In a violin, guitar, etc., the strip of wood on the neck against which the strings are stopped by the fingers; in a piano, organ, etc., the keyboard.—**fin'ger=bowl,** *n.* A bowl to hold water for rinsing the fingers at table.—**fin'ger-breadth,** *n.* The breadth of a finger ($\frac{3}{4}$ inch).—**fin'gered,** *a.* Having fingers; in *bot.*, digitate.—**fin'ger-er,** *n.* One who fingers; esp., a pilferer.—**fin'ger=glass,** *n.* A glass finger-bowl.

fin-ger-ing[1] (fing'gėr-ing), *n.* [Earlier *fingram*; perhaps < F. *fin grain*, 'fine grain': cf. *grogram* and *grosgrain*.] A kind of woolen yarn, used esp. for knitting.

fin-ger-ing[2] (fing'gėr-ing), *n.* The act of one who fingers; esp., in *music*, the action or method of using the fingers in playing on an instrument; the indication of the way the fingers are to be used in performing a piece of music.

fin-ger-less (fing'gėr-les), *a.* Without fingers.

fin-ger-ling (fing'gėr-ling), *n.* [See *-ling*[1].] Something very small; esp., a very small salmon or a small trout.

fin-ger-mark (fing'gėr-märk), *n.* A mark, esp. a smudge or stain, made by a finger.

fin-ger=nail (fing'gėr-nāl), *n.* The nail growing on each of the fingers of the hand.

fin-ger=plate (fing'gėr-plāt), *n.* A plate of metal, etc., on a door as a protection from fingermarks.

fin-ger=post (fing'gėr-pōst), *n.* A guide-post, as where roads cross or divide, bearing an arm terminating in the shape of an index-finger.

fin-ger-print (fing'gėr-print), *n.* An impression, as with ink, of the markings of the inner surface of the last joint of the thumb or a finger, taken esp. for purposes of identification, as of criminals.—**fin'ger-print,** *v. t.* To take the finger-prints of.

fin-ger's=breadth (fing'gėrz-bredth), *n.* Same as *finger-breadth.*

fin-ger=shaped (fing'gėr-shāpt), *a.* Shaped like a finger; slenderly oblong.

fin-ger=stall (fing'gėr-stâl), *n.* [See *stall*[2], *n.*] A sheath, as of leather, worn to protect a finger.

fin-i-al (fin'i-ạl), *n.* [L. *finis*, end.] In *arch.*, the ornamental termination of a pinnacle, gable, etc., usually foliated.

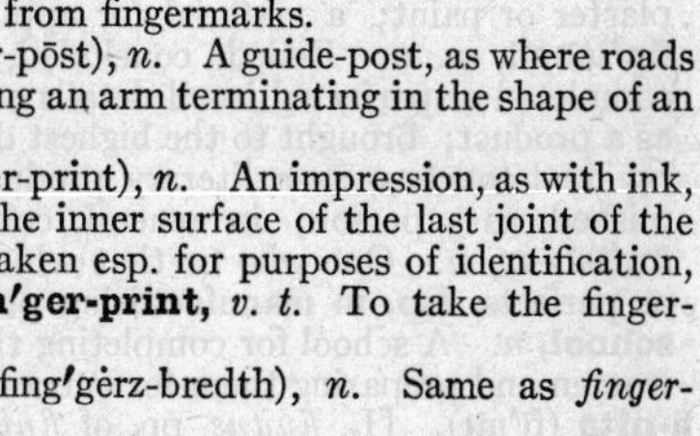

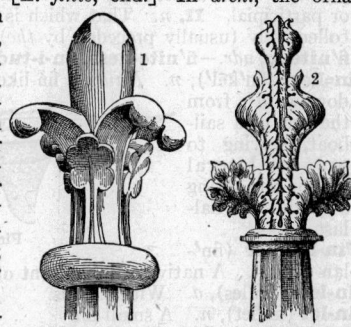

1. Finial, A.D. 1230, Cathedral of Amiens, France. 2. Finial, 15th century.

fin-i-cal (fin'i-kạl), *a.* [Appar. < *fine*[2]; recorded earlier than the var. *finikin*, later *finicking*.] Affectedly fine, refined, or nice; excessively fastidious or particular about trifles; pettily dainty or precise; mincing.—**fin-i-cal'i-ty** (-kal'i-ti), **fin'i-cal-ness,** *n.*—**fin'i-cal-ly,** *adv.*

fin-ick-ing, fin-ick-y, fin-i-kin (fin'i-king, -ki, -kin), *a.* Same as *finical*.—**fin'ick-ing-ly,** *adv.*

fi-nis (fī'nis), *n.* [L.] End; conclusion: a word occasionally, and in former times commonly, placed at the end of a book.

fin-ish (fin'ish), *v.* [OF. F. *finir* (*finiss-*), < L. *finire* (pp. *finitus*), bound, limit, terminate, finish, end, < *finis*, boundary, border, end.] **I.** *tr.* To bring (action, speech, etc.) to an end; come to the end of (a course, period of time, etc.); conclude; end; also, to bring (work, affairs, etc.) to completion; complete; also, to dispose of completely, use up, or consume (as, to *finish* a book that one is reading; to *finish* a spool of thread or a plate of food); also, to put an end to, terminate the existence of, destroy, or kill (as, "God hath numbered thy kingdom, and *finished* it," Dan. v. 26; to *finish* a wounded beast in hunting or an enemy in battle); fig., to give a quietus to, settle, or overcome completely (colloq.: as, this retort *finished* him); also, to complete or perfect in detail, as by final touches (sometimes with *off*); give the final smoothness, polish, nicety or elegance of effect, etc., to (any product of labor or art); perfect (a person) in education, accomplishments, social graces, etc.; also, to complete in preparation with specified features, fittings, ornamentation, etc., or with a particular effect (as, to *finish* cloth with a nap; to *finish* metal with a dull surface; to *finish* a room with wainscoting, or in shades of brown). **II.** *intr.* To come to an end, as of action, speech, a course, etc.; leave off; cease; also, to terminate or end (as, "Exeter doth wish His days may *finish* ere that hapless time": Shakspere's "1 Henry VI.," iii. 1. 201); terminate existence†, or die† (see Shakspere's "Cymbeline," v. 5. 36); also, to complete a course, etc. (as, he started in the race but did not *finish*).—**fin'ish,** *n.* The end or conclusion; the last stage; esp., the end of a hunt, race, etc.; also, a decisive ending (as, a fight to a *finish*); also, the quality of being finished, or completed with smoothness, nicety, elegance, etc.; perfected excellence of workmanship or execution; often, educational or social polish; also, the manner in which a thing is finished in preparation, or an effect imparted in finishing (as, cloth with a smooth or a soft *finish*; a lustrous or a dull *finish* for kid, metal, gilding, etc.); also, something used or serving to finish, complete, or perfect a thing; any completing feature or decoration (as, a *finish* for a costume); woodwork, etc., esp. in the interior of a building, not essential to the structure, but used for purposes of ornament, neatness, etc.; a final coat of plaster or paint; a material for application in finishing.—**fin'ished,** *p. a.* Ended, concluded, or completed; esp., completed or perfected in all details or processes of making, as a product; brought to the highest degree of excellence, as by final touches, as a literary production; highly accomplished, as a person; in general, consummate; perfect.—**fin'ish-er,** *n.* One who or that which finishes, completes, or perfects, esp. in manufacturing processes.—**fin'ish-ing=school,** *n.* A school for completing the education of young women and preparing them for entrance into society.

fi-nite (fī'nīt). [L. *finitus*, pp. of *finire*: see *finish.*] **I.** *a.* Having bounds or limits; not too great or too small to be naturally susceptible of measurement; not infinite or infinitesimal; hence, subject to limitations or conditions, as of space, time, circumstances, or the laws of nature; in *gram.*, of verbs, limited by person and number; not infinitival or participial. **II.** *n.* That which is finite, or finite things collectively (usually preceded by *the*); something finite.—**fi'nite-ly,** *adv.*—**fi'nite-ness, fin-i-tude** (fin'i-tūd), *n.*

fin=keel (fin'kēl'), *n.* *Naut.*, a fin-like projection extending downward from the keel of a sailboat, serving to prevent lateral motion and acting as additional ballast.

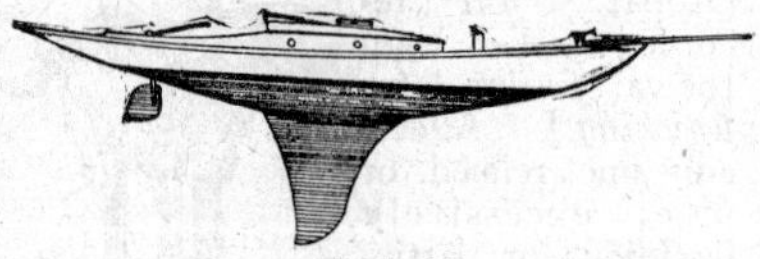

Fin-keel.

Fin-land-er (fin'lạn-dėr), *n.* A native or inhabitant of Finland.

fin-less (fin'les), *a.* Without fins.

fin-let (fin'let), *n.* A small fin.

Finn (fin), *n.* [AS. *Finnas*, pl.] A native or inhabitant of Finland; also, one of a people inhabiting Finland and other parts of northern Europe; also, a member of a race or ethnological group including this people and allied peoples (cf. *Finno-Ugrian*).

fin-nan=had-dock, fin-nan=had-die (fin'ạn-had'ọk, -had'i), *n.* [For *Findon haddock*, named from a village in eastern Scotland, where they were first cured.] A smoked haddock.

finned (find), *a.* Having a fin or fins.

Finn-ic (fin'ik), *a.* Of or pertaining to the Finns, esp. as an ethnological group; pertaining to the languages spoken by them.

fin'nick-ing, etc. See *finicking*, etc.

Finn-ish (fin'ish). **I.** *a.* Of or pertaining to Finland, its inhabitants, or their language; also, Finnic. **II.** *n.* The language of the Finns of Finland.

Fin-no=U-gri-an (fin'ọ-ö'gri-ạn), *a.* Pertaining to the Finns and the Ugrians; noting or pertaining to a division of the Ural-Altaic family of languages containing Finnish, Esthonian, Lapp, and related languages, and also Magyar and related languages. Also **Fin'no=U'gric** (-grik).

fin-ny (fin'i), *a.* Having fins; finned; also, of the nature of a fin; fin-like; also, of, pertaining to, or containing fish (as, "the *finny* deep": Goldsmith's "Traveller," 187).

Fin-sen (fin'sen) **light.** [From N. R. *Finsen* (1860–1904), Danish physician, who devised this form of treatment.] Light composed of violet and ultra-violet rays, used in the treatment of cutaneous diseases.

fiord, fjord (fyôrd), *n.* [Norw. and Dan. *fjord* = Icel. *fjördhr*: cf. *firth, frith.*] A long, relatively narrow arm of the sea, bordered by steep cliffs, as on the coast of Norway.

fip-pence, fip-pen-ny (fip'ẹns, fip'ẹ-ni). Colloquial forms of *fivepence, fivepenny.*

fir (fėr), *n.* [ME. *firr*; prob. from Scand.] Any of the pyramidal pinaceous evergreen trees or shrubs constituting the genus *Abies*, as *A. balsamea*, the balsam-fir; any of various similar pinaceous trees; the wood of such a tree.—**fir'=bal''sam,** *n.* The balsam-fir, *Abies balsamea.*

Fir (*Abies fraseri*).

fire (fīr), *n.* [AS. *fȳr* = D. *vuur* = G. *feuer* = Icel. *fūrr*, fire; akin to Gr. πῦρ, fire.] The active principle of burning or combustion, manifested by the evolution of light and heat; also, burning or combustion (as, on *fire*, ignited or burning; to take *fire*, to become ignited); also, a burning mass of material, as on a hearth or in a furnace; also, the destructive burning of any large mass, as a building or a forest; a conflagration; also, torture by burning; exposure to fire by way of ordeal; fig., severe trial (as, the *fires* of affliction); also, a composition or device for producing a conflagration or a fiery display (as, Greek *fire*: see under *Greek, a.*); also, lightning, or a thunderbolt (archaic: as, "Vapours, from whose solid atmosphere Black rain, and *fire*, and hail will burst," Shelley's "Ode to the West Wind"); a spark or sparks; flashing light; luminous appearance like that of fire (as, "his sparkling eyes, replete with wrathful *fire*": Shakspere's "1 Henry VI.," i. 1. 12); brilliancy, as of a gem; a luminous object, as a star (as, "the *fires* of heaven": Shakspere's "Coriolanus," i. 4. 39); also, heating quality, as of strong drink; also, bodily heat, as from disease (as, "the raging *fire* of fever": Shakspere's "Comedy of Errors," v. 1. 75); fever; inflammation; in fig. use, burning passion, as of love or rage (as, "With an inward *fire* possessed, They raged": Shelley's "Revolt of Islam," x. 40); ardor, fervor, or enthusiasm (as, a man full of *fire* and courage); liveliness of imagination, vigor of fancy, or inspiration (as, "a poet's *fire*": Pope's "Essay on Criticism," 676); also, the discharge of firearms (as, to open *fire*; under *fire*: often fig.).—**fire,** *v.*; *fired, firing.* **I.** *tr.* To set on fire; kindle; also, to expose to the action of fire; subject to heat; bake, as bricks; also, to supply (a furnace, etc.) with fuel; attend to the fire of (a boiler, etc.); also, to drive out or away by or as by fire† (as, "He that parts us shall bring a brand from heaven, And *fire* us hence like foxes": Shakspere's "King Lear," v. 3. 23); also, to light or illuminate, or cause to glow as if on fire (as, "The sun, with ruddy orb Ascending, *fires* th' horizon": Cowper's "Task," v. 2); also, to inflame, as with passion; fill with ardor; inspire (as, a scene to *fire* a poet's imagination); also, to subject to explosion or explosive force, as a mine; discharge, as a gun; project (a missile) by discharging from a gun, etc.; hence, to project or hurl as if from a gun (colloq.: as, to *fire* a stone through a window); eject or dismiss forcibly or peremptorily (slang); in *vet. surg.*, to cauterize. **II.** *intr.* To take fire; be kindled; also, to glow as if on fire; also, to become inflamed with passion; become excited; also, to go off, as a gun; discharge a gun, etc. (as, to *fire* at a fleeing enemy); hence, to hurl a missile (colloq.).—**to fire away,** to begin; go ahead; go on. [Colloq.]—**to fire up,** to start a fire in a furnace, a locomotive, etc.; also, to become irritated or angry.

fire=a-larm (fīr'ạ-lärm''), *n.* An alarm of fire; also, an apparatus for giving the alarm.

fire-arm (fīr'ärm), *n.* A weapon from which a missile is discharged by gunpowder or other explosive.

fire=ar-row (fīr'ar''ō), *n.* An arrow with combustible matter attached, formerly used, by shooting from a hand-bow or an engine, for incendiary purposes.

Fire-arrows, 14th and 15th centuries.

fire=ball (fīr'bâl), *n.* A ball of fire, as the sun; esp., a luminous meteor, sometimes exploding; also, lightning having the appearance of a globe of fire; also, a ball filled with explosive or combustible material, used as a projectile, as for injuring the enemy by explosion or for setting fire to their works.

fire=bal-loon (fīr'bạ-lön''), *n.* A balloon made buoyant by air heated by a fire attached beneath an opening at the bottom; also, a balloon sent up at night with fireworks which ignite at a regulated height.

fire=bee-tle (fīr'bē''tl), *n.* Any of various beetles, esp. of the genus *Pyrophorus* of tropical America, having light-producing organs.

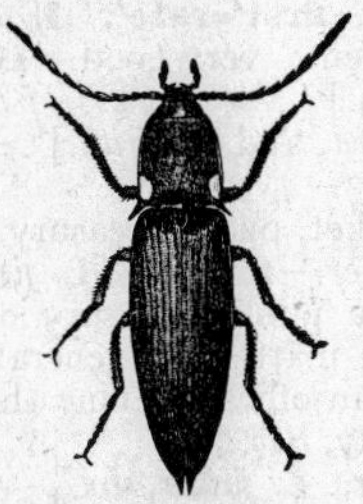

Fire-beetle (*Pyrophorus noctilucus*).

fire=bird (fīr'bėrd), *n.* The Baltimore oriole (see *oriole*).

fire-board (fīr'bōrd), *n.* A board used to close a fire-place.

fire=boat (fīr'bōt), *n.* A steamboat fitted with apparatus for extinguishing fires.

fire=box (fīr'boks), *n.* The box or chamber in which the fire of a furnace, steam-boiler, etc., is placed.

fire-brand (fīr'brand), *n.* A piece of burning wood or other material (as, "I took up a great *firebrand,* and in I rushed . . . with the stick flaming in my hand": Defoe's "Robinson Crusoe," i. 12); fig., one who or that which kindles strife, inflames the passions, etc.

fire=brick (fīr'brik), *n.* A brick made of fire-clay.

fire-bug (fīr'bug), *n.* An incendiary. [U. S.]

fire=clay (fīr'klā), *n.* A kind of clay capable of resisting high temperature: used for making crucibles, fire-bricks, etc.

fire=com-pa-ny (fīr'kum''pạ-ni), *n.*; pl. *-nies* (-niz). A company of men organized or employed to extinguish fires; also, a fire-insurance company.

fire=crack-er (fīr'krak''ėr), *n.* A paper cylinder filled with an explosive and furnished with a fuse, and discharged to make a noise.

fire=damp (fīr'damp), *n.* A combustible gas, consisting chiefly of methane, formed esp. in coal-mines, and dangerously explosive when mixed with certain proportions of atmospheric air.

fire=dog (fīr'dog), *n.* An andiron.

fire-drake (fīr'drāk), *n.* [AS. *fȳrdraca:* see *drake*².] A mythical fiery dragon; a luminous meteor†; an ignis fatuus†; a kind of firework†.

fire=drill (fīr'dril), *n.* A practice drill for a company of firemen, the crew of a ship, etc., to accustom them to the duties proper to each in case of fire; also, a drill for pupils in a school, employees in a factory, etc., to train them in the manner of exit to be followed in case of fire.

fire=eat-er (fīr'ē''tėr), *n.* A juggler who pretends to eat fire; also, one who seeks occasion to fight or quarrel; a hotspur.—**fire'=eat''ing,** *a.*

fire=en-gine (fīr'en''jin), *n.* An apparatus (usually mounted on wheels, and commonly moved by horses or a motor) for throwing a continuous stream of water through a hose to extinguish fires, consisting essentially of a pump operated usually by steam but sometimes by hand; also, an apparatus fitted with chemical fire-extinguishing devices, moved by horses or otherwise.

fire=es-cape (fīr'es-kāp''), *n.* An apparatus or structure to afford escape from a burning building.

fire=flaught (fīr'flât), *n.* [See *flaught.*] Lightning; a flash of lightning; also, a fiery glance; also, a sudden burst or rush; also, the aurora borealis. [Chiefly Sc.]

fire-fly (fīr'flī), *n.*; pl. *-flies* (-flīz). Any of various winged insects, esp. beetles of the genera *Photinus* and *Photuris,* having light-producing organs.

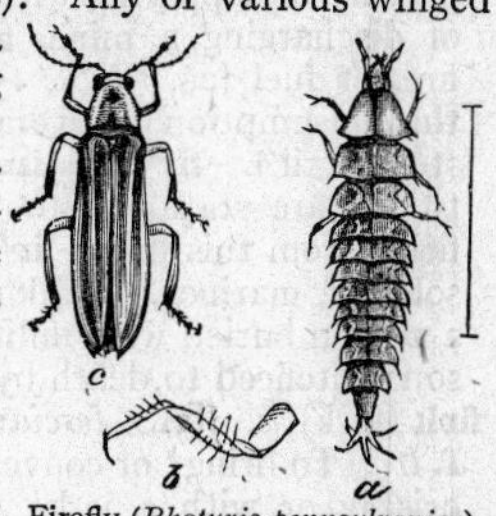

Firefly (*Photuris pennsylvanica*). — *a,* larva (line shows natural size); *b,* leg of larva, magnified; *c,* beetle.

fire=house (fīr'hous), *n.* A building where apparatus for extinguishing fires is kept, or one forming the headquarters of a fire-company.

fire-less (fīr'les), *a.* Lacking fire; without a fire; fig., without life or animation.

fire-light (fīr'līt), *n.* The light from a fire, as on a hearth.

fire=line (fīr'līn), *n.* A strip of forest land cleared to prevent the spread of fire; also, a police cordon round the scene of a fire.

fire-lock (fīr'lok), *n.* An old type of gun-lock, as a flintlock, which ignites the priming by means of sparks; a gun with such a gun-lock; a soldier armed with such a gun.

fire-man (fīr'mạn), *n.*; pl. *-men.* A man employed to extinguish or prevent fires; also, a man employed to tend fires; a stoker.

fire=new (fīr'nū'), *a.* Fresh from the fire or forge; hence, brand-new. See Shakspere's "Richard III.," i. 3. 256. [Archaic.]

fire=o-pal (fīr'ō''pạl), *n.* In *mineral.*, girasol.

fire=pink (fīr'pingk), *n.* A caryophyllaceous plant, *Silene virginica,* with brilliant scarlet flowers.

fire-place (fīr'plās), *n.* That part of a chimney which opens into an apartment and in which fuel is burned; a hearth.

fire-proof (fīr'pröf), *a.* Proof against fire; comparatively incombustible.—**fire'proof,** *v. t.* To render fireproof.—**fire'proof''ing,** *n.* Material for use in making anything fireproof.

fir-er (fīr'ėr), *n.* One who fires, or sets on fire, treats with fire or heat, discharges a firearm, etc.; also, a firearm with reference to its firing (as, a single-*firer;* a rapid-*firer*).

fire=room (fīr'röm), *n.* A room containing a fireplace; also, a space in front of a furnace or steam-boiler, from which coal is supplied; also, a fire-box.

fire=ship (fīr'ship), *n.* A vessel freighted with combustibles and explosives and set adrift to destroy an enemy's ships, etc.

fire-side (fīr'sīd), *n.* The side of a fireplace; the space about a fire or hearth, considered esp. as the place of a family's social enjoyment: as, "There is no *fireside* . . . But has one vacant chair" (Longfellow's "Resignation").

fire=stone (fīr'stōn), *n.* A flint†; also, iron pyrites†; also, a fire-resisting stone, esp. a kind of sandstone used in fireplaces, furnaces, etc.

fire=tow-er (fīr'tou''ėr), *n.* A tower with a beacon at its top, as for service as a lighthouse; also, a fireproof tower, or separately constructed tower-like portion of a building, with stairs, for use as a fire-escape.

fire=trap (fīr'trap), *n.* A building in which, as from the material or arrangement of the structure, life is especially exposed to peril in case of fire.

fire=war-den (fīr'wâr''dn), *n.* An officer having authority in the prevention or extinguishing of fires, as in towns or camps.

fire=wa-ter (fīr'wâ''tėr), *n.* Strong liquor: a term used by American Indians.

fire-weed (fīr'wēd), *n.* Any of various plants appearing in recently burned clearings or districts, as an asteraceous weed, *Erechtites hieracifolia,* of North America.

fire-wood (fīr'wůd), *n.* Wood for fuel.

fire-work (fīr'wėrk), *n.* A combustible or explosive device for producing in combustion a striking display of light (sometimes a pictorial or ornamental design) or a loud noise, or to be used in signaling at night or for various other purposes, as in war (usually in *pl.*); *pl.*, a pyrotechnic display.

fire=worm (fīr'wėrm), *n.* A glow-worm; also, the larva of an American tortricid (moth), *Eudemis vacciniana,* so injurious to cranberry-vines as to give them a burned appearance.

fir-ing (fīr′ing), *n.* The act of one who or that which fires; a setting on fire; a taking fire; exposure to heat, as in order to bake; the application of fire or of a cautery; the act or manner of supplying with fuel, or of tending a fire; the act of discharging a mine, firearm, etc.; also, material for a fire, or fuel (as, "I . . . brought home *firing* sufficient for the consumption of several days": Mrs. Shelley's "Frankenstein," xii.).—**fir′ing=line,** *n.* *Milit.*, the line along which troops are stationed to fire upon the enemy; the troops firing from this line.—**fir′ing=par″ty,** *n.* A detachment of soldiers, marines, or sailors detailed to fire over the grave of a person buried with military honors, or to execute any person sentenced to death by shooting.

firk (fėrk), *v.* [AS. *fercian*, bring; perhaps akin to E. *fare.*] **I.** *tr.* To bring† or convey†; also, to move, drive, pull, etc., briskly or with a jerk; stir (*up*); also, to beat soundly; trounce. [Obs. or archaic or prov.] **II.** *intr.* To go quickly†; also, to move about briskly or in a jerky manner; stir about; poke about in something. [Obs. or prov.]

fir-kin (fėr′kin), *n.* [ME. *ferdekyn*, appar. a dim. form < D. *vierde*, fourth.] A measure of capacity, usually the fourth part of a barrel; also, a small wooden vessel for butter, etc.

firm (fėrm), *a.* [OF. F. *ferme*, < L. *firmus*, firm, stable, steadfast, strong.] Able or tending to maintain form or cohesion of substance (as, *firm* ground or snow; *firm* flesh; a *firm* jelly; a *firm* fabric; *firm* consistence or texture); comparatively solid, hard, stiff, or rigid; also, securely fixed in place, fast, or immovable (as, a candle *firm* in its socket; "Hope, as an anchor *firm* and sure, holds fast The Christian vessel, and defies the blast," Cowper's "Hope," 167); fixed, settled, or unalterable, as a belief or conviction, a decree, etc.; also, steady, or not shaking, trembling, quivering, etc. (as, a *firm* step, grasp, hand, or voice); not fluctuating or falling, as prices or the market; steadfast or unwavering, as persons or the purpose, resolution, principles, attachments, etc.; unfaltering; resolute; constant.—**firm,** *v. t.* [OF. *fermer*, make firm, fix (F. close), < L. *firmare*, make firm, confirm, < *firmus.*] To make firm in substance or consistence; render more solid; also, to fix securely in place; make or hold fast; also, to establish, ratify, or confirm (obs. or archaic); sign (a document)†.—**firm,** *n.* [It. and Sp. *firma*, signature, < L. *firmare*, confirm, E. *firm*, *v.*] Signature†; also, the name or style under which associated persons do business; also, a partnership or association of two or more persons for carrying on a business; a commercial house.

fir-ma-ment (fėr′mạ-mẹnt), *n.* [LL. *firmamentum*, firmament, L. a support, prop, < L. *firmare*, E. *firm*, *v.*] The vault of heaven; the sky: now chiefly rhetorical or literary. —**fir-ma-men′tal** (-men′tạl), *a.*

fir-man (fėr′mạn or fėr-män′), *n.*; pl. *-mans.* [Pers. *fermān.*] An edict or order issued by an Oriental sovereign.

firm-ly (fėrm′li), *adv.* In a firm manner.—**firm′ness,** *n.*

firn (firn), *n.* [G., prop. adj., of last year.] Névé.

fir-ry (fėr′i), *a.* Of or pertaining to the fir; made of fir; abounding in firs (as, "in *firry* woodlands": Tennyson's "Miller's Daughter," 42).

first (fėrst), *a.* [AS. *fyrst* = OHG. *furist* (G. *fürst*, prince) = Icel. *fyrstr*, foremost, first; a superl. form akin to E. *fore.*] Being before all others with respect to time, order, rank, importance, etc.: used as the ordinal of *one.*—**at first blush,** at the first view; on first consideration.—**at first hand,** from the first or original source.—**first aid,** emergency aid or treatment given to persons suffering from accident, etc., before the services of a physician can be obtained.—**first,** *n.* That which or something that is first in time, order, rank, etc.; the beginning (as, at *first*, or at the *first*, at the beginning or outset; from the *first*, from the beginning or outset); the first part; the first member of a series; a place in the first or highest group in an examination for honors; the first place in a race, etc.; *pl.*, the best quality of certain articles of commerce.—**first,** *adv.* Before all others or anything else in time, order, rank, etc. (as, "The good die *first*," Wordsworth's "Excursion," i. 500; "The consent of the historians . . . makes him, *first* and foremost, a legislator and administrator," Stubbs's "Constitutional Hist. of Eng.," xii. § 147); in the first place, or firstly (as, "*First* of all I would have them seriously think of the shortness of their time": Addison, in "Spectator," 89); also, before some other thing, event, etc., specified or implied (as, "Thou shalt not see my face, except thou *first* bring Michal Saul's daughter": 2 Sam. iii. 13); hence, in preference to something else, rather, or sooner (as, "Die? He'll bribe a gaoler or break prison *first!*" Browning's "Ring and the Book," x.); also, for the first time (as, "For as you were when *first* your eye I eyed, Such seems your beauty still": Shakspere's "Sonnets," civ.).—**first and last,** at one time and another; altogether; in all.—**first or last,** at one time or another; sooner or later. —**first′=born′.** **I.** *a.* First in the order of birth; eldest. **II.** *n.* One that is born first; a first-born child; fig., the first result or product.—**first′=class′,** *a.* Of the highest or best class or quality; first-rate.—**first′=fruit′,** *n.* The earliest fruit of the season; hence, the first product or result of anything; in *feudal* and *eccles. law*, the first year's income of a holding or benefice, formerly paid to some superior: usually in *pl.*—**first′=hand′.** **I.** *a.* Of or pertaining to the first or original source; obtained directly from the original source, and not through an intermediate agency. **II.** *adv.* From the first or original source.—**first′ling,** *n.* The first of its kind to be produced or to appear; the first product or result; esp., the first offspring of an animal.—**first′ly,** *adv.* In the first place; first.—**first′=night′er,** *n.* One who makes a practice of attending the theater on the nights of the first public performance of plays.—**first′=rate′.** **I.** *a.* Of the first rate or class; hence, excellent; very good. **II.** *adv.* Excellently; very well. [Colloq.]

firth (fėrth), *n.* [Icel. *fjördhr*: see *fiord*, and cf. *frith.*] A narrow arm of the sea; a frith.

fisc (fisk), *n.* [F. *fisc*, < L. *fiscus*, basket, purse, treasury.] A royal or state treasury; an exchequer.—**fis′cal.** [L. *fiscalis.*] **I.** *a.* Of or pertaining to the public treasury or revenues; also, pertaining to financial matters in general; financial. **II.** *n.* In some countries, an official having the function of public prosecutor.—**fis′cal-ly,** *adv.*

fish[1] (fish), *n.* [F. *fiche*, peg, counter, < *ficher*, fix.] A counter used in various games.

fish[2] (fish), *n.*; pl. *fishes* or (esp. collectively) *fish.* [AS. *fisc* = D. *visch* = G. *fisch* = Icel. *fiskr* = Goth. *fisks*, fish; akin to L. *piscis*, fish.] In popular use, any animal that lives entirely in water (as, a shell-*fish*); specif., any of various cold-blooded, completely aquatic vertebrates (generally regarded as comprising the group or class *Pisces*), having gills, commonly fins, and typically an elongated body usually covered with scales; also, the flesh of fishes used as food; also, a fish-tackle; also, a long strip of wood, iron, etc., used to strengthen a mast, joint, etc.; *pl.* [*cap.*], the zodiacal constellation or sign Pisces ('the Fishes').—**fish**[2], *v.* [AS. *fiscian.*] **I.** *intr.* To catch or attempt to catch fish, as by angling or drawing a net; also, to search for or attempt to lay hold on something under water, in mud, etc., by the use of a dredge, rake, hook, or the like; also, to seek to obtain something by artifice or indirectly (as, to *fish* for compliments). **II.** *tr.* To catch or attempt to catch (fish or the like); hence, to draw (*up*, *out*, etc.) as by fishing; specif., to hoist the flukes of (an anchor) up to the gunwale by means of a tackle; also, to try to catch fish in (a stream, etc.); search through as by fishing; also, to strengthen (a mast, joint, etc.) by a fish.—**fish′a-ble,** *a.* That may be fished in, as a stream.—**fish′=ball,** *n.* A fried ball or cake of shredded fish, esp. salt codfish, and mashed potato; a fish-cake.—**fish′=bolt,** *n.* A bolt which secures a fish-plate.—**fish′=cake,** *n.* A fish-ball.

fish-er (fish′ėr), *n.* [AS. *fiscere.*] One who or that which fishes; a fisherman; an animal that catches fish for food; also, a kind of marten, *Mustela pennanti*, of a dark-brown or blackish color and a somewhat fox-like appearance, inhabiting the northern parts of North America;

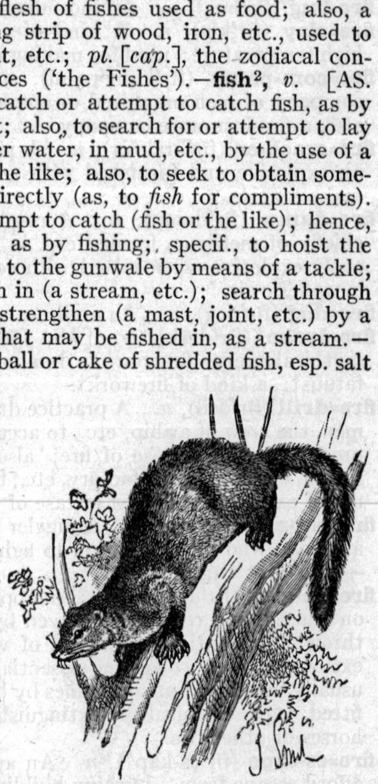

Fisher (*Mustela pennanti*).

its fur.—**fish'er-man** (-mạn), *n.*; pl. *-men.* One engaged in fishing, whether for profit or pleasure; an animal that catches fish; a vessel employed in fishing.—**fish'er-y,** *n.*; pl. *-ies* (-iz). The occupation or industry of catching fish or taking other products of the sea or streams from the water; also, a place where such an industry is regularly carried on; also, those engaged in fishing at such a place; a fishing establishment; also, a fishing venture; also, the right of fishing in certain waters.

fish=hawk (fish'hâk), *n.* The osprey.

fish=hook (fish'hůk), *n.* A hook used for catching fish; also, a hook used with a fish-tackle.

fish-i-fy (fish'i-fī), *v. t.*; *-fied, -fying.* [See *-fy.*] To change (flesh) to fish. See Shakspere's "Romeo and Juliet," ii. 4. 40.

fish-i-ly (fish'i-li), *adv.* In a fishy manner.—**fish'i-ness,** *n.*

fish=joint (fish'joint), *n.* A joint formed by one or more rigid plates fastened to the side or sides of rails, beams, etc., meeting end to end: used esp. in connecting the rails of railroads.

fish-less (fish'les), *a.* Without fish.

fish=line (fish'līn), *n.* A line used in fishing.

fish=louse (fish'lous), *n.*; pl. *-lice* (-līs). Any of numerous small crustaceans parasitic on fishes.

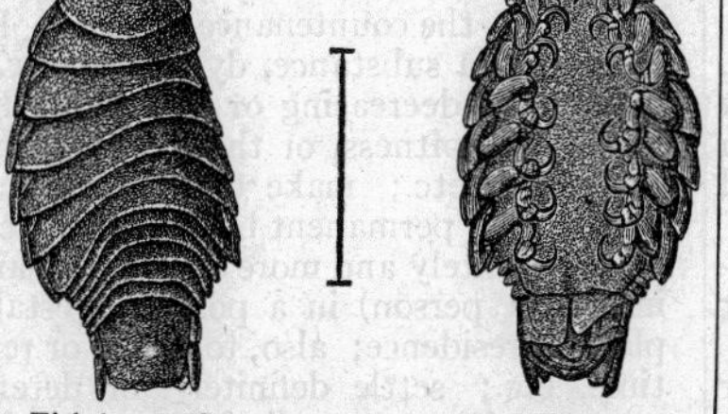

Fish-louse (*Cymothoa ovalis*), upper and under views. (Line shows natural size.)

fish-mong-er (fish'-mung"gėr), *n.* A dealer in fish.

fish=plate (fish'-plāt), *n.* One of the plates used in a fish-joint.

fish=slice (fish'slīs), *n.* A kitchen implement with a broad, thin blade and a long handle, for turning fish in frying; also, a broad-bladed implement for serving fish at table.

fish=spear (fish'spēr), *n.* A spear or lance, often having more than one tine, for spearing fish through ice or from a boat.

fish=sto-ry (fish'stō"ri), *n.* An extravagant or incredible story or tale. [Colloq.]

fish=tack-le (fish'tak"l), *n.* The tackle used for fishing an anchor.

fish=tail (fish'tāl), *a.* Like a fish's tail in shape or action.

fish-way (fish'wā), *n.* An arrangement for enabling fish to ascend a fall or dam.

fish-wife (fish'wīf), *n.*; pl. *-wives* (-wīvz). A woman who sells fish. Also **fish'wom"an;** pl. *-women* (-wim"en).

fish-y (fish'i), *a.*; compar. *fishier*, superl. *fishiest.* Abounding in fish (as, "the *fishy* flood": Pope's tr. Homer's "Odyssey," iv.); also, consisting of fish (as, "*fishy* food": Pope's tr. Homer's "Odyssey," v.); also, fish-like in shape, smell, taste, etc.; dull and expressionless (as, *fishy* eyes); also, of questionable character (colloq.); improbable, as a story (colloq.).

fis-sile (fis'il), *a.* [L. *fissilis*, < *findere*: see *fission.*] Capable of being split or divided; cleavable.—**fis-sil-i-ty** (fi-sil'i-ti), *n.*

fis-sion (fish'ọn), *n.* [L. *fissio(n-)*, < *findere* (pp. *fissus*), cleave, split: cf. *-fid.*] The act of cleaving or splitting into parts; in *biol.*, the automatic division of a cell or organism into new cells or organisms as a process of reproduction; cell-division; sometimes, splitting or division in general, as of a chromatin granule.

fis-si-pal-mate (fis-i-pal'māt), *a.* [L. *fissus*, pp., cleft (see *fission*), + *palma*, palm: cf. *palmate.*] Semipalmate.

fis-sip-a-rous (fi-sip'ạ-rus), *a.* [L. *fissus*, pp., cleft (see *fission*), + *parere*, bring forth.] Reproducing by fission. — **fis-sip'a-rism** (-rizm), **fis-si-par-i-ty** (fis-i-par'i-ti), *n.*

fis-si-ros-tral (fis-i-ros'trạl), *a.* [L. *fissus*, pp., cleft (see *fission*), + *rostrum*, beak.] Having a broad, deeply cleft beak or bill, as the swallows, goatsuckers, and other birds; of the bill, deeply cleft. See cut in preceding column.

Fissirostral Bill of Goatsucker.

fis-sle (fis'l), *v. i.*; *-sled, -sling.* [Imit.] To rustle; also, to fidget. [Prov. Eng. and Sc.]

fis-sure (fish'ụr), *n.* [L. *fissura*, < *findere*: see *fission.*] A narrow opening produced by cleavage, or separation of parts; a cleft; also, the act of cleaving, or the state of being cleft; cleavage.—**fis'sure,** *v. t.* or *i.*; *-sured, -suring.* To make fissures in, or open in fissures; cleave; split.

fist[1] (fīst), *n.* See *fice.*

fist[2] (fist), *n.* [AS. *fȳst* = D. *vuist* = G. *faust*, fist.] The hand closed tightly, with the fingers doubled into the palm, as for the purpose of striking, or in order to grasp or hold something; also, the hand (now colloq.); also, a person's handwriting (now colloq.); in *printing*, the index sign (☞).—**fist**[2], *v. t.* To strike with the fist (as, "The boy would *fist* me hard": Tennyson's "Harold," i. 1); also, to grasp with the fist (as, "We have been down together . . . *fisting* each other's throat": Shakspere's "Coriolanus," iv. 5. 131).—**fist'ed,** *a.* Having fists: as, hard-*fisted.*—**fis'tic,** *a.* Of or pertaining to the fists; pugilistic. [Colloq.]

fis-ti-cuff (fis'ti-kuf), *n.* A cuff or blow with the fist; *pl.*, combat with the fists.—**fis'ti-cuff,** *v. t.* or *i.* To strike or fight with the fists.—**fis'ti-cuff-er,** *n.*

fis-tle (fis'l), *v. i.* See *fissle.*

fis-tu-la (fis'ṭụ-lạ̈), *n.*; pl. *-las* or *-læ* (-lē). [L., pipe, tube, reed, ulcer: cf. *fester.*] A reed or pipe; a tube; in *pathol.*, a narrow passage or duct formed by disease or injury, as one leading from an abscess to a free surface, or one forming an abnormal means of communication with some normal cavity; in *vet. science*, any of various suppurative inflammations, as in the withers of a horse.—**fis'tu-lar** (-lạ̈r), **fis'tu-lous,** *a.* Tube-like; tubular; also, containing tubes or tube-like parts; in *pathol.*, pertaining to or of the nature of a fistula.

fit[1] (fit), *n.* [AS. *fitt*, fight, struggle.] A sudden, acute attack or manifestation of a disease (as, a *fit* of gout, ague, or colic); also, a sudden morbid seizure characterized by loss of consciousness or by convulsions (as, a fainting-*fit*; an apoplectic *fit*; epileptic *fits*; to fall down in a *fit*); also, an attack of any physical disturbance (as, a *fit* of coughing, sneezing, or nosebleed); fig., an access, spell, or period of emotion or feeling, inclination, activity, idleness, etc.—**by fits, or by fits and starts,** by irregular spells; fitfully; intermittently.

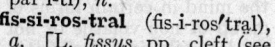

fit[2] (fit), *a.*; compar. *fitter*, superl. *fittest.* [ME. *fyt*; origin uncertain: cf. *feat*[2].] Well adapted or suited by nature or character, as for a purpose, use, or occasion (as, a *fit* choice, plan, or opportunity; berries *fit* for food, or *fit* to be eaten; those *fittest* to survive in the struggle for existence); suitable; meet; often, suitable on grounds of propriety or right, worthy, or deserving (as, a story not *fit* to be repeated; *fit* to be hanged; not *fit* to live); proper, becoming, or right as a course of action (as, to do as one sees or thinks *fit*; "Is it *fit* to say to a king, Thou art wicked?" Job, xxxiv. 18); also, suitable by reason of qualifications, abilities, etc., as for a position, office, or function; qualified or competent; also, in a suitable condition, prepared, or ready (as, crops *fit* for gathering; men *fit* for active service); in good physical condition, as an athlete, a race-horse, military troops, etc.; hence, in general, in good health (colloq.); also, in a condition, ready, or inclined, to do something specified (now chiefly colloq.: as, to be *fit* to explode with wrath); also, of the right size or shape, as a garment†.—**fit**[2], *v.*; *fitted, fitting.* **I.** *tr.* To be adapted or suited to (a purpose, object, occasion, etc.); be suitable or meet for; accord with; also, to be proper, becoming, or right for (as, "It *fitteth* not a prelate so to plead": Shakspere's "1 Henry VI.," iii. 1. 57); become; befit; also, to be of the right size or shape for (as, garments that *fit* the wearer; a key that *fits* the lock); conform to in a specified way in adjustment (as, this coat *fits* the figure loosely); also, to adapt or suit to a purpose, object, etc. (as, "We'll *fit* him to our turn": Shakspere's "Taming of the Shrew," iii. 2. 134); also, to render qualified or competent (as, qualities that *fit* one for leadership; his learning *fits* him to speak on the subject); also, to bring to a suitable condition, or prepare (as, this school *fits* students for college); also, to conform, adjust, or apply with exact conformity, to something (as, to *fit* a dress to the figure; to *fit* a ring to the finger or a cork to a bottle); put (*in, into, on, over, together,* etc.) with nice adjustment; also, to supply suitably with something specified (as, to *fit* one with gloves; to *fit* a door with a new handle); provide, furnish, or equip; furnish with clothing, equipments, furniture, fixtures, or other requisites (usually with *out* or *up*: as, to *fit* out a person for a hunting trip; to *fit* up a house). **II.** *intr.* To be fit or suitable (now chiefly as in *fitting, p. a.*); accord or agree (*with*)†; also, to be proper, becoming, or right (now chiefly as in *fitting, p. a.*); also, to be of the right size or shape, as a garment for the wearer or any object or part for a thing to which it is applied; conform (*to*) when worn or applied (as "Gown'd in pure white, that *fitted* to the shape . . . she stood": Tennyson's "Gardener's Daughter," 125); go (*in, into, on,* etc.) with nice adjustment.—**fit**², *n.* The process or a process of fitting, adapting, preparing, adjusting, etc.; also, the manner in which a thing fits (as, the fit of a coat; the *fit* of a wheel on the axle; a loose, tight, poor, or perfect *fit*); often, a good or satisfactory manner of fitting; also, something that fits in a manner indicated (as, the coat is a poor *fit*; the ring is a good *fit*); often, something that fits well (as, this coat is a *fit*).

fit³, **fytte** (fit), *n.* [AS. *fitt.*] A division of a song, poem, or story. [Archaic.]

fitch¹ (fich), *n.* Same as *vetch.* [Now prov.]

fitch² (fich), *n.* [MD. *fisse, visse, vitsche,* polecat: cf. *fitchew.*] The European polecat, *Putorius fœtidus,* or its fur; also, a fitch-brush.—**fitch′=brush,** *n.* A small brush made of the hair of the fitch, or sometimes of the hog: used for painting, etc.—**fitch′et** (-et), *n.* Same as *fitch*².

fitch-ew (fich′ö), *n.* [OF. *fichau,* also *fissel,* a dim. form connected with MD. *fisse, visse*: see *fitch*².] The fitch, or European polecat; also, its fur.

fit-ful (fit′fůl), *a.* Characterized by or occurring in fits or occasional attacks, as a disease (archaic: as, "After life's *fitful* fever he sleeps well," Shakspere's "Macbeth," iii. 2. 23); hence, in general, coming, appearing, acting, etc., by spells (as, *fitful* gusts, gleams, or sounds; *fitful* conversation; *fitful* impulses or zeal); irregularly intermittent.—**fit′ful-ly,** *adv.*—**fit′ful-ness,** *n.*

fit-ly (fit′li), *adv.* In a fit manner; also, at a fit time.

fit-ment (fit′mẹnt), *n.* That with which something is fitted or furnished; dress† or equipment† (see Shakspere's "Cymbeline," v. 5. 409); a fitting, fixture, or the like, as of a house (often in *pl.*); also, that which is fitting for one† (see Shakspere's "Pericles," iv. 6. 6).

fit-ness (fit′nes), *n.* The state or quality of being fit.

fit-ter (fit′ėr), *n.* One who or that which fits; one who fits articles of dress on persons; one who fits together or adjusts the parts of machinery; one who supplies and fixes fittings or fixtures (as, a gas-*fitter*); one who furnishes or equips with whatever is necessary for some purpose.

fit-ters (fit′ėrz), *n. pl.* [Origin obscure: cf. *flitters* and *fritter*².] Fragments; bits; shreds. [Obs. or prov. Eng.]

fit-ting (fit′ing), *n.* The act of one who or that which fits; also, anything with which something is fitted by way of furnishing, equipping, completing, etc.; *pl.,* furnishings, fixtures, or the like (as, *fittings* for an office; gas-*fittings*).—**fit′ting,** *p. a.* That fits; suitable or appropriate; proper or becoming.—**fit′ting-ly,** *adv.*—**fit′ting-ness,** *n.*

fitz (fits), *n.* [AF., for OF. *fiz, filz* (F. *fils*), < L. *filius,* son.] A son: now occurring only as an element in certain surnames, as *Fitzgerald* ('son of Gerald'). Some such surnames were given specifically to illegitimate sons and daughters of kings or princes: as, Henry *Fitzroy* ('son of the king'), son of Charles II. and the Countess of Castlemaine; Lady Mary *Fitzclarence,* daughter of the Duke of Clarence (afterward William IV.) and Mrs. Jordan.

five (fīv), *a.* [AS. *fīf* = D. *vijf* = G. *fünf* = Icel. *fimm* = Goth. *fimf,* five; akin to L. *quinque,* Gr. πέντε, Skt. *pañca,* five.] One more than four.—**Five Nations,** a powerful confederacy of Iroquoian Indians comprising the Mohawks, Oneidas, Onondagas, Cayugas, and Senecas, prominent in American history.—**five,** *n.* A number composed of five units, or a symbol, as 5 or v, representing it; a set of five persons or things; a playing-card, die-face, etc., with five pips.—**five′fin″ger** (-fing″gėr), *n.* Any of certain species of potentilla with leaves of five leaflets, as *Potentilla canadensis*; also, the Virginia creeper, *Parthenocissus quinquefolia*; also, a starfish with five rays.—**five′fold** (-fōld). **I.** *a.* Comprising five parts or members; five times as great or as much. **II.** *adv.* In fivefold measure.—**five-pence** (fiv′pẹns or fip′ẹns), *n.* A sum of money of the value of five English pennies, or about 10 U. S. cents.—**five-pen-ny** (fiv′pẹ-ni or fip′ẹ-ni), *a.* Of the amount or value of fivepence.—**fiv-er** (fī′vėr), *n.* A five-dollar bill or a five-pound note; also, anything that counts as five. [Colloq.]—**fives** (fīvz), *n.* [Orig. pl. of *five, n.*] An English game, of two varieties, similar to handball.—**fives′=court,** *n.* A court where the game of fives is played.

fix (fiks), *v.* [L. *fixus,* pp. of *figere,* fix, fasten, drive in, pierce.] **I.** *tr.* To make fast, firm, or stable; place, attach, or insert so as to secure against displacement (as, to *fix* bayonets, to attach them to the end of the barrel of muskets or rifles); fasten; fig., to implant firmly, as principles, etc.; put or place (responsibility, blame, etc.) on a person; also, to make constant or steadfast; render unchangeable in purpose or conviction (as, "I am *fix'd,* not to part hence without him": Milton's "Samson Agonistes," 1481); also, to direct (the eyes, the attention, etc.) steadily or unwaveringly; look at with a steady gaze (as, to *fix* a person with one's eyes); attract and hold (the eye, the attention, etc.); render set or rigid, as the countenance in death; hold spellbound; also, to render (a substance, dye, color, etc.) stable or more permanent by decreasing or destroying its volatility, fluidity, solubility, softness, or the like, through chemical combination, cold, etc.; make (a photographic negative, positive, image, etc.) permanent by chemical treatment, etc.; also, to place definitely and more or less permanently; set or station; install (a person) in a position; establish (a person) in a place of residence; also, to assign or refer to a definite place, time, etc.; settle definitely, or determine (as, to *fix* the amount of an appropriation); settle or determine the form of (a language, etc.); put into permanent form (as, to *fix* one's thoughts on paper); also, to put into due condition; put in order; adjust or arrange; repair; also, to arrange matters with, or with respect to, esp. privately or dishonestly, so as to secure favorable action (colloq.: as, to *fix* a jury; to *fix* a series of baseball games); also, to put in a condition or position to make no further trouble (colloq.); get even with (colloq.). **II.** *intr.* To become fixed; become firmly attached or implanted; become steadily directed, as the eyes or the attention; become set, as the features; assume a rigid or solid form; become stable or permanent; also, to settle down; take up a position, esp. a permanent one; also, to settle one's choice, or decide (*on* or *upon*: as, to *fix* on a time).—**fix,** *n.* A position from which it is difficult to escape; a predicament; a bad plight: as, "If we get left on this wreck we are in a *fix*" (Mark Twain's "Huckleberry Finn," xiii.).—**fix′a-ble,** *a.* Capable of being fixed.

fix-ate (fik′sāt), *v.*; *-ated, -ating.* [Appar. a back-formation from *fixation.*] **I.** *tr.* To fix; render stable, as a sensation; determine the position of, as a star. **II.** *intr.* To become fixed.

fix-a-tion (fik-sā′shọn), *n.* [ME., < ML. *fixatio(n-),* < *fixare,* freq. of L. *figere*: see *fix.*] The act of fixing, or the state of being fixed; establishment in a fixed, stable, or permanent position or condition; reduction from a volatile or fluid to a stable or solid form; a rendering fast or unfading, as of colors.—**fix-a-tive** (fik′sạ-tiv). **I.** *a.* Serving to fix; making fixed or permanent. **II.** *n.* A fixative substance, as a mordant for fixing colors.

fixed (fikst), *p. a.* Made fast or firm; firmly implanted (as, a *fixed* idea: see below); set or intent upon something, as the mind; steadily directed, as the gaze; set or rigid, as the countenance in death; non-volatile, or not easily volatilized (as, a *fixed* oil: see below); rendered stable or permanent, as color; definitely and permanently placed, or stationary (as, the *fixed* stars: see *star, n.*); definitely assigned or appointed, or not fluctuating or varying (as, *fixed* charges); put in order; arranged with, or arranged, privately or dishonestly (colloq.).—**fixed idea,** a persistent or obsessing idea, often delusional, which the subject cannot escape; specif., a delusional idea which dominates the mind in certain forms of insanity.—**fixed oil,** any of a group of non-volatile or not easily volatilized natural oils, as lard-oil, linseed-oil, etc., occurring in the cellular membranes, etc., of animals, and in the seeds, capsules, etc., of plants.—**fix-ed-ly** (fik′sed-li), *adv.*—**fix′ed-ness,** *n.*

fix-er (fik′sėr), *n.* One who or that which fixes.—**fix′ing,** *n.* The act of one who or that which fixes; the process by which anything is fixed; *pl.* (colloq.), appliances; trimmings.

fix-i-ty (fik′si-ti), *n.*; pl. *-ties* (-tiz). [= F. *fixité.*] The state or quality of being fixed; stability; permanence; also, something fixed.

fix-ture (fiks′ṭūr), *n.* [For *fixure.*] The act of fixing, or the state of being fixed (now rare); also, something securely fixed in position; an appendage, or part of the equipment, of a house, etc., permanently attached to it (as, a gas-*fixture*); also, a person or thing long established in the same place or position; also, a fixed or appointed time or event, as a date set for a race, or the race itself; in *law*, a personal chattel annexed to real property.

fix-ure (fik′ṣūr), *n.* [LL. *fixura*, < L. *figere*: see *fix.*] Fixed position or condition. See Shakspere's "Troilus and Cressida," i. 3. 101. [Obs. or archaic.]

fiz-gig (fiz′gig), *n.* [Cf. *fizz* and *gig*¹.] A frivolous, gadding girl or woman (as, "My husband . . . prefers to me . . . this *fizgig* called Fifine!" Browning's "Fifine at the Fair," xxxiii.); also, a kind of hissing firework; also, a fish-spear.

fizz, fiz (fiz), *v. i.* [Imit.] To make a hissing or sputtering sound.—**fizz, fiz,** *n.* A hissing sound; effervescence; spirit or go (colloq.); an effervescent drink, as champagne (colloq.).

fiz-zle (fiz′l), *v. i.*; *-zled, -zling.* [Imit.: cf. *fizz* and *fissle.*] To make a hissing or sputtering sound, esp. one that dies out weakly; hence (colloq.), to fail ignominiously after a more or less brilliant start; come to a lame conclusion; fail.—**fiz′zle,** *n.* A fizzling, hissing, or sputtering (as, "The chicken and ham had a cheerful and joyous *fizzle* in the pan": Mrs. Stowe's "Uncle Tom's Cabin," xiii.); also (colloq.), a fiasco; a failure.

fiz-zy (fiz′i), *a.*; compar. *fizzier*, superl. *fizziest.* That fizzes; fizzing.

fjeld (fyeld), *n.* [Norw.: cf. *fell*⁵.] A high, almost barren plateau on the Scandinavian range.

fjord (fyôrd), *n.* See *fiord.*

flab-ber-gast (flab′ėr-gast), *v. t.* [Origin obscure: cf. *flabby* or *flap* and *aghast.*] To overcome with surprise and bewilderment; astound: as, "The aldermen . . . were what is sometimes emphatically styled *flabbergasted*; they were speechless from bewilderment" (Disraeli's "Coningsby," v. 3). [Colloq.]

flab-by (flab′i), *a.*; compar. *flabbier*, superl. *flabbiest.* [For earlier *flappy*, < *flap.*] Hanging loosely or limply, as flesh, muscles, etc., or having such flesh, as persons or animals; flaccid; fig., lacking firmness, force, pith, etc., as character or persons, principles, utterances, etc.; feeble.—**flab′bi-ly,** *adv.*—**flab′bi-ness,** *n.*

fla-bel-late (flạ-bel′āt), *a.* [See *flabellum.*] Fan-shaped. Also **fla-bel′li-form** (-bel′i-fôrm).

fla-bel-lum (flạ-bel′um), *n.*; pl. *flabella* (-ạ̈). [L., fan, < *flare*, blow.] A fan, esp. one used in religious ceremonies; also, a fan-shaped part.

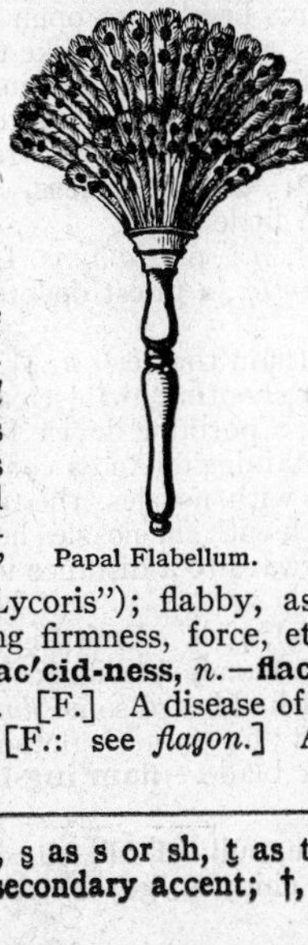

Papal Flabellum.

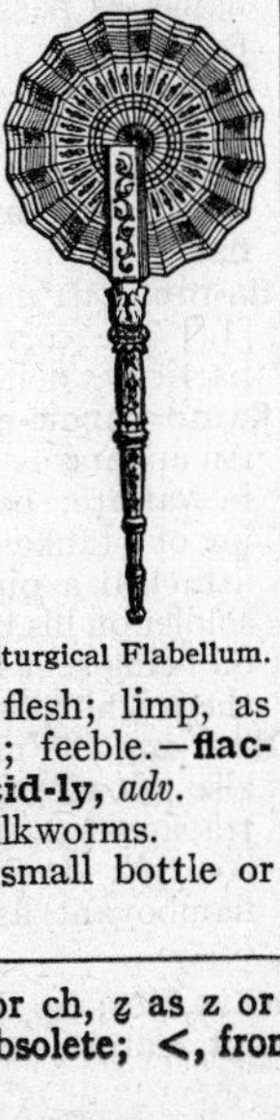

Liturgical Flabellum.

flac-cid (flak′sid), *a.* [L. *flaccidus*, < *flaccus*, flabby.] Drooping or hanging loosely, as from want of stiffness or firmness of substance (as, a balloon becomes *flaccid* with the escape of its gas; "*Flaccid* threads of ivy, in the still And sultry air, depending motionless," Wordsworth's "To Lycoris"); flabby, as flesh; limp, as garments; fig., lacking firmness, force, etc.; feeble.—**flac-cid′i-ty** (-sid′i-ti), **flac′cid-ness,** *n.*—**flac′cid-ly,** *adv.*

flache-rie (flȧsh-rē), *n.* [F.] A disease of silkworms.

fla-con (flȧ-kôṅ), *n.* [F.: see *flagon.*] A small bottle or flask with a stopper.

flag¹ (flag), *v.*; *flagged, flagging.* [Appar. a later form of ME. *flacken*, flap, flutter, = Icel. *flaka*, flap, hang loose.] **I.** *intr.* To hang loosely or limply, as sails, wings, etc.; become limp or flaccid; droop, as plants; hence, to fall off in vigor, energy, activity, etc. (as, dogs *flagging* in the chase; the conversation *flags*; the zeal, attention, or imagination *flags*); grow languid; slacken; fail, as the spirits; fall off in interest, as a diversion. **II.** *tr.* To droop (the wings, etc.)†; also, to cause or allow to fall off in vigor, activity, etc. (obs. or archaic).

flag² (flag), *n.* [= D. *vlag* = Dan. *flag* = Sw. *flagg* = G. *flagge*; appar. recorded first in Eng.: cf. *flag*¹.] A piece of cloth, commonly bunting, of varying size, shape, color, and device, usually attached by one edge to a staff or cord, and used as an ensign, standard, symbol, signal, etc. (as, the *flag* of a nation, state, or city; a military or naval *flag*; a Red Cross *flag*; the *flag* of a yacht club; a danger *flag*; a weather *flag*; the black *flag* of pirates; the red *flag* of socialists; the white *flag*, used in token of truce, surrender, etc.; the yellow *flag* of quarantine); also, something resembling a flag, as the tail of a deer or of a setter dog.—**Flag Day,** June 14, as the anniversary of the day (June 14, 1777) when Congress adopted the Stars and Stripes as the national emblem of the United States of America: now widely observed with patriotic exercises.—**flag of truce,** *milit.*, a white flag displayed as an invitation to the enemy to confer, or carried as a sign of peaceful intention by one sent to communicate with the enemy.—**flag**², *v. t.*; *flagged, flagging.* To place a flag or flags over or on; decorate with flags; also, to signal or warn (a person, etc.), or communicate (information), by means of a flag; also, to decoy, as game, by waving a flag or the like to excite attention or curiosity.

flag³ (flag), *n.* [ME. *flagge*; origin uncertain.] Any of various plants with long, sword-shaped leaves, as the sweet-flag (which see) or, esp., a plant of the genus *Iris*, as *I. versicolor* or *I. prismatica* (both known as 'blue flag'); also, the long, slender leaf of such a plant or of a cereal.

flag⁴ (flag), *n.* [ME. *flagge*, a turf: cf. Icel. *flag*, spot where a turf has been cut out, *flaga*, flag or slab of stone.] A flat slab of stone used for paving, etc.; a flagstone; *pl.*, a walk paved with such slabs.—**flag**⁴, *v. t.*; *flagged, flagging.* To lay or pave with flags.

fla-gel-la (flạ-jel′ạ̈), *n.* Plural of *flagellum.*

flag-el-lant (flaj′e-lạnt). [L. *flagellans* (*-ant-*), ppr. of *flagellare*: see *flagellate*².] **I.** *a.* Flagellating; scourging. **II.** *n.* One who flagellates; usually, one who flagellates or scourges himself for religious discipline; esp. [*l. c.* or *cap.*], one of a medieval European sect of fanatics that practised scourging in public.

flag-el-late¹ (flaj′e-lāt), *a.* [See *flagellum.*] Having flagella; also, flagelliform.

flag-el-late² (flaj′e-lāt), *v. t.*; *-lated, -lating.* [L. *flagellatus*, pp. of *flagellare*, < *flagellum*, a whip, scourge: see *flagellum.*] To whip; scourge; flog; lash.—**flag-el-la′tion** (-lā′shọn), *n.*—**flag′el-la-tor,** *n.*

fla-gel-li-form (flạ-jel′i-fôrm), *a.* [L. *flagellum*, a whip: see *-form.*] Long, slender, and flexible, like the lash of a whip.

fla-gel-lum (flạ-jel′um), *n.*; pl. *flagella* (-ạ̈). [L., a whip, scourge, dim. of *flagrum*, a whip.] A whip or lash; in *bot.*, a runner; in *biol.*, a long, lash-like appendage serving as an organ of locomotion in certain reproductive bodies, bacteria, protozoa, etc.

flag-eo-let (flaj-ọ-let′ or flaj′ọ-let), *n.* [F., dim. of OF. *flageol*, *flajol*, flute.] A small wind-instrument of the flute type, having a tubular mouthpiece at one end, six or more holes, and sometimes keys.

Flageolet.

flag-ging¹ (flag′ing), *p. a.* Drooping; failing.

flag-ging² (flag′ing), *n.* Flagstones collectively; a pavement of flagstones.

flag-gy¹ (flag′i), *a.* Flagging; drooping; limp.

flag-gy² (flag′i), *a.* Abounding in, consisting of, or resembling the plants called flags.

flag-gy³ (flag′i), *a.* Pertaining to flags or flagstone; having a structure like flagstone; laminate.

flag-i-tate (flaj′i-tāt), *v. t.*; *-tated, -tating.* [L. *flagitatus*, pp. of *flagitare*, demand, entreat, akin to *flagrare*, burn: see *flagrant.*] To entreat earnestly; importune. [Obs. or rare.]

fla-gi-tious (flạ-jish′us), *a.* [L. *flagitiosus*, < *flagitium*, a shameful act or thing.] Shamefully wicked, as persons, actions, life, character, times, etc.; heinous or flagrant, as crime; infamous.—**fla-gi′tious-ly,** *adv.*—**fla-gi′tious-ness,** *n.*

flag-man (flag′mạn), *n.*; pl. *-men.* One who has charge of or carries a flag; one who signals with a flag, as at a railroad-crossing.

flag=of-fi-cer (flag′of″i-sėr), *n.* A naval officer, as an admiral, vice-admiral, or rear-admiral, entitled to display a flag indicating his rank; an officer in command of a fleet, squadron, or group of ships.

flag-on (flag′ọn), *n.* [OF. F. *flacon*, < ML. *flasco(n-)*: see *flask.*] A large bottle for wine, etc.; also, a vessel for holding liquids, as for use at table, esp. one with a handle, a spout, and usually a cover.

fla-grant (flā′grạnt), *a.* [L. *flagrans* (*flagrant-*), ppr. of *flagrare*, blaze, burn, akin to Gr. φλέγειν, burn.] Blazing, burning, or glowing (now rare: as, a *flagrant* brand); fig., ardent or fervent (now rare: as, "He burns with most intense and *flagrant* zeal To serve his country," Cowper's "Task," iii. 794); also, glaring, notorious, or scandalous, as an offense or an offender (as, "You're an old, *flagrant* heathen": Synge's "Tinker's Wedding," i.); conspicuous in a reprehensible way; also, actually going on, or in progress (a Latinism: as, in *flagrant* war, L. *flagrante bello*); also, red from blows† (as, "*flagrant* from the scourge": Pope's "Dunciad," ii. 148).—**fla′grance, fla′gran-cy,** *n.*—**fla′grant-ly,** *adv.*

flag=ship (flag′ship), *n.* The ship which bears the flag-officer of a fleet, squadron, or the like, and displays his flag.

flag-staff (flag′ståf), *n.* A staff or pole on which a flag is displayed.

flag=sta-tion (flag′stā″shọn), *n.* A railroad-station where trains stop only when a signal is displayed.

flag-stone (flag′stōn), *n.* A flat slab of stone used for paving, etc.; a flag; *pl.*, a walk paved with such slabs; *sing.*, rock, such as sandstone, shale, etc., which can be split up into such slabs.

flail (flāl), *n.* [ME. *flegl, flayel*, in part through OF. *flaiel* (F. *fléau*), < LL. *flagellum*, flail, L. whip, scourge: see *flagellum.*] An instrument for threshing grain by hand, consisting of a staff or handle to one end of which is attached a freely swinging stick or bar; also, a weapon resembling this in construction or action.—**flail,** *v. t.* To strike with or as with a flail; thresh.

flair (flãr), *n.* [F., < *flairer*, smell, scent, OF. *flairier*, emit an odor, < L. *fragrare*: see *fragrant*, and cf. *flavor.*] Power of detecting as by smell; scent; keen perception.

flak (flak), *n.* Anti-aircraft fire.

flake[1] (flāk), *n.* [ME. *flake, fleke*: cf. Icel. *flaki, fleki*, hurdle, wickerwork shield, = D. *vlaak*, hurdle.] A hurdle (prov. Eng. and Sc.); also, a frame, as for drying fish.

flake[2] (flāk), *n.* [ME. *flake*: cf. Icel. *flōki*, felt, hair, wool, and E. *flock*[2], also *flaw*[2] and *flay*[2].] A small, loosely cohering piece or mass, as of falling snow or of cloud; a small detached bit of burning matter; a scale, or a small, flat exfoliated particle; a thin piece split off from the surface of anything; a stratum or layer; a loose sheet of ice; a lock of hair (archaic); among florists, a carnation whose petals have a white or yellow ground marked by stripes of a single color (as, a purple *flake*, one striped with purple).—**flake**[2], *v.*; *flaked, flaking.* **I.** *intr.* To fall in flakes, as snow; fall like flakes of snow; also, to peel off or separate in flakes. **II.** *tr.* To cover with or as with flakes of snow; fleck; also, to form into flakes; also, to remove in flakes; also, to break flakes or chips from.—**flak-er** (flā′kėr), *n.* One who or that which flakes; esp., one who strikes off flakes of flint for use in flintlocks.—**flake′=white′,** *n.* Pure white lead in the form of flakes or scales, used as a pigment.—**flak′y,** *a.*; compar. *flakier*, superl. *flakiest.* Consisting of flakes; also, lying, or cleaving off, in flakes or layers; flake-like.—**flak′i-ly,** *adv.*—**flak′i-ness,** *n.*

flam[1] (flam), *n.* [Origin uncertain: cf. *flimflam.*] A fanciful notion or composition†; also (now prov. or colloq.), a fabrication or falsehood; a deception or trick; a humbug (as, "They told me . . . about liberty and property . . . and I find it is all a *flam*": Godwin's "Caleb Williams," xxvi.).—**flam**[1], *v. t.*; *flammed, flamming.* To deceive by a flam; delude; cheat. [Now prov. or colloq.]

flam[2] (flam), *n.* [Prob. imit.] A drum-beat made by striking the drum with the two sticks almost at the same instant, but so as to produce separate sounds.

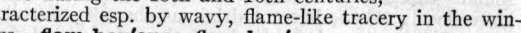

Bronze Flambeau, Florence.

flam-beau (flam′bō), *n.*; pl. *-beaux* (-bōz). [F., < OF. *flambe*: see *flame.*] A flaming torch; a torch for use at night in illuminations, processions, etc.; also, a large decorated candlestick, as of bronze.

flam-boy-ant (flam-boi′ạnt), *a.* [F., ppr. of *flamboyer*, to flame, flare, < OF. *flambe*: see *flame.*] Flaming, flaring, or gorgeous (as, *flamboyant* red hair; *flamboyant* colors or dress); showily striking (as, "that *flamboyant* but egotistical figure Alexander the Great": H. G. Wells's "Outline of History," xxxiv. § 3); also, florid or ornate (as, *flamboyant* rhetoric); also, of wavy form, like the outline of flame, as the blades of some swords; in *arch.*, noting or pertaining to the highly ornate Gothic style prevalent in France during the 15th and 16th centuries, characterized esp. by wavy, flame-like tracery in the windows.—**flam-boy′ance, flam-boy′an-cy,** *n.*—**flam-boy′ant-ly,** *adv.*

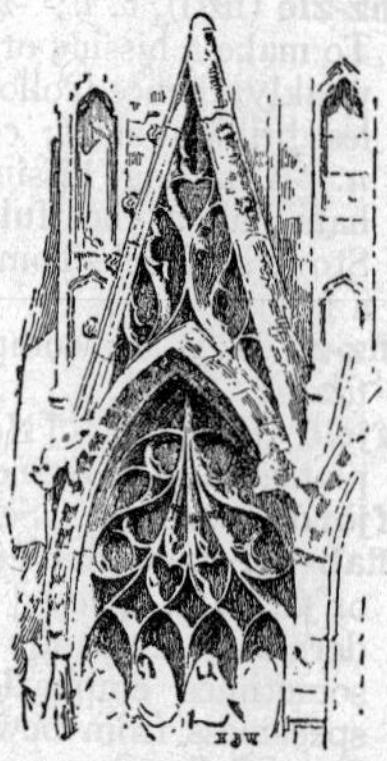
Flamboyant Tracery, Rouen Cathedral, Normandy.

flame (flām), *n.* [OF. *flame, flambe* (F. *flamme*), < L. *flamma*, flame, perhaps akin to *flagrare*, blaze, burn: see *flagrant.*] Burning gas or vapor, as from wood, etc., undergoing combustion; a portion of ignited gas or vapor; *pl.*, with *the*, fire, with reference to destruction or death by burning (as, to commit a thing to the *flames*; condemned to the *flames*); also, *sing.* or *pl.*, the state or condition of blazing combustion (as, to set in *flame*; to burst into *flames*); hence, any flame-like condition; glow; inflamed condition; also, *sing.*, something resembling flame or a flame; bright light (as, "The moon began To show her silver *flame*": Longfellow's "Spanish Student," iii. 5); a beam of light; bright coloring; a streak or patch of color; also, fig., heat or ardor, as of zeal or passion; a burning feeling of love (as, "Ah youth ungrateful to a *flame* like mine!" Pope's "Sappho to Phaon," 20); hence, an object of the passion of love (as, she was an old *flame* of his).—**flame,** *v.*; *flamed, flaming.* [OF. *flamer*, < L. *flammare*, < *flamma.*] **I.** *intr.* To burn with a flame or flames; burst into flames; blaze; fig., to burn as with flame, as passion; break into open anger, indignation, etc. (with *out* or *up*); also, to glow like flame; shine brilliantly; flash. **II.** *tr.* To burn†; also, to inflame†; also, to subject to the action of flame or fire; also, to send forth by flaming.—**flame′=col″or,** *n.* A vivid reddish-orange color.—**flame′=col″ored,** *a.*—**flame′less,** *a.* Without flame.—**flame′let,** *n.* A little flame.

fla-men (flā′men), *n.*; pl. *flamens*, L. *flamines* (flam′i-nēz). [L.] In *Rom. antiq.*, a priest devoted to the service of one particular deity.

flame=throw-er (flām′thrō″ėr), *n.* [Tr. G. *flammenwerfer.*] An apparatus for shooting forth streams of fire at the enemy in warfare; esp., a portable device for this purpose, consisting of a tank containing oil and a compressed gas, to which is attached a pipe with nozzles, the tank being carried by a soldier on his back with the nozzles held in his hands, and the oil being sent forward to a distance in the form of spray and there ignited.

flam-ing (flā′ming), *p. a.* Emitting flames; blazing; fiery; also, glowing like flame; brilliant; very bright; hence, extravagant (as, "I had heard some *flaming* stories of Captain Avery": Defoe's "Captain Singleton," xi.); glaring; also, flamboyant, as a blade.—**flam′ing-ly,** *adv.*

fla-min-go (flą-ming′gō), *n.*; pl. *-gos* or *-goes* (-gōz). [Pg. *flamingo* = Sp. *flamenco*, < L. *flamma*, E. *flame.*] Any of the aquatic birds constituting the genus *Phœnicopterus*, of tropical and semitropical regions, with very long neck and legs, webbed feet, and pinkish to scarlet plumage.

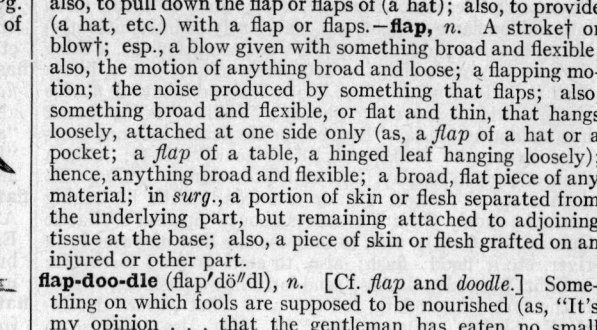

Red Flamingo (*Phœnicopterus ruber*).

flam-ma-ble (flam′ą-bl), *a.* [L. *flammare*, E. *flame*, *v.*] Inflammable.

flam-mu-lat-ed (flam′ū-lā-ted), *a.* [L. *flammula*, dim. of *flamma*, E. *flame.*] In *ornith.*, reddish; ruddy.

flam-y (flā′mi), *a.* Pertaining to, consisting of, or resembling flame: as, "And look! that flash of *flamy* wings, —The fire-plumed oriole!" (Holmes's "After a Lecture on Wordsworth").

flâne-rie (flän-rē), *n.* [F., < *flâner*, stroll, lounge.] Strolling; lounging; idling.—**flâ-neur** (flä-nėr), *n.* [F.] A stroller or lounger; an idler.

flange (flanj), *n.* [Cf. *flank.*] A projecting rim, collar, edge, ridge, or the like, on an object, for keeping it in place, attaching it to another object, strengthening it, etc.—**flange,** *v.*; *flanged, flanging.* **I.** *intr.* To project like, or take the form of, a flange. **II.** *tr.* To furnish with a flange.

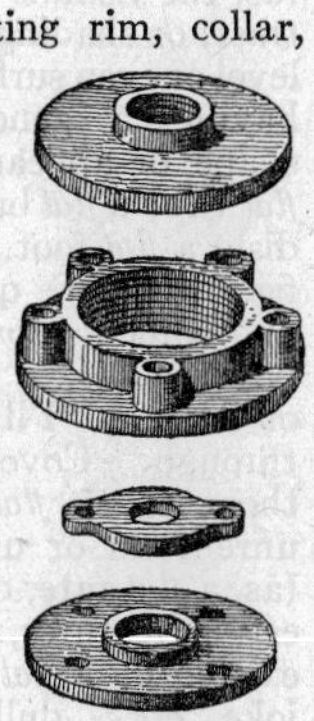

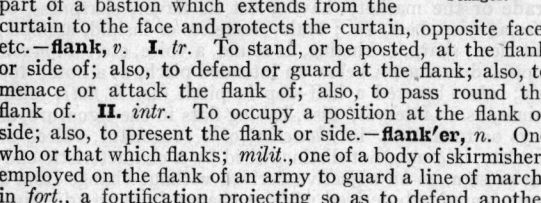

Various forms of Flanges.

flank (flangk), *n.* [OF. F. *flanc*; prob. from Teut.] The side of an animal or a human being between the ribs and hip; the thin piece of flesh constituting this part; also, the side of anything, as of a building; the extreme right or left side of an army or fleet, or of a subdivision of an army or fleet; in *fort.*, the right or left side of a work or fortification; also, a part of a work that defends another work by a fire along the outside of its parapet; esp., the part of a bastion which extends from the curtain to the face and protects the curtain, opposite face, etc.—**flank,** *v.* **I.** *tr.* To stand, or be posted, at the flank or side of; also, to defend or guard at the flank; also, to menace or attack the flank of; also, to pass round the flank of. **II.** *intr.* To occupy a position at the flank or side; also, to present the flank or side.—**flank′er,** *n.* One who or that which flanks; *milit.*, one of a body of skirmishers employed on the flank of an army to guard a line of march; in *fort.*, a fortification projecting so as to defend another work, or to command the flank of an assailing body.

flan-nel (flan′ęl), *n.* [Origin uncertain.] A warm, soft woolen fabric in many varieties, used for clothing, bed-coverings, etc.; a similar fabric made of cotton (as, outing *flannel*, outing cloth; Canton *flannel*, a strong cotton cloth with a long, soft nap, usually on one side only); *pl.*, outer garments made of the woolen fabric, as for boating, tennis, etc.; also, woolen undergarments.—**flan′nel,** *v. t.*; *-neled* or *-nelled*, *-neling* or *-nelling.* To cover or clothe with flannel; also, to rub with flannel: chiefly in *flanneled*, *flannelled*, pp. —**flan-nel-ette′** (-et′), *n.* A light cotton flannel; outing cloth.—**flan′nel-ly,** *a.* Of or like flannel.

flap (flap), *v.*; *flapped, flapping.* [ME. *flappen*; prob. imit.] **I.** *intr.* To strike a sudden blow†; esp., to strike a blow with something broad and flexible; also, to fall or plump down suddenly, esp. with noise (colloq.); also, to swing or sway loosely, as in the wind; make a noise in doing this, as when striking against something else; also, to move up and down, as wings; flap the wings, or make similar movements. **II.** *tr.* To strike with a sudden blow (now prov.); esp., to strike with something broad and flexible (as, "Yet let me *flap* this bug with gilded wings": Pope's "Prologue to the Satires," 309); also, to toss, fold, shut, etc., smartly, roughly, or noisily (colloq.); also, to cause to swing or sway loosely, esp. with noise; also, to move (wings, etc.) up and down; also, to pull down the flap or flaps of (a hat); also, to provide (a hat, etc.) with a flap or flaps.—**flap,** *n.* A stroke† or blow†; esp., a blow given with something broad and flexible; also, the motion of anything broad and loose; a flapping motion; the noise produced by something that flaps; also, something broad and flexible, or flat and thin, that hangs loosely, attached at one side only (as, a *flap* of a hat or a pocket; a *flap* of a table, a hinged leaf hanging loosely); hence, anything broad and flexible; a broad, flat piece of any material; in *surg.*, a portion of skin or flesh separated from the underlying part, but remaining attached to adjoining tissue at the base; also, a piece of skin or flesh grafted on an injured or other part.

flap-doo-dle (flap′dö″dl), *n.* [Cf. *flap* and *doodle.*] Something on which fools are supposed to be nourished (as, "It's my opinion . . . that the gentleman has eaten no small quantity of *flap-doodle*": Marryat's "Peter Simple," xxviii.); food for fools; hence, specious nonsense, bosh, or humbug (as, "a speech, all full of tears and *flapdoodle* about its being a sore trial for him": Mark Twain's "Huckleberry Finn," xxv.). [Colloq.]

flap-drag-on (flap′drag″ǫn), *n.* An old game in which the players snatch raisins, plums, etc., out of burning brandy, and eat them; the object so caught and eaten.

flap=eared (flap′ērd), *a.* Having broad, loose, flapping ears: as, "A . . . *flap-ear'd* knave!" (Shakspere's "Taming of the Shrew," iv. 1. 160).

flap-jack (flap′jak), *n.* [Cf. *slapjack.*] A griddle-cake. See Shakspere's "Pericles," ii. 1. 87.

flap=mouthed (flap′mouᴛʜd), *a.* Having loose, hanging lips, as a dog. See Shakspere's "Venus and Adonis," 920.

flap-per (flap′ėr), *n.* One who or that which flaps; something broad and flat for striking with, or for making a noise by striking; something flat and loose; a broad fin or flipper; the hand (slang); a young bird, esp. a wild duck, when first trying its wings or just able to fly; a young, half-grown girl, often one who is extreme in dress, speech, etc. (colloq.).

flare (flãr), *v.*; *flared, flaring.* [Origin uncertain.] **I.** *intr.* To spread or stream out, as the hair, head-dress, etc.† (as, "Quaint in green she shall be loose enrobed, With ribands pendent, *flaring* 'bout her head": Shakspere's "Merry Wives of Windsor," iv. 6. 42); also, to burn with an unsteady, swaying flame, as a torch or candle in the wind; blaze with a sudden burst of flame, as a fire or something burning (often with *up*); flame; fig., to start up or burst out in sudden, fierce activity, passion, etc. (usually with *up* or *out*: as, the persecutions *flared* up afresh; to *flare* up or out in anger); also, to shine or glow like flame (as, "The blood-red light of dawn *Flared* on her face": Tennyson's "Lancelot and Elaine," 1019); be glaringly bright or showy (used esp. as in *flaring*, *p. a.*); also, to spread gradually outward in form toward the edge or rim, as the bell-shaped end of a trumpet or the walls of a basin; incline outward from a perpendicular, as a ship's sides or bows. **II.** *tr.* To spread out (the hair)†; also, to wave or flourish (something) in the air; display conspicuously or ostentatiously; also, to cause (a candle, etc.) to burn with a swaying flame; signal by flares of fire or light; light up (the sky, etc.) as with flame; also, to cause (something) to spread gradually outward in form.—**flare,** *n.* The act or the effect of flaring; a flaring or swaying flame or light, as of torches in the wind; a sudden blaze or burst of flame; a sudden blaze of fire or light used as a signal or for illumination or guidance, or a combustible for burning to produce such a blaze; fig., a sudden burst, as of zeal or of temper; also, glaring brightness or show; glare; also, a gradual spread outward in form; in *photog.*, a spot of light (as the image of the diaphragm) cast by the lens of a camera on the plate, etc.—**flare′=back,** *n.* A blast of flame which sometimes issues from the breech of a large gun or cannon when it is opened after firing; fig., an outburst of something coming back (as, a *flare-back* of winter).—**flare′=up,** *n.* A sudden flaring up of flame or light; fig., a sudden outburst of anger (colloq.).—**flar-ing** (flãr′ing), *p. a.* That flares; flaming; glaringly bright or showy; spreading gradually outward in form.—**flar′ing-ly,** *adv.*

flash (flash), *v.* [ME. *flaschen*; prob. imit.] **I.** *intr.* To dash or splash, as the sea or waves (now rare: as, "The tortured wave . . . Now *flashes* o'er the scattered fragments,"

(variable) ḑ as d or j, ș as s or sh, ţ as t or ch, ẓ as z or zh; *o*, F. cloche; ü, F. menu; ċh, Sc. loch; ṅ, F. bonbon; **′**, primary accent; **″**, secondary accent; †, obsolete; <, from; +, and; =, equals. See also lists at beginning of book.

Thomson's "Seasons," Summer, 601); also, to break forth into sudden flame or light, esp. transiently or intermittently; hence, to burst suddenly into view or perception (as, a thing *flashes* upon one's sight, or into one's mind); move like a flash (as, "Bear me to thine abode When desolation *flashes* o'er a world destroyed": Shelley's "Hellas," 956); break into sudden action (as, "Every hour He *flashes* into one gross crime or other": Shakspere's "King Lear," i. 3. 4); make a flash or sudden display (now colloq. or slang). **II.** *tr.* To dash or splash (water: obs. or rare: as, "With his raging armes he rudely *flasht* The waves about," Spenser's "Faerie Queene," ii. 6. 42); also, to increase the flow of water in (a river, etc.); flood; flush; also, to emit or send forth (fire or light) in sudden flashes; send forth like a flash (as, "Stern is the tyrant's mandate, red the gaze That *flashes* desolation": Shelley's "Queen Mab," iii. 145); also, to cause to flash, as powder by ignition or a sword by waving; also, to express or communicate by or as by a flash or flashes; convey by instantaneous communication, as by telegraph; also, to make a sudden or ostentatious display of (slang: as, to *flash* one's roll, that is, of money); in *glass-making,* to cause (a blown globe or mass of glass) to expand into a flat disk; also, to coat (plain glass or a glass object) with a film of colored glass; apply (a film of colored glass) to glass or a glass object; in *arch.*, to protect by flashing (see *flashing*).—**flash,** *n.* A dash or splash of water†; also, an extra volume or rush of water, as that produced by a dam and sluiceway, utilized to float a boat over shoals or for other purposes; the device, as a lock or sluice, used for this purpose; also, a sudden, transitory outburst of flame or light; a sudden blaze instantly disappearing; a gleam; hence, the brief period occupied by a flash of light; an instant; also, a telegraphic despatch (chiefly in journalistic use); also, a sudden, brief outburst or display of joy, wit, etc.; also, ostentatious display (as, "Pedants . . . are apt to decry the writings of a polite author, as *flash* and froth": Addison, in "Spectator," 59); an ostentatious or showy person†; also, the cant or jargon of thieves, vagabonds, etc. (colloq.); also, a preparation for coloring, and giving a factitious strength to, brandy, rum, etc.—**a flash in the pan,** a flashing of the priming in the pan of a flintlock, without discharge of the weapon; fig., a sudden showy or pretentious outburst or effort, without any result.—**flash,** *a.* Showy or ostentatious; vulgarly ostentatious or gaudy; also, counterfeit or sham; also, belonging or pertaining to the class of sporting men; also, belonging to or connected with the class of thieves, vagabonds, etc., or pertaining to the cant or jargon spoken by thieves, etc. [Colloq.]—**flash'=back,** *n.* A representation, in the course of presenting a story by moving pictures, of some event or scene of a previous time; a cut-back.—**flash'=board,** *n.* A board, or one of a series of boards, as on a mill-dam, used to increase the depth or force of a stream of water.—**flash'er,** *n.*—**flash'i-ly,** *adv.* In a flashy manner.—**flash'i-ness,** *n.*—**flash'ing,** *n.* The act of one who or that which flashes; the producing of an artificial flash or flood of water; in *glass-making,* the process or method by which glass is flashed; in *arch.*, pieces of sheet-metal, etc., used to cover and protect certain joints and angles, as where a roof comes in contact with a wall or chimney.—**flash'ing=point,** *n.* The temperature at which a mineral oil or the like gives off inflammable vapor in sufficient quantity to flash, or ignite momentarily, on the application of a flame or spark.—**flash'=light,** *n.* A flash of light, or a light that flashes; a device for giving forth flashes of light, as in a lighthouse or for signaling; a preparation which on ignition emits a brilliant flash of light, as for use in taking photographs at night.—**flash'y,** *a.*; compar. *flashier,* superl. *flashiest.* Flashing with light; fig., sparkling or brilliant, esp. in a superficial way or for the moment; pretentiously smart; showy; often, vulgarly showy, as dress, ornaments, etc., or the wearer; gaudy.

flask (flȧsk), *n.* [F. *flasque,* < It. *fiasca,* < ML. *flasca,* also *flasco(n-), flascus* (see *flagon* and *fiasco*), perhaps < L. *vasculum,* dim. of *vas,* vessel.] A bottle or bottle-shaped vessel, of glass, metal, leather, or other material, esp. one of some special form, as a long-necked, bulbous glass bottle (sometimes protected by wickerwork) for wine, etc., a flat glass or metal bottle for holding a supply of drink, suitable for carrying in the pocket, or a leather or other vessel carried by sportsmen to contain gunpowder; in *founding,* the box or frame holding together the sand, etc., which forms the mold.

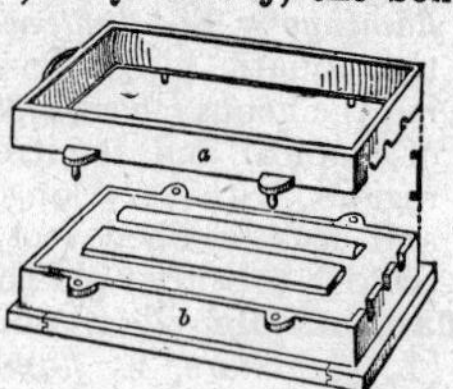

Two-part Molding-flask.—*a,* top part; *b,* bottom part.

flas-ket (flȧs'ket), *n.* [Cf. OF. *flasquet, flachet,* a small flask, also E. *flask.*] A small flask (as, "a *flasket* richly chased": Scott's "Harold the Dauntless," v. 18); also, a long, shallow basket.

flat[1] (flat), *n.* [Var. of obs. *flet,* < AS. *flet,* floor, house, hall; akin to E. *flat*[2].] A floor or story of a building; esp., a floor, or a suite of rooms on one floor, forming a complete residence, as for a family.

flat[2] (flat), *a.*; compar. *flatter,* superl. *flattest.* [ME. *flat,* from Scand.: cf. Icel. *flatr,* Sw. *flat,* Dan. *flad,* OHG. *flaz,* flat, and E. *flat*[1].] Horizontally level, or not sloping or tilted, as the ground, a roof, etc.; lying at full length on the ground or the like, as a person; prostrate, rather than upright or erect; thrown down, laid low, or level with the ground, as fallen trees or buildings; lying wholly on or against something (as, a ladder *flat* against a wall); also, level, even, or without inequalities of surface, as land, areas, surfaces, etc.; comparatively lacking in projection or depression of surface (as, the Eskimo has a broad, *flat* face); lacking relief, contrast, or shading, as a painting; disposed so as to present a level or even surface, as an unrolled map, the open hand, etc.; having a generally level shape or appearance (as, a *flat* cap; a *flat* button; a *flat* dish; a *flat* foot, cf. *flatfoot*); fig., without qualification, unqualified, downright, or positive (as, a *flat* refusal or denial; "I'll not march through Coventry with them, that's *flat,*" Shakspere's "1 Henry IV.," iv. 2. 43); unrelieved or unbroken, as a calm; without modification (as, a *flat* rate, one not subject to discount); without interesting features, uninteresting, dull, or tedious (as, a *flat* existence; a *flat* discourse or book); pointless, as a remark, joke, etc.; dull-witted or stupid, as persons; spiritless, apathetic, or depressed, as persons; commercially dull, as trade or the market; having lost its flavor, sharpness, or life, as wine, beer, etc.; stale; tasteless or insipid, as food; not clear, sharp, or ringing, as sound, a voice, etc.; in *music* (opposed to *sharp*), below an intended pitch, as a note; too low; also, lowered a half-step in pitch (as, B *flat*); also, minor, as an interval; also, having flats in the signature, as keys or tonalities; in *phonetics,* of a consonant, voiced or sonant; in *gram.*, not distinguished by a characteristic ending or sign, as an adjective derived without change from a noun, an adverb derived without change from an adjective, or an infinitive used without *to.*—**flat wheel,** in *railroading,* a car-wheel or engine-wheel in which the tread has been worn flat in one or more places. Also called *square wheel.*—**flat**[2], *n.* That which is flat; the flat surface, side, or part of anything (as, the *flat* of a sword-blade; the *flat* of the hand, the inside surface of the open hand; to lie on the *flat* of one's back); flat or level ground; a flat area, stretch of country, or plain; a level tract near water or covered by shallow water (often in *pl.*: as, "The naked shore, Wide *flats,* where nothing but coarse grasses grew," Tennyson's "Holy Grail," 791); a marsh; a shallow; an object or thing having a generally flat shape, as a flat-bottomed boat, a platform-car, a low-crowned and broad-brimmed hat, or a shallow basket or box; fig., a stupid person, or simpleton (colloq.: as, "You wouldn't be such a *flat* as to let three thousand a year go out of the family?" Thackeray's "Vanity Fair," x.); in *music,* a tone one half-step below a given tone; in musical notation, the character (♭) which indicates this.—**flat**[2], *v.*; *flatted, flatting.* **I.** *tr.* To make flat; in *music,* to lower in pitch, esp. one half-step. **II.** *intr.* To become flat; in *music,* to sound below the true pitch.—**flat**[2], *adv.* In a flat position; horizontally; levelly; also, in a flat manner; without qualification; positively; absolutely; entirely or quite; in *finance,* without interest; in *music,* below the true pitch; *naut.*, used in various phrases to indicate that a sail has been

Flat Caps of the 16th century.

flattened against a mast or has been brought nearly in the direction of the keel, or that a sheet or other part has been brought as far as possible in a particular direction (as, to haul a sheet *flat* aft, to haul a sheet aft as far as possible, as when making a fore-and-aft sail lie like a board without protuberance; to brace a yard *flat* aback, to put it in such a position that the wind is nearly at right angles to the forward surface of the sail).

flat-boat (flat′bōt), *n.* A large flat-bottomed boat, as for use in shallow water, esp. one for floating merchandise, etc., down a river.

flat-fish (flat′fish), *n.*; pl. *-fishes* or (esp. collectively) *-fish.* Any of a group of fishes (often considered as constituting the suborder *Heterosomata*), including the halibut, flounder, sole, etc., having a greatly compressed body, and swimming on one side, and (in the adult) having both eyes on the upper side.

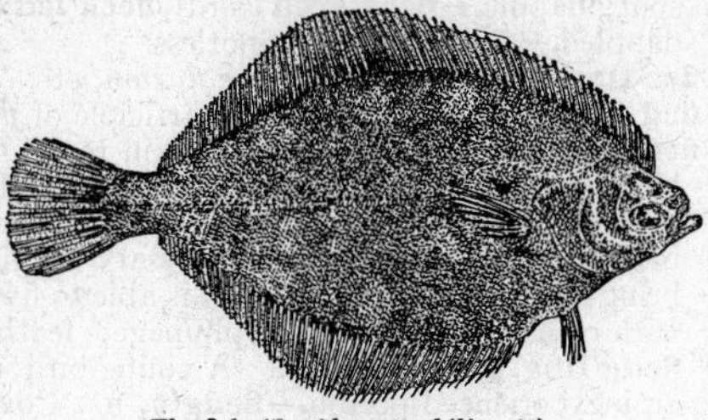

Flatfish (*Lepidopsetta bilineata*).

flat-foot (flat′-fůt), *n.* In *pathol.*, a condition in which the arch of the foot is flattened so that the entire sole rests upon the ground.

flat=foot-ed (flat′fůt′ed), *a.* Having flat feet; also (colloq.), taking or showing an uncompromising stand in a matter; firm and explicit.—**flat′=foot′ed-ly,** *adv.*

Flat-head (flat′hed), *n.* One of a small tribe of American Indians of northwestern Montana, specifically so called, though not having flattened heads; also, a Chinook Indian.

flat=head-ed (flat′hed′ed), *a.* Having a flat head or top.

flat=i-ron (flat′ī″ėrn), *n.* An iron with a flat face, for smoothing cloth.

flat-ling, flat-lings (flat′ling, -lingz), *adv.* [From *flat*² + *-ling*².] In a flat position; with the flat side, as of a sword; also, flatly or positively. [Archaic or prov.] Also **flat′-long†.**

flat-ly (flat′li), *adv.* In a flat position or manner; horizontally; levelly; unqualifiedly; positively; dully; insipidly.—**flat′ness,** *n.*

flat=nosed (flat′nōzd), *a.* Having a flat nose.

flat-ten (flat′n), *v. t.* or *i.* To make or become flat.—**to flatten out,** in *aëronautics*, of an aviator, to bring an aëroplane into a horizontal position, as after a dive; of an aëroplane, to assume such a position.—**flat′ten-er,** *n.*

flat-ter¹ (flat′ėr), *n.* One who or that which makes something flat; esp., a hammer with a broad face, used by smiths.

flat-ter² (flat′ėr), *v.* [ME. *flateren*: cf. OF. *flater* (F. *flatter*), stroke, caress, flatter, *flatere*, a flatterer, prob. from Teut. and akin to E. *flat*².] **I.** *tr.* To seek to please by complimentary speech or attentions; compliment or praise insincerely; also, to gratify by compliments or attentions, or as a compliment does (as, to feel *flattered* by an invitation); hence, to play upon the vanity or susceptibilities of, as by artful blandishments; cajole, wheedle, or beguile; often, to beguile with hopes; encourage (hopes); please (one's self) with the thought or belief (*that*: with a clause); also, to gratify (the eye, ear, etc.); also, to represent too favorably, as in portrayal. **II.** *intr.* To use flattery.—**flat′ter-er,** *n.*—**flat′ter-ing-ly,** *adv.*—**flat′ter-y,** *n.*; pl. *-ies* (-iz). [OF. *flaterie* (F. *flatterie*).] The act of flattering; adulation; obsequious or insincere compliment or praise; artful blandishment or cajolery; a flattering tribute or speech; also, a pleasing hope or belief† (as, "She is persuaded I will marry her, out of her own love and *flattery*, not out of my promise": Shakspere's "Othello," iv. 1. 133).

flat-tish (flat′ish), *a.* Somewhat flat.

flat-u-lent (flat′ū-lent), *a.* [F. *flatulent*, < L. *flatus*: see *flatus*.] Full of, or of the nature of, wind or gas; also, generating gas in the alimentary canal, as food; attended with or caused by, or suffering from, such an accumulation of gas; fig., inflated; pretentious; empty.—**flat′u-lence, flat′u-len-cy,** *n.*—**flat′u-lent-ly,** *adv.*

fla-tus (flā′tus), *n.* [L., a blowing, < *flare*, blow: see *blow*³.] A puff of wind; a breath; in *pathol.*, an accumulation of gas in the stomach, intestines, or other body-cavity.

flat=ware (flat′wãr), *n.* Vessels for the table, or for other use, that are more or less flat, as plates, saucers, etc.: distinguished from *hollow-ware.*

flat-ways, flat-wise (flat′wāz, -wīz), *adv.* With the flat side (not the edge) foremost or in contact.

flat-worm (flat′wėrm), *n.* Any platyhelminth: sometimes restricted to the turbellarians.

flaught (flât, Sc. flächt), *n.* [ME. *flaght*; akin to *flake*².] A flake, as of snow; also, a flash, as of fire or lightning. [Archaic or Sc.]

flaunt (flânt or flänt), *v.* [Origin uncertain.] **I.** *intr.* To wave conspicuously in the air, as a banner or a plume; hence, to make a gay or showy appearance, as a flower or plant; parade or display one's self in fine clothes or showy finery, or in any conspicuous and pretentious manner, as a person (as, "The Miss Lambs might now be seen *flaunting* along the streets in French bonnets, with unknown beaux": Irving's "Sketch-Book," Little Britain); parade one's self boldly or brazenly in public; be obtrusively conspicuous. **II.** *tr.* To parade or display ostentatiously (as, to *flaunt* one's self or one's finery; to *flaunt* one's vices or one's radical opinions); make a bold or brazen parade of.—**flaunt,** *n.* The act of flaunting; also, something flaunted, as finery† (see Shakspere's "Winter's Tale," iv. 4. 23).—**flaunt′er,** *n.*—**flaunt′ing-ly,** *adv.*—**flaunt′y,** *a.* Flaunting; ostentatious; showy.

flau-tist (flâ′tist), *n.* [It. *flautista.*] A flutist.

fla-ves-cent (flạ-ves′ent), *a.* [L. *flavescens* (*-ent-*), ppr. of *flavescere*, turn yellow, < *flavere*, be yellow, < *flavus*, yellow.] Turning yellow; yellowish.

Fla-vi-an (flā′vi-an). **I.** *a.* Pertaining to members of the Flavius gens, or group of families, of ancient Rome, esp. to the three Roman emperors, Vespasian and his sons Titus and Domitian, who reigned A.D. 70–96: as, the *Flavian* amphitheater (the Colosseum, which was built by Vespasian and Titus). **II.** *n.* Any of the Flavian emperors.

fla-vin (flā′vin), *n.* [L. *flavus*, yellow.] A yellow dyestuff obtained from quercitron bark.—**fla′vone** (-vōn), *n.* In *chem.*, an organic compound, $C_{15}H_{10}O_2$, which is the parent substance of various (yellow) dyes.—**fla-vo-pur-pu-rin** (flā-vọ-pėr′pū-rin), *n.* A yellowish crystalline compound (isomeric with purpurin): used in dyeing.

fla-vor (flā′vọr), *n.* [ME. *flavor*, appar. < OF. *flaur*, *fraor*, *flairor*, odor, < L. *fragrare* (OF. *flairier*), emit an odor: see *fragrant*, and cf. *flair*.] Smell, odor, or aroma; now, more commonly, taste, esp. a characteristic taste, or a noticeable element in the taste, of a thing (as, water without *flavor*; a sweet, bitter, or mild *flavor*; the *flavor* of the peach; ice-cream with a vanilla *flavor*); fig., the characteristic quality of a thing as affecting the mental taste or perception (as, the *flavor* of a book; the whole *flavor* of the transaction is objectionable); a particular quality noticeable in a thing (as, language with a strong nautical *flavor*); also, a flavoring substance or extract.—**fla′vor,** *v. t.* To give flavor to; season; render of a particular flavor by adding some ingredient (as, to *flavor* food with herbs, spices, fruit-juice, etc.).—**fla′vor-er,** *n.*—**fla′vor-ing,** *n.* The act of one who or that which flavors; also, something that gives flavor; a substance or preparation used to give a particular flavor to food or drink.—**fla′vor-less,** *a.* Without flavor; tasteless.—**fla′vor-ous,** *a.* Full of flavor; pleasant to the smell or taste.

fla′vour, fla′vour-er, fla′vour-ing, fla′vour-less. British preferred forms of *flavor*, etc.

flaw¹ (flâ), *n.* [= D. *vlaag* = LG. and Dan. *flage*.] A sudden gust or brief, sharp storm of wind (as, "The hulk flew . . . before rapidly succeeding *flaws* of wind": Poe's "MS. Found in a Bottle"); a short spell of rough weather; fig., a gust or storm of feeling, passion, fury, etc.† (see Shakspere's "Macbeth," iii. 4. 63).

flaw² (flâ), *n.* [ME. *flaw*, flake; prob. from Scand., and akin to E. *flay*²: cf. *flake*².] A flake, as of snow†; a fragment† (as, "This heart Shall break into a hundred thousand *flaws*, Or ere I'll weep": Shakspere's "King Lear," ii. 4. 288); also, a crack, break, breach, or rent in a thing; any defect in an object, whether occurring as a natural imperfection in the substance or due to accident or fault in making (as, a *flaw* in a diamond; a *flaw* in a casting); an imperfection; fig., a defect impairing beauty, excellence, logical soundness, etc.; a marring feature; a fault; often, a defect impairing legal soundness or validity (as, a *flaw* in a lease or a will; a *flaw* in a title); sometimes, a fault in conduct (as, "death for ev'ry *flaw*": Cowper's "Truth," 550).—**flaw**², *v.* **I.** *tr.* To produce a flaw, crack, or defect in; impair or mar by a flaw. **II.** *intr.* To contract a flaw; become cracked or defective.—**flaw'less,** *a.* Without flaw, defect, or imperfection.—**flaw'less-ly,** *adv.*—**flaw'less-ness,** *n.*

flawn (flân), *n.* [OF. *flaon* (F. *flan*); from Teut. (cf. G. *fladen*, flat cake).] A kind of custard-pie. [Archaic or prov.]

flaw-y (flâ'i), *a.* Characterized by flaws or gusts, as wind.

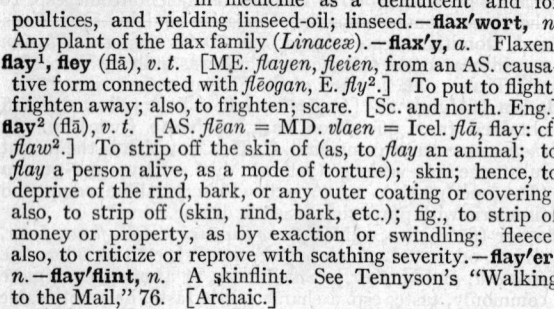

flax (flaks), *n.* [AS. *fleax* = D. *vlas* = G. *flachs*, flax.] Any plant of the genus *Linum*, esp. *L. usitatissimum*, a slender, erect annual plant with narrow, lance-shaped leaves and blue flowers, much cultivated for its fiber and seeds; the fiber of this plant, used in the manufacture of linen thread and fabrics; also, any of various plants resembling flax.—**flax'=bush,** *n.* A liliaceous plant, *Phormium tenax*, of New Zealand, with erect, sword-shaped leaves which yield a strong fiber.—**flax'en,** *a.* Made of flax; also, resembling flax; of the pale yellowish color of dressed flax; also, pertaining to flax.—**flax'=plant,** *n.* The plant flax; also, the flax-bush.—**flax'seed,** *n.* The seed of flax, used in medicine as a demulcent and for poultices, and yielding linseed-oil; linseed.—**flax'wort,** *n.* Any plant of the flax family (*Linaceæ*).—**flax'y,** *a.* Flaxen.

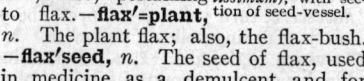

Flax (*Linum usitatissimum*), with section of seed-vessel.

Flax-bush.

flay¹, **fley** (flā), *v. t.* [ME. *flayen*, *fleien*, from an AS. causative form connected with *flēogan*, E. *fly*².] To put to flight; frighten away; also, to frighten; scare. [Sc. and north. Eng.]

flay² (flā), *v. t.* [AS. *flēan* = MD. *vlaen* = Icel. *flā*, flay: cf. *flaw*².] To strip off the skin of (as, to *flay* an animal; to *flay* a person alive, as a mode of torture); skin; hence, to deprive of the rind, bark, or any outer coating or covering; also, to strip off (skin, rind, bark, etc.); fig., to strip of money or property, as by exaction or swindling; fleece; also, to criticize or reprove with scathing severity.—**flay'er,** *n.*—**flay'flint,** *n.* A skinflint. See Tennyson's "Walking to the Mail," 76. [Archaic.]

flea (flē), *n.* [AS. *flēah*, *flēa*, = D. *vloo* = G. *floh* = Icel. *flō*, flea; prob. from the root of E. *flee*.] Any of numerous small, wingless, blood-sucking insects, typically of the genus *Pulex*, parasitic upon mammals and birds, and noted for their powers of leaping; also, any of various small beetles and crustaceans which leap like a flea.—**a flea in one's ear,** a stinging utterance that disturbs the serenity or complacency of the hearer; a discomfiting rebuke or rebuff; a sharp hint.—**flea'bane,** *n.* Any of various asteraceous plants, as *Pulicaria dysenterica* of Europe or *Erigeron philadelphicus* of the U. S., reputed to destroy or drive away fleas.—**flea'bite,** *n.* The bite of a flea, or the red spot caused by it; hence, a trifling wound, pain, annoyance, etc.; a mere trifle; also, a mark resembling that caused by the bite of a flea.—**flea'-bit"ten,** *a.* Bitten by a flea or fleas; also, of a horse, etc., having small reddish spots or streaks upon a lighter ground.

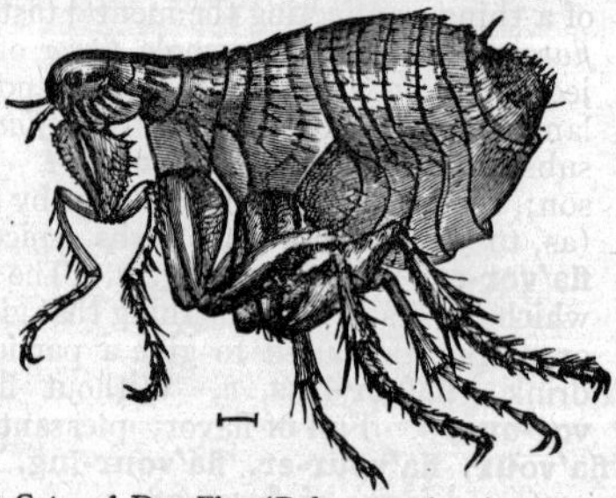

Cat and Dog Flea (*Pulex serraticeps*). (Line shows natural size.)

fleam (flēm), *n.* [OF. *flieme* (F. *flamme*), < LL. *phlebotomus*, lancet, < Gr. φλεβοτόμος, opening veins: cf. *phlebotomy*.] In *surg.*, a kind of lancet, as for opening veins.

flea-wort (flē'wėrt), *n.* Any of certain plants supposed to destroy or drive away fleas, as *Inula conyza*, a rough-leaved asteraceous herb of Europe; also, a European plantain, *Plantago psyllium*, whose seeds resemble fleas.

flèche (flesh), *n.* [F.] An arrow; in *arch.*, a spire; esp., a slender spire rising from the junction of the nave and transepts of a church; in *fort.*, a field-work consisting of two faces forming a salient angle.—**flé-chette** (flā-shet), *n.* [F., dim. of *flèche*.] A little arrow; a steel dart thrown from an aëroplane.

fleck (flek), *n.* [Cf. Icel. *flekkr*, Sw. *fläck*, D. *vlek*, G. *fleck*, spot.] A spot or mark on the skin, as a freckle; hence, any spot or patch of color, light, etc.; also, a speck or small bit of something.—**fleck,** *v. t.* [Cf. Icel. *flekka*.] To mark with a fleck or spot; diversify with spots, as of color or light; spot; dapple.—**fleck'ered** (-ėrd), **fleck'led** (-ld), *a.* Flecked; dappled.—**fleck'less,** *a.* Spotless.

flec-tion (flek'shọn), etc. See *flexion*, etc.

fled (fled). Preterit and past participle of *flee*.

fledge† (flej), *a.* [ME. *flegge*; akin to E. *fly*².] Of young birds, able to fly; having the wings developed for flight; fledged.—**fledge,** *v.*; *fledged*, *fledging*. **I.** *intr.* Of a young bird, to acquire the feathers necessary for flight. **II.** *tr.* To bring up (a young bird) until it is able to fly; also, to furnish with or as with feathers or plumage; feather (an arrow).—**fledg'ling, fledge'ling,** *n.* A young bird just fledged; fig., an inexperienced person.—**fledg'y,** *a.* Covered with feathers; feathery.

flee (flē), *v.*; *fled*, *fleeing*. [AS. *flēon* = G. *fliehen* = Icel. *flȳja* = Goth. *thliuhan*, flee; long confused with the unrelated word *fly*².] **I.** *intr.* To run away, as from danger, pursuers, or any cause or place of danger or embarrassment; seek escape or safety by flight; take flight; depart or withdraw hastily; often, to withdraw or go hastily (*to*, *into*, etc.), as for refuge, protection, etc. (as, "To whom will ye *flee* for help?" Isa. x. 3); also, to pass quickly away, or vanish, as shadows, clouds, bloom, beauty, etc. (often with *away*); also, to move swiftly along, fly, or speed, as a missile (as, "Arrows *fled* not swifter toward their aim Than did our soldiers . . . Fly from the field": Shakspere's "2 Henry IV.," i. 1. 123). **II.** *tr.* To run away from (a place, person, etc.); depart hastily from; also, to avoid by flight; shun; also, to escape (now rare).

fleece (flēs), *n.* [AS. *flēos* = D. *vlies* = G. *fliess*.] The coat of wool that covers a sheep or some similar animal; also, the wool shorn from a sheep at one time; also, something resembling a fleece of wool, as in quality or appearance (as, "the *fleeces* of descending snows": Pope's tr. Homer's "Iliad," iii.); a head of hair (as, "the Aboriginal Savage, glaring fiercely from under his *fleece* of hair": Carlyle's "Sartor Resartus," i. 5); a soft nap or pile.—**golden fleece.** See under *golden*, *a.*—**fleece,** *v. t.*; *fleeced*, *fleecing*. To deprive (a sheep) of the fleece; hence, to strip of money or belongings; plunder; victimize; swindle; also, to overspread as with a fleece; fleck with fleece-like masses.—**fleece'a-ble,** *a.* That may be fleeced.—**fleeced,** *a.* Provided with a fleece: as, thick-*fleeced*.—**flee-cer** (flē'sėr), *n.*

fleech (flēch), *v.* [Origin obscure.] **I.** *tr.* To cajole; wheedle; also, to beseech. [Sc. and north. Eng.] **II.** *intr.* To speak in a cajoling or beseeching manner. [Sc. and north. Eng.]

flee-cy (flē'si), *a.*; compar. *fleecier*, superl. *fleeciest*. Covered with, consisting of, or resembling a fleece or wool.—**flee'ci-ly,** *adv.*

fle-er¹ (flē'ėr), *n.* One who flees.

fleer² (flēr), *v.* [ME. *fleryen*; prob. from Scand.] **I.** *intr.* To grimace†; also, to grin or laugh coarsely or rudely; also, to smile or laugh mockingly; jeer. **II.** *tr.* To fleer at; deride.—**fleer**², *n.* A fleering look; a jeer or gibe.—**fleer'er,** *n.*—**fleer'ing-ly,** *adv.*

fleet¹ (flēt), *v.* [AS. *flēotan*, float, = Icel. *fljōta*, float, flow, = D. *vlieten*, G. *fliessen*, flow; akin to L. *pluere*, rain, Gr. πλεῖν, sail, Skt. *plu-*, float.] **I.** *intr.* To float†; drift†; swim†; sail†; also, to fluctuate† or waver†; also, to flow, as water†; hence, to glide away like a stream; slip away; fade; vanish; also, to move swiftly; fly; *naut.*, to change position; shift. **II.** *tr.* To cause (time) to pass lightly or swiftly (see Shakspere's "As You Like It," i. 1. 124); *naut.*, to change the position of; shift.

fleet[2] (flēt), *n.* [AS. *flēot*, ship, craft, < *flēotan*, float: see *fleet*[1].] A number of armed vessels, or vessels carrying armed men; a number of war-ships under the command of a single chief officer (as an admiral or rear-admiral), with other officers in command of single vessels or groups of vessels; a naval armament; hence, any group of ships or boats sailing in company, employed in the same service, or otherwise associated; also, a number of aëroplanes, automobiles, or the like, moving or operating in company.

fleet[3] (flēt), *n.* [AS. *flēot*, flowing water, = Icel. *fljōt*, river, = D. *vliet*, G. *fliess*, brook; akin to E. *fleet*[1].] An arm of the sea; an inlet; a creek. [Now prov. Eng., or in place-names.]—**the Fleet,** a former London prison, long used for debtors: so called from its situation near a run of water (now a covered sewer) also known as 'the Fleet,' flowing into the Thames at Blackfriars Bridge.

fleet[4] (flēt), *a.* [Cf. Icel. *fljōtr*, swift, akin to E. *fleet*[1].] Swift of motion; rapid; also, fleeting; evanescent. [Chiefly in literary use.]—**fleet′=foot′ed,** *a.*

fleet-ing (flē′ting), *p. a.* That fleets; gliding swiftly away; passing swiftly, as time; evanescent or transitory, as joys.—**fleet′ing-ly,** *adv.*—**fleet′ing-ness,** *n.*

fleet-ly (flēt′li), *adv.* In a fleet manner; swiftly; rapidly.—**fleet′ness,** *n.*

fleg (fleg), *v. t.*; *flegged, flegging.* [Cf. *flay*[1], *fley*.] To frighten; frighten away. [Sc.]—**fleg,** *n.* A fright; a scare: as, "One dark night we got a *fleg* in sober earnest" (Moir's "Mansie Wauch," xii.). [Sc.]

Flem-ing (flem′ing), *n.* [MD. *Vlaming*.] A native of Flanders; esp., a Flemish-speaking Belgian.

Flem-ish (flem′ish). [MD. *Vlaemisch*.] **I.** *a.* Of or pertaining to Flanders, its people, or their language. **II.** *n.* The people of Flanders; the Flemings; also, the language of the Flemings, a form of Low German closely related to Dutch.

flense (flens), *v. t.*; *flensed, flensing.* [Dan. *flense*.] To strip the blubber or the skin from (a whale, seal, etc.); also, to strip off (blubber or skin).

flesh (flesh), *n.* [AS. *flǣsc* = D. *vleesch* = G. *fleisch*, flesh, = Icel. *flesk*, pork.] The soft substance of an animal body, consisting of muscle and fat, or, in a more restricted sense, of muscular tissue alone; also, such substance of animals as an article of food, usually excluding fish and sometimes fowl; meat; also, the surface of the body, esp. with respect to color; also, the body, esp. as distinguished from the spirit or soul (as, to see a person in the *flesh*; "The spirit indeed is willing, but the *flesh* is weak," Mat. xxvi. 41); man's physical or animal nature, as distinguished from his moral or spiritual nature (as, to yield to the promptings of the *flesh*; "From all the deceits of the world, the *flesh*, and the devil, Good Lord, deliver us," Book of Common Prayer, Litany); also, mankind, or living creatures generally (as, to go the way of all *flesh*; "And all *flesh* died . . . both of fowl, and of cattle . . . and every man," Gen. vii. 21); also, one's kindred or family, or a member of it (as, "He is our brother and our *flesh*," Gen. xxxvii. 27: now commonly in the phrase 'one's own flesh and blood'); also, the pulpy portion of a fruit, vegetable, or the like.—**flesh,** *v. t.* To feed (a hound or hawk) with flesh in order to make it more eager for the chase; make (an animal) eager for prey, as the taste of flesh or blood does; hence, to incite and accustom (persons) to bloodshed or battle by an initial experience; fig., to inflame the ardor or passions of by a taste of indulgence; also, to plunge (a weapon) into the flesh; also, to clothe (a skeleton, etc.) with flesh; make fleshy; also, to remove adhering flesh, etc., from (hides, etc.).—**flesh′=col″or,** *n.* A pinkish-white color with a tinge of yellow; a pinkish cream-color.—**flesh′=col″ored,** *a.*—**fleshed,** *a.* Having flesh: as, white-*fleshed*.—**flesh′er,** *n.* A butcher (chiefly Sc.); also, one who fleshes hides; a tool for fleshing hides.—**flesh′=fly,** *n.* Any of various true flies, as the blow-fly, whose eggs or larvæ are deposited on flesh.—**flesh′=hook,** *n.* A hook for use in lifting meat, as from a pot; also, a hook to hang meat on.—**flesh′i-ness,** *n.* The state of being fleshy.—**flesh′ings,** *n. pl.* Flesh-colored tights; also, bits of flesh, etc., scraped from hides.—**flesh′-less,** *a.* Destitute of flesh, as a skeleton; also, emaciated; lean.—**flesh′ly,** *a.*; compar. *fleshlier*, superl. *fleshliest*. [AS. *flǣsclīc*.] Of or pertaining to the flesh or body (as, the *fleshly* form or eye); bodily, corporeal, or physical; also, of or pertaining to man's physical or animal nature (as, *fleshly* appetites or indulgences); carnal or sensual; given to sensual indulgences; sometimes, worldly, rather than spiritual; also, consisting of flesh (now rare); having much flesh†, or fleshy†.—**flesh′li-ness,** *n.*—**flesh′ment**†, *n.* The state of being fleshed or stimulated, as by a taste of something. See Shakspere's "King Lear," ii. 2. 130.—**flesh′pot,** *n.* A pot or vessel containing flesh or meat; hence, good food or fare; good living; luxuries or substantial advantages that are the object of longing regret or covetous desire: from the Biblical use, "Would to God we had died . . . in the land of Egypt, when we sat by the *flesh pots*, and when we did eat bread to the full" (Ex. xvi. 3).—**flesh′y,** *a.*; compar. *fleshier*, superl. *fleshiest*. Having much flesh; plump; fat; also, of, pertaining to, or consisting of flesh; also, of flesh-like substance; pulpy, as a fruit; thick and tender, as a leaf.

fletch (flech), *v. t.* [Prob. < *fletcher*.] To provide (an arrow) with a feather.

fletch-er (flech′ėr), *n.* [OF. *flechier*, < *fleche* (F. *flèche*), arrow.] One who makes or deals in arrows, or bows and arrows. [Archaic.]

Fletch-er-ism (flech′ėr-izm), *n.* The practice of chewing food until it is reduced to a finely divided, liquefied mass, as advocated by Horace Fletcher (1849–1919) as a nutritional measure.—**Fletch′er-ize,** *v. t.* or *i.*; *-ized, -izing.* To masticate (food) thoroughly.

fleur=de=lis (flėr-dė-lē′), *n.*; pl. *fleurs-de-lis* (flėr-). [F. *fleur de lis*, 'flower of lily.'] The iris (flower or plant); also, a heraldic device somewhat resembling three petals or floral segments assembled in a cluster by an encircling band, explained by some as having originally represented an iris, by others the head of an arrow, spear, scepter, or the like, esp. used as the distinctive bearing of the royal family of France. Cf. *giglio*.

fleu-ron (flė-rôṅ), *n.* [F., < *fleur*: see *flower*.] A flower-shaped ornament, used esp. in architectural decoration, on coins, etc.

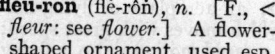

Various forms of the Fleur-de-lis.

fleu-ry, flo-ry (flö′ri, flō′-), *a.* [F. *fleuré*, OF. *floré*, < OF. *flor* (F. *fleur*), E. *flower*.] In *her.*, decorated with fleurs-de-lis; of a cross, having each arm ending in a fleur-de-lis, or the upper part of one.

flew (flö). Preterit of *fly*[2].

flews (flöz), *n. pl.* [Origin unknown.] The large pendulous upper lip of certain dogs, as bloodhounds.—**flewed,** *a.*

flex (fleks), *v. t.* or *i.* [L. *flexus*, pp. of *flectere*, bend.] To bend, as a part of the body.

flex-i-ble (flek′si-bl), *a.* [F. *flexible*, < L. *flexibilis*, < *flectere*, bend.] Capable of being bent; easily bent; pliable; pliant; also, willing or disposed to yield; compliant; tractable; also, susceptible of modification or adaptation; adaptable.—**flex-i-bil′i-ty** (-bil′i-ti), **flex′i-ble-ness,** *n.*—**flex′i-bly,** *adv.*

flex-ile (flek′sil), *a.* [L. *flexilis*.] Flexible; pliant; tractable; adaptable.—**flex-il-i-ty** (flek-sil′i-ti), *n.*

flex-ion, flec-tion (flek′shọn), *n.* [L. *flexio(n-)*, < *flectere*, bend.] The act of bending, or the state of being bent; a bend; a bent part; in *gram.*, inflection.—**flex′ion-al, flec′tion-al,** *a.*—**flex′ion-less, flec′tion-less,** *a.* Without (grammatical) flexion.

flex-or (flek′sọr), *n.* [NL.] A muscle which serves to flex or bend a part of the body.

flex-u-ous (flek′ṣū-us), *a.* [L. *flexuosus*, < *flexus*, a bending, < *flectere*, bend.] Full of bends or curves; winding; sinuous; also, waving or undulating.—**flex-u-os′i-ty** (-os′i-ti), *n.*—**flex′u-ous-ly,** *adv.*

flex-ure (flek′ṣūr), *n.* [L. *flexura*.] The act of flexing or bending; the state of being flexed or bent; a bend; a fold; a bent part or thing.—**flex′ur-al,** *a.*

fley (flā), *v. t.* See *flay*[1].

flib-ber-ti-gib-bet (flib″ėr-ti-jib′et), *n.* [Appar. a made word.] A chattering or flighty person: commonly applied to a woman, and also formerly used [*cap.*] as the name of a fiend (see Shakspere's "King Lear," iii. 4. 120).

flic-flac (flik'flak), *n.* [F.; imit. of the sound made.] A step in dancing in which the feet strike rapidly together.

flick (flik), *n.* [Appar. imit.] A sudden light blow or stroke, as with a whip or the finger; also, the sound thus made; also, something thrown off with or as with a jerk (as, a *flick* of spray).—**flick,** *v.* **I.** *tr.* To strike lightly with a whip, the finger, etc.; remove with such a stroke (as, "He would . . . *flick* away the remaining particles of dust with a graceful wave of his hand": Thackeray's "Vanity Fair," xxxviii.); also, to move with a sudden stroke or jerk. **II.** *intr.* To move with a jerk or jerks; also, to flutter.

flick-er[1] (flik'ėr), *n.* [Imit. of the bird's note.] Any of several handsomely colored woodpeckers; esp., the golden-winged woodpecker, *Colaptes auratus*, of eastern North America.

Flicker, or Golden-winged Woodpecker (*Colaptes auratus*).

flick-er[2] (flik'ėr), *v. i.* [AS. *fliccerian*; prob. imit.] To flutter, as a bird; hover; flap the wings rapidly; also, to wave to and fro; vibrate; quiver; also, to burn unsteadily (as, "A chain-droop'd lamp was *flickering* by each door": Keats's "Eve of St. Agnes," xl.); flash up and die down alternately, as a flame; shine with a wavering light.—**flick'er**[2], *n.* A flickering; a flickering movement; an unsteady flame or light.—**flick'er-ing-ly,** *adv.*—**flick'er-tail,** *n.* A destructive rodent or gopher, *Citellus* (or *Spermophilus*) *richardsoni*, from which North Dakota is called the 'Flickertail State.' See *gopher*.

fli-er, fly-er (flī'ėr), *n.* [See *fly*[2], *v.*] Something that flies, as a bird or insect; an aviator; an aëroplane or flying-machine; also, one who or that which moves with great speed; some part of a machine having a rapid motion; also, a flying jump or leap; hence, a financial venture outside of one's ordinary business (U. S.); also, a single one of a straight flight of steps; also, a small handbill (U. S.); also, one who flees; a fugitive.

flight[1] (flīt), *n.* [ME. *fliht*, < AS. *flēon*, E. *flee*.] The act of fleeing; hasty departure.

flight[2] (flīt), *n.* [AS. *flyht*, < *flēogan*, E. *fly*[2].] The act, manner, or power of flying with or as with wings; also, swift movement in general, as of a missile; fig., a soaring above or transcending ordinary bounds (as, a *flight* of fancy; a *flight* of ambition); also, the distance covered or the course pursued by a flying object; also, a number of beings or things flying or passing through the air together (as, "a *flight* of doves or swallows," Irving's "Sketch-Book," Christmas Day; "*flights* of angels," Shakspere's "Hamlet," v. 2. 371; "a *flight* of fairy arrows," Tennyson's "Aylmer's Field," 94); also, a light arrow for long-distance shooting; a contest with such arrows; also, the series of steps or stairs between two adjacent landings; hence, a series of steps, etc., ascending without change of direction.—**flight**[2], *v. i.* Of wild-fowl, to fly in flights: as, "The wild geese are *flighting*" (Kipling's "Irish Guards").—**flight'=feath''er,** *n.* In *ornith.*, one of the large, stiff feathers which form most of the extent of a bird's wing, and which are essential to flight.—**flight'-less,** *a.* Incapable of flying.—**flight'=path,** *n.* In *aëronautics*, the path (with reference to the earth) taken by the center of gravity of an aircraft.—**flight'y,** *a.*; compar. *flightier*, superl. *flightiest*. Swift or fleet (obs. or rare); also, given to flights or sallies of fancy, caprice, etc.; volatile; frivolous; also, slightly delirious, or light-headed; mildly crazy.—**flight'i-ly,** *adv.*—**flight'i-ness,** *n.*

flim-flam (flim'flam), *n.* [Origin uncertain: cf. *flam*.] A trifling fancy or conceit†; also, a piece of nonsense; mere nonsense; also, a trick or deception; mere trickery or humbug. [Now colloq.]—**flim'flam,** *v. t.*; *-flammed, -flamming*. To trick; delude; humbug; cheat. [Colloq.]—**flim'-flam''mer,** *n.*

flim-sy (flim'zi). [Perhaps connected with *film*.] **I.** *a.*; compar. *flimsier*, superl. *flimsiest*. Without material strength or solidity; frail; unsubstantial; also, without force or value; trivial; paltry; frivolous. **II.** *n.* A flimsy or thin kind of paper, esp. for use in making several copies of a writing, telegraphic despatch, etc., at once (as in newspaper work); a copy of a report or despatch on such paper; also, a bank-note (slang).—**flim'si-ly,** *adv.*—**flim'si-ness,** *n.*

flinch (flinch), *v.* [Prob. < OF. *flenchir*, var. of *flechir* (F. *fléchir*), bend, turn aside, appar. < L. *flectere*, bend.] **I.** *intr.* To draw back from an undertaking, duty, etc., as from want of courage or endurance; shrink from what is dangerous, difficult, or unpleasant; also, to shrink under pain; wince; in *croquet*, to let the foot slip from the ball in the act of croqueting. **II.** *tr.* To draw back or withdraw from.—**flinch,** *n.* The act or an act of flinching.—**flinch'er,** *n.*—**flinch'ing-ly,** *adv.*

flin-der (flin'dėr), *n.* [Cf. Norw. *flindra*, splinter.] A splinter; a small piece or fragment: usually in *pl.*: as, "The tough ash spear, so stout and true, Into a thousand *flinders* flew" (Scott's "Lay of the Last Minstrel," iii. 6).

fling (fling), *v.*; *flung*, *flinging*. [Cf. Icel. *flengja*, whip, mod. ride furiously, Sw. *flänga*, fly, race, tear, romp.] **I.** *tr.* To throw, cast, or hurl; throw with force or violence; throw with impatience, disdain, etc.; also, to put suddenly or violently (as, to *fling* one into prison); send forth suddenly and rapidly (as, to *fling* fresh troops into a battle); also, to throw to the ground, as in wrestling or from horseback. **II.** *intr.* To fling a missile; also, to move with haste or violence; rush; dash; sometimes, to be driven forcibly or swiftly; also, to fly into violent and irregular motions, as a horse; throw the body about, as a person; also, to caper or dance (Sc.).—**fling,** *n.* An act of flinging; a throw; a cast from the hand; fig., an attack upon or attempt at something, as in passing; a severe or contemptuous remark, or gibe, uttered in passing or incidentally; also, a rush or dash (obs. or rare); also, a violent, irregular movement, as of an animal; a throw or twist of the body; also, a lively Scotch dance characterized by flinging movements of the legs and arms (commonly called 'Highland fling'); also, a spell of unrestrained indulgence of one's impulses (as, to have one's *fling*).—**fling'er,** *n.*

flint (flint), *n.* [AS. *flint* = MLG. *vlins* = OHG. *flins* = Dan. *flint*.] A hard kind of stone, a form of silica resembling chalcedony but more opaque and less lustrous; a piece of this, esp. as used, as with a piece of steel, for striking fire; hence, something very hard or obdurate.—**flint'=glass',** *n.* A glass of great brilliancy containing silicon, potassium or sodium, and lead: used for making tableware, lenses, etc.—**flint'i-ly,** *adv.* In a flinty manner.—**flint'i-ness,** *n.*—**flint'-lock,** *n.* A gun-lock in which a piece of flint striking against steel produces sparks which ignite the priming; also, a fire-arm with such a lock.—**flint'y,** *a.*; compar. *flintier*, superl. *flintiest*. Of, like, or containing flint; hard as flint.

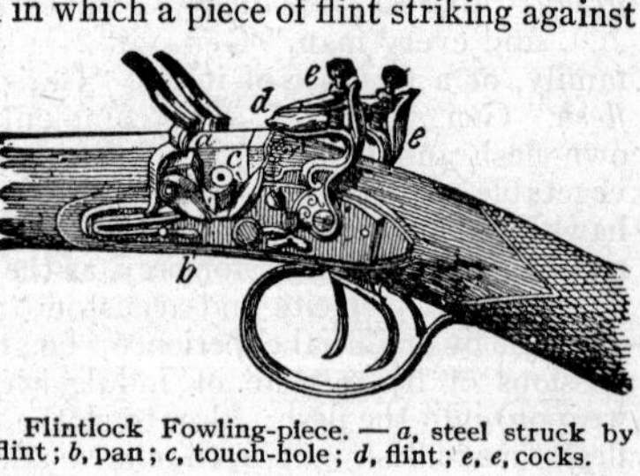

Flintlock Fowling-piece. — *a*, steel struck by flint; *b*, pan; *c*, touch-hole; *d*, flint; *e, e*, cocks.

flip[1] (flip), *v.*; *flipped*, *flipping*. [Appar. a variant of *fillip* (recorded earlier).] **I.** *tr.* To fillip; flick; put into motion by or as by a fillip with the fingers; toss (a coin) with a fillip or flip; also, to move with a jerk or jerks; flirt. **II.** *intr.* To make a fillip; strike smartly at something; also, to move with a jerk or jerks.—**flip**[1], *n.* A fillip; a smart tap or stroke; also, a sudden jerk.—**flip**[1], *a.*; compar. *flipper*, superl. *flippest*. Smart; pert; flippant. [Colloq.]

flip[2] (flip), *n.* [Origin uncertain; perhaps < *flip*[1].] A beverage made of beer or ale, cider, or the like, sweetened, spiced, and heated with a hot iron: as, "The minister himself heated two little old andirons red-hot . . . and therewith . . . stirred up a mighty bowl of *flip*" (Mrs. Stowe's "Oldtown Folks," xxxvii.).

flip-pant (flip′ant), *a.* [Perhaps < *flip*[1]: cf. Icel. *fleipa,* babble, prattle.] Nimble, limber, or pliant (obs. or prov. Eng.); also, voluble† or talkative†; also, smart or pert in speech; characterized by a shallow or disrespectful levity.—**flip′pan-cy, flip′pant-ness,** *n.*—**flip′pant-ly,** *adv.*

flip-per (flip′ėr), *n.* [From *flip*[1].] A broad, flat limb, as of a seal, whale, etc., especially adapted for swimming; also, the hand (slang).

flirt (flėrt), *v.* [Prob. imit.] **I.** *tr.* To throw or propel with a toss or jerk; fling suddenly; also, to give a sudden or brisk motion to; wave smartly, as a fan. **II.** *intr.* To move with a jerk or jerks; dart about; also, to play at courtship; trifle in love; coquet; also, in general, to trifle.—**flirt,** *n.* A quick throw or toss; a sudden jerk; a darting motion; also, a giddy or wanton woman†; also, a person (woman or man) given to flirting; sometimes, a person to flirt with (as, "General Tufto is a great *flirt* of mine": Thackeray's "Vanity Fair," xxv.).—**flir-ta-tion** (flėr-tā′shọn), *n.* A flirting; playing at courtship; amorous trifling or adventure.—**flir-ta′tious** (-shus), *a.* Given to flirtation; also, of, pertaining to, or of the nature of flirtation.—**flir-ta′tious-ly,** *adv.*—**flir-ta′tious-ness,** *n.*—**flirt′er,** *n.*—**flirt′=gill**† (-jil), *n.* A giddy or wanton woman. See Shakspere's "Romeo and Juliet," ii. 4. 162.—**flirt′ing-ly,** *adv.*—**flirt′y,** *a.* Flirtatious.

flit (flit), *v.*; *flitted, flitting.* [Cf. Icel. *flytja,* carry, convey, akin to E. *fleet*[1].] **I.** *tr.* To remove; transfer; oust or dispossess. [Chiefly Sc.] **II.** *intr.* To shift position; move; depart or be gone, or die (chiefly north. Eng. and Sc.); change one's residence (chiefly north. Eng. and Sc.); also, to move lightly and swiftly; fly, dart, or skim along; also, to pass away quickly, as time; also, to flutter, as a bird.—**flit,** *n.* A flitting; a removal (chiefly north. Eng. and Sc.); a light, swift movement; a flutter.

flitch (flich), *n.* [AS. *flicce* = MLG. *vlicke* = Icel. *flikki,* flitch.] The side of a hog (or, formerly, some other animal) salted and cured ('flitch of bacon'); a side of bacon; also, a steak cut from a halibut; also, a slab cut lengthwise from the trunk of a tree; specif., one of several planks fastened together to form a compound beam.

flite, flyte (flīt), *v.*; *flited, flyted, fliting, flyting.* [AS. *flītan,* strive, contend.] **I.** *intr.* To dispute; wrangle; rail; scold; flout; jeer. [Now Sc. and north. Eng.] **II.** *tr.* To berate; scold; jeer at. [Now Sc. and north. Eng.]—**flite, flyte,** *n.* [AS. *flīt,* strife.] A dispute; a wrangle; an abusive speech; a scolding; a flout. [Now Sc. and north. Eng.]

flit-ter[1] (flit′ėr), *n.* One who or that which flits.

flit-ter[2] (flit′ėr), *v. i.* or *t.* [Freq. of *flit.*] To flutter.

flit-ter-mouse (flit′ėr-mous), *n.*; pl. *-mice* (-mīs). [From *flitter*[2] + *mouse*: cf. G. *fledermaus.*] A bat (animal). [Now chiefly prov.]

flit-ters (flit′ėrz), *n. pl.* [Var. of *fitters*: cf. *fritter*[2].] Fragments; bits; shreds. [Prov. or colloq.]

flit-ting (flit′ing), *p. a.* That flits; moving; moving lightly and swiftly; passing quickly; fluttering.—**flit′ting-ly,** *adv.*

fliv-ver (fliv′ėr), *n.* [Origin obscure.] A bungle or fizzle; a failure; also, something of unsatisfactory quality or inferior grade, as an automobile (sometimes applied humorously to any automobile); something small of its kind, as a small naval destroyer (vessel). [Slang.]—**fliv′ver,** *v. i.* To fail ignominiously; fizzle; also, to go or be conveyed in a flivver (automobile). [Slang.]

float (flōt), *v.* [AS. *flotian,* < *flēotan,* float: see *fleet*[1].] **I.** *intr.* To rest on the surface of a liquid; be buoyant; also, to move gently on the surface of a liquid; drift along; also, to rest or move in a liquid, the air, etc.; in fig. use, to move or hover before the eyes or in the mind (as, "Faded ideas *float* in the fancy like half-forgotten dreams": Sheridan's "Rivals," Preface); pass from one to another, as a rumor; move or drift about free from attachment; in *com.,* to be in circulation, as an acceptance; be awaiting maturity; also, to be launched or floated, as a company, scheme, etc. **II.** *tr.* To cause to float; also, to cover with water; flood; irrigate; also, to launch (a company, scheme, etc.); set going; also, to make smooth or level, as the surface of plaster; also, to subject (pigments, etc.) to a process in which the powdered material is put into slowly moving water in order to carry the suspended finer particles to some distance and thus separate them from the coarser.—**float,** *n.* [AS. *flot,* a floating, *flota,* a ship, fleet.] The act or state of floating (now rare); also, a wave†, or the sea† (see Shakspere's "Tempest," i. 2. 234); also, something that floats, as a raft; something for buoying up, as a piece of cork for supporting a baited line in the water and showing by its movement when a fish bites, or an inflated organ that supports an animal in the water; in certain apparatuses, cisterns, etc., a device, as a hollow metal ball, which through its buoyancy automatically regulates the level, supply, or outlet of a liquid; a float-board of a water-wheel or a paddle-wheel; also, *pl.* or *sing.,* the footlights of a theater†; also, *sing.,* a platform on wheels, bearing a tableau or other display, and drawn in a procession; a low-bodied dray for transporting heavy goods; also, any of various tools for smoothing, leveling, or the like, as a kind of file, a plasterer's trowel, etc.—**float′a-ble,** *a.* Capable of floating; that may be floated; also, that can be floated on, as a river.—**float-a-bil′i-ty** (-bil′i-ti), *n.*—**float′age** (-āj), *n.* The act or state of floating; also, floating power; buoyancy; also, anything that floats; flotsam; the vessels that float on a stream.

float-a-tion (flō-tā′shọn), *n.* See *flotation.*

float=board (flōt′bōrd), *n.* One of the boards of an undershot water-wheel; also, one of the boards (paddles) at the circumference of a paddle-wheel.

float-er (flō′tėr), *n.* One who or that which floats; one who is continually changing his place of abode, employment, etc.; a voter not attached to any party, esp. one whose vote may be purchased (U. S.); one who fraudulently votes in different places in the same election (U. S.).

float-ing (flō′ting), *p. a.* That floats; resting or moving on or in water, air, etc.; free from attachment, or having but little attachment; not fixed or settled in a definite place or state (as, the *floating* population; the *floating* vote, the voters not definitely attached to any political party); in circulation or use, or not permanently invested, as capital; not funded, as a debt.—**floating dock.** See *dock*[3], *n.*—**floating heart,** any of certain perennial aquatic herbs of the genus *Limnanthemum,* with floating, more or less heart-shaped leaves.—**floating island,** a floating island-like mass of earth held together by driftwood, interlacing roots, etc.; also, a dish consisting of boiled custard with portions of meringue or whipped cream, and often bits of jelly, etc., floating upon it.—**floating kidney,** in *pathol.,* a kidney which has become loose and displaced in the abdomen.—**floating ribs.** See *rib, n.*—**float′ing-ly,** *adv.*

float-y (flō′ti), *a.* Able to float; buoyant; of a boat, drawing little water.

floc-cil-la-tion (flok-si-lā′shọn), *n.* [L. *floccus,* flock of wool.] In *pathol.,* a delirious picking of the bedclothes, etc., by the patient, as in certain fevers.

floc-cose (flok′ōs), *a.* [LL. *floccosus,* < L. *floccus,* flock of wool.] In *bot.,* consisting of or bearing woolly tufts.

floc-cu-late (flok′ū-lāt), *v.*; *-lated, -lating.* [NL. *flocculus*: see *flocculus.*] **I.** *tr.* To form into flocculent masses. **II.** *intr.* To form flocculent masses, as cloud, a chemical precipitate, etc.; form aggregated or compound masses of particles.—**floc-cu-la′tion** (-lā′shọn), *n.*

floc-cule (flok′ūl), *n.* [NL. *flocculus*: see *flocculus*] Something resembling a small flock or tuft of wool; a bit of flocculent matter, as in a liquid.

floc-cu-lent (flok′ū-lẹnt), *a.* [L. *floccus,* flock of wool.] Like a flock or flocks of wool; consisting of or containing loose woolly masses; covered with a soft, woolly substance.—**floc′cu-lence,** *n.*—**floc′cu-lent-ly,** *adv.*

floc-cu-lus (flok′ū-lus), *n.*; pl. *-li* (-lī). [NL., dim. of L. *floccus,* flock of wool.] A small flock of wool, or something resembling it; a floccule; a flake.

flock[1] (flok), *n.* [AS. *flocc* = Icel. *flokkr.*] A band or company of persons (now somewhat rare); also, a number of animals of one kind keeping, feeding, or herded together, now esp. of sheep or goats or of birds; fig., in Biblical and ecclesiastical use, the Christian church in relation to Christ, or a single congregation in relation to its pastor; sometimes, in general, an assemblage, collection, or multitude (as, "*flocks* of churches": Wordsworth's "Prelude," iii. 33).—**flock**[1], *v. i.* To gather or go in a flock, company, or crowd.

flock[2] (flok), *n.* [ME. *flokke,* appar. < OF. F. *floc,* < L. *floccus,* flock of wool: cf. MD. and MLG. *vlocke,* OHG. *floccho,* flock, flake, Icel. *flōki,* felt, hair, wool, and E. *flake*[2].]

A lock or tuft of wool, hair, etc.; *pl.* or *sing.*, wool refuse, shearings of cloth, old cloth torn to pieces, etc., used for stuffing mattresses, upholstering furniture, etc.; also, finely powdered wool, cloth, etc., used in making flock-paper; *sing.*, a tuft-like mass, as in a chemical precipitate.—**flock**², *v. t.* To stuff with flock, as a mattress; also, to cover or coat with flock, as wall-paper.—**flock′=pa″per,** *n.* Wall-paper coated or figured with flock, or powdered wool.—**flock′y,** *a.* Like flocks or tufts; flocculent.

floe (flō), *n.* [Cf. Norw. *flo*, Icel. *flō*, layer.] A field of floating ice formed on the surface of the sea, etc.; a detached floating portion of such a field.

flog (flog), *v. t.*; *flogged, flogging.* [Origin obscure.] To beat or whip; chastise with repeated blows, as of a rod or whip.—**flog′ger,** *n.*—**flog′ging,** *n.* The act of one that flogs; chastisement; a beating or whipping.

flood (flud), *n.* [AS. *flōd* = D. *vloed* = G. *flut* = Icel. *flōdh* = Goth. *flōdus*, flood; from the root of E. *flow*².] The flowing in of the tide (opposed to *ebb*); also, a great flowing or overflowing of water, esp. over land not usually submerged; an inundation; a deluge; [often *cap.*] with *the*, the universal deluge recorded as having occurred in the days of Noah (see Gen. vii.); also [*l. c.*], a body of flowing water, as a river (now poetic); the water or the sea as opposed to the land (now poetic); also, any great outpouring or stream, as of lava, light, etc.; an overflowing abundance (as, "You see this confluence, this great *flood* of visitors": Shakspere's "Timon of Athens," i. 1. 42).—**flood,** *v.* **I.** *tr.* To overflow in or cover with a flood; inundate; deluge; cover with water, as grassland; fill to overflowing, as a river; fig., to cover as with a flood (as, "The moon is at her full and, riding high, *Floods* the calm fields with light": Bryant's "Tides"); overwhelm with an abundance of something (as, the new governor is *flooded* with applications for office); also, to pour in a flood. **II.** *intr.* To flow or pour in or as in a flood; rise in a flood, or overflow (as, "The Nilus would have risen before his time And *flooded* at our nod": Tennyson's "Dream of Fair Women," 144); in *pathol.*, to have an excessive menstrual flow; also, to suffer uterine hemorrhage, esp. in connection with parturition.—**flood′a-ble,** *a.* That may be flooded.—**flood′er,** *n.*—**flood′=gate,** *n.* A gate designed to control the flow of water; hence, anything serving to control indiscriminate flow or passage.—**flood′=light,** *n.* Artificial light so directed or diffused as to give a comparatively uniform illumination throughout a room or the like.—**flood′=light,** *v. t.* To illuminate with flood-light.—**flood′=tide,** *n.* The inflow of the tide; the rising tide.

floor (flōr), *n.* [AS. *flōr* = D. *vloer* = G. *flur* = Icel. *flōr*, floor.] That part of a room or the like (consisting of boards, planks, tiles, stone, concrete, etc.) which forms its lower inclosing surface, and upon which one walks; the part of a legislative chamber, etc., where the members sit, and from which they speak; the right of one member to speak from such a place at a particular time in preference to other members (as, to get or have the *floor*); the main part of an exchange or the like, in distinction from galleries, etc.; also, a story of a building (as, to occupy the second *floor*); also, a level supporting surface in any structure (as, the *floor* of a bridge or of an elevator); a platform or prepared level area for a particular use (as, a threshing-*floor*); also, the flat bottom of any more or less hollow place (as, the *floor* of a cave or of the ocean); a flat extent of surface (as, "For Lycidas your sorrow is not dead, Sunk though he be beneath the watery *floor*": Milton's "Lycidas," 167); in *mining*, an underlying stratum; also, a stratum or layer, as of ore; *naut.*, that part of the bottom of a vessel on each side of the keelson which is most nearly horizontal.—**floor,** *v. t.* To furnish with a floor; also, to bring down to the floor or ground; knock down; hence, to beat or defeat (colloq.); confound or nonplus (colloq.: as, to be *floored* by a problem); also, to place upon a floor; base.—**floor′age** (-āj), *n.* Floor space.—**floor′=cloth,** *n.* A piece of cloth or some substitute material for covering a floor (with or without carpet); any material, as crash, drugget, oilcloth, linoleum, etc., used for this purpose; also, a cloth for washing or wiping floors.—**floor′er,** *n.* One who lays floors; also, a person or thing, as a blow, that knocks to the floor or ground; hence, something that beats, overwhelms, or confounds (colloq.).—**floor′ing,** *n.* A floor; floors collectively; materials for making floors.—**floor′less,** *a.* Having no floor.—**floor′=walk″er,** *n.* A person employed in a large retail store to walk about as an overseer, to direct customers, etc.

flop (flop), *v.*; *flopped, flopping.* [Var. of *flap.*] **I.** *intr.* To fall or plump down suddenly, esp. with noise; drop or turn with a sudden bump or thud; hence, to change suddenly, as from one side or party to another (often with *over*); yield or break down suddenly; also, to flap, as in the wind. [Colloq.] **II.** *tr.* To drop, throw, etc., with a sudden bump or thud; also, to flap clumsily and heavily, as wings. [Colloq.]—**flop,** *n.* The act or sound of flopping; a thud. [Colloq.]—**flop′per,** *n.*—**flop′py,** *a.*; compar. *floppier*, superl. *floppiest.* Tending to flop. [Colloq.]—**flop′pi-ly,** *adv.*—**flop′pi-ness,** *n.*

flo-ra (flō′rạ), *n.*; pl. *-ras* or *-ræ* (-rē). [L. *Flora*, < *flos* (*flor-*), flower.] [*cap.*] The Roman goddess of flowers; [*l. c.*] the plants of a particular region or period, taken collectively; a work systematically describing such plants.—**flo′ral,** *a.* [L. *Floralis.*] [*cap.*] Of or pertaining to the goddess Flora; [*l. c.*] pertaining to a flora; also, of, pertaining to, or consisting of flowers.—**floral circle,** in *bot.*, a ring of like organs, as petals, round the axis of a flower; one of the whorls of a flower.—**floral envelop** or **envelops,** in *bot.*, the floral leaves (petals or sepals, or both) of a flower, collectively; a perianth.—**floral leaf,** in *bot.*, one of the divisions of a perianth; a petal or sepal; also, less properly, a bract.—**flo′ral-ly,** *adv.*

Flo-ré-al (flo-rā-âl), *n.* [F. *floréal*, < L. *floreus*, of flowers, < *flos* (*flor-*), flower.] In the calendar of the first French republic, the eighth month of the year, extending from April 20 to May 19.

Flor-en-tine (flor′ẹn-tēn or -tīn). [L. *Florentinus*, < *Florentia*, Florence.] **I.** *a.* Of or pertaining to Florence, in Italy: as, the *Florentine* lily (see *giglio*). **II.** *n.* A native or inhabitant of Florence; [*l. c.*] a twilled silk fabric, used for wearing apparel.

flo-res-cence (flō-res′ẹns), *n.* [NL. *florescentia*, < L. *florescens*, ppr. of *florescere*, begin to flower, < *florere*: see *flourish.*] The act, state, or period of flowering; bloom.—**flo-res′cent,** *a.* [L. *florescens* (*-ent-*), ppr.] Flowering.

flo-ret (flō′ret), *n.* [Dim. < L. *flos* (*flor-*), flower.] A small flower, or floweret (as, "acres of houstonia, whose innumerable *florets* whiten and ripple before the eye": Emerson's "Essays," Nature); in *bot.*, one of the closely clustered small flowers that make up the flower-head in asteraceous plants, as the daisy.

flo-ri-at-ed (flō′ri-ā-ted), *a.* [L. *flos* (*flor-*), flower.] Decorated with floral ornamentation: as, *floriated* capitals of columns.—**flo-ri-a′tion** (-ā′shọn), *n.*

flo-ri-cul-ture (flō′ri-kul-ţūr or flor′i-), *n.* [L. *flos* (*flor-*), flower, + *cultura*, culture.] The cultivation of flowers or flowering plants.—**flo-ri-cul′tur-al,** *a.*—**flo-ri-cul′tur-ist,** *n.*

flor-id (flor′id), *a.* [L. *floridus*, < *flos* (*flor-*), flower.] Abounding in or consisting of flowers†; fig., flowery or highly ornate, as language, composition, style, or a speaker or writer; abounding in decorative features or work, as architecture; of a highly embellished or showily elaborate kind, as music; in general, ornate; showy; pretentiously fine; also, bright in color, esp. bright-red, as arterial blood†; high-colored or ruddy, as complexion, cheeks, persons, etc.

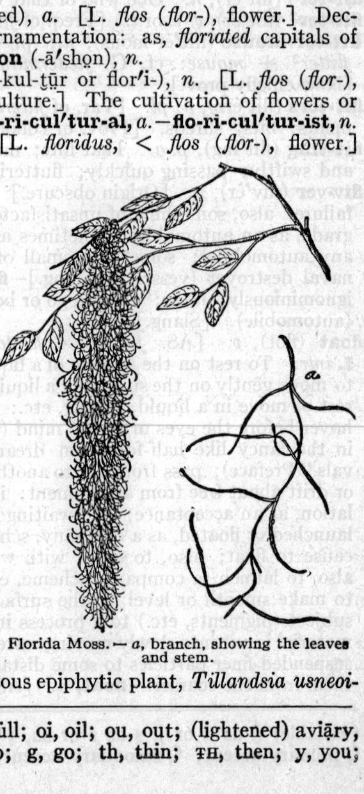

Florida Moss.—*a*, branch, showing the leaves and stem.

Flor-i-da (flor′i-dạ) **moss.** A bromeliaceous epiphytic plant, *Tillandsia usneoi-*

des, of the southern U. S., forming pendulous tufts which drape the branches of trees.

flo-rid-i-ty (flǫ-rid′i-ti), *n.* The state or quality of being florid.—**flor-id-ly** (flor′id-li), *adv.* In a florid manner.—**flor′id-ness,** *n.* Floridity.

flo-rif-er-ous (flǫ-rif′ę-rus), *a.* [L. *florifer*, < *flos* (*flor-*), flower, + *ferre*, bear.] Flower-bearing.

flo-ri-le-gi-um (flō-ri-lē′ji-um), *n.*; pl. *-gia* (-ji-ạ̈). [NL., < L. *florilegus*, flower-culling, < *flos* (*flor-*), flower, + *legere*, gather, choose.] A collection of flowers†; fig., an anthology.

flor-in (flor′in), *n.* [OF. F. *florin*, < It. *fiorino*, a Florentine coin stamped with a lily, < *fiore*, < L. *flos* (*flor-*), flower.] A former gold coin weighing about 55 grains, first issued at Florence in 1252; a former English gold coin of Edward III., worth 6 shillings; an Austrian silver coin, equal to 2 krones, not coined since 1892; the gulden of the Netherlands; an English silver coin worth 2 shillings, first minted in 1849.

Obverse. Reverse.
Gold Florin of Florence.— British Museum.

flo-rist (flō′rist or flor′ist), *n.* [L. *flos* (*flor-*), flower.] One who cultivates flowers, esp. for sale; a dealer in flowers.

-florous. Adjective termination from L. *flos* (*flor-*), flower, as in *biflorous*, *noctiflorous*, *tubuliflorous*.

flor-u-it (flor′ū-it). [L.] 'He (or she) flourished': used in giving the date of the most successful or effective period, or the accepted period, of a person's life and activity.

flo-ry (flō′ri), *a.* See *fleury*.

flos-cule (flos′kūl), *n.* [L. *flosculus*, dim. of *flos*, flower.] In *bot.*, a floret.—**flos-cu-lar, flos-cu-lous** (flos′kū-lär, -lus), *a.*

floss (flos), *n.* [F. *floche*, earlier *flosche*, soft, not twisted (as silk), < It. *floscio*, soft, flaccid, < L. *fluxus*, pp. of *fluere*, flow.] Silk or other fiber in untwisted filaments; silk, linen, etc., in untwisted strands for use in embroidery; also, the outer rough or broken silk fibers of cocoons; also, the cottony fiber yielded by the silk-cotton trees; in general, any silky filamentous matter, as the silk of maize.—**floss′=silk,** *n.* Silk in untwisted filaments or strands; also, the floss of cocoons.—**floss′y,** *a.*; compar. *flossier*, superl. *flossiest*. Of or like floss.

flot-age (flōt′ā̤j), *n.* See *floatage*.

flo-ta-tion (flǫ-tā′shǫn), *n.* [For *floatation*: cf. F. *flottaison* (see *flotsam*).] The act or state of floating (see *float*, *v.*); esp., the floating or launching of a commercial venture, a loan, etc.

flo-til-la (flǫ-til′ạ̈), *n.* [Sp., dim. of *flota*, fleet; prob. akin to E. *float*.] A small fleet; a fleet of small vessels.

flot-sam (flot′sạm), *n.* [AF. *floteson*, flotsam, = OF. *flotaison*, flooding (F. *flottaison*, flotation), < *floter*, float, flood; prob. akin to E. *float*.] Such part of the wreckage of a ship and its cargo as is found floating on the water. Also fig. Cf. *jetsam*.

flounce[1] (flouns), *v. i.*; *flounced*, *flouncing*. [Cf. Sw. dial. *flunsa*, plunge.] To plunge, as into water, a hole, etc.†; also, to make plunging or heavy, violent movements of the body, as a horse or other animal or a person; throw the body about, as in floundering or struggling; sometimes, to fling one's self about in dancing; also, to go (*away*, *off*, *out*, etc.) with an indignant or angry fling of the body.—**flounce**[1], *n.* A flouncing movement; esp., a sudden fling of the body in indignation or anger.

flounce[2] (flouns), *n.* [Var. of *frounce*.] A strip of material, wider than a ruffle, gathered and attached at one edge and with the other edge left hanging: used for trimming, esp. on women's skirts.—**flounce**[2], *v. t.*; *flounced*, *flouncing*. To trim with a flounce or flounces.—**floun-cing** (floun′sing), *n.* Trimming consisting of a flounce; also, material for flounces.

floun-der[1] (floun′dėr), *v. i.* [Origin uncertain: cf. *founder*[3].] To stumble†; slip, plunge, or tumble about, as in mud or snow, with strong efforts to maintain or regain the footing or balance (as, "The foot-passengers had a hard time of it *floundering* in the arctic drifts": Aldrich's "Story of a Bad Boy," xii.); struggle (*along*, *on*, *through*, etc.) with stumbling or plunging movements; fig., to struggle clumsily or helplessly in embarrassment or confusion; go (*along*, *on*, *through*, etc.) in action, speech, writing, etc., with clumsy slips and painful efforts to retrieve one's self (as, to *flounder* through a dance or an apology).—**floun′der**[1], *n.* A floundering movement or action.

floun-der[2] (floun′dėr), *n.* [ME.; prob. from Scand.] Any flatfish; esp., one of various flatfishes of the genus *Pleuronectes* and allied genera, as *P. platessa* of England, and *Pseudopleuronectes americana* and *Paralichthys oblongus* of the eastern U. S.

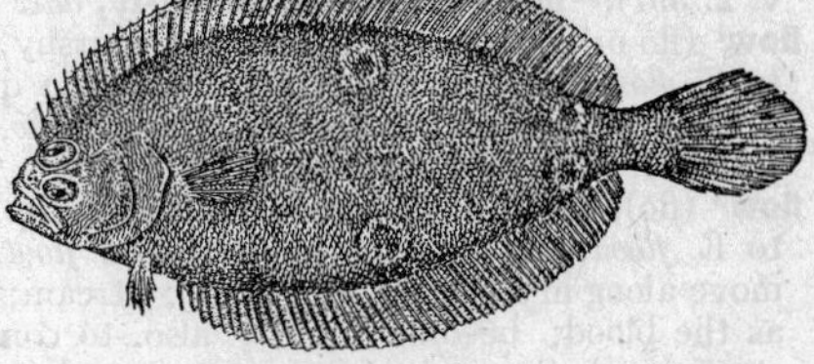

Four-spotted Flounder (*Paralichthys oblongus*).

flour (flour), *n.* [An earlier spelling of *flower*, as meaning the 'finest part' of meal.] The finely ground meal of grain, esp. the finer meal separated by bolting; commonly, the finely ground and bolted meal of wheat; hence, any fine, soft powder (as, *flour* of emery).—**flour,** *v. t.* To sprinkle or dredge with flour, as food or utensils in cookery; powder (a wig); also, to make (grain, etc.) into flour; grind and bolt.—**flour′=bee″tle,** *n.* Any of various beetles that live on flour or farinaceous substances, as *Tenebrio molitor*, whose larva is a common meal-worm.

Flour-beetle (*Tenebrio molitor*). (Line shows natural size.)

flour-ish (flur′ish), *v.* [OF. *florir* (*floriss-*) (F. *fleurir*), < L. *florere*, flower, bloom, flourish, < *flos* (*flor-*), E. *flower*.] **I.** *intr.* To flower† or blossom†; also, to grow luxuriantly, or thrive in growth, as a plant; hence, in general, to thrive, do well, or prosper (as, an age when art and learning *flourished*; the enterprise *flourishes*; churches and kingdoms *flourish*; "The stars shall fade away, the sun . . . Grow dim . . . But thou shalt *flourish* in immortal youth," Addison's "Cato," v. 1); be in its or one's prime; often, of persons, to be in the most successful or effective period, or the best-known or the accepted period, of life and activity, at a date specified (as, Sappho, the Greek poetess, *flourished* about 600 B.C.: cf. *floruit*); also, to add embellishments or flourishes to writing, letters, etc.; make fanciful strokes with a pen or the like; speak or write in flowery or pretentious language; descant (*on* or *upon*); also, to make strokes or flourishes with a brandished weapon or the like; hence, to make a parade or ostentatious display; in *music*, to play a showy passage; play in a showy manner; also, to sound a trumpet-call or fanfare. **II.** *tr.* To cause to bloom, thrive, or prosper†; also, to adorn with decorative work or designs, color, etc. (now only as in next sense); embellish (writing, letters, etc.) with sweeping or fanciful curves or lines; embellish (discourse, etc.) with flowery or pretentious language†; also, to brandish or wave (a sword, a stick, the limbs, etc.) about in the air; hence, to parade, flaunt, or display ostentatiously (as, to *flourish* one's wealth or authority).—**flour′ish,** *n.* The state of flowering or blossoming†; a blossom, or blossoms collectively (Sc. and north. Eng.); also, the condition of flourishing or thriving; the bloom of youth or life (as, "A Prince In the mid might and *flourish* of his May, Gawain, surnamed The Courteous, fair and strong": Tennyson's "Lancelot and Elaine," 552); prosperity; also, a decoration or embellishment, now esp. one of sweeping or fanciful curves, etc., about writing, an initial letter, or the like; also, rhetorical embellishment, or an instance of it; a parade of fine language; an expression used merely for effect; also, a brandishing or waving, as of a sword, a stick, or the like; hence, a parade or ostentatious display; in *music*, an elaborate passage or addition merely for display; also, a trumpet-call or fanfare.—**flour′ish-er,** *n.*—**flour′ish-ing,** *p. a.* That flourishes; vigorous in growth; thriving; prosperous.—**flour′ish-ing-ly,** *adv.*

flour-y (flour′i), *a.* Of, pertaining to, or resembling flour; covered or white with flour.

flout (flout), *v.* [Origin uncertain: cf. *flite, flyte.*] **I.** *intr.* To mock, gibe, or scoff (often with *at*); behave with disdain or contumely. **II.** *tr.* To mock; scoff at; treat with disdain or contempt.—**flout,** *n.* A flouting speech or action; a mocking insult; a gibe: as, "Bruise me with scorn, confound me with a *flout*" (Shakspere's "Love's Labour's Lost," v. 2. 397).—**flout′er,** *n.*—**flout′ing-ly,** *adv.*

flow[1] (flō or flou), *n.* [Cf. Icel. *flōi*, marshy moor, bay, akin to E. *flow*[2].] A marshy tract; a bog; a quicksand; also, a basin or arm of the sea (as, Scapa *Flow*, in the Orkney Islands). [Sc. and north. Eng.]

flow[2] (flō), *v.* [AS. *flōwan* = D. *vloeien* = Icel. *flōa*; akin to E. *flood*, and perhaps to *fleet*[1] and *float*.] **I.** *intr.* To move along in a stream, as a liquid; stream; run; circulate, as the blood; become liquid†; also, to come or go as in a stream, as persons or things; proceed continuously and smoothly, like a stream, as thought, speech, or verse; fall or hang loosely at full length, as hair; also, to stream or well forth; gush out; issue or proceed from a source; discharge a stream, as of blood; also, to rise and advance, as the tide (opposed to *ebb*); be in flood or overfull, as a river†; overflow or abound with something (as, "a land *flowing* with milk and honey": Ex. iii. 8). **II.** *tr.* To cause or permit to flow; also, to cover with water or other liquid; flood.—**flow**[2], *n.* The act of flowing; movement in or as in a stream; any continuous movement, as of thought, speech, trade, etc., like that of a stream of water; an outpouring or discharge of something, as in a stream (as, to check a *flow* of blood); the rise of the tide (opposed to *ebb*); an overflowing (as, "regions fatten'd with the *flows* of Nile": Pope's tr. Homer's "Odyssey," iv.); also, that which flows; a stream, as of water or other fluid or of anything regarded as flowing (as, to cross a lava-*flow*; "A most silver *flow* Of subtle-paced counsel in distress," Tennyson's "Isabel"); also, the rate of flowing; the volume of fluid that flows through a passage of any given section in a unit of time.—**flow′age** (-āj), *n.* The act of flowing; flow; the state of being flowed or flooded; also, the flowing or overflowing liquid.

flow-er (flou′ėr), *n.* [OF. *flor, flour* (F. *fleur*), < L. *flos* (*flor-*), flower; akin to E. *blow*[2].] The blossom or bloom of a plant; in botanical use, that part of a seed-plant comprising the reproductive organs and their envelops (if any), esp. when such envelops are more or less conspicuous in form and color (in scientific use, usually applied to a single complex structure consisting typically of pistil, stamens, corolla, and calyx, but in popular use applied also to a complete inflorescence or cluster of such structures); an analogous reproductive structure in other plants, as the mosses; a plant considered with reference to its blossom or cultivated for its floral beauty; also, an ornament representing a flower; any ornament or adornment; an ornament or figure of speech; also, the best or finest member or part of a number, body, or whole (as, to be the *flower* of the family); the finest or choicest product of anything (as, this work was the *flower* of his genius); the best or finest example of some quality (as, "Lancelot, the *flower* of bravery": Tennyson's "Lancelot and Elaine," 113); also, the state of efflorescence or bloom (as, plants in *flower*); the finest or most flourishing state or period, as of life or beauty; the prime; *pl.*, in *chem.*, a substance in the form of a fine powder, esp. as obtained by sublimation (as, *flowers* of sulphur).—**flow′er,** *v.* **I.** *intr.* To produce flowers, or blossom, as a plant; abound in flowers, as ground; come into full bloom, as a flower; fig., to come out into full development or display (often with *out*); froth, as beer†; also, to flourish† or prosper†; sometimes, to flourish, or be alive and active, at a specified time†. **II.** *tr.* To cause (a plant) to blossom or bloom; also, to cover or deck with flowers; embellish with a design of flowers, as by embroidery (as, "A queenlier thing Than to weave silk and *flower* it with fine gold": Swinburne's "Bothwell," i. 5); in general, to decorate† or adorn†.—**flow′er-age** (-āj), *n.* The process or state of flowering; also, flowers collectively; an assemblage of flowers; floral ornament or decoration.

flow-er=de=luce (flou″ėr-dẹ-lūs′), *n.* [Old var. of *fleur-de-lis*, conformed to *flower*.] The iris (flower or plant); also, the heraldic fleur-de-lis. [Archaic.]

flow-ered (flou′ėrd), *a.* Having or bearing flowers (as, pink-*flowered*); also, covered or decked with flowers; embellished with a design of flowers, as fabrics, wall-paper, etc.

flow-er-er (flou′ėr-ėr), *n.* A plant that flowers.

flow-er-et (flou′ėr-et), *n.* A small flower; a floret.

flow-er=head (flou′ėr-hed), *n.* In *bot.*, an inflorescence consisting of a dense cluster of sessile florets; a capitulum.

flow-er-i-ly (flou′ėr-i-li), *adv.* In a flowery manner.—**flow′er-i-ness,** *n.*

flow-er-ing (flou′ėr-ing), *p. a.* Bearing flowers; being in bloom.—**flowering almond,** a shrub, *Amygdalus japonica*, much cultivated for its pink flowers.—**flowering maple,** the abutilon.

flow-er-less (flou′ėr-les), *a.* Without flowers; in *bot.*, cryptogamous.

flow-er=pot (flou′ėr-pot), *n.* A pot to hold earth for a plant to grow in: commonly made of burned clay, unglazed, and tapering a little toward the bottom, which is perforated for drainage.

flow-er-y (flou′ėr-i), *a.* Abounding in, consisting of, or pertaining to flowers (as, *flowery* meadows; *flowery* garlands; *flowery* fragrance); also, embellished with a design of flowers, as a fabric; flowered; also, abounding in or given to flowers of speech, or fine or showy words and expressions, as language or a speaker; highly ornate; florid.

flow-ing (flō′ing), *p. a.* That flows; moving in or as in a stream; proceeding smoothly or with ease, as language, eloquence, the pen, etc.; smoothly and gracefully continuous throughout the length, as lines or curves; falling or hanging loosely at full length, as hair.—**flow′ing-ly,** *adv.*—**flow′ing-ness,** *n.*

flown[1] (flōn). Past participle of *fly*[2].

flown[2] (flōn), *p. a.* [Obs. pp. of *flow*[2].] Swollen, as a river in flood†; filled to excess (archaic: as, "The sons Of Belial, *flown* with insolence and wine," Milton's "Paradise Lost," i. 502).

flu (flö), *n.* Shortened form of *influenza*. [Colloq.]

flub-dub (flub′dub), *n.* [Prob. a made word.] Pretentious nonsense or show; airs. [Colloq.]

fluc-tu-ant (fluk′ṭū-ạnt), *a.* Fluctuating; varying.

fluc-tu-ate (fluk′ṭū-āt), *v.*; *-ated, -ating.* [L. *fluctuatus*, pp. of *fluctuare*, < *fluctus*, a wave, < *fluere*, flow.] **I.** *intr.* To move in waves or like waves, as the sea, a flag, etc.; hence, to change continually, as by turns, from one course, position, condition, amount, etc., to another, as the mind, opinion, policy, prices, temperature, etc.; often, to vary with alternating tendencies, as between opposite courses, positions, etc. (as, to *fluctuate* between hope and fear; the election returns *fluctuated* between the two candidates); waver. **II.** *tr.* To put into wave-like motion (as, "A breeze began to tremble o'er The large leaves of the sycamore, And *fluctuate* all the still perfume": Tennyson's "In Memoriam," xcv.); also, to cause to waver. [Rare.]—**fluc-tu-a′tion** (-ā′shọn), *n.* [L. *fluctuatio*(*n*-).] The act of fluctuating; wave-like motion; continual change from one course, position, condition, etc., to another; alternating variation, as between opposite courses, etc.; wavering.

flue[1] (flö), *n.* [Origin obscure.] Formerly, a chimney; now, the smoke-passage in a chimney; any duct or passage for air, gases, or the like; in certain steam-boilers, any of the pipes or tubes through which hot gases, etc., are conveyed in order to heat surrounding or adjacent water.

flue[2] (flö), *n.* [Origin uncertain; perhaps akin to *fly*[2]: cf. *fluff*.] Downy matter; fluff.

flue[3] (flö), *n.* [Cf. *fluke*[1].] The fluke of an anchor; a barb or fluke of a harpoon; a barb of a feather.—**flued,** *a.* Having a flue or flues.

flu-ent (flö′ẹnt), *a.* [L. *fluens* (*fluent-*), ppr. of *fluere*, flow.] Flowing, as a stream; capable of flowing, or fluid, as liquids or gases; fig., not fixed or stable in form; also, proceeding smoothly and easily, as speech, a speaker or writer, the pen, etc.; characterized by readiness of expression, as style; also, falling loosely, or flowing, as hair.—**flu′en-cy, flu′ent-ness,** *n.*—**flu′ent-ly,** *adv.*

flue-y (flö′i), *a.* Covered with flue; fluffy; downy.

fluff (fluf), *n.* [Appar. var. of *flue*[2].] Light, downy particles, as of cotton; also, a downy mass; something downy or fluffy.—**fluff,** *v.* **I.** *tr.* To make into fluff; shake or puff out (feathers, hair, etc.) into a fluffy mass; also, to buff (leather). **II.** *intr.* To become fluffy; move, float, or settle down like fluff.—**fluff'y,** *a.*; compar. *fluffier*, superl. *fluffiest.* Of, like, or covered with fluff; soft and light as fluff.—**fluff'i-ness,** *n.*

flu-id (flö'id), *a.* [L. *fluidus*, < *fluere*, flow.] Capable of flowing; liquid or gaseous; fig., changing readily; shifting; not fixed, stable, or rigid. Also, of or pertaining to fluids: see phrases following.—**fluid dram,** the eighth part of a fluid ounce: often written *fluidrachm.*—**fluid measure,** apothecaries' measure. See under *apothecary.*—**fluid ounce,** a measure of capacity equal to one sixteenth of a pint in the U. S., and to one twentieth of an imperial pint (28.4 cubic centimeters) in Great Britain: often written *fluidounce.*—**flu'id,** *n.* One of a class of substances (including liquids and gases) whose particles move freely among themselves and thus yield readily to pressure; also, any of various hypothetical subtle substances, as that to which electrical phenomena were formerly attributed.—**flu-id-ic** (flö-id'ik), *a.* Of, pertaining to, or of the nature of a fluid; fluid.—**fluidic body,** in *spiritualism*, a supposed fluid double of the physical body.—**flu-id'i-ty,** *n.* Fluid state or quality.—**flu'id-ly,** *adv.*—**flu'id-ness,** *n.*—**flu'id-ounce** (-ouns), *n.* See *fluid ounce*, under *fluid*, *a.*—**flu'i-drachm** (-i-dram), *n.* See *fluid dram*, under *fluid*, *a.*

fluke[1] (flök), *n.* [Origin uncertain.] The flat triangular piece at the end of each arm of an anchor, forming the part which catches in the ground; also, a barb, or the barbed head, of a harpoon, etc.; also, either half of the triangular tail of a whale.

fluke[2] (flök), *n.* [AS. *flōc.*] Any of various flatfishes, as the common British flounder; also, any of several trematode worms (which in certain stages resemble flounders in shape) parasitic in man and certain animals, esp. sheep; sometimes, any trematode.

fluke[3] (flök), *n.* [Origin uncertain.] An accidentally successful stroke in billiards; hence, any accidental advantage; a lucky chance; also, a failure; a fiasco. [Colloq.]—**fluke**[3], *v.*; *fluked, fluking.* **I.** *tr.* To hit, make, or gain by a fluke. [Colloq.] **II.** *intr.* To make a fluke in billiards; gain an advantage as by chance; also, to make a failure. [Colloq.]—**fluk-y** (flö'ki), *a.* Of the nature of a fluke; obtained by chance rather than skill; also, uncertain, as a wind. [Colloq.]—**fluk'i-ness,** *n.*

flume (flöm), *n.* [OF. *flum*, < L. *flumen*, stream, river, < *fluere*, flow.] A stream†; also, a deep, narrow defile, esp. one containing a mountain torrent; also, an artificial channel or trough for conducting water, as one in which logs, etc., are transported.—**flume,** *v. t.*; *flumed, fluming.* To transport, as lumber, in a flume, also, to divert, as a river, etc., by a flume.

flum-mer-y (flum'ėr-i), *n.* [W. *llymru.*] Oatmeal or flour boiled with water until thick (prov. Eng., Sc., and Ir.); any of various dishes made of flour, milk, eggs, sugar, etc.; fig., agreeable humbug; empty compliment; nonsense.

flum-mox, flum-mux (flum'ǫks, -uks), *v. t.* [Origin obscure.] To bewilder; confound; bring to confusion. [Slang.]

flump (flump), *v. i.* or *t.* [Imit.] To plump down suddenly or heavily; flop. [Colloq.]—**flump,** *n.* The act or sound of flumping. [Colloq.]

flung (flung). Preterit and past participle of *fling.*

flunk (flungk), *v.* [Origin uncertain: cf. *funk*[2].] **I.** *intr.* To fail, as a student in a recitation or examination; give up; back (*out*). [Colloq., U. S.] **II.** *tr.* To fail in (a recitation, etc.); also, to cause to fail. [Colloq., U. S.]—**flunk,** *n.* A flunking; a failure. [Colloq., U. S.]

flun-ky, flun-key (flung'ki), *n.*; pl. *-kies, -keys* (-kiz). [Orig. Sc.; perhaps akin to *flank.*] A male servant in livery (as, "His *flunkies* answer at the bell": Burns's "Twa Dogs," 54); a lackey; also, a servile follower; a toady.—**flun'ky-ism, flun'key-ism,** *n.* Servility; toadying.

fluo-. Form of *fluorine* used in combination.

flu-or (flö'ǫr), *n.* [So called from its use as a flux, < L. *fluor*, a flowing, < *fluere*, flow.] Fluor-spar; fluorite. See *fluor-spar.*

flu-or-esce (flö-ǫr-es'), *v. i.*; *-esced, -escing.* [From *fluorescence.*] To exhibit fluorescence.

flu-or-es-cence (flö-ǫr-es'ẹns), *n.* [From *fluor(-spar).*] The property possessed by certain transparent substances, such as fluor-spar, of emitting light of a certain color, or becoming self-luminous, upon exposure to the ultra-violet and other rays; also, the light or luminosity so produced.—**flu-or-es'cent,** *a.* Characterized by or pertaining to fluorescence.

flu-or-ic (flǫ-or'ik), *a.* Pertaining to or obtained from fluor or fluorine.

flu-or-ide, flu-or-id (flö'ǫr-īd or -id, -id), *n.* In *chem.*, a compound of fluorine with another element or a radical.

flu-or-ine, flu-or-in (flö'ǫr-in), *n.* [From *fluor.*] Chem. sym., F; at. wt., 19.0. A non-metallic element, a pale greenish-yellow corrosive gas, occurring combined, esp. in fluor-spar and other minerals.

flu-or-ite (flö'ǫr-īt), *n.* Fluor-spar.

flu-or-o-scope (flö'ǫr-ǫ-skōp or flǫ-or'-), *n.* [From *fluor(escence)* + *-scope.*] A tube or box fitted with a screen coated with a fluorescent substance, used for viewing objects exposed to the Röntgen rays.—**flu″or-o-scop'ic** (-skop'ik), *a.* Pertaining to the fluoroscope or to fluoroscopy.—**flu″or-o-scop'i-cal-ly,** *adv.*—**flu-or-os'co-py** (-os'kǫ-pi), *n.* [See *-scopy.*] The art of using the fluoroscope, or of examining by means of a fluorescent screen the shadows of bodies exposed to the Röntgen rays.

Fluoroscope.

flu-or=spar (flö'ǫr-spär'), *n.* [See *fluor.*] A native fluoride of calcium, CaF_2, sometimes colorless and transparent, but more often in tints of yellow, green, blue, and red, used as a flux and for ornamental purposes.

flu-o-sil-i-cate (flö-ǫ-sil'i-kāt), *n.* [See *fluo-.*] In *chem.*, a salt of fluosilicic acid.—**flu″o-si-li'cic** (-si-lis'ik), *a.* In *chem.*, noting or pertaining to an acid (H_2SiF_6) containing silicon and fluorine, and obtained only as an aqueous solution.

flur-ry (flur'i), *n.*; pl. *flurries* (-iz). [Origin uncertain; perhaps imit.] A sudden gusty blowing of wind; also, a light gusty shower or snowfall; also, a sudden commotion; agitation; perturbation; also, the spasmodic movements of a dying whale.—**flur'ry,** *v. t.*; *-ried, -rying.* To put (a person) into a flurry; agitate; perturb: as, "O lud! now, Mr. Fag—you *flurry* one so" (Sheridan's "Rivals," ii. 2).

flush[1] (flush), *v.* [ME. *flusshen*; appar. imit.: cf. *flash.*] **I.** *intr.* To fly out or start up suddenly, as a bird when disturbed. **II.** *tr.* To cause (birds, etc.) to start up.—**flush**[1], *n.* The act of flushing; also, a flushed bird, or flock of birds.

flush[2] (flush), *v.* [Cf. *flush*[1] and *flash.*] **I.** *intr.* To flow with a rush; flow and spread suddenly; also, to become suffused with color; blush; redden; also, to send out shoots, as a tea-plant. **II.** *tr.* To flood with water, as for cleansing purposes; wash out (a sewer, etc.); also, to suffuse with color; redden; also, to animate or elate (as, "armies *flushed* with conquest": Addison's "Cato," i. 2).—**flush**[2], *n.* A rushing or overspreading flow, as of water; also, a suffusion with color; a blush; a rosy glow; glowing freshness or vigor (as, the *flush* of youth); also, a rush of emotion (as, a *flush* of joy); elation (as, in the first *flush* of victory); also, a fresh growth, as of shoots and leaves.

flush[3] (flush). [Perhaps < *flush*[2].] **I.** *a.* Quite full; full to overflowing; also, full of vigor; lusty; also, well supplied, as with money; affluent; prosperous; sometimes, abundant or plentiful, as money; also, flushed with color; blushing; also, even or level, as with a surface; in one plane (as, a *flush* deck, one which is unbroken by deck-houses, etc., and has an even surface fore and aft or from stem to stern). **II.** *adv.* So as to be flush or even.—**flush**[3], *v. t.* To make flush or even.

flush[4] (flush), *n.* [F. (obs.) *flus*, for *flux*, flow, flush (cf. '*run* of cards'), < L. *fluxus*, E. *flux.*] In *card-playing*, a hand or set of cards all of the same suit.

flus-ter (flus'tėr), *v.* [Cf. Icel. *flaustra*, be flustered, *flaustr*, fluster, hurry.] **I.** *tr.* To excite and confuse with drink (as, "Three lads of Cyprus . . . Have I to-night *fluster'd* with flowing cups": Shakspere's "Othello," ii. 3. 60); also, to render agitated and confused; flurry. **II.** *intr.* To become confused; move with agitation or flurry (as, "At Miltoun's approach two blackbirds *flustered* out through the netting and flew away": Galsworthy's "Patrician," ii. 4).—**flus'ter,** *n.* Confusion; flurry.—**flus'trate** (-trāt), *v. t.*; *-trated, -trating.* To fluster. [Colloq.]—**flus-tra'tion** (-trā'shon), *n.*

Ancient Greek Double Flute.

flute (flöt), *n.* [OF. *fleute, flehute, flaute, flahute*; origin unknown.] A musical wind-instrument consisting of a tube with a series of finger-holes or keys for producing tone variations, in early forms blown through a mouthpiece at the upper end, but in the form now in common use having a hole in the side near the upper end across the edge of which a current of air is blown; also, a channel or furrow with rounded section, as in a pillar.—**flute,** *v.*; *fluted, fluting.* **I.** *intr.* To play on a flute; also, to produce or utter flute-like sounds (as, "The thrushes are in song there, *fluting* from the nest": Masefield's "West Wind"). **II.** *tr.* To utter in flute-like tones; also, to form flutes, grooves, or furrows in.—**flut-ed** (flö'ted), *p. a.* Uttered in flute-like tones; also, having flutes or grooves, as a pillar; furrowed.—**flut'er,** *n.*—**flut'ing,** *n.* The act of one who flutes; a flute-like sound; also, the act of making flutes, or ornamenting with flutes; fluted work; a flute, groove, or furrow.—**flut'ing=i''ron,** *n.* A specially shaped iron for pressing ruffles, etc., into a fluted form.—**flut'-ist,** *n.* A flute-player.

Modern Flute.

Fluting-iron.

flut-ter (flut'ėr), *v.* [AS. *floterian*, a freq. form connected with *flēotan*, float, E. *fleet*[1].] **I.** *intr.* To float or toss on waves†; also, to toss or wave in air, as a flag; move in quick, irregular motions; beat fast and irregularly, as the heart; be tremulous or agitated (as, "With this my lady swept out of the room, *fluttering* with her own audacity": Thackeray's "Vanity Fair," lv.); also, to go with irregular motions or aimless course (as, "One flaunts in rags, one *flutters* in brocade": Pope's "Essay on Man," iv. 196); also, of birds, etc., to flap the wings, or fly with flapping movements. **II.** *tr.* To cause to flutter; vibrate; agitate; throw into confusion or tremulous excitement (as, to *flutter* one's nerves).—**flut'-ter,** *n.* A fluttering movement or state; agitation; confused excitement.—**flut'ter-er,** *n.*—**flut'ter-ing-ly,** *adv.*—**flut'ter-y,** *a.* Fluttering; apt to flutter.

flut-y (flö'ti), *a.* Flute-like, as in tone.

flu-vi-al (flö'vi-al), *a.* [L. *fluvialis*, < *fluvius*, river, < *fluere*, flow.] Of, pertaining to, or produced by a river.

flu-vi-a-tile (flö'vi-a-til), *a.* [L. *fluviatilis*, < *fluvius*, river: see *fluvial*.] Pertaining or peculiar to rivers; found in or near rivers.

fluvio-. Form of L. *fluvius*, river, used in combination.—**flu-vi-o-graph** (flö'vi-ō-grȧf), *n.* [+ *-graph*.] An instrument which measures and records automatically the rise and fall of a river.—**flu-vi-ol'o-gy** (-ol'ō-ji), *n.* [+ *-logy*.] The science of rivers and streams.—**flu''vi-o-ma-rine'** (-ō-ma-rēn'), *a.* Noting or pertaining to deposits formed by rivers in estuaries or on the bottom of the sea.—**flu-vi-om'e-ter** (-om'e-tėr), *n.* [+ *-meter*.] An apparatus for determining the height of water in a river.

flux (fluks), *n.* [OF. F. *flux*, < L. *fluxus*, a flowing, < *fluere*, flow.] A flowing or flow; the flowing in of the tide; a stream (often fig.); specif., an abnormal or morbid discharge of blood or other matter from the body; dysentery ('bloody flux'); also, the rate of flow of a fluid, heat, or the like; also, continuous passage; continuous change (as, "The matter is in a perpetual *flux*, and never at a stay": Bacon's "Essays," Of Vicissitude of Things); also, fusion; also, a substance, as borax or fluor-spar, used to promote the fusion of metals or minerals.—**magnetic flux.** See under *magnetic*.—**flux,** *v.* **I.** *tr.* To purge†; also, to fuse; treat with a flux. **II.** *intr.* To flow; also, to change.—**flux-ion** (fluk'shon), *n.* [F. *fluxion*, < L. *fluxio(n-)*, < *fluere*.] The act of flowing; a flow or flux; in *math.*, the rate of change of a continuously varying quantity.—**flux'ion-al, flux'ion-a-ry** (-ā-ri), *a.*—**flux'ion-al-ly,** *adv.*—**flux'me''ter** (-mē''tėr), *n.* In *elect.*, an instrument for measuring magnetic flux.

fly[1] (flī), *n.*; pl. *flies* (flīz). [AS. *flēoge* = D. *vlieg* = G. *fliege*, a fly; from the root of E. *fly*[2].] Orig., any winged insect (as, a butter*fly*); now, any of the two-winged insects constituting the order *Diptera* ('true flies'), and esp. the family *Muscidæ*, as *Musca domestica* (the common 'house-fly'); also, a fish-hook dressed with silk, tinsel, etc., so as to resemble an insect.

fly[2] (flī), *v.*; pret. *flew*, pp. *flown*, ppr. *flying*. [AS. *flēogan* = D. *vliegen* = G. *fliegen* = Icel. *fljūga*, fly: cf. *flee*.] **I.** *intr.* To move through the air on wings, as a bird; travel through the air in an aëroplane or the like, or as an aëroplane does; be borne through the air by the wind or any other force or agency; also, to float or flutter in the air, as a flag, the hair, etc.; also, to move or pass swiftly (as, the ship *flies* before the wind); move with a start or rush (as, to *fly* to arms); spring with violence (as, a dog *flies* at an intruder); be forced or driven suddenly (as, "From the cold stone sparks of fire do *fly*": Shakspere's "Lucrece," 177); be thrown (*open, up*, etc.: as, "Up *flew* the windows all," Cowper's "John Gilpin," 110); burst (*apart, in pieces*, etc.); also, to flee, run away, or take flight (as, "For those that *fly* may fight again, Which he can never do that's slain": Butler's "Hudibras," iii. 3); withdraw hastily; pass quickly away. **II.** *tr.* To cause to fly (as, "I'll *fly* my hawk with yours": Heywood's "Woman Killed with Kindness," i. 1); pilot (an aëroplane or the like) in flight; carry in an aëroplane or the like, as a passenger; perform by flying (as, "Ere the bat hath *flown* His cloister'd flight": Shakspere's "Macbeth," iii. 2. 40); traverse or cross by flying (as, to *fly* the Atlantic in an aëroplane); also, to cause to float or flutter in the air, as a kite or a flag; also, to chase with a hawk; attack by flying, as a hawk does; also, to flee from; shun.—**fly**[2], *n.*; pl. *flies* (flīz). The act or an act of flying; a flight; the course of a flying object, as a ball; also, something that flies, as a ball batted high in the air; a light public carriage for passengers (Eng.: as, "She came . . . driving up from the station in a *fly*," Galsworthy's "Patrician," ii. 3); a regulating device for clockwork, etc., consisting of an arrangement of vanes on a revolving axis; a fly-wheel; the extent of a flag from the staff to the outer end, or the outer end itself; a piece of canvas extending over the ridge-pole of a tent and forming an outer roof; a flap forming the door of a tent; a strip sewed along one edge to a garment, to aid in concealing the buttons; *pl.*, the space and apparatus above the stage in a theater.—**fly**[2], *a.* [Appar. < *fly*[2], *v.*] Knowing; sharp; smart. [Slang.]

fly=ag-a-ric (flī'ag''a-rik), *n.* A very poisonous mushroom, *Amanita muscaria*: sometimes used for making a poison for flies. Cf. *amanita*. Also **fly'=am-a-ni''ta** (-am-a-nī''tä).

fly-a-way (flī'a-wā''), *a.* Fluttering; streaming; also, flighty; volatile; frivolous.

fly-blow (flī'blō), *n.* The egg or young larva of a flesh-fly, deposited on meat, etc.—**fly'-blow,** *v. t.* To taint with or as with flyblows.—**fly'blown,** *a.* Tainted with flyblows; spoiled; corrupt.

fly-boat (flī'bōt), *n.* [Cf. D. *vlieboot*.] A kind of fast sailing-vessel formerly in use; a flat-bottomed Dutch coaster; a swift boat for canal transportation.

fly=book (flī'bůk), *n.* An angler's book-like case for holding artificial flies.

Fly-book.

fly-catch-er (flī′kach″ėr), *n.* One who or that which catches flies; usually, a bird that captures insects on the wing; esp., a bird of the family *Muscicapidæ*, as *Muscicapa grisola* (the 'spotted fly-catcher' of Europe) and *Seisura inquieta* (the 'restless flycatcher' of Australia), or a bird of the American family *Tyrannidæ*, as the kingbird.

Spotted Flycatcher (*Muscicapa grisola*).

fly′er, *n.* See *flier.*

fly=fish (flī′fish), *v. i.* To fish with flies, natural or artificial, as bait.—**fly′=fish″ing,** *n.*

fly-ing (flī′ing), *p. a.* That flies; making flight through the air (as, "a fiery *flying* serpent," Isa. xiv. 29; a *flying* circus, see *circus*); passing through the air (as, *flying* sand); floating, fluttering or waving, or hanging or moving freely, in the air (as, *flying* kites; *flying* colors, or flags, esp. as ensigns of victory; a *flying* jib, a triangular sail set outside of the jib); extending through the air (as, a *flying* buttress: see under *buttress, n.*); moving swiftly (as, "Earth rolls back beneath the *flying* steed": Pope's "Windsor Forest," 158); made while moving swiftly (as, a *flying* start, a start, as of a race, made at full speed, as after a preparatory run; a *flying* jump, one made after a run or while running); hasty (as, to make a *flying* trip; to pay one a *flying* visit); designed for swiftness (as, *flying* artillery); also, fleeing, running away, or taking flight.—**fly′ing=boat′,** *n.* A hydro-aëroplane whose main body consists of a single hull or boat.—**fly′ing=drag′on,** *n.* Any of the small arboreal lizards of the genus *Draco.* See *dragon.*—**Fly′ing Dutch′man.** A legendary spectral Dutch ship supposed to be seen at sea, esp. near the Cape of Good Hope; also, the captain of this ship, supposed to have been condemned to sail the sea, beating against the wind, till the day of judgment.—**Fly′ing Fish.** In *astron.*, the southern constellation Piscis Volans.—**fly′ing=fish,** *n.* Any of certain fishes with wing-like pectoral fins which help them to glide for some distance through the air after leaping from the water; esp., a fish of the genus *Exocœtus,* as *E. volitans,* common in open seas.—**fly′ing=fox′,** *n.* Any large fruit-eating bat of the family *Pteropodidæ,* esp. of the genus *Pteropus,* as *P. edulis,* of old-world tropical regions: so called from the fox-like head.—**fly′ing=frog′,** *n.* An East Indian frog of the genus *Rhacophorus,* with large webbed toes which enable it to glide through the air.—**fly′ing=gur′nard,** *n.* Any of several fishes of the acanthopterygian genus *Cephalacanthus,* esp. *C. volitans,* having wing-like pectoral fins which enable them to move for some distance through the air after leaping from the water.—**fly′ing=le′mur,** *n.* An East Indian lemur-like mammal of the family *Galeopithecidæ,* having a fold of skin on each side of the body, which acts like a parachute as the animal leaps from tree to tree.—**fly′ing=ma-chine″,** *n.* A contrivance which sustains itself in and propels itself through the air; an aëroplane or the like.—**fly′ing=mouse′,** *n.* A very small Australian flying-phalanger of the genus *Acrobates.*—**fly′ing=pha-lan′ger,** *n.* A phalanger (marsupial quadruped) with a parachute-like fold of skin at each side, which assists it in leaping.—**fly′ing=squir′rel,** *n.* A squirrel-like animal, esp. of the genus *Sciuropterus,* as *S. volans* of the eastern U. S., with folds of skin connecting the fore and hind legs, enabling it to take long flying leaps; also, a flying-phalanger.

Flying-fox (*Pteropus edulis*).

Flying-frog (*Rhacophorus marmoratus*).

Flying-squirrel (*Sciuropterus volans*).

fly=leaf (flī′lēf), *n.*; pl. *-leaves* (-lēvz). A blank leaf at the beginning or the end of a book or the like.

fly=pa-per (flī′pā″pėr), *n.* Paper prepared to destroy flies by poisoning them or by catching them on its sticky surface.

flysch (flish), *n.* [Swiss.] In *geol.*, a partly Tertiary, partly Cretaceous formation, consisting chiefly of sandstones, soft marls, and sandy shales, found in the Alps, etc.

fly=speck (flī′spek), *n.* A speck or tiny stain from the excrement of a fly; a minute spot.—**fly′=speck,** *v. t.* To mark with fly-specks.

flyte (flīt), *v.* and *n.* See *flite.*

fly=trap (flī′trap), *n.* A trap for flies; also, any of various plants which entrap insects, as *Apocynum androsæmifolium,* a species of dogbane, or *Dionæa muscipula* (see *Venus's fly-trap*).

fly=weight (flī′wāt), *n.* A boxer or other contestant of very light weight, lighter than a feather-weight and a bantam-weight.

fly=wheel (flī′hwēl), *n.* A heavy wheel which by its momentum tends to equalize the speed of machinery with which it is connected.

foal (fōl), *n.* [AS. *fola* = OHG. *folo* = Icel. *foli* = Goth. *fula,* foal; akin to L. *pullus,* Gr. πῶλος, young animal, foal.] The young of the horse, ass, or any allied animal; a colt or filly.—**foal,** *v. t.* or *i.* To bring forth (a foal).

foam (fōm), *n.* [AS. *fām* = G. *feim*: cf. Skt. *phena,* foam.] An aggregation of minute bubbles formed on the surface of a liquid by agitation, fermentation, etc.; froth formed in the mouth, as in epilepsy and rabies; the froth of perspiration formed on the skin of a horse or other animal from great exertion; spume.—**foam,** *v.* **I.** *intr.* To form or gather foam; emit foam; froth. **II.** *tr.* To cause to foam; also, to cover with foam; also, to emit in or like foam.—**foam′-ing-ly,** *adv.*—**foam′less,** *a.* Free from foam.—**foam′y,** *a.*; compar. *foamier,* superl. *foamiest.* Covered with or full of foam; consisting of foam; resembling foam; of or pertaining to foam.

fob[1] (fob), *v. t.*; *fobbed, fobbing.* [Appar. a var. of *fop, v.*] To fool; trick; cheat; also, to bring, put, or foist, as into a position, by trickery; pass or palm off, as on a person; put (*off*), as a person, by pretenses or deceit.—**fob**[1], *n.* A trick; an artifice.

fob[2] (fob), *n.* [Origin uncertain.] A small pocket just below the waist-line in trousers or breeches, to hold a watch, etc.; also, a short chain or ribbon with a seal or the like, attached to a watch and worn hanging from the pocket.

fo-cal (fō′kal), *a.* Of or pertaining to a focus: as, the *focal* distance or length of a lens (the distance from its center to its principal focus).—**fo′cal-ize** (-īz), *v. t.*; *-ized, -izing.* To focus.—**fo″cal-i-za′tion** (-i-zā′shon), *n.*—**fo′cal-ly,** *adv.*

fo-cus (fō′kus), *n.*; pl. *-cuses* or *-ci* (-sī). [L., hearth, fireplace.] A point at which rays of light, heat, or the like, meet after being reflected or refracted; a point from which diverging rays appear to proceed, or a point at which converging rays would meet if they could be prolonged in the same direction ('virtual focus'); the point to which parallel rays are brought upon striking a converging lens or mirror ('principal focus'), or the point from which they appear to diverge upon striking a diverging lens or mirror ('principal virtual focus'); either of two points ('conjugate foci') so situated in relation to a lens or mirror that the rays emitted from a luminous body at either point are refracted or reflected to the other; also, the position of an object, or the adjustment of an optical device, necessary to produce a clear image (as, in *focus*; out of *focus*); clear and sharply defined condition of an image, etc., resulting from such position or adjustment; also, the focal length of a lens; in fig. use, a central point, as of attraction, attention, or activity (as, "Every upstart of fortune . . . presents himself at Bath, as in the very *focus* of observation": Smollett's "Humphry Clinker," April 23); in *geom.*, one of the points from which the distances to any point of a given curve are in a linear relation.—**fo'cus,** *v.*; *-cused* or *-cussed, -cusing* or *-cussing.* **I.** *tr.* To bring (rays of light, etc.) to a focus; fig., to concentrate (as, to *focus* one's attention on a matter); also, to adjust (a lens, the eye, etc.) to a focus; also, to bring (an image, etc.) into focus. **II.** *intr.* To become focused.—**fo'cus-er,** *n.*

fod-der (fod'ėr), *n.* [AS. *fōdor* = D. *voeder* = G. *futter* = Icel. *fōdhr*, fodder; akin to E. *food*.] Food for cattle, horses, etc., esp. such food as hay, straw, vegetables, etc.; specif., in the U. S., the stalks and leaves of Indian corn or maize as fed to cattle, etc.—**fod'der,** *v. t.* To feed with or as with fodder.

foe (fō), *n.* [AS. *gefā*, < *ge-*, together, mutually, + *fāh*, hostile: cf. *feud*¹.] One who entertains enmity, hatred, or malice against another; an enemy; also, an adversary in combat; sometimes, an adversary or opponent in a game or contest; also, an enemy in war; one belonging to a hostile army or nation; a hostile army or force (as, "Whispering, with white lips—'The *foe!* they come! they come!'" Byron's "Childe Harold," iii. 25); also, a person who is opposed in feeling, principle, etc., to something (as, to be a *foe* to all measures of reform); a thing that is opposed or inimical (as, intemperance is a *foe* to thrift).

foehn (fėn), *n.* See *föhn*.

foe-man (fō'mạn), *n.*; pl. *-men.* [AS. *fāhman*, < *fāh*, hostile, + *man*, man.] A foe, as in war.

fœ'tal, etc., **fœt'id,** etc. See *fetal*, etc., *fetid*, etc.

fog¹ (fog), *n.* [ME. *fogge*; origin unknown.] A second growth of grass, as after mowing; aftergrass; also, long grass left standing in fields during the winter; also, moss. [Prov.]

fog² (fog), *n.* [Cf. Dan. *fog*, spray, shower, drift, Icel. *fok*, spray, drift (of snow, sand, ashes, etc.), *fjūk*, snow-storm, *fjūka*, be driven by the wind, as spray, snow, etc.] A cloud-like mass or layer of minute globules of water in the air near the earth's surface; thick mist; hence, any darkened state of the atmosphere, or the diffused substance which causes it; a dark mass, as of smoke; fig., an influence or a condition that prevents clear mental perception (as, to dispel the *fog* of ignorance; to be in a *fog* of doubt); in *photog.*, a (usually uniform) darkening or opacity of the whole or of parts of a developed plate or a print.—**fog**², *v.*; *fogged, fogging.* **I.** *tr.* To envelop with or as with fog; befog; confuse; in *photog.*, to affect (a plate or print) by fog. **II.** *intr.* To become enveloped or obscured with or as with fog.—**fog'=bank,** *n.* A stratum of fog as seen from a distance.—**fog'=bell,** *n.* A bell, as on a rocky coast, for warning vessels in foggy weather.—**fog'=bow** (-bō), *n.* A whitish or slightly colored bow or appearance analogous to a rainbow, sometimes seen in fog.—**fog'=dog,** *n.* A bright spot sometimes seen in a fog-bank.—**fog'=fruit,** *n.* A procumbent verbenaceous plant, *Lippia lanceolata*, with small pale-blue flowers; any of certain other plants of this genus.

fog-gage (fog'ạj), *n.* [See *fog*¹.] The pasturing of cattle on fog or aftergrass, or the right of such pasturing; also, fog or aftergrass. [Chiefly prov.]

fog-gy (fog'i), *a.*; compar. *foggier*, superl. *foggiest.* Abounding in, thick with, or resembling fog; misty; dim; obscure; in *photog.*, affected by fog.—**fog'gi-ly,** *adv.*—**fog'gi-ness,** *n.*

fog=horn (fog'hôrn), *n.* A horn for sounding warning signals, as to vessels, in foggy weather.

fog-less (fog'les), *a.* Free from fog.

fo-gy (fō'gi), *n.*; pl. *-gies* (-giz). [Orig. Sc.: origin uncertain.] A slow or dull fellow; an old-fashioned or excessively conservative person: usually preceded by *old*: as, "My part . . . is always that of the old *Fogy* who sees nothing to admire in the young folks" (George Eliot's "Adam Bede," xxii.). [Colloq.]—**fo'gy-ish,** *a.* Inclined to be a fogy; fogy-like.—**fo'gy-ism,** *n.*

foh (fō), *interj.* [Cf. *faugh* and *fie*.] An exclamation of disgust.

föhn (fėn), *n.* [G.] A warm, dry south wind of the valleys on the north side of the Alps.

foi-ble (foi'bl), *n.* [F. *foible*, obs. form of *faible*, E. *feeble*.] A weak point; a weakness or failing of character; also, the weaker part of a sword-blade, being the portion between the middle and the point (opposed to *forte*).

foil¹ (foil), *n.* [OF. *foil* (also fem. *foille*, F. *feuille*), < L. *folium*, leaf; akin to Gr. φύλλον.] A leaf of a plant†; also, metal hammered or rolled into a very thin sheet (as, gold-*foil*; tin-*foil*); the metallic backing applied to glass to form a mirror; a thin layer of metal placed under a gem to improve its color or brilliancy; the setting of a jewel† (see Shakspere's "Richard II.," i. 3. 266); fig., anything that serves to set off another thing distinctly or to advantage by contrast (as, "gray duennas, *foils* of younger maids": Holmes's "Old Player"); in *arch.*, an arc or a rounded space between cusps, as in the tracery of a window or in other ornamentation.—**foil**¹, *v. t.* To cover or back with foil; also, to set off by contrast; in *arch.*, to ornament with foils.

foil² (foil), *v. t.* [OF. F. *fouler*, trample, full (cloth): see *full*².] To tread under foot†; trample (the ground, track, etc.) or spoil (the scent) by trampling, as an animal does, so as to baffle the hounds in hunting; also, to give (a person) an incomplete fall in wrestling† (see Shakspere's "As You Like It," ii. 2. 14); fig., to defeat, discomfit, or balk (an adversary, enemy, etc.); frustrate or baffle (efforts, attempts, etc.); disappoint (hopes, etc.).—**foil**², *n.* The track or trail of hunted game; also, an incomplete or partial fall given in wrestling†; fig., a defeat, discomfiture, or baffling check (archaic).

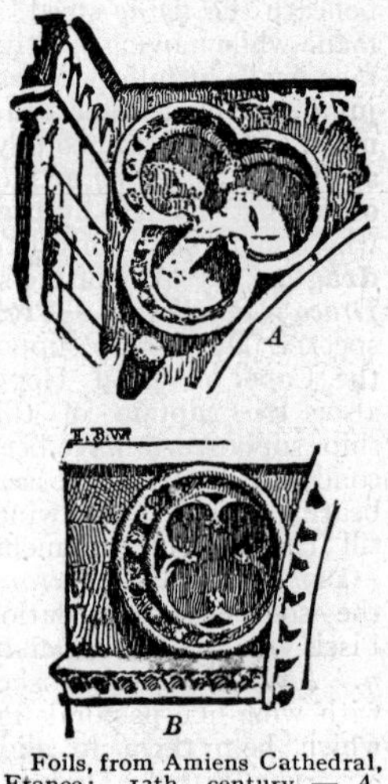

Foils, from Amiens Cathedral, France; 13th century.— *A*, trefoil; *B*, quatrefoil.

foil³ (foil), *n.* [Appar. < *foil*².] A blunt sword with a button at the point, for use in fencing; *pl.*, the art or exercise of fencing with such swords.

foil-er (foi'lėr), *n.* One who or that which foils, defeats, balks, or baffles.

foils-man (foilz'mạn), *n.*; pl. *-men.* One who is expert at fencing with foils.

foin (foin), *v. i.* [ME. *foynen*, appar. < OF. *foine* (F. *fouine*), fish-spear, < L. *fuscina*, trident.] To thrust with a weapon; lunge. See Shakspere's "Merry Wives of Windsor," ii. 3. 24. [Obs. or archaic.]—**foin,** *n.* A thrust with a weapon. See Shakspere's "King Lear," iv. 6. 251. [Obs. or archaic.]

foi-son (foi'zọn), *n.* [OF. F. *foison*, < L. *fusio(n-)*, a pouring out, E. *fusion*.] Abundance or plenty of something, esp. abundant harvest (archaic or prov.: as, "Earth's increase, *foison* plenty, Barns and garners never empty," Shakspere's "Tempest," iv. 1. 110); also, vigor, strength, or ability (chiefly Sc.); also, nourishing power, or nourishment, as in food (chiefly Sc.).

foist (foist), *v. t.* [Prob. < D. *vuisten*, take in the hand, < *vuist*, fist.] To palm, or bring (*in*) when palmed, as a false die in dicing†; hence, to bring or put (*in* or *into*) surreptitiously or fraudulently (as, to *foist* spurious passages into a text); palm off or impose fraudulently or unwarrantably (*on* or *upon*: as, to *foist* inferior goods on a customer; to *foist* an unworthy governor upon a province).

fold[1] (fōld), *v.* [AS. *fealdan* = OHG. *faldan* = Icel. *falda* = Goth. *falthan*, fold: cf. *-fold*.] **I.** *tr.* To double or bend (cloth, paper, etc.) over upon itself; bend (*back, down, over*, etc.), as one part upon another; bring into a compact form, or shut, by bending and laying parts together (often with *up*: as, to *fold* up a map); also, to bend or wind (*about, round*, etc.: as, to *fold* one's arms about a person's neck); bring together (the arms, hands, legs, etc.) with parts disposed one about or within another; bring (the wings) close to the body, as a bird; also, to inclose, wrap, or envelop in something (as, "Hast thou a knife? . . . Here, Marcus, *fold* it in the oration": Shakspere's "Titus Andronicus," iv. 3. 116); clasp or embrace, as in the arms; also, to be disposed about, surround, or cover (poetic: as, "Light and shadow ever wander O'er the green that *folds* thy grave," Tennyson's "Dirge"); shut (*in*: as, "This blind haze, which . . . Hath *folded* in the passes of the world," Tennyson's "Passing of Arthur," 78); in *cookery*, to mix (*in*), as beaten egg-whites added to a batter or the like, by gently turning one part over another with strokes of a spoon. **II.** *intr.* To become folded or doubled, with one part upon another; also, to pass or wind about something.—**fold**[1], *n.* A folded disposition, form, or part of anything (as, a garment hanging in loose *folds*); a pleat; a flexure; a bend, winding, or sinuosity (as, the *folds* of the mountains); a coil, as of the body of a serpent; a leaf of a door or gate (as, "The doors, Opening their brazen *folds*": Milton's "Paradise Lost," i. 724); also, an act of folding or doubling over; also, a clasp† or embrace† (see Shakspere's "Troilus and Cressida," iii. 3. 223); also, an enveloping layer or thickness of something (as, to wrap a mummy in many *folds* of cloth); a band of material applied to a garment or the like by way of trimming or finish; in *geol.*, a portion of strata which is folded or bent (as an anticline or syncline), or which connects two horizontal or parallel portions of strata of different levels (as a monocline).

fold[2] (fōld), *n.* [AS. *fald, falod*, fold, = MLG. *valt*, inclosure, yard.] An inclosure for domestic animals, esp. sheep; the sheep contained in it, or a flock of sheep; fig., the church, or a particular church.—**fold**[2], *v. t.* To confine (sheep, etc.) in a fold.

-fold (-fōld). [AS. *-feald* = OHG. G. *-falt* = Icel. *-faldr* = Goth. *-falths*, -fold; akin to E. *fold*[1]: see *double*.] A suffix appended to numerals, or other quantitative words or word-elements, to denote formation or division into so many parts or members, and also used with multiplicative force to form words meaning '(so many) times as great or as much,' as in *twofold, bifold, threefold, fourfold, manifold*.

fold-er (fōl′dėr), *n.* One who or that which folds; also, a folded printed sheet, as a circular or a time-table.

fol-de-rol (fol′dẹ-rol), *n.* [Orig. meaningless syllables used in songs.] Mere nonsense; foolish talk or ideas (as, "She had no *fol-de-rol* about woman's rights": Mrs. Stowe's "Oldtown Folks," xxxiii.); also, a silly trifle; a piece of trumpery; a gimcrack; a gewgaw.

Medieval Conventionalized Foliage, Notre Dame, Paris; end of 13th century.

fo-li-a (fō′li-ạ̈), *n.* Plural of *folium*.

fo-li-a-ceous (fō-li-ā′shius), *a.* [L. *foliaceus*, < *folium*, leaf.] Of the nature of a leaf; leaf-like; bearing leaves or leaf-like parts; pertaining to or consisting of leaves; consisting of leaf-like plates or laminæ.

fo-li-age (fō′li-ạ̄j), *n.* [Altered (to conform to L. *folium*) from F. *feuillage*, < *feuille*, < L. *folium*, leaf.] The leaves of a plant, collectively; leaves in general; also, the representation of leaves, flowers, and branches, as in architectural ornament.—**fo′li-aged,** *a.* Having foliage; also, decorated with foliage.—**fo′-li-age=plant,** *n.* Any plant cultivated for ornament for the sake of its foliage rather than its flowers.

fo-li-ar (fō′li-ạ̈r), *a.* [L. *folium*, leaf.] Of, pertaining to, or of the nature of a leaf or leaves.

fo-li-ate (fō′li-āt), *v.*; *-ated, -ating.* [ML. *foliatus*, pp. of *foliare*, put forth leaves, < L. *folium*, leaf.] **I.** *intr.* To put forth leaves; also, to split into thin leaf-like layers or laminæ. **II.** *tr.* To furnish with leaves; also, to shape like a leaf or leaves; also, to form into thin sheets; also, to spread over with a thin metallic backing; also, to number consecutively the folios or leaves of (a book, etc.); in *arch.*, to decorate with foils, or with foliage.—**fo′li-ate** (-ạ̄t), *a.* [L. *foliatus*, < *folium*.] Having leaves; leaf-like.—**fo′li-at-ed** (-ā-ted), *p. a.* Furnished with leaves; shaped like a leaf or leaves; consisting of thin leaf-like layers or laminæ; backed with foil, as glass; in *arch.*, ornamented with foils, or with foliage.—**fo-li-a′tion** (-ā′shọn), *n.* The act of foliating, or bursting into leaf; the state of being in leaf; the arrangement of leaves within the bud; leaves or foliage; also, formation into thin sheets; also, the application of foil to glass; also, the consecutive numbering of the folios or leaves of a book, etc.; in *geol.*, the splitting up or the arrangement of certain rocks in leaf-like layers; in *arch.*, ornamentation with foils, or tracery so formed; ornamentation with foliage, or an arrangement of foliage.—**fo′li-a-ture** (-ạ̄-tūr), *n.* [L. *foliatura*.] A cluster of leaves; foliage; also, foliar ornamentation.

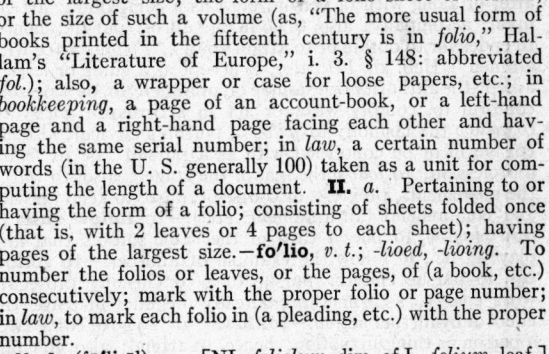

Foliations in Tracery.— Sainte Chapelle, Paris; 13th century.

fo-lio (fō′liō). [L., abl. of *folium*, leaf.] **I.** *n.*; pl. *-lios* (-liōz). A leaf of paper, parchment, etc., as of a manuscript or book, esp. one of a collection of such leaves numbered consecutively on the front side only; also, the number of a page, as of a book, inserted at the top or the bottom; also, a sheet of paper folded once; a volume consisting of sheets folded once (that is, with 2 leaves or 4 pages to each sheet); a volume having pages of the largest size; the form of a folio sheet or volume, or the size of such a volume (as, "The more usual form of books printed in the fifteenth century is in *folio*," Hallam's "Literature of Europe," i. 3. § 148: abbreviated *fol.*); also, a wrapper or case for loose papers, etc.; in *bookkeeping*, a page of an account-book, or a left-hand page and a right-hand page facing each other and having the same serial number; in *law*, a certain number of words (in the U. S. generally 100) taken as a unit for computing the length of a document. **II.** *a.* Pertaining to or having the form of a folio; consisting of sheets folded once (that is, with 2 leaves or 4 pages to each sheet); having pages of the largest size.—**fo′lio,** *v. t.*; *-lioed, -lioing.* To number the folios or leaves, or the pages, of (a book, etc.) consecutively; mark with the proper folio or page number; in *law*, to mark each folio in (a pleading, etc.) with the proper number.

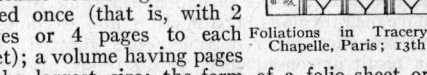

fo-li-ole (fō′li-ōl), *n.* [NL. *foliolum*, dim. of L. *folium*, leaf.] In *bot.*, a division of a compound leaf; a leaflet; in *zoöl.*, a small leaf-like part or organ.—**fo′li-o-late** (-ọ-lāt), *a.*

fo-li-ose (fō′li-ōs), *a.* [L. *foliosus*, < *folium*, leaf.] Abounding in leaves; leafy.

fo-li-um (fō′li-um), *n.*; pl. *folia* (-ạ̈). [L., leaf: see *foil*[1].] A leaf or sheet, as of paper (as, "protocols and memoranda in ten thousand *folia*": Motley's "Dutch Republic," vi. 3); also, a thin leaf-like stratum or layer; a lamella.

folk (fōk), *n.*; pl. *folks*. [AS. *folc* = D. and G. *volk* = Icel. *fōlk* = Sw. and Dan. *folk*, folk, people.] A people or tribe (archaic); an aggregation of people in relation to a superior, as God or a king (archaic); the common people (archaic); people in general, or people of a specified class or group (archaic in *sing.*; now usually, and chiefly colloq., in *pl.*

in same sense as *sing.*); *pl.* (colloq.), the persons of one's own family; one's relatives.—**folk′=dance,** *n.* A dance which originated among, and has been transmitted through, the common people; a piece of music for such a dance. —**folk′land** (-land), *n.* [AS. *folcland.*] In *old Eng. law,* land held by folkright or customary law, as distinguished from *bookland,* which was held by charter or deed.—**folk′-lore** (-lōr), *n.* The lore of the common people; the traditional beliefs, legends, customs, etc., of a people, or the study of these.—**folk′lor-ist** (-lōr-ist), *n.* One versed or engaged in the study of folklore.—**folk-lor-is′tic,** *a.* —**folk′moot, folk′mote** (-möt, -mōt), *n.* [AS. *folcmōt,* 'folk meeting.'] Formerly, in England, a general assembly of the people of a shire, town, etc.—**folk′=mu″sic,** *n.* Music, usually of simple character, originating and handed down among the common people.—**folk′right,** *n.* [AS. *folcryht.*] In *old Eng. hist.*, the right of the people under the customary law; customary or common law.—**folk′=song,** *n.* A song, usually of simple or artless character, originating and handed down among the common people; also, a song in imitation of this type.—**folk′=speech,** *n.* Popular language; the dialect spoken by the common people of a country or district, as distinguished from the speech of the educated people or from the literary language.—**folk′=sto″ry,** *n.* A folk-tale.—**folk′=tale,** *n.* A tale or legend originating and handed down among the common people.

fol-li-cle (fol′i-kl), *n.* [L. *folliculus,* dim. of *follis,* bellows, bag.] In *anat.*, etc., a small cavity, sac, or gland; in *bot.*, a dry one-celled seed-vessel consisting of a single carpel, and dehiscent only by the ventral suture, as the fruit of larkspur.—**fol-lic-u-lar** (fo-lik′ū-lạ̈r), *a.* Pertaining to, consisting of, or like a follicle or follicles; provided with follicles; in *pathol.*, affecting, or originating in, a follicle or follicles.—**fol-lic′u-late, fol-lic′u-lat-ed** (-lāt, -lā-ted), *a.* Provided with or consisting of a follicle or follicles.—**fol-lic-u-lo′sis** (-lō′sis), *n.* [NL.] In *pathol.*, an abnormal or diseased condition of follicles, as of the inner surface of an eyelid.

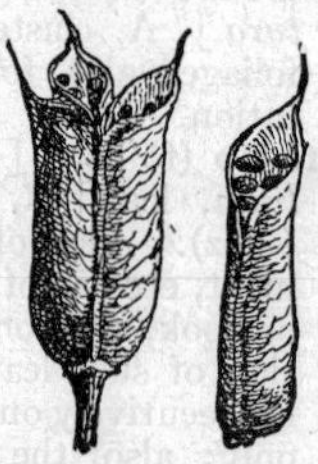
Follicle. — Fruit of larkspur.

fol-low (fol′ō), *v. t.* [AS. *folgian,* also *fylgan,* = D. *volgen* = G. *folgen* = Icel. *fylgja,* follow; perhaps akin to E. *full*¹.] To go or come after; move behind in the same direction; also, to move forward along (a path, etc.); also, to come after in natural sequence, order of time, etc.; succeed; come after as a result or consequence; result from; also, to go after or along with (a person, etc.) as a companion; attend upon; accompany; also, to go in pursuit of; pursue; hence, to endeavor to obtain or to attain to (as, "*Follow* peace with all men": Heb. xii. 14); also, to accept as a guide or leader, accept the authority or example of, or adhere to, as a person; conform to, comply with, or act in accordance with (as, to *follow* the fashion; to *follow* a person's advice); also, to engage in or be concerned with as a pursuit (as, to *follow* a profession; to *follow* the sea, or the stage); also, to watch the movements, progress, or course of; also, to keep up with and comprehend (an argument, etc.).—**to follow suit,** in *card-playing,* to play a card of the same suit as that first played; fig., to follow the example of another.—**to follow up,** to pursue closely; pursue to a conclusion; prosecute with energy, as something already begun; increase the effect of by further action.—**fol′low,** *v. i.* To go or come after a person or thing in motion; hence, to attend; also, to come after something else in natural sequence, order of time, etc.; ensue; also, to result as an effect; occur as a consequence; also, to go in pursuit; hence, to strive for attainment. —**fol′low,** *n.* The act of following; in *billiards,* a stroke which causes the player's ball to roll on after the ball struck by it.—**fol′low-a-ble,** *a.* That may be followed.—**fol′-low-er,** *n.* One who or that which follows; an attendant, retainer, or servant; an adherent; an imitator; a male admirer and frequent visitor of a young woman, esp. a maid-servant (colloq.); in *mach.*, a part of a machine that receives motion from, or follows the motion of, another part.—**fol′low-ing,** *n.* A body of followers, attendants, adherents, etc.—**fol′low-ing,** *p. a.* That follows; esp., that comes after or next in order or time (as, "Living carcases design'd For death, the *following* day, in bloody fight": Milton's "Paradise Lost," x. 278); succeeding; also, that is now to follow; now to be mentioned, described, related, or the like.—**fol′-low=up′,** *n.* The act of following up; also, a letter or circular sent to a person to enhance the effect of a previous one, as in advertising.

fol-ly (fol′i), *n.*; pl. *follies* (-iz). [OF. F. *folie,* < *fol*: see *fool*¹.] The state or quality of being foolish; want of understanding or sense (as, "Where ignorance is bliss, 'Tis *folly* to be wise": Gray's "On a Distant Prospect of Eton College"); also, unwise or light-minded conduct; also, a foolish action, practice, idea, etc.; an absurdity; also, a costly but foolish undertaking; a more or less pretentious building left unfinished for want of means, or, when finished, too expensive to be properly maintained, or inconveniently situated or otherwise inadequate for practical use; also, wickedness† (see Josh. vii. 15); wantonness† (see Shakspere's "Othello," v. 2. 132).

fo-ment (fọ-ment′), *v. t.* [F. *fomenter,* < LL. *fomentare,* < L. *fomentum,* a warm application, < *fovere,* keep warm.] To apply warm water or medicated liquid, cloths dipped in such liquid, or the like to (the surface of the body); also, to cherish with heat† (as, "All things . . . these soft fires . . . with kindly heat . . . *foment* and warm": Milton's "Paradise Lost," iv. 669); also, to promote the growth or development of; foster; esp., to foster or instigate (discord, rebellion, etc.).—**fo-men-ta-tion** (fō-men-tā′shọn), *n.* [LL. *fomentatio(n-).*] The act of fomenting; the application of warm liquid, etc., to the surface of the body; the liquid, etc., so applied; also, encouragement; instigation.—**fo-ment′er,** *n.* One who or that which foments; a device for applying heat to some part of the body.

fond (fond), *a.* [ME. *fonned,* pp. of *fonnen,* be foolish; origin uncertain: cf. *fun.*] Foolish or silly (archaic or prov.); esp., foolishly credulous or confident; also, foolishly tender or loving; doting; hence, loving or affectionate (without implication of foolishness); also, cherished or prized highly or too highly; doted on; also, having affection or liking for a person or thing (as, to be *fond* of children; to be *fond* of sports); also, desirous (of something, or of doing something)†; pleased or glad (to do something: now chiefly Sc.).—**fond†,** *v.* **I.** *intr.* To be fond; dote: as, "My master loves her dearly; And I . . . *fond* as much on him" (Shakspere's "Twelfth Night," ii. 2. 35). **II.** *tr.* To show fondness for; fondle: as, "The Tyrian hugs and *fonds* thee on her breast" (Dryden's tr. Virgil's "Æneid," i. 962).

fon-da (fon′dä), *n.* [Sp.; from Ar.] In Spain or Spanish-speaking countries, an inn or hotel.

fon-dant (fon′dạnt, F. fôṅ-däṅ), *n.* [F., prop. ppr. of *fondre,* melt: see *found*².] Thick, creamy sugar paste, the basis of many candies.

fon-dle (fon′dl), *v.*; *-dled, -dling.* [Freq. of *fond, v.*] **I.** *tr.* To treat with fond indulgence†; also, to handle or touch fondly; caress. **II.** *intr.* To show fondness, as by manner, words, or caresses: as, "*Fondling* together, as I'm alive! . . . Ah! have I caught you, my pretty doves?" (Goldsmith's "She Stoops to Conquer," iv.).—**fon′dler,** *n.*

fond-ling (fond′ling), *n.* [From *fond, a.*] A fool or simpleton (now prov. Eng.); also, a person or thing fondly treated; a pet.

fond-ly (fond′li), *adv.* In a fond manner; foolishly (now prov.); with complacent credulity; lovingly or affectionately.—**fond′ness,** *n.* The state or quality of being fond; foolishness (now prov.); complacent credulity; doting affection; affectionateness or tenderness; instinctive liking.

fon-du (fôṅ-dü), *a.* [F., pp. of *fondre,* melt: see *found*².] Blended; characterized by blending of colors, one into another, through delicate gradations.

fon-due (fôṅ-dü), *n.* [F., prop. fem. of *fondu,* pp.: see *fondu.*] A dish composed of grated cheese melted with butter, eggs, etc.

font¹ (font), *n.* [F. *fonte,* < *fondre,* melt, cast: see *found*².] The act or process of founding or casting; in *printing,* a complete assortment of type of one style and size, as required for ordinary printed work.

font² (font), *n.* [AS. *font,* < ML. *fons* (*font-*), baptismal font, L. spring, fountain, E. *fount*².] A receptacle, usually of stone, as in a baptistery or a church, for the water used in baptism; also, a receptacle for holy water; a stoup; a bénitier; also, the reservoir for oil in a lamp; also, a fount or fountain (archaic).—**fon-tal** (fon′tạl), *a.* Of or pertaining to a font, as of baptism; also, pertaining to or issuing as from a fount or spring; fig., pertaining to or being the source of something.

Baptismal Font.— Cathedral of Langres, France.

fon-ta-nelle, fon-ta-nel (fon-tạ-nel′), *n.* [F. *fontanelle*, < *fontaine*, E. *fountain*.] In *pathol.*, an opening for the discharge of pus†; in *anat.*, one of the spaces, covered with a membranous structure, between certain bones of the fetal or young skull.

fon-ti-nal (fon′ti-nạl), *a.* [L. *fontinalis*, < *fons* (*font-*), E. *fount*[2].] Growing in or about springs, as certain plants.

food (föd), *n.* [AS. *fōda*, food; akin to OHG. *fuotan*, Icel. *fædha*, Goth. *fōdjan*, feed, and to Gr. *πατεῖσθαι*, eat: cf. *feed*, *fodder*, and *foster*.] What is eaten, or taken into the body, for nourishment (as, *food* for man and beast); more broadly, whatever supplies nourishment to organic bodies (as, the *food* of plants); aliment; nutriment; often, more or less solid nutriment, as opposed to *drink*; also, a particular kind or article of nutriment (as, animal *food*, meat, etc.; breakfast *foods*, as various cereal preparations); fig., that on which anything subsists (as, intellectual *food*); something that sustains, or keeps in existence (as, *food* for hope); anything serving as material for consumption or use (as, "*Prince*. I did never see such pitiful rascals. *Fal.* Tut, tut . . . *food* for powder, *food* for powder; they'll fill a pit as well as better": Shakspere's "1 Henry IV.," iv. 2. 71); matter (for thought, etc.); also, the process of feeding or eating† (see Shakspere's "Comedy of Errors," v. 1. 83).—**food′less,** *a.* Without food.—**food′stuff,** *n.* A substance or material suitable for food.

fool[1] (föl), *n.* [OF. *fol* (F. *fol*, *fou*), n. and a., < L. *follis*, bellows, bag or ball inflated with air: cf. *windbag*.] One who is deficient in judgment or sense; a silly or stupid person; a simpleton; also, a professional jester or buffoon; a retainer dressed in motley, wearing a cap often hung with bells, and carrying a bauble or mock scepter in his hand, formerly kept by a person of rank for the purpose of making sport; also, one who is made to appear deficient in sense or ridiculously simple-minded (as, to make a *fool* of a person); the victim of some trick, imposition, or the like (as, an April *fool*: see under *April*); a butt or dupe (as, to be fortune's *fool*); also, a weak-minded or idiotic person.—**fool's cap,** a kind of cap or hood, usually hung with bells, formerly worn by professional fools or jesters; also, a conical paper cap sometimes worn by dunces at school as a punishment. See also *foolscap*.—**fool's errand,** an absurd or useless errand or undertaking.—**fool's gold,** iron pyrites, which is sometimes mistaken for gold.—**fool's paradise,** a state of illusory happiness; enjoyment based on false beliefs or hopes.—**fool's parsley,** a fetid, poisonous apiaceous plant, *Æthusa cynapium*, resembling common parsley.—**fool**[1], *a.* Foolish; silly. [Now colloq.]—**fool**[1], *v.* **I.** *intr.* To play the fool; play, trifle, dally, or toy; jest, or make believe; potter; idle. **II.** *tr.* To make a fool of; impose on; dupe; deceive; also, to make foolish†, or infatuate†; also, with *away*, to spend foolishly, as time or money.

fool[2] (föl), *n.* [Prob. another use of *fool*[1].] A dish made of fruit scalded or stewed, crushed, and mixed with cream, etc.: as, gooseberry *fool*.

fool-er-y (fö′lėr-i), *n.*; pl. *-ies* (-iz). Foolish action or conduct (as, "We've had about enough of this *foolery*": Stevenson's "Treasure Island," xxvi.); fooling; a piece of fooling; a foolish action, performance, or thing.

fool-har-dy (föl′här″di), *a.* [OF. *fol hardi*: see *fool*[1] and *hardy*[1].] Bold without judgment; foolishly rash or venturesome.—**fool′har″di-ly,** *adv.*—**fool′har″di-ness,** *n.*

fool-ing (fö′ling), *n.* The act of one who fools; trifling; jesting; foolery.

fool-ish (fö′lish), *a.* Like or befitting a fool; unwise or silly; also, ridiculous (as, to cut a *foolish* figure); also, trifling, insignificant, or paltry (obs. or archaic: as, "a trifling *foolish* banquet," Shakspere's "Romeo and Juliet," i. 5. 124).—**fool′ish-ly,** *adv.*—**fool′ish-ness,** *n.*

fool=proof (föl′pröf), *a.* Proof against fools; involving no risk, even from the handling or meddling of foolish or ignorant persons.

fools-cap (fölz′kap), *n.* Paper for writing (usually folded) or for printing, in sheets varying in size from 12 by 15 to 13½ by 17 inches: named from an old watermark consisting of a fool's cap. See also *fool's cap*, under *fool*[1], *n.*

foot (fu̇t), *n.*; pl. *feet* (fēt). [AS. *fōt* = D. *voet* = G. *fuss* = Icel. *fōtr* = Goth. *fōtus*, foot; akin to L. *pes* (*ped-*), Gr. *πούς* (*ποδ-*), and Skt. *pad*, foot.] In vertebrates, the terminal part of the leg, below the ankle-joint, on which the body stands and moves; in invertebrates, any part similar in position or function; often, such a part considered as the organ of locomotion; hence, walking or running motion; step; pace; also, foot-soldiers or infantry (as, "Single or in array of battle ranged Both horse and *foot*": Milton's "Paradise Lost," xi. 645); also, the end of a bed, grave, etc., toward which the feet are placed; the part of a stocking, etc., covering the foot; also, some thing or part resembling an animal's foot, as in function; also, the lowest part, or bottom, as of a hill, ladder, column, page, etc.; the lower edge of a sail; the part of anything opposite to the top or head; the last, as of a series; that which is written at the bottom, as the total of an account; also (often in pl. *foots*), sediment or dregs; also, foothold†; status† or footing†; also, a unit of length derived from the length of the human foot, in English-speaking countries equivalent to 12 inches, or 30.48 centimeters; in *pros.*, a group of syllables constituting a metrical unit of a verse.—**on foot,** on one's own feet (as, to come *on foot*); also, in motion; astir; also, in active existence or operation.—**foot,** *v.* **I.** *intr.* To move the feet as in walking, or go on foot (often with indefinite *it*); also, to move the feet to measure or music, or dance (often with indefinite *it*); also, to total (*up*), as an account. **II.** *tr.* To set foot on; walk or dance on; traverse on foot; also, to settle or establish (as, "What confederacy have you with the traitors Late *footed* in this kingdom?" Shakspere's "King Lear," iii. 7. 45); also, to kick†; seize with the talons, as a hawk does; also, to make or attach a foot to (as, to *foot* a stocking); also, to add (*up*), as a column of figures, and set the sum at the foot; hence, to pay or settle, as a bill (colloq.).

foot-age (fu̇t′ạj), *n.* Length or extent in feet (as, the *footage* of a moving-picture film); in *mining*, payment by the running foot of work done, or the amount so paid.

foot=and=mouth (fu̇t′ạnd-mouth′) **dis-ease′.** A contagious disease of cattle and other animals, communicable to man, characterized by a vesicular eruption about the hoofs and in the mouth.

foot-ball (fu̇t′bâl), *n.* A large, oval or round, inflated ball designed for propulsion with the foot; also, an outdoor game played with such a ball by two sets of players, each of which endeavors to kick or convey it to or through a goal defended by the opposing side. See *Rugby football* and *soccer*.—**foot′ball″er, foot′ball″ist,** *n.*

foot-board (fu̇t′bōrd), *n.* A board or small platform on which to support the foot or feet; also, a treadle; also, an upright piece across the foot of a bedstead.

foot-boy (fu̇t′boi), *n.* A boy in livery employed as a servant; a page; a lackey.

foot=bridge (fu̇t′brij), *n.* A bridge intended for pedestrians only.

foot=can-dle (fu̇t′kan″dl), *n.* A unit of illumination equivalent to that produced by a standard candle at the distance of one foot.

foot=cloth (fu̇t′klôth), *n.* A richly ornamented caparison for a horse, hanging down to the ground†; also, a carpet or rug.

foot=drop (fu̇t′drop), *n.* In *pathol.*, dropping of the anterior portion of the foot when the limb is raised from the ground, due to paralysis of the flexor muscles.

foot-ed (fu̇t′ed), *a.* Provided with a foot or feet: as, a four-*footed* animal.

foot-er (fůt′ẽr), *n.* One who goes on foot; a walker; also, with a numeral prefixed, a person or thing of the height or length in feet indicated by that number (as, a six-*footer*).
foot-fall (fůt′fâl), *n.* A footstep.
foot=gear (fůt′gēr), *n.* Covering for the feet, as shoes, boots, etc.
foot=guard (fůt′gärd), *n.* A boot or pad worn by a horse to prevent wounding the feet by interfering or overreaching; also, one of a body of infantry soldiers forming a guard; *pl.*, any of certain British infantry regiments.
foot=hill (fůt′hil), *n.* A minor elevation at the base of a mountain or mountain-range.
foot-hold (fůt′hōld), *n.* A hold or support for the feet; a place where one may stand or tread securely; firm footing; secure position.
foot-ing (fůt′ing), *n.* The act of one that foots, or moves on foot, as in walking or dancing; also, a firm placing or stable position of the feet; hence, place or support for the feet; surface to stand on; fig., secure position; established place; foothold; also, the basis or foundation on which anything is established; position or status assigned to a person, etc., in estimation or treatment; relation with reference to intercourse (as, to be on a friendly *footing* with a person); also, entrance into a new position or relationship; a fee demanded from a person upon his entrance into a trade, society, etc. (as, "Fork out the tin and pay your *footing*": Kingsley's "Alton Locke," ii.); also, the act of putting a foot to anything, as a stocking; that which is added as a foot; also, the act of adding up a column of figures, or the amount of such a column as footed up; in *arch.*, a projecting course or courses at the base of a wall, etc.
foot=jaw (fůt′jâ), *n.* One of those limbs of crustaceans and other arthropods which are modified into accessory mouth-parts.
foot-less (fůt′les), *a.* Without a foot or feet; hence, unsupported or unsubstantial; also, awkward, helpless, or inefficient (colloq.).
foot-lights (fůt′līts), *n. pl.* In *theaters*, etc., a row of lights at the front of the stage, nearly on a level with the feet of the performers.
foot-ling (fůt′ling), *adv.* and *a.* [See *-ling*[2].] In *obstetrics*, with the feet foremost.
foot=loose (fůt′lös), *a.* Free to go or travel about at will; not confined to any one place, etc., by ties, responsibilities, or other circumstances.
foot-man (fůt′mạn), *n.*; pl. *-men.* A pedestrian (archaic or prov.); also, a foot-soldier; also, a runner in attendance upon a rider of rank†; a servant who ran before his master's carriage†; also, a male servant in livery who attends the carriage, waits at table, etc.; also, a metal stand to hold anything before a fire; also, any moth of the family *Lithosiidæ* (also called *footman-moth*).

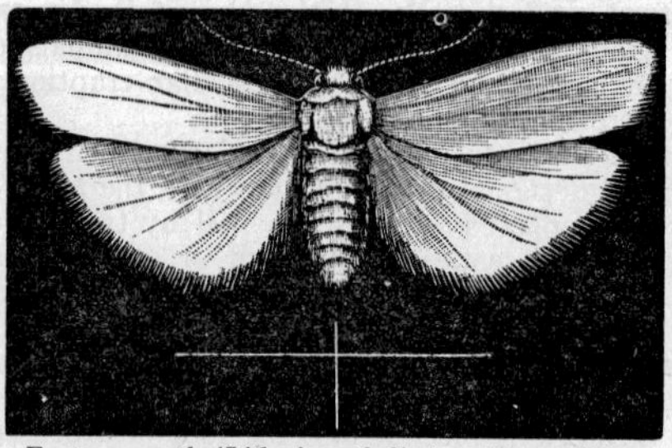
Footman-moth (*Lithosia cephalica*). (Cross shows natural size.)

foot-mark (fůt′märk), *n.* A mark made by the foot; a footprint.
foot=note (fůt′nōt), *n.* A note or comment at the foot of a page, referring to something in the text.
foot-pace (fůt′pās), *n.* A walking pace (as, to go at a *foot-pace*); also, something on which to tread, or place the feet; a raised portion of a floor; a landing or resting-place at the end of a short flight of steps.
foot-pad (fůt′pad), *n.* A highwayman who robs on foot.
foot=path (fůt′pȧth), *n.* A path for pedestrians only.
foot=pound (fůt′pound), *n.* In *mech.*, a unit of energy or work equivalent to the energy required to raise the weight of one pound avoirdupois to the height of one foot.—**foot′=pound″al,** *n.* A unit of energy equivalent to that of an avoirdupois pound moving with the velocity of one foot per second.
foot=pow-er (fůt′pou″ẽr), *n.* Power applied by the motion and pressure of the foot, as for running a machine.
foot-print (fůt′print), *n.* An impression left by the foot.
foot=rope (fůt′rōp), *n.* *Naut.*, the portion of the bolt-rope to which the lower edge of a sail is sewed; also, a rope extended under a yard, for the men to stand on while reefing or furling.

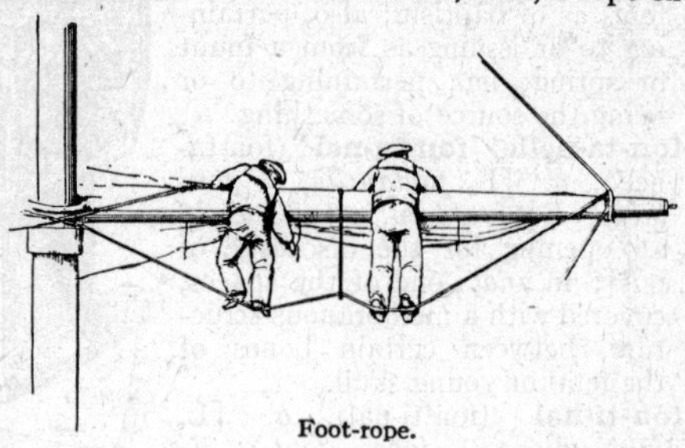
Foot-rope.

foot=sec-ond (fůt′-sek″ọnd), *n.* In *mech.*, a unit of velocity equal to one linear foot per second, used in stating the velocity of a projectile; also, a unit for measuring the flow of liquids, equal to a flow of one cubic foot per second.
foot=sol-dier (fůt′sōl″jẽr), *n.* A soldier who serves and fights on foot; an infantryman.
foot=sore (fůt′sōr), *a.* Having the feet sore or tender, as from much walking.
foot-stalk (fůt′stâk), *n.* In *bot.* and *zoöl.*, a petiole; a pedicel; a peduncle.
foot-step (fůt′step), *n.* A step or tread of the foot, or the sound produced by it; a footfall; also, the distance traversed by the foot in stepping; a pace; also, the mark or impression of a foot; a footprint; also, a step by means of which to ascend or descend (as, "the *footsteps* of a throne": Wordsworth's "Miscellaneous Sonnets," i. 28).
foot-stone (fůt′stōn), *n.* A stone placed at the foot of a grave.
foot-stool (fůt′stöl), *n.* A low stool upon which to rest the foot or feet.
foot=ton (fůt′tun), *n.* In *mech.*, a unit of work equivalent to the energy expended in raising a ton of 2,240 pounds one foot.
foot=warm-er (fůt′wâr″mẽr), *n.* Any of various contrivances for keeping the feet warm.
foot-way (fůt′wā), *n.* A way or path for pedestrians only: as, "Mr. Ferris took his way through the devious *footways*" (Howells's "Foregone Conclusion," ii.).
foot-wear (fůt′wãr), *n.* Articles for wearing on the feet, esp. shoes, slippers, gaiters, etc.
foot=worn (fůt′wôrn), *a.* Worn by the feet (as, a *foot-worn* pavement); also, foot-sore.
foot-y (fůt′i). [Cf. F. *foutu.*] **I.** *a.* Poor; mean; worthless; paltry; insignificant; silly or ridiculous. [Prov. or colloq.] **II.** *n.*; pl. *footies* (-iz). A worthless person or thing. [Prov., U. S.]
foo-zle (fö′zl), *v. t.* or *i.*; *-zled, -zling.* [Origin uncertain.] To bungle; play clumsily (as, to *foozle* a stroke in golf).—**foo′zle,** *n.* An act of foozling; a badly played stroke in golf; also, an old-fashioned person; a fogy.
fop (fop), *n.* [ME. *foppe*, fool: see *fop, v.*] A fool†; a foolish, pretentious person†; now, an empty-headed dandy.—**fop†,** *v. t.*; *fopped, fopping.* [Appar. < *fop, n.* (recorded earlier): cf. *fob*[1], *v.*, also G. *foppen*, befool, hoax, mock, deride.] To fool; cheat. See Shakspere's "Othello," iv. 2. 197.—**fop′ling,** *n.* A petty fop.—**fop′per-y,** *n.*; pl. *-ies* (-iz). Foolishness†; a foolish action or thing†; now, the manners, practices, dress, etc., of a fop; something characteristic of a fop.—**fop′pish,** *a.* Foolish† (as, "Wise men are grown *foppish*": Shakspere's "King Lear," i. 4. 182); now, resembling or befitting a fop.—**fop′pish-ly,** *adv.*—**fop′pish-ness,** *n.*
for (fôr). [AS. *for*, also *fore*, before, for: see *fore, prep.*] **I.** *prep.* Before†; in the interest of (as, to act *for* a client); in place of, or instead of (as, a substitute *for* butter); in consideration of, or in requital of (as, three *for* a dollar; to be thanked *for* one's efforts); as an offset to (as, blow *for* blow); in favor of, or on the side of (as, to stand *for* honest government); in honor of (as, to give a dinner *for* a person); with the object or purpose of (as, to go *for* a

walk, or, now archaic or vulgar, to go *for* to walk); in order to become (as, to go *for* a soldier); conducive to (as, *for* the advantage of everybody); in order to obtain (as, a suit *for* damages); in order to save (as, to flee *for* one's life); with inclination or tendency toward (as, to long *for* a thing; an eye *for* beauty); with the purpose of reaching (as, to start *for* London); intended to belong to, suit the purposes or needs of, or be used in connection with (as, this is *for* you; a book *for* children; a box *for* gloves); in assignment or attribution to (as, an engagement *for* this evening; it is *for* you to decide); appropriate or adapted to (as, a subject *for* speculation; he is no match *for* his opponent); to allow of, or to require (as, too many *for* separate mention; important enough *for* separate treatment); such as results in (as, his reason *for* going); with regard or respect to (as, so much *for* that; pressed *for* time; weather too warm *for* April); as affecting the interests or circumstances of (as, bad *for* one's health); in the character of, or as being (as, to know a thing *for* a fact); by reason of, or because of (as, to shout *for* joy; famed *for* its beauty); in spite of (as, *for* all that); during the continuance of (as, *for* a long time); to the extent or amount of (as, to walk *for* a mile). Sometimes used to govern a noun or pronoun followed by an infinitive, in a construction equivalent to a clause with *that* and the auxiliary *should*, etc. (as, it is time *for* him to go, or that he should go). **II.** *conj.* Because (archaic); also, seeing that; since; also, in order that†.

for-. [AS. *for-* = D. and G. *ver-* = Icel. *for-* = Goth. *fra-*; akin to E. *for, fore,* and *from.*] A prefix meaning 'away,' 'off,' 'to the uttermost,' 'extremely,' 'to detriment or destruction,' or imparting a negative or privative force, occurring in words of Anglo-Saxon or Middle English origin, many of which are now obsolete or archaic.

for-age (for'āj), *n.* [OF. *forrage* (F. *fourrage*), < *forre, fuerre,* fodder; from Teut., and akin to E. *fodder.*] Food for horses and cattle; fodder; provender; also, the seeking or obtaining of such food; hence, the act of searching for provisions of any kind; sometimes, a raid.—**for'age,** *v.*; *-aged, -aging.* [OF. *forragier* (F. *fourrager*).] **I.** *intr.* To wander in search of supplies; hence, to make a raid; also, to hunt or search about. **II.** *tr.* To collect forage from; strip of supplies; plunder; also, to obtain by foraging (as, "*foraged* corn": Whittier's "Yorktown"); also, to supply with forage.—**for'age=cap,** *n.* A small, low undress cap worn by soldiers.—**for'ag-er** (-ā-jėr), *n.*

fo-ra-men (fō-rā'men), *n.*; pl. *foramina* (fō-ram'i-nạ). [L., hole, < *forare,* pierce; akin to E. *bore*[1].] An opening, orifice, or short passage, as in a bone or in the integument of the ovule of a plant.—**fo-ram-i-nate, fo-ram-i-nat-ed** (fō-ram'i-nāt, -nā-ted), *a.* [LL. *foraminatus,* < L. *foramen.*] Furnished with foramina; perforated.

fo-ra-min-i-fer (fō-rạ-min'i-fėr), *n.* [NL. *Foraminifera,* pl., < L. *foramen,* hole, + *ferre,* bear.] Any of the *Foraminifera,* an extensive order of rhizopods commonly having a calcareous shell which in many species is perforated by small holes or pores (foramina).—**fo-ram-i-nif-er-al** (fō-ram-i-nif'ẹ-rạl), **fo-ram-i-nif'er-ous,** *a.*

fo-rane (fō-rān'), *a.* [ML. *foraneus,* < L. *foras,* out of doors, outside: cf. *foreign.*] Pertaining to places or things remote: as, vicar *forane* (in the *Rom. Cath. Ch.,* an ecclesiastical dignitary appointed by a bishop to exercise limited jurisdiction in a particular district of his diocese).

for-as-much (fôr-ạz-much'), *adv.* Followed by *as*: In view of the fact that; seeing that; since.

for-ay (for'ā), *v.* [ME. *forray*: cf. OF. *forrer,* forage, ravage, *forreor, forrier,* forager, < *forre,* fodder (see *forage*).] **I.** *tr.* To ravage in search of forage or booty; pillage. **II.** *intr.* To make a raid; forage; pillage.—**for'ay,** *n.* A predatory incursion or inroad; a raid.—**for'ay-er,** *n.*

for-bade, for-bad (for-bad'). Preterit of *forbid.*

for'bear[1], *n.* See *forebear.*

for-bear[2] (for-bãr'), *v.*; pret. *-bore,* pp. *-borne,* ppr. *-bearing.* [AS. *forberan*: see *for-* and *bear*[1].] **I.** *tr.* To endure†; also, to endure the absence of†; also, to keep away from†; also, to refrain from; desist from; cease; also, to refrain from using, etc. (as, "Yet stay a while; *forbear* thy bloody hand": Marlowe's "Edward II.," v. 5); keep back; withhold; also, to show mercy or indulgence to (now rare); refrain from insisting on or exacting (now rare). **II.** *intr.* To refrain; hold back; also, to be patient; show forbearance.—**for-bear'ance,** *n.* The act of forbearing; a refraining from something; also, forbearing conduct or quality; patient endurance; lenity; also, an abstaining from the enforcement of something due.—**for-bear'ing-ly,** *adv.*

for-bid (for-bid'), *v.*; pret. *-bade,* also *-bad,* pp. *-bidden,* also *-bid,* ppr. *-bidding.* [AS. *forbēodan*: see *for-* and *bid.*] **I.** *tr.* To command (a person, etc.) not to do, have, use, etc., something, or not to enter some place; also, to put an interdiction against (something); prohibit; also, to hinder or prevent; render impossible; exclude; repel; also, to curse† (as, "He shall live a man *forbid*": Shakspere's "Macbeth," i. 3. 21). **II.** *intr.* To utter a prohibition: as, "*Forbid* who will, none shall from me withhold Longer thy offer'd good" (Milton's "Paradise Lost," v. 62).—**for-bid'dance,** *n.* The act of forbidding, or the state of being forbidden; prohibition.—**for-bid'den,** *p. a.* Prohibited; interdicted.—**forbidden degrees,** degrees of consanguinity or affinity within which marriage is not allowed.—**forbidden fruit,** the fruit of the tree of the knowledge of good and evil, of which Adam and Eve partook (see Gen. ii. 17 and Gen. iii.); hence, unlawful pleasure, esp. illicit love.—**for-bid'den-ly,** *adv.*—**for-bid'der,** *n.*—**for-bid'ding,** *p. a.* That forbids; keeping one back from a nearer approach; repellent; repulsive; causing aversion or dislike.—**for-bid'ding-ly,** *adv.*—**for-bid'ding-ness,** *n.*

for-bode† (for-bōd'), *n.* [AS. *forbod,* < *forbēodan,* E. *forbid.*] Forbidding; prohibition.

for-bore (for-bōr'). Preterit of *forbear*[2].—**for-borne'** (-bôrn'). Past participle of *forbear*[2].

for-by, for-bye (for-bī'), *prep.* and *adv.* [See *for* and *by.*] Close by; near; also, besides. [Now chiefly Sc. and prov. Eng.]

force[1]† (fōrs), *v. t.* [=*farce.*] To stuff. See Shakspere's "Troilus and Cressida," v. 1. 64.

force[2] (fōrs), *n.* [Icel. *fors.*] A waterfall. [North. Eng.]

force[3] (fōrs), *n.* [OF. F. *force,* < ML. *fortia,* < L. *fortis,* strong.] Strength or power, esp. active power; impetus; intensity of effect; also, might, as of a ruler or realm; strength for war; also, a body of armed men (often in *pl.*); hence, any body of persons combined for joint action (as, a police *force*; an office *force*); also, strength or power exerted upon an object; physical coercion; violence; specif., in legal use, unlawful violence offered to persons or things; also, mental or moral strength; power of overcoming resistance; power to influence or control (as, "Let not her cries or tears have *force* to move you": Addison's "Cato," iv. 2); power to convince; also, binding power, as of an agreement; hence, operation (as, a law now in *force*); also, value, significance, meaning, or import; also, any influence or agency analogous to physical force (as, social *forces*); in *physics,* etc., an influence which produces or tends to produce motion or change of motion, or the intensity of such an influence (sometimes loosely used as equivalent to *energy* or *power,* or to indicate a natural phenomenon, as electricity).—**force**[3], *v.*; *forced, forcing.* [OF. F. *forcer,* < *force.*] **I.** *tr.* To use force upon; overcome the resistance of; ravish or violate (a woman); also, to compel by force; constrain; also, to drive or propel against resistance; also, to press, urge, or exert to violent effort or to the utmost; also, to put or impose forcibly (*on* or *upon*); enforce (a law, etc.)†; also, to take or enter by force (as, to *force* a stronghold, a ship, etc.); effect a passage through or across (mountains, a river, etc.) by force; break open (a door, a lock, etc.); also, to bring about or effect by force; produce by unnatural effort; bring about of necessity; make (one's way, etc.) by force; also, to obtain or draw forth by or as by force; extort; also, to cause (plants, fruits, etc.) to grow or mature by artificial means; also, to give force to†; strengthen†; reinforce†; also, to attach importance to†; care for†; in *card-playing,* to compel (a player) to trump, by leading a suit of which he has no cards; compel (a player) to play so as to make known the strength of his hand; also, to compel a player to play (a particular card). **II.** *intr.* To use force; also, to make one's way by force; also, to scruple† or hesitate†.—**forced,** *p. a.* Subjected to force; also, enforced or compulsory (as, *forced* labor); also, effected by unusual force or effort (as, a *forced* march); strained, unnatural, or affected (as, a *forced* smile).—**for-ced-ly** (fōr'sed-li), *adv.*—**force'ful,** *a.* Full of force; powerful; vigorous; effective; also, acting or driven with force.—**force'ful-ly,** *adv.* —**force'ful-ness,** *n.*—**force'less,** *a.* Without force; impotent; feeble: as, "feeble heart and *forceless* hand" (Scott's "Rokeby," i. 24).

force-meat (fōrs'mēt), *n.* [See *force*[1].] In *cookery*, meat chopped fine and seasoned, used as stuffing, etc.

for-ceps (fôr'seps), *n.*; pl. *-ceps* or *-cepses* (-sep-sez). [L.] An instrument, as pincers or tongs, for seizing and holding objects, as in surgical operations; in *anat.* and *zoöl.*, a part or process resembling a forceps: sometimes used as *pl.* in same sense as *sing.*, and also called a *pair of forceps.*

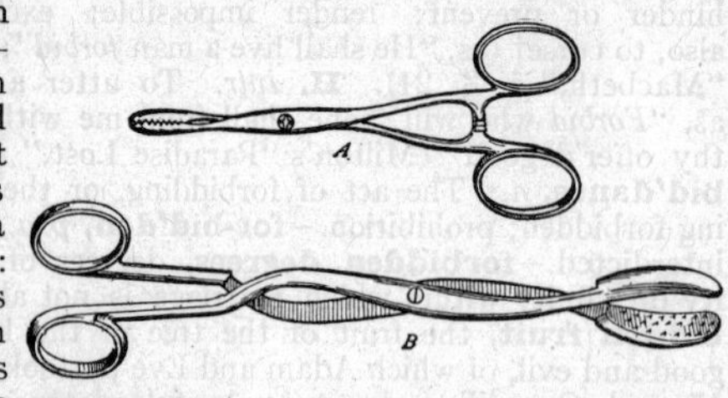

Surgical Forceps. — *A*, for compression of an artery to control hemorrhage; *B*, for removing stone from the bladder in lithotomy.

force=pump (fōrs'pump), *n.* Any pump which delivers a liquid under pressure, so as to eject it forcibly: distinguished from *lift-pump*.

for-cer (fōr'sėr), *n.* One who or that which forces.

for-ci-ble (fōr'si-bl), *a.* [OF. *forcible.*] Characterized by the use of force or violence; effected by force; also, possessing force; producing a powerful effect; effective; convincing, as reasoning.—**for'ci-ble-ness,** *n.*—**for'ci-bly,** *adv.*

for-cite (fōr'sīt), *n.* [See *force*[3].] A powerful explosive containing nitroglycerin, soluble guncotton, and potassium nitrate.

ford (fōrd), *n.* [AS. *ford* = G. *furt*, ford; akin to E. *fare.*] A place where a river or other body of water may be crossed by wading; also, a stream to be crossed†.—**ford,** *v. t.* To cross (a river, etc.) by a ford: as, "The streams rose so rapidly that we could hardly *ford* them" (Parkman's "Oregon Trail," i.).—**ford'a-ble,** *a.* That may be forded.—**ford'-less,** *a.* Without a ford; not fordable.

for-do (for-dö'), *v. t.*; pret. *-did*, pp. *-done*, ppr. *-doing.* [AS. *fordōn*: see *for-* and *do*[1].] To do away with; kill; destroy; ruin; undo; also, to wear out or exhaust (only in *pp.*: as, "The heavy ploughman snores, All with weary task *fordone*," Shakspere's "Midsummer Night's Dream," v. 1. 381). [Archaic.]

fore (fōr). [AS. *fore* = D. *voor* = G. *vor* = Goth. *faura*, before, for; akin to L. *præ*, before, *pro*, Gr. πρό, before, for, Skt. *pra*, before: cf. *for* and *from.*] **I.** *prep.* and *conj.* Before: now only prov., or regarded as a shortened form of *before* or *afore*, and written *'fore.* **II.** *adv.* Before (now prov., except as in composition); forward (now prov.); *naut.*, at or toward the bow.—**fore and aft,** *naut.*, at or toward both bow and stern; alternately toward the bow and the stern (as, to walk *fore and aft*); also, from stem to stern, or in line with the keel (as, a vessel rigged *fore and aft*, that is, having fore-and-aft sails); lengthwise.—**fore,** *interj.* In *golf*, a cry of warning to persons ahead who are liable to be struck by the ball.—**fore.** [From *fore-*, prefixal use of *fore, adv.*, in noun compounds: cf. *forepart*, also written *fore-part* and *fore part.*] **I.** *a.* Situated at or toward the front, as compared with something else; first in place, time, order, rank, etc.; forward; earlier. **II.** *n.* The fore part of anything; the front.—**to the fore,** to or at the front; to or in a conspicuous place or position; also (orig. Sc., Ir., and north. Eng.), within call, or present; still surviving, or alive; ready at hand, or available.

fore=and=aft (fōr'ąnd-áft'), *a.* and *adv.* *Naut.*, in a line with the keel: as, a *fore-and-aft* sail.—**fore'=and=aft'er,** *n.* *Naut.*, a vessel with fore-and-aft sails; as a schooner.

fore-arm[1] (fōr'ärm), *n.* The part of the arm between the elbow and the wrist.

fore-arm[2] (fōr-ärm'), *v. t.* To arm beforehand.

fore-bear (fōr'bãr or fōr-bãr'), *n.* [Orig. Sc., < *fore, adv.*, + *be, v.*, + *-ar* for *-er*[1].] An ancestor, a forefather.

fore-bode (fōr-bōd'), *v.*; *-boded, -boding.* **I.** *tr.* To bode beforehand; foretell or predict; portend or foreshadow; also, to have a presentiment of (esp. evil: as, "My heart *forebodes* Danger or death awaits thee on this field," M. Arnold's "Sohrab and Rustum"). **II.** *intr.* To prophesy; presage; also, to have a presentiment.—**fore-bode'ment,** *n.* A foreboding.—**fore-bod'er** (-bō'dėr), *n.*—**fore-bod'ing,** *n.* A prediction or presage; a portent; also, a presentiment.—**fore-bod'ing-ly,** *adv.*

fore-brain (fōr'brān), *n.* The prosencephalon.

fore-cast (fōr-kȧst'), *v.*; *-cast* or *-casted, -casting.* **I.** *tr.* To cast, contrive, or plan beforehand; prearrange; also, to conjecture beforehand; predict; also, to make a forecast of (the weather, etc.); also, to serve as a forecast of; foreshadow. **II.** *intr.* To plan or arrange beforehand; also, to conjecture beforehand; make a forecast.—**fore'cast,** *n.* The act, practice, or faculty of forecasting; foresight in planning; also, a conjecture as to something in the future; a prediction, esp. as to the weather; also, a foreshadowing, as by one thing, of something else to come.—**fore-cast'er,** *n.*

fore-cas-tle (fōr'kȧs-l, naut. fōk'sl), *n.* *Naut.*, a short raised deck in the fore part of a ship†; also, that part of the upper deck forward of the foremast; also, the seamen's quarters in the forward part of a merchant vessel.

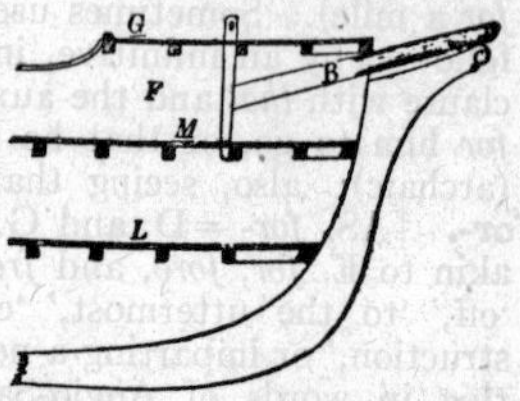

Diagram of Ship's Bow. — *B*, bowsprit; *F*, forecastle; *G*, forecastle-deck; *L*, lower deck; *M*, main deck or spar-deck.

fore-cit-ed (fōr'sī'ted), *a.* Previously cited.

fore-close (fōr-klōz'), *v.*; *-closed, -closing.* [OF. *forclos*, pp. of *forclore*, exclude, < *for-* (< L. *foris*), outside, + *clore*, < L. *claudere*, shut: cf. *close*[1].] **I.** *tr.* To shut out; exclude or bar; also, to hinder or prevent, as from doing something; also, to establish an exclusive claim to; also, to close, settle, or answer beforehand (as, to *foreclose* a case; to *foreclose* objections); in *law*, to deprive (a mortgager) of the right to redeem his mortgaged estate; also, to take away the right to redeem (a mortgage). **II.** *intr.* To foreclose a mortgage.—**fore-clos'a-ble** (-klō'-zą-bl), *a.*—**fore-clo'sure** (-klō'zhụr), *n.* The act of foreclosing; esp., the act of foreclosing a mortgage, as on an estate.

fore-court (fōr'kōrt), *n.* A front or outer court.

fore-date (fōr-dāt'), *v. t.*; *-dated, -dating.* To antedate.

fore-do', *v. t.* See *fordo.*

fore-doom (fōr'döm), *n.* A doom ordained beforehand. —**fore-doom',** *v. t.* To doom beforehand.

fore-fa-ther (fōr'fä"ᴛʜėr), *n.* An ancestor.—**Forefathers' Day,** the anniversary of the day (Dec. 21, 1620, in Old Style Dec. 11) on which the Pilgrims landed at Plymouth, Mass.: owing to an error in changing the date from the Old Style to the New, generally observed on Dec. 22.

fore-feel (fōr-fēl'), *v. t.* To feel or perceive beforehand; have a presentiment of.—**fore'feel,** *n.* A feeling beforehand. —**fore-feel'ing,** *n.* A feeling beforehand; a presentiment: as, "a strong *forefeeling* that much of my destined life . . . was yet to come" (Kinglake's "Eothen," xviii.).

fore-fend', *v. t.* See *forfend.*

fore-fin-ger (fōr'fing"gėr), *n.* The first finger, or that next to the thumb.

fore-foot (fōr'fu̇t), *n.*; pl. *-feet* (-fēt). One of the front feet of a quadruped, or of an insect, etc. (also written *fore foot*); *naut.*, the forward end of the keel.

fore-front (fōr'frunt), *n.* The foremost part or place.

fore-gath'er, *v. i.* See *forgather.*

fore-glow (fōr'glō), *n.* A glow often seen in the sky before sunrise.

fore-go'[1], *v. t.* See *forgo.*

fore-go[2] (fōr-gō'), *v. t.* or *i.*; pret. *-went*, pp. *-gone*, ppr. *-going.* [AS. *foregān.*] To go before; precede.—**fore-go'er,** *n.*—**fore-go'ing,** *p. a.* Going before; preceding; antecedent. —**fore-gone'** (-gôn'), *p. a.* That has gone before; previous; past.—**foregone conclusion,** a conclusion, opinion, or decision formed in advance; also, an inevitable conclusion or result. See Shakspere's "Othello," iii. 3. 428.—**fore-gone'ness,** *n.*

fore-ground (fōr′ground), *n.* The ground or parts situated, or represented as situated, in the front; the nearer portion of a scene: opposed to *background.*

fore-hand (fōr′hand). **I.** *n.* Position in front or above; superior position; advantage; also, the mainstay† (as, "The great Achilles . . . The sinew and the *forehand* of our host": Shakspere's "Troilus and Cressida," i. 3. 143); also, the part of a horse which is in front of the rider. **II.** *a.* Being in front or ahead; foremost or leading; also, done beforehand; anticipative; given or made in advance, as a payment; also, made with the hand turned palm forward, as a stroke in tennis, etc.—**fore′hand′ed,** *a.* Providing for the future; prudent; thrifty; hence, in easy circumstances; well-to-do; also, of a horse, formed (in a specified manner) in the forehand; also, forehand, as a stroke in tennis, etc.—**fore′hand′ed-ness,** *n.*

fore-head (for′ed), *n.* [AS. *forhēafod.*] The fore or front upper part of the head; the part of the face above the eyes; the brow; also, the fore or front part of anything; also, decency† or modesty†; also, assurance† or audacity†.

for-eign (for′ẹn), *a.* [OF. F. *forain,* < L. *foras, foris,* out of doors, outside, connected with *foris,* door: see *door.*] Outside† or outer†; also, not of one's household or family†; also, belonging to or proceeding from other persons or things (as, a statement supported by *foreign* testimony); also, situated outside a district, province, etc.; belonging to or coming from another district, province, society, etc.; esp., external to one's own country or nation (as, a *foreign* country; *foreign* regions); pertaining to, characteristic of, or derived from another country or nation; not native or domestic; hence, strange or unfamiliar; also, carried on abroad, or with other countries (as, *foreign* service; *foreign* trade); also, pertaining to relations or dealings with other countries (as, the *foreign* office of a government; a *foreign* money-order); also, not related to or connected with the thing under consideration (as, *foreign* to his nature; *foreign* from our discussion); alien in character; irrelevant or inappropriate; remote; also, not belonging to the place or body where found (as, a *foreign* substance in the flesh).—**foreign legion,** a military body in the service of a state, consisting of foreign volunteers; specif. [*caps.*], a military body in the French service, consisting of foreigners of all nationalities, with a small proportion of Frenchmen, which was formed about 1830 for service in the conquest of Algeria, and was employed, up to the time of the World War, in the French colonial service and in distant expeditions.—**for′eign-er,** *n.* An outsider, as one from another district, province, society, etc. (now only prov.); also, a person not native or naturalized in the country or jurisdiction under consideration; an alien; also, a thing produced in or brought from a foreign country; esp., a foreign vessel.—**for′eign-ism,** *n.* Foreign quality; imitation of anything foreign; a foreign custom, trait, idiom, term, or the like.—**for′eign-ly,** *adv.*—**for′eign-ness,** *n.*

fore-judge′[1], *v. t.* See *forjudge.*

fore-judge[2] (fōr-juj′), *v. t.*; *-judged, -judging.* To judge beforehand; prejudge.—**fore-judg′ment,** *n.* A judgment formed or rendered beforehand.

fore-know (fōr-nō′), *v. t.*; pret. *-knew,* pp. *-known,* ppr. *-knowing.* To know beforehand.—**fore-know′a-ble,** *a.* That may be foreknown.—**fore-knowl′edge** (-nol′ej), *n.* Knowledge of a thing before it exists or happens; prescience.

fore-land (fōr′lạnd), *n.* A cape, headland, or promontory (as, "Now the *forelands* took the shapes they knew": H. Newbolt's "Admiral Blake"); also, land or territory lying in front (in some uses, opposed to *hinterland*).

fore-leg (fōr′leg), *n.* One of the front legs of a quadruped, or of an insect, etc.: also written *fore leg.*

fore-lock[1] (fōr′lok), *n.* The lock of hair that grows from the fore part of the head; a prominent or somewhat detached lock above the forehead: as, to take time by the *forelock* (fig., to anticipate an emergency or occasion by suitable action; act in anticipation or with promptness).

fore-lock[2] (fōr′lok), *n.* A wedge or pin passed through a hole in the end of a bolt or the like, to keep it in place. —**fore′lock**[2], *v. t.* To secure (a bolt, etc.) by a forelock.

fore-man (fōr′mạn), *n.*; pl. *-men.* The chief or head man, as the spokesman of a jury or the overseer of a group of workmen.—**fore′man-ship,** *n.*

fore-mast (fōr′mȧst), *n.* *Naut.,* the mast nearest the bow of a ship.

fore-men-tioned (fōr′men′shọnd), *a.* Previously mentioned; aforesaid.

fore-most (fōr′mōst), *a.* and *adv. superl.* [Altered (to conform to *most*) from AS. *formest, fyrmest,* superl. < *forma,* first, which is itself superl. < *fore,* before: see *fore* and *-most.*] First in place, order, rank, etc.

fore-moth-er (fōr′muᴛʜ″ėr), *n.* A female ancestor.

fore-name (fōr′nām), *n.* A name that precedes the family name, or surname; a first name; a prænomen.

fore-nent, fore-nenst (fọr-nent′, -nenst′), *prep.* [See *fore* and *anent.*] Opposite to; directly in front of; over against; in the direction or neighborhood of; also, with respect to. [Now prov.]

fore-noon (fōr′nön′), *n.* The period of daylight before noon; often, the latter part of the morning, esp. the part ordinarily employed in transacting business.

fo-ren-sic (fọ-ren′sik), *a.* [L. *forensis,* < *forum,* forum.] Pertaining to, connected with, or used in courts of law or public discussion and debate; adapted or suited to argumentation; argumentative.—**forensic medicine.** Same as *medical jurisprudence.*—**fo-ren′sic,** *n.* A spoken or written exercise in argumentation, as in a college.—**fo-ren′si-cal-ly,** *adv.*

fore-or-dain (fōr-ôr-dān′), *v. t.* To ordain or appoint beforehand; predestinate.—**fore-or-dain′ment,** *n.*

fore-or-di-na-tion (fōr″ôr-di-nā′shọn), *n.* Previous ordination or appointment; predestination.

fore-part (fōr′pärt), *n.* The fore, front, or early part.

fore-peak (fōr′pēk), *n.* *Naut.,* the part of the hold in the angle formed by the bow.

fore-post (fōr′pōst), *n.* An advanced post; an outpost.

fore-reach (fōr-rēch′), *v.* **I.** *intr.* To gain, as one ship on another; shoot or glide ahead, as a ship after coming into the wind. **II.** *tr.* To gain upon; pass; sail beyond.

fore=room (fōr′röm), *n.* The front room or parlor of a house. [Local, U. S.]

fore-run (fōr-run′), *v. t.*; pret. *-ran,* pp. *-run,* ppr. *-running.* To run in front of; precede; hence, to be the precursor of (as, "These signs *forerun* the death or fall of kings": Shakspere's "Richard II.," ii. 4. 15); anticipate or forestall; also, to outrun or outstrip.—**fore-run′ner,** *n.* One who or that which foreruns; a herald or harbinger; a predecessor; an ancestor; a prognostic or portent.

fore-said (fōr′sed), *a.* Forementioned; aforesaid.

fore-sail (fōr′sāl, naut. -sl), *n.* *Naut.,* the sail bent to the foreyard of a square-rigged vessel; also, the principal fore-and-aft sail set on the foremast of a schooner; also, the forestaysail of a sloop, cutter, etc.

fore-say (fōr-sā′), *v. t.*; *-said, -saying.* [AS. *foresecgan.*] To say beforehand; predict; also, to foreordain (as, "Let ordinance Come as the gods *foresay* it": Shakspere's "Cymbeline," iv. 2. 146).

fore-see (fōr-sē′), *v.*; pret. *-saw,* pp. *-seen,* ppr. *-seeing.* [AS. *foresēon.*] **I.** *tr.* To see beforehand; have prescience of; foreknow; also, to provide for or against†. **II.** *intr.* To exercise foresight.—**fore-see′a-ble,** *a.* That may be foreseen.—**fore-see′ing-ly,** *adv.*—**fore-se′er,** *n.*

fore-shad-ow (fōr-shad′ō), *v. t.* To shadow or indicate beforehand; prefigure.—**fore′shad″ow,** *n.* An indication or prefiguration of something to come: as, "to impart some outline or *foreshadow* of this Doctrine" (Carlyle's "Sartor Resartus," i. 8).—**fore-shad′ow-er,** *n.*

fore=sheet (fōr′shēt), *n.* *Naut.,* a sheet of a foresail; *pl.,* the forward part of an open boat.

fore-ship (fōr′ship), *n.* *Naut.,* the fore part of a ship.

fore-shore (fōr′shōr), *n.* The fore part of the shore; the part of the shore between the ordinary high-water mark and low-water mark; also, the ground between the water's edge and the land cultivated or built upon.

fore-short-en (fōr-shôr′tn), *v. t.* To represent (a line, part, object, or the like, which lies in a plane not perpendicular to the line of sight) as of less than its true length in order to give the proper impression to the eye; shorten, or delineate as shortened, because of perspective.

fore-show (fōr-shō′), *v. t.* To show beforehand; foretell; foreshadow.

fore-side (fōr′sīd), *n.* The front side or part; also, the upper side; also, a stretch of land fronting the sea (New Eng.).

fore-sight (fōr′sīt), *n.* The act or power of foreseeing; prevision; prescience; also, the act or an act of looking forward; perception gained by or as by looking forward; prospect; a view into the future; also, care or provision for the future; provident care; also, the sight nearest the muzzle of a firearm; in *surv.*, a sight or reading taken in a forward direction.

fore-skin (fōr′skin), *n.* In *anat.*, the fold of skin which covers the head of the penis; the prepuce.

fore-spend′, *v. t.* See *forspend.*

for-est (for′est), *n.* [OF. *forest* (F. *forêt*), < ML. *forestis*, an uninclosed wood (as opposed to a park), < L. *foris*, outside: see *foreign.*] A large tract of land covered with trees; an extensive wood; sometimes, the trees alone (as, to cut down a *forest*); in *Eng. law*, a tract of woody grounds and pastures, generally belonging to the sovereign, set apart for game. —**for′est,** *v. t.* To cover with trees; convert into a forest. —**for′es-tal** (-es-tạl), *a.*

fore-stall (fōr-stâl′), *v. t.* [ME. *forstallen*, < AS. *foresteall*, a standing before, intercepting, waylaying: see *fore* and *stall*[2].] To lie in wait for†; intercept†; also, to buy up (goods) in advance, in order to enhance the price; prevent sales at (a fair, market, etc.) by buying up or diverting goods; also, to prevent, hinder, or thwart by action in advance (as, "Her foresight could not *forestall* their will": Shakspere's "Lucrece," 728); debar (*from*) or deprive (*of*) by previous action† (as, "May This night *forestall* him of the coming day!" Shakspere's "Cymbeline," iii. 5. 69); in general, to be beforehand with or get ahead of (a person, etc.) in action (as, to *forestall* another in recording a claim; to *forestall* one by bestowing a favor before it is asked); take measures concerning or deal with (a thing) in advance (as, to *forestall* the action of others; to *forestall* objections by explaining a case); anticipate; sometimes, to deal with, meet, or realize in advance of the natural or proper time (as, "What need a man *forestall* his date of grief, And run to meet what he would most avoid?" Milton's "Comus," 362). —**fore-stall′er,** *n.* —**fore-stal′ment, fore-stall′ment,** *n.*

for-es-ta-tion (for-es-tā′shọn), *n.* The planting or establishment of forests.

fore-stay (fōr′stā), *n.* *Naut.*, a stay running from the head of the most forward mast of a schooner, etc., or the single mast of a cutter, etc., to the bowsprit or stem, and serving to support the mast. —**fore′stay″sail** (-sāl, naut. -sl), *n.* *Naut.*, a triangular sail set on the forestay, being the first sail in front of the forward (or single) mast.

for-est-er (for′es-tėr), *n.* [OF. F. *forestier.*] An officer having charge of a forest; also, one who practises, or is versed in, forestry; also, one who lives in a forest; an animal of the forest; also, any of various moths of the family *Agaristidæ*, as *Alypia octomaculata* (the 'eight-spotted forester'), a black moth with large yellow spots, whose larva devours the foliage of grape-vines. —**for′est-ine** (-es-tin), *a.* Of or belonging to the forest. —**for′est-less,** *a.* Without forests. —**for′est-ry,** *n.* The art or science of forming or cultivating forests; the economic management of trees; also, forest land.

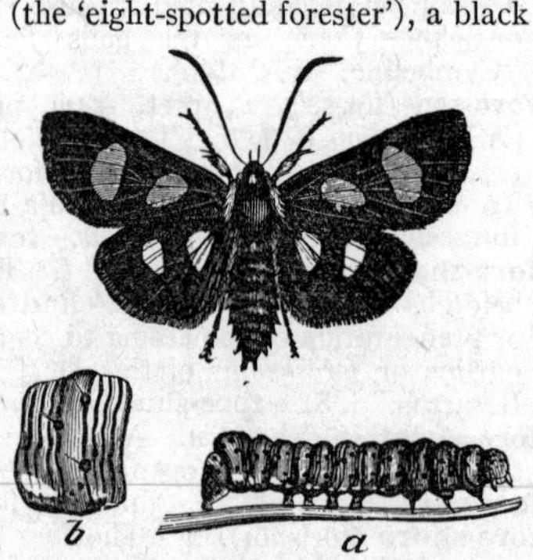

Eight-spotted Forester, natural size. — *a*, larva; *b*, side view of one joint, enlarged.

fore-taste (fōr-tāst′), *v. t.*; *-tasted, -tasting.* To taste beforehand; enjoy by anticipation. —**fore′taste,** *n.* A taste beforehand; an anticipation.

fore-tell (fōr-tel′), *v.*; *-told, -telling.* **I.** *tr.* To tell of beforehand; predict or prophesy; of things, to foreshow. **II.** *intr.* To utter prediction or prophecy. —**fore-tell′er,** *n.*

fore-think (fōr-thingk′), *v. t.*; *-thought, -thinking.* [AS. *forethencean.*] To think of or contemplate beforehand (now rare); also, to think out beforehand†; plan†. —**fore-think′er,** *n.*

fore-thought (fōr′thôt), *n.* A thinking of something beforehand; previous consideration; anticipation; also, a thinking out beforehand (as, "His good was mainly an intent, His evil not of *forethought* done": Whittier's "My Namesake"); planning; premeditation; also, provident care; prudence. —**fore′thought″ful,** *a.* Full of or having forethought; provident. —**fore′thought″ful-ly,** *adv.* —**fore′thought″ful-ness,** *n.*

fore-time (fōr′tīm), *n.* Former or past time; the past.

fore-to-ken (fōr′tō″kn), *n.* [AS. *foretācn.*] A premonitory token or sign; a prognostic. —**fore-to′ken,** *v. t.* To betoken beforehand; foreshadow.

fore-top (fōr′top), *n.* The fore part of the crown of the head†; a lock of hair on this part of the head, or on the front of a wig† (as, "a periwig with an high *foretop*": Steele, in "Spectator," 17); the forelock of an animal, esp. a horse; also, the front seat on the top of a vehicle; *naut.*, a platform at the head of a foremast.

fore-top-gal-lant-mast (fōr-top-gal′ạnt-mȧst, naut. -tọ-gal′ạnt-mạst), *n.* *Naut.*, the mast next above the foretopmast. —**fore-top-gal′lant=sail** (-sāl, naut. -sl), **fore-top-gal′lant=yard,** *n.* *Naut.*, the sail or the yard belonging to the foretopgallantmast.

fore-top-mast (fōr-top′mȧst), *n.* *Naut.*, the mast erected at the head of the foremast, above the foretop.

fore-top-sail (fōr-top′sāl, naut. -sl), *n.* *Naut.*, the sail set on the foretopmast.

for-ev-er (for-ev′ėr), *adv.* For ever; eternally; continually. See *ever.* —**for-ev′er-more′,** *adv.* See *evermore.*

fore-warn (fōr-wârn′), *v. t.* To warn, admonish, or advise beforehand. —**fore-warn′er,** *n.* —**fore-warn′ing-ly,** *adv.*

fore-went (fōr-went′). Preterit of *forego*[2].

fore-wom-an (fōr′wu̇m″ạn), *n.*; pl. *-women* (-wim″en). The chief or head woman; esp., the woman overseer of a number of women in a workshop or factory.

fore-word (fōr′wėrd), *n.* A word said beforehand; hence, an introduction or preface.

fore-worn′, *pp.* See *forworn.*

fore-yard (fōr′yärd), *n.* *Naut.*, the lower yard on the foremast.

for-feit (fôr′fit), *n.* [OF. F. *forfait*, < ML. *forisfactum*, transgression, prop. pp. neut. of *forisfacere*, transgress, < L. *foris*, outside, + *facere*, do, make.] A transgression† or crime†; also, something to which the right is lost by the commission of a crime or misdeed, the neglect of a duty, a breach of contract, etc.; hence, a fine; a penalty; also, an article deposited in a game because of a mistake and redeemable by a sportive fine or penalty; *pl.*, a game so played; also, *sing.*, the act of forfeiting; forfeiture. —**for′feit,** *v. t.* To lose as a forfeit; lose, or become liable to lose, in consequence of crime, fault, breach of engagement, etc.; hence, to yield up (as, "So should we save a valiant gentleman By *forfeiting* a traitor and a coward": Shakspere's "1 Henry VI.," iv. 3. 27); also, to cause the forfeiture of; also, to subject to forfeiture or confiscation (now rare). —**for′feit,** *a.* Forfeited: as, "Thy wealth being *forfeit* to the state, Thou hast not left the value of a cord" (Shakspere's "Merchant of Venice," iv. 1. 365). —**for′feit-a-ble,** *a.* Liable to be forfeited. —**for′feit-er,** *n.* —**for′feit-ure** (-fi-tụr), *n.* [OF. F. *forfaiture.*] The act of forfeiting; also, that which is forfeited; a fine or mulct.

for-fend (for-fend′), *v. t.* [See *for-* and *fend.*] To fend off, avert, or prevent (archaic); also, to forbid† or prohibit†; sometimes, to defend, secure, or protect.

for-fi-cate (fôr′fi-kāt), *a.* [L. *forfex* (*forfic-*), scissors.] Deeply forked, as the tail of certain birds. —**for-fi-ca′tion** (-kā′shọn), *n.* Forficate state or form.

for-fought-en (for-fô′tn), *a.* [See *for-* and *foughten.*] Exhausted with fighting, or by labor. [Sc. and north. Eng.]

for-gath-er (for-gaᴛʜ′ėr), *v. i.* [See *for-* and *gather.*] To gather together; convene; assemble; also, to encounter or meet, esp. by accident; also, to associate or fraternize (*with*). [Orig. and chiefly Sc.]

for-gave (for-gāv′). Preterit of *forgive.*

forge[1] (fōrj), *v. i.*; *forged, forging.* [Origin uncertain: cf. *forge*[2], also *force*[3], *v.*] To move ahead, esp. slowly or with difficulty: usually with *ahead.*

forge[2] (fōrj), *n.* [OF. F. *forge*, < L. *fabrica*, workshop: see *fabric.*] A workshop or establishment where metal, as iron, is heated and hammered or worked into form; a smithy; also, the special fireplace, hearth, or furnace (fitted with a bellows or other device for producing a blast) in which metal is heated before hammering; also, a hearth, furnace, or establishment where metal is melted, refined, or the like, as one for producing wrought-iron directly from the ore; a bloomery; a puddling and shingling mill.—**forge**[2], *v.*; *forged, forging.* [OF. *forgier* (F. *forger*), < L. *fabricare*, < *fabrica*: cf. *fabricate.*] **I.** *tr.* To form by heating and hammering; beat into shape; hence, to form or make in any way; esp., to invent or devise (a fictitious story, a lie, etc.); sometimes, to pretend (something) to have happened; also, to make (a thing) in fraudulent imitation of something else; make (something spurious) in order to pass it off as genuine; also, to imitate (a signature, seal, etc.) fraudulently. **II.** *intr.* To work at a forge; do a smith's work; also, to commit forgery.—**forge′a-ble,** *a.* That may be forged. —**for′ger,** *n.* One who forges metals; a smith; also, a maker or author, now only of false stories, etc. (as, "Ye are *forgers* of lies": Job, xiii. 4); also, one guilty of forgery. —**for′ger-y,** *n.*; pl. *-ies* (-iz). The act of forging metal† (as, "The *forgery* Of brazen shield and spear": Milton's "Samson Agonistes," 131); also, invention or devising, often fictitious invention, or deception or artifice (now only poetic); also, the act of fabricating or producing falsely; the making of a fraudulent imitation of a thing, or of something spurious which is put forth as genuine, as a coin, a work of art, a literary production, etc.; esp., the fraudulent making or altering of a writing to the prejudice of the right of another; also, something, as a coin, a work of art, a writing, etc., produced by forgery.

for-get (for-get′), *v. t.*; pret. *-got* (archaic *-gat*), pp. *-gotten* (sometimes *-got*), ppr. *-getting.* [AS. *forgitan, forgietan*: see *for-* and *get.*] To lose remembrance of; cease to remember; fail to remember; be unable to recall; also, to omit or neglect unintentionally (to do something); omit to take, or leave behind inadvertently (as, "A plague upon it! I have *forgot* the map": Shakspere's "1 Henry IV.," iii. 1. 6); omit to mention, or leave unnoticed; also, to omit to think of, or take no note of (as, "How happy is the blameless Vestal's lot! The world *forgetting*, by the world *forgot*": Pope's "Eloisa to Abelard," 208); hence, to neglect wilfully; overlook, disregard, or slight.—**to forget one's self,** to fail to remember one's station, position, or character; lose sight of what is due from one; say or do something improper; also, to become absent-minded; also, to lose consciousness, as in sleep; also, to neglect or slight one's self. —**for-get′,** *v. i.* To cease or omit to think of something. —**for-get′a-ble,** etc. See *forgettable*, etc.—**for-get′ful,** *a.* Apt to forget; that forgets; also, heedless or neglectful; also, causing to forget, or inducing oblivion (poetic).—**for-get′ful-ly,** *adv.*—**for-get′ful-ness,** *n.*

for-ge-tive (fōr′je-tiv), *a.* [Appar. < *forge*[2], *v.*] Inventive; creative: as, "A good sherris-sack . . . ascends me into the brain . . . makes it apprehensive, quick, *forgetive*, full of nimble fiery and delectable shapes" (Shakspere's "2 Henry IV.," iv. 3. 107). [Archaic.]

for-get=me=not (for-get′mē-not), *n.* A small boraginaceous plant, *Myosotis palustris*, which bears a light-blue flower commonly regarded as the emblem of constancy and friendship; any of several other plants of the same genus, or any of various similar plants.

for-get-ta-ble (for-get′a̦-bl), *a.* That may be forgotten. —**for-get′ta-ble-ness,** *n.*

for-get-ter (for-get′ėr), *n.* One who forgets; a heedless person.

for-ging (fōr′jing), *n.* Something forged; a piece of forged work in metal.

for-give (for-giv′), *v.*; pret. *-gave*, pp. *-given*, ppr. *-giving.* [AS. *forgifan, forgiefan*: see *for-* and *give.*] **I.** *tr.* To give† or grant†; also, to give up† or resign†; also, to grant free pardon for or remission of (an offense, debt, etc.); pardon; give up all claim on account of; also, to grant free pardon to (a person); cease to feel resentment against. **II.** *intr.* To pardon an offense or an offender (as, "To err is human, to *forgive*, divine": Pope's "Essay on Criticism," 525); remit a debt, etc.—**for-giv′a-ble,** *a.*—**for-give′ness,** *n.* [AS. *forgifnes.*] The act of forgiving, or the state of being forgiven; also, disposition or willingness to forgive. —**for-giv′er,** *n.*—**for-giv′ing,** *p. a.* That forgives; disposed to forgive; indicating forgiveness.—**for-giv′ing-ly,** *adv.*—**for-giv′ing-ness,** *n.*

for-go (for-gō′), *v. t.*; pret. *-went*, pp. *-gone*, ppr. *-going.* [AS. *forgān*: see *for-* and *go.*] To go or pass by†; hence, to neglect or overlook (archaic); also, to quit or leave (archaic); also, to abstain or refrain from; do without; give up, renounce, or resign.—**for-go′er,** *n.*

for-got (for-got′). Preterit of *forget.*—**for-got′ten, for-got′.** Past participles of *forget.*

for-judge (for-juj′), *v. t.*; *-judged, -judging.* [OF. *forjugier*, < *for-* (< L. *foris*, outside) + *jugier*, E. *judge, v.*] To exclude, expel, dispossess, or deprive by a judgment. [Now only in law.]

fork (fôrk), *n.* [AS. *forca*, < L. *furca*, a fork.] An instrument having two or more prongs or tines, for holding, lifting, etc., as any of various agricultural tools or an implement for handling food at table or in cooking; also, something resembling or suggesting this in form; a tuning-fork; the forked tongue of a snake†; the barbed head of an arrow†; also, a forking, or dividing into branches; the point or part at which a thing, as a river or a road, divides into branches; each of the branches into which a thing forks.—**fork,** *v.* **I.** *tr.* To make fork-shaped; also, to pierce, raise, pitch, dig, etc., with a fork; hence, to hand (*over* or *out*: slang). **II.** *intr.* To form a fork; divide into branches.—**forked** (fôrkt or fôr′ked), *a.* Having a fork or bifurcation, or forking branches; also, zigzag, as lightning.—**fork′ed-ly,** *adv.*—**fork′ed-ness,** *n.*—**fork′y,** *a.* Forked: as, "A Python . . . With *forky* tongue" (Browning's "Pippa Passes," iii.).

for-la-na (fôr-lä′nä), *n.* Same as *furlana.*

for-lorn (for-lôrn′), *a.* [ME. *forlorn* (= D. *verloren*), pp. of *forlesen*, < AS. *forlēosan* (pp. *forloren*), lose utterly, destroy: see *for-* and *lorn.*] Lost†; also, desperate or hopeless (as, a *forlorn* cause); also, abandoned, deserted, or forsaken (sometimes followed by *of*); bereft (*of*: as, "Dreamland lies *forlorn* of light," Rossetti's "Love's Nocturn"); desolate or dreary; unhappy, miserable, or wretched, as in feeling, condition, or appearance.—**forlorn hope.** [D. *verloren hoop*, 'lost troop.'] A body of men appointed to lead in an assault, storm a fortification, enter a breach, or perform some other unusually perilous service; a member of such a body; also, a perilous or desperate enterprise; also (with a play upon words, or through misunderstanding of 'hope'), a vain hope; an undertaking almost certain to fail.—**for-lorn′ly,** *adv.* —**for-lorn′ness,** *n.*

form (fôrm), *n.* [OF. F. *forme*, < L. *forma*, form, shape, figure, plan, model, mold, frame, sort, kind, ML. seat, bench.] Definite shape; external shape or appearance considered apart from color or material; configuration; also, a particular shape; the shape of a thing or person; hence, a particular structural condition, character, or mode of being exhibited by a thing (as, sulphur in the crystalline or the amorphous *form*; water in the *form* of steam or of ice; electricity is a *form* of energy; a mild *form* of a disease; a novel in the *form* of letters); a particular character as to spelling, inflection, etc., exhibited by a word, or a word considered as exhibiting such a character (as, an archaic, Anglicized, or abbreviated *form* of a word; 'his' is the possessive *form* of 'he'); also, due or proper shape; orderly arrangement of parts; good order; also, the manner or style of arranging and coördinating parts for a pleasing or effective result, as in literary or musical composition; also, a set, prescribed, or customary order or method of doing something (as, "The citadel was defended in *form*, and at length, in proper *form*, surrendered at discretion": Fielding's "Tom Jones," i. 11); a set order of words, as for use in religious ritual or in a legal document; also, a formulary document with blank spaces to be filled in with particulars; a sample or specimen document to be used as a guide in framing others for like cases (as, a *form* for a deed, lease, or contract); also, a conventional method of procedure or behavior; a formality or ceremony, often with implication of absence of real meaning (as, "For who would keep an ancient *form* Thro' which the spirit breathes no more?" Tennyson's

"In Memoriam," cv.); also, procedure according to a set order or method; formality; ceremony; conformity to the usages of society; often, in depreciation, mere outward formality or ceremony; conventional observance of social usages; also, procedure or conduct as judged by social standards (as, it is bad *form* to do such a thing); also, manner or method of performing something (as, he is a fast runner, but his *form* is bad); also, condition, esp. good condition, with reference to fitness for performing (colloq.: as, an athlete in good *form*, or in *form*); also, something having a definite shape or arrangement; a figure; a body, esp. that of a human being; also, an image† or likeness†; also, a rank or class of pupils in a school; also, a bench or long seat; also, an assemblage of types, etc., secured in a chase to print from or make plates from (in Great Britain, often spelled *forme*); also, the bed or lair of a hare; also, something that gives or determines shape; a mold; in *crystal.*, the combination of all the like faces possible on a crystal of given symmetry; in *philos.*, that element which determines the mode in which a thing is, or is perceived.—**form,** *v.* [OF. F. *former*, < L. *formare*, < *forma.*] **I.** *tr.* To give form or shape to; shape; fashion; give a particular form to, or fashion in a particular manner; also, to mold by discipline or instruction (as, "The most skilful masters . . . had labored to *form* the mind and body of the young prince": Gibbon's "Decline and Fall of the Roman Empire," xxvii.); train; also, to place in order; arrange; organize; also, to construct or frame; make or produce; frame in the mind (ideas, opinions, etc.); also, to contract (habits, friendships, etc.); also, to serve to make up, or compose; serve for, or constitute. **II.** *intr.* To take or assume form; be formed or produced; assume a particular form or arrangement.

-form. [L. *-formis*, < *forma*, form.] A termination of adjectives expressing form, shape, or likeness, as *aëriform*, *cruciform*, *cuneiform*, *deiform*, *pisciform*, or denoting the number of forms, as *biform*, *triform*, *quadriform*, *multiform*, *omniform*.

form-a-ble (fôr′mạ-bl), *a.* That may be formed.

for-mal (fôr′mạl), *a.* [L. *formalis.*] Of or pertaining to the form, shape, structural condition, or mode of being of a thing, esp. as distinguished from the matter; also, being such in form, esp. in mere outward form; also, being in accordance with prescribed or customary forms (as, a *formal* siege); made or done in accordance with forms ensuring validity (as, a *formal* authorization); being in accordance with conventional requirements; conventional; academic; rigorously methodical; excessively regular or symmetrical; also, marked by form or ceremony (as, a *formal* call; a *formal* occasion); observant of form, as persons; ceremonious; sometimes, excessively ceremonious; punctilious or precise to affectation; also, being a matter of form only; perfunctory; also, normal or sound in intellect† (as, "With wholesome syrups, drugs and holy prayers, To make of him a *formal* man again": Shakspere's "Comedy of Errors," v. 1. 105); in *philos.*, pertaining to form.

for-mal-de-hyde (fôr-mal′dẹ-hīd), *n.* [From *formic* + *aldehyde.*] In *chem.*, a gas, CH_2O, used, often in the form of an aqueous solution, as a disinfectant and preservative.

for-ma-lin (fôr′mạ-lin), *n.* [From *formal*(*dehyde*) + *-in.*] An aqueous solution of formaldehyde.

for-mal-ism (fôr′mạl-izm), *n.* [See *formal.*] Strict adherence to or observance of prescribed or customary forms; esp., in religion, excessive attachment to external forms and observances.—**for′mal-ist,** *n.*—**for-mal′i-ty** (-mal′i-ti), *n.*; pl. *-ties* (-tiz). The condition or quality of being formal; accordance with prescribed, customary, or due forms; conventionality; rigorously methodical character; excessive regularity, or stiffness; observance of form or ceremony; sometimes, marked or excessive ceremoniousness; also, an established order or mode of proceeding (as, the *formalities* of judicial process); a formal act or observance; also, something done merely for form's sake; a requirement of custom or etiquette.—**for′mal-ize** (-īz), *v.*; *-ized*, *-izing.* **I.** *tr.* To give a definite form or shape to; also, to render formal. **II.** *intr.* To be formal; act with formality.—**for″mal-i-za′tion** (-i-zā′shọn), *n.*—**for′mal-ly,** *adv.*—**for′mal-ness,** *n.*

for-mat (fôr′mat, F. fôr-mä), *n.* [F., < L. *formatus*, pp. of *formare*, E. *form*, *v.*] The shape and size of a book; the form or style generally, in which a book is made.

for-mate (fôr′māt), *n.* In *chem.*, a salt of formic acid.

for-ma-tion (fôr-mā′shọn), *n.* [L. *formatio*(*n-*).] The act or process of forming, or the state of being formed; also, the manner in which a thing is formed; disposition of parts; formal structure or arrangement; specif., a particular disposition of troops, as in columns, squares, etc.; also, something formed; in *geol.*, strata formed during some subdivision (usually minor) of geological time; a body of sedimentary rock of practically the same kind throughout; also, a mass or deposit of rock or mineral of a particular composition or origin (as, the siliceous *formation* around a geyser).

for-ma-tive (fôr′mạ-tiv). [OF. F. *formatif.*] **I.** *a.* Giving form or shape; forming; shaping; fashioning; molding; also, pertaining to formation or development (as, the *formative* period of a nation); in *gram.*, serving to form words (as, a *formative* termination); in *biol.*, *anat.*, etc., concerned with the formation of an embryo, organ, or the like (as, *formative* yolk: see *yolk*); capable of developing new cells or tissue by cell-division (as, *formative* tissue). **II.** *n.* In *gram.*, a formative element of a word, as a prefix or a suffix; also, a word formed, as from a root.—**for′ma-tive-ly,** *adv.*—**for′ma-tive-ness,** *n.*

forme (fôrm), *n.* See *form* (assemblage of types, etc.).

form-er[1] (fôr′mėr), *n.* One who or that which forms or serves to form.

for-mer[2] (fôr′mėr), *a.* [ME. *former*, a compar. formed to correspond to ME. and AS. *formest*, superl.: see *foremost.*] Being before in place†; forward†; foremost†; also, preceding in time; prior or earlier; past; long past, or ancient; also, preceding in order; being the first of two; esp., being the first mentioned of two.—**for′mer-ly,** *adv.* Before something else†; first†; also, in time past; heretofore; of old; also, in time just past†; just now†.

for-mic (fôr′mik), *a.* [L. *formica*, ant.] Pertaining to or derived from ants: as, *formic* acid (a colorless, irritant, vesicatory acid, HCO.OH, existing in ants, other insects, certain plants, etc.).

for-mi-ca-ry (fôr′mi-kā-ri), *n.*; pl. *-ries* (-riz). [ML. *formicarium*, < L. *formica*, ant.] An ants' nest.

for-mi-cate (fôr′mi-kāt), *v. i.*; *-cated*, *-cating.* [L. *formicatus*, pp. of *formicare*, < *formica*, ant.] To crawl like ants; also, to swarm with moving beings.—**for-mi-ca′tion** (-kā′shọn), *n.* [L. *formicatio*(*n-*).] In *pathol.*, an abnormal sensation as of ants creeping over the body.

for-mi-da-ble (fôr′mi-dạ-bl), *a.* [F. *formidable*, < L. *formidabilis*, < *formidare*, fear, dread.] That is to be feared or dreaded, esp. in encounters or dealings; of alarming strength, power, size, difficulty, appearance, etc. (as, "a most *formidable* fellow to look at": Defoe's "Robinson Crusoe," i. 12); such as to inspire apprehension of defeat or failure.—**for′mi-da-ble-ness,** *n.*—**for′mi-da-bly,** *adv.*

form-less (fôrm′les), *a.* Wanting form or shape; shapeless; without a determinate or regular form.—**form′less-ly,** *adv.*—**form′less-ness,** *n.*

for-mu-la (fôr′mū-lạ̈), *n.*; pl. *-las* or *-læ* (-lē). [L., dim. of *forma*, E. *form*, *n.*] A set form of words, as for stating or declaring something definitely or authoritatively, for indicating procedure to be followed, or for prescribed use on some ceremonial occasion; a rule; a recipe or prescription; a formal statement of religious doctrine; in scientific use, a group of symbols, etc., by which something is expressed; specif., in *math.*, a rule or principle expressed in algebraic symbols; in *chem.*, an expression of the constituents of a compound by symbols and figures.—**for′mu-lar** (-lạ̈r), *a.* Of or pertaining to a formula; formulary.—**for′mu-lar-ize** (-īz), *v. t.*; *-ized*, *-izing.* To formulate.—**for″mu-lar-i-za′tion** (-i-zā′shọn), *n.*—**for′mu-la-ry** (-lạ-ri). [F. *formulaire*, n., < L. *formula.*] **I.** *n.*; pl. *-ries* (-riz). A collection or system of formulas; also, a set form of words; a formula. **II.** *a.* Of or pertaining to a formula or formulas; of the nature of a formula.

for-mu-late (fôr′mū-lāt), *v. t.*; *-lated*, *-lating.* [Cf. F. *formuler.*] To reduce to a formula; express in or as in a formula; state definitely or systematically.—**for-mu-la′tion** (-lā′shọn), *n.*

for-mu-lism (fôr′mụ̄-lizm), *n.* Adherence to or systematic use of formulas; also, a system of formulas.—**for′mu-list,** *n.* One who adheres to or favors the use of formulas.—**for-mu-lis′tic,** *a.*

for-mu-lize (fôr′mụ̄-līz), *v. t.*; *-lized, -lizing.* To formulate. —**for″mu-li-za′tion** (-li-zā′shọn), *n.*

for-myl (fôr′mil), *n.* [See *formic* and *-yl.*] In *chem.*, the hypothetical radical, CHO, of formic acid.

for-nent′, for-nenst′, *prep.* See *forenent, forenenst.*

for-ni-cate[1] (fôr′ni-kāt), *a.* [L. *fornicatus,* < *fornix,* arch, vault.] Arched; vaulted.

for-ni-cate[2] (fôr′ni-kāt), *v. i.*; *-cated, -cating.* [LL. *fornicatus,* pp. of *fornicari,* < L. *fornix,* arch, vault, (underground) brothel.] To commit fornication.—**for-ni-ca′tion** (-kā′shọn), *n.* [LL. *fornicatio(n-).*] Voluntary sexual intercourse on the part of an unmarried person with a person of the opposite sex; also, esp. in Scripture, adultery; fig., idolatry.—**for′ni-ca-tor,** *n.*—**for′ni-ca-tress,** *n.*

for-nix (fôr′niks), *n.*; pl. *-nices* (-ni-sēz). [L., arch, vault.] In *anat.*, any of various arched or vaulted structures, as an arching fibrous formation in the brain.

for-sake (for-sāk′), *v. t.*; pret. *-sook,* pp. *-saken,* ppr. *-saking.* [AS. *forsacan,* < *for-* (see *for-*) + *sacan,* contend: see *sake*[1].] To deny†; repudiate†; also, to decline† or refuse†; avoid† or shun†; also, to give up or renounce; also, to quit or leave entirely; desert; abandon.—**for-sak′en** (-sā′kn), *p. a.* Deserted; abandoned; forlorn; also, morally abandoned†. —**for-sak′en-ly,** *adv.*—**for-sak′er,** *n.*

for-slow (for-slō′), *v.* [AS. *forslāwian,* < *for-* (see *for-*) + *slāwian,* be slow, < *slāw,* E. *slow.*] **I.** *tr.* To be slow or dilatory about; put off; also, to make slow; delay; obstruct. [Obs. or archaic.] **II.**† *intr.* To be slow or dilatory: as, "*Forslow* no longer, make we hence amain" (Shakspere's "3 Henry VI.," ii. 3. 56).

for-sook (for-sůk′). Preterit of *forsake.*

for-sooth (for-söth′), *adv.* [AS. *forsōth,* 'for sooth.'] In truth; in fact; indeed: now commonly used ironically or derisively.

for-speak (for-spēk′), *v. t.*; pret. *-spoke,* pp. *-spoken* or *-spoke,* ppr. *-speaking.* [See *for-* and *speak.*] To speak against† (as, "Thou hast *forspoke* my being in these wars, And say'st it is not fit": Shakspere's "Antony and Cleopatra," iii. 7. 3); also, to bewitch (now only Sc. and north. Eng.).

for-spend (for-spend′), *v. t.*; *-spent, -spending.* [AS. *forspendan*: see *for-* and *spend.*] To spend or use up completely, as strength; wear out or exhaust, as with exertion: chiefly in *forspent, pp.*

for-swear (for-swãr′), *v.*; pret. *-swore,* pp. *-sworn,* ppr. *-swearing.* [AS. *forswerian*: see *for-* and *swear.*] **I.** *tr.* To reject or renounce upon oath or with protestations; abjure; also, to deny upon oath or with strong asseveration; also, to perjure (one's self). **II.** *intr.* To swear falsely; commit perjury.—**for-swear′er,** *n.*—**for-sworn′** (-swôrn′), *p. a.* Perjured.

for-sy-thi-a (for-sī′thi-ạ̈ or -sith′i-ạ̈), *n.* [NL.; from W. *Forsyth* (1737–1804), British horticulturist.] Any shrub of the oleaceous genus *Forsythia,* native in China and southeastern Europe, species of which are much cultivated for their showy yellow flowers, appearing in early spring before the leaves.

fort (fōrt), *n.* [F. *fort,* noun use of *fort,* adj., < L. *fortis,* strong.] A strong or fortified place; an armed place surrounded by defensive works and occupied by troops; a fortification; also, in North America, a trading-post (so called because such posts were originally fortified).—**fort,** *v. t.* To fortify; inclose in a fort.

for-ta-lice (fôr′tạ-lis), *n.* [OF. *fortalice, fortelesse,* < ML. *fortalitia, fortalitium,* < L. *fortis,* strong.] A fortress†; also, a small fort; an outwork.

forte[1] (fōrt), *n.* [F. *fort,* noun use of *fort,* adj.: see *fort.*] A strong point, as of a person; that in which one excels; also, the stronger part of a sword-blade, being the portion between the middle and the hilt (opposed to *foible*).

for-te[2] (fôr′tā). [It., < L. *fortis,* strong.] In *music*: **I.** *a.* Loud. **II.** *adv.* Loudly.

forth (fōrth). [AS. *forth* = D. *voort* = G. *fort;* akin to E. *fore* and *further.*] **I.** *adv.* Forward; onward or outward in place or space; also, onward in time, in order, or in a series (as, from that day *forth;* and so *forth,* that is, and so on, and others, or et cetera); also, out, as from concealment or inaction; into view or consideration; also, away, as from a place or country; abroad. **II.** *prep.* Out of; forth from: as, "Steal *forth* thy father's house to-morrow night" (Shakspere's "Midsummer Night's Dream," i. 1. 164). [Archaic.]

forth-come (fōrth-kum′), *v. i.* [AS. *forthcuman.*] To come forth; appear.—**forth-com′ing,** *p. a.* Coming forth, or about to come forth; about to appear; approaching in time; often, ready or available when required or expected (as, "Still no Christian was *forthcoming*": J. H. Newman's "Callista," xvii.).

forth-put-ting (fōrth-pủt′ing), *a.* That puts forth; esp., putting one's self forward; obtrusive; presumptuous; meddlesome. [Now chiefly U. S.]

forth-right (fōrth′rīt or fōrth-rīt′), *adv.* [AS. *forthrihte.*] Straight or directly forward; in a direct manner; also, straightway; at once; immediately.—**forth′right. I.** *a.* Proceeding in a straight course; direct; straightforward; fig., going straight to the point; outspoken. **II.** *n.* A straight course or path.—**forth′right-ness,** *n.*

forth-with (fōrth-wiᴛʜ′ or -with′), *adv.* Immediately; at once; without delay; as soon as can reasonably be expected.

for-ti-eth (fôr′ti-eth). [AS. *fēowertigotha.*] **I.** *a.* Next after the thirty-ninth; also, being one of forty equal parts. **II.** *n.* The fortieth member of a series; also, a fortieth part.

for-ti-fi-a-ble (fôr′ti-fī-ạ-bl), *a.* That may be fortified.

for-ti-fi-ca-tion (fôr″ti-fi-kā′shọn), *n.* [F. *fortification,* < LL. *fortificatio(n-).*] The act of fortifying or strengthening; specif., the art or science of constructing defensive military works; also, that which fortifies or protects; specif., a military work constructed for the purpose of strengthening a position; a fortified place; a fort; a castle.

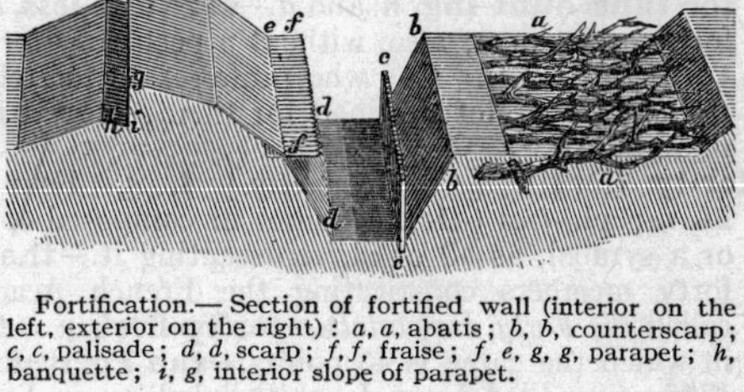

Fortification.— Section of fortified wall (interior on the left, exterior on the right): *a, a,* abatis; *b, b,* counterscarp; *c, c,* palisade; *d, d,* scarp; *f, f,* fraise; *f, e, g, g,* parapet; *h,* banquette; *i, g,* interior slope of parapet.

for-ti-fy (fôr′ti-fī), *v.*; *-fied, -fying.* [OF. F. *fortifier,* < LL. *fortificare,* < L. *fortis,* strong, + *facere,* make.] **I.** *tr.* To make strong; impart strength or vigor to, as the body; strengthen mentally or morally (as, courage *fortified* by prayer); confirm or corroborate (as, a charge *fortified* by particulars); furnish with a means of resisting force or standing strain, wear, etc. (as, a barrel *fortified* with metal hoops); specif., to strengthen against attack; surround with defenses; provide with defensive military works; protect with fortifications. **II.** *intr.* To set up defensive works; erect fortifications.—**for′ti-fi-er** (-fī-ėr), *n.*—**for′ti-fy-ing-ly,** *adv.*

for-tis-si-mo (fôr-tis′i-mō). [It., superl. of *forte*: see *forte*[2].] In *music*: **I.** *a.* Very loud. **II.** *adv.* Very loudly.

for-ti-tude (fôr′ti-tūd), *n.* [L. *fortitudo,* < *fortis,* strong.] Physical strength†; firmness†; also, moral strength or endurance (as, "adamantine *fortitude,* which sustained without flinching a mountain of responsibility": Motley's "Dutch Republic," iii. 2); patient courage under affliction, privation, or temptation.

fort-night (fôrt′nīt or -nit), *n.* [ME. *fourtenight,* < AS. *fēowertȳne niht,* fourteen nights.] The space of fourteen nights and days; two weeks.—**fort′night-ly. I.** *a.* Occurring or appearing once a fortnight. **II.** *n.*; pl. *-lies* (-liz). A fortnightly publication. **III.** *adv.* Once a fortnight.

for-tress (fôr′tres), *n.* [OF. *forterece* (F. *forteresse*), appar. var. of *fortalice*: see *fortalice.*] A fortified place; a fort; esp., a large permanent fortification, often including a town; hence, any place of security.—**Flying Fortress.** A U. S. high-altitude, long-range heavy bomber (Boeing).—**for′tress,** *v. t.* To furnish with a fortress; fortify.

for-tu-i-tism (fôr-tū′i-tizm), *n.* [See *fortuitous.*] The doctrine or belief that adaptations in nature are produced by the fortuitous operations of natural causes, and not by design.—**for-tu′i-tist,** *n.*

for-tu-i-tous (fôr-tū′i-tus), *a.* [L. *fortuitus*, < *fors* (*fort-*), chance: see *fortune.*] Happening or produced by chance; accidental; casual.—**for-tu′i-tous-ly,** *adv.*—**for-tu′i-tous-ness,** *n.*—**for-tu′i-ty** (-ti), *n.*; pl. *-ties* (-tiz). Fortuitous character; the fact of being accidental or casual; accident or chance; an accidental occurrence.

for-tu-nate (fôr′tū-nāt), *a.* [L. *fortunatus*, pp. of *fortunare*, E. *fortune, v.*] Having good fortune; receiving good from uncertain or unexpected sources; lucky; also, bringing or presaging good fortune; resulting favorably; auspicious. —**Fortunate Islands,** the Islands of the Blessed (see under *island*); also, the Canary Islands.—**for′tu-nate-ly,** *adv.* —**for′tu-nate-ness,** *n.*

for-tune (fôr′tūn), *n.* [OF. F. *fortune*, < L. *fortuna*, chance, luck, fortune, < *fors* (*fort-*), chance, akin to *ferre*, bear.] Chance, hap, or luck; [often *cap.*] chance personified, commonly regarded as a goddess distributing arbitrarily or capriciously the lots of life; also [*l. c.*], that which falls or is to fall to one as his portion in life or in any particular proceeding (often in *pl.*); lot; destiny; esp., good luck; success; prosperity; also, position in life as determined by wealth; amount of wealth; a person's possessions collectively; a stock of wealth; often, great wealth; an ample stock of wealth; also, a person of wealth, esp. a woman; an heiress.—**for′tune,** *v.*; *-tuned, -tuning.* [L. *fortunare*, make fortunate, < *fortuna.*] **I.** *tr.* To make fortunate†; also, to determine or control the lot or destiny of†; also, to endow with a fortune. **II.** *intr.* To chance or happen; come by chance: as, "It *fortuned*, out of the thickest wood A ramping Lyon rushed suddeinly" (Spenser's "Faerie Queene," i. 3. 5). [Now rare.]—**for′tune=hunt″er,** *n.* One who seeks to win a fortune, esp. through marriage.—**for′tune=hunt″ing,** *n.* and *a.*—**for′tune-less,** *a.* Without fortune; luckless; also, without a pecuniary fortune.—**for′tune=tell″er,** *n.* One who professes to foretell to persons the fortune or lot destined for them.—**for′tune=tell″ing,** *n.* and *a.*

for-ty (fôr′ti). [AS. *fēowertig.*] **I.** *a.* Four times ten. **II.** *n.*; pl. *-ties* (-tiz). A number composed of forty units, or a symbol, as 40 or xl, representing it.—**the Forty,** the forty members constituting the French Academy. Also called *the Forty Immortals.*—**for′ty=five′,** *n.* A card-game in which the game is 45 points.—**the Forty=five,** the year 1745 as marked by a Jacobite rebellion in Scotland; the rebellion itself.—**for′ty=nin′er** (-nī′nėr), *n.* One of those who went to California in 1849, during the gold fever, in search of fortune. Cf. *Argonaut.*

fo-rum (fō′rum), *n.*; pl. *-rums*, L. *-ra* (-rạ̈). [L.] The market-place or public place of an ancient Roman city, the center of judicial and other public business and a place of assembly for the people; hence, a court or tribunal (often fig.: as, the *forum* of conscience; the *forum* of public opinion); also, an assembly for the discussion of questions of public interest.

for-ward (fôr′wạ̈rd), *adv.* [AS. *forweard*, < *for, fore*, before, + *-weard*: see *fore* and *-ward.*] Toward or at a place, point, or time in advance; onward; ahead; also, to the front, into view or consideration, or forth (as, to bring *forward* new evidence).—**for′ward. I.** *a.* Situated in the front or fore part; lying in advance; fore; also, directed toward a point in advance; moving ahead; onward; also, of or pertaining to the future (as, *forward* buying); prospective; also, being in a condition of advancement; well advanced; often, advanced beyond one's years; precocious; also, ready, prompt, or eager (as, "I killed a sea-fowl or two . . . but was not very *forward* to eat them": Defoe's "Robinson Crusoe," i. 6); also, presumptuous, pert, or bold (as, "Your cousin Sophy is a *forward*, impertinent gipsy": Sheridan's "School for Scandal," iii. 1); also, radical or extreme, as persons or opinions. **II.** *n.* A player stationed in advance of others on his team, as, in *football*, any player in the forward line.—**for′ward,** *v. t.* To send forward; transmit, esp. to an ulterior destination (as, to *forward* a letter); also, to advance or help onward (as, to *forward* the growth of a plant); promote; hasten; in *bookbinding*, to prepare (a book) for the finisher by fitting it with back and covers, etc. —**for′ward-er,** *n.*—**for′ward-ly,** *adv.*—**for′ward-ness,** *n.* —**for′wards,** *adv.* Forward.

for-wear (for-wãr′), *v. t.* [See *for-* and *wear*².] To wear out; exhaust: now only in *forworn, pp.* [Archaic.]

for-wear-y (for-wēr′i), *v. t.*; *-wearied, -wearying.* [See *for-* and *weary, v.*] To weary utterly; tire out. [Obs. or archaic.]

for-went (for-went′). Preterit of *forgo.*

for-worn (for-wôrn′). Past participle of *forwear.*

foss (fos), *n.* See *fosse.*

fos-sa (fos′ạ̈), *n.*; pl. *fossæ* (-ē). [L., a ditch, trench, prop. pp. fem. of *fodere*, dig.] In *anat.*, a pit, cavity, or depression in a bone, etc.

fosse (fos), *n.* [OF. F. *fosse*, < L. *fossa*: see *fossa.*] A ditch, trench, or canal; esp., a moat in a fortification.

fos-sette (fo-set′), *n.* [F. *fossette*, dim. of *fosse*: see *fosse.*] A little hollow; a depression; a dimple.

fos-sick (fos′ik), *v.* [Origin obscure.] **I.** *intr.* To search for gold in relinquished workings, washing-places, etc.; hence, to search about or rummage. [Australia.] **II.** *tr.* To dig; hunt. [Australia.]—**fos′sick-er,** *n.*

fos-sil (fos′il). [L. *fossilis*, < *fodere*, dig.] **I.** *a.* Dug out of the earth, or obtained by digging (as, *fossil* fuel); also, of the nature of a fossil; hence, belonging to a past epoch or discarded system; antiquated. **II.** *n.* Any rock or mineral substance dug out of the earth†; also, any remains, impression, or trace of an animal or plant of a former geological age, found in the earth's crust or strata; hence, a fossilized or antiquated person or thing; a person of antiquated ideas or ways.—**fos-sil-if-er-ous** (fos-i-lif′ẹ-rus), *a.* [See *-ferous.*] Bearing or containing fossils, as rocks or strata.—**fos′sil-ist,** *n.* A student of fossils; a paleontologist.—**fos′sil-ize** (-īz), *v.*; *-ized, -izing.* **I.** *tr.* To convert into a fossil (as, to *fossilize* animal remains); fig., to change as if into mere lifeless remains or traces of the past; render rigidly antiquated, as persons, ideas, etc. **II.** *intr.* To become fossilized (lit. or fig.); also, to search for fossils. —**fos″sil-i-za′tion** (-i-zā′shọn), *n.*

fos-so-ri-al (fo-sō′ri-ạl), *a.* [LL. *fossorius*, < L. *fossor*, digger, < *fodere*, dig.] Digging or burrowing, or adapted for digging or burrowing: as, a *fossorial* animal; a *fossorial* limb.

fos-ter (fos′tėr), *n.* [AS. *fōstor*, akin to *fōda*, E. *food.*] Nourishment: now chiefly as in *foster-father, foster-mother, foster-parent, foster-child, foster-brother*, etc., implying relationship through nursing or rearing, not by blood. —**fos′ter,** *v. t.* To feed† or nourish† (as, "*foster'd* with cold dishes": Shakspere's "Cymbeline," ii. 3. 119); also, to bring up or rear, as a foster-child; hence, to care for or cherish tenderly (as, "He gave them charge about the Queen, To guard and *foster* her for evermore": Tennyson's "Guinevere," 588); also, to promote the growth or development of (as, to *foster* a plant; to *foster* trade or friendly relations); further; encourage.—**fos′ter-age** (-āj), *n.* The act of fostering or rearing another's child as one's own; the condition of being a foster-child; also, the act of promoting or encouraging.—**fos′ter-er,** *n.*—**fos′ter-ling,** *n.* A foster-child.—**fos′tress,** *n.* A woman who fosters. Also fig.

foth-er¹ (foᴛʜ′ėr), *n.* [AS. *fōther.*] A cart-load, or any large quantity (now chiefly Sc. and north. Eng.); also, an old unit of weight for lead, lime, coal, etc., that for lead being now usually 19½ hundredweight.

foth-er² (foᴛʜ′ėr), *v. t.* [Cf. D. *voederen, voeren*, LG. *fodern*, Icel. *fōdhra*, line.] To cover (a sail) with oakum, rope-yarn, etc., fastened upon it, for placing over and stopping a leak in a ship; also, to stop (a leak) with a sail prepared thus.

Fou-cault (fö-kō) **cur′rent.** [From J. B. L. *Foucault* (1819–68), French physicist.] In *elect.*, an eddy current.

fou-droy-ant (fọ-droi′ạnt, F. fö-drwo-yäṅ), *a.* [F., ppr. of *foudroyer*, strike with lightning, < *foudre*, < L. *fulgur*, lightning.] Striking as with lightning; sudden and overwhelming in effect; stunning; dazzling.

fou-gasse (fọ-gas′), *n.* [F., earlier *fougade*; from It.] *Milit.*, a small, well-like mine sunk in the ground.

fought (fôt). Preterit and past participle of *fight.*—**fought′en,** *p. a.* [Old pp. of *fight.*] That has been the scene of fighting (archaic: as, a *foughten* field); also, forfoughten (Sc. and north. Eng.).

foul (foul). [AS. *fūl* = D. *vuil* = G. *faul* = Icel. *fūll* = Goth. *fūls*, foul; akin to L. *pus*, Gr. πύον, pus, Gr. πύθειν, rot, L. *putere*, Skt. *pū-*, stink.] **I.** *a.* Grossly offensive to the senses, or disgusting (as, *foul* matter; a *foul* exudation; a *foul* smell); loathsome; noisome; also, charged with or characterized by offensive or noisome matter (as, a *foul* pond; *foul* air; a *foul* ulcer); filthy or dirty, as places, vessels, or clothes; muddy, as a road; abounding in errors or in marks of correction, as a printer's proof; clogged or obstructed with foreign matter (as, a *foul* chimney, one choked with soot; a ship with a *foul* bottom, one having the bottom clogged with seaweed, barnacles, etc.); in collision or obstructing contact (as, a ship *foul* of another or of a rock); entangled, caught, or jammed (as, a *foul* rope or anchor); also, not fair; ugly or unattractive (now chiefly prov.); disfigured† (as, "My face is *foul* with weeping": Job, xvi. 16); contrary to the rules or established usages, as of a sport or game; unfair (as, *foul* play, unfair conduct in a game, or any unfair or treacherous dealing, often such as involves murder); unfavorable or stormy, as weather; contrary, as the wind; also, grossly offensive in a moral sense; abominable, wicked, or vile, as deeds, crime, slander, etc.; scurrilous, profane, or obscene, as language; in *baseball*, noting a hit or batted ball which is not a fair ball (see *fair ball*, under *fair*[1], *a.*); noting the lines from home to first base and from home to third base, with their indefinite continuations. **II.** *n.* That which is foul; a collision or entanglement; a violation of the rules of a sport or game; in *baseball*, a foul ball.—**foul,** *adv.* In a foul manner; foully; unfairly.—**foul,** *v.* **I.** *tr.* To make foul; defile; soil; clog or obstruct, as a chimney or the bore of a gun; encumber (a ship's bottom) with seaweed, barnacles, etc.; collide with (as, one boat *fouled* another); cause to become entangled or caught, as a rope; also, to defile in a moral sense; dishonor; disgrace. **II.** *intr.* To become foul; collide, as ships; become entangled or caught, as a rope; also, to make a foul play, give a foul blow, knock a foul ball, etc.

fou-lard (fọ̈-lärd′), *n.* [F.; origin unknown.] A soft, light-weight silk or satin, plain or with a printed pattern, used for women's dresses, etc.

foul-ly (foul′li), *adv.* In a foul manner.

foul=mind-ed (foul′mīn′ded), *a.* Foul or unclean in mind or thoughts.

foul=mouthed (foul′mouᴛʜd′), *a.* Using scurrilous, profane, or obscene language; given to filthy or abusive speech.

foul-ness (foul′nes), *n.* The state or quality of being foul; also, that which is foul; foul matter; filth; wickedness.

foul=spok-en (foul′spō′kn), **foul=tongued** (foul′tungd′), *a.* Foul-mouthed.

fou-mart (fö′märt), *n.* [ME. *fulmard*, < AS. *fūl*, foul, + *mearth*, marten.] The European polecat.

found[1] (found). Preterit and past participle of *find*.

found[2] (found), *v. t.* [OF. F. *fondre*, melt, cast, < L. *fundere*, pour, melt, cast: cf. *fuse*[1].] To melt and pour (metal, etc.) into a mold; form or make (an article) of molten material in a mold; cast.

found[3] (found), *v.* [OF. F. *fonder*, < L. *fundare*, lay the bottom of, found, < *fundus*, bottom: cf. *fund*.] **I.** *tr.* To lay the lowest part of, fix, or build (a structure) on a firm base or ground (as, a house *founded* upon a rock: see Mat. vii. 25); hence, to set up or establish on a firm basis or for enduring existence (as, to *found* a city, colony, or institution; to *found* a family or dynasty; to *found* a system of philosophy); also, to base or ground (*on* or *upon*: as, a story *founded* on fact; to *found* a claim on right or justice); sometimes, to afford a basis or ground for. **II.** *intr.* To be founded or based (*on* or *upon*); also, to base one's opinion (*on* or *upon*).

foun-da-tion (foun-dā′shọn), *n.* [OF. F. *fondation*, < L. *fundatio(n-)*.] The act of founding, setting up, establishing, etc., or the state of being founded; also, that on which something is founded; the natural or prepared ground or base on which some structure rests; the lowest division of a building, wall, or the like, usually of masonry and partly or wholly below the surface of the ground; the basis or ground of anything (as, a report that has no *foundation* of fact); also, a donation or legacy for the support of an institution; an endowment; an endowed institution.—**foun-da′tion-er,** *n.* In Great Britain, one who is supported on the foundation or endowment of a college or school.—**foun-da′tion-less,** *a.* Without foundation; baseless; unfounded.

found-er[1] (foun′dėr), *n.* One who founds or casts metal, etc.

found-er[2] (foun′dėr), *n.* One who founds or establishes.

foun-der[3] (foun′dėr), *v.* [OF. *fondrer*, < L. *fundus*, bottom: cf. *found*[3].] **I.** *intr.* To fall or sink down, as buildings, ground, etc.; sink in mire, a quicksand, etc.; esp., to fill with water and sink, as a ship; fig., to suffer wreck, or fail utterly (as, "In this point All his tricks *founder*": Shakspere's "Henry VIII.," iii. 2. 40); also, to stumble, break down, or go lame, as a horse. **II.** *tr.* To cause to fall or sink down†; undermine, as a structure†; cause to sink in mire, etc. (as, "A boggy Syrtis, neither sea, Nor good dry land: nigh *founder'd* on he fares": Milton's "Paradise Lost," ii. 940); cause to fill with water and sink, as a ship; also, to cause (a horse, etc.) to break down, go lame, or suffer from founder; in *golf*, to drive (the ball) into the ground.—**foun′der**[3], *n.* Lameness or inflammation in the foot of a horse, mule, etc., as from overwork; laminitis.—**foun′der-ous,** *a.* Apt to cause foundering, as roads, ground, etc.; miry; swampy. [Now chiefly prov. Eng.]

found-ling (found′ling), *n.* An infant found abandoned; a child without a parent or claimant.

found-ress (foun′dres), *n.* A woman who founds or establishes.

foun-drous (foun′drus), *a.* See *founderous*.

foun-dry (foun′dri), *n.*; pl. *-dries* (-driz). [F. *fonderie*, < *fondre*, E. *found*[2].] The founding of metal, etc.; also, things made by founding; castings; also, an establishment for founding (as, an iron-*foundry*; a type-*foundry*; a glass-*foundry*).

fount[1] (fount), *n.* In *printing*, same as *font*[1]. [Chiefly Eng.]

fount[2] (fount), *n.* [L. *fons* (*font-*), spring, fountain: cf. *font*[2].] A spring of water; a fountain; fig., a source or origin.

foun-tain (foun′tān), *n.* [OF. F. *fontaine*, < LL. *fontana*, prop. fem. of L. *fontanus*, of or from a spring, < *fons*, E. *fount*[2].] A spring or source of water; the source or head of a stream; fig., the source or origin of anything (as, "Almighty God, the *fountain* of all wisdom": Book of Common Prayer, Communion); also, a jet or stream of water (or other liquid) issuing or spouted forth, esp. one made by mechanical means to spout or rise from an orifice or structure, as to afford water for use, or to cool the air, or to serve for ornament (as, "And drew, from butts of water . . . The *fountain* of the moment, playing, now A twisted snake, and now a rain of pearls, Or steep-up spout whereon the gilded ball Danced like a wisp": Tennyson's "Princess," Prologue, 61); hence, a structure for discharging such a jet or a number of jets, often an elaborate or artistic work with basins, sculptures, etc.; an erection, as in a public place, for furnishing a constant supply of fresh water for drinking; a soda-fountain; also, a reservoir for a liquid to be supplied gradually or continuously, as one for oil in certain kinds of lamp or one for ink in a printing-press (cf. *fountain-pen*).—**foun′tained,** *a.* Having a fountain or fountains.—**foun′tain-head,** *n.* A fountain or spring from which a stream flows; the head or source of a stream; fig., a primary source.—**foun′tain-less,** *a.* Without fountains.—**foun′tain=pen′,** *n.* A writing-pen with a reservoir for supplying ink continuously.

four (fōr), *a.* [AS. *fēower* = D. and G. *vier* = Icel. *fjōrir* = Goth. *fidwōr*, four; akin to L. *quattuor*, Gr. τέτταρες, Skt. *catur*, four.] One more than three.—**the four freedoms,** freedom of speech, freedom of worship, freedom from want, and freedom from fear: listed by Franklin D. Roosevelt.—**the four seas.** See under *sea*.—**four,** *n.* A number composed of four units, or a symbol, as 4 or iv, representing it; a set of four things or persons, as a team of four horses or the crew of a four-oared boat; also, the boat; also, a playing-card, die-face, etc., with four pips.—**on all fours,** on the hands and feet (or knees).

four-ché, four-chée (för-shā′), *a.* [F. *fourché*, masc., *fourchée*, fem., < *fourche*, a fork: see *fourchette*.] In *her.*, forked; having the extremity or extremities divided into two parts: said of a bearing, esp. a cross having each arm divided into two square ends at its extremity.

Cross Fourché.

four-chette (fōr-shet′), *n.* [F., dim. of *fourche*, < L. *furca*, E. *fork*.] A fork, or something resembling a fork; the strip of material forming the sides of two adjacent fingers of a glove; in *anat.*, the furcula of a bird; also, the frog of an animal's foot; also, a small fold of membrane just within the posterior commissure of the vulva; in *card-playing*, the combination in one hand of the card immediately above and that immediately below a given card.

four=cy-cle (fōr′sī″kl), *n.* In an internal-combustion engine, a cycle in which one piston stroke out of every four is a working stroke.

Four-dri-nier (fōr-dri-nēr′) **ma-chine′.** [From H. and S. *Fourdrinier*, English inventors.] A machine for making paper in a continuous strip or web.

four=flush (fōr′flush′), *n.* In the game of poker, four cards of a possible flush, which, with one card of a different suit, make up a hand; an imperfect flush (which, as such, is of no value); hence (slang), a mere bluff or empty pretense. —**four′=flush′**, *v. i.* To act as a four-flusher. [Slang.] —**four′=flush′er,** *n.* One who bluffs on or as on the strength of a four-flush; one who makes pretensions that he cannot or does not bear out. [Slang.]

four-fold (fōr′fōld). **I.** *a.* Comprising four parts or members; four times as great or as much. **II.** *adv.* In fourfold measure.

four=foot-ed (fōr′fu̇t″ed), *a.* Having four feet.

four-gon (fōr-gôn), *n.* [F.; origin uncertain.] A long covered wagon for carrying baggage, goods, military supplies, etc.; a van; also, a baggage-car.

four=hand-ed (fōr′han″ded), *a.* Having four hands, or four feet adapted for use as hands; quadrumanous; also, intended for four hands, as a piece of music for the piano; also, involving four hands or players, as a game at cards.

Fou-ri-er-ism (fö′ri-ėr-izm), *n.* The communistic system propounded by the French socialist F. M. Charles Fourier (1772–1837), according to which society was to be organized into associations or communities called phalanxes, each with a membership of about 1,800.—**Fou′ri-er-ist, Fou′-ri-er-ite** (-īt), *n.*

four=in=hand (fōr′in-hand), *n.* A vehicle drawn by four horses driven by one person; also, a team of four horses; also, a long scarf or necktie to be tied in a slip-knot with the ends left hanging.

four=leaved (fōr′lēvd), *a.* Having four leaves or leaflets.

four=o'clock (fōr′ọ-klok″), *n.* A common nyctaginaceous garden-plant, *Mirabilis jalapa*, with red, white, yellow, or variegated flowers which open late in the afternoon; any plant of the same genus; also, the friar-bird.

four-pence (fōr′pẹns), *n.* A sum of money of the value of four English pennies, or about 8 U. S. cents; also, a British silver coin of this value.—**four′pen-ny** (-pẹ-ni), *a.* Of the amount or value of fourpence.

Obverse. Reverse.
Fourpence of Queen Victoria.

four=post-er (fōr′pōs′tėr), *n.* A bed with four posts, as for supporting curtains.

four-ra-gère (fö-rä-zhãr), *n.* [F., said to have originated in the *corde à fourrage*, 'cord for forage,' carried by mounted men for binding and transporting forage: see *forage*.] In French military use, an ornament of cord worn on the shoulder; specif., such a cord awarded as an honorary decoration, as to the members of a regiment or other unit that has received a requisite number of citations.

four-score (fōr′skōr), *a.* Four times twenty; eighty.

four-some (fōr′sum). **I.** *a.* Consisting of four; performed by four persons together. [Chiefly Sc.] **II.** *n.* A company or set of four (chiefly Sc.); in *golf*, etc., a match played by four persons, two against two.

four-square (fōr′skwãr). **I.** *a.* Having its four sides and angles equal; square. **II.** *n.* A foursquare figure; a square.

four-teen (fōr′tēn′). [AS. *fēowertȳne*.] **I.** *a.* Four more than ten. **II.** *n.* A number composed of fourteen units, or a symbol, as 14 or xiv, representing it.—**four′teenth′.** **I.** *a.* Next after the thirteenth; also, being one of fourteen equal parts. **II.** *n.* The fourteenth member of a series; also, a fourteenth part.—**Fourteenth of July,** the date of the fall of the Bastille, in Paris, in 1789, observed as the national holiday of France.

fourth (fōrth), *a.* [AS. *fēortha*.] Next after the third; also, being one of four equal parts.—**fourth arm.** See *arm*², *n.*—**fourth dimension.** See *dimension*, *n.*—**fourth estate.** See under *estate*, *n.*—**fourth,** *n.* The fourth member of a series; [*cap.*] the Fourth of July (see phrase below); also [*l. c.*], a fourth part; in *music*, a tone on the fourth degree from a given tone (counted as the first); the interval between such tones; the harmonic combination of such tones; in a scale, the subdominant.—**Fourth of July,** the date of the adoption of the Declaration of Independence, in 1776, observed as a public holiday of the U. S. Often called *the Fourth*.—**fourth′ly,** *adv.*

four=wheeled (fōr′hwēld), *a.* Having, or running on, four wheels.—**four′=wheel′er,** *n.* A vehicle with four wheels; esp., a four-wheeled cab.

fous-sa (fös′ạ̈), *n.* [Native name.] A cat-like carnivorous quadruped, *Cryptoprocta ferox*, of Madagascar; the galet.

Foussa.

fou-tre, fou-ter (fö′tėr), *n.* [Cf. F. *se foutre de*, care nothing for, *foutre* (< L. *futuere*), have sexual commerce with.] A word formerly used in expressions of contemptuous indifference (as, to care not a *foutre*; "A *foutre* for the world and worldlings base!" Shakspere's "2 Henry IV.," v. 3. 103); also, a term of the deepest contempt for a person (chiefly Sc. and north. Eng.).

fo-ve-a (fō′vẹ-ạ̈), *n.*; pl. *foveæ* (-ē). [L., a small pit.] In *anat.*, *bot.*, etc., a small pit or depression, as one in the center of the yellow spot on the retina of the eye.—**fo′ve-al,** *a.* Of, pertaining to, or situated in a fovea.—**fo′ve-ate, fo′ve-at-ed** (-āt, -ā-ted), *a.* Having foveæ; pitted.

fo-ve-o-la (fọ-vē′ọ̄-lạ̈), *n.*; pl. *-læ* (-lē). [NL., dim. of L. *fovea*: see *fovea*.] In *anat.*, *bot.*, etc., a small fovea; a very small pit or depression.—**fo-ve-o-late, fo-ve-o-lat-ed** (fō′vẹ-ọ̄-lāt, -lā-ted), *a.* Having foveolæ, or very small pits.

fowl (foul), *n.*; pl. *fowls* or (esp. collectively) *fowl*. [AS. *fugel* = D. and G. *vogel* = Icel. *fugl* = Goth. *fugls*, fowl, bird; possibly akin to E. *fly*².] Any bird (now chiefly in combination, as in sea-*fowl*, water-*fowl*, wild-*fowl*); specif., the domestic or barnyard cock or hen ('domestic fowl'), a gallinaceous bird (often designated as *Gallus domesticus*) of the pheasant family, descended from wild species of *Gallus*, esp. *G. ferrugineus*; any of various other gallinaceous or similar birds, as the turkey or duck; *pl.*, poultry; *sing.*, in market and household use, a full-grown domestic fowl for food purposes (as distinguished from a chicken, or young fowl); the flesh or meat of a domestic fowl.—**fowl,** *v. i.* [AS. *fuglian*.] To hunt or take wild-fowl.—**fowl′er,** *n.* One who hunts or takes wild-fowl.—**fowl′ing=piece,** *n.* A light gun for shooting wild-fowl; also, a picture of wild-fowl.

fox (foks), *n.* [AS. *fox* = D. *vos* = G. *fuchs*, fox.] Any of certain carnivorous quadrupeds of the dog family (*Canidæ*), esp. those constituting the genus *Vulpes*, smaller than the wolves, characterized by pointed muzzle, erect ears, and long, bushy tail (commonly called the *brush*), and proverbially noted for cunning (see cut on following page); also, the fur of the fox; also, some animal likened to the fox, as the flying-fox; in the English Bible, sometimes, the jackal;

fig., a cunning or crafty person; also, a kind of sword†; *naut.*, a seizing or the like made by twisting rope-yarns together.—**fox and geese,** a game played on a cross-shaped board or a checker-board with pins, checkers, or the like, one representing a fox and the rest geese, the object of the geese being to surround the fox, and that of the fox to capture or to escape from the geese; also, a boys' game in which one player tries to catch others as they run from one goal to another.

Red Fox (*Vulpes vulgaris* or *fulvus*).

—**fox,** *v.* **I.** *intr.* To hunt the fox; also, to act cunningly or craftily; also, to become discolored through decay, etc., as timber or the leaves of a book; also, to turn sour, as beer. **II.** *tr.* To intoxicate or befuddle; also, to cause (timber, book-leaves, etc.) to fox; also, to make sour, as beer; also, to repair, finish, or make (a shoe) with a piece or pieces of leather or other material applied so as to cover or form part of the upper next above the sole.—**foxed,** *p. a.* Intoxicated or befuddled; also, discolored by decay, as timber or paper; also, turned sour, as beer.

fox-fire (foks′fīr), *n.* The phosphorescent light emitted by foxed or decaying timber.

fox-glove (foks′gluv), *n.* Any plant of the scrophulariaceous genus *Digitalis*, esp. *D. purpurea* (the common foxglove), a native of Europe, bearing tall racemes of drooping, tubular, purple or white flowers, and leaves that are used in medicine as the drug digitalis; also, any of various plants of other genera.

Foxglove (*Digitalis purpurea*).

fox=grape (foks′grāp), *n.* Either of two species of grape, *Vitis labrusca* of the northern U. S. and *V. rotundifolia* of the southern U. S., from which various cultivated varieties have been derived.

fox-hound (foks′hound), *n.* One of a breed of fleet, keen-scented hounds trained to hunt foxes.

fox-i-ness (fok′si-nes), *n.* Foxy quality or character.

fox-ing (fok′sing), *n.* The piece or pieces of leather or other material with which a shoe is foxed.

Northern Fox-grape (*Vitis labrusca*).

fox=squir-rel (foks′skwur′el), *n.* Any of several North American arboreal squirrels varying in color and remarkable for large size.

Black Fox-squirrel (*Sciurus niger*).

fox-tail (foks′tāl), *n.* The tail of a fox; also, any of various grasses with soft, brush-like spikes of flowers.—**foxtail millet,** an annual grass, *Chætochloa italica*, of numerous varieties, introduced into the U. S. from Europe and Asia, and grown somewhat for its seed but chiefly for hay. Also called *Italian millet*.

fox=ter-ri-er (foks′ter′i-ėr), *n.* One of a breed of small active terriers, sometimes used for driving foxes from their holes, but kept chiefly as pets.

fox=trot (foks′trot), *n.* A pace, as of a horse, consisting of a series of short steps, as in slackening from a trot to a walk; also, a kind of dance performed by couples, characterized by various combinations of short, quick steps.

fox-wood (foks′wůd), *n.* Foxed or decayed wood.

fox-y (fok′si), *a.*; compar. *foxier*, superl. *foxiest*. Fox-like; cunning or crafty; also, of the color of the common red fox; of a yellowish or reddish brown; marked by an excess of reddish tints, as a painting; also, discolored or foxed; also, impaired or defective in quality; having turned sour in fermentation, as beer; also, having the musky flavor of the fox-grape.

foy (foi), *n.* [MD. *foye*, prob. < OF. *voie*, < L. *via*, way.] A feast, gift, etc., given by or to a person about to start on a journey; also, a feast held on some special occasion, as at the end of the harvest. [Now Sc. and prov. Eng.]

foy-er (foi′ėr, F. fwo-yā), *n.* [F., hearth, fireside, foyer (to which orig. the audience went for warmth from the unheated hall between the acts), < ML. *focarium*, < L. *focus*, hearth.] A corridor or outer public room in a theater, opera-house, or the like, used by the audience as a promenade, etc., during intermissions.

fra (frä), *n.* [It., for *frate*: see *frate*.] Brother: a title of a friar: as, *Fra* Giovanni ('Brother John').

fra-cas (frā′kạs, F. frȧ-kä), *n.* [F., < It. *fracasso*, < *fracassare*, smash.] A disorderly noise or disturbance; an uproar; a noisy quarrel or fight.

fract-ed (frak′ted), *a.* [L. *fractus*, pp. of *frangere*, break: see *fraction*.] Broken† (as, "My reliances on his *fracted* dates Have smit my credit": Shakspere's "Timon of Athens," ii. 1. 22); in *her.*, having a part displaced, as if broken.

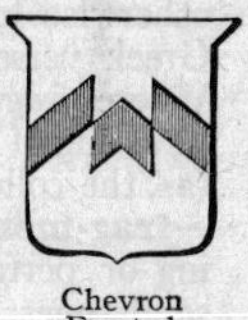

Chevron Fracted.

frac-tion (frak′shọn), *n.* [OF. F. *fraction*, < LL. *fractio(n-)*, < L. *frangere*, break; akin to E. *break*.] The act of breaking (as, *eccles.*, the *fraction* of the bread in the eucharist); a broken state or place†; a fracture, as of a bone†; fig., a rupture of harmony, friendly relations, etc.†; discord†; also, a piece broken off, fragment, or bit (see Shakspere's "Troilus and Cressida," v. 2. 158); a part, as distinct from the whole of anything (as, a mere *fraction* of the regiment came back); in *math.*, a part of unity; one or more of a number of equal parts into which a unit is divided, or an arithmetical representation of such a part or parts, as $\frac{1}{2}$ or $\frac{3}{4}$ (as, a common or vulgar *fraction*, one having the numerator above and the denominator below a horizontal or diagonal line; a proper *fraction*, one having the numerator less than the denominator; an improper *fraction*, one having the numerator greater than the denominator; a simple *fraction*, one expressing a ratio between two whole numbers; a complex *fraction*, one expressing a ratio between fractions or mixed numbers, or between a fraction or mixed number and a whole number; a compound *fraction*, a complex fraction, or a fraction of a fraction); also, an analogous ratio of algebraic quantities.—**frac′tion,** *v. t.* To divide into fractions; also, to fractionate.—**frac′tion-al,** *a.* Of or pertaining to a fraction or fractions; constituting a fraction; hence, partial, inconsiderable, or insignificant.—**fractional crystallization,** a process by which a substance, as a mixture of salts, is separated into its ingredients, or into portions having different properties, by means of repeated crystallizations.—**fractional currency,** current coins or paper money of a smaller denomination than the monetary unit.—**fractional distillation.** See *distillation*.—**frac′tion-al-ly,** *adv.*—**frac′tion-a-ry** (-ā-ri), *a.* Fractional.—**frac′tion-ate** (-āt), *v. t.*; *-ated, -ating.* To separate (a mixture) into its ingredients, or into portions having different properties, as by distillation or crystallization; subject to fractional distillation, crystallization, or the like; also, to obtain by such a process.—**frac-tion-a′tion** (-ā′shọn), *n.*

frac-tious (frak′shus), *a.* [Cf. *fraction* in the obs. sense 'discord.'] Refractory or unruly; also, cross, fretful, or peevish.—**frac′tious-ly,** *adv.*—**frac′tious-ness,** *n.*

frac-ture (frak'ţūr), *n.* [F. *fracture*, < L. *fractura*, < *frangere*, break: see *fraction.*] The act of breaking, or the state of being broken; breakage; specif., the breaking of a bone, cartilage, etc., or the resulting condition (in the case of a bone, called *simple* when the bone only is divided, and *compound* when there is also a laceration of the integuments); in general, a break, breach, or split; also, the characteristic manner of breaking, or the characteristic appearance of a broken surface, as of a mineral.—**frac'ture,** *v.*; *-tured, -turing.* **I.** *tr.* To break or crack; specif., to cause or to suffer a fracture in (a bone, etc.). **II.** *intr.* To undergo fracture; break.

frae (frā), *prep.* [=*fro.*] From. [Sc.]

fræ-num (frē'num), *n.* See *frenum.*

frag-ile (fraj'il), *a.* [F. *fragile*, < L. *fragilis*, < *frangere*, break: see *fraction*, and cf. *frail*².] Easily broken or shattered; hence, in general, easily damaged or destroyed; delicate; frail (as, "This city is for the King, whose body is *fragile*, a very unhealthy city": Dunsany's "Laughter of the Gods," i.).—**frag'ile-ly,** *adv.*—**frag'ile-ness,** *n.*—**fra-gil-i-ty** (fra̤-jil'i-ti), *n.* [OF. *fragilite* (F. *fragilité*), < L. *fragilitas.*] Fragile character; liability to be broken or damaged; delicacy.

frag-ment (frag'me̤nt), *n.* [F. *fragment*, < L. *fragmentum*, < *frangere*, break: see *fraction.*] A part broken off (as, scattered *fragments* of rock; to reduce glass to *fragments*); hence, a detached portion of anything, esp. a portion that is incomplete or imperfect in character, as if separated by accident or chance (as, *fragments* of a letter or a picture; to overhear *fragments* of conversation); an odd piece, bit, or scrap; often, an extant or surviving portion of something otherwise lost or no longer in existence (as, *fragments* of Greek verse attributed to Sappho; "A land of old . . . Where *fragments* of forgotten peoples dwelt," Tennyson's "Passing of Arthur," 84); often, a part of an unfinished whole (as, the collected poems of Shelley include many *fragments*).—**frag-men'tal** (-men'ta̤l), *a.* Fragmentary; in *geol.*, noting or pertaining to rock or rocks (as the conglomerates, sandstones, shales, etc.) made up of fragments or particles of older rocks.—**frag'men-ta-ry** (-me̤n-tā̤-ri), *a.* Of the nature of a fragment; incomplete; also, composed of fragments; broken; disconnected; in *geol.*, fragmental.—**frag'men-ta-ri-ly,** *adv.*—**frag'men-ta-ri-ness,** *n.*—**frag-men-ta'tion** (-tā'sho̤n), *n.* A breaking up into fragments or parts; in *biol.*, amitosis.—**frag'ment-ed,** *a.* Reduced to fragments.

fra-grance (frā'gra̤ns), *n.* Fragrant quality or odor; sweet scent. Also **fra'gran-cy.**

fra-grant (frā'gra̤nt), *a.* [L. *fragrans* (*fragrant-*), ppr. of *fragrare*, emit an odor, smell sweet.] Emitting a pleasing odor; sweet-smelling; sweet-scented.—**fra'grant-ly,** *adv.*

frail¹ (frāl), *n.* [OF. *fraiel, freel*; origin unknown.] A flexible basket made of rushes, used esp. for dried fruits, as dates, figs, or raisins; also, the quantity, as of figs or raisins, contained in such a basket.

frail² (frāl), *a.* [OF. *fraile* (F. *frêle*), < L. *fragilis*, E. *fragile.*] Easily broken, damaged, or destroyed; fragile; hence, weak in any way; having little capacity for enduring or lasting (as, "*Frail* is our happiness, if this be so": Milton's "Paradise Lost," ix. 340); esp., physically delicate, or weakly, as a person, the constitution, etc.; often, morally weak, or not strong against temptation; specif., of a woman, infirm in virtue, or unchaste.—**frail'ly,** *adv.*—**frail'ness,** *n.*—**frail'ty** (-ti), *n.*; pl. *-ties* (-tiz). [OF. *frailete*, < L. *fragilitas*: cf. *fragility.*] The quality or state of being frail; esp., moral weakness; liability to yield to temptation; also, a fault proceeding from moral weakness; a weakness or failing.

fraise (frāz), *n.* [F.] A ruff worn around the neck; in *fort.*, a defense consisting of pointed stakes projecting from the ramparts in a horizontal or an inclined position.

fram-a-ble (frā'ma̤-bl), *a.* That may be framed.

fram-bœ-sia (fram-bē'zia̤), *n.* [NL., < F. *framboise*, raspberry; origin uncertain.] In *pathol.*, a contagious disease prevalent in certain tropical regions, characterized by an eruption of raspberry-like excrescences; yaws.

frame (frām), *v.*; *framed, framing.* [AS. *framian*, avail, profit, < *fram*, adv., forward, forth, also prep.: see *from.*] **I.** *intr.* To avail† or profit†; also, to succeed, get on, or fare (now prov.); also, to betake one's self, or resort (now prov.); also, to prepare, attempt, give promise, or manage to do something (now chiefly prov.). **II.** *tr.* To fashion or shape; esp., to shape or adapt to a particular purpose (as, "to *frame* and fashion your own lives . . . according to the Doctrine of Christ": Book of Common Prayer, Ordering of Deacons); dispose; also, to direct, as one's steps (obs. or rare: as, "A stately Castle far away she spyde, To which her steps directly she did *frame*," Spenser's "Faerie Queene," iii. 1. 20); also, to form or make, as by fitting and uniting parts together; construct; hence, to contrive, devise, or compose, as a plan, law, poem, etc.; conceive or imagine, as ideas, etc.; also, in recent slang use (often with *up*), to contrive or devise fraudulently or falsely, as a plot, a charge, etc.; prearrange the result of fraudulently, as a race or a boxing-match; incriminate unjustly by a plot, as a person. Also, to provide with or put into a frame, as a picture.—**frame,** *n.* The act of framing, fashioning, or constructing†; also, manner or method of framing; form, constitution, or structure; also, an established system or order, as of government; also, natural or habitual temper or disposition (as, "I am a fellow of a very odd *frame* of mind": Steele, in "Spectator," 167); more commonly, temporary state of mind (as, "In this *frame* of thankfulness I went home to my castle," Defoe's "Robinson Crusoe," i. 12: now usually in the phrase 'frame of mind'); also, anything composed of parts fitted and joined together; a structure; often, the body, esp. the human body, with reference to its make or build; also, the sustaining parts of a structure fitted and joined together; a framework or skeleton; also, a frame-house; also, a structure for admitting or inclosing something; an inclosing border or case, as for a picture; in *pool*, the triangular form used to set up the balls for a game; the balls as so set up; the period of play required to pocket them; in *American bowling*, a turn to bowl, each player usually having ten turns, of three shots each, in a game.—**frame'=house',** *n.* A house constructed with a skeleton frame of timber, as the ordinary wooden house.—**frame'less,** *a.* Having no frame.—**fram-er** (frā'mėr), *n.*—**frame'=up,** *n.* The act of framing up; that which is framed up, as a plot, or a contest the result of which has been fraudulently prearranged. [Slang.]—**frame'work,** *n.* A structure composed of parts fitted and united together; esp., one designed to support or inclose something; a frame or skeleton; also, frames collectively; also, work done in, on, or with a frame.—**fram'ing,** *n.* The act of one who or that which frames; the act, process, or manner of constructing or contriving anything; the act of providing with a frame; also, framed work; a frame or a system of frames.

fram-pold† (fram'po̤ld), *a.* [Origin uncertain.] Ill-tempered, fretful, or quarrelsome (see Shakspere's "Merry Wives of Windsor," ii. 2. 94); also, high-spirited or fiery, as a horse.

franc (frangk), *n.* [OF. F. *franc*, said to be so called from the legend, ML. *Francorum rex*, king of the Franks (or French), on the first coin.] Either of two old coins of

Obverse. Reverse.
Silver Franc of Henry III. of France.— British Museum.

France, one of gold and the other of silver; now, a French silver coin and money of account, the monetary unit of France, equal to 19.3 U. S. cents.

fran-chise (fran'chīz or -chiz), *n.* [OF. F. *franchise*, < *franc*, free, E. *frank*².] Freedom†; also, a legal immunity or exemption from a particular burden, exaction, or the like; also, a privilege arising from the grant of a sovereign or government, or from prescription, which presupposes a grant; a privilege of a public nature conferred on an individual or a body of individuals by a governmental grant (as, a *franchise* for a street railway); specif., the right of suffrage (as, the U. S. granted the *franchise* to women in 1920); also, the district or jurisdiction to which the privilege of an individual or corporation extends†; also, the privilege or right of affording asylum or sanctuary to fugitives†, or a place of asylum or sanctuary†.—**fran′chise†**, *v. t.*; *-chised*, *-chising*. To set free; invest with a franchise; enfranchise.

fran-cisc (fran-sisk′), *n.* Same as *francisca*.

fran-cis-ca (fran-sis′kạ̈), *n.* [ML., prop. fem. of *Franciscus*, Frankish.] A battle-ax used by the (ancient) Franks, commonly having a head long in proportion to the width and expanding toward a convex curved edge.

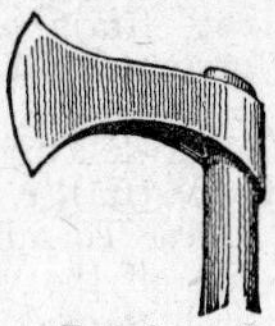

Francisca.

Fran-cis-can (fran-sis′kạn). [ML. *Franciscus*, Francis.] **I.** *a.* Of or pertaining to St. Francis of Assisi (1181 or 1182–1226), or the mendicant religious order founded by him. **II.** *n.* A member of the order of St. Francis.

fran-cisque (fran-sisk′), *n.* [F.] Same as *francisca*.

Fran-co- (frang′kọ̄-). Form of LL. *Francus*, Frank, used in combination, often in the sense of 'French,' as in *Franco-American*, *Franco-German*.

fran-co-lin (frang′kọ̄-lin), *n.* [F. *francolin*, < It. *francolino*.] Any of the old-world gallinaceous birds of the partridge kind constituting the genus *Francolinus* and allied genera, esp. *F. vulgaris*, a species formerly common in southern Europe but now chiefly confined to Asia.

Francolin (*Francolinus vulgaris*).

Fran-co-phil, Fran-co-phile (frang′kọ̄-fil). [See *Franco-* and *-phil*.] **I.** *a.* Friendly to France or the French. **II.** *n.* One who is friendly to France or the French.

Fran-co=Prus-sian (frang′kọ̄-prush′ạn), *a.* [See *Franco-*.] Pertaining to France and Prussia: as, the *Franco-Prussian* War of 1870–71.

franc=ti-reur (frän-tē-rėr), *n.*; pl. *francs-tireurs* (F. frän-tē-rėr). [F., 'free shooter.'] A sharpshooter in the French service, sometimes forming part of a corps of light troops and sometimes of a separate body of guerrillas, during the Franco-Prussian War largely the latter; in general, a guerrilla combatant.

fran-gi-ble (fran′ji-bl), *a.* [OF. F. *frangible*, < L. *frangere*, break: see *fraction*.] Capable of being broken; breakable.—**fran-gi-bil′i-ty** (-bil′i-ti), *n.*

fran-gi-pa-ni (fran-ji-pä′ni), *n.* [Said to be named from the inventor.] A perfume prepared from, or imitating the odor of, the flower of the red jasmine, *Plumeria rubra*, an apocynaceous tree or shrub of tropical America; also, the tree or shrub itself.

Frank[1] (frangk), *n.* [LL. *Francus*, usually explained as from the name of the national weapon (cf. AS. *franca*, spear, javelin): see *frank*[2].] A member of a group of ancient Germanic peoples dwelling in the regions of the Rhine, one division of whom, the Salians, conquered Gaul about A.D. 500, founded an extensive kingdom ruled successively by the Merovingian and Carolingian dynasties, and gave origin to the name France; also, a designation in the Levant for any native or inhabitant of western Europe.

frank[2] (frangk), *a.* [OF. F. *franc* (fem. *franche*), < ML. *francus*, free, < LL. *Francus*, Frank: see *Frank*[1].] Free with respect to condition or rights, or the absence of restraints, restrictions, obligations, etc.†; also, liberal or generous (now rare: see Shakspere's "King Lear," iii. 4. 20); also, free from concealment or dissimulation, as persons, the nature or disposition, manner, etc.; open, ingenuous, or sincere; often, open or unreserved in utterance; candid or outspoken; also, undisguised, manifest, or plain (as, *frank* mutiny; a *frank* imitation); also, good or fine in quality† (cf. *frankincense*).—**frank**[2], *v. t.* To mark (a letter, package, etc.) for transmission by public conveyance free of the usual charge, by virtue of official or special privilege; send free of charge, as mail; also, to send or convey (a person) gratuitously, as on a journey; fig., to enable to pass or go freely (as, "English . . . will now *frank* the traveller through the most of North America": Stevenson's "Memories and Portraits," i.); also, to secure exemption for.—**frank**[2], *n.* A signature or mark affixed by special privilege to a letter, package, or the like, to ensure its transmission free of charge, as by mail; also, a franked letter, package, etc.; also, the privilege of franking letters, etc.

frank[3]† (frangk), *n.* [OF. *franc*.] A pen, as for hogs; a sty. See Shakspere's "2 Henry IV.," ii. 2. 160.—**frank**[3]†, *v. t.* To shut up in a pen or sty, as for fattening (see Shakspere's "Richard III.," iv. 5. 3); hence, to cram with food; fatten by feeding.

frank-a-ble (frang′kạ-bl), *a.* That may be franked, as a letter.—**frank-a-bil′i-ty** (-bil′i-ti), *n.*

frank-al-moin, frank-al-moigne (frangk′al-moin), *n.* [AF. *franke almoigne*, < OF. *franc*, free (see *frank*[2]), + *almosne*, < LL. *eleemosyna*, E. *alms*.] In *Eng. law*, a tenure by which a religious corporation holds lands, on condition of praying for the soul of the donor and his heirs or performing other religious service.

Frank-en-stein (frangk′ẹn-stīn), *n.* [From the hero of Mrs. Shelley's story "Frankenstein," a young student who creates a destructive being, in human form, that he cannot control.] One who creates a 'monster' or a destructive agency that he cannot control or that brings about his own ruin; often, incorrectly, the 'monster' or destructive agency itself.

frank-er (frang′kėr), *n.* One who franks letters, etc.

frank-furt-er (frangk′fėr-tėr), *n.* [G.,'Frankfort (sausage).'] A reddish variety of sausage, of German origin: commonly cooked by steaming or boiling.

frank-in-cense (frangk′in-sens), *n.* [OF. *franc encens*: see *frank*[2] and *incense*[1].] An aromatic gum-resin from various Asiatic and African trees of the genus *Boswellia*, used chiefly for burning as incense or ceremonially (see Lev. ii. 1, 2); also, any of various similar resinous exudations.

Frank-ish (frang′kish), *a.* Of or pertaining to the Franks.

frank-lin (frangk′lin), *n.* [ME. *frankeleyn*, < ML. *francus*, free, E. *frank*[2].] A freeman†; formerly, in England, a freeholder; in the 14th and 15th centuries, one of a class of landowners, of free but not noble birth, ranking next below the gentry.

frank-lin-ite (frangk′lin-īt), *n.* [From *Franklin*, N. J., where it is found.] A black native oxide of iron, zinc, and manganese: used as a zinc ore and in the manufacture of spiegeleisen.

frank-ly (frangk′li), *adv.* In a frank manner; freely; openly; unreservedly; candidly; plainly.—**frank′ness**, *n.*

frank=pledge (frangk′plej), *n.* [AF. *franc plege*: cf. *frank*[2] and *pledge*.] In *old Eng. law*, a system by which the members of a tithing were made responsible for one another's conduct; also, each of these mutually responsible members; also, the tithing itself.

fran-tic (fran′tik), *a.* [OF. *frenetique* (F. *frénétique*), < L. *phreneticus*, < Gr. φρενιτικός, < φρενῖτις, inflammation of the brain: see *phrenitis*.] Insane or mad (obs. or archaic); also, wild with excitement, passion, fear, pain, etc.; frenzied; characterized by or pertaining to frenzy.—**fran′ti-cal-ly, fran′tic-ly**, *adv.*—**fran′tic-ness**, *n.*

frap (frap), *v. t.*; *frapped*, *frapping*. [OF. *fraper*, strike, F. *frapper*, strike, fasten, chill: cf. *frappé*.] To strike (obs. or prov. Eng.); *naut.*, to bind securely.

frap-pé (fra-pā′). [F., pp. of *frapper*: see *frap*.] **I.** *a.* Artificially chilled, as with ice; iced; frozen. **II.** *n.* An iced or frozen refreshment.

frat (frat), *n.* [Short for *fraternity.*] A college or school fraternity. See *fraternity.* [Slang.]—**frat house,** a fraternity house. [Slang.]

fratch (frach), *v. i.* [ME. *fracchyn,* creak, as a cart; appar. imit.] To quarrel; wrangle. [Prov. Eng.]—**fratch,** *n.* A quarrel; a wrangle. [Prov. Eng.]

fra-te (frä'tā), *n.*; pl. *frati* (-tē). [It., < L. *frater,* brother: cf. *fra.*] In Italian use, a friar.

fra-ter (frā'tėr), *n.* [L., brother; akin to E. *brother.*] A brother; a comrade.

fra-ter-nal (fra-tėr'nal), *a.* [L. *fraternus,* brotherly, < *frater,* brother: see *frater.*] Of, pertaining to, or befitting a brother or brothers; brotherly; also, being, or pertaining to, a society of men associated in brotherly union, as for mutual aid or benefit (as, a *fraternal* organization; *fraternal* insurance).—**fra-ter'nal-ism,** *n.* The state or character of being fraternal; also, the principle or practice of association in fraternal organizations.—**fra-ter'nal-ly,** *adv.*

fra-ter-ni-ty (fra-tėr'ni-ti), *n.*; pl. *-ties* (-tiz). [OF. *fraternite* (F. *fraternité*), < L. *fraternitas,* < *fraternus*: see *fraternal.*] The relation of a brother or between brothers; brotherhood; also, the relation of persons associated on the footing of brothers (as, 'liberty, equality, *fraternity,*' F. *liberté, égalité, fraternité,* the motto of the French Republic); also, a body of persons associated as by ties of brotherhood; any body or class of persons having common purposes, interests, etc. (as, the medical *fraternity*; the sporting *fraternity*); in American colleges and schools, a student society organized for social and other purposes, commonly composed of affiliated branches or chapters in various institutions and designated by two or more letters of the Greek alphabet ('Greek-letter fraternity').—**fraternity house,** a house occupied by a college or school fraternity.

frat-er-nize (frat'ėr-nīz), *v.*; *-nized, -nizing.* [F. *fraterniser,* < ML. *fraternizare,* < L. *fraternus*: see *fraternal.*] **I.** *intr.* To associate, or hold intercourse, in a fraternal or brotherly way. **II.** *tr.* To bring into fraternal association or sympathy.—**frat"er-ni-za'tion** (-ni-zā'shon), *n.*—**frat'er-niz-er** (-nī-zėr), *n.*

frat-ri-cide (frat'ri-sīd), *n.* [L. *fratricida, fratricidium,* < *frater,* brother: see *-cide.*] One who kills his or her brother; also, the act of killing one's own brother.—**frat'ri-ci-dal** (-sī-dal), *a.*

frau (frou), *n.*; pl. *fraus* (frouz), G. *frauen* (frou'en). [G.] In German use, a woman; a married woman; a wife; a lady; as a title, equivalent to *Mrs.*

fraud (frâd), *n.* [OF. F. *fraude,* < L. *fraus* (*fraud-*), cheating, deceit.] Deceit or trickery deliberately practised in order to gain some advantage or end unfairly, dishonestly, or to the prejudice of another's right or interest (as, to obtain a prize or carry an election by *fraud*; to allege *fraud* in a bankruptcy case or in the administration of an estate); a particular instance of such deceit or trickery (as, election *frauds*; to uncover *frauds* in business operations); in general, deceit or trickery of any kind (as, "Artificer of *fraud* . . . the first That practised falsehood under saintly show, Deep malice to conceal, couch'd with revenge": Milton's "Paradise Lost," iv. 121); a deception, artifice, or trick (as, a pious *fraud*: see *pious*); anything contrived or intended to deceive (as, the letter is a *fraud*); sometimes, a person who makes deceitful pretenses, or a humbug or impostor (colloq.).—**fraud'ful,** *a.* Full of fraud; deceitful; treacherous; fraudulent.—**fraud'ful-ly,** *adv.*

frau-du-lent (frâ'dū-lent), *a.* [L. *fraudulentus,* < *fraus,* E. *fraud.*] Given to or using fraud, as a person; cheating; dishonest; also, characterized by, involving, or proceeding from fraud, as actions, enterprises, methods, gains, etc. —**frau'du-lence, frau'du-len-cy,** *n.*—**frau'du-lent-ly,** *adv.*

fraught (frât), *n.* [MD. or MLG. *vracht,* also *vrecht* (see *freight*), freight, freight money: cf. OHG. *frēht,* earnings, gain.] The freight or cargo of a vessel† (see Shakspere's "Titus Andronicus," i. 1. 71); in general, a load carried (obs. or Sc.).—**fraught,** *v. t.*; *fraught* or *fraughted, fraughting.* To freight (a vessel); in general, to load, charge, store, or fill with something: now only in *fraught, pp.,* as in the following phrase.—**fraught with,** freighted with (a cargo, etc.), as a vessel (archaic); hence, loaded, stored, or filled with (something material: archaic: as, "waggons, *fraught with* utensils of war," Milton's "Paradise Regained," iii. 336); fig., filled with (something immaterial: as, words *fraught with* wisdom or deep meaning); attended with, involving, or producing (as, memories *fraught with* pain; scenes *fraught with* horror); sometimes, pregnant with, or destined or likely to produce (as, an act *fraught with* momentous consequences).

fräu-lein (froi'līn), *n.*; pl. *fräuleins,* G. *fräulein.* [G., dim. of *frau.*] In German use, an unmarried woman; a young lady; as a title, equivalent to *Miss.*

Fraun-ho-fer's (froun'hō"fėrz) **lines.** The dark lines of the solar spectrum, first accurately studied by Joseph von Fraunhofer (1787–1826), a German optician.

frax-i-nel-la (frak-si-nel'ä), *n.* [NL., dim. of L. *fraxinus,* ash-tree.] The dittany, *Dictamnus albus.*

fray[1] (frā), *v.* [For *affray.*] **I.** *tr.* To frighten. [Archaic or prov.] **II.** *intr.* To fight; brawl. [Archaic or prov.] —**fray**[1], *n.* Fright (obs. or Sc.); also, a noisy quarrel; a brawl; a fight, skirmish, or battle.

fray[2] (frā), *v.* [F. *frayer,* < L. *fricare,* rub: see *friction.*] **I.** *tr.* To rub (as, a stag *frays* its horns against a tree to rub off the velvet); also, to wear by rubbing (sometimes with *through*); esp., to wear (cloth, rope, etc.) to loose, raveled threads or fibers at the edge or end; cause to ravel out. **II.** *intr.* To rub against something; also, to become frayed, as cloth, etc.; ravel out.—**fray**[2], *n.* A frayed part, as in cloth.

fraz-zle (fraz'l), *v. i.* or *t.*; *-zled, -zling.* [Var. of *fazel,* perhaps by association with *fray*[2].] To ravel; fray; wear to threads or shreds. Also fig. [Prov. or colloq.]—**fraz'zle,** *n.* A frazzled state or remnant; a shred. [Prov. or colloq.]

freak[1] (frēk), *n.* [Origin uncertain: cf. AS. *frīcian,* dance.] A sudden and apparently causeless change or turn of the mind; a capricious notion or humor; a whim; a vagary; also, capriciousness; also, a capricious prank; also, a product of capricious fancy; any abnormal product or curiously unusual object; an abnormal organism; a monstrosity; a person or animal on exhibition in a show as an example of some strange deviation from nature.—**freak**[1], *v. i.* To indulge in freaks; frolic: as, "Then glad they left their covert lair, And *freaked* about in the midnight air" (J. R. Drake's "Culprit Fay," xxvi.).

freak[2] (frēk), *v. t.* [Appar. < *freak*[1], but cf. *freck, freckle.*] To fleck, streak, or variegate: as, "the pansy *freak'd* with jet" (Milton's "Lycidas," 144).—**freak**[2], *n.* A fleck or streak of color.

freak-ish (frē'kish), *a.* Addicted to or characterized by freaks; whimsical; capricious; also, of the nature of a freak; queer; grotesque.—**freak'ish-ly,** *adv.*—**freak'ish-ness,** *n.*

freak-y (frē'ki), *a.*; compar. *freakier,* superl. *freakiest.* Freakish.

freck (frek), *v. t.* [Appar. < *freckle*: cf. *freak*[2].] To mark with spots or freckles; dapple.

freck-le (frek'l), *n.* [Var. of earlier *frecken*: cf. Icel. *freknur,* pl., freckles.] A small brownish-yellow spot in the skin, esp. on the face, neck, or arms; also, any small spot or discoloration.—**freck'le,** *v. t.* or *i.*; *-led, -ling.* To mark or become marked with or as with freckles.—**freck'ly,** *a.* Marked or covered with freckles.

free (frē), *a.*; compar. *freer* (frē'ėr), superl. *freest* (frē'est). [AS. *frēo* = D. *vrij* = G. *frei* = Goth. *freis,* free; orig. meaning 'dear, favored,' and akin to Skt. *priya,* dear: cf. *friend.*] Enjoying personal rights or liberty, as one not in bondage or slavery; pertaining to or reserved for those who enjoy personal liberty (as, *free* labor; *free* soil, see *free-soil*); also, possessed of, characterized by, or existing under civil liberty as opposed to arbitrary or despotic government, as a country or state, or its citizens, institutions, etc.; also, enjoying political liberty or independence, as a people or country not under foreign rule; also, at liberty, or not in confinement or under physical restraint (as, to set a prisoner *free*); released from confinement or restraint; disengaged (as, he will be *free* presently, if you care to wait); in general, exempt from external authority, control, interference, restriction, hampering conditions, etc., as a person, the will, thought, choice, action, etc.; independent; unfettered; not bound by legal or moral ties or obligations; not subject to special regulation or restrictions, as trade (see *free trade*, below); not subject to rules, set forms, etc. (as, the *free* song of a bird; *free* verse, see *vers libre*); not literal, as a translation; clear of obstructions or obstacles, as a place, passage, etc.; vacant or unoccupied; often, exempt or released from something specified that controls, restrains, burdens, etc. (with *from* or *of*: as, *free* from foreign domination; *free* from interference, obligation, responsibility, or matrimonial ties; *free* of taxes or customs-duties); having immunity or being safe (usually with *from*: as, *free* from criticism, reproach, or suspicion); in general, exempt from the presence of something specified, usually something objectionable or unnecessary (with *from*, sometimes *of*: as, roads *free* from snow; to be *free* from jealousy; *free* from any trace of human occupation; "Infirmities that honesty Is never *free* of," Shakspere's "Winter's Tale," i. 2. 264); clear or void (*of*); guiltless† or innocent† (sometimes with *of*: see Shakspere's "Hamlet," v. 2. 343); also, at liberty, permitted, or able at will (to do something: as, to be *free* to come and go; *free* to choose, object, or decline; to be left *free* to stir up trouble); permissible or allowable (to do something: as, it is *free* to, or for, him to go); open (*to* or *for*: as, privileges *free* to all; a race *free* for all competitors); open to all comers, users, etc. (as, a *free* port, see phrase below); general or promiscuous (as, a *free* fight); also, unimpeded, as motion or movements; easy, firm, or swift in movement (as, a *free* step; a *free* sweep): able to move without restraint (as, a *free* polyp; a *free* balloon, as distinguished from a captive balloon); also, loose, or not held fast or attached (as, a rope *free* at one end; to get one's arm *free*; a nut may work *free* in time); not joined to or in contact with something else (as, a *free* surface; a column standing *free*); uncombined chemically (as, *free* oxygen); also, acting spontaneously or readily (as, a *free* horse); ready or willing (to do something: as, to be *free* to confess a thing); acting without self-restraint or reserve (as, too *free* in the use of liquor; too *free* with one's tongue); frank and open in intercourse; unconstrained, unceremonious, or familiar; sometimes, unduly familiar (hence, 'to make free with,' to treat or use too familiarly, or take liberties with); plain-spoken or candid; unrestrained by decency, loose, or licentious; also, ready in giving, liberal, or lavish (as, to be *free* with one's money or advice); given readily or in profusion, or unstinted; more frequently, given without consideration of a return, as a gift; hence, provided without, or not subject to, a charge or payment (as, *free* schools; admission *free*; a *free* pass or passenger); gratuitous; also, easily worked, as stone or land; also, invested with all the rights, privileges, or immunities (*of*: as, to be made *free* of a city); fig., admitted to entry and enjoyment at will (*of*: as, to be *free* of a friend's house); also, of gentle birth or breeding†, noble†, or honorable† (formerly much used as a term of compliment); noble in spirit or character, or magnanimous (archaic: as, "Ring in the valiant man and *free*, The larger heart, the kindlier hand," Tennyson's "In Memoriam," cvi.); *naut.*, of a wind, blowing so that a boat can sail free.—**free and easy,** unconstrained; unconventional; showing little regard for conventional formalities; sometimes, careless.—**free church,** a church in which the pews or sittings are not rented, but are open to all; also, a church free from state control; esp. [*caps.*], a Presbyterian church in Scotland, organized in 1843 by secession from the established Presbyterian church, the majority of the members uniting in 1900 with the United Presbyterian Church to form the 'United Free Church of Scotland,' and the name 'Free Church of Scotland' still being borne by the congregations who opposed this union.—**free city,** a city having an independent government and forming a sovereign state by itself, as Hamburg, Bremen, and Lübeck, in Germany.—**free coinage,** the unrestricted coinage of bullion, or of a specified metal, as silver, into money acceptable as legal tender, for any person bringing it to the mint.—**free companion,** a member of a band of mercenary soldiers of the middle ages; a free-lance.—**free company,** a band of free companions.—**free kick,** in *football*, an unhampered kick at the ball, during which the opponents are prohibited from advancing upon the kicker.—**free love,** the doctrine or practice of free choice in sexual relations, without restraint of legal marriage or of any continuing obligations independent of individual will.—**free port,** a port open under equal conditions to all traders, or one where no customs-duties are collected.—**free thought,** thought unrestrained by deference to authority, esp. in matters of religion.—**free trade,** unrestricted trade or commerce; specif., trade or commerce between different countries, free from governmental restrictions, duties, or differences of treatment; esp., international trade free from protective duties, etc., and subject only to such tariffs as are necessary for revenue (cf. *protection*); also, the system, principles, or maintenance of such trade; also, smuggling.—**free verse.** Same as *vers libre*.—**free,** *adv.* In a free manner; freely; without cost or charge; *naut.*, further from the wind than when close-hauled (as, to sail *free*).—**free,** *v. t.*; *freed, freeing.* [AS. *frēon.*] To make free; set at liberty; release from bondage, imprisonment, or restraint; exempt or deliver (*from*); relieve or rid (*of*); disengage (*from*); clear (with *from* or *of*).

free=board (frē′bōrd), *n.* *Naut.*, the part of a ship's side between the water-line and the deck or gunwale.

free-boot (frē′böt), *v. i.* [Back-formation from *freebooter*.] To act as a freebooter.

free-boot-er (frē′bö″tėr), *n.* [D. *vrijbuiter*, < *vrij*, free, + *buit*, booty.] One who goes about in search of plunder; esp., a pirate or buccaneer.

free=born (frē′bôrn), *a.* Born free, rather than in slavery, bondage, or vassalage; also, pertaining to or befitting persons born free.

freed-man (frēd′man), *n.*; pl. *-men*. A man who has been freed from slavery.

free-dom (frē′dom), *n.* [AS. *frēodōm*.] The state of being free; personal liberty, as opposed to bondage or slavery; civil liberty, as opposed to subjection to an arbitrary or despotic government; political or national independence; the state of being at liberty rather than in confinement or under physical restraint; in general, exemption from external control, interference, regulation, etc. (as, to claim *freedom* of choice); power of determining one's or its own action (as, to exercise complete *freedom* in the management of an affair; to maintain the doctrine of the *freedom* of the will); absence of or release from ties, obligations, etc. (as, to win one's *freedom* by divorce); often, exemption or immunity (*from*: as, *freedom* from control or obligation; *freedom* from taxation or arrest); in general, exemption from the presence of anything specified (with *from*: as, *freedom* from vanity or prejudice); also, ease or facility of movement or action; frankness of manner or speech; absence of ceremony or reserve; familiarity, often undue familiarity; sometimes, a liberty taken; also, a particular immunity or other privilege enjoyed, as by a city or corporation; the right of enjoying all the privileges or peculiar rights of citizenship, membership, or the like (as, to present a foreign visitor with the *freedom* of the city); fig., the right of frequenting, enjoying, or using at will (as, to have the *freedom* of a friend's library).

freed-wom-an (frēd′wům″an), *n.*; pl. *-women* (-wim″en). A woman who has been freed from slavery.

free=hand (frē′hand), *a.* Done by the hand without guiding instruments, measurements, or other artificial aid: as, *free-hand* drawing.

free=hand-ed (frē′han′ded), *a.* Having the hands free; also, open-handed; generous; liberal.

free=heart-ed (frē′här′ted), *a.* Having a free heart; light-hearted; spontaneous; frank; generous.

free-hold (frē′hōld), *n.* In *law*, a tenure by which an estate is held in fee simple or fee tail, or for life; a similar tenure of an office; an estate or office held by this tenure.—**free′-hold″er,** *n.* One who possesses a freehold estate.—**chosen freeholder.** See under *chosen*.

free=lance (frē′láns), *n.* A mercenary soldier or military adventurer, often of knightly rank, of the middle ages, who offered his services to any state, party, or cause; hence, one who contends in any cause, or in a succession of various causes, as he chooses, without personal attachment or allegiance; often, an unattached journalist or writer who sells his work wherever opportunity offers.—**free′=lance,** *v. i.*; *-lanced, -lancing.* To act as a free-lance.

free=liv-er (frē′liv′ėr), *n.* One who in his mode of life freely indulges his appetites.—**free′=liv′ing,** *a.*

free=lov-er (frē′luv′ėr), *n.* One who advocates or practises free love. See *free love*, under *free, a.*
free-ly (frē′li), *adv.* [AS. *frēolīce.*] In a free manner.
free-man (frē′mạn), *n.*; pl. *-men.* [AS. *frēoman.*] A man who is free; a man who enjoys personal, civil, or political liberty; one who possesses the freedom of a city, corporation, etc.
free-ma-son (frē′mā′sn), *n.* One of a class of skilled stone-workers of the middle ages and later†; later, a member of a society composed of such workers, with honorary members (known as 'accepted masons') who were not connected with the building trades†; now [often *cap.*], a member of a widely distributed secret order ('Free and Accepted Masons') developed from societies of this kind, having for its object mutual assistance and the promotion of brotherly love among its members.—**free′ma-son′ic** (-mạ-son′ik), *a.* —**free′ma′son-ry,** *n.* [Often *cap.*] The principles, practices, and institutions of freemasons; hence [*l. c.*], secret or tacit brotherhood; instinctive sympathy.
free-ness (frē′nes), *n.* The state or quality of being free; freedom.
fre-er¹ (frē′ėr), *n.* One who frees.
fre-er² (frē′ėr). Comparative of *free, a.*
free-sia (frē′ẓịạ), *n.* [NL.; from E. M. *Fries* (1794–1878), Swedish botanist.] Any plant of the iridaceous genus *Freesia* (or *Nymanina*), native in South Africa, esteemed in cultivation for its fragrant white, yellow, or sometimes rose-colored, tubular flowers.
free=soil (frē′soil′), *a.* In *U. S. hist.*, pertaining to or in favor of 'free soil,' or the non-extension of slavery into the Territories, or those parts of the country not yet erected into States: used [*cap.*] as the epithet of a political party active 1848–56.—**free′=soil′er,** *n.*—**free′=soil′ism,** *n.*
free=spok-en (frē′spō′kn), *a.* Given to speaking freely or without reserve.—**free′=spok′en-ness,** *n.*
fre-est (frē′est). Superlative of *free, a.*
free-stone (frē′stōn). **I.** *n.* Any stone, as a sandstone, which can be freely worked or quarried, esp. one which cuts well in all directions without splitting; also, a freestone peach. **II.** *a.* Having a stone from which the pulp is easily separated, as certain peaches.
free=swim-mer (frē′swim′ėr), *n.* An animal, as a fish, that swims about freely.—**free′=swim′ming,** *a.* Capable of swimming about freely: said specif. of aquatic animals that are not fixed or attached.
free-think-er (frē′thing′kėr), *n.* One who forms his opinions independently of authority or tradition, esp. in matters of religion: as, "A *free-thinker* I will be, and believe nothing but what I know and understand" (Kingsley's "Alton Locke," v.).—**free′think′ing,** *n.* and *a.*
free=trad-er (frē′trā′dėr), *n.* One who trades without restriction; sometimes, a smuggler; specif., an advocate of the principle or system of free trade.
free=wheel (frē′hwēl), *n.* That form of rear wheel (driving-wheel) on a bicycle, which has a clutch-like device ('free-wheel clutch') for freeing or releasing it from the driving mechanism, as when the pedals are stopped in coasting.
free-will (frē′wil′), *a.* Made or done freely or of one's own accord; voluntary: as, "a *freewill* offering" (Deut. xvi. 10).
freez-a-ble (frē′zạ-bl), *a.* That may be frozen.
freeze (frēz), *v.*; pret. *froze*, pp. *frozen*, ppr. *freezing.* [AS. *frēosan* = D. *vriezen* = G. *frieren* = Icel. *frjōsa*, freeze.] **I.** *intr.* To be congealed by cold, as a liquid; be hardened into ice by the abstraction of heat; become covered with ice, as a river or pond; become obstructed by the formation of ice, as pipes; become hard or rigid under the influence of cold, as objects containing moisture; become fixed to something by or as by the action of frost (as, "My very lips might *freeze* to my teeth": Shakspere's "Taming of the Shrew," iv. 1. 7); also, to be of the degree of cold at which water freezes (often used impersonally to describe the state of the weather: as, it is *freezing* to-night); also, to suffer the effects of intense cold; have the sensation of extreme cold; die of frost or cold; fig., to lose warmth of feeling; be chilled with fear, etc. **II.** *tr.* To congeal by cold, as a liquid; harden into ice; form ice on the surface of, as a river or pond; obstruct or close by the formation of ice, as pipes (often with *up*); fix fast in ice (with *in* or *up*); shut (*in*) or keep (*out*) by a barrier of ice; fig., to exclude, or compel to withdraw, from society, business, etc., as by chilling behavior, severe competition, etc. (with *out*: colloq., U. S.); also, to harden or stiffen by cold, as objects containing moisture; also, to cause to suffer the effects of intense cold; produce the sensation of extreme cold in; kill by frost or cold; fig., to congeal as if by cold; chill with fear, etc.; quench warmth of feeling in; paralyze with dismay, etc.; sometimes, to render (credit given or loans made) impossible of liquidation, as business conditions do (colloq.)—**freeze,** *n.* The act of freezing, or the state of being frozen; a frost. —**freez′er,** *n.*—**freez′ing,** *p. a.* That freezes; tending to freeze; very cold; chilling.—**freez′ing-ly,** *adv.*—**freez′ing=mix″ture,** *n.* A mixture, as of salt and snow, whose temperature becomes low enough to cool or freeze substances in contact with it.—**freez′ing=point,** *n.* The temperature at which a liquid freezes: as, the *freezing-point* of water (32° F., 0° C., or 0° R.).
freight (frāt), *n.* [= *fraught*: cf. MD. and MLG. *vrecht*, for *vracht*, also the related OF. *fret.*] Transportation of goods by water or (esp. in the U. S. and Canada) by land; esp., the ordinary conveyance or means of transport of goods afforded by common carriers, as opposed to *express*; also, the price paid for such transportation; also, the cargo, or any part of the cargo, of a vessel; in the U. S. and Canada, cargo or lading carried for pay either by water or by land; also, in the U. S. and Canada, a train of cars for transporting goods or merchandise.—**freight,** *v. t.* To load with goods for transportation; let out for the transportation of freight; in general, to load; burden; also, to transport as freight; send by freight.—**freight′age** (-āj), *n.* The transportation of goods, or the price paid for this; also, freight, cargo, or lading.—**freight′er,** *n.* One who loads a ship, or who charters it for the transportation of goods; also, one whose occupation it is to receive and forward freight; also, a vessel engaged chiefly in the transportation of goods; also, one for whom freight is transported.
frei-herr (frī′her), *n.*; pl. *-herren* (-her′en). [G., 'free lord.'] In German use, a nobleman ranking below a graf (or count), and corresponding to an English baron.
fremd (fremd), *a.* [AS. *fremde* = D. *vreemd* = G. *fremd* = Goth. *framaths*, foreign, strange; akin to E. *from.*] Foreign; strange; unrelated; unfamiliar; unusual or unnatural; unfriendly or estranged. [Now only Sc. and north. Eng.]
fre-mes-cent (frẹ-mes′ẹnt), *a.* [L. *fremere*, murmur, growl, roar: see *-escent.*] Beginning to murmur; growing noisy. —**fre-mes′cence,** *n.*
frem-i-tus (frem′i-tus), *n.*; pl. *fremitus.* [L., < *fremere*: see *fremescent.*] In *med.*, palpable vibration, as of the walls of the chest.
French (french), *a.* [AS. *Frencisc*, < *Franca*, a Frank.] Of, pertaining to, or characteristic of France, its inhabitants, or their language.—**French Academy.** See *academy.*—**French and Indian War,** the war between France and England in America, 1754–60, in which the French were aided by Indian allies.—**French bean,** the common kidney-bean or haricot, *Phaseolus vulgaris.*—**French chalk,** a variety of talc used for marking lines on cloth, etc.—**French horn.** See *horn, n.*—**French leave,** departure without ceremony, permission, or notice.—**French Revolution.** See *revolution.* —**French roof,** a form of roof resembling the mansard roof. —**French window,** a long window having two sashes hinged at the sides and opening in the middle.—**French,** *n.* The people of France and their immediate descendants elsewhere, collectively; also, the chief language spoken by the French people (divided for convenience into Old French, extending to about 1500, and modern French, from about 1500 on, to which is sometimes added Middle French, extending from 1500, or 1400, to 1600).—

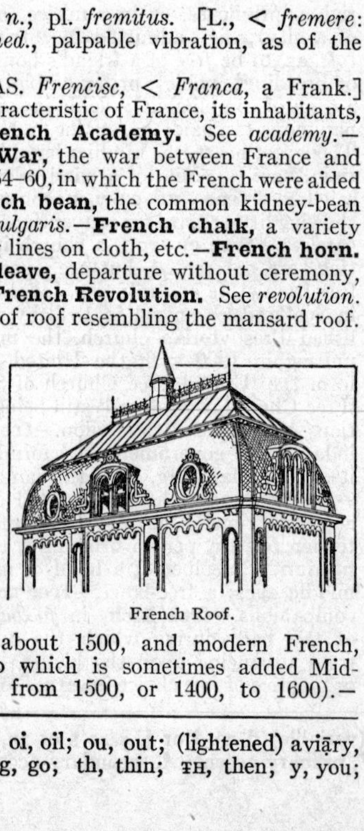
French Roof.

French, *v. t.* To give a French form to; render into French; also, to prepare according to the French mode.—**French'i-fy** (-i-fī), *v. t.*; *-fied, -fying.* [See *-fy.*] To make French; imbue with French qualities.—**French'man** (-ma̤n), *n.*; pl. *-men.* A man belonging to the French race; also, a French ship.—**French'wom"an,** *n.*; pl. *-women* (-wim"en).—**French'y,** *a.* Characteristic or suggestive of the French.

fre-net-ic, phre-net-ic (frē̤-net'ik), *a.* [OF. *frenetique* (F. *frénétique*), < L. *phreneticus*: see *frantic.*] Insane† or mad†; also, frantic; frenzied.—**fre-net'i-cal-ly, phre-net'i-cal-ly,** *adv.*

fre-num (frē'num), *n.*; pl. *-na* (-nä̤). [L. *frenum,* also *frænum,* bridle, curb, bit.] In *anat.*, a ligament or fold of membrane which checks or restrains the motion of a part, as the one which binds down the under side of the tongue.

fren-zied (fren'zid), *p. a.* Affected with frenzy; characterized by, due to, or suggestive of frenzy; frantic.

fren-zy (fren'zi), *n.*; pl. *-zies* (-ziz). [OF. *frenesie* (F. *frénésie*), < L. *phrenesis,* for Gr. *φρενῖτις*: see *phrenitis.*] Mental derangement; delirium; the violent excitement of a paroxysm of mania; fig., violent mental agitation resembling temporary madness; wild excitement or enthusiasm.—**fren'zy,** *v. t.*; *-zied, -zying.* To affect with or drive to frenzy; render frantic.

fre-quence (frē'kwe̤ns), *n.* [L. *frequentia.*] Assemblage, or an assembly (archaic: as, "In full *frequence* bright Of angels," Milton's "Paradise Regained," i. 128); also, frequent occurrence; frequency.—**fre'quen-cy,** *n.* The state or fact of being frequent; frequent occurrence, or rate of recurrence (as, "The *frequency* of his colds had somewhat diminished": Arnold Bennett's "Clayhanger," iv. 1); in *physics,* the number of regularly recurring events of any given kind in a given time; of an alternating electric current, the number of cycles, that is, complete or double alternations or reversals, per second (as, an alternating current of high *frequency,* or of low *frequency,* one having a comparatively large, or comparatively small, number of cycles per second; hence, a high-*frequency,* or low-*frequency,* current); of electric or other waves, the number occurring or passing per second.—**audio frequency.** [That is, 'hearing frequency': *audio,* < L. *audire,* hear.] In *wireless teleg.* and *teleph.*, a frequency or variation corresponding to that of audible or sound vibrations, commonly any below 10,000 cycles per second: opposed to *radio frequency.*—**radio frequency,** in *wireless teleg.* and *teleph.*, a frequency or variation greater than that of sound vibrations or audio frequency, commonly any with 10,000 or more cycles per second, as that of the continuous oscillations or waves produced by radio apparatus: opposed to *audio frequency.*

fre-quent (frē'kwe̤nt), *a.* [L. *frequens* (*frequent-*), akin to *farcire,* stuff: cf. *farce.*] Assembled in great numbers, as persons†; filled or crowded, as with persons, as a place†; also, found at short distances apart (as, a coast with *frequent* lighthouses); numerous; abundant; usually, happening or occurring at short intervals (as, to make *frequent* trips to a place); often recurring; coming in close succession; sometimes, in common use, of common occurrence, or usual (now rare); also, accustomed to do or indulge in something often (now rare: as, to be *frequent* in one's remonstrances); given to repetition in something (now rare); also, constant, habitual, or regular (as, "The tim'rous hare, Grown so familiar with her *frequent* guest, Scarce shuns me": Cowper's "Task," vi. 306).—**fre-quent** (frē̤-kwent'), *v.* [L. *frequentare,* < *frequens.*] **I.** *tr.* To crowd† or fill†; also, to visit often, as a place; resort to habitually; also, to associate with, as a person (now rare); also, to use habitually†. **II.** *intr.* To resort, as to a place (obs. or rare: as, "Nor track nor pathway might declare That human foot *frequented* there," Scott's "Lady of the Lake," i. 25); also, to associate, as with a person†.—**fre-quen-ta-tion** (frē-kwen-tā'sho̤n), *n.* [L. *frequentatio(n-).*] The practice of frequenting.—**fre-quen-ta-tive** (frē̤-kwen'ta̤-tiv). [L. *frequentativus.*] In *gram.*: **I.** *a.* Of a verb, serving to express the frequent repetition of an action. **II.** *n.* A frequentative verb.—**fre-quent'er,** *n.*—**fre'quent-ly,** *adv.*—**fre'quent-ness,** *n.*

fres-co (fres'kō), *n.*; pl. *-coes* or *-cos* (-kōz). [It. *fresco*: see *fresh.*] Coolness†; fresh air†; also, a method of painting on a wall, ceiling, or the like, before the plaster is dry ('true fresco'), or, less properly, after the plaster has dried ('dry fresco'), in which the colors sink in and become incorporated; loosely, painting on plaster in any manner; also, a picture or design so painted.—**fres'co,** *v. t.*; *-coed, -coing.* To paint in fresco.—**fres'co-er,** *n.*—**fres'co-ing,** *n.* The process of painting in fresco; frescoed decoration.

fresh (fresh), *a.* [OF. *fres,* fem. *fresche* (F. *frais,* fem. *fraîche*), = It. *fresco,* fresh, cool; from Teut. (cf. G. *frisch*).] New; not previously known, met with, etc.; novel; also, additional or further (as, *fresh* supplies); also, newly made, arrived, obtained, etc. (as, *fresh* footprints; a book *fresh* from the press); also, inexperienced or unsophisticated (as, "How green you are and *fresh* in this old world!" Shakspere's "King John," iii. 4. 145); forward or presumptuous (slang); also, not preserved by pickling, salting, drying, etc.; also, not salt, as water; fit for drinking; also, pure, cool, or refreshing, as air or water; also, retaining the original properties unimpaired; not deteriorated in any way; not stale, musty, etc.; also, not faded, worn, obliterated, etc.; not sullied or tarnished; looking youthful and healthy (as, "a *fresh* and fair old man": Campbell's "Ritter Bann"); also, not exhausted or fatigued (as, to feel *fresh* after long exertion); brisk; vigorous; also, in a refreshed condition; freshened; renewed; also, moderately strong or brisk, as the wind; also, sober (Sc.); also, tipsy (colloq.).—**fresh blood,** blood of another strain, as for imparting new strength or vigor in breeding; fig., any accession of new elements or members bringing fresh force, ideas, etc.—**fresh,** *n.* The fresh or early part of the day, season, etc.; also, a spring, pool, or stream of fresh water; also, a stream of fresh water running into tide-water; the part of a tidal river above the salt water; also, a flood of fresh water flowing into the sea; also, a freshet or flood; also, a freshman (college slang).

fresh-en (fresh'n), *v.* **I.** *intr.* To become or grow fresh, bright, strong, brisk, etc.: as, "The gentle morning breeze had a little *freshened*" (De Quincey's "Revolt of the Tartars"). **II.** *tr.* To make fresh; refresh, revive, or renew; remove saltness from; *naut.*, to relieve, as a rope, by altering the position of a part exposed to friction.—**fresh'en-er,** *n.*

fresh-et (fresh'et), *n.* [Dim. of *fresh.*] A small stream of fresh water†; also, a stream or rush of fresh water flowing into the sea; also, a flood or overflowing of a stream, due to heavy rains or melted snow.

fresh-ly (fresh'li), *adv.* In a fresh manner; newly; afresh.

fresh-man (fresh'ma̤n), *n.*; pl. *-men.* A novice; esp., a student in the first year of the course at a university, college, or school.

fresh-ness (fresh'nes), *n.* The condition or quality of being fresh.

fresh=wa-ter (fresh'wâ"tėr), *a.* Of or pertaining to water that is fresh, or not salt; living in fresh water, or pertaining to animals doing this; also, accustomed to fresh water only, and not to the sea (as, "You're but a *fresh-water* sailor": Defoe's "Robinson Crusoe," i. 1); hence, of little experience, green, or raw, as soldiers; crude; of slight attainments; of minor standing.

fret[1] (fret), *n.* [Origin uncertain.] Any of the ridges of wood, metal, etc., set across the finger-board of a guitar or similar instrument, to serve as fixed points against which the strings may be pressed by the fingers in regulating the tone.—**fret**[1], *v. t.*; *fretted, fretting.* To provide with frets.

fret[2] (fret), *n.* [OF. *frete* (F. *frette*), interlaced work: origin uncertain.] Ornamental interlaced work; fretwork; also, a band-like ornament of which the pattern is composed of straight (not curved) lines bending or combined at right or other angles (cf. *guilloche*).—**fret**[2], *v. t.*; *fretted, fretting.* [OF. *freter.*] To ornament with or as with fretwork.

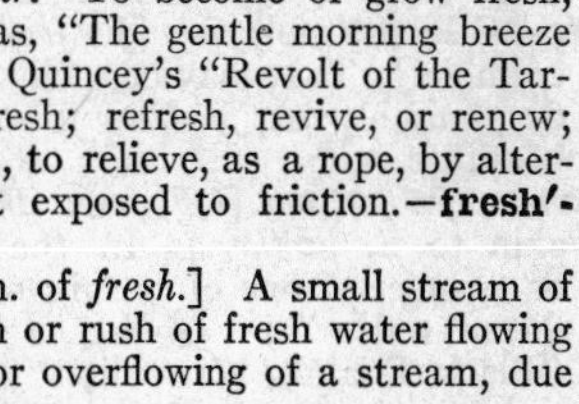

Greek Frets. — *a,* from the Parthenon, above cella frieze; *b,* from vases.

fret[3] (fret), *v.*; *fretted, fretting.* [AS. *fretan* = D. *vreten* = G. *fressen* = Goth. *fraitan,* eat up, devour; from elements represented by E. *for-* and *eat.*] **I.** *tr.* To eat† or devour†; also, to gnaw; wear away or consume by gnawing (as, "Rich robes are *fretted* by the moth": Wordsworth's "Egyptian Maid"); hence, to wear away or consume by friction, rust, chemical corrosives, etc.; fig., to torment; irritate, annoy, or vex; also, to form or make (a passage, etc.) by wearing away a substance; also, to throw (water) into agitation. **II.** *intr.* To gnaw; cause corrosion; make a way by gnawing or corrosion; also, to become eaten, worn, or corroded; fig., to give one's self up to feelings of irritation, resentful discontent, regret, worry, or the like; often, to express such feelings in a peevish, complaining way; also, to move in agitation or commotion, as water (as, "I love the Brooks which down their channels *fret*": Wordsworth's "Intimations of Immortality," xi.).—**fret**³, *n.* A gnawing or wearing away; erosion; corrosion; also, a worn or eroded place; fig., an irritated state of mind; annoyance; vexation; peevish complaining.—**fret′ful,** *a.* Gnawing†; corroding†; also, disposed to fret; irritable or peevish; impatient; also, in agitation or commotion, as water; gusty, as wind; also, characterized by or producing fretting (as, "The *fretful* days Of prejudice and error": Thomson's "To the Memory of Lord Talbot," 340).—**fret′ful-ly,** *adv.*—**fret′ful-ness,** *n.*—**fret′less,** *a.* Free from fret; untroubled; unruffled: as, "*fretless* and free" (Browning's "La Saisiaz").—**fret′ter,** *n.*—**fret′ty,** *a.* Fretful.

fret-work (fret′wėrk), *n.* Ornamental work in an interlaced or openwork design.

Freud-i-an (froid′i-ạn). **I.** *a.* Of or pertaining to the Austrian physician, psychoanalyst, and psychopathologist Sigmund Freud (born 1856), or his doctrines, esp. respecting the causes and treatment of neurotic and psychopathic states, the interpretation of dreams, etc. **II.** *n.* An adherent of the doctrines of Freud.—**Freud′i-an-ism,** *n.* The Freudian doctrines. Also **Freud′ism.**—**Freud′ist,** *n.*

fri-a-ble (frī′ạ-bl), *a.* [F. *friable*, < L. *friabilis*, < *friare*, crumble.] That may be easily crumbled or reduced to powder; crumbly: as, *friable* soil.—**fri-a-bil′i-ty** (-bil′i-ti), **fri′a-ble-ness,** *n.*

fri-ar (frī′ạ̈r), *n.* [OF. *frere* (F. *frère*), < L. *frater*, brother; akin to E. *brother.*] In the *Rom. Cath. Ch.*, a brother or member of one of certain religious orders, esp. the mendicant orders of Franciscans ('Gray Friars'), Dominicans ('Black Friars'), Carmelites ('White Friars'), and Augustinians ('Austin Friars').—**Friars Minor,** the Franciscan friars, esp. the Observants.—**fri′ar=bird,** *n.* Any of various Australasian honey-eaters, esp. *Philemon corniculatus*: so called from the bare head and neck.—**fri′ar′s=lan′tern,** *n.* The ignis fatuus or will-o'-the-wisp. See Milton's "L'Allegro," 104.—**fri′ar-y,** *n.*; pl. *-ies* (-iz). A convent of friars; also, a brotherhood of friars.

Friar-bird (*Philemon corniculatus*).

frib-ble (frib′l), *v.*; *-bled, -bling.* [Origin uncertain: cf. F. *frivole*, frivolous.] **I.** *intr.* To totter†; falter†; also, to act in a trifling or frivolous manner. **II.** *tr.* To waste foolishly.—**frib′ble.** **I.** *n.* A trifler; also, anything trifling or frivolous; also, frivolousness. **II.** *a.* Trifling; frivolous.—**frib′bler,** *n.*

fric-an-deau (frik-ạn-dō′), *n.*; pl. *-deaux* (-dōz′). [F.] Veal or other meat larded, stewed, and served with a sauce.

fric-as-see (frik-ạ-sē′), *n.* [F. *fricassée*, < *fricasser*, cook as a fricassee.] Meat, as chicken or veal, cut up, stewed, and served in a sauce made of its own gravy.—**fric-as-see′,** *v. t.*; *-seed, -seeing.* To prepare as a fricassee.

fric-a-tive (frik′ạ-tiv). [= F. *fricatif*, < L. *fricare*, rub.] In *phonetics*: **I.** *a.* Characterized by a frictional rustling of the breath in utterance, as *f, v, s, sh,* and certain other consonants. **II.** *n.* A fricative consonant.

fric-tion (frik′shọn), *n.* [F. *friction*, < L. *frictio(n-)*, < *fricare*, rub: cf. Gr. χρίειν, rub, anoint.] The act of rubbing or chafing, as the body or limbs; also, the rubbing of the surface of one body against that of another; fig., clashing or conflict, as of temperaments, opinions, etc. (as, "Fresh *friction* was created by Alexander's objection to Napoleon's matrimonial ambitions": H. G. Wells's "Outline of History," xxxviii. § 4); in *mech.* and *physics*, the resistance to the relative motion (sliding or rolling) of surfaces of bodies in contact; sometimes, such resistance of the particles of a body among themselves ('internal friction').—**fric′tion-al,** *a.* Of, pertaining to, or of the nature of friction; moved, worked, or produced by friction.—**fric′tion-al-ly,** *adv.*—**fric′tion-less,** *a.* Free from or unattended with friction.—**fric′tion=match,** *n.* A kind of match tipped with a compound that ignites by friction.—**fric′tion=tight,** *a.* In *mech.*, fitting so tightly or closely, as a joint, that a desired effect of friction, as the prevention of slipping, is produced.

Fri-day (frī′dā̤), *n.* [AS. *Frīgedæg*, < *Frīg*, name of a Teutonic goddess in part identified with the Roman Venus (akin to E. *free* and *friend*), + *dæg*, E. *day.*] The sixth day of the week, following Thursday.—**Black Friday.** See under *black, a.*—**Good Friday.** See under *good, a.*—**man Friday.** See under *man, n.*

fried (frīd). Preterit and past participle of *fry*².

friend (frend), *n.* [AS. *frēond* = D. *vriend* = G. *freund* = Icel. *frændi* = Goth. *frijōnds*, all orig. ppr. of a verb (AS. *frēon*, love, free) from the source of E. *free.*] One attached to another by feelings of personal regard; an intimate; also, a kinsman (now only in *pl.* except in prov. use: as, "She . . . is promised by her *friends* Unto a youthful gentleman of worth," Shakspere's "Two Gentlemen of Verona," iii. 1. 106); also, a favorer or well-wisher; a patron or supporter; also, one who is on good terms with another; one not hostile; a member of the same nation, party, etc.; specif. [*cap.*], a member of the 'Society of Friends,' the proper designation of the Christian sect commonly called *Quakers*, founded by George Fox about 1650, and opposed to oath-taking and all war.—**friend at** (or **in**) **court,** a friend who is in a position to further one's interests with others: as, "A *friend i' the court* is better than a penny in purse" (Shakspere's "2 Henry IV.," v. 1. 34).—**friend,** *v. t.* To make friendly†; also, to befriend (*archaic*).—**friend′less,** *a.* Without friends; forlorn.—**friend′less-ness,** *n.*—**friend′ly,** *a.*; compar. *friendlier*, superl. *friendliest.* [AS. *frēondlīc.*] Like a friend; disposed to act as a friend; kind; also, characteristic of or befitting a friend; manifesting friendship; hence, favorably disposed; inclined to approve, help, or support; favorable or propitious, as things or influences; suitable to one's comfort or convenience (as, "Neighb'ring trees with *friendly* shade invite The troops": Dryden's tr. Virgil's "Georgics," iv. 33); also, not hostile or at variance; without hostility; amicable.—**friend′li-ly,** *adv.*—**friend′li-ness,** *n.*—**friend′ly,** *adv.* [AS. *frēondlīce.*] In a friendly manner; like a friend.—**friend′ship,** *n.* [AS. *frēondscipe.*] The state of being a friend; association as friends; also, a friendly relation or intimacy (as, "And softly, thro' a vinous mist, My college *friendships* glimmer": Tennyson's "Will Waterproof's Lyrical Monologue," 40); also, friendly feeling or disposition; also, a friendly act†; friendly aid† (as, "Hard by here is a hovel; Some *friendship* will it lend you 'gainst the tempest": Shakspere's "King Lear," iii. 2. 62).

fri-er, fry-er (frī′ėr), *n.* One who or that which fries; also, something, as a chicken, for frying.

Frie-sian, Fris-ian (frē′zịan, friz̤′ịạn). **I.** *a.* Of or pertaining to Friesland, a province of the Netherlands, or its inhabitants or their language. **II.** *n.* One of the people of Friesland, or one of their ancient Low German ancestors; also, Friesic.

Frie-sic (frē′zik). **I.** *a.* Friesian. **II.** *n.* The language of the Friesians, belonging to the Low German group.

frieze¹ (frēz), *n.* [F. *frise*, appar. < It. *fregio*, decoration, border, frieze, < L. *Phrygius*, Phrygian.] That part of an entablature which is between the architrave and the cornice, and which is commonly ornamented with sculpture; hence, any similar longitudinal or horizontal decorative band or feature, as on a wall.

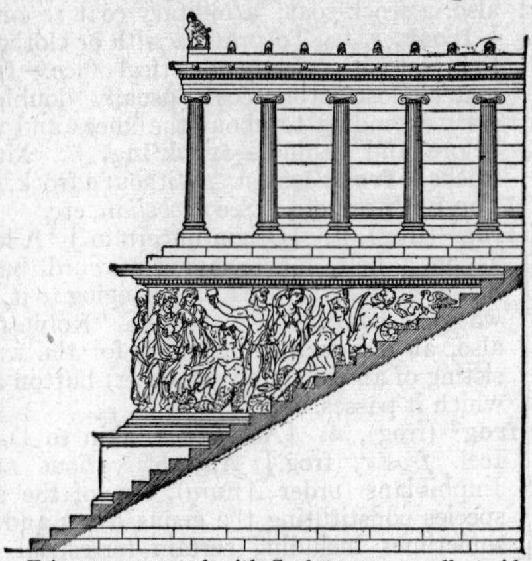

Frieze ornamented with Sculpture, on wall at side of stairway of the great altar of Pergamum, Asia Minor.

frieze[2] (frēz), *n.* [OF. *frize* (F. *frise*), perhaps < *Frise,* Friesland: cf. F. *friser,* curl (hair, etc.), not recorded in OF.] A thick woolen cloth finished with a shaggy nap on one side. —**frieze**[2], *v. t.*; *friezed, friezing.* To raise a nap on (cloth).

frig-ate (frig′ạt), *n.* [F. *frégate,* < It. *fregata.*] Orig., a small, swift vessel; later, an old type of sailing war-vessel, larger than a corvette; hence, any of various more modern war-vessels.—**frig′ate=bird,** *n.* Either of two species of rapacious marine birds, *Fregata aquila* and *F. minor,* noted for their powers of flight.

Frigate-bird (*Fregata aquila*).

fright (frīt), *n.* [AS. *fryhto,* for *fyrhto,* akin to G. *furcht* and Goth. *faurhtei,* fear.] Sudden and extreme fear; a sudden terror; also, something that frightens; hence, a person or thing of shocking, grotesque, or ridiculous appearance.—**fright,** *v. t.* [AS. *fyrhtan.*] To affect with fright; terrify; also, to scare (*away,* etc.). [Now chiefly poetic or prov.]—**fright′en,** *v. t.* To throw into a fright; terrify; scare; also, to drive (*away, off,* etc.) by scaring. —**fright′en-er,** *n.*—**fright′ful,** *a.* Full of fright or fear†; also, such as to cause fright; dreadful, terrible, or alarming; horrible, shocking, or revolting; also, hyperbolically, 'awful' (colloq.).—**fright′ful-ly,** *adv.* In a frightful manner, or to a frightful degree; dreadfully; 'awfully' (colloq.). —**fright′ful-ness,** *n.* The quality of being frightful; sometimes, terrifying methods or measures intended as a means of coercion, as in war; terrorism.

frig-id (frij′id), *a.* [L. *frigidus,* < *frigere,* be cold, < *frigus,* cold, coldness.] Very cold in temperature (as, the *frigid* zones, the regions between the poles and the polar circles); devoid of heat or warmth; fig., destitute of warmth of feeling, or without ardor or enthusiasm; cold or indifferent, as persons or their manners, etc.; stiff or formal, as a bow; chilling or depressing, as circumstances or surroundings; failing to excite feeling or interest, dull, or flat, as literary efforts.—**frig-i-da′ri-um** (-i-dā′ri-um), *n.*; pl. *-ria* (-ri-ạ). [L., prop. neut. of *frigidarius,* of or for cooling, < *frigidus.*] The cooling-apartment of the ancient Roman thermæ, usually furnished with a cold bath; the cold bath itself; hence, any room kept at a low temperature. —**fri-gid-i-ty** (fri-jid′i-ti), **frig′id-ness,** *n.*—**frig′id-ly,** *adv.*

frig-o-rif-ic (frig-ọ-rif′ik), *a.* [L. *frigorificus,* < *frigus* (*frigor-*), cold, + *facere,* make.] Causing or producing cold.

fri-jol (frē′hōl), *n.*; pl. *frijoles* (-hō′lās). [Sp. *fríjol.*] A cultivated bean of the genus *Phaseolus,* much used for food in Mexico, etc.

frill (fril), *n.* [Origin uncertain.] A trimming consisting of a strip of cloth, lace, or the like, gathered at one edge and left loose at the other; a ruffle; also, something resembling such a trimming, as the projecting fringe of hair on the chest of some dogs; fig., an affectation of manner, style, etc. (colloq.).—**frill,** *v.* **I.** *tr.* To trim or ornament with a frill or frills; form into a frill; in *photog.,* to cause to frill. **II.** *intr.* In *photog.,* to become wrinkled at the edge, as the gelatin coating of a dry plate.—**frill′ing,** *n.* Frilled trimming; frills collectively.—**frill′=liz″ard,** *n.* An Australian lizard, *Chlamydosaurus kingi,* which grows to a length of 3 feet, remarkable for a broad, frill-like, erectile fold of skin about the neck, and for a habit of running, when startled, upon its hind legs. Also called *frilled lizard.*

Frill-lizard.

Fri-maire (frē-mãr), *n.* [F. *frimaire,* < *frimas,* hoar-frost.] In the calendar of the first French republic, the third month of the year, extending from Nov. 21 to Dec. 20.

fringe (frinj), *n.* [OF. *fringe, frenge* (F. *frange*), < LL. *fimbria,* border, fringe, for L. *fimbriæ,* pl., threads, fringe: cf. L. *fibra,* E. *fiber.*] An ornamental bordering having projecting lengths of thread, cord, etc., either loose or variously arranged or combined; also, anything resembling or suggesting this (as, a *fringe* of hair over the forehead; a *fringe* of trees about a field); a border or margin.—**fringe,** *v. t.*; *fringed, fringing.* To furnish with or as with a fringe; also, to serve as a fringe for.—**fringe′less,** *a.* Without fringe. —**fringe′=tree,** *n.* An oleaceous shrub or small tree, *Chionanthus virginica,* of the southern U. S., bearing panicles of white flowers with long, narrow petals.

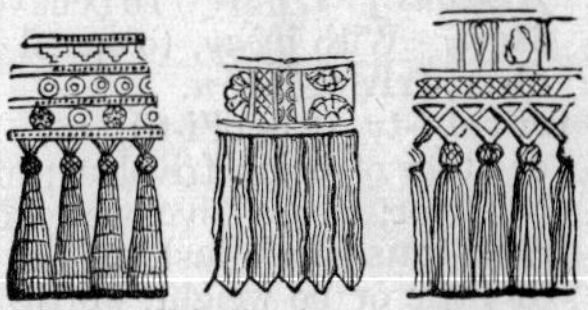

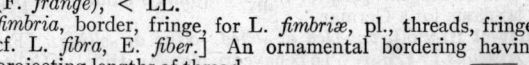

Assyrian Fringes, from ancient bas-reliefs.

frin-gil-line (frin-jil′in), *a.* [L. *fringilla,* kind of bird.] Of or pertaining to the finch family of birds; finch-like.

frin-gy (frin′ji), *a.* Like a fringe; adorned with fringe.

frip-per-y (frip′ėr-i), *n.*; pl. *-ies* (-iz). [F. *friperie,* OF. *freperie,* < *frepe,* rag.] Old or cast-off clothes†, or a place where they are sold†; also, finery in dress, esp. when tawdry; an article of this kind; in general, tawdry ornamentation; also, trifling articles, or something trifling; fig., empty display; ostentation.

fri-sette (fri-zet′), *n.* [F., little curl, frizz, < *friser,* to curl, E. *frizz*[2].] A fringe of curled or frizzed hair, esp. artificial, worn on the forehead by women.

fri-seur (frē-zėr), *n.* [F., < *friser*: see *frisette.*] A hair-dresser.

Fris-ian (friz′ian), *a.* and *n.* See *Friesian.*

frisk (frisk), *a.* [OF. F. *frisque*; origin uncertain.] Lively; brisk; frisky. [Obs. or archaic.]—**frisk,** *v.* **I.** *intr.* To dance, leap, skip, or gambol, as in frolic: as, "We were as twinn'd lambs that did *frisk* i' the sun" (Shakspere's "Winter's Tale," i. 2. 67). **II.** *tr.* To search (a person), as for stolen property, concealed weapons, or other articles carried. [Slang.]—**frisk,** *n.* A leap, skip, or caper; a sportive movement; a frolic.—**frisk′er,** *n.*

fris-ket (fris′ket), *n.* [F. *frisquette.*] In *printing,* a thin framework of iron hinged to the tympan of a hand-press, for holding in place the sheet to be printed; later, a sheet with parts cut out, or a frame for holding such a sheet, for placing over a form so that only certain parts may print.

frisk-y (fris′ki), *a.*; compar. *friskier,* superl. *friskiest.* Given to frisking; lively; frolicsome; playful.—**frisk′i-ly,** *adv.* —**frisk′i-ness,** *n.*

frit (frit), *n.* [F. *fritte*, < It. *fritta*, prop. pp. fem. of *friggere*, < L. *frigere*, roast, E. *fry*².] In *glass-making*, a calcined, partly fused material ready for complete fusion to form glass; in *ceramics*, a partially fused material used as a basis for glazes; also, the composition from which artificial soft-paste porcelain is made.—**frit,** *v. t.*; *fritted, fritting.* To make into frit; fuse partially.

frit=fly (frit′flī), *n.*; pl. *-flies* (-flīz). [Cf. *fret*³.] A dipterous insect, *Oscinis frit*, of Europe, whose larva damages growing wheat, etc.

frith (frith), *n.* [Var. of *firth*.] A narrow arm of the sea; a firth.

frit-il-la-ri-a (frit-i-lā′ri-ạ), *n.* [NL., < L. *fritillus*, dice-box.] Any plant of the liliaceous genus *Fritillaria*, comprising bulbous herbs with drooping, bell-shaped flowers, as *F. imperialis*, the crown-imperial.—**frit′il-la-ry** (-lạ-ri), *n.*; pl. *-ries* (-riz). A fritillaria; also, any of several butterflies of the genus *Argynnis* and allied genera.

frit-ter¹ (frit′ėr), *n.* [OF. F. *friture*, < *frire*, fry, < L. *frigere*, E. *fry*².] A small cake of batter, sometimes containing fruit, clams, or some other ingredient, fried in deep boiling lard or the like or in a frying-pan.

frit-ter² (frit′ėr), *n.* [Appar. < *flitters*.] A small piece, fragment, or shred; also, a trifle.—**frit′ter**², *v. t.* To break or tear into small pieces or shreds (now rare); hence, to disperse or squander piecemeal, or waste little by little (now usually with *away*: as, to *fritter* away one's money or energies on trifles; "The allies . . . *frittered* away precious time in . . . rapacious disputes," H. G. Wells's "Outline of History," xxxviii. § 5).—**frit′ter-er,** *n.*

Fritz (frits), *n.* [G., for *Friedrich*, man's name.] A popular name for a German.

friv-ol (friv′ọl), *v.*; *-oled* or *-olled, -oling* or *-olling.* [From *frivolous*.] **I.** *intr.* To behave frivolously; trifle. [Colloq.] **II.** *tr.* With *away*, to spend frivolously. [Colloq.]—**friv′-ol-er, friv′ol-ler,** *n.*

fri-vol-i-ty (fri-vol′i-ti), *n.*; pl. *-ties* (-tiz). The quality or state of being frivolous; disposition to trifle; frivolous behavior; also, a frivolous act or thing.

friv-o-lous (friv′ọ-lus), *a.* [L. *frivolus*, silly, trifling, paltry.] Of little or no weight, worth, or importance (as, a *frivolous* matter; a *frivolous* objection or pretext); paltry or trivial; not worthy of serious notice; also, characterized by lack of seriousness or sense, as conduct; given to trifling or levity, as persons.—**friv′o-lous-ly,** *adv.*—**friv′o-lous-ness,** *n.*

frizz¹ (friz), *v.* [Imit.] **I.** *intr.* To make a sizzling or sputtering noise, as in frying. **II.** *tr.* To frizzle (meat, etc.).

frizz², **friz** (friz), *v.*; *frizzed, frizzing.* [F. *friser*, curl (hair, etc.); origin uncertain.] **I.** *tr.* To curl or crisp (the hair); form into small, crisp curls; also, to form into little tufts, as the nap of cloth. **II.** *intr.* To form short, crisp curls.—**frizz**², **friz,** *n.* The state of being frizzed; also, something frizzed; a curl, fringe, or wig of frizzed hair.

friz-zle¹ (friz′l), *v.*; *-zled, -zling.* [Freq. of *frizz*¹.] **I.** *intr.* To make a sizzling or sputtering noise in frying or the like; frizz. **II.** *tr.* To fry or cook with a sizzling noise; crisp (meat, etc.) by frying; also, to prepare (dried beef sliced thin) in a white sauce.—**friz′zle**¹, *n.* The act or sound of frizzling; a dish of something frizzled.

friz-zle² (friz′l), *v. t.* or *i.*; *-zled, -zling.* [Appar. freq. of *frizz*².] To curl in small, crisp curls; frizz.—**friz′zle**², *n.* The state of being frizzled; frizz; also, frizzled hair; a short, crisp curl.—**friz′zly,** *a.* Frizzled.

friz-zy (friz′i), *a.* Frizzed, as hair; frizz-like.

fro (frō). [ME. *fro, fra*, from Scand.: cf. Icel. *frā*, also E. *from*.] **I.** *prep.* From. [Archaic or prov.] **II.** *adv.* Away; back: now only in the phrase 'to and fro' (forward and backward; hither and thither).

Frö-bel-i-an, Froe-bel-i-an (frė-bel′i-ạn), *a.* Of or pertaining to Friedrich Fröbel (1782–1852), the German educational reformer, or the kindergarten system of instruction, originated by him.—**Frö′bel-ism, Froe′bel-ism,** *n.* The Fröbelian or kindergarten system of instruction.

frock (frok), *n.* [OF. F. *froc*; origin uncertain.] A coarse outer garment with large sleeves, worn by monks; hence, the priestly or clerical office; also, a long coat or mantle; also, a loose outer garment worn by peasants and workmen; a smock-frock; also, a sailor's woolen jersey (chiefly Sc.); also, the principal outer garment of women; a gown or dress; also, a frock-coat; a military coat resembling a frock-coat.—**frock,** *v. t.* To provide with or clothe in a frock; hence, to invest with priestly or clerical office.—**frock′=coat′,** *n.* A man's close-fitting coat, usually double-breasted, with a skirt extending to about the knees and of the same length before and behind.—**frock′ing,** *n.* Material for making frocks.—**frock′less,** *a.* Without a frock.

Froe-bel′i-an, etc. See *Fröbelian*, etc.

frog¹ (frog), *n.* [Origin uncertain.] A loop or attachment, as on a belt, for receiving a sword, bayonet, etc. (as, "I made him a belt, with a *frog* hanging to it, such as in England we wear hangers in": Defoe's "Robinson Crusoe," i. 15); also, an ornamental fastening for the front of a coat, consisting of an elongated (or other) button and a loop through which it passes.

frog² (frog), *n.* [AS. *frogga*, akin to D. *vorsch*, G. *frosch*, Icel. *froskr*, frog.] Any of various anurous or tailless amphibians (order *Anura*), esp. of the web-footed aquatic species constituting the genus *Rana* and allied genera, but sometimes including certain terrestrial species which are more commonly called *toads*; also, any of various animals somewhat resembling frogs; also, a slight hoarseness due to mucus on the vocal cords ('frog in the throat'); also, a triangular mass of elastic, horny substance in the middle of the sole of the foot of a horse or related animal; also, an arrangement or device in the rail of a railroad for connecting one track with another branching from it or crossing it.—**frog**², *v. i.*; *frogged, frogging.* To catch, or search for, frogs.

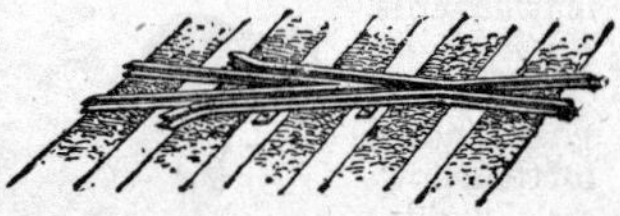

Railroad Frog.

frog-bit (frog′bit), *n.* A floating aquatic plant, *Hydrocharis morsus-ranæ*, of Europe, with white flowers; also, a similar plant, *Limnobium spongia*, of the United States.

frog=eye (frog′ī), *n.* A disease which affects tobacco-leaves, producing small white spots: attributed to a fungus.—**frog′=eyed,** *a.* Affected with frog-eye.

frog-fish (frog′fish), *n.* Any of the fishes constituting the family *Antennariidæ*, characterized by a wide frog-like mouth and broad limb-like fins; also, the angler, *Lophius piscatorius*.

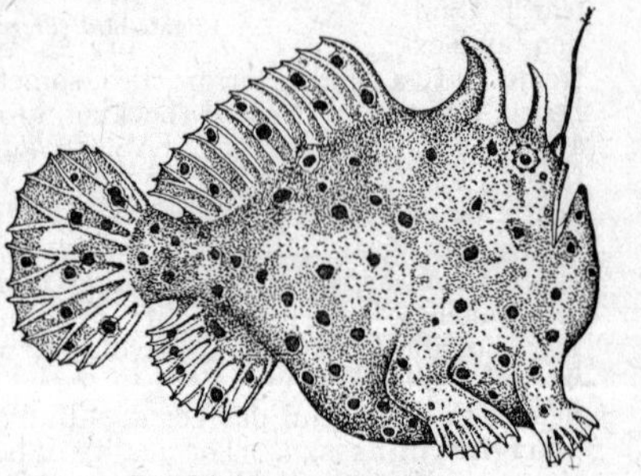

Frogfish (*Antennarius pictus*).

frogged (frogd), *a.* [See *frog*¹.] Fastened or ornamented with frogs.—**frog′ging,** *n.* Fastenings or ornamentation consisting of frogs.

frog-gy (frog′i), *a.* [See *frog*².] Abounding in frogs; frog-like.

frog-hop-per (frog′hop″ėr), *n.* Any of various small, leaping, frog-like homopterous insects (family *Cercopidæ*) whose young are inclosed in a frothy secretion called cuckoo-spit.

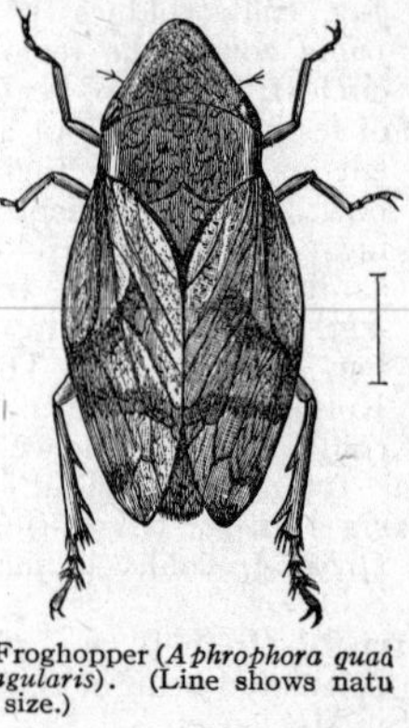

Froghopper (*Aphrophora quadrangularis*). (Line shows natural size.)

frog=lil-y (frog′lil″i), *n.* The yellow pond-lily.

frog-mouth (frog′mouth), *n.* Any of the Australian and East Indian goatsuckers (birds) constituting the family *Podargidæ*, or, according to some classifications, the subfamily *Podarginæ*: so called from their wide, flat, frog-like mouth. See *goatsucker*.

frog=spawn (frog′spân), *n.* Frog-spit (alga); also, a micro-organism, *Streptococcus mesenteri* *oides*, causing fermentation and the formation of slimy masses in saccharine solutions.

frog=spit, frog=spit-tle (frog′spit, -spit″l), *n.* Any of several filamentous fresh-water algæ, esp. of the genus *Spirogyra*, forming floating masses; also, cuckoo-spit.

frol-ic (frol′ik), *a.* [D. *vroolijk* (= G. *fröhlich*), < MD. *vro* = G. *froh*, glad, joyous.] Joyous or merry; sportive; full of pranks. [Archaic.]—**frol′ic,** *v. i.*; *-icked, -icking.* To play merrily; sport; gambol; play pranks. —**frol′ic,** *n.* A frolicking; a fit of merry play; a frolicsome performance; a merrymaking; also, sportive gaiety; merry play.—**frol′ick-er,** *n.*—**frol′ick-y,** *a.* Frolicsome.—**frol′ic-some** (-sum), *a.* Disposed to frolic; sportive; merrily playful. —**frol′ic-some-ly,** *adv.*—**frol′ic-some-ness,** *n.*

from (from or from), *prep.* [AS. *fram*, prep., from, as adv. forward, forth (see *frame*), = OHG. and Goth. *fram*, prep. and adv., = Icel. *frā*, prep. (cf. *fro*), *fram*, adv.; ult. akin to E. *fore.*] A particle specifying a starting-point, and hence used to express removal or separation in space, time, order, etc., discrimination or distinction, source or origin, instrumentality, and cause or reason: as, a train running west *from* New York; to leap *from* a seat; *from* that time onward; to count *from* 0 to 10; to wander *from* one's purpose; he is often *from* home; a long way *from* being rich; to tell one tree *from* another; *from* one point of view; a gift *from* his wife; sketches drawn *from* nature; a blow *from* one's fist; to suffer *from* measles; to act *from* a sense of duty.

fro-mage (fro-mäzh), *n.* [F. *fromage*, OF. *formage*, < L. *forma*, E. *form.*] Cheese.

fro-men-ty (frō′men-ti), *n.* Same as *frumenty*.

frond (frond), *n.* [L. *frons* (*frond-*), leafy branch.] In *bot.*, a large compound leaf, as of a palm; in specif. use, a leaf-like expansion not differentiated into stem and foliage, as in lichens; also, the leaf of a fern; in *zoöl.*, a leaf-like expansion in certain animal organisms.—**frond-age** (fron′dāj), *n.* Fronds collectively; loosely, foliage.—**frond′ed,** *a.* Having fronds: as, "*fronded* palms" (Whittier's "Eternal Goodness").

fron-dent (fron′dent), *a.* [L. *frondens* (*frondent-*), ppr. of *frondere*, have leaves, < *frons*, E. *frond.*] Abounding in leaves; leafy.

fron-desce (fron-des′), *v. i.*; *-desced, -descing.* [L. *frondescere*, < *frondere*: see *frondent.*] To put forth leaves. —**fron-des′cence** (-des′ens), *n.* The process or period of coming into leaf; also, foliage.—**fron-des′cent,** *a.* Putting forth leaves or fronds.

fron-dif-er-ous (fron-dif′e-rus), *a.* [L. *frondifer*: see *frond* and *-ferous.*] Bearing leaves or fronds.

fron-dose (fron′dōs or fron-dōs′), *a.* [L. *frondosus*, < *frons*: see *frond.*] Leafy; frondiferous; frond-like.

front (frunt). [OF. F. *front*, < L. *frons* (*front-*), forehead, front.] **I.** *n.* The forehead, or the entire face; hence, bearing or demeanor in confronting anything (as, a calm *front*); sometimes, cool assurance, or impudence (as, "Men of *front* carry things before them with little opposition": Steele, in "Tatler," 168); also, the part or side of anything, as a house, which seems to look out or be directed forward; the foremost part or surface of anything; any side or face, as of a house; the beginning; land facing a road, river, etc.; the line between cold and warm masses of air; also, something attached or worn at the fore part, as a shirt-front, a dicky, etc.; also, a place or position directly before anything, or that place to which one's view is directed (as, in *front* of it or him); *milit.*, the foremost line or part of an army, etc., or the direction in which it faces; a line of battle; the place where active operations are carried on. **II.** *a.* Of or pertaining to the front; situated in or at the front. —**front,** *v.* **I.** *tr.* To have the front toward; face; also, to meet face to face; confront; esp., to face in opposition, hostility, or defiance (as, "With Stupidity and sound Digestion man may *front* much": Carlyle's "Sartor Resartus," ii. 7); oppose; also, to set face to face, as with some one or something; also, to furnish or adorn in front; supply with a front; also, to serve as a front to. **II.** *intr.* To have or turn the front in some specified direction.

fron-tage (frun′tāj), *n.* Land abutting on a river, street, etc.; also, the space lying between a building and the street, etc.; also, the front of a building or lot; the lineal extent of this front; also, the act or fact of fronting in a certain direction; outlook; exposure.—**fron′tag-er** (-tā-jėr), *n.* One who owns land fronting on a stream, road, etc.; also, one who lives on a frontier.

fron-tal[1] (frun′tal), *a.* [NL. *frontalis*, < L. *frons*, E. *front.*] Of or pertaining to the forehead; noting or pertaining to the bone (or pair of bones) forming the forehead; also, pertaining to, or being in or at, the front.

fron-tal[2] (frun′tal), *n.* [OF. *frontel*, < ML. *frontale*, < L. *frons*, E. *front.*] Something worn on or applied to the forehead, as an ornamental band for the hair†; also, the façade of a building; *eccles.*, a movable cover or hanging for the front of an altar; in *anat.*, the frontal bone.

front-ed (frun′ted), *a.* Having a front; formed with a front.

fron-tier (fron′tēr, fron-tēr′, or frun-tēr′). [OF. *frontiere* (F. *frontière*), < ML. *frontaria*, < L. *frons*, E. *front.*] **I.** *n.* That part of a country which fronts or faces another country; the border; also, that part of a country which forms the border of its settled or inhabited regions; also, a border town or fortress†. **II.** *a.* Of or pertaining to a frontier; situated on the frontier.—**fron-tiers-man** (fron′tērz-man or frun-tērz′-), *n.*; pl. *-men.* A man who lives on the frontier.

fron-tis-piece (frun′tis-pēs or fron′-), *n.* [An altered form, simulating *piece*, of *frontispice*, < F. *frontispice*, < ML. *frontispicium*, < L. *frons*, front, + *specere*, look at.] The part which is seen in front, or which first strikes the eye; specif., the principal face of a building; the decorated entrance of a building; also, the pediment over a door, gate, etc.; also, a sculptured or engraved panel; also, the first page of a book†, or what is printed on it†; now, usually, an illustration facing the title-page of a book or of a division of a book; in humorous use, the face or the forehead.—**fron′tis-piece,** *v. t.*; *-pieced, -piecing.* To furnish (a book) with a frontispiece; also, to represent on a frontispiece; also, to provide as a frontispiece.

front-less (frunt′les), *a.* Without a front; also, without shame or modesty, shameless, or audacious (now rare: as, "For vice, though *frontless* and of hardened face, Is daunted at the sight of awful grace," Dryden's "Hind and the Panther," iii. 1040).

front-let (frunt′let), *n.* [OF. *frontelet*, dim. of *frontel*, E. *frontal*[2].] Something worn on the forehead, as an ornament, band, or the like; also, the forehead, esp. of an animal; in *ornith.*, the forehead when marked by a different color or texture of the plumage.

fron-to- (fron′tō-). Form of L. *frons* (*front-*), forehead, in combination: used esp. in anatomical terms, often with reference to the frontal bone, as in *frontomalar* (pertaining to the frontal and the malar bone), *frontoparietal*, *frontotemporal*.

fron-tol-y-sis (frun-tol′i-sis), *n.* [See *front* and *-lysis.*] The dissolution of a front between masses of air.

fron-ton (frun′ton, F. frôn-tôn), *n.* [F., < It. *frontone*, < *fronte*, < L. *frons*, E. *front.*] In *arch.*, a pediment.

front-ward, front-wards (frunt′wärd, -wärdz), *adv.* Toward the front.

frore (frōr), *a.* [Old pp. of *freeze.*] Frozen; also, frosty; intensely cold. [Archaic.]

frost (frôst), *n.* [AS. *frost*, *forst*, = D. *vorst* = G. and Icel. *frost*, frost; from the verb represented by E. *freeze.*] The act or process of freezing, or the state of being frozen; a state of the temperature which occasions the freezing of water (as, degrees of *frost*, degrees below the freezing-point, forty degrees of frost, Fahrenheit, for example, corresponding to −8° F.); also, a covering of minute ice-needles formed from the atmosphere at night upon the ground and exposed objects when these have cooled by radiation below the dew-point and when the dew-point is below the freezing-point ('white frost' or 'hoar-frost'); frozen vapor; fig., coldness of manner or temperament; a coolness between persons (slang); also, a failure (slang).—**frost,** *v.* **I.** *tr.* To freeze; frost-bite; also, to cover with hoar-frost; also, to give a frost-like surface to (glass, etc.); ice (a cake, etc.). **II.** *intr.* To freeze; hence, to become like frost.—**frost′=bite,** *v. t.*; pret. *-bit*, pp. *-bitten*, ppr. *-biting.* To injure by frost; blight with frost; affect by severe cold so as to cause inflammation or gangrene.—**frost′=bite,** *n.* The condition or effect of being frost-bitten.—**frost′ed,** *p. a.* Frozen; frost-bitten; also, covered with hoar-frost; also, having a frost-like surface; iced, as cake.—**frost′=fish,** *n.* The tomcod, *Microgadus tomcod* (so called because it appears on the coast of North America as frost sets in); also, the American smelt, *Osmerus mordax.*—**frost′i-ly,** *adv.* In a frosty manner.—**frost′i-ness,** *n.*—**frost′ing,** *n.* A preparation of powdered sugar beaten together with whites of eggs, etc., or a preparation of sugar and water boiled together, for covering cakes or the like; also, a lusterless finish, as of metal or glass.—**frost′less,** *a.* Without frost.—**frost′=plant,** *n.* Any of various plants on whose stems crystals of ice form in autumn, as the frostweed, *Helianthemum canadense,* or the American dittany, *Cunila origanoides.*—**frost′weed,** *n.* Any of the woody herbs or low shrubs constituting the cistaceous genus *Helianthemum,* as *H. canadense,* a yellow-flowered species notable for the crystals of ice which shoot from the bursting bark near the base of the stem in autumn.—**frost′work,** *n.* The delicate tracery formed by hoar-frost, esp. on glass; ornamentation in imitation of this as on metal.—**frost′y,** *a.*; compar. *frostier,* superl. *frostiest.* Attended with or producing frost; freezing; very cold; fig., lacking warmth of feeling; chilling; also, consisting of or covered with hoar-frost; also, resembling hoar-frost; white or gray, as the hair; hence, pertaining to or characteristic of old age.

froth (frôth), *n.* [ME. *frothe*: cf. Icel. *frodha,* froth, also AS. *āfrēothan,* form froth.] An aggregation of bubbles, as on a fermented liquid or at the mouth of a hard-driven horse; foam; fig., something unsubstantial or evanescent (as, "a *froth* of fleeting joy": Shakspere's "Lucrece," 212).—**froth,** *v.* **I.** *intr.* To give out froth; foam. **II.** *tr.* To cause to foam; also, to emit like froth; also, to cover with froth.—**froth′y,** *a.*; compar. *frothier,* superl. *frothiest.* Of, like, or having froth; foamy; fig., unsubstantial; trifling; vain.—**froth′i-ly,** *adv.*—**froth′i-ness,** *n.*

frot-té (fro-tā), *n.* [F., prop. pp. of *frotter,* rub.] In *art,* a picture, or a part of a picture, executed by means of very slight and more or less transparent washes of color, as in producing hazy effects of atmosphere in landscape.

frou=frou (frö′frö), *n.* [F.] A rustling, as of silk.

frounce (frouns), *n.* [OF. F. *fronce,* a wrinkle, fold; origin uncertain.] A wrinkle†; a fold†; a flounce†; a furbelow or showy ornament (archaic).—**frounce,** *v. t.*; *frounced, frouncing.* [OF. *froncier* (F. *froncer*).] To wrinkle†; gather into folds†; curl (the hair)†; adorn with furbelows (archaic).

frou′zy, etc. See *frowzy,* etc.

frow (frou), *n.* [D. *vrouw* = G. *frau.*] A woman; a wife: used esp. with reference to the Dutch or Germans.

fro-ward (frō′wạrd), *a.* [See *fro* and *-ward.*] Perverse; wilfully contrary; refractory; untoward.—**fro′ward-ly,** *adv.*—**fro′ward-ness,** *n.*

frown (froun), *v.* [OF. *froignier, frongnier* (cf. F. *renfrogner,* contract in a frown); origin uncertain.] **I.** *intr.* To contract the brow as in displeasure or deep thought; scowl; also, to look disapprovingly (as, to *frown* on a scheme); also, to have a threatening aspect; lower. **II.** *tr.* To force (*away, off, into,* etc.) by a frown; also, to express by a frown.—**frown,** *n.* A frowning look; a scowl; also, any expression or show of disapproval.—**frown′er,** *n.*—**frown′ing-ly,** *adv.*—**frown′less,** *a.* Without a frown.

frow-y (frou′i), *a.* [Cf. *frowzy.*] Musty; stale; not fresh and sweet: said of articles of food. [Prov. Eng. and U. S.]

frow-zy (frou′zi), *a.*; compar. *frowzier,* superl. *frowziest.* [Origin obscure.] Ill-smelling (as, "a thousand *frouzy* steams which I could not analyze": Smollett's "Humphry Clinker," May 8); musty; also, dirty and untidy; slovenly; dingy; unkempt.—**frow′zi-ly,** *adv.*—**frow′zi-ness,** *n.*

froze (frōz). Preterit of *freeze.*—**froz-en** (frō′zn), *p. a.* Subjected to freezing; congealed by cold; covered with ice, as a stream; obstructed by the formation of ice, as pipes; injured or killed by frost or cold; frigid, or very cold; chilly or cold in manner (as, a *frozen* stare); rendered impossible of liquidation, as by business conditions (colloq.: as, *frozen* credits; *frozen* loans).—**froz′en-ly,** *adv.*—**froz′en-ness,** *n.*

fruc-tes-cence (fruk-tes′ẹns), *n.* [NL. *fructescentia,* < L. *fructus,* E. *fruit.*] The fruiting of a plant; the fruiting season.

Fruc-ti-dor (frük-tē-dôr), *n.* [F. *fructidor,* < L. *fructus,* fruit, + Gr. δῶρον, gift.] In the calendar of the first French republic, the twelfth month of the year, extending from Aug. 18 to Sept. 16.

fruc-tif-er-ous (fruk-tif′ẹ-rus), *a.* [L. *fructifer,* < *fructus,* fruit, + *ferre,* bear.] Fruit-bearing; producing fruit.

fruc-ti-fi-ca-tion (fruk″ti-fi-kā′shọn), *n.* [LL. *fructificatio(n-).*] The act of fructifying; the fruiting of a plant; also, the fruit of a plant; the organs of fruiting.

fruc-ti-fy (fruk′ti-fī), *v.*; *-fied, -fying.* [OF. F. *fructifier,* < L. *fructificare,* < *fructus,* fruit, + *facere,* make.] **I.** *intr.* To bear fruit. **II.** *tr.* To make fruitful or productive; fertilize.—**fruc′ti-fi-er** (-fī-ėr), *n.*

fruc-tiv-o-rous (fruk-tiv′ọ-rus), *a.* [L. *fructus,* fruit, + *vorare,* devour.] Feeding on fruits; frugivorous.

fruc-tose (fruk′tōs), *n.* [L. *fructus,* fruit: see *-ose*[2].] In *chem.,* a sugar occurring in three optically different isomeric forms, the best known being levulose.

fruc-tu-ous (fruk′tụ̄-us), *a.* [OF. *fructuous* (F. *fructueux*), < L. *fructuosus,* < *fructus,* E. *fruit.*] Fruitful; productive; profitable.

fru-gal (frö′gạl), *a.* [L. *frugalis,* < *frugi,* useful, worthy, frugal, prop. dative of *frux* (*frug-*), fruit, profit, akin to *fructus,* E. *fruit.*] Economical in use or expenditure (as, "Though on pleasure she was bent, She had a *frugal* mind": Cowper's "John Gilpin," 32); prudently saving or sparing; also, entailing little expense (as, a *frugal* meal).—**fru-gal-i-ty** (frọ-gal′i-ti), *n.*; pl. *-ties* (-tiz). [L. *frugalitas.*] The quality of being frugal; prudent economy; *pl.,* frugal practices or resources.—**fru′gal-ly,** *adv.*—**fru′gal-ness,** *n.*

fru-giv-o-rous (frọ-jiv′ọ-rus), *a.* [L. *frux* (*frug-*), fruit, + *vorare,* devour.] Feeding on fruits, as certain animals.

fruit (fröt), *n.* [OF. F. *fruit,* < L. *fructus,* enjoyment, proceeds, fruit, < *frui,* enjoy, akin to E. *brook*[1].] Any product of vegetable growth useful to men or animals (commonly in *pl.*: as, the *fruits* of the earth); usually, an edible seed-containing plant-product, esp. one in which the seed is contained in a succulent pulp, as the apple, orange, or plum, a melon, or a berry; such products collectively; in botanical use, the matured ovary of a plant with its contents and appendages (as, an aggregate *fruit,* see *aggregate, a.*; a collective or multiple *fruit,* see *collective, a.*); also, the spores of a cryptogam; in fig. use, offspring; also, anything produced or accruing; a product, result, or effect; return or profit.—**fruit,** *v. i.* or *t.* To bear or bring to bear fruit.—**fruit′age** (-ạ̄j), *n.* The bearing of fruit; also, fruit borne (as, "Greedily they pluck'd The *fruitage* fair to sight": Milton's "Paradise Lost," x. 561); fig., product or result.—**fruit′=cake,** *n.* A rich cake containing raisins, currants, citron, etc.—**fruit′=crow,** *n.* Any of various South American birds of the family *Cotingidæ* that feed largely on fruits.—**fruit′ed,** *a.* Having fruit; laden with fruit.—**fruit′er,** *n.* A fruit-bearing tree; also, a fruit-grower; also, a ship employed in transporting fruit.—**fruit′er-er,** *n.* A dealer in fruit; a fruit-seller.—**fruit′er-y,** *n.*; pl. *-ies* (-iz). [F. *fruiterie.*] A place for raising or storing fruit; also, fruit collectively.—**fruit′ful,** *a.* Abounding in fruit, as trees or other plants; bearing fruit abundantly; conducing to abundance of fruit, as soil or showers; also, producing offspring, esp. abundantly; prolific; fecund; also, abundantly productive (*of* or *in*: as, "golden days, *fruitful* of golden deeds," Milton's "Paradise Lost," iii. 337; *fruitful* in expedients); often, productive of results (as, a *fruitful* journey; *fruitful* investigations); profitable; also, abundant† or

Fruit-crow (*Querula purpurata*).

plenteous† (as, "One *fruitful* meal would set me to 't": Shakspere's "Measure for Measure," iv. 3. 161).—**fruit′ful-ly,** *adv.*—**fruit′ful-ness,** *n.*

fru-i-tion (frö̤-ish′o̤n), *n.* [OF. *fruition*, < LL. *fruitio(n-)*, < L. *frui*, enjoy: see *fruit.*] Enjoyment, as of something attained or realized: as, "an object of desire placed out of the possibility of *fruition*" (Addison, in "Spectator," 256).

fruit-less (fröt′les), *a.* Without fruit; barren; hence, unproductive; vain.—**fruit′less-ly,** *adv.*—**fruit′less-ness,** *n.*

fruit-let (fröt′let), *n.* A small fruit.

fruit=sug-ar (fröt′shůg′ä̤r), *n.* In *chem.*, levulose.

fruit-y (frö′ti), *a.* Fruit-like, as in flavor: as, "The Madeira . . . is a trifle too *fruity* for my taste" (F. H. Smith's "Colonel Carter of Cartersville," iii.).

fru-men-ta-ceous (frö-men-tā′shius), *a.* [LL. *frumentaceus*, < L. *frumentum*, grain.] Of the nature of or resembling wheat or other grain.

fru-men-ty (frö′me̤n-ti), *n.* [OF. *frumentee*, < *frument*, < L. *frumentum*, grain.] Hulled wheat boiled in milk and seasoned with sugar, etc.

frump (frump), *v. t.* [Origin obscure.] To mock; flout; also, to vex. [Archaic or prov. Eng.]—**frump,** *n.* A flout (now prov.); ill humor (often in *pl.*: now prov.); also, an ill-natured, old-fashioned woman; a dowdy.—**frump′ish, frump′y,** *a.* Ill-natured; cross; also, dowdy.

frush† (frush), *v. t.* [OF. *fruissier* (F. *froisser*), < L. *frustum*, piece, bit.] To break to pieces; crush; batter. See Shakspere's "Troilus and Cressida," v. 6. 29.—**frush,** *a.* Brittle; also, not firm; soft. [North. Eng. and Sc.]

frus-trate (frus′trāt), *v. t.*; *-trated, -trating.* [L. *frustratus*, pp. of *frustrari, frustrare*, < *frustra*, in vain.] To disappoint or thwart (a person); also, to make (plans, efforts, etc.) of no avail; defeat; baffle; nullify.—**frus′trate,** *a.* Frustrated; hence, futile; vain. [Archaic.]—**frus-tra′tion** (-trā′sho̤n), *n.*

frus-tule (frus′tūl), *n.* [L. *frustulum*, dim. of *frustum*, piece, bit.] In *bot.*, the siliceous shell of a diatom.

frus-tum (frus′tum), *n.*; pl. *-tums* or *-ta* (-tä̤). [L., piece, bit.] A piece or portion; in *geom.*, the part of a solid left after cutting off a top portion by a plane parallel to the base; the part of a solid between two cutting planes.

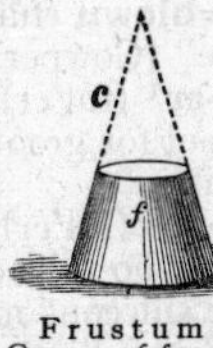

Frustum of a Cone.—*f*, frustum; *c*, part cut off.

fru-tes-cent (frö̤-tes′e̤nt), *a.* [Irreg. < L. *frutex*, shrub, bush: see *-escent.*] In *bot.*, shrub-like; shrubby.—**fru-tes′cence,** *n.*

fru-ti-cose (frö′ti-kōs), *a.* [L. *fruticosus*, < *frutex* (*frutic-*), shrub, bush.] In *bot.*, having the form of a shrub; shrub-like.

fry[1] (frī), *n.* [ME. *fry*: cf. Icel. *frjō, fræ*, Goth. *fraiw*, seed.] Offspring, as of human beings†; also, the young of fishes, or of some other animals, as frogs; young or small fishes or other young creatures, as children, collectively, or, fig., lesser persons or minor things (chiefly in 'young fry,' 'small fry'); a swarm, crowd, or multitude of such.

fry[2] (frī), *v.*; *fried, frying.* [OF. F. *frire*, < L. *frigere*, roast, parch, fry.] **I.** *tr.* To cook in fat over a fire. **II.** *intr.* To undergo cooking in fat. Also fig.—**fry**[2], *n.*; pl. *fries* (frīz). A dish of something fried; also, any of various internal parts of animals, usually eaten fried.—**fry′er,** *n.* See *frier.*—**fry′ing=pan,** *n.* A shallow pan, commonly of iron, with a long handle, used for frying food.

fu (fö), *n.* [Chinese.] In China, a prefecture or department; also, the chief city of a department.

fu' (fö), *a.* Scotch form of *full*[1].

fub[1] (fub), *v. t.*; *fubbed, fubbing.* [Var. of *fob*[1].] To trick; also, to put (*off*) by a trick or pretense (see Shakspere's "2 Henry IV.," ii. 1. 37).

fub[2]†, **fubs**† (fub, fubz), *n.* [Prob. imit.] A small, chubby person.—**fub′sy,** *a.* Chubby; short and fat or thick. [Prov. or colloq., Eng.]

fuch-sia (fū′shiä̤ or fök′si-ä̤), *n.* [NL.; from Leonhard *Fuchs* (1501–66), German botanist.] Any plant of the onagraceous genus *Fuchsia*, which includes many varieties cultivated for their handsome drooping flowers.

fuch-sin, fuch-sine (fök′sin), *n.* [From G. *Fuchs* (lit. 'fox'), tr. F. *Renard*, name of the introducers of the dye.] A coal-tar dyestuff occurring as a greenish solid which forms deep-red solutions; magenta.

fu-coid (fū′koid). **I.** *a.* Resembling, or allied to, seaweeds of the genus *Fucus* (see *fucus*); of sandstone, etc., containing seaweed-like forms or markings. **II.** *n.* A fucoid seaweed.

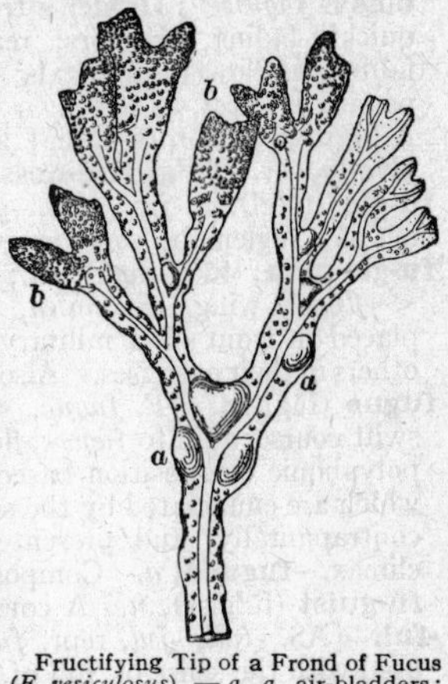

Fructifying Tip of a Frond of Fucus (*F. vesiculosus*).—*a, a*, air-bladders; *b, b*, conceptacles.

fu-cus (fū′kus), *n.*; pl. *fuci* (-sī). [L., rock lichen.] Any seaweed of the genus *Fucus*, which comprises leathery olive-brown algæ with branching fronds and often air-bladders; rockweed.

fud-dle (fud′l), *v.*; *-dled, -dling.* [Origin obscure.] **I.** *tr.* To make stupid with drink; intoxicate; also, to muddle or confuse. **II.** *intr.* To tipple.—**fud′dler,** *n.* A tippler.—**fud′dling=cup,** *n.* An old English drinking-vessel, as of earthenware, formed of a group of cups with communicating interiors, so that to empty one it was necessary to empty all.

Fuddling-cup.

fudge (fuj), *v. t.*; *fudged, fudging.* [Origin obscure: cf. *fadge.*] To adjust or perform clumsily, perfunctorily, or dishonestly; make or get (*up*).—**fudge,** *n.* A made-up story; also, nonsense or bosh (sometimes used as a contemptuous interjection: as, "Mr. Burchell . . . at the conclusion of every sentence would cry out *fudge*, an expression which displeased us all," Goldsmith's "Vicar of Wakefield," xi.); also, a mass of printed matter (often in color), as a piece of late news, inserted in a page of a newspaper; a machine or attachment for printing masses of this kind; also, a kind of candy (often home-made) composed of sugar, butter, milk, and chocolate, or maple sugar, sometimes nuts, etc., boiled together, poured into a shallow pan, and when cool cut into small blocks.

fu-el (fū′e̤l), *n.* [OF. *fouaille*, < ML. *focalia*, pl. of *focale*, fuel, < L. *focus*, hearth, fireplace.] Combustible matter used to maintain fire, as coal, wood, oil, etc.; fig., means of sustaining or increasing passion, ardor, etc. (as, "Each party is always laying up *fuel* for dissension": Steele, in "Tatler," 150).—**fu′el,** *v. t.*; *-eled* or *-elled, -eling* or *-elling.* To supply with fuel.—**fu′el=oil,** *n.* An oil used for fuel, esp. one used as a substitute for coal, as crude petroleum.

fuerst (fürst), *n.* See *fürst.*

fuff (fuf), *v. i.* or *t.* [Imit.] To puff; whiff. [Sc. and north. Eng.]—**fuff,** *n.* A puff; a whiff; a sputter; an angry fume or huff. [Sc. and north. Eng.]

fu-ga-cious (fṳ̄-gā′shus), *a.* [L. *fugax* (*fugac-*), < *fugere*, flee: see *fugitive.*] Tending to flee; fleeting; transitory; in *bot.*, falling or fading early.—**fu-ga′cious-ly,** *adv.*—**fu-ga′cious-ness, fu-ga′ci-ty** (-gas′i-ti), *n.*

fu-gal (fū′ga̤l), *a.* Pertaining to or in the style of a fugue.—**fu′gal-ly,** *adv.*

-fuge. [F. *-fuge*, < L. *fugare*, put to flight.] A termination of adjectives meaning 'driving away (something),' and of nouns denoting some agent that drives away, dispels, or expels something (esp. disease or disease-producing organisms), as in *febrifuge, tænifuge, vermifuge.*

fu-gi-tive (fū′ji-tiv). [OF. F. *fugitif*, < L. *fugitivus*, < *fugere* = Gr. φεύγειν, flee: see *bow*[1].] **I.** *a.* Fleeing, or tending to flee (as, "A *fugitive* and gracious light he seeks, Shy to illumine": M. Arnold's "Thyrsis"); having taken flight, or runaway (as, a *fugitive* slave); also, wandering, roving, or vagabond; fig., fleeting or transitory (as, "In youth alone, unhappy mortals live; But, ah! the mighty bliss is *fugitive*": Dryden's tr. Virgil's "Georgics," iii. 109); quickly fading, as colors; readily escaping, as odors; soon falling, as flowers or petals; also, dealing with subjects of passing interest, as writings; ephemeral; occasional. **II.** *n.* A fugitive person or thing; a runaway; a refugee.—**fu′gi-tive-ly,** *adv.*—**fu′gi-tive-ness,** *n.*

fu-gle (fū′gl), *v. i.*; *-gled, -gling.* [From *fugleman.*] To act as a fugleman; serve as guide or director; make signals.

fu-gle-man (fū′gl-mạn), *n.*; pl. *-men.* [G. *flügelmann,* < *flügel,* wing, + *mann,* man.] A well-drilled soldier placed in front of a military company as a model for the others in their exercises. Also fig.

fugue (fūg), *n.* [F. *fugue,* < It. *fuga,* < L. *fuga,* flight, swift course, akin to *fugere,* flee: see *fugitive.*] In *music,* a polyphonic composition based on one, two, or more themes, which are enunciated by the several parts in turn, developed contrapuntally, and presented finally in a conclusion or climax.—**fugued,** *a.* Composed in the style of a fugue.—**fu-guist** (fū′gist), *n.* A composer or performer of fugues.

-ful. [AS. *-full, -ful,* repr. *full, ful,* E. *full*[1], *a.*] A suffix used with the sense of 'full of,' 'fraught with,' 'characterized by,' or with less definite signification, to form adjectives, as *artful, careful, grateful, masterful, mournful, thankful,* or with the sense of 'enough to fill,' to form nouns, as *handful, roomful, spoonful.*

ful-crum (ful′krum), *n.*; pl. *-crums* or *-cra* (-krạ̈). [L., bedpost, < *fulcire,* prop up.] A prop; in *mech.,* the support, or point of rest, on which a lever turns in moving a body.—**ful′crum,** *v. t.*; *-crumed, -cruming.* To furnish with a fulcrum; place on something as a fulcrum; also, to establish as a fulcrum.

F, Fulcrum; L, Lever.

ful-fil, ful-fill (fu̇l-fil′), *v. t.*; *-filled, -filling.* [AS. *fullfyllan,* < *full,* E. *full*[1], *a.,* + *fyllan,* E. *fill*[2], *v.*] To fill full or make full (archaic: as, "I hear it now, that tender strain *Fulfilled* with all of sorrow save its pain," R. W. Gilder's "Music and Words"); make complete, or supply what is lacking in (archaic); hence, to carry out, or bring to consummation, as a prophecy, promise, etc.; also, to perform, execute, or do, as duty; obey or follow, as commands; also, to satisfy (requirements, etc.); answer (a purpose); also, to bring to an end, finish, or complete, as a period of time or a course of procedure (archaic).—**ful-fil′ler,** *n.*—**ful-fil′ment,** *n.*

ful-gent (ful′jẹnt), *a.* [L. *fulgens* (*fulgent-*), ppr. of *fulgere,* flash, shine.] Shining brightly; resplendent: as, "Then issued Vesper from the *fulgent* west" (Wordsworth's "Gipsies").—**ful′gent-ly,** *adv.*

ful-gid (ful′jid), *a.* [L. *fulgidus,* < *fulgere,* flash, shine.] Glittering; gleaming: as, "Through the brown shade the *fulgid* weapons shined" (Pope's tr. Homer's "Iliad," x.).

ful-gor (ful′gọr), *n.* [L. *fulgor,* < *fulgere,* flash, shine.] Dazzling brightness; splendor.—**ful′gor-ous,** *a.*

ful-gu-ral (ful′gū̦-rạl), *a.* [L. *fulguralis,* < *fulgur,* lightning, < *fulgere,* flash, shine.] Of or pertaining to lightning.

ful-gu-rant (ful′gū̦-rạnt), *a.* Fulgurating; flashing like lightning: as, "that erect form, flashing brow, *fulgurant* eye" (Browning's "Ring and the Book," vi.).

ful-gu-rate (ful′gū̦-rāt), *v. i.*; *-rated, -rating.* [L. *fulguratus,* pp. of *fulgurare,* < *fulgur,* lightning: see *fulgural.*] To flash or dart like lightning.—**ful-gu-ra′tion** (-rā′shọn), *n.*

ful-gu-rite (ful′gū̦-rīt), *n.* [L. *fulgur,* lightning.] A tube formed in sand or rock by lightning; also, rocky matter fused by lightning; also, an explosive of the nitroglycerin class, used for blasting.

ful-gu-rous (ful′gū̦-rus), *a.* [L. *fulgur,* lightning: see *fulgural.*] Flashing with or like lightning; lightning-like.

ful-ham (fu̇l′ạm), *n.* See *fullam.*

fu-lig-i-nous (fū̦-lij′i-nus), *a.* [LL. *fuliginosus,* < L. *fuligo,* soot.] Sooty; soot-like; smoky; dusky.—**fu-lig-i-nos′i-ty** (-nos′i-ti), *n.*—**fu-lig′i-nous-ly,** *adv.*

full[1] (fu̇l), *a.* [AS. *full, ful,* = D. *vol* = G. *voll* = Icel. *fullr* = Goth. *fulls,* full; akin to L. *plenus,* Gr. πλήρης, full, L. *plere,* Gr. πιμπλάναι, Skt. *pur-,* fill: see *plus* and *poly-.*] Containing all that can be held (*of*); containing a plentiful amount or number (*of*); filled (with contents understood: as, a *full* cup; *full* sails; a *full* stomach; a *full* heart); having had one's fill, as of food; drunk (slang); sated (now with *up,* as slang); filled with the thought or subject (*of*); also, filled or rounded out, as in form; of garments, draperies, etc., wide, ample, or having ample folds; also, of the maximum size, amount, extent, volume, etc. (as, a *full* mile; *full* pay; *full* growth; the *full* moon); complete; entire; perfect; unqualified; also, ample in detail; copious; also, of dress, suited for occasions of the utmost state; esp., of the style customary for formal evening wear; also, of wines, having considerable body; not thin.—**full blood,** pure extraction (as, an Indian of *full blood*); also, whole blood, or relationship through both parents (as, brothers of *full blood,* male children of the same father and the same mother).—**full hand** or **full house,** in *poker,* a hand consisting of three of a kind and a pair, as three queens and two tens.—**full stop,** in *punctuation,* a period.—**full tilt.** See under *tilt*[2], *n.*—**in full blast,** in full operation; at full force.—**in full cry,** in full pursuit, as dogs in the chase.—**full**[1], *n.* Full measure, or utmost extent; the height, as of a season; of the moon, the stage of complete illumination.—**full**[1], *adv.* [AS. *full.*] Fully, completely, or entirely; also, exactly or directly (as, "*Full* in the middle way there stood a lake": Pope's "Dunciad," ii. 69); also, very (now chiefly poetic: as, "*Full* many a gem of purest ray serene, The dark unfathom'd caves of ocean bear," Gray's "Elegy," xiv.).—**full**[1], *v. t.* or *i.* To make or become full.

full[2] (fu̇l), *v.* [OF. F. *fouler,* < ML. *fullare,* full (cloth), < L. *fullo(n-),* a fuller: cf. *fuller*[2].] **I.** *tr.* To cleanse and thicken (cloth, etc.) by special processes in manufacture. **II.** *intr.* Of cloth, etc., to become compacted or felted.

ful-lam, ful-ham (fu̇l′ạm), *n.* [Earlier *fullam;* origin uncertain.] A loaded die. See Shakspere's "Merry Wives of Windsor," i. 3. 94. [Slang.]

full=back (fu̇l′bak), *n.* In *football,* etc., the back furthest behind the forward line. See *back*[2], *n.*

full=blood-ed (fu̇l′blud′ed), *a.* Having a full supply of blood; also, of pure extraction; thoroughbred.

full=blown (fu̇l′blōn′), *a.* In full bloom: as, "the *full-blown* rose" (Cowper's "Task," i. 36). Also fig.

full-er[1] (fu̇l′ėr), *n.* [Appar. < *full*[1], *v.*] In blacksmithing, a tool for grooving and spreading iron; also, a groove made by it.

full-er[2] (fu̇l′ėr), *n.* [AS. *fullere,* < L. *fullo(n-)*: see *full*[2].] One who fulls cloth.—**fullers' earth,** a mixture of clay and fine siliceous material, used for removing grease from cloth, etc., in fulling.

full=face (fu̇l′fās), *n.* In *printing,* bold-face.—**full′=faced,** *a.* Having a plump or round face; also, facing squarely toward the spectator or in a given direction; in *printing,* of type, bold-faced.

full=fledged (fu̇l′flejd′), *a.* Fully developed; fully organized; of full rank or standing (as, a *full-fledged* professor).

full=grown (fu̇l′grōn′), *a.* Fully grown; mature.

full=heart-ed (fu̇l′här′ted), *a.* Full of courage and confidence, as a person; carried on zealously, as a work; also, full of emotion.

full-ness, ful-ness (fu̇l′nes), *n.* The state of being full.—**the fullness of time,** the proper or destined time: as, "When *the fulness of the time* was come, God sent forth his Son" (Gal. iv. 4).—**ful′ly,** *adv.* In a full manner; completely; entirely; wholly; exactly; quite.

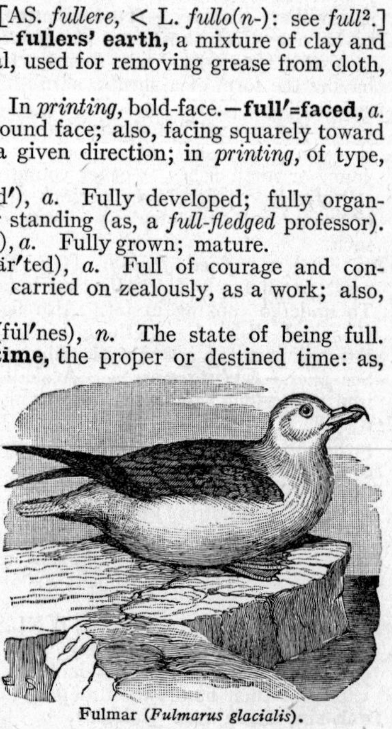

Fulmar (*Fulmarus glacialis*).

ful-mar (fu̇l′mär), *n.* [Perhaps < Icel. *fūll,* foul (with allusion to odor), + *mār,* gull.] Any of certain oceanic birds of the petrel family, esp. *Fulmarus glacialis,* a gull-like arctic species.

ful-mi-nant (ful′mi-nạnt), *a.* Fulminating.

ful-mi-nate (ful′mi-nāt), *v.*; *-nated, -nating.* [L. *fulminatus*, pp. of *fulminare*, < *fulmen* (*fulmin-*), lightning, thunderbolt, < *fulgere*, flash, shine.] **I.** *intr.* To lighten and thunder; also, to explode with a loud noise; detonate; also, to issue denunciations or the like. **II.** *tr.* To cause to explode; also, to send forth (denunciations, etc.); also, to denounce vehemently.—**ful′mi-nate,** *n.* A salt of fulminic acid (as, mercuric *fulminate*, an explosive used in percussion-caps); also, an explosive powder.—**ful-mi-na′tion** (-nā′shọn), *n.* [L. *fulminatio*(*n-*).] The act of fulminating; also, that which is fulminated, or thundered forth; a violent denunciation or censure.—**ful′mi-na-to-ry** (-nạ-tō-ri), *a.* Fulminating; denunciatory.

ful-mine (ful′min), *v. i.* or *t.*; *-mined, -mining.* [L. *fulminare*: see *fulminate.*] To fulminate; thunder: as, "Orators . . . whose resistless eloquence . . . Shook the arsenal, and *fulmined* over Greece" (Milton's "Paradise Regained," iv. 270). [Archaic.]

ful-min-ic (ful-min′ik), *a.* [L. *fulmen* (*fulmin-*): see *fulminate.*] Pertaining to detonation.—**fulminic acid,** in *chem.*, an acid, CNOH, whose salts are extremely explosive.

ful-mi-nous (ful′mi-nus), *a.* [L. *fulmen* (*fulmin-*): see *fulminate.*] Of or like lightning or a thunderbolt.

ful-ness (fůl′nes), *n.* See *fullness.*

ful-some (fůl′sum or ful′-), *a.* [ME. *fulsum*; < *full*[1] + *-some*[1].] Full†; also, plump†; also, surfeiting† or cloying†; also, disgusting†; esp., offensive to good taste, esp. as being excessive; gross, as flattery; also, lustful†; obscene†.—**ful′some-ly,** *adv.*—**ful′some-ness,** *n.*

ful-vous (ful′vus), *a.* [L. *fulvus.*] Reddish-yellow; tawny.

fu-ma-role (fū′mạ-rōl), *n.* [It. *fumaruola*, < L. *fumus*, smoke, E. *fume, n.*] A hole, as in a volcano, from which vapor issues.

fu-ma-to-ri-um (fū-mạ-tō′ri-um), *n.*; pl. *-ria* (-ri-ạ̈). [NL., < L. *fumare* (pp. *fumatus*), E. *fume, v.*] A structure in which plants are fumigated, to destroy insects.—**fu′ma-to-ry** (-tọ-ri). **I.** *a.* Of or pertaining to smoking. **II.** *n.*; pl. *-ries* (-riz). A place set apart for smoking or fumigating.

fum-ble (fum′bl), *v.*; *-bled, -bling.* [= D. *fommelen* = LG. *fummeln* = Sw. *fumla.*] **I.** *intr.* To feel or grope about clumsily; search awkwardly; also, to stammer; mumble. **II.** *tr.* To handle clumsily; catch or stop (a ball) in a clumsy or ineffectual way; also, to utter in a hesitating or indistinct manner.—**fum′ble,** *n.* A fumbling.—**fum′bler,** *n.*—**fum′bling-ly,** *adv.*

fume (fūm), *n.* [OF. *fum*, < L. *fumus*, smoke, steam, fume.] Smoke (archaic in the general sense); now, esp., a portion or cloud of smoke, esp. odorous smoke (as of incense or tobacco), or smoke of stifling or otherwise powerful (and often useful) properties (now commonly in *pl.*: cf. *fumigate*); also, any smoke-like or vaporous exhalation from matter or substances (often in *pl.*); sometimes, an odorous exhalation, as from flowers; fig., something comparable to an exhalation, as in being unsubstantial or evanescent (as, "Love is a smoke raised with the *fume* of sighs": Shakspere's "Romeo and Juliet," i. 1. 196); also, an irritable or angry mood (as, to be in a *fume*).—**fume,** *v.*; *fumed, fuming.* [OF. F. *fumer*, < L. *fumare*, < *fumus.*] **I.** *intr.* To emit fumes; also, to rise, or pass off, as fumes; fig., to show irritation or anger. **II.** *tr.* To treat with fumes; fumigate; also, to burn incense before; also, to send forth as fumes.—**fumed,** *p. a.* Darkened or colored by exposure to ammonia fumes, as oak and other wood.

fu-mi-gate (fū′mi-gāt), *v. t.*; *-gated, -gating.* [L. *fumigatus*, pp. of *fumigare*, < *fumus*, smoke, + *agere*, drive.] To expose to smoke or fumes, as in coloring wood or in disinfecting; also, to perfume.—**fu-mi-ga′tion** (-gā′shọn), *n.* The act of fumigating, as in disinfecting; the generation of odorous smoke or fumes, as in magic rites; also, the smoke or fumes generated in fumigating; also, a preparation used for fumigating.—**fu′mi-ga-tor,** *n.* One who or that which fumigates; a brazier or pan in which something is burned for the purpose of fumigating or perfuming rooms, etc.—**fu′mi-ga-to-ry** (-gạ-tọ-ri). **I.** *a.* Serving to fumigate. **II.** *n.*; pl. *-ries* (-riz). A room or apparatus for fumigating.

fum-ing (fū′ming), *p. a.* That fumes.—**fum′ing-ly,** *adv.*

fu-mi-to-ry (fū′mi-tọ-ri), *n.*; pl. *-ries* (-riz). [OF. F. *fumeterre*, < ML. *fumus terræ*, 'smoke of the earth.'] Any plant of the genus *Fumaria*, of the poppy family, esp. *F. officinalis*, a delicate herb with finely dissected leaves and racemes of small purplish flowers.

fu-mous (fū′mus), *a.* [L. *fumosus.*] Fumy; smoky; in *bot.*, smoke-colored.

fum-y (fū′mi), *a.* Full of fumes; fuming; fume-like.

fun (fun), *n.* [Prob. < ME. *fonnen*, be foolish: see *fond.*] Mirthful sport or diversion; merry amusement; drollery.—**figure of fun.** See *figure, n.*—**to make fun of,** to ridicule.—**fun,** *v. i.*; *funned, funning.* To make fun; joke. [Colloq.]

fu-nam-bu-list (fụ-nam′bụ-list), *n.* [L. *funambulus*, < *funis*, rope, + *ambulare*, walk.] One who performs feats of walking, dancing, etc., on a stretched rope.—**fu-nam′bu-lism,** *n.*

func-tion (fungk′shọn), *n.* [F. *function* (now *fonction*), < L. *functio*(*n-*), < *fungi*, perform.] The act of performing†; also, action† or behavior†; also, the kind of action or activity proper to a person or thing; office; duty; also, a religious ceremony; any ceremonious public or social gathering or occasion (as, "He . . . set out to attend the last gathering of the season at Valleys House, a *function* . . . almost perfectly political": Galsworthy's "Patrician," ii. 6); in *math.*, a quantity having a definite value when any special value is given to another quantity to which it is related.—**func′tion,** *v. i.* To perform a function, or one's or its functions; act; serve; operate.—**func′tion-al,** *a.* Of or pertaining to a function or functions; in *biol.*, having the function or functions usual to the part or organ (as, the *functional* wings of an insect, those used for flying).—**functional disease,** a disease in which there is a morbid change in the function of an organ, but no structural alteration in the tissues involved: opposed to *organic disease.*—**func′tion-al-ly,** *adv.*—**func′tion-a-ry** (-ạ-ri), *n.*; pl. *-ries* (-riz). One invested with a function or office; an official.—**func′tion-ate** (-āt), *v. i.*; *-ated, -ating.* To fulfil a function; act; operate; function.—**func′tion-less,** *a.* Having no function.

fund (fund), *n.* [= F. *fond*, bottom, foundation, *fonds*, land, capital, stock, fund, < L. *fundus*, bottom, piece of land, estate.] Bottom†; also, foundation†; basis†; also, a store or stock of something, now often of something immaterial (as, a *fund* of knowledge or experience); esp., a stock of money or pecuniary resources, as for some purpose; *pl.*, money in hand; pecuniary resources; also, *pl.*, with *the*, the stock of a national debt, considered as a form of investment (as in Great Britain: as, to have money in *the funds*).—**fund,** *v. t.* To put into a fund or store; store up; also, to invest, as in the funds; also, to provide a fund to pay the interest or principal of (debt); hence, to convert (general outstanding debts) into a more or less permanent debt or loan, represented by interest-bearing bonds; also, to provide funds for (a work, etc.); finance.—**fund′a-ble,** *a.* That may be funded.

fun-da-ment (fun′dạ-mẹnt), *n.* [OF. F. *fondement*, < L. *fundamentum*, < *fundare*, E. *found*[3].] The foundation, as of a building†; also, the buttocks; specif., the anus.—**fun-da-men′tal** (-men′tạl), *a.* Of or pertaining to the foundation or basis; serving as, or being a component part of, a foundation or basis; basic; underlying; elementary; original; essential.—**fundamental unit,** in *physics*, one of the units (esp. those of mass, length, and time) taken as a basis for a system of units.—**fun-da-men′tal,** *n.* A leading or primary principle, rule, law, or the like, which serves as the groundwork of a system; an essential part.—**fun-da-men′tal-ism,** *n.* The principle of accepting the fundamental teachings of Christianity as beyond question or not subject to criticism. See *modernism.*—**fun-da-men′tal-ist,** *n.* and *a.*—**fun″da-men-tal′i-ty** (-tal′i-ti), *n.* The quality of being fundamental.—**fun-da-men′tal-ly,** *adv.*

fun-dus (fun′dus), *n.* [L.: see *fund.*] The bottom or foundation; in *anat.*, the base of an organ, or the part opposite to or remote from an aperture.

fu-ner-al (fū′nẹ-rạl), *a.* [ML. *funeralis* (as n., neut. pl., *funeralia*), < L. *funus* (*funer-*), funeral.] Of or pertaining to the ceremonial burial (or, sometimes, cremation) of the dead; used, spoken, etc., on such an occasion (as, *funeral* rites; a *funeral* sermon).—**funeral pile,** a pile of wood or other combustible material upon which a dead body is burned.—**fu'ner-al,** *n.* The ceremonies connected with the disposition of the body of a dead person; obsequies; also, a funeral procession (as, "A *funeral*, with plumes and lights And music, went to Camelot": Tennyson's "Lady of Shalott," ii.).

fu-ner-a-ry (fū'ne-rā-ri), *a.* [LL. *funerarius*, < L. *funus* (*funer-*), funeral.] Of or pertaining to a funeral or burial: as, a *funerary* urn.

fu-ne-re-al (fū-nē'rē-al), *a.* [L. *funereus*, < *funus* (*funer-*), funeral.] Of or pertaining to a funeral (as, "the sad *funereal* feast": Pope's tr. Homer's "Odyssey," iv.); appropriate to or suggestive of a funeral (as, *funereal* garb; *funereal* gloom); hence, mournful; gloomy; dismal.—**fu-ne're-al-ly,** *adv.*

fu-nest (fū-nest'), *a.* [L. *funestus*, < *funus*, funeral, also death, murder, destruction.] Causing or portending death; deadly; fatal; dire. [Now rare.]

fun-gal (fung'gal), *a.* Of, pertaining to, or of the nature of a fungus; consisting of fungi.

fun-gi (fun'jī), *n.* Plural of *fungus*.

fungi-. Form of L. *fungus*, mushroom, fungus, used in combination.

fun-gi-ble (fun'ji-bl). [ML. *fungibilis*, < L. *fungi*, perform, discharge.] In *law*: **I.** *a.* Of such a nature that one instance or portion may be replaced by another in respect of function, office, or use. **II.** *n.* A fungible thing, as money or grain.

fun-gi-cide (fun'ji-sīd), *n.* [See *fungi-* and *-cide*.] An agent for destroying fungi.—**fun'gi-ci-dal** (-sī-dal), *a.*

fun-gi-form (fun'ji-fôrm), *a.* [See *fungi-* and *-form*.] Having the form of a fungus or mushroom.

fun-giv-o-rous (fun-jiv'ō-rus), *a.* [See *fungi-* and *-vorous*.] Feeding on fungi, as certain insects.

fun-goid (fung'goid), *a.* [See *-oid*.] Resembling a fungus; of the nature of a fungus; in *pathol.*, characterized by spongy morbid growths, as certain diseases.

fun-gous (fung'gus), *a.* [L. *fungosus*, < *fungus*, fungus.] Of or pertaining to fungi; of the nature of or resembling a fungus; fig., springing up suddenly like a mushroom, but not enduring; in *pathol.*, fungoid.—**fun-gos'i-ty** (-gos'i-ti), *n.*

fun-gus (fung'gus), *n.*; pl. *fungi* (-jī) or *funguses*. [L., mushroom, fungus.] Any of the *Fungi*, a group of thallophytes including the mushrooms, molds, mildews, smuts, etc., characterized chiefly by absence of chlorophyl and by subsisting upon dead or living organic matter; in *pathol.*, a spongy morbid growth, as proud flesh formed in a wound.—**fun'gus=bee"tle,** *n.* Any of various beetles that feed on fungi, esp. beetles of the family *Endomychidæ*, as *Endomychus biguttatus* of North America.

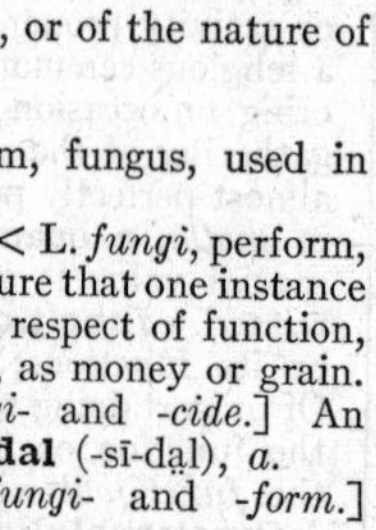

Fungus-beetle (*Endomychus biguttatus*). (Line shows natural size.)

fu-ni-cle (fū'ni-kl), *n.* [L. *funiculus*, dim. of *funis*, rope.] A small cord, or cord-like part or process; in *bot.*, the stalk of an ovule or seed.—**fu-nic-u-lar** (fū-nik'ū-lār), *a.* Of, pertaining to, or of the nature of a funicle or funiculus; also, of or pertaining to a rope or cord, or its tension; worked by a rope or the like (as, a *funicular* railway, one operated by a moving cable; a cable-railroad).—**fu-nic'u-lus** (-lus), *n.*; pl. *-li* (-lī). [L.] In bot., a funicle; in *anat.*, the umbilical cord; also, one of the small bundles of fibers that make up the larger nerves.

Funicle. — Pod showing funicles, *a, a, a.*

funk[1] (fungk), *v.* [Cf. OF. *funkier*, *fungier*, emit smoke, < L. *fumigare*: see *fumigate*.] **I.** *tr.* To blow smoke upon; annoy with smoke; also, to smoke (a pipe, etc.). **II.** *intr.* To smoke: as, "But there my triumph's straw-fire flared and *funked*" (Browning's "Fra Lippo Lippi").—**funk**[1], *n.* A strong and offensive smell, esp. of smoke.

funk[2] (fungk), *v.* [Origin uncertain.] **I.** *intr.* To shrink or quail in fear. [Colloq.] **II.** *tr.* To shrink from; try to shirk; also, to be afraid of; also, to frighten. [Colloq.]—**funk**[2], *n.* Cowering fear; a state of fright or terror (as, to be in a *funk*, or, more emphatically, a blue *funk*); also, a coward. [Colloq.]—**funk'=hole,** *n.* In soldiers' use, a rough shelter dug in the ground for protection against the enemy's fire; a dugout; hence, a safe situation for one shirking military duty. [Colloq.]—**funk'y,** *a.* Shrinking in fear; timid. [Colloq.]

fun-nel (fun'el), *n.* [ME. *funell*, prob., through OF., < LL. *fundibulum*, funnel, < L. *fundere*, pour.] A cone-shaped utensil with a tube at the apex, for conducting liquids, etc., through a small opening, as into a bottle; also, a flue, tube, or shaft, as for ventilation; a smoke-stack, esp. of a steamship or a locomotive.—**fun'neled, fun'nelled,** *a.* Having a funnel or funnels (as, "The red-*funnelled* tug has gone": Masefield's "Valediction"); also, funnel-shaped.—**fun'nel-form,** *a.* Having the form or shape of a funnel.—**fun'nel=shaped,** *a.* Shaped like a funnel; of a corolla or a flower, having the form of a tube enlarging gradually upward and expanding widely at the summit.

Funnel-shaped Corolla.

fun-ny (fun'i), *a.*; compar. *funnier*, superl. *funniest*. Affording fun; amusing; comical; also, curious, strange, or queer (colloq.).—**fun'ni-ly,** *adv.*—**fun'ni-ness,** *n.*—**fun'ny=bone,** *n.* The part of the elbow where the ulnar nerve passes by the internal condyle of the humerus, which when struck causes a peculiar, tingling sensation in the arm and hand; the crazy-bone.

fur (fėr), *v. t.*; *furred*, *furring*. [OF. *forrer*, *furrer* (F. *fourrer*), line, face, orig. encase, < *forre*, *fuerre*, case, sheath; from Teut.] To line, face, or trim (a garment, etc.) with fur; clothe (a person) with fur; also, to coat with foul or deposited matter, as the tongue or the inside of a boiler; in *building*, to apply furring to.—**fur,** *n.* [Appar. < *fur*, *v.*: cf. OF. *forreure*, fur lining or trimming, F. *fourrure*, fur.] The skin of certain animals (as the sable, ermine, beaver, etc.), covered with a fine, soft, thick hairy coating, used for lining or trimming garments or for entire garments; such skins as a material; an article of apparel made of or with this material (usually in *pl.*); the hairy coating on such a skin; also, fur-bearing animals collectively; also, any of a class of heraldic tinctures representing tufts upon a plain ground, or patches of different colors supposed to be sewed together; also, any coating resembling or suggesting fur, as one of morbid matter on the tongue.

fur-be-low (fėr'bē-lō), *n.* [Var. of *falbala*.] Orig., a pleated or gathered trimming on a woman's gown or the like; a flounce; hence, any bit of elaborate trimming or showy finery, esp. in women's dress.—**fur'be-low,** *v. t.* To ornament with or as with furbelows.

fur-bish (fėr'bish), *v. t.* [OF. *forbir* (*forbiss-*) (F. *fourbir*), polish, clean; from Teut.] To rub or scour (armor, weapons, etc.) to brightness; polish; burnish; hence, in general, to restore to freshness of appearance or condition (often with *up*); renovate; revive; brush (*up*).—**fur'bish-er,** *n.*—**fur'bish-ment,** *n.*

fur-cate (fėr'kāt), *v. i.*; *-cated*, *-cating*. [L. *furca*, fork.] To form a fork; divide into branches.—**fur'cate,** *a.* Forked.—**fur-ca'tion** (-kā'shon), *n.* A forking or branching; also, a branch.

fur-cu-la (fėr'kū-lą), *n.*; pl. *-læ* (-lē). [L., dim. of *furca*, fork.] The forked clavicular bone of a bird; the wish-bone. Also **fur'cu-lum** (-lum); pl. *-la* (-lą).

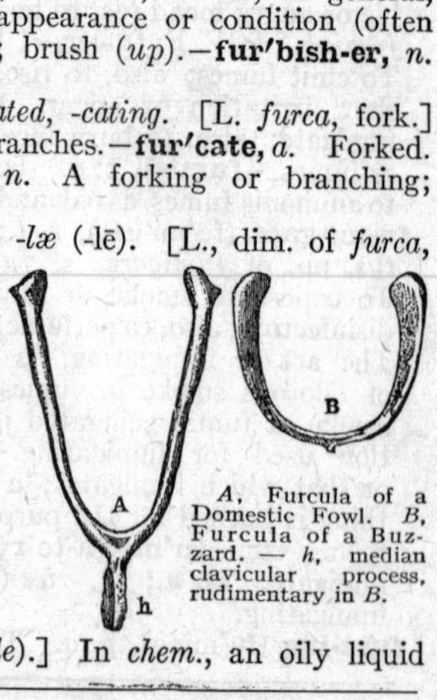

A, Furcula of a Domestic Fowl. *B*, Furcula of a Buzzard. — *h*, median clavicular process, rudimentary in *B*.

fur-fur (fėr'fėr), *n.*; pl. *furfures* (-ēz). [L., bran, scurf.] Dandruff; scurf; *pl.*, scales or particles of scurf.—**fur-fu-ra'ceous** (-fū-rā'shius), *a.* [LL. *furfuraceus*.] Bran-like; scaly; scurfy.—**fur'fu-ral** (-ral), *n.* [L. *furfur*, bran, + E. *al*(*dehyde*).] In *chem.*, an oily liquid aldehyde, $C_5H_4O_2$, with an aromatic odor, obtained by distilling bran, sugar, wood, corncobs, etc., with dilute sulphuric acid, and used in the manufacture of dyes. Also **fur′fu-rol** (-rol or -rōl).

fu-ri-bund (fū′ri-bund), *a.* [L. *furibundus*, < *furere*, rage, rave.] Raging; furious.

fu-ri-ous (fū′ri-us), *a.* [OF. F. *furieux*, < L. *furiosus*, < *furia*, E. *fury*.] Full of fury, violent passion, or rage, as a person or animal, temper, action, speech, etc.; also, fiercely vehement or violent, as battle, onslaughts, blows, etc.; in general, intensely violent, as wind, storms, etc.; of unrestrained energy, speed, etc. (as, *furious* activity; a *furious* pace or gallop); sometimes, unrestrainedly boisterous (as, the fun grew fast and *furious*).—**fu′ri-ous-ly,** *adv.*—**fu′ri-ous-ness,** *n.*

furl (fėrl), *v. t.* [Prob. a contr. of obs. *furdel*, var. of obs. *fardel*, furl, < *fardel*, a bundle: see *fardel*.] To draw into a compact roll, as a sail against a spar or a flag against its staff; in general, to draw or fold into small compass (as, to *furl* an umbrella or a tent; the eagle *furls* its wings).

fur-la-na (för-lä′nä), *n.* [It.; from the *Furlanei* or Friuli district in Italy, north of the Adriatic Sea.] A lively Italian dance in sextuple rhythm, common esp. among Venetian gondoliers; also, a piece of music written for, or in the rhythm of, this dance.

fur-long (fėr′lông), *n.* [AS. *furlang*, < *furh*, furrow, + *lang*, long.] A measure of length equal to the eighth part of a mile (equivalent to 40 rods, 220 yards, or 201.17 meters).

fur-lough (fėr′lō), *n.* [D. *verlof*, leave, furlough: cf. G. *verlaub*, leave, permission.] Leave of absence, esp. to a soldier.—**fur′lough,** *v. t.* To grant a furlough to.

fur-men-ty, fur-me-ty (fėr′mẹn-ti, -mẹ-ti), *n.* Same as *frumenty*.

fur-nace (fėr′nās), *n.* [OF. *fornais*, *fornaise* (F. *fournaise*), < L. *fornax* (*fornac-*), < *fornus*, *furnus*, oven.] A structure or apparatus in which to generate and maintain heat, as for melting ores, baking pottery, heating houses, etc.; fig., a place of severe trial (as, "the *furnace* of affliction": Isa. xlviii. 10); also, a place of burning heat.—**fur′nace,** *v. t.*; *-naced*, *-nacing*. To subject to the heat of a furnace; also, to emit like a furnace† (as, "He *furnaces* The thick sighs from him": Shakspere's "Cymbeline," i. 6. 66).

fur-nish (fėr′nish), *v. t.* [OF. *furnir* (*furniss-*) (F. *fournir*), accomplish, complete, supply, furnish; from Teut., and akin to E. *frame* and *from*.] To accomplish or perform, as an undertaking†; also, to provide or supply with something specified, usually something necessary, useful, appropriate, or desired (as, to *furnish* one with money, food, information, or an excuse; to *furnish* a boat with oars; to *furnish* a cane with a ferrule); also, to provide or supply with what is necessary or proper; now, esp., to fit up (a house, room, etc.) with necessary appliances, esp. furniture; formerly, to equip with dress, harness, trappings, etc., as a person or a horse†; fit out, as a ship†; also, to serve for supplying, fitting up, etc. (sometimes formerly with *forth*: as, "The funeral baked meats Did coldly *furnish* forth the marriage tables," Shakspere's "Hamlet," i. 2. 181); also, to provide or supply (something), as for use or consideration (as, to *furnish* money to one for a special purpose; to *furnish* heat for tenants; to *furnish* proof or an instance of something); give, afford, or yield.—**fur′nish-er,** *n.*—**fur′nish-ing,** *n.* The act of one who or that which furnishes; also, that with which anything is furnished; esp., *pl.*, fittings, appliances, articles of furniture, etc., for a house or room; accessories of dress (as, to deal in gentlemen's *furnishings*).—**fur′nish-ment,** *n.* The act of furnishing, or the state of being furnished; also, that which is furnished; *pl.*, supplies.

fur-ni-ture (fėr′ni-ṭūr), *n.* [F. *fourniture*, < *fournir*, furnish: see *furnish*.] The act of furnishing, or the state of being furnished†; also, that with which anything is furnished; equipment; outfit; harness, trappings, etc., of a horse or other animal; fittings, apparatus, or necessary accessories for something; specif., the movable articles, as tables, chairs, bedsteads, desks, cabinets, etc., required for use or ornament in a house, office, or the like; in *printing*, pieces of wood or metal, less than type-high, set in and about pages of type to fill them out and hold the type in place.

fu-ror (fū′rôr), *n.* [L., < *furere*, rage, rave.] Fury; rage; madness; also, inspired frenzy (as, the poetic *furor*); also, a prevailing mania or craze for something; a general outburst of enthusiasm or excitement.

fu-ro-re (fö-rō′rā), *n.* [It., < L. *furor*: see *furor*.] A furor, as of enthusiasm or excitement.

furred (fėrd), *p. a.* Made with or of fur, as garments; clad in fur or furs, as persons; covered with or having fur, as animals; also, coated with morbid matter, as the tongue; in *building*, furnished with furring.

fur-ri-er (fur′i-ėr), *n.* A dealer in or dresser of furs.—**fur′ri-er-y,** *n.*; pl. *-ies* (-iz). The business or trade of a furrier; also, furs in general.

fur-ring (fėr′ing), *n.* The act of lining, trimming, or clothing with fur, or the fur used; also, the formation of a coating of matter on something, as on the tongue or the inside of a boiler; in *building*, the nailing on of thin strips of board, as to furnish a level surface for lathing or plastering, to provide air-space between a wall and plastering, etc.; the strips thus nailed on.

fur-row (fur′ō), *n.* [AS. *furh* = D. *voor* = G. *furche*, furrow, = Icel. *for*, drain.] A narrow trench made in the ground, esp. by a plow; hence, a narrow, trench-like depression in any surface (as, the *furrows* between waves of the sea; the *furrows* of a wrinkled face); a long, narrow hollow; a groove or channel.—**fur′row,** *v.* **I.** *tr.* To make a furrow or furrows in; plow (land, etc.); cleave (the sea, etc.); make wrinkles in (the face, etc.); groove; also, to hollow out (a way) as by a furrow. **II.** *intr.* To make a furrow or furrows.—**fur′row-er,** *n.*—**fur′row-less,** *a.* Without furrows.—**fur′row-y,** *a.* Full of furrows; furrowed.

fur-ry (fėr′i), *a.* Consisting of or resembling fur; made of or with fur; wearing fur; covered with fur.

fur=seal (fėr′sēl), *n.* Any of various species of eared seal, as *Callorhinus ursinus* ('northern fur-seal'), which have under the outer hair a thick coat of fur, of great commercial value: distinguished from *hair-seal*.

Northern Fur-seal (*Callorhinus ursinus*).

fürst (fürst), *n.*; pl. *fürsten* (fürst′-en). [G.: see *first*.] In German use, a nobleman ranking below a herzog and above a graf: the word is commonly represented in English by *prince*.

fur-ther (fėr′ᴛʜėr), *adv. compar.* [AS. *furthor*, compar. of *fore*, before, E. *fore*.] At or to a more advanced point; to a greater extent; also, at or to a greater distance; farther; also, in addition; moreover.—**fur′ther,** *a. compar.* [AS. *furthra*.] More extended; additional; more; also, more distant or remote; farther.—**fur′ther,** *v. t.* [AS. *fyrthrian*.] To help forward (a work, undertaking, cause, etc.); promote; advance; forward; also, to help or assist (a person)†.—**fur′ther-ance,** *n.* The act of furthering; promotion; advancement.—**fur′ther-er,** *n.*—**fur′ther-more′,** *adv.* Moreover; besides; in addition.—**fur′ther-most,** *a. superl.* Most distant or remote.

fur-thest (fėr′ᴛʜest), *adv.* and *a.* [ME.; formed to correspond to *further*.] Superl. of *further*.

fur-tive (fėr′tiv), *a.* [L. *furtivus*, < *furtum*, theft, < *fur*, thief.] Obtained by theft, or stolen; also, thieving or thievish; more commonly, fig., taken, done, used, etc., by stealth, or in the manner of one wishing to escape observation (as, a *furtive* glance, movement, or effort); surreptitious; clandestine; secret; also, showing or suggesting a wish to escape observation (as, a *furtive* manner; "That *furtive* mien, that scowling eye . . . The traitor Judas," M. Arnold's "St. Brandan").—**fur′tive-ly,** *adv.*—**fur′tive-ness,** *n.*

fu-run-cle (fū′rung-kl), *n.* [L. *furunculus*, a petty thief, a boil, dim. of *fur*, thief.] A boil, or inflammatory sore.—**fu-run-cu-lar** (fū-rung′kū-lạr), *a.*—**fu-run-cu-lo′sis** (-lō′sis), *n.* [NL.] In *pathol.*, the morbid state characterized by the presence of furuncles.

fu-ry (fū′ri), *n.*; pl. *-ries* (-riz). [OF. F. *furie*, < L. *furia*, < *furere*, rage, rave.] Frenzied or unrestrainedly violent passion, esp. anger; rage; a fit of rage; also, frenzied or fierce vehemence or violence in action (as, the *fury* of battle); a course or period of fierce violence (as, the Spanish *Fury* at Antwerp in 1576, characterized by wholesale plundering, burning, and massacre by Spanish soldiery); in general, intense violence, as of wind, storms, waves, fire, disease, etc.; unrestrained energy, speed, etc. (as, to work with *fury*); also, the frenzy of one supernaturally possessed or inspired (as, "A sibyl . . . In her prophetic *fury* sew'd the work": Shakspere's "Othello," iii. 4. 72); [*cap.*] one of the avenging deities of classical mythology (in female form, with serpents twined in their hair), in later accounts three in number and called Alecto, Megæra, and Tisiphone; [*l. c.*] any avenging spirit, or minister of vengeance; also, a fierce and violent person, esp. a woman; a termagant; a virago.

furze (fėrz), *n.* [AS. *fyrs.*] Any plant of the fabaceous genus *Ulex*, esp. *U. europæus*, a low, much-branched, spiny shrub with yellow flowers, common on waste lands in Europe; gorse; whin.—**furz′y,** *a.* Of or pertaining to furze; overgrown with furze (as, "the *furzy* hills of Braid": Scott's "Marmion," iv. 23).

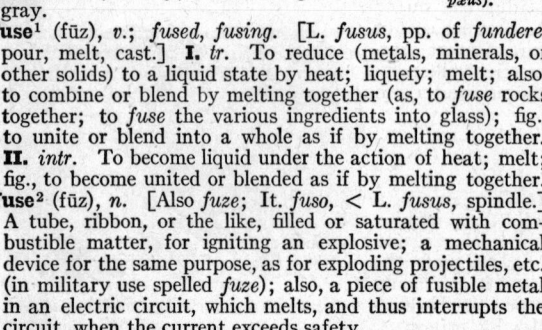

Furze (*Ulex europæus*).

fu-sain (fü-zaṅ), *n.* [F., spindle-tree, charcoal made from its wood, < L. *fusus*, spindle.] A fine charcoal used in drawing, made from the wood of the spindle-tree; also, a drawing made with it.

fus-ces-cent (fu-ses′ẹnt), *a.* Somewhat fuscous.

fus-cous (fus′kus), *a.* [L. *fuscus.*] Of a dark color; dusky; brown tinged with gray.

fuse[1] (fūz), *v.*; *fused, fusing.* [L. *fusus*, pp. of *fundere*, pour, melt, cast.] **I.** *tr.* To reduce (metals, minerals, or other solids) to a liquid state by heat; liquefy; melt; also, to combine or blend by melting together (as, to *fuse* rocks together; to *fuse* the various ingredients into glass); fig., to unite or blend into a whole as if by melting together. **II.** *intr.* To become liquid under the action of heat; melt; fig., to become united or blended as if by melting together.

fuse[2] (fūz), *n.* [Also *fuze*; It. *fuso*, < L. *fusus*, spindle.] A tube, ribbon, or the like, filled or saturated with combustible matter, for igniting an explosive; a mechanical device for the same purpose, as for exploding projectiles, etc. (in military use spelled *fuze*); also, a piece of fusible metal in an electric circuit, which melts, and thus interrupts the circuit, when the current exceeds safety.

fu-see (fụ-zē′), *n.* [F. *fusée*, < ML. *fusata*, spindleful, orig. pp. fem. of *fusare*, work with a spindle, < L. *fusus*, spindle.] A conical pulley or wheel; esp., a device in a clock or watch for counteracting the diminishing power of the uncoiling mainspring, consisting essentially of a spirally grooved conical pulley wound with a chain or cord whose other end winds round the barrel containing the mainspring; also, a fuse; a kind of match with a large head, for igniting by friction; a kind of firework, usually a tube filled with combustible matter, lighted on a railroad as a signal.

fu-se-lage (fū′zẹ-lạj), *n.* [F., < *fuselé*, spindle-shaped, < *fuseau*, < L. *fusus*, spindle.] The framework of the body of a flying-machine or aëroplane.

fu-sel=oil (fū′zẹl-oil′), *n.* [G. *fusel*, inferior liquor or spirits.] An acrid, oily, poisonous liquid consisting chiefly of amyl alcohol, often obtained as a by-product in the manufacture of spirits.

fu-si-ble (fū′zi-bl), *a.* [OF. F. *fusible*, < L. *fundere*: see *fuse*[1].] Capable of being fused or melted.—**fusible metal** or **alloy,** any of various alloys, as one of bismuth, lead, and tin, which melt at comparatively low temperatures, and hence can be used for making various safety devices, such as a plug which melts when a certain temperature is reached.—**fu-si-bil′i-ty** (-bil′i-ti), *n.*

fu-si-form (fū′si-fôrm), *a.* [L. *fusus*, spindle: see *-form.*] Spindle-shaped; rounded, and tapering from the middle toward each end, as some roots.

fu′sil[1], *a.* See *fusile.*

fu-sil[2] (fū′zil), *n.* [F. *fusil*, OF. *foisil*, steel for striking fire with flint, < ML. *focus*, fire, L. hearth.] A light flintlock musket.

fu-sile (fū′zil), *a.* [L. *fusilis*, < *fundere*: see *fuse*[1].] Capable of being fused; fusible; also, fused or molten (as, "*fusile* gold": Pope's tr. Homer's "Odyssey," vi.); also, made by fusing; founded or cast, as type. [Archaic.]

fu-si-lier (fū-zi-lēr′), *n.* [F.] Orig., a soldier armed with a fusil: a term still used (without reference to weapons) in the names of certain British regiments.

fu-sil-lade (fū-zi-lād′), *n.* [F., < *fusiller*, shoot, < *fusil*: see *fusil*[2].] A simultaneous or continuous discharge of firearms; a wholesale execution by this means; fig., a general discharge or outpouring of anything.—**fu-sil-lade′,** *v. t.*; *-laded, -lading.* To attack or shoot by a fusillade.

fu-sion (fū′zhọn), *n.* [L. *fusio(n-)*, < *fundere*: see *fuse*[1].] The act of fusing, or the state of being fused; a melting, or a melting together; the uniting or blending of various elements into a whole as if by melting together; also, something formed by or resulting from fusing; in *politics*, the coalition of parties or factions; the body or group resulting from such coalition.—**fu′sion-ism,** *n.* In *politics*, the principle, policy, or practice of fusion.—**fu′sion-ist,** *n.* In *politics*, one who advocates or supports a coalition of parties or factions.

fuss (fus), *n.* [Origin uncertain: cf. *fuzz.*] An excessive display of anxious activity (as, "The king and queen meant to treat this *fuss* about the national finance as a terrible bore": H. G. Wells's "Outline of History," xxxvii. § 8); needless or useless bustle; to-do; also, a disturbance or commotion; a 'rumpus'; also, a person given to fussing.—**fuss,** *v.* **I.** *intr.* To make a fuss; make much ado about trifles; busy one's self in an anxious way, with little effect; move restlessly (*about, in and out*, etc.); fidget; worry; also, to pay complimentary attentions to a girl (college slang, U. S.). **II.** *tr.* To put into a fuss; disturb with trifles; bother; worry; also, to pay complimentary attentions to (college slang, U. S.).—**fuss′=budg″et,** *n.* A fussy or fidgety person. [Colloq.]—**fuss′er,** *n.*—**fuss′y,** *a.*; compar. *fussier*, superl. *fussiest.* Given to fuss; excessively busy about trifles; anxious or particular about petty details; also, full of petty details; of clothes, etc., elaborately made or trimmed.—**fuss′i-ly,** *adv.*—**fuss′i-ness,** *n.*

fust (fust), *n.* [OF. *fust* (F. *fût*), cask, wood, < L. *fustis*, cudgel.] A wine-cask†; also, mold, or a moldy or strong smell (obs. or prov.).—**fust,** *v. i.* To become or smell moldy or musty. See Shakspere's "Hamlet," iv. 4. 39. [Obs. or prov.]

fus-ta-nel-la (fus-tạ-nel′ạ̈), *n.* [A dim. form prob. < It. *fustagno*, fustian.] A kind of skirt or kilt of white cotton or linen, very full and stiffened, worn by men in modern Greece.

fus-tian (fus′chạn). [OF. *fustagne* (F. *futaine*); said to be named from *Fostat* (old Cairo), Egypt.] **I.** *n.* Formerly, a stout fabric of cotton and flax; now, a stout twilled cotton fabric with a short nap or pile; fig., inflated or turgid language in writing or speaking; bombast; rant; claptrap. **II.** *a.* Made of fustian; fig., pompous or bombastic, as language; also, worthless.

fus-tic (fus′tik), *n.* [F. and Sp. *fustoc*, < Ar. *fustuq*, akin to Gr. πιστάκη, pistachio-tree; from Pers.] The wood of a large moraceous tree, *Chlorophora tinctoria*, of tropical America, yielding a light-yellow dye; the tree itself, or the dye; also, any of several other dyewoods.

fus-ti-gate (fus′ti-gāt), *v. t.*; *-gated, -gating.* [LL. *fustigatus*, pp. of *fustigare*, < L. *fustis*, cudgel.] To cudgel; beat.—**fus-ti-ga′tion** (-gā′shọn), *n.*—**fus′ti-ga-tor,** *n.*

fust-y (fus′ti), *a.*; compar. *fustier*, superl. *fustiest.* [See *fust.*] Moldy; musty; having a stale smell; stuffy; also, old-fashioned; fogyish.—**fust′i-ly,** *adv.*—**fust′i-ness,** *n.*

fu-thorc (fö′thôrk), *n.* [So called from the first six letters, equivalent to *f, u, th, o, r, c.*] The runic alphabet.

fu-tile (fū′til, Brit. often -tīl), *a.* [L. *futilis, futtilis*, untrustworthy, vain, lit. 'that easily pours out,' related to *fundere*, pour.] Addicted to talking†; also, incapable of producing any result; ineffective; useless; vain; trifling or frivolous.—**fu′tile-ly,** *adv.*—**fu′tile-ness,** *n.*—**fu-til-i-ty** (fụ-til′i-ti), *n.*; pl. *-ties* (-tiz). Disposition to talk or tattle†; also, the quality of being futile (as, "The chief characteristic of her existence seemed to be a tragic *futility*": Arnold Bennett's "Clayhanger," iv. 9); ineffectiveness; uselessness; frivolousness; also, something futile.

fut-tock (fut'ọk), *n.* [Said to be for *foot-hook.*] *Naut.*, one of the curved timbers which form the middle sections of a compound rib in a ship.—**fut'tock=plates,** *n. pl. Naut.*, iron plates at the top of a lower mast, to which are secured the deadeyes of the topmast rigging and into which are fastened the upper ends of the futtock-shrouds; also, similar plates at the top of a topmast.—**fut'tock=shrouds,** *n. pl. Naut.*, the short iron rods extending downward from the futtock-plates to an iron band on the mast.

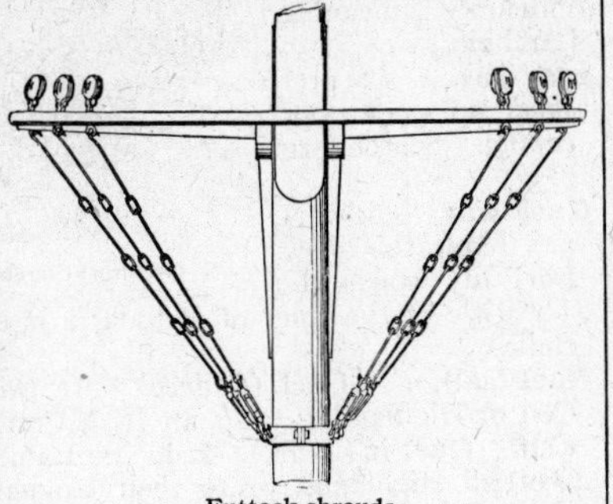
Futtock-shrouds.

fu-ture (fū'ṭụr). [OF. F. *futur*, < L. *futurus*, future participle of *esse*, be.] **I.** *a.* That is to be or come hereafter (as, *future* events; a *future* king; at some *future* day); also, pertaining to or connected with time to come (as, one's *future* prospects; "*future* hopes," Shakspere's "Two Gentlemen of Verona," i. 1. 50); in *gram.*, relating to or expressing action or being in time to come (as, the *future* tense). **II.** *n.* Future time; also, what will exist or happen in future time; future condition, as of a person, institution, etc.; often, a future condition of success or prosperity; a prospect of future betterment or prosperity; also, goods or stocks purchased or sold for future receipt or delivery, or a purchase or sale on such terms (usually in *pl.*); in *gram.*, the future tense, or a verb-form in it.—**fu'ture-less,** *a.* Without a future; having no prospect of future betterment or prosperity.—**fu'ture=per'fect.** In *gram.*: **I.** *a.* Denoting an action or state viewed as completed before a given future time: as, the *future-perfect* tense. **II.** *n.* The future-perfect tense; a verb-form in this tense, as Latin *amavero*, 'I shall have loved.'—**fu'tur-ism,** *n.* A recent doctrine or movement (orig. Italian) requiring complete abandonment of traditional usage and reconstruction of art and life on the basis of the present and the future: having reference esp. to painting, literature, and music. Cf. *post-impressionism.* —**fu'tur-ist,** *n.* An advocate of futurism.—**fu-tur-is'tic,** *a.* —**fu-tu-ri-ty** (fū-tū'ri-ti), *n.*; pl. *-ties* (-tiz). The state of being future; also, future time; also, what will exist or happen in the future; future state or condition; a future event.—**futurity race,** a race, as for horses, to be run long after the entries are made.—**futurity stakes,** the stakes in a futurity race.

fuze, fu-zee (fūz, fụ-zē'). See *fuse*[2], *fusee.*

fuzz (fuz), *n.* [Origin uncertain.] Loose, light fibrous or fluffy matter; a mass or coating of such matter.—**fuzz,** *v.* **I.** *intr.* To form, or take on, fuzz; become fuzzy. **II.** *tr.* To form into or cover with fuzz; make fuzzy.—**fuzz'ball,** *n.* A puffball.—**fuzz'y,** *a.*; compar. *fuzzier*, superl. *fuzziest.* Of the nature of or resembling fuzz; covered with fuzz. —**fuzz'i-ly,** *adv.*—**fuzz'i-ness,** *n.*

-fy. [F. *-fier*, prop. < L. *-ficare*, verb suffix (orig. through *-ficus*, adj. suffix: see *-fic*), < *facere*, do, make; but used also, like E. *-fy*, to form verbs directly from L. *facere.*] A verb suffix meaning 'to make,' 'render,' or 'convert into,' or 'to be made,' or 'become,' as in *acetify, beatify, deify, indemnify, liquefy, rarefy, speechify, terrify.*

fyke[1] (fīk), *v.* and *n.* See *fike.*

fyke[2] (fīk), *n.* [D. *fuik.*] A bag-shaped net for catching fish.

fyl-fot (fil'fot), *n.* [A word of doubtful meaning found once in a late ME. manuscript.] Same as *swastika.*

fytte (fit), *n.* See *fit*[3].

G

G, g (jē); pl. *G's, g's* (jēz). A consonant, the 7th letter of the English alphabet.

gab[1] (gab), *v. i.*; *gabbed, gabbing.* [Appar. imit.: cf. OF. *gaber* and Icel. *gabba*, mock.] To talk idly or much; chatter. [Colloq.]—**gab**[1], *n.* Idle talk; chatter; also, fluent or glib speech (as, "We knew well enough that he had the gift of the *gab*": Godwin's "Caleb Williams," iv.). [Colloq.]

gab[2] (gab), *n.* [Var. of *gob*[2].] The mouth. See Burns's "Jolly Beggars," 23. [Sc.]

gab[3] (gab), *n.* [Origin obscure.] In *mech.*, a hook, esp. on the rod transmitting the motion of an eccentric.

gab-ar-dine, gab-er-dine (gab-ạr-dēn', -ėr-dēn'), *n.* [Sp. *gabardina* or OF. *gavardine, galvardine*; origin uncertain.] A man's long, loose cloak or frock, formerly worn distinctively by Jews (as, "You . . . spit upon my Jewish *gaberdine*": Shakspere's "Merchant of Venice," i. 3. 113); also, a closely woven woolen fabric with fine diagonal ribs on the face; a fabric of like weave made of some other fiber, as cotton.

gab-bart (gab'ạrt), *n.* [F. *gabare*, < Pr. *gabarra.*] A barge or lighter, esp. for inland navigation. [Sc.]

gab-ble (gab'l), *v.*; *-bled, -bling.* [Imit.: cf. *gab*[1].] **I.** *intr.* To talk rapidly and unintelligently or foolishly; jabber; of geese, etc., to cackle (as, "the noisy geese that *gabbled* o'er the pool": Goldsmith's "Deserted Village," 119). **II.** *tr.* To utter rapidly and unintelligently.—**gab'ble,** *n.* Rapid, unintelligent talk; senseless chatter; also, inarticulate chatter, as of birds.—**gab'bler,** *n.*

gab-bro (gab'rō), *n.*; pl. *gabbros* (-rōz). [It.] Any one of a particular class of granular igneous rocks.

gab-by (gab'i), *a.* Full of gab; loquacious. [Colloq.]

ga-belle (gạ-bel'), *n.* [F.; prob. akin to E. *gavel*[2].] A tax; an excise; esp., in France before the Revolution, a tax on salt.

gab-er-dine (gab-ėr-dēn'), *n.* See *gabardine.*

gab-er-lun-zie (gab-ėr-lun'zi or -lūn'yi), *n.* [Origin uncertain.] A beggar; a mendicant. [Sc.]

ga-bi-on (gā'bi-ọn), *n.* [F. *gabion*, < It. *gabbione*, aug. of *gabbia*, < L. *cavea*, E. *cage.*] A cylinder of wickerwork

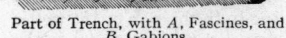

Part of Trench, with *A*, Fascines, and *B*, Gabions.

filled with earth, used as a military defense; also, a similar cylinder filled with stones and sunk in water, as in laying the foundations of a dam or jetty.—**ga"bi-on-ade'** (-ọ-nād'), *n.* [F. *gabionnade.*] A work formed of or with gabions.—**ga'bi-oned,** *a.* Furnished with gabions.

Ornamental Gable of the South Transept Door of Notre Dame, Paris; 13th century.

ga-ble (gā'bl), *n.* [OF. *gable*: cf. Icel. *gafl*, gable, OHG. *gabala*, G. *gabel*, fork.] The end of a ridged roof which at its extremity is not hipped or returned on itself but cut off in a vertical plane, together with the triangular expanse of wall from the level of the eaves to the apex; a similar end, as of a gambrel-roof, not of triangular shape; an architectural member resembling the triangular end of a roof, as an ornamental structure over a doorway (see cut on preceding page); also, an end-wall with a gable; a gable-end.—**ga′ble,** *v. t.*; *-bled, -bling.* To build with a gable or gables; form as a gable: chiefly in *gabled, pp.*—**ga′ble=end′,** *n.* An end-wall with a gable.—**ga′ble=roof′,** *n.* A ridged roof terminating at one or both ends in a gable.—**ga′blet,** *n.* A small gable or gable-like architectural ornament.—**ga′ble=win′dow,** *n.* A window in or under a gable; a window having its upper part shaped like a gable.

Gablet. — From a buttress of York Minster, England.

ga-by (gā′bi), *n.*; pl. *-bies* (-biz). [Origin uncertain.] A simpleton; a fool: as, "She is still whimpering after that *gaby* of a husband" (Thackeray's "Vanity Fair," lxvii.). [Colloq.]

gad[1] (gad), *n.* A minced form of *God*: often used interjectionally, as a mild oath.

gad[2] (gad), *n.* [= Icel. *gaddr*, spike, = Goth. *gazds*, sting; akin to E. *yard*[2].] A pointed bar or rod; a spike; a goad for driving cattle; a thick, pointed nail; a pointed mining tool for breaking up rock, coal, etc.—**gad**[2], *v. t.*; *gadded, gadding.* To break up with a mining gad.

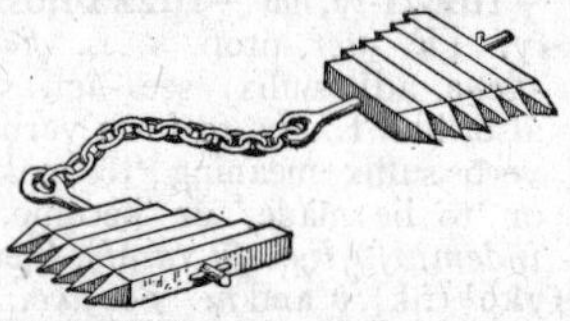

Mining Gads, fastened together for convenience in carrying.

gad[3] (gad), *v. i.*; *gadded, gadding.* [Origin uncertain.] To move restlessly or idly about; go about in pursuit of amusement or excitement; ramble or wander (sometimes fig.); sometimes, to straggle in growth (as, "Now *gads* the wild vine o'er the pathless ascent": Wordsworth's "Fort Fuentes").—**gad**[3], *n.* The act of gadding (as, always on the *gad*); also, a gadabout.—**gad′a-bout″,** *n.* One given to gadding about.

gad-bee (gad′bē), *n.* A gadfly.

gad-der (gad′ėr), *n.* One who gads; a gadabout.

gad-fly (gad′flī), *n.*; pl. *-flies* (-flīz). [See *gad*[2].] A fly that goads or stings domestic animals; esp., some member of the family *Tabanidæ*, the females of which have a piercing proboscis and suck the blood of horses, cattle, etc.

gadg-et (gaj′et), *n.* [Origin obscure.] A contrivance, device, or 'contraption'; any ingenious article or interesting object or trifle; a gimcrack. [Colloq.]

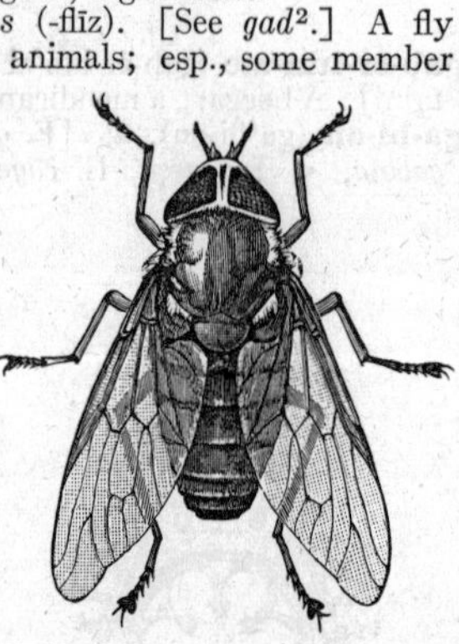

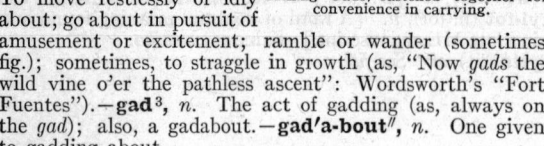

Gadfly (*Tabanus ruficornis*), natural size.

Ga-dhel-ic (gą-del′ik). [Ir. *Gaedheal*, Gael. *Gaidheal*, E. *Gael.*] **I.** *a.* Of or pertaining to the branch of the Celtic race comprising the Irish, the Gaels of Scotland, and the Manx of the Isle of Man: distinguished from *Cymric.* **II.** *n.* The group of dialects or languages spoken by the Gadhelic Celts.

ga-doid (gā′doid). [NL. *gadus*, cod, < Gr. γάδος, kind of fish: see *-oid.*] **I.** *a.* Resembling a cod; belonging to the *Gadidæ*, a family of soft-finned fishes including the cod, haddock, pollack, etc. **II.** *n.* A gadoid fish.

gad-o-lin-i-a (gad-ǫ-lin′i-ạ̈), *n.* [NL., < *gadolinium.*] Oxide of gadolinium.

gad-o-lin-ite (gad′ǫ-lin-īt), *n.* [From J. *Gadolin* (1760–1852), Finnish chemist.] A silicate mineral containing iron, yttrium, cerium, beryllium, etc.

gad-o-lin-i-um (gad-ǫ-lin′i-um), *n.* [NL.: see *gadolinite.*] Chem. sym., Gd; at. wt., 157.3. A rare metallic element found associated with yttrium.

ga-droon (gą-drön′), etc. Same as *godroon*, etc.

gad-wall (gad′wâl), *n.* [Origin unknown.] A fresh-water wild duck, *Chaulelasmus streperus*, much esteemed for the table; also, some allied species.

Gadwall (*Chaulelasmus streperus*).

gad-zooks (gad′-zöks′), *interj.* [See *gad*[1]; second element uncertain.] An emphatic expletive of indefinite meaning. [Archaic.]

gae (gā), *v. i.*; pret. *gaed*, pp. *gaen*, ppr. *gaeing.* Scotch form of *go.*

Gaek-war (gīk′wär), *n.* [Marathi *gāekwār*, lit. 'cowherd.'] The title of the ruler of Baroda, a native state of western India.

Gael (gāl), *n.* [Gael. *Gaidheal* = Ir. *Gaedheal.*] A Scottish Celt or Highlander; also, an Irish Celt; also, any Gadhelic Celt.—**Gael-ic** (gā′lik). **I.** *a.* Pertaining to the Gaels of the Scottish Highlands, or to their language; also, Irish; also, Gadhelic. **II.** *n.* The Celtic language of the Highlanders of Scotland; Erse; also, Irish; also, Gadhelic.

gaff[1] (gaf), *n.* [OF. F. *gaffe*, boat-hook.] A strong hook with a handle, used for landing large fish; also, a barbed fish-spear; also, a metal spur for a game-cock; *naut.*, the spar extending the upper edge of a fore-and-aft sail.—**gaff**[1], *v. t.* To hook or land with a gaff.

gaff[2] (gaf), *n.* [Origin unknown.] A cheap place of amusement; a theater or music-hall of the lowest class. [Slang, Eng.]

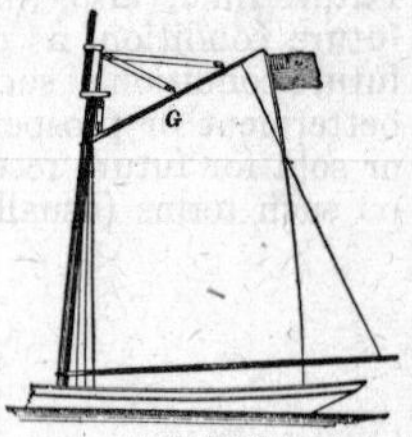

G, Gaff.

gaff[3] (gaf), *n.* [Origin obscure: cf. *gaff*[1].] The hardship, suffering, or strain occasioned by something: chiefly in the phrase 'to stand the gaff.' [Slang.]

gaff[4] (gaf), *n.* [Origin obscure; appar. first in rogues' slang.] A word occurring in the phrase 'to blow the gaff,' to disclose or betray the secret, reveal the plot, or inform on others. [Slang.]

gaf-fer (gaf′ėr), *n.* [Also formerly *gaffar*; appar. a contr. of *grandfather.*] A rustic title or term for an old man (as, "the only son of *Gaffar* and Gammer Andrews," Fielding's "Joseph Andrews," i. 2: cf. *gammer*); also, a master, or employer of labor (now prov. Eng.); an overseer or foreman (Eng.).

gaf-fle (gaf′l), *n.* [Prob. < D. *gaffel* = G. *gabel*, fork: cf. *gable.*] A lever for bending a crossbow; also, an artificial spur for a game-cock.

gaff=top-sail (gaf′top′sāl, naut. -sl), *n.* *Naut.*, a light triangular or quadrilateral sail set above a gaff, by which its foot is extended; also, in *ichth.*, a sea catfish, *Felichthys felis*, of the Atlantic and Gulf coasts of the U. S. (so called from the elevated dorsal fin).

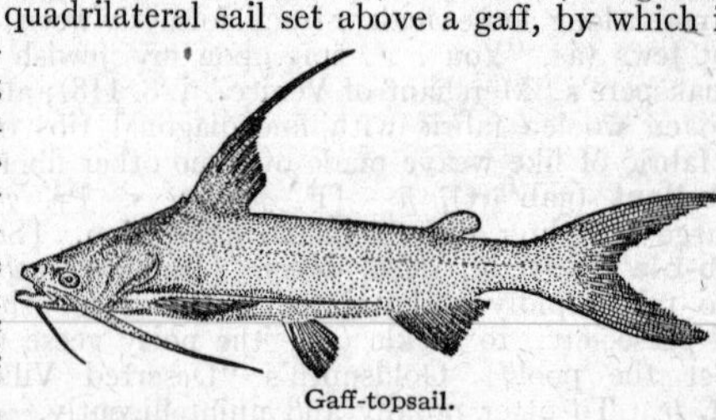

Gaff-topsail.

gag (gag), *v.*; *gagged, gagging.* [Prob. imit. of the sound made in choking.] **I.** *tr.* To stop up the mouth of (a person) with something, so as to prevent speech; hence, to silence, as by force or authority (as, "The time was not yet come when eloquence was to be *gagged*": Macaulay's "Essays," Machiavelli); also, to choke up (a valve, etc.); also, to fasten open the jaws of, as in surgical operations; also, to cause to heave with nausea; also, to introduce interpolations into (a stage part, etc.: slang); also, to ply with talk, false stories, etc., or take in by such means (slang). **II.** *intr.* To heave with nausea; also, to introduce interpolations or gags in acting (slang); also, to play on one's credulity by false stories, etc. (slang).—**gag,** *n.* Something thrust into the mouth to prevent speech (also fig.); a surgical device for distending the jaws; also, an interpolation introduced by an actor into his part (slang); also, a joke (slang); a hoax (slang).

gage[1] (gāj), *n.* [OF. *gage, guage, wage* (F. *gage*), pledge, security; from Teut.: see *wage.*] A pledge or pawn; security; also, something, as a glove, thrown down in token of challenge to combat; hence, a challenge.—**gage**[1], *v. t.*; *gaged, gaging.* [OF. *gagier* (F. *gager*).] To pledge, stake, or wager (archaic: as, "And 'gainst an oaken bough I'll *gage* my silver wand of state," Scott's "Lord of the Isles," ii. 7); also, to engage†.

gage[2] (gāj), *n.* [Named about 1725 from Sir W. *Gage.*] A name given to several varieties of plum: as, the green *gage*; the golden *gage.*

gage[3], **gauge** (gāj), *n.* [OF. *gauge, jauge* (F. *jauge*); origin uncertain.] A standard of measure; a standard dimension, quantity, or amount; in general, measure; extent or capacity; specif., the distance between the rails of a railroad (as, standard *gage,* 4 feet 8½ inches; broad *gage,* or narrow *gage,* a gage greater, or less, than standard gage); the distance between the opposite wheels of a vehicle; also, the exposed part or length of a shingle or tile; also, the depth to which a loaded vessel sinks in the water; also, the position of one ship with reference to another and to the wind (as, to have the weather-*gage* of a ship, to be to the windward of it; to have the lee-*gage*); also, any of various instruments for determining, testing, or adjusting dimensions, capacity, force, or the like; in *joinery,* a tool for marking lines parallel to an edge. —**gage**[3], **gauge,** *v. t.*; *gaged, gauged, gaging, gauging.* [OF. *gaugier, jaugier* (F. *jauger*).] To measure, as with a gage; determine the dimensions, capacity, quantity, or force of; hence, to appraise, estimate, or judge (as, "But I bar to-night: you shall not *gauge* me By what we do to-night": Shakspere's "Merchant of Venice," ii. 2. 208); also, to make conformable to a standard; in *sewing,* to gather in parallel rows.—**gage′a-ble, gauge′a-ble,** *a.* That may be gaged.—**ga-ger, gau-ger** (gā′jėr), *n.* One who or that which gages; esp., an officer who ascertains the contents of casks, etc.; an exciseman.

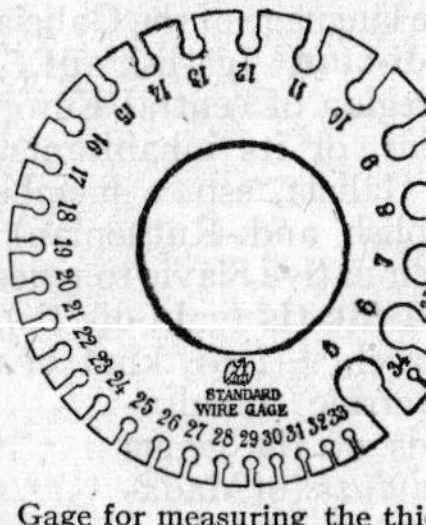

Gage for measuring the thickness of Wire.

gag-ger (gag′ėr), *n.* One who gags.

gag-gle (gag′l), *v. i.*; *-gled, -gling.* [Imit.] To utter the cry of a goose; cackle.—**gag′gle,** *n.* A flock of geese; also, gaggling; cackle.

gag=law, gag=rule (gag′lâ, -röl), *n.* A law or rule made and enforced for the purpose of preventing or restricting discussion or expression of opinion, as in a deliberative body.

gahn-ite (gän′īt), *n.* [From J. G. *Gahn* (1745–1818), Swedish chemist.] A dark-colored mineral containing aluminium and zinc.

gai-e-ty, gay-e-ty (gā′ẹ-ti), *n.*; pl. *-ties* (-tiz). [F. *gaieté, gaîté.*] The state of being gay or cheerful; gay spirits; cheerful liveliness; also, merrymaking or festivity (often in *pl.*); also, showiness; finery.

Gaik-war (gīk′wär), *n.* See *Gaekwar.*

gail-lar-di-a (gą-lär′di-ą), *n.* [NL.; named from M. *Gaillard* de Marentonneau.] Any plant of the American asteraceous genus *Gaillardia,* several species of which are cultivated for their showy flowers with yellow, purple, or variegated rays.

gai-ly, gay-ly (gā′li), *adv.* In a gay manner; cheerfully or merrily; brightly or showily.

gain[1] (gān), *a.* [Icel. *gegn.*] Straight or direct; convenient or advantageous; handy or skilful; active; graceful. [Now Sc. and prov. Eng.]

gain[2] (gān), *n.* [Origin uncertain.] A mortise; a groove or notch, as in a timber.—**gain**[2], *v. t.* To make a gain or gains in; also, to unite or fasten by a gain or gains, as timbers; mortise.

gain[3] (gān), *v.* [OF. *gaignier, waignier* (F. *gagner*), gain, from an OHG. verb meaning 'to pasture, hunt for food,' < OHG. *weida* (G. *weide*), pasture, hunting, = AS. *wāth,* Icel. *veidhr,* hunting.] **I.** *tr.* To obtain as a profit or advantage; succeed in getting; win; also, to attain or reach by effort (as, "Now spurs the lated traveller apace To *gain* the timely inn": Shakspere's "Macbeth," iii. 3. 7); also, to win over to one's friendship or purposes (as, "To come, with presents laden, from the port, To gratify the queen, and *gain* the court": Dryden's tr. Virgil's "Æneid," i. 953); also, to make an increase of (as, the clock *gains* a minute a day). **II.** *intr.* To profit; benefit; also, to improve; make progress.—**to gain on** or **upon,** to encroach gradually on (as, "oceans daily *gaining on* the land": Tennyson's "Golden Year," 29); also, to win favor or influence with (as, "Such a one . . . *gains upon* you, not by a fulsome way of commending you . . . but liking whatever you propose or utter": Steele, in "Tatler," 208); also, to advance nearer to (a person or thing pursued).—**gain**[3], *n.* [OF. F. *gain.*] Profit or advantage; esp., pecuniary profit, or, *pl.,* sums constituting profit; also, an increase or advance; also, a gaining or winning.—**gain′a-ble,** *a.* That may be gained.

gaine (gān), *n.* [F., < L. *vagina,* sheath.] The lower part of a sculptured figure, below the bust or the head, having the appearance of a quadrangular sheath inclosing the body and contracting toward the feet; also, a kind of pedestal of the same general shape, for holding a statuette or other ornamental object.

gain-er (gā′nėr), *n.* One who or that which gains.

gain-ful (gān′fůl), *a.* Profitable; lucrative. —**gain′ful-ly,** *adv.*—**gain′ful-ness,** *n.*

gain-giv-ing (gān′giv″ing), *n.* [Cf. *gain-* in *gainsay.*] A misgiving. See Shakspere's "Hamlet," v. 2. 226. [Obs. or archaic.]

gain-less (gān′les), *a.* Without gain; unprofitable; useless.

gain-ly (gān′li), *a.* [See *gain*[1].] Proper, becoming, or suitable (now Sc. and prov. Eng.); also, graceful, shapely, or comely. Cf. *ungainly.*—**gain′li-ness,** *n.*

gain-say (gān′sā′), *v. t.*; *-said* (-sād′ or -sed′), also *-sayed* (-sād′), *-saying.* [ME., for *againsay,* lit. 'say against': see *again* and *say*[3].] To deny; contradict; dispute; also, to oppose; act against.—**gain′say,** *n.* A gainsaying; contradiction: as, "He . . . was the umpire in all disputes . . . giving his decisions with an air and tone admitting of no *gainsay* or appeal" (Irving's "Sketch-Book," Sleepy Hollow).—**gain′say′er,** *n.*

Gaine.— Renaissance sculpture; Maison de Pierre, Toulouse, France.

gainst, 'gainst (genst), *prep.* Against. [Poetic.]

gair-ish (gãr′ish), etc. See *garish,* etc.

gait (gāt), *n.* [Scotch and north. Eng. spelling of *gate*[2] in various senses, but current in general literary use only in the following.] Manner of going, walking, or stepping: as, a slow *gait*; a limping *gait*; the various *gaits* of a horse. —**gait′ed,** *a.* Having a gait: as, slow-*gaited*; "heavy-*gaited* oxen" (Parkman's "Oregon Trail," vi.).

gai-ter (gā′tėr), *n.* [F. *guêtre*; origin unknown.] A covering of cloth, leather, etc., for the ankle and instep, and sometimes also the lower leg, worn over the shoe, etc.; also, a cloth or leather shoe with elastic insertions at the sides.—**gai′tered,** *a.* Wearing gaiters.

ga-la (gā′lą). [F., < It. *gala,* festal pomp, finery; akin to E. *gallant.*] **I.** *n.* Festal pomp or dress; festivity; also, a festive occasion. **II.** *a.* Festive; festal.

ga-lac-ta-gogue (gą-lak′tą-gog). [Gr. γάλα (γαλακτ-), milk, + ἀγωγός, leading, < ἄγειν, lead.] **I.** *a.* Promoting the flow or secretion of milk; galactopoietic. **II.** *n.* A galactagogue agent or medicine.

ga-lac-tic (gą-lak′tik), *a.* [Gr. γαλακτικός, < γάλα (γαλακτ-), milk, akin to L. *lac* (*lact-*), milk: cf. *lacteal.*] Of, pertaining to, or obtained from milk; also, in *astron.,* pertaining to the Galaxy.

galacto-. Form of Gr. γάλα (γαλακτ-), milk, used in combination.—**gal-ac-tom-e-ter** (gal-ak-tom′e-tėr), *n.* [See *-meter.*] An instrument for determining the richness of milk by its specific gravity.—**gal-ac-toph′o-rous** (-tof′ọ-rus), *a.* [See *-phorous.*] Conveying or producing milk.—**gal-ac-to-poi-et-ic** (gạ-lak″tō-poi-et′ik). [+ Gr. ποιεῖν, make.] **I.** *a.* Producing milk; increasing the secretion of milk; galactagogue. **II.** *n.* A galactopoietic agent or medicine.—**ga-lac-tor-rhe′a, ga-lac-tor-rhœ′a** (-tọ-rē′ạ̈), *n.* [NL. (Gr. ῥοία, a flow, < ῥεῖν, flow).] In *pathol.*, an excessive flow of milk.

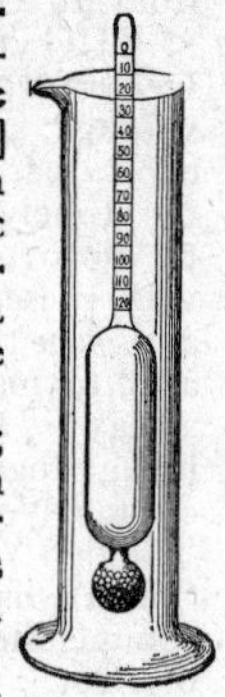

Galactometer.

ga-la-go (gạ-lā′gō), *n.*; pl. *-gos* (-gōz). [NL.; from native African name.] Any lemur of the African genus *Galago* and allied genera.

Thick-tailed Galago (*G. crassicaudatus*).

Gal-a-had (gal′ạ-had), *n.* [From Sir *Galahad*, the pure, of King Arthur's Round Table.] A man of ideal purity of heart and life.

ga-lan-gal, gal-in-gale (gạ-lang′gạl or gal′ạn-gạl, gal′in-gāl), *n.* [OF. *galingal*, < Ar. *khalanjān*, said to be from Chinese.] The aromatic, medicinal rhizome of certain plants of the ginger family, esp. of China and the East Indies; also, any sedge of the genus *Cyperus*, esp. *C. longus*, an English plant with aromatic roots.

gal-an-tine (gal′ạn-tin or -tēn), *n.* [OF. F. *galantine*, earlier *galatine*; origin uncertain.] A kind of sauce for fish, etc.†; also, veal, chicken, or other white meat boned, tied up, boiled, and served cold with its own jelly.

ga-lan-ty=show (gạ-lan′ti-shō), *n.* [Cf. It. *galante*, gallant.] A miniature pantomime produced by throwing shadows of puppets on a wall or screen.

gal-a-te-a (gal-ạ-tē′ạ̈), *n.* [From the *Galatea*, a vessel in the British navy.] A stout striped cotton fabric used for clothing.

Ga-la-tian (gạ-lā′shạn). **I.** *a.* Of or pertaining to Galatia, an ancient inland division of Asia Minor, or its inhabitants. **II.** *n.* A native or inhabitant of Galatia; *pl.*, the book of the New Testament called in full "The Epistle of Paul the Apostle to the Galatians."

gal-a-vant (gal-ạ-vant′), *v. i.* See *gallivant.*

ga-lax (gā′laks), *n.* [NL., < Gr. γάλα (γαλακτ-), milk; so called from the white flowers.] An evergreen herb, *Galax aphylla*, of southeastern U. S., with a raceme of small white flowers.

Gal-ax-y (gal′ạk-si), *n.* [F. *galaxie*, < LL. *galaxias*, < Gr. γαλαξίας, < γάλα (γαλακτ-), milk.] The Milky Way (as, "The *galaxy*, that milky way, Which nightly, as a circling zone, thou seest Powder'd with stars": Milton's "Paradise Lost," vii. 579); hence [*l. c.*; pl. *galaxies* (-siz)], any brilliant or splendid assemblage, as of persons.

gal-ba-num (gal′bạ-num), *n.* [L.; prob. from Heb.] A gum-resin with a peculiar disagreeable odor, obtained esp. from certain Asiatic plants of the apiaceous genus *Ferula*: used in medicine and the arts. See Ex. xxx. 34.

gale[1] (gāl), *n.* [Origin uncertain.] A strong wind, esp. one between a stiff breeze and a tempest; also, a breeze (poetic: as, "Wanton *gales* along the valleys play," Wm. Collins's "Oriental Eclogues," i. 15); fig., a noisy fit or outburst of laughter or the like (colloq.).

gale[2] (gāl), *n.* [AS. *gagel* = D. and G. *gagel.*] A shrub, *Myrica gale*, with a pleasant aromatic odor, growing in marshy places: often called *sweet-gale.*

gale[3] (gāl), *n.* [Prob. a contr. of *gavel*[2].] A periodical payment of rent, interest, or the like; the amount paid.

ga-le-a (gā′lẹ-ạ̈), *n.*; pl. *galeæ* (-ē). [L., helmet.] In *zoöl.*, *bot.*, etc., a helmet-like part.—**ga′le-ate, ga′le-at-ed** (-āt, -ā-ted), *a.* [L. *galeatus*, pp. of *galeare*, cover with a helmet, < *galea.*] Having a galea (as, the *galeated* curassow, of the South American genus *Pauxi*, having a horny protuberance on the head); also, helmet-shaped.—**ga′le-i-form** (-i-fôrm), *a.* Helmet-shaped.

Galeated Curassow.

Ga-len (gā′lẹn), *n.* [From *Galen*, the Greek physician (born about A.D. 130).] A physician. See Shakspere's "Merry Wives of Windsor," ii. 3. 29.

ga-le-na (gạ-lē′nạ̈), *n.* [L., lead ore.] Native lead sulphide: a valuable ore of lead.—**ga-len′ic**[1] (-len′ik), *a.* Pertaining to or containing galena.

Ga-len-ic[2] (gạ-len′ik), *a.* Of or pertaining to Galen, the celebrated Greek physician, or his principles or methods. Also **Ga-len′i-cal.**

ga-le-nite (gạ-lē′nīt), *n.* Same as *galena.*

ga-let (gā′let), *n.* [Gr. γαλέη, weasel.] Same as *foussa.*

Ga-li-cian[1] (gạ-lish′ạn). **I.** *a.* Of or pertaining to Galicia, a district of northwestern Spain, or its inhabitants or their language. **II.** *n.* A native or inhabitant of Galicia; also, the language of the Galicians, a dialect of Portuguese.

Ga-li-cian[2] (gạ-lish′ạn). **I.** *a.* Of or pertaining to Galicia, a region of central Europe north of the Carpathian Mountains, or its inhabitants. **II.** *n.* A native or inhabitant of Galicia, esp. a member of one of the indigenous Slavic (Polish and Ruthenian) peoples of this region, speaking their native Slavic tongues.

gal-i-dic-tis (gal-i-dik′tis), *n.* [NL., < Gr. γαλιδεύς, young weasel, + ἴκτις, kind of marten.] Any of the carnivorous viverrine quadrupeds of the genus *Galidictis*, of Madagascar.

Galidictis (*G. striata*).

Gal-i-læ-an (gal-i-lē′ạn), *a.* and *n.* See *Galilean*[1].

Gal-i-le-an[1] (gal-i-lē′ạn). **I.** *a.* Of or pertaining to Galilee, the northernmost division of Palestine in the time of Christ. **II.** *n.* A native or inhabitant of Galilee, as Jesus Christ ('the Galilean'); hence, a Christian.

Gal-i-le-an[2] (gal-i-lē′ạn), *a.* Of or pertaining to Galileo Galilei (1564–1642), the celebrated Italian physicist and astronomer.

gal-i-lee (gal′i-lē), *n.* [OF. *galilee*, < ML. *Galilæa*, a galilee, orig. (L.) the province of Galilee: said to refer to the "Galilee of the Gentiles" in Mat. iv. 15.] A chapel or porch at the entrance of some medieval churches.

gal-i-ma-tias (gal-i-mā′shiạs or -mat′i-ạs), *n.* [F.; origin unknown: cf. *gallimaufry.*] Confused or unintelligible talk; gibberish.

gal-in-gale (gal′in-gāl), *n.* See *galangal.*

gal-i-ot, gal-li-ot (gal′i-ọt), *n.* [OF. F. *galiote*, < OF. *galie*, E. *galley.*] A small galley propelled by both sails and oars; also, a kind of Dutch cargo vessel.

gal-i-pot (gal′i-pot), *n.* [F. *galipot*; origin unknown.] A kind of turpentine which concretes on the stem of certain species of pine.

gall[1] (gâl), *n.* [AS. *gealla* = D. *gal* = G. *galle* = Icel. *gall*; akin to L. *fel*, Gr. χολή, gall, bile.] Bile, esp. that of the ox; also, the gall-bladder; fig., something very bitter or severe; also, bitterness of spirit; rancor; also, impudence or effrontery (slang).

gall[2] (gâl), *n.* [AS. *gealla*, perhaps = *gealla*, E. *gall*[1].] A sore on the skin, esp. of a horse, due to rubbing; an excoriation; fig., something irritating or exasperating; a state of irritation; also, a bare spot; a spot of ground from which the soil has been washed away or which is unfit for cultivation (southern U. S.); an imperfection, blemish, or flaw. —**gall**[2], *v.* **I.** *tr.* To make sore by rubbing; also, to impair the surface of by rubbing; fig., to vex or irritate (as, "The sarcasms of the King soon *galled* the sensitive temper of the poet [Voltaire]": Macaulay's "Essays," Frederic the Great); harass or annoy (as, "Where bowmen might in ambush wait . . . To *gall* an entering foe": Scott's "Lord of the Isles," i. 29). **II.** *intr.* To become chafed; also, to make galling or irritating remarks† (see Shakspere's "Henry V.," v. 1. 78).

gall[3] (gâl), *n.* [OF. F. *galle*, < L. *galla*.] Any abnormal vegetable growth or excrescence developed on plants by the action of certain parasites, esp. insects; esp., a nut-like excrescence on the oak due to certain insects of the hymenopterous genus *Cynips*, yielding tannin, and used in dyeing and medicine.

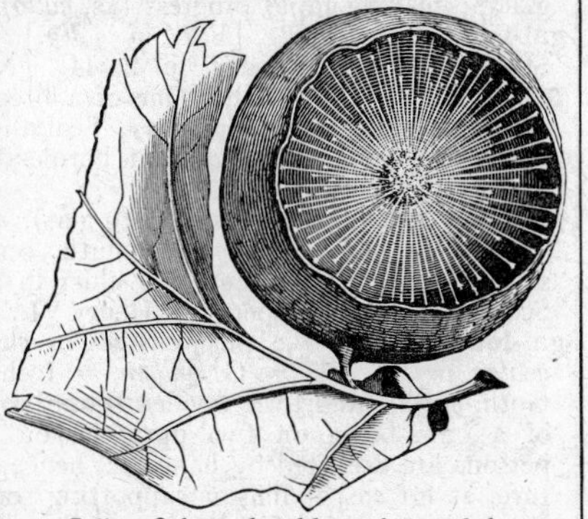
Gall on Oak, produced by an insect of the genus *Cynips*.

gal-lant (gal′ạnt). [OF. F. *galant*, ppr. of OF. *galer*, be gay, make merry, connected with *gale*, gaiety, festivity, = It. *gala*, E. *gala*.] **I.** *a.* Gay or showy, as in dress; also, splendid or fine; stately (as, "a *gallant* bark from Albion's coast": Cowper's "My Mother's Picture," 88); also, brave, high-spirited, or chivalrous (as, a *gallant* soldier; *gallant* conduct); also (pron. gal′ạnt or gạ-lant′), polite and attentive to women; courtly; sometimes, amorous; erotic. **II.** *n.* A gay, dashing person, now always of the male sex; a man of fashion; sometimes, a man of spirit or mettle; also (pron. gal′ạnt or gạ-lant′), a man particularly attentive to women; also, a suitor or lover; sometimes, a paramour.—**gal′lant**, *v.* **I.** *tr.* To make gallant or fine; also (pron. gạ-lant′), to play the gallant to; escort with courtly attentions. **II.** *intr.* (Pron. gạ-lant′.) To play the gallant.—**gal′lant-ly**, *adv.*—**gal′lant-ness**, *n.*—**gal′lant-ry**, *n.*; pl. *-ries* (-riz). [F. *galanterie*.] Gay or fine appearance; finery; also, dashing courage; heroic bravery; sometimes, a gallant deed; also, the conduct of a gallant; gallant or courtly attention to women; a polite or courtly action or speech; sometimes, amorous intrigue; also, gallants collectively†; fashionable people†.

gal-lan-ty=show (gạ-lan′ti-shō), *n.* See *galanty-show*.

gal-late (gal′āt), *n.* In *chem.*, a salt of gallic acid.

gall=blad-der (gâl′blad″ėr), *n.* The sac which receives the gall or bile from the liver.

gal-le-ass, gal-li-ass (gal′ẹ̄-as, -i-as), *n.* [OF. *galeace*, *galiace*, < It. *galeazza*, aug. of *galea*, < ML. *galea*, E. *galley*.] A kind of large galley or ship formerly used in war.

gal-le-on (gal′ẹ̄-ọn), *n.* [Sp. *galeón*, < ML. *galeo(n-)*, < *galea*, E. *galley*.] A kind of large ship, usually with several decks, formerly used by the Spaniards and others: as, "three very great *galleons*, or Spanish ships, from the south seas" (Defoe's "Captain Singleton," xiv.).

gal-le-ry (gal′ẹ-ri), *n.*; pl. *-ries* (-riz). [OF. F. *galerie*, < ML. *galeria*; origin unknown.] A covered walk or promenade; a piazza or portico; a veranda; also, a raised platform or passageway along the outside or inside of the wall of a building; a balcony; specif., a balcony-like structure or platform at the stern or quarters of ships of the older type; also, a platform projecting from the interior walls of a church, theater, or the like, to provide seats or room for a part of the audience; specif., the highest of such platforms in a theater; also, the occupants of a gallery, esp. in a theater; hence, the less refined or cultured part of the public; also, any body of spectators or auditors, as the spectators of a golf-match; also, a long narrow apartment; a corridor; often, a room or building devoted to the exhibition of works of art; a collection of such works for exhibition; also, a room or building in which to take photographs, practise shooting, etc.; also, a passageway made or dug by an animal; in *fort.*, an underground or covered passage; in *mining*, a level or drift; also, in *jewelry*, a setting having the sides perforated.—**gallery gods,** those who occupy seats in the gallery of a theater. [Colloq.]—**to play to the gallery,** to address one's self to those in the gallery, as an actor; hence, to seek popular applause or favor.—**gal′le-ry,** *v. t.*; *-ried, -rying.* To provide with a gallery; dispose like a gallery.—**gal′le-ry-ite,** *n.* One who occupies a seat in a gallery, as of a theater. [Colloq.]

gal-ley (gal′i), *n.*; pl. *galleys* (-iz). [OF. *galie* (F. *galée*), < ML. *galea*, < MGr. γαλέα; origin unknown.] An early form of sea-going vessel propelled by oars or by oars and sails; also, a state or pleasure barge; also, a large rowboat; also, the kitchen of a ship, or its stove or range; in *printing*, a long, narrow tray, usually of metal, for holding type which has been set; also, a galley-proof.—**gal′ley=proof,** *n.* In *printing*, a proof taken from type on a galley.—**gal′ley=slave,** *n.* A person condemned to work at the oar on a galley. Also fig.—**gal′ley=worm,** *n.* A myriapod: so called from its resemblance to a many-oared vessel.

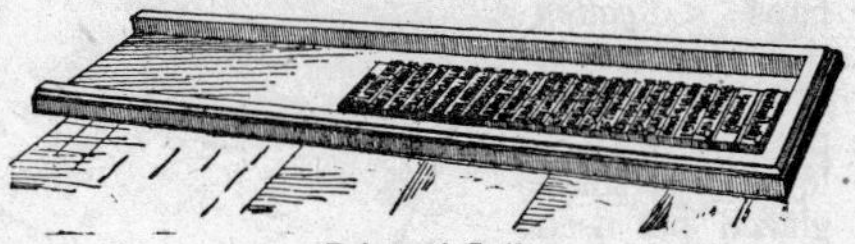
Printers' Galley.

gall=fly (gâl′flī), *n.*; pl. *-flies* (-flīz). An insect, esp. of the hymenopterous genus *Cynips*, that causes galls on oaks, etc.

gal-liard (gal′yạrd). [OF. F. *gaillard*; origin uncertain.] **I.** *a.* Sturdy, hardy, or valiant; also, lively or gay. [Archaic.] **II.** *n.* A galliard fellow (archaic); also, a spirited dance in triple rhythm, common in the 16th and 17th centuries; a piece of music written for, or in the rhythm of, this dance.—**gal-liar-dise** (gal′yạr-dis), *n.* [F. *gaillardise*.] Gaiety, merriment, or revelry; also, a merry trick, or joke (as, "My budget bursteth sure with this! This were a crowning *galliardise* For king himself to tell in hall": Leigh Hunt's "Palfrey," v.). [Archaic.]

gal′li-ass, *n.* See *galleass*.

gal-lic[1] (gal′ik), *a.* Pertaining to or derived from galls (vegetable growths): as, *gallic* acid (used esp. in making ink).

gal-lic[2] (gal′ik), *a.* Of or pertaining to gallium.

Gal-lic[3] (gal′ik), *a.* [L. *Gallicus*, < *Gallus*, a Gaul.] Of or pertaining to the Gauls or Gaul (see *Gaul*); hence, of or pertaining to the French or France; French.—**Gal-li-can** (gal′i-kạn), *a.* Gallic; hence, French; specif., *eccles.*, noting or pertaining to the Roman Catholic Church in France; esp., noting or pertaining to a school or party of French Roman Catholics advocating a restriction of the papal authority in favor of the authority of general councils and of the bishops and temporal rulers (cf. *ultramontane*).—**Gal′li-cè** (-sē), *adv.* [L., in the Gallic language.] In French.—**Gal′li-cism** (-sizm), *n.* A French usage or idiom; also, the use of French idioms or expressions.—**Gal′li-cize** (-sīz), *v. t.* or *i.*; *-cized, -cizing.* To make or become Gallic; conform to French usage.

gal-li-gas-kins (gal-i-gas′kinz), *n. pl.* [Corruption of obs. F. *garguesques*, for *greguesques*, < It. *Grechesco*, Greek.] A kind of loose hose or breeches worn in the 16th and 17th centuries; hence, loose breeches in general; also, leggings or gaiters.

gal-li-mau-fry (gal-i-mâ′fri), *n.*; pl. *-fries* (-friz). [F., a ragout made of remnants; origin unknown.] A ragout or hash of various ingredients (obs. or prov. Eng.); hence, any heterogeneous mixture; a hodgepodge; a jumble; a confused medley.

gal-li-na-cean (gal-i-nā′shi̤an). **I.** *a.* Gallinaceous. **II.** *n.* A gallinaceous bird.

gal-li-na-ceous (gal-i-nā′shius), *a.* [L. *gallinaceus*, < L. *gallina*, hen.] Belonging to or resembling the domestic fowls; belonging to the group or order *Gallinaceæ*, which includes the common poultry, also pheasants, grouse, partridges, etc.

gall-ing (gâ′ling), *p. a.* That galls; chafing; irritating; distressing.—**gall′ing-ly,** *adv.*—**gall′ing-ness,** *n.*

gal-li-nip-per (gal′i-nip-ėr), *n.* [Origin obscure.] A large mosquito. [U. S.]

gall=in-sect (gâl′in″sekt), *n.* Any insect which causes galls, as a gall-fly.

gal-li-nule (gal′i-nūl), *n.* [NL. *Gallinula*, the typical genus, L. *gallinula*, chicken, dim. of *gallina*, hen.] Any of certain long-toed aquatic birds of the rail family, as *Gallinula galeata* ('Florida gallinule'), or *G. chloropus*, the moor-hen of Europe.

Florida Gallinule.

gal′li-ot, *n.* See *galiot.*

gal-li-pot[1] (gal′-i-pot), *n.* [Perhaps < *galley* + *pot* (as if brought or imported in galleys).] A small glazed pot used by apothecaries for holding medicines, etc.

gal′li-pot[2], *n.* See *galipot.*

gal-li-um (gal′i-um), *n.* [NL., < L. *gallus*, cock, tr. F. *coq*, from the name of the discoverer, Lecoq de Boisbaudran.] Chem. sym., Ga; at. wt., 69.9; sp. gr., 5.935. A rare, bluish-white, highly fusible metallic element.

gal-li-vant (gal-i-vant′), *v. i.* [Perhaps a humorous variation of *gallant.*] To gad about in a gay or frivolous manner.

gal-li-wasp (gal′i-wosp), *n.* [Origin uncertain.] A lizard, *Celestus occiduus*, about a foot long, found in the West Indies and Central America; also, a fish, *Synodus fœtens*, of the Atlantic coast of North America, having a scaly lizard-like head.

gal-lize (gal′īz), *v. t.*; *-lized, -lizing.* [From L. *Gall*, who developed the process.] In *wine-making*, to add water and sugar to (the unfermented grape-juice) in order to increase the quantity of the wine produced.—**gal-li-za-ti̤on** (gal-i-zā′sho̤n), *n.*

gall-nut (gâl′nut), *n.* Same as *gall*[3].

Gal-lo- (gal′ō̤-). Form of L. *Gallus*, a Gaul, used in combination, often in the sense of 'French,' as in *Gallo-American*, *Gallo-Celtic.*

gal-lo-glass (gal′ō̤-glȧs), *n.* See *gallowglass.*

Gal-lo-ma-ni-a (gal-ō̤-mā′ni-ä̤), *n.* [See *Gallo-.*] A mania or passion for what is French.—**Gal-lo-ma′ni-ac** (-ak), *n.*

gal-lon (gal′o̤n), *n.* [OF. *galon, jalon*, = ML. *galo(n-)*: cf. OF. *jalle* (F. *jale*), large bowl, *jalaie*, measure for wine, etc.] A dry or, esp., liquid measure of capacity containing 4 quarts, the liquid measure being equivalent in the U. S. to 231 cubic inches (old English 'wine-gallon'), and in Great Britain to 277.274 cubic inches ('imperial gallon'). See *liquid measure*, under *liquid, a.*; *apothecaries' measure*, under *apothecary*; and *dry measure*, under *dry, a.*

gal-loon (ga̤-lön′), *n.* [F. *galon*, < *galonner*, trim with galloon, orig. adorn (the head or hair) with bands or ribbons; origin uncertain.] A braid or band-like trimming of worsted, silk, tinsel, gold or silver, etc.—**gal-looned′,** *a.* Trimmed with galloon.

gal-loot (ga̤-löt′), *n.* See *galoot.*

gal-lop (gal′o̤p), *v.* [OF. *galoper, waloper* (F. *galoper*); from Teut.: cf. *wallop*[1].] **I.** *intr.* To move or run by leaps, as a horse; go at a gallop; hence, to ride at a gallop, or at full speed; in general, to go fast, as a person on foot, the pulse, the tongue, or time (see Shakspere's "As You Like It," iii. 2. 329, 344); race; hurry (*through, over*, etc.) in reading, reciting, etc. **II.** *tr.* To cause (a horse, etc.) to gallop; also, to drive or convey at a gallop; also, to traverse at a gallop† (as, "The golden sun . . . *Gallops* the zodiac in his glistering coach": Shakspere's "Titus Andronicus," ii. 1. 7).—**gal′lop,** *n.* [OF. F. *galop*: cf. *galop.*] A fast gait of the horse (or other quadruped) in which in the course of each stride all four feet are off the ground at once; a run or ride at this gait; in general, a rapid rate of going, or a course of going at a rapid rate.

gal-lop-ade (gal-o̤-pād′), *n.* [F. *galopade*, < *galoper*: see *gallop.*] A sidelong or curvetting kind of gallop; also, a sprightly kind of dance, or the music for it; a galop.—**gal-lop-ade′,** *v. i.*; *-aded, -ading.* To dance a gallopade.

gal-lop-er (gal′o̤p-ėr), *n.* An animal or a person that gallops.

Gal-lo-phil, Gal-lo-phile (gal′ō̤-fil), *n.* [See *Gallo-* and *-phil.*] A friend or admirer of the French; a Francophil.

Gal-lo-phobe (gal′ō̤-fōb), *n.* [See *Gallo-* and *-phobe.*] One who fears or hates the French, or French influences, tendencies, etc.—**Gal-lo-pho′bi-a** (-fō′bi-ä̤), *n.* [See *-phobia.*] Fear or hatred of the French.

gal-lop-ing (gal′o̤p-ing), *p. a.* That gallops; going at a gallop; making rapid progress (as, *galloping* consumption).

gal-low (gal′ō), *v. t.* [Var. of *gally.*] To frighten. See Shakspere's "King Lear," iii. 2. 44. [Now prov. Eng.]

Gal-lo-way (gal′ō̤-wā), *n.* One of a breed of small, strong horses first raised in Galloway, Scotland; hence, a small horse; also, one of a breed of hornless cattle peculiar to Galloway.

gal-low-glass, gal-lo-glass (gal′ō̤-glȧs), *n.* [Ir. *galloglach*, < *gall*, foreigner, + *oglach*, youth, servant, soldier.] A soldier or armed retainer of a chief in ancient Ireland or Scotland. See Shakspere's "2 Henry VI.," iv. 9. 26.

gal-lows (gal′ōz), *n.*; pl. *gallowses* or *gallows.* [AS. *galga, gealga*, = D. *galg* = G. *galgen* = Icel. *gālgi*, gallows, = Goth. *galga*, cross.] A wooden frame, consisting commonly of a cross-beam on two uprights, on which condemned persons are executed by hanging; hence, any similar structure, as for suspending or supporting something or for use in gymnastic exercise; *pl.*, suspenders (now prov. or colloq.); also, *sing.*, a gallows-bird or rascal (now prov. Eng.: see Shakspere's "Love's Labour's Lost," v. 2. 12).—**gal′lows. I.** *a.* Fit for the gallows; villainous or rascally; hence, mischievous or wild, as children; spirited or smart; fine; great (as, a *gallows* lot of anything). [Prov. or slang.] **II.** *adv.* Extremely; exceedingly; very. [Prov. or slang.] —**gal′lows=bird,** *n.* A person who deserves to be hanged. [Colloq.]—**gal′lows=bitts,** *n. pl. Naut.*, a frame on the deck of a ship for supporting spare topmasts, etc.—**gal′lows=tree,** *n.* A gallows (for hanging). [Archaic.]

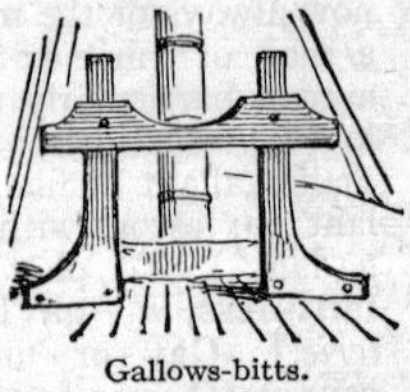

Gallows-bitts.

gall=stone (gâl′stōn), *n.* A calculus or concretion formed in the gall-bladder; a biliary calculus.

gal-lus (gal′us), *n., a.,* and *adv.* Prov. form of *gallows.*

gal-ly (gal′i), *v. t.*; *-lied, -lying.* [Cf. AS. *āgælwan*, alarm.] To frighten or scare (as, "He [a whale] was frightened, or '*gallied*,' as they call it": H. Melville's "Omoo," xix.); also, to frighten away. [Now chiefly prov. or in whaling.]

gal-ly-gas′kins, *n. pl.* See *galligaskins.*

ga-loche (ga̤-losh′), *n.* See *galosh.*

ga-loot (ga̤-löt′), *n.* [Origin obscure.] A fellow: often used in good-natured depreciation. [Slang.]

gal-op (gal′o̤p), *n.* [F., = E. *gallop, n.*] A kind of lively round dance in duple time; also, a piece of music for, or in the rhythm of, this dance.

ga-lore (ga̤-lōr′). [Ir. *go leor*, Gael. *gu leor*, to sufficiency.] **I.** *adv.* In abundance. **II.** *n.* Abundance or plenty.

ga-losh (ga̤-losh′), *n.* [OF. F. *galoche*, prob., through L., < Gr. καλόπους, shoemaker's last, < κᾶλον, wood, + πούς, foot.] Formerly, a kind of patten or clog; now, an overshoe or rubber (usually in *pl.*).

galt (gâlt), *n.* See *gault.*

ga-lumph (ga̤-lumf′), *v. i.* [Coined by C. L. Dodgson ("Lewis Carroll"), possibly < *gallop* + *triumph*, in "Through the Looking-Glass" (1871).] To gallop, prance, or go as in triumph. [Humorous.]

gal-van-ic (gal-van′ik), *a.* [See *galvanism.*] Of, pertaining to, or produced by galvanism; voltaic; also, affecting or affected as if by galvanism.—**galvanic battery,** a voltaic battery (see *battery*).—**galvanic pile.** See *pile*², *n.*—**gal-van′i-cal-ly,** *adv.*

gal-va-nism (gal′vạ-nizm), *n.* [From L. *Galvani* (1737–98), Italian physician, discoverer of galvanism.] Current electricity, esp. as produced by chemical action; the science treating of this; in *med.*, the application of the ordinary voltaic or battery current (in distinction from that produced by an induction-coil, static apparatus, etc.) to the body, for therapeutic purposes.—**gal′va-nist,** *n.* One versed in galvanism.—**gal″va-ni-za′tion** (-ni-zā′shọn), *n.* The act of galvanizing, or the state of being galvanized.—**gal′va-nize** (-nīz), *v. t.*; *-nized, -nizing.* To subject to galvanism; stimulate by or as by a galvanic current; also, to plate, as with gold, by means of galvanic electricity; by extension, to coat (iron) with zinc.—**gal′va-niz-er** (-nī-zėr), *n.*

galvano-. Form of *galvanic* or *galvanism* used in combination.—**gal-va-no-cau-ter-y** (gal″vạ-nọ-kâ′tėr-i), *n.*; pl. *-ies* (-iz). A cautery heated by a galvanic current; also, cauterization by such means.—**gal″va-no-cau″ter-i-za′tion** (-i-zā′shọn), *n.*—**gal-va-nog′ra-phy** (-nog′rạ-fi), *n.* [+ *-graphy.*] A process for producing by electrical deposition plates which can be printed from in the same way as etched copper plates.—**gal-va-nom′e-ter** (-nom′e-tėr), *n.* [+ *-meter.*] An instrument for determining the strength, presence, or direction of an electric current.—**gal″va-no-met′ric** (-met′rik), *a.*—**gal-va-nom′e-try,** *n.*—**gal′va-no-plas″ty** (-plas″ti), *n.* [+ *-plasty.*] The process of coating things with metal by means of electrolysis; esp., electrotypy.—**gal″va-no-plas′tic,** *a.*—**gal′va-no-scope** (-skōp), *n.* [+ *-scope.*] An instrument for detecting the existence and direction of an electric current.—**gal″va-no-scop′ic** (-skop′ik), *a.*—**gal-va-nos′-co-py** (-nos′kọ-pi), *n.*

gam (gam), *n.* [Origin obscure.] In whalers' speech, a herd or school of whales; also, a social meeting, visit, or the like, as between vessels at sea.—**gam,** *v.*; *gammed, gamming.* **I.** *intr.* In whalers' speech, to herd together or form a school, as whales; also, to have a social gam. **II.** *tr.* In whalers' speech, to have a social gam with.

Gama-grass.—1, the plant; 2, the spikes; 3, lower part of the spikes, showing male and female spikelets; *a*, a male spikelet; *b*, a female spikelet.

ga-ma=grass (gä′mạ-gràs), *n.* [Cf. *grama.*] A tall, stout grass, *Tripsacum dactyloides*, one of the largest grasses in the United States, used for fodder.

ga-mash-es (gạ-mash′ez), *n. pl.* [F. *gamaches*; from Sp. and prob. Ar.] A kind of leggings or gaiters worn for protection against mud and wet. [Archaic or prov.]

gam-bade (gam-bād′), *n.* [F.: see *gambol.*] A leap, as of a horse; hence, a caper, prank, or frolic; a freakish action. Also **gam-ba′do**[1] (-bā′dō); pl. *-dos* or *-does* (-dōz).

gam-ba-do² (gam-bā′dō), *n.*; pl. *-dos* or *-does* (-dōz). [It. *gamba*, leg: see *gambol.*] One of a pair of large boots or gaiters fixed to a saddle instead of stirrups; hence, any long gaiter or legging.

gam-be-son (gam′bẹ-sọn), *n.* [OF. *gambeson*, *wambizon*; from Teut., and akin to E. *womb.*] A medieval military garment of leather or cloth, sometimes padded, worn orig. under the haubergeon but later as the principal garment of defense.

Gambeson (about 1375).

gam-bier, gam-bir (gam′bēr), *n.* [Malay *gambīr.*] An astringent extract obtained from the leaves and young shoots of *Ouroouparia gambir*, a tropical Asiatic rubiaceous shrub: used in medicine, dyeing, tanning, etc.

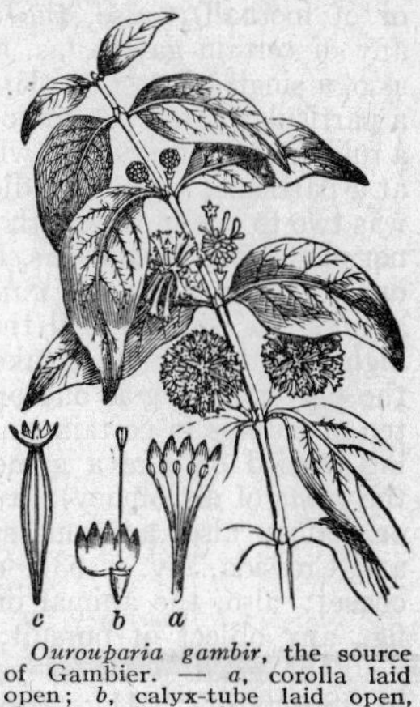

Ourouparia gambir, the source of Gambier.—*a*, corolla laid open; *b*, calyx-tube laid open, showing the style and stigma; *c*, fruit with persistent calyx.

gam-bist (gam′bist), *n.* A player on the viola da gamba.

gam-bit (gam′bit), *n.* [It. *gambetto*, lit. 'a tripping up the legs,' < *gamba*, leg: see *gambol.*] In *chess*, a method of opening in which the player seeks by the sacrifice of a pawn or piece to obtain some advantage.

gam-ble (gam′bl), *v.*; *-bled, -bling.* [Prob. from a var. of ME. *gamenen*, < AS. *gamenian*, play, < *gamen*, E. *game*².] **I.** *intr.* To play at any game of chance for stakes; hence, in general, to stake or risk money, or anything of value, on the issue of something involving chance or unknown contingencies (as, to *gamble* on the result of a race; to *gamble* in stocks). **II.** *tr.* To stake, as on the issue of a game; also, to squander (*away*) on games or matters of chance.—**gam′ble,** *n.* An act or process of gambling; a venture in or as in gambling; hence, any matter or thing involving risk or uncertainty. [Chiefly colloq.]—**gam′bler,** *n.* One who gambles, esp. habitually or professionally.—**gam′-bling,** *n.* The act or practice of one who gambles; the playing of games of chance for stakes; the staking or risking of money or anything of value on a matter of chance or uncertainty.—**gam′bling=house,** *n.* A house in which gambling is carried on as a business.

gam-boge (gam-bōj′ or -böj′), *n.* [From *Camboja*, *Cambodia*, in Indo-China.] A gum-resin from various trees of the clusiaceous genus *Garcinia*, esp. *G. hanburii*, native in Cambodia, Siam, etc.: used as a yellow pigment and also medicinally as a cathartic.

gam-bol (gam′bọl), *n.* [Earlier *gambold*, *gambald*, < F. *gambade*, a leap, < It. *gambata*, a kick, < *gamba*, leg, < LL. *gamba*, hoof.] A leap, spring, or skip, as in dancing or sport; a frolicsome movement; also, a skipping or frisking about; a frolic.—**gam′bol,** *v. i.*; *-boled* or *-bolled, -boling* or *-bolling.* To leap or skip about, as in dancing or sport; frisk; frolic.

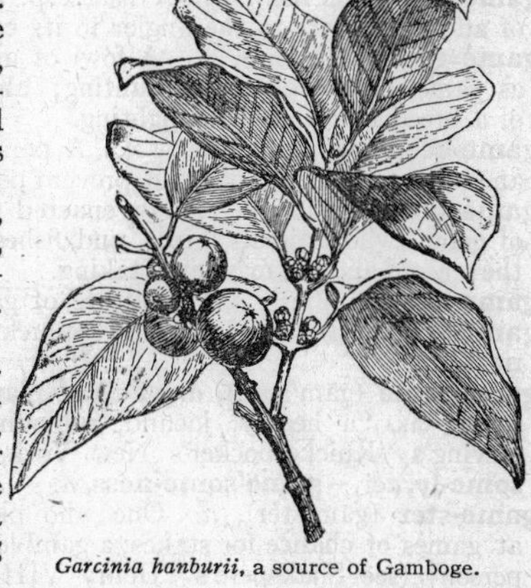

Garcinia hanburii, a source of Gamboge.

gam-brel (gam′brẹl), *n.* [OF. *gamberel*, butcher's gambrel; origin uncertain.] A bent piece of wood or iron used by butchers to extend and hang a carcass on; also, the hock of an animal, esp. of a horse; also, a gambrel-roof.—**gam′brel=roof′,** *n.* A roof whose ends are cut off in a vertical plane, and whose sides have two slopes (likened to a horse's gambrel), the lower one being the steeper.—**gam′brel=roofed′,** *a.*

game¹ (gām), *a.* [Origin uncertain.] Lame, as a leg or arm: as, "Once I had a *game* leg, and then I went limping" (J. H. Newman's "Callista," iv.). [Colloq.]

game² (gām). [AS. *gamen* = OHG. and Icel. *gaman*, amusement, sport.] **I.** *n.* Fun, sport, or jest (now chiefly in 'to make game of,' to make fun of, or ridicule); also, an amusement or pastime (as, children's *games*; the *game* of blindman's-buff); often, a diversion in the form of a trial of chance, skill, or endurance, conducted according to set rules (as, card-*games*; the *game* of roulette; the *game* of chess, of billiards, or of golf; the *game* of baseball, of handball, or of football); also, the apparatus employed in playing any of certain games (as, a store selling toys and *games*); also, a single contest at play, or a definite portion of play in a particular game (as, to go to see a baseball-*game*; to play a rubber of three *games* at whist); the state of such a contest at a particular time, as indicated by the score (as, the *game* was two to one in the ninth inning); also, a particular manner of playing a game (as, he plays a good *game*; to be off one's *game*); also, the number of points required to win a game (as, in handball the *game* is 21 points); also, the highest count for cards taken in certain card-games, giving the player having it one or more points in the score; the ten of trumps in certain card-games; in fig. use, a proceeding carried on like a game (as, to play a waiting *game*; the *game* of diplomacy); a person's plan of action; a trick or dodge; also, amorous sport† (see Shakspere's "Troilus and Cressida," iv. 5. 63); also, the sport of hunting†; the chase†; also, the animal or animals pursued in the chase; fig., any object of pursuit, attack, etc. (as, "Widows are . . . the great *game* of your fortune-hunters": Addison, in "Spectator," 311); also, wild animals, including birds and fishes (cf. *game-bird* and *game-fish*), such as are hunted or taken for sport or profit; the flesh of wild animals, including game-birds, used for food; sometimes, a game-fowl or game-cock; also, fighting spirit, or pluck; also, a flock or herd of animals, now esp. swans, kept for pleasure. **II.** *a.*; compar. *gamer*, superl. *gamest*. Of or pertaining to animals hunted or taken as game; also, having the fighting spirit of a game-cock; plucky; courageous; also, having the spirit or will (for or to do something: colloq.).—**game**[2], *v.*; *gamed, gaming*. **I.** *intr.* To play, sport, or jest (now prov. Eng.); also, to play games, esp. games of chance for stakes; gamble. **II.** *tr.* To squander (*away*) in gaming: as, to *game* away one's patrimony.

game=bird (gām'bėrd), *n.* A bird hunted for sport or profit, or protected by law.

game=cock (gām'kok), *n.* A cock bred and trained for fighting, or one of a fighting breed.

game=fish (gām'fish), *n.* A fish, esp. a food-fish, capable of affording sport to the angler in its capture.

game=fowl (gām'foul), *n.* A fowl of any species regarded as game, or the object of hunting; also, a domestic fowl of a breed much used for fighting.

game-keep-er (gām'kē″pėr), *n.* A person employed as on an estate, to take care of game, prevent poaching, etc.

game=law (gām'lâ), *n.* A law enacted for the preservation of game (wild animals, birds, and fishes), as by restricting the seasons and the manner of taking.

game-less (gām'les), *a.* Destitute of game, as a region.

game-ly (gām'li), *adv.* In a game or plucky manner.—**game'-ness**, *n.*

game-some (gām'sum), *a.* Full of play; sportive; frolicsome: as, "a hearty, jocund, rubicund, *gamesome* wag" (Irving's "Knickerbocker's New York," vii. 4).—**game'-some-ly**, *adv.*—**game'some-ness**, *n.*

game-ster (gām'stėr), *n.* One who plays at games, esp. at games of chance for stakes; a gambler; also, a frolicsome person† (see Shakspere's "Henry VIII.," i. 4. 45); also, a lewd person†.

gam-e-tal (gam'ę-tal), *a.* In *biol.*, pertaining to, or having the character of, a gamete; reproductive; generative.

gam-e-tan-gi-um (gam-ę-tan'ji-um), *n.*; pl. *-gia* (-ji-ä). [NL., < Gr. γαμετή, wife, γαμέτης, husband, + ἀγγεῖον, vessel.] In *bot.*, an organ or body producing gametes.

gam-ete (gam'ēt or ga-mēt'), *n.* [Gr. γαμετή, wife, γαμέτης, husband, < γαμεῖν, marry, < γάμος, marriage.] In *biol.*, either of the two germ-cells which unite to form a new organism.—**ga-met-ic** (ga-met'ik), *a.*—**gam-e-to-phore** (gam'ę-tǫ-fōr or ga-mē'-), *n.* [See *-phore.*] In *bot.*, a part or structure producing gametes.—**gam-e-to-phyte** (gam'ę-tǫ-fīt or ga-mē'-), *n.* [See *-phyte.*] In *bot.*, the sexual form of a plant in the alternation of generations: opposed to *sporophyte.*

gam-ic (gam'ik), *a.* [Gr. γαμικός, of or for marriage, < γάμος, marriage.] In *biol.*, sexual: opposed to *agamic.*

gam-in (gam'in, F. gȧ-maṅ), *n.* [F.; origin uncertain.] A neglected boy left to run about the streets; a street Arab. —**ga-mine** (gȧ-mēn), *n.* [F.] Fem. of *gamin.*—**ga-mine-rie** (gȧ-mēn-rē), *n.* [F.] The spirit, action, or language of a gamin.

gam-ing (gā'ming), *n.* The act or practice of one who games; the playing of games of chance for stakes; gambling. —**gam'ing=house**, *n.* A gambling-house.

gam-ma (gam'ä), *n.* [Gr. γάμμα.] The third letter (Γ, γ, = English G, g) of the Greek alphabet; the third of any series (esp. in scientific classification).—**gamma rays.** See under *ray*[3], *n.*

gam-ma-di-on (ga-mā'di-on), *n.*; pl. *-dia* (-di-ä). [MGr. γαμμάδιον, γαμμάτιον, dim. of Gr. γάμμα, gamma.] An ornamental figure consisting of combinations of the Greek capital gamma, esp. in the form of a swastika or fylfot, or of a voided Greek cross.

gam-mer (gam'ėr), *n.* [Appar. a contr. of *grandmother.*] A rustic title or term for an old woman: as, "*Gammer* Gurton's Needle" (the title of a celebrated English comedy, published in 1575, the authorship of which has been attributed to several different persons, latterly to a certain William Stevenson). Cf. *gaffer.*

gam-mon[1] (gam'ǫn), *n.* [Appar. < ME. and AS. *gamen*, E. *game*[2].] The game of backgammon; also, in this game, a victory in which the winner throws off all his men before his opponent throws off any.—**gam'mon**[1], *v. t.* In backgammon, to win a gammon over.

gam-mon[2] (gam'ǫn), *n.* [Origin obscure: cf. *gammon*[1].] Deceitful nonsense; humbug; bosh. [Colloq.]—**gam'-mon**[2], *v.* **I.** *intr.* To talk gammon; also, to make pretense. [Colloq.] **II.** *tr.* To ply with or deceive by gammon; humbug. [Colloq.]

gam-mon[3] (gam'ǫn), *n.* [OF. *gambon, jambon* (F. *jambon*), < *gambe, jambe*, leg, < LL. *gamba*, hoof.] The haunch or ham of a swine†; also, a smoked or cured ham; also, the lower end of a side of bacon.—**gam'mon**[3], *v. t.* To cure by salting and smoking; make into bacon.

gam-mon[4] (gam'ǫn), *v. t.* [Origin unknown.] *Naut.*, to fasten (a bowsprit) to the stem of a ship.

gam-mon-er (gam'ǫn-ėr), *n.* One who gammons.

gam-mon-ing (gam'ǫn-ing), *n.* *Naut.*, the arrangement of ropes, chains, or iron bands serving to gammon a bowsprit.

Gammoning. — 1, rope gammoning; 2, chain gammoning; 3, iron-strap gammoning.

gamo-. Form of Gr. γάμος, marriage, in combination: used chiefly in biological and botanical terms, to denote sexual union, union of parts, etc.—**gam-o-gen-e-sis** (gam-ǭ-jen'e-sis), *n.* In *biol.*, sexual reproduction.—**gam″o-ge-net'ic** (-ję-net'ik), *a.*—**gam″o-ge-net'i-cal-ly**, *adv.*—**gam-o-pet'a-lous** (-pet'a̤-lus), *a.* In *bot.*, having the petals united.—**gam-o-phyl'-lous** (-fil'us), *a.* [+ *-phyllous.*] In *bot.*, having the leaves of the perianth united.—**gam-o-sep'a-lous** (-sep'a̤-lus), *a.* In *bot.*, having the sepals united.

-gamous. [Gr. -γαμος, < γάμος, marriage.] An adjective termination meaning 'marrying,' 'married,' as in *monogamous*, *polygamous*, and used also with figurative applications in botanical and biological terms, as *dichogamous, heterogamous, isogamous.* Cf. *-gamy.*

gamp (gamp), *n.* [Said to be from the umbrella of Mrs. Sarah *Gamp*, in Dickens's "Martin Chuzzlewit."] An umbrella. [Humorous.]

gam-ut (gam'ut), *n.* [ML. *gamma ut*, < *gamma*, used to represent the first or lowest tone (G) in the medieval scale, and *ut*, later *do.*] The lowest note in the medieval scale of music; also, the whole series of recognized musical notes; sometimes, the major scale; fig., the whole range of anything.

gam-y (gā'mi), *a.*; compar. *gamier*, superl. *gamiest*. Abounding in game; also, having the flavor of game, esp. game that has been kept uncooked until slightly tainted (when it is considered by connoisseurs to be in proper condition for the table); also, game or plucky.

-gamy. [Gr. -γαμία, < -γαμος, marrying, married, < γάμος, marriage.] A noun termination meaning 'marriage,' as in *monogamy*, *polygamy*, and used figuratively in botanical and biological terms, as *allogamy*, *apogamy*, *cleistogamy*. Cf. *-gamous*.

gan (gan). Preterit of *gin*[1].

gan-der (gan'dėr), *n.* [AS. *gandra*: see *gannet*.] The male of the goose.

gang (gang), *v.* [AS. *gangan* = OHG. *gangan* = Goth. *gaggan*, go: cf. *go*.] **I.** *intr.* To walk; go. [Now Sc. and prov. Eng.] **II.** *tr.* To arrange in gangs.—**gang,** *n.* [AS. *gang*.] A walking† or going†; ability to walk†; also, a way or passage (now Sc. and north Eng.); also, a pasture for cattle, or the right of pasturing (Sc.); also, a set of things such as are ordinarily taken together; a number of similar tools, machines, or the like, arranged to work together (as, a *gang* of saws or of plows); also, a set or company of persons employed or working together (as, a *gang* of laborers; a press-*gang*); a company of convicts, slaves, or the like (as, a chain-*gang*); any set of persons associated or going about together (usually with a disparaging force: as, a *gang* of roughs or of thieves; a political *gang*; "a *gang* of crazy heretics," Macaulay's "Hist. of Eng.," iv.); also, a herd, as of elk or buffalo (U. S.).—**gang'=drill,** *n.* A machine having several drills so arranged that they may be operated together or independently.—**gang'er**[1], *n.* One who walks or goes. [Now Sc. and prov. Eng.]—**gang'er**[2], *n.* The foreman of a gang of workmen.

Gan-get-ic (gan-jet'ik), *a.* Of or along the river Ganges in India: as, *Gangetic* cities; the *Gangetic* crocodile (the gavial).

gan-gli-a (gang'gli-ạ̈), *n.* Plural of *ganglion*.

gan-gli-ate, gan-gli-at-ed (gang'gli-āt, -ā-ted), *a.* Having ganglia.

gan-gling (gang'gling), *a.* [From *gang*, *v.*] Straggling, as a plant; also, awkwardly tall and slender, as a person; lank and loosely built.

gan-gli-on (gang'gli-ọn), *n.*; pl. *ganglia* (-ạ̈) or *-ons*. [LL., kind of swelling, < Gr. γάγγλιον, tumor under the skin, on or near a tendon.] In *pathol.*, an encysted tumor or enlargement in connection with the sheath of a tendon; also, an enlarged bursa; in *anat.*, any aggregation of nerve-cells or mass of gray matter forming a nerve-center; in fig. use, a center of force, activity, or the like.—**gan-gli-on'ic** (-on'ik), *a.*

gang=plank (gang'plangk), *n.* A plank, often with cleats, or a long, narrow, flat structure, used as a temporary bridge in passing into and out of a ship, etc.

gang=plow (gang'plou), *n.* A plow with several shares, or a combination of plows in one frame.

gan-grel (gang'grẹl), *n.* [From *gang*, *v.*: cf. *gangling*.] A vagabond or vagrant; also, a lank, loosely built person. [Archaic or prov.]

gan-grene (gang'grēn), *n.* [L. *gangræna*, < Gr. γάγγραινα, < γράειν, gnaw.] In *pathol.*, the dying of tissue, as from interruption of circulation; mortification.—**gan'grene,** *v. t.* or *i.*; *-grened, -grening.* To affect or become affected with gangrene.—**gan-gre-nous** (gang'grẹ̄-nus), *a.* Of the nature of, or affected with, gangrene.

gang-ster (gang'stėr), *n.* A member of a gang of roughs, criminals, or the like, or of a political gang. [Colloq., U. S.]

gangue (gang), *n.* [F., < G. *gang*, mineral vein, lode.] The stony or earthy minerals occurring with the metallic ore in a vein or deposit.

gang-way (gang'wā), *n.* A passageway; *naut.*, any of various passageways on a ship, as that between the rail and the cabins or houses on the deck; an opening in the rail or bulwarks for passing into or out of a ship; a gang-plank; in *mining*, a main passage or level.

gan-is-ter (gan'is-tėr), *n.* [Origin unknown.] A hard siliceous rock occurring in some English coal-seams, or an artificial mixture resembling it, used esp. as a refractory material in the lining of furnaces, etc.

gan-net (gan'et), *n.* [AS. *ganot*, akin to D. *gent*, gander, and AS. *gandra*, E. *gander*.] Any of the large totipalmate swimming birds of the genus *Sula*, as the solan, *S. bassana*, of the Atlantic coasts of Europe and North America, or the booby, *S. leucogastra*, of the southern Atlantic coast of the U. S.

Gannet (*Sula bassana*), adult and young.

gan-oid (gan'oid). [Gr. γάνος, brightness, + εἶδος, form, appearance.] **I.** *a.* Of fish-scales, having a smooth, shining enameled surface; also, belonging or pertaining to the *Ganoidei*, a group of fishes many of which have such scales, including the sturgeons, etc. **II.** *n.* A ganoid fish.

gant-let[1], **gaunt-let**[1] (gȧnt'let, gȧnt'let or gänt'-), *n.* [Earlier *gantlope*, < Sw. *gatlopp*, < *gata*, way, lane, + *lopp*, a running, course.] A former punishment, chiefly military, in which the offender, stripped to the waist, was compelled to run between two rows of men who struck at him with switches or other weapons as he passed: used chiefly in the phrase 'to run the gantlet' (often fig., to proceed under attacks from both sides, or under any like trying conditions: as, to *run the gantlet* of hostile or curious glances, or of criticism or ridicule).

gant-let[2] (gȧnt'let), *n.* Same as *gauntlet*[2].

gan-try, gaun-try (gan'tri, gȧn'-), *n.*; pl. *-tries* (-triz). [Cf. OF. *gantier*, var. of *chantier*, < L. *cantherius*, a supporting framework.] A frame for supporting a barrel or cask; also, a spanning framework or platform, as a bridge-like portion of certain cranes.

Gan-y-mede (gan'i-mēd), *n.* [L. *Ganymedes*, < Gr. Γανυμήδης.] A Trojan youth of classical mythology who was carried off (according to one legend, by an eagle) to become cup-bearer to Zeus; hence, any youth who serves liquor; a cup-bearer; a pot-boy; in *astron.*, the largest satellite of the planet Jupiter.

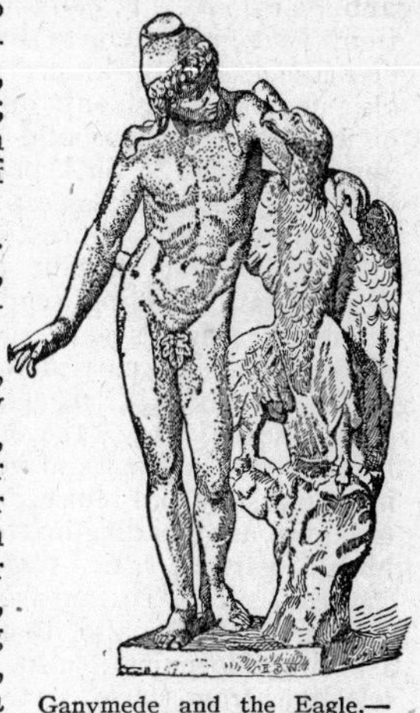

Ganymede and the Eagle.—Museo Nazionale, Naples.

gaol (jāl), **gaol-er** (jā'lėr), etc. Archaic spellings of *jail*, *jailer*, etc., still current in Great Britain, esp. in official use.

gap (gap), *n.* [ME. *gap*, *gappe*, from Scand.: cf. Icel. *gap*, empty space, connected with *gapa*, gape: see *gape*.] A break or opening, as in a fence, wall, or the like; a breach; also, an opening between high rocks or in a mountain-range; a deep, sloping ravine or cleft cutting a mountain-ridge; in general, a vacant space or interval; a hiatus; a blank or deficiency in something; sometimes, a wide divergence; in *aëronautics*, the distance between one supporting plane of an aëroplane and another directly above or below it.—**gap,** *v. t.*; *gapped*, *gapping.* To make a gap, opening, or breach in: as, "Ready! take aim at their leaders—their masses are *gapp'd* with our grape" (Tennyson's "Defence of Lucknow," iii.).

gape (gāp, U. S. also gäp, popularly gap: cf. *gaup*, *gawp*), *v. i.*; *gaped*, *gaping.* [ME. *gapen*, prob. from Scand.: cf. Icel. *gapa*, Sw. *gapa*, Dan. *gabe*, also D. *gapen*, G. *gaffen*, gape.] To open the mouth wide, as if to swallow something, or as the result of weariness, sleepiness, absorbed attention, astonishment, etc.; yawn; hence, to stare with open mouth, as in wonder; stare in wonder; also, to open like a mouth (as, "May that ground *gape* and swallow me alive, Where I shall kneel to him that slew my father!" Shakspere's "3 Henry VI.," i. 1. 161); of a gap, etc., to be or become open wide.—**gape,** *n.* The act of gaping; a yawn; a stare, as with open mouth; also, the width of the open mouth:

also, a breach or rent; *pl.*, a fit of yawning; also, a disease of poultry and other birds, attended with frequent gaping, due to infestation of the trachea and bronchi with a nematoid worm, *Syngamus trachealis.*—**gap-er** (gā′pėr, also gä′-), *n.* One who or that which gapes; specif., any of various broad-billed or fissirostral birds, as *Cymbirhynchus macrorhynchus*, an East Indian broadbill ('blue-billed gaper').—**gape′=seed,** *n.* An imaginary seed supposed to yield something to gape or stare at in wonder; hence, something to gape or stare at; an opportunity for gaping or staring; also, gaping or staring; also, one who gapes or stares.—**gape′=worm,** *n.* A nematoid worm, *Syngamus trachealis*, which causes the gapes in birds.—**gap′ing-ly,** *adv.*—**gap′ing=stock,** *n.* An object of gaping or open-mouthed wonder.

Blue-billed Gaper.

gap-py (gap′i), *a.* Having gaps, breaks, or hiatuses.

gap=toothed (gap′tötht), *a.* Having gaps in the rows of teeth; having the teeth set wide apart.

gap-y (gā′pi, also gä′-), *a.* Affected with the gapes.

gar[1] (gär), *n.*; pl. *gars* or (esp. collectively) *gar.* [Short for *garfish.*] A garfish.

gar[2] (gär), *v. t.*; *garred* or *gart, garring.* [From Scand.: cf. Icel. *gera, göra*, make, do, akin to E. *gear* and *yare.*] To make, cause, or compel. [Chiefly Sc. and north. Eng.]

ga-rage (ga-räzh′, also gar′āj), *n.* [F., < *garer*, put in shelter.] A building for sheltering, cleaning, or repairing motor-cars; also, a shelter for flying-machines.—**ga-rage′,** *v. t.*; *-raged, -raging.* To put or keep in a garage.

garb (gärb), *n.* [F. *garbe* (now *galbe*), < It. *garbo*, grace; from Teut., and akin to E. *gear.*] Grace or elegance, as of manners or appearance†; also, bearing† or demeanor†; also, manner†, fashion†, or style† (as, "The appurtenance of welcome is fashion and ceremony: let me comply with you in this *garb*": Shakspere's "Hamlet," ii. 2. 390); now, fashion or mode of dress, esp. of a distinctive or characteristic kind, or the dress or costume itself (as, official, military, or priestly *garb*; peasant *garb*; in the *garb* of a beggar); fig., outward covering, semblance, or form (as, "false rules prank'd in reason's *garb*": Milton's "Comus," 759).—**garb,** *v. t.* To dress in a particular garb or manner.

gar-bage (gär′bāj), *n.* [ME.; possibly < OF. *garbe, gerbe*, sheaf.] Orig., the entrails or offal from an animal; hence, refuse animal and vegetable matter from a kitchen; in general, any foul refuse, or vile or worthless matter (sometimes fig., as of reading-matter).

gar-ble (gär′bl), *v. t.*; *-bled, -bling.* [It. *garbellare*, < Ar. *gharbala*, sift.] To free (spices, etc.) from refuse or dirt†; sift† or cleanse†; also, to take out the best of (now rare: as, to *garble* coins); also, to make unfair or misleading selections from (facts, statements, writings, etc.); mutilate so as to misrepresent.—**gar′ble,** *n.* Refuse, as of spices†; also, merchandise containing an admixture of waste†; also, a mixture of base and precious metal; also, the process of garbling.—**gar′bler,** *n.*

gar-board (gär′bōrd), *n.* [D. *gaarboord.*] In *ship-building*, one of the planks or plates on a ship's bottom, next to the keel.

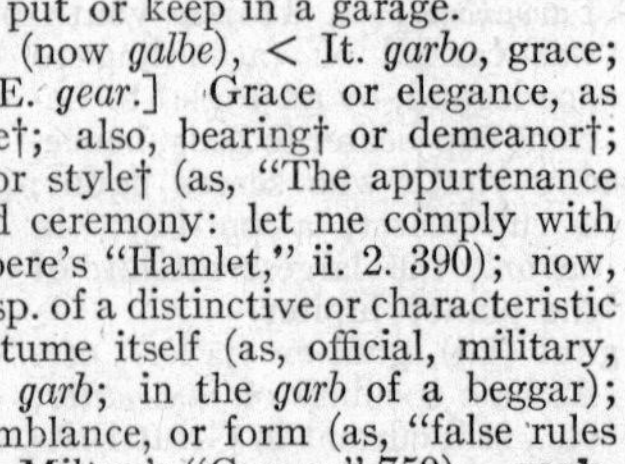

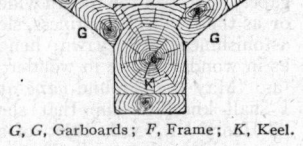

G, G, Garboards; *F*, Frame; *K*, Keel.

gar-boil (gär′boil), *n.* [Obs. F. *garbouil*, < It. *garbuglio.*] Commotion; disorder; a tumult or disturbance (see Shakspere's "Antony and Cleopatra," ii. 2. 67). [Obs. or archaic.]

gar-çon (gär-sôṅ), *n.* [F. *garçon*, OF. *garçun*, = ML. *garcio(n-)*; origin unknown.] A boy or young man; a fellow; often, a male employee or servant; esp., a waiter.

gar-den (gär′dn), *n.* [OF. *gardin, jardin* (F. *jardin*); from Teut. (cf. G. *garten*), and akin to E. *yard*[1] and *garth.*] A plot of ground devoted to the cultivation of useful or ornamental plants, or the raising of herbs, vegetables, fruits, flowers, etc.; often, an inclosed plot of this kind adjoining a dwelling; also, a piece of ground, or other space, commonly with ornamental plants, trees, etc., used as a place of public resort (as, a botanical or zoölogical *garden*; a beer-*garden*; a roof-*garden*); also, a region of luxuriant vegetation or high cultivation (as, "Fruitful Lombardy, The pleasant *garden* of great Italy": Shakspere's "Taming of the Shrew," i. 1. 4); a fertile and delightful spot.—**garden of Eden.** See *Eden.*—**gar′den,** *v.* **I.** *intr.* To cultivate or tend a garden. **II.** *tr.* To cultivate as a garden.—**gar′den-er,** *n.* One who lays out, cultivates, or tends gardens, esp. as a regular occupation; often, a person employed to take care of a garden.—**gar′den-er=bird,** *n.* A bird, *Amblyornis inornata*, of New Guinea, which builds a bower-like structure for pleasure or play, scattering flowers, fruits, and other bright objects on the ground before it. Cf. *bower-bird.*—**gar-den-esque′** (-esk′), *a.* [See *-esque.*] In the style or manner of a garden; garden-like.

Gardener-bird.

gar-de-ni-a (gär-dē′ni-ä), *n.* [NL.; from Dr. Alexander *Garden* (1730–91).] Any of the evergreen trees and shrubs of the rubiaceous genus *Gardenia*, native in the warmer parts of the Old World, including species, as *G. florida*, the Cape jasmine, cultivated for their fragrant, wax-like white flowers.

gar-den-ing (gär′dn-ing), *n.* The cultivating of a garden; the work or art of a gardener.

gar-den=par-ty (gär′dn-pär″ti), *n.*; pl. *-ties* (-tiz). A party or social gathering held in a garden or on the lawn or grounds of a house.

garde-robe (gärd′rōb), *n.* [OF. *garderobe, warderobe* (F. *garde-robe*), < *garder*, guard, keep, + *robe*, robe.] A room or place for keeping articles of dress, etc.; a wardrobe; also, its contents. [Archaic.]

gare-fowl (gãr′foul), *n.* [Icel. *geirfugl.*] The great auk.

gar-fish (gär′fish), *n.* [AS. *gār*, spear.] Any of various fishes with a long, sharp (spear-like) snout or beak, esp. those of the family *Belonidæ* (as *Tylosurus marinus*, a species of the eastern U. S., frequently ascending rivers), and of the ganoid family *Lepisosteidæ* (as *Lepisosteus osseus*, the 'long-nosed garfish,' and *L. platystomus*, the 'broad-nosed garfish' or 'short-nosed garfish,' both common in the central U. S.).

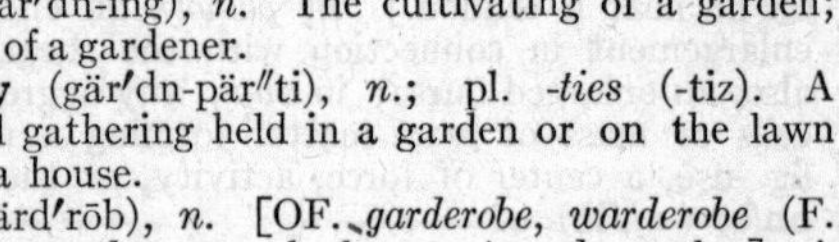

Broad-nosed Garfish.

gar-ga-ney (gär′ga-ni), *n.* [From It.] An old-world species of teal (duck), *Querquedula circia.*

Gar-gan-tu-an (gär-gan′tū-an), *a.* Of, like, or befitting Gargantua, the amiable giant and king, of enormous capacity for eating and drinking, in Rabelais's satire; hence, gigantic; enormous; prodigious.

gar-get (gär′get), *n.* [Cf. OF. *gargate*, throat.] An inflamed condition of the head or throat of cattle and swine; also, inflammation of the udder in cows, ewes, etc.; also, the pokeweed, *Phytolacca decandra.*

gar-gle (gär′gl), *v.*; *-gled, -gling.* [OF. F. *gargouiller*, < *gargouille*, throat: cf. L. *gurgulio*, gullet.] **I.** *tr.* To wash or rinse (the throat or mouth) with a liquid held in the throat and agitated by a gentle expiration of air. **II.** *intr.* To gargle the throat or mouth.—**gar′gle,** *n.* Any liquid used for gargling.

gar-goyle (gär′goil), *n.* [OF. *gargouille, gargoule* (F. *gargouille*), appar. the same word as *gargouille,* throat: see *gargle.*] A spout, often terminating in a grotesque head (animal or human) with open mouth, projecting from the gutter of a building for discharging rain-water clear of the wall.—**gar′goyled,** *a.* Provided with gargoyles.

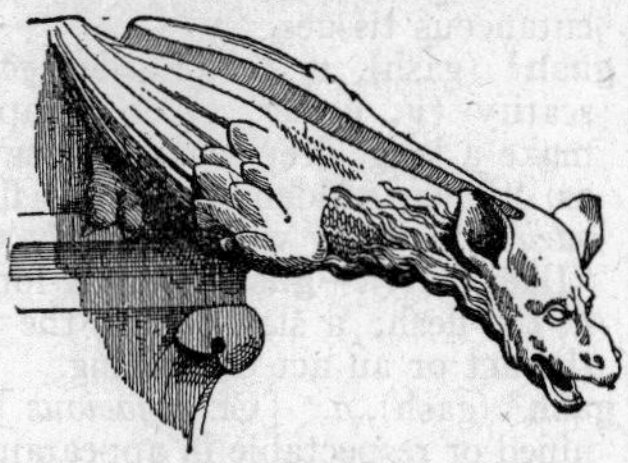
Gargoyle, 13th century. — Sainte Chapelle, Paris.

gar-i-bal-di (gar-i-bâl′di), *n.* [From *Garibaldi* (1807–82), the Italian patriot.] A loose waist worn by women and children, made in imitation of the red shirts worn by the soldiers of Garibaldi; also, a fish, *Hypsypops rubicundus,* of a bright scarlet color, found along the coast of California.

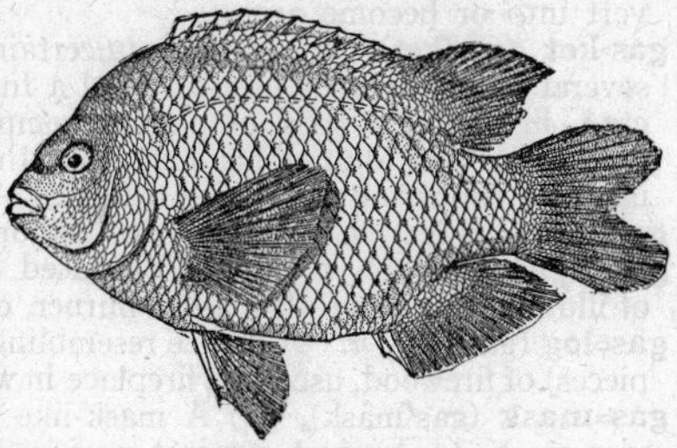
Garibaldi.

gar-ish (gãr′ish), *a.* [Origin uncertain; cf. ME. *gauren,* stare.] Glaring, or excessively bright (as, "the *garish* sun," Shakspere's "Romeo and Juliet," iii. 2. 25; "the *garish* day," J. H. Newman's "Lead, Kindly Light"); esp., glaringly or unpleasantly bright, as colors or anything colored; crudely or vulgarly gay or showy, as dress, ornaments, etc.; gaudy; fig., pretentious, or excessively ornate, as structures, writings, etc.—**gar′ish-ly,** *adv.*—**gar′ish-ness,** *n.*

gar-land (gär′lạnd), *n.* [OF. *garlande* = It. *ghirlanda* (whence F. *guirlande*); origin unknown.] A wreath or chaplet of flowers, leaves, or other material, for the head, worn for ornament or serving as a mark of distinction or honor (as, a *garland* of roses; the poet's *garland* of laurel); any wreath, festoon, or string of flowers, leaves, or the like, hung on something as a decoration, as on occasions of rejoicing (as, Christmas *garlands*); a decorative representation of such a wreath, festoon, or the like; sometimes, formerly, a crown, as of sovereignty† (see Shakspere's "Richard III.," iii. 2. 40); fig., the crowning or chief ornament† (as, "Bellay, first *garland* of free Poësie That France brought forth": Spenser's "Ruines of Rome," L'Envoy); also, a collection of choice short literary pieces, esp. in verse; an anthology; *naut.,* a band, collar, or grommet, as of rope, for various purposes.—**gar′land,** *v. t.* To crown with a garland; deck with garlands; also, to form into a garland.—**gar′land-age** (-ạj), **gar′land-ry** (-ri), *n.* A decoration of garlands: as, "gayest *garlandage* of flowers" (Tennyson's "Balin and Balan," 80).

gar-lic (gär′lik), *n.* [AS. *gārlēac,* < *gār,* spear, + *lēac,* leek.] A hardy liliaceous plant, *Allium sativum,* whose strong-scented, pungent bulb is used in cookery and medicine; any of various other species of the same genus; also, the bulb of any such plant.—**gar′lick-y,** *a.* Of, like, or containing garlic.

gar-ment (gär′mẹnt), *n.* [OF. *garniment, garnement,* < *garnir,* equip: see *garnish.*] Any article of clothing; a vestment.—**gar′ment,** *v. t.* To clothe: chiefly in *garmented,* *pp.*: as, "Earth was gaily *garmented*" (Joaquin Miller's "Walker in Nicaragua," ii. 1).—**gar′ment-less,** *a.* Without garments.—**gar′ment-ure** (-mẹn-ţūr), *n.* Clothing; dress.

gar-ner (gär′nėr), *n.* [OF. *gernier, garnier, granier* (F. *grenier*), < L. *granarium*: see *granary.*] A storehouse for grain; a granary; fig., a store of anything.—**gar′ner,** *v.* **I.** *tr.* To store in a garner; fig., to collect or deposit as in a garner. **II.** *intr.* To be stored up; accumulate: as, "the wrath that *garners* in my heart" (Tennyson's "In Memoriam," lxxxii.).

gar-net[1] (gär′net), *n.* [ME. *garnett*; origin obscure.] *Naut.,* a form of hoisting-tackle.

gar-net[2] (gär′net), *n.* [OF. F. *grenat,* appar. (by reason of the red color) < L. *granatum,* pomegranate, prop. neut. of *granatus,* having grains or seeds, < *granum,* E. *grain*[2].] A hard, vitreous silicate mineral occurring in a number of varieties all of which have the same general formula but differ more or less in composition, the common deep-red transparent variety used as a gem being a silicate of iron and aluminium; also, the deep-red color of this gem.—**gar-net-if′er-ous** (-ne-tif′ẹ-rus), *a.* [See *-ferous.*] Yielding or containing garnets.

gar-nier-ite (gär′niėr-īt), *n.* [From Jules *Garnier,* French geologist.] A native hydrous silicate of nickel and magnesium: an important ore of nickel.

gar-nish (gär′nish), *v. t.* [OF. *garnir* (*garniss-*), *warnir,* fortify, equip, prepare, warn, F. *garnir,* furnish, garnish; from Teut.: cf. *warn.*] To equip or furnish with something; now, esp., to fit out with something that adorns or decorates; ornament; embellish; often, to decorate (a dish) for the table, as with parsley; in *law,* to serve with a garnishment; garnishee.—**gar′nish,** *n.* Adornment or decoration; an ornament or embellishment; esp., something placed around or added to a dish for decorative effect; also, a fee, esp. one formerly paid in English jails by a new prisoner.—**gar-nish-ee′** (-ē′), *n.* In *law,* a person served with a garnishment.—**gar-nish-ee′,** *v. t.*; *-eed, -eeing.* In *law,* to make (a person) a garnishee; also, to attach (money or property) by garnishment.—**gar′nish-er,** *n.* One who garnishes or decorates; in *law,* one who serves with a garnishment.—**gar′nish-ment,** *n.* Adornment; decoration; an ornament or embellishment; in *law,* a warning or notice, esp. a summons to appear in litigation already pending between others, or a warning served on a person, at the suit of a creditor plaintiff, to hold, subject to the court's direction, money or property in his possession belonging to the defendant.

gar-ni-ture (gär′ni-ţūr), *n.* [F. *garniture,* < *garnir*: see *garnish.*] Anything that garnishes, furnishes, or decorates; appurtenances or outfit; adornment or embellishment.

ga-rote′, etc., **ga-rotte′,** etc. See *garrote,* etc.

gar-pike (gär′pīk), *n.* A garfish, esp. one of the family *Lepisosteidæ.*

gar-ran (gar′ạn), *n.* [Ir. and Gael. *gearran.*] A kind of small, hardy horse bred in Ireland and Scotland: hence applied to similar horses elsewhere.

gar-ret (gar′et), *n.* [OF. *garite* (F. *guérite*), watch-tower, < *garir,* defend: see *garrison.*] A watch-tower†; also, that part of a house which is on the uppermost floor, esp. under a sloping roof; an attic.—**gar-ret-eer** (gar-e-tēr′), *n.* One who lives in a garret; esp., an impecunious author (as, "He . . . ate and drank with the keen appetite of a *garreteer*": Irving's "Tales of a Traveler," ii. 2).

gar-ri-son (gar′i-sọn), *n.* [OF. *garison, warison,* defense, deliverance (F. *guérison,* cure), < *garir, warir,* defend, save (F. *guérir,* cure); from Teut. (cf. G. *wehren,* defend): cf. F. *garnison,* garrison, < *garnir,* E. *garnish.*] Defense†; means of defense†; also, a body of troops stationed in a fortified place; hence, the place where they are stationed.—**gar′ri-son,** *v. t.* To provide (a fort, town, etc.) with a garrison, for defense; defend by fortresses manned with troops, as a region; also, to occupy (a fort, etc.) as a garrison, as troops do; also, to put (troops, etc.) on duty in a garrison.

gar-ron (gar′ọn), *n.* Same as *garran.*

gar-rot (gar′ọt), *n.* [F. *garrot.*] The goldeneye (duck).

gar-rote (gạ-rōt′), *n.* [Sp. *garrote,* orig. a stick (formerly used in drawing the cord tight in strangling), = F. *garrot,* cudgel, stick for tightening the cord about a pack.] A Spanish mode of capital punishment orig. by means of an instrument causing death by strangulation, later by one injuring the spinal column at the base of the brain; the instrument used; also, strangulation or throttling, esp. as a means of robbery.—**gar-rote′,** *v. t.*; *-roted, -roting.* [Sp. *garrotear.*] To execute by the garrote; also, to throttle, esp. for the purpose of robbery.—**gar-rot′er** (-rō′tėr), *n.*

gar-rotte (ga-rot′), etc. [After F. *garrotte*, n., *garrotter*, v., < Sp. *garrote*.] Same as *garrote*, etc.
gar-ru-lous (gar′ǫ-lus), *a.* [L. *garrulus*, < *garrire*, chatter.] Given to much talking, esp. about trifles; talkative; chattering; also, wordy or diffuse, as speech.—**gar-ru-li-ty** (ga-rö′li-ti), **gar′ru-lous-ness,** *n.*—**gar′ru-lous-ly,** *adv.*
gar-ter (gär′tėr), *n.* [OF. *gartier, jartier*, < *garet* (F. *jarret*), the bend of the knee; prob. from Celtic.] A fastening, often in the form of a band passing round the leg, to keep the stocking up; also, the badge of the Order of the Garter, the highest order of knighthood in Great Britain; membership in the order; [*cap.*] the order itself; also [*cap.*], the principal king-of-arms in England (more fully, 'Garter king-of-arms').—**gar′ter,** *v. t.* To fasten with a garter; also, to invest with the garter of the Order of the Garter (as, "*garter'd* earls": Byron's "Don Juan," xiii. 68). —**gar′ter=snake,** *n.* Any of various harmless snakes of the genus *Eutænia*, having a brownish or greenish body with long yellow stripes.—**gar′ter=stitch,** *n.* The simplest knitting stitch, done without purling.
garth (gärth), *n.* [Icel. *gardhr* = AS. *geard*, E. *yard*[1].] A yard or garden (archaic or prov. Eng.); esp., the open court inclosed by a cloister (in full, 'cloister-garth'); also, a dam or weir for catching fish.
gas (gas), *n.*; pl. *gases* (gas′ez). [Coined by J. B. van Helmont (1577–1644), Flemish chemist; suggested by Gr. χάος, chaos.] An aëriform elastic fluid possessing perfect molecular mobility and the property of indefinite expansion; in popular usage, any such fluid or mixture of fluids except air, as laughing-gas, or some combustible gaseous fluid burned for illuminating and heating purposes; sometimes, a material suspended in the air, etc., in the form of fine, mist-like particles; specif., an aëriform fluid, or a mist-like assemblage of fine particles suspended in the air, used in warfare as a means of asphyxiating, poisoning, or stupefying the enemy; also, empty talk (slang); also, gasoline (colloq.). —**gas,** *v.*; *gassed, gassing.* **I.** *tr.* To supply with gas; also, to treat or impregnate with gas (as, to *gas* lime with chlorine in the manufacture of bleaching-powder); also, to singe (fabrics, etc.) with a gas-flame to remove superfluous fibers; also, to affect, overcome, or asphyxiate with gas or fumes, as in an attack in battle (sometimes fig.). **II.** *intr.* To give off gas, as a storage-battery while being charged; also, to indulge in empty talk, or talk idly (slang).—**gas′=at-tack″,** *n.* *Milit.*, an attack in which asphyxiating or poisonous gases are employed, as by liberating the gases from cylinders and allowing the wind to carry the fumes to the enemy, or by the use of gas-shells.—**gas′=bag,** *n.* A bag for holding gas, as for the use of dentists; a bag to be inserted empty into a gas-main during repairs or alterations, and there inflated to serve as a plug; fig., an empty, voluble talker, or windbag (slang).—**gas′=burn″er,** *n.* The tip, jet, or end-piece of a gas-fixture, where the gas is caused to issue to be ignited.
Gas-con (gas′kǫn), *n.* [F.] A native of Gascony, a former province of southwestern France, the inhabitants of which were noted for their boastfulness; hence [*l. c.*], a boaster or braggart.—**gas-con-ade′** (-kǫ-nād′), *n.* [F. *gasconnade.*] Extravagant boasting; a boast or vaunt.—**gas-con-ade′,** *v. i.*; *-aded, -ading.* To boast extravagantly; bluster.—**gas-con-ad′er** (-kǫ-nā′dėr), *n.*
gas-e-i-ty (ga-sē′i-ti), *n.* Gaseous state.
gas-e-lier (gas-ẹ-lēr′), *n.* [From *gas* + *-elier* in *chandelier.*] A chandelier adapted for burning gas.
gas=en-gine (gas′en″jin), *n.* An internal-combustion engine operated by illuminating gas, natural gas, or other gas supplied from without; often, any internal-combustion engine.
gas-e-ous (gas′ẹ-us), *a.* Of the nature of, in the form of, or pertaining to gas; specif., in *engin.*, noting steam in the superheated condition.—**gas′e-ous-ness,** *n.*
gas=fit-ter (gas′fit″ėr), *n.* One whose business is the fitting up of buildings with apparatus for the use of gas.—**gas′=fit″ting,** *n.* The work or business of a gas-fitter; *pl.*, fittings for the employment of gas for illuminating and heating purposes.
gas=fix-ture (gas′fiks″tūr), *n.* A permanent fixture attached to a gas-pipe in the ceiling or wall of a room, as a more or less ornamental pipe (without or with branches) bearing a burner or burners and regulating devices.
gas=gan-grene (gas′gang″grēn), *n.* In *pathol.*, a gangrenous infection developing in wounds, esp. deep wounds with closed spaces, due to bacteria which form gases in the subcutaneous tissues.
gash[1] (gash), *v. t.* [Earlier *garse*, < OF. *garser, jarser*, scarify (F. *gercer*, crack, chap); origin uncertain.] To make a long, deep wound or cut in (the flesh, etc.); slash: as, "Then sudden waved his flaming falchion round, And *gash'd* his belly with a ghastly wound" (Pope's tr. Homer's "Iliad," iv.).—**gash**[1], *n.* A long, deep wound or cut, esp. in the flesh; a slash; also, the mouth (slang, U. S.); also, the act or an act of gashing.
gash[2] (gash), *a.* [Cf. *sagacious.*] Sagacious; wise; also, dignified or respectable in appearance; trim. [Sc.]
gas-i-fi-ca-tion (gas″i-fi-kā′shǫn), *n.* The process of gasifying; conversion into a gas.
gas-i-form (gas′i-fôrm), *a.* Having the form of a gas.
gas-i-fy (gas′i-fī), *v. t.* or *i.*; *-fied, -fying.* [See *-fy.*] To convert into or become a gas.
gas-ket (gas′ket), *n.* [Origin uncertain.] *Naut.*, one of several bands or lines used to bind a furled sail to a yard, etc.; in *mech.*, a strip of plaited hemp, tow, or the like, used to make a joint tight; hence, anything used as a packing, as a rubber or metal ring or disk. Also **gas′kin** (-kin).
gas-less (gas′les), *a.* Without gas, as for illumination.
gas=light (gas′līt), *n.* Light produced by the combustion of illuminating gas; also, a gas-burner, or the light from it.
gas=log (gas′log), *n.* A device resembling a piece (or several pieces) of firewood, used in a fireplace in which gas is burned.
gas=mask (gas′måsk), *n.* A mask-like or helmet-like device worn to protect against noxious gases, fumes, etc., as those employed in warfare or those incidental to certain industries, the air inhaled by the wearer being filtered through charcoal and chemicals.
gas=me-ter (gas′mē″tėr), *n.* An apparatus for measuring and recording the amount of gas produced or consumed.
gas-o-gene (gas′ǫ-jēn), *n.* Same as *gazogene.*
gas-o-lier (gas-ǫ-lēr′), *n.* Same as *gaselier.*
gas-o-line, gas-o-lene (gas′ǫ-lēn), *n.* [From *gas* + L. *oleum*, oil.] A volatile, inflammable liquid, consisting of a mixture of hydrocarbons, obtained in the distillation of petroleum, and used as a solvent, as fuel for internal-combustion engines, etc.: a term usually restricted to distillates having comparatively low boiling-points, those of higher boiling-points being usually known as *naphtha* or *benzine.* —**gasoline engine** or **motor,** an internal-combustion engine using gasoline for fuel.
gas-om-e-ter (gas-om′e-tėr), *n.* [= F. *gazomètre*: see *gas* and *-meter.*] An apparatus for measuring, holding and measuring, or holding gas; commonly, a reservoir or storehouse for gas.—**gas-om′e-try** (-tri), *n.* [See *-metry.*] The art of measuring gases, or the science dealing with such measurements.—**gas-o-met′ric** (-ǫ-met′rik), *a.*
gasp (gåsp), *v.* [ME. *gaspen*, from Scand.: cf. Icel. *geispa*, Sw. *gäspa*, yawn.] **I.** *intr.* To catch the breath, or labor for breath, with open mouth; respire convulsively; pant, as for air; fig., to long with breathless eagerness (*for* or *after*). **II.** *tr.* To breathe or emit with gasps (often with *away*); also, to utter with gasps (often with *out*).—**gasp,** *n.* A gasping, as for breath; a short, convulsive effort to breathe (as, to be at the last *gasp*, to be at the point of expiring, ceasing, etc.); also, a short, convulsive utterance (as, "Then Balin told him brokenly, and in *gasps*, All that had chanced": Tennyson's "Balin and Balan," 592).—**gasp′er,** *n.*—**gasp′ing-ly,** *adv.*
gas=range (gas′rānj), *n.* A cooking-stove or range in which gas is used as fuel.
gas-ser (gas′ėr), *n.* One who or that which gasses; a workman engaged in gassing fabrics, etc.; a well or boring yielding natural gas.
gas=shell (gas′shel), *n.* *Milit.*, an explosive shell containing a liquid or other material which, when the shell bursts, is converted into an asphyxiating or poisonous gas or vapor.
gas-sing (gas′ing), *n.* The act of one who or that which gasses; the process by which a material is gassed; an affecting or overcoming with gas or fumes, as in battle.

gas-sy (gas′i), *a.*; compar. *gassier*, superl. *gassiest.* Full of or containing gas (as, "Big *gassy* . . . bubbles burst on the ooze": Masefield's "Daffodil Fields," iii.); of the nature of gas; also, given to or characterized by empty talk (slang). —**gas′si-ness,** *n.*

gast† (gȧst), *v. t.* [AS. *gǣstan*, terrify: see *aghast, ghastly*, and *ghost.*] To strike aghast; terrify. See Shakspere's "King Lear," ii. 1. 57.—**gast,** *n.* A fright. [Sc.]

gas-ter-o-pod (gas′tẹ-rọ̄-pod), etc. Same as *gastropod*, etc.

gast-ness† (gȧst′nes), *n.* [See *gast.*] Terror; fright. See Shakspere's "Othello," v. 1. 106.

gas-tral-gia (gas-tral′jiạ̈), *n.* [NL., < Gr. γαστήρ (γαστρ-), belly, stomach, + ἄλγος, pain.] In *pathol.*, pain in the stomach; esp., neuralgia of the stomach.

gas-trec-to-my (gas-trek′tọ̄-mi), *n.* [Gr. γαστήρ (γαστρ-), belly, stomach, + ἐκ, out of, + -τομία, E. *-tomy.*] In *surg.*, the excision of a portion of the stomach.

gas-tric (gas′trik), *a.* [Gr. γαστήρ (γαστρ-), belly, stomach.] Of or pertaining to the stomach; also, of the nature of a stomach.—**gastric juice,** in *physiol.*, the digestive liquid secreted by the glands of the stomach, and containing pepsin and other enzymes.

gas-tril-o-quism (gas-tril′ọ̄-kwizm), *n.* [Gr. γαστήρ (γαστρ-), belly, + L. *loqui*, speak.] Ventriloquism.—**gas-tril′o-quist** (-kwist), *n.* A ventriloquist.—**gas-tril′o-quy** (-kwi), *n.* Ventriloquy.

gas-tri-tis (gas-trī′tis), *n.* [NL., < Gr. γαστήρ (γαστρ-), belly, stomach.] In *pathol.*, inflammation of the stomach, esp. of its mucous membrane.—**gas-trit′ic** (-trit′ik), *a.*

gastro-. Form of Gr. γαστήρ, belly, stomach, used in combination.

gas-tro-lith (gas′trọ̄-lith), *n.* [See *gastro-* and *-lith.*] A calculus or stony concretion in the stomach.

gas-trol-o-gy (gas-trol′ọ̄-ji), *n.* [Gr. γαστρολογία: see *gastro-* and *-logy.*] The science of catering to the stomach; gastronomy; also, the science of the structure, functions, and diseases of the stomach.—**gas-trol′o-ger, gas-trol′o-gist,** *n.*—**gas-tro-log′i-cal** (-trọ̄-loj′i-kạl), *a.*

gas-tro-nome (gas′trọ̄-nōm), *n.* [F.] One versed in gastronomy; an epicure. Also **gas-tron′o-mer** (-tron′ọ̄-mėr).

gas-tro-nom-ic, gas-tro-nom-i-cal (gas-trọ̄-nom′ik, -i-kạl), *a.* [F. *gastronomique.*] Of or pertaining to gastronomy. —**gas-tro-nom′i-cal-ly,** *adv.*

gas-tron-o-mist (gas-tron′ọ̄-mist), *n.* A gastronome.

gas-tron-o-my (gas-tron′ọ̄-mi), *n.* [F. *gastronomie*, < Gr. γαστρονομία: see *gastro-* and *-nomy.*] The art or science of good eating.

gas-tro-pod (gas′trọ̄-pod). [NL. *Gastropoda*, pl., < Gr. γαστήρ, belly, + πούς (ποδ-), foot.] **I.** *n.* Any of the *Gastropoda*, a class of mollusks including the snails, whelks, slugs, etc., the members of which usually have a muscular, disk-like foot on the ventral surface of the body by means of which they move about. **II.** *a.* Pertaining to the gastropods; belonging to the *Gastropoda.*—**gas-trop′o-dous** (-trop′ọ̄-dus), *a.*

gas-tro-scope (gas′trọ̄-skōp), *n.* [See *gastro-* and *-scope.*] An instrument for inspecting the interior of the stomach. —**gas-tro-scop′ic** (-skop′ik), *a.*—**gas-tros′co-py** (-tros′kọ̄-pi), *n.*

gas-trot-o-my (gas-trot′ọ̄-mi), *n.* [See *gastro-* and *-tomy.*] In *surg.*, the operation of cutting into the abdomen or the stomach.

gas-tro-vas-cu-lar (gas-trọ̄-vas′kụ̄-lạ̈r), *a.* [See *gastro-* and *vascular.*] In *zoöl.*, serving alike for the functions of digestion and of circulation, as a cavity.

gas-tru-la (gas′trọ̈-lạ̈), *n.*; pl. *-læ* (-lē). [NL., dim. < Gr. γαστήρ (γαστρ-), belly, stomach.] In *embryol.*, an embryo of a metazoan, consisting in typical cases of a cup-like body (developed from the blastula) with a wall formed by two layers of cells.—**gas′tru-lar** (-lạ̈r), *a.*—**gas-tru-la′tion** (-lā′shọn), *n.* In *embryol.*, the formation of a gastrula; any process (as that of invagination) by which a blastula or other form of embryo is converted into a gastrula.

gas=works (gas′wėrks), *n. pl.* or *sing.* An establishment where illuminating gas is manufactured.

gat[1] (gat). Old preterit of *get.*

gat[2] (gat), *n.* [=*gate*[1].] An opening between banks or cliffs, as along a coast. [Chiefly Eng.]

gat[3] (gat), *n.* [Humorous abbr. of *Gatling gun.*] A gun, pistol, or revolver. [Slang.]

gate[1] (gāt), *n.* [AS. *geat*, gate, = D. and LG. *gat* = Icel. *gat*, hole, opening.] An opening for passage into and out of an inclosure such as a fenced yard, walled city, or fortification, esp. an opening closed by a movable barrier; also, a structure built about such an opening and containing the barrier; also, the barrier itself, as a swinging frame, often of openwork, in a fence or wall; a movable structure used to close any passageway, as a road, bridge, etc.; a contrivance for regulating the passage of water, steam, or the like, as in a dam, pipe, etc.; also, any means of access or entrance, as a pass or defile in a mountain-range; also, a sash or frame for a saw or a gang of saws; also, the number of persons who pay at the gate or entrance for admission to an athletic contest or other exhibition; hence, the total amount of money received from them; gate-money; in *founding*, a channel or opening in a mold, as the opening through which metal is poured; the waste piece of metal cast in it.—**gate**[1], *v. t.*; *gated, gating.* To punish (an undergraduate) by confinement to the precincts of the college, etc.: as, "The Dean . . . *gated* him for a fortnight" (Hughes's "Tom Brown at Oxford," xii.). [Eng.]

gate[2] (gāt), *n.* [From Scand.: cf. Icel. *gata*, way, path, road, Sw. *gata*, Dan. *gade*, also G. *gasse*, Goth. *gatwō*, street.] A way, path, road, or street (now Sc. and prov. Eng., or as retained locally in street-names: as, Canon*gate* and Cow*gate*, in Edinburgh, Scotland; Mickle*gate* and Walm*gate*, in York, England); fig., way of proceeding, acting, or doing (now Sc. and prov. Eng.); also, manner of going, walking, or stepping (now usually spelled *gait*: see *gait*); also, the act of going or proceeding†; a journey, trip, or course (now north. Eng.).

gate-age (gāt′ạ̄j), *n.* The use of gates, as in controlling the flow of water; the gates used; area of gate-opening, as of a turbine-gate.

gâ-teau (gä-tō), *n.*; pl. *gâteaux* (-tō). [F. *gâteau*, OF. *gastel, wastel*; prob. from Teut.] A cake.

Gate-house. — Vitré, France.

gat-ed (gā′ted), *a.* [See *gate*[1].] Provided with a gate or gates: as, "thy hundred-*gated* capitals" (Young's "Night Thoughts," ix. 922).

gate=house (gāt′hous), *n.* A house at or over a gate, used as the keeper's quarters, a fortification, a prison, etc.; specif., a house or structure at the gate of a dam, reservoir, etc., with apparatus for regulating the flow of the water.

gate=keep-er (gāt′kē″pėr), *n.* One who has charge of a gate.

gate=legged, gate=leg (gāt′legd, -leg), *a.* Having the legs connected by crosspieces so as to look somewhat like a number of gates: applied esp. to a kind of table with folding flaps, each flap being supported when in use by a hinged gate-like arrangement of legs that may be pushed back to lower the flap.

gate-less (gāt′les), *a.* Having no gate, as a wall.

gate-man (gāt′mạn), *n.*; pl. *-men.* A gate-keeper.

gate=mon-ey (gāt′mun″i), *n.* The receipts taken in at the gate or entrance, for admission to an athletic contest or other exhibition.

gate=post (gāt′pōst), *n.* The post on which a gate is hung, or the one against which it is closed.

gate=tow-er (gāt′tou″ėr), *n.* A tower built beside or over a gate, as of a city, as for the purpose of defending the passage.

Gate-tower or Barbican, Walmgate Bar, York, England.

gate-ward (gāt′wârd), *n.* [AS. *geatweard.*] A gate-keeper: as, "the heedful *gate-ward*" (Scott's "Lay of the Last Minstrel," iv. 4). [Archaic.]

gate-way (gāt′wā), *n.* A passage or entrance which is or may be closed by a gate; also, a frame or arch in which a gate is hung; a structure built at or over a gate; also, any means of ingress or egress.

gate-wom-an (gāt′wu̇m″ạn), *n.*; pl. *-women* (-wim″en). A woman who has charge of a gate.

gath-er (gaᴛʜ′ėr), *v.* [AS. *gaderian,* < *gador, geador,* together, akin to *gæd,* fellowship: cf. *together* and *good.*] **I.** *tr.* To bring (persons, animals, or things) together into one place, company, body, mass, or aggregate (as, "*Gather* the elders and all the inhabitants of the land into the house of the Lord": Joel, i. 14); assemble; add or join, as to an assemblage, company, or body (as, to be *gathered* to one's fathers, to die: see Judges, ii. 10); take (*in*) for addition to a company or body (as, to *gather* in a recruit); also, to get together from various places or sources, or gradually (as, to *gather* an army; to *gather* sticks for a fire; to *gather* materials for a book; to *gather* a store of knowledge); collect; accumulate; amass; also, to take (any crop or natural yield) from its place of growth or formation (as, to *gather* grain, fruit, or mushrooms; to *gather* honey, gums, or resins); pick or pluck (flowers, or a single flower, spray, fruit, etc.); in general, to take (as, to *gather* a person into one's arms; "Cast up the highway; *gather* out the stones," Isa. lxii. 10); take or pick (*up*), as from the ground or other place; also, to take on or acquire gradually, as by natural process (as, to *gather* dust or stains; a rolling stone *gathers* no moss; standing water *gathers* filth); acquire or gain in increasing measure (as, to *gather* speed or momentum; to *gather* strength or courage); also, to learn, or (more commonly) to conclude or infer, from observation, indications, evidence, etc. (as, "*Gather* the sequel by that went before," Shakspere's "Comedy of Errors," i. 1. 96; we *gathered* from his letter that he was not satisfied); also, to assemble or collect (one's energies, faculties, thoughts, etc., or one's self), as for an effort or to meet some emergency (often with *up*); also, to draw into smaller compass (as, to *gather* the hair into a coil, or a garment into folds; to *gather* up the legs under one when sitting); contract (the brow) into wrinkles; draw (cloth, etc.) into fine folds or puckers on a thread run through; make narrower, as a drain. **II.** *intr.* To come together or assemble (as, to *gather* about the fire; to *gather* in crowds in the streets); also, to collect, accumulate, or form as by the collecting or accumulating of parts (as, tears *gather* in the eyes; clouds, storms, and darkness *gather*); grow as by accretion; come to a head, as a sore in suppurating; also, to become contracted into wrinkles, as the brow; contract or grow narrower, as a drain; *naut.*, to make way; gain.—**gath′er,** *n.* A drawing together; a contraction; also, a fold or pucker in gathered cloth, etc. (usually in *pl.*). —**gath′er-a-ble,** *a.* That may be gathered.—**gath′er-er,** *n.*—**gath′er-ing,** *n.* The act of one who or that which gathers, or that which is gathered; esp., an assembly or meeting of persons, as for social or other purposes, or the persons present; a collecting or accumulating, or that which is collected (as, the book represents the *gatherings* of years); an inflamed and suppurating swelling; a contracted or narrower part, as of a drain.

gat-ing (gā′ting), *n.* The compulsory confinement of an undergraduate within the precincts of the college, etc., as a punishment. [Eng.]

Gat-ling (gat′ling) **gun.** [From R. J. *Gatling* (1818-1903), American inventor.] A machine-gun consisting of a revolving cluster of barrels around a central axis, each barrel being automatically loaded and fired during every revolution of the cluster.

gauche (gōsh), *a.* [F.; from Teut.] Left (as opposed to right); hence, awkward; clumsy; tactless; in *math.*, skew; not plane; not perfectly symmetrical.—**gauche-rie** (gōsh-rē), *n.* [F.] Awkwardness, or an awkward movement, act, etc.: as, "if ever she committed an extreme *gaucherie*, calculated to set her aunt's teeth on edge" (H. Kingsley's "Geoffry Hamlyn," vii.).

Gau-cho (gou′chō), *n.*; pl. *-chos* (-chōz). [Sp.] A native of the South American pampas, of mixed Spanish and Indian descent.

gaud (gâd), *n.* [ME. *gaude,* prob. < L. *gaudium,* joy, gladness: see *joy.*] A prank†; a trick†; also, a plaything or toy (as, "An idle *gawd* Which in my childhood I did dote upon": Shakspere's "Midsummer Night's Dream," iv. 1. 172); now, esp., a showy ornament; a piece of finery; sometimes, a showy ceremony; vain display or ceremony (as, "with pomp and *gaud*": Campbell's "Lines on Poland"). —**gaud**†, *v.* **I.** *intr.* To make merry; sport; jest. **II.** *tr.* To adorn with showy ornament; paint, as the cheeks (see Shakspere's "Coriolanus," ii. 1. 233).—**gaud′er-y,** *n.*; pl. *-ies* (-iz). Finery; fine or showy things; also, ostentatious show; also, something showy.—**gaud′y,** *a.*; compar. *gaudier,* superl. *gaudiest.* Joyful† or festive† (as, "Let's have one other *gaudy* night . . . fill our bowls once more": Shakspere's "Antony and Cleopatra," iii. 13. 183); also, brilliant, bright, or showy (as, "*gaudy* plumage": Cowper's "On a Goldfinch"); usually, excessively showy (as, "Costly thy habit as thy purse can buy, But not express'd in fancy; rich, not *gaudy*": Shakspere's "Hamlet," i. 3. 71); showy without taste; vulgarly showy; flashy.—**gaud′i-ly,** *adv.* —**gaud′i-ness,** *n.*—**gaud′y,** *n.*; pl. *-ies* (-iz). [L. *gaudium,* joy.] A festival or merrymaking; now, chiefly, an annual college feast or banquet. [Eng.]

gauf-fer (gâ′fėr), *v. t.* Same as *goffer.*

gauge (gāj), etc. See *gage*[3], etc.

Gaul (gâl), *n.* [L. *Gallus.*] An inhabitant of ancient Gaul (equivalent to modern France and Belgium, with adjoining regions), esp. a member of the Celtic race as distinguished from other races settled there; hence, a Frenchman (humorous).—**Gaul′ish,** *a.*

gault (gâlt), *n.* [Cf. Norw. *gald,* hard ground, Icel. *gald,* hard snow.] A thick, heavy clay (prov. Eng.); in *geol.*, a series of beds of clay and marl of the Cretaceous system, occurring in southern England.

gaul-the-ri-a (gâl-thē′ri-ạ̈), *n.* [NL.; named from Dr. *Gaultier,* Canadian physician.] Any of the aromatic evergreen shrubs constituting the ericaceous genus *Gaultheria,* as *G. procumbens,* the American wintergreen; in *phar.*, oil of wintergreen.

gaum (gâm), *v. t.* [Cf. *gum*[2].] To smear, as with something sticky; daub (something sticky) on a surface.

gaun (gân), *ppr.* Going. [Sc.]

gaunt (gânt or gänt), *a.* [ME. *gawnt;* origin uncertain.] Slim or slender, as persons†; also, abnormally thin, as from hunger; lean; emaciated; haggard; often, tall, thin, and angular; lank; also, such as to cause leanness or emaciation (as, *gaunt* poverty); also, bleak, desolate, or grim, as places or things.

gaunt′let[1], *n.* See *gantlet*[1].

gaunt-let[2] (gânt′let or gänt′-), *n.* [OF. F. *gantelet,* dim. of *gant,* glove; from Teut.] A medieval glove, as of mail or plate, to protect the hand from wounds; also, a glove with a cuff-like extension covering the wrist; also, the extension itself.—**to take up the gauntlet,** to take up from the ground a gaunt-

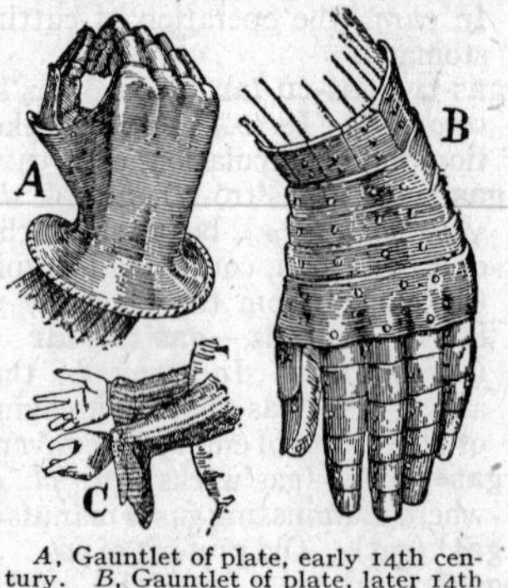

A, Gauntlet of plate, early 14th century. *B*, Gauntlet of plate, later 14th century. *C*, Gauntlet of mail forming part of the hauberk, 13th century.

let thrown down by another in token of challenge (see phrase following); hence, in general, to accept a challenge; esp., to undertake to meet attacks on some opinion, cause, person, etc.—**to throw down the gauntlet,** to cast one's gauntlet to the ground in token of challenge, to be taken up by a person accepting the challenge (a custom of medieval times: see phrase preceding); hence, in general, to issue a challenge.—**gaunt'let-ed,** *a.* Wearing or having a gauntlet.

gaunt-ly (gânt'li or gänt'-), *adv.* In a gaunt manner. —**gaunt'ness,** *n.*

gaun-try (gân'tri), *n.* See *gantry.*

gaup (gâp), *v. i.* See *gawp.*

gaur (gour), *n.* [Hind.] A large wild ox, *Bos gaurus,* of India, having a broad, protuberant forehead.

gauss (gous), *n.* [From K. F. *Gauss*: see *Gaussian.*] In *elect.*, a unit used to measure the intensity of a magnetic field, equal to the intensity produced by a magnetic pole of unit strength at a distance of one centimeter.

Gauss-i-an (gous'i-ạn), *a.* In *math.*, pertaining to or named after Karl Friedrich Gauss (1777–1855), the German mathematician.

gauze (gâz), *n.* [F. *gaze*; origin uncertain.] A very thin, slight, transparent textile fabric of silk, cotton, or other fiber; also, some similar open fabric, as of wire; hence, a thin haze (as, "And in circles, Purple *gauzes,* golden hazes, liquid mazes, Flung the torrent rainbow round": Tennyson's "Vision of Sin," ii.).—**gauz'y,** *a.*; compar. *gauzier,* superl. *gauziest.* Like gauze; thin as gauze.—**gauz'i-ness,** *n.*

ga-vage (gȧ-väzh), *n.* [F., < *gaver,* gorge with food.] Forced feeding, as of poultry or human beings, as by means of a flexible tube and a force-pump.

gave (gāv). Preterit of *give.*

gav-el[1] (gav'ẹl), *n.* [Origin uncertain.] A small mallet used by a presiding officer to signal for attention or order.

gav-el[2] (gav'ẹl), *n.* [AS. *gafol,* tribute, tax: cf. *gabelle.*] Rent: as, "a socager, paying rent or *gavel*" (Stubbs's "Constitutional Hist. of Eng.," vii. § 75). [Obs. or hist.]

gav-el-kind (gav'ẹl-kīnd), *n.* [ME. *gavelkynde, gavelikind,* < AS. *gafol,* E. *gavel*[2], + *gecynd,* E. *kind*[1].] The tenure in old English law of land let out for rent payable in forms other than military service; also, a land-tenure, chiefly in Kent, England, by which estates are divided equally among all the heritable heirs; the custom of such division.

ga-vi-al (gā'vi-ạl), *n.* [Hind. *ghariyāl.*] A large crocodile, *Gavialis gangeticus,* with elongated jaws, found in the Ganges and certain other rivers of India.

Head of Gavial.

ga-votte (gạ-vot'), *n.* [F., < Pr. *gavoto,* dance of the *gavots* (Alpine mountaineers).] A minuet-like dance in moderately quick duple rhythm; also, a piece of music for, or in the rhythm of, this dance, often forming one of the movements in the suite, usually following the saraband.

gawd†, *n.* and *v.* See *gaud.*

gawk (gâk), *n.* [Origin uncertain.] An awkward person; a fool or simpleton.—**gawk,** *v. i.* To act like a gawk; stare idly or stupidly. [Colloq.]—**gawk'y. I.** *a.*; compar. *gawkier,* superl. *gawkiest.* Awkward, clumsy, or clownish: as, "A lanky, *gawky* fellow . . . tumbles over everybody. I know him" (Thackeray's "Vanity Fair," xiv.). **II.** *n.*; pl. *-ies* (-iz). A gawk: as, "She is . . . an awkward *gawky*" (Sheridan's "School for Scandal," ii. 2).—**gawk'i-ness,** *n.*

gawp (gâp), *v. i.* [Var. of *gape.*] To gape or yawn; stare with the mouth open.

gay (gā), *a.*; compar. *gayer,* superl. *gayest.* [OF. F. *gai*; from Teut.] Having or showing lightness of heart or a joyous liveliness of mood, as persons or the spirits, bearing, actions, etc.; in general, cheerfully lively, as scenes, occasions, pleasures, music, etc.; also, given to or abounding in social or other pleasures, festivities, etc., as a person or a set of persons, a city, a social season, etc.; sometimes, given over to pleasure; dissipated; licentious; also, bright or showy, as colors, flowers, ornaments, dress, etc.; brightened or showily adorned (*with*: as, *gay* with color, flowers, or ribbons; "when all is *gay* with lamps," Tennyson's "In Memoriam," xcviii.); finely or showily dressed; fig., brilliant† (as, "Enjoy your dear wit, and *gay* rhetorick, That hath so well been taught her dazzling fence": Milton's "Comus," 790); also, in good health or condition (prov. or colloq.); also, fairly large or great, or considerable (Sc. and prov. Eng.).—**the gay science** [tr. Pr. *gai saber*], the art of poetry: so named with reference to the poetry of the troubadours: as, "He presented . . . Blondel, as king of minstrelsy, and his master in *the gay science*" (Scott's "Talisman," xxvi.).—**gay,** *adv.* In a gay, lively, or showy manner (obs. or rare); also, fairly, considerably, or very (Sc. and prov. Eng.).

gay-al (gā'ạl or gạ-yäl'), *n.* [Hindi *gayāl.*] A domesticated ox, *Bos frontalis,* with slender horns and white legs, common in parts of India: supposed to be a domesticated descendant of the gaur.

Gayal.

gay-e-ty (gā'ẹ-ti), **gay-ly** (gā'li). See *gaiety, gaily.*

gay-ness (gā'nes), *n.* The state or quality of being gay.

ga-za-bo (gạ-zā'bō), *n.*; pl. *-bos* (-bōz). [Var. of *gazebo.*] A gazebo (as, "that old *gazabo* on the top of the market-place": Thackeray's "Vanity Fair," xxviii.); also, a person gazed or stared at, as because of odd appearance (prov. or slang); a fellow (slang: as, the main *gazabo,* the chief person).

gaze (gāz), *v.*; *gazed, gazing.* [ME.; perhaps from Scand.: cf. Sw. dial. *gasa,* gaze, stare.] **I.** *intr.* To look steadily or intently; look with curiosity, wonder, etc. **II.** *tr.* To look steadily at: as, "Straight toward heaven my wondering eyes I turn'd, And *gazed* awhile the ample sky" (Milton's "Paradise Lost," viii. 258). [Poetic.]—**gaze,** *n.* The act of gazing; a steady or intent look; also, the object gazed at†, or a gazing-stock† (as, "Then yield thee, coward, And live to be the show and *gaze* o' the time": Shakspere's "Macbeth," v. 8. 24).

ga-ze-bo (gạ-zē'bō), *n.*; pl. *-bos* (-bōz). [Origin uncertain; now associated with *gaze.*] A structure commanding an extensive prospect, as a turret, belvedere, balcony, projecting window, or the like; also, a gazabo (prov. or slang).

gaze-hound (gāz'hound), *n.* A hound that pursues by sight rather than by scent.

ga-zelle, ga-zel (gạ-zel'), *n.* [F. *gazelle,* < Ar. *ghazāl.*] Any of various small antelopes of the genus *Gazella* and allied genera, noted for their graceful movements and lustrous eyes.

gaz-er (gā'zėr), *n.* One who gazes.

ga-zette (gạ-zet'), *n.* [F., < It. *gazzetta,* gazette, orig. a Venetian coin (as the price of the gazette), dim. < L. *gaza,* treasure.] A newspaper (now chiefly or only in names of newspapers); also, an official government journal, esp. in Great Britain, containing lists of government appointments and promotions, of persons declared bankrupt, etc.; also, an official announcement (rare).—**ga-zette',** *v. t.*; *-zetted, -zetting.* To publish, announce, or list in a gazette.—**gaz-et-teer** (gaz-e-tēr'), *n.* [F. *gazettier,* now *gazetier.*] A

Gazelle (*Gazella dorcas*).

writer in a gazette or newspaper (obs. or hist.); a journalist appointed and paid by the government to publish news (as, "Steele had been appointed *Gazetteer* . . . and thus had access to foreign intelligence earlier and more authentic than was . . . within the reach of an ordinary newswriter": Macaulay's "Essays," Addison); also, a geographical dictionary; an account of the divisions, places, seas, mountains, etc., of the world or any part of it, under their names, in alphabetic order.

gaz-ing=stock (gā′zing-stok), *n.* A person or thing gazed at, as with curiosity, wonder, or contempt.

gaz-o-gene (gaz′ǫ-jēn), *n.* [F. *gazogène*, < *gaz*, gas, + *-gène*: see *-gen.*] An apparatus for manufacturing aërated water.

gean (gēn), *n.* [F. *guigne*; origin uncertain.] The wild cherry, *Prunus avium*, of Europe.

ge-an-ti-cli-nal (jē″an-ti-klī′nạl). [Gr. γῆ, earth, + E. *anticlinal.*] In *geol.*: **I.** *a.* Noting or pertaining to an anticlinal fold which embraces a notable part of the earth's surface. **II.** *n.* A geanticlinal fold.—**ge-an′ti-cline** (-klīn), *n.* In *geol.*, a geanticlinal fold.

gear (gēr), *n.* [ME. *gere*, prob. from Scand.: cf. Icel. *gervi*, *görvi*, gear, apparel, akin to AS. *gearwe*, pl., clothes, ornaments, armor, *gearu*, ready: see *yare*, also *gar*^{2} and *garb.*] Apparel or attire (as, "From every side came noisy swarms Of Peasants in their homely *gear*": Wordsworth's "White Doe of Rylstone," iii.); armor or arms (archaic); harness or furniture for horses, etc.; also, apparatus or appliances generally; implements or tools; specif., the ropes, blocks, etc., belonging to a particular sail or spar; also, the appliances connected with the acting parts of a piece of machinery; a mechanism for transmitting or changing motion, as by toothed wheels; toothed wheels collectively; a toothed wheel which engages with another wheel or part; the connection or engagement of toothed wheels with each other, or of a machine or a machine part with a motor, shaft, or the like (as, in *gear*, or out of *gear*, fig., in, or out of, working order); also, movable property, or goods; possessions in general (Sc. and north. Eng.); matter, business, or an affair (archaic or prov.).—**gear,** *v.* **I.** *tr.* To provide with gear; harness (a draft-animal); esp., in *mach.*, to provide with gearing; connect by gearing; put (machinery) into gear. **II.** *intr.* In *mach.*, to fit exactly, as one part of gearing into another; come into or be in gear.—**gear′ing,** *n.* The parts collectively by which motion is transmitted in machinery, esp. a train of toothed wheels.—**gear′=wheel,** *n.* A wheel having teeth or cogs which engage with the teeth of another wheel or part to transmit or receive motion.

geck (gek), *n.* [MLG. *geck* = D. *gek.*] A fool; a dupe: as, "The most notorious *geck* and gull That e'er invention play'd on" (Shakspere's "Twelfth Night," v. 1. 351). [Obs. or prov. Eng.]—**geck,** *v. i.* To mock or scoff; look derisively; toss the head, as in scorn: as, "Ye *geck* at me because I'm poor" (Burns's "Tibbie"). [Sc. and prov. Eng.]

geck-o (gek′ō), *n.*; pl. *-os* or *-oes* (-ōz). [Malay *gēkoq.*] A small, harmless lizard of the family *Geckonidæ*, having toes with adhesive disks: common in warm countries.

Gecko.

gee^1 (jē), *interj.* A word of command to horses, etc., usually directing them to turn to the right. Cf. *haw*^{3}.—**gee**^{1}, *v. i.* or *t.*; *geed, geeing.* To turn to the right.—**gee**^{1}, *n.* A horse. [Colloq., Eng.]

gee^2 (jē), *v. i.*; *geed, geeing.* [Origin obscure.] To work well, or answer the purpose; also, to agree, as persons or things or as one with another; get on or go well together: commonly in negative statements. [Colloq.]

geese (gēs), *n.* Plural of *goose.*

geest (gēst), *n.* [LG., dry or sandy soil.] In *geol.*, old deposits produced by flowing water; coarse drift; gravel.

gee-zer (gē′zėr), *n.* [Dial. pron. of *guiser.*] A queer character; hence, in general, in vague, often good-natured depreciation, a fellow (as, a queer old *geezer*; who was that *geezer* with you last night?). [Slang, orig. prov. Eng.]

ge-gen-schein (gā′gen-shīn), *n.* [G., counter-glow.] In *astron.*, same as *counter-glow.*

Ge-hen-na (gẹ-hen′ạ̈), *n.* [LL., < Gr. Γέεννα, < Heb. *Gē-Hinnōm.*] The valley of Hinnom, near Jerusalem, regarded as a place of abomination (see 2 Kings, xxiii. 10), and used as a dumping-place for refuse, with fires kept burning to prevent pestilence; hence, the place of the future torment of the wicked; hell; also [*l. c.*], a place where prisoners are tortured (as, "the '*gehenna*' or torture-room [at Tournay]": Motley's "Dutch Republic," ii. 8); in general, a place of extreme discomfort or suffering.

gei-sha (gā′shạ̈), *n.*; pl. *-sha* or *-shas* (-shạ̈z). [Jap.] A Japanese singing and dancing girl.

Geiss-ler's (gīs′lėrz) **tube.** [From H. *Geissler* (1814–79), the (German) inventor.] A sealed glass tube with platinum connections at the ends, containing rarefied gas, which is made luminous by an electrical discharge.

gei-to-nog-a-my (gī-tǫ-nog′ạ-mi), *n.* [Gr. γείτων, neighbor, + γάμος, marriage.] In *bot.*, fertilization in which the pollination of a flower is effected by pollen from another flower on the same plant.

gel-a-da (jel′ạ-dạ̈), *n.* [Native name.] An Abyssinian baboon, *Theropithecus gelada*, notable for the long, heavy mane of the full-grown male.

Gelada.

gel-a-tin, gel-a-tine (jel′ạ-tin), *n.* [F. *gélatine*, < L. *gelare* (pp. *gelatus*), freeze, congeal.] A brittle, nearly transparent, faintly yellow, inodorous and almost tasteless organic substance obtained by boiling in water the ligaments, bones, skin, etc., of animals, and forming the basis of jellies, glues, and the like; a preparation or product in which this substance is the essential constituent.—**gel-a-ti-nate** (jel′ạ-ti-nāt or jẹ-lat′i-), *v. i.* or *t.*; *-nated, -nating.* To become or make gelatinous.—**gel″a-ti-na′tion** (-nā′shǫn), *n.*—**gel″a-ti-nif′er-ous** (-nif′ẹ-rus), *a.* [See *-ferous.*] Yielding gelatin.—**gel-a-tin′i-form** (-i-fôrm), *a.* [See *-form.*] Having the form or appearance of gelatin.—**gel-a-ti-nize** (jel′ạ-ti-nīz or jẹ-lat′i-), *v.*; *-nized, -nizing.* **I.** *intr.* To become gelatinous. **II.** *tr.* To make gelatinous; also, to coat with gelatin, as paper.—**gel″a-ti-ni-za′tion** (-ni-zā′shǫn), *n.*—**gel-a-ti-noid** (jel′ạ-ti-noid or jẹ-lat′i-). [See *-oid.*] **I.** *a.* Resembling gelatin; gelatinous. **II.** *n.* A gelatinoid substance.—**ge-lat-i-nous** (jẹ-lat′i-nus), *a.* Pertaining to or consisting of gelatin; also, of the nature or consistence of jelly; jelly-like.—**ge-lat′i-nous-ly,** *adv.*—**ge-lat′i-nous-ness,** *n.*

ge-la-tion (jẹ-lā′shǫn), *n.* [L. *gelatio(n-)*, < *gelare*, freeze, congeal.] Solidification by cold; freezing.

geld^1 (geld), *n.* [AS. *geld, gield, gild*, payment, tribute, also gild (see *gild*^{1}), = D. and G. *geld*, money, = Icel. *gjald*, payment, = Goth. *gild*, tribute; from the Teut. verb represented by E. *yield.*] In *Eng. hist.*, a payment; a tax; esp., the tax paid to the crown by landholders under the Anglo-Saxon and Norman kings.

geld^2 (geld), *v. t.*; *gelded* or *gelt, gelding.* [From Scand.: cf. Icel. *gelda.*] To castrate (used esp. of animals); sometimes, to spay; hence, to deprive of something essential†; weaken†; expurgate, as a book†.—**geld′ing,** *n.* A castrated animal, esp. a horse; also, a eunuch†.

gel-id (jel′id), *a.* [L. *gelidus*, < *gelus*, frost, icy cold.] Cold as ice; frosty; very cold; in general, cold; refreshingly cool, as water.—**ge-lid-i-ty** (jẹ-lid′i-ti), **gel′id-ness,** *n.*—**gel′id-ly,** *adv.*

gel-ig-nite (jel′ig-nīt), *n.* [From *gelatin* + L. *lignum*, wood.] A powerful explosive containing nitroglycerin, soluble guncotton, powdered wood, and potassium or sodium nitrate.

gel-se-mi-um (jel-sē′mi-um), *n.* [NL., < It. *gelsomino*, jasmine.] A twining shrub of the genus *Gelsemium*, esp. the yellow jasmine, *G. sempervirens*, of the southern U. S., which has evergreen leaves and fragrant yellow flowers; also, the root of the yellow jasmine, or the tincture from it, used as a drug.

Flowering Branch of Gelsemium (*G. sempervirens*).

gem (jem), *n.* [OF. F. *gemme*, < L. *gĕmma*, bud, gem.] A bud or gemma; also, a precious stone, esp. when cut and polished for ornament; a jewel; also, a precious or semiprecious stone carved or engraved; fig., something likened to a gem because of its beauty, brilliance, perfection, worth, etc., often something small; something greatly prized; in *cookery*, a kind of muffin; in *printing*, a printing-type (4 point) of a size between brilliant and diamond (Eng.).—**gem,** *v. t.*; *gemmed, gemming.* To put forth in buds† (as, "The stately trees . . . *gemm'd* Their blossoms": Milton's "Paradise Lost," vii. 325); also, to adorn with or as with gems; also, to extract gems from; search for gems in.

Ge-ma-ra (ge-mä′rạ), *n.* [Aram. *gemārā*, completion.] In *Jewish lit.*, a rabbinical commentary on the Mishnah, and with it forming the Talmud, or, as viewed by some, itself constituting the Talmud.—**Ge-mar′ic** (-mar′ik), *a.*

gem-el (jem′ẹl), *n.* [OF. *gemel* (F. *jumeau*), < L. *gemellus*, dim. of *geminus*, twin.] A twin†; also, a hinge; also, a gemel-ring.—**gem′el=ring,** *n.* A finger-ring formed of two or more separable or interlocked circlets.

gem-i-nate (jem′i-nāt), *v. t.* or *i.*; *-nated, -nating.* [L. *geminatus*, pp. of *geminare*, to double, < *geminus*, twin.] To make or become double.—**gem′i-nate,** *a.* Combined in a pair or pairs; coupled; binate.—**gem-i-na′tion** (-nā′shọn), *n.* [L. *geminatio(n-)*.] A doubling; duplication; repetition; in *rhet.*, the immediate repetition of a word, phrase, etc., for rhetorical effect; in *philol.*, the doubling of an originally single consonant sound; also, an orthographic doubling.

Gem-i-ni (jem′i-nī), *n. pl.* [L., pl. of *geminus*, twin.] The Twins, a zodiacal constellation containing the bright stars Castor and Pollux; also, as *sing.*, the third sign of the zodiac (see *zodiac*); also [*l. c.*], as *sing.*, a pair† (as, "Else you had looked through the grate, like a *geminy* of baboons": Shakspere's "Merry Wives of Windsor," ii. 2. 8).

gem-ma (jem′ä), *n.*; pl. *gemmæ* (-ē). [L., bud, gem: cf. *gem.*] In *bot.*, a bud, esp. a leaf-bud; also, a bud-like body which separates from the mother plant and forms a new plant, as in mosses, liverworts, etc.; in *zoöl.*, a bud or protuberance which develops into a new organism.

gem-mate (jem′āt), *v. i.*; *-mated, -mating.* [L. *gemmatus*, pp. of *gemmare*, to bud, < *gemma*, bud: see *gemma.*] To put forth buds; increase by budding.—**gem′mate,** *a.* Having buds; increasing by budding.—**gem-ma-tion** (je-mā′shọn), *n.* The act of putting forth buds; the arrangement of the leaf in the bud, or of the buds on the stalk; also, the process of reproduction by gemmæ.

gem-mif-er-ous (je-mif′ẹ-rus), **gem-mip-a-rous** (je-mip′ạ-rus), *a.* [L. *gemma*, bud: see *-ferous, -parous.*] Producing buds; increasing by gemmation.

gem-mu-la-tion (jem-ū-lā′shọn), *n.* [See *gemmule.*] The formation of gemmules.

gem-mule (jem′ūl), *n.* [L. *gemmula*, dim. of *gemma*, bud: see *gemma.*] In *bot.*, a small bud or gemma; in *zoöl.*, a small gemma; a germinal mass of spores, as of sponges; the ciliated embryo of some cœlenterates; in *biol.*, one of the hypothetical living units conceived by Darwin as the bearers of the hereditary attributes of animals and plants.

gem-my (jem′i), *a.* Set with or as with gems (as, "The *gemmy* bridle glitter'd free": Tennyson's "Lady of Shalott," iii.); jeweled; also, gem-like; brilliant.

ge-mot (gẹ-mōt′), *n.* [AS. *gemōt*, < *ge-*, together, + *mōt*, meeting: see *moot.*] In *Anglo-Saxon hist.*, a meeting; an assembly, as for judicial or legislative purposes.

gems-bok (gemz′bok), *n.* [S. Afr. D., 'chamois buck.'] A large antelope, *Oryx capensis* (or *gazella*), of South Africa, having long, straight horns and a long, tufted tail.

Gemsbok.

-gen. [F. *-gène*, < Gr. -γενής, born, produced, < γεν-, bear, produce: see *genius.*] A noun termination meaning 'something produced, or growing,' as in *acrogen, endogen, exogen*, and used also to mean 'something that produces,' as in *hydrogen, oxygen, plasmogen.*

gen-darme (zhoṅ-därm), *n.*; pl. *-darmes* (-därmz, F. -därm). [F., formed as sing. < *gens d'armes*, men of arms (*gens*, pl. of *gent*, < L. *gens*: see *gens*).] Orig., in France, a mounted soldier in full armor, commanding a troop; later, a cavalryman; now, one of a corps of military police, esp. in France.—**gen-dar-me-rie** (zhoṅ-där-mė-rē), *n.* [F.] Gendarmes collectively; the body of gendarmes. Also **gen-dar-me-ry** (jen-där′mẹ-ri).

gen-der (jen′dėr), *n.* [OF. *gendre* (F. *genre*), < L. *genus* (*gener-*), race, kind, sort, gender: cf. *genus* and *genre.*] Kind†, sort†, or class†; also, sex, male or female (now only humorous); in *gram.*, each of the classes into which the words of a language are distinguished with reference to sex, actual or ascribed, or lack of sex (as, the masculine, feminine, or neuter *gender*); the property of belonging to, or having the form required by, one of these classes; the formal distinction of words into such classes, as a grammatical principle.—**gen′der,** *v.* [OF. *gendrer*, < L. *generare*, < *genus*: cf. *generate.*] **I.** *tr.* To beget or procreate (offspring); in general, to give rise to (as, "Foolish and unlearned questions avoid, knowing that they do *gender* strifes": 2 Tim. ii. 23). [Archaic.] **II.**† *intr.* To copulate; breed.—**gen′der-less,** *a.* In *gram.*, without distinction of gender.

gene (jēn), *n.* [Gr. γεν-, bear, produce: see *genius*, and cf. *-gen.*] In *biol.*, a hypothetical agent or element considered as being transmitted from parent to offspring, and regarded as determining, or entering into, the development of some particular character in the offspring.

gen-e-a-log-ic, gen-e-a-log-i-cal (jen″ẹ-ạ-loj′ik or jē″nẹ-, -i-kạl), *a.* [See *genealogy.*] Pertaining to genealogy.—**gen″e-a-log′i-cal-ly,** *adv.*—**gen-e-al′o-gist** (-al′ọ-jist), *n.* One who traces genealogies; one versed in genealogy.—**gen-e-al′o-gize** (-jīz), *v.*; *-gized, -gizing.* **I.** *tr.* To draw up a genealogy of. **II.** *intr.* To trace genealogies.

gen-e-al-o-gy (jen-ẹ-al′ọ-ji or jē-nẹ-), *n.*; pl. *-gies* (-jiz). [OF. *genealogie* (F. *généalogie*), < LL. *genealogia*, < Gr. γενεαλογία, < γενεά, race, family, + λέγειν, speak.] An account of the descent of a person or family from an ancestor or ancestors; a pedigree; hence, a similar account of the descent of animals or plants from ancestral forms; also, lineage†; also, progeny†; also, the investigation of pedigrees as a department of study or knowledge.

gen-er-a (jen′ẹ-rạ), *n.* Plural of *genus.*

gen-er-a-ble (jen′ẹ-rạ-bl), *a.* [L. *generabilis.*] Capable of being generated or produced.

gen-er-al (jen′ẹ-rạl), *a.* [OF. *general* (F. *général*), < L. *generalis*, < *genus*, race, kind: see *genus.*] Pertaining to, affecting, including, or participated in by, all members of a class or group (as, the *general* welfare); not partial or particular; also, of or pertaining to a whole region or body (as, a *general* election); not local or sectional; also, common to many or most of a community, though not universal (as, a subject of *general* remark; the *general* practice); prevalent; usual; also, not limited to a precise application (as, *general* instructions or directions); not specific or special; applicable to a variety of cases, or to most cases (as, *general* principles; a *general* rule); applicable to all of the individuals forming a class (as, a *general* term); also, not restricted to one class, field, department, etc. (as, the *general* public; a *general* practitioner; a *general* dealer, store, or cargo); miscellaneous; also, considered with reference to, or comprising, the main elements, features, etc., irrespective of details and unimportant exceptions (as, the *general* tendency; a *general* knowledge of a subject); indefinite or vague (as, to refer to a matter in a *general* way); also, having extended command, or superior or chief rank (as, a *general* officer, see below; adjutant-*general*; attorney-*general*).—**general officer,** *milit.*, an officer, as a brigadier-general, major-general, etc., ranking above a colonel, and entitled to command a force larger than a regiment.—**general staff,** *milit.*, a body of officers whose duties include the consideration or preparation of plans for war, national defense, etc.: in the U. S. army called the *General Staff Corps.*—**gen′er-al,** *n.* The total† or whole†; the most part†; the general public (archaic: as, "The play . . . pleased not the million; 'twas caviare to the *general*," Shakspere's "Hamlet," ii. 2. 457); also, a general fact, statement, principle, notion, etc. (now chiefly in *pl.*, and as opposed to *particulars*, etc.: as, "It is by means of our knowledge of particulars that we ascend to *generals*," Hallam's "Literature of Europe," iii. 3. § 104); *milit.*, a drum-beat or other signal calling troops to prepare to march; also, a general officer; in address and common speech, any officer whose title contains the term *general*, as a major-general, brigadier-general, adjutant-general, surgeon-general, etc.; in a restricted sense, in the U. S. army, an officer of the hightest rank except the President, the title being conferred only by a special act of Congress; in European armies, an officer of a definite high rank, in Great Britain being just below a field-marshal; *eccles.*, the chief of a religious order. —**in general,** with respect to the whole class referred to; also, as a general rule; commonly; usually; also, without exception†; also, in all things†.—**gen′er-al,** *v. t.*; *-aled* or *-alled*, *-aling* or *-alling*. To serve as general to.—**gen′er-al-cy,** *n.*; pl. *-cies* (-siz). The office or rank of a general.

gen-er-a-lis-si-mo (jen″ę-rą-lis′i-mō), *n.*; pl. *-mos* (-mōz). [It., superl. of *generale*, general, < L. *generalis*: see *general*.] The supreme commander of all the forces of a country, or of several armies acting together.

gen-er-al-i-ty (jen-ę-ral′i-ti), *n.*; pl. *-ties* (-tiz). [LL. *generalitas*.] The state or quality of being general; also, something that is general; a general principle or proposition; a general or vague statement; also, the main body, greater part, or majority (as, "the *generality* of travellers": Jane Austen's "Pride and Prejudice," xxvii.); formerly, in France, a fiscal and administrative district.

gen-er-al-i-za-tion (jen″ę-rąl-i-zā′shǫn), *n.* The act or process of generalizing; an instance of this; also, a result of this process; a general inference.

gen-er-al-ize (jen′ę-rąl-īz), *v.*; *-ized*, *-izing*. **I.** *tr.* To make general; bring into general use or knowledge; also, to give a general (rather than specific or special) character to; sometimes, to make indefinite or without distinctive features; also, to infer inductively, as a general rule from particular facts; also, to infer a general principle, etc., from (facts, etc.). **II.** *intr.* To form general notions; also, to make general inferences; also, to deal or indulge in generalities.—**gen′er-al-iz-er** (-ī-zėr), *n.*

gen-er-al-ly (jen′ę-rąl-i), *adv.* All together†, in a body†, or collectively†; also, universally†; with respect to the larger part, or for the most part (as, a claim *generally* recognized); in most cases, usually, or commonly (as, he *generally* comes at noon); also, in a general (rather than specific) way, or without reference to particular persons or things (as, *generally* speaking; a charge made against a class of persons *generally*; interested in all sports *generally*).—**gen′er-al-ness,** *n.*

gen-er-al-ship (jen′ę-rąl-ship), *n.* The office or rank of a general; also, the exercise of a general's functions; also, skill as a general; hence, management or tactics generally.

gen-er-ant (jen′ę-rąnt). **I.** *a.* Generating; producing. **II.** *n.* A generator.

gen-er-ate (jen′ę-rāt), *v. t.*; *-ated*, *-ating*. [L. *generatus*, pp. of *generare*, < *genus*, race, kind: see *genus*, and cf. *gender*, *v.*] To produce (offspring); procreate; hence, to bring into existence; produce; evolve; also, to bring about; give rise to; in *math.*, to form (a line, surface, figure, or solid) by the motion of a point, line, or figure.—**gen-er-a′tion** (-ę-rā′shǫn), *n.* [L. *generatio(n-)*.] The act or process of generating; procreation; reproduction; the fact of being generated; descent or genealogy (now rare: as, "the book of the *generation* of Jesus Christ," Mat. i. 1); also, production by natural or artificial processes; evolution, as of heat or sounds; also, offspring† or progeny†; descendants†; also, the offspring of a given parent or of given parents, considered as a single degree or step in descent; a single degree or step in natural descent, as of human beings, animals, or plants; specif., a form or phase of a plant or animal, with reference to the manner of its reproduction (as, the asexual *generation* and the sexual *generation*: see *alternation of generations*, under *alternation*); also, the whole body of individuals born about the same general period (as, the last, present, or next *generation*; the rising *generation*); the time covered by their lives; a term of years (commonly 30) accepted as the average difference of age between one generation of a family and the next; also, a family†; a race†; a class of persons†.—**gen′er-a-tive** (-ę-rą-tiv), *a.* Having the power of generating; pertaining to generation.—**gen′er-a-tor** (-ę-rā-tǫr), *n.* [L.] One who generates; also, something that generates or produces; specif., an apparatus for producing a gas or vapor; also, a machine by which mechanical energy is converted into electrical energy; a dynamo.—**gen-er-a′trix** (-ę-rā′triks), *n.* [L.] A female generator†; in *math.*, a point, line, or figure whose motion gives rise to a line, surface, figure, or solid.

ge-ner-ic (jē-ner′ik), *a.* [= F. *générique*, < L. *genus* (*gener-*), race, kind, E. *genus*.] Pertaining to or characteristic of a genus, kind, or class, esp. a zoölogical or botanical genus (as, *generic* characters or differences); applicable or referring to all of the individuals forming a genus or class (as, a *generic* name or term). Also **ge-ner′i-cal.**—**ge-ner′i-cal-ly,** *adv.* With reference to genus, kind, or class, esp. to zoölogical or botanical genus (as, *generically* identical or distinct; *generically* related or different); with reference to all of the members of a genus or class, rather than to a particular member of it (as, to use a term *generically*).

gen-er-os-i-ty (jen-ę-ros′i-ti), *n.*; pl. *-ties* (-tiz). [L. *generositas*.] The quality of being generous; excellence of race or stock (archaic); freedom from meanness or smallness of mind or character; magnanimity; readiness or liberality in giving; munificence; also, a generous act.

gen-er-ous (jen′ę-rus), *a.* [F. *généreux*, < L. *generosus*, < *genus*, race, kind: see *genus*.] Of good birth or stock (archaic); also, gallant, spirited, or courageous (archaic); also, noble-minded or magnanimous, as persons; indicative of freedom from meanness or smallness of mind or character, as actions, etc.; also, munificent, liberal, or bountiful, as a giver or a gift; sometimes, fertile, as soil; hence, in general, furnished liberally (as, a *generous* table; a *generous* portion); abundant; full; ample; also, rich or strong, as wine.—**gen′er-ous-ly,** *adv.*—**gen′er-ous-ness,** *n.*

gen-e-sis (jen′e-sis), *n.*; pl. *geneses* (-sēz). [L., < Gr. γένεσις, origin, origination, production, creation, < γεν-, bear, produce: see *genius*.] Origin; production; creation; mode of generation or formation; [*cap.*] the first book of the Old Testament, so named as containing an account of the creation of the world.

gen-et[1] (jen′et), *n.* See *jennet*.

gen-et[2] (jen′et or ję-net′), *n.* [OF. *genete* (F. *genette*), < Sp. *gineta*; from Ar.] Any of the small old-world carnivorous quadrupeds constituting the genus *Genetta*, esp. *G. vulgaris*, allied to the civet-cats but without a scent-pouch, and yielding a soft fur; also, the fur of such an animal, or an imitation of it, as from cat's fur.

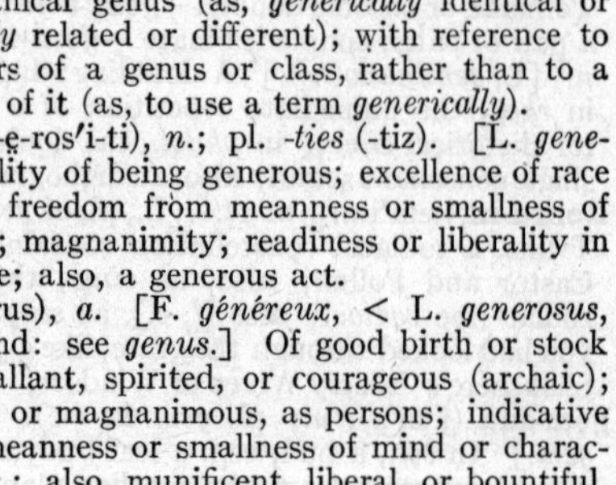

Genet (*Genetta vulgaris*).

ge-neth-li-ac (jē-neth′li-ak). [L.

genethliacus, < Gr. γενεθλιακός, pertaining to birth or nativity, < γενέθλη, birth, < γεν-, bear, produce: see *genius*.] **I.** *a.* Of or pertaining to the casting of nativities; also, pertaining to a birthday. **II.** *n.* One who is versed in genethlialogy (as, "Strange turns, in the world's affairs, Foreseen b' astrologers, soothsayers, Chaldeans, learned *Genethliacs*": Butler's "Hudibras," ii. 3); also, a birthday ode.—**gen-eth-li-a-con** (jen-eth-lī′ą-kon), *n.*; pl. *-ca* (-ką). [L., < Gr. γενεθλιακόν, neut. of γενεθλιακός.] A birthday ode.—**ge-neth-li-al′o-gy** (-li-al′ǫ-ji), *n.* [Gr. γενεθλιαλογία, < γενέθλη, birth, + λέγειν, speak.] The art of casting nativities; astrology.

ge-net-ic (ję-net′ik), *a.* [From *genesis*.] Of or pertaining to genesis or origin. Also **ge-net′i-cal.**—**ge-net′i-cal-ly,** *adv.*—**ge-net′ics,** *n.* The science of genesis, esp. the genesis of living organisms; in *biol.*, that portion of evolutionary science which deals with natural development uncomplicated by artificial process.

gen-e-trix, gen-i-trix (jen′ę-triks, jen′i-), *n.* [L., fem. of *genitor*: see *genitor*.] A female parent; a mother.

ge-ne-va (je-nē′vą), *n.* [D. *genever, jenever*, < F. *genièvre*, < L. *juniperus*, E. *juniper*.] An alcoholic liquor flavored with juniper-berries; Holland gin. See *gin*³.

Ge-ne-va (je-nē′vą) **bands.** [From *Geneva*, city in Switzerland.] Two bands, or pendent strips, worn at the throat as part of a clerical garb: worn orig. by the Swiss Calvinist clergy.—**Ge-ne′va Bi′ble.** See under *Bible*.—**Ge-ne′va Con-ven′tion.** An international convention, orig. adopted at a conference at Geneva in 1864 but subsequently altered, providing for the neutrality of ambulances and hospitals, the protection of sanitary officers, military and naval chaplains, and civilians rendering help to the sick and wounded, etc., during war.—**Ge-ne′va cross.** A red Greek cross on a white ground, displayed in war, etc., to distinguish ambulances and hospitals, and persons serving them. Also called *red cross*.—**Ge-ne′va gown.** A loose, large-sleeved black preaching-gown worn by Protestant clergymen: so named from its use by the Swiss Calvinist clergy.

Ge-ne-van (je-nē′vąn). **I.** *a.* Of or pertaining to Geneva in Switzerland or, esp., its ecclesiastical organization; Calvinistic. **II.** *n.* A native or inhabitant of Geneva; also, an adherent of Genevan or Calvinistic theology; a Calvinist.

Gen-e-vese (jen-ę-vēs′ or -vēz′). **I.** *a.* Of or pertaining to Geneva in Switzerland. **II.** *n.*; pl. *-vese*. A native or inhabitant of Geneva.

ge-ni-al¹ (ję-nī′ąl), *a.* [Gr. γένειον, chin, < γένυς, jaw; akin to E. *chin*.] In *anat.*, of or pertaining to the chin.

ge-nial² (jē′nią l), *a.* [L. *genialis*, pertaining to generation or to marriage, festive, jovial, pleasant, < *genius*: see *genius*.] Pertaining to generation, or generative (now rare); pertaining to marriage, or nuptial (now rare); also, conducive to growth, as climate, sunshine, etc.; hence, pleasantly warm, or mild (as, "a soft sunny morning in the *genial* month of May": Irving's "Sketch-Book," Royal Poet); also, cheering or enlivening (as, "I hail Thy *genial* loved return": Wm. Collins's "Ode to Evening," 20); also, sympathetically cheerful; kindly; jovial; also, natural† or innate† (as, "a theologue more by need than *genial* bent": Dryden's "Hind and the Panther," iii. 1147); also, of, pertaining to, or characterized by genius, or exalted natural capacity and aptitude.—**ge-ni-al′i-ty** (-ni-al′i-ti), *n.* Genial quality; mildness, as of weather; sympathetic cheerfulness, or kindliness.—**ge′nial-ize,** *v. t.*; *-ized, -izing.* To render genial.—**ge′nial-ly,** *adv.*—**ge′nial-ness,** *n.*

-genic. [Gr. γεν-, bear, produce; or from E. *-gen* (or *-geny*) + *-ic*.] An adjective termination meaning 'producing,' 'produced,' or 'pertaining to production,' as in *carpogenic, eugenic, hepatogenic, pathogenic, psychogenic, pyrogenic, saprogenic, toxicogenic*.

ge-nic-u-late, ge-nic-u-lat-ed (ję-nik′ū-lāt, -lā-ted), *a.* [L. *geniculatus*, < *geniculum*, dim. of *genu*, knee: see *genu*.] Having knee-like joints or bends; bent at a joint like the knee.—**ge-nic-u-la′tion** (-lā′shǫn), *n.* Geniculate state; a geniculate formation.

ge-nie (jē′ni), *n.* [F. *génie*, < L. *genius*: see *genius*.] A tutelary genius†; also, a jinni or spirit of Mohammedan mythology.

ge-nii (jē′nii), *n.* Latin plural of *genius*.

gen-i-pap (jen′i-pap), *n.* [From native name.] The edible fruit of a tropical American rubiaceous tree, *Genipa americana*, about the size of an orange and having an agreeable vinous flavor; also, the tree.

Genipap. — Flowering branch and fruit.

gen-i-tal (jen′i-tąl), *a.* [L. *genitalis*, < *gignere* (pp. *genitus*), beget, bear: see *genius*.] Pertaining to generation, or to the organs of generation.—**gen-i-ta′li-a** (-tā′li-ą), *n. pl.* [L.] The genitals.—**gen′i-tals,** *n. pl.* The genital organs, esp. the external genital organs, usually of the male.

gen-i-tive (jen′i-tiv). [L. *genitivus, genetivus*, lit. 'pertaining to generation' (< *gen-*, beget, produce: see *genius*), used to render Gr. γενικός, generic (ἡ γενικὴ πτῶσις, the generic or genitive case), < γένος, race, kind: see *genus*.] In *gram.*: **I.** *a.* Pertaining to or indicating origin, source, possession, or the like: applied to a case in declension in Latin and other languages (corresponding in part to the possessive in English), or to its forms, constructions, etc. **II.** *n.* The genitive case, or a word in that case.—**gen-i-ti′val** (-tī′vąl), *a.*

gen-i-tor (jen′i-tǫr), *n.* [L., < *gignere* (pp. *genitus*), beget, bear: see *genius*.] A male parent; a father; a progenitor. [Now rare.]

gen-i-to=u-ri-na-ry (jen″i-tǫ-ū′ri-ną-ri), *a.* Noting or pertaining to the genital and urinary organs.

gen-i-trix (jen′i-triks), *n.* See *genetrix*.

ge-nius (jē′nius), *n.*; pl. *geniuses* or (in senses meaning 'attendant spirit' and 'genie') *genii* (jē′nii). [L., tutelary spirit, taste, inclination, talent, genius, orig. a male generative or creative principle, < *gen-* (as in *gignere*, pp. *genitus*, beget, bear) = Gr. γεν- (as in γίγνεσθαι, γενέσθαι, be born) = Skt. *jan-*, beget, bear, produce: see *genial*², *genital, genus, genesis*, and *kin*.] A tutelary or attendant spirit which, according to ancient belief, was allotted to each person at his birth; the attending or controlling spirit of a place, institution, etc.; also, either of two mutually opposed spirits, one good and the other evil, supposed to attend a person throughout his life; hence, a person who strongly influences for good or evil the character, conduct, or destiny of another; also, a personification of something immaterial, esp. as represented in art; a person or thing regarded as an embodied type of something (as, "I do remember him . . . like a man made after supper of a cheese-paring . . . a' was the very *genius* of famine": Shakspere's "2 Henry IV.," iii. 2. 337); also, any demon or spirit, esp. a genie or jinni (now chiefly or only in pl. *genii*); also, a person's characteristic disposition or bent; distinctive character or spirit, as of a nation, period, language, or institution; the peculiar character or associations belonging to a place; also, natural ability or capacity (as, a task suited to one's *genius*); natural aptitude for something (as, to have a *genius* for finance, for politics, or for making friends); also, exalted or phenomenal natural capacity and aptitude, as for creative and original conceptions, esp. in literature, art, or science; also, a person having such capacity and aptitude (as, "Homer was the greater *genius*, Virgil the better artist": Pope's Preface, in tr. Homer's "Iliad").

Gen-o-ese (jen-ǫ-ēs′ or -ēz′). **I.** *a.* Of or pertaining to Genoa, in northwestern Italy. **II.** *n.*; pl. *-ese*. A native or inhabitant of Genoa. Also **Gen-o-vese′** (-vēs′ or -vēz′), *a.* and *n.*

-genous. [Gr. -γενής, born, produced, or γεν-, bear, produce (see *-gen*); or from E. *-gen* + *-ous*.] An adjective termination meaning 'produced' or 'producing,' as in *alkaligenous, autogenous, isogenous*.

genre (zhoṅr), *n.* [F.: see *gender.*] Genus; kind; sort; style; esp., style of art or literature with reference to subject, treatment, etc.; also, the style or kind of painting (or other art) that represents scenes from ordinary life (as distinguished from landscapes, historical subjects, etc.).

gens (jenz), *n.*; pl. *gentes* (jen′tēz). [L., clan, race, people, < *gen-*, beget, produce: see *genius.*] A group of families in ancient Rome claiming descent from a common ancestor and united by a common name and common religious rites; in general, a tribe or clan.

gent[1]† (jent), *a.* [OF. *gent,* < L. *genitus,* pp. of *gignere,* beget, bear: see *genius.*] Well-born or noble; hence, well-bred; also, elegant, graceful, or pretty (as, "He lov'd . . . a Lady *gent*": Spenser's "Faerie Queene," i. 9. 27).

gent[2] (jent), *n.* Shortened form of *gentleman.* [Now chiefly humorous or vulgar.]

gen-teel (jen-tēl′), *a.* [F. *gentil*: see *gentle.*] Of gentle birth (archaic); hence, belonging or suited to polite society, as persons, manners, pursuits, dress, dwellings, etc. (as, "Do now send a *genteel* conveyance for them, for . . . they were most of them used to ride in their own carriages": Sheridan's "School for Scandal," iv. 1); well-bred or refined; gentlemanly or ladylike; elegant or stylish; nice or fine. [Now often used playfully or ironically, with implication of excessive reverence for or careful affectation of characteristics indicated by the word, which by many is now regarded with disfavor.]—**gen-teel′ly,** *adv.*—**gen-teel′ness,** *n.*

gen-tes (jen′tēz), *n.* Plural of *gens.*

gen-tian (jen′shạn), *n.* [L. *gentiana*; said to be named from *Gentius,* an Illyrian king.] Any plant of the large genus *Gentiana,* comprising herbs having commonly blue flowers, less frequently yellow, white, or red, as *G. crinita* (one of the 'fringed gentians'), of eastern North America, with blue, delicately fringed corolla, and *G. lutea,* a yellow-flowered European species whose root is used in medicine; also, the root of *G. lutea,* or a preparation of it, used as a stomachic and tonic; also, any of various plants resembling the gentian.—**gen″ti-a-na′ceous** (-shi-ạ-nā′shius), *a.* Belonging to the *Gentianaceæ,* or gentian family of plants.

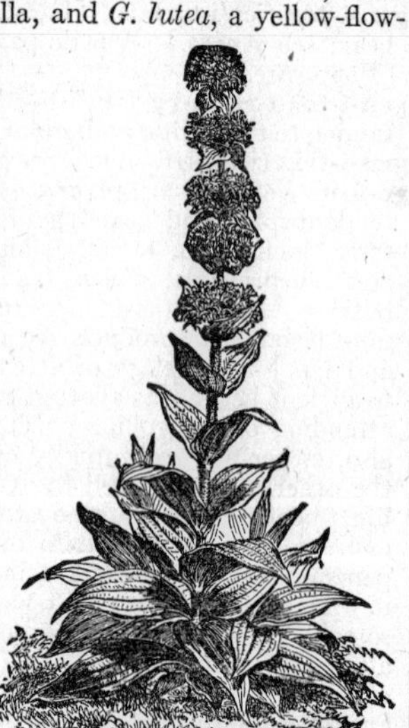
Gentian (*Gentiana lutea*).

gen-ti-a-nel-la (jen″shi-ạ-nel′ạ̈), *n.* [NL., dim. of L. *gentiana,* E. *gentian.*] Any of several species of gentian (sometimes regarded as being the typical members of a subgenus, *Gentianella,* or as comprising a single species, *Gentiana acaulis*), esp. a dwarf species native in the Alps and bearing large, intensely blue flowers.

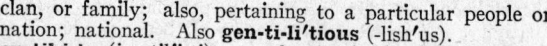

gen-tile (jen′til or -tīl). [L. *gentilis,* belonging to a clan, race, or people, national, LL. foreign, pagan, heathen, < L. *gens,* clan, race, people: see *gens.*] **I.** *a.* Of or pertaining to a gens, tribe, or nation (as, *gentile* divisions; a *gentile* group); of a word, expressing race, nationality, or local extraction (as, a *gentile* noun or adjective, such as 'Arab,' 'Greek,' 'Peruvian'); also [often *cap.*, and pron. only jen′tīl], of or pertaining to any people not Jewish; also, heathen or pagan; also, among Mormons, of or pertaining to those outside the Mormon community. **II.** *n.* A member of a gens; also, a noun or adjective indicating race, nationality, or local extraction; also [often *cap.*, and pron. only jen′tīl], a person belonging to a non-Jewish nation; also, one neither a Jew nor a Christian; a heathen or pagan; also, among Mormons, one not a Mormon.—**gen-til′ic** (-til′ik), *a.* Tribal or national, as a name.—**gen′til-ism** (-tīl-izm), *n.* Heathenism; paganism.

gen-ti-li-tial (jen-ti-lish′ạl), *a.* [L. *gentilitius, gentilicius,* < *gentilis*: see *gentile.*] Pertaining to a particular gens, clan, or family; also, pertaining to a particular people or nation; national. Also **gen-ti-li′tious** (-lish′us).

gen-til-i-ty (jen-til′i-ti), *n.*; pl. *-ties* (-tiz). [OF. *gentilite,* gentilism, heathenism, also (with sense from *gentil*: see *gentle*) gentle birth (F. *gentilité,* gentilism, the gentiles), < L. *gentilitas,* clan relationship, LL. paganism, heathenism, < L. *gentilis*: see *gentile* and *gentle.*] The relation of those belonging to the same Roman gens or clan; also, gentilism† or heathenism†; also, gentle birth; people of gentle birth†, or the gentry†; gentle manners† or courtesy†; also, the state or quality of being genteel (see note added to *genteel*); superior refinement, elegance, etc., as possessed or affected; *pl.*, genteel ways, niceties, appearances, etc. (as, "Let him forsake a decent craft that he may pursue the *gentilities* of a profession to which nature never called him": George Eliot's "Silas Marner," ix.).

gen-tle (jen′tl), *a.*; compar. *gentler,* superl. *gentlest.* [OF. *gentil,* of good family, noble, excellent (F. *gentil,* nice, graceful, pretty), < L. *gentilis*: see *gentile,* and cf. *genteel* and *jaunty.*] Of good birth or family, or well-born, as persons (often opposed to *simple*); of excellent breed, as an animal (now only of a falcon: cf. *falcon-gentle*); good, superior, or honorable, as birth, blood, or family; also (from the association of certain characteristics with gentle birth), noble, gallant, or chivalrous (archaic: as, a *gentle* knight); courteous (archaic: as, "There fayrely them receives a *gentle* Squyre, Of myld demeanure and rare courtesee," Spenser's "Faerie Queene," i. 10. 7); refined, as manners or breeding; polite or fine, as a pursuit (as, the *gentle* art of angling; the *gentle* craft, see phrase below); mild, kindly, or amiable (as, a *gentle* lady; a *gentle* disposition; *gentle* words); considerate or forbearing (as, "For I have let men be, and have their way; Am much too *gentle,* have not used my power": Tennyson's "Marriage of Geraint," 467); of things, mild, or not severe, rough, or violent (as, a *gentle* wind, current, or stream; a *gentle* tap; *gentle* measures); soft or low, as sound; moderate, as heat; gradual, as a slope; of animals, tame, or easily handled or managed; of plants, cultivated (archaic: opposed to *wild*).—**gentle reader,** courteous or kind reader: an old expression still sometimes used by the author in addressing or mentioning the reader in the course of a book or the like.—**the gentle craft,** the trade of shoemaking (as in the title of Dekker's play, "The Shoemakers' Holiday; or, *The Gentle Craft*"); also, the sport of angling.—**the gentle** (or **gentler**) **sex,** the female sex.—**gen′tle,** *n.* A person of gentle birth or good family (archaic); also, a falcon-gentle; also, a maggot or larva of a flesh-fly, used as bait by anglers.—**gen′tle,** *v. t.*; *-tled, -tling.* To make gentle or honorable† (as, "Be he ne'er so vile, This day shall *gentle* his condition": Shakspere's "Henry V.," iv. 3. 63); also, to make mild; soften; also, to tame (a horse, etc.).—**gen′tle-folk,** *n.* Persons of good family and breeding: often (as orig.) in *pl.*, *gentlefolks.*—**gen′tle=heart′ed,** *a.* Gentle in heart or disposition; mild; kindly.—**gen′tle-hood** (-hůd), *n.* The character or breeding proper to gentle birth.

gen-tle-man (jen′tl-mạn), *n.*; pl. *-men.* [ME. *gentil man*: cf. F. *gentilhomme.*] A man of gentle birth, or above the social rank of yeoman, esp. one who bears a coat of arms though not ranking among the nobility (Eng.); also, a man of gentle birth who recognizes and fulfils the obligations of honor attaching to his station (as, "And thus he bore without abuse The grand old name of *gentleman*": Tennyson's "In Memoriam," cxi.); also, a man of good breeding or polite manners (as, "With such true breeding of a *gentleman,* You never could divine his real thought": Byron's "Don Juan," iii. 41); often, a man of fine feelings or instincts (irrespective of social position or training), as shown by behavior and esp. by nice or generous consideration for others (as, "It is almost a definition of a *gentleman* to say he is one who never inflicts pain": J. H. Newman's "Idea of a University," i. 8); also, a man of superior social position or advantages; a man who lives on independent means without engaging in business, professional work, etc.; a polite term for any man (as a term of address, now only in the *pl.*, as in addressing an audience, the term in the *sing.* being *sir*); also, a male personal servant, or valet, of a man of social position (sometimes called 'gentleman's gentleman').

—**gentlemen's agreement,** an agreement binding as a matter of honor alone, as one not reduced to legal form or one whose terms could not be enforced at law.—**gen'tle-man=at=arms',** *n.* In England, one of a guard of forty gentlemen with their officers who attend the sovereign on state occasions.—**gen'tle-man-hood** (-hůd), *n.* The condition or character of a gentleman.—**gen'tle-man-like,** *a.* Gentlemanly.—**gen'tle-man-ly,** *a.* Like or befitting a gentleman; well-bred; polite.—**gen'tle-man-li-ness,** *n.*

gen-tle-ness (jen'tl-nes), *n.* The state or quality of being gentle.

gen-tle-wom-an (jen'tl-wům″ạn), *n.*; pl. -*women* (-wim″en). [ME. *gentil womman.*] A woman of good family or breeding; also, a woman who attends upon a lady of rank.—**gen'tle-wom″an-hood** (-hůd), *n.* The condition or character of a gentlewoman.—**gen'tle-wom″an-like, gen'tle-wom″an-ly,** *a.* Like or befitting a gentlewoman.—**gen'tle-wom″an-li-ness,** *n.*

gen-tly (jen'tli), *adv.* In a gentle manner.

Gen-too[1] (jen-tö'). [Anglo-Ind., < Pg. *gentio,* gentile, pagan (applied to the Hindus as contrasted with the Mohammedans), < L. *gentilis*: see *gentile.*] **I.** *n.* An adherent of the Hindu religion; esp., a Telugu; also, the language of the Telugus. **II.** *a.* Of or pertaining to the Gentoos.

gen-too[2] (jen-tö'), *n.* [Cf. *Gentoo*[1].] A penguin, *Pygoscelis tæniata,* of the Falkland Islands.

Gentoo.

gen-trice (jen'tris), *n.* [OF. *genterise,* var. of *gentilise,* < *gentil,* E. *gentle.*] Gentle birth, or persons of gentle birth; also, good breeding; honorable or noble feeling; generosity. [Archaic or Sc.]

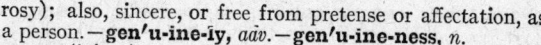

gen-try (jen'tri), *n.* [ME.; appar. a var. of *gentrice.*] Gentle birth (archaic); the quality or rank of gentleman (archaic); also, the class of well-born and well-bred people, esp., as in England, the class next below the nobility; also, 'gentlemen' or persons of any particular class (used in playful or ironical civility: as, "Reader, if thou meetest one of these small *gentry* . . . it is good to give him a penny," Lamb's "Praise of Chimney-Sweepers"); also, courtesy† (see Shakspere's "Hamlet," ii. 2. 22).

ge-nu (jē'nū), *n.*; pl. *genua* (jen'ū-ạ). [L., the knee; akin to E. *knee.*] In *anat.,* the knee; a knee-like part or bend. —**genu valgum** (val'gum). [L., properly, 'knee bent outward,' bow-leg (not knock-knee).] Knock-knee. Cf. *genu varum.*—**genu varum** (vā'rum). [L., properly, 'knee bent inward,' knock-knee.] Bow-leg. Cf. *genu valgum.*—

gen-u-al (jen'ū-ạl), *a.* Of or pertaining to the knee; knee-like.

gen-u-flect (jen-ū-flekt' or jen'ū-flekt), *v. i.* [ML. *genuflectere,* < L. *genu,* knee, + *flectere,* bend.] To bend the knee, as in worship; perform a genuflexion.—**gen-u-flec'tor** (-flek'tǫr), *n.*—**gen-u-flex'ion, gen-u-flec'tion** (-flek'shǫn), *n.* [ML. *genuflexio(n-).*] The act of genuflecting; esp., a momentary sinking downward by bending one knee or both as a gesture of reverence or worship.

gen-u-ine (jen'ū-in), *a.* [L. *genuinus,* native, natural, authentic, genuine, < *gen-,* beget, produce: see *genius.*] Native or natural, rather than foreign or acquired†; also, belonging to or proceeding from the original stock (as, a *genuine* Celtic people; a dog of the *genuine* Newfoundland breed); pure in race or breed; also, actually proceeding from the reputed source or author, as a relic, painting, signature, writing, etc. (as, "The political correspondence of Machiavelli, first published in 1767, is unquestionably *genuine*": Macaulay's "Essays," Machiavelli); authentic, or not spurious; also, being truly such, rather than counterfeit, pretended, or merely seeming (as, *genuine* regret; *genuine* worth or benefit; *genuine* cause for satisfaction); real or true; properly so called (as, a case of *genuine* leprosy); also, sincere, or free from pretense or affectation, as a person.—**gen'u-ine-ly,** *adv.*—**gen'u-ine-ness,** *n.*

ge-nus (jē'nus), *n.*; pl. *genera* (jen'ẹ-rạ) or *genuses.* [L. *genus* (= Gr. γένος), race, stock, kind, sort, gender, < *gen-* (= Gr. γεν-), beget, bear, produce: see *genius,* and cf. *gender.*] A kind, sort, or class; in *logic,* a class or group of individuals including subordinate groups called *species*; in *zoöl.* and *bot.,* a group or category ranking below a family and above a species; a group of animal or plant species (sometimes a single species) possessing certain structural characters different from those of any other.

-geny. [Gr. -γένεια, < -γενής, born, produced; or Gr. γεν-, bear, produce: see *-gen.*] A noun termination meaning 'production,' 'genesis,' 'origination,' or 'evolution,' as in *autogeny, cosmogeny, epirogeny, phylogeny.*

geo-. Form of Gr. γῆ, earth, used in combination.—**ge-o-cen-tric** (jē-ǭ-sen'trik), *a.* In *astron.,* as viewed or measured from the center of the earth (as, the *geocentric* latitude of a planet); also, having or representing the earth as a center (as, a *geocentric* theory of the universe).—**ge-o-cen'tri-cal-ly,** *adv.*—**ge-o-chem'is-try,** *n.* The science dealing with the chemical changes in, and the composition of, the earth's crust.—**ge-o-chem'i-cal,** *a.*—**ge-o-cyc'lic** (-sik'lik), *a.* [See *cyclic.*] Of or pertaining to the revolutions of the earth (as, a *geocyclic* machine, a machine for illustrating processes by which day and night and the seasons are produced); also, circling the earth periodically.

ge-ode (jē'ōd), *n.* [L. *geodes,* < Gr. γεώδης, earth-like, < γῆ, earth, + εἶδος, form.] A hollow concretionary or nodular stone frequently lined with crystals.—**ge-o-dal** (jē-ō'dạl), *a.*

Geode (Quartz).

ge-o-des-ic (jē-ǭ-des'ik), *a.* Of or pertaining to geodesy; pertaining to the extension of theorems of plane geometry to figures drawn on curved surfaces (as, a *geodesic* line, a line so drawn upon a curved surface, or any surface, as to coincide with the position of a string stretched across the surface between any two points in the line). Also **ge-o-des'i-cal.**

ge-od-e-sist (jẹ-od'e-sist), *n.* One versed in geodesy; a geodetic surveyor.

ge-od-e-sy (jẹ-od'e-si), *n.* [Gr. γεωδαισία, < γῆ, earth, + δαίειν, divide.] That branch of applied mathematics which determines the shape and area of large tracts of country, the exact position of geographical points, and the curvature, shape, and dimensions of the earth; also, that branch of surveying which involves such applied mathematics.—**ge-o-det-ic** (jē-ǭ-det'ik), *a.* Pertaining to geodesy; geodesic. Also **ge-o-det'i-cal.**—**ge-o-det'i-cal-ly,** *adv.*—**ge-o-det'ics,** *n.* Geodesy.

ge-od-ic (jẹ-od'ic), *a.* Of, pertaining to, or resembling a geode.

ge-o-duck (jē'ǭ-duk), *n.* Erroneous form of *goeduck* for *gweduc.*

ge-o-dy-nam-ic (jē″ǭ-dī-nam'ik), *a.* [See *geo-* and *dynamic.*] Noting or pertaining to the natural forces and processes (volcanic, seismic, etc.) of the earth's interior and crust.—**ge″o-dy-nam'ics,** *n.* The science dealing with geodynamic phenomena.

ge-og-e-ny (jẹ-oj'e-ni), *n.* [See *geo-* and *-geny.*] Geogony; also, that branch of geology which treats of the formation of the earth's crust.—**ge-o-gen-ic** (jē-ǭ-jen'ik), *a.*

ge-og-nost (jē'og-nost), *n.* [G. *geognost,* < Gr. γῆ, earth, + γνώστης, one who knows.] One versed in geognosy. —**ge-og-nos'tic** (-nos'tik), *a.* Of or pertaining to geognosy. —**ge-og-nos'ti-cal-ly,** *adv.*

ge-og-no-sy (jẹ-og'nǭ-si), *n.* [G. *geognosie,* < Gr. γῆ, earth, + γνῶσις, knowledge.] That branch of geology which treats of the constituent parts of the earth, its envelop of air and water, its crust, and the probable condition of its interior.

ge-og-o-ny (jẹ-og'ǭ-ni), *n.* [See *geo-* and *-gony.*] The genesis or origination of the earth; a theory or account of the origin of the earth.

ge-og-ra-pher (jẹ-og'rạ-fėr), *n.* One versed in geography.

ge-o-graph-ic, ge-o-graph-i-cal (jē-ọ-graf′ik, -i-kạl), *a.* [Gr. γεωγραφικός.] Of or pertaining to geography; having reference to position, extent, area, etc., on the earth.—**geographical mile.** See under *mile.*—**ge-o-graph′i-cal-ly,** *adv.*

ge-og-ra-phize (jẹ̄-og′rạ-fīz), *v.*; *-phized, -phizing.* **I.** *intr.* To pursue geographical researches. **II.** *tr.* To determine or describe the geographical character of.

ge-og-ra-phy (jẹ̄-og′rạ-fi), *n.*; pl. *-phies* (-fiz). [L. *geographia,* < Gr. γεωγραφία, < γῆ, earth, + γράφειν, draw, write.] The science of the description of the earth in its external aspects, dealing with its form and movements, physical features, climate and products, inhabitants, and natural and political divisions, and the population, industries, etc., of the various countries; also, a treatise on this science; also, the topographical features of a region: properly referring to the earth, but sometimes used with reference to Mars, the moon, etc.

ge-oid (jē′oid), *n.* [Gr. γεοειδής, earth-like, var. of γεώδης: see *geode.*] An imaginary surface which coincides with the mean sea-level over the ocean and its extension under the continents; the geometrical figure formed by this surface.—**ge-oi-dal** (jē-oi′dạl), *a.*

ge-o-log-ic, ge-o-log-i-cal (jē-ọ-loj′ik, -i-kạl), *a.* Of or pertaining to geology.—**ge-o-log′i-cal-ly,** *adv.*

ge-ol-o-gist (jẹ̄-ol′ọ-jist), *n.* One versed in geology; specif., one employed in the investigation or exposition of the structure of the earth, or of any part of it (as, the *geologist* of an exploring expedition; a state *geologist*).

ge-ol-o-gize (jẹ̄-ol′ọ-jīz), *v.*; *-gized, -gizing.* **I.** *intr.* To make geological investigations. **II.** *tr.* To study or describe the geological character of.

ge-ol-o-gy (jẹ̄-ol′ọ-ji), *n.*; pl. *-gies* (-jiz). [NL. *geologia,* < Gr. γῆ, earth, + -λογία, < λέγειν, speak.] The science which treats of the earth's crust, the strata of which it is composed, and the physical changes which it has undergone or is still undergoing; also, a treatise on this science.

ge-o-man-cy (jē′ọ-man-si), *n.* [OF. *geomancie* (F. *géomancie*), < ML. *geomantia,* < Gr. γῆ, earth, + μαντεία, divination.] Divination by means of signs connected with the earth, as by the figure made by a handful of earth thrown down at random; hence, divination by means of figures or lines formed by a number of dots jotted down at random.—**ge′o-man-cer** (-sėr), *n.*—**ge-o-man′tic,** *a.*

ge-om-e-ter (jẹ̄-om′e-tėr), *n.* [L. *geometra, geometres,* < Gr. γεωμέτρης, land-measurer, geometer, < γῆ, earth, + μέτρον, measure.] One versed in geometry; a geometrician; also, a geometrid moth or its larva.

ge-o-met-ric, ge-o-met-ri-cal (jē-ọ-met′rik, -ri-kạl), *a.* [L. *geometricus,* < Gr. γεωμετρικός, < γεωμετρία: see *geometry.*] Of or pertaining to geometry; according to the principles of geometry; also, resembling or employing the lines or figures in geometry.—**ge-o-met′ri-cal-ly,** *adv.*—**ge-om-e-tri-cian** (jẹ̄-om-e-trish′ạn), *n.* One versed in geometry.

ge-om-e-trid (jẹ̄-om′e-trid). [NL. *Geometridæ,* < L. *geometra*: see *geometer.*] **I.** *n.* Any of the *Geometridæ,* a family of moths whose larvæ (called *measuring-worms*) progress by bringing the rear end of the body forward, thus forming a loop, and then advancing the front end. **II.** *a.* Belonging to the *Geometridæ* (family of geometrids).

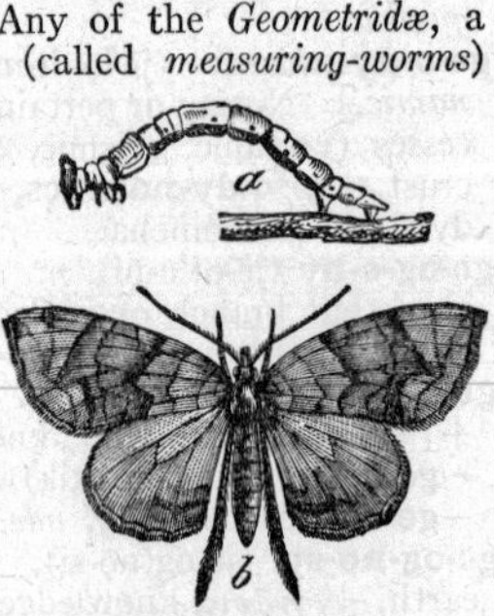

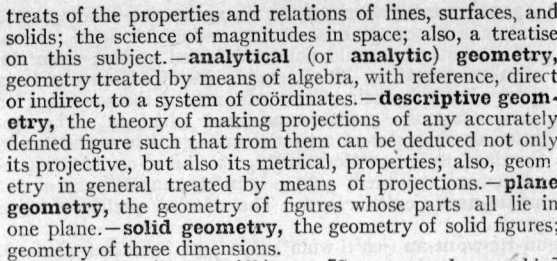

Geometrid, natural size.—*a,* larva; *b,* moth.

ge-om-e-trism (jẹ̄-om′e-trizm), *n.* A movement in pictorial art, subsequent to cubism and first attracting attention in 1922, which characteristically involves representation by geometrical lines and figures.

ge-om-e-trize (jẹ̄-om′e-trīz), *v.*; *-trized, -trizing.* **I.** *intr.* To work by geometrical methods; practise geometry. **II.** *tr.* To form geometrically.

ge-om-e-try (jẹ̄-om′e-tri), *n.*; pl. *-tries* (-triz). [OF. *geometrie* (F. *géométrie*), < L. *geometria,* < Gr. γεωμετρία, < γεωμέτρης: see *geometer.*] That branch of mathematics which treats of the properties and relations of lines, surfaces, and solids; the science of magnitudes in space; also, a treatise on this subject.—**analytical** (or **analytic**) **geometry,** geometry treated by means of algebra, with reference, direct or indirect, to a system of coördinates.—**descriptive geometry,** the theory of making projections of any accurately defined figure such that from them can be deduced not only its projective, but also its metrical, properties; also, geometry in general treated by means of projections.—**plane geometry,** the geometry of figures whose parts all lie in one plane.—**solid geometry,** the geometry of solid figures; geometry of three dimensions.

ge-o-mor-phic (jē-ọ-môr′fik), *a.* [See *geo-* and *-morphic.*] Of or pertaining to the figure of the earth or the contours and forms of its surface; resembling the earth in form.

ge-oph-a-gy (jẹ̄-of′ạ-ji), *n.* [See *geo-* and *-phagy.*] The practice of eating earthy matter, as clay or chalk. Also **ge-oph′a-gism** (-jizm).—**ge-oph′a-gist** (-jist), *n.*

ge-oph-i-lous (jẹ̄-of′i-lus), *a.* [See *geo-* and *-philous.*] In *zoöl.*, terrestrial, as certain snails; in *bot.*, growing or rooting in the ground; fruiting underground.

ge-o-phone (jē′ọ-fōn), *n.* [See *geo-* and *-phone.*] A device with which to detect sounds transmitted through the ground, and to determine their kind and the direction or location of their source: invented and used by the French, during the World War, for locating mining operations of the Germans, and afterward (with various modifications) employed in locating fires in coal-mines, rescuing imprisoned miners, etc.

ge-o-phys-ics (jē-ọ-fiz′iks), *n.* [See *geo-.*] The physics of the earth; the science dealing with the relations between the features of the earth and the agencies that produce them.—**ge-o-phys′i-cal,** *a.*—**ge-o-phys′i-cist** (-sist), *n.*

ge-o-pon-ic (jē-ọ-pon′ik), *a.* [Gr. γεωπονικός, < γεωπονία, tillage, < γεωπόνος, husbandman, < γῆ, earth, + πένεσθαι, work.] Of or pertaining to tillage or agriculture; agricultural; hence, rustic; countrified.—**ge-o-pon′ics,** *n.* The art or science of agriculture.

ge-o-ra-ma (jē-ọ-rä′mạ̈), *n.* [F. *géorama,* < Gr. γῆ, earth, + ὅραμα, view.] A large hollow globe on the inside of which is depicted a map of the earth's surface, to be viewed by a spectator within the globe.

George (jôrj), *n.* A jewel showing a figure of St. George (the patron saint of England) on horseback encountering the dragon, worn as part of the insignia of the Order of the Garter (as, "Look on my *George*; I am a gentleman": Shakspere's "2 Henry VI.," iv. 1. 29); also, an English coin bearing the image of St. George†.

geor-gette (jôr-jet′), *n.* [For *Georgette crêpe,* so called from Mme. *Georgette,* French modiste.] A fine, thin, transparent variety of silk crape, with minute irregularities of surface.

Geor-gian[1] (jôr′jiạn). **I.** *a.* Of or pertaining to the four Georges, kings of Great Britain and Ireland (1714–1830), or the period of their reigns; also, of or pertaining to George V. (acceded to the throne in 1910), or the period of his reign; also, of or pertaining to the State of Georgia in the U. S. (named after George II.). **II.** *n.* A person, esp. a writer, of either of the Georgian periods in England; also, a native or inhabitant of the State of Georgia.

Geor-gian[2] (jôr′jiạn). **I.** *a.* Of or pertaining to Georgia in Transcaucasia, east of the Black Sea; also, of or pertaining to the Georgians or their language. **II.** *n.* A native or inhabitant of Georgia in Transcaucasia; one of a handsome race, of purest Caucasian type, inhabiting a large part of Transcaucasia, and speaking an agglutinative language which has no known connection with any other tongue; also, the language itself.

geor-gic (jôr′jik). [L. *georgicus,* < Gr. γεωργικός, < γεωργία, tillage, < γεωργός, husbandman, < γῆ, earth, + -εργός, working, worker.] **I.** *a.* Pertaining to husbandry; agricultural. **II.** *n.* A poem on husbandry or agricultural matters: as, Virgil's "Georgics" (L. *Georgica*).

ge-o-stat-ic (jē-ọ-stat′ik), *a.* [See *geo-* and *static.*] Capable of sustaining the pressure of superincumbent earth or the like, as a type of arch.—**ge-o-stat′ics,** *n.* The statics of rigid bodies.

ge-o-syn-cli-nal (jē″ọ-sin-klī′nạl). [See *geo-* and *synclinal.*] In *geol.*: **I.** *a.* Noting or pertaining to a synclinal fold which embraces a notable part of the earth's surface. **II.** *n.*

A geosynclinal fold.—**ge-o-syn′cline** (-klīn), *n.* In *geol.*, a geosynclinal fold.

ge-o-tec-ton-ic (jē″ō-tek-ton′ik), *a.* [See *geo-* and *tectonic.*] Pertaining to the structure of the earth's crust or to the arrangement and form of the materials composing it.

ge-o-ther-mal, ge-o-ther-mic (jē-ō-thėr′mal, -mik), *a.* [See *geo-* and *thermal.*] Of or pertaining to the internal heat of the earth.

ge-o-trop-ic (jē-ō-trop′ik), *a.* [See *geo-* and *-tropic.*] In *bot.*, tending toward the earth, or the center of the earth, as the roots of plants in growing; in general, taking a particular direction with reference to the earth (as, positively *geotropic*, see def. preceding; negatively *geotropic*, directed upward, away from the center of the earth; transversely *geotropic*, directed horizontally).—**ge-o-trop′i-cal-ly,** *adv.* —**ge-ot-ro-pism** (jē-ot′rō-pizm), *n.* In *bot.*, geotropic tendency or growth.

ge-rah (gē′rä), *n.* [Heb.] An ancient Jewish weight and coin, equivalent to the twentieth part of a shekel.

ge-ra-ni-a-ceous (je-rā-ni-ā′shius), *a.* [See *geranium.*] Belonging to the *Geraniaceæ*, or geranium family of plants.

ge-ra-ni-um (je-rā′ni-um), *n.* [L., < Gr. γεράνιον, crane's-bill, < γέρανος, crane.] Any of the plants of the genus *Geranium*, most of which have pink or purple flowers, and some of which, as *G. maculatum*, have an astringent root used in medicine; crane's-bill; also, a plant of the allied genus *Pelargonium*, of which many species are well known in cultivation for their showy flowers (as the 'scarlet geranium' and the 'Lady Washington geranium') or their fragrant leaves (as the 'rose-geranium').

ger-a-tol-o-gy (jer-a-tol′ō-ji), *n.* [Gr. γῆρας (γηρατ-), old age: see *-logy.*] The science that treats of the decline of life, as in animals approaching extinction.

ger-bil, ger-bille (jėr′bil), *n.* [F. *gerbille*, < NL. *gerbillus*, dim. < *jerboa*, E. *jerboa.*] Any of numerous jerboa-like rodents (genus *Gerbillus*, etc.) of Asia, Africa, and southern Russia, belonging to the mouse family, and forming the subfamily *Gerbillinæ*.

Gerbil (*Gerbillus longifrons*).

ge-rent (jē′rent), *n.* [L. *gerens* (*gerent-*), ppr. of *gerere*, bear, conduct, manage.] A manager; a ruler.

ger-fal-con (jėr′fâ″kn or -fâl″kon), *n.* [OF. *gerfaucon*: cf. OHG. *gīr* (G. *geier*), vulture, and E. *falcon.*] Any of various large falcons of the cold regions of the north.

Gerfalcon (*Falco gyrfalco*).

germ (jėrm), *n.* [F. *germe*, < L. *germen*, sprout.] The earliest rudiment of a living organism; an embryo in its early stages; a seed; a bud; also, a micro-organism, esp. when disease-producing; a microbe; in fig. use, that from which anything springs as if from a seed (as, "By thy first step awry thou didst plant the *germ* of evil": Hawthorne's "Scarlet Letter," xiv.); a formative principle.—**germ theory,** in *biol.*, the theory of biogenesis; in *pathol.*, the theory that infectious diseases, etc., are due to the agency of germs or micro-organisms.

ger-man[1] (jėr′man). [OF. F. *germain*, < L. *germanus*, german.] **I.** *a.* Sprung from the same father and mother (as, a brother *german*; sisters *german*); sprung from the brother or sister of one's father or mother, or from brothers or sisters (as, a cousin *german*; cousins *german*, see under *cousin*); hence, akin or related, as persons†; fig., related†, relevant†, or germane†; also, genuine or true (obs. or archaic). **II.**† *n.* One sprung from the same stock; a brother or sister; a near relative.

Ger-man[2] (jėr′man), *a.* [L. *Germanus*; prob. from Celtic.] Of or pertaining to Germany, its inhabitants, or their language; sometimes, pertaining to Germany, the Netherlands, etc., or to the group of related peoples or languages of these regions (as, High *German*; Low *German*: cf. the phrases under *German*[2], *n.*).—**German Baptist Brethren.** See *Dunker.*—**German measles,** in *pathol.*, rubella.—**German silver,** a white alloy of copper, zinc, and nickel, used for making utensils, drawing-instruments, wire of high electrical resistance, etc.—**German text,** in *printing*, the modern German type, or an ornamental type resembling it. See *type.*—**Ger′man**[2], *n.*; pl. *-mans.* A native or inhabitant of Germany; also, the language, esp. the literary language, of Germany; sometimes, a member of any of the group of related peoples of Germany, the Netherlands, etc., or the group of languages, or a particular member of the group, spoken by them (see the phrases below); also [*l. c.*], an elaborate kind of dance; a cotillion; a party at which it is danced.—**High German,** an inhabitant of the more elevated parts of Germany, in the center and south; also, the language spoken there, including many dialects, one of which, the court and official dialect of Saxony, became and is now the literary language throughout the whole of Germany (divided into Old High German, extending from about 800 to about 1100; Middle High German, from about 1100 to about 1500; and modern German, from about 1500 on).—**Low German,** an inhabitant of the more low-lying parts of Germany in the north, or of the Netherlands, etc.; also, the group of dialects spoken by the Low Germans (divided into Old Low German, Middle Low German, and modern Low German, corresponding substantially to the periods of High German).—**Ger′man=A-mer′i-can. I.** *a.* Pertaining to Germany and America; also, noting or pertaining to Americans of German birth or descent. **II.** *n.* An American of German birth or descent.

ger-man-der (jėr-man′dėr), *n.* [ML. *germandra*, by corruption < Gr. χαμαίδρυς, < χαμαί, on the ground, + δρῦς, tree, oak.] Any of the herbs or shrubs constituting the menthaceous genus *Teucrium*, as *T. chamædrys*, a purple-flowered European species, and *T. canadense*, an American species; also, a species of speedwell ('germander speedwell': see *speedwell*).

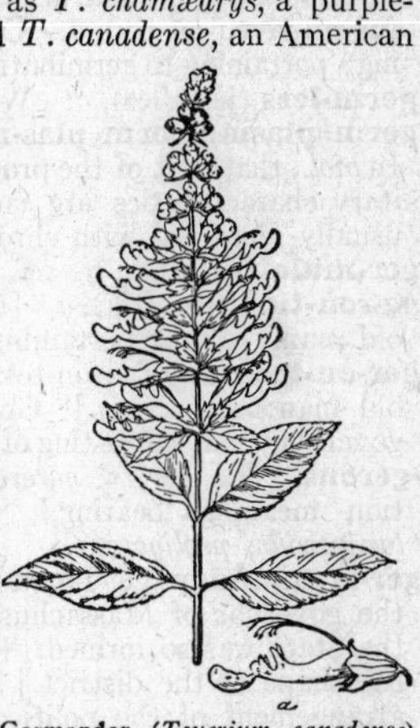

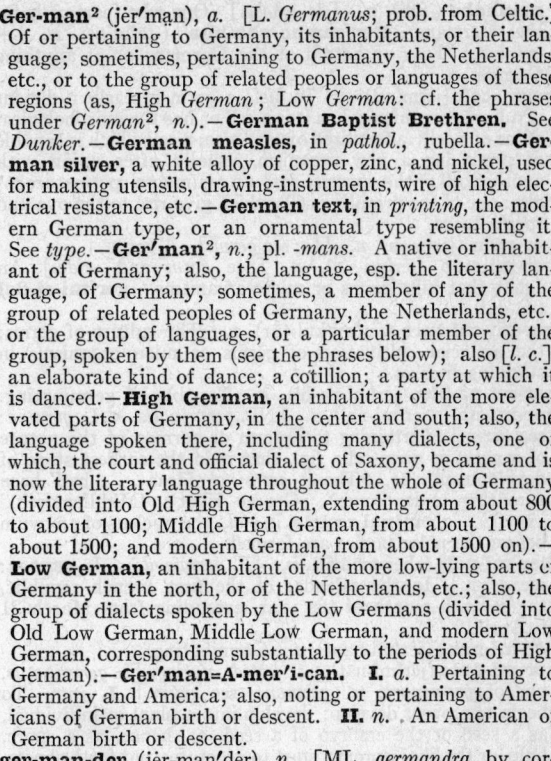

Germander (*Teucrium canadense*) — *a*, a flower.

ger-mane (jėr-mān′), *a.* [Var. of *german*[1]: cf. *humane* and *human.*] German†, or akin†; fig., closely related; relevant; pertinent.

Ger-man-ic (jėr-man′ik). [L. *Germanicus.*] **I.** *a.* Of or pertaining to the Germans; German; also, pertaining to the Teutonic race or any of the peoples belonging to it, or to the group of languages spoken by these peoples; Teutonic. **II.** *n.* The language or languages of the Germanic or Teutonic peoples.

Ger-man-ism (jėr′man-izm), *n.* Characteristic German quality; German modes of thought, action, etc.; attachment to or affectation of what is German; also, a German characteristic, usage, or idiom.

ger-ma-ni-um (jėr-mā′ni-um), *n.* [NL., < L. *Germania*, country of the Germans.] Chem. sym., Ge; at. wt., 72.5; sp. gr., 5.469. A rare metallic element with a grayish-white color.

Ger-man-ize (jėr′man-īz), *v.*; *-ized, -izing.* **I.** *tr.* To render German in character, sentiment, etc.; also, to translate into German. **II.** *intr.* To become German in habits, sympathies, etc.—**Ger″man-i-za′tion** (-i-zā′shon), *n.*

Ger-ma-no- (jėr′ma-nō-). Form of L. *Germanus*, German, used in combination.—**Ger″ma-no-ma′ni-a** (-mā′ni-ä), *n.* A mania or passion for what is German.—**Ger′ma-no-phil, Ger′ma-no-phile** (-fil). [+ *-phil, -phile.*] **I.** *a.* Friendly to Germany or the Germans. **II.** *n.* One who is friendly to Germany or the Germans.—**Ger′ma-**

no-phobe (-fōb), *n.* [+ *-phobe.*] One who fears or hates the Germans.—**Ger″ma-no-pho′bi-a** (-fō′bi-ạ̈), *n.* [+ *-phobia.*] Fear or hatred of the Germans or of anything German.

germ=cell (jėrm′sel), *n.* In *biol.*, a germ or early rudiment of a living organism when it is a cell or has the morphological value of a cell; a fertilized ovum; also, a cell which is capable of producing a new organism, usually after union with another cell of the opposite sex; an ovum or a spermatozoön; also, one of the primitive cells which give rise to the ova and spermatozoa.

ger-men (jėr′men), *n.* [L.: see *germ.*] A germ.

ger-mi-cide (jėr′mi-sīd), *n.* [See *germ* and *-cide.*] An agent that kills germs or micro-organisms.—**ger′mi-ci-dal** (-sī-dạl), *a.*

ger-mi-cul-ture (jėr′mi-kul-ṭụ̄r), *n.* The culture of germs; the artificial cultivation of germs or micro-organisms in studying diseases.

ger-mi-na-ble (jėr′mi-nạ-bl), *a.* Capable of germinating.

ger-mi-nal[1] (jėr′mi-nạl), *a.* [NL. *germinalis*, < L. *germen*: see *germ.*] Pertaining to a germ or germs; of the nature of a germ or germ-cell; fig., that is in the earliest stage of development (as, "Those *germinal* ideas . . . had been sprouting under cover": George Eliot's "Middlemarch," xxxvii.).—**germinal vesicle,** in *biol.*, the nucleus of an ovum before the polar bodies are formed.

Ger-mi-nal[2] (zher-mē-nȧl), *n.* [F. *germinal*, < L. *germen*: see *germ.*] In the calendar of the first French republic, the seventh month of the year, extending from March 21 to April 19.

ger-mi-nant (jėr′mi-nạnt), *a.* Germinating.

ger-mi-nate (jėr′mi-nāt), *v.*; *-nated, -nating.* [L. *germinatus*, pp. of *germinare*, < *germen*: see *germ.*] **I.** *intr.* To begin to grow or develop; develop into a plant or individual, as a seed or the embryo of a seed, or, hence, as a spore, bulb, or the like; sprout; start to vegetate; put forth shoots. Also fig. **II.** *tr.* To cause to sprout; fig., to cause to develop; produce.—**ger-mi-na′tion** (-nā′shọn), *n.* [L. *germinatio(n-).*] The act or process of germinating.—**ger′mi-na-tive** (-nạ-tiv), *a.* Capable of germinating or developing; pertaining to germination.—**ger′mi-na-tor** (-nā-tọr), *n.*

germ-less (jėrm′les), *a.* Without germs.

germ=plasm, germ=plas-ma (jėrm′plazm, -plaz″mạ̈), *n.* In *biol.*, that part of the protoplasm of a cell by which hereditary characteristics are supposed to be transmitted: now usually identified with chromatin.

ger-mule (jėr′mūl), *n.* A small or incipient germ.

ge-ron-tic (jẹ-ron′tik), *a.* [Gr. γεροντικός, < γέρων (γεροντ-), old man.] Of or pertaining to old age; senile.

ger-on-toc-ra-cy (jer-ọn-tok′rạ-si), *n.* [Gr. γέρων (γεροντ-), old man: see *-cracy.*] Government by old men; also, a governing body consisting of old men.

-gerous. [L. *-ger*, < *gerere*, bear.] An adjective termination meaning 'bearing,' 'producing,' as in *dentigerous, lanigerous, proligerous.*

ger-ry-man-der (ger′i-man-dėr), *n.* [From Elbridge *Gerry*, the governor of Massachusetts in 1812 when a district in the State was so formed, + *(sala)mander*, with allusion to the shape of the district.] In *U. S. politics*, an arbitrary arrangement of the political divisions of a State, county, etc., made so as to give one party an unfair advantage in elections.—**ger-ry-man′der,** *v. t.* To subject (a State, county, etc.) to a gerrymander; hence, in general, to manipulate unfairly.—**ger-ry-man′der-er,** *n.*

ger-und (jer′und), *n.* [LL. *gerundium*, < L. *gerere*, bear, conduct, carry on.] In *gram.*, a form of the Latin verb used as a substantive in the oblique cases of the singular, but retaining certain functions of the verb, as that of governing an object or taking adverbial qualifiers, as *audiendi* ('of hearing') in *cupidus te audiendi* ('desirous of hearing you'); hence, any of various analogous forms in other languages, as the English verbal noun in *-ing* in certain uses, as in 'a man noted for readily *overcoming* difficulties.'—**ger′und=grind″er,** *n.* A teacher of Latin grammar; a pedagogue. [Humorous or contemptuous.]—**ge-run-di-al** (jẹ-run′di-ạl), *a.*—**ge-run′dive** (-div). [LL. *gerundivus.*] In *gram.*: **I.** *a.* Resembling a gerund. **II.** *n.* A Latin verbal adjective, of the nature of a future passive participle, having the same suffix as the gerund, and expressing necessity, fitness, etc., as *legendus* ('to be read') in *liber legendus* ('a book to be read,' or 'a book that should be read'); also, an analogous verbal adjective in other languages.—**ger-un-di′val** (-un-dī′vạl), *a.*—**ge-run′dive-ly,** *adv.*

ges-so (jes′ō), *n.* [It., < L. *gypsum*: see *gypsum.*] Gypsum, or plaster of Paris, now esp. as prepared for use in painting, sculpture, etc.; any plaster-like preparation applied to a surface to fit it for painting, gilding, or the like; a prepared surface of plaster or plaster-like material as a ground for painting, etc.

gest[1] (jest), *n.* [OF. F. *geste*, < ML. *gesta*, pl., deeds, prop. pp. neut. pl. of L. *gerere*, bear, conduct, carry on.] A deed or exploit (as, the *gests* of Alexander the Great, a favorite theme of poets in the middle ages); hence, a narrative, esp. in verse, of deeds or events; a metrical romance or history; in general, a story or tale. [Archaic.]

gest[2] (jest), *n.* [OF. F. *geste*, < L. *gestus*, < *gerere*: see *gest*[1].] Bearing or deportment; also, a gesture. [Archaic.]

gest[3]† (jest), *n.* [Earlier *gist*, < OF. *giste* (F. *gîte*), < *gesir*, lie: see *gist.*] A stopping-place in or a stage or distinct portion of a journey, esp. a royal progress (usually in *pl.*); also, the time of stopping, as in the course of a journey (see Shakspere's "Winter's Tale," i. 2. 41).

Ge-sta-po (gẹ-stä′pō), *n.* [From syllables of German name.] A German secret police understood to be directed by Hitler.

ges-tate (jes′tāt), *v. t.*; *-tated, -tating.* [L. *gestatus*, pp. of *gestare*, carry, freq. of *gerere*, bear.] To carry in the womb during the period from conception to delivery; fig., to form and gradually mature (a project, etc.) in the mind.—**ges-ta′tion** (-tā′shọn), *n.* [L. *gestatio(n-).*] A carrying or being carried (now rare); also, the act or period of carrying young in the womb from conception to delivery; pregnancy.—**ges′ta-tive** (-tạ-tiv), *a.* Of or pertaining to gestation.

ges-ta-to-ri-al (jes-tạ-tō′ri-ạl), *a.* [L. *gestatorius*, < *gestare*, carry: see *gestate.*] Of or for carrying: applied to a chair in which the Pope is carried on certain occasions.

geste (jest), *n.* See *gest*[1].

ges-tic (jes′tik), *a.* [See *gest*[2].] Of or pertaining to bodily action or motion, esp. dancing: as, "And the gay grandsire, skill'd in *gestic* lore, Has frisk'd beneath the burden of threescore" (Goldsmith's "Traveller," 253).

ges-tic-u-lant (jes-tik′ụ̄-lạnt), *a.* Gesticulating.

ges-tic-u-late (jes-tik′ụ̄-lāt), *v.*; *-lated, -lating.* [L. *gesticulatus*, pp. of *gesticulari*, < *gesticulus*, a gesticulation, dim. of *gestus*, bearing, gesture, E. *gest*[2].] **I.** *intr.* To make or use gestures, esp. in an animated or excited manner. **II.** *tr.* To express by gesticulation.—**ges-tic-u-la′tion** (-lā′shọn), *n.* [L. *gesticulatio(n-).*] The act of gesticulating; an animated or excited gesture.—**ges-tic′u-la-tive** (-lạ-tiv), **ges-tic′u-la-to-ry** (-tọ-ri), *a.* Characterized by or making gesticulations.—**ges-tic′u-la-tor** (-lā-tọr), *n.*

ges-tion (jes′chọn), *n.* [L. *gestio(n-)*, < *gerere*, bear, conduct, manage.] Conduct or management. [Archaic.]

ges-ture (jes′ṭụ̄r), *n.* [ML. *gestura*, < L. *gerere*, bear, conduct.] Carriage or posture of the body†; also, a movement of the body or of any part of it, as the hand, to express thought, feeling, or meaning or to emphasize or illustrate speech (as, a *gesture* of impatience; a *gesture* of command or warning; the *gestures* of an orator); the use of such movements, as in speaking; also, in recent use, any action or proceeding intended for effect or to impress others; a demonstration, as of power, purpose, principles, spirit, etc., often a mere demonstration or empty show; sometimes, a more or less spectacular action affording a display of fine spirit or feeling, high-mindedness, generosity, pride, etc. (as, this refusal of special honors was viewed as a *gesture*, or as a fine or superb *gesture*).—**ges′ture,** *v.*; *-tured, -turing.* **I.** *intr.* To make or use gestures; gesticulate. **II.** *tr.* To express by gestures.—**ges′tur-er,** *n.*

get (get), *v. t.*; pret. *got* (archaic *gat*), pp. *got* or (now less frequently, and chiefly in U. S.) *gotten*, ppr. *getting.* [ME. *geten*, from Scand.: cf. Icel. *geta* = AS. *-gitan, -gietan* (in compounds: see *beget, forget*) = OHG. *-gezzan* (G. *-gessen* in *vergessen*, forget) = Goth *-gitan*, akin to L. *-hendere* in *prehendere*, seize, take, and to Gr. χανδάνειν, hold, contain.] To become possessed of or obtain by effort or contrivance; earn, as one's living; gain or win (as, to *get* little for one's trouble; to *get* the start of a competitor); attain or achieve, as reputation, etc.; learn, or commit to memory, as lessons or a part in a play; ascertain by calculation, experiment, etc.; obtain by entreaty, insistence, etc., as permission or a confession; also, to receive, as a gift, salary, payment, etc.; acquire, or come to have (as, one gradually *gets* skill through practice); catch or contract (a disease or illness); receive, meet with, or suffer (a blow, defeat, etc.); receive as punishment or penalty (as, to *get* a thrashing; to *get* ten days in jail); also, to seek out and obtain, or procure, or secure (something required); succeed in finding, as a thing or a person; lay hold on, or capture; corner, as in an argument (colloq.); get into one's power, or do for (slang, U. S.); also, to reach, or arrive at (a place)†; also, to succeed in bringing, taking, putting, sending, etc. (*away, in, into, out, over, through,* etc.); betake (one's self: archaic: as, "Go *get* thee hence," Shakspere's "Two Gentlemen of Verona," iv. 4. 64); bring into a particular position, situation, or condition (as, to *get* one's self into trouble; to *get* a fire under control; to *get* dinner ready); cause (a person or thing) to be (as specified: as, to *get* a friend appointed to an office; to *get* one's hair cut); induce or cause to do something (as, we *got* him to speak; we could not *get* the fire to burn; you must *get* the janitor to fix that lock); also, to beget (now usually of animals). The past participle *got* is often used colloquially after *have* ('have got,' 'has got') in the sense of *have* alone: as, I *have got* (have) a cold; I *have got* (have, or am obliged) to go.—**to get up,** to prepare, arrange, or organize; contrive, devise, or concoct; work up, as an emotion or feeling; acquire a knowledge of, as a subject; do up, as linen; dress or array, as the person; produce in a specified manner or style with respect to appearance or externals, as a book.—**get,** *v. i.* To succeed in coming or going (*away, in, into, out, over, through,* etc.); make one's way (as specified); come to or arrive in a place specified or implied (as, he will *get* to Bombay in May; his boat *got* in yesterday; he *got* here last night); bring one's self into a particular place, situation, or condition (as, to *get* into position; to *get* into a rage); come or attain (followed by an infinitive: as, I did not *get* to see him; they never *got* to be friends); come to be, or become (as, to *get* sick; to *get* well; conditions are *getting* better); also, to be off (slang: often in the form *git*).—**to get along.** Same as *to get on,* below.—**to get away,** to escape; also, to start, as in a race.—**to get even with,** to square accounts with; retaliate upon.—**to get off,** to escape; evade consequences; also, to start, as on a journey.—**to get on,** to make progress; proceed; advance; also, to fare in a specified manner; often, to succeed or prosper; manage, as without something specified; also, to maintain harmonious relations, or agree, as with a person.—**to get over,** to surmount or overcome (a difficulty, etc.); cease to be troubled by (something); recover from (a shock, illness, etc.).—**to get round,** to circumvent or outwit; also, to cajole.—**to get up,** to arise; raise one's self to a sitting or standing posture; rise from bed; also, to ascend or mount; also, as a command to a horse ('get up!'), go! go ahead!—**get,** *n.* A getting, or what is got, obtained, or gained (now chiefly prov. or colloq.); also, a begetting, or an offspring, or progeny (now usually of animals); contemptuously, a child or brat (Sc. and north. Eng.).—**get′a-way″,** *n.* A getting away; an escape; the start, as of a race. [Colloq.]—**get′ta-ble, get′a-ble,** *a.* That can be got or procured; obtainable. —**get′ter,** *n.*—**get′=up,** *n.* Style of dress, equipment, etc.; style of production with respect to appearance or externals, as of a book. [Colloq.]

gew-gaw (gū′gâ). [Origin uncertain.] **I.** *n.* A showy trifle; a trumpery ornament; a bit of gaudy or useless finery; a bauble; a gimcrack. **II.** *a.* Showy but trifling; trumpery.—**gew′gawed,** *a.* Decked with gewgaws.

gey (gā), *a.* and *adv.* Scotch form of *gay.*

gey-ser (gī′sėr or -zėr), *n.* [Icel. *Geysir,* name of a hot spring in Iceland, < *geysa,* rush furiously, gush.] A hot spring which intermittently sends up fountain-like jets of water and steam into the air.—**gey′ser-ic,** *a.* Pertaining to or of the nature of a geyser.—**gey′ser-ite** (-īt), *n.* A variety of opaline silica deposited about the orifices of geysers and hot springs.

Giant Geyser, Yellowstone National Park, United States.

Geyserite.

ghaist (gāst), *n.* Scotch form of *ghost.*

ghar-ry (gar′i), *n.*; pl. *gharries* (-iz). [Hind. *gārī.*] A cart, carriage, or other wheeled vehicle. [Anglo-Ind.]

ghast[1]† (gȧst), *v. t.* See *gast.*

ghast[2] (gȧst), *a.* [From *ghastly.*] Ghastly. [Archaic or poetic.]

ghast-ful (gȧst′fụl), *a.* [ME. *gastful,* < AS. *gǣstan*: see *ghastly.*] Fearful, frightened, or timid; also, frightful or dreadful. [Obs. or archaic.]

ghast-ly (gȧst′li), *a.*; compar. *ghastlier,* superl. *ghastliest.* [ME. *gastly,* < AS. *gǣstan,* terrify, E. *gast*: cf. *ghost.*] Orig., terrifying or terrible, as fiends, furies, etc.†; later, exciting horror, as from association with or suggestion of death (as, *ghastly* wounds or carnage; *ghastly* traces of a struggle; *ghastly* shrieks); horrible, frightful, or dreadful, esp. in a sickening way (as, a *ghastly* threat; a *ghastly* tale); shocking (sometimes used in exaggeration: as, a *ghastly* failure); also, like or suggestive of a dead person or a ghost, as the face, appearance, color, etc. (as, "faces . . . *ghastly* with guilt and fear": Hawthorne's "Twice-Told Tales," David Swan); pallid; also, terrified†.—**ghast′li-ly,** *adv.*—**ghast′li-ness,** *n.*—**ghast′ly,** *adv.* In a ghastly manner; horribly; with a death-like aspect; deathly (pale, sick, etc.).

ghat, ghaut (gât), *n.* [Hind. *ghāt.*] In India, a mountain-pass, or a path of descent from a mountain; hence (incorrectly, as used by Europeans), a mountain-range (as, the Eastern and Western *Ghats,* parallel respectively with the eastern and western coasts of southern India); also, a passage or stairway descending to a river (as, the *ghats* along the Ganges at Benares, down which the Hindus come to bathe in the sacred river); a landing-place.

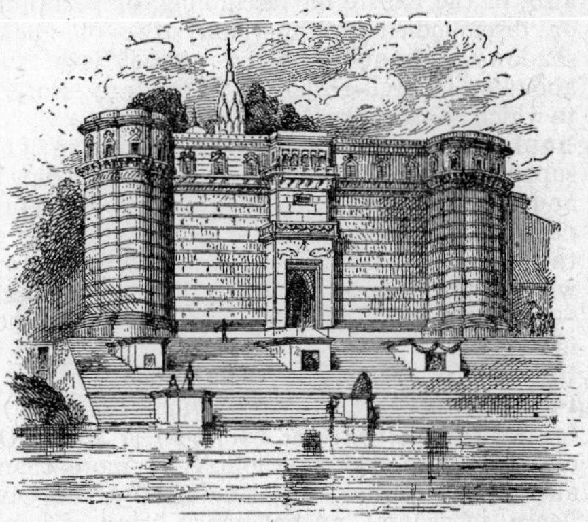

Ghat, Benares.

gha-wa-zi (gạ-wä′zē), *n. pl.* [Ar. *ghawāzī.*] In Egypt, a class of public dancing-girls. Cf. *almah.*

ghaz-al (gaz′ạl), *n.* [Pers. and Ar. *ghazal.*] A kind of short Oriental poem, usually of erotic character, in which the first two lines rime, with a corresponding rime in the second line of each succeeding couplet.

gha-zi (gä′zē), *n.*; pl. *-zis* (-zēz). [Ar. *ghāzī.*] Among Mohammedans, a warrior or champion fighting against infidels; a fanatic who has devoted himself to the destruction of infidels; also, a title of honor conferred for distinguished military service against infidel enemies.

Ghe-ber (gē′bėr or gā′-), *n.* See *Gueber.*

ghee (gē), *n.* [Hind. *ghī.*] In the East Indies, a kind of liquid butter, clarified by boiling, made from the milk of cows and buffaloes.

gher-kin (gėr′kin), *n.* [D. *agurkje*; from Slavic.] The small, immature fruit of some common variety of cucumber, or the fruit of some small-fruited variety, used for pickling; also, the small, spiny fruit of a cucurbitaceous vine, *Cucumis anguria,* of the West Indies, the southern U. S., etc., used in pickling as a substitute for the ordinary cucumber; the plant yielding this fruit.

ghet-to (get′ō), *n.*; *pl. ghettos* (-ōz), It. *ghetti* (-tē). [It.] A quarter in a city, as formerly in Italy, in which Jews were required to live; hence, any quarter inhabited chiefly by Jews.

Ghib-el-line (gib′e-lin). [It. *Ghibellino*, < G. *Waiblingen*, name of an estate belonging to the imperial family.] **I.** *n.* A member of the imperial and aristocratic party of medieval Italy, opposed to the Guelphs. **II.** *a.* Of or pertaining to the Ghibellines.

Ghoor-ka (gör′kạ̈), *n.* See *Gurkha.*

ghost (gōst), *n.* [AS. *gāst* = D. *geest* = G. *geist*, spirit; prob. akin to E. *gast* and *ghastly*.] The spirit, as the vital or the psychical principle (now chiefly in 'to give up the ghost,' to die); also, a spirit, or spiritual being (as, the Holy *Ghost*, the third person of the Trinity); sometimes, an evil spirit†, or demon†; also, a spirit conceived as surviving bodily death and manifesting itself to the living; a specter or apparition; fig., a mere shadow or semblance (as, the *ghost* of a smile; not the *ghost* of an idea, or of a chance); also, one who does literary or other work for a person who takes the credit; in *optics*, a bright spot or secondary image, as from a defect of the instrument.—**the ghost walks,** the salaries are paid or forthcoming: as, this is the day *the ghost walks.* [Orig. theatrical slang.]—**ghost,** *v.* **I.** *intr.* To give up the ghost†, or die†; also, to go (*about*, etc.) like a ghost or disembodied spirit. **II.** *tr.* To appear to or haunt, as a ghost does: as, "Julius Cæsar, Who at Philippi the good Brutus *ghosted*" (Shakspere's "Antony and Cleopatra," ii. 6. 13).—**ghost′=dance,** *n.* A religious dance of western North American Indian tribes, originating in connection with a Messianic doctrine which was put forth about 1888 and led to serious disturbances in 1890, and which prophesied the return of the dead and the extinction of the whites.—**ghost′hood** (-hůd), *n.* The state of a ghost.—**ghost′land** (-land), *n.* The land or region of ghosts.—**ghost′like,** *a.* and *adv.*—**ghost′ly,** *a.*; compar. *ghostlier*, superl. *ghostliest.* [AS. *gāstlīc.*] Spiritual (archaic or literary: as, *ghostly* counsel; *ghostly* father, a father confessor); also, of the nature of, resembling, or pertaining to a ghost or disembodied spirit; suggestive of ghosts; spectral; shadowy.—**ghost′li-ness,** *n.*—**ghost′=sto″ry,** *n.* A story about or involving ghosts; hence, any story or statement to which no credence should be given.

ghoul (göl), *n.* [Ar. *ghūl.*] An evil demon of Oriental story, supposed to feed on human beings, and esp. to rob graves and prey on corpses; hence, any one who preys upon the dead, as a body-snatcher or grave-robber or one who robs the unburied dead after some great catastrophe; fig., one who revels in what is revolting to ordinary human instincts.—**ghoul′ish,** *a.* Of, like, or befitting a ghoul.—**ghoul′ish-ly,** *adv.*

ghyll (gil), *n.* See *gill*².

gi-ant (jī′ạnt). [OF. *geant, jaiant* (F. *géant*), < L. *gigas* (*gigant-*), < Gr. γίγας (γιγαντ-).] **I.** *n.* One of a race of beings in Greek mythology, of more than human size and strength, who were subdued by the Olympian gods; hence, in general, an imaginary being of human form but superhuman size, strength, etc.; also, a person or thing of unusually great size; fig., one who towers or is eminent above others in endowments, achievements, importance, etc. (as, an intellectual *giant*; *giants* in the field of science or industry). **II.** *a.* Giant-like; gigantic; of extraordinary size (as, the *giant* cactus, *Cereus giganteus*, see *cereus*; the *giant* fennel, see *fennel*); fig., great or eminent above others.—**gi′ant-ess,** *n.* A female giant.—**gi′ant-ism,** *n.* The state of being a giant, or of gigantic size; in *physiol.*, etc., abnormally great development in size or stature; gigantism.—**gi′ant=pow″der,** *n.* A form of dynamite composed of nitroglycerin and kieselguhr.

giaour (jour), *n.* [Turk. *giaur*, < Pers. *gaur*, var. of *gabr*: see *Gueber.*] In Mohammedan use, an infidel, esp. a Christian: as, "Who falls in battle 'gainst a *Giaour* Is worthiest an immortal bower" (Byron's "Giaour").

gib¹ (gib), *n.* [Origin obscure.] A hook (prov.); in a machine, etc., a piece of metal fitted in to hold parts together or in place.—**gib**¹, *v. t.*; *gibbed, gibbing.* To secure with a gib or gibs.

gib² (gib), *n.* [From *Gib*, for *Gilbert*, man's name.] A cat, esp. a male cat, often one that has been castrated. [Now prov. Eng. and Sc.]

gib-ber¹ (jib′ėr or gib′ėr), *v. i.* [Imit.: cf. *gibberish* (recorded earlier), also *jabber.*] To speak rapidly and inarticulately; chatter senselessly: as, "The graves stood tenantless and the sheeted dead Did squeak and *gibber* in the Roman streets" (Shakspere's "Hamlet," i. 1. 116).—**gib′ber**¹, *n.* Gibbering utterance.

gib-ber² (gib′ėr), *n.* [Native Australian.] A large stone; a boulder. [Australia.]

gib-ber-ish (gib′ėr-ish), *n.* [Cf. *gibber*¹.] Rapid, unintelligible talk; meaningless chatter; jargon.

gib-bet (jib′et), *n.* [OF. F. *gibet*, appar. dim. of OF. *gibe*, staff, bill-hook.] A gallows; esp., an upright post with a projecting arm at the top, from which formerly the bodies of criminals were suspended after execution; also, the projecting beam of a crane.—**gib′bet,** *v. t.* To put (a person) to death by hanging on a gallows; also, to hang or expose (a body after execution) on a gibbet; hence, fig., to hold up to public scorn (as, "Was he to be *gibbeted* in the press?" Trollope's "Warden," v.); also, to hang or suspend (something) on a support (as, "swifter than he that *gibbets* on the brewer's bucket": Shakspere's "2 Henry IV.," iii. 2. 282).

gib-bon (gib′ọn), *n.* [F. *gibbon*; origin unknown.] Any of the small, slender, long-armed anthropoid apes of the genus *Hylobates*, of arboreal habits, found in the East Indies: in some respects closely approaching man.

Gibbon (*Hylobates lar*).

gib-bose (gib′ōs or gi-bōs′), *a.* [L. *gibbosus*, < *gibbus*, hump.] In *bot.*, *zoöl.*, etc., protuberant; having a protuberance; gibbous.

gib-bos-i-ty (gi-bos′i-ti), *n.*; pl. *-ties* (-tiz). The state of being gibbous or gibbose; also, a protuberance or swelling.

gib-bous (gib′us), *a.* [See *gibbose.*] Protuberant; convex; of a heavenly body, so illuminated as to be convex on both margins, as the moon when more than half full but less than full; also, humpbacked.—**gib′bous-ly,** *adv.*—**gib′bous-ness,** *n.*

gib=cat (gib′kat), *n.* Same as *gib*², *n.* [Archaic or prov.]

gibe (jīb), *v.*; *gibed, gibing.* [Origin uncertain.] **I.** *intr.* To jest in a bantering or derisive way (as, "He would familiarly *gybe* and jest with him": E. K., in Spenser's "Shepheardes Calender," Feb., Embleme); utter a mocking fling; scoff; jeer. **II.** *tr.* To gibe at; banter; deride; also, to dismiss with gibes (as, "You . . . with taunts Did *gibe* my missive out of audience": Shakspere's "Antony and Cleopatra," ii. 2. 74).—**gibe,** *n.* A gibing remark; a derisive or mocking fling.

Gib-e-on-ite (gib′ẹ̄-ọn-īt), *n.* [From the inhabitants of Gibeon, whom Joshua, to punish them for deception, made "hewers of wood and drawers of water" for the Israelites: see Josh. ix.] One compelled to toil for others; a drudge.

gib-er (jī′bėr), *n.* One who gibes.

gib-ing (jī′bing), *p. a.* That gibes; deriding; mocking; jeering.—**gib′ing-ly,** *adv.*

gib-let (jib′let), *n.* [OF. *gibelet*, dish of game.] The heart, liver, gizzard, or some other edible part, as the end of the wing, removed from a fowl before cooking: usually in *pl.*

Gi-bral-tar (ji-brâl′tạ̈r), *n.* [From *Gibraltar*, the British fortress on the Mediterranean coast of Spain.] An impregnable stronghold; also, a kind of candy.

gi-bus (jī′bus, F. zhē-büs), *n.* [From *Gibus*, the first (French) maker.] An opera-hat or crush-hat.

gid (gid), *n.* [From *giddy.*] A kind of staggers in sheep, etc., due to infestation of the brain with a larval form of the tapeworm *Tænia cœnurus.*

gid-dy (gid′i), *a.*; compar. *giddier*, superl. *giddiest.* [AS. *gidig*, mad; perhaps orig. 'possessed by a god,' and akin to

E. *god.*] Mad† or insane†; hence, furious or wild (prov. Eng.); also, having a confused, whirling sensation; affected with vertigo; dizzy; attended with or causing dizziness (as, a *giddy* climb; "*giddy* precipices," Irving's "Conquest of Granada," lxxxviii.); also, whirling, as motion or something moving; fig., unstable† (as, "An habitation *giddy* and unsure Hath he that buildeth on the vulgar heart": Shakspere's "2 Henry IV.," i. 3. 89); also, frivolously light, unsteady, or changeable, as the mind, fancy, persons, etc.; esp., readily swayed by wild impulses, exuberant spirits, etc.; flighty; volatile.—**gid′di-ly,** *adv.*—**gid′di-ness,** *n.*—**gid′dy,** *v. t.* or *i.*; *-died, -dying.* To make or become giddy.

gier=ea-gle† (jēr′ē″gl), *n.* [D. *gier*=G. *geier*, vulture: cf. *gerfalcon.*] A bird mentioned in the Authorized Version of the Bible (Lev. xi. 18, and Deut. xiv. 17): called *vulture* in the Revised Version.

gift (gift), *n.* [ME. *gift*, prob. from Scand.: cf. Icel. *gift*, *gipt*, gift, = AS. *gift*, payment for a wife, pl. marriage, related to Icel. *gefa*, AS. *gifan*, E. *give.*] The act of giving (as, to get a thing by *gift*; "I will not take her on *gift* of any man," Shakspere's "As You Like It," iii. 3. 69); also, the power or right of giving (as, certain offices are in his *gift*); also, something given; a present; sometimes, formerly, a bribe† (see 2 Chron. xix. 7); often, a quality, faculty, or special ability regarded as bestowed by God or nature; a natural endowment; a talent.—**gift,** *v. t.* To present with a gift or gifts; endow with natural gifts (chiefly as in *gifted*, *p. a.*); sometimes, to present or endow (*with*: as, to be *gifted* by nature with a sense of humor); also, to give (something) as a gift (chiefly Sc.).—**gift′ed,** *p. a.* Endowed with natural gifts; talented.—**gift′ed-ness,** *n.* —**gift′=horse,** *n.* A horse given as a present.—**to look a gift=horse in the mouth,** to criticize, or find fault with, a present or favor received: with allusion to the custom of ascertaining the age of horses by examining their teeth. —**gift′ie,** *n.* A Scotch diminutive form of *gift* (special faculty): as, "O wad some Pow'r the *giftie* gie us To see oursels as others see us!" (Burns's "To a Louse").—**gift′less,** *a.* Having no gift to offer; also, having received no gift; also, destitute of natural gifts or endowments.

gig[1] (gig), *n.* [Origin obscure; perhaps imit.] Something that whirls, as a top†; a machine for teazeling cloth; also, a giddy or flighty girl†; an odd character or figure (slang, Eng.); also, a joke or trick, or sport or fun (now prov. Eng. and Sc.); also, a light, two-wheeled, one-horse carriage; also, a ship's boat for either rowing or sailing; a long rowboat used chiefly for racing; also, a special combination of three numbers in the game of policy.—**gig**[1], *v.*; *gigged, gigging.* **I.** *intr.* To ride in a gig. **II.** *tr.* To teazel (cloth) with a gig.

gig[2] (gig), *n.* [From *fizgig.*] A fish-spear; also, a device, commonly four barbless hooks secured back to back, for dragging through a school of fish in order to hook them through the body.—**gig**[2], *v. t.* or *i.*; *gigged, gigging.* To spear or take (fish) with a gig.

gi-gan-te-an (jī-gan-tē′ạn), *a.* [L. *giganteus.*] Gigantic.

gi-gan-tesque (jī-gan-tesk′), *a.* [F. *gigantesque*, < It. *gigantesco*, < *gigante*, < L. *gigas*: see *giant.*] Of a gigantic kind; befitting a giant.

gi-gan-tic (jī-gan′tik), *a.* [L. *gigas* (*gigant-*): see *giant.*] Of, like, or befitting a giant; hence, huge; enormous; immense.—**gi-gan′ti-cal-ly,** *adv.*—**gi-gan′ti-cide** (-sīd), *n.* [See *-cide.*] The killer, or the killing, of a giant.—**gi-gan′tic-ness,** *n.*—**gi-gan′tism** (-tizm), *n.* In *physiol.*, etc., gigantic development; giantism.—**gi-gan′tize** (-tīz), *v. t.*; *-tized, -tizing.* To cause to appear gigantic.

gi-gan-tom-a-chy (jī-gan-tom′ạ-ki), *n.*; pl. *-chies* (-kiz). [LL. *gigantomachia*, < Gr. γιγαντομαχία, < γίγας (γιγαντ-), giant, + μάχεσθαι, fight.] A war of giants, esp. the war of the giants of Greek mythology against the Olympian gods; also, a representation of this, as in sculpture.

gi-gan-to-sau-rus (jī-gan-tộ-sâ′rus), *n.* [NL., < Gr. γίγας (γιγαντ-), giant, + σαῦρος, lizard.] An extremely large dinosaurian reptile of the extinct genus *Gigantosaurus.*

gig-gle (gig′l), *v. i.*; *-gled, -gling.* [Imit.] To laugh in a light, silly or undignified way, as from levity, youthful spirits, or ill-controlled amusement; titter.—**gig′gle,** *n.* A giggling laugh; a titter.—**gig′gler,** *n.*—**gig′gle-some** (-sum), **gig-gly** (gig′li), *a.* Inclined to giggle.

gig=lamp (gig′lamp), *n.* A lamp attached to a gig; hence, a firefly (local); also, *pl.*, spectacles (slang).

gig-let, gig-lot (gig′let, -lot), *n.* [Appar. < *gig*[1].] A wanton woman†; also, a giddy girl.

gi-glio (jē′lyō), *n.* [It., < L. *lilium*, E. *lily.*] The heraldic lily of the arms of Florence, Italy, a form of the fleur-de-lis with two slender added members issuing one at each side of the central petal, between it and the side petals.

gig-o-lo (jig′ộ-lō), *n.*; pl. *-los* (-lōz). [F.] A male professional dancing-partner employed to dance with women.

gig-ot (jig′ọt), *n.* [F. *gigot*; origin unknown.] A leg of mutton, veal, or the like. [Now Sc. and prov. Eng.]

gigue (zhēg), *n.* [F., < E. *jig.*] In *music*, a jig, often forming the concluding movement in the suite.

Gi-la (hē′lạ̈) **mon′ster.** [From the *Gila* River, in Arizona.] A large, venomous lizard, *Heloderma suspectum*, of New Mexico, Arizona, etc., having the skin studded with tubercles like nail-heads in a yellow or orange and black coloration; sometimes, a closely allied lizard, the caltetepon, *H. horridum*, of Mexico.

Gila Monster (*Heloderma suspectum*).

gil-bert (gil′bėrt), *n.* [From W. *Gilbert* (1540–1603), English scientist.] In *elect.*, a unit of magnetomotive force equal to .7958 ampere-turn.

gild[1], **guild** (gild), *n.* [AS. *gild, gield*, or the related Icel. *gildi*, gild, also payment, tribute: see *geld*[1].] A society of persons organized to further common interests and purposes; esp., one of the associations, numerous in the middle ages, each composed of persons belonging to and regulating a particular trade or industry (as, a *gild* of merchants or of craftsmen; "In the 11th century *gilds* of wool weavers existed at Cologne and Mainz," Encyc. Brit., 11th ed., XXVI. 404); in modern use, often, a charitable or benevolent society, as in a church.—**gild socialism.** See under *socialism.*—**national gild.** See *gild socialism*, under *socialism.*

gild[2] (gild), *v. t.*; *gilded* or *gilt, gilding.* [AS. *gyldan*, < *gold*, E. *gold.*] To coat with gold, gold-leaf, or some gold-colored finishing substance; also, to color like gold (as, the sun *gilds* the clouds); fig., to give a bright, pleasing, or specious aspect to (as, "Love *gilds* the scene," Sheridan's "Rivals," Epilogue; to *gild* folly or vice); sometimes, to render attractive as wealth does (as, "Cursed be the gold that *gilds* the straiten'd forehead of the fool!" Tennyson's "Locksley Hall," 62); also, to make red, as with blood (obs. or archaic: see Shakspere's "Macbeth," ii. 2. 56).—**gild′ed,** *p. a.* Coated with or as with gold; also, colored like gold; fig., presented under a fair or specious aspect (as, *gilded* vice); also, wealthy (as, the *gilded* youth of the period). —**gild′er,** *n.*

gild-hall, guild-hall (gild′hâl), *n.* The hall where a gild assembles; often, a town hall.

gild-ing (gil′ding), *n.* The act of one who or that which gilds; also, the gold-leaf or other material with which anything is gilded, or the golden surface produced.

gilds-man, guilds-man (gildz′mạn), *n.*; pl. *-men.* A member of a gild; also, an advocate of gild socialism.

gi-let (zhē-lā), *n.* [F.] A waistcoat; a vest.

gil-guy (gil′gī), *n.* [From *gil-* (origin and meaning uncertain) + *guy*[1].] *Naut.*, a temporary or makeshift contrivance of rope, as about the rigging of a ship; in general (indefinitely and more or less contemptuously), a contrivance or 'contraption'; a gimcrack.

gill[1] (gil), *n.* [ME.: cf. Sw. *gäl*, Dan. *gjælle.*] A respiratory organ of a fish or other animal that breathes in or under water (usually in *pl.*); also, *pl.*, the wattles of a fowl; the flesh under the jaws in man; the radiating plates on the under side of the cap of a mushroom.—**gill**[1], *v. t.* To gut or clean (fish); also, to catch (fish) by the gills in a gill-net; also, to cut away the gills of (a mushroom).

gill[2] (gil), *n.* [Icel. *gil.*] A narrow valley, esp. one with a stream running through it; a ravine; a glen; also, a stream in a ravine; a mountain stream; a brook. [Sc. and north. Eng.]

gill[3] (jil), *n.* [OF. *gille, gelle,* vessel or measure for wine: cf. *gallon.*] A liquid measure equal to one fourth of a pint.

Gill[4], **Jill** (jil), *n.* [From *Gill,* for *Gillian* (= *Juliana*), woman's name.] A popular name for a girl or woman, often used, in connection with *Jack,* to denote a girl friend, a sweetheart, or a wife; [*l. c.*] a girl or woman; also, the ground-ivy.

gilled (gild), *a.* Having gills, as fishes.

gill=flirt (jil'flėrt), *n.* [See *Gill*[4].] A giddy girl or young woman. [Archaic.]

gil-lie (gil'i), *n.* [Gael. *gille, giolla,* lad, servant.] Orig., a male attendant on a Highland chieftain; now, commonly, a sportsman's attendant. [Sc.]

gill=net (gil'net), *n.* A curtain-like net, suspended vertically in the water, with meshes of such a size as to catch by the gills a fish that has thrust its head through.

gil'ly, *n.* See *gillie.*

gil-ly-flow-er (jil'i-flou''ėr), *n.* [Corruption of ME. *gilofre,* < OF. *gilofre, girofre* (F. *girofle*), clove, < L. *caryophyllon,* < Gr. καρυόφυλλον, clove-tree, < κάρυον, nut, + φύλλον, leaf.] The clove-pink (archaic or prov.); also, one of various other flowers, as the wallflower, *Cheiranthus cheiri,* or the common stock-gillyflower, *Matthiola incana.*

gil-py (gil'pi), *n.*; pl. *-pies* (-piz). [Origin obscure.] A frolicsome young fellow†; also, a lively young girl (see Burns's "Halloween," 129). [Sc.]

gil-rav-age (gil-rav'āj), *n.* [Origin obscure.] Boisterous merrymaking; riotous sport. [Sc.]—**gil-rav'age,** *v. i.*; *-aged, -aging.* To make merry in a riotous or disorderly way. [Sc.]—**gil-rav'ag-er,** *n.*

gil-son-ite (gil'sọn-īt), *n.* [From S. H. *Gilson,* of Salt Lake City, Utah.] Same as *uintahite.*

gilt (gilt). Preterit and past participle of *gild*[2].—**gilt,** *p. a.* Gilded; golden in color.—**gilt,** *n.* The gold or other material applied in gilding; gilding.—**gilt'=edged',** *a.* Having the edges gilded, as paper; fig., of the highest order or quality, as securities.—**gilt'head,** *n.* Any of various fishes with golden spots or streaks on the head, as several species of bonito.

gim-bal (jim'bạl), *n.* [Var. of *gimmal,* for *gemel.*] A gimmal† or gemel-ring†; *pl.,* a contrivance for keeping a suspended object, as a ship's compass, horizontal, being usually a pair of rings pivoted to swing, one within the other, on axes at right angles to each other.

gim-crack (jim'krak). [Origin uncertain.] **I.** *n.* A showy, useless trifle; a trivial knickknack; any trumpery article or object; a toy; a contrivance or 'contraption' (as, "He has great doubts of those new *gimcracks,* the steamboats": Irving's "Sketch-Book," Little Britain). **II.** *a.* Showy but unsubstantial or useless; trumpery.—**gim'crack''er-y** (-ėr-i), *n.* Gimcracks collectively; gimcrack articles or ornaments.

gim-let (gim'let), *n.* [OF. *guimbelet* (F. *gibelet*); from Teut., and akin to E. *wimble.*] A small tool for boring holes, consisting of a steel shaft with a pointed screw at one end and a transverse handle at the other.—**gim'let,** *v. t.*; *-leted* or *-letted, -leting* or *-letting.* To pierce with or as with a gimlet; also, to turn round like a gimlet.

gim-mal (jim'ạl), *n.* [= *gemel.*] A gemel-ring.

gimp[1] (gimp), *n.* [Origin uncertain.] A flat trimming made of silk, worsted, or other cord, sometimes stiffened with wire, used on garments, curtains, furniture, etc.

gimp[2] (gimp), *n.* [Origin unknown.] Energy; vim. [Colloq.]

gin[1], **'gin** (gin), *v.*; pret. *gan,* pp. *gun,* ppr. *ginning.* Shortened form of *begin.* [Archaic or poetic.]

gin[2] (jin), *n.* [= *engine.*] Ingenuity†; artifice†; also, a scheme† or device†; also, a mechanical contrivance (archaic); an engine of war†; an engine of torture†; an apparatus for hoisting; a machine for separating cotton from its seeds ('cotton-gin'); also, a trap or snare for game, etc. (often fig.). —**gin**[2], *v. t.*; *ginned, ginning.* To clear (cotton) of seeds with a gin; also, to catch (game, etc.) in a gin (also fig.: as, "Destiny has her nets round him . . . soon he will be *ginned!*" Carlyle's "Essays," Count Cagliostro, ii.).

gin[3] (jin), *n.* [Abbr. of *geneva.*] A distilled alcoholic liquor made in Holland from rye or other grain, and flavored with juniper-berries; a similar liquor made in imitation of it.

ging† (ging), *n.* [AS. *genge*; akin to *gang.*] A company; a gang. See Shakspere's "Merry Wives of Windsor," iv. 2. 123.

gin-ger[1] (jin'jėr), *n.* [OF. *gingibre* (F. *gingembre*), < L. *zingiber,* < Gr. ζιγγίβερις, ginger; of Eastern origin.] The pungent, spicy rhizome of any of the reed-like plants of the genus *Zinziber,* esp. of *Z. zingiber* (or *officinale*), variously used in cookery and medicine; any of these plants, native in the East Indies, but now cultivated in most tropical countries; hence, spiciness or piquancy (colloq.); spirit or animation (colloq.); also, a light sandy or tawny color.—**gin'ger**[1], *v. t.* To treat or flavor with ginger; hence (colloq.), to impart spiciness or piquancy to; make spirited or lively.

Ginger-plant (*Zinziber zingiber*).—*a,* flower on larger scale.

gin-ger[2] (jin'jėr), *a.* [Back-formation from *gingerly.*] Gingerly. [Now chiefly prov.]

gin-ger=ale (jin'jėr-āl'), *n.* A non-alcoholic effervescing drink similar to ginger-beer.

gin-ger=beer (jin'jėr-bēr'), *n.* A non-alcoholic effervescing drink containing water, sugar or molasses, yeast, etc., flavored with ginger.

gin-ger-bread (jin'jėr-bred). **I.** *n.* A kind of cake flavored with ginger: often made in fanciful shapes, and sometimes gilded (as, "As if the poet, purposing to wed, Should carve himself a wife in *gingerbread*": Cowper's "Table Talk," 555). **II.** *a.* Showy; gaudy; tawdry.—**gin'ger-bread=tree,** *n.* The doom-palm; also, a tree, *Parinarium macrophyllum,* of western Africa, with a large, edible farinaceous fruit ('gingerbread-plum').

gin-ger-ly (jin'jėr-li). [Cf. OF. *gensor, gentior,* pretty, orig. compar. of *gent,* E. *gent*[1].] **I.** *adv.* Daintily† or mincingly† (as, to dance *gingerly*); hence, with extreme care or caution in stepping, handling, proceeding, etc.; cautiously; warily. **II.** *a.* Dainty† or mincing†; also, cautious or wary.—**gin'ger-li-ness,** *n.*

gin-ger-snap (jin'jėr-snap), *n.* A small, thin, brittle cake spiced with ginger.

gin-ger-y (jin'jėr-i), *a.* Ginger-like; hot; pungent; spicy; also, of the color ginger.

ging-ham (ging'ạm), *n.* [Malay *ginggang,* lit. 'striped.'] A cotton fabric woven of dyed yarns, esp. in striped, checked, or plaid patterns.

gin-gi-li (jin'ji-li), *n.* [Hind. *jinjalī,* < Ar. *juljulān.*] The sesame (plant), or its oil.

gin-gi-val (jin-jī'vạl), *a.* [L. *gingiva,* gum.] Of or pertaining to the gums.—**gin-gi-vi'tis** (-ji-vī'tis), *n.* [NL.] In *pathol.,* inflammation of the gums.

ging-ko (ging'kō or jing'-), *n.* See *ginkgo.*

gin-gly-mus (jing'gli-mus or ging'-), *n.*; pl. *-mi* (-mī). [NL., < Gr. γίγγλυμος.] In *anat.,* a hinge-like joint, as that of the elbow.—**gin'gly-moid,** *a.*

gink (gingk), *n.* [Origin obscure.] A person; a fellow. [Slang.]

gink-go (gingk'gō or jingk'-), *n.* [Jap. *gingko.*] A large, ornamental gymnospermous tree, *Ginkgo biloba,* native in Japan and China, yielding an edible fruit or nut.

gin=mill (jin'mil), *n.* A liquor-saloon. [Slang, U. S.]

gin-ner (jin'ėr), *n.* One who gins cotton.—**gin'ner-y,** *n.*; pl. *-ies* (-iz). A mill for ginning cotton.—**gin'ning,** *n.* The act of separating the fiber of cotton from the seeds; *pl.,* the fiber, or the amount of fiber, so separated.

gin-ny (gin'i), *n.*; pl. *ginnies* (-iz). [See *guinea.*] An Italian, or any foreigner of similar appearance; a guinea. [Slang, U. S.]

gin-seng (jin'seng), *n.* [From Chinese.] Either of two araliaceous plants, *Panax ginseng* of China, Korea, etc., and *P. quinquefolium* of North America, yielding an aromatic root which is extensively used in medicine by the Chinese; also, the root itself, or a preparation made from it.

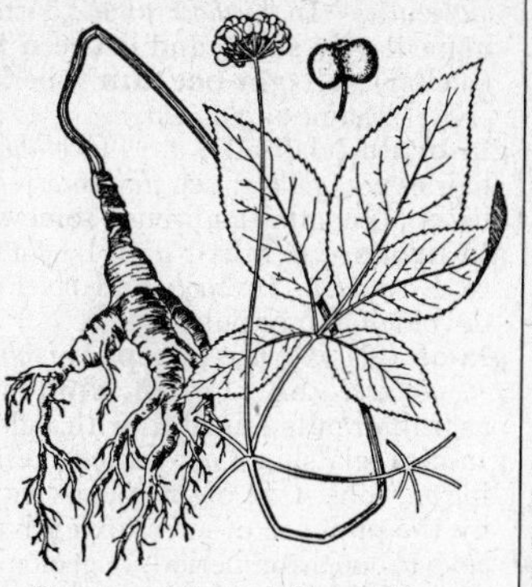

Branch and Root of Ginseng (*Panax ginseng*).

gip (jip), *n.* and *v.* See *gyp.*

gip-on (jip'on), *n.* A jupon or tunic: as, "With nought to fence his dauntless breast But the close *gipon's* under-vest" (Scott's "Bridal of Triermain," iii. 18). [Archaic.]

Gip-sy, Gyp-sy (jip'si), *n.*; pl. *-sies* (-siz). [Corruption of *Egyptian.*] [Also *l. c.*] One of a nomadic, tawny-skinned, black-haired race of Hindu origin, now found in many parts of the world; [*cap.*] the language of these people; Romany; hence [*l. c.*], any person of similar vagrant life; a dark-complexioned person; an artful girl.—**gipsy ring,** a finger-ring having a stone or stones set low within a comparatively broad, flat band.—**gip'sy, gyp'sy,** *v. i.*; *-sied, -sying.* To live or rove like a Gipsy; often, to picnic (as, "There is to be a village picnic—a *gypsying* they call it—at East Egdon": Hardy's "Return of the Native," iv. 3).—**gip'sy-dom** (-dọm), *n.* The life or habits of Gipsies; also, Gipsies collectively.—**gip'sy-fy** (-fī), *v. t.*; *-fied, -fying.* To make like a Gipsy in appearance or character.—**gip'sy-hood** (-hụd), *n.* The state of a Gipsy; also, Gipsies collectively.—**gip'sy-ish,** *a.* Gipsy-like.—**gip'sy-ism,** *n.* The life or habits of Gipsies.—**gip'sy=moth,** *n.* A moth *Porthetria* (or *Ocneria*) *dispar*, whose larva is very destructive to trees.—**gip'sy-ry** (-ri), *n.*; pl. *-ries* (-riz). A colony of Gipsies; a place of encampment of Gipsies.

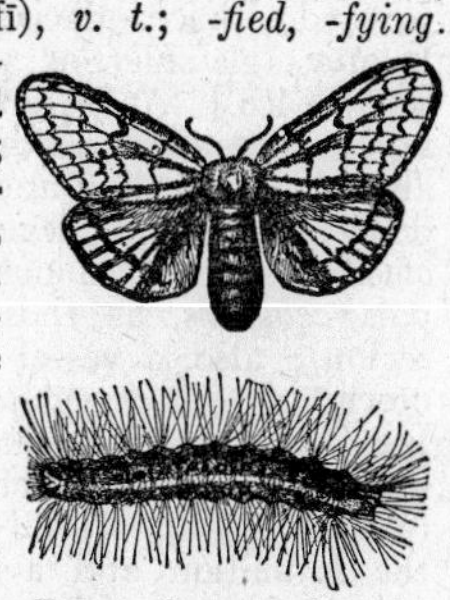

Female Gipsy-moth, with Larva. (Reduced.)

gi-raffe (ji-raf'), *n.* [F. *giraffe* (now *girafe*), < Ar. *zarāfah.*] A tall, long-necked, spotted ruminant quadruped, *Giraffa camelopardalis*, of Africa, the tallest of existing quadrupeds; the camelopard; [*cap.*] in *astron.*, the northern constellation Camelopardalis.—**gi-raf'fine** (-raf'in), *a.*

Giraffe.

gir-an-dole (jir'ạn-dōl), *n.* [F. *girandole*, < It. *girandola*, < *girare*, turn, < L. *gyrare*: see *gyrate.*] A kind of rotating and radiating firework; also, a jet of water, or series of jets, of similar character; also, a branched support for candles or other lights.

gir-a-sol, gir-a-sole (jir'ạ-sol, -sōl), *n.* [F. *girasol*, < It. *girasole*, < *girare*, turn, + *sole*, sun.] A variety of opal which reflects a reddish glow in a bright light.

gird[1] (gėrd), *v. t.*; *girt* or *girded, girding.* [AS. *gyrdan* = D. *gorden* = G. *gürten* = Icel. *gyrdha*, gird; prob. akin to E. *yard*[1].] To bind or encircle (a person, the waist, etc.) with a belt or girdle; also, to equip with a sword or weapon at the belt; also, to attach (a weapon) at one's belt; put on (clothing, armor, etc.: as, "Warn Lanark's knights to *gird* their mail," Scott's "Lord of the Isles," v. 34); in fig. use, to equip (one's self) for action (as, to *gird* one's self for a task); also, to invest or indue (as, "The Son On his great expedition now appear'd, *Girt* with omnipotence": Milton's "Paradise Lost," vii. 194); also, in general, to surround; confine; hem in.

gird[2] (gėrd), *v.* [ME. *girden*; origin uncertain.] **I.** *tr.* To strike† or smite†; also, to gibe or jeer at; taunt. **II.** *intr.* To rush or spring (now prov.); also, to gibe; jeer.—**gird**[2], *n.* A stroke†; also, a gibe.

gird-er[1] (gėr'dėr), *n.* One who or that which girds, binds, etc.; specif., one of the principal horizontal timbers which support the joists in certain floors; in structural work, any main horizontal supporting member or beam, as of wood or iron.

gird-er[2] (gėr'dėr), *n.* One who girds or gibes.

gir-dle[1] (gėr'dl), *n.* A griddle. [Sc. and prov. Eng.]

gir-dle[2] (gėr'dl), *n.* [AS. *gyrdel*, < *gyrdan*, E. *gird*[1].] A belt, cord, sash, or the like, worn about the waist; hence, any encircling band; a zone or ring of something; compass or circuit (as, "Suppose within the *girdle* of these walls Are now confined two mighty monarchies": Shakspere's "Henry V.," Prologue, 19); specif., the line about a brilliant or other cut stone at the junction of the upper and lower faces; also, a ring made about a tree-trunk, etc., by cutting the bark.—**gir'dle**[2], *v. t.*; *-dled, -dling.* To encircle with or as with a girdle; encompass; specif., to cut away the bark in a ring about (a tree, branch, etc.), thus causing decay.—**gir'dler,** *n.* A maker of girdles or belts; also, one who girdles; specif., a beetle, as *Oncideres cingulatus*, which girdles twigs on which it has deposited eggs.

girl (gėrl), *n.* [ME. *gurle, girle*, child; origin obscure.] A child or young person of either sex†; now, a child or young person of the female sex; often, a young unmarried woman; sometimes, a familiar term for any woman; also, a female servant (colloq.); also, a sweetheart (colloq.).—**Girl Guide,** a member of an organization of girls (Girl Guides), in England and elsewhere, a sister organization of the Boy Scouts. See *Boy Scout*, under *boy.*—**Girl Scout,** a member of an organization of girls (Girl Scouts), founded in the U. S. in 1912, and patterned after the Girl Guides (see above), and aiming to develop in its members good health, good citizenship, knowledge of home-making, and high womanly character.—**girl'hood** (-hụd), *n.* The state or time of being a girl; also, girls collectively.—**girl'ish,** *a.* Of, like, or befitting a girl.—**girl'ish-ly,** *adv.*—**girl'ish-ness,** *n.*

girn (gėrn), *v. i.* [Var. of *grin*[1].] To show the teeth, as in pain or rage; snarl; whine. [Now only Sc. and north. Eng.]

Gi-ron-dist (ji-ron'dist), *n.* [F. *Girondiste.*] A member of a French political party of moderate republicans (1791–1793), whose leaders were deputies from the department of the Gironde.

girt[1] (gėrt). Preterit and past participle of *gird*[1].

girt[2] (gėrt), *v. t.* Same as *gird*[1].

girt[3] (gėrt), *n.* and *v.* Same as *girth*[1].

girth[1] (gėrth), *n.* [ME. *girth, gerth*, from Scand.: cf. Icel. *gjördh*, girdle, girth; akin to E. *gird*[1].] A band or girdle; specif., a band passed under the belly of a horse, etc., to secure a saddle or pack on its back; also, the measure around anything; circumference; compass.—**girth**[1], *v.* **I.** *tr.* To girdle; encircle; also, to equip, bind, or fasten with a girth. **II.** *intr.* To measure a specified amount in girth.

girth[2] (gėrth), *n.* Same as *grith.* [Obs. or archaic.]

gi-sarme, gui-sarme (gi-zärm'), *n.* [OF.; origin uncertain.] A long-handled medieval military weapon in various forms, esp. one having a long blade prolonged into a straight, sharp point, with a hook on one side of the blade and a projecting point on the other.

gist (jist), *n.* [OF. *gist* (F. *gît*), 3d pers. sing. pres. ind. of *gesir* (F. *gésir*), lie, rest, < L. *jacere*, lie.] The ground on which a legal action rests; hence, the substance or pith of a matter (as, to give one the *gist* of an argument in a few words); the essential part.

git (git), *v.* Prov. or vulgar form of *get.*

gi-ta-na (ji-tä'nạ, Sp. ʜē-tä'nä), *n.*; pl. *-nas* (-nạz, Sp. -näs). [Sp., orig. 'Egyptian': cf. *Gipsy.*] In Spanish use, a

Gipsy woman.—**gi-ta-no** (ji-tä'nō, Sp. hē-tä'nō), *n.*; pl. *-nos* (-nōz, Sp. -nōs). [Sp.] In Spanish use, a Gipsy man: as, "The *Gitano*, or gipsy of Spain, is not the mere vagrant we see on our commons and road-sides" (Bulwer-Lytton's "Caxtons," xvi. 3).

git-ter (git'ėr), *n.* [G., grating.] A diffraction grating. See *grating*[1].

git-tern (git'ėrn), *n.* [OF. *guiterne*: cf. *guitar*.] An old musical instrument of the guitar kind.

gius-to (jös'tō), *a.* [It., < L. *justus*, just.] In *music*, just; regular; suitable; strict.

give (giv), *v. t.*; pret. *gave*, pp. *given*, ppr. *giving*. [AS. *gifan*, *giefan*, = D. *geven* = G. *geben* = Icel. *gefa* = Goth. *giban*, give: cf. *gift*.] To deliver or hand over to another gratuitously (as, to *give* one a present); deliver to another in exchange for something (as, I *gave* it to him for $5; I *gave* a good price for it); deliver to another without reference to ownership (as, please *give* me a drink); grant, bestow, or confer, as power, permission, etc.; commit (as, to *give* a person into custody); deliver as a pledge (as, to *give* one's word of honor); present or offer (as, to *give* a toast); furnish or provide (as, to *give* aid to the enemy); set forth or show (as, the newspaper *gave* a long account; the house *gave* no sign of life); deal or administer (as, to *give* one a blow); impart or communicate (as, to *give* advice; to *give* a twist to a rope); assign, allot, or award (as, to *give* a contract to a person); designate or appoint (a day or time); assign as a basis of calculation, reasoning, etc. (as, *given* these premises, only one conclusion is possible); attribute or ascribe (as, to *give* credit to another); account† or consider† (as, "Men's reports *Give* him much wrong'd": Shakspere's "Antony and Cleopatra," i. 4. 40); deliver or produce (a lecture, play, etc.); afford or yield (as, to *give* satisfaction); make (a movement: as, to *give* a start); put forth, emit, or utter (as, to *give* a cry); issue or deliver (a command, decision, etc.); execute (only in *pp.*, in and of documents: as, *given* under my hand Feb. 1, 1787); cause or occasion (as, to *give* trouble); do or perform (as, to *give* battle or chase); relinquish or surrender (as, to *give* ground, to *give* place, or to *give* way: see below); sacrifice (as, to *give* one's life for one's country); dedicate or devote (as, to *give* one's mind to a subject).—**to give a good account of one's self,** to bear one's self creditably.—**to give away,** to give as a present, etc.; make over to another; hand over (the bride) to the bridegroom at a wedding; also (slang), to cause or permit (a secret, etc.) to be known; let out; betray (a person).—**to give ground,** to retire before a superior force; hence, to yield place; relax efforts.—**to give place,** to give ground; hence, to yield precedence; resign or relinquish one's or its place (to another).—**to give rise to,** to give origin to; occasion; result in.—**to give up,** to surrender; hand over or part with; forsake or abandon, as a person; desist from or relinquish, as labors or a task; abandon as hopeless or useless, as a contest, etc.; abandon hope of seeing (a person), solving (a problem), performing (a feat), curing (a sick person), etc.; also, to devote entirely (*to*); addict (*to*).—**to give way,** to retreat before an advancing force; make way or give place, as to another; yield, as under pressure; break down, or fail; yield to emotional strain, as a person; abandon one's self, as to despair, etc.—**give,** *v. i.* To make a gift or gifts; also, to yield, as to pressure, strain, etc.; draw back; relax; break down, or fail; also, to afford a passage or view (a French use: as, a window that *gives* upon a court).—**to give in,** to yield; submit.—**to give out,** to break down, or fail; become exhausted, as a supply.—**to give up,** to leave off, or stop; abandon effort, hope, etc.; succumb.—**give,** *n.* The act of giving; esp., the act or fact of yielding to pressure, strain, etc.; elasticity.—**giv'en,** *p. a.* Bestowed as a gift; conferred (as, a *given* name, a Christian name: see under *Christian*, *a.*); also, stated, fixed, or specified (as, at a *given* time); assigned as a basis of calculation, reasoning, etc.; also, addicted or disposed (often with *to*).—**giv'er,** *n.*

giz-zard (giz'ạrd), *n.* [OF. *giser* (F. *gésier*), < L. *gigeria*, pl., entrails of poultry.] The grinding or muscular stomach of birds, the organ in which the food is triturated after leaving the preceding glandular stomach. Cf. *stomach.*

gla-bel-la (glạ-bel'ạ), *n.*; pl. *glabellæ* (-ē). [NL., prop. fem. of L. *glabellus*, smooth, hairless, dim. of *glaber*: see *glabrous*.] In *human anat.*, a small space on the forehead immediately above and between the eyebrows.—**gla-bel'lar** (-bel'ạr), *a.*—**gla-bel'lum** (-bel'um), *n.*; pl. *glabella* (-ạ). [NL.] Same as *glabella.*

gla-brate (glā'brāt), *a.* [L. *glabratus*, pp. of *glabrare*, make hairless, < *glaber*: see *glabrous*.] In *zoöl.*, smooth; glabrous; in *bot.*, becoming glabrous; somewhat glabrous.

gla-brous (glā'brus), *a.* [L. *glaber*, smooth, hairless; akin to E. *glad*.] In *zoöl.* and *bot.*, smooth; having a surface devoid of hair or pubescence.

gla-cé (glȧ-sā), *a.* [F., pp. of *glacer*, < L. *glaciare*, freeze, < *glacies*, ice.] Frozen; frosted or iced, as cake; candied, as fruit or nuts; finished with a gloss, as kid or silk.

gla-cial (glā'shiạl), *a.* [L. *glacialis*, < *glacies*, ice.] Abounding in, consisting of, or cold as ice; icy; specif., characterized by the presence of ice in extensive masses or glaciers (as, the *glacial* epoch or period, a geological epoch, the Pleistocene, during which much of the northern hemisphere was covered by great ice-sheets); due to or associated with the action of ice or glaciers; of or pertaining to glaciers or the glacial epoch; in *chem.*, having or tending to assume an ice-like form, as certain acids.—**gla'cial-ist,** *n.* A specialist in glacial geology; also, one who explains geological phenomena by the action of ice.—**gla'cial-ly,** *adv.*

gla-ci-a-ri-um (glā-shi-ā'ri-um), *n.*; pl. *-ria* (-ri-ạ). [NL., < L. *glacies*, ice.] A skating-rink having a floor of artificial ice.

gla-ci-ate (glā'shi-āt), *v. t.*; *-ated*, *-ating*. [L. *glaciatus*, pp. of *glaciare*, freeze, < *glacies*, ice.] To freeze†; also, to cover with ice or glaciers; affect by glacial action.—**gla-ci-a'tion** (-ā'shọn), *n.* Freezing†; also, a covering or being covered with ice; glacial action or effect.

gla-cier (glā'shiėr or glas'i-ėr), *n.* [F., < *glace*, < L. *glacies*, ice.] An extended mass of ice formed from snow falling and accumulating on high mountains or elsewhere above the snow-line, and moving (in most cases, very slowly) downward to lower levels (as, the river-like alpine or valley *glaciers* of mountainous regions; the broad continental or polar *glaciers*, as those of Greenland and the antarctic region); also, a vessel for holding ice to cool wine.—**gla'-ciered,** *a.* Having glaciers.

glacio-. Form of L. *glacies*, ice, in combination: sometimes used with special reference to glaciers.—**gla-ci-ol-o-gy** (glā-shi-ol'ọ-ji), *n.* [+ *-logy*.] The science that treats of the formation and action of glaciers.—**gla''ci-o-na'tant** (-ọ-nā'tạnt), *a.* [See *natant*.] Pertaining to or produced by floating ice.

gla-cis (glā'sis, F. glȧ-sē), *n.* [F., orig. 'icy or slippery place,' < *glacer*, freeze, make icy: see *glacé*.] A gentle slope; in *fort.*, a bank of earth in front of a counterscarp or covered way, having an easy slope toward the field or open country.

glad (glad), *a.*; compar. *gladder*, superl. *gladdest*. [AS. *glæd* = Icel. *gladhr*, bright, glad, = D. *glad* and G. *glatt*, smooth; akin to L. *glaber*, smooth, hairless (see *glabrous*).] Bright, as in luster or color†; also, cheerful, joyous, or merry (as, "a troop of damsels *glad*": Tennyson's "Lady of Shalott," ii.); joyful or happy, as for a special reason (as, "A wise son maketh a *glad* father": Prov. x. 1); delighted or pleased (with *of*, *at*, etc., or an infinitive or clause: as, *glad* of one's success; *glad* at the news; *glad* to go; *glad* that one has come); characterized by or showing cheerfulness, joy, or pleasure, as feelings, looks, smiles, utterances, etc.; attended with or causing joy or pleasure (as, a *glad* occasion; *glad* tidings); also, of natural scenes, seasons, circumstances, etc., delightful, pleasant, or genial (as, *glad* climes; the *glad* month of May; the *glad* sunshine).—**glad,** *v.*; *gladded*, *gladding*. **I.** *tr.* To make glad: as, "The hour's gone by, When Albion's lessening shores could grieve or *glad* mine eye" (Byron's "Childe Harold," iii. 1). [Archaic.] **II.**† *intr.* To be glad.

glad-den (glad'n), *v.* **I.** *tr.* To make glad; cheer; delight; brighten. **II.** *intr.* To be glad; rejoice.—**glad'den-er,** *n.*

glade (glād), *n.* [Perhaps related to *glad*, as meaning a bright (open) space.] An open space or passage, natural or artificial, in a wood or forest (as, "She guided them through . . . the wood to a little open *glade* . . . surrounded by trees and bushes": Scott's "Guy Mannering," liii.); also, an opening, or a place left unfrozen, in the ice of a river or lake (local, U. S.); also, a stretch of smooth ice (local, U. S.); also, an everglade (local, U. S.).

glad-ful (glad′fu̇l), *a.* Full of gladness; joyful; gladsome. [Archaic.]

glad-i-ate (glad′i-āt or glā′di-), *a.* [NL. *gladiatus*, < L. *gladius*, sword.] In *bot.*, sword-shaped.

glad-i-a-tor (glad′i-ā-to̦r), *n.* [L., < *gladius*, sword.] Among the ancient Romans, a person (often a slave or a captive) who fought in public, with a sword or other weapon, against other gladiators or against wild beasts, for the entertainment of the people; also, in general, a professional swordsman or fencer†; fig., a skilled contender in any field or cause.—**glad″i-a-to′ri-al** (-a̦-tō′ri-a̦l), *a.*—**glad′i-a-tor-ship,** *n.*

gla-di-o-lus (gla̦-dī′o̦-lus, commonly glad-i-ō′lus), *n.*; pl. *-luses* or *-li* (-lī). [L., dim. of *gladius*, sword.] Any plant of the iridaceous genus *Gladiolus*, native esp. in South Africa, with erect, gladiate leaves and spikes of handsome, variously colored flowers: familiar in gardens.

glad-ly (glad′li), *adv.* In a glad manner.—**glad′ness,** *n.*

glad-some (glad′sum), *a.* Glad; cheerful or joyous; joyful or happy; delightful or pleasant. [Now poetic or literary.]—**glad′some-ly,** *adv.*—**glad′some-ness,** *n.*

Glad-stone (glad′sto̦n), *n.* [From W. E. *Gladstone* (1809–98), English statesman.] A kind of four-wheeled pleasure-carriage with a calash-top, two inside seats, and seats for driver and footman; also, a kind of light traveling-bag opening into compartments (short for *Gladstone bag*).

Glag-o-lit-ic (glag-o̦-lit′ik), *a.* [Slav. *glagol*, word.] Denoting an ancient Slavic alphabet still used in service-books in some Roman Catholic dioceses in Dalmatia, etc.

glair (glãr), *n.* [OF. F. *glaire*, < L. *clarus*, clear.] The (uncooked) white of an egg; a size or glaze made from it; also, any similar viscous substance.—**glair,** *v. t.* To smear with glair.—**glair′e-ous** (-ē̦-us), *a.* Glairy.—**glair′y,** *a.* Of the nature of glair; viscous; also, covered with glair.—**glair′i-ness,** *n.*

glaive (glāv), *n.* [OF. *glaive*, lance, sword (F. sword): cf. L. *gladius*, sword.] A lance†; also, a kind of halberd†; also, a sword, esp. a broadsword (archaic).—**glaived,** *a.* Armed with a glaive.

glam-or-ous (glam′o̦r-us), *a.* Full of glamour, magic influence, or alluring charm: as, "That thought shone out . . . like a *glamorous* flower" (Galsworthy's "Patrician," ii. 11).—**glam′or-ous-ly,** *adv.*

glam-our (glam′o̦r), *n.* [Orig. Sc., corruption of *grammar*: cf. *gramary*.] Magic or enchantment (as, "Like that maiden in the tale, Whom Gwydion made by *glamour* out of flowers": Tennyson's "Marriage of Geraint," 743); magic influence; spell; witchery; hence, alluring and often illusory charm.—**glam′our,** *v. t.* To affect with glamour; bewitch; charm.—**glam′our-ous,** etc. See *glamorous*, etc.

glance[1] (glȧns), *v.*; *glanced, glancing.* [ME. *glaunche, glench*: cf. the earlier *glent*.] **I.** *intr.* To glide off in an oblique direction from an object struck, as a weapon, missile, etc.; dart off or aside; also, to allude obliquely or in passing, often by way of censure or satire; also, to look quickly or briefly (as, to *glance* at or over something); also, to gleam or flash. **II.** *tr.* To direct obliquely, as something aimed or cast; also, to direct (the eye, etc.) in a glance or brief look; convey by a glance of the eye; also, to cast or reflect, as a gleam; also, to glance at or allude to in speaking† (see Shakspere's "Comedy of Errors," v. i. 66); also, to cast a glance or brief look at; catch a glimpse of.—**glance**[1], *n.* A glancing off, as of a missile after striking; a stroke in cricket in which the ball is allowed to glance off from the bat; also, an allusion or reference, as in passing; also, a quick or brief look; also, a gleam or flash, as of light (as, "swift as the lightning *glance*": Milton's "Samson Agonistes," 1284).

glance[2] (glȧns), *n.* [G. *glanz*, lit. 'brightness,' 'luster.'] In *mining* and *mineral.*, any of various ores having a luster which indicates their metallic nature.—**glance′=coal,** *n.* [G. *glanzkohle*.] Any hard, lustrous coal, esp. anthracite.

gland[1] (gland), *n.* [F. *glande*, OF. *glandre*, < L. *glandula*, gland, dim. of *glans* (*gland-*), acorn.] In *anat.*, an organ by which certain constituents are separated from the blood for use in the body or for ejection from it, or by which certain changes are produced in the blood or lymph; also, any of various organs or structures likened to true glands; in *bot.*, a secreting organ or structure, esp. one on or near a surface; also, any similar prominence or appendage which does not secrete.

gland[2] (gland), *n.* [Origin uncertain.] In *mach.*, the cover or adjustable member of a stuffing-box, by which the packing is compressed; also, any of various devices for clamping parts together.

glan-der (glan′dėr), *n.* [OF. *glandre*, glandular swelling, gland: see *gland*[1].] A glandular swelling†; *pl.* (construed as *sing.*), in *pathol.*, a contagious disease of horses, mules, etc., communicable to man, due to a micro-organism (*Bacillus mallei*), and characterized by swellings beneath the jaw and a profuse mucous discharge from the nostrils.—**glan′dered,** *a.* Affected with glanders.—**glan′der-ous,** *a.* Pertaining to or affected with glanders.

glan-dif-er-ous (glan-dif′e̦-rus), *a.* [L. *glandifer*, < *glans* (*gland-*), acorn, + *ferre*, bear.] Acorn-bearing; producing mast or nuts.

glan-di-form (glan′di-fôrm), *a.* [L. *glans* (*gland-*), acorn: see *-form*.] Acorn-shaped; also, gland-like.

glan-du-lar (glan′d̦ū-lạ̈r), *a.* Of, pertaining to, or resembling a glandule or gland; consisting of, containing, or bearing glands.—**glan′du-lar-ly,** *adv.*

glan-dule (glan′d̦ūl), *n.* [L. *glandula*: see *gland*[1].] A gland; a small gland.—**glan-du-lif′er-ous** (-d̦ū-lif′e̦-rus), *a.* [See *-ferous*.] Bearing glandules.—**glan′du-lous, glan′du-lose** (-lōs), *a.* [L. *glandulosus*.] Containing glands; gland-like; glandular.

glans (glanz), *n.*; pl. *glandes* (glan′dēz). [L., lit. 'acorn.'] In *anat.*, the head of the penis (more fully *glans penis*) or of the clitoris (more fully *glans clitoridis*).

glare[1] (glãr), *v.*; *glared, glaring.* [ME. *glaren* = MLG. *glaren*; prob. akin to E. *glass*.] **I.** *intr.* To shine with a strong, dazzling light; hence, to be intensely bright in color; be too brilliantly ornamented; fig., to be obtrusively conspicuous (as, "a writer . . . whose ungenerous prejudice against the house of Stuart *glares* in misrepresentation": Boswell's "Johnson," 1778); also, to look with a fierce or piercing stare (as, "Each upon his rival *glared*": Scott's "Lady of the Lake," ii. 34). **II.** *tr.* To send forth or express with a glare.—**glare**[1], *n.* A strong, dazzling light; dazzling brilliance of light; shine; hence, dazzling or showy appearance; showiness; also, a fierce or piercing look.

glare[2] (glãr). [Origin uncertain: cf. mod. Icel. *glerungr*, glassy sheet of ice, *gler*, glass.] **I.** *n.* A bright, smooth surface, as of ice. [U. S.] **II.** *a.* Bright and smooth, as ice; glassy. [U. S.]

glar-ing (glãr′ing), *p. a.* That glares; dazzling; excessively bright, as color; obtrusively conspicuous, as defects or errors; staring fiercely or piercingly, as the eyes.—**glar′ing-ly,** *adv.*—**glar′ing-ness,** *n.*

glar-y[1] (glãr′i), *a.* Of a dazzling brilliance or luster; glaring.

glar-y[2] (glãr′i), *a.* Smooth and slippery, as ice. [U. S.]

glass (glȧs), *n.* [AS. *glæs* = D. and G. *glas*, glass: cf. *glare*[1].] A hard, brittle, more or less transparent, artificially prepared substance, usually consisting of a silicate or a mixture of silicates (the ordinary variety used for windows, etc., being a silicate of calcium and sodium: cf. *crown-glass* and *flint-glass*); also, any artificial or natural substance having similar properties or composition, as fused borax, obsidian ('volcanic glass'), etc.; also, things made of glass, collectively; glassware; also, something made of glass; a glass vessel, esp. one to drink from, or the contents of such a vessel; an hour-glass, or the like, or the length of time measured by it; a pane or plate of glass; a looking-glass; a crystal for a watch; a lens; an optical instrument, as a telescope, etc.; *pl.*, eye-glasses; *sing.*, a barometer; a thermometer.—**liquid glass, soluble glass.** See *water-glass*.—**stained glass.** See under *stained*.—**glass,** *a.* Made of glass; also, furnished or fitted with panes of glass; glazed.—**glass,** *v. t.* To fit with panes of glass; also, to cover or protect with glass; put (fruit, vegetables, or other food commodities) into glass jars, especially with vacuum sealing; put (drugs, etc.) into glass containers; also, to make glassy; also, to reflect in or as in a glass mirror.

glass=blow-er (glȧs′blō″ėr), *n.* One who fashions glass by glass-blowing.—**glass′=blow″ing,** *n.* The art or process of inflating, and thus shaping, a mass of glass by taking it up while hot and soft on the end of a hollow tube and then blowing through the tube; loosely, the making of ornaments, etc., by the twisting, drawing out, uniting, etc., of pieces of hot, soft glass.

glass=eye (glȧs′ī), *n.* A thrush, *Turdus jamaicensis*, of Jamaica; also, the wall-eyed pike-perch, *Stizostedion vitreum*.

glass-ful (glȧs′fu̇l), *n.*; pl. *-fuls*. As much as a glass holds.

glass=house (glȧs′hous), *n.* An establishment where glass is made; also, a building made chiefly of glass, esp. a green-house; a glass-roofed room, as for use in photography.

glass-i-ly (glȧs′i-li), *adv.* In a glassy manner.—**glass′i-ness,** *n.*

glass-ine (glȧs-ēn′), *n.* A thin, transparent paper used for book-wrappers, transparent panels in envelopes, etc.

glass=pa-per (glȧs′pā″pėr), *n.* Paper covered with finely powdered glass, used for polishing, etc.

glass=snake (glȧs′snāk), *n.* A limbless, snake-like lizard, *Ophiosaurus ventralis*, of the southern U. S., having an extremely fragile tail; also, any of certain similar lizards of Europe and Asia.

Glass-snake (*Ophiosaurus ventralis*).

glass-ware (glȧs′wãr), *n.* Articles made of glass.

glass-work (glȧs′wėrk), *n.* The manufacture of glass and glassware; also, the fitting of glass; glazing; also, articles of glass collectively; glassware; ornamentation made of glass.—**glass′=works,** *n. pl.* or *sing.* An establishment where glass is made.

glass-wort (glȧs′wėrt), *n.* Any of the herbs with succulent leafless stems constituting the chenopodiaceous genus *Salicornia*, growing in salt-water marshes, alkaline regions, etc., and formerly much used (when burned to ashes) as a source of soda for glass-making; also, the saltwort, *Salsola kali* ('prickly glasswort').

glass-y (glȧs′i), *a.*; compar. *glassier*, superl. *glassiest*. Of the nature of glass; vitreous; also, resembling glass, as in transparency, smoothness, etc.; often, having a fixed, unintelligent stare, as the eye or glance.

Glau-ber's (glou′bėrz) **salt.** [From J. R. *Glauber* (1604–68), German chemist.] Sodium sulphate, used as a cathartic, etc.

glau-ces-cent (glâ-ses′ent), *a.* [See *glaucous* and *-escent*.] Somewhat glaucous.

glau-co-ma (glâ-kō′mạ), *n.* [L., < Gr. γλαύκωμα, < γλαυκός, gray: see *glaucous*.] In *pathol.*, a disease of the eye, characterized by increased tension within the eyeball with progressive diminution or loss of vision.—**glau-com′a-tous** (-kom′ạ-tus), *a.*

glau-co-nite (glâ′kọ-nīt), *n.* [Gr. γλαυκός, bluish-green: see *glaucous*.] A greenish mineral consisting essentially of a hydrous silicate of iron and potassium, and occurring in greensand, clays, etc.—**glau-co-nit′ic** (-nit′ik), *a.*

glau-co-sis (glâ-kō′sis), *n.* [NL., < Gr. γλαύκωσις, < γλαυκός, gray: see *glaucous*.] Same as *glaucoma*.

glau-cous (glâ′kus), *a.* [L. *glaucus*, < Gr. γλαυκός, gleaming, silvery, gray, bluish-green.] Of a light bluish-green or greenish-blue color (as, "the *glaucous* caverns of old Ocean": Shelley's "Prometheus Unbound," ii. 1. 44); in *bot.*, covered with a whitish bloom, as a plum.

glave, glaved. See *glaive, glaived*.

glaze (glāz), *v.*; *glazed, glazing*. [ME. *glasen*; < *glass*.] **I.** *tr.* To furnish or fit with glass, as a window; cover with glass, as a picture; also, to produce a vitreous or glossy surface on (pottery, biscuit, etc.), as by coating the ware with the proper materials and then firing in a kiln, or by throwing salt into the kiln at a certain stage of the firing, or by other methods; in general, to cover with a smooth and lustrous coating; give a glassy surface to, as by polishing; in *oil-painting*, to cover (a painted surface) with a thin layer of transparent color; lay (a transparent color) over a painted surface. **II.** *intr.* To become glazed or glassy.—**glaze,** *n.* The vitreous or glossy surface or coating on glazed pottery, etc., or the substance or material used to produce such a surface; also, any smooth, glossy surface or coating or a substance for producing it; a glassy coating of ice, esp. as formed by rain which freezes upon striking the ground, etc.; in *oil-painting*, a thin layer of transparent color spread over a painted surface; in *cookery*, stock cooked down to a thin paste, for applying to the surface of meats.—**glaz-er** (glā′zėr), *n.* One who or that which glazes.

gla-zier (glā′zhėr), *n.* [ME. *glasier*, < *glas*, E. *glass*.] One who fits windows, picture-frames, etc., with glass.—**gla′-zier-y,** *n.* Glaziers' work.

glaz-ing (glā′zing), *n.* The act of furnishing or fitting with glass; the business of a glazier; glass set, or to be set, in frames, etc.; also, the act of applying a glaze; the glaze applied; the glassy surface or appearance of anything glazed.

glaz-y (glā′zi), *a.* Glaze-like; glazed; glossy; shiny.

gleam (glēm), *n.* [AS. *glǣm*, akin to OS. *glīmo*, brightness, OHG. *glīmo*, glow-worm, and E. *glimmer*.] Brightness; shine; esp., a transient or partial shining; a flash or beam of light; an interval of sunshine, as between showers (now prov. Eng); fig., a brief or slight manifestation or appearance, as of feeling, intelligence, hope, etc.—**gleam,** *v.* **I.** *intr.* To send forth a gleam or gleams; shine, esp. with a flash or beam of light; fig., to appear suddenly and clearly, like a flash of light. **II.** *tr.* To send forth in gleams.—**gleam′-ing-ly,** *adv.*—**gleam′y,** *a.* Gleaming; shining; intermittently bright; of weather, etc., having intervals of sunshine (now chiefly prov. Eng.: as, "antique castles seen through *gleamy* showers," Wordsworth's "Descriptive Sketches," 225).

glean (glēn), *v.* [OF. *glener* (F. *glaner*), < LL. *glenare*; origin uncertain.] **I.** *tr.* To gather (grain, etc.) after the reapers or regular gatherers; strip (a field, vineyard, etc.) of what is left by the reapers or regular gatherers; hence, to collect in scattered or fragmentary quantities; gather slowly and assiduously. **II.** *intr.* To gather what is left by reapers (as, "The poor are allowed to enter and *glean* upon another's ground after the harvest without being guilty of trespass": Blackstone's "Commentaries," III. 212); hence, to collect or gather anything little by little or slowly.—**glean′a-ble,** *a.* That may be gleaned.—**glean′er,** *n.*—**glean′ing,** *n.* The act of one who gleans; also, that which is gleaned (usually in *pl.*).

glebe (glēb), *n.* [L. *gleba*, *glæba*, clod, soil, land.] The soil (now only poetic: as, "The *glebe* of fifty kingdoms shall be till'd To feed his dazzling, desolating train," Campbell's "Power of Russia"); a cultivated field (now only poetic); a portion of land belonging to an ecclesiastical benefice.

gled (gled), *n.* Scotch form of *glede*.

glede (glēd), *n.* [AS. *glida* = Icel. *gledha*; akin to E. *glide*.] The common European kite, *Milvus ictinus*; also, any related bird, as the osprey.

gledge (glej), *v. i.*; *gledged, gledging*. [Var. of *gleg*[1].] To look obliquely, furtively, or slyly. [Sc.]—**gledge,** *n.* A side glance; a sly look. [Sc.]

glee[1] (glē), *n.* [AS. *glēo* = Icel. *glȳ*.] Entertainment†, sport†, or pleasure†; also; merriment or mirth (as, "Full well they laugh'd with counterfeited *glee* At all his jokes": Goldsmith's "Deserted Village," 201); joy or delight; also, musical entertainment† or music†; specif., a kind of unaccompanied part-song, grave or gay, for three or more voices.

glee[2] (glē), *v.* and *n.* See *gley*.

glee=club (glē′klub), *n.* A club or company organized to sing glees and other songs.

gleed[1] (glēd), *p. a.* See *gleyed*.

gleed[2] (glēd), *n.* [AS. *glēd* = D. *gloed* = G. *glut* = Icel. *glōdh*; akin to E. *glow*.] A live or burning coal (archaic or prov.); a fire or flame (obs. or prov.); *pl.*, cinders or coke (prov. Eng.).

glee-ful (glē′fu̇l), *a.* Full of glee; merry; joyous.—**glee′-ful-ly,** *adv.*—**glee′ful-ness,** *n.*

gleek[1] (glēk), *n.* [Origin uncertain.] A gibe, gird, or jest (obs. or Sc.); also, a coquettish glance†.—**gleek**[1], *v.*

I. *tr.* To ridicule; also, to trick. [Obs. or prov.] **II.** *intr.* To gibe; jest: as, "I have seen you *gleeking* and galling at this gentleman" (Shakspere's "Henry V.," v. 1. 78). [Obs. or Sc.]

gleek[2] (glēk), *n.* [OF. *glic.*] An old game at cards, played by three persons.

glee-man (glē′mạn), *n.*; pl. *-men.* [AS. *glēomann.*] A professional entertainer, esp. a singer or minstrel. [Now only hist.]

glee-some (glē′sum), *a.* Gleeful.—**glee′some-ly,** *adv.*—**glee′some-ness,** *n.*

gleet (glēt), *n.* [OF. *glette,* slime, mucus, pus, foul matter (F. litharge).] Slimy matter (now only Sc.); also, a thin, morbid discharge, as from a wound; specif., a morbid discharge from the urethra.

gleg[1] (gleg), *v. i.*; *glegged, glegging.* [=*gley.*] To squint; look obliquely or furtively; peep. [Prov. Eng.]—**gleg**[1], *n.* A squint; a side glance; a peep. [Prov. Eng.]

gleg[2] (gleg), *a.* [Icel. *gleggr, glöggr,* clear-sighted, = AS. *glēaw,* wise.] Quick of perception or apprehension; sharp-sighted; quick-witted; also, quick in action; also, lively or cheerful (as, "Dr. Dinwiddie was a *gleg* man, of a jocose nature": Galt's "Annals of the Parish," xxxvii.); also, sharp, as a knife. [Sc. and north. Eng.]—**gleg′ly,** *adv.* —**gleg′ness,** *n.*

glen (glen), *n.* [Gael. *gleann* = W. *glyn.*] A narrow valley; a depression or hollow between hills.

glen-gar-ry (glen-gar′i), *n.* [From *Glengarry,* valley in Inverness-shire, Scotland.] A Scotch cap with straight sides diminishing in height toward the back, a hollow or crease along the top, and sometimes short ribbon streamers at the back: sometimes worn as part of military dress.

gle-noid (glē′noid). [Gr. γληνοειδής, < γλήνη, socket of a joint, + εἶδος, form.] In *anat.*: **I.** *a.* Shallow or slightly cupped, as the articular cavities of the scapula and the temporal bone; pertaining to such a cavity. **II.** *n.* A glenoid cavity.

glent (glent), *v. i.* [ME. *glenten*; prob. from Scand.] To glance, glide, or dart off or aside; also, to glance or look quickly or briefly; also, to gleam or flash, as something bright; glint. [Now prov. Eng. and Sc.]—**glent,** *n.* A darting movement; also, a glance or look; a glimpse; also, a gleam or flash; a glint. [Now prov. Eng. and Sc.]

gley, glee[2] (glī or glē, glē), *v. i.* [ME. *gleyen, gleien, glien*; origin uncertain.] To squint; look obliquely or sideways. [Sc. and north. Eng.]—**gley, glee**[2], *n.* A squint; a side glance. [Sc. and north. Eng.]—**gleyed, gleed**[1] (glīd or glēd, glēd), *p. a.* Squint-eyed; also, crooked; wrong. [Sc. and north. Eng.]

glib (glib), *a.*; compar. *glibber,* superl. *glibbest.* [Cf. D. *glibberen,* slide, slip.] Smooth and slippery, as ice (now chiefly prov.); fig., easy, as action or manner; also, ready and fluent, as speakers, utterance, etc.; plausibly voluble. —**glib′ly,** *adv.*—**glib′ness,** *n.*

glide (glīd), *v.*; *glided, gliding.* [AS. *glīdan* = D. *glijden* = G. *gleiten,* glide: cf. *glede.*] **I.** *intr.* To move smoothly along, as if without effort or difficulty, as a flying bird, a flowing stream, a boat, a carriage, a skater, etc.; also, to go quietly, stealthily, or unperceived (*in, out,* etc.); slip; steal; also, to pass quietly or imperceptibly (*along, away, by,* etc.), as time, life, etc.; pass by gradual or insensible change, as into a state, or as one thing into another; in *aëronautics,* to move in the air, esp. at an easy angle downward, by the action of gravity or of air-currents, or by virtue of momentum already acquired, as a gliding-machine, or an aëroplane with the engine shut off (as, the *gliding* angle, the angle the path of an aëroplane makes with the horizontal when it is gliding to earth in still air without any action of the propeller). **II.** *tr.* To cause to glide.—**glide,** *n.* The act of gliding; a gliding movement, as in dancing, or a dance in which such movements are employed; in *music,* a slur; in *phonetics,* a fleeting sound produced in passing from one definite speech-sound to another, or in entering upon or passing from a definite speech-sound.—**glid-er** (glī′dėr), *n.* One who or that which glides; in *aëronautics,* a gliding-machine.—**glid′ing-ly,** *adv.*—**glid′ing=ma-chine″,** *n.* In *aëronautics,* an apparatus (commonly a structure built more or less like an aëroplane but having no motor) for gliding through the air from a higher to a lower level by the action of gravity, or from a lower to a higher level by the action of air-currents.

gliff (glif), *v.* [Origin obscure.] **I.** *intr.* To glance. [Obs. or Sc.] **II.** *tr.* To glance at; also, to frighten. [Sc. and north. Eng.]—**gliff,** *n.* A glimpse or slight view; also, a touch, trace, or suggestion of something; also, a moment or brief time; also, a fright or scare. [Sc. and north. Eng.]

glim (glim), *n.* [Cf. *glimmer.*] A light, as a lamp or candle; also, an eye. [Slang or prov.]

glim-mer (glim′ėr), *v. i.* [ME. *glimeren, glemeren,* = G. *glimmern* = Sw. *glimra* = Dan. *glimre*; a freq. form akin to D. and G. *glimmen,* Sw. *glimma,* glimmer, glow, and E. *gleam.*] To shine faintly or unsteadily; twinkle; flicker, as a candle about to go out; fig., to fail gradually and perceptibly; also, to appear faintly or dimly.—**to go glimmering,** to be gradually extinguished, like a candle flickering out: said of hopes, prospects, etc.—**glim′mer,** *n.* A faint or unsteady shining; a tremulous play of light; a faint gleam; also, a faint glimpse; a dim perception or notion; an inkling.—**glim′mer-ing,** *n.* The act or the light of something that glimmers; a glimmer; also, a faint glimpse; an inkling.—**glim′mer-ing-ly,** *adv.*

glimpse (glimps), *v.*; *glimpsed, glimpsing.* [ME. *glimsen* = MHG. *glimsen*; akin to E. *glimmer.*] **I.** *intr.* To shine briefly, gleam, or flash (archaic); also, to appear momentarily or slightly (archaic: as, "And *glimpsing* over these, just seen, High up, the topmost palace spire," Tennyson's "Day-Dream," 67); also, to look briefly, or glance. **II.** *tr.* To show in a glimpse; also, to catch a glimpse of.—**glimpse,** *n.* A gleam, as of light (archaic: as, "the *glimpses* of the moon," Shakspere's "Hamlet," i. 4. 53); also, a momentary or slight appearance or show of something (as, "With looks . . . wherein appear'd Obscure some *glimpse* of joy": Milton's "Paradise Lost," i. 524); a slight touch or trace shown; also, a momentary or slight view or sight of something (as, to catch a *glimpse* of a house through the trees).—**glimps′er,** *n.*

glint (glint), *v.* [Var. of *glent.*] **I.** *intr.* To glance or glide off (archaic or prov.); also, to glance or look (now prov. Eng. and Sc.); also, to gleam or flash, as light or something bright (as, "Ruddy arrows of the sun *glinted* among the boughs": Tarkington's "Gentleman from Indiana," xix.); show a sudden brief or varying brightness, as something that catches the light on one part or another. **II.** *tr.* To cause to glint; cast or reflect (light) in glints (as, "The sun's last glance was *glinted* back, From spear and glaive, from targe and jack": Scott's "Lady of the Lake," v. 10). —**glint,** *n.* A glance, look, or glimpse (prov. Eng. and Sc.); also, a gleam or flash; a glinting brightness.

gli-o-ma (glī-ō′mạ̈), *n.*; pl. *-mas* or *-mata* (-mạ-tạ̈). [NL., < Gr. γλία, glue: see *-oma.*] In *pathol.,* a tumor arising from and consisting largely of neuroglia.—**gli-om′a-tous** (-om′ạ-tus), *a.*

glis-sade (gli-säd′ or -säd′), *n.* [F., < *glisser,* slip, slide; from Teut.] The act of sliding, as down a slope of ice or snow or on any surface (as, "The figure . . . descended . . . with the *glissade* of a water-drop down a bud": Hardy's "Return of the Native," i. 2); a slide; in *dancing,* a sliding or gliding step to the right or left.—**glis-sade′,** *v. i.*; *-saded, -sading.* To perform a glissade.

glis-san-do (glē-sän′dō). [It., < F. *glissant,* ppr. of *glisser,* slide: see *glissade.*] In *music*: **I.** *a.* Performed with a gliding effect, as, on a pianoforte, by sliding the back of the finger rapidly over the white keys. **II.** *n.* A gliding effect; a glissando passage.

glis-ten (glis′n), *v. i.* [AS. *glisnian*: cf. *glister* and *glitter.*] To shine with a sparkling light or luster, as snow, dew, armor, satin, the eyes, etc.; sparkle.—**glis′ten,** *n.* A glistening; a sparkling luster; sparkle.—**glis′ten-ing-ly,** *adv.*

glis-ter (glis′tėr), *v. i.* [ME. *glistren*; akin to *glisten* and prob. *glitter.*] To glisten; sparkle; glitter: as, "All that *glisters* is not gold" (Shakspere's "Merchant of Venice," ii. 7. 65). [Archaic or prov.]—**glis′ter,** *n.* A glistering or glistening; glitter. [Archaic or prov.]

glit-ter (glit′ėr), *v. i.* [ME. *gliteren* = Icel. *glitra* = G. *glitzern*; a freq. form akin to Icel. *glita,* OS. *glītan,* OHG. *glīzan,* G. *gleissen,* shine, glitter, and prob. to E.

glister and *glisten*.] To shine with a brilliant, sparkling light or luster (as, "The gemmy bridle *glitter'd* free, Like to some branch of stars we see Hung in the golden Galaxy": Tennyson's "Lady of Shalott," iii.); sparkle vividly or with intense brightness; fig., to make a brilliant or splendid appearance or show.—**glit′ter,** *n.* A glittering; glittering light or luster; brilliance; splendor.—**glit′ter-ing-ly,** *adv.* —**glit′ter-y,** *a.* Glittering; sparkling.

gloam (glōm), *v. i.* [Back-formation from *gloaming*.] To become dusk; grow dark. [Chiefly Sc. and north. Eng.] —**gloam,** *n.* The gloaming. See Keats's "La Belle Dame sans Merci," xi. [Prov. or poetic.]

gloam-ing (glō′ming), *n.* [AS. *glōmung*, < *glōm*, twilight.] Evening twilight; dusk: now chiefly poetic and literary.

gloat (glōt), *v. i.* [Cf. Icel. *glotta*, grin, smile scornfully, G. *glotzen*, stare.] To cast sidelong or furtive glances†; also, to cast amorous glances†; also, to gaze intently or dwell mentally upon something with satisfaction, esp. upon something that gratifies an evil passion or a corrupt propensity.—**gloat′er,** *n.*—**gloat′ing-ly,** *adv.*

glo-bal (glō′bạl), *a.* Spherical; globe-shaped; also, pertaining to the earth; world-wide (as, the *Global* War, a term applied to the present world-wide war to indicate a condition more entire and total than any previous war).

glo-bate (glō′bāt), *a.* [L. *globatus*, pp. of *globare*, form into a ball, < *globus*, E. *globe*.] Having the form of a globe. Also **glo′bat-ed** (-bā-ted).

globe (glōb), *n.* [F. *globe*, < L. *globus*, round body or mass, ball, globe.] A spherical body; a sphere; a ball; often, the earth (usually with *the*); hence, any planet or other celestial body; also, a sphere on whose surface is depicted a map of the earth ('terrestrial globe') or of the heavens ('celestial globe'); also, a golden ball borne as an emblem of sovereignty (as, "With crown, with sceptre, and with *globe*, Emblems of empery": Scott's "Bridal of Triermain," iii. 35); also, anything more or less spherical in shape, as the eyeball, a kind of glass lamp-shade, or a glass vessel for holding water in which to exhibit living fish.—

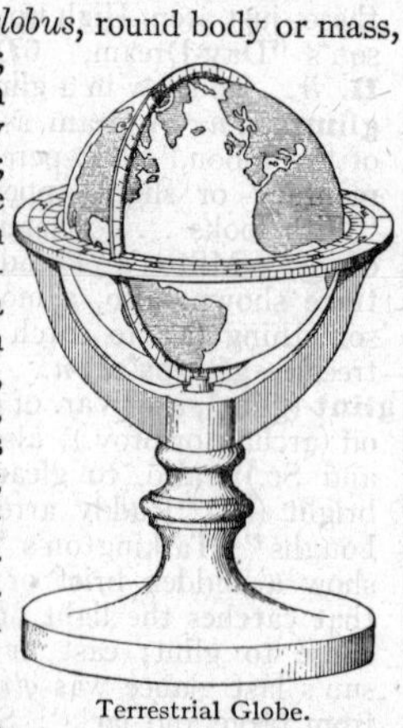

Terrestrial Globe.

globe, *v.*; *globed, globing.* **I.** *tr.* To form into a globe; also, to provide with a globe or globes. **II.** *intr.* To take the form of a globe.—**globe′=fish,** *n.* Any of various fishes (genera *Tetraodon, Diodon*, etc.) which can assume a more or less globular form by inflating the body.—**globe′=flow″er,** *n.* A ranunculaceous plant, *Trollius europæus*, of Europe, having pale-yellow globe-like flowers; also, an American species, *T. laxus*, with spreading sepals.—**globe′let,** *n.* A little globe; a drop.—**globe′=trot″ter,** *n.* One who travels rapidly and widely over the world, esp. for sight-seeing. [Colloq.]—**globe′=trot″ting,** *n.* and *a.*

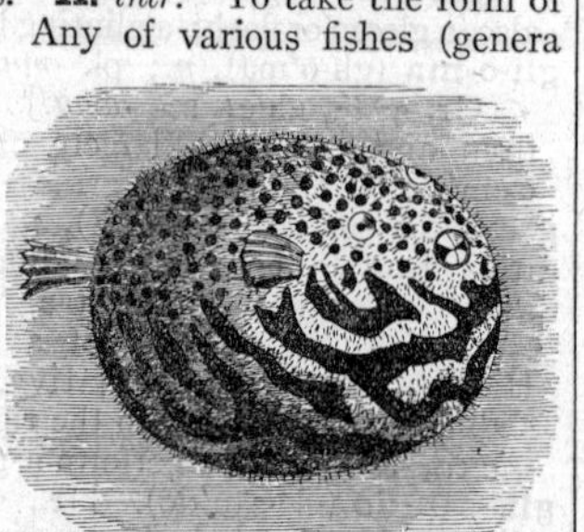

Globe-fish (*Tetraodon lineatus*).

Globe-flower (*Trollius europæus*).

glo-bi-ge-ri-na (glō″bi-jẹ-rī′nạ̈), *n.*; pl. *-næ* (-nē). [NL., < L. *globus*, globe, + *gerere*, bear.] Any member of the genus *Globigerina*, which comprises small foraminifers of pelagic habits, having a shell with globular chambers which forms the chief constituent of large deposits ('globigerina ooze' or 'globigerina mud') on the bottom of the ocean. —**glo-big-er-ine** (glọ-bij′ẹ-rin), *a.* and *n.*

glo-bin (glō′bin), *n.* [L. *globus*, E. *globe*.] In *physiol. chem.*, a proteid substance formed in the decomposition of hemoglobin.

glo-boid (glō′boid). [L. *globus*, E. *globe*: see *-oid*.] **I.** *a.* Approximately globular. **II.** *n.* A globoid figure or body.

glo-bose (glọ-bōs′ or glō′bōs), *a.* [L. *globosus*, < *globus*, E. *globe*.] Globe-like in form; globular, or approximately so.—**glo-bose′ly,** *adv.*—**glo-bos′i-ty** (-bos′i-ti), *n.*—**glo-bous** (glō′bus), *a.* Globose.

glob-u-lar (glob′ụ-lạ̈r), *a.* Having the form of a globule or globe; spherical; round; also, composed of globules.—**glob-u-lar′i-ty** (-lar′i-ti), *n.*—**glob′u-lar-ly,** *adv.*

glob-ule (glob′ūl), *n.* [F. *globule*, < L. *globulus*, dim. of *globus*, E. *globe*.] A globe or sphere of small size; a small spherical body or structure, as a pill, a blood-corpuscle, etc. —**glob′u-lin** (-ụ-lin), *n.* In *physiol. chem.*, any of a group of proteids which are insoluble in pure water.—**glob′u-lite** (-līt), *n.* One of the minute rounded bodies seen in vitreous igneous rocks, etc., when examined under the microscope: supposed by some authorities to represent a rudimentary stage in crystallization.—**glob-u-lit′ic** (-lit′ik), *a.*

glo-chid-i-ate (glọ-kid′i-āt), *a.* [Gr. γλωχίς, point of an arrow.] In *bot.* and *zoöl.*, barbed at the tip, as a hair or bristle; bearing barbs.

glock-en-spiel (glok′ẹn-spēl), *n.* [G., < *glocke*, bell, + *spiel*, play.] A musical instrument consisting of a series of small bells, or of metal bars or tubes, mounted on a support or in a frame and struck with hammers.

glom-er-ate (glom′ẹ-rāt), *a.* [L. *glomeratus*, pp. of *glomerare*, wind or form into a ball, < *glomus*, ball: see *glomerule*.] Gathered into a rounded mass; compactly clustered.—**glom-er-a′tion** (-ẹ-rā′shọn), *n.* Glomerate condition; also, a glomerate mass.

glom-er-ule (glom′ẹ-röl), *n.* [NL. *glomerulus*, dim. of L. *glomus*, ball (of yarn, thread, etc.).] A compact cluster, as of capillary blood-vessels; in *bot.*, a cyme condensed into a head-like cluster.—**glo-mer-u-lar** (glọ-mer′ọ-lạ̈r), *a.*

glon-o-in (glon′ọ-in), *n.* [Said to be < *gl(ycerin)* + *o(xygen)* + *n(itrogen)*.] Nitroglycerin: esp. so called in medicine.

gloom (glöm), *v.* [ME. *gloumen, gloumben*, frown, lower: cf. MLG. *glomen*, make turbid.] **I.** *intr.* To frown or scowl; also, to look dismal or dejected; also, to become dark or cloudy, as the sky; lower; also, to appear as a dark object; have a dark or somber appearance. **II.** *tr.* To make gloomy; also, to make dark or somber.—**gloom,** *n.* A frown or scowl (Sc.); also, a despondent look, as on a person's countenance; a state of melancholy or depression; *pl.*, low spirits; also, *sing.*, darkness; deep shade; a dark or deeply shaded place.—**gloom′i-ly,** *adv.* In a gloomy manner.—**gloom′i-ness,** *n.*—**gloom′ing,** *n.* [Prob. in part associated with *gloaming*.] The action of one that glooms; a frown; a fit of sullenness; sometimes, gloaming or twilight (poetic).—**gloom′less,** *a.* Free from gloom. —**gloom′y,** *a.*; compar. *gloomier*, superl. *gloomiest*. Affected with, characterized by, or expressive of gloom, or depression of spirits; melancholy; causing gloom, or depressing (as, a *gloomy* prospect); also, full of gloom or darkness; dark; deeply shaded.

Glo-ri-a (glō′ri-ạ̈), *n.* [L., glory.] In Christian liturgical worship, the great, or greater, doxology beginning "Gloria in excelsis Deo" (Glory be to God on high), the lesser doxology beginning "Gloria Patri" (Glory be to the Father), or the response "Gloria tibi, Domine" (Glory be to thee, O Lord); [also *l. c.*] a repetition of any one of these; a musical setting for any one of these, esp. the first; also [*l. c.*], a halo, nimbus, or aureola, or an ornament in imitation of one; also, a fabric made of silk and wool (or cotton), used for umbrellas, dresses, etc.

glo-ri-ette (glō-ri-et′), *n.* [F., < L. *gloria*, E. *glory*, *n.*] A pavilion or kiosk, as in a park; a summer-house.

glo-ri-fi-a-ble (glō′ri-fī-ạ-bl), *a.* That may be glorified.

glo-ri-fi-ca-tion (glō″ri-fi-kā′shọn), *n.* The act of glorifying, or the state of being glorified; exaltation to the glory of heaven; ascription of glory or praise; sometimes, a doxology; also, a celebration or jubilation (colloq.); also, a glorified or more splendid form of something (colloq.).

glo-ri-fied (glō′ri-fīd), *p. a.* Made glorious; often, invested with a glory, magnificence, or dignity not naturally belonging.

glo-ri-fy (glō′ri-fī), *v. t.*; *-fied, -fying.* [OF. F. *glorifier,* < LL. *glorificare,* < L. *gloria,* glory, + *facere,* make.] To render glorious; invest with glory; sometimes, to exalt to the glory of heaven; often, to promote the glory of (God); ascribe glory and praise in adoration to (God); in general, to magnify with praise; extol; also, to invest with radiance or beauty (as, "The bright sun *glorifies* the sky": Shakspere's "Venus and Adonis," 485); also, to transform into something more splendid; present in a highly favorable aspect.—**glo′ri-fi-er** (-fī-ėr), *n.*

glo-ri-ole (glō′ri-ōl), *n.* [F. *gloriole,* < L. *gloriola,* dim. of *gloria,* E. *glory, n.*] A petty glory or distinction†; also, a halo, nimbus, or aureola.

glo-ri-ous (glō′ri-us), *a.* [OF. *glorios* (F. *glorieux*), < L. *gloriosus,* < *gloria,* E. *glory, n.*] Full of glory; entitled to renown; illustrious; also, conferring glory (as, a *glorious* victory); entitling to renown; also, splendid or magnificent (as, "the *glorious* planet Sol": Shakspere's "Troilus and Cressida," i. 3. 89); admirable, delightful, or fine (as, to have a *glorious* time; "The weather was *glorious,*" Lever's "Harry Lorrequer," xlv.); also, elated or hilarious from drink (colloq.); also, vainglorious†.—**glo′ri-ous-ly,** *adv.*—**glo′ri-ous-ness,** *n.*

glo-ry (glō′ri), *n.*; pl. *-ries* (-riz). [OF. *glorie* (F. *gloire*), < L. *gloria,* glory, fame, vainglory, boasting.] Exalted praise, honor, or distinction, accorded by common consent (as, "The paths of *glory* lead but to the grave": Gray's "Elegy," ix.); renown; also, something that renders honored or illustrious; a distinguished ornament; an object of pride; also, adoring praise or thanksgiving (as, "Fear God, and give *glory* to him": Rev. xiv. 7); also, majesty and splendor, as of God (as, "He . . . looked up stedfastly into heaven, and saw the *glory* of God, and Jesus standing on the right hand of God": Acts, vii. 55); the splendor and bliss of heaven (as, "Thou, bright saint, high sit'st in *glory*": Milton's "Epitaph on the Marchioness of Winchester"); heaven (as, to go to *glory*); also, brightness, brilliance, or radiant beauty (as, "One star differeth from another star in *glory,*" 1 Cor. xv. 41; "What will be the morning *glory,* when at dusk thus gleams the lake?" Browning's "La Saisiaz"); some feature or thing characterized by such beauty; also, a state of splendor, magnificence, or greatest prosperity (as, the Spanish monarchy in the days of its *glory*); a state of fullest gratification or enjoyment (as, to be in one's *glory*); also, a ring, circle, or surrounding radiance of light represented about the head or the whole figure of a sacred person, as Christ, a saint, etc.; a halo, nimbus, or aureola; hence, any ring or circle of light; also, vainglory† (as, "In military commanders and soldiers, vain glory is an essential point; for as iron sharpens iron, so by *glory* one courage sharpeneth another": Bacon's "Essays," Of Vain Glory).—**glo′ry,** *v. i.*; *-ried, -rying.* [L. *gloriari,* pride one's self, boast, < *gloria.*] To exult with triumph; rejoice proudly; also, to boast†.—**glo′ry=hole,** *n.* A receptacle or place, as a drawer or a room, into which things are put without attempt at order; *naut.,* a lazaretto.—**glo′ry-ing-ly,** *adv.*—**glo′ry=pea,** *n.* Same as *clianthus.*

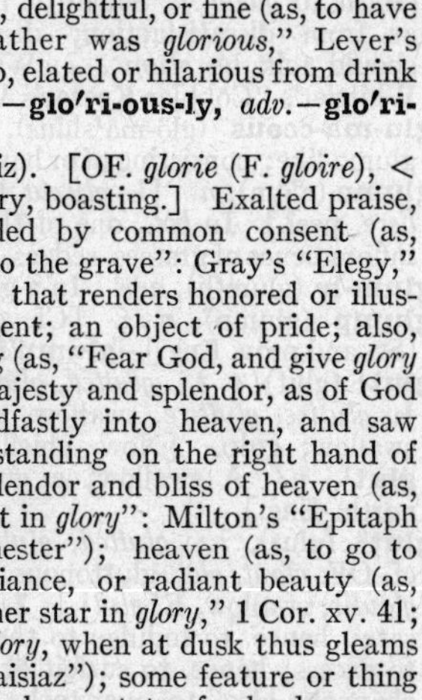

Glory. — Figure of Christ, façade of Cathedral of Angoulême, France; 12th century.

glose (glōz), *n.* and *v.* See *gloze*[2].

gloss[1] (glos), *n.* [Cf. D. (obs.) *gloos* and MHG. *glose,* a gleam, glow, Icel. *glossi,* a blaze.] A superficial luster, as of satin; also, an external show; a specious appearance; also, the glow of a fire (Sc. and north. Eng.).—**gloss**[1], *v. t.* To put a gloss or luster upon; also, to give a fair or specious appearance to (often with *over*).

gloss[2] (glos), *n.* [Later form (conformed to L. *glossa*) of *glose, gloze,* < OF. *glose,* < L. *glossa,* a word needing explanation, the explanation, < Gr. γλῶσσα, tongue, language, foreign or other word needing explanation: cf. *gloze*[2].] An interlinear or marginal interpretation of a foreign or otherwise difficult word, phrase, etc., in a text; also, an interpretation or definition of a word, phrase, etc., given in a glossary or dictionary; in general, an explanation or comment; also, a series of verbal interpretations of a text; an interlinear translation of a text; a collection or list of verbal explanations of a text; a glossary; sometimes, an artfully misleading or false interpretation.—**gloss**[2], *v.* **I.** *tr.* To insert glosses on; annotate; also, to give a specious interpretation of; explain away. **II.** *intr.* To make glosses; comment.

glos-sal (glos′ạl), *a.* [Gr. γλῶσσα, tongue.] Of or pertaining to the tongue.

glos-sa-ri-al (glo-sā′ri-ạl), *a.* [See *glossary.*] Of, pertaining to, or of the nature of a glossary.—**glos-sa′ri-an,** *n.* A glossarist.—**glos-sa-rist** (glos′ạ-rist), *n.* A writer of glosses; a commentator; the compiler of a glossary.—**glos′sa-rize** (-rīz), *v. t.*; *-rized, -rizing.* To enter and explain in a glossary.

glos-sa-ry (glos′ạ-ri), *n.*; pl. *-ries* (-riz). [L. *glossarium,* < *glossa,* E. *gloss*[2].] A collection of glosses; a list with explanations, as of difficult, dialectal, or technical terms; a vocabulary or dictionary of limited scope: as, a *glossary* to Shakspere's works; a *glossary* of Scottish words and phrases; a *glossary* of the mining and mineral industry.

glos-sa-tor (glo-sā′tọr), *n.* [ML., < *glossare,* to gloss, < L. *glossa,* E. *gloss*[2].] A writer of glosses; a commentator; esp., one of the medieval commentators on the texts of the civil and canon law.

gloss-er[1] (glos′ėr), *n.* One who puts a gloss or luster on something.

gloss-er[2] (glos′ėr), *n.* A writer of glosses; a glossarist.

gloss-i-ly (glos′i-li), *adv.* In a glossy manner.—**gloss′i-ness,** *n.*

glos-si-tis (glo-sī′tis), *n.* [NL., < Gr. γλῶσσα, tongue.] In *pathol.,* inflammation of the tongue.

gloss-less (glos′les), *a.* Without gloss or luster.

glos-so-graph (glos′ọ-gráf), *n.* [Gr. γλωσσογράφος, < γλῶσσα (see *gloss*[2]) + γράφειν, write.] A writer of glosses; a commentator. Also **glos-sog-ra-pher** (glo-sog′rạ-fėr).—**glos-sog′ra-phy,** *n.* The writing of glosses.

glos-sol-o-gy (glo-sol′ọ-ji), etc. Same as *glottology,* etc.

gloss-y (glos′i), *a.*; compar. *glossier,* superl. *glossiest.* Having a gloss; lustrous; smooth and shining; also, having a specious appearance (as, "*glossy* duplicity": Boswell's "Johnson," 1754); plausible.

glost (glost), *n.* [Var. of *gloss*[1].] In *ceram.,* glaze.—**glost′=kiln, glost′=ov″en,** *n.* A kiln or oven in which pottery or biscuit is fired in the glazing process.

glot-tal (glot′ạl), *a.* Of, pertaining to, or produced in the glottis. Also **glot′tic**[1].

glot-tic[2] (glot′ik), *a.* [Gr. γλωττικός, < γλῶττα, γλῶσσα, tongue, language.] Pertaining to language; linguistic.

glot-tis (glot′is), *n.* [NL., < Gr. γλωττίς, < γλῶττα, γλῶσσα, tongue.] In *anat.,* the opening at the upper part of the larynx, between the vocal cords.

glot-tol-o-gy (glo-tol′ọ-ji), *n.* [Gr. γλῶττα, γλῶσσα, tongue, language: see *-logy.*] The science of language; comparative philology.—**glot-to-log-ic, glot-to-log-i-cal** (glot-ọ-loj′ik, -i-kạl), *a.*—**glot-tol′o-gist,** *n.*

glove (gluv), *n.* [AS. *glōf* = Icel. *glōfi.*] A covering for the hand, esp. one having a separate sheath for each finger (cf. *mitten*); sometimes, specif., a boxing-glove.—**glove,** *v. t.*; *gloved, gloving.* To cover with or as with a glove; provide with gloves; also, to serve as a glove for.—**glove′less,** *a.* Without a glove; not gloved.—**glov-er** (gluv′ėr), *n.* One who makes or sells gloves.

glow (glō), *v.* [AS. *glōwan* = D. *gloeien* = G. *glühen* = Icel. *glōa,* glow: cf. *gleed*[2].] **I.** *intr.* To emit bright light and heat without flame; be incandescent; also, to shine like something intensely heated; also, to exhibit a strong, bright color; be lustrously red or brilliant; also, to be excessively hot (as, "The torrid zone *Glows* with the passing and repassing sun": Dryden's tr. Virgil's "Georgics," i. 323); feel an intense sensation of heat; burn or be animated as with emotion or passion (as, to *glow* with resentment). **II.** *tr.* To cause to glow†.—**glow,** *n.* The state of glowing; light such as is emitted by a body heated to luminosity; incandescence; also, brightness of color; vivid redness; also, a state of bodily heat; warmth of emotion or passion.—**glow'er**[1], *n.* One who or that which glows; specif., the light-giving rod in a Nernst lamp.

glow-er[2] (glou'ėr), *v. i.* [Origin uncertain: cf. ME. *gloren*, stare, glare.] To stare or gaze intently (Sc.); also, to look angrily or with sullen dislike or discontent (as, "He . . . stood *glowering* in sullen suspense": Galsworthy's "Patrician," ii. 5); scowl.—**glow'er**[2], *n.* A glowering look.—**glow'er-ing-ly,** *adv.*

glow-ing (glō'ing), *p. a.* That glows; incandescent; brilliantly luminous; rich and warm in coloring; exhibiting the glow of health, excitement, etc.; ardent or impassioned.—**glow'ing-ly,** *adv.*

glow=lamp (glō'lamp), *n.* An incandescent electric lamp.

glow=worm (glō'wėrm), *n.* Any of various luminous insects or insect larvæ; esp., a European beetle, *Lampyris noctiluca*, the wingless female of which emits a greenish light from the end of the abdomen.

glox-in-i-a (glok-sin'i-ạ̈), *n.* [NL.; from B. P. *Gloxin*, German botanist.] Any of the tropical American plants constituting the genus *Gloxinia* (family *Gesneriaceæ*), little known in cultivation; also, a widely cultivated plant, *Sinningia speciosa*, of the same family, having large white, red, or purple bell-shaped flowers (so called because orig. referred to the genus *Gloxinia*).

Gloxinia (*Sinningia speciosa*).

gloze[1] (glōz), *v. i.*; *glozed, glozing.* [Cf. *gloss*[1].] To blaze, as a fire. [Sc.]—**gloze**[1], *n.* The blaze or clear flame of a fire. [Sc.]

gloze[2] (glōz), *n.* [ME. *glose*, < OF. *glose*: see *gloss*[2].] A gloss, or explanatory note; also, flattery or deceit; a flattering speech, etc.; also, a specious show; a pretense; a disguise. [Now rare.]—**gloze**[2], *v.*; *glozed, glozing.* [ME. *glosen*, < OF. *gloser*, < *glose.*] **I.** *tr.* To make glozes or glosses upon†; interpret†; also, to palliate with specious representations (as, "Fawning fools . . . With the tongue of flattery *glozing* deeds which God and Truth condemn": Whittier's "Lines Suggested by a Visit to Washington"); explain away; extenuate; also, to flatter or wheedle (archaic). **II.** *intr.* To make glosses†; comment†; also, to talk speciously, or use flattering language (now rare).

glu-case (glö'kās), *n.* [See *glucose* and *-ase.*] In *chem.*, an enzyme present in certain species of yeast, etc., and capable of converting maltose into glucose.

glu-ci-num (glọ-sī'num), *n.* [NL., < Gr. γλυκύς, sweet (some of the salts having a sweet taste).] Chem. sym., Gl (or Be); at. wt., 9.1; sp. gr., 1.85. A white metallic element occurring combined in certain minerals. Also called *beryllium.*—**glu-cin'ic** (-sin'ik), *a.*

glu-co-pro-te-id (glö-kọ-prō'tẹ-id), *n.* [Gr. γλυκύς, sweet, + E. *proteid.*] In *physiol. chem.*, any of a class of proteid compounds which contain a carbohydrate group.

glu-cose (glö'kōs), *n.* [F. *glucose*, perhaps < Gr. γλεῦκος, must, sweet new wine (cf. *grape-sugar* as a name for the common form of glucose), but usually referred to γλυκύς, sweet: cf. *-ose*[2].] In *chem.*, a sugar, $C_6H_{12}O_6$, having three optically different forms, the common or dextrorotatory form occurring in many fruits, animal tissues and fluids, etc., and having a sweetness about one half that of ordinary sugar; in *com.*, a syrup obtained by the incomplete conversion of starch into common glucose.—**glu-co-side** (glö'kọ-sīd or -sid), *n.* In *chem.*, any of an extensive group of compounds which yield a sugar (usually glucose) and some other substance or substances when treated with a dilute acid or alkali, or when decomposed by a ferment or enzyme.—**glu-co-su'ri-a** (-sū'ri-ạ̈), *n.* Same as *glycosuria.*

glue (glö), *n.* [OF. F. *glu*, < LL. *glus* (*glut-*), glue: cf. *gluten.*] An impure gelatin obtained by boiling skins, hoofs, and other animal substances, in water, and used for various purposes in the arts, esp. as an adhesive medium in uniting substances; any of various preparations of this substance; also, any similar adhesive material.—**glue,** *v. t.*; *glued, gluing.* To join or fasten with glue or other viscous substance; hence, to fix or attach firmly as if with glue; cause to adhere closely.—**glu'er,** *n.*—**glue'y,** *a.* Like glue; viscid; sticky; also, full of or smeared with glue.

glum (glum), *a.*; compar. *glummer*, superl. *glummest.* [Akin to *gloom.*] Sullen or frowning, as persons; gloomy as from dissatisfaction; dismal or dejected (as, "Why should folk be *glum* . . . When Nature herself is glad?" Whittier's "Cobbler Keezar's Vision").

glu-ma-ceous (glọ-mā'shius), *a.* [See *-aceous.*] In *bot.*, glume-like; consisting of or having glumes.

glume (glöm), *n.* [L. *gluma*, hull or husk (of grain), < *glubere*, peel.] In *bot.*, one of the characteristic bracts of the inflorescence of grasses, sedges, etc.

glum-ly (glum'li), *adv.* In a glum manner.—**glum'ness,** *n.*

glump (glump), *v. i.* [Cf. *glum.*] To be sullen; sulk. [Sc. and prov. Eng.]—**glump'ish, glump'y,** *a.* Glum.

glut[1] (glut), *v. t.*; *glutted, glutting.* [OF. *gloutir, glotir*, < L. *glutire, gluttire*, swallow, gulp down: cf. *glutton.*] To swallow; gulp. [Now chiefly Sc. and north. Eng.]—**glut**[1], *n.* A swallow; a gulp; a draft. [Now Sc. and north. Eng.]

glut[2] (glut), *v.*; *glutted, glutting.* [ME. *glouten, glotten*: cf. OF. *glout, glot*, gluttonous, greedy, *glouton*, glutton, also *gloutir*, swallow, E. *glut*[1].] **I.** *tr.* To feed or fill to satiety; sate; hence, to indulge to the utmost; also, to feed or fill to excess; hence, to surfeit or cloy; also, to choke up, as a channel; also, to overstock, as a market. **II.** *intr.* To eat to satiety.—**glut**[2], *n.* The act of glutting, or the state of being glutted; also, a full supply; a surfeit, or excessive supply (as, "They had had a *glut* of Christian blood": J. H. Newman's "Callista," xxvii.); in *com.*, a supply of mercantile goods greatly in excess of the demand.

glu-tæ-us, glu-te-us (glọ-tē'us), *n.*; pl. *glutæi, glutei* (-ī). [NL., < Gr. γλουτός, rump, pl. buttocks.] In *anat.*, any of several muscles of the buttocks.—**glu-te'al** (-ạl), *a.* In *anat.*, pertaining to the buttock muscles, or to the buttocks.

glu-ten (glö'ten), *n.* [L. *gluten*, glue, akin to LL. *glus*, E. *glue.*] Glue, or some gluey substance; esp., the tough, viscid nitrogenous substance which remains behind when the flour of wheat or other grain is washed with water to remove the starch.—**gluten bread,** bread made from gluten flour.—**gluten flour,** wheat flour from which a part of the starch has been removed, thus increasing the proportion of gluten.

glu-te-us (glọ-tē'us), *n.* See *glutæus.*

glu-ti-nous (glö'ti-nus), *a.* [L. *glutinosus*, < *gluten*, glue.] Of the nature of glue; gluey; viscid; sticky.—**glu-ti-nos'i-ty** (-nos'i-ti), **glu'ti-nous-ness,** *n.*—**glu'ti-nous-ly,** *adv.*

glut-ton (glut'n), *n.* [OF. F. *glouton*, < L. *gluto(n-)*, *glutto(n-)*, < *glutire*, swallow, E. *glut*[1].] One who eats to excess; a gormandizer; hence, one who indulges in something excessively or inordinately; one who is excessively fond of a specified object, etc.; in *zoöl.*, a thick-set, voracious mammal, *Gulo luscus*, of the weasel family, measuring from 2 to 3 feet in length, and inhabit-

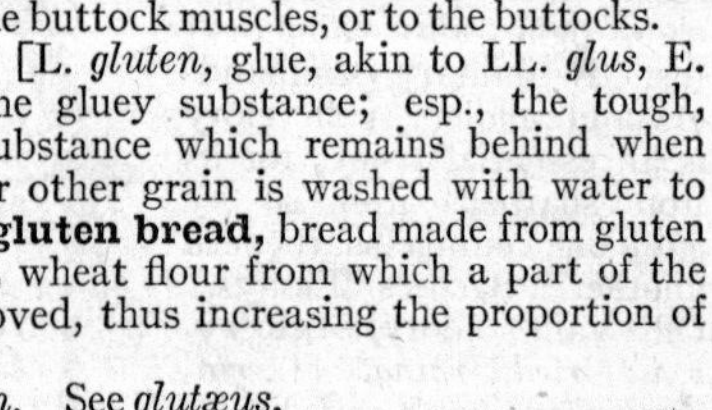
Glutton (*Gulo luscus*).

ing northern regions (the kind found in America, usually called the *wolverene*, being practically identical with that of Europe and Asia).—**glut′ton-ize,** *v. i.* or *t.*; *-ized, -izing.* To feast or devour like a glutton.—**glut′ton-ous,** *a.* Given to or characterized by excessive eating; voracious; hence, greedy; insatiable.—**glut′ton-ous-ly,** *adv.* —**glut′ton-ous-ness,** *n.*—**glut′ton-y,** *n.*; pl. *-ies* (-iz). Excess in eating; voracity.

gly-cer-ic (gli-ser′ik or glis′ẹ-rik), *a.* Pertaining to or derived from glycerin: as, *glyceric* acid (an acid obtained by the oxidation of glycerin).

gly-cer-ide (glis′ẹ-rīd or -rid), *n.* In *chem.*, an ester of glycerin.

gly-cer-in, gly-cer-ine (glis′ẹ-rin), *n.* [F. *glycérine*, < Gr. γλυκερός, sweet.] A clear, colorless, odorless liquid ($C_3H_5.O_3H_3$, a compound of the alcohol class), of thick, syrupy consistence and sweet taste, obtained by the saponification of natural fats and oils, and used in the arts, in medicine, etc.—**gly′cer-in-ate** (-āt), *v. t.*; *-ated, -ating.* To mix or treat with glycerin.—**gly-cer-ite** (glis′ẹ-rīt), *n.* In *phar.*, any of a class of preparations consisting of a medicinal substance dissolved or suspended in glycerin.—**gly-cer-ol** (glis′ẹ-rol or -rōl), *n.* Same as *glycerin.*—**gly-cer-o-late** (glis′ẹ-rọ-lāt), *n.* Same as *glycerite.*—**gly-cer-yl** (glis′ẹ-ril), *n.* [See *-yl.*] In *chem.*, the hypothetical trivalent radical (C_3H_5) in glycerin and the glycerides.

gly-co-gen (glī′kọ-jen), *n.* [Gr. γλυκύς, sweet: see *-gen.*] In *chem.*, a white, amorphous, tasteless carbohydrate found in the liver and other animal tissues.—**gly-co-gen′ic,** *a.*

gly-col (glī′kol), *n.* [From *glyc(erin)* + *(alcoh)ol.*] In *chem.*, a colorless, sweet-tasting liquid, $C_2H_4(OH)_2$, of the alcohol class, regarded as intermediate between glycerin and ethyl alcohol; also, any of a group of alcohols of a similar type.—**gly′co-late** (-kọ-lāt), *n.* In *chem.*, a salt or ester of glycolic acid.—**gly-col′ic,** *a.* Pertaining to or derived from glycol: as, *glycolic* acid (a crystalline compound produced from glycol).

Gly-con-ic (glī-kon′ik). [From *Glycon*, Greek lyric poet.] [Also *l. c.*] In *anc. pros.*: **I.** *a.* Noting or pertaining to a form of verse, usually catalectic, consisting of four feet (three trochees and one dactyl, the dactyl commonly being the second foot) or of three feet (a spondee and two dactyls). **II.** *n.* The Glyconic meter; a Glyconic verse.

gly-cose (glī′kōs), *n.* Same as *glucose.*

gly-co-su-ri-a (glī-kọ-sū′ri-ạ̈), *n.* [NL., < E. *glycose* (*glucose*) + Gr. οὖρον, urine.] In *pathol.*, a condition in which glucose is present in the urine, as in diabetes.—**gly-co-su′ric,** *a.*

glyph (glif), *n.* [Gr. γλυφή, carving, < γλύφειν, carve: cf. *cleave*[2].] In *arch.*, an ornamental channel or groove, usually vertical, as in a Doric frieze; in *archæol.*, a pictograph or hieroglyph.—**glyph′ic,** *a.* [Gr. γλυφικός.] Of or pertaining to carving; sculptured.

gly-phog-ra-phy (gli-fog′rạ-fi), *n.* [Gr. γλυφή, carving: see *-graphy.*] An electrotype process by which a plate with a raised surface suitable for printing is made from an engraved plate.

glyp-tic (glip′tik), *a.* [Gr. γλυπτικός, < γλύφειν, carve.] Of or pertaining to carving or engraving, esp. on precious stones.—**glyp-ti′cian** (-tish′ạn), *n.* A cutter of precious stones; a lapidary.—**glyp′tics,** *n.* The art of carving or engraving, esp. on precious stones.

glyp-to-don (glip′tọ-don), *n.* [NL., < Gr. γλυπτός, carved, + ὀδούς (ὀδοντ-), tooth.] Any animal of the extinct genus *Glyptodon*, comprising large, armadillo-like edentate mammals with solid carapace and fluted teeth, found in the Pleistocene deposits of South America, Mexico, etc.—**glyp′to-dont** (-dont), *a.* and *n.*

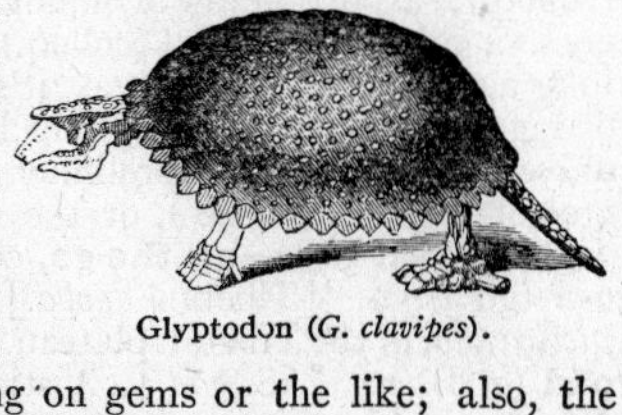
Glyptodon (*G. clavipes*).

glyp-tog-ra-phy (glip-tog′rạ-fi), *n.* [Gr. γλυπτός, carved: see *-graphy.*] The art or process of engraving on gems or the like; also, the description or study of engraved gems, etc.

glyp-to-thek (glüp-tō-tāk′), *n.* [G., < Gr. γλυπτός, carved, + θήκη, case, repository.] A gallery or museum of sculpture.

gnar, gnarr (när), *v. i.*; *gnarred, gnarring.* [Imit.] To snarl; growl.

gnarl[1] (närl), *v. i.* [Freq. of *gnar.*] To snarl. See Shakspere's "2 Henry VI.," iii. 1. 192. [Obs. or prov.]

gnarl[2] (närl), *n.* [Cf. *knarl* and *knurl.*] A knotty protuberance on a tree; a knot in wood.—**gnarled,** *a.* [Cf. *knurled.*] Full of or covered with gnarls, as a tree; knotted; twisted; rugged. Also fig. Also **gnarl′y.**

gnash (nash), *v.* [Var. of earlier *gnast*: cf. Icel. *gnastan*, a gnashing.] **I.** *tr.* To strike or grind (the teeth) together, esp. in rage or pain; also, to strike or grind the teeth together upon; bite with grinding teeth (as, "I strove . . . To rend and *gnash* my bonds in twain": Byron's "Prisoner of Chillon," vii.). **II.** *intr.* To gnash the teeth; of the teeth, to strike or grind together.

gnat (nat), *n.* [AS. *gnæt.*] In English use, any of certain small dipterous insects (mosquitoes) of the family *Culicidæ*, esp. *Culex pipiens*; in American use, any of various small dipterous insects of the families *Simuliidæ*, *Chironomidæ*, etc., as the black-fly, *Simulium venustum*, a small black-bodied blood-sucking fly of the wooded regions of the northern U. S. and Canada; a midge.—**to strain at a gnat and swallow a camel,** fig., to make difficulties over something small or easy and have no trouble with something large or difficult. See Mat. xxiii. 24.—**gnat′-catch″er,** *n.* Any of various small American insectivorous birds of the genus *Polioptila.*

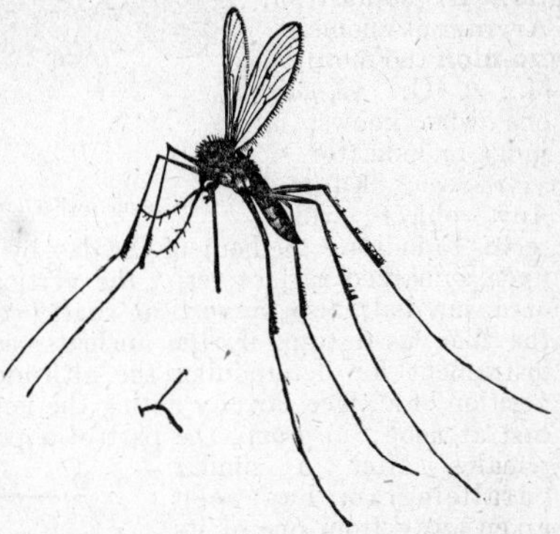
Gnat (*Culex pipiens*). (Small figure natural size.)

gnath-ic (nath′ik), *a.* [Gr. γνάθος, jaw.] Of or pertaining to the jaw.

gnath-i-on (nath′i-on), *n.* [NL., dim. < Gr. γνάθος, jaw.] In *craniol.*, the foremost median point of the lower border of the lower jaw.

-gnathous. Adjective termination from Gr. γνάθος, jaw, as in *orthognathous, prognathous.*

Blue-gray Gnatcatcher (*Polioptila cærulea*).

gnaw (nâ), *v.*; pret. *gnawed*, pp. *gnawed* or *gnawn*, ppr. *gnawing.* [AS. *gnagan* = G. *nagen* = Icel. *gnaga*, gnaw.] **I.** *tr.* To bite persistently, esp. so as to remove portions; wear away or remove by persistent biting; also, to corrode; consume. Often fig. **II.** *intr.* To bite persistently; also, to produce an effect as of persistent biting; cause corrosion. Often fig.—**gnaw′er,** *n.*—**gnaw′ing,** *n.* The act of one who or that which gnaws; also, a persistent pain suggesting gnawing, as in the bowels (as, the *gnawings* of hunger). —**gnaw′ing-ly,** *adv.*

gneiss (nīs), *n.* [G.] A metamorphic rock consisting essentially of the same mineral elements as granite, but having a more or less distinctly foliated arrangement of the constituent elements, esp. of the mica.—**gneiss′ic,** *a.* Pertaining to, of the nature of, or resembling gneiss.—**gneiss′oid,** *a.* Resembling gneiss, as in structure.—**gneiss′ose** (-ōs), *a.* Gneissic.

gnome[1] (nōm), *n.* [F., < NL. *gnomus* (used by Paracelsus); origin uncertain: cf. *sylph.*] One of a race of diminutive beings fabled to inhabit the interior of the earth and to act as the guardians of its treasures; a kobold; hence, an odd-looking, dwarfish person.

gnome² (nōm), *n.* [L., < Gr. γνώμη, judgment, opinion, maxim, < γιγνώσκειν, know.] A short, pithy expression of a general truth; an aphorism; a maxim.

gnome=owl (nōm′oul), *n.* [See *gnome*¹.] Any owl of the genus *Glaucidium*, of both hemispheres, comprising small species with imperfect facial disk, as *G. gnoma* of western North America.

Gnome-owl (*Glaucidium gnoma*).

gno-mic (nō′mik), *a.* [Gr. γνωμικός.] Dealing in, containing, or pertaining to gnomes; aphoristic; sententious. Also **gno′mi-cal.**—**gno′mi-cal-ly,** *adv.*

gnom-ist (nō′mist), *n.* A writer of gnomes.

gno-mon (nō′mon), *n.* [L., < Gr. γνώμων, one who knows, a judge, an indicator, < γιγνώσκειν, know.] Any object which serves to indicate the hour of the day by casting its shadow upon a marked surface; esp., the vertical triangular plate of a sun-dial; also, a vertical shaft, column, obelisk, or the like, used (esp. by the ancients) as an astronomical instrument for determining the altitude of the sun, the position of a place, etc., by noting the length of the shadow cast at noon; in *geom.*, the part of a parallelogram which remains after a similar parallelogram has been taken away from one of its corners.—**gno-mon-ic** (nō-mon′ik), *a.* [L. *gnomonicus*, < Gr. γνωμονικός.] Pertaining to the gnomon or the sun-dial, or to the art of dialing.—**gno-mon′ics,** *n.* The art or science of dialing.

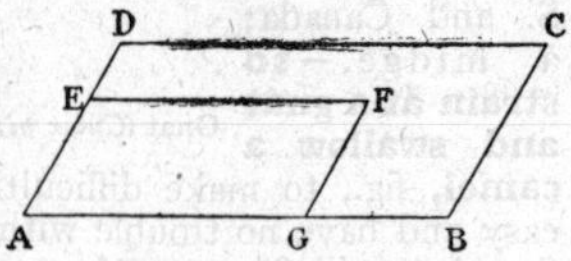

Gnomon, *EFGBCD.*

gno-sis (nō′sis), *n.* [NL., < Gr. γνῶσις, < γιγνώσκειν, know.] Knowledge; esp., a special knowledge of spiritual things; mystical knowledge.

-gnost. Noun termination from Gr. γνώστης, one who knows, as in *bibliognost, geognost.*

gnos-tic (nos′tik). [Gr. γνωστικός, < γιγνώσκειν, know.] **I.** *a.* Pertaining to knowledge; also, possessing knowledge, esp. esoteric knowledge of spiritual things; also [*cap.*], pertaining to or characteristic of the Gnostics. **II.** *n.* [*cap.*] A member of any of certain sects among the early Christians who claimed to have superior knowledge of spiritual things, and who explained the world as created by powers or agencies arising as emanations from the Godhead.—**Gnos′ti-cism** (-ti-sizm), *n.* The doctrines of the Gnostics.—**Gnos′ti-cize** (-sīz), *v.*; *-cized, -cizing.* **I.** *intr.* To adopt or maintain Gnostic views. **II.** *tr.* To explain on Gnostic principles; give a Gnostic coloring to.

-gnosy. Noun termination from Gr. γνῶσις, knowledge, as in *astrognosy, geognosy.*

gnu (nö or nū), *n.* [Kafir *nqu.*] Any of several African antelopes constituting the genus *Catoblepas* (or *Connochætes*), characterized by an ox-like head, curved horns, and a long, flowing tail; a wildebeest.

Gnu (*Catoblepas gnu*).

go (gō), *v. i.*; pret. *went*, pp. *gone*, ppr. *going.* [AS. *gān* = D. *gaan* = MLG. *gān* = OHG. *gān*, *gēn*, G. *gehen*, go: cf. *gang*, *v.*] To move or pass along; walk, run, ride, travel, etc.; proceed; take a specified direction (as, to *go* straight); continue, or be habitually, in particular circumstances (as, to *go* in rags); keep or be in motion, act, or work, as a clock or other mechanism; act or operate with sound, as a bell or a gun; pass or elapse, as time; circulate, pass current, or be accepted, as coin or notes; be known (as, to *go* by a name, or under an alias); have a general course, tendency, character, etc. (as, good as things *go*; as prices *go*); harmonize, or be compatible (as, colors that *go* well together); turn out or result (as, how did the match *go?*); prove successful, as a play; also, to move or pass away or out, or depart (opposed to *come* or *arrive*); begin, or come into, action (as, here *goes!*); be loosed or freed (as, let *go* his hand); pass, or pass away, by sale, expenditure, etc.; be given up or relinquished (as, Greek is *going*, Latin will *go* next); be lost, or come to an end (as, his eyesight is *going*); die (as, his wife *went* first); fail, or give way (as, when he stooped over, the stitches *went*); wear through, as a garment; also, to move or proceed toward or to a particular place, destination, etc. (as, to *go* to Jericho: see *Jericho*); resort, or have recourse (as, to *go* to court over a dispute); carry an action to a given point or stage (as, to *go* as high as $10 for a thing); be capable of passing, entering, or being contained (as, a book that will *go* into one's pocket; four *goes* in twelve three times); belong as to place (as, this book *goes* on the top shelf); pass, be awarded, or be transferred to a particular recipient (as, the first prize *went* to a dark horse; the property *went* to his son); be applied or appropriated (as, all the income *went* to making repairs); contribute to a result (as, the items which *go* to make up a total); conduce or tend (as, this *goes* to show that you cannot depend on appearances); reach or extend (as, his memory does not *go* back very far); pass into a particular condition (as, to *go* to ruin); become (as, to *go* mad). Also used in the present participle *going*, followed by an infinitive, to express futurity ('about, intending, or destined' to do something): as, it is *going* to rain; he is *going* to write; who is *going* to win?—**go to!** formerly, set to work! begin! (as, "*Go to*, let us make brick": Gen. xi. 3); now, an expression of disapprobation, protest, or derision (archaic: as, "*Go to, go to*, thou art a foolish fellow," Shakspere's "Twelfth Night," iv. 1. 3).—**to go about,** to change the course of a vessel by tacking or wearing.—**to go for,** to be taken or valued as; also, to attack or assail (colloq.).—**to go in for,** to make (a thing) one's particular object, principle, interest, amusement, etc.—**to go off,** to be discharged, as firearms; explode, as powder, etc.—**to go through,** to proceed to the end of; also, to undergo or experience; also, to exhaust, as a fortune; also, to subject to a search, as for valuables.—**to go under,** to be submerged or overwhelmed; succumb; be ruined.—**to go up,** to rise or ascend; advance or increase; also (colloq.), to go to ruin; become bankrupt.—**to go west,** to die. [Colloq., first in British soldiers' use.]—**to go with,** to accompany; associate with; also, to frequent the society of, as an admirer or lover (vulgar); also, to harmonize with.—**to go without,** to get along without; do without.—**go,** *v. t.* To go or proceed on, through, etc.; also, to go to the extent of, or venture as far as (colloq.); endure or tolerate (colloq.); risk or wager (colloq.: as, to *go* $5 on a thing; to *go* a person one better, fig., to go beyond or surpass him in some respect).—**go,** *n.*; pl. *goes* (gōz). The act of going (as, the come and *go* of the seasons); energy, spirit, or animation (colloq.); a proceeding, turn of affairs, or state of things (colloq.: as, this is a pretty *go!*); a turn, chance, or attempt at something (colloq.); a portion, as of liquor (colloq.); something that goes, or proves successful (colloq.); a compact, or something fully agreed upon (colloq.: as, it's a *go!*); the fashion, style, or rage (colloq.: as, a thing which is all the *go*); in English universities, the first or preliminary examination for the degree of B. A. ('little go'), or the final examination for this degree ('great go').—**on the go,** constantly going. [Colloq.]

go-a (gō′ạ), *n.* [Tibetan *dgoba.*] An antelope, *Procapra picticauda*, of the Tibetan plateau.

goad (gōd), *n.* [AS. *gād.*] A stick with a pointed end, for driving cattle, etc.; hence, anything that pricks or wounds like such a stick; a stimulus.—**goad,** *v. t.* To prick or drive with a goad; hence, to irritate; incite; urge by harassing.

goaf (gōf), *n.*; pl. *goaves* (gōvz) or *goafs.* [Origin obscure.] In *coal-mining,* a space from which coal has been worked away; also, the refuse left in old workings.

go=a-head (gō′ạ-hed′), *a.* Energetic; enterprising; progressive: as, "You would fancy that the *go-ahead* party try to restore order, and help business on" (Kingsley's "Two Years Ago," xiv.). [Colloq.]

goal (gōl), *n.* [ME. *gol,* boundary, limit: cf. AS. *gǣlan,* hinder, impede.] A boundary† or limit†; also, the terminal point in a race; a pole or other object by which this is marked; hence, that toward which effort is directed; the aim or end; also, in various games, a bound or structure toward which the players strive to advance the ball, etc.; the advancement of the ball, etc., to, through, or into the goal; the score made by accomplishing this.

Go-a (gō′ạ̈) **pow′der.** [From *Goa,* Portuguese territory in southwestern India.] A bitter powder obtained from the interspaces of the wood of a large leguminous tree, *Vouacapoua* (or *Andira*) *araroba,* of Brazil, and used in the preparation of remedies for skin-diseases: so called from its being exported from Brazil to Goa in India.

Wild Goat (*Capra ægagrus*).

goat (gōt), *n.* [AS. *gāt* = D. *geit* = G. *geiss* = Icel. *geit* = Goth. *gaits,* goat; akin to L. *hædus,* kid.] Any animal of the genus *Capra* (family *Bovidæ*), comprising various agile hollow-horned ruminants closely related to the sheep, found native in rocky and mountainous regions of the Old World, and including domesticated forms common throughout the world; also, any of various allied animals, as *Creamnos montanus* ('Rocky Mountain goat'), a ruminant of western North America; also, a lustful man; also, one who serves as a scape-goat, or suffers in the place of others (slang); also [*cap.*], in *astron.,* the zodiacal constellation or sign Capricorn.

Rocky Mountain Goat (*Oreamnos montanus*).

goat-ee (gō-tē′), *n.* [From *goat.*] A man's beard trimmed to a tuft hanging from the chin, like that of the he-goat.

goat=fish (gōt′fish), *n.* Any of certain mullets (family *Mullidæ*) with barbels at the chin, as *Pseudupeneus maculatus,* a food-fish of tropical American seas.

goat-herd (gōt′hėrd), *n.* One who tends goats.

goat-ish (gō′tish), *a.* Like, or characteristic of, a goat; lustful.—**goat′ish-ness,** *n.*

goat-ling (gōt′ling), *n.* A young goat.

goat's=beard (gōts′bērd), *n.* A cichoriaceous plant, *Tragopogon pratensis,* with a long and coarse pappus; also, a rosaceous herb, *Aruncus aruncus,* with long, slender spikes of small flowers in large panicles.

goat-skin (gōt′skin), *n.* The skin or hide of a goat, or leather made from it.

goat's=rue (gōts′rö), *n.* A European leguminous herb, *Galega officinalis,* formerly used in medicine; also, an American leguminous herb, *Cracca virginiana.*

goat-suck-er (gōt′suk″ėr), *n.* A non-passerine nocturnal bird, *Caprimulgus europæus,* of Europe, with flat head and wide mouth, formerly supposed to suck the milk of goats; also, any of the group of chiefly nocturnal or crepuscular birds to which this species belongs, sometimes regarded as including two families, the *Caprimulgidæ* ('true goatsuckers') and the *Podargidæ* (frogmouths), and sometimes only one family, the *Caprimulgidæ,* which is then divided into the subfamilies *Caprimulginæ* and *Podarginæ.* See *whippoorwill* and *frogmouth.*

Goatsucker (*Caprimulgus europæus*).

goat-y (gō′ti), *a.* Goat-like; goatish.

gob[1] (gob), *n.* [ME. *gobbe,* lump, mass: cf. *gobbet.*] A mass or lump; also, a large mouthful. [Now prov. or colloq.]

gob[2] (gob), *n.* [Cf. Gael. and Ir. *gob,* beak, mouth.] The mouth. [Prov. or slang.]

gob[3] (gob), *n.* Same as *goaf.*

gob[4] (gob), *n.* [Cf. *gob*[1].] A sailor in the naval service. [Slang.]

go-bang (gō-bang′), *n.* [Jap. *goban,* checker-board.] A game of Japanese origin, played on a checker-board by two players, each endeavoring to get five pieces in a row before his opponent does.

gobbe (gob), *n.* [Surinam name.] A creeping leguminous plant, *Voandzeia subterranea,* which ripens its edible pods and seeds underground, and is extensively cultivated in Africa and South America.

gob-bet (gob′et), *n.* [OF. F. *gobet,* mouthful, morsel, piece, akin to *gober,* swallow, gulp down; said to be from Celtic.] A portion or piece, as of raw flesh; a lump or mass. [Now chiefly prov. or archaic.]

gob-ble[1] (gob′l), *v. t.*; *-bled, -bling.* [Appar. < *gob*[1].] To swallow hastily in large pieces; gulp; also, to seize upon greedily or eagerly (colloq.).

gob-ble[2] (gob′l), *v. i.*; *-bled, -bling.* [Imit.] To utter the characteristic throaty cry of a turkey-cock, or some sound resembling it: as, "Regiments of turkeys were *gobbling* through the farm-yard" (Irving's "Sketch-Book," Sleepy Hollow).—**gob′ble**[2], *n.*

gob-bler[1] (gob′lėr), *n.* One who or that which gobbles food, etc.

gob-bler[2] (gob′lėr), *n.* A turkey-cock.

Gob-e-lin (gob′ẹ-lin or gō′bẹ-, F. gob-laṅ), *a.* Made at the French national tapestry factory, in Paris, of the Gobelins (orig. a dye-house of a family named Gobelin); resembling, or suggestive of, the tapestry made at the Gobelins.

gobe-mouche (gob-mösh), *n.* [F. *gobe-mouches,* 'swallow-flies.'] A credulous person.

go=be-tween (gō′bẹ-twēn″), *n.* One who goes to and fro as agent between persons or parties: as, "A prophet . . . is the *go-between* of gods and men" (Dunsany's "Laughter of the Gods," iii.).

go-bi-oid (gō′bi-oid). **I.** *a.* Resembling the goby (fish). **II.** *n.* A gobioid fish.

gob-let (gob′let), *n.* [OF. F. *gobelet,* dim. of OF. *gobel,* cup; origin uncertain.] A bowl-shaped drinking-vessel without a handle (archaic); now, specif., a drinking-glass with a foot and stem.

gob-lin (gob′lin), *n.* [OF. F. *gobelin*: cf. ML. *cobalus,* < Gr. κόβαλος, rogue, mischievous goblin.] A grotesque, mischievous sprite or elf.—**gob′lin-ize,** *v. t.*; *-ized, -izing.* To transform into a goblin.—**gob′lin-ry,** *n.* The acts or practices of goblins.

gob-stick (gob′stik), *n.* [See *gob*².] A stick for removing a hook from a fish's mouth or gullet.

go-by (gō′bi), *n.*; pl. *-bies* (-biz). [L. *gobius, cobius,* < Gr. κωβιός, kind of fish.] Any member of the *Gobiidæ,* a family of acanthopterygian marine and fresh-water fishes, mostly small and usually having the ventral fins united to form a suctorial disk that enables them to cling to rocks.

go=by (gō′bī), *n.* A going by; a passing, esp. without noticing or being noticed: as, to give one the *go-by.*

go=cart (gō′kärt), *n.* A small framework with casters, in which children learn to walk; also, a kind of small wheeled chair or vehicle for small children to ride in; also, a child's cart or wagon; also, a hand-cart; also, a kind of light carriage.

god (god or gôd), *n.* [AS. *god* = D. *god* = G. *gott* = Icel. *godh* = Goth. *guth,* god: cf. Skt. *hū-,* call upon, invoke.] A personal being conceived as superior to nature and mankind and entitled to worship; a deity, esp. a male deity, presiding over some portion of worldly affairs; also, an image of a deity, to which worship is addressed; an idol; hence, any person or thing made the object of adoration or supreme respect (as, "Sir Aylmer Aylmer, that almighty man, The county *God*": Tennyson's "Aylmer's Field," 14); also, one of the occupants of the gallery in a theater (colloq.); also [*cap.*], the one Supreme Being, the creator and ruler of the universe; sometimes, the Supreme Being considered with reference to a particular attribute (as, the *God* of justice; the *God* of mercy); also [*cap.* or *l. c.*], a supreme being according to some particular conception (as, the *God* of pantheism).—**god,** *v. t.*; *godded, godding.* To make into a god; deify; idolize.—**god′child,** *n.*; pl. *-children.* One for whom a person (godparent) stands sponsor at baptism.—**god′-daugh″ter,** *n.* A female godchild.

god=den (god-den′), *n.* and *interj.* See *good-den.*

god-dess (god′es), *n.* A female god or deity; hence, a woman of extraordinary or stately beauty; also, a woman whom one adores.—**god′dess-hood** (-hůd), **god′dess=ship,** *n.*

go=dev-il (gō′dev″l), *n.* A rough sled for holding one end of a log or the like while it is being dragged.

god-fa-ther (god′fä″ᴛʜėr), *n.* A man who stands sponsor for a child at baptism; hence, a male sponsor, as at confirmation; *pl.,* jocularly, jurymen who convict a person of a capital offense† (cf. Shakspere's "Merchant of Venice," iv. 1. 398).—**god′fa″ther,** *v. t.* To act as godfather to; be sponsor for.

God=fear-ing (god′fēr″ing), *a.* Having a reverential fear of God.

God=for-sak-en (god′fọr-sā″kn), *a.* Forsaken, or seemingly forsaken, by God; abandoned to evil and its penalties (as, a band of *God-forsaken* robbers); forlorn, desolate, or miserable (as, a *God-forsaken* spot or place).

god-head (god′hed), *n.* Godhood or godship; also, a god; [*cap.*] the essential being of God; the Supreme Being.

god-hood (god′hůd), *n.* Divine character; godship.

god-less (god′les), *a.* Having or acknowledging no God; having or showing no reverence for God; irreligious; ungodly.—**god′less-ly,** *adv.*—**god′less-ness,** *n.*

god-like (god′līk), *a.* Like or befitting a god, or God.—**god′-like-ness,** *n.*

god-ling (god′ling), *n.* A little god; a minor or petty deity.

god-ly (god′li), *a.*; compar. *godlier,* superl. *godliest.* Divine (archaic); also, conforming to God's laws; pious; religious; righteous.—**god′li-ly,** *adv.*—**god′li-ness,** *n.*—**god′ly,** *adv.* In a godly manner.

god-moth-er (god′muᴛʜ″ėr), *n.* A woman who stands sponsor for a child at baptism; hence, in general, a female sponsor.

go-down (gō-doun′), *n.* [Malay *gadong.*] In India and eastern Asia, a warehouse.

god-par-ent (god′pãr″ẹnt), *n.* A godfather or godmother.

go-droon (gō-drön′), *n.* [F. *godron,* OF. *goderon;* origin unknown.] A convex rounded ornament of great variety in form, repeated in a band or the like, as in a molding, on silverware, etc.; also, a convex rounded fold or plait in cloth, etc.—**go-drooned′,** *a.* Ornamented with godroons.

God's=a-cre (godz′ā′kėr), *n.* [= G. *Gottesacker,* 'God's field.'] A churchyard; a burial-ground: as, "the churchyard, or, as the Germans more devoutly say, *God's-acre*" (Longfellow's "Hyperion," ii. 9).

god-send (god′send), *n.* [For the earlier *God's send.*] A thing regarded as sent by God; an unexpected but particularly welcome acquisition or advantage; a timely piece of good fortune.

god-ship (god′ship), *n.* The rank or character of a god; with *his, your,* etc., a title for a god.

god-son (god′sun), *n.* A male godchild.

God=speed (god′spēd′), *n.* [From the expression 'God speed (you).'] A wish of success to one setting out on a journey or undertaking.

God-ward, God-wards (god′wärd, -wärdz), *adv.* Toward God.

god-wit (god′wit), *n.* [Origin uncertain.] Any bird of the genus *Limosa,* which comprises wading birds of the snipe family, characterized by a long bill curved slightly upward.

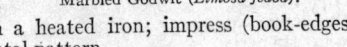

Marbled Godwit (*Limosa fedoa*).

goe-duck (gwē′duk), *n.* See *gweduc.*

go-er (gō′ėr), *n.* One who or that which goes.

goe-thite (gė′tīt), *n.* See *göthite.*

gof-fer (gof′ėr), *v. t.* [F. *gaufrer,* < *gaufre,* honeycomb, waffle: see *wafer.*] To flute (a frill, etc.), as with a heated iron; impress (book-edges, etc.) with an ornamental pattern.

gog-gle (gog′l), *v.*; *-gled, -gling.* [ME. *gogelen;* perhaps from Celtic.] **I.** *intr.* To turn or roll the eyes to one side or another; roll the eyes staringly; stare; of eyes, to roll or bulge and stare. **II.** *tr.* To roll (the eyes).—**gog′gle,** *n.* A goggling look; also, *pl.,* a kind of protective spectacles with the glasses set in short tubes that spread at the base (toward the face); hence, any large or conspicuous spectacles.—**gog′gle=eye,** *n.* A rolling or bulging staring eye.—**gog′gle=eyed,** *a.*

gog-let (gog′let), *n.* [Pg. *gorgoleta.*] In India, etc., a long-necked vessel, usually of porous earthenware, used as a water-cooler.

go-ing (gō′ing), *n.* The act of a person or thing that goes; proceeding or course (usually in *pl.*: as, "His eyes are upon the ways of man, and he seeth all his *goings,*" Job, xxxiv. 21); gait†; departure (as, "The day is placid in its *going*": Wordsworth's "White Doe of Rylstone," i.); also, the manner or kind (good, bad, rough, etc.) of walking, driving, sledding, etc., esp. from the condition of the ground.—**go′ing,** *p. a.* That goes; moving or working, as machinery; in operation; in existence; departing.—**go′ings=on′,** *n. pl.* Actions; conduct; behavior: used chiefly with depreciative force. [Colloq.]

goi-ter, goi-tre (goi′tėr), *n.* [F. *goitre,* < *goitreux,* goitrous, < L. *guttur,* throat.] In *pathol.,* a morbid enlargement of the thyroid gland, on the front and side of the neck.—**goi′tered, goi′tred,** *a.* Affected with or as with goiter.—**goi′trous,** *a.* Pertaining to, abounding in, or affected with goiter.

Gol-con-da (gol-kon′dạ), *n.* [From *Golconda,* an ancient city of India, famed for diamond-cutting.] A mine or source of wealth.

gold (gōld). [AS. *gold* = D. *goud* = G. *gold* = Icel. *gull* = Goth. *gulth,* gold; prob. akin to E. *yellow.*] **I.** *n.* Chem. sym., Au (see *aurum*); at. wt., 197.2; sp. gr., 19.3. A precious yellow metal, highly malleable and ductile, and free from liability to rust; also, coin made of it; hence, money; wealth; also, something likened to this metal in brightness, preciousness, etc. (as, "The king's a bawcock, and a heart of *gold*": Shakspere's "Henry V.," iv. 1. 44); also, a bright or lustrous yellow. **II.** *a.* Consisting or made of gold; also, like gold; of the color of gold; gilded; also, pertaining to gold.—**gold brick.** See entry below.—**gold certificate.** See under *certificate, n.*—**gold standard.** See *standard, n.*

—gold′=bear″ing, *a.* Containing or yielding gold; auriferous.—**gold′=beat″er,** *n.* One who beats gold into thin sheets.—**gold=beaters' skin,** the prepared outside membrane of the large intestine of the ox, used by gold-beaters to lay between the leaves of the metal while they beat it. —**gold′=beat″ing,** *n.*—**gold′=bee″tle,** *n.* Any of certain beetles characterized by a golden luster, as *Coptocycla aurichalcea*, a small beetle which feeds on the sweet potato and allied plants.—**gold brick.** A brick-shaped mass of gold for which a swindler receives a price but delivers a spurious substitute; also, a brick of base metal or the like sold as gold; hence, anything of supposed value which turns out to be spurious or worthless. [Colloq.]—**gold′=brick,** *v. t.* To swindle, as by means of a gold brick. [Colloq.]—**gold′=bug,** *n.* A gold-beetle; also, an advocate of the single gold standard in finance (slang).—**gold′crest,** *n.* A kinglet with a yellow crest, esp. *Regulus cristatus*, a small European bird.—**gold′=cure,** *n.* A treatment for the drink habit in which the chief remedy employed is said to be chloride of gold.—**gold′=dig″ger,** *n.* One who digs or seeks for gold in a gold-field; hence (colloq.), one who seeks to get money or profit by calculated, often unscrupulous, ways; esp., a woman who uses her feminine arts or seductions to extract profit from men.—**gold′=dig″ging,** *n.* The action or work of digging for gold; also, *pl.*, a region where digging or seeking for gold, esp. by placer mining, is carried on.—**gold′=dust,** *n.* Gold in fine particles.

Goldcrest (*Regulus cristatus*).

gold-en (gōl′dn), *a.* Made or consisting of gold (as, "Every door is barr'd with gold, and opens but to *golden* keys": Tennyson's "Locksley Hall," 100); also, containing or yielding gold; also, of the color of gold; yellow; bright or shining, like gold; also, resembling gold in value; most excellent; exceedingly favorable, as an opportunity; of great utility or importance, as a rule or precept; flourishing or joyous, as a time or period. —**golden age,** the finest or most flourishing period. See *ages in mythology*, under *age*, *n.*—**golden calf,** the golden idol set up by Aaron (see Ex. xxxii.), or either of the two similar idols set up by Jeroboam (see 1 Kings, xii. 28, 29); hence, wealth as an object of undue regard.—**golden eagle,** a large eagle, *Aquila chrysaëtus*, of both eastern and western hemispheres: so called because of the ruddy-brown feathers on the back of the neck.—**golden fleece,** in *Gr. myth.*, the fleece of gold taken from the ram on which Phrixus was carried to Colchis, recovered from King Æetes by the Argonautic expedition under Jason. Also used in the title of the *Order of the Golden Fleece*, an order of knighthood for royalty and the highest nobility, founded by Philip the Good of Burgundy in 1429, and subsequently maintained separately in Austria and Spain.—**golden mean,** the happy medium between extremes.—**golden number,** the number of any year in the Metonic cycle of 19 years (see *Metonic*), so called because important in calculating the date of Easter: found for any year of the Christian era by adding 1 to the number of the year and dividing by 19, when the remainder, or 19 if there is no remainder, will be the golden number.—**golden robin,** the Baltimore oriole (see *oriole*).—**golden rose,** a rose made of pure gold, blessed by the Pope on the fourth Sunday of Lent, and occasionally sent as a mark of special honor to some Catholic sovereign or other notable person, or to some church, city, etc.—**golden rule,** the rule, "Whatsoever ye would that men should do to you, do ye even so to them" (Mat. vii. 12). —**gold′en,** *v. t.* or *i.* To make or become golden.—**gold′en-eye,** *n.* Any duck of the genus *Clangula*; a garrot; esp., *C. clangula*, found throughout the northern hemisphere.—**gold′en-ly,** *adv.*—**gold′en-ness,** *n.*—**gold′en-rod,** *n.* Any plant of the asteraceous genus *Solidago*, most species of which bear numerous small yellow flowers, often arranged in panicles; also, any of various related asteraceous plants, as *Brachychæta sphacelata* ('false goldenrod'). —**gold′en-seal,** *n.* A ranunculaceous herb, *Hydrastis canadensis*, with a thick yellow rootstock.

Golden Eagle.

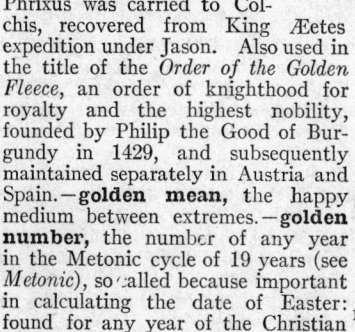

Badge of the Order of the Golden Fleece.

Goldeneye. — Rocky Mountain Garrot (*Clangula islandica*).

Goldenrod (*Solidago nemoralis*).

gold=field (gōld′fēld), *n.* A district in which gold is mined.

gold=filled (gōld′fild′), *a.* Containing a filling of cheaper metal within a layer of gold.

gold-finch (gōld′finch), *n.* A European fringilline song-bird, *Carduelis elegans*, having wings marked with yellow; also, any of certain small American finches, esp. *Chrysomitris* (or *Spinus*) *tristis*, the male of which has yellow body-plumage in summer.

gold-fin-ny (gōld′fin″i), *n.*; pl. *-finnies* (-fin″iz). The cunner, *Crenilabrus melops*, which is beautifully colored; also, any of various related fishes.

gold-fish (gōld′fish), *n.* A small fish, *Carassius auratus*, of the carp family, and orig. native in China, prized for aquariums, etc., because of its golden coloring (produced by artificial selection); also, a red marine fish, *Hypsypops rubicundus*, of California; the garibaldi. See cut below.

gold=foil (gōld′foil′), *n.* Gold beaten into a thin sheet.

American Goldfinch (*Chrysomitris tristis*).

gold-i-locks (gōl′di-loks), *n.* A person with golden hair; also, a species of buttercup, *Ranunculus auricomus*; also, any of several cultivated plants of the genus *Chrysocoma*, with heads of yellow flowers.

gold=leaf (gōld′lēf), *n.* Gold beaten into a very thin sheet: used for gilding, etc.

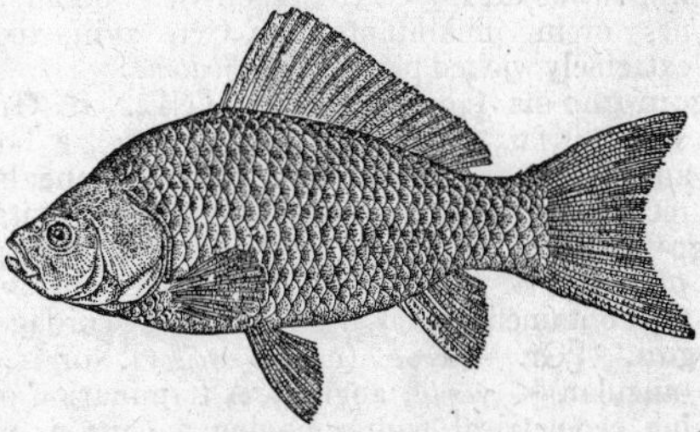

Goldfish (*Carassius auratus*).

gold-less (gōld′les), *a.* Without gold: as, "the *goldless* age, where gold disturbs no dreams" (Byron's "Island," i. 10).

gold=mine (gōld′mīn), *n.* A mine yielding gold; fig., a source of great wealth.

gold=of=pleas-ure (gōld′ọv-plezh′ụ̈r), *n.* A brassicaceous herb, *Camelina sativa*, with small yellowish flowers.

gold-smith (gōld′smith), *n.* [AS. *goldsmith.*] One who makes articles of gold (formerly often acting also as a banker: as, "He gave me a bill upon his *goldsmith*, in London, of two thousand pounds," Steele, in "Guardian," 2).—**gold′smith=bee″tle,** *n.* A large yellowish scarabæid beetle, *Cotalpa lanigera.*

gold=stick (gōld′stik), *n.* In England, a gilded rod carried on state occasions by certain members of the royal household; also, the bearer of it.

gold-stone (gōld′stōn), *n.* Aventurine (glass).

gold-thread (gōld′thred), *n.* A white-flowered ranunculaceous herb, *Coptis trifolia*, with a slender yellow root; also, the root itself, used in medicine.

gold-y-locks (gōl′di-loks), *n.* See *goldilocks.*

go-lem (gō′lem), *n.* [Heb., embryo, something unformed or incomplete.] In Jewish legend, a figure constructed to represent a human being, and endowed with life, by human agency; hence, fig., an automaton; a blockhead.

golf (golf, also gof), *n.* [Origin uncertain.] An outdoor game, which was popular in Scotland as early as the middle of the 15th century, in which a small resilient ball is driven with special clubs into a series of holes distributed over a course, or links, having natural or artificial obstacles, or hazards, the object being to get the ball into each hole in as few strokes as possible. Cf. *match-play* and *medal-play.*—**golf,** *v. i.* To play golf.—**golf′=club,** *n.* Any of the various implements for striking the ball in golf; also, a club of golf-players.—**golf′er,** *n.*—**golf′=links,** *n. pl.* The ground or course over which golf is played: sometimes construed as *sing.*

Gol-go-tha (gol′gọ-thạ̈), *n.* [From *Golgotha*, repr. the Aramaic name for Calvary (Aram. *gogolthā*, Heb. *gulgōleth*, skull): see John, xix. 17.] A place of interment; a graveyard; a charnel.

go-li-ard (gō′li-ärd), *n.* [OF. *goliard*, appar. lit. 'glutton,' < L. *gula*, throat, palate, gluttony.] One of a class of wandering students in Germany, France, and England, chiefly in the 12th and 13th centuries, noted for their rioting and intemperance, and as the authors of satirical Latin verse.—**go-li-ar′dic** (-är′dik), *a.*

Go-li-ath (gọ-lī′ạth), *n.* [From the Philistine champion: see 1 Sam. xvii. 4.] A giant; also [*l. c.*], any of the large lamellicorn African beetles constituting the genus *Goliathus*, esp. *G. giganteus* which sometimes grows to the length of four inches; any of various large beetles of related genera.

gol-ly (gol′i), *n.* A minced form of *God*: often used interjectionally, as a mild oath: as, "My folks to hum air full ez good ez his'n be, by *golly!*" (Lowell's "Biglow Papers," i. 2. 25).

go-losh (gọ-losh′), *n.* Same as *galosh.*

go-lup-tious (gọ-lup′shus), *a.* [Made word.] Delicious; delightful. [Slang.]

gom-been (gom-bēn′), *n.* [Ir. *gaimbín.*] Usury. [Ir.]

gom-er-el (gom′ẹ-rel), *n.* [Also *gomeril*; origin obscure.] A fool, simpleton, or blockhead: as, "our auld daft laird here and his *gomerils* o' sons" (Scott's "Rob Roy," xiv.). [Sc. and prov. Eng.]

Go-mor-rah, Go-mor-rha (gọ-mor′ạ̈), *n.* An ancient city which was destroyed (together with Sodom) for the wickedness of its inhabitants (see Gen. xviii.–xix.); hence, any extremely wicked place. See *Sodom.*

gom-pho-sis (gom-fō′sis), *n.* [NL., < Gr. γόμφωσις, < γομφοῦν, fasten with bolts, < γόμφος, a bolt.] In *anat.*, an immovable articulation in which one bone or part is received in a cavity in another, as a tooth in its socket.

go-mu-ti (gọ-mö′ti), *n.* [Malay.] A sago-palm, *Saguerus pinnatus*, of the East Indies; also, a black, horsehair-like fiber obtained from it, used for making cordage, etc.

-gon. [Gr. -γωνος (neut. -γωνον), or -γώνιος, -angled, -angular, < γωνία, angle.] A termination of nouns denoting geometrical figures having a certain number or kind of angles, as in *hexagon, orthogon, pentagon, polygon.*

gon-do-la (gon′dọ-lạ̈), *n.* [It. *gondola*, dim. of *gonda*, boat; origin uncertain.] A long, narrow boat with a high peak at each end and often a small cabin near the middle, used on the Venetian canals and usually propelled at the stern by a single oar or pole; also, a kind of lighter (U. S.); also, a railway freight-car with low sides and no top (U. S.); also, a car of a dirigible balloon.—**gon-do-lier′** (-lēr′), *n.* [It. *gondoliere.*] A man who rows or poles a gondola.

Venetian Gondola.

gone (gôn). Past participle of *go.*—**gone,** *p. a.* That has departed or passed away (as, *gone* ages); lost, undone, or hopeless (as, a *gone* case); much advanced or deeply involved (chiefly in 'far gone'); weak and faint (as, a *gone* feeling); infatuated or enamoured (usually followed by *on* or *upon*: colloq.).—**gone′ness,** *n.* Gone state; a sinking sensation; faintness.—**gon-er** (gôn′ėr), *n.* A person or thing that is dead, lost, or past recovery: as, "Tom, we're *goners!* Can you pray?" (Mark Twain's "Tom Sawyer," ix.). [Colloq.]

gon-fa-lon (gon′fạ-lon), *n.* [It. *gonfalone* = F. *gonfalon, gonfanon*, OF. *gonfanon, gunfanun*, < OHG. *gundfano*, 'war banner': cf. *fanon.*] A banner suspended from a cross-bar, and often having several streamers or tails: the form of standard used esp. by the medieval Italian republics.—**gon″fa-lo-nier′** (-lọ-nēr′), *n.* [It. *gonfaloniere.*] The bearer of a gonfalon; a standard-bearer; esp., the chief magistrate or some other official in several medieval Italian republics.

gon-fa-non (gon′fạ-non), *n.* [OF.: see *gonfalon.*] Same as *gonfalon.* [Obs. or archaic.]

gong (gong), *n.* [Malay.] A shallow, bowl-shaped metallic instrument which produces a sonorous sound when struck with a stick having a padded or covered head; also, a saucer-shaped bell sounded by a hammer.

go-nid-i-um (gọ-nid′i-um), *n.*; pl. *-ia* (-i-ạ̈). [NL., dim. < Gr. γόνος, offspring, seed, < γεν-, bear, produce: see *genius.*] In *bot.*, among thallophytes, a reproductive body produced asexually; also, one of the algal cells inclosed in the thallus of a lichen.—**go-nid′i-al,** *a.*

go-ni-om-e-ter (gō-ni-om′e-tėr), *n.* [Gr. γωνία, angle: see *-meter.*] An instrument for measuring solid angles, as of crystals; also, a radiogoniometer.—**go-ni-om′e-try,** *n.* [See *-metry.*] The measurement of angles.—**go″ni-o-met′ric, go″ni-o-met′ri-cal** (-ọ-met′rik, -ri-kạl), *a.*

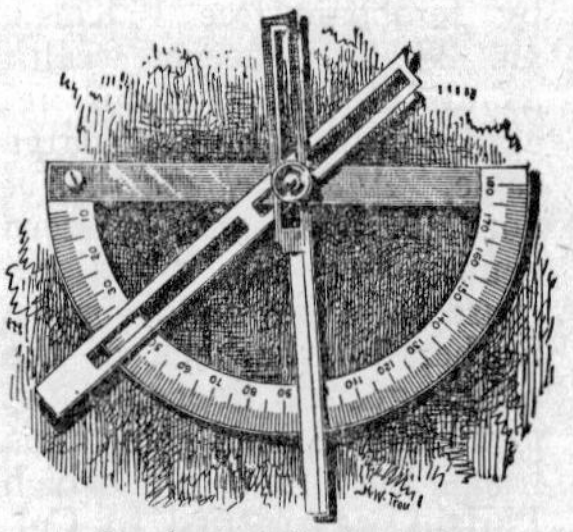
One form of Goniometer.

go-ni-on (gō′ni-on), *n.*; pl. *gonia* (-ạ̈). [NL., < Gr. γωνία, angle.] In *craniol.*, that point on either side of the lower jaw at the vertex of the angle made by the inferior and posterior borders.

go-ni-o-sta-tion (gō′ni-ọ-stā″shọn), *n.* [Gr. γωνία, angle, + E. *station.*] A place where observations are made with a radiogoniometer.

gon-o-coc-cus (gon-ọ-kok′us), *n.*; pl. *-cocci* (-kok′sī). [NL., < Gr. γόνος, offspring, seed, + NL. *coccus*: see *coccus.*] The micro-organism *Micrococcus gonorrhœæ*, which causes gonorrhea.

gon-of, gon-oph (gon′ọf), *n.* [Heb. *gannābh*, thief.] A thief; a pickpocket: as, "He's as obstinate a young *gonoph* as I know" (Dickens's "Bleak House," xix.). [Slang.]

gon-o-phore (gon′ọ-fōr), *n.* [Gr. γόνος, offspring, seed: see *-phore.*] In *bot.*, a prolongation of the axis of a flower above the perianth, bearing the stamens and pistil; in *zoöl.*, one of the generative buds or receptacles of the reproductive elements in hydrozoans.

gon-or-rhe-a, gon-or-rhœ-a (gon-o-rē'ä), *n.* [LL. *gonorrhœa*, < Gr. γονόρροια, < γόνος, offspring, seed, + ῥοία, a flow, < ῥεῖν, flow.] In *pathol.*, a contagious, purulent inflammation of the urethra or the vagina, due to the gonococcus.—**gon-or-rhe'al, gon-or-rhœ'al,** *a.*

-gony. [Gr. -γονία, < γεν-, bear, produce: cf. *-geny.*] A noun termination meaning 'production,' 'genesis,' 'origination,' as in *cosmogony, theogony.*

goo (gö), *n.* [Origin unknown.] Sticky matter. [Slang.]

goo-ber (gö'bėr), *n.* [Angola *nguba.*] The peanut. [Southern U. S.]

good (gůd), *a.*; compar. *better*, superl. *best.* [AS. *gōd* = D. *goed* = G. *gut* = Icel. *gōdhr* = Goth. *gōths*, good; perhaps orig. meaning 'fitting, suitable,' and akin to E. *gather.*] In general, of commendable quality or character; satisfactory, fair, excellent, or fine (with varying force, increased by emphatic utterance or by context: as, a *good* horse, pen, or farm; *good* wine, music, or drawing; a really *good* book, game, or performance); genuine, as money, jewels, etc.; sound or valid, as judgment, reasons, excuses, claims, etc.; reliable, safe, or sure, as a trader or debtor, securities, promises, etc.; often, morally excellent, righteous, or virtuous, as persons, conduct, motives, intentions, etc.; well-behaved, as a child; right or proper (as, do whatever seems *good* to you in the matter); kind, beneficent, or friendly (as, to be *good* to the poor; to say a *good* word for one; a *good* turn; mutual *good* feeling); honorable or worthy (much used, esp. formerly, as an epithet of respect: as, *good* sir; my *good* friend; Mr. Hood and his *good* lady: cf. *goodman*); of fair repute, social standing, etc. (as, a *good* name; *good* birth or family); holy (as, *Good* Friday: see phrase below); also, satisfactory for the wishes or purposes (cf. *good day*, below); favorable, as news, weather, conditions, etc.; advantageous, beneficial, or useful (as, a *good* idea or plan; drugs *good* for fever: cf. *good-for-nothing*); wholesome, as food; sound or unimpaired, as the health, condition, etc.; cheerful or courageous, as the spirits, heart, etc.; agreeable or pleasant (as, to have a *good* time); genial or jovial (as, a *good* fellow); competent or skilful (as, a *good* manager; a *good* doctor, draftsman, or driver); skilful or clever (*at*: as, to be *good* at arithmetic); to be relied on (*for*: as, his credit is *good* for the sum specified); also, satisfactory in quantity or degree; adequate, sufficient, or ample (as, to give *good* measure or weight; a *good* supply of provisions); full (as, a *good* day's journey); fairly great (as, a *good* deal; a *good* while).—**Good Book,** the Bible.—**good cheer,** cheerful spirits, or courage (as, to be of *good cheer*); also, feasting and merrymaking (as, to make *good cheer*); good fare or food, as for feasting (as, to be fond of *good cheer*).—**good day, evening, morning,** etc., short for *I wish you* (or *I bid you*, or *God give you*) *a good day, evening*, etc.: used in salutation at the time of day appropriate, upon meeting or parting.—**Good Friday,** the Friday before Easter, a holy day of the Christian church, observed as the anniversary of Christ's crucifixion.—**good graces.** See under *grace, n.*—**good morrow,** good morning: a salutation used at meeting in the morning. [Archaic.]—**good night,** a salutation used at night upon parting or going to sleep.—**good Samaritan.** See *Samaritan, n.*—**Good Shepherd,** a title given to Jesus Christ (see John, x. 11).—**good speed,** good fortune, or success (as, to wish a person *good speed*); also, a good rate of progress or motion.—**to make good.** See under *make*², *v. t.* and *i.*—**good,** *n.* That which is good; excellence or merit (as, to discern the *good* in a book); righteousness (as, to be a power for *good* in the world); kindness or good deeds (as, to do *good*); well-being, advantage, or benefit (as, to work for the common *good*); profit, worth, use, or service (as, that knife is of no *good*, or, elliptically, that knife is no *good*; what is the *good* of that? what *good* will that do?); also, a good, commendable, excellent, or desirable thing (as, "And cherished peaceful days For their own sakes, as mortal life's chief *good*": Wordsworth's "Excursion," iii. 365); *pl.*, possessions, esp. movable effects or personal chattels (as, household *goods*); also, articles of trade, wares, or merchandise (as, to sell *goods*: cf. *dry-goods*); also, cloth or textile material (U. S., and often construed as *sing.*: as, will these *goods*, or this *goods*, wash well?).—**for good (and all),** finally and permanently; forever: as, to leave a place *for good*, or *for good and all.*—**to the good,** to or on the side of profit or advantage, as an excess in one's favor: as, to come out $5 *to the good* in a transaction; to have two points *to the good* in a game.—**good,** *interj.* That is good: an elliptical expression of commendation or satisfaction.—**good,** *adv.* Well. [Now colloq. or vulgar.]

good=by, good=bye (gůd-bī'). [Contr. of *God be with you.*] **I.** *interj.* Farewell: a conventional expression used at parting. **II.** *n.*; pl. *-bys, -byes* (-bīz'). A farewell.

good=den (gůd-den'), *n.* and *interj.* Contraction of *good even*, 'good evening,' as used in salutation. [Obs. or prov.]

good=fel-low-ship (gůd'fel'ō-ship), *n.* Agreeable or jovial companionship; conviviality; also, friendly fellowship.

good=for=noth-ing (gůd'for-nuth''ing). **I.** *a.* Worthless. **II.** *n.* A worthless person.—**good'=for=noth''ing-ness,** *n.*

good=hu-mored (gůd'hū'mord), *a.* Having or showing good humor, or a pleasant or amiable temper or mood.—**good'=hu'mored-ly,** *adv.*—**good'=hu'mored-ness,** *n.*

good-ish (gůd'ish), *a.* Rather good; fairly good: as, a *goodish* horse; a *goodish* distance.

good=look-ing (gůd'lůk'ing), *a.* Of good appearance; comely; handsome.

good-ly (gůd'li), *a.*; compar. *goodlier*, superl. *goodliest.* [AS. *gōdlīc.*] Of good or fine appearance (as, "A *goodly* apple rotten at the heart: O, what a *goodly* outside falsehood hath!" Shakspere's "Merchant of Venice," i. 3. 102); also, of a good quality or kind (as, a *goodly* gift; a *goodly* place or time); excellent or fine; also, of good size or ample amount (as, a *goodly* stature; a *goodly* sum); rather large; considerable. [Now chiefly literary.]—**good'li-ness,** *n.*

good-man (gůd'man or gůd'man'), *n.*; pl. *-men.* The master of a household; also, a husband; also, a title of respect applied esp. to a farmer or yeoman. [Archaic or prov.]

good=na-tured (gůd'nā'tūrd), *a.* Having or showing good nature, or a pleasant or complaisant disposition or mood; good-humored.—**good'=na'tured-ly,** *adv.*—**good'=na'tured-ness,** *n.*

good-ness (gůd'nes), *n.* [AS. *gōdnes.*] The quality or state of being good; excellence; virtue; kindness; beneficence. Also used, now more or less vaguely but orig. with reference to the goodness of God, or to God, in various exclamatory or emphatic expressions: as, for *goodness'* sake! *goodness* gracious! my *goodness!* *goodness* knows! thank *goodness!*

goods (gůdz), *n. pl.* See *good, n.*

good=tem-pered (gůd'tem'pėrd), *a.* Having or showing a good temper; amiable.—**good'=tem'pered-ly,** *adv.*

good-wife (gůd'wīf'), *n.*; pl. *-wives* (-wīvz'). The mistress of a household; also, a title of respect for a woman. [Archaic or prov.]

good=will (gůd'wil'), *n.* Friendly disposition; benevolence; favor; cheerful acquiescence; readiness or zeal; in business, the advantage due to custom or patronage, as distinct from the value of stock, property, etc.

good-y¹ (gůd'i). [From *good, a.*] **I.** *a.* Weakly or sentimentally good or pious; ostentatiously affecting goodness; goody-goody. **II.** *n.*; pl. *-ies* (-iz). A goody person; also, something considered especially good to eat, as a sweetmeat or bonbon (usually in *pl.*).

good-y² (gůd'i), *n.*; pl. *-ies* (-iz). [From *goodwife.*] A term of civility formerly applied to a woman in humble life (as, "Old *Goody* Blake was old and poor": Wordsworth's "Goody Blake and Harry Gill," 21); hence, any such woman; at Harvard University, a woman who takes care of students' rooms.

good-y=good-y (gůd'i-gůd'i). **I.** *a.* Same as *goody*¹, *a.*: as, "*goody-goody* expressions" (G. B. Shaw's "Man and Superman," i.). **II.** *n.* A goody person.—**good'y=good'i-ness,** *n.*

goo-ey (gö'i), *a.* Like goo; sticky; viscid. [Slang.]

goo-ral (gö'ral), *n.* Same as *goral.*

Goor-kha (gör'kä), *n.* See *Gurkha.*

goo-roo (gö'rö), *n.* See *guru.*

goo-san-der (gö-san'dėr), *n.* [Origin uncertain.] Either of the two common mergansers, *Mergus americanus* and *M. merganser.*

goose (gös), *n.*; pl. *geese* (gēs). [AS. *gōs* (pl. *gēs*) = D. and G. *gans* = Icel. *gās*, goose; akin to L. *anser*, Gr. *χήν*, Skt. *hansa*, goose.] Any of numerous wild or domesticated web-footed birds of the family *Anatidæ*, esp. of the genus *Anser* and allied genera, mostly larger and with a longer neck than the ducks; the female of this bird, as distinguished from the male (or *gander*); the flesh of the goose; also, a silly or foolish person; a simpleton; also, a tailors' smoothing-iron with a curved handle (pl. *gooses*); also, a game played with counters†.

Chinese Goose (*Cygnopsis cygnoides*).

goose-ber-ry (gös′ber″i or göz′-), *n.*; pl. *-berries* (-iz). [Appar. < *goose* + *berry*.] The small, edible, acid, globular fruit or berry of certain wild or cultivated shrubs of the grossulariaceous genus *Ribes* (which includes also the currant), esp. *R. grossularia*; the shrub itself; also, any of various similar fruits or shrubs; also, a chaperon or third person accompanying an unmarried pair.
goose=egg (gös′eg), *n.* The egg of a goose; also, in athletic and other contests, a zero, indicating a miss or a failure to score.
goose=fish (gös′fish), *n.* The angler, *Lophius piscatorius.* [U. S.]
goose=flesh (gös′flesh), *n.* A rough condition of the skin, resembling that of a plucked goose, induced by cold or fear.
goose-foot (gös′fůt), *n.*; pl. *-foots.* Any plant of the genus *Chenopodium*, containing many widely distributed herbs with toothed or entire, often mealy leaves and clusters of minute green flowers; hence, any chenopodiaceous plant.
goose=girl (gös′gėrl), *n.* A girl in charge of geese.
goose=grease (gös′grēs), *n.* The melted fat of the goose: used in domestic medicine as an ointment.
goose-herd (gös′hėrd), *n.* One who takes care of geese.
goose-neck (gös′nek), *n.* Something curved like the neck of a goose, as an iron hook for attaching a boom to a mast, or a kind of movable stand for an incandescent electric lamp.

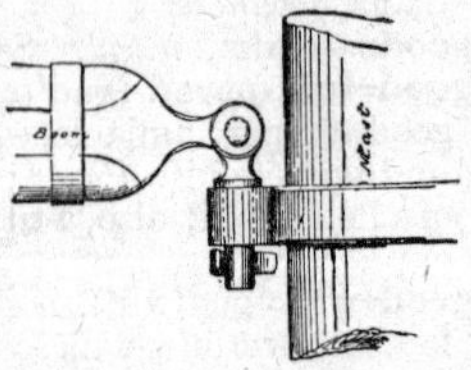

Gooseneck of a Spanker-boom.

goose=quill (gös′kwil), *n.* One of the large feathers or quills of a goose; hence, a pen made from such a feather (as, "Many wearing rapiers are afraid of *goose-quills*": Shakspere's "Hamlet," ii. 2. 359).
goose=skin (gös′skin), *n.* Same as *goose-flesh.*
goose=step (gös′step), *n.* A military exercise in which the body is balanced on one foot (without advancing) while the other foot is swung forward and back; also, a marching step of the German infantry, in which the legs are swung high with straight, stiff knees.
go-pher (gō′fėr), *n.* [F. *gaufre*, honeycomb (with allusion to the burrow).] Any of various burrowing rodents of the genera *Geomys*, *Thomomys*, etc. (family *Geomyidæ*), of western and southern North America, with large cheek-pouches (also called *pocket-gopher* and *pouched rat*); also, any of various ground-squirrels of western North America, as *Citellus* (or *Spermophilus*) *tridecemlineatus* (the destructive rodent from which Minnesota is named the 'Gopher State'), and *Citellus* (or *Spermophilus*) *richardsoni* (a destructive rodent, the so-called flickertail, from which North Dakota is called the 'Flickertail State'); also, an edible, burrowing land-tortoise, *Xerobates* (or *Testudo*) *polyphemus*, of the southern U. S.; also, a burrowing snake, *Compsosoma corais*, of the southern U. S.

Pocket-gopher (*Thomomys talpoides*).

go-pher=wood (gō′fėr-wůd), *n.* [Heb. *gōpher.*] An unidentified wood used in the construction of Noah's ark (see Gen. vi. 14); also, the yellow-wood, *Cladrastis lutea*, of the U. S.
go-pu-ra (gō′pö-rą̈), *n.* [Skt. *gōpura*, city gate.] In southern India, a temple gateway surmounted by a massive pyramidal tower arranged in stories.

Gopura of the Great Temple, Srirangam, India.

go-ral (gō′rąl), *n.* [E. Ind.] A goat-like antelope, *Cemas goral*, of central Asia.

Goral.

gor-bel-ly (gôr′bel″i), *n.*; pl. *-bellies* (-iz). [Cf. *gore*[1].] A prominent belly, or a person having one. [Obs. or prov.]—**gor′bel″lied,** *a.*
gor-cock (gôr′kok), *n.* [Origin of *gor-* obscure.] The moor-cock, or male red grouse.
gor-crow (gôr′krō), *n.* [See *gore*[1].] The carrion-crow, *Corvus corone.*
Gor-di-an (gôr′di-ạn), *a.* Pertaining to Gordius, an ancient king of Phrygia, who tied a knot (the 'Gordian knot') which was to be undone only by one who should rule Asia, and which was summarily cut by Alexander the Great; hence, resembling this knot; intricate.
gore[1] (gōr), *n.* [AS. *gor*, dung, dirt.] Dirt, slime, or mire (now prov. Eng.); also, blood, esp. when clotted.
gore[2] (gōr), *n.* [AS. *gāra*, point of land, = D. *geer* = G. *gehre* = Icel. *geiri*, gore; akin to AS. *gār*, spear.] A triangular piece or tapering strip of land, as between fields; also, a triangular piece of cloth, etc., inserted in a garment, a sail, etc., to give greater width or secure the desired shape or adjustment; one of the breadths (mostly more or less tapering, or shaped) of a woman's skirt; hence, a triangular or tapering piece of anything.—**gore**[2], *v. t.*; *gored, goring.* To shape like a gore; also, to make or furnish with a gore or gores.
gore[3] (gōr), *v. t.*; *gored, goring.* [ME. *goren*, *gorren*, pierce, stab: cf. AS. *gār*, spear.] To stab or pierce deeply†; specif., of an animal, to pierce with the horns or tusks.
gored (gōrd), *a.* Having a gore or gores: as, a five-*gored* skirt.
gorge (gôrj), *n.* [OF. F. *gorge*, throat; origin uncertain.] The throat (archaic); the crop of a hawk (archaic); the maw (archaic); also, that which is swallowed; the contents of the stomach (also fig.: as, one's *gorge* rises in disgust or resentment); hence, a choking mass, as of ice in a river; also, a gorging or gluttonous meal; also, a narrow passage between steep, rocky walls, esp. one through which a stream runs; in *fort.*, the rear entrance or part of a bastion or outwork; in *mech.*, the groove in the circumference of a pulley.—**gorge,** *v.*; *gorged, gorging.* [OF. F. *gorger.*] **I.** *tr.* To fill the gorge of; stuff with food; satiate; glut; hence, to choke up; also, to swallow, esp. greedily (as, "Though they see the hook and the string . . . they *gorge* the bait never-

theless": Thackeray's "Vanity Fair," xiv.). **II.** *intr.* To fill the gorge; eat greedily: as, "They . . . like hounds of a base breed, *Gorge* from a stranger's hand, and rend their master" (Shelley's "Hellas," 469).—**gorged,** *a.* Having a gorge or throat; in *her.*, having the neck encircled with a collar, coronet, or the like.

gor-geous (gôr′jus), *a.* [OF. *gorgias*; origin uncertain.] Splendid in dress, appearance, or coloring; showily rich or ornate; sumptuous; magnificent.—**gor′geous-ly,** *adv.* —**gor′geous-ness,** *n.*

gor-ger (gôr′jėr), *n.* One who or that which gorges, or eats to repletion; a glutton.

gor-ger-in (gôr′jẹ-rin), *n.* [F., < *gorge*, throat.] In *arch.*, the neck-like portion of a capital of a column, or a feature forming the junction between a shaft and its capital.

gor-get (gôr′jet), *n.* [OF. *gorgete*, dim. of *gorge*, throat.] A piece of armor for the throat (as, "Unfix the *gorget's* iron clasp, And give him room for life to gasp!" Scott's "Lay of the Last Minstrel," v. 22); hence, a collar; also, a kind of covering for the neck and breast, formerly worn by women; also, a necklace; also, a crescent-shaped badge suspended from the neck, formerly worn by military officers; also, a patch on the throat of a bird or other animal, distinguished by its color or otherwise (as, "the golden-winged woodpecker, with . . . his broad black *gorget*": Irving's "Sketch-Book," Sleepy Hollow); also, a grooved surgical instrument used in operations for stone, etc.

1, Gorget (*a*) attached to the brigandine; 15th century. 2, Gorget (*a*) worn over mail; early 15th century.

gor-gi-o (gôr′ji-ō). **I.** *n.*; pl. *os* (-ōz). The Romany name for any one not of the Gipsy race. See Borrow's "Romany Rye," x. **II.** *a.* Of or pertaining to the gorgios: as, "Out of the dark of the *gorgio* camp . . . Gipsy, come away!" (Kipling's "Gipsy Trail").

Gor-gon (gôr′gọn), *n.* [L. *Gorgo(n-)*, < Gr. Γοργώ, < γοργός, grim, terrible.] Any of three sisters, Stheno, Euryale, and Medusa, of Greek legend, whose heads were covered with snakes instead of hair, and whose terrific aspect turned the beholder to stone; esp., Medusa, the only mortal one of the three, who was slain by Perseus, and whose head was fixed on the shield of Athene; [*l. c.*] a gorgoneion; also, a terrible or repulsive woman.—**gor-go-nei′on** (-gọ-nī′on), *n.*; pl. *-neia* (-nī′ạ̈). [NL., < Gr. Γοργόνειον.] A representation of the head of a Gorgon, esp. that of Medusa.—**gor-go′ni-an** (-gō′ni-ạn), *a.* Of, pertaining to, or characteristic of a Gorgon, esp. Medusa; Gorgon-like; terrible; petrifying; also, of a shield, bearing a gorgoneion.—**gor′gon-ize,** *v. t.*; *-ized, -izing.* To petrify as by the look of a Gorgon; also, to stare at with a Gorgon's look (as, "He . . . *Gorgonised* me from head to foot With a stony British stare": Tennyson's "Maud," i. 13. 2).

Gor-gon-zo-la (gôr-gọn-zō′lạ̈) **cheese.** [From *Gorgonzola*, town in northern Italy.] A strongly flavored, hard-pressed variety of milk cheese veined with mold.

gor-hen (gôr′hen), *n.* [See *gorcock*.] The female red grouse.

go-ril-la (gọ-ril′ạ̈), *n.* [NL., < Gr. γορίλλα; of African origin.] A large, fierce, powerful anthropoid ape, *Gorilla gorilla* (or *savagei*), of western equatorial Africa; also, as applied contemptuously to persons, an ugly brute; a brutal fellow.

Gorilla.

gor-i-ly (gōr′i-li), *adv.* In a gory manner.—**gor′i-ness,** *n.*

gor-ing (gōr′ing), *n.* A making or furnishing with a gore or gores; also, the gore or gores. See *gore*[2].

gor-mand (gôr′mạnd), *n.* [= *gourmand.*] A glutton†; also, a gourmand.—**gor′man-dize** (-mạn-dīz), *n.* [=*gourmandise.*] Gluttony†; also, luxury in eating (obs. or rare). —**gor′man-dize,** *v. i.* or *t.*; *-dized, -dizing.* To eat like a glutton; feed or devour voraciously.—**gor′man-diz-er** (-dī-zėr), *n.*

gorse (gôrs), *n.* [AS. *gorst.*] Furze.—**gors′y,** *a.* Abounding in or overgrown with gorse.

gor-y (gōr′i), *a.*; compar. *gorier*, superl. *goriest.* Covered or stained with gore; bloody; also, resembling gore.

gosh (gosh), *n.* A minced form of *God*: often used interjectionally, as a mild oath.

gos-hawk (gos′hâk), *n.* [AS. *gōshafoc*, 'goose hawk.'] Any of various powerful, short-winged hawks, esp. *Astur palumbarius*, of Europe, formerly much used in falconry, and *A. atricapillus*, of America.

American Goshawk (*Astur atricapillus*).

Go-shen (gō′shẹn), *n.* [From *Goshen*, in Egypt, where the Israelites were permitted to dwell, exempt from the plagues.] A land or place of plenty and comfort, free from ills.

gos-let (goz′let), *n.* [Dim. of *goose*: cf. *gosling.*] A very small goose of the genus *Nettapus*, of several species, found in India, Africa, Australia, etc.

gos-ling (goz′ling), *n.* [ME.; dim. of *goose.*] A young goose; also, a foolish, inexperienced person; also, a catkin.

gos-pel (gos′pel). [AS. *godspel*, appar. orig. *gōd spel*, 'good tidings': see *good* and *spell*[2], and cf. *evangel.*] **I.** *n.* Glad tidings, esp. concerning salvation and the kingdom of God as announced to the world by Christ; hence, the body of doctrine taught by Christ and the apostles; Christian revelation; also, the story of Christ's life and teachings, esp. as contained in the first four books of the New Testament; [usually *cap.*] one of these books; hence [*l. c.*], something taken as a guide to action (as, "The law of the land is his *gospel*": Steele, in "Spectator," 456); a doctrine regarded as of prime importance (as, "the propagators of this political *gospel*": Burke's "Revolution in France," 18); also, something infallibly true or implicitly believed (colloq.: as, "Those holier mysteries which the wise and just Receive as *gospel*," Byron's "Don Juan," xvi. 6); specif. [often *cap.*], *eccles.*, an extract from one of the four Gospels, forming part of the eucharistic service in certain churches. **II.** *a.* Pertaining to the gospel; accordant with the gospel; evangelical.—**gos′pel†,** *v. t.*; *-peled* or *-pelled, -peling* or *-pelling.* To evangelize. See Shakspere's "Macbeth," iii. 1. 88.—**gos′pel-er, gos′pel-ler,** *n.* One of the four evangelists†; also, one who professes the faith of the gospel, or claims for his party the exclusive possession of the true gospel; specif., *eccles.*, one who reads or sings the gospel in the eucharistic service.—**gos′pel-ize,** *v. t.*; *-ized, -izing.* To make accordant with the gospel†; also, to instruct in the gospel; evangelize.

gos-sa-mer (gos′ạ-mėr). [ME. *gossomer*, *gosesomer*, appar. orig. 'goose summer,' for a mild late autumn period when geese were in season, and hence for the filmy matter seen in the air at that period.] **I.** *n.* A fine filmy substance, consisting of cobweb formed by various small spiders, seen on grass and bushes, or floating in the air in calm weather esp. in autumn; a thread or a web of this substance; hence, an extremely delicate variety of gauze; any thin, light fabric; in England, a very light silk hat, or, facetiously, any hat; in the U. S., a thin waterproof outer garment, esp.

for women. **II.** *a.* Of or like gossamer; thin and light. —**gos′sa-mer-y,** *a.* Of or like gossamer; filmy; flimsy.

gos-san (gos′ạn or goz′-), *n.* [Cornish.] In *mining,* decomposed rock of a reddish or ferruginous color, which often forms a large part of the outcrop of a metallic vein.

gos-sip (gos′ip), *n.* [AS. *godsibb,* < *god,* God, + *sibb,* related, E. *sib.*] A godparent, in relation either to the child baptized (archaic or prov.) or to the child's parents (obs.); a friend or familiar acquaintance, esp. a woman (archaic); a person, esp. a woman, given to tattle or idle talk or the spreading of reports about others (as, "a set of malicious, prating, prudent *gossips,* both male and female, who murder characters to kill time": Sheridan's "School for Scandal," ii. 3); also, current talk, rumor, or scandal; also, light, familiar talk or writing.—**gos′sip,** *v.*; *-siped, -siping.* **I.** *tr.* To stand godparent to† (see Shakspere's "All's Well," i. 1. 189); also, to repeat like a gossip (as, to *gossip* scandal). **II.** *intr.* To act as a familiar acquaintance or boon companion† (as, "With all my heart, I'll *gossip* at this feast": Shakspere's "Comedy of Errors," v. 1. 407); also, to talk idly, esp. about other people; go about tattling.—**gos′-sip-er,** *n.*—**gos′sip-ing,** *n.* A christening or christening-feast (prov. Eng.); a meeting of friends, as at a woman's lying-in (prov. Eng.); a merrymaking (prov. Eng.); also, indulgence in gossip or idle talk; idle talk; a meeting of which gossip is the chief feature.—**gos′sip-ing-ly,** *adv.* —**gos′sip-mong″er** (-mung″gėr), *n.* One who retails gossip or current talk.—**gos′sip-red** (-red), *n.* The relation of a gossip; also, gossip; idle talk.—**gos′sip-ry,** *n.* Gossipred; also, gossip or small talk; also, a body of gossips. —**gos′sip-y,** *a.* Given to or characterized by gossip.

gos-soon (go-sön′), *n.* [F. *garçon.*] A boy; a male servant. [Ireland.]

got (got). Preterit and past participle of *get.*

Goth (goth), *n.* [LL. *Gothi,* pl.: cf. Goth. *Gut-thiuda,* 'Goth people.'] One of a Teutonic race which in the 3d, 4th, and 5th centuries overran the greater part of the Roman Empire; hence, a barbarian, or rude, ignorant person (as, "He must be a *Goth* and a barbarian if he did not enter into the spirit of such a happy . . . contrivance": Smollett's "Humphry Clinker," Oct. 3). See *Ostrogoth* and *Visigoth.*

Go-tham (gō′thạm or goth′ạm), *n.* [So called by Washington Irving, in "Salmagundi," after an English village of *Gotham* (pron. got′ạm), proverbial for the foolishness of its inhabitants.] The city of New York.—**Go′tham-ite** (-īt), *n.* An inhabitant of Gotham.

Goth-ic (goth′ik). [LL. *Gothicus.*] **I.** *a.* Of or pertaining to the Goths or their language; also, Teutonic† or Germanic†; also [also *l. c.*], of, pertaining to, or characteristic of the middle ages; medieval; romantic, as opposed to classical; disparagingly, of or pertaining to the dark ages, barbarous, or rude (as, "O! more than *Gothic* ignorance": Fielding's "Tom Jones," vii. 3); [*cap.*] in *arch.,* noting or pertaining to a style, prevalent in western Europe from the 12th to the 16th century, characterized chiefly by the pointed arch and the comparatively great height of many of the buildings. **II.** *n.* [*cap.*] The language of the Goths, perhaps the earliest recorded of the Teutonic tongues, preserved chiefly in the remains of the translation of the Bible made by Ulfilas in the 4th century; also, Gothic architecture or decoration; [*l. c.*] a square-cut printing-type, without serifs or hair-lines (see *type*).—**Goth′i-cal-ly,** *adv.*—**Goth′i-cism** (-i-sizm), *n.* Adherence to Gothic ideas, etc.; a Gothic idiom; also, conformity or devotion to the Gothic style of architecture; also [also *l. c.*], barbarism; rudeness.—**Goth′i-cize** (-sīz), *v. t.*; *-cized, -cizing.* [Also *l. c.*] To make Gothic, as in character or style; render medieval.

gö-thite, goe-thite (gė′tīt), *n.* [From *Goethe,* the German poet.] A mineral consisting of a hydrous oxide of iron.

got-ten (got′n). Past participle of *get.* See *get.*

gouache (gwȧsh), *n.* [F., < It. *guazzo.*] A method of painting with opaque colors prepared by mixing pigments with water, gum, and honey; also, an opaque color used in, or a painting executed by, this method.

gouge (gouj or göj), *n.* [OF. F. *gouge,* < ML. *gubia, gulbia*; prob. from Celtic.] A chisel whose blade has a concavo-convex cross-section; also, the act or an act of gouging, or a groove or hole made by gouging; fig., an imposition or swindle (colloq., U. S.).—**gouge,** *v. t.*; *gouged, gouging.* To work upon with or as with a gouge, as in making grooves or holes; make with or as with a gouge, as a channel; also, to dig or force out with or as with a gouge; force out (a person's eye), as with the thumb; force out the eye of (a person), as with the thumb; also, fig., to impose upon or swindle (colloq., U. S.).—**gou-ger** (gou′jėr or gö′-), *n.*

gou-lash (gö′läsh), *n.* [Hung. *gulyas-hus,* 'herdsman's meat.'] A stew of beef, veal, vegetables, etc., with paprika or other seasoning.

goum (göm), *n.* [F.; from Ar.] An Arab tribal contingent in the French military service.

gou-pen (gou′pẹn), *n.* See *gowpen.*

gou-ra (gö′rạ̈), *n.* [NL.; from native name.] Any bird of the genus *Goura,* comprising large pigeons (the crowned pigeons) of New Guinea, etc., with immense erect crests.

Goura (*G. coronata*).

gourd (gōrd or gōrd), *n.* [OF. F. *gourde,* < L. *cucurbita,* gourd.] The fruit of any of various cucurbitaceous plants, esp. the fruit of *Lagenaria vulgaris* (or *lagenaria*) ('bottle-gourd'), whose dried shell is used for bottles, bowls, etc., or that of certain forms of *Cucurbita pepo* sometimes cultivated for ornament; also, a plant bearing such a fruit; also, the dried shell of, or a vessel made from, such a fruit; hence, a gourd-shaped vessel.—**gourd′=shaped,** *a.* Having the shape of a gourd; typically, having a globular body and a long, slender neck, as a flask or bottle.

gour-mand (gör′mạnd, F. gör-mäṅ), *n.* [OF. F. *gourmand,* gluttonous; origin unknown.] A glutton†; also, one fond of good eating; an epicure.—**gour-man-dise** (gör-mäṅ-dēz), *n.* [F., < *gourmand.*] The tastes or practices of a gourmand.—**gour-man-dize** (gör′mạn-dīz), *v.,* etc. Same as *gormandize, v.,* etc.

gour-met (gör-mā), *n.* [F. *gourmet,* OF. *gourmet, groumet,* wine-taster, wine-merchant's man: cf. *groom*[1].] A connoisseur in the delicacies of the table; an epicure.

gous-ty (gous′ti), *a.* [Origin obscure.] Large and empty; dreary; desolate. [Sc. and north. Eng.]

goût[1] (gö), *n.* [F., < L. *gustus,* taste.] Taste (in various senses).

gout[2] (gout), *n.* [OF. *goute* (F. *goutte*), < L. *gutta,* a drop, ML. gout.] A drop of liquid; a splash; a clot of blood; also, a constitutional disease characterized by painful inflammation of the joints (chiefly those in the feet and hands, and esp. in the great toe), and by excess of uric acid in the blood.—**gout′y,** *a.* Diseased with or subject to gout; also, pertaining to or of the nature of gout; causing gout; also, swollen as if from gout.—**gout′i-ly,** *adv.*—**gout′i-ness,** *n.*

gov-ern (guv′ėrn), *v.* [OF. *governer* (F. *gouverner*), < L. *gubernare,* < Gr. κυβερνᾶν, steer, guide, govern.] **I.** *tr.* To rule by right of authority, as a sovereign does; direct and control the actions and affairs of (a people, state, etc.); also, to exercise a directing or restraining influence over (as, the motives *governing* a person's decision); guide in conduct or action; regulate; also, to hold in check (as, to *govern* the temper); also, to serve as or constitute a law or rule for (as, the principles *governing* a case); in *gram.,* to require (a word) to be in a particular case or mode; necessitate (a particular case or mode). **II.** *intr.* To exercise the function of government; also, to have predominating influence.—**gov′ern-a-ble,** *a.* That may be governed. —**gov′ern-ance,** *n.* [OF. F. *gouvernance.*] Government; exercise of authority; control; method or system of government or management; also, conduct† or behavior†.

gov-er-ness (guv'ėr-nes), *n.* [For earlier *governeress*, < OF. *gouverneresse*, fem. of *gouverneur*, *governeor*, E. *governor*.] A female governor or ruler (obs. or rare); an instructress or female teacher, esp. in a private household; also, the wife of a governor (now only humorous).

gov-ern-ment (guv'ėrn-mẹnt), *n.* [F. *gouvernement*.] The act of governing; rule; control; regulation; specif., the direction of the affairs of a state, etc.; political rule and administration; also, the function or office of governing (as, "The *government* I cast upon my brother": Shakspere's "Tempest," i. 2. 75); also, the form or system of rule by which a state, community, or the like is governed (as, monarchical or republican *government*; episcopal *government*); form of polity; also, the governing body of persons in a state, etc.; the administration; also, a body politic, or state; also, a country governed; more frequently, a portion of a country, ruled by a governor; a province; also, conduct† or behavior†; in *gram.*, the influence of one word in determining the case or mode of another word, according to established usage. —**gov-ern-men'tal** (-men'tạl), *a.* Of or pertaining to government or a government.—**gov-ern-men'tal-ly**, *adv.*

gov-er-nor (guv'ėr-nọr), *n.* [OF. *governeor* (F. *gouverneur*), < L. *gubernator*, steersman, director, < *gubernare*, E. *govern*.] A steersman† (as, "Behold also the ships, which though they be so great . . . yet are they turned about with a very small helm, whithersoever the *governor* listeth": Jas. iii. 4); also, one who governs; a ruler or chief magistrate; one appointed to govern a province, town, fort, or the like; the executive head of a State in the U. S.; the representative of the crown in a British colony or dependency; one charged with the direction or control of an institution, society, etc.; a tutor†; a person regarded as governing, as an employer, one's father, etc. (colloq.); in *mach.*, a device for regulating a supply of steam, gas, etc., esp. for insuring uniform speed, as in a steam-engine.—**gov'er-nor=gen'er-al**, *n.*; pl. *governors-general*. A governor who has under him subordinate or deputy governors.—**gov'er-nor=gen'er-al-ship**, *n.*—**gov'er-nor-ship**, *n.*

gow-an (gou'ạn), *n.* [Origin uncertain.] Any of various yellow or white field-flowers, esp. the English daisy, *Bellis perennis*. [Sc. and north. Eng.]—**gow'aned, gow'an-y**, *a.*

gowk (gouk), *n.* [From Scand.: cf. Icel. *gaukr* and AS. *gēac*, cuckoo, G. *gauch*, cuckoo, fool.] The cuckoo; also, a fool or simpleton. [Chiefly Sc. and north. Eng.]

gown (goun), *n.* [OF. *goune*, *gone*, < ML. *gunna*; origin uncertain.] A loose, flowing outer garment in various forms, worn by men or women as an article of ordinary attire or as distinctive of office, profession, or status (as, a dressing-*gown*; a night*gown*; a judge's *gown*; an academic *gown*); also, a flowing outer garment worn by the ancients, esp. the Roman toga; hence, the dress of peace (as, "He Mars depos'd, and arms to *gowns* made yield": Dryden's "Stanzas on Oliver Cromwell," xx.); also, a woman's dress, robe, or frock, comprising waist and skirt (either joined or separate).—**gown**, *v. t.* or *i.* To dress in, or put on, a gown. —**gowns'man** (-mạn), *n.*; pl. *-men*. A man who wears a gown as an indication of his office, profession, or status, as a judge, lawyer, clergyman, or member of a university; also, a beadsman (Sc.); also, a civilian, in distinction from a soldier.

gow-pen (gou'pẹn), *n.* [= Icel. *gaupn*.] The two hands held together in the form of a bowl; also, as much as can be contained in the hands held thus; a double handful; hence, a great quantity. [Sc. and north. Eng.]

goz-zan (goz'ạn), *n.* See *gossan*.

Graaf-i-an (gräf'i-ạn), *a.* Pertaining to or named after Regnier de Graaf (1641–73), a Dutch physician and anatomist.—**Graafian follicle** or **vesicle**, in *anat.*, one of the small ovum-containing sacs or bodies present in an ovary.

grab[1] (grab), *n.* [Ar. *gharāb*.] A vessel used on the Malabar coast, etc., having a long, sharp prow and usually two masts.

grab[2] (grab), *v.*; *grabbed*, *grabbing*. [= MLG. *grabben* = Sw. *grabba*; perhaps akin to E. *grasp*.] **I.** *tr.* To seize suddenly and eagerly; snatch; hence, to take possession of in an unscrupulous manner (as, to *grab* land); also, to capture or arrest (a person). **II.** *intr.* To make a grab or snatch, as at something.—**grab**[2], *n.* The act of grabbing; a sudden, eager grasp or snatch; seizure or acquisition by violent or unscrupulous means; also, that which is grabbed; also, one who or that which grabs; a mechanical device for gripping objects.—**grab'ba-ble**, *a.* That may be grabbed. —**grab'=bag**, *n.* A bag or receptacle containing various articles from which a person is permitted to 'grab' or draw one (without seeing or examining it), usually on payment of a small sum, as at a fair. Also fig.—**grab'ber**, *n.*

grab-ble (grab'l), *v.*; *-bled*, *-bling*. [Freq. of *grab*[2]: cf. D. *grabbelen*.] **I.** *intr.* To feel or search with the hands; grope; also, to sprawl or scramble. **II.** *tr.* To catch hold of; clutch: as, "The speaker slowly rose, *grabbling* the face of the rock" (G. W. Cable's "John March, Southerner," xxii.).

grab=line (grab'līn), *n.* *Naut.*, any of certain lines or ropes on a ship for taking hold of if necessary, as one for boatmen to hold on to when coming alongside. Also **grab'=rope.**

grace (grās), *n.* [OF. *grace* (F. *grâce*), < L. *gratia*, < *gratus*, dear, pleasing, agreeable, thankful, grateful.] That quality of form, manner, movement, deportment, language, or anything else, which renders it pleasing or agreeable; elegance or beauty of form, manner, motion, or act (as, "*Grace* was in all her steps": Milton's "Paradise Lost," viii. 488); a pleasing or attractive quality or endowment (as, "Chastity, good-nature, and affability are the *graces* that play in her countenance": Steele, in "Spectator," 4); also, aspect or demeanor with reference to pleasingness, creditableness, graciousness, willingness, etc. (as, to do a thing with a good *grace*; to yield with a bad or ill *grace*); also, favor or good-will, or the manifestation of it, esp. as by a superior (as, to enjoy the *grace* of the sovereign; king by the *grace* of God); honor† (as, to do a person *grace*); a particular favor accorded, offered, or sought (archaic); a privilege or dispensation bestowed by authority (obs. or hist.); a fate or destiny allotted†; also, the free, unmerited favor and love of God; the influence of God operating in man to regenerate or strengthen (as, "But where sin abounded, *grace* did much more abound": Rom. v. 20); the condition of one under this influence; a virtue or excellence of divine origin (as, the Christian *graces*); moral strength (to do something: as, *grace* to perform a duty or to endure affliction); sense of right or propriety (as, to have the *grace* to blush for a fault); virtue, potency, or efficacy, as in herbs†; also, favor shown in granting a delay or temporary immunity, or the time allowed (as, "Stay a little! One golden minute's *grace!*" Tennyson's "Lancelot and Elaine," 680; days of *grace*, see under *day*); mercy, clemency, or pardon (as, a parliamentary act of *grace*); also, *pl.*, thanks†; *sing.* (formerly *pl.*), a short prayer before or after a meal, in which thanks are given and a blessing is asked; also [usually *cap.*], with *your*, *his*, etc., a formal title used in addressing or mentioning a duke, duchess, or archbishop, and formerly also a sovereign; [*l. c.*] in *music*, an embellishment consisting of a note or notes not essential to the harmony or melody, as an appoggiatura, a trill, etc.; [*cap.*] in *class. myth.*, one of three sister goddesses, commonly given as Aglaia ('brilliance'), Euphrosyne ('joy'), and Thalia ('bloom'), presiding over all beauty and charm in nature and humanity.—**good graces**, favor or liking: as, to be in the *good graces* of a person.—**grace**, *v. t.*; *graced*, *gracing*. To lend or add grace to; adorn, as with something added, or as the thing added does; embellish; also, to show favor or be gracious to†; favor or honor with something specified (as, "Please 't your highness To *grace* us with your royal company": Shakspere's "Macbeth," iii. 4. 45); gratify† or delight†; in *music*, to add grace-notes, cadenzas, etc., to.—**grace'=cup**, *n.* A cup of wine or the like passed round, after the saying of grace at table, for a last draft or health; also, the draft itself; a parting draft.—**grace'ful**, *a.* Characterized by grace, as of form, manner, movement, verbal expression, etc.; pleasingly elegant; admirably easy or effective; felicitous; also, full of spiritual grace†.—**grace'ful-ly**, *adv.*—**grace'ful-ness**, *n.*—**grace'less**, *a.* Wanting grace, pleasing elegance, or charm; also, destitute of spiritual grace; unregenerate or ungodly; without any sense of or regard for right or propriety (as, a *graceless* young scamp; "She knows very well what *graceless* dogs sailors are," H. Melville's "Omoo," lxxvii.: cf. *scapegrace*).—**grace'less-ly**, *adv.*—**grace'less-ness**, *n.*—**grace'=note**, *n.* In *music*, a note not essential to the harmony or melody, added as an embellishment; esp., an appoggiatura.

gra-cile (gras′il), *a.* [L. *gracilis*, slender, thin.] Slender; thin; lean; sometimes, in recent use (by erroneous association with *grace*), gracefully slender.—**gra-cil-i-ty** (gra-sil′i-ti), *n.*

gra-cious (grā′shus), *a.* [OF. *gracios* (F. *gracieux*), < L. *gratiosus*, < *gratia*, E. *grace*.] Pleasing, agreeable, or graceful (archaic: as, a *gracious* scene; "Then playing with the blade he prick'd his hand, 'A *gracious* gift to give a lady, this!'" Tennyson's "Aylmer's Field," 240); also, enjoying grace or favor†; fortunate† or happy†; also, characterized by or disposed to show grace or favor; kind, benevolent, or courteous; now, usually, kind, indulgent, or beneficent in a condescending or patronizing way (as, to be *gracious* to inferiors; to vouchsafe a *gracious* reply; a *gracious* smile); also, merciful or compassionate (as, "Thou art a God ready to pardon, *gracious* and merciful": Neh. ix. 17); also, full of spiritual grace†, righteous†, or virtuous†.—**gra-ci-os′i-ty** (-shi-os′i-ti), **gra′cious-ness**, *n.*—**gra′cious-ly**, *adv.*

grack-le (grak′l), *n.* [L. *graculus*, jackdaw.] Any of various birds of the old-world family *Sturnidæ* (starlings), or of the American family *Icteridæ* (American starlings, blackbirds, etc.), as the crow-blackbird, *Quiscalus purpureus* ('purple grackle').

Rusty Grackle (*Scolecophagus ferrugineus*), of eastern North America.

gra-date (grā′dāt), *v.*; *-dated*, *-dating*. [Back-formation from *gradation*.] **I.** *intr.* To pass by insensible degrees, as one color into another. **II.** *tr.* To cause to gradate; also, to arrange in steps or grades.

gra-da-tim (grạ-dā′tim), *adv.* [L., < *gradus*, step, E. *grade*.] Step by step; by degrees; gradually.

gra-da-tion (grạ-dā′shọn), *n.* [L. *gradatio(n-)*, < *gradus*, step, E. *grade*.] An advancing, step by step†; a gradual progress†; hence, any process or change taking place or conducted through a series of stages, by degrees, or gradually; the passing of one tint or shade of color into another by insensible degrees, as in painting; occurrence or arrangement in a series of degrees or grades (as, a variety of forms exhibiting *gradation*); also, a series of successive stages, degrees, or grades (obs. or rare); a stage, degree, or grade in such a series (usually in *pl.*: as, to pass by *gradations* from one form or condition into another; *gradations* of color); also, succession† (as, "Preferment goes by letter and affection, And not by old *gradation*, where each second Stood heir to first": Shakspere's "Othello," i. 1. 37); in *philol.*, ablaut.—**gra-da′tion-al**, *a.* Pertaining to or exhibiting gradation.—**gra-da′tion-al-ly**, *adv.*

gra-da-tive (grạ-dā′tiv), *a.* [L. *gradus*, step, E. *grade*.] Proceeding step by step, or by degrees or grades. Also **grad-a-to-ry** (grad′ạ-tọ-ri).

grade (grād), *n.* [L. *gradus*, step, stage, degree.] A step or stage in a course or process; hence, a degree in a scale, as of rank, advancement, quality, value, intensity, etc.; a class of persons or things of the same relative rank, quality, etc.; a single division of a school classified according to the progress of the pupils (American public schools commonly being divided into eight grades below the high school division); also, a hybrid animal; an animal, particularly a cow or bull or a sheep, resulting from a cross between a parent of ordinary breed and one of superior breed; also, the degree of inclination from the horizontal, or the rate of ascent or descent, in a road, railroad, etc.; an inclined portion of a road, etc.; a slope or gradient; also, degree of altitude; level.—**at grade,** on the same level: as, a railroad which crosses a highway or another railroad *at grade*.—**grade crossing,** a crossing of a railroad and a highway or another railroad at grade, or on the same level.—**grade,** *v.*; *graded*, *grading*. **I.** *tr.* To arrange in a series of grades; class according to rank, advancement, merit, etc.; sort according to size, quality, etc.; determine the grade of; also, to cause to pass by degrees, as from one color or shade to another; also, to reduce (the line of a road, railroad, etc.) to a level or to practicable degrees of inclination; also, to cross (an animal) with one of a better breed; improve (a stock, etc.) by crossing with animals of purer blood. **II.** *intr.* To be graded; be of a particular grade or quality.

-grade. [L. *-gradus*, < *gradi*, walk, go: see *gradient*.] An adjective (and noun) termination meaning 'walking,' 'moving,' 'going,' as in *cirrigrade*, *plantigrade*, *retrograde*.

grade-ly (grād′li), *a.* [Var. of *graithly*.] Orderly, decent, or respectable; proper; good; also, handsome, comely, or fine; also, great; thorough. [Sc. and prov. Eng.]—**grade′ly,** *adv.* Decently; properly; well; also, thoroughly; very. [Sc. and prov. Eng.]

grad-er (grā′dėr), *n.* One who or that which grades.

gra-di-ent (grā′di-ẹnt). [L. *gradiens* (*-ent-*), ppr. of *gradi* (pp. *gressus*), walk, go, < *gradus*, step, E. *grade*.] **I.** *a.* Progressing by taking steps with the feet, as an animal; walking; gressorial; also, rising or descending by regular degrees of inclination. **II.** *n.* The degree of inclination, or the rate of ascent or descent, in a railroad, etc.; grade; also, an inclined portion of a road, etc.; a grade; in *physics*, the rate at which a variable quantity, as temperature or pressure, changes in value; a curve representing such a rate of change.—**gra′di-ent-er,** *n.* A surveyors' instrument for fixing grades, etc., consisting essentially of a telescope, a spirit-level, and a graduated vertical arc, mounted on a tripod.

gra-din (grā′din, F. grȧ-daṅ), *n.* [F., < It. *gradino*, dim. of *grado*, < L. *gradus*, step, E. *grade*.] One of a series of steps or seats raised one above another; *eccles.*, a shelf or one of a series of shelves behind and above an altar. Also **gra-dine** (grạ-dēn′).

grad-u-al (grad′ū-ạl). [ML. *gradualis* (as n., *graduale*), < L. *gradus*, step, E. *grade*.] **I.** *a.* Consisting of or arranged in steps, stages, or degrees, as a scale†; also, proceeding step by step, or by orderly stages or degrees, as a process; taking place, changing, moving, etc., by degrees or little by little; rising or descending at an even, moderate inclination, as a slope. **II.** *n.* *Eccles.*, an antiphon sung between the epistle and the gospel in the eucharistic service (so called because orig. sung on the steps of the ambo: see etym.); also, a book containing the words and music of the graduals, the introits, and the other parts of the eucharistic service which are sung by the choir.—**grad′u-al-ly,** *adv.* In a gradual manner; by orderly stages; by degrees; little by little.—**grad′u-al-ness,** *n.*

grad-u-ate (grad′ū-āt), *v.*; *-ated*, *-ating*. [ML. *graduatus*, pp. of *graduare*, admit to an academic degree, < L. *gradus*, step, E. *grade*.] **I.** *tr.* To confer a degree or diploma upon at the close of a course of study, as in a university, college, or school; also, to divide into or mark with degrees, as the scale of a thermometer; arrange in grades or gradations; establish gradation in. **II.** *intr.* To receive a degree or diploma on completing a course of study; also, to pass by degrees; change gradually.—**grad′u-ate.** **I.** *a.* That has been graduated (as, a *graduate* student); of or pertaining to graduates (as, a *graduate* school). **II.** *n.* One who has received a degree or diploma on completing a course of study, as in a university, college, or school; also, a graduated vessel, as of glass, for measuring.—**grad′u-at-ed** (-ā-ted), *p. a.* Marked so as to indicate degrees or quantities; arranged in grades or gradations.—**grad-u-a′tion** (-ā′shọn), *n.* [ML. *graduatio(n-)*.] The act of graduating, or the state of being graduated; the ceremony of conferring degrees or diplomas, as at a college or school; also, marks or a mark, as on an instrument or a vessel, for indicating degree, quantity, etc.—**grad′u-a-tor,** *n.*

gra-dus (grā′dus), *n.* [Short for L. *gradus ad Parnassum*, 'steps to Parnassus.'] A dictionary of prosody, for aid in writing Latin or Greek verses: as, "instead of sweet knowledge . . . doggrel grammars and *graduses*" (Kinglake's "Eothen," iv.).

Græ-cism (grē′sizm), **Græ-cize** (grē′sīz), **Græco-**, etc. See *Grecism, Grecize, Greco-*, etc.

graf (gräf), *n.*; pl. *grafen* (grä′fen). [G. *graf* = D. *graaf*: cf. *burgrave, landgrave, margrave*.] In German use, a nobleman ranking below a fürst, and corresponding to an English earl; a count.

graff (gráf), *n.* and *v.* Older form of *graft*[1].

graf-fi-to (gräf-fē′tō), *n.*; pl. *-ti* (-tē). [It., ult. < Gr. γράφειν, mark, draw, write.] In *archæol.*, an ancient drawing or writing scratched on a wall or other surface; in *art*, a method of decoration in which designs are scratched through a superficial layer, as of plaster, showing a ground of different color beneath.

Graffito, found on wall of the Domus Gelotiana, Rome.

graft[1] (gráft), *n.* [Earlier *graff*, < OF. *grafe, greife* (F. *greffe*), orig. stylus, pencil, < L. *graphium*, < Gr. γραφεῖον, stylus, < γράφειν, write.] A shoot or part of a plant (the scion) inserted in a groove, slit, or the like in another plant or tree (the stock) so as to become nourished by and united with it, the scion usually bearing flowers, fruit, etc., like the plant from which it was taken, and the stock usually retaining its own characteristics; the plant or tree (the united stock and scion) resulting from such an operation; the place where the scion is inserted; also, a portion of living tissue transplanted by surgery from one part of an individual to another, or from one individual to another, with a view to its adhesion and growth; in fig. use, anything inserted in or fixed upon something else to which it did not originally belong; an extraneous addition; also, the act of grafting.—**graft**[1], *v.* **I.** *tr.* To insert (a graft) into a plant or tree; insert a scion of (one plant) into another plant; fix a graft or grafts upon (a plant or tree); in *surg.*, to transplant (a portion of living tissue) as a graft; in fig. use, to insert or fix as if by grafting (as, to *graft* a pagan custom upon Christian institutions). **II.** *intr.* To insert a graft or grafts; also, to become grafted.

graft[2] (gráft), *n.* [Cf. prov. Eng. or slang *graft*, work, a job or trade, perhaps orig. 'digging': cf. *grave*[1].] The acquisition of gain or advantage by dishonest, unfair, or sordid means, esp. through the abuse of one's position or influence in politics, business, etc., as by corrupt agreement or connivance or private or secret practices; a particular instance, method, or means of thus acquiring gain; also, the gain or advantage acquired. [Colloq.]—**graft**[2], *v. i.* or *t.* To practise graft, or obtain by graft. [Colloq.]

graft-age (gráf′tāj), *n.* The process of grafting on trees, etc.

graft-er[1] (gráf′tėr), *n.* One who grafts on trees, etc.; also, the original plant from which a scion has been taken for grafting†; also, a saw designed specially for use in grafting.

graft-er[2] (gráf′tėr), *n.* One who practises graft; one who accepts or obtains graft. [Colloq.]

Gra-ham (grā′am) **bread.** [From Sylvester *Graham* (1794–1851), American dietetic reformer.] Bread of a light brownish color made of unbolted wheat flour (*Graham flour*).—**Gra′ham-ism,** *n.* The vegetarian system of diet.

Grail (grāl), *n.* [OF. *graal*, < ML. *gradalis*, dish, vessel; origin uncertain.] A platter (also taken as a chalice) which according to medieval legend was used by Christ at the Last Supper, and in which Joseph of Arimathea received the last drops of Christ's blood at the cross: often called *Holy Grail*.

grain[1] (grān), *n.* [From Scand.: cf. Icel. *grein*, Sw. and Dan. *gren*, branch.] A bough or branch (now prov.); one of the prongs of a fork (now prov.); *pl.*, an iron instrument with barbed prongs, for spearing or harpooning fish (often construed as *sing.*).

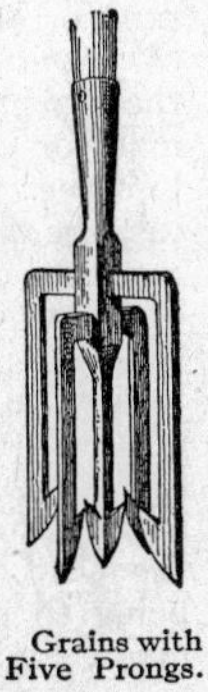
Grains with Five Prongs.

grain[2] (grān), *n.* [OF. F. *grain*, also *graine*, < L. *granum*, grain, seed.] A small, hard seed; specif., the seed-like fruit, or caryopsis, of a cereal plant, as wheat, rice, maize, etc.; a corn; collectively, the seed-like fruits of wheat and other cereal plants in mass, or the plants themselves (in British use, commonly called *corn*); a particular species of such fruits or plants; *pl.*, the refuse of grain after brewing or distilling; also, *sing.*, any small, hard particle, as of sand, gold, pepper, gunpowder, etc.; also, a unit of weight (orig. the weight of a plump grain of wheat) equal in apothecaries' weight to one twentieth of a scruple, and in troy weight to one twenty-fourth of a pennyweight (27.34 or $27\frac{11}{32}$ grains being equivalent to 1 dram avoirdupois) (there are 5,760 grains to the pound in both apothecaries' weight and troy weight, and 7,000 to the pound in avoirdupois weight); fig., the smallest possible amount of anything (as, there is not a *grain* of truth in that statement); also, kermes or cochineal, or the red dye made from either; any red dye; dye or color in general, esp. when fast; color or hue (as, "a robe of darkest *grain*": Milton's "Il Penseroso," 33); also, granular texture or appearance; specif., the side of leather from which the hair has been removed, the marking on such a side, or a more or less similar superficial finish or marking produced artificially; also, the size and arrangement of constituent particles of any substance; texture; also, fibrous constitution; the fibers in a piece of wood; the arrangement or direction of fibers in wood, or the resulting appearance or markings; lamination or cleavage of stone, coal, etc.; fig., temper or natural character (as, it goes against the *grain* to submit to this).—**grains of paradise,** the pungent, peppery seeds of either of two zingiberaceous plants, *Amomum melegueta* and *A. granum-paradisi*, of Africa: used to strengthen cordials, etc., and in veterinary medicine.—**in grain,** in kermes or other red dye, or in a fast color, or through the fiber (as, to dye a thing *in grain*); hence, indelible, firmly fixed, or ingrained (see Shakspere's "Twelfth Night," i. 5. 255); also, in substance or nature (as, a scoundrel *in grain*).—**with a grain of salt,** with some reserve or allowance, as in accepting or believing a statement.—**grain**[2], *v. t.* To form into grains; granulate; also, to dye in grain; also, to give a granular appearance to; also, to paint in imitation of the grain of wood, etc.; in *tanning*, to remove the hair from (skins); soften and raise the grain of (leather); finish with a particular grain.—**grained,** *a.* Having grains or a granular structure; also, having a fibrous structure or appearance.—**grain′=el″e-va-tor,** *n.* See *elevator*.—**grain′er,** *n.*—**grain′ing,** *n.* Painting in imitation of the grain of wood, etc.—**grain′less,** *a.* Without grains or grain; not grained.

grains (grānz), *n. pl.* or *sing.* See *grain*[1].

grain-y (grā′ni), *a.* Grain-like or granular; also, full of grains or grain; also, resembling the grain of wood, etc.

graith (grāth), *v. t.* [From Scand.: cf. Icel. *greidha*, make ready, < *greidhr* (= AS. *gerǣde*), ready: cf. *ready*.] To make ready; prepare; equip. [Now Sc. and prov. Eng.]—**graith,** *n.* [Cf. Icel. *greidhi*.] Readiness; order; preparation; also, equipment; harness; apparatus; also, possessions; also, material; stuff. [Now Sc. and prov. Eng.]—**graith′ly,** *a.* [Cf. *gradely*.] Tidy; trim; decent; good. [Now prov. Eng.]

gral-la-to-ri-al (gral-a-tō′ri-al), *a.* [L. *grallator*, one who goes on stilts, < *grallæ*, stilts.] Belonging or pertaining to the wading birds, as the storks, herons, etc., many species of which are remarkable for their long legs.

Grallatorial Birds. — 1, stork; 2, heron; 3, crane.

gram[1] (gram), *n.* [Pg. *grão*, < L. *granum*, E. *grain*[2].] In the East Indies, the chick-pea, *Cicer arietinum*, there used as a food for both man and cattle; also, any of various other plants, as *Phaseolus mungo* ('green gram'), a bean cultivated in India as a food crop.

gram², **gramme** (gram), *n.* [F. *gramme*, < LL. *gramma*, < Gr. γράμμα, a small weight, orig. something drawn or written, a character or letter, < γράφειν, write.] In the *metric system*, a unit of mass (weight), intended to be, and being very nearly, equal to the mass (weight) of a cubic centimeter of water at its maximum density, but actually being equal to one thousandth of a certain platinum-iridium block, forming the standard kilogram, preserved at the International Bureau of Weights and Measures, near Paris: equivalent to a weight of 15.432 grains.

-gram. [Gr. -γραμμα, something drawn or written, γράμμα, something drawn or written, character, letter, or γραμμή, line, all < γράφειν, mark, draw, write.] A termination of nouns denoting something drawn or written, as *diagram, epigram, monogram, pentagram, radiogram, telegram.* Cf. *-graph* and *-graphy.* [For *-gram* in terms of the metric system, see *gram²*.]

gra-ma (grä'mạ̈), *n.* [Sp. *grama*, kind of grass.] Any of various pasture grasses of the western and southwestern U. S., esp. those of the genus *Bouteloua*, as *B. oligostachya* ('blue grama'), the commonest species. Also **gra'ma=grass.**

gram-a-ry, gram-a-rye (gram'ạ-ri), *n.* [ME. *grammarie, gramarye*: cf. OF. *gramaire*, grammar (see *grammar*), also magic.] Grammar†; learning†; occult learning, or magic (archaic: as, "dark words of *gramarye*," Scott's "Lay of the Last Minstrel," iii. 14).

gram=at-om (gram'at'ọm), *n.* In *chem.*, that quantity of an element whose weight in grams is numerically equal to the number which expresses the atomic weight of the element.

gra-mer-cy (grạ-mėr'si), *interj.* [OF. *grant merci*: see *grand* and *mercy.*] Great thanks; many thanks; also, an exclamation of surprise or sudden feeling (as, "*Gramercy!* they for joy did grin": Coleridge's "Ancient Mariner," iii.). [Archaic.]

gram-i-na-ceous (gram-i-nā'shius), *a.* Gramineous.

gra-min-e-ous (grạ-min'ẹ̄-us), *a.* [L. *gramineus*, < *gramen* (*gramin-*), grass.] Of or like grass; belonging to the *Gramineæ* (or *Poaceæ*), the grass family of plants.

gram-i-niv-o-rous (gram-i-niv'ọ̄-rus), *a.* [L. *gramen* (*gramin-*), grass, + *vorare*, devour.] Feeding or subsisting on grass.

gram-ma-logue (gram'ạ-log), *n.* [Gr. γράμμα, character, letter, + λόγος, word.] In *shorthand*, a word represented by a single sign; also, a logogram.

gram-mar (gram'ạ̈r), *n.* [OF. *gramaire* (F. *grammaire*), < L. *grammatica*, < Gr. γραμματική, grammar, prop. fem. of γραμματικός: see *grammatic*, and cf. *gramary* and *glamour.*] The study or science of the usages of language or of a particular language, esp. as regards the classes, forms, and inflections of words, the combination of words into sentences, the principles of correct usage, etc.; a treatise on this subject; also, manner of speech or writing with reference to conformity to established or correct usage (as, "He had German enough to scold his servants . . . but his *grammar* and pronunciation were extremely bad": Macaulay's "Essays," Frederic the Great); speech or writing in accordance with established grammatical usage (as, that sentence is not *grammar*); also, grammatical forms and usages collectively (as, a language having little *grammar*); also, the elements of any science, art, or subject (as, the *grammar* of painting); a book presenting them (as, a *grammar* of ornament).—**gram-ma-ri-an** (grạ-mā'ri-ạn), *n.* One versed in grammar. —**gram'mar-less,** *a.* Destitute of grammar or grammatical forms, as a language; also, not conforming to grammatical rules, as speech; ignorant of grammar, as a person.—**gram'mar=school,** *n.* Formerly, a school for teaching Latin; now, esp. in England, a secondary school in which Latin and Greek are among the principal subjects taught; in the U. S., a graded public school intermediate between a primary school and a high school.

gram-mat-ic (grạ-mat'ik), *a.* [L. *grammaticus*, < Gr. γραμματικός, pertaining to letters, language, or grammar, < γράμμα, character, letter, orig. something written, < γράφειν, write.] Of or pertaining to grammar.—**gram-mat'i-cal,** *a.* Of or pertaining to grammar (as, a *grammatical* rule; a *grammatical* error); also, in accordance with the rules of grammar (as, that sentence is not *grammatical*).—**gram-mat'i-cal-ly,** *adv.*

gram-mat-i-cas-ter (grạ-mat'i-kas-tėr), *n.* [ML., < L. *grammaticus*, a grammarian, orig. adj.: see *grammatic.*] A petty grammarian.

gramme (gram), *n.* See *gram²*.

gram=mol-e-cule (gram'mol'e-kūl), *n.* In *chem.*, that quantity of a substance whose weight in grams is numerically equal to the number which expresses the molecular weight of the substance.

gram-o-phone (gram'ọ̄-fōn), *n.* [Gr. γράμμα, something written, + φωνή, sound.] An instrument invented in 1887 by Emile Berliner, for recording and reproducing speech, music, and other sounds, differing from the original phonograph and the original graphophone in employing for its record, instead of a rotating cylinder with indentations or incisions of varying depth in a line of one direction, a thin rotating disk with a groove of even depth and varying (zigzag) direction; in general, any sound-reproducing machine employing a disk record, whether with a groove of even depth and varying direction or with incisions of varying depth in a line of one direction. Cf. *phonautograph, phonograph*, and *graphophone.*

gram-pus (gram'pus), *n.* [For ME. *grapeys, graspeys*, < OF. *graspeis, craspois*, < ML. *crassus piscis*, 'fat fish.'] A cetacean, *Grampus griseus*, of the dolphin family, widely distributed in northern seas; also, any of various related cetaceans, as the caaing-whale, *Globicephalus melas*, or the killer, *Orca gladiator.*

Grampus (*Grampus griseus*).

gran-a-dil-la (gran-ạ-dil'ạ̈), *n.* [Sp., dim. of *granada*, pomegranate: see *grenade.*] The large edible fruit of certain species of passion-flower, esp. *Passiflora quadrangularis*; also, a plant yielding this fruit.

gran-a-ry (gran'ạ-ri), *n.*; pl. *-ries* (-riz). [L. *granarium*, < *granum*, E. *grain²*.] A storehouse or repository for grain, esp. after it has been threshed or husked; fig., a region abounding in grain.

grand (grand), *a.* [OF. *grand, grant* (F. *grand*, fem. *grande*), < L. *grandis*, large, full-grown, advanced in years, great, grand.] Of great, notable, or imposing size (as, "I was of late as petty to his ends As is the morn-dew on the myrtle-leaf To his *grand* sea": Shakspere's "Antony and Cleopatra," iii. 12. 10); imposing in size and appearance or general effect (as, *grand* old trees; *grand* mountain scenery; buildings or statues on a *grand* scale); hence (without reference to size), stately, majestic, or elegantly dignified, as persons or their appearance, manner, air, etc.; lofty, as ideas, language, or style; magnificent or splendid, as a palace, a coach, festivities, display, etc.; noble or fine (as, a *grand* old man; "the *grand* old name of gentleman," Tennyson's "In Memoriam," cxi.); first-rate, capital, or 'splendid' (colloq. or vulgar: as, to have a *grand* time; *grand* weather; the dinner was just *grand*); also, highest, or very high, in rank or official dignity (as, a *grand* marshal; a *grand* jury: cf. *grand duke*, below); chief or arch (as, "Sin and Death, the two *grand* foes": Milton's "Paradise Regained," i. 159); main or principal (as, the *grand* entrance or staircase of a building: cf. *grand stand*, below); of the highest importance (as, the *grand* elixir of the alchemists; the *grand* question, resource, or desideratum); of great importance, distinction, or pretensions (as, *grand* personages; a *grand* international congress); also, complete or comprehensive (as, a *grand* total); in *genealogy*, one degree more remote in ascent or descent (used in compounds: see *grandaunt, grandchild*, etc., and cf. *great*).—**Grand Army of the Republic,** a society, founded in 1866, composed of men who served in the U. S. army or navy during the Civil War, its objects being to preserve fraternal feeling, strengthen loyal sentiment, and aid needy families of members. Abbreviated

G. A. R.—**grand climacteric.** See *climacteric.*—**grand duchess,** the wife or widow of a grand duke; also, a woman who governs a grand duchy in her own right; in Russia, a daughter of a czar or of a czar's son.—**grand duchy,** a territory ruled by a grand duke or grand duchess.—**grand duke,** the sovereign of a territory called a grand duchy (ranked next below a king); in Russia, a son of a czar or of a czar's son.—**grand jury.** See under *jury.*—**Grand Lama.** See *lama*².—**grand larceny.** See *larceny.*—**grand opera.** See under *opera*².—**grand piano.** See under *piano*², *n.*—**grand stand,** the principal stand for spectators at a race-course, athletic field, etc.—**grand tour.** See under *tour, n.*—**grand vizier.** See *vizier.*

gran-dam, gran-dame (gran′dam, -dām), *n.* [OF. *grand,* grand, + *dame,* E. *dame.*] A grandmother; hence, an ancestress; in general, an old woman. [Archaic or prov.]

grand-aunt (grand′änt), *n.* [See *grand,* def.] An aunt of one's father or mother; a great-aunt.—**grand′child,** *n.*; pl. *-children.* A child of one's son or daughter.—**grand′-daugh″ter,** *n.* A daughter of one's son or daughter.

grande dame (gräṅd däm). [F.] A grand or great lady.

gran-dee (gran-dē′), *n.* [Sp. and Pg. *grande,* < L. *grandis,* E. *grand.*] A Spanish or Portuguese nobleman of the highest rank; hence, any person of high rank or great eminence (as, political *grandees*).

gran-deur (gran′dụ̄r), *n.* [F. *grandeur,* < *grand*: see *grand.*] The state or quality of being grand; imposing greatness; majesty; sublimity; magnificence; exalted rank, dignity, or importance.

grand-fa-ther (grand′fä″ᴛʜėr), *n.* The father of one's father or mother; hence, a forefather.—**grand′fa″ther-ly,** *a.*

gran-dil-o-quent (gran-dil′ọ-kwẹnt), *a.* [L. *grandis,* great, grand, + *loquens* (*loquent-*), ppr. of *loqui,* speak.] Speaking or expressed in a lofty or pompous style; bombastic.—**gran-dil′o-quence,** *n.*—**gran-dil′o-quent-ly,** *adv.*—**gran-dil′o-quous** (-kwus), *a.* [L. *grandiloquus.*] Grandiloquent.

gran-di-ose (gran′di-ōs), *a.* [F. *grandiose,* < It. *grandioso,* < L. *grandis,* E. *grand.*] Grand in an imposing or impressive way; also, affectedly grand or stately, or pompous (as, "a *grandiose* aping of Cæsar, Alexander, and Charlemagne": H. G. Wells's "Outline of History," xxxviii. § 3).—**gran′di-ose-ly,** *adv.*—**gran-di-os′i-ty** (-os′i-ti), *n.*

gran-di-o-so (grän-dē-ō′sō), *a.* [It.: see *grandiose.*] In *music,* grand or stately.

Gran-di-so-ni-an (gran-di-sō′ni-ạn), *a.* Pertaining to or characteristic of Sir Charles Grandison, the hero of a novel of that name by Samuel Richardson (published in 1753), represented by the author as his ideal of the perfect gentleman.

grand-ly (grand′li), *adv.* In a grand manner; imposingly; majestically; magnificently; splendidly.

grand-ma (grand′mä), *n.* [See *grand,* def.] Shortened form of *grandmamma.* [Colloq.]—**grand′mam-ma″,** *n.* A familiar equivalent of *grandmother.*—**grand′moth″er,** *n.* The mother of one's father or mother; hence, an ancestress.—**grand′moth″er-ly,** *a.*—**grand′neph″ew,** *n.* A son of one's nephew or niece.

grand-ness (grand′nes), *n.* The quality of being grand.

grand-niece (grand′nēs), *n.* [See *grand,* def.] A daughter of one's nephew or niece.—**grand′pa,** *n.* Shortened form of *grandpapa.* [Colloq.]—**grand′pa-pa″,** *n.* A familiar equivalent of *grandfather.*—**grand′par″ent,** *n.* A parent of a parent.—**grand′sire,** *n.* A grandfather; hence, a forefather; in general, an old man. [Archaic or prov.]—**grand′son,** *n.* A son of one's son or daughter.—**grand′-un″cle,** *n.* An uncle of one's father or mother; a great-uncle.

grane (grān), *v.* and *n.* Scotch form of *groan.*

grange (grānj), *n.* [OF. F. *grange,* < ML. *granea,* < L. *granum,* E. *grain*².] A granary (archaic: as, "For their teeming flocks and *granges* full, In wanton dance they praise the bounteous Pan," Milton's "Comus," 175); also, a farm; often, a country dwelling-house with its various farm-buildings; formerly, an outlying farm-house with barns, etc., belonging to a feudal manor or a religious establishment, where crops and tithes in kind were stored; also, in the U. S., a lodge or local branch of the "Patrons of Husbandry," a secret association for promoting the interests of agriculture; also [*cap.*], with *the,* in popular use, the association itself.—**gran-ger** (grān′jėr), *n.* A farm-steward; in the U. S., a member of a grange; also, a farmer.—**gran′ger-ism**¹, *n.* The principles and methods of the association of grangers in the U. S.

gran-ger-ism² (grān′jėr-izm), *n.* The practice of grangerizing books.

gran-ger-ize (grān′jėr-īz), *v. t.*; *-ized, -izing.* [From J. *Granger,* whose "Biographical History of England" (1769) was arranged for such illustration.] To illustrate (a book) with additional prints, engravings, etc., as from other books.—**gran″ger-i-za′tion** (-i-zā′shọn), *n.*—**gran′ger-iz-er** (-ī-zėr), *n.*

gran-ite (gran′it), *n.* [It. *granito,* orig. pp., 'grained,' of *granire,* < *grano,* < L. *granum,* E. *grain*².] A granular igneous rock composed chiefly of feldspar (orthoclase) and quartz, usually with one or more other minerals, as mica, hornblende, etc.: much used in building, and for monuments, etc.—**gran′ite=ware,** *n.* Pottery with a speckled appearance like granite; also, a variety of pottery of unusual hardness; also, a kind of ironware with a gray, stone-like enamel.—**gra-nit-ic** (gra-nit′ik), *a.* Of or like granite.—**gran-i-toid** (gran′i-toid), *a.* [See *-oid.*] Granite-like.

gra-niv-o-rous (gra-niv′ọ-rus), *a.* [L. *granum,* grain, seed, + *vorare,* devour.] Feeding on grain or seeds.

gran-ny (gran′i), *n.*; pl. *grannies* (-iz). [Dim. of *grandam,* or of *grandmother.*] A grandmother (colloq.); an old woman (colloq.); a nurse or midwife (southern U. S.); one exhibiting the fussiness, mental weakness, or other traits of an old woman (colloq.).—**gran′ny=knot,** *n.* The ordinary knot tied by landsmen, derided by seamen because difficult to untie when jammed.

gran-o-phyre (gran′ọ-fīr), *n.* [G. *granophyr,* < *granit,* granite, + *porphyr,* porphyry.] Any of a class of porphyritic igneous rocks in which the ground-mass is a mixture of crystals.—**gran-o-phyr′ic** (-fir′ik), *a.*

grant (grȧnt), *v.* [OF. *graanter, creanter,* promise, assure, authorize, grant, confirm, approve, < L. *credens* (*credent-*), ppr. of *credere,* trust, believe.] **I.** *tr.* To agree or accede to (a request, etc.); also, to give or accord, esp. in answer to a request (as, to *grant* permission); also, to bestow or confer (a right, etc.), esp. by a formal act; transfer or convey (property), esp. by deed or writing; also, to admit or concede, as for the sake of argument. **II.**† *intr.* To agree or consent: as, "The soldiers should have toss'd me on their pikes Before I would have *granted* to that act" (Shakspere's "3 Henry VI.," i. 1. 245).—**grant,** *n.* The act of granting; also, that which is granted, as a privilege or right, a sum of money, or a tract of land; in *law,* a transfer or conveyance of property by deed or writing.—**grant′a-ble,** *a.* That may be granted.—**grant-ee′,** *n.* In *law,* one to whom a grant is made.—**grant′er,** *n.* One who grants.—**grant′or,** *n.* In *law,* one who makes a grant.

gran-u-lar (gran′ụ̄-lạ̈r), *a.* [LL. *granulum*: see *granule.*] Composed of, containing, or bearing granules or grains; also, of the nature of granules.—**granular lids** or **eyelids,** eyelids affected with trachoma.—**gran-u-lar′i-ty** (-lar′i-ti), *n.*—**gran′u-lar-ly,** *adv.*

gran-u-late (gran′ụ̄-lāt), *v.*; *-lated, -lating.* [LL. *granulum*: see *granule.*] **I.** *tr.* To form into granules or grains; also, to raise in granules; make rough on the surface. **II.** *intr.* To become granular; in *pathol.,* to develop granulations, as a wound.—**gran′u-lat-ed** (-lā-ted), *p. a.* Formed into or consisting of grains; also, having the surface raised in small grain-like elevations; hence, mottled; in *pathol.,* characterized by the presence of small grain-like bodies; having granulations.—**gran-u-la′tion** (-lā′shọn), *n.* The act or process of granulating; granulated condition; also, a granular formation; one of the grains of a granulated surface; in *pathol.,* the formation of small grain-like bodies, esp. in the process of healing; also, a small grain-like body or elevation, esp. one of those which form on the surface of wounds, etc., during healing.—**gran′u-la-tor,** *n.*

gran-ule (gran′ūl), *n.* [LL. *granulum,* dim. of L. *granum,* E. *grain*².] A little grain; a small particle; a pellet; a corpuscle; a sporule; a small grain-like elevation.—**gran′-u-lite** (-ụ̄-līt), *n.* In *petrog.,* any of various fine-grained or even-grained gneisses and granites, consisting chiefly of feldspar and quartz.—**gran-u-lit′ic** (-lit′ik), *a.*—**gran′u-lose** (-lōs), *n.* That portion of the starch-granule which is acted upon by diastase and the saliva.—**gran′u-lous,** *a.* Granular.

grape (grāp), *n.* [OF. *grape*, *crape* (F. *grappe*), cluster of fruit or flowers, orig. hook; from Teut. (cf. G. *krapf*, hook), and akin to E. *cramp*[1]: cf. *grapnel* and *grapple.*] The edible, pulpy, smooth-skinned berry or fruit which grows in clusters on vines of the genus *Vitis*, and from which wine is made; any vine bearing this fruit; also, *milit.*, grape-shot (as, "a fire of musketry and *grape*": Byron's "Don Juan," vii. 29); also, *pl.*, in *vet. science*, a morbid growth on the leg of a horse, resembling a bunch of grapes.—**grape′=fruit,** *n.* The roundish, usually pale-yellow, edible fruit yielded by certain varieties of the tropical or semitropical tree *Citrus decumana*, resembling the orange but larger, and having a bitter rind and an acid pulp (also called *shaddock*, which term however is usually restricted to the pear-shaped fruit yielded by other varieties of this tree). See *shaddock* and *citrus.*—**grape′=hy′a-cinth,** *n.* Any plant of the liliaceous genus *Muscari*, as *M. botryoides*, a species whose globular blue flowers resemble minute grapes.—**grap-er-y** (grā′pėr-i), *n.*; pl. *-ies* (-iz). An inclosure, as a glass-house, where grapes are grown; a plantation of grape-vines.—**grape′=shot,** *n.* A cluster of small cast-iron balls used as a charge for a cannon.—**grape′=stone,** *n.* A seed of a grape.—**grape′=sug′ar,** *n.* Dextroglucose.—**grape′=vine,** *n.* A vine that bears grapes; also, an imaginary telegraph line by which mysterious reports are popularly said to be transmitted (commonly 'grape-vine telegraph'); hence, an unauthenticated or baseless report; a canard; also, a complicated movement or figure in dancing.

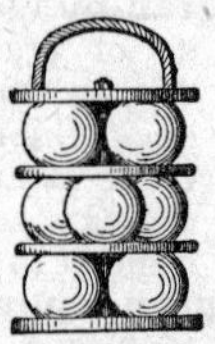
Grape-shot.

graph (grȧf), *n.* [Gr. γραφή, drawing, delineation, writing, < γράφειν, mark, draw, write.] A diagrammatic representation of a system of connections or relations by means of a number of spots or circles; in *math.*, a curve as representing an equation or function.—**graph,** *v. t.* In *math.*, to draw or plot (a curve) from its equation or function; also, to draw a curve representing (an equation or function).

-graph. [Gr. -γραφος, drawn or written, something drawn or written, -γράφος, drawing or writing, one who draws or writes, or γραφή, a drawing or writing, all < γράφειν, mark, draw, write; many E. words in *-graph* being referred directly to Gr. γράφειν.] A termination of adjectives meaning 'drawn or written' (in some manner), as *autograph*, *holograph*, and of nouns meaning 'something drawn or written,' 'writer,' 'apparatus for drawing, writing, recording, etc.,' as *allograph*, *bibliograph*, *digraph*, *paragraph*, *phonograph*, *photograph*, *radiograph*, *seismograph*, also of verbs, as *aërograph*. Cf. *-gram* and *-graphy*.

graph-ic (graf′ik), *a.* [L. *graphicus*, < Gr. γραφικός, pertaining to drawing, painting, or writing, < γραφή: see *graph.*] Of or pertaining to drawing, engraving, painting, etc. (as, the *graphic* arts); also, exhibiting as in a picture (as, a *graphic* description of a person or a scene); lifelike; vivid; also, of or pertaining to writing (as, *graphic* symbols); presenting an appearance like writing or printing (as, *graphic* gold, ore, or tellurium, same as *sylvanite*); noting, pertaining to, or possessing that kind of texture produced in a rock when certain constituents crystallize in such a way as to appear like written characters on the surfaces or sections of the rock; also, pertaining to the use of diagrams, graphs, mathematical curves, or the like; diagrammatic; pertaining to the determination of values, solving of problems, etc., by direct measurement on diagrams instead of by ordinary calculations. Also **graph′i-cal.**—**graph′i-cal-ly,** **graph′ic-ly,** *adv.*—**graph′ic-ness,** *n.*—**graph′ics,** *n.* The art of drawing, esp. as concerned with mathematics, engineering, etc.; the science of calculating by means of diagrams.

graph-ite (graf′īt), *n.* [G. *graphit*, < Gr. γράφειν, mark, draw, write.] Soft native carbon, having an iron-gray color and metallic luster, used in lead-pencils and crucibles, as a lubricant, etc.—**gra-phit-ic** (gra-fit′ik), *a.*—**graph′i-tize** (-i-tīz), *v. t.*; *-tized*, *-tizing*. To convert into graphite; also, to cover (the surface of an object) with graphite.—**graph″i-ti-za′tion** (-ti-zā′shọn), *n.*—**graph′i-toid, graph-i-toi′dal** (-toid, -toi′dạl), *a.* Resembling graphite.

gra-phol-o-gy (gra-fol′ọ-ji), *n.* [Gr. γραφή, writing: see *-logy.*] The study of handwriting, esp. as regarded as an expression of the writer's character.—**gra-phol′o-gist,** *n.*

graph-o-ma-ni-a (graf-ọ-mā′ni-ä), *n.* [NL., < Gr. γραφή, writing, + μανία, E. *mania.*] A mania for writing.—**graph-o-ma′ni-ac** (-ak), *n.*

graph-o-phone (graf′ọ-fōn), *n.* [Gr. γράφειν, write, + φωνή, sound.] An instrument invented in 1886 by Charles S. Tainter and Chichester A. Bell, for recording and reproducing speech, music, and other sounds, being of the phonograph type but substituting for the tin-foil cylinder of the original phonograph, into which the record was merely indented, a wax or similar cylinder into which the record of the sound-vibrations is cut or engraved in a line of one direction but of varying depth; in later use, any of various sound-reproducing machines employing either a cylinder record or a disk record (the term having at times been loosely used, but being now restricted to a particular make of machines and constituting a proprietary name, registered as a trade-mark in the U. S. in 1921). Cf. *phonograph* and *gramophone.*

-graphy. [Gr. -γραφία, < -γράφος, drawing or writing, one who draws or writes, < γράφειν, mark, draw, write; many E. words in *-graphy* being referred directly to Gr. γράφειν.] A termination of nouns denoting some process or form of drawing, representing, writing, recording, describing, etc., or an art or science concerned with some such thing, as in *biography*, *choregraphy*, *geography*, *hydrography*, *orthography*, *photography*, *telegraphy*, *topography*. Cf. *-gram* and *-graph*.

grap-nel (grap′nel), *n.* [ME. *grapenel*, dim. < OF. *grapin*, kind of hook, dim. of *grape*, hook: see *grape.*] An instrument with one or more hooks for seizing and holding something, as one thrown by a rope for catching on an enemy's ship; also, a small anchor with three or more flukes; also, any of various implements for clutching or grasping.

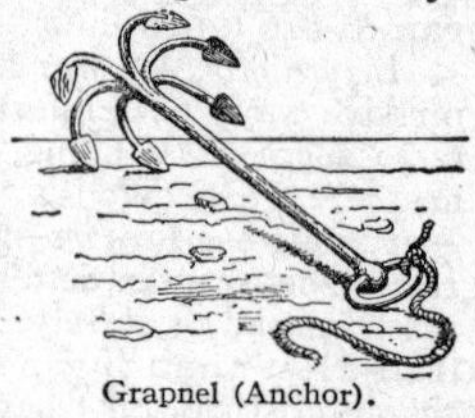
Grapnel (Anchor).

grap-ple (grap′l), *n.* [Appar. a dim. form < OF. *grape*, hook (see *grape* and *grapnel*); in later senses, < *grapple, v.*] A grapnel; also, the act of grappling; a grip or close hold, as in wrestling; a close encounter.—**grap′ple,** *v.*; *-pled*, *-pling*. **I.** *tr.* To seize, hold, or fasten with a grapple; fig., to fasten as with a grapple, or attach firmly (as, "Those friends thou hast, and their adoption tried, *Grapple* them to thy soul with hoops of steel": Shakspere's "Hamlet," i. 3. 63); also, to seize and hold (an opponent) firmly in a struggle; engage in a struggle or close encounter with. **II.** *intr.* To use a grapple; also, to hold or make fast to something as with a grapple; also, to seize another, or each other, in a firm grip, as in wrestling; clinch; contend (*with*) in a close encounter (often fig.).—**grap′pler,** *n.*—**grap′pling,** *n.* That by which anything is seized and held; a grapnel.—**grap′pling=i″ron,** *n.* A device with one or more iron claws or hooks for grappling; a grapnel.

grap-to-lite (grap′tọ-līt), *n.* [Gr. γραπτός, marked, written, + λίθος, stone.] Any of a group of Paleozoic cœlenterate organisms whose fossils found in hard shales resemble hieroglyphics.—**grap-to-lit′ic** (-lit′ik), *a.*

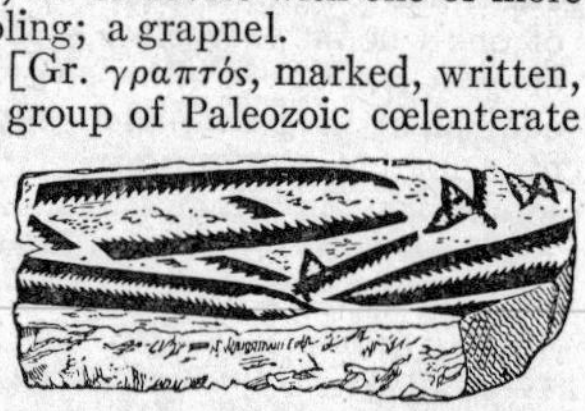
Block of Stone containing Graptolites.

grap-y (grā′pi), *a.* Of or like grapes.

grasp (grȧsp), *v.* [ME. *graspen*, *grapsen*; prob. akin to AS. *grāpian*, E. *grope.*] **I.** *tr.* To seize and hold by or as by clasping with the fingers; seize upon; hold firmly; also, to lay hold of with the mind; comprehend. **II.** *intr.* To make the motion of seizing; seize something firmly or eagerly.—**grasp,** *n.* A grasping or gripping; a grip of the hand; power of seizing and holding (as, to have a thing within one's *grasp*); also, hold, possession, or mastery (as, to wrest power from the *grasp* of a usurper); also, mental hold or comprehension (as, a subject beyond one's *grasp*); esp., broad or thorough comprehension.—**grasp'a-ble,** *a.* That may be grasped.—**grasp'er,** *n.*—**grasp'ing,** *p. a.* That grasps; fig., avaricious or greedy (as, "Stelling is moderate in his terms—he's not a *grasping* man": George Eliot's "Mill on the Floss," i. 3).—**grasp'ing-ly,** *adv.*—**grasp'ing-ness,** *n.*—**grasp'less,** *a.* Without grasp or grip; incapable of grasping; also, not to be grasped.

grass (gràs), *n.* [AS. *græs, gærs,* = D., G., Icel., and Goth. *gras,* grass; from the Teut. root whence E. *grow* and *green.*] Herbage in general, or the plants on which grazing animals pasture; specif., any plant of the family *Gramineæ* (or *Poaceæ*), characterized by jointed stems, sheathing leaves, flower-spikelets, and fruit consisting of a seed-like grain or caryopsis ('true grasses'); popularly, any of the plants of this family on which animals are pastured or which are cut and dried as hay; any of various similar plants, as sedges, rushes, etc., of related and other families; also, a blade of grass (now rare); also, pasture, or the condition of being at pasture (as, to put animals to *grass*); pasture-land (as, half of the farm is *grass*); also, the yearly growth of grass; hence, the season of the new growth of grass (as, a horse five years old next *grass*); also, the grass-covered ground. —**grass,** *v.* **I.** *tr.* To feed with growing grass; pasture; also, to cover with grass or turf; also, to lay on the grass, as for the purpose of bleaching; also, to knock, throw, or bring to the grass or ground (colloq.). **II.** *intr.* To produce grass; become covered with grass; also, to feed on growing grass; graze.

grass=cloth (gràs'klôth), *n.* Any of several kinds of cloth made from the fibers of grasses or other plants; esp., a thin, light fabric woven in China and the East from the fiber of the ramie and other urticaceous plants.

grass-finch (gràs'finch), *n.* A common sparrow, *Poœcetes gramineus,* of North America; also, any of various weaver-birds, esp. of the Australian genus *Poëphila.*

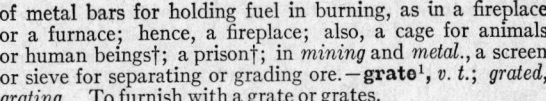

Grassfinch (*Poœcetes gramineus*).

grass=green (gràs'-grēn'). **I.** *a.* Of the green color of grass; also, green with grass. **II.** *n.* The green color of grass.

grass=grown (gràs'grōn), *a.* Overgrown with grass.

grass-hop-per (gràs'hop"ėr), *n.* Any of numerous orthopterous insects with hind legs fitted for leaping, as the locusts, certain katydids, etc.

Female Red-legged Grasshopper (*Melanoplus femur-rubrum*), a locust of the family *Acrididæ.*

grass-land (gràs'land), *n.* Land kept under grass; meadow-land; permanent pasture.

grass-less (gràs'les), *a.* Without grass.

grass=plot, grass=plat (gràs'plot, -plat), *n.* A plot of ground covered with grass; a lawn.

grass=snipe (gràs'snīp), *n.* The pectoral sandpiper.

grass=tree (gràs'trē), *n.* Any member of the Australian liliaceous genus *Xanthorrhœa,* comprising plants with a stout, woody stem bearing a tuft of long, grass-like leaves and a dense flower-spike; also, any of various similar plants of Australasia.

grass=widow (gràs'wid'ō), *n.* [From *grass* + *widow*; the original force of *grass* being uncertain.] A discarded mistress, or an unmarried mother of a child (now prov. Eng.); also, a woman who is separated or who lives apart from her husband (whether by reason of divorce or otherwise). —**grass'=wid'ow-er,** *n.* A man who is separated or who lives apart from his wife.

grass-y (gràs'i), *a.* Covered with grass; pertaining to or consisting of grass; grass-like.

grate[1] (grāt), *n.* [ML. *grata,* < L. *cratis,* wickerwork, hurdle: cf. *crate.*] A framework of parallel or crossed bars used as a partition, guard, cover, or the like; also, a frame of metal bars for holding fuel in burning, as in a fireplace or a furnace; hence, a fireplace; also, a cage for animals or human beings†; a prison†; in *mining* and *metal.,* a screen or sieve for separating or grading ore.—**grate**[1], *v. t.*; *grated, grating.* To furnish with a grate or grates.

grate[2] (grāt), *v.*; *grated, grating.* [OF. *grater* (F. *gratter*); from Teut. (cf. G. *kratzen,* scratch).] **I.** *tr.* To scratch†, scrape†, or scarify†; hence, to wear down or away by rough friction (archaic); more commonly, to reduce to small particles by rubbing against a rough surface or instrument (as, to *grate* a nutmeg); pulverize with a grater; also, to rub harshly together, as the teeth; rub against with a harsh, jarring sound (as, a boat *grates* the shore); produce by rough friction (poetic: as, "Open fly . . . The infernal doors, and on their hinges *grate* Harsh thunder," Milton's "Paradise Lost," ii. 881); declare or utter with harsh sound; also, fig., to fret, irritate, or vex (now rare: as, "*Grating* so harshly all his days of quiet With turbulent and dangerous lunacy," Shakspere's "Hamlet," iii. 1. 3). **II.** *intr.* To scrape or rub with rough or noisy friction, as one thing on or against another; make a sound as of rough scraping; sound harshly, or jar, as on the ear; fig., to have an irritating or unpleasant effect, as on the feelings.

grate-ful (grāt'fůl), *a.* [Obs. *grate,* pleasing, also thankful (< L. *gratus*: see *grace*), + *-ful.*] Pleasing to the mind or the senses; agreeable or welcome (as, a *grateful* task; *grateful* news); refreshing (as, *grateful* shade or breezes; *grateful* slumber; *grateful* fruits); also, warmly or deeply appreciative of kindness shown to one's self or to any person or thing that one is interested in; pleasurably sensible of indebtedness for benefits received; thankful; actuated by or betokening gratitude, as feelings, actions, or words.—**grate'ful-ly,** *adv.*—**grate'ful-ness,** *n.*

grat-er (grā'tėr), *n.* One who or that which grates; esp., an implement for grating; an instrument with a rough, indented surface for rubbing off small particles of a substance (as, a nutmeg-*grater*).

grat-i-cule (grat'i-kūl), *n.* [F., < ML. *graticula,* for L. *craticula,* gridiron: see *grille.*] A design or plan divided into squares to facilitate copying.

grat-i-fi-ca-tion (grat"i-fi-kā'shọn), *n.* [L. *gratificatio(n-).*] The act of gratifying, or the state of being gratified; also, something that gratifies; a source of pleasure or satisfaction; a reward, recompense, or gratuity (archaic).

grat-i-fi-er (grat'i-fī-ėr), *n.* One who gratifies.

grat-i-fy (grat'i-fī), *v. t.*; *-fied, -fying.* [F. *gratifier,* < L. *gratificari,* do a favor to, oblige, gratify, < *gratus,* pleasing, thankful, + *facere,* make.] To give pleasure to (persons) by satisfying desires or humoring inclinations or feelings; please by something especially desired or acceptable; satisfy (desires, appetites, etc.); indulge or humor (tastes, feelings, etc.); also, to reward or requite as in gratitude† (as, "to *gratify* his noble service": Shakspere's "Coriolanus," ii. 2. 44); remunerate, or give a gratuity to (archaic).—**grat'i-fy-ing-ly,** *adv.*

gra-tin (grà-taṅ), *n.* [F., < *gratter,* scrape: see *grate*[2].] A browned crust, as of bread-crumbs with butter or grated cheese on a baked dish of food; a dish with such a crust; this manner of preparing food.—**grat-i-nate** (grat'i-nāt), *v. t.*; *-nated, -nating.* [= F. *gratiner.*] To prepare or cook (food) in the gratin manner.

grat-ing[1] (grā'ting), *n.* A grate, or framework of parallel or crossed bars; a lattice cover for a ship's hatchway in fair weather; in *optics,* a series of fine parallel lines or scratches ruled very close together on a glass or polished metal surface, used to produce spectra by diffraction ('diffraction grating').

grat-ing[2] (grā'ting), *p. a.* That grates; harsh or jarring in sound, or as sound; irritating or unpleasant in effect. —**grat'ing-ly,** *adv.*

gra-tis (grā'tis). [L. *gratis,* for *gratiis,* by favor or kindness, abl. pl. of *gratia,* favor, E. *grace.*] **I.** *adv.* For nothing; without charge or pay; gratuitously. **II.** *a.* Free of cost; gratuitous.

grat-i-tude (grat'i-tūd), *n.* [OF. F. *gratitude,* < ML. *gratitudo,* < L. *gratus,* pleasing, thankful: see *grace.*] The quality or feeling of being grateful or thankful; grateful sense of indebtedness for kindness or benefits enjoyed.

gra-tu-i-tous (gra̤-tū′i-tus), *a.* [L. *gratuitus,* < *gratia,* favor: cf. *gratis.*] Freely bestowed or obtained; costing the recipient nothing; free; also, being without reason, cause, or justification (as, "He has indulged in *gratuitous* suppositions," H. James's "Portrait of a Lady," xlix.; a *gratuitous* insult); unwarranted; uncalled-for.—**gra-tu′i-tous-ly,** *adv.*—**gra-tu′i-tous-ness,** *n.*

gra-tu-i-ty (gra̤-tū′i-ti), *n.*; pl. *-ties* (-tiz). [F. *gratuité,* < ML. *gratuitas,* < L. *gratia,* favor: cf. *gratuitous* and *gratis.*] A gift or present, usually of money; a bounty, as to soldiers; often, a gift of money, over and above payment due for service, to a servant, porter, cabman, etc. (as, "Rainscourt . . . dismissed the post-boys with a handsome *gratuity*": Marryat's "King's Own," xviii.); a tip; a douceur.

grat-u-lant (grat̤′ū-la̤nt), *a.* Gratulating; expressing joy. [Archaic.]

grat-u-late (grat̤′ū-lāt), *v. t.*; *-lated, -lating.* [L. *gratulatus,* pp. of *gratulari,* express joy, congratulate, thank, < *gratus,* pleasing, thankful: see *grace.*] To express joy at; greet, salute, or hail with joy (as, "Where this night are met in state Many a friend to *gratulate* His wish'd presence": Milton's "Comus," 949); offer congratulations or felicitations upon (some happy event, etc.); also, to express joy or offer congratulations to; congratulate or felicitate. [Archaic.]—**grat-u-la′tion** (-lā′sho̤n), *n.* [L. *gratulatio(n-).*] The expression of joy at something welcome or fortunate; congratulation or felicitation; a speech of congratulation; also, a feeling of joy at something welcome or gratifying; gratification.—**grat′u-la-to-ry** (-la̤-tō̤-ri), *a.* Expressing joy or gratification; congratulatory.

grau-wack-e (grou′väk″ė), *n.* [G.] Graywacke.

gra-va-men (gra̤-vā′men), *n.*; pl. *-vamina* (-vam′i-nä̤). [LL., < L. *gravare,* load, weigh down: see *grieve.*] A grievance; also, that part of an accusation which weighs most heavily against the accused; the burden or substantial part of a charge or complaint.

grave[1] (grāv), *v. t.*; pret. *graved,* pp. *graved* or *graven,* ppr. *graving.* [AS. *grafan* = D. *graven* = G. *graben* = Icel. *grafa* = Goth. *graban,* dig: cf. *grave*[2], *groove,* and *gravure.*] To dig (archaic or prov.); also, to bury (archaic or prov.); also (archaic), to carve or sculpture (an image, etc.); incise or engrave (letters, designs, etc.), as on a surface; fig., to impress deeply, as on the mind or memory (as, "Until my heart shall cease to beat . . . That kind blue eye, and golden hair, Eternally are *graven* there": Praed's "Reminiscences of My Youth").

grave[2] (grāv), *n.* [AS. *græf* = D. *graf* = G. *grab,* grave; from the Teut. root seen in E. *grave*[1].] An excavation made in the earth to receive a dead body in burial; the place of interment of a corpse; a tomb or sepulcher; any place that becomes the receptacle of what is dead (lit. or fig.: as, a watery or a fiery *grave*; the province became the *grave* of dead reputations); also, death (sometimes personified: as, "O *grave,* where is thy victory?" 1 Cor. xv. 55).

grave[3] (grāv). [F. *grave,* < L. *gravis,* heavy, weighty, important, grievous, low in pitch.] **I.** *a.*; compar. *graver,* superl. *gravest.* Heavy to lift or carry (obs. or archaic); fig., weighty, momentous, or important (as, *grave* cares or responsibilities; *grave* matters or considerations); involving important or critical issues or serious consequences (as, *grave* questions, doubts, symptoms, or news; a *grave* situation); also, of great personal importance or authority (archaic: as, "most potent, *grave,* and reverend signiors," Shakspere's "Othello," i. 3. 76); also, dignified, sedate, or sober, as persons or their aspect, deportment, speech, etc.; solemn, as ceremonies, music, etc.; serious, earnest, or in earnest (rather than gay, smiling, or jesting); also, sober or somber, as colors, dress, etc.; also, low in pitch, as sound (opposed to *acute*); noting or having a particular accent (\`) indicating orig. a comparatively low pitch (as in ancient Greek), later quality of sound (as in the French *père*), distinct syllabic value (as in *belovèd*), etc. **II.** *n.* The grave accent.

grave[4] (grāv), *v. t.*; *graved, graving.* [Origin obscure.] *Naut.,* to clean (a ship's bottom or a ship) by burning or scraping off accretions and paying it over with pitch.

gra-ve[5] (grä′vā), *a.* [It., < L. *gravis*: E. *grave*[3].] In *music,* grave; solemn; slow.

grave=clothes (grāv′klōᴛʜz), *n. pl.* The clothes or dress in which a dead body is interred; cerements: as, "Like a ghost he seem'd whose *grave-clothes* were unbound" (Spenser's "Faerie Queene," ii. 11. 20).

grav-el (grav′e̤l), *n.* [OF. *gravele* (F. *gravelle*), dim. of *grave,* gravel, sandy shore; from Celtic.] Sand†; also, small stones and pebbles, or a mixture of these with sand; in *pathol.,* small calculi or concretions formed in the kidneys; the disease characterized by such concretions.—**grav′el,** *v. t.*; *-eled* or *-elled, -eling* or *-elling.* To cover or lay with gravel, as walks, roads, etc.; also, to bury under or choke with gravel or sand†; also, to run (a vessel) aground, as on a beach†; fig., to 'stick,' or bring to a standstill from perplexity or embarrassment; puzzle, pose, or nonplus (as, "The wisest doctor is *gravelled* by the inquisitiveness of a child": Emerson's "Essays," Intellect); also, to be a cause of irritation to (colloq., U. S.).—**grav′el=blind,** *a.* Blind or dim-sighted to a degree greater than sand-blind and less than stone-blind: orig. a humorous Shaksperian use ("O heavens, this is my true-begotten father! who, being more than sand-blind, high-gravel blind, knows me not": "Merchant of Venice," ii. 2. 38).

grave-less (grāv′les), *a.* Without a grave; unburied: as, "Till . . . my brave Egyptians all . . . Lie *graveless*" (Shakspere's "Antony and Cleopatra," iii. 13. 166).

grav-el-ly (grav′e̤l-i), *a.* Abounding in, consisting of, or resembling gravel.

grave-ly (grāv′li), *adv.* In a grave manner; seriously.

grav-en (grā′vn). Past participle of *grave*[1].—**grav′en,** *p. a.* Carved; sculptured; engraved. [Archaic.]

grave-ness (grāv′nes), *n.* Grave character; seriousness; gravity.

gra-ve-o-lent (gra̤-vē′ō̤-le̤nt), *a.* [L. *graveolens* (*-ent-*), < *gravis,* heavy, + *olens,* ppr. of *olere,* emit a smell.] Having a strong, unpleasant smell; rank; fetid.

grav-er (grā′vėr), *n.* One who carves or engraves (archaic); also, any of various tools for cutting, engraving, etc., as an engraver's burin.

grave=rob-ber (grāv′rob″ėr), *n.* One who robs graves, as of bodies or valuables buried in them; esp., one who steals dead bodies from graves; a body-snatcher.—**grave′=rob″bing,** *n.*

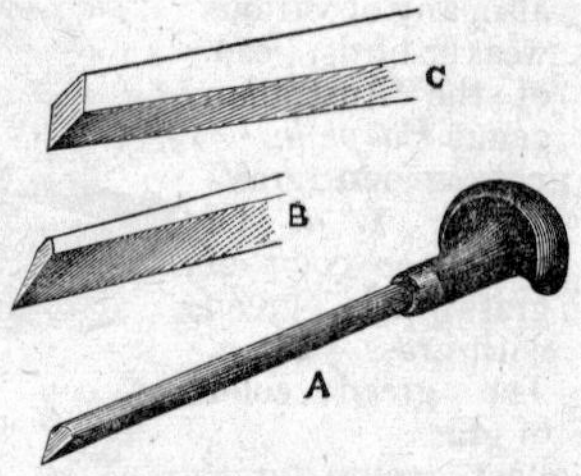

Wood-engraver's Gravers. — *A,* ordinary graver; *B,* tint-tool or liner; *C,* lozenge-graver.

Graves[1] (gräv), *n.* [From the *Graves,* gravelly districts in the Gironde department, France.] A class of Bordeaux wines, red and white, esp. the white.

graves[2], **greaves** (grāvz, grēvz), *n. pl.* [LG. *greve* = G. *griebe.*] The sediment of melted tallow or animal fat, pressed into cakes for dogs' food, fish-bait, etc.

grave-stone (grāv′stōn), *n.* A stone placed upon or at a grave, to mark the spot.

grave-ward (grāv′wä̤rd), *adv.* and *a.* Toward the grave.

grave-yard (grāv′yärd), *n.* A yard for graves; a cemetery.

grav-id (grav′id), *a.* [L. *gravidus,* < *gravis,* heavy, E. *grave*[3].] Heavy with young; pregnant.—**gra-vid-i-ty** (gra̤-vid′i-ti), *n.*

gra-vif-ic (gra-vif′ik), *a.* [L. *gravis,* heavy, + *facere,* make.] Making heavy; producing weight.

grav-i-grade (grav′i-grād). [L. *gravis,* heavy, + *gradi,* walk.] **I.** *a.* Walking with heavy steps; specif., of or pertaining to the *Gravigrada,* a group of extinct edentate animals including the megathere and the mylodon. **II.** *n.* A gravigrade animal.

gra-vim-e-ter (gra-vim′e-tėr), *n.* [L. *gravis,* heavy: see *-meter.*] An instrument for determining specific gravities. —**grav-i-met-ric, grav-i-met-ri-cal** (grav-i-met′rik, -ri-ka̤l), *a.* Of or pertaining to gravimetry.—**grav-i-met′ri-cal-ly,** *adv.*—**gra-vim′e-try,** *n.* [See *-metry.*] The measurement of weight; the determination of specific gravities.

grav-ing=dock (grā′ving-dok), *n.* A dry-dock: so called because used in graving or cleaning the bottoms of ships.

grav-i-tate (grav′i-tāt), *v.*; *-tated, -tating.* [NL. *gravitatus,* pp. of *gravitare,* < L. *gravitas,* E. *gravity.*] **I.** *intr.* To move or tend to move toward a body by the force of gravity or of gravitation; esp., to tend toward the lowest level; settle down; fig., to have a natural tendency, or be strongly attracted, toward some point or object of influence. **II.** *tr.* To cause to move downward by the force of gravity.—**grav-i-ta′tion** (-tā′shọn), *n.* [NL. *gravitatio(n-).*] The act or process of gravitating; also, the attraction or force by which all bodies in the universe tend to move toward one another, and to which, in the case of the earth, the fall of bodies is due; also, fig., natural tendency toward some point or object of influence (as, the *gravitation* of population toward the cities).—**grav-i-ta′tion-al,** *a.* Of or pertaining to gravitation.—**grav-i-ta′tion-al-ly,** *adv.*—**grav′i-ta-tive** (-tạ-tiv), *a.* Of or pertaining to gravitation; tending or causing to gravitate.

grav-i-tom-e-ter (grav-i-tom′e-tėr), *n.* [From *gravity* + *-meter.*] An instrument for determining specific gravities.

grav-i-ty (grav′i-ti), *n.*; pl. *-ties* (-tiz). [F. *gravité,* < L. *gravitas,* < *gravis,* heavy, E. *grave*[3].] Heaviness or weight (as, the center of *gravity*; specific *gravity*); specif., terrestrial gravitation; the attraction or force by which terrestrial bodies tend to move toward the center of the earth; precisely, the downward acceleration of terrestrial bodies due to the gravitation of the earth modified by centrifugal force, etc.; also, loosely, gravitation in general; also, fig., the quality or state of being grave; weightiness or importance; serious or critical character, as of news, occurrences, a case or situation, etc.; personal importance or authority†; dignity or sedateness of aspect, deportment, etc.; solemnity, as of ceremonies; seriousness, earnestness, or unsmiling demeanor (as, to find it difficult to preserve one's *gravity*); lowness in pitch, as of sounds; also, something grave, serious, or solemn, as a remark, subject, or matter.—**center of gravity.** See under *center*[2], *n.*—**specific gravity.** See under *specific, a.*

gra-vure (grạ-vūr′ or grā′vụr), *n.* [F., engraving, < *graver,* engrave; from Teut., and akin to E. *grave*[1].] Photogravure; a plate or print produced by photogravure.

gra-vy (grā′vi), *n.*; pl. *-vies* (-viz). [ME. *gravey, grave*; origin obscure.] The fat and juices that drip from meat in cooking; these juices made into a dressing for meat, vegetables, etc.—**gra′vy=boat,** *n.* A small boat-shaped (or other) vessel for serving gravy or sauce.

gray, grey (grā), *a.* [AS. *grǣg* = D. *grauw* = G. *grau* = Icel. *grār,* gray.] Of a color between white and black, having little or no positive hue; ash-colored; lead-colored; hence, not bright (as, a *gray* day); dismal or gloomy (as, a *gray* existence); also, dressed or habited in gray (as, a *gray* friar: see below); also, gray-haired (as, "Who knows not this, tho' *grey,* is still a child": Young's "Night Thoughts," ii. 386); hence, old or ancient (as, "Who pious gather'd each tradition *grey,* That floats your solitary wastes along": Scott's "Vision of Don Roderick," Introd., v.); pertaining to old age; mature, as experience.—**gray friar,** a Franciscan friar: from the gray color of the original habit of the order.—**gray goose,** the graylag.—**gray mare,** a wife who rules her husband: in allusion to the proverb 'the gray mare is the better horse,' referring to such a wife.—**gray matter,** in *anat.,* nervous tissue, esp. of the brain and spinal cord, containing both fibers and nerve-cells, and of a dark reddish-gray color (cf. *white matter,* under *white, a.*); hence (colloq.), brains or intellect.—**gray, grey,** *n.* A gray color; also, something of this color; a gray or subdued light (as, "in the *gray* of the daybreak": Longfellow's "To the Driving Cloud," 30); gray material or clothing; a gray horse (as, "Mrs. Mantrap . . . who drives her *greys* in the park": Thackeray's "Vanity Fair," xxxvii.).—**gray, grey,** *v.* **I.** *intr.* To become gray. **II.** *tr.* To make gray; also, to make dull in appearance, as glass, a photograph, etc.—**gray′-back, grey′back,** *n.* A Confederate soldier during the American Civil War (in allusion to the gray uniform: colloq.); also, any of various animals, as a bird, the knot, *Tringa canutus,* and a whale, *Rhachianectes glaucus,* of the northern Pacific.—**gray′beard, grey′beard,** *n.* A man with a gray beard; hence, an old man; also, a large jug for holding spirits; a bellarmine.—**gray′fish, grey′fish,** *n.* The common dogfish, *Squalus acanthias.*—**gray′=head′ed, grey′=head′ed,** *a.* Having a gray head of hair; hence, old or ancient (as, a *gray-headed* error); of or pertaining to old age or old men (as, *gray-headed* wisdom).

gray-hound (grā′hound), *n.* See *greyhound.*

gray-ish, grey-ish (grā′ish), *a.* Having a tinge of gray.

gray-lag, grey-lag (grā′lag), *n.* [Perhaps named from its lagging behind other species in migrating.] The common gray wild goose, *Anser cinereus* (or *ferus*), of Europe.

Graylag.

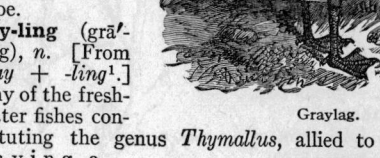

gray-ling (grā′-ling), *n.* [From *gray* + *-ling*[1].] Any of the fresh-water fishes constituting the genus *Thymallus,* allied to the trout, but having a longer and higher dorsal fin.

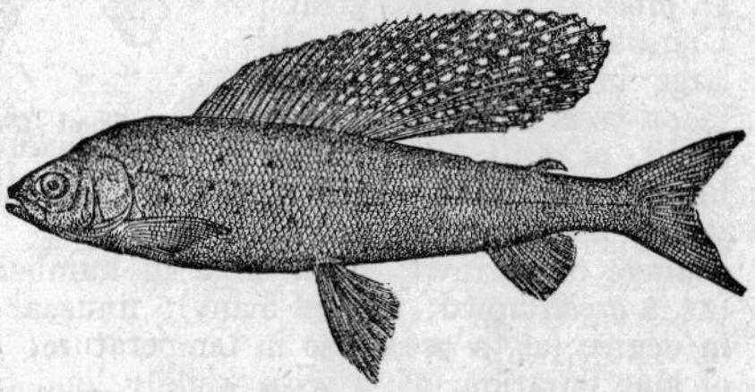

Alaska Grayling (*Thymallus signifer*).

gray-ly, grey-ly (grā′li), *adv.* With a gray hue or tinge: as, "A hazy light Spread *greyly* eastward" (Keats's "Endymion," i.).—**gray′ness, grey′ness,** *n.*

gray-wack-e, grey-wack-e (grā′wak″ė), *n.* [G. *grauwacke,* 'gray wacke': see *wacke.*] In *geol.,* a compact aggregate of grains of various siliceous rocks, held together by a paste which is usually siliceous.

graze[1] (grāz), *v.*; *grazed, grazing.* [Origin obscure.] **I.** *tr.* To touch or rub lightly in passing; also, to scrape the skin from (a part of the body). **II.** *intr.* To touch or rub something lightly, or so as to produce slight abrasion, in passing.—**graze**[1], *n.* A grazing, or touching or rubbing lightly in passing; a slight abrasion.

graze[2] (grāz), *v.*; *grazed, grazing.* [AS. *grasian,* < *græs,* E. *grass.*] **I.** *intr.* To feed on growing herbage, as cattle, etc., do; also, to pasture cattle, etc. **II.** *tr.* To feed on (growing grass, etc.: as, "Flocks *Grazing* the tender herb," Milton's "Paradise Lost," iv. 253); put cattle, etc., to feed on (grass, land, etc.: as, "You may *graze* the ground, when the trees are grown up," Johnson, in Boswell's "Johnson," April 18, 1783); also, to put (cattle, etc.) to pasture; tend (cattle, etc.) while at pasture.—**graze**[2], *n.* A grazing, or feeding on grass.—**graz-er** (grā′zėr), *n.* An animal that grazes.—**gra-zier** (grā′zhėr), *n.* One who grazes cattle for the market.—**graz′ing,** *n.* The act of one who or that which grazes or pastures; also, pasture-land; a pasture.

gra-zi-o-so (grä-tsē-ō′sō), *a.* [It., < L. *gratiosus,* E. *gracious.*] In *music,* graceful.

grease (grēs), *n.* [OF. *graisse, craisse* (F. *graisse*), < L. *crassus,* fat.] The melted or rendered fat of animals, esp. when in a soft state; hence, fatty or oily matter in general; also, wool as shorn, before being cleansed of the oily matter; in *hunting,* the fat or fatness of game, with reference to the season for killing; in *vet. science,* an inflammation of a horse's skin in the fetlock region, attended with an oily secretion.—**grease** (grēs or grēz), *v. t.*; *greased, greasing.* To smear or anoint with grease; also, to soil with grease; also, to lubricate with grease; hence, to cause to run easily; often, to bribe (as, "Envy not the store Of the *greas'd* advocate, that grinds the poor": Dryden's tr. Persius's "Satires," iii. 139); in *vet. science,* to cause (a horse) to become affected with grease.—**grease′=bush,** *n.* Greasewood.—**grease′=paint′,** *n.* A mixture of tallow or hard grease and a pigment, used by actors for painting their faces.—**greas-er** (grē′sėr or grē′zėr), *n.* One who or that which greases; also, a

Mexican or Spanish-American (slang, U. S.).—**grease′-wood,** *n.* A chenopodiaceous shrub, *Sarcobatus vermiculatus,* of the alkaline regions of the western U. S., containing a small amount of oil and used for fuel; also, any of various similar shrubs. —**greas-y** (grē′si or grē′zi), *a.*; compar. *greasier,* superl. *greasiest.* Composed of or containing grease; oily; unctuous; often, containing much grease, as food; also, smeared or soiled with grease; also, grease-like, as in appearance or feel; hence, slippery; also, dirty, as the weather; also, indecent, as language; in *vet. science,* affected with the disease called grease. —**greas′i-ly,** *adv.*—**greas′i-ness,** *n.*

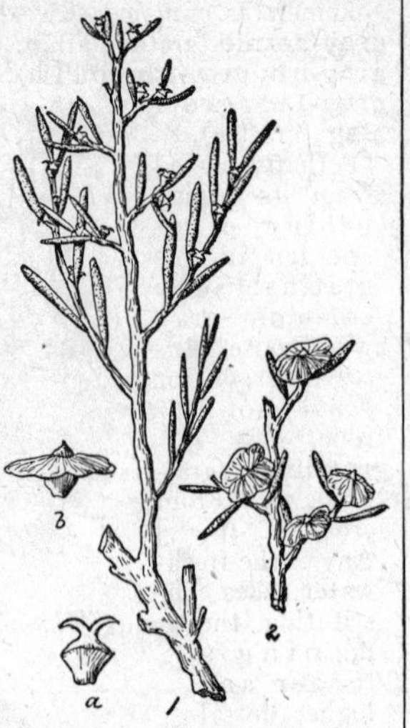
Greasewood (*Sarcobatus vermiculatus*).—1, branch with female flowers; 2, branch with fruits; *a*, a female flower; *b*, the fruit.

great (grāt), *a.* [AS. *grēat* = D. *groot* = G. *gross,* great.] Unusually or comparatively large in size or dimensions (as, a *great* house, tree, lake, cloud, or fire); big; large; hence, big with child or young; pregnant; full, as with courage or sorrow†; also, large in number, or numerous (as, a *great* crowd; a *great* many); unusual or considerable in degree (as, a *great* rise in temperature; *great* velocity); of long duration (as, a *great* while); loud (as, a *great* cry; a *great* noise); in general, beyond what is ordinary, as in extent, scope, character, etc. (as, *great* kindness; *great* authority; *great* ignorance; a *great* joke); of much consequence, or important (as, the *great* point to be noted; *great* issues are at stake; no *great* matter); chief or principal (as, the *great* seal: see phrase below); notable or remarkable (as, a *great* occasion; a *great* miracle); distinguished, illustrious, or famous, as persons or things (often in titles: as, Alexander the *Great*); of high rank, official position, social standing, etc. (as, *great* nobles; *great* personages; the *great* man of the town); of extraordinary powers, abilities, or achievements (as, a *great* poet or composer; a *great* statesman; a *great* race-horse); of unusual excellence or merit, admirable, or fine (as, a *great* poem; *great* achievements); of noble or lofty character, as persons, thoughts, utterances, acts, ends, etc.; in general (often playful) characterization, first-rate, capital, fine, amusing, etc. (colloq.: as, we had a *great* time; he is a *great* old fellow); also, being such in an extreme degree (as, *great* friends; a *great* rogue); incessant or persistent (as, a *great* talker; a *great* traveler); also, skilful or expert (*at*: colloq.: as, to be *great* at golf or at mathematics); having the taste or interest strongly fixed (*on*: colloq.: as, to be *great* on art or on social reform); much addicted to something (with *on*: colloq.: as, to be *great* on finding fault); also, much in use or favor (as, 'humor' was a *great* word with the old physiologists); intimate or friendly (now prov. Eng. and Sc.); in *genealogy,* one degree more remote in ascent (through a parent or ancestor) or in descent (through a direct descendant, a nephew or niece, etc.) than a relationship specified (used in compounds: as, *great-grandfather,* a parent's grandfather; *great-great-grandfather,* a parent's great-grandfather; *great-grandson,* a son's or daughter's grandson; *great-great-grandson,* a son's or daughter's great-grandson; *great-aunt,* a father's or mother's aunt, a grandaunt; *great-niece,* a nephew's or niece's daughter, a grandniece; *great-uncle,* a granduncle; *great-nephew,* a grandnephew: cf. *grand*).—**Great Bear.** See *bear*[2], *n.*—**great circle.** See under *circle, n.* —**great Dane.** See *Dane.*—**Great Dog.** See *dog, n.*—**great go.** See *go, n.*—**great gross.** See under *gross, n.*—**Great Lakes,** a chain of five large fresh-water lakes (Superior, Michigan, Huron, Erie, and Ontario) between the U. S. and Canada.—**Great Mogul.** See *Mogul.*—**great primer.** See under *primer*[2].—**Great Russians.** See under *Russian, n.*—**great seal,** the principal seal of a government or state.—**Great War.** Same as *World War* (see under *world*). —**Great White Way,** a popular name for Broadway, New York, for some distance north and south from 42d Street, in allusion to the brilliant illumination at night.

great-coat (grāt′kōt), *n.* A heavy overcoat. [Chiefly Eng.]

great-en (grā′tn), *v.* **I.** *tr.* To make great or greater; enlarge; increase. **II.** *intr.* To become great or greater: as, "Life *greatens* in these later years" (Whittier's "Snow-Bound").

great=heart-ed (grāt′här′ted), *a.* Having or showing a great, noble, or generous heart; magnanimous.—**great′=heart′ed-ness,** *n.*

great-ly (grāt′li), *adv.* In a great manner or degree.—**great′-ness,** *n.*

greave (grēv), *n.* [OF. *greve,* shin, greave; origin unknown.] A piece of armor for the leg below the knee.

greaves, *n. pl.* See *graves*[2].

grebe (grēb), *n.* [F. *grèbe.*] Any of the diving birds constituting the family *Podicipedidæ,* related to the loons, but having lobate instead of webbed toes, and a merely rudimentary tail, as *Podiceps cristatus* ('crested grebe') or *P. fluviatilis* ('little grebe') of Europe, or *Podilymbus podiceps* ('pied-billed grebe') of America; also, the plumage of the breast of these birds, of a silvery luster and satiny texture, much used for millinery, etc.

Horned Grebe (*Podiceps cornutus,* or *Colymbus auritus*), of the northern hemisphere.

Gre-cian (grē′shạn). [L. *Græcia,* Greece, < *Græcus,* Greek.] **I.** *a.* Of or pertaining to Greece or its inhabitants; Greek. **II.** *n.* A Greek; also, a Hellenized Jew (as, "There arose a murmuring of the *Grecians* [Revised Version *Grecian Jews*] against the Hebrews": Acts, vi. 1); also, one versed in the Greek language or literature.—**Gre′-cism** (-sizm), *n.* [L. *Græcus,* Greek.] An idiom or peculiarity of the Greek language; also, the spirit of Greek thought, art, etc.; adoption or imitation of this.—**Gre′cize** (-sīz), *v.*; *-cized, -cizing.* **I.** *tr.* To impart Greek characteristics to; also, to translate into Greek. **II.** *intr.* To conform to what is Greek; adopt Greek speech, idioms, customs, etc.

Gre-co-, Græ-co- (grē′kọ-). Form of L. *Græcus,* Greek, used in combination, as in *Greco-Latin, Greco-Roman, Greco-Turkish.*—**Gre-co-ma′ni-a** (-mā′ni-ạ̈), *n.* A mania or passion for what is Greek.—**Gre-co-ma′ni-ac** (-ak), *n.* —**Gre′co-phil, Gre′co-phile** (-fil), *n.* [See *-phil.*] A lover or admirer of Greece or the Greeks.

gree[1] (grē), *n.* [OF. *gre,* < L. *gradus,* step, E. *grade.*] A step†, stage†, or degree†; also, superiority, mastery, or victory, or the prize for a victory (now only Sc.: as, "That sense and worth, o'er a' the earth, May bear the *gree,*" Burns's "For A' That," 36).

gree[2] (grē), *n.* [OF. *gre* (F. *gré*), < L. *gratus,* pleasing.] Favor or good-will (as, to take a thing in *gree*); also, will, accord, or consent (as, by one's *gree*); also, satisfaction, as for an injury done (as, to make *gree*). [Obs. or archaic.]

gree[3] (grē), *v. t.* or *i.*; *greed, greeing.* [For *agree.*] To bring or come into accord; harmonize; agree. [Now Sc. and prov. Eng.]

greed (grēd), *n.* [Back-formation from *greedy.*] Greedy desire; inordinate or rapacious longing, esp. for wealth.

greed-y (grē′di), *a.*; compar. *greedier,* superl. *greediest.* [AS. *grǣdig,* akin to *grǣdum,* with greed, Icel. *grādhr,* hunger, greed, Goth. *grēdus,* hunger.] Having an inordinate desire for food or drink; ravenous; voracious; also, eager for gain, wealth, etc.; avaricious; covetous; in general, having eager desire (as, *greedy* of praise); keenly desirous; eager. —**greed′i-ly,** *adv.*—**greed′i-ness,** *n.*

gree-gree (grē′grē), *n.* [Afr.] An African charm, amulet, or fetish.

Greek (grēk), *n.* [AS. *Grēcas*, also *Crēcas*, pl., < L. *Græcus*, < Gr. Γραικός, a Greek.] A native or inhabitant of Greece, ancient or modern; a member of the Greek race; also, a member of the Greek Church; also, a wily person; a swindler or sharper; a cheat at cards; also, a merry fellow; a boon companion; also, the language of the people of Greece (divided for convenience into ancient or classical Greek, extending to A.D. 200; Late Greek, from 200 to 600; Middle Greek, from 600 to 1500; and modern, or New, Greek, from 1500 on), esp. that of the classical period; hence, anything unintelligible, as speech, statements, etc. (colloq.: as, the letter, being in French, was *Greek* to him).

⁂ Since Greek is the only language printed in this dictionary in other than Roman (or English) letters, the Greek alphabet, with the Roman equivalents, is here given:

Form.	Equivalent.	Name.	Form.	Equivalent.	Name.
Α α	a	alpha	Ν ν	n	nu
Β β	b	beta	Ξ ξ	x	xi
Γ γ	g	gamma	Ο ο	o (short)	omicron
Δ δ	d	delta	Π π	p	pi
Ε ε	e (short)	epsilon	Ρ ρ	r	rho
Ζ ζ	z	zeta	Σ σ, ς	s	sigma
Η η	e (long)	eta	Τ τ	t	tau
Θ θ, ϑ	th	theta	Υ υ	u, y	upsilon
Ι ι	i	iota	Φ φ	ph	phi
Κ κ	k, c	kappa	Χ χ	kh, ch	chi
Λ λ	l	lambda	Ψ ψ	ps	psi
Μ μ	m	mu	Ω ω	o (long)	omega

—**Greek,** *a.* Of or pertaining to Greece, the Greeks, or their language; also, pertaining to the Greek Church. —**Greek calends.** See under *calends.*—**Greek Church,** the Christian church of the countries in communion or doctrinal agreement with the patriarch of Constantinople, comprising the former Eastern (Roman) Empire, and countries evangelized from it, as Russia (also called *Eastern Church*: cf. *Western Church,* under *western, a.*); also, that part of this church which constitutes the established church in Greece.—**Greek cross,** a cross consisting of an upright crossed in the middle by a horizontal piece of the same length.—**Greek fire,** any of various combustible compositions (consisting of substances such as pitch, asphalt, inflammable oils, sulphur, etc.) used by the Greeks and others in medieval warfare.—**Greek′ish,** *a.* Greek or Grecian (archaic); also, like what is Greek; after the Greek type.

green (grēn), *a.* [AS. *grēne* = D. *groen* = G. *grün* = Icel. *grœnn, grænn,* green; from the Teut. root whence E. *grow* and *grass.*] Of the color of growing herbage and foliage (in the spectrum, being intermediate between yellow and blue); also, covered with a growth of herbage or foliage (as, *green* fields); verdant; characterized by the presence of verdure (as, a *green* Christmas); hence, mild or temperate (as, a *green* winter); also, having a pale or sickly color, as from fear, jealousy, or illness; also, full of life and vigor (as, "His *green* old age seemed to be the result of health and benevolence": Goldsmith's "Vicar of Wakefield," xiv.); vigorous; undecayed; also, not fully developed or perfected in growth or condition; unripe or immature; unseasoned, as timber; not dried, cured, etc.; raw or underdone, as meat; not fired, as bricks or pottery; also, immature in age, judgment, etc.; untrained; inexperienced; hence, simple or gullible; also, fresh, recent, or new (as, a *green* wound). —**green cheese,** new or fresh cheese; also, cheese colored green, as by means of sage. In popular expressions the belief that the moon is made of green cheese is taken as a type of foolish credulity or utter absurdity.—**green corn,** the unripe and tender ears of maize, esp. when used as a table vegetable.—**green dragon,** an American araceous herb, *Arisæma dracontium,* with a greenish or whitish spathe. —**green goose,** a young goose, suitable for market.—**green monkey,** a monkey, *Cercopithecus sabæus* (or *callitrichus*), of western Africa, with a greenish-gray back.—**green soap.** See under *soap, n.*—**green tea.** See under *tea.*—**green,** *n.* A green color; also, a green dye or pigment; also, any of various things of green color; green material or clothing; grassy land; a plot of grassy ground; a piece of grassy ground constituting a town or village common; the whole course or links on which golf is played, or a putting-green alone; *pl.,* fresh leaves or branches of trees, shrubs, etc., used for decoration; the leaves and stems of plants, as spinach, used for food.—**green,** *v. i.* or *t.* To become or make green: as, "Spring came again *greening* the hawthorn buds" (Masefield's "Daffodil Fields," iii.).

green-back (grēn′bak), *n.* A U. S. legal-tender note (officially called 'United States note') issued against the credit of the country and not against gold or silver on deposit (so called because the back is printed in green); by extension, any piece of U. S. paper money having the back printed in green; also, any of various animals, as the American golden plover (*Charadrius dominicus*), a European garfish (*Belone vulgaris*), etc.—**Greenback party,** in *U. S. hist.,* a former political party, organized in 1874, opposed to the retirement, or the reduction in amount, of the greenback currency, and aiming to make such notes the only paper currency.—**Green′back″er,** *n.*

green-bri-er (grēn′brī″ėr), *n.* Any plant of the genus *Smilax* (see *smilax*), esp. *S. rotundifolia,* of the eastern U. S., a climbing plant with prickly stem and thick leaves.

green=cod (grēn′kod), *n.* The cultus-cod.

green-er (grē′nėr), *n.* A green or inexperienced workman, esp. a foreigner. [Slang, Eng.]

green-er-y (grē′nėr-i), *n.*; pl. *-ies* (-iz). Green foliage or vegetation; verdure; also, a place where green plants are reared or kept.

green=eyed (grēn′īd), *a.* Having green eyes (as, the *green-eyed* monster, jealousy: see Shakspere's "Othello," iii. 3. 166); hence, having the mental perception disturbed by jealousy.

green-finch (grēn′finch), *n.* A European finch, *Ligurinus chloris,* with green and yellow plumage; also, the Texas sparrow.

green-gro-cer (grēn′grō″sėr), *n.* A retailer of fresh vegetables and fruit.—**green′gro″cer-y,** *n.*; pl. *-ies* (-iz).

green-heart (grēn′härt), *n.* The bebeeru (tree), or its hard, durable wood.

green-horn (grēn′hôrn), *n.* [In allusion to the immature horns of a young animal.] A raw, inexperienced person (as, "mere *greenhorns,* men unused to Indian life": Irving's "Captain Bonneville," vii.); a foreigner lately arrived; hence, one easily imposed upon.

green-house (grēn′hous), *n.* A glass-house for the cultivation or protection of tender plants; in *ceram.,* a house where pottery is dried before being placed in the kiln.

green-ing (grē′ning), *n.* A kind of apple the ripe skin of which is green.

green-ish (grē′nish), *a.* Somewhat green; having a tinge of green.

green-let (grēn′let), *n.* [See *-let.*] A vireo (bird).

green-ling (grēn′ling), *n.* Any of the acanthopterygian fishes constituting the family *Hexagrammidæ,* found about rocks and kelp in the northern Pacific Ocean.

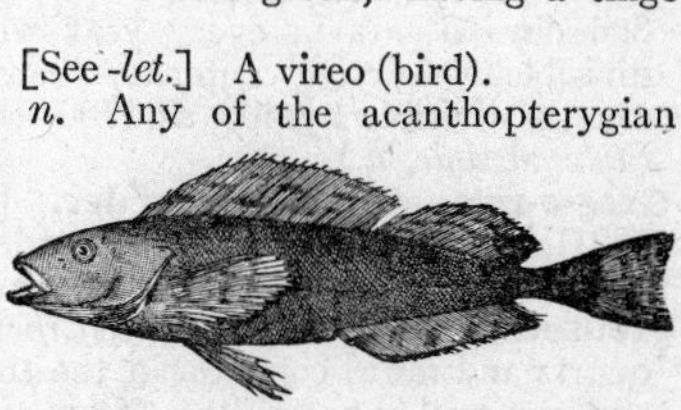

Greenling (*Hexagrammos stelleri*).

green-ly (grēn′li), *adv.* With a green color or tinge; also, with vigorous growth or life; also, with inexperience; with the awkwardness or simplicity of inexperience (as, "I must assist you, I reckon, for you are setting very *greenly* about this gear": Scott's "Monastery," xxx.).—**green′ness,** *n.*

green-ock-ite (grē′nọk-īt), *n.* [Named (1840) from Lord *Greenock.*] A rare mineral consisting of cadmium sulphide.

green-room (grēn′röm), *n.* A retiring-room in a theater, for the use of the actors and actresses when not required on the stage; also, a room for the reception of new cloth from the weaving factory, or one in which to dry pottery before burning.

green-sand (grēn′sand), *n.* A variety of sandstone containing a silicate of iron and potassium (glauconite) which imparts to it a greenish hue. See *marl*[1], *n.*

green-shank (grēn′shangk), *n.* An old-world sandpiper, *Totanus glottis* (or *nebularius*).

Greenshank.

green-sick-ness (grēn′sik″nes), *n.* Chlorosis.—**green′-sick,** *a.*

green-stone (grēn′-stōn), *n.* Any of various dark-greenish eruptive rocks; also, nephrite.

green-sward (grēn′-swârd), *n.* Turf green with grass.—**green′sward″ed,** *a.*

greenth (grēnth), *n.* Green color, as of vegetation; verdure.

Green-wich (grin′ij) **time.** The mean solar time of the meridian of Greenwich, near London.

green-wood (grēn′wůd), *n.* A wood or forest when green, as in summer.

green-y (grē′ni). **I.** *a.* Greenish. **II.** *n*; pl. *greenies* (-niz). A greenhorn; a freshman at a college, etc. (as, "He was entered among the *greenies* of this famous university [at Leyden]": Southey's "Doctor," ch. l.). [Colloq.]

greet[1] (grēt), *v. i.* [AS. *grǣtan, grētan,* = Icel. *grāta* = Goth. *grētan,* weep.] To cry; weep; lament. [Now Sc. and north. Eng.]

greet[2] (grēt), *v.* [AS. *grētan* = D. *groeten* = G. *grüssen,* greet.] **I.** *tr.* To address with some form of salutation; salute; hail; welcome; also, to meet (the eye, etc.). **II.** *intr.* To give salutations on meeting.—**greet′er,** *n.*—**greet′ing,** *n.* The act or words of one who greets; a salutation; a welcome.

greg-a-rine (greg′ą-rin), *n.* [NL. *Gregarina,* the typical genus, < L. *gregarius,* E. *gregarious.*] One of the *Gregarinida,* a group of protozoans which are parasitic in insects, worms, crustaceans, etc.

gre-ga-ri-ous (grę-gā′ri-us), *a.* [L. *gregarius,* < *grex* (*greg-*), flock, herd.] Living in flocks or herds, as animals; hence, disposed to associate with others, as persons; also, pertaining to a flock or crowd; in *bot.,* growing in open clusters.—**gre-ga′ri-ous-ly,** *adv.*—**gre-ga′ri-ous-ness,** *n.*

Gre-go-ri-an (grę-gō′ri-ąn), *a.* Of or pertaining to Gregory I., pope from 590 to 604 (as, *Gregorian* music, the liturgical music of the Roman Catholic and other churches), or Gregory XIII., pope from 1572 to 1585 (as, the *Gregorian* calendar, the reformed Julian calendar now in use, according to which the ordinary year consists of 365 days, and a leap-year of 366 days occurs in every year whose number is exactly divisible by 4 except centenary years whose numbers are not exactly divisible by 400, as 1700, 1800, and 1900: see *New Style,* at *style, n.*).

Greg-o-ry's (greg′ǫ-riz) **pow′der.** [From J. *Gregory* (1753–1821), Scotch physician.] A powder composed of rhubarb, magnesium oxide, and ginger: used as a laxative.

grei-sen (grī′zn), *n.* [G.] A rock composed chiefly of quartz and mica, common in the tin mines of Saxony, etc., and supposed to be an altered form of granite.

gre-mi-al (grē′mi-ąl). [LL. *gremialis* (as n., ML. *gremiale*), < L. *gremium,* lap, bosom.] **I.** *a.* Of or pertaining to the lap or bosom; hence, intimate; also, dwelling within the bosom of a university, society, etc.; resident; also, of or pertaining to the internal affairs of a corporation or society, or confined to its members. **II.** *n.* A cloth placed on a bishop's lap when he sits in celebrating mass or in conferring orders; also, a resident member of a university, society, etc.

Grem-lin (grem′lin), *n.* One of the imaginary elf-like beings which supposedly trouble the pilots of war planes.

gre-nade (grę-nād′), *n.* [F. *grenade* = Sp. *granada,* pomegranate, grenade, < L. *granatus,* having grains or seeds (*granatum,* pomegranate), < *granum,* E. *grain*[2].] A pomegranate†; also, a small explosive shell, usually thrown by hand; also, a glass missile for scattering chemicals.

gren-a-dier (gren-ą-dēr′), *n.* [F., < *grenade,* E. *grenade.*] Orig., a soldier who threw grenades; later, a member of a company composed of the tallest men of a regiment (hence applied contemptuously to a tall, masculine woman); now, in the British army, a member of the first regiment of household infantry ('Grenadier Guards').

British Grenadier of 1745, blowing his fuse to light a grenade.

gren-a-dil-la (gren-ą-dil′ä), *n.* Same as *granadilla.*

gren-a-dine (gren-ą-dēn′), *n.* [F. *grenadine,* < *grenade,* pomegranate: see *grenade.*] A syrup made from pomegranate juice; also, a thin openwork fabric of silk, wool, or other fiber, used for women's dresses, etc.

Gresh-am's (gresh′ąmz) **law.** [From Sir T. *Gresham* (died 1579), English financier.] In *polit. econ.,* the tendency of the inferior of two forms of currency in circulation together to circulate more freely than, or to the exclusion of, the superior, due to the hoarding of the latter: observed and commented on by Gresham, but well explained by earlier economic writers.

gres-so-ri-al (gre-sō′ri-ąl), *a.* [NL. *gressorius,* < L. *gradi,* walk, go: see *gradient.*] Having the habit of walking; adapted for walking, as the feet of some birds. Also **gres-so′ri-ous.**

grew (grö). Preterit of *grow.*

grew′some, etc. See *gruesome, etc.*

grey (grā), etc. See *gray,* etc.

grey-hound (grā′hound), *n.* [AS. *grīghund* = Icel. *greyhundr,* greyhound (Icel. *grey,* dog); not connected with *gray.*] One of a breed of tall, slender dogs notable for keen sight and for fleetness; fig., a swift ship, esp. an ocean steamship.

grib-ble (grib′l), *n.* [Origin obscure.] A small marine isopod crustacean, *Limnoria terebrans,* which destroys submerged timber by boring into it; also, any of certain related species.

grice (grīs), *n.* [ME. *grise,* from Scand.: cf. Icel. *grīss,* Sw. and Dan. *gris.*] A young pig. [Now Sc. and prov. Eng.]

grid (grid), *n.* [Back-formation from *gridiron.*] A grating; also, a gridiron; in *elect.,* a ridged or perforated lead plate used in a storage-battery; in *wireless teleg.* and *teleph.,* one of the interior elements of a vacuum-tube (see *vacuum-tube*).

grid-dle (grid′l), *n.* [OF. *gredil,* var. of *greil,* gridiron: see *grill*[1].] A gridiron (now prov.); also, a plate, as of iron or soapstone, on which cakes are cooked over a fire.—**grid′-dle,** *v. t.*; *-dled, -dling.* To cook on a griddle.—**grid′dle=cake,** *n.* A thin cake of batter cooked on a griddle; a flapjack.

gride (grīd), *v. t.* or *i.*; *grided, griding.* [Var. of *gird*[2].] To pierce or cut (archaic); also, to grate or scrape harshly.—**gride,** *n.* A griding or grating sound: as, "The *gride* of hatchets fiercely thrown, On wigwam-log and tree and stone" (Whittier's "Mogg Megone," iii.).

grid-i-ron (grid′ī″ėrn), *n.* [ME. *gredirne,* earlier *gredire,* appar. an altered form of *gredil,* E. *griddle.*] A utensil having parallel bars to broil meat, etc., on; also, something resembling this; a framework on which victims were formerly tortured by fire; a frame for supporting a ship undergoing repairs, etc.; a structure above the stage of a theater, from which the drop-scenes, etc., are manipulated; in *football,* the field of play, so called on account of the transverse white lines crossing it every five yards (U. S.).—**grid′i″ron,** *v. t.* To mark with parallel bars or lines like those of a gridiron.

grid=leak (grid′lēk), *n.* In *wireless teleg.* and *teleph.,* a high-resistance device which permits excessive charges on the grid to leak off or escape.

grief (grēf), *n.* [OF. F. *grief,* < *grever,* E. *grieve.*] Hardship or trouble caused or endured†; an injury†, wrong†, or grievance†; displeasure† or offense†; also, a wound†, sore†, or ailment†; physical suffering or pain† (as, "Can honour . . . take away the *grief* of a wound? no": Shakspere's "1 Henry IV.," v. i. 134); now, keen mental suffering or distress over affliction or loss; sharp sorrow; painful regret; a cause or occasion of keen distress or sorrow (as, "A foolish son is a *grief* to his father": Prov. xvii. 25); also, mischance or disaster (as, to come to *grief*).—**grief′ful,** *a.* Full of grief; sorrowful.—**grief′less,** *a.* Free from grief.—**grief′=strick″en,** *a.* Stricken or smitten with grief or sorrow; afflicted.

griev-ance (grē′vạns), *n.* [OF. *grevance*, < *grever*, E. *grieve*.] Oppression† or injury†; suffering† or distress†; also, something oppressive or annoying; a wrong (real or fancied); a matter for resentment or complaint.

grieve (grēv), *v.*; *grieved, grieving.* [OF. F. *grever*, < L. *gravare*, load, weigh down, oppress, < *gravis*, heavy, E. *grave*[3].] **I.** *tr.* To oppress†, injure†, or wrong†; vex†, displease†, or offend†; also, to hurt or pain physically†; also, to visit with affliction or trouble (obs. or archaic: as, "He doth not afflict willingly nor *grieve* the children of men," Lam. iii. 33); in later use, to distress mentally, or cause to feel grief or sorrow (as, to be *grieved* by sad news, unkind words, or wrong-doing); also, to feel or show grief for (poetic). **II.** *intr.* To feel grief; sorrow; mourn.—**griev′er,** *n.* —**griev′ing-ly,** *adv.*

griev-ous (grē′vus), *a.* [OF. *grevos*, < *grever*, E. *grieve*.] Burdensome or oppressive, as a tax; hence, bringing serious suffering or distress, as injury, wrong, trouble, etc.; severe, as pain, wounds, etc.; heinous, as a fault or crime; also, causing grief or sorrow (as, "This news is bad indeed . . . 'Tis very *grievous* to be thought upon": Shakspere's "Richard III.," i. 1. 141); full of or expressing grief (as, a *grievous* cry); sorrowful.—**griev′ous-ly,** *adv.*—**griev′ous-ness,** *n.*

griff[1] (grif), *n.* [Origin obscure.] A deep, narrow glen or ravine. [North. Eng.]

griff[2] (grif), *n.* [F. *griffe*.] A claw; also, part of a loom. See *griffe*[1].

griff[3] (grif), *n.* See *griffe*[2].

griff[4] (grif), *n.* Same as *griffin*[3].

griffe[1] (grif), *n.* [F. *griffe*, claw; from Teut., and akin to E. *gripe*[2].] In looms, a series of horizontal parallel bars for raising and lowering the hooks that lift the warp threads; in *arch.*, an ornament at the base of a column, projecting from the torus toward a corner of the plinth.

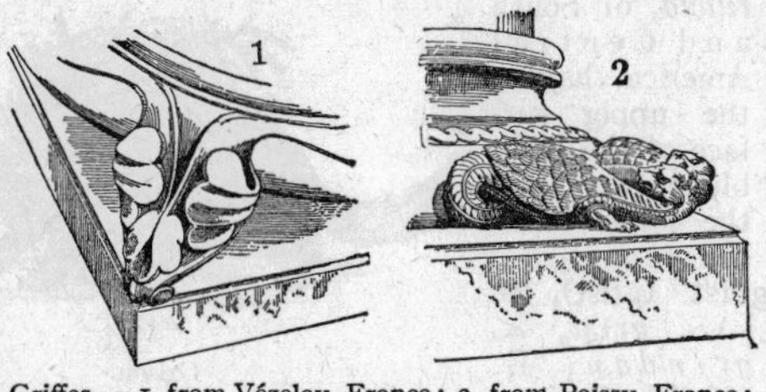

Griffes. — 1, from Vézelay, France; 2, from Poissy, France; end of 12th century.

griffe[2] (grif), *n.* [F.] The offspring of a negro and a mulatto; also, a mulatto; also, a person of mixed negro and American Indian blood. [Southern U. S.]

grif-fin[1] (grif′in), *n.* [OF. *grifon, gripon* (F. *griffon*), < L. *gryphus*, for *gryps*, < Gr. γρύψ, (fabulous) griffin.] A fabulous monster usually having the head and wings of an eagle and the body of a lion; also, a vulture of the genus *Gyps*, esp. *G. fulvus* of southern Europe.

grif-fin[2] (grif′in), *n.* Same as *griffe*[2].

grif-fin[3] (grif′in), *n.* [Origin uncertain: cf. *griffin*[1].] In India and the East, a new-comer or greenhorn; also, a racehorse that runs for the first time.—**grif′fin-age** (-ạ̄j), **grif′fin-hood** (-hůd), *n.* The state or time of being a griffin.

Medieval Griffin. — Porch of the Duomo, Verona, Italy.

grif-fon (grif′ọn), *n.* [F. *griffon*: see *griffin*[1].] A griffin (either fabulous monster or vulture); also, one of a breed of coarse-haired hunting-dogs combining the qualities of the pointer and the setter; also, a small, wiry-haired pet dog of Belgian origin, resembling a Scotch terrier.

grig (grig), *n.* [Origin uncertain.] A small or young eel; also, a cricket or a grasshopper; also, a cheerful, lively person.

gri-gri[1] (grē′grē), *n.* See *greegree*.

gri-gri[2] (grē′grē), *n.* Same as *grugru*.

grill[1] (gril), *n.* [F. *gril*, gridiron, OF. *greil, grail*, gridiron, grating, < L. *craticulum*, dim. of *cratis*, wickerwork, hurdle: cf. *grille*. Later senses of *grill*[1], *n.*, are from *grill*[1], *v.*] A gridiron; also, a grill-room; also, the act of grilling; also, a dish of grilled meat, etc.—**grill**[1], *v.* [F. *griller*, < *gril*.] **I.** *tr.* To broil on a gridiron or other apparatus over or before a fire; hence, to torment with heat; fig., to subject, as a witness, to severe examination or questioning; also, to mark with a series of parallel bars like those of a grill. **II.** *intr.* To undergo broiling.

grill[2] (gril), *n.* See *grille*.

grill-age (gril′ạ̄j), *n.* [F. *grillage*, < *grille*: see *grille*.] A heavy framework of crossed timbers, used for foundations in soft soils or the like.

grille (gril), *n.* [F. *grille*, grating, OF. *greille*, gridiron, < ML. *graticula*, for L. *craticula*, gridiron, dim. of *cratis*, wickerwork, hurdle: cf. *grate*[1] and *grill*[1].] A grating or openwork barrier, as for a gate, usually of metal and often of decorative design.—**grilled,** *a.* Furnished with a grille.

Grille. — San Giacomo di Rialto, Venice.

grill-er (gril′ėr), *n.* One who or that which grills.

grill=room (gril′röm), *n.* A room or restaurant where meats, etc., are grilled and served.

grilse (grils), *n.* [Origin uncertain.] A salmon which has ceased to be a smolt and is ready to return, or has returned, from the sea to the river for the first time, and which subsequently develops into an adult.

grim (grim), *a.*; compar. *grimmer*, superl. *grimmest.* [AS. *grim* = OS. and OHG. *grim* = Icel. *grimmr*, grim.] Fierce, savage, or cruel in a stern, merciless way, as persons or animals; sternly harsh, as necessity; merciless, as strife; stern or uncompromising, as determination; involving, threatening, or suggesting harshness or severity, as measures, purposes, words, etc.; also, of a fierce, stern, or forbidding aspect (as, "Or, with countenance *grim*, Glared on him passing": Milton's "Paradise Lost," x. 713); repellent or uninviting to the view; also, of a sinister or ghastly character or suggestiveness (as, a *grim* pastime; "*grim* jokes about graves, worms, and epitaphs," Peacock's "Nightmare Abbey," iii.).

gri-mace (gri-mās′), *n.* [F. *grimace*; origin uncertain.] A wry face; a facial contortion; hence, an affected look; affectation or pretense.—**gri-mace′,** *v. i.*; *-maced, -macing.* To make grimaces.—**gri-ma′cer** (-mā′sėr), *n.*

gri-mal-kin (gri-mal′kin or -mâl′kin), *n.* [Appar. for *gray malkin*: see *malkin*.] A cat, esp. an old female cat: as, "A strange *grimalkin* . . . clambered hastily over the fence, and vanished" (Hawthorne's "House of the Seven Gables," xix.).

grime (grīm), *v. t.*; *grimed, griming.* [ME.: cf. MLG. *grimet*, black-streaked, spotted.] To cover with dirt: soil; begrime: as, "My face I'll *grime* with filth" (Shakspere's "King Lear," ii. 3. 9).—**grime,** *n.* Dirt or foul matter, esp. on or ingrained in a surface.

grim-i-ly (grī′mi-li), *adv.* In a grimy manner.—**grim′i-ness,** *n.*

grim-ly (grim′li), *adv.* In a grim manner.—**grim′ness,** *n.*

grim-y (grī′mi), *a.*; compar. *grimier*, superl. *grimiest.* Covered with grime; dirty: as, "In his *grimy* hands he held a knotted stick" (Dickens's "Barnaby Rudge," xxxvii.).

grin[1] (grin), *v.*; *grinned, grinning.* [AS. *grennian*, grin: cf. G. *greinen* and *grinsen*, grin.] **I.** *intr.* To draw back the lips so as to show the teeth, as a snarling dog or a person in pain; also, to smile broadly, or with a wide distention of the mouth. **II.** *tr.* To express or produce by grinning. —**grin**[1], *n.* The act or an act of grinning; a broad smile.

grin[2] (grin), *n.* [AS. *grin.*] A snare, gin, or noose. [Archaic or prov.]

grind (grīnd), *v.*; *ground,* also *grinded, grinding.* [AS. *grindan,* grind: cf. L. *frendere,* gnash the teeth, grind to pieces.] **I.** *tr.* To reduce to fine particles, as by pounding or crushing; bray, triturate, or pulverize; also, to wear, smooth, or sharpen by friction (as, to *grind* a lens; to *grind* an ax or a knife); also, to rub harshly or gratingly; rub or grate together (as, to *grind* one's teeth); also, to operate by turning a crank, as a coffee-mill or a hand-organ; also, to oppress or torment (as, "Laws *grind* the poor, and rich men rule the law": Goldsmith's "Traveller," 386); also, to teach in a dull, laborious manner (as, "to get their living . . . by *grinding* Latin and Greek": Thackeray's "Vanity Fair," lvi.); study or learn by close application (college slang); also, to produce by pulverizing, turning a crank, etc. (as, to *grind* flour; to *grind* out a tune). **II.** *intr.* To perform the act or operation of grinding something (as, "Though the mills of God *grind* slowly, yet they *grind* exceeding small": Longfellow's tr. Logau's "Retribution"); also, to be or become ground; also, to rub harshly; grate; also, to work or study laboriously (colloq.).—**grind,** *n.* The act of grinding; a grinding sound; also, laborious work (colloq.: as, the *grind* of toil); also, a laborious student (college slang).

grin-de-lia (grin-dē'liạ), *n.* [NL.; from D. H. *Grindel* (1777–1836), Russian scientist.] Any of the coarse, yellow-flowered asteraceous herbs constituting the genus *Grindelia;* also, the dried leaves and flowering tops of certain species of this plant, used in medicine.

grind-er (grīn'dėr), *n.* One who or that which grinds; a sharpener of tools; a molar tooth; sometimes, a tutor or coach.

grind-er-y (grīn'dėr-i), *n.*; pl. *-ies* (-iz). A place where tools, etc., are ground; also, leather-workers' materials, tools, etc. (Eng.).

grind-ing (grīn'ding), *p. a.* That grinds; grating or strident, as sounds; burdensome or oppressive, as toil; excruciating or racking, as pain.—**grind'ing-ly,** *adv.*

grind-stone (grīnd'stōn), *n.* A rotating solid stone wheel used for grinding, sharpening, etc.

grin-go (gring'gō), *n.*; pl. *-gos* (-gōz). [Mex. Sp. use of Sp. *gringo,* gibberish.] Among Spanish-Americans, a foreigner, esp. an American or Englishman.

grin-ner (grin'ėr), *n.* One who grins.

grip[1] (grip), *n.* [AS. *gripe* = G. *griff,* grasp, hold, = Icel. *gripr,* possession; from the root of E. *gripe*[2].] The act of grasping; a seizing and holding fast; specif., a special mode of clasping hands, as among members of a secret society; fig., grasp, hold, or control (as, to be in the *grip* of poverty; to lose one's *grip* on some situation or affair); mental or intellectual hold (as, to have a *grip* of a subject); also, something which seizes and holds, as a clutching device on a cable-car; also, a handle or hilt; also, a gripsack (U. S.). —**at grips,** hand to hand; in close combat.—**grip**[1], *v.*; *gripped, gripping.* **I.** *tr.* To grasp or seize firmly; gripe; hold fast; fig., to take hold on (the mind, etc.); hold the interest or attention of (a person); also, to attach by a grip or clutch. **II.** *intr.* To take firm hold; hold fast, as an anchor; fig., to take hold on the mind; hold the interest or attention (as, a story which *grips*).

grip[2], *n.* See *grippe.*

gripe[1]† (grīp), *n.* [L. *gryps*: see *griffin*[1].] A griffin (fabulous monster); also, a vulture (as, "a white hind under the *gripe's* sharp claws": Shakspere's "Lucrece," 543).

gripe[2] (grīp), *v.*; *griped, griping.* [AS. *grīpan* = D. *grijpen* = G. *greifen* = Icel. *grīpa* = Goth. *greipan,* gripe, seize: cf. *grip*[1], *griffe*[1], *grippe,* and *grope.*] **I.** *tr.* To seize and hold firmly; grip; grasp; clutch; also, to clench (the hand, etc.)†; also, to distress or oppress; also, to produce pain in, as if by constriction. **II.** *intr.* To grasp or clutch, as a miser at gain; also, to produce pain in the bowels as if by constriction; also, to suffer pain in the bowels; *naut.,* to tend to come up into the wind.—**gripe**[2], *n.* The act of griping, grasping, or clutching; a fast hold; fig., grasp, hold, or control; also, that which grips or clutches; also, a handle, hilt, etc.; in *pathol.,* an intermittent spasmodic pain in the bowels; *naut.,* the forefoot; *pl.,* lashings for securing boats.—**grip-er** (grī'pėr), *n.*

grip-man (grip'mạn), *n.*; pl. *-men.* The man who works the grip on a cable-car.

grippe (grip, F. grēp), *n.* [F., < *gripper,* seize; from Teut., and akin to E. *gripe*[2].] Influenza.—**grip-pal** (grip'-ạl), *a.*

grip-per (grip'ėr), *n.* One who grips; a gripping device.

grip-ping (grip'ing), *p. a.* That grips; esp., that catches and holds the attention or interest.—**grip'ping-ly,** *adv.*

grip-ple (grip'l), *a.* [AS. *gripul,* akin to *grīpan,* E. *gripe*[2].] Griping; grasping; avaricious: as, "While *gripple* owners still refuse To others what they cannot use" (Scott's "Marmion," vi., Introd.). [Archaic or prov.]

grip-sack (grip'sak), *n.* A traveler's handbag or valise. [U. S.]

gri-saille (gri-zāl', F. grē-zä-y'), *n.* [F., < *gris,* gray: see *grizzle*[2].] A method of decorative painting in monochrome in various shades of gray, as for representing objects as if in relief; a painting so executed.

Gri-sel-da (gri-zel'dạ), *n.* [From *Griselda,* a heroine of old romance, famed for her patience under cruel ordeals imposed upon her as a wife and mother.] A woman of exemplary meekness and patience.

gris-e-ous (gris'ē-us or griz'-), *a.* [ML. *griseus* = F. *gris;* from Teut.: see *grizzle*[2].] Gray; esp., pearl-gray.

gri-sette (gri-zet', F. grē-zet), *n.* [F., a common gray fabric worn by working-girls, a working-girl, < *gris,* gray: see *grizzle*[2].] A French working-girl or shop-girl: as, "The beautiful *grisette* rose up . . . and, going behind the counter, reached down a parcel" (Sterne's "Sentimental Journey," The Gloves).

gris-ly[1] (griz'li), *a.*; compar. *grislier,* superl. *grisliest.* [AS. *grislic,* horrible: cf. AS. *āgrīsan,* shudder.] Such as to cause a shuddering horror; frightful or dreadful in an appalling or ghastly way, as a monster, demon, or specter; horrible; gruesome; ghastly; also, less definitely, terrible; formidable; grim.—**gris'li-ness,** *n.*

gris-ly[2] (griz'li), *a.* See *grizzly.*

gri-son (grī'sọn or griz'ọn), *n.* [F. *grison,* < *gris,* gray: see *grizzle*[2].] A carnivorous musteline quadruped, *Galictis vittata,* of South and Central America, having the upper surface of the body bluish-gray and the lower dark-brown.

Grison.

grist (grist), *n.* [AS. *grīst,* < *grindan,* E. *grind.*] Grain to be ground; also, ground grain; also, a quantity of grain for grinding at one time, or the meal produced from it; fig., a quantity or lot (colloq., U. S.).

gris-tle (gris'l), *n.* [AS. *gristle.*] Cartilage.—**gris-tly** (gris'li), *a.* Of the nature of, containing, or pertaining to gristle; cartilaginous.

grist=mill (grist'mil), *n.* A mill for grinding grain.

grit[1] (grit), *a.* Scotch form of *great.*

grit[2] (grit), *n.* [AS. *grēot* = OHG. *grioz,* G. *griess,* grit, = Icel. *grjōt,* stones, rubble.] Formerly, sand or gravel; now, fine, stony or hard particles such as are deposited like dust from the air or occur as impurities in food, etc.; also, a coarse-grained siliceous rock, as sandstone; also, the structure of stone with regard to fineness, coarseness, etc.; also, firmness of character; indomitable spirit; pluck.—**grit**[2], *v.*; *gritted, gritting.* **I.** *intr.* To give forth a grating sound; grate. **II.** *tr.* To grate or grind (the teeth).

grith (grith), *n.* [AS. *grith,* from Scand.: cf. Icel. *gridh,* peace, truce, sanctuary, orig. domicile, home.] Security or protection; safe-conduct; esp., peace or protection guaranteed under particular conditions as to time, place, or person; also, a place of security or protection; a sanctuary or asylum. [Archaic or hist.]

grits (grits), *n. pl.* [AS. *grytt*, pl. *grytta*, *gryttan*, = G. *grütze*, grits: cf. *groats*.] Grain, esp. oats or wheat, hulled and often coarsely ground.

grit-ty (grit'i), *a.*; compar. *grittier*, superl. *grittiest*. Consisting of, containing, or resembling grit; sandy; of the nature of or containing fine, stony or hard particles; also (colloq., U. S.), resolute and courageous; plucky.—**grit'ti-ness**, *n.*

griv-et (griv'et), *n.* [F. *grivet*: cf. F. *gris*, gray, and *vert*, green.] A small African monkey, *Cercopithecus griseiviridis*, with a greenish-gray back.

griz-zle[1] (griz'l), *v. i.*; *-zled*, *-zling*. [Origin obscure.] To show the teeth; grin or laugh, esp. mockingly; also, to fret or sulk; whine; whimper. [Prov. or colloq.]

griz-zle[2] (griz'l). [OF. *grisel*, < (OF. and F.) *gris*, gray; from Teut. (cf. G. *greis*, gray, hoary).] **I.** *a.* Gray; grizzled. **II.** *n.* The color gray; also, a gray-haired old man†; a gray animal, esp. a horse; also, gray hair; a gray wig.—**griz'zle**[2], *v. t.* or *i.*; *-zled*, *-zling*. To make or become gray.—**griz'zled**, *a.* Gray; grizzly.—**griz'zly**. **I.** *a.*; compar. *grizzlier*, superl. *grizzliest*. Somewhat gray; grayish: as, the *grizzly* bear (a large, ferocious bear, *Ursus horribilis*, of western North America, varying in color from grayish to brownish). **II.** *n.*; pl. *grizzlies* (-liz). A grizzly bear.

Grizzly Bear.

groan (grōn), *v.* [AS. *grānian*; perhaps akin to E. *grin*[1].] **I.** *intr.* To utter a deep inarticulate sound expressive of grief or pain; moan; hence, to make a deep sound resembling a groan; resound harshly; also, to suffer lamentably (*beneath*, etc.: as, "As Atlas *groan'd* The world beneath, we *groan* beneath an hour," Young's "Night Thoughts," ii. 129); be overburdened; also, to call painfully or urgently (*for*: often fig.). **II.** *tr.* To utter or salute with groans.—**groan**, *n.* A groaning utterance or sound.—**groan'er**, *n.*—**groan'ing-ly**, *adv.*

groat (grōt), *n.* [OD. *groot*, lit. 'great' or 'thick' (coin).] An English silver coin, issued 1351–1662, worth fourpence.

Obverse. Reverse.
Groat of Edward III. — British Museum.

groats (grōts), *n. pl.* [ME. *grotes*, pl.: cf. AS. *grot*, fragment, particle, also E. *grit*[2], *grits*, and *grout*[1].] Hulled and crushed (or whole) grain, as wheat or oats.

gro-bi-an (grō'bi-an), *n.* [G., < ML. *Grobianus*, a fictitious personage in old German literature, < G. *grob*, coarse, rude: cf. *gruff*.] A clownish, slovenly person. [Archaic or literary.]

gro-cer (grō'sėr), *n.* [OF. *grossier*, < ML. *grossarius*, wholesale dealer, < LL. *grossus*, E. *gross*.] A wholesale dealer†; also, a dealer in general supplies for the table, as flour, sugar, coffee, etc., and in other articles of household use.—**gro'cer-y**, *n.*; pl. *-ies* (-iz). The commodities sold by grocers (usually in *pl.*); also, the business of a grocer; also, a grocer's shop (U. S.).

grog (grog), *n.* [Said to be from 'Old *Grog*,' the English Admiral Vernon (with allusion to his *grogram* cloak), who in 1740 ordered the mixture to be served, instead of pure spirits, to sailors.] A mixture of spirits and water; hence, strong drink.—**grog'ger-y**, *n.*; pl. *-ies* (-iz). A grog-shop. [U. S.]—**grog'gy**, *a.*; compar. *groggier*, superl. *groggiest*. Tipsy; hence, staggering from exhaustion or blows, as in a fight; shaky or unsteady. [Colloq.]—**grog'gi-ness**, *n.*

grog-ram (grog'ram), *n.* [F. *gros grain*: see *grosgrain*.] A coarse fabric of silk, of silk and mohair or wool, or of wool, formerly in use.

grog=shop (grog'shop), *n.* A shop where grog or spirituous liquor is sold.

groin (groin), *n.* [Earlier *gryne*, ME. *grynde*: cf. AS. *grynde*, abyss, akin to *grund*, bottom, E. *ground*[2].] The fold or hollow on either side of the body where the thigh joins the abdomen; in *arch.*, the curved line or edge formed by the intersection of two vaults; also, in *civil engin.*, a structure of timber, masonry, or other material, built out into the sea from a beach or shore, for the purpose of retaining the sand, etc., washed up by the tide and raising up a barrier against the waves (as, "Our foreshore stretches far through sea-gate, dyke, and *groin*," Kipling's "The Dykes": also spelled *groyne*).—**groin**, *v. t.* In *arch.*, to form with groins (as, "He *groined* his arches and matched his beams": Lowell's "Vision of Sir Launfal," ii., Prelude); also, in *civil engin.* (also spelled *groyne*), to furnish with groins, as a beach; raise groins against, as the sea.—**groin'ing**, *n.* In *arch.*, groined vaulting; in *civil engin.* (also spelled *groyning*), the building of groins; also, groins collectively; a system of groins.

Medieval Groins, in early 12th century vaulting. — *A*, *A*, groins.

Gro-lier (grō-lyā), *a.* Of or pertaining to Jean Grolier de Servières (1479–1565), a French bibliophile, noted for his bindings: as, *Grolier* design (a style of decoration in book-binding, consisting of bold lines of gold curiously interlaced in geometrical forms and intermixed with delicate leaves and sprays).

grom-met, grum-met (grom'et, grum'et), *n.* [F. (obs.) *gromette*, var. of *gourmette*, curb of bridle, < *gourmer*, curb; origin unknown.] A ring of rope, used for various nautical purposes, etc.; an eyelet of rope, metal, or the like, as on the edge of a sail.

Grommet.

grom-well (grom'wel), *n.* [OF. *gromil* (F. *grémil*); origin uncertain.] Any plant of the boraginaceous genus *Lithospermum*, comprising hairy herbs with white, yellow, or blue flowers and smooth, stony nutlets.

groo-groo (grö'grö), *n.* See *grugru*.

groom[1] (gröm), *n.* [ME. *grom*, *grome*, boy, man, groom; origin uncertain.] A boy†; also, a man, esp. of low station (archaic: as, "What sprinklings of blithe company! Of lasses and of shepherd *grooms*," Wordsworth's "White Doe of Rylstone," i.); also, a man-servant, now usually one in charge of horses; also, any of several officers of the English royal household.—**groom**[1], *v. t.* To tend (horses) as a groom; hence, to tend carefully as to person and dress; in general, to make neat or tidy.

groom[2] (gröm), *n.* Shortened form of *bridegroom*.—**grooms'man** (-man), *n.*; pl. *-men*. A man who attends the bridegroom at a wedding.

groove (gröv), *n.* [ME. *grofe* = D. *groef* = G. *grube* = Icel. *grōf* = Goth. *grōba*, lit. 'something dug'; from the root of E. *grave*[1].] A pit, shaft, or mine (now prov. Eng.); also, a furrow or channel, esp. as cut by a tool; fig., a fixed routine.—**in the groove**, absolutely perfect (slang).—**groove**, *v. t.*; *grooved*, *grooving*. To cut a groove in; furrow; also, to form by furrowing.—**groov'y**, *a.* Of, pertaining to, or resembling a groove; also (colloq.), having a tendency to a routine of action or life; inclined to a narrow course.

grope (grōp), *v.*; *groped*, *groping*. [AS. *grāpian*, < *grāp*, the grip or grasp, < *grīpan*, E. *gripe*[2].] **I.** *intr.* To feel about with the hands; feel one's way; fig., to search blindly or uncertainly. **II.** *tr.* To feel with the hands†; also, to seek or find by or as by feeling (as, "I *groped* my way out of the room": Irving's "Tales of a Traveler," i. 7).—**grop-er** (grō'pėr), *n.*—**grop'ing-ly**, *adv.*

gros-beak (grōs′bēk), *n.* [F. *gros-bec*, 'large beak.'] Any of various finches or similar birds having a large, stout conical bill.

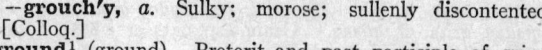

Rose-breasted Grosbeak (*Zamelodia*, or *Habia, ludoviciana*).

grosch-en (grosh′en), *n.* [G., < MHG. *gros*, < ML. *grossus*, name of a coin, < LL. *grossus*, thick, E. *gross*.] A small silver coin of Germany, no longer current; also, the current 10-pfennig German nickel coin (colloq.).

gros-grain (grō′grān), *n.* [F. *gros grain*, 'large grain': cf. *grogram*.] A closely woven silk fabric with heavy transverse threads and but little luster.

gross (grōs). [OF. F. *gros*, large (as n., *grosse*, twelve dozen), < LL. *grossus*, thick.] **I.** *a.* Large, big, or bulky (as, "The crows and choughs that wing the midway air Show scarce so *gross* as beetles": Shakspere's "King Lear," iv. 6. 14); burly, corpulent, or fat, as a person, esp. in a coarse or repulsive way; rank, as vegetation; thick or dense, as vapor; compact or solid, as a body of troops†; also, coarse in grain, fiber, or texture, as meal, sand, stone, cloth, etc.†; of coarse or inferior quality, as food, dress, wares, etc.†; now, of food, a feeder, etc., uncleanly or disgusting; fig., dull or stupid (archaic: as, "For this people's heart is waxed *gross*, and their ears are dull of hearing," Mat. xiii. 15); rude, unrefined, or ignorant (archaic); morally coarse, indelicate, or indecent, as persons, manners, language, pleasures, etc. (as, "The terms which are delicate in one age become *gross* in the next": Macaulay's "Essays," Leigh Hunt); also, plain†, evident†, or palpable†; glaring or flagrant (as, a *gross* error; *gross* injustice); also, whole, entire, or total, esp. without having been subjected to deduction, as for charges, loss, etc. (as, *gross* profits: cf. *net*); general (opposed to *particular*). **II.** *n.* The main body, the bulk, or the mass (as, in the *gross*, or in *gross*); also (pl. *gross*), a unit consisting of twelve dozen, or 144 (as, five *gross*; a great *gross*, twelve gross, or 144 dozen).—**gross′ly,** *adv.*—**gross′ness,** *n.*

gros-su-la-ri-a-ceous (gros″ū-lā-ri-ā′shius), *a.* [NL. *grossularia*, gooseberry bush, < F. *groseille*, gooseberry or currant; from Teut.] Belonging to the *Grossulariaceæ*, a family of plants comprising the gooseberry and currant.

grot (grot), *n.* [F. *grotte*, < It. *grotta*: see *grotto*.] A grotto: as, "mermaid's alabaster *grot*" (Scott's "Lord of the Isles," iii. 28). [Now poetic.]

gro-tesque (grō-tesk′). [F. *grotesque*, < It. *grottesco* (as n., *grottesca*, grotesque decoration, such appar. as was found in ancient excavated dwellings), < *grotta*: see *grotto*.] **I.** *a.* Fantastic in the shaping and combination of forms, as decorative work combining incongruously human and animal figures with scrolls, foliage, etc. (as, "'Tis *grotesque* painting; the fine woman ends in a fish's tail": Dryden's Dedication, in tr. Virgil's "Æneid"); hence, odd or unnatural in shape, appearance, or character; fantastically ugly or absurd; bizarre. **II.** *n.* Grotesque decorative work; a grotesque design or figure; hence, any grotesque object or thing.—**gro-tesque′ly,** *adv.*—**gro-tesque′ness,** *n.*—**gro-tes′quer-y, gro-tes′quer-ie** (-tes′kėr-i), *n.*; pl. *-ies* (-iz). Grotesque work; something grotesque; grotesque character.

Grotesque Work (Italian); 16th century.

grot-to (grot′ō), *n.*; pl. *grottoes* or *grottos* (-ōz). [It. *grotta*, < L. *crypta*, subterranean passage or chamber, cave, E. *crypt*.] A cave or cavern; also, an artificial cavern-like recess or structure.

grouch (grouch), *v. i.* [Cf. *grudge*.] To be sulky or morose; show discontent. [Colloq.]—**grouch,** *n.* A sulky or morose mood; also, a morose person. [Colloq.]—**grouch′y,** *a.* Sulky; morose; sullenly discontented. [Colloq.]

ground[1] (ground). Preterit and past participle of *grind*.—**ground**[1], *p. a.* Reduced to fine particles by grinding; also, having the surface abraded or roughened by or as by grinding (as, *ground* glass, which is so treated in order to destroy its transparency).

ground[2] (ground). [AS. *grund* = D. *grond* = G. *grund*, bottom, ground: cf. Goth. *grundu-waddjus*, 'ground-wall,' foundation.] **I.** *n.* The bottom† (as, the *ground* of a vessel; the *ground* of the heart); specif., the solid bottom underlying a body of water (now chiefly *naut.*: as, to strike *ground* in taking soundings); also, the underlying or main surface, or background, in painting, decorative work, lace, etc.; also, the foundation or basis of anything (now only fig.: as, the *ground* on which a theory rests); a reason or motive (as, to be dismissed on the *ground* of incompetence; one's *grounds* for an action); sometimes, a valid reason (as, to have no *grounds* for a statement); also, the earth as an underlying surface (as, to fall to the *ground*); the earth's solid surface (as, above or under *ground*); firm or dry land as opposed to the water or sea; land as owned, occupied, used, etc., or as having a special character (as, a tract of *ground*; a stretch of hilly *ground*); a particular portion or extent of land (as, a rising *ground*); a tract of land occupied, or appropriated to a special use (often in *pl.*: as, a house and *grounds*; baseball *grounds*); a particular tract or area on the globe (as, fishing-*grounds*); a space or position taken or defended (as, to hold one's *ground*); also, area or distance on the earth (as, to gain *ground*; to cover considerable *ground* in a search: often fig.); also, earth or soil (as, *stony* ground); also, *pl.*, dregs or sediment (as, coffee-*grounds*); also, *sing.*, in *elect.*, a connection (accidental or intentional) of a conductor with the earth. **II.** *a.* Pertaining to the ground; situated on or at, or adjacent to, the surface of the earth (as, the *ground* floor of a building); also, fundamental or basic (as, *ground* bass, in *music*, a fundamental bass part of four or eight bars, continually repeated throughout a whole movement).—**ground**[2], *v.* **I.** *tr.* To place on a foundation; found; fix firmly; settle or establish; fig., to instruct in elements or first principles; also, to lay or set on the ground (as, to *ground* arms); also, to furnish with a ground or background, as decorative work, etc.; *naut.*, to run aground; in *elect.*, to connect (a conductor, etc.) with the ground. **II.** *intr.* To have a basis; depend or rely; also, to come to or strike the ground; run aground (as, "Romero, himself, whose ship had *grounded*, sprang out of a port-hole and swam ashore": Motley's "Dutch Republic," iv. 1).

ground=bait (ground′bāt), *n.* Bait dropped to the bottom of the water to attract fish.

ground=con-nec-tion (ground′kọ-nek″shọn), *n.* In *elect.*, a connection of a conductor with the earth; a ground.

ground=dove (ground′duv), *n.* Any of certain small doves or pigeons of terrestrial habits, esp. *Columbigallina passerina*, of the southern U. S.

Ground-dove (*Columbigallina passerina*).

ground-ed-ly (groun′ded-li), *adv.* In a well-grounded or well-founded manner; with good reason.

ground-er (groun′dėr), *n.* One who or that which grounds; in *baseball*, etc., a ball knocked or thrown along the ground and not rising into the air.

ground=hog (ground′hog), *n.* The woodchuck; also, the aardvark.—**ground=hog day,** a popular name for Candlemas Day, Feb. 2, in allusion to the popular belief that the ground-hog (woodchuck) first comes out of his hole after hibernation on that day, and, if the sun is shining and he sees his shadow, retires to his hole for six weeks longer, which points to so much more wintry weather.

ground=ice (ground′īs), *n.* Ice formed at the bottom of a river or other body of water: supposed to be due to excessive radiation of heat from river bottoms, etc., on cold, clear nights.

ground=i-vy (ground'ī''vi), *n.* A trailing menthaceous plant, *Glecoma hederacea*, bearing blue flowers.

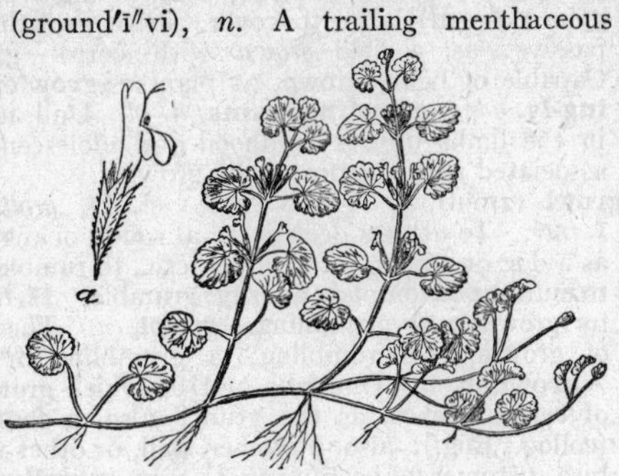

Ground-ivy. — *a*, a flower.

ground=lau-rel (ground'-lâ''rel), *n.* Trailing arbutus (see *arbutus*).

ground-less (ground'les), *a.* Without ground, basis, or reason.—**ground'less-ly,** *adv.*—**ground'less-ness,** *n.*

ground-ling (ground'ling), *n.* [See *-ling*[1].] Anything that lives on the ground; also, any of various fishes that live at the bottom of the water; also, a spectator in the pit of a theater, which formerly was literally on the ground, having neither floor nor benches† (see Shakspere's "Hamlet," iii. 2. 12); hence, a spectator, reader, or other person of crude or uncultivated tastes; an uncritical or uncultured person.

ground=mass (ground'mȧs), *n.* The crystalline, granular, or glassy base or matrix of a porphyry, in which the more prominent crystals are embedded.

ground-nut (ground'nut), *n.* Any of various plants with edible underground portions, as the earthnut, *Conopodium denudatum*, and the peanut, *Arachis hypogæa*, and the American climbing fabaceous vine *Apios apios*, which has an edible tuberous root; also, the edible tuber, pod, or the like, of such a plant.

ground=pig (ground'pig), *n.* The ground-hog or aardvark; also, the ground-rat.

ground=pine (ground'pīn), *n.* A European menthaceous herb, *Ajuga chamæpitys*, having a resinous odor; also, a club-moss, *Lycopodium obscurum*, or some allied species.

ground=plan (ground'plan), *n.* The plan of anything as it is disposed on the ground (as, the *ground-plan* of a fieldwork); specif., the plan of the ground floor, or of any floor, of a building; fig., any first or fundamental plan.

ground=plate (ground'plāt), *n.* A groundsill; also, a bedplate under railroad-ties; in *elect.*, a metal plate sunk in the ground to form the connection from a circuit to the earth.

ground=plum (ground'plum), *n.* A leguminous plant, *Astragalus crassicarpus*, of the American prairie regions, or its edible plum-shaped fruit; also, any of certain related species or the fruit.

ground=rat (ground'rat), *n.* Any of several large African rodents of the genus *Aulacodus* (or *Thryonomys*); a ground-pig.

Ground-rat (*Aulacodus swinderianus*).

ground=rent (ground'-rent), *n.* The rent at which land is let for building purposes.

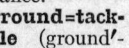

ground=sea (ground'sē), *n.* A heavy sea or swell on the ocean, occurring without apparent cause but thought to be due usually to distant gales.

ground-sel[1] (ground'sel), *n.* [AS. *grundeswelge*, earlier *gundeswelge*, appar. < *gund*, matter, pus, + *swelgan*, swallow (from its use in medicine).] Any plant of the genus *Senecio*, of the aster family, as *S. vulgaris*, a weed bearing small yellow flowers and seeds with a white pappus.

ground-sill, ground-sel[2] (ground'sil, -sel), *n.* [See *ground*[2].] The lowest horizontal timber of a frame or building, lying next to the ground; the sill.

ground=squir-rel (ground'skwur''el), *n.* Any of various terrestrial rodents of the squirrel family, as of the genus *Tamias* (chipmunks), and of the genus *Citellus* (or *Spermophilus*) (see *gopher*).

African Ground-squirrel (*Xerus rutilans*).

ground=swell (ground'swel), *n.* A broad, deep swell or rolling of the sea, due to a distant storm, gale, or seismic disturbance.

ground=tac-kle (ground'-tak''l), *n.* Cables, anchors, etc., for securing a vessel at anchor.

ground-work (ground'wėrk), *n.* The foundation, base, or basis.

group (gröp), *n.* [F. *groupe*, < It. *gruppo*, *groppo*, knot, mass, heap, group; from Teut., and akin to E. *crop*.] An assemblage of figures arranged together in a work of art (as, "The huddled *group* of those who stand most distant are admirable representations of men abashed with their late unbelief": Steele, in "Guardian," 21); also, any assemblage of persons or things; a cluster; an aggregation; also, a number of persons or things ranged or considered together as being related in some way; often, a number of persons, as in a community, united by common ties or interests, as of race, class, occupation, or the like; specif., a number of individuals ranged together as being naturally related, in scientific classification; in *geol.*, a division in the classification of stratified deposits, usually comprising those of a given geological era; in *chem.*, a number of atoms in a molecule connected or arranged together in some special manner; a radical.—**group,** *v.* **I.** *tr.* To arrange in or form into a group or groups (as, "On the terrace were *grouped* perhaps a dozen people": H. G. Wells's "Mr. Britling," i. 2. § 3); also, to place in a group, as with others. **II.** *intr.* To form a group; be part of a group.—**group'age** (-āj), *n.* Grouping; arrangement in a group or groups.

group-er (grö'pėr), *n.* [Pg. *garupa*, appar. from some S. Amer. name.] Any of various serranoid fishes, esp. of the genus *Epinephelus*, as *E. morio* ('red grouper'), an important food-fish of the southern Atlantic coast of the U. S.

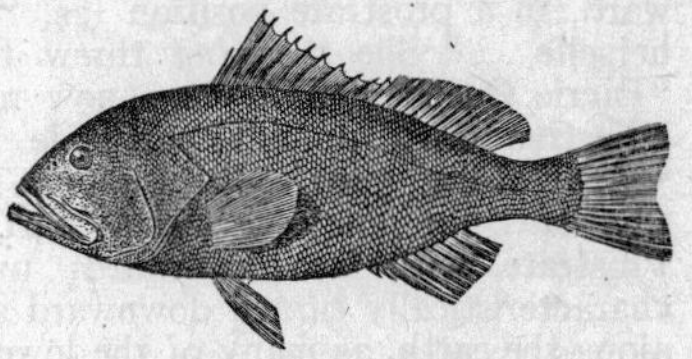
Red Grouper (*Epinephelus morio*).

group-ing (grö'ping), *n.* Placing or manner of being placed in a group or groups; relative arrangement of persons, things, parts, etc., viewed or considered together.

grouse[1] (grous), *n.*; pl. *grouse.* [Origin uncertain.] A reddish gallinaceous game-bird with feathered legs, *Lagopus scoticus*, of the British Isles ('red grouse'); also, any bird of the same subfamily, *Tetraoninæ* (or of the same family, *Tetraonidæ*), including many important game-birds, as *Lyrurus tetrix* ('black grouse') common on British heaths, *Tetrao urogallus* (the capercaillie, or wood-grouse) of the Old World, *Canace canadensis* ('Canada grouse') of the forests of northern North America, and *Bonasa umbellus* ('ruffed grouse') of the eastern U. S. and Canada.—**grouse**[1], *v. i.*; *groused, grousing.* To hunt or shoot grouse.

Red Grouse (*Lagopus scoticus*).

grouse[2] (grous), *v. i.*; *groused, grousing.* [Cf. *grouch*.] To grumble; complain: as, "They didn't *grouse* an' shirk at an hour's extry work" (Kipling's "Men That Fought at Minden"). [Prov. or slang, Eng.]—**grouse**[2], *n.* An act of grousing; a complaint. [Prov. or slang, Eng.]—**grous'er**[1], *n.*

grous-er[2] (grou'zėr or -sėr), *n.* [Origin unknown.] A temporary pile or iron-shod pole driven into the bottom of a stream, etc., to hold a floating object in position, esp. such a pole passing through the hull or down the side of a boat; also, one of a series of projecting pieces, cleats, or lugs attached to the surface of the endless chain or belt (track) of the track-laying type of tractor (see *caterpillar, n.*), to prevent slipping when mud, sand, snow, or ice is encountered.

grout[1] (grout), *n.* [AS. *grūt*; akin to *grits, groats,* and *grit*[2].] Coarse meal; *pl.*, groats; also, *sing.*, coarse porridge; also, wort before and during fermentation (obs. or prov.); also, *sing.* or *pl.*, lees or grounds.

grout[2] (grout), *n.* [Appar. another use of *grout*[1].] A thin, coarse mortar; also, a finishing or setting coat of plaster for walls and ceilings.—**grout**[2], *v. t.* To fill up, form, or finish with grout; also, to use as grout.

grout-y (grou'ti), *a.* [See *grout*[1].] Dreggy or muddy (prov. Eng.); threatening, as the weather (prov. Eng.); also, sulky or surly (colloq., U. S.).

grove (grōv), *n.* [AS. *grāf.*] A small wood or plantation of trees, esp. one used as a shady resort (as, "See there the olive *grove* of Academe, Plato's retirement": Milton's "Paradise Regained," iv. 244); also, in the Authorized Version of the Bible, an erroneous rendering of a Hebrew word now explained as meaning a wooden post set up near the altar of a Semitic god (see 2 Kings, xxi. 7); a rendering of a Hebrew word translated *tamarisk tree* in the Revised Version (see Gen. xxi. 33).

grov-el (grov'l), *v. i.*; *-eled* or *-elled, -eling* or *-elling.* [From *groveling, adv.*, taken as present participle.] To lie or move with the face downward and the body prostrate, esp. in abject humility, fear, etc.; fig., to humble one's self or act in an abject manner, as in fear or in mean servility; continue, esp. willingly or contentedly, in an abject condition; take pleasure in mean or base things.—**grov'el-er, grov'el-ler,** *n.*

grov-el-ing, grov-el-ling (grov'l-ing), *adv.* [ME. *groveling, grufelynge,* < *grufe,* as in *on grufe,* in a groveling position, + *-ling,* E. *-ling*[2]: cf. Icel. *ā grūfu,* in a groveling position, face downward, also *grūfa,* to grovel, cower.] Face downward, in a prostrate position (as, "Streight downe againe herselfe . . . She *groveling* threw to ground": Spenser's "Faerie Queene," ii. 1. 45): now regarded as a predicate adjective or a present participle (see following entry).—**grov'el-ing, grov'el-ling,** *a.* or *p. a.* [Adj. use of *groveling, adv.*, but now regarded as participial, from *grovel, v.*] Prostrate, with face downward; prone; having the face characteristically turned downward and the body extended along the earth, as many of the lower animals; fig., abject, base, or low; without moral elevation, dignity, or aspirations.—**grov'el-ing-ly, grov'el-ling-ly,** *adv.*

grov-y (grō'vi), *a.* Of, belonging to, or situated in a grove; abounding in groves; grove-like.

grow (grō), *v. i.*; pret. *grew,* pp. *grown,* ppr. *growing.* [AS. *grōwan* = D. *groeien* = OHG. *gruoan* = Icel. *grōa,* grow: cf. *grass* and *green.*] To undergo the process of development characteristic of living plants; undergo the vital processes, or exist, as plants (as, all the herbs that *grow*; trees *growing* only in the tropics); also, to germinate, sprout, or spring, as a seed, shoot, or plant; be produced by natural process, as leaves, fruit, etc.; arise or issue as from a germ, stock, or originating source (as, the whole affair *grew* out of an indiscreet letter; "How *grew* your quarrel?" Shakspere's "King Lear," ii. 2. 66); also, to increase by natural development, as any living organism or part by assimilation of nutriment; in general, to increase gradually, or become greater (as, a heap, flood, or sum *grows*; heat or sound *grows*; power, fame, zeal, or fear *grows*); increase in influence or effect (*on* or *upon*: as, a habit that *grows* on one; the book will *grow* upon you as you read); also, to become gradually attached or united by or as by growth (as, to *grow* fast to a thing; to *grow* together); also, to come or pass by degrees (with *into, to,* or an infinitive); come to be, or become, by degrees (as, to *grow* old or rich; to *grow* scarce).—**to grow up,** to spring up; arise; also, to increase in growth; advance toward maturity; attain maturity.—**grow,** *v. t.* To cause to grow; cultivate, produce, or raise; also, to allow to grow (as, to *grow* a beard); also, to cover with a growth (used in the passive: as, a field *grown* with corn).—**grow'a-ble,** *a.* Capable of being grown, as plants.—**grow'er,** *n.*—**grow'ing-ly,** *adv.*—**grow'ing=pains,** *n. pl.* Dull, indefinite pains in the limbs during childhood and adolescence, commonly associated with the process of growing.

growl (groul), *v.* [Prob. imit.: cf. D. *grollen,* grumble.] **I.** *intr.* To utter a deep guttural sound of anger or hostility, as a dog or a bear; of thunder, etc., to rumble; of a person, to murmur or complain angrily; grumble. **II.** *tr.* To express by growling or grumbling.—**growl,** *n.* The act or sound of growling; a rumbling; a grumbling or complaining.—**growl'er,** *n.* One who or that which growls; also, any of certain fishes, as the grunt; also, a four-wheeled cab (colloq., Eng.); also, a pitcher, pail, or other vessel brought by a customer for beer (slang, U. S.).—**growl'ing-ly,** *adv.*

grown (grōn). Past participle of *grow.*—**grown,** *p. a.* Advanced in growth; also, arrived at full growth or maturity (as, a *grown* man); adult.

growth (grōth), *n.* The act, process, or manner of growing; development; gradual increase; production; also, the condition or size attained in growth, esp. at maturity (as, to come to the full *growth*); also, something that has grown, sprung up, or developed by or as by a natural process (as, a *growth* of weeds or of hair; a *growth* of legend); a product; in *pathol.*, a morbid mass of tissue, as a tumor.—**growth'ful,** *a.* Vigorous in growth.—**growth'less,** *a.* Deficient in growth.—**growth'y,** *a.* Of good growth; growing well or fast; well grown or developed.

groyne (groin), etc. See *groin,* etc.

grub (grub), *v.*; *grubbed, grubbing.* [ME. *grubben,* dig: cf. G. *grübeln,* grub, rake, rack (the brains), also E. *grave*[1].] **I.** *tr.* To dig; clear (ground) of roots, etc.; dig up (trees, etc.) by the roots; uproot; extract by or as by digging; also, to provide with 'grub' or food (slang). **II.** *intr.* To dig; search by or as by digging; rummage; also, to lead a laborious or groveling life; drudge; also, to take 'grub' or food (slang).—**grub,** *n.* The larva of an insect, esp. of a beetle; a worm (now prov.); also, a dull, plodding person; a drudge; a literary hack; sometimes, a sloven; also, food or victuals (slang).—**grub'ber,** *n.* One who grubs; a digger; a laborious worker; also, an implement for breaking up ground, etc.; also, an eater or feeder (slang).—**grub'by,** *a.*; compar. *grubbier,* superl. *grubbiest.* Infested with or affected by grubs or larvæ; like a grub or larva; also, stunted or dwarfish (now prov.); also, dirty; slovenly.—**grub'bi-ness,** *a.*—**grub'=stake,** *n.* Provisions, outfit, etc., furnished to a prospector on condition of participating in the profits of his discoveries. [Mining slang, U. S.]—**grub'=stake,** *v. t.* To furnish with a grub-stake. [Mining slang, U. S.]

Grub (grub) **Street.** A London street (now Milton Street) described by Dr. Samuel Johnson as "much inhabited by writers of small histories, dictionaries, and temporary poems"; hence, petty and needy authors, or literary hacks, collectively.

grudge (gruj), *v.*; *grudged, grudging.* [Earlier *grutch,* < OF. *gruchier, groucier,* murmur, grumble; origin uncertain.] **I.** *intr.* To grumble† or complain†; also, to feel dissatisfaction or ill-will. **II.** *tr.* To be reluctant to give or allow (something: as, to *grudge* the cost of a thing); be dissatisfied at seeing (a person) have (something: as, to *grudge* a man his success); begrudge.—**grudge,** *n.* Grumbling† or complaining†; also, dissatisfaction† or reluctance†; also, a feeling of ill-will or resentment excited by some special cause, as a personal injury or insult, the success of an opponent or rival, etc. (as, "He ne'er bore *grudge* for stalwart blow, Ta'en in fair fight from gallant foe": Scott's "Lay of the Last Minstrel," v. 28); resentful ill-will.—**grudg'er,** *n.*—**grudg'ing-ly,** *adv.*

grue (grö), *v. i.*; *grued, gruing.* [ME.: cf. D. *gruwen,* shudder, G. *grauen,* feel horror, also E. *gruesome.*] To shudder; shiver; feel horror. [Sc. and north. Eng.]

gru-el (grö'ẹl), *n.* [OF. *gruel* (F. *gruau*), meal; from Teut., and akin to E. *grits, groats,* and *grout*[1].] A light, usually thin, liquid food made by boiling meal, esp. oatmeal, in water or milk; hence, any similar substance.—**to take one's gruel,** fig., to take one's punishment. [Colloq.]—**gru′el,** *v. t.*; *-eled* or *-elled, -eling* or *-elling.* To 'punish,' or use severely; exhaust; disable. [Colloq.]—**gru′el-ing, gru′el-ling,** *n.* Any trying or exhausting procedure or experience; defeat, as in an athletic contest. [Colloq.]

grue-some (grö′sum), *a.* [From *grue*: cf. G. *grausam*, horrible.] Such as to make one shudder; inspiring horror; now, esp., revolting in a ghastly way, as the scene, evidences, or details of a brutal murder; disturbing or unpleasant from weird character or sinister suggestiveness, as shadows, sounds, places, etc.; also, ugly or hideous (Sc. and north. Eng.).—**grue′some-ly,** *adv.*—**grue′some-ness,** *n.*

gruff (gruf), *a.* [D. *grof* = G. *grob*, coarse, rough, rude: cf. *grobian.*] Coarse (now chiefly technical, as in 'gruff saltpeter'); also, rough, harsh, or surly, as persons, manner, aspect, speech, etc.; often, of voice, tone, etc., rough or harsh in sound, rather than smooth, soft, clear, etc.—**gruff′ly,** *adv.*—**gruff′ness,** *n.*

gru-gru (grö′grö), *n.* [Native name.] The grub of a large weevil, *Rhynchophorus* (or *Calandra*) *palmarum*, of tropical America, which lives in the stems of palm-trees, etc., and is regarded by the natives as a delicacy ('grugru worm'); also, any of various spiny palms of the West Indies, as *Acrocomia sclerocarpa.*

gru-i-form (grö′i-fôrm), *a.* [L. *grus*, crane, + *forma*, form.] Crane-like; of the crane type of birds.

grum (grum), *a.*; compar. *grummer*, superl. *grummest.* [Appar. a mixture of *glum* and *grim.*] Morose; surly; glum.

grum-ble (grum′bl), *v.*; *-bled, -bling.* [Cf. F. *grommeler*, MD. *grommelen*, G. *grommeln*, murmur, grumble.] **I.** *intr.* To utter or make low, indistinct sounds, as persons or animals; murmur; growl; of thunder, storms, etc., to rumble; now, commonly, to murmur in discontent; complain in a sulky, ill-humored, or peevish way. **II.** *tr.* To express or utter with murmuring or complaining.—**grum′ble,** *n.* The act or sound of grumbling; a murmur; a growl; a rumble; an ill-humored complaining; *pl.*, a grumbling, discontented mood.—**grum′bler,** *n.*—**grum′bling-ly,** *adv.*

grume (gröm), *n.* [L. *grumus*, little heap, hillock.] A clot, as of blood; clotted blood; any thick or viscous fluid.

grum′met, *n.* See *grommet.*

gru-mous (grö′mus), *a.* [See *grume.*] Containing, consisting of, or resembling grume; clotted; thick; viscous; in *bot.*, formed of clustered grains, granules, or the like, as certain roots.

grum-py (grum′pi). [Cf. *grum* and *glumpy.*] **I.** *a.*; compar. *grumpier*, superl. *grumpiest.* Surly; ill-humored; gruff. **II.** *n.*; pl. *-pies* (-piz). A grumpy person.—**grum′pi-ly,** *adv.*—**grum′pi-ness,** *n.*

Grun-dy (grun′di), *n.* A name (commonly *Mrs. Grundy*) taken as representing society at large in regard to its censorship of personal conduct: from the question "What will Mrs. Grundy say?" frequently asked by Dame Ashfield, a character in Thomas Morton's play "Speed the Plough" (1798).

grunt (grunt), *v.* [AS. *grunnettan*, freq. of *grunian*, grunt: cf. G. *grunzen* and L. *grunnire*, grunt.] **I.** *intr.* To utter the deep guttural sound characteristic of a hog; utter a similar sound; also, to grumble, as in discontent; also, to groan† (as, "Who would fardels bear, To *grunt* and sweat under a weary life?" Shakspere's "Hamlet," iii. 1. 77). **II.** *tr.* To express with a grunt.—**grunt,** *n.* The characteristic deep guttural sound uttered by a hog; some similar utterance; also, any of various chiefly marine fishes of the genus *Hæmulon* and allied genera, which emit a grunting sound when taken from the water.—**grunt′er,** *n.* An animal or person that grunts, esp. a hog; also, any of various fishes that make a grunting noise; a grunt.—**grunt′ing-ly,** *adv.* With grunting.

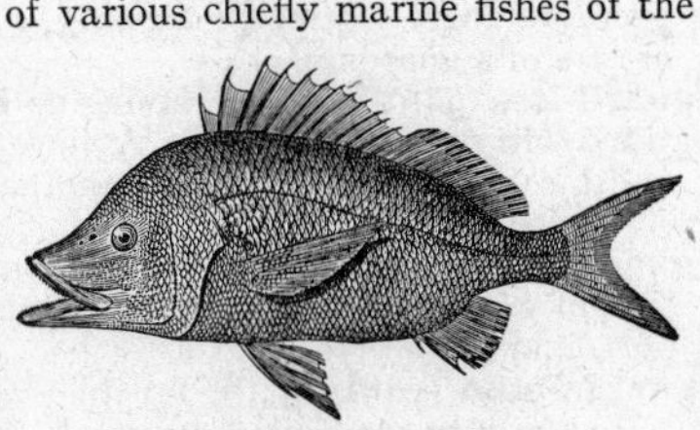
Grunt (*Hæmulon plumieri*).

grun-tle (grun′tl), *v. i.*; *-tled, -tling.* [Dim. of *grunt.*] To utter a low grunt; fig., to murmur; grumble.

grutch (gruch), *v.* and *n.* Older form of *grudge.* [Now prov. Eng.]

Gru-yère (grü-yãr) **cheese.** [From *Gruyère*, district in Switzerland.] A firm, pale-yellow variety of cheese containing many holes; Swiss cheese.

gryph-on (grif′on), *n.* Same as *griffin*[1].

grys-bok (grīs′bok), *n.* [S. Afr. D. *grijsbok*, 'gray buck.'] A small reddish-brown South African antelope, *Neotragus melanotis.*

gua-cha-ro (gwä′chä-rō), *n.*; pl. *-ros* (-rōz). [Sp.; prob. from native name.] A nocturnal fruit-eating South American bird, *Steatornis caripensis*, related to the goatsuckers: valued by the natives for the oil produced from the fat of the young, which is used as a substitute for butter.

Guacharo.

gua-co (gwä′kō), *n.* [Sp.; from native name.] A climbing asteraceous plant, *Mikania guaco*, of tropical America; its medicinal leaves, or a substance obtained from them, used as an antidote for snake-bites; also, a tropical American plant, *Aristolochia maxima*, also used for snake bites.

guai-ac (gwī′ak), *n.* [See *guaiacum.*] The wood or resin of the guaiacum (tree).—**guai-a′cic** (-as′ik), *a.* Pertaining to or obtained from guaiacum.—**guai′a-col** (-a-kol or -kōl), *n.* In *chem.*, a colorless liquid resembling creosote, obtained by distillation from guaiacum resin, and in other ways, used in phthisis, bronchitis, etc.

guai-a-cum (gwī′a-kum), *n.* [NL., < Sp. *guayaco*; from Haitian.] Any of the hard-wooded tropical American trees and shrubs constituting the zygophyllaceous genus *Guaiacum*, esp. *G. officinale*, of the West Indies and South America, and *G. sanctum*, of the West Indies and Florida (see *lignum-vitæ*); also, the hard, heavy wood of such a tree (see *lignum-vitæ*); also, a greenish-brown resin obtained from trees of this genus, used as a stimulant and alterative, and as a remedy for rheumatism, cutaneous eruptions, etc.

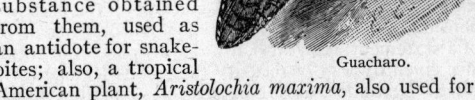

Flowering Branch of Guaiacum (*G. sanctum*).

guan (gwän), *n.* [W. Ind.] Any of various large gallinaceous birds constituting the subfamily *Penelopinæ* (family *Cracidæ*), chiefly of Central and South America, allied to the curassows.

gua-na (gwä′nä), *n.* [For *iguana.*] An iguana; in Australasia, any of various large lizards.

Texas Guan (*Ortalis vetula maccalli*).

gua-na-co (gwä-nä′kō), *n.*; pl. *-cos* (-kōz). [Sp., < Peruvian *huanacu.*] A wild South American ruminant animal, *Lama* (or *Auchenia*) *huanaco*, of which the llama and alpaca are thought to be varieties.

Guanaco.

gua-ni-dine (gwä′-ni-din), *n.* [From *guanine*.] In *chem.*, a crystalline compound formed by the oxidation of guanine.

gua-nine (gwä′-nin), *n.* [From *guano*.] In *chem.*, a white amorphous substance found in guano, the liver and pancreas of mammals, and the scales of certain fishes.

gua-no (gwä′nō), *n.*; pl. *-nos* (-nōz). [Sp., < Peruvian *huanu*, dung.] A natural manure composed chiefly of the excrement of sea-birds, found esp. on islands near the Peruvian coast; also, any similar substance, as an artificial fertilizer made from fish.

gua-ra-na (gwä-rä′nạ), *n.* [Native name.] A paste prepared from the seeds of a climbing, sapindaceous Brazilian shrub, *Paullinia cupana*: used for both food and medicine.

guar-an-tee (gar-ạn-tē′), *n.* [Appar. for *guaranty*: cf. Sp. *garante*, one who warrants.] One who warrants, or gives a formal assurance or guaranty, as for the fulfilment of obligations; also, the giving of a guaranty; the assuming of responsibility for the fulfilment of some obligation, the truth of a statement, etc.; also, a warrant, pledge, or formal assurance given by way of security (as, goods stamped with the maker's *guarantee*, as for genuineness, quality, or durability); fig., something that has the force or effect of a guaranty, as for the fulfilment or realization of something (as, wealth is no *guarantee* of happiness); also, one to whom a guaranty is made.—**guar-an-tee′**, *v. t.*; *-teed*, *-teeing*. To be or become a guarantee for, as by giving a formal assurance or guaranty (as, Russia *guaranteed* the treaty of Teschen, in 1779, between Austria and Prussia); warrant by formal assurance or guaranty (as, to *guarantee* safe-conduct, immunity, or satisfaction; to *guarantee* the genuineness or the durability of a thing; gloves *guaranteed* by the maker, being returnable if not reasonably satisfactory); specif., to make one's self answerable for in behalf of one primarily responsible (as, to *guarantee* the carrying out of a contract or the fulfilment of obligations by another); also, to undertake to secure to another, as rights or possessions; engage to uphold or maintain (as, to *guarantee* peace between nations); engage to protect or indemnify (with *from*, *against*, etc.); in general, to engage (to do something: as, I will *guarantee* to prove every statement); warrant (with a clause: as, I will *guarantee* that he is wrong); fig., to serve as a warrant or guaranty for (as, such actions *guarantee* his good faith).

guar-an-tor (gar′ạn-tôr), *n.* One who makes or gives a guaranty.

guar-an-ty (gar′ạn-ti), *n.*; pl. *-ties* (-tiz). [F. *garantie*, OF. *guarantie*, < *guarant*, *warant*, warrant; from Teut.: see *warrant*.] The act of warranting, or giving a formal assurance or pledge (as, treaties of *guaranty*, whereby other powers promise to give aid to secure the carrying out of the agreement between the treaty-making powers); also, a warrant, pledge, or promise given by way of security; specif., a formal or written assurance by which one person or party undertakes to be responsible for the carrying out of a contract, the payment of a debt, or the fulfilment of some obligation, by another; fig., something that serves as a warrant (as, his character is a *guaranty* for his assertions); also, one who warrants, or gives a formal assurance of being responsible for something†.—**guar′an-ty**, *v. t.*; *-tied*, *-tying*. To guarantee.

guard (gärd), *v.* [OF. *guarder*, *garder*, *warder* (F. *garder*), guard; from Teut.: see *ward*, *n.* and *v.*] **I.** *tr.* To keep safe from harm, attack, wrong, etc. (as, "Mercy *guard* me!" Milton's "Comus," 695); protect or defend (often with *from* or *against*); also, to watch over in order to protect (as, to *guard* the gates of a city; to *guard* a grave); attend or escort, as a guard does (archaic); also, to keep under close watch in order to prevent escape, outbreaks, etc. (as, to *guard* a prisoner or a madman); keep in check, as in caution or prudence (as, to *guard* the tongue or the thoughts); also, to provide with some safeguard, protective appliance, or the like (as, to *guard* the body with armor); also, to border or trim (archaic: as, "a long motley coat *guarded* with yellow," Shakspere's "Henry VIII.," Prologue, 16). **II.** *intr.* To give protection (as, "Disorder wounds Where it should *guard*": Shakspere's "2 Henry VI.," v. 2. 33); also, to keep guard or watch; be on one's guard; hence, to take precautions (*against*: as, to *guard* against errors).—**guard**, *n.* [OF. *guarde*, *garde* (F. *garde*), < *guarder*: cf. *ward*, *n.*] Keeping† or guardianship†; also, protection or defense (as, "I was dispatch'd for their defence and *guard*": Milton's "Comus," 42); a posture of defense, as in fencing, boxing, etc., or the weapon or arms in such a posture (as, to beat down a person's *guard*); protective watch, as to detect threatened attack or danger (as, to keep *guard* as a sentry); vigilant care or heed, as against anything adverse (as, to be on one's *guard*: see phrase below); caution†; a precaution (obs. or rare); also, restraining watch, as over a prisoner or other person under restraint (as, to be kept under close *guard*); cautious restraint (as, to keep a careful *guard* over one's tongue); also, one who guards, protects, or keeps protecting or restraining watch; a sentry; a member of a guarding force, as of soldiers; one who keeps watch over prisoners or others under restraint; the conductor of a railroad-train, etc. (in British use); a person in charge of the gates or doors of a train on an elevated or subway railroad; a player holding a position of defense, as either of two, at the right and the left of the center, in the forward line in football; *pl.*, the name of certain bodies of troops in the British army; *sing.*, a body of men, esp. soldiers, charged with guarding a person or place from attack, acting as escort, watching over prisoners, or the like; also, something intended or serving to guard or protect; a safeguard; a contrivance, appliance, or attachment designed for guarding against injury, loss, etc. (as, a watch-*guard*); also, an ornamental border or trimming, as on a garment (archaic).—**National Guard.** See under *national*, *a.*—**off one's guard**, unprepared to meet a sudden attack; unwary.—**on one's guard**, in a position of readiness to meet attack; also, watchful or vigilant against attack; cautious; wary.—**guard′a-ble**, *a.* Capable of being guarded.—**guard′age**† (-āj), *n.* Guardianship. See Shakspere's "Othello," i. 2. 70.

guard-ant (gär′dạnt). [F. *gardant*, ppr. of *garder*: see *guard*, *v.*] **I.** *a.* Guarding; protecting. **II.**† *n.* A guard or guardian. See Shakspere's "1 Henry VI.," iv. 7. 9.

guard-ed (gär′ded), *p. a.* Protected or watched, as by a guard; also, cautious; careful.—**guard′ed-ly**, *adv.*—**guard′ed-ness**, *n.*

guard-er (gär′dėr), *n.* One who or that which guards.

guard=house (gärd′hous), *n.* A building for the accommodation of a guard; also, a building in which prisoners are detained under guard, esp. one in which soldiers are confined for misconduct.

guard-i-an (gär′di-ạn). [OF. F. *gardien*, < *garde*, E. *guard*, *n.*] **I.** *n.* One who guards, protects, or preserves; one to whom the care or preservation of something is committed; in *law*, one to whom the law intrusts the care of the person or property, or both, of another, as of a minor or of some other person legally incapable of managing his own affairs. **II.** *a.* Guarding; protecting; tutelary: as, a *guardian* angel.—**guard′i-an-ship**, *n.* The position, office, or care of a guardian.

guard-less (gärd′les), *a.* Having no guard; unguarded.

guard=ring (gärd′ring), *n.* A finger-ring, usually narrow and inconspicuous, worn with another ring to keep it from slipping off.

guard=room (gärd′röm), *n.* A room for the accommodation of a guard; also, a room in which military prisoners are confined.

guards-man (gärdz′mạn), *n.*; pl. *-men*. A man who acts as a guard; a member of a guard; also, a member of any body of troops called guards; also, a member of the National Guard (see under *national*, *a.*).

gua-va (gwä′vą̈), *n.* [Sp. *guayabo*, the tree, *guayaba*, the fruit; from S. Amer. name.] Any of various trees or shrubs of the myrtaceous genus *Psidium*, esp. *P. guajava*, natives of tropical or subtropical America, with a fruit used for jelly, etc.; also, the fruit; also, any of certain other plants, as *Inga vera* of the West Indies.

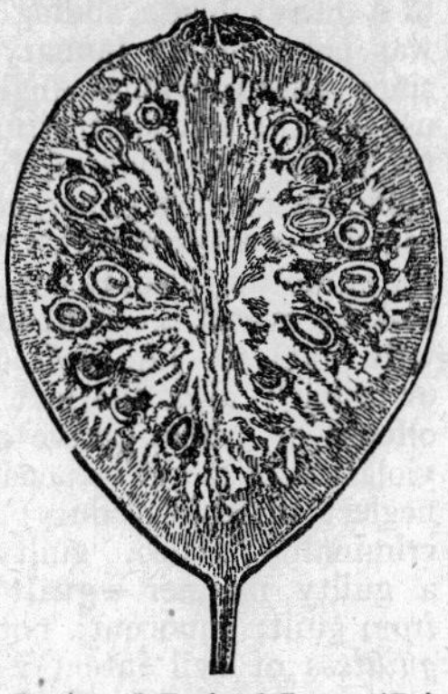

Section of Fruit of Guava (*Psidium guajava*).

gua-yu-le (gwä-ū′lą̄), *n.* [Sp.] A rubber-yielding bush-like plant of northern Mexico, etc.

gu-ber-na-to-ri-al (gū″bėr-nạ-tō′ri-ạl), *a.* [L. *gubernator*, steersman, director, E. *governor*.] Pertaining to a governor or to government.

gude (güd), *a.*, *n.*, and *adv.* Sc. and prov. Eng. form of *good*.

gudg-eon[1] (guj′ọn), *n.* [OF. F. *goujon*, < L. *gobio(n-)*, var. of *gobius*, E. *goby*.] A small European fresh-water fish, *Gobio gobio*, of the carp family, easily caught, and much used for bait; also, a minnow; in fig. use, one who is easily duped or cheated (as, "So golden a conjecture . . . was too tempting not to be immediately snapped at by the *gudgeons* of learning": Irving's "Knickerbocker's New York," i. 4); also, a bait or allurement.—**gudg′eon**[1], *v. t.* To dupe; cheat.

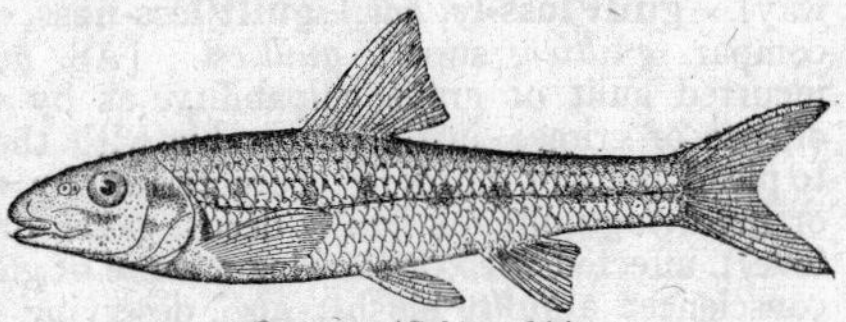

Gudgeon (*Gobio gobio*).

gudg-eon[2] (guj′ọn), *n.* [OF. F. *goujon*, pin, gudgeon: cf. *gouge*.] A metal pin or the like attached to the end of a wooden shaft to act as a journal; hence, a pivot; a journal; also, a socket or eye for a pivot or the like; also, a metallic pin for securing together blocks or slabs of stone, etc.

Gue-ber, Gue-bre (gē′bėr or gā′-), *n.* [F. *guèbre*, < Pers. *gebr*, *gabr*, a Gueber; commonly explained as meaning 'unbeliever' (Ar. *kāfir*), from the Mohammedan point of view: cf. *giaour*.] A member of the Persian sect of fire-worshipers, the remnant in Persia of the ancient Zoroastrians. See *Zoroastrian*, *n.*

guel-der=rose (gel′dėr-rōz′), *n.* [From *Guelders*, or *Gelderland*, province of the Netherlands.] The snowball, a cultivated variety of the cranberry-tree.

Guelph, Guelf (gwelf). [It. *Guelfo* = ML. *Guelphus*, < G. *Welf*, name of the founder of a princely German family.] **I.** *n.* A member of the papal and popular party in medieval Italy, opposed to the Ghibellines. **II.** *a.* Of or pertaining to the Guelphs.—**Guelph′ic, Guelf′ic,** *a.*

gue-non (gė-nôṅ), *n.* [F.; origin unknown.] Any of the agile, long-tailed African monkeys constituting the genus *Cercopithecus*, as the grivet and the green monkey.

guer-don (gėr′dọn), *n.* [OF. *guerdon*, *werdoun*, by alteration (prob. by association with L. *donum*, gift) < OHG. *widarlōn*, < *widar*, again, back, + *lōn*, reward.] A reward, recompense, or requital: as, "Verse, like the laurel, its immortal meed, Should be the *guerdon* of a noble deed" (Cowper's "Charity," 293). [Now chiefly poetic.]—**guer′don,** *v. t.* To reward; recompense: as, "Him we gave a costly bribe To *guerdon* silence" (Tennyson's "Princess," i. 201). [Now chiefly poetic.]

guer-e-za (ger′ẹ-zą̈), *n.* [Native name.] A large Abyssinian monkey, *Colobus guereza*, having a thick growth of long white hair on the sides of the otherwise black body and on the end of the tail; also, any of several related species. See cut in next column.

gue-ril′la, *n.* and *a.* See *guerrilla*.

Guern-sey (gėrn′zi), *n.*; pl. *-seys* (-ziz). One of a celebrated breed of dairy cattle, slightly larger than the Jersey, originating on the island of Guernsey, in the English Channel; also [*l. c.*], a close-fitting knitted woolen shirt much worn by seamen.

guer-ril-la (gẹ-ril′ą̈). [Sp. *guerrilla* (F. *guérilla*), dim. of *guerra*, war; from Teut., and akin to E. *war*.] **I.** *n.* An irregular war carried on by independent bands (now rare); also, an independent and generally predatory fighter in a war, esp. a member of a band of such fighters. **II.** *a.* Of or pertaining to guerrillas: as, a *guerrilla* band; *guerrilla* warfare.

Guereza (*Colobus guereza*).

guess (ges), *v.* [ME. *gessen* = D. and LG. *gissen* = Sw. *gissa* = Dan. *gisse*, guess; from the root of E. *get*, prob. through Scand.] **I.** *tr.* To judge of approximately (as, to *guess* the height of a building; to *guess* the number of people in a crowd); estimate; also, to form an opinion of at random or from evidence admittedly uncertain (as, *guess* whom I saw to-day; we can only *guess* what will happen next); conjecture; also, to estimate correctly (as, to win a prize by *guessing* the number of beans in a bowl); conjecture rightly (as, to *guess* the answer to a question by mere chance); discover by conjecture, or divine (as, to *guess* a person's designs); solve by a correct conjecture (as, to *guess* a riddle); also, loosely, to think, believe, or suppose (as, I *guess* I can get there in time; I *guess* I know what you mean: hence often used colloquially, esp. in the U. S., to soften the form of statement in cases in which no uncertainty is involved, as in 'I *guess* I'll go now,' for the more blunt 'I will go now'). **II.** *intr.* To form an estimate or conjecture (often with *at*: as, to *guess* at the height of a building; to *guess* at what a thing means); also, to estimate or conjecture correctly.—**guess,** *n.* The act of guessing (as, by *guess*, by rough estimate, or by conjecture); also, an act of guessing; a rough estimate; a conjecture; a supposition based on uncertain evidence.—**guess′a-ble,** *a.* That may be guessed.—**guess′er,** *n.*—**guess′ing-ly,** *adv.* —**guess′work,** *n.* Work or procedure based on or consisting in guessing; conjecture.

guest (gest), *n.* [AS. *gæst*, *giest*, = D. and G. *gast* = Icel. *gestr* = Goth. *gasts*, orig. 'stranger'; akin to L. *hostis*, stranger, enemy, and *hospes*, host, guest, stranger.] A stranger†; also, a person entertained gratuitously at the house or table of another; hence, one who received the hospitality of a club, a city, or the like; also, a person entertained for pay, as at a hotel or boarding-house; also, in *zoöl.* and *bot.*, an inquiline; a commensal; a parasite.—**guest,** *v. t.* or *i.* To entertain as or be a guest: as, "Be merry together . . . *Guesting* awhile in the rooms of a beautiful inn" (Masefield's "Laugh and Be Merry").—**guest′=cham″ber, guest′=room,** *n.* A room for the lodging or entertainment of guests. —**guest′less,** *a.* Without guests.—**guest′ship,** *n.* The position or relation of a guest.

guff (guf), *n.* [Origin obscure.] Empty or foolish talk; stuff; humbug; nonsense. [Slang.]

guf-faw (gu-fâ′), *n.* [Imit.; orig. Sc.] A loud, coarse burst of laughter.—**guf-faw′,** *v. i.* To laugh loudly and boisterously.

gug-gle (gug′l), *v. i.*; *-gled*, *-gling*. [Imit.: cf. *gurgle*.] To make a gurgling sound; gurgle.

guid-a-ble (gī′dạ-bl), *a.* Capable of being guided.

guid-ance (gī′dạns), *n.* The act of guiding; leadership; direction; also, something that guides.

guide (gīd), *v. t.*; *guided*, *guiding*. [OF. F. *guider*, for earlier *guier*, guide; from Teut., and prob. akin to E. *wit* and *wise*[1].] To lead or conduct on the way, as to a place or through a region; go with in order to show the way, as a guide does; sometimes, to show the way to or for, as stars, light, etc., do; also, to lead or show (the way); hence, to direct the movement or course of (the hand, a pen, a horse, a plow, etc.); fig., to lead or direct in any course of action (as, to be *guided* by advice, by one's own wishes, or by prudence); determine the course or direction of (actions, events, etc.); conduct the affairs of (a state, institution, etc.); manage (property, money, etc.: now Sc.); also, to treat or use, as in a particular manner (Sc. and north. Eng.: as, "There are few—very few, either of fools or of wise men, ken how to *guide* a woman," Scott's "Fortunes of Nigel," xxxv.).—**guide,** *n.* [OF. F. *guide.*] One who guides; one who leads or conducts others on the way; one employed to guide travelers, tourists, hunters, etc.; one who directs some course of action or procedure; also, something that guides or directs; a guide-book; a book of instruction or information in an art, etc.; a mark or the like to direct the eye; a mechanical appliance or part for directing or regulating motion or action; also, guidance (now rare: as, "Give them *guide* to us," Shakspere's "Timon of Athens," i. 1. 252). —**guide'=board,** *n.* A board, as on a guide-post, containing directions to travelers.—**guide'=book,** *n.* A book of directions and information for travelers, tourists, etc.—**guide'-less,** *a.* Without a guide or means of guidance.—**guide'=post,** *n.* A post, as at the intersection of two or more roads, bearing a sign for the guidance of travelers.—**guid-er** (gī'dėr), *n.*—**guide'=rope,** *n.* A rope used for guiding something, as one for steadying an object which is being hoisted; also, a long rope hung downward from a balloon and trailing along the ground, for regulating automatically the altitude of the balloon.—**guide'way,** *n.* In *mech.*, a track, channel, slot, framework, or the like, on or in which a part slides or moves.

gui-don (gī'dọn), *n.* [F. *guidon*, < It. *guidone*; akin to E. *guide.*] A small flag or streamer carried as a guide by troops (as cavalry or mounted batteries of artillery), or used for marking or signaling; also, the officer carrying it.

guild (gild), *n.* See *gild*[1].

guil-der (gil'dėr), *n.* [For *gulden.*] A gulden.

guild'hall, guilds'man. See *gildhall, gildsman.*

guile (gīl), *n.* [OF. *guile*, guile; from Teut., and akin to E. *wile.*] Insidious cunning; craft; deceit; treachery; also, a stratagem†; a wile†.—**guile,** *v. t.*; *guiled, guiling.* To deceive or beguile (archaic); also, to make guileful or treacherous† (as, "Ornament is but the *guiled* shore To a most dangerous sea": Shakspere's "Merchant of Venice," iii. 2. 97).—**guile'ful,** *a.* Full of guile; wily; deceitful; treacherous.—**guile'ful-ly,** *adv.*—**guile'ful-ness,** *n.*—**guile'-less,** *a.* Free from guile: as, "The plain ox, That harmless, honest, *guileless* animal" (Thomson's "Seasons," Spring, 363).—**guile'less-ly,** *adv.*—**guile'less-ness,** *n.*

guil-le-mot (gil'ẹ-mot), *n.* [F. *guillemot*, appar. dim. of *Guillaume*, William.] Any of various birds of the auk family constituting the genera *Cepphus* and *Uria*, natives of the northern coasts and characterized by a relatively narrow bill, as *Cepphus grylle* ('black guillemot') and *Uria troile* ('foolish guillemot').

Black Guillemot (*Cepphus grylle*). — Right-hand figure, summer plumage; left-hand figure, winter plumage.

guil-loche (gi-lōsh'), *n.* [F. *guillochis*; origin uncertain.] A band-like ornament composed of curved lines or strands interlacing or otherwise combined in a pattern. Cf. *fret*[2], *n.*

Ionic Guilloche, from a column-base of the north porch of the Erechtheum, Athens.

guil-lo-tine (gil'ọ-tēn or gil-ọ-tēn'), *n.* [F.; from J. I. *Guillotin* (1738-1814), French physician, who, although not the inventor of the machine adopted, urged the use of such a means of decapitation.] A machine for beheading persons by means of a heavy blade sliding in two grooved posts (as, "Louis was beheaded in January, 1793. He was guillotined—for since the previous August the *guillotine* had been in use as the official instrument in French executions": H. G. Wells's "Outline of History," xxxvii. § 10); also, a machine for cutting paper, etc.; an instrument for cutting the tonsils.—**guil-lo-tine',** *v. t.*; *-tined, -tining.* To behead by the guillotine; also, to cut, as paper, with a guillotine.—**guil-lo-tine'ment,** *n.*—**guil-lo-tin'er** (-tē'nėr), *n.*

guilt (gilt), *n.* [AS. *gylt*, offense, crime, fault.] An offense† or crime†; also, the fact or state of having committed an offense or crime; grave culpability, as for some conscious violation of moral or penal law, either by positive act or by neglect of known duty; responsibility for heinous fault; criminality; also, guilty conduct.—**guilt'i-ly,** *adv.* In a guilty manner.—**guilt'i-ness,** *n.*—**guilt'less,** *a.* Free from guilt; innocent; not liable to the imputation (*of*: as, *guiltless* of evil intent); hence, having no knowledge or experience (*of*: as, "Such gardening-tools as art, yet rude, *Guiltless* of fire, had form'd," Milton's "Paradise Lost," ix. 392); destitute or devoid (*of*: as, a street *guiltless* of a footway).—**guilt'less-ly,** *adv.*—**guilt'less-ness,** *n.*—**guilt'y,** *a.*; compar. *guiltier*, superl. *guiltiest.* [AS. *gyltig.*] Having incurred guilt or grave culpability, as by committing an offense or crime; justly chargeable with the guilt (*of*: as, to plead *guilty* of murder); characterized by, connected with, or involving guilt (as, *guilty* deeds, gains, or intent; *guilty* love); affected with or showing a sense of guilt (as, a *guilty* conscience; a *guilty* blush); also, deserving (*of*) by reason of guilt† (as, "He is *guilty* of death": Mat. xxvi. 66); also, conscious† (with *of* or a clause: as, "Farewell, ye never-opening gates . . . And threshold *guilty* of my midnight moans!" Dryden's tr. Theocritus, Idyl xxiii.).

guimpe (gamp), *n.* [F. *guimpe*, OF. *guimple*, wimple; from Teut., and akin to E. *wimple.*] A kind of chemisette or yoke of lace, embroidery, or other material, worn with a dress cut out at the neck.

guin-ea (gin'ẹ), *n.* [From *Guinea*, in western Africa, the first of the coins being made of gold from Guinea and for use in African trade.] A British gold coin issued from 1663 to 1813, at first of a nominal value of 20 shillings, but from 1717 of a fixed value of 21 shillings; also, a British monetary unit equal to the value of this coin (now to 21 shillings, or $5.11), still employed in certain cases (as, a fee or a subscription of 20 *guineas*; a prize of 2,000 *guineas* in a horse-race); also, a guinea-fowl (colloq.); also, an Italian, or any foreigner of similar appearance (slang, U. S.).—**guin'ea=corn,** *n.* Durra.—**guin'ea=fowl,** *n.* An African gallinaceous bird, *Numida meleagris*, which has (usually) dark-gray plumage with small white spots, and which is now domesticated throughout the world and valued for its flesh and eggs; also, any of a group of birds of which this species is the type.—**guin'ea=grains,** *n. pl.* Grains of paradise (see under *grain*[2], *n.*).—**guin'ea=hen,** *n.* The female of the guinea-fowl; also, a guinea-fowl without regard to sex; also, a courtezan†.

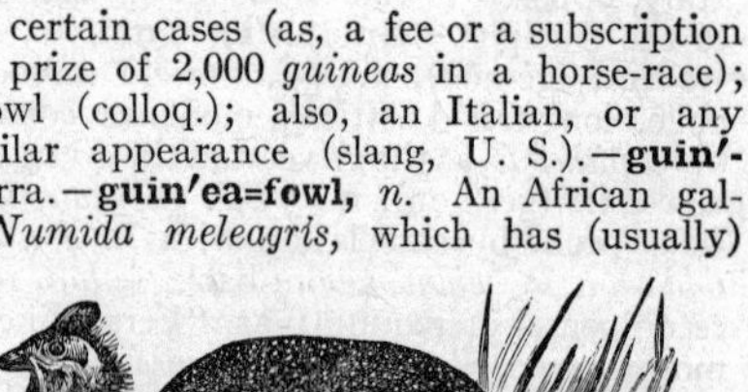

Obverse. Reverse.

Guinea of Charles II., 1663. — British Museum.

Common Guinea-fowl (*Numida meleagris*).

guin-ea=pig (gin'ẹ-pig), *n.* [First element of name uncertain, and variously explained.] A short-eared, short-tailed rodent of the genus *Cavia*, usually white, black, and tawny in color, sometimes kept as a pet and much used in bacteriological experiments: commonly regarded as the domesticated form of one of the South American wild species of cavy.

guin-ea=worm (gin′ḛ-wėrm), *n.* A slender nematode worm, *Filaria* (or *Dracunculus*) *medinensis*, parasitic in man, horses, etc.: common on the Guinea coast and in other warm regions.

Guinea-worm.

gui-pure (gi-pūr′, F. gē-pür), *n.* [F., < *guiper*, cover or whip with silk, etc.; from Teut.] Any of various laces or trimmings formerly in use, made with cords or heavy threads, metal, etc.; in later use, any of various laces, often heavy, made of linen, silk, etc., with the pattern connected by brides (rather than by a net ground).

gui-sarme (gi-zärm′), *n.* See *gisarme*.

guise (gīz), *n.* [OF. F. *guise*; from Teut., and akin to E. *wise*[2].] Manner†, mode†, or fashion† (as, "stately pillours fram'd after the Doricke *guize*": Spenser's "Faerie Queene," iv. 10. 6); habit† or custom† (as, "It never was our *guise* To slight the poor": Pope's tr. Homer's "Odyssey," xiv.); behavior† or conduct† (as, "By their *guise* Just men they seem'd": Milton's "Paradise Lost," xi. 576); also, style of dress, or garb (as, in the *guise* of a shepherdess); also, external appearance in general, aspect, or semblance (as, an old principle in a new *guise*); sometimes, assumed appearance or mere semblance (as, to put on a *guise* of simplicity or virtue); also, a disguise (obs. or prov.); a dance or entertainment in disguises, or a masquerade (obs. or Sc.).—**guise,** *v.*; *guised, guising.* **I.** *tr.* To dress, attire, or garb (archaic); also, to disguise (obs. or prov.). **II.** *intr.* To go in disguise; masquerade; go about as a mummer or guiser. [Chiefly Sc. and north. Eng.]—**guis-er** (gī′zėr), *n.* A masquerader; a mummer. [Chiefly Sc. and north. Eng.]

French Guitar of the 17th century.

gui-tar (gi-tär′), *n.* [F. *guitare*, < Sp. *guitarra*, < L. *cithara*: see *cithara*.] A musical instrument of the lute class, with a long, fretted neck and a violin-like body, and six strings plucked or twanged by the fingers.—**gui-tar′-ist,** *n.* A player on the guitar.

Blue Guitguit.

guit-guit (gwit′gwit), *n.* [Imit. of its note.] Any of various small, usually brilliantly colored, oscine birds (family *Cœrebidæ*) of the warmer parts of America, as *Cœreba cyanea* ('blue guitguit'), a brilliant species found in Guiana.

gu-lar (gū′lạr). [L. *gula*, throat.] **I.** *a.* Of, pertaining to, or situated on the throat. **II.** *n.* A gular plate or shield beneath the throat of a serpent or fish.

gu-lash (gö′läsh), *n.* See *goulash*.

gulch (gulch), *n.* [Origin uncertain.] A deep, narrow ravine, esp. one marking the course of a stream or torrent; a gorge. [Chiefly western U. S.]

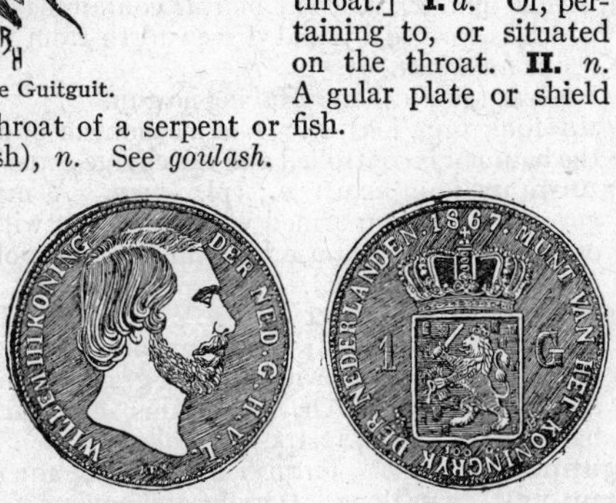

Obverse. Reverse.
Silver Gulden of William III., King of the Netherlands, 1867. — British Museum.

gul-den (gůl′-den), *n.*; pl. *-dens* or *-den.* [D. and G., lit. 'golden.'] Any of various obsolete gold coins of Germany and the Netherlands; also, the gold monetary unit of the Netherlands, equal to 40.2 U. S. cents; a Dutch silver coin of this value (also called *florin*: see cut in preceding column); also, the Austrian florin.

gules (gūlz), *n.* [OF. F. *gueules*; origin uncertain.] In *her.*, the color red.

gulf (gulf). [OF. F. *golfe*, < It. *golfo*, < LGr. κόλφος, Gr. κόλπος, bosom, hollow, gulf.] **I.** *n.* A portion of an ocean or sea extending into the land (as, the *Gulf* of Mexico); also, a deep hollow; a chasm or abyss; also, any wide separation, as in station, education, etc. (cf. Luke, xvi. 26); also, something that engulfs or swallows up; a whirlpool. **II.** *a.* Of or pertaining to a gulf, esp. [*cap.*] the Gulf of Mexico.—**Gulf States,** those States of the U. S. bordering on the Gulf of Mexico.—**Gulf Stream,** a warm oceanic current issuing from the Gulf of Mexico, flowing northward along the U. S. coast, and thence in a northeasterly direction toward the British Isles.—**gulf,** *v. t.* To swallow like a gulf, or as in a gulf; cast into or as into a gulf; engulf.—**gulf′weed,** *n.* A coarse olive-brown seaweed, *Sargassum bacciferum*, found in the Gulf Stream and elsewhere, characterized by numerous berry-like air-vessels by which it is buoyed up; also, some related species.—**gulf′y,** *a.* Full of gulfs or hollows; also, full of whirlpools; like a whirlpool.

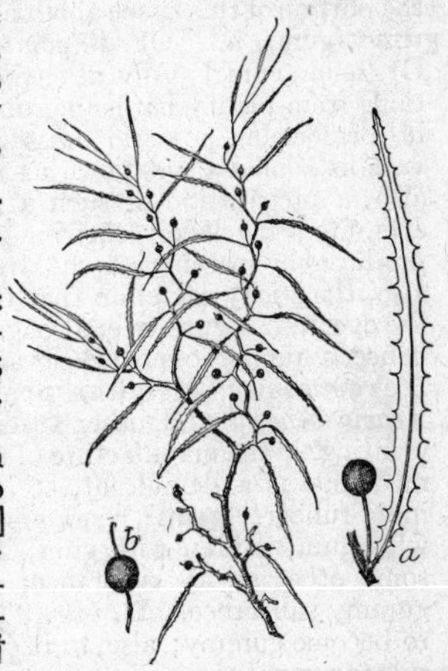

Branch of Gulfweed (*Sargassum bacciferum*). — *a*, vesicle with leaf; *b*, mucronate vesicle.

gull[1] (gul), *n.* [ME. *goll*: cf. ME. *gull*, Icel. *gulr*, yellow.] An unfledged bird; esp., an unfledged gosling. [Now prov. Eng.]

gull[2] (gul), *v. t.* [Origin uncertain: cf. *gull*[1], also obs. *gull*, to swallow, guzzle.] To deceive; trick; cheat.—**gull**[2], *n.* One easily deceived or cheated; a simpleton; a dupe; also, a trick† or fraud† (see Shakspere's "Much Ado about Nothing," ii. 3. 123).

gull[3] (gul), *n.* [ME. *gull*; from Celtic.] Any of the long-winged, web-footed aquatic birds constituting the subfamily *Larinæ* (family *Laridæ*), esp. of the genus *Larus*, usually white with dark back and wings; also, any bird of this family, as a tern or a jäger.

Gull (*Larus argentatus*).

gull-a-ble (gul′ạ-bl), etc. See *gullible*, etc.

gul-let (gul′et), *n.* [OF. *goulet*, dim. of *goule* (F. *gueule*), < L. *gula*, throat.] The esophagus, or tube by which food and drink swallowed pass to the stomach (as, "I'm going down to cool my *gullet* at the blessed well": Synge's "Tinker's Wedding," ii.); loosely, the throat or neck; also, something like or likened to the gullet or esophagus; a channel for water; a gully or ravine; a pass or defile; a preparatory cut in excavations.

gull-i-ble (gul′i-bl), *a.* Easily gulled, deceived, or cheated. —**gull-i-bil′i-ty** (-bil′i-ti), *n.*—**gull′i-bly,** *adv.*

gul-ly (gul′i), *n.*; pl. *gullies* (-iz). [Appar. an altered form of *gullet*.] The gullet†; also, a channel worn in the earth by a current of water; a narrow ravine; also, a ditch or gutter. —**gul′ly,** *v. t.*; *-lied, -lying.* To make gullies or channels in; also, to form (channels) by the action of water.

gulp (gulp), *v.* [ME. *gulpen*: cf. D. *gulpen*, gulp.] **I.** *tr.* To swallow eagerly, or in large drafts or morsels (as, "He does not swallow, but he *gulps* it down": Cowper's "Conversation," 340); also, fig. (often with *down*), to take in as by swallowing eagerly; sometimes, to repress (sobs, rage, etc.) as by swallowing. **II.** *intr.* To gasp as when taking large drafts of liquid.—**gulp,** *n.* An act of gulping; a swallow; also, the amount swallowed at one time; a mouthful.—**gulp'er,** *n.* One who or that which gulps; specif., a long-tailed deep-sea fish, *Saccopharynx ampullaceus,* remarkable for its powers of gulping and distention, whereby it sometimes swallows fishes larger than itself; any fish belonging to the same family, the *Saccopharyngidæ.*

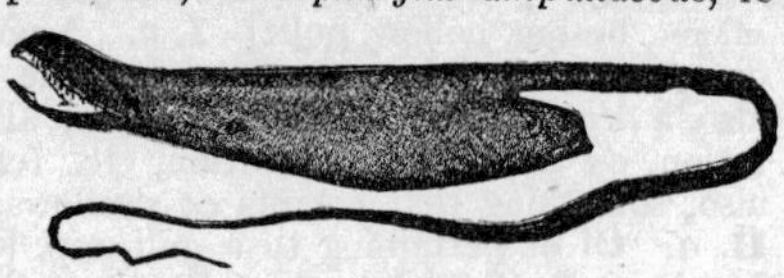

Gulper (*Saccopharynx ampullaceus*).

gum[1] (gum), *n.* [AS. *gōma,* palate, inside of the mouth, akin to G. *gaumen,* palate.] The firm, fleshy tissue covering the alveolar parts of either jaw and enveloping the necks of the teeth (when present) (often in *pl.*); sometimes, the portion of this tissue about a single tooth.

gum[2] (gum), *n.* [OF. F. *gomme,* < L. *gummi, cummi,* < Gr. *κόμμι,* gum.] Any of various viscid, amorphous exudations from plants, hardening on exposure to air, and soluble in, or forming a viscid mass with, water; loosely, any of various similar exudations, as resin, gum-resin, or the like; also, a preparation of such a substance, as for use in the arts, etc.; mucilage; chewing-gum; also, a form of dextrin produced by roasting starch ('artificial gum' or 'British gum'); also, the sticky secretion that collects in the inner corner of the eye; also, a gum-tree; also, gum elastic (see phrase below); hence, a rubber overshoe (local, U. S.).—**gum ammoniac.** See *ammoniac, a.*—**gum arabic,** a gum obtained from *Acacia senegal* and other species of acacia, used in calico-printing, in the manufacture of mucilage, ink, and the like, in medicine as a demulcent, etc.—**gum elastic,** caoutchouc; india-rubber.—**gum**[2], *v.*; *gummed, gumming.* **I.** *tr.* To smear with gum; stiffen with gum; fasten or unite with gum or some other sticky substance; clog with or as with some gummy substance. **II.** *intr.* To exude or form gum; also, to become gummy; also, to become clogged by some gummy substance.

gum-bo[1] (gum'bō), *n.* [From Angola name.] The okra plant, or its mucilaginous pods; also, a soup, usually of chicken, thickened with these pods; also, a kind of silty soil in the southern and western U. S., becoming very sticky when wet.

gum-bo[2] (gum'bō), *n.* [Appar. of some native origin.] A patois spoken by negroes and creoles of the French West Indies and Louisiana.

gum=boil (gum'boil), *n.* A small abscess on the gum.

gum=drop (gum'drop), *n.* A drop-like or molded confection of gum arabic, gelatin, or the like, sweetened and flavored.

gum-ma (gum'ạ̈), *n.*; pl. *gummas* or *gummata* (gum'ạ-tạ̈). [NL., < L. *gummi,* E. *gum*[2].] In *pathol.,* a kind of tumor with gum-like contents, produced by syphilis.—**gum'ma-tous** (-tus), *a.* Of the nature of or resembling a gumma; pertaining to a gumma.

gum-mif-er-ous (gu-mif'ẹ-rus), *a.* [L. *gummi,* gum: see *-ferous.*] Producing gum.

gum-mi-ness (gum'i-nes), *n.* Gummy quality or state; also, gummy matter.

gum-mo-sis (gu-mō'sis), *n.* [NL., < L. *gummi,* E. *gum*[2].] In *bot.,* an abnormal condition of certain trees such as the cherry, plum, etc., which causes the formation of gum and its exudation through the bark.

gum-mous[1] (gum'us), *a.* [L. *gummosus.*] Of the nature of or resembling gum; gummy.

gum-mous[2] (gum'us), *a.* Gummatous.

gum-my[1] (gum'i), *a.*; compar. *gummier,* superl. *gummiest.* Of the nature of gum; gum-like; viscid; also, exuding gum; also, covered with or clogged by gum or sticky matter; also, swollen as if by gum-like matter, as the ankles.

gum-my[2] (gum'i), *a.* Gummatous.

gump (gump), *n.* [Origin obscure.] A foolish person; a dolt. [Prov. or colloq.]

gump-tion (gump'shọn), *n.* [Orig. Sc.; origin obscure.] Shrewd, practical sense: as, "He has mair *gumption* in him than most people" (Scott's "Redgauntlet," ch. x.). [Colloq.]

gum=res-in (gum'rez'in), *n.* Any of various natural mixtures of gum and resin, obtained from certain plants.

gum=shoe (gum'shö'), *n.* A shoe made of gum elastic or india-rubber; a rubber overshoe.—**gum'=shoe,** *v. i.*; *-shoed, -shoeing.* To go softly, as if wearing rubber shoes; move or act stealthily. [Colloq., U. S.]

gum=tree (gum'trē), *n.* Any tree that exudes gum, as a eucalyptus, the sour-gum, the sweet-gum, etc.

gun[1] (gun). Past participle of *gin*[1].

gun[2] (gun), *n.* [ME. *gunne, gonne,* perhaps from a Scand. feminine proper name (cf. Icel. *Gunna,* woman's name).] A military engine for hurling stones†; also, a metallic tube, with its stock or carriage and attachments, from which heavy missiles are thrown by the force of gunpowder, etc. ('great gun'); a piece of ordnance, esp. a long cannon; also, any portable firearm except a pistol or revolver, as a rifle; hence, any similar device for projecting a missile (as, an air-*gun*); a device for projecting something else (see *cement-gun*); sometimes, a pistol or revolver (colloq., U. S.); also, the discharge of a gun, as in a salute, or as a signal; also, one who carries a gun; an artilleryman or gunner; also, a thief or pickpocket (slang).—**gun**[2], *v. i.*; *gunned, gunning.* To shoot with a gun; hunt with a gun.—**gun'boat,** *n.* A small vessel carrying mounted guns; esp., a small, armed war-vessel of light draft, used for visiting minor ports, etc. —**gun'=car''riage,** *n.* The carriage or structure on which a gun is mounted or moved, and on which it is fired: as, a disappearing *gun-carriage* (one so arranged that the gun after being fired descends to the loading position behind the protection of a parapet).—**gun'-cot''ton,** *n.* Any of a number of substances composed of one or more cellulose nitrates, as the high explosive produced by treating cotton or the like with a mixture of nitric and sulphuric acids, or the more soluble and less explosive material ('soluble gun-cotton') used in making collodion, celluloid, etc. Cf. *cellulose nitrate,* under *cellulose*[1].

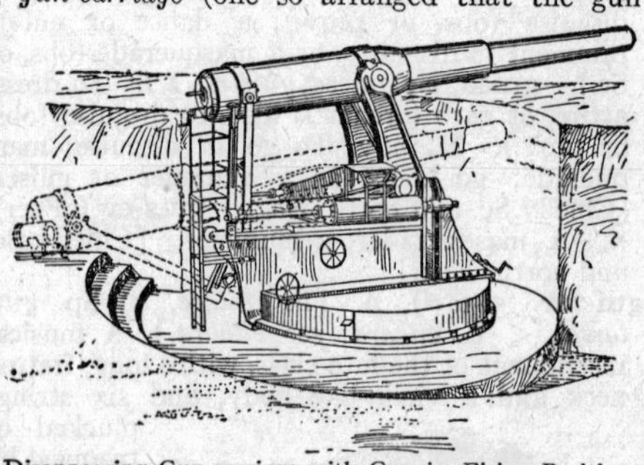

Disappearing Gun-carriage with Gun in Firing Position, Loading Position being shown in dotted outline.

gun-de-low (gun'dẹ-lō), *n.* A corruption of *gondola.* See Whittier's "Snow-Bound."

gun-di (gun'di), *n.*; pl. *-dis* (-diz). [N. Afr.] Same as *ctenodactyl.*

gun=fire (gun'fīr), *n.* The firing of a gun or guns; also, the hour at which the morning or evening gun is fired, as in the navy or the army.

gun=flint (gun'flint), *n.* The piece of flint in a flintlock.

gun-ite (gun'īt), *n.* The mortar containing cement and sand which is formed by and driven forth from the cement-gun. See *cement-gun.*

gun-less (gun'les), *a.* Having no gun.

gun=lock (gun'lok), *n.* The mechanism of a gun by which the hammer is controlled and the charge exploded.

gun-man (gun'mạn), *n.*; pl. *-men.* A man who makes guns; also, a man armed with, or expert with, a gun; esp., one who is ready to use his skill with a revolver unlawfully for hire (colloq., U. S.).

gun=met-al (gun'met''ạl), *n.* A bronze formerly much employed for cannon; also, any of various other alloys or metallic substances with a dark-gray or blackish color or finish, used for watchcases, chains, belt-buckles, umbrella-handles, etc.; also, a dark-gray color.

gunned (gund), *a.* Furnished with guns, as a ship.

gun-nel[1] (gun'l), *n.* [Origin unknown.] Any of certain blennies (fishes), esp. *Pholis gunnellus,* which is found in the northern Atlantic.

gun-nel[2] (gun′l), *n.* See *gunwale.*

gun-ner (gun′ėr), *n.* One who works a gun or cannon; also, a warrant-officer in the navy having charge of the ordnance, etc., on a ship, or engaged in other duties; also, one who hunts with a gun.

gun-ner-y (gun′ėr-i), *n.* The art and science of constructing and managing guns, esp. large guns; also, the use of guns; the firing of guns; also, guns collectively.

gun-ning (gun′ing), *n.* The act, practice, or art of shooting with guns; esp., the hunting of game with guns.

gun-ny (gun′i), *n.*; pl. *gunnies* (-iz). [Hind. *gōnī.*] A strong, coarse material made commonly from jute, used for bagging, etc.; also, a bag or sack of this material.—**gun′ny=bag, gun′ny=sack,** *n.*

gun=port (gun′pōrt), *n.* A port-hole for a gun.

gun-pow-der (gun′pou″dėr), *n.* An explosive mixture of saltpeter (potassium nitrate), sulphur, and charcoal, used esp. in gunnery; also, any of various other explosives.—**Gunpowder Plot,** in *Eng. hist.*, a plot to blow up the king (James I.) and the Lords and Commons in the Parliament House, on Nov. 5, 1605, in revenge for the laws against Roman Catholics: it was discovered in time and defeated, and its agents, Guy Fawkes and others, were put to death.—**gunpowder tea,** a fine variety of green tea, each leaf of which is rolled into a little ball.

gun=room (gun′röm), *n.* In a British man-of-war, orig. an apartment occupied by the gunner and his mates, now one devoted to the use of the junior officers; also, in a house or other building, a room in which guns are kept.

gun=run-ning (gun′run″ing), *n.* The practice of illegally conveying firearms and ammunition into a country.—**gun′=run″ner,** *n.*

gun-shot (gun′shot), *n.* The shooting of a gun; also, the range of a gun; also, shot fired from a gun.

gun=shy (gun′shī), *a.* Frightened at the report of a gun.

gun-smith (gun′smith), *n.* One whose occupation it is to make or repair small firearms.

gun=stock (gun′stok), *n.* The stock or wooden support in which the barrel of a gun is fixed.

Gun-ter's (gun′tėrz) **chain.** [From E. *Gunter* (1581-1626), English mathematician.] A surveyor's chain. See *chain, n.*—**Gunter's scale.** A plane rule containing scales of sines, tangents, etc., on one side, and corresponding scales of logarithms on the other: used for solving mechanically problems in trigonometry, navigation, etc.

gun-wale (gun′l or gun′wāl), *n.* [From *gun*[2] + *wale*[2]; so called because formerly guns were set upon it.] *Naut.*, the upper edge of a vessel's or boat's side; the uppermost wale of a ship, next below the bulwarks.

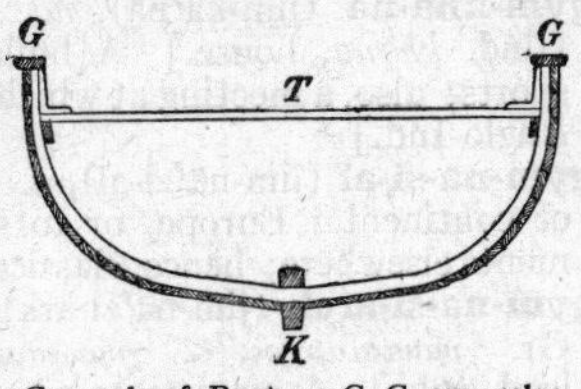

Gunwale of Boat. — *G, G,* gunwale; *K,* keel; *T,* thwart.

gun-yah (gun′yä), *n.* [Native name.] A native Australian hut.

gurge (gėrj), *n.* [L. *gurges.*] A whirlpool: as, "A black bituminous *gurge* Boils out from under ground" (Milton's "Paradise Lost," xii. 41). [Poetic.]

gur-gi-ta-tion (gėr-ji-tā′shon), *n.* [LL. *gurgitare* (pp. *gurgitatus*), engulf, flood, < L. *gurges,* whirlpool, gulf.] Surging rise and fall; ebullient motion, as of water.

gur-gle (gėr′gl), *v.*; *-gled, -gling.* [Appar. imit.; perhaps orig. a varied form of *gargle.*] **I.** *intr.* To gargle†; also, to flow in a broken, irregular, noisy current, as water from a bottle or a small stream on a stony bottom; make a sound as of water doing this (often used with reference to the utterance of birds or of human beings). **II.** *tr.* To utter with a gurgling sound.—**gur′gle,** *n.* A gargle†; also, the act or the noise of gurgling; a gurgling sound.—**gur′gling-ly,** *adv.*

gur-goyle (gėr′goil); *n.* Same as *gargoyle.*

gur-jun (gėr′jun), *n.* [E. Ind.] A large tree, *Dipterocarpus alatus,* of the East Indies, valued for its balsam and wood; also, the balsam of this tree and of certain other species of the same genus, used as a medicine, a varnish, etc.; also, the wood.

Gur-kha (gör′kä), *n.* One of a Hindu race dominant in Nepal and noted as warriors.

gur-nard (gėr′närd), *n.* [OF. *gornart,* prob. lit. 'grunter' (from the sound made by the fish when taken out of the water), = F. *grognard,* grumbler, < *grogner,* grunt.] Any of various marine acanthopterygian fishes, esp. of the genus *Trigla* of Europe and the genus *Prionotus* of America, having a spiny head with mailed cheeks, and three pairs of free pectoral rays; any of various similar fishes (see *flying-gurnard*). Also **gur′net.**

Gurnard (*Trigla gurnardus*).

gu-ru (gö′rö or gu̇-rö′), *n.* [Hind. *gurū,* < Skt. *guru,* teacher, orig. adj., heavy, weighty, worthy of honor.] In India, a religious teacher or guide.

gush (gush), *v.* [ME. *guschen;* appar. imit.] **I.** *intr.* To issue with force, as a fluid from confinement; flow suddenly or copiously; also, to have a copious flow of something, as of blood, tears, etc.; also, to express one's self in an effusive or extravagantly emotional manner; talk effusively or sentimentally. **II.** *tr.* To emit suddenly, forcibly, or copiously: as, "The gaping wound *gush'd* out a crimson flood" (Dryden's tr. Virgil's "Æneid," x. 1117).—**gush,** *n.* A sudden and violent emission, as of fluid; the fluid emitted; also, gushing or effusive language.—**gush′er,** *n.* One who or that which gushes; specif., an oil-well which sends out oil in abundance without pumping.—**gush′ing-ly,** *adv.*—**gush′y,** *a.*; compar. *gushier,* superl. *gushiest.* Given to or marked by gush or effusiveness.

gus-set (gus′et), *n.* [OF. *gousset, gouchet* (F. *gousset*): cf. F. *gousse,* pod, husk.] A flexible piece, as of mail, in armor, used to protect the armpit; hence, an angular piece of material inserted in a shirt, etc., at the under part of the armhole; in general, an angular or shaped piece serving to fill an opening, afford more room, adjust shape, give strength, etc.—**gus′set,** *v. t.*; *-seted, -seting.* To furnish or make with a gusset or gussets.

gust[1] (gust), *n.* [Prob. from Scand.: cf. Icel. *gustr,* a gust, blast.] A sudden, strong blast of wind; hence, a sudden rush of water, fire, smoke, etc.; a burst of sound; an outburst of passionate feeling.

gust[2] (gust), *n.* [L. *gustus,* a tasting, taste: see *choose.*] The sense of taste; also, individual taste or liking (as, to find a thing little to one's *gust*); also, relish, enjoyment, zest, or gusto (as, "He drinks his simple bev'rage with a *gust*": Cowper's "Table Talk," 240); also, flavor, esp. pleasing flavor (as, "The whole vegetable tribe have lost their *gust* with me": Lamb's "Grace before Meat"). [Archaic.]—**gust**[2], *v. t.* [L. *gustare,* < *gustus.*] To taste; relish. [Archaic or Sc.]—**gust′a-ble.** [LL. *gustabilis.*] **I.** *a.* That may be tasted; perceptible by the sense of taste; also, pleasing to the taste; savory. [Archaic.] **II.** *n.* Something that may be tasted; also, something pleasing to the taste; a savory food. [Archaic.]—**gus-ta-tion** (gus-tā′shon), *n.* [L. *gustatio(n-).*] The act or the faculty of tasting; taste.—**gus′ta-tive** (-ta-tiv), **gus′ta-to-ry** (-tō-ri), *a.* Of or pertaining to gustation or tasting.—**gustatory bud** or **corpuscle,** in *anat.,* any of a number of small, flask-shaped bodies in the epithelium of the tongue, etc., believed to be special organs of taste.

gust-ful[1] (gust′fu̇l), *a.* Gusty; windy: as, "on a *gustful* April morn" (Tennyson's "Holy Grail," 14). [Poetic.]

gust-ful[2] (gust′fu̇l), *a.* Pleasant to the taste; palatable; hence, agreeable to the mind; also, characterized by relish or gusto. [Archaic.]—**gust′ful-ly,** *adv.*

gust-i-ly (gus′ti-li), *adv.* In a gusty manner.

gus-to (gus′tō), *n.*; pl. *-tos* (-tōz). [It., < L. *gustus,* E. *gust*[2].] Individual taste or liking; also, now usually, keen relish or hearty enjoyment, as in eating or drinking or in action or speech generally (as, to carry out a joke or to tell a story with *gusto*); zest.

gust-y (gus′ti), *a.*; compar. *gustier,* superl. *gustiest.* Blowing or coming in gusts, as wind, rain, storms, etc.; affected or marked by gusts of wind, etc.; windy; also, occurring or characterized by sudden bursts or outbursts, as sound, laughter, passion, etc.

gut (gut), *n.* [AS. *guttas*, pl., akin to *gēotan*, pour, flow, G. *giessen*, pour.] The alimentary canal between the pylorus and the anus, or some portion of it; sometimes, the whole alimentary canal; *pl.*, the bowels or entrails (now vulgar, except of animals); fig., insides (slang); substantial contents or qualities (slang: as, a book or a play with no *guts* to it); also, *sing.*, the intestines of animals prepared for various purposes, as for violin-strings; also, the silken substance taken from a silkworm killed when about to spin its cocoon, used in making snells for fish-hooks ('silk-worm gut'); also, a narrow passage, as a channel of water or a defile between hills.—**gut**, *v. t.*; *gutted*, *gutting*. To take out the guts or entrails of; disembowel; hence, to clear or plunder of contents (as, "We *gutted* him [a ship] of the pearl": Defoe's "Captain Singleton," xii.); destroy the interior of.

gut-ta (gut'ä̤), *n.*; pl. *guttæ* (-ē). [L., a drop.] A drop, or something resembling one; in *arch.*, one of a series of pendent ornaments, generally in the form of a frustum of a cone, attached to the under side of the mutules, etc., of the Doric entablature.

Guttæ in Doric Architecture. — *A*, form of gutta beneath regula; *G*, *G*, guttæ beneath mutules and regulæ.

gut-ta=per-cha (gut'ä̤-pėr'chä̤), *n.* [Malay *getah*, gum, balsam, + *percha*, kind of tree producing the substance.] The concrete milky juice, nearly white when pure, of various Malaysian sapotaceous trees, esp. *Palaquium gutta*: variously used in the arts and manufactures, as for insulating electric wires.

gut-tate (gut'āt), *a.* [L. *guttatus*, < *gutta*, a drop.] In the form of drops; containing drops or drop-like masses; spotted as if by drops. Also **gut-tat-ed** (gut'-ā-ted).

gut-ter (gut'ėr), *n.* [OF. *goutiere* (F. *gouttière*), < *goute* (F. *goutte*), < L. *gutta*, a drop.] A channel at the eaves or on the roof of a building, for carrying off rain-water; also, a channel at the side (or in the middle) of a road or street, for leading off surface water (often taken figuratively as the abode or resort of the lowest class of persons in the community: as, to raise a person out of the *gutter*; children of the *gutter*; the language of the *gutter*); hence, any channel, trough, or the like, for carrying off fluid; also, a furrow or channel made by running water; also, any channel or groove; also, a watercourse†; a brook†.—**gut'ter**, *v.* **I.** *tr.* To furnish with a gutter or gutters; make gutters in; channel or furrow as if with gutters. **II.** *intr.* To form gutters, as water does; also, to flow in streams (as, "Their lab'ring sides Are swell'd, and sweat runs *gutt'ring* down in tides": Dryden's tr. Virgil's "Æneid," v. 261); also, to become channeled, as a burning candle does by the flow of the melted tallow or wax down its side (as, "The candles flickered and *guttered* down, and made long winding-sheets": Dickens's "Barnaby Rudge," lv.).—**gut'ter=snipe**, *n.* A gatherer of rags, paper, etc., from street gutters; also, a street child of the lowest class; a street Arab; a gamin. [Colloq.]

gut-ti-fer (gut'i-fėr), *n.* [NL., < L. *gutta*, a drop, + *ferre*, bear.] A plant yielding gum or resin; a clusiaceous plant. —**gut-tif-er-ous** (gu-tif'e̤-rus), *a.* Yielding gum or resin; clusiaceous.

gut-tle (gut'l), *v. i.* or *t.*; *-tled*, *-tling*. [Appar. a freq. < *gut*.] To eat or swallow greedily or voraciously.—**gut'-tler**, *n.*

gut-tu-la (gut'ū-lä̤), *n.*; pl. *-læ* (-lē). [L., dim. of *gutta*, a drop.] In *bot.* and *zoöl.*, a small (drop-like) spot, as of color.—**gut'tu-late** (-lāt), *a.* In *bot.* and *zoöl.*, composed of, containing, or resembling small drop-like vesicles, spots, or the like.

gut-tur-al (gut'u-ra̤l). [NL. *gutturalis*, < L. *guttur*, throat.] **I.** *a.* Of or pertaining to the throat; esp., of sounds, etc., produced, or regarded as produced, in the throat; noting any harsh or rasping vocal sound; in *phonetics*, formed between the tongue and the soft palate, as the sound of *k*, and of *g* in *go*. **II.** *n.* A guttural sound. —**gut'tur-al-ize**, *v. t.*; *-ized*, *-izing*. To utter in a guttural manner; also, to make (a sound) guttural in character. —**gut'tur-al-ly**, *adv.*—**gut'tur-al-ness**, *n.*

gut-tur-o- (gut'u-rō̤-). Form of L. *guttur*, throat, used in combination, as in *gutturolabial* (involving both throat and lips; both guttural and labial), *gutturonasal* (both guttural and nasal), *gutturosibilant*, etc.

gut-ty (gut'i), *n.*; pl. *gutties* (-iz). [From *gutta-percha*.] In *golf*, a gutta-percha ball. [Colloq.]

guy[1] (gī), *n.* [OF. *guis*, *guie*, a guide, < *guier*, guide: see *guide*.] A guide†; also, a rope or appliance used to guide and steady a thing being hoisted or lowered, or to steady or secure anything liable to shift its position.—**guy**[1], *v. t.* To guide, steady, or secure with a guy or guys.

guy[2] (gī), *n.* [From *Guy* Fawkes.] A grotesque effigy of Guy Fawkes (see *Gunpowder Plot*) carried about and burned in England (esp. formerly) on the anniversary of the defeat of the Gunpowder Plot (Nov. 5, 1605); hence, a person of grotesque appearance; a fright; also, a fellow or person (slang: as, he's a queer *guy*).—**guy**[2], *v. t.* To jeer at or make fun of; ridicule. [Colloq.]

guz-zle (guz'l), *v. t.* or *i.*; *-zled*, *-zling*. [Perhaps connected with F. *gosier*, throat, gullet: cf. obs. F. *desgouziller*, gulp down.] To drink greedily or to excess.—**guz'zle**, *n.* Drink or liquor; also, a drinking-bout or debauch; also, the throat (now prov.); also, a gutter or drain (now prov.).—**guz'zler**, *n.*

gwe-duc (gwē'duk), *n.* [N. Amer. Ind., lit. 'come deep' or 'dig deep.'] A large edible clam, *Glycymeris generosa*, of the northwest coast of the U. S., sometimes 3 feet or more in length with the siphons extended.

Gweduc.

gy-as-cu-tus (jī-a̤s-kū'tus), *n.* [A made word, simulating Latin.] An imaginary quadruped supposed to be of tremendous size, to have the legs on one side of the body much shorter than those on the other, and thus to be able to keep its balance in feeding on the side of a steep mountain.

gybe (jīb), *v.* See *jibe*[1].

gym (jim), *n.* Short for *gymnasium*. [Colloq.]

gym-kha-na (jim-kä'nä̤), *n.* [Appar. < *gym*(*nastics*) + Hind. *khāna*, house.] A building or grounds for athletic sports; also, a meeting at which such sports are held. [Orig. Anglo-Ind.]

gym-na-si-al (jim-nā'zi-a̤l), *a.* Pertaining to the gymnasia of continental Europe, or to similar educational establishments elsewhere; hence, classical, as opposed to scientific, etc.

gym-na-si-arch (jim-nā'zi-ärk), *n.* [L. *gymnasiarchus*, < Gr. γυμνασίαρχος, < γυμνάσιον, E. *gymnasium*, + ἄρχειν, lead, rule.] A magistrate who superintended the gymnasia and certain public games in ancient Athens; also, a leader among athletes; also, a head instructor in a school or college.

gym-na-si-ast (jim-nā'zi-ast), *n.* [G.] A gymnast; also, a student in a gymnasium or classical school in continental Europe.

gym-na-si-um (jim-nā'zi-um), *n.*; pl. *-siums* or *-sia* (-zi-ä̤). [L., < Gr. γυμνάσιον, < γυμνάζειν, train, exercise, < γυμνός, naked, stripped, lightly clad.] A place or building for athletic exercises; a school for gymnastics; also (as G., pron. güm-nä'zē-ům), in continental Europe, esp. Germany, a classical school preparatory to the universities.

gym-nast (jim'nast), *n.* [Gr. γυμναστής, trainer of professional athletes, < γυμνάζειν, train: see *gymnasium*.] One skilled in athletic exercises: as, "leaping back . . . with the speed and security of a trained *gymnast*" (Stevenson's "Treasure Island," xiv.).—**gym-nas'tic**, *a.* [L. *gymnasticus*, < Gr. γυμναστικός.] Of or pertaining to athletic exercises, as for health, defense, or diversion (as, "*gymnastic* feats": Du Maurier's "Trilby," iii.); athletic; also, pertaining to disciplinary exercises for the mind. —**gym-nas'ti-cal-ly**, *adv.*—**gym-nas'tics**, *n.* As *pl.*, gymnastic exercises; as *sing.*, the practice or art of gymnastic exercises.

Gym-nos-o-phist (jim-nos'ọ-fist), *n.* [L. *gymnosophistæ*, pl., < Gr. γυμνοσοφισταί, < γυμνός, naked, + σοφιστής, wise man, E. *sophist.*] One of a sect of ancient Hindu philosophers who wore little or no clothing, ate no flesh, and devoted themselves to mystical contemplation.

gym-no-sperm (jim'nọ-spėrm), *n.* [NL. *gymnospermus*, < Gr. γυμνόσπερμος, having naked seeds, < γυμνός, naked, + σπέρμα, seed.] A plant having its seeds exposed or naked (not inclosed in an ovary): opposed to *angiosperm.*—**gym-no-sper'mous,** *a.* Of the gymnosperm class; having naked seeds.

gyn-æ-ce-um (jin-ẹ-sē'um or jī-nẹ-), *n.*; pl. *-cea* (-sē'ạ). [L., < Gr. γυναικεῖον, prop. neut. of γυναικεῖος, of or for women, < γυνή, woman: see *quean.*] Among the ancients, the part of a dwelling devoted to the use of the women.

gy-nan-drous (ji-nan'drus or jī-), *a.* [Gr. γύνανδρος, of doubtful sex, < γυνή, woman, + ἀνήρ (ἀνδρ-), man.] In *bot.*, having the gynœcium and andrœcium united in a column, as in orchids.

gyn-ar-chy (jin'ạ̈r-ki or jī'nạ̈r-), *n.*; pl. *-chies* (-kiz). [Gr. γυνή, woman: see *-archy.*] Government by a woman or women.

gy-ne'ci-um, *n.* See *gynœcium.*

gyn-e-coc-ra-cy, gyn-æ-coc-ra-cy (jin-ẹ-kok'rạ-si or jī-nẹ-), *n.* [Gr. γυναικοκρατία, < γυνή (γυναικ-), woman, + κρατεῖν, rule.] Government by a woman or women; female government; petticoat rule.—**gyn"e-co-crat'ic, gyn"æ-co-crat'ic** (-kọ-krat'ik), *a.*

gyn-e-col-o-gy, gyn-æ-col-o-gy (jin-ẹ-kol'ọ-ji or jī-nẹ-), *n.* [Gr. γυνή (γυναικ-), woman: see *-logy.*] That department of medical science which deals with the functions and diseases peculiar to women.—**gyn"e-co-log'i-cal, gyn"æ-co-log'i-cal** (-kọ-loj'i-kạl), *a.*—**gyn-e-col'o-gist, gyn-æ-col'o-gist,** *n.*

gyn-e-co-mor-phous, gyn-æ-co-mor-phous (jin"ẹ-kọ-môr'-fus or jī"nẹ-), *a.* [Gr. γυναικόμορφος, < γυνή (γυναικ-), woman, + μορφή, form.] In *biol.*, having the form, appearance, or attributes of a female.

gyn-e-oc-ra-cy, gyn-æ-oc-ra-cy (jin-ẹ-ok'rạ-si or jī-nẹ-), *n.* Same as *gynecocracy.*

gyn-e-ol-a-try, gyn-æ-ol-a-try (jin-ẹ-ol'ạ-tri or jī-nẹ-), *n.* [Gr. γυνή, woman, + λατρεία, worship.] Extravagant devotion to or worship of woman.

gyn-i-at-rics (jin-i-at'riks or jī-ni-), *n.* [Gr. γυνή, woman, + ἰατρικός, E. *iatric.*] The treatment of diseases peculiar to women.

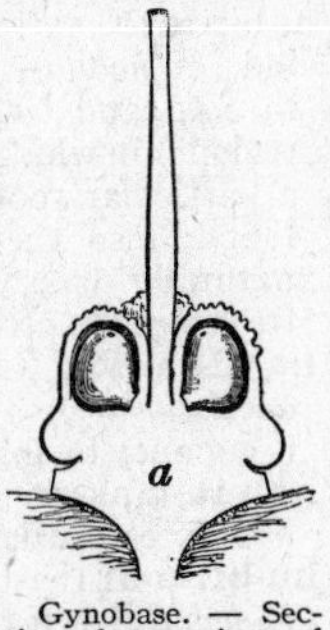

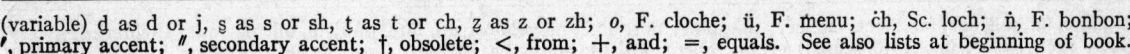

Gynobase. — Section of gynœcium of borage, enlarged, showing gynobase (*a*) bearing the carpels and style.

gyn-o-base (jin'ọ-bās or jī'nọ-), *n.* [Gr. γυνή, woman, + E. *base*².] In *bot.*, a short conical or flat elevation of the receptacle of a flower, bearing the gynœcium.

gy-nœ-cium (ji-nē'shium or jī-), *n.*; pl. *-cia* (-shiạ). [NL., orig. *gynæceum* (see *gynæceum*), but now regarded as < Gr. γυνή, woman, + οἶκος, house.] In *bot.*, the pistil, or the pistils collectively, of a flower. Cf. *andrœcium.*

gyn-o-phore (jin'ọ-fōr or jī'nọ-), *n.* [Gr. γυνή, woman: see *-phore.*] In *bot.*, the elongated pedicel or stalk bearing the gynœcium in some flowers.

-gynous. [Gr. -γυνος, < γυνή, woman.] An adjective termination involving the idea of 'woman,' 'wife,' 'female,' and hence used in botanical terms to imply 'female organ,' 'pistil,' as in *monogynous, polygynous.* Cf. *-androus.*

gyp (jip), *n.* [Perhaps for *gypsy* (*gipsy*).] A male college servant, as at Cambridge, England; also (slang), a swindler, as in horse-dealing; a cheat; a thief.—**gyp,** *v. t.*; *gypped, gypping.* To swindle; cheat; defraud or rob by some sharp practice; also, to obtain by swindling or cheating; steal. [Slang.]—**gyp'per,** *n.*

gyp-se-ous (jip'sẹ-us), *a.* [LL. *gypseus.*] Of the nature of, resembling, or containing gypsum.

gyp-sif-er-ous (jip-sif'ẹ-rus), *a.* [See *-ferous.*] Containing or yielding gypsum.

Flower, with Gynophore (*a*).

gyp-sum (jip'sum), *n.* [L., < Gr. γύψος, chalk, gypsum.] A mineral, a hydrous sulphate of calcium, occurring in both crystalline and massive varieties: used to make plaster of Paris, as an ornamental material, as a fertilizer, etc. Cf. *alabaster* and *selenite*².

Gyp'sy, gyp'sy-dom, etc. See *Gipsy,* etc.

gy-ral (jī'rạl), *a.* Moving in a gyre; gyratory; in *anat.*, pertaining to a cerebral gyrus.—**gy'ral-ly,** *adv.*

gy-rate (jī'rāt), *v. i.*; *-rated, -rating.* [L. *gyratus*, pp. of *gyrare*, turn, wheel round, < *gyrus*: see *gyre.*] To move in a circle or spiral; revolve round a fixed point or on an axis; rotate; whirl.—**gy'rate,** *a.* In *bot.*, circinate; in *zoöl.*, having convolutions.—**gy-ra'tion** (-rā'shọn), *n.* The act of gyrating; circular or spiral motion; revolution; rotation; whirling; a continually wheeling movement, as in dancing.—**gy'ra-to-ry** (-rạ-tọ-ri), *a.* Moving in a circle or spiral; gyrating.

gyre (jīr), *n.* [L. *gyrus*, < Gr. γῦρος, ring, circle.] A ring or circle (as, "She rushing through . . . Perforce disparted their compacted *gyre*": Spenser's "Faerie Queene," iii. 1. 23); also, a circular, spiral, or wheeling course or motion; a circular or spiral turn (as, "The lark Shot up and shrill'd in flickering *gyres*": Tennyson's "Princess," vii. 31); in *anat.*, a gyrus.—**gyre,** *v. t.* or *i.*; *gyred, gyring.* To turn round; revolve; wheel. [Now chiefly poetic.]

gyr-fal-con (jėr'fâ"kn or -fâl"kọn), *n.* See *gerfalcon.*

gy-ri (jī'rī), *n.* Plural of *gyrus.*

gyro-. Form of Gr. γῦρος, ring, circle, used in combination.

gy-ro (jī'rō), *n.*; pl. *-ros* (-rōz). Shortened form of *gyroscope*, also of *gyro-compass.*—**gy'ro=car,** *n.* A motor-car running on a monorail, and kept in an upright position by means of a gyroscope or gyroscopes.—**gy'ro=com'pass,** *n.* A device used like the ordinary compass for determining directions, but employing a continuously driven gyroscope instead of a magnetized needle or bar, the gyroscope being so mounted that its axis constantly maintains its position with reference to the geographical north, thus dealing with true geographical meridians used in navigation instead of magnetic meridians (which, contrary to the usual understanding, are never directly used for navigation): applied esp. to the device invented by Elmer A. Sperry.

gy-ro-cop-ter (jī-rọ-kop'tėr), *n.* [Coined by E. Berliner, from *gyro-* + (*heli*)*copter.*] A form of helicopter provided with means for tilting forward, thereby causing forward flight the speed of which depends on the tilting-angle: designed by Henry A. and Emile Berliner.

gy-roi-dal (jī-roi'dạl), *a.* [Gr. γυροειδής, like a circle, round: see *gyro-* and *-oid.*] Spiral in arrangement or movement.—**gy-roi'dal-ly,** *adv.*

gy-ro-plane (jī'rọ-plān), *n.* [See *gyro-* and *plane*².] A form of flying-machine employing rotating planes (horizontal or nearly so) for support and balance.

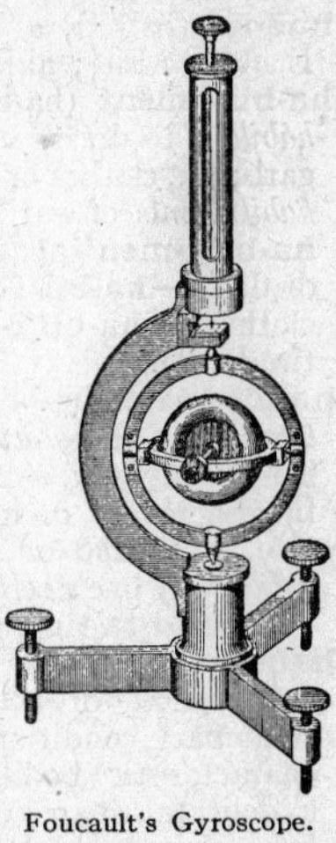
Foucault's Gyroscope.

gy-ro-scope (jī'rọ-skōp), *n.* [F. *gyroscope*: see *gyro-* and *-scope.*] An apparatus consisting of a rotating wheel which is so mounted that its axis can turn freely in certain or all directions, and which is capable of maintaining the same absolute direction in space in spite of movements of the mountings or surrounding parts: based on the principle that a body rotating steadily about an axis tends to resist change in the direction of the axis, and used to illustrate the dynamics of rotating bodies, to maintain equilibrium (see *gyro-car* and *gyro-stabilizer*), to determine direction (see *gyro-compass*), etc.—**gy-ro-scop'ic** (-skop'ik), *a.* Of or pertaining to the gyroscope.—**gyroscopic compass.** Same as *gyro-compass.*—**gyroscopic stabilizer.** Same as *gyro-stabilizer.*—**gy-ro-scop'ics,** *n.* The principles of the operation of the gyroscope.

gy-ro=stab-i-liz-er (jī'rọ-stab'i-lī-zėr), *n.* A device for stabilizing a sea-going vessel by counteracting its rolling motion from side to side, consisting essentially of a rotating gyroscope weighing about 1 per cent of the displacement of the vessel: invented by Elmer A. Sperry. [Proprietary name.]

gy-ro-stat (jī'rō-stat), *n.* [See *gyro-* and *-stat.*] A modification of the gyroscope, consisting of a rotating wheel pivoted within a rigid case: used for illustrating the dynamics of rotating bodies.—**gy-ro-stat'ic,** *a.* Pertaining to the gyrostat or to gyrostatics; connected with the dynamic principle that a rotating body tends to preserve its plane of rotation.—**gy-ro-stat'i-cal-ly,** *adv.*—**gy-ro-stat'ics,** *n.* The science which deals with the laws of rotating solids.

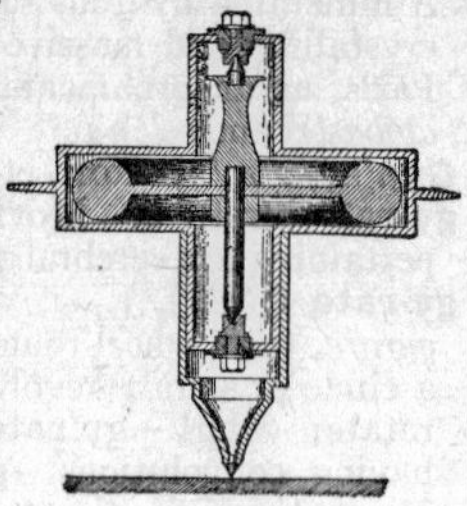
Gyrostat.

gy-rus (jī'rus), *n.*; pl. *gyri* (-rī). [L.: see *gyre.*] In *anat.*, a convolution, esp. of the brain.

gyte (gīt), *a.* [Origin unknown.] Crazy; mad: as, "Ye're surely gaun *gyte*" (Moir's "Mansie Wauch," xxvi.). [Sc.]

gyve (jīv), *n.* [ME. *gives, gyves*; origin uncertain.] A shackle, esp. for the leg; a fetter: chiefly in *pl.*: as, "The villains march wide betwixt the legs, as if they had *gyves* on; for indeed I had the most of them out of prison" (Shakspere's "1 Henry IV.," iv. 2. 44). [Archaic.]—**gyve,** *v. t.*; *gyved, gyving.* To shackle; fetter: as, "Those yron fetters wherewith he was *gyv'd*, The badges of reproach, he threw away" (Spenser's "Faerie Queene," v. 4. 35). [Archaic.]

H

H, h (āch); pl. *H's, h's* (āch'ez). A consonant, the 8th letter of the English alphabet.

ha (hä), *interj.* An exclamation of surprise, interrogation, suspicion, triumph, etc.; also, a sound marking hesitation in speech; often, when repeated (*ha! ha!* or *ha, ha!*), a word imitative of the sound of laughter.

ha-be-as cor-pus (hā'bē-as kôr'pus). [L., 'have thou the body.'] In *law*, a writ requiring the body of a person to be brought before a judge or court, esp. for investigation of a restraint of the person's liberty.

hab-er-dash-er (hab'ėr-dash"ėr), *n.* [ME. *haberdassher*: cf. AF. *hapertas*, appar. the name of a fabric.] A dealer in small wares, as accessories of dress, trimmings, buttons, pins, needles, thread, etc.; sometimes, formerly, a dealer in hats and caps†; in the U. S., a dealer in men's furnishings, as shirts, collars, neckties, gloves, etc.—**hab'er-dash"er-y,** *n.*; pl. *-ies* (-iz). The goods, business, or shop of a haberdasher.

hab-er-geon (hab'ėr-jon or ha-bėr'-), *n.* Same as *haubergeon.*

ha-bil-a-to-ry (ha-bil'a-tō-ri), *a.* [Irreg. < F. *habiller*, to dress: see *habiliment.*] Pertaining to dressing or clothing: as, "*habilatory* art" (Bulwer-Lytton's "Pelham," lxxix.).

hab-ile (hab'il), *a.* [OF. F. *habile*, < L. *habilis*, fit, apt, E. *able.*] Fit†; able†; also, skilful; ready.

ha-bil-i-ment (ha-bil'i-ment), *n.* [OF. F. *habillement*, < *habiller*, to dress, < *habile*, fit: see *habile.*] Dress; attire; garb; *pl.*, clothes or garments; accoutrements (as, "plated in *habiliments* of war": Shakspere's "Richard II.," i. 3. 28).—**ha-bil-i-men'tal** (-men'tal), *a.* Pertaining to habiliments or dress.—**ha-bil"i-men-ta'tion** (-tā'shon), *n.* Dressing or clothing.—**ha-bil'i-ment-ed** (-men-ted), *a.* Dressed; attired; clad.

ha-bil-i-tate (ha-bil'i-tāt), *v.*; *-tated, -tating.* [ML. *habilitatus*, pp. of *habilitare*, < L. *habilis*: see *habile.*] **I.** *tr.* To qualify† or capacitate†; also (after Sp. *habilitar*), to furnish money or means to work (a mine: western U. S.); also, to clothe or dress. **II.** *intr.* [Cf. G. *habilitieren.*] To qualify one's self, esp. as teacher in a German university.—**ha-bil-i-ta'tion** (-tā'shon), *n.*—**ha-bil'i-ta-tor,** *n.*

hab-it[1] (hab'it), *n.* [OF. F. *habit*, < L. *habitus*, condition, appearance, dress, < *habere*, have.] Characteristic or customary condition, constitution, or mode of being; esp., characteristic bodily or physical condition (as, to be of a delicate, spare, or apoplectic *habit*); the characteristic form, aspect, mode of growth, etc., of an animal or plant (as, a slender or erect *habit*; a twining *habit*); also, the mental character or disposition (as, the book reveals the *habit* of mind of the author); also, a disposition or tendency constantly shown to act in a certain way, esp. such a disposition acquired by frequent repetition of an act (as, "How use doth breed a *habit* in a man!" Shakspere's "Two Gentlemen of Verona," v. 4. 1); a particular practice, custom, or usage (as, the *habit* of smoking tobacco; to fall into a *habit* of faultfinding); customary practice, use, or wont (as, to act from force of *habit*; inured by *habit*; to be the slave of *habit*); also, bearing† or deportment†; also, dress, attire, or garb, or a garment or robe (archaic, except as in following senses); the dress or costume proper to a particular rank, profession, etc., esp. the dress of a religious order; a woman's riding-dress.—**hab'it**[1], *v. t.* To dress; clothe; array: as, "I discerned Jack Waller, *habited* in a very accurate black frock and dark trousers" (Lever's "Harry Lorrequer," xi.).

hab-it[2] (hab'it), *v.* [OF. F. *habiter*, < L. *habitare*, have frequently, inhabit, dwell, freq. of *habere*, have: cf. *habit*[1].] **I.**† *intr.* To dwell; reside. **II.** *tr.* To dwell in; inhabit. [Archaic.]—**hab'it-a-ble,** *a.* [OF. F. *habitable*, < L. *habitabilis.*] Capable of being inhabited; suitable for a habitation.—**hab"it-a-bil'i-ty** (-bil'i-ti), **hab'it-a-ble-ness,** *n.*—**hab'it-a-bly,** *adv.*—**hab'it-an-cy** (-i-tan-si), *n.* Inhabitance; residence; also, inhabitants collectively.—**hab'it-ant,** *n.* [OF. F. *habitant*, < L. *habitans* (*-ant-*), ppr. of *habitare.*] An inhabitant; also (F. pron. ȧ-bē-täṅ), a French settler, or a descendant of a French settler, in Canada or Louisiana, esp. one of the farming class.

hab-i-tat (hab'i-tat), *n.* [L., 'it dwells,' 3d pers. sing. pres. ind. of *habitare*, E. *habit*[2].] Place of abode; habitation; in *zoöl.* and *bot.*, the locality (the geographical region or regions) in which an animal or plant naturally lives or grows; a particular spot or place where a given animal or plant is found; also, the kind of place where a given animal or plant naturally lives or grows, as warm seas, mountain-tops, fresh waters, etc.

hab-i-ta-tion (hab-i-tā'shon), *n.* [OF. F. *habitation*, < L. *habitatio(n-)*, < *habitare*, E. *habit*[2].] The act of inhabiting; occupancy by inhabitants; also, a place of abode; a dwelling.

hab-it=mak-er (hab'it-mā"kėr), *n.* A tailor who makes habits, esp. women's riding-habits.

ha-bit-u-al (ha-bit'ū-al), *a.* [ML. *habitualis*, < L. *habitus*, E. *habit*[1].] Of the nature of a habit, or fixed by or resulting from habit (as, a *habitual* tendency or practice; *habitual* courtesy; a *habitual* smile); customary; also, being such by habit (as, a *habitual* theater-goer; a *habitual* drunkard); also, commonly used, occurring, seen, etc., or usual (as, a *habitual* resort; a *habitual* experience or sight).—**ha-bit'u-al-ly,** *adv.*—**ha-bit'u-al-ness,** *n.*

ha-bit-u-ate (ha-bit'ū-āt), *v. t.*; *-ated, -ating.* [LL. *habituatus*, pp. of *habituare*, < L. *habitus*, E. *habit*[1].] To accustom (a person, the mind, etc.), as to something; render used (*to*).—**ha-bit-u-a'tion** (-ā'shon), *n.* The act of habituating, or the state of being habituated.

hab-i-tude (hab'i-tūd), *n.* [OF. F. *habitude*, < L. *habitudo*, < *habere* (pp. *habitus*), have.] Habit, or customary condition or character (as, "His real *habitude* gave life and grace To appertainings and to ornament": Shakspere's "Lover's Complaint," 114); also, a habit or custom (as, "The wilderness required . . . *habitudes* of which they were totally deficient": Irving's "Captain Bonneville," vi.); also, relation†; relationship†; association† or intercourse†.

ha-bit-u-é (ha-bit-ū-ā', F. ȧ-bē-tü-ā), *n.* [F., pp. of *habituer*, < LL. *habituare*: see *habituate.*] A habitual frequenter of a place; also, one addicted to some habit, as the taking of a drug.

hab-ro-come (hab'rō-kōm), *n.* [NL. *Habrocoma*, < Gr. ἁβρός, graceful, delicate, + κόμη, hair.] Any animal of the

South American genus *Habrocoma*, comprising hystricomorphic rodents with fine, soft fur and large, rounded ears, as *H. bennetti*, of Chile.

Habrocome (*H. bennetti*).

hab-u-tai (hab′-u̇-tī), *n.* [Jap.] A soft, plain-woven Japanese silk of even texture.

ha-chure (hȧ-shör′), *n.* [F., < *hacher*, E. *hatch*[3].] In *drawing, engraving*, etc., a line used in shading or the like, esp. one of the short lines representing the slopes of mountains, etc., on maps.—**ha-chure′**, *v. t.*; *-chured, -churing.* To mark or shade with, or indicate by, hachures.

ha-cien-da (ä-syen′dä), *n.* [Sp., landed property, estate, domestic work, < L. *facienda*, things to be done, neut. pl. gerundive of *facere*, do, make.] A landed estate; a farming, stock-raising, mining, or manufacturing establishment in the country; a farm-house or country-house. [Spanish-American.]

hack[1] (hak), *v.* [AS. *haccian* (recorded in the compound *tōhaccian*, hack to pieces) = D. *hakken* = G. *hacken*, hack.] **I.** *tr.* To make irregular cuts in or upon, as with heavy blows; cut or notch at random; cut or chop (*to pieces, off*, etc.); also, to roughen or dress (stone), as with a hack-hammer; also, to break up the surface of (the ground); plant (seed) as with a hoe; cut or reap, or uproot, with a hack, sickle, or the like; also, to kick the shins of (an opponent) intentionally, as in football. **II.** *intr.* To make rough cuts or notches; deal cutting blows; also, to kick an opponent's shins intentionally, as in football; also, to emit short, frequently repeated coughs.—**hack**[1], *n.* A tool or instrument, as an ax, hoe, mattock, pick, etc., for hacking or cutting; also, a cut, gash, or notch; a cut or notch made in a tree to indicate a particular spot or to mark a path in a forest; a gash in the skin produced by a kick, as in football; also, an act of hacking; a cutting blow; a short, broken cough; sometimes, a hesitation in speech.

hack[2] (hak), *n.* [= *hatch*[1].] A frame or rack, as for holding fodder for cattle, or for drying fish, cheese, or bricks.

hack[3] (hak). [Short for *hackney*.] **I.** *n.* A horse kept for common hire, or adapted for general work, esp. ordinary riding; specif., a saddle-horse for the road; sometimes, an old or worn-out horse; a jade; also, a coach or carriage kept for hire; a hackney; also, a person who hires himself out for general work, esp. general literary work; a drudge. **II.** *a.* Hired; of a hired sort; also, much in use; hackneyed or trite (as, "When the old world grows dull, And we are sick of its *hack* sounds and sights": Byron's "Don Juan," iv. 17).—**hack**[3], *v.* **I.** *tr.* To make a hack of; let out for hire; put to indiscriminate use; hence, to render trite or stale by frequent use; hackney. **II.** *intr.* To ride on the road, or to ride at an ordinary pace, as distinguished from cross-country or military riding.

Hackberry (*Celtis occidentalis*). — 1 and 2, branches with male and female flowers; 3, branch with fruit; *a*, flower; *b*, stamen; *c*, fruit; *d*, fruit cut longitudinally; *e*, embryo.

hack-a-more (hak′ạ-mōr), *n.* [Sp. *jáquima*.] Any of several forms of halter used esp. for breaking horses. [Western U. S.]

hack-ber-ry (hak′-ber″i), *n.*; pl. *-berries* (-iz). [Var. of *hagberry*.] The hagberry (Sc. and north. Eng.); also, the small, edible, cherry-like fruit of American trees of the ulmaceous genus *Celtis*; a tree bearing this fruit. See cut in preceding column.

hack-but (hak′but), *n.* Same as *harquebus*.—**hack-but-eer′, hack′but-ter,** *n.* Same as *harquebusier*.

hack-er (hak′ėr), *n.* One who or that which hacks.

hack=ham-mer (hak′ham″ėr), *n.* An adz-like tool for dressing stone.

hack-le[1] (hak′l), *n.* [= *heckle*.] A comb for dressing flax or hemp; also, one of the long, slender feathers on the neck or saddle of certain birds, as the domestic cock, much used in making artificial flies for anglers; the neck plumage of the domestic cock, etc.; also, a kind of artificial fly for anglers; a palmer.—**hack′le**[1], *v. t.*; *-led, -ling.* To comb (flax or hemp) with a hackle; also, to dress (an artificial fly) with a hackle.

hack-le[2] (hak′l), *v. t.*; *-led, -ling.* [Freq. of *hack*[1].] To cut roughly; hack; mangle.—**hack′ly,** *a.* Rough or jagged as if hacked.

hack-man (hak′mạn), *n.*; pl. *-men.* The driver or keeper of a hack or public carriage.

hack-ma-tack (hak′mạ-tak), *n.* [N. Amer. Ind.] The tamarack, *Larix laricina*, an American larch; also, its wood.

hack-ney (hak′ni). [OF. *haquenee*: cf. OF. *haque, haquet*, horse; origin unknown.] **I.** *n.*; pl. *-neys* (-niz). A horse for ordinary riding or (later) driving; also, a horse kept for hire†; fig., a hired drudge†; also, a carriage kept for hire. **II.** *a.* Let out, employed, or done for hire; also, hackneyed†; trite†.—**hack′ney,** *v. t.*; *-neyed, -neying.* To make a hackney of, as a horse; use as a hack; hence, to make common or stale by frequent use; render commonplace or trite; also, to render habituated or experienced.—**hack′neyed,** *p. a.* Made commonplace or trite; stale; also, habituated or experienced (as, "His foreign accent . . . showed him not to be a *hackneyed* inhabitant of Paris": Irving's "Tales of a Traveler," i. 6).

hack=saw (hak′sâ), *n.* A saw used for cutting metal, consisting typically of a narrow fine-toothed blade fixed in a frame.—**hack′=saw,** *v. t.* To cut with a hack-saw.

hack=work (hak′wėrk), *n.* Work done by a hack, esp. a literary hack.

hacque-ton, haque-ton (hak′tọn), *n.* Same as *acton*.

had (had). Preterit and past participle of *have*.—**had better** [a form with a personal subject substituted for the earlier impersonal form, (*him*, etc.) *were better*, 'it were better (for him, etc.)'], would find it better to; would better: as, he *had better* be careful; perhaps I *had better* go. Similarly, *had liefer*, and the later phrases *had rather, had sooner* (would preferably), and hence *had liefest, had as lief, had as soon*, etc.

had-die (had′i), *n.* Same as *haddock*. [Sc.]

had-dock (had′ọk), *n.*; pl. *haddocks* or (esp. collectively) *haddock*. [ME. *haddok*; origin unknown.] A food-fish, *Melanogrammus æglefinus*, of the northern Atlantic, allied to but smaller than the cod; also, any of various allied fishes.

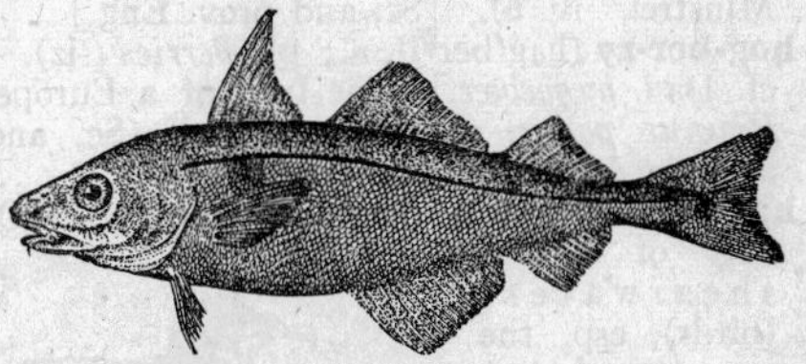

Haddock (*Melanogrammus æglefinus*).

hade (hād), *v. i.*; *haded, hading.* [Origin uncertain.] In *mining* and *geol.*, to incline from a vertical position.—**hade,** *n.* In *mining* and *geol.*, the inclination of a vein or the like from a vertical position; the complement of the dip.

Ha-des (hā′dēz), *n.* [Gr. Ἅιδης (ᾅδης).] The lord of the lower world of Greek mythology; Pluto; also, the gloomy subterranean abode of departed spirits or shades over which he ruled (as, "the enthroned Persephone in *Hades*": Tennyson's "Princess," iv. 419); also, esp. in the Revised Version of the New Testament, the abode or state of the dead; also [*cap.* or *l. c.*], hell, the abode of evil and condemned spirits (colloq.).—**Ha-de-an** (hā′dẹ-ạn or hā-dē′ạn), *a.*

hadj, hadj-i (haj, haj′ē). See *hajj, hajji.*

had-ro-saur (had′rọ-sâr), *n.* [NL. *hadrosaurus,* < Gr. ἁδρός, thick, stout, + σαῦρος, lizard.] An extinct dinosaurian reptile of the genus *Hadrosaurus,* of gigantic size.

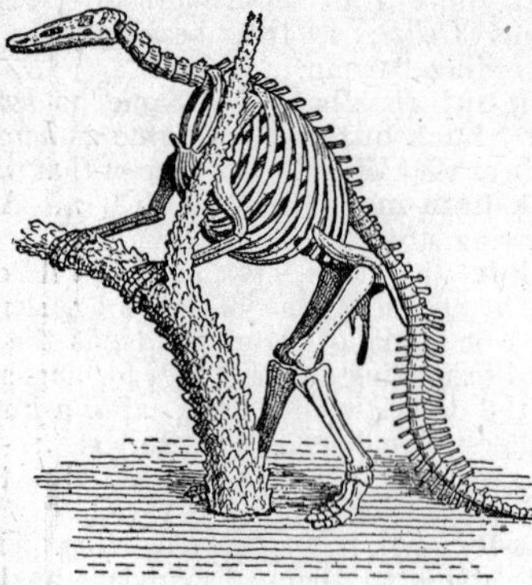

Hadrosaur.

hae (hā), *v.* Scotch form of *have.*

hæma-, etc., hæmato-, etc., hæmo-, etc. See *hema-,* etc., *hemato-,* etc., *hemo-,* etc.

ha-fiz (hä′fiz), *n.* [Ar. *hāfiz.*] A title of a Mohammedan who knows the Koran by heart.

haft[1] (håft), *n.* [AS. *hæft* = D. and G. *heft* = Icel. *hepti,* haft.] A handle, esp. of a cutting or thrusting instrument, as a knife, sword, dagger, etc.—**haft**[1], *v. t.* To furnish with a haft or handle; set in a haft.

haft[2] (håft), *v. t.* [Origin uncertain: cf. *haft*[1], *v.*] To fix; settle; establish. [Sc. and north. Eng.]—**haft**[2], *n.* A fixed or established place of abode. [Sc. and north. Eng.]

hag[1] (hag), *n.* [ME. *hagge, hegge*: cf. AS. *hægtesse,* G. *hexe,* witch.] A female evil spirit, demon, goblin, or ghost (archaic); also, a witch (as, "How now, you secret, black, and midnight *hags!*" Shakspere's "Macbeth," iv. 1. 48); hence, a repulsive (and often vicious or malicious) old woman; also, any of the eel-like marine cyclostomes constituting the group or order *Hyperotreta* (or *Myxinoidei*), notable esp. for their circular suctorial mouth and their habit of boring into the bodies of fishes.—**hag**[1], *v. t.*; *hagged, hagging.* To torment, worry, or harass (as, "That makes them in the dark see visions, And *hag* themselves with apparitions": Butler's "Hudibras," iii. 3); also, to tire; fag. [Now prov.]

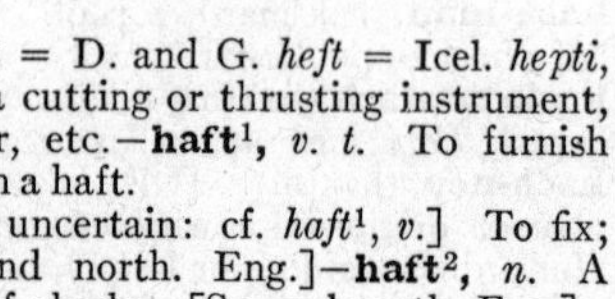

Hag (*Myxine glutinosa*).

hag[2] (hag), *v. t.*; *hagged, hagging.* [Cf. Icel. *höggva,* strike, hew, akin to E. *hew.*] To hew; chop; hack; cut. [Now Sc. and prov. Eng.]—**hag**[2], *n.* A hewing or cutting; a heavy cutting stroke; a notch or mark. [Sc. and prov. Eng.]

hag[3] (hag), *n.* [Cf. Icel. *högg,* a stroke, hewing, gap, ravine, and E. *hag*[2].] An abrupt, cliff-like eminence; also, wild, broken ground; rocky moorland; also, a break or cutting in a peat-bog; a soft spot in boggy land; also, a firm spot in a bog (as, "A small and shaggy nag, That through a bog, from *hag* to *hag,* Could bound": Scott's "Lay of the Last Minstrel," iv. 5). [Sc. and prov. Eng.]

hag-ber-ry (hag′ber″i), *n.*; pl. *-berries* (-iz). [From Scand.: cf. Dan. *hæggebær.*] The fruit of a European cherry-tree, *Prunus padus,* or the tree itself (Sc. and prov. Eng.); also, the American hackberry.

hag-den, hag-don (hag′dẹn, -dọn), *n.* [Origin obscure.] Any of various shearwaters (birds), esp. the greater shearwater, *Puffinus major.*

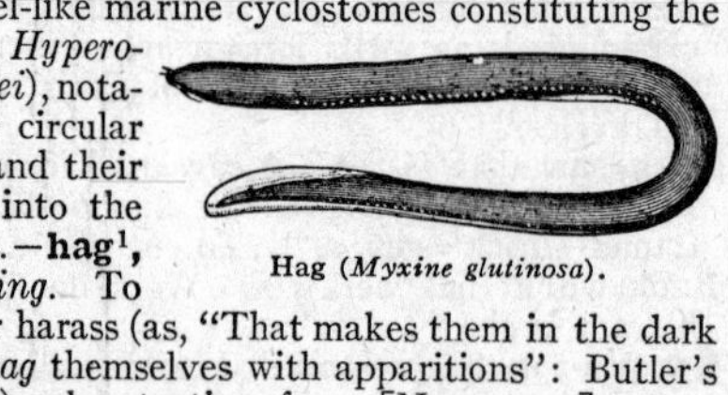

Hagden, or Greater Shearwater (*Puffinus major*).

hag-fish (hag′fish), *n.* A hag (cyclostome).

hag-ga-dah (hạ-gä′dạ), *n.*; pl. *-doth* (-dōth). [Heb. *haggādah,* 'narrative,' < *higgīd,* tell.] In *Jewish lit.,* a legend, anecdote, parable, or the like; hence [*cap.*], the non-legal portion of rabbinical literature; esp., the free exposition or illustration, chiefly homiletical, of the Scripture. Cf. *halakah* and *midrash.*—**hag-gad-ic, hag-gad-i-cal** (hạ-gad′ik, -i-kạl), *a.* Pertaining to or of the nature of a haggadah; of or pertaining to the Haggadah.—**hag-ga′dist** (-dist), *n.* A writer of haggadoth; also, a student of the Haggadah.—**hag-ga-dis-tic** (hag-ạ-dis′tik), *a.*

hag-gard (hag′ärd). [F. *hagard,* wild (orig. of a falcon); perhaps from Teut. (cf. G. *hag,* hedge, wood).] **I.** *a.* Wild or untamed (used esp., in *falconry,* of a hawk caught after it has assumed adult plumage); also, wild-looking, as from prolonged suffering, anxiety, exertion, want, etc.; careworn; gaunt. **II.** *n.* A haggard hawk. Cf. *eyas.*—**hag′gard-ly,** *adv.*—**hag′gard-ness,** *n.*

hag-ged (hag′ed), *a.* [See *hag*[1].] Hag-like; also, haggard. [Chiefly prov. Eng.]

hag-gis (hag′is), *n.* [ME. *hagese, hagas*: cf. *hag*[2].] A dish made of the pluck of a sheep, etc., minced with suet and oatmeal, seasoned, and boiled in the stomach of the animal. [Now chiefly Sc.]

hag-gish (hag′ish), *a.* Of or like a hag; old and ugly: as, "On us both did *haggish* age steal on" (Shakspere's "All's Well," i. 2. 29).—**hag′gish-ness,** *n.*

hag-gle (hag′l), *v.*; *-gled, -gling.* [Freq. of *hag*[2].] **I.** *tr.* To mangle in cutting; hack; also, to harass with wrangling or haggling. **II.** *intr.* To hack; also, to wrangle, dispute, or cavil; esp., to make difficulties in bargaining; bargain in a petty and tedious manner (as, "He went marketing in the morning to *haggle* with tradesmen over fish . . . tapioca, and so forth": Kipling's "Light That Failed," xiv.).—**hag′gle,** *n.* The act or an act of haggling.—**hag′gler,** *n.*

hagio-. Form of Gr. ἅγιος, sacred, holy, used in combination.

ha-gi-oc-ra-cy (hā-ji-ok′rạ-si or hag-i-), *n.*; pl. *-cies* (-siz). [See *hagio-* and *-cracy.*] Government by a body of persons esteemed as holy; a sacred or sacerdotal government.

Ha-gi-og-ra-pha (hā-ji-og′rạ-fạ̈ or hag-i-), *n. pl.* [LL., < Gr. ἁγιόγραφα, < ἅγιος, sacred, + γράφειν, write.] The books which form the third of the three Jewish divisions of the Old Testament, comprising Psalms, Proverbs, Job, Canticles, Ruth, Lamentations, Ecclesiastes, Esther, Daniel, Ezra, Nehemiah, and 1 and 2 Chronicles. Cf. *law* and *prophet.*—**ha-gi-og′ra-pher,** *n.* A writer of sacred books; esp., one of the writers of the Hagiographa; also, a writer of lives of the saints; a hagiologist.—**ha-gi-og′ra-phy,** *n.*; pl. *-phies* (-fiz). [See *-graphy.*] The writing of the lives of the saints; hagiology.—**ha″gi-o-graph′ic, ha″gi-o-graph′i-cal** (-ọ-graf′ik, -i-kạl), *a.*

ha-gi-ol-a-try (hā-ji-ol′ạ-tri or hag-i-), *n.* [See *hagio-* and *-latry.*] The worship of saints.—**ha-gi-ol′a-ter,** *n.*—**ha-gi-ol′a-trous,** *a.*

ha-gi-ol-o-gy (hā-ji-ol′ọ-ji or hag-i-), *n.*; pl. *-gies* (-jiz). [See *hagio-* and *-logy.*] That branch of literature which deals with the lives and legends of the saints; the list and legends of the saints, and, by extension, of popular heroes; also, a work on the lives and legends of the saints.—**ha″gi-o-log′ic, ha″gi-o-log′i-cal** (-ọ-loj′ik, -i-kạl), *a.*—**ha-gi-ol′o-gist,** *n.*

ha-gi-o-scope (hā′ji-ọ-skōp or hag′i-), *n.* [See *hagio-* and *-scope.*] In *arch.,* an opening in a wall or other barrier in a church, to afford a view of the chief altar to worshipers in the chapels, side aisles, or the like.—**ha-gi-o-scop′ic** (-skop′ik), *a.*

hag=moth (hag′môth), *n.* A North American moth, *Phobetron pithecium,* whose larva, which has curious hairy appendages somewhat suggesting disheveled locks of hair, feeds on a great variety of trees and plants.

Larva of Hag-moth, natural size.

hag=ride (hag′rīd), *v. t.*; pret. *-rode,* pp. *-ridden,* ppr. *-riding.* To ride as a hag does; oppress with or as with nightmare: chiefly in *hag-ridden, pp.*

hag=ta-per (hag′tā″pėr), *n.* [Appar. orig. *Hig's* or *Hick's taper*: see *hick.*] The common mullen (weed), *Verbascum thapsus.*

hah (hä), *interj.* See *ha.*

ha=ha (hä′hä), *n.* [F. *haha*; said to represent an exclamation of surprise at such a hindrance to passage.] A barrier consisting of a trench or ditch; a sunk fence.

Hah-ne-mann-i-an (hä-nẹ-man′i-ạn), *a.* Pertaining to S. C. F. Hahnemann (1755–1843), a German physician, founder of the homeopathic system of medicine.—**Hah′ne-mann-ism** (-mạn-izm), *n.* The medical theories of Dr. Hahnemann; homeopathy.

Hai-duk (hī′dụ̈k), *n.* [= G. *heiduck*, < Hung. *hajdu*, pl. *hajduk*, prob. < Turk. *haidūd*, marauder, brigand.] A brigand or bandit among the Balkan Slavs; also, one of a former class of mercenary foot-soldiers of Magyar stock, distinguished for their bravery; also [*cap.* or *l. c.*], a male servant or attendant dressed in Hungarian semi-military costume; a lackey.

haik (hīk), *n.* [Ar.] An oblong piece of cloth used as an outer garment by the Arabs.

hai-kwan (hī-kwän′), *n.* [Chinese.] Maritime customs in China.

hail[1] (hāl), *n.* [AS. *hægl, hagol*, = D. and G. *hagel* = Icel. *hagl*, hail.] Pellets or small (usually rounded) masses of ice falling from the clouds in a shower; also, a shower or storm of such masses; hence, a shower of anything, as shot.—**hail**[1], *v.* **I.** *intr.* To pour down hail; fall as hail. **II.** *tr.* To pour down as or like hail.

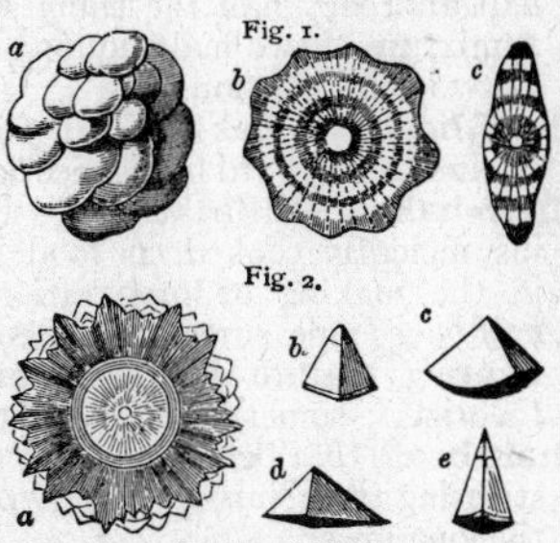

Forms of Hail.
Fig. 1. *a*, hailstone which fell at Bonn in 1822, diameter 1 1-2 inches; *b, c*, sections of differently shaped hailstones which fell on the same occasion. Fig. 2. *a*, section of hailstone with minute pyramids on its surface; *b, c, d, e*, fragments of same when burst asunder.

hail[2] (hāl), *interj.* [ME. *hail, heyl*, prop. adj., hale, sound, well, < Icel. *heill*, hale, whole: see *hale*[2] and *whole*.] An exclamation of salutation or greeting: used absolutely, or followed by *to*: as, "*Hail*, King of the Jews!" (Mark, xv. 18); "*Hail* to the Chief who in triumph advances!" (Scott's "Lady of the Lake," ii. 19).—**hail**[2], *n.*[1] [Icel. *heill*, good luck, happiness.] Luck; fortune: now only in the phrase 'all hail,' used in salutation.—**hail**[2], *v.* **I.** *tr.* To salute with 'hail!' hence, in general, to salute or greet; welcome; also, to call out to, in order to attract attention (as, "The huge Earl Doorm . . . like one that *hails* a ship, Cried out with a big voice": Tennyson's "Geraint and Enid," 540). **II.** *intr.* To call out in order to attract attention.—**to hail from,** to come from as the port of registry, or of departure on a voyage, as a ship; hence, to belong to as the place of birth or residence.—**hail**[2], *n.*[2] An exclamation of 'hail!' (as, "On whom the angel *Hail* Bestow'd; the holy salutation used Long after to blest Mary, second Eve": Milton's "Paradise Lost," v. 385); a salutation or greeting; also, the act of hailing; a shout or call to attract attention.—**within hail,** near enough to be hailed; within reach of the sound of the voice.—**hail′er,** *n.*—**hail′=fel″low,** *a.* and *adv.* On terms of familiar accost or intercourse: often in the form *hail-fellow-well-met.*—**Hail Ma-ry** (mā′ri). Same as *Ave Maria*, which see.

hail-stone (hāl′stōn), *n.* A pellet of hail.

hail=storm (hāl′stôrm), *n.* A storm with hail; a precipitation of hail.

hail-y (hā′li), *a.* Consisting of or characterized by hail.

hair (hãr). [AS. *hǣr* = D. and G. *haar* = Icel. *hār*, hair.] **I.** *n.* One of the numerous fine, usually cylindrical filaments growing from the skin and forming the characteristic coat of most mammals; a similar fine, filamentous outgrowth from the body of insects, etc.; also, the aggregate of hairs which grow on an animal; the natural covering of the human head (as, "My *hair* is grey, but not with years": Byron's "Prisoner of Chillon," i.); hairs collectively or in the mass (as, a mattress stuffed with *hair*); also, something resembling a hair or a mass of hair; often, a hair taken to represent very small magnitude, measure, etc.; a jot or tittle; the least degree; also, sort† or kind†; character† or quality†; also, cloth made of hair; haircloth; a mat or wrapping of such cloth; in *bot.*, a filamentous outgrowth of the epidermis. **II.** *a.* Made of or with hair (as, *hair* jewelry; a *hair* shirt, a garment of coarse haircloth, made in the form of a shirt or a girdle, worn next the skin by ascetics and penitents); stuffed with hair (as, a *hair* mattress).—**hair,** *v.* **I.** *intr.* To produce or grow hair; form hair-like fibers. **II.** *tr.* To free from hair.

Section of Skin, showing the roots of two Hairs. (Highly magnified.) — *a*, cuticle; *b*, deeper parts of skin; *c*, a hair; *d*, erecting muscle; *e*, sebaceous glands.

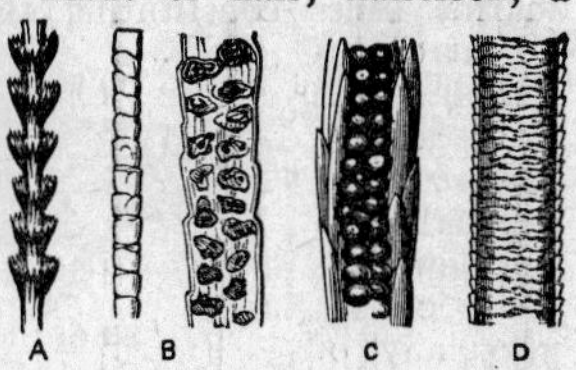

Hairs of Various Animals, magnified. — *A*, bat; *B*, mouse; *C*, sable; *D*, man.

hair-breadth (hãr′bredth). **I.** *n.* The breadth or diameter of a hair; a very small space or distance. **II.** *a.* Extremely narrow or close: as, a *hairbreadth* escape.

hair=brush (hãr′brush), *n.* A brush for dressing the hair.

hair-cloth (hãr′klôth), *n.* Fabric made of hair, as of the camel; also, something made of such cloth, as a shirt.

hair=do (hãr′dö), *n.* Any method of doing, arranging, or modifying a woman's hair; hair so dressed.

hair=dress-er (hãr′dres″ėr), *n.* One whose business it is to dress or trim the hair.—**hair′=dress″ing,** *n.*

haired (hãrd), *a.* Having hair; covered with hair.

hair-i-ness (hãr′i-nes), *n.* Hairy condition.

hair-less (hãr′les), *a.* Without hair.—**hair′less-ness,** *n.*

hair=line (hãr′līn), *n.* A line or rope of hair; also, a very slender line, as a stroke made in writing or a stripe on a textile fabric; also, a fabric woven with very fine lines or stripes; in *printing*, a very thin line on the face of a type; also, a style of type consisting entirely of such lines.

hair=oil (hãr′oil), *n.* An oil or oily preparation for dressing the hair.

hair=pin (hãr′pin), *n.* A pin used by women for fastening up the hair or adjusting a head-dress: in a common form, a slender U-shaped piece of wire, shell, or other material.

hair's=breadth (hãrz′bredth), *n.* and *a.* Same as *hairbreadth.*

hair=seal (hãr′sēl), *n.* Any of various seals with coarse hair and no soft underlying fur: distinguished from *fur-seal.*

hair=space (hãr′spās), *n.* In *printing*, the thinnest metal space used to separate words, etc.

hair=split-ter (hãr′split″ėr), *n.* One who makes minute or excessively fine distinctions, as in reasoning.—**hair′=split″-ting,** *n.* and *a.*

hair=spring (hãr′spring), *n.* A fine hair-like spring in a timepiece, for regulating the motion of the balance-wheel.

hair=stroke (hãr′strōk), *n.* A fine stroke or line in writing or printing.

hair-tail (hãr′tāl), *n.* An acanthopterygian marine fish, *Trichiurus lepturus*, with a silvery band-like body terminating in a hair-like tail, common in tropical and subtropical Atlantic waters; any fish of the family *Trichiuridæ.*

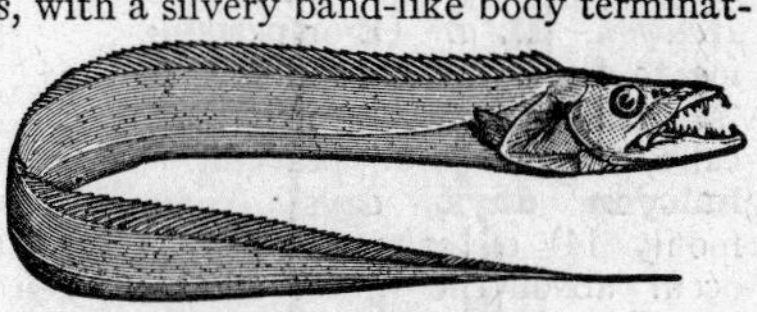
Hairtail (*Trichiurus lepturus*).

hair=trig-ger (hãr′trig″ėr), *n.* A trigger that allows the firing mechanism of a firearm to be operated by very slight pressure.

hair-y (hãr′i), *a.*; compar. *hairier*, superl. *hairiest.* Covered with hair; having much hair; characterized by hair-like growths, as a plant; also, consisting of or resembling hair.

Hai-ti-an (hā′ti-ạn). **I.** *a.* Of or pertaining to Haiti. **II.** *n.* A native or inhabitant of Haiti; also, the language of Haiti.

hajj, hadj (haj), *n.* [Ar. *hajj*, < *hajja*, set out, go on a pilgrimage.] A pilgrimage to Mecca, as enjoined upon Mohammedans.—**haj-ji, hadj-i** (haj′ē), *n.*; pl. *hajjis, hadjis* (-ēz). [Ar. *hājjī.*] A Mohammedan who has performed his hajj (as, "I greeted him as poor Arabs in a desert village greet the *Hadji* or pilgrim who returns from Mecca, and has seen the Prophet's tomb and the holy stone," G. W. Curtis's "Howadji in Syria," i. 3: often used as a title); also, a Greek or Armenian who has visited the Holy Sepulcher at Jerusalem.

hake (hāk), *n.* [ME. *hake*; origin uncertain.] Any of the marine fishes constituting the genus *Merlucius*, related to and resembling the cod, as *M. bilinearis* ('silver hake') of the New England coast; also, any of various related marine fishes, esp. of the genus *Urophycis*, as *U. tenuis* ('white hake') of the New England coast.

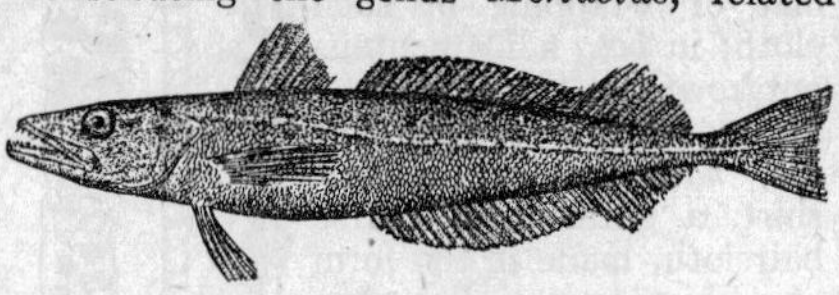

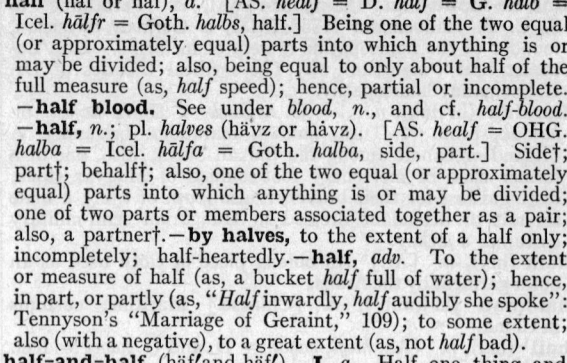

Silver Hake (*Merlucius bilinearis*).

ha-kim[1] (ha-kēm′), *n.* [Ar. *hakīm.*] In Mohammedan countries, a wise or learned man; a physician.

ha-kim[2] (hä′kim), *n.* [Ar. *hākim.*] In Mohammedan countries, a ruler; a governor; a judge.

ha-la-kah, ha-la-chah (ha-lä′kä), *n.*; pl. *-koth, -choth* (-kōth). [Heb. *halākāh*, 'rule to go by,' < *hālak*, walk, go.] In *Jewish lit.*, usage, custom, or tradition; [*cap.*] the body of traditional or oral laws of the Jews, as explained by the rabbis, supplementing or interpreting the law of the Scripture; also [*l. c.*], a single tradition or law; an explanation or decision by a rabbi. Cf. *haggadah, midrash,* and *mishnah.* —**ha-lak′ic, ha-lach′ic** (-lak′ik), *a.* Of or pertaining to the *Halakah.*—**ha-la′kist, ha-la′chist** (-lä′kist), *n.* One who gives or renders halakoth.

ha-la-tion (hā-lā′shon), *n.* [From *halo.*] In *photog.*, the effect of excess of light, or of adventitious reflected light, on some part of a negative, as when an interior view includes a window the light-rays from which produce a fog which spreads over the neighboring parts of the picture.

hal-berd (hal′bėrd), *n.* [OF. F. *hallebarde*; from Teut.] A long-handled, ax-like military weapon in various forms, surmounted by a long point: esp. used in the 15th and 16th centuries.—**hal-ber-dier′** (-bėr-dēr′), *n.* [F. *hallebardier.*] A soldier, guard, or attendant armed with a halberd.

A, German Halberd, early 17th century. *B*, Halberd, 15th century.

hal-bert (hal′bėrt), *n.* Same as *halberd.*

hal-cy-on (hal′si-on). [L. *halcyon*, prop. *alcyon*, < Gr. ἀλκυών, kingfisher.] **I.** *n.* A bird, usually identified with the kingfisher, fabled by the ancients to breed in a nest floating on the sea, about the time of the winter solstice, and to have the power of charming winds and waves so as to calm the sea; hence, any of various kingfishers, esp. of the genus *Halcyon.* **II.** *a.* Of or pertaining to the halcyon or kingfisher (see *halcyon days*, below); also, calm, tranquil, or peaceful.—**halcyon days,** days (commonly 14) of calm weather supposed by the ancients to occur about the winter solstice when the halcyon was brooding; hence, days of tranquillity or peace; a quiet, happy period.

hale[1] (hāl), *v.*; *haled, haling.* [OF. F. *haler*, hale, haul; from Teut. (cf. G. *holen*, fetch, haul): cf. *haul.*] **I.** *tr.* To haul, pull, or draw with force (as, "Galling His kingly hands *haling* ropes": Shakspere's "Pericles," iv. 1. 55); also, to drag along, or bring as by dragging (as, to *hale* an evil-doer to prison). [Archaic.] **II.** *intr.* To haul, pull, or tug: as, "A yoke of great-necked stolid oxen were patiently *haling* at the plough" (Stevenson's "Travels with a Donkey," i. 3). [Archaic.]

hale[2] (hāl), *a.*; compar. *haler*, superl. *halest.* [AS. *hāl* = Icel. *heill*, hale, whole: see *hail*[2] and *whole.*] Free from disease or bodily infirmity, robust, or vigorous (as, "I was strong and *hale* of body then," Tennyson's "St. Simeon Stylites," 28; a *hale* old age); also, free from injury, unhurt, or sound (now Sc. and north. Eng.); also, whole, complete, or entire (now Sc. and north. Eng.).—**hale′ness,** *n.*

hal-er (hā′lėr), *n.* One who hales or hauls. [Archaic.]

half (häf or håf), *a.* [AS. *healf* = D. *half* = G. *halb* = Icel. *hālfr* = Goth. *halbs*, half.] Being one of the two equal (or approximately equal) parts into which anything is or may be divided; also, being equal to only about half of the full measure (as, *half* speed); hence, partial or incomplete. —**half blood.** See under *blood, n.*, and cf. *half-blood.* —**half,** *n.*; pl. *halves* (hävz or håvz). [AS. *healf* = OHG. *halba* = Icel. *hālfa* = Goth. *halba*, side, part.] Side†; part†; behalf†; also, one of the two equal (or approximately equal) parts into which anything is or may be divided; one of two parts or members associated together as a pair; also, a partner†.—**by halves,** to the extent of a half only; incompletely; half-heartedly.—**half,** *adv.* To the extent or measure of half (as, a bucket *half* full of water); hence, in part, or partly (as, "*Half* inwardly, *half* audibly she spoke": Tennyson's "Marriage of Geraint," 109); to some extent; also (with a negative), to a great extent (as, not *half* bad).

half=and=half (häf′and-häf′). **I.** *a.* Half one thing and half another; half the thing specified and half not. **II.** *n.* A mixture of two malt liquors, esp. porter and ale. **III.** *adv.* In two equal portions.

half=back (häf′bak), *n.* In *football*, etc., one of the players behind the forward line. See *back*[2], *n.*

half=baked (häf′bākt′), *a.* Baked only half enough, or insufficiently cooked, as food; fig., not properly completed in the making or preparation; ill-digested or crude (as, *half-baked* measures or schemes); imperfectly educated; wanting mature judgment or experience (as, *half-baked* theorists); sometimes, half-witted.

half-beak (häf′bēk), *n.* Any of certain marine fishes constituting the genus *Hemirhamphus* and allied genera, having the long lower jaw extending far beyond the short upper jaw.

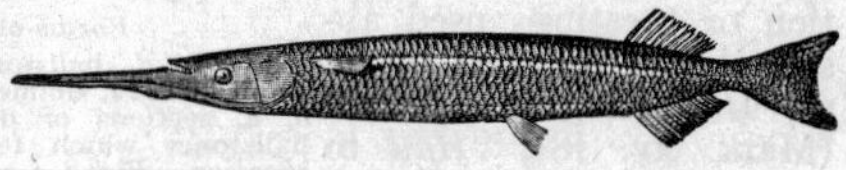

Halfbeak (*Hyporhamphus*, or *Hemirhamphus*, *unifasciatus*).

half=blood (häf′blud), *n.* [See *half blood*, under *blood, n.*] A person whose parents are of different races; a half-breed.—**half′=blood′ed,** *a.* Having parents of different races or breeds; esp., of superior race or breed by one parent only.

half=boot (häf′böt), *n.* A boot reaching about half-way to the knee.

half=bred (häf′bred), *a.* Of mixed breed; mongrel; also, imperfectly acquainted with the rules of good breeding. —**half′=breed,** *n.* The offspring of parents of different races; one who is half-blooded; esp., the offspring of a white person and an American Indian; also [*cap.*], in *U. S. politics*, a member of that faction of the Republican party in New York State in 1881 which opposed the Stalwarts, the faction in control.

half=broth-er (häf′bruᴛʜ″ėr), *n.* A brother by one parent only.

half=caste (häf′kåst), *n.* A person of mixed race; esp., one of mixed European and East Indian parentage.

half=cock (häf′kok′), *n.* The position of the hammer of a firearm when raised only half-way and there held by the mechanism so that the trigger will not operate.—**to go off at half=cock,** fig., to act prematurely; take action without due preparation or forethought.—**half′=cock′,** *v. t.* To set (a firearm) at half-cock.

Obverse. Reverse.
Half-crown of Queen Anne, 1704. — British Museum.

half=crown (häf′kroun′), *n.* A British silver coin of half the value of the crown, or worth two shillings and sixpence.

half=grown (häf′grōn′), *a.* Having reached only half the full growth; at an intermediate stage of physical development.

half=heart-ed (häf′här′ted), *a.* Having or showing little heart, enthusiasm, or ardor (as, *half-hearted* supporters or support); lukewarm.—**half′=heart′ed-ly,** *adv.*—**half′=heart′ed-ness,** *n.*

half=hitch (häf′hich′), *n.* *Naut.*, a hitch formed by passing the end of a rope round its standing part and then through the bight.

half=hol-i-day (häf′hol′i-dā), *n.* The half, usually the latter half, of a working-day, given up to recreation; also, a day on which work is carried on only during half or a part of the usual working-hours.

half=hose (häf′hōz), *n. pl.* Short hose or stockings; socks.

half=hour (häf′our′), *n.* The half of an hour, a period of thirty minutes.—**half′=hour′ly,** *a.* and *adv.*

half-ling (häf′ling). **I.** *n.* A half-grown person; also, a halfpenny. [Sc.] **II.** *a.* Half-grown. [Sc.]—**half′ling, half′lings,** *adv.* Half; partly, or to some extent. [Sc.]

half=mast (häf′måst′), *n.* A position half-way (or a smaller distance) below the top of a mast, staff, etc.: as, a flag at *half-mast* (as a mark of respect for the dead, or as a signal of distress).—**half′=mast′,** *v. t.* To hang at half-mast, as a flag.

half=meas-ure (häf′mezh″ūr), *n.* A measure inadequate for the full accomplishment of a purpose; an only partially effective measure.

half=moon (häf′mön′), *n.* The moon at the quadratures, when half its disk appears illuminated; hence, something of the shape of a half-moon, or, loosely, of a crescent; in *fort.*, a demilune (as, "The *half moon* . . . rose before them bristling with cannon": Motley's "Dutch Republic," iii. 8).

half=mourn-ing (häf′mōr′ning), *n.* The style of dress, esp. as to color (black with white, lavender, or gray), appropriated to the latter half of a period of formal mourning, or adopted for use less extreme than full or deep mourning.

half=note (häf′nōt), *n.* In *music*, a note equivalent to one half of a whole-note; a minim.

half=pay (häf′pā′). **I.** *n.* Half the full wages or salary; reduced pay (not literally half of the full pay); a reduced allowance paid to an officer in the army or navy when not in actual service, or after retirement at a prescribed time. **II.** *a.* Receiving, or entitled to, half-pay: as, a *half-pay* officer.

half-pen-ny (hā′pe-ni, sometimes häf′-). **I.** *n.*; pl. *-pennies* (-pe-niz) or *-pence* (-pens) (see *penny*). A British coin (at first of silver, later of copper, now of bronze) of half the value of a penny; the sum of half a penny. **II.** *a.* Of the price or value of a halfpenny; hence, of trifling value, or paltry (as, "a *halfpenny* matter": Sterne's "Tristram Shandy," i. 1).

Obverse. Reverse.
Halfpenny of Charles II. — British Museum.

half=seas o-ver (häf′sēz ō′vėr). Half-way across the sea; hence, half-way on any course (esp. fig.); often, half drunk (humorous: as, "a quarrelsome toper . . . who, when *half-seas-over*, plays the very devil," Irving's "Tales of a Traveler," iv. 1).

half=shell (häf′shel′), *n.* One valve of a bivalve: as, oysters on the *half-shell* (as when served raw at table).

half=sis-ter (häf′sis″tėr), *n.* A sister by one parent only.

half=sole (häf′sōl′), *n.* That part of the sole of a boot or shoe which extends from the shank to the end of the toe.—**half′=sole′,** *v. t.*; *-soled*, *-soling*. To repair by putting on a new half-sole.

half=step (häf′step), *n.* In *music*, a semitone.

half=tide (häf′tīd′), *n.* The state of the tide when at half the height of high water.

half=tim-bered (häf′tim′bėrd), *a.* Of a house or building, having the frame and principal supports of timber, but with the interstices filled in with masonry, plaster, or the like.

half=tint (häf′tint), *n.* An intermediate tint or color; a tone intermediate between the high light and the deep shade of a painting, etc.

half=ti-tle (häf′tī′tl), *n.* In *printing*, a shortened or short title of a book used at the head of the first page of text; also, a bastard title; also, the title of any subdivision of a book that immediately precedes that subdivision, when printed on a full page.

half=tone (häf′tōn), *n.* In *music*, a semitone; in *painting*, etc., a half-tint; in *photo-engraving*, a process in which gradation of tone, as in a photograph, is obtained by means of a system of minute dots between fine intersecting blank lines produced by a screen placed in the camera a short distance in front of the sensitized plate; a metal plate made by this process, or a print from it.

half=way (häf′wā′), *adv.* Half over the way (as, to go *half-way* to Rome); to or at half the distance (as, the rope reaches only *half-way*; at a point *half-way* to the goal); to half the full extent (as, the morning is *half-way* over).—**half′=way,** *a.* Midway, as between two places or points (as, a *half-way* house); going to or covering only half the full extent, or partial (as, *half-way* measures).

half=wit-ted (häf′wit′ed), *a.* Not having all the wits or mental faculties; mentally defective; imbecile.—**half′=wit′ted-ness,** *n.*

half=year (häf′yēr′), *n.* Half of a year; a period or term of six months; also, half of a school or other year, whatever its length.—**half′=year′ly.** **I.** *a.* Happening every half-year, or twice in each year; semiannual. **II.** *adv.* Twice in each year; semiannually.

hal-i-but (hal′i-but), *n.*; pl. *halibuts* or (esp. collectively) *halibut*. [ME. *halybutte*, appar. < *haly*, holy, + *butte*, kind of fish; perhaps so called as being eaten on holy days.] The largest species of flatfish, *Hippoglossus hippoglossus*, of northern seas, sometimes weighing several hundred pounds, and much used for food; also, any of various other similar flatfishes.

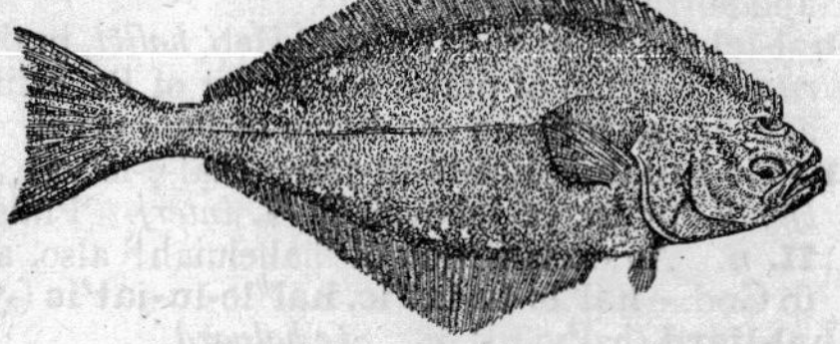
Halibut (*Hippoglossus hippoglossus*).

hal-ide (hal′īd or -id, or hā′līd or -lid). [Gr. ἅλς (ἁλ-), salt.] In *chem.*: **I.** *n.* A binary compound formed by the direct union of a halogen with an element or radical; a haloid salt. **II.** *a.* Of the nature of, or pertaining to, a halide; haloid.

hal-i-dom, hal-i-dome (hal′i-dom, -dōm), *n.* [AS. *hāligdōm*, < *hālig*, holy: see *-dom*.] Holiness† or sanctity†; also, a holy place, or sanctuary (archaic); also, a thing regarded as holy, as a relic (archaic: formerly much used in oaths and asseverations: as, "Now sure, and by my *hallidome* . . . Ye a great master are," Spenser's "Mother Hubberds Tale," 545).

hal-i-eu-tic (hal-i-ū′tik), *a.* [L. *halieuticus*, < Gr. ἁλιευτικός, < ἁλιεύειν, to fish, < ἅλς, sea.] Of or pertaining to fishing.—**hal-i-eu′tics,** *n.* The art or practice of fishing.

hal-ite (hal′īt or hā′līt), *n.* [Gr. ἅλς (ἁλ-), salt.] Native rock-salt.

hal-i-to-sis (hal-i-tō′sis), *n.* [NL., < L. *halitus*, breath.] Bad or offensive breath.

hal-i-tus (hal′i-tus), *n.* [L., < *halare*, breathe.] The breath; also, an exhalation; a vapor.

hall (hâl), *n.* [AS. *heall* = OS. and OHG. *halla* = Icel. *hall*, *höll*, hall; akin to AS. *helan*, cover, hide, L. *celare*, hide, Gr. καλύπτειν, cover: cf. *hell*, *helm*[2], and *hull*[1].] A large, roofed place, as a temple, palace, etc.†; also, the large main room in a castle, palace, mansion, or the like, devoted to common use, or used for receptions, banquets, etc.; a large room in a house, for common use (as, the servants' *hall*, in which the servants dine); also, the proprietor's residence on a large landed estate, esp. in Great Britain; a mansion or residence (used esp. in the proper names of residences of imposing or stately character, and in certain phrases, as 'bachelor's hall,' and 'liberty hall,' which see below); also, a large building for residence, instruction, or other purposes, as in a university or college; the occupants of such a building; in some American colleges, a room or building appropriated to the use of a students' literary or other society, or the society itself; in English colleges, a large room in which the members and students dine in common, or dinner in such a room (as, "You ought to dine in *hall* perhaps four days a week. *Hall* is at five o'clock": Hughes's "Tom Brown at Oxford," i.); also, a building belonging to a trade, gild, or society, used for the transaction of its business (as, Stationers' *Hall*, London: see under *stationer*); the society itself; also, a large public building, as for the transaction of public business, the holding of assemblies or entertainments, or other use; also, a large room devoted to such uses; an assembly-room; also, the entrance-room or vestibule of a house or building; a corridor or passageway in a building (U. S.: as, "Minnie . . . led her through the dark *hall* to the parlor," Tarkington's "Gentleman from Indiana," ix.). —**a hall! a hall!** an exclamation formerly used to call for room in a crowd as for an exhibition or a dance, or to call people together for any ceremony or spectacle, or to summon servants: as, "*A hall, a hall!* give room! and foot it, girls" (Shakspere's "Romeo and Juliet," i. 5. 28). —**bachelor's hall** or **bachelor hall,** the abode of a bachelor, or of a man or men only: as, "a worthy fox-hunting old Baronet, who kept *bachelor's hall* in jovial style in an ancient, rook-haunted family mansion" (Irving's "Tales of a Traveler," i. 2).—**liberty hall,** a house where every one is allowed or expected to do as he likes: as, "Gentlemen—pray be under no constraint in this house. This is *Liberty Hall*, gentlemen. You may do just as you please here" (Goldsmith's "She Stoops to Conquer," ii. 1).

hal-lan (hal'ạn), *n.* [Origin uncertain.] A partition between the door of a cottage and the fireplace, to keep off drafts; also, the space at the door thus partitioned off. [Sc. and north. Eng.]

hal-lel (hal'el or hạ-lāl'), *n.* [Heb. *hallēl*, praise.] In *Jewish ritual*, a hymn of praise consisting of Ps. cxiii.–cxviii.; also, another such hymn consisting of Ps. cxxxvi. ('great hallel').

hal-le-lu-iah, hal-le-lu-jah (hal-ē-lö'yạ). [Heb. *hallelūyāh*, 'praise ye Jehovah.'] **I.** *interj.* Praise ye the Lord! **II.** *n.* An exclamation of 'halleluiah!' also, a song of praise to God.—**hal″le-lu-iat'ic, hal″le-lu-jat'ic** (-yat'ik), *a.*

hal-liard (hal'yärd), *n.* See *halyard*.

hall=mark (hâl'märk), *n.* [From Goldsmiths' *Hall* in London, the seat of the Goldsmiths' Company.] An official mark or stamp indicating standard of purity, used in marking gold and silver articles assayed by the Goldsmiths' Company of London; any official or authoritative mark similarly used; fig., any mark or special indication of genuineness, good quality, etc.—**hall'=mark,** *v. t.* To mark with a hall-mark. Also fig.

hal-lo, hal-loa (hạ-lō'), **hal-loo** (hạ-lö'), *interj., n.,* and *v.* Same as *hollo*.

hal-low (hal'ō), *n.* [AS. *hālga*, < *hālig*, E. *holy*.] A holy person; a saint: now only as in *All-hallows*, *Hallowe'en*, etc.—**hal'low,** *v. t.* [AS. *hālgian*, < *hālig*.] To make holy, or sanctify; invest with a holy or sacred character (as, a place *hallowed* by memories or associations); also, to declare holy, consecrate, or bless (archaic: as, to *hallow* a church; "Sword, I will *hallow* thee for this thy deed," Shakspere's "2 Henry VI.," iv. 10. 72); also, to honor as holy (as, "Our Father which art in heaven, *Hallowed* be thy name": Mat. vi. 9); keep or observe (a day, etc.) as holy.—**hal'lowed,** *p. a.* Made holy; sacred; consecrated; honored or observed as holy.—**hal'lowed-ness,** *n.*

Hal-low-e'en, Hal-low-een (hal-ō-ēn'), *n.* [For *All-hallows even* (eve).] The evening of Oct. 31st, the eve of All-hallows or All Saints' Day.

Hal-low-mas (hal'ō-mạs), *n.* [For *Allhallowmas*.] The feast of All-hallows or All Saints, celebrated on Nov. 1.

Hall-statt-i-an (häl-stät'i-ạn), *a.* Of or pertaining to Hallstatt, a village in Austria; noting or pertaining to a variously dated pre-Christian stage of culture in central Europe, characterized by the use of bronze, the introduction of iron, artistic work in pottery, jewelry, etc., as shown by the contents of a burial-ground of the period found near Hallstatt.

hal-lu-cal (hal'ū-kạl), *a.* Of or pertaining to the hallux.

hal-lu-ci-nate (ha-lū'si-nāt), *v.*; *-nated, -nating.* [L. *hallucinatus*, pp. of *hallucinari*, better *alucinari*, wander in mind, dream: cf. Gr. ἀλύειν, wander in mind.] **I.** *intr.* To suffer from illusion or misconception; entertain false notions. [Obs. or archaic.] **II.** *tr.* To affect with hallucination. —**hal-lu-ci-na'tion** (-nā'shọn), *n.* [L. *hallucinatio(n-)*.] A suffering from illusion or false notions; an unfounded notion; a belief in an unreality; specif., an apparent perception, as by sight or hearing, for which there is no real external cause (cf. *illusion*).—**hal-lu'ci-na-to-ry** (-nạ-tō-ri), *a.* Pertaining to or characterized by hallucination.

hal-lux (hal'uks), *n.*; pl. *halluces* (-ū-sēz). [NL., for L. *allex*, great toe.] The innermost of the five digits normally present in the hind foot of air-breathing vertebrates; in man, the great toe; in birds, usually, the hind toe or inner-toe. Cf. *pollex*.

hall-way (hâl'wā), *n.* An entrance-hall; also, a corridor, as in a building. [U. S.]

halm, haulm (hâm), *n.* [AS. *healm* = D. and G. *halm* = Icel. *hālmr*, halm, straw: cf. L. *culmus*, stem, stalk, E. *culm*², and L. *calamus*, Gr. κάλαμος, reed, E. *calamus*.] Stems or stalks collectively, as of grain or of peas, beans, hops, etc., esp. as used for litter or thatching (chiefly Eng.); also, a single stem or stalk.

hal-ma (hal'mạ), *n.* [Gr. ἅλμα, a leap, < ἅλλεσθαι, to leap.] A game played with pieces on a special board by two or four persons.

ha-lo (hā'lō), *n.*; pl. *-los* or *-loes* (-lōz). [L. *halos*, < Gr. ἅλως, threshing-floor (on which the oxen trod out a circular path), disk, halo.] A white or colored circle of light seen round a luminous body, esp. the moon or the sun (in meteorology, restricted to circles due to the refraction produced by ice particles in the upper atmosphere, and not, as with the true coronas, to the diffraction produced by thin clouds or mist); also, a circle or disk of light represented about the head of a sacred person, as a saint; hence, an ideal glory investing an object as viewed through the medium of feeling or sentiment (as, "My head was in the clouds. I . . . fancied it already encircled by a *halo* of literary glory": Irving's "Tales of a Traveler," ii. 4).—**ha'lo,** *v.*; *-loed, -loing.* **I.** *tr.* To surround with a halo. **II.** *intr.* To form a halo, as about something.

hal-o-gen (hal'ō-jen), *n.* [Gr. ἅλς (ἁλ-), salt: see *-gen*.] In *chem.*, any of the elements chlorine, iodine, bromine, and fluorine, and sometimes the radical cyanogen, which form a salt by direct union with a metal.

hal-oid (hal'oid or hā'loid). [Gr. ἅλς (ἁλ-), salt: see *-oid*.] In *chem.*: **I.** *a.* Noting or pertaining to a salt formed by the union of a halogen with a metal, or a compound formed by the union of a halogen with a hydrocarbon radical. **II.** *n.* A haloid salt.

ha-loph-i-lous (ha-lof'i-lus), *a.* [Gr. ἅλς (ἁλ-), salt: see *-philous*.] Salt-loving; of plants and animals, growing in or inhabiting marshes or regions abounding in salt.

hal-o-phyte (hal'ō-fīt), *n.* [Gr. ἅλς (ἁλ-), salt: see *-phyte*.] A plant growing naturally in soil impregnated with common salt or other salts, as various chenopodiaceous plants of maritime and alkaline regions.—**hal-o-phyt'ic** (-fit'ik), *a.*

halt¹ (hâlt), *a.* [AS. *healt* = OHG. *halz* = Icel. *haltr* = Goth. *halts*, lame.] Lame; crippled; limping: as, "It is better for thee to enter *halt* into life, than having two feet to be cast into hell" (Mark, ix. 45). [Archaic.]—**halt**¹, *v. i.* [AS. *healtian*.] To be lame; walk lamely; limp; fig., to stand in doubt, waver, or hesitate (as, "How long *halt* ye between two opinions?" 1 Kings, xviii. 21); also, to proceed in a lame or faulty way, as reasoning, verse, rime, utterance, etc.—**halt**¹, *n.* A halting movement or gait; a limp.

halt² (hâlt), *n.* [G. *halt*, < *halten*, hold: see *hold*².] A temporary stop, as in marching, traveling, or any onward course: as, to make a *halt*; to come to a *halt*; to call a *halt* (to order a halt, as by troops on the march; hence, to require the discontinuance of any proceeding).—**halt**², *v.* **I.** *intr.* To make a halt or temporary stop, as in marching, traveling, etc. **II.** *tr.* To cause to halt.

hal-ter¹ (hâl'tėr), *n.* [AS. *hælfter* = G. *halfter*, halter; akin to E. *helve*.] A rope or strap with a noose or head-stall, for leading or fastening horses or cattle; also, a rope with a noose for hanging malefactors; hence, death by hanging. —**hal′ter**[1], *v. t.* To put a halter on; restrain as by a halter; catch with a noose; also, to hang (a person).

halt-er[2] (hâl′tėr), *n.* One who halts, limps, or hesitates.

halt-ing (hâl′ting), *p. a.* That halts; limping; lame; fig., wavering or hesitating; also, feeble, ineffective, or faulty. —**halt′ing-ly**, *adv.*—**halt′ing-ness**, *n.*

halve (häv or hȧv), *v. t.*; *halved, halving.* [ME. *halven, halfen,* < *half,* E. *half, n.*] To divide into halves; share equally; give or take the half of; complete the half of; reduce to half; also, to join, as one piece of timber with another, by cutting out half the thickness of each, so that each may be let into the other; in *golf,* to play (a hole, match, etc.) in the same number of strokes, as two opponents.

Halving.

halves (hävz or hȧvz), *n.* Plural of *half.*

hal-yard (hal′yąrd), *n.* [For ME. *halier, hallyer,* 'that which hales or hauls': cf. *hale*[1].] A rope or tackle used to hoist or lower a sail, yard, flag, etc.

ham[1] (ham), *n.* [AS. *hamm* = D. *ham* = G. dial. *hamme,* ham.] The part of the leg back of the knee; sometimes, the back of the hock, or the hock itself, of a quadruped; also, the back of the thigh, or the thigh and the buttock together (often in *pl.*: as, to squat on one's *hams*); also, the thigh of a slaughtered animal as used for food; specif., that of a hog either fresh or salted and cured; the meat of this part.

ham[2] (ham), *n.* [Short for *hamfatter.*] A theatrical performer of low grade; an inferior actor. [Slang.]

ham-a-dry-ad (ham-ą-drī′ad), *n.* [L. *Hamadryas* (pl. *Hamadryades*), < Gr. Ἁμαδρυάς (pl. Ἁμαδρυάδες), < ἅμα, together, + δρῦς, tree, oak.] In *class. myth.,* a wood-nymph fabled to live and die with the tree which she inhabited.

ha-mal, ham-mal (hą-mäl′), *n.* [Ar. *hammāl,* < *hamala,* carry.] An Oriental porter; in western India, a palanquin-bearer; a male house-servant.

ham-a-me-li-da-ceous (ham-ą-mē-li-dā′shius), *a.* [See *hamamelis.*] Belonging to the *Hamamelidaceæ,* a family of shrubs and trees including the witch-hazel, sweet-gum, etc.

ham-a-me-lis (ham-ą-mē′lis), *n.* [NL., < Gr. ἀμαμηλίς, kind of fruit-tree, < ἅμα, together, + μῆλον, fruit, apple.] Any of the shrubs or small trees constituting the genus *Hamamelis,* as the witch-hazel, *H. virginiana.*

Ham-ble-to-ni-an (ham-bl-tō′ni-ąn). [From *Hambletonian,* a horse (foaled in 1849) said to be so named from Black *Hambleton,* a race-course in Yorkshire, England.] **I.** *a.* Noting or pertaining to a superior breed of American trotting-horses descended from Hambletonian (see etym.), and more remotely from Messenger, an English thoroughbred imported to America in 1788. **II.** *n.* A horse of this breed.

Ham-burg (ham′bėrg), *n.* [From *Hamburg,* city in Germany.] A choice black variety of grape, well adapted for hothouse cultivation; also, a small-sized variety of the domestic fowl; also [*l. c.*], a machine-made cotton embroidery (edging, insertion, etc.).—**Ham′burg steak.** Beef chopped while raw, seasoned, and fried or broiled in cakes.

hame[1] (hām), *n.* [ME. *hame* = D. *haam.*] Either of two curved pieces lying upon the collar in the harness of a horse, etc., to which the traces are fastened.

hame[2] (hām), *n.* Scotch form of *home.*

ham-fat-ter (ham′fat″ėr), *n.* [Said to be from an old negro-minstrel song called "The Ham-Fat Man."] A theatrical performer of low grade; a ham. [Slang.]

Ham-ite (ham′īt), *n.* A descendant of Ham, the second son of Noah (see Gen. x. 1, 6–20); a member of any of various races of northern and eastern Africa supposed to be descended from Ham, as the native Egyptians.—**Ham-it′ic** (-it′ik), *a.* Of or pertaining to the Hamites; noting or pertaining to a group of languages of northern and eastern Africa, including the ancient Egyptian and the Coptic, Libyan, Somali, etc.

ham-let (ham′let), *n.* [OF. *hamelet,* dim. of *hamel* (F. *hameau*), hamlet; from Teut., and akin to E. *home.*] A small village; a little cluster of houses in the country; esp., in England, a village without a church of its own, but belonging to the parish of another village or a town.

ham-mal (hą-mäl′), *n.* See *hamal.*

ham-mam (hą-mäm′), *n.* [Ar. *hammām,* hot bath.] A Turkish or Oriental bathing establishment.

ham-mer (ham′ėr), *n.* [AS. *hamor* = D. *hamer* = G. *hammer* = Icel. *hamarr,* hammer.] An instrument consisting of a solid head, usually of metal, set crosswise on a handle, used for beating metals, driving nails, etc.; sometimes, a mallet or gavel, esp. one used by an auctioneer; in fig. use, an aggressive and destructive foe (as, Edward I., of England, the *Hammer* of the Scots; St. Augustine, the *Hammer* of Heretics); also, any of various instruments or devices resembling a hammer in form, action, or use; one of the padded devices by which the strings of a piano are struck; in *firearms,* that part of the lock which by its fall or action causes the discharge, as by exploding the percussion-cap; the cock; in *athletics,* a metal ball attached to a long, flexible handle, used in throwing-contests; in *anat.,* the malleus.—**ham′mer,** *v.* **I.** *tr.* To beat or drive with or as with a hammer; also, to fasten by or as by using a hammer, as in driving nails (as, "All that long morn the lists were *hammer'd* up": Tennyson's "Princess," v. 358); also, to form with a hammer (often with *out*); fig., to contrive or work out laboriously (often with *out*). **II.** *intr.* To strike blows with or as with a hammer; fig., to make persistent or laborious attempts.

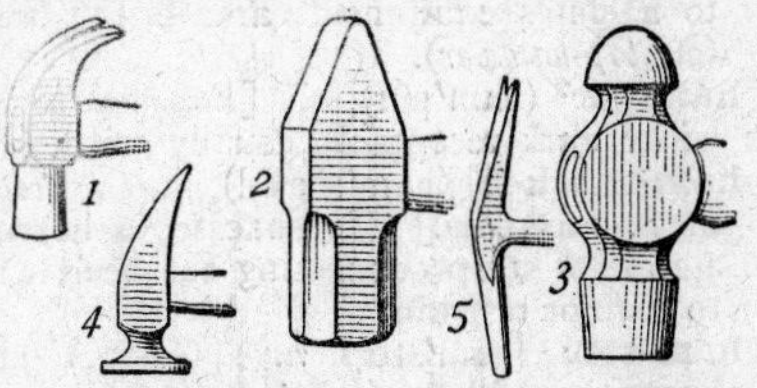

1, Nail Hammer; 2, Engineer's Hammer; 3, Machinist's Hammer; 4, Shoemaker's Hammer; 5, Carpet-layer's Hammer.

ham-mer=cloth (ham′ėr-klôth), *n.* [Origin uncertain.] A cloth which covers the driver's seat in some kinds of carriage.

ham-mer-er (ham′ėr-ėr), *n.* One who hammers.

ham-mer=hard-en (ham′ėr-här″dn), *v. t.* To harden (metals) by hammering.

ham-mer-head (ham′ėr-hed), *n.* Any of the sharks constituting the family *Sphyrnidæ,* characterized by a head expanded laterally so as to resemble a double-headed hammer, esp. *Sphyrna zygæna,* a widely distributed species; also, an American fresh-water fish, *Hypentelium nigricans,* of the sucker family, with a curiously shaped head.

Hammerhead (*Sphyrna zygæna*).

ham-mer-less (ham′ėr-les), *a.* Having no hammer or no visible hammer: applied esp. to firearms in which the hammer or striking device is concealed.

ham-mer-smith (ham′ėr-smith), *n.* One who works metal with a hammer.

ham-mock[1] (ham′ǫk), *n.* [Sp. *hamaca;* of W. Ind. origin.] A kind of hanging bed or couch made of canvas, netted cord, or the like.

Sailor's Hammock.

ham-mock[2] (ham′ǫk), *n.* [= *hummock.*] A tract of more or less elevated, thickly wooded land within a marshy region; a wooded tract within a region of different character: common in the southeastern U. S., esp. Florida.

ha-mose, ha-mous (hā′mōs, -mus), *a.* [L. *hamus,* a hook.] In *bot.,* hooked.

ham-per[1] (ham′pėr), *v. t.* [ME. *hampren;* origin uncertain.] To impede the movements of (a person, animal, etc.), or impede (movement, etc.), by means of some fastening, clog, entanglement, or the like, or as the fastening or other thing does (as, clothing *hampers* a swimmer); fetter;

entangle; catch, or hold fast (as, "Goats . . . I made snares to *hamper* them, and believe they were more than once taken in them": Defoe's "Robinson Crusoe," i. 10); in general, to impede or embarrass in action or procedure (as, to be *hampered* by debt, ill health, restrictions, or interference).—**ham′per**[1], *n.* Something that hampers, as a shackle (obs. or rare); *naut.*, articles which, while necessary to a ship's equipment, are in the way at certain times (cf. *top-hamper*).

ham-per[2] (ham′pėr), *n.* [For *hanaper.*] A large basket or wickerwork receptacle, usually with a cover.

ham-shack-le (ham′shak-l), *v. t.*; *-led*, *-ling.* [First element uncertain.] To shackle (a horse, etc.) by means of a rope or strap connecting the head with one foreleg; fig., to curb or restrain.

ham-ster (ham′stėr), *n.* [G.] A short-tailed, rat-like, burrowing rodent, *Cricetus frumentarius* (or *cricetus*), with large cheek-pouches, inhabiting parts of Europe and Asia; also, any of various other rodents of the same genus and allied genera; also, the fur.

Common Hamster (*Cricetus frumentarius*).

ham-string (ham′-string), *n.* In man, any of the tendons which bound the ham, or part behind the knee; in quadrupeds, the great tendon at the back of the hock.—**ham′string,** *v. t.*; *-strung* or *-stringed*, *-stringing.* To cut the hamstring or hamstrings of and thus disable; hence, to cripple or disable.

ham-u-late (ham′ū-lāt), *a.* [See *hamulus.*] In *anat.* and *zoöl.*, hooked; in *bot.*, hooked at the tip; covered with little hooks.

ham-u-lus (ham′ū-lus), *n.*; pl. *-li* (-lī). [L., dim. of *hamus*, a hook.] In *anat.*, *zoöl.*, *bot.*, etc., a small hook or hook-like process.

han-ap (han′ap), *n.* [OF. *hanap*; from Teut.] A goblet or drinking-vessel, often large and ornate. [Obs. or hist.]

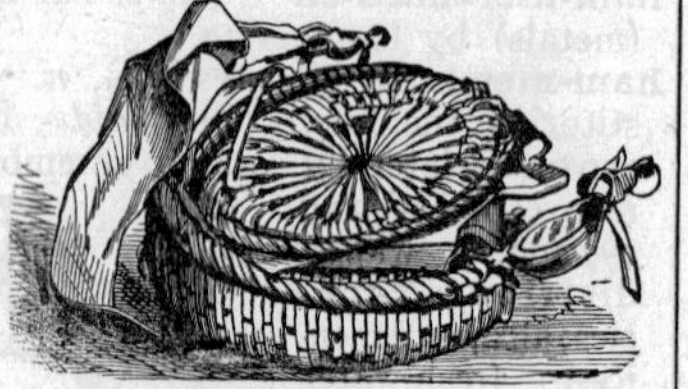
Hanaper.

han-a-per (han′ạ-pėr), *n.* [OF. *hanaper*, *hanapier*, hanap case, < *hanap*: see *hanap.*] A case for hanaps, etc.†; a repository for treasure or money†; also, a receptacle, often of wickerwork, for holding documents; also [*cap.*], a former office or department of the English Court of Chancery, into which fees were paid for the sealing and enrolment of charters, etc.

hance (håns), *n.* [Cf. F. *hausse*, a raising, rise, something serving to raise, and E. *enhance.*] A lintel†; in *arch.*, the sharply curving portion nearest the impost at either side of an elliptical or similar arch; also, the haunch of an arch; *naut.*, a curved rise from a lower to a higher part, as of the bulwarks from the waist to the quarter-deck.

Han-cock (han′kok). See *John Hancock*, under *John.*

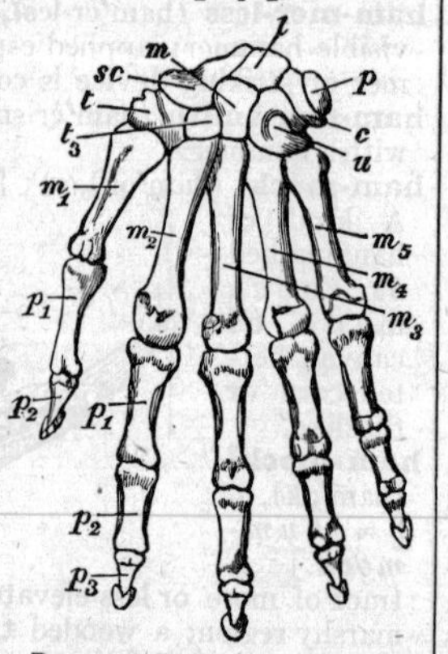

Bones of Right Human Hand, palmar surface, being the third segment of the fore limb, divided into carpus, metacarpus, and phalanges. — *sc*, scaphoid; *l*, semilunar; *c*, cuneiform; *p*, pisiform; *t*, trapezium; *t*3, trapezoid; *m*, magnum; *u*, unciform: these being the carpal bones, in two series, proximal and distal; — m_1 to m_5, the first to the fifth metacarpals, constituting the metacarpus; — P_1 to P_3, the 14 phalanges.

hand (hand), *n.* [AS. *hand* = D. and G. *hand* = Icel. *hönd* (*hand-*) = Goth. *handus*, hand.] In man, the terminal, prehensile part of the arm, consisting of the palm and five digits; hence, the corresponding part of the fore limb in any of the higher vertebrates; loosely, the terminal part of any limb when prehensile, as the hind foot of a monkey, the chela of a crustacean, or (in *falconry*) the foot of a hawk; hence, possession or power, disposal or control, or custody or care (usually in *pl.*: as, to put a thing into a person's *hands*); also, agency or instrumentality (as, to die by one's own *hand*); also, part or share in something (as, to have a *hand* in a matter); also, side (right, left, or other: as, on the right *hand*; on every *hand*); fig., a side of a subject, question, etc. (as, on the other *hand*); also, the hand as used in making a promise, taking an oath, etc., and esp. as representing a woman promised, given, or won in marriage; also, a person who does a specified thing, esp. with the hands (as, a book by several *hands*); also, a person employed in manual labor, as in a factory; a workman or workwoman; specif., each of the members of a ship's crew (as, all *hands*, the whole crew, or, by extension, all the persons of any company or number); also, a person with reference to action, ability, or skill (colloq.: as, to be a poor *hand* at writing letters); also, a person considered as a source, as of information or of supply (as, knowledge obtained at second *hand*; to buy goods at first *hand*: cf. *first-hand* and *second-hand*); also, skill or knack at doing something, whether with the hands or otherwise; also, work, execution, or touch (as, painting that shows a master's *hand*); also, a turn or inning of play in certain games; also, a round or outburst of applause, as for an actor; also, style of handwriting; hence, a person's signature (archaic); also, something resembling a hand in shape, function, etc.; a sign (☞) used in writing or printing to draw attention to something; a pointer or index on the dial of a clock or watch; a palmate root of ginger; a bundle of tobacco-leaves tied together; one of the clusters forming a bunch of bananas, etc.; also, a lineal measure used in giving the height of horses, etc., equal to four inches; in *card-playing*, the cards dealt to or held by each player at one time; the person holding the cards; a single part of a game, in which all the cards dealt at one time are played.—**at hand,** within reach; near by; also, near in time.—**from hand to mouth,** with consumption of food as soon as it is obtained; with attention to immediate wants only; without provision for the future; improvidently: hence the adjective *hand-to-mouth* (as, a *hand-to-mouth* existence).—**hand and glove** or **hand in glove,** in close relations; on very intimate terms: as, "I am sorry to say it, but you are *hand and glove* with a set of traitors" (J. H. Newman's "Callista," xxii.).—**hand in hand,** with hands mutually clasped; hence, conjointly or concurrently (as, the two processes go forward *hand in hand*).—**hand to hand,** with close approach of hands, as in fighting; in close combat; at close quarters: hence the adjective *hand-to-hand* (as, a *hand-to-hand* combat).—**in hand,** in immediate possession (as, cash *in hand*); also, in process (as, keep to the matter *in hand*); also, under control (as, to keep a horse, or one's passions, *in hand*).—**off one's hands,** out of one's responsible charge or care; so as to relieve or rid one of a burden, task, etc.—**on hand,** in immediate possession (as, cash *on hand*); subject to disposal (as, goods *on hand*); also, before one for performance or attention, as a task, duty, or engagement; also, in attendance, or present (U. S.: as, be *on hand* early).—**on one's hands,** resting on one as a burden, responsibility, or task.—**out of hand,** no longer in process; over and done with; also, beyond control (as, to let one's temper get *out of hand*); also, at once; without delay; suddenly.—**to change hands.** See under *change*, *v. t.*—**to hand,** within reach; at hand; also, into one's immediate presence or possession (as, your letter came *to hand* to-day).—**to have one's hands full,** fig., to have all one can do or manage; be fully occupied, as with a troublesome task.—**hand,** *v. t.* To grasp, touch, manage, or work with the hands (now only technical); hence, to deal with†; also, to lead or conduct with the hand (as, to *hand* a lady to a carriage); also, to deliver or pass with the hand or hands; fig., to pass, transfer, or transmit (as, a story *handed* down by tradition from generation to generation); also, *naut.*, to furl, as a sail.

hand-bag (hand′bag), *n.* A bag for carrying in the hand, as a valise or a woman's small bag for carrying small purchases, toilet articles, etc.

hand-ball (hand′bâl), *n.* A game (orig. and properly played in an inclosed court) in which a small ball is batted against a wall with the (usually gloved) hand (cf. *fives*); also, the kind of ball used in this game.

hand=bar-row (hand′bar″ō), *n.* A barrow or frame with handles at each end by which it is carried; also, a hand-cart.

hand-bill (hand′bil), *n.* A printed bill or announcement, as for distribution by hand.

hand-book (hand′bůk), *n.* A small book or treatise, properly one that may easily be held in the hand; a manual; esp., a book or treatise serving for guidance, as in an occupation or study; also, a guide-book for travelers.

hand-breadth (hand′bredth), *n.* The breadth of the hand; a unit of linear measure varying from 2½ to 4 inches; a palm; as, "The good sword stood a *hand-breadth* out Behind the Tuscan's head" (Macaulay's "Horatius," xlv.).

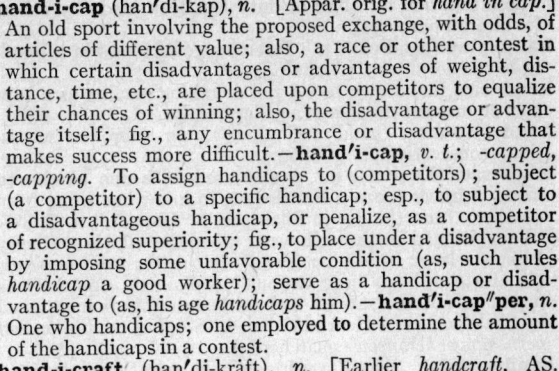

Hand-cannon, close of 15th century.

hand=can-non (hand′kan″-ọn), *n.* An early form of portable firearm, having the barrel mounted on a stock, and fired by means of a match.

hand=car (hand′kär), *n.* A light car propelled by a mechanism worked by hand, used on railroads in inspecting and repairing the tracks.

hand=cart (hand′kärt), *n.* A small cart drawn or pushed by hand.

hand-cuff (hand′kuf), *n.* [See *cuff*².] A shackle for the hand or wrist, esp. one of a pair connected by a short chain or the like; a manacle: usually in *pl.*—**hand′cuff,** *v. t.* To put handcuffs on; manacle.

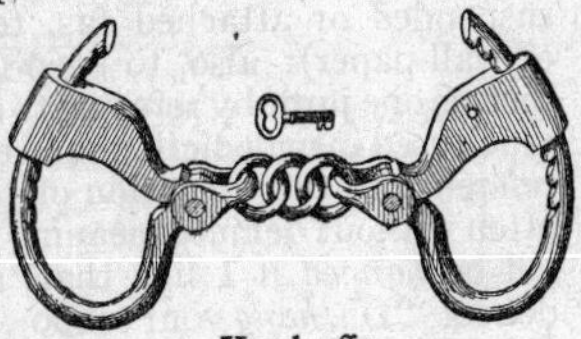
Handcuffs.

hand-ed (han′ded), *a.* Having a hand or hands; having the hands (as specified: as, empty-*handed*; white-*handed*); also, done with the hands (as specified: as, cross-*handed* piano-playing); played, used, etc., with a specified number of hands, or by a specified number of persons (as, a four-*handed* piece of music for the piano, a two-*handed* sword; a three-*handed* game at cards); also, joined hand in hand (archaic: as, "Into their inmost bower *Handed* they went," Milton's "Paradise Lost," iv. 739).

hand-fast (hand′fâst), *v. t.* [Cf. Icel. *handfesta,* strike a bargain by joining hands (*festa,* fasten, settle, pledge).] To betroth, orig. by the joining of hands (obs. or archaic); also, to take fast hold of†.—**hand′fast,** *n.* A covenant or contract, esp. of marriage (obs. or archaic); also, fast hold†, or custody† (as, "If that shepherd be not in *hand-fast,* let him fly": Shakspere's "Winter's Tale," iv. 4. 795).

hand-ful (hand′fůl), *n.*; pl. *-fuls.* As much or as many as the hand can grasp or contain; also, a small quantity or number (as, "All that tread The globe are but a *handful* to the tribes That slumber in its bosom": Bryant's "Thanatopsis"); also, a thing or a person that is as much as one can manage (colloq.: as, that child is a *handful*).

hand=gal-lop (hand′gal″ọp), *n.* An easy gallop, with the horse kept well in hand.

hand=glass (hand′glâs), *n.* A glass, or a framework of glass, placed over plants for protection, etc.; also, a small mirror with a handle; also, a magnifying glass for holding in the hand, as when reading.

hand=gre-nade (hand′grẹ-nād″), *n.* A grenade or explosive shell which is thrown by hand and exploded by impact or by means of a fuse; also, a grenade, or glass missile containing a chemical, for extinguishing fire.

hand=grip (hand′grip), *n.* [AS. *handgripe.*] A grasping with the hand; a grip of the hand, as in greeting; *pl.*, hand-to-hand combat (as, to come to *hand-grips* with a person); also, *sing.*, a handle by which a thing is gripped.

hand-i-cap (han′di-kap), *n.* [Appar. orig. for *hand in cap.*] An old sport involving the proposed exchange, with odds, of articles of different value; also, a race or other contest in which certain disadvantages or advantages of weight, distance, time, etc., are placed upon competitors to equalize their chances of winning; also, the disadvantage or advantage itself; fig., any encumbrance or disadvantage that makes success more difficult.—**hand′i-cap,** *v. t.*; *-capped, -capping.* To assign handicaps to (competitors); subject (a competitor) to a specific handicap; esp., to subject to a disadvantageous handicap, or penalize, as a competitor of recognized superiority; fig., to place under a disadvantage by imposing some unfavorable condition (as, such rules *handicap* a good worker); serve as a handicap or disadvantage to (as, his age *handicaps* him).—**hand′i-cap″per,** *n.* One who handicaps; one employed to determine the amount of the handicaps in a contest.

hand-i-craft (han′di-krâft), *n.* [Earlier *handcraft,* AS. *handcræft.*] Manual skill, as in work; skilled work with the hands; also, a manual art or occupation; also, a handicraftsman† (as, "We *handicrafts* best love the folks we live by": Scott's "Fair Maid of Perth," vi.).—**hand′i-crafts-man** (-mạn), *n.*; pl. *-men.* A man skilled in a handicraft; an artisan.

hand-i-ly (han′di-li), *adv.* In a handy manner.—**hand′i-ness,** *n.*

hand-i-work (han′di-wėrk), *n.* [AS. *handgeweorc.*] Work done or a thing or things made by the hands, or the labor or action, of a particular doer or maker (as, the *handiwork* of man, of nature, or of God); in general, the result of one's action or agency (as, this whole trouble is his *handiwork*); also, work done with the hands, rather than with the head or brain; manual work.

hand-ker-chief (hang′kėr-chif), *n.* A small piece of linen, silk, or other fabric, usually square, carried about the person for wiping the face, nose, etc., or used as a neckerchief or a kerchief.

han-dle (han′dl), *n.* [AS. *handle,* < *hand,* E. *hand.*] A part of a thing which is intended to be grasped by the hand in using or moving it; fig., that by which anything may be taken hold of; something that may be taken advantage of in effecting a purpose.—**a handle to one's name,** a title, as of honor, rank, or profession (as *Lord, General,* or *Doctor*), prefixed to a person's name. [Colloq.]—**han′dle,** *v. t.*; *-dled, -dling.* [AS. *handlian,* < *hand.*] To touch or feel with the hand; use the hands on, as in picking up, turning over, etc.; also, to manage in use with the hands; manipulate; hence, to manage, direct, or control (as, to *handle* troops in battle); wield, employ, or use (as, to *handle* one's fists well in a fight); also, to deal with or treat, as a matter or subject; esp., to deal with or treat in a particular way (as, to *handle* a case or a person with discretion); also, to deal or trade in (goods, etc.).—**han′dle-a-ble,** *a.* Capable of being handled.—**han′dle=bar,** *n.* A bar fitted with a handle or handles; esp., in a bicycle, etc., the (curved) bar in front of the rider, by which the vehicle is guided; either half of this bar.—**han′dled,** *a.* Having a handle: as, long-*handled.*—**han′dle-less,** *a.* Without a handle. —**han′dler,** *n.*

hand-less (hand′les), *a.* Without a hand or hands; also, unhandy, awkward, or inefficient (now Sc.).

han-dling (han′dling), *n.* The act of one who handles; a touching, grasping, or using with the hands; manipulation; management; treatment.

hand=made (hand′mād′), *a.* Made by hand, rather than by machine; also, made by man, or artificial, rather than natural†.

hand-maid (hand′mād), *n.* A female servant or personal attendant. Also **hand′maid″en.** [Archaic.]

hand=or-gan (hand′ôr″gạn), *n.* A portable barrel-organ played by means of a crank turned by hand.

hand=out (hand′out), *n.* A portion of food or the like handed out to a beggar, as at a house-door. [Slang, U. S.]

hand=pick (hand′pik′), *v. t.* [Back-formation from *hand-picked.*] To pick by hand; hence, to select carefully; often, to select for ulterior purposes, as a candidate for office. —**hand′=picked′,** *a.* Picked by hand; hence, carefully selected or chosen (often used disparagingly, as of persons whose selection for office or duty has been made by others for ulterior purposes).

hand=play (hand′plā), *n.* Interchange of blows in a hand-to-hand encounter. [Archaic.]

hand=rail (hand′rāl), *n.* A rail or railing serving as a support or guard at the edge of a gallery, stairs, etc.

hand=run-ning (hand′run′ing), *adv.* In unbroken succession; consecutively. [Colloq.]

hand=saw (hand′sâ), *n.* A saw used with one hand.—**to know a hawk from a hand=saw,** to know one thing from another: from the use in Shakspere's "Hamlet," ii. 2. 397, "I am but mad north-north-west: when the wind is southerly I know a hawk from a handsaw." In this the word *handsaw* (as also *hawk*) has been variously explained, commonly as meaning, not the saw or tool (although this is mentioned by Shakspere in "1 Henry IV.," ii. 4. 187), but the bird called *hernshaw* or *heronsew* (small heron).

hand-saw=fish (hand′sâ-fish), *n.* A voracious deep-sea fish, *Alepidosaurus* (or *Plagyodus*) *ferox*, having a long, high dorsal fin.

Handsaw-fish.

hand's=breadth (handz′bredth), *n.* Same as *hand-breadth.*

hand-sel, han-sel (hand′sel, han′-), *n.* [Cf. AS. *handselen*, a giving into the hand, Icel. *handsal*, the binding of a bargain by joining hands, Sw. *handsöl*, Dan. *handsel*, handsel, earnest.] A gift or token for good luck or as an expression of good wishes, as at the beginning of the new year, at entering upon a new condition, situation, or enterprise, etc.; also, anything given or taken as an earnest of what is to come; a first instalment of payment; also, the first use or experience of anything; a foretaste.—**hand′sel, han′sel,** *v. t.*; *-seled* or *-selled*, *-seling* or *-selling.* To give a handsel to; also, to inaugurate auspiciously; also, to use, try, or experience for the first time (as, "He carries his griefs on a shoulder That *handselled* them long before": A. E. Housman's "Shropshire Lad," l.).

hand-some (han′sum), *a.*; compar. *handsomer*, superl. *handsomest.* Easy to handle†; also, conveniently placed†, or handy†; also, appropriate, apt, or to the purpose, as speech or action (obs. or archaic: as, "an honest method . . . and by very much more *handsome* than fine," Shakspere's "Hamlet," ii. 2. 466); proper or seemly, as dress or conduct†; clever, graceful, or fine, as a speech or speaker, a performance or performer, etc. (now colloq.); gracious, generous, or magnanimous, as treatment, acknowledgments, apologies, etc.; also, considerable, ample, or liberal in amount, as a fortune, income, contribution, or price; also, of persons, of fine or admirable appearance, as from advantages of form, features, coloring, bearing, etc.; good-looking or comely, esp. in a dignified, spirited, or dashing way; in general, of strikingly fine appearance, as a horse, a tree, flowers or foliage, etc.; often, tastefully or elegantly fine, as a building, avenue, equipage, or costume, jewels, plate, furniture, etc.—**hand′some-ly,** *adv.*—**hand′some-ness,** *n.*

hand-spike (hand′spīk), *n.* [D. *handspaak*, 'hand bar.'] A bar, as of wood, used as a lever for various purposes.

hand-spring (hand′spring), *n.* A kind of somersault in which the body is supported upon one or both hands while turning in the air.

hand=to=hand (hand′tö-hand′), *a.* See *hand to hand*, under *hand*, *n.*

hand=to=mouth (hand′tö-mouth′), *a.* See *from hand to mouth*, under *hand*, *n.*

hand=work (hand′wėrk′), *n.* Work done by hand, now esp. as distinguished from that done by machine.

hand-writ-ing (hand′rī″ting), *n.* Writing done with the hand; a kind or style of writing done by hand, esp. that of a particular person.

hand-y (han′di), *a.*; compar. *handier*, superl. *handiest.* Done by the hand†; also, ready to hand; conveniently accessible; also, convenient to handle; easily manipulated or managed; convenient or useful; also, ready or skilful with the hands; deft; dexterous.

hand-y=dan-dy (han′di-dan′di). [Varied redupl. of *handy* for *hand.*] **I.** *n.* A children's game in which one guesses in which hand another holds some small object, as a pebble or a coin. **II.** *adv.* An expression used in offering the alternative for guessing in this game, and hence in general any alternative of choice. [Obs. or prov.]

hand′y-work, *n.* See *handiwork.*

hang (hang), *v. t.*; *hung*, also *hanged* (esp. for the capital punishment and for suicide), *hanging.* [In part AS. *hōn* (pret. *hēng*, pp. *hangen*), tr., hang, suspend, execute by hanging on a cross or gibbet, in part the derived AS. *hangian* (pret. *hangode*), intr., hang, depend; akin to D. *hangen*, G. *hangen*, *hängen*, Icel. *hanga*, *hengja*, and Goth. *hāhan.*] To fasten or attach (a thing) so that it is supported only from above; suspend; specif., to suspend so as to allow free movement, as on a hinge, etc.; also, to fasten or suspend (a person) on a cross, gallows, or the like, as a mode of capital punishment, esp. to suspend by the neck until dead (as, sentenced to be *hanged* by the neck until dead); suspend (one's self) thus as a means of suicide (as, "Judas . . . departed, and went and *hanged* himself": Mat. xxvii. 5); also, to let droop or bend downward (as, to *hang* one's head in shame); also, to fasten in position, as the blade of a scythe; attach (paper, etc.) to walls; also, to furnish or decorate with something suspended or attached (as, to *hang* a room with pictures or wall-paper); also, to keep (a jury) from rendering a verdict, as one juror by refusing to agree with the others. *Hang* is much used in maledictions and emphatic expressions, orig. with reference to the execution of persons by hanging, and later often without definite meaning: as, go, and be *hanged* to you! I'll be *hanged* if I like that! *hang* the fellow, or his impudence! "Oh, *hang* your taboo . . . talk taboo to the marines" (H. Melville's "Typee," xxix.).—**to hang fire,** to be slow in firing, as a gun; fig., to hesitate or be slow in acting, as a person; be delayed, or remain unsettled or unfinished, as a matter or undertaking.—**to hang up,** to suspend on a hook, peg, etc.; also, to put into or hold in abeyance; keep back or delay.—**hang,** *v. i.* To be suspended; depend; dangle; specif., to swing freely, as on a hinge; also, to be suspended from a cross, gallows, etc.; suffer death by suspension by the neck, esp. as a form of punishment; also, to bend forward or downward; lean over; incline downward; also, to rest, float, or hover in the air; fig., to impend; be imminent; also, to rest for support, etc. (*on* or *upon*); be conditioned or contingent; be dependent; remain in attention or consideration, as upon a person's words; also, to hold fast, cling, or adhere; often, to cling or adhere as an encumbrance (as, "Most heavily remorse *hangs* at my heart!" Shelley's "Prometheus Unbound," i. 436); be burdensome, as time (as, "Several hours of the day *hang* upon our hands": Addison, in "Spectator," 93); also, to remain in doubtful suspense (as, "He *hangs* between; in doubt to act, or rest": Pope's "Essay on Man," ii. 7); be doubtful or undecided; waver or hesitate; also, to remain with motion or action suspended; remain unsettled or unfinished; sometimes, to fail to agree, as a jury; also, to loiter or linger, as in expectation (as, to *hang* about a place).—**to hang back,** to resist advance; be reluctant to proceed; be backward.—**to hang out,** to have one's abode, or place of customary resort, as at a particular place. [Slang.]—**to hang over,** to remain behind from a former period, state of affairs, etc. [Colloq.]—**to hang together,** to hold together; remain united (often fig.: as, "We must all *hang together*, or assuredly we shall all hang separately," a remark attributed to Benjamin Franklin at the signing of the Declaration of Independence); also, to be consistent (as, his statements do not *hang together*).—**hang,** *n.* The action of hanging; the way in which a thing hangs; also, a slope or declivity; also (colloq., U. S.), the precise manner of using or doing something (as, to get the *hang* of a tool, a process, or a trick); meaning or force (as, to get the *hang* of a sentence or a subject).

han-gar (hang′är, F. äṅ-gär), *n.* [F.; origin uncertain.] A shed or shelter, as for vehicles or for an airship or aëroplane.

hang-bird (hang′bėrd), *n.* A bird that builds a hanging nest; esp., any of the American orioles.

hang-dog (hang′dog). **I.** *n.* A degraded fellow, fit only to hang dogs or to be hanged like a dog. **II.** *a.* Of or pertaining to a hangdog (as, a *hangdog* look); of persons, having a mean or sneaking appearance.

hang-er (hang′ėr), *n.* One who hangs something (as, a paper-*hanger*); also, something that hangs; a kind of short sword; also, something by which a thing is hung, as a loop on a garment or a shaped support for a coat or other garment when not in use; a chain or bent iron rod on which a pot or kettle is hung by means of a pothook, as in old-fashioned open fireplaces; also, a stroke with a double curve (turned reversely from the pothook), as made by children in learning to write (cf. *pothook*); a crooked stroke in writing.—**hang′er=on′,** *n.*; pl. *hangers-on.* A dependent or follower; a self-seeking adherent, or parasite; a persistent frequenter of a place; one who persistently clings to a service, connection, etc.

hang-ing (hang′ing), *n.* The action of one who or that which hangs; suspension; capital punishment by suspension on a gallows; also, something that hangs or is hung, as a curtain or drapery, a piece of tapestry, a wall-covering of paper, etc. (usually in *pl.*).—**hang′ing,** *p. a.* That hangs; pendent; pendulous; also, leaning over or overhanging; inclining downward, or steep or declivitous, as ground; situated on a steep slope or at a height, as a wood, a garden, etc.; also, directed downward, as the look; downcast.—**hanging indention,** in *printing*, etc., an indention of uniform amount at the beginning of each line except the first, which is of full width.

hang-man (hang′mạn), *n.*; pl. *-men.* One whose office is to hang persons condemned to death; a public executioner.

hang-nail (hang′nāl), *n.* [For *agnail.*] A small piece of partly detached epidermis at the side or base of a nail, as of a finger.

hang=out (hang′out), *n.* A place where one 'hangs out'; a place of abode, resort, or the like. [Slang.]

hang=o-ver (hang′ō″vėr), *n.* Something that 'hangs over,' or remains behind from a former period, state of affairs, etc.; sometimes, the effects left on a person after excessive indulgence in strong drink. [Colloq. or slang.]

hank (hangk), *n.* [ME.: cf. Icel. *hönk*, hank, coil, skein.] A coil, knot, or loop (as, "A rag and a bone and a *hank* of hair . . . But the fool he called her his lady fair": Kipling's "Vampire"); also, a skein, as of thread or yarn; a definite length of thread or yarn (a hank of cotton yarn measuring 840 yards); also, a loop of string, wire, or the like used to fasten something or hold or hang a thing by; *naut.*, a ring, as of iron or wood, round a stay, to which a sail is attached.

han-ker (hang′kėr), *v. i.* [Origin uncertain: cf. D. *hunkeren*, dial. *hankeren*, hanker; perhaps akin to E. *hang.*] To linger about a place or person, esp. with expectation or longing (as, "We . . . *hankered* about the Rio de la Plata a long time," Defoe's "Captain Singleton," xi.: now prov.); also, to have an uneasy, restless, or incessant longing (often with *after*, *for*, or an infinitive: as, to *hanker* after forbidden pleasures; "What business had he to be *hankering* after this girl at all!" Galsworthy's "Patrician," ii. 6).—**han′ker,** *n.* A hankering.—**han′ker-er,** *n.*—**han′ker-ing,** *n.* An uneasy or incessant longing.

han-ky=pan-ky (hang′ki-pang′ki), *n.* [A made word: cf. *hocus-pocus.*] Jugglery or legerdemain; hence, trickery; underhand dealing. [Colloq.]

Han-o-ve-ri-an (han-ọ-vē′ri-ạn). **I.** *a.* Of or pertaining to Hanover, formerly an electorate of northern Germany, later a kingdom, and since 1866 a province of Prussia; also, of or pertaining to the former ruling house of Hanover, to which belonged the sovereigns of Great Britain and Ireland from George I. (reigned 1714–27) to Victoria (all of them except Victoria being rulers of Hanover also, but she, as a woman, being unable to succeed to the Hanoverian throne: cf. *Windsor*). **II.** *n.* A native or inhabitant of Hanover; also, in *Eng. politics*, a supporter of the house of Hanover.

Hans (häns), *n.* [G. and D., for *Johannes*, John.] A popular name for a German or a Dutchman.

hanse (hans), *n.* [OF. *hanse* = ML. *hansa*, < OHG. *hansa* = Goth. *hansa*, multitude, company, band.] A company or gild of merchants; [*cap.*] a medieval league of towns of northern Germany and adjacent countries for the promotion and protection of commerce; also [*l. c.*], a fee paid to a medieval trading-gild.—**Han-se-at-ic** (han-sẹ̄-at′ik), *a.* Of or pertaining to the German Hanse: as, the *Hanseatic* League.

han-sel (han′sẹl), *n.* and *v.* See *handsel.*

han-som (han′sọm), *n.* [From J. A. *Hansom*, English patentee (1834).] A low-hung, two-wheeled, covered vehicle drawn by one horse, for two passengers, the driver being mounted on an elevated seat behind, and the reins running over the roof. Also called *hansom cab.*

Hansom.

han-tle (hän′tl), *n.* [Origin obscure.] A considerable number or quantity; a great deal. [Sc. and north. Eng.]

Ha-nuk-kah (ḉhä′nụk-kä), *n.* [Heb.] The Feast of the Dedication, a Jewish festival commemorating the dedication of the new altar on the occasion of the purifying of the Temple at Jerusalem after its pollution by Antiochus Epiphanes (see 1 Mac. i. 41–64, iv. 41–59; 2 Mac. i. 18, x. 1–8), beginning on the 25th day of the month Kislev, and lasting for eight days (mostly in December): called also 'Festival of Lights,' from the lights burned specially during this period.

Modern Russian Hanukkah Lights (one light being burned the first night, two the second, and so on until the eighth night, the two higher lights being additional).

hap[1] (hap), *v. t.*; *happed*, *happing.* [ME. *happen*; origin obscure.] To cover or wrap. [Sc. and prov. Eng.]

hap[2] (hap), *n.* [ME. *hap*, from Scand.: cf. Icel. *happ*, hap, chance, good luck.] The chance or fortune that falls to one (as, "Hard is his *hap* that first fals in his jeopardee": Spenser's "Faerie Queene," ii. 4. 43); one's luck or lot; also, an occurrence, happening, or accident (as, to narrate the *haps* and mishaps of the day); also, good fortune or good luck; also, mere chance or fortuity (as, "Be it art or *hap*, He hath spoken true: the very dice obey him": Shakspere's "Antony and Cleopatra," ii. 3. 32). [Archaic or prov.]—**hap**[2], *v. i.*; *happed*, *happing.* [ME. *happen.*] To chance, occur, or happen (as, "Make yourself ready . . . for the mischance of the hour, if it so *hap*": Shakspere's "Tempest," i. 1. 28); also, to have the fortune or lot (to do something); come or light by chance (*on* or *upon*). [Archaic or prov.]

hap-ax-an-thous (hap-ak-san′thus), *a.* [Gr. ἅπαξ, once, + ἄνθος, flower.] In *bot.*, having a single period of flowering.

hap-haz-ard (hap′haz′ärd). [From *hap*[2] + *hazard.*] **I.** *n.* Mere chance or accident as determining events, actions, etc.: as, to proceed at, or by, *haphazard.* **II.** *a.* Determined by or dependent on mere chance: as, a *haphazard* performance; a *haphazard* remark. **III.** *adv.* In a haphazard manner.—**hap′haz′ard-ly,** *adv.*—**hap′haz′ard-ness,** *n.*

haph-ta-rah (haf-tä′rạ̈), *n.*; pl. *-roth* (-rōth). [Heb.] A portion of the Prophets read immediately after the parashah in the Jewish synagogue on Sabbaths and festivals.

hap-less (hap′les), *a.* [From *hap*[2], *n.*] Luckless; unfortunate; unlucky.—**hap′less-ly,** *adv.*

hap-lite (hap′līt), *n.* [Gr. ἁπλόος, single, simple.] A kind of granite consisting essentially of quartz and some variety of feldspar.—**hap-lit′ic** (-lit′ik), *a.*

hap-log-ra-phy (hap-log′ra̤-fi), *n.* [Gr. ἁπλόος, single: see *-graphy.*] The unintentional writing of a letter or word, or of a series of letters or words, but once when it should have been written twice or more; also, the resulting passage or reading: opposed to *dittography.*

hap-lol-o-gy (hap-lol′ō̤-ji), *n.* [Gr. ἁπλόος, single: see *-logy.*] The utterance of only one of two similar adjacent syllables or sounds, resulting in the contraction of a word, as in *idly* for *idlely*, and *symbolatry* for *symbololatry.*

hap-ly (hap′li), *adv.* [From *hap*[2], *n.*] Perhaps; perchance: as, "And seeing a fig tree afar off . . . he came, if *haply* he might find any thing thereon" (Mark, xi. 13). [Archaic.]

hap-pen (hap′n), *v. i.* [ME. *happenen*, < *happen*, E. *hap*[2], *v.*] To come to pass by chance or without apparent reason or design; chance; hence, in general, to come to pass, take place, or occur (as, "It hath *happened* all as I would have had it": Shakspere's "All's Well," iii. 2. 1); befall or betide, as to a person or thing (as, "It was a chance that *happened* to us": 1 Sam. vi. 9); often, to befall with unfortunate effect (as, something has *happened* to the lock—the key will not turn); also, to have the fortune or lot (to do or be as specified: as, I *happened* to see him, or to be present); come or light by chance (*on* or *upon*: as, to *happen* on a clue to a mystery); be, come, or go (as specified) by some chance or casually (as, to *happen* in to see a friend).—**hap′pen-ing,** *n.* The process or fact of chancing, occurring, or befalling; also, something that happens; a chance; an occurrence; an event.

hap-pi-ly (hap′i li), *adv.* Haply or perchance (obs. or archaic); also, in a happy manner; fortunately or luckily; with pleasure or gladness; aptly or felicitously.—**hap′pi-ness,** *n.* The quality or state of being happy; good fortune, or a piece of good fortune; pleasure, content, or gladness, as from the possession or enjoyment of what is considered good; aptness or felicity, as of expression.

hap-py (hap′i), *a.*; compar. *happier*, superl. *happiest.* [From *hap*[2], *n.*] Coming or happening by chance†; also, characterized by or attended with good fortune (as, a *happy* accident or event; a *happy* omen); favored by fortune, as a person; fortunate or lucky; also, having a feeling of great pleasure or pleasurable content, as from a sense of good fortune, gratified desires, or agreeable conditions (as, "*happy* souls, that love to live," Tennyson's "Œnone," 236; "How *happy* could I be with either, Were t' other dear charmer away!" Gay's "Beggar's Opera," ii. 2); delighted, pleased, or glad, as over a particular thing (as, to be *happy* to see a person); characterized by or indicative of pleasure, content, or gladness (as, a *happy* mood, life, or home; *happy* faces or smiles); also, fortunate, successful, or dexterous in performance (as, to be *happy* at repartee); apt or felicitous, as actions, utterances, ideas, etc.—**hap′py=go=luck′y. I.** *adv.* As luck may have it; haphazard. **II.** *a.* Taking things easily, as they happen to come; trusting cheerfully to luck.

haque-ton (hak′to̤n), *n.* See *hacqueton* and *acton.*

ha-ra=ki-ri (hä′ra̤-kē′rē), *n.* [Jap., 'belly cutting.'] Suicide by ripping open the abdomen with a dagger or knife: the national form of honorable suicide in Japan, formerly practised by the higher classes when in disgrace or under sentence of death.

ha-rangue (ha̤-rang′), *n.* [F. *harangue*, < OHG. *hring*, ring, circle of people, arena, = E. *ring*[2].] A formal speech or address, as to an assembly (as, "Gray-headed men and grave . . . Assemble, and *harangues* are heard": Milton's "Paradise Lost," xi. 663); now, esp., a passionate, vehement, or noisy and intemperate address; also, any long, declamatory or pompous speech.—**ha-rangue′,** *v.*; *-rangued, -ranguing.* [F. *haranguer.*] **I.** *tr.* To address in a harangue. **II.** *intr.* To deliver a harangue: as, "He did not discourse, but *harangue*" (Smollett's "Humphry Clinker," June 2).—**ha-ran′guer** (-rang′ėr), *n.*

ha-ras (å-rä), *n.* [F.; origin uncertain.] A stud of horses for breeding purposes; an establishment for breeding horses.

har-ass (har′a̤s), *v. t.* [F. *harasser*, perhaps < OF. *harier, herier*, harry, harass: cf. *harry.*] To trouble by repeated attacks, incursions, etc., as in war or hostilities; harry; hence, to disturb or torment persistently or incessantly, as with troubles, cares, importunities, etc., or as troubles or cares do; worry; also, to wear out or exhaust with fatigue, trouble, care, etc.†.—**har′ass-er,** *n.*—**har′ass-ing-ly,** *adv.*—**har′ass-ment,** *n.* The act of harassing, or the state of being harassed; worry; also, something that harasses.

har-bin-ger (här′bin-jėr), *n.* [OF. *herbergeor*, < *herbergier*, provide lodging for, < *herberge*, lodging, < OHG. *heriberga*: see *harbor*, and cf. *auberge.*] One who provides lodgings†; also, one sent in advance of troops, a royal train, etc., to provide or secure lodgings and other accommodations (obs. or hist.); hence, one who goes before and makes known the approach of another (now chiefly fig. and literary: as, "the boding cry of the tree-toad, that *harbinger* of storm," Irving's "Sketch-Book," Sleepy Hollow).—**har′bin-ger,** *v. t.* To act as harbinger to; herald the coming of: chiefly fig. and literary.

har-bor (här′bo̤r), *n.* [ME. *herbore, herboru, hereberge*, = Icel. *herbergi* = OLG. and OHG. *heriberga*, lit. 'army shelter'; from elements equivalent to AS. *here*, army, + *beorgan*, protect: see *harry* and *bury*, and cf. *harbinger.*] Shelter, lodging, or refuge (as, to give, take, or find *harbor*); also, a place of shelter, sojourn, or refuge (as, "*Harbour* of many a stranger, free to friend . . . O thou house": Browning's "Balaustion's Adventure"); the retreat or covert of a deer or other wild animal; esp., a place of shelter for ships afforded by a recess of the shore or by breakwaters or other artificial works; a haven; a port.—**har′bor,** *v.* **I.** *tr.* To provide with shelter, lodgings, or quarters, as troops†; also, to give shelter or refuge to (now usually fugitives, offenders, etc.); give storage or concealment for (now usually smuggled or stolen goods, etc.); afford covert for (animals, vermin, etc.); fig., to entertain within the mind (a thought, feeling, design, etc., now usually one that is unfavorable or evil: as, to *harbor* suspicion, resentment, or malice); cherish; also, to shelter (a ship) in a harbor or haven; also, to track (a deer, etc.) to its harbor or retreat (as, "If I do know how to *harbour* a stag, you do know how to hunt him": Whyte-Melville's "Katerfelto," xvi.). **II.** *intr.* To take or have shelter or lodging (obs. or archaic: as, "Now, for this night, let's *harbour* here in York," Shakspere's "3 Henry VI.," iv. 7. 79); have a retreat or covert, as a deer or other animal; fig., to be entertained or cherished in the mind, as a thought or feeling; also, of a ship, etc., to take shelter in a harbor.—**har′bor-age** (-ā̤j), *n.* Shelter or lodging, or a place of shelter; also, shelter for ships, as in a harbor.—**har′bor-er,** *n.*—**har′bor-less,** *a.* Without a harbor; shelterless; without a haven or port.—**har′bor=mas″ter,** *n.* An officer who has charge of a harbor or port, and enforces the regulations respecting it.—**har′bor=seal,** *n.* The common (earless) seal of northern coasts, *Phoca vitulina.*

Harbor-seal.

har′bour, etc. British preferred form of *harbor*, etc.

hard (härd), *a.* [AS. *heard* = D. *hard* = G. *hart* = Icel. *hardhr* = Goth. *hardus*, hard; akin to Gr. κρατύς, strong, mighty.] Solid and firm to the touch; not easily penetrated, or divided, or altered in shape; not soft; specif., in coin or specie rather than paper currency, or, sometimes, in coin, bills, or actual money as distinguished from other property, debts, etc. (as, *hard* money; *hard* cash); also, firmly formed, tight, or not easily loosed (as, a *hard* knot); sometimes, capable of great endurance and exertion, as persons (as, "men, a *hard* laborious kind": Dryden's tr. Virgil's "Georgics," i. 95); also, difficult to do or accomplish, fatiguing, or troublesome, as a task; difficult or troublesome with respect to an action specified (as, *hard* to please; *hard* to be found; food *hard* of digestion); having difficulty in doing something (now only in 'hard of hearing'); difficult to deal with, manage, control, or overcome (as, "I am this day weak . . . and these men . . . be too *hard* for me": 2 Sam. iii. 39); irreclaimable, incorrigible, or disreputable, as persons (colloq.: as, a *hard* case; a *hard* character); difficult to understand, explain, or solve (as, a *hard* subject; a *hard* question or problem); also, difficult to bear or endure (as, to lead a *hard* life; to have a *hard* time); severe or rigorous (as, a *hard* winter); rude or coarse (as, *hard* fare); also, not easily impressed or moved, as persons; obdurate; unfeeling or pitiless; sometimes, not swayed by sentiment or sophistry (as, *hard* sense; to have a *hard* head: cf. *hardhead*); of a shrewd, practical nature; sometimes, not easily moved to part with money; niggardly; stingy; also, harsh or severe in dealing with others (as, a *hard* master; to be *hard* upon a person); harsh or unfriendly (as, to cherish *hard* feelings toward a person; to use *hard* words to a person, or call him *hard* names); severe or rigorous in provisions, etc. (as, a *hard* bargain); also, carried on or performed with great exertion, energy, or persistence (as, *hard* work; *hard* labor; *hard* study); carrying on work in this manner (as, a *hard* worker; a *hard* student); vigorous or violent (as, a *hard* run; a *hard* rain); also, harsh or unpleasant to the eye, ear, or esthetic sense (as, a *hard* face, or *hard* features; *hard* outlines in a painting); also, of water, containing mineral salts which interfere with the action of soap; also, acid or sour, as liquors; now, esp., strong, spirituous, or intoxicating, as liquors (U. S.); also, high and unyielding, as prices; in *phonetics*, having a guttural sound, as the *c* and *g* in *corn* and *get* (as distinguished from the 'soft' *c* and *g* in *cite* and *gin*); also, surd or breathed, as *k*, *p*, and *t*, in distinction from *g*, *b*, and *d*, which are soft, sonant, or voiced.—**hard and fast,** firm and secure; fig., strongly binding, strictly obligatory, or not to be set aside or violated (as, *hard and fast* rules).—**hard coal,** anthracite.—**hard rays.** See under *ray*³, *n.*—**hard tube.** See under *tube*, *n.*—**hard,** *n.* A firm beach; also, a sloping stone roadway or jetty at the water's edge (Eng.).—**hard,** *adv.* [AS. *hearde.*] So as to be hard, solid, or firm (as, the river is frozen *hard*; eggs boiled *hard*: cf. *hard-boiled*, below); also, firmly or tightly (as, "He took me by the wrist and held me *hard*": Shakspere's "Hamlet," ii. 1. 87); also, with difficulty (as, "*Hard* his labouring breath he drew": Scott's "Lady of the Lake," iii. 11); also, harshly or severely (as, to use, treat, or press *hard*; taxes that bear *hard* upon the poor); so as to involve severity or hardship (as, to be *hard* put to it to keep going; it will go *hard* with him if he is caught); also, with great exertion or energy, or with vigor or violence (as, to work *hard*; to run *hard*; to ride *hard*; it is raining *hard*); earnestly or intently (as, to look *hard* at a thing or a person); also, close or near, as in place, amount, or time (as, to follow *hard* after a person; a town *hard* by; to weigh *hard* upon 200 pounds; to be *hard* upon 60 years old; it is *hard* upon five o'clock); *naut.*, closely, fully, or to the extreme limit (as, *hard* alee; *hard* aport).—**hard and fast,** firmly and securely (as, bound, or held, *hard and fast*); fig., strictly or rigorously.—**hard up,** distressingly or urgently in want of something (with *for*: as, a caravan *hard up* for water; to be *hard up* for amusement); esp., urgently in want of money. [Colloq.]

hard=bit-ten (härd′bit″n), *a.* Given to hard biting, as a horse; hence, unyielding; dogged.

hard=boiled (härd′boild′), *a.* Boiled until hard, as an egg; hence (slang), stiff or hard (as, a *hard-boiled* hat, a derby or stiff hat, or a helmet); also (slang), hardened by experience, as a person; not easily impressed or moved; unyielding or uncompromising; stern, unfeeling, or pitiless; rough or tough.

hard-en (här′dn), *v.* **I.** *tr.* To make hard or harder; indurate; make hardy, robust, or capable of endurance; make obdurate or unyielding; make unfeeling or pitiless. **II.** *intr.* To become hard or harder; become inured or toughened; become obdurate, or unfeeling or pitiless; of prices, the market, etc., to become higher; rise in price.—**hard′ened,** *p. a.* Rendered hard; indurated; inured; obdurate; unfeeling.—**hard′en-er,** *n.*

hard=fa-vored (härd′fā′vọrd), *a.* Having a hard, unpleasant, or repellent appearance or countenance.

hard=fea-tured (härd′fē′tụ̄rd), *a.* Having hard or harsh features: as, "*hard-featured* women, weather-beaten brown" (Masefield's "Daffodil Fields," i.).

hard=fist-ed (härd′fis′ted), *a.* Niggardly; stingy.

hard-hack (härd′hak), *n.* A woolly-leaved rosaceous shrub, *Spiræa tomentosa*, of North America, having terminal panicles of rose-colored or white flowers and astringent roots.

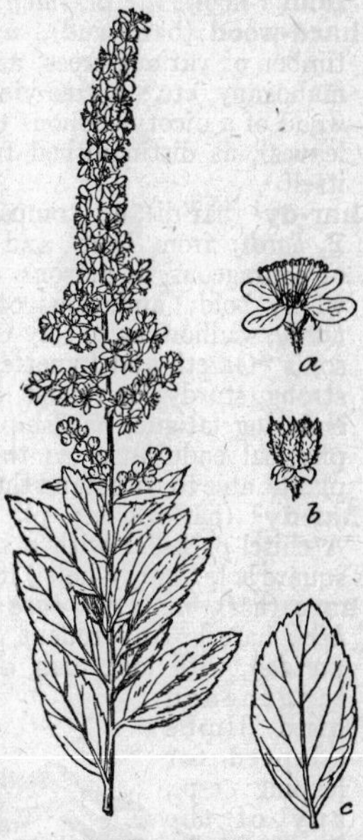

Flowering Branch of Hardhack. *a*, flower; *b*, fruit; *c*, leaf.

hard=hand-ed (härd′han′ded), *a.* Having hands hardened by toil; also, ruling with a strong or cruel hand; severe.—**hard′=hand′ed-ness,** *n.*

hard-head (härd′hed), *n.* One who is not moved by sentiment or sophistry; a shrewd, practical person; also, a blockhead; also, any of various fishes, as a gurnard, *Trigla gurnardus*, and the menhaden.—**hard′=head′ed,** *a.* Not easily moved or deceived; matter-of-fact; practical; shrewd.—**hard′=head′ed-ness,** *n.*

hard=heart-ed (härd′här′ted), *a.* Unfeeling; unmerciful; pitiless.—**hard′=heart′ed-ly,** *adv.*—**hard′=heart′ed-ness,** *n.*

har-di-hood (här′di-hůd), *n.* Hardy spirit or character; boldness or daring (as, "With dauntless *hardihood*, And brandish'd blade, rush on him": Milton's "Comus," 650); audacity or effrontery; temerity or rashness; also, sturdiness or robustness, as of body.

har-di-ly (här′di-li), *adv.* In a hardy manner; with hardihood.

har-di-ment (här′di-mẹnt), *n.* [OF., < *hardi*, E. *hardy*¹.] Boldness, daring, or hardihood (archaic: as, "Vanguard of Liberty, ye men of Kent . . . Now is the time to prove your *hardiment!*" Wordsworth's "To the Men of Kent"); also, a bold exploit† (see Shakspere's "Cymbeline," v. 4. 75).

har-di-ness (här′di-nes), *n.* The quality or state of being hardy; now, esp., robustness; capability of endurance.

hard-ly (härd′li), *adv.* In a hard manner; harshly or severely (as, to deal *hardly* with a person); with trouble or difficulty (as, pleasures *hardly* earned); hence, barely, or only just (as, I had *hardly* reached there, when it began to rain); almost not (as, *hardly* any; *hardly* ever); also, not quite (as, it is *hardly* strong enough; that is *hardly* true); also, with little likelihood (as, he will *hardly* come now).

hard=mouthed (härd′mouᴛʜd′), *a.* Having a hard mouth, as a horse; not easily controlled by the bit or rein; hence, self-willed; obstinate.

hard-ness (härd′nes), *n.* [AS. *heardnes.*] The state or quality of being hard; sometimes, an instance of this quality.

hard=pan (härd′pan′), *n.* [See *pan*¹.] Any layer of firm detrital matter, as of clay, underlying soft soil; also, hard, unbroken ground; also, in fig. use, firm bottom or solid foundation; hard underlying reality (as, to get down to *hard-pan*); the lowest level (as, prices have reached *hard-pan*). [Chiefly U. S.]

hards (härdz), *n. pl.* [AS. *heordan*, pl.] The refuse or coarser parts of flax or hemp, separated in hackling.

hard=set (härd′set′), *a.* Firmly or rigidly set; fig., determined or obstinate; also, in a hard or difficult position; beset with difficulties; hard put to it, or finding it hard (to do something: as, "It's *hard set* I am to know what would be right," Synge's "Well of the Saints," iii.).

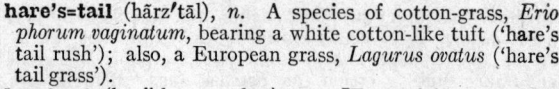

hard=shell (härd′shel), *a.* Having a hard shell (as, the *hard-shell* crab, the common edible crab, *Callinectes hastatus,* when its shell is hard: cf. *soft-shell*); fig., rigid or uncompromising, as in religious orthodoxy.

hard-ship (härd′ship), *n.* A condition that bears hard upon one; severe toil, trial, oppression, or want; also, an instance of this; something hard to bear.

hard=spun (härd′spun′), *a.* Compactly twisted in spinning, as yarn.

hard-tack (härd′tak), *n.* [See *tack*[2].] A kind of hard biscuit much used by sailors and soldiers; ship-biscuit.

hard-ware (härd′wãr), *n.* Metal ware or articles, as tools, locks, hinges, cutlery, kitchen utensils, etc.—**hard′ware-man** (-mạn), *n.*; pl. *-men.*

hard-wood (härd′wůd), *n.* The hard, compact wood or timber of various trees, as the oak, cherry, maple, ebony, mahogany, etc.; a tree yielding such wood; in *forestry,* the wood of a dicotyledonous tree (or one with relatively broad leaves), as distinguished from a conifer, etc.; such a tree itself.

har-dy[1] (här′di), *a.*; compar. *hardier,* superl. *hardiest.* [OF. F. *hardi*; from Teut., and akin to E. *hard.*] Bold, daring, or courageous, as persons, actions, etc.; also, unduly or unwisely bold; audacious or presumptuous (as, "Be not so *hardy,* scullion, as to slay One nobler than thyself": Tennyson's "Gareth and Lynette," 956); foolhardy or rash; also, strong, sturdy, or robust, as persons or animals; fitted for enduring fatigue, hardship, exposure, etc.; requiring great physical endurance, as the mode of life, sports, etc.; of plants, able to withstand the cold of winter in the open air.

har-dy[2] (här′di), *n.*; pl. *-dies* (-diz). [Appar. < *hard.*] A chisel or fuller with a square shank for insertion into a square hole ('hardy-hole') in a blacksmith's anvil.

hare (hãr), *n.* [AS. *hara* = D. *haas* = G. *hase* = Icel. *hēri,* hare.] Any rodent of the genus *Lepus* (family *Leporidæ*), with long ears, divided upper lip, short tail, and lengthened hind limbs adapted for leaping; esp., any of the larger species of this genus, certain of the smaller ones being known as *rabbits*; also, any of various other animals of the same family; [*cap.*] in *astron.,* the southern constellation Lepus.—**hare and hounds,** an outdoor sport in which certain players known as hares start off in advance on a long run, scattering behind them small pieces of paper called scent, the other players, known as hounds, following the trail so marked in an effort to catch the hares before they reach home.

American Varying Hare (*Lepus americanus*).

hare-bell (hãr′bel), *n.* [Appar. < *hare* + *bell*[1].] A low campanulaceous herb, the bluebell of Scotland, *Campanula rotundifolia,* with blue bell-shaped flowers; also, a liliaceous plant, *Scilla nonscripta,* with bell-shaped flowers.

hare-brained, hare-brain (hãr′brānd, -brān), *a.* Having or showing no more brains than a hare; giddy; heedless; reckless.

hare-lip (hãr′lip′), *n.* A congenitally deformed lip, usually the upper one, in which there is a vertical fissure causing it to resemble somewhat the cleft lip of a hare; also, the deformity itself.—**hare′lipped′,** *a.*

ha-rem (hā′rem), *n.* [Ar. *haram,* also *harīm,* lit. 'forbidden place,' < *harama,* forbid.] The part of a Mohammedan dwelling-house appropriated to the women of the household; also, its occupants collectively.

Harebell (*Campanula rotundifolia*).

hare's=tail (hãrz′tāl), *n.* A species of cotton-grass, *Eriophorum vaginatum,* bearing a white cotton-like tuft ('hare's-tail rush'); also, a European grass, *Lagurus ovatus* ('hare's-tail grass').

har-i-cot (har′i-kō or -kot), *n.* [F.; origin uncertain.] A ragout of meat and vegetables; also, a plant of the genus *Phaseolus,* esp. *P. vulgaris,* the common kidney-bean or string-bean; also, its edible seed or green pod.

ha-ri=ka-ri (hä′rẹ-kä′rẹ), *n.* Erroneous form of *hara-kiri.*

hark (härk), *v.* [ME. *harkien, herkien,* from an AS. verb not recorded, but implied in the derivative AS. *hercnian,* E. *harken*; from the source of E. *hear.*] **I.** *tr.* To listen to; hear: as, "*Hark* the clock within" (Tennyson's "Maud," i. 18. 8). [Archaic.] **II.** *intr.* To listen; harken: often used interjectionally, in the imperative (as, "*Hark, hark!* the lark at heaven's gate sings": Shakspere's "Cymbeline," ii. 3. 21).—**to hark back,** of hounds, to return along the course in order to regain a lost scent; hence, fig., to return to a previous point or subject, as in discourse or thought; revert.—**hark,** *n.* The act of harking; also, a hunters' cry to hounds (as, "With *hark* and whoop and wild halloo, No rest Benvoirlich's echoes knew": Scott's "Lady of the Lake," i. 3).

hark-en, heark-en (här′kn), *v.* [AS. *hercnian, heorcnian,* extended form of the AS. verb represented by E. *hark.*] **I.** *intr.* To listen; hence, to give heed or attend; also, to seek attentively† or inquire† (as, "*Hearken* after their offence, my lord": Shakspere's "Much Ado about Nothing," v. 1. 216); also, to wait attentively† (as, "They did me too much injury That ever said I *hearken'd* for your death": Shakspere's "1 Henry IV.," v. 4. 52). **II.** *tr.* To listen to; hear; hence, to give heed to. [Now poetic.]—**hark′en-er, heark′en-er,** *n.*

harl[1] (härl), *v.* [ME. *harlen*; origin obscure.] **I.** *tr.* To drag; also, to rough-cast (walls, etc.) with lime. [Chiefly Sc.] **II.** *intr.* To be dragged; drag one's self along; trail. [Chiefly Sc.]

harl[2] (härl), *n.* [Also *herl,* ME. *herle,* = MLG. *herle, harle,* filament of flax, etc.] A filament of flax, hemp, etc.; filamentous matter; also, a barb, or the barbs, of a feather, much used in dressing anglers' flies; a fly so dressed.

Har-le-ian (här′lẹ-ạn or här-lē′-), *a.* Of or pertaining to Robert Harley (1661–1724) and his son Edward (1689–1741), 1st and 2d Earls of Oxford, or their collection of books, pamphlets, and manuscripts, of which the manuscripts are now in the British Museum.

har-le-quin (här′lẹ-kwin or -kin). [F. *harlequin* (now *arlequin*), < It. *arlecchino*: cf. OF. *Helequin, Hellekin, Herlequin,* name of a devil, or a troop of demons (*mesnie Helequin*), of medieval legend.] **I.** *n.* [*cap.* or *l. c.*] A droll character in comedy (orig. the early Italian) and pantomime, usually masked, dressed in party-colored spangled tights, and bearing a wooden sword or magic wand; [*l. c.*] a buffoon. **II.** *a.* Party-colored; fantastically or strikingly variegated in color (as, the *harlequin* duck, a sea-duck, *Histrionicus minutus,* of northern regions, with variegated plumage; a *harlequin* snake, a coral-snake); fancifully varied in color, decoration, etc., as a set of dishes; also, of furniture, ingeniously contrived to combine or conceal in one piece parts or articles for various uses (applied esp. to furniture of the latter part of the 18th century).—**har″le-quin-ade′** (-ād′), *n.* A piece, or part of a piece, of pantomime or the like in which the harlequin plays the principal part; hence, any fantastic procedure; buffoonery.—**har″le-quin-esque′** (-esk′), *a.* [See *-esque.*] In the style or manner of a harlequin; harlequin-like.

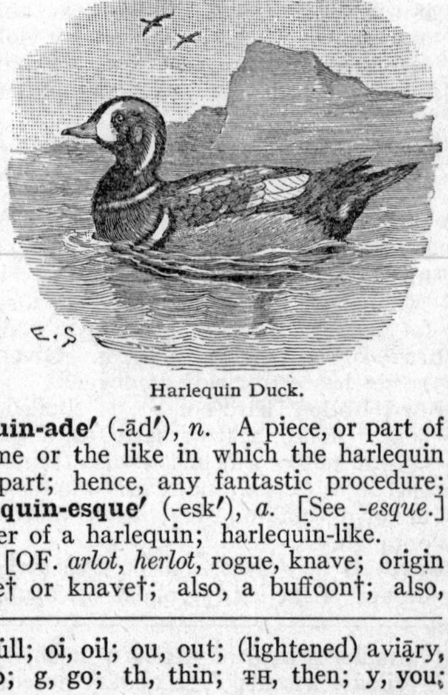

Harlequin Duck.

har-lot (här′lọt), *n.* [OF. *arlot, herlot,* rogue, knave; origin uncertain.] A rogue† or knave†; also, a buffoon†; also, a lewd woman; a prostitute; a strumpet.—**har′lot-ry** (-ri), *n.*; pl. *-ries* (-riz). Buffoonery†; ribaldry†; also, lewdness or unchastity; the practice or trade of prostitution; fig., meretriciousness; also, a harlot.

harm (härm), *n.* [AS. *hearm* = G. *harm* = Icel. *harmr*, harm, grief.] Evil of any kind, done or suffered, that impairs soundness, health, value, quality or character, etc.; injury, whether physical or moral; mischief, damage, hurt, or wrong; a form or instance of injury (as, "diffusing blessings, or averting *harms*": Pope's "Essay on Man," iii. 212); also, grief† or distress†.—**harm,** *v. t.* [AS. *hearmian.*] To do harm to; injure; damage; hurt.

har-mat-tan (här-mat′ạn), *n.* [W. Afr.] A dry, parching land-wind, charged with dust, on the west coast of Africa.

harm-er (här′mėr), *n.* One who or that which harms.

harm-ful (härm′fůl), *a.* Fraught with or doing harm; injurious; hurtful.—**harm′ful-ly,** *adv.*—**harm′ful-ness,** *n.*

harm-less (härm′les), *a.* Free from harm, unharmed, or uninjured (now rare); free from liability or loss (as, to hold or save one *harmless*, as by the terms of an agreement); also, having done no harm, or innocent (archaic); now, commonly, destitute of power or tendency to harm; innocuous; inoffensive.—**harm′less-ly,** *adv.*—**harm′less-ness,** *n.*

har-mon-ic (här-mon′ik). [L. *harmonicus*, < Gr. ἁρμονικός, < ἁρμονία, E. *harmony*.] **I.** *a.* Pertaining to or marked by harmony, agreement, or concord; concordant; consonant; also, pertaining to music; musical; now, esp., sounding together with pleasing effect; in harmony; specif., pertaining to musical harmony, as distinguished from melody and rhythm; in *acoustics*, pertaining to harmonics or overtones; also, in *math.*, having relations resembling those of musical concords (as, a *harmonic* progression, a series of numbers the reciprocals of which are in arithmetical progression). **II.** *n.* In *acoustics*, one of the secondary tones (overtones) accompanying a fundamental tone, and produced by the vibration of a sonorous body in aliquot parts of its length; one of these tones produced separately, as by lightly stopping a vibrating string; in *elect.*, a series of oscillations or waves of higher frequency accompanying a fundamental series of lower frequency, the frequency of the former being a multiple of that of the latter. See also *harmonics.*

har-mon-i-ca (här-mon′i-kạ̈), *n.* [NL., prop. fem. of L. *harmonicus*, E. *harmonic.*] Any of various musical instruments; esp., one having a set of small metallic reeds mounted in a case and played by the breath; a mouth-organ.

har-mon-i-cal (här-mon′i-kạl), *a.* Harmonic.—**har-mon′i-cal-ly,** *adv.*

har-mon-i-con (här-mon′i-kọn), *n.* [NL., < Gr. ἁρμονικόν, neut. of ἁρμονικός, E. *harmonic.*] Any of various musical instruments, as a harmonica or mouth-organ or an orchestrion.

har-mon-ics (här-mon′iks), *n.* The science of musical sounds.

har-mo-ni-ous (här-mō′ni-us), *a.* [F. *harmonieux*, < *harmonie*, E. *harmony.*] Exhibiting harmony; being in harmony; forming a pleasingly consistent whole; also, marked by agreement in feeling or action (as, *harmonious* consent; a *harmonious* meeting); also, agreeable to the ear; tuneful; free from discord.—**har-mo′ni-ous-ly,** *adv.*—**har-mo′ni-ous-ness,** *n.*

har-mo-nist (här′mọ-nist), *n.* One who reduces something to harmony; also, one who makes a harmony, as of the Gospels; also, one skilled in musical harmony; a musician; a composer.—**har-mo-nis′tic** (-nis′tik), *a.* Pertaining to a harmonist or harmony; pertaining to the collation and harmonizing of parallel passages, as of the Gospels.—**har-mo-nis′ti-cal-ly,** *adv.*

har-mo-ni-um (här-mō′ni-um), *n.* [NL., < L. *harmonia*, E. *harmony.*] A reed-organ, esp. one in which the air is forced outward through the reeds.

har-mo-nize (här′mọ-nīz), *v.*; *-nized, -nizing.* [OF. F. *harmoniser*, < *harmonie*, E. *harmony.*] **I.** *intr.* To be in harmony, accord, or agreement; in *music*, to form a concord. **II.** *tr.* To bring into harmony, accord, or agreement; also, to make musically harmonious; specif., in *music*, to set accompanying parts to, as a melody.—**har″mo-ni-za′tion** (-ni-zā′shọn), *n.*—**har′mo-niz-er** (-nī-zėr), *n.*

har-mo-ny (här′mọ-ni), *n.*; pl. *-nies* (-niz). [OF. F. *harmonie*, < L. *harmonia*, < Gr. ἁρμονία, a joining, joint, frame, arrangement, concord, music, akin to ἁρμόζειν, fit together, and ἁρμός, joint: see *arm*[1].] A consistent, orderly, or pleasing arrangement of parts; agreement; congruity; concord; also, accord, as in sentiments or action (as, "*Harmony* to behold in wedded pair More grateful than harmonious sound to the ear": Milton's "Paradise Lost," viii. 605); harmonious relations; also, a collated assemblage of passages on the same subject from different works, showing their points of agreement (as, a *harmony* of the Gospels); also, harmonious or musical sound; melodious sound; in *music*, any simultaneous combination of consonant tones, as in a chord; a concord; specif., a triad; also, the simultaneous combination of such tones; chordal structure, as distinguished from melody and rhythm; also, the science of the structure, relations, and practical combination of chords. —**harmony of the spheres.** See *music of the spheres*, under *music.*

har-ness (här′nes), *n.* [OF. *harnas, herneis* (F. *harnais*); origin uncertain.] Armor or defensive equipments for men or horses (or other animals) in war, or a suit of armor, etc. (archaic: as, "Arm, arm, and out! . . . At least we'll die with *harness* on our back," Shakspere's "Macbeth," v. 5. 52; "one of the beasts [elephants], armed with the royal *harness*," 1 Mac. vi. 43); in general, equipments, accoutrements, trappings, or dress (obs. or rare); now, commonly, the combination of straps, bands, and other parts forming the working-gear of a horse or other draft-animal (except the ox); fig., the equipments, constraining conditions, or routine of work (as, to live or die in *harness*); also, the heddles and connected parts in a loom; also, the mechanism by which a large bell is suspended and rung.—**har′ness,** *v. t.* To array in armor or equipments of war (archaic); in general, to equip, accoutre, or dress (obs. or rare); now, commonly, to put harness on (a horse, etc.); attach by a harness, as to a vehicle to be drawn; fig., to bring under conditions for working (as, to *harness* water-power).—**har′nessed,** *p. a.* Equipped with or being in harness; hence, marked with streaks of color, as if wearing a harness (as, the *harnessed* antelope, any of various antelopes of the genus *Tragelaphus*).—**har′ness-er,** *n.*—**har′ness=mak″er,** *n.*

Horse's Harness.

1, crown; 2, cheek-piece; 3, front; 4, 4, blinds; 5, nose-band; 6, bit; 7, curb; 8, check; 9, throat-latch; 10, rein; 11, collar; 12, hame; 13, hame-link; 14, hame-strap; 15, pole-strap; 16, martingale; 17, trace-tug; 18, trace; 19, saddle; 20, terret; 21, belly-band; 22, 23, crupper; 24, 24, breeching; 25, hip-strap; 26, trace-bearer.

Harnessed Antelope (*Tragelaphus bor*).

harns (härnz), *n. pl.* [Late AS. *hærnes*, pl.: cf. Icel. *hjarni*, G. *hirn*, brain.] Brains. [Sc. and north. Eng.]

harp (härp), *n.* [AS. *hearpe* = D. *harp* = G. *harfe* = Icel. *harpa*, harp: cf. LL. *harpa*, from Teut.] A musical instrument with strings, which are commonly set in a triangular frame and plucked with the fingers (see cut on following page); also, a representation of this instrument (the national device of Ireland); hence, an Irishman (slang, U. S.); also [*cap.*], in *astron.*, the northern constellation Lyra.—**Æolian harp.** See *Æolian*[1].—**harp,** *v.* [AS. *hearpian.*] **I.** *intr.* To play on a harp (as, to *harp* on one string, fig., to dwell persistently on one subject); fig., to dwell persistently or tediously (*on* or *upon*) in speaking or writing. **II.** *tr.* To play (music, etc.) on a harp†; also, to bring, put, etc., by playing on a harp (poetic: as, to *harp* one to sleep); also, to give voice or utterance to (archaic: as, "Thou hast *harp'd* my fear aright," Shakspere's "Macbeth," iv. 1. 74).—**harp'er,** *n.*

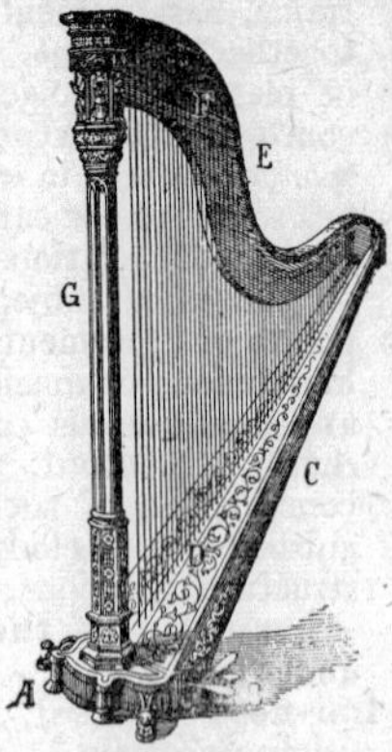

Modern Harp.
A, pedestal; *B*, pedals; *C*, back; *D*, sounding-board; *E*, neck; *F*, pins to which the strings are fastened; *G*, pillar.

harp-ings (här'pingz), *n. pl.* [Cf. F. *harpe, harpon*, cramp-iron: see *harpoon.*] *Naut.*, the stout wales about the bow of a ship. Also **harp'ins.**

harp-ist (här'pist), *n.* One who plays on the harp.

har-poon (här-pön'), *n.* [F. *harpon*, harpoon, earlier grappling-iron, cramp-iron, < *harpe*, cramp-iron, cramp, < L. *harpe*, < Gr. ἅρπη, sickle, simitar.] A barbed, spear-like missile attached to a rope, and thrown by hand or shot from a gun, used in capturing whales and large fish.—**har-poon',** *v. t.* To strike, catch, or kill with or as with a harpoon. —**har-poon'er,** *n.*—**har-poon'=gun,** *n.* A gun for shooting a harpoon, as at a whale.

Harp-seal.

harp=seal (härp'sēl), *n.* A large whitish seal, *Phoca grœnlandica*, with a dark harp-like figure on its back, common from Newfoundland northward.

harp-si-chord (härp'si-kôrd), *n.* [Obs. F. *harpechorde*, < It. *arpicordo*, < *arpa*, harp, + *corda*, string, cord.] A piano-like instrument in use from the 16th to the 18th century, in which the strings were plucked by leather or quill points connected with the keys.

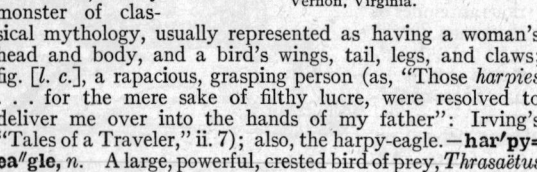

Harpsichord in the Washington Mansion, Mount Vernon, Virginia.

har-py (här'pi), *n.*; pl. *-pies* (-piz). [F. *harpie*, < L. *harpyia*, < Gr. ἅρπυια, lit. 'snatcher,' akin to ἁρπάζειν, snatch, seize.] [*l. c.* or *cap.*] A ravenous, filthy monster of classical mythology, usually represented as having a woman's head and body, and a bird's wings, tail, legs, and claws; fig. [*l. c.*], a rapacious, grasping person (as, "Those *harpies* . . . for the mere sake of filthy lucre, were resolved to deliver me over into the hands of my father": Irving's "Tales of a Traveler," ii. 7); also, the harpy-eagle.—**har'py=ea"gle,** *n.* A large, powerful, crested bird of prey, *Thrasaëtus harpyia*, of South and Central America and Mexico, with strong beak and talons, rounded wings, and fan-like tail.

har-que-bus (här'kẹ-bus or här'kwẹ-), *n.* [F. (obs.) *harquebuse*, later *arquebuse* (forms derived through It. from Teut.), for OF. *hacquebute, haquebusche*, harquebus; from Teut. (cf. MD. *haeckbusse*, MLG. *hakebusse*, MHG. *hakenbühse*), and meaning 'hook gun,' perhaps from a hook on the weapon for attaching it to a rest or support.] An old form of portable gun, provided at first with a matchlock, afterward with a wheel-lock, and superseded by the musket. —**har"que-bus-ier'** (-ēr'), *n.* [F.] A soldier armed with a harquebus.

har-ri-dan (har'i-dạn), *n.* [Cf. F. *haridelle*, sorry horse, jade.] A vicious old hag; a hardened, violent woman.

har-ri-er¹ (har'i-ėr), *n.* [Appar. < *hare.*] One of a breed of small hounds employed in hunting the hare; also, a member of a hare and hounds team; a cross-country runner.

har-ri-er² (har'i-ėr), *n.* [See *harry.*] One who or that which harries; specif., any of the hawks of the genus *Circus* (family *Falconidæ*), which prey on small animals.

har-row¹ (har'ō), *v. t.* [= *harry.*] To harry; ravage; despoil. See *harrowing¹*. [Archaic.]

har-row² (har'ō), *n.* [ME. *haru, harwe*: cf. Icel. *herfi*, harrow, MLG. *harke*, rake.] An agricultural implement set with teeth, upright disks, etc., usually of iron, drawn over plowed land to level it, break clods, etc.—**har'row²,** *v. t.* To draw a harrow over (land, etc.); hence, to cut, scratch, or lacerate (flesh, etc.); fig., to distress or disturb keenly or painfully, as a person, the mind, feelings, etc. (as, "Amazed I stood, *harrow'd* with grief and fear": Milton's "Comus," 565); work (*up*) to a mental state of acute discomfort or uneasiness. —**har'row-er,** *n.*

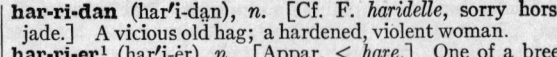

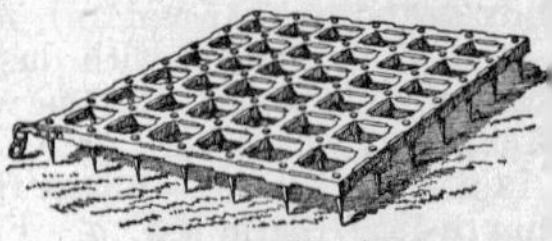
Common Harrow.

har-row-ing¹ (har'ọ̄-ing), *n.* Harrying, ravaging, or despoiling: as, the *harrowing* of hell by Christ (according to apocryphal account) in his descent thither, after his crucifixion, in order to rescue the captive souls of the just (a familiar subject of allusion and literary treatment in medieval and later times). [Archaic.]

har-row-ing² (har'ọ̄-ing), *p. a.* That harrows; keenly distressing or disturbing; heartrending.—**har'row-ing-ly,** *adv.*

har-ry (har'i), *v.*; *-ried, -rying.* [AS. *hergian*, ravage as an army does, < *here* = OHG. *heri, hari*, G. *heer*, = Icel. *herr* = Goth. *harjis*, army, host.] **I.** *tr.* To ravage (places), as in war; devastate, pillage, or despoil; also, to harass (persons) by repeated attacks, forced exactions, rapacious demands, etc.; in general, to harass, trouble, torment, or worry (as, "Thou their tool, set on to plague And play upon and *harry* me, petty spy And traitress!" Tennyson's "Guinevere," 358); also, to carry off, as in a raid (now Sc.). **II.** *intr.* To make harassing incursions.

harsh (härsh), *a.* [ME. *harsk*: cf. Dan. *harsk*, Sw. *härsk*, rancid, G. *harsch*, harsh, rough, hard.] Unpleasantly rough to the touch (as, a *harsh* towel; fruit with a *harsh* rind); hence, unpleasant to other senses; rough, sharp, or acrid to the tongue, as taste, flavor, fruit, etc.; grating, jarring, or discordant to the ear, as sounds, voices, etc.; unpleasing to the eye, as outlines, colors, features, etc.; jarring upon the esthetic sense, hard, or inartistic, as contrasts, effects, etc.; also, unpleasant in action or effect, severe, ungentle, or cruel, as persons, measures, treatment, utterances, etc.; stern, grim, or forbidding, as faces, expression, etc.; rugged or bleak, as places, scenery, climate, etc. —**harsh'en,** *v. t.* To render harsh.—**harsh'ly,** *adv.*—**harsh'ness,** *n.*

hars-let (härs'let), *n.* Same as *haslet.*

hart (härt), *n.* [AS. *heort* = D. *hert* = G. *hirsch* = Icel. *hjörtr*, hart, stag.] The male of the deer, commonly the red deer (*Cervus elaphus*), esp. after its fifth year.

harte-beest (härt'bēst), *n.* [S. Afr. D., 'hart beast.'] A large South African antelope, *Bubalis caama*, of a red color, having a long face with naked muzzle; also, any of various allied African antelopes.

harts-horn (härts'hôrn), *n.* The antler of the hart, formerly much used as a source of ammonia; also, an aqueous solution of ammonia ('spirit of hartshorn'); ammonium carbonate, or sal volatile ('volatile salt of hartshorn').

hart's=tongue (härts'tung), *n.* Any of various ferns, esp. *Phyllitis scolopendrium*, which has long simple fronds.

har-um=scar-um (hãr'um-skãr'um). [Appar. from obs. *hare*, harry, harass, + *scare.*] **I.** *adv.* Recklessly; wildly. **II.** *a.* Reckless; rash. **III.** *n.* A reckless person; also reckless conduct.

ha-rus-pex (ha-rus'peks), *n.*; pl. *haruspices* (-pi-sēz). [L., < *haru-* (= Skt. *hira*), entrails, + *specere*, look at.] In ancient Rome, one of a class of minor priests who practised divination, esp. from the entrails of animals killed in sacrifice.

—**ha-rus-pi-ca′tion** (-pi-kā′shọn), *n.* Divination by or as by a haruspex. Also **ha-rus′pi-cy** (-si).

har-vest (här′vest), *n.* [AS. *hærfest* = D. *herfst* = G. *herbst*, autumn; perhaps akin to L. *carpere*, pick, Gr. *καρπός*, fruit.] The third season of the year†; autumn†; hence, the season of gathering ripened crops, esp. of grain; also, the gathering of crops (as, "A field Of Ceres, ripe for *harvest*": Milton's "Paradise Lost," iv. 981); also, a crop or yield, as of grain; hence, the product or result of any labor or process. —**har′vest,** *v. t.* To gather, as a crop; also, to gather the crop from (as, "And, side by side . . . *Harvest* the fields wherein they fought": Whittier's "Snow-Bound").—**har′vest=bug,** *n.* A harvest-fly; also, a harvest-tick.—**har′vest-er,** *n.* One who harvests (as, "a *harvester* of hay": Whittier's "Maud Muller"); a reaper; also, any of various machines for harvesting or gathering field-crops, such as grain, beans, flax, potatoes, etc.; esp., a machine for harvesting grain, often fitted with an attachment for tying or binding the grain in bundles or sheaves; also, a harvestman (arachnid).—**har′vest=fly,** *n.* Any of certain cicadas, as *Cicada tibicen* ('dog-day harvest-fly'), noted for its sharp trill. —**har′vest=home′,** *n.* The bringing home of the harvest, or the time of doing it; the close of the harvesting; also, an English festival celebrated at the close of the harvest; also, a harvest song.—**har′vest-man** (-mạn), *n.*; pl. *-men.* A man engaged in harvesting; also, any of the arachnids of the order *Phalangidea*, comprising spider-like creatures with small rounded body and usually very long legs; the daddy-long-legs of the U. S.—**har′vest=moon′,** *n.* The moon which is full nearest to the autumnal equinox, esp. at and about the period of fullness.—**har′vest=mouse,** *n.*; pl. *-mice* (-mīs). A very small European field-mouse, *Mus minutus*, which builds its nest on the stalks of growing grain.—**har′vest=tick,** *n.* Any of various acarids in an immature stage, common in late summer and autumn, which attach themselves to the skin of man and animals.

Harvest-mouse and its Nest.

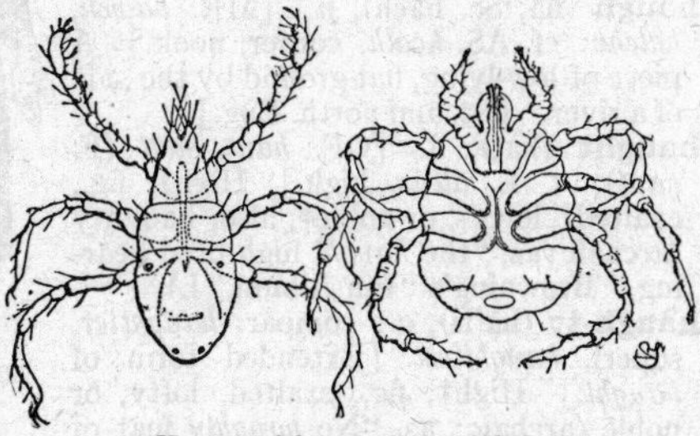

Harvest-ticks, much magnified.

Har-vey-ize (här′vi-īz), *v. t.*; *-ized, -izing.* [From H. A. *Harvey* (1824–93), American inventor.] To harden the face of (steel armor-plate, etc.) by a process involving cementation and chilling.

has (haz). Third person sing. pres. ind. of *have*.—**has′=been,** *n.* A person or thing that has been but is no longer, that belongs to the past, or whose period of flourishing or effectiveness is over. [Colloq.]

hash (hash), *v. t.* [F. *hacher*, < *hache*, ax: see *hatchet*, and cf. *hatch*³.] To chop into small pieces; mince; make into a hash.—**hash,** *n.* Something hashed or chopped up; esp., a dish of chopped cooked meat, and often potatoes, seasoned, and cooked again; hence, any preparation of old material worked over; also, a mess, jumble, or muddle (as, to make a *hash* of a matter).

hash-ish, hash-eesh (hash′ēsh or ha-shēsh′), *n.* [Ar. *hashīsh.*] The flowering tops, leaves, etc., of Indian hemp (see under *hemp*), smoked, chewed, or otherwise used in the Orient as a narcotic and intoxicant; any of certain preparations made from this plant. Cf. *bhang.*

has-let (has′let), *n.* [OF. *hastelet* (F. *hâtelette*), roasted bit of meat, < *haste*, spit, < L. *hasta*, spear.] The heart, liver, etc., of a hog or other animal, as used for food.

hasp (hȧsp), *n.* [AS. *hæpse* = G. *haspe* = Icel. *hespa*, hasp.] A clasp or fastening for a door, window, trunk, etc.; esp., a piece of metal fitting over a staple or into a hole and then made fast.—**hasp,** *v. t.* To fasten with or as with a hasp.

has-sock (has′ọk), *n.* [AS. *hassuc*, tussock of grass.] A rank tuft of coarse grass or sedge, as on boggy ground; a tussock; also, a shock of hair; also, a thick, firm cushion used as a footstool or to kneel on (as, "In order to make them kneel and join in the responses, he gave every one of them a *hassock* and a Common Prayer Book": Addison, in "Spectator," 112).

hast (hast). Second person sing. pres. ind. of *have*: now only in poetic or solemn use.

has-tate (has′tāt), *a.* [NL. *hastatus*, hastate, L. armed with a spear, < L. *hasta*, spear.] Spear-like, as weapons; also, shaped like the head of a spear; in *bot.*, of a leaf, triangular, with two spreading lobes at the base.—**has′tate-ly,** *adv.*

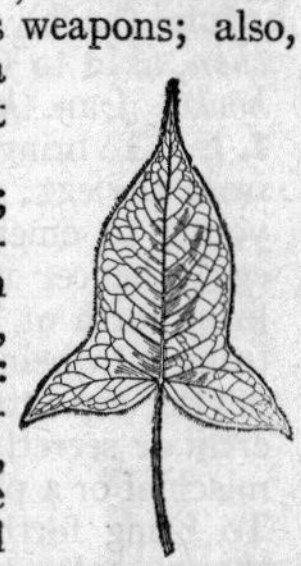

Hastate Leaf.

haste (hāst), *n.* [OF. *haste* (F. *hâte*), haste; from Teut. (cf. AS. *hǣst*, violence).] Energetic speed in motion or action, as from eagerness, fear, urgency of circumstances, etc. (as, "The king's business required *haste*": 1 Sam. xxi. 8); celerity, expedition, or despatch; often, thoughtless or rash speed (as, *haste* makes waste; "Married in *haste*, we may repent at leisure," Congreve's "Old Bachelor," v. 3); hurry or precipitance; also, eager or quickened effort to do something with speed (as, to be breathless with *haste*; to make *haste*, see phrase below); also, need or sense of need of, or eagerness for, speed (as, to be in great *haste*; to be in no *haste*, or to show no *haste*, to begin).—**to make haste,** to exert one's self to do something with speed; sometimes, with adjunct, to go or proceed with haste or speed (as, to *make haste* to a place; to *make haste* to reply).—**haste,** *v. i.* or *t.*; *hasted, hasting.* [OF. *haster* (F. *hâter*).] To hasten. [Now chiefly poetic.]—**haste′ful,** *a.* Full of haste; hurrying. —**haste′less,** *a.* Without haste or hurry.

hast-en (hā′sn), *v.* [From *haste*.] **I.** *intr.* To move or act with haste; make haste; go or proceed with haste (as, to *hasten* away; to *hasten* to a place; to *hasten* to explain); hurry. **II.** *tr.* To cause to make haste (as, "Bid her *hasten* all the house to bed": Shakspere's "Romeo and Juliet," iii. 3. 156); urge or impel to greater speed; accelerate (a process); bring about (an event, etc.) more speedily.—**hast′en-er,** *n.*

hast-y (hās′ti), *a.*; compar. *hastier*, superl. *hastiest.* Moving or acting with haste; speedy; quick; hurried; often, unduly quick in movement or action; precipitate; rash; also, easily excited to anger; quick-tempered; passionate; also, eager† or impatient† (as, "Where now the throng That . . . *hasty* to depart, Look'd to the sea for safety?" Cowper's "Task," ii. 118); of fruit, etc., ripening early†; also, made, done, etc., with haste or speed (as, a *hasty* visit, glance, or letter: cf. *hasty-pudding*); often, done with or characterized by thoughtless or angry haste, as actions, words, etc.—**hast′i-ly,** *adv.*—**hast′i-ness,** *n.*—**hast′y=pud′ding,** *n.* A dish made of flour or oatmeal stirred into boiling water or milk and quickly cooked; in the U. S., usually, mush made with Indian meal.

hat (hat), *n.* [AS. *hæt*, head-covering, = Icel. *höttr*, hood, = Sw. *hatt*, Dan. *hat*, hat; akin to E. *hood*.] A shaped covering for the head, esp. one with a crown and a brim (see cut on following page); specif., in Roman Catholic use, the distinctive red head-covering of a cardinal; hence, the office or dignity of cardinal.—**hat,** *v. t.*; *hatted, hatting.* To provide with a hat; put a hat on.

hat-a-ble (hā′tạ-bl), *a.* Capable or worthy of being hated.

hat-band (hat′band), *n.* A band or ribbon placed about the crown of a hat, just above the brim.

hat=box (hat′boks), *n.* A box for holding a hat; also, a small, nearly cubical trunk.

hatch[1] (hach), *n.* [AS *hæc*, gate, hatch: cf. D. and LG. *hek*, fence, gate, Sw. *häck*, Dan. *hæk*, rack.] A door, gate, or wicket with an opening over it; the lower half of a divided door; also, a floodgate; also, a cover for an opening in a ship's deck, a floor, a roof, or the like; hence, a hatchway; also, *pl.*, a ship's deck (now only in 'under hatches,' that is, below deck).—**hatch**[1], *v. t.* To close with or as with a hatch: as, "Sleep begins with heavy wings To *hatch* mine eyes" (Sidney's "Astrophel and Stella," xxxviii.).

Forms of Hats worn in England in the 16th, 17th, and 18th centuries.
1, 2, time of Henry VIII.; 3, time of Mary; 4, time of Elizabeth; 5, 6, time of James I. and Charles I.; 7, 8, time of the Commonwealth; 9, 10, time of William III.; 11-16, 18th century.

hatch[2] (hach), *v.* [ME. *hacchen*, akin to G. *hecken*, Sw. *häcka*, Dan. *hække*, hatch.] **I.** *tr.* To bring forth (young) from the egg; also, to cause young to emerge from (the egg); hence, in general, to bring forth or breed; fig., to bring into being; contrive or devise; esp., to contrive covertly or secretly (as, to *hatch* mischief or a plot). **II.** *intr.* To bring forth young from the egg; also, to be hatched.—**hatch**[2], *n.* The act of hatching; also, that which is hatched, as a brood (also fig.: as, "the *hatch* and brood of time," Shakspere's "2 Henry IV," iii. 1. 86).

hatch[3] (hach), *v. t.* [F. *hacher*, chop, hash, hatch: see *hash*.] To mark with lines, esp. closely set parallel lines, as for shading in drawing or engraving; also, to inlay with lines or fine strips of a different material.—**hatch**[3], *n.* A line or stroke, as for shading.

hatch-el (hach′el), *n.* [= *hackle*[1], *heckle*.] A hackle for flax or hemp.—**hatch′el**, *v. t.*; *-eled* or *-elled*, *-eling* or *-elling*. To hackle (flax or hemp); fig., to harass or torment. —**hatch′el-er, hatch′el-ler**, *n.*

hatch-er (hach′ėr), *n.* One that hatches, as a bird or an incubator; fig., a contriver; a plotter.—**hatch′er-y**, *n.*; pl. *-ies* (-iz). A place for hatching eggs, esp. those of fish.

hatch-et (hach′et), *n.* [OF. F. *hachette*, dim. of *hache*, ax; from Teut.] A small, short-handled ax for use with one hand; sometimes, a tomahawk.—**to bury the hatchet,** to make peace: in allusion to a practice of American Indians of burying a tomahawk upon making peace.—**to dig up the hatchet,** to prepare for war.—**hatch′et=face,** *n.* A sharp, narrow face.—**hatch′et=faced,** *a.*

hatch-ett-in, hatch-ett-ine (hach′et-in), *n.* [From C. *Hatchett* (died 1847), English chemist.] A soft waxy mineral substance of a yellowish-white or greenish-yellow color, consisting of carbon and hydrogen in combination, and occurring in Wales, Scotland, etc. Also, **hatch′ett-ite** (-īt).

hatch-et-y (hach′et-i), *a.* Hatchet-like; thin and sharp, as the face.

hatch-ing (hach′ing), *n.* A marking with lines, esp. closely set parallel lines, as for shading; also, the lines made.

hatch-ment (hach′ment), *n.* [Corruption of *achievement.*] An escutcheon or armorial shield granted for some achievement; esp., a square tablet set diagonally, bearing the arms of a deceased person (see cut in preceding column).

Hatchment of an Esquire — his arms impaled with those of his wife, the wife surviving.

hatch-way (hach′wā), *n.* An opening (covered by a hatch) in a ship's deck, for passage to parts below; also, a similar opening in a floor, roof, etc.

hate (hāt), *v. t.*; *hated*, *hating*. [AS. *hatian* = D. *haten* = G. *hassen* = Icel. *hata* = Goth. *hatan*, hate: cf. *heinous.*] To regard with a strong or passionate dislike (as, "Love your enemies, do good to them which *hate* you": Luke, vi. 27); detest; also, in a weakened sense, to dislike.—**hate,** *n.* [AS. *hete.*] Hatred; also, the object of hatred (poetic). —**hate′a-ble,** *a.* See *hatable.*—**hate′ful,** *a.* Full of hate; malignant; malevolent; also, exciting hate; detestable; odious. —**hate′ful-ly,** *adv.*—**hate′ful-ness,** *n.*—**hate′less,** *a.* Free from hate.—**hat-er** (hā′tėr), *n.*

hath (hath). Third person sing. pres. ind. of *have*: now only in poetic or solemn use.

Ha-thor-ic (ha-thor′ik), *a.* Of or pertaining to the goddess Hathor of Egyptian mythology, usually represented with the head, horns, or ears of a cow; esp., decorated with a face or head assumed to represent this goddess, as the capital of a column.

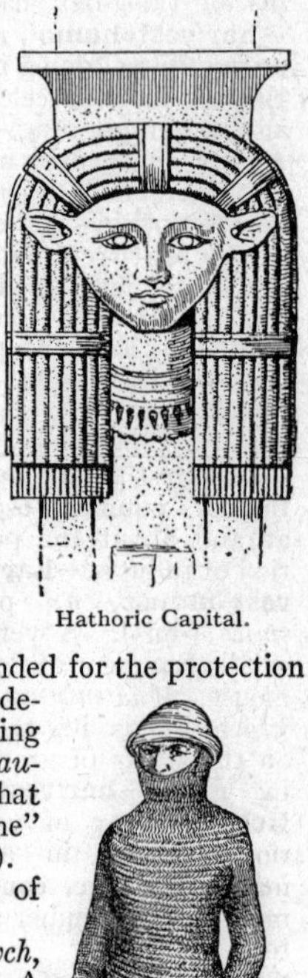
Hathoric Capital.

ha-tred (hā′tred), *n.* [ME. *hatrede.*] The feeling of one who hates; passionate dislike; detestation.

hat-ted (hat′ed), *a.* Wearing a hat.

hat-ter (hat′ėr), *n.* A maker or seller of hats.—**hat′ter-y**, *n.*; pl. *-ies* (-iz). The goods of a hatter; also, the factory or the store of a hatter.

hat=tree (hat′trē), *n.* A stand with spreading arms or pegs on which hats, coats, etc., may be hung.

hau-ber-geon (hâ′bėr-jon), *n.* [OF. F. *haubergeon*, < OF. *hauberc*, E. *hauberk.*] A short hauberk, reaching to the middle of the thighs; hence, any hauberk.

hau-berk (hâ′bėrk), *n.* [OF. *hauberc*, *halberc* (F. *haubert*), < OHG. *halsberg*, < *hals*, neck, + *bergan*, protect.] A piece of armor orig. intended for the protection of the neck and shoulders, but early developed into a long coat of mail reaching below the knees: as, "And on the *haubergh* stroke the Prince so sore, That quite disparted all the linked frame" (Spenser's "Faerie Queene," ii. 8. 44).

Hauberk, 12th and 13th centuries.

haud (hâd), *v.* and *n.* Scotch form of *hold*[2].

haugh (hâ, Sc. häċh), *n.* [ME. *hawch*, *halche*: cf. AS. *healh*, corner, nook.] A piece of low-lying, flat ground by the side of a river. [Sc. and north. Eng.]

haught (hât), *a.* [OF. *haut*, *halt* (F. *haut*), < L. *altus*, high.] High†; fig., exalted†, lofty†, or noble†; also, haughty (archaic: as, "the *haught* high-bred bearing," Browning's "Inn Album," i.).

haugh-ty (hâ′ti), *a.*; compar. *haughtier*, superl. *haughtiest*. [Extended form of *haught.*] High†; fig., exalted, lofty, or noble (archaic: as, "No *haughty* feat of arms I tell," Scott's "Lay of the Last Minstrel," vi. 23); also, having or showing a feeling of lofty dignity; disdainfully proud; arrogant; supercilious.—**haugh′ti-ly,** *adv.*—**haugh′ti-ness,** *n.*

haul (hâl), *v. t.* [Var. of *hale*[1].] To pull or draw with force; move or transport by drawing; *naut.*, to change the course of (a ship), esp. so as to sail closer to the wind; also, to cause a ship to sail closer to (the wind).—**to haul over the coals,** fig., to take severely to task; reprimand severely. —**to haul up,** to bring up, as before a superior, for reprimand; call to account. [Colloq.]—**haul,** *v. i.* To pull or tug (as, "The skipper *hauled* at the heavy sail": Whittier's "Wreck of Rivermouth"); *naut.*, to change a ship's course, esp. so as to sail closer to the wind; loosely, to sail, as in a particular direction; hence, in general use, to change one's course of procedure or action; make one's way in a particular direction; of the wind, to change direction, shift, or veer.—**to haul off,** to change the course of a ship so as to get further off from an object; hence, in general, to draw off or away; also, to draw back the arm in preparation for a blow.—**to haul up,** to change a ship's course so as to sail closer to the wind; also, to bring one's self to a position of rest by hauling or drawing action (as, the boat *hauled up* at the pier).—**haul,** *n.* The act or an act of hauling; a strong pull or tug; the draft of a fishing-net; also, the distance through which anything is hauled; also, that which is hauled; the quantity of fish taken at one draft of the net (as, "The bulging nets swept shoreward, With their silver-sided *haul*": Whittier's "Sycamores"); also, in fig. use, the taking or acquisition of anything, or that which is taken (colloq.: as, "That [silver] . . . would ha' been a *haul* for Congress, if they could ha' got hold on 't in war-time," Mrs. Stowe's "Oldtown Folks," xxvi.).—**haul'age** (-ạj), *n.* The act or labor of hauling; the amount of force expended in hauling; also, a charge for hauling; also, a charge made by a railroad for the use of a line of track.—**haul'er,** *n.*

haulm (hâm), *n.* See *halm.*

haunch (hânch or hänch), *n.* [OF. F. *hanche*; from Teut.] The fleshy part of the body about the hip; the hip; also, a hind quarter of an animal; the leg and loin of an animal, as used for food; in *arch.*, either side of an arch, extending from the vertex or crown to the impost.—**haunch'=bone,** *n.* The innominate bone; also, the ilium.

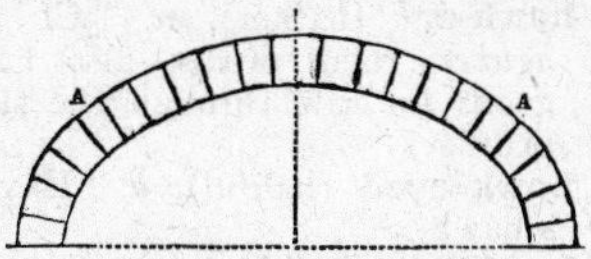

A, A, Haunches of an Arch.

haunt (hânt or hänt), *v.* [OF. F. *hanter*; origin uncertain.] **I.** *tr.* To practise habitually†; use habitually or frequently†; also, to resort to much, or visit frequently (as, "I *haunt* the pine-dark solitudes," Lowell's "L'Envoi: To the Muse"; "*Haunt* less the plays, and more the public pray'rs," T. Parnell's "Elegy to an Old Beauty"); frequent the company of (a person: as, to *haunt* the rich); hence, to intrude upon (a person) continually, as memories, thoughts, cares, etc., do; recur to persistently; specif., of ghosts, etc., to visit (a place or a person) frequently or habitually, with manifested presence. **II.** *intr.* To resort habitually (as, "I have charged thee not to *haunt* about my doors": Shakspere's "Othello," i. 1. 96); associate, as with a person.—**haunt,** *n.* Habit, custom, or usage (now prov. Eng. and Sc.); habitual practice† (as, "Of clooth-making she hadde swiche an *haunt*, She passed hem of Ypres and of Gaunt": Chaucer's "Prologue to the Canterbury Tales," 447); also, the practice of resorting to or frequently visiting a place, etc.† (as, "This our life exempt from public *haunt* Finds tongues in trees, books in the running brooks": Shakspere's "As You Like It," ii. 1. 15); also, a place of frequent resort (as, to revisit one's old *haunts*); also, a ghost (local, Eng. and U. S.).—**haunt'ed,** *p. a.* Much resorted to; specif., frequented or visited by ghosts (as, a *haunted* room; a *haunted* man).—**haunt'er,** *n.*—**haunt'ing-ly,** *adv.*

hause, hawse[1] (hâs), *n.* [AS. *heals* = Icel. *hāls* = OHG. and Goth. *hals*, neck.] A narrow passage between mountains; a narrow connecting ridge. [Sc. and north. Eng.]

hau-sen (hâ'zn, G. hou'zen), *n.* [G., < OHG. *hūso*: cf. *isinglass.*] A large sturgeon, *Acipenser huso*, of the Black Sea and Caspian Sea and their rivers.

haus-mann-ite (hous'mạn-īt), *n.* [From J. F. L. *Hausmann* (1782–1859), German mineralogist.] A native oxide of manganese found in Germany, etc.

Hauss-mann-ize (hous'mạn-īz), *v. t.*; *-ized, -izing.* To remodel (a city, its streets, etc.) after the manner of Baron Haussmann (1809–91) in Paris, as by providing broad, straight thoroughfares, fine architectural effects, etc.—**Hauss"mann-i-za'tion** (-i-zā'shọn), *n.*

haus-tel-lum (hâs-tel'um), *n.*; pl. *haustella* (-ạ̈). [NL., dim. of L. *haustrum*, machine for drawing water, < *haurire*, draw, drain.] In certain insects and crustaceans, a proboscis or organ adapted for sucking blood or plant-juices.—**haus'tel-late** (-te-lāt), *a.*

haus-to-ri-um (hâs-tō'ri-um), *n.*; pl. *-ria* (-ri-ạ̈). [NL., < L. *haustor*, drawer, drinker, < *haurire*, draw, drain.] In *bot.*, one of the small suckers or other appendages on a parasitic plant, which penetrate the host and absorb nutriment.

haut-boy (hō'boi), *n.* [F. *hautbois*, < *haut*, high, + *bois*, wood; named with reference to its high notes.] An oboe.—**haut'boy-ist,** *n.* An oboist.

hau-teur (hō-tėr'), *n.* [F., < *haut*, high: see *haught.*] Haughty manner or spirit; haughtiness.

ha-üy-nite, ha-üyne (hä'wi-nīt, -win), *n.* [From R. J. *Haüy* (1743–1822), French mineralogist.] A silicate and sulphate mineral containing aluminium, calcium, and sodium, and having usually a bluish or greenish color: found embedded in igneous rocks.

Ha-van-a (hạ-van'ạ̈), *n.* A cigar made at Havana or in Cuba, or one made elsewhere of Cuban tobacco.

have (hav), *v.*; pres. 1 *have*, 2 *hast*, 3 *has* or *hath*, pl. *have*; pret. and pp. *had*; ppr. *having.* [AS. *habban* = D. *hebben* = G. *haben* = Icel. *hafa* = Goth. *haban*, have; appar. akin to L. *habere*, have.] **I.** *tr.* To hold or possess in ownership, or own (as, to *have* much property or money); hold or possess in some other relation, as of kindred, relative position, etc. (as, a man who *has* two sons; to *have* one's opponent down); possess as a part or appendage, or as the constituent parts (as, true flies *have* two wings; the year *has* twelve months); possess as an attribute, quality, right, effect, etc. (as, to *have* a dark complexion; to *have* a cheerful disposition; to *have* special privileges; to *have* beneficial results); possess by acquiring or receiving (as, to *have* no news); get, receive, or take (as, there are few to be *had*; do *have* one); hold in mind, sight, etc. (as, to *have* a journey in contemplation); entertain (an opinion, feeling, etc.: as, to *have* doubts); show or exhibit in action (as, to *have* regard, heed, a care, etc.); assert or maintain (as, rumor *has* it so); engage in or perform (as, to *have* a talk, a dance, or a party); know or understand (as, to *have* neither Latin nor Greek); experience, enjoy, or suffer (as, to *have* a pleasant time; to *have* a headache or bad health); undergo or encounter as an experience (with an adjunct: as, to *have* one's hopes fulfilled; to *have* one's fingers burned); hold in estimation (archaic: as, to *have* in reverence or in contempt); hold in one's power or at a disadvantage, as in an argument (colloq.: as, he *has* you there); outwit, deceive, or cheat (slang: as, a person not easily *had*); bring, take, or put (archaic: as, "I was *had* into a whole room full of women," Fielding's "Tom Jones," xvii. 3); require or cause (to do something, be done, or be as specified: as, *have* him saddle my horse; to *have* one's horse saddled; *have* the horse here at five); permit or allow (as, I will not *have* it; I would not *have* them lose by it); be required, compelled, or under obligation (followed by an infinitive with *to*: as, I *have* to stop now). See also *had better*, under *had.* **II.** *intr.* To get, go, or be: in archaic phrases: as, *have at* them! (as in attack); *have with* you! (on with you!); *had like* (was or came near: now colloq.). **III.** *auxiliary.* Used with the past participle of a principal verb to form a compound or perfect tense, sometimes with another auxiliary: as, I *have, had,* or *shall have* done it; you *should* or *would* not *have* gone.

have-lock (hav'lok), *n.* [From Sir H. *Havelock* (1795–1857), British general.] A white cloth cap-cover with a flap hanging over the neck, for protection from the sun.

Havelock.

ha-ven (hā'vn), *n.* [AS. *hæfen* = D. *haven* = G. *hafen* = Icel. *höfn*, haven: cf. AS. *hæf*, Icel. *haf*, sea.] A harbor or port; fig., any place of shelter and safety.—**ha'ven,** *v. t.* To shelter as in a haven.—**ha'ven-less,** *a.* Without a haven; harborless.

hav-er[1] (hav'ėr), *n.* One who has; a possessor: as, "Valour is the chiefest virtue, and Most dignifies the *haver*" (Shakspere's "Coriolanus," ii. 2. 89).

ha-ver[2] (hā'vėr), *v. i.* [Origin unknown.] To talk foolishly; prate. [Sc. and north. Eng.]—**ha'ver**[2], *n.* Foolish talk; nonsense: usually in *pl.* [Sc. and north. Eng.]

hav-er[3] (hav'ėr), *n.* [ME. *haver* = G. *hafer* = Sw. *hafre* = Dan. *havre.*] The oat; oats. [Sc. and north. Eng.]

have-rel (hāv'rẹl), *n.* [See *haver*[2].] A foolish talker; a silly chatterer; a fool. [Sc. and north. Eng.]

hav-er-sack (hav′ėr-sak), *n.* [F. *havresac*, < G. *habersac*, lit. 'oat sack': cf. *haver*[3].] A soldier's bag for carrying rations, as when on the march (as, "We bore two days' rations in our *haversacks*": Conan Doyle's "Exploits of Brigadier Gerard," v.); also, any similar bag used for a like purpose.

Ha-ver-sian (ha-vėr′ṣian), *a.* Pertaining to or discovered by Clopton Havers (died 1702), a London anatomist: as, a *Haversian* canal (a cylindrical hollow in bone, through which a blood-vessel runs).

hav-il-dar (hav′il-där), *n.* [Hind. *havildār*, < Pers. *hawāldār*.] In India, a native or sepoy sergeant.

hav-ing (hav′ing), *n.* Possession; also, that which one possesses; *pl.*, belongings; also, now usually in *pl.*, behavior or manners (Sc.).

hav-ior, hav-iour (hāv′yọr), *n.* [OF. *aveir* (F. *avoir*), possession, property, orig. inf., < L. *habere*, have: cf. *aver*[2].] Possession†; property†; also, behavior, deportment, or, *pl.*, manners (archaic or prov.).

hav-oc (hav′ọk), *n.* [AF. *havok*, OF. *havot*, a word used esp. in the phrase *crier havot*, 'cry havoc,' give the call for pillaging; prob. from Teut.] Orig., a word used as the signal for pillage in warfare (as, "Cæsar's spirit . . . Shall . . . Cry '*Havoc*,' and let slip the dogs of war": Shakspere's "Julius Cæsar," iii. 1. 273); hence, devastation; ruinous damage.—**hav′oc,** *v.*; *-ocked, -ocking.* **I.** *tr.* To work havoc upon. **II.** *intr.* To work havoc.—**hav′ock-er,** *n.*

Havoc. A U. S. attack bomber and night fighter (Douglas).

haw[1] (hâ), *n.* [AS. *haga*.] The fruit of the hawthorn, *Cratægus oxyacantha*, or of other species of the same genus; hence, any of various shrubs or small trees of this genus, as *C. coccinea* ('scarlet haw'), of North America; also, any of certain other shrubs or trees, as *Viburnum prunifolium* (see *black-haw*).

haw[2] (hâ), *n.* [Origin uncertain.] The nictitating membrane of a horse, dog, etc.: formerly so called only when inflamed and then regarded as an excrescence.

haw[3] (hâ), *interj.* A word of command to horses, etc., usually directing them to turn to the left. Cf. *gee*[1].—**haw**[3], *v. i.* or *t.* To turn to the left.

haw[4] (hâ). **I.** *interj.* An unmeaning utterance marking hesitation in speech. **II.** *n.* The utterance 'haw.'—**haw**[4], *v. i.* To use the utterance 'haw,' as in hesitating speech.

Ha-wai-ian (hä-wī′yạn). **I.** *a.* Pertaining to Hawaii, the largest of the Hawaiian Islands, in the Pacific, or to the whole group. **II.** *n.* A native or inhabitant of Hawaii or the Hawaiian Islands; also, the Hawaiian language.

Hawfinch.

haw-finch (hâ′finch), *n.* [See *haw*[1].] A European grosbeak, *Coccothraustes vulgaris.*

haw=haw (hâ′hâ′). [Cf. *ha*.] **I.** *interj.* A word representing the sound of a loud, boisterous laugh. **II.** *n.* A loud, boisterous laugh; a guffaw.—**haw′=haw′,** *v. i.* To laugh loudly and boisterously; guffaw.

Cooper's Hawk (*Accipiter cooperi*).

hawk[1] (hâk), *n.* [AS. *hafoc* = D. *havik* = G. *habicht* = Icel. *haukr*, hawk; perhaps from the root of E. *heave*.] Any of various diurnal birds of prey of the family *Falconidæ*, as the falcons, buzzards, kites, harriers, etc. (but not the eagles and vultures); esp., any of the short-winged birds of the genera *Accipiter* and *Astur*, as the European sparrow-hawk and the goshawks; also, any of certain other birds, as the goatsucker, *Caprimulgus europæus* (see *night-hawk*); fig., a person who preys on others, as a sharper.—**to know a hawk from a hand=saw.** See under *hand-saw*.—**hawk**[1], *v. i.* To hunt with hawks trained to pursue game; also, to fly, or hunt on the wing, like a hawk.

hawk[2] (hâk), *v. i.* or *t.* [Appar. < *hawker*[2].] To carry about or offer (wares) for sale in the manner of a hawker; peddle.

hawk[3] (hâk), *v.* [Imit.] **I.** *intr.* To make an effort to raise phlegm from the throat; clear the throat noisily. **II.** *tr.* To raise (phlegm, etc.) from the throat by hawking.—**hawk**[3], *n.* A noisy effort to clear the throat.

hawk[4] (hâk), *n.* [Origin uncertain.] A small board with a handle underneath, used by plasterers to hold mortar.

hawk-bill (hâk′bil), *n.* A sea-turtle, *Chelone imbricata*, having a mouth shaped like the bill of a hawk, and yielding tortoise-shell.—**hawk′=billed,** *a.* Having a mouth like a hawk's bill or beak.

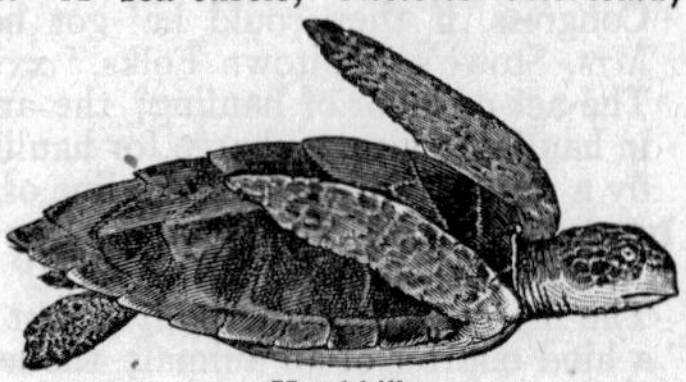

Hawkbill.

hawk-er[1] (hâ′kėr), *n.* One who hawks; a falconer.

hawk-er[2] (hâ′kėr), *n.* [Cf. MLG. *hoker*, G. *höker*, D. *heuker*, retail dealer, also E. *huckster*.] One who offers goods for sale through the streets or country districts; a peddler.

hawk=eyed (hâk′īd), *a.* Having keen eyes, like those of a hawk.

hawk-ing (hâ′king), *n.* The practice or sport of hunting with trained hawks; falconry.

hawk-ish (hâ′kish), *a.* Resembling, characteristic of, or suggesting a hawk.

hawk=moth (hâk′môth), *n.* A sphinx-moth: named from its flight, which resembles the hovering of a hawk.

hawk=nose (hâk′nōz), *n.* A nose curved like the beak of a hawk.—**hawk′=nosed,** *a.*

hawk=par-rot (hâk′par″ọt), *n.* A South American short-tailed parrot, *Deroptyus accipitrinus* (or *coronatus*), with a large erectile nuchal crest.

Hawk-parrot.

hawk's=beard (hâks′bērd), *n.* Any of the herbs constituting the cichoriaceous genus *Crepis*, having yellow or orange flowers and a copious white pappus.

hawk's=bill (hâks′bil), *n.* Same as *hawkbill*.

hawk's=eye (hâks′ī), *n.* A dark-blue chatoyant stone formed like tiger's-eye by the alteration of crocidolite: used for ornamental purposes.

Hawk-shaw (hâk′shâ), *n.* [From *Hawkshaw*, a detective in Tom Taylor's play, "The Ticket-of-Leave Man" (1863).] [Also *l. c.*] A detective.

hawk-weed (hâk′wēd), *n.* Any of the herbs with yellow, orange, or red flowers, constituting the cichoriaceous genus *Hieracium*; also, any of various related plants.

hawse[1] (hâs), *n.* See *hause*.

hawse[2] (hâz), *n.* [ME. *halse*, prob. from Scand.: cf. Icel. *hāls*, part of ship's bow, front sheet of sail, orig. neck, = E. *hause*.] The part of a ship's bow having holes for the cables to pass through; hence, a hawse-hole; also, the space between a ship at anchor and her anchors; also, the situation of a ship's cables when she is moored with both bow anchors.—**hawse′=hole,** *n.* A hole in the bow of a ship, through which a cable is passed.

haw-ser (hâ′zėr), *n.* [ME. *haucer*, hawser, < OF. *haucier* (F. *hausser*), raise, < L. *altus*, high.] *Naut.*, a small cable or large rope used in warping, mooring, towing, etc.—**haw′ser=laid,** *a.* Plain-laid; sometimes, cable-laid.

haw-thorn (hâ′thôrn), *n.* [AS. *hagathorn*: cf. *haw*[1].] A malaceous thorny shrub or small tree, *Cratægus oxyacantha*, with white or pink flowers and red berries, native in the Old World, but introduced in the U. S., and used in hedges; also, any species of *Cratægus*.—**hawthorn pattern,** a decorative pattern on Chinese and hence other porcelain, consisting of a branching, scattered, or clustered arrangement of white flowers (in Chinese use, plum-blossoms) on a ground of blue or some other color. See cut below.

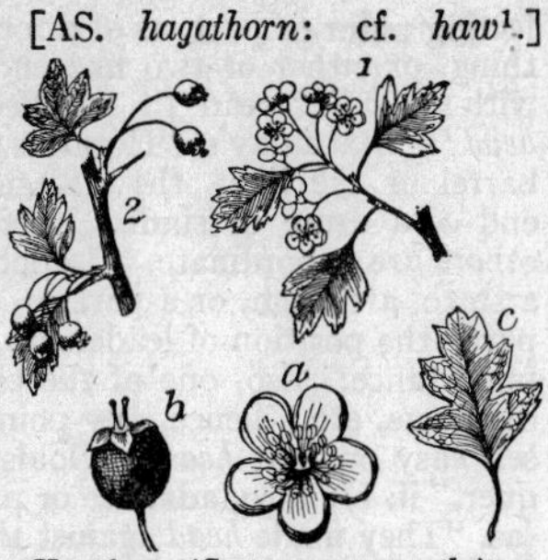

Hawthorn (*Cratægus oxyacantha*). — 1, 2, branches with flowers and fruit; *a*, *b*, flower and fruit on larger scale; *c*, leaf.

hay[1] (hā), *n.* [AS. *hege*, akin to *hecg*, E. *hedge*.] A hedge; a fence; also, an inclosed space; an inclosure; a park. [Archaic or prov. Eng.]

hay[2] (hā), *n.* [OF. *haye*, kind of dance.] A kind of old country-dance with winding movements.

hay[3]† (hā). [It. *hai*, 'thou hast (it).'] In *fencing*: **I.** *interj.* An exclamation on hitting an opponent. **II.** *n.* A hit, or home thrust. See Shakspere's "Romeo and Juliet," ii. 4. 27.

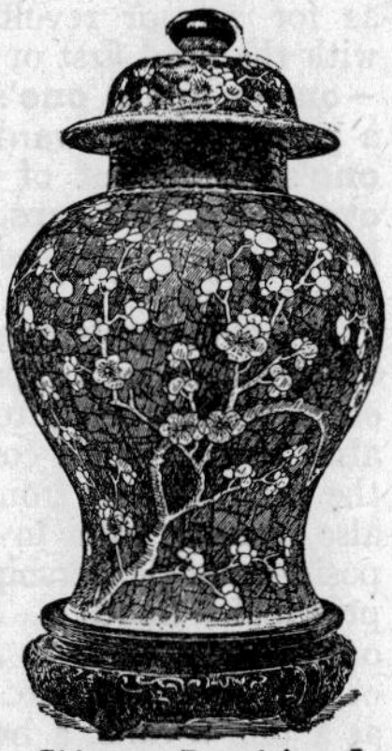
Chinese Porcelain Jar with Hawthorn Pattern Decoration.— Pennsylvania Museum, Philadelphia.

hay[4] (hā), *n.* [AS. *hīeg* = D. *hooi* = G. *heu* = Icel. *hey* = Goth. *hawi*, hay; from the root of E. *hew*.] Grass mowed or fit or intended for mowing; esp., grass cut and dried for use as fodder.—**hay**[4], *v.* **I.** *tr.* To furnish (horses, etc.) with hay; put (land) under hay; also, to convert (grass) into hay. **II.** *intr.* To cut and dry or cure grass for use as fodder.

hay[5] (hā), *interj.* See *hey*.

hay-cock (hā′kok), *n.* A small conical pile of hay thrown up in a hay-field, as while it is being cured or is awaiting removal to a barn.

hay=fe-ver (hā′fē′vėr), *n.* A catarrhal affection of the mucous membranes of the eyes and respiratory tract, attacking susceptible persons (usually) during the summer, and due to the action of the pollen of certain plants.

hay=field (hā′fēld), *n.* A field in which grass is grown for making into hay, or a field in which grass is being cut for hay: as, "From the sun-burnt *hay-field* homeward creeps The loaded wain" (Cowper's "Task," i. 295).

hay-ing (hā′ing), *n.* The act or process of making hay.

hay=loft (hā′lôft), *n.* A loft in a stable or barn, for the storage of hay.

hay-mak-er (hā′mā″kėr), *n.* One who makes hay; esp., one who tosses and spreads hay to dry after it is mowed; also, an apparatus for drying and curing hay; also, in *pugilism*, a knock-out blow.—**hay′mak″ing,** *n.*

hay=mar-ket (hā′mär″ket), *n.* A place for the sale of hay.

hay-mow (hā′mou), *n.* A mow or mass of hay stored in a barn; the place in a barn where hay is stored; also, a rick or stack of hay.

hay=rack (hā′rak), *n.* A rack for holding hay for feeding horses or cattle; also, a rack or framework mounted on a wagon, for use in carrying hay, straw, etc.; also, the wagon and rack together.

hay=rake (hā′rāk), *n.* A rake for raking hay; an apparatus for this purpose, drawn by a horse or horses.

hay-rick (hā′rik), *n.* A haystack.

hay=seed (hā′sēd), *n.* Grass-seed, esp. that shaken out of hay; also, small bits of the chaff, etc., of hay; also, a countryman or rustic (slang, U. S.).

hay-stack (hā′stak), *n.* A stack or large pile of hay with a conical or ridged top, built up in the open air for preservation, and sometimes thatched or covered with a cap.

hay=ted-der (hā′ted″ėr), *n.* [See *ted*.] A machine for spreading newly mown hay so as to expose it to the sun and air.

Hay-tedder.

Hay-ti-an (hā′ti-an), *a.* and *n.* See *Haitian*.

hay-ward (hā′wârd), *n.* [See *hay*[1] and *ward*.] An officer having charge of hedges and fences, esp. to keep cattle from breaking through, and to impound estrays; also, the herdsman of cattle feeding on a common.

hay-wire (hā′wīr). **I.** *n.* Wire used to bind bales of hay. **II.** *adv.* and *a.* [Said to refer orig. to the use of such wire for repairs about ranches, etc.] In an ill-repaired or ill-kept condition; in disorder; awry; wrong; out of order; out of control; wild or crazy: as, to be all *haywire*; to go *haywire*. [Slang.]

haz-ard (haz′ạrd), *n.* [OF. *hasard*, *hasart* (F. *hasard*); prob. from Ar.] A game played with two dice in which the caster, having called out the 'main' (any number from 5 to 9, inclusive), throws a 'nick' (the 'main' or some other winning number), or 'crabs' (a losing number), or his 'chance,' a number which neither wins nor loses but entitles the caster to continue throwing until he throws either his 'chance' again, now the winning number, or the 'main,' now the losing number; hence, the uncertainty of the result in throwing a die; in general, chance, or a chance; also, exposure to danger or harm; risk; a risk or peril (as, at all *hazards*, at all risks, or in spite of every peril); also, something risked or staked; in *billiards*, a stroke by which the player pockets the object-ball ('winning hazard') or his own ball after contact with another ball ('losing hazard'); in *court-tennis*, any of certain openings in the walls of the court, the striking of a ball into which scores the striker a point; also, that side of the court into which the ball is served ('hazard side'); in *golf*, a bunker, a road, a bush, water, or the like on the course.—**haz′ard,** *v. t.* [F. *hasarder*.] To put to the risk of being lost, as in a game of chance; stake; expose to hazard or risk; also, to take or run the risk of (a misfortune, penalty, etc.: as, to *hazard* the loss of one's reputation); also, to venture upon (anything of doubtful issue); venture to offer (a statement, conjecture, etc.).—**haz′ard-a-ble,** *a.* That may be hazarded; also, hazardous†.—**haz′ard-er,** *n.*—**haz′ard-ous,** *a.* Dependent on hazard or chance (as, a *hazardous* contract); also, full of hazard or risk; perilous; risky; also, inclined to run risks†.—**haz′ard-ous-ly,** *adv.*—**haz′ard-ous-ness,** *n.*

haze[1] (hāz), *n.* [Origin obscure.] An aggregation of minute suspended particles of vapor, dust, etc., near the surface of the earth, causing an appearance of thin mist in the atmosphere; hence, something appearing like a mist or obscuring the view; fig., obscurity or vagueness, as of mind.—**haze**[1], *v.*; *hazed*, *hazing*. **I.** *intr.* To drizzle; be foggy. [Prov. Eng.] **II.** *tr.* To obscure with haze.

haze[2] (hāz), *v. t.*; *hazed*, *hazing*. [Cf. OF. *haser*, irritate, annoy.] To harass with unnecessary or disagreeable tasks (chiefly *naut.*); hence, to subject to rough or severe treatment, as because of unpopularity; often, to subject to abusive or ridiculous tricks, as freshmen in a college or newcomers generally.

ha-zel (hā′zl). [AS. *hæsel* = G. *hasel* = Icel. *hasl*, hazel.] **I.** *n.* Any of the shrubs or small trees of the betulaceous genus *Corylus*, which bear edible nuts, as *C. abellana* of Europe or *C. americana* and *C. rostrata* of America (see cut on following page); the wood of such a shrub or tree; a stick of this wood; also, the hazelnut; hence, the light-brown color of the hazelnut; also, any of certain other shrubs or trees (as *Pomaderris apetala*, a rhamnaceous shrub of Australia, etc.), or their wood. **II.** *a.* Of or pertaining to the hazel; made of the wood of the hazel; also, of the color hazel (as, "her . . . eye of *hazel* hue": Scott's "Rokeby," iv. 5).—**ha′zel-ly,** *a.* Abounding in hazels; also, of a hazel color.—**ha′zel-nut,** *n.* The nut of the hazel.

haz-er (hā′zėr), *n.* One who hazes, as on a ship or in a college, school, or the like.

haz-i-ly (hā′zi-li), *adv.* In a hazy manner.—**haz′i-ness,** *n.*

haz-ing (hā′zing), *n.* The act or practice of one who hazes.

haz-y (hā′zi), *a.*; compar. *hazier,* superl. *haziest.* Characterized by the presence of haze (as, "*hazy* weather": Defoe's "Robinson Crusoe," i. 10); misty; fig., lacking distinctness, as of perception; vague, indistinct, or confused.

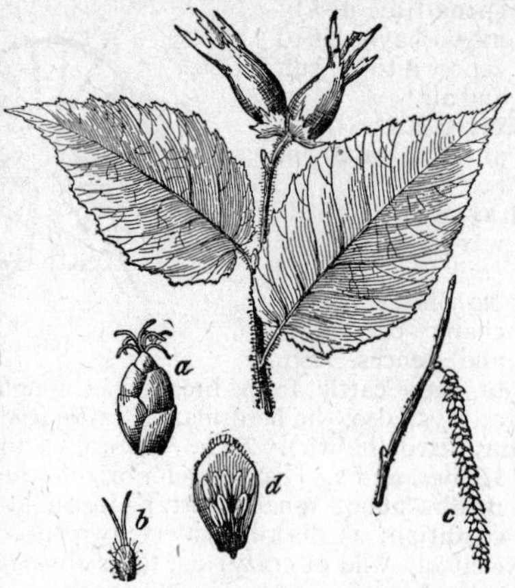

Hazel (*Corylus americana*).—*a,* female catkin; *b,* female flower; *c,* male catkin; *d,* male flower.

he (hē), *pron.*; nom. *he,* poss. *his,* obj. *him,* pl. nom. *they,* poss. *their* or *theirs,* obj. *them.* [AS. *hē* (gen. *his,* dat. *him,* acc. *hine*) = OS. *he, hi,* = OFries. *hi,* he: cf. *her, it, hence, here,* and *hither.*] A personal pronoun of the third person, being the nominative singular masculine, and standing (1) for the male being in question or last mentioned, or (2) for 'the man or male' or 'any one' (as, *he* who hesitates is lost).—**he,** *n.*; pl. *hes* (hēz). A man or any male person; a male, esp. of an animal (often used attributively or in composition: as, a *he*-goat).

head (hed), *n.* [AS. *hēafod* = D. *hoofd* = G. *haupt* = Icel. *höfudh* = Goth. *haubith,* head.] The upper part of the human body, joined to the trunk by the neck; the corresponding part of an animal's body; also, this part of the human body considered as the seat of thought, memory, etc. (often in contrast to the *heart* as the seat of the emotions); hence, mind or understanding (as, to have a good *head;* out of one's *head,* see phrase below); a mental aptitude (for something: as, to have a *head* for mathematics); presence of mind, or self-possession (as, to keep or lose one's *head*); also, the obverse of a coin, as bearing a head or other principal figure (opposed to the *tail,* or reverse: as, *head* or tail, or *heads* or tails, said in tossing up a coin to decide a choice or chance; to be unable to make *head* or tail of a thing, to be unable to gain any definite idea from it); also, the hair covering the head (as, "I curl'd and comb'd his comely *head*": Tennyson's "Sisters"); the antlers of a deer; also, a person considered with reference to his mind, disposition, attributes, etc. (as, wise *heads;* crowned *heads*); a person or animal considered merely as one of a number (often with pl. *head:* as, ten *head* of cattle); an aggregation or collection of animals, esp. of game (as, a *head* of pheasants); also, something resembling a head in form or position (as, the *head* of a pin or of a cane); a rounded or compact part of a plant, usually at the top of the stem, as of leaves (as in the cabbage or lettuce), leafstalks (as in the celery), flower-buds (as in the cauliflower), sessile florets (see *flower-head*), etc.; froth or foam on beer, etc.; cream on milk; also, that part of anything which forms or is regarded as forming the top, summit, or upper end (as, the *head* of a mast or a staircase, or of a lake); the end of a bed, grave, etc., toward which the head is placed; the top of a page or piece of writing or printing; something, as a title, written at the top of a page, section, etc.; the upper edge (or corner) of a sail; the maturated part of an abscess, boil, etc.; the source of a river or stream; also, a body of water at a height above a particular level, or its height, the force of its fall, or its pressure; hence, the pressure of a confined body of steam, etc., per unit of area; also, the foremost part or end of anything; the front, as of a procession; the outer or projecting end of a fortification, etc.; the fore part of a ship, etc. (as, a ship which is by, or down by, the *head,* that is, so loaded as to draw more water forward than aft); a projecting point of a coast, esp. when high, as a cape, headland, or promontory; any projecting point or part, as of a rock; an end or extremity of a thing, or either of two like ends (as, "As that great host, with measured tread . . . Rolled slowly towards the bridge's *head*": Macaulay's "Horatius," xxxv.); either end of a barrel or the like; the stretched membrane covering the end of a drum or similar instrument; also, one to whom others are subordinate, a leader, or a chief (as, the *head* of a state, a church, or a party); the chief or most important part; the position of leadership, chief command, or greatest importance; also, one of the chief points or divisions of a discourse, etc.; hence, any point or topic (as, "Make yourself easy on that *head*": Goldsmith's "She Stoops to Conquer," ii. 1); also, advance or progress, as against resistance (as, "They made *head* against the wind as they best could": Dickens's "Barnaby Rudge," xxxiv.); also, strength or force gradually attained (as, the movement gathered *head*); also, culmination or crisis (as, to bring matters to a *head*); issue or result; conclusion; also, a body or force gathered, as for war or revolt†.—**head first** or **head foremost,** with the head first or foremost; fig., precipitately; hastily.—**on** (or **upon**) **one's head,** falling or resting upon one as a punishment, reward, responsibility, or the like.—**out of one's head,** out of one's mind; demented; delirious.—**over head and ears,** completely immersed (as, "The poor lad plumped *over head and ears* into the water": Fielding's "Tom Jones," iv. 3); fig., deeply involved, as in debt or in love.—**over one's head,** passing over or ignoring one having a prior claim or a superior position (as, to promote a junior *over a senior's head;* to go *over a superior's head* in a matter); also, beyond one's comprehension.—**head,** *a.* Situated at the head, top, or front (as, the *head* division of a parade); also, coming from in front, as a wind; also, being in the position of leadership, command, or superiority; chief; principal.—**head,** *v.* **I.** *tr.* To behead or decapitate (now only animals: as, to *head* a fish); lop off the top branches of, or poll (a tree, etc.); also, to furnish or fit with a head, as a pin, a cane, a barrel, etc.; start (a page, a list, etc.) with something as a head or beginning; also, to form or constitute the head or top of (something); stand at the head of (a page, a list, etc.); also, to collect (water) so as to form a head; also, to go at the head of or in front of; lead; precede; hence, to outdo or excel; also, to be the head or chief of (as, to *head* a company, a party, etc.); also, to turn the head or front of in a specified direction; direct the course of as specified (as, to *head* one's boat for the shore); also, to advance directly against, or in opposition to the course of (as, to *head* the wind); get in front of so as to cause to turn back or aside (often with *off*); also, to go round the head of (a stream, etc.). **II.** *intr.* To form a head; come to a head; also, to have the head or source where specified, as a river or stream; rise; also, to have the head or front directed as specified; move forward toward a point or in a direction specified.

-head. [ME. *-hede, -hed,* < *hede,* rank, condition, character, akin to AS. *hād,* whence E. *-hood.*] A suffix of nouns denoting state, condition, character, etc., as in *maidenhead, godhead, lowlihead, drowsihead,* and other words, now mostly archaic or obsolete, many being superseded by forms in *-hood.*

head-ache (hed′āk), *n.* [AS. *hēafodece.*] A pain in the cranial part of the head.—**head′ach″y** (-ā″ki), *a.* Suffering from headache; inclined or subject to headache; also, attended with or causing headache.

head=band (hed′band), *n.* A band worn around the head; a fillet; in *printing,* a band of decoration at the head of a chapter or at the top of a page in a book; in *bookbinding,* an ornamental band, as of silk, attached at the head and tail of the inner back of a bound book.

head-board (hed′bōrd), *n.* A board or boarding which forms, or is placed at, the head of anything, as of a bed or a grave.

head-bor-ough (hed′bur″ō), *n.* [ME. *heed borow:* see *borrow.*] In England, orig., the head of a frank-pledge or tithing; later, a parish officer having the functions of a petty constable; also, a similar official elsewhere.

head-cheese (hed′chēz), *n.* A preparation of parts of the head and feet of hogs cut up, cooked, and seasoned, and forming when cold a jellied mass or loaf.

head=dress (hed′dres), *n.* A covering or decoration for the head; also, an ornamental arrangement of the hair.

head-ed (hed′ed), *a.* Having a head: as, long-*headed*; gray-*headed*.

Head-dress of Isabeau of Bavaria, Queen of France; about 1395.

head-er (hed′ėr), *n.* One who or that which removes the head from something; also, one who or an apparatus which puts a head on something; also, one who or that which stands at the head of something; one who leads a party, etc.; also, a plunge or dive head foremost, as into water, or, involuntarily, from a horse or a bicycle (colloq.); in *building*, a brick or stone laid with its length across the thickness of a wall; also, a timber or beam in the framing about an opening in a floor or roof, placed so as to fit between two long beams and support the ends of short ones.

head-ful (hed′fůl), *n.* As much as the head can hold.

head=gate (hed′gāt), *n.* The up-stream gate of a canal-lock; also, a flood-gate of a race, sluice, or the like.

head=gear (hed′gēr), *n.* Any covering for the head; also, the parts of a harness about the animal's head.

head=hunt-er (hed′hun″tėr), *n.* One given to the practice of seeking human heads, as for trophies, characteristic of various savage tribes, esp. in Borneo and the Philippines. —**head′=hunt″ing,** *n.* and *a.*

head-i-ly (hed′i-li), *adv.* In a heady manner; headlong; precipitately; rashly.—**head′i-ness,** *n.*

head-ing (hed′ing), *n.* The act of one who or that which heads; also, something that serves as a head, top, or front; esp., a title or caption of a page, chapter, etc.; also, a section of a subject of discourse; a topic; also, a horizontal passage in the earth, as for an intended tunnel, for working a mine, for ventilation or drainage, etc.; a drift.

head=ker-chief (hed′kėr″chif), *n.* A kerchief worn on the head.

head-land (hed′land), *n.* A strip of unplowed land at the ends of furrows or near a fence or border; also, a cape or promontory (as, "an high *headland* thrust far into the sea": Spenser's "Colin Clout," 281).

head-less (hed′les), *a.* [AS. *hēafodlēas.*] Having no head; deprived of the head; also, destitute of a leader or chief; also, wanting in brains; foolish; stupid; in *aëronautics*, of an aëroplane, having no front elevator.

head-light (hed′līt), *n.* A light carried on the front of a locomotive, electric car, etc.

head=line (hed′līn), *n.* The line at the top of a page, containing the title, pagination, etc.; also, a title line over an article, etc., as in a newspaper.—**head′=line,** *v. t.*; *-lined, -lining.* To furnish with a head-line.—**head′=lin″er** (-lī″nėr), *n.* One who writes head-lines, as for a newspaper; also, one whose name is displayed at the head of a bill, or in larger letters than the rest, as in a theatrical announcement (colloq.).

head-long (hed′lông). **I.** *adv.* Head foremost (as, to fall or plunge *headlong* from a height); also, with uncontrolled or precipitate onward course (lit. or fig.: as, to rush *headlong* to destruction); precipitately; hurriedly and rashly. **II.** *a.* Done or going with the head foremost (as, a *headlong* plunge or dive; a *headlong* diver); also, descending steeply, or precipitous, as a hill; also, done or proceeding with, or characterized by, uncontrolled speed or rash impetuosity (as, a *headlong* rush, course, or flight; a *headlong* rider; *headlong* haste or folly); violently or rashly impetuous; precipitate; rash.—**head′long-ness,** *n.*

head=man (hed′man′), **head-man** (hed′man or -mạn), *n.*; pl. *-men.* [AS. *hēafodman.*] A chief man; a chief or leader: often written as two words.

head=mon-ey (hed′mun″i), *n.* A tax of so much per head or person; also, a reward paid for each person captured or brought in; also, a reward for the production of the head of an outlaw or enemy.

head-most (hed′mōst), *a. superl.* Most advanced; most forward; foremost.

head=on (hed′on′), *a.* With the head foremost: said esp. of a collision between trains, ships, etc., meeting head to head.

head=phone (hed′fōn), *n.* A head-set.

head=piece (hed′pēs), *n.* A piece of armor for the head; a helmet; also, any covering for the head, as a cap; also, the head, esp. as the seat of the intellect; also, the top piece or part of any of various things; in *printing*, a decorative piece at the head of a page, chapter, etc.

head-quar-ters (hed′kwâr′tėrz), *n. pl.* or *sing.* The quarters or residence of a military or other chief; the place from which orders are issued; any center of operations (as, "Harrowgate . . . is our *headquarters*, from whence we shall make some excursions": Smollett's "Humphry Clinker," June 23).

head-race (hed′rās), *n.* The race, flume, or channel which leads water to a water-wheel or the like. Cf. *tailrace.*

head-right (hed′rīt), *n.* The inheritable right to a tract of the public land of the State, formerly granted by Texas, Georgia, and other States, upon certain conditions, to heads of families, resident or immigrant; also, a tract of land so granted.—**head′right,** *v. t.* To grant or acquire (land) by headright.

head-room (hed′röm), *n.* Clear space in height, as in a doorway or under an arch; headway.

head=set (hed′set), *n.* A device, as in radio outfits, consisting of two telephone receivers with attachments for holding them over the ears, for listening to messages, etc.

head-ship (hed′ship), *n.* The position of head or chief; chief authority; leadership; supremacy.

heads-man (hedz′mạn), *n.*; pl. *-men.* An executioner who beheads condemned persons.

head-spring (hed′spring), *n.* The fountainhead or source of a stream; fig., the source of anything.

head=stall (hed′stâl), *n.* That part of a bridle or halter which encompasses the head.

head=stock (hed′stok), *n.* The part of a machine containing the revolving or working members; in a lathe, the frame supporting the live spindle.

head-stone (hed′stōn), *n.* The principal stone in a foundation; also, a stone set at the head of a grave.

head-strong (hed′strông), *a.* Bent on having one's own way; wilful; obstinate; also, marked by or proceeding from wilfulness or obstinacy (as, "Thus I'll curb her mad and *headstrong* humour": Shakspere's "Taming of the Shrew," iv. 1. 212).—**head′strong-ness,** *n.*

head=tire (hed′tīr), *n.* Attire for the head; a head-dress. [Archaic.]

head=tone (hed′tōn), *n.* In *singing*, a tone so produced as to bring the cavities of the nose and head into sympathetic vibration.

head=voice (hed′vois), *n.* In *singing*, that method of using the voice, or that portion of the singer's compass or register, which tends to produce head-tones.

head-ward (hed′wạrd), *adv.* and *a.* Toward the head.—**head′wards,** *adv.*

head=wa-ter (hed′wâ″tėr), *n.* One of the upper tributaries of a river: usually in *pl.* (as, the *head-waters* of the Mississippi).

head-way (hed′wā), *n.* Motion forward or ahead; advance; progress in general; rate of progress; also, the interval between two trains, etc., traveling in the same direction over the same route; also, clear space in height, as in a doorway or under an arch; headroom.

head=word (hed′wėrd′), *n.* A word serving as a heading or title, as of a paragraph, article, etc.

head=work (hed′wėrk), *n.* Mental labor: as, "The worthy pedagogue . . . was thought, by all who understood nothing of the labor of *headwork*, to have a wonderfully easy life of it" (Irving's "Sketch-Book," Sleepy Hollow).—**head′=work″er,** *n.*

head-y (hed′i), *a.*; compar. *headier*, superl. *headiest.* Headlong; precipitate; rash; rashly impetuous (as, "this *heady*, imaginative young enthusiast": H. G. Wells's "Outline of History," xxxv. § 5); also, apt to affect the head; intoxicating; also, intelligent (colloq.).

heal (hēl), *v.* [AS. *hǣlan*, < *hāl*, hale, whole: see *whole.*] **I.** *tr.* To make whole or sound; restore to health; free from ailment; hence, to free from anything evil or distressing; cleanse or purify; comfort or strengthen; also, to overcome by remedial means; cure, as a disease or wound; hence, to remedy or amend (any evil or distressing condition). **II.** *intr.* To effect a cure (as, "I kill, and I make alive; I wound, and I *heal*": Deut. xxxii. 39); also, to become whole or sound; get well.—**heal,** *n.* [AS. *hǣlu*, *hǣl*, < *hāl.*] Health; welfare. [Obs. or archaic.]—**heal'a-ble,** *a.* That may be healed.—**heal'=all,** *n.* A cure-all; a panacea; also, any of various plants reputed to have healing properties.

heald (hēld), *n.* [AS. *hefeld.*] Same as *heddle.*

heal-er (hē'lėr), *n.* One who or that which heals; specif., one who practises healing by Christian Science or some form of faith-cure.—**heal'ing,** *p. a.* That heals; curing; curative; salutary; also, growing sound; getting well.—**heal'ing-ly,** *adv.*

heal-some (hēl'sum), *a.* [See *heal, n.*] Wholesome. [Sc.]

health (helth), *n.* [AS. *hǣlth*, < *hāl*, hale, whole: see *whole.*] Soundness of body; freedom from disease or ailment; also, the general condition of the body with reference to soundness and vigor (as, good *health*; ill *health*); also, spiritual, moral, or mental soundness; more generally, well-being or welfare (obs. or archaic: as, "On his choice depends The safety and *health* of this whole state," Shakspere's "Hamlet," i. 3. 21); also, a polite or complimentary wish for a person's health; a toast drunk in a person's honor.—**health'ful,** *a.* Full of health, or healthy, as a person, the body or mind, etc.; also (now commonly), conducive to health, wholesome, or salutary, as air, diet, exercise, etc.—**health'ful-ly,** *adv.* —**health'ful-ness,** *n.*—**health'y,** *a.*; compar. *healthier*, superl. *healthiest.* Possessing or enjoying health; hale; also, pertaining to or characteristic of health (as, a *healthy* state or appearance); also, conducive to health, or healthful.—**health'i-ly,** *adv.*—**health'i-ness,** *n.*

heap (hēp), *n.* [AS. *hēap*, heap, multitude, troop, = D. *hoop* = MLG. *hōp* = OHG. *houf* (G. *haufe*).] An assemblage of things lying one on another; a raised mass of things or matter; a pile; hence, a great mass, quantity, or number (now colloq.); also, a troop, multitude, or crowd (now colloq.).—**heap,** *v.* [AS. *hēapian.*] **I.** *tr.* To gather, put, or cast in a heap (often with *up, on, together*, etc.); pile; fig., to accumulate or amass (often with *up*: as, to *heap* up riches); also, to cast or bestow in great quantity (as, to *heap* blessings or reproaches upon a person); also, to fill (a vessel, measure, etc.) with contents rising above the brim; load or cover (a surface, ground, etc.) with a heap or heaps of something; fig., to load or supply abundantly with something (as, to *heap* a person with benefits). **II.** *intr.* To become heaped or piled, as sand, snow, etc.; rise in a heap or heaps.—**heap'er,** *n.*—**heap'y,** *a.* Forming a heap or heaps: as, "with wither'd foliage strew'd, a *heapy* store" (Pope's tr. Homer's "Odyssey," xix.).

hear (hēr), *v.*; *heard* (hėrd), *hearing.* [AS. *hīeran, hēran*, = D. *hooren* = G. *hören* = Icel. *heyra* = Goth. *hausjan*, hear: cf. *hark.*] **I.** *tr.* To perceive by the ear (as, to *hear* sounds, voices, etc.); perceive the sound made by (as, to *hear* a person moving or speaking; to *hear* the wind, waves, birds, bells, etc.); also, to listen to (as, to refuse to *hear* a person or his explanations; "*Hear* me to the close," Tennyson's "Lover's Tale," iv. 241); give a formal, official, or judicial hearing to, as a sovereign, a teacher, an assembly, or a judge does; be among the audience at or of (as, to *hear* a sermon or the preacher; to *hear* an opera); also, to listen to with favor, assent, or compliance (as, "O thou that *hearest* prayer, unto thee shall all flesh come": Ps. lxv. 2); also, to learn by the ear or by being told (as, to *hear* news or facts; to *hear* that prices are falling); be informed of. **II.** *intr.* To have perception of sound by the ear; also, to listen or harken (often used in the imperative 'hear, hear!' in applauding a speaker, as in a parliamentary assembly); also, to listen with favor or assent (in prov. or colloq. use sometimes followed by *to*: as, he would not *hear* to any such plan); also, to receive news or information by the ear or otherwise (as, to *hear* from a friend by telephone, telegraph, or letter; to *hear* of an accident).—**hear'a-ble,** *a.* That may be heard; audible.—**hear'er,** *n.*—**hear'ing,** *n.* The act of perceiving sound; the faculty or sense by which sound is perceived; also, a listening, as to a speaker or to one seeking to be heard (as, to grant a person a *hearing*; to gain a *hearing*); a formal or official listening or an audience given; esp., a judicial listening to testimony and arguments, as in a suit at law; also, range or distance within which one may hear sound or be heard by others (as, to be within *hearing* of a conversation; to talk freely in the *hearing* of others; to pass out of *hearing*); earshot; also, something heard, as a piece of news (now chiefly prov.); a scolding (Sc.).

heark-en (här'kn), etc. See *harken*, etc.

hear-say (hēr'sā). **I.** *n.* Report heard, common talk, or gossip (as, all this is mere *hearsay*); sometimes, a report or rumor (as, "Sometimes a rumor, a *hearsay* . . . Came with its airy hand to point and beckon her forward": Longfellow's "Evangeline," ii. 1); also, hearsay evidence. **II.** *a.* Of the nature of hearsay; pertaining to or depending on hearsay.—**hearsay evidence,** evidence at second hand; testimony whose relevancy does not consist in what the witness giving it himself perceived, but in what he derived by information from another person, the credibility of which, therefore, cannot be estimated from the credit to be given to the witness, but depends on the veracity or competency of the other person.

hearse (hėrs), *n.* [OF. *herce* (F. *herse*), harrow, frame for holding candles in church, < L. *hirpex, irpex*, large rake used as a harrow.] A triangular frame for holding candles, used at the service of Tenebræ in Holy Week; also, a framework (orig. for holding candles) formerly set over a bier or a tomb; hence, a bier, a coffin, or a tomb (archaic: as, "And daffadillies fill their cups with tears, To strew the laureat *herse* where Lycid lies," Milton's "Lycidas," 151); now, commonly, a funeral vehicle for conveying a dead person to the place of burial.—**hearse,** *v. t.*; *hearsed, hearsing.* To place on a bier or in a coffin or tomb (archaic: as, "Tell Why thy canonized bones, *hearsed* in death, Have burst their cerements," Shakspere's "Hamlet," i. 4. 47); also, to inclose as a tomb does, or entomb (archaic); also, to cover or surround with something funereal (archaic: as, "I only see . . . The hill-top *hearsed* with pines," Longfellow's "Hawthorne"); also, to convey in a hearse (vehicle), as to the place of burial.

heart (härt), *n.* [AS. *heorte* = D. *hart* = G. *herz* = Icel. *hjarta* = Goth. *hairtō*, heart; akin to L. *cor* (*cord-*), Gr. καρδία and κῆρ, heart.] A hollow muscular organ which by alternate contractions and dilatations (pulsations: see *heart-beat*) keeps the blood in circulation throughout the body, in man being conoidal in shape and lying obliquely in the chest, between the lungs, with the apex downward, forward, and to the left; this organ considered as the seat of life or vital powers, or of thought, feeling or emotion, etc. (as, "The whole head is sick, and the whole *heart* faint," Isa. i. 5; to die of a broken *heart*; to feel cut to the *heart*); hence, the mind or soul (as, beliefs or feelings deeply seated in the human *heart*; to be dissatisfied in one's *heart*; to speak from the *heart*); moral nature (as, to be pure in *heart*); disposition (as, to have a good or kind *heart*, or a cruel *heart*); will or inclination (as, a task after one's own *heart*); spirit, courage, or enthusiasm (as, his *heart* failed him at the prospect; to pluck up or take *heart*); conscience (as, his *heart* smote him); memory (as, to know a poem by *heart*); esp., the seat of the emotions and affections (often in contrast to the *head* as the seat of the intellect: as, to appeal to the *heart* rather than to the head; deeds that stir the *heart*; an affair of the *heart*, a love-affair); hence, one's affection or love (as, to win one's *heart*); feeling, sensibility, or capacity for sympathetic emotions (as, a man of *heart*; to have no *heart*); also, a person (esp. in expressions of praise or affection, often with *brave, true, noble, dear*, etc.); also, the breast or bosom (as, to clasp a person to one's *heart*); also, the stomach (now prov. Eng. and Sc.: cf. *heartburn*); also, the innermost or middle part of anything (as, in the *heart* of a wilderness; in the *heart* of winter); the core, or central portion or substance (as, the *heart* of a cabbage, or of lettuce or celery; the *heart* of a tree); also, the vital or essential part (as, this idea is the very *heart* of the matter); also, good (or other) condition for production, growth, etc., as of land or crops (as, to be in *heart*, or good *heart*, as good soil; to be in bad *heart*, as poor soil); also, a figure or an object with rounded sides meeting in an obtuse point at the bottom and curving inward to a cusp at the top; hence, a playing-card of a suit marked with such figures in red; *pl.* (construed as *sing.*), a kind of card-game in which the players try to avoid taking tricks containing hearts; also, *sing.*, a heart-cherry.—**at heart,** in one's heart, thoughts, or feelings; inwardly or secretly (as, to be disloyal *at heart*); also, in one's actual character or disposition, or in reality (as, to be good *at heart*).—**in one's heart of hearts,** in the depths of one's heart; in one's inmost thoughts or feelings.—**to break the heart of,** to crush with sorrow or grief; sometimes, to disappoint grievously in love.—**to lay to heart,** to take into the mind as something to be remembered; take to heart.—**to take to heart,** to take as a serious matter; think seriously about; be deeply affected by; grieve over.—**with all one's heart,** with all willingness or enthusiasm; heartily.—**heart,** *v.* **I.** *tr.* To hearten or encourage; also, to fix in the heart (as, "I hate the Moor: my cause is *hearted*": Shakspere's "Othello," i. 3. 373). [Obs. or archaic.] **II.** *intr.* To form a heart, core, or compact central portion, as cabbages or lettuce.

Heart.

heart-ache (härt'āk), *n.* Mental anguish; sorrow; grief.

heart=beat (härt'bēt), *n.* A pulsation of the heart, including one complete systole (contraction) and diastole (dilatation).

heart=block (härt'blok), *n.* In *pathol.*, a condition of the heart in which the ventricular pulsations are less frequent than the auricular, owing to some defect or condition which blocks the stimulus for contraction conveyed from auricle to ventricle by the muscular fibers connecting the auricular and ventricular portions of the heart.

heart-break (härt'brāk), *n.* Sorrow or grief that breaks the heart; crushing sorrow.—**heart'break"er,** *n.* One who or that which breaks the heart; also, a curl or love-lock (humorous).—**heart'break"ing,** *a.* Causing great sorrow or grief; extremely distressing.—**heart'break"ing-ly,** *adv.*—**heart'brok"en,** *a.* Broken-hearted; crushed with sorrow or grief.—**heart'brok"en-ly,** *adv.*—**heart'brok"en-ness,** *n.*

heart-burn (härt'bėrn), *n.* An uneasy, burning sensation in the stomach, often extending toward the esophagus; cardialgia; also, heartburning.—**heart'burn"ing,** *n.* Rankling discontent, esp. from envy or jealousy; a grudge.

heart=cher-ry (härt'cher"i), *n.* A heart-shaped kind of cherry with soft, sweet flesh.

heart=dis-ease (härt'di-zēz"), *n.* Any morbid condition of the heart, whether nervous or organic.

heart-ed (här'ted), *a.* Having a heart (as, hard-*hearted*); also, heart-shaped.

heart-en (här'tn), *v.* **I.** *tr.* To give heart or courage to; inspirit; cheer. **II.** *intr.* To take heart or courage; cheer up.—**heart'en-er,** *n.*

heart-felt (härt'felt), *a.* Deeply or sincerely felt, as joy, regret, etc.; characterized by or proceeding from deep or sincere feeling, as utterances; earnest; sincere.

heart=free (härt'frē'), *a.* Having the heart free from the influence of love; heart-whole.

heart-ful (härt'fůl), *a.* Hearty; cordial; earnest; sincere.—**heart'ful-ly,** *adv.*—**heart'ful-ness,** *n.*

hearth (härth), *n.* [AS. *heorth* = D. *haard* = G. *herd*, hearth.] That part of the floor of a room on which the fire is made or above which is a grate or the like for fire; the floor of a fireplace; a similar part in a furnace, stove, etc.; also, the fireside, or home (as, "sweet household talk, and phrases of the *hearth*": Tennyson's "Princess," ii. 294); in *metal.*, etc., the bottom of a reverberatory furnace, etc.; the lower part of a blast-furnace; a bloomery; the fireplace of a forge, etc.; in *soldering*, a brazier, chafing-dish, or box for charcoal.

heart=heav-y (härt'hev"i), *a.* Heavy-hearted; sad.

hearth=mon-ey (härth'mun"i), *n.* A tax upon hearths or chimneys; esp., an annual tax of two shillings on each hearth, imposed in England from 1662 to 1689. Also called *hearth-tax*.

hearth=pen-ny (härth'pen"i), *n.* A tax formerly paid by a householder to the papal see. See *Peter's pence*.

hearth=stone (härth'stōn), *n.* A stone forming a hearth; hence, the fireside; the home; also, a soft stone, or a preparation of powdered stone and clay, used to whiten or scour hearths, steps, floors, etc.

hearth=tax (härth'taks), *n.* Same as *hearth-money*.

heart-i-ly (här'ti-li), *adv.* In a hearty manner; earnestly or sincerely; cordially; zealously; thoroughly; with a hearty appetite.—**heart'i-ness,** *n.*

heart-less (härt'les), *a.* Without a heart; also, without heart or feeling, unfeeling, or cruel (as, a *heartless* coquette; *heartless* words); also, without spirit, courage, or enthusiasm (as, "a *heartless* mood": Wordsworth's "Prelude," ix. 515).—**heart'less-ly,** *adv.*—**heart'less-ness,** *n.*

heart=quake (härt'kwāk), *n.* Palpitation of the heart; also, a sudden tremor of emotion (as, "How a lip's mere tremble, Look's half hesitation . . . effect a *heartquake*": Browning's "Two Camels").

heart-rend-ing (härt'ren"ding), *a.* Causing acute mental anguish; grievously distressing.—**heart'rend"ing-ly,** *adv.*

heart's=ease, hearts-ease (härts'ēz), *n.* Peace of mind (now usually *heart's-ease* or as two words); also, the pansy, or some other plant of the genus *Viola*.

heart=shaped (härt'shāpt), *a.* Having the shape of a heart (esp. the figure so called); cordate.

heart=sick (härt'sik), *a.* Sick at heart; grievously depressed or unhappy; also, characterized by or showing grievous depression (as, a *heart-sick* condition or tone).—**heart'=sick"ness,** *n.*

heart-some (härt'sum), *a.* Giving heart, spirit, or cheer (as, "Overhead the *heartsome* stars were set in the face of the night": Stevenson's "Travels with a Donkey," v. 5); inspiriting; exhilarating; also, cheerful; merry. [Chiefly Sc.]—**heart'some-ly,** *adv.*

heart=sore (härt'sōr), *a.* Sore at heart; grieved; also, characterized by or showing grief (as, "*heart-sore* sighs": Shakspere's "Two Gentlemen of Verona," i. 1. 30).

heart=stir-ring (härt'stėr"ing), *a.* Stirring or rousing the heart; animating; inspiriting; inspiring: as, *heart-stirring* words or memories; *heart-stirring* music.

heart=strick-en (härt'strik"n), *a.* Stricken to the heart, as with grief.

heart-strings (härt'stringz), *n. pl.* Nerves or tendons formerly supposed to brace and sustain the heart; hence, the deepest feelings; the strongest affections.

heart=struck (härt'struk), *a.* Heart-stricken; also, inflicted on or distressing the heart† (as, "*heart-struck* injuries": Shakspere's "King Lear," iii. 1. 17).

heart=throb (härt'throb), *n.* A throb or pulsation of the heart. Sometimes fig., with reference to passionate or sentimental emotion.

heart=wa-ter (härt'wâ"tėr), *n.* A serious infectious disease of sheep, goats, etc., in South Africa, transmitted through the bont-tick.

heart=whole (härt'hōl'), *a.* Whole or sound of heart; fig., having the heart untouched by love (as, "Cupid hath clapped him o' the shoulder, but I'll warrant him *heart-whole*": Shakspere's "As You Like It," iv. 1. 49); also, in good spirits (now prov. Eng.); also, whole-hearted, hearty, or sincere.—**heart'=whole'ness,** *n.*

heart=wood (härt'wůd), *n.* The hard central wood of the trunk of an exogenous tree; the duramen.

heart-y (här'ti). **I.** *a.*; compar. *heartier*, superl. *heartiest*. Heartfelt, earnest, sincere, or whole-souled (as, *hearty* faith or satisfaction); warmly cordial or friendly (as, a *hearty* welcome); also, courageous† or bold†; also, ardent, enthusiastic, or zealous (as, *hearty* supporters or support); unrestrained or vigorous (as, a *hearty* laugh; a *hearty* blow); also, physically vigorous, or strong and well (as, to be hale and *hearty*); requiring substantial or abundant food, as an eater or the appetite; of food, a meal, etc., substantial or satisfying; also, of land, soil, etc., in good heart, or fertile. **II.** *n.*; pl. *hearties* (-tiz). A brave or good fellow (used esp. in familiar address to and by sailors: as, come, my *hearties*; "Look out, my *hearty*, for squalls," Marryat's "Peter Simple," xxxiii.); hence, a sailor.

heat (hēt), *n.* [AS. *hǣtu*, *hǣte*, < *hāt*, E. *hot.*] The quality or condition of being hot; hotness; high temperature; warmth; specif., a form of energy due to oscillatory or other

(variable) ḏ as d or j, ş as s or sh, ţ as t or ch, ẕ as z or zh; *o*, F. cloche; ü, F. menu; ċh, Sc. loch; ṅ, F. bonbon; ', primary accent; ", secondary accent; †, obsolete; <, from; +, and; =, equals. See also lists at beginning of book.

motion of the molecules of a substance, made manifest to the senses in various ways, as by the sensation or effect produced by nearness to or contact with fire (cf. *temperature*, also *radiant heat*, under *radiant*, *a.*); also, degree of hotness; temperature; also, the sensation of hotness or warmth, such as is experienced from nearness to fire; also, hot condition of the atmosphere or physical environment; hot weather; a hot period or season; also, the natural warmth of the living body; a heated bodily condition (as, to get into a *heat* by running); flushed or heightened color, as of the face; inflamed or feverish state of the body; a redness or eruption of the skin, accompanied by a sensation of hotness (cf. *prickly heat*); also, warmth or intensity of feeling (as, "The *heat* of his spirit Struck warm through all lands": Kipling's "Great-Heart: Theodore Roosevelt in 1919"); ardor or fervor; vehemence; excitement; passion or rage; sometimes, a fit of passion; also, the height or greatest intensity of any action (as, "to come upon them in the *heat* of their division": Shakspere's "Coriolanus," iv. 3. 19); also, sexual excitement in animals, esp. in the female; also, a single operation of heating, as of metal in a furnace; the quantity heated; also, a single intense effort, or one continuous operation (as, to do a thing at a *heat*); a single course in or division of a race or other contest.—**specific heat.** See under *specific*, *a.*—**heat,** *v.* [AS. *hǣtan*, < *hāt*, E. *hot.*] **I.** *tr.* To communicate heat to; make hot; warm; cause to feel hot, or warm; fig., to excite in mind or feeling; inspire with ardor; inflame with passion. **II.** *intr.* To become hot or warm; fig., to become excited in mind or feeling.—**heat'ed,** *p. a.* Hot; inflamed; vehement; angry. —**heat'ed-ly,** *adv.*—**heat'er,** *n.* One who or that which heats; esp., an apparatus for heating, as a furnace for heating a house.

heath (hēth), *n.* [AS. *hǣth* = D. and G. *heide* = Icel. *heidhr* = Goth. *haithi*, heath.] A tract of open and uncultivated or waste land; esp., such a tract overgrown with low shrubs; also, any of various low evergreen ericaceous shrubs common on waste land, as *Calluna vulgaris*, the common heather of England and Scotland, with small pinkish-purple flowers, or an allied species, *Erica cinerea* ('fine-leaved heath'), also common in Great Britain, with slightly larger flowers; any plant of the genus *Erica*, or of the family *Ericaceæ* (see *ericaceous*); also, any of several heath-like but not ericaceous shrubs, as *Frankenia lævis* ('sea-heath') of the European coasts.—**heath'=bell,** *n.* The bell-shaped flower of the heath.—**heath'=bird,** *n.* The black grouse.—**heath'=cock,** *n.* The male heath-bird.

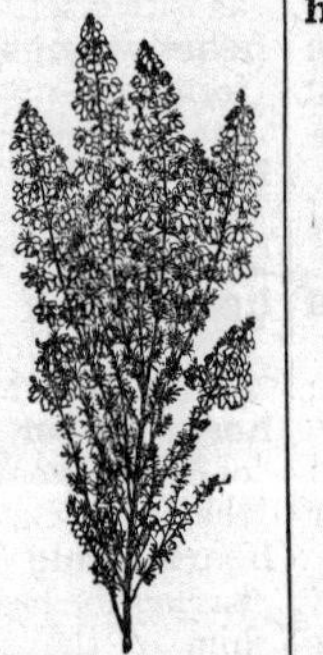
Branch of Heath (*Erica cinerea*).

hea-then (hē'ᴛʜẹn). [AS. *hǣthen*, n. and a., = D. *heiden*, n., = G. *heide*, n., = Icel. *heidhinn*, a., = Goth. *haithnō*, n. fem.; commonly explained as meaning orig. 'heath dweller': see *heath*, and cf. *pagan*.] **I.** *n.*; pl. *heathen* or *heathens*. An unconverted individual of a people which does not acknowledge the God of the Bible, esp. when uncivilized or uncultured; a Gentile, pagan, or idolater; hence, an irreligious or unenlightened person. **II.** *a.* That is a heathen; pagan; pertaining to the heathen; hence, irreligious or unenlightened.—**hea'then-dom** (-dọm), *n.* [AS. *hǣthendōm.*] Heathenism; also, heathen lands or people.—**hea'then-esse''** (-es''), *n.* [AS. *hǣthennes.*] Heathenism; also, heathendom. [Archaic.]—**hea'then-ish,** *a.* [AS. *hǣthenisc.*] Being a heathen†; pagan†; also, pertaining to the heathen (as, *heathenish* rites); hence, like or befitting the heathen; unchristian; barbarous; sometimes, abominable (colloq.). —**hea'then-ish-ly,** *adv.*—**hea'then-ish-ness,** *n.*—**hea'then-ism,** *n.* The condition, belief, or practice of heathen; hence, irreligion; unchristian barbarism.—**hea'then-ize** (-īz), *v.*; *-ized*, *-izing.* **I.** *tr.* To make heathen or heathenish. **II.** *intr.* To become heathen or heathenish; practise heathenism.—**hea'then-ry,** *n.* Heathenism (as, "In black blind pride and anger and all kinds of *heathenry* . . . I called on the fiends and they obeyed": Chesterton's "Magic," iii.); also, heathen people; the heathen.

heath-er (heᴛʜ'ẽr), *n.* [ME. *hathir*, *haddyr*; origin uncertain: commonly associated with *heath.*] Any of various heaths (plants), esp. *Calluna vulgaris* (often called 'Scotch heather'); also, a heather mixture.—**heather mixture,** a fabric woven of yarn combining various colors (with any particular color predominating): so called from the supposed resemblance of some mixtures to a tract of heather.—**heath'er=bell,** *n.* The heath-bell.—**heath'er=grass,** *n.* Heath-grass.—**heath'er-y,** *a.* Of, like, or abounding in heather.

Scotch Heather (*Calluna vulgaris*).

heath=grass (hēth'gràs), *n.* A European grass, *Sieglingia decumbens*, growing in spongy, wet, cold soils.

heath=hen (hēth'hen), *n.* The female heath-bird.

heath-y (hē'thi), *a.* Of or like a heath; heathery.

heat=light-ning (hēt'līt''ning), *n.* Flashes of light unaccompanied by thunder, seen near the horizon on summer evenings: thought to be reflections of distant lightning.

hea-tron-ic (hẹ-tron'ik), *a.* [*hea*(*t*) + (*elec*)*tronic.*] Noting or pertaining to a molding process in which high-frequency radio waves are used to heat the plastic material prior to or during the molding process.

heaume (hōm), *n.* [F.: see *helmet.*] A large helmet reaching down to the shoulders, worn in the 12th, 13th, and 14th centuries, usually over an inner defense, such as a coif of mail.

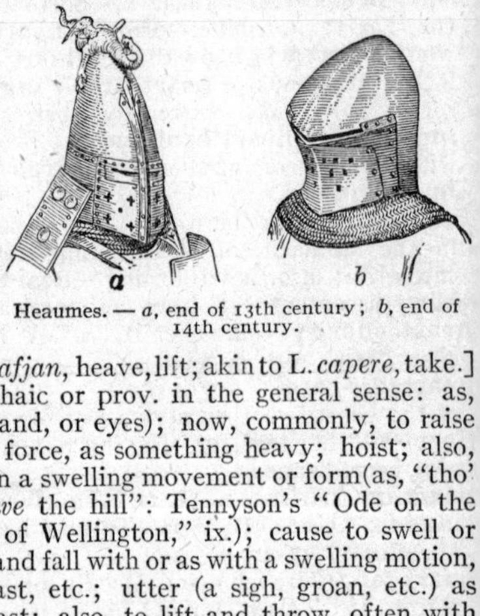

Heaumes. — *a*, end of 13th century; *b*, end of 14th century.

heave (hēv), *v. t.*; *heaved* or *hove*, *heaving.* [AS. *hebban* (pret. *hōf*, *hefde*, pp. *hafen*) = D. *heffen* = G. *heben* = Icel. *hefja* = Goth. *hafjan*, heave, lift; akin to L. *capere*, take.] To raise or lift (archaic or prov. in the general sense: as, to *heave* the head, hand, or eyes); now, commonly, to raise or lift with effort or force, as something heavy; hoist; also, to raise or force up in a swelling movement or form (as, "tho' the Giant Ages *heave* the hill": Tennyson's "Ode on the Death of the Duke of Wellington," ix.); cause to swell or bulge; cause to rise and fall with or as with a swelling motion, as the sea, the breast, etc.; utter (a sigh, groan, etc.) as from a swelling breast; also, to lift and throw, often with effort or force (now colloq. or naut.: as, to *heave* a brick at a window; to *heave* a dead body overboard); thrust, drive, or carry (*away*, *out*, etc.)†; *naut.*, to haul, draw, or pull, as by a cable; in *geol.*, to thrust (a vein, etc.) out of place. —**to heave to,** to stop the headway of (a vessel), esp. by bringing the head to the wind and arranging the sails so that they act against one another.—**heave,** *v. i.* To rise as if thrust up, as a hill; swell or bulge; rise and fall with or as with a swelling motion, as the sea, the breast in hard breathing, the earth in an earthquake, etc.; hence, to breathe with effort, or pant; sometimes, to retch; also, to labor†, struggle†, or strive†; aim (*at*)†; *naut.*, to haul or pull, as at a cable, or push, as at the bar of a capstan; move a ship, or move as a ship does, by such action; move or go (*about*, *ahead*, etc.).—**heave ho!** an exclamation used by sailors when heaving the anchor up, etc.—**to heave in sight,** to rise into view as from below the horizon, as land or a ship seen at sea; hence, in general, to come into view.—**to heave to,** of persons, to heave a vessel to (see transitive phrase *to heave to*, above); of a vessel, to come to a standstill, as from being brought into the wind.—**heave,** *n.* The act or an act of heaving; a lifting movement, or an effort to lift or move something; a swelling movement; an alternately rising and falling motion, as of the waves of the sea; a throw or cast; also, a rise of ground, a knoll, or a mound (prov. Eng. and Sc.); in *geol.*, a horizontal displacement of a vein or stratum at a fault. See also *heaves*.

heav-en (hev′n), *n.* [AS. *hefen*, *heofon*, = OS. *hebhan* = MLG. *heven*, sky, heaven; not connected with E. *heave*.] The sky, firmament, or expanse of space surrounding the earth, appearing as a great arch or vault in which the sun, moon, and stars seem to be set (in prose use now commonly in *pl.*: as, a map of the *heavens*); sometimes, a particular kind or region of sky, with reference to clearness or cloud, climate, the land beneath, etc. (as, "flowers of all *heavens*": Tennyson's "Princess," Prologue, 12); also, any of a (varying) number of concentric spheres, or spherical shell-like divisions, into which the space about the earth was divided according to old systems of cosmography or astronomy (cf. *empyrean*, *n.*); also, the celestial abode of immortal beings; in Christian use, the abode of God, the angels, and the spirits of the righteous after death; the place or state of existence of the blessed after the mortal life; in various non-Christian doctrines, any of a number of celestial abodes or realms (as, the seven *heavens* of the Talmud or of the Mohammedans; the seventh *heaven*, or the *heaven* of *heavens*, see phrases below); in general, a place or state of supreme bliss (as, "a *heaven* on earth": Milton's "Paradise Lost," iv. 208); also, the Supreme Being, or God (usually *cap.* in reverent or solemn use, but commonly *l. c.* in various merely emphatic expressions: as, for *heaven's* sake; in *heaven's* name; *heaven* only knows!); *pl.*, the celestial powers, as ruling over mankind (as, "*Heavens* keep him from these beasts!" Shakspere's "Tempest," ii. 1. 324; in exclamation, good *heavens!*).—**heaven of heavens,** in Biblical use, the highest heaven, the abode of God: as, "Behold, the heaven and the *heaven of heavens* is the Lord's thy God" (Deut. x. 14). Also fig. —**seventh heaven,** the highest heaven, the abode of God and the most exalted angels, according to rabbinical doctrine; hence, fig., the highest attainable place or state of joy or felicity (as, to feel one's self raised to the *seventh heaven* with delight).—**heav′en=born,** *a.* Of heavenly birth or origin; hence, sent, as it were, from heaven, as for a special work or purpose (as, a *heaven-born* teacher).—**heav′en-ly,** *a.* [AS. *heofonlīc.*] Of or in the heavens (as, the *heavenly* bodies, the sun, planets, stars, comets, etc.); also, of, belonging to, or coming from the heaven of God, the angels, etc. (as, our *heavenly* Father, God; the *heavenly* Jerusalem, see Heb. xii. 22; *heavenly* bread); celestial or divine; also, resembling or befitting heaven (as, a *heavenly* spot; *heavenly* peace or joy); supremely blissful or excellent.—**heav′en-li-ness,** *n.*—**heav′en-ly,** *adv.* [AS. *heofonlīce.*] In a heavenly manner.—**heav′en-ly=mind′ed,** *a.* Having the thoughts and affections fixed on heavenly things; pious; devout.—**heav′en-ward** (-wạrd), *adv.* and *a.* Toward heaven.—**heav′en-wards,** *adv.*

heave=of-fer-ing (hēv′of″ėr-ing), *n.* In the Jewish priestly law, an offering which was lifted up ('heaved') by the priest when presented, and which became the portion of the priests and their families. See Ex. xxix. 27.

heav-er (hē′vėr), *n.* One who or that which heaves.

heaves (hēvz), *n. pl.* [Pl. of *heave*, *n.*] A disease of horses, characterized by difficult breathing; broken wind.

heav-i-er=than=air (hev′i-ėr-ᴛʜạn-ãr′), *a.* In *aëronautics*, of greater specific gravity than the air, as aircraft (such as aëroplanes); of or pertaining to such aircraft. Cf. *lighter-than-air*.

heav-i-ly (hev′i-li), *adv.* In a heavy manner.—**heav′i-ness,** *n.*

heav-y (hev′i). [AS. *hefig*, < *hefe*, weight, < *hebban*, E. *heave*.] **I.** *a.*; compar. *heavier*, superl. *heaviest*. Of great weight, hard to lift or carry, or ponderous (as, a *heavy* load); having much weight in proportion to bulk, or being of high specific gravity (as, a *heavy* metal; *heavy* earth, baryta); of more than the usual, average, or specified weight (as, a *heavy* grade of paper or silk; *heavy* freight; *heavy* guns); also, weighted or laden with something (lit. or fig.: as, wagons *heavy* with booty; air *heavy* with moisture or perfume); big with young, gravid, or pregnant; weighed down or drooping with drowsiness or weariness, as the eyelids, head, etc., or the person; depressed with trouble, sorrow, care, etc., as the heart or the person; showing depression or sorrow, as the countenance, utterances, etc.; overcast or cloudy, as the sky; also, exceptionally dense in substance; insufficiently raised or leavened, as bread; having much body, as liquor; thick, as vapor; also, of great amount, force, intensity, etc. (as, a *heavy* vote; a *heavy* strain; a *heavy* sea; *heavy* sleep); severe or violent, as a blow, an onslaught, a storm, etc.; loud and deep, as sound; being such in an unusual degree (as, a *heavy* buyer; a *heavy* drinker); also, weighing or bearing hard, as upon persons; burdensome, as taxes or expenses; harsh or severe, as censure, penalties, punishment, etc.; grievous or distressing, as affliction, sorrow, (bad) news, etc.; oppressive, as odors, air, etc.; hard to deal with, trying, or difficult, as a task; hard to travel over, as roads, or to work, as soil; not easily digested, as food; also, of great import or moment, or weighty (archaic: as, "Some *heavy* business hath my lord in hand," Shakspere's "1 Henry IV.," ii. 3. 66); grave or serious, as a fault, offense, etc.; sober, serious, or somber (as, a *heavy* part, *heavy* villain, or *heavy* father, in a play); also, lacking lightness, delicacy, grace, etc.; broad, thick, or coarse, as lines, handwriting, decorative designs, features, etc.; clumsy, sluggish, or slow in movement or action, or as movement, gait, etc.; without vivacity or interest, ponderous, dull, or tedious (as, a *heavy* book or style); *milit.*, heavily armed or equipped (as, *heavy* cavalry or infantry; *heavy* marching order, the condition of soldiers fully equipped for field-service). **II.** *n.*; pl. *-ies* (-iz). One who or that which is heavy; esp., a gun of great weight or large caliber; *pl.*, heavy cavalry; *sing.*, in *theatrical use*, a heavy part or character, or an actor who plays such parts.—**heav′y,** *adv.* [AS. *hefige.*] In a heavy manner; heavily.

heav-y=armed (hev′i-ärmd), *a.* Equipped with heavy arms or armor, as troops.

heav-y=hand-ed (hev′i-han′ded), *a.* Having the hands heavily laden; also, having the hands heavy from weariness, weakness, etc.; also, clumsy of hand, touch, etc.; also, oppressive or harsh in action or treatment.—**heav′y=hand′ed-ness,** *n.*

heav-y=head-ed (hev′i-hed′ed), *a.* Having the head heavy, as with weight; also, drowsy or sleepy; also, dull or stupid.

heav-y=heart-ed (hev′i-här′ted), *a.* Having, proceeding from, or showing a heavy heart; sorrowful; sad; melancholy; gloomy.—**heav′y=heart′ed-ness,** *n.*

heav-y=lad-en (hev′i-lā′dn), *a.* Laden with a heavy burden; also, weighed down with weariness, trouble, sorrow, etc. (as, "Come unto me, all ye that labour and are *heavy laden*, and I will give you rest": Mat. xi. 28).

heav-y=spar (hev′i-spär), *n.* Barite.

heav-y=weight (hev′i-wāt), *n.* One of more than average weight; esp., a boxer or other contestant of the heaviest class; fig., a person of considerable mental powers or of influence or importance (colloq.).

heb-do-mad (heb′dọ-mad), *n.* [L. *hebdomas* (*hebdomad-*), < Gr. ἑβδομάς (ἑβδομαδ-), < ἑπτά, seven.] The number seven; also, a group of seven; esp., a period of seven days; a week.—**heb-dom′a-dal** (-dom′ạ-dạl), *a.* [LL. *hebdomadalis.*] Weekly.—**heb-dom′a-dal-ly,** *adv.*—**heb-dom′a-da-ry** (-dạ-ri). [ML. *hebdomadarius.*] **I.** *a.* Weekly; hebdomadal. **II.** *n.*; pl. *-ries* (-riz). In the *Rom. Cath. Ch.*, the member of a chapter, monastery, etc., whose turn it is for a week to perform certain services, as officiating in the choir.

He-be (hē′bẹ), *n.* [L., < Gr. Ἥβη, personification of ἥβη, youth, youthful prime.] The Grecian goddess of youth and spring, cup-bearer (before Ganymede) of Olympus; hence, a blooming young woman; also, a waitress.

heb-e-non† (heb′ẹ-nọn), *n.* [Origin uncertain.] Some unidentified substance with a poisonous juice. See Shakspere's "Hamlet," i. 5. 62.

heb-e-tate (heb′ẹ-tāt), *v. t.*; *-tated*, *-tating*. [L. *hebetatus*, pp. of *hebetare*, < *hebes* (*hebet-*), blunt, dull.] To blunt; dull.—**heb′e-tate,** *a.* In *bot.*, having a blunt, soft point, as awns.—**heb-e-ta′tion** (-tā′shọn), *n.*

heb-e-tude (heb′ẹ-tūd), *n.* [LL. *hebetudo*, < L. *hebes*: see *hebetate*.] The state of being blunt or dull; dullness; lethargy; stupidity.

He-bra-ic (hẹ̄-brā′ik), *a.* [LL. *Hebraicus*, < Gr. Ἑβραϊκός, < Ἑβραῖος, E. *Hebrew*.] Pertaining to the Hebrews or their language; Hebrew.—**He-bra′i-cal-ly,** *adv.*—**He-bra-ism** (hē′brạ̄-izm), *n.* A Hebrew usage or idiom; also, Hebrew character, spirit, thought, or practice.—**He′bra-ist,** *n.* One versed in the Hebrew language and learning; also, one imbued with the Hebraic spirit; also, one of the ancient Jews, as in Palestine, who used the Hebrew or Aramaic tongue (opposed to *Hellenist*).—**He-bra-is′tic,** *a.* Pertaining to Hebraists; marked by Hebraism; Hebraic. —**He′bra-ize** (-īz), *v. i.* or *t.*; *-ized, -izing.* To become or make Hebraic; conform to the Hebrew usage or type.

He-brew (hē′brö). [OF. *Hebreu* (F. *Hébreu*), < L. *Hebræus*, < Gr. Ἑβραῖος, Hebrew; from Aramaic, and meaning lit. 'one from beyond.'] **I.** *n.* A member of that branch of the Semitic race descended from the line of Abraham; an Israelite; a Jew; also, the language of the ancient Israelites, which became extinct as a vernacular tongue before the Christian era, but has been preserved or revived in religious, literary, and scholarly use; in the New Testament, the Aramaic dialect spoken by the Jews at the time of Christ; also, *pl.*, a New Testament book of disputed authorship, called in full "The Epistle of Paul the Apostle to the Hebrews." **II.** *a.* Of or pertaining to the Hebrews or their language.

He-bri-cian (hẹ̄-brish′ạn), *n.* One versed in Hebrew; a Hebraist.

Hec-a-te (hek′ạ̄-tē), *n.* [L., < Gr. Ἑκάτη, prop. fem. of ἕκατος, far-darting (epithet of Apollo), < ἑκάς, far.] A Greek goddess of the moon, earth, and infernal regions, also associated with sorcery and witchcraft (in art, often represented in three forms standing back to back); hence, a witch; a hag.

The Triple Hecate. — Relief from Ægina.

hec-a-tomb (hek′ạ̄-tom or -töm), *n.* [L. *hecatombe*, < Gr. ἑκατόμβη, < ἑκατόν, hundred, + βοῦς, ox.] A great public sacrifice, orig. of a hundred oxen, as to the Greek gods; hence, any sacrifice of many victims; a great slaughter; also, a great number sacrificed or offered at one time; hence, a great number or quantity (as, "There were barrels of oysters, *hecatombs* of lobsters": Trollope's "Warden," xvi.).

heck-el-phone (hek′ẹl-fōn), *n.* [From *Heckel*, name of the (German) inventor: see *-phone*.] A wooden wind-instrument of the oboe class, intended to serve as a barytone or tenor oboe.

heck-le (hek′l), *n.* [ME. *hekele, hechele*, = MLG. *hekele* = D. *hekel* = G. *hechel*, heckle; prob. from the root of E. *hook*.] Same as *hackle*[1], *n.*—**heck′le,** *v. t.*; *-led, -ling.* To hackle (flax, etc.); hence, to badger or torment; harass (a public speaker) with questions, etc.—**heck′ler,** *n.*

hec-tare (hek′tãr), *n.* [F. *hectare*: see *hecto-*.] In the *metric system*, a surface measure equal to 100 ares, 10,000 square meters, or 2.471 acres.

hec-tic (hek′tik). [F. *hectique*, < ML. *hecticus*, < Gr. ἑκτικός, habitual, hectic, < ἕξις, habit, < ἔχειν, have.] **I.** *a.* Habitual†; also, marking a particular habit or condition of body, as the fever of phthisis, which is attended with flushed cheeks, hot skin, and emaciation; also, pertaining to or affected with such fever; consumptive; hence, flushed; feverish; wasting; often, characterized by great heat of excitement, passions, etc. (as, *hectic* pleasures; a *hectic* romance; a man with a *hectic* past). **II.** *n.* A hectic fever; also, a hectic flush; hence, any flush, or flushed appearance (as, "A *hectic* of a moment pass'd across his cheek": Sterne's "Sentimental Journey," The Monk, Calais); also, a consumptive person.—**hec′ti-cal-ly,** *adv.*

hecto-, hect-. Forms of Gr. ἑκατόν, hundred, used in combination.—**hec-to-cot-y-lus** (hek-tọ̄-kot′i-lus), *n.* [NL. (Gr. κοτύλη, cup).] In *zoöl.*, a modified arm of the male of certain cephalopods which is concerned in the process of reproduction.—**hec′to-gram, hec′to-gramme** (-gram), *n.* [F. *hectogramme*.] In the *metric system*, a unit of weight equal to 100 grams, or 3.527 ounces avoirdupois.—**hec′to-graph** (-grȧf), *n.* [+ *-graph*.] A process for making copies of a writing, etc., from a prepared gelatin surface to which the original writing has been transferred; also, the apparatus used.—**hec′to-graph,** *v. t.* To copy with the hectograph.—**hec′to-li-ter, hec′to-li-tre** (-lē-tėr), *n.* [F. *hectolitre*.] In the *metric system*, a unit of capacity equal to 100 liters, 2.8377 U. S. bushels, or 26.417 U. S. gallons.—**hec′to-me-ter, hec′to-me-tre** (-mē-tėr), *n.* [F. *hectomètre*.] In the *metric system*, a measure of length equal to 100 meters, or 328.08 feet.

hec-tor (hek′tọr), *n.* [From *Hector*, the Trojan hero, celebrated in Homer's "Iliad."] A blustering, domineering fellow; a swashbuckler; a bully.—**hec′tor,** *v. t.* or *i.* To treat or act in a blustering domineering way; bully.

hec-to-stere (hek′tọ̄-stēr), *n.* [F. *hectostère*: see *hecto-*.] In the *metric system*, a unit of volume equal to 100 steres.

hed-dle (hed′l), *n.* [= *heald*.] In a loom, one of the two or more sets of vertical cords or wires, usually in pairs, forming the principal part of the harness which guides the warp-threads; also, a single pair of such cords or wires.

hed-er-a-ceous (hed-ẹ-rā′shius), *a.* [L. *hederaceus*, < *hedera*, ivy.] Of or like ivy; of the ivy family.

hed-er-i-form (hed′ẹ-ri-fôrm), *a.* [L. *hedera*, ivy: see *-form*.] Resembling ivy.

hedge (hej), *n.* [AS. *hecg* = D. *hegge* = G. *hecke*, hedge: cf. *hay*[1].] A row of bushes or small trees planted close together to form a fence or boundary; any similar row of bushes or small trees; hence, any barrier or boundary; also, an act or a means of hedging a bet or the like. Often in composition, esp. with reference to vagrant life, low status or character, meanness, etc., as in 'hedge-priest' (see below), 'hedge-tavern,' etc.—**hedge,** *v.*; *hedged, hedging.* **I.** *tr.* To fence (*in, off, about*, etc.) with a hedge (as, "There was a certain householder, which planted a vineyard, and *hedged* it round about": Mat. xxi. 33); surround as with a hedge (as, "England, *hedged* in with the main": Shakspere's "King John," ii. 1. 26); also, to surround so as to prevent escape or hinder free movement (often with *in*: as, to be *hedged* in by difficulties); shut or keep (*out*)†; also, to obstruct with a hedge or any barrier (as, "I will *hedge* up thy way with thorns": Hos. ii. 6); also, to protect (a bet, etc.) by taking some offsetting risk. **II.** *intr.* To make or repair hedges (as, "To *hedge*, or dig the ditch, To lop or fell the tree": Hood's "Lay of the Labourer," 9); also, to turn aside, or swerve (as, "If you . . . *hedge* aside from the direct forthright . . . they all rush by And leave you hindmost": Shakspere's "Troilus and Cressida," iii. 3. 158); dodge; shuffle; avoid an open or decisive course; also, to protect a bet, speculation, etc., by taking some offsetting risk.

hedge=gar-lic (hej′gär″lik), *n.* An erect brassicaceous herb, *Alliaria alliaria*, with a garlic-like odor.

hedge-hog (hej′hog), *n.* An old-world insectivorous quadruped of the genus *Erinaceus*, having the upper part of the body covered with spines, and able to roll itself into a ball; also, any of various other spined animals, as the Canada porcupine.

Common European Hedgehog (*Erinaceus europæus*).

hedge′=hop″ping, *n.* Flying a plane very low.

hedge=hys-sop (hej′his″ọp), *n.* Any of the low herbs constituting the scrophulariaceous genus *Gratiola*, as *G. officinalis*, a medicinal species of Europe; also, any of certain similar plants, as *Scutellaria minor*, an English species of skullcap.

hedge=par-son (hej′pär″sọn), *n.* A hedge-priest.

hedge-pig (hej′pig), *n.* A hedgehog.

hedge=priest (hej′prēst), *n.* An illiterate or unworthy priest.

hedg-er (hej′ėr), *n.* One who hedges; one who makes or

repairs hedges; one who dodges or shuffles; one who hedges in betting, etc.

hedge=row (hej′rō), *n.* A row of bushes or trees forming a hedge.

hedge=spar-row (hej′spar″ō), *n.* A small European warbler, *Accentor modularis*, which frequents hedges.

Hedge-sparrow.

hedg-y (hej′i), *a.* Abounding in hedges.

he-don-ic (hē-don′ik), *a.* [Gr. ἡδονικός, < ἡδονή, pleasure, < ἥδεσθαι, be pleased, akin to ἡδύς, sweet.] Pertaining to or consisting in pleasure; also, pertaining to hedonism or to hedonics. —**he-don′i-cal-ly,** *adv.* —**he-don′ics,** *n.* The branch of ethics which treats of pleasure; also, that part of psychology which treats of pleasurable and painful states of consciousness.

he-do-nism (hē′dǫ-nizm), *n.* [Gr. ἡδονή, pleasure: see *hedonic.*] The doctrine that pleasure or happiness is the highest good.—**he′do-nist,** *n.* An advocate of hedonism. —**he-do-nis′tic,** *a.* Of or pertaining to hedonists or hedonism.—**he-do-nis′ti-cal-ly,** *adv.*

-hedron. [Gr. -εδρον, neut. of -εδρος, having bases, -sided, < ἕδρα, seat, base.] A termination of nouns denoting geometrical solid figures having a certain number of faces, as *dodecahedron, octahedron, polyhedron.*

heed (hēd), *v.* [AS. *hēdan* = D. *hoeden* = G. *hüten*, attend to, mind.] **I.** *tr.* To give attention to; regard; notice; mind: as, "They pass, and *heed* each other not" (Bryant's "Crowded Street"). **II.** *intr.* To give attention; have regard.—**heed,** *n.* Attention; regard; care: as, "Full slowly pacing o'er the stones, With caution and good *heed*" (Cowper's "John Gilpin," 80).—**heed′er,** *n.*—**heed′ful,** *a.* Attentive; regardful; mindful: as, "*heedful* of advice" (Pope's tr. Homer's "Odyssey," i.).—**heed′ful-ly,** *adv.*—**heed′ful-ness,** *n.*—**heed′less,** *a.* Regardless; unmindful; careless; thoughtless: as, "Hobbling down stairs with *heedless* haste, I set my foot full in a pail of water" (Steele, in "Tatler," 266).—**heed′less-ly,** *adv.*—**heed′less-ness,** *n.*

hee-haw (hē′hâ′), *n.* [Imit.] The braying sound made by an ass: as, "asinine *hee-haws*" (Browning's "Two Poets of Croisic," cxx.). Also fig., as of rude laughter.—**hee′haw′,** *v. i.* To utter heehaws; bray.

heel[1] (hēl), *v.* [Earlier *heeld*, < AS. *hieldan*, bend, incline, < *heald*, bent, inclined.] **I.** *intr.* Of a ship, etc., to lean to one side; cant; tilt. **II.** *tr.* To cause (a ship, etc.) to lean or cant.—**heel**[1], *n.* A heeling movement; a cant.

heel[2] (hēl), *n.* [AS. *hēla* = D. *hiel*, heel; akin to E. *hock*[1].] The hinder part of the foot in man, below and behind the ankle; an analogous part in other vertebrates; sometimes, the foot as a whole (as, "Fauns with cloven *heel*": Milton's "Lycidas," 34); also, either hind foot or hoof of some quadrupeds, as the horse (as, the horse kicked up his *heels* and threw his rider); also, the human foot as fitted with a riding-spur (as, to give a horse a touch of the *heel*); also, the part of a stocking, shoe, or the like, covering the heel; a solid part, as of several thicknesses of leather, or of rubber, projecting downward from the hinder part of the sole of a shoe, etc.; also, something resembling or suggestive of the human heel, as in position, shape, etc.; the crook in the head of a golf-club; the part of a knife-blade or tool next to the handle; the hinder part of a plowshare; the after end of a ship's keel; an end or crust of a loaf of bread, remaining after cutting; the latter or concluding part of anything, as of a session or a discourse.—**at one's heels,** close behind one.—**down at (the) heel,** having the shoe-heels worn down; also, having the back parts of the uppers (about the heels), as of slippers, negligently crushed down by the feet; in fig. use, shabby; slipshod or slovenly.—**heels over head,** with the heels in the air and the head down; upside down.—**to take to one's heels,** to take to flight.—**heel**[2], *v.* **I.** *tr.* To furnish with heels, as shoes; also, to arm (a game-cock) with spurs; hence, in general, to arm or equip (a person slang, U. S.); also, to catch or secure by the heel; also, to follow at the heels of; chase by running at the heels; also, to perform (a dance) with the heels; also, in *golf*, to strike the (ball) with the heel of the club. **II.** *intr.* To follow at one's heels; also, to move on or tap with the heels, as in dancing.

heel=and=toe (hēl′ąnd-tō′), *a.* Noting a kind of pace, as in walking-contests, in which the heel of the front foot touches the ground before the toes of the rear one leave it.

heeled (hēld), *a.* Having heels (as, high-*heeled*); also, armed, equipped, supplied with money, etc. (slang, U. S.).

heel-er (hē′lėr), *n.* One who heels; esp., a servile follower or hanger-on of a political boss (slang, U. S.).

heel=fly (hēl′flī), *n.*; pl. *-flies* (-flīz). A warble-fly, *Hypoderma lineata*, which flies about the heels of cattle and lays its eggs in the hair, whence they are licked by the animal.

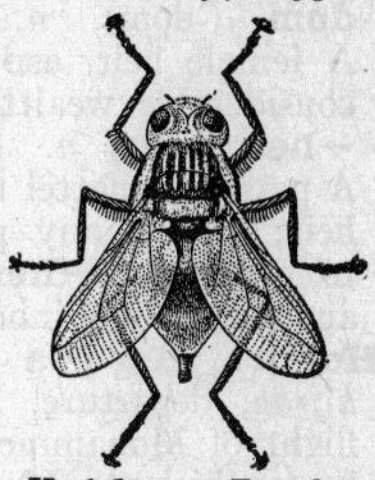

Heel-fly. — Female, slightly enlarged.

heel=piece (hēl′pēs), *n.* A piece serving as or fitted to a heel, as of a shoe; also, a piece, as of armor, covering the heel of the foot; fig., a terminal piece or part.

heel=post (hēl′pōst), *n.* A post forming or fitted to the heel or end of something, as the post on which a gate or door is hinged.

heel=tap (hēl′tap), *n.* A layer of leather or the like in a shoe-heel; also, a small portion of liquor left in a glass after drinking.

heft (heft), *n.* [From *heave.*] A heaving movement or effort (now prov.); also, weight (colloq. or prov.: as, "Constitoounts air hendy to help a man in, But arterwards don't weigh the *heft* of a pin," Lowell's "Biglow Papers," i. 4. 134); also, the bulk or main part (colloq., U. S.).—**heft,** *v. t.* To heave or lift; also, to try the weight of by lifting. [Prov. or colloq.]—**heft′y,** *a.* Heavy; weighty. [Prov. or colloq.]

He-ge-lian (hē-gē′lian or hā-gā′-), *a.* Of or pertaining to the German philosopher Georg Wilhelm Friedrich Hegel (1770–1831), or his system of philosophy.—**He-ge′lian-ism,** *n.*

he-ge-mo-ny (hē′jē-mō-ni, hej′ē-, or hē-jem′ǫ-), *n.*; pl. *-nies* (-niz). [Gr. ἡγεμονία, < ἡγεμών, leader, < ἡγεῖσθαι, lead.] Leadership; predominance; esp., leadership or predominant influence exercised by one state over others, as in a confederation.—**he-ge-mon-ic** (hē-jē-mon′ik or hej-ē-), *a.*

Heg′i-ra, *n.* See *Hejira.*

Hei-duc, Hei-duk (hī′dụk), *n.* See *Haiduk.*

heif-er (hef′ėr), *n.* [AS. *heahfore.*] A young cow that has not had a calf.

heigh (hā or hī), *interj.* [Cf. *hey.*] An exclamation used to call attention, give encouragement, etc.—**heigh′=ho′,** *interj.* An exclamation of surprise, exultation, etc.; a sighing utterance expressing melancholy, weariness, etc.

height (hīt), *n.* [AS. *hīehtho, hēahthu*, < *hēah*, E. *high.*] The state of being high; extent upward, altitude, or stature; distance upward, or elevation, as of an object above the ground; considerable or great altitude or elevation (as, a mountain famed for its *height*); high rank, as of persons; high degree, as of a quality; sometimes, loftiness, as of mind (archaic); also, a high place or level; a hill or mountain; also, the highest part, top, or summit of anything; the highest or culminating point, or utmost degree (as, at the *height* of one's popularity; the *height* of the season; the *height* of fashion; the *height* of absurdity).

height-en (hī′tn), *v.* **I.** *tr.* To increase the height of; make higher; also, to augment; intensify; also, to exalt†; elate†. **II.** *intr.* To become higher; also, to increase; augment.—**height′en-er,** *n.*

heim-weh (hīm′vā), *n.* [G.: see *home* and *woe.*] Homesickness.

Hein-ie (hī′ni), *n.* [For G. *Heinrich*, Henry (man's name).] A popular name for a German.

hei-nous (hā′nus), *a.* [OF. *hainos* (F. *haineux*), < *haine*, hatred, < *hair* (F. *haïr*), hate; from Teut., and akin to E. *hate.*] Hateful, odious, or gravely reprehensible, as offenses or the offenders; wicked or criminal in a high degree; flagitious; atrocious.—**hei'nous-ly,** *adv.*—**hei'nous-ness,** *n.*

heir (âr), *n.* [OF. *heir, eir* (F. *hoir*), < L. *heres*, heir.] One who inherits or is entitled to inherit; one who receives or is entitled to receive possession of property or a vested right on the death of its owner, either as his natural or as his legal successor; hence, one who receives or is entitled to receive any gift, endowment, etc., by inheritance or transmission; one to whom something falls, comes, or is due; also, an offspring† or product†.—**heir apparent,** an heir whose right is indefeasible, provided he survives the ancestor. —**heir presumptive,** an heir whose expectation may be defeated by the birth of a nearer relative.—**heir,** *v. t.* To inherit: as, "When falls a mate in battle broil, His comrade *heirs* his portion'd spoil" (Scott's "Rokeby," i. 21).—**heir'-dom** (-dọm), *n.* Heirship; inheritance.—**heir'ess,** *n.* A female heir, esp. one inheriting or expected to inherit considerable wealth.—**heir'less,** *a.* Destitute of an heir. —**heir'loom,** *n.* [See *loom*¹, orig. tool or implement.] A personal chattel that descends with an inheritance to the heir; hence, any possession transmitted from generation to generation.—**heir'ship,** *n.* The position or rights of an heir; right of inheritance; inheritance.

Hej-i-ra, Heg-i-ra (hej'i-rä̤, commonly hẹ-jī'rä̤), *n.* [Ar. *hijrah*, departure, migration, < *hajara*, go away.] The flight of Mohammed from Mecca to Medina, in A.D. 622, from which the Mohammedan era is reckoned; hence, this era itself; also [*l. c.*], any flight or departure.

hek'tare, hekto-, etc. See *hectare, hecto-*, etc.

held (held). Preterit and past participle of *hold*².

he-li-ac (hē'li-ak), *a.* [LL. *heliacus*, < Gr. ἡλιακός, < ἥλιος, sun: see *Sol*¹.] Pertaining to the sun; solar; heliacal. —**he-li-a-cal** (hẹ-lī'ạ-kạl), *a.* Pertaining to or occurring near the sun: applied esp. to such risings and settings of a star as are most nearly coincident with those of the sun while yet being visible.—**he-li'a-cal-ly,** *adv.*

he-li-an-thus (hē-li-an'thus), *n.* [NL., < Gr. ἥλιος, sun, + ἄνθος, flower.] Any plant of the asteraceous genus *Helianthus*; a sunflower.

hel-i-cal (hel'i-kạl), *a.* [L. *helix* (*helic-*): see *helix*.] Pertaining to or having the form of a helix.—**hel'i-cal-ly,** *adv.*

hel-i-coid (hel'i-koid). [Gr. ἑλικοειδής, < ἕλιξ, helix, + εἶδος, form.] **I.** *a.* Helix-like; coiled or curving like a helix. **II.** *n.* In *geom.*, a warped surface generated by a straight line so moving as always to cut or touch a fixed helix.—**hel-i-coi'dal,** *a.*

Hel-i-con (hel'i-kọn), *n.* [L., < Gr. Ἑλικών.] A mountain in Bœotia, Greece, sacred to the Muses, from which flowed the fountains of Aganippe and Hippocrene, regarded as sources of poetic inspiration. Hence fig., with reference to poetry and poetic inspiration.—**Hel-i-co'ni-an** (-kō'ni-ạn), *a.*

hel-i-cop-ter (hel-i-kop'tėr), *n.* [F. *hélicoptère*, < Gr. ἕλιξ, helix, + πτερόν, wing.] Any of a class of flying-machines which are lifted and sustained in the air by helicoid surfaces or propellers turning on vertical axes.

he-lic-tis (he-lik'tis), *n.* [NL.] Any of the small carnivorous animals constituting the genus *Helictis*, of southern and eastern Asia, belonging to the family *Mustelidæ* (the weasels, badgers, martens, etc.).

Helictis (*H. moschata*).

helio-. Form of Gr. ἥλιος, sun, used in combination.

he-li-o (hē'li-ō), *n.*; pl. *-os* (-ōz). Shortened form of *heliograph* or *heliogram*. See Kipling's "Code of Morals."

he-li-o-cen-tric (hē''li-ọ-sen'trik), *a.* [See *helio-*.] In *astron.*, as viewed or measured from the center of the sun (as, the *heliocentric* latitude of a planet); also, having or representing the sun as a center (as, the *heliocentric* theory of the universe). —**he''li-o-cen'tri-cal-ly,** *adv.*

he-li-o-chrome (hē'li-ọ-krōm), *n.* [From *helio-* + Gr. χρῶμα, color.] A photograph in the natural colors.—**he'li-o-chro-my** (-krō-mi), *n.* Photography in the natural colors.—**he''li-o-chro'mic,** *a.*

he-li-o-gram (hē'li-ọ-gram), *n.* A heliographic message.

he-li-o-graph (hē'li-ọ-grȧf), *n.* [See *helio-* and *-graph.*] A device for signaling by means of a movable mirror which flashes beams of light to a distance; also, an apparatus for taking photographs of the sun.—**he'li-o-graph,** *v.* **I.** *tr.* To communicate by heliograph: as, "With damnatory dot and dash he *heliographed* his wife Some interesting details of the General's private life" (Kipling's "Code of Morals"). **II.** *intr.* To signal by heliograph.—**he-li-og'ra-pher** (-og'rạ-fėr), *n.*—**he''li-o-graph'ic** (-graf'ik), *a.* —**he-li-og'ra-phy,** *n.* [See *-graphy.*] The system of signaling with the heliograph.

he-li-o-gra-vure (hē''li-ọ-grạ-vūr' or -grā'vūr), *n.* [F. *héliogravure*, < Gr. ἥλιος, sun, + F. *gravure*, engraving.] Any of various photomechanical processes, esp. photogravure; also, a plate or print made by such a process.

he-li-ol-a-ter (hē-li-ol'ạ-tėr), *n.* [See *helio-* and *-later.*] A sun-worshiper.—**he-li-ol'a-try,** *n.* [See *-latry.*] Sun-worship.

he-li-ol-o-gy (hē-li-ol'ọ-ji), *n.* [See *helio-* and *-logy.*] The science of the sun.—**he-li-ol'o-gist,** *n.*

he-li-om-e-ter (hē-li-om'e-tėr), *n.* [See *helio-* and *-meter.*] An astronomical instrument orig. designed for measuring the sun's diameter, but now used esp. in determining the angular distance between two stars.—**he''li-o-met'ric, he''li-o-met'ri-cal** (-met'rik, -ri-kạl), *a.* Pertaining to the heliometer or to heliometry.—**he''li-o-met'ri-cal-ly,** *adv.*—**he-li-om'e-try,** *n.* [See *-metry.*] The art of making measurements with the heliometer.

he-li-oph-i-lous (hē-li-of'i-lus), *a.* [See *helio-* and *-philous.*] Sun-loving; attracted by sunlight.

he-li-o-scope (hē'li-ọ-skōp), *n.* [See *helio-* and *-scope.*] A device for viewing the sun without injury to the eyes, or a telescope fitted with such a device.—**he''li-o-scop'ic** (-skop'ik), *a.*

he-li-o-stat (hē'li-ọ-stat), *n.* [See *helio-* and *-stat.*] An instrument consisting of a mirror moved by clockwork, for reflecting the sun's rays in a fixed direction.

he-li-o-ther-a-py (hē''li-ọ-ther'ạ-pi), *n.* [See *helio-* and *therapy.*] Treatment of disease by means of sunlight.

he-li-o-trope (hē'li-ọ-trōp), *n.* [F. *héliotrope*, < L. *heliotropium*, < Gr. ἡλιοτρόπιον, < ἥλιος, sun, + τρέπειν, turn.] Any herb or shrub of the boraginaceous genus *Heliotropium*, esp. *H. peruvianum*, a garden-plant with small, fragrant purple flowers; also, a purple color, esp. one with a reddish tinge; also, bloodstone, a form of quartz; in *surv.*, etc., an instrument for reflecting the sun's rays to a distant point.

he-li-o-trop-ic (hē''li-ọ-trop'ik), *a.* [See *helio-* and *-tropic.*] In *bot.*, turning or tending toward the light; taking a particular direction under the influence of light.—**he''li-o-trop'i-cal-ly,** *adv.*—**he-li-ot'ro-pism** (-ot'rọ-pizm), *n.* In *bot.*, heliotropic tendency or growth.

he-li-o-type (hē'li-ọ-tīp), *n.* [See *helio-* and *-type.*] A picture or print produced by a photomechanical process in which the impression in ink is taken directly from a prepared gelatin film which has been exposed under a negative; also, the process itself.—**he'li-o-type,** *v. t.*; *-typed, -typing.* To make a heliotype of.—**he''li-o-typ'ic** (-tip'ik), *a.*—**he'li-o-ty-py** (-tī-pi), *n.* The heliotype process.

hel-i-spher-i-cal (hel-i-sfer'i-kạl), *a.* [From *helix* + *spherical.*] Of a line, etc., winding spirally on a sphere.

he-li-um (hē'li-um), *n.* [NL., < Gr. ἥλιος, sun.] Chem. sym., He; at. wt., 4.00. An inert gaseous element present in the sun's atmosphere, certain minerals, natural gas, etc., and also occurring as a decomposition product of radium and niton: used, because of its non-inflammability, as a substitute for inflammable gases in dirigible balloons.

he-lix (hē'liks), *n.*; pl. *helixes* (hē'lik-sez) or *helices* (hel'i-sēz). [L. *helix* (pl. *helices*), < Gr. ἕλιξ (pl. ἕλικες), spiral, curl, coil, convolution, < ἑλίσσειν, turn round, roll, wind.] An ascending or advancing curve proceeding as if wound round and along a cylinder (like a screw-thread) or a cone; hence, any spiral; also, a spiral object or part; in *arch.*, a spiral ornament, esp. a volute under the abacus of the Corinthian capital; in *anat.*, the curved fold forming most of the rim of the external ear.

Helices (*H, H*), as used in a Corinthian Capital.

hell (hel), *n.* [AS. *hell* = D. *hel* = G. *hölle* = Icel. *hel* = Goth. *halja*, hell; from the root of AS. *helan*, cover, hide: see *hall.*] The abode of the dead; the place of departed spirits; the grave; Sheol or Hades; also, the abode of evil and condemned spirits; the place or state of punishment of the wicked after death; Gehenna or Tartarus; hence, the infernal powers; also, any place or state of torment or misery (as, a *hell* on earth; "No civilised troops in the world could have endured the *hell* through which they came," Kipling's "Light That Failed," ii.); often, a gambling-house; also, a receptacle into which a tailor throws his shreds or a printer his broken type.—**hell′bend″er,** *n.* A large aquatic salamander, *Menopoma alleghaniensis,* common in the Ohio valley.—**hell′=broth,** *n.* A magical broth prepared for an infernal purpose.—**hell′=cat,** *n.* A furious vixen; a hag or witch.

Hellbender.

Hellcat. A U. S. Navy fighter plane (Grumman).

hel-le-bore (hel′ē-bōr), *n.* [L. *helleborus, elleborus,* < Gr. ἑλλέβορος, hellebore.] Any plant of the ranunculaceous genus *Helleborus*, esp. *H. niger* ('black hellebore'), a European herb with showy flowers; a cathartic made from the root of the black hellebore; also, any of the coarse herbs constituting the melanthiaceous genus *Veratrum*, as *V. album* (European 'white hellebore') and *V. viride* (American 'white hellebore'); an insecticide or a cardiac medicine made from the root of the European or the American white hellebore.—**hel-le-bo′re-in** (-bō′rē-in), *n.* In *chem.*, a poisonous crystalline glucoside occurring along with helleborin in species of hellebore (genus *Helleborus*): used in veterinary medicine.—**hel-le-bo-rin** (hel′ē-bō-rin or he-leb′ọ-rin), *n.* In *chem.*, a poisonous crystalline glucoside occurring in species of hellebore (genus *Helleborus*).

Black Hellebore.

Hel-lene (hel′ēn), *n.* [Gr. Ἕλλην.] A Greek.—**Hel-len-ic** (he-len′ik or -lē′nik), *a.* [Gr. Ἑλληνικός.] Grecian; Greek.—**Hel-len-ism** (hel′en-izm), *n.* [Gr. Ἑλληνισμός.] A peculiarity of the Greek language; also, conformity to or adoption of Greek speech, ideas, or customs; also, the character or spirit of the Greeks; ancient Greek culture or ideals.—**Hel′len-ist,** *n.* [Gr. Ἑλληνιστής.] One who adopts the Greek language, or Greek ideas or customs; esp., one of the ancient Jews, as in Asia Minor, Greece, and Egypt, who used Greek as their mother-tongue (opposed to *Hebraist*); also, one versed in the Greek language and literature; also, one of the learned Byzantine Greeks who disseminated the knowledge of the Greek language and literature in Europe at the Renaissance.—**Hel-len-is′tic,** *a.* Pertaining to Hellenists; following or resembling Hellenic usage; esp., pertaining to the Greeks or their language, culture, etc., after the time of Alexander the Great (356–323 B.C.) when Hellenic characteristics were modified by foreign elements.—**Hel-len-is′ti-cal-ly,** *adv.*—**Hel′len-ize** (-īz), *v.*; *-ized, -izing.* [Gr. Ἑλληνίζειν.] **I.** *intr.* To use the Greek language; adopt Greek ideas or customs. **II.** *tr.* To make Greek in character.—**Hel″len-i-za′tion** (-i-zā′shọn), *n.*—**Hel′len-iz-er** (-ī-zėr), *n.*

hel-ler (hel′ėr), *n.*; pl. *heller.* [G.] A small coin formerly current in Germany, worth half a pfennig; also, a modern Austrian copper coin equal to one hundredth of a krone.

Obverse. Reverse.
Heller of Count William VIII. of Hanau. British Museum.

hell-gram-mite, hell-gra-mite (hel′grạ-mit), *n.* [Origin uncertain.] The larva of a large neuropterous insect, *Corydalus cornutus*: used as a bait by anglers.

hell=hound (hel′hound), *n.* A hound or dog of hell; also, a fiend; a fiendish person.

hel-li-cat (hel′i-kat). [Cf. Sc. *hallockit*, giddy, also E. *hell-cat.*] **I.** *a.* Light-headed; giddy; wild. [Sc.] **II.** *n.* A wicked or cruel creature. [Sc.]

hell-ish (hel′ish), *a.* Of, like, or befitting hell; infernal; diabolical; fiendish; wicked.—**hell′ish-ly,** *adv.*—**hell′ish-ness,** *n.*

hell=kite (hel′kīt), *n.* A kite of hell; a person of hellish cruelty; a fiend. See Shakspere's "Macbeth," iv. 3. 217.

hel-lo (he-lō′). [= *hallo, hollo.*] **I.** *interj.* An exclamation to attract attention or express greeting (much used in calling through the telephone); also, an exclamation of surprise, etc. **II.** *n.*; pl. *hellos* (-lōz′). The call 'hello.'—**hel-lo′,** *v. i.*; *-loed, -loing.* To call 'hello,' as to attract attention or in greeting.—**hel-lo′=girl,** *n.* A girl employed as a telephone operator. [Colloq.]

helm[1] (helm), *n.* [AS. *helma* = G. *helm* = Icel. *hjālm*, rudder.] The handle or tiller, or the wheel, by which the rudder of a vessel is managed; the entire steering apparatus; hence, any thing or part for a similar purpose; fig., that by which affairs are guided; the place or post of direction or control.—**helm**[1], *v. t.* To steer; direct.

helm[2] (helm), *n.* [AS. *helm* = D. and G. *helm* = Icel. *hjālmr* = Goth. *hilms*, helmet; from the root of AS. *helan*, cover, hide: see *hall*, and cf. *helmet.*] A helmet. [Archaic.]—**helm**[2], *v. t.* To furnish or cover with a helmet. [Archaic.]

hel-met (hel′met), *n.* [OF. *helmet*, dim. of *helme* (F. *heaume*), helm, helmet; from Teut., and akin to E. *helm*[2].] A piece of armor for the head; also, any of various forms of protective head-covering worn by soldiers, firemen, divers, etc.; hence, anything resembling these, as in form or position; in *bot.* and *zoöl.*, a galea.—**hel′met,** *v.t.* To furnish or cover with a helmet: chiefly in *helmeted*, *pp.*—**hel′met=quail,** *n.* Any of the American gallinaceous birds constituting the genus *Lophortyx*, characterized by a recurved crest.

Medieval Helmets.
a, conical helmet with nasal, 12th century; *b*, conical basinet with camail secured to it, middle of 14th century; *c*, vizored basinet, early years of 15th century; *d*, cylindrical helmet with hinged vizor, middle of 13th century.

Helmet-quail (*Lophortyx californicus*).

hel-minth (hel′minth), *n.* [Gr. ἕλμινς (ἑλμινθ-), worm.] A worm; esp., an intestinal worm, as the tapeworm, roundworm, etc.—**hel-min′thic** (-min′thik), *a.* Pertaining to worms; also, expelling intestinal worms.—**hel-min-thol′o-gy** (-thol′ǫ-ji), *n.* [See *-logy.*] The science of helminths or worms.

helm-less (helm′les), *a.* Without a helm or steering apparatus; rudderless.

helms-man (helmz′mạn), *n.*; pl. *-men.* The man at the helm, who steers a ship; a steersman.

he-lo-derm (hē′lǭ-dėrm), *n.* [NL. *Heloderma,* < Gr. ἧλος, nail, stud, wart, + δέρμα, skin.] Either of two venomous lizards constituting the genus *Heloderma,* the Gila monster and the caltetepon.

Hel-ot (hel′ọt), *n.* [L. *Helotes, Hilotæ,* pl., < Gr. Εἵλως, Εἱλώτης, a Helot.] One of a class of serfs in ancient Sparta; hence [*l. c.*], a serf or slave; a bondman.—**hel′ot-ism,** *n.* Serfdom, as of the Helots in ancient Sparta; a system of serfage, as that of ancient Sparta.—**hel′ot-ry,** *n.* Helots collectively; also, serfdom; slavery.

help (help), *v.*; pret. *helped* (archaic *holp*), pp. *helped* (archaic *holpen*), ppr. *helping.* [AS. *helpan* = D. *helpen* = G. *helfen* = Icel. *hjālpa* = Goth. *hilpan,* help.] **I.** *tr.* In general, to furnish with or benefit by anything that furthers efforts or advances purposes or welfare (as, to *help* a person with one's strength, money, influence, or advice, by affording an opportunity, by keeping silence, etc.); be of service or advantage to (as, his training or his good eyesight *helps* him); further, promote, or facilitate (a process, etc.: as, remedies that *help* digestion); esp., to coöperate effectively with (a person, etc.) in efforts, labor, etc. (as, to *help* a man in his work; *help* me to move this trunk); aid; assist; assist in going, coming, getting, etc. (*down, in, off, out, up,* etc.: as, *help* me to the door; *help* him out of his difficulty; to *help* the work along); assist to attain to or obtain something specified (with *to*: as, "*Help* me to a candle, and pen, ink and paper," Shakspere's "Twelfth Night," iv. 2. 87; to *help* one's self to a thing, to take or appropriate it at will); hence, to serve with food at table (with *to*: as, to *help* a guest or one's self to a salad); serve or distribute (food), as at table; also, to relieve (a person, etc.) in want, trouble, or distress; succor; save; sometimes, to relieve from pain, disease, etc., as a physician, treatment, or remedy does; mitigate or cure (pain, disease, etc.); hence, to remedy, stop, or prevent (as, mistakes that it is too late to *help* now; I cannot *help* your thinking so); refrain from or forbear (as, "Nothwithstanding his vices, one can't *help* feeling for him": Sheridan's "School for Scandal," i. 1). **II.** *intr.* To give aid, assistance, or help; be of service or advantage (as, every little *helps*); also, to serve food, as at table.—**help,** *n.* [AS. *help.*] The act of helping; useful service in behalf of a person, cause, object, etc.; anything done or given in helping; aid or assistance; relief or succor; a single serving of food, or the portion served, as at table; also, a person or thing that helps; a source of aid, assistance, relief, or succor; a hired helper, esp., in the U. S., a household servant or a farm-laborer; a body of such helpers; also, means of remedying, stopping, or preventing (as, the thing is done, and there is no *help* for it).—**help′a-ble,** *a.* That may be helped.—**help′er,** *n.* —**help′ful,** *a.* Full of help; giving or affording help; serviceable; useful.—**help′ful-ly,** *adv.*—**help′ful-ness,** *n.* —**help′ing,** *n.* The act of one who or that which helps; the serving of food, as at table, or a portion served to a person at one time.—**help′ing-ly,** *adv.*—**help′less,** *a.* Destitute of help, aid, or succor (as, "Against the unarmed weakness of one virgin, Alone and *helpless*": Milton's "Comus," 583); also, unable to help one's self, weak, or dependent (as, a *helpless* cripple; a *helpless* child); sometimes, incapable, inefficient, or shiftless; also, affording no help (now rare); also, beyond help or remedy†.—**help′less-ly,** *adv.*—**help′less-ness,** *n.*—**help′mate,** *n.* [Cf. *helpmeet.*] A companion and helper; a partner in effort, work, or life: applied esp. to a wife or a husband.—**help′-meet,** *n.* [From the use (two words) in Gen. ii. 18, "It is not good that the man should be alone; I will make him an *help meet* for him" (that is, a helper meet for him).] A meet or fitting helper; a helpmate, esp. a wife.

hel-ter=skel-ter (hel′tėr-skel′tėr). [Origin obscure; appar. imit.] **I.** *adv.* In headlong, disorderly haste; hurry-scurry; pell-mell: as, "*Helter-skelter* have I rode to thee" (Shakspere's "2 Henry IV.," v. 3. 98). **II.** *a.* Characterized by headlong and disorderly haste. **III.** *n.* A helter-skelter flight, course, or performance; also, tumultuous haste or disorder.

helve (helv), *n.* [AS. *hielf, helfe,* handle; akin to E. *halter*[1].] The handle of an ax, hatchet, hammer, or the like.—**to throw** (**fling,** etc.) **the helve after the hatchet,** to send what is left to share or risk the fate of what is already gone; take further risk in a losing venture.—**helve,** *v. t.*; *helved, helving.* To furnish with a helve.

Hel-ve-tia (hel-vē′shiạ̈), *n.* [ML., < L. *Helvetii,* pl., a Celtic people of ancient Switzerland.] An ancient name of Switzerland. [Now chiefly poetic.]—**Hel-ve′tian. I.** *a.* Of or pertaining to the Helvetii (see *Helvetia,* etym.); also, Swiss. **II.** *n.* One of the Helvetii; also, a Swiss.—**Hel-vet′ic** (-vet′ik), *a.* [L. *Helveticus.*] Helvetian; Swiss.

hem[1] (hem), *n.* [AS. *hem,* prob. akin to *ham,* inclosure.] The edge or border of a garment, etc. (as, "They . . . besought him that they might only touch the *hem* of his garment": Mat. xiv. 36); specif., the edge made by folding back the margin of cloth and sewing it down; in general, the edge, border, or margin of anything (archaic: as, "the very *hem* o' the sea," Shakspere's "Timon of Athens," v. 4. 66).—**hem**[1], *v. t.*; *hemmed, hemming.* To edge or border (a garment, etc.) with something (obs. or archaic: as, "All the skirt about Was *hemd* with golden fringe," Spenser's "Faerie Queene," ii. 3. 26); also, to fold back and sew down the edge of (cloth, a garment, etc.); also, to form an edge or border to or about; go or stand (*round* or *about*) so as to inclose or confine (as, "The angelic squadron . . . began to *hem* him round With ported spears": Milton's "Paradise Lost," iv. 979); shut (*in* or *up*) closely (as, to be *hemmed* in by floods or by enemies).

hem[2] (hem). **I.** *interj.* An utterance resembling a slight clearing of the throat, used to attract attention, express doubt or hesitation, etc. **II.** *n.* The utterance or sound of 'hem.'—**hem**[2], *v. i.*; *hemmed, hemming.* To utter the sound expressed by 'hem' (as, "If any one is about, come to the foot of the stairs and *hem*": C. Brontë's "Jane Eyre," xx.); hence, to hesitate or stammer in speaking.

hema-, hæma-. Forms of Gr. αἷμα, blood, used in combination. Cf. *hemato-* (or *hæmato-*) and *hemo-* (or *hæmo-*), better forms as representing the regular Greek usage.

hem-a-chrome, hæm-a-chrome (hem′ạ-krōm or hē′mạ-), *n.* [From *hema-, hæma-,* + Gr. χρῶμα, color.] Coloring matter of the blood; hematin.

he-mal, hæ-mal (hē′mạl), *a.* [Gr. αἷμα, blood.] Of or pertaining to the blood or blood-vessels; also, noting, pertaining to, or situated on that side of the body containing the heart and great blood-vessels (cf. *neural*); ventral.

hem-a-poi-e-sis, hæm-a-poi-e-sis (hem″ạ-poi-ē′sis or hē″-mạ-), etc. Same as *hematopoiesis,* etc.

hem-a-tem-e-sis, hæm-a-tem-e-sis (hem-ạ-tem′e-sis or hē-mạ-), *n.* [NL. *hæmatemesis,* < Gr. αἷμα (αἱματ-), blood, + ἔμεσις, E. *emesis.*] In *pathol.*, the vomiting of blood. —**hem″a-te-met′ic, hæm″a-te-met′ic** (-tę-met′-ik), *a.*

he-mat-ic, hæ-mat-ic (hę-mat′ik). [Gr. αἱματικός, < αἷμα, blood.] **I.** *a.* Of or pertaining to blood; containing blood; of the color of blood; acting on the blood, as a medicine. **II.** *n.* A hematic medicine.

hem-a-ti-dro-sis, hæm-a-ti-dro-sis (hem″ạ-ti-drō′sis or hē″mạ-), *n.* [NL. *hæmatidrosis,* < Gr. αἷμα (αἱματ-), blood, + ἵδρωσις, E. *hidrosis.*] In *pathol.*, the sweating of blood or a bloody fluid.

hem-a-tim-e-ter, hæm-a-tim-e-ter (hem-ạ-tim′e-tėr or hē-mạ-), *n.* [Gr. αἷμα (αἱματ-), blood, + μέτρον, measure.] A device for counting blood-corpuscles, consisting essentially of a microscope-slide having a cell which contains a known amount of blood.

hem-a-tin, hæm-a-tin (hem′ạ-tin or hē′mạ-), *n.* [Gr. αἷμα (αἱματ-), blood.] A pigment containing iron, produced in the decomposition of hemoglobin.—**hem-a-tin′ic, hæm-a-tin′ic,** *n.* A medicine, as a compound of iron, which tends to increase the amount of hematin or hemoglobin in the blood.—**hem″a-ti-nom′e-ter, hæm″a-ti-nom′e-ter**

(-tī-nom′e-tėr), *n.* [See *-meter.*] A device for determining the amount of hematin or hemoglobin in the blood.

hem-a-tite, hæm-a-tite (hem′ạ-tīt or hē′mạ-), *n.* [L. *hæmatites*, hematite, < Gr. αἱματίτης, blood-like, < αἷμα, blood.] A native oxide of iron, Fe_2O_3, having a reddish color when powdered: an important ore.—**hem-a-tit′ic, hæm-a-tit′ic** (-tit′ik), *a.*

hemato-, hæmato-. Forms of Gr. αἷμα (αἱματ-), blood, used in combination. Cf. *hema-* and *hemo-.*—**hem-a-to-blast, hæm-a-to-blast** (hem′ạ-tọ-blast or hē′mạ-), *n.* [+ *-blast.*] A protoplasmic mass, as in bone-marrow, from which a red blood-corpuscle is supposed to develop.—**hem′a-to-cele, hæm′a-to-cele** (-sēl), *n.* [+ *-cele.*] In *pathol.*, a tumor containing blood.—**hem′a-to-crit, hæm′a-to-crit** (-krit), *n.* [+ Gr. κριτής, decider, judge.] A centrifugal device for determining the volume of blood-corpuscles in a given quantity of blood.—**hem′a-to-gen, hæm′a-to-gen** (-jen), *n.* [+ *-gen.*] An iron-containing compound obtained from the yolk of hens' eggs, and supposed to be concerned in the production of hemoglobin; also, any of various preparations used in the treatment of anemia, etc. —**hem″a-to-gen′e-sis, hæm″a-to-gen′e-sis** (-jen′e-sis), *n.* The formation of blood.—**hem-a-tog′e-nous, hæm-a-tog′e-nous** (-toj′e-nus), *a.* [+ *-genous.*] Originating in the blood; also, blood-producing.—**hem′a-toid, hæm′a-toid,** *a.* [Gr. αἱματοειδής: see *-oid.*] Resembling blood; blood-like.—**hem-a-tol′o-gy, hæm-a-tol′o-gy** (-tol′ọ-ji), *n.* [+ *-logy.*] The branch of biology dealing with the blood. —**hem-a-tol′y-sis, hæm-a-tol′y-sis** (-i-sis), etc. Same as *hemolysis*, etc.—**hem-a-to′ma, hæm-a-to′ma** (-tō′mä), *n.*; pl. *-mas* or *-mata* (-mạ-tạ). [NL. *hæmatoma*: see *-oma.*] In *pathol.*, a swelling or tumor filled with extravasated blood.—**hem-a-tom′e-ter, hæm-a-tom′e-ter** (-tom′e-tėr), *n.* [+ *-meter.*] Any of various blood-testing devices, as for determining the percentage of hemoglobin, estimating the number of blood-corpuscles present, or measuring the blood-pressure.—**hem″a-to-poi-e′sis, hæm″a-to-poi-e′sis** (-poi-ē′sis), *n.* [NL. *hæmatopoiesis*, < Gr. αἱματοποίησις (ποιεῖν, make).] The formation of blood.—**hem″a-to-poi-et′ic, hæm″a-to-poi-et′ic** (-et′ik), *a.*

hem-a-to-sis, hæm-a-to-sis (hem-ạ-tō′sis or hē-mạ-), *n.* [NL. *hæmatosis*, < Gr. αἱμάτωσις, < αἱματοῦν, make into blood, < αἷμα, blood.] The formation of blood; also, the conversion of venous into arterial blood; arterialization.

hem-a-tox-y-lin, hæm-a-tox-y-lin (hem-ạ-tok′si-lin or hē-mạ-), *n.* [NL. *Hæmatoxylon*, the logwood genus, < Gr. αἷμα (αἱματ-), blood, + ξύλον, wood.] A crystalline compound obtained from logwood: used in microscopy for staining.

hem-a-to-zo-ön, hæm-a-to-zo-ön (hem″ạ-tọ-zō′on or hē″mạ-), *n.*; pl. *-zoa* (-zō′ä). [NL. *hæmatozoön*, < Gr. αἷμα (αἱματ-), blood, + ζῷον, animal.] An animal parasite living in the blood.—**hem″a-to-zo′ic, hæm″a-to-zo′ic,** *a.*

hem-el-y-trum (hem-el′i-trum), etc. Same as *hemielytrum*, etc.

hem-e-ra-lo-pi-a (hem″ẹ-rạ-lō′pi-ä), *n.* [NL., < Gr. ἡμεράλωψ, blind by day, < ἡμέρα, day, + ἀλαός, blind, + ὤψ, eye.] A condition of the eyes in which distinct vision is possible only at night or in dim light; day-blindness; also, nyctalopia, a visual condition exactly opposite; night-blindness.

hemi-. [Gr. ἡμι-: see *semi-.*] A prefix meaning 'half.' Cf. *semi-.*

hem-i-al-gia (hem-i-al′jiä), *n.* [NL.: see *hemi-* and *-algia.*] In *pathol.*, pain or neuralgia involving only one side of the body or head.

hem-i-a-nop-si-a (hem″i-ạ-nop′si-ä), *n.* [NL., < Gr. ἡμι-, half, + ἀν- priv. + ὄψις, sight.] In *pathol.*, complete or partial loss of sight in one half of the field of vision, affecting one or both eyes.

he-mic, hæ-mic (hē′mik), *a.* [Gr. αἷμα, blood.] Of or pertaining to the blood.

hem-i-cra-ni-a (hem-i-krā′ni-ä), *n.* [LL., < Gr. ἡμικρανία, < ἡμι-, half, + κρανίον, skull.] In *pathol.*, a kind of severe headache, limited usually to one side of the head, and often accompanied with nausea; migraine; megrim.

hem-i-cy-cle (hem′i-sī-kl), *n.* [L. *hemicyclium*, < Gr. ἡμικύκλιον, < ἡμι-, half, + κύκλος, circle.] The half of a circle; a semicircle; a semicircular or approximately semicircular structure.

hem-i-cy-lin-dri-cal (hem″i-si-lin′dri-kạl), *a.* [See *hemi-.*] Having the form of half of a cylinder divided in the direction of its axis.

hem-i-dem-i-sem-i-qua-ver (hem′i-dem′i-sem′i-kwā″vėr), *n.* [See *hemi-.*] In *music*, a note having half the time-value of a demisemiquaver; a sixty-fourth-note. See note under *note, n.*

hem-i-el-y-trum, hem-i-el-y-tron (hem-i-el′i-trum, -tron), *n.*; pl. *-tra* (-trä). [See *hemi-* and *elytrum.*] One of the fore wings of hemipterous and especially heteropterous insects, coriaceous at the base and membranous at the tip.—**hem-i-el′y-tral** (-trạl), *a.*

hem-i-he-dral (hem-i-hē′drạl), *a.* [Gr. ἡμι-, half, + ἕδρα, seat, base.] Of a crystal, having only half the planes or faces required by the maximum symmetry.—**hem-i-he′drism,** *n.* The property of being hemihedral.—**hem-i-he′dron** (-drọn), *n.* A hemihedral crystal or form.

hem-i-mor-phic (hem-i-môr′fik), *a.* [Gr. ἡμι-, half, + μορφή, form.] Of a crystal, having the two ends of an axis unlike in their planes or modifications.—**hem-i-mor′phism,** *n.* The property of being hemimorphic.—**hem-i-mor′phite** (-fīt), *n.* Calamin (hydrous silicate of zinc): so called from its hemimorphic crystals.

he-min, hæ-min (hē′min), *n.* [Gr. αἷμα, blood.] The hydrochloride of hematin, occurring in reddish-brown crystals, which in tests serve to indicate the presence of blood.

hem-i-par-a-site (hem-i-par′ạ-sīt), *n.* [See *hemi-.*] A partially parasitic plant.—**hem″i-par-a-sit′ic** (-sit′ik), *a.*

hem-i-ple-gi-a (hem-i-plē′ji-ä), *n.* [NL., < Gr. ἡμι-, half, + -πληγία as in παραπληγία, E. *paraplegia.*] In *pathol.*, paralysis affecting only one side of the body.—**hem-i-pleg′ic** (-plej′ik or -plē′jik), *a.*

he-mip-ter (hẹ-mip′tėr), *n.* [NL. *Hemiptera*, pl., < Gr. ἡμι-, half, + πτερόν, wing.] Any of the *Hemiptera*, an order of insects (certain of which have the fore wings half or in part thickened or coriaceous) which includes the true bugs (bedbug, water-bugs, etc.), lice, and aphids.—**he-mip′ter-an,** *a.* and *n.*—**he-mip′ter-ous,** *a.* Having the fore wings half (or in part) thickened or coriaceous, as most of the true bugs; belonging to the *Hemiptera* (see *hemipter*).

hem-i-sect (hem′i-sekt), *v. t.* [Gr. ἡμι-, half, + L. *sectus*, pp. of *secare*, cut: cf. *bisect.*] To cut into halves; bisect, esp. longitudinally, or into equal right and left parts: as, to *hemisect* an animal body.—**hem-i-sec′tion** (-sek′shọn), *n.*

hem-i-sphere (hem′i-sfēr), *n.* [L. *hemisphærium*, < Gr. ἡμισφαίριον, < ἡμι-, half, + σφαῖρα, E. *sphere.*] The half of a sphere; esp., half of the terrestrial globe or the celestial sphere, or a map or projection of either of these (as, the eastern and western *hemispheres*, the eastern and western halves of the terrestrial globe, the former including the continents of Europe, Asia, and Africa and their islands, and the latter the two American continents and their islands; the northern and southern *hemispheres*, the halves of the terrestrial globe north and south of the equator, or the corresponding divisions of the celestial sphere); in *anat.*, either of the lateral halves of the cerebrum.—**hem-i-spher′ic, hem-i-spher′i-cal** (-sfer′ik, -i-kạl), *a.* Of, pertaining to, or having the form of a hemisphere.—**hem-i-spher′i-cal-ly,** *adv.*—**hem-i-sphe′roid** (-sfē′roid), *n.* The half of a spheroid.—**hem″i-sphe-roi′dal** (-sfẹ-roi′dạl), *a.*

hem-i-stich (hem′i-stik), *n.* [L. *hemistichium*, < Gr. ἡμιστίχιον, < ἡμι-, half, + στίχος, row, line.] In *pros.*, the exact or approximate half of a stich, or poetic verse or line, esp. as divided by a cæsura or the like; also, an incomplete line, or a line of less than the usual length.

hem-i-sys-to-le (hem-i-sis′tọ-lē), *n.* [See *hemi-* and *systole.*] In *physiol.*, a contraction of only one ventricle of the heart.

hem-i-trope (hem′i-trōp). [F. *hémitrope*, < Gr. ἡμι-, half, + -τροπος, turned, < τρέπειν, turn.] **I.** *a.* Half-turned: specif. applied in mineralogy to a compound or twin crystal which has two similar parts or halves, one of which is turned half way round upon the other. **II.** *n.* A hemitrope crystal.—**hem-i-trop′ic** (-trop′ik), *a.*

hem-lock (hem′lok), *n.* [AS. *hemlic, hymlice.*] A poisonous apiaceous herb, *Conium maculatum,* with spotted stems, finely divided leaves, and small white flowers, used medicinally as a powerful sedative; a poisonous drink made from this herb (as, "A drowsy numbness pains My sense, as though of *hemlock* I had drunk": Keats's "Ode to a Nightingale"); also, any of various other apiaceous herbs, esp. species of the genus *Cicuta* ('water-hemlock'); also the hemlock-spruce, or its wood.—**hem′lock=spruce′,** *n.* Any of the trees of the pinaceous genus *Tsuga,* esp. *T. canadensis,* a tree of eastern North America whose bark is used in tanning. See cut below.

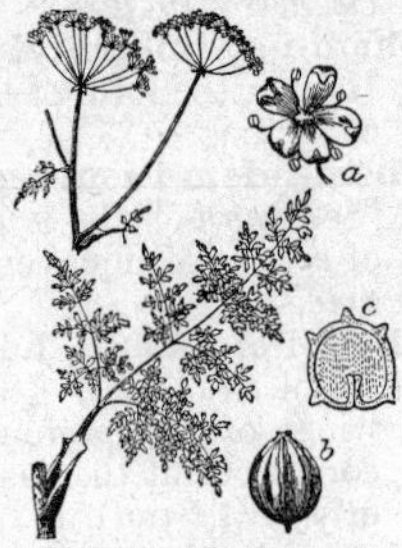

Hemlock (*Conium maculatum*). — *a,* flower; *b,* fruit; *c,* carpel, cut transversely.

hem-mer (hem′ėr), *n.* One who or that which hems; a sewing-machine attachment for hemming edges.

hemo-, hæmo-. Shorter forms of *hemato-, hæmato-* (Gr. αἱματο- contracted to αἱμο-). Cf. *hema-.*—**hem-o-gas-tric, hæm-o-gas-tric** (hem-ǫ-gas′trik or hē-mǫ-), *a.* [See *gastric.*] Characterized by the effusion of blood into the stomach: as, *hemogastric* fever (yellow fever).—**hem-o-glo′bin, hæm-o-glo′bin** (-glō′bin), *n.* [+ L. *globus,* E. *globe.*] The coloring matter of the red blood-corpuscles, which serves to convey oxygen to the tissues: occurring in its simplest form (hemoglobin proper) in venous blood, and in combination with oxygen (oxyhemoglobin) in arterial blood.—**hem″o-glo-bi-nu′ri-a, hæm″o-glo-bi-nu′ri-a,** (-bi-nū′ri-ą), *n.* [NL.: see *-uria.*] In *pathol.,* the presence of hemoglobin in the urine.—**he-moid, hæ-moid** (hē′moid), *a.* [Gr. αἱμοειδής: see *-oid.*] Blood-like; hematoid.

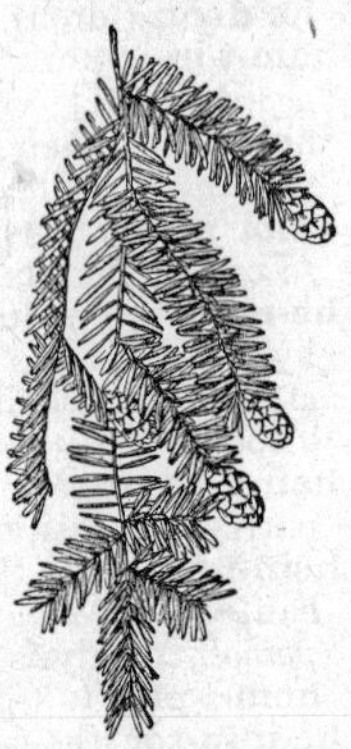
Branch with Cones of Hemlock-spruce (*Tsuga canadensis*).

he-mol, hæ-mol (hē′mol or -mōl), *n.* [Gr. αἷμα, blood.] An iron-containing product derived from hemoglobin: used as a hematinic.

he-mol-y-sin, hæ-mol-y-sin (hę̄-mol′i-sin), *n.* [See *hemolysis.*] A substance which causes the dissolution of the red corpuscles of the blood.

he-mol-y-sis, hæ-mol-y-sis (hę̄-mol′i-sis), *n.* [See *hemo-* and *-lysis.*] The process of dissolution of the blood-corpuscles.—**hem-o-lyt-ic, hæm-o-lyt-ic** (hem-ǫ-lit′ik or hē-mǫ-), *a.*

hem-o-phil-i-a, hæm-o-phil-i-a (hem-ǫ-fil′i-ą or hē-mǫ-), *n.* [NL. *hæmophilia,* < Gr. αἷμα, blood, + φιλία, affection, fondness.] In *pathol.,* a morbid condition, usually congenital, characterized by a tendency to bleed immoderately, as from an insignificant wound: due to the blood not coagulating properly.—**hem-o-phil′ic, hæm-o-phil′ic,** *a.*

he-mop-ty-sis, hæ-mop-ty-sis (hę̄-mop′ti-sis), *n.* [NL. *hæmoptysis,* < Gr. αἷμα, blood, + πτύσις, spitting.] In *pathol.,* the expectoration of blood or bloody mucus.

hem-or-rhage, hæm-or-rhage (hem′ǫ-rāj), *n.* [L. *hæmorrhagia,* < Gr. αἱμορραγία, < αἷμα, blood, + ῥηγνύναι, break, burst forth.] A discharge of blood, as from a ruptured blood-vessel; profuse bleeding.—**hem-or-rhag′ic, hæm-or-rhag′ic** (-raj′ik), *a.*

hem-or-rhoid, hæm-or-rhoid (hem′ǫ-roid), *n.* [L. *hæmorrhoida,* < Gr. αἱμορροΐς (pl. -ΐδες), < αἷμα, blood, + ῥεῖν, flow.] A swelling formed by the dilatation of a blood-vessel at the anus: usually in *pl.*—**hem-or-rhoi′dal, hæm-or-rhoi′dal** (-roi′dąl), *a.*

hem-o-spa-sia, hæm-o-spa-sia (hem-ǫ-spā′zią or hē-mǫ-), *n.* [NL. *hæmospasia,* < Gr. αἷμα, blood, + σπᾶν, draw.] In *med.,* the drawing or attracting of blood to a part, as by cupping.—**hem-o-spas′tic, hæm-o-spas′tic** (-spas′tik), *a.*

hem-o-sta-sia, hæm-o-sta-sia (hem-ǫ-stā′zią or hē-mǫ-), *n.* [NL. *hæmostasia,* < Gr. αἷμα, blood, + ἱστάναι, cause to stand.] In *med.,* stagnation of blood in a part; also, any operation for arresting hemorrhage, as the ligation of an artery. Also **he-mos-ta-sis, hæ-mos-ta-sis** (hę̄-mos′tą-sis).—**hem′o-stat, hæm′o-stat** (-stat), *n.* [See *-stat.*] An instrument used to compress a bleeding vessel in order to arrest hemorrhage.—**hem-o-stat′ic, hæm-o-stat′ic. I.** *a.* Pertaining to stagnation of the blood; also, arresting hemorrhage, as a drug; styptic. **II.** *n.* A hemostatic agent or substance.

hem-o-tho-rax, hæm-o-tho-rax (hem-ǫ-thō′raks or hē-mǫ-), *n.* [See *hemo-.*] In *pathol.,* the presence of blood in a pleural cavity.

hemp (hemp), *n.* [AS. *henep, hænep,* = D. *hennep* = G. *hanf* = Icel. *hampr,* hemp; akin to Gr. κάνναβις, L. *cannabis.*] A tall, annual moraceous herb, *Cannabis sativa,* native in Asia, but cultivated in many parts of the world (see *carl-hemp* and *fimble*); the tough fiber of this plant, used for making coarse fabrics, ropes, etc.; also, a narcotic drug obtained from the Indian hemp (see below); also, any of various plants resembling hemp, or any of various fibers similar to that of hemp (cf. *manila,* also *Sisal hemp*); also, a hangman's rope.—**Indian hemp,** an East Indian variety, *Cannabis sativa indica* (or *Cannabis indica*), of common hemp, having narcotic and poisonous properties and yielding hashish, bhang, cannabin, etc.; also, a North American apocynaceous herb, *Apocynum cannabinum,* yielding a strong fiber, which was used by American Indians for making nets (also called *Canadian,* or *Canada, hemp*).—**hemp′=ag′ri-mo-ny,** *n.* A European asteraceous herb, *Eupatorium cannabinum,* with dull purplish or reddish flowers; also, any of various related species.—**hemp′en,** *a.* Made of hemp; of or pertaining to hemp; resembling hemp.

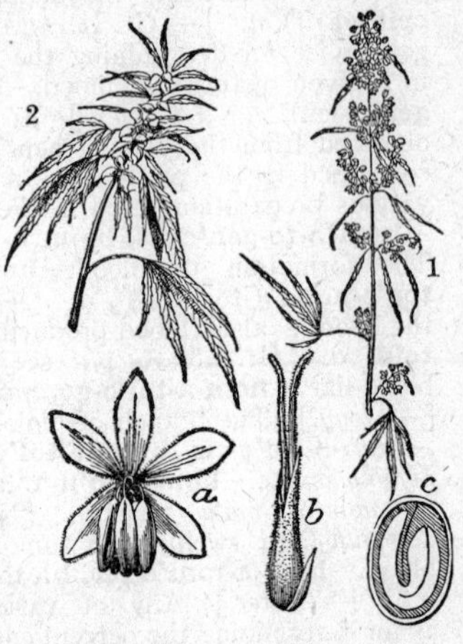

Male (1) and Female (2) Plants of Hemp (*Cannabis sativa*). — *a,* male flower; *b,* female flower; *c,* embryo.

hemp-ie, hemp-y (hem′pi). [From *hemp* (as the material of the rope).] **I.** *a.* Deserving of the hangman's rope; liable to be hanged; hence, wild, mischievous, or giddy (as, "I was a daft *hempie* lassie then, and little thought what was to come o't": Scott's "Old Mortality," xlii.). [Sc. and north. Eng.] **II.** *n.*; pl. *hempies* (-piz). One deserving to be hanged; hence, a wild or giddy young person (as, "When I was a *hempie* of nineteen or twenty, it wasna my fault if I wasna at a' the merry-makings": Scott's "Monastery," iv.). [Sc. and north. Eng.]

hemp=net-tle (hemp′net″l), *n.* A coarse menthaceous weed, *Galeopsis tetrahit,* likened to the hemp from its general appearance and to the nettle from its bristly hairs; loosely, any plant of the same genus.

hemp=palm (hemp′päm), *n.* A palm, *Chamærops humilis,* of the Mediterranean region, yielding a fiber of commercial value; also, a palm, *Trachycarpus excelsus,* of China and Japan, also valued for its fiber.

hemp=seed (hemp′sēd), *n.* The seed of hemp, used as a food for cage-birds; also, a gallows-bird (see Shakspere's "2 Henry IV.," ii. 1. 64).

hemp-weed (hemp′wēd), *n.* Same as *hemp-agrimony.*

hem-stitch (hem′stich), *v. t.* To hem along a line from which threads have been drawn out, drawing the cross-threads into a series of little groups.—**hem′stitch,** *n.* The stitch used or the needlework done in hemstitching.

hen (hen), *n.* [AS. *henn* (= D. *hen* = G. *henne*), hen, fem. of AS. *hana* = D. *haan* = G. *hahn* = Icel. *hani* = Goth. *hana,* cock; prob. akin to L. *canere,* sing.] The female of the domestic fowl; sometimes, the domestic fowl without reference to sex; also, the female of any bird (as, "I will be more jealous of thee than a Barbary cock-pigeon over his *hen*": Shakspere's "As You Like It," iv. 1. 151); a female fish or the like.—**hen′bane,** *n.* A coarse solanaceous herb, *Hyoscyamus niger*, native in Europe and Asia, bearing sticky, hairy foliage of a disagreeable odor, and yellowish-brown flowers, and possessing narcotic and poisonous properties: esp. destructive to domestic fowls.—**hen′bit,** *n.* A weed, *Lamium amplexicaule*, with small purplish flowers.

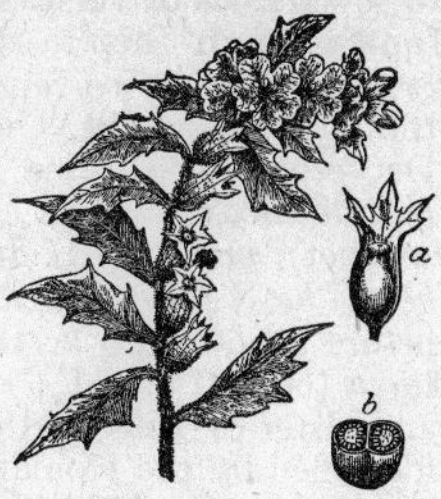

Henbane. — *a*, fruit; *b*, capsule, cut transversely.

hence (hens), *adv.* [ME. *hennes* (with adverbial suffix -*s*), < *henne*, < AS. *heonan*, *hionan*, = G. *hinnen*, hence; from the pronominal stem represented by E. *he.*] From here, away from this place, or to a distance (as, to go *hence*: often used, by ellipsis of *go*, *depart*, or other verb of motion, with the effect of a verb, esp. as a command, as in 'hence!' go hence, or depart, or 'hence with it!' go hence with it, or take it away); at a distance from here, or away (as, "I have a kinsman not past three quarters of a mile *hence*": Shakspere's "Winter's Tale," iv. 3. 86); sometimes, specif., from this world or this life, or in the next world (as, "before I go *hence*, and be no more," Ps. xxxix. 13; "Both here and *hence* pursue me lasting strife, If, once a widow, ever I be wife!" Shakspere's "Hamlet," iii. 2. 232); also, from this time onward, or henceforth (as, "That the rule of men was over now, And *hence*, the subject world to woman's will must bow": Shelley's "Revolt of Islam," ix. 16); at the end of a specified period from now in the future (as, he will come again a month *hence*); also, from this source or origin (as, "The sun's orb . . . great palace now of light . . . *hence* the morning planet gilds her horns": Milton's "Paradise Lost," vii. 366); as a result from this fact or circumstance (as, he is ill, and *hence* unable to come); as an inference from this fact or these data, for this reason, or therefore (as, it is of the best quality, and *hence* probably satisfactory). —**from hence,** hence: a pleonasm.—**hence′forth′,** *adv.* From this time forth; from now on: as, "Hitherto he had been merely a soldier . . . *Henceforth* he is to be chiefly regarded as a statesman" (Macaulay's "Essays," Lord Clive). Sometimes preceded by *from*.—**hence′for′ward, hence′for′wards,** *adv.* Henceforth: as, "*Henceforward* we must consider them as a kind of privileged persons" (Burke's "Revolution in France," 4).

hench-man (hench′ma̤n), *n.*; pl. -*men*. [ME. *henchemanne*, *henxtman*, prob. orig. meaning 'groom,' and appar. < AS. *hengest*, stallion, horse, + *mann*, man.] A squire† or page† (as, "I do but beg a little changeling boy, To be my *henchman*": Shakspere's "Midsummer Night's Dream," ii. 1. 121); also, a trusty attendant or follower; now, usually, a close and obedient adherent, esp. one who carries out without demur or scruple the instructions of a leader, as in politics (as, "You will become the catspaw of corrupt functionaries and the *henchman* of ambitious humbugs": G. B. Shaw's "Man and Superman," iii.); a servile and unscrupulous follower.—**hench′wom″an,** *n.*; pl. -*women* (-wim″en).

hendeca-. Form of Gr. ἕνδεκα, eleven, used in combination.

hen-dec-a-gon (hen-dek′a̤-gon), *n.* [See *hendeca-* and *-gon.*] A plane figure having eleven angles and eleven sides. —**hen-de-cag′o-nal** (-de-kag′o̤-na̤l), *a.*

hen-dec-a-syl-la-ble (hen″dek-a̤-sil′a̤-bl), *n.* [L. *hendecasyllabus*, < Gr. ἑνδεκασύλλαβος, of eleven syllables (συλλαβή, syllable).] In *pros.*, a metrical line of eleven syllables. —**hen″dec-a-syl-lab′ic** (-si-lab′ik), *a.*

hen-di-a-dys (hen-dī′a̤-dis), *n.* [NL., < Gr. ἓν διὰ δυοῖν, 'one through two.'] In *rhet.*, a figure in which a single complex idea is expressed by two words connected by a copulative conjunction, as in 'to pour from *cups and gold*' instead of 'from *golden cups*.'

hen-e-quen (hen′ḗ-ken), *n.* [Sp. *jeniquên*; from native name.] The fiber of an agave, *Agave rigida sisalana*, of Yucatan, used for making ropes, coarse fabrics, etc.; the fiber of certain related species; also, a plant yielding such fiber. Cf. *Sisal hemp.*

hen=hawk (hen′hâk), *n.* Any of various hawks or buzzards that prey on poultry, esp. *Buteo borealis*, the red-tailed buzzard, common in the U. S.

hen=heart-ed (hen′här″ted), *a.* Chicken-hearted; cowardly.

hen-na (hen′a̤), *n.* [Ar. *hennā*, *hinnā*.] A lythraceous shrub or small tree, *Lawsonia inermis*, of Asia and the Levant, cultivated for its leaves, which are used for making a reddish-orange dye and a cosmetic; a dye or cosmetic so made; also, a brownish-red color.

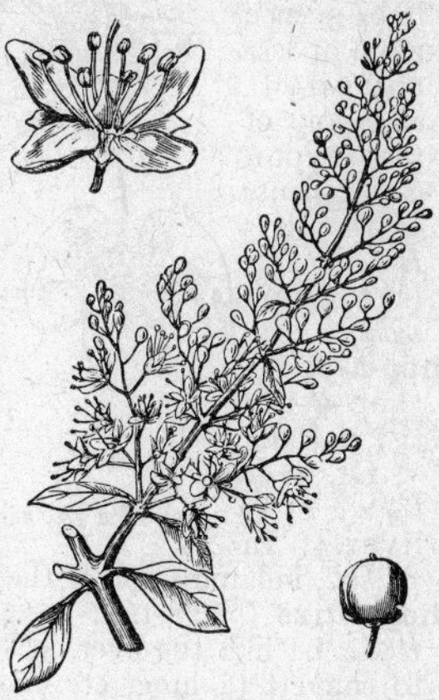
Branch of Henna, with flower and fruit.

hen-ner-y (hen′ėr-i), *n.*; pl. -*ies* (-iz). A place where fowls are kept.

hen-nin (hen′in), *n.* [OF.] A high, conical head-dress with a veil depending from it, worn by women in the 15th century.

hen-o-the-ism (hen′o̤-thē-izm), *n.* [Gr. εἷς (ἑν-), one, + θεός, god.] The belief in one god as the deity of a race, tribe, etc., without denial of the existence of other gods.—**hen′o-the-ist,** *n.*—**hen″o-the-is′tic,** *a.*

he-not-ic (he-not′ik), *a.* [Gr. ἑνωτικός, < ἑνοῦν, unite, < εἷς (ἑν-), one.] Tending to make one; unifying; harmonizing.

hen-peck (hen′pek), *v. t.* [Back-formation from *henpecked.*] To domineer over, as a wife over her husband: as, "Ye lords of ladies intellectual, Inform us truly, have they not *henpeck'd* you all?" (Byron's "Don Juan," i. 22).

hen-pecked (hen′pekt), *a.* [Lit., 'pecked by the hen,' as a domestic cock.] Of a man, domineered over or kept in meek submission by his wife or some other woman of his household.

hen-ri-et-ta (hen-ri-et′a̤), *n.* [From *Henrietta*, woman's name.] A soft, lustrous fabric of wool, usually with a silk warp, having a twilled face and resembling a fine cashmere. Also called *Henrietta cloth.*

hen=roost (hen′röst), *n.* A place where poultry roost at night.

hen-ry (hen′ri), *n.*; pl. -*ries* or -*rys* (-riz). [From Joseph *Henry* (1797–1878), American physicist.] In *elect.*, the practical unit of inductance, equivalent to the inductance of a circuit in which an electromotive force of one volt is produced by an inducing current which varies at the rate of one ampere per second.

hent (hent), *v. t.*; *hent*, *henting*. [AS. *hentan*, seize.] To seize, grasp, catch, or take, as with the hand (archaic or prov.); fig., to take possession of† or affect powerfully† (as, "What hellish fury hath . . . thee *hent?*" Spenser's "Faerie Queene," ii. 6. 49); also, to reach or occupy, as a place†; also, to 'take' or clear, as a barrier† (as, "Jog on, jog on, the foot-path way, And merrily *hent* the stile-a": Shakspere's "Winter's Tale," iv. 3. 133); also, to encounter†, experience†, or find†.—**hent†,** *n.* A seizing or grasping; also, a purpose or intention (as, "Up, sword; and know thou a more horrid *hent*": Shakspere's "Hamlet," iii. 3. 88).

he-or-tol-o-gy (hē-ôr-tol′o̤-ji), *n.* [Gr. ἑορτή, feast, festival: see *-logy*. Cf. MGr. ἑορτολόγιον, calendar of festivals.] Systematic study or knowledge of feasts or festivals, specif. those of the church, including their origin, history, significance, etc.—**he-or-to-log-i-cal** (hḗ-ôr-to̤-loj′i-ka̤l), *a.*

hep (hep), *n.* Same as *hip*².

he-par (hē′pär), *n.* [L., < Gr. ἧπαρ, liver.] In *old chem.*, any of various liver-colored or reddish-brown substances, consisting wholly or in part of a sulphur compound, esp. a metallic sulphide.

he-pat-ic (hḗ-pat′ik). [L. *hepaticus*, < Gr. ἡπατικός, < ἧπαρ (ἡπατ-), liver.] **I.** *a.* Of or pertaining to the liver; acting on the liver, as a medicine; also, liver-colored; dark reddish-brown; also, belonging or pertaining to the class *Hepaticæ* of cryptogamic plants (see *liverwort*). **II.** *n.* A medicine acting on the liver; also, a plant of the class *Hepaticæ* (see *liverwort*).

he-pat-i-ca (hḗ-pat′i-kä), *n.*; pl. -*cas*, L. -*cæ* (-sē). [NL., prop. fem. of L. *hepaticus*: see *hepatic.*] Any of the ranunculaceous herbs, with three-lobed leaves and delicate purplish, pink, or white flowers, constituting the genus *Hepatica*, as *H. hepatica*, whose leaf-lobes are more or less rounded; also, any of the cryptogamic plants of the class *Hepaticæ* (see *liverwort*).

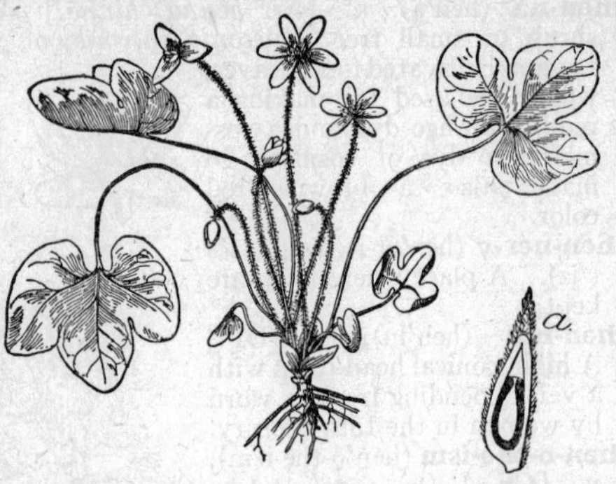

Hepatica (*H. hepatica*). — *a*, fruit, cut longitudinally.

hep-a-ti-tis (hep-ą-tī′tis), *n.* [NL., < Gr. ἧπαρ (ἡπατ-), liver.] In *pathol.*, inflammation of the liver.

hep-a-tize (hep′ą-tīz), *v. t.*; *-tized, -tizing.* [Cf. Gr. ἡπατίζειν, be like the liver, < ἧπαρ (ἡπατ-), liver.] In *pathol.*, to convert (a lung, etc.) into liver-like tissue by engorgement.—**hep″a-ti-za′tion** (-ti-zā′shǫn), *n.*

hepato-. Form of Gr. ἧπαρ (ἡπατ-), liver, used in combination.—**hep-a-to-cir-rho-sis** (hep″ą-tō-si-rō′sis), *n.* In *pathol.*, cirrhosis of the liver.—**hep″a-to-gen′ic** (-tǫ-jen′ik), *a.* [+ *-genic.*] Produced in or arising from the liver. Also **hep-a-tog′e-nous** (-toj′e-nus).—**hep″a-to-pex′i-a** (-pek′si-ą), **hep′a-to-pex″y,** *n.* [NL. *hepatopexia* (Gr. πῆξις, a making fast).] Surgical fixation of a floating liver.

He-phæs-tus (hē-fes′tus), *n.* [Gr. Ἥφαιστος.] The Greek god of fire and metal-working, identified by the Romans with Vulcan.

Hep-ple-white (hep′l-hwīt), *a.* Pertaining to George Hepplewhite (died 1786), an English furniture-maker; in the style of Hepplewhite.

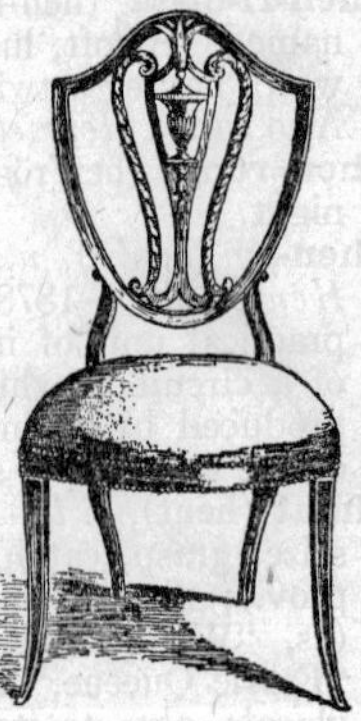

Hepplewhite Chair.

hepta-, hept-. Forms of Gr. ἑπτά, seven, used in combination.

hep-ta-chord (hep′tą-kôrd), *n.* [Gr. ἑπτάχορδος, seven-stringed: see *hepta-* and *chord*[1].] In *music*, an instrument with seven strings; also, a diatonic series of seven tones; also, the interval of a major seventh.

hep-tad (hep′tad), *n.* [LL. *heptas* (*heptad-*), < Gr. ἑπτάς (ἑπταδ-), < ἑπτά, seven.] The number seven; also, a group of seven; in *chem.*, an element, atom, or radical having a valence of seven.

hep-ta-gon (hep′tą-gon), *n.* [Gr. ἑπτάγωνος, heptangular: see *hepta-* and *-gon.*] A plane figure having seven angles and seven sides.—**hep-tag′o-nal** (-tag′ǫ-nąl), *a.*

hep-ta-he-dron (hep-tą-hē′drǫn), *n.*; pl. *-drons* or *-dra* (-drą). [See *hepta-* and *-hedron.*] A solid figure having seven faces.—**hep-ta-he′dral,** *a.*

hep-tam-er-ous (hep-tam′ę-rus), *a.* [See *hepta-* and *-merous.*] Consisting of or divided into seven parts; in *bot.*, of flowers, having seven members in each whorl.

hep-tam-e-ter (hep-tam′e-tėr), *n.* [LL. *heptametrum*, < Gr. ἑπτάμετρον, < ἑπτά, seven, + μέτρον, measure.] In *pros.*, a verse consisting of seven metrical feet.—**hep-ta-met′ri-cal** (-tą-met′ri-kąl), *a.*

hep-tane (hep′tān), *n.* [Gr. ἑπτά, seven (with reference to the atoms of carbon).] In *chem.*, any of several isomeric hydrocarbons with the formula C_7H_{16}.

hep-tan-gu-lar (hep-tang′gū-lär), *a.* [See *hepta-.*] Having seven angles.

hep-tarch (hep′tärk), *n.* [See *hepta-* and *-arch.*] One of the rulers of a heptarchy.—**hep′tar-chy** (-tär-ki), *n.*; pl. *-chies* (-kiz). [See *-archy.*] A government by seven persons; also, a group of seven states or kingdoms, each under its own ruler; esp. [often *cap.*], the seven principal Anglo-Saxon kingdoms.—**hep-tar′chic** (-kik), *a.*

hep-ta-stich (hep′tą-stik), *n.* [Gr. ἑπτά, seven, + στίχος, row, line.] In *pros.*, a strophe, stanza, or poem consisting of seven lines or verses.

Hep-ta-teuch (hep′tą-tūk), *n.* [LL. *Heptateuchos*, < Gr. ἑπτά, seven, + τεῦχος, book.] The first seven books of the Old Testament, Genesis, Exodus, Leviticus, Numbers, Deuteronomy, Joshua, and Judges. Cf. *Pentateuch* and *Hexateuch.*

her (hėr), *pron.* [AS. *hire*, gen. and dat. of *hēo*, she, fem. of *hē*, E. *he.*] The possessive form corresponding to *she*, used before a noun (cf. *hers*); also, the objective case of *she.*

He-ra (hē′rą), *n.* [L., < Gr. Ἥρα.] A Greek goddess, wife and sister of Zeus and queen of heaven, identified by the Romans with Juno.

Hera. — Statue in Museo Nazionale, Naples.

Her-a-cles (her′ą-klēz), *n.* [Gr. Ἡρακλῆς: see *Hercules.*] Greek name of the hero Hercules.

her-ald (her′ąld), *n.* [OF. *herault, heraut* (F. *héraut*), herald; prob. from Teut.] Orig., a royal or official proclaimer or messenger (as, "A *herald* is arrived From Cæsar's camp": Addison's "Cato," ii. 1); later, such an officer employed also to arrange and supervise tourneys, public processions and funerals, etc., and to regulate the use of armorial bearings; now, esp., in Great Britain, an officer who exercises jurisdiction over and keeps record of armorial matters, etc. (see phrase *Heralds' College*, below); hence, in general, one who proclaims or announces (often used as the name of a newspaper); a messenger; also, a forerunner, precursor, or harbinger (as, "It was the lark, the *herald* of the morn": Shakspere's "Romeo and Juliet," iii. 5. 6).—**Heralds' College,** a royal corporation in England, instituted in 1483, consisting of the earl marshal, kings-of-arms, heralds, and pursuivants, and occupied chiefly with armorial bearings, genealogies, honors, and precedence.—**her′ald,** *v. t.* To give tidings of, as or by a herald; proclaim; announce; also, to usher (*in*).—**he-ral-dic** (he-ral′dik), *a.* Of or pertaining to heralds or heraldry.—**he-ral′di-cal-ly,** *adv.* —**her′ald-ry,** *n.*; pl. *-ries* (-riz). The office or duty of a herald; the science of armorial bearings, or of distinctive devices as borne by persons, communities, states, etc.; the art of blazoning armorial bearings, of settling the right of persons to bear arms or to use certain bearings, of tracing and recording genealogies, of recording honors, and of deciding questions of precedence; also, heraldic title or precedence† (see Shakspere's "All's Well," ii. 3. 280); also, a heraldic device, or a collection of such devices; a coat of arms; armorial bearings; heraldic symbolism; also, heraldic pomp or ceremony (as, "He would proclaim it far and wide, With trump and solemn *heraldry*": Coleridge's "Christabel," ii.).

herb (ėrb or hėrb), *n.* [OF. *erbe, herbe* (F. *herbe*), < L. *herba*, vegetation, grass, an herb.] A flowering plant whose stem above ground does not become woody and persistent (as, an annual *herb*, one that lasts but one year, growing, flowering, fruiting, and dying in the same season; a biennial *herb*, one that lasts but two years, growing and storing up food, as in a corm, the first year, and flowering, fruiting, and dying the second year; a perennial *herb*, one that lasts year after year); specif., such a plant when valued for its medicinal properties, flavor, scent, or the like; also, herbage (as, "On the flowery *herb* . . . he lay": Pope's tr. Homer's "Odyssey," v.).—**her-ba-ceous** (hėr-bā′shius), *a.* [L. *herbaceus.*] Of, pertaining to, or of the nature of an herb; herb-like; of stems, soft and not woody; of flowers, sepals, etc., having the texture, color, etc., of an ordinary foliage leaf.—**her-bage** (ėr′bąj or hėr′-), *n.* [OF. F.] Herbs collectively; herbaceous vegetation; pasturage; also, the succulent parts (leaves and stems) of herbaceous plants. —**her-bal** (hėr′bąl). **I.** *a.* Of or pertaining to herbs. **II.** *n.* A treatise on herbs or plants; also, a herbarium. —**her′bal-ist,** *n.* Orig., one versed in herbs or plants; now, one who collects or deals in herbs, esp. medicinal herbs. —**her-ba-ri-um** (hėr-bā′ri-um), *n.*; pl. *-riums* or *-ria* (-ri-ą). [LL., < L. *herba*: cf. *arbor*[1].] A collection of dried plants systematically arranged; also, a book or other contrivance for preserving such plants, or a room or building in which such a collection is kept.

Her-bar-ti-an (hėr-bär′ti-ạn), *a.* Of or pertaining to the German philosopher Johann Friedrich Herbart (1776–1841), or his system of philosophy.—**Her-bar′ti-an-ism,** *n.*

herb=ben-net (ėrb′ben′et), *n.* [OF. *herbe beneite,* < ML. *herba benedicta,* 'blessed herb.'] A European perennial rosaceous herb, *Geum urbanum,* having yellow flowers and an aromatic, tonic, and astringent root.

her-bes-cent (hėr-bes′ẹnt), *a.* [L. *herbescens* (*-ent-*), ppr. of *herbescere,* grow into green stalks, < *herba,* E. *herb.*] Becoming or tending to become herbaceous; growing like an herb; herbaceous.

her-bif-er-ous (hėr-bif′ẹ-rus), *a.* [L. *herbifer,* < *herba,* herb, + *ferre,* bear.] Bearing or producing herbs.

her-biv-o-rous (hėr-biv′ọ-rus), *a.* [NL. *herbivorus,* < L. *herba,* herb, + *vorare,* devour.] Eating herbs; feeding on plants.

herb-less (ėrb′les or hėrb′-), *a.* Without herbs or herbage.

her-bo-rize (hėr′bọ-rīz), *v. i.*; *-rized, -rizing.* [F. *herboriser,* irreg. (prob. after *arboriser,* cultivate or study trees, < L. *arbor,* tree) < L. *herba,* E. *herb.*] To seek or gather herbs for purposes of study; botanize.—**her″bo-ri-za′tion** (-ri-zā′shọn), *n.*—**her′bo-riz-er** (-rī-zėr), *n.*

herb=par-is (ėrb′par′is), *n.* A European liliaceous herb, *Paris quadrifolia,* formerly used in medicine.

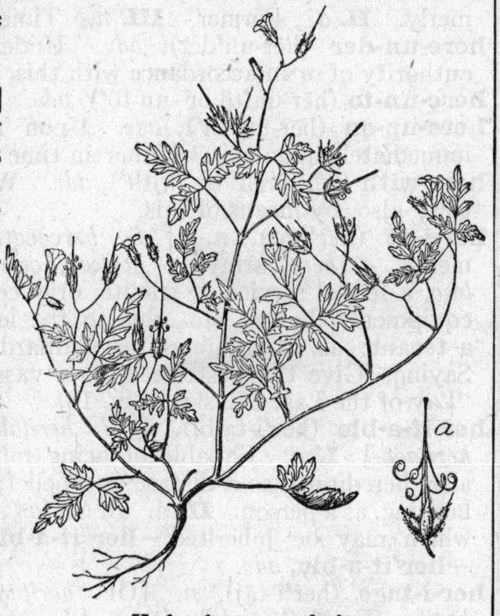

Herb-robert. — *a,* fruit.

herb=rob-ert (ėrb′rob′ėrt), *n.* A species of geranium, *Geranium robertianum,* with reddish-purple flowers.

herb-y (ėr′bi or hėr′bi), *a.* Abounding in herbs; grassy; also, pertaining to herbs; herblike.

Her-cu-le-an (hėr-kū′lẹ-ạn or hėr-kū-lē′ạn), *a.* Of or pertaining to Hercules; [now commonly *l. c.*] like or characteristic of Hercules; prodigious in strength, courage, or size, as persons (as, "*Herculean* Samson": Milton's "Paradise Lost," ix. 1060); prodigiously powerful or vigorous, as efforts; also, requiring the strength of a Hercules, as a task; very hard to perform.

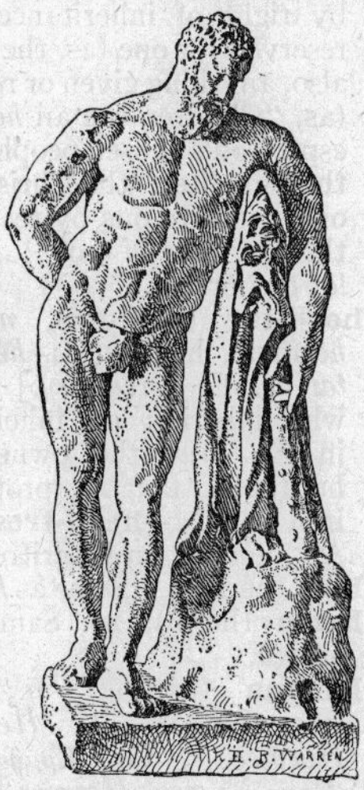
The Farnese Hercules. — Statue of the school of Lysippus, in Museo Nazionale, Naples.

Her-cu-les (hėr′kụ-lēz), *n.* [L., < Gr. Ἡρακλῆς, Ἡρακλέης, < Ἥρα, Hera, + κλέος, glory.] A celebrated hero of Greek and Roman mythology, who possessed great physical strength and courage, and performed twelve extraordinary tasks or labors, and who is usually represented as armed with a club; hence, one who resembles Hercules, as in great strength or size; in *astron.,* one of the northern constellations.—**Her′cu-les=bee′tle,** *n.* A Brazilian lamellicorn beetle, *Dynastes hercules,* sometimes attaining a length of 6 inches. See cut in next column.—**Her′cu-les′=club′,** *n.* A prickly araliaceous shrub or small tree, *Aralia spinosa,* with medicinal bark, root, and berries.

Her-cyn-i-an (hėr-sin′i-ạn), *a.* [L. *Hercynia* (*silva*), Hercynian (forest).] Noting or pertaining to the forest-covered mountain-system of Germany, or various parts of it.

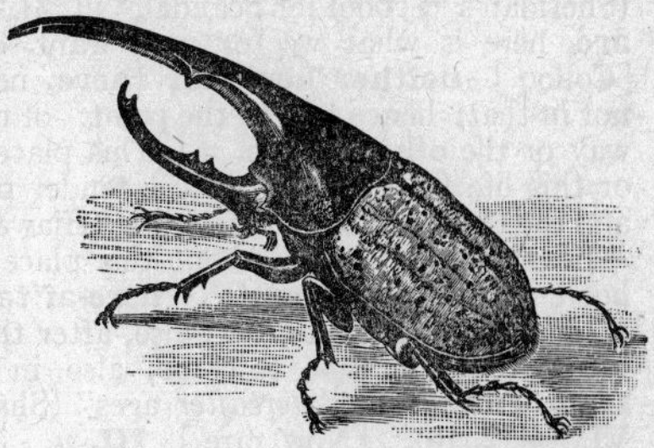
Hercules-beetle, about one third natural size.

herd[1] (hėrd), *n.* [AS. *heord* = G. *herde* = Icel. *hjördh* = Goth. *hairda,* herd: cf. Skt. *çardha,* troop, host.] A number of animals, esp. large animals, of one kind, kept, feeding, or traveling together (as, "The lowing *herd* winds slowly o'er the lea": Gray's "Elegy," i.); hence, a multitude or large company of people, etc. (now in a disparaging sense); with *the,* the common people, or the rabble (as, "Who o'er the *herd* would wish to reign, Fantastic, fickle, fierce, and vain!" Scott's "Lady of the Lake," v. 30).—**herd**[1], *v.* **I.** *intr.* To unite or go in a herd; form or join a herd; hence, in disparagement, to associate like beasts in a herd, as persons; in general, to join together in a band or company; associate one's self with a party, faction, or the like (as, "I'll *herd* among his friends, and seem One of the number": Addison's "Cato," iii. 4). **II.** *tr.* To form into a herd; place in a herd. Also fig.

herd[2] (hėrd), *n.* [AS. *hirde, hierde, hyrde,* = G. *hirte* = Icel. *hirdhir* = Goth. *hairdeis,* herdsman; from the Teut. stem represented by E. *herd*[1].] The keeper of a herd; a herdsman: now esp. in composition, as in cow*herd,* goat*herd,* etc.—**herd**[2], *v. t.* To tend, drive, or lead as a herdsman does; take care of (cattle or sheep).—**herd′=book,** *n.* A book containing the pedigree of and other information concerning a herd or herds, as of choice cattle or pigs.—**herd′er,** *n.*

her-dic (hėr′dik), *n.* [From P. *Herdic,* the inventor.] A low-hung cab or carriage with two or four wheels, having the entrance at the back and the seats at the sides. [U. S.]

herd-man† (hėrd′mạn), *n.*; pl. *-men.* A herdsman.

herd's=grass (hėrdz′gràs), *n.* Any of certain grasses esteemed for pasture or hay, as timothy-grass, *Phlẹum pratense,* or redtop, *Agrostis alba.*

herds-man (hėrdz′mạn), *n.*; pl. *-men.* The keeper of a herd; a man employed in tending a herd of cattle; also [*cap.*], in *astron.,* the northern constellation Boötes.—**herds′-wom″an,** *n.*; pl. *-women* (-wim″en).

here (hēr), *adv.* [AS. *hēr* = D. and G. *hier* = Icel. and Goth. *hēr,* here; from the pronominal stem represented by E. *he.*] In this place; in this spot or locality; hence, by ellipsis, often employed in the sense of 'I am, or we are, in this place, or present,' as in answer to a summons, roll-call, etc. (as, "*Mast.* Boatswain! *Boats. Here,* master: what cheer?" Shakspere's "Tempest," i. 1. 2); also, often used in indicating some person or thing present (as, my friend *here* knows the circumstances), in directing the attention to something (as, *here* is a letter for you; *here* is July already), and in emphasizing *this* and *these* as used before a noun or absolutely (as, this pen *here* is broken, these pens *here* are not very good, or these *here* are satisfactory; hence, in illiterate use, appended to *this* and *these* used adjectivally, as in 'this *here* pen' and 'these *here* pens'); also, in the present life or state (as, "Man wants but little *here* below, Nor wants that little long": Goldsmith's "Hermit," viii.); also, at this point or period in an action, speech, etc. (as, *here* the speaker paused); at this juncture; also, in this case or particular (as, "*Here* can then be no injustice, where no one is injured": Steele, in "Tatler," 76); also, to or toward this place, or hither (as, come *here* quickly; or, elliptically, *here,* quick!).—**here and there,** in this place and in that; in various places; at intervals, usually of space, sometimes of time; also, hither and thither; to and fro.—**here goes!** an exclamation calling attention to one's resolution or actual beginning to do some act, esp. one of bold, rash, or unpleasant character. [Colloq.]—**here's to,** a formula used in offering a toast, a health, or a wish of success, as to a person: as, "*Here's to* the maiden of bashful fifteen; *Here's to* the widow of fifty . . . Let the toast pass,—Drink to the lass" (Sheridan's "School for Scandal," iii. 3).—**here we** (or **you**) **are,** here is what we (or you) want, or are looking for. [Colloq.]—**neither here nor there,** neither in this place nor in that; hence, not to the point; of no matter either one way or the other.—**here,** *n.* This place; also, this world, or this life (as, "Full of all the tender pathos Of the *Here* and the Hereafter": Longfellow's "Hiawatha," Introd., 113). —**here′a-bout′,** *adv.* About this place; in this neighborhood. Also **here′a-bouts′.**—**here-af′ter.** [AS. *hērǣfter.*] **I.** *adv.* After this in order; also, after this in time; at some future time; in time to come; also, in the world to come. **II.** *a.* Future: as, "*hereafter* ages" (Shakspere's "1 Henry VI.," ii. 2. 10). [Now rare.] **III.** *n.* Time to come; the future; also, a future life; the world to come.—**here-at′,** *adv.* At this; by reason of this.—**here′a-way″,** *adv.* In this neighborhood (as, "They told us below, we should find settlers something thinnish, *hereaway*": Cooper's "Prairie," ii.); also, hither. [Now colloq.]—**here-by′,** *adv.* Near by†; also, by this; by this means; as a result of this.

he-red-i-ta-ble (hẹ-red′i-tạ-bl), *a.* [ML. *hereditabilis,* < LL. *hereditare,* inherit, < L. *heres,* E. *heir.*] Heritable. —**he-red″i-ta-bil′i-ty** (-bil′i-ti), *n.*—**he-red′i-ta-bly,** *adv.*

her-e-dit-a-ment (her-ẹ-dit′ạ-mẹnt), *n.* [ML. *hereditamentum,* < LL. *hereditare*: see *hereditable.*] In *law,* any property that can be inherited: as, "all the landed possessions, houses, mills, baths, and other *hereditaments* which formed the royal patrimony" (Irving's "Conquest of Granada," xcvii.).

he-red-i-ta-ry (hẹ-red′i-tā-ri), *a.* [L. *hereditarius,* < *hereditas,* E. *heredity.*] Descending by inheritance; transmitted or transmissible in the line of descent by force of law; also, holding a title, position, etc., by inheritance (as, a *hereditary* peer; a *hereditary* proprietor); also, passing or capable of passing naturally from parents to offspring, as a disease or an instinct; coming to one from one's parents or predecessors (as, *hereditary* beliefs; *hereditary* hatred; "that ignorance and superstitiousness *hereditary* to all sailors," H. Melville's "Moby-Dick," xli.); also, being such from natal endowment or tendency, or through feelings, etc., derived from parents or predecessors (as, a *hereditary* musician; a *hereditary* enemy to a country); also, pertaining to inheritance or heredity (as, *hereditary* descent; *hereditary* transmission).—**he-red′i-ta-ri-ly,** *adv.*—**he-red′i-ta-ri-ness,** *n.*

he-red-i-ty (hẹ-red′i-ti), *n.* [L. *hereditas,* heirship, inheritance, < *heres,* E. *heir.*] Heirship† or inheritance†; also, the state or fact of being heritable; also, the descent or transmission of physical or mental qualities or characteristics from parents to offspring; the tendency in organisms by which qualities or characteristics are transmitted from parents or ancestors to offspring.

Her-e-ford (her′ẹ-fọrd), *n.* One of a breed of beef cattle, orig. from Herefordshire, England, having usually a reddish body and a whitish face, throat, etc.

here-from (hēr-from′), *adv.* From here; from this place; also, from this fact, circumstance, etc.

here-in (hēr-in′), *adv.* [AS. *hērinne.*] In here; in or into this place; also, in this fact, circumstance, etc.—**here-in-af′ter,** *adv.* Afterward in this document, statement, etc. —**here-in″be-fore′,** *adv.* Before in this document, statement, etc.

here-in-to (hēr-in′tọ̈), *adv.* Into this.

here-of (hēr-ov′), *adv.* [AS. *hērof.*] Of this (as, upon the receipt *hereof*); concerning this (as, more *hereof* later); also, from this† (as, "*Hereof* comes it that Prince Harry is valiant": Shakspere's "2 Henry IV.," iv. 3. 126).

here-on (hēr-on′), *adv.* [AS. *hēron.*] On or upon this; also, following on the occurrence of this; hereupon.

her-e-si-arch (her′e-si-ärk or hẹ-rē′-), *n.* [LL. *hæresiarcha,* < Gr. αἱρεσιάρχης, < αἵρεσις, heresy, + ἄρχειν, lead, rule.] A leader in heresy; the chief of a heretical sect.

her-e-si-ol-o-gy (her″e-si-ol′ọ̄-ji), *n.*; pl. *-gies* (-giz). [Gr. αἵρεσις, heresy: see *-logy.*] The study of or a treatise on heresies.—**her″e-si-ol′o-gist,** *n.*

her-e-sy (her′e-si), *n.*; pl. *-sies* (-siz). [OF. *heresie* (F. *hérésie*), < L. *hæresis,* < Gr. αἵρεσις, a taking, choice, principles, sect, heresy, < αἱρεῖν, take.] Opinion or doctrine at variance with the orthodox or accepted doctrine of a church or religious system; also, an instance of this; a heretical opinion or doctrine; hence, in general, opinion or doctrine opposed to what is generally accepted as authoritative, as in philosophy, science, art, etc.; a particular opinion or doctrine of this kind; also, opinion or doctrine peculiar to particular individuals or parties; a school of thought; a sect.

her-e-tic (her′e-tik). [OF. *hereticque* (F. *hérétique*), < LL. *hæreticus,* a. and n., < Gr. αἱρετικός, able to choose, heretical, < αἱρεῖν, take.] **I.** *a.* Maintaining a heresy; heretical. **II.** *n.* One who maintains a heresy; esp., in *theol.,* a professed believer who maintains religious opinions contrary to those accepted by his church or rejects doctrines prescribed by his church.—**he-ret-i-cal** (hẹ-ret′i-kạl), *a.* Of or pertaining to heretics or heresy; characterized by or of the nature of heresy.—**he-ret′i-cal-ly,** *adv.*

here-to (hēr-tö′), *adv.* To this (place, thing, document, circumstance, proposition, etc.: as, adjoining *hereto*; attached *hereto*; to give evidence *hereto*; to accord *hereto*); also, hitherto† (see Shakspere's "Coriolanus," ii. 2. 64).

here-to-fore (hēr′tọ̈-fōr′). **I.** *adv.* Before this time; formerly. **II.** *a.* Former. **III.** *n.* Time past.

here-un-der (hēr-un′dėr), *adv.* Under this; also, under authority of or in accordance with this.

here-un-to (hēr-un′tọ̈ or -un-tö′), *adv.* Unto this; hereto.

here-up-on (hēr-u-pon′), *adv.* Upon this; also, following immediately upon this, whether in time or consequence.

here-with (hēr-wiŧħ′ or -with′), *adv.* With this; along with this; also, by means of this.

her-i-ot (her′i-ọt), *n.* [AS. *heregeatwa,* military equipments, < *here,* army, + *geatwa,* equipments.] In *Eng. law,* a feudal service or tribute, orig. consisting of military equipments, horses, etc., due to the lord on the death of a tenant: as, "Of Gilbert the Galliard a *heriot* he sought, Saying, 'Give thy best steed, as a vassal ought' " (Scott's "Lay of the Last Minstrel," iv. 10).

her-it-a-ble (her′i-tạ-bl). [OF. *heritable,* < *heriter*: see *heritage.*] **I.** *a.* Capable of being inherited; inheritable; also, hereditary, as a disease or a belief; also, capable of inheriting, as a person. **II.** *n.* In *Sc. law,* a possession or right which may be inherited.—**her″it-a-bil′i-ty** (-bil′i-ti), *n.* —**her′it-a-bly,** *adv.*

her-i-tage (her′i-tāj), *n.* [OF. *heritage* (F. *héritage*), < *heriter* (F. *hériter*), inherit, < LL. *hereditare*: see *hereditable.*] That which has been or may be inherited by legal descent or succession; any property, esp. land, that devolves by right of inheritance; hence, something allotted to or reserved for one (as, the *heritage* of the righteous in heaven); also, anything given or received to be a permanent possession (as, "Children are an *heritage* of the Lord": Ps. cxxvii. 3); esp., God's chosen people, regarded as his peculiar possession; the Israelites; the Christian church; also, that which comes or belongs to one by reason of birth (as, "Lord of himself,—that *heritage* of woe": Byron's "Lara," i. 2); an inherited lot or portion.

her-i-tor (her′i-tọr), *n.* [AF. *heriter,* OF. *heritier* (F. *héritier*), heir, < L. *hereditarius,* E. *hereditary.*] One who inherits; an inheritor; in *Sc. law,* the owner of heritable, taxable property in a parish.—**her′i-tress,** *n.* An heiress; an inheritress.

herl (hėrl), *n.* Same as *harl*[2].

herm (hėrm), *n.* Same as *herma.*

her-ma (hėr′mạ̈), *n.*; pl. *-mæ* (-mē). [L. *Herma, Hermes,* < Gr. Ἑρμῆς (pl. Ἑρμαῖ): see *Hermes.*] In *Gr. antiq.,* a kind of monument or statue, common in ancient Athens, consisting of a head, usually that of the god Hermes, supported on a quadrangular pillar corresponding roughly in mass to the absent body.

Upper part of a Double Herma.

Her-ma-ic (hėr-mā′ik), *a.* [Gr. Ἑρμαϊκός.] Pertaining to Hermes or Mercury, or [also *l. c.*] to a herma; also [*cap.*], pertaining to Hermes Trismegistus; Hermetic.

her-maph-ro-dite (hėr-maf′rǭ-dīt). [L. *hermaphroditus*, < Gr. ἑρμαφρόδιτος, < Ἑρμαφρόδιτος, Hermaphroditus (son of Hermes and Aphrodite), who became united in body with the nymph Salmacis while bathing in her fountain.] **I.** *n.* A human or animal monstrosity in which the reproductive organs characteristic of both sexes are to some extent, really or apparently, combined; also, an animal or a flower having normally both the male and the female organs of generation; a plant having normally both stamens and pistils in the same flower; fig., a person or thing in which two opposite attributes or qualities are combined; *naut.*, a hermaphrodite brig (see phrase below). **II.** *a.* Of the nature of or pertaining to a hermaphrodite; of a flower, monoclinous; in general, combining two opposite attributes or qualities.—**hermaphrodite brig,** *naut.*, a two-masted vessel square-rigged on the foremast and schooner-rigged on the mainmast.—**her-maph-ro-dit′ic** (-dit′ik), *a.* Of, pertaining to, or of the nature of a hermaphrodite.—**her-maph-ro-dit′i-cal-ly,** *adv.*—**her-maph′ro-dit-ism** (-dī-tizm), *n.* The condition of a hermaphrodite; union of the two sexes in the same individual.

her-me-neu-tic (hėr-mę-nū′tik), *a.* [Gr. ἑρμηνευτικός, < ἑρμηνεύειν, interpret, < ἑρμηνεύς, interpreter, said to be < Ἑρμῆς, Hermes, as the messenger of the gods.] Of, pertaining to, or concerned with interpretation; interpretative; explanatory.—**her-me-neu′ti-cal-ly,** *adv.*—**her-me-neu′tics,** *n.* The science of interpretation, esp. of the Scriptures; that branch of theology which treats of the principles of Biblical exegesis.

Her-mes (hėr′mēz), *n.* [L., < Gr. Ἑρμῆς, Hermes, also a herma.] A Greek deity, herald and messenger of the gods, and god of roads, commerce, invention, cunning, and theft, identified by the Romans with Mercury; [*l. c.*] in *Gr. antiq.*, a herma.—**Hermes Trismegistus** (tris-me-jis′tus). [Gr. Ἑρμῆς τρισμέγιστος, 'thrice greatest Hermes.'] A name given by Neoplatonists and others to the Egyptian god Thoth, who was to some extent identified with the Grecian Hermes, and to whom were attributed various works embodying mystical, theosophical, astrological, and alchemical doctrines.

her-met-ic (hėr-met′ik), *a.* [ML. *hermeticus*, < L. *Hermes*: see *Hermes.*] [*cap.* or *l. c.*] Of or pertaining to Hermes or a herma; also [*cap.*], of or pertaining to Hermes Trismegistus or the writings, doctrines, etc., ascribed to him; hence [*l. c.*], pertaining to occult science; magical; esp., alchemical; also, made air-tight by fusion or sealing. Also **her-met′i-cal.**—**her-met′i-cal-ly,** *adv.* In a hermetic manner; esp., so as to render air-tight (as, a vessel *hermetically* sealed); fig., closely or tightly (closed).

her-mit (hėr′mit), *n.* [OF. *hermite, ermite* (F. *ermite*), < LL. *eremita*, E. *eremite.*] One who has retired to a solitary place for a life of religious seclusion; an eremite; hence, any person living in seclusion; a solitary; also, a beadsman† (as, "In thy dumb action will I be as perfect As begging *hermits* in their holy prayers": Shakspere's "Titus Andronicus," iii. 2. 41); also, any of various animals of solitary habits; also, a spiced molasses cooky, often containing raisins and sometimes nuts.—**her′mit-age** (-āj), *n.* [OF.] The habitation of a hermit; hence, any secluded habitation; also [*cap.*], a French wine made in the region of Valence, in the department of Drôme.—**her′mit=crab′,** *n.* Any of numerous decapod crustaceans of the genera *Pagurus*, *Eupagurus*, etc., which protect their soft uncovered rear by occupying the cast-off shell of a univalve mollusk.—**her-mit′ic, her-mit′i-cal** (-ik, -i-kạl), *a.* Of or pertaining to a hermit; eremitic.—**her-mit′i-cal-ly,** *adv.*—**her′mit=thrush′,** *n.* A North American thrush, *Turdus aonalaschkæ* (or *Hylocichla guttata*), of which there are several distinct varieties: noted for its song, and often found secluded in the undergrowth.

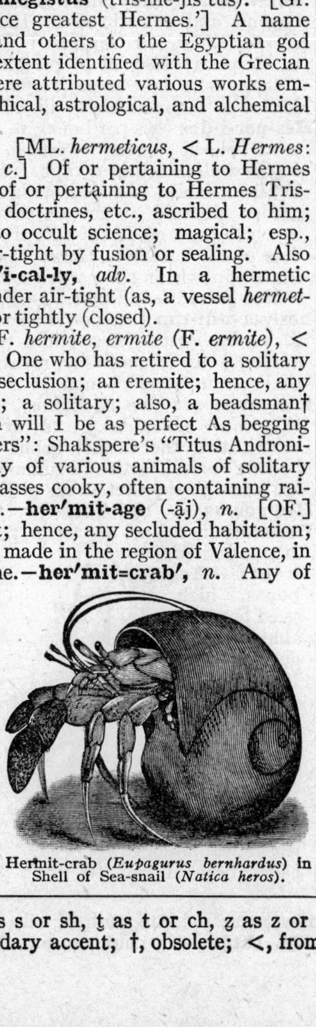
Hermit-crab (*Eupagurus bernhardus*) in Shell of Sea-snail (*Natica heros*).

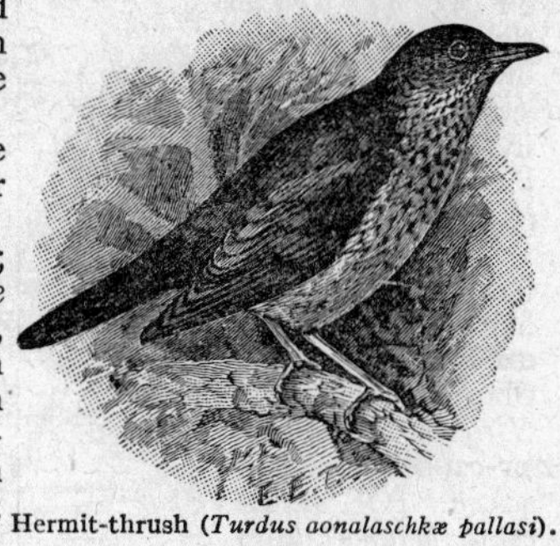
Hermit-thrush (*Turdus aonalaschkæ pallasi*).

hern (hėrn), *n.* Same as *heron.* [Archaic or prov.]

her-ni-a (hėr′ni-ạ̈), *n.*; pl. *hernias*, L. *herniæ* (-ē). [L.] In *pathol.*, the protrusion of an organ or tissue through an opening in its surrounding walls, esp. in the abdominal region; rupture.—**her′ni-al,** *a.*—**her-ni-ot′o-my** (-ot′ǭ-mi), *n.* [See *-tomy.*] In *surg.*, the operation of cutting for relief of hernia.

hern-shaw (hėrn′shâ), *n.* Same as *heronsew.* [Archaic or prov.]—**to know a hawk from a hernshaw.** See phrase under *hand-saw.*

he-ro (hē′rō), *n.*; pl. *-roes* (-rōz). [L. *heros*, < Gr. ἥρως.] In the Homeric period, a man of superhuman strength, courage, or ability; in later periods of antiquity, an immortal being intermediate in nature between gods and men; a demigod; hence, a man of distinguished valor, intrepidity, or fortitude; a central or prominent personage in any remarkable action or course of events; a man admired and venerated for his noble deeds or qualities; hence, one invested with heroic qualities in the opinion of others (as, no one is a *hero* to his valet); also, the principal male character in a poem, story, play, or the like, in whom the chief interest of the plot is centered (as, "I want a *hero* . . . I'll therefore take our ancient friend Don Juan," Byron's "Don Juan," i. 1; "Vanity Fair: A Novel without a *Hero*," the title of a work by Thackeray).

he-ro-ic (hę-rō′ik), *a.* [L. *heroicus*, < Gr. ἡρωικός.] Of or pertaining to the heroes of antiquity (as, the *heroic* age: see phrase below); also, pertaining to heroes, or men of distinguished valor, etc.; characteristic of or befitting a hero, as conduct, etc.; intrepid; brave; bold; of the nature of a hero, as a person; also, of a size larger than life and, usually, less than colossal, as a statue; also, dealing with the deeds of heroes (as, *heroic* poetry); also, used in heroic poetry (as, *heroic* verse: see phrase below); also, resembling heroic poetry in language or style; magniloquent; grand; hence, extravagant or bombastic; also, having or involving recourse to extreme measures (as, *heroic* treatment); boldly experimental; daring.—**heroic age,** the time when the heroes of Greek antiquity are supposed to have lived. See *ages in mythology*, under *age, n.*—**heroic verse,** in classical poetry, the dactylic hexameter (see *hexameter, n.*); in English, German, and Italian, the iambic pentameter; in French, the Alexandrine.—**he-ro′ic,** *n.* Heroic verse (usually in *pl.*); a heroic poem; also, *pl.*, extravagant language or sentiment; bombast.—**he-ro′i-cal,** *a.* Heroic.—**he-ro′i-cal-ly,** *adv.*—**he-ro′ic-ness, he-ro′i-cal-ness,** *n.*

her-o-in (her′ǭ-in or hę-rō′in), *n.* [Appar. < *hero*: cf. G. *heroin.*] In *phar.*, a derivative of morphine used (usually in the form of a hydrochloride) as a sedative, etc., and constituting a dangerous habit-forming drug.

her-o-ine (her′ǭ-in), *n.* [L. *heroina*, < Gr. ἡρωίνη, fem. of ἥρως, E. *hero.*] A female hero; a woman of heroic character or qualities; also, the principal female character in a poem, story, play, or the like, in whom the chief interest of the plot is centered (as, "Take Lilia, then, for *heroine* . . . And make her some great princess": Tennyson's "Princess," Prologue, 217).—**her′o-ine-ship, her′o-in-ism,** *n.*

her-o-ism (her′ǭ-izm), *n.* [F. *héroïsme*, < *héros*, < L. *heros*, E. *hero.*] The qualities of a hero or heroine; heroic conduct; a heroic trait or action.

he-ro-ize (hē′rǭ-īz), *v. t.*; *-ized, -izing.* To make a hero of; render heroic; treat or represent as a hero.—**he″ro-i-za′tion** (-i-zā′shǭn), *n.*

her-on (her′ǫn), *n.* [OF. *hairon* (F. *héron*); from Teut.: cf. *aigrette.*] Any of the long-legged, long-necked, long-billed wading birds constituting the subfamily *Ardeinæ* ('true herons'), as *Ardea cinerea* ('gray heron') of Europe or *A. herodias* ('great blue heron') of America; also, any bird of the family *Ardeidæ*, as the bittern or the boatbill.—**her′on-ry** (-ri), *n.*; pl. *-ries* (-riz). A place where herons breed.—**her′on's=bill,** *n.* The plant stork's-bill (*Erodium*).

Great Blue Heron (*Ardea herodias*).

her-on-sew (her′on-sū), *n.* [OF. *heronceau, heroncel*, dim. of *heron, hairon*, E. *heron.*] A small or young heron; any heron. Also **her′on-shaw** (-shâ). [Archaic or prov.]

he-ro=wor-ship (hē′rō-wėr″ship), *n.* The worship of deified heroes, as practised by the ancients; hence, profound reverence for great men or their memory, or for persons accepted as heroes (as, "On Heroes, *Hero-Worship*, and the Heroic in History": the title of a work by Carlyle, published in 1841).—**he′ro=wor″ship-er,** *n.*

her-pes (hėr′pēz), *n.* [L., < Gr. ἕρπης (ἑρπητ-), herpes, < ἕρπειν, creep: see *serpent.*] In *pathol.*, any of certain inflammatory affections of the skin or mucous membrane, characterized by clusters of vesicles, which tend to spread; esp., herpes zoster.—**her′pes zos-ter** (zos′tėr). [L.: see *zoster.*] In *pathol.*, a form of herpes characterized by vesicles which sometimes form a girdle about the body; shingles.—**her-pet′ic** (-pet′ik), *a.*

her-pe-tol-o-gy (hėr-pe-tol′ō-ji), *n.* [Gr. ἑρπετόν, reptile (< ἕρπειν, creep): see *-logy* and *serpent.*] The branch of zoölogy that treats of reptiles.—**her″pe-to-log′i-cal** (-tō-loj′i-kal), *a.*—**her-pe-tol′o-gist,** *n.*

herr (her), *n.*; pl. *herren* (her′en). [G.] In German use, lord; master; gentleman; sir: as a title, equivalent to *Mister* (*Mr.*).

her-ring (her′ing), *n.*; pl. *herrings* or (esp. collectively) *herring.* [AS. *hǣring* = D. *haring* = G. *häring*, herring.] An important food-fish, *Clupea harengus*, occurring in great numbers in the northern Atlantic; also, any of various closely related fishes; also, any fish of the family *Clupeidæ*, which includes also the shad, sardine, etc.—**her′ring=bone,** *a.* Resembling the spine of a herring: applied esp. to masonry or paving in which the stones, bricks, or the like, in alternate courses, are set obliquely at like angles in opposite directions, to a similar pattern in fabrics, and to a similar stitch, or a kind of cross-stitch, in embroidery, etc.—**her′ring=bone,** *v. t.* or *i.*; *-boned, -boning.* To embroider or sew with the herring-bone stitch.—**her′ring=pond,** *n.* The sea or ocean. [Humorous.]

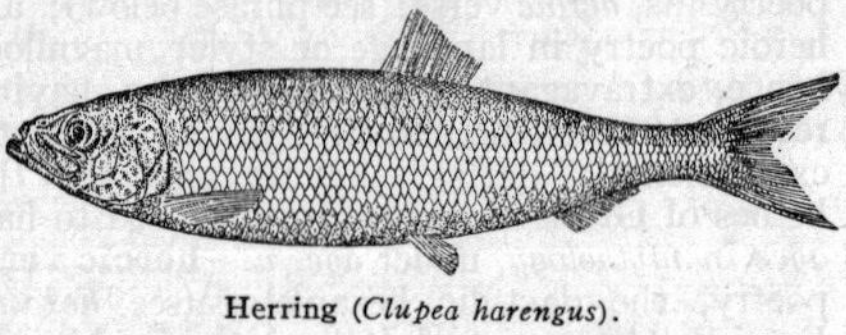

Herring (*Clupea harengus*).

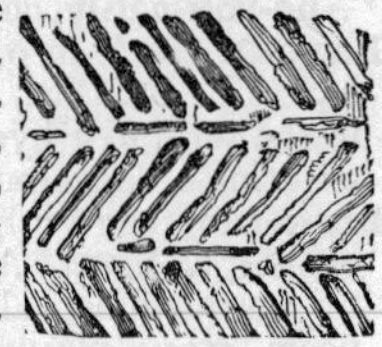

Herring-bone Masonry.

hers (hėrz), *pron.* Form of the possessive *her* used predicatively or without a noun following.

her-self (hėr-self′), *pron.* An emphatic form of *her* or *she*; also, a reflexive form of *her.*

her-ship (hėr′ship), *n.* [ME. *heirschip*: cf. AS. *here*, army, and E. *-ship*, also Icel. *herskapr*, warfare, harrying.] Harrying or pillage; a foray or warlike incursion, as to steal cattle; also, ruin or distress, as from pillage; also, booty or plunder, as cattle stolen in a foray. [Obs. or archaic, Sc.]

Hertz-i-an (hert′si-an), *a.* Of or pertaining to the German physicist Heinrich Hertz (1857–94).—**Hertzian wave,** an electromagnetic disturbance or wave produced in the luminiferous ether, serving as a means of transmission in wireless telegraphy and telephony: first fully investigated by Hertz.

her-zog (her′tsōch), *n.*; pl. *-zoge* (-tsō-gė). [G., = D. *hertog*, duke, = AS. *heretoga*, army leader.] In German use, a sovereign prince ruling over a small state, or a member of the highest rank of nobility: equivalent to English *duke.*

Hesh-van (hesh′van), *n.* [Heb.] In the Jewish calendar, the second month (29 or 30 days) of the civil year and the eighth of the ecclesiastical year, beginning in October or in the first part of November.

hes-i-tant (hez′i-tant), *a.* Hesitating; irresolute; undecided; also, wanting readiness of speech.—**hes′i-tance, hes′i-tan-cy,** *n.*—**hes′i-tant-ly,** *adv.*

hes-i-tate (hez′i-tāt), *v.*; *-tated, -tating.* [L. *hæsitatus*, pp. of *hæsitare*, stick fast, hesitate, intensive of *hærere*, stick.] **I.** *intr.* To hold back in doubt or indecision; also, to halt or falter in speech (as, "His [Henry Fox's] delivery was *hesitating*; he was often at a stand for want of a word": Macaulay's "Essays," William Pitt, Earl of Chatham); stammer. **II.** *tr.* To utter or express with indecision or reluctance: as, "Willing to wound, and yet afraid to strike, Just hint a fault, and *hesitate* dislike" (Pope's "Prologue to the Satires," 204).—**hes′i-tat-er** (-tā-tėr), **hes′i-tat-or,** *n.*—**hes′i-tat-ing-ly,** *adv.*—**hes-i-ta′tion** (-tā′shon), *n.* [L. *hæsitatio(n-).*] The act of hesitating; a state of doubt or indecision; also, a halting or faltering in speech.—**hes′i-ta-tive** (-tā-tiv), **hes′i-ta-to-ry** (-tō-ri), *a.* Characterized by hesitation; hesitating.

Hes-per, Hes-per-us (hes′pėr, -pe-rus), *n.* [L. *Hesperus*, < Gr. Ἕσπερος, the evening star, orig. adj., ἕσπερος, of or at evening, western: cf. *vesper.*] The evening star, esp. Venus: as, "Some shed a mild and silver beam Like *Hesperus* o'er the western sea" (Shelley's "Queen Mab," i. 259).

Hes-pe-ri-a (hes-pē′ri-ä), *n.* [L., < Gr. Ἑσπερία, prop. fem. of ἑσπέριος, toward or at evening, western, < ἕσπερος: see *Hesper.*] The land of the west: a name applied by Greek poets to Italy, and by Roman poets to Spain or regions beyond and sometimes to Italy.—**Hes-pe′ri-an,** *a.* [L. *Hesperius*, < Gr. ἑσπέριος.] Western; of or pertaining to Hesperia; also, of or pertaining to the Hesperides (as, "Happy isles, Like those *Hesperian* gardens, famed of old": Milton's "Paradise Lost," iii. 568). [Poetic.]

Hes-per-i-des (hes-per′i-dēz), *n. pl.* [L., < Gr. Ἑσπερίδες, prop. pl. of ἑσπερίς, western, < ἕσπερος: see *Hesper.*] In *Gr. myth.*, certain nymphs, variously given as from three to seven, fabled to guard, with the aid of a fierce serpent, a garden situated at the western extremity of the world, in which grew golden apples, the wedding-gift of Gæa (goddess of the earth) to Hera; also, the garden itself, or the islands in which the garden was supposed to be situated.—**Hes-pe-rid′i-an** (-pe-rid′i-an), *a.*

hes-per-i-di-um (hes-pe-rid′i-um), *n.*; pl. *-ia* (-i-ä). [NL., < L. *Hesperides*, Hesperides (with allusion to the golden apples).] In *bot.*, a fleshy, many-celled fruit with a leathery rind, as the orange, lemon, etc.

hes-per-or-nis (hes-pe-rôr′nis), *n.* [NL., < Gr. ἕσπερος, western, + ὄρνις, bird.] Any of the very large diving birds constituting the extinct genus *Hesperornis*, characterized by long conical teeth and rudimentary wings, whose remains are found in the Cretaceous of Kansas.

Hes′per-us, *n.* See *Hesper.*

Hes-sian (hesh′an), *a.* Of or pertaining to Hesse, in Germany, or its inhabitants.—**Hessian boots,** high tasseled boots fashionable in England during the early 19th century, orig. worn by Hessian troops.—**Hessian fly,** a small dipterous insect, *Cecidomyia destructor*, whose larva is very destructive to wheat: supposed to have been intro-

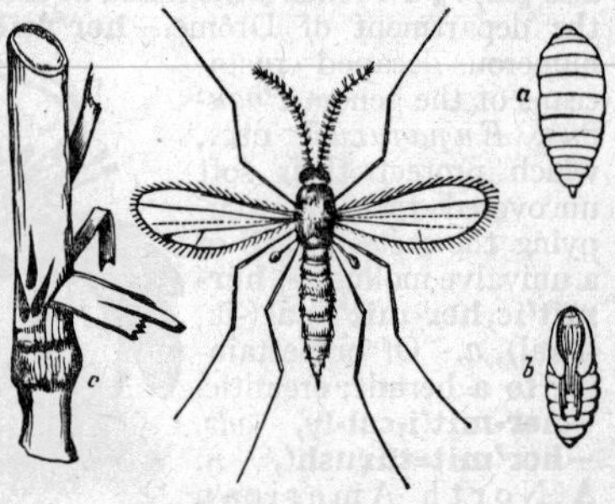

Hessian Fly.—*a*, larva; *b*, pupa; *c*, infested stalk of wheat.

duced into America by Hessian troops.—**Hes′sian,** *n.* A native or inhabitant of Hesse; hence, in the U. S. (in allusion to the Hessian mercenaries employed by England during the American Revolution), a hireling; a ruffian; also [*l. c.*], *pl.*, Hessian boots; also, *sing.*, a coarse cloth made of hemp or of a mixture of hemp and jute, used chiefly for bagging.

hes-son-ite (hes′o̧n-īt), *n.* [Gr. ἥσσων, less, inferior, < ἦκα, slightly.] A yellowish or brownish variety of garnet, found in Ceylon, etc., and sometimes used in jewelry.

hest (hest), *n.* [AS. *hǣs*, < *hātan*, bid: see *hight.*] Bidding, injunction, or behest (archaic: as, "Female attendance shall obey Your *hest*, for service or array," Scott's "Lady of the Lake," vi. 10); also, a vow† or promise†.

hes-ter-nal (hes-tėr′na̧l), *a.* [L. *hesternus.*] Of or pertaining to yesterday: as, "enervating slumbers, from the *hesternal* dissipation or debauch" (Bulwer-Lytton's "Pelham," lvii.).

Hes-y-chast (hes′i-kast), *n.* [Gr. ἡσυχαστής, a recluse, < ἡσυχάζειν, be quiet, < ἥσυχος, quiet.] One of a sect of mystics which originated in the 14th century among the monks living on Mount Athos, Greece.—**Hes-y-chas′tic** (-kas′tik), *a.*

het (het). Obs. or prov. pret. and pp. of *heat.*

he-tæ-ra, he-tai-ra (he-tē′rä̧, -tī′rä̧), *n.*; pl. *hetæræ* (-rē), *hetairai* (-rī). [NL., < Gr. ἑταίρα, fem. of ἑταῖρος, companion.] A female paramour, or concubine, in ancient Greece; hence, in general, a concubine; a courtezan.

he-tæ-ri-o (he-tē′ri-ō), *n.*; pl. *-os* (-ōz). [Gr. ἑταιρία, association, < ἑταῖρος, companion.] In *bot.*, a fruit consisting of a number of distinct indehiscent carpels produced by a single flower.

he-tæ-rism, he-tai-rism (he-tē′rizm, he-tī′-), *n.* [See *hetæra.*] The practice of concubinage; in *anthropol.*, common intercourse between the sexes, as among primitive races.

het-er-ize (het′ę-rīz), *v. t.*; *-ized, -izing.* [Gr. ἕτερος, other, different: see *other.*] To make other or different; change. —**het″er-i-za′tion** (-ę-ri-zā′sho̧n), *n.*

hetero-. Form of Gr. ἕτερος, other, different, used in combination.—**het-er-o-cer-cal** (het″ę-rō̧-sėr′ka̧l), *a.* [+ Gr. κέρκος, tail.] In *ichth.*, noting, pertaining to, or having a form of tail which is unsymmetrical as to its upper and lower halves. Cf. *homocercal.*—**het″er-o-chro′mous** (-krō′mus), *a.* [Gr. ἑτερόχρωμος (χρῶμα, color).] Of different colors, as florets; of a composite flower or flower-head, having the florets of the disk different in color from those of the margin. Cf. *homochromous.*—**het-er-och′thon** (-ę-rok′tho̧n), *n.* [NL. (Gr. χθών, earth).] One of the animals of a region which have evidently been derived by immigration from another region.

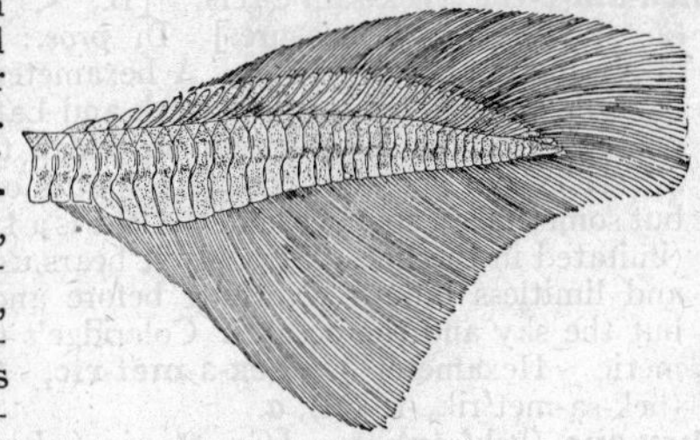

Heterocercal Tail of Fish.

het-er-o-clite (het′ę-rō̧-klīt). [LL. *heteroclitus*, < Gr. ἑτερόκλιτος, < ἕτερος, other, different, + κλίνειν, incline, inflect.] **I.** *a.* In *gram.*, irregular in declension or inflection, as a noun; hence, fig., exceptional or anomalous. **II.** *n.* In *gram.*, a word irregular in declension or inflection; hence, fig., a person or thing that deviates from the ordinary rule or form.

het-er-o-dox (het′ę-rō̧-doks), *a.* [Gr. ἑτερόδοξος, < ἕτερος, other, different, + δόξα, opinion.] Not in accordance with established or accepted doctrines or opinions, esp. in theology; not orthodox; also, holding unorthodox doctrines or opinions, as persons.—**het′er-o-dox″ly,** *adv.*—**het′er-o-dox″y,** *n.*; pl. *-doxies* (-dok″siz). [Gr. ἑτεροδοξία.] The state or quality of being heterodox; deviation from what is orthodox; also, a heterodox doctrine, opinion, etc.

het-er-od-ro-mous (het-ę-rod′rō̧-mus), *a.* [Gr. ἕτερος, other, different, + δρόμος, a running, course.] In *bot.*, having the spiral arrangement of the leaves on the stem in one direction and of those on the branches in the opposite direction. Cf. *homodromous.*

het-er-o-dyne (het′ę-rō̧-dīn), *a.* [Gr. ἕτερος, other, different, + δύναμις, power.] In *wireless teleg.* and *teleph.*, noting or pertaining to a method of receiving continuous-wave wireless-telegraph signals by impressing upon the continuous radio-frequency oscillations another set of radio-frequency oscillations of a slightly different frequency, the interference resulting in fluctuations or beats with audio frequency.—**het′er-o-dyne,** *v. i.*; *-dyned, -dyning.* In *wireless teleg.* and *teleph.*, to produce a heterodyne effect.

het-er-œ-cious (het-ę-rē′shus), *a.* [Gr. ἕτερος, other, different, + οἶκος, house.] In *bot.*, passing througl different stages of growth on different hosts, as certain parasitic fungi.—**het-er-œ′cism** (-sizm), *n.*

het-er-og-a-mous (het-ę-rog′a̧-mus), *a.* [Gr. ἕτερος, other, different, + γάμος, marriage.] In *bot.*, having flowers or florets of two sexually different kinds (opposed to *homogamous*); in *biol.*, having unlike gametes, or reproducing by the union of such gametes (opposed to *isogamous*); also, characterized by heterogenesis (a kind of reproduction).—**het-er-og′a-my,** *n.* The state of being heterogamous; also, heterogenesis (a kind of reproduction).

het-er-o-ge-ne-ous (het″ę-rō̧-jē′nę-us), *a.* [ML. *heterogeneus*, < Gr. ἑτερογενής, < ἕτερος, other, different, + γένος, race, kind.] Different in kind; widely dissimilar; unlike; incongruous; also, composed of parts of different kinds; having widely unlike elements or constituents; not homogeneous; in *math.*, of different kinds and incommensurable; also, of different degrees or dimensions.—**het″er-o-ge-ne′i-ty** (-ję-nē′i-ti), **het″er-o-ge′ne-ous-ness,** *n.*—**het″er-o-ge′ne-ous-ly,** *adv.*

het-er-o-gen-e-sis (het″ę-rō̧-jen′e-sis), *n.* [See *hetero-* and *genesis.*] In *biol.*, abiogenesis; also, that kind of reproduction in which the parent produces offspring differing from itself, but in which after one or more generations the original form reappears.—**het″er-o-ge-net′ic** (-ję-net′ik), *a.*

het-er-og-o-nous (het-ę-rog′ō̧-nus), *a.* [Gr. ἕτερος, other, different, + γόνος, offspring, generation.] In *bot.*, noting or pertaining to monoclinous flowers of two or more kinds occurring on different individuals of the same species, the kinds differing in the relative length of stamens and pistils (opposed to *homogonous*); in *biol.*, characterized by irregular reproduction, as in the alternation of generations.—**het-er-og′o-nism, het-er-og′o-ny,** *n.*

het-er-og-ra-phy (het-ę-rog′ra̧-fi), *n.* [See *hetero-* and *-graphy.*] Spelling different from that in current use; incorrect spelling; also, spelling in which the same letter is used to represent different sounds.—**het″er-o-graph′ic** (-ę-rō̧-graf′ik), *a.*

het-er-og-y-nal (het-ę-roj′i-na̧l), *a.* Heterogynous.

het-er-og-y-nous (het-ę-roj′i-nus), *a.* [NL. *heterogynus*, < Gr. ἕτερος, other, different, + γυνή, woman, female.] In *zoöl.*, having females of two different kinds, one sexual and the other abortive or neuter, as the ants.

het-er-ol-o-gous (het-ę-rol′ō̧-gus), *a.* [Gr. ἕτερος, other, different, + λόγος, proportion, relation.] Having a different relation; not corresponding; not homologous; in *pathol.*, abnormal; consisting of tissue unlike the normal tissue of a part, as a tumor.—**het-er-ol′o-gy** (-ji), *n.*

het-er-om-er-ous (het-ę-rom′ę-rus), *a.* [Gr. ἕτερος, other, different, + μέρος, part.] Having or consisting of parts which differ in quality, number of elements, or the like (as, a *heteromerous* flower, having the members of one or more whorls differing in number from those of the others); in *chem.*, unrelated as to chemical composition.

het-er-o-mor-phic (het″ę-rō̧-môr′fik), *a.* [Gr. ἑτερόμορφος, < ἕτερος, other, different, + μορφή, form.] Of different or dissimilar form; also, deviating from the normal structure, type, or the like; specif., in *entom.*, undergoing complete metamorphosis; in *bot.*, heterogonous. Also **het″er-o-mor′phous.**—**het″er-o-mor′phism, het′er-o-mor″phy,** *n.*

het-er-on-o-mous (het-ę-ron′ō̧-mus), *a.* [Gr. ἕτερος, other, different, + νόμος, law.] Subject to or involving different laws; also, subject to the law or will of another; in *biol.*, having different laws or modes of growth, as parts or organs. —**het-er-on′o-my,** *n.*

het-er-o-nym (het′ẹ-rǭ-nim), *n.* [Gr. ἑτερώνυμος, of different name, < ἕτερος, other, different, + ὄνυμα, name.] A word having a different sound and meaning from another, but the same spelling, as *lead*, to conduct, and *lead*, a metal. —**het-er-on′y-mous** (-ẹ-ron′i-mus), *a.* [Gr. ἑτερώνυμος.] Pertaining to or of the nature of a heteronym; also, having different names, as a pair of correlatives; in *optics*, noting or pertaining to the images formed in a kind of double vision in which the image seen by the right eye is on the left side and that seen by the left eye is on the right (cf. *homonymous*). —**het-er-on′y-my,** *n.*

het-er-o-pel-mous (het″ẹ-rǭ-pel′mus), *a.* [Gr. ἕτερος, other, different, + πέλμα, sole of the foot.] In *ornith.*, having one of the two deep flexor tendons of the toes dividing and going to the first and second digits, and the other dividing and going to the third and fourth digits.

het-er-o-phyl-lous (het″ẹ-rǭ-fil′us), *a.* [NL. *heterophyllus*, < Gr. ἕτερος, other, different, + φύλλον, leaf.] In *bot.*, having different kinds of leaves on the same plant.—**het′er-o-phyl″ly,** *n.*

het-er-o-plas-ty (het′ẹ-rǭ-plas″ti), *n.* [See *hetero-* and *-plasty.*] In *surg.*, the repairing of lesions with tissue taken from another individual.

het-er-op-ter (het-ẹ-rop′tėr), *n.* [NL. *Heteroptera*, pl., < Gr. ἕτερος, other, different, + πτερόν, wing.] Any of the *Heteroptera*, a suborder of hemipterous insects having wings composed of distinct parts, comprising the true bugs.—**het-er-op′ter-an,** *a.* and *n.*—**het-er-op′ter-ous,** *a.* Having wings composed of distinct parts; belonging to the *Heteroptera* (see *heteropter*).

het-er-os-po-rous (het-ẹ-ros′pǭ-rus), *a.* [See *hetero-* and *-sporous.*] In *bot.*, having more than one kind of asexual spores. Cf. *homosporous.*—**het-er-os′po-ry,** *n.*

het-er-o-stat-ic (het″ẹ-rǭ-stat′ik), *a.* [See *hetero-* and *static.*] In *elect.*, noting or pertaining to the measurement of potential by electrostatic methods employing an auxiliary electrification.

het-er-o-tax-is (het″ẹ-rǭ-tak′sis), *n.* [NL., < Gr. ἕτερος, other, different, + τάξις, arrangement.] Abnormal or irregular arrangement, as of parts of the body, geological strata, etc. Also **het′er-o-tax″y.**—**het″er-o-tax′ic,** *a.*

het-er-ot-o-py, het-er-ot-o-pism (het-ẹ-rot′ǭ-pi, -pizm), *n.* [Gr. ἕτερος, other, different, + τόπος, place.] Disarrangement in position or order; misplacement or displacement, as of an organ; the formation of tissue in a part where it is abnormal.—**het″er-o-top′ic** (-ẹ-rǭ-top′ik), **het-er-ot′o-pous,** *a.*

het-er-o-zy-gote (het″ẹ-rǭ-zī′gōt or -zig′ōt), *n.* [See *hetero-* and *zygote.*] In Mendelian phraseology, an animal or plant (a hybrid) which will not always breed true to type. Cf. *homozygote.*—**het″er-o-zy′gous** (-zī′gus), *a.*

het-man (het′mạn), *n.*; pl. *-mans.* [Pol. *hetman* = Russ. *ataman*, prob. < G. *hauptmann*, captain.] Orig., a Polish military chief; hence, a Cossack chief; an ataman.

heugh, heuch (hūch), *n.* [Cf. AS. *hōh*, ridge, promontory.] A crag; a precipice; also, a glen with steep, overhanging sides; also, the shaft of a coal-mine (as, "three new coal-*heughs* . . . in the Douray moor": Galt's "Annals of the Parish," vi.); a pit. [Sc. and north. Eng.]

heu-land-ite (hū′lạnd-īt), *n.* [Named (1822) from H. *Heuland*, English collector of minerals.] A mineral consisting of a hydrous silicate of aluminium and calcium.

heu-ris-tic (hū-ris′tik), *a.* [Irreg. < Gr. εὑρίσκειν, find, discover.] Serving to find out or discover: as, a *heuristic* principle.—**heu-ris′ti-cal-ly,** *adv.*

hew (hū), *v.*; pret. *hewed*, pp. *hewed* or *hewn*, ppr. *hewing.* [AS. *hēawan* = D. *houwen* = G. *hauen* = Icel. *höggva*, hew: cf. *hag*[2], *hay*[4], and *hoe.*] **I.** *tr.* To strike forcibly with a cutting tool; cut with a blow or blows of a sharp instrument, as an ax, sword, etc.; chop; hack; also, to cut down, as trees; fell with cutting blows; also, to shape with cutting blows of an ax, hammer and chisel, etc., as timber or stone; cut roughly into form with such blows; also, to make or produce with cutting blows, as a passage. **II.** *intr.* To deal cutting blows, as with an ax or a sword.—**hew′er,** *n.* One who or that which hews.—**hewers of wood and drawers of water,** those who perform work of the humblest kind; drudges: with allusion to Josh. ix. 21. Cf. *Gibeonite.*

hex-, hexa-. Forms of Gr. ἕξ, six, used in combination. —**hex-a-ba-sic** (hek-sạ-bā′sik), *a.* In *chem.*, of an acid, having six atoms of hydrogen replaceable by basic atoms or radicals.—**hex′a-chord** (-kôrd), *n.* [+ Gr. χορδή, string.] In *music*, an instrument with six strings; also, a diatonic series of six tones, having in medieval music a half-step between the third and fourth tones and whole steps between the others; also, the interval of a major sixth.—**hex-a-cid** (hek-sas′id), *a.* In *chem.*, capable of combining with six molecules of a monobasic acid.

hex-ad (hek′sad), *n.* [LL. *hexas* (*hexad-*), < Gr. ἑξάς (ἑξαδ-), < ἕξ, six.] The number six; also, a group or series of six; in *chem.*, an element, atom, or radical whose valence is six.—**hex-ad′ic,** *a.*

hex-a-ëm-e-ron (hek-sạ-em′ẹ-rǫn), *n.* [LL., < Gr. ἑξαήμερον, neut. of ἑξαήμερος, of six days, < ἕξ, six, + ἡμέρα, day.] The six days of the creation of the world; a history of this period, as contained in Genesis, or a treatise on it. —**hex″a-ë-mer′ic** (-ẹ-mer′ik), *a.*

hex-a-gon (hek′sạ-gon), *n.* [L. *hexagonum*, < Gr. ἑξάγωνος, hexangular: see *hexa-* and *-gon.*] A plane figure having six angles and six sides.—**hex-ag-o-nal** (hek-sag′ǭ-nạl), *a.* Of, pertaining to, or having the form of a hexagon; having a hexagon as base or cross-section (as, a *hexagonal* pyramid); divided into hexagons, as a surface; in *crystal.*, noting or pertaining to a system of crystallization characterized by three equal lateral axes intersecting at angles of 60° and a vertical axis of different length at right angles to them. —**hex-ag′o-nal-ly,** *adv.*

hex-a-gram (hek′sạ-gram), *n.* [See *hexa-* and *-gram.*] A six-pointed star-like figure formed of two equilateral triangles placed concentrically with their sides parallel and on opposite sides of the center; in *geom.*, a figure of six lines.

hex-a-he-dron (hek-sạ-hē′drǫn), *n.*; pl. *-drons* or *-dra* (-drạ̈). [See *hexa-* and *-hedron.*] A solid figure having six faces. —**hex-a-he′dral,** *a.*

hex-a-hem-e-ron (hek-sạ-hem′ẹ-rǫn), etc. Same as *hexaëmeron*, etc.

hex-am-er-ous (hek-sam′ẹ-rus), *a.* [See *hexa-* and *-merous.*] Consisting of or divided into six parts; in *bot.*, of flowers, having six members in each whorl.

hex-am-e-ter (hek-sam′e-tėr). [L., < Gr. ἑξάμετρος, < ἕξ, six, + μέτρον, measure.] In *pros.*: **I.** *a.* Consisting of six metrical feet. **II.** *n.* A hexameter verse; esp., the dactylic verse of six feet, of Greek and Latin epic and other poetry ('dactylic hexameter'), in which the first four feet are dactyls or spondees, the fifth foot is ordinarily a dactyl but sometimes a spondee, and the last is a trochee or spondee (imitated in the lines "Strongly it bears us along in swelling and limitless billows, Nothing before and nothing behind but the sky and the ocean": Coleridge's tr. Schiller's "Homeric Hexameter").—**hex-a-met-ric, hex-a-met-ri-cal** (hek-sạ-met′rik, -ri-kạl), *a.*

hex-ane (hek′sān), *n.* [Gr. ἕξ, six (with reference to the atoms of carbon).] In *chem.*, any of five isomeric hydrocarbons, C_6H_{14}.

hex-an-gu-lar (hek-sang′gū-lạ̈r), *a.* [See *hex-.*] Having six angles.

Hex-a-pla (hek′sạ-plạ̈), *n.* [Gr. ἑξαπλᾶ, neut. pl. of ἑξαπλόος, sixfold, < ἕξ, six, + -πλόος as in διπλόος, double.] An edition of the Old Testament containing six texts or versions in parallel columns, compiled by Origen in the 3d century; hence [*l. c.*], a similar edition of any work.—**hex′a-plar** (-plạ̈r), *a.*

hex-a-pod (hek′sạ-pod). [NL. *Hexapoda*, pl., < Gr. ἑξάπους (-ποδ-), six-footed, < ἕξ, six, + πούς (ποδ-), foot.] **I.** *n.* One of the *Hexapoda* (or *Insecta*), a class of arthropods having six feet, comprising the true insects. **II.** *a.* Having six feet; belonging to the *Hexapoda.*—**hex-ap-o-dous** (hek-sap′ǭ-dus), *a.*

hex-ap-o-dy (hek-sap′ǭ-di), *n.*; pl. *-dies* (-diz). [Gr. ἑξάπους (-ποδ-), of six metrical feet, also six-footed: see *hexapod.*] In *pros.*, a line or verse consisting of six metrical feet.

hex-a-stich (hek′sạ-stik), *n.* [Gr. ἑξάστιχος, of six rows or lines, < ἕξ, six, + στίχος, row, line.] In *pros.*, a strophe, stanza, or poem consisting of six lines or verses.

hex-a-style (hek′sạ-stīl). [Gr. ἑξάστυλος, < ἕξ, six, + στῦλος, pillar, column.] **I.** *a.* Having six columns in front, as a temple or a portico. **II.** *n.* A hexastyle structure.

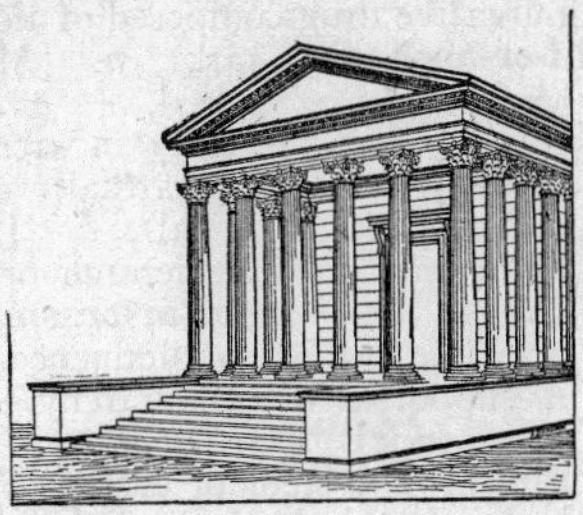

Hexastyle ancient Roman Temple (called the Maison Carrée), at Nîmes, France.

Hex-a-teuch (hek′sạ-tūk), *n.* [Gr. ἕξ, six, + τεῦχος, book.] The first six books of the Old Testament, Genesis, Exodus, Leviticus, Numbers, Deuteronomy, and Joshua. Cf. *Pentateuch.*—**Hex′a-teuch-al,** *a.*

hex-ath-lon (hek-sath′lon), *n.* [Gr. ἕξ, six, + ἆθλον, ἆθλος, contest.] An athletic contest comprising six different exercises or events, and won by the contestant having the highest total score.

hex-a-tom-ic (hek-sạ-tom′ik), *a.* [See *hex-*.] In *chem.*, having six atoms in the molecule; also, containing six replaceable atoms or groups.

hex-a-va-lent (hek-sạ-vā′lẹnt or hek-sav′ạ-), *a.* [See *hexa-* and *-valent.*] In *chem.*, having a valence of six.

hex-en-be-sen (hek′sen-bā″zen), *n.* [G.] Witches'-broom.

hex-ite (hek′sīt), *n.* [Gr. ἕξ, six.] In *chem.*, an alcohol containing six hydroxyl groups.

hex-oc-ta-he-dron (hek-sok-tạ-hē′drọn), *n.*; pl. *-drons* or *-dra* (-drạ̈). [See *hex-* and *octahedron.*] An isometric crystal with 48 equal triangular faces.—**hex-oc-ta-he′dral,** *a.*

hex-ode (hek′sōd), *a.* [Gr. ἕξ, six, + ὁδός, way.] Noting or pertaining to a system of telegraphy in which six messages can be sent simultaneously over the same wire.

hex-one (hek′sōn), *n.* [Gr. ἕξ, six.] In *chem.*, any of various organic bases which contain six atoms of carbon in the molecule.—**hex-ose** (hek′sōs), *n.* [See *-ose*[2].] In *chem.*, any of a class of sugars containing six atoms of carbon, as glucose.—**hex-yl** (hek′sil), *n.* [See *-yl.*] In *chem.*, the univalent radical, C_6H_{13}, of the alcohols, etc., derived from hexane.

hey (hā), *interj.* [Cf. D. and G. *hei*, Sw. *hej*, also E. *heigh* and *hi.*] An exclamation of pleasure, surprise, etc., also used to call attention, and as an interrogative.

hey-day[1] (hā′dā), *interj.* [Cf. *hey*, also D. *heidaar*, G. *heida.*] An exclamation of cheerfulness, surprise, wonder, etc.

hey-day[2] (hā′dā), *n.* [Perhaps < *heyday*[1].] High spirits; a state of exaltation; also, the stage or period of highest vigor or fullest strength (as, "The *heyday* of life is over with him": Longfellow's "Hyperion," iv. 2); the acme.

hi (hī), *interj.* [Cf. *hey* and *hoy*[2].] An exclamation used to call attention.

hi-a-tus (hī-ā′tus), *n.*; pl. *-tuses*, L. *-tus.* [L., < *hiare*, gape.] A gap or opening; a break, with a part missing; also, an interruption of continuity, as in a series; a lacuna; in *gram.* and *pros.*, a break or slight pause due to the coming together without contraction of two vowels in successive words or syllables.

hi-ba-chi (hē-bä′chē), *n.* [Jap., 'fire bowl.'] In Japanese use, a receptacle in which charcoal is kept burning, to warm a room, etc.; a brazier.

Hibachi, with Tongs.

hi-ber-nac-u-lum (hī-bėr-nak′ū-lum), *n.*; pl. *-la* (-lạ̈). [L., a winter residence, < *hibernus*: see *hibernate.*] That which serves for shelter or protection in winter; winter quarters, as of a hibernating animal; a covering for protection in winter, as of an animal or a bud; in *zoöl.*, in colonies of polyzoans, an encysted bud which is capable of surviving the winter and germinating the following spring.

hi-ber-nal (hī-bėr′nạl), *a.* [LL. *hibernalis*, < L. *hibernus*: see *hibernate.*] Of or pertaining to winter; wintry.

hi-ber-nate (hī′bėr-nāt), *v. i.*; *-nated, -nating.* [L. *hibernatus*, pp. of *hibernare*, < *hibernus*, of winter, wintry: cf. L. *hiems*, Gr. χεῖμα, Skt. *hima*, winter.] To winter; specif., to spend the winter in close quarters, in a torpid condition, as certain animals; fig., to remain in seclusion, or torpid or inactive; lie dormant.—**hi-ber-na′tion** (-nā′shọn), *n.*

Hi-ber-ni-a (hī-bėr′ni-ạ̈), *n.* [L.] An ancient name of Ireland. [Now poetic.]—**Hi-ber′ni-an. I.** *a.* Of or pertaining to Ireland; Irish. **II.** *n.* A native or inhabitant of Ireland; a member of the Irish race.—**Hi-ber′ni-an-ism, Hi-ber′ni-cism** (-sizm), *n.* Irish character; also, an Irish characteristic; an idiom or expression peculiar to the Irish; often, an Irish bull.

hi-bis-cus (hī-bis′kus or hi-), *n.* [L., < Gr. ἰβίσκος, mallow.] Any of the herbs, shrubs, or trees of the malvaceous genus *Hibiscus*, many of which, as the althæa, *H. syriacus*, have large, showy flowers.

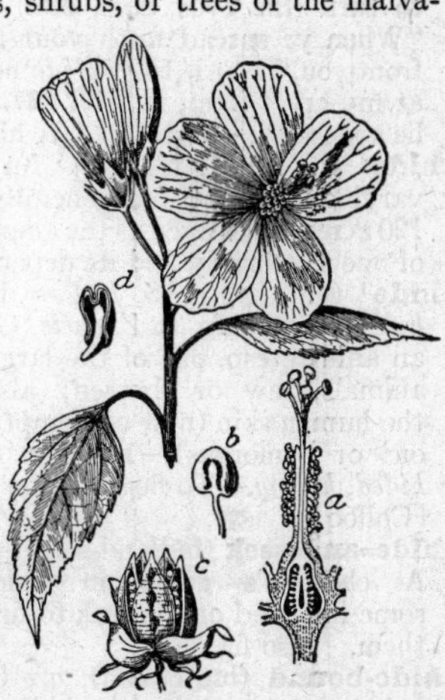

Flowering Branch of Hibiscus (*H. moscheutos*). — *a*, flower cut longitudinally; *b*, stamen; *c*, fruit; *d*, embryo.

hic (hik), *interj.* A syllable used to express the sound of a hiccup, esp. as interrupting the speech of a drunken person.

hic-cup, hic-cough (hik′up), *n.* [Imit.; the form *hiccough* being due to association with *cough.*] A quick, involuntary inspiration suddenly checked by closure of the glottis, producing a characteristic sound; also, the affection of having such spasms (usually in *pl.*).—**hic′cup, hic′cough,** *v.* **I.** *intr.* To make the sound of a hiccup; be affected with hiccups. **II.** *tr.* To utter with hiccups.

hic ja-cet (hik jā′set). [L.] 'Here lies': words often used to begin epitaphs on tombstones.

hick (hik). [From *Hick*, for *Richard*, man's name.] **I.** *n.* A countryman; an ignorant or stupid rustic. [Slang.] **II.** *a.* Pertaining to or characteristic of countrymen or rustics. [Slang.]

hick-o-ry (hik′ọ-ri), *n.*; pl. *-ries* (-riz). [N. Amer. Ind.] Any of the North American trees constituting the juglandaceous genus *Hicoria*, certain of which, as the shagbark, *H. ovata*, yield valuable hard wood and sweet, edible nuts; the wood of such a tree; also, a switch, stick, etc., of this wood.—**hick′o-ry-nut,** *n.* The nut of the hickory.

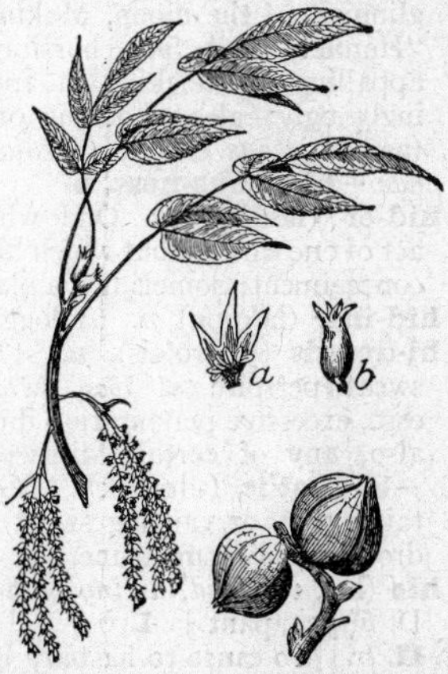

Flowering Branch and Fruit of Hickory (*Hicoria ovata*). — *a*, male flower; *b*, female flower.

Hicks-ite (hiks′īt), *n.* One of a seceding body of American Quakers, founded by Elias Hicks (1748–1830), holding Socinian doctrines.

hick-wall (hik′wâl), *n.* [Prob. orig. imit. of its note: cf. *highhole.*] Any of certain European woodpeckers, esp. the green woodpecker, *Gecinus viridis.*

hid (hid). Preterit and past participle of *hide*[1].

hi-dal-go (hi-dal′gō), *n.*; pl. *-gos* (-gōz). [Sp., for *hijo de algo*, 'son of something.'] In Spain, a man of the lower nobility; a gentleman by birth.

hid-at-ed (hī′dā-ted), *a.* [See *hide*[2].] Measured or reckoned by hides (measure of land).—**hid-a-tion** (hī-dā′shọn), *n.* Measurement or assessment by hides.

hid-den (hid′n). Past participle of *hide*[1].—**hid′den,** *p. a.* Concealed; secret; latent; obscure.

hid-den-ite (hid′n-īt), *n.* [From W. E. *Hidden,* who discovered it (1879).] A transparent emerald-green or yellowish-green variety of spodumene, highly esteemed as a gem.

hide[1] (hīd), *v.*; pret. *hid,* pp. *hidden* or *hid,* ppr. *hiding.* [AS. *hȳdan* = MLG. *hūden,* hide; perhaps akin to Gr. κεύθειν, cover, hide.] **I.** *tr.* To conceal intentionally from the sight, or prevent from being seen (as, to *hide* a stain or a scar); conceal from discovery, or secrete (as, to *hide* money beneath the floor); also, to obstruct the view of, or cover up (as, "A huge town, continuous and compact, *Hiding* the face of earth for leagues": Wordsworth's "Excursion," viii. 121); also, to conceal from knowledge, or keep secret (as, "Tell me now what thou hast done; *hide* it not from me": Josh. vii. 19); also, in Biblical language, to turn (the eyes, ears, etc.) away, as in displeasure (as, "When ye spread forth your hands, I will *hide* mine eyes from you," Isa. i. 15; "*Hide* not thine ear at my breathing, at my cry," Lam. iii. 56). **II.** *intr.* To conceal one's self; lie concealed.—**hide**[1], *n.* A hiding-place.

hide[2] (hīd), *n.* [AS. *hīd.*] An old English measure of land, varying in extent, but generally taken as normally equal to 120 acres, considered as the amount adequate for the support of one free family and its dependents.

hide[3] (hīd), *n.* [AS. *hȳd* = D. *huid* = G. *haut* = Icel. *hūdh,* hide; akin to L. *cutis,* Gr. κύτος, skin.] The skin of an animal, esp. one of the larger animals, raw or dressed; also, the human skin (now contemptuous or humorous).—**hide**[3], *v. t.*; *hided, hiding.* To flog or thrash. [Colloq.]

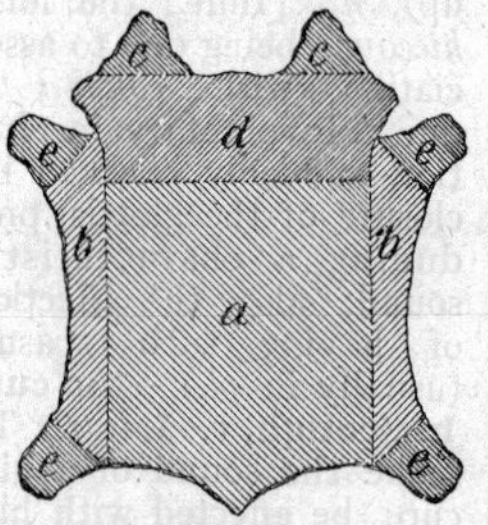

Diagram showing Divisions of a Tanned Hide. — *a,* butt; *b, b,* belly; *c, c,* cheek; *d,* neck; *e, e, e, e,* shank.

hide=and=seek (hīd′ạnd-sēk′), *n.* A children's game in which some hide and others seek to find them. Also fig.

hide-bound (hīd′bound), *a.* Of a horse, etc., having the hide or skin adhering closely to the back and ribs; of a tree, etc., having the bark so close or unyielding as to impede growth; hence, fig., of a person, the mind, etc., narrow and rigid in opinion; hardened or confirmed in narrow views.

hid-ed (hī′ded), *a.* Having a hide: as, thick-*hided.*

hid-e-ous (hid′ē-us), *a.* [OF. *hidos* (F. *hideux*), < *hide, hisde,* horror, fear; origin uncertain.] Horrible or frightful to the sight, hearing, or feelings generally (as, a *hideous* monster; *hideous* wounds; *hideous* cries; "What may this mean, That thou, dead corse . . . Revisit'st thus the glimpses of the moon, Making night *hideous?*" Shakspere's "Hamlet," i. 4. 54); horribly unpleasant; dreadful; esp., appalling or shocking in appearance; horribly or revoltingly ugly; also, shocking or revolting to the moral sense (as, a *hideous* crime; *hideous* debauchery).—**hid′e-ous-ly,** *adv.*—**hid′e-ous-ness,** *n.*

hid-er (hī′dėr), *n.* One who hides.—**hid′ing**[1], *n.* The act of one who or that which hides; the state of being hidden; concealment; sometimes, a place or means of concealment.

hid-ing[2] (hī′ding), *n.* A flogging or thrashing. [Colloq.]

hi-dro-sis (hi-drō′sis), *n.* [NL., < Gr. ἵδρωσις, < ἱδροῦν, sweat, perspire, < ἶδος, sweat: see *sweat.*] Perspiration; esp., excessive perspiration due to drugs, disease, or the like; also, any of certain diseases characterized by sweating.—**hi-drot′ic** (-drot′ik). [Gr. ἱδρωτικός.] **I.** *a.* Of, pertaining to, or causing sweat or perspiration. **II.** *n.* A hidrotic agent or medicine.

hie (hī), *v.*; *hied, hieing* or *hying.* [AS. *hīgian,* strive: cf. D. *hijgen,* pant.] **I.** *intr.* To hasten; speed; go in haste. **II.** *tr.* To cause to hasten; incite to action.

hi-e-mal (hī′ẹ-mạl), *a.* [L. *hiemalis,* < *hiems,* winter: see *hibernate.*] Of or belonging to winter.

hi-e-ra-co-sphinx (hī-ẹ-rā′kǭ-sfingks), *n.* [Gr. ἱέραξ (ἱερακ-), hawk, + σφίγξ, sphinx.] A sphinx with the head of a hawk.

hi-er-a=pic-ra (hī″ẹ-rạ-pik′rạ), *n.* [ML. *hiera picra,* < Gr. ἱερά, a name for various medicines (prop. fem. of ἱερός, sacred), + πικρά, fem. of πικρός, bitter.] In *phar.,* a purgative drug composed of aloes and canella.

hi-er-arch (hī′ẹ-rärk), *n.* [ML. *hierarcha,* < Gr. ἱεράρχης, < ἱερός, sacred, + ἄρχειν, lead, rule.] One who rules or has authority in sacred things; a chief priest.—**hi-er-ar-chal** (hī-ẹ-rär′kạl), *a.*—**hi-er-ar′chic, hi-er-ar′chi-cal** (-kik, -ki-kạl), *a.* [Gr. ἱεραρχικός.] Pertaining or belonging to a hierarch or a hierarchy.—**hi-er-ar′chi-cal-ly,** *adv.*—**hi′er-ar-chism** (-kizm), *n.* Hierarchical principles, rule, or influence.—**hi′er-ar-chist** (-kist), *n.* A supporter of a hierarchy.—**hi′er-ar-chy** (-ki), *n.*; pl. *-chies* (-kiz). [Gr. ἱεραρχία.] Rule or authority in sacred things; a system of ecclesiastical rule; also, an organized body of ecclesiastical officials in successive ranks or orders (as, the Roman Catholic *hierarchy*); also, one of the three divisions of the angels, each made up of three orders (see *angel*), conceived as constituting a graded body; often, the collective body of angels ('celestial hierarchy'); also, any system of persons or things in graded orders, classes, etc.

hi-er-at-ic (hī-ẹ-rat′ik), *a.* [L. *hieraticus,* < Gr. ἱερατικός, priestly, sacerdotal, < ἱερᾶσθαι, be a priest, < ἱερός, sacred.] Of or pertaining to the priestly class; sacerdotal; specif., noting or pertaining to a form of ancient Egyptian writing consisting of abridged forms of hieroglyphics, used by the priests in their records; also, noting or pertaining to certain styles in art which are characterized by types or methods fixed by religious tradition. Also **hi-e-rat′i-cal.**

hiero-. Form of Gr. ἱερός, sacred, used in combination.

hi-er-oc-ra-cy (hī-ẹ-rok′rạ-si), *n.*; pl. *-cies* (-siz). [See *hiero-* and *-cracy.*] Rule or government by priests or ecclesiastics; also, a hierarchy.—**hi″er-o-crat′ic** (-ẹ-rǭ-krat′ik), *a.*

hi-er-o-dule (hī′ẹ-rǭ-dūl), *n.* [Gr. ἱερόδουλος, < ἱερός, sacred, + δοῦλος, slave.] In *Gr. antiq.,* a slave dwelling in a temple and dedicated to the service of a deity.—**hi″er-o-du′lic** (-dū′lik), *a.*

hi-er-o-glyph (hī′ẹ-rǭ-glif), *n.* [Back-formation from *hieroglyphic.*] A hieroglyphic character; fig., a figure or device with a hidden meaning.—**hi′er-o-glyph,** *v. t.* To represent by or inscribe with hieroglyphs: as, "*hieroglyphed* limestone tablets" (Amelia B. Edwards's "Thousand Miles up the Nile," xxi.).

hi-er-o-glyph-ic (hī″ẹ-rǭ-glif′ik). [LL. *hieroglyphicus,* < Gr. ἱερογλυφικός, < ἱερός, sacred, + γλύφειν, carve.] **I.** *a.* Pertaining to or of the nature of, or inscribed in or with, the symbolic characters used for ancient Egyptian sacred and other records, or similar characters used by other peoples; hence, having a hidden meaning; mysteriously symbolic; also, hard to decipher. **II.** *n.* A picture or character standing for or representing a word, idea, etc., in the writing found on the monuments and other records of the ancient Egyptians, and in similar writing of other peoples, or the mode of writing in such characters (usually in *pl.*); hence, a figure or device with a hidden meaning (as, "He was the first to imprint New-Year cakes with the mysterious *hieroglyphics* of the Cock and Breeches": Irving's "Knickerbocker's New York," vii. 9); *pl.,* writing difficult to decipher.—**hi″er-o-glyph′i-cal,** *a.* Hieroglyphic.—**hi″er-o-glyph′i-cal-ly,** *adv.*

Hieroglyphics, from mummy-case in the Museum of Fine Arts, Boston.

hi-er-o-gram (hī′ẹ-rǭ-gram), *n.* [See *hiero-* and *-gram.*] A hierograph.

hi-er-o-graph (hī′ẹ-rǭ-gráf), *n.* [See *hiero-* and *-graph.*] A sacred inscription or symbol; a hieroglyph.—**hi″er-o-graph′ic** (-graf′ik), *a.*

hi-er-ol-a-try (hī-ẹ-rol′ạ-tri), *n.* [See *hiero-* and *-latry.*] The worship of saints or holy beings; hagiolatry.

hi-er-ol-o-gy (hī-ẹ-rol′ǭ-ji), *n.* [See *hiero-* and *-logy.*] Sacred literature or learning; the history of religions as a study; also, hagiology; also, hieroglyphic lore†.

hi-er-o-phant (hī′ẹ-rǭ-fant or hī-ėr′ǭ-), *n.* [LL. *hierophantes,* < Gr. ἱεροφάντης, < ἱερός, sacred, + φαίνειν, show.] In ancient Greece, etc., an official expounder of rites of worship and sacrifice; specif., the chief priest of the Eleusinian mysteries; in general, any interpreter of sacred mysteries or esoteric principles.—**hi″er-o-phan′tic** (-fan′-tik), *a.*

hi-fa-lu-tin (hī′fa̤-lö′tin), *n.* and *a.* See *highfalutin.*

hig-gle (hig′l), *v. i.*; *-gled, -gling.* [Appar. a varied form of *haggle.*] To dispute as to terms; strive for advantage in bargaining, esp. in a petty way; haggle; also, to go about with small wares or provisions for sale.

hig-gle-dy=pig-gle-dy (hig′l-di-pig′l-di). [Origin obscure.] **I.** *adv.* In jumbled confusion; in a disorderly manner. **II.** *a.* Confused; jumbled: as, "narrow uneven alleys leading to *higgledy-piggledy* workshops and kilns" (Arnold Bennett's "Clayhanger," i. 2). **III.** *n.* Confusion or disorder; a disorderly jumble.

hig-gler (hig′lėr), *n.* One who higgles.

high (hī), *a.* [AS. *hēah* = D. *hoog* = G. *hoch* = Icel. *hār* = Goth. *hauhs,* high.] Having a great or considerable reach or extent upward (as, a *high* mountain; a *high* building; *high* boots); lofty; tall; rising considerably from a surface (as, *high* relief: see *relief* and *alto-rilievo*); having a specified reach or extent upward (as, a mountain 29,000 feet *high*; a dog 10 inches *high*); also, situated far above the ground or some base (as, the *high* top of a sky-scraper; a balloon *high* in the air); elevated or raised in position; lying above the general level, as a tract of land; designating or pertaining to highland or inland regions as opposed to those near the sea-level or the sea (as, the *High* Germans: see under *German*[2], *n.*); situated a specified distance above some level (as, an aëroplane 10,000 feet *high*; a roof 50 feet *high*); also, extending to or from an elevation (as, a *high* leap; a *high* dive); also, elevated or exalted in rank, station, estimation, etc. (as, a *high* official; a person *high* in public esteem); of exalted character, or of a lofty or superior kind (as, *high* resolves; "Plain living and *high* thinking are no more," Wordsworth's "O Friend! I know not which way I must look"); grave or serious (as, *high* crimes; *high* treason, see phrase below); advanced or abstruse (as, "To speculations *high* or deep I turn'd my thoughts": Milton's "Paradise Lost," ix. 602); also, chief, principal, or main (as, the *high* altar of a church; a *high* priest; the *high* sheriff); also, rich or luxurious (as, *high* living); also, of great amount, degree, force, etc. (as, a *high* number; a *high* price; a *high* temperature; a *high* speed; a *high* wind); deep or intense (as, a *high* color); powerful or quick-acting (as, *high* explosives, those such as nitroglycerin, dynamite, etc.); denoted by a high number (as, a *high* latitude, one at a great distance from the equator); for large stakes (as, *high* play); expensive, costly, or dear (as, food is *high*); also, produced by relatively rapid vibrations, as sounds; acute in pitch, as a note; shrill; sometimes, loud; also, advanced to the utmost extent, or to the culmination (as, *high* noon; *high* summer); fully advanced or come (as, it is *high* time to start, or to begin work); also, of early date (as, of *high* antiquity); also, lofty, haughty, or arrogant, as manner or expression; angry (as, *high* words); also, extreme in opinion or doctrine, esp. religious or political (cf. *High-church*); also, exalted in feeling; elated, merry, or hilarious (as, *high* spirits); sometimes, excited with drink (slang); also, of meat, esp. game, tending toward decomposition, or slightly tainted (used esp. when this is considered a desirable quality).—**high comedy,** comedy of a high or superior kind, attaining its effects without the use of broad humor; esp., comedy dealing with polite or refined society, and depending on the wit of its dialogue rather than on action or striking plot. Cf. *low comedy,* under *low*[4], *a.*—**high jinks.** See under *jink, n.* —**high life,** life in high or fashionable society; also, persons in such society.—**high light,** an effect or representation of bright light, as in a picture; a part of a picture on which the light is represented as falling with full force; fig., a conspicuous or striking part, as of a speech or a book.—**high mass.** See under *mass*[1].—**high school,** in the U. S., a free public school intermediate between a grammar-school and a college; in late use, either of two free public schools, one ('junior high school') corresponding to the upper grades or grade of the ordinary grammar-school together with one or more years of the ordinary high school, and another ('senior high school') corresponding to the remainder of the ordinary high school; also, a school of corresponding grade but not belonging to a public school system, as among Roman Catholics.—**high seas,** the open seas or ocean. —**high tea,** a tea at which meat is served: in distinction from an ordinary tea with bread, butter, cake, etc. —**high tide,** the tide at high water; the time of high water; fig., the culminating point.—**high treason,** treason against the sovereign or state. See *treason.*—**high water,** water at its greatest elevation, as in a river; the highest state of the tide; the time when the highest point of the tide is reached.—**high=water mark,** a mark showing the highest level reached by a body of water; esp., the mark left or the limit reached by the tide at high water; fig., the highest point attained, as in intensity, excellence, etc.—**on high,** at or to a height, aloft, or above (often with reference to heaven); also, in automobiling, with the transmission-gears set to obtain the highest speed (as, to drive up a hill *on high*).—**with a high hand,** with a vigorous or arrogant display of power; overbearingly; domineeringly.—**high,** *adv.* [AS. *hēah.*] At or to a high point, place, or level, or a high rank or estimate, a high amount or price, or a high degree; for high stakes (as, to play *high*); at or to a high pitch (as, to sing *high*); richly or luxuriously (as, to live *high*); haughtily† or arrogantly†.—**high and low,** up and down; here and there; everywhere: as, I have looked *high and low* for it.

high=ball (hī′bâl), *n.* A drink of whisky or other liquor diluted with soda-water or the like and served with ice in a tall glass.

high-bind-er (hī′bīn″dėr), *n.* A rowdy† or ruffian†; also, a member of a secret band or society of Chinese said to exist in California and other parts of the U. S., associated for purposes of blackmailing, assassination, etc., in the employ of others. [U. S.]

high=born (hī′bôrn), *a.* Of high rank by birth; of noble birth.

high=boy (hī′boi), *n.* A tall chest of drawers supported on legs. Cf. *low-boy.*

high=bred (hī′bred), *a.* Of superior breed or stock; also, characterized by superior breeding or highly refined manners, as persons; characteristic of superior breeding, as manners.

high-brow (hī′brou). **I.** *n.* A person of intellectual tastes or pretensions: used humorously or disparagingly. Cf. *lowbrow.* [Slang.] **II.** *a.* Being a highbrow; pertaining or proper to highbrows. [Slang.]

High=church (hī′chėrch′), *a.* Laying great stress on church authority and jurisdiction, ritual, etc.: used of a party in the Anglican Church, and opposed to *Low-church.*—**High′=church′man** (-ma̤n), *n.*; pl. *-men.*

high=col-ored (hī′kul′o̤rd), *a.* Having a high color; deep in color; esp., florid or red, as complexion, the person, etc.

high=day (hī′dā), *n.* A day of high celebration; a holy day; a festal day; also, heyday.

high-er (hī′ėr), *a.* Comparative of *high, a.*: esp., more high, elevated, advanced, etc., than the average or ordinary: as, the *higher* Alps; the *higher* classes of society; the *higher* education of women; *higher* mathematics, see under *mathematics*; *higher* criticism, see *criticism.*—**high′er,** *adv.* Comparative of *high, adv.*—**higher up,** further up, lit. or fig.; esp., in a higher position as to rank or importance, as in an organization or the like: as, to trace a crime from the ostensible perpetrator to persons *higher up*; to look for the man *higher up* behind the wrong-doing of a subordinate. Hence, as a noun, **high′er=up′** (pl. *higher-ups*), a person in a higher position, esp. as instigating wrong-doing by a subordinate. —**high′er,** *v. t.* or *i.* To raise or rise higher.

high-fa-lu-tin (hī′fa̤-lö′tin). [From *high, a.* or *adv.*, with *-falutin* of unknown origin.] **I.** *n.* Pompous speech or writing; bombast. [Colloq.] **II.** *a.* Pompous or bombastic. [Colloq.]

high=fli-er, high=fly-er (hī′flī″ėr), *n.* One who or that which flies high; fig., one who is extravagant or goes to extremes in aims, pretensions, opinions, etc.—**high′=flown,** *a.* Soaring, aspiring, or extravagant in aims, pretensions, or character (as, "filled up with *high-flown* ideas above and beyond her place in life": W. De Morgan's "Alice-for-Short," l.); also, pretentiously lofty or elevated, as language, sentiments, a speaker or writer, etc. (as, "Sir Ulic . . . made her a great many *high-flown* compliments": Smollett's "Humphry Clinker," April 26); bombastic.—**high′=fly″ing,** *a.* That flies high, as a bird; fig., extravagant or extreme in aims, pretensions, opinions, etc.

high=hand-ed (hī′han′ded), *a.* Acting or done in a bold, arbitrary way; domineering; arbitrary: as, "A race *high-handed*, strong of heart, Sea-rovers, conquerors" (H. Newbolt's "Non-Combatant").—**high′=hand′ed-ness,** *n.*
high=heart-ed (hī′här′ted), *a.* Courageous; high-spirited.
high=heeled (hī′hēld), *a.* Having high heels, as boots or shoes, or, occasionally, the wearer.
high-hole, high-hold-er (hī′hōl, -hōl″dėr), *n.* [Cf. *hick-wall.*] The flicker (bird), *Colaptes auratus.*
high-land (hī′lạnd). **I.** *n.* An elevated region; a plateau; *pl.* [usually *cap.*], a mountainous region or part of a country (as, the *Highlands* of Scotland, in the northern and western parts of the country). **II.** *a.* Of, pertaining to, or characteristic of highlands, esp. [usually *cap.*] the Highlands of Scotland.—**high′land-er,** *n.* An inhabitant of high land; esp. [*cap.*], a member of the Gaelic race of the Highlands of Scotland; also, a soldier of a Highland regiment.
high=low (hī′lō), *n.* A boot reaching up over the ankle.
high=low=jack (hī′lō′jak′), *n.* The card-game of seven-up.
high-ly (hī′li), *adv.* At or to a high place or level, or a high rank, or a high amount or price; in or to a high degree (as, *highly* amusing); with high appreciation or praise (as, to speak *highly* of a person); haughtily† or arrogantly†.
high=mind-ed (hī′mīn′ded), *a.* Having or showing high, elevated, or exalted principles or feelings; magnanimous; also, proud or arrogant.—**high′=mind′ed-ness,** *n.*
high-most (hī′mōst), *a. superl.* Highest. [Now prov.]
high=necked (hī′nekt), *a.* Of a garment, high at the neck; covering the shoulders and neck.
high-ness (hī′nes), *n.* The state of being high; loftiness; dignity; also [usually *cap.*], with *his, your,* etc., a title of honor given to royal or princely personages.
high=pres-sure (hī′presh′ụr), *a.* Having or involving a pressure (as of steam, water, etc.) above the normal.
high=proof (hī′pröf), *a.* Containing a high percentage of alcohol: as, *high-proof* spirits.
high-road (hī′rōd), *n.* A chief or main road; a highway.
high=souled (hī′sōld′), *a.* Having exalted principles or feelings.
high=sound-ing (hī′soun′ding), *a.* High or loud in sound; also, having an imposing or pretentious sound.
high=spir-it-ed (hī′spir′i-ted), *a.* Having a high, lofty, proud, or bold spirit; mettlesome.
high=strung (hī′strung′), *a.* Strung to a high pitch, as a musical instrument; fig., at great tension, as nerves; highly sensitive or nervous, as persons.
hight (hīt), *v.*; pret. and pp. *hight.* [AS. *hātan* = D. *heeten* = G. *heissen* = Icel. *heita* = Goth. *haitan*, call, name, bid, command: cf. *hest.*] **I.** *tr.* To call or name (now chiefly in pp.: archaic or prov.: as, "Childe Harold was he *hight*," Byron's "Childe Harold," i. 3); also, to bid† or command†; also, to promise or vow (now Sc.); also, to threaten (Sc.). **II.** *intr.* To be called. [Archaic.]
highth (hītth or hīth), *n.* Obs. or prov. var. of *height.*
high=toned (hī′tōnd′), *a.* High in tone or pitch; also, having high or lofty character or principles; also, fashionable or stylish (colloq., U. S.).
high-ty=tigh-ty (hī′ti-tī′ti), *a.* and *interj.* Hoity-toity.
high-way (hī′wā), *n.* A main road, as between one town and another; any public road; hence, any main or ordinary route, track, or course.—**high′way-man** (-mạn), *n.*; pl. *-men.* One who frequents the highway for the purpose of robbing persons, esp. one who does this on horseback.
high=wrought (hī′rôt), *a.* Wrought with a high degree of skill; highly finished; also, highly agitated.
hi-jack (hī′jak), *v. t.* or *i.* [Said to have come from *hi, Jack!* as used by a robber in accosting an intended victim.] To rob (a person) or take (goods, etc.) by force or trickery, esp. on the way or in transit: commonly said of those who prey on bootleggers.—**hi′jack″er,** *n.*—**hi′jack″ing,** *n.*
hike (hīk), *v.*; *hiked, hiking.* [Perhaps connected with *hitch.*] **I.** *tr.* To move, draw, or raise as with a jerk; hitch; jerk; twitch; pull; throw; toss; jolt. [Prov. or colloq.] **II.** *intr.* To move suddenly; go hastily; decamp; also, to march or tramp, as soldiers; also, to be drawn (*up*) unevenly, as a garment. [Prov. or colloq.]—**hike,** *n.* The act of hiking; a march or tramp. [Prov. or colloq.]—**hik-er** (hī′kėr), *n.*
hi-la (hī′lạ̈), *n.* Plural of *hilum.*
hi-lar (hī′lạ̈r), *a.* Of or pertaining to a hilum.
hi-la-ri-ous (hi-lā′ri-us or hī-), *a.* [L. *hilaris*, < Gr. ἱλαρός, cheerful, gay.] Cheerful or gay; now, esp., demonstratively or boisterously gay; merry; mirthful.—**hi-la′ri-ous-ly,** *adv.*—**hi-la′ri-ous-ness,** *n.*—**hi-lar′i-ty** (-lar′i-ti), *n.* [L. *hilaritas.*] Cheerfulness or gaiety; now, esp., demonstrative or boisterous gaiety; merriment; mirth.
Hil-a-ry (hil′ạ-ri) **sit′ting.** [From St. *Hilary* of Poitiers, whose feast is celebrated on Jan. 13.] In England, a session of the High Court of Justice, held in the same part of the year as the former Hilary term.—**Hil′a-ry term.** In England, formerly, a period extending from Jan. 11 to Jan. 31, being one of the four terms during which the superior courts were in session; also, one of the university terms at Oxford and Dublin.
hil-ding (hil′ding). [Perhaps < AS. *hieldan*, bend, incline: see *heel*[1].] **I.** *n.* A mean, worthless person. See Shakspere's "All's Well," iii. 6. 4. [Archaic.] **II.** *a.* Worthless; base: as, "He was some *hilding* fellow that had stolen The horse he rode on" (Shakspere's "2 Henry IV.," i. 1. 57). [Archaic.]
hill (hil), *n.* [AS. *hyll* = MD. *hille*, hill; akin to L. *collis*, hill, *columen*, top, *columna*, column: see *column.*] A conspicuous natural elevation of the earth's surface, esp. one smaller than a mountain; also, an artificial heap or pile, as of earth; specif., a little heap of earth raised about a cultivated plant or a cluster of such plants; also, the plant or plants so surrounded.—**seven hills of Rome.** See under *seven, a.*—**hill,** *v. t.* To form into a hill or heap; also, to surround with hills, as plants.—**hill′bil″ly,** *n.*; pl. *-billies* (-bil″iz). [Cf. *billy*[2].] A countryman from the hills; in general, an uncouth, raw, or rough rustic: used contemptuously or humorously. [Colloq., orig. southern U. S.]—**hilled,** *a.* Having a hill or hills: as, the seven-*hilled* city (Rome).—**hill′er,** *n.* One who or that which hills; specif., a device or attachment for hilling plants.—**hill′i-ness,** *n.* Hilly character.—**hill′man** (-mạn), *n.*; pl. *-men.* An inhabitant of a hilly country; also, a frequenter or climber of hills.—**hill′=mi″na** (-mī″nạ̈), *n.* Any of the Asiatic birds constituting the genus *Eulabes* (of the starling family, *Sturnidæ*), esp. *E. religiosa*, which is easily tamed and taught to articulate words.

Hill-mina (*Eulabes religiosa*).

hil-lo, hil-loa (hil′ō or hi-lō′), *interj.*, *n.*, and *v.* Same as *hollo.*
hil-lock (hil′ọk), *n.* A little hill; a mound.—**hil′lock-y,** *a.*
hill=par-tridge (hil′pär″trij), *n.* Any of the gallinaceous birds constituting the genus *Galloperdix*, of India and Ceylon.

Hill-partridge (*Galloperdix lunulatus*).

hill-side (hil′sīd), *n.* The side or slope of a hill.
hill-top (hil′top), *n.* The top or summit of a hill.
hill-y (hil′i), *a.*; compar. *hillier*, superl. *hilliest.* Abounding in hills; also, hill-like; elevated; steep.
hilt (hilt), *n.* [AS. *hilt, hilte.*] The handle of a sword or dagger; hence, the handle of any weapon or tool.—**hilt,** *v. t.* To furnish with a hilt.—**hilt′ed,** *a.* Having a hilt: as, golden-*hilted*; basket-*hilted.*
hi-lum (hī′lum), *n.*; pl. *hila* (-lạ̈). [L., little thing, trifle.] In *bot.*, the mark or scar on a seed produced by separation

from its funicle or placenta; also, the nucleus of a granule of starch; in *anat.*, that part of an organ or gland at which the vessels, nerves, etc., enter or emerge.

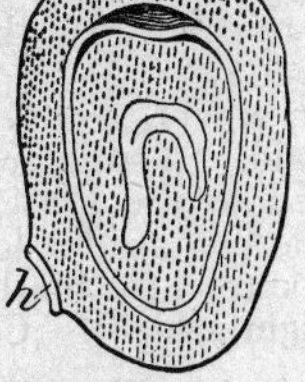

Vertical Section of a Seed, magnified. — *h*, hilum.

him (him), *pron.* [AS. *him*, dat. of *hē*, E. *he*.] Objective case of *he*.

hi-mat-i-on (hi-mat′i-on), *n.*; pl. *-ia* (-i-ạ̈). [Gr. ἱμάτιον.] In *Gr. antiq.*, a garment consisting of a rectangular piece of cloth thrown over the left shoulder and wrapped about the body.

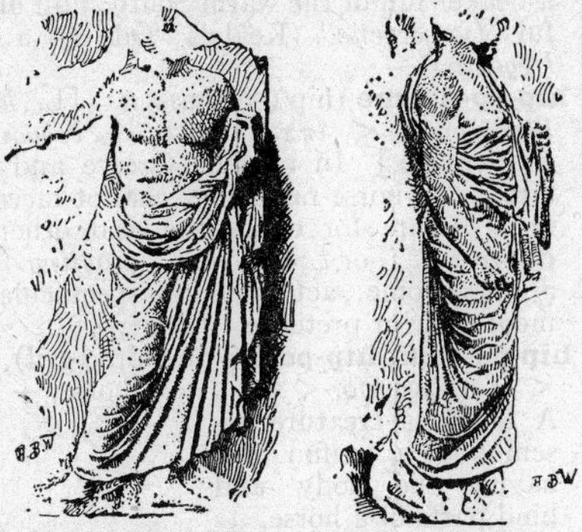
Front and Side Views of Himation, showing two methods of wearing it. — From the frieze of the Parthenon.

him-self (him-self′), *pron.* An emphatic form of *him* or *he*; also, a reflexive form of *him*.

Him-yar-ite (him′-yạr-īt), *n.* [Said to be named from an ancient king *Himyar*.] One of an ancient people of southern Arabia, of an advanced civilization, speaking an Arabic dialect closely akin to Ethiopic.—**Him-yar-it′ic** (-it′ik), *a.*

hin (hin), *n.* [Heb. *hīn*.] A Hebrew liquid measure, the sixth part of the bath.

hind[1] (hīnd), *n.* [AS. *hind* = Icel. *hind*, hind: cf. D. and G. *hinde*.] The female of the deer, chiefly the red deer (*Cervus elaphus*), esp. in and after the third year; also, any of various serranoid food-fishes of the West Indies, etc., as *Epinephelus maculosus* ('red hind').

hind[2] (hīnd), *n.* [ME. *hine*, sing., < AS. *hīna*, pl., gen. of *hīwan*, members of a household, domestics; akin to G. *heirat*, marriage.] A farm-servant or agricultural laborer; also, a bailiff or steward on a farm; also, a peasant or rustic. [Now chiefly prov.]

hind[3] (hīnd), *a.* [Appar. < *hinder*[1] (taken as a comparative) or possibly < *behind*; but cf. AS. *hindan*, adv., from behind, behind, = Goth. *hindana*, prep., behind, beyond, = OHG. *hintana*, G. *hinten*, adv., behind, all perhaps from the source of E. *hence*.] Situated in the rear or at the back; posterior: as, the *hind* legs of an animal.—**hind′brain,** *n.* The epencephalon.

hind-er[1] (hīn′dėr), *a.* [ME. *hindere*, appar. < AS. *hinder*, adv., behind, back, = Goth. *hindar*, prep., behind, beyond, = OHG. *hintar*, G. *hinter*, prep., behind; all orig. comparative forms from the base of AS. *hindan*, Goth. *hindana*, etc.: see *hind*[3].] Situated at the rear or back; hind; posterior: as, "the *hinder* part of the ship" (Mark, iv. 38).

hin-der[2] (hin′dėr), *v.* [AS. *hindrian*, < *hinder*, behind, back: see *hinder*[1].] **I.** *tr.* To hold or keep back by delaying or stopping progress or action (as, to be *hindered* by storms throughout a journey; to *hinder* a person in his work, or from working; "My tears must stop, for every drop *Hinders* needle and thread!" Hood's "Song of the Shirt"); impede or stop (movement, progress, action, etc.); sometimes, to prevent from acting, taking place, etc., as by measures in advance (as, to *hinder* a man from committing a crime; to *hinder* a crime). **II.** *intr.* To impede or stop progress or action; be an obstacle or impediment.—**hin′der-ance,** *n.* See *hindrance*.—**hin′der-er,** *n.*—**hin′der-ing-ly,** *adv.*

hind-er-most (hīn′dėr-mōst), *a. superl.* Hindmost.

Hin-di (hin′dē), *n.* [Hind. and Pers. *Hindī*, < Pers. *Hind*, India.] The Aryan vernacular language of northern India, in two main divisions (eastern and western Hindi) comprising various dialects (cf. *Hindustani*); also, a form of Hindustani composed of Sanskritic and other Indo-Aryan elements (excluding Persian and Arabic); also, a native of India.

hind-most (hīnd′mōst), *a. superl.* Furthest behind; last in position; also, last in order, succession, or time (chiefly Sc.).

Hin′doo, etc. See *Hindu*, etc.

hin-drance, hin-der-ance (hin′drạns, -dėr-ạns), *n.* The act of hindering, or the state of being hindered; an impeding, stopping, or preventing; also, a means or cause of hindering (as, "an attachment that would be a *hindrance* to him in any honourable career": Hardy's "Two on a Tower," xxv.); an obstacle or impediment.

hind-sight (hīnd′sīt), *n.* Perception of the nature and exigencies of a case after the event (opposed to *foresight*); also, the sight nearest the breech of a firearm.

Hin-du (hin′dö or hin-dö′). [Hind. and Pers. *Hindū*, < Pers. *Hind*, India.] **I.** *a.* Of or pertaining to a native race in India descended from the ancient Aryan conquerors, or their languages or religion; also, of or pertaining to the people of Hindustan generally. **II.** *n.* One of the Hindu race; also, any adherent of Hinduism; in general, a member of any of the native peoples of Hindustan.—**Hin′du-ism,** *n.* The religious and social system of the Hindus, a development of ancient Brahmanism with the accretion of Buddhistic and other elements.—**Hin′du-ize,** *v. t.*; *-ized*, *-izing*. To render Hindu in character, customs, religion, etc.

Hin-du-stan-i, Hin-do-stan-i (hin-dọ̈-stàn′ē, hin-dọ̄-). [Hind. and Pers. *Hindūstānī*, *Hindōstānī*.] **I.** *a.* Of or pertaining to Hindustan, its people, or their languages, esp. the language called Hindustani (see below). **II.** *n.* A native of Hindustan; also, one of the languages of Hindustan, orig. a dialect of western Hindi spoken in the neighborhood of Delhi, taken into use in the camps of the Mohammedan conquerors of India, and later, with copious additions from Persian, Arabic, and other foreign sources, becoming current throughout nearly all India; Urdu.

hind-ward (hīnd′wạ̈rd), *adv.* and *a.* Backward; rearward.

hinge (hinj), *n.* [ME. *heng*, *hing*; akin to E. *hang*.] The movable joint or device on which a door, gate, shutter, lid, or the like, turns or moves; also, a natural joint moving in only one plane, as the joint of the knee (also called *hinge-joint*); also, the axis of the earth†, or, *pl.*, the four cardinal points† (as, "Nor slept the winds Within their stony caves, but rush'd abroad From the four *hinges* of the world": Milton's "Paradise Regained," iv. 415); also, *sing.*, fig., that on which something turns or depends (as, "We usually call reward and punishment the two *hinges* upon which all government turns": Swift's "Gulliver's Travels," i. 6); a central point, principle, or rule; a turning-point or crisis.—**hinge,** *v.*; *hinged*, *hinging*. **I.** *tr.* To furnish with a hinge or hinges; attach by or as by a hinge; also, to bend (the knee: as, "Be thou a flatterer now . . . *hinge* thy knee," Shakspere's "Timon of Athens," iv. 3. 211). **II.** *intr.* To hang or turn on or as on a hinge; depend.

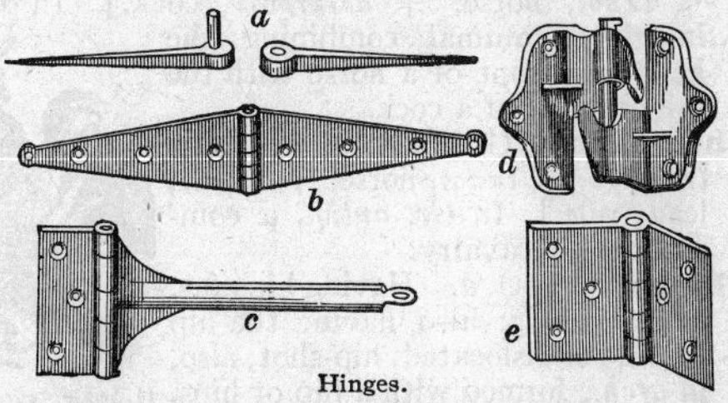

Hinges.
a, hook-and-eye or gate hinge; *b*, strap-hinge; *c*, T-shaped hinge; *d*, blind or self-shutting hinge; *e*, butt-hinge.

hin-ny[1] (hin′i), *n.*; pl. *hinnies* (-iz). [L. *hinnus*.] The offspring of a stallion and a she-ass. Cf. *mule*[2].

hin-ny[2] (hin′i), *n.* and *a.* Sc. and north. Eng. form of *honey*.

hint (hint), *n.* [Prob. < *hent*.] An occasion† or opportunity† (as, "Of antres vast and deserts idle . . . It was my *hint* to speak": Shakspere's "Othello," i. 3. 142); also, an indirect or covert suggestion or implication; an intimation.—**hint,** *v.* **I.** *tr.* To give a hint of; suggest or indicate in an indirect or covert manner. **II.** *intr.* To make indirect suggestion or allusion.—**hint′er,** *n.*

hin-ter-land (hin′tėr-land), *n.* [G., < *hinter*, behind, back, + *land*, land.] Land lying behind a coast district; interior or back country; fig., background; remote parts.

hip[1] (hip), *n.* [AS. *hype* = D. *heup* = G. *hüfte* = Goth. *hups*, hip.] The projecting part on each side of the body formed by the side of the pelvis and the upper part of the femur, with the flesh covering them; the haunch; also, the hip-joint; also, the coxa of arthropods; in *arch.*, the inclined projecting angle formed by the junction of a sloping side and a sloping end, or of two adjacent sloping sides, of a roof. —**hip and thigh,** with overwhelming blows, afflictions, etc.; unsparingly: as, "He smote them *hip and thigh* with a great slaughter" (Judges, xv. 8).—**on** (or **upon**) **the hip,** at a disadvantage (orig. in wrestling): as, "I'll have our Michael Cassio *on the hip*" (Shakspere's "Othello," ii. 1. 314). —**hip,**[1] *v. t.*; *hipped, hipping.* To injure or dislocate the hip of; in *arch.*, to form (a roof) with a hip or hips.

hip[2] (hip), *n.* [AS. *hēope.*] The fruit of a rose, esp. of a wild rose: as, "The oaks bear mast, the briers scarlet *hips*" (Shakspere's "Timon of Athens," iv. 3. 422).

hip[3] (hip), *interj.* An exclamation used in applauding or in signaling for applause: as, *hip, hip,* hurrah!

hip[4] (hip), *n.* [For *hyp,* < *hypochondria.*] Hypochondria; the blues: often in *pl.*: as, "Will Hazard has got the *hipps,* having lost to the tune of five hund'rd pound" (Swift, in "Tatler," 230). [Colloq.]—**hip**[4], *v. t.*; *hipped, hipping.* To render hypochondriac, melancholy, or depressed. [Colloq.]

hip=bath (hip'bȧth), *n.* A sitz-bath.

hip=bone (hip'bōn), *n.* The innominate bone; sometimes, the ilium; sometimes, the ischium.

hip=dis-ease (hip'di-zēz''), *n.* A disease of the hip-joint, characterized by caries, the formation of abscesses, the production of deformities, etc.

hip=joint (hip'joint), *n.* The articulation between the femur and the innominate bone.

hip=knob (hip'nob), *n.* In *arch.*, a knob or other ornament placed on the top of the hip of a roof, or on the apex of a gable.

hip-less (hip'les), *a.* Without hips.

hip-pa-lec-try-on (hip-ạ-lek'tri-ọn), *n.* [Gr. ἱππαλεκτρυών, < ἵππος, horse, + ἀλεκτρυών, cock.] In *Gr. antiq.*, an imaginary animal combining the head and front of a horse with the tail and feet of a cock.

Hippalectryon. — From an amphora in the Louvre.

hip-parch (hip'ärk), *n.* [Gr. ἵππαρχος, < ἵππος, horse, + ἄρχειν, lead, rule.] In *Gr. antiq.*, a commander of cavalry.

hipped[1] (hipt), *a.* Having hips (as, large-*hipped*); also, having the hip injured or dislocated; hip-shot; also, in *arch.*, formed with a hip or hips, as a roof.

hipped[2] (hipt), *p. a.* Rendered hypochondriac; melancholy; depressed; also, out of temper; vexed; offended; also, having a mental obsession, as on a particular subject. [Colloq.]

hip-pic (hip'ik), *a.* [Gr. ἱππικός, < ἵππος, horse.] Of or pertaining to horses or horse-racing.

hip-pish (hip'ish), *a.* [See *hip*[4].] Somewhat hipped; mopish; low-spirited: as, "To divert my thoughts a little space, Because I'm rather *hippish*" (Byron's "Beppo," lxiv.). [Colloq.]

hip-po (hip'ō), *n.*; pl. *hippos* (-ōz). Shortened form of *hippopotamus.*

hip-po-cam-pus (hip-ọ-kam'pus), *n.*; pl. *-pi* (-pī). [L., < Gr. ἱππόκαμπος, < ἵππος, horse, + κάμπος, sea-monster.] In *myth.*, a sea-horse with two fore feet and a body ending in the tail of a dolphin or fish; in *zoöl.*, a sea-horse of the genus *Hippocampus*; in *anat.*, either of two ridges in each of the two large upper cavities in the interior of the brain.

hip-po-cas-ta-na-ceous (hip''ọ-kas-tạ-nā'shius), *a.* [NL. *Hippocastanum,* the genus *Æsculus,* < Gr. ἵππος, horse, + κάστανα, pl., chestnuts.] In *bot.*, same as *æsculaceous.*

hip-po-cen-taur (hip-ọ-sen'târ), *n.* [L. *hippocentaurus,* < Gr. ἱπποκένταυρος, < ἵππος, horse, + κένταυρος, centaur.] A fabulous creature, part man and part horse; a centaur.

hip-po-cras (hip'ọ-kras), *n.* [OF. *ypocras* (F. *hypocras*), < *Hippocras,* Hippocrates: see *Hippocratic.*] An old medicinal cordial made of wine mixed with spices, etc.

Hip-po-crat-ic (hip-ọ-krat'ik), *a.* Of or pertaining to Hippocrates, a celebrated Greek physician, born about 460 B.C.—**Hippocratic face,** the face as it appears immediately before death, or after an exhausting sickness or the like, characterized by sunken eyes, pinched nose, livid complexion, etc.: vividly described by Hippocrates.—**Hippocratic oath,** an oath embodying the duties and obligations of physicians, formerly taken by those about to enter upon the practice of medicine.

Hip-po-crene (hip'ọ-krēn or hip-ọ-krē'nē), *n.* [L., < Gr. Ἱπποκρήνη, < ἵππος, horse, + κρήνη, fountain.] A spring on Mount Helicon, in Bœotia, Greece, sacred to the Muses, and regarded as a source of poetic inspiration: as, "O for a beaker full of the warm South, Full of the true, the blushful *Hippocrene*" (Keats's "Ode to a Nightingale"). Cf. *Pegasus.*

hip-po-drome (hip'ọ-drōm), *n.* [L. *hippodromos,* < Gr. ἱππόδρομος, < ἵππος, horse, + δρόμος, a running, course, race-course.] In ancient Greece and Rome, a course or circus for horse-races and chariot-races; hence, any arena or structure for equestrian and other displays.—**hip'po-drome,** *v. i.* or *t.*; *-dromed, -droming.* To perform as if in a hippodrome; act or do in a spectacular way, sometimes in mere show or pretense. [Slang.]

hip-po-griff, hip-po-gryph (hip'ọ-grif), *n.* [F. *hippogriffe,* < It. *ippogrifo,* < Gr. ἵππος, horse, + L. *gryphus,* griffin.] A fabulous creature resembling a griffin but having the body and hind parts of a horse.

Hippogriff. (After Tiepolo and Ingres.)

hip-pol-o-gy (hi-pol'ọ-ji), *n.* [Gr. ἵππος, horse: see *-logy.*] The study of horses.—**hip-pol'o-gist,** *n.*

hip-poph-a-gous (hi-pof'ạ-gus), *a.* [Gr. ἱπποφάγος, < ἵππος, horse, + φαγεῖν, eat.] Eating horse-flesh.—**hip-poph'a-gy** (-ji), *n.* The practice of eating horse-flesh.

hip-po-pot-a-mus (hip-ọ-pot'ạ-mus), *n.*; pl. *-muses,* L. *-mi* (-mī). [L., < Gr. ἱπποπόταμος, < ἵππος, horse, + ποταμός, river.] A large herbivorous mammal, *Hippopotamus amphibius,* having a thick hairless body, short legs and large head and muzzle, which is found in and near the rivers, lakes, etc., of Africa, and which is able to remain under water for a considerable time; also, a smaller and markedly different species, *H.* (or *Chœropsis*) *liberiensis,* of western Africa.

Hippopotamus (*H. amphibius*).

hip=roof (hip'röf'), *n.* In *arch.*, a roof with a hip or hips; a hipped roof; a roof with sloping ends and sides.

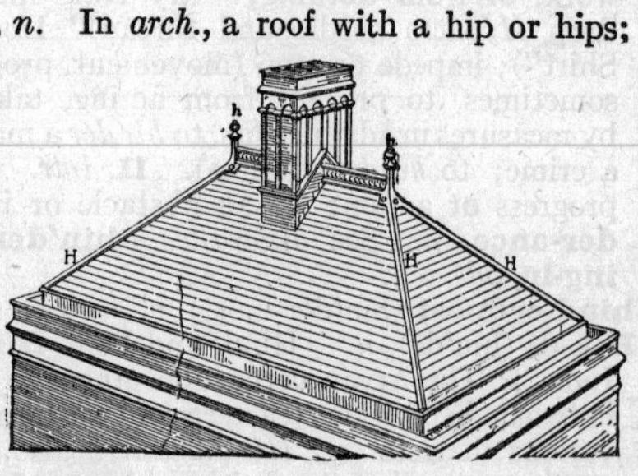

Hip-roof. — *H, H, H,* hips; *h, h,* hip-knobs.

hip=shot (hip'shot), *a.* Having the hip dislocated; hence, fig., lame; awkward.

hir-cine (hėr'sin or -sīn), *a.* [L. *hircinus,* < *hircus,* he-goat.] Of, pertaining to, or resembling a goat; often, having a goatish odor; sometimes, lustful.

hire (hīr), *n.* [AS. *hȳr* = MLG. *hūre* = D. *huur* = G.

heuer, hire.] The price or compensation paid or contracted to be paid for the temporary use of something or for personal services or labor (as, money paid as boat-*hire* or carriage-*hire*; "The labourer is worthy of his *hire*," Luke, x. 7); hence, reward or compensation in general; also, the act of hiring, or the fact of being hired.—**hire,** *v.*; *hired, hiring.* [AS. *hȳrian.*] **I.** *tr.* To engage the temporary use of for hire; also, to engage the services or labor of for hire; engage to do something for payment; also, to grant the temporary use of, or the services of, for a compensation (as, "He left his father's house, And *hired* himself to work within the fields": Tennyson's "Dora," 36). **II.** *intr.* To engage one's self for a compensation: commonly with *out.*—**hire′ling.** [AS. *hȳrling.*] **I.** *n.* One serving for hire (now usually in contempt); hence, one acting only with a view to reward or material benefit; a mercenary. **II.** *a.* Serving or to be had for hire (now usually in contempt); hence, venal; mercenary.—**hir-er** (hīr′ėr), *n.*

hir-ple (hėr′pl), *v. i.*; *-pled, -pling.* [Origin unknown.] To walk lamely or with difficulty; hobble. [Chiefly Sc. and north. Eng.]

hir-sute (hėr′sūt or hėr-sūt′), *a.* [L. *hirsutus.*] Having rough or shaggy hair; hairy; also, of, pertaining to, or of the nature of hair; also, in fig. use, rough or untrimmed; uncouth or unpolished; also, in *bot.* and *zoöl.*, covered with long, rather stiff hairs.—**hir-sute′ness,** *n.*

hi-run-dine (hi-run′din), *a.* [L. *hirundo* (*-din-*), swallow.] Of or pertaining to the swallow; swallow-like.

his (hiz), *pron.* [AS. *his*, gen. of *hē*, E. *he*, also of neut. *hit*, E. *it.*] The possessive form of *he*, used either with or without a noun following (as, this is *his* book; this book is *his*: cf. *her* and *hers*); sometimes, after a noun, an equivalent of the possessive or genitive inflection *'s* (archaic: as, John Smith *his* book); also, its† (as, "the tent, and all *his* furniture": Ex. xxxix. 33).

His-pa-ni-a (his-pā′ni-ą), *n.* [L., the Spanish peninsula (with Portugal), < *Hispanus*, Spanish.] Spain. [Poetic.] —**His-pan′ic** (-pan′ik), *a.* Spanish; sometimes, pertaining to both Spain and Portugal.—**His-pan′i-cism** (-i-sizm), *n.* A Spanish phrase or idiom.—**His-pan′i-cize** (-sīz), *v. t.*; *-cized, -cizing.* To render Spanish, as in character.—**His-pan′i-o-late, His-pan′i-o-lize** (-ǫ-lāt, -ǫ-līz), *v. t.* To make Spanish; imbue with Spanish sentiments.

His-pan-o- (his-pan′ǫ-). Form of L. *Hispanus*, Spanish, used in combination, as in *Hispano-American.*

his-pid (his′pid), *a.* [L. *hispidus.*] In *bot.* and *zoöl.*, rough with stiff hairs, bristles, or minute spines.—**his-pid-u-lous** (his-pid̦′ū-lus), *a.* Slightly hispid.

hiss (his), *v.* [ME.; imit.] **I.** *intr.* To make or emit a sharp sound like that of the letter *s* prolonged, as a goose or a serpent does, or as steam does in rushing through a small orifice; also, to express disapproval or contempt by making this sound. **II.** *tr.* To express disapproval of by hisses (as, "If the tag-rag people did not clap him and *hiss* him . . . as they used to do the players in the theatre, I am no true man": Shakspere's "Julius Cæsar," i. 2. 261); force or drive (*away, down*, etc.) by hisses; also, to utter with a hiss.—**hiss,** *n.* A sharp sound like that of the letter *s* prolonged, as made by geese, escaping steam, etc.; also, a hissing sound as an expression of disapproval, etc. —**hiss′ing,** *n.* The act of or sound of one who or that which hisses; also, an occasion or object of scorn (archaic: as, "I will make this city desolate, and an *hissing*," Jer. xix. 8).

hist (hist), *interj.* A sibilant exclamation used to attract attention, command silence, etc.—**hist,** *v. t.* To use the exclamation 'hist' to.

histo-. Form of Gr. ἱστός, web, tissue, used in combination.

his-to-gen-e-sis (his-tǫ-jen′e-sis), *n.* [See *histo-*.] In *biol.*, the origination and development of organic tissues. Also **his-tog′e-ny** (-toj′e-ni).

his-toid (his′toid), *a.* [See *histo-* and *-oid.*] Resembling or involving organic tissue, esp. normal tissue or connective tissue; in *pathol.*, noting a tumor composed of connective tissue or its equivalent.

his-tol-o-gy (his-tol′ǫ-ji), *n.* [See *histo-* and *-logy.*] The science of organic tissues; the study of the structure, esp. the microscopic structure, of organic tissues.—**his-to-log′i-cal** (-tǫ-loj′i-kąl), *a.*—**his-tol′o-gist,** *n.*

his-tol-y-sis (his-tol′i-sis), *n.* [See *histo-* and *-lysis.*] In *biol.*, disintegration or dissolution of organic tissue.—**his-to-lyt′ic** (-tǫ-lit′ik), *a.*

his-tone (his′tōn), *n.* [Gr. ἱστός, web, tissue.] In *physiol. chem.*, any of a class of proteid substances, as globin, having marked basic properties.

his-to-ri-an (his-tō′ri-ąn), *n.* A writer of history; sometimes, one versed in history.

his-to-ri-at-ed (his-tō′ri-ā-ted), *a.* [ML. *historiatus*, pp. of *historiare*, decorate with historical or other representations, < L. *historia*, E. *history.*] Decorated with figures of men, animals, etc., as ornamental letters or borders.

his-tor-ic (his-tor′ik), *a.* [L. *historicus*, < Gr. ἱστορικός, < ἱστορία, E. *history.*] Pertaining to or of the nature of history, sometimes as opposed to legend or fiction; historical; also, dealing with history, recording past events, or using history as a basis (in this sense *historical* is the usual word); also, noted or celebrated in history (as, the *historic* meeting between Livingstone and Stanley in central Africa in 1871; Waterloo, the *historic* spot where Napoleon met final defeat in 1815; "Let him pick out the most *historic* house, castle or abbey that England contains," G. B. Shaw's "Man and Superman," iv.); in *gram.*, same as *historical.*—**his-tor′i-cal,** *a.* Of or pertaining to history; of the nature of or constituting history; following, or in accordance with, history; sometimes, specif., pertaining to or of the nature of history as opposed to legend or fiction (as, the *historical* King Arthur); also, dealing with or treating of history (as, a *historical* work; a *historical* writer); using history as a basis (as, a *historical* novel; a *historical* novelist); also, noted or celebrated in history (in this sense *historic* is the usual word); also, preserved as a term in history (though otherwise obsolete), as many words denoting customs, officials, weapons, garments, fabrics, etc., belonging to a past time; in *gram.*, used in the statement of past facts or the narration of past events (as, the *historical* present, the present tense used in vividly narrating a past event as if it were happening at the time of narration). —**his-tor′i-cal-ly,** *adv.*—**his-tor′i-cal-ness,** *n.*—**his-to-ri′ci-ty** (-tǫ-ris′i-ti), *n.* Historic quality.—**his-tor′i-cize** (-sīz), *v. t.*; *-cized, -cizing.* To make historical; record or represent as history.

his-to-ried (his′tǫ-rid), *a.* Having a history (as specified: as, "some great-*historied* land," M. Arnold's "Resignation"); also, recorded or celebrated in history; historic.

his-to-ri-ette (his-tō-ri-et′), *n.* [F.] A short history or story; an anecdote.

his-tor-i-fy (his-tor′i-fī), *v. t.*; *-fied, -fying.* [See *-fy.*] To treat of or record in history.

his-to-ri-og-ra-pher (his-tō-ri-og′rą-fėr), *n.* [LL. *historiographus*, < Gr. ἱστοριογράφος, < ἱστορία, history, + γράφειν, write.] A historian; esp., an official historian, as of a court, a public institution, etc.—**his-to-ri-og′ra-phy,** *n.*

his-to-ry (his′tǫ-ri), *n.*; pl. *-ries* (-riz). [L. *historia*, < Gr. ἱστορία, a learning or knowing by inquiry, information, narrative, history, < ἵστωρ, knowing, learned, from the root of εἰδέναι, know, ἰδεῖν, see: see *wit.*] A narrative or story; now, esp., a continuous, systematic written narrative, in order of time, of past events as connected with a particular people, country, period, person, etc.; also, a systematic account of any set of natural phenomena, without reference to time (as, "An *History* of the Earth and Animated Nature": the title of a work by Goldsmith, published in 1774); also, a drama representing historical events (as, "Mr. William Shakespeares Comedies, *Histories*, & Tragedies": the title of the first folio edition of Shakspere's works, published in 1623); also, a historical picture†; also, the branch of knowledge dealing with past events; the record of past events, esp. in connection with the human race; also, the aggregate of past events; esp., the aggregate of such events connected with a particular people, country, person, etc.; career; sometimes, a past worthy of record or out of the ordinary (as, a ship with a *history*; "Somehow, I rather think she has a *history*," Henley's "In Hospital," ix.); an eventful career. —**natural history.** See under *natural, a.*

his-tri-on (his′tri-ǫn), *n.* [F. *histrion*, < L. *histrio*(*n-*).] A stage-player; an actor: as, "a *histrion* angular and profound" (Henley's "Ballade of a Toyokuni Colour-Print"). [Now rare.]—**his-tri-on′ic** (-on′ik), *a.* [LL. *histrionicus.*]

Of or pertaining to actors or acting; dramatic; theatrical. —**his-tri-on'i-cal-ly,** *adv.*—**his-tri-on'i-cism** (-sizm), *n.* Histrionic action; acting.—**his-tri-on'ics,** *n.* Dramatic representation; theatricals; acting.

hit (hit), *v. t.*; *hit, hitting.* [Late AS. *hyttan* = Icel. *hitta* = Sw. *hitta* = Dan. *hitte*, hit on, find.] To come or light upon, meet with, or find (as, to *hit* the right road in the dark; to *hit* a happy medium); reach, as an intended point or object; hence, to succeed in representing, imitating, or producing exactly (as, to *hit* a likeness in a portrait; to *hit* a person's mannerisms in mimicry; to *hit* a tune: see phrase *to hit off*, below); also, to conform to, agree with, or suit exactly (as, this *hits* my fancy; "Something jarr'd . . . He scarcely *hit* my humour," Tennyson's "Edwin Morris," 76); also, to come against with an impact or collision, as a missile, a flying fragment, a falling body, or the like does; also, to reach with a missile, a weapon, a blow, or the like (intentionally or otherwise), as one throwing, shooting, or striking; esp., to succeed in striking (as, to *hit* the mark); deal a blow to (as, to *hit* an adversary in a fight); strike intentionally; strike (a ball) with a bat, as in baseball; drive or propel by a stroke, as in a particular direction; bring forcibly into collision (as, to *hit* the head against a shelf); deal (a blow, stroke, etc.); also, fig., to reach or touch directly and effectively (as, "Dear Countess! you have charms all hearts to *hit!*" Pope's "Satires of Donne," iv. 232); esp., to assail effectively and sharply (as, to be *hit* by satire or innuendo); affect severely (as, to be badly *hit* in a financial panic); also, to guess, judge, or say rightly (as, "Thou hast *hit* it": Shakspere's "2 Henry VI.," iv. 2. 21).—**to hit it off,** to agree; get on, as with a person, or with each other. [Colloq.] —**to hit off,** to represent, reproduce, or describe aptly (as, to *hit off* a person's character in a few words); also, to produce readily or offhand (as, to *hit off* a sonnet).—**hit,** *v. i.* To come or light (*upon* or *on*: as, to *hit* upon a passage in reading; to *hit* on a new way of doing a thing); also, to agree, as persons or things (now prov. or colloq.); also, to come into collision (often with *against, on,* or *upon*); also, to strike with a missile, a weapon, or the like; deal a blow or blows; fig., to realize an aim or purpose, or succeed (now rare: as, "Oft expectation fails . . . and oft it *hits* Where hope is coldest," Shakspere's "All's Well," ii. 1. 146).—**hit or miss,** whether one hits or misses; regardless of results; at haphazard.—**hit,** *n.* An impact or collision, as of one thing against another; also, a stroke that reaches an object; a blow; fig., a stroke of satire, censure, etc. (as, the letter contained severe *hits* at the administration); also, a successful stroke, performance, or production (as, to make a *hit* with a new play; the play is the *hit* of the season); a success; sometimes, a successful guess; also, an effective or telling expression or saying (as, a speech abounding in happy *hits*); also, a stroke of luck or chance (as, "What late he call'd a blessing, now was wit, And God's good providence, a lucky *hit*": Pope's "Moral Essays," iii. 378); in *backgammon*, a victory won by a player after his opponent has thrown off one or more men from the board, as distinguished from a *gammon* and a *backgammon*; in *baseball*, a ball so hit that even when fielded without error it enables the batter to reach first base safely and without forcing out another base-runner.

hitch (hich), *v.* [ME. *hytchen*; origin obscure: cf. *hike*.] **I.** *tr.* To move or draw (something) with a jerk or jerks, or with short, successive changes of position (as, to *hitch* one's chair over the floor); often, to raise with a jerk (commonly with *up*: as, to *hitch* up one's trousers); also, to make fast, esp. temporarily, by means of a hook, ring, rope, strap, etc.; tether, as a horse to a post; harness to a vehicle, as a horse (often with *up*). **II.** *intr.* To move with a jerk or jerks; hobble or limp; also, to become fastened or caught, as on something; stick, as when caught (as, "Knots and impediments make something *hitch*": Cowper's "Conversation," 108); also, to fasten one's self or itself to something (often with *on*); also, to harness a horse or horses to a vehicle (with *up*: colloq.); also, to get on together, or agree (colloq.). —**hitch,** *n.* A hitching movement; a jerk or pull; also, a hitching gait; a hobble or limp; also, a making fast, as to something, esp. temporarily; also, a sticking or stoppage, as if from catching; an unexpected impediment to progress; also, in nautical and other use, any of various forms of knot or fastening made with rope or the like (as, the clove-*hitch* or the half-*hitch*, see the entries; the diamond *hitch*, see phrase under *diamond, n.*).—**hitch'er,** *n.*

hitch=hike (hich'hīk'), *v. i.* [Cf. *hitch* and *hike*.] To travel by hiking or walking with rides in passing automobiles. [Colloq.]—**hitch'=hik'er,** *n.*

hitch-ing=post (hich'ing-pōst), *n.* A post to which horses, etc., are to be hitched or tethered.

hithe, hythe (hīᴛʜ), *n.* [AS. *hȳth.*] A port or haven; esp., a landing-place on a river. [Archaic, or in place-names.]

hith-er (hiᴛʜ'ėr), *adv.* [AS. *hider* = Icel. *hēdhra* = Goth. *hidrē*, hither; from the pronominal stem represented by E. *he.*] To or toward this place or point (as, to come *hither*; the journey *hither*); also, up to this time†, or hitherto†; also, to this matter, subject, or end†, or hereto†.—**hither and thither,** to this place and that; first in one direction and then in another.—**hith'er,** *a.* On or toward this side; on the side or in the direction of the person speaking; nearer. —**hith'er-most,** *a. superl.* Nearest in this direction. —**hith-er-to'** (-tö'), *adv.* To this place or point (archaic); also, up to this time, or until now (as, a fact *hitherto* unknown).—**hith'er-ward, hith'er-wards** (-wärd, -wärdz), *adv.* Toward this place; in this direction; hither.

hit-ter (hit'ėr), *n.* One who or that which hits.

Hit-tite (hit'īt), *n.* One of a powerful, civilized ancient people who flourished for centuries in Asia Minor and adjoining regions until subjugated by the Assyrians in the 8th century B.C.

Hit-torf (hit'ôrf) **rays.** [From J. W. *Hittorf* (1824-1914), German physicist.] In *elect.*, all the rays (chiefly cathode rays) observed when an electric discharge takes place in a Hittorf tube.—**Hit'torf tube.** In *elect.*, a highly exhausted vacuum-tube fitted with two terminals.

hive (hīv), *n.* [AS. *hȳf*, perhaps akin to Icel. *hūfr*, ship's hull, and L. *cupa*, tub, cask: see *coop.*] An artificial shelter for the habitation of a swarm of honey-bees, orig. and still often made of straw or the like in a characteristic conical or dome-like form; also, something resembling or suggesting this, as in structure, shape, or use; often, a place swarming with busy occupants (as, a *hive* of industry); also, the bees inhabiting a hive; hence, a swarming or teeming multitude. —**hive,** *v.*; *hived, hiving.* **I.** *tr.* To gather into or cause to enter a hive; fig., to shelter as in a hive; also, to store up in a hive, as honey; fig., to lay up for future use or enjoyment. **II.** *intr.* To enter a hive, as bees; also, to live together in the manner of bees; dwell as in a hive (as, "Little legends do not *hive* in the sacred ears of kings; nevertheless they hum among lesser men from generation unto generation": Dunsany's "Laughter of the Gods," i.).—**hive'=nest,** *n.* A large nest, or an aggregation of nests, occupied by a number of pairs of birds forming a colony or community.

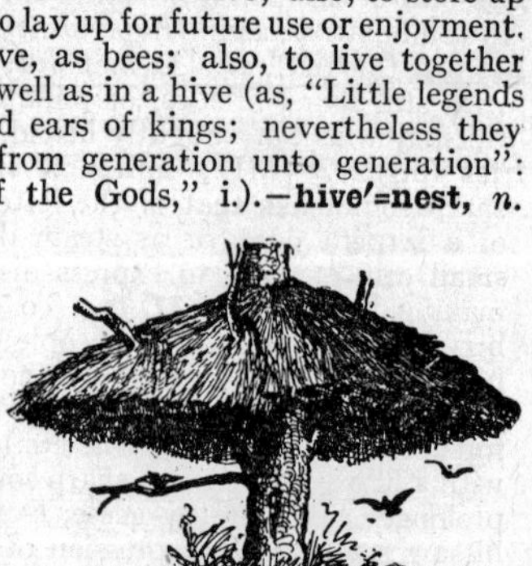

Hive-nest of Republican Grosbeak or Sociable Weaver-bird (*Philetærus socius*).

hives (hīvz), *n.* [Origin uncertain.] Any of various eruptive diseases of the skin, as urticaria; also, croup or laryngitis.

h'm (h'm), *interj.* Same as *hem*².

ho¹ (hō), *interj.* An exclamation expressing surprise, exultation, etc., or, when repeated, derisive laughter; also, a cry or call uttered to attract attention (sometimes specially used after a word denoting destination: as, "*Oli.* There lies your way, due west. *Vio.* Then westward-*ho!*" Shakspere's "Twelfth Night," iii. 1. 146).

ho² (hō), *interj.* [Cf. *whoa.*] Stop!—now used only to stop a horse, etc.

ho-act-zin (hō-akt'zin), *n.* [Native name.] A South American crested bird, *Opisthocomus cristatus*, somewhat smaller than a pheasant and remarkable for its peculiar structural characteristics. See cut on following page.

hoar (hōr). [AS. *hār* = Icel. *hārr*, hoary, old, = OHG. *hēr*, venerable, G. *hehr*, august, sublime.] **I.** *a.* Gray-haired with age, as persons; gray or white with age, as the hair or beard; hence, old; ancient; also, in general, gray or white (used esp. of frost and of objects covered with frost: cf. *hoar-frost*); also, gray or white with mold (obs. or prov. Eng.). **II.** *n.* Hoariness; also, a hoary coating or appearance; esp., hoar-frost or rime.

Hoactzin.

hoard (hōrd), *n.* [AS. *hord* = OHG. *hort* = Icel. *hodd* = Goth. *huzd*, treasure; perhaps from the root of E. *hide*[1].] An accumulation of something laid by for preservation or future use; a stock or store, as of money; a treasure.—**hoard,** *v. t.* [AS. *hordian.*] To amass and put away for preservation or future use; store or lay up, as money; treasure up.—**hoard′er,** *n.*—**hoard′ing**[1], *n.* The act of one who hoards; also, *pl.*, that which is hoarded; money laid by.

hoard-ing[2] (hōr′ding), *n.* [F. *hourd*, scaffolding, framework; from Teut., and akin to E. *hurdle.*] A temporary fence inclosing a building during erection or while undergoing repairs, often used for posting bills; hence, any boarding on which bills are posted (as, "There was a great quantity of recruiting posters on the *hoardings* and in windows": H. G. Wells's "Mr. Britling," ii. 2. § 1).

hoar=frost (hōr′frôst), *n.* White frost (see *frost*); rime.

hoar-hound, hore-hound (hōr′hound), *n.* [AS. *hārhūne*, < *hār*, hoary, + *hūne*, kind of plant.] Any of various plants of the mint family; esp., a perennial herb, *Marrubium vulgare*, native in the Old World, with downy leaves and small whitish flowers and containing a bitter medicinal juice; also, a medicinal extract or preparation made from this plant, or a confection containing it (used esp. for coughs, etc.).

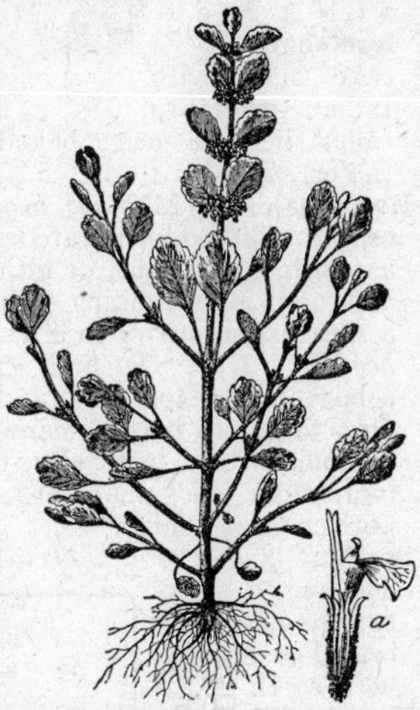

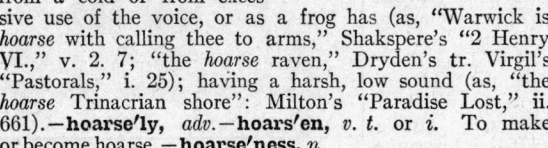

Hoarhound (*Marrubium vulgare*). *a*, flower.

hoar-i-ness (hōr′i-nes), *n.* Hoary state or color.

hoarse (hōrs), *a.*; compar. *hoarser*, superl. *hoarsest.* [ME. *hors*, also *hos*, AS. *hās*, akin to Icel. *hāss*, MD. *heersch*, D. *heesch*, OHG. *heis*, G. *heisch*, *heiser*, hoarse.] Rough and deep in sound, as the voice when affected with a cold, or the voice of a frog; harsh and low in pitch; raucous; also, having a raucous voice, as a person suffering from a cold or from excessive use of the voice, or as a frog has (as, "Warwick is *hoarse* with calling thee to arms," Shakspere's "2 Henry VI.," v. 2. 7; "the *hoarse* raven," Dryden's tr. Virgil's "Pastorals," i. 25); having a harsh, low sound (as, "the *hoarse* Trinacrian shore": Milton's "Paradise Lost," ii. 661).—**hoarse′ly,** *adv.*—**hoars′en,** *v. t.* or *i.* To make or become hoarse.—**hoarse′ness,** *n.*

hoar-y (hōr′i), *a.*; compar. *hoarier*, superl. *hoariest.* [From *hoar.*] Gray-haired or white-haired, as persons; gray or white with age, as the hair; hence, ancient or venerable (as, "Windsor's *hoary* tow'rs": Cowper's "Expostulation," 596); also, in general, gray or white; in *bot.* and *entom.*, covered with short, dense, grayish-white hairs.

hoast (hōst), *n.* [From Scand.] A cough. [Sc. and north. Eng.]

ho-at-zin (hō̤-at′zin), *n.* Same as *hoactzin.*

hoax (hōks), *n.* [Appar. a contracted form of *hocus.*] A humorous or mischievous deception, esp. in the form of a fabricated story.—**hoax,** *v. t.* To deceive by a hoax.

hob[1] (hob), *n.* [Origin obscure: cf. *hub.*] A rounded peg or pin used as a target in certain games, as quoits; hence, any of these games; also, a hobnail; also, a projection or shelf at the back or side of a fireplace (as, "an old-fashioned English grate set into the chimney with wide *hobs*": F. H. Smith's "Colonel Carter of Cartersville," i.).

hob[2] (hob), *n.* [From *Hob*, for *Robert*, or *Robin*, man's name.] A countryman or rustic; also, a hobgoblin, elf, or sprite; also, the male ferret.—**to play** (or **raise**) **hob,** fig., to cause mischief; create trouble or confusion.

hob[3] (hob), *v.* See *hobnob, v.*

hob-ble (hob′l), *v.*; *-bled, -bling.* [ME. *hobelen* = D. *hobbelen*, toss, rock, stammer; a freq. form related to E. *hop*[1], and with sense in part affected by *hopple.*] **I.** *intr.* To move unsteadily; wabble; also, to walk lamely; limp; fig., to proceed irregularly and haltingly, as in action or speech. **II.** *tr.* To cause to limp; also, to fasten together the legs of (a horse, etc.) so as to prevent free motion; also, to embarrass; impede; perplex.—**hob′ble,** *n.* The act or an act of hobbling; an uneven, halting gait; a limp; also, an awkward or difficult situation (as, "Pray get out of this *hobble* as fast as you can": Byron's "The Blues," i.); also, a rope, strap, etc., used to hobble an animal; a fetter.—**hob′ble=bush,** *n.* A caprifoliaceous shrub, *Viburnum alnifolium*, with cymes of white flowers, and a red berry-like fruit.

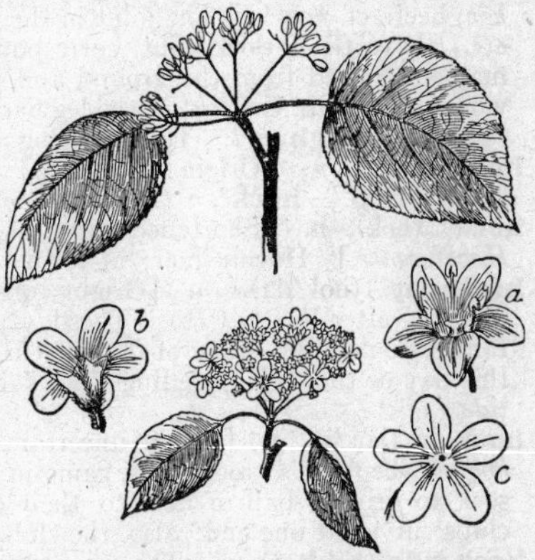

Branches of Hobble-bush, with flowers and fruit. — *a*, fertile flower, front view; *b*, same, back view; *c*, sterile flower.

hob-ble-de-hoy (hob′l-dē̤-hoi′), *n.* [Origin obscure.] A youth between boyhood and manhood; a stripling; esp., an awkward or clumsy youth (as, "Dick had grown into a lanky *hobbledehoy* more than ever conscious of his bad clothes": Kipling's "Light That Failed," i.).

hob-bler (hob′lėr), *n.* One who or that which hobbles.—**hob′bling,** *p. a.* That hobbles; wabbling; limping.—**hob′bling-ly,** *adv.*

hob-by[1] (hob′i), *n.*; pl. *hobbies* (-iz). [OF. *hobé*, *hobet*, dim. of *hobe*, hobby (falcon): cf. OF. *hober*, move, stir (from Teut.: cf. *hobble*).] A small old-world falcon, *Falco subbuteo*, formerly flown at small game, as larks.

hob-by[2] (hob′i), *n.*; pl. *hobbies* (-iz). [ME. *hoby*, *hobyn*, prob. for *Robin*, or *Robert*, man's name: cf. *Dobbin* and *hob*[2].] A small or medium-sized horse (now chiefly prov. Eng.); also, a child's hobby-horse; also, a favorite occupation, subject, topic, or the like, pursued for the amusement or interest it affords (likened to a hobby-horse as ridden by children: as, to ride one's *hobby*); any favorite pursuit, object, topic, etc.—**hob′by=horse,** *n.* A figure of a horse, made of wickerwork or other light material, and furnished with a deep housing, supported about the waist of a performer in a morris-dance, pantomime, etc.; the performer himself (as, "Captain Coxe . . . executed . . . a gambade, the like whereof had never been practised by two-legged *hobby-horse*": Scott's "Kenilworth," xxxix.); also, a foolish fellow†; a buffoon†; also, a lewd person†; also, a stick with a horse's head, or a figure of a horse, ridden by children; also, a hobby, or favorite occupation, etc. (now rare: as, "I will draw my uncle Toby's character from his *Hobby-Horse*," Sterne's "Tristram Shandy," i. 23).

hob-gob-lin (hob-gob′lin or hob′gob″lin), *n.* [See *hob*[2].] A mischievous sprite or elf; [*cap.*] the fairy Puck, or Robin Goodfellow (as, "Those that *Hobgoblin* call you and sweet Puck, You do their work, and they shall have good luck": Shakspere's "Midsummer Night's Dream," ii. 1. 40); also [*l. c.*], an alarming or terrifying apparition; also, anything causing superstitious fear or dread; a bogy; a bugbear.

hob-nail (hob′nāl), *n.* [See *hob*[1].] A short, large-headed nail for protecting the soles of heavy boots and shoes; hence, a man wearing such shoes; a rustic; a clown.—**hob′-nailed,** *a.* Furnished with hobnails; also, rustic or clownish (as, "a *hobnailed* slave": Scott's "Kenilworth," xviii.).

hob-nob (hob′nob′), *adv.* [Earlier *hab nab, hab or nab,* 'have or not have' (AS. *habban,* have; *nabban,* for *ne habban,* not have).] Hit or miss; anyhow; haphazard. [Now prov. Eng.]—**hob′nob′,** *v. i.*; *-nobbed, -nobbing.* [From the phrase *hob or nob* (also *hob a nob* and *hob and nob*), used by persons drinking to each other; from *hab or nab* (see *hobnob, adv.*), but with the particular application now uncertain.] To drink together; also, to associate or consort on terms of intimacy; converse familiarly.

ho-bo (hō′bō), *n.*; pl. *-bos* or *-boes* (-bōz). [Origin uncertain.] A tramp (vagrant). [Slang, U. S.]—**ho′bo-ism,** *n.*

Hob-son's (hob′sọnz) **choice.** The choice of taking either the thing offered or nothing: said to refer to the practice of Thomas Hobson (about 1544–1631), of Cambridge, England, who let horses, and obliged each customer to take in his turn the horse nearest the stable-door or none at all. See Steele, in "Spectator," 509.

Hoch-heim-er (hok′hī″mėr, G. hōch′-), *n.* [G.: cf. *hock*[3].] A Rhine wine produced at Hochheim, near Mainz, Germany.

hock[1], **hough** (hok), *n.* [ME. *hoch, hogh, howh,* < AS. *hōh,* heel: cf. *heel*[2].] The joint in the hind leg of the horse, etc., above the fetlock-joint, corresponding to the ankle in man but raised from the ground and protruding backward when bent; also, the part of the leg back of the knee in man.—**hock**[1], **hough,** *v. t.* To hamstring.

hock[2] (hok), *n.* [Origin uncertain.] Pawn: as, in *hock.* [Slang, U. S.]—**hock**[2], *v. t.* To pawn. [Slang, U. S.]

hock[3] (hok), *n.* [Shortened form of obs. *hockamore,* for *Hochheimer.*] Hochheimer; also, any white Rhine wine.

hock=day (hok′dā), *n.* [Origin obscure.] The second Tuesday after Easter ('Hock Tuesday'), formerly an important term-day and a day of festivity in England; also, either this day or the day preceding ('Hock Monday'). See *hock-tide.*

hock-ey (hok′i), *n.* [Origin uncertain: cf. *hook,* also OF. *hoquet,* shepherd's crook.] A game in which opposing sides seek to drive a ball or disk to their opponents' goal with clubs curved at one end; also, the club so used.

hock-tide (hok′tīd), *n.* The time of the hock-days, Hock Monday and Hock Tuesday (see *hock-day*), observed formerly in England with popular festivities during which money was collected for parish or church purposes, and associated with various traditional customs, some of which have survived or been from time to time revived. See Scott's "Kenilworth," xxxix.

ho-cus (hō′kus), *n.* [Short for *hocus-pocus.*] A conjurer† or juggler†; also, jugglery, trickery, or deception; also, drugged liquor.—**ho′cus,** *v. t.*; *-cused* or *-cussed, -cusing* or *-cussing.* To play a trick upon; hoax; cheat; also, to stupefy with drugged liquor (as, "He was *hocussed* at supper and lost eight hundred pounds to Major Loder": Thackeray's "Vanity Fair," lxiv.); also, to drug (liquor).

ho-cus=po-cus (hō′kus-pō′kus), *n.* [From jugglers' jargon, simulating Latin.] A conjurer† or juggler†; also, a juggler's trick; sleight of hand; trickery or deception; also, a formula used in conjuring or incantation.—**ho′cus=po′cus,** *v.*; *-cused* or *-cussed, -cusing* or *-cussing.* **I.** *intr.* To perform tricks; practise deception. **II.** *tr.* To play tricks upon or with.

hod (hod), *n.* [Cf. prov. *hot,* basket for carrying earth, manure, etc., < F. *hotte,* basket for carrying on the back.] A portable trough for carrying mortar, bricks, etc., fixed crosswise on the top of a pole and borne on the shoulder; also, a scuttle for coal.—**hod′=car″ri-er,** *n.* A laborer who carries mortar, bricks, etc., in a hod.

hod-den (hod′n), *n.* [Origin unknown.] A coarse cloth of undyed wool: sometimes called *hodden gray* (for *gray hodden*) or *hodden-gray*: as, "What tho' on hamely fare we dine, Wear *hodden-gray,* and a' that" (Burns's "For A' That," 10). [Sc.]

Hodge (hoj), *n.* [For *Roger,* man's name.] The typical English farm-laborer or rustic; [*l. c.*] a rustic; a countryman.

hodge-podge (hoj′poj), *n.* [Var. of *hotchpotch,* for *hotchpot.*] A hotchpotch; a heterogeneous mixture; a medley; a jumble.

hodge=pud-ding† (hoj′pu̇d″ing), *n.* [Cf. *hodgepodge.*] A pudding with a variety of ingredients. See Shakspere's "Merry Wives of Windsor," v. 5. 159.

ho-di-er-nal (hō-di-ėr′nạl), *a.* [L. *hodiernus,* < *hodie,* for *hoc die,* on this day, to-day.] Of or pertaining to the present day: as, "The rule and *hodiernal* life of a good man is benefaction" (Emerson's "Essays," Character).

hod-man (hod′mạn), *n.*; pl. *-men.* A man who carries a hod.

ho-dom-e-ter (họ-dom′e-tėr), *n.* [Gr. ὁδόμετρον, < ὁδός, way, + μέτρον, measure.] A device attached to a wheeled vehicle for recording the number of revolutions of a wheel and thus indicating the distance traveled; a similar instrument for measuring distances in surveying; also, a pedometer.

Hoes.—*a* and *b*, Dutch hoes; *c*, hoe and rake combined; *d*, common hoe.

hoe (hō), *n.* [OF. F. *houe*; from Teut. (cf. G. *haue*), and akin to E. *hew.*] A long-handled implement with a thin, flat blade usually set transversely, used for breaking up the surface of the ground, removing weeds, etc.; also, an implement with blades, pushed over the ground or drawn by a horse, used for the same purpose.—**hoe,** *v.*; *hoed, hoeing.* **I.** *tr.* To dig, scrape, weed, cultivate, etc., with a hoe. **II.** *intr.* To work with a hoe.—**hoe′=cake,** *n.* A cake made with Indian meal: so called because orig. baked on a hoe. [U. S.]—**ho-er** (hō′ėr), *n.*

Horse-hoe.

hog (hog), *n.* [ME. *hog, hogge*; origin unknown.] A swine, esp. an adult domesticated swine raised for slaughter; fig., a selfish, gluttonous, or filthy person (colloq.); also, a sort of broom for scrubbing a ship's bottom under water; also, a mechanical stirrer in a paper-pulp vat.—**hog,** *v.*; *hogged, hogging.* **I.** *tr.* To arch (the back) upward like that of a hog; hence, to cause (a ship, etc.) to droop at the ends; also, to cut (a horse's mane) short; also, to clean (a ship's bottom) with a hog; also, to appropriate selfishly, or take more than one's share of (slang). **II.** *intr.* To droop at both ends, as a ship.

ho-gan (hō-gan′), *n.* [Navaho *qoghân.*] A Navaho Indian dwelling, a structure of posts and branches covered with earth.

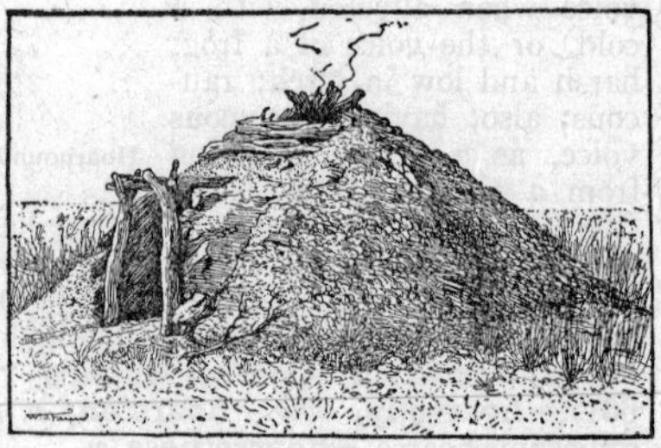
Hogan.

Ho-garth-i-an (họ-gär′thi-ạn), *a.* Of, pertaining to, or suggestive of the English painter and engraver William Hogarth (1697–1764) or his work: as, the *Hogarthian* line of beauty (a serpentine curve, somewhat like a slender, elongated letter S); *Hogarthian* humor or satire.

hog-back (hog′bak), *n.* An arching back like that of a hog; in *geol.,* a low, sharply crested ridge.

hog=deer (hog′dēr), *n.* A small deer, *Cervus porcinus,* abundant in India.

hog-fish (hog′fish), *n.* Any of various fishes, as *Lachnolæmus maximus,* a crimson labroid food-fish of the Florida coast and the West Indies, and *Percina caprodes,* a darter of American lakes and streams. See cut on following page.

hog-gish (hog′ish), *a.* Like or befitting a hog; swinish; selfish; gluttonous; filthy. —**hog′gish-ly,** *adv.* —**hog′gish-ness,** *n.*

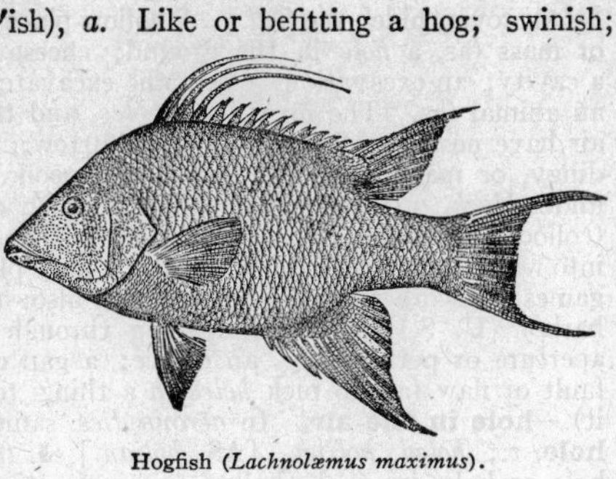

Hogfish (*Lachnolæmus maximus*).

hog=mil-let (hog′mil″et), *n.* Same as *proso.*

hog-nose (hog′nōz), *n.* Any of the harmless American snakes constituting the genus *Heterodon,* notable for their hog-like snouts and their curious actions and contortions when disturbed. —**hog′=nosed,** *a.* Having a snout like that of a hog: as, a *hog-nosed* snake (a hognose).

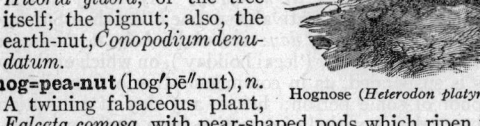

Hognose (*Heterodon platyrhinus*).

hog-nut (hog′nut), *n.* The nut of the brown hickory, *Hicoria glabra,* or the tree itself; the pignut; also, the earth-nut, *Conopodium denudatum.*

hog=pea-nut (hog′pē″nut), *n.* A twining fabaceous plant, *Falcata comosa,* with pear-shaped pods which ripen in or on the ground.

hog=reeve (hog′rēv), *n.* An officer charged with the prevention or appraising of damage by stray swine. [U. S.]

hogs-head (hogz′hed), *n.* [Reason of name unknown.] A large cask, esp. one containing from 100 to 140 gallons; also, a liquid measure containing 63 wine-gallons.

hog-skin (hog′skin), *n.* The skin of a hog; leather made from this; also, the skin of a hog used as a bottle.

hog=tie (hog′tī), *v. t.*; *-tied, -tying.* To tie as a hog is tied, with all four feet together.

hog-wash (hog′wosh), *n.* Refuse given to hogs; swill; hence, any worthless stuff.

hoicks, hoick (hoiks, hoik), *interj.* [Origin unknown: cf. *yoicks.*] A cry used to incite hounds in hunting. —**hoicks, hoick,** *v. t.* or *i.* To incite (hounds) by the cry 'hoicks.'

hoi-den (hoi′dn), etc. See *hoyden,* etc.

hoi pol-loi (hoi po-loi′). [Gr. *οἱ πολλοί.*] The many; the multitude; the common herd: sometimes preceded improperly by *the* (improperly, because *hoi* means 'the').

hoise (hoiz), *v. t.*; *hoised* or *hoist, hoising.* [Earlier *hyse, hysse*: cf. D. *hijschen,* LG. *hissen,* Sw. *hissa,* Dan. *hisse,* F. *hisser,* hoist.] To hoist. [Now prov.]

hoist (hoist), *v. t.* [Later form of *hoise.*] To raise or lift, esp. by some mechanical appliance. —**hoist,** *n.* The act or an act of hoisting; a lift; also, an apparatus for hoisting, as an elevator; also, the perpendicular height of a sail or flag. —**hoist′er,** *n.*

hoi-ty=toi-ty (hoi′ti-toi′ti). [Cf. obs. or prov. *hoit,* indulge in riotous mirth.] **I.** *n.* Giddy behavior; also, a fuss; also, haughtiness. **II.** *a.* Giddy; flighty; also, assuming; haughty. **III.** *interj.* An exclamation denoting surprise with some degree of contempt, as at what is considered undue assumption: as, "*Hoity toity!* . . . madam is in her airs, I protest" (Fielding's "Tom Jones," vii. 8).

ho-key (hō′ki), *n.* [Origin obscure.] Used in 'by the hokey!' a mild oath or meaningless expletive: as, "By the *hokey,* they'd better take care!" (Lover's "Handy Andy," xiv.). [Prov. or slang.]

ho-kum (hō′kum), *n.* [Cf. *hocus-pocus.*] Elements of low comedy or crude humor introduced into a play or the like for the laughs they may bring; also, sentimental or pathetic matter of an elementary or stereotyped kind introduced into a play or the like. [Slang.]

ho-ky=po-ky, ho-key=po-key (hō′ki-pō′ki), *n.* [For *hocus-pocus.*] Hocus-pocus; trickery; also, ice-cream sold by street venders.

Hol-arc-tic (hol-ärk′tik), *a.* [Gr. ὅλος, whole, + ἀρκτικός, E. *arctic.*] In *zoögeog.,* belonging to a division comprising the Nearctic division of the New World and the Palearctic division of the Old World.

hold[1] (hōld), *n.* [Var. of *hole,* prob. by association with *hold*[2].] *Naut.,* the interior of a ship below the deck, or below the lower deck, where the cargo is stowed.

hold[2] (hōld), *v. t.*; pret. *held,* pp. *held* (archaic *holden*), ppr. *holding.* [AS. *haldan, healdan,* = D. *houden* = G. *halten* = Icel. *halda* = Goth. *haldan,* hold: cf. *halt*[2].] To keep fast, or from getting away, with the grasp of the hand or by any means; prevent or control the motion or movement of by grasping or by any means of detention or constraint; keep or retain (as, to be *held* until called for); keep back or detain; arrest and retain (the attention), or the attention of (a person); keep back from action, hinder, or restrain (as, to *hold* one's breath; to *hold* one's tongue); refrain from (as, "I wish you'd *hold* your noise!" Dickens's "Martin Chuzzlewit," xxv.); keep in a specified state, relation, etc. (as, to *hold* the enemy in check; to *hold* one's self aloof); oblige (a person) to adhere to a promise, etc.; also, to have or keep in the hand; bear, sustain, or support with the hand, arms, etc., or by any means; also, to bear or carry in a certain position or attitude (as, to *hold* one's self erect); also, to bear or endure (some treatment)†; also, to keep or retain (something) within itself, as a vessel does; contain; be capable of containing (as, this basket *holds* two bushels; that theater *holds* two thousand people); also, to have or keep as one's own, either absolutely or temporarily; have the ownership or use of; occupy (a position, office, etc.); keep forcibly, as against an adversary; remain in occupation or possession of (as, a play that long *held* the boards); also, to have or keep in the mind; entertain (a belief, etc.); think or believe (as, "It is *held* That valour is the chiefest virtue": Shakspere's "Coriolanus," ii. 2. 87); regard or consider (as, to *hold* an idea to be absurd; to *hold* human life cheap; to *hold* a person responsible); decide legally (as, the court *held* that the plaintiff was entitled to damages); also, to maintain or carry on (dealings, communication, etc.: as, "There are few . . . who dwell in the maritime parts, but what can *hold* conversation in both tongues," Swift's "Gulliver's Travels," i. 5); pursue or prosecute (as, to *hold* one's course); engage in or have (a meeting, assembly, etc.); go through or perform (a proceeding, etc.); observe or celebrate (a festival, etc.); sustain (a musical tone), esp. in one part while the other parts progress; also, to abide by (one's word, etc.)†; also, to offer or accept as a wager†; also, to oblige† or constrain†; in *law,* to bind (to or in bail: as, the prisoner was *held* in $2,500 bail). —**to hold copy,** to act as a copy-holder. —**to hold in,** to restrain, check, or curb. —**to hold one's own,** to maintain one's position or condition, as against opposition or competition. —**to hold one's peace,** to keep silent; cease or refrain from speaking. —**to hold out,** to extend or stretch forth; fig., to offer or present; also, to keep out; keep back; also, to continue to endure or resist†. —**to hold over,** to keep for future consideration or action; postpone. —**to hold up,** to keep in an erect position; fig., to support or uphold; also, to present to notice; exhibit; display; also, to stop; specif., to stop by force in order to rob (colloq.). —**to hold water,** to retain water (and not let it run through); fig., to prove sound, tenable, or valid, as a theory or an argument. —**hold**[2], *v. i.* To keep or maintain a grasp on something; keep hold; adhere or cling as if by grasping; maintain connection, or remain fast; keep from becoming loose or giving way; also, to remain attached, faithful, or steadfast (as, to *hold* to one's purpose); also, to side or agree (*with*); also, to maintain one's position against opposition; continue in resistance; also, to refrain or forbear (now usually in the imperative: as, "Lay on, Macduff, And damn'd be him that first cries '*Hold,* enough!'" Shakspere's "Macbeth," v. 8. 34); also, to hold property by some tenure (as, a tenant *holding* under a long lease); derive title to something (*of* or *from*: as, to *hold* directly of the crown); also, to remain or continue in a specified state, relation, etc. (as, "Fair *held* the breeze behind us," Kipling's "Three-Decker"; please *hold* still; to *hold* aloof); last or endure (as, winter still *holds*); remain valid or be in force (as, the rule does not *hold* in this case);

also, to keep on or continue in a course (as, "Beneath the moon's unclouded light I *held* awa to Annie": Burns's "Rigs o' Barley"); also, to prevail (as, the rainy season now *holds*).—**to hold forth,** to discourse; preach; harangue: often used in disparagement: as, "He is able to *hold forth* upon canes longer than upon any one subject in the world" (Steele, in "Tatler," 142).—**to hold in,** to restrain or contain one's self: as, "I am full of the fury of the Lord; I am weary with *holding in*" (Jer. vi. 11).—**to hold off,** to keep aloof or at a distance (as, "Some thought that Philip did but trifle with her; Some that she but *held off* to draw him on": Tennyson's "Enoch Arden," 473); also, to refrain from action (as, the rain still *holds off*).—**to hold on,** to keep fast hold on something; also, to continue; keep going; also, to stop or halt (chiefly in the imperative: colloq.).—**to hold out,** to maintain resistance; refuse to yield or submit; also, to continue; endure; last; also, to keep back something expected or due (slang).—**to hold over,** to remain in possession or in office beyond the regular term.—**to hold up,** to keep up; maintain one's position, condition, etc.; endure; also, to stop; cease; esp., to cease from raining; keep from raining.—**hold**[2], *n.* The act or an act of holding fast by a grasp of the hand or by some other physical means (as, to catch, lay, or take *hold*; to release one's *hold*); grasp; grip; hence, a non-physical grasp, control, controlling force, or dominating influence (as, to have a secret *hold* on a person; the idea has a strong *hold* on the imagination); also, confinement or imprisonment (archaic: as, "They laid hands on them, and put them in *hold* unto the next day," Acts, iv. 3); also, possession or occupation, as of land†; legal tenure (now Sc. and north. Eng.: cf. *copyhold, freehold,* etc.); also, a thing that holds fast or supports something else; a receptacle for something; a prison or prison-cell; also, something grasped for support (as, "He that stands upon a slippery place Makes nice of no vile *hold* to stay him up": Shakspere's "King John," iii. 4. 138); something to hold a thing by, as a handle; also, a piece of property held, or a holding (now Sc. and north. Eng.: cf. *copyhold, freehold,* etc.); a dwelling or habitation (Sc. and north. Eng.); a place of refuge or shelter (see Shakspere's "Cymbeline," iii. 3. 20); a fortified place, or stronghold (archaic); in *music*, a pause (symbol).

hold-a-ble (hōl′dạ-bl), *a.* That may be held.

hold=all (hōld′âl), *n.* A portable case or bag for miscellaneous articles, used by soldiers, travelers, etc.

hold-back (hōld′bak), *n.* Something that holds one back; a restraint; a hindrance; also, the iron or strap on the shaft of a vehicle to which the breeching of the harness is attached, enabling the horse to hold back or to back the vehicle.

hold-er (hōl′dėr), *n.* One who or that which holds (in any sense); esp., one who has the ownership, possession, or use of something; an owner; a possessor; an occupier; a tenant; specif., one in actual or constructive possession of a bill, note, etc., whether as payee, indorsee, or bearer; also, something to hold a thing with (as, a pen*holder*; an iron-*holder*).

hold-fast (hōld′fȧst), *n.* Something used to hold or secure a thing in place, as a catch, hook, or clamp.

hold-ing (hōl′ding), *n.* The act of one who or that which holds (in any sense); specif., tenure, as of land; also, that which lays hold on or holds something; a means of laying hold; also, land, or a piece of land, held, esp. of a superior; in general, property owned, esp. stocks and bonds (often in *pl.*).—**hold′ing,** *p. a.* That holds.—**holding company,** in *finance*, a company which owns stocks or securities of other companies, deriving income from the dividends or interest yielded by these.

hold=out (hōld′out), *n.* One who holds out, maintains resistance, or refuses to submit; one who withholds consent, as in the hope of securing better terms. [Colloq.]

hold=o-ver (hōld′ō″vėr), *n.* A lockup or cell for prisoners awaiting trial; also, one who remains in possession or in office beyond the regular term; something which remains behind from a former period. [Colloq.]

hold=up (hōld′up), *n.* A forcible stopping of a person, etc., as by a highwayman, for the purpose of robbery; any proceeding likened to this; also, one who robs in this manner. [Colloq.]

hole (hōl), *n.* [AS. *hol*, hole, cave, den, orig. neut. of *hol*, adj., = D. *hol* = G. *hohl* = Icel. *holr*, hollow; perhaps akin to AS. *helan*, cover, hide: see *hall*.] A hollow place in a solid body or mass (as, a *hole* in the ground; cheese full of *holes*); a cavity; an excavation; often, the excavated habitation of an animal (as, "The foxes have *holes*, and the birds of the air have nests": Mat. viii. 20); a burrow; hence, a small, dingy, or mean abode; a cell or dungeon (cf. *black hole*, under *black, a.*); an embarrassing position or predicament (colloq.: as, to find one's self in a *hole*); also, a small cavity into which a marble, ball, or the like is to be played in various games; a score made by so playing; also, a cove or small harbor (U. S.); also, an opening through anything; an aperture or perforation; an orifice; a gap or rent; fig., a fault or flaw (as, to pick *holes* in a thing, to find faults in it).—**hole in the air.** In *aëronautics*, same as *air-hole*.—**hole,** *v.*; *holed, holing.* [AS. *holian*.] **I.** *tr.* To make a hole or holes in; make hollows or perforations in; also, to make (a hole); sink (a shaft), bore (a tunnel), etc.; also, to put or drive into a hole, as the ball in golf; also, in *golf*, to drive the ball into (a hole). **II.** *intr.* To make a hole or holes; also, to go into a hole; retire into a hole for the winter, as a hibernating animal (usually with *up*); also, in *golf* (with or without *out*), to drive the ball into a hole.—**hole′=and=cor′ner,** *a.* Clandestine; underhand.—**hol′ey,** *a.* Having holes or a hole.

hol-i-but (hol′i-but), *n.* Same as *halibut*.

hol-i-day (hol′i-dā), *n.* [AS. *hāligdæg*, 'holy day.'] A consecrated day or religious festival, esp. one other than Sunday (now usually written *holy day*: see under *holy, a.*); also, a day, esp. one fixed by law ('legal holiday'), on which ordinary business is suspended, as in commemoration of some event or in honor of some person; hence, any day of exemption from labor; also, a period of cessation from work, or of recreation; a vacation; also, any day or time of festivity.

ho-li-ly (hō′li-li), *adv.* In a holy manner; sacredly; piously or devoutly.—**ho′li-ness,** *n.* The state or character of being holy; also [*cap.*], with *his* or *your*, a title of the Pope, and formerly also of other high ecclesiastical dignitaries, etc.

hol-la (hǫ-lä′ or hol′ạ̈), *interj.* [F. *holà*, 'ho there!' Cf. *hollo*.] A shout to attract attention; also, an exclamation of exultation, etc.; also, a call to stop or halt†.—**hol′la,** *n.*; pl. *hollas* (-ạ̈z). A cry of 'holla'; a shout.—**hol′la,** *v.*; *-laed, -laing.* **I.** *intr.* To cry 'holla'; call out; shout. **II.** *tr.* To call 'holla' to; shout to; also, to shout (something).

hol-land (hol′ạnd), *n.* A plain linen fabric, usually unbleached, or light-brown and sometimes glazed, orig. made in Holland.

Hol-land-er (hol′ạn-dėr), *n.* A native of Holland; a Dutchman; also, a Dutch ship.

hol-lands (hol′ạndz), *n.* Holland gin. See *gin*[3].

hol-ler (hol′ėr), *n.* and *v.* Provincial or vulgar form of *holla* or *hollo*.

hol-lo (hǫ-lō′ or hol′ǭ), *interj.* [= *holla*: cf. *hallo, hello, hillo,* and *hullo*.] A call to attract attention or express greeting (cf. *hello*); also, an exclamation of surprise, etc.—**hol′lo,** *n.*; pl. *hollos* (-ǭz). A cry of 'hollo'; a shout.—**hol′lo,** *v.*; *-loed, -loing.* **I.** *intr.* To cry 'hollo'; call out; shout. **II.** *tr.* To cry 'hollo' to; call out to; urge or incite by shouting; also, to shout (something).

hol-loa (hǫ-lō′), *interj., n.,* and *v.* Same as *hollo*.

hol-low (hol′ō). [AS. *holh*, a hollow, hole, connected with *hol*, hollow: see *hole*.] **I.** *n.* An empty space within anything; a hole; a cavity; an excavation; also, a depression in a surface; a concavity; specif., a low part of land, as between hills (as, "This sequestered glen has long been known by the name of Sleepy *Hollow*": Irving's "Sketch-Book," Sleepy Hollow); a valley; a basin. **II.** *a.* Having a hole or cavity within, or not solid (as, a *hollow* ball; a *hollow* tree); also, having a depression or concavity, as a surface; depressed or concave, as a part or place; sunken, as the cheeks or eyes; having deep troughs between the waves, as the sea; also, empty, or without contents (as, "a *hollow* walnut": Shakspere's "Merry Wives of Windsor," iv. 2. 171); sometimes, empty as to the stomach, or hungry (as, to feel *hollow*); fig., without substantial or real worth, or vain (as, *hollow* joys; a *hollow* victory); insincere or false (as, *hollow* hearts; *hollow* compliments or promises); unreal (as, "O *hollow* wraith of dying fame, Fade wholly": Tennyson's "In Memoriam," lxxiii.); also, of sound, not full, sonorous, or resonant (as, a *hollow* voice; *hollow* groans); dull, muffled, or deep (as, a *hollow* roar). **III.** *adv.* Thoroughly or completely: as, to beat a competitor *hollow*. [Colloq.]—**hol′low,** *v.* **I.** *tr.* To make hollow; excavate; also, to form by making a hollow: often with *out*, in both senses. **II.** *intr.* To become hollow.—**hol′low=eyed′,** *a.* Having sunken eyes. —**hol′low=heart′ed,** *a.* Insincere; false: as, "doubtful *hollow-hearted* friends" (Shakspere's "Richard III.," iv. 4. 435).—**hol′low=horned,** *a.* Having hollow horns, borne on a bony core of the frontal bone, as the ox and sheep.—**hol′low-ly,** *adv.*—**hol′low-ness,** *n.*—**hol′low=ware,** *n.* Vessels for the table, or for other use, that are hollow or more or less deep, as bowls, cups, etc.: distinguished from *flat-ware.*

hol-ly (hol′i), *n.*; pl. *hollies* (-iz). [ME. *holi, holin,* < AS. *holen, holegn,* holly; akin to D. and G. *hulst,* F. *houx,* holly.] Any of the trees or shrubs of the aquifoliaceous genus *Ilex,* having glossy, spiny-edged leaves and small, whitish flowers succeeded by bright-red berries; the foliage and berries, much used for decoration, esp. during the Christmas season; also, the holm-oak.

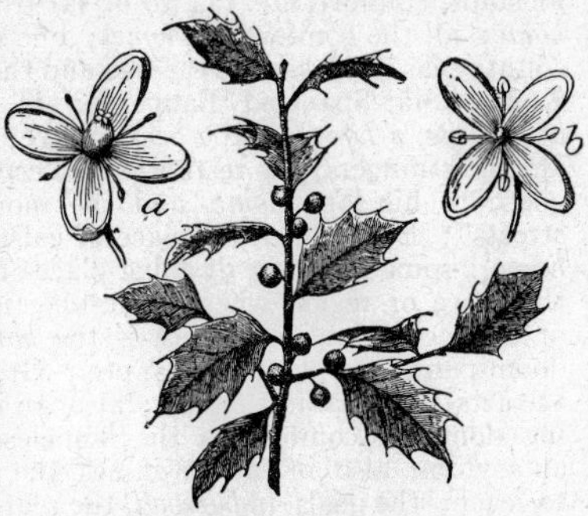

American Holly (*Ilex opaca*). — *a, b,* female and male flowers.

hol-ly-hock (hol′i-hok), *n.* [ME. *holihoc,* < *holi,* holy, + *hoc,* mallow.] A tall malvaceous plant, *Althæa rosea,* having large, rounded leaves and showy flowers of various colors.

hol-ly=oak (hol′i-ōk), *n.* The holm-oak.

holm[1] (hōm), *n.* [AS. *holm* = Icel. *holmr,* islet.] A small island in a river or lake, or near a larger island or the mainland (now chiefly in British place-names, or in the Orkney and Shetland Islands); also, a low, flat tract of land beside a river or stream (Eng. and Sc.: as, "O Derwent! winding among grassy *holms,*" Wordsworth's "Prelude," i. 275).

holm[2] (hōm), *n.* [ME. *holm,* for *holin,* holly: see *holly.*] The holly (now prov. Eng.); also, the holm-oak.

hol-mi-a (hol′mi-ạ or hōl′-), *n.* [NL.; named from (*Stock*)-*holm,* Sweden.] In *chem.,* oxide of holmium.—**hol′mi-um** (-um), *n.* [NL.] Chem. sym., Ho; at. wt., 163.5. A rare element found in the mineral gadolinite.—**hol′mic,** *a.*

holm=oak (hōm′ōk), *n.* [See *holm*[2].] An evergreen oak, *Quercus ilex,* of southern Europe, with foliage resembling that of the holly.

holo-. Form of Gr. ὅλος, whole, entire, used in combination. —**hol-o-blast** (hol′ọ-blast), *n.* [+ *-blast.*] In *biol.,* an ovum the contents of which consist entirely or mostly of formative or germinal matter: opposed to *meroblast.*—**hol-o-blas′tic** (-blas′tik), *a.*—**ho-lo-ca-ine** (họ-lō′kạ-in or hol-ọ-kā′in), *n.* [+ E. (*co*)*caine.*] A local anesthetic resembling cocaine in its action: used chiefly for the eye.

hol-o-caust (hol′ọ-kâst), *n.* [LL. *holocaustum,* < Gr. ὁλόκαυστον, neut. of ὁλόκαυστος, burnt whole, < ὅλος, whole, + καυστός, burnt, < καίειν, burn.] An offering or sacrifice devoted wholly, or without reservation of parts, to burning, or the burning of such an offering; hence, anything offered or sacrificed unreservedly, as to a person or a cause, or a sacrificing of something unreservedly; also, something entirely consumed by fire (as, "Like that self-begotten bird [the phenix] . . . That . . . lay erewhile a *holocaust*": Milton's "Samson Agonistes," 1702); more commonly, a process of complete consumption by fire; a great and destructive fire; a great or wholesale destruction of life, by fire or otherwise.—**hol-o-caus′tic** (-kâs′tik), *a.*

hol-o-graph (hol′ọ-grȧf). [LL. *holographus,* < Gr. ὁλόγραφος, < ὅλος, whole, + γράφειν, write.] **I.** *a.* Wholly written by the person in whose name it appears, as a letter, deed, etc. **II.** *n.* A holograph writing.—**hol-o-graph′ic** (-graf′ik), *a.*

hol-o-he-dral (hol-ọ-hē′drạl), *a.* [Gr. ὅλος, whole, + ἕδρα, seat, base.] Of a crystal, having all the planes or faces required by the maximum symmetry.—**hol-o-he′drism,** *n.* The property of being holohedral.—**hol-o-he′dron** (-drọn), *n.*; pl. *-drons* or *-dra* (-drạ). A holohedral crystal or form.

hol-o-mor-phic (hol-ọ-môr′fik), *a.* [Gr. ὅλος, whole, + μορφή, form.] Holohedral: esp. as opposed to *hemimorphic.* —**hol-o-mor′phism,** *n.* The property of being holomorphic.

hol-o-phote (hol′ọ-fōt), *n.* [Gr. ὅλος, whole, + φῶς (φωτ-), light.] An optical apparatus by which practically all the light from a lighthouse lamp, etc., is made available for illumination by reflection or refraction or both.—**hol-o-pho′tal** (-fō′tạl), *a.*

ho-loph-ra-sis (họ-lof′rạ-sis), *n.* [NL., < Gr. ὅλος, whole, + φράσις, speech, expression: see *phrase.*] The expression of a whole phrase or sentence in a single word, as in agglutinative languages.—**hol-o-phras-tic** (hol-ọ-fras′tik), *a.* Pertaining to or characterized by holophrasis; expressing a whole phrase or sentence in a single word.

hol-o-phyte (hol′ọ-fīt), *n.* [Gr. ὅλος, whole, + φυτόν, plant.] In *bot.,* a plant which manufactures its own food, being in no sense parasitic or saprophytic.—**hol-o-phyt′ic** (-fit′ik), *a.*

hol-o-thu-ri-an (hol-ọ-thū′ri-ạn), *n.* [NL. *Holothuria,* a genus of echinoderms, < L. *holothuria,* neut. pl., < Gr. ὁλοθούριον, a kind of zoöphyte.] Any of the *Holothurioidea,* a class or group of echinoderms having an elongated body and a leathery integument; a sea-cucumber.

holp (hōlp), **holp-en** (hōl′pn). Archaic preterit and past participle of *help.*

Hol-stein (hōl′stīn), *a.* and *n.* Same as *Holstein-Friesian.*

Hol-stein=Frie-sian (hōl′stīn-frē′zịạn). **I.** *a.* Noting a breed of dairy cattle of large size, originating in North Holland and Friesland, and usually having a coat of pure white and jet black in irregular patches. **II.** *n.* One of the Holstein-Friesian breed of cattle.

hol-ster (hōl′stėr), *n.* [D. *holster* = Sw. *hölster* = Dan. *hylster,* holster, case; from the same root as AS. *helan,* cover, hide: see *hall.*] A leather case for a pistol, worn on the belt or attached to a horseman's saddle: as, "In th' *holsters,* at his saddle-bow, Two aged pistols he did stow" (Butler's "Hudibras," i. 1).—**hol′ster,** *v. t.* To put into the holster: as, "He *holstered* his pistol with a jerk" (Wister's "Virginian," xv.).—**hol′stered,** *a.* Bearing holsters.

holt[1] (hōlt), *n.* [AS. *holt* = G. *holz* = Icel. *holt,* wood.] A wood or grove (as, "She sent her voice thro' all the *holt*": Tennyson's "Talking Oak," 123); also, a wooded hill. [Now chiefly prov. Eng. and Sc., or poetic, or in place-names, surnames, etc.]

holt[2] (hōlt), *n.* [Cf. *hold*[2], *n.*] Hold, grasp, or grip (now prov.); also, a stronghold†; also, the retreat or lair of an animal, as an otter; a lurking-place of fish, as trout, in a stream.

ho-lus=bo-lus (hō′lus-bō′lus), *adv.* [A formation simulating Latin, appar. < *whole* + *bolus.*] All in a lump; all at once: as, to swallow a thing *holus-bolus.* [Colloq.]

ho-ly (hō′li), *a.*; compar. *holier,* superl. *holiest.* [AS. *hālig* = D. and G. *heilig* = Icel. *heilagr,* holy; akin to E. *hale*[2] and *heal.*] Entitled (or regarded as entitled) to worship or profound religious reverence because of divine character or origin, or connection with God or divinity (esp. in Christian use: as, the *Holy* Ghost; our *Holy* Saviour; the *Holy* Virgin; the *Holy* Bible; the *Holy* Cross; the *holy* communion); in general, invested with a sacred character, hallowed, or held in profound reverence (whether by a particular church, sect, or body, or by persons generally, or by an individual); also, specially recognized as or declared sacred by religious use or authority, or consecrated (as, a *holy* day; *holy* ground; *holy* water); also, dedicated or devoted to the service of God, the church, or religion (as, a *holy* man; a *holy* house; a *holy* life); saintly or godly; pious or devout; of religious purity, exaltation, solemnity, etc., as desires, feelings, etc.; religiously observed, or not desecrated or profaned (as, "Remember the sabbath day, to keep it *holy*": Ex. xx. 8); religious (as, *holy* rites or hymns); also, consecrated (*to*: as, "woodlands *holy* to the dead," Tennyson's "In Memoriam," xcix.: poetic).—**Holy Alliance,**

a league formed by the sovereigns of Russia, Austria, and Prussia in 1815, after the fall of Napoleon, with the professed object of uniting their respective governments in a Christian brotherhood.—**Holy Cross,** the cross on which Christ died.—**holy day,** a day, esp. one other than Sunday, set apart by the church for religious observance; a religious festival or anniversary.—**Holy Father,** a title of the Pope.—**Holy Ghost,** the third person of the Trinity. Also used in the title of the *Order of the Holy Ghost*, a former high order of knighthood in France, founded by Henry III. in 1578.—**Holy Grail.** See *Grail*.—**Holy Innocents' Day,** a day of religious observance, Dec. 28, commemorating the slaughter of the children of Bethlehem by Herod's order (Mat. ii. 16); Childermas.—**Holy Land,** Palestine.—**Holy Office,** the Inquisition.—**holy order,** *eccles.*, the rank or status of an ordained Christian minister (usually called *holy orders*); also, any of the degrees or grades of the Christian ministry, esp. one of the major orders (usually in *pl.*); also, the rite or sacrament of ordination (usually called *holy orders*).—**holy place,** the outer and larger chamber of the Jewish tabernacle and temple, adjoining the holy of holies. See Ex. xxvi. 33.—**Holy Roman Empire,** the empire in western and central Europe which began with the coronation of Otto the Great, king of Germany, as Roman emperor in 962, and ended with the renunciation of the Roman imperial title by Francis II. in 1806, regarded theoretically as the continuation of the Western Empire and as the temporal form of a universal dominion whose spiritual head was the Pope: sometimes regarded as originating with Charlemagne, king of the Franks, who was crowned Roman emperor in 800.—**Holy Rood,** the cross on which Christ died; also [*l. c.*], a crucifix, esp. one placed above the middle of a rood-screen.—**Holy Saturday,** the Saturday in Holy Week.—**Holy See,** the see of Rome; the office or jurisdiction of the Pope; the papal court.—**Holy Sepulcher,** the sepulcher in which the body of Christ lay between his burial and his resurrection: its traditional location is marked by the Church of the Holy Sepulcher at Jerusalem.—**Holy Spirit,** the Holy Ghost.—**Holy Thursday,** Ascension Day; also, as in the *Rom. Cath. Ch.*, the Thursday in Holy Week; Maundy Thursday.—**holy water,** water blessed by a priest for religious uses.—**Holy Week,** the week immediately preceding Easter Sunday; Passion Week.—**Holy Writ,** the Scriptures.—**ho'ly,** *n.*; pl. *-lies* (-liz). That which is holy; something holy.—**holy of holies,** the inner and smaller chamber of the Jewish tabernacle and temple (cf. *holy place*, under *holy*, *a.*), entered only by the high priest, and by him only once a year; also, a similar part of any temple; the sanctuary or bema of a Christian church; fig., a place of special sacredness.

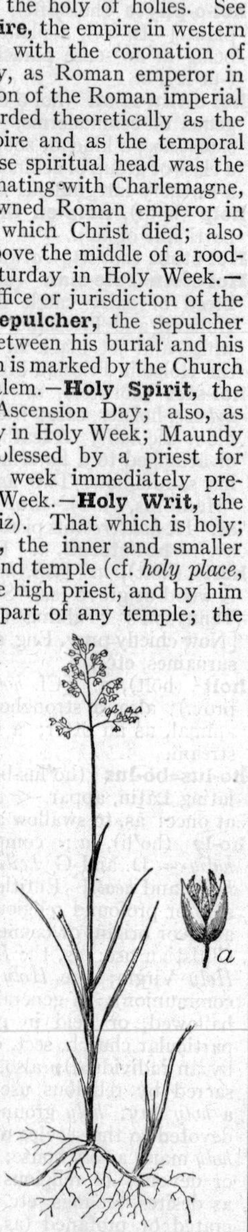

Holy-grass (*Hierochloë odorata*). — *a*, spikelet.

ho-ly=grass (hō'li-gràs), *n.* Any of several fragrant grasses of the genus *Hierochloë* (or *Savastana*), esp. *H. odorata* of northern Europe and America: named from the European custom of strewing the grass about churches on festival days.

ho-ly-stone (hō'li-stōn), *n.* [Origin uncertain: cf. *holey*.] A soft sandstone used for scrubbing the decks of a ship.—**ho'ly-stone,** *v. t.*; *-stoned*, *-stoning*. To scrub with a holy-stone.

ho-ly-tide (hō'li-tīd), *n.* A holy season. [Archaic.]

hom-age (hom'āj), *n.* [OF. *homage* (F. *hommage*), < ML. *hominaticum*, < *homo* (*homin-*), vassal, L. man.] The formal acknowledgment by which a feudal tenant or vassal declared himself to be the man of his lord, owing him faith and service; the relation thus established of a vassal to his lord; something done or given in acknowledgment or consideration of vassalage; fig., respect or reverence paid or rendered; honor; respectful or complimentary attentions.—**hom'ag-er** (-ā-jėr), *n.* One who owes or does homage; one who holds land of another by homage.

ho-mat-ro-pine, ho-mat-ro-pin (hō-mat'rō-pin), *n.* [See *homo-* and *atropine*.] In *chem.*, a crystalline alkaloid derived from atropine: used in medicine.

hom-bre (om'brā), *n.*; pl. *-bres* (-brās). [Sp., < L. *homo*, man.] A man.

home (hōm), *n.* [AS. *hām*, home, dwelling, = G. *heim* = Icel. *heimr*, abode, village, = Goth. *haims*, village.] A dwelling or abode; a house that is the fixed residence of a person, a family, or a household (as, "Ancient *homes* of lord and lady, Built for pleasure and for state": Tennyson's "Lord of Burleigh"); a seat of domestic life and interests (as, "O happy day, When a new household finds its place Among the myriad *homes* of earth": Longfellow's "Hanging of the Crane," i.); the accustomed or familiar place of abode, often as the place of birth, youthful residence, loved companionships, comfort, etc. (as, to be far from *home*; to long for *home*; all the comforts of *home*); one's native place or own country (as, "the land of the free and the *home* of the brave": Key's "Star-Spangled Banner"); in general, a place of abode (as, a *home* on the ocean wave; to make one's *home* among strangers); a resting-place, esp. in death (as, "Man goeth to his long *home*, and the mourners go about the streets": Eccl. xii. 5); a place of existence (as, a heavenly *home*); sometimes, the dwelling-place or retreat of an animal; the place or region where something is native, indigenous, or most common (as, Africa is the *home* of the zebra, the doom-palm, the plant freesia, etc.; Greece was the *home* of the arts); the habitat or seat; also, an institution for affording domestic comfort to the homeless, sick, infirm, etc.; an asylum; also, in various games, the point which one tries to reach; the goal; in *baseball*, the plate at which the batter stands, and which he must return to and touch, after running around the bases, in order to score a run.—**at home,** at or in one's own house or place of abode (as, to find a person *at home*); in the place, region, or country of customary residence (as, to keep an army *at home*; affairs *at home* and abroad); also, in a situation familiar to one, or in one's element (as, to be *at home* in a canoe, in society, or in a science); at one's ease (as, to be, or to make one's self, *at home* in a friend's house); also, prepared to receive social visits, or accessible to visitors (cf. *at-home*).—**home,** *a.* Of, pertaining to, or connected with one's home, place of abode, or country; domestic; not foreign; also, that strikes home, or to the mark aimed at; effective; to the point; also, in various games, pertaining to or situated at or near the home; reaching, or enabling a player to reach, home.—**home rule,** management of the affairs of a country, province, district, city, or place by its own citizens or people; local self-government; administrative autonomy: used esp. with reference to Ireland. Hence **home'=rul'er,** an advocate of home rule.—**home run,** in *baseball*, a run made by a player on a hit which enables him without aid from fielding errors of the opponents, to make the entire circuit of the bases without a stop.—**home,** *adv.* [AS. *hām*.] To, toward, or at home (as, to go *home*; he will be *home* to-night); also, to the mark or point aimed at (as, to strike or thrust *home*); quite into or to something (as, to drive a nail *home*; the cavalry charged *home*); hence, so as to reach effectually (as, to bring a lesson *home* to a person, to make him feel its force; to bring a charge *home* to the actual offender, to fix it upon him); directly and effectively (as, to speak *home*).—**home,** *v.*; *homed*, *homing*. **I.** *intr.* To go or return home (see *homing*, *p. a.*); also, to have the home or abode (where specified). **II.** *tr.* To provide with a home; also, to bring or send home.

home=born (hōm'bôrn), *a.* Born or originating at home; native; domestic.

home=bred (hōm'bred), *a.* Bred or reared at home; native; indigenous; domestic; also, of homely breeding; unpolished; unsophisticated.

home=brew (hōm'brö), *n.* Beer or other beverage brewed at home, as for home consumption.—**home'=brewed,** *a.*

home=keep-ing (hōm'kē"ping), *a.* Staying at home: as, "*Home-keeping* youth have ever homely wits" (Shakspere's "Two Gentlemen of Verona," i. 1. 2).—**home'=keep"ing,** *n.*

home-land (hōm'land), *n.* The land that is one's home.

home-less (hōm′les), *a.* Destitute of a home, as persons or animals; also, affording no home, as a place.—**home′less-ness,** *n.*

home-like (hōm′līk), *a.* Like, or suggestive of, home; familiar; comfortable.—**home′like-ness,** *n.*

home-ly (hōm′li), *a.*; compar. *homelier,* superl. *homeliest.* Of or belonging to the home or household†; hence, familiar or intimate, or friendly or kindly (archaic or prov.); also, proper or suited to the home or to ordinary domestic life; common, plain, simple, or unpretentious (as, *homely* fare, dress, or language; "the excellent and *homely* type of house architecture that still prevails in Philadelphia," H. G. Wells's "Outline of History," xxxvii. § 6); not having or affecting any particular elegance, refinement, or cultivation, as persons; also, of commonplace or plain appearance, or without pretensions to beauty (often as a mild substitute for *ugly*: as, "Let time, that makes you *homely,* make you sage," T. Parnell's "Elegy to an Old Beauty").—**home′li-ness,** *n.*

home=made (hōm′mād), *a.* Made at home; of domestic manufacture.

homeo-, etc. See *homœo-,* etc.

ho-me-o-path, ho-mœ-o-path (hō′mẹ-ọ-path), *n.* [See *homeopathy.*] A homeopathist.—**ho″me-o-path′ic, ho″-mœ-o-path′ic,** *a.* Of, pertaining to, or according to the principles of, homeopathy; practising or advocating homeopathy.—**ho″me-o-path′i-cal-ly, ho″mœ-o-path′i-cal-ly,** *adv.*—**ho-me-op′a-thist, ho-mœ-op′a-thist** (-op′ạ-thist), *n.* One who practises or favors homeopathy.

ho-me-op-a-thy, ho-mœ-op-a-thy (hō-mẹ-op′ạ-thi), *n.* [Gr. ὅμοιος, like, + παθεῖν, suffer.] The method of treating disease by drugs, given in minute doses, which would produce in a healthy person symptoms similar to those of the disease: opposed to *allopathy.*

hom-er[1] (hō′mėr), *n.* A homing pigeon; in *baseball,* a home run (colloq.).

ho-mer[2] (hō′mėr), *n.* [Heb. *khōmer.*] A Hebrew dry measure equal to 10 ephahs; also, a Hebrew liquid measure equal to 10 baths. See Ezek. xlv. 11.

Ho-mer-ic (họ-mer′ik), *a.* Of, pertaining to, or suggestive of Homer, the great epic poet of ancient Greece, or his poetry.—**Homeric laughter,** 'inextinguishable laughter,' or loud, hearty laughter, such as Homer describes. See "Iliad," i. 599; "Odyssey," xx. 346.—**Ho-mer′i-cal-ly,** *adv.*

Bust of Homer, Museo Nazionale, Naples.

home-sick (hōm′sik), *a.* Ill or depressed from a longing for home while absent from it: as, "I long to see my master's face again, For I turn *home-sick*" (W. B. Yeats's "Countess Cathleen," iii.).—**home′sick″-ness,** *n.*

home-spun (hōm′spun). **I.** *a.* Spun or made at home, as yarn or cloth; made of such cloth, as garments; hence, of homely origin or character; plain or simple; unpolished or rude. **II.** *n.* Cloth made at home, or of homespun yarn; hence, cloth of similar appearance, commonly of somewhat loose texture but stout and durable; hence, anything of a homely or plain kind; also, a person clad in homespun garments, as a rustic (as, "What hempen *home-spuns* have we swaggering here?" Shakspere's "Midsummer Night's Dream," iii. 1. 79).

home-stead (hōm′sted), *n.* [AS. *hāmstede.*] The place, as a town or village, in which one's home is†; also, a home or dwelling, esp. a house with the ground and buildings immediately connected with it; in the U. S., a dwelling with its land and buildings, occupied by the owner as a home, and exempted by a State law ('homestead law') from seizure or forced sale for debt; also, a parcel of 160 acres of the unappropriated public land granted to a settler on certain conditions, in accordance with a special U. S. statute ('Homestead Act').—**home′stead-er,** *n.* One who holds a homestead; esp., a settler holding a homestead under the Homestead Act (western U. S.).

home-ward (hōm′wạrd). [AS. *hāmweard.*] **I.** *adv.* Toward home. **II.** *a.* Being in the direction of home.—**home′wards** (-wạrdz), *adv.* Homeward.

hom-i-cide (hom′i-sīd), *n.* [OF. F. *homicide,* < L. *homicida, homicidium,* < *homo,* man: see *-cide.*] One who kills a human being; a manslayer; also, the killing of a human being by a human being (in a broad sense, including suicide and accidental killing); commonly, the killing of one human being by another.—**hom′i-ci-dal** (-sī-dạl), *a.*

hom-i-let-ic (hom-i-let′ik), *a.* [Gr. ὁμιλητικός, < ὁμιλεῖν, consort, converse, speak, < ὅμιλος, assembly: see *homily.*] Pertaining to preaching, or to sermons or homilies; of the nature of a homily; of or pertaining to homiletics. Also **hom-i-let′i-cal.**—**hom-i-let′i-cal-ly,** *adv.*—**hom-i-let′ics,** *n.* The art of preaching; the branch of practical theology that treats of homilies or sermons.

hom-i-list (hom′i-list), *n.* One who writes or delivers homilies.

hom-i-ly (hom′i-li), *n.*; pl. *-lies* (-liz). [OF. *omelie* (F. *homélie*), < ML. *homilia,* < Gr. ὁμιλία, intercourse, conversation, discourse, < ὅμιλος, assembly, < ὁμός, same, + ἴλη, company.] A religious discourse addressed to a congregation; a sermon; esp., a discourse which expounds and applies a particular passage of Scripture, with a view to the spiritual edification of the hearers; hence, in general, an admonitory or moralizing discourse.

hom-ing (hō′ming), *p. a.* Returning home: applied esp. to pigeons trained to fly home from a distance and employed to carry messages.

hom-i-ny (hom′i-ni), *n.* [N. Amer. Ind.] Maize hulled and crushed or coarsely ground: prepared for use as food by boiling.

ho-mo (hō′mō), *n.* [L.] Man.

homo-. Form of Gr. ὁμός, same, used in combination.—**hom-o-cen-tric** (hom-ọ-sen′trik or hō-mọ-), *a.* Concentric.—**hom-o-cer′cal** (-sėr′kạl), *a.* [+ Gr. κέρκος, tail.] In *ichth.,* noting, pertaining to, or having a form of tail which is symmetrical as to its upper and lower halves. Cf. *heterocercal.*—**hom-o-chro′mous** (-krō′-mus), *a.* [Gr. ὁμόχρωμος (χρῶμα, color).] Of the same color, as florets; of a composite flower or flower-head, having all the florets of the same color. Cf. *heterochromous.*—**ho-mod-ro-mous** (họ-mod′rọ-mus), *a.* [+ Gr. δρόμος, a running, course.] In *bot.,* having the spiral arrangement of the leaves on the stem and of those on the branches in the same direction. Cf. *heterodromous.*—**hom′o-dyne** (-dīn), *a.* [+ δύναμις, power.] In *wireless teleph.,* noting or pertaining to a method by which the modulated oscillations in the receiving apparatus are reinforced by locally produced oscillations of the same frequency.

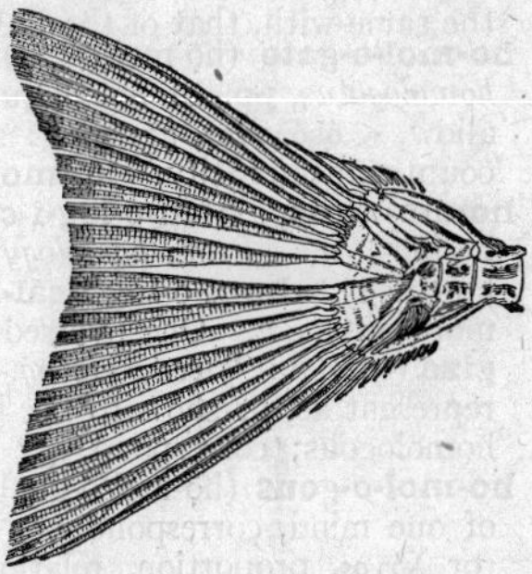

Homocercal Tail of a Fish.

homœo-, homeo-. Forms of Gr. ὅμοιος, like, used in combination.—**ho-mœ-o-crys-tal-line, ho-me-o-crys-tal-line** (hō″mẹ-ọ-kris′tạ-lin or hom″ẹ-), *a.* In *petrog.,* composed of crystals or grains of equal size.—**ho″mœ-o-mor′phous, ho″me-o-mor′phous** (-môr′fus), *a.* [Gr. ὁμοιόμορφος, of like form (μορφή, form).] Crystallizing in the same or a related form: said esp. of substances not having an analogous chemical composition. Cf. *isomorphous.*—**ho″mœ-o-mor′-phism, ho″me-o-mor′phism,** *n.*—**ho′mœ-o-path** (-path), etc. See *homeopath,* etc.

ho-mog-a-mous (họ-mog′ạ-mus), *a.* [Gr. ὁμός, same, + γάμος, marriage.] In *bot.,* having flowers or florets which do not differ sexually (opposed to *heterogamous*); also, having the stamens and pistils maturing simultaneously, as a monoclinous flower (opposed to *dichogamous*).—**ho-mog′a-my,** *n.*

hom-o-ge-ne-ous (hom-ọ-jē′nẹ-us or hō-mọ-), *a.* [ML. *homogeneus,* < Gr. ὁμογενής, < ὁμός, same, + γένος, race, kind.] Of the same kind or nature; essentially alike; similar; congruous; also, composed of parts all of the same kind; not heterogeneous; in *math.*, of the same kind and commensurable; also, of the same degree or dimensions.—**homogeneous function,** in *math.*, a polynomial in two or more variables, all the terms being of the same degree.—**hom″o-ge-ne′i-ty** (-jē-nē′i-ti), **hom-o-ge′ne-ous-ness,** *n.* —**hom-o-ge′ne-ous-ly,** *adv.*

hom-o-gen-e-sis (hom-ǫ-jen′e-sis or hō-mǫ-), *n.* [See *homo-* and *genesis.*] In *biol.*, the ordinary course of generation, in which the offspring is like the parent and runs through the same cycle of development.—**hom″o-ge-net′ic** (-jē-net′ik), *a.* In *biol.*, pertaining to homogenesis; also, having a common origin; derived from the same structure however modified.

ho-mog-e-nize (hǫ-moj′e-nīz), *v. t.* To make homogeneous; form by mixing and emulsifying (as, *homogenized* milk).

ho-mog-e-nous (hǫ-moj′e-nus), *a.* [Gr. ὁμογενής: see *homogeneous.*] In *biol.*, of organs or the like, corresponding in structure because of a common origin.—**ho-mog′e-ny,** *n.*

ho-mog-o-nous (hǫ-mog′ǫ-nus), *a.* [Gr. ὁμός, same, + γόνος, offspring, generation.] In *bot.*, noting or pertaining to monoclinous flowers which do not differ in the relative length of stamens and pistils (opposed to *heterogonous*); in *biol.*, characterized by regular reproduction, without metamorphosis or alternation of generations.—**ho-mog′o-ny,** *n.*

hom-o-graph (hom′ǫ-grȧf or hō′mǫ-), *n.* [See *homo-* and *-graph.*] In *philol.*, a word of the same form as another, but of different origin and signification, as *base* the adjective and *base* the noun.—**hom-o-graph′ic** (-graf′ik), *a.* Pertaining to homographs; also, pertaining to homography.—**ho-mog-ra-phy** (hǫ-mog′rạ-fi), *n.* [See *-graphy.*] In *geom.*, the relation between two figures (as two representations of the same thing in different perspective) such that for every point, line, or the like in one there is a corresponding point, line, or the like in the other.

Ho-moi-ou-si-an (hō-moi-ö′si-ạn), *n.* [LGr. ὁμοιούσιος, of like substance, < Gr. ὅμοιος, like, + οὐσία, being, substance.] One of a 4th century church party which maintained that the essence of the Son is similar to, but not the same with, that of the Father. Cf. *Homoousian.*

ho-mol-o-gate (hǫ-mol′ǫ-gāt), *v. t.*; *-gated, -gating.* [ML. *homologatus*, pp. of *homologare*, < Gr. ὁμολογεῖν, agree to, allow, < ὁμόλογος, agreeing: see *homologous.*] To approve; countenance; ratify.—**ho-mol-o-ga′tion** (-gā′shǫn), *n.*

hom-o-log-ic, hom-o-log-i-cal (hom-ǫ-loj′ik, -i-kạl, or hō-mǫ-), *a.* [From *homology.*] Pertaining to or involving homology.—**hom-o-log′i-cal-ly,** *adv.*—**ho-mol-o-gist** (hǫ-mol′ǫ-jist), *n.* One versed in homologies.—**ho-mol′o-gize** (-jīz), *v.*; *-gized, -gizing.* **I.** *tr.* To make homologous; represent as, or show to be, homologous. **II.** *intr.* To be homologous; correspond.

ho-mol-o-gous (hǫ-mol′ǫ-gus), *a.* [Gr. ὁμόλογος, agreeing, of one mind, correspondent, < ὁμός, same, + λέγειν, speak (or λόγος, proportion, relation).] Having the same or a similar relation; corresponding, as in relative position, proportion, value, or structure; in *biol.*, corresponding in type of structure and in origin, but not necessarily in function (as, the wing of a bird and the fore leg of a horse are *homologous*).—**hom-o-logue** (hom′ǫ-log or hō′mǫ-), *n.* [F., < Gr. ὁμόλογος.] Something homologous; a thing or part that corresponds in position, structure, etc., to another thing or part; in *biol.*, an organ or part which is homologous with another.—**ho-mol′o-gy** (-ji), *n.*; pl. *-gies* (-jiz). [Gr. ὁμολογία, agreement, assent, conformity, < ὁμόλογος.] The state of being homologous; sameness of relation; correspondence, or an instance of correspondence; in *biol.*, homologous relation or correspondence.

hom-o-mor-phic (hom-ǫ-môr′fik or hō-mǫ-), *a.* [Gr. ὁμός, same, + μορφή, form.] Of the same or similar form; in *entom.*, noting or pertaining to insects in which the larva resembles the imago to some extent; in *bot.*, homogonous; in *biol.*, alike in form or external appearance but not in type of structure and in origin. Also **hom-o-mor′phous.**—**hom-o-mor′phism, hom′o-mor-phy,** *n.*

ho-mon-o-mous (hǫ-mon′ǫ-mus), *a.* [Gr. ὁμόνομος, under the same laws, < ὁμός, same, + νόμος, law.] Subject to the same or a constant law; in *biol.*, having the same law or mode of growth, as parts or organs.—**ho-mon′o-my,** *n.*

hom-o-nym (hom′ǫ-nim or hō′mǫ-), *n.* [L. *homonymus*, < Gr. ὁμώνυμος, having the same name, < ὁμός, same, + ὄνυμα, name.] A single word applied as a name to different things; also, a person or thing in relation to some other person or thing having the same name; in *philol.*, a word like another in sound, and perhaps in spelling, but different in meaning, as *meat* and *meet*; in *biol.*, a name given to a species, genus, or the like, which has been used at an earlier date for a different species, genus, or the like, and which is therefore rejected.—**ho-mon-y-mous** (hǫ-mon′i-mus), *a.* [Gr. ὁμώνυμος.] Having the same name; also, similar in sound but not in meaning; of the nature of homonyms; in *optics*, noting or pertaining to the images formed in a kind of double vision in which the image seen by the right eye is on the right side and that seen by the left eye is on the left (cf. *heteronymous*).—**ho-mon′y-my,** *n.*

Ho-mo-ou-si-an (hō-mǫ-ö′si-ạn), *n.* [LGr. ὁμοούσιος, of the same substance, < Gr. ὁμός, same, + οὐσία, being, substance.] One of a 4th century church party which maintained that the essence or substance of the Father and the Son is the same. Cf. *Homoiousian.*

hom-o-phone (hom′ǫ-fōn or hō′mǫ-), *n.* [Gr. ὁμόφωνος, of the same sound, < ὁμός, same, + φωνή, sound.] In *philol.*, a letter or character expressing a like sound with another; also, a homonym.—**hom-o-phon′ic** (-fon′ik), *a.* In *music*, formerly, in unison (opposed to *antiphonic*); now, having one part or melody predominating (opposed to *polyphonic*); in *philol.*, expressing the same sound; also, alike in sound but not in meaning. Also **ho-moph-o-nous** (hǫ-mof′ǫ-nus).—**ho-moph′o-ny,** *n.* [Gr. ὁμοφωνία, unison, < ὁμόφωνος.] The quality of being homophonic; also, homophonic music.

hom-o-plas-tic (hom-ǫ-plas′tik or hō-mǫ-), *a.* [Gr. ὁμός, same, + πλαστός, formed, < πλάσσειν, form, mold.] In *biol.*, of organs or the like, similar but of different origin.—**ho-mop-la-sy** (hǫ-mop′lạ-si), *n.*

ho-mop-ter (hǫ-mop′tėr), *n.* [NL. *Homoptera*, pl., < Gr. ὁμός, same, + πτερόν, wing.] Any of the *Homoptera*, a suborder of hemipterous insects having wings of the same texture throughout, comprising the aphids, cicadas, etc.—**ho-mop′ter-an,** *a.* and *n.*—**ho-mop′ter-ous,** *a.* Having wings of the same texture throughout; belonging to the *Homoptera* (see *homopter*).

hom-o-sex-u-al-i-ty (hom″ǫ-sek-shṳ-al′i-ti or hō″mǫ-), *n.* [See *homo-.*] In *pathol.*, perverted sexual desire for a person of the same sex.—**hom-o-sex′u-al** (-ạl), *a.*

ho-mos-po-rous (hǫ-mos′pǫ-rus), *a.* [See *homo-* and *-sporous.*] In *bot.*, having only one kind of asexual spores. Cf. *heterosporous.*—**ho-mos′po-ry,** *n.*

hom-o-tax-is (hom-ǫ-tak′sis or hō-mǫ-), *n.* [NL., < Gr. ὁμός, same, + τάξις, arrangement.] Similarity of arrangement, as of geological strata which, though not necessarily contemporaneous, have the same relative position, or of the fossiliferous deposits found in them.—**hom-o-tax′i-al, hom-o-tax′ic,** *a.*—**hom-o-tax′i-al-ly,** *adv.*

hom-o-type (hom′ǫ-tīp or hō′mǫ-), *n.* [See *homo-* and *type.*] In *biol.*, that which has the same type of structure as something else; specif., any of two or more serially homologous parts or organs in an animal, as successive vertebræ; also, a part or organ homologous with another part or organ which is on the opposite side of the body or across a given axis (as, the right arm and right leg are *homotypes*).—**hom′o-ty-pal** (-tī-pạl), **hom-o-typ′ic** (-tip′ik), *a.*—**hom′o-ty-py** (-tī-pi), *n.* The relation of homotypes.

hom-o-zy-gote (hom-ǫ-zī′gōt or hō-mǫ-, or -zig′ōt), *n.* [See *homo-* and *zygote.*] In Mendelian phraseology, an animal or plant which breeds true to type. Cf. *heterozygote.*—**hom-o-zy′gous** (-zī′gus), *a.*

ho-mun-cu-lus (hǫ-mung′kṳ-lus), *n.*; pl. *-li* (-lī). [L., dim. of *homo*, man.] A little man; a dwarf; a manikin: as, "The same little grey *homunculus* . . . stood behind the counter" (Lever's "Harry Lorrequer," xii.).

hone[1] (hōn), *n.* [AS. *hān*, stone, rock, = Icel. *hein*, hone.] A whetstone of fine, compact texture, esp. one for sharpening razors.—**hone**[1], *v. t.*; *honed, honing.* To sharpen on or as on a hone.

hone[2] (hōn), *v. i.*; *honed, honing.* [F. *hogner*, OF. *hoignier*, *vuignier*, grumble, growl: cf. *whine.*] To grumble, whine, or moan; also, to pine or yearn (*for* or *after*). [Now prov. Eng., Sc., and southern U. S.]

hon-est (on′est), *a.* [OF. *honeste* (F. *honnête*), < L. *honestus*, honorable, respectable, worthy, virtuous, decent, < *honor*, *honos*, E. *honor*.] Honorable, or held in honor, as persons†; respectable or reputable (now chiefly Sc. and prov. Eng.); estimable or worthy (now usually with a patronizing force: as, these *honest* fellows); creditable, commendable, or seemly (obs. or archaic: as, "Provide things *honest* in the sight of all men," Rom. xii. 17); also, honorable in principles, intentions, and actions, upright, or without deceit or fraud, as persons; that does not lie, cheat, or steal; straightforward and fair in business or other dealings; showing uprightness, probity, straightforwardness, fairness, etc., as actions, methods, work, etc.; gained by fair means (as, *honest* profits; to turn an *honest* penny, see under *turn*, *v. t.*); also, truthful or sincere, as persons, utterances, feelings, etc.; frank, open, or without disguise (as, an *honest* rogue; *honest* opposition); genuine or unadulterated, as commodities; also, chaste or virtuous (said usually of a woman: archaic).—**hon′est-ly,** *adv.*—**hon-es-ty** (on′es-ti), *n.* [OF. *honeste*, < L. *honestas*.] Honorable standing†, respectability†, or credit†; also, seemliness† or decency†; also, the quality or fact of being honest; uprightness, probity, or integrity; freedom from deceit or fraud, esp. as shown in conduct or dealings; truthfulness, sincerity, or frankness; chastity, as of a woman (archaic); in *bot.*, a brassicaceous herb, *Lunaria annua*, with purple flowers and semitransparent, satiny pods (cf. *satin-pod*); also, any of various other plants.

hon-ey (hun′i). [AS. *hunig* = D. and G. *honig* = Icel. *hunang* = Sw. *honung* = Dan. *honning*, honey.] **I.** *n.*; pl. *-eys* (-iz). A sweet, viscid fluid elaborated by bees from the nectar collected from flowers, and stored in their nests or hives as food; the nectar of flowers; any of various similar products produced by insects or in other ways; fig., sweetness, or something sweet, delicious, or delightful (as, the *honey* of flattery); sweet one (a term of endearment). **II.** *a.* Of or like honey; sweet; dear.—**hon′ey,** *v.*; *honeyed, honeying.* **I.** *tr.* To sweeten with or as with honey; also, to talk sweetly to; flatter. **II.** *intr.* To become sweet or agreeable (as, "Discuss'd his tutor, rough to common men, But *honeying* at the whisper of a lord": Tennyson's "Princess," Prologue, 115); also, to talk sweetly; use endearments (see Shakspere's "Hamlet," iii. 4. 93).

hon-ey=bear (hun′i-bãr), *n.* The sloth-bear; also, the kinkajou.

hon-ey=bee (hun′i-bē), *n.* Any of various bees that produce honey, esp. the common bee, *Apis mellifica*.

hon-ey-comb (hun′i-kōm). [AS. *hunigcamb*.] **I.** *n.* A structure of wax containing rows of hexagonal cells, formed by bees for the reception of honey and of their eggs; also, something resembling this; a substance having cells like those of the bees' honeycomb; the reticulum of a ruminant. **II.** *a.* Having the structure or appearance of a honeycomb (as, the *honeycomb* coral, a coral of the genus *Favosites*; a *honeycomb* coil, a coil of wire wound in a lattice-like arrangement, used in wireless telegraphy and telephony for tuning, etc.); characterized by small depressions of surface (as, a *honeycomb* weave, used esp. for towels, quilts, etc.; a *honeycomb* pattern in needlework or knitting).—**hon′ey-comb,** *v. t.* To reduce to the condition or form of a honeycomb; pierce with many holes or cavities (as, a rock *honeycombed* with passages; "Each bastion was *honeycombed* with casemates and subterranean storehouses," Motley's "Dutch Republic," iii. 1); fig., to penetrate, in all parts, with harmful results (as, a city *honeycombed* with vice).

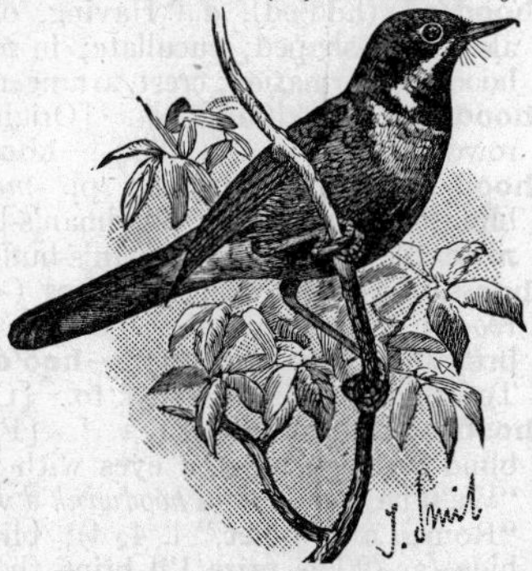
Honey-creeper (*Diglossa pectoralis*).

hon-ey=creep-er (hun′i-krē″pėr), *n.* Any of the small, usually brilliantly colored, tropical or semitropical American oscine birds of the family *Cœrebidæ*; a guitguit.

hon-ey-dew (hun′i-dū), *n.* A sweet substance which exudes from the leaves of certain plants in hot weather; also, a sweet substance, found on leaves and bark, secreted by aphids and other homopterous insects (cf. *aphis-sugar*).

hon-ey=eat-er (hun′i-ē″tėr), *n.* An eater of honey; esp., an animal given to eating honey; specif., any of the numerous oscine birds constituting the family *Meliphagidæ*, chiefly of Australasia, with a bill and tongue adapted for extracting the nectar from flowers; a honey-sucker.

hon-eyed (hun′id), *a.* Mixed or sweetened with honey (as, *honeyed* drinks); laden with honey (as, "the bee with *honied* thigh": Milton's "Il Penseroso," 142); abounding in, consisting of, or resembling honey; fig., sweet as honey; dulcet or mellifluous (as, *honeyed* tones); agreeable or ingratiating (as, *honeyed* words; "courtiers whispering *honied* nothings," M. Arnold's "Tristram and Iseult," ii.).

hon-ey=guide (hun′i-gīd), *n.* Any of various small, dull-colored non-passerine birds (genus *Indicator*, etc.) of Africa, Asia, and the East Indies, said to guide men or animals to places where honey may be found.

hon-ey-less (hun′i-les), *a.* Destitute of honey.

hon-ey=lo-cust (hun′i-lō″kust), *n.* A thorny North American cæsalpiniaceous tree, *Gleditsia triacanthos*, bearing pods with a sweet pulp.

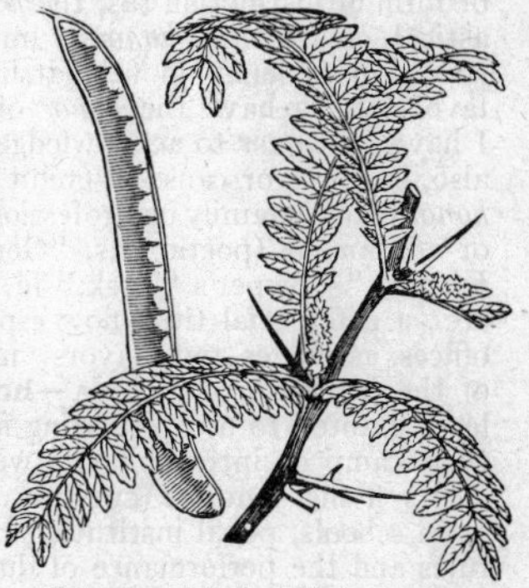
Branch and Pod of Honey-locust.

hon-ey=mes-quite (hun′i-mes-kēt′), *n.* The common mesquite, *Prosopis glandulosa*.

hon-ey-moon (hun′i-mön), *n.* [Said to have referred orig. to the moon which when at the full is nevertheless about to wane.] The first month (or more or less) after marriage, before love begins to calm or cool; also, a holiday spent by a newly married couple in traveling, visiting, or otherwise before settling down in their new life.—**hon′ey-moon,** *v. i.* To spend or have a honeymoon.—**hon′ey-moon″er,** *n.*

hon-ey=suck-er (hun′i-suk″ėr), *n.* Any of the honey-eaters (birds).

hon-ey-suck-le (hun′i-suk″l), *n.* [Cf. AS. *hunisūce*, privet, lit. 'honey-suck.'] Any of the upright or climbing shrubs constituting the caprifoliaceous genus *Lonicera*, some species of which are cultivated for their fragrant white, yellow, or red tubular flowers (cf. *woodbine*); also, any of various other fragrant or ornamental plants.—**hon′ey-suck″led,** *a.* Abounding in or fragrant with honeysuckle.

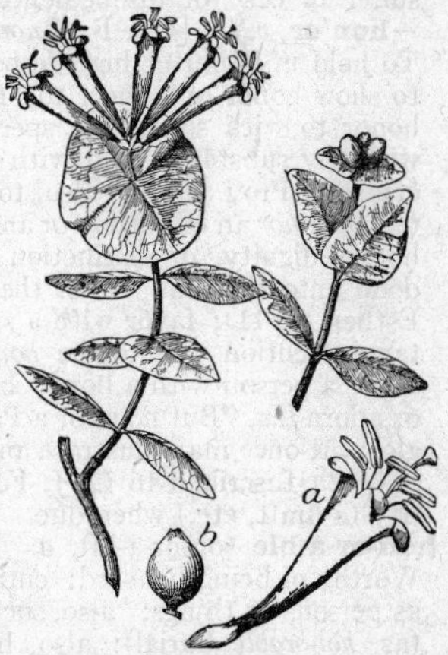

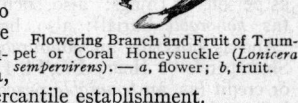

Flowering Branch and Fruit of Trumpet or Coral Honeysuckle (*Lonicera sempervirens*). — *a*, flower; *b*, fruit.

hong (hong), *n.* [Chinese.] In China, a succession of rooms or buildings forming a warehouse, factory, or the like; one of the foreign factories formerly maintained at Canton; also, formerly, a corporation of Chinese merchants at Canton who had the exclusive privilege of trading with the Europeans; also, in China, Japan, etc., any foreign mercantile establishment.

hon-ied (hun′id), *a.* See *honeyed*.

honk (hongk), *n.* [Imit.] The cry of the wild goose; any similar sound, as of an automobile horn.—**honk,** *v. i.* To emit a honk.—**honk′er,** *n.* That which honks; specif., the common wild goose, *Bernicla canadensis*, of North America.

hon-ky=tonk (hong′ki-tongk″), *n.* [Also *honkatonk*; origin uncertain.] A low drinking-resort. [Slang, U. S.]

hon-or (on′ọr), *n.* [ME. *onur, honour, honor,* < OF. *onur, onor, honur, honor* (F. *honneur*), < L. *honor, honos,* honor, repute, official dignity, mark of honor, ornament.] High respect, as for worth, merit, or rank (as, to be held in *honor*; to be worthy of *honor*); admiring or deferential respect; reverence; also, such respect manifested (as, to show or do one *honor*; to be received with *honor*); the manifestation of respect (as, a dinner in *honor* of a person); a particular manifestation or mark of respect; *pl.*, courtesies or civilities (as, to do the *honors* of a house to visitors); also, *sing.*, high public esteem, credit, exalted fame, or glory (as, to seek or win *honor*; a roll of *honor*; the field of *honor*, the battle-field); credit or reputation for becoming or worthy action (as, a choice greatly to one's *honor*; to assert a thing upon one's *honor*; to seek safety with *honor*); hence, personal title to high respect or esteem; high-minded character or principles, or fine sense of obligations as to conduct (as, a man of *honor*; to make it a point of *honor* to fulfil a promise; there is *honor* among thieves); chastity or purity in a woman; also, high rank, dignity, or distinction (as, "The burthen of an *honour* Unto which she was not born": Tennyson's "Lord of Burleigh"); a particular rank, dignity, or form of distinction (as, the *honor* of knighthood; ecclesiastical or political *honors*; university *honors*, gained by special proficiency in scholarship); a special privilege or favor (as, to have the *honor* of being presented at court; I have the *honor* to acknowledge the receipt of your letter); also, a source or cause of credit or distinction (as, to be an *honor* to one's family or profession); sometimes, a decoration or adornment (poetic: as, "Geranium boasts Her crimson *honours*," Cowper's "Task," iii. 578); also, with *his, your,* etc., a deferential title, now esp. for the holders of certain offices, as judges and mayors; in *whist* and *bridge*, any one of the highest trump-cards.—**honors of war,** *milit.*, privileges granted to a capitulating force, as of marching out of their camp or intrenchments with all their arms and with colors flying.—**honor system,** a system of management, as in schools, penal institutions, etc., whereby obedience to rules and the performance of duty generally are sought (as far as possible) by putting persons upon their honor, rather than by using special guards and constraints. See *to put a person upon his honor*, below.—**to do honor to,** to show honor or respect to; treat with honor; also, to do credit to; be a source of honor to.—**to put a person upon** (or **on**) **his honor,** to put him solely under the obligation imposed by his honor or credit, or leave him to do (or refrain from doing) a thing because his own honor requires it and would suffer in case of disobedience. See *honor system*, above. —**hon′or,** *v. t.* [OF. F. *honorer*, < L. *honorare*, < *honor*.] To hold in honor or high respect; reverence; revere; also, to show honor or respect to; treat with honor; show or do honor to with something specified (as, "*Honour* the Lord with thy substance, and with the firstfruits of all thine increase": Prov. iii. 9); also, to show a courteous regard for (as, to *honor* an invitation or an introduction); also, to confer honor, dignity, or distinction upon (as, "Thus shall it be done unto the man whom the king delighteth to *honour*": Esther, vi. 11); favor with a specified honor or complimentary attention (as, to be *honored* with a royal visit; to *honor* a person with a bow); be a source of honor to, grace, or adorn (as, "But now for a Patron, whose name and whose glory At once may illustrate and *honour* my story": Burns's "Sketch Inscribed to C. J. Fox"); in *com.*, to accept and pay (a draft, etc.) when due.

hon-or-a-ble (on′ọr-ạ-bl), *a.* [OF. F., < L. *honorabilis*.] Worthy of being honored; entitled to honor or high respect, as persons or things; also, such as to show honor or respect (as, *honorable* burial); also, bringing honor or credit (as, "And is not this an *honourable* spoil? A gallant prize?" Shakspere's "1 Henry IV.," i. 1. 74); consistent with honor or credit (as, an *honorable* peace); also, characterized by or in accordance with principles of honor (as, an *honorable* man; *honorable* conduct or intentions); scrupulously upright, or showing a fine regard for obligations as to conduct; also, of high rank, dignity, or distinction; noble, illustrious, or distinguished; specif., a title of honor or distinction prefixed to the names of certain officials and others (as, in Great Britain, the sons and daughters of peers below the rank of marquis).—**hon′or-a-ble-ness,** *n.*—**hon′or-a-bly,** *adv.*

hon-o-ra-ri-um (on-ọ-rā′ri-um), *n.*; pl. *-riums* or *-ria* (-ri-ạ̈). [L., prop. neut. of *honorarius*, E. *honorary*.] An honorary reward, as in recognition of professional services on which no price may be set; hence, a fee for services rendered, esp. by a professional person.

hon-o-ra-ry (on′ọ-rạ̄-ri), *a.* [L. *honorarius*, < *honor*, E. *honor, n.*] Given, made, or serving as a token of honor (as, an *honorary* gift or reward); specif., given or intended for honor only (as, an *honorary* title or position, one not accompanied with the usual duties, privileges, emoluments, etc.; an *honorary* degree, a complimentary degree, as from a university; an *honorary* monument, a cenotaph); also, holding a title or position conferred for honor only (as, an *honorary* vice-president; an *honorary* member of a society); sometimes, holding the title but serving without compensation or without the full powers or obligations of the office (as, an *honorary* secretary or treasurer); also, of an obligation, depending on one's honor for fulfilment, but not enforceable otherwise.

hon-or-er (on′ọr-ėr), *n.* One who honors.

hon-o-rif-ic (on-ọ-rif′ik). [L. *honorificus*: see *honor, n.*, and *-fic*.] **I.** *a.* Doing or conferring honor; of words, etc., expressing respect or deference. **II.** *n.* An honorific word or phrase, as in Chinese and Japanese.

hon-or-less (on′ọr-les), *a.* Destitute or devoid of honor.

hon′our, hon′our-a-ble, hon′our-er, hon′our-less. British preferred forms of *honor*, etc.

hon-véd (hon′vād), *n.* [Hung.] The landwehr of Hungary.

hoo (hö), *interj.* An exclamation used to express excitement, delight, contempt, etc.; also, an imitation of an owl's cry, the wind, etc.

hooch (höch), *n.* [Short for *hoochinoo*, orig. the name (for *Hutsnuwu*, lit. 'grizzly bear fort') of an Indian tribe on Admiralty Island, Alaska, who made liquor.] Illicitly distilled liquor; smuggled liquor; surreptitiously sold liquor; alcoholic beverages in general. [Slang.]

hood (hu̇d), *n.* [AS. *hōd*, hood, = D. *hoed* = G. *hut*, hat; akin to E. *hat*.] A soft or flexible covering for the head and neck, either separate or attached to a cloak or the like; also, something resembling or suggesting this, as the cover of a carriage, the bonnet of an automobile, a hood-shaped petal or sepal, etc.; in *falconry*, a cover for the entire head of a hawk, used to blind the hawk when not in pursuit of game.—**hood,** *v. t.* To cover with or as with a hood; furnish with a hood.

Hoods. — *A*, hood of the middle ages; *B*, hood like *A*, but worn by fitting the face-opening around the head and twisting the cape into a wreath; *C*, hawk's hood with long tail; *D*, hawk's hood without the tail.

-hood. [ME. *-hode, -hod,* < AS. *-hād*, < *hād*, rank, condition, character: cf. *-head*.] A suffix of nouns denoting state, condition, character, nature, etc., or a body of persons of a particular character or class, as in *brotherhood, childhood, fatherhood, godhood, likelihood, priesthood, sisterhood*.

hood-ed (hu̇d′ed), *a.* Having, or covered with, a hood; also, hood-shaped; cucullate; in *zoöl.*, having on the head a hood-like formation, crest, arrangement of colors, or the like.

hood-lum (höd′lum), *n.* [Origin uncertain.] A young rowdy; a ruffian. [Colloq.]—**hood′lum-ism,** *n.*

hood-man (hu̇d′mạn), *n.*; pl. *-men.* A hooded man; the blindfolded person in blindman's-buff. [Archaic.]—**hood′-man=blind′,** *n.* Blindman's-buff. [Archaic.]

hoo-doo (hö′dö), *n.*; pl. *-doos* (-döz). [Appar. a var. of *voodoo*.] Voodoo; also (colloq.), a person or thing that brings bad luck; bad luck.—**hoo′doo,** *v. t.*; *-dooed, -dooing.* To bring or cause bad luck to. [Colloq.]

hood-wink (hu̇d′wingk), *v. t.* [From *hood* + *wink*.] To blind by covering the eyes with a hood or otherwise (as, "We'll have no Cupid *hoodwink'd* with a scarf": Shakspere's "Romeo and Juliet," i. 4. 4); blindfold; also, to cover or hide (as, "The prize I'll bring thee to Shall *hoodwink* this

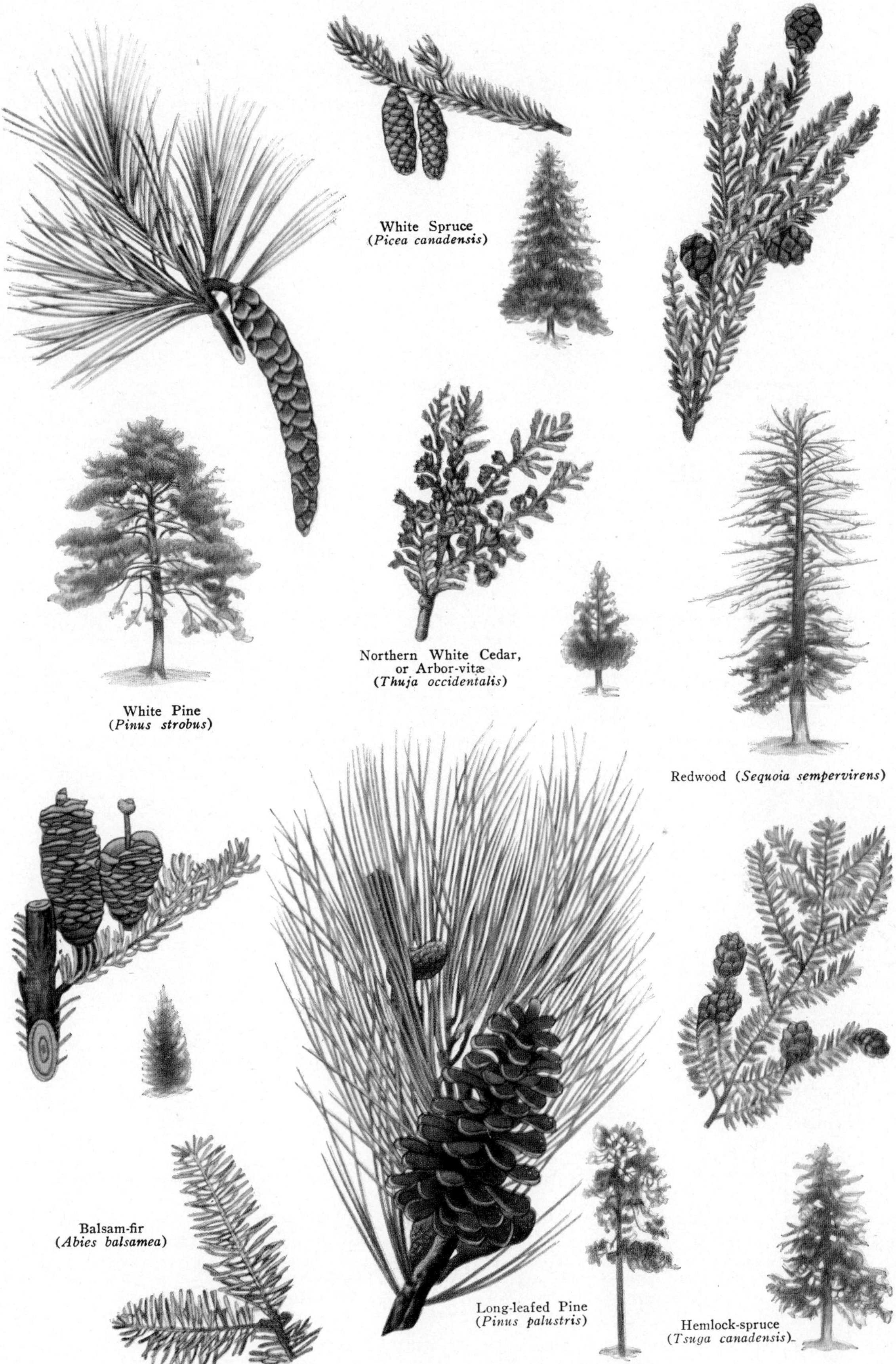

Taken from the collection of Romeyn B. Hough, B. A.

EVERGREENS OF NORTH AMERICA

mischance": Shakspere's "Tempest," iv. 1. 206); also, to blind mentally, deceive, or humbug (as, "Some to the fascination of a name Surrender judgment, *hood-wink'd*": Cowper's "Task," vi. 102).—**hood'wink''er,** *n.*

hoof (höf), *n.*; pl. *hoofs* (höfs), also *hooves* (hövz). [AS. *hōf* = D. *hoef* = G. *huf* = Icel. *hōfr*, hoof.] The horny covering protecting the ends of the digits or incasing the foot in certain animals, as the ox, horse, etc. (as, the cleft or cloven *hoof* of the ox and other ruminants, each half of which is a complete hoof for its own digit; the solid *hoof* of the horse, ass, etc.; a false *hoof*, the hoof of a functionless digit, on which an animal does not walk, as one of a pair behind and above the other hoofs of the ox, deer, pig, etc.); also, a hoofed animal (as, "Our cattle also shall go with us; there shall not an *hoof* be left behind": Ex. x. 26); sometimes, the human foot (humorous); in *geom.*, an ungula.—**on the hoof,** alive; not butchered: used of live stock.—**hoof,** *v. i.* To go on foot; walk. [Colloq.]—**hoof'=and=mouth' disease'.** Same as *foot-and-mouth disease.*—**hoof'=bound,** *a.* Having a dry and contracted hoof, causing lameness.—**hoofed,** *a.* Having hoofs; ungulate.—**hoof'let,** *n.* A small hoof terminating a rudimentary digit, as one of the pair behind and above the regular hoofs of the deer, pig, etc.

hook (hůk), *n.* [AS. *hōc*, hook, = D. *hoek*, hook, angle, corner, point of land: cf. *heckle.*] A curved or angular piece of metal or other firm substance, adapted to catch, hold, pull, or sustain something; esp., a fish-hook; also, a curved instrument for cutting or lopping, as a sickle; also, something curved or bent like a hook, as a curved spit of land (as, the *Hook* of Holland, or Sandy *Hook*), a recurved and pointed organ or appendage of an animal or plant, a curved or bent mark or symbol, or a stroke or line attached to the stem of eighth-notes, sixteenth-notes, etc.; a sharp curve or angle in the length or course of anything; also, an act of hooking, as in cricket or golf; a swinging stroke or blow, as in boxing.—**by hook or by crook,** by one means or another; by any means, fair or foul.—**hook and eye,** a fastening for garments, etc., consisting of a hook and an eye or loop into which the hook fits, both commonly of wire.—**hook=and=ladder truck,** a vehicle equipped with a ladder or ladders, hooked instruments, axes, etc., and manned by its own crew ('hook-and-ladder company'), employed in fire departments for gaining access to and making rescues from burning buildings.—**on one's own hook,** on one's own account or responsibility; by or for one's self. [Colloq.]—**hook,** *v.* **I.** *tr.* To make hook-shaped; crook; also, to catch, seize, fasten, or catch hold of and draw, with or as with a hook; esp., to catch (fish) with a fish-hook; fig., to catch or secure by or as by artifice; also, to seize by stealth, pilfer, or steal (colloq.); also, to catch on the horns, or attack with the horns, as a horned animal does; also, to strike with a swinging stroke, as in boxing; in *cricket* and *golf*, same as *pull*, *v. t.* **II.** *intr.* To curve or bend like a hook; also, to move with a sudden turn (as, "always *hooking* about on mysterious voyages": Irving's "Tales of a Traveler," iv. 2); depart, or make off (slang); also, to become attached or fastened by or as by a hook; join (*on*).

hook-a, hook-ah (hůk'ạ), *n.* [Ar. *huqqah*, box, vase, pipe for smoking.] A smoking-pipe with a long, flexible tube by which the smoke is drawn through a vase of water and cooled.

Hooka.

hooked (hůkt or hůk'ed), *a.* Bent like a hook; hook-shaped; also, furnished with a hook or hooks; also, made with a hook (as, a *hooked* rug: see below).—**hooked rug,** a kind of hand-made rug made by drawing yarn or some substitute, by means of a hook, or hooked implement, through a foundation of canvas, burlap, or the like, a pattern being formed according to the combination of colors used.—**hook'ed-ness,** *n.*

hook-er[1] (hůk'ėr), *n.* One who or that which hooks; a pilferer or thief (colloq.).

hook-er[2] (hůk'ėr), *n.* [D. *hoeker*, < *hoek*: see *hook.*] A two-masted Dutch vessel; also, a kind of small fishing smack; also, any old-fashioned or clumsy vessel; in general, a vessel (used familiarly or depreciatively: as, "A long pull, a strong pull, and warp the *hooker* out," Masefield's "Valediction").

hook=mon-ey (hůk'mun''i), *n.* Money consisting of pieces of silver in the form of fish-hooks: formerly used in Ceylon, Persia, etc.

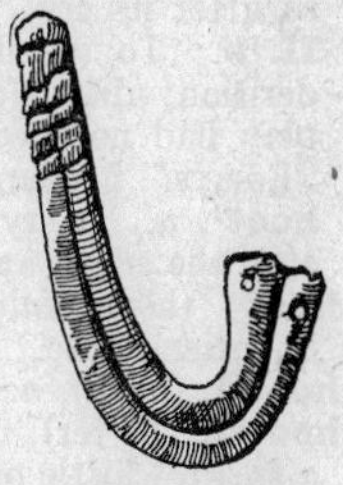

Hook-money.—British Museum.

hook=nose (hůk'nōz), *n.* An aquiline nose.—**hook'=nosed,** *a.*

hook=rug (hůk'rug'), *n.* A hooked rug. See under *hooked.*

hook=up (hůk'up), *n.* In *wireless teleg.* and *teleph.*, a diagram of a radio receiving or transmitting apparatus, showing the arrangement and connection of the different elements.

hook-worm (hůk'wėrm), *n.* Any of certain blood-sucking nematode worms, as *Ancylostoma duodenale* and *Uncinaria americana*, with hooks about the mouth, parasitic in the intestine of man and certain animals and causing a disease characterized esp. by severe anemia ('hookworm disease,' ancylostomiasis, or uncinariasis).

hook-y[1] (hůk'i), *a.* Full of hooks; also, hook-shaped.

hook-y[2] (hůk'i), *n.* [See *hook*, *v. i.*] A word used in the phrase *to play hooky*, to run away or be absent, as a truant from school.

hoo-li-gan (hö'li-gạn). [Prob. from a personal name.] **I.** *n.* A young street ruffian; a hoodlum. [Slang, orig. Eng.] **II.** *a.* Pertaining to, characteristic of, or having the character of hooligans: as, *hooligan* performances; "what we should call nowadays a *hooligan* class . . . ready to turn out to fight and loot on either side" (H. G. Wells's "Outline of History," xxxvii. § 12). [Slang, orig. Eng.]—**hoo'li-gan-ism,** *n.*

hoop[1] (höp), *n.* [Late AS. *hōp* = OFries. *hōp* = D. *hoep*, hoop.] A circular band or ring of metal, wood, or other stiff material; esp., such a band to hold together the staves of a cask, tub, etc.; also, a large ring of iron or wood for a child to trundle; also, a circular band of stiff material used to expand a woman's skirt (as, "the petticoat . . . stiff with *hoops*, and arm'd with ribs of whale": Pope's "Rape of the Lock," ii. 120); hence, a hoop-skirt; also, a finger-ring; also, something resembling a hoop; a hoop-like or ring-like structure; also, one of the iron arches used in croquet.—**hoop**[1], *v. t.* To bind or fasten with a hoop or hoops; hence, to encircle; embrace.

hoop[2] (höp), *v.* and *n.* Same as *whoop.*

hooped (höpt), *a.* Having a hoop or hoops; expanded with hoops, as a woman's skirt; also, wearing a hoop-skirt.

hoop-er[1] (hö'pėr), *n.* One who hoops casks, etc.; a cooper.

hoop-er[2] (hö'pėr), *n.* A common European swan. See *whooper.*

hoop-ing=cough (hö'ping-kôf), *n.* See *whooping-cough.*

hoo-poe (hö'pö), *n.* [Earlier *hoop*, < F. *huppe*, < L. *upupa*, hoopoe; so called from its cry.] Any of the old-world non-passerine birds constituting the family *Upupidæ*, esp. *Upupa epops*, a common species with a semicircular erectile crest.

Hoopoe (*Upupa epops*).

hoop=skirt (höp'skėrt'), *n.* A skirt-like combination of flexible hoops connected by tapes, worn to expand a woman's skirt.

hoose-gow, hoos-gow (hös-gou′), *n.* [Sp. *juzgado*, tribunal, court of justice, in Mexico a jail.] A jail or lockup. [Slang, orig. southwestern U. S.]

Hoo-sier (hö′zhėr), *n.* [Origin obscure.] An inhabitant of Indiana: a nickname.

hoot[1] (höt), *v.* [ME. *huten, hoten*; prob. imit.] **I.** *intr.* To cry out or shout, esp. in disapproval or derision (as, "A troop of strange children ran at his heels, *hooting* after him": Irving's "Sketch-Book," Rip Van Winkle); also, of an owl, to utter its cry; hence, to utter or make a similar sound. **II.** *tr.* To assail with cries or shouts of disapproval or derision; drive (*out, away, off*, etc.) by hooting (as, "His play had not been *hooted* from the boards": Macaulay's "Essays," Madame d'Arblay); also, to express in hoots.—**hoot**[1], *n.* A cry or shout, esp. of disapproval or derision; also, the cry of an owl; hence, any similar sound.

hoot[2] (höt), *interj.* An exclamation of dissatisfaction, impatience, etc. [Chiefly Sc.]

hootch (höch), *n.* See *hooch.*

hoot-er (hö′tėr), *n.* One who or that which hoots; an owl; a steam-whistle or siren; an automobile horn.

Hoo-ver-ize (hö′vėr-īz), *v.* [From Herbert C. *Hoover*, U. S. food administrator 1917–19.] **I.** *tr.* To use economically, as food; economize. [Colloq.] **II.** *intr.* To be economical or sparing in the use of food, etc.; practise economy. [Colloq.]—**Hoo′ver-ism,** *n.*

hop[1] (hop), *v.*; *hopped, hopping.* [AS. *hoppian* = Icel. and Sw. *hoppa* = Dan. *hoppe* = G. *hopfen*, hop: cf. *hobble.*] **I.** *intr.* To leap; move by a short leap, or by a succession of such leaps; specif., to move by leaps with both or all the feet at once, as a bird, frog, etc.; of a person, to spring or leap on one foot; also, to dance (now colloq.); also, to limp (as, "the limping smith . . . *hopping* here and there": Dryden's tr. Homer's "Iliad," i. 769); also (colloq.), of an aëroplane, etc., to leave the ground in beginning a flight or ascent (often with *off*); make a flight or trip. **II.** *tr.* To hop about (a place), off (something elevated), or over (a fence, ditch, etc.) (colloq.); of an aëroplane, etc., to cross by a flight or trip (colloq.: as, to *hop* the Atlantic); also, to cause to hop.—**hop**[1], *n.* An act of hopping; a short leap; esp., a spring or leap on one foot; also, a dance, or dancing-party (colloq.: as, "The vulgar . . . now thrust themselves into all assemblies, from a ridotto at St. James's to a *hop* at Rotherhithe," Smollett's "Humphry Clinker," June 5); also, a flight or trip of an aëroplane, etc. (colloq.).

hop[2] (hop), *n.* [MD. *hoppe* (D. *hop*) = LG. *hoppe* = G. *hopfen*, the hop.] A twining moraceous plant, *Humulus lupulus*, the male flowers of which grow in panicles, and the female in cones or strobiles; *pl.*, the dried ripe cones of the female plant, used in brewing, medicine, etc.; also, *sing.*, opium (slang).—**hop**[2], *v.*; *hopped, hopping.* **I.** *tr.* To treat or flavor with hops. **II.** *intr.* To pick or gather hops.—**hop′bine** (-bīn), *n.* The twining stem of the hop.—**hop′=clo″ver,** *n.* A trefoil, *Trifolium procumbens*, whose yellow flowers when withered resemble the strobiles of the hop; also, any of certain related species.

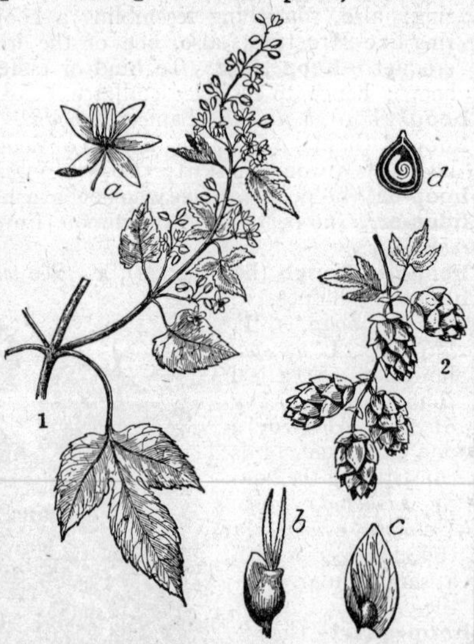

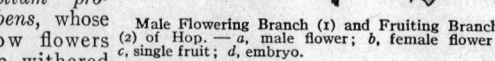

Male Flowering Branch (1) and Fruiting Branch (2) of Hop. — *a*, male flower; *b*, female flower; *c*, single fruit; *d*, embryo.

hope[1] (hōp), *n.* [ME. *hope*: cf. AS. *fenhop, mōrhop*, piece of land in a fen or marsh, also Icel. *hōp*, bay, inlet.] A small inclosed valley; a hollow among hills; also, a small bay, inlet, or haven. [Sc. and prov. Eng., or in place-names.]

hope[2] (hōp), *n.* [D. *hoop*, heap, lot, troop.] See *forlorn hope*, under *forlorn.*

hope[3] (hōp), *v.*; *hoped, hoping.* [AS. *hopian* = MLG. and D. *hopen* = G. *hoffen*, hope.] **I.** *intr.* To entertain an expectation of something desired (as, to *hope* for brighter days); also, to trust or rely, esp. confidently (archaic: as, "*Hope* thou in God," Ps. xlii. 5). **II.** *tr.* To hope for, or look forward to with desire and more or less confidence (as, this is more than we dared to *hope*; "Within what space *Hopest* thou my cure?" Shakspere's "All's Well," ii. 1. 163); expect with desire, or desire with expectation (with a clause or an infinitive: as, we *hope* that you will consent; we *hope* to hear from you soon); hence, to trust as to the actual fact or truth in a case (with a clause: as, I *hope* that you are satisfied; I *hope* I know what I'm talking about).—**hope**[3], *n.* [AS. *hopa.*] Expectation of something desired, or desire accompanied by expectation; a particular instance of such expectation or desire (as, a *hope* of success; swayed by *hopes* and fears); hence, ground for expecting something desired (as, there is no *hope* of his recovery); promising character, or promise (as, a land of *hope*); a person or thing that expectations are centered in (as, he is the *hope* of the family; this measure is our chief *hope*); that which is hoped for (as, "Lavinia is thine elder brother's *hope*": Shakspere's "Titus Andronicus," ii. 1. 74); also, confidence or trust (archaic: as, "Happy is he . . . whose *hope* is in the Lord his God," Ps. cxlvi. 5); that in which one puts his confidence or trust (archaic: as, "Blessed is the man . . . whose *hope* the Lord is," Jer. xvii. 7).—**hope′=chest,** *n.* A chest or the like in which a young unmarried woman, esp. one not yet engaged to be married, collects articles which may be of use to her in a home of her own in the event of her future marriage.—**hope′ful. I.** *a.* Full of hope, as a person, the mood, disposition, etc.; expressing or showing hope, as words, looks, etc.; also, inspiring or affording hope, as prospects, circumstances, etc.; promising, as a person, esp. a young person (often used humorously or ironically). **II.** *n.*; pl. *-fuls.* A hopeful or promising young person: commonly humorous or ironical.—**hope′ful-ly,** *adv.*—**hope′ful-ness,** *n.*—**hope′less,** *a.* Without hope; despairing; also, affording no hope; despaired of; desperate.—**hope′less-ly,** *adv.*—**hope′less-ness,** *n.*—**hop-er** (hō′pėr), *n.*—**hop′ing-ly,** *adv.*

hop-lite (hop′līt), *n.* [Gr. **ὁπλίτης, < ὅπλον,** tool, implement, pl. arms.] A heavy-armed foot-soldier of ancient Greece.

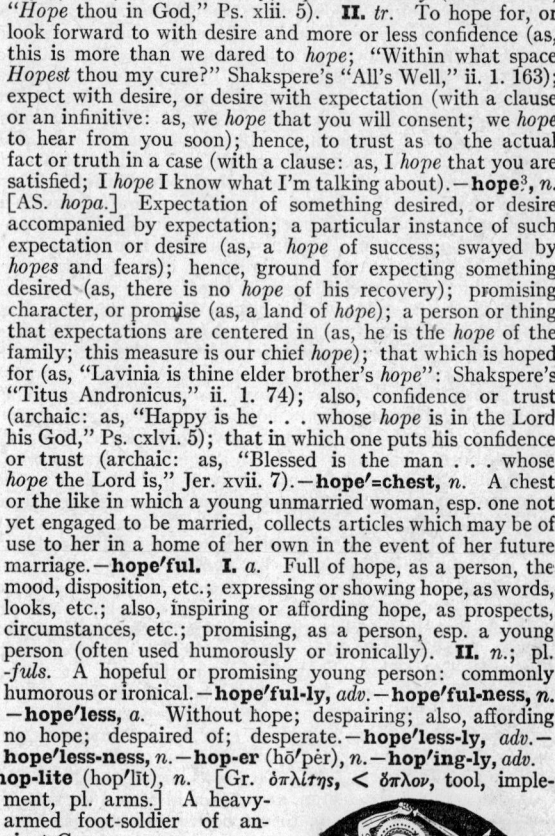

Hoplite. — From a cup, 5th century B.C.

hop=off (hop′ôf), *n.* Of an aëroplane, etc., the act of leaving the ground in beginning a flight or ascent. [Colloq.]

hop=o′=my=thumb (hop′ǫ-mī-thum″), *n.* [Orig. *hop on* (or *upon*) *my thumb.*] A diminutive person; a dwarf.

hop-per[1] (hop′ėr), *n.* One who or that which hops; specif., any of various saltatorial larvæ or insects, as a maggot found in cheese, a grasshopper, etc.; also, a receiver, usually shaped like an inverted cone, for feeding material to a mill, machine, etc.; also, something shaped like or provided with such a receiver, as a car for carrying coal, etc., or a barge for receiving and depositing the mud from a dredging-machine; also, in the action of a pianoforte, a part which raises a hammer.

hop-per[2] (hop′ėr), *n.* A hop-picker.

hop-ple (hop′l), *v. t.*; *-pled, -pling.* [Cf. *hop*[1] and *hobble.*] To fasten together the legs of (a horse or other animal) to prevent leaping or straying; hobble; hence, to fetter.—**hop′ple,** *n.* A hobble for a horse, etc.; hence, a fetter.

hop=sack-ing (hop′sak′ing), *n.* A coarse sacking or bagging used for hops; also, a woolen fabric of loose texture, woven of heavy thread, used for clothing.

hop=scotch (hop′skoch′), *n.* [See *scotch*[1], *n.*] A children's game in which the player, while hopping on one foot, with that foot drives a flat stone or the like from one compartment to another of an oblong figure traced on the ground, neither the stone nor the foot being allowed to rest on a line (scotch).

hop=toad (hop′tōd), *n.* A toad. [Colloq.]

hop=tree (hop′trē), *n.* A North American rutaceous shrub or small tree, *Ptelea trifoliata*, with trifoliolate leaves, cymes of small greenish-white flowers, and a bitter winged fruit (samara) said to be used as a substitute for hops.

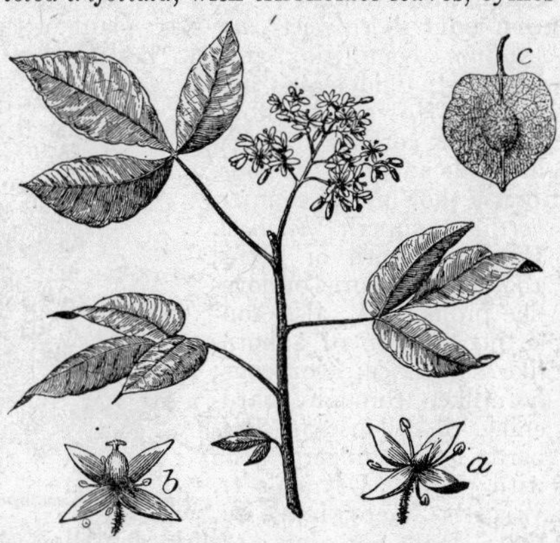

Hop-tree. — *a*, male flower; *b*, female flower; *c*, fruit.

hop=tre-foil (hop′trē″foil), *n.* Hop-clover; also, black medic.

Ho-ræ (hō′rē), *n. pl.* [L., < Gr. Ὧραι, pl.] In *class. myth.*, the Hours.

ho-ral (hō′ra̤l), *a.* [LL. *horalis*, < L. *hora*, E. *hour*.] Pertaining to an hour or hours; hourly.

ho-ra-ry (hō′ra̤-ri), *a.* [ML. *horarius*, < L. *hora*, E. *hour*.] Pertaining to an hour; indicating the hours; also, occurring every hour; hourly.

horde (hōrd), *n.* [F. *horde* = G. *horde* = Pol. *horda*, < Turki *ordā*, *ordū*, *urdū*, camp: cf. *Urdu*.] A tribe or troop of Asiatic nomads; hence, some other nomadic group; also, a great company or multitude (often in disparagement: as, "Society is now one polish'd *horde*, Form'd of two mighty tribes, the Bores and Bored," Byron's "Don Juan," xiii. 95).—**horde**, *v. i.*; *horded*, *hording*. To gather in a horde: as, "My fathers' house shall never be a cave For wolves to *horde* and howl in" (Byron's "Sardanapalus," v. 1).

hore′hound, *n.* See *hoarhound*.

ho-ri-zon (hō̤-rī′zo̤n), *n.* [OF. *orizon* (F. *horizon*), < L. *horizon*, < Gr. ὁρίζων, bounding circle, horizon, prop. ppr. of ὁρίζειν, bound, < ὅρος, boundary, limit.] The line or circle which forms the apparent boundary between earth and sky ('apparent horizon' or 'visible horizon'); fig., the limit or range of perception, knowledge, or the like; in *astron.*, the plane which is tangent to the earth at the place of the observer and extends to the celestial sphere ('sensible horizon'); also, the great circle of the celestial sphere whose plane is parallel to the sensible horizon of a particular place and passes through the center of the earth, or the plane itself ('astronomical horizon,' 'celestial horizon,' or 'rational horizon'); in *geol.*, a stratum or group of strata differing, as in fossils, from the deposits above or below.—**artificial horizon**, a level reflector, as the surface of mercury in a dish, used in determining the altitudes of stars, etc.—**horizon blue**, a light grayish blue: used during the World War for French military uniforms.—**ho-ri′zon-less**, *a.* Without a perceptible horizon; apparently boundless.

hor-i-zon-tal (hor-i-zon′ta̤l). [= F. *horizontal*, < L. *horizon*, E. *horizon*.] **I.** *a.* Of or pertaining to the horizon; situated on or occurring at the horizon; also, parallel to the plane of the horizon; at right angles to the vertical; neither vertical nor inclined; measured or contained in a plane parallel to the horizon (as, a *horizontal* distance); specif., of various mechanical contrivances, etc., placed, or acting or working, wholly or with respect to the main parts, in a plane parallel to the horizon. **II.** *n.* A horizontal line, plane, or the like; also, horizontal position.—**hor″i-zon-tal′i-ty** (-tal′i-ti), **hor-i-zon′tal-ness**, *n.*—**hor-i-zon′tal-ly**, *adv.*

hor-mone (hôr′mōn), *n.* [Gr. ὁρμῶν, ppr. of ὁρμᾶν, set in motion, < ὁρμή, impulse, start.] In *physiol.*, any of various substances which are formed in certain organs and which produce functional activity in other organs when transported to them by the blood.—**hor-mo-no-poi-et-ic** (hôr″mo̤-no̤-poi-et′ik), *a.* [+ Gr. ποιεῖν, make.] In *physiol.*, producing hormones, as certain organs; pertaining to the production of hormones.

horn (hôrn), *n.* [AS. *horn* = OHG. G. *horn* = Icel. *horn* = Goth. *haurn*, horn; akin to L. *cornu* and Gr. κέρας, horn.] A hard, projecting, often curved and pointed, hollow and permanent growth (usually one of a pair, a right and a left) on the head of certain mammals, as cattle, sheep, goats, antelopes, etc. ('true horn'); each of the pair of solid, deciduous, usually branched, bony growths, or antlers, on the head of a deer; also, some similar growth, as the tusk of a narwhal; also, a growth or part like a horn of an animal attributed to deities, demons, etc. (as, "the devil's *horn*": Shakspere's "Measure for Measure," ii. 4. 16); an imaginary projection on the brow of a cuckold; also, a process projecting from the head of an animal and suggestive of a horn, as a feeler, tentacle, crest, etc. (as, "The snail, whose tender *horns* being hit, Shrinks backward in his shelly cave": Shakspere's "Venus and Adonis," 1033); also, a symbol of power, might, etc., as in the Bible; also, something formed from or resembling the hollow horn of an animal, as a powder-horn, a drinking-vessel, etc.; hence, a drink of liquor; esp., an instrument for producing sound or music by blowing, orig. formed from the hollow horn of an animal but now usually made of brass or other metal or material, and occurring in various forms more or less resembling the horn of an animal (as, a hunting-*horn*; a coaching-*horn*); specif., an orchestral metallic wind-instrument of the trumpet class, consisting of a long, coiled tube terminating in a flaring bell, and producing mellow tones (called more fully *French horn*); also, any horn-like projection or extremity; a projection or angle at the corner of an altar; one of the extremities of the moon when waxing or waning, and hence of any crescent-shaped object (as, "The moon Wears a wan circle round her blunted *horns*": Thomson's "Seasons," Winter, 125); the beak of an anvil; any of certain short, arm-like levers on an aëroplane; also, each of the alternatives of a dilemma; also, the substance of which true horns are composed; any similar substance, as that of hoofs, nails, corns, etc.; also, an article made of horn, as a thimble, a spoon, or a shoe-horn.—**English horn** [tr. F. *cor anglais*], the tenor oboe (wooden musical wind-instrument).—**French horn.** See *horn*, *n.*—**horn of plenty**, the cornucopia.—**horn**, *v.* **I.** *tr.* To furnish with horns; also, to cuckold†; also, to butt or gore with the horns; also, to provide, fit, etc., with horn. **II.** *intr.* To thrust one's self obtrusively (*in* or *into*): as, to *horn* in with a remark; to *horn* into an affair. [Slang, orig. western U. S.]

Horns. — 1, coaching-horn; 2, French or orchestral horn; 3, 4, military bugles, with and without keys; 5, hunting-horn.

horn-beam (hôrn′bēm), *n.* Any of the shrubs or small trees constituting the betulaceous genus *Carpinus*, with

Rhinoceros Hornbill (*Buceros rhinoceros*).

a heavy, hard wood, as the old-world species *C. betulus*, or the American species *C. caroliniana* ('American hornbeam,' or ironwood).

horn-bill (hôrn′bil), *n.* Any of the large non-passerine birds constituting the family *Bucerotidæ*, characterized by a very large bill surmounted by a horny protuberance, sometimes of enormous size. See cut on preceding page.

Hornbook.

horn-blende (hôrn′blend), *n.* [G.] Amphibole; esp., any of the common black or dark-colored aluminous varieties of amphibole.—**horn-blen′dic** (-blen′dik), *a.*

horn-book (hôrn′bu̇k), *n.* A leaf or page containing the alphabet, etc., covered with a sheet of transparent horn and fixed in a frame with a handle, formerly used in teaching children to read (see Shakspere's "Love's Labour's Lost," v. 1. 49); hence, a primer, or book of rudiments.

Great Horned Owl of North America (*Bubo virginianus*).

horned (hôrnd), *a.* Having a horn or horns; also, provided or fitted with horn.—**horned frog,** any of various South American frogs (genus *Ceratophrys*) with a horn-like process over the eye; also, a horned toad.—**horned owl,** any of various owls (genus *Bubo*, etc.) with horn-like tufts of feathers on the head.—**horned pout,** a horn-pout.—**horned toad,** any of various small, harmless lizards (genera *Phrynosoma* and *Anota*) of western North America, with horn-like spines on the head.—**horned viper.** See *viper*.

horn-er (hôr′nėr), *n.* One who horns; esp., one who works or deals in horn; also, one who blows or plays a horn.

hor-net (hôr′net), *n.* [AS. *hyrnetu* = MLG. *hornte* = OHG. *hornuz*, G. *hornisse*, hornet.] A large, strong social wasp having an exceptionally severe sting, esp. *Vespa crabro* ('European hornet') or *V. maculata* ('American hornet' or 'white-faced hornet').

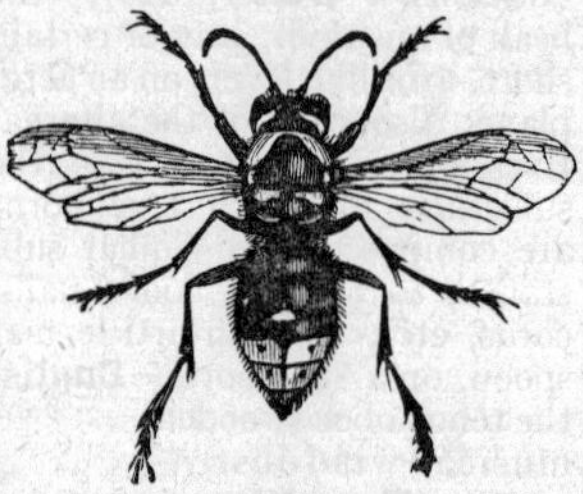

American Hornet (*Vespa maculata*), natural size.

horn-i-ness (hôr′ni-nes), *n.* Horny quality.

horn-ing (hôr′ning), *n.* The act of one who or that which horns; also, a charivari, or mock serenade with tin horns and other discordant instruments (U. S.); also, in *Sc. law*, the act of proclaiming a person a rebel by blowing three blasts on a horn.

horn-ist (hôr′nist), *n.* One who plays a horn, esp. the French horn.

hor-ni-to (hôr-nē′tō, Sp. ôr-nē′tō), *n.*; pl. *-tos* (-tōz, Sp. -tōs). [Sp., dim. of *horno*, < L. *furnus*, oven.] In *geol.*, a low oven-shaped mound, common in the volcanic districts of South America, etc., usually emitting hot smoke and vapors from its sides and summit.

horn-less (hôrn′les), *a.* Having no horns, as some cattle.—**horn′less-ness,** *n.*

horn=mad (hôrn′mad′), *a.* Enraged enough to gore with the horns, as a bull; hence, raging mad; furious; stark mad.

horn-pipe (hôrn′pīp), *n.* An old kind of musical wind-instrument; also, a lively dance (orig. to hornpipe music), usually performed by a single person, and popular among sailors; a piece of music for, or in the style of, such a dance.

horn=pout (hôrn′pout), *n.* Any of certain fresh-water catfishes. See *pout*[1].

horn=sil-ver (hôrn′sil′vėr), *n.* Native chloride of silver.

horn-stone (hôrn′stōn), *n.* A variety of quartz resembling flint.

horn-tail (hôrn′tāl), *n.* Any of various hymenopterous insects of the genus *Tremex*, etc.: so called from the horn-like protuberance at the end of the abdomen.

horn=worm (hôrn′wėrm), *n.* Any of various sphingid larvæ, as the tobacco-worms, characterized by a horn-like caudal projection.

horn-wort (hôrn′wėrt), *n.* Any plant of the genus *Ceratophyllum*, comprising aquatic herbs with whorled, finely dissected, rigid leaves and minute flowers without calyx or corolla, common in ponds and slow streams.

Hornwort (*Ceratophyllum demersum*).

horn-y (hôr′ni), *a.*; compar. *hornier*, superl. *horniest*. Having a horn or horns; abounding in horns or horn-like projections; also, consisting of horn or a horn-like substance; corneous; horn-like through hardening, or callous (as, "His hard *horny* fingers ache with pain": Dryden's tr. Virgil's "Georgics," iv. 172); more or less translucent like horn.—**horn′y=hand′ed,** *a.* Having the hands hardened, as by labor.

ho-rog-ra-phy (hō-rog′rạ-fi), *n.* [F. *horographie*, < Gr. ὥρα, time, hour, + γράφειν, mark, write.] The art of constructing instruments for marking the hours.

hor-o-loge (hor′ọ-lōj), *n.* [OF. F. *horloge*, < L. *horologium*, < Gr. ὡρολόγιον, < ὥρα, time, hour, + λέγειν, tell.] An instrument for indicating the hours; a timepiece; a clock: as, "On the left stands the slender octagon tower of the *horologe*" (Longfellow's "Hyperion," i. 6).—**ho-rol-o-ger, ho-rol-o-gist** (hō-rol′ọ-jėr, -jist), *n.* One versed in horology; a maker of timepieces.—**hor-o-log′ic, hor-o-log′i-cal** (-loj′ik, -i-kạl), *a.* Pertaining to a horologe or to horology.—**ho-rol′o-gy,** *n.* The art or science of making timepieces or of measuring time.

ho-rop-ter (hō-rop′tėr), *n.* [Gr. ὅρος, boundary, limit, + ὀπτήρ, one who looks.] In *optics*, the line or surface containing all the points in space which in any position of the eyes are projected on corresponding points of the two retinas; the aggregate of points which are seen single while the position of the two eyes remains unchanged.—**hor-op-ter-ic** (hor-op-ter′ik), *a.*

hor-o-scope (hor′ọ-skōp), *n.* [F. *horoscope*, < L. *horoscopus*, < Gr. ὡροσκόπος, < ὥρα, time, hour, + σκοπεῖν, view.] In *astrol.*, the appearance or a representation of the heavens, with the relative positions of the planets, at a particular hour, esp. that of a person's birth, regarded as influencing future events; a nativity; also, that part of the ecliptic which is on the eastern horizon at the time of a birth, etc.; the ascendant; also, a diagram of the heavens for use in calculating nativities, etc.—**ho-ros-co-py** (hō-ros′kọ-pi), *n.* The casting or taking of horoscopes; also, the aspect of the heavens at a given moment, esp. that of a person's birth.

hor-ren-dous (ho-ren′dus), *a.* [L. *horrendus*, gerundive of *horrere*: see *horrent*.] To be regarded with horror; dreadful; terrible; horrible.

hor-rent (hor′ẹnt), *a.* [L. *horrens* (*horrent-*), ppr. of *horrere*, bristle, shudder: cf. *abhor*.] Bristling, or standing erect like bristles (as, "Him round A globe of fiery seraphim inclosed, With . . . *horrent* arms": Milton's "Paradise Lost," ii. 513); rough as if with bristles; also, shuddering, horrified, or expressing horror (poetic).

hor-ri-ble (hor′i-bl), *a.* [OF. F. *horrible*, < L. *horribilis*, < *horrere*: see *horrent*.] Such as to excite horror, or a shuddering fear or abhorrence (as, a *horrible* monster; a *horrible* sight, crime, or disease); frightful, hideous, or dreadful; shocking or revolting; in a milder sense, extremely unpleasant (as, a *horrible* noise); deplorable or objectionable (as, "A most *horrible* system of extravagance had found its way into my lord the count's establishment": Malkin's tr. Le

Sage's "Gil Blas," vii. 15); unpleasantly large, great, etc. (now colloq.: as, a *horrible* price).—**hor′ri-ble-ness,** *n.* —**hor′ri-bly,** *adv.*

hor-rid (hor′id), *a.* [L. *horridus*, < *horrere*: see *horrent.*] Bristling or rough (archaic: as, "The forest . . . *Horrid* with fern, and intricate with thorn," Dryden's tr. Virgil's "Æneid," ix. 519); also, such as to excite horror, or dreadful (as, "Moloch, *horrid* king, besmear'd with blood Of human sacrifice," Milton's "Paradise Lost," i. 392; *horrid* wars; a *horrid* spectacle); shocking; abominable; hence (now colloq.), extremely unpleasant or disagreeable (as, *horrid* weather; a *horrid* thing to say; we had a *horrid* time; "I am not quite such a *horrid* girl as I used to be," Barrie's "Tommy and Grizel," xv.); objectionable or obnoxious; 'awful.'—**hor′rid-ly,** *adv.*—**hor′rid-ness,** *n.*

hor-rif-ic (ho-rif′ik), *a.* [L. *horrificus*, < *horrere*, shudder, + *facere*, make.] Causing horror; horrifying: as, "that ungodly and *horrific* spectacle of the scalped head" (Stevenson's "Master of Ballantrae," xi.).

hor-ri-fy (hor′i-fī), *v. t.*; *-fied*, *-fying*. [L. *horrificare*, < *horrificus*, E. *horrific.*] To cause to feel horror; strike with horror; shock intensely.—**hor″ri-fi-ca′tion** (-fi-kā′shọn), *n.*

hor-ri-pi-la-tion (hor″i-pi-lā′shọn), *n.* [LL. *horripilatio(n-)*, < L. *horripilare*, bristle with hairs, < *horrere*, bristle, + *pilus*, hair.] A bristling of the hair on the skin from cold, fear, etc.; goose-flesh.

hor-ror (hor′ọr), *n.* [OF. *orror* (F. *horreur*), < L. *horror*, a bristling, shuddering, horror, < *horrere*: see *horrent.*] A bristling or roughness, or a bristling mass or growth, as of branches and foliage (obs. or archaic: see Milton's "Comus," 38); also, a shuddering, or convulsive trembling, now esp. in a cold fit in disease; also, a shuddering fear or abhorrence; a painful emotion excited by something frightful or shocking (as, to shrink back in *horror*; the crime aroused universal *horror*); often, a painful or intense aversion or repugnance (as, to have a *horror* of cats; a *horror* of publicity or scandal); also, a character, aspect, etc., such as to excite a shuddering fear or abhorrence (as, a scene of *horror*); anything that excites such a feeling (as, the *horrors* of war; a book full of *horrors*); an object of intense aversion (as, cats are his particular *horror*); something considered especially objectionable, atrocious, or bad (colloq.: as, most of the pictures were *horrors*; that hat is a *horror*).—**the horrors,** a fit of horror, as in delirium tremens; also, extreme depression; the blues. [Colloq.]

hors (hôr), *adv.* and *prep.* [F., < L. *foris*, out of doors: see *foreign.*] Out (of).—**hors concours** (kôṅ-kör). [F.] Out of competition; not competing for a prize: said of pictures, etc., in an exhibition.—**hors de combat** (dė kôṅ-bä). [F.] Out of the fight; disabled from further effort. —**hors=d'œuvre** (-dėvr), *n.* [F., 'out of (the) work.'] A relish such as olives or radishes, or any light supplementary dish, served before or between the regular courses of a meal.

horse (hôrs), *n.*; pl. *horses*, also, esp. formerly, *horse* (now chiefly as used collectively, in military language, in sense of 'cavalry'). [AS. *hors* = OS. *hros* = OHG. *hros*, G. *ross*, = Icel. *hross*, horse.] A large, solid-hoofed quadruped, *Equus caballus*, domesticated since prehistoric times, and employed as a beast of draft and burden and for carrying a rider; specif., the male of this animal, in distinction from the female, or mare; a stallion or a gelding; also, any animal of the family *Equidæ* ('horse family'), which includes the ass, zebra, etc.; also, a representation or figure of a horse (as, a rocking-*horse*); also, soldiers serving on horseback,

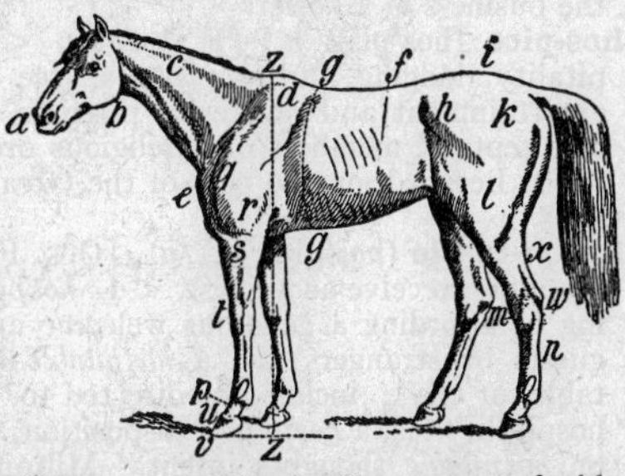

Horse. — *a*, muzzle; *b*, gullet; *c*, crest; *d*, withers; *e*, chest; *f*, loins; *gg*, girth; *h*, hip or ilium; *i*, croup; *k*, haunch; *l*, thigh; *m*, hock; *n*, cannon; *o*, fetlock; *p*, pastern; *q*, shoulder-bone; *r*, elbow-joint; *s*, arm; *t*, knee; *u*, coronet; *v*, hoof; *w*, point of hock; *x*, hamstring; *zz*, height.

or cavalry (as, a thousand *horse*; a troop of *horse*; *horse* and foot); also, an opprobrious or playful term applied to a man (as, "If I tell thee a lie, spit in my face, call me *horse*": Shakspere's "1 Henry IV.," ii. 4. 215); also, something on which a person rides, sits, or exercises, as if on a horse's back; also, a frame, block, etc., on which something is mounted or supported; any of various instruments, appliances, or devices employed for services suggesting or supposed to suggest those of a horse, as a foot-rope, or a rope or bar for a sail or other part to travel on; also, a crib, or translation or other illicit aid (school and college slang, U. S.); also, in *mining*, a mass of rock inclosed within a lode or vein.—**dark horse.** See under *dark, a.*—**wild horse.** See under *wild, a.*—**horse,** *v.*; *horsed, horsing.* **I.** *tr.* To provide with a horse or horses; also, to set on horseback; hence, to set or carry on a person's back; carry on one's own back; also, to place on a person's back or on a wooden horse or the like to be flogged; hence, to flog (as, "The schoolmaster . . . gave me a sound . . . flogging . . . I felt . . . indignant at the ignominious *horsing* I had incurred": Irving's "Tales of a Traveler," ii. 7); also, to bestride (see Shakspere's "Coriolanus," ii. 1. 227); also, to drive or urge (a person) at work, esp. unfairly or tyrannically (colloq. or slang: as, to *horse* a ship's crew); hence, to torment or plague in sport (slang); also, to perform boisterously, as a part or a scene in a play (slang). **II.** *intr.* To mount on a horse; go on horseback.

horse-back (hôrs′bak). **I.** *n.* The back of a horse (now chiefly in the phrase 'on horseback'); also, a low ridge of sand, gravel, or rock (U. S.). **II.** *adv.* On horseback: as, to ride *horseback*.

horse=block (hôrs′blok), *n.* A block or stage for the convenience of horsemen in mounting or dismounting.

horse=car (hôrs′kär), *n.* A street-car drawn by a horse or horses. [U. S.]

horse=chest-nut (hôrs′ches′nut), *n.* The shiny, brown nut-like seed of *Æsculus hippocastanum*, an ornamental tree bearing large digitate leaves and upright clusters of showy white flowers; also, the tree itself.

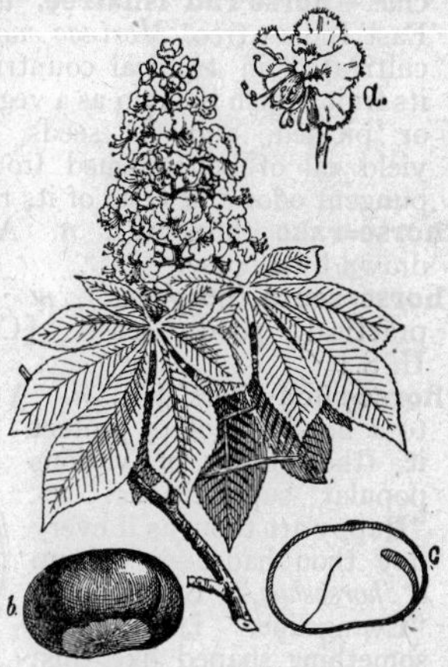

Horse-chestnut. — *a*, flower; *b*, seed; *c*, seed cut longitudinally.

horse=doc-tor (hôrs′dok″tọr), *n.* A veterinary surgeon. [Colloq.]

horse=flesh (hôrs′flesh), *n.* The flesh of a horse; also, horses collectively, esp. for riding, driving, and racing (as, "a person . . . profoundly learned in *horse-flesh*": Steele, in "Spectator," 157).

horse=fly (hôrs′flī), *n.*; pl. *-flies* (-flīz). A fly that bites or stings horses; a gadfly or breeze; a bot-fly.

horse=god-moth-er (hôrs′god′muᴛʜ″ėr), *n.* A big, coarse, masculine woman. [Prov. or vulgar, Eng.]

horse=guards (hôrs′gärdz), *n. pl.* A body of cavalry serving as a guard; also, the barracks or guard-house of such cavalry.

horse-hair (hôrs′hãr), *n.* A hair, or the hair, of a horse, esp. from the mane or tail; also, a wiry fabric made of this hair.

horse-hide (hôrs′hīd), *n.* The hide of a horse, or leather made from it.

horse=jock-ey (hôrs′jok″i), *n.* A professional rider of race-horses: now used more commonly in the shortened form *jockey*.

horse=lat-i-tudes (hôrs′lat″i-tūdz), *n. pl. Naut.*, a belt of the northern Atlantic Ocean between the region of westerly winds of higher latitudes and the region of the trade-winds of the torrid zone, notorious for tedious calms; also, a similar belt elsewhere.

horse=laugh (hôrs′läf), *n.* A loud, coarse, boisterous laugh.

horse=leech (hôrs′lēch), *n.* A veterinary surgeon†; also, a large leech, as *Hæmopsis sanguisorba,* said to attack the mouth of horses while they are drinking; hence, an extortionate, insatiable person.

horse-less (hôrs′les), *a.* Without a horse; also, not requiring a horse, being self-propelled (as, a *horseless* carriage).

horse=mack-er-el (hôrs′mak″ẹ-rẹl), *n.* Any of various fishes allied to the mackerel, esp. the common tunny.

horse-man (hôrs′mạn), *n.*; pl. *-men.* A rider on horseback; one skilled in managing horses; also, a cavalryman†; also, one who attends to horses.—**horse′man-ship,** *n.* The management of horses; equestrian skill.

horse=ma-rine (hôrs′mạ-rēn″), *n.* A marine mounted on horseback, or a cavalryman doing duty on shipboard; also, a member of an imaginary corps of mounted marine soldiers; hence, a person out of his element.

horse-mint (hôrs′mint), *n.* A wild mint, *Mentha longifolia,* orig. a native of Europe but now found in parts of America; also, any of various other menthaceous plants, as *Monarda punctata,* an erect odorous herb of America.

horse=net-tle (hôrs′net″l), *n.* A prickly solanaceous weed, *Solanum carolinense,* of America.

horse=pis-tol (hôrs′pis″tọl), *n.* A kind of large pistol formerly carried by horsemen.

horse=play (hôrs′plā), *n.* Rough or boisterous play.

horse=pow-er (hôrs′pou″ėr), *n.* The power of a horse; specif., a unit for measuring power, or rate of work, equivalent to 550 foot-pounds per second; also, rate of work in terms of this unit; also, the power or agency of a horse or horses as employed to drive machinery; also, a machine worked by a horse, as a treadmill.

horse=race (hôrs′rās), *n.* A race by horses; a match of horses in running.—**horse′=ra″cing,** *n.*

horse=rad-ish (hôrs′rad″ish), *n.* A cultivated brassicaceous plant, *Roripa armoracia;* also, its pungent root, used as a condiment and in medicine.—**horse′rad″ish=tree,** *n.* An East Indian tree, *Moringa moringa,* cultivated in tropical countries for its fruit, which is eaten as a vegetable or pickled, and its seeds, which yield oil of ben: named from the pungent odor and taste of its root.

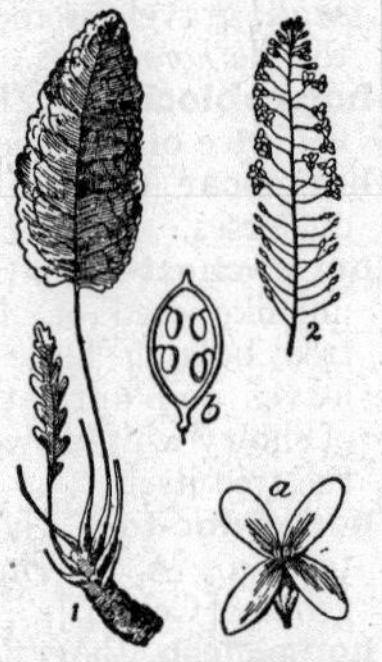

Horse-radish (*Roripa armoracia*). — 1, rhizome, with two leaves; 2, part of the inflorescence, with flowers and fruit; *a,* flower; *b,* fruit, opened to show the seeds.

horse=rake (hôrs′rāk), *n.* A rake drawn by a horse.

horse=sense (hôrs′sens′), *n.* Plain, practical good sense. [Colloq., U. S.]

horse-shoe (hôrs′shö), *n.* A U-shaped iron plate nailed to a horse's hoof to protect it (the object of various popular superstitions: as, "Happy art thou, as if every day thou hadst picked up a *horseshoe,*" Longfellow's "Evangeline," i. 2); also, something shaped like this; specif., a horseshoe-crab.—**horse′shoe=crab,** *n.* A king-crab.

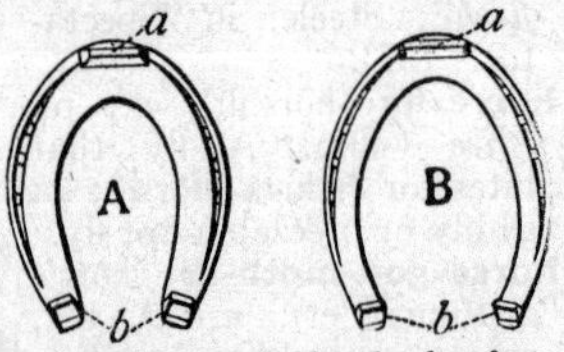

Horseshoes. — *A,* shoe for fore foot; *B,* shoe for hind foot; *a, a,* toe-calks; *b, b,* heel-calks.

horse-tail (hôrs′tāl), *n.* A horse's tail; specif., a horse's tail used as a Turkish military standard or as an ensign denoting the rank of pasha; also, any of the perennial, herbaceous pteridophytic plants constituting the widely distributed genus *Equisetum,* characterized by hollow, jointed stems, with leaves reduced to sheaths at the joints; also, in *anat.,* the collection of nerves in which the spinal cord ends.

horse-way (hôrs′wā), *n.* A way or passage for horses: as, "*Glou.* Know'st thou the way to Dover? *Edg.* Both stile and gate, *horse-way* and foot-path" (Shakspere's "King Lear," iv. 1. 58).

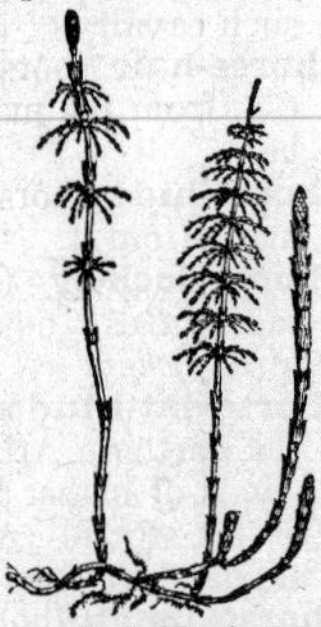
Horsetail (*Equisetum sylvaticum*).

horse-weed (hôrs′wēd), *n.* A troublesome asteraceous weed, *Leptilon canadense;* also, any of various other plants, as *Lactuca canadensis,* an herb of the lettuce genus.

horse-whip (hôrs′hwip), *n.* A whip for driving or controlling horses.—**horse′whip,** *v. t.*; *-whipped, -whipping.* To chastise with a horsewhip.

horse-wom-an (hôrs′wům″ạn), *n.*; pl. *-women* (-wim″en). A woman who rides on horseback.

horse=wran-gler (hôrs′rang″glėr), *n.* A herder having charge of a string of ponies. [Western U. S.]

hors-y (hôr′si), *a.* Pertaining to, characteristic of, or of the nature of a horse or horses; also, dealing with horses; interested in or devoted to horses, horse-breeding, horse-racing, etc.—**hors′i-ness,** *n.*

hor-ta-tive (hôr′tạ-tiv). [L. *hortativus,* < *hortari,* urge, exhort, < *hori,* urge.] **I.** *a.* Giving exhortation; urging; inciting. **II.** *n.* An exhortation: as, "Generals commonly, in their *hortatives,* put men in mind of their wives and children" (Bacon's "Essays," Of Marriage and Single Life).—**hor′ta-tive-ly,** *adv.*

hor-ta-tor (hôr-tā′tọr), *n.* [L., < *hortari*: see *hortative.*] One who exhorts.

hor-ta-to-ry (hôr′tạ-tō-ri), *a.* [LL. *hortatorius,* < L. *hortator*: see *hortator.*] Of, pertaining to, or characterized by exhortation; giving exhortation; hortative.

hor-ti-cul-ture (hôr′ti-kul-tūr), *n.* [L. *hortus,* garden, + *cultura,* culture.] The cultivation of a garden; the art of cultivating gardens; the growing of flowers and ornamental plants, fruits, vegetables, etc.—**hor-ti-cul′tur-al,** *a.*—**hor-ti-cul′tur-ist,** *n.*

hor-tus sic-cus (hôr′tus sik′us). [L., 'dry garden.'] A collection of dried plants; a herbarium.

Hor-wat (hôr′wot), *n.* [= Croatian *Hrvat.*] A Croat. [U. S.]

ho-san-na (hō-zan′ạ). [LL., < Gr. ὡσαννά, < Heb. *hōshī'āh-nnā,* 'save, pray!'] **I.** *interj.* An exclamation, orig. an appeal to God for deliverance (cf. Ps. cxviii. 25), used as an acclamation or ascription of praise to God or Christ: as, "And the multitudes . . . cried, saying, *Hosanna* to the son of David . . . *Hosanna* in the highest" (Mat. xxi. 9). **II.** *n.* A cry of 'hosanna!' hence, a shout of praise or adoration; an acclamation.

hose (hōz), *n.*; pl. *hose,* archaic *hosen* (hō′zẹn). [AS. *hosa* = D. *hoos* = G. *hose* = Icel. *hosa,* hose.] An article of clothing for the leg, esp., in modern use, for the foot and lower part of the leg; a stocking; formerly, a garment for the legs and waist, as tights or breeches, worn by men (as, "O fine villain! A silken doublet! a velvet *hose!* a scarlet cloak!" Shakspere's "Taming of the Shrew," v. i. 69); also (pl. also *hoses*), a flexible tube for conveying water, etc., to a desired point (as, a garden *hose*; a fire-engine *hose*); also, a sheath, or sheathing part, as that inclosing the ear of grain; also, a socket, esp. one receiving the shaft or handle of a tool, golf-club, or the like.—**hose,** *v. t.*; *hosed, hosing.* To furnish with hose for wearing; also, to water, wash, or drench by means of a hose or tube.—**ho-sier** (hō′zhėr), *n.* One who makes or deals in hose or stockings, or goods knitted or woven like hose.—**ho′sier-y,** *n.* Hose or stockings of any kind; the class of goods in which a hosier deals; also, the business of a hosier.

hos-pice (hos′pis), *n.* [F. *hospice,* < L. *hospitium,* hospitality, lodging, inn, < *hospes*: see *host*[2].] A house of entertainment and refuge for pilgrims, strangers, etc., esp. one kept by members of a religious order: as, the *hospice* of St. Bernard, on the pass of the Great St. Bernard in the Alps.

hos-pi-ta-ble (hos′pi-tạ-bl), *a.* [Obs. F. *hospitable,* < ML. *hospitare,* receive as a guest, < L. *hospes*: see *host*[2].] Giving or affording a generous welcome and entertainment to guests or strangers (as, a *hospitable* host, family, house, table, or city); inclined or directed to, or characterized by, hospitality (as, a *hospitable* disposition; "In haste She turns, on *hospitable* thoughts intent," Milton's "Paradise Lost," v. 332; a *hospitable* reception); hence, favorably receptive or open (with *to*: as, a people *hospitable* to new ideas).—**hos′pi-ta-ble-ness,** *n.*—**hos′pi-ta-bly,** *adv.*

hos-pi-tal (hos′pi-tạl), *n.* [OF. *hospital* (F. *hôpital*), < ML. *hospitale,* inn, hospice, prop. neut. of L. *hospitalis,* pertaining to guests, hospitable, < *hospes*: see *host*[2].] A hospice†; also, a charitable institution for the shelter and maintenance of the needy, infirm, or aged, or for the maintenance and education of the young (now chiefly in the names of old institutions in Great Britain: as, Greenwich *Hospital*, a home for retired seamen at Greenwich, England, since 1873 used as a royal naval college; Christ's *Hospital*, a famous English educational institution, orig. in London, afterward removed to Horsham, Sussex); now, esp., an institution in which sick or injured persons are given medical or surgical treatment; also, a similar establishment for the care of animals.

hos-pi-tal-er, hos-pi-tal-ler (hos'pi-tạl-ėr), *n.* [OF. F. *hospitalier*, < ML. *hospitalarius*, < *hospitale*: see *hospital*.] The person receiving and attending upon pilgrims, strangers, etc., in a hospice or religious house; also, a person devoted to the care of the sick or needy in hospitals, esp. a member of a religious order devoted to this charity; also [*cap.*], a member of a religious and military order ('Knights Hospitalers,' also called 'Knights of St. John of Jerusalem') taking its origin, about the time of the first Crusade (1096–99), from a hospital at Jerusalem; also [*l. c.*], in some London hospitals orig. religious foundations, the chief resident official, who was formerly also religious superintendent; hence, sometimes, a hospital chaplain; also, sometimes, an inmate of a hospital.

hos-pi-tal-i-ty (hos-pi-tal'i-ti), *n.*; pl. *-ties* (-tiz). [OF. *hospitalite* (F. *hospitalité*), < L. *hospitalitas*, < *hospitalis*, hospitable: see *hospital*.] The reception and entertainment of guests or strangers with liberality and kindness; *pl.*, hospitable courtesies (as, "Women are always more cautious in their casual *hospitalities* than men": Hawthorne's "Blithedale Romance," iv.).

hos-pi-tal-ize (hos'pi-tạl-īz), *v. t.*; *-ized*, *-izing*. To place for care or treatment in a hospital.—**hos"pi-tal-i-za'tion** (-i-zā'shọn), *n.*

hos-pi-tal=ship (hos'pi-tạl-ship), *n.* A vessel fitted up as a hospital, as one accompanying a fleet of war-ships.

hos-po-dar (hos'pọ-där), *n.* [Rumanian.] A title formerly borne by the governors or princes of Wallachia and Moldavia (now included in Rumania).

host[1] (hōst), *n.* [OF. *host*, *ost*, < ML. *hostis*, army, L. stranger, enemy: see *guest* and *host*[2].] An army (archaic: as, "Nebuchadnezzar king of Babylon came, he, and all his *host*, against Jerusalem, and pitched against it," 2 Kings, xxv. 1); hence, a multitude or great body or number of persons or things (as, to have a *host*, or *hosts*, of friends; a *host* of books; a *host* of details).—**host** (or **hosts**) **of heaven,** the sun, moon, and stars, or heavenly bodies (see Deut. iv. 19); also, the angels of heaven (see 1 Kings, xxii. 19).—**to be a host in one's self,** to have in one's self the power or effectiveness of a whole host (cf. "Ajax the great . . . Himself a host: the Grecian strength and pride," Pope's tr. Homer's "Iliad," iii.); be the equivalent of a whole multitude or great body or number.—**host**[1], *v. t.* or *i.* To assemble in a host. Cf. *hosting*. [Obs. or archaic.]

host[2] (hōst), *n.* [OF. *hoste*, *oste* (F. *hôte*), < L. *hospes*, host, guest, stranger: see *guest* and *host*[1].] One who entertains a guest or guests in his own home or elsewhere (as, the *host* at a house-party, a dinner, or a theater-party); also, the landlord of an inn or hotel (as, "mine *host* of the Garter": Shakspere's "Merry Wives of Windsor," i. 1. 143); also, an animal or plant in or on which a parasite or commensal lives.—**to reckon without one's host.** See under *reckon*.—**host**[2]†, *v.* **I.** *tr.* To receive or entertain as a host does: as, "Such was that Hag, unmeet to *host* such guests" (Spenser's "Faerie Queene," iv. 8. 27). **II.** *intr.* To sojourn as a guest; lodge: as, "Come, pilgrim, I will bring you Where you shall *host*" (Shakspere's "All's Well," iii. 5. 97).

host[3] (hōst), *n.* [OF. *hoiste*, *oiste*, < L. *hostia*, animal sacrificed: cf. L. *hostire*, strike.] A victim for sacrifice†; a sacrifice†; hence [often *cap.*], *eccles.*, esp. in the *Rom. Cath. Ch.*, the bread consecrated in the celebration of the eucharist, regarded as the body of Christ offered in sacrifice; a consecrated wafer.

hos-tage (hos'tạj), *n.* [OF. *hostage*, *ostage* (F. *otage*), < LL. *obsidatus*, hostageship, < L. *obses*, hostage.] The condition of a person given or held as a security for the performance of something†; also, a person thus given or held as a security; anything serving as a security or pledge (as, "He that hath wife and children hath given *hostages* to fortune; for they are impediments to great enterprises, either of virtue or mischief": Bacon's "Essays," Of Marriage and Single Life).—**hos'tage-ship,** *n.* The condition of a hostage.

hos-tel (hos'tel), *n.* [OF. *hostel*, *ostel* (F. *hôtel*), < ML. *hospitale*: see *hospital*.] An inn, as for travelers (archaic: as, "We . . . enter'd an old *hostel*, call'd mine host," Tennyson's "Princess," i. 171); also, a house of residence for students at a university or elsewhere, esp. one at a university but not under direct university control and not sharing like a college in the government of the university (Eng.); some similar house of residence, as for incapacitated soldiers (Eng.).—**hos'tel-er,** *n.* [OF. *hostelier* (F. *hôtelier*).] An innkeeper. [Archaic.]—**hos'tel-ry,** *n.*; pl. *-ries* (-riz). [OF. *hostelerie* (F. *hôtellerie*).] A hostel or inn (archaic); also, esp. in journalistic language, a modern hotel, as in a city.

host-ess (hōs'tes), *n.* [OF. *hostesse* (F. *hôtesse*), fem. of *hoste*, E. *host*[2].] A female host; a woman who entertains a guest or guests; the mistress of an inn or the like (as, "my *hostess* of the tavern": Shakspere's "1 Henry IV.," i. 2. 45).—**host'-ess=ship,** *n.*

hos-tile (hos'til or, chiefly Brit., -tīl). [L. *hostilis*, < *hostis*, enemy: see *host*[1].] **I.** *a.* Of or pertaining to an enemy, as in war or arms (as, *hostile* ground or positions; "The hooked chariot stood Unstain'd with *hostile* blood," Milton's "On the Morning of Christ's Nativity," 57); characteristic of or carried on by an enemy (as, *hostile* incursions or operations); acting as or being an enemy (as, a *hostile* force, army, or nation); hence, in general, opposed in feeling, action, tendency, or character (as, to be *hostile* to a measure; *hostile* criticism, remarks, or intentions); unfriendly; antagonistic; inimical; adverse. **II.** *n.* A hostile person; an enemy; esp., an American Indian hostile to the whites.—**hos'tile-ly,** *adv.*—**hos-til'i-ty** (-til'i-ti), *n.*; pl. *-ties* (-tiz). [LL. *hostilitas*.] Hostile state, feeling, or action; enmity; antagonism; also, a hostile act; *pl.*, acts of warfare.

host-ing (hōs'ting), *n.* An assembling of a host or armed multitude; hence, a hostile expedition or encounter (as, "Strange to us it seem'd . . . that angel should with angel war, And in fierce *hosting* meet": Milton's "Paradise Lost," vi. 93). [Obs. or archaic.]

hos-tler (hos'lėr or os'lėr), *n.* [For *hosteler*.] An innkeeper†; also, one who has the care of horses at an inn; any person who takes care of horses; a groom.

hot (hot), *a.*; compar. *hotter*, superl. *hottest*. [AS. *hāt* = D. *heet* = G. *heiss* = Icel. *heitr*, hot: cf. Goth. *heito*, fever, and E. *heat*.] Being in the condition or of the temperature characteristic of things that have stood for a time near a fire or under the rays of the summer sun; having or communicating sensible heat, esp. in a high degree (as, a *hot* stove, bath, or room; coffee too *hot* to swallow; *hot* springs; *hot* winds); very warm, as weather, climate, etc.; also, having a sensation of great bodily heat, as from nearness to fire, or from heavy clothing, vigorous exercise, fever, etc.; attended with or producing such a sensation, as a blush, swelling, fever, etc.; also, having an effect as of burning on the tongue, skin, etc., as pepper, mustard, a blister, etc.; peppery, biting, pungent, or acrid; also, having or showing intense feeling; ardent or fervent (as, "I know thy works, that thou art neither cold nor *hot*": Rev. iii. 15); passionate, vehement, or fiery, as persons, the temper, wrath, haste, words, etc.; lustful; inflamed (*with*: as, to be *hot* with rage); violent, furious, or intense (as, "Set ye Uriah in the forefront of the *hottest* battle": 2 Sam. xi. 15); also, uncomfortable or unpleasant (colloq.: as, his opponents soon made the town too *hot* for him); also, strong or fresh, as a scent or trail.—**hot air,** empty, pretentious talk or writing. [Slang.]—**hot and hot,** served hot from the fire to the table, without delay, as food.—**hot dog,** a hot frankfurter (sausage), esp. as served in a split roll. [Colloq.]—**in hot water,** fig., in trouble or difficulties. [Colloq.]—**hot,** *adv.* In a hot manner; with great heat; hotly.—**hot,** *v. t.*; *hotted*, *hotting*. To heat; warm. [Now prov. or colloq., Eng.]

hot-bed (hot′bed), *n.* A bed of earth, heated by fermenting manure, etc., and usually covered with glass, for raising or forcing plants; fig., a place favoring rapid growth, esp. of something bad (as, a *hotbed* of sedition or vice).

hot-blood (hot′blud), *n.* A hot-blooded person.—**hot′=blood′ed,** *a.* Having hot blood; impetuous; excitable; passionate.

hot=brained (hot′brānd), *a.* Hot-headed; fiery; passionate; rash.

hotch-pot (hoch′pot), *n.* [OF. F. *hochepot*, ragout, < *hocher*, shake, + *pot*, pot.] A ragout or other dish of various ingredients; a hotchpotch; in *law*, the aggregating of shares or properties in order to secure equality of division.

hotch-potch (hoch′poch), *n.* [For *hotchpot.*] A ragout or stew of meat with vegetables, etc.; a cooked dish containing a variety of ingredients; fig., a medley or hodgepodge; in *law*, hotchpot.

ho-tel (hō-tel′, F. ō-tel), *n.* [F. *hôtel*: see *hostel.*] A public house for the lodging and entertainment of travelers, strangers, or others, esp. a more or less pretentious establishment with modern appointments, etc. (cf. *inn*, a much older word); in French use, a large private residence in a city, or a public building.—**hôtel de ville** (ō-tel dė vēl). [F.] A city hall or town hall.—**hô-tel=Dieu** (-dyė), *n.* [F., 'hotel (of) God.'] A hospital.

hot-foot (hot′fůt), *adv.* With great speed in going; in hot haste.—**hot′foot,** *v.* **I.** *intr.* To go hotfoot; run in hot haste: often with indefinite *it* (as, to *hotfoot* it to a place). [Colloq.] **II.** *tr.* To pursue or follow hotfoot. [Colloq.]

hot-head (hot′hed), *n.* A hot-headed person.—**hot′=head′ed,** *a.* Hot or fiery in spirit or temper; impetuous; passionate; rash: as, "We're both a little *hot-headed*, I guess, and do things we're sorry for" (W. Churchill's "Coniston," ii. 20).—**hot′=head′ed-ness,** *n.*

hot-house (hot′hous), *n.* A house for sweating, bathing, etc.†; also, a brothel†; also, an artificially heated glass-house for the cultivation of tender plants.

hot-ly (hot′li), *adv.* In a hot manner; with great heat; ardently; passionately; vehemently.—**hot′ness,** *n.*

hot=plate (hot′plāt), *n.* A simple, portable appliance for cooking, etc., consisting of a flat iron frame mounted on short legs and having gas-burners beneath to supply heat.

hot=pot (hot′pot), *n.* Mutton or beef cooked with potatoes, etc., in a covered pot.

hot=press (hot′pres), *n.* A machine in which heat is applied in conjunction with mechanical pressure, as one for producing a smooth, glassy surface on paper or cloth, or one for expressing oil.—**hot′=press,** *v. t.* To subject to treatment in a hot-press.—**hot′=press″er,** *n.*

hot=room (hot′röm), *n.* A room specially heated to a high temperature, esp. for inducing sweating as in a bathing establishment.

hot=short (hot′shôrt), *a.* Of iron, brittle at a forging temperature.

hot-spur (hot′spėr), *n.* A person who drives or pushes recklessly onward, like a rider keeping his spurs hot with use; an impetuous or reckless person; a hothead: as, Sir Henry Percy (1364–1403), surnamed *Hotspur* for his zeal in border warfare against the Scots; "I am not yet of Percy's mind, the *Hotspur* of the north; he that kills me some six or seven dozen of Scots at a breakfast, washes his hands, and says to his wife 'Fie upon this quiet life! I want work'" (Shakspere's "1 Henry IV.," ii. 4. 114).

Hot-ten-tot (hot′n-tot), *n.* A member of a native South African race of dark yellowish-brown complexion, low stature, and ungainly build, probably of mixed Bushman and Bantu (negro) origin; also, their language.

Hou-dan (hö′dan), *n.* [From *Houdan*, town in France, near Paris.] One of a breed of domestic fowls of French origin, having a heavy, globular crest and evenly mottled black and white plumage.

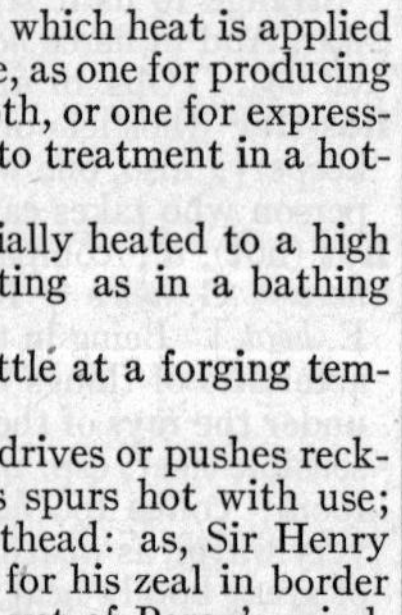

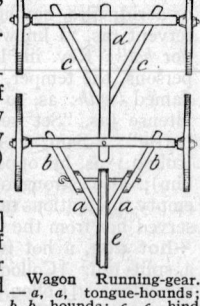

Wagon Running-gear. — *a, a,* tongue-hounds; *b, b,* hounds; *c, c,* hind hounds; *d,* coupling-pole, or reach; *e,* tongue.

hough (hok), *n.* and *v.* See *hock*[1].

hound[1] (hound), *n.* [Cf. Icel. *hūnn*, knob at the masthead.] A projection at a masthead, serving to support rigging or trestletrees; also, either of a pair of horizontal braces for reinforcing some part of the running-gear of a vehicle (see cut in preceding column).

hound[2] (hound), *n.* [AS. *hund* = D. *hond* = G. *hund* = Icel. *hundr* = Goth. *hunds*, dog: cf. L. *canis*, Gr. κύων, Skt. *çvan*, dog.] A dog, now esp. one of any of various breeds used in the chase and commonly hunting by scent (as, a fox*hound*; a stag*hound*); also, a mean, despicable fellow; also, a person who constantly pursues a particular object of liking, or is inordinately addicted to something specified (slang: as, a rum-*hound*; a movie-*hound*).—**hare and hounds.** See under *hare*.—**hound**[2], *v. t.* To hunt or track with hounds, or as a hound does; hence, in general, to pursue or drive unrelentingly; also, to incite (a hound, etc.) to pursuit or attack; hence, in general, urge (*on*).—**hound′er,** *n.*—**hound′fish,** *n.* Any of various fishes, as certain small sharks of the genus *Scyliorhinus* and certain large voracious fishes of the genus *Tylosurus*.—**hound's′=tongue,** *n.* A troublesome boraginaceous weed, *Cynoglossum officinale*, with prickly nutlets and tongue-like leaves.

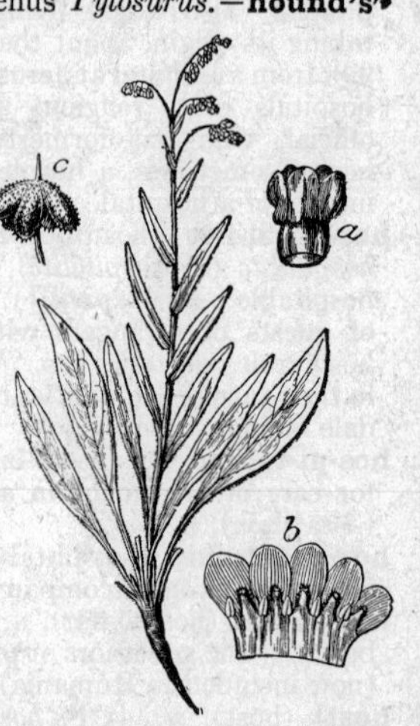

Hound's-tongue. — *a,* corolla; *b,* same, opened; *c,* fruit.

hour (our), *n.* [OF. *ure, ore, hore* (F. *heure*), < L. *hora*, < Gr. ὥρα, time, season, hour; akin to E. *year*.] A space of time equal to the 24th part of a mean solar day or civil day; 60 minutes; also, indefinitely, a short or limited period of time (as, "Sad *hours* seem long": Shakspere's "Romeo and Juliet," i. 1. 167); also, one of the 24 points (12 after midnight and 12 after noon) measuring off the periods of 60 minutes in the course of a day (as, trains leave every hour on the *hour*; a clock which strikes the *hours*); hence, any definite time of day, or the time indicated by a timepiece (as, what is the *hour?*); *pl.*, customary time of going to bed and getting up (as, to keep early *hours* or good *hours*, or late *hours* or bad *hours*); also, *sing.*, a particular or appointed time (as, "In an ill *hour* . . . I went on board a ship bound for London," Defoe's "Robinson Crusoe," i. 1; "Mine *hour* is not yet come," John, ii. 4); the present time (with *the*: as, the question of the *hour*; the man of the *hour*); also, *pl.*, *eccles.*, the seven stated times of the day set apart for prayer and devotion ('canonical hours': see under *canonical*); the offices or services prescribed for these times, or a book containing them; also, *pl.* [*cap.*], in *class. myth.*, the goddesses presiding over the changes of the seasons; the Horæ; also, *sing.* [*l. c.*], in *astron.*, etc., a unit of measure of right ascension, etc., representing 15 degrees, or the 24th part of a great circle.—**sidereal hour.** See *sidereal*.—**solar hour.** See *solar*.—**hour′=glass,** *n.* An instrument for measuring time, consisting of two bulbs of glass joined by a narrow passage through which a quantity of sand (or mercury) runs in just an hour.—**hour′=hand,** *n.* The hand that indicates the hours on a clock or watch. Cf. *minute-hand*.

hou-ri (hö′ri or hou′-), *n.*; pl. *-ris* (-riz). [F. *houri*, < Pers. *hūri*, < Ar. *haurā*, fem., black-eyed.] A nymph of the Mohammedan paradise: as, "Happy he who falls fighting in the cause of the prophet! he will at once be transported to the paradise of the faithful, and surrounded by immortal *houris*" (Irving's "Conquest of Granada," xlviii.). Also fig.

hour-ly (our′li), *a.* Of, pertaining to, occurring, or done each successive hour; hence, frequent; continual.—**hour′ly,** *adv.* Every hour; hour by hour; hence, frequently.

house[1] (hous), *n.* [OF. *houce* (F. *housse*); origin uncertain.] A covering of cloth or the like, esp. one for the back and flanks of a horse, etc.; a housing. [Obs. or archaic.]—**house**[1] (houz), *v. t.*; *housed, housing.* To equip (a horse, etc.) with a house or housing.

house² (hous), *n.*; pl. *houses* (hou′zez). [AS. *hūs* = D. *huis* = G. *haus* = Icel. and Goth. *hūs*, house; perhaps akin to E. *hide*¹.] A building for human habitation; also, a building or structure designed or used for any purpose (as, a *house* of worship; a coffee-*house*; a ware*house*; a green-*house*; a cow-*house*); specif., the building in which a legislative or deliberative body meets, or the body itself (as, the *House* of Commons, of Lords, or of Representatives: see *commons, lord, n.*, and *representative, n.*); hence, a quorum of such a body; also, a place of business, or a business firm or establishment; also, a place of entertainment, as a theater, or the audience at such a place; also, a household (as, "Bid her hasten all the *house* to bed": Shakspere's "Romeo and Juliet," iii. 3. 156); also, a family regarded as consisting of ancestors and descendants, esp. a noble family or race (as, the *house* of Hapsburg); also, a habitation or abiding-place (as, "An heav'nly mind May be indiff'rent to her *house* of clay": Cowper's "Task," ii. 458); a place of lodgment, rest, etc., as of an animal; in *astrol.*, a twelfth part of the heavens as divided by great circles drawn through the north and south points of the horizon; also, a sign of the zodiac as the seat of the greatest influence of a particular planet.—**house of correction,** a place for the confinement and reform of persons convicted of minor offenses and not regarded as confirmed criminals.—**house of ill fame,** a disorderly house; esp., a house of prostitution.—**to put,** or **set, one's house in order,** fig., to put one's affairs into good order or condition, as by amending or reforming whatever is amiss: as, "The Prussians, after the disaster of Jena in 1807, had set to work to *put their house in order*" (H. G. Wells's "Outline of History," xxxviii. § 4).—**house**² (houz), *v.*; *housed, housing.* [AS. *hūsian.*] **I.** *tr.* To put or receive into a house; provide with a house; also, to cause to take shelter† (see Shakspere's "Comedy of Errors," v. 1. 188); also, to give shelter to; harbor; lodge; *naut.*, to place in a secure or protected position; in *carp.*, to fix in a socket or the like. **II.** *intr.* To take shelter; dwell: as, "He wends unfollow'd, he must *house* alone" (M. Arnold's "Thyrsis").

house=boat (hous′bōt), *n.* A boat fitted up for use as a dwelling, esp. one having a flat bottom and a house-like structure built on the deck.

house-break-er (hous′brā″kėr), *n.* One who breaks open and enters a house with felonious intent.—**house′break″ing,** *n.*

house-carl (hous′kärl), *n.* [AS. *hūscarl*, from Scand.: cf. Icel. *hūscarl*, 'house man.'] A member of the household troops or body-guard of a Danish or early English king or noble.

house-fa-ther (hous′fä″ᴛʜėr), *n.* The father of a household or family; also, the male head of a community or number of persons living together as a family.

house=fly (hous′flī), *n.*; pl. *-flies* (-flīz). A dipterous insect, *Musca domestica*, common in houses, etc., and found in nearly all parts of the world. Cf. *fly*¹.

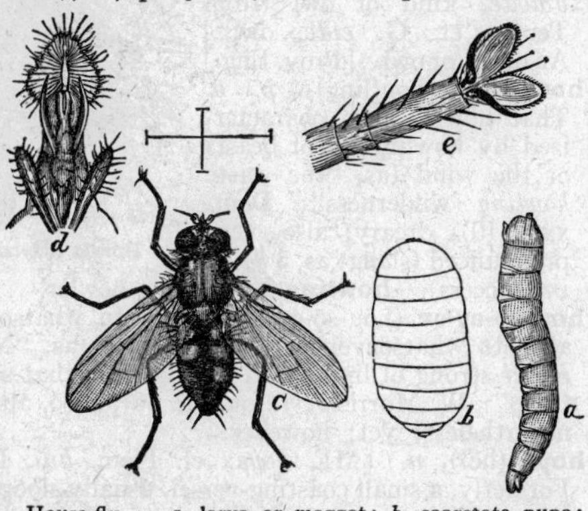

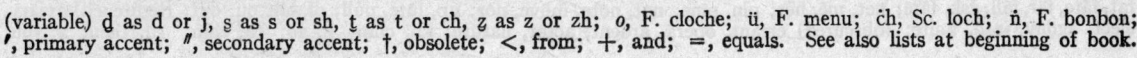

House-fly. — *a*, larva or maggot; *b*, coarctate pupa; *c*, adult fly (cross shows natural size); *d*, mouth-parts; *e*, foot. (All magnified.)

house-ful (hous′fụl), *n.*; pl. *-fuls.* A number or quantity sufficient to fill a house.

house-hold (hous′hōld, commonly hous′ōld). **I.** *n.* The inmates of a house collectively; a family, including servants, etc.; a domestic establishment; specif., the domestic establishment of a king or other royal personage (as, "He had two good places, one in the Treasury, the other in the *household*": Macaulay's "Hist. of Eng.," xviii.). **II.** *a.* Of or pertaining to a household; domestic; specif., of or pertaining to a royal household (as, *household* troops; *household* infantry).

house-hold-er (hous′hōl″dėr), *n.* One who holds or occupies a house; the head of a family.—**house′hold″ing,** *n.* and *a.*

house-keep (hous′kēp), *v. i.*; *-kept, -keeping.* [Back-formation from *housekeeper.*] To act as housekeeper; keep house.

house-keep-er (hous′kē″pėr), *n.* A householder (obs. or rare); also, a person in charge of a house or building; esp., a woman who does the work or manages the affairs of a household; also, a watch-dog† (see Shakspere's "Macbeth," iii. 1. 97); also, one who stays much at home.—**house′keep″ing,** *n.* The maintaining of a house or domestic establishment (as, to go to *housekeeping*); also, the management of household affairs.

hou-sel (hou′zẹl), *n.* [AS. *hūsl* = Icel. *hūsl*, housel, = Goth. *hunsl*, sacrifice.] The eucharist (consecrated elements); the administering or receiving of the eucharist. [Archaic.]—**hou′sel,** *v. t.*; *-seled* or *-selled, -seling* or *-selling.* [AS. *hūslian.*] To administer the eucharist to. [Archaic.]

house-leek (hous′lēk), *n.* A crassulaceous herb, *Sempervivum tectorum*, with pink flowers and thick, succulent leaves, found growing on the roofs and walls of houses; also, any plant of the genus *Sempervivum.*

Houseleek (*Sempervivum tectorum*). — *a*, fruit.

house-less (hous′les), *a.* Having no house to dwell in; without habitation or shelter; also, destitute of houses (as, "the *houseless* ocean's heaving field": Tennyson's "Voyage," iv.).—**house′less-ness,** *n.*

house=line (hous′līn), *n.* *Naut.*, a small line of three strands, used for seizings, etc.

house-maid (hous′mād), *n.* A female servant employed in a household.—**housemaid's knee,** in *pathol.*, an acute or chronic inflammation of the bursa over the knee-pan: so called because of its supposed prevalence among housemaids who work much upon the knees.

house-mate (hous′māt), *n.* One who lives in the same house with another; a fellow-member of a household.

house-moth-er (hous′muᴛʜ″ėr), *n.* The mother of a household or family; also, the female head of a community or number of persons living together as a family.

house=or-gan (hous′ôr″gạn), *n.* A periodical publication issued by a business house or the like for circulation among its employees or patrons, presenting news of its activities, etc.

house=par-ty (hous′pär″ti), *n.* A company or an entertainment of guests for some days at a host's house, esp. in the country.

house=phy-si-cian (hous′fi-zish″ạn), *n.* A resident physician in a hospital or other public institution.

house=room (hous′röm), *n.* Room or accommodation in a house.

house-smith (hous′smith), *n.* A mechanic who works upon the ironwork or steelwork of houses, etc.

house=sur-geon (hous′sėr″jọn), *n.* A resident surgeon in a hospital.

house-top (hous′top), *n.* The top or roof of a house.

house-warm-ing (hous′wâr″ming), *n.* An entertainment given in a house to celebrate the beginning of one's occupancy.

house-wife (hous′wīf), *n.*; pl. *-wives* (-wīvz). The mistress of a household; also, a hussy†; also (commonly pron. huz′if), a small case for needles, thread, etc.—**house′wife″ly,** *a.* Of, like, or befitting a housewife; thrifty or skilled as to household affairs.—**house′wife″li-ness,** *n.*—**house′wife″ry,** *n.* The function or work of a housewife.

house-work (hous′wėrk), *n.* The (manual) work to be done in housekeeping; household work.

house=wreck-er (hous′rek″ėr), *n.* One whose business it is to demolish old houses.

hous-ing[1] (hou′zing), *n.* [See *house*[1], *v.*] A covering of cloth or the like; esp., such a covering for the back and flanks of a horse or other animal, for protection or ornament; a caparison or trapping (often in *pl.*).

hous-ing[2] (hou′zing), *n.* [See *house*[2], *v.*] The act of one who houses; a putting or receiving into a house or under shelter; a dwelling in a house; specif., the providing of houses as homes for the community; also, shelter, as in a house; lodging; also, houses collectively; sometimes, a single house; hence, something serving as a shelter, covering, or the like; *naut.*, a roofing for a vessel laid up in dock; also, a house-line; also, the inboard end of a bowsprit; the part of a mast which is below deck; in *arch.*, a niche for a statue; in *carp.*, the space or cavity made in one piece of wood or the like for the insertion of another; in *mach.*, a frame, plate, or the like, that supports a part of a machine, etc.

hous-to-ni-a (hös-tō′ni-ạ̈), *n.* [NL.; from Dr. W. *Houston* (died 1733), English botanist.] Any herb of the rubiaceous genus *Houstonia*, as *H. cærulea*, the common bluet or innocence, a small, delicate plant with bluish or white flowers.

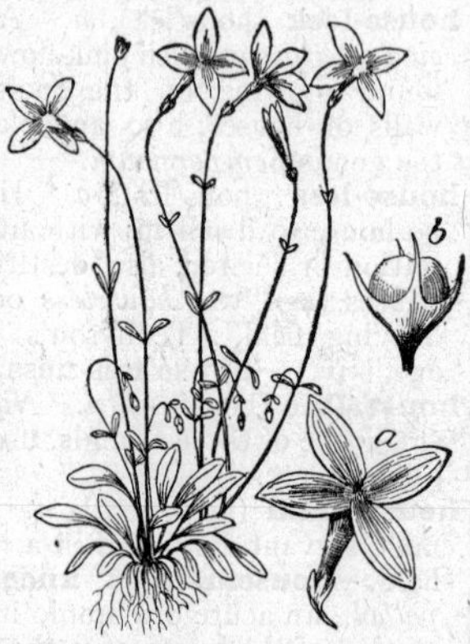

Houstonia (*H. cærulea*). — *a*, flower; *b*, fruit.

Houyhn-hnm (hwin′m), *n.* [Appar. intended to suggest a whinnying sound.] In Swift's "Gulliver's Travels," iv., one of a race of horses endowed with reason, who bear rule over the Yahoos, a race of degraded, brutish creatures having the form of man; hence, a horse considered as having human characteristics.

hove (hōv). Preterit and past participle of *heave*.

hov-el (hov′ẹl, also huv′-), *n.* [ME. *hovel*, *hovyl*; origin uncertain.] An open shed, as for sheltering cattle, tools, etc.; also, a small, mean dwelling-house; a wretched hut.—**hov′el,** *v. t.*; *-eled* or *-elled*, *-eling* or *-elling*. To shelter or lodge as in a hovel.

hov-er (huv′ėr or hov′-), *v.* [ME. *hoveren*, freq. of *hoven*, hover, hang; origin uncertain.] **I.** *intr.* To hang fluttering or suspended in the air, as a bird or a cloud; hence, to keep lingering (*about*, etc.); wait near at hand; also, to remain in an uncertain or irresolute state; waver. **II.** *tr.* To cover (the young) with wings and body: said of a brooding fowl.—**hov′er,** *n.* The action or state of hovering; also, an overhanging shelter, as of a fish.—**hov′er-er,** *n.*—**hov′er-ing-ly,** *adv.*

how[1] (hou), *n.* [From Scand.: cf. Icel. *haugr*, mound, akin to E. *high*.] A mound, knoll, or hillock; a small detached hill. [Prov. Eng., or in place-names.]

how[2] (hou). [AS. *hū* = OS. *hwō* = OFries. *hū* = D. *hoe*, how; from the pronominal stem represented by E. *who*.] **I.** *interrog. adv.* In what way or manner? (as, *how* did it happen?); by what means? (as, *how* did you come?); also, for what reason?† (as, "She is thy wife: and *how* saidst thou, She is my sister?" Gen. xxvi. 9); also, in what state or condition? (as, *how* are you?); also, to what effect? or with what meaning? (as, "*Sir Oliver.* Is there nothing you could dispose of? *Chas. How* do you mean?" Sheridan's "School for Scandal," iii. 3); by what name? (as, "*How* art thou call'd?" Shakspere's "2 Henry VI.," v. 1. 73); also, what? (as, " '*How*,' cried I, ' is that all you are to have for your two shillings?' " Goldsmith's "Vicar of Wakefield," x.); also, to what extent, degree, etc.? (as, *how* much? *how* many? *how* old? *how* long?); also, at what price? (as, *how* do you sell these apples?). **II.** *rel. conj.* In what way, state, etc. (as, "*How* we all came to disregard so material a point is inconceivable," Goldsmith's "Vicar of Wakefield," xvi.; tell us *how* matters stand); to what extent, or in what degree (as, I wonder *how* late it is); also, in the or any way, etc., that (as, "He would go as a merchant, or *how* I pleased to order him": Defoe's "Robinson Crusoe," ii. 13).—**how**[2], *n.* A question beginning with 'how'; also, way or manner of doing, etc.

how-adj-i (hou-aj′ē), *n.*; pl. *howadjis* (-ēz). [Ar. *khawājah*; from Pers.] In the East, a merchant; a rich man; a gentleman; in respectful address, sir.

how-be-it (hou-bē′it), *adv.* However it may be; nevertheless; however.

how-dah (hou′dạ̈), *n.* [Hind. *haudah*, < Ar. *haudaj*.] In the East Indies, a seat, commonly with a railing and a canopy, placed on the back of an elephant.

how-e'er (hou-âr′). Contraction of *however*.

how-ev-er (hou-ev′ėr). **I.** *conj.* In whatever manner (as, it is his, *however* he came by it); also, to whatever extent or degree; no matter how (far, much, etc.); also, although†; also, nevertheless, or yet (as, "They might have wholly abolished their monarchy . . . *However*, they did not think such bold changes within their commission": Burke's "Revolution in France," 27). **II.** *adv.* In any case† (see Shakspere's "Two Gentlemen of Verona," i. 1. 34); also, interrogatively, how under any circumstances? (as, *however* did you manage to get here?).

howff (houf), *n.* [Origin uncertain.] A haunt or resort. [Sc.]—**howff,** *v. i.* To haunt or frequent a place. [Sc.]

how-it-zer (hou′it-sėr), *n.* [G. *haubitze*, < Bohem. *houfnice*, catapult.] A comparatively short and light cannon, used esp. for indirect or curved fire, as in reaching troops behind cover.

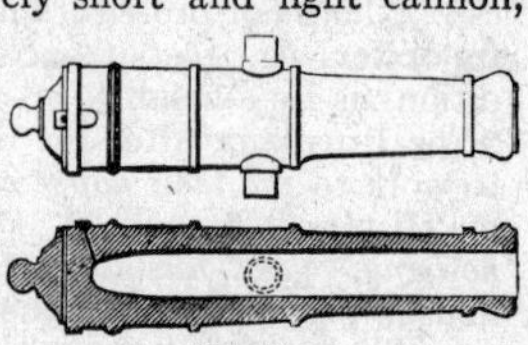
Howitzer.

howl (houl), *v.* [ME. *houlen* = D. *huilen* = G. *heulen*, howl; imit.] **I.** *intr.* To utter a loud, prolonged, mournful cry, as that of a dog or wolf; hence, to utter a similar cry, as a person in distress; wail; also, to make a loud, prolonged sound like wailing, as the wind (as, "The wind is *howling* in turret and tree": Tennyson's "Sisters"). **II.** *tr.* To utter with howls; also, to drive or force by howls.—**howl,** *n.* The prolonged, mournful cry of a dog, wolf, etc.; also, a loud cry or wail, as of pain or rage; also, a prolonged sound like wailing, as of the wind.—**howl′er,** *n.* One who or that which howls; specif., any of the large tropical American monkeys of the genus *Mycetes* (or *Alouatta*), notable for their loud howling cries; also (slang), something pronounced or excessive; esp., an especially ludicrous blunder, as in a school recitation or examination (Eng.).

Howler (*Mycetes ursinus*).

how-let (hou′let), *n.* [Cf. F. *hulotte*, kind of owl (from Teut.: cf. G. *eule*, owl).] An owlet or owl. [Prov. Eng.]

howl-ing (hou′ling), *p. a.* That howls; also, characterized by howling, as of beasts or the wind (as, "the waste *howling* wilderness": Deut. xxxii. 10); dreary; also, very pronounced (slang: as, a *howling* success).—**howling monkey,** a howler.

how-so-ev-er (hou-sọ̄-ev′ėr), *conj.* In whatsoever manner; also, to whatsoever extent or degree (as, "No man, *howsoever* strong of limb, Had dared across that swollen stream to go": W. Morris's "Jason," ii. 56); also, although†; also, nevertheless; yet; however.

hoy[1] (hoi), *n.* [ME. *hoye*: cf. Flem. *hui*, D. *heu*, hoy.] Formerly, a small coasting-vessel, usually sloop-rigged; now, a heavy lighter.

hoy[2] (hoi). [Cf. *hi*, *hey*, and *ahoy*.] **I.** *interj.* An exclamation used to call attention. **II.** *n.* A cry of 'hoy!' as, "I see your young man . . . and I give him a *Hoy!*" (Dickens's "Our Mutual Friend," i. 8).

hoy-den, hoi-den (hoi′dn). [Origin uncertain: cf. D. *heiden*, heathen.] **I.** *n.* A rude, ignorant fellow†; also, a rude or ill-bred girl or woman; now, usually, a boisterous, romping girl (as, "a fine, fresh *hoyden* just from boarding school": Irving's "Tales of a Traveler," iii. 4). **II.** *a.* Pertaining to or characteristic of a hoyden; hoydenish.—**hoy'den-ish, hoi'den-ish,** *a.* Having the manners of a hoyden; characteristic of a hoyden; boisterous; romping.—**hoy'den-ish-ness, hoi'den-ish-ness,** *n.*

hsien (shyen), *n.* [Chinese.] In China, an administrative subdivision of a prefecture or department; also, its seat of government.

hub (hub), *n.* [Origin obscure: cf. *hob*[1].] The central part of a wheel, as that part of a wagon-wheel into which the spokes are inserted; hence, something resembling this, as in central position or in importance (as, the *hub* of the universe, or the *Hub*, a humorous designation of Boston, Mass.); also, the peg or hob used as a target in quoits, etc.

hub-ble=bub-ble (hub'l-bub''l), *n.* [Varied redupl. of *bubble.*] A tobacco-pipe in which the smoke passes through water with a bubbling sound; also, a bubbling or gurgling sound; confused talk or noise.

Hubble-bubble.

hub-bub (hub'ub), *n.* [Prob. of Irish origin.] A loud, confused noise, as of many voices or sounds (as, "A universal *hubbub* wild Of stunning sounds and voices all confused": Milton's "Paradise Lost," ii. 951); a confused din; also, a noisy tumult, or uproar (as, the whole place was in a *hubbub*); turmoil or commotion.

hub-by (hub'i), *n.*; pl. *hubbies* (-iz). Familiar form of *husband.*

huck[1] (huk), *n.* [Cf. MLG. *huken*, Icel. *hūka*, squat, sit on the haunches.] The hip or haunch. [Now prov.]

huck[2] (huk), *n.* Shortened form of *huckaback.*

huck-a-back (huk'ạ-bak), *n.* [Origin unknown.] A coarse, durable fabric of linen, linen and cotton, or cotton only, woven in a small pattern with a rough surface, much used for towels.

huck-le (huk'l), *n.* [Appar. a dim. of *huck*[1].] The hip or haunch.

huck-le-ber-ry (huk'l-ber''i), *n.*; pl. *-berries* (-iz). [Appar. a corruption of *hurtleberry.*] The dark-blue or black edible berry of any of various shrubs of the vacciniaceous genus *Gaylussacia*; a shrub yielding such a berry; sometimes, the berry (blueberry) yielded by any of certain shrubs of the related genus *Vaccinium*, or any of these shrubs.

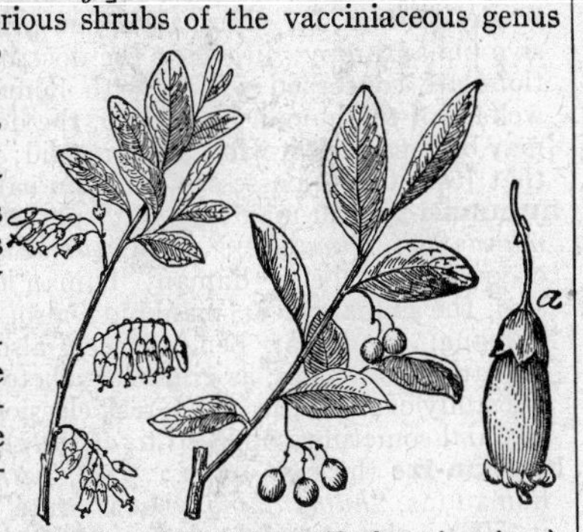

Branches of Huckleberry (*Gaylussacia resinosa*), with flowers and fruit. — *a*, single flower on larger scale.

huck-le-bone (huk'l-bōn), *n.* [See *huckle.*] The hip-bone; also, the ankle-bone or astragalus.

huck-ster (huk'stẽr), *n.* [ME. *huccster, hokester,* huckster (of either sex): cf. D. *heukster*, fem. of *heuker*, retail dealer, D. *heuken*, MLG. *hoken*, G. *höken*, to retail goods, also E. *hawker*[2].] A retailer of small articles; a hawker; a peddler; esp., a small dealer in agricultural produce; fig., one who makes petty or mean bargains; a mean trafficker.—**huck'ster,** *v.* **I.** *intr.* To act as a huckster; bargain or haggle. **II.** *tr.* To deal in, retail, or expose for sale as a huckster does; bargain over.—**huck'ster-er,** *n.*—**huck'ster-ess, huck'stress,** *n.* A female huckster.

hud-dle (hud'l), *v.*; *-dled, -dling.* [Perhaps akin to *hide*[1].] **I.** *tr.* To hide†, cover (*up*)†, or hush (*up*)†; also, to heap or crowd together in a confused way (as, the children were *huddled* together for warmth); draw (one's self) into a disorderly heap; put on (clothes) with careless haste; get (*over, through,* or *up*) in a hurried, slovenly manner (as, "The English ministry hastened to *huddle* up a peace with France and Holland at Breda": Macaulay's "Essays," Sir William Temple). **II.** *intr.* To gather or crowd together in a confused mass.—**hud'dle,** *n.* A confused heap, mass, or crowd (as, a *huddle* of houses; a *huddle* of frightened animals; "The soldiers were crowded together in a *huddle*," B. Franklin's "Autobiography," xi.); a jumble, as of ideas; also, confusion or disorder; slovenly hurry.—**hud'dler,** *n.*

Hu-di-bras-tic (hū-di-bras'tik), *a.* Of or pertaining to, or resembling the style of, Samuel Butler's "Hudibras," a mock-heroic satirical poem directed against the Puritans, published 1663–78; mock-heroic.

Hud-son (hud'sọn) **seal.** See *seal*[2], *n.*

hue[1] (hū), *n.* [OF. *hu*, < *huer*, cry out, shout; prob. imit.] Outcry, as of pursuers; clamor: now only in *hue and cry* (orig., an outcry calling for the pursuit of a felon; also, the pursuit; in general, an outcry or clamor raised publicly against or over something).

hue[2] (hū), *n.* [AS. *hīw*, form, appearance, color, = Goth. *hiwi*, form, appearance, = Sw. *hy*, color, complexion.] Form† or appearance†; also, complexion, or color of the skin (archaic); hence, in general, color or coloring (as, "Coloured with the florid *hue* Of rainbows," Milton's "Paradise Lost," vii. 445; "bays, the peacock's neck in *hue*," Tennyson's "Daisy," 14); technically, the distinctive quality of a color, or that quality whereby one color (as red) differs from other colors (as green, blue, etc.); also, a particular color, or variety of a color (as, silks of many *hues*; a crimson, golden, or greenish *hue*; pale *hues*); a tint.—**hued,** *a.* Having a hue (as specified): as, bright-*hued.*—**hụe'less,** *a.* Lacking color; colorless: as, "when *hueless* is the west" (A. E. Housman's "Shropshire Lad," lv.).

huff (huf), *v.* [Imit.] **I.** *intr.* To puff or blow (now prov. Eng.); also, to swell up (now prov. Eng.); fig., to swell with pride or arrogance, swagger, or bluster (obs. or archaic); also, to take offense; in *checkers,* to huff a piece. **II.** *tr.* To puff or swell (now prov. Eng.); also, to treat with arrogance or contempt; bluster at, hector, or bully; also, to give offense to, or put into a huff; in *checkers,* to remove from the board (a piece with which one's opponent could have jumped but did not: from the old custom of blowing on the piece when removing it).—**huff,** *n.* A puff, as of wind†; also, swagger† or bluster†, or a swaggering or blustering person†; also, a sudden swell of anger; a fit of offended feeling or petulant resentment (as, "He had a great dispute with the congressmen about politics, and left the place in a *huff*": Irving's "Knickerbocker's New York," Account of the Author); in *checkers,* the act of huffing.—**huff'i-ly,** *adv.* In a huffy manner.—**huff'i-ness,** *n.*—**huff'ish,** *a.* Huffy.—**huff'ish-ly,** *adv.*—**huff'ish-ness,** *n.*—**huff'y,** *a.*; compar. *huffier*, superl. *huffiest.* Arrogant or blustering (obs. or archaic); also, offended (as, "You're not *huffy* with myself": Synge's "Well of the Saints," i.); easily offended, or touchy.

hug (hug), *v.*; *hugged, hugging.* [Origin obscure.] **I.** *tr.* To clasp tightly in the arms, esp. with affection; embrace closely or warmly; sometimes, to squeeze with the fore limbs, as a bear does; fig., to cling firmly or fondly to (an opinion, hope, etc.); also, to keep close to (the shore, the wall, etc.), as in sailing or going along; also, to congratulate (one's self) warmly. **II.** *intr.* To cling together; lie close (as, "to *hug* with swine": Shakspere's "King John," v. 2. 142).—**hug,** *n.* An act of hugging; a tight clasp with the arms; a warm embrace; a squeeze by a bear.

huge (hūj), *a.*; compar. *huger*, superl. *hugest.* [ME. *huge, hoge*: cf. OF. *ahuge, ahoge*, great, large, high, *hoge*, hill, height (from Teut.: cf. E. *high*).] Extraordinarily large or big, as in bulk, size, or dimensions (as, a *huge* giant; a *huge* mountain; a *huge* cake; a *huge* bonfire; a *huge* wave); enormous; immense; also, extraordinarily large in quantity or number (as, a *huge* sum, amount, or debt; a *huge* army; a *huge* list of names); also, extraordinarily great in extent, scope, degree, capacity, etc. (as, a *huge* undertaking; a *huge* success or joke; *huge* satisfaction; "Your mynheers are *huge* sleepers," Irving's "Tales of a Traveler," i. 5).—**huge'ly,** *adv.*—**huge'ness,** *n.*

hu-geous (hū'jus), *a.* Huge: as, "My master is close by . . . beside the *hugeous* oak" (Scott's "Woodstock," xiv.). [Prov. or archaic.]

hug-ger (hug'ẽr), *n.* One who hugs.

hug-ger=mug-ger (hug'ẽr-mug'ẽr). [Origin obscure.] **I.** *n.* Secrecy or concealment (as, "We have done but greenly, In *hugger-mugger* to inter him": Shakspere's "Hamlet,"

(variable) ḍ as d or j, ș as s or sh, ț as t or ch, ẓ as z or zh; *o*, F. cloche; ü, F. menu; ċh, Sc. loch; ṅ, F. bonbon; **'**, primary accent; **''**, secondary accent; †, obsolete; <, from; +, and; =, equals. See also lists at beginning of book.

iv. 5. 84); also, disorder or confusion; a medley; a muddle. **II.** *a.* Secret or clandestine; also, disorderly or confused. —**hug'ger=mug'ger,** *v.* **I.** *tr.* To keep secret or concealed. **II.** *intr.* To act secretly; take secret counsel.

Hu-gue-not (hū'gẹ-not), *n.* [F., earlier *eiguenot*, appar. < G. *eidgenoss*, confederate, < *eid*, oath, + *genoss*, companion, associate.] A member of the Reformed or Calvinistic communion of France in the 16th and 17th centuries; a French Protestant. See *Edict of Nantes*, under *edict*.

hu-ia (hö'iạ̈), *n.* [Maori.] A New Zealand bird, *Heteralocha acutirostris*, whose black tail-feathers tipped with white are prized for ornament by the Maoris. Also **hu'ia=bird.**

Huia-birds: male, short bill; female, long curved bill.

hu-la, hu-la=hu-la (hö'lä, hö'lä-hö'lä), *n.* [Native name.] A kind of native Hawaiian dance.

hulk (hulk), *n.* [AS. *hulc* = ML. *hulcus*: cf. Gr. ὁλκάς, towed vessel, ship of burden, < ἕλκειν, draw, drag.] A ship, esp. a heavy, unwieldy vessel (archaic); hence, a big, unwieldy person; a bulky or unwieldy mass of anything; also, the hull of a ship†; also, the body of an old or dismantled ship used as a storehouse, a prison (chiefly in *pl.*), or otherwise; a vessel specially built for such purposes, and not for sea-service; sometimes, a dismasted wreck.—**hulk,** *v. i.* To be bulky or unwieldy; loom (*up*) in bulky form; also, to lounge or slouch in a heavy, loutish manner.—**hulk'ing,** *a.* Bulky; unwieldy; heavy and clumsy: as, a big, *hulking* fellow. Also **hulk'y,** *a.*

hull[1] (hul), *n.* [AS. *hulu*, akin to *helan*, cover, hide: see *hall*.] The husk, shell, or outer covering of a seed or fruit; the calyx of certain fruits, as the strawberry and raspberry; fig., any covering or envelop.—**hull**[1], *v. t.* To remove the hull of.

hull[2] (hul), *n.* [Origin uncertain: cf. *hull*[1], also *hold*[1] and *hole*.] The frame or body of a ship, exclusive of masts, yards, sails, and rigging.—**hull**[2], *v.* **I.**† *intr.* Of a ship, to float or drift on the water without the aid of sails: as, "There they *hull*, expecting but the aid Of Buckingham to welcome them ashore" (Shakspere's "Richard III.," iv. 4. 438). **II.** *tr.* To strike or pierce the hull of (a ship), as with a cannon-ball or a torpedo.

hul-la-ba-loo (hul''ạ-bạ-lö'), *n.* [Perhaps a mixture of *hurly-burly* and *halloo* or *hollo*.] A clamorous noise or disturbance; an uproar.

hulled[1] (huld), *a.* Having a hull or husk, as grain; also, deprived of the hull.

hulled[2] (huld), *a.* Having a hull or body, as a ship.

hull-er (hul'ėr), *n.* One who or that which removes hulls or husks.

hul-lo (hu-lō'), *interj.*, *n.*, and *v.* Same as *hello, hollo*.

hum[1] (hum), *v.*; *hummed, humming.* [ME. *hummen* = G. *hummen*, hum; imit.] **I.** *intr.* To make a low, continuous, droning sound, as a bee in flight or a spinning top; hence, to sing with closed lips, without articulating words; also, to utter an inarticulate or indistinct sound, in hesitation, embarrassment, dissatisfaction, etc. (as, "Don't stand *humming* and hawing, but speak out": Fielding's "Tom Jones," viii. 11); hem; also, to give forth an indistinct sound of mingled voices or noises, as a crowd or a place; murmur; buzz; hence, to be in a state of busy activity (colloq.). **II.** *tr.* To sound, sing, or utter by humming; also, to bring, put, etc., by humming (as, to *hum* a child to sleep).—**hum**[1], *n.* The act or the sound of humming (as, the *hum* of bees; to sing in a low *hum*; the *hum* of city streets); an inarticulate or indistinct murmur; a hem.—**hum**[1], *interj.* An inarticulate sound uttered in hesitation, dissatisfaction, etc.

hum[2] (hum), *n.* and *v.* Same as *humbug*. [Colloq.]

hu-man (hū'mạn). [OF. F. *humain*, < L. *humanus*, akin to *homo*, man.] **I.** *a.* Of, pertaining to, or characteristic of man (as, a *human* head, voice, or life; the *human* form; the *human* heart; *human* nature); natural to man (as, *human* weaknesses); also, having the nature of man (as, the *human* animal; a *human* being; the *human* race); being a man or men; sometimes, having or showing qualities (good or bad) natural to man (as, "You are . . . more *human* in your moods, Than your twin-sister": Tennyson's "Margaret," iv.); also, belonging, pertaining, or relative to man, with his powers and limitations, as opposed to what is superhuman or divine (as, *human* agency; beyond *human* foresight; in all *human* probability); also, of or pertaining to mankind generally (as, *human* affairs or events; *human* history). **II.** *n.* A human being. [Now colloq. or humorous.]

hu-mane (hū-mān'), *a.*; compar. *humaner*, superl. *humanest.* [Var. of *human*: cf. *germane* and *german*[1].] Having or showing the feelings befitting a man, esp. with respect to other human beings or to the lower animals; characterized by tenderness and compassion for the suffering or distressed (as, a *humane* man; *humane* feelings; *humane* measures); kind; benevolent; also, of branches of learning or literature (see *humanity*), tending to refine; polite.—**hu-mane'ly,** *adv.* —**hu-mane'ness,** *n.*

hu-man-ism (hū'mạn-izm), *n.* Human character or quality; also, any system or mode of thought or action in which human interests predominate; also, devotion to or study of the humanities; polite learning; literary culture; esp. [sometimes *cap.*], the studies, principles, or culture of the humanists of the Renaissance.—**hu'man-ist,** *n.* A student of human nature or affairs; also, one devoted to or versed in the humanities; often, a classical scholar; esp. [sometimes *cap.*], one of the scholars of the Renaissance who pursued and disseminated the study and a truer understanding of the literatures, ideas, etc., of ancient Rome and Greece.—**hu-man-is'tic,** *a.*

hu-man-i-ta-ri-an (hū-man-i-tā'ri-ạn). **I.** *a.* Having regard to the interests of humanity or all mankind; broadly philanthropic; also, pertaining to ethical or theological humanitarianism. **II.** *n.* One who professes or practises humanitarian doctrines; a philanthropist; also, one who professes ethical or theological humanitarianism.—**hu-man-i-ta'ri-an-ism,** *n.* Humanitarian principles; comprehensive philanthropy; in *ethics*, the doctrine that man's obligations are concerned wholly with human relations and the welfare of the human race; also, the doctrine that mankind may become perfect without divine aid; in *theol.*, the doctrine that Jesus Christ possessed a human nature only.

hu-man-i-ty (hū-man'i-ti), *n.*; pl. *-ties* (-tiz). [OF. *humanite* (F. *humanité*), < L. *humanitas*.] The condition or quality of being human; human character or nature; also, the human race; mankind; also, the quality of being humane; kindness; benevolence; also, polite learning in its various branches, as grammar, rhetoric, poetry, etc., esp. the study of the Latin and Greek classics (usually in *pl.*, with *the*, and sometimes opposed to *divinity*).

hu-man-ize (hū'mạn-īz), *v.*; *-ized, -izing.* **I.** *tr.* To make human (as, "*humanizing* what is brute": Cowper's "Task," v. 700); also, to make humane, kind, or gentle; soften; civilize; refine. **II.** *intr.* To become human or humane. —**hu''man-i-za'tion** (-i-zā'shọn), *n.*

hu-man-kind (hū'mạn-kīnd'), *n.* The human race; mankind: as, "Far From all the ways of *humankind*" (Southey's "Thalaba," x. 13).

hu-man-ly (hū'mạn-li), *adv.* In a human manner; after the manner of men; by human means; with the feelings natural to or befitting man; also, according to human knowledge or experience (as, *humanly* speaking, it is impossible).—**hu'man-ness,** *n.*

hum-ble (hum'bl), *a.*; compar. *humbler*, superl. *humblest.* [OF. F. *humble*, < L. *humilis*, low, lowly, humble, < *humus*, earth, ground.] Low in height, level, etc.†; fig., low in station, grade of importance, etc. (as, a *humble* family; *humble* origin; a *humble* post); lowly; modest or unpretentious in character (as, "Be it ever so *humble*, there's no place like home": J. H. Payne's "Home, Sweet Home"); also, modest, meek, or abased in spirit or feeling (as, "Show me thy *humble* heart, and not thy knee": Shakspere's "Richard II.," ii. 3. 83); devoid of pride or arrogance; characterized by humility; sometimes, esp. in conventional expressions, deeply or courteously respectful (as, your *humble* servant; in my *humble* opinion).—**hum'ble,** *v. t.*; *-bled, -bling.* To lower in height or level†; bow down†; fig., to lower in condition, importance, dignity, etc. (as, "The mighty man shall be *humbled*": Isa. v. 15); abase; also, to lower the pride of (a person), or lower (pride); humiliate; also, to make humble or meek in spirit or feeling (as, to *humble* one's heart); induce humility in.

hum-ble-bee (hum'bl-bē), *n.* [ME. *humbylbee* = MLG. *hummelbe*: cf. G. *hummel*, humblebee, and E. *hum*[1].] The bumblebee.

hum-ble-ness (hum'bl-nes), *n.* Humble condition, character, or spirit; unpretentiousness; humility.

hum-ble=pie (hum'bl-pī'), *n.* [Orig. < *umbles*, for *numbles*, but later associated with *humble, a.*] A pie made of the umbles (inward parts) of deer, etc.†; fig., something unpalatable and humiliating that one is forced to 'eat' (submit to or do).

hum-bler (hum'blėr), *n.* One who or that which humbles. —**hum'bling,** *p. a.* That humbles; humiliating.—**hum'bling-ly,** *adv.*

hum-bly (hum'bli), *adv.* In a humble manner.

hum-bug (hum'bug), *n.* [Origin unknown.] A deluding trick; a hoax; a fraud; also, pretense or sham (as, there is too much *humbug* about him); also, one who seeks to impose deceitfully upon others; a cheat; an impostor; a deceitful pretender (as, "What a *humbug* that woman is": Thackeray's "Vanity Fair," xxix.).—**hum'bug,** *v.*; *-bugged, -bugging.* **I.** *tr.* To impose upon by humbug or false pretense; delude. **II.** *intr.* To practise humbug.—**hum'bug"ger,** *n.*—**hum'bug"ger-y,** *n.* Humbugging; false pretense.

hum-ding-er (hum'ding'ėr), *n.* [Appar. a made word.] A person or thing remarkable of its kind. [Slang.]

hum-drum (hum'drum). [Varied redupl. of *hum*[1].] **I.** *a.* Lacking variety; monotonous; commonplace; dull: as, a *humdrum* existence; *humdrum* talk; "the honest *humdrum* man" (Masefield's "Daffodil Fields," v.). **II.** *n.* Humdrum character or routine; monotony; also, monotonous or tedious talk; also, a commonplace, dull fellow.—**hum'drum,** *v. i.*; *-drummed, -drumming.* To proceed in a humdrum way.

hu-mer-us (hū'me-rus), *n.*; pl. *humeri* (-rī). [L., prop. *umerus*, akin to Gr. ὦμος, shoulder.] In man, the single long bone in the arm which extends from the shoulder to the elbow; also, the brachium; also, a corresponding bone in the fore limb of other animals or in the wing of birds. —**hu'mer-al,** *a.*

hu-mid (hū'mid), *a.* [L. *humidus*, prop. *umidus*, < *umere*, be moist: see *humor*.] Moist or damp (as, *humid* eyes; "*Humid* flowers, that breathed Their morning incense," Milton's "Paradise Lost," ix. 193); esp., moist with aqueous vapor (as, *humid* air); characterized by much moisture in the air, as weather, climate, a region, etc.—**hu-mid-i-fy** (hū-mid'i-fī), *v. t.*; *-fied, -fying.* [See *-fy*.] To make humid, moist, or damp.—**hu-mid"i-fi-ca'tion** (-fi-kā'shon), *n.* —**hu-mid'i-fi-er** (-fī-ėr), *n.*—**hu-mid'i-ty** (-ti), *n.*; pl. *-ties* (-tiz). Humid condition; moistness or dampness; also, moisture, or watery matter diffused through anything; in *meteor.*, the amount (or percentage) of aqueous vapor in the atmosphere compared with that which is required to saturate it at the given temperature, the humidity of complete saturation being expressed at 100, and lesser amounts by lower numbers (called specifically 'relative humidity').—**hu'mid-ly,** *adv.*—**hu'mid-ness,** *n.*

hu-mi-dor (hū'mi-dôr), *n.* [From *humid*.] A box, jar, case, or storage-room for cigars or other preparations of tobacco, fitted with means for keeping the tobacco suitably moist; also, a device, as a holder containing a damp sponge or the like, for supplying moisture for this purpose.

hu-mil-i-ate (hū-mil'i-āt), *v. t.*; *-ated, -ating.* [LL. *humiliatus*, pp. of *humiliare*, < L. *humilis*, E. *humble*.] To humble or abase in condition, dignity, etc.†; also, to lower the pride or self-respect of, as by some offense to dignity; treat or affect in such a manner as to cause a painful sense of loss of dignity; mortify.—**hu-mil'i-at-ing** (-ā-ting), *p. a.* That humiliates; mortifying.—**hu-mil'i-at-ing-ly,** *adv.*—**hu-mil-i-a'tion** (-ā'shon), *n.* [LL. *humiliatio(n-)*.] The act of humiliating; the state or the feeling of being humiliated; mortification.—**hu-mil'i-a-tor,** *n.*

hu-mil-i-ty (hū-mil'i-ti), *n.*; pl. *-ties* (-tiz). [OF. *humilite* (F. *humilité*), < L. *humilitas*, < *humilis*, E. *humble*.] Humble or lowly condition or character (obs. or rare); also, the quality of being humble in spirit or feeling; modest or meek sense of one's own insignificance, inferiority, weaknesses, faults, etc. (opposed to *pride* or *arrogance*); *pl.*, acts showing a humble spirit.

hum-mer (hum'ėr), *n.* One who or that which hums; a very rapid, energetic, or otherwise extraordinary person or thing (slang).

hum-ming (hum'ing), *p. a.* That hums; buzzing; resounding with busy activity (colloq.); extraordinarily active, intense, great, or big (slang); foaming, strong, or heady, as liquor (colloq.: as, "*humming* ale," Irving's "Tales of a Traveler," i. 7).—**hum'ming=bird,** *n.* Any of the small American birds constituting the family *Trochilidæ*, characterized by long and narrow bills, narrow wings whose rapid vibration produces a humming sound, and usually by brilliant plumage.

Humming-birds. — Upper figure, *Trochilus colubris*; lower figure, *Amazilia fuscocaudata.*

hum-mock (hum'ok), *n.* [Origin obscure: cf. *hammock*[2], also *hump*.] A knoll or hillock; also, a protuberance or ridge, as on a floe of ice; also, an elevated tract rising above the general level of a marshy region; a hammock.—**hum'mock-y,** *a.* Abounding in hummocks; also, like a hummock.

hum-mum (hum'um), *n.* Same as *hammam*.

hu-mor (hū'mor or ū'-), *n.* [OF. *humor*, *umor* (F. *humeur*), < L. *humor*, prop. *umor*, moisture, liquid, < *umere*, be moist: cf. Gr. ὑγρός, wet, moist, Skt. *uksh-*, sprinkle.] Moisture†; vapor†; also, any animal or plant fluid, whether natural or morbid; in the old physiology, one of the four chief bodily fluids, blood (see *sanguine*), choler or yellow bile, phlegm, and melancholy or black bile ('cardinal humors'), regarded as determining, by their relative proportions in the system, a person's physical and mental constitution (see *temperament*); hence, mental disposition or tendency (as, "that rash *humour* which my mother gave me": Shakspere's "Julius Cæsar," iv. 3. 120); also, temporary state or frame of mind (as, good or bad *humor*; in the *humor* for fighting); temper; mood; inclination; sometimes, capricious or freakish inclination, or a fancy, whim, or caprice (as, "There is no crossing him in 's *humour*," Shakspere's "Timon of Athens," i. 2. 166; "according as his *humours* lead," Tennyson's "Day-Dream," 207); *pl.*, whimsical or odd traits, ways, or actions (as, "And so well could paint The village-folk, with all their *humors* quaint": Whittier's "Countess"); also, *sing.*, the quality in anything whereby it excites amusement (as, to fail to see the *humor* of a situation; a speech abounding in unconscious *humor*, that is, in an amusing quality not perceived or intended by the speaker); *pl.*, amusing or comical features (as, to be alive to the *humors* of the occasion); also, *sing.*, the faculty of perceiving what is amusing, comical, or ludicrous ('sense of humor'), or of expressing it in speech, or of imagining and expressing it as in literary work; speech or writing showing this faculty; sometimes, speech, writing, action, etc., intended to excite amusement (as, to introduce *humor* into a play; to indulge in crude *humor*); in *pathol.*, any chronic skin-disease ascribed to a disordered condition of the blood.—**aqueous humor.** See under *aqueous*.—**out of humor,** displeased or dissatisfied; cross.—**vitreous humor.** See under *vitreous*.—**hu'mor,** *v. t.* To comply with the humor, inclination, or fancy of (as, to *humor* a child, an exacting person, or a madman, as by assenting to everything; "We must *humour* his madness," Dunsany's "Laughter of the Gods," iii.); indulge;

fig., to comply with the exigencies of (as, "Thou shalt be writ the man, That with smooth air couldst *humour* best our tongue": Milton's "Sonnets," To H. Lawes); accommodate one's self to.—**hu′mor-al,** *a.* Pertaining to or proceeding from the bodily humors.—**hu′mored,** *a.* Having a (specified) humor: as, good-*humored.*

hu-mor-esque (hū-mo̤-resk′), *n.* [G. *humoreske,* < L. *humor,* E. *humor.*] A musical composition of humorous or capricious character.

hu-mor-ist (hū′mo̤r-ist), *n.* One subject to humors or whims†; also, one who possesses or exercises the faculty of humor; a humorous talker, writer, actor, lecturer, or the like; esp., a writer devoted particularly to producing books, articles, paragraphs, etc., in a humorous vein.—**hu-mor-is′tic,** *a.*

hu-mor-less (hū′mo̤r-les), *a.* Destitute of humor.

hu-mor-ous (hū′mo̤r-us), *a.* [LL. *humorosus,* prop. *umorosus,* moist, < L. *humor, umor:* see *humor.*] Moist†; also, pertaining or due to the bodily humors† (as, *humorous* disorders); also, out of humor†, or ill-humored†; also, full of or characterized by humors or whims (obs. or archaic: as, "a vain, giddy, shallow, *humorous* youth," Shakspere's "Henry V.," ii. 4. 28); also, characterized by humor or amusing quality, amusing, comical, or funny (as, the affair has its *humorous* aspect or features; to be able to see the *humorous* side of things); having or showing the faculty of humor, as a person, speech, writing, action, etc.; droll; facetious.—**hu′mor-ous-ly,** *adv.*—**hu′mor-ous-ness,** *n.*

hu-mor-some (hū′mo̤r-sum), *a.* Out of humor, or ill-humored; also, subject to humors or whims; capricious; also, humorous, amusing, or droll (chiefly prov. Eng. and Sc.).

hu′mour, hu′moured, hu′mour-less, hu′mour-some. British preferred forms of *humor,* etc.

hump (hump), *n.* [Origin uncertain: cf. D. *homp,* lump, chunk, LG. *hump,* heap, hill, stump.] A rounded protuberance, esp. on the back, as that due to abnormal curvature of the spine in man, or that normally present in certain animals, such as the camel and bison; also, with *the,* a fit of ill humor or gloomy dissatisfaction (slang: as, to have or get the *hump;* to give one the *hump*).—**hump,** *v.* **I.** *tr.* To raise (the back, etc.) in a hump; also, to exert (one's self) in a great effort (slang, U. S.). **II.** *intr.* To rise in a hump; also, to exert one's self, as in running (slang, U. S.).—**hump′back,** *n.* A back with a hump; also, one who has such a back; also, a whale of the genus *Megaptera,* with a hump-like dorsal fin.—**hump′backed,** *a.* Having a hump on the back.—**humped,** *a.* Having a hump or humps: as, the two-*humped* (Bactrian) camel.

humph (humf or hmf). **I.** *interj.* An utterance expressive of disbelief, dissatisfaction, contempt, etc. **II.** *n.* An utterance of 'humph.'

hump-less (hump′les), *a.* Without a hump.

hump-ty=dump-ty (hump′ti-dump′ti). [Cf. *hump* and *dump*[2].] **I.** *a.* Short and thick-set or stout. **II.** *n.;* pl. *-ties* (-tiz). A short, clumsily stout person; also (written *Humpty-Dumpty* or *Humpty Dumpty*), the hero of a familiar riming nursery riddle (who fell from a wall, and could not be put up or together again), commonly explained as meaning an egg.

hump-y (hum′pi), *a.* Full of humps; also, hump-like.

hu-mus (hū′mus), *n.* [L., earth, ground.] The brown or black organic constituent of soils, which is produced by the partial decomposition of vegetable or animal matter: a source of nitrogenous food for plants.

Hun (hun), *n.* [LL. *Hunni,* pl.] One of an Asiatic race of warlike nomads who in the 5th century, under their king Attila, overran and devastated Europe; hence, an uncivilized or barbarous devastator; in recent use, a German.

hunch (hunch), *v. t.* [Origin obscure: cf. *hump.*] To push or thrust (now prov.); also, to thrust out or up in a hump.—**hunch,** *n.* A protuberance or hump; also, a lump or thick piece; also, a premonition or suspicion (slang, U. S.).—**hunch′back,** *n.* A back with a hunch; also, one who has such a back; a humpback.—**hunch′backed,** *a.*

hun-dred (hun′dre̤d), *n.;* pl. *hundreds* or (as after a numeral) *hundred.* [AS. *hundred* (= D. *honderd* = G. *hundert* = Icel. *hundradh*), < *hund* = OS. *hund* = OHG. *hunt* = Goth. *hund,* hundred; akin to L. *centum,* Gr. ἑκατόν, Skt. *çata,* hundred. For the final element, *-red,* cf. Goth. *rathjō,* number.] A number composed of ten times ten units, or a symbol, as 100 or c, representing it; a set of a hundred persons or things; also, an administrative division of an English county; a similar division in colonial Pennsylvania, Delaware, Maryland, and Virginia, still surviving in Delaware. Also used as a quasi-adjective, by omission of *of* before a noun following: as, a *hundred* (of) miles; five *hundred* (of) men.—**Hundred Days,** the closing period of Napoleon Bonaparte's career in France, in 1815, after his escape from Elba, variously reckoned as approximately 100 days, his actual second reign beginning with his reëntry into Paris, March 19, and ending with his abdication, June 22.—**Hundred Years' War,** the series of wars in France between England and France, from 1337 to 1453, the English, generally the victors, and rulers of a great part of France, being finally expelled except from Calais, which they retained for about a century longer.—**Old Hundred.** See under *old, a.*—**hun′dred-al** (-a̤l), *a.* Of or pertaining to a hundred (administrative division).—**hun′dred-er, hun′dred-or,** *n.* The chief officer, or bailiff, of a hundred; also, an inhabitant of a hundred, esp. one liable to service on a jury.—**hun′dred-fold** (-fōld), *a.* and *n.* A hundred times as great or as much.—**hun′dredth. I.** *a.* Next after the ninety-ninth; also, being one of a hundred equal parts. **II.** *n.* The hundredth member of a series; also, a hundredth part.—**hun′dred-weight,** *n.;* pl. *hundredweights* or (as after a numeral) *hundredweight.* A unit of avoirdupois weight commonly equivalent to 100 pounds in the U. S. and 112 pounds ('long hundredweight') in England.

hung (hung). Preterit and past participle of *hang.*

Hun-ga-ri-an (hung-gā′ri-a̤n). **I.** *a.* Of or pertaining to Hungary or its people; pertaining to the language of the predominant race of Hungary; also, freebooting† or thieving† (sometimes with implication of hunger: see Shakspere's "Merry Wives of Windsor," i. 3. 23). **II.** *n.* A native or inhabitant of Hungary; esp., a member of the predominant race of Hungary; a Magyar; also, the language of this race; Magyar.

hun-ger (hung′gėr), *n.* [AS. *hungor* = D. *honger* = G. *hunger* = Icel. *hungr,* hunger.] The uneasy or painful sensation caused by want of food; craving appetite; also, famine (archaic); also, fig., strong or eager desire (as, *hunger* for praise).—**hun′ger,** *v.* [AS. *hyngran.*] **I.** *intr.* To feel hunger; be hungry; fig., to have a strong desire. **II.** *tr.* To subject to hunger; starve.—**hun′gered,** *a.* Hungry; starved.—**hun′ger-er,** *n.*—**hun′ger-ly,** *a.* Having a hungry look. [Archaic.]—**hun′ger=strike,** *n.* A persistent refusal to eat, as a protest against imprisonment or other forms of restraint or compulsion.—**hun′ger=strike,** *v. i.* To enter upon or engage in a hunger-strike.—**hun′ger=strik″er,** *n.*—**hun′gry,** *a.;* compar. *hungrier,* superl. *hungriest.* [AS. *hungrig.*] Having the sensation of hunger; craving food; having a keen appetite; indicating, characteristic of, or characterized by hunger (as, "Cassius has a lean and *hungry* look," Shakspere's "Julius Cæsar," i. 2. 194; "And stop and eat, for well you may Be in a *hungry* case," Cowper's "John Gilpin," 192); fig., strongly or eagerly desirous for something; also, rarely, causing hunger (as, a *hungry* place); that leaves one hungry, or unsatisfying (as, *hungry* fare); also, lacking needful or desirable elements, as land, etc.; not rich or fertile; poor.—**hun′gri-ly,** *adv.*—**hun′gri-ness,** *n.*

hunk[1] (hungk), *n.* [Cf. *hunch.*] A large piece or lump; a chunk. [Colloq.]

hunk[2] (hungk), *n.* [D. *honk,* post, station, home.] In children's games, the goal, base, or home: as, to be on *hunk.* [Local, U. S.]—**hunk**[2], *adv.* or *a.* On hunk (local, U. S.); hence, in a safe or satisfactory position or condition (slang, U. S.).

Hunk-er[1] (hung′kėr), *n.* [Perhaps < D. *honk,* post, home: see *hunk*[2].] Orig., a member of the conservative section of the Democratic party in the State of New York, about 1845; hence [*l. c.*], one who opposes innovation or change; a fogy. Cf. *Barnburner.*

hunk-er[2] (hung′kėr), *v. i.* [Origin obscure: cf. *huck*[1].] To squat on one's haunches, or with the haunches brought near the heels: as, "The road . . . is so steep . . . that in a sharp frost children *hunker* at the top and are blown down . . . on rails of ice" (Barrie's "Auld Licht Idylls," ii.). [Sc. and prov. Eng.]—**hunk'ers,** *n. pl.* The haunches or hams: in the phrase 'on one's hunkers' (in a squatting posture, with the knees sharply bent). [Prov. or colloq.]

hunks (hungks), *n.* [Origin obscure.] A crabbed, disagreeable person (as, "some old *hunks* of a sea-captain": H. Melville's "Moby-Dick," i.); also, a covetous, sordid man; a miser.

hunk-y[1] (hung'ki), *n.*; pl. *hunkies* (-kiz). A Hungarian. [Slang, U. S.]

hunk-y[2] (hung'ki), *a.* [See *hunk*[2], *adv.* or *a.*] In a satisfactory position or condition; well; right. Also **hunk'y=do'ry** (-dō'ri). [Slang.]

hunt (hunt), *v.* [AS. *huntian*, prob. akin to *hentan*, seize, E. *hent*.] **I.** *tr.* To chase (game or other wild animals) for the purpose of catching or killing; hence, in general, to pursue with force, hostility, etc. (as, "Evil shall *hunt* the violent man to overthrow him": Ps. cxl. 11); drive (*out*, etc.); also, to search for, or seek; endeavor to obtain or find; also, to scour (a region) in pursuit of game; hence, to search (a place) thoroughly; also, to use or manage (a horse, etc.) in the chase. **II.** *intr.* To engage in the chase; also, to make a search or quest (often with *for* or *after*); in *mach.*, to jump back and forth or move abnormally instead of remaining steady, as a part of a mechanism.—**hunt,** *n.* The act or practice, or an act, of hunting game or other wild animals; the chase; hence, a pursuing with hostility, etc.; also, the act of seeking or endeavoring to find something; a search; also, a body of persons associated for the purpose of hunting; an association of huntsmen; also, a district hunted with hounds.—**hunt'a-ble,** *a.* Capable of or suitable for being hunted.

hunt-er (hun'tėr), *n.* One who hunts game or other wild animals; a huntsman; a horse or a dog used in hunting; also, an animal that hunts its prey; also, one who searches or seeks for something (as, a fortune-*hunter*).—**hunter's moon,** the full moon next after the harvest-moon.

hunt-ing (hun'ting), *n.* The act of one who or that which hunts; esp., the pursuing of game or other wild animals in order to catch or kill them; the chase.—**hunt'ing=box,** *n.* A small house for use during the hunting-season; a shooting-box.—**hunt'ing=case,** *n.* A watchcase with a hinged cover to protect the crystal, orig. against accident in hunting.—**hunt'ing=dog,** *n.* A dog employed in hunting; also, any of various dog-like animals that hunt their prey in packs, as *Lycaon pictus*, of South Africa, and the dhole, of India; also, *pl.* [*cap.*], in *astron.*, the constellation Canes Venatici.—**hunt'ing=ground,** *n.* A place or region for hunting: as, the happy *hunting-grounds* (the American Indians' heaven).—**hunt'ing=leop''ard,'** *n.* The chetah.

Hunting-dog (*Lycaon pictus*).

hunt-ress (hun'tres), *n.* A woman who hunts; also, a mare employed in hunting.

hunts-man (hunts'man), *n.*; pl. *-men*. A man who practises hunting; also, the manager of a hunt.

hunt's=up (hunts'up), *n.* A song sung or tune played to awaken huntsmen in the morning. Also fig. [Archaic.]

Hu-on (hū'on) **pine.** [From the river *Huon*, in Tasmania.] A large taxaceous tree, *Dacrydium franklinii*, of Tasmania, whose wood is used for boat-building, carving, etc.

hur-dle (hėr'dl), *n.* [AS. *hyrdel*, akin to D. *horde*, G. *hürde*, hurdle, Icel. *hurdh*, Goth. *haurds*, door, L. *cratis*, wickerwork, Gr. *κύρτος*, basket, cage.] A movable rectangular frame of interlaced twigs, crossed bars, or the like, as for a temporary fence; also, a frame or sledge on which criminals were formerly drawn to the place of execution; also, a barrier in a race-course, to be leaped by the contestants; *pl.* (with *the*), a race in which such barriers are leaped.—**hur'dle,** *v.*; *-dled*, *-dling*. **I.** *tr.* To construct with hurdles; inclose with hurdles; also, to leap over (a hurdle, etc.), as in a race. **II.** *intr.* To leap over a hurdle or other barrier.—**hur'dler,** *n.*

hurds (hėrdz), *n. pl.* Same as *hards*.

hur-dy=gur-dy (hėr'di-gėr''di), *n.*; pl. *-dies* (-diz). [Appar. imit. of the sound of the instrument.] Orig., a lute-shaped stringed musical instrument sounded by the revolution, against the strings, of a rosined wheel turned by a crank; now, usually, a barrel-organ, street-piano, or similar instrument played by turning a handle.

hurl (hėrl), *v.* [ME. *hurlen*; origin uncertain: cf. *hurtle*.] **I.** *tr.* To drive or throw with great force; cast or fling violently; hence, to utter with vehemence (as, "*hurling* defiance toward the vault of heaven": Milton's "Paradise Lost," i. 669). **II.** *intr.* To rush impetuously (archaic: as, "The very streams . . . impatient seem To *hurl* into the covert of the grove," Thomson's "Seasons," Summer, 450); also, to throw a missile; specif., to play at the game of hurling.—**hurl,** *n.* A forcible or violent throw; a fling.—**hurl'er,** *n.*—**hurl'ey,** *n.* The Irish game of hurling; also, the stick or club used in this game.—**hurl'ing,** *n.* An old game, once popular in Cornwall, between opposite parties each striving to hurl or carry a ball to a goal; in Ireland, a game similar to hockey.

hur-ly (hėr'li), *n.* [See *hurly-burly*.] Commotion; hurly-burly.

hur-ly=bur-ly (hėr'li-bėr'li), *n.*; pl. *-lies* (-liz). [Appar. a reduplicated formation < *hurl*: cf. F. *hurluberlu*, a hare-brained person.] Commotion; tumult; bustle; confusion.

hur-rah (hů-rä' or -râ'). [Cf. G. *hurra*, hurrah, in MHG. a cry used in chasing, connected with *hurren*, rush. Cf. also *huzza*.] **I.** *interj.* An exclamation of joy, exultation, applause, or the like. **II.** *n.* The exclamation 'hurrah.'—**hurrah's nest,** a tangled or disorderly mass; a scene or state of disorder: as, "Here you've got our clock all to pieces, and have been keeping up a perfect *hurrah's nest* in our kitchen for three days" (Mrs. Stowe's "Oldtown Folks," iv.). [U. S.]—**hur-rah',** *v.* **I.** *intr.* To shout 'hurrah.' **II.** *tr.* To salute with shouts of 'hurrah'; cheer.

hur-ri-cane (hur'i-kān), *n.* [Sp. *huracán*; from Carib.] A violent tropical cyclonic storm; any great windstorm; fig., anything suggesting such a storm.—**hur'ri-cane=deck',** *n.* A light upper deck on passenger-steamers, etc.

Hurricane. A British fighter plane (Hawker).

hur-ried (hur'id), *p. a.* Driven or impelled to hurry, as a person; also, characterized by or done with hurry, as actions, work, etc.; hasty.—**hur'ried-ly,** *adv.*—**hur'ried-ness,** *n.*

hur-ri-er (hur'i-ėr), *n.* One who hurries.

hur-ry (hur'i), *v.*; *-ried*, *-rying*. [Prob. orig. imit.: cf. MHG. *hurren*, rush, G. whir, Dan. *hurre*, hum, buzz, and E. *whir*.] **I.** *tr.* To drive, carry, send, or move with more than a natural or easy speed, often with confused or precipitated haste (as, to *hurry* a person along the street; to *hurry* a thing out of sight; "A second fear . . . madly *hurries* her she knows not whither," Shakspere's "Venus and Adonis," 904); impel or force with haste, esp. undue haste, in action, mental processes, etc. (as, to be *hurried* into an imprudent action or decision); urge to a greater or undue rapidity of movement or action (as, to *hurry* a horse; to *hurry* a worker; don't let me *hurry* you); also, to hasten or accelerate (a process, etc.); bring about (an event, etc.) more speedily; also, to agitate or disturb (now prov. Eng.). **II.** *intr.* To move, proceed, or act with haste, often undue haste.—**hur'ry,** *n.*; pl. *hurries* (-iz). Hurried movement or action; haste, esp. undue or precipitate haste; sometimes, eager haste (as, to be in no *hurry* to begin); also, need of haste (as, there is no *hurry* for this); also, agitation, disturbance, or tumult (now prov. Eng. and Sc.).—**hur'ry-ing-ly,** *adv.*

hur-ry=scur-ry (hur'i-skur'i). **I.** *adv.* With hurrying and scurrying; in headlong, disorderly flight or haste. **II.** *a.* Characterized by headlong, disorderly flight or haste. **III.** *n.* A hurry-scurry flight, rush, or performance; also, headlong, disorderly haste; hurry and confusion.—**hur'ry=scur'ry,** *v.i.* To rush or go hurry-scurry.

hurst (hėrst), *n.* [AS. *hyrst* = G. *horst.*] A grove or small wood; a wooded eminence; a knoll, hill, or bank; a sandbank. [Sc. and prov. Eng., or in place-names.]

hurt (hėrt), *v.*; *hurt, hurting.* [Prob. < OF. *hurter* (F. *heurter*), strike against something; origin uncertain.] **I.** *tr.* To strike or dash (a thing) against something†; hence, to injure or damage (a material object, etc.) by striking rough use, or otherwise (as, the hail *hurt* the young plants; to *hurt* walls or furniture; the cup fell without being *hurt*); in general, to injure, harm, or affect detrimentally (as, to *hurt* credit, business, or a cause; to *hurt* a person financially, socially, or morally); esp., to cause bodily injury to (with or without consequent pain: as, to be *hurt* in battle; to be *hurt* in the arm; "if one man's ox *hurt* another's, that he die," Ex. xxi. 35); hence, to cause bodily pain to or in (as, the wound still *hurts* him; tight shoes *hurt* the feet; the cough *hurts* my throat); fig., to cause mental pain to (as, to *hurt* a person, or his feelings, by unkind words; to feel *hurt* by neglect); wound in feelings; grieve. **II.** *intr.* To strike or dash, as against something†; also, to cause injury, damage, or harm; also, to cause or occasion pain (bodily or mental). —**hurt,** *n.* [OF. *hurte, hurt* (F. *heurt*).] A stroke† or blow†; also, injury, damage, or harm; often, a bodily injury, as a wound; also, pain (bodily or mental) from a particular cause.—**hurt′er,** *n.*—**hurt′ful,** *a.* Such as to cause hurt or injury; injurious; harmful.—**hurt′ful-ly,** *adv.*—**hurt′ful-ness,** *n.*

hur-tle (hėr′tl), *v.*; *-tled, -tling.* [Freq. of *hurt.*] **I.** *tr.* To dash or knock, as one thing against another; drive violently, or fling; also, to dash against; collide with. **II.** *intr.* To strike together or against something; meet in collision; also, to rush or dash, esp. noisily (as, "The bowstrings twang'd, and arrows hiss'd, And javelins *hurtled* by": Southey's "Roderick," xxv. 165); also, to resound as in collision or rapid motion.—**hur′tle,** *n.* The act or an act of hurtling; collision; clashing sound.

hur-tle-ber-ry (hėr′tl-ber″i), *n.*; pl. *-berries* (-iz). [= *whortleberry.*] The whortleberry; also, the huckleberry.

hurt-less (hėrt′les), *a.* Receiving or doing no hurt.

hus-band (huz′band), *n.* [AS. *hūsbonda*, < *hūs*, house, + *bonda*, householder: see *bond*[2].] The master of a house†; also, a man joined in marriage to a woman as wife; also, a husbandman†; also, a manager or steward (archaic: cf. *ship's husband*, under *ship, n.*).—**hus′band,** *v. t.* To till, as soil; cultivate, as plants; also, to manage or administer, esp. with prudent economy (as, to *husband* one's resources); economize; also, to provide with a husband; also, to act as a husband to; marry (a woman).—**hus′band-hood** (-hůd), *n.* The position or relation of a husband.—**hus′band-less,** *a.* Destitute or bereft of a husband.—**hus′band-ly,** *a.* Of, like, or befitting a husband; marital; also, frugal†.—**hus′band-man** (-man), *n.*; pl. *-men.* One who tills the soil; a farmer.—**hus′band-ry,** *n.* The management of domestic affairs, or of resources generally (as, good *husbandry*; bad *husbandry*); economy, good or bad; often, careful or thrifty management; frugality; thrift; also, the business of a husbandman or farmer; agriculture; farming; also, agricultural produce†.

hush (hush), *v.* [Appar. < ME. *husst*, also *hust, huyst*, adj. (orig. interj., as a natural utterance calling for silence), taken as a pp.: cf. *whist*[1].] **I.** *tr.* To make silent; silence; quiet; still; also, to calm or allay (as, "All her fears were *hush'd* together": Cowper's "Fable"); also, to procure silence concerning (usually with *up*: as, "The thing was *hushed* up, and never known at court," Swift's "Gulliver's Travels," ii. 5). **II.** *intr.* To become or be silent or quiet. —**hush,** *interj.* A command to be silent or quiet.—**hush,** *n.* Silence or quiet, esp. after noise.—**hush,** *a.* Silent; quiet: as, "The bold winds speechless and the orb below As *hush* as death" (Shakspere's "Hamlet," ii. 2. 508). [Archaic.] —**hush′ful,** *a.* Silent; still.—**hush′ful-ly,** *adv.*—**hush′=mon″ey,** *n.* Money paid to secure silence or prevent disclosure.—**hush′=ship,** *n.* One of a class of light cruisers of very high speed, provided with long-range guns, built by the British during the World War: so called because of the secrecy in regard to their construction.

husk[1] (husk), *n.* [ME. *huske*; origin uncertain.] The dry external covering of certain fruits or seeds, esp. (U. S.) of an ear of maize or Indian corn; hence, the enveloping or outer part of anything, esp. when dry or worthless.—**husk**[1], *v. t.* To remove the husk from.

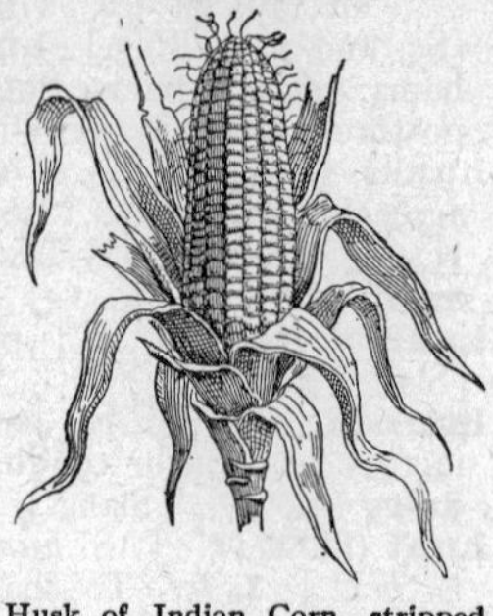
Husk of Indian Corn, stripped down about the ear.

husk[2] (husk), *n.* [Prob. < *husky.*] A husky quality or state, as of the voice.

husk[3] (husk), *n.* [Origin uncertain: cf. *husk*[2].] A disease of cattle, characterized by a hacking cough, due to round-worms in the bronchial tubes.

husk-er (hus′kėr), *n.* One who or that which husks.

husk-i-ly (hus′ki-li), *adv.* In a husky voice; hoarsely.—**husk′i-ness,** *n.*

husk-ing (hus′king), *n.* The act of removing husks, esp. (U. S.) those of maize or Indian corn; also, a husking-bee.—**husk′ing=bee,** *n.* A gathering of persons to assist in husking Indian corn: usually a kind of merrymaking. [U. S.]

husk-y[1] (hus′ki). **I.** *a.*; compar. *huskier*, superl. *huskiest.* Of, like, or abounding in husks; dry as husks; also, dry in the throat, as a person; hoarse; rough in tone, as the voice; also, burly, or big and strong (colloq., U. S.). **II.** *n.*; pl. *huskies* (-kiz). A husky, or big and strong, person. [Colloq., U. S.]

Hus-ky[2] (hus′ki), *n.*; pl. *-kies* (-kiz). [Said to be a corruption of *Eskimo.*] An Eskimo; also, the Eskimo language; also [*l. c.*], an Eskimo dog (as, "skulking furry forms,—starving *huskies* . . . from some Indian village": Jack London's "Call of the Wild," iii.).

hus-sar (hů-zär′), *n.* [Hung. *huszár*, orig. freebooter; akin to E. *corsair.*] Orig., one of a body of light Hungarian cavalry formed during the 15th century; hence, one of a class of similar troops, usually with striking or showy uniforms, in European armies.

Huss-ite (hus′īt), *n.* A follower of John Huss (1369?–1415), the Bohemian religious reformer, whose teachings were largely founded on those of Wyclif, and who was adjudged a heretic and burned alive at Constance.

hus-sy (huz′i), *n.*; pl. *hussies* (-iz). [From *housewife* (ME. *huswif*).] The mistress of a household†; also, a pert, mischievous, or ill-behaved girl (as, "Alice may only turn out a story-telling little *hussy*, after all!" W. De Morgan's "Alice-for-Short," vii.: often used jocosely); a worthless woman; also, a small case for needles, etc.

hus-tings (hus′tingz), *n. pl.* or *sing.* [AS. *hūsting*, from Scand.: cf. Icel. *hūsthing*, 'house assembly,' council summoned by a king or leader.] [*cap.*] An ancient court of the city of London, still infrequently held; also [*l. c.*], the temporary platform from which candidates for Parliament were formerly nominated and addressed the electors; in general, an electioneering platform; hence, election proceedings. [Eng.]—**hustings court,** a local court in various cities of Virginia.

hus-tle (hus′l), *v.*; *-tled, -tling.* [D. *hutselen*, freq. of *hutsen*, shake, jog.] **I.** *tr.* To shake, push, or shove roughly; jostle; often, to force roughly or hurriedly, as into, out of, or through a place (as, "The orator . . . was . . . most unceremoniously *hustled* out of the city": Motley's "Dutch Republic," iii. 6). **II.** *intr.* To push or force one's way (as, "Here in the ruck, anyhow . . . *Hustles* the Class!" Henley's "In Hospital," xi.); also, to proceed or work rapidly or energetically (colloq.).—**hus′tle,** *n.* The act of one who hustles; esp., energetic activity, as in work or business (colloq.).—**hus′tler,** *n.* One who hustles; esp., one who is active and energetic, as in work or business (colloq.).—**hus′tling,** *p. a.* That hustles; energetic; strenuous. [Colloq.]

hut (hut), *n.* [F. *hutte*, < G. *hütte*, hut; prob. from the root of E. *hide*[1].] A small, rude, or humble dwelling; *milit.*, a rude wooden structure for the temporary housing of troops.—**hut,** *v.*; *hutted, hutting.* **I.** *tr.* To place in or furnish with a hut or huts: as, "There was a sawmill near, round which were left several piles of boards, with which we

soon *hutted* ourselves" (B. Franklin's "Autobiography," xii.). **II.** *intr.* To take shelter in a hut or huts.
hutch (huch), *n.* [OF. F. *huche*, < ML. *hutica*, chest; perhaps from Teut.] A chest, box, or trough; also, a pen for confining small animals, as rabbits; also, a hut or cabin. —**hutch,** *v. t.* To put in or as in a hutch.
hut-ment (hut'mẹnt), *n.* Accommodation in huts; a camp of huts; a hut, as for troops.
huz-za (hu-zä'). [Cf. G. *hussa*, huzza, also E. *hurrah.*] **I.** *interj.* An exclamation of exultation, applause, or the like. **II.** *n.*; pl. *-zas* (-zäz'). The exclamation 'huzza.'— **huz-za',** *v.*; *-zaed, -zaing.* **I.** *intr.* To shout 'huzza'; hurrah. **II.** *tr.* To salute with shouts of 'huzza.'
hy-a-cinth (hī'ạ-sinth), *n.* [L. *hyacinthus*, < Gr. ὑάκινθος, kind of flower, also a gem: cf. *jacinth.*] Among the ancients, a plant variously identified as iris, gladiolus, larkspur, etc.; now, any of the bulbous liliaceous plants constituting the genus *Hyacinthus*, esp. *H. orientalis*, widely cultivated for its spikes of fragrant, white or colored, bell-shaped flowers; any of various similar plants; also, among the ancients, a bluish gem; now, a reddish-orange gem, the jacinth.—**hy-a-cin'thine** (-sin'-thin), *a.* [L. *hyacinthinus*, < Gr. ὑακίνθινος.] Of or like the hyacinth (flower or gem); adorned with hyacinths.

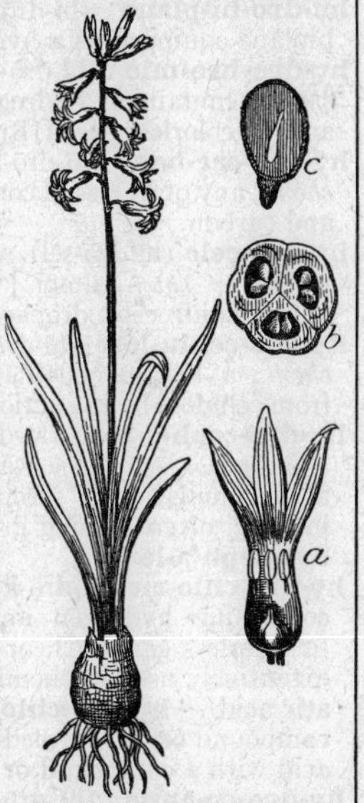

Hyacinth (*Hyacinthus orientalis*). — *a*, flower cut longitudinally; *b*, fruit cut transversely; *c*, seed cut longitudinally, showing the embryo.

Hy-a-des (hī'ạ-dēz), *n. pl.* [L., < Gr. Ὑάδες, Hyades, popularly associated with ὕειν, rain, but perhaps < ὗς, hog.] In *astron.*, a group of stars in the constellation Taurus, supposed by the ancients to portend rain when they rose with the sun.
hy-æ-na (hī-ē'nạ), *n.* See *hyena.*
hy-a-line (hī'ạ-lin). [LL. *hyalinus*, < Gr. ὑάλινος, < ὕαλος, glass.] **I.** *a.* Glassy; crystalline; transparent: as, *hyaline* cartilage (in *anat.*, the typical translucent form of cartilage, containing little fibrous tissue). **II.** *n.* Something glassy or transparent; the clear sea (poetic: as, "the clear *hyaline*, the glassy sea," Milton's "Paradise Lost," vii. 619); in *anat.*, the hyaloid membrane of the eye; also, hyaline cartilage.
hy-a-lite (hī'ạ-līt), *n.* [Gr. ὕαλος, glass.] A colorless variety of opal, sometimes transparent like glass, and sometimes whitish and translucent.
hy-a-loid (hī'ạ-loid). [Gr. ὑαλοειδής, < ὕαλος, glass, + εἶδος, form.] **I.** *a.* Glassy; hyaline: as, the *hyaloid* membrane of the eye (investing the vitreous humor). **II.** *n.* In *anat.*, the hyaloid membrane of the eye.
hy-a-lo-plasm (hī'ạ-lọ-plazm), *n.* [Gr. ὕαλος, glass, + πλάσμα, E. *plasma, plasm.*] In *biol.*, the pellucid portion of the protoplasm of a cell, as distinguished from the granular and reticular portions.
Hy-blæ-an (hī-blē'ạn), *a.* [L. *Hyblæus.*] Of or pertaining to the town of Hybla in ancient Sicily, celebrated for its honey; hence, honeyed; mellifluous.
hy-brid (hī'brid). [L. *hybrida, hibrida.*] **I.** *n.* The offspring of two animals or plants of different races, varieties, species, or genera (sometimes restricted to those produced by individuals of different species: cf. *mongrel*); a half-breed; a mongrel; hence, anything derived from heterogeneous sources, or composed of elements of different or incongruous kinds; specif., a word composed of elements belonging to different languages. **II.** *a.* Bred from two distinct races, varieties, species, or genera; hence, derived from heterogeneous sources, or of a mixed character (as, "The historians use a *hybrid* jargon intermixed with modern words": Hallam's "Literature of Europe," i. 1. § 87).— **hy'brid-ism,** *n.* Hybrid character; also, the production of hybrids.—**hy'brid-ist,** *n.* One who produces hybrids by crossing different species, etc.—**hy-brid'i-ty,** *n.* Hybrid character.—**hy'brid-ize** (-īz), *v.*; *-ized, -izing.* **I.** *tr.* To cause to produce hybrids; cross; also, to form in a hybrid manner, as words. **II.** *intr.* To cause the production of hybrids by crossing different species, etc.; also, to produce hybrids by crossing with a different species, etc.—**hy"brid-i-za'tion** (-i-zā'shọn), *n.*—**hy'brid-iz-er** (-ī-zėr), *n.*
hy-da-tid (hī'dạ-tid), *n.* [Gr. ὑδατίς (ὑδατιδ-), watery vesicle, < ὕδωρ (ὑδατ-), water.] A cyst with watery contents, produced in man and animals by a tapeworm in the larval state; hence, the encysted larva of a tapeworm, esp. of *Tænia echinococcus*; a cysticercus.
hy-dra (hī'drạ), *n.*; pl. *-dras* (-drạz), L. *-dræ* (-drē). [L. *hydra*, < Gr. ὕδρα, water serpent, < ὕδωρ, water: see *water.*] [*cap.* or *l. c.*] A monstrous serpent of Greek mythology, slain by Hercules, represented as having nine heads, each of which was replaced by two after being cut off unless the wound was cauterized; hence [*l. c.*], any persistent evil arising from many sources or difficult to extirpate; in *zoöl.*, any of the fresh-water polyps constituting the genus *Hydra*, so called because when the tube-like body is cut into pieces each piece forms a new individual; [*cap.*] in *astron.*, a southern constellation represented as a serpent.

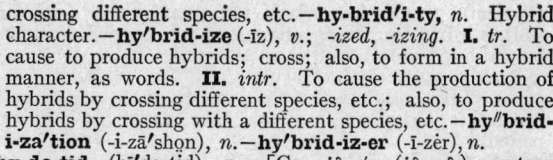

Combat between Hercules and the Hydra. — From a Greek amphora.

hy-dra-cid (hī-dras'id), *n.* [See *hydro-*[2].] In *chem.*, an acid which contains no oxygen, as hydrochloric acid, which is composed of hydrogen and chlorine.
hy-dræ'mi-a, *n.* See *hydremia.*
hy-dra-gogue (hī'drạ-gog). [LL. *hydragogus*, < Gr. ὑδραγωγός, < ὕδωρ, water, + ἀγωγός, leading, < ἄγειν, lead.] In *med.*: **I.** *a.* Having the property of removing water or serum from the body, or of causing watery alvine evacuations. **II.** *n.* A hydragogue medicine.
hy-dra=head-ed (hī'drạ-hed"ed), *a.* Having many heads, like the Hydra; also, self-renewing, like the Hydra; difficult to extirpate.
hy-dran-ge-a (hī-dran'jē-ạ), *n.* [NL., < Gr. ὕδωρ, water, + ἀγγεῖον, vessel: so called from the cup-shaped fruit.] Any shrub of the genus *Hydrangea*, various species of which are cultivated for their large, showy, white or pink or blue flower-clusters. —**hy-dran-ge-a'ceous** (-ā'shius), *a.* Belonging to the *Hydrangeaceæ*, or hydrangea family of shrubs and trees.

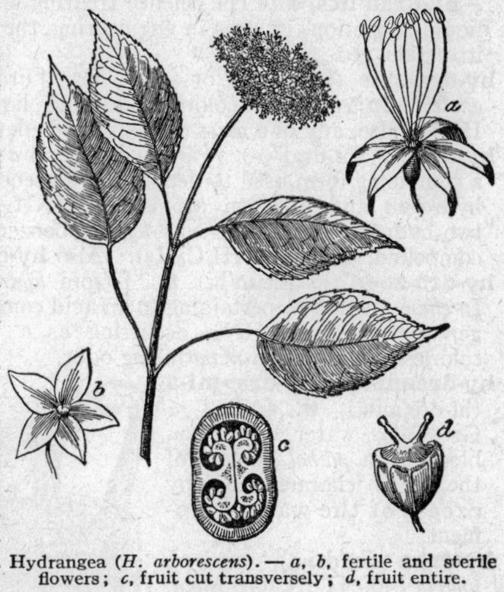

Hydrangea (*H. arborescens*). — *a*, *b*, fertile and sterile flowers; *c*, fruit cut transversely; *d*, fruit entire.

hy-drant (hī'-drạnt), *n.* [Gr. ὕδωρ, water.] An upright pipe with a spout, nozzle, or other outlet, usually in the street or elsewhere out of doors, for drawing water from a main.
hy-dranth (hī'dranth), *n.* [NL. *Hydra*, genus of polyps, + Gr. ἄνθος, flower.] In *zoöl.*, one of the distinct elements, individuals, or zoöids, which make up a compound hydrozoan.
hy-drar-gy-ri-a-sis (hī-drär-ji-rī'ạ-sis), *n.* [NL., < *hydrargyrum*: see *hydrargyrum.*] In *pathol.*, a morbid condition due to the introduction of mercury into the system; mercurial poisoning.
hy-drar-gyr-ic (hī-drär-jir'ik), *a.* [See *hydrargyrum.*] Of or pertaining to mercury; mercurial.—**hy-drar'gy-rism**

(-ji-rizm), *n.* Hydrargyriasis.—**hy-drar′gy-rol** (-rol or -rōl), *n.* In *phar.*, an organic salt of mercury, occurring in brownish-red scales: used as an antiseptic.

hy-drar-gy-rum (hī-drär′ji-rum), *n.* [NL., < L. *hydrargyrus*, < Gr. ὑδράργυρος, < ὕδωρ, water, + ἄργυρος, silver.] Mercury; quicksilver: in *chem.*, abbreviated *Hg* (without period).

hy-dras-tine (hī-dras′tin), *n.* [NL. *Hydrastis* (see def.), < Gr. ὕδωρ, water, + δρᾶν, do (perhaps from the active properties of the juice).] In *chem.*, a crystalline alkaloid found in the rootstock of the goldenseal, *Hydrastis canadensis*: used in medicine.—**hy-dras′ti-nine** (-ti-nin), *n.* In *chem.*, a colorless crystalline compound formed by the oxidation of hydrastine: used in medicine.

hy-drate (hī′drāt), *n.* [Gr. ὕδωρ, water.] In *chem.*, any of a class of compounds produced when certain substances, as metallic salts, unite with water, often represented in formulas as actually containing water (because when heated they usually break down into the original substance and water), but now commonly regarded as true molecular compounds (cf. *water of hydration*, and *water of crystallization*, under *water, n.*); less properly, a hydroxide.—**hy′drate,** *v. t.* or *i.*; *-drated, -drating.* To combine chemically with water; form into a hydrate.—**hy-dra′tion** (-drā′shǫn), *n.* —**hy′dra″tor,** *n.*

hy-drau-lic (hī-drâ′lik), *a.* [L. *hydraulicus*, < Gr. ὑδραυλικός, < ὕδραυλις, hydraulic organ, < ὕδωρ, water, + αὐλός, flute, pipe.] Pertaining to water or other liquid in motion, or to hydraulics; also, operated by or employing water; also, hardening under water, as a cement.—**hydraulic press,** a press in which a pressure exerted by a small piston, as one worked by hand, is communicated through a confined liquid to a larger piston, the force being multiplied as many times as the area of the smaller piston must be multiplied to equal that of the larger.—**hydraulic ram,** a device by which the energy of descending water is utilized to raise a part of the water to a height greater than that of the source.—**hy-drau′lic,** *v. t.*; *-licked, -licking.* In *mining*, to work (gravelly auriferous deposits, etc.) by means of a powerful jet of water, which breaks up the material and washes it down into a sluice.—**hy-drau′li-cal-ly,** *adv.*—**hy-drau-li′cian** (-lish′ąn), *n.* One skilled in hydraulics.—**hy-drau-li′ci-ty** (-lis′i-ti), *n.* The quality or property, as of cement, of being hydraulic, or hardening under water. —**hy-drau′lics,** *n.* The science treating of water or other liquid in motion, its uses in engineering, the laws governing its action, etc.

hy-dra-zine (hī′drą-zin or -zēn), *n.* [From *hydrogen* + *azote.*] In *chem.*, a colorless, fuming liquid compound, H_4N_2; also, any of a class of compounds derived from it.

hy-draz-o- (hī-draz′ǫ-). [See *hydro-*[2] and *azo-*.] In *chem.*, a combining form used to denote the presence of a group of hydrogen and nitrogen atoms, —HNNH—, united with two hydrocarbon radicals: as, *hydrazo*benzene (a crystalline compound, $C_6H_5.HNNH.C_6H_5$). Also **hy-draz′o,** *a.*

hy-dra-zo-ic (hī-drą-zō′ik), *a.* [From *hydrogen* + *azote.*] In *chem.*, noting or pertaining to an acid composed of hydrogen and nitrogen, HN_3, occurring as a very explosive, colorless liquid with a penetrating odor.

hy-dre-mi-a, hy-dræ-mi-a (hī-drē′mi-ą), *n.* [NL., < Gr. ὕδωρ, water, + αἷμα, blood.] In *pathol.*, a state of the blood characterized by excess of the watery element.

hy-dri-a (hī′dri-ą), *n.*; *pl. hydriæ* (-ē). [L., < Gr. ὑδρία, water-pot, < ὕδωρ, water.] In *Gr. antiq.*, a kind of vase for carrying water, with capacious body, narrow mouth, and one large handle at the back and a small one at each side.

Hydria. — Museum of Fine Arts, Boston.

hy-dric (hī′drik), *a.* [From *hydrogen.*] Of or pertaining to hydrogen.

hy-drics (hī′driks), *n.* [Gr. ὕδωρ, water.] The branch of physics that treats of the properties of water.

hy-dride, hy-drid (hī′drīd or -drid, -drid), *n.* [From *hydrogen.*] In *chem.*, a compound of hydrogen with another element or a radical.

hy-dri-od-ic (hī-dri-od′ik), *a.* [See *hydro-*[2].] In *chem.*, containing hydrogen and iodine: as, *hydriodic* acid (a colorless gas, HI, with a suffocating odor).

hydro-[1], **hydr-**[1]. Forms of Gr. ὕδωρ, water, used in combination.

hydro-[2], **hydr-**[2]. Forms of *hydrogen* used in combination.

hy-dro (hī′drō), *n.* Shortened form of *hydropathic, n.*, also of *hydro-aëroplane.*

hy-dro=a-ër-o-plane (hī-drǫ-ā′ẹ-rǫ-plān″), *n.* [See *hydro-*[1].] An aëroplane provided with floats, or with a boat-like under part, enabling it to alight upon or ascend from water.

hy-dro=air-plane (hī-drǫ-ãr′plān), *n.* [See *hydro-*[1].] A hydro-aëroplane.

hy-dro-bi-plane (hī-drǫ-bī′plān), *n.* [See *hydro-*[1].] A biplane equipped as a hydro-aëroplane for use on the water.

hy-dro-bro-mic (hī-drǫ-brō′mik), *a.* [See *hydro-*[2].] In *chem.*, containing hydrogen and bromine: as, *hydrobromic* acid (a colorless gas, HBr, with a pungent odor).

hy-dro-car-bon (hī-drǫ-kär′bǫn), *n.* [See *hydro-*[2].] In *chem.*, any of a class of compounds containing only hydrogen and carbon.

hy-dro-cele (hī′drǫ-sēl), *n.* [L., < Gr. ὑδροκήλη, < ὕδωρ, water, + κήλη, tumor.] In *pathol.*, an accumulation of serous fluid; esp., dropsy of the testicle or scrotum.

hy-dro-cel-lu-lose (hī-drǫ-sel′ū-lōs), *n.* [See *hydro-*[1].] In *chem.*, a brittle colloidal substance, $C_{12}H_{22}O_{11}$, obtained from cellulose by the action of dilute mineral acid.

hy-dro-ceph-a-lus (hī-drǫ-sef′ą-lus), *n.* [NL., < Gr. ὑδροκέφαλον, < ὕδωρ, water, + κεφαλή, head.] In *pathol.*, an accumulation of serous fluid within the cranium, esp. in infancy, often causing great enlargement of the head.—**hy-dro-ceph′a-lous,** *a.*

hy-dro-chlo-ric (hī-drǫ-klō′rik), *a.* [See *hydro-*[2].] In *chem.*, containing hydrogen and chlorine: as, *hydrochloric* acid (a colorless gas, HCl, or an aqueous solution of it which is extensively used in chemical and industrial processes; muriatic acid).—**hy-dro-chlo′ride** (-rīd or -rid), *n.* In *chem.*, a compound or salt formed by the direct union of hydrochloric acid with a compound or radical.

hy-dro-cy-an-ic (hī″drǫ-sī-an′ik), *a.* [See *hydro-*[2].] In *chem.*, containing hydrogen and cyanogen: as, *hydrocyanic* acid (a colorless liquid, HCN, with an odor like that of bitter almonds; prussic acid: a prompt and virulent poison).

hy-dro-drome (hī′drǫ-drōm), *n.* [From *hydro-*[1] + *-drome* (Gr. -δρόμος, running) as in *aërodrome* (first sense).] A kind of motor-boat fitted with submerged planes which enable it to travel with great speed over the surface of the water after the manner of a hydroplane.

hy-dro-dy-nam-ic (hī″drǫ-dī-nam′ik), *a.* [See *hydro-*[1].] Pertaining to the force or motion of fluids, or to hydrodynamics. —**hy″dro-dy-nam′ics,** *n.* The dynamics of fluids: commonly restricted to hydrokinetics, but in a wider sense including hydrokinetics, hydrostatics, and sometimes hydraulics.

hy-dro=e-lec-tric (hī″drǫ-ẹ-lek′trik), *a.* [See *hydro-*[1].] Pertaining to or effecting the generation of electricity by the friction of water or steam, or by water-power.

hy-dro-flu-or-ic (hī″drǫ-flǫ-or′ik), *a.* [See *hydro-*[2].] In *chem.*, containing hydrogen and fluorine: as, *hydrofluoric* acid (a colorless, corrosive, volatile liquid, HF, used for etching glass).

hy-dro-gen (hī′drǫ-jen), *n.* [F. *hydrogène*, < Gr. ὕδωρ, water, + γεν-, bear, produce (from its generating water by combining with oxygen).] Chem. sym., H; at. wt., 1.008. A colorless, odorless, inflammable gas, which combines chemically with oxygen to form water: the lightest of the known elements.—**hydrogen dioxide** or **peroxide,** a colorless, unstable, oily liquid, H_2O_2, the aqueous solution of which is used as a bleaching agent and an antiseptic. —**hydrogen sulphide,** a colorless, inflammable poisonous gas, H_2S, smelling like rotten eggs.—**hy′dro-gen-ate** (-āt), *v. t.*; *-ated, -ating.* To combine or treat with hydrogen.—**hy″dro-gen-a′tion** (-ā′shǫn), *n.*—**hy′dro-gen-ize**

(-īz), *v. t.*; *-ized, -izing.* To hydrogenate.—**hy-drog′e-nous** (-droj′e-nus), *a.* Pertaining to or containing hydrogen.

hy-dro-graph (hī′drō-grȧf), *n.* [See *hydro-*¹ and *-graph.*] A hydrographic record, diagram, or chart.—**hy-drog′ra-pher** (-drog′ra-fėr), *n.* One versed in hydrography or engaged in hydrographic work.—**hy-dro-graph′ic, hy-dro-graph′i-cal** (-graf′ik, -i-kal), *a.* Of or pertaining to hydrography.—**hy-dro-graph′i-cal-ly,** *adv.*—**hy-drog′ra-phy,** *n.* [See *-graphy.*] The science of the measurement and description of the sea, lakes, rivers, etc., with special reference to their use for the purposes of navigation and commerce.

hy-droid (hī′droid). [See *hydra* and *-oid.*] In *zoöl.*: **I.** *a.* Noting, pertaining to, or resembling the hydras, or the hydrozoans; specif., noting or pertaining to that form of hydrozoan which is asexual and grows into branching colonies by budding (cf. *Medusa*). **II.** *n.* A hydroid hydrozoan; specif., the hydroid form of a hydrozoan.

hy-dro-ki-net-ic (hī″drō-ki-net′ik), *a.* [See *hydro-*¹.] Pertaining to the motion of fluids, or to hydrokinetics.—**hy″dro-ki-net′ics,** *n.* The kinetics of fluids: a branch of science usually confined to the theory of the motion of liquids.

hy-drol-o-gy (hī-drol′ō-ji), *n.* [See *hydro-*¹ and *-logy.*] The science dealing with water, its properties, laws, geographical distribution, etc.—**hy-dro-log′ic, hy-dro-log′i-cal** (-drō-loj′ik, -i-kal), *a.*—**hy-drol′o-gist,** *n.*

hy-drol-y-sis (hī-drol′i-sis), *n.* [See *hydro-*¹ and *-lysis.*] A kind of chemical decomposition by which a compound is resolved into other compounds by taking up the elements of water.—**hy′dro-lyte** (-drō-līt), *n.* [See *-lyte.*] A compound subjected to hydrolysis.—**hy-dro-lyt′ic** (-lit′ik), *a.* —**hy′dro-lyze** (-līz), *v. t.*; *-lyzed, -lyzing.* To subject to hydrolysis.—**hy′dro-lyz-a-ble,** *a.*

hy-dro-man-cy (hī′drō-man-si), *n.* [L. *hydromantia*, < Gr. ὕδωρ, water, + μαντεία, divination.] Divination by means of water.—**hy-dro-man′tic,** *a.*

hy-dro-me-chan-i-cal (hī″drō-mē-kan′i-kal), *a.* [See *hydro-*¹.] Pertaining to mechanical devices in which water is employed, or to hydromechanics.—**hy″dro-me-chan′ics,** *n.* The mechanics of fluids: usually considered as embracing hydrokinetics (hydrodynamics), hydrostatics, and hydraulics.

hy-dro-me-du-sa (hī″drō-mē-dū′sạ), *n.*; pl. *-sæ* (-sē). [NL.: see *hydra* and *Medusa.*] One of the *Hydromedusæ*, a variously limited group of cœlenterates, comprising all or a portion of the hydrozoans.—**hy″dro-me-du′san,** *a.* and *n.*

hy-dro-mel (hī′drō-mel), *n.* [L., < Gr. ὑδρόμελι, < ὕδωρ, water, + μέλι, honey.] A liquor consisting of honey and water: when fermented, known also as *mead.*

hy-dro-met-al-lur-gy (hī-drō-met′a-lėr-ji), *n.* [See *hydro-*¹.] The assay or reduction of ores by means of liquid reagents.—**hy″dro-met-al-lur′gi-cal,** *a.*

hy-drom-e-ter (hī-drom′e-tėr), *n.* [See *hydro-*¹ and *-meter.*] An instrument for determining the specific gravity of liquids (also of solids) and hence the strength of solutions, usually consisting of a graduated tube made to float vertically in a liquid by means of a hollow bulb and of a counterpoise at the lower end; also, an instrument for measuring the velocity or discharge of water.—**hy-dro-met′ric, hy-dro-met′ri-cal** (-drō-met′rik, -ri-kal), *a.*—**hy-drom′e-try,** *n.* [See *-metry.*] The art of using the hydrometer; the determination of specific gravity, density, purity, etc., by means of hydrometers.

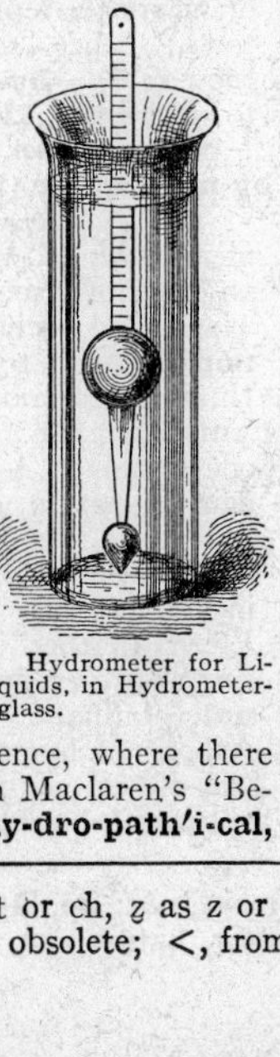

Hydrometer for Liquids, in Hydrometer-glass.

hy-dro-mon-o-plane (hī-drō-mon′ō-plān), *n.* [See *hydro-*¹.] A monoplane equipped as a hydro-aëroplane for use on the water.

hy-dro-path (hī′drō-path), *n.* [From *hydropathy.*] A hydropathist.—**hy-dro-path′ic. I.** *a.* Of or pertaining to hydropathy or water-cure. **II.** *n.* A hydropathic establishment; a sanatorium in which the treatment is chiefly by water-cure: as, "the Dunleith sphere of influence, where there were four doctors and a *hydropathic*" (Ian Maclaren's "Beside the Bonnie Brier Bush," vii. 1).—**hy-dro-path′i-cal,** *a.*—**hy-drop′a-thist** (-drop′a-thist), *n.* One who practises or favors hydropathy.

hy-drop-a-thy (hī-drop′a-thi), *n.* [See *hydro-*¹ and *-pathy.*] The treatment of disease by the external or internal use of water; hydrotherapy.

hy-dro-phane (hī′drō-fān), *n.* [Gr. ὕδωρ, water, + φαίνεσθαι, appear.] A partly translucent variety of opal, which becomes more translucent or transparent when immersed in water.—**hy-droph′a-nous** (-drof′a-nus), *a.*

hy-droph-i-lous (hī-drof′i-lus), *a.* [See *hydro-*¹ and *-philous.*] In *bot.*, pollinated by the agency of water.

hy-dro-pho-bi-a (hī-drō-fō′bi-ạ), *n.* [LL., < Gr. ὑδροφοβία, < ὑδροφόβος, fearing water, < ὕδωρ, water, + φέβεσθαι, flee in fear.] In *pathol.*, a morbid dread of water, as in rabies; hence, the disease rabies, esp. in man.—**hy-dro-pho′bic,** *a.*

hy-dro-phone (hī′drō-fōn), *n.* [See *hydro-*¹ and *-phone.*] An instrument employing the principles of the microphone, used to detect the flow of water through a pipe, as in locating waste; also, any of various devices for locating causes or sources of sound under water, as for determining the presence and position of submarines from the noise made by their engines, etc.; in *med.*, an instrument used in auscultation, whereby sounds are conveyed through a column of water.

hy-dro-phyte (hī′drō-fīt), *n.* [See *hydro-*¹ and *-phyte.*] A plant growing in water or very moist ground.—**hy-dro-phyt′ic** (-fit′ik), *a.*

hy-drop-ic (hī-drop′ik), *a.* Pertaining to hydrops; dropsical.

hy-dro-plane (hī′drō-plān), *n.* [See *hydro-*¹ and *plane*².] A kind of motor-boat provided with a plane or planes by means of which it can reduce its displacement at high speed or skim along the surface of the water; a plane on such a boat, or a similar attachment to an aëroplane enabling it to glide on the water; also, a horizontal rudder for submerging or elevating a submarine boat.

hy-dro-pneu-mat-ic (hī″drō-nū-mat′ik), *a.* [See *hydro-*¹.] Pertaining to, involving, or produced by the action or use of both water and air or water and gas.

hy-dro-pon-ics (hī-drō-pon′iks), *n.* [*hydro-* + **Gr.** πόνος, work.] Soilless growth of plants. See *soilless.*

hy-drops (hī′drops), *n.* [L., < Gr. ὕδρωψ, < ὕδωρ, water.] In *pathol.*, dropsy. Also **hy′drop-sy.**

hy-dro-quin-one (hī-drō-kwin′ōn), *n.* [See *hydro-*² and *quinone.*] In *chem.*, a white, sweetish crystalline compound, $C_6H_4(OH)_2$, formed by the reduction of quinone.

hy-dro-scope (hī′drō-skōp), *n.* [See *hydro-*¹ and *-scope.*] An ancient device which measured the lapse of time by the subsidence of water in a graduated tube perforated at the bottom; also, an optical apparatus which enables the observer to view objects below the surface of the sea.—**hy-dro-scop′ic** (-skop′ik), *a.*

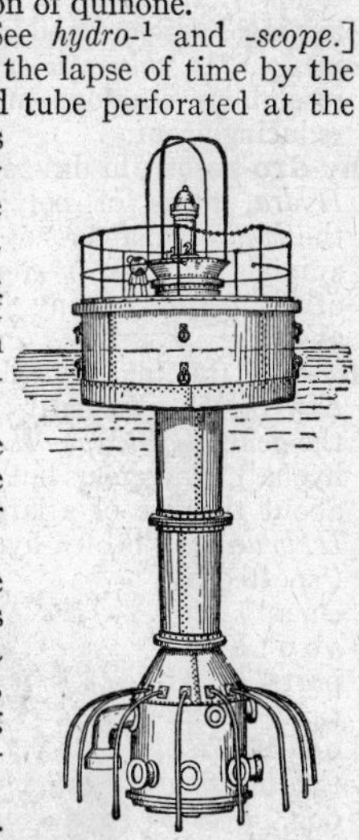

Hydroscope, for observing objects in the sea.

hy-dro-some (hī′drō-sōm), *n.* [NL. *hydrosoma*, < *Hydra*, genus of polyps, + Gr. σῶμα, body.] In *zoöl.*, the entire body of a compound hydrozoan.

hy-dro-sphere (hī′drō-sfēr), *n.* [See *hydro-*¹.] The water on the surface of the globe; also, the aqueous vapor in the atmosphere.

hy-dro-stat (hī′drō-stat), *n.* [See *hydro-*¹ and *-stat.*] Any of various devices for preventing injury to a steam-boiler from low water; also, an electrical device for detecting the presence of water, as from overflow or leakage.

hy-dro-stat-ic (hī-drō-stat′ik), *a.* [See *hydro-*¹ and *static.*] Pertaining to fluids in equilibrium, their properties, pressure, etc., or to hydrostatics.—**hydrostatic press,** a hydraulic press.—**hy-dro-stat′i-cal-ly,** *adv.*—**hy-dro-stat′ics,** *n.* The statics of fluids: a branch of science usually confined to the theory of the equilibrium and pressure of liquids.

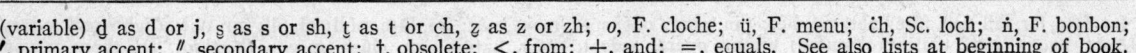

hy-dro-sul-phide (hī-drō-sul′fīd or -fid), *n.* [See *hydro-*².] In *chem.*, a compound formed when one of the hydrogen atoms of hydrogen sulphide (H_2S) has been replaced by a more strongly electropositive element or radical: as, sodium *hydrosulphide* (NaHS).—**hy-dro-sul′phite** (-fīt), *n.* In *chem.*, a salt of hydrosulphurous acid.—**hy″dro-sul-phu′-ric** (-fū′rik), *a.* In *chem.*, containing hydrogen and sulphur: as, *hydrosulphuric* acid (hydrogen sulphide).—**hy″dro-sul-phu′rous,** *a.* In *chem.*, containing hydrogen and sulphur: as, *hydrosulphurous* acid (hyposulphurous acid, $H_2S_2O_4$).

hy-dro-tech-ny (hī′drǭ-tek-ni), *n.* [Gr. ὕδωρ, water, + τέχνη, art.] Hydraulic engineering, esp. when applied to the storage and distribution of water; the technics of water-supply.—**hy-dro-tech′nic, hy-dro-tech′ni-cal,** *a.*

hy-dro-ther-a-peu-tics (hī″drǭ-ther-ạ-pū′tiks), *n.* [See *hydro-*[1].] That branch of therapeutics which deals with the curative use of water.—**hy″dro-ther-a-peu′tic,** *a.*—**hy-dro-ther′a-py,** *n.* Treatment of disease by means of water.—**hy″dro-the-rap′ic** (-the-rap′ik), *a.*

hy-dro-ther-mal (hī-drǭ-thėr′mạl), *a.* [Gr. ὕδωρ, water, + θερμός, hot.] Of or pertaining to heated water: applied esp. to the action of heated waters in producing geological changes by dissolving and redepositing mineral substances.

hy-dro-tho-rax (hī-drǭ-thō′raks), *n.* [NL., < Gr. ὕδωρ, water, + θώραξ, chest.] In *pathol.*, the presence of serous fluid in one or both pleural cavities.—**hy″dro-tho-ra′cic** (-thǭ-ras′ik), *a.*

hy-dro-trop-ic (hī-drǭ-trop′ik), *a.* [See *hydro-*[1] and *-tropic.*] In *bot.*, turning or tending toward moisture, as growing organs; taking a particular direction with reference to moisture.—**hy-drot′ro-pism** (-drot′rǭ-pizm), *n.* In *bot.*, hydrotropic tendency or growth.

hy-drous (hī′drus), *a.* [Gr. ὕδωρ, water.] Containing water; in *chem.* and *mineral.*, containing water or its elements in some kind of union, as in hydrates or in hydroxides.

hy-drox-ide (hī-drok′sīd or -sid), *n.* [See *hydro-*[1].] In *chem.*, a compound consisting of an element or radical (esp. a metal or basic radical) combined with one or more hydroxyl groups.

hy-drox-y- (hī-drok′si-). [From *hydr*(*ogen*) + *oxy*(*gen*).] In *chem.*, a combining form indicating the presence of the hydroxyl group: as, *hydroxy*benzene (a compound formed from benzene by substituting one or more hydroxyl groups for its hydrogen atoms). Also **hy-drox′y,** *a.*

hy-drox-yl (hī-drok′sil), *n.* [From *hydr*(*ogen*) + *ox*(*ygen*) + *-yl.*] In *chem.*, a univalent radical or group, OH, containing hydrogen and oxygen.—**hy-drox″yl-am′ine** (-am′-in), *n.* In *chem.*, a crystalline basic compound, NH_2OH, resembling ammonia in chemical properties, and used as a reducing agent.

hy-dro-zo-ön (hī-drǭ-zō′on), *n.*; pl. *-zoa* (-zō′ạ̈). [NL., < *Hydra*, genus of polyps, + Gr. ζῷον, animal.] Any of the *Hydrozoa*, a class of cœlenterate aquatic (mostly marine) animals, simple or compound, including the hydras and other polyps, many jellyfishes, etc.—**hy-dro-zo′an,** *a.* and *n.*

hy-e-na (hī-ē′nạ̈), *n.* [L. *hyæna*, < Gr. ὕαινα, < ὗς, hog.] Any of the nocturnal carnivorous quadrupeds constituting the genus *Hyæna*, as *H. striata* ('striped hyena' or 'laughing hyena'), a ravenous but cowardly African and Asiatic species about the size of a large dog, living chiefly on carrion, or *H. brunnea* ('brown hyena'), of South Africa, or *H. crocuta* ('spotted hyena'), of southern parts of Africa.—**painted hyena,** the hunting-dog, *Lycaon pictus.*—**hy-e′na=dog,** *n.* The hunting-dog, *Lycaon pictus.*

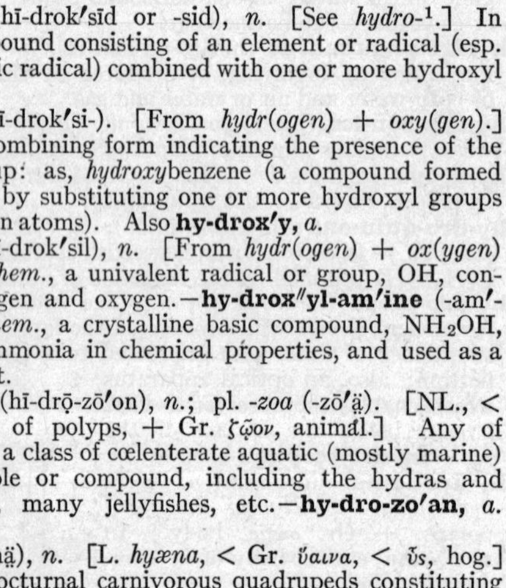

Spotted Hyena (*Hyæna crocuta*).

hyeto-. Form of Gr. ὑετός, rain, used in combination.—**hy-e-to-graph** (hī′e-tǭ-gråf), *n.* [+ *-graph.*] A chart showing the rainfall.—**hy-e-tog′ra-phy** (-tog′rạ-fi), *n.* [+ *-graphy.*] The branch of meteorology dealing with the distribution of rain.—**hy″e-to-graph′ic, hy″e-to-graph′i-cal** (-graf′ik, -i-kạl), *a.*—**hy-e-tol′o-gy** (-tol′ǭ-ji), *n.* [+ *-logy.*] The branch of meteorology dealing with rain, snow, etc.—**hy″e-to-log′i-cal** (-loj′i-kạl), *a.*

Hy-ge-ia (hī-jē′ạ̈), *n.* [Gr. Ὑγίεια, personification of ὑγίεια, ὑγεία, health, < ὑγιής, sound, healthy.] In *class. myth.*, the goddess of health, daughter of Æsculapius.—**Hy-ge′ian,** *a.* Pertaining to the goddess Hygeia; [*l. c.*] pertaining to health or to hygiene; hygienic.—**hy′ge-ist** (-ję̄-ist), *n.* A hygienist.

hy-gi-ene (hī′ji-ēn), *n.* [F. *hygiène*, < Gr. ὑγιεινός, healthful, sanitary, < ὑγιής, sound, healthy.] The science which deals with the preservation of health; sanitary science.—**hy-gi-en′ic** (-en′ik), *a.* Pertaining to hygiene; sanitary.—**hy-gi-en′i-cal-ly,** *adv.*—**hy-gi-en′ics,** *n.* Hygiene.—**hy′gi-en-ist** (-ę-nist), *n.* One versed in hygiene.

hygro-. Form of Gr. ὑγρός, wet, moist, used in combination.—**hy-gro-graph** (hī′grǭ-gråf), *n.* [+ *-graph.*] An instrument which registers automatically the variations in atmospheric humidity.—**hy-grol′o-gy** (-grol′ǭ-ji), *n.* [+ *-logy.*] The science which treats of humidity, as that of the atmosphere.—**hy-grom′e-ter** (-grom′e-tėr), *n.* [+ *-meter.*] An instrument for determining the humidity of the atmosphere.—**hy-gro-met′ric** (-met′rik), *a.* Pertaining to the hygrometer or hygrometry; also, hygroscopic.—**hy-grom′e-try,** *n.* [+ *-metry.*] The branch of physics that treats of the determination of the humidity of air and gases.—**hy-groph′i-lous** (-grof′i-lus), *a.* [+ *-philous.*] In *bot.*, growing in water or moist places.—**hy′gro-scope** (-skōp), *n.* [+ *-scope.*] An instrument which shows the variations in the humidity of the air.—**hy-gro-scop′ic** (-skop′ik), *a.* Pertaining to or perceptible by the hygroscope; also, absorbing or attracting moisture from the air; in *bot.*, sensitive to or caused by moisture.

hy-ing (hī′ing). Present participle of *hie.*

hy-lic (hī′lik), *a.* [Gr. ὑλικός, < ὕλη, wood, matter.] Of or pertaining to matter; material.—**hy′li-cism** (-li-sizm), **hy′lism,** *n.* Materialism.—**hy′li-cist** (-sist), *n.* A materialist.

hylo-. Form of Gr. ὕλη, wood, matter, used in combination.—**hy-loph-a-gous** (hī-lof′ạ-gus), *a.* [Gr. ὑλοφάγος: see *-phagous.*] Eating wood, as certain beetles.—**hy-lo-the-ism** (hī′lǭ-thē-izm), *n.* [+ Gr. θεός, god.] The doctrine that matter or the material universe is God.—**hy-lo-zo′ic** (-zō′ik), *a.* Pertaining to or characterized by hylozoism.—**hy-lo-zo′ism,** *n.* [+ Gr. ζωή, life.] The doctrine that all matter is endowed with life.—**hy-lo-zo′ist,** *n.* A believer in hylozoism.—**hy″lo-zo-is′tic** (-zǭ-is′tik), *a.* Of or pertaining to hylozoists or hylozoism.—**hy″lo-zo-is′ti-cal-ly,** *adv.*

hy-men[1] (hī′men), *n.* [Gr. ὑμήν, thin skin, membrane.] In *anat.*, a fold of mucous membrane extending across and partly closing the external orifice of the vagina.

Hy-men[2] (hī′men), *n.* [L., < Gr. Ὑμήν.] The Greek god of marriage, represented as a young man bearing a bridal torch; hence [*cap.* or *l. c.*], marriage or a marriage-song (now rare).—**hy-me-ne-al** (hī-mę-nē′ạl). **I.** *a.* Pertaining to marriage. **II.** *n.* A marriage-song; also, *pl.*, nuptials.—**hy-me-ne′an,** *a.*

hy-me-nop-ter (hī-mę-nop′tėr), *n.* [NL. *Hymenoptera*, pl., < Gr. ὑμενόπτερος, having membranous wings, < ὑμήν, membrane, + πτερόν, wing.] Any of the *Hymenoptera*, an order of insects having (when winged) four membranous wings, and including the wasps, bees, ants, etc.—**hy-me-nop′ter-an** (-tę-rạn), *a.* and *n.*—**hy-me-nop′ter-ous,** *a.* Having membranous wings; belonging to the hymenopters.

hymn (him), *n.* [LL. *hymnus*, < Gr. ὕμνος, festive song, ode, hymn.] A song or ode in praise or honor of God, a deity, a nation, etc.; esp., a metrical composition designed to be sung in religious worship.—**hymn,** *v.*; *hymned, hymning* (him′ing or him′ning). **I.** *tr.* To praise or celebrate in a hymn (as, "As sons of one great Sire, *Hymning* the Eternal Father": Milton's "Paradise Lost," vi. 96); also, to sing or express in a hymn. **II.** *intr.* To sing hymns.—**hym-nal** (him′nạl). **I.** *a.* Of or pertaining to hymns. **II.** *n.* A book of hymns for use in divine worship.—**hym′na-ry** (-nạ-ri), *n.*; pl. *-ries* (-riz). [ML. *hymnarium.*] A hymnal.—**hymn′=book,** *n.* A hymnal.—**hym′nic,** *a.* Of or pertaining to hymns; having the character of a hymn.—**hym'nist,** *n.* A composer of hymns.

hym-no-dy (him'nọ-di), *n.* [ML. *hymnodia,* < Gr. ὑμνῳδία, < ὕμνος, hymn, + ἀείδειν, sing.] The singing or the composition of hymns or sacred songs; also, hymns collectively.—**hym'no-dist,** *n.*

hym-nog-ra-phy (him-nog'rạ-fi), *n.* [Gr. ὕμνος, hymn: see *-graphy.*] The writing of hymns.—**hym-nog'ra-pher,** *n.*

hym-nol-o-gy (him-nol'ọ-ji), *n.* [Gr. ὕμνος, hymn: see *-logy.*] The study of hymns, their history, classification, etc.; also, the composition of hymns; also, hymns collectively.—**hym-no-log'ic, hym-no-log'i-cal** (-nọ-loj'ik, -i-kạl), *a.*—**hym-nol'o-gist,** *n.*

hy-oid (hī'oid). [NL. *hyoides,* < Gr. ὑοειδής, < ὗ, the letter upsilon, + εἶδος, form.] **I.** *a.* Shaped like the Greek letter υ (upsilon); in *anat.,* noting or pertaining to a bone of this shape at the root of the tongue in man, or a corresponding bone or collection of bones in animals. **II.** *n.* In *anat.,* the hyoid bone.

hy-os-cine (hī'ọ-sin), *n.* [L. *hyoscyamus*: see *hyoscyamine.*] In *chem.,* an alkaloid occurring with hyoscyamine in henbane, etc., and chemically identical with scopolamine: used as a mydriatic, etc.

hy-os-cy-a-mine (hī-ọ-sī'ạ-min), *n.* [L. *hyoscyamus,* < Gr. ὑοσκύαμος, henbane, lit. 'hog's bean,' < ὗς, hog, + κύαμος, bean.] In *chem.,* a poisonous alkaloid obtained from henbane and other solanaceous plants, used as a sedative, mydriatic, etc.

hyp (hip), *n.* and *v.* See *hip*[4].

hyp-æs-the-sia (hip-es-thē'ziạ), *n.* [NL.: see *hypo-* and *æsthesia.*] In *pathol.,* diminished capacity for sensation.—**hyp-æs-the'sic** (-zik), *a.*

hy-pæ'thral, *a.* See *hypethral.*

hy-pal-la-ge (hi-pal'ạ-jē or hī-), *n.* [LL., < Gr. ὑπαλλαγή, < ὑπαλλάσσειν, exchange, < ὑπό, under, + ἀλλάσσειν, change.] In *rhet.,* a figure which consists in an inversion of syntactical relation between two words, as in 'to give the winds to the fleets' (L. *dare classibus austros*: Virgil's "Æneid," iii. 61), instead of 'to give the fleets to the winds.'

hy-pax-i-al (hī-pak'si-ạl), *a.* [See *hypo-* and *axis*[1].] In *anat.,* beneath or anterior to an axis, esp. the vertebral axis.

hyper-. [Gr. ὑπερ-, repr. ὑπέρ, prep., over, above, beyond, as adv. overmuch, beyond measure; akin to L. *super* and E. *over*: see *super-* and *over.*] A prefix of Greek origin, meaning 'over,' 'above,' 'beyond,' and hence 'exceedingly,' 'to excess,' freely used as an English formative, as in *hyperacute, hypermature, hypernormal, hypersecretion.* In chemical terms *hyper-* (like *super-*), as indicating the highest of a series of compounds or the largest amount of an element, is now commonly replaced by *per-.* Cf. *hypo-.*

hy-per-a-cid (hī-pėr-as'id), *a.* Excessively acid.—**hy"per-a-cid'i-ty** (-a-sid'i-ti), *n.* Excessive acidity, as of the gastric juice. Cf. *hypoacidity.*

hy-per-æ'mi-a, etc. See *hyperemia,* etc.

hy-per-æs-the-sia (hī"pėr-es-thē'ziạ), *n.* [NL.: see *hyper-* and *æsthesia.*] In *pathol.,* increased or excessive capacity for sensation.—**hy"per-æs-thet'ic** (-thet'ik), *a.*

hy-per-al-ge-sia (hī"pėr-al-jē'ziạ), *n.* [NL., < Gr. ὑπέρ, over, + ἀλγεῖν, feel pain.] In *pathol.,* an abnormally great sensitiveness to pain.—**hy"per-al-ge'sic** (-zik), *a.*

hy-per-ba-ton (hī-pėr'bạ-ton), *n.*; pl. *-ta* (-tạ). [L., < Gr. ὑπέρβατον, < ὑπερβαίνειν, pass over, < ὑπέρ, over, + βαίνειν, go.] In *rhet.,* inversion of the natural or logical order of words, as for emphasis, as in "Great is Diana of the Ephesians" (Acts, xix. 28).

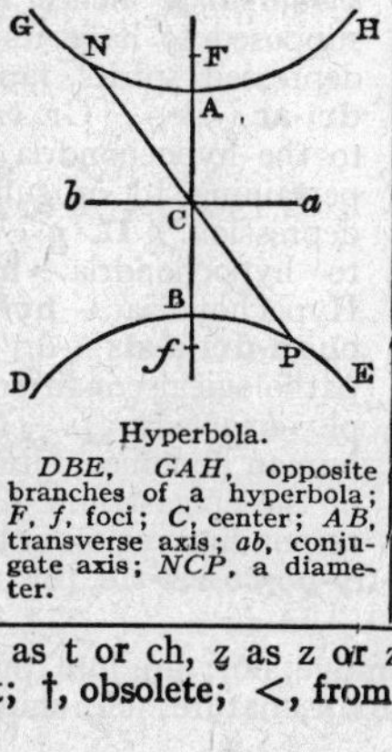

Hyperbola.
DBE, GAH, opposite branches of a hyperbola; *F, f,* foci; *C,* center; *AB,* transverse axis; *ab,* conjugate axis; *NCP,* a diameter.

hy-per-bo-la (hī-pėr'bọ-lạ), *n.*; pl. *-las* (-lạz). [NL., < Gr. ὑπερβολή, hyperbola, lit. 'a throwing beyond': see *hyperbole.*] In *geom.,* a curve consisting of two distinct and similar branches, formed by the intersection of a plane with two similar cones placed apex to apex.

hy-per-bo-le (hī-pėr'bọ-lē), *n.* [L., < Gr. ὑπερβολή, a throwing beyond, excess, hyperbole, also a hyperbola, < ὑπερβάλλειν, throw beyond, exceed, < ὑπέρ, over, beyond, + βάλλειν, throw.] In *rhet.,* obvious exaggeration, as for effect; an extravagant statement not intended to be understood literally.—**hy-per-bol'ic** (-bol'ik), *a.* [Gr. ὑπερβολικός.] Pertaining to or of the nature of hyperbole; exaggerated; using hyperbole, or exaggerating; also, of or pertaining to the hyperbola. Also **hy-per-bol'i-cal.**—**hy-per-bol'i-cal-ly,** *adv.*—**hy-per'bo-lism,** *n.* The use of hyperbole.—**hy-per'bo-list,** *n.* One who uses hyperbole.—**hy-per'bo-lize,** *v.*; *-lized, -lizing.* **I.** *intr.* To use hyperbole; exaggerate. **II.** *tr.* To represent or express with hyperbole or exaggeration.

Hy-per-bo-re-an (hī-pėr-bō'rẹ-ạn). [LL. *Hyperboreanus,* < L. *Hyperborei,* < Gr. Ὑπερβόρεοι, pl., the Hyperboreans, < ὑπέρ, beyond, + Βορέας, the north wind, Boreas.] **I.** *a.* Of or pertaining to the Hyperboreans; hence [*l. c.*], of the far north; arctic; frigid. **II.** *n.* One of a people described in Greek legend as living in a land of perpetual sunshine and plenty beyond the north wind; hence [*l. c.*], an inhabitant of the far north.

hy-per-cat-a-lec-tic (hī"pėr-kat-ạ-lek'tik), *a.* [LL. *hypercatalecticus,* < Gr. ὑπερκατάληκτος, < ὑπέρ, beyond, + καταλήγειν, leave off: see *catalectic.*] In *pros.,* having an additional syllable after the last complete dipody.

hy-per-crit-ic (hī-pėr-krit'ik), *n.* [See *hyper-.*] One who is excessively or captiously critical.—**hy-per-crit'i-cal,** *a.* Excessively or captiously critical; overcritical.—**hy-per-crit'i-cal-ly,** *adv.*—**hy-per-crit'i-cism** (-sizm), *n.* Excessively minute or severe criticism.

hy-per-du-li-a (hī"pėr-dụ-lī'ạ), *n.* [ML., < Gr. ὑπέρ, beyond, + δουλεία, E. *dulia.*] In *Rom. Cath. theol.,* the veneration offered to the Virgin Mary as the most exalted of mere creatures. Cf. *dulia* and *latria.*

hy-per-e-mi-a, hy-per-æ-mi-a (hī-pėr-ē'mi-ạ), *n.* [NL., < Gr. ὑπέρ, over, + αἷμα, blood.] In *pathol.,* an excessive accumulation of blood in any part.—**hy-per-e'mic, hy-per-æ'mic** (-ē'mik or -em'ik), *a.*

hy"per-es-the'sia, etc. See *hyperæsthesia,* etc.

hy-per-eu-tec-tic (hī"pėr-ụ-tek'tik), *a.* [See *hyper-* and *eutectic.*] Noting or pertaining to steel whose combined carbon content is over 4.3%, which is the amount contained in the eutectic alloy of carbon and iron.

hy-per-hi-dro-sis, hy-per-i-dro-sis (hī"pėr-hi-drō'sis, -i-drō'sis), *n.* [NL., < Gr. ὑπέρ, over, + ἵδρωσις, E. *hidrosis.*] In *pathol.,* excessive sweating.

hy-pe-ri-ca-ceous (hī"pẹ-ri-kā'shius), *a.* [L. *hypericum,* < Gr. ὑπέρεικον, St.-John's-wort, < ὑπό, under, + ἐρείκη, heath.] Belonging to the *Hypericaceæ,* or St.-John's-wort family of plants.

hy-per-ki-ne-sia (hī"pėr-ki-nē'ziạ), *n.* [NL., < Gr. ὑπέρ, over, + κινεῖν, move.] In *pathol.,* abnormal amount of muscular action; spasm. Also **hy"per-ki-ne'sis** (-sis).—**hy"per-ki-net'ic** (-net'ik), *a.*

hy-per-me-ter (hī-pėr'me-tėr), *n.* [LL., < Gr. ὑπέρμετρος, beyond measure, beyond the meter, < ὑπέρ, beyond, + μέτρον, measure.] In *pros.,* a verse or line having one or more syllables in addition to those proper to the meter.—**hy-per-met'ric, hy-per-met'ri-cal** (-met'rik, -ri-kạl), *a.*

hy-per-met-rope (hī-pėr-met'rōp), *n.* [Gr. ὑπέρμετρος, beyond measure, + ὤψ, eye.] A person affected with hypermetropia.—**hy"per-me-tro'pi-a** (-me-trō'pi-ạ), *n.* [NL.] In *pathol.,* a condition of the eye in which parallel rays are focused behind the retina, distant objects being seen more distinctly than near ones; far-sightedness: opposed to *myopia.*—**hy"per-me-trop'ic** (-trop'ik), *a.* Pertaining to or affected with hypermetropia; far-sighted.

hy-perm-ne-sia (hī-pėrm-nē'ziạ), *n.* [NL., < Gr. ὑπέρ, over, + μνᾶσθαι, remember.] Unusual power of recollection. Also **hy-perm-ne'sis** (-sis).

hy-per-o-pi-a (hī-pėr-ō'pi-ạ), *n.* [NL., < Gr. ὑπέρ, over, + ὤψ, eye.] Hypermetropia.—**hy-per-op'ic** (-op'ik), *a.*

hy-per-os-mi-a (hī-pėr-os'mi-ạ), *n.* [NL., < Gr. ὑπέρ, over, + ὀσμή, smell.] An abnormally acute sense of smell.—**hy-per-os'mic,** *a.*

hy-per-os-to-sis (hī"pėr-os-tō'sis), *n.*; pl. *-toses* (-tō'sēz). [NL., < Gr. ὑπέρ, over, beyond, + ὀστέον, bone.] A morbid outgrowth of bone from a bone; also, a normal increase or outgrowth of bony tissue.

hy-per-ox-ide (hī-pėr-ok′sīd or -sid), *n.* [See *hyper-*.] Same as *peroxide.*

hy-per-phe-nom-e-nal (hī″pėr-fẹ-nom′e-nạl), *a.* [See *hyper-*.] Superior to the phenomenal; transcendental; noumenal.

hy-per-phys-i-cal (hī-pėr-fiz′i-kạl), *a.* [See *hyper-*.] Above or beyond the physical; immaterial; supernatural.

hy-per-pla-sia (hī-pėr-plā′ẓiạ̈), *n.* [NL., < Gr. ὑπέρ, over, + πλάσσειν, form.] In *pathol.* and *bot.*, abnormal multiplication of cells or structural elements.—**hy-per-pla′sic** (-zik), **hy-per-plas′tic,** *a.*

hy-perp-nœ-a (hī-pėrp-nē′ạ̈), *n.* [NL., < Gr. ὑπέρ, over, + πνεῖν, blow, breathe.] In *pathol.*, energetic or labored respiration.

hy-per-py-rex-i-a (hī″pėr-pī-rek′si-ạ̈), *n.* [NL.: see *hyper-* and *pyrexia.*] In *pathol.*, an abnormally high degree of fever.—**hy″per-py-rex′i-al,** *a.*

hy-per-sen-si-tive (hī-pėr-sen′si-tiv), *a.* [See *hyper-*.] Excessively sensitive.—**hy-per-sen′si-tive-ness,** *n.*

hy-per-space (hī′pėr-spās), *n.* [See *hyper-*.] Space of more than three dimensions.

hy-per-sthene (hī′pėr-sthēn), *n.* [Gr. ὑπέρ, over, + σθένος, strength (with reference to difficult frangibility).] A native silicate of iron and magnesium, usually of a grayish or greenish-black color.—**hy-per-sthen′ic** (-sthen′ik), *a.*

hy-per-sus-cep-ti-bil-i-ty (hī″pėr-su-sep-ti-bil′i-ti), *n.* [See *hyper-*.] Increased or abnormal susceptibility; in *pathol.*, anaphylaxis.

hy-per-tro-phy (hī-pėr′trọ-fi), *n.* [NL. *hypertrophia*, < Gr. ὑπέρ, over, + τρέφειν, nourish.] In *pathol.* and *bot.*, enlargement of a part or organ, as through excessive nutrition; excessive growth. Also fig.—**hy-per-troph′ic** (-trof′ik), *a.* —**hy-per′tro-phy,** *v. t.* or *i.*; *-phied, -phying.* To affect with or undergo hypertrophy.

hyp-es-the′sia, etc. See *hypæsthesia*, etc.

hy-pe-thral, hy-pæ-thral (hī-pē′thrạl or hi-), *a.* [L. *hypæthrus*, < Gr. ὕπαιθρος, < ὑπό, under, + αἰθήρ, sky, E. *ether.*] Open to the sky, or having no roof, as a building; also, in the open air.

hy-pha (hī′fạ̈), *n.*; pl. *hyphæ* (-fē). [NL., < Gr. ὑφή, web.] In *bot.*, one of the thread-like elements of the thallus in fungi, consisting of a membrane inclosing protoplasm, and developing by apical growth.—**hy′phal,** *a.*

hy-phen (hī′fen), *n.* [LL. *hyphen*, < Gr. ὑφέν, a sign for joining syllables, < ὑφέν, adv., for phrase ὑφ᾽ ἕν, under one, in one, together.] A short line (-) used to connect the parts of a compound word, or the parts of a word divided for any purpose, as for syllabication or etymological analysis; specif., recently, in the U. S., this mark as used in designations (as *German-American*, etc.) of American citizens of foreign birth or descent (often with opprobrious force as implying incomplete allegiance to their adopted country and undue loyalty to that of their origin).—**hy′phen,** *v. t.* To hyphenate.—**hy′phen-ate** (-āt), *v. t.*; *-ated, -ating.* To join by a hyphen; write with a hyphen.—**hy′phen-ate. I.** *a.* Joined by or written with a hyphen; specif., in the U. S., noting American citizens of foreign birth or descent as designated by a hyphenated term (as *German-American*, etc.), esp. those of this class whose complete allegiance to their adopted country is questionable; pertaining to such citizens. **II.** *n.* In the U. S., a hyphenate citizen.—**hy′phen-at-ed** (-ā-ted), *p. a.* Joined by or written with a hyphen; specif., in the U. S., hyphenate.—**hy-phen-a′tion** (-ā′shọn), *n.* The act of joining by or writing with a hyphen; also, in the U. S., the practices or principles of hyphenates.—**hy′phen-ism,** *n.* In the U. S., the spirit or practices of hyphenates.—**hy′phen-ize** (-īz), *v. t.*; *-ized, -izing.* To hyphenate.—**hy″phen-i-za′tion** (-i-zā′shọn), *n.*

hyp-na-gogue (hip′nạ-gog), *n.* [Gr. ὕπνος, sleep, + ἀγωγός, leading, < ἄγειν, lead.] Something that induces sleep; a hypnotic.—**hyp-na-gog′ic** (-goj′ik), *a.*

hyp-nic (hip′nik), *a.* [Gr. ὑπνικός, < ὕπνος, sleep.] Of, pertaining to, or inducing sleep; hypnotic.

hypno-. Form of Gr. ὕπνος, sleep, used in combination: sometimes used to mean the hypnotic sleep, or hypnosis.—**hyp-no-gen-e-sis** (hip-nọ-jen′e-sis), *n.* Induction of the hypnotic state.—**hyp″no-ge-net′ic** (-jẹ-net′ik), *a.*—**hyp-nog′e-ny** (-noj′e-ni), *n.* [+ *-geny.*] Hypnogenesis.—**hyp-no-gen′ic, hyp-nog′e-nous,** *a.*—**hyp′noid,** *a.* [See *-oid.*] Resembling hypnosis.—**hyp-nol′o-gy** (-nol′ọ-ji), *n.* [+ *-logy.*] The science dealing with the phenomena of sleep.—**hyp-no-log′ic, hyp-no-log′i-cal** (-loj′ik, -i-kạl), *a.*—**hyp-nol′o-gist,** *n.*—**hyp-no-pho′bi-a** (-fō′bi-ạ̈), *n.* [NL.: see *-phobia.*] In *pathol.*, a morbid dread of falling asleep.

hyp-no-sis (hip-nō′sis), *n.* [NL., < Gr. ὑπνοῦν, put to sleep, < ὕπνος, sleep: see *sopor.*] A condition or state, allied to normal sleep, which can be artificially induced and is characterized by marked susceptibility to suggestion, loss of will-power, more or less loss of sensation, etc.; the hypnotic state; also, hypnotism.

hyp-nos-o-phy (hip-nos′ọ-fi), *n.* [Gr. ὕπνος, sleep, + σοφία, wisdom.] Knowledge or the science of the phenomena of sleep.—**hyp-nos′o-phist,** *n.*

hyp-no-ther-a-py (hip-nọ-ther′ạ-pi), *n.* [See *hypno-* and *therapy.*] Treatment of disease by means of hypnotism.

hyp-not-ic (hip-not′ik). [LL. *hypnoticus*, < Gr. ὑπνωτικός, < ὑπνοῦν, put to sleep: see *hypnosis.*] **I.** *a.* Inducing sleep; also, pertaining to hypnosis or hypnotism; also, susceptible to hypnotism, as a person. **II.** *n.* An agent or drug that produces sleep; a sedative; also, a person under the influence of hypnotism; one subject to hypnotic influence. —**hyp-not′i-cal-ly,** *adv.*—**hyp′no-tism** (-nọ-tizm), *n.* The induction of hypnosis; also, the science dealing with the induction of hypnosis; loosely, hypnosis.—**hyp′no-tist,** *n.* One who hypnotizes.—**hyp′no-tiz-a-ble** (-tī-zạ-bl), *a.* Capable of being hypnotized.—**hyp′no-tize** (-tīz), *v. t.*; *-tized, -tizing.* To put in the hypnotic state. —**hyp″no-ti-za′tion** (-ti-zā′shọn), *n.*—**hyp′no-tiz-er** (-tī-zėr), *n.*

hypo-, hyp-. [Gr. ὑπο-, ὑπ-, repr. ὑπό, prep. and adv., under; akin to L. *sub*, under: see *sub-*.] A prefix of Greek origin, meaning 'under,' 'in a lower position,' 'in a lesser degree,' 'slightly,' 'somewhat,' freely used as an English formative, esp. in scientific words, as in *hypæsthesia*, *hypoacidity*, *hyposecretion*, *hypotoxicity*. In chemical terms *hypo-* indicates a lower place in a series of compounds or a lesser amount of an element. Cf. *hyper-*.

hy-po (hī′pō), *n.* Shortened form of *hypochondria*, also of *sodium hyposulphite* (see *hyposulphite*).

hy-po-a-cid-i-ty (hī″pọ-a-sid′i-ti), *n.* [See *hypo-*.] Acidity in a lesser degree than is usual or normal, as of the gastric juice. Cf. *hyperacidity.*

hy-po-blast (hī′pọ-blast), *n.* [See *hypo-* and *-blast.*] In *embryol.*, the endoderm.—**hy-po-blas′tic** (-blas′tik), *a.*

hyp-o-caust (hip′ọ-kâst or hī′pọ-), *n.* [L. *hypocaustum*, < Gr. ὑπόκαυστον, < ὑποκαίειν, heat from below, < ὑπό, under, + καίειν, burn.] In *anc. arch.*, a chamber for the reception or distribution of heat; a hollow space or flue in the floor or wall of a building, which received and distributed the heat from a furnace.

hy-po-chlo-rite (hī-pọ-klō′rīt), *n.* [See *hypo-*.] In *chem.*, a salt of hypochlorous acid.—**hy-po-chlo′rous,** *a.* In *chem.*, noting or pertaining to an acid, HClO, whose solutions have marked bleaching properties.

hy-po-chon-dri-a (hī-pọ-kon′dri-ạ̈ or hip-ọ-), *n.* [LL. *hypochondria*, pl., < Gr. ὑποχόνδρια, neut. pl. of ὑποχόνδριος, under the cartilage (of the breast-bone), < ὑπό, under, + χόνδρος, cartilage.] Orig., as *pl.*, the parts of the body under the cartilage of the breast-bone and above the navel (see *hypochondrium*); hence, as *sing.*, a morbid condition, formerly supposed to have its seat in those parts, characterized by depressed spirits, fancies of ill health, etc.—**hy-po-chon′dri-ac** (-ak). [Gr. ὑποχονδριακός.] **I.** *a.* Of or pertaining to the hypochondria (as, the *hypochondriac* regions); also, pertaining to or suffering from hypochondria or morbid depression. **II.** *n.* A person suffering from or subject to hypochondria.—**hy″po-chon-dri′a-cal** (-drī′ạ-kạl), *a.* Hypochondriac.—**hy″po-chon-dri′a-cal-ly,** *adv.*—**hy″po-chon-dri′a-sis** (-drī′ạ-sis), *n.* [NL.] Hypochondria as a pathological condition.—**hy-po-chon′dri-um** (-dri-um), *n.*; pl. *-dria* (-dri-ạ̈). [NL.] Either of two regions of the human abdomen, situated on opposite sides (left and right) of the epigastrium, above the lumbar regions; also, a corresponding region in lower animals.

hy-po-co-ris-tic (hī″pọ-kọ-ris′tik or hip″ọ-), *a.* [Gr. ὑποκοριστικός, < ὑποκορίζεσθαι, use endearing or fair terms, < ὑπό, under, + κόρος, boy, κόρη, girl.] Endearing, as a pet name; diminutive; euphemistic.—**hy″po-co-ris′ti-cal-ly,** *adv.*

hy-po-cot-yl (hī-pō-kot′il), *n.* [From *hypo-* + *cotyl(edon).*] In *bot.*, in the embryo of a plant, that part of the stem below the cotyledons.—**hy″po-cot-y-le′don-a-ry** (-i-lē′don-ā-ri), *a.* In *bot.*, below the cotyledons.

hy-po-cra-ter-i-form (hī″pō-krā-ter′i-fôrm), *a.* [Gr. ὑποκρατήριον, the stand of a crater or bowl (< ὑπό, under, + κρατήρ, E. *crater*): see *-form.*] In *bot.*, salver-shaped: applied to a corolla consisting of a straight tube surmounted by a flat and spreading border. Also **hy″po-cra-ter-i-mor′phous** (-môr′fus).

hy-poc-ri-sy (hi-pok′ri-si), *n.*; pl. *-sies* (-siz). [OF. *ypocrisie* (F. *hypocrisie*), < LL. *hypocrisis,* < Gr. ὑπόκρισις, < ὑποκρίνεσθαι, reply, play a part, feign, < ὑπό, under, + κρίνειν, decide.] The feigning of a character or of beliefs, principles, etc., that one does not possess; esp., false assumption of virtue or piety; sanctimonious pretense.

hyp-o-crite (hip′ō-krit), *n.* [OF. *ypocrite* (F. *hypocrite*), < LL. *hypocrita,* < Gr. ὑποκριτής, actor, pretender, hypocrite, < ὑποκρίνεσθαι: see *hypocrisy.*] One given to hypocrisy; one who feigns virtue or piety; a pretender.—**hyp-o-crit′i-cal,** *a.* [Gr. ὑποκριτικός.] Of, like, or befitting a hypocrite; marked by hypocrisy.—**hyp-o-crit′i-cal-ly,** *adv.*

hy-po-cy-cloid (hī-pō-sī′kloid), *n.* [From *hypo-* + *-cycloid* as in *epicycloid.*] In *geom.*, a curve generated by the motion of a point on the circumference of a circle which rolls upon the concave side of another circle.

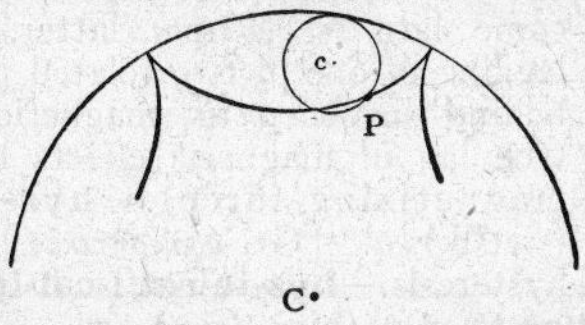

Hypocycloid. — *C* is the center of the fixed circle, *c* of the moving circle; *P* is the point of the latter whose path is traced.

hy-po-der-ma (hī-pō-dėr′mä), *n.* [NL., < Gr. ὑπό, under, + δέρμα, skin.] In *bot.*, a tissue or layer of cells beneath the epidermis; in *zoöl.*, the hypodermis.—**hy-po-der′mal,** *a.* Of or pertaining to the hypoderma; also, hypodermic.—**hy″po-der-mat′ic** (-mat′ik), *a.* and *n.* Same as *hypodermic.* —**hy-po-der′mic.** [Gr. ὑπό + δέρμα.] **I.** *a.* Pertaining to parts under the skin; characterized by the introduction of medical remedies under the skin (as, *hypodermic* injection); introduced under the skin (as, a *hypodermic* remedy; a *hypodermic* syringe); also, lying under the skin, as tissue; of the nature of or pertaining to the hypodermis; also, burrowing or living under the skin, as certain parasites. **II.** *n.* A hypodermic remedy; a hypodermic injection; also, a hypodermic syringe.—**hy-po-der′mi-cal-ly,** *adv.*—**hy-po-der′mis,** *n.* [NL.] In *zoöl.*, a layer of tissue lying under the outer integument of certain invertebrates, as the reticulated tissue lying beneath the cuticle of earthworms.

hy-po=eu-tec-tic (hī″pō-ū-tek′tik), *a.* [See *hypo-* and *eutectic.*] Noting or pertaining to steel whose combined carbon content is under 4.3%, which is the amount contained in the eutectic alloy of carbon and iron.

hy-po-gæ′al, etc. See *hypogeal,* etc.

hy-po-gas-tri-um (hī-pō-gas′tri-um), *n.* [NL., < Gr. ὑπογάστριον, prop. neut. of ὑπογάστριος, abdominal, < ὑπό, under, + γαστήρ, belly, stomach.] In *human anat.*, the lower part of the abdomen, esp. the region between the right and left iliac regions.—**hy-po-gas′tric,** *a.*

hy-po-ge-al, hy-po-ge-an (hī-pō-jē′al, -an), *a.* [See *hypogeous.*] Underground; subterranean; in *bot.*, hypogeous.

hy-po=gene (hī′pō-jēn), *a.* [Gr. ὑπό, under, + -γενής, produced.] In *geol.*, formed beneath the earth's surface, as granite: opposed to *epigene.*

hy-pog-e-nous (hī-poj′e-nus), *a.* [See *hypogene.*] In *bot.*, growing beneath, or on the under surface, as fungi on leaves. Cf. *epigenous.*

hy-po-ge-ous (hī-pō-jē′us), *a.* [L. *hypogeus,* < Gr. ὑπόγειος, ὑπόγαιος, < ὑπό, under, + γῆ, earth.] Underground; subterranean; in *bot.*, growing or remaining underground.

hy-po-ge-um, hy-po-gæ-um (hī-pō-jē′um), *n.*; pl. *-gea, -gæa* (-jē′ä). [L., < Gr. ὑπόγειον, ὑπόγαιον, neut. of ὑπόγειος, ὑπόγαιος, underground: see *hypogeous.*] In *anc. arch.*, the underground part of a building; an underground structure or chamber.

hy-po-glos-sal (hī-pō-glos′al). [Gr. ὑπό, under, + γλῶσσα, tongue.] In *anat.* and *zoöl.*: **I.** *a.* Situated under the tongue, wholly or in part: as, a *hypoglossal* nerve (either of the pair of cranial nerves which give rise to the movements of the tongue). **II.** *n.* A hypoglossal nerve.

hy-pog-y-nous (hī-poj′i-nus), *a.* [Gr. ὑπό, under, + γυνή, woman, female.] In *bot.*, situated on the receptacle beneath the pistil, as stamens, etc.; having stamens, etc., so arranged, as a flower.—**hy-pog′y-ny,** *n.*

hy-po-nas-ty (hī′pō-nas-ti), *n.* [Gr. ὑπό, under, + ναστός, pressed close, compact, < νάσσειν, press close.] In *bot.*, increased growth along the lower surface of an organ or part, causing the part to bend upward.—**hy-po-nas′tic,** *a.*

hy-po-ni-trite (hī-pō-nī′trīt), *n.* [See *hypo-.*] In *chem.*, a salt of hyponitrous acid.—**hy-po-ni′trous,** *a.* In *chem.*, noting or pertaining to an unstable crystalline acid, $H_2N_2O_2$.

hy-po-phos-phate (hī-pō-fos′fāt), *n.* [See *hypo-.*] In *chem.*, a salt of hypophosphoric acid.—**hy-po-phos′phite** (-fīt), *n.* In *chem.*, a salt of hypophosphorous acid.—**hy″po-phos-phor′ic** (-for′ik), *a.* In *chem.*, noting or pertaining to a tetrabasic acid, $H_4P_2O_6$, produced by the slow oxidation of phosphorus in moist air.—**hy-po-phos′pho-rous** (-fō-rus), *a.* In *chem.*, noting or pertaining to a monobasic acid of phosphorus, H_3PO_2, having salts which are used in medicine.

hy-poph-y-ge (hī-pof′i-jē or hi-), *n.* [NL., < Gr. ὑποφυγή, < ὑποφεύγειν, withdraw, < ὑπό, under, + φεύγειν, flee.] In *arch.*, a depression of curved profile, as a hollow molding beneath some Doric capitals.

hy-poph-y-sis (hī-pof′i-sis or hi-), *n.*; pl. *-yses* (-i-sēz). [NL., < Gr. ὑπόφυσις, anatomical process, < ὑποφύεσθαι, grow from below, < ὑπό, under, + φύειν, produce.] In *anat.*, the pituitary body of the brain.

hy-po-scope (hī′pō-skōp), *n.* [Gr. ὑπό, under, + σκοπεῖν, view.] An attachment for a rifle or the like, consisting of a number of mirrors so arranged that the piece can be aimed from behind a breastwork without exposing the head.

hy-pos-ta-sis (hī-pos′ta-sis or hi-), *n.*; pl. *-tases* (-ta-sēz). [LL., < Gr. ὑπόστασις, substance, nature, essence, also sediment, < ὑφίστασθαι, stand under, subsist, < ὑπό, under, + ἱστάναι, cause to stand.] In *metaph.*, the underlying or essential part of anything, as distinguished from attributes or from what is unsubstantial; substance, essence, or essential principle; also, a hypothetical substance; a phenomenon or state of things conceived of as a real substance; in *theol.*, a real personal subsistence; a personality; one of the three real and distinct subsistences in the one undivided substance or essence of God; a person of the Trinity; the one personality of Christ in which his two natures, human and divine, are united; in *med.*, a sediment or deposit, as from urine; also, an excessive accumulation of blood in a dependent part.—**hy-pos′ta-size** (-sīz), *v. t.*; *-sized, -sizing.* To hypostatize.—**hy-po-stat-ic** (hī-pō-stat′ik), *a.* [Gr. ὑποστατικός.] Of or pertaining to a hypostasis or hypostases. Also **hy-po-stat′i-cal.**—**hy-po-stat′i-cal-ly,** *adv.*—**hy-pos′ta-tize** (-tīz), *v. t.*; *-tized, -tizing.* To treat or regard as a distinct substance or reality.

hy-po-style (hī′pō-stīl or hip′ō-). [Gr. ὑπόστυλος, < ὑπό, under, + στῦλος, pillar, column.] In *arch.*: **I.** *a.* Having the roof supported by pillars. **II.** *n.* A hypostyle structure; a covered colonnade.

hy-po-sul-phite (hī-pō-sul′fīt), *n.* [See *hypo-.*] In *chem.*, a salt of hyposulphurous acid: as, sodium *hyposulphite* (a crystalline compound, $Na_2S_2O_3$, used in photography, etc., and properly called 'sodium thiosulphate').—**hy″po-sul-phu′rous** (-fū′rus), *a.* Designating an acid, $H_2S_2O_4$, next in a series below sulphurous acid; also, less properly, thiosulphuric.

hy-po-tax-is (hī-pō-tak′sis), *n.* [NL., < Gr. ὑπόταξις, subjection, < ὑποτάσσειν, place under, < ὑπό, under, + τάσσειν, arrange.] In *gram.*, dependent relation or construction, as of clauses.—**hy-po-tac′tic** (-tak′tik), *a.*

hy-pot-e-nuse (hī-pot′e-nūs or hi-), *n.* [L. *hypotenusa,* < Gr. ὑποτείνουσα, ppr. fem. of ὑποτείνειν, subtend, < ὑπό, under, + τείνειν, stretch.] In *geom.*, the side of a right-angled triangle opposite the right angle.

hy-poth-ec (hī-poth′ek or hi-), *n.* [= F. *hypothèque*, < LL. *hypotheca*, < Gr. ὑποθήκη, a deposit, pledge, mortgage, < ὑποτιθέναι, put under, lay down: see *hypothesis*.] In *Roman* and *civil law*, a contract lien given by a debtor to his creditor as security, without giving him possession of the property.—**hy-poth′e-ca-ry** (-ẹ̄-kā̤-ri), *a.* [LL. *hypothecarius*.] Of or pertaining to a hypothec; created or secured by a hypothec.—**hy-poth′e-cate** (-kāt), *v. t.*; *-cated, -cating.* [ML. *hypothecatus*, pp. of *hypothecare*, < LL. *hypotheca*.] To pledge to a creditor as security, without delivering over; mortgage; also, to put in pledge by delivery, as stocks given as security for a loan.—**hy-poth-e-ca′tion** (-kā′shọn), *n.*—**hy-poth′e-ca-tor,** *n.*

hy-poth-e-nuse (hī-poth′e-nūs or hi-), *n.* Erroneous form of *hypotenuse*.

hy-poth-e-sis (hī-poth′e-sis or hi-), *n.*; pl. *-eses* (-e-sēz). [NL., < Gr. ὑπόθεσις, supposition, postulate, < ὑποτιθέναι, put under, lay down, suppose, < ὑπό, under, + τιθέναι, put.] A proposition put forth as a basis for reasoning; also, a supposition or theory presented as an explanation of facts, as in the sciences; hence, in general, a supposition; an assumption; often, a mere assumption or guess.—**hy-poth′e-size** (-sīz), *v.*; *-sized, -sizing.* **I.** *intr.* To form a hypothesis or hypotheses. **II.** *tr.* To assume by hypothesis.—**hy-po-thet-i-cal, hy-po-thet-ic** (hī-pọ̄-thet′i-kạl, -ik, or hip-ọ̄-), *a.* [Gr. ὑποθετικός.] Pertaining to, involving, or of the nature of hypothesis (as, *hypothetical* reasoning; a *hypothetical* statement); supposititious; conjectural; assumed by hypothesis, or supposed (as, a *hypothetical* case; a *hypothetical* type of prehistoric man); given to making hypotheses, as a person; in *logic*, involving a hypothesis or condition, as a proposition; conditional; of a syllogism, having a hypothetical proposition for one of its premises.—**hy-po-thet′i-cal-ly,** *adv.*—**hy-poth′e-tize** (-tīz), *v. i.* or *t.*; *-tized, -tizing.* To hypothesize.

hy-po-tra-che-li-um (hī″pọ̄-trạ-kē′li-um), *n.*; pl. *-lia* (-li-ä̤). [L., < Gr. ὑποτραχήλιον, < ὑπό, under, + τράχηλος, neck.] In *arch.*, the neck of a column, between the echinus and the shaft; also, in the Doric order, the junction of this member with the shaft, marked by a bevel or cut.

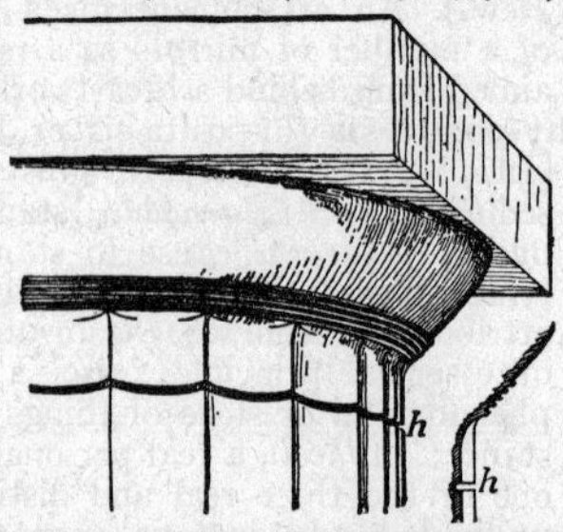

Hypotrachelium (*h, h*), from a column of the Parthenon (Doric architecture).

hy-po-tro-choid (hī-pọ̄-trō′koid or hī-pot′rọ̄-), *n.* [See *hypo-* and *trochoid*.] In *geom.*, a curve which can be traced by a point rigidly connected with a circle which rolls upon the interior of another circle.

hy-po-xan-thine (hī-pọ̄-zan′thin), *n.* [See *hypo-* and *xanthine*.] In *chem.*, a crystalline nitrogenous compound related to xanthine, and found in animal and vegetable tissues.—**hy-po-xan′thic,** *a.*

hypped, hyp-pish (hipt, hip′ish). See *hipped*², *hippish*.

hyp-si-ce-phal-ic (hip″si-se-fal′ik), *a.* [Gr. ὕψι, on high, + κεφαλή, head.] In *craniol.*, characterized by a high skull.

hypso-. Form of Gr. ὕψος, height, used in combination.—**hyp-sog-ra-phy** (hip-sog′rạ-fi), *n.* [+ *-graphy*.] The science dealing with the form or relief of the earth's surface, esp. with regard to differences of elevation; topographic relief.—**hyp-so-graph′ic, hyp-so-graph′i-cal** (-sọ̄-graf′ik, -i-kạl), *a.*—**hyp-som′e-ter** (-som′e-tėr), *n.* [+ *-meter*.] An instrument for measuring altitude by determining the boiling-point of a liquid at the given height.—**hyp-so-met′ric, hyp-so-met′ri-cal** (-met′rik, -ri-kạl), *a.* Of or pertaining to hypsometry.—**hyp-so-met′ri-cal-ly,** *adv.*—**hyp-som′e-try,** *n.* [+ *-metry*.] The measuring of altitudes.

hy-ra-coid (hī′rạ-koid), *a.* [See *hyrax* and *-oid*.] Resembling the hyrax; of or belonging to the suborder *Hyracoidea*, comprising the hyraxes.—**hy-ra-coi′de-an** (-koi′dẹ̄-ạn), *a.* and *n.*

hy-rax (hī′raks), *n.* [NL., < Gr. ὕραξ (ὑρακ-), shrew-mouse.] Any animal of the genus *Procavia* (or *Hyrax*), comprising small, timid, rabbit-like ungulate mammals of Asia and Africa, which live mostly in rocky places; also, any animal belonging to the same suborder (*Hyracoidea*).

Hyr-ca-ni-an (hėr-kā′ni-ạn), *a.* Of or pertaining to Hyrcania, an ancient country or province of Asia, south of the Caspian Sea.

hy-son (hī′sn), *n.* [From Chinese, and meaning lit. 'blooming spring.'] A Chinese green tea.

hys-sop (his′ọp), *n.* [L. *hyssopus*, < Gr. ὕσσωπος, kind of aromatic plant.] An aromatic menthaceous herb, *Hyssopus officinalis*, with blue flowers; also, in the Bible and derived use, a plant, perhaps the caper, whose twigs were used in ceremonial sprinkling (as, "Purge me with *hyssop*, and I shall be clean," Ps. li. 7; "They all went into the church, each one stopping, as he passed the grave, to throw a handful of earth into it, and sprinkle it with the *hyssop*," Longfellow's "Hyperion," iv. 8); also, any of various other plants (as, giant *hyssop*, any plant of the menthaceous genus *Agastache*, esp. *A. anethiodora*, a tall, fragrant herb).

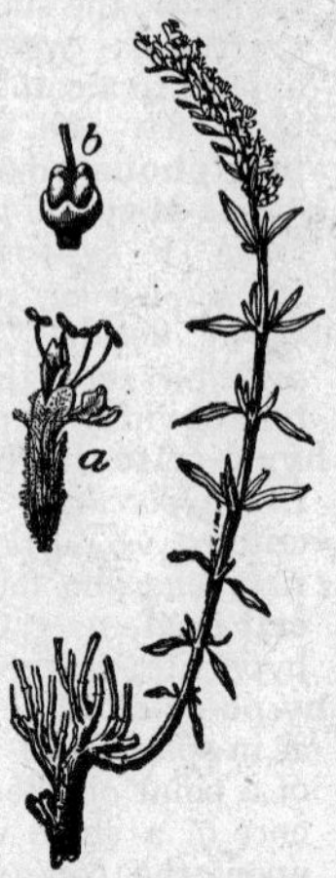

Hyssop (*Hyssopus officinalis*).—*a*, flower; *b*, fruit.

hys-te-rec-to-my (his-tẹ-rek′tọ̄-mi), *n.* [Gr. ὑστέρα, uterus, + ἐκ, out of, + -τομία, E. *-tomy*.] In *surg.*, the excision of the uterus.

hys-te-re-sis (his-tẹ-rē′sis), *n.* [NL., < Gr. ὑστέρησις, < ὑστερεῖν, be behind, come late, < ὕστερος, latter, later.] A lagging of one of two related phenomena behind the other: as, magnetic *hysteresis* (the lag of magnetic effects behind the magnetizing force).—**hys-te-ret′ic** (-ret′ik), *a.* [Gr. ὑστερητικός.] Pertaining to or exhibiting hysteresis.—**hys-te-ret′i-cal-ly,** *adv.*

hys-te-ri-a (his-tē′ri-ä̤), *n.* [NL., < Gr. ὑστέρα, uterus: cf. *hysteric*.] In *pathol.*, nervous disorder occurring most often in women and formerly attributed to disturbances of the uterus, characterized esp. by violent emotional outbreaks, perversion of sensation, and various morbid effects due to autosuggestion; hence, fig., morbid or senseless emotionalism; emotional frenzy.

hys-ter-ic (his-ter′ik). [L. *hystericus*, < Gr. ὑστερικός, pertaining to or suffering in the uterus, hysterical, < ὑστέρα, uterus.] **I.** *a.* Hysterical: as, "She often broke into a little, nervous, *hysteric* laugh" (Hawthorne's "House of the Seven Gables," vii.). **II.** *n.* One subject to hysteria; also, *pl.* (occasionally *sing.*), a fit of hysteria; hysteria.—**hys-ter′i-cal,** *a.* Of, pertaining to, or characteristic of hysteria (as, a *hysterical* fit); suffering from or subject to hysteria (as, a *hysterical* girl); hence, fig., resembling or suggesting hysteria; morbidly or senselessly emotional; emotionally disordered.—**hys-ter′i-cal-ly,** *adv.*

hys-te-ri-tis (his-tẹ-rī′tis), *n.* [NL., < Gr. ὑστέρα, uterus.] In *pathol.*, inflammation of the uterus; metritis.

hystero-. Form of Gr. ὑστέρα, uterus, in combination: used also to represent *hysteria*.—**hys-te-ro=ep-i-lep-sy** (his″tẹ-rọ̄-ep′i-lep-si), *n.* In *pathol.*, a form of hysteria with epileptiform attacks.—**hys″te-ro=ep-i-lep′tic,** *a.* and *n.*—**hys″te-ro-gen′ic** (-jen′ik), *a.* [+ *-genic*.] Producing, or concerned in the production of, hysteria.—**hys′te-roid,** *a.* [See *-oid*.] Resembling hysteria. Also **hys-te-roi′dal.**—**hys-te-rom′e-ter** (-rom′e-tėr), *n.* [+ *-meter*.] An instrument for measuring the uterus; a uterine sound.

hys-te-ron=prot-e-ron (his″tẹ-ron-prot′ẹ-ron), *n.* [LL., < Gr. ὕστερον, neut. of ὕστερος, latter, + πρότερον, neut. of πρότερος, being before, sooner.] In *rhet.*, a figure by which a word, phrase, or clause that logically should come last is put first.

hys-te-ro-pex-i-a, hys-te-ro-pex-y (his″tẹ-rọ̄-pek′si-ä̤, his′tẹ-rọ̄-pek″si), *n.* [NL. *hysteropexia*, < Gr. ὑστέρα, uterus, + πῆξις, a making fast.] In *surg.*, the fixation of the uterus by suturing it to the anterior wall of the abdomen.

hys-te-rop-to-sis (his″tẹ-rop-tō′sis), *n.* [NL., < Gr. ὑστέρα, uterus, + πτῶσις, a falling.] In *pathol.*, a downward displacement of the uterus; falling of the womb.

hys-te-ror-rha-phy (his-tẹ-ror′ạ-fi), *n.* [Gr. ὑστέρα, uterus, + ῥαφή, a sewing.] In *surg.*, the closing of a wound in the uterus by sutures; also, hysteropexia.

hys-te-rot-o-my (his-tẹ-rot′ọ-mi), *n.* [NL. *hysterotomia*, < Gr. ὑστέρα, uterus, + -τομία, E. *-tomy*.] In *surg.*, the operation of cutting into the uterus; sometimes, the Cæsarean operation.
hys-tri-co-morph (his′tri-kọ-môrf), *n.* [NL. *Hystricomorpha*, pl., < Gr. ὕστριξ, porcupine, + μορφή, form.] Any of the *Hystricomorpha*, a group of rodents including the porcupines and their allies.—**hys″tri-co-mor′phic** (-môr′-fik), *a.*
hythe (hīᴛʜ), *n.* See *hithe*.

I

I[1], **i**[1] (ī); pl. *I's*, *i's* (īz). A vowel, the 9th letter of the English alphabet.
I[2] (ī), *pron.*; nom. *I*, poss. *my* or *mine*, obj. *me*, pl. nom. *we*, poss. *our* or *ours*, obj. *us*. [AS. *ic* = D. *ik* = G. *ich* = Icel. *ek* = Goth. *ik*, I; akin to L. *ego*, Gr. ἐγώ, Skt. *aham*, I.] The nominative case singular of the pronoun of the first person, used by a speaker or writer to denote himself.—**I**[2], *n.*; pl. *I's* (īz). The pronoun *I* used as a substantive; also, the ego.
i-amb (ī′amb), *n.* [L. *iambus*, < Gr. ἴαμβος, said to be < ἰάπτειν, throw, shoot, assail, the iambus having been first used in satiric verse.] In *pros.*, an iambus or iambic.—**i-am-bic** (ī-am′bik). [LL. *iambicus*, < Gr. ἰαμβικός.] In *pros.*: **I.** *a.* Pertaining to the iambus; consisting of or employing an iambus or iambi. **II.** *n.* An iambus; also, a verse or poem consisting of iambi (usually in *pl.*).—**i-am′bus** (-bus), *n.*; pl. *-bi* (-bī) or *-buses*. [L.] In *pros.*, a metrical foot of two syllables, a short followed by a long, or an unaccented by an accented.
-iasis. [L. *-iasis*, < Gr. -ιασις, in nouns from verbs with infinitive in -ιάειν, -ιᾶν.] A suffix of nouns denoting state or condition, esp. a morbid condition or a form of disease, as in *elephantiasis*, *hydrargyriasis*, *leontiasis*, *phthiriasis*, and *trypanosomiasis*.
i-at-ric (ī-at′rik), *a.* [Gr. ἰατρικός, < ἰατρός, physician, < ἰᾶσθαι, heal.] Pertaining to a physician or to medicine. Also **i-at′ri-cal.**
i-a-tro-chem-i-cal (ī-ā″trọ-kem′i-kạl or ī-at″rọ-), *a.* [Gr. ἰατρός, physician, + E. *chemical*.] Noting or pertaining to a period in the history of chemistry (the 16th century and the first half of the 17th century), during which the leading chemists held that the main purpose of this science is the preparation of medicine; also, noting or pertaining to a school of medicine of the 17th century, which held that physiological and pathological phenomena are due to chemical action, disturbances, etc.—**i-a″tro-chem′is-try,** *n.*
i-a-trol (ī′ạ-trol or -trōl), *n.* [Gr. ἰατρός, physician.] In *phar.*, an organic compound containing iodine, used as an antiseptic.
i-a-tro-phys-i-cal (ī-ā″trọ-fiz′i-kạl or ī-at″rọ-), *a.* [Gr. ἰατρός, physician, + E. *physical*.] Noting or pertaining to a school of medicine of the 17th century, which employed the laws of physics and mechanics in explaining the functions of the body and in applying remedies.—**i-a″tro-phys′ics,** *n.*
I=bar (ī′bär), *n.* A metal bar having a cross-section like the capital letter I.
I-be-ri-a (ī-bē′ri-ạ), *n.* [L., < Gr. Ἰβηρία, < Ἴβηρες, the Iberians.] An ancient name for the Spanish peninsula (Spain and Portugal: as, "The Musselmen upon *Iberia's* shore Descend," Southey's "Roderick," i. 15), also for a country of Asia south of the Caucasus.—**I-be′ri-an. I.** *a.* Of or pertaining to Iberia in Europe or its inhabitants (as, "Better be first, he [Julius Cæsar] said, in a little *Iberian* village, Than be second in Rome": Longfellow's "Courtship of Miles Standish," ii.); specif., noting or pertaining to a dark dolichocephalic race inhabiting a great part of southern Europe and parts of northern Africa, comprising the ancient Iberians and other peoples, and their descendants; also, of or pertaining to ancient Iberia in Asia or its inhabitants. **II.** *n.* One of the ancient inhabitants of Iberia in Europe, from whom the Basques are supposed to be descended; specif., a member of the Iberian race; also, one of the ancient inhabitants of Iberia in Asia.
I-be-ro- (ī-bē′rọ-). Form of L. *Iberus*, Iberian, used in combination, often in the sense of 'Spanish and Portuguese,' as in *Ibero-American*.
i-bex (ī′beks), *n.*; pl. *ibexes* or (esp. collectively) *ibex*. [L.] Any of various wild goats with large recurved horns, esp. *Capra ibex*, of the Alps and Apennines.

Alpine Ibex (*Capra ibex*).

i-bi-dem (i-bī′dem), *adv.* [L.] In the same place.
i-bis (ī′bis), *n.*; pl. *ibises*. [L., < Gr. ἶβις.] Any of various large wading birds of warm regions, allied to the herons and storks, esp. *Ibis æthiopica* (or *religiosa*) of Egypt and other parts of Africa, with white and black plumage, an object of veneration among the ancient Egyptians ('sacred ibis'), or any bird of the genus *Plegadis*, comprising species with dark, more or less metallic or iridescent plumage ('glossy ibis'), as *P. falcinellus*, an old-world species sometimes found in America.—**i-bi-dine** (ī′bi-din), *a.*

Glossy Ibis (*Plegadis falcinellus*).

-ible. [L. *-ibilis*, suffix forming adjectives from verbs with infinitive in *-ere* and *-ire*, being one form of the suffix *-bilis*: see *-ble*, and cf. *-able*.] An adjective suffix equivalent to *-able*, occurring in words taken from the Latin, as *credible*, *horrible*, *legible*, *visible*, or formed after the Latin type, as *addible* (for *addable*), *reducible*. See *-able* and *-ble*.
-ic. [= F. *-ique*, < L. *-icus*, < Gr. -ικός.] A suffix meaning 'of or pertaining to,' 'characteristic of,' 'of the nature of,' 'like,' 'due to,' etc., occurring in numerous adjectives, as *artistic*, *Attic*, *civic*, *electric*, *graphic*, *historic*, *metallic*, *poetic*, also in many nouns derived from such adjectives in English, or ultimately of adjectival origin, as *attic*, *critic*, *heretic*, *magic*, *mechanic*, *music*, *rhetoric*. In chemical terms, as compared with *-ous*, *-ic* implies a smaller proportion of the element indicated, that is, a higher valence (see *-ous*).
-ical. [= *-ic* + *-al*[1].] A compound suffix of adjectives usually interchangeable with forms in *-ic*, as in *geometrical* and *geometric*, *poetical* and *poetic*, but sometimes differentiated in sense, as in *economical* and *economic*, *historical* and *historic*, *political* and *politic*. In another class of adjectives, *-ical* represents *-al* attached to *-ic* of nouns, as in *musical*, *rhetorical*.
I-ca-ri-an (ī-kā′ri-ạn), *a.* Pertaining to or characteristic of Icarus, who, according to Greek legend, flew so high that the sun melted the wax with which his artificial wings were fastened on, causing him to fall into the Ægean Sea; hence, presumptuously ambitious, venturesome, or foolhardy (as, an *Icarian* undertaking).

ice (īs), *n.* [AS. *īs* = D. *ijs* = G. *eis* = Icel. *īss*, ice.] The solid form of water, produced by freezing; frozen water; the frozen surface of a body of water; hence, some substance resembling this; esp., a confection made of water and fruit-juice or of variously flavored cream, custard, etc., sweetened and frozen; also, icing.—**ice age,** the glacial epoch (see *glacial*).—**ice,** *v.*; *iced, icing.* **I.** *tr.* To cover with ice; also, to convert into ice; freeze; also, to refrigerate with ice; cool with ice, as a drink; hence, to make cold as if with ice; deprive of warmth of feeling; also, to cover (cakes, etc.) with icing; frost. **II.** *intr.* To turn to ice; freeze.

ice=a-pron (īs′ā″prọn), *n.* A pointed structure on the upstream side of a bridge-pier to protect it from floating ice.

Portion of Bridge showing Ice-aprons (*a*, *a*, *a*) on the bank and in midstream.

ice-berg (īs′bėrg), *n.* [Cf. D. *ijsberg*, G. *eisberg*, Sw. *isberg*, Dan. and Norw. *isbjerg*, 'ice mountain.'] A large floating mass of ice, detached from a glacier and carried out to sea.

ice=blink (īs′blingk), *n.* A luminous appearance near the horizon, due to the reflection of light from ice.

ice=boat (īs′bōt), *n.* A triangular frame with runners, fitted with a mast, sails, etc., for sailing on ice; also, a strong boat used to break a channel through ice, as in a river.

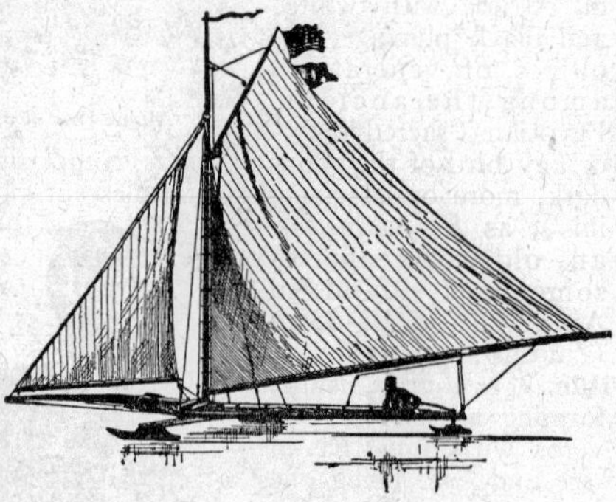
Ice-boat, for sailing on ice.

ice=bound (īs′bound), *a.* Held fast by ice; frozen in; hemmed in by ice; also, obstructed by ice, as a harbor.

ice=box (īs′boks), *n.* A box or chest for containing ice to keep food, etc., cool.

ice=break-er (īs′brā″kėr), *n.* Anything used or serving to break up ice; a tool or machine for breaking ice into conveniently small pieces for various uses; an ice-boat for breaking channels through ice; a structure of masonry or timber for protection against moving ice.

ice=cap (īs′kap), *n.* A permanent cap or covering of ice over an area (sometimes of vast extent), sloping on all sides from an elevated center; in *med.*, a bag containing ice for application to the head.

ice=chest (īs′chest), *n.* An ice-box.

ice=cold (īs′kōld′), *a.* [AS. *īs-cald.*] Cold as ice.

ice=cream (īs′krēm′), *n.* A confection made of cream, custard, etc., sweetened, variously flavored, and frozen.

iced (īst), *p. a.* Covered with ice; also, cooled by means of ice; also, covered with icing.

ice=floe (īs′flō), *n.* A large sheet of floating ice.

ice=foot (īs′fụt), *n.* A belt or wall of ice extending along the shore in arctic regions: due chiefly to the accumulation of snow, which becomes converted into ice when it meets the sea-water.

ice=house (īs′hous), *n.* A building for the storage of ice.

Ice-land-er (īs′lạn-dėr), *n.* A native or inhabitant of Iceland.

Ice-land-ic (īs-lan′dik). **I.** *a.* Pertaining to Iceland, or to its inhabitants or their language. **II.** *n.* The language of Iceland, the oldest and best-preserved member of the Scandinavian branch of the Teutonic family of languages, in its older form accepted as representative of the old Scandinavian (or Old Norse) tongue, and having an extensive and important literature. See *Edda* and *saga.*

Ice-land (īs′lạnd) **moss.** An edible lichen, *Cetraria islandica*, of arctic regions, used to some extent in medicine.—**Ice′land spar.** A transparent variety of calcite, used extensively for optical purposes.

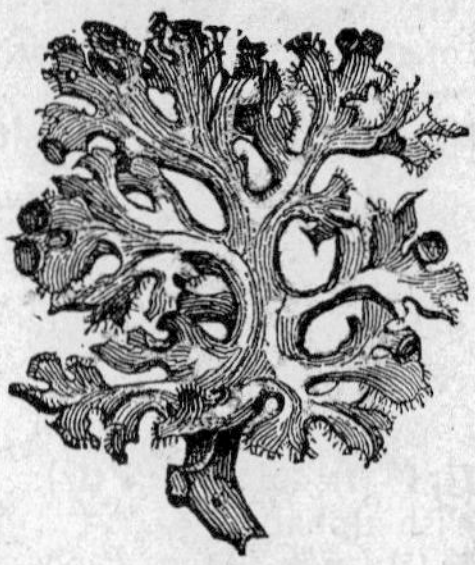
Iceland Moss.

ice-less (īs′les), *a.* Free from ice, as a river; also, requiring no ice, as a refrigerating device.

ice=ma-chine (īs′mạ-shēn″), *n.* A machine for the artificial production of ice.

ice-man (īs′mạn or -man), *n.*; pl. *-men.* A man skilled in traveling over ice; also, a man engaged in the industry of gathering and storing ice, or in selling or delivering it to customers; also, a man in charge of the ice on a skating-pond, etc.

ice=pack (īs′pak), *n.* A large area of floating ice, consisting of separate masses more or less packed together, as in the arctic seas.

ice=pick (īs′pik), *n.* A pick, or a small awl-like tool, for breaking ice.

ice=pitch-er (īs′pich″ėr), *n.* A pitcher for holding ice-water: often made of metal, with double or non-conducting walls.

ice=plant (īs′plant), *n.* A low-growing, spreading plant, *Mesembryanthemum crystallinum*, native in southern Africa, the Mediterranean regions, etc., having leaves covered with pellucid watery vesicles that glisten in the sun.

ice=plow (īs′plou), *n.* An implement for cutting grooves in ice to facilitate division into blocks for harvesting.

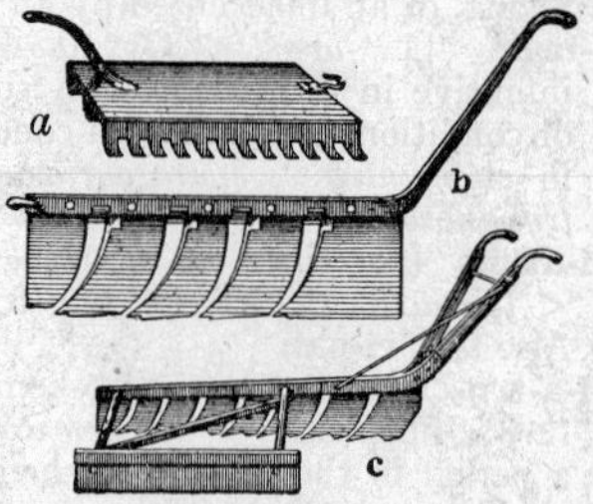

Ice-plows.

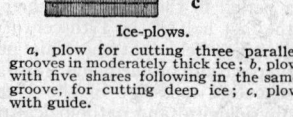

a, plow for cutting three parallel grooves in moderately thick ice; *b*, plow with five shares following in the same groove, for cutting deep ice; *c*, plow with guide.

ice=quake (īs′kwāk), *n.* The rending and crashing which precede or accompany the breaking up of great masses of ice.

ice=sheet (īs′shēt), *n.* A broad, thick sheet of ice covering an extensive area for a long period of time; a continental glacier: as, "It appears that during the glacial period a series of great *ice-sheets* covered enormous areas in North America and, north-west Europe" (Encyc. Brit., 11th ed., XII. 59).

ice=storm (īs′stôrm), *n.* A storm of rain turning to hail or ice, or freezing on the objects or surfaces that it strikes.

ice=wa-ter (īs′wâ″tėr), *n.* Water obtained from or cooled by ice.

Ich-a-bod (ik′ạ-bod), *n.* [Heb. *Ikābōd*, < ī, not, + *kābōd*, glory.] A Hebrew proper name (see 1 Sam. iv. 21, also etym.): used allusively to imply that the "glory" of something "is departed" (see Whittier's poem entitled "Ichabod!" also Browning's "Waring," i. 6).

ich-neu-mon (ik-nū′mọn), *n.* [L., < Gr. *ἰχνεύμων*, lit. 'tracker,' < *ἰχνεύειν*, to track, < *ἴχνος*, track, trace.] A slender carnivorous mammal, *Herpestes ichneumon*, of Egypt, of the same genus as the common mongoos of India, resembling the weasel in form and habits, and feeding on rats, mice, reptiles, etc., but esp. noted for devouring crocodiles' eggs, for which reason it was held in great regard by the ancient Egyptians (also called *Pharaoh's rat*); hence, any animal of the same genus; a mongoos; also, an ichneumon-fly.—**ich-neu′mon=fly,** *n.* Any of a large group of hymenopterous insects (genera *Ophion*, *Thalessa*, etc.) which in

Ichneumon (*Herpestes ichneumon*).

larval form are parasitic on or in and destructive to the larvæ of other insects.

ich-nite (ik′nīt), *n.* [Gr. ἴχνος, track, trace.] A fossil footprint; an ichnolite.

ichno-. Form of Gr. ἴχνος, track, footprint, trace, used in combination.—**ich-no-graph** (ik′nǫ-gráf), *n.* [+ *-graph.*] A ground-plan.—**ich-nog′ra-phy** (-nog′rą-fi), *n.* [Gr. ἰχνογραφία: see *-graphy.*] The drawing of ground-plans; also, a ground-plan; a map.—**ich-no-graph′ic, ich-no-graph′i-cal** (-graf′ik, -i-kąl), *a.*—**ich′no-lite** (-līt), *n.* [+ *-lite.*] A footprint preserved in rock; a fossil footprint.—**ich-nol′o-gy** (-nol′ǫ-ji), *n.* [+ *-logy.*] The branch of paleontology that treats of fossil footprints.

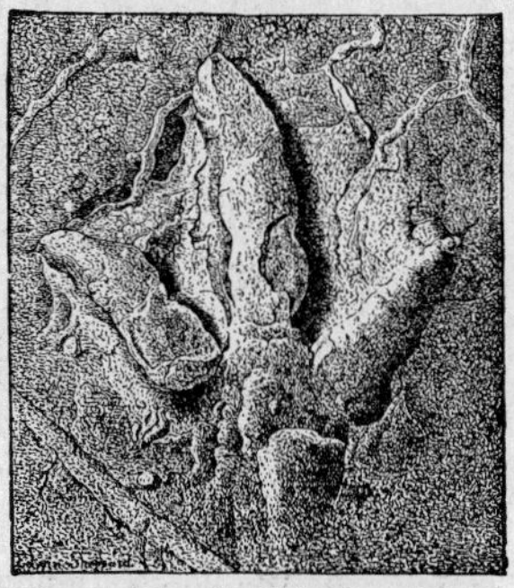
Ichnolite from the Triassic rocks near Boonton, New Jersey.

i-chor (ī′kôr), *n.* [NL., < Gr. ἰχώρ.] In *class. myth.*, an ethereal fluid supposed to flow in the veins of the gods; in *pathol.*, an acrid watery discharge, as from an ulcer or wound.—**i-chor-ous** (ī′kǫr-us), *a.*

ich-thy-ic (ik′thi-ik), *a.* [Gr. ἰχθυϊκός, < ἰχθύς, fish.] Of or pertaining to fishes; piscine.

ichthyo-, ichthy-. Forms of Gr. ἰχθύς, fish, used in combination.—**ich-thy-oid** (ik′thi-oid), *a.* [Gr. ἰχθυοειδής: see *-oid.*] Fish-like. Also **ich-thy-oi′dal.**—**ich′thy-ol** (-ol or -ōl), *n.* [+ *-ol.*] In *phar.*, a reddish-brown syrupy liquid obtained from a bituminous shale rich in fossil fishes, used externally as an alterative and discutient.

ich-thy-ol-o-gy (ik-thi-ol′ǫ-ji), *n.* [See *ichthyo-* and *-logy.*] The branch of zoölogy that treats of fishes.—**ich″thy-o-log′ic, ich″thy-o-log′i-cal** (-ǫ-loj′ik, -i-kąl), *a.*—**ich-thy-ol′o-gist,** *n.*

ich-thy-o-mor-phic (ik″thi-ǫ-môr′fik), *a.* [See *ichthyo-* and *-morphic.*] Having the form or characteristics of a fish.

ich-thy-oph-a-gous (ik-thi-of′ą-gus), *a.* [Gr. ἰχθυοφάγος, < ἰχθύς, fish, + φαγεῖν, eat.] Fish-eating; feeding on fish.—**ich-thy-oph′a-gy** (-ji), *n.*

ich-thy-or-nis (ik-thi-ôr′nis), *n.* [NL., < Gr. ἰχθύς, fish, + ὄρνις, bird.] Any of an extinct genus (*Ichthyornis*) of toothed birds with vertebræ resembling those of fishes.

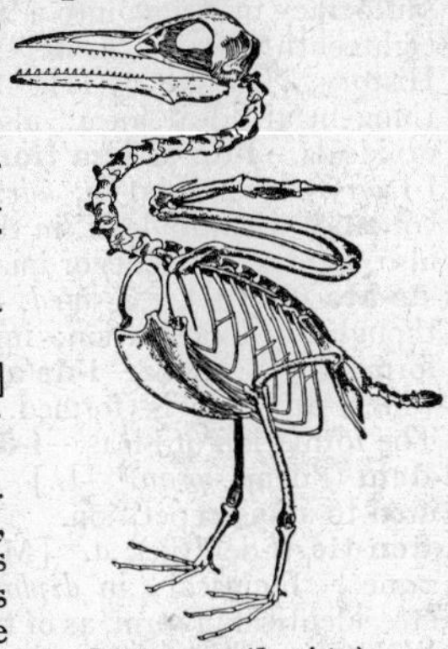
Ichthyornis (*I. victor*).

ich-thy-o-saur (ik′thi-ǫ-sâr), *n.* [NL. *ichthyosaurus*, < Gr. ἰχθύς, fish, + σαῦρος, lizard.] Any of an extinct order (*Ichthyosauria*) of marine fish-like reptiles ranging from 4 to 40 feet in length, and having a round tapering body, a large head, four paddle-like flippers, and a vertical caudal fin. Also **ich″thy-o-sau′rus** (-sâ′rus); pl. *-ri* (-rī).

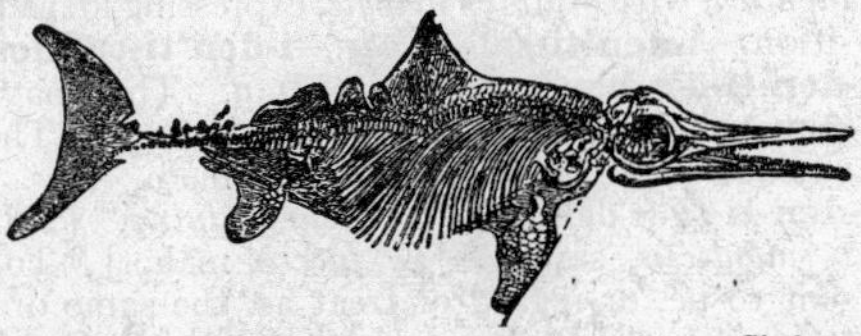
Ichthyosaur (*Ichthyosaurus quadricissus*). — Skeleton showing outline of integument and dorsal and caudal fins.

ich-thy-o-sis (ik-thi-ō′sis), *n.* [NL., < Gr. ἰχθύς, fish.] In *pathol.*, a disease in which the skin becomes hard, dry, and scaly.—**ich-thy-ot′ic** (-ot′ik), *a.*

i-ci-cle (ī′si-kl), *n.* [ME. *ysse-ikkle*, < AS. *īs*, ice, + *gicel*, icicle.] A pendent tapering mass of ice formed by the freezing of dripping water.—**i′ci-cled,** *a.* Hung with icicles.

i-ci-ly (ī′si-li), *adv.* In an icy manner.—**i′ci-ness,** *n.*

i-cing (ī′sing), *n.* A preparation of sugar, often made with whites of eggs, for covering cakes, etc.; frosting.

i-con (ī′kon), *n.* [L., < Gr. εἰκών, likeness, image.] A picture, image, or other representation; in the *Greek Ch.*, a representation in painting, mosaic, etc., of some sacred personage, as Christ or a saint or angel, itself regarded as sacred and honored with a relative worship.—**i-con′ic,** *a.* [L. *iconicus*, < Gr. εἰκονικός.] Pertaining to or of the nature of an icon, portrait, or image; specif., in *art*, of statues, etc., executed according to conventional type.

icono-. Form of Gr. εἰκών, likeness, image, used in combination.

i-con-o-clasm (ī-kon′ǫ-klazm), *n.* [See *iconoclast.*] The action or spirit of iconoclasts; the breaking or destroying of images, esp. those set up for religious veneration; the attacking of cherished beliefs or institutions as based on error or superstition.

i-con-o-clast (ī-kon′ǫ-klast), *n.* [MGr. εἰκονοκλάστης, < Gr. εἰκών, image, + κλᾶν, break.] A breaker or destroyer of images, esp. those set up for religious veneration; one hostile to image-worship; specif. [often *cap.*], one of a sect or party in the Eastern or Greek Church in the 8th and 9th centuries which opposed the use and veneration of images, and, when in power, destroyed them; also, one of those Protestants of the 16th and 17th centuries, esp. in the Netherlands during the reign of Philip II., who practised or approved the destruction of images in the churches; also [*l. c.*], in fig. use, one who attacks cherished beliefs or institutions as based on error or superstition (as, "I have become a reformer, and, like all reformers, an *iconoclast* . . . I shatter creeds and demolish idols": G. B. Shaw's "Man and Superman," i.).—**i-con-o-clas′tic** (-klas′tik), *a.* Pertaining to iconoclasts or iconoclasm.—**i-con-o-clas′ti-cal-ly,** *adv.*

i-con-o-graph (ī-kon′ǫ-gráf), *n.* [See *icono-* and *-graph.*] A drawing, engraving, or other picture, as for illustrating a book.

i-co-nog-ra-pher (ī-kǫ-nog′rą-fėr), *n.* One skilled or versed in iconography.

i-co-nog-ra-phy (ī-kǫ-nog′rą-fi), *n.*; pl. *-phies* (-fiz). [Gr. εἰκονογραφία: see *icono-* and *-graphy.*] The art of representing objects by pictures, images, or the like, as in painting, sculpture, etc.; also, the illustration of a subject by means of drawings, figures, etc.; a book or the like in which a subject is so illustrated.—**i-con-o-graph-ic, i-con-o-graph-i-cal** (ī-kon-ǫ-graf′ik, -i-kąl), *a.*

i-co-nol-a-try (ī-kǫ-nol′ą-tri), *n.* [See *icono-* and *-latry.*] The worship of images.—**i-co-nol′a-ter,** *n.*

i-co-nol-o-gy (ī-kǫ-nol′ǫ-ji), *n.* [See *icono-* and *-logy.*] The branch of knowledge concerned with pictorial or sculptural representations; such representations collectively; also, symbolical representation; symbolism.—**i-co-nol′o-gist,** *n.*—**i-con-o-log-i-cal** (ī-kon-ǫ-loj′i-kąl), *a.*

i-co-nom-a-chy (ī-kǫ-nom′ą-ki), *n.* [Gr. εἰκονομαχία: see *icono-* and *-machy.*] Hostility to images, esp. as objects of religious veneration: as, "the celebrated *iconomachy* of the Netherlands" (Motley's "Dutch Republic," ii. 7).—**i-co-nom′a-chist** (-kist), *n.*

i-con-o-phile (ī-kon′ǫ-fil), *n.* [See *icono-* and *-phil.*] A lover or connoisseur of pictures, engravings, etc.—**i-co-noph-i-lism** (ī-kǫ-nof′i-lizm), *n.* A liking or taste for pictures, engravings, etc.—**i-co-noph′i-list,** *n.* An iconophile.

i-co-nos-ta-sis (ī-kǫ-nos′tą-sis), *n.*; pl. *-tases* (-tą-sēz). [NL., < NGr. εἰκονόστασις, < Gr. εἰκών, image, + στάσις, a standing, station.] In the *Greek Ch.*, a partition or screen on which the icons are placed, separating the sanctuary from the main part of the church.

i-co-sa-he-dron (ī″kǫ-są-hē′drǫn), *n.*; pl. *-drons* or *-dra* (-drą). [Gr. εἰκοσάεδρον, < εἴκοσι, twenty, + ἕδρα, seat, base.] A solid figure having twenty faces.—**i″co-sa-he′dral,** *a.*

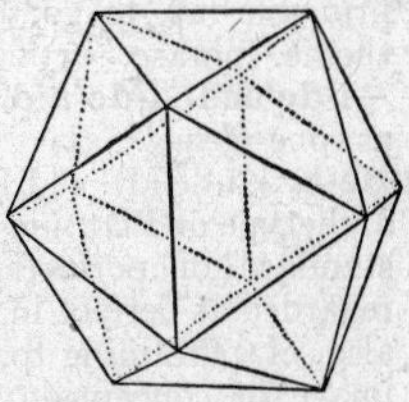
Regular Icosahedron.

-ics. [Pl. form of *-ic*, orig. rendering L. *-ica*, Gr. -ικά, neut. pl. ending.] A suffix of nouns, originally plural, as denoting things pertaining to a particular subject, but now mostly used as singular, as denoting the body of matters, facts, knowledge, principles, etc., pertaining to a subject, and hence a science or art, as in *economics, ethics, physics, politics, tactics.*

ic-ter-ic (ik-ter′ik). [L. *ictericus*, < Gr. ἰκτερικός.] **I.** *a.* Pertaining to or affected with icterus; jaundiced. **II.** *n.* One affected with jaundice; also, a remedy for jaundice.

ic-te-rus (ik′tẹ-rus), *n.* [NL., < Gr. ἴκτερος.] In *pathol.*, the disease jaundice; in *bot.*, a yellow appearance assumed by wheat and certain other plants when exposed to excess moisture and cold.

ic-tus (ik′tus), *n.*; pl. *ictuses*, L. *ictus*. [L., < *icere*, strike.] A stroke; in *pros.*, rhythmical or metrical stress.

i-cy (ī′si), *a.*; compar. *icier*, superl. *iciest*. Abounding in, or characterized by the presence of, ice; covered with ice; consisting of ice; resembling ice; extremely cold, like ice; slippery, like ice; fig., without warmth of feeling; chilling.

id (id), *n.* [G., < Gr. ἴδιος, own: cf. *idioplasm*.] In *biol.*, a hypothetical unit of germ-plasm regarded as an aggregation of determinants: usually identified with a chromatin granule.

I'd (īd). Contraction of *I would, I should*, or *I had*.

-id[1]. [L. *-id-*, nom. *-is*, < Gr. -ιδ-, nom. -ις, fem. patronymic ending.] A noun suffix meaning 'daughter of,' as in *Nereid*, and used also, in *astron.*, to form names of meteors appearing to radiate in showers from particular constellations, etc., as in *Andromedid, Bielid, Leonid, Orionid, Perseid*.

-id[2]. [NL. *-idæ*, in zoölogical family names, pl. of L. *-ides*, < Gr. -ίδης, masc. patronymic ending; sometimes, NL. *-ida*, in group names, taken as neut. pl. of L. *-ides*.] A suffix of nouns and adjectives indicating members of a zoölogical family, as in *cichlid, culicid, echinid, elaterid, muscid, noctuid*, or of some other group or division, as in *acarid, arachnid, araneid, eurypterid*.

-id[3]. See *-ide*.

i-dant (ī′dạnt), *n.* [G.] In *biol.*, a hypothetical unit of germ-plasm regarded as an aggregation of ids: usually identified with a chromosome.

-ide, -id[3]. [From *oxide*.] A noun suffix in names of chemical compounds, as in *bromide, chloride, hydride, saccharide*.

i-de-a (ī-dē′ạ̈), *n.* [L., < Gr. ἰδέα, form, look, semblance, kind, sort, idea, < ἰδεῖν, see: see *wit*.] In the Platonic philosophy, an archetype or pattern of which the individual objects in any natural class are imperfect copies and from which they derive their being ('Platonic idea'); hence, in general, the conception of anything in its highest perfection (obs. or archaic); also, a conception of what is desirable, or what ought to be; a governing conception or principle; the plan or design in accordance with which a thing is created or constructed (as, "To behold this new-created world . . . how good, how fair, Answering his great *idea*": Milton's "Paradise Lost," vii. 557); hence, any conception or notion of a thing to be done or put into practice; a plan of action; an intention; also, a representation†, likeness†, or figure† (as, "I did infer your lineaments, Being the right *idea* of your father, Both in your form and nobleness of mind": Shakspere's "Richard III.," iii. 7. 13); also, a mental picture of something previously seen or known† (as, "Though I despaired of possessing you . . . I doated still on your charming *idea*": Fielding's "Tom Jones," xiii. 11); hence, a mental picture or conception of anything (as, to have an *idea* how a thing looks); sometimes, something merely imagined without corresponding reality; a fantasy; also, thought or imagination (in the phrase 'in idea'); also, any conception existing in the mind as the result of mental apprehension or activity; a thought, conception, or notion; an impression; an opinion, view, or belief; a particular way of thinking (as, old-fashioned *ideas*); often, a more or less indefinite or vague notion (as, I had no *idea* of such a state of affairs); a peculiar or fanciful notion (as, what an *idea!*); sometimes, an abstract principle (as, to go to war for an *idea*); also, in *music*, a theme, phrase, or figure.—**fixed idea.** See under *fixed*. —**i-de′aed, i-de′a'd** (-ạ̈d), *a.* Having an idea or ideas: as, one-*ideaed*.

i-de-al (ī-dē′ạl). [LL. *idealis*.] **I.** *a.* Existing as an archetype or Platonic idea; also, conceived as constituting a standard of perfection or excellence (as, *ideal* beauty); regarded as perfect in its kind (as, an *ideal* spot for a home); also, of, pertaining to, or of the nature of an idea, or mental image or conception; representing an idea rather than a material object; also, existing only in idea, thought, or imagination (as, things having only *ideal* existence); imaginary; hence, not real or practical; visionary; in *philos.*, regarding ideas as the only real entities; pertaining to or of the nature of idealism. **II.** *n.* A conception of something in its highest perfection; a standard of perfection or excellence; a person or thing regarded as realizing such a conception or conforming to such a standard, and taken as a model for imitation (as, the Chevalier Bayard, the *ideal* of chivalry); often, an ideal end or object to be realized by attainment (as, to have high or low *ideals* in politics or business; to strive toward one's *ideals*); an ultimate object or aim of endeavor, esp. one of high or noble character (as, to sacrifice *ideals* to practical or sordid considerations).—**i-de′al-ism,** *n.* Any philosophical system or theory which maintains that the real is of the nature of thought or ideas, or that the object of external perception consists of ideas (cf. *realism*); also, the practice of idealizing; the tendency to represent things in an ideal form, or as they might be rather than as they are; specif., the imaginative treatment of subjects in literature or art (as opposed to *realism*); also, something idealized; an ideal representation; also, the cherishing or pursuing of ideals, as for attainment.—**i-de′al-ist,** *n.* One who holds some form of philosophical idealism; also, one who idealizes; one who represents things as they might be rather than as they are; a writer or artist who treats subjects imaginatively; also, one who cherishes or pursues ideals, as for attainment; hence, a visionary or unpractical person. —**i-de-al-is′tic,** *a.* Pertaining or proper to an idealist; characterized by idealism.—**i-de-al-is′ti-cal-ly,** *adv.*—**i-de-al-i-ty** (ī-dẹ-al′i-ti), *n.*; pl. *-ties* (-tiz). Ideal quality or character; also, capacity to idealize; also, something ideal or imaginary.—**i-de′al-ize** (-ạl-īz), *v.*; *-ized, -izing*. **I.** *tr.* To make ideal; represent in an ideal form or character; exalt to an ideal perfection or excellence; represent, or exalt in representation, in accordance with some preconceived ideal: as, "He [Gibbon] *idealized* the crude and gross plutocracy of Rome into a world of fine gentlemen upon the eighteenth-century model" (H. G. Wells's "Outline of History," xxxvi. § 11). **II.** *intr.* To represent something in an ideal form; also, to imagine or form an ideal or ideals.—**i-de″al-i-za′tion** (-i-zā′shọn), *n.*—**i-de′al-iz-er** (-ī-zėr), *n.*—**i-de′al-ly,** *adv.* In an ideal manner; in accordance with an ideal; in the highest perfection; perfectly; also, in idea, thought, or imagination.—**i-de′al-ness,** *n.*

i-de-ate (ī-dē′āt), *v.*; *-ated, -ating*. **I.** *tr.* To form in idea, thought, or imagination; imagine; conceive. **II.** *intr.* To form ideas; think.—**i-de′ate,** *n.* The external object of which an idea is formed.—**i-de-a-tion** (ī-dẹ-ā′shọn), *n.* The formation of ideas.—**i-de-a′tion-al,** *a.*

i-dem (ī′dem), *pron.* [L.] The same (as previously given): used to avoid repetition.

i-den-tic (ī-den′tik), *a.* [ML. *identicus*, irreg. < L. *idem*, same.] Identical: in *diplomacy*, applied to action, notes, etc., identical in form, as of two or more governments dealing simultaneously with another government.—**i-den′ti-cal,** *a.* The same, or being the same one (as, he is the *identical* man we saw here last week); also, of the same kind, nature, meaning, etc., or agreeing exactly (as, our experience was *identical* with yours); in *logic*, expressing identity, as a proposition.—**i-den′ti-cal-ly,** *adv.*—**i-den′ti-cal-ness,** *n.*

i-den-ti-fi-a-ble (ī-den′ti-fī-ạ-bl), *a.* That may be identified.

i-den-ti-fi-ca-tion (ī-den″ti-fi-kā′shọn), *n.* The act of identifying, or the state of being identified.

i-den-ti-fy (ī-den′ti-fī), *v. t.*; *-fied, -fying*. [ML. *identificare*, < *identicus*, same, + L. *facere*, make.] To make, represent to be, or regard or treat as, the same or identical (as, to *identify* the Roman god Mars with the Greek Ares); also, to recognize or establish as being a particular person or thing (as, to *identify* a man as a neighbor; to *identify* handwriting as one's own); attest or prove to be as purported or asserted (as, to *identify* the presenter of a check); determine who (a person) is or what or whose (a thing) is (as, to *identify* a victim of aphasia; to *identify* a strange plant; to *identify* the body of a drowned person); establish the identity of; also, to associate in feeling, interest, action, etc. (*with*: as, to *identify* one's self with a party or a cause; "I tried to *identify* my mind with the old fellow's, and take his view of the world," Hawthorne's "Blithedale Romance," x.); link or connect inseparably (*with*: as, a doctrine *identified* with the name of President Monroe).—**i-den'ti-fi-er** (-fī-ėr), *n.*

i-den-ti-ty (ī-den'ti-ti), *n.*; pl. *-ties* (-tiz). [LL. *identitas*, irreg. < L. *idem*, same.] The state or fact of being the same one (as, to establish the *identity* of a person seen to-day with one seen yesterday); also, the state or fact of remaining the same one, as under varying aspects or conditions; the condition of being one's self or itself, and not another (as, "He doubted his own *identity*, and whether he was himself or another man": Irving's "Sketch-Book," Rip Van Winkle); condition or character as to who a person or what a thing is (as, to veil one's *identity* under a pseudonym; to discover the *identity* of a stranger, or of some strange substance; a case of mistaken *identity*); also, sameness in nature or qualities (as, there is complete *identity* between the two cases); exact likeness; an instance or point of sameness or likeness (as, to note the *identities* in the two cases).

ideo-. Form of Gr. ἰδέα, idea, used in combination.

i-de-o-gram (ī'dē-ō-gram or id'ē-), *n.* [See *ideo-* and *-gram.*] An ideograph.

i-de-o-graph (ī'dē-ō-gräf or id'ē-), *n.* [See *ideo-* and *-graph.*] A graphic symbol representing the idea of a thing without expressing its name, as most Egyptian hieroglyphics.—**i''de-o-graph'ic, i''de-o-graph'i-cal** (-graf'ik, -i-kal), *a.*—**i''de-o-graph'i-cal-ly,** *adv.*—**i-de-og'ra-phy** (-og'ra-fi), *n.* [See *-graphy.*] The representation of ideas by ideographs.

i-de-o-log-i-cal (ī''dē-ō-loj'i-kal or id''ē-), *a.* [See *ideology.*] Pertaining to ideology, or the study of ideas; also, pertaining to ideas, esp. of a visionary nature; dealing with ideas rather than facts; speculative; visionary.—**i''de-o-log'i-cal-ly,** *adv.* —**i-de-ol'o-gist** (-ol'ō-jist), *n.* One versed in ideology; also, one occupied with ideas, esp. of a visionary or unpractical nature; one who indulges in theories or speculations; a mere theorist; a visionary.—**i-de-o-logue** (ī-dē'ō-log), *n.* [F. *idéologue.*] One occupied with ideas, esp. of an unpractical nature; a visionary; an ideologist.

i-de-ol-o-gy (ī-dē-ol'ō-ji or id-ē-), *n.*; pl. *-gies* (-jiz). [F. *idéologie*: = E. *ideo-* + *-logy.*] The science of ideas; specif., the system of philosophy (of the French philosopher Condillac) which derives ideas exclusively from sensation; sensationalism; also, abstract speculation; esp., theorizing or speculation of a visionary or unpractical nature; also, a particular system of ideas; the characteristic way of thinking of a people, group, or person, as on social or political subjects.

i-de-o-mo-tor (ī''dē-ō-mō'tor or id''ē-), *a.* [See *ideo-* and *motor.*] In *psychol.*, noting or pertaining to muscular movement which is the result of complete engrossment by an idea, and is neither voluntary nor purely reflex.

ides (īdz), *n. pl.* [L. *idus*, pl.] In the ancient Roman calendar, the 15th day of March, May, July, and October, and the 13th day of the other months.

idio-. Form of Gr. ἴδιος, own, private, peculiar, used in combination.

id-i-o-blast (id'i-ō-blast), *n.* [See *idio-* and *-blast.*] In *bot.*, a cell which differs greatly from the surrounding cells or tissue; in *biol.*, one of the hypothetical ultimate elements of living protoplasm (equivalent to *biophore*).

id-i-o-cy (id'i-ō-si), *n.*; pl. *-cies* (-siz). The condition of being an idiot; mental imbecility; hence, senseless folly (as, "the bottomless *idiocy* of the world": H. James's "Portrait of a Lady," lv.).

id-i-o-e-lec-tric (id''i-ō-ē-lek'trik). [See *idio-.*] **I.** *a.* Capable of being electrified by friction: a practically obsolete term used orig. of substances such as sealing-wax, glass, etc., other substances, as metals, being then thought to be incapable of such electrification. Cf. *anelectric.* **II.** *n.* An idioelectric substance.

id-i-o-graph (id'i-ō-gräf), *n.* [Gr. ἰδιόγραφος, autographic, < ἴδιος, own, + γράφειν, mark, write.] A private mark or signature; a trade-mark.—**id''i-o-graph'ic** (-graf'ik), *a.*

id-i-om (id'i-om), *n.* [LL. *idioma*, < Gr. ἰδίωμα, a peculiarity, property, idiom, < ἰδιοῦσθαι, make one's own, < ἴδιος, own.] The language peculiar to a people; a variety or form of a language; a dialect; also, the peculiar character or genius of a language; also, a form of expression peculiar to a language.—**id''i-o-mat'ic** (-ō-mat'ik), *a.* [Gr. ἰδιωματικός.] Peculiar to or characteristic of a particular language; also, exhibiting the characteristic modes of expression of a language; given to or marked by the use of idioms.—**id''i-o-mat'i-cal-ly,** *adv.*

id-i-o-mor-phic (id''i-ō-môr'fik), *a.* [See *idio-* and *-morphic.*] Having its own form; specif., noting or pertaining to a mineral constituent of a rock, which has its own characteristic crystalline form, and not one forced upon it by the other constituents of the rock. Cf. *xenomorphic.*—**id''i-o-mor'phi-cal-ly,** *adv.*

id-i-op-a-thy (id-i-op'a-thi), *n.*; pl. *-thies* (-thiz). [Gr. ἰδιοπάθεια, < ἴδιος, own, + παθεῖν, suffer.] In *pathol.*, a disease not preceded or occasioned by any other.—**id''i-o-path'ic** (-ō-path'ik), *a.*

id-i-o-plasm (id'i-ō-plazm), *n.* [See *idio-* and *-plasm.*] In *biol.*, that kind of protoplasm which is regarded as the physical basis of inheritance; germ-plasm.—**id''i-o-plas-mat'ic** (-plaz-mat'ik), **id''i-o-plas'mic,** *a.*

id-i-o-stat'ic (id''i-ō-stat'ik), *a.* [See *idio-* and *static.*] In *elect.*, noting or pertaining to the measurement of potential by electrostatic methods in which no auxiliary electrification is employed.

id-i-o-syn-cra-sy (id''i-ō-sing'kra-si), *n.*; pl. *-sies* (-siz). [Gr. ἰδιοσυγκρασία, < ἴδιος, own, + σύγκρασις, a mixing together, tempering, < σύν, with, + κεραννύναι, mix.] The physical constitution peculiar to an individual; also, a peculiarity of the physical or the mental constitution; any tendency, characteristic, mode of expression, or the like, peculiar to an individual.—**id''i-o-syn-crat'ic** (-krat'ik), *a.* Pertaining or due to idiosyncrasy.—**id''i-o-syn-crat'i-cal-ly,** *adv.*

id-i-ot (id'i-ot), *n.* [OF. F. *idiot*, < L. *idiota*, < Gr. ἰδιώτης, a private, non-professional, or ignorant person, < ἴδιος, own, private.] A private or non-professional person†; also, an unlearned or ignorant person†; also, one hopelessly deficient, esp. from birth, in the ordinary mental powers; hence, an utterly foolish or senseless person (as, "You *idiot*, do you know what peril you stand in?" Dickens's "Barnaby Rudge," li.); also, a professional fool† or jester† (as, "the head of an *idiot* dressed in a cap and bells": Addison, in "Spectator," 47).—**id'i-ot-cy** (-si), *n.* Idiocy.—**id-i-ot'ic** (-ot'ik), *a.* [LL. *idioticus*, < Gr. ἰδιωτικός.] Of or like an idiot; senselessly foolish.—**id-i-ot'i-cal-ly,** *adv.*—**id'i-ot-ism,** *n.* [F. *idiotisme*, < L. *idiotismus*, < Gr. ἰδιωτισμός, < ἰδιωτίζειν, put into common language, < ἰδιώτης.] A peculiarity of phrase; an idiom; also, idiocy or mental imbecility; also, idiotic or senselessly foolish conduct; an idiotic proceeding.

i-dle (ī'dl), *a.*; compar. *idler*, superl. *idlest.* [AS. *īdel* = D. *ijdel* = G. *eitel*, idle.] Empty†, vacant†, or void†; hence, of no real worth, importance, or significance, or trivial (as, *idle* talk; *idle* dreams; an *idle* whim; "For manners are not *idle*, but the fruit Of loyal nature and of noble mind," Tennyson's "Guinevere," 333); baseless or groundless (as, *idle* fears; *idle* rumors); frivolous or vain (as, *idle* pleasures); futile or ineffective (as, *idle* threats); useless (as, *idle* weeds; "Caught in the meshy snare, in vain they beat Their *idle* wings," Thomson's "Seasons," Autumn, 371); also, unoccupied, as time (as, a pastime for *idle* hours); also, unemployed, or doing nothing, as a person (as, *idle* workmen; "Why stand ye here all the day *idle*?" Mat. xx. 6); not kept busy or in use or operation (as, *idle* hands; money lying *idle*; *idle* machinery); inactive; sometimes, habitually doing nothing or avoiding work (as, a shiftless, *idle* fellow); lazy; indolent.—**idle pulley,** a loose pulley made to press or rest on a belt in order to tighten or guide it.—**idle wheel,** a cog-wheel placed between two other cog-wheels in order to transfer the motion of one to the other without changing the direction of rotation; also, an idle pulley.—**i'dle,** *v.*; *idled, idling.* **I.** *intr.* To move, loiter, or saunter idly (as, "Presently a vagrant poodle dog came

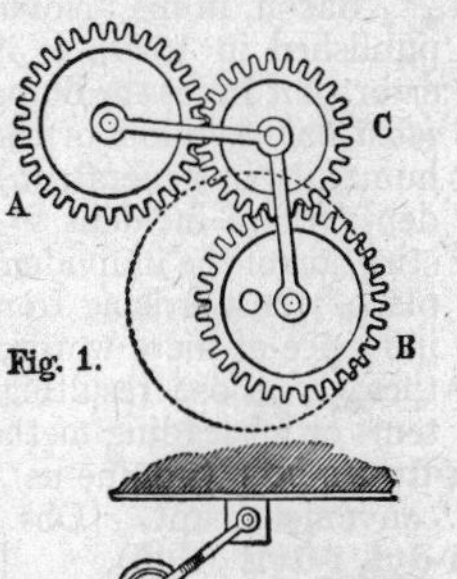

Fig. 1.

Fig. 2.

Fig. 1 shows Idle Wheel (*C*) between two other cog-wheels (*A* and *B*). Fig. 2 shows Idle Pulley resting on a belt in order to maintain the tension.

idling along . . . lazy with the summer softness": Mark Twain's "Tom Sawyer," v.); also, to pass time in idleness. **II.** *tr.* To pass (time) in idleness; also, to cause (a person) to be idle.—**i′dle-ness,** *n.*—**i′dler,** *n.* One who idles; *naut.*, a member of a ship's crew who is liable to constant day duty and therefore is not required to keep night-watch; in *mach.*, an idle pulley or wheel; in *railroading*, an empty car; an empty.—**i′dlesse, i′dless** (-dles), *n.* [A pseudo-archaic formation appar. due to Spenser: see "Faerie Queene," vi. 2. 31.] The state of being idle; idleness: as, "The tables were drawn, it was *idlesse* all" (Scott's "Lay of the Last Minstrel," i. 2). [Poetic.]—**i′dly,** *adv.* In an idle manner; vainly; uselessly; inactively; indolently.

I-do (ē′dō), *n.* An artificial language designed as an international medium, and put forth in 1907, being a revised and simplified form of Esperanto.

i-do-crase (ī′dọ-krās), *n.* [F., < Gr. εἶδος, form, + κρᾶσις, mixture, E. *crasis.*] The mineral vesuvianite.

i-dol (ī′dọl), *n.* [OF. F. *idole*, < L. *idolum, idolon*, < Gr. εἴδωλον, image, phantom, idol, < εἶδος, form, < ἰδεῖν, see: see *wit.*] An image or other material object to which religious worship is addressed; hence, a false god or fictitious divinity, as of a heathen people (as, "All the gods of the nations are *idols*": Ps. xcvi. 5); fig., any person or thing that is the object of blindly adoring regard or inordinate devotion (as, to be the *idol* of one's family; a popular *idol*; gold was his *idol*); also, an image, effigy, or likeness of something†; hence, a mere image or semblance of something, visible but without substance, as an image in a mirror, or a phantom; also, a figment of the mind or imagination; esp., a false conception or notion, or fallacy (as, *idols* of the tribe, cave, market-place, or theater: see *idolum*, note).

i-dol-a-ter (ī-dol′ạ-tėr), *n.* [OF. *idolatre* (F. *idolâtre*), < LL. *idololatres*, < Gr. εἰδωλολάτρης, < εἴδωλον, idol, + -λάτρης, < λατρεύειν, serve.] A worshiper of idols; fig., an adorer or devotee.—**i-dol′a-tress,** *n.* A female idolater.—**i-dol′a-trize** (-trīz), *v. t.*; *-trized, -trizing.* To worship as an idolater does; idolize.—**i-dol′a-trous,** *a.* Pertaining to or of the nature of idolatry; also, given to idolatry; idolizing; blindly adoring.—**i-dol′a-trous-ly,** *adv.*—**i-dol′a-trous-ness,** *n.*—**i-dol′a-try** (-tri), *n.*; pl. *-tries* (-triz). [OF. *idolatrie* (F. *idolâtrie*), < LL. *idololatria*, < Gr. εἰδωλολατρεία, < εἰδωλολάτρης: see *idolater.*] The worship of idols; fig., blindly adoring regard or inordinate devotion.

i-dol-ism (ī′dọl-izm), *n.* Idolatry; idolizing; also, an idol or fallacy (obs. or archaic).—**i′dol-ist,** *n.*

i-dol-ize (ī′dọl-īz), *v. t.*; *-ized, -izing.* To worship as an idol; regard with blindly adoring regard or inordinate devotion; adore.—**i″dol-i-za′tion** (-i-zā′shọn), *n.*—**i′dol-iz-er** (-ī-zėr), *n.*

i-dol-o-clast (ī-dol′ọ-klast), *n.* [Gr. εἴδωλον, idol, with *-clast* as in *iconoclast.*] A breaker of idols; an iconoclast.—**i-dol-o-clas′tic** (-klas′tik), *a.*

i-do-lum, i-do-lon (ī-dō′lum, -lon), *n.*; pl. *-la* (-lạ̈). [L.: see *idol*, and cf. *eidolon.*] An image; a phantom; also, a false conception or notion; a fallacy or idol.

⁂ Bacon, in his "Novum Organum" (written in Latin, and published in 1620), i. 39, divides the fallacies or forms of error that beset the human mind into four classes: (*a*) [Latin] *idola tribus*, 'idols of the tribe (or race),' those incident to humanity in general; (*b*) *idola specus*, 'idols of the cave (or den),' those incident to the peculiar mental or bodily constitution of the individual; (*c*) *idola fori*, 'idols of the market-place,' those arising from human intercourse, or due to the influence of mere words; and (*d*) *idola theatri*, 'idols of the theater,' those resulting from imperfect philosophical systems or misleading methods of demonstration.

i-do-ne-ous (ī-dō′nē-us), *a.* [L. *idoneus.*] Fit; suitable; convenient; apt. [Obs. or rare.]

i-dyl, i-dyll (ī′dil), *n.* [L. *idyllium*, < Gr. εἰδύλλιον, dim. of εἶδος, form: see *idol.*] A poem or prose composition describing pastoral scenes or events or any charmingly simple episode, appealing incident, or the like (as, the *idyls* of Theocritus, Bion, or Moschus; Austin Dobson's "Old-World *Idylls*"; Barrie's "Auld Licht *Idylls*"); less definitely, a simple descriptive or narrative piece in verse or prose (as, Tennyson's "*Idylls* of the King"); also, an episode or scene of idyllic simplicity or charm; also, a musical composition of like character.—**i′dyl-ist, i′dyll-ist,** *n.* A writer of idyls.—**i-dyl-li-an** (ī-dil′i-ạn), *a.* Idyllic.—**i-dyl′lic,** *a.* Of, pertaining to, or of the nature of an idyl (as, an *idyllic* poem or description); also, suitable for or suggestive of an idyl (as, an *idyllic* scene; *idyllic* simplicity or charm); of a charmingly simple, poetic character. Also **i-dyl′li-cal.**—**i-dyl′li-cal-ly,** *adv.*

-ie. [Sc. form of *-y*².] A diminutive suffix of nouns, same as *-y*², as in *beastie, dearie, laddie, lassie, Lizzie, Willie.*

i-er=oe (ē″ėr-ō′), *n.* [From Gael.] A great-grandchild. [Sc.]

if (if). [AS. *gif* = D. *of* = G. *ob* = Icel. *ef*, if, whether, = Goth. *ibai*, whether, lest; prob. akin to OHG. *iba*, condition, stipulation, doubt, Icel. *if, ef*, doubt.] **I.** *conj.* On condition that; in case that; granting or supposing that; also, even though (as, *if* he is little, he is strong); also, whether (as, "He sent forth a dove from him, to see *if* the waters were abated": Gen. viii. 8). **II.** *n.* The word 'if' as introducing a condition or a supposition; a condition; a supposition.

ig-loo (ig′lö), *n.*; pl. *-loos* (-löz). [Eskimo.] An Eskimo hut, dome-shaped, and often built of blocks of hard snow; also, an excavation made by a seal in the snow over its breathing-hole in the ice.

Seal's Igloo (shown in section).

ig-ne-ous (ig′nē-us), *a.* [L. *igneus*, < *ignis*, fire.] Pertaining to or of the nature of fire; also, produced by fire or intense heat, as rocks of volcanic origin.

ig-nes-cent (ig-nes′ẹnt). [L. *ignescens* (*-ent-*), ppr. of *ignescere*, take fire, < *ignis*, fire.] **I.** *a.* Bursting into flame; emitting sparks of fire, as certain stones when struck with steel. **II.** *n.* An ignescent substance.

ig-nic-o-list (ig-nik′ọ-list), *n.* [L. *ignis*, fire, + *colere*, worship.] A worshiper of fire.

ig-nif-er-ous (ig-nif′ẹ-rus), *a.* [L. *ignifer*, < *ignis*, fire, + *ferre*, bear.] Bringing or producing fire.

ig-ni-fy (ig′ni-fī), *v. t.*; *-fied, -fying.* [L. *ignis*, fire: see *-fy.*] To set on fire.

ig-nip-o-tent (ig-nip′ọ-tẹnt), *a.* [L. *ignipotens* (*-ent-*), < *ignis*, fire, + *potens*, E. *potent.*] Ruling over fire; potent in fire.

ig-ni-punc-ture (ig′ni-pungk-ṭūr), *n.* [L. *ignis*, fire, + *punctura*, puncture.] In *surg.*, puncture or pricking with white-hot needles.

ig-nis fat-u-us (ig′nis faṭ′ū-us); pl. *ignes fatui* (ig′nēz faṭ′ū-ī). [NL., 'foolish fire.'] A flitting phosphorescent light seen at night, chiefly over marshy ground, and supposed to be due to spontaneous combustion of gas from decomposed organic matter; a jack-o'-lantern; a will-o'-the-wisp; hence, something deluding or misleading.

ig-nit-a-ble (ig-nī′tạ-bl), etc. See *ignitible*, etc.

ig-nite (ig-nīt′), *v.*; *-nited, -niting.* [L. *ignitus*, pp. of *ignire*, < *ignis*, fire.] **I.** *tr.* To set on fire; kindle; also, to make intensely hot; cause to glow with heat. **II.** *intr.* To take fire; begin to burn.—**ig-nit′er** (-nī′tėr), *n.* One who or that which ignites; specif., in an internal-combustion engine, a device for producing an electric spark which ignites the charge of gas or vapor in the cylinder.—**ig-nit′i-ble** (-nī′ti-bl), *a.* Capable of being ignited.—**ig-nit-i-bil′i-ty** (-bil′i-ti), *n.*—**ig-ni′tion** (-nish′ọn), *n.* The act of igniting, or the state of being ignited; a kindling or burning; a heating to a glow; specif., in an internal-combustion engine, the igniting of the charge in the cylinder.

ig-niv-o-mous (ig-niv′ọ-mus), *a.* [LL. *ignivomus*, < L. *ignis*, fire, + *vomere*, vomit.] Vomiting fire.

ig-no-ble (ig-nō′bl), *a.* [F. *ignoble*, < L. *ignobilis*, < *in-*, not, + *gnobilis*, later *nobilis*, E. *noble.*] Not noble; of low birth or station; lowly, humble, or obscure; also, of low character, aims, etc.; mean; base; also, of low grade or quality; inferior.—**ig-no-bil′i-ty** (-nọ-bil′i-ti), **ig-no′ble-ness,** *n.*—**ig-no′bly,** *adv.*

ig-no-min-i-ous (ig-nọ-min′i-us), *a.* [L. *ignominiosus.*]

Marked by or attended with ignominy (as, "a precipitate and *ignominious* retreat": Gibbon's "Decline and Fall of the Roman Empire," xviii.); disgraceful; discreditable; shameful; often, injurious to one's dignity, or humiliating (as, "The blundering weapon recoiled and gave the valiant Kip an *ignominious* kick, which laid him prostrate": Irving's "Knickerbocker's New York," ii. 4); also, of persons, covered with or deserving ignominy; infamous; contemptible.—**ig-no-min′i-ous-ly,** *adv.*—**ig-no-min′i-ous-ness,** *n.*

ig-no-min-y (ig′nǫ-min-i), *n.*; pl. *-ies* (-iz). [L. *ignominia*, < *in-*, not, + *nomen*, name, reputation.] Disgrace; dishonor; public contempt; also, base quality or conduct; a cause of disgrace or contempt.

ig-no-ra-mus (ig-nǫ-rā′mus), *n.*; pl. *-muses.* [L., 'we do not know,' or 'we take no notice.'] An indorsement formerly made by a grand jury on a bill presented to them, to signify that they ignored or rejected it for want of sufficient evidence; hence, an answer or declaration admitting ignorance†; also, an ignorant person (as, "I am quite an *ignoramus.* I know nothing—nothing in the world": C. Brontë's "Villette," vi.).

ig-no-rance (ig′nǫ-rąns), *n.* [OF. F. *ignorance*, < L. *ignorantia.*] The state or fact of being ignorant; want of knowledge, learning, or information; also, a fault or offense due to want of knowledge (archaic: as, "Our sins are multiplied above our heads, and our *ignorances* have reached up unto heaven," 1 Esdras, viii. 75).

ig-no-rant (ig′nǫ-rąnt), *a.* [OF. F. *ignorant*, < L. *ignorans* (*-ant-*), ppr. of *ignorare*: see *ignore.*] Destitute of knowledge; unlearned; often, lacking knowledge or information as to a particular subject or fact (esp. with *of* or a dependent clause: as, "The Dutch governor was . . . *ignorant* of the existence of a war between England and Holland," Lecky's "Hist. of Eng. in the 18th Century," xiv.; "She was *ignorant* what sort of man Harold had become now," George Eliot's "Felix Holt," i.); uninformed; unaware; also, due to or showing lack of knowledge (as, an *ignorant* statement); also, keeping one in ignorance† (as, "If you know aught . . . imprison 't not In *ignorant* concealment": Shakspere's "Winter's Tale," i. 2. 397).

Ig-no-ran-tine (ig-nǫ-ran′tin). [F. *ignorantin*, < *ignorant*, E. *ignorant.*] **I.** *a.* An epithet assumed in humility by the Brothers of St. John of God, a religious community founded in 1540 to minister to the sick poor: also applied, by confusion or in disparagement, to the Brothers of the Christian Schools (founded in 1680), a religious community devoted to the Christian education of youth, esp. of the children of the poor. **II.** *n.* A member of the Ignorantine community.

ig-no-rant-ly (ig′nǫ-rąnt-li), *adv.* In an ignorant manner; in ignorance.

ig-no-ra-tion (ig-nǫ-rā′shǫn), *n.* [L. *ignoratio*(*n-*).] The act of ignoring, or the state or fact of being ignored.

ig-nore (ig-nōr′), *v. t.*; *-nored, -noring.* [F. *ignorer*, < L. *ignorare*, not to know, disregard, < *in-*, not, + *gno-*, a stem occurring also in *gnoscere, noscere*, know: see *know.*] To be without knowledge of (now rare); also, to refrain from noticing or recognizing; disregard; in *law*, of a grand jury, to reject (a bill of indictment) as without sufficient evidence.—**ig-nor′er,** *n.*

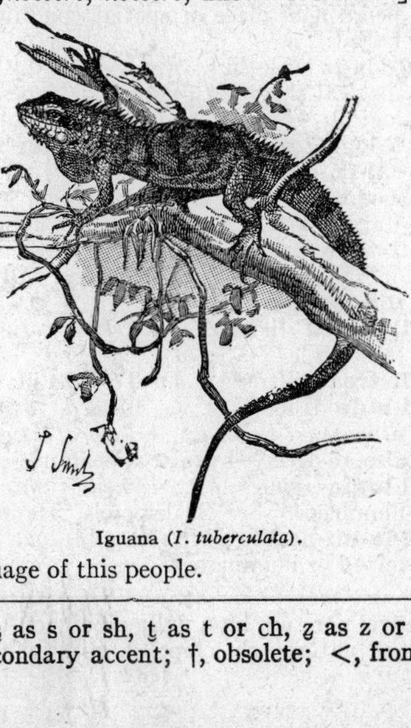
Iguana (*I. tuberculata*).

I-go-rot (ē-go-rōt′), *n.* Same as *Igorrote.*

I-gor-ro-te (ē-gor-rō′tā), *n.* [Sp.; from native name.] A member of a people of the Malay stock in northern Luzon, Philippine Islands, comprising various tribes, some noted as head-hunters; also, the language of this people.

i-gua-na (i-gwä′ną), *n.* [Sp.; from Carib name.] Any lizard of the genus *Iguana*, of tropical America, esp. *I. tuberculata*, a large, arboreal, herbivorous species 5 feet or more in length, esteemed as food (see cut in preceding column); also, some lizard of a related genus.—**i-gua′ni-an** (-ni-ąn), *a.* and *n.*

i-guan-o-don (i-gwan′ǫ-don), *n.* [NL., < *iguana*, iguana, + Gr. ὀδούς (ὀδοντ-), tooth.] Any member of the extinct genus *Iguanodon*, found fossil in Europe, comprising reptiles from 15 to 30 feet long, having teeth like the iguana's and walking on the hind limbs.—**i-guan′o-dont** (-dont). **I.** *a.* Having teeth like the iguana's; belonging to the fossil family *Iguanodontidæ.* **II.** *n.* An iguanodont reptile.

Iguanodon (*I. bernissartensis*).

ih-ram (i-räm′), *n.* [Ar.] The dress assumed by Mohammedan pilgrims to Mecca, consisting of two white cotton cloths, one girded round the waist, the other thrown over the left shoulder and knotted at the right side.

IHS or **I. H. S.** A contraction or abbreviation of Gr. ΙΗΣΟΥΣ, Jesus: sometimes taken as representing (*a*) L. *Iesus Hominum Salvator*, Jesus, Saviour of Men, (*b*) L. *In Hoc Signo* (*vinces*), in this sign [the cross] (shalt thou conquer), (*c*) L. *In Hac Salus*, in this [cross] is salvation, or (*d*), popularly, *I* [Christ] *Have Suffered.*

il-[1]**.** A form of *in-*[1] used before *l.*

il-[2]**.** A form of *in-*[2] used before *l.*

i-lang=i-lang (ē′lang-ē′lang), *n.* See *ylang-ylang.*

-ile. [L. *-ilis*, used to form adjectives, esp. from verbs.] A suffix of adjectives expressing capability or susceptibility, liability, aptitude, adaptedness, etc., as in *agile, docile, ductile, fragile, prehensile, tensile, volatile.*

il-e-ac (il′ę-ak), *a.* Of or pertaining to the ileum. Cf. *iliac.*

il-e-os-to-my (il-ę-os′tǫ-mi), *n.* [NL. *ileum*, ileum, + Gr. στόμα, mouth.] In *surg.*, the formation of an artificial opening into the ileum.

il-e-um (il′ę-um), *n.* [NL., < L. *ileum, ilium*, groin, flank, usually pl. *ilia*, flanks, also entrails.] In *anat.*, the third and lowest division of the small intestine, continuous with the jejunum and ending at the cæcum.

il-e-us (il′ę-us), *n.* [NL., < L. *ileos*, < Gr. εἰλεός, ἰλεός, ileus, prob. < εἴλειν, roll up, pack close.] In *pathol.*, severe colic attended with vomiting, etc., due to intestinal obstruction.

i-lex (ī′leks), *n.* [L. *ilex*, the holm-oak, NL. *Ilex*, the holly genus.] The holm-oak; also, any tree or shrub of the aquifoliaceous genus *Ilex*; holly.

il-i-ac (il′i-ak), *a.* [F. *iliaque*, < LL. *iliacus*, pertaining to ileus or colic (L. *ileos*), later pertaining to the flank (L. *ilium*): see *ileum, ileus*, and *ilium.*] Pertaining to ileus or to the ileum (as, the *iliac* passion, ileus); also, pertaining to the flank or to the ilium.

Il-i-ad (il′i-ąd), *n.* [L. *Ilias* (*Iliad-*), < Gr. Ἰλιάς (Ἰλιαδ-), < Ἴλιον, Ilium, Troy.] A Greek epic poem attributed to Homer, describing the siege of Ilium or Troy by the Greeks; hence, any similar poem; a long narrative or account; also, a long series of woes, etc.—**Il-i-ad′ic** (-ad′ik), *a.*

il-i-ca-ceous (il-i-kā′shius), *a.* [NL. *Ilex* (*Ilic-*): see *ilex.*] Belonging to the *Ilicaceæ* (or *Aquifoliaceæ*), the holly family of plants.

i-li-cic (i-lis′ik), *a.* [NL. *Ilex* (*Ilic-*): see *ilex.*] Pertaining to or derived from holly: as, *ilicic* acid.

il-i-um (il′i-um), *n.*; pl. *ilia* (-ą). [NL., < L. *ilium*, flank: see *ileum.*] In *anat.*, the ileum†; also, the broad upper portion of either innominate bone.

ilk[1] (ilk), *a.* [AS. *ilca.*] Same: now chiefly in the phrase (orig. Sc.) *of that ilk*, of that same (family or estate name, etc.) (as, Kinloch *of that ilk*, Kinloch of Kinloch; "Cosmo Comyne Bradwardine, Esq., *of that ilk*, commonly called Baron of Bradwardine," Scott's "Waverley," lxvi.). Hence sometimes used erroneously, as if a noun, to mean 'family,' 'class,' or 'kind': as, men of that *ilk*; he and all his *ilk.*

ilk² (ilk), *a.* [= *each.*] Each; every. Also **il-ka** (il′kạ). [Sc. and north. Eng.]

ill (il). [ME. *ill*, from Scand.: cf. Icel. *īllr, illr*, ill, bad; origin unknown.] **I.** *a.*; compar. *worse*, superl. *worst.* Evil, wicked, or bad (formerly often used of persons, now chiefly of actions, estimation, etc.: as, *ill* deeds; *ill* repute); also, hostile or unkindly (as, *ill* feeling; *ill* nature); also, unfavorable or adverse (as, *ill* winds; *ill* luck); also, of an objectionable, unsatisfactory, poor, or faulty kind (as, *ill* effects; *ill* manners; *ill* success); also, physically disordered, as the health; unwell, sick, or indisposed, as persons. Except with reference to health, and in certain established expressions, the adjective *ill* is now less common in general use than *bad* and other equivalents. **II.** *n.* Evil, as opposed to good (as, "O, yet we trust that somehow good Will be the final goal of *ill*": Tennyson's "In Memoriam," liv.); sometimes, wickedness or sin (archaic: as, "Many people call themselves virtuous, from no other pretence to it but an absence of *ill*," Steele, in "Spectator," 79); also, harm or injury (as, "Love worketh no *ill* to his neighbour": Rom. xiii. 10); also, trouble or misfortune (as, the fear of future *ill*); a misfortune (as, "No sense have they of *ills* to come": Gray's "On a Distant Prospect of Eton College"); also, a disease or ailment (as, "Peter now grew old, and had An *ill* no doctor could unravel": Shelley's "Peter Bell the Third," i. 3).—**ill,** *adv.* In an ill manner; wickedly or blamefully; in a hostile or unfriendly manner (as, to use a person *ill*); with displeasure or offense (as, a suggestion *ill* received; to take a thing *ill*); unfavorably or unfortunately (as, "*Ill* blows the wind that profits nobody," Shakspere's "3 Henry VI.," ii. 5. 55; things have gone *ill* with him); faultily or improperly (as, to perform one's task *ill*); unsatisfactorily or poorly (as, conduct that *ill* becomes one; *ill* at ease, uncomfortable or uneasy); hence, with trouble, difficulty, or inconvenience (as, an expense we can *ill* afford; a man he can *ill* spare). The adverb *ill* is much used in composition, as in *ill-pleased, ill-satisfied, ill-smelling,* etc., only the most common of such combinations being entered separately below.

I'll (īl). Contraction of *I will* or *I shall.*

ill=ad-vised (il′ad-vīzd′), *a.* Acting or done without due consideration; injudicious; imprudent.—**ill′=ad-vis′ed-ly** (-vī′zed-li), *adv.*

il-lapse (i-laps′), *v. i.*; *-lapsed, -lapsing.* [L. *illapsus*, pp. of *illabi*, < *in*, in, + *labi*, fall, slide.] To fall, glide, or slip in. [Now rare.]—**il-lapse′,** *n.* [L. *illapsus*, n.] A gliding in; a gentle influx. [Now rare.]

il-la-tion (i-lā′shọn), *n.* [L. *illatio(n-)*, < *illatus*, pp. of *inferre*, E. *infer.*] The act of inferring; an inference or conclusion.—**il-la-tive** (il′ạ-tiv), *a.* [L. *illativus.*] Pertaining to or expressing illation; inferential: as, an *illative* particle or word (such as *then* or *therefore*).—**il′la-tive-ly,** *adv.*

il-laud-a-ble (i-lâ′dạ-bl), *a.* [L. *illaudabilis.*] Not laudable; unworthy of praise; blameworthy: as, "sentiments which were not in themselves *illaudable*" (Jane Austen's "Sense and Sensibility," xi.).—**il-laud′a-bly,** *adv.*

ill=bred (il′bred′), *a.* Badly brought up, as persons; also, showing, or due to, lack of proper breeding, as actions; unmannerly; rude.—**ill′=breed′ing,** *n.*

ill=con-di-tioned (il′kọn-dish′ọnd), *a.* Having bad qualities or undesirable characteristics (as, "an ugly, *ill-conditioned* cur, that snarls and snaps at everybody": Smollett's "Humphry Clinker," May 6); also, in a bad condition.

ill=dis-posed (il′dis-pōzd′), *a.* Wickedly or unfavorably disposed; unfriendly; also, indisposed† or unwell† (see Shakspere's "Troilus and Cressida," ii. 3. 84).

il-le-gal (i-lē′gạl), *a.* [ML. *illegalis.*] Not legal; unlawful; illicit.—**il-le-gal-i-ty** (il-ē̦-gal′i-ti), **il-le′gal-ness,** *n.*—**il-le′gal-ize** (-gạl-īz), *v. t.*; *-ized, -izing.* To render illegal.—**il-le′gal-ly,** *adv.*

il-leg-i-ble (i-lej′i-bl), *a.* [See *il-*².] Not legible; impossible or hard to read or decipher.—**il-leg-i-bil′i-ty** (-bil′i-ti), **il-leg′i-ble-ness,** *n.*—**il-leg′i-bly,** *adv.*

il-le-git-i-mate (il-ē̦-jit′i-mạt), *a.* [See *il-*².] Not legitimate; unlawful; hence, unauthorized or unwarranted; irregular or improper; in specific use, born out of wedlock; bastard; hence, spurious; also, not in accordance with the laws of reasoning (as, an *illegitimate* inference); also, in *biol.*, abnormal, as fertilization; produced by irregular or abnormal fertilization.—**il-le-git′i-ma-cy** (-mạ-si), *n.*—**il-le-git′i-mate** (-māt), *v. t.*; *-mated, -mating.* To render or declare illegitimate; bastardize.—**il-le-git′i-mate-ly** (-mạt-li), *adv.*—**il-le-git-i-ma′tion** (-mā′shọn), *n.* The act of illegitimating; the state of being illegitimate.

ill=fat-ed (il′fā′ted), *a.* Destined to an unhappy fate (as, an *ill-fated* person); also, bringing bad fortune (as, an *ill-fated* hour).

ill=fa-vored (il′fā′vọrd), *a.* Unpleasing in appearance, or uncomely, as a person (as, "a poor virgin, sir, an *ill-favoured* thing, sir, but mine own": Shakspere's "As You Like It," v. 4. 60); hence, offensive; unpleasant; objectionable.—**ill′=fa′vored-ness,** *n.*

ill=got-ten (il′got′n), *a.* Acquired by evil means: as, *ill-gotten* gains.

ill=hu-mored (il′hū′mọrd), *a.* Having or showing ill humor, or an unamiable temper or mood.—**ill=hu′mored-ly,** *adv.*

il-lib-er-al (i-lib′ẹ-rạl), *a.* [L. *illiberalis.*] Not liberal; without liberal culture; unscholarly; mean or vulgar; also, not generous in giving; niggardly; also, not generous in habit of thought; narrow-minded; bigoted.—**il-lib′er-al-ism,** *n.* Illiberal principles.—**il-lib-er-al′i-ty** (-ẹ-ral′-i-ti), *n.*—**il-lib′er-al-ly,** *adv.*

il-li-cit (i-lis′it), *a.* [L. *illicitus*, < *in-*, not, + *licitus*, permitted, E. *licit.*] Not permitted or authorized; unlicensed; unlawful: as, the *illicit* sale of intoxicating beverages; "There are lawful religions, there are *illicit*" (J. H. Newman's "Callista," xxii.).—**il-li′cit-ly,** *adv.*—**il-li′cit-ness,** *n.*

il-lim-it-a-ble (i-lim′i-tạ-bl), *a.* [See *il-*².] Not limitable; limitless; boundless: as, "the void *illimitable* space" (Pope's tr. Homer's "Odyssey," xx.).—**il-lim″it-a-bil′i-ty** (-bil′i-ti), **il-lim′it-a-ble-ness,** *n.*—**il-lim′it-a-bly,** *adv.*

il-li-quid (i-lik′wid), *a.* [See *il-*².] In *civil* and *Sc. law*, of a debt, claim, etc., not liquid; not clear or manifest; not ascertained and constituted either by a written obligation or by the decree of a court.

il-lit-er-ate (i-lit′ẹ-rạt). [L. *illiteratus*, < *in-*, not, + *literatus*, lettered, E. *literate.*] **I.** *a.* Not literate or lettered; deficient in education; specif., unable to read; also, showing want of culture (as, an *illiterate* literary style). **II.** *n.* An illiterate person.—**il-lit′er-a-cy** (-ẹ-rạ-si), **il-lit′er-ate-ness,** *n.*—**il-lit′er-ate-ly,** *adv.*

ill=judged (il′jujd′), *a.* Done with or resulting from bad judgment; injudicious; unwise.

ill=na-tured (il′nā′ţụ̄rd), *a.* Having or showing ill nature, or an unamiable or unkindly disposition or mood; spiteful.—**ill′=na′tured-ly,** *adv.*—**ill′=na′tured-ness,** *n.*

ill-ness (il′nes), *n.* Wickedness†; badness†; also, a state of ill health; sickness; an attack of sickness (as, "He soon contracted a slow *illness*": Gibbon's "Decline and Fall of the Roman Empire," xiii.).

il-lo-cal (i-lō′kạl), *a.* [LL. *illocalis.*] Not local; independent of place or spatial conditions.—**il-lo-cal-i-ty** (il-ō̦-kal′i-ti), *n.*

il-log-ic (i-loj′ik), *n.* [See *il-*².] The reverse of logic; illogical character; unreasonableness.—**il-log′i-cal,** *a.* Not logical; contrary to or disregardful of the rules of logic.—**il-log-i-cal′i-ty** (-kal′i-ti), **il-log′i-cal-ness,** *n.*—**il-log′i-cal-ly,** *adv.*

ill=starred (il′stärd′), *a.* Under the influence of an evil star; ill-fated; unfortunate; of actions, etc., disastrous.

ill=tem-pered (il′tem′pėrd), *a.* Distempered†; also, having or showing ill temper; cross.—**ill′=tem′pered-ly,** *adv.*—**ill′=tem′pered-ness,** *n.*

ill=timed (il′tīmd′), *a.* Badly timed; inopportune; unseasonable.

ill=treat (il′trēt′), *v. t.* To treat ill; ill-use; maltreat.

il-lude (i-lūd′), *v. t.*; *-luded, -luding.* [L. *illudere* (pp. *illusus*), < *in*, in, on, + *ludere*, play.] To mock† or deride†; also, to deceive by false appearances; trick.

il-lume (i-lūm′), *v. t.*; *-lumed, -luming.* [For *illumine.*] To illuminate. See Shakspere's "Hamlet," i. 1. 37. [Poetic.]

il-lu-mi-na-ble (i-lū′mi-nạ-bl), *a.* Capable of being illumined or illuminated.

il-lu-mi-nant (i-lūʹmi-nạnt). **I.** *a.* Illuminating; affording illumination. **II.** *n.* An illuminating agent or material.

il-lu-mi-nate (i-lūʹmi-nāt), *v.*; *-nated, -nating.* [L. *illuminatus*, pp. of *illuminare*, < *in*, in, on, + *lumen* (*lumin-*), light.] **I.** *tr.* To supply with light; light up; also, to decorate with lights, as in celebration; also, to set alight, or kindle (rare: as, "The butler . . . *illuminated* the antique gothic chandelier," Thackeray's "Pendennis," i. 38); also, fig., to enlighten, as with knowledge; also, to throw light on (a subject); make lucid or clear; also, to render illustrious; also, to decorate (a letter, manuscript, etc.) with color, gold, or the like. **II.** *intr.* To display lights, as in celebration; also, to become illuminated.—**il-luʹmi-nate. I.** *a.* Illuminated. [Archaic.] **II.** *n.* One who is, or affects to be, specially enlightened.

il-lu-mi-na-ti (i-lū-mi-nāʹtī), *n. pl.* [L.] Illuminates; persons possessing, or affecting to possess, superior enlightenment: used [*cap.*] as a name for various sects or societies (as the deistic and republican 'Order of the Illuminati,' founded in Bavaria in 1776 and suppressed there in 1785).

il-lu-mi-nat-ing (i-lūʹmi-nā-ting), *p. a.* That illuminates; shedding light; enlightening.—**il-luʹmi-nat-ing-ly,** *adv.*

il-lu-mi-na-tion (i-lū-mi-nāʹshọn), *n.* [LL. *illuminatio*(*n-*).] The act of illuminating, or supplying with light, or the fact or condition of being illuminated; the intensity of the light falling on a surface; a supply of light; often, a decorating with lights, as in celebration; a decoration consisting of lights; also, intellectual or spiritual enlightenment; also, decoration, as of a letter or manuscript, in color, gold, or the like; an embellishment in color, gold, or the like.—**il-luʹmi-na-tive** (-nạ-tiv), *a.* Serving to illuminate.

il-lu-mi-na-tor (i-lūʹmi-nā-tọr), *n.* [LL.] One who or that which illuminates; any of various instruments for illuminating, as a lens for concentrating light, or a mirror for reflecting light; one who decorates manuscripts, books, etc., with color, gold, or the like.

il-lu-mine (i-lūʹmin), *v. t.* or *i.*; *-mined, -mining.* [OF. F. *illuminer*, < L. *illuminare*: see *illuminate.*] To illuminate or be illuminated.

il-lu-mi-nism (i-lūʹmi-nizm), *n.* [F. *illuminisme*, < *illuminer*, E. *illumine.*] The doctrines or claims of illuminati; also, a doctrine advocating enlightenment.—**il-luʹmi-nist,** *n.*

ill=use (il'ūzʹ), *v. t.*; *-used, -using.* To use badly; treat unjustly or cruelly; ill-treat.

il-lu-sion (i-lūʹzhọn), *n.* [OF. F. *illusion*, < L. *illusio*(*n-*), < *illudere*, E. *illude.*] The act of deceiving by false appearances†; also, the state of being so deceived, or an instance of this; a false impression or belief; a delusion or delusive fancy; specif., false perception or conception of some object of sense; a perception of a thing which misrepresents it, or gives it qualities not present in reality (cf. *hallucination*); sometimes, any false or apparent perception, including a hallucination; also, something that deceives by producing a false impression; a deceptive appearance; often, formerly, an apparition or phantom (as, "Stay, *illusion!* If thou hast any sound, or use of voice, Speak to me": Shakspere's "Hamlet," i. 1. 127); also, a very thin, delicate kind of tulle.—**il-luʹsion-a-ry** (-ạ-ri), *a.* Characterized by illusion; of the nature of an illusion; illusory.—**il-luʹsion-ism,** *n.* A theory or doctrine that the material world is an illusion.—**il-luʹsion-ist,** *n.* One subject to illusions; also, one who produces illusions, as by sleight of hand; a conjurer; also, an adherent of illusionism.

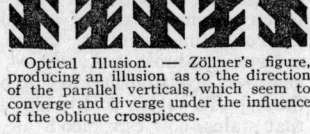

Optical Illusion. — Zöllner's figure, producing an illusion as to the direction of the parallel verticals, which seem to converge and diverge under the influence of the oblique crosspieces.

il-lu-sive (i-lūʹsiv), *a.* Illusory.—**il-luʹsive-ly,** *adv.*—**il-luʹsive-ness,** *n.*

il-lu-so-ry (i-lūʹsọ-ri), *a.* [LL. *illusorius*, < L. *illudere*, E. *illude.*] Causing illusion; deceptive; of the nature of an illusion; unreal.—**il-luʹso-ri-ly,** *adv.*—**il-luʹso-ri-ness,** *n.*

il-lus-trate (ilʹus-trāt or i-lusʹ-), *v. t.*; *-trated, -trating.* [L. *illustratus*, pp. of *illustrare*, illuminate, make illustrious, make clear, < *illustris*: see *illustrious.*] To illuminate or light (archaic); also, to enlighten (archaic); also, to shed luster on (archaic); also, to embellish†; also, to make clear or intelligible, as by examples; exemplify; also, to furnish (a book, etc.) with drawings or pictorial representations intended for elucidation or adornment; of drawings, etc., to elucidate or adorn (a book, etc.).—**il-lusʹtrate†,** *a.* Illustrious: as, "this most gallant, *illustrate*, and learned gentleman" (Shakspere's "Love's Labour's Lost," v. 1. 128).—**il-lus-traʹtion** (-trāʹshọn), *n.* [L. *illustratio*(*n-*).] The act of illustrating; the state of being illustrated; also, that which illustrates, as an example or a pictorial representation; esp., a picture used to illustrate a book, etc. —**il-lusʹtra-tive** (-trạ-tiv), *a.* Serving to illustrate.—**il-lusʹtra-tive-ly,** *adv.*—**ilʹlus-tra-tor** (-trā-tọr), *n.* [LL.] One who or that which illustrates; esp., an artist who makes illustrations for books, etc.

il-lus-tri-ous (i-lusʹtri-us), *a.* [L. *illustris*, lighted up, bright, illustrious, < *in*, in, on, + *-lustris*, prob. akin to *lux*, light: cf. *luster*³.] Luminous†; bright†; also, highly distinguished, as persons, etc.; renowned; famous; glorious, as deeds, etc.—**il-lusʹtri-ous-ly,** *adv.*—**il-lusʹtri-ous-ness,** *n.*

ill=will (ilʹwilʹ), *n.* Hostile or unfriendly feeling.

ill=wish-er (ilʹwishʹėr), *n.* One who wishes ill or evil to another: as, "If he was left to his *ill-wishers* he would be a bloody corpse ere morn" (Scott's "Guy Mannering," xlvii.).

il-ly (ilʹi), *adv.* Ill: a form occasionally used but commonly objected to, preference being given to the older and better established *ill.*

Il-lyr-i-an (i-lirʹi-ạn). **I.** *a.* Pertaining to ancient Illyria, a region on the eastern shore of the Adriatic, or to modern Illyria, a former titular kingdom of Austria comprising territories on or near the northern Adriatic. **II.** *n.* A native or inhabitant of Illyria; also, the language of ancient Illyria.

il-men-ite (ilʹmen-īt), *n.* [From the *Ilmen* Mountains, in the southern Urals.] A black mineral composed of iron, titanium, and oxygen.

I'm (īm). Contraction of *I am.*

im-¹. A form of *in-*¹ used before *b*, *m*, and *p*, as in *imbrute*, *immingle*, *impearl.*

im-². A form of *in-*² used before *b*, *m*, and *p*, as in *immoral*, *imparity*, *imperishable.*

im-age (imʹạj), *n.* [OF. F. *image*, < L. *imago* (*imagin-*), copy, likeness, image, semblance, apparition, conception, idea, akin to *imitari*, E. *imitate.*] A likeness or similitude of something, esp. a representation in the solid form, as a statue or effigy; also, an optical counterpart of an object as produced by reflection, refraction, etc. (see phrases below); also, form, appearance, or semblance (as, "God created man in his own *image*, in the *image* of God created he him": Gen. i. 27); also, an illusion or apparition (archaic); also, a counterpart or copy (as, the child is the *image* of its mother); also, anything considered as representing something else; a symbol or emblem; also, a type or embodiment (as, "An awful *image* of calm power . . . now thou sittest": Shelley's "Prometheus Unbound," i. 296); also, a mental picture or representation, as formed by the memory or imagination; an idea or conception; also, a description of something in speech or writing; in *rhet.*, a figure of speech, esp. a metaphor or a simile.—**real image.** See *real*¹, *a.*—**virtual image.** See *virtual.*—**imʹage,** *v. t.*; *-aged, -aging.* To form an image of; figure; portray; also, to reflect the likeness of; mirror; also, to symbolize or typify (as, "O stream! . . . Thou *imagest* my life": Shelley's "Alastor," 505); also, to picture or represent in the mind; imagine; conceive; also, to set forth in speech or writing, or describe (as, "The flight of Satan to the gates of hell is finely *imaged* [in "Paradise Lost"]": Addison, in "Spectator," 309).—**imʹage-ry** (-ri), *n.*; pl. *-ries* (-riz). The formation of images, figures, or likenesses of things, or such images collectively; also, the work of the imagination or fancy; mental images collectively (as, "a dream's dim *imagery*": Shelley's "Mask of Anarchy," lii.); also, the use of rhetorical images; figurative description or illustration; rhetorical images collectively. —**im-a-ge′ri-al** (-ạ-jē′ri-ạl), *a.*

i-mag-i-na-ble (i-maj′i-nạ-bl), *a.* Capable of being imagined or conceived: as, "He ran into all the extravagancies *imaginable*" (Steele, in "Spectator," 82).—**i-mag′i-na-ble-ness,** *n.*—**i-mag′i-na-bly,** *adv.*

i-mag-i-nal (i-maj′i-nạl), *a.* In *entom.*, of or pertaining to, or in the form of, an imago.

i-mag-i-na-ry (i-maj′i-nā-ri), *a.* [L. *imaginarius*, < *imago*: see *image*.] Existing only in the imagination or fancy (as, "Besides real diseases, we are subject to many that are only *imaginary*": Swift's "Gulliver's Travels," iv. 6); not real; fancied; also, imaginative† (as, "My soul's *imaginary* sight Presents thy shadow to my sightless view": Shakspere's "Sonnets," xxvii.); in *math.*, noting or pertaining to a quantity or expression involving the square root of a negative quantity, and thus having no real existence.—**i-mag′i-na-ri-ly,** *adv.*—**i-mag′i-na-ri-ness,** *n.*

i-mag-i-na-tion (i-maj-i-nā′shọn), *n.* [OF. F. *imagination*, < L. *imaginatio(n-)*, < *imaginari*: see *imagine*.] The action of imagining, or of forming mental images or concepts of what is not actually present to the senses; also, the faculty of forming such images or concepts; the power of the mind of reproducing images or concepts stored in the memory under the suggestion of associated images ('reproductive imagination'), or of recombining former experiences in the creation of new images different from any known by experience ('productive imagination' or 'creative imagination'); specif., the faculty of producing ideal creations consistent with reality, as in poetical or literary composition (distinguished from *fancy*); also, the product of imagining; a conception or mental creation, often a baseless or fanciful one; also, the act of planning or scheming, or a plan, scheme, or plot (archaic: as, "Thou hast seen all their vengeance and all their *imaginations* against me," Lam. iii. 60); also, mind, or thinking or thought (now rare).—**i-mag-i-na′tion-al,** *a.*

i-mag-i-na-tive (i-maj′i-nā-tiv), *a.* [OF. F. *imaginatif*, < LL. *imaginativus*.] Given to imagining, as persons; having exceptional powers of imagination; sometimes, fanciful; also, pertaining to or concerned with imagination (as, the *imaginative* faculty); also, characterized by or bearing evidence of imagination (as, "the *imaginative* tale of Sintram and his companions, by Mons. Le Baron de la Motte Fouqué": Scott's "Guy Mannering," Introd.).—**i-mag′i-na-tive-ly,** *adv.*—**i-mag′i-na-tive-ness,** *n.*

i-mag-i-na-tor (i-maj′i-nā-tọr), *n.* One who imagines.

i-mag-ine (i-maj′in), *v.*; *-ined, -ining.* [OF. F. *imaginer*, < L. *imaginari*, picture to one's self, fancy, imagine, < *imago*: see *image*.] **I.** *tr.* To form a mental image of (something not actually present to the senses: as, "And far beyond, *Imagined* more than seen, the skirts of France," Tennyson's "Princess," Conclusion, 48); represent to one's self in imagination; conceive; hence, to assume or suppose (as, for the sake of argument *imagine* this to be the case); conjecture or guess (as, I cannot *imagine* whom you mean); think, believe, or fancy (as, "I doubt not of the facts which you relate, but *imagine* that you impute them to mistaken motives": Johnson's "Rasselas," ix.); also, to plan, scheme, or plot (archaic: as, "How long will ye *imagine* mischief against a man?" Ps. lxii. 3). **II.** *intr.* To form mental images of things not present to the senses; exercise the imagination.—**i-mag′in-er,** *n.*

im-ag-ism (im′ạj-izm), *n.* A method or movement in poetic composition, originating about 1912, which aims particularly at 'images' or clear presentments of what the poet has in mind (without vagueness or symbolism), and uses rhythm or cadence rather than the conventional metrical forms (cf. *vers libre*).—**im′ag-ist.** **I.** *n.* An adherent of imagism. **II.** *a.* Pertaining to imagists or imagism.—**im-ag-is′tic,** *a.*

i-ma-go (i-mā′gō), *n.*; pl. *-gos* (-gōz), L. *imagines* (i-maj′i-nēz). [NL. use of L. *imago*: see *image*.] In *entom.*, an insect in the final, perfect stage or form, after it has undergone complete metamorphosis.

i-mam, i-maum (i-mäm′, i-mâm′), *n.* [Ar. *imām*, leader, guide.] The title of any of various Mohammedan leaders and chiefs; also, the officiating priest of a mosque.

i-ma-ret (i-mä′ret), *n.* [Turk.] Among the Turks, a kind of hospice for pilgrims and other travelers.

im-bal-ance (im-bal′ạns), *n.* [See *im-*².] Lack of balance; specif., inequality in the action of the muscles of the eyes; failure of the muscles of the eyes to keep the optical axes parallel.

im-be-cile (im′bę-sil, Brit. also -sēl or -sīl). [F. *imbecille*, now *imbécile*, < L. *imbecillus*, weak, feeble.] **I.** *a.* Weak or feeble, as persons or things (as, "his stunted stature and *imbecile* frame": Shelley's "Queen Mab," viii. 152); now, esp., mentally feeble, as persons; feeble-minded (as, "The man became *Imbecile* . . . Dead for two years before his death was he": Tennyson's "Aylmer's Field," 836); showing mental feebleness or incapacity, as actions; hence, silly; fatuous; absurd. **II.** *n.* An imbecile person; a person in a condition of imbecility.—**im′be-cile-ly,** *adv.*—**im-be-cil′i-ty** (-sil′i-ti), *n.*; pl. *-ties* (-tiz). [F. *imbécillité*, < L. *imbecillitas*.] The condition or quality of being imbecile; weakness or feebleness, or an instance or point of weakness; now, esp., feebleness of mind; mental weakness (usually) that falls short of absolute idiocy; hence, silliness or absurdity, or an instance of it.

im-bed (im-bed′), etc. Same as *embed*, etc.

im-ber=goose (im′bėr-gös), *n.* Same as *ember-goose.*

im-bibe (im-bīb′), *v.*; *-bibed, -bibing.* [L. *imbibere*, < *in*, in, + *bibere*, drink.] **I.** *tr.* To drink in, or drink (as, "He filled a quart flagon from a barrel . . . Oliver . . . *imbibed* the contents": Scott's "Fair Maid of Perth," xvi.); hence, to absorb or take in as if by drinking (as, "So barren sands *imbibe* the show'r": Cowper's "Friendship," 184); often, to take or receive into the mind, as knowledge, ideas, etc. (as, "They had *imbibed* some notions of the Christian faith from Catholic missionaries": Irving's "Captain Bonneville," ix.); also, to soak† or saturate†; imbue†. **II.** *intr.* To drink; absorb liquid, moisture, etc.—**im-bib′er** (-bī′bėr), *n.*—**im-bi-bi′tion** (-bi-bish′ọn), *n.* The act of imbibing; absorption.

im-bos-om (im-bůz′ọm), *v. t.* Same as *embosom.*

im-bow-er (im-bou′ėr), *v. t.* Same as *embower.*

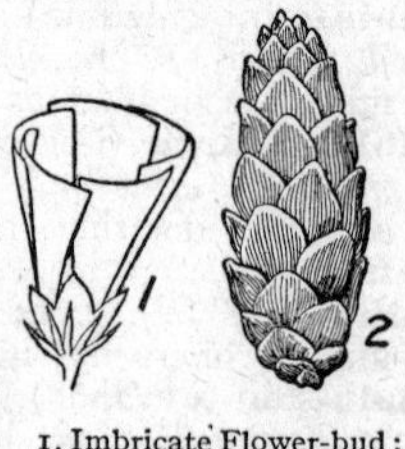

1, Imbricate Flower-bud; 2, Imbricate Scales (of cone of hemlock-spruce).

im-bri-cate (im′bri-kāt), *v. t.* or *i.*; *-cated, -cating.* [L. *imbricatus*, pp. of *imbricare*, cover with tiles, < *imbrex*, tile, < *imber*, rain.] To overlap like tiles or shingles.—**im′bri-cate,** *a.* Overlapping like tiles or shingles, as scales, leaves, etc.; also, characterized by or as by overlapping scales.—**im-bri-ca′tion** (-kā′shọn), *n.* An overlapping as of tiles or shingles; a decorative pattern in imitation of this.

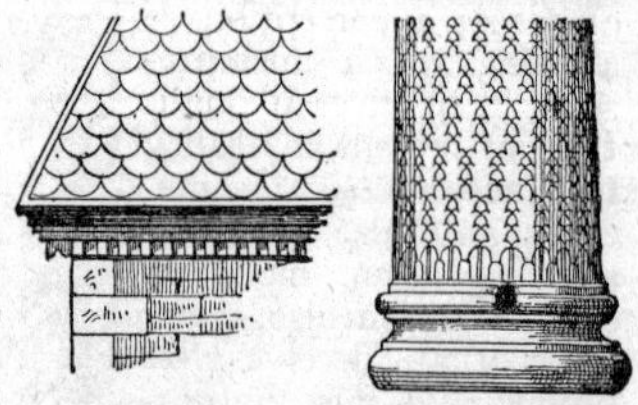

Imbrication. — Roof and Column.

im-bro-glio (im-brō′lyō), *n.*; pl. *-glios* (-lyōz). [It., < *imbrogliare*, confuse, = E. *embroil*.] A confused heap (as, "I keep my prints, an *imbroglio*, Fifty in one portfolio": Browning's "A Likeness"); fig., an intricate and perplexing state of affairs; a complicated or difficult situation; esp., a misunderstanding or disagreement of a complicated nature, as between persons or nations; an embroilment.

im-brown (im-broun′), *v.* Same as *embrown.*

im-brue (im-brö′), *v. t.*; *-brued, -bruing.* [OF. *embreuver*, *embevrer*, give to drink, wet, imbrue, < L. *in*, in, + *bibere*, drink.] To wet† or soak†; also, to wet in or with something that stains, now esp. blood (as, "Who has not heard how brave O'Neale In English blood *imbrued* his steel?" Scott's "Rokeby," iv. 6); of blood, etc., to wet or stain.—**im-brue′ment,** *n.*

im-brute (im-bröt′), *v. t.* or *i.*; *-bruted, -bruting.* [See *im-*¹.] To degrade or sink to the level of a brute: as, "They have been ground down and debased and *imbruted* till human nature can bear no longer" (Mrs. Stowe's "Oldtown Folks," xxxviii.).—**im-brute′ment,** *n.*

im-bue (im-bū′), *v. t.*; *-bued, -buing.* [L. *imbuere,* wet, tinge, imbue.] To saturate with moisture; impregnate with color, etc.; sometimes, to imbrue, as with blood; often, fig., to impregnate or inspire, as with feelings, opinions, etc. (as, "Thy words, with grace divine *Imbued*": Milton's "Paradise Lost," viii. 216).—**im-bue′ment,** *n.*

im-burse (im-bėrs′), *v. t.*; *-bursed, -bursing.* [ML. *imbursare,* < L. *in,* in, + ML. *bursa,* bag, purse.] To put into a purse; store up; also, to pay, as a person; reimburse.—**im-burse′ment,** *n.*

im-ide (im′īd or -id), *n.* [Varied form of *amide.*] In *chem.,* any of a class of compounds regarded as ammonia with two of its hydrogen atoms replaced by a bivalent acid radical, or as a combination of a bivalent acid radical with the imidogen radical NH.—**im-i-do-** (im′i-dō-, also i-mē′dō-). A form of *imide* in compounds. Also **im′i-do,** *a.*—**i-mid-o-gen** (i-mid′ọ-jen), *n.* [See *-gen.*] In *chem.,* the bivalent hydrogen and nitrogen radical NH, present in imides.

im-i-ta-ble (im′i-tạ-bl), *a.* [L. *imitabilis.*] That may be imitated (as, "simple and *imitable* virtues, which are within every man's reach": Irving's "Sketch-Book," Roscoe); also, worthy of imitation†.—**im″i-ta-bil′i-ty** (-bil′i-ti), *n.*

im-i-tate (im′i-tāt), *v. t.*; *-tated, -tating.* [L. *imitatus,* pp. of *imitari,* copy, imitate: cf. *image.*] To follow or endeavor to follow in manner (as, "If our betters play at that game, we must not dare To *imitate* them": Shakspere's "Timon of Athens," i. 2. 13); copy in action; follow the example of; sometimes, to mimic or counterfeit; also, to make a copy of; copy; reproduce more or less closely; also, to have or assume the aspect or semblance of, or simulate (as, "The diseases of the mind do in almost every particular *imitate* those of the body," Fielding's "Tom Jones," iv. 12; wood painted to *imitate* stone).—**im-i-ta′tion** (-tā′shọn). [L. *imitatio(n-).*] **I.** *n.* The act or an act of imitating; the practice of imitating; also, a result or product of imitating; a copy, or more or less close reproduction, of something; a counterfeit, made to look like something else which it is not; in *music,* the repetition of a melodic phrase or theme at a different pitch or key from the original, or in a different voice-part, or with some modification of rhythm or intervals not so great as to destroy the resemblance. **II.** *a.* Made in imitation of something else; esp., made to imitate a genuine or superior article or thing (as, *imitation* pearls; *imitation* lace, machine-made lace as imitating the hand-made).—**im-i-ta′tion-al,** *a.*—**im′i-ta-tive** (-tạ-tiv), *a.* [LL. *imitativus.*] Imitating or copying, or given to imitating, as persons or some animals; characterized by or involving imitation or copying (as, the *imitative* arts); also, reproducing more or less closely the appearance, character, sound, etc., of something (as, *imitative* coloration in animals; *imitative* words, such as *bobolink* and *whiz*); also, made in imitation of something; imitation; counterfeit.—**im′i-ta-tive-ly,** *adv.*—**im′i-ta-tive-ness,** *n.*—**im′i-ta-tor** (-tā-tọr), *n.*

im-mac-u-late (i-mak′ū-lạt), *a.* [L. *immaculatus,* < *in-,* not, + *maculatus,* spotted.] Free from spot or stain; spotlessly clean, as linen; esp., in fig. use, free from moral blemish or impurity, pure, or undefiled (as, "She was a woman . . . of . . . *immaculate* and inaccessible virtue": Irving's "Conquest of Granada," iii.); also, free from fault or flaw; free from errors, as a text; in *zoöl.* and *bot.,* without spots or colored marks; unicolor.—**immaculate conception,** the conception of the Virgin Mary by her mother free from the taint of original sin: formally proclaimed on Dec. 8, 1854, as a dogma of the Roman Catholic Church.—**im-mac′u-la-cy** (-lạ-si), **im-mac′u-late-ness,** *n.*—**im-mac′u-late-ly,** *adv.*

im-mal-le-a-ble (i-mal′ẹ̄-ạ-bl or im-mal′-), *a.* [See *im-*[2].] Not malleable; incapable of being extended by hammering or the like.

im-mane (i-mān′), *a.* [L. *immanis.*] Monstrous; huge; prodigious; also, monstrously cruel or savage.

im-ma-nent (im′ạ-nẹnt), *a.* [LL. *immanens* (*-ent-*), ppr. of *immanere,* remain in, < L. *in,* in, + *manere,* remain.] Remaining within; indwelling; inherent; specif., of a mental act or action, taking place entirely within the mind of the subject, and producing no effect outside of it.—**im′ma-nence, im′ma-nen-cy,** *n.*—**im′ma-nent-ly,** *adv.*

im-man-tle (i-man′tl or im-man′tl), *v. t.*; *-tled, -tling.* [See *im-*[1].] To envelop with or as with a mantle: as, "O joy to him in this retreat, *Immantled* in ambrosial dark" (Tennyson's "In Memoriam," lxxxix.). [Poetic.]

Im-man-u-el, Em-man-u-el (i-man′ū-el, e-man′-), *n.* [LL. *Emmanuel,* < Gr. Ἐμμανουήλ, < Heb. *ʻImmānūēl,* 'God with us.'] A Scriptural name of Christ. See Isa. vii. 14, and Mat. i. 23.

im-ma-te-ri-al (im-ạ-tē′ri-ạl), *a.* [ML. *immaterialis.*] Not material; incorporeal; spiritual; also, of no essential consequence, or unimportant (as, the discrepancy is *immaterial*).—**im-ma-te′ri-al-ism,** *n.* Immateriality; also, the doctrine that there is no material world, but that all things exist only in the mind.—**im-ma-te′ri-al-ist,** *n.*—**im″ma-te-ri-al′i-ty** (-al′i-ti), *n.*; pl. *-ties* (-tiz). The state or character of being immaterial, or not of the nature of matter (as, "All the conclusions of reason enforce the *immateriality* of mind": Johnson's "Rasselas," xlviii.); also, something immaterial; also, the state of being unessential or unimportant.—**im-ma-te′ri-al-ize** (-ạl-īz), *v. t.*; *-ized, -izing.* To make immaterial.—**im-ma-te′ri-al-ly,** *adv.*—**im-ma-te′ri-al-ness,** *n.*

im-ma-ture (im-ạ-tūr′), *a.* [L. *immaturus.*] Not mature, ripe, developed, or perfected; also, premature (archaic: as, a person's *immature* death); in *phys. geog.,* youthful.—**im-ma-ture′ly,** *adv.*—**im-ma-ture′ness, im-ma-tu′ri-ty** (-tū′ri-ti), *n.*

im-meas-ur-a-ble (i-mezh′ūr-ạ-bl), *a.* [See *im-*[2].] Incapable of being measured; limitless; immense.—**im-meas″ur-a-bil′i-ty** (-bil′i-ti), **im-meas′ur-a-ble-ness,** *n.*—**im-meas′ur-a-bly,** *adv.*

im-me-di-ate (i-mē′di-ạt), *a.* [ML. *immediatus.*] Not mediate; being or acting without intervening medium or agent; in direct connection or relation; direct; also, intuitive (as, *immediate* knowledge); also, having a direct bearing (as, *immediate* considerations); also, having no object or space intervening; nearest or next; hence, close or near (as, in the *immediate* vicinity); also, having no time intervening; present or next adjacent (as, our *immediate* age; the *immediate* future); pertaining to the present time or moment (as, our *immediate* plans); also, occurring or accomplished without delay (as, an *immediate* effect; an *immediate* reply); instant.—**im-me′di-a-cy** (-ạ-si), **im-me′di-ate-ness,** *n.*—**im-me′di-ate-ly,** *adv.* Without intervening medium or agent; in direct relation; so as to concern or affect directly; also, with no object or space intervening; next (as, *immediately* adjoining); closely (as, *immediately* in the vicinity); directly (as, "*Immediately* in the route of the travellers lay a high mountain": Irving's "Captain Bonneville," xxx.); also, without lapse of time, or without delay (as, "He had only dipped his head into the water, and *immediately* taken it out again": Addison, in "Spectator," 94); instantly; at once.

im-med-i-ca-ble (i-med′i-kạ-bl), *a.* [L. *immedicabilis.*] Incapable of being healed; incurable: as, "wounds *immedicable*" (Milton's "Samson Agonistes," 620).

im-me-lo-di-ous (im-e-lō′di-us), *a.* [See *im-*[2].] Not melodious.

im-mem-o-ra-ble (i-mem′ọ-rạ-bl), *a.* [L. *immemorabilis.*] Not memorable; unworthy of remembrance; also, immemorial†.

im-me-mo-ri-al (im-ẹ̄-mō′ri-ạl), *a.* [ML. *immemorialis.*] Extending or dating back beyond the bounds of memory; ancient beyond record or knowledge: as, dating from time *immemorial*; "*immemorial* elms" (Tennyson's "Princess," vii. 206); "keeping only one anna in each rupee . . . the *immemorial* commission of Asia" (Kipling's "Kim," ii.).—**im-me-mo′ri-al-ly,** *adv.*

im-mense (i-mens′). [OF. F. *immense,* < L. *immensus,* < *in-,* not, + *mensus,* pp. of *metiri,* measure.] **I.** *a.* Immeasurable; boundless; hence, vast; huge; very great; also, very good or fine (slang). **II.** *n.* An immense extent or quantity; the boundless expanse of space (as "When . . . the solid shores of sense Melt into the vague *immense*": Whittier's "Andrew Rykman's Prayer").—**im-mense′ly,** [illegible]—**im-mense′ness,** *n.*—**im-men-si-ty** (i-men′si-ti), *n.*; [illegible] (-tiz). The state of being immense; boundless or [illegible]; infinity; vastness; also, infinite space; a vast expanse; an immense quantity (as, "rough-looking desperadoes, with . . . an *immensity* of beard": Hawthorne's "Scarlet Letter," xxi.).

im-men-su-ra-ble (i-men′shų-rạ-bl), *a.* [LL. *immensurabilis.*] Not mensurable; immeasurable.

im-merge (i-mėrj′), *v.*; *-merged, -merging.* [L. *immergere* (pp. *immersus*), < *in,* in, + *mergere,* dip, plunge, E. *merge.*] **I.** *tr.* To immerse. **II.** *intr.* To plunge, as into a fluid; disappear as by plunging.—**im-mer-gence** (i-mėr′jẹns), *n.*

im-merse (i-mėrs′), *v. t.*; *-mersed, -mersing.* [L. *immersus,* pp. of *immergere*: see *immerge.*] To plunge into or place under a liquid; dip; sink; specif., to baptize by immersion; hence, to embed; bury; fig., to involve deeply; absorb.—**im-mersed′,** *p. a.* Plunged or sunk in or as in a liquid; in *bot.,* growing wholly under water; in *biol.,* somewhat or wholly sunk in the surrounding parts, as an organ.—**im-mer-si-ble** (i-mėr′si-bl), *a.* Capable of being immersed.—**im-mer′sion** (-shọn), *n.* [LL. *immersio(n-).*] The act of immersing, or the state of being immersed; specif., baptism by plunging the whole person into water; in *astron.,* the disappearance of a celestial body by passing either behind another or into its shadow.—**im-mer′sion-ism,** *n.* The doctrine that immersion is essential to Christian baptism; also, the practice of baptism by immersion.—**im-mer′sion-ist,** *n.*

im-mesh (i-mesh′), *v. t.* Same as *enmesh.*

im-me-thod-i-cal (im-e-thod′i-kạl or im-me-), *a.* [See *im-*².] Not methodical; having no method; irregular; disorderly: as, "My reading has been lamentably desultory and *immethodical*" (Lamb's "The Old and the New Schoolmaster").—**im-me-thod′i-cal-ly,** *adv.*

im-met-ri-cal (i-met′ri-kạl or im-met′-), *a.* [See *im-*².] Not metrical.—**im-met′ri-cal-ly,** *adv.*

im-mi-grant (im′i-grạnt). **I.** *a.* Immigrating. **II.** *n.* One who or that which immigrates; esp., a person who migrates into a country for permanent residence.

im-mi-grate (im′i-grāt), *v.*; *-grated, -grating.* [L. *immigratus,* pp. of *immigrare,* < *in,* in, + *migrare,* migrate.] **I.** *intr.* To pass or come into a new habitat or place of residence; esp., to come into a country of which one is not a native for the purpose of permanent residence. **II.** *tr.* To introduce as settlers.—**im-mi-gra′tion** (-grā′shọn), *n.* The act of immigrating; entrance into a foreign country for permanent residence; also, immigrants, or a body of immigrants, collectively.—**im′mi-gra-tor.** *n.*

im-mi-nence (im′i-nẹns), *n.* The state or fact of being imminent or impending (as, "The very *imminence* of the emergency paralyzed his invention": Mark Twain's "Tom Sawyer," xx.); also, that which is imminent; impending evil or danger.—**im′mi-nen-cy,** *n.* The state of being imminent.

im-mi-nent (im′i-nẹnt), *a.* [L. *imminens (-ent-),* ppr. of *imminere,* overhang, < *in,* in, on, + *-minere,* project: see *eminent.*] Projecting or leaning forward, or overhanging (as, "Flake by flake, the beetling avalanches Build up their *imminent* crags of noiseless snow": Lowell's "Ode to France," i.); also, likely to occur at any moment (as, changes are *imminent*); impending; usually, of evil or danger, impending threateningly (as, "the gloom of *imminent* war," Tennyson's "Idylls of the King," Dedication, 12; "You have defended me from *imminent* death," Shakspere's "2 Henry VI.," v. 3. 19).—**im′mi-nent-ly,** *adv.*

im-min-gle (i-ming′gl), *v. t.* or *i.*; *-gled, -gling.* [See *im-*¹.] To mingle in; intermingle.

im-mis-ci-ble (i-mis′i-bl), *a.* [See *im-*².] Not miscible; incapable of being mixed.—**im-mis-ci-bil′i-ty** (-bil′i-ti), *n.*—**im-mis′ci-bly,** *adv.*

im-mit (i-mit′), *v. t.*; *-mitted, -mitting.* [L. *immittere* (pp. *immissus*), < *in,* in, + *mittere,* send.] To send or let in; inject; introduce.—**im-mis-sion** (i-mish′ọn), *n.*

im-mit-i-ga-ble (i-mit′i-gạ-bl), *a.* [LL. *immitigabilis.*] Not mitigable; not to be mitigated, softened, or made more mild: as, "the *immitigable* end" (Henley's "Echoes," xlvi.).—**im-mit″i-ga-bil′i-ty** (-bil′i-ti), *n.*—**im-mit′i-ga-bly,** *adv.*

im-mix (i-miks′), *v. t.* [L. *immixtus,* pp. of *immisce*- *in,* in, + *miscere,* mix.] To mix in; mix intimately: as, "amongst her teares *immixing* prayers me- ser's "Faerie Queene," iv. 3. 47).—**im-mix′ture** (-tụr), *n.*

im-mo-bile (i-mō′bil), *a.* [L. *immobilis.*] Not mobile; immovable; fixed; also, that does not move; motionless.—**im-mo-bil-i-ty** (im-ọ-bil′i-ti), *n.*—**im-mo′bi-lize** (-bi-līz), *v. t.*; *-lized, -lizing.* To render immobile.—**im-mo″bi-li-za′tion** (-li-zā′shọn), *n.*

im-mod-er-ate (i-mod′ẹ-rạt), *a.* [L. *immoderatus.*] Not moderate; exceeding just or reasonable limits; excessive; extreme.—**im-mod′er-ate-ly,** *adv.*—**im-mod′er-ate-ness,** *n.*—**im-mod-er-a′tion** (-ẹ-rā′shọn), *n.* [L. *immoderatio(n-).*] Want of moderation; excess.

im-mod-est (i-mod′est), *a.* [L. *immodestus.*] Not modest in assertion or pretension; forward; impudent; also, not modest in conduct, utterance, etc.; wanting in delicacy or decency; indelicate; indecent.—**im-mod′est-ly,** *adv.*—**im-mod′es-ty,** *n.*

im-mo-late (im′ọ-lāt), *v. t.*; *-lated, -lating.* [L. *immolatus,* pp. of *immolare,* sacrifice, orig. sprinkle (a victim) with sacrificial meal, < *in,* in, on, + *mola,* meal mixed with salt.] To kill as a sacrificial victim; offer in sacrifice; sacrifice.—**im-mo-la′tion** (-lā′shọn), *n.* [L. *immolatio(n-).*] The act of immolating, or the state of being immolated; sacrifice; also, a sacrificial offering; a sacrifice.—**im′mo-la-tor,** *n.*

im-mor-al (i-mor′ạl), *a.* [See *im-*².] Not moral; not conforming to the moral law; unprincipled; vicious; licentious.—**im-mo-ral-i-ty** (im-ọ-ral′i-ti), *n.*; pl. *-ties* (-tiz). Immoral quality, character, or conduct; wickedness; vice; specif., sexual impurity; unchastity; also, an immoral act or practice; a vice.—**im-mor′al-ly,** *adv.*

im-mor-tal (i-môr′tạl). [L. *immortalis.*] **I.** *a.* Not mortal; not liable or subject to death; undying; hence, not liable to perish or decay; imperishable; everlasting; often, remembered or celebrated through all time (as, *immortal* fame; "*immortal* verse," Milton's "L'Allegro," 137); sometimes, perpetual, lasting, or constant; also, pertaining to immortal beings or immortality (as, "These be they that have put off the mortal clothing, and put on the *immortal*": 2 Esdras, ii. 45). **II.** *n.* An immortal being (as, "She thought she saw Christian her husband in a place of bliss, among many *immortals,* with a harp in his hand": Bunyan's "Pilgrim's Progress," ii.); esp., one of the gods of classical mythology (usually in *pl.*); also, fig., a member of a body of persons regarded as immortal, as of the royal guard of ancient Persia ('the Immortals,' whose number was constantly kept full), or of the French Academy ('the Forty Immortals,' so called in allusion to the perpetuity of their number and succession, and to their supposed enduring fame); a person, esp. an author, of enduring fame.—**im-mor-tal-i-ty** (im-ôr-tal′i-ti), *n.* [L. *immortalitas.*] The condition or quality of being immortal; unending life or existence; enduring fame (as, "In Fate's defiance—in the world's great eye, Poland has won her *immortality*": Campbell's "Lines on Poland").—**im-mor′tal-ize** (-tạl-īz), *v. t.*; *-ized, -izing.* To render immortal; exempt from death; perpetuate; bestow enduring fame upon (as, "Drive them from Orleans and be *immortalized*": Shakspere's "1 Henry VI.," i. 2. 148).—**im-mor″tal-i-za′tion** (-i-zā′shọn), *n.*—**im-mor′tal-iz-er** (-ī-zėr), *n.*—**im-mor′tal-ly,** *adv.*

im-mor-telle (im-ôr-tel′), *n.* [F., prop. fem. of *immortel,* < L. *immortalis,* E. *immortal.*] An everlasting (plant or flower).

im-mo-tile (i-mō′til), *a.* [See *im-*².] Not motile; incapable of movement.

im-mov-a-ble (i-mö′vạ-bl). [See *im-*².] **I.** *a.* Incapable of being moved; fixed; stationary; sometimes, not moving; motionless; fig., not subject to change, or unalterable; not changing from one date to another in different years (as, an *immovable* feast); incapable of being moved from one's purpose, opinion, etc., or steadfast or unyielding (as, "Mr. Jorkins has his opinions on these subjects . . . Mr. Jorkins is *immovable*": Dickens's "David Copperfield," xxiii.); incapable of being affected with feeling, emotionless, or impassive (as, an *immovable* countenance); in *law,* not liable to be removed, or permanent in place; real, as distinguished from personal. **II.** *n.* Something immovable; *pl.,* in *law,* lands and the appurtenances thereof, as trees, buildings, etc.—**im-mov-a-bil′i-ty** (-bil′i-ti), **im-mov′a-ble-ness,** *n.*—**im-mov′a-bly,** *adv.*

im-mund (i-mund′), *a.* [L. *immundus*, < *in-*, not, + *mundus*, clean.] Unclean; impure; foul; filthy.—**im-mun-di-ty** (i-mun′di-ti), *n.*

im-mune (i-mūn′). [L. *immunis*, < *in-*, not, + *-munis*, bound, under obligation, akin to *munia*, duties, functions, *munus*, service, duty, *munis*, obliging: cf. *common.*] **I.** *a.* Exempt; specif., protected from a disease or the like, as by inoculation. **II.** *n.* One who is immune; specif., one who is immune from a particular disease or the like.—**im-mu-ni-ty** (i-mū′ni-ti), *n.*; pl. *-ties* (-tiz). [L. *immunitas.*] Exemption from obligation, service, or duty; freedom from liability to taxation, jurisdiction, etc.; sometimes, special privilege; also, a particular exemption or privilege (as, "He is the Provost of Perth, and for his own honour must see the freedoms and *immunities* of the burgh preserved": Scott's "Fair Maid of Perth," vii.); specif., in ecclesiastical use, the exemption of ecclesiastical persons and things from secular or civil liabilities, duties, and burdens; a particular exemption of this kind; also, exemption from any natural or usual liability, or from anything evil (as, "But man is frail, and can but ill sustain A long *immunity* from grief and pain": Cowper's "Expostulation," 82); specif., the state of being immune from or insusceptible to a particular disease or the like.—**im-mu-nize** (i-mū′nīz or im′ū̦-), *v. t.*; *-nized*, *-nizing.* To render immune.—**im-mu-ni-za′tion** (-ni-zā′shọn), *n.*—**im-mu-nol-o-gy** (im-ū̦-nol′ọ̄-ji), *n.* [See *-logy.*] That branch of medical science which deals with immunity from disease and the production of such immunity.—**im-mu-no-log-ic, im-mu-no-log-i-cal** (i-mū-nọ̄-loj′ik, -i-kạl), *a.*—**im-mu-nol′o-gist,** *n.*

im-mure (i-mūr′), *v. t.*; *-mured*, *-muring.* [ML. *immurare*, < L. *in*, in, + *murus*, wall.] To inclose within walls; imprison; hence, in general, to shut in; confine; also, to build into or entomb in a wall.—**im-mure′ment,** *n.*

im-mu-si-cal (i-mū′zi-kạl or im-mū′-), *a.* [See *im-*².] Unmusical.

im-mu-ta-ble (i-mū′tạ-bl), *a.* [L. *immutabilis.*] Not mutable; not capable or susceptible of change; unchangeable; unalterable; changeless.—**im-mu-ta-bil′i-ty** (-bil′i-ti), **im-mu′ta-ble-ness,** *n.*—**im-mu′ta-bly,** *adv.*

imp (imp), *n.* [AS. *impa*, shoot, graft.] A shoot of a plant (obs. or prov.); a shoot or slip used in grafting (obs. or prov.); also, a person as a scion or offshoot, as of a noble house (archaic); an offspring, usually a male child (archaic: as, "My *imps* . . . hard, bold and wild, As best befits the mountain child," Scott's "Marmion," i., Introd.); esp., a child of the devil; a little devil or demon; an evil spirit; hence, a mischievous child (as, "The little *imp* fell a squalling, and scratching, and biting": Swift's "Gulliver's Travels," iv. 8); also, something added or united to something else to lengthen, enlarge, or repair it (chiefly prov. Eng.).—**imp,** *v. t.* [AS. *impian.*] To graft (archaic); implant (archaic); esp., as in falconry, to graft (feathers) into a wing, or furnish (a wing, etc.) with feathers, as to make good losses or deficiencies and improve powers of flight (often fig.); also, to fasten (wings) on; equip with wings (as, "*Imp'd* with wings, The grubs proceed to bees with pointed stings": Dryden's tr. Virgil's "Georgics," iv. 439); also, to extend or enlarge; eke out; add a piece to; mend or repair.

im-pact (im-pakt′), *v. t.* [L. *impactus*, pp. of *impingere*, drive in, strike against: see *impinge.*] To drive or press closely or firmly into something; pack in something.—**im′pact,** *n.* The striking of one body against another; a collision; specif., in *physics*, *mech.*, etc., the striking of a moving body against another body; an impinging; the single instantaneous blow of a moving body (as a projectile) when it meets another body.—**im-pac′tion** (-pak′shọn), *n.* [L. *impactio(n-).*] The act of impacting; impacted state.—**im-pac′tion-ize** (-īz), *v. t.*; *-ized*, *-izing.* To render (an aëroplane, etc.) useless by plugging up or damaging machinery or parts.—**im-pac′tu-al** (-ṭū-ạl), *a.* Pertaining to or resulting from impact.

im-pair (im-pâr′), *v. t.* or *i.* [OF. *empeirier* (F. *empirer*), < ML. *impejorare*, < L. *in*, in, + *pejorare*, make worse: see *pejorate.*] To make or become worse; diminish in value, excellence, etc.; weaken.—**im-pair′er,** *n.*—**im-pair′ment,** *n.*

im-pale (im-pāl′), *v. t.*; *-paled*, *-paling.* [F. *empaler*, < ML. *impalare*, < L. *in*, in, on, + *palus*, stake, E. *pale*¹.] To fix upon a sharpened stake or the like (as, "His head, crowned in mockery . . . is said to have been *impaled* on the walls of York": Green's "Short Hist. of the Eng. People," vi. 2); pierce with a sharpened stake thrust up through the body, as for torture or punishment; hence, to fix upon, or pierce through with, anything pointed; fig., to render helpless as if pierced through; also, to inclose or surround with or as with pales or stakes; fence in; hem in; hence, to surround or encircle (archaic); also, in *her.*, to display or combine side by side, separated palewise, as two coats of arms on one shield.—**im-pale′ment,** *n.* The act of impaling, or the state of being impaled; also, a paling or inclosure; also, an inclosed space; specif., in *her.*, the impaling of two coats of arms; also, two coats of arms marshaled side by side on one shield.

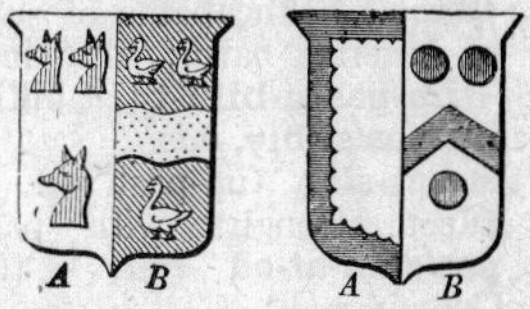

Impalement. — The arms of the wife (*B*) impaled with those of the husband (*A*).

im-pal-pa-ble (im-pal′pạ-bl), *a.* [ML. *impalpabilis.*] Not palpable; incapable of being perceived by the sense of touch; intangible; of powder, so fine that when rubbed between the fingers no grit is perceptible; fig., incapable of being readily grasped by the mind (as, *impalpable* distinctions).—**im-pal-pa-bil′i-ty** (-bil′i-ti), *n.*—**im-pal′pa-bly,** *adv.*

im-pa-nate (im-pā′nāt), *v. t.*; *-nated*, *-nating.* [ML. *impanatus*, pp. of *impanare*, < L. *in*, in, + *panis*, bread.] In *theol.*, to embody in bread. See *impanation.*—**im-pa-na′tion** (-pạ-nā′shọn), *n.* [ML. *impanatio(n-).*] In *theol.*, a local presence or inclusion of the body of Christ in the bread of the eucharist after consecration. Cf. *consubstantiation* and *transubstantiation.*

im-pan-el (im-pan′ẹl), *v. t.*; *-eled* or *-elled*, *-eling* or *-elling.* [AF. *empaneller*, < *em-* (< L. *in*, in) + *panel*, panel.] To enter on a panel or list for jury duty; also, to select (a jury) from the panel.—**im-pan′el-ment,** *n.*

im-par-a-dise (im-par′ạ-dīs), *v. t.*; *-dised*, *-dising.* [See *im-*¹.] To put in or as in paradise; make supremely happy (as, "*imparadised* in one another's arms": Milton's "Paradise Lost," iv. 506); also, to make a paradise of.

im-par-i-pin-nate (im-par-i-pin′āt), *a.* [L. *impar*, unequal, + *pinna*, E. *pinna.*] In *bot.*, unevenly pinnate; pinnate with an odd terminal leaflet; odd-pinnate.

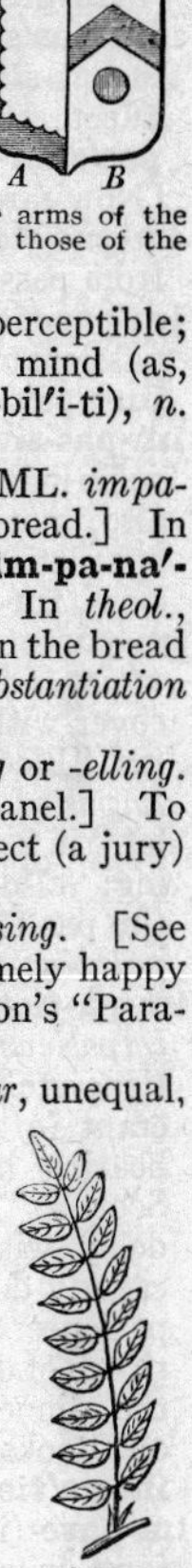
Imparipinnate Leaf.

im-par-i-ty (im-par′i-ti), *n.*; pl. *-ties* (-tiz). [See *im-*².] Lack of parity or equality; disparity; an inequality.

im-park (im-pärk′), *v. t.* [OF. *emparquer*, < *em-* (< L. *in*, in) + *parc*, E. *park.*] To shut up as in a park; also, to inclose as a park.—**im-par-ka′tion** (-pär-kā′shọn), *n.*

im-parl (im-pärl′), *v. i.* [OF. *emparler*, < *em-* (< L. *in*, in) + *parler*, speak, E. *parl.*] To confer† or parley†; in *law*, to confer for amicable adjustment.—**im-par′lance** (-pär′lạns), *n.* Conference†; a parley†; in *law*, a delay granted to a party before pleading, orig. to effect an amicable adjustment; any delay or continuance of a suit, or a petition or leave for such delay.

im-part (im-pärt′), *v.* [OF. *impartir*, < L. *impartire*, < *in*, in, + *partire*, divide: see *part*, *v.*] **I.** *tr.* To grant a part or share of; hence, to give, bestow, or communicate (esp. something immaterial, as a condition, quality, etc.); also, to make known, tell, or relate (as, "I came to *impart* a secret to you": Congreve's "Way of the World," ii.). **II.** *intr.* To grant a part or share; give: as, "He that hath two coats, let him *impart* to him that hath none" (Luke, iii. 11).—**im-par-ta′tion** (-pär-tā′shọn), *n.*—**im-part′er,** *n.*

im-par-tial (im-pär′shạl), *a.* [See *im-*².] Not partial; unbiased; fair; just.—**im-par-ti-al′i-ty** (-shi-al′i-ti), **im-par′tial-ness,** *n.*—**im-par′tial-ly,** *adv.*

im-par-ti-ble¹ (im-pär′ti-bl), *a.* [LL. *impartibilis.*] Not partible; indivisible.—**im-par-ti-bil′i-ty**¹ (-bil′i-ti), *n.*

im-par-ti-ble² (im-pär′ti-bl), *a.* Capable of being imparted; communicable.—**im-par-ti-bil′i-ty**² (-bil′i-ti), *n.*

im-part-ment (im-pärt′mẹnt), *n.* The act of imparting; also, a communication or disclosure.

im-pass-a-ble (im-pȧs′ạ-bl), *a.* [See *im-*².] Not passable; that cannot be passed over, through, or along: as, "The roads, which were difficult before, were now quite *impassable*" (Defoe's "Robinson Crusoe," i. 19).—**im-pass-a-bil′i-ty** (-bil′i-ti), **im-pass′a-ble-ness,** *n.*—**im-pass′a-bly,** *adv.*

im-passe (im-pȧs′, F. aṅ-päs), *n.*; pl. *impasses* (im-pȧs′ez, F. aṅ-päs). [F., < *im-* (< L. *in-*), not, + *passer*, E. *pass*, *v.*] A road or way that has no outlet; fig., a position from which there is no escape.

im-pas-si-ble (im-pas′i-bl), *a.* [LL. *impassibilis*: cf. *passible.*] Incapable of suffering or pain; also, incapable of suffering harm; also, incapable of emotion; impassive. —**im-pas-si-bil′i-ty** (-bil′i-ti), **im-pas′si-ble-ness,** *n.*—**im-pas′si-bly,** *adv.*

im-pas-sion (im-pash′ọn), *v. t.* [See *im-*¹.] To fill, or affect strongly, with passion.—**im-pas′sion-ate**¹, **im-pas′sion-at-ed** (-ạt, -ā-ted), *a.* Impassioned; ardent. [Now rare.]

im-pas-sion-ate² (im-pash′ọn-ạt), *a.* [See *im-*².] Free from passion; dispassionate. [Now rare.]

im-pas-sioned (im-pash′ọnd), *p. a.* Filled with passion; passionate; vehement; ardent.—**im-pas′sioned-ly,** *adv.*—**im-pas′sioned-ness,** *n.*

im-pas-sive (im-pas′iv), *a.* [See *im-*².] Not subject to suffering; hence, insensible or unconscious; also, inanimate; also, not susceptible of injury; also, without emotion; apathetic; unmoved.—**im-pas′sive-ly,** *adv.*—**im-pas′sive-ness, im-pas-siv′i-ty** (-pa-siv′i-ti), *n.*

im-paste (im-pāst′), *v. t.*; *-pasted, -pasting.* [It. *impastare*, < *im-* (< L. *in*, in) + *pasta*, < LL. *pasta*, E. *paste.*] To cover with or inclose in a paste; also, to form into a paste (as, "Blood of fathers, mothers, daughters, sons, Baked and *impasted* with the parching streets": Shakspere's "Hamlet," ii. 2. 481); also, to lay on thickly the colors of, in painting; also, to lay on thickly, as paste.—**im-pas-ta-tion** (im-pas-tā′shọn), *n.*—**im-pas-to** (im-pȧs′tō), *n.* [It.] In *painting*, the laying on of colors thickly; also, color so laid on.

im-pa-tient (im-pā′shẹnt), *a.* [OF. F. *impatient*, < L. *impatiens* (*-ent-*).] Not patient; not bearing pain, opposition, etc., with composure; wanting in endurance; intolerant (*of*: as, "The knight . . . became . . . *impatient* of hearing his misery made . . . the ground of proverbs," Scott's "Talisman," xxii.); often, that does not endure delay with composure; restless in desire or expectation; eagerly desirous (to do something); also, indicating lack of patience (as, an *impatient* answer); attended with impatience of delay (as, "the five or six *impatient* minutes before the dinner is quite ready": Lamb's "Detached Thoughts on Books and Reading").—**im-pa′tience** (-shẹns), *n.*—**im-pa′tient-ly,** *adv.*

im-pave (im-pāv′), *v. t.*; *-paved, -paving.* [See *im-*¹.] To form in a pavement. See Wordsworth's "On Revisiting Dunolly Castle."

im-pav-id (im-pav′id), *a.* [L. *impavidus*: cf. *pavid.*] Fearless; undaunted.—**im-pav′id-ly,** *adv.*

im-pawn (im-pân′), *v. t.* [See *im-*¹.] To put in pawn; pledge. See Shakspere's "1 Henry IV.," iv. 3. 108.

im-pay-able (aṅ-pā-yäbl), *a.* [F.] Priceless; invaluable; hence, extraordinary.

im-peach (im-pēch′), *v. t.* [OF. *empechier* (F. *empêcher*), hinder, < LL. *impedicare*, catch, entangle, < L. *in*, in, + *pedica*, fetter, < *pes*, foot.] To hinder†; also, to affect injuriously†; also, to call in question, or cast an imputation upon (as, to *impeach* a person's motives; "a conclusive proof of accuracy wrongly *impeached*," W. De Morgan's "Alice-for-Short," ix.); challenge the credibility of (as, to *impeach* a witness); also, to bring an accusation against; charge with wrong-doing (as, "I *impeach* thee of treason": Scott's "Talisman," xxiv.); specif., to accuse (a public official), before a competent tribunal, of misconduct in office.—**im-peach′,** *n.* Impeachment: as, "It is war's prize to take all 'vantages; And ten to one is no *impeach* of valour" (Shakspere's "3 Henry VI.," i. 4. 60).—**im-peach′a-ble,** *a.* Liable to be impeached; rendering one liable to impeachment, as an offense.—**im-peach-a-bil′i-ty** (-bil′i-ti), *n.*—**im-peach′er,** *n.*—**im-peach′ment,** *n.* The act of impeaching, or the state of being impeached; specif., the impeaching of a public official before a competent tribunal.

im-pearl (im-pėrl′), *v. t.* [See *im-*¹.] To form into pearl-like drops (as, "Dew-drops, which the sun *Impearls* on every leaf and every flower": Milton's "Paradise Lost," v. 747); also, to make pearl-like or pearly; also, to adorn with pearls or pearl-like drops (as, "Proud be the rose, with rains and dews Her head *impearling*": Wordsworth's "To the Daisy"). [Poetic.]

im-pec-ca-ble (im-pek′ạ-bl), *a.* [L. *impeccabilis*: cf. *peccable.*] Not liable to sin; exempt from the possibility of doing wrong; also, in general, faultless or irreproachable (as, *impeccable* manners; an *impeccable* appearance; "He was an *impeccable* young man, and the avowed delight of his tailor," Arnold Bennett's "Helen with the High Hand," x.).—**im-pec-ca-bil′i-ty** (-bil′i-ti), *n.*—**im-pec′ca-bly,** *adv.*

im-pec-cant (im-pek′ạnt), *a.* [See *im-*² and *peccant.*] Not sinning; sinless; unerring.—**im-pec′can-cy,** *n.*

im-pe-cu-ni-ous (im-pẹ-kū′ni-us), *a.* [See *im-*² and *pecunious.*] Having no money; penniless; poor: as, "Certainly an *impecunious* Subaltern was not a catch" (Kipling's "Post That Fitted").—**im-pe-cu-ni-os′i-ty** (-os′i-ti), *n.*—**im-pe-cu′ni-ous-ly,** *adv.*

im-ped-ance (im-pē′dạns), *n.* In *elect.*, the apparent resistance, or total opposition to current, of an alternating-current circuit, consisting of two components, reactance and true or ohmic resistance.

im-pede (im-pēd′), *v. t.*; *-peded, -peding.* [L. *impedire* (pp. *impeditus*), entangle, hamper, orig. as to the feet, < *in*, in, + *pes* (*ped-*), foot: cf. *expedite.*] To retard in movement or progress by means of obstacles or hindrances, or as obstacles or hindrances do; obstruct; hinder: as, "It is one of the principal tenets of the Utilitarians that sentiment and eloquence serve only to *impede* the pursuit of truth" (Macaulay's "Essays," Mill on Government). —**im-ped′er** (-pē′dėr), *n.*—**im-pe′di-ent** (-pē′di-ẹnt), *a.* [L. *impediens* (*-ent-*), ppr. of *impedire.*] Impeding; hindering.

im-ped-i-ment (im-ped′i-mẹnt), *n.* [L. *impedimentum* (pl. *-ta*), < *impedire*, E. *impede.*] Obstruction or hindrance; also, an obstacle; a hindrance; also, a physical or bodily defect, now only a defect which prevents distinct speech (as, "They bring unto him one that was deaf, and had an *impediment* in his speech": Mark, vii. 32); also (usually in *pl.*), baggage, esp. of an army; impedimenta. —**im-ped-i-men′ta** (-men′tạ), *n. pl.* [L.] Things which impede or encumber progress, as baggage; *milit.*, supplies carried along with an army.—**im-ped-i-men′tal, im-ped-i-men′ta-ry** (-tạ-ri), *a.* Of the nature of an impediment; impeditive.

im-ped-ing (im-pē′ding), *p. a.* That impedes; obstructing; hindering.—**im-ped′ing-ly,** *adv.*

im-ped-i-tive (im-ped′i-tiv), *a.* Tending to impede; obstructive; hindering.

im-pel (im-pel′), *v. t.*; *-pelled, -pelling.* [L. *impellere* (pp. *impulsus*), < *in*, in, on, + *pellere*, drive.] To drive, or cause to move, onward (as, "The wave behind *impels* the wave before": Dryden's tr. Ovid's "Metamorphoses," xv. 271); propel; impart motion to; fig., to constrain to, or to do, something, as by acting on the mind (as, "I cannot tell what *impels* me to speak thus boldly": Scott's "Fair Maid of Perth," xxxi.); incite.—**im-pel′lent. I.** *a.* Impelling. **II.** *n.* An impelling agency or force.—**im-pel′ler,** *n.*

im-pend (im-pend′), *v. i.* [L. *impendere*, < *in*, in, on, + *pendere*, hang.] To hang or be suspended (*over*); overhang; fig., to hang or hover (*over*) as if about to fall, as evil or danger (as, "Destruction sure o'er all your heads *impends*": Pope's tr. Homer's "Odyssey," ii.); hence, to be about to happen, be imminent, or be near at hand (as, "I saw, alas! some dread event *impend*," Pope's "Rape of the Lock," i. 109; "Now the same glad task *Impends*," Akenside's "Pleasures of Imagination," ii. 68).—**im-pend′ent,** *a.* Impending.—**im-pend′ence, im-pend′en-cy,** *n.*—**im-pend′ing,** *p. a.* Overhanging (as, "Aquiline his nose, And overbuilt with most *impending* brows": Cowper's "Task," iii. 193); fig., about to fall or happen; imminent.

im-pen-e-tra-bil-i-ty (im-pen″ẹ̄-trạ-bil′i-ti), *n.* Impenetrable quality; in *physics*, that property of matter in virtue of which two bodies cannot occupy the same space at the same time.

im-pen-e-tra-ble (im-pen′ẹ̄-trạ-bl), *a.* [L. *impenetrabilis.*] Not penetrable; that cannot be penetrated, pierced, or entered; fig., inaccessible to ideas, influences, etc., as persons; also, incapable of being comprehended, inscrutable, or unfathomable (as, "an *impenetrable* mystery that mocked investigation": George Eliot's "Silas Marner," x.); in *physics*, of a body, excluding all other bodies from the space it occupies.—**im-pen′e-tra-ble-ness,** *n.*—**im-pen′e-tra-bly,** *adv.*

im-pen-e-trate (im-pen′ẹ̄-trāt), *v. t.*; *-trated, -trating.* [See *im-*¹.] To penetrate within; permeate.—**im-pen-e-tra′tion** (-trā′shọn), *n.*

im-pen-i-tent (im-pen′i-tẹnt), *a.* [LL. *impænitens* (*-ent-*).] Not penitent; having no contrition for sin; obdurate.—**im-pen′i-tence, im-pen′i-ten-cy,** *n.*—**im-pen′i-tent-ly,** *adv.*

im-pen-nate (im-pen′āt), *a.* [See *im-*² and *pennate.*] Featherless or wingless; specif., having short wings covered with scale-like feathers, as the penguins.

im-per-a-tive (im-per′ạ-tiv). [L. *imperativus,* < *imperare,* command: see *empire.*] **I.** *a.* Of the nature of or expressing a command; commanding; peremptory; also, not to be avoided or evaded (as, an *imperative* duty; *imperative* necessity); obligatory; urgent; in *gram.*, noting or pertaining to that mode of the verb which expresses command, exhortation, advice, or entreaty. **II.** *n.* Something imperative; a command; in *gram.*, the imperative mode, or a verb-form belonging to it.—**im-per-a-ti′val** (-tī′vạl), *a.*—**im-per′a-tive-ly,** *adv.*—**im-per′a-tive-ness,** *n.*

im-pe-ra-tor (im-pẹ-rā′tọr), *n.* [L.: see *emperor.*] Orig., a Roman military commander; later, the Roman emperor; hence, an absolute or supreme ruler; also, a gastropod of the genus *Imperator* (family *Turbinidæ*).—**im-per-a-to′ri-al** (-per-ạ-tō′ri-ạl), *a.*

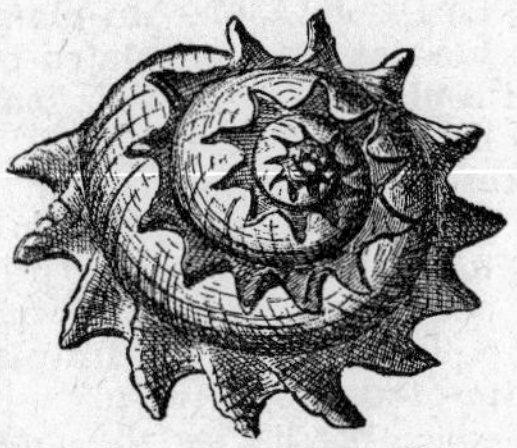

Imperator (*I. imperialis*).

im-per-cep-ti-ble (im-pėr-sep′ti-bl), *a.* [ML. *imperceptibilis.*] Not perceptible; not affecting the perceptive faculties; hence, very slight, gradual, or subtle.—**im-per-cep-ti-bil′i-ty** (-bil′i-ti), **im-per-cep′ti-ble-ness,** *n.*—**im-per-cep′ti-bly,** *adv.*

im-per-cep-tion (im-pėr-sep′shọn), *n.* [See *im-*².] Want of perception.—**im-per-cep′tive,** *a.* Not perceptive; lacking perception.—**im-per-cip′i-ent** (-sip′i-ẹnt), *a.* Not percipient; imperceptive.

im-per-fect (im-pėr′fekt). [L. *imperfectus.*] **I.** *a.* Not perfect; incomplete; defective; in *bot.*, of a flower, wanting certain parts; esp., diclinous; in *gram.*, denoting incompleted action or state, esp. in past time (as, the *imperfect* tense); in *music*, noting the consonances of a normal third and sixth (cf. *perfect*); of an interval, diminished; of a chord or triad, involving a diminished fifth; of a cadence or period, not complete or fully satisfactory. **II.** *n.* In *gram.*, the imperfect tense; a verb-form in this tense, as Latin *amabam,* 'I was loving.'—**im-per-fec′tion** (-fek′shọn), *n.* [LL. *imperfectio*(*n-*).] Lack of perfection; imperfect condition or character; incompleteness; defectiveness; also, a defect or fault (as, "Sent to my account With all my *imperfections* on my head": Shakspere's "Hamlet," i. 5. 79).—**im-per′fect-ly,** *adv.*—**im-per′fect-ness,** *n.*

im-per-fo-rate (im-pėr′fọ-rāt), *a.* [See *im-*².] Not perforate; having no perforation. Also **im-per′fo-rat-ed** (-rā-ted).—**im-per-fo-ra′tion** (-rā′shọn), *n.* Imperforate state.

im-pe-ri-al (im-pē′ri-ạl), *a.* [OF. *imperial* (F. *impérial*), < L. *imperialis,* < *imperium*: see *empire.*] Of or pertaining to an empire, or an emperor or empress; also, of the nature or rank of an emperor or supreme ruler; supreme in authority; also, of a commanding quality, manner, or aspect (as, "The Lily's height bespoke command—A fair *imperial* flow'r": Cowper's "Lily and the Rose"); majestic; sometimes, domineering; imperious; also, befitting an emperor or empress; very fine or grand; magnificent; also, of special size or quality, as various products, commodities, etc.; also, of weights and measures, conforming to the standards legally established in Great Britain.—**Imperial Chamber,** a supreme court of justice of the old German Empire, or Holy Roman Empire, acting for the empire as the Aulic Council acted for the emperor.—**im-pe′ri-al,** *n.* A member of an imperial party or of imperial troops; also, an emperor or empress (as, "I . . . am going with Sir Proteus to the *Imperial's* court": Shakspere's "Two Gentlemen of Verona," ii. 3. 5); also, a Russian gold coin worth 15 rubles; also, the top of a carriage, esp. of a diligence; a case for luggage carried there (as, "The *imperials* were packed, and the post-chariot was at the door": Peacock's "Nightmare Abbey," iii.); also, any of various articles of special size or quality; a size of paper, 23 × 31 inches, in England 22 × 30 inches; also, a small part of the beard left growing beneath the under lip (said to be named from the emperor Napoleon III., who wore an imperial).—**im-pe′ri-al-ism,** *n.* Imperial government; an imperial system of government; also, advocacy of imperial interests; specif., the policy of extending the rule or authority of an empire or nation over foreign countries, or of acquiring and holding colonies and dependencies; also, as in British use, the policy of so uniting the separate parts of an empire with separate governments as to secure for certain purposes practically a single state.—**im-pe′ri-al-ist,** *n.* An adherent of an imperial cause; also, an advocate of imperial rule; also, an advocate of imperialism.—**im-pe″ri-al-is′tic,** *a.*—**im-pe-ri-al′i-ty** (-al′i-ti), *n.*; pl. *-ties* (-tiz). Imperial rank or power; also, one possessing it.—**im-pe′ri-al-ize** (-ạl-īz), *v. t.*; *-ized, -izing.* To make imperial; invest with imperial character or form.—**im-pe″ri-al-i-za′tion** (-i-zā′shọn), *n.*—**im-pe′ri-al-ly,** *adv.*—**im-pe′ri-al-ness,** *n.*

im-per-il (im-per′il), *v. t.*; *-iled* or *-illed, -iling* or *-illing.* [See *im-*¹.] To put in peril; endanger.—**im-per′il-ment,** *n.*

im-pe-ri-ous (im-pē′ri-us), *a.* [L. *imperiosus,* < *imperium*: see *empire.*] Imperial† (as, "*imperious* Cæsar, dead and turn'd to clay": Shakspere's "Hamlet," v. 1. 236); also, domineering, dictatorial, or overbearing (as, "A youthful face, *Imperious,* and of haughtiest lineaments": Tennyson's "Marriage of Geraint," 190); also, urgent, overmastering, or imperative (as, "*imperious* need, which cannot be withstood": Dryden's "Hind and the Panther," iii. 837).—**im-pe′ri-ous-ly,** *adv.*—**im-pe′ri-ous-ness,** *n.*

im-per-ish-a-ble (im-per′ish-ạ-bl), *a.* [See *im-*².] Not perishable; indestructible; enduring.—**im-per″ish-a-bil′i-ty** (-bil′i-ti), **im-per′ish-a-ble-ness,** *n.*—**im-per′ish-a-bly,** *adv.*

im-pe-ri-um (im-pē′ri-um), *n.*; pl. *-ria* (-ri-ạ̈). [L.: see *empire.*] Command; supreme power; empire; specif., in *law,* the right to command the force of the state in order to enforce the law.

im-per-ma-nent (im-pėr′mạ-nẹnt), *a.* [See *im-*².] Not permanent; not enduring; transient.—**im-per′ma-nence, im-per′ma-nen-cy,** *n.*

im-per-me-a-ble (im-pėr′mẹ̄-ạ-bl), *a.* [LL. *impermeabilis.*] Not permeable; impassable; esp., of substances, not permitting the passage of a fluid through the pores, interstices, etc.—**im-per″me-a-bil′i-ty** (-bil′i-ti), **im-per′me-a-ble-ness,** *n.*—**im-per′me-a-bly,** *adv.*

im-per-mis-si-ble (im-pėr-mis′i-bl), *a.* [See *im-*².] Not permissible or allowable.

im-per-son-al (im-pėr′sọn-ạl), *a.* [LL. *impersonalis.*] Not personal; without personal reference or connection (as, an *impersonal* remark); having no personality (as, an *impersonal* deity); in *gram.*, of verbs, constructions, etc., having the non-personal or non-specific subject *it* expressed or understood, as in 'it rains.'—**im-per-son-al′i-ty** (-al′i-ti), *n.*; pl. *-ties* (-tiz). Impersonal character; absence of personal quality; also, an impersonal being or thing.—**im-per′son-al-ly,** *adv.*

im-per-son-ate (im-pėr′sọn-āt), *v. t.*; *-ated, -ating.* [L. *in,* in, + *persona,* E. *person.*] To embody in a person†; hence, to represent in personal or bodily form; personify; typify; also, to assume the character of; personate, esp. on the stage.—**im-per′son-ate,** *a.* Embodied in a person; invested with personality: as, "Love *impersonate*" (Keats's

"Isabella," l.).—**im-per-son-a′tion** (-ā′shọn), *n.* The act of impersonating, or the state of being impersonated; personification; dramatic personation; also, a person or thing impersonating or representing a principle, quality, etc. (as, "the face of a pretty, laughing girl . . . the very *impersonation* of good-humour and blooming beauty": Dickens's "Barnaby Rudge," iv.).—**im-per′son-a-tive** (-ạ-tiv), *a.* That impersonates; pertaining to dramatic impersonation.—**im-per′son-a-tor** (-ā-tọr), *n.* One who impersonates; esp., an actor who impersonates on the stage particular persons or types; a professional mimic.

im-per-ti-nence (im-pėr′ti-nẹns), *n.* Impertinent quality or action; irrelevance; inappropriateness or incongruity; triviality or absurdity; unmannerly intrusion or presumption; presumptuous rudeness of behavior or speech, esp. to a superior; insolence; also, something impertinent; an irrelevance; an incongruity; a triviality; a presumptuous, rude, or insolent act or speech. Also **im-per′ti-nen-cy,** *n.*; pl. *-cies* (-siz).

im-per-ti-nent (im-pėr′ti-nẹnt). [LL. *impertinens* (*-ent-*).] **I.** *a.* Not pertinent or relevant; irrelevant; hence, inappropriate or incongruous; trivial, silly, or absurd; also, intrusive or presumptuous, as persons or their actions; presumptuously rude in behavior or speech, esp. to a superior; insolent or saucy. **II.** *n.* An impertinent person: as, "when an *impertinent* in tragedy . . . breaks in upon the serious passions of the scene" (Lamb's "Stage Illusion"). —**im-per′ti-nent-ly,** *adv.*

im-per-turb-a-ble (im-pėr-tėr′bạ-bl), *a.* [LL. *imperturbabilis.*] Incapable of being perturbed or agitated; not easily excited; calm: as, "A man . . . Cool, and quite English, *imperturbable*" (Byron's "Don Juan," xiii. 14); "*imperturbable* gravity" (Scott's "Talisman," xviii.).—**im-per-turb-a-bil′i-ty** (-bil′i-ti), **im-per-turb′a-ble-ness,** *n.*—**im-per-turb′a-bly,** *adv.*—**im-per-tur-ba′tion** (-tėr-bā′-shọn), *n.* [LL. *imperturbatio(n-).*] Freedom from perturbation; tranquillity; calmness.—**im-per-turbed′,** *a.* Not perturbed; undisturbed; calm.

im-per-vi-a-ble (im-pėr′vi-ạ-bl), *a.* Impervious.

im-per-vi-ous (im-pėr′vi-us), *a.* [L. *impervius.*] Not pervious; impassable; impermeable; fig., impenetrable (as, "He was no more *impervious* than others to Miltoun's caustic, thinly-veiled contempt for the commonplace": Galsworthy's "Patrician," ii. 5).—**im-per′vi-ous-ly,** *adv.*—**im-per′vi-ous-ness,** *n.*

im-pe-ti-go (im-pē-tī′gō), *n.* [L., < *impetere,* attack: see *impetus.*] In *pathol.*, a skin disease marked by small pustules.—**im-pe-tig′i-nous** (-tij′i-nus), *a.*

im-pe-trate (im′pē-trāt), *v. t.*; *-trated, -trating.* [L. *impetratus,* pp. of *impetrare,* < *in,* in, + *patrare,* bring to pass.] To obtain by entreaty; also, to entreat, or ask urgently for (as, "a slight testimonial, sir, which I thought fit to *impetrate* from that worthy nobleman": Scott's "Rob Roy," ix.).—**im-pe-tra′tion** (-trā′shọn), *n.*

im-pet-u-os-i-ty (im-pet-ū-os′i-ti), *n.*; pl. *-ties* (-tiz). Impetuous quality or character; violence; sudden or rash energy; also, an impetuous action.

im-pet-u-ous (im-pet′ū-us), *a.* [LL. *impetuosus,* < L. *impetus*: see *impetus.*] Having great impetus; moving with great force; violent; also, acting with or characterized by sudden or rash energy; passionate; ardent.—**im-pet′u-ous-ly,** *adv.*—**im-pet′u-ous-ness,** *n.*

im-pe-tus (im′pē-tus), *n.* [L., < *impetere,* rush upon, attack, < *in,* in, on, + *petere,* fall on, rush at, seek.] The force with which a moving body tends to maintain its velocity and overcome resistance; energy of motion; hence, moving force; impulse; stimulus.

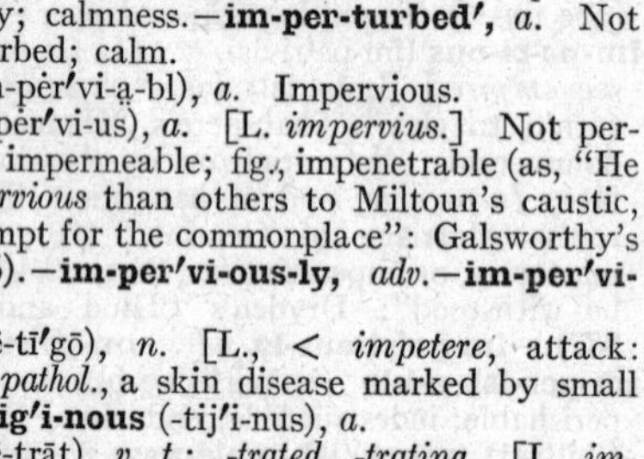

Impeyan Pheasant (*Lophophorus impeyanus*).

Im-pey-an (im′pi-ạn) **pheas′ant.** [Named (1787) from Sir E. or Lady *Impey,* who tried to bring living specimens of the bird to England.] An East Indian pheasant, *Lophophorus impeyanus,* the male of which has remarkably brilliant plumage; sometimes, any of certain related species. See cut in preceding column.

im-pi (im′pi), *n.* [Zulu.] A band of Kafir warriors.

im-pic-ture (im-pik′tūr), *v. t.*; *-tured, -turing.* [See *im-*¹.] To represent as in a picture: as, "like passing clouds *impictured* on thy breast" (Coleridge's "Lines to a Beautiful Spring").

im-pi-e-ty (im-pī′ẹ-ti), *n.*; pl. *-ties* (-tiz). [L. *impietas.*] Lack of piety; want of reverence for God; ungodliness; wickedness; also, an impious or ungodly act, practice, etc.; also, lack of dutifulness or respect, as toward parents (as, filial *impiety*).

im-pig-no-rate (im-pig′nọ-rāt), *v. t.*; *-rated, -rating.* [ML. *impignoratus,* pp. of *impignorare,* < L. *in,* in, + *pignus* (*pignor-*), a pledge.] To pledge; pawn. [Chiefly Sc.] —**im-pig-no-ra′tion** (-rā′shọn), *n.*

im-pinge (im-pinj′), *v. i.*; *-pinged, -pinging.* [L. *impingere* (pp. *impactus*), drive in or at, strike against, < *in,* in, on, + *pangere,* fix, drive in.] To strike or dash (*on, upon,* or *against*); collide; also, to encroach or infringe (*on* or *upon*: as, "Heaven forbid that I should do aught that might . . . *impinge* upon the right of my kinsman," Scott's "Waverley," xiv.).—**im-pinge′ment,** *n.*

im-pi-ous (im′pi-us), *a.* [L. *impius.*] Not pious; wanting in reverence for God; ungodly; irreligious; wicked; profane.—**im′pi-ous-ly,** *adv.*—**im′pi-ous-ness,** *n.*

imp-ish (im′pish), *a.* Like, or characteristic of, an imp; mischievous.—**imp′ish-ly,** *adv.*—**imp′ish-ness,** *n.*

im-pla-ca-ble (im-plā′kạ-bl), *a.* [L. *implacabilis.*] Not placable, not to be appeased or pacified, or inexorable (as, an *implacable* enemy; *implacable* malice); also, not to be assuaged† (as, "Pain *Implacable*": Milton's "Paradise Lost," vi. 658).—**im-pla-ca-bil′i-ty** (-bil′i-ti), **im-pla′ca-ble-ness,** *n.*—**im-pla′ca-bly,** *adv.*

im-pla-cen-tal (im-plạ-sen′tạl), *a.* [See *im-*².] In *zoöl.*, having no placenta.

im-plant (im-plant′), *v. t.* [F. *implanter,* < L. *in,* in, + *plantare,* E. *plant, v.*] To plant in something; infix; hence, to instil or inculcate (principles, opinions, etc.); also, to plant (ground, etc.) with something.—**im-plan-ta′tion** (-plan-tā′shọn), *n.*—**im-plant′er,** *n.*

im-plau-si-ble (im-plâ′zi-bl), *a.* [See *im-*².] Not plausible; not having the appearance of truth or credibility.—**im-plau′si-bly,** *adv.*

im-pleach (im-plēch′), *v. t.* [See *im-*¹ and *pleach.*] To interweave. See Shakspere's "Lover's Complaint," 205. [Poetic.]

im-plead (im-plēd′), *v. t.* [OF. *emplaidier,* < *em-* (< L. *in,* in) + *plaidier,* E. *plead.*] To sue in a court of justice; also, to accuse; impeach; also, to plead (a suit, etc.). [Now rare.]

im-pledge (im-plej′), *v. t.*; *-pledged, -pledging.* [See *im-*¹.] To pledge.

im-ple-ment (im′plẹ-mẹnt), *n.* [LL. *implementum,* a filling up (hence, prob., a thing that completes, or supplies a want), < L. *implere*: see *impletion.*] An article of equipment or outfit; an article of household furniture, wearing apparel, etc.; now, usually, an instrument, tool, or utensil (as, "The *implements* of Scottish fray, The buckler, lance, and brand," Scott's "Marmion," iii. 3; agricultural *implements*); fig., an instrument, agent, or tool (as, "This old man was a most useful *implement* to us everywhere": Defoe's "Robinson Crusoe," ii. 13); also, fulfilment, performance, or execution, as of a contract (Sc.).—**im′ple-ment** (-ment), *v. t.* To provide with implements; also (chiefly Sc.), to fulfil or carry out, as an engagement, agreement, etc.; execute, as a piece of work; satisfy, as requirements or conditions; fill out or supplement.—**im-ple-men′tal** (-men′tạl), *a.*

im-ple-tion (im-plē′shọn), *n.* [LL. *impletio(n-),* < L. *implere,* fill up, < *in,* in, + *plere,* fill.] The act of filling; the state of being filled.

im-pli-cate (im′pli-kāt), *v. t.*; *-cated, -cating.* [L. *implicatus,* pp. of *implicare,* infold, entangle, involve, < *in,* in, + *plicare,* fold: cf. *imply* and *employ.*] To fold or twist together, one thing or part within another; intertwine, interlace, or entangle (as, "The meeting boughs and *implicated* leaves Wove twilight o'er the Poet's path": Shelley's "Alastor," 426); also, to imply as a necessary circumstance, or as something to be inferred or understood; also, to involve as being concerned in a matter, affair, condition, etc. (as, to be *implicated* in a crime or a scandal; the disease may *implicate* various organs).—**im′pli-cate,** *n.* A thing implied.—**im-pli-ca′tion** (-kā′shǫn), *n.* [L. *implicatio(n-)*.] The act of implicating, intertwining, or entangling, or the resulting condition; also, the act of implying, or the state of being implied (as, to admit a thing by *implication* rather than by express statement); something implied, or suggested as naturally to be inferred, without being expressly stated; also, the act of involving or the state of being involved in some matter, condition of affairs, etc. (as, to acquit one of the charge of *implication* in a conspiracy).—**im′pli-ca-tive** (-kā-tiv), *a.* Tending to implicate or imply; characterized by or involving implication.

im-pli-cit (im-plis′it), *a.* [L. *implicitus*, var. of *implicatus*, pp. of *implicare*: see *implicate*.] Intertwined† or entangled† (as, "Th' humble shrub, And bush with frizzled hair *implicit*": Milton's "Paradise Lost," vii. 323); also, implied, rather than expressly stated (as, an *implicit* consent: cf. *explicit*); tacitly included or understood; virtually contained (*in*); existing in the mind without being clearly formulated, as ideas or feelings; also, of faith, involved in the general belief of the church, rather than proper to the individual; hence, in general, of faith, belief, confidence, obedience, etc., unquestioning, unreserved, or absolute; of persons, blindly credulous or obedient†.—**im-pli′cit-ly,** *adv.*—**im-pli′cit-ness,** *n.*

im-plied (im-plīd′), *p. a.* [See *imply*.] Involved, indicated, or suggested by implying; so indicated as naturally to be inferred, though without express statement (as, an *implied* contract; an *implied* rebuke); tacitly understood.—**im-pli′ed-ly** (-plī′ed-li), *adv.* By implication, rather than expressly.

im-plode (im-plōd′), *v. i.*; *-ploded, -ploding.* [From *im-*[1] + *-plode* as in *explode*.] To burst inward: opposed to *explode*.

im-plo-ra-tion (im-plǫ-rā′shǫn), *n.* [L. *imploratio(n-)*.] The act of imploring; earnest supplication; beseechment. —**im-plor′a-to-ry** (-plōr′ą-tǫ-ri), *a.* Imploring; beseeching.

im-plore (im-plōr′), *v.*; *-plored, -ploring.* [L. *implorare*, < *in*, in, on, + *plorare*, cry out, wail.] **I.** *tr.* To call upon (a person, a deity, etc.) in urgent or piteous supplication, as for aid or mercy; beseech; entreat earnestly (to do something); also, to make urgent supplication for (aid, mercy, pardon, etc.). **II.** *intr.* To make urgent or piteous supplication.—**im-plor′er** (-plōr′ėr), *n.*—**im-plor′ing-ly,** *adv.*—**im-plor′ing-ness,** *n.*

im-plo-sion (im-plō′zhǫn), *n.* [From *im-*[1] + *-plosion* as in *explosion*.] A bursting inward: opposed to *explosion*.

im-plu-vi-um (im-plö′vi-um), *n.*; pl. *-via* (-vi-ä). [L., < *impluere*, rain in, < *in*, in, + *pluere*, rain.] In ancient Roman houses, a rectangular basin or tank in the middle of the atrium or hall, for receiving the rain-water from an opening (the compluvium) in the roof above.

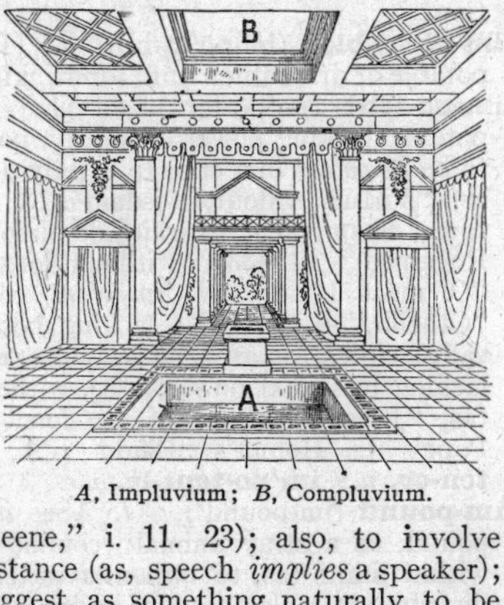

A, Impluvium; *B*, Compluvium.

im-ply (im-plī′), *v. t.*; *-plied, -plying.* [OF. *emplier*, < L. *implicare*, infold, entangle, involve: see *implicate*, and cf. *employ*.] To infold†, inwrap†, or entangle† (as, "Striving to loose the knott . . . Himselfe in streighter bandes too rash *implyes*": Spenser's "Faerie Queene," i. 11. 23); also, to involve as a necessary circumstance (as, speech *implies* a speaker); also, to indicate or suggest, as something naturally to be inferred, without express statement (as, "Your smooth eulogium, to one crown address'd, Seems to *imply* a censure on the rest," Cowper's "Table Talk," 92: opposed to *express*); express indirectly, or insinuate; also, of words, to signify or mean.

im-pol-i-cy (im-pol′i-si), *n.* [See *im-*[2].] Bad policy; inexpediency: as, "The danger and the *impolicy* of such pledges were very clearly shown by the event" (Lecky's "Hist. of Eng. in the 18th Century," i.).

im-po-lite (im-pǫ-līt′), *a.* [L. *impolitus*.] Unpolished, as of surface†; fig., without refinement or elegance†; now, not polite or courteous; uncivil; rude.—**im-po-lite′ly,** *adv.* —**im-po-lite′ness,** *n.*

im-pol-i-tic (im-pol′i-tik), *a.* [See *im-*[2].] Not politic; inexpedient; injudicious: as, "a provision as *impolitic* as it was barbarous" (Lecky's "Hist. of Eng. in the 18th Century," i.).—**im-pol′i-tic-ly,** *adv.*

im-pon-der-a-ble (im-pon′dėr-ą-bl). [See *im-*[2].] **I.** *a.* Not ponderable; that cannot be weighed; without appreciable weight: formerly used esp. of heat, light, electricity, etc., on the supposition that they were material substances, but now chiefly of moral forces or agencies. **II.** *n.* An imponderable thing, force, or agency.—**im-pon″der-a-bil′i-ty** (-bil′i-ti), **im-pon′der-a-ble-ness,** *n.*—**im-pon′der-a-bly,** *adv.*

im-pon-der-ous (im-pon′dėr-us), *a.* [See *im-*[2].] Not ponderous; imponderable.

im-pone† (im-pōn′), *v. t.*; *-poned, -poning.* [L. *imponere* (pp. *impositus*), < *in*, in, on, + *ponere*, place, put: cf. *impose*.] To impose, or place on something; also, to stake or wager (see Shakspere's "Hamlet," v. 2. 155).—**im-po′nent** (-pō′nęnt). **I.** *a.* That imposes. **II.** *n.* One who imposes.

im-port (im-pōrt′), *v.* [L. *importare*, bring in, bring about, occasion, cause, < *in*, in, + *portare*, carry. Some E. senses come through F. *importer*, be of consequence, matter, signify.] **I.** *tr.* To bring in; introduce from without or abroad (as, "Others *import* yet nobler arts from France": Pope's "Dunciad," iv. 597); esp., to bring in from a foreign country, as merchandise or commodities, for sale or use; also, to convey as a meaning or implication, as words, statements, actions, etc., do; mean, signify, betoken, or imply; make known or express; also, to be of consequence or importance to (as, "It doth *import* him much to speak with me": Shakspere's "Troilus and Cressida," iv. 2. 52); concern; hence, to behoove (as, "Yet first, let me say . . . what it *imports* thee to know": Scott's "Ivanhoe," xxxi.). **II.** *intr.* To be of consequence or importance; matter.—**im′port,** *n.* The act of importing or bringing in; importation, as of merchandise from abroad; that which is imported from abroad; an imported commodity or article; also, meaning, implication, or purport (as, "There's letters from my mother: what the *import* is, I know not yet": Shakspere's "All's Well," ii. 3. 294); significance; also, consequence or importance (as, matters of great *import*).—**im-port′a-ble,** *a.* That may be imported.

im-por-tance (im-pôr′tąns), *n.* [F. *importance*, < ML. *importantia*.] The quality or fact of being important; significance, consequence, or moment; notable character; important position or standing; personal or social consequence; consequential air or manner; also, an important matter†; also, importunity† (as, "At our *importance* hither is he come": Shakspere's "King John," ii. 1. 7); also, import† or meaning† (see Shakspere's "Winter's Tale," v. 2. 20).

im-por-tant (im-pôr′tąnt), *a.* [F. *important*, < ML. *importans (-ant-)*, ppr. of *importare*, be of consequence, L. bring in, cause: see *import*.] Of much significance or consequence (as, an *important* event, circumstance, or decision; "The great, the *important* day, big with the fate Of Cato and of Rome," Addison's "Cato," i. 1); having great consequences, momentous, or weighty; mattering much (*to*: as, details *important* to a clear understanding of the case); hence, of more than ordinary title to consideration or notice, as for character, merit, interest, etc. (as, an *important* subject, book, or discovery; an *important* example of a painter's work); noteworthy or notable; prominent (as, an *important* character or part in a play); also, of considerable influence or authority, as a person, official, committee, position or office, etc.; influential; also, of social consequence or distinction, as a personage, family, etc.; also, consequential, pompous, or self-important (as, "*important* triflers," Cowper's "Conversation," 250; an *important* air or manner); also, importunate† (as, "If the prince be too *important*, tell him there is measure in every thing": Shakspere's "Much Ado about Nothing," ii. 1. 74).—**im-por′tant-ly,** *adv.*

im-por-ta-tion (im-pọr-tā′shọn), *n.* The act of importing or bringing in, as from abroad; esp., the bringing in of merchandise or commodities from foreign countries, for sale or use; also, something imported (as, the book is a recent *importation*).

im-port-er (im-pōr′tėr), *n.* One who imports; esp., a merchant or a mercantile house that imports goods from foreign countries.

im-por-tu-nate (im-pôr′tū-nāt), *a.* [L. *importunus*: see *importune, a.*] Inopportune†; also, troublesome†; also, urgent or persistent in solicitation (as, "*Importunate* hours . . . Each clamorous with its own sharp need": Whittier's "Snow-Bound"); pertinacious, as solicitations or demands. —**im-por′tu-na-cy** (-nā-si), **im-por′tu-nate-ness,** *n.*—**im-por′tu-nate-ly,** *adv.*

im-por-tune (im-pôr-tūn′ or -pôr′tūn), *a.* [OF. F. *importun*, < L. *importunus*, unfit, inconvenient, troublesome: cf. *opportune*.] Inopportune† or unseasonable†; also, troublesome† or grievous†; also, importunate, persistent in solicitation, or pertinacious (now rare: as, "the *importune* tempter," Milton's "Paradise Regained," ii. 404).—**im-por-tune′,** *v.*; *-tuned, -tuning.* [F. *importuner*, < ML. *importunari*, < L. *importunus*.] **I.** *tr.* To trouble† or annoy† (as, "Nicholas the Fifth, the last [pope] who was *importuned* by the presence of a Roman emperor": Gibbon's "Decline and Fall of the Roman Empire," lxx.); also, to harass or beset (a person, etc.) with solicitations; beg urgently or persistently (as, to *importune* one for money; to *importune* one to consent); also, to beg for (something) urgently or persistently. **II.** *intr.* To make urgent or persistent solicitations.—**im-por-tun′er** (-tū′nėr), *n.*—**im-por-tu′ni-ty** (-tū′ni-ti), *n.*; pl. *-ties* (-tiz). [OF. *importunite* (F. *importunité*), < L. *importunitas*.] The state of being importune or importunate; persistence in solicitation; *pl.*, importunate solicitations or demands.

im-pos-a-ble (im-pō′zạ-bl), *a.* That may be imposed.

im-pose (im-pōz′), *v.*; *-posed, -posing.* [OF. F. *imposer*, < *im-* (< L. *in*, in, on) + *poser*, put (see *pose*[1]), but associated with derivatives of L. *imponere*: see *imposition*.] **I.** *tr.* To put or place on something, or in a particular place (obs. or archaic); hence, to lay on (the hands) ceremonially, as in confirmation or ordination; also, to put or set by or as by authority (as, to *impose* a name on a place; to *impose* an arbitrary meaning or construction upon words); esp., to lay on or set as something to be borne, endured, obeyed, fulfilled, etc. (as, to *impose* taxes, penalties, laws, or tasks; to *impose* one's authority or opinions upon others); inflict or force (*on* or *upon*); obtrude or thrust (one's self, one's company, etc.) upon others; pass or palm off fraudulently or deceptively (as, "My son is either married, or going to be so, to this lady, whom he *imposed* upon me as his sister": Goldsmith's "Good-Natured Man," v.); also, to subject to some penalty, etc. (now rare: as, "*Impose* me to what penance your invention Can lay upon my sin," Shakspere's "Much Ado about Nothing," v. 1. 283); in *printing*, to lay (type-pages, etc.) in proper order on an imposing-stone or the like and secure in a chase for printing. **II.** *intr.* To impose one's or its authority or influence, esp. on the mind (as, "When it [truth] is found, it *imposeth* upon men's thoughts": Bacon's "Essays," Of Truth); make an impression on the mind (see *imposing*); also, to obtrude one's self or one's requirements, as upon others; presume, as upon patience, good nature, etc.; also, to pass off something fraudulent, as upon a person; perpetrate some fraud or deception (*upon* or *on*); of something fraudulent, to produce a false impression or act with a delusive effect (*upon* or *on*).—**im-pos′er** (-pō′zėr), *n.*—**im-pos′ing,** *p. a.* That imposes; making an impression on the mind, as by great size, stately appearance or dignity, etc.—**im-pos′ing-ly,** *adv.* —**im-pos′ing-ness,** *n.*—**im-pos′ing=stone,** *n.* In *printing*, a slab, orig. of carefully leveled stone but now often of metal, resting upon a frame, on which pages of type or plates are imposed, and on which type-correcting in the page is done.—**im-pos′ing=ta″ble,** *n.* In *printing*, an imposing-stone.

im-po-si-tion (im-pọ-zish′ọn), *n.* [L. *impositio(n-)*, < *imponere*, place or put upon, impose: see *impone* and *impose*.] The act of putting, placing, or laying on, esp. the ceremonial laying on of hands, as in confirmation; also, the act of imposing by or as by authority; the laying on of something as a burden, obligation, etc. (as, the *imposition* of taxes or laws); something imposed, as a tax, duty, or impost; a task; a charge† or injunction† (see Shakspere's "Merchant of Venice," iii. 4. 33); also, an imposing upon a person as by taking undue advantage of his good nature, or something that has the effect of doing this (as, this demand is a downright *imposition*); also, the act of imposing fraudulently or deceptively on others; a passing off of something false as genuine or true; an imposture.

im-pos-si-bil-i-ty (im-pos-i-bil′i-ti), *n.*; pl. *-ties* (-tiz). The quality of being impossible; also, something impossible.

im-pos-si-ble (im-pos′i-bl), *a.* [L. *impossibilis*.] Not possible; that cannot be, exist, or happen (as, an *impossible* monster; an accident that had seemed *impossible*); that cannot be done or effected (as, "Few things are *impossible* to diligence and skill": Johnson's "Rasselas," xii.); that cannot be true, as a rumor or story; also, not to be done, endured, tolerated, etc., with any degree of reason or propriety (as, an *impossible* performance or situation; an *impossible* match or suitor); utterly impracticable; intolerable; hopelessly unsuitable, undesirable, or objectionable (as, an *impossible* hat; an *impossible* person).—**im-pos′si-bly,** *adv.*

im-post (im′pōst), *n.* [In part, OF. *impost* (F. *impôt*), < ML. *impostus*, a tax, < L. *imponere*, impose (see *impone*); in part, F. *imposte*, < It. *imposta*, architectural impost, from the same L. source.] A tax, tribute, or duty; esp., a customs-duty; also, in *arch.*, the uppermost part of a column, etc., on which the end of an arch rests.

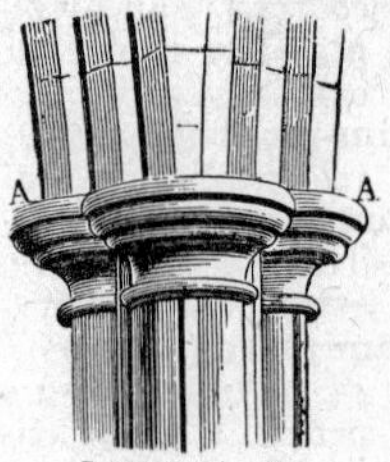

Impost (*A, A*).

im-pos-tor (im-pos′tọr), *n.* [LL., < L. *imponere*, impose: see *impone*.] One who imposes fraudulently upon others; a deceiver or cheat; esp., one who practises deception under an assumed character or name.

im-pos-tume, im-pos-thume (im-pos′tūm), *n.* [OF. *empostume*, for *apostume*, < L. *apostema*, < Gr. ἀπόστημα, lit. 'separation' (of pus), < ἀπό, from, + ἱστάναι, stand.] An abscess. [Obs. or archaic.]

im-pos-ture (im-pos′tūr), *n.* [LL. *impostura*, < L. *imponere*, impose: see *impone*.] The action or practice of imposing fraudulently upon others; esp., deception practised under an assumed character or name, as by an impostor; an instance or piece of fraudulent imposition; anything deliberately passed off for what it is not.—**im-pos′tur-ous,** *a.*

im-po-sure (im-pō′zhūr), *n.* The act of imposing; imposition.

im-po-ta-ble (im-pō′tạ-bl), *a.* [LL. *impotabilis*.] Not potable or drinkable; unfit for drinking.

im-po-tent (im′pọ-tẹnt), *a.* [L. *impotens* (*-ent-*).] Not potent; lacking power or ability, powerless, or helpless (as, to be *impotent* in a crisis); utterly unable (to do something: as, "Virtue, valour, wisdom . . . wealth, without these three, is *impotent* to gain dominion," Milton's "Paradise Regained," ii. 433); without force or effectiveness (as, "O most lame and *impotent* conclusion!" Shakspere's "Othello," ii. 1. 162); lacking bodily strength, or physically helpless, as an aged person or a cripple; specif., wholly lacking in sexual power; also, without control or restraint† (as, "Juno, *impotent* of passion . . . with fury spoke": Pope's tr. Homer's "Iliad," iv.).—**im′po-tence, im′po-ten-cy,** *n.*—**im′po-tent-ly,** *adv.*

im-pound (im-pound′), *v. t.* [See *im-*[1].] To shut up in a pound, as a stray animal; confine within an inclosure or within limits (as, to *impound* water in a reservoir, as for distribution); also, to seize and retain in custody of the law, as a document for evidence; hence, to seize, take, or appropriate summarily, as for one's own use.—**im-pound′a-ble,** *a.* Liable to be impounded.—**im-pound′er,** *n.*

im-pov-er-ish (im-pov'ėr-ish), *v. t.* [OF. *empovrir* (*empovriss-*), < *em-* (< L. *in*, in) + *povre*, E. *poor.*] To reduce to poverty (as, a country *impoverished* by war); also, to make poor in quality, productiveness, etc. (as, to *impoverish* the blood or the soil); exhaust the strength or richness of.—**im-pov'er-ish-er,** *n.*—**im-pov'er-ish-ment,** *n.*

im-prac-ti-ca-ble (im-prak'ti-ka-bl), *a.* [See *im-*².] Not practicable; that cannot be put into practice, carried out, or done, esp. with the available means or with the sanction of reason or good judgment (as, an *impracticable* measure, plan, or attempt; "my fellowship of toil and *impracticable* schemes with the dreamy brethren of Brook Farm," Hawthorne's "Scarlet Letter," The Custom House); unsuitable for practical use or purposes, as a device, material, etc.; of ground, places, etc., impassable; of persons, etc., that one cannot do anything with, as because of stubbornness, stupidity, unpractical ideas, etc. (as, "The man was dull . . . A poor *impracticable* creature!" Goldsmith's "Good-Natured Man," ii.; "You are so utterly unreasonable and *impracticable*," G. B. Shaw's "Man and Superman," ii.).—**im-prac"ti-ca-bil'i-ty** (-bil'i-ti), **im-prac'ti-ca-ble-ness,** *n.* —**im-prac'ti-ca-bly,** *adv.*

im-prac-ti-cal (im-prak'ti-kal), *a.* [See *im-*².] Not practical; unpractical.

im-pre-cate (im'prē-kāt), *v. t.*; *-cated, -cating.* [L. *imprecatus*, pp. of *imprecari*, < *in*, in, on, + *precari*, pray.] To call down or invoke (esp. evil or curses), as upon a person (as, "I on them Did *imprecate* quick ruin, and it came": Shelley's "Cenci," iv. 1. 111); sometimes, to pray or make entreaty for (anything desired); also, to invoke evil upon, or curse (a person, etc.: now rare); also, to invoke or supplicate (a deity, etc.), as for something desired (now rare). —**im-pre-ca'tion** (-kā'shon), *n.* [L. *imprecatio*(*n*-).] The act of imprecating; the invoking of evil, as upon a person; cursing; a curse or malediction.—**im'pre-ca-tor,** *n.* —**im'pre-ca-to-ry** (-ka-tō-ri), *a.* Expressing imprecation; invoking evil; maledictory.

im-pre-cise (im-prē-sīs'), *a.* [See *im-*².] Not precise; lacking precision.—**im-pre-ci'sion** (-sizh'on), *n.*

im-pregn (im-prēn'), *v. t.* [LL. *impraegnare*: see *impregnate.*] To impregnate: as, "Persuasive words, *impregn'd* With reason" (Milton's "Paradise Lost," ix. 737). [Obs. or poetic.]

im-preg-na-ble (im-preg'na-bl), *a.* [OF. F. *imprenable*, < *im-*, not, + *prenable*, E. *pregnable.*] Not pregnable, as a fortress; not to be taken by force; proof against attack; fig., not to be overcome or overthrown (as, *impregnable* virtue; an *impregnable* basis of argument).—**im-preg-na-bil'i-ty** (-bil'i-ti), *n.*—**im-preg'na-bly,** *adv.*

im-preg-nate (im-preg'nāt), *v. t.*; *-nated, -nating.* [LL. *impraegnatus*, pp. of *impraegnare*, < L. *in*, in, + *praegnans*, E. *pregnant.*] To make pregnant; get with child or young; hence, to render capable of development by the introduction of the male germ-element or reproductive cell, as an ovum; fecundate; fertilize; also, to charge with something infused or permeating throughout, or to permeate as something infused does (as, water *impregnated* with mineral salts; "airs *impregnated* with incense," Cowper's "My Mother's Picture," 94); saturate; fig., to furnish with some actuating or modifying element infused or introduced (as, to *impregnate* the mind with new ideas; a district *impregnated* with discontent or vice; a book *impregnated* with optimism); imbue, infect, or tincture.—**im-preg'nate,** *a.* Impregnated.—**im-preg-na'tion** (-nā'shon), *n.* The act of impregnating, or the state of being impregnated; also, that with which something is impregnated.

im-pre-sa-ri-o (im-pre-sä'ri-ō), *n.*; pl. *-os* (-ōz). [It., < *impresa*, enterprise: see *imprese.*] The organizer or manager of an opera or concert company.—**im-pre-sa'ri-o-ship,** *n.*

im-pre-scrip-ti-ble (im-prē-skrip'ti-bl), *a.* [See *im-*².] Not subject to prescription; existing independently of law or convention; not legally to be taken away or violated, as rights.—**im-pre-scrip'ti-bly,** *adv.*

im-prese† (im-prēz'), *n.* [Obs. F. *imprese*, < It. *impresa*, device, also enterprise, = E. *emprise.*] A device or emblem (see Shakspere's "Richard II.," iii. 1. 25); also, a motto.

im-press¹ (im-pres'), *v. t.* [See *im-*¹ and *press*².] To press or force into public service, as seamen (as, "The captain applied to the port-admiral, and obtained permission to send parties on shore to *impress* seamen": Marryat's "Peter Simple," x.); seize or take for public use, as necessaries; hence, in general, to take into service or use as by force or constraint, as the occasion arises (as, to *impress* a passer-by, or a vehicle, into service in an emergency).—**im'press**¹, *n.* Impressment, as into service: as, "Tell me . . . Why such *impress* of shipwrights, whose sore task Does not divide the Sunday from the week" (Shakspere's "Hamlet," i. 1. 75).

im-press² (im-pres'), *v. t.* [L. *impressus*, pp. of *imprimere*, < *in*, in, on, + *premere*, press.] To press (a thing) into or on something (as, to *impress* a seal into wax; "But he . . . his foot *impress'd* On the strong neck of that destructive beast," Dryden's "Meleager and Atalanta," 210); apply with pressure, esp. so as to leave a mark; also, to produce (a mark, figure, etc.) by pressure; stamp; imprint; bestow (a kiss), as by pressure on the lips; fig., to impart or cause as if by pressure, as qualities, conditions, motion, etc.; fix deeply or firmly on the mind or memory, as ideas, facts, circumstances, etc.; urge, as something to be remembered or done; also, to subject to, or mark or indent by, pressure with something; furnish with a mark, figure, etc., by or as by stamping (as, a document *impressed* with a seal; leather *impressed* with an ornamental pattern); fig., to affect or invest with something as if by pressure or stamping (as, a literature strongly *impressed* with the national characteristics); affect deeply or strongly in mind or feelings (as, he *impressed* us with his earnestness, or his earnestness *impressed* us); make an impression on; influence in opinion (favorably or otherwise).—**im'press**², *n.* The act of impressing; also, a mark made by or as by pressure; a stamp or imprint; fig., a distinctive character or effect imparted (as, a work that bears the *impress* of its origin); an impression on the mind or feelings (now rare).—**im-press'er,** *n.*— **im-press'i-ble,** *a.* Capable of being impressed; sensitive to impressions; impressionable.—**im-press-i-bil'i-ty** (-bil'i-ti), *n.*

im-pres-sion (im-presh'on), *n.* [OF. F. *impression*, < L. *impressio*(*n*-), < *imprimere*: see *impress*².] The act of impressing, or the state of being impressed; also, a mark, indentation, figure, etc., produced by pressure; hence, the effect produced by any agency or influence (as, time has left its *impression* on the structure; remonstrances made little *impression* on the action of the leaders); often, an effect produced on the senses or mind; a strong effect produced on the intellect, feelings, or conscience; a notion, remembrance, or belief, often one that is vague or indistinct; in *printing*, etc., the process or result of printing from type, plates, etc.; a printed copy from type, a plate, an engraved block, etc.; the aggregate of copies of a book, etc., printed at one time; esp., one of a number of printings made at different times from the same set of types, without alteration (as distinguished from an *edition*, which see: as, a copy of the second *impression* of the third edition of a book).—**im-pres'sion-a-ble,** *a.* Capable of being impressed; liable to be easily impressed or influenced; susceptible.—**im-pres"sion-a-bil'i-ty** (-bil'i-ti), **im-pres'sion-a-ble-ness,** *n.*—**im-pres'sion-al,** *a.* Of or pertaining to impression or impressions; also, impressionable.—**im-pres'sion-ism,** *n.* A method of painting in which scenes and objects are represented as they first strike the eye, in their immediate and momentary effect, without attention to details; also, a corresponding mode of treatment in literature; also, a recent method in musical composition, diverging markedly from classical methods by its great freedom of form and by employing various unorthodox or unusual means to express impressions or emotions (exemplified in the work of Debussy). —**im-pres'sion-ist,** *n.* One who practises the method of impressionism.—**im-pres-sion-is'tic,** *a.* Of, pertaining to, or characteristic of impressionists; hence, conveying only a general or hasty impression; sketchy.

im-pres-sive (im-pres'iv), *a.* Such as to impress, or make a deep impression on the mind; arousing serious or solemn feelings or a degree of awe: as, an *impressive* discourse or ceremony; an *impressive* scene.—**im-pres'sive-ly,** *adv.*— **im-pres'sive-ness,** *n.*

im-press-ment (im-pres'mẹnt), *n.* The act or practice of impressing men, property, etc., as for public service or use.

im-pres-sure (im-presh'ụr), *n.* Impression. [Archaic.]

im-prest (im-prest'), *v. t.* [See *im-*[1] and *prest*[1].] To advance (money), esp. for use in carrying out some public business. [Obs. or hist., Eng.]—**im'prest,** *n.* An advance of money, esp. for use in carrying out some public business; formerly, an advance payment made to a soldier or sailor at enlistment. [Eng.]

im-pri-ma-tur (im-pri-mā'tėr), *n.* [NL., 'let it be printed.'] An official license to print or publish a book, etc.

im-pri-mis (im-prī'mis), *adv.* [L. *imprimis, in primis,* in or among the first.] In the first place; first.

im-print (im'print), *n.* [OF. F. *empreinte,* < *empreindre,* < L. *imprimere*: see *impress*[2].] A mark made by pressure (as, the *imprint* of a foot in sand); any impression or impressed effect (as, the *imprint* of suffering on the face); also, something printed, as from type; specif., the name of the publisher, with the place of issue, and often the date, printed on the title-page or elsewhere (formerly at the end) in a book or other publication, or the printer's name and address as printed on any printed matter; sometimes, the printing of a book or the like.—**im-print',** *v. t.* To produce (a mark, etc.) on something by pressure; impress; stamp; bestow (a kiss); fix as by pressure or stamping, as on the aspect, character, mind, or memory; also, to make an imprint upon (as, "I . . . may tread a land never before *imprinted* by the foot of man": Mrs. Shelley's "Frankenstein," letter i.); mark (a thing) with or as with something impressed or stamped upon it; formerly, specif., to print from type, as letters, words, etc., or a book†.—**im-print'er,** *n.*

im-pris-on (im-priz'n), *v. t.* [OF. *emprisoner* (F. *emprisonner*), < *em-* (< L. *in,* in) + *prison,* E. *prison.*] To put into or keep in prison; incarcerate; hence, to shut up as if in a prison; confine closely; hold in restraint.—**im-pris'on-ment,** *n.* The act of imprisoning, or the state of being imprisoned; incarceration; confinement or restraint as if in prison.

im-prob-a-bil-i-ty (im-prob-ạ-bil'i-ti), *n.*; pl. *-ties* (-tiz). The quality or fact of being improbable; unlikelihood; also, something improbable or unlikely.

im-prob-a-ble (im-prob'ạ-bl), *a.* [L. *improbabilis.*] Not probable; unlikely to be true or to happen: as, "If this were played upon a stage now, I could condemn it as an *improbable* fiction" (Shakspere's "Twelfth Night," iii. 4. 141).—**im-prob'a-bly,** *adv.*

im-prob-i-ty (im-prob'i-ti), *n.* [L. *improbitas,* < *improbus,* bad, < *in-,* not, + *probus,* good.] The reverse of probity; dishonesty; wickedness.

im-promp-tu (im-promp'tū). [L. *in promptu,* in readiness.] **I.** *adv.* Without preparation; offhand; extempore: as, verses written *impromptu.* **II.** *a.* Made or done without previous preparation (as, *impromptu* verses; an *impromptu* address); improvised, or having the character of an improvisation, as music; also, suddenly or hastily prepared, arranged, made, etc. (as, an *impromptu* dinner; an *impromptu* costume); extemporized; makeshift. **III.** *n.*; pl. *-tus* (-tūz). Something impromptu; an impromptu composition, speech, or performance; an improvisation.

im-prop-er (im-prop'ėr), *a.* [F. *impropre,* < L. *improprius.*] Not proper; not strictly belonging, applicable, or right (as, an *improper* name for a thing; to use a word in an *improper* sense); incorrect, erroneous, or wrong; abnormal or irregular (as, an *improper* fraction, one in which the numerator is greater than the denominator); metaphorical or figurative, rather than literal†; unsuitable or inappropriate, as for the purpose, object, or occasion; often, not in accordance with propriety of behavior, manners, etc.; unbecoming or unseemly; indecorous; sometimes, immoral or indecent.—**im-prop'er-ly,** *adv.*—**im-prop'er-ness,** *n.*

im-pro-pri-ate (im-prō'pri-āt), *v. t.*; *-ated, -ating.* [ML. *impropriatus,* pp. of *impropriare,* < L. *in,* in, + *proprius,* one's own, E. *proper.*] To appropriate†; in *Eng. eccles. law,* to place (ecclesiastical property, tithes, etc.) in lay hands.—**im-pro-pri-a'tion** (-ā'shọn), *n.* The act of impropriating; also, that which is impropriated.—**im-pro'pri-a-tor,** *n.* A layman in possession of church property or revenues.

im-pro-pri-e-ty (im-prọ-prī'ẹ-ti), *n.*; pl. *-ties* (-tiz). [F. *impropriété,* < L. *improprietas.*] The quality of being improper; incorrectness; inappropriateness; unseemliness; also, improper conduct; an improper act, expression, etc.; a breach of propriety.

im-prov-a-ble (im-prö'vạ-bl), *a.* That may be improved.—**im-prov-a-bil'i-ty** (-bil'i-ti), *n.*

im-prove (im-pröv'), *v.*; *-proved, -proving.* [AF. *emprouer,* < *em-* (< L. *in,* in) + OF. *prou, pro, prod,* profit: cf. L. *prodesse,* be of profit.] **I.** *tr.* To turn (money, land, etc.) to profit†; hence, to turn to account, or make good use of (an opportunity, occasion, time, etc.); utilize, use, or employ (things, persons, places, etc.: now rare); also, to make (land) more profitable or valuable by inclosure, cultivation, etc.; increase the value of (real property) by betterments, as buildings or additions to buildings; in general, to bring into a more desirable or excellent condition (as, to *improve* the health by exercise, or the mind by study; to *improve* breeds of cattle; to *improve* a poem by polishing); make better; ameliorate, as conditions; also, to increase in amount or degree†; augment†. **II.** *intr.* To make improvements, as on real property; also, to make an advance in excellence or achievement on something previous (with *on* or *upon*: as, to *improve* on one's earlier work; this plan could hardly be *improved* upon); also, to increase in value, excellence, etc., or become better (as, the land *improves* in value every year; wine *improves* with age; the situation is *improving*); also, to increase† or grow† (as, "Intimacy *improves* with time": Irving's "Knickerbocker's New York," i. 3).—**im-prove'-ment,** *n.* The act of improving, or the state of being improved; profitable use, now esp. of an opportunity or occasion, time, etc.; a bringing into a more valuable or desirable condition, as of land or real property; a making or becoming better, or betterment; also, a change or addition whereby a thing is improved; specif., something done or added to real property whereby its value is increased; also, one thing or person that represents an advance on another in excellence or achievement (as, this book is a great *improvement* on the others; this cook is an *improvement* on the last; "To fall by the sword, however ungracefully, was still an *improvement* on the gallows," Stevenson's "David Balfour," viii.).—**im-prov'er** (-prö'vėr), *n.*

im-prov-i-dent (im-prov'i-dẹnt), *a.* [See *im-*[2].] Not provident; wanting foresight; incautious or unwary (as, "*Improvident* soldiers! had your watch been good, This sudden mischief never could have fall'n": Shakspere's "1 Henry VI.," ii. 1. 58); now, esp., neglecting to provide for future needs; spending freely without thought of the future; thriftless.—**im-prov'i-dence,** *n.*—**im-prov'i-dent-ly,** *adv.*

im-prov-ing (im-prö'ving), *p. a.* That improves; making or becoming better; often, such as to improve the mind or character (as, "a book of travels . . . very *improving* too," Weir Mitchell's "Hugh Wynne," iii.; *improving* conversation or company); instructive; elevating.—**im-prov'-ing-ly,** *adv.*

im-prov-i-sate (im-prov'i-zāt), *v. t.* or *i.*; *-sated, -sating.* Same as *improvise.*

im-prov-i-sa-tion (im-prov-i-zā'shọn), *n.* The act of improvising; also, something improvised, as verse, music, etc.

im-prov-i-sa-tor (im-prov'i-zā-tọr), *n.* One who improvises.—**im-prov"i-sa-to'ri-al** (-zạ-tō'ri-ạl), **im-prov'i-sa-to-ry** (-tọ-ri), *a.* Of or pertaining to an improvisator or improvisation.—**im-prov"i-sa-to'ri-al-ly,** *adv.*

im-pro-vise (im-prọ-vīz'), *v.*; *-vised, -vising.* [F. *improviser,* < It. *improvvisare,* < *improvviso,* < L. *improvisus,* unforeseen, unexpected, < *in-,* not, + *provisus,* pp. of *providere,* foresee, E. *provide.*] **I.** *tr.* To compose (verse, music, etc.) on the spur of the moment; recite, sing, etc., extemporaneously; also, to prepare or provide offhand or hastily; extemporize. **II.** *intr.* To compose, utter, or execute anything extemporaneously.—**im-pro-vis'er** (-vī'zėr), *n.*

im-prov-vi-sa-to-re (ēm-prōv-vē-zä-tō'rā), *n.*; pl. *-ri* (-rē). [It.] An improvisator.—**im-prov-vi-sa-tri'ce** (-trē'chā), *n.*; pl. *-ci* (-chē). [It.] Fem. of *improvvisatore.*

im-pru-dence (im-prö'dẹns), *n.* [L. *imprudentia.*] The quality or fact of being imprudent; also, imprudent conduct; an imprudent act.

im-pru-dent (im-prö'dẹnt), *a.* [L. *imprudens* (*-ent-*).]

Not prudent; wanting in prudence or discretion; indiscreet; injudicious; rash.—**im-pru'dent-ly,** *adv.*

im-pu-dence (im'pū-dens), *n.* [L. *impudentia.*] The quality or fact of being impudent; shamelessness†; effrontery; insolence; also, impudent conduct or language; an impudent thing. Also **im'pu-den-cy.**

im-pu-dent (im'pū-dent), *a.* [L. *impudens* (*-ent-*), < *in-*, not, + *pudens*, ppr. of *pudere*, feel shame.] Shameless† or brazenly immodest†; also, characterized by a shameless boldness, assurance, or effrontery (as, an *impudent* rogue; *impudent* behavior, language, or pretensions); offensively impertinent; insolent.—**im'pu-dent-ly,** *adv.*

im-pu-di-ci-ty (im-pū-dis'i-ti), *n.* [F. *impudicité*: cf. *pudicity.*] Shamelessness; immodesty.

im-pugn (im-pūn'), *v. t.* [OF. F. *impugner*, < L. *impugnare*, < *in*, in, on, + *pugnare*, fight.] To fight against†; fig., to assail by words or arguments, as statements, opinions, motives, veracity, etc.; call in question; challenge as false; sometimes, to assail the statements or actions of (a person, etc.: as, "The Venetian law Cannot *impugn* you as you do proceed," Shakspere's "Merchant of Venice," iv. 1. 179).—**im-pugn'a-ble,** *a.* That may be impugned.—**im-pug-na'tion** (-pug-nā'shon), **im-pugn'ment,** *n.* The act of impugning, assailing, or calling in question.—**im-pugn'er,** *n.*

im-pu-is-sant (im-pū'i-sant), *a.* [F. *impuissant*: cf. *puissant.*] Impotent; powerless; feeble; weak.—**im-pu'is-sance,** *n.*

im-pulse (im'puls), *n.* [L. *impulsus*, < *impellere*, E. *impel.*] An impelling action or force, driving onward or inducing motion (as, "instruments of soft music . . . played by the *impulse* of the wind": Johnson's "Rasselas," vi.); a thrust or push; also, the effect of an impelling force; motion induced; impetus given; fig., constraining or inciting action or influence on the mind or conduct (as, "So without least *impulse* . . . They trespass, authours to themselves in all": Milton's "Paradise Lost," iii. 120); often, the inciting influence of a particular feeling, mental state, etc. (as, to act under the *impulse* of pity, curiosity, or passion); hence, sudden, involuntary inclination prompting to action, or a particular instance of it (as, to be swayed by *impulse*, or by contrary *impulses*); in *mech.*, the product obtained by multiplying the value of a force by the time during which it acts (sometimes restricted to cases in which the force is great and the time very short, as in the blow of a hammer).

im-pul-sion (im-pul'shon), *n.* [OF. F. *impulsion*, < L. *impulsio*(*n-*), < *impellere*, E. *impel.*] The act of impelling, driving onward, or pushing, or the resulting state or effect; impulse; impetus; fig., constraining or inciting action on the mind or conduct (as, "Thou didst plead Divine *impulsion* prompting how thou might'st Find some occasion to infest our foes": Milton's "Samson Agonistes," 422); the inciting influence of some feeling or motive; mental impulse.

im-pul-sive (im-pul'siv), *a.* [ML. *impulsivus.*] Having the power or effect of impelling; driving onward, or inducing motion; characterized by impulsion; fig., inciting to action, as a cause or motive; esp., actuated or controlled by mental impulse, as a person, the disposition, conduct, etc.; swayed by emotional or involuntary impulses; in *mech.*, of forces, acting momentarily; not continuous.—**im-pul'sive-ly,** *adv.* —**im-pul'sive-ness,** *n.*

im-pu-ni-ty (im-pū'ni-ti), *n.* [L. *impunitas*, < *impunis*, unpunished, < *in-*, not, + *pœna*, penalty, punishment.] Exemption from punishment or ill consequences: as, "The *impunity* with which outrages were committed . . . can now hardly be realised" (Lecky's "Hist. of Eng. in the 18th Century," iii.); "children . . . playing a thousand tricks on him with *impunity*" (Irving's "Sketch-Book," Rip Van Winkle).

im-pure (im-pūr'), *a.* [L. *impurus.*] Not pure; mixed with extraneous matter, esp. of an inferior or contaminating kind (as, *impure* native salt; *impure* water or air); modified by admixture, as color; marked by foreign and unsuitable or objectionable elements or characteristics, as a style of art or of literary expression; ceremonially unclean, as things, animals, etc.; not morally pure, as persons, the mind, thoughts, life, etc.; corrupt; depraved; unchaste. —**im-pure'ly,** *adv.*—**im-pure'ness,** *n.*—**im-pu'ri-ty** (-pū'ri-ti), *n.*; pl. *-ties* (-tiz). [L. *impuritas.*] The quality or state of being impure; also, that which is or makes impure (often in *pl.*: as, *impurities* in drinking-water).

im-pur-ple (im-pėr'pl), *v. t.* Same as *empurple.*

im-pu-ta-ble (im-pū'ta-bl), *a.* That may be imputed; attributable.—**im-pu-ta-bil'i-ty** (-bil'i-ti), *n.*—**im-pu'ta-bly,** *adv.*

im-pu-ta-tion (im-pū-tā'shon), *n.* [LL. *imputatio*(*n-*).] The act of imputing; an attribution, esp. of fault, crime, etc., whether expressly or by implication; a charge or insinuation of something discreditable.

im-pu-ta-tive (im-pū'ta-tiv), *a.* [LL. *imputativus.*] That imputes; making imputations; also, imputed; belonging or existing by imputation.—**im-pu'ta-tive-ly,** *adv.*

im-pute (im-pūt'), *v. t.*; *-puted, -puting.* [OF. F. *imputer*, < L. *imputare*, bring into the reckoning. < *in*, in, + *putare*, reckon: see *putative.*] To attribute or ascribe (as, "Abraham believed God, and it was *imputed* unto him for righteousness": James, ii. 23); commonly, to attribute (fault, crime, or something discreditable), as to a person; also, to charge (a person) with fault, etc. (archaic: as, "They . . . that most impute a crime Are pronest to it, and *impute* themselves," Tennyson's "Merlin and Vivien," 824); also, to reckon†, regard†, or consider† (as, "if we *impute* this last humiliation as the cause of his death": Gibbon's "Decline and Fall of the Roman Empire," lxiv.); in *theol.*, to attribute (righteousness, guilt, etc.) vicariously; ascribe as derived from another.—**im-put'er** (-pū'tėr), *n.*

in (in), *prep.* [AS. *in* = D. and G. *in* = Icel. *ī* = Goth. *in*, in; akin to L. *in*, Gr. ἐν, in.] A particle expressing inclusion, situation, presence, existence, action, etc., within limits, as of place, time, state, circumstances, etc.: in particular, used to express (1) inclusion within space or limits, a whole, material or immaterial surroundings, etc.: as, *in* the city; *in* the army; dressed *in* white; *in* politics; (2) inclusion within, or occurrence during the course of or at the expiration of, a period or limit of time: as, *in* ancient times; to do a task *in* an hour; to return *in* ten minutes; (3) situation, state, condition, occupation, action, manner, relation or respect, etc.: as, *in* darkness; *in* sickness; *in* tears; *in* service; *in* crossing the Alps; to tell *in* confidence; to write *in* French; (4) object or purpose: as, *in* honor of the event; (5) motion or direction from without to a point within (now usually *into*), or transition from one state to another: as, to put *in* operation; to break *in* two.—**in,** *adv.* [AS. *inn, in.*] In or into some place, position, state, relation, etc.; on the inside, or within; in one's house or office; in office or power; in possession or occupancy; having the turn to play, in a game; in season, or in fashion; in addition, or into the bargain; to the good, or in pocket.—**in. I.** *a.* That is in; internal; inward. **II.** *n.* In *pl.*, those who are in, as the political party in power; also, nooks or recesses (in the phrase 'ins and outs,' nooks and corners, turns and windings, or, fig., intricacies).—**in,** *v. t.*; *inned, inning.* To put, take, or bring in; harvest, as grain; include or inclose, as waste land. [Now chiefly prov. Eng.]

in-¹. [In part, E. *in*, prep. and adv.; in part, L. *in-*, repr. *in*, prep., in, into, on, to: cf. *en-*, *em-*, and *im-¹*.] A prefix in part representing E. *in*, as in *income, indwelling, inland, insight*, in part of Latin origin and meaning primarily 'in,' but used also (like, or interchangeably with, its equivalent *en-*) as an English verb-formative with transitive, intensive, or sometimes little apparent force, as in *inarch, incase, ingulf, insnare, intrench, intrust.* See *en-*, and cf. *em-* and *im-¹*.

in-². [L. *in-*, akin to Gr. ἀν-, ἀ- (see *a-¹*) and E. *un-¹*.] A prefix of Latin origin, having a negative or privative force, freely used as an English formative, esp. of adjectives and their derivatives and of nouns, as in *inapt, inattention, incaution, indefensible, indevout, inexpensive, inoccupation, inorganic, insolvent, invariable.* See *un-¹*, and cf. *il-²*, *im-²*, and *ir-²*.

-in. [= *-ine²*.] A noun suffix used in chemical terms, esp. names of neutral substances, as *albumin, gelatin, lecithin.* Cf. *-ine²*.

in-a-bil-i-ty (in-a-bil'i-ti), *n.* [See *in-²*.] Lack of ability; want of power, capacity, or means: as, *inability* to perform a task, or to pay one's debts.

in-ac-ces-si-ble (in-ak-ses′i-bl), *a.* [LL. *inaccessibilis.*] Not accessible; not to be reached; inapproachable.—**in-ac-ces-si-bil′i-ty** (-bil′i-ti), **in-ac-ces′si-ble-ness,** *n.*—**in-ac-ces′si-bly,** *adv.*

in-ac-cu-ra-cy (in-ak′ū̦-rą̄-si), *n.*; pl. *-cies* (-siz). The quality of being inaccurate; also, an error or mistake.

in-ac-cu-rate (in-ak′ū̦-rą̄t), *a.* [See *in-*².] Not accurate; inexact; incorrect.—**in-ac′cu-rate-ly,** *adv.*—**in-ac′cu-rate-ness,** *n.*

in-ac-quaint-ance (in-ą-kwān′tąns), *n.* [See *in-*².] Lack of acquaintance.

in-ac-tion (in-ak′shǫn), *n.* [See *in-*².] Absence of action; inertness; idleness: as, "He soon grew impatient . . . of the quiet and *inaction* of his mimic kingdom" (Irving's "Conquest of Granada," lxxxv.).—**in-ac′tive,** *a.* Not active; inert; indolent; sluggish; passive.—**in-ac′tive-ly,** *adv.*—**in-ac′tive-ness, in-ac-tiv′i-ty,** *n.*

in-a-dapt-a-ble (in-ą-dap′tą-bl), *a.* [See *in-*².] Not adaptable; incapable of being adapted.—**in-a-dapt-a-bil′i-ty** (-bil′i-ti), *n.*

in-ad-e-quate (in-ad′ē̦-kwą̄t), *a.* [See *in-*².] Not adequate; not equal to requirement; insufficient.—**in-ad′e-qua-cy** (-kwą̄-si), **in-ad′e-quate-ness,** *n.*—**in-ad′e-quate-ly,** *adv.*

in-ad-mis-si-ble (in-ad-mis′i-bl), *a.* [See *in-*².] Not admissible.—**in-ad-mis-si-bil′i-ty** (-bil′i-ti), *n.*—**in-ad-mis′si-bly,** *adv.*

in-ad-vert-ence (in-ad-vėr′tęns), *n.* The quality of being inadvertent; inattention; heedlessness; also, an act or effect of inattention; an oversight. Also **in-ad-vert′en-cy.**

in-ad-vert-ent (in-ad-vėr′tęnt), *a.* [See *in-*².] Not advertent or attentive, as persons; heedless; also, characterized by want of attention, as actions, etc.; hence, unintentional.—**in-ad-vert′ent-ly,** *adv.*

in-ad-vis-a-ble (in-ad-vī′zą-bl), *a.* [See *in-*².] Not advisable; inexpedient.—**in-ad-vis-a-bil′i-ty** (-bil′i-ti), *n.*

in-al-ien-a-ble (in-āl′yęn-ą-bl), *a.* [See *in-*².] Not alienable; that cannot be transferred to another.—**in-al″ien-a-bil′i-ty** (-bil′i-ti), *n.*—**in-al′ien-a-bly,** *adv.*

in-al-ter-a-ble (in-âl′tėr-ą-bl), *a.* [See *in-*².] Not alterable; unalterable; unchangeable.—**in-al″ter-a-bil′i-ty** (-bil′i-ti), *n.*—**in-al′ter-a-bly,** *adv.*

in-am-o-ra-ta (in-am-ǫ-rä′tą), *n.*; pl. *-tas* (-tąz). [It. *innamorata,* fem. of *innamorato*: see *inamorato.*] A female lover; a woman with whom one is in love; a sweetheart: as, "I know not how the lover had behaved . . . so as to decline in the favour of his *inamorata*" (Smollett's "Humphry Clinker," July 18).—**in-am-o-ra′to** (-tō), *n.*; pl. *-tos* (-tōz). [It. *innamorato,* pp. masc. of *innamorare,* enamour, < *in,* in, + *amore,* love.] A (male) lover: as, "the chivalrous *inamorato*" (Scott's "Quentin Durward," xxiv.).

in and in (in ąnd in). Repeatedly within the same limits, as of family or strain: as, to breed stock *in and in.*—**in′=and=in′,** *a.*

in-ane (in-ān′). [L. *inanis,* empty, vain.] **I.** *a.* Empty; void; fig., void of sense or ideas, or silly (as, "asking *inane* questions": Kipling's "Kim," viii.). **II.** *n.* That which is inane, empty, or void; empty space; the void of infinite space: as, "the illimitable *inane*" (Tennyson's "Lucretius," 40).—**in-ane′ly,** *adv.*

in-an-i-mate (in-an′i-mą̄t), *a.* [LL. *inanimatus.*] Not animate; destitute of life, or lifeless; not endowed with animal life (as, *inanimate* nature; "He then fell, like an *inanimate* log, to the earth," Cooper's "Prairie," xxvi.); hence, without the activity of life; spiritless; sluggish; dull.—**in-an′i-mate-ly,** *adv.*—**in-an′i-mate-ness,** *n.*

in-a-ni-tion (in-ą-nish′ǫn), *n.* [LL. *inanitio(n-),* < L. *inanire,* make empty, < *inanis,* empty, E. *inane.*] The condition of being empty; specif., exhaustion from lack of nourishment; starvation.

in-an-i-ty (in-an′i-ti), *n.*; pl. *-ties* (-tiz). [L. *inanitas.*] The state of being inane, empty, or void; emptiness; fig., want of substance, or vanity or worthlessness; lack of sense or ideas, or senselessness or silliness; emptiness of existence, or idleness or inaction; also, something inane; an inane or silly practice, remark, etc.

in-ap-peas-a-ble (in-ą-pē′zą-bl), *a.* [See *in-*².] Not appeasable; not to be appeased: as, an *inappeasable* appetite or longing; *inappeasable* anger.

in-ap-pel-la-ble (in-ą-pel′ą-bl), *a.* [See *in-*².] Not appellable; not admitting of appeal; from which there is no appeal.—**in-ap-pel-la-bil′i-ty** (-bil′i-ti), *n.*

in-ap-pe-tence (in-ap′ē̦-tęns), *n.* [See *in-*².] Lack of appetence or appetite. Also **in-ap′pe-ten-cy.**

in-ap-pli-ca-ble (in-ap′li-ką-bl), *a.* [See *in-*².] Not applicable; unsuitable.—**in-ap″pli-ca-bil′i-ty** (-bil′i-ti), **in-ap′pli-ca-ble-ness,** *n.*—**in-ap′pli-ca-bly,** *adv.*—**in-ap-pli-ca′tion** (-kā′shǫn), *n.* Want of application, or assiduous effort or attention; negligence; inattention; also, the quality of being inapplicable.

in-ap-po-site (in-ap′ǭ-zit), *a.* [See *in-*².] Not apposite; not pertinent.—**in-ap′po-site-ly,** *adv.*

in-ap-pre-ci-a-ble (in-ą-prē′shi-ą-bl), *a.* [See *in-*².] Not appreciable; imperceptible; insignificant.—**in-ap-pre′ci-a-bly,** *adv.*—**in-ap-pre-ci-a′tion** (-si-ā′shǫn), *n.* Want of appreciation.—**in-ap-pre′ci-a-tive** (-shi-ą̄-tiv), *a.* Not appreciative; wanting in appreciation.—**in-ap-pre′ci-a-tive-ly,** *adv.*—**in-ap-pre′ci-a-tive-ness,** *n.*

in-ap-pre-hen-si-ble (in-ap-rē̦-hen′si-bl), *a.* [See *in-*².] Not apprehensible; not to be grasped by the senses or intellect.—**in-ap-pre-hen′sion** (-shǫn), *n.* Want of apprehension.—**in-ap-pre-hen′sive** (-siv), *a.* Not apprehensive; without apprehension.

in-ap-proach-a-ble (in-ą-prō′chą-bl), *a.* [See *in-*².] Not approachable; unapproachable.—**in-ap-proach-a-bil′i-ty** (-bil′i-ti), *n.*—**in-ap-proach′a-bly,** *adv.*

in-ap-pro-pri-ate (in-ą-prō′pri-ą̄t), *a.* [See *in-*².] Not appropriate; unsuitable; unfitting.—**in-ap-pro′pri-ate-ly,** *adv.*—**in-ap-pro′pri-ate-ness,** *n.*

in-apt (in-apt′), *a.* [See *in-*² and *apt,* and cf. *inept.*] Not apt or fitted; unsuited; inappropriate; inapposite; also, without aptitude or capacity; unskilful; awkward.—**in-ap′ti-tude** (-ap′ti-tūd), *n.* Want of aptitude; unfitness; unskilfulness.—**in-apt′ly,** *adv.*—**in-apt′ness,** *n.*

in-arch (in-ärch′), *v. t.* [See *in-*¹.] To graft by uniting a growing branch to a stock without separating the branch from its parent stock.

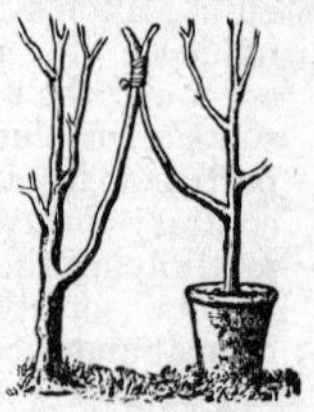
Inarching.

in-arm (in-ärm′), *v. t.* [See *in-*¹.] To encircle with or as with the arms.

in-ar-tic-u-late (in-är-tik′ū̦-lą̄t), *a.* [LL. *inarticulatus.*] Not articulate or jointed; not composed of distinct segments united by joints, as an animal; also, not of the nature of articulate speech, as musical notes or a groan; imperfectly articulated, as words; also, unable to use articulate speech (as, "She . . . was found by the maids in the morning, *inarticulate,* but still alive": Thackeray's "Newcomes," v.); dumb.—**in-ar-tic′u-late-ly,** *adv.*—**in-ar-tic′u-late-ness,** *n.*

in-ar-ti-fi-cial (in-är-ti-fish′ąl), *a.* [L. *inartificialis.*] Not artificial; natural; artless or unaffected; plain or simple; rude or inartistic.—**in-ar-ti-fi′cial-ly,** *adv.*

in-ar-tis-tic (in-är-tis′tik), *a.* [See *in-*².] Not artistic; esthetically crude or poor: as, "*inartistic* figures crowding the canvas of life without adequate effect" (George Eliot's "Adam Bede," v.). Also **in-ar-tis′ti-cal.**—**in-ar-tis′ti-cal-ly,** *adv.*

in-as-much (in-ąz-much′), *adv.* Followed by *as*: In so far as, or to such a degree as; also, in view of the fact that, seeing that, or since (as, "He was not worthy of death, *inasmuch* as he hated him not in time past": Deut. xix. 6).

in-as-sim-i-la-tion (in-ą-sim-i-lā′shǫn), *n.* [See *in-*².] Want of assimilation.

in-at-ten-tion (in-ą-ten′shǫn), *n.* [See *in-*².] Lack of attention; want of observant notice; heedlessness; negligence.—**in-at-ten′tive,** *a.* Not attentive; not fixing the mind attentively; heedless; negligent.—**in-at-ten′tive-ly,** *adv.*—**in-at-ten′tive-ness,** *n.*

in-au-di-ble (in-â′di-bl), *a.* [LL. *inaudibilis.*] Not audible; incapable of being heard: as, "the *inaudible* and noiseless foot of Time" (Shakspere's "All's Well," v. 3. 41).—**in-au-di-bil′i-ty** (-bil′i-ti), *n.*—**in-au′di-bly,** *adv.*

in-au-gu-ral (in-â′gū̦-rąl). [F. *inaugural,* < *inaugurer,* < L. *inaugurare*: see *inaugurate.*] **I.** *a.* Of or pertaining to an inauguration. **II.** *n.* An inaugural address, as of a governor or president. [U. S.]

in-au-gu-rate (in-â′gụ̄-rāt), *v. t.*; *-rated, -rating.* [L. *inauguratus*, pp. of *inaugurare*, consecrate or install with augural ceremonies, < *in*, in, + *augurare*, take auguries.] To induct into office with formal ceremonies; install; also, to make a formal beginning of; initiate; commence or begin; also, to introduce into public use by some formal ceremony.—**in-au-gu-ra′tion** (-rā′shọn), *n.* [LL. *inauguratio(n-).*] The act or ceremony of inaugurating.—**Inauguration Day,** the day upon which the President of the United States is inaugurated, being Jan. 20 of every year next after a year whose number is divisible by four (but March 4 before 1937).—**in-au′gu-ra-tive** (-rạ-tiv), **in-au′gu-ra-to-ry** (-tọ-ri), *a.* Inaugural.—**in-au′gu-ra-tor** (-rā-tọr), *n.*

in-aus-pi-cious (in-âs-pish′us), *a.* [See *in-*[2].] Not auspicious; unfavorable; unlucky.—**in-aus-pi′cious-ly,** *adv.*—**in-aus-pi′cious-ness,** *n.*

in-au-then-tic (in-â-then′tik), *a.* [See *in-*[2].] Not authentic.—**in-au-then-ti′ci-ty** (-tis′i-ti), *n.*

in-au-thor-i-ta-tive (in-â-thor′i-tạ-tiv), *a.* [See *in-*[2].] Not authoritative.—**in-au-thor′i-ta-tive-ness,** *n.*

in-bark (in′bärk), *n.* In *forestry*, a condition of wood in which portions of the external bark are included within the wood: often produced by the trunk and a branch growing together at the fork.

in-be-ing (in′bē″ing), *n.* The condition of being or existing in something else; immanence; also, inward nature.

in-board (in′bōrd), *adv.* and *a.* *Naut.*, within the hull or interior, or toward the center, of a ship or boat.

in-born (in′bôrn), *a.* Implanted by nature; innate: as, *inborn* virtue; an *inborn* sense of courtesy.

in-bound (in′bound), *a.* Inward bound: as, an *inbound* vessel.

in-break (in′brāk), *n.* A breaking in; irruption; invasion.—**in′break″ing,** *n.* and *a.*

in-breathe (in-brēᴛʜ′), *v. t.*; *-breathed, -breathing.* To breathe in; infuse; also, to inspire.—**in-breath′er** (-brē′ᴛʜėr), *n.*

in-bred (in′bred), *a.* Bred within; innate; native.

in-breed (in′brēd or in-brēd′), *v. t.*; *-bred, -breeding.* To breed within; engender; also, to breed (animals) in and in, as from one family or strain.

in-burst (in′bėrst), *n.* A bursting in; irruption.—**in′burst″ing,** *n.* and *a.*

In-ca (ing′kạ), *n.* One of the dominant race of South American Indians who occupied Peru prior to the Spanish conquest; also, the chief ruler of the race; also [*l. c.*], a sea-bird, *Inca mystacalis*, a species of tern, having dark plumage with a bundle of white plumes on each side of the head (also called *inca tern*).—**In-ca-ic** (ing-kā′ik), *a.*

Inca Tern.

in-cage (in-kāj′), *v. t.* Same as *encage.*

in-cal-cu-la-ble (in-kal′kụ̄-lạ-bl), *a.* [See *in-*[2].] That cannot be calculated; beyond calculation: as, "In an instant, a treasure of *incalculable* value lay gleaming before us" (Poe's "Gold-Bug").—**in-cal″cu-la-bil′i-ty** (-bil′i-ti), **in-cal′cu-la-ble-ness,** *n.*—**in-cal′cu-la-bly,** *adv.*

in-ca-les-cent (in-kạ-les′ẹnt), *a.* [L. *incalescens* (*-ent-*), ppr. of *incalescere*, grow hot, < *in*, in, + *calescere*: see *calescent.*] Increasing in heat.—**in-ca-les′cence,** *n.*

In-can (ing′kạn), *a.* Of or pertaining to the Incas of Peru.

in-can-desce (in-kan-dẹs′), *v. i.* or *t.*; *-desced, -descing.* [L. *incandescere*, grow hot, glow, < *in*, in, + *candescere*: see *candescent.*] To glow or cause to glow with heat.—**in-can-des′cence,** *n.* Incandescent state; a glowing with heat. Also **in-can-des′cen-cy.**—**in-can-des′cent,** *a.* Glowing or white with heat; hence, intensely bright; brilliant; also, pertaining to an incandescent lamp or light.—**incandescent lamp,** a lamp whose light is due to the glowing of some special material, as a gas-lamp using a mantle (see *Welsbach burner*), or the common electric lamp which consists of an exhausted glass bulb containing a carbon or other filament rendered luminous by the current.—**incandescent light,** light produced from an incandescent object, lamp, or the like; also, an incandescent lamp.—**in-can-des′cent-ly,** *adv.*

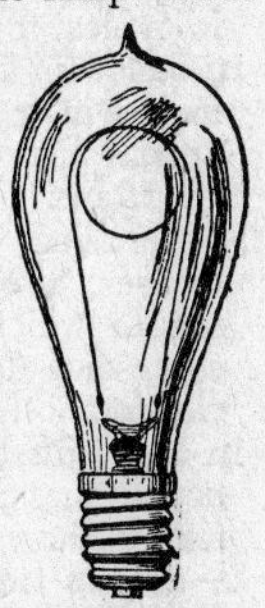

Incandescent Electric Lamp.

in-can-ta-tion (in-kan-tā′shọn), *n.* [OF. F. *incantation*, < LL. *incantatio(n-)*, < L. *incantare*, chant a magic formula against, enchant, < *in*, in, on, + *cantare*, sing, E. *chant.*] The chanting or uttering of words purporting to have magical power; also, the formula employed; a spell or charm; also, in general, magical ceremonies; magic; sorcery.—**in′can-ta-tor,** *n.* [LL., < L. *incantare.*] One who uses incantation.—**in-can′ta-to-ry** (-tạ-tọ-ri), *a.* Of or pertaining to incantation.

in-ca-pa-ble (in-kā′pạ-bl). [See *in-*[2].] **I.** *a.* Not capable; unable to be a container (*of*)†; not open to the influence, or not susceptible or admitting (*of*: as, *incapable* of pleasure; *incapable* of exact measurement); not having the capacity or power (with *of* or formerly an infinitive: as, "a claim, which they were *incapable* of supporting, either by reason or by arms," Gibbon's "Decline and Fall of the Roman Empire," xxix.); not having the depravity, weakness, etc., for the doing, experiencing, etc. (*of*: as, *incapable* of sin; *incapable* of fear); without ordinary capability or ability, or incompetent (as, *incapable* workers); without qualification, esp. legal qualification (often with *of*: as, *incapable* of holding public office). **II.** *n.* One without capacity or ability; one thoroughly incompetent.—**in-ca-pa-bil′i-ty** (-bil′i-ti), **in-ca′pa-ble-ness,** *n.*—**in-ca′pa-bly,** *adv.*

in-ca-pa-cious (in-kạ-pā′shus), *a.* [See *in-*[2].] Not capacious; lacking capacity; narrow; limited; often, mentally incapable.—**in-ca-pa′ci-tate** (-pas′i-tāt), *v. t.*; *-tated, -tating.* To deprive of capacity; render incapable or unfit; disqualify.—**in-ca-pa-ci-ta′tion** (-tā′shọn), *n.*—**in-ca-pa′ci-ty** (-pas′i-ti), *n.*; pl. *-ties* (-tiz). Lack of capacity; incapability (as, "a leaden *incapacity* of motion that seized him": Reade's "Peg Woffington," i.); incompetence (as, "His *incapacity* and ignorance were equal to his presumption": Gibbon's "Decline and Fall of the Roman Empire," xxi.); legal disqualification; also, a disability.

in-car-cer-ate (in-kär′sẹ-rāt), *v. t.*; *-ated, -ating.* [ML. *incarceratus*, pp. of *incarcerare*, < L. *in*, in, + *carcer*, prison.] To imprison; confine.—**in-car-cer-a′tion** (-sẹ-rā′shọn), *n.*—**in-car′cer-a-tor,** *n.*

in-car-di-nate (in-kär′di-nāt), *v. t.*; *-nated, -nating.* [ML. *incardinatus*, pp. of *incardinare*, < L. *in*, in, on, + *cardo*, hinge: cf. *cardinal.*] To institute or attach as chief presbyter, priest, etc., in a particular church or place; also, to institute as a cardinal.—**in-car-di-na′tion** (-nā′shọn), *n.*

in-car-na-dine (in-kär′nạ-din), *a.* [F. *incarnadin*, < It. *incarnatino*, < *incarnato*, flesh-colored, < LL. *incarnatus*: see *incarnate.*] Flesh-colored; pale-red; also, blood-colored. [Archaic.]—**in-car′na-dine,** *v. t.*; *-dined, -dining.* To dye or tinge with the color of flesh, or (now usually) of blood. See Shakspere's "Macbeth," ii. 2. 62. [Archaic.]

in-car-nate (in-kär′nāt), *v. t.*; *-nated, -nating.* [LL. *incarnatus*, pp. of *incarnare*, < L. *in*, in, + *caro* (*carn-*), flesh.] To embody in flesh; invest with a bodily, esp. a human, form; hence, to put into or represent in a concrete form, as an idea; also, to be the embodiment or type of.—**in-car′nate** (-nạt), *a.* Embodied in flesh; invested with a bodily, esp. a human, form (as, "You look on him almost with a shudder, as on some *incarnate* Mephistopheles": Carlyle's "Sartor Resartus," i. 4); hence, personified or typified, as a quality or idea (as, "Liberty and independence itself seemed *incarnate* in his name": Green's "Short Hist. of the Eng. People," ii. 2); also, flesh-colored; red.—**in-car-na′tion** (-nā′shọn), *n.* [LL. *incarnatio(n-).*] The act of incarnating, or the state of being incarnated; esp., assumption of human form or nature, as by a divine being (as, the *incarnation* of God in Christ, often called simply 'the Incarnation'); also, an incarnate being or form (as, "When shall my soul her *incarnation* quit, And . . . Obtain her apotheosis in Thee?" Young's "Night Thoughts," ix. 1341); hence, a person or thing representing or exhibiting some quality, idea, etc., in typical form; a personification or embodiment.

in-case (in-kās′), *v. t.*; *-cased, -casing.* [See *in-*[1].] To inclose in or as in a case: as, "In that portal should the chief appear . . . In radiant panoply his limbs *incased*" (Pope's tr. Homer's "Odyssey," i.).—**in-case′ment,** *n.* The act of incasing, or the state of being incased; also, that which incases; also, in *biol.*, a former theory of reproduction according to which successive generations are produced by the successive development of innumerable germs incased one within another.

in-cau-tion (in-kâ′shọn), *n.* [See *in-*[2].] Want of caution; heedlessness; carelessness: as, "I blamed myself bitterly for my *incaution*" (Stevenson's "Master of Ballantrae," v.).—**in-cau′tious** (-shus), *a.* Not cautious; heedless; unwary; rash: as, "The ostrich . . . Commits her eggs, *incautious*, to the dust, Forgetful that the foot may crush the trust" (Cowper's "Tirocinium," 791).—**in-cau′tious-ly,** *adv.*—**in-cau′tious-ness,** *n.*

in-cave (in-kāv′), *v. t.* Same as *encave.*

in-cen-di-a-ry (in-sen′di-ạ-ri). [L. *incendiarius*, < *incendium*, a burning, fire, < *incendere*: see *incense*[2].] **I.** *a.* Of or pertaining to the malicious or criminal setting on fire of buildings or other property; used or adapted for setting property on fire, as in war (as, "He had seen houses flaring, set afire by *incendiary* bombs": H. G. Wells's "Mr. Britling," ii. 2. § 8); fig., tending to arouse strife, sedition, etc.; inflammatory. **II.** *n.*; pl. *-ries* (-riz). One who maliciously sets fire to buildings or other property; fig., one who stirs up strife, sedition, etc.; an agitator.—**in-cen′di-a-rism** (-ạ-rizm), *n.*

in-cen-sa-tion (in-sen-sā′shọn), *n.* The act of incensing, or perfuming with incense.

in-cense[1] (in′sens), *n.* [OF. F. *encens*, < LL. *incensum*, incense, prop. pp. neut. of L. *incendere*: see *incense*[2].] An aromatic gum or other substance producing a sweet odor when burned, used esp. in religious ceremonies; also, the perfume or smoke arising from such a substance when burned; hence, any pleasant perfume or fragrance (as, "The matin winds from the expanded flowers Scatter their hoarded *incense*": Shelley's "Ginevra," 126); fig., homage or adulation (as, the *incense* of flattery).—**in′cense**[1], *v.*; *-censed, -censing.* [OF. F. *encenser.*] **I.** *tr.* To burn incense for; perfume with incense. **II.** *intr.* To burn or offer incense.

in-cense[2] (in-sens′), *v. t.*; *-censed, -censing.* [L. *incensus*, pp. of *incendere*, set on fire, kindle, inflame, < *in*, in, on, + *-cendere*, akin to *candere*, shine, glow.] To set on fire†; hence, to kindle or excite (passion, etc.: obs. or rare: as, "Will God *incense* his ire For such a petty trespass?" Milton's "Paradise Lost," ix. 692); also, to inflame or excite (a person) with passion; now, to inflame with wrath; make angry; enrage.

in-cense=burn-er (in′sens-bėr″nėr), *n.* A vessel or receptacle, often highly ornamental, for holding incense when burned.

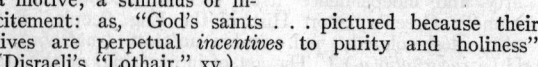

Japanese Incense-burner.

in-cense-ment (in-sens′-mẹnt), *n.* The act of incensing or inflaming, as with wrath, or the state of being incensed; wrath; anger.

in-cen-tive (in-sen′tiv). [L. *incentivus*, setting the tune, later inciting, < *incinere*, sing, sound, < *in*, in, on, + *canere*, sing.] **I.** *a.* Inciting, as to action; stimulating; provocative. **II.** *n.* That which incites to action, etc.; a motive; a stimulus or incitement: as, "God's saints . . . pictured because their lives are perpetual *incentives* to purity and holiness" (Disraeli's "Lothair," xv.).

in-cept (in-sept′), *v.* [L. *inceptus*, pp. of *incipere*, begin, commence, < *in*, in, on, + *capere*, take.] **I.** *tr.* To begin or commence (obs. or rare); also, to take in; intussuscept. **II.** *intr.* To complete the taking of a degree in a university. [Eng.]—**in-cep′tion** (-sep′shọn), *n.* [L. *inceptio(n-)*.] Beginning; commencement; also, the action of incepting in a university (Eng.); also, a taking in or receiving within.—**in-cep′tive.** **I.** *a.* Beginning; initial; in *gram.*, of verbs, etc., expressing the beginning of action. **II.** *n.* In *gram.*, an inceptive verb.—**in-cep′tive-ly,** *adv.*—**in-cep′tor,** *n.* [LL., beginner.] A beginner (rare); also, one who incepts in a university (Eng.).

in-cer-tain† (in-sėr′tạn), *a.* [OF. F. *incertain.*] Uncertain.—**in-cer′tain-ty**†, *n.*

in-cer-ti-tude (in-sėr′ti-tūd), *n.* [F. *incertitude*, < ML. *incertitudo*, < L. *incertus*, uncertain, < *in-*, not, + *certus*, certain.] Uncertainty; doubtfulness; insecurity; also, want of assurance or confidence; doubt.

in-ces-sant (in-ses′ạnt), *a.* [LL. *incessans (-ant-)*, < L. *in-*, not, + *cessans*, ppr. of *cessare*, E. *cease.*] Continuing without interruption; ceaseless; continual: as, "an *incessant* noise like that of a water-mill" (Swift's "Gulliver's Travels," i. 2).—**in-ces′san-cy, in-ces′sant-ness,** *n.*—**in-ces′sant-ly,** *adv.*

in-cest (in′sest), *n.* [L. *incestus, incestum*, < *incestus*, unchaste, < *in-*, not, + *castus*, E. *chaste.*] The crime of sexual intercourse between persons related within the degrees in which marriage is prohibited.—**in-ces′tu-ous** (-ses′tụ-us), *a.* [LL. *incestuosus.*] Guilty of incest; also, pertaining to or involving incest.—**in-ces′tu-ous-ly,** *adv.*—**in-ces′tu-ous-ness,** *n.*

inch (inch), *n.* [AS. *ynce*, < L. *uncia*, twelfth part, inch, ounce: cf. *ounce*[1].] A measure of length, the twelfth part of a foot, or 2.54 centimeters; as a unit of rainfall or precipitation, the amount of water, melted (or frequently unmelted) snow, or the like, which would cover a surface to the depth of one inch; as a unit of atmospheric or other pressure, a degree of pressure which balances the weight of a vertical column of mercury or other liquid one inch in height in a barometer or the like; also, a very small measure or amount of anything (as, "I'll flog you within an *inch* of your life": Dickens's "Nicholas Nickleby," xiii.).—**by inches,** or **inch by inch,** by small or slow degrees; very gradually: as, "Don't kill him at once . . . starve him gradually, *inch by inch*" (Congreve's "Way of the World," iv.).—**every inch,** every bit; in every respect; completely: as, "*every inch* a king" (Shakspere's "King Lear," iv. 6. 109).—**inch,** *v. i.* or *t.* To move by inches or small degrees: as, "I crawled aboard and *inched* along and got in among some bundles of shingles" (Mark Twain's "Life on the Mississippi," iii.).—**inch′meal** (-mēl), *adv.* [With *-meal* as in *limbmeal.*] By inches; inch by inch; little by little. Also used as a quasi-noun, after *by.*

in-cho-ate (in′kọ-āt), *v. t.* or *i.*; *-ated, -ating.* [L. *inchoatus*, pp. of *inchoare, incohare.*] To begin; commence; start.—**in′cho-ate,** *a.* Just begun; in an early stage; incipient; hence, rudimentary; incomplete.—**in′cho-ate-ly,** *adv.*—**in′cho-ate-ness,** *n.*—**in-cho-a′tion** (-ā′shọn), *n.* [LL. *inchoatio(n-)*.] Beginning; commencement; rudimentary or early stage.—**in-cho′a-tive** (-kō′ạ-tiv). [LL. *inchoativus.*] **I.** *a.* Rudimentary; inchoate; in *gram.*, inceptive. **II.** *n.* In *gram.*, an inchoative or inceptive verb.

inch-worm (inch′wėrm), *n.* The larva of any geometrid moth; a measuring-worm.

in-ci-dence (in′si-dẹns), *n.* The fact or the manner of being incident; the falling, or manner of falling, of a ray of light, etc., on a surface; also, a falling upon, affecting, or befalling; the range of occurrence or influence of a thing, or the extent of its effects (as, the *incidence* of the disease is general, or is limited to one locality); often, the fall of taxation upon individuals; also, something incidental†.—**angle of incidence,** the angle which a line, ray of light, etc., falling upon a surface, makes with a perpendicular to that surface at the point of incidence.

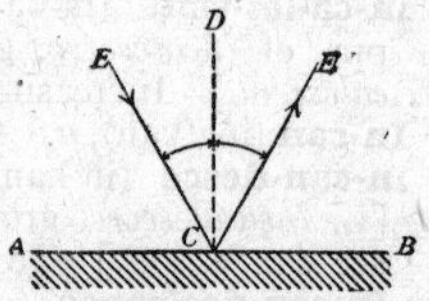

Angle of Incidence.—Ray *EC* (at left) impinges on surface *AB* at point *C*, *CD* being the perpendicular and angle *ECD* (at left) the angle of incidence; the ray being shown reflected at right, the angle *ECD* (at right) being the angle of reflection.

in-ci-dent (in′si-dẹnt). [L. *incidens (-ent-)*, ppr. of *incidere*, fall on, befall, < *in*, in, on, + *cadere*, fall.] **I.** *a.* Falling or striking on something; impinging, as rays of light on a surface; also, befalling; liable or apt to happen (*to*: as, "All natural and almost all political evils are *incident* alike to the bad and good," Johnson's "Rasselas," xxvii.);

hence, naturally appertaining (as, the hardships *incident* to the life of an explorer); also, conjoined or attaching, esp. as subordinate to a principal thing; also, incidental or casual (obs. or rare). **II.** *n.* Something that befalls in connection with a person or thing; something that occurs casually in connection with something else; an event or matter of accessory or subordinate character; sometimes, an occurrence or event considered separately or independently; in specif. use, a distinct piece of action, or an episode, as in a story, play, etc. (as, "A tale should be judicious, clear, succinct; The language plain, and *incidents* well link'd": Cowper's "Conversation," 236); a separate or single feature in a painting, etc.; also, something appertaining or attaching to something else; a natural or characteristic accompaniment; a secondary feature.—**in-ci-den′tal** (-den′tạl). **I.** *a.* Occurring or liable to occur in connection with something else; happening in fortuitous or subordinate conjunction with something else; casual or accidental; often, incurred casually and in addition to the regular or main amount, as expenses or charges; also, liable to happen or naturally appertaining (*to*); incident (*to*); also, casually met with or encountered (rare: as, an *incidental* acquaintance). **II.** *n.* Something incidental, as a circumstance; often, in *pl.*, incidental items, esp. of expense.—**in-ci-den′tal-ly,** *adv.*

in-cin-e-rate (in-sin′ẹ-rāt), *v. t.*; *-rated, -rating.* [ML. *incineratus*, pp. of *incinerare*, < L. *in*, in, + *cinis* (*ciner-*), ashes.] To burn or reduce to ashes; cremate.—**in-cin-e-ra′tion** (-rā′shọn), *n.*—**in-cin′e-ra-tor,** *n.* A furnace or apparatus for incinerating.

in-cip-i-ent (in-sip′i-ẹnt), *a.* [L. *incipiens* (*-ent-*), ppr. of *incipere*, begin: see *incept.*] Beginning to exist or appear; in an initial stage.—**in-cip′i-ence, in-cip′i-en-cy,** *n.*—**in-cip′i-ent-ly,** *adv.*

in-cise (in-sīz′), *v. t.*; *-cised, -cising.* [L. *incisus*, pp. of *incidere*, cut into, < *in*, in, + *cædere*, cut.] To cut into; cut marks, etc., upon; also, to make (marks, etc.) by cutting; engrave; carve.—**in-cised′,** *p. a.* Cut into; made by cutting; in *bot.* and *entom.*, having the margin deeply notched, as certain leaves or insect wings.—**in-ci′sion** (-sizh′ọn), *n.* [L. *incisio*(*n-*).] The act of incising; a cutting into, esp. for surgical purposes; also, a cut, gash, or notch; also, fig., incisiveness; keenness.—**in-ci′sive** (-sī′siv), *a.* Adapted for cutting, as the incisor teeth; fig., penetrating, trenchant, or biting; sharp; keen; acute.—**in-ci′sive-ly,** *adv.*—**in-ci′sive-ness,** *n.*—**in-ci′sor** (-sọr or -zọr), *n.* [NL.] A tooth adapted for cutting, esp. one of the front teeth situated between the canine teeth in either jaw.—**in-ci′so-ry** (-sọ-ri), *a.* Adapted for cutting, as the incisor teeth.—**in-cis′ure** (-sizh′ụ̄r), *n.* [L. *incisura.*] An incision, cleft, or notch; a deep indentation.—**in-cis′ur-al** (-sizh′ụ̄-rạl), *a.*

in-cite (in-sīt′), *v. t.*; *-cited, -citing.* [L. *incitare*, < *in*, in, on, + *citare*, drive, urge, call, E. *cite.*] To urge on; stimulate or prompt to action; instigate: as, "Each host now joins, and each a god inspires, These Mars *incites*, and those Minerva fires" (Pope's tr. Homer's "Iliad," iv.).—**in-ci-ta′tion** (-si-tā′shọn), *n.*—**in-cite′ment,** *n.* The act of inciting; also, that which incites; a stimulus or incentive.—**in-cit′er** (-sī′tėr), *n.*—**in-cit′ing-ly,** *adv.*

in-ci-vil-i-ty (in-si-vil′i-ti), *n.*; pl. *-ties* (-tiz). [LL. *incivilitas*, < L. *incivilis*, uncivil, < *in-*, not, + *civilis*, E. *civil.*] The quality or fact of being uncivil; uncivil behavior or treatment; discourtesy; rudeness; also, an uncivil act.

in-civ-il-i-za-tion (in-siv″i-li-zā′shọn), *n.* [See *in-*².] Want of civilization; uncivilized condition; barbarism.

in-civ-ism (in′si-vizm), *n.* [F. *incivisme*: cf. *civism.*] Bad citizenship; neglect of civic duties.

in-clem-ent (in-klem′ẹnt), *a.* [L. *inclemens* (*-ent-*).] Not clement; severe in temper or disposition; harsh; also, of the weather, etc., rough or stormy.—**in-clem′en-cy,** *n.*—**in-clem′ent-ly,** *adv.*

in-clin-a-ble (in-klī′nạ-bl), *a.* [OF. *inclinable*, < L. *inclinabilis.*] Inclining; tending; disposed; favorable.

in-cli-na-tion (in-kli-nā′shọn), *n.* [OF. F. *inclination*, < L. *inclinatio*(*n-*).] The act or an act of inclining; a leaning, bending, or bowing; also, the state of being inclined; deviation or amount of deviation from a normal, esp. horizontal or vertical, direction or position; slant; also, an inclined surface; also, tendency, now esp. of the mind or will; a disposition more favorable to one thing or person than to another; propensity; preference; specif., in *geom.*, the mutual approach of two lines or planes that tend to meet and form an angle ('angle of inclination'); also, the difference of direction of the lines or planes as measured by the angle.—**in-cli-na′tion-al,** *a.*

in-cline (in-klīn′), *v.*; *-clined, -clining.* [OF. F. *incliner*, < L. *inclinare*, incline, < *in*, in, on, + *-clinare*, bend, incline: see *decline.*] **I.** *tr.* To cause to lean or bend in a particular direction; give a slanting direction or position to; also, to bow (the head, body, etc.); turn (the ear) toward a speaker in order to listen attentively; also, to give a particular tendency to (the mind, heart, will, etc.); dispose (a person) in mind, will, habit, etc. (often with *to*). **II.** *intr.* To lean; bend; deviate from the vertical or horizontal; slant; also, to bow the head or body†; also, to tend in course or character; have a mental tendency; be disposed.—**in-cline** (in-klīn′ or in′klīn), *n.* An inclined surface; a slope.—**in-clined′,** *p. a.* Deviating in direction from the horizontal or vertical; sloping; slanting; hence, having a direction making an angle with anything else; also, having a tendency; disposed, esp. favorably.—**inclined plane,** a plane surface inclined to the horizon, or forming with a horizontal plane any angle but a right angle: one of the so-called simple machines.—**in-clin′er** (-klī′nėr), *n.*—**in-cli-nom′e-ter** (-kli-nom′e-tėr), *n.* [See *-meter.*] An instrument for determining the vertical component of the earth's magnetic force, as shown by the dip of the magnetic needle; also, an instrument for measuring the inclination or slope of anything; in *aëronautics*, an instrument for measuring the angle an aircraft makes with the horizontal.

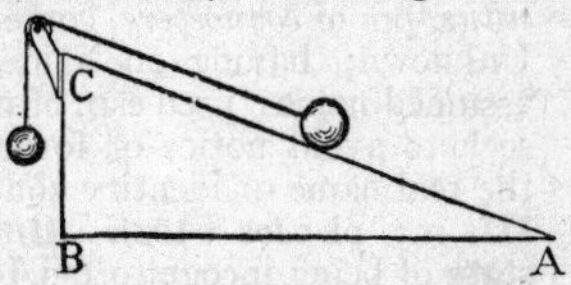

Inclined Plane. — *AC*, the plane; *CB*, its height; *BA*, its base; *BAC*, angle of inclination or elevation.

in-close, en-close (in-klōz′, en-), *v. t.*; *-closed, -closing.* [OF. F. *enclos*, pp. of *enclore*, inclose, < ML. *inclaudere*, L. *includere*: see *include*, and cf. *close*¹ and *close*².] To shut in; close in on all sides; insert in something that encompasses, surrounds, or confines; form an encompassing or confining medium about (something), as things do; esp., to surround as with a fence or wall; specif., to fence in (waste or common land) with the intention of cultivating it or of appropriating it to individual ownership; also, to shut up in a case, envelop, etc.; specif., to insert for transmission in the same cover with a letter, parcel, etc.; contain (the thing transmitted), as the letter or parcel does (as, we have received your letter *inclosing* your check).—**in-clos′er, en-clos′er** (-klō′zėr), *n.*—**in-clo′sure, en-clo′sure** (-klō′zhụ̄r), *n.* [OF. *enclosure.*] The act of inclosing, or the state of being inclosed; also, that which incloses, as a fence or wall, or an outer covering; also, that which is inclosed, as land, or a paper sent in a letter, or a parcel sent in a larger parcel.

in-clud-a-ble (in-klö′dạ-bl), *a.* Same as *includible.*

in-clude (in-klöd′), *v. t.*; *-cluded, -cluding.* [L. *includere* (pp. *inclusus*), shut in, < *in*, in, + *cludere*, *claudere*, shut, close: cf. *close*¹ and *inclose.*] To shut in†; also, to put within limits; hold or inclose within limits; also, to place in an aggregate, class, category, or the like; reckon in a calculation; also, to contain, embrace, or comprise, as a whole does parts or any part or element; often, to contain as a subordinate element; involve as a factor.—**in-clud′ed** (-klö′ded), *p. a.* Inclosed; embraced; comprised; in *bot.*, not projecting beyond the mouth of the corolla, as stamens or a style.—**in-clud′i-ble,** *a.* That may be included.—**in-clu′sion** (-klö′zhọn), *n.* [L. *inclusio*(*n-*).] The act of including, or the state of being included; also, that which is included; specif., in *mineral.*, a body of gas or liquid or a crystal inclosed within the mass of a mineral.—**in-clu′sive** (-siv), *a.* That includes; inclosing;

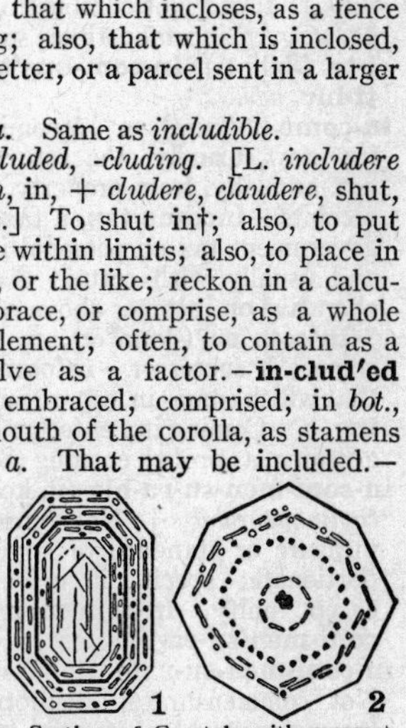

Sections of Crystals, with symmetrically arranged Inclusions. — 1, augite; 2, leucite.

embracing; comprising; often, including a great deal, or including everything concerned; comprehensive; also, including in consideration or account as the stated limit or extremes (often used adverbially: as, from Monday to Saturday *inclusive*, that is, taking in both Monday and Saturday).—**in-clu′sive-ly,** *adv.*—**in-clu′sive-ness,** *n.*

in-co-ag-u-la-ble (in-kō-ag′ū-lạ-bl), *a.* [See *in-*².] Not coagulable.

in-co-er-ci-ble (in-kō-ėr′si-bl), *a.* [See *in-*².] Not coercible.

in-cog (in-kog′). Colloquial abbreviation of *incognita* or *incognito*: as, "a Foreign Count, — who came *incog.*" (Hood's "Miss Kilmansegg," 1464).

in-cog-i-ta-ble (in-koj′i-tạ-bl), *a.* [LL. *incogitabilis.*] Not cogitable; unthinkable.—**in-cog″i-ta-bil′i-ty** (-bil′i-ti), *n.*

in-cog-i-tant (in-koj′i-tạnt), *a.* [L. *incogitans* (*-ant-*), < *in-*, not, + *cogitans*, ppr. of *cogitare*, think: see *cogitate.*] Unthinking; thoughtless; inconsiderate; also, not having the faculty of thinking.

in-cog-ni-ta (in-kog′ni-tạ̈). [It., fem. of *incognito*: see *incognito.*] **I.** *a.* Of a woman or girl, unknown; having the real name or identity concealed. **II.** *n.*; pl. *-tas* (-tạ̈z). A woman or girl who is incognita.—**in-cog′ni-to** (-tō). [It., masc., < L. *incognitus*, unknown, < *in-*, not, + *cognitus*, pp. of *cognoscere*, come to know: see *cognition.*] **I.** *a.* Unknown; having one's identity concealed, as under an assumed name: used esp. of persons of distinction who thus seek to avoid notice or formal attentions. **II.** *adv.* With the real name or identity concealed: as, to travel *incognito*. **III.** *n.*; pl. *-tos* (-tōz). One who is incognito; also, the state of being incognito (as, to preserve, or to discard, one's *incognito*).

in-cog-ni-za-ble (in-kog′ni-zạ-bl or in-kon′i-), *a.* [See *in-*².] Not cognizable; beyond cognizance or knowledge; unrecognizable.—**in-cog′ni-zant** (-zạnt), *a.* Not cognizant; without perception or knowledge (*of*); unaware.—**in-cog′ni-zance,** *n.*

in-co-her-ence, in-co-her-en-cy (in-kō-hēr′ẹns, -ẹn-si), *n.*; pl. *-ences* (-ẹn-sez), *-encies* (-siz). The state of being incoherent; also, something incoherent; an incoherent statement, proceeding, etc.

in-co-her-ent (in-kō-hēr′ẹnt), *a.* [See *in-*².] Not coherent or cohering; without physical cohesion, unconnected, or loose, as matter; also, without unity or harmony of elements, as an assemblage; without congruity of parts, or uncoördinated, as a system; without logical connection, disjointed, or rambling, as thought, language, etc.; characterized by such thought or language, as a person; also, naturally different, or incompatible, as things.—**in-co-her′ent-ly,** *adv.*

in-co-he-sion (in-kō-hē′zhọn), *n.* [See *in-*².] Want of cohesion.—**in-co-he′sive** (-siv), *a.* Not cohesive.

in-com-bus-ti-ble (in-kọm-bus′ti-bl). [ML. *incombustibilis.*] **I.** *a.* Not combustible; incapable of being burned. **II.** *n.* An incombustible substance.—**in-com-bus-ti-bil′i-ty** (-bil′i-ti), **in-com-bus′ti-ble-ness,** *n.*—**in-com-bus′ti-bly,** *adv.*

in-come (in′kum), *n.* A coming in, or something that comes in; now, usually, the returns that come in periodically, esp. annually, from property, business, labor, etc.; revenue; receipts.—**income tax,** a tax levied on incomes; an annual government tax on personal incomes, commonly graduated, and usually with certain deductions and exemptions and operative on incomes above a comparatively low fixed limit. —**in′com″er** (-kum″ėr), *n.* One who comes in; a newcomer; a successor.—**in′com″ing,** *n.* A coming in; also, that which comes in, esp. revenue (usually in *pl.*).—**in′com″ing,** *a.* Coming in; entering, as a tenant or an office-holder; accruing, as profit; ensuing (Sc.: as, the *incoming* week).

in-com-men-su-ra-ble (in-kọ-men′shụ̄-rạ-bl), *a.* [ML. *incommensurabilis.*] Not commensurable; having no common measure or standard of comparison; also, utterly disproportionate; specif., in *arith.*, having no common divisor except unity.—**in-com-men″su-ra-bil′i-ty** (-bil′i-ti), **in-com-men′su-ra-ble-ness,** *n.*—**in-com-men′su-ra-bly,** *adv.*

in-com-men-su-rate (in-kọ-men′shụ̄-rạt), *a.* [See *in-*².] Not commensurate; disproportionate; inadequate; also, incommensurable.—**in-com-men′su-rate-ly,** *adv.*—**in-com-men′su-rate-ness,** *n.*

in-com-mode (in-kọ-mōd′), *v. t.*; *-moded, -moding.* [F. *incommoder*, < L. *incommodare*, < *incommodus*, inconvenient, < *in-*, not, + *commodus*: see *commode.*] To subject to inconvenience, discommode, or trouble (as, "an interregnum *incommoded* with an abundance of sleek parsons and sly priests": H. G. Wells's "Outline of History," xxxvi. § 11); also, to impede; hinder.

in-com-mo-di-ous (in-kọ-mō′di-us), *a.* [See *in-*².] Not commodious; inconvenient; now, usually, not affording sufficient room; inconveniently or uncomfortably small.—**in-com-mo′di-ous-ly,** *adv.*—**in-com-mo′di-ous-ness,** *n.*

in-com-mod-i-ty (in-kọ-mod′i-ti), *n.*; pl. *-ties* (-tiz). [OF. *incommodite* (F. *incommodité*), < L. *incommoditas*, inconvenience, < *incommodus*: see *incommode.*] Inconvenience; disadvantage; discomfort; also, something inconvenient or disadvantageous; a discomfort or annoyance.

in-com-mu-ni-ca-ble (in-kọ-mū′ni-kạ-bl), *a.* [LL. *incommunicabilis.*] Not communicable; incapable of being communicated, imparted, or told to others; sometimes, incommunicative; also, without communication.—**in-com-mu″ni-ca-bil′i-ty** (-bil′i-ti), **in-com-mu′ni-ca-ble-ness,** *n.* —**in-com-mu′ni-ca-bly,** *adv.*

in-com-mu-ni-ca′do, *a.* See *incomunicado*.

in-com-mu-ni-ca-tive (in-kọ-mū′ni-kā-tiv), *a.* [See *in-*².] Not communicative; uncommunicative; reserved.—**in-com-mu′ni-ca-tive-ly,** *adv.*—**in-com-mu′ni-ca-tive-ness,** *n.*

in-com-mu-ta-ble (in-kọ-mū′tạ-bl), *a.* [L. *incommutabilis.*] Not commutable; not exchangeable; also, unchangeable.—**in-com-mu-ta-bil′i-ty** (-bil′i-ti), **in-com-mu′ta-ble-ness,** *n.*—**in-com-mu′ta-bly,** *adv.*

in-com-pact (in-kọm-pakt′), *a.* [See *in-*².] Not compact; loose in structure or consistence.—**in-com-pact′ly,** *adv.*—**in-com-pact′ness,** *n.*

in-com-pa-ra-ble (in-kom′pạ-rạ-bl), *a.* [L. *incomparabilis.*] Not comparable; admitting of no comparison; esp., matchless or unequaled (as, "Her words do show her wit *incomparable*": Shakspere's "3 Henry VI.," iii. 2. 85). —**in-com″pa-ra-bil′i-ty** (-bil′i-ti), **in-com′pa-ra-ble-ness,** *n.*—**in-com′pa-ra-bly,** *adv.*

in-com-pat-i-ble (in-kọm-pat′i-bl). [See *in-*².] **I.** *a.* Not compatible; incapable of existing together in harmony; contrary or opposed in character; discordant; inconsistent. **II.** *n.* An incompatible person or thing: usually in *pl.*: as, "In the inevitable jangle of these *incompatibles* the church had become dogmatic" (H. G. Wells's "Outline of History," xxxiii. § 13).—**in-com-pat-i-bil′i-ty** (-bil′i-ti), *n.*—**in-com-pat′i-bly,** *adv.*

in-com-pe-tent (in-kom′pē-tẹnt). [F. *incompétent*, < LL. *incompetens* (*-ent-*).] **I.** *a.* Not competent; lacking qualification or ability; incapable; not legally qualified; also, not admissible. **II.** *n.* An incompetent person.—**in-com′pe-tence, in-com′pe-ten-cy,** *n.*—**in-com′pe-tent-ly,** *adv.*

in-com-plete (in-kọm-plēt′), *a.* [LL. *incompletus.*] Not complete; lacking some part; unfinished; imperfect; defective.—**in-com-plete′ly,** *adv.*—**in-com-plete′ness,** *n.*

in-com-ple-tion (in-kọm-plē′shọn), *n.* [See *in-*².] Lack of completion; incomplete state.

in-com-pli-ant (in-kọm-plī′ạnt), *a.* [See *in-*².] Not compliant; unyielding; unaccommodating.—**in-com-pli′ance,** *n.*

in-com-pre-hen-si-ble (in-kom-prē-hen′si-bl), *a.* [L. *incomprehensibilis.*] Not comprehensible; not to be comprehended within limits, or illimitable (archaic: as, "The firmament . . . And all her number'd stars, that seem to roll Spaces *incomprehensible*," Milton's "Paradise Lost," viii. 20); not to be grasped by the mind; not to be understood, or unintelligible (as, "She was perfectly *incomprehensible* to me": Dickens's "Great Expectations," ix.). —**in-com-pre-hen-si-bil′i-ty** (-bil′i-ti), **in-com-pre-hen′si-ble-ness,** *n.*—**in-com-pre-hen′si-bly,** *adv.*

in-com-pre-hen-sion (in-kom-prē-hen′shọn), *n.* [See *in-*².] Want of comprehension or understanding.—**in-com-pre-hen′sive** (-siv), *a.* Not comprehensive; unduly limited or restricted; lacking mental comprehension (as, "Thou art an *incomprehensive* coxcomb!" Sheridan's "Trip to Scarborough," i. 2).—**in-com-pre-hen′sive-ly,** *adv.*—**in-com-pre-hen′sive-ness,** *n.*

in-com-press-i-ble (in-kọm-pres′i-bl), *a.* [See *in-*².] Not compressible.—**in-com-press-i-bil′i-ty** (-bil′i-ti), *n.*

in-com-pu-ta-ble (in-kọm-pū'tạ-bl), *a.* [See *in-*[2].] Not computable; incalculable.

in-co-mu-ni-ca-do (ēn-kō-mö-nē-kä'ᴛʜō), *a.* [Sp.] Of a prisoner, deprived of communication or intercourse with others.

in-con-ceiv-a-ble (in-kọn-sē'vạ-bl), *a.* [See *in-*[2].] Not conceivable; unimaginable; unthinkable; incredible.—**in-con-ceiv-a-bil'i-ty** (-bil'i-ti), **in-con-ceiv'a-ble-ness,** *n.* —**in-con-ceiv'a-bly,** *adv.*

in-con-clu-sion (in-kọn-klö'zhọn), *n.* [See *in-*[2].] Absence of conclusion or final decision; also, something inconclusive. —**in-con-clu'sive** (-siv), *a.* Not conclusive; not such as to settle a question or case; without decisive force or effect; indecisive; ineffective.—**in-con-clu'sive-ly,** *adv.*—**in-con-clu'sive-ness,** *n.*

in-con-dens-a-ble (in-kọn-den'sạ-bl), *a.* [See *in-*[2].] Not condensable. Also **in-con-dens'i-ble.**

in-con-dite (in-kon'dit or in'kọn-dīt), *a.* [L. *inconditus,* < *in-,* not, + *conditus,* pp. of *condere,* put together: see *condiment.*] Unformed; ill constructed; crude; rude. [Now rare.]

in-con-du-cive (in-kọn-dū'siv), *a.* [See *in-*[2].] Not conducive.

in-con-form-a-ble (in-kọn-fôr'mạ-bl), *a.* [See *in-*[2].] Not conformable; unconformable.—**in-con-for'mi-ty** (-fôr'mi-ti), *n.* Lack of conformity; failure or refusal to conform.

in-con-gru-ent (in-kong'grö-ẹnt), *a.* [L. *incongruens* (*-ent-*).] Not congruent; disagreeing; incongruous.—**in-con'gru-ence,** *n.*

in-con-gru-i-ty (in-kọn-grö'i-ti), *n.*; pl. *-ties* (-tiz). The quality of being incongruous; also, something incongruous.

in-con-gru-ous (in-kong'grö-us), *a.* [L. *incongruus.*] Not congruous; inharmonious in character; inconsonant; inconsistent; out of keeping or place; inappropriate; unbecoming; also, lacking harmony of parts.—**in-con'gru-ous-ly,** *adv.*—**in-con'gru-ous-ness,** *n.*

in-con-nu (in-kọ-nū', F. aṅ-ko-nü), *n.* [F., 'unknown': the fish being unknown to the Canadian voyageurs who first saw it.] A large salmonoid food-fish, *Stenodus mackenzii,* of the rivers of northwestern Canada and of Alaska. Also called *Mackenzie River salmon.*

Inconnu.

in-con-scious (in-kon'shus), *a.* [LL. *inconscius.*] Not conscious; unconscious. [Now rare.]—**in-con'scious-ly,** *adv.*

in-con-sec-u-tive (in-kọn-sek'ū-tiv), *a.* [See *in-*[2].] Not consecutive; disconnected.—**in-con-sec'u-tive-ly,** *adv.*—**in-con-sec'u-tive-ness,** *n.*

in-con-se-quent (in-kon'sē-kwent), *a.* [L. *inconsequens* (*-ent-*).] Not consequent; not following from the premises, or illogical (as, an *inconsequent* deduction); out of proper relation, or irrelevant (as, an *inconsequent* remark); not in keeping with the general character or design (as, *inconsequent* features of a work; *inconsequent* ornamentation); also, characterized by lack of logical sequence (as, *inconsequent* reasoning); disconnected; of persons, characterized by lack of sequence in thought, speech, or action.—**in-con'se-quence,** *n.*—**in-con-se-quen'tial** (-kwen'shạl), *a.* Inconsequent; illogical; irrelevant; also, of no consequence (as, "As my time is not wholly *inconsequential,* I should not be sorry to have an early opportunity of being heard": Miss Burney's "Cecilia," ix. 3).—**in-con-se-quen'tial-ly,** *adv.*—**in-con'se-quent-ly,** *adv.*—**in-con'se-quent-ness,** *n.*

in-con-sid-er-a-ble (in-kọn-sid'ėr-ạ-bl), *a.* [See *in-*[2].] Not considerable; not worthy of consideration or notice; unimportant; trivial; insignificant; small, as in value, amount, size, etc.—**in-con-sid'er-a-ble-ness,** *n.*—**in-con-sid'er-a-bly,** *adv.*

in-con-sid-er-ate (in-kọn-sid'ėr-ạt), *a.* [L. *inconsideratus.*] Not considerate; done or acting without consideration; thoughtless; heedless; also, without due regard for the rights or feelings of others.—**in-con-sid'er-ate-ly,** *adv.*—**in-con-sid'er-ate-ness,** *n.*—**in-con-sid-er-a'tion** (-ẹ-rā'shọn), *n.* [LL. *inconsideratio(n-).*] Want of due consideration; thoughtlessness.

in-con-sist-en-cy (in-kọn-sis'tẹn-si), *n.*; pl. *-cies* (-siz). The quality of being inconsistent; also, something inconsistent.

in-con-sist-ent (in-kọn-sis'tẹnt), *a.* [See *in-*[2].] Not consistent; lacking agreement, as one thing with another, or two or more things in relation to each other; at variance; discrepant; incongruous; also, wanting in harmony between the different parts or elements; self-contradictory; also, of persons, not consistent in principles, conduct, etc. (as, "Man is a creature very *inconsistent* with himself": Steele, in "Tatler," 7); acting at variance with professed principles or former conduct.—**in-con-sist'ent-ly,** *adv.*

in-con-sol-a-ble (in-kọn-sō'lạ-bl), *a.* [L. *inconsolabilis.*] Not consolable; disconsolate.—**in-con-sol'a-ble-ness,** *n.*—**in-con-sol'a-bly,** *adv.*

in-con-so-nant (in-kon'sọ-nạnt), *a.* [LL. *inconsonans* (*-ant-*).] Not consonant or in accord.—**in-con'so-nance,** *n.* —**in-con'so-nant-ly,** *adv.*

in-con-spic-u-ous (in-kọn-spik'ū-us), *a.* [LL. *inconspicuus.*] Not conspicuous, noticeable, or prominent.—**in-con-spic'u-ous-ly,** *adv.*—**in-con-spic'u-ous-ness,** *n.*

in-con-stant (in-kon'stạnt), *a.* [OF. F. *inconstant,* < L. *inconstans* (*-ant-*).] Not constant; changeable; fickle; variable: as, "O, swear not by the moon, the *inconstant* moon, That monthly changes in her circled orb" (Shakspere's "Romeo and Juliet," ii. 2. 109).—**in-con'stan-cy,** *n.*—**in-con'stant-ly,** *adv.*

in-con-sum-a-ble (in-kọn-sū'mạ-bl), *a.* [See *in-*[2].] Not consumable; incapable of being consumed.

in-con-test-a-ble (in-kọn-tes'tạ-bl), *a.* [See *in-*[2].] Not contestable; not admitting of dispute; incontrovertible: as, "The genius and daring of Bolingbroke were . . . *incontestable*" (Lecky's "Hist. of Eng. in the 18th Century," i.).—**in-con-test'a-ble-ness,** *n.*—**in-con-test'a-bly,** *adv.*

in-con-ti-nent[1] (in-kon'ti-nẹnt), *a.* [L. *incontinens* (*-ent-*).] Not continent; lacking in restraint, esp. over the sexual appetite; also, unable to contain or retain (usually with *of*: as, "Melantho with imperious mien Renew'd the attack, *incontinent* of spleen," Pope's tr. Homer's "Odyssey," xix.).—**in-con'ti-nence, in-con'ti-nen-cy,** *n.*—**in-con'ti-nent-ly**[1], *adv.*

in-con-ti-nent[2] (in-kon'ti-nẹnt), *adv.* [OF. F. *incontinent,* < LL. *in continenti* (*tempore*), 'in continuous (time),' or without pause.] Straightway; immediately; at once: as, "He will be here *incontinent*" (Scott's "Kenilworth," xix.). [Archaic.] Also **in-con'ti-nent-ly**[2].

in-con-tin-u-ous (in-kọn-tin'ū-us), *a.* [See *in-*[2].] Not continuous; discontinuous.—**in-con-ti-nu'i-ty** (-kon-ti-nū'i-ti), *n.*

in-con-trol-la-ble (in-kọn-trō'lạ-bl), *a.* [See *in-*[2].] Not controllable; uncontrollable.

in-con-tro-vert-i-ble (in-kon-trọ-vėr'ti-bl), *a.* [See *in-*[2].] Not controvertible; indisputable.—**in-con-tro-vert-i-bil'i-ty** (-bil'i-ti), **in-con-tro-vert'i-ble-ness,** *n.*—**in-con-tro-vert'i-bly,** *adv.*

in-con-ve-nience (in-kọn-vē'niẹns), *n.* [OF. *inconvenience,* < LL. *inconvenientia.*] The quality of being inconvenient; disagreement†; unsuitableness†; impropriety†; now, troublesomeness; disadvantageousness; inopportune character; unfavorableness to comfort; trouble or discomfort caused or experienced (as, "She could have spared him without the smallest *inconvenience*": Dickens's "Pickwick Papers," xxvii.); also, something inconvenient; something that causes trouble, disadvantage, or discomfort.—**in-con-ve'nience,** *v. t.*; *-nienced, -niencing.* To put to inconvenience; incommode.—**in-con-ve'nien-cy** (-niẹn-si), *n.*; pl. *-cies* (-siz). Inconvenience; also, something inconvenient.

in-con-ve-nient (in-kọn-vē'niẹnt), *a.* [OF. *inconvenient* (F. *inconvénient*), < L. *inconveniens* (*-ent-*).] Not convenient; not agreeing or consonant†; unsuitable† or inappropriate†; now, giving trouble or annoyance; disadvantageous; embarrassing; inopportune; unfavorable to comfort.—**in-con-ve'nient-ly,** *adv.*

in-con-vert-i-ble (in-kọn-vėr'ti-bl), *a.* [See *in-*[2].] Not convertible; incapable of being converted or exchanged; specif., of paper money, not capable of being converted into specie.—**in-con-vert-i-bil′i-ty** (-bil′i-ti), **in-con-vert′i-ble-ness,** *n.*—**in-con-vert′i-bly,** *adv.*

in-con-vin-ci-ble (in-kọn-vin′si-bl), *a.* [See *in-*[2].] Not convincible; incapable of being convinced.—**in-con-vin-ci-bil′i-ty** (-bil′i-ti), *n.*—**in-con-vin′ci-bly,** *adv.*

in-con-y† (in-kun′i), *a.* [Origin uncertain.] Rare; fine; pretty. See Shakspere's "Love's Labour's Lost," iv. 1. 144.

in-co-ör-di-nate (in-kọ̄-ôr′di-nạ̄t), *a.* [See *in-*[2].] Not coördinate.—**in-co-ör′di-nat-ed** (-nā-ted), *a.* Not coördinated.—**in-co-ör-di-na′tion** (-nā′shọn), *n.* Lack of coördination.

in-cor-po-rate[1] (in-kôr′pọ̄-rạ̄t), *a.* [LL. *incorporatus*: cf. *corporate.*] Not embodied; incorporeal. [Obs. or rare.]

in-cor-po-rate[2] (in-kôr′pọ̄-rāt), *v.*; *-rated, -rating.* [LL. *incorporatus*, pp. of *incorporare*, < L. *in*, in, + *corporare*, embody: see *corporate.*] **I.** *tr.* To form or combine into one body or uniform substance, as, ingredients; unite intimately; also, to put or introduce into a body or mass as an integral part or integral parts; take in or include as a part or parts, as the body or mass does; also, to form into a society or organization; esp., to constitute as a legal corporation; also, to admit as a member of an association or corporation; also, to give material form to, or embody (as, "some actual Air-maiden, *incorporated* into tangibility and reality": Carlyle's "Sartor Resartus," ii. 5). **II.** *intr.* To unite or combine so as to form one body; also, to form a corporation.—**in-cor′po-rate**[2] (-rạ̄t), *a.* Incorporated; combined into one body, mass, or substance (as, "Gazing on thee, sullen tree . . . I seem to fail from out my blood And grow *incorporate* into thee": Tennyson's "In Memoriam," ii.); also, constituted as a corporation; admitted into a corporation, as a person; also, embodied.—**in-cor-po-ra′tion** (-rā′shọn), *n.* [LL. *incorporatio(n-).*] The act of incorporating, or combining into one body; incorporated state; also, the act or process of forming into a corporation; an incorporated society, or a corporation (as, "an eminent member of the Goldsmiths' *Incorporation*": Scott's "Fortunes of Nigel," ix.); also, embodiment; an embodied form of something.—**in-cor′po-ra-tor,** *n.* One who incorporates; specif., one of the original members of a corporation.

in-cor-po-re-al (in-kôr-pō′rẹ̄-ạl), *a.* [L. *incorporeus.*] Not corporeal; immaterial; also, pertaining to immaterial beings; in *law*, without material existence, but existing in contemplation of law, as a franchise or a right of way.—**in-cor-po-re-al′i-ty** (-al′i-ti), **in-cor-po-re′i-ty** (-pọ̄-rē′i-ti), *n.*—**in-cor-po′re-al-ly,** *adv.*

in-corpse (in-kôrps′), *v. t.* [See *in-*[1].] To form or combine into one body; incorporate. See Shakspere's "Hamlet," iv. 7. 88. [Archaic.]

in-cor-rect (in-kọ-rekt′), *a.* [L. *incorrectus.*] Not correct; faulty or improper; erroneous or inaccurate.—**in-cor-rect′ly,** *adv.*—**in-cor-rect′ness,** *n.*

in-cor-ri-gi-ble (in-kor′i-ji-bl), *a.* [L. *incorrigibilis.*] Not corrigible; bad beyond correction or reform; irreclaimable: as, "If Tavy were not in love with you . . . he'd have found out what an *incorrigible* liar you are" (G. B. Shaw's "Man and Superman," ii.).—**in-cor″ri-gi-bil′i-ty** (-bil′i-ti), **in-cor′ri-gi-ble-ness,** *n.*—**in-cor′ri-gi-bly,** *adv.*

in-cor-rupt (in-kọ-rupt′), *a.* [L. *incorruptus.*] Not corrupt; free from decomposition or putrefaction; not debased or perverted; morally upright; not to be bribed; not vitiated by errors or alterations, as a text.—**in-cor-rup′ti-ble** (-rup′ti-bl), *a.* [LL. *incorruptibilis.*] Not corruptible; incapable of physical or moral corruption; that cannot be perverted or bribed.—**in-cor-rup-ti-bil′i-ty** (-bil′i-ti), **in-cor-rup′ti-ble-ness,** *n.*—**in-cor-rup′ti-bly,** *adv.*—**in-cor-rup′tion** (-shọn), *n.* [LL. *incorruptio(n-).*] Incorrupt condition. See 1 Cor. xv. 42–54.—**in-cor-rupt′ly,** *adv.*—**in-cor-rupt′ness,** *n.*

in-cras-sate (in-kras′āt), *v. t.*; *-sated, -sating.* [LL. *incrassatus*, pp. of *incrassare*, < L. *in*, in, + *crassare*, thicken, < *crassus*, thick.] To thicken; in *phar.*, to make (a liquid) thicker by addition of another substance or by evaporation.—**in-cras′sate,** *a.* In *bot.* and *entom.*, thickened or swollen.—**in-cras-sa′tion** (-kra-sā′shọn), *n.*

in-creas-a-ble (in-krē′sạ-bl), *a.* That may be increased.

in-crease (in-krēs′), *v.*; *-creased, -creasing.* [OF. *encreistre*, < L. *increscere*, < *in*, in, on, + *crescere*, grow.] **I.** *intr.* To become greater in any respect; augment; grow; wax, as the moon; multiply by propagation; formerly, often, to grow richer, more prosperous, or more powerful. **II.** *tr.* To make greater in any respect; augment; add to; make more numerous; formerly, often, to make richer, more prosperous, or more powerful.—**in′crease,** *n.* The act or process of increasing, or becoming or making greater; augmentation; growth; enlargement; growth or augmentation in numbers; specif., multiplication by propagation; the production of offspring; also, the result of increasing, or that by which something is increased; an addition or increment; also, offspring or progeny (as, "All the *increase* of thine house shall die in the flower of their age": 1 Sam. ii. 33); also, produce of the earth; also, product; profit; interest.—**in-creas′er,** *n.*—**in-creas′ing-ly,** *adv.*

in-cre-ate (in′krẹ̄-āt), *a.* [ML. *increatus.*] Not created; existing without having been created.

in-cred-i-ble (in-kred′i-bl), *a.* [L. *incredibilis.*] Not credible; surpassing the possibility of belief; also, surpassing belief as to what is possible, or seemingly too extraordinary to be possible (as, "Experienced as he was, he had never come across a fact so *incredible* as this fact": Arnold Bennett's "Helen with the High Hand," iv.).—**in-cred-i-bil′i-ty** (-bil′i-ti), *n.*—**in-cred′i-bly,** *adv.*

in-cred-u-lous (in-kreḍ′ū-lus), *a.* [L. *incredulus.*] Not credulous; indisposed to believe; skeptical; also, indicating unbelief (as, an *incredulous* smile); also, incredible† (see Shakspere's "Twelfth Night," iii. 4. 88).—**in-cre-du′li-ty** (-krẹ̄-dū′li-ti), *n.*—**in-cred′u-lous-ly,** *adv.*

in-cre-mate (in′krẹ̄-māt), *v. t.*; *-mated, -mating.* [See *in-*[1].] To cremate.—**in-cre-ma′tion** (-mā′shọn), *n.*

in-cre-ment (in′krẹ̄-mẹnt), *n.* [L. *incrementum*, < *increscere*: see *increase.*] The act or process of increasing, or becoming greater; augmentation; growth; increase; also, something added or gained; an addition or increase; profit; in *math.*, a small increase (positive or negative) in an independent variable, or the increase of a function due to this.—**in-cre-men′tal** (-men′tạl), *a.*

in-cres-cent (in-kres′ẹnt), *a.* [L. *increscens* (*-ent-*), ppr. of *increscere*: see *increase.*] Increasing or waxing, as the moon.

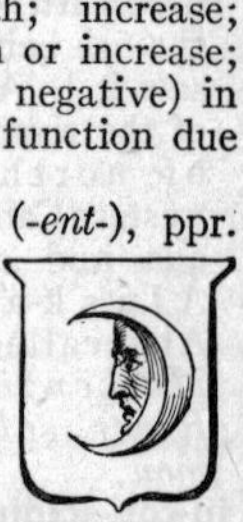

Heraldic representation of Increscent Moon.

in-crim-i-nate (in-krim′i-nāt), *v. t.*; *-nated, -nating.* [ML. *incriminatus*, pp. of *incriminare*, < L. *in*, in, on, + *criminare*: see *criminate.*] To charge with a crime or fault; also, to involve in an accusation.—**in-crim-i-na′tion** (-nā′shọn), *n.* The act of incriminating, or the state or fact of being incriminated.—**in-crim′i-na-tor,** *n.*—**in-crim′i-na-to-ry** (-nạ̄-tọ̄-ri), *a.* Tending to incriminate.

in-croy-able (aṅ-krwo-yäbl), *n.* [F., 'incredible': so called from their frequent use of this word.] One of a class of French men and women of fashion during the period of the Directory (1795–99), who affected extravagant modes of dress, peculiarities of speech, etc.

in-crust (in-krust′), *v. t.* [L. *incrustare* (pp. *incrustatus*), < *in*, in, on, + *crusta*, E. *crust.*] To cover or line with a crust or hard coating; also, to form into a crust; deposit as a crust; also, specif., to overlay (a surface) with a crust of precious material; apply or inlay (mosaic, marble slabs, etc.) as a decorative covering. Also **in-crus′tate** (-krus′tāt); *-tated, -tating.*—**in-crus-ta′tion** (-tā′shọn), *n.* [LL. *incrustatio(n-).*] An incrusting or being incrusted; also, a crust or hard coating; specif., an outer hard layer or facing of fine material placed over a common substance.

in-cu-bate (in′kū-bāt), *v.*; *-bated, -bating.* [L. *incubatus*, pp. of *incubare*, lie on, sit or rest on, < *in*, in, on, + *cubare*, lie.] **I.** *tr.* To sit upon (eggs) for the purpose of hatching; hatch (eggs) as by sitting upon them; fig., to brood; produce as if by hatching; also, to hatch (eggs) by artificial heat, as in an incubator; maintain (bacterial cultures, etc.) at a temperature suitable for development. **II.** *intr.* To sit upon eggs; brood (sometimes fig.); also, to undergo incubation; in *pathol.*, to go through the process of incubation.—**in-cu-ba′tion** (-bā′shọn), *n.* [L. *incubatio(n-).*] The act or process of incubating (often fig.); in *pathol.*, the development of a disease between infection and the appearance of its symptoms.—**in′cu-ba-tive** (-bạ-tiv), **in′cu-ba-to-ry** (-tọ-ri), *a.* Of or pertaining to incubation.—**in′cu-ba-tor** (-bā-tọr), *n.* One who or that which incubates; an apparatus for hatching eggs artificially, consisting essentially of a case heated by a lamp or the like; a similar apparatus for rearing children prematurely born; a device in which bacterial cultures, etc., are developed.

in-cu-bus (in′kụ̄-bus), *n.*; pl. *-buses*, L. *-bi* (-bī). [LL., < L. *incubare*, lie on: see *incubate*.] An imaginary demon or evil spirit supposed to descend upon sleeping persons; esp., a male demon supposed to consort with women in their sleep (cf. *succuba* and *succubus*); hence, the nightmare; also, something that weighs upon or oppresses one like a nightmare (as, "There sat upon my very heart an *incubus* of utterly causeless alarm," Poe's "Fall of the House of Usher"; "the hateful *incubus* of debt," George Eliot's "Mill on the Floss," iv. 2).

in-cul-cate (in-kul′kāt or in′kul-), *v. t.*; *-cated, -cating.* [L. *inculcatus*, pp. of *inculcare*, tread in, impress, < *in*, in, + *calcare*, tread, press, E. *calk*[1].] To impress by repeated statement or admonition; urge on the mind; teach persistently and earnestly: as, "When learning, virtue, piety, and truth, Were precious, and *inculcated* with care" (Cowper's "Task," ii. 701).—**in-cul-ca′tion** (-kā′shọn), *n.* The act of inculcating; the impressing of principles, etc., on the mind by persistent urging or teaching.—**in-cul′ca-tor,** *n.*—**in-cul′ca-to-ry** (-kạ-tọ-ri), *a.* Serving to inculcate.

in-cul-pa-ble (in-kul′pạ-bl), *a.* [LL. *inculpabilis*.] Not culpable; blameless.—**in-cul′pa-bly,** *adv.*

in-cul-pate (in′kul-pāt or in-kul′-), *v. t.*; *-pated, -pating.* [ML. *inculpatus*, pp. of *inculpare*, < L. *in*, in, + *culpa*, fault.] To charge with fault; blame; accuse; also, to involve in a charge; incriminate.—**in-cul-pa′tion** (-pā′shọn), *n.*—**in-cul′pa-to-ry** (-pạ-tọ-ri), *a.* Tending to inculpate; imputing blame; incriminating.

in-cult (in-kult′), *a.* [L. *incultus*, < *in-*, not, + *cultus*, pp. of *colere*, cultivate, till.] Uncultivated; untilled; wild; rude; unrefined. [Now rare.]

in-cum-ben-cy (in-kum′bẹn-si), *n.*; pl. *-cies* (-siz). The state of being incumbent; also, that which is incumbent; an incumbent weight or mass; a duty or obligation; also, the position or term of an incumbent.

in-cum-bent (in-kum′bẹnt). [L. *incumbens* (*-ent-*), ppr. of *incumbere*, < *in*, in, on, + *-cumbere*, lie: cf. *accumbent*.] **I.** *a.* Lying, leaning, or pressing on something; also, resting on one as a duty (as, "It . . . appeared a duty *incumbent* upon me to attempt to reclaim them": Goldsmith's "Vicar of Wakefield," xxvi.); obligatory. **II.** *n.* The holder of an office; esp., one who holds an ecclesiastical benefice.—**in-cum′bent-ly,** *adv.*

in-cum-ber (in-kum′bėr), etc. Same as *encumber*, etc.

in-cu-nab-u-la (in-kụ̄-nab′ụ̄-lạ̈), *n. pl.* [L., swaddling-clothes, cradle, beginning, < *in*, in, + *cunabula*, cradle: see *cunabula*.] The earliest stages or first traces of anything; the beginnings; commonly, books produced in the infancy of printing, esp. before the year 1500.—**in-cu-nab′u-lar** (-lạ̈r), *a.*

in-cur (in-kėr′), *v. t.*; *-curred, -curring.* [L. *incurrere* (pp. *incursus*), < *in*, in, on, + *currere*, run.] To run or fall into (some consequence, usually an undesirable or injurious consequence); become liable or subject to through one's own action; bring upon one's self: as, to *incur* liabilities or penalties; "They are in danger of *incurring* his royal displeasure" (Swift's "Gulliver's Travels," iii. 9).

in-cur-a-ble (in-kūr′ạ-bl). [LL. *incurabilis*.] **I.** *a.* Not curable; incapable of being cured or corrected; irremediable: as, an *incurable* invalid; an *incurable* disease; an *incurable* evil. **II.** *n.* One suffering from an incurable disease.—**in-cur-a-bil′i-ty** (-bil′i-ti), **in-cur′a-ble-ness,** *n.*—**in-cur′a-bly,** *adv.*

in-cu-ri-ous (in-kū′ri-us), *a.* [L. *incuriosus*.] Not curious; careless, negligent, or heedless (*of*: archaic); inattentive or unobservant (as, an *incurious* observer; "listless and *incurious* eyes," Cooper's "Prairie," ii.); devoid of curiosity, or indifferent; also, deficient in interest or novelty (usually with a negative: as, a not *incurious* anecdote).—**in-cu-ri-os′i-ty** (-os′i-ti), **in-cu′ri-ous-ness,** *n.*—**in-cu′ri-ous-ly,** *adv.*

in-cur-sion (in-kėr′shọn), *n.* [L. *incursio*(*n-*), < *incurrere*: see *incur*.] A running in; usually, a hostile entrance into or invasion of a place or territory, esp. one of sudden character (as, "There had been repeated *incursions* of the Highlanders into the very town of Perth": Scott's "Fair Maid of Perth," xiv.); a sudden attack; fig., a harmful inroad, as of the sea, of disease, etc.—**in-cur′sive** (-siv), *a.* Making incursions; invading.

in-cur-vate (in-kėr′vāt), *v. t.*; *-vated, -vating.* [L. *incurvatus*, pp. of *incurvare*, < *in*, in, + *curvare*, bend, E. *curve*, *v.*] To make curved; turn from a straight line or course; curve; esp., to curve inward.—**in-cur′vate,** *a.* Curved, esp. inward.—**in-cur-va′tion** (-vā′shọn), *n.*

in-curve (in-kėrv′), *v. t.* or *i.*; *-curved, -curving.* [L. *incurvare*: see *incurvate*.] To curve, esp. inward.

in-cus (ing′kus), *n.*; pl. *incudes* (in-kū′dēz). [L. *incus* (*incud-*), anvil, < *incudere*: see *incuse*.] In *anat.*, the middle one of a chain of three small bones in the middle ear of man and other mammals: so called from a fancied resemblance to an anvil. See *malleus* and *stapes*.

in-cuse (in-kūz′), *v. t.*; *-cused, -cusing.* [L. *incusus*, pp. of *incudere*, forge with a hammer, < *in*, in, on, + *cudere*, strike, beat.] To impress by striking or stamping, as a coin.—**in-cuse′. I.** *a.* Hammered or stamped in, as a figure on a coin. **II.** *n.* An incuse figure or impression.

1 2

1. Reverse of Coin of Ægina, with early Incuse Square. — British Museum. 2. Reverse of Coin of Phocis, with later Incuse Square (inclosing the device). — British Museum.

Ind (ind), *n.* [OF. F. *Inde*.] India (now poetic: as, "this . . . golden realm of *Ind*," Byron's "Sardanapalus," i. 2); also, the Indies (East or West)†.

in-da-ba (in-dä′bạ̈), *n.* [Zulu.] A conference or consultation between or with South African natives.

in-da-gate (in′dạ-gāt), *v. t.*; *-gated, -gating.* [L. *indagatus*, pp. of *indagare*, track, investigate.] To trace out; search out; investigate. [Now rare.]—**in-da-ga′tion** (-gā′shọn), *n.*—**in′da-ga-tor,** *n.*

in-dam-ine (in-dam′in), *n.* [From *indigo* + *amine*.] In *chem.*, any of a certain series of basic organic compounds which form bluish and greenish salts: used in the manufacture of dyes.

in-debt (in-det′), *v. t.* [First used in pp., ME. *endetted*, < OF. *endeter* (F. *endetter*), < *en-* (< L. *in*, in) + *dete*, E. *debt*.] To put in debt; render (one) a debtor, as for money due; place under obligation for benefits, favors, assistance, etc., received; render beholden; bind by obligations of duty†: used chiefly in *indebted*, *pp.*—**in-debt′ed-ness,** *n.* The state or condition of being indebted; also, an amount owed; debts collectively. Also **in-debt′ment.**

in-de-cen-cy (in-dē′sẹn-si), *n.*; pl. *-cies* (-siz). The quality of being indecent; unbecomingness; impropriety; indelicacy or immodesty; obscenity; also, something indecent; an unseemly act, practice, etc.; a highly immodest or an obscene action, speech, etc.

in-de-cent (in-dē′sẹnt), *a.* [L. *indecens* (*-ent-*).] Not decent; unbecoming or unseemly; offending against recognized standards of propriety or good taste; highly indelicate or immodest; offensive to the sense of decency; obscene.—**in-de′cent-ly,** *adv.*

in-de-cid-u-ate (in-dẹ-sid′ụ̄-āt), *a.* [See *in-*[2].] Not deciduate; having no decidua.

in-de-cid-u-ous (in-dẹ-sid′ụ̄-us), *a.* [See *in-*[2].] Not deciduous; not falling or shed at a particular time, as leaves; of trees, evergreen.

in-de-ci-pher-a-ble (in-dẹ-sī′fėr-ạ-bl), *a.* [See *in-*[2].] Not decipherable.—**in-de-ci″pher-a-bil′i-ty** (-bil′i-ti), *n.*

in-de-ci-sion (in-dẹ-sizh′ọn), *n.* [See *in-*[2].] Want of decision; irresolution: as, "the strange *indecision* of mind . . . which we may observe in some people" (Boswell's "Johnson," April 17, 1778).—**in-de-ci′sive** (-sī′siv), *a.* Not decisive or conclusive (as, "Several severe but *indecisive* naval battles were fought in the Indian seas": Lecky's "Hist. of Eng. in the 18th Century," xiv.); also, characterized by indecision, as persons; irresolute; undecided.—**in-de-ci'sive-ly,** *adv.*—**in-de-ci'sive-ness,** *n.*

in-de-clin-a-ble (in-dę̄-klī'nạ-bl), *a.* [LL. *indeclinabilis.*] In *gram.*, not declinable.—**in-de-clin'a-bly,** *adv.*

in-de-com-pos-a-ble (in-dē-kọm-pō'zạ-bl), *a.* [See *in-*[2].] Not decomposable.

in-de-co-rous (in-dę̄-kō'rus or in-dek'ọ̄-), *a.* [L. *indecorus.*] Not decorous; violating propriety; unseemly.—**in-de-co'rous-ly,** *adv.*—**in-de-co'rous-ness,** *n.*—**in-de-co-rum** (in-dę̄-kō'rum), *n.* [L., neut. of *indecorus.*] Something indecorous; a breach of decorum; an indecorous proceeding; also, indecorous behavior or character; impropriety.

in-deed (in-dēd'), *adv.* [Orig. two words, *in deed.*] In fact; in reality; in truth; truly: much used (*a*) for emphasis (as, I am very glad *indeed*; "Do you believe it?" "Yes, *indeed*"); (*b*) to confirm and amplify a previous statement (in the sense of 'as a matter of fact': as, he is a good workman, *indeed* an excellent one); (*c*) to indicate a concession or admission (in the sense of 'it must be admitted': as, it is *indeed* poor work, but it might be worse); (*d*) interrogatively, for the purpose of obtaining confirmation (equivalent to 'is it so?': as, "I fear that he is very ill." "*Indeed?*"); and (*e*) as an interjection, expressing surprise, incredulity, etc., or used in irony (as, "The prisoner has escaped." "*Indeed!*" — "I will stand this no longer." "*Indeed!*").

in-de-fat-i-ga-ble (in-dę̄-fat'i-gạ-bl), *a.* [L. *indefatigabilis,* < *in-*, not, + *defatigare*, tire out, < *de-*, utterly, + *fatigare*, E. *fatigue, v.*] Incapable of being tired out; not yielding to fatigue; tireless; untiring; unwearying; unflagging: as, "The French were *indefatigable* in their efforts to obtain a naval ascendency on the coast" (Lecky's "Hist. of Eng. in the 18th Century," xiv.); "His diligence was *indefatigable*" (Gibbon's "Decline and Fall of the Roman Empire," xviii.).—**in-de-fat"i-ga-bil'i-ty** (-bil'i-ti), **in-de-fat'i-ga-ble-ness,** *n.*—**in-de-fat'i-ga-bly,** *adv.*

in-de-fea-si-ble (in-dę̄-fē'zi-bl), *a.* [See *in-*[2].] Not defeasible; not to be annulled or made void; not forfeitable: as, "the doctrine of the *indefeasible* right of the legitimate sovereign, and of the absolute sinfulness of resistance" (Lecky's "Hist. of Eng. in the 18th Century," i.).—**in-de-fea-si-bil'i-ty** (-bil'i-ti), *n.*—**in-de-fea'si-bly,** *adv.*

in-de-fec-ti-ble (in-dę̄-fek'ti-bl), *a.* [See *in-*[2].] Not defectible; not liable to defect or failure; unfailing; not liable to fault or imperfection; faultless.—**in-de-fec-ti-bil'i-ty** (-bil'i-ti), *n.*—**in-de-fec'ti-bly,** *adv.*

in-de-fen-si-ble (in-dę̄-fen'si-bl), *a.* [See *in-*[2].] Not defensible; that cannot be defended by force of arms (as, an *indefensible* frontier); that cannot be defended in argument; unjustifiable; inexcusable.—**in-de-fen-si-bil'i-ty** (-bil'i-ti), **in-de-fen'si-ble-ness,** *n.*—**in-de-fen'si-bly,** *adv.*

in-de-fin-a-ble (in-dę̄-fī'nạ-bl), *a.* [See *in-*[2].] Not definable; incapable of being defined or exactly described: as, "*indefinable* longings" (Longfellow's "Evangeline," ii. 3).—**in-de-fin'a-ble-ness,** *n.*—**in-de-fin'a-bly,** *adv.*

in-def-i-nite (in-def'i-nit), *a.* [L. *indefinitus.*] Not definite; without fixed or specified limit; unlimited; not clearly defined or determined; not precise; vague; in *gram.*, not specifying precisely (as, the *indefinite* article 'a'); in *logic*, without designation of extent; in *bot.*, very numerous or not easily counted, as stamens; of an inflorescence, indeterminate.—**in-def'i-nite-ly,** *adv.*—**in-def'i-nite-ness,** *n.*

in-de-fin-i-tive (in-dę̄-fin'i-tiv), *a.* [See *in-*[2].] Not definitive.—**in-de-fin'i-tive-ness,** *n.*

in-de-his-cent (in-dę̄-his'ẹnt), *a.* [See *in-*[2].] In *bot.*, not dehiscent; not opening at maturity.—**in-de-his'cence,** *n.*

in-del-i-ble (in-del'i-bl), *a.* [L. *indelebilis*: see *in-*[2] and *delible.*] Not delible; incapable of being deleted or obliterated; ineffaceable; permanent: as, *indelible* ink; an *indelible* disgrace; an *indelible* impression.—**in-del-i-bil'i-ty** (-bil'i-ti), *n.*—**in-del'i-bly,** *adv.*

in-del-i-cate (in-del'i-kạ̄t), *a.* [See *in-*[2].] Not delicate; lacking delicacy; offensive to a refined sense of propriety, or to purity of mind; coarse; unrefined.—**in-del'i-ca-cy** (-kạ̄-si), *n.*—**in-del'i-cate-ly,** *adv.*

in-dem-ni-fi-ca-tion (in-dem"ni-fi-kā'shọn), *n.* The act of indemnifying, or the state of being indemnified; also, that which serves to indemnify; a compensation or recompense (as, "What *indemnification* is one great man for populations of pigmies!" Emerson's "Representative Men," i.).

in-dem-ni-fy (in-dem'ni-fī), *v. t.*; *-fied, -fying.* [L. *indemnis*, unharmed (see *indemnity*), + *facere*, make.] To preserve from or secure against damage or loss; secure against legal responsibility for actions, events, etc. (as, "The act *indemnified* the peace-officers . . . if they killed any of the mob in endeavouring to suppress such riot": Blackstone's "Commentaries," IV. 142); also, to compensate for damage or loss sustained, expense incurred, etc.; recompense for annoyances, disadvantages, hardships, etc. (as, "Here they found deer and other game in abundance, and *indemnified* themselves for past famine": Irving's "Captain Bonneville," xxxviii.).—**in-dem'ni-fi-er** (-fī-ėr), *n.*

in-dem-ni-tee (in-dem-ni-tē'), *n.* [Irreg. < *indemnity.*] One to whom indemnity is given.—**in-dem'ni-tor,** *n.* One who gives indemnity.

in-dem-ni-ty (in-dem'ni-ti), *n.*; pl. *-ties* (-tiz). [LL. *indemnitas,* < L. *indemnis*, unharmed, < *in-*, not, + *damnum*, harm, loss.] Protection or security against damage or loss; specif., legal exemption from liabilities or penalties incurred by one's actions (as, "He has . . . an *indemnity* granted him of being free and discharged forever from all debts owing by him at the time he became a bankrupt": Blackstone's "Commentaries," II. 483); legal exemption from penalties attaching to unconstitutional or illegal actions, granted to public officers and other persons (as, an act or bill of *indemnity*); also, compensation for damage or loss sustained; something paid by way of such compensation.

in-de-mon-stra-ble (in-dę̄-mon'strạ-bl), *a.* [L. *indemonstrabilis.*] Not demonstrable; incapable of being demonstrated; not subject to demonstration (said of primary truths, etc.).—**in-de-mon-stra-bil'i-ty** (-bil'i-ti), *n.*

in-dent[1] (in-dent'), *v. t.* [See *in-*[1] and *dent*[1].] To form as a dent or depression (as, "Deep scars were seen *indented* on his breast": Dryden's tr. Juvenal's "Satires," vi. 151); also, to drive or force into something so as to form a dent (as, "Deep in the neck his fangs *indent* their hold": Pope's tr. Homer's "Odyssey," xix.); also, to make a dent or depression in (as, "shields *indented* deep in glorious wars": Pope's tr. Homer's "Odyssey," xix.).—**in'dent**[1], *n.* A dent or depression in the surface of anything, as from a blow.

in-dent[2] (in-dent'), *v.* [OF. F. *endenter*, < ML. *indentare*, < L. *in*, in, + *dens* (*dent-*), tooth.] **I.** *tr.* To make tooth-like notches in; notch; hence, to form deep recesses in; penetrate deeply; also, to make an incision or incisions in (a board, etc.) for the purpose of dovetailing; join together by dovetailing; also, to divide (a document drawn up in duplicate) by a zigzag line as a means of identification; cut the edge of (copies of a document) in an exactly corresponding shape; hence, to draw up (a document) in duplicate; also, to indenture, as an apprentice; also, to draw an order upon; order, as commodities; in *printing*, etc., to set in or back from the margin, as the first line of a paragraph. **II.** *intr.* To form a recess; also, to enter into an agreement by indenture; make a compact; also, to make out an order or requisition in duplicate; hence, to draw upon a person or thing for something.—**in-dent**[2] (in-dent' or in'dent), *n.* A tooth-like notch or deep recess; an indentation; also, an indenture; specif., a certificate issued by the U. S. government at the close of the Revolutionary War, for the principal or interest of the public debt; also, an official requisition for stores; also, an order for goods; in *printing*, etc., an indention.—**in-den-ta'tion** (-den-tā'shọn), *n.* A notching or being notched; also, a cut, notch, or deep recess, as in a margin; a series of incisions or notches; in *printing*, etc., an indention.—**in-dent'ed,** *p. a.* Having a notched edge or serrate outline; having a zigzag direction or course; also, indentured, as an apprentice (as, "I lead the life of an *indented* slave": Smollett's "Humphry Clinker," April 28); in *printing*, etc., set in or back from the margin.—**in-dent'er,** *n.*—**in-den'tion** (-shọn), *n.* An indenting; an indentation; in *printing*, etc., an indenting of a line or lines, and leaving of blank space; also, the blank space so left.

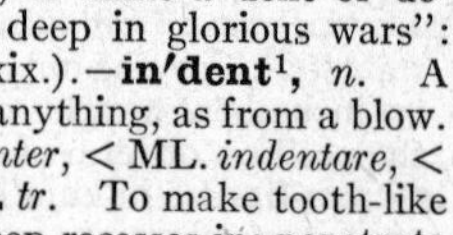

Indented Molding.

in-den-ture (in-den′ṭụr), *n.* [OF. *endenteure* (F. *endenture*).] Indentation; also, a deed or agreement executed in two or more copies with edges correspondingly indented as a means of identification; hence, any deed or sealed agreement; specif., a contract by which a person, as an apprentice, is bound to service; also, any official or formal list, certificate, etc., authenticated for use as a voucher or the like.—**in-den′ture,** *v. t.*; *-tured, -turing.* To bind by indenture, as an apprentice.

in-de-pend-ence (in-dẹ-pen′dẹns), *n.* The state or quality of being independent; exemption from external control or support; freedom from subjection, or from the influence of others; also, a competency (as, "In old-fashioned times, an '*independence*' was hardly ever made without a little miserliness as a condition": George Eliot's "Mill on the Floss," i. 12).—**Independence Day,** in the U. S., July 4, a holiday commemorating the adoption of the Declaration of Independence on July 4, 1776; the Fourth of July.—**in-de-pend′en-cy,** *n.* Independence; specif. [*cap.*], *eccles.*, the principle that the individual congregation or church is an autonomous society free from any external ecclesiastical control; the system of polity based on this principle.

in-de-pend-ent (in-dẹ-pen′dẹnt). [See *in-*[2].] **I.** *a.* Not dependent; not depending or contingent on something else for existence, operation, etc.; also, not subject to another's authority; autonomous; free; also, not relying on another or others for aid or support (as, "With his horse and his rifle, he is *independent* of the world": Irving's "Captain Bonneville," i.); hence, possessing a competency (as, "the only *independent* gentleman of the neighborhood": Irving's "Sketch-Book," Little Britain); sufficient for a competency (as, a gentleman of *independent* means); also, declining others' aid or support; refusing to be under obligations to others; also, not influenced by others in matters of opinion, conduct, etc.; thinking or acting for one's self; not influenced by that of others, as thought or action; also, expressive of a spirit of independence (as, an *independent* air or manner); self-confident; unconstrained; also, adverbially, independently (*of*); in *math.*, of a quantity or function, not depending upon another for value; [*cap.*] *eccles.*, of or pertaining to the Independents. **II.** *n.* An independent person or thing; in *politics*, one who votes without regard to any organized party; also, a member of any party called 'Independent'; [*cap.*] *eccles.*, an adherent of Independency; specif., a Congregationalist (Eng.).—**in-de-pend′ent-ly,** *adv.* In an independent manner; with *of*, apart from; without regard to.

in-de-scrib-a-ble (in-dẹ-skrī′bạ-bl), *a.* [See *in-*[2].] Not describable; beyond or transcending description.—**in-de-scrib-a-bil′i-ty** (-bil′i-ti), **in-de-scrib′a-ble-ness,** *n.*—**in-de-scrib′a-bly,** *adv.*

in-de-sert (in-dẹ-zėrt′), *n.* [See *in-*[2].] Want of desert or merit: as, "a man in power, who can . . . raise obscure merit, and discountenance successful *indesert*" (Steele, in "Tatler," 69).

in-de-struc-ti-ble (in-dẹ-struk′ti-bl), *a.* [See *in-*[2].] Not destructible; incapable of being destroyed: as, "Even if all these orchids died to-night yet their beauty is an *indestructible* memory" (Dunsany's "Laughter of the Gods," iii.).—**in-de-struc-ti-bil′i-ty** (-bil′i-ti), **in-de-struc′ti-ble-ness,** *n.*—**in-de-struc′ti-bly,** *adv.*

in-de-ter-mi-na-ble (in-dẹ-tėr′mi-nạ-bl), *a.* [LL. *indeterminabilis.*] Not determinable; incapable of being determined, decided, or ascertained.—**in-de-ter′mi-na-bly,** *adv.*

in-de-ter-mi-nate (in-dẹ-tėr′mi-nạt), *a.* [LL. *indeterminatus.*] Not determinate; undetermined; indefinite; uncertain; vague; unsettled or undecided; in *bot.*, of an inflorescence, having the axis or axes not ending in a flower or bud, thus allowing further elongation.—**in-de-ter′mi-nate-ly,** *adv.*—**in-de-ter′mi-nate-ness,** *n.*

in-de-ter-mi-na-tion (in-dẹ-tėr-mi-nā′shọn), *n.* [See *in-*[2].] Want of determination; unsettledness; an unsettled state, as of the mind.

in-de-ter-min-ism (in-dẹ-tėr′min-izm), *n.* [See *in-*[2] and *determinism.*] The doctrine that human actions, though somewhat influenced by preëxisting psychological and other conditions, are not entirely governed by them, but have a certain freedom and spontaneity; the theory that the will is to some extent independent of the strength of motives, or may itself determine their strength.—**in-de-ter′min-ist,** *n.*

in-de-vo-tion (in-dẹ-vō′shọn), *n.* [LL. *indevotio*(*n*-).] Want of devotion; impiety; irreligion.

in-de-vout (in-dẹ-vout′), *a.* [See *in-*[2].] Not devout; irreligious.

in-dex (in′deks), *n.*; pl. *indexes* or *indices* (in′di-sēz). [L. *index* (*indic-*), < *indicare*, point out, show: see *indicate.*] Something used or serving to point out; the forefinger, or index-finger; a piece of wood, metal, or the like, serving as a pointer or indicator; a pointer or indicator in a scientific instrument; an alidade; a hand of a clock, etc.; also, something that serves to direct attention to some fact, condition, etc. (as, "The State Constitutions . . . are . . . instructive . . . as an *index* to the present tendencies of American democracy": Bryce's "American Commonwealth," xxxviii.); a guiding principle; a sign, token, or indication (as, the face is an *index* of the heart); also, a table of contents, or a summary or argument, as of a book† (as, "Even as an *index* to a book, So to his mind was young Leander's look": Marlowe's "Hero and Leander," ii.); a preface† or prologue† (see Shakspere's "Othello," ii. 1. 263); an alphabetic or classified list for facilitating reference, as one placed at the end of a book, or a series of books, and containing topics, names, etc., occurring in it, with indication of the places where they occur; specif. [*cap.*], a list of books which Roman Catholics are forbidden by ecclesiastical authority to read, or which are not to be read unless expurgated or corrected (L. *Index Librorum Prohibitorum*, 'Index of Prohibited Books'), or a list of books of the latter class only, with specification of objectionable passages (L. *Index Expurgatorius*, 'Expurgatory Index'); also [*l. c.*], in *printing*, etc., a sign (☞) used to point out a particular note, paragraph, etc.; in *alg.*, an exponent; in *science*, a number or formula expressing some property, ratio, etc., of a thing indicated.—**in′dex,** *v. t.* To provide with an index, as a book; enter in an index, as a word; also, to serve to indicate.—**in′dex-er,** *n.*—**in′dex=fin″ger,** *n.* The forefinger: so called because used in pointing.—**in-dex′i-cal,** *a.* Pertaining to or of the nature of an index.—**in′dex-less,** *a.* Having no index, as a book.

In-di-a (in′di-ạ) **ink.** A black pigment, made chiefly in China and Japan, consisting of lampblack mixed with a binding material and molded into sticks or cakes; also, a liquid ink prepared from this.

In-di-a-man (in′di-ạ-mạn), *n.*; pl. *-men.* A ship in the India trade, esp. a large one belonging to the East India Company.

In-di-an (in′di-ạn), *a.* Of or pertaining to India or the East Indies (often 'East Indian': see *East Indian, a.*); also, noting, belonging to, or pertaining to the race embracing the aborigines of America (from the usage of Columbus and the people of his day, who believed that the lands he had discovered were a part of India or the East Indies: see *American, a.*); also, made of Indian corn (as, *Indian* meal: see phrase below).—**Indian club,** a bottle-shaped wooden club used in gymnastic exercises.—**Indian corn,** maize: so called because cultivated orig. by the American Indians.—**Indian cucumber,** a convallariaceous plant, *Medeola virginica*, growing in damp woods in eastern North America, having a fleshy rootstock with a flavor somewhat like that of a cucumber.—**Indian file,** single file (see under *single, a.*): as, "The party . . . moved up the pathway in single or *Indian file*" (Scott's "Waverley," xxxviii.).—**Indian giver,** one who takes back a gift after having bestowed it. [Colloq.]—**Indian hemp.** See under *hemp.*—**Indian licorice,** a fabaceous woody shrub, *Abrus abrus*, of India, etc., whose seeds (see *jequirity*) are

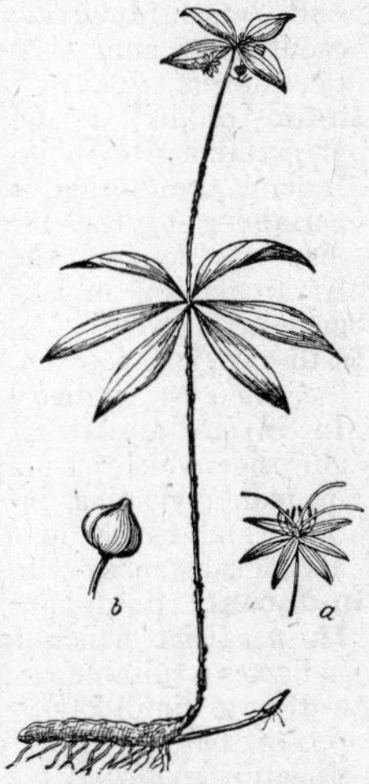

Flowering Plant of Indian Cucumber. — *a*, flower; *b*, fruit.

used for beads, and whose root is employed as a substitute for licorice.—**Indian mallow,** a malvaceous plant, *Abutilon abutilon,* with yellow flowers and velvety leaves, introduced into America, etc., from southern Asia; sometimes, any of certain related species.—**Indian meal,** meal made from Indian corn.—**Indian millet,** durra.—**Indian Mutiny.** Same as *Sepoy Mutiny,* under *sepoy.*—**Indian physic,** either of two American rosaceous herbs, *Porteranthus trifoliatus* and *P. stipulatus,* whose roots have emetic properties.—**Indian pudding,** a sweet pudding made with Indian meal: an old New England dish.—**Indian summer,** a period of mild, dry weather, usually accompanied by a hazy atmosphere, occurring in the U. S. in late autumn or early winter.—**Indian tobacco,** a common American herb, *Lobelia inflata,* with small blue flowers and inflated capsules: used medicinally.—**Indian turnip,** the plant jack-in-the-pulpit.—**In'di-an,** *n.* A member of any of the native races of India or the East Indies (an 'East Indian'); also, a European, esp. an Englishman, who resides or has resided in India or the East Indies (as, "He [Colonel Newcome] appeared at Bath and at Cheltenham, where . . . there are many old *Indians*": Thackeray's "Newcomes," xxi.); also, a member of the aboriginal race of America (see *Indian, a.*), or of any of the aboriginal North and South American stocks, often excepting the Eskimos (an 'American Indian'); also, the language, or any of the languages, of the American Indians.—**In'di-an-ist,** *n.* One versed in the languages, history, and customs of India.—**In'di-an=pipe',** *n.* A leafless parasitic plant, *Monotropa uniflora,* of North America and Asia, having a solitary flower, and resembling a tobacco-pipe.

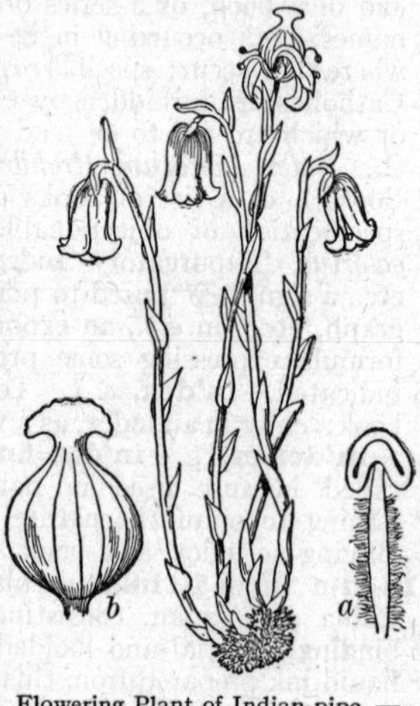

Flowering Plant of Indian-pipe. — *a,* stamen; *b,* fruit.

In-di-a (in'di-ą) **pa'per.** A thin, soft, absorbent paper, made chiefly in China and Japan, used for the first or finest impressions of engravings, etc.; also, a thin, tough, opaque printing-paper, used for Bibles, prayer-books, etc. —**In'di-a proof.** A proof or first impression of an engraving, etc., on India paper.

in-di-a=rub-ber (in'di-ą-rub'ėr), *n.* A highly elastic substance obtained from the milky juice of numerous tropical plants, used for rubbing out pencil marks, and variously in the arts and manufactures; caoutchouc; gum elastic; rubber.

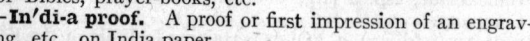

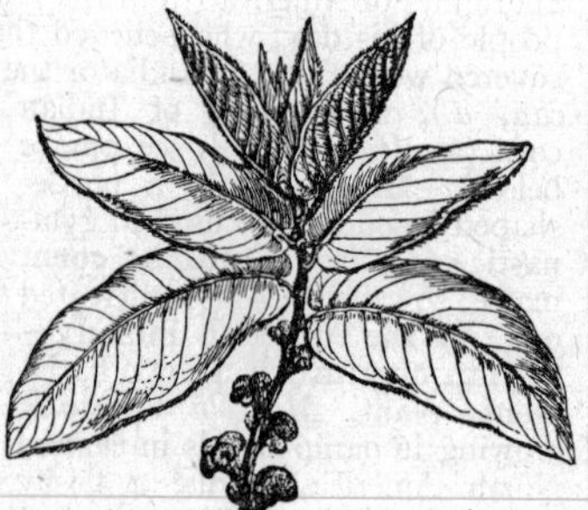
Flowering Branch of *Castilla elastica,* a Central American Tree yielding India-rubber.

In-dic (in'dik), *a.* Of or pertaining to India; Indian; also, noting or pertaining to the Indian division of the Aryan family of languages.

in-di-can (in'di-kąn), *n.* [L. *indicum,* indigo.] In *chem.,* a natural glucoside which occurs in plants yielding indigo, and which upon decomposition forms indigo blue; also, a substance occurring in urine and other bodily fluids.

in-di-cant (in'di-kąnt). **I.** *a.* Indicating; indicative. **II.** *n.* That which indicates; in *med.,* something that indicates a suitable remedy or treatment, as a symptom.

in-di-cate (in'di-kāt), *v. t.*; *-cated, -cating.* [L. *indicatus,* pp. of *indicare,* point out, show, < *in,* in, on, + *dicare,* declare: see *diction.*] To point out or point to (as, to *indicate* a place on a map; an arrow *indicates* the direction); direct attention to; hence, in general, to show, or make known (as, the thermometer *indicates* temperature; to *indicate* a face by outlines; "Viewing all she sees, As meant to *indicate* a God to man," Cowper's "Task," iii. 246); be a sign of, or betoken (as, the asterisk *indicates* a foot-note; his hesitation *indicates* unwillingness); signify or imply, as words do; state or express, esp. briefly or in a general way (as, to *indicate* one's views or intentions); intimate or suggest; in *med.,* of symptoms, etc., to point out (a particular remedy, treatment, operation, etc.) as suitable or necessary; show the presence of (a disease, etc.).—**in-di-ca'tion** (-kā'shǫn), *n.* [L. *indicatio(n-).*] The act of indicating; a pointing out, showing, or betokening; a suggestion or hint; also, anything serving to indicate or point out, as a sign, token, or symptom; in *med.,* a special symptom or the like which points out a suitable remedy or treatment or shows the presence of a disease.

in-dic-a-tive (in-dik'ą-tiv). [LL. *indicativus.*] **I.** *a.* That indicates; pointing out; giving intimation or knowledge of something not visible or obvious; suggestive; in *gram.,* stating or expressing something regarded as actual, and not merely possible or desirable, as a mode of the verb used in predicating, affirming, asking questions, etc.; of or pertaining to this mode. **II.** *n.* In *gram.,* the indicative mode, or a verb-form belonging to it.—**in-dic'a-tive-ly,** *adv.*

in-di-ca-tor (in'di-kā-tǫr), *n.* [LL.] One who or that which indicates; specif., a pointing or directing device, as a pointer or hand on the dial of an instrument; any of various mechanical devices or gages for indicating or recording something, as an apparatus for recording (by means of a diagram) the variations of pressure or vacuum in the cylinder of a steam-engine; in *chem.,* a substance used (esp. in volumetric analysis) to indicate (as by a change in color) the condition of a solution, the point at which a certain reaction ends and another begins, or the like.—**in'di-ca-to-ry** (-ką-tō-ri), *a.* Serving to indicate.

in-di-ces (in'di-sēz), *n.* A plural of *index.*

in-di-ci-a (in-dish'i-ą), *n. pl.* [L., pl. of *indicium,* < *index*: see *index.*] Indications; signs, tokens, or symptoms: as, "The corpse afforded no other *indicia* respecting the fate of Kennedy" (Scott's "Guy Mannering," x.).—**in-di'cial** (-dish'ąl), *a.*

in-dict (in-dīt'), *v. t.* [AF. *enditer,* accuse, indict, = OF. *enditer,* make known, dictate, write: see *indite.*] To charge with an offense or crime; accuse; esp., of a grand jury, to bring a formal accusation against, as a means of bringing to trial.—**in-dict'a-ble** (-dī'tą-bl), *a.* Liable to be indicted, as a person; also, rendering one liable to be indicted, as an offense.—**in-dict'er** (-dī'tėr), *n.*

in-dic-tion (in-dik'shǫn), *n.* [L. *indictio(n-),* < *indicere,* declare, appoint, < *in,* in, + *dicere,* say.] Authoritative declaration or appointment; proclamation; esp., a proclamation made every 15 years in the ancient Roman Empire, fixing the valuation of property to be used as a basis for taxation; hence, a tax based on such valuation; also, the recurring fiscal period of 15 years in the Roman Empire, long used for dating ordinary events; also, a specified year in this period, or the number indicating it.

in-dict-ment (in-dīt'mȩnt), *n.* The act of indicting, or the state of being indicted; an accusation; esp., a formal accusation presented by a grand jury.

in-dif-fer-ence (in-dif'ȩ-rȩns), *n.* The quality or fact of being indifferent; impartiality; want of interest or concern (as, to regard a thing with *indifference*); unimportance (as, a matter of complete *indifference* to us); mediocre quality; absence of difference (obs. or rare). Also **in-dif'fer-en-cy.**

in-dif-fer-ent (in-dif'ȩ-rȩnt). [L. *indifferens* (*-ent-*), < *in-,* not, + *differens* (*-ent-*), E. *different.*] **I.** *a.* Making no difference or distinction, as between persons or things; impartial, unbiased, or without preference (as, an *indifferent* judge, juror, or arbitrator); also, having no feeling favorable or unfavorable to some thing or person (as, to be *indifferent* to an advantage offered, or to an admirer); without interest or concern, not caring, or apathetic; also, not making a difference, or mattering, either way, as to a person (as, the hour for the meeting is *indifferent* to me; the details are *indifferent*); immaterial or unimportant; not essential or obligatory, as an observance; also, neutral in character or quality; neither good nor bad (as, an *indifferent* specimen or quality; an *indifferent* player; things good, bad, and *indifferent*); mediocre; only passable, or not very good; sometimes, of only moderate amount, extent, etc. (as, an *indifferent* supply); also, neutral in chemical, electrical, or magnetic quality; also, not different, dissimilar, or distinct†; in *biol.*, not differentiated or specialized, as cells or tissues. **II.** *n.* One who is indifferent in feeling, as to some matter or cause; a neutral; *pl.*, things that are indifferent; non-essentials; adiaphora.—**in-dif′fer-ent,** *adv.* Passably or moderately; not exceptionally: as, "I am myself *indifferent* honest" (Shakspere's "Hamlet," iii. 1. 123). [Obs. or archaic.]—**in-dif′fer-ent-ism,** *n.* Systematic indifference (as, "Often . . . was I blamed . . . for my so-called Hardness . . . my *Indifferentism* towards men": Carlyle's "Sartor Resartus," ii. 4); esp., the principle that differences of religious belief are essentially unimportant; adiaphorism.—**in-dif′fer-ent-ist,** *n.*—**in-dif′fer-ent-ly,** *adv.*

in-di-gence (in′di-jẹns), *n.* Indigent state; poverty; also, indigent persons collectively (as, "aiding helpless *indigence*": Cowper's "Task," vi. 964).

in-di-gene (in′di-jēn), *n.* [L. *indigena*, < *indu*, old form of *in*, in, + *gen-*, beget, produce: see *genius*.] One who or that which is indigenous or native; a native; an autochthon.

in-dig-e-nous (in-dij′e-nus), *a.* [L. *indigenus*, < *indigena*: see *indigene*.] Born or originating in a particular region or country (as, the *indigenous* races, animals, or plants of South America; the *indigenous* school of Spanish poetry); produced or arising naturally in a region; native (*to*); fig., innate; inherent; natural (*to*).—**in-di-gen′i-ty** (-jen′i-ti), **in-dig′e-nous-ness,** *n.*—**in-dig′e-nous-ly,** *adv.*

in-di-gent (in′di-jẹnt), *a.* [OF. F. *indigent*, < L. *indigens* (*-ent-*), ppr. of *indigere*, be in need, < *indu* (see *indigene*) + *egere*, be needy, want.] Wanting, lacking, or deficient in what is requisite (archaic: as, "How low, how little are the proud, How *indigent* the great!" Gray's "On the Spring"); destitute or in want (*of*: archaic: as, "How do I see that our sex is naturally *indigent* of protection?" Steele's "Funeral," ii. 2); now, usually, lacking the necessaries of life; needy; poor.—**in′di-gent-ly,** *adv.*

in-di-gest-ed (in-di-jes′ted), *a.* [See *in-*[2].] Not digested; undigested; without arrangement or order; unformed or shapeless (as, "Foul *indigested* lump, As crooked in thy manners as thy shape!" Shakspere's "2 Henry VI.," v. 1. 157); not duly considered, as a scheme; of food, not having undergone digestion.

in-di-gest-i-ble (in-di-jes′ti-bl), *a.* [LL. *indigestibilis*.] Not digestible; not capable of being digested; not easily digested.—**in-di-gest-i-bil′i-ty** (-bil′i-ti), **in-di-gest′i-ble-ness,** *n.*—**in-di-gest′i-bly,** *adv.*

in-di-ges-tion (in-di-jes′chọn), *n.* [LL. *indigestio(n-)*.] Want of digestion; incapability of or difficulty in digesting food; dyspepsia.—**in-di-ges′tive,** *a.* Attended with or suffering from indigestion; dyspeptic.

in-dign (in-dīn′), *a.* [OF. F. *indigne*, < L. *indignus*, < *in-*, not, + *dignus*, worthy.] Unworthy or undeserving (as, "She her selfe was of his grace *indigne*": Spenser's "Faerie Queene," iv. 1. 30); also, unbecoming or disgraceful (as, "*indign* and base adversities": Shakspere's "Othello," i. 3. 274); also, undeserved, as suffering. [Now poetic.]

in-dig-nant (in-dig′nạnt), *a.* [L. *indignans* (*-ant-*), ppr. of *indignari*, deem unworthy, be displeased at, < *indignus*, unworthy: see *indign*.] Displeased or incensed by something deemed unworthy, unjust, or base; affected with or characterized by indignation.—**in-dig′nant-ly,** *adv.*

in-dig-na-tion (in-dig-nā′shọn), *n.* [L. *indignatio(n-)*, < *indignari*: see *indignant*.] Displeasure at something deemed unworthy, unjust, or base; anger mingled with contempt or abhorrence; righteous anger.—**indignation meeting,** a meeting held for the purpose of expressing indignation, as at some public abuse.

in-dig-ni-ty (in-dig′ni-ti), *n.*; pl. *-ties* (-tiz). [L. *indignitas*, < *indignus*, unworthy: see *indign*.] Unworthiness†; also, disgrace†, or disgraceful action†; also, injury to dignity; slighting or contemptuous treatment; a humiliating affront, insult, or injury (as, "We, the most aristocratic of people . . . were we, by voluntarily going outside, to court *indignities?*" De Quincey's "English Mail-Coach," i.).

in-di-go (in′di-gō), *n.*; pl. *-gos* or *-goes* (-gōz). [Sp. or Pg., < L. *indicum*, indigo, lit. 'Indian (dye).'] A blue dyestuff obtained from various plants, esp. of the fabaceous genus *Indigofera*; also, indigo blue or indigotin, the coloring principle of this dyestuff; also, a plant yielding this dyestuff; also, a deep violet-blue color, one of the seven prismatic colors.—**in-digo blue,** the essential coloring principle (a chemical compound, $C_{16}H_{10}N_2O_2$), which is contained, along with other substances, in the dyestuff indigo, and which can also be prepared artificially (also called *indigotin*); also, the color indigo. Hence, adjectively, *indigo-blue*.—**in′di-go=bird,** *n.* A North American finch, *Cyanospiza cyanea*, the male of which is indigo-blue: often kept as a cage-bird. Also **in′di-go=bun′ting** and **in′di-go=finch.**—**in-di-got′ic** (-got′ik), *a.* Pertaining to or derived from indigo or indigotin; also, of a deep-blue color.—**in′di-go-tin** (-gọ-tin), *n.* In *chem.*, indigo blue, the coloring principle of the dyestuff indigo.

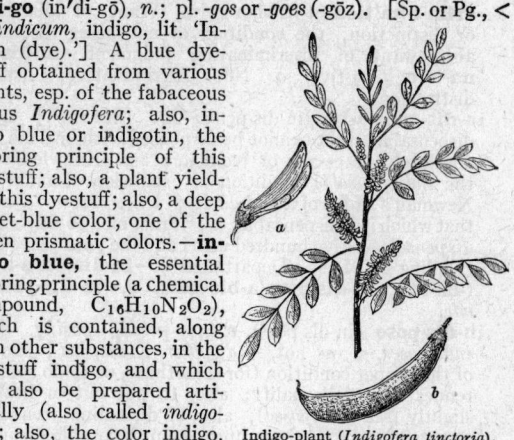

Indigo-plant (*Indigofera tinctoria*). *a*, flower; *b*, fruit.

Indigo-bird.

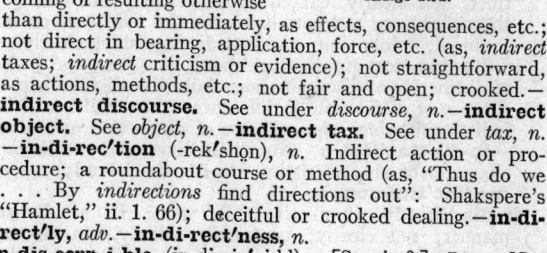

in-di-rect (in-di-rekt′), *a.* [L. *indirectus*.] Not direct; not straight, as a way or course; circuitous, roundabout, or devious; not descending in a direct line of succession, as a title or inheritance; coming or resulting otherwise than directly or immediately, as effects, consequences, etc.; not direct in bearing, application, force, etc. (as, *indirect* taxes; *indirect* criticism or evidence); not straightforward, as actions, methods, etc.; not fair and open; crooked.—**indirect discourse.** See under *discourse*, *n.*—**indirect object.** See *object*, *n.*—**indirect tax.** See under *tax*, *n.*—**in-di-rec′tion** (-rek′shọn), *n.* Indirect action or procedure; a roundabout course or method (as, "Thus do we . . . By *indirections* find directions out": Shakspere's "Hamlet," ii. 1. 66); deceitful or crooked dealing.—**in-di-rect′ly,** *adv.*—**in-di-rect′ness,** *n.*

in-dis-cern-i-ble (in-di-zėr′ni-bl). [See *in-*[2].] **I.** *a.* Not discernible; imperceptible. **II.** *n.* Something indiscernible.—**in-dis-cern′i-ble-ness,** *n.*—**in-dis-cern′i-bly,** *adv.*

in-dis-cerp-ti-ble (in-di-sėrp′ti-bl), *a.* [See *in-*[2].] Not discerptible; indivisible; not to be destroyed by dissolution of parts.—**in-dis-cerp-ti-bil′i-ty** (-bil′i-ti), *n.*

in-dis-ci-pline (in-dis′i-plin), *n.* [See *in-*[2].] Want of discipline; lack of systematic training or regulating control.

in-dis-cov-er-a-ble (in-dis-kuv′ėr-ạ-bl), *a.* [See *in-*[2].] Not discoverable; undiscoverable.

in-dis-creet (in-dis-krēt′), *a.* [OF. F. *indiscret*: cf. *discreet*.] Not discreet; injudicious; imprudent.—**in-dis-creet′ly,** *adv.*—**in-dis-creet′ness,** *n.*

in-dis-crete (in-dis-krēt′), *a.* [L. *indiscretus*: cf. *discrete*.] Not discrete; not consisting of distinct parts.

in-dis-cre-tion (in-dis-kresh′ọn), *n.* [OF. *indiscretion* (F. *indiscrétion*), < LL. *indiscretio(n-)*.] Want of discretion; imprudence; also, an indiscreet act or step.

in-dis-crim-i-nate (in-dis-krim′i-nạt), *a.* [See *in-*[2].] Not discriminate; confused; promiscuous; also, not discriminating (as, to be *indiscriminate* in one's friendships).—**in-dis-crim′i-nate-ly,** *adv.*—**in-dis-crim′i-nate-ness,** *n.*—**in-dis-crim′i-nat-ing** (-nā-ting), *a.* Not discriminating; undiscriminating.—**in-dis-crim′i-nat-ing-ly,** *adv.*—**in-dis-**

crim-i-na′tion (-nā′shọn), *n.* Want of discrimination or distinction; the condition of not being discriminated; also, want of discriminating judgment.—**in-dis-crim′i-na-tive** (-nạ-tiv), *a.* Not discriminative; making no distinctions.

in-dis-pens-a-ble (in-dis-pen′sạ-bl). [See *in-*[2].] **I.** *a.* Not dispensable; that cannot be dispensed with or done without; absolutely necessary or requisite: as, "Knowledge then is the *indispensable* condition of expansion of mind" (J. H. Newman's "Idea of a University," i. 6). **II.** *n.* One who or that which is indispensable: as, "Trust me, To-day's Most *Indispensables*, Five hundred men can take your place or mine" (Kipling's "Last Department").—**in-dis-pens-a-bil′i-ty** (-bil′i-ti), **in-dis-pens′a-ble-ness,** *n.*—**in-dis-pens′a-bly,** *adv.*

in-dis-pose (in-dis-pōz′), *v. t.*; *-posed, -posing.* [OF. F. *indisposer*, < *in-*, not, + *disposer*, E. *dispose.*] To put out of the proper condition (for something, or to do something); render unfit; disqualify; also, to put out of health, esp. slightly (see *indisposed*); also, to disincline; render averse or unwilling; sometimes, to make unfavorable or unfriendly (now rare); also, to render not liable or subject, as to disease. —**in-dis-posed′,** *p. a.* Sick or ill, esp. slightly (as, "Mr. Allworthy had been for some days *indisposed* with a cold": Fielding's "Tom Jones," v. 7); also, disinclined or unwilling; sometimes, unfavorable (now rare).—**in-dis-po-si′tion** (-pọ-zish′ọn), *n.* [OF. F. *indisposition.*] The state of being indisposed; derangement of health; a slight or passing illness; disinclination; unfavorable disposition.

in-dis-pu-ta-ble (in-dis′pū-tạ-bl or in-dis-pū′-), *a.* [LL. *indisputabilis.*] Not disputable; incontestable; unquestionable.—**in-dis″pu-ta-bil′i-ty** (-bil′i-ti), **in-dis′pu-ta-ble-ness,** *n.*—**in-dis′pu-ta-bly,** *adv.*

in-dis-so-cia-ble (in-di-sō′shạ-bl), *a.* [See *in-*[2].] Not dissociable; incapable of being dissociated.

in-dis-so-lu-ble (in-dis′ọ-lū-bl or in-di-sol′ū-), *a.* [L. *indissolubilis.*] Not dissoluble; incapable of being dissolved, decomposed, undone, or destroyed; firm or stable, as ties; perpetually binding or obligatory, as a covenant.—**in-dis″-so-lu-bil′i-ty** (-bil′i-ti), **in-dis′so-lu-ble-ness,** *n.*—**in-dis′so-lu-bly,** *adv.*

in-dis-tinct (in-dis-tingkt′), *a.* [L. *indistinctus.*] Not distinct; not clearly marked off or defined; not clearly distinguishable or perceptible, as to the eye, ear, or mind; confused; faint; dim; also, not distinguishing clearly.

in-dis-tinc-tion (in-dis-tingk′shọn), *n.* [See *in-*[2].] Want of distinction or discrimination; failure to distinguish; also, absence of distinction or difference; the condition of being indistinguishable; also, absence of distinction or eminence. —**in-dis-tinc′tive,** *a.* Not distinctive; without distinctive character or characteristics.—**in-dis-tinc′tive-ly,** *adv.*—**in-dis-tinc′tive-ness,** *n.*

in-dis-tinct-ly (in-dis-tingkt′li), *adv.* In an indistinct manner; not clearly; confusedly; dimly.—**in-dis-tinct′-ness,** *n.*

in-dis-tin-guish-a-ble (in-dis-ting′gwish-ạ-bl), *a.* [See *in-*[2].] Not distinguishable; incapable of being discriminated as different, one from another; indiscernible or imperceptible.—**in-dis-tin′guish-a-ble-ness,** *n.*—**in-dis-tin′guish-a-bly,** *adv.*

in-dite (in-dīt′), *v. t.*; *-dited, -diting.* [OF. *enditer*, make known, dictate, write, < L. *in*, in, + *dictare*, pronounce, dictate, compose: see *dictate, v.*, and cf. *ditty* and *indict.*] To dictate or utter, as something to be written down†; also, to dictate† or prescribe† (as, "Hear how learn'd Greece her useful rules *indites*": Pope's "Essay on Criticism," 92); also, to frame in words, compose, or write, as a speech, poem, tale, letter, etc. (now chiefly archaic or literary); also, to treat of or describe in a literary composition (obs. or archaic: as, "Not sedulous by nature to *indite* Wars, hitherto the only argument Heroic deem'd," Milton's "Paradise Lost," ix. 27).—**in-dite′ment,** *n.*—**in-dit′er** (-dī′tėr), *n.*

in-di-um (in′di-um), *n.* [NL., < L. *indicum*, indigo.] Chem. sym., In; at. wt., 114.8; sp. gr., 7.4. A rare metallic element, soft, white, malleable, and easily fusible, found combined in various ores, esp. zinc-blende: so called from the two indigo-blue lines in its spectrum.

in-di-vert-i-ble (in-di-vėr′ti-bl), *a.* [See *in-*[2].] Not dive ible; not to be turned aside.—**in-di-vert′i-bly,** *adv.*

in-di-vid-u-al (in-di-vid′ū-ạl). [ML. *individualis*, < L. *i dividuus*, indivisible, < *in-*, not, + *dividuus*, divisible: *dividual.*] **I.** *a.* Indivisible†; also, existing as a distinct, i divisible entity, or considered as such (as, each *individu* person; *individual* members may refuse to subscribe to t party policy; *individual* groups in a classification); sing particular, or separate; also, pertaining or peculiar to a sing person or thing (as, *individual* characteristics or tendencie *individual* property, tastes, efforts, or losses); intended f the use of one person only (as, an *individual* cup or sa cellar; food served in *individual* portions); also, distinguish by peculiar and marked characteristics (as, to be *individu* in one's work, utterances, or views; a highly *individu* writer or style); exhibiting individuality. **II.** *n.* A distinc indivisible entity; a single thing, being, instance, or iter or a group considered as a unit; often, a single human bein as distinguished from a group, the community, or socie (as, "views about the functions of government and i relations to the *individual*": Bryce's "American Commo wealth," xcii.); hence, in general, a person (as, he is a stran *individual*; this *individual* gave us some trouble: no chiefly colloq., and humorous or disparaging); in *bio* a single or simple organism capable of independent existenc a member of a compound organism or colony, as one of t distinct elements or zoöids which make up a compour hydrozoan, or sometimes (when a whole plant or tree regarded as a colony or compound organism) a single sho or bud; any of the morphological units known as morphon embracing forms ranging from the plastid to the compou organism; any of the functional or physiological units know as bions.

in-di-vid-u-al-ism (in-di-vid′ū-ạl-izm), *n.* The princip or habit of individual or independent thought or action; t pursuit of individual rather than common or collecti interests; egoism; also, a social theory advocating the li erty, rights, or independent action of the individual; es the theory of the economic independence of the individu (cf. *collectivism*, also *socialism*); also, individual characte or individuality.—**in-di-vid′u-al-ist,** *n.* One characteriz by individualism in thought or action; also, an advoca of a theory of individualism.—**in-di-vid″u-al-is′tic,** Of or pertaining to individualists or individualism; characte ized by or tending to individualism.

in-di-vid-u-al-i-ty (in-di-vid-ū-al′i-ti), *n.*; pl. *-ties* (-tiz The state or quality of being individual; existence as distinct individual; also, individual or distinctive characte the particular character, or aggregate of qualities, whic distinguishes one person or thing from others; often, strong marked individual character (as, a person or a work havin *individuality*); *pl.*, individual characteristics (as, "The twain . . . Distinct in *individualities*, But like each oth even as those who love": Tennyson's "Princess," v 275); also, *sing.*, a person or thing of individual or distinctiv character.

in-di-vid-u-al-ize (in-di-vid′ū-ạl-īz), *v.*; *-ized, -izing.* **I.** *t* To make individual; give an individual or distinctive chara ter to (as, Carlyle's peculiar style strongly *individualiz* his works); also, to mention, indicate, or consider indivi ually; specify; particularize. **II.** *intr.* To become ind vidual; specialize; also, to mention or consider individual particularize.—**in-di-vid″u-al-i-za′tion** (-i-zā′shọn), *n.*—**in-di-vid′u-al-iz-er** (-ī-zėr), *n.*

in-di-vid-u-al-ly (in-di-vid′ū-ạl-i), *adv.* In an individu manner; singly or separately; also, in an individual capacit

in-di-vid-u-ate (in-di-vid′ū-āt), *v. t.*; *-ated, -ating.* [M *individuatus*, pp. of *individuare*, < L. *individuus*: s *individual.*] To form into an individual or distinct entit also, to give an individual or distinctive character to; i dividualize.—**in-di-vid-u-a′tion** (-ā′shọn), *n.* The act individuating, or the state of being individuated; individu existence; individuality; also, an individualized state form of something.

in-di-vis-i-ble (in-di-viz′i-bl). [LL. *indivisibilis.*] **I.** Not divisible. **II.** *n.* Something indivisible; esp., infinitely small quantity.—**in-di-vis-i-bil′i-ty** (-bil′i-ti **in-di-vis′i-ble-ness,** *n.*—**in-di-vis′i-bly,** *adv.*

In-do- (in′dǭ-). Form of L. *Indus,* Gr. Ἰνδός, of or in India, Indian, used in combination, as in *Indo-African* (of India and Africa), *Indo-Malayan, Indo-Malaysian, Indo-Aryan* (Aryan of India), *Indo-British* (British in India), *Indo-French, Indo-Portuguese.*—**In′do=Chi-nese′,** *a.* Of or pertaining to Indo-China (or Farther India), the southeastern peninsula of Asia; also, of or pertaining to the Mongoloid peoples of Indo-China or their languages; also, designating or pertaining to the language family comprising these languages and the Tibetan and Chinese groups of languages.

in-do-cile (in-dos′il, Brit. also -dō′sīl), *a.* [L. *indocilis.*] Not docile; not amenable to teaching, discipline, or guidance; intractable: as, "He had been *indocile* and restive to the pedant who held the office of his tutor" (Godwin's "Caleb Williams," iii.).—**in-do-cil-i-ty** (in-dǭ-sil′i-ti), *n.*

in-doc-tri-nate (in-dok′tri-nāt), *v. t.*; *-nated, -nating.* [L. *in,* in, + *doctrina,* teaching, E. *doctrine.*] To imbue (a person, etc.) with learning, or with a doctrine, principle, etc.; instruct; also, to teach or inculcate (a doctrine, etc.). —**in-doc-tri-na′tion** (-nā′shǫn), *n.*—**in-doc′tri-na-tor,** *n.*

In-do=Eu-ro-pe-an (in′dǭ-ū-rǭ-pē′ạn), *a.* [See *Indo-.*] Of India and Europe: esp. applied to the peoples of Aryan descent and to the Aryan family of languages (including both Asiatic and European branches). See *Aryan.*—**In′do=Ger-man′ic,** *a.* Indian and Germanic (Teutonic); Indo-European.—**In′do=I-ra′ni-an,** *a.* Indian and Iranian; noting or pertaining to the Indian and Iranian divisions of the Aryan family of languages.

in-dol (in′dol or -dōl), *n.* [From *indigo.*] In *chem.,* a white crystalline compound obtained by the reduction of indigo derivatives, and also formed within the intestines.

in-do-lent (in′dǭ-lẹnt), *a.* [LL. *indolens* (*-ent-*), < L. *in-,* not, + *dolens,* suffering, painful, E. *dolent.*] Causing little or no pain (as, an *indolent* tumor); also, having or showing a disposition to avoid exertion (as, an *indolent* person; *indolent* repose); lazy; slothful.—**in′do-lence,** *n.* —**in′do-lent-ly,** *adv.*

in-dom-i-ta-ble (in-dom′i-tạ-bl), *a.* [LL. *indomitabilis,* < L. *in-,* not, + *domitare,* freq. of *domare,* tame: see *tame.*] That cannot be tamed or made gentle†; fig., that cannot be subdued or overcome, as persons, pride, courage, energy, determination, etc.; bravely or stubbornly unyielding.—**in-dom′i-ta-ble-ness,** *n.*—**in-dom′i-ta-bly,** *adv.*

In-do-ne-sian (in-dǭ-nē′shiạn or -zhiạn). [Gr. Ἰνδός, Indian, + νῆσος, island.] **I.** *a.* Of or pertaining to the Malay Archipelago; also, pertaining to the Indonesians. **II.** *n.* An inhabitant of the Malay Archipelago; esp., a member of a light-colored (mixed Caucasian and Mongoloid?) race supposed to have been dominant in the Malay Archipelago before the Malays, and believed to constitute one element of the present mixed population of Malaysia and Polynesia, and to be found in a nearly pure state on some of the islands.

in-door (in′dōr), *a.* Occurring, used, passed, etc., in a house or building, rather than out of doors (as, *indoor* amusements or dress; an *indoor* life); also, within a poorhouse, hospital, etc. (as, *indoor* paupers or patients; *indoor* relief). —**in′doors′,** *adv.* In or into a house or building: as, "Till then he must keep close *in-doors*" (J. H. Newman's "Callista," xviii.).

in-do-phe-nol (in-dǭ-fē′nol or -nōl), *n.* [From *ind(ig)o* + *phenol.*] A coal-tar dyestuff resembling indigo in appearance and giving indigo-blue shades; also, any of various related dyes.

in-dors-a-ble, en-dors-a-ble (in-dôr′sạ-bl, en-), *a.* That may be indorsed.

in-dor-sa-tion, en-dor-sa-tion (in-dôr-sā′shǫn, en-), *n.* The act of indorsing, or something written by way of indorsing; indorsement. [Chiefly Sc.]

in-dorse, en-dorse (in-dôrs′, en-), *v. t.*; *-dorsed, -dorsing.* [ML. *indorsare,* < L. *in,* in, on, + *dorsum,* back.] To write (something) on the back of a document, etc.; also, to inscribe (a document, etc.) with one's name or other writing on the back (or elsewhere), as in docketing papers, approving contents, guaranteeing payment of a note, or authorizing payment of a check; fig., to approve, support, or sustain (as, to *indorse* a statement, plan, or opinion); also, to load with something placed on the back† (as, "Elephants *indorsed* with towers Of archers": Milton's "Paradise Regained," iii. 329).—**in-dors-ee′, en-dors-ee′,** *n.* One to whom a note, bill, or the like is indorsed, or assigned by indorsement.—**in-dorse′ment, en-dorse′ment,** *n.* The act of indorsing, or that which is written by way of indorsing, as on a note or bill; fig., approval or sanction.—**in-dors′er, en-dors′er,** *n.* One who indorses. Also (in *law*) **in-dor′sor.**

in-draft, in-draught (in′dråft), *n.* A draft or drawing inward; an inward current; an inflow: as, "There is sometimes a strong *indraught* setting up St. George's Channel, which deceives seamen" (B. Franklin's "Autobiography," xiv.).

in-draw-al (in′drâ″ạl), *n.* A drawing in; indraft.—**in′draw″ing,** *a.* Drawing in.—**in′drawn,** *a.* Drawn in; introspective; abstracted.

in-dri (in′dri), *n.* [Malagasy, said to be an exclamation, 'lo! see!' erroneously taken as the name of the animal.] A short-tailed lemur, *Indris brevicaudatus,* of Madagascar, about two feet in length.

Indri.

in-du-bi-ta-ble (in-dū′bi-tạ-bl), *a.* [L. *indubitabilis.*] Not dubitable; that cannot be doubted; unquestionable; certain: as, "Between vague wavering Capability and fixed *indubitable* Performance, what a difference!" (Carlyle's "Sartor Resartus," ii. 7).—**in-du′bi-ta-bly,** *adv.*

in-duce (in-dūs′), *v. t.*; *-duced, -ducing.* [L. *inducere* (pp. *inductus*), lead in, bring in, persuade, < *in,* in, + *ducere,* lead: cf. *induct.*] To lead or bring in†; introduce†; bring forward† or adduce†; also, to lead by persuasion or influence, as to some action, state of mind, etc. (as, to *induce* a person to consent; "Pray what could *induce* him to commit so rash an action?" Goldsmith's "Good-Natured Man," i.); prevail upon, influence, or move; also, to bring about, produce, or cause (as, this measure *induced* discontent; opium *induces* sleep); also, to infer, as by logical induction; in *physics,* to produce (an electric current, etc.) by induction.—**in-duce′ment,** *n.* The act of inducing; also, something that induces or persuades; an incentive; in *law,* a statement which leads to the main statement; facts or circumstances stated by way of introduction.—**in-du′cer** (-dū′sėr), *n.*—**in-du′ci-ble,** *a.* Capable of being induced.

in-duct (in-dukt′), *v. t.* [L. *inductus,* pp. of *inducere:* see *induce.*] To lead or bring in; introduce, as into a place, seat, position, etc.; esp., to put formally in possession of an office or benefice; install; also, to initiate (*into*); introduce in knowledge or experience (*to:* as, "the pleasures to which the footman *inducted* him," Thackeray's "Vanity Fair," lvi.).—**in-duct′ance,** *n.* In *elect.,* that property of a circuit by virtue of which induction takes place.

in-duc-tile (in-duk′til), *a.* [See *in-*[2].] Not ductile; not pliable or yielding.—**in-duc-til′i-ty** (-til′i-ti), *n.*

in-duc-tion (in-duk′shǫn), *n.* [L. *inductio(n-),* < *inducere:* see *induce* and *induct.*] The act of inducting; introduction or initiation; esp., formal introduction into an office or benefice; installation; also, an introductory act, stage, or part, or beginning (archaic: see Shakspere's "Richard III.," iv. 4. 5); a preface or prologue (archaic: as, Sackville's *Induction,* 1563, to the "Mirror for Magistrates"; Shakspere's *Induction* to "The Taming of the Shrew"); also, a bringing forward or adducing, as of facts, evidence, etc.; also, the act of inducing, bringing about, or causing (as, *induction* of the hypnotic state); production; in *logic,* inference by reasoning from particulars to generals (opposed to *deduction*); a conclusion thus reached; in *physics*, the process by which a body having electrical or magnetic properties calls forth similar properties in a neighboring body without direct contact.—**in-duc'tion=coil,** *n.* An electrical apparatus in which an ordinary battery current running through a coil of coarse wire (the *primary coil*) and having its circuit opened and closed in rapid succession, produces an induced current of high voltage in a surrounding coil of fine wire (the *secondary coil*).

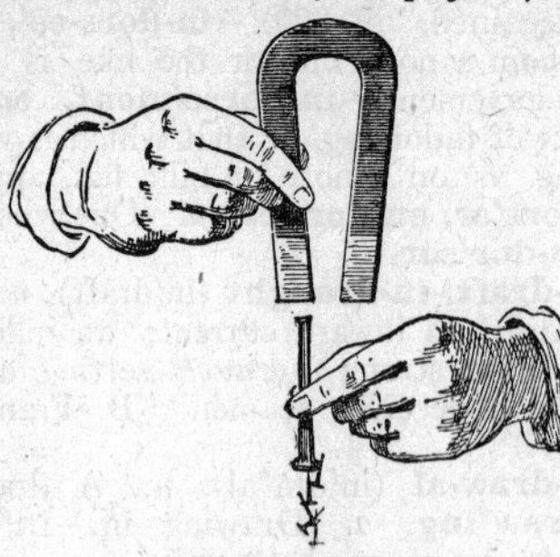

Magnetic Induction.

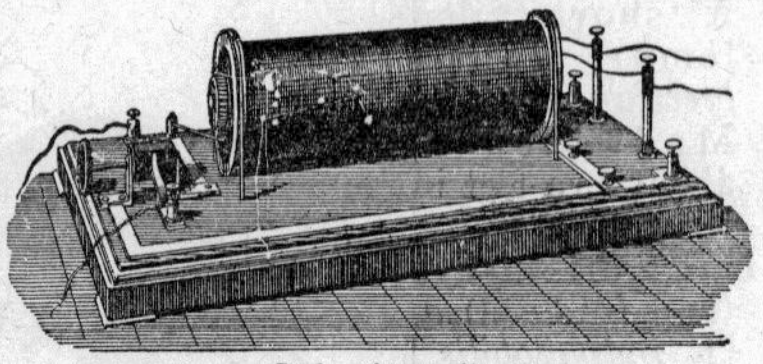

Induction-coil.

in-duc-tive (in-duk'tiv), *a.* [LL. *inductivus*, < L. *inducere*: see *induce* and *induct.*] Serving to induce; leading or influencing (*to*: as, "A brutish vice, *Inductive* mainly to the sin of Eve," Milton's "Paradise Lost," xi. 519); also, introductory; also, pertaining to or employing logical induction; also, pertaining to or involving electrical or magnetic induction.—**in-duc'tive-ly,** *adv.*—**in-duc'tive-ness,** *n.*—**in-duc-tiv'i-ty** (-tiv'i-ti), *n.* Inductive property; capacity for induction.

in-duc-tor (in-duk'tọr), *n.* [L.] One who inducts, as into office; in *elect.*, any part of an apparatus which causes or is affected by induction.

in-duc-to-ri-um (in-duk-tō'ri-um), *n.*; pl. *-riums* or *-ria* (-ri-ạ̈). [NL.] An induction-coil.

in-due (in-dū'), *v. t.*; *-dued, -duing.* [L. *induere*, put on (cf. *exuere*, put off): cf. *endue*, also *endow.*] To put on (a garment, etc.: as, "By this time the Baron . . . had *indued* a pair of jack-boots," Scott's "Waverley," xii.); also, to clothe (a person, etc.), as with a garment (as, "*Indued* with robes of various hue she flies": Dryden's "Ceyx and Alcyone," 264); fig., to invest or endow, as with qualities, powers, etc.

in-dulge (in-dulj'), *v.*; *-dulged, -dulging.* [L. *indulgere* (pp. *indultus*), be kind, yield, grant.] **I.** *tr.* To yield to the wishes or whims of (as, to *indulge* a child); show favoring or complaisant allowance to, or humor (*in*: as, "Pelham . . . felt that an ally so little used to control . . . might well be *indulged* in an occasional fit of waywardness," Macaulay's "Essays," William Pitt, Earl of Chatham); allow (one's self) to follow one's will (*in*: as, to *indulge* one's self in folly, pleasing fancies, or vain hopes); gratify (*with*: as, will you not *indulge* us with a song?); also, to yield to, satisfy, or gratify (desires, feelings, etc.); give free scope to (qualities, activities, etc.: as, to *indulge* one's candor; "Useful rules . . . When to repress, and when *indulge* our flights," Pope's "Essay on Criticism," 93); also, to grant or accord (something) by favor or complaisance, as to a person (now rare); also, to grant special privileges to, as in matters of religion; in *com.*, to grant an extension of time, for payment or performance, to (a person, etc.) or on (a bill, etc.). **II.** *intr.* To indulge one's self, or yield to an inclination or impulse (with *in*: as, to *indulge* in pleasures or hopes; to *indulge* in a sneer); allow one's self something desired or pleasurable (with *in* specifying the object, or elliptically without *in*: as, to *indulge* in a new hat; to *indulge* in a social glass; no, thanks, I never *indulge*).—**in-dul'gence** (-dul'jẹns), *n.* [L. *indulgentia.*] The act or practice of indulging; indulgent allowance or tolerance (as, "some degree of *indulgence* towards human frailty": Burke's "Conciliation with the Colonies"); humoring; gratification of desire; also, something granted or taken in gratification of desire (as, "to have a cup of tea, an *indulgence* which she rarely allowed herself": George Eliot's "Adam Bede," x.); a grant of special privileges, esp. in religious matters; in the *Rom. Cath. Ch.*, a remission of the punishment still due to sin after sacramental absolution; in *com.*, an extension, through favor, of time for payment or performance. Also **in-dul'gen-cy.**—**in-dul'gent,** *a.* Indulging or humoring wishes, whims, etc. (as, an *indulgent* parent or master); laxly kind or complaisant; sometimes kindly lenient (as, "Mrs. Jamieson was kindly *indulgent* to Miss Barker's want of knowledge of the customs of high life": Mrs. Gaskell's "Cranford," vii.); also, characterized by or showing indulgence (as, *indulgent* treatment; an *indulgent* smile).—**in-dul'gent-ly,** *adv.*—**in-dul'ger,** *n.*

in-du-line (in'dụ̄-lin), *n.* [From *indigo.*] Any of a large class of dyes yielding colors similar to indigo.

in-dult (in-dult'), *n.* [LL. *indultum*, indulgence, permission, favor, prop. neut. of L. *indultus*, pp. of *indulgere*: see *indulge.*] In the *Rom. Cath. Ch.*, a license from the Pope granting some privilege not authorized by the common law of the church.

in-du-na (in-dö'nạ̈), *n.* [Zulu.] Among the Zulus and other South African tribes, an officer under the chief or king.

in-du-pli-cate (in-dū'pli-kạt), *a.* [NL. *induplicatus*, < L. *in*, in, + *duplicatus*, doubled: see *duplicate.*] In *bot.*, folded or rolled inward: said of the parts of the calyx or corolla in estivation when the edges are bent abruptly toward the axis, or of leaves in vernation when the edges are rolled inward and then arranged about the axis without overlapping.—**in-du-pli-ca'tion** (-kā'shọn), *n.*

in-du-rate (in'dụ̄-rāt), *v. t.* or *i.*; *-rated, -rating.* [L. *induratus*, pp. of *indurare*, < *in*, in, + *durare*, harden, < *durus*, hard.] To make or become hard; harden. Also fig.—**in'du-rate** (-rạt), *a.* Hardened; fig., callous; unfeeling.—**in-du-ra'tion** (-rā'shọn), *n.* The act of hardening, or a hardened condition; also, a hardened part or mass.—**in'du-ra-tive** (-rạ̄-tiv), *a.* Tending to harden.

in-du-si-al (in-dū'ẓi-ạl), *a.* Pertaining to, composed of, or containing indusia, or the coverings of larval insects: as, *indusial* limestone (a limestone found in France, supposed to be composed of the agglomerated indusia of the larvæ of caddis-flies).

in-du-si-um (in-dū'ẓi-um), *n.*; pl. *-sia* (-ẓi-ạ̈). [L., tunic, < *induere*, put on, E. *indue.*] In *anat.* and *zoöl.*, an enveloping layer or membrane; specif., the covering of a larval insect; in *bot.*, the covering of a sorus; also, a cup-like collection of hairs inclosing a stigma.

in-dus-tri-al (in-dus'tri-ạl), *a.* [ML. *industrialis.*] Of or pertaining to, of the nature of, or resulting from industry or productive labor; pertaining to or connected with the industries, trades, or manufactures (as, *industrial* activity or depression; an *industrial* exhibition); engaged in an industry or industries (as, *industrial* workers); pertaining to the workers in industries; specif., noting or pertaining to a form of life insurance for the working classes, with policies for comparatively low sums and with premiums payable weekly.—**industrial school,** a school for teaching one or more branches of industry; also, a school for educating neglected children committed to its care and training them to some form of industry.—**Industrial Workers of the World,** an international industrial union, organized in Chicago in 1905, aiming to supersede trade-unions and bring together within itself as an unaffiliated organization the workers in all industries, for the purposes of promoting industrial unity, combating effectually the employing class, doing away with capitalism and abolishing the wage system, and taking possession of the machinery of production. Abbreviated *I. W. W.*—**in-dus'tri-al,** *n.* A worker in some industry, esp. a manufacturing industry; also, one who conducts or owns an industrial enterprise; also, *pl.*, stocks, bonds, etc., of industrial enterprises.—**in-dus'tri-al-ism,** *n.* The predominance of industrial activities or interests; the system of things in which industrial interests predominate; the modern system of great industries; also, the industrial branch of work or labor (as, "In 1765 Watt's steam engine was constructed, a very important date in the history of *industrialism*": H. G. Wells's "Outline of History," xxxvi. § 12).—**in-dus'tri-al-ist,** *n.* A person employed in or concerned with some branch of industry; **an industrial worker;**

one who conducts or owns an industrial enterprise.—**in-dus′tri-al-ize,** *v. t.*; *-ized, -izing.* To imbue with the spirit of industrialism; interest in industrial pursuits; organize industrially.—**in-dus′tri-al-ly,** *adv.* In an industrial manner; with respect to industry.

in-dus-tri-ous (in-dus′tri-us), *a.* [L. *industriosus*, also *industrius.*] Given to or characterized by industry, as a person, the disposition or habits, activity or labor, etc.; diligent; busy; also, zealous, as in a cause† (as, "Here is a dear, a true *industrious* friend . . . new lighted from his horse": Shakspere's "1 Henry IV.," i. 1. 62); studious† (with *in, of, to,* or an infinitive: as, "*industrious* of the common good," Dryden's "To John Driden," 53); also, skilful† or clever†.—**in-dus′tri-ous-ly,** *adv.*—**in-dus′tri-ous-ness,** *n.*

in-dus-try (in′dus-tri), *n.*; pl. *-tries* (-triz). [OF. F. *industrie*, < L. *industria*, diligence, industry.] Assiduous activity at any work or task; diligence; busy application; also, systematic work or labor; productive labor, esp. in manufacturing; a particular branch of productive labor; a trade or manufacture (as, the steel *industry*; the cotton *industry*); also, skill†, cleverness†, or ingenuity†.

in-dwell (in-dwel′), *v.*; *-dwelt, -dwelling.* **I.** *tr.* To dwell within; inhabit. **II.** *intr.* To dwell (*in*).—**in′dwell″er,** *n.* —**in′dwell″ing,** *a.* Dwelling within; esp., abiding in the mind or soul (as, an *indwelling* faith).

-ine[1]. [L. *-īnus*, also L. *-inus*, < Gr. *-ινος.*] An adjective suffix meaning 'of or pertaining to,' 'of the nature of,' 'made of,' 'like,' as in *asinine, crystalline, equine, marine, murrine, vulpine.*

-ine[2]. [F. *-ine*, < L. *-īna*, orig. fem. of *-īnus*, adj. suffix: see *-ine*[1].] A noun suffix, orig. in words of Latin origin denoting some action, procedure, art, place, etc., as in *discipline, doctrine, medicine, rapine, latrine,* occurring also in many nouns of later formation and various meanings, as *famine, routine, vitrine, grenadine, brilliantine, vaseline, gasoline,* and particularly in chemical terms, as *bromine, chlorine,* and esp. names of basic substances, as *amine, aniline, caffeine, quinine, quinoline* (cf. *-in*).

in-earth (in-ėrth′), *v. t.* To bury in the earth; inter: as, "Refusing rest, Till I had seen in holy ground *inearth'd* My poor lost brother" (Southey's "Madoc," i. 3. 161). [Chiefly poetic.]

in-e-bri-ant (in-ē′bri-ạnt). **I.** *a.* Inebriating; intoxicating. **II.** *n.* An intoxicant.

in-e-bri-ate (in-ē′bri-āt), *v. t.*; *-ated, -ating.* [L. *inebriatus*, pp. of *inebriare*, < *in*, in, + *ebrius*, drunk.] To make drunk, or intoxicate (sometimes used absolutely: as, "While the . . . urn Throws up a steamy column, and the cups, That cheer but not *inebriate*, wait on each," Cowper's "Task," iv. 40); fig., to intoxicate mentally; excite beyond self-control; stupefy.—**in-e′bri-ate** (-ạt). **I.** *a.* Inebriated; intoxicated. **II.** *n.* An intoxicated person; esp., a habitual drunkard.—**in-e-bri-a′tion** (-ā′shọn), *n.* [LL. *inebriatio(n-).*] Intoxication; drunkenness. Also fig.

in-e-bri-e-ty (in-ẹ-brī′ẹ-ti), *n.* [From *in-*, as in *inebriate*, + *ebriety.*] The state or the habit of being inebriated; drunkenness, esp. habitual drunkenness.—**in-e′bri-ous** (-ē′bri-us), *a.* [Cf. *ebrious.*] Drunken; addicted to drunkenness.

in-ed-i-ble (in-ed′i-bl), *a.* [See *in-*[2].] Not edible; unfit to be eaten.—**in-ed-i-bil′i-ty** (-bil′i-ti), *n.*

in-ed-it-ed (in-ed′i-ted), *a.* [See *in-*[2].] Not edited; unpublished.

in-ed-u-ca-ble (in-eḍ′ū-kạ-bl), *a.* [See *in-*[2].] Not educable; incapable of being educated.

in-ef-fa-ble (in-ef′ạ-bl), *a.* [L. *ineffabilis*: cf. *effable.*] That cannot be uttered or expressed (as, "orgies of *ineffable* demoralisation": Disraeli's "Lothair," xv.); unutterable, inexpressible, or unspeakable; also, that must not be uttered (as, the *ineffable* name: see *Jehovah*).—**in-ef′fa-ble-ness,** *n.* —**in-ef′fa-bly,** *adv.*

in-ef-face-a-ble (in-e-fā′sạ-bl), *a.* [See *in-*[2].] Not effaceable; indelible.—**in-ef-face-a-bil′i-ty** (-bil′i-ti), *n.*—**in-ef-face′a-bly,** *adv.*

in-ef-fec-tive (in-e-fek′tiv), *a.* [See *in-*[2].] Not effective; without due effect; ineffectual, as efforts; inefficient, as a person; lacking in artistic effect, as a design or work.—**in-ef-fec′tive-ly,** *adv.*—**in-ef-fec′tive-ness,** *n.*

in-ef-fec-tu-al (in-e-fek′ţū-ạl), *a.* [See *in-*[2].] Not effectual; without satisfactory or decisive effect, as efforts, actions, means, etc.; unavailing, futile, or vain; sometimes, powerless or impotent (as, "He [a ghost] lifts his *ineffectual* hand, and tries the frame": Hawthorne's "House of the Seven Gables," xviii.).—**in-ef-fec′tu-al-ly,** *adv.*—**in-ef-fec′tu-al-ness,** *n.*

in-ef-fi-ca-cious (in-ef-i-kā′shus), *a.* [See *in-*[2].] Not efficacious; without efficacy or effective virtue; of inadequate force.—**in-ef-fi-ca′cious-ly,** *adv.*—**in-ef-fi-ca′cious-ness, in-ef-fi-ca′ci-ty** (-kas′i-ti), *n.* Inefficacy.—**in-ef′fi-ca-cy** (-kạ-si), *n.* Lack of efficacy, effective virtue, or force: as, "The prince . . . went away convinced of the emptiness of rhetorical sound, and the *inefficacy* of polished periods and studied sentences" (Johnson's "Rasselas," xviii.).

in-ef-fi-cient (in-e-fish′ẹnt), *a.* [See *in-*[2].] Not efficient; without ability to effect or accomplish; incapable; incompetent.—**in-ef-fi′cien-cy,** *n.*—**in-ef-fi′cient-ly,** *adv.*

in-e-las-tic (in-ẹ-las′tik), *a.* [See *in-*[2].] Not elastic; lacking elasticity; unyielding.—**in″e-las-ti′ci-ty** (-tis′i-ti), *n.*

in-el-e-gant (in-el′ẹ-gạnt), *a.* [L. *inelegans* (*-ant-*).] Not elegant; not in accordance with a nice or refined taste; unrefined; crude; vulgar.—**in-el′e-gance, in-el′e-gan-cy,** *n.*—**in-el′e-gant-ly,** *adv.*

in-el-i-gi-ble (in-el′i-ji-bl). [See *in-*[2].] **I.** *a.* Not eligible; not proper or suitable for choice; legally or otherwise disqualified, as for an office. **II.** *n.* One who is ineligible, esp. as a suitor or husband.—**in-el″i-gi-bil′i-ty** (-bil′i-ti), *n.* —**in-el′i-gi-bly,** *adv.*

in-el-o-quent (in-el′ọ-kwẹnt), *a.* [See *in-*[2].] Not eloquent; lacking eloquence: as, "Nor are thy lips ungraceful, sire of men, Nor tongue *ineloquent*" (Milton's "Paradise Lost," viii. 219).—**in-el′o-quence,** *n.*—**in-el′o-quent-ly,** *adv.*

in-e-luc-ta-ble (in-ẹ-luk′tạ-bl), *a.* [L. *ineluctabilis*, < *in-*, not, + *eluctabilis*, escapable, < *eluctari*, struggle out of, < *e*, out of, + *luctari*, wrestle, struggle.] That cannot be escaped from, as a fate.—**in-e-luc′ta-bly,** *adv.*

in-e-lud-i-ble (in-ẹ-lū′di-bl), *a.* [See *in-*[2].] Not eludible; inescapable.—**in-e-lud′i-bly,** *adv.*

in-ept (in-ept′), *a.* [L. *ineptus*, < *in-*, not, + *aptus*, E. *apt*: cf. *inapt.*] Not apt, fitted, or suitable; unsuitable; inappropriate; out of place; also, absurd or foolish, as a proceeding, remark, etc.—**in-ep′ti-tude** (-ep′ti-tūd), *n.* [L. *ineptitudo.*] The quality of being inept; unfitness; foolishness; also, an inept act or remark.—**in-ept′ly,** *adv.*—**in-ept′ness,** *n.*

in-e-qual-i-ty (in-ẹ-kwol′i-ti), *n.*; pl. *-ties* (-tiz). [L. *inæqualitas*, < *inæqualis*, unequal, < *in-*, not, + *æqualis*, E. *equal.*] The condition of being unequal; lack of equality; disparity; disproportion; inadequacy; unevenness, as of surface; irregularity; variableness; an instance of unevenness; a deviation from uniformity; in *math.*, an expression of two unequal quantities connected by either of the signs of inequality > or < (as, $a > b$, 'a is greater than b'; $a < b$, 'a is less than b').

in-e-qui-lat-er-al (in-ē-kwi-lat′ẹ-rạl), *a.* [See *in-*[2].] Not equilateral; having unequal sides.—**in-e-qui-lat′er-al-ly,** *adv.*

in-e-qui-ta-ble (in-ek′wi-tạ-bl), *a.* [See *in-*[2].] Not equitable; unfair.—**in-e′qui-ta-bly,** *adv.*

in-e-qui-ty (in-ek′wi-ti), *n.*; pl. *-ties* (-tiz). [See *in-*[2].] Want of equity; unfairness; injustice; also, an unfair circumstance or proceeding.

in-e-rad-i-ca-ble (in-ẹ-rad′i-kạ-bl), *a.* [See *in-*[2].] Not eradicable; that cannot be eradicated, rooted out, or removed utterly.—**in-e-rad′i-ca-bly,** *adv.*

in-e-ras-a-ble (in-ẹ-rā′sạ-bl), *a.* [See *in-*[2].] Not erasable; not to be erased or effaced.—**in-e-ras′a-bly,** *adv.*

in-er-ra-ble (in-er′ạ-bl), *a.* [L. *inerrabilis*, < *in-*, not, + *errare*, wander, err.] Incapable of erring; infallible.—**in-er-ra-bil′i-ty** (-bil′i-ti), *n.*—**in-er′ra-bly,** *adv.*

in-er-rant (in-er′ạnt), *a.* [L. *inerrans* (*-ant-*), < *in-*, not, + *errans*, ppr. of *errare*, wander, err.] Of stars, not wandering†; fixed†; fig., not erring; free from error.—**in-er′ran-cy,** *n.*

in-ert (in-ėrt′), *a.* [L. *iners* (*inert-*), unskilled, idle, inert, < *in-*, not, + *ars*, E. *art*[2].] Having no inherent power of action, motion, or resistance (as, *inert* matter; an *inert* mass); inactive, inanimate, or without life; also, without active properties, as a drug; also, of an inactive or sluggish habit or nature (as, "The Honourable Mrs. Jamieson . . . was fat and *inert*, and very much at the mercy of her old servants": Mrs. Gaskell's "Cranford," iii.); without energy; indolent or slothful (as, "The favour'd isles . . . *inert* Through plenty . . . victims of luxurious ease": Cowper's "Task," i. 623).

in-er-tia (in-ėr′shiạ̈), *n.* [L., < *iners*: see *inert.*] That property of matter by virtue of which it retains its state of rest or of uniform rectilinear motion so long as it is not acted upon by an external force; hence, an analogous property of a force (as, electric *inertia*); fig., inactivity; sluggishness; inert condition.—**in-er′tial** (-shiạl), *a.*

in-er-tion (in-ėr′shọn), *n.* [Irreg. < *inert.*] A being or remaining inert; inaction; sluggishness.

in-ert-ly (in-ėrt′li), *adv.* In an inert manner.—**in-ert′-ness,** *n.*

in-er-u-dite (in-er′ö̦-dīt), *a.* [L. *ineruditus.*] Not erudite; unlearned: as, "Others again will blame . . . my collections, for crude . . . verbose, *inerudite*" (Lamb's "Curious Fragments," i.).—**in-er′u-dite-ly,** *adv.*

in-es-cap-a-ble (in-es-kā′pạ-bl), *a.* [See *in-*[2].] That cannot be escaped; unescapable.

in-es-cutch-eon (in-es-kuch′ọn), *n.* In *her.*, a small escutcheon borne as a charge upon a larger escutcheon.

Inescutcheon.

in-es-sen-tial (in-e-sen′shạl), *a.* [See *in-*[2].] Not essential; without essence or substantial quality, or insubstantial (as, "His *inessential* figure cast no shade Upon the golden floor": Shelley's "Queen Mab," vii. 71); not necessary, not indispensable, or nonessential.—**in-es-sen-ti-al′i-ty** (-shi-al′i-ti), *n.*

in-es-sive (in-es′iv), *a.* [Irreg. < L. *inesse*, be in, < *in*, in, + *esse*, be.] In *gram.*, expressing the place in which a thing is; locative.

in-es-ti-ma-ble (in-es′ti-mạ-bl), *a.* [L. *inæstimabilis*: cf. *estimable.*] That cannot be estimated, or too great to be estimated (as, "The people . . . fancied that a privilege so dearly purchased must be of *inestimable* value": Lecky's "Hist. of Eng. in the 18th Century," iii.); incalculable; also, of incalculable value (as, "Heaps of pearl, *Inestimable* stones, unvalued jewels": Shakspere's "Richard III.," i. 4. 27); now more commonly, of immaterial things, of surpassing worth or excellence (as, an *inestimable* boon or privilege).—**in-es′ti-ma-bly,** *adv.*

in-ev-i-ta-ble (in-ev′i-tạ-bl), *a.* [L. *inevitabilis*: cf. *evitable.*] That cannot be avoided, evaded, or escaped (as, "Alcides . . . bending his *inevitable* bow, Reach'd him in air": Dryden's tr. Ovid's "Metamorphoses," xii. 744); admitting of no evasion, as necessity; esp., sure to befall, happen, or come, by the very nature of things (as, one's *inevitable* fate; "The boast of heraldry, the pomp of power . . . Await alike th' *inevitable* hour: The paths of glory lead but to the grave," Gray's "Elegy," ix.); certain or necessary, as an effect, result, or conclusion.—**in-ev″i-ta-bil′i-ty** (-bil′i-ti), **in-ev′i-ta-ble-ness,** *n.*—**in-ev′i-ta-bly,** *adv.*

in-ex-act (in-eg-zakt′), *a.* [See *in-*[2].] Not exact; not strictly accurate or correct; not precise.—**in-ex-ac′ti-tude** (-eg-zak′ti-tūd), **in-ex-act′ness,** *n.*—**in-ex-act′ly,** *adv.*

in-ex-cus-a-ble (in-eks-kū′zạ-bl), *a.* [L. *inexcusabilis.*] Not excusable; unpardonable; indefensible.—**in-ex-cus-a-bil′i-ty** (-bil′i-ti), **in-ex-cus′a-ble-ness,** *n.*—**in-ex-cus′a-bly,** *adv.*

in-ex-e-cut-a-ble (in-ek′sẹ-kū-tạ-bl), *a.* [See *in-*[2].] Not executable; incapable of being executed.—**in-ex-e-cu′tion** (-kū′shọn), *n.* Lack or neglect of execution.

in-ex-er-tion (in-eg-zėr′shọn), *n.* [See *in-*[2].] Want or absence of exertion; inaction.

in-ex-haust-ed (in-eg-zâs′ted), *a.* [See *in-*[2].] Not exhausted; unfailing: as, "a new and *inexhausted* fund of matter" (Addison, in "Spectator," 420).—**in-ex-haust′i-ble,** *a.* Not exhaustible; incapable of being exhausted; unfailing; tireless.—**in-ex-haust-i-bil′i-ty** (-bil′i-ti), **in-ex-haust′i-ble-ness,** *n.*—**in-ex-haust′i-bly,** *adv.*—**in-ex-haus′tive,** *a.* Not exhaustive; failing to exhaust; also, inexhaustible.—**in-ex-haus′tive-ly,** *adv.*

in-ex-ist (in-eg-zist′), *v. i.* [See *in-*[1].] To exist in something else; inhere.—**in-ex-ist′ence**[1], *n.* Existence in something else.

in-ex-ist-ence[2] (in-eg-zis′tẹns), *n.* [See *in-*[2].] Absence of existence; non-existence.—**in-ex-ist′ent,** *a.* Not existent; having no existence.

in-ex-o-ra-ble (in-ek′sọ̄-rạ-bl), *a.* [L. *inexorabilis*: cf. *exorable.*] Not to be persuaded, moved, or affected by prayers or entreaties (as, an *inexorable* judge or avenger; *inexorable* justice; an *inexorable* doom; "Cynthia was *inexorable* — she would have none of him," W. Churchill's "Coniston," ii. 8); unrelenting; fig., unyielding or unalterable (as, *inexorable* law; *inexorable* facts).—**in-ex″o-ra-bil′i-ty** (-bil′i-ti), **in-ex′o-ra-ble-ness,** *n.*—**in-ex′o-ra-bly,** *adv.*

in-ex-pan-si-ble (in-eks-pan′si-bl), *a.* [See *in-*[2].] Not expansible.—**in-ex-pan′sive** (-siv), *a.* Not expansive.

in-ex-pect-ant (in-eks-pek′tạnt), *a.* [See *in-*[2].] Not expectant; without expectation.—**in-ex-pect′an-cy,** *n.*

in-ex-pe-di-ent (in-eks-pē′di-ẹnt), *a.* [See *in-*[2].] Not expedient; not conducive to purposes, advantage, etc.; inadvisable; impolitic.—**in-ex-pe′di-ence, in-ex-pe′di-en-cy,** *n.*—**in-ex-pe′di-ent-ly,** *adv.*

in-ex-pen-sive (in-eks-pen′siv), *a.* [See *in-*[2].] Not expensive; costing little.—**in-ex-pen′sive-ly,** *adv.*—**in-ex-pen′sive-ness,** *n.*

in-ex-pe-ri-ence (in-eks-pē′ri-ẹns), *n.* [LL. *inexperientia.*] Want of experience, or of knowledge or skill gained from experience.—**in-ex-pe′ri-enced,** *a.* Not experienced; without knowledge or skill gained from experience.

in-ex-pert (in-eks-pėrt′), *a.* [L. *inexpertus.*] Not expert; unskilled.—**in-ex-pert′ly,** *adv.*—**in-ex-pert′ness,** *n.*

in-ex-pi-a-ble (in-eks′pi-ạ-bl), *a.* [L. *inexpiabilis.*] Not expiable, as an offense; not admitting of expiation or atonement; also, not to be settled or appeased, as by expiation (as, *inexpiable* war; "*inexpiable* hate," Milton's "Samson Agonistes," 839); implacable.—**in-ex′pi-a-ble-ness,** *n.*—**in-ex′pi-a-bly,** *adv.*

in-ex-plain-a-ble (in-eks-plā′nạ-bl), *a.* [See *in-*[2].] Not explainable; inexplicable.

in-ex-pli-ca-ble (in-eks′pli-kạ-bl), *a.* [L. *inexplicabilis.*] Not explicable; incapable of being explained.—**in-ex″pli-ca-bil′i-ty** (-bil′i-ti), **in-ex′pli-ca-ble-ness,** *n.*—**in-ex′pli-ca-bly,** *adv.*

in-ex-pli-cit (in-eks-plis′it), *a.* [L. *inexplicitus.*] Not explicit; not clearly expressed.—**in-ex-pli′cit-ly,** *adv.*—**in-ex-pli′cit-ness,** *n.*

in-ex-plo-sive (in-eks-plō′siv), *a.* [See *in-*[2].] Not explosive.

in-ex-press-i-ble (in-eks-pres′i-bl). [See *in-*[2].] **I.** *a.* Not expressible; beyond expression; unutterable; unspeakable. **II.** *n.* Something inexpressible; *pl.*, breeches or trousers (colloq.: as, "*inexpressibles* of the best Saxon cloth at 7s. 6d. a pair," Bulwer-Lytton's "Caxtons," ii. 2).—**in-ex-press-i-bil′i-ty** (-bil′i-ti), **in-ex-press′i-ble-ness,** *n.*—**in-ex-press′i-bly,** *adv.*

in-ex-pres-sive (in-eks-pres′iv), *a.* [See *in-*[2].] Not expressive; lacking in expression; also, inexpressible (archaic).—**in-ex-pres′sive-ly,** *adv.*—**in-ex-pres′sive-ness,** *n.*

in-ex-pug-na-ble (in-eks-pug′nạ-bl or in-eks-pū′-), *a.* [L. *inexpugnabilis*, < *in-*, not, + *expugnabilis*, capable of being taken by storm, < *expugnare*, storm, capture, < *ex-*, out, + *pugnare*, fight.] That cannot be taken by storm or overcome by force; impregnable; unconquerable. Often fig.—**in-ex-pug-na-bil′i-ty** (-bil′i-ti), **in-ex-pug′na-ble-ness,** *n.*—**in-ex-pug′na-bly,** *adv.*

in-ex-tend-ed (in-eks-ten′ded), *a.* [See *in-*[2].] Not extended; without extension.—**in-ex-ten′si-ble** (-ten′si-bl), *a.* Not extensible; incapable of being extended.—**in-ex-ten-si-bil′i-ty** (-bil′i-ti), *n.*—**in-ex-ten′sion** (-shọn), *n.* Want of extension.

in-ex-tin-guish-a-ble (in-eks-ting′gwish-ạ-bl), *a.* [See *in-*[2].] Not extinguishable; not to be extinguished, quenched, suppressed, or brought to an end: as, *inextinguishable* fire or light; *inextinguishable* rage; *inextinguishable* laughter (derived from a Greek expression used by Homer: see *Homeric laughter*, under *Homeric*).—**in-ex-tin′guish-a-bly,** *adv.*

in-ex-tri-ca-ble (in-eks′tri-kạ-bl), *a.* [L. *inextricabilis*, < *in-*, not, + *extricare*, E. *extricate*.] From which one cannot extricate one's self (as, an *inextricable* maze; *inextricable* difficulty); hence, hopelessly intricate, involved, or perplexing (as, *inextricable* confusion); also, that cannot be disentangled, undone, or loosed, as a tangle, knot, grasp, etc.—**in-ex″tri-ca-bil′i-ty** (-bil′i-ti), **in-ex′tri-ca-ble-ness,** *n.*—**in-ex′tri-ca-bly,** *adv.*

in-fall (in′fâl), *n.* An incursion or inroad (now rare); also, the junction of one stream, road, etc., with another; also, the place where water enters a reservoir, canal, etc.

in-fal-li-bi-lism (in-fal′i-bi-lizm), *n.* The principle of infallibility, esp. of the infallibility of the Pope.—**in-fal′li-bi-list,** *n.*

in-fal-li-bil-i-ty (in-fal-i-bil′i-ti), *n.* [ML. *infallibilitas*.] The quality of being infallible; exemption from liability to error: as, the *infallibility* of the Pope (when speaking officially on matters of faith or morals: proclaimed by the Vatican Council in 1870).

in-fal-li-ble (in-fal′i-bl). [ML. *infallibilis*.] **I.** *a.* Not fallible; exempt from liability to error, as persons, the judgment, pronouncements, etc.; absolutely trustworthy or sure (as, an *infallible* rule; an *infallible* sign; "*infallible* proofs," Acts, i. 3); unfailing in operation (as, an *infallible* remedy); certain or indubitable (as, "most *infallible* disobedience": Shakspere's "All's Well," i. 1. 150). **II.** *n.* An infallible person or thing.—**in-fal′li-ble-ness,** *n.*—**in-fal′li-bly,** *adv.*

in-fa-mize (in′fạ-mīz), *v. t.*; *-mized*, *-mizing*. To make infamous; also, to defame.

in-fa-mous (in′fạ-mus), *a.* [OF. *infameux*, < ML. *infamosus*, for L. *infamis*, infamous, < *in-*, not, + *fama*, E. *fame*.] Of evil fame or repute (as, "*infamous* for plunder'd provinces": Pope's "Essay on Man," iv. 298); notoriously bad or vile; also, such as to deserve or to cause evil repute (as, an *infamous* deceiver; *infamous* character; an *infamous* deed); detestable; shamefully bad; in *law*, deprived of credit and of certain rights as a citizen, in consequence of conviction of certain offenses; of offenses, etc., involving such deprivation.—**in′fa-mous-ly,** *adv.*—**in′fa-my** (-mi), *n.*; pl. *-mies* (-miz). [L. *infamia*, < *infamis*.] Evil fame, shameful notoriety, or public reproach; also, infamous character (as, to reveal the *infamy* of a proceeding); also, infamous conduct; an infamous act or circumstance; in *law*, the loss of credit and rights incurred by conviction of an infamous offense.

in-fan-cy (in′fạn-si), *n.* [L. *infantia*.] The state or period of being an infant; babyhood; early childhood; hence, the corresponding period in the existence of anything (as, the *infancy* of the world; an art yet in its *infancy*); also, infants collectively; in *law*, the period of life to the age of majority (in the common law, to the end of the twenty-first year); minority; nonage.

in-fant (in′fạnt). [L. *infans* (*infant-*), young child, prop. adj., 'not speaking,' < *in-*, not, + *fans*, ppr. of *fari*, speak.] **I.** *n.* A child during the earliest period of its life, or a baby (as, "As soon as the helpless *infant* sees the light, though in every other eye it appears a despicable and a miserable creature, it is regarded by its fond parent with the utmost affection": Hume's "Essays," The Sceptic); hence, anything in the first period of existence or the first stage of progress; a beginner, as in learning; formerly, a youth of noble or gentle birth† (see Spenser's "Faerie Queene," vi. 8. 25, and cf. *child*, *childe*); in *law*, a minor. **II.** *a.* Being in infancy or babyhood (as, an *infant* child); hence, being in the earliest period or stage (as, *infant* colonies; an *infant* industry); incipient, nascent, or of recent origin; also, of or pertaining to infants or infancy (as, *infant* hand; *infant* years); in *law*, minor.

in-fan-ta (in-fan′tạ), *n.* [Sp. and Pg., fem. of *infante*.] A royal princess of Spain or Portugal.—**in-fan′te** (-tạ), *n.* [Sp. and Pg., < L. *infans*, E. *infant*.] A royal prince of Spain or Portugal, not heir to the throne.

in-fant-hood (in′fạnt-hủd), *n.* Infancy; babyhood.

in-fan-ti-cide (in-fan′ti-sīd), *n.* [LL. *infanticida*, *infanticidium*: see *-cide*.] One who kills an infant; also, the killing of an infant.—**in-fan′ti-ci-dal** (-sī-dạl), *a.*

in-fan-tile (in′fạn-til or -tīl), *a.* [L. *infantilis*.] Of or pertaining to infants; characteristic of or befitting an infant; babyish or childish; infant-like; also, being in the earliest stage.—**infantile paralysis,** in *pathol.*, an acute disease, most common in infants but often attacking older children and adults, characterized by inflammation of the anterior horns of the gray matter of the spinal cord, and by motor paralysis, muscular atrophy, etc., and often resulting in permanent deformities. Also called *acute anterior poliomyelitis*.—**infantile scurvy,** in *pathol.*, a disease of childhood, due to improper diet, characterized by progressive anemia, mental apathy, spongy gums, hemorrhages into various structures, etc.—**in′fan-til-ism** (-til-izm), *n.* Abnormal persistence or recurrence of childish characteristics (physical or mental) in an adult.

in-fan-tine (in′fạn-tin or -tīn), *a.* Infantile; babyish; childish: as, "an *infantine* flow of tears" (Irving's "Tales of a Traveler," i. 9).

in-fan-try (in′fạn-tri), *n.*; pl. *-tries* (-triz). [F. *infanterie*, < It. *infanteria*, < *infante*, infant, youth, foot-soldier, < L. *infans*: see *infant*.] Soldiery or troops regularly serving on foot, and commonly carrying small arms, now esp. rifles. —**in′fan-try-man** (-mạn), *n.*; pl. *-men*. A soldier of the infantry; a foot-soldier.

in-farct (in-färkt′), *n.* [L. *infarctus*, *infartus*, pp. of *infarcire*, stuff in, < *in*, in, + *farcire*, stuff.] In *pathol.*, a circumscribed portion of tissue that has become stuffed or filled with extraneous matter, as extravasated blood, or has become otherwise morbidly affected, through obstructed circulation, infiltration of salts, or the like; also, the morbid condition of such tissue; also, the matter which fills or obstructs such tissue; an embolus.—**in-farct′ed,** *a.* In *pathol.*, characterized by or exhibiting infarction.—**in-farc′tion** (-färk′shọn), *n.* In *pathol.*, the formation of an infarct; also, an infarct.

in-fare (in′fãr), *n.* [AS. *infær*, entrance, < *in*, in, + *faran*, go, E. *fare*, *v.*] A housewarming, esp. upon the entrance of a bride into her new home. [Sc., Ir., north. Eng., and local, U. S.]

in-fat-u-ate (in-fat′ū-āt), *v. t.*; *-ated*, *-ating*. [L. *infatuatus*, pp. of *infatuare*, < *in*, in, + *fatuus*, foolish, E. *fatuous*.] To affect with senseless folly; esp., to inspire or possess with a foolish or unreasoning passion, as of love, admiration, enthusiasm, etc. (as, to be *infatuated* with a woman, or with an idea; "Some to the fascination of a name Surrender judgment, hood-wink'd. Some the style [of a book] *infatuates*," Cowper's "Task," vi. 103); also, to reduce to foolishness†, or bring to naught†.—**in-fat′u-ate,** *a.* Infatuated.—**in-fat′u-at-ed-ly** (-ā-ted-li), *adv.*—**in-fat-u-a′tion** (-ā′shọn), *n.* [LL. *infatuatio*(*n*-).] The act of infatuating, or the state of being infatuated; a foolish or unreasoning passion.

in-faust (in-fâst′), *a.* [L. *infaustus*, < *in-*, not, + *faustus*, favorable, < *favere*, be favorable.] Unfavorable; inauspicious; unlucky: as, "It was an *infaust* and sinister augury for Austin Caxton" (Bulwer-Lytton's "Caxtons," vii. 1). [Now rare.]

in-fea-si-ble (in-fē′zi-bl), *a.* [See *in-*[2].] Not feasible; impracticable.—**in-fea-si-bil′i-ty** (-bil′i-ti), *n.*

in-fect (in-fekt′), *v. t.* [L. *infectus*, pp. of *inficere*, put in, dye, imbue, infect, < *in*, in, + *facere*, do, make.] To dye†, color†, or tinge†; hence, to impregnate with something that affects quality, character, or condition, esp. unfavorably (as, to *infect* the air with noisome gases or noxious germs); often, to permeate and affect, as the entering element does (as, noisome gases have *infected* the air); specif., to impregnate (a person, organ, wound, etc.) with disease-producing or septic germs; affect with disease; fig., to taint, contaminate, or affect morally, as with vice or evil; imbue with some pernicious belief, opinion, etc.; also, to affect so as to influence feeling or action, as if by infection, or contagion (as, to *infect* others with one's own zeal; his courage *infected* his followers); in *law*, to taint with illegality, or expose to penalty, forfeiture, etc.—**in-fec′tion** (-fek′shọn), *n.* [LL. *infectio*(*n*-).] The act of infecting, or the state of being infected; esp., an infecting with the germs of disease, as through the medium of infected insects, air, water, clothing, etc. (sometimes distinguished from *contagion*); also, an infectious disease; an epidemic; also, an infecting agency or influence; fig., an influence or impulse passing from one to another and affecting feeling or action (as, "While her tears deplored the godlike man, Through all her train the soft *infection* ran": Pope's tr. Homer's "Iliad," vi.).—**in-fec'tious** (-shus), *a.* Causing or communicating infection; also, communicable by infection, as diseases; tending to spread from one to another, as feelings, actions, etc. (as, "They say cowardice is *infectious*": Stevenson's "Treasure Island," iv.); contagious; catching.—**in-fec'tious-ly,** *adv.*—**in-fec'tious-ness,** *n.*—**in-fec'tive,** *a.* Infectious.—**in-fec'tive-ness, in-fec-tiv'i-ty,** *n.*—**in-fec'tor,** *n.*

in-fec-und (in-fek'und or -fē'kund), *a.* [L. *infecundus.*] Not fecund; unfruitful; barren.—**in-fe-cun'di-ty** (-fẹ-kun'di-ti), *n.*

in-fe-li-ci-tous (in-fẹ-lis'i-tus), *a.* [See *in-*[2].] Not felicitous; unhappy or unfortunate; inapt or inappropriate.—**in-fe-li'ci-tous-ly,** *adv.*

in-fe-li-ci-ty (in-fẹ-lis'i-ti), *n.*; pl. *-ties* (-tiz). [L. *infelicitas,* < *infelix,* unhappy, < *in-,* not, + *felix,* happy.] The state of being unhappy; unhappiness; ill fortune; an unfortunate circumstance; a misfortune; also, inaptness or inappropriateness, as of expression or style; something inapt or infelicitous.

in-felt (in'felt), *a.* Felt within; heartfelt.

in-fer (in-fėr'), *v.*; *-ferred, -ferring.* [L. *inferre* (pp. *illatus*), bring in or on, infer, < *in,* in, on, + *ferre,* bear: cf. *illation.*] **I.** *tr.* To bring on or about†, or cause† (as, "Who . . . fled fast away, afeard Of villany to be to her *inferd*": Spenser's "Faerie Queene," vi. 8. 31); also, to adduce† or allege† (as, "Full well hath Clifford play'd the orator, *Inferring* arguments of mighty force": Shakspere's "3 Henry VI.," ii. 2. 44); also, to derive by reasoning, or conclude or judge from premises or evidence (as, to *infer* a conclusion; from the facts known we *infer* his innocence, or that he is innocent, or we *infer* him to be innocent); deduce; also, of facts, circumstances, statements, etc., to indicate or involve as a conclusion, or imply (as, "Consider first, that great Or bright *infers* not excellence": Milton's "Paradise Lost," viii. 91). **II.** *intr.* To draw a conclusion, as by reasoning.—**in-fer-a-ble** (in'fẹ-rạ-bl or in-fėr'ạ-), *a.* That may be inferred; deducible.—**in'fer-a-bly,** *adv.*—**in'fer-ence** (-fẹ-rẹns), *n.* [ML. *inferentia.*] The act or process, or a particular act, of inferring (as, to form a judgment by *inference* from known facts; to make rash *inferences*); also, that which is inferred; a conclusion drawn from premises or evidence; a deduction.—**in-fer-en'tial** (-fẹ-ren'shạl), *a.* Pertaining to or depending on inference; deduced or deducible by inference.—**in-fer-en'tial-ly,** *adv.* In an inferential manner; by way of inference; as may be inferred.

in-fe-ri-or (in-fē'ri-ọr), *a.* [L., compar. of *inferus,* being below, under, nether: cf. *under.*] Lower in place or position (now chiefly in scientific or technical use); hence, lower in station, rank, degree, or grade; less important, valuable, or excellent; of lower grade or poorer quality; hence, of comparatively low grade; poor in quality; also, of lower status, grade, etc., as opposed (*to*); in *bot.,* situated below some other organ; of a calyx, inserted below the ovary; of an ovary, having a superior calyx; in *printing,* lower than the main line of type, as the figures in chemical formulæ.—**inferior planets.** See under *planet.*—**in-fe'ri-or,** *n.* One inferior to another or others, as in rank, merit, or some specified particular; in *printing,* an inferior letter or figure.—**in-fe-ri-or'i-ty** (-or'i-ti), *n.* The state or quality of being inferior.—**in-fe'ri-or-ly,** *adv.* In an inferior position, degree, or manner.

in-fer-nal (in-fėr'nạl), *a.* [OF. F. *infernal,* < LL. *infernalis,* < L. *infernus,* being below, of the lower regions, < *inferus*: see *inferior.*] Of or pertaining to the lower world, or regions of the dead, of classical mythology; also, of, inhabiting, or befitting hell, the abode of evil and condemned spirits; hellish; fiendish; diabolical; hence, execrable or outrageous (colloq.: as, "If you go ashore, you will get into some *infernal* row," H. Melville's "Typee," v.).—**infernal machine,** an explosive mechanical apparatus intended to destroy life or property.—**in-fer-nal'i-ty** (-nal'i-ti), *n.* The quality of being infernal.—**in-fer'nal-ly,** *adv.*

in-fer-no (in-fėr'nō), *n.*; pl. *-nos* (-nōz). [It., hell (esp. as the subject and title of a part of Dante's "Divina Commedia"), < L. *infernus*: see *infernal.*] An infernal or hell-like region; a place of hellish torment.

in-fe-ro- (in'fẹ-rọ-). Form of L. *inferus,* being below, used in combination, as in *infero-anterior* (situated below and in front), *inferoposterior* (situated below and behind), *inferolateral* (situated below and to one side).

in-fer-ri-ble (in-fėr'i-bl), *a.* Same as *inferable.*

in-fer-tile (in-fėr'til), *a.* [LL. *infertilis.*] Not fertile; unfruitful; unproductive; barren.—**in-fer-til'i-ty,** *n.*

in-fest (in-fest'), *v. t.* [L. *infestare,* < *infestus,* disturbed, unsafe, hostile, < *in,* in, on, + *-festus,* akin to *-fendere,* strike: see *defend.*] To attack or molest persistently, or harass (now rare: as, "How thou might'st Find some occasion to *infest* our foes," Milton's "Samson Agonistes," 423); also, to haunt or overrun in a troublesome manner, as predatory bands, destructive animals, vermin, etc., do (as, "mountains *infested* by barbarians," Johnson's "Rasselas," vi.; jungles *infested* with snakes); be numerous in, as anything troublesome (as, seas *infested* with icebergs; "the cares that *infest* the day," Longfellow's "The Day Is Done").—**in-fes-ta'tion** (-fes-tā'shọn), *n.* The act of infesting, or the state of being infested; a harassing or troublesome invasion.—**in-fest'er,** *n.*

in-feu-da-tion (in-fū-dā'shọn), *n.* [ML. *infeudatio(n-),* < *infeudare,* enfeoff, < *in,* in, + *feudum,* fee: see *fee*[2].] In *Eng. law,* the conferring of an estate in fee; also, the granting of tithes to laymen.

in-fi-del (in'fi-del). [F. *infidèle,* < L. *infidelis,* unfaithful, later unbelieving, < *in-,* not, + *fidelis,* faithful: see *fidelity.*] **I.** *a.* Without religious faith; unbelieving; commonly, not accepting a particular faith, esp. Christianity or Mohammedanism; heathen; also, of or pertaining to unbelievers or infidels. **II.** *n.* An unbeliever; commonly, one who does not accept a particular faith, esp. Christianity (formerly applied by Christians esp. to a Mohammedan); also (to Mohammedans), one who does not accept the Mohammedan faith (as, "As long as he wore a cap . . . blessed by Mahomet, he deemed himself invulnerable amidst the darts of the *infidels*": Gibbon's "Decline and Fall of the Roman Empire," li.).—**in-fi-del'i-ty,** *n.*; pl. *-ties* (-tiz). [F. *infidélité,* < L. *infidelitas.*] Lack of religious faith; disbelief in religion, esp. in Christianity; also, unfaithfulness; a breach of trust; esp., unfaithfulness to the marriage vows.

in-field (in'fēld), *n.* That part of farm-lands nearest to the buildings; in *baseball,* the diamond; also, the three basemen and the shortstop.—**in'field"er,** *n.* In *baseball,* an infield player.

in-fight-ing (in'fī"ting), *n.* In *boxing,* fighting at close quarters, where only short-range blows can be delivered.

in-fill (in'fil or in-fil'), *v. t.* To fill in; fill up.—**in'fill"ing,** *n.* A filling in or up; also, that which serves to fill in or up.

in-fil-ter (in-fil'tėr), *v. t.* or *i.* To filter in.

in-fil-trate (in-fil'trāt), *v.*; *-trated, -trating.* **I.** *tr.* To cause to pass in by or as by filtering; also, to filter into or through; permeate. **II.** *intr.* To pass in or through a substance, etc., by or as by filtering.—**in-fil'trate,** *n.* That which infiltrates; in *pathol.,* a substance which passes into the tissues and forms a morbid accumulation.—**in-fil-tra'tion** (-trā'shọn), *n.* The act or process of infiltrating, or the state of being infiltrated; also, that which infiltrates; an infiltrate; specif., *milit.,* a method of attack in which small bodies of men penetrate into the enemy's lines at various weak points, in order to bring fire eventually upon the enemy's flanks or rear.—**in-fil'tra-tive** (-trạ-tiv), *a.*

in-fin-i-tate (in-fin'i-tāt), *v. t.*; *-tated, -tating.* [ML. *infinitatus,* pp. of *infinitare,* < L. *infinitus,* E. *infinite.*] To render infinite; in *logic,* to render (a positive term, etc.) indefinite by attaching a sign of negation to it.—**in-fin-i-ta'tion** (-tā'shọn), *n.*

in-fi-nite (in'fi-nit). [L. *infinitus,* unbounded, unlimited, < *in-,* not, + *finitus,* E. *finite.*] **I.** *a.* Unbounded or unlimited, or not finite (as, *infinite* space; *infinite* time; the *infinite* wisdom of God); immeasurably great; boundless, endless, or innumerable; inexhaustible; also, indefinitely or exceedingly great (as, "He . . . told him that the treasury in Jerusalem was full of *infinite* sums of money," 2 Mac. iii. 6; "All my devices . . . failed me, though they cost *infinite* labour too," Defoe's "Robinson Crusoe," i. 9); immense; vast. **II.** *n.* That which is infinite; the boundless regions of space; an immeasurably or an indefinitely great extent or amount; an infinite quantity or magnitude; [*cap.*] with *the*, the Infinite Being, God.—**in′fi-nite-ly,** *adv.* —**in′fi-nite-ness,** *n.*

in-fi-ni-tes-i-mal (in″fi-ni-tes′i-mạl). [NL. *infinitesimus*, < L. *infinitus*: see *infinite*.] **I.** *a.* Immeasurably small; less than any assignable quantity; also, indefinitely or exceedingly small; minute; also, pertaining to or involving infinitesimals (as, *infinitesimal* calculus: see *calculus*). **II.** *n.* An infinitesimal quantity.—**in″fi-ni-tes′i-mal-ly,** *adv.*

in-fin-i-ti-val (in-fin-i-tī′vạl), *a.* In *gram.*, of or pertaining to the infinitive mode.—**in-fin-i-ti′val-ly,** *adv.*

in-fin-i-tive (in-fin′i-tiv). [LL. *infinitivus*, < L. *in-*, not, + *finitivus*, defining, definite, < *finire*, bound, limit: see *finish*.] In *gram.*: **I.** *a.* Unlimited or indefinite: applied to a certain mode or form of the verb (by origin a verbal noun, and in English commonly preceded by the preposition *to*) which expresses the general sense of the verb without restriction as to person or number, as (*to*) *give* (F. *donner*, G. *geben*, L. *dare*). **II.** *n.* The infinitive mode; also, an infinitive verb-form.—**split infinitive.** See under *split, p. a.* —**in-fin′i-tive-ly,** *adv.* As an infinitive.

in-fin-i-tude (in-fin′i-tūd), *n.* The state of being infinite; infinity; also, an infinite extent, amount, or number.

in-fin-i-ty (in-fin′i-ti), *n.*; pl. *-ties* (-tiz). [OF. *infinite* (F. *infinité*), < L. *infinitas*, boundlessness, < *in-*, not, + *finis*, boundary, E. *fine*[1].] The state of being infinite; also, that which is infinite; infinite space, time, or quantity; an infinite extent, amount, or number; sometimes, an indefinitely great amount or number (as, "an *infinity* of rumors": Cooper's "Prairie," xv.); in *math.*, an infinite quantity or magnitude; in *geom.*, infinite distance, or an infinitely distant part of space.

in-firm (in-fėrm′), *a.* [L. *infirmus*.] Not firm, solid, or strong (as, "*Infirm* the stalks, unsolid are the leaves": Dryden's tr. Ovid's "Metamorphoses," xv. 307); feeble in body or health, esp. from age (as, "Here I stand . . . A poor, *infirm*, weak, and despised old man": Shakspere's "King Lear," iii. 2. 20); physically weak or enfeebled; fig., not steadfast, unfaltering, or resolute, as persons, the mind, etc.; also, unsound or invalid, as an argument, a title, etc.—**in-fir-ma′ri-an** (-fėr-mā′ri-ạn), *n.* One in charge of an infirmary, as in a monastic institution.—**in-fir′ma-ry** (-mạ-ri), *n.*; pl. *-ries* (-riz). [ML. *infirmaria*.] A place for the care of the infirm, sick, or injured; a hospital; esp., in an institution, as a school, a hospital for the members or inmates; also, a dispensary or establishment for treating or advising outdoor patients.—**in-fir′mi-ty** (-mi-ti), *n.*; pl. *-ties* (-tiz). [L. *infirmitas*.] The state of being infirm; want of strength; feebleness in body or health; a physical weakness or ailment (as, the *infirmities* of age); a moral weakness or failing (as, "Fame is the spur that the clear spirit doth raise (That last *infirmity* of noble mind)": Milton's "Lycidas," 71).—**in-firm′ly,** *adv.*—**in-firm′ness,** *n.*

in-fix (in-fiks′), *v. t.* [L. *infixus*, pp. of *infigere*, < *in*, in + *figere*, fix, drive in.] To fix, fasten, or drive in (as, "Meges in the rear Full in his nape *infix'd* the fatal spear": Pope's tr. Homer's "Iliad," v.); implant; fig., to fix in the mind or memory, as a fact or idea; impress; in *gram.*, to insert (a formative element) in the body of a word.—**in′fix,** *n.* In *gram.*, an infixed word-element.—**in-fix′ion** (-fik′shọn), *n.* The act of infixing, or the state of being infixed.

in-flame (in-flām′), *v.*; *-flamed*, *-flaming*. [OF. *enflamer* (F. *enflammer*), < L. *inflammare*, < *in*, in, + *flamma*, E. *flame*.] **I.** *tr.* To set aflame, ablaze, or afire (as, "Old wood *inflam'd* doth yield the bravest fire": Sidney's "Arcadia," ii. 1); light or redden with or as with flames (as, the setting sun *inflames* the sky); also, to raise (the blood, bodily tissue, etc.) to a morbid or feverish heat; excite inflammation in; also, to rouse to a high degree of passion or feeling (as, to *inflame* a person, or the mind, with ardor or rage); kindle or excite (passions, desires, etc.); make more violent, or aggravate (as, "The happy place . . . *inflames* thy torment; representing Lost bliss": Milton's "Paradise Regained," i. 418); sometimes, to affect in appearance by passion, etc. (as, a face *inflamed* with wrath). **II.** *intr.* To burst into flame; take fire; also, to become morbidly inflamed, or affected with inflammation; also, to become hot with passion, as the heart; be kindled, as passion.—**in-flamed′,** *p. a.* In *her.*, represented as in flames or burning; decorated with flames along the edge, as a bend.—**in-flam′er** (-flā′mėr), *n.*

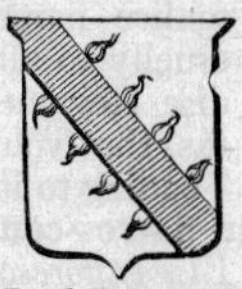
Bend Inflamed.

in-flam-ma-ble (in-flam′ạ-bl), *a.* [= F. *inflammable*, < L. *inflammare*, E. *inflame*.] Capable of being set on fire; combustible; also, easily roused to passion; excitable.—**in-flam-ma-bil′i-ty** (-bil′i-ti), **in-flam′ma-ble-ness,** *n.*—**in-flam′ma-bly,** *adv.*

in-flam-ma-tion (in-flạ-mā′shọn), *n.* [L. *inflammatio*(*n*-), < *inflammare*, E. *inflame*.] The act of inflaming, or the state of being inflamed; in *gunnery*, the propagation of ignition from grain to grain when a charge of powder is set off; in *pathol.*, a morbid condition of some part of the body, characterized by heat, redness, swelling, pain, etc.—**in-flam′ma-to-ry** (-flam′ạ-tọ-ri), *a.* Tending to inflame; kindling passion, anger, etc.; in *pathol.*, pertaining to or attended with inflammation.—**in-flam′ma-to-ri-ly,** *adv.*

in-flat-a-ble (in-flā′tạ-bl), *a.* That may be inflated.

in-flate (in-flāt′), *v.*; *-flated*, *-flating*. [L. *inflatus*, pp. of *inflare*, < *in*, in, + *flare*, blow.] **I.** *tr.* To distend with air or gas (as, to *inflate* an air-cushion or a balloon); hence, to distend in any manner; swell or puff out; dilate; fig., to puff up with pride, self-importance, satisfaction, etc.; elate; also, to expand (currency, prices, etc.) unduly; raise above the just or proper amount or value. **II.** *intr.* To cause inflation; also, to become inflated.—**in-flat′ed** (-flā′ted), *p. a.* Distended with air or gas; swollen; fig., puffed up, as with pride; turgid or bombastic, as language; also, unduly expanded, as currency.—**in-flat′ed-ness,** *n.*—**in-flat′er, in-flat′or,** *n.*—**in-fla′tile** (-flā′til), *a.* [LL. *inflatilis*.] Sounded by blowing, as a wind-instrument.—**in-fla′tion** (-shọn), *n.* [L. *inflatio*(*n*-).] The act of inflating, or the state of being inflated; specif., expansion or increase of the currency of a country by the issuing of paper money, esp. paper money not redeemable in specie or insufficiently secured by precious metal.—**in-fla′tion-ism,** *n.* The process or practice of inflation of currency.—**in-fla′tion-ist,** *n.* An advocate of inflation of currency.

in-flect (in-flekt′), *v. t.* [L. *inflectere* (pp. *inflexus*), < *in*, in, + *flectere*, bend.] To bend in; hence, simply, to bend; fig., to incline or dispose; also, to modulate (the voice); in *gram.*, to vary (a noun, verb, etc.) in form, whether in the word-ending or the stem, to indicate number, case, mode, tense, etc.; decline; conjugate.—**in-flec′tion, in-flex′ion** (-flek′shọn), *n.* [L. *inflexio*(*n*-).] The act of inflecting, or the state of being inflected; hence, a bend or angle; also, modulation of the voice; change in pitch or tone of voice; in *gram.*, the process of inflecting; also, an inflected form of a word; also, a suffix or other element used in inflecting. —**in-flec′tion-al, in-flex′ion-al,** *a.* Of or pertaining to inflection, esp. grammatical inflection; exhibiting inflection. —**in-flec′tion-al-ly, in-flex′ion-al-ly,** *adv.*—**in-flec′tion-less, in-flex′ion-less,** *a.* Without inflection.—**in-flec′tive,** *a.* Tending to inflect or bend; in *gram.*, pertaining to or characterized by inflection.—**in-flec′tor,** *n.*

in-flex (in-fleks′), *v. t.* [L. *inflexus*, pp. of *inflectere*: see *inflect*.] To bend in; incurve; hence, to bend: chiefly in *inflexed, p. a.*

in-flex-i-ble (in-flek′si-bl), *a.* [L. *inflexibilis*.] Not flexible; incapable of being bent, or stiff or rigid (as, "The bow *inflexible* resists their pain": Pope's tr. Homer's "Odyssey," xxi.); unyielding in temper or purpose (as, to remain *inflexible* to both threats and promises; *inflexible* integrity); unalterable (as, "In religion the law is written, and *inflexible*, never to do evil": Goldsmith's "Vicar of Wakefield," xxi.).—**in-flex-i-bil′i-ty** (-bil′i-ti), **in-flex′i-ble-ness,** *n.*—**in-flex′i-bly,** *adv.*

in-flex′ion, etc. See *inflection*, etc.

in-flict (in-flikt′), *v. t.* [L. *inflictus*, pp. of *infligere*, < *in*, in, on, + *fligere*, strike.] To lay on as a stroke, blow, or wound; impose as something that must be borne or suffered, as punishment or a penalty; hence, to impose as something unwelcome (as, to *inflict* one's presence on a person); also, to afflict or trouble (a person, etc.) with something (obs. or rare).—**in-flict'a-ble,** *a.* That may be inflicted.—**in-flict'er, in-flict'or,** *n.*—**in-flic'tion** (-flik'shọn), *n.* [LL. *inflictio(n-).*] The act of inflicting; also, something inflicted, as punishment, suffering, etc. (as, "What but thy malice moved thee to misdeem Of righteous Job, then cruelly to afflict him With all *inflictions?*" Milton's "Paradise Regained," i. 426); hence, an annoyance or nuisance (as, that young man is a terrible *infliction*).—**in-flic'tive,** *a.* Tending to inflict; pertaining to infliction.

in-flo-res-cence (in-flǫ-res'ẹns), *n.* [NL. *inflorescentia,* < LL. *inflorescere,* come into flower, < L. *in,* in, + *florescere,* begin to flower: see *florescence.*] A flowering or blossoming; in *bot.*, the arrangement of flowers on the axis; the method of development of flowers; also, the flowering part of a plant; a flower cluster.

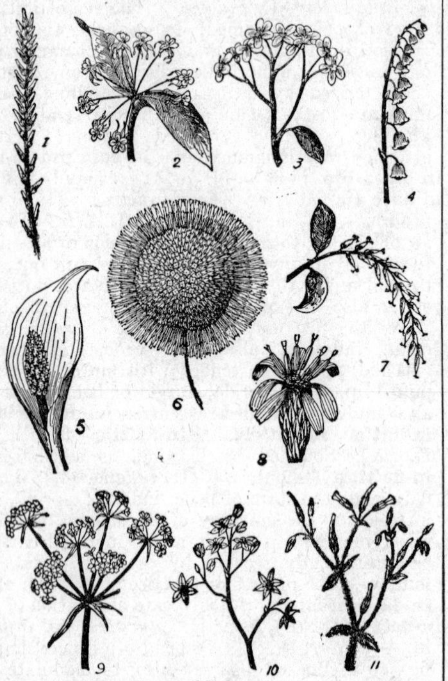

Forms of Inflorescence.

1, spike (plantain, *Plantago*); 2, simple umbel (milkweed, *Asclepias*); 3, corymb (chokeberry, *Aronia*); 4, raceme (lily-of-the-valley, *Convallaria*); 5, spadix within the spathe (calla, *Calla*); 6, flower-head (button-bush, *Cephalanthus*); 7, female catkin (willow, *Salix*); 8, anthodium (goldenrod, *Solidago*); 9, compound umbel (water-parsnip, *Sium*); 10, panicle (blue cohosh, *Caulophyllum*); 11, cyme (a chickweed, *Cerastium*).

in-flow (in'-flō), *n.* The act of flowing in; also, that which flows in.

in-flu-ence (in'flǫ-ẹns), *n.* [OF. F. *influence,* < ML. *influentia,* lit. 'a flowing in,' < L. *influens*: see *influent.*] A flowing in†; inflow†; also, the supposed radiation of an ethereal fluid from the stars, regarded in astrology as affecting human actions and destinies, etc.; hence, the exercise of occult power by the stars, or such power as exercised; fig., the exercise of similar power by human beings (now poetic: as, "Store of ladies, whose bright eyes Rain *influence,*" Milton's "L'Allegro," 122); also, the inflow or infusion of some spiritual, moral, or like power or principle†, or such power or principle as flowing in or infused† (as, "So spake the false archangel, and infused Bad *influence* into the unwary breast Of his associate": Milton's "Paradise Lost," v. 695); hence, invisible or insensible action exerted by one thing or person on another (as, the *influence* of the moon on the tides; the *influence* of example on the young); power of producing effects by invisible or insensible means (as, the drug in time loses its *influence* on the system); esp., personal power independent of force or authority enabling one to produce effects or gain ends (as, to obtain a position through *influence*; to have *influence* with those in authority); often, power or authority due to favor, position, etc. (as, a man of great *influence*); also, a thing or person that exerts action by invisible or insensible means (as, "These prejudices . . . are to be considered as *influences* of a like kind to enthusiasm": J. Butler's "Analogy of Religion," ii. 7); specif., in *elect.*, induction.—**in'flu-ence,** *v. t.*; *-enced, -encing.* To exert influence upon; affect by invisible or insensible means (as, the moon *influences* the tides); esp., to affect (a person, etc.) by influence (as, "These prejudices are often scarce known or reflected upon by the persons themselves who are *influenced* by them": J. Butler's "Analogy of Religion," ii. 7); affect the mind or action of in some particular way; move or impel to, or to do, something; sometimes, to move by improper or undue influence.—**in'flu-en-cer** (-ẹn-sėr), *n.*

in-flu-ent (in'flǫ-ẹnt), *a.* [L. *influens* (*-ent-*), ppr. of *influere,* flow in, < *in,* in, + *fluere,* flow.] Flowing in; also, exerting influence†.

in-flu-en-tial (in-flǫ-en'shạl), *a.* Having or exerting influence, esp. great influence; often, possessed of great personal influence (as, to have *influential* friends).—**in-flu-en'tial-ly,** *adv.*

in-flu-en-za (in-flǫ-en'zạ), *n.* [It., influence, also influx of disease, epidemic, influenza, < ML. *influentia*: see *influence.*] An acute, extremely contagious, commonly epidemic disease characterized by general prostration, and occurring in several forms with varying symptoms, usually with nasal catarrh and bronchial inflammation, and due to a specific micro-organism; grippe; also, a contagious specific fever of horses, characterized by alterations of the blood, depression of the vital forces, and inflammatory complications.—**in-flu-en'zal,** *a.*

in-flux (in'fluks), *n.* [LL. *influxus,* < L. *influere,* flow in: see *influent.*] The act of flowing in; an inflow; an inpouring; a continuous coming or going of persons or things into some place, etc. (as, "The *influx* of this wandering trade has had its effects on the habits of the mountain tribes": Irving's "Captain Bonneville," i.); also, the mouth of a stream. Also **in-flux'ion** (-fluk'shọn).

in-fold, en-fold (in-fōld', en-), *v. t.* [See *in-*[1].] To wrap up; inclose; encompass; embrace; also, to fold in or inward; form into a fold or folds.—**in-fold'er, en-fold'er,** *n.*—**in-fold'ment, en-fold'ment,** *n.*

in-form[1] (in-fôrm'), *v.* [OF. *enformer* (F. *informer*), < L. *informare,* give form to, shape, instruct, < *in,* in, + *forma,* E. *form.*] **I.** *tr.* To put into form or shape† (as, "Infinite shapes of creatures men doe fynd *Informed* in the mud on which the Sunne hath shynd": Spenser's "Faerie Queene," iii. 6. 8); also, to endow or imbue with something that determines character (as, "The god of soldiers . . . *inform* Thy thoughts with nobleness": Shakspere's "Coriolanus," v. 3. 71); of the determining agency, to give character to; pervade with determining effect on the character; specif., to animate or inspire, as a spirit or soul does (as, "The breath Of life *informing* each organic frame": Akenside's "Pleasures of Imagination," i. 74); also, to train or instruct (now rare); give instruction in†; also, to direct† or guide† (as, "Where else Shall I *inform* my unacquainted feet In the blind mazes of this tangled wood?" Milton's "Comus," 180); also, to impart knowledge of a fact or circumstance to (usually with *of* or a clause); apprise, notify, or tell; often, to supply (one's self) with knowledge of a matter or subject; also, to impart knowledge of† (a fact, etc.: as, "Haply thou mayst *inform* Something to save thy life," Shakspere's "All's Well," iv. 1. 91). **II.** *intr.* To take form† (as, "It is the bloody business which *informs* Thus to mine eyes": Shakspere's "Macbeth," ii. 1. 48); also, to give intelligence or information, esp. as in accusation (as, "Even though it may benefit the public, you must not *inform* against him": Goldsmith's "Vicar of Wakefield," xxi.).

in-form[2] (in-fôrm'), *a.* [L. *informis,* < *in-,* not, + *forma,* E. *form.*] Without form, or formless; shapeless; misshapen or deformed. [Archaic.]

in-for-mal (in-fôr'mạl), *a.* [See *in-*[2].] Not formal; not according to prescribed or customary forms, or irregular (as, *informal* proceedings); without formality, or unceremonious (as, an *informal* visit).—**in-for-mal'i-ty** (-mal'i-ti), *n.*; pl. *-ties* (-tiz). The state of being informal; absence of formality; also, an informal act or procedure.—**in-for'mal-ly,** *adv.*

in-form-ant (in-fôr'mạnt), *n.* [L. *informans* (*-ant-*), ppr. of *informare*: see *inform*[1].] One who informs, or gives information: as, "Those came who wished to gain information on a subject new to them, from *informants* whom they . . . regarded as authorities" (J. H. Newman's "Idea of a University," ii. 9).

in-for-ma-tion (in-fôr-mā'shọn), *n.* [OF. *enformacion* (F. *information*), < L. *informatio(n-)*, < *informare*: see *inform*¹.] The act of informing, training, or instructing (now rare: as, "our reason and affections, which God has given us for the *information* of our judgment and the conduct of our lives," J. Butler's "Analogy of Religion," ii. 7); also, the act of informing of some fact or circumstance, or the state of being so informed (as, for your *information* the names are given); also, knowledge communicated or received concerning some fact or circumstance (as, to get *information* of a shipwreck); news; intelligence; an item of information or intelligence†; knowledge on various subjects, however acquired (as, a man of wide *information* rather than of learning); also, the act or an act of informing against, or laying a charge against, a person; specif., in *law*, a complaint or charge against a person for the institution of criminal proceedings otherwise than by formal indictment.—**in-for'ma-tive** (-mạ-tiv), **in-for'ma-to-ry** (-tọ-ri), *a.* Affording information; informing; instructive.

in-form-er (in-fôr'mėr), *n.* One who or that which informs, animates, or inspires (as, "O Sun! . . . *Informer* of the planetary train!" Thomson's "Seasons," Summer, 104); also, one who communicates information; an informant; also, one who informs against another; specif., one who informs of a violation of law; a person who makes it his business to detect violations of law and to lay informations against the offenders.

in-for-mi-da-ble (in-fôr'mi-dạ-bl), *a.* [LL. *informidabilis.*] Not formidable; not to be dreaded.

in-form-ing (in-fôr'ming), *p. a.* That informs; affording information; instructive.—**in-form'ing-ly,** *adv.*

in-for-tune (in-fôr'tūn), *n.* [OF. F. *infortune.*] Misfortune†; in *astrol.*, a planet or aspect of evil influence, esp. either of the planets Saturn and Mars.

in-fra (in'frạ̈), *adv.* and *prep.* [L.] Below; beneath: esp. used (adverbially) in making reference to parts of a text. Cf. *supra.* Also used as a prefix, esp. in scientific words, as in *infra-axillary* (below the axilla or axil), *infracostal* (below the costæ or ribs), *infrahyoid* (below the hyoid bone), *infra-orbital, infraspinal,* etc. Cf. *supra-.*—**in-fra dig.** (dig). Colloquial abbreviation of L. *infra dignitatem*, beneath (one's) dignity: as, "It would be *infra dig.* in the Provost of this most flourishing and loyal town to associate with Redgauntlet" (Scott's "Redgauntlet," ch. xi.).

in-fract (in-frakt'), *v. t.* [L. *infractus*, pp. of *infringere*: see *infringe.*] To break; violate or infringe.—**in-frac'tion** (-frak'shọn), *n.* [L. *infractio(n-).*] The act of infracting; a breakage; breach, violation, or infringement, as of a law.—**in-frac'tor,** *n.* One who infracts or infringes; a violator: as, "The states-general formally declared that Don John was . . . an *infractor* of the peace which he had sworn to maintain" (Motley's "Dutch Republic," v. 4).

in-fra-nat-u-ral (in-frạ̈-nat'ū-rạl), *a.* [See *infra.*] Below what is natural.

in-fran-gi-ble (in-fran'ji-bl), *a.* [See *in-*².] Not frangible; not to be broken; unbreakable; also, inviolable.—**in-fran-gi-bil'i-ty** (-bil'i-ti), *n.*—**in-fran'gi-bly,** *adv.*

in-fra=red (in'frạ̈-red'), *a.* [See *infra.*] Below the red, as the invisible rays of the spectrum lying outside the red end of the visible spectrum; pertaining to these rays.

in-fre-quent (in-frē'kwẹnt), *a.* [L. *infrequens* (*-ent-*).] Not frequent; found at wide distances apart, or not plentiful (as, a coast with *infrequent* lighthouses; a plant which is *infrequent* in this region); happening or occurring at long intervals or not often (as, words of *infrequent* occurrence; *infrequent* visits); not constant, habitual, or regular (as, an *infrequent* visitor to a place).—**in-fre'quence, in-fre'quen-cy,** *n.*—**in-fre'quent-ly,** *adv.*

in-fringe (in-frinj'), *v.*; *-fringed, -fringing.* [L. *infringere* (pp. *infractus*), < *in*, in, + *frangere*, break.] **I.** *tr.* To break down†; frustrate†; invalidate†; now, to commit a breach or infraction of, violate, or transgress (as, "The ancient limits of the constitution which had been grievously *infringed* . . . were reasserted by the Declaration of Rights": Lecky's "Hist. of Eng. in the 18th Century," i.). **II.** *intr.* To encroach or trespass (*on* or *upon*).—**in-fringe'ment,** *n.* The act of infringing; a breach or infraction, as of a law; a violation of a right or privilege of another; an encroaching or trespassing upon rights.—**in-frin'ger** (-frin'jėr), *n.*

in-fruc-tu-ous (in-fruk'tū-us), *a.* [L. *infructuosus*: cf. *fructuous.*] Unfruitful; fruitless.—**in-fruc'tu-ous-ly,** *adv.*

in-fun-dib-u-lar (in-fun-dib'ū-lạ̈r), *a.* [L. *infundibulum*, funnel.] Infundibuliform.

in-fun-dib-u-li-form (in-fun-dib'ū-li-fôrm), *a.* [L. *infundibulum*, funnel: see *-form.*] Funnel-shaped: specif. in *bot.*, as of a flower.

in-fun-dib-u-lum (in-fun-dib'ū-lum), *n.*; pl. *-la* (-lạ̈). [L., funnel, < *infundere*, pour in: see *infuse.*] A funnel-shaped part or organ.

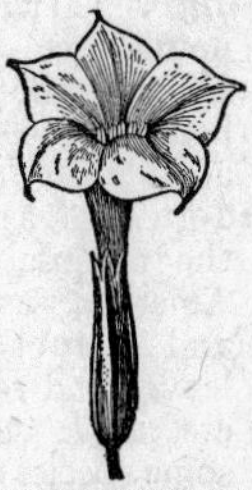

Infundibuliform Corolla.

in-fu-ri-ate (in-fū'ri-āt), *v. t.*; *-ated, -ating.* [ML. *infuriatus*, pp. of *infuriare*, < L. *in*, in, + *furia*, E. *fury.*] To put into a fury; render furious; enrage.—**in-fu'ri-ate** (-ạt), *a.* Infuriated: as, "Inflamed beyond the most *infuriate* wrath Of the worst monster that e'er roamed the waste" (Thomson's "Seasons," Autumn, 392).—**in-fu'ri-at-ing-ly** (-ā-ting-li), *adv.*—**in-fu-ri-a'tion** (-ā'shọn), *n.*

in-fus-cate (in-fus'kāt), *a.* [L. *infuscatus*, pp. of *infuscare*, darken, < *in*, in, + *fuscus*, E. *fuscous.*] Darkened with a fuscous or brownish shade or cloud: said esp. of the wings of insects.

in-fuse (in-fūz'), *v. t.*; *-fused, -fusing.* [L. *infusus*, pp. of *infundere*, pour in or on, < *in*, in, on, + *fundere*, pour.] To pour in; hence, to introduce as by pouring (as, "He *infused* his own intrepid spirit into the troops": Gibbon's "Decline and Fall of the Roman Empire," xviii.); instil; insinuate; also, to shed† or diffuse† (as, "those clear rays which she *infused* on me": Shakspere's "1 Henry VI.," i. 2. 85); also, to steep or soak (a plant, etc.) in a liquid so as to extract its soluble properties or ingredients; also, to imbue or inspire (*with*).—**in-fus'er** (-fū'zėr), *n.*—**in-fu'si-ble**¹ (-fū'zi-bl), *a.* Capable of being infused.

in-fu-si-ble² (in-fū'zi-bl), *a.* [See *in-*².] Not fusible; incapable of being fused or melted.—**in-fu-si-bil'i-ty** (-bil'i-ti), **in-fu'si-ble-ness,** *n.*

in-fu-sion (in-fū'zhọn), *n.* [L. *infusio(n-)*, < *infundere*: see *infuse.*] The act of infusing; also, that which is infused; an introduced element or admixture (as, "He was a gentleman with a slight *infusion* of the footman": Lamb's "On Some of the Old Actors"); also, a liquid extract obtained from a substance by steeping or soaking it in water; hence, any liquid containing dissolved organic matter, as that in which infusoria are found; in *med.*, the introduction of a saline or other solution into a vein.—**in-fu'sion-ism,** *n.* The doctrine that the soul has existed in a previous state and is infused into the body at conception or birth. Cf. *creationism* and *traducianism.*—**in-fu'sion-ist,** *n.*—**in-fu'sive** (-siv), *a.* Infusing; pertaining to infusion.

in-fu-so-ri-a (in-fū-sō'ri-ạ̈), *n. pl.* [NL., < L. *infundere*: see *infuse.*] Orig., certain minute or microscopic animal and vegetable organisms (constituting the old group *Infusoria*) frequently developed in infusions of decaying organic matter; now, certain protozoans (constituting the modern class *Infusoria*), mostly microscopic and aquatic, having vibratile cilia or flagella.—**in-fu-so'ri-al,** *a.* Of or pertaining to the infusoria; also, consisting of infusoria (as, *infusorial* earth, a fine white earth composed chiefly of the siliceous shells of diatoms, minute vegetable organisms formerly called infusoria).—**in-fu-so'ri-an. I.** *a.* Belonging to the infusoria. **II.** *n.* Any of the infusoria.—**in-fu-so'ri-um** (-um), *n.* [NL.] Occasional singular of *infusoria.*

ing (ing), *n.* [= Icel. *eng.*] A meadow; esp., a low meadow beside a river. [Prov. Eng., or in place-names.]

-ing¹. [ME. *-ing*, < AS. *-ing, -ung.*] A suffix of nouns formed from verbs ('verbal nouns'), and expressing the action of the verb or its result, product, material, etc., as in 'the art of *building*,' 'a new *building*,' 'fine *sewing*,' 'cotton *wadding*': hence used also to form nouns from other words than verbs, as in *lobstering, offing, overcoating, shirting.* Verbal nouns in *-ing* are often used attributively, as in '*building* operations,' 'the *drinking* habit,' 'the *printing* trade,' and in composition, as in *drinking-song*, *meeting-house*. In some compounds, as *printing-press*, *sewing-machine*, the first element might reasonably be regarded as the participial adjective (see *-ing*[2]), the compound thus meaning 'a press that prints,' or 'a machine that sews'; but it is commonly taken as the verbal noun, the compound being explained as 'a press for printing,' or 'a machine for sewing.'

-ing[2]. [ME. *-ing*, *-inge* (by confusion with *-ing* in verbal nouns: see *-ing*[1]), for *-inde*, *-ende*, < AS. *-ende*.] A suffix forming the present participle of verbs, such participles being often used as adjectives ('participial adjectives'), as in 'a *coming* man,' '*warring* factions.' Cf. *-ing*[1].

in-ga (ing'gạ̈), *n.* [NL.; of S. Amer. origin.] Any plant of the mimosaceous genus *Inga*, of tropical and subtropical America, comprising trees and shrubs with pinnate leaves and red or white flowers, as *I. vulpina*, a handsome species sometimes cultivated in conservatories.

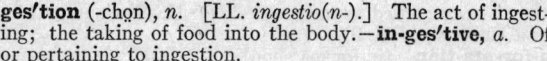

Flowering Branch of Inga (*I. vulpina*). — *a*, flower; *b*, fruit.

in-gath-er (in-gaᴛʜ'ėr), *v. t.* To gather in; collect; bring in, as a harvest.—**in-gath'-er-er,** *n.*

in-gem-i-nate (in-jem'i-nāt), *v. t.*; *-nated*, *-nating*. [L. *ingeminatus*, pp. of *ingeminare*, < *in*, in, + *geminare*, double, E. *geminate*.] To repeat; reiterate.—**in-gem-i-na'tion** (-nā'shọn), *n.*

in-gen-er-a-ble (in-jen'ẹ-rạ-bl), *a.* [See *in-*[2].] Not generable; incapable of being generated.

in-gen-er-ate[1] (in-jen'ẹ-rāt), *a.* [LL. *ingeneratus*, < *in-*, not, + *generatus*, pp., generated: see *generate*.] Not generated; unbegotten; self-existent.

in-gen-er-ate[2] (in-jen'ẹ-rāt), *v. t.*; *-ated*, *-ating*. [L. *ingeneratus*, pp. of *ingenerare*, < *in*, in, + *generare*, E. *generate*: cf. *engender*.] To generate within; breed or produce in one; engender. [Now rare.]—**in-gen'er-ate**[2], *a.* Ingenerated; inborn; innate. [Now rare.]—**in-gen-er-a'-tion** (-ẹ-rā'shọn), *n.*

in-ge-nious (in-jē'nius), *a.* [L. *ingeniosus*, < *ingenium*, natural capacity, cleverness: see *engine*.] Possessed of genius†; also, having inventive faculty; apt or skilful in contriving or constructing; also, of things, actions, etc., showing cleverness of invention or construction; skilfully or cleverly contrived or devised; clever; also, ingenuous†. —**in-ge'nious-ly,** *adv.*—**in-ge'nious-ness,** *n.*

in-gé-nue (aṅ-zhā-nü), *n.* [F.] An ingenuous or artless girl, esp. as represented on the stage; also, the actress who plays such a part.

in-ge-nu-i-ty (in-jẹ̄-nū'i-ti), *n.*; pl. *-ties* (-tiz). [L. *ingenuitas*, < *ingenuus*: see *ingenuous*. The senses corresponding to *ingenious* are due to a former confusion of *ingenuous* and *ingenious*.] Ingenuous or free-born condition†; frankness or candor (archaic); also, the quality of being ingenious; inventive or constructive capacity, as of a person; skilfulness of contrivance or design, as of things, actions, etc.; also, an ingenious contrivance.

in-gen-u-ous (in-jen'ū-us), *a.* [L. *ingenuus*, native, innate, free-born, noble, frank, < *in*, in, + *gen-*, beget, produce: see *genius*.] Of free or honorable birth; also, generous or noble (archaic); also, free from reserve, restraint, or dissimulation; frank or candid; hence, artless; guileless; innocent; also, erroneously, ingenious† (see Shakspere's "Love's Labour's Lost," iv. 2. 80: cf. *ingenuity*).—**in-gen'u-ous-ly,** *adv.*—**in-gen'u-ous-ness,** *n.*

in-gest (in-jest'), *v. t.* [L. *ingestus*, pp. of *ingerere*, < *in*, in, + *gerere*, bear.] To put or take (food, etc.) into the body; opposed to *egest*.—**in-ges'ta** (-jes'tạ̈), *n. pl.* [L.] Substances ingested, as through the alimentary passage.—**in-ges'tion** (-chọn), *n.* [LL. *ingestio(n-)*.] The act of ingesting; the taking of food into the body.—**in-ges'tive,** *a.* Of or pertaining to ingestion.

in-gle (ing'gl), *n.* [Orig. Sc.; origin obscure.] Fire; a fire burning upon the hearth; sometimes, a fireplace (as, "The Indian women . . . grouped themselves about the end of the *ingle* already occupied by black Cæsar": Mrs. Stowe's "Oldtown Folks," vi.).—**in'gle=nook,** *n.* A nook or corner by the fire: as, "Old Feyther Taft . . . had some time ago gone back to his *ingle-nook*" (George Eliot's "Adam Bede," ii.). [Orig. Sc.]—**in'gle-side,** *n.* A fireside: as, "It's an auld story now, and everybody tells it . . . by the *ingleside*" (Scott's "Guy Mannering," xii.). [Orig. Sc.]

in-glo-ri-ous (in-glō'ri-us), *a.* [L. *ingloriosus*.] Not glorious, famous, or renowned (as, "Some mute *inglorious* Milton here may rest": Gray's "Elegy," xv.); also, conferring no glory, as actions, etc.; hence, bringing disgrace; ignominious.—**in-glo'ri-ous-ly,** *adv.*—**in-glo'ri-ous-ness,** *n.*

in-go-ing (in'gō''ing), *n.* A going in; entrance.—**in'go''-ing,** *a.*

in-got (ing'gọt), *n.* [ME. *ingot*, mold for metal, perhaps < AS. *in*, in, + *gēotan*, pour: see *gut*.] A mold in which metal is cast†; also, a mass of metal, esp. of gold or silver, or of steel, cast into convenient shape in a mold.

in-graft (in-gráft'), *v. t.* [See *in-*[1].] To insert as a graft, as a scion of one tree or plant into or upon another, for propagation; fig., to implant or introduce so as to make part of something; incorporate (*into*); add (*on* or *upon*); also, to subject to grafting, as a tree; furnish with a graft. —**in-graft'ment,** *n.*

in-grain (in-grān' or in'grān), *v. t.* [See *in-*[1].] To dye scarlet or crimson with or as with grain (the dye from the kermes or the cochineal insect) (obs. or archaic); also, to dye in grain, or through the fiber, as yarn, wool, etc., esp. before manufacture; also, to cause (a dye, stain, etc.) to sink into the fiber or substance; fig., to fix deeply and firmly, as in the nature or mind (as, beliefs or prejudices *ingrained* in the human heart; a habit becomes *ingrained* in us).—**in'grain. I.** *a.* Dyed in grain, or through the fiber; hence, dyed in the yarn, or in a raw state, before manufacture; of carpets, made of yarn dyed before weaving, and so woven as to show the pattern on both sides; of colors, imparted by dyeing in the fiber or yarn; fig., ingrained, or firmly fixed. **II.** *n.* Yarn, wool, etc., dyed with fast colors before manufacture; also, ingrain carpet.—**in-grained** (in'grānd or in-grānd'), *p. a.* Fixed firmly, as in the very fiber, nature, or being (as, *ingrained* qualities, beliefs, or habits); also, being such in the very fiber or nature (as, an *ingrained* rebel; an *ingrained* optimist); thorough; out-and-out.

in-grate (in'grāt). [L. *ingratus*, < *in-*, not, + *gratus*, grateful: see *grace*.] **I.** *a.* Ungrateful; unthankful. [Archaic.] **II.** *n.* An ungrateful person: as, "This is worse than your treachery and deceit, you base *ingrate*" (Sheridan's "Rivals," iv. 2).

in-gra-ti-ate (in-grā'shi-āt), *v. t.*; *-ated*, *-ating*. [L. *in*, in, + *gratia*, favor, E. *grace*.] To bring (a person, now one's self) into favor (*with*: as, "I wanted . . . only to *ingratiate* myself with Lady Teazle, that she might not be my enemy with Maria," Sheridan's "School for Scandal," ii. 2); establish (one's self) in the favor or good graces of others; insinuate (one's self), as into favor; also, to render (a thing) agreeable or acceptable†.—**in-gra'ti-at-ing-ly** (-ā-ting-li), *adv.*—**in-gra-ti-a'tion** (-ā'shọn), *n.* The act of ingratiating one's self.—**in-gra'ti-a-to-ry** (-ạ-tọ̄-ri), *a.* Serving or intended to ingratiate.

in-grat-i-tude (in-grat'i-tūd), *n.* [LL. *ingratitudo*, < L. *ingratus*, E. *ingrate*.] The state of being ungrateful; indisposition to acknowledge or reciprocate favors; unthankfulness.

in-gra-ves-cent (in-grạ-ves'ẹnt), *a.* [L. *ingravescens* (*-ent-*), ppr. of *ingravescere*, grow heavier, < *in*, in, + *gravescere*, grow heavy, < *gravis*, heavy, E. *grave*[3].] In *pathol.*, increasing in gravity or severity, as a disease.—**in-gra-ves'cence,** *n.*

in-gre-di-ent (in-grē'di-ẹnt), *n.* [L. *ingrediens* (*-ent-*), ppr. of *ingredi*, enter: see *ingress*.] Something that enters as an element into a mixture or combination of substances or materials (as, an *ingredient* in a medicine; the *ingredients* of a cake); hence, a constituent element of anything (as, wit is an effective *ingredient* in a speech; the *ingredients* of one's mental make-up); a component part.

in-gress (in′gres), *n.* [L. *ingressus*, < *ingredi*, go in, enter, < *in*, in, + *gradi*, walk, go: see *gradient.*] The act of going in or entering; entrance; also, the right of going in (as, to have free *ingress* to a place); also, a means or place of going in; an entrance.—**in-gres′sion** (-gresh′ọn), *n.* [L. *ingressio(n-)*, < *ingredi.*] A going in or entering; entrance.—**in-gres′sive** (-gres′iv), *a.* Entering; pertaining to entrance; in *gram.*, inceptive.—**in-gres′sive-ness,** *n.*

in-grow-ing (in′grō″ing), *a.* Growing within or inward; of a nail, growing into the flesh.—**in′grown,** *a.* Grown within or inward; innate; of a nail, having grown into the flesh.—**in′growth,** *n.* Growth inward; also, something formed by growth inward.

in-gui-nal (ing′gwi-nạl), *a.* [L. *inguinalis*, < *inguen*, groin.] Of, pertaining to, or situated in the groin.

in-gulf (in-gulf′), etc. Same as *engulf*, etc.

in-gur-gi-tate (in-gėr′ji-tāt), *v. t.*; *-tated*, *-tating.* [L. *ingurgitatus*, pp. of *ingurgitare*, < *in*, in, + *gurges*, whirlpool, gulf.] To swallow greedily or in great quantity, as food or drink; also, to engulf (as, "There is only . . . a momentary eddy — very small, as compared with the apparent magnitude of the *ingurgitated* object": Hawthorne's "House of the Seven Gables," xxi.).—**in-gur-gi-ta′tion** (-tā′shọn), *n.*

in-hab-it (in-hab′it), *v.* [OF. *inhabiter*, *enhabiter*, < L. *inhabitare*, < *in*, in, + *habitare*, dwell, E. *habit* [2].] **I.** *tr.* To live or dwell in (a place, region, house, cave, tree, the sea, etc.), as persons or animals; have the regular or natural abode in; fig., to have its seat, or exist, in (as, the soul *inhabits* the body; thoughts that *inhabit* the mind); also, to establish in a place of abode† (as, "O knowledge ill-*inhabited*, worse than Jove in a thatched house!" Shakspere's "As You Like It," iii. 3. 10). **II.** *intr.* To live, dwell, or abide, as in a place. [Archaic.]—**in-hab′it-a-ble,** *a.* [LL. *inhabitabilis.*] That may be inhabited; habitable.—**in-hab′it-ance, in-hab′it-an-cy,** *n.* Residence as an inhabitant.—**in-hab′it-ant,** *n.* [OF., < L. *inhabitans* (*-ant-*), ppr. of *inhabitare.*] A person or an animal that inhabits a place; a permanent resident.—**in-hab-i-ta′tion** (-i-tā′shọn), *n.* [LL. *inhabitatio(n-)*.] The act of inhabiting, or the state of being inhabited; also, a place inhabited†, or habitation†; also, inhabitants† or population†.—**in-hab′i-ta-tive-ness** (-tạ-tiv-nes), *n.* Inhabitiveness.—**in-hab′it-er,** *n.*—**in-hab′i-tive-ness,** *n.* Propensity to remain in one place of residence; fondness for home: in *phren.*, a special faculty.

in-hal-a-ble (in-hā′lạ-bl), *a.* Capable of being inhaled.

in-hal-ant (in-hā′lạnt). **I.** *a.* Inhaling; used for inhaling. **II.** *n.* An apparatus or a medicine used for inhaling.

in-ha-la-tion (in-hạ-lā′shọn), *n.* The act of inhaling; also, a medicinal preparation to be inhaled.

in-hale (in-hāl′), *v. t.*; *-haled*, *-haling.* [L. *in*, in, + *halare*, breathe: cf. *exhale.*] To breathe in; draw in by or as by breathing: as, to *inhale* air, fragrance, or poisonous gases; to *inhale* medicinal vapors.—**in-hale′ment,** *n.*—**in-hal′er** (-hā′lėr), *n.* One who inhales; also, an apparatus used in inhaling medicinal vapors, etc.; also, a respirator.

in-har-mon-ic (in-här-mon′ik), *a.* [See *in-* [2].] Not harmonic; inharmonious. Also **in-har-mon′i-cal.**—**in-har-mo′ni-ous** (-mō′ni-us), *a.* Not harmonious; discordant; disagreeing.—**in-har-mo′ni-ous-ly,** *adv.*—**in-har-mo′ni-ous-ness,** *n.*—**in-har′mo-ny** (-mọ-ni), *n.* Want of harmony; discord.

in-haul (in′hâl), *n.* *Naut.*, a rope for hauling in a sail or spar.

in-hearse (in-hėrs′), *v. t.*; *-hearsed*, *-hearsing.* To put into a hearse. See Shakspere's "Sonnets," lxxxvi. [Archaic.]

in-here (in-hēr′), *v. i.*; *-hered*, *-hering.* [L. *inhærere* (pp. *inhæsus*), < *in*, in, + *hærere*, stick.] To stick or remain fixed (*in*: obs. or rare); hence, to exist permanently and inseparably (*in*), as a quality, attribute, or element; belong intrinsically; be inherent.—**in-her′ence** (-hēr′ẹns), *n.* The state or fact of inhering or being inherent. Also **in-her′en-cy.**—**in-her′ent,** *a.* Existing in something as a permanent and inseparable quality or attribute (as, the *inherent* justice of a cause; faults *inherent* in a system); forming an essential or characteristic element; intrinsic; essential.—**in-her′ent-ly,** *adv.*

in-her-it (in-her′it), *v.* [OF. *enheriter*, < LL. *inhereditare*, make (one) heir, < L. *in*, in, + *heres* (*hered-*), E. *heir.*] **I.** *tr.* To make (one) heir†; put in possession†; also, to take or receive (property, a right, a title, etc.) as being the heir of the former possessor; fig., to receive (qualities, traits, etc.) as by natural right from progenitors; receive (anything) as by succession from predecessors (as, to *inherit* the duties or difficulties of an office; to *inherit* the office furniture); receive as one's portion (as, "Good Master, what shall I do to *inherit* eternal life?" Luke, xviii. 18); also, to succeed (a person) as heir (as, "Our sons *inherit* us": Tennyson's "Choric Song," vi.). **II.** *intr.* To take or receive property, etc., as being heir to it; have succession as heir; fig., to receive qualities, powers, duties, etc., as by inheritance (*from*).—**in-her′it-a-ble,** *a.* [AF. *enheritable.*] Capable of being inherited; also, capable of inheriting; qualified to inherit.—**in-her″it-a-bil′i-ty** (-bil′i-ti), **in-her′it-a-ble-ness,** *n.*—**in-her′it-a-bly,** *adv.*—**in-her′it-ance,** *n.* [AF. *enheritance.*] The act or fact of inheriting (as, to receive property, or, fig., qualities or abilities, by *inheritance*); also, the right of inheriting, or succession to property; also, that which is or may be inherited; any property passing, as at the owner's death, to the heir or those entitled to succeed; fig., anything received from progenitors or predecessors as if by a process of succession (as, an *inheritance* of family pride; he is an *inheritance* from the last administration); portion, peculiar possession, or heritage (as, "meet to be partakers of the *inheritance* of the saints in light": Col. i. 12).—**in-her′i-tor,** *n.* One who inherits; an heir.—**in-her′i-tress,** *n.* A female inheritor; an heiress. Also **in-her′i-trix.**

in-he-sion (in-hē′zhọn), *n.* [LL. *inhæsio(n-)*.] The state or fact of inhering; inherence.

in-hib-it (in-hib′it), *v. t.* [L. *inhibitus*, pp. of *inhibere*, hold back, restrain, < *in*, in, on, + *habere*, have, hold.] To prohibit (a person) from doing something; forbid; interdict; also, to prohibit the doing or use of (something: as, "A practiser Of arts *inhibited* and out of warrant," Shakspere's "Othello," i. 2. 79); also, to restrain, hinder, arrest, or check, as action, esp. functional activity (now used esp. in *physiol.*).—**in-hi-bi′tion** (-hi-bish′ọn), *n.* [L. *inhibitio(n-)*.] The act of inhibiting, or the state of being inhibited; prohibition; restraining, arresting, or checking, as of action (specif. in *physiol.*).—**in-hib′i-tor,** *n.*—**in-hib′i-to-ry** (-tọ-ri), *a.* Serving or tending to inhibit.

in-hos-pi-ta-ble (in-hos′pi-tạ-bl), *a.* [See *in-* [2].] Not hospitable; not inclined to or characterized by hospitality, as persons, actions, etc.; of a region, climate, etc., not offering favorable conditions for visitors or travelers.—**in-hos′pi-ta-ble-ness,** *n.*—**in-hos′pi-ta-bly,** *adv.*—**in-hos-pi-tal′i-ty** (-tal′i-ti), *n.* Want of hospitality; inhospitable attitude toward visitors or strangers.

in-hu-man (in-hū′mạn), *a.* [L. *inhumanus*: cf. *human* and *humane.*] Not human; not of the ordinary human type or kind; not having the qualities natural to a human being; esp., destitute of natural human feeling or sympathy for others; unfeeling, brutal, or barbarously cruel.—**in-hu-mane′** (-hụ-mān′), *a.* [L. *inhumanus.*] Inhuman† or barbarously cruel†; now, in a milder sense, not humane; without compassion for the suffering or distressed; wanting in humanity or kindness.—**in-hu-mane′ly,** *adv.*—**in-hu-man′i-ty** (-man′i-ti), *n.*; pl. *-ties* (-tiz). [L. *inhumanitas.*] The quality of being inhuman or inhumane; brutality, cruelty, or want of humanity (as, "Man's *inhumanity* to man Makes countless thousands mourn!" Burns's "Man Was Made to Mourn," 55); also, an inhuman or inhumane act.—**in-hu′man-ize,** *v. t.*; *-ized*, *-izing.* To make inhuman.—**in-hu′man-ly,** *adv.*

in-hume (in-hūm′), *v. t.*; *-humed*, *-huming.* [L. *inhumare*, < *in*, in, + *humus*, earth, ground.] To bury in the earth (esp. a dead body); inter: as, "No hand his bones shall gather, or *inhume*" (Pope's tr. Homer's "Iliad," xxi.).—**in-hu-ma′tion** (-hụ-mā′shọn), *n.*

in-im-i-cal (in-im′i-kạl), *a.* [LL. *inimicalis*, < L. *inimicus*, unfriendly, an enemy, < *in-*, not, + *amicus*, friendly, a friend: cf. *enemy.*] Unfriendly or hostile in spirit (as, to be *inimical* to a proposed candidate; *inimical* opinions or utterances); hence, adverse in tendency or effect (as, conditions *inimical* to the success of an undertaking; a climate *inimical* to health); unfavorable; injurious.—**in-im-i-cal′i-ty** (-kal′i-ti), *n.*—**in-im′i-cal-ly,** *adv.*

in-im-i-ta-ble (in-im′i-ta-bl), *a.* [L. *inimitabilis.*] Not imitable; incapable of being imitated or reproduced (as, "Thick with sparkling orient gems The portal shone, *inimitable* on earth By model or by shading pencil drawn": Milton's "Paradise Lost," iii. 508); surpassing imitation; matchless.—**in-im″i-ta-bil′i-ty** (-bil′i-ti), **in-im′i-ta-ble-ness,** *n.*—**in-im′i-ta-bly,** *adv.*

in-i-on (in′i-on), *n.* [NL., < Gr. ἰνίον, back of the head, < ἴς, muscle.] In *craniol.*, a point at the external occipital protuberance of the skull.

i-ni-qui-tous (i-nik′wi-tus), *a.* Characterized by iniquity; grossly unjust; unrighteous; wicked.—**i-ni′qui-tous-ly,** *adv.*—**i-ni′qui-tous-ness,** *n.*

i-ni-qui-ty (i-nik′wi-ti), *n.*; pl. *-ties* (-tiz). [OF. *iniquite* (F. *iniquité*), < L. *iniquitas*, < *iniquus*, unequal, unjust, < *in-*, not, + *æquus*, equal.] Gross injustice, or unrighteousness (as, the *iniquity* of the transaction aroused general indignation); also, unrighteous action or practices (as, "If I have done *iniquity*, I will do no more": Job, xxxiv. 32); wickedness; sin; an unrighteous act or proceeding (as, "Blessed are they whose *iniquities* are forgiven": Rom. iv. 7).

in-isle (in-īl′), *v. t.* Same as *enisle.*

i-ni-tial (i-nish′al). [L. *initialis*, < *initium*, beginning, < *inire*, go into, enter upon, < *in*, in, + *ire*, go.] **I.** *a.* Of, pertaining to, or constituting the beginning (as, the *initial* act or stage of a proceeding); standing at the beginning (as, the *initial* letter of a word). **II.** *n.* An initial letter, as of a word; often, the first letter of a proper name (as, to sign a note with one's *initials*, as 'J. S.' for 'John Smith'); also, a letter of extra size or ornamental character used at the beginning of a chapter or other division of a book, etc.—**i-ni′tial,** *v. t.*; *-tialed* or *-tialled*, *-tialing* or *-tialling.* To mark or sign with an initial or initials.—**i-ni′tial-ly,** *adv.*

i-ni-ti-ate (i-nish′i-āt), *v. t.*; *-ated*, *-ating.* [L. *initiatus*, pp. of *initiare*, begin, initiate, < *initium*: see *initial.*] To begin, set going, or originate (as, to *initiate* a course of action; to *initiate* reforms); introduce by some initial step; also, to admit with formal rites into mysteries, secret knowledge, a society, etc.; introduce into the knowledge of some art or subject (as, to *initiate* a person into business methods).—**i-ni′ti-ate** (-āt). **I.** *a.* Initiated; begun, or set going; admitted into mysteries, a society, etc., or into the knowledge of a subject. **II.** *n.* One who has been initiated, as into mysteries or knowledge.—**i-ni-ti-a′tion** (-ā′shon), *n.* [L. *initiatio(n-)*.] The act of initiating, or the fact of being initiated; beginning or origination; formal admission into mysteries, a society, etc.; introduction into the knowledge of some art or subject.—**i-ni′ti-a-tive** (-a-tiv). **I.** *a.* Serving to initiate; pertaining to initiation; initiatory. **II.** *n.* That which initiates; the introductory or first step in some process or enterprise (as, "'Good evening, Sir Gervaise,' called out the earl, as usual taking the *initiative* in the discourse": Cooper's "Two Admirals," xxvi.); hence, the taking of the first step (as, to act on one's own *initiative*); also, readiness and ability in initiating action (as, to lack *initiative*); enterprise; also, the right or power of initiating or originating something; esp., the right by which a sufficient number of citizens outside of the legislative body may originate or demand specific legislation to be submitted to popular vote.—**i-ni′ti-a-tive-ly,** *adv.*—**i-ni′ti-a-tor** (-ā-tor), *n.* [LL.] One who or that which initiates.—**i-ni′ti-a-to-ry** (-a-tō-ri), *a.* Pertaining to initiation or beginning; introductory; initial; also, serving to initiate or admit, as into mysteries or knowledge.—**i-ni′ti-a-tress** (-ā-tres), **i-ni′ti-a-trix,** *n.* A female initiator.

i-ni-tis (i-nī′tis), *n.* [NL., < Gr. ἴς (ἰν-), muscle, fiber.] In *pathol.*, inflammation of the muscular or fibrous tissue.

in-ject (in-jekt′), *v. t.* [L. *injectus*, pp. of *injicere*, throw or put in, < *in*, in, + *jacere*, throw.] To throw in; specif., to force (a fluid, etc.) into a passage, cavity, or tissue (as, to *inject* a drug into the body with a syringe; to *inject* coloring matter into anatomical specimens for the study of the structure); hence, to charge or fill (a cavity, etc.) with fluid matter forced in; also, fig., to introduce (something new or different) into a thing (as, to *inject* an element of comedy into a situation); interject (a remark, suggestion, etc.), as into conversation.—**in-ject′a-ble,** *a.* Capable of being injected.—**in-ject′ed,** *p. a.* Thrown or forced in; also, charged or filled by injection; in *pathol.*, affected with hyperemia; bloodshot.—**in-jec′tion** (-jek′shon), *n.* [L. *injectio(n-)*.] The act or an act of injecting (as, hypodermic *injections* of morphine); also, injected state; the condition of being charged with injected matter; also, that which is injected; esp., a liquid injected into the body, as for medicinal purposes.—**in-jec′tor,** *n.* One who or that which injects; specif., a device for forcing water into a steam-boiler.

in-ju-di-cious (in-jö-dish′us), *a.* [See *in-*[2].] Not judicious; showing lack of judgment; unwise; imprudent; ill-advised.—**in-ju-di′cious-ly,** *adv.*—**in-ju-di′cious-ness,** *n.*

in-junc-tion (in-jungk′shon), *n.* [LL. *injunctio(n-)*, < L. *injungere*, E. *enjoin.*] The act of enjoining; a command, order, or direction; in *law*, a judicial process or order requiring the person or persons to whom it is directed to do or (more commonly) not to do a particular thing.—**in-junc′tive,** *a.* Serving to enjoin.

in-jure (in′jör), *v. t.*; *-jured*, *-juring.* [Earlier *injury*, < OF. F. *injurier*, < L. *injuriari*, injure, < *injuria*: see *injury.*] To do wrong or injustice to (as, "Those that are not favoured will think themselves *injured*": Johnson's "Rasselas," xxvii.); treat unjustly; wrong; hence, to do or cause harm of any kind to; damage (as, to *injure* a knife-blade, a fabric, or a book-cover); hurt physically (as, to *injure* the hand or eyes; to be *injured* in a railroad accident); affect detrimentally, as in character, standing, prospects, etc.; impair, as credit, chances, etc.; wound or offend, as feelings, vanity, etc.—**in′jured,** *p. a.* Wronged; harmed, damaged, or hurt; offended.—**in′jur-er,** *n.*

in-ju-ri-ous (in-jö′ri-us), *a.* [OF. *injurious* (F. *injurieux*), < L. *injuriosus*, < *injuria*: see *injury.*] Doing or involving injury or wrong, as to a person (as, "Call him my king by whose *injurious* doom My elder brother . . . Was done to death?" Shakspere's "3 Henry VI.," iii. 3. 101); also, harmful, hurtful, or detrimental, as in effect (as, acids *injurious* to color; rumors *injurious* to credit); also, insulting or abusive, as speech or a speaker†.—**in-ju′ri-ous-ly,** *adv.*—**in-ju′ri-ous-ness,** *n.*

in-ju-ry (in′jö-ri), *n.*; pl. *-ries* (-riz). [L. *injuria*, wrong, harm, insult, < *injurius*, wrongful, unjust, < *in-*, not, + *jus* (*jur-*), right, law.] Wrong or injustice done or suffered, or a wrong (as, "with lifelong *injuries* burning unavenged": Tennyson's "Geraint and Enid," 695); hence, harm of any kind done or sustained; damage, hurt, or detriment (as, to escape without *injury*); a particular form or instance of harm (as, an *injury* to a painting; severe bodily *injuries*; an *injury* to reputation); also, insulting language†, or an insulting speech†.

in-jus-tice (in-jus′tis), *n.* [OF. F. *injustice*, < L. *injustitia*, < *injustus*, unjust, < *in-*, not, + *justus*, E. *just*[1].] The quality or fact of being unjust; also, unjust action; violation of another's rights; unjust or unfair treatment; an act or circumstance that is unjust or unfair (as, "A scientific man must expect his little disappointments and *injustices*": Kingsley's "Alton Locke," xv.).

ink (ingk), *n.* [OF. *enque* (F. *encre*), < LL. *encaustum*, < LGr. ἔγκαυστον, purple ink used by Greek and Roman emperors, < Gr. ἐγκαίειν, burn in: see *encaustic.*] A fluid or viscous substance, black or colored, used for writing or printing; also, a dark protective fluid ejected by the cuttlefish and other cephalopods.—**sympathetic ink.** See under *sympathetic.*—**ink,** *v. t.* To mark with ink; stain or smear with ink (as, "a poor gentleman who *inks* the seams of his coat": H. Melville's "Omoo," lxvii.); cover (type, etc.) with ink to print with.—**ink′ber″ry,** *n.* An aquifoliaceous shrub, *Ilex glabra*, with leathery evergreen leaves and black berries; its berry; also, any of various other plants, as the pokeweed, or the berry.—**ink′er,** *n.* One who or that which inks something; a telegraphic recording device using ink; a roller of a printing-press, by which ink is applied to the type.—**ink′horn,** *n.* A small portable vessel of horn or other material, formerly used to hold writing-ink: as, "Pulling out an old *inkhorn*, he proceeded to fill out a bill of sale" (Mrs. Stowe's "Uncle Tom's Cabin," xiv.).

ink-i-ness (ing'ki-nes), *n.* Inky quality or state.

in-kle[1] (ing'kl), *v. t.*; *-kled, -kling.* [ME. *incle*; origin uncertain: cf. *inkling.*] To give a hint or inkling of†; also, to get an inkling or notion of (prov. Eng.: as, "She *inkled* what it was," Blackmore's "Lorna Doone," lii.).

in-kle[2] (ing'kl), *n.* [Origin uncertain.] A kind of linen tape; also, the linen thread or yarn from which this tape is made.

in-kling (ing'kling), *n.* [See *inkle*[1].] A hint, intimation, or slight suggestion (as, to give a person an *inkling* of what is going on); also, a vague idea or notion, or a suspicion (as, "They have had *inkling* this fortnight what we intend to do": Shakspere's "Coriolanus," i. 1. 59).

ink=sling-er (ingk'sling"ėr), *n.* A writer; one who makes a business of writing. [Slang.]—**ink'=sling"ing,** *n.*

ink-stand (ingk'stand), *n.* A stand for holding ink, pens, etc.; also, a cup-like receptacle for ink used in writing.

ink=well (ingk'wel), *n.* A receptacle or reservoir for ink in use.

ink-wood (ingk'wu̇d), *n.* A sapindaceous tree, *Exothea paniculata*, of the West Indies and Florida, with hard reddish-brown wood.

ink-y (ing'ki), *a.*; compar. *inkier*, superl. *inkiest.* Of or pertaining to ink; consisting of or containing ink; written with ink; stained with ink; resembling ink; black as ink (as, "*inky* shadows": Parkman's "Oregon Trail," v.).

in-lace (in-lās'), *v. t.* Same as *enlace.*

in-laid (in-lād' or in'lād). Pret. and pp. of *inlay.*—**in'-laid,** *p. a.* Laid or set in the surface of a thing (as, an *inlaid* decorative design in wood); also, decorated or made with a design set in the surface (as, an *inlaid* table or box; *inlaid* work).

in-land (in'lạnd or -land). **I.** *n.* The interior part of a country, away from the border or the coast: as, "A wall sufficient to defend Our *inland* from the pilfering borderers" (Shakspere's "Henry V.," i. 2. 142). **II.** *a.* Pertaining to or situated in the interior part of a country or region (as, *inland* cities; an *inland* sea); within and remote from the border or the coast; also, carried on, proceeding, or effective within the limits of a country (as, *inland* trade; an *inland* bill of exchange); domestic, or not foreign. **III.** *adv.* In or toward the interior of a country.—**in'land-er** (-lạn-dėr), *n.* An inhabitant of an inland region.

in-law (in-lâ'), *v. t.* [AS. *inlagian*, < *in*, in, + *lagu*, E. *law*[3].] To clear of outlawry or attainder; restore to the protection of the law. [Now hist.]

in=law (in-lâ'), *n.* A person connected with one by marriage and designated by a name ending in *-in-law*, as a father-in-law, mother-in-law, brother-in-law, sister-in-law, etc. [Colloq.]

in-lay (in-lā' or in'lā), *v. t.*; *-laid, -laying.* To lay or insert in something; specif., to lay, set, or fix decoratively in the surface substance of a thing (as, to *inlay* ivory, shell, or metal in wood; to *inlay* gold wire in iron or steel); decorate (a surface, furniture, objects of art, etc.) with material or a design thus set in (also fig.); be set, as or like such materials, in (as, "The sea-girt isles, That, like to rich and various gems, *inlay* The unadorned bosom of the deep": Milton's "Comus," 22); also, to insert (a leaf, plate, etc.) in a book, esp. in a space cut in a larger leaf which thus serves as a frame or margin; furnish (a book) with matter so inserted.—**in-lay** (in'lā or in-lā'), *n.* The act or process of inlaying; also, that which is inlaid; material inlaid, or used for inlaying, in a surface (as, an ivory *inlay*; mother-of-pearl is used as an *inlay*); a design or decoration made by inlaying (also fig.: as, an *inlay* of flowers in a meadow); inlaid work.—**in'lay"er,** *n.*

in-let (in-let'), *v. t.*; *-let, -letting.* To let in† or admit†; also, to put in; insert.—**in'let,** *n.* A letting in, or admission; a place of admission or ingress; an entrance; also, a narrow strip of water running from a larger body into the land or between islands; a recess in a shore; also, something put in or inserted.

in-li-er (in'lī"ėr), *n.* In *geol.*, a part of one formation completely surrounded by another of later date.

in-look (in'lu̇k), *n.* A looking in; introspection.

in-ly† (in'li), *a.* Inward; internal: as, "the *inly* touch of love" (Shakspere's "Two Gentlemen of Verona," ii. 7. 18).—**in'ly,** *adv.* Inwardly, internally, or within (as, "What warm, poetic heart but *inly* bleeds, And execrates man's savage, ruthless deeds!" Burns's "Brigs of Ayr," 38); hence, privately; intimately; deeply or thoroughly. [Now chiefly poetic.]

in-mate (in'māt), *n.* One who dwells as a mate or associate with another or others in the same house; one of a group occupying the same abode; often, one of those confined in a hospital, prison, etc.; also, a single or solitary occupant, as of an abode, cell, or other place (as, "So spake the enemy of mankind, enclosed In serpent, *inmate* bad!" Milton's "Paradise Lost," ix. 495).

in-mesh (in-mesh'), *v. t.* Same as *enmesh.*

in-most (in'mōst). [AS. *innemest*, a double superlative < *inne*, within, < *in*, in: see *-most.*] **I.** *a. superl.* Situated furthest within; most remote from the outside; hence, most intimate (as, one's *inmost* thoughts); deepest. **II.** *n.* The inmost part.

inn (in), *n.* [AS. *inn*, house, < *inn*, E. *in*, *adv.*] A house†, dwelling†, or abode†; also, a public house for the lodging and entertainment of travelers and others (a much older word than the modern *hotel*, and usually implying an older type of house, often one on a road of common travel: as, a wayside *inn*; "take mine ease in mine *inn*," Shakspere's "1 Henry IV.," iii. 3. 93); a hostelry or hostel; also, a house or place of residence for students (now only in names of buildings derived from such use: as, the *Inns* of Court, see phrase below); hence, a legal society occupying such a house or any buildings bearing the name of 'inn' (as, "The King's *Inns*, Dublin, the legal school in Ireland, corresponds closely to the English *Inns* of Court": Encyc. Brit., 11th ed., XIV. 587).—**Inns of Court,** the buildings, or sets of buildings, in London, Lincoln's Inn, the Inner Temple, the Middle Temple, and Gray's Inn, belonging respectively to the four legal societies which have the exclusive privilege of calling candidates to the English bar, and maintain instruction and examinations for them; also, these societies themselves.—**inn,** *v.* **I.** *tr.* To lodge in or as in an inn; find lodging for. [Archaic.] **II.** *intr.* To stop at an inn; lodge; sojourn. [Archaic.]

in-nate (in'nāt or i-nāt'), *a.* [L. *innatus*, pp. of *innasci*, be born in, < *in*, in, + *nasci*, be born.] Inborn, or existing in one from birth (as, *innate* modesty or good sense); native, esp. to the mind; of ideas, arising from the constitution of the mind, rather than acquired from experience; also, existing naturally or originating in anything; inherent.—**in'nate-ly,** *adv.*—**in'nate-ness,** *n.*

in-na-tive (i-nā'tiv), *a.* [From *innate*, with *-ive* as in *native.*] Innate; native: as, "Some *innative* weakness there must be In him" (Lowell's "Commemoration Ode," vi.). [Now rare.]

in-nav-i-ga-ble (i-nav'i-gạ-bl), *a.* [L. *innavigabilis.*] Not navigable: as, "th' *innavigable* lake" (Dryden's tr. Virgil's "Æneid," vi. 205).

in-ner (in'ėr), *a.* [AS. *innera*, compar. of *inne*, within: cf. *inmost.*] Situated further within or inward; interior; inward; internal; hence, more intimate, private, or secret (as, "What delights can equal those That stir the spirit's *inner* deeps?" Tennyson's "In Memoriam," xlii.); also, mental or spiritual (as, the *inner* life; "This attracts the soul, Governs the *inner* man, the nobler part," Milton's "Paradise Regained," ii. 477).—**in'ner-most.** **I.** *a. superl.* Furthest inward; inmost. **II.** *n.* The innermost part.—**in'ner-ness,** *n.*

in-ner-vate (i-nėr'vāt), *v. t.*; *-vated, -vating.* [L. *in*, in, + *nervus*, E. *nerve.*] To supply with nerves; also, to communicate nervous energy to; stimulate through nerves.—**in-ner-va-tion** (in-ėr-vā'shọn), *n.* The act of innervating, or the state of being innervated; in *physiol.*, the communicating of nervous energy by means of nerves; the stimulation of some part or organ through its nerves; in *anat.*, the disposition of nerves in an animal body or some part of it.—**in-nerve** (i-nėrv'), *v. t.*; *-nerved, -nerving.* To supply with nervous energy; invigorate; animate.

inn-hold-er (in'hōl"dėr), *n.* An innkeeper. [Now rare.]

in-ning (in′ing), *n.* [See *in*, *v.*] The act of putting, taking, or bringing in; harvesting, as of crops; inclosure, as of waste land; reclaiming, as of marsh or flooded land; also, something taken or brought in; land reclaimed from the sea, etc.; also (often, esp. in British use, in plural form with singular sense and construction), that part of a game of cricket, baseball, etc., played while one side, or each side in turn, is at the bat; hence, the time during which a party, person, etc., is in power; an opportunity for activity; a turn.

inn-keep-er (in′kē″pėr), *n.* The keeper of an inn.

in-no-cence (in′ọ-sẹns), *n.* [OF. F. *innocence*, < L. *innocentia.*] The state or fact of being innocent; freedom from sin or moral wrong; freedom from specific wrong or guilt, or guiltlessness of that with which one is charged; simplicity, artlessness, or guilelessness (as, "The girl . . . was . . . a mixture of *innocence* and astuteness": W. Churchill's "Coniston," ii. 6); want of knowledge or sense; harmlessness or innocuousness; freedom from illegality, as of a cargo that might be contraband; also, an innocent person or thing; also, the common bluet or houstonia, *Houstonia cærulea*; also, a scrophulariaceous herb, *Collinsia verna*, with a blue and white flower.—**in′no-cen-cy** (-sẹn-si), *n.* The state or fact of being innocent; innocence. [Now rare.]

in-no-cent (in′ọ-sẹnt). [OF. F. *innocent*, < L. *innocens* (*-ent-*), < *in-*, not, + *nocens*, ppr. of *nocere*, harm, hurt.] **I.** *a.* Doing no wrong or evil; free from sin or moral wrong; sinless; often, unacquainted with evil, as a child; also, free from specific wrong or guilt; free from the guilt of a particular offense or crime; blameless; guiltless; hence, devoid (with *of*: colloq.: as, a book *innocent* of merit); also, having or showing the simplicity, artlessness, or unsuspecting nature of a child or one unacquainted with the world (as, "For all she looks so *innocent* . . . take my word for it she is no fool": Steele, in "Spectator," 118); guileless; ingenuous or naïve; hence, silly or half-witted (now prov.); also, not involving evil intent or motive (as, an *innocent* action; *innocent* misrepresentation); also, producing no morally bad result (as, an *innocent* amusement); morally harmless; hence, in general, harmless in effect (as, "The shaft with brazen head Fell *innocent*, and on the dust lay dead": Pope's tr. Homer's "Iliad," xv.); not injurious; innocuous; also, free from illegality, or lawful (as, *innocent* goods carried to a belligerent). **II.** *n.* An innocent person; one not disposed to do wrong; one unacquainted with evil; esp., a young child; specif. [*cap.*], *pl.*, the young children of Bethlehem slain by Herod's order after the birth of Jesus (see Mat. ii. 16: as, *Innocents'* Day, or Holy *Innocents'* Day, see under *holy*, *a.*); also [*l. c.*], *sing.*, a simple or guileless person; also, a simpleton or idiot.—**in′no-cent-ly**, *adv.*

in-noc-u-ous (i-nok′ụ̄-us), *a.* [L. *innocuus*, < *in-*, not, + *nocuus*, harmful, < *nocere*, hurt.] Not harmful or injurious; harmless.—**in-noc′u-ous-ly**, *adv.*—**in-noc′u-ous-ness**, *n.*

in-nom-i-nate (i-nom′i-nāt), *a.* [LL. *innominatus*, < L. *in-*, not, + *nominatus*, pp., named: see *nominate.*] Unnamed; nameless.—**innominate bone**, in *anat.*, either of the two bones forming the sides of the pelvis, each consisting of three consolidated bones, known as ilium, ischium, and pubis; the hip-bone.

in-no-vate (in′ọ-vāt), *v.*; *-vated*, *-vating*. [L. *innovatus*, pp. of *innovare*, renew, alter, < *in*, in, + *novare*, make new, < *novus*, new.] **I.**† *tr.* To change into something new; alter; also, to bring in (something new) for the first time (as, "Every moment alters what is done, And *innovates* some act till then unknown": Dryden's tr. Ovid's "Metamorphoses," xv. 277). **II.** *intr.* To introduce novelties; make changes in something established: as, "It were good . . . that men in their innovations would follow the example of time itself, which indeed *innovateth* greatly, but quietly" (Bacon's "Essays," Of Innovations).—**in-no-va′tion** (-vā′shọn), *n.* [L. *innovatio*(*n-*).] The act of innovating; the introduction of novelties; also, a change made in an established arrangement of any kind; an unwonted variation; something new or different introduced (as, "The scheme of a Colony revenue by British authority appeared therefore to the Americans in the light of a great *innovation*": Burke's "American Taxation").—**in′no-va-tive** (-vā-tiv), *a.* Tending to innovate; characterized by innovation.—**in′no-va-tor** (-vā-tọr), *n.*

in-nox-ious (i-nok′shus or in-nok′-), *a.* [L. *innoxius.*] Not noxious; harmless; innocuous.—**in-nox′ious-ly**, *adv.*—**in-nox′ious-ness**, *n.*

in-nu-en-do (in-ụ̄-en′dō), *n.*; pl. *-does* (-dōz). [L., 'intimating,' 'meaning' (in legal documents, used to introduce explanatory matter), abl. gerund of *innuere*, give a nod, intimate, < *in*, in, on, + *-nuere*, nod.] In legal use, a parenthetic explanation or specification, esp., as in an action for slander or libel, of a word or expression thereby declared to be of injurious meaning; also, the word or expression thus explained; hence, in general, an oblique hint; an indirect intimation about a person or thing; esp., an indirect intimation of a derogatory nature.—**in-nu-en′do**, *v.*; *-doed*, *-doing*. **I.** *tr.* To explain by an innuendo, as in law; also, to convey by an innuendo or insinuation; insinuate. **II.** *intr.* To make innuendoes or insinuations.

In-nu-it (in′ụ̄-it), *n. pl.* [Eskimo, 'the people.'] The native name of the Eskimos; as *sing.*, an Eskimo.

in-nu-mer-a-ble (i-nū′mẹ-rạ-bl or in-nū′-), *a.* [L. *innumerabilis.*] Not numerable; incapable of being numbered or counted; countless; hence, very numerous.—**in-nu′mer-a-ble-ness**, *n.*—**in-nu′mer-a-bly**, *adv.*

in-nu-mer-ous (i-nū′mẹ-rus or in-nū′-), *a.* [LL. *innumerosus*: cf. *numerous.*] Numberless; innumerable: as, "The huge *innumerous* mass [of locusts] . . . began its career, darkening the face of day" (J. H. Newman's "Callista," xv.). [Archaic.]

in-nu-tri-ent (i-nū′tri-ẹnt or in-nū′-), *a.* [See *in-*[2].] Not nutrient or nourishing; innutritious.—**in-nu-tri-tion** (in-ụ̄-trish′ọn or in-nụ̄-), *n.* Lack of nutrition; failure of nourishment.—**in-nu-tri′tious** (-trish′us), *a.* Not nutritious.—**in-nu′tri-tive** (-tri-tiv), *a.* Not nutritive.

in-ob-ser-vance (in-ọb-zėr′vạns), *n.* [L. *inobservantia.*] Want of observance or noticing; inattention; also, neglect or failure to observe, adhere to, or keep (as, "They justly blame . . . his *inobservance* of propriety": Hallam's "Literature of Europe," i. 4. § 69); non-observance.—**in-ob-ser′vant**, *a.* [LL. *inobservans* (*-ant-*).] Not observant; not quick or keen in observing; unobservant.

in-ob-tru-sive (in-ọb-trö′siv), *a.* [See *in-*[2].] Not obtrusive; unobtrusive.

in-oc-cu-pa-tion (in-ok-ụ̄-pā′shọn), *n.* [See *in-*[2].] Lack of occupation.

in-o-cer-a-mus (in-ọ-ser′ạ-mus), *n.* [NL., < Gr. ἴς (ἰν-), muscle, fiber, + κέραμος, pottery, tile, shell.] Any of the genus *Inoceramus* of fossil bivalve mollusks, characteristic of the Cretaceous period.

Inoceramus (*I. sulcatus*).

in-oc-u-la-ble (in-ok′ụ̄-lạ-bl), *a.* Capable of being inoculated.—**in-oc″u-la-bil′i-ty** (-bil′i-ti), *n.*

in-oc-u-late (in-ok′ụ̄-lāt), *v.*; *-lated*, *-lating*. [L. *inoculatus*, pp. of *inoculare*, ingraft, implant, < *in*, in, + *oculus*, eye, bud.] **I.** *tr.* To insert (a bud or scion) in a plant for propagation; fig., to ingraft; also, to subject (a plant) to this operation; also, to introduce (micro-organisms) into surroundings suited to their growth, esp. into the body; specif., to implant (a disease) in a person or animal by the introduction of germs or virus, as through a puncture, in order to produce a mild form of the disease and thus secure immunity; also, to impregnate in this manner; specif., to impregnate (a person or animal) thus, in order to render immune from the disease; fig., to imbue (a person, etc.), as with ideas (as, "My parents had tried in vain to *inoculate* me with wisdom": Irving's "Tales of a Traveler," i. 8). **II.** *intr.* To perform inoculation.—**in-oc-u-la′tion** (-lā′shọn), *n.* [L. *inoculatio*(*n-*).] The act of inoculating; esp., the introduction of micro-organisms into surroundings suited to their growth; specif., the introduction of the germs or virus of a disease into a person or animal in order to produce the disease in a mild form and thus render the subject immune from future contagion.—**in-oc′u-la-tive** (-lạ-tiv), *a.* Of or pertaining to inoculation.—**in-oc′u-la-tor** (-lā-tọr), *n.*

in-o-dor-ous (in-ō′dọr us), *a.* [See *in-*².] Not odorous; odorless.—**in-o′dor-ous-ness,** *n.*

in-of-fen-sive (in-ọ-fen′siv), *a.* [See *in-*².] Not offensive; doing no harm, harmless, or unoffending (as, an *inoffensive* animal; "a mild, *inoffensive* man," Bret Harte's "Tennessee's Partner"); not objectionable, or not being a cause of offense (as, an *inoffensive* odor or taste).—**in-of-fen′sive-ly,** *adv.* —**in-of-fen′sive-ness,** *n.*

in-of-fi-cial (in-ọ-fish′ạl), *a.* [See *in-*².] Not official; unofficial.

in-of-fi-cious (in-ọ-fish′us), *a.* [L. *inofficiosus*: cf. *officious.*] Not ready to do one's duty†; not inclined to do good offices†; disobliging†; also, in *law*, not in accordance with moral duty (as, an *inofficious* testament or will, one disposing of property contrary to the dictates of natural affection or to just expectations).

in-op-er-a-ble (in-op′ẹ-rạ-bl), *a.* [See *in-*².] Not operable; not admitting of a surgical operation.

in-op-er-a-tive (in-op′ẹ-rā-tiv), *a.* [See *in-*².] Not operative; not in operation; without effect.—**in-op′er-a-tive-ness,** *n.*

in-op-por-tune (in-op-ọr-tūn′), *a.* [LL. *inopportunus.*] Not opportune; inappropriate, esp. with regard to time; unseasonable.—**in-op-por-tune′ly,** *adv.*—**in-op-por-tune′-ness,** *n.*—**in-op-por-tun′ist** (-tū′nist), *n.* One who disapproves of a particular course or policy as being inopportune; esp. [*cap.*], one who opposed the declaration of the dogma of papal infallibility at the Vatican Council in 1870, on the ground that its publication was inopportune.—**in-op-por-tu′ni-ty** (-tū′ni-ti), *n.* The state or fact of being inopportune.

in-orb (in-ôrb′), *v. t.* [See *in-*¹.] To inclose in or surround as with an orb; encircle. [Poetic.]

in-or-di-nate (in-ôr′di-nạt), *a.* [L. *inordinatus*: cf. *ordinate.*] Not properly ordered or regulated; irregular; also, not kept within proper limits, or immoderate or excessive (as, *inordinate* vanity; *inordinate* demands); also, of persons, not conforming to order or rule, or disorderly; unrestrained in conduct, passions, etc. (as, "Marcus Antonius . . . was indeed a voluptuous man, and *inordinate*": Bacon's "Essays," Of Love).—**in-or′di-na-cy** (-nạ-si), **in-or′di-nate-ness,** *n.*—**in-or′di-nate-ly,** *adv.*

in-or-gan-ic (in-ôr-gan′ik), *a.* [See *in-*².] Not organic; not having the organization which characterizes living bodies; not characterized by vital processes; specif., noting or pertaining to chemical compounds not containing carbon, or other than those classed in chemistry as 'organic' (see *organic*); also, not belonging or pertaining to the constitution or structure of a thing; not fundamental; extraneous. —**in-or-gan′i-cal-ly,** *adv.*

in-or-gan-iz-a-ble (in-ôr′gạn-ī-zạ-bl), *a.* [See *in-*².] Not organizable; incapable of being organized.—**in-or″gan-i-za′tion** (-i-zā′shọn), *n.* Absence of organization; unorganized condition.—**in-or′gan-ized** (-īzd), *a.* Not organized; unorganized.

in-or-nate (in-ôr-nāt′), *a.* [L. *inornatus.*] Not ornate; unadorned; plain: as, *inornate* language; a literary style that is simple yet not *inornate.*

in-os-cu-late (in-os′kū-lāt), *v. i.* or *t.*; *-lated, -lating.* [L. *in*, in, + LL. *osculare* (pp. *osculatus*), supply with a mouth or outlet, < L. *osculum*, dim. of *os*, mouth: cf. *osculate.*] To unite by openings, as arteries; also, to connect or join so as to become or make continuous, as fibers; hence, to unite intimately.—**in-os-cu-la′tion** (-lā′shọn), *n.*

in-o-site (in′ọ̄-sīt), *n.* [Gr. ἴς (ἰν-), muscle, fiber.] In *chem.*, a white, sweetish compound found in certain muscle tissues, plants, etc.

in-ox-id-iz-a-ble (in-ok′si-dī-zạ-bl), *a.* [See *in-*².] Not oxidizable; incapable of being oxidized.—**in-ox′id-ize** (-ok′si-dīz), *v. t.*; *-ized, -izing.* To render inoxidizable.—**in-ox′id-ized,** *a.* Not oxidized.

in=pa-tient (in′pā″shẹnt), *n.* A patient who is lodged and fed as well as treated in a hospital.

in-pour (in′pōr), *n.* A pouring in; an influx.—**in′pour″-ing,** *n.* and *a.*

in-put (in′put), *n.* That which is put in; the power supplied to a machine; a contribution (Sc.).

in-quest (in′kwest), *n.* [OF. *enqueste* (F. *enquête*), < L. *inquirere* (pp. *inquisitus*): see *inquire.*] An inquiry, investigation, or quest (obs. or rare); esp., a legal or judicial inquiry, esp. before a jury; now, commonly, one made by a coroner ('coroner's inquest'); also, the body of men appointed to hold such an inquiry, esp. a coroner's jury.

in-qui-et (in-kwī′et), *a.* [L. *inquietus.*] Not quiet; restless; disturbed; unquiet.—**in-qui′et-ly,** *adv.*—**in-qui′e-tude** (-e-tūd), *n.* [LL. *inquietudo.*] Inquiet state; restlessness; uneasiness; disquietude; *pl.*, disquieting thoughts or feelings, or anxieties (as, "As the evening advanced, my father's *inquietudes* increased": C. B. Brown's "Wieland," ii.).

in-qui-line (in′kwi-lin or -līn), *n.* [L. *inquilinus*, lodger, < *in*, in, + *colere*, inhabit.] In *zoöl.*, an animal that lives in an abode properly belonging to another, as certain hymenopterous insects that inhabit the galls made by the true gall-insects; a guest.—**in-qui-lin′i-ty** (-lin′i-ti), *n.* In *zoöl.*, the condition or the mode of life of an inquiline.—**in-qui-li′nous** (-lī′nus), *a.*

in-quire (in-kwīr′), *v.*; *-quired, -quiring.* [OF. *enquerre* (F. *enquérir*), < L. *inquirere* (pp. *inquisitus*), < *in*, in, + *quærere*, seek.] **I.** *tr.* To search into†; seek information concerning†; also, to seek to learn by asking (as, to *inquire* a person's name or business; to *inquire* when a person will be in); request to be told; also, to question† or interrogate† (a person); also, to seek†, search for†, or try to find† (often with *out*: as, "Well known to me the palace you *inquire*," Pope's tr. Homer's "Odyssey," vii.; "*Inquire* her out . . . and tell her, her nephew . . . is in the house," Congreve's "Way of the World," iii.). **II.** *intr.* To make investigation (*into*); esp., to seek information by questioning, or ask (as, to *inquire* of a person about a matter; to *inquire* after a person, to make inquiries concerning his welfare); make inquiry (*for*: as, to *inquire* for a person, to ask to see him).—**in-quir′er** (-kwīr′ėr), *n.*—**in-quir′ing-ly,** *adv.*—**in-quir-y** (in-kwīr′i, also in′kwi-ri), *n.*; pl. *-ies* (-iz). A seeking for truth, information, or knowledge; examination into facts or principles; investigation; research; an investigation, as into a matter (as, to spend one's leisure in *inquiries* into antiquity); also, the act of inquiring, or seeking information by questioning; interrogation; a question or query.

in-qui-si-tion (in-kwi-zish′ọn), *n.* [L. *inquisitio(n-)*, < *inquirere*: see *inquire.*] The act or process of inquiring or searching into matters, in order to learn the truth or the facts; inquiry; investigation; research; also, an investigation, or process of inquiry; esp., a judicial or official inquiry or investigation; an inquest; also, the finding of such an inquiry; also [*cap.*], in the *Rom. Cath. Ch.*, a tribunal, officially styled the Holy Office, for the discovery and suppression of heresy and the punishment of heretics (as, the Spanish *Inquisition*, a branch of this tribunal in Spain, now suppressed, which was reorganized and put under the control of the state at the end of the 15th century, and which was particularly active in Spain, the Netherlands, etc., during the 16th century, and noted for its severity and the number of its victims).—**in-qui-si′tion-al,** *a.* Pertaining to inquisition; inquisitorial; also, pertaining to the Inquisition.—**in-qui-si′tion-ist,** *n.* One who makes inquisition; an inquisitor; esp., a member of the Inquisition.

in-quis-i-tive (in-kwiz′i-tiv), *a.* [LL. *inquisitivus*, < L. *inquirere*: see *inquire.*] Given to inquiry or research; desirous of or eager for knowledge; curious; now, usually, unduly curious (as, "Remember, no revolvers. The police are, I believe, proverbially *inquisitive*": Dunsany's "Night at an Inn"); prying.—**in-quis′i-tive-ly,** *adv.*—**in-quis′i-tive-ness,** *n.*

in-quis-i-tor (in-kwiz′i-tọr), *n.* [L., < *inquirere*: see *inquire.*] One who makes inquisition; an investigator; esp., one who investigates by virtue of his office; specif., a member of the Inquisition; also, a questioner, esp. an inquisitive one.—**in-quis-i-to′ri-al** (-tō′ri-ạl), *a.* Pertaining to an inquisitor or inquisitors, or to inquisition; exercising the office or functions of an inquisitor; hence, suggestive of an inquisitor; resembling an inquisitor; unduly curious, or inquisitive.—**in-quis-i-to′ri-al-ly,** *adv.*—**in-quis′i-tor-ship,** *n.* The office of inquisitor.—**in-quis′i-tress,** *n.* A female inquisitor.

in-ro (in'rō), *n.* [Jap.] A set of small ornamental boxes, fitting one upon another, carried at the girdle by Japanese, to hold medicines, perfumes, etc.

in-road (in'rōd), *n.* [From *in* + *road* ('riding, raid').] A hostile or predatory incursion; a raid; a foray; fig., a forcible encroachment (as, "The face . . . had once been handsome . . . though intemperance was making sad *inroads* on its comeliness": Cooper's "Two Admirals," ii.).—**in'road,** *v. i.* To make inroads.

in-run (in'run), *n.* A running in; an influx or inrush.—**in'run"ning,** *n.* and *a.*

in-rush (in'rush), *n.* A rushing in; an influx: as, "since the Roman Imperial system dissolved under the barbarian *inrush*" (H. G. Wells's "Outline of History," xxxvii. § 6).—**in'rush"ing,** *n.* and *a.*

in-sal-i-vate (in-sal'i-vāt), *v. t.*; *-vated, -vating.* [See *in-*[1].] To mix with saliva, as food.—**in-sal-i-va'tion** (-vā'shọn), *n.*

in-sa-lu-bri-ous (in-sạ-lū'bri-us), *a.* [L. *insalubris.*] Not salubrious; unfavorable to health.—**in-sa-lu'bri-ty** (-bri-ti), *n.*

in-sal-u-ta-ry (in-sal'ụ-tạ-ri), *a.* [LL. *insalutaris.*] Not salutary; unwholesome; unfavorable; prejudicial.

in-sane (in-sān'), *a.* [L. *insanus.*] Not sane; not of sound mind; mentally deranged; mad; also, characteristic of one mentally deranged; hence, wild; utterly senseless; also, set apart for the use of mentally deranged persons (as, an *insane* asylum); also, causing insanity† (as, "Have we eaten on the *insane* root That takes the reason prisoner?" Shakspere's "Macbeth," i. 3. 84).—**in-sane'ly,** *adv.*—**in-sane'ness,** *n.*

in-san-i-ta-ry (in-san'i-tạ-ri), *a.* [See *in-*[2].] Not sanitary; unhealthful.—**in-san'i-ta-ri-ness,** *n.*

in-san-i-ta-tion (in-san-i-tā'shọn), *n.* [See *in-*[2].] Want of sanitation or sanitary regulation; insanitary condition.

in-san-i-ty (in-san'i-ti), *n.*; pl. *-ties* (-tiz). [L. *insanitas.*] The condition of being insane; more or less permanent derangement of one or more psychical functions, due to disease of the brain; madness or lunacy; hence, extreme folly, or an instance of it; specif., in *law,* such unsoundness of mind as affects legal responsibility or capacity.

in-sa-ti-a-ble (in-sā'shi-ạ-bl), *a.* [L. *insatiabilis,* < *in-,* not, + *satiare,* E. *satiate.*] Not satiable; incapable of being satisfied or appeased; inordinately greedy.—**in-sa"ti-a-bil'i-ty** (-bil'i-ti), **in-sa'ti-a-ble-ness,** *n.*—**in-sa'ti-a-bly,** *adv.*

in-sa-ti-ate (in-sā'shi-āt), *a.* [L. *insatiatus,* < *in-,* not, + *satiatus,* pp., satiated: see *satiate.*] Not satiated; never satisfied; insatiable: as, "the *insatiate* greediness of his desires" (Shakspere's "Richard III.," iii. 7. 7).—**in-sa'ti-ate-ly,** *adv.*—**in-sa'ti-ate-ness,** *n.*

in-scient (in'shient), *a.* [L. *insciens* (*-ent-*), < *in-,* not, + *sciens,* ppr. of *scire,* know.] Not knowing; nescient; ignorant. [Now rare.]—**in'science** (-shiens), *n.*

in-scribe (in-skrīb'), *v. t.*; *-scribed, -scribing.* [L. *inscribere* (pp. *inscriptus*), < *in,* in, on, + *scribere,* write.] To write or engrave (words, characters, etc.), or mark (a surface) with words, characters, etc., esp. in a durable or conspicuous way; fig., to imprint or impress deeply (as, to *inscribe* something on the memory); also, to enroll, as on an official list; also, to address or dedicate (a book, etc.) informally to a person; in *geom.,* to draw or delineate (one figure) within another figure so that the inner lies in the boundary of the outer at as many points as possible.—**in-scrib'a-ble** (-skrī'bạ-bl), *a.*—**in-scrib'er,** *n.*

in-scrip-tion (in-skrip'shọn), *n.* [L. *inscriptio(n-).*] The act of inscribing; also, something inscribed; a description, record, or the like, written, engraved, or otherwise traced, esp. upon something durable, as a monument, coin, etc.; also, a brief, more or less informal dedication, as of a book or a work of art.—**in-scrip'tion-al,** *a.*—**in-scrip'tion-less,** *a.* Without an inscription.

in-scrip-tive (in-skrip'tiv), *a.* Pertaining to or of the nature of an inscription.—**in-scrip'tive-ly,** *adv.*

in-scroll (in-skrōl'), *v. t.* [See *in-*[1].] To write on a scroll.

in-scru-ta-ble (in-skrö'tạ-bl), *a.* [LL. *inscrutabilis,* < L. *in-,* not, + *scrutari,* search, examine: see *scrutiny.*] Incapable of being searched into, or of being understood by inquiry or investigation (as, "the doctrine of the Trinity, which theologians agree to call *inscrutable*": Hallam's "Literature of Europe," ii. 2. § 27); impenetrable or unfathomable to investigation; incomprehensible; also, sometimes, impenetrable or unfathomable physically (as, "A locust sang once or twice in some *inscrutable* seclusion of the tree," Hawthorne's "House of the Seven Gables," xix.; "deep holes, — *inscrutable* cavities of the earth," Lamb's "Two Races of Men").—**in-scru-ta-bil'i-ty** (-bil'i-ti), **in-scru'ta-ble-ness,** *n.*—**in-scru'ta-bly,** *adv.*

in-sculp (in-skulp'), *v. t.* [L. *insculpere* (pp. *insculptus*), < *in,* in, on, + *sculpere,* carve.] To carve in or on something; engrave. [Obs. or rare.]

in-sculp-sit (in-skulp'sit). [L.] '(The person indicated) engraved it': a word sometimes inscribed on an engraving, with the engraver's name or initials prefixed.

in-sculp-ture (in-skulp'tụr), *n.* [See *insculp.*] A carved or engraved figure or inscription. See Shakspere's "Timon of Athens," v. 4. 67. [Obs. or rare.]—**in-sculp'ture,** *v. t.*; *-tured, -turing.* To carve or sculpture (figures, etc.) on something.

in-sect (in'sekt), *n.* [L. *insectum* (so called from the segmented form), prop. neut. of *insectus,* pp. of *insecare,* cut in or up, < *in,* in, + *secare,* cut.] Popularly, any of numerous small, often winged, invertebrate creatures whose body generally appears to consist of several segments, as flies, spiders, centipedes, etc.; in *zoöl.,* any of the *Insecta,* a class of arthropods (including flies, bugs, beetles, etc.) with three pairs of legs, usually two pairs of wings, and a body divided into head, thorax, and abdomen.

in-sec-ta-ri-um (in-sek-tā'ri-um), *n.*; pl. *-riums* or *-ria* (-ri-ạ). [NL.] A place in which a collection of living insects is kept; also, the collection itself. Also **in'sec-ta-ry** (-tạ-ri); pl. *-ries* (-riz).

in-sec-ti-cide (in-sek'ti-sīd), *n.* [See *-cide.*] A killer of insects; a substance or preparation used for killing insects; also, the killing of insects.—**in-sec'ti-ci-dal** (-sī-dạl), *a.*

in-sec-tile (in-sek'til), *a.* Of or pertaining to an insect; of the nature of an insect; consisting of insects; resembling an insect.

in-sec-ti-vore (in-sek'ti-vōr), *n.* [See *-vore.*] An insectivorous animal or plant; specif., one of the *Insectivora,* an order of small mammals including the shrews, moles, hedgehogs, and flying-lemurs.—**in-sec-tiv'o-rous** (-tiv'ọ-rus), *a.* [See *-vorous.*] Insect-eating, as certain animals and plants; specif., belonging or pertaining to the *Insectivora* (see *insectivore*).

in-sec-tol-o-gy (in-sek-tol'ọ-ji), *n.* [See *-logy.*] The science of insects.

in-se-cure (in-sẹ-kūr'), *a.* [See *in-*[2].] Not secure; not free from apprehension or uncertainty (as, "*insecure* delight": Wordsworth's "White Doe of Rylstone," i. 195); exposed to danger, or unsafe (as, a region where life is *insecure*); liable to fail or give way (as, an *insecure* support or fastening).—**in-se-cure'ly,** *adv.*—**in-se-cu'ri-ty** (-kū'ri-ti), *n.*; pl. *-ties* (-tiz). The state of being insecure; want of assurance or confidence; unsafe condition; liability to fail or give way; also, an instance of this; something insecure.

in-sem-i-nate (in-sem'i-nāt), *v. t.*; *-nated, -nating.* [L. *inseminatus,* pp. of *inseminare,* < *in,* in, + *seminare,* sow, E. *seminate.*] To sow as seed in something; implant; also, to inject seed into; impregnate.—**in-sem-i-na'tion** (-nā'shọn), *n.*

in-sen-sate (in-sen'sāt), *a.* [LL. *insensatus*: cf. *sensate*[1].] Not endowed with sense or sensation, or inanimate (as, "Hers the silence and the calm Of mute *insensate* things": Wordsworth's "Three Years She Grew"); also, devoid of sensibility or feeling, or unfeeling (as, "the *insensate* barbarous trade of war": Thomson's "Seasons," Winter, 844); also, devoid of sense, understanding, or judgment, or senseless (as, an *insensate* person; *insensate* folly).—**in-sen'sate-ly,** *adv.*—**in-sen'sate-ness,** *n.*

in-sen-si-ble (in-sen'si-bl), *a.* [L. *insensibilis.*] Not sensible, or not actually or readily perceptible by the senses or mind (as, *insensible* changes; *insensible* gradations or degrees); imperceptible; inappreciable; also, incapable of feeling or perceiving; not endowed with feeling or sensation, as matter; deprived of sensation, or unconscious, as a person after a violent blow; also, incapable or devoid of, or not subject to, a particular feeling (as, *insensible* of, or to, pain or shame); unconscious, unaware, or inappreciative (as, we are not *insensible* of your kindness); unresponsive in feeling, or indifferent (as, "Nothing disturbs the tranquillity of their souls, equally *insensible* to disasters and to prosperity": Irving's "Knickerbocker's New York," i. 5); unfeeling; callous; apathetic.—**in-sen-si-bil′i-ty** (-bil′i-ti), *n.*—**in-sen′si-bly,** *adv.* In an insensible manner; by imperceptible degrees; imperceptibly.

in-sen-si-tive (in-sen′si-tiv), *a.* [See *in-*².] Not sensitive; without sensation or feeling; not susceptible to agencies or influences; deficient in sensibility or acuteness of feeling. —**in-sen′si-tive-ness,** *n.*

in-sen-tient (in-sen′shiẹnt), *a.* [See *in-*².] Not sentient; not endowed with sensation or feeling; inanimate.—**in-sen′tience,** *n.*

in-sep-a-ra-ble (in-sep′ạ-rạ-bl). [L. *inseparabilis.*] **I.** *a.* Not separable; incapable of being separated, parted, or disjoined: as, *inseparable* companions; an *inseparable* prefix; parts *inseparable* from the whole. **II.** *n.* Something inseparable; an inseparable companion or friend: usually in *pl.*—**in-sep″a-ra-bil′i-ty** (-bil′i-ti), *n.*—**in-sep′a-ra-bly,** *adv.*

in-sert (in-sėrt′), *v. t.* [L. *insertus,* pp. of *inserere,* < *in,* in, + *serere,* join.] To put or set in (as, to *insert* a key in, or into, a lock; to *insert* a cut in a page of type); place in a hole or space, or between parts; introduce into the body of something (as, to *insert* a letter in a word; to *insert* an advertisement in a newspaper); in *bot., zoöl.,* etc., to attach (used only in *pp.*: as, an organ *inserted* on its support, that is, fixed there by natural growth).—**in′sert,** *n.* Something inserted, or to be inserted; an extra leaf or extra leaves inserted between the pages of a book, etc.; an inset; a circular or the like placed within the leaves of a book, etc., or within the folds of a newspaper.—**in-sert′er,** *n.*—**in-ser′tion** (-sėr′shọn), *n.* [LL. *insertio(n-).*] The act of inserting; also, something inserted; lace, embroidery, or the like, in band-like form, to be sewed at each edge between parts of other material; in *bot., zoöl.,* etc., manner or place of attachment, as of an organ.

in-ses-so-ri-al (in-se-sō′ri-ạl), *a.* [NL. *Insessores,* pl., the perching birds (considered as an order), < L. *insidere,* sit in or on, < *in,* in, on, + *sedere,* sit.] Of or pertaining to birds that perch; habitually perching, as a bird; adapted for perching, as a bird's foot.

in-set (in-set′), *v. t.*; *-set, -setting.* To set in; insert; specif., to insert as an inset; also, to insert an inset in.—**in′set,** *n.* The act of setting in; also, something set in or inserted; an extra leaf or series of leaves inserted in a folded sheet or a book, esp. before binding; a smaller picture, map, etc., inserted within the border of a larger one.

in-sev-er-a-ble (in-sev′ėr-ạ-bl), *a.* [See *in-*².] Not severable; incapable of being severed.—**in-sev′er-a-bly,** *adv.*

in-sheathe (in-shēᴛʜ′), *v. t.*; *-sheathed, -sheathing.* [See *in-*¹.] To inclose in or as in a sheath; sheathe.

in-shoot (in′shöt), *n.* In *baseball,* a curve which shoots or bends in toward the batter as it approaches the home base.

in-shore (in′shōr′), *adv.* and *a.* In toward or near the shore.

in-shrine (in-shrīn′), *v. t.* Same as *enshrine.*

in-side (in′sīd′ or in-sīd′), *n.* The inner side or surface; also, the inner part, or interior; specif., the inward parts of the body, esp. the stomach and intestines (often in *pl.*: colloq.); fig., the inward nature; also, an inside passenger or place in a coach, etc. (colloq.: as, "I . . . hurried . . . to the coach-office, to book myself an *inside* in the mail of that night," Lever's "Harry Lorrequer," xiv.); in *printing,* that side of a sheet of paper which contains the second page.—**in-side** (in′sīd′ or in′sīd), *a.* Situated or being on or in the inside; interior; internal; also, acting, employed, done, or originating within a building or place (as, *inside* workers or work; the robbery was an *inside* job); of information, etc., derived from the inner circle of those concerned in and having private knowledge of a case.—**in-side′. I.** *adv.* On the inside; in or into the inner part; within; also, within the space or period (*of*: as, to break down *inside* of a mile or a year: colloq.). **II.** *prep.* Inside of; within. —**in-sid′er** (-sī′dėr), *n.* One who is inside, or within the limits of some place, society, organization, etc.; one who is within a limited circle of persons who understand the actual conditions or facts in a case.

in-sid-i-ous (in-sid′i-us), *a.* [L. *insidiosus,* < *insidiæ,* ambush, artifice, < *insidere,* sit in or on: see *insessorial.*] Seeking or intended to entrap or beguile (as, an *insidious* foe; *insidious* designs or attempts); stealthily treacherous or deceitful; wily, crafty, or sly; also, operating or proceeding inconspicuously but with grave effect, as poison, a disease, etc.—**in-sid′i-ous-ly,** *adv.*—**in-sid′i-ous-ness,** *n.*

in-sight (in′sīt), *n.* Inner or mental vision†; understanding†; also, penetrating mental vision or discernment; faculty of seeing into inner character or underlying truth; also, a sight had or given into something; a view beneath the surface of a thing.

in-sig-ni-a (in-sig′ni-ä̤), *n. pl.* [L., pl. of *insigne,* mark, badge, prop. neut. of *insignis,* distinguished by a mark, < *in,* in, + *signum,* mark, E. *sign, n.*: cf. *ensign.*] Badges or distinguishing marks of office or honor (as, military *insignia*; the *insignia* of an order of knighthood); hence, distinguishing marks or signs of anything (as, "Rags . . . are the Beggar's robes, and graceful *insignia* of his profession": Lamb's "Decay of Beggars").

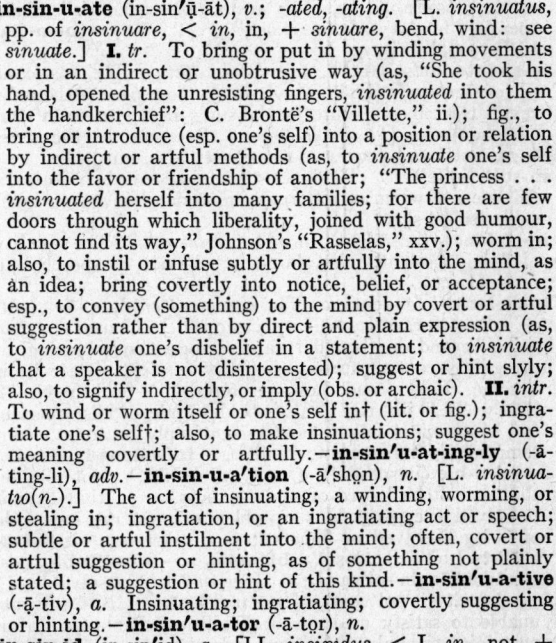

Insignia of the Order of St. Michael and St. George.

in-sig-nif-i-cant (in-sig-nif′i-kạnt), *a.* [See *in-*².] Not significant; meaningless, as terms; unimportant, trifling, or petty, as things, matters, details, etc.; of no consequence, influence, or distinction, as persons; sometimes, too small to be important (as, an *insignificant* sum).—**in-sig-nif′i-cance, in-sig-nif′i-can-cy,** *n.* —**in-sig-nif′i-cant-ly,** *adv.*

in-sin-cere (in-sin-sēr′), *a.* [L. *insincerus.*] Not sincere; wanting in sincerity; not honest or candid in the expression of actual feeling; disingenuous; deceitful.—**in-sin-cere′ly,** *adv.*—**in-sin-cer′i-ty** (-ser′i-ti), *n.*

in-sin-u-ate (in-sin′ụ̄-āt), *v.*; *-ated, -ating.* [L. *insinuatus,* pp. of *insinuare,* < *in,* in, + *sinuare,* bend, wind: see *sinuate.*] **I.** *tr.* To bring or put in by winding movements or in an indirect or unobtrusive way (as, "She took his hand, opened the unresisting fingers, *insinuated* into them the handkerchief": C. Brontë's "Villette," ii.); fig., to bring or introduce (esp. one's self) into a position or relation by indirect or artful methods (as, to *insinuate* one's self into the favor or friendship of another; "The princess . . . *insinuated* herself into many families; for there are few doors through which liberality, joined with good humour, cannot find its way," Johnson's "Rasselas," xxv.); worm in; also, to instil or infuse subtly or artfully into the mind, as an idea; bring covertly into notice, belief, or acceptance; esp., to convey (something) to the mind by covert or artful suggestion rather than by direct and plain expression (as, to *insinuate* one's disbelief in a statement; to *insinuate* that a speaker is not disinterested); suggest or hint slyly; also, to signify indirectly, or imply (obs. or archaic). **II.** *intr.* To wind or worm itself or one's self in† (lit. or fig.); ingratiate one's self†; also, to make insinuations; suggest one's meaning covertly or artfully.—**in-sin′u-at-ing-ly** (-ā-ting-li), *adv.*—**in-sin-u-a′tion** (-ā′shọn), *n.* [L. *insinuatio(n-).*] The act of insinuating; a winding, worming, or stealing in; ingratiation, or an ingratiating act or speech; subtle or artful instilment into the mind; often, covert or artful suggestion or hinting, as of something not plainly stated; a suggestion or hint of this kind.—**in-sin′u-a-tive** (-ạ-tiv), *a.* Insinuating; ingratiating; covertly suggesting or hinting.—**in-sin′u-a-tor** (-ā-tọr), *n.*

in-sip-id (in-sip′id), *a.* [LL. *insipidus,* < L. *in-,* not, + *sapidus,* having a taste, savory, E. *sapid.*] Without taste or flavor; esp., without sufficient taste to be pleasing to the palate, as food or drink; fig., without distinctive, interesting, or attractive qualities (as, an *insipid* tale; "A faded beauty

. . . *Insipid* as the queen upon a card," Tennyson's "Aylmer's Field," 28); flat; dull; uninteresting.—**in-si-pid′i-ty** (-si-pid′i-ti), *n.*; pl. *-ties* (-tiz). The quality of being insipid; also, something insipid; an insipid person or being (as, "His face looks out at us across an interval of thirty-four centuries, a man amidst ranks of divine *insipidities*": H. G. Wells's "Outline of History," xix. § 7).—**in-sip′id-ly,** *adv.*—**in-sip′id-ness,** *n.*

in-sip-i-ent (in-sip′i-ent), *a.* [L. *insipiens* (*-ent-*), < *in-*, not, + *sapiens*, E. *sapient*.] Not sapient or wise; destitute of wisdom; foolish. [Now rare.]—**in-sip′i-ence,** *n.*

in-sist (in-sist′), *v. i.* [L. *insistere*, stand or press upon, insist, < *in*, in, + *sistere*, stand.] To stand or rest (*on* or *upon*: now rare); fig., to dwell with earnestness or emphasis (*on* or *upon*: as, to *insist* on a point in a discourse); lay emphasis in assertion (as, to *insist* on the justice of a claim); assert or maintain positively (as, to *insist* that a claim is just); often, to be emphatic, firm, or pertinacious on some matter of desire, demand, intention, etc. (as, to *insist* on, or upon, having or doing something; he *insisted* that we should come; "Sharply thou hast *insisted* on rebuke," Milton's "Paradise Regained," i. 468); also, to continue firmly, or persist, as in a course†.—**in-sist′ence,** *n.* The act or fact of insisting (as, *insistence* on the moral side of a question); also, the quality of being insistent; urgency; pertinacity.—**in-sist′en-cy,** *n.* The quality of being insistent; insistence.—**in-sist′ent,** *a.* Insisting; earnest or emphatic in dwelling upon, maintaining, or demanding something; urgent; pertinacious; persistent; of things, compelling attention or notice.—**in-sist′ent-ly, in-sist′ing-ly,** *adv.*—**in-sist′er,** *n.*

in-si-ti-tious (in-si-tish′us), *a.* [L. *insiticius*, < *inserere* (pp. *insitus*), ingraft, < *in*, in, + *serere*, sow, plant.] Ingrafted or inserted; introduced from without: as, *insititious* passages in a text.

in situ (in sī′tū). [L.] In its original situation or place.

in-snare, en-snare (in-snãr′, en-), *v. t.*; *-snared, -snaring.* [See *in-*¹.] To take in or as in a snare; entrap; catch; entangle.—**in-snare′ment, en-snare′ment,** *n.*—**in-snar′er, en-snar′er** (-snãr′ėr), *n.*

in-so-bri-e-ty (in-sọ-brī′ẹ-ti), *n.* [See *in-*².] Want of sobriety; intemperance; drunkenness.

in-so-cia-ble (in-sō′shạ-bl), *a.* [L. *insociabilis.*] Not sociable; unsociable: as, "this austere *insociable* life" (Shakspere's "Love's Labour's Lost," v. 2. 809).—**in-so-cia-bil′i-ty** (-bil′i-ti), *n.*

in-so-late (in′sọ-lāt), *v. t.*; *-lated, -lating.* [L. *insolatus*, pp. of *insolare*, < *in*, in, + *sol*, sun.] To expose to the sun's rays; treat by exposure to the sun's rays.—**in-so-la′tion** (-lā′shọn), *n.* [L. *insolatio*(*n-*).] Exposure to the sun's rays, specif. as a process of treatment; also, sunstroke.

in-sole (in′sōl), *n.* The inner sole of a shoe or boot; also, a thickness of warm or waterproof material laid as an inner sole within a shoe.

in-so-lence (in′sọ-lẹns), *n.* [L. *insolentia.*] The quality of being insolent; also, insolent behavior or speech; an insolent act.

in-so-lent (in′sọ-lẹnt), *a.* [L. *insolens* (*-ent-*), < *in-*, not, + *solens*, ppr. of *solere*, be accustomed.] Unusual†; also, going beyond due bounds†; also, arrogant, overbearing, or arrogantly contemptuous (as, "How *insolent* of late he is become, How proud, how peremptory": Shakspere's "2 Henry VI.," iii. 1. 7); also, boldly rude or disrespectful (as, an *insolent* fellow; an *insolent* reply or tone); contemptuously impertinent; insulting.—**in′so-lent-ly,** *adv.*

in-sol-u-ble (in-sol′ụ̄-bl), *a.* [L. *insolubilis.*] Not soluble; that cannot be loosed or undone (now rare); that cannot be solved or explained, as a problem or mystery; incapable of being dissolved or liquefied, as a substance.—**in-sol-u-bil′i-ty** (-bil′i-ti), **in-sol′u-ble-ness,** *n.*—**in-sol′u-bly,** *adv.*

in-solv-a-ble (in-sol′vạ-bl), *a.* [See *in-*².] Not solvable.

in-sol-vent (in-sol′vẹnt). [See *in-*².] **I.** *a.* Not solvent; unable to satisfy creditors or liabilities; bankrupt; also, pertaining to bankrupt persons or bankruptcy (as, *insolvent* laws). **II.** *n.* One who is insolvent.—**in-sol′ven-cy,** *n.*

in-som-ni-a (in-som′ni-ạ̈), *n.* [L., < *insomnis*, sleepless, < *in-*, not, + *somnus*, sleep.] Inability to sleep, esp. when chronic; sleeplessness.—**in-som′ni-ac** (-ak), *n.* One who suffers from insomnia.—**in-som′ni-ous,** *a.* Affected with insomnia; unable to sleep.

in-so-much (in-sọ-much′), *adv.* To such an extent or degree (*that* or *as*: as, "The lover was thunder-struck . . . *insomuch* that . . . he lost his senses," Addison, in "Spectator," 60); so (*that* or *as*: as, "He answered him to never a word; *insomuch* that the governor marvelled greatly," Mat. xxvii. 14); also, followed by *as*, inasmuch as, seeing that, or since.

in-sou-ci-ant (in-sö′si-ạnt, F. aṅ-sö-syäṅ), *a.* [F., < *in-*, not, + *souciant*, ppr. of *soucier*, refl., concern one's self, care, < L. *sollicitare*, disturb, E. *solicit*.] Free from concern or care; unconcerned; without solicitude or anxiety; care-free: as, "This *insouciant* light-tempered, gay, and thoughtless disposition conducted René . . . to a hale and mirthful old age" (Scott's "Anne of Geierstein," xxix.).—**in-sou-ci-ance** (in-sö′si-ạns, F. aṅ-sö-syäṅs), *n.*

in-soul (in-sōl′), *v. t.* Same as *ensoul.*

in-span (in-span′), *v.*; *-spanned, -spanning.* [D. *inspannen.*] **I.** *tr.* To yoke or harness, as oxen or horses to a wagon; attach animals to (a vehicle); span. [South Africa.] **II.** *intr.* To attach animals to a vehicle, as in preparation for a journey. [South Africa.]

in-spect (in-spekt′), *v. t.* [L. *inspectus*, pp. of *inspicere*, < *in*, in, on, + *specere*, look at.] To look carefully at or over; view closely and critically; esp., to view or examine formally or officially, in order to ascertain condition or quality or ensure conformity to standards or laws (as, to *inspect* troops; to *inspect* goods for trade; to *inspect* buildings or mines).—**in-spec′tion** (-spek′shọn), *n.* [L. *inspectio*(*n-*).] The act of inspecting; careful or critical viewing; esp., formal or official viewing or examination; the action of an inspector; also, a district under an inspector.—**in-spec′tion-al,** *a.* Of or pertaining to inspection; of an instrument, showing results directly on being inspected, without calculation or the like.—**in-spec′tive,** *a.* Given to or making inspection; pertaining to inspection.

in-spec-tor (in-spek′tọr), *n.* [L., < *inspicere*: see *inspect.*] One who inspects; an officer appointed to inspect; an officer of police, usually ranking next below a superintendent.—**in-spec′tor-ate** (-ạ̄t), *n.* The office or function of an inspector; also, a body of inspectors; also, a district under an inspector.—**in-spec-to′ri-al** (-tō′ri-ạl), *a.* Of or pertaining to an inspector.—**in-spec′tor-ship,** *n.* The office of an inspector.—**in-spec′tress,** *n.* A female inspector.

in-sphere (in-sfēr′), *v. t.* Same as *ensphere.*

in-spir-a-ble (in-spīr′ạ-bl), *a.* Capable of being inspired.

in-spi-ra-tion (in-spi-rā′shọn), *n.* [LL. *inspiratio*(*n-*).] The act of inspiring, or the state of being inspired; the drawing of air into the lungs; inhalation; fig., the infusing of some animating, quickening, or exalting influence into the mind or soul; the arousing of some feeling, thought, or impulse, esp. of an exalted kind; inspiring or animating action or influence (as, "I cannot write without *inspiration.* And nobody can give me that except Ann": G. B. Shaw's "Man and Superman," ii.); also, something inspired, as a thought or impulse (as, "Holy men at their death have good *inspirations*": Shakspere's "Merchant of Venice," i. 2. 31); a product or result of inspired activity (as, the device was a happy *inspiration*); also, a thing or person that inspires; a source of inspiring influence; in *theol.*, a divine influence directly and immediately exerted upon the mind or soul of man; esp., the direct influence of God under which the books of Scripture are regarded as having been written.—**in-spi-ra′tion-al,** *a.* Of or pertaining to inspiration; also, imparting inspiration; also, under the influence of inspiration, or inspired.—**in-spi-ra′tion-al-ly,** *adv.*

in-spir-a-to-ry (in-spīr′ạ-tọ-ri or in′spi-rạ-), *a.* Pertaining to inspiration or inhalation.

in-spire (in-spīr′), *v.*; *-spired, -spiring.* [L. *inspirare*, < *in*, in, + *spirare*, breathe.] **I.** *tr.* To breathe or blow into or upon (obs. or archaic: as, to *inspire* a musical instrument); also, to breathe or blow (air, etc.) into or upon something (archaic); infuse (breath, life, a soul, etc.) into by breathing (archaic: as, "That pure breath of life, the spirit of man Which God *inspired*," Milton's "Paradise Lost," x. 785); also, to take (air, gases, etc.) into the lungs in breathing; inhale; also, fig., to infuse an animating, quickening, or exalting influence into (as, his courage, or his example, *inspired* his followers; the orator, or his eloquence, *inspires* his hearers); animate or actuate by a divine or supernatural influence (as, to *inspire* a prophet or an oracle; "*Inspire* me, Phœbus, in my Delia's praise," Pope's "Spring," 45); affect with a specified feeling, thought, etc. (as, to *inspire* a person with distrust); animate, as an influence, feeling, thought, or the like does; influence or impel to, or to do, something (as, opposition *inspired* him to greater efforts; this hope *inspires* us to persevere); also, to infuse (something) into the mind; produce or arouse (a feeling, thought, etc.: as, to *inspire* distrust in a person; to *inspire* fear, pleasure, or pleasant thoughts); also, to communicate or suggest by divine or supernatural influence, or inform with a sacred or lofty character (as, writings *inspired* by God; "I call no Goddess to *inspire* my strains," Burns's "To Robert Graham"); also, to give rise to, occasion, or cause (as, "Behold in Ætna's emblematic fires The mischiefs your ambitious pride *inspires!*" Cowper's "Heroism," 46); sometimes, to prompt or instigate (utterances, etc.) by influence without avowal of responsibility. **II.** *intr.* To draw air into the lungs, as in breathing; also, to infuse an animating or exalting influence; give inspiration.—**in-spired′,** *p. a.* Breathed in, or inhaled; also, animated or actuated by, or communicated or produced under, divine or supernatural influence (as, an *inspired* teacher or prophet; an *inspired* poet; the *inspired* writings of Scripture); sometimes, prompted by or emanating from an influential person, the authorities, etc., but without avowal of responsibility (as, an *inspired* editorial).—**in-spir′er** (-spīr′ėr), *n.*—**in-spir′ing,** *p. a.* That inspires; animating; infusing fresh ardor, enthusiasm, confidence, etc.—**in-spir′ing-ly,** *adv.*

in-spir-it (in-spir′it), *v. t.* [See *in-*[1].] To infuse spirit or life into; animate or enliven; cheer or encourage.—**in-spir′-it-ing-ly,** *adv.*

in-spis-sate (in-spis′āt), *v. t.* or *i.*; *-sated, -sating.* [LL. *inspissatus*, pp. of *inspissare*, < L. *in*, in, + *spissare*, thicken, < *spissus*, thick.] To thicken, as by evaporation; make or become dense; condense.—**in-spis-sa′tion** (-spi-sā′shọn), *n.*

in-sta-bil-i-ty (in-stạ-bil′i-ti), *n.* [L. *instabilitas.*] The state of being instable; want of stability or firmness; liability to fall, fail, give way, or suffer change.

in-sta-ble (in-stā′bl), *a.* [L. *instabilis.*] Not stable; lacking stability; unstable.

in-stall (in-stâl′), *v. t.* [ML. *installare*, < *in*, in, + *stallum*, place, seat, stall (from Teut.: see *stall*[2]).] To invest with office by seating in a stall or official seat; hence, to induct into an office, etc., with ceremonies or formalities; also, to establish in any office, position, or place (as, "Mrs. John Dashwood now *installed* herself mistress of Norland": Jane Austen's "Sense and Sensibility," ii.); also, to place in position for service or use, as a system of electric lighting, etc.—**in-stal-la′tion** (-stâ-lā′shọn), *n.* [ML. *installatio(n-)*.] The act of installing, or the fact of being installed; also, a system of machinery or apparatus placed in position for service or use.—**in-stall′er,** *n.*—**in-stal′ment, in-stall′ment,** *n.* The act of installing, or the fact of being installed; installation; also, a seat or place in which one is installed† (see Shakspere's "Merry Wives of Windsor," v. 5. 67); also, any of several parts into which a debt or other sum payable is divided for payment at successive fixed times (as, to pay for furniture by *instalments*; to buy furniture on the *instalment* plan, that is, on condition of paying for it by fixed instalments); a single portion of something furnished or issued by parts at successive times (as, a serial published in six *instalments*).

in-stance (in′stạns), *n.* [OF. F. *instance*, < L. *instantia*, < *instans*: see *instant*.] Urgency in speech or action (archaic); hence, solicitation, instigation, or suggestion (as, to do a thing at the *instance* of some one); also, an impelling motive† (as, "Tell him his fears are shallow, wanting *instance*": Shakspere's "Richard III.," iii. 2. 25); also, the present time†; an instant† or moment†; also, an example put forth in proof or illustration (as, "We may take, perhaps, a foreign *instance* to illustrate this fundamental point in our municipal history," Green's "Short Hist. of the Eng. People," iv. 4; for *instance*, that is, as an example of what has been said); hence, an example or case of anything (as, "Some fresh *instance* of misery or oppression forced itself upon me," Kingsley's "Alton Locke," xxiv.; he is an *instance* of the man who succeeds without effort); sometimes, a case occurring or considered (as, this has happened in three *instances*; it was correct in the first *instance*); also, a proof†, evidence†, sign†, or token† (as, "I beg you to accept a guinea as a small *instance* of my gratitude": Fielding's "Tom Jones," viii. 9); also, legal process (now chiefly in certain expressions: as, a court of first, or of higher, or of last, *instance*).—**in′stance,** *v.*; *-stanced, -stancing.* **I.** *tr.* To exemplify by an instance or as an instance does; also, to cite as an instance or example. **II.** *intr.* To cite an instance.—**in′stan-cy,** *n.* The quality of being instant; urgency or pressing nature; immediateness.

in-stant (in′stạnt). [OF. F. *instant*, < L. *instans* (*instant-*), ppr. of *instare*, stand upon, insist, be at hand, < *in*, in, on, + *stare*, stand.] **I.** *a.* Pressing or urgent (as, "Preach the word; be *instant* in season, out of season," 2 Tim. iv. 2; *instant* necessity); also, present, current, or now passing (as, the 10th *instant*, or *inst.*, the tenth day of the present month); also, close at hand in time, or imminent (as, "The evil which to men in other stations may seem far distant, to him is *instant*, and ever before his eyes": Steele, in "Guardian," 18); also, succeeding without any interval of time, immediate, or instantaneous (as, "The shame itself doth speak For *instant* remedy": Shakspere's "King Lear," i. 4. 268). **II.** *n.* The point of time now present, or present with reference to some action or event; a particular moment; also, an infinitesimal or very short space of time (as, he hesitated for an *instant* only); a moment.—**in′stant,** *adv.* Instantly; at once: as, "You, my sinews, grow not *instant* old, But bear me stiffly up" (Shakspere's "Hamlet," i. 5. 94). [Obs. or archaic.]

in-stan-ta-ne-ous (in-stạn-tā′nē-us), *a.* [From L. *instans* (*instant-*), E. *instant*, + *-aneus* as in *momentaneus*, E. *momentaneous*.] Occurring, done, or completed in an instant (as, "His reason saw With *instantaneous* view the truth of things," Thomson's "To the Memory of Lord Talbot," 27; *instantaneous* photography); also, existing at or pertaining to a particular instant (as, the *instantaneous* position, velocity, or acceleration of something).—**in-stan-ta′ne-ous-ly,** *adv.*—**in-stan-ta′ne-ous-ness,** *n.*

in-stan-ter (in-stan′tėr), *adv.* [L.] Immediately; without delay; at once: as, "I was led *instanter* into the apartment" (Bulwer-Lytton's "Pelham," lxiii.).

in-stant-ly (in′stạnt-li), *adv.* Urgently (archaic: as, "When they came to Jesus, they besought him *instantly*," Luke, vii. 4); also, immediately; at once.

in-star (in-stär′), *v. t.*; *-starred, -starring.* [See *in-*[1].] To place as a star; make a star of; also, to set with or as with stars (as, "The shining circlets of his golden hair . . . *Instarr'd* with gems and gold": Pope's tr. Homer's "Iliad," xvii.).

in-state (in-stāt′), *v. t.*; *-stated, -stating.* [See *in-*[1].] To put into a certain state, condition, or position; install; also, to invest or endow with something† (see Shakspere's "Measure for Measure," v. 1. 429).—**in-state′ment,** *n.*

in-stau-ra-tion (in-stâ-rā′shọn), *n.* [L. *instauratio(n-)*, < *instaurare*, renew, restore, < *in*, in, + *-staurare*, occurring also in *restaurare*, E. *restore*[2]: cf. *store*.] Renewal; restoration; renovation; repair.—**in′stau-ra-tor,** *n.* [LL.] A restorer or renovator.

in-stead (in-sted′), *adv.* [Orig. two words, *in stead*.] In the stead or place (*of*); in lieu (*of*); also, in one's (its, their, etc.) stead.

in-steep (in-stēp′), *v. t.* [See *in-*[1].] To steep in something; imbrue. See Shakspere's "Henry V.," iv. 6. 12. [Poetic.]

in-step (in′step), *n.* [Appar. < *in* + *step*, but with orig. notion uncertain.] The arched upper surface of the human foot between the toes and the ankle; also, the front of the hind leg of a horse, etc., between the hock and the pastern-joint; also, the part of a shoe, stocking, etc., over the instep.

in-sti-gate (in′sti-gāt), *v. t.*; *-gated, -gating.* [L. *instigatus*, pp. of *instigare*, < *in*, in, on, + *-stigare*, akin to *-stinguere*, prick, and prob. to *stimulus*, goad: see *stick*[2], and cf. *dis-*

tinguish, *instinct*, and *stimulus*.] To spur on, set on, or incite to some action or course, now usually to wrong-doing; stimulate; induce; also, to bring about by incitement or persuasion; stir up; foment.—**in-sti-ga′tion** (-gā′shọn), *n.* The act of instigating; incitement, esp. to wrong-doing; also, an incentive.—**in′sti-ga-tor,** *n.*

in-stil, in-still (in-stil′), *v. t.*; *-stilled, -stilling.* [L. *instillare*, < *in*, in, + *stillare*, drop, drip, < *stilla*, a drop.] To put in by drops; introduce drop by drop; hence, to infuse by degrees or slowly into the mind, etc. (as, "How hast thou *instill'd* Thy malice into thousands!" Milton's "Paradise Lost," vi. 269); cause to enter gradually; insinuate.—**in-stil-la′tion** (-sti-lā′shọn), *n.* [L. *instillatio*(*n*-).] The act of instilling; also, something instilled.—**in-stil′ler,** *n.* —**in-stil′ment, in-still′ment,** *n.*

in-stinct (in-stingkt′), *a.* [L. *instinctus*, pp. of *instinguere*, instigate, impel, < *in*, in, on, + *-stinguere*, prick: see *stick*[2], and cf. *distinguish* and *instigate*.] Impelled† or animated† (as, "Thou . . . in the loamy clod Swelling, with vegetative force *instinct* Didst burst thine egg": Cowper's "Yardley Oak," 34); also, imbued or pervaded with something (as, *instinct* with life, grace, beauty, or feeling).—**in′stinct,** *n.* [L. *instinctus*, n., < *instinguere*.] Instigation†; also, innate impulse or natural inclination, or a particular natural inclination or tendency (as, a man who is by *instinct* a musician; "He had . . . neither the grander nor the meaner *instincts* of the born tyrant," Green's "Short Hist. of the Eng. People," viii. 5); specif., the involuntary, unreasoning tendency in animals and human beings, or a particular tendency of this character, whether merely natural (or inherited) or modified by experience, to act in a specific way under given conditions (as, "those almighty *instincts* that propel the migrations of the swallow and the lemming, or the life-withering marches of the locust": De Quincey's "Revolt of the Tartars"); also, a natural aptitude or gift for something (as, to have an *instinct* for color, or for the choice of words).—**in-stinc′tive** (-stingk′tiv), *a.* Pertaining to or of the nature of instinct; prompted by or resulting from instinct.—**in-stinc′tive-ly,** *adv.*

in-sti-tute (in′sti-tūt), *v. t.*; *-tuted, -tuting.* [L. *institutus*, pp. of *instituere*, < *in*, in, on, + *statuere*, set up, set, establish: see *statute*.] To set up or establish; bring into use or practice; hence, to set in operation, as an investigation or legal proceedings; set on foot; inaugurate; initiate; also, to establish in an office or position; specif., in ecclesiastical use, to assign to or invest with a spiritual charge; also, to train† or instruct†.—**in′sti-tute,** *n.* [L. *institutum*, prop. pp. neut.] Something instituted; an established principle, law, custom, or organization; an institution; often, a principle or element of a subject, esp. of jurisprudence; *pl.*, a digest of the elements of a subject, esp. of jurisprudence (as, the *Institutes* of Justinian, an elementary treatise on Roman law compiled under the authority of the emperor Justinian in the 6th century); also, *sing.*, a society or organization for carrying on a particular work, as of literary, scientific, or educational character; hence, the building occupied by such a society.

in-sti-tu-tion (in-sti-tū′shọn), *n.* [L. *institutio*(*n*-).] The act of instituting, or the fact of being instituted; establishment; foundation; specif., the investment of a clergyman with a spiritual charge; formerly, training† or instruction†; also, an established law, custom, usage, practice, organization, etc.; hence, any familiar practice or object (colloq.); esp., an organization or establishment instituted for the promotion of a particular object, usually one for some public, educational, charitable, or similar purpose; hence, the building devoted to its work; also, a principle of a subject†, or (*sing.* or *pl.*) a book of first principles†.—**in-sti-tu′tion-al,** *a.* Of, pertaining to, or established by institution; pertaining to or of the nature of an institution; often, pertaining to institutions or organized societies, or to the buildings devoted to their work (as, *institutional* charity; *institutional* life); also, pertaining to institutes or principles, esp. of jurisprudence.—**in-sti-tu′tion-al-ism,** *n.* Strong attachment to established institutions, as of religion; also, the system of institutions or organized societies for public, charitable, or similar purposes.—**in-sti-tu′tion-al-ize,** *v. t.*; *-ized, -izing.* To render institutional; make into or treat as an institution.—**in-sti-tu′tion-al-ly,** *adv.*—**in-sti-tu′tion-a-ry** (-ā-ri), *a.* Of or pertaining to institution, esp. ecclesiastical institution; pertaining to an institution or institutions; pertaining to instruction or education†; pertaining to legal institutes or principles.

in-sti-tu-tive (in′sti-tū-tiv), *a.* Tending to institute; pertaining to institution; also, instituted or established.—**in′sti-tu-tive-ly,** *adv.*

in-sti-tu-tor (in′sti-tū-tọr), *n.* [L.] One who institutes.

in-stream-ing (in′strē″ming), *n.* A streaming in; an influx; an inflow.—**in′stream″ing,** *a.* Streaming in.

in-struct (in-strukt′), *v. t.* [L. *instructus*, pp. of *instruere*, build, prepare, furnish, instruct, < *in*, in, + *struere*, pile up, build, make.] To prepare† or equip†; also, to furnish with knowledge, esp. by a systematic method; teach; train; educate; also, to furnish with information, inform, or apprise (as, "A power I have, but of what strength and nature I am not yet *instructed*": Shakspere's "Measure for Measure," i. 1. 81); also, to furnish with authoritative directions, direct, or command (as, "If thou dost As this *instructs* thee, thou dost make thy way To noble fortunes": Shakspere's "King Lear," v. 3. 29).—**in-struct′i-ble,** *a.* Capable of being instructed; teachable.—**in-struc′tion** (-struk′shọn), *n.* [L. *instructio*(*n*-).] The act or practice of instructing or teaching; education; enlightenment; knowledge or information imparted, or an item of such knowledge or information; also, a furnishing with authoritative directions; an order or direction (usually in *pl.*: as, "My *instructions* are that this boy is to move on," Dickens's "Bleak House," xix.).—**in-struc′tion-al, in-struc′tion-a-ry** (-ā-ri), *a.* Of or pertaining to instruction; educational. —**in-struc′tive,** *a.* Serving to instruct or inform; conveying instruction, knowledge, or information.—**in-struc′tive-ly,** *adv.*—**in-struc′tive-ness,** *n.*—**in-struc′tor,** *n.* [L.] One who instructs; a teacher; specif., in American colleges, a teacher inferior in rank to a professor.—**in-struc′tor-ship,** *n.* The office or position of an instructor. —**in-struc′tress,** *n.* A female instructor.

in-stru-ment (in′strọ̈-mẹnt), *n.* [OF. F. *instrument*, < L. *instrumentum*, < *instruere*: see *instruct*.] A thing with or by which something is effected (as, "The gods are just, and of our pleasant vices Make *instruments* to plague us": Shakspere's "King Lear," v. 3. 171); a means; an agency; sometimes, a person made use of by another or others for the accomplishment of a purpose (as, "When the Protector wished to put his own brother to death . . . he found a ready *instrument* in Cranmer": Macaulay's "Essays," Hallam); also, a mechanical device or contrivance; a tool; an implement; specif., a contrivance for producing musical sounds (as, a stringed *instrument*; a wind-*instrument*); also, a formal legal document, as a contract, deed, grant, etc.—**in′stru-ment** (-ment), *v. t.* In *music*, to score or arrange (a piece of music) for instruments, esp. for an orchestra.—**in-stru-men′tal** (-men′tạl), *a.* Of or pertaining to an instrument; also, performed on or written for a musical instrument or musical instruments (as, *instrumental* music); also, serving as an instrument or means (as, "My chief inducement . . . was to be *instrumental* in forwarding your happiness": Goldsmith's "She Stoops to Conquer," ii.); conducive; serviceable; in *gram.*, noting or pertaining to a case in some languages, as Sanskrit, serving to indicate the instrument or means.—**in-stru-men′tal-ism,** *n.* In *philos.*, the theory that the function of thought is to be instrumental to control of the environment, or that ideas have value according to their function in human experience or progress.—**in-stru-men′tal-ist,** *n.* One who performs on a musical instrument; in *philos.*, an advocate of instrumentalism.—**in-stru-men-tal-is′tic,** *a.* In *philos.*, pertaining to instrumentalists or instrumentalism.—**in″stru-men-tal′i-ty** (-tal′i-ti), *n.*; pl. *-ties* (-tiz). The quality of being instrumental; the fact or function of serving for the accomplishment of some purpose; agency; also, a means or agency.—**in-stru-men′tal-ly,** *adv.*—**in′stru-men-tate** (-tāt), *v. t.*; *-tated, -tating.* In *music*, to instrument.—**in″stru-men-ta′tion** (-tā′shọn), *n.* The use of, or work done by, instruments; also, instrumental agency; instrumentality; also, the composing or arranging of music for instruments, esp. for an orchestra.

in-sub-or-di-nate (in-sub-ôr′di-nạt). [See *in-*²·] **I.** *a.* Not subordinate; not submitting to authority; disobedient. **II.** *n.* One who is insubordinate.—**in-sub-or-di-na′tion** (-nā′shọn), *n.*

in-sub-stan-tial (in-sub-stan′shạl), *a.* [ML. *insubstantialis.*] Not substantial; lacking substance; slight; without reality; unreal.—**in-sub-stan-ti-al′i-ty** (-shi-al′i-ti), *n.*

in-suf-fer-a-ble (in-suf′ėr-ạ-bl), *a.* [See *in-*².] Not sufferable; intolerable; unbearable: as, "A sense of *insufferable* gloom pervaded my spirit" (Poe's "Fall of the House of Usher").—**in-suf′fer-a-ble-ness,** *n.*—**in-suf′fer-a-bly,** *adv.*

in-suf-fi-cient (in-su-fish′ẹnt), *a.* [LL. *insufficiens* (*-ent-*).] Not sufficient; lacking in what is necessary or required; deficient in force, quality, or amount; inadequate.—**in-suf-fi′cience, in-suf-fi′cien-cy,** *n.*—**in-suf-fi′cient-ly,** *adv.*

in-suf-flate (in-suf′lāt or in′su-flāt), *v. t.*; *-flated, -flating.* [LL. *insufflatus*, pp. of *insufflare*, < L. *in*, in, on, + *sufflare*, blow up, blow: see *sufflate.*] To blow or breathe (something) in; also, to breathe upon, as in exorcism; specif., in *med.*, to blow (air or a medicinal substance) into some opening or upon some part of the body; treat by insufflation.—**in-suf-fla′tion** (-su-flā′shọn), *n.* [LL. *insufflatio*(*n-*).] The act of insufflating; also, the condition of being distended with air; specif., *eccles.*, the act or ceremony of breathing upon a person or thing to symbolize the influence of the Holy Ghost and the expulsion of evil spirits; in *med.*, the blowing of air into the lungs to induce respiration, or of a gas, vapor, etc., into some opening or upon some part of the body.—**in′suf-fla-tor,** *n.* One who or that which insufflates; an injector for blowing air into a furnace; a medical instrument for use in insufflation.

in-su-lar (in′ṣụ̄-lạ̈r), *a.* [LL. *insularis*, < L. *insula*, island.] Of or pertaining to an island or islands; dwelling or situated on an island (as, "There now is your *insular* city of the Manhattoes, belted round by wharves": H. Melville's "Moby-Dick," i.); also, forming an island; hence, detached, or standing alone; also, characteristic or suggestive of inhabitants of an island; often, narrow or illiberal (as, *insular* prejudices); specif., in *pathol.*, occurring in or characterized by one or more isolated spots, patches, or the like.—**in′su-lar-ism,** *n.* Insular quality or character; narrowness of ideas or opinions.—**in-su-lar′i-ty** (-lar′i-ti), *n.* Insular state or character; the condition of being an island; the condition of living on an island; narrowness of mind, views, etc., suggestive of inhabitants of an island.—**in′su-lar-ly,** *adv.*

in-su-late (in′ṣụ̄-lāt), *v. t.*; *-lated, -lating.* [L. *insulatus*, made into an island, < *insula*, island.] To make into an island; hence, to cause to stand detached from surroundings; set or place apart; isolate; in *physics*, etc., to separate by the interposition of a non-conductor, in order to prevent the transfer of electricity or heat; cover or surround (an electric wire, etc.) with non-conducting material.—**in-su-la′tion** (-lā′shọn), *n.* The act of insulating, or the resulting state; also, material used for insulating; non-conducting material.—**in′su-la-tor,** *n.* One who or that which insulates; a non-conductor; a contrivance, as of glass or porcelain, for supporting electric wires without carrying off the current.

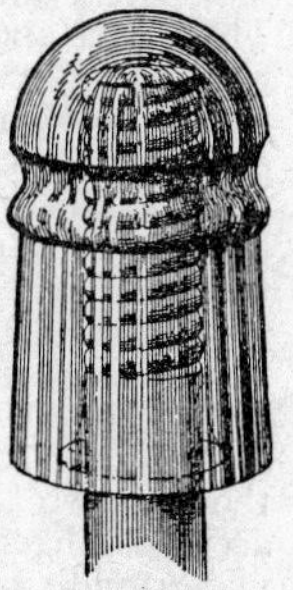
Glass Insulator for Electric Wires.

in-su-lin (in′ṣụ̄-lin), *n.* [L. *insula*, island: with reference to the islands of the pancreas.] In *med.*, an extract obtained from the pancreas of animals (which apparently contains the internal secretion of this organ, furnished by its 'islands'), used in the treatment of diabetes, and causing a reduction of the amount of sugar in the blood and urine. [Proprietary name.]

in-sult (in-sult′), *v.* [L. *insultare*, leap on or at, insult, freq. of *insilire*, leap into or on, < *in*, in, on, + *salire*, leap.] **I.** *intr.* To behave with insolent triumph; exult arrogantly or contemptuously: as, "So he walks, *insulting* o'er his prey" (Shakspere's "3 Henry VI.," i. 3. 14). [Obs. or archaic.] **II.** *tr.* To treat insolently or with contemptuous rudeness; offer a scornful or wanton affront to, whether by action or by speech; also, to attack, assault, or assail (obs. or rare).—**in′sult,** *n.* The act or an act of insulting; an insolent or contemptuously rude action or speech; a wanton affront; something having the effect of an affront (as, "Ten shillings would have been an *insult* to the old fellow": Dunsany's "If," i. 2); also, an attack or assault (obs. or rare: as, "Many a rude tower and rampart there Repell'd the *insult* of the air," Scott's "Marmion," vi. 2).—**in-sult′a-ble,** *a.* That may be insulted; quick to feel insult.—**in-sul-ta′tion** (-sul-tā′shọn), *n.* [L. *insultatio*(*n-*).] The act of insulting; insulting behavior or speech. [Obs. or archaic.]—**in-sult′er,** *n.*—**in-sult′ing-ly,** *adv.*

in-su-per-a-ble (in-sū′pėr-ạ-bl), *a.* [L. *insuperabilis*: cf. *superable.*] Not superable; not to be passed over or overcome; insurmountable: as, an *insuperable* barrier; "an *insuperable* aversion to all kinds of profitable labor" (Irving's "Sketch-Book," Rip Van Winkle).—**in-su″per-a-bil′i-ty** (-bil′i-ti), **in-su′per-a-ble-ness,** *n.*—**in-su′per-a-bly,** *adv.*

in-sup-port-a-ble (in-su-pōr′tạ-bl), *a.* [LL. *insupportabilis*, < L. *in-*, not, + *supportare*, E. *support.*] That cannot be supported or endured; insufferable; intolerable.—**in-sup-port′a-ble-ness,** *n.*—**in-sup-port′a-bly,** *adv.*

in-sup-pos-a-ble (in-su-pō′zạ-bl), *a.* [See *in-*².] Not supposable; that cannot be supposed.

in-sup-press-i-ble (in-su-pres′i-bl), *a.* [See *in-*².] Not suppressible; not to be suppressed; irrepressible.—**in-sup-press′i-bly,** *adv.*—**in-sup-pres′sive,** *a.* Insuppressible: as, "*insuppressive* joy on every face" (Browning's "Colombe's Birthday," ii.). [Obs. or archaic.]

in-sur-a-ble (in-shör′ạ-bl), *a.* Capable of being insured, as against risk of loss or harm; proper to be insured.—**in-sur-a-bil′i-ty** (-bil′i-ti), *n.*

in-sur-ance (in-shör′ạns), *n.* The act of insuring; specif., the act, system, or business of insuring property, life, the person, etc., against loss or harm arising in specified contingencies, as fire, accident, death, disablement, or the like, in consideration of a payment proportioned to the risk involved; the contract thus made, set forth in a written or printed agreement (*policy*); also, the sum (*premium*) paid for insuring a thing; also, the amount for which anything is insured.—**in-sur′ant,** *n.* The person who takes out an insurance policy.

in-sure (in-shör′), *v.*; *-sured, -suring.* [Var. of *ensure.*] **I.** *tr.* To ensure, or make sure, secure, or certain (see *ensure*); specif., to guarantee against risk of loss or harm; secure indemnity to or on, in case of loss, damage, or death; issue or procure an insurance policy on. **II.** *intr.* To issue or procure an insurance policy.—**in-sur′er,** *n.*

in-sur-gent (in-sėr′jẹnt). [L. *insurgens* (*-ent-*), ppr. of *insurgere* (pp. *insurrectus*), rise on or up, < *in*, in, on, + *surgere*, rise.] **I.** *a.* Rising in revolt; rebellious. **II.** *n.* One who is insurgent; a rebel; in *U. S. politics*, a member of a section of a political party that revolts against the methods of the party.—**in-sur′gence, in-sur′gen-cy,** *n.*

in-sur-mount-a-ble (in-sėr-moun′tạ-bl), *a.* [See *in-*².] Not surmountable; that cannot be surmounted, passed over, or overcome.—**in-sur-mount′a-bly,** *adv.*

in-sur-rec-tion (in-su-rek′shọn), *n.* [LL. *insurrectio*(*n-*), < L. *insurgere*: see *insurgent.*] The act of rising in arms or open resistance against civil or established authority; also, an instance of this; a revolt; an incipient or limited rebellion.—**in-sur-rec′tion-al,** *a.* Of or pertaining to insurrection.—**in-sur-rec′tion-al-ly,** *adv.*—**in-sur-rec′tion-a-ry** (-ā-ri). **I.** *a.* Pertaining to or of the nature of insurrection; given to insurrection. **II.** *n.*; pl. *-ries* (-riz). One who engages in insurrection; an insurgent.—**in-sur-rec′tion-ism,** *n.* The principle of insurrection against constituted authority.—**in-sur-rec′tion-ist,** *n.* One who engages in or advocates insurrection.

in-sur-rec-to (ēn-sör-rek′tō), *n.*; pl. *-tos* (Sp. -tōs). [Sp.] An insurgent.

in-sus-cep-ti-ble (in-su-sep′ti-bl), *a.* [See *in-*².] Not susceptible; not admitting (*of*); not accessible or sensitive (*to*); unsusceptible.—**in-sus-cep-ti-bil′i-ty** (-bil′i-ti), *n.*

in-swathe (in-swāᴛʜ′), *v. t.* Same as *enswathe.*

in-tact (in-takt′), *a.* [L. *intactus*, < *in-*, not, + *tactus*, pp. of *tangere*, touch.] Untouched or unaffected by anything that might harm or impair; remaining uninjured, unaltered, sound, or whole: as, dishes left *intact* after a fall; the main body of the text is *intact*; this sum is still *intact*.—**in-tact′-ness,** *n.*

in-ta-glio (in-tal′yō), *n.*; pl. *intaglios* (-yōz). [It., < *intagliare*, cut in, engrave, < L. *in*, in, + ML. *taliare*, cut: see *tail*[1].] Incised carving, as opposed to carving in relief; ornamentation with a figure or design sunk below the surface; also, a figure or design so produced; also, a gem, seal, piece of jewelry, or the like cut with an incised or sunken design (as, "He had also a seal ring, a veritable antique *intaglio*": Irving's "Tales of a Traveler," iii. 2).—**in-ta′-glio,** *v. t.*; pp. *-glioed*. To carve or execute in intaglio.

in-take (in′tāk), *n.* The act of taking in; also, that which is taken in; a piece of land inclosed from a moor, common, etc., or reclaimed from tidal waters (chiefly north. Eng.); also, the point at which a fluid is taken into a channel, pipe, etc.; also, a narrowing or contraction, as in a tube or a stocking, or the point at which this begins.

in-tan-gi-ble (in-tan′ji-bl), *a.* [See *in-*[2].] Not tangible; incapable of being perceived by the sense of touch, as incorporeal or immaterial things; fig., not to be grasped mentally, or not definite or clear to the mind.—**in-tan-gi-bil′i-ty** (-bil′i-ti), **in-tan′gi-ble-ness,** *n.*—**in-tan′gi-bly,** *adv.*

in-te-ger (in′tẹ-jėr), *n.* [L. *integer*, untouched, whole, entire, sound, pure, upright, < *in-*, not, + *tag-*, root of *tangere*, touch: cf. *entire*.] A complete entity; specif., a whole number, as distinguished from a fraction or a mixed number.

in-te-gra-ble (in′tẹ-grạ-bl), *a.* Capable of being integrated. —**in″te-gra-bil′i-ty** (-bil′i-ti), *n.*

in-te-gral (in′tẹ-grạl). [ML. *integralis*, < L. *integer*: see *integer*.] **I.** *a.* Of or pertaining to a whole; belonging as a part to the whole; constituent or component; often, necessary to the completeness of the whole; also, made up of parts which together constitute a whole; hence, entire or complete; in *math.*, pertaining to or being an integer; not fractional; also, pertaining to or involving integrals (as, *integral* calculus: see *calculus*). **II.** *n.* An integral whole; a whole, either as made up of parts or as lacking no part; in *math.*, the result of the operation inverse to differentiation (see *integration*); an expression from which a given function, equation, or system of equations is derived by differentiation.—**in-te-gral′i-ty** (-gral′i-ti), *n.* Integral state or character; entirety.—**in′te-gral-ly,** *adv.*

in-te-grand (in′tẹ-grand), *n.* [L. *integrandus*, gerundive of *integrare*: see *integrate*.] In *math.*, the expression to be integrated.

in-te-grant (in′tẹ-grạnt). [L. *integrans* (*-ant-*), ppr. of *integrare*: see *integrate*.] **I.** *a.* Making up, or belonging as a part to, a whole; constituent; component. **II.** *n.* An integrant part; a component.

in-te-grate (in′tẹ-grāt), *v. t.*; *-grated*, *-grating*. [L. *integratus*, pp. of *integrare*, make whole, < *integer*: see *integer*.] To make up or complete as a whole, as parts do; also, to bring together (parts) into a whole; also, to indicate the total amount or the mean value of; in *math.*, to find the integral of.—**in′te-grate,** *a.* Entire; complete; also, composite.—**in-te-gra′tion** (-grā′shọn), *n.* [L. *integratio*(*n-*).] The act of integrating; combination into an integral whole; in specif. uses, unification of diverse elements into a complex whole or a harmonious relation; harmonization; behavior, as of the individual, in harmony with the environment; in *math.*, the operation of finding the integral of a function or equation; the inverse of differentiation.—**in′te-gra-tive** (-grạ-tiv), *a.* Tending to integrate.—**in′te-gra-tor** (-grā-tọr), *n.* One who or that which integrates; esp., an instrument for indicating the total amount or mean value of something, as area, temperature, etc.

in-teg-ri-ty (in-teg′ri-ti), *n.* [L. *integritas*, < *integer*: see *integer*.] The state of being whole, entire, or undiminished (as, to preserve the *integrity* of an empire); also, sound, unimpaired, or perfect condition; also, soundness of moral principle and character; uprightness; honesty.

in-teg-u-ment (in-teg′ū-mẹnt), *n.* [L. *integumentum*, < *integere*, cover, < *in*, in, on, + *tegere*, cover.] A covering or investment, esp. of an animal or vegetable body; a skin, shell, rind, or the like.—**in-teg-u-men′ta-ry** (-men′tạ-ri), *a.* Of, pertaining to, or of the nature of an integument.

in-tel-lect (in′te-lekt), *n.* [L. *intellectus*, < *intellegere*: see *intelligent*.] The power or faculty of the mind by which one knows or understands, in distinction from that by which one feels and that by which one wills; the understanding; also, understanding or mental capacity, esp. of a high order (as, men of *intellect*; "The only human quality that interested Sidonia was *Intellect*," Disraeli's "Coningsby," iv. 10); also, a particular mind or intelligence, esp. of a high order, or the person possessing it (as, a problem that occupied the greatest *intellects* of the time); sometimes, minds collectively, as of a number of persons, or the persons themselves (as, the *intellect* of the time); also, *pl.*, the mental faculties, or wits (archaic: as, "Our unfortunate patron was at times disordered in his *intellects*," Godwin's "Caleb Williams," i.).

in-tel-lec-tion (in-te-lek′shọn), *n.* [ML. *intellectio*(*n-*), < L. *intellegere*: see *intelligent*.] The action or process of understanding; the exercise of the intellect; a particular act of the intellect (as, "The immortality of man is as legitimately preached from the *intellections* as from the moral volitions": Emerson's "Essays," Intellect); also, a conception or idea as the result of such an act.—**in-tel-lec′-tive,** *a.* Having power to understand; intelligent; also, of or pertaining to the intellect.

in-tel-lec-tu-al (in-te-lek′tū-ạl). [L. *intellectualis*, < *intellectus*, E. *intellect*.] **I.** *a.* Of or pertaining to the intellect (as, *intellectual* powers or processes); appealing to or engaging the intellect (as, *intellectual* pleasures or pursuits); directed or inclined toward things that involve the intellect (as, *intellectual* tastes; "ladies *intellectual*," Byron's "Don Juan," i. 22); also, possessing or showing intellect or mental capacity, esp. to a high degree (as, an *intellectual* being; an *intellectual* writer or book); characterized by or suggesting a predominance of intellect (as, an *intellectual* type of mind; an *intellectual* face). **II.** *n.* The intellectual faculty†, or mind†; *pl.*, the mental faculties, or wits (archaic: as, "those instructions . . . being too refined for the *intellectuals* of their workmen," Swift's "Gulliver's Travels," iii. 2); also, things pertaining to the intellect; also, *sing.*, an intellectual being or person; specif., a person of the intellectual class, as in a community; a member of a class or group professing or supposed to possess enlightened judgment and opinions with respect to public or political questions (often in *pl.*).—**in-tel-lec′tu-al-ism,** *n.* The doctrine that knowledge is wholly or chiefly derived from pure reason; also, the exercise of the intellect; devotion to intellectual pursuits. —**in-tel-lec′tu-al-ist,** *n.*—**in-tel-lec-tu-al′i-ty** (-al′i-ti), *n.*; pl. *-ties* (-tiz). [LL. *intellectualitas*.] The quality of being intellectual; intellectual character or power; also, an intellectual person.—**in-tel-lec′tu-al-ize** (-ạl-īz), *v. t.* or *i.*; *-ized*, *-izing*. To make or become intellectual.—**in-tel-lec″tu-al-i-za′tion** (-i-zā′shọn), *n.*—**in-tel-lec′tu-al-ly,** *adv.* —**in-tel-lec′tu-al-ness,** *n.*

in-tel-li-gence (in-tel′i-jẹns), *n.* [L. *intelligentia*, *intellegentia*, < *intelligens*, *intellegens*: see *intelligent*.] The faculty of understanding; the mind; also, a mind or intelligent agency (as, "having recourse to a mind or supreme *intelligence* as the first cause of all": Hume's "Natural Hist. of Religion," iv.); hence, an intelligent being, esp. an incorporeal one, or spirit (as, "The great *Intelligences* fair That range above our mortal state": Tennyson's "In Memoriam," lxxxv.); also, capacity for understanding (as, a person of great or of little *intelligence*); esp., good mental capacity; quickness in grasping truth, facts, meaning, etc. (as, to display *intelligence*; a task requiring *intelligence*); also, understanding or knowledge of a thing or subject (archaic: as, "Of lakes he had *intelligence*, He knew something of heath and fell," Shelley's "Peter Bell the Third," v. 11); also, knowledge of an event, circumstance, state of affairs, etc., received or imparted; news or tidings; information (see phrases following); also, interchange of information, thoughts, etc., or communication (obs. or rare: as, to be accused of having *intelligence* with the enemy); also, mutual understanding, or relations between persons or parties (obs. or rare: as, to maintain good *intelligence* with an ally).—**intelligence bureau,** a bureau of information on particular matters.—**intelligence department,** a department of information; esp., a governmental department charged with obtaining information, as for the use of the army or navy.—**intelligence office,** an intelligence bureau; esp., an office where servants or other employees may be hired.—**intelligence officer,** an officer in the service of an intelligence department.—**intelligence quotient,** in *psychol.*, of a child (under the age of the normal or average limit of the growth of intelligence), the mental age divided by the actual age: as, a child with a mental age of 12 years and an actual age of 10 years has an *intelligence quotient* of 1.2 (or 120%), and is above the average intelligence for his age. Cf. *mental age*, under *mental*^{2}, *a.*—**in-tel′li-gen-cer** (-jẹn-sėr), *n.* One who or that which conveys intelligence or information (sometimes used, esp. formerly, as the name of a newspaper); specif., an informer; a spy.

in-tel-li-gent (in-tel′i-jẹnt), *a.* [L. *intelligens* (*-ent-*), for *intellegens*, ppr. of *intellegere*, also *intelligere*, discern, understand, < *inter*, between, + *legere*, gather, choose, see, read.] Having the faculty of understanding (as, an *intelligent* being); also, having a good understanding or mental capacity, or quick to understand, as persons or animals; acute, sagacious, or bright; showing quickness of understanding, as actions, utterances, etc.; also, having understanding or knowledge (*of*: obs. or rare: as, "The association of these masters with each other, and with men *intelligent* of their merits, is mutually agreeable and stimulating," Emerson's "Essays," Manners); also, imparting or conveying intelligence or information† (as, "Our posts shall be swift and *intelligent* betwixt us": Shakspere's "King Lear," iii. 7. 12).

in-tel-li-gen-tial (in-tel-i-jen′shạl), *a.* Of or pertaining to the intelligence or understanding; also, endowed with intelligence (as, an *intelligential* being); also, conveying intelligence or information.

in-tel-li-gent-ly (in-tel′i-jẹnt-li), *adv.* In an intelligent manner; with intelligence or quickness of understanding.

in-tel-li-gen-tsi-a (in-tel-i-gent′si-ạ̈), *n.* [Russ., < L. *intelligentia*, E. *intelligence*.] In Russian use, the class or body of persons representing, or professing to represent, the superior intelligence or enlightened opinion of the country on public or political questions; the intellectuals; hence, in general use, a class or group of persons professing or affecting special enlightenment in views or principles.

in-tel-li-gi-ble (in-tel′i-ji-bl), *a.* [L. *intelligibilis*, for *intellegibilis*, < *intellegere*: see *intelligent*.] Capable of being understood; comprehensible; in *philos.*, capable of being apprehended by the understanding only, not by the senses.—**in-tel″li-gi-bil′i-ty** (-bil′i-ti), **in-tel′li-gi-ble-ness,** *n.*—**in-tel′li-gi-bly,** *adv.*

in-tem-er-ate (in-tem′ẹ-rạt), *a.* [L. *intemeratus*, < *in-*, not, + *temeratus*, pp. of *temerare*, violate.] Inviolate; undefiled; unsullied; pure. [Now rare.]

in-tem-per-ance (in-tem′pėr-ạns), *n.* [L. *intemperantia*.] Lack of temperance, moderation, or due restraint, as in action or speech; immoderation; excess; esp., excessive indulgence of a natural appetite or passion (as, "*Intemperance* . . . In meats and drinks": Milton's "Paradise Lost," xi. 472); specif., immoderate indulgence in intoxicating drink; excessive drinking of alcoholic liquors; also, severity of climate, weather, or the like†.

in-tem-per-ate (in-tem′pėr-ạt), *a.* [L. *intemperatus*.] Not temperate; immoderate, unrestrained, or unbridled (as, "Use not thy mouth to *intemperate* swearing": Ecclus. xxiii. 13); immoderate as regards indulgence of appetite or passion; given to or characterized by immoderate indulgence in intoxicating drink; extreme in temperature, as climate, etc.—**in-tem′per-ate-ly,** *adv.*—**in-tem′per-ate-ness,** *n.*

in-tem-pes-tive (in-tem-pes′tiv), *a.* [L. *intempestivus*, < *in-*, not, + *tempestivus*, timely, < *tempestas*, time, season: see *tempest*.] Untimely; unseasonable; inopportune.

in-tend (in-tend′), *v.* [OF. F. *entendre*, < L. *intendere* (pp. *intentus*, also *intensus*), stretch out, extend, direct, attend, purpose, intend, < *in*, in, on, + *tendere*, stretch, E. *tend*^{1}.] **I.** *tr.* To stretch out† or extend†; stretch† or strain†; also, to direct (one's course, etc.: archaic: as, "Cæsar through Syria *Intends* his journey," Shakspere's "Antony and Cleopatra," v. 2. 201); direct (the eyes, mind, etc.: archaic: as, "Let him *intend* his mind without respite, without rest, in one direction," Emerson's "Essays," Intellect); also, to direct or devote the attention to† (as, "Herodicus, who did nothing all his life long but *intend* his health": Bacon's "Advancement of Learning," ii. 20. 11); now, commonly, to have in mind as something willed to be done or brought about (as, to *intend* an action; to *intend* to do a thing, or that a thing shall be done; "I *intend* the good of mine own countrymen," 2 Mac. xiv. 8); purpose, design, or mean; often, to design or mean for a particular purpose, use, lot, recipient, etc., or destine (as, a book *intended* for reference or for advanced students; nature *intended* him for a better fate); design to express or indicate, or mean (as, what, or whom, did you *intend* by that last speech?); of words, etc., to signify or indicate (obs. or rare: as, "The thesis which thy words *intend* — That to begin implies to end," Tennyson's "Two Voices," 338); also, to assert†, profess†, or pretend† (as, "*Intend* a kind of zeal both to the prince and Claudio": Shakspere's "Much Ado about Nothing," ii. 2. 35). **II.** *intr.* To direct one's course†, or set out on one's course† (as, to *intend* homeward; to *intend* for France); also, to direct or devote the attention, as to a matter†; also, to have a purpose or design (as, he may *intend* otherwise).

in-tend-ance (in-ten′dạns), *n.* [F.] The function of an intendant; superintendence; also, a department of the public service, as in France, or the officials in charge of it; also, the official quarters of an intendant.—**in-tend′an-cy** (-ten′dạn-si), *n.*; pl. *-cies* (-siz). The office or function of an intendant; also, a body of intendants; also, a district under the charge of an intendant.

in-tend-ant (in-ten′dạnt), *n.* [F., < L. *intendens* (*-ent-*), ppr. of *intendere*: see *intend*.] One who has the direction or management of some public business, the affairs of an establishment, etc.; a superintendent: specif. used as the title of various public officials in France and other countries.

in-tend-ed (in-ten′ded). **I.** *p. a.* Purposed or designed (as, to produce the *intended* effect); determined upon; hence, prospective (as, one's *intended* husband or wife). **II.** *n.* An intended husband or wife. [Colloq.]—**in-tend′ed-ly,** *adv.* Purposely; designedly.

in-tend-er (in-ten′dėr), *n.* One who intends.

in-tend-ment (in-tend′mẹnt), *n.* [OF. F. *entendement*, < *entendre*, E. *intend*.] Understanding† or intelligence†; also, manner of understanding, construing, or viewing something (now legal: as, in the *intendment* of law, according to the understanding or view of the law); also, signification or import (obs. or rare); also, intention† or design† (as, "We . . . fear the main *intendment* of the Scot": Shakspere's "Henry V.," i. 2. 144).

in-ten-er-ate (in-ten′ẹ-rāt), *v. t.*; *-ated*, *-ating*. [L. *in*, in, + *tener*, soft, E. *tender*^{2}.] To make soft or tender; soften: as, "Thus she [nature] contrives to *intenerate* the granite and felspar" (Emerson's "Essays," Compensation). [Now rare.]—**in-ten-er-a′tion** (-ẹ-rā′shọn), *n.*

in-ten-sate (in-ten′sāt), *v. t.*; *-sated*, *-sating*. To intensify.—**in-ten-sa′tion** (-sā′shọn), *n.*—**in-ten′sa-tive** (-sạ-tiv), *a.* and *n.* Same as *intensive*.

in-tense (in-tens′), *a.* [OF. F. *intense*, < L. *intensus*, stretched tight, intense, pp. of *intendere*: see *intend*.] Existing or occurring in a high or extreme degree (as, *intense* light, color, heat, or cold; an *intense* strain); hence, having the characteristic qualities in a high degree (as, "the *intense*, clear, star-sown vault of heaven," M. Arnold's "Self-Dependence"; "All is concenter'd in a life *intense*, Where not a beam, nor air, nor leaf is lost, But hath a part of being," Byron's "Childe Harold," iii. 89); in general, of an extreme kind; very great, strong, keen, severe, etc.; strenuous or earnest, as activity, exertion, diligence, thought, etc.; acute, strong, or vehement, as sensations, feelings, or emotions; hence, having or showing great strength or vehemence of feeling, as a person, the face, language, etc.; in *photog.*, dense.—**in-tense′ly,** *adv.*—**in-tense′ness,** *n.*

in-ten-si-fi-ca-tion (in-ten″si-fi-kā′shọn), *n.* The act of intensifying, or the state of being intensified.

in-ten-si-fy (in-ten′si-fī), *v. t.* or *i.*; *-fied*, *-fying*. [See *-fy*.] To make or become intense or more intense; in *photog.*, to make or become denser or more opaque, as a negative.—**in-ten′si-fi-er** (-fī-ėr), *n.*

in-ten-sion (in-ten′shọn), *n.* [L. *intensio*(*n-*), < *intendere*: see *intend*.] A stretching or straining (obs. or rare); fig., exertion of the mind; attention; determination; also, intensification, or increase in degree; intensity, or high degree; relative intensity, or degree; in *logic*, the sum of the attributes contained in a concept or connoted by a term (cf. *extension*).

in-ten-si-ty (in-ten′si-ti), *n.*; pl. *-ties* (-tiz). The quality or condition of being intense; high or extreme degree, as of light or cold; great energy, strength, vehemence, etc., as of activity, thought, or feeling; also, the degree or extent to which something is intense; relative force or strength; in *physics*, magnitude, as of a force, per unit of area, volume, etc.; in *elect.*, the strength of an electric current in amperes; in *photog.*, density.

in-ten-sive (in-ten′siv). [F. *intensif*, < L. *intendere*: see *intend.*] **I.** *a.* Of, pertaining to, or characterized by intensity; specif., noting or pertaining to a system involving operations carried on by more laborious or more expensive methods designed to result in a high degree of effectiveness, as in the cultivation of land (as of a small area, where land is expensive) by thorough tillage, the application of fertilizers, etc., so as to secure the most from each acre (opposed to *extensive*); also, increasing in intensity or degree, as successive inoculations of a virus; also, increasing the intensity; intensifying; in *gram.*, expressing increase of intensity; serving to give force or emphasis. **II.** *n.* Something that intensifies; in *gram.*, an intensive word, prefix, etc.—**in-ten′sive-ly,** *adv.*—**in-ten′sive-ness,** *n.*

in-tent[1] (in-tent′), *a.* [L. *intentus*, stretched, strained, attentive, intent, pp. of *intendere*: see *intend.*] Fixed with strained or earnest attention, as the eyes or gaze, the mind or thoughts, etc. (often with *on* or *upon*); earnest; also, having the gaze or thoughts earnestly fixed on something (as, to be *intent* on, or upon, one's book or reading; to be *intent* on a task); attentively or sedulously engaged; often, bent, as on some object or purpose in view (as, to be *intent* on gain, or on revenge).

in-tent[2] (in-tent′), *n.* [OF. *entent*, *entente* (F. *entente*), < L. *intendere*: see *intend.*] An intending or purposing, as to commit some act (as, to do a thing with *intent*, or with criminal *intent*; to shoot with *intent* to kill); intention; a particular intention or design (as, "The word of God . . . is a discerner of the thoughts and *intents* of the heart": Heb. iv. 12); also, the end or object intended (as, "Jehu did it in subtilty, to the *intent* that he might destroy the worshippers of Baal," 2 Kings, x. 19; to all *intents* and purposes, see phrase following); also, meaning or import (as, "I have received New-dated letters . . . Their cold *intent*, tenour and substance, thus": Shakspere's "2 Henry IV.," iv. 1. 9).—**to all intents and purposes,** for all the ends and purposes in view; for all practical purposes; practically: as, the revised edition is *to all intents and purposes* a new book.

in-ten-tion (in-ten′shọn), *n.* [OF. *entencion* (F. *intention*), < L. *intentio(n-)*, < *intendere*: see *intend.*] The directing of the eyes, mind, or attention on something (obs. or rare); also, the act or fact of intending or purposing (as, to do a thing without *intention*; to seek proof of *intention* in the case of damage done); a determining mentally upon some action or result; a purpose or design (as, to reveal or to carry out an *intention*; "Sir, Hell is paved with good *intentions*," Johnson, in Boswell's "Johnson," April, 1775); *pl.*, purposes with respect to a proposal of marriage (colloq.); *sing.*, the end or object intended (as, the chief *intention* of the builders, or of the structure, was stability); also, meaning or import, as of words or statements; in *surg.* and *med.*, a manner or process of healing, as in the healing of a lesion or fracture without granulation ('healing by first intention') or the healing of a wound by granulation after suppuration ('healing by second intention'); in *logic*, a general concept.—**in-ten′tion-al,** *a.* Of or pertaining to intention or purpose; esp., done with intention or on purpose; intended; designed.—**in-ten′tion-al-ly,** *adv.*—**in-ten′tioned,** *a.* Having intentions (as specified): as, well-*intentioned*.—**in-ten′tion-less,** *a.* Without intention.

in-ten-tive (in-ten′tiv), *a.* [OF. *ententif*, < L. *intendere*: see *intend.*] Attentive; intent. [Obs. or archaic.]

in-tent-ly (in-tent′li), *adv.* In an intent manner; with earnest attention.—**in-tent′ness,** *n.*

in-ter (in-tėr′), *v. t.*; *-terred*, *-terring*. [OF. F. *enterrer*, < ML. *interrare*, < L. *in*, in, + *terra*, earth.] To put into the earth or ground (now only as in the following use); esp., to deposit (a dead body, etc.) in a grave or tomb; bury, esp. with ceremonies; inhume.

inter-. [L. *inter-*, repr. *inter*, adv. and prep., between, among, during, a compar. form < *in*, in: cf. Skt. *antar*, within, between.] A prefix of Latin origin, meaning 'between,' 'among,' 'mutually,' 'reciprocally,' 'together,' freely used as an English formative, as in *interblend*, *intercellular*, *intercity*, *interflow*, *intergrowth*, *interlay*, *intermarry*, *inter-oceanic*, *interstate*, *interweave*.

in-ter-act (in′tėr-akt), *n.* [See *inter-*.] An interval between two acts of a play, etc.; a short performance between two acts; hence, any intermediate time or employment.—**in-ter-act′,** *v. i.* To act on each other.—**in-ter-ac′tion** (-ak′shọn), *n.* Action on each other; reciprocal action.—**in-ter-ac′tive,** *a.* Interacting; reciprocally active.

in-ter-a-gent (in-tėr-ā′jẹnt), *n.* [See *inter-*.] An intermediate agent; an intermediary.—**in-ter-a′gen-cy,** *n.*

in-ter-al-lied (in″tėr-ạ-līd′), *a.* Between or among allied powers or nations, esp. the Allies of the World War: as, an *interallied* conference; *interallied* debts.

in-ter-am-ni-an (in-tėr-am′ni-ạn), *a.* [LL. *interamnus*, < L. *inter*, between, + *amnis*, river.] Lying or situated between rivers (as Mesopotamia).

in-ter-bed (in-tėr-bed′), *v. t.*; *-bedded*, *-bedding*. [See *inter-*.] To interstratify: used chiefly in the passive.

in-ter-blend (in-tėr-blend′), *v. t.* or *i.*; *-blended* or *-blent*, *-blending*. [See *inter-*.] To blend, one with another.

in-ter-bor-ough (in-tėr-bur′ọ̄, also in′tėr-bur″ọ̄), *a.* [See *inter-*.] Between boroughs: as, an *interborough* railway.

in-ter-bra-chi-al (in-tėr-brā′ki-ạl), *a.* [See *inter-* and *brachium.*] In *zoöl.*, between the brachia or arms, as of a starfish or a cephalopod.

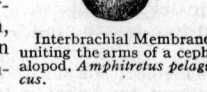

Interbrachial Membrane, uniting the arms of a cephalopod. *Amphitretus pelagicus.*

in-ter-breed (in-tėr-brēd′), *v. t.* or *i.*; *-bred*, *-breeding*. [See *inter-*.] To breed by the crossing of different animal or plant species, varieties, or the like.

in-ter-ca-la-ry (in-tėr′kạ-lā-ri), *a.* [L. *intercalarius*, *intercalaris*, < *intercalare*: see *intercalate.*] Inserted or interpolated in the calendar, as an extra day, month, etc.; having such an inserted day, month, etc., as a particular year; hence, in general, interpolated; interposed; intervening.

in-ter-ca-late (in-tėr′kạ-lāt), *v. t.*; *-lated*, *-lating*. [L. *intercalatus*, pp. of *intercalare*, < *inter*, between, + *calare*, call, proclaim.] To insert (an extra day, month, etc.) in the calendar; hence, in general, to interpolate; interpose.—**in-ter-ca-la′tion** (-lā′shọn), *n.* [L. *intercalatio(n-)*.] The act of intercalating; insertion or interpolation, as in a series (as, "He was obliged to submit to the *intercalation* of the disastrous siege of Metz in the long history of his successes": Motley's "Dutch Republic," iii. 1); also, that which is intercalated; an interpolation.

in-ter-cede (in-tėr-sēd′), *v. i.*; *-ceded*, *-ceding*. [L. *intercedere* (pp. *intercessus*), < *inter*, between, + *cedere*, go.] To go or come between, as in space or time†; also, to interpose in behalf of one in difficulty or trouble, as by pleading or petition (as, to *intercede* with the governor for a condemned man); also, in *Rom. hist.*, of a tribune or other magistrate, to interpose a veto.—**in-ter-ced′er** (-sē′dėr), *n.*

in-ter-cel-lu-lar (in-tėr-sel′ū-lạ̈r), *a.* [See *inter-*.] Situated between or among cells or cellules.

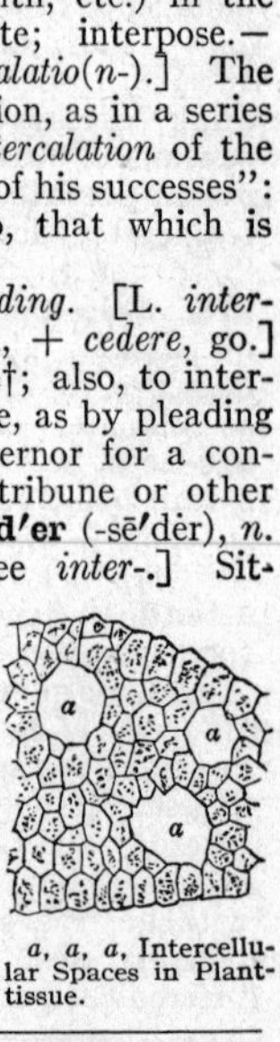

a, a, a, Intercellular Spaces in Plant-tissue.

in-ter-cen-sal (in-tėr-sen′sạl), *a.* [See *inter-*.] Between censuses: as, an *intercensal* period; the *intercensal* increase in population.

in-ter-cen-tral (in-tėr-sen′trạl), *a.* [See *inter-*.] Between centers.

in-ter-cept (in-tėr-sept′), *v. t.* [L. *interceptus*, pp. of *intercipere*, < *inter*, between, + *capere*, take.] To take or seize on the way from one place to another (as, to *intercept* a letter or a messenger); cut off from the intended destination; hence, to stop the natural course of (light, water, etc.); stop or check (passage, etc.: as, to *intercept* a person's flight); formerly, to interrupt, as a speaker, a narrative, etc.† (as, "They will not *intercept* my tale": Shakspere's "Titus Andronicus," iii. 1. 40); also, to prevent or hinder from accomplishing a purpose (obs. or rare: as, "O, she that might have *intercepted* thee . . . From all the slaughters, wretch, that thou hast done!" Shakspere's "Richard III.," iv. 4. 137); prevent or cut off the operation or effect of (as, to *intercept* the view); also, to cut off (one thing) from another; cut off from access, sight, etc. (as, "When I saw the gate which *intercepted* the tomb, my heart glowed within me," Sterne's "Tristram Shandy," vii. 40; "Thick clouds of dust . . . *intercept* the skies," Pope's tr. Homer's "Iliad," xi.); also, to mark off or include, as between two points or lines (chiefly in *math.*).—**in'ter-cept,** *n.* An interception; in *math.*, the part of a line lying between the two points at which it is intersected by two other lines or the like.—**in-ter-cep'tion** (-sep'shọn), *n.* [L. *interceptio(n-).*] The act or an act of intercepting, or the state or fact of being intercepted: as, the *interception* of letters; the *interception* of light.—**in-ter-cep'tive,** *a.* Serving to intercept.—**in-ter-cept'or, in-ter-cept'er,** *n.*

in-ter-ces-sion (in-tėr-sesh'ọn), *n.* [L. *intercessio(n-)*, < *intercedere*: see *intercede.*] The act of interceding; an interposing or pleading in behalf of one in difficulty or trouble; rarely, a pleading against others (see Rom. xi. 2); often, in religious use, an interposing or pleading with God in behalf of another or others, as that of Christ (see Heb. vii. 25) or that of the saints in behalf of men; also, in *Rom. hist.*, the interposing of a veto, as by a tribune.—**in-ter-ces'sion-al,** *a.*

in-ter-ces-sor (in-tėr-ses'ọr), *n.* [L., < *intercedere*: see *intercede.*] One who intercedes, or makes intercession; often, one who intercedes with God in behalf of men.—**in-ter-ces'so-ry** (-ses'ō-ri), *a.* Making intercession.

in-ter-chain† (in-tėr-chān'), *v. t.* [See *inter-*.] To chain or link, one to another. See Shakspere's "Midsummer Night's Dream," ii. 2. 49.

in-ter-change (in-tėr-chānj'), *v.*; *-changed, -changing.* [OF. *entrechangier*, < *entre-* (< L. *inter*, between) + *changier*, E. *change.*] **I.** *tr.* To give and receive (things) reciprocally (as, two persons *interchange* gifts or blows; one person *interchanges* courtesies with another); exchange; also, to put each of (two things) in the place of the other; cause (one thing) to change places with another; transpose; also, formerly, to exchange (a thing) for something else† (as, "Once more I shall *interchange* My waned state for Henry's regal crown": Shakspere's "3 Henry VI.," iv. 7. 3); also, to cause to occur by turns, in succession (as, to *interchange* severity and indulgence, or to *interchange* severity with indulgence, in the treatment of children); alternate. **II.** *intr.* To change places, as two persons or things, or as one with another; also, to occur by turns, in succession; alternate.—**in'ter-change,** *n.* [OF. *entrechange.*] The act or an act of interchanging, or giving and receiving reciprocally (as, the *interchange* of commodities; an *interchange* of blows); reciprocal exchange; also, the putting of each of two things in the place of the other, or of causing one thing to change places with another; a changing of places, as between two persons or things, or of one with another; also, alternation; alternate succession.—**in-ter-change'a-ble,** *a.* Capable of being interchanged; esp., capable of being put or used in the place of each other, as two things; admitting of mutual substitution; of one thing, that may be put in the place of, or may change places with, something else (as, one term *interchangeable* with another).—**in-ter-change-a-bil'i-ty** (-bil'i-ti), **in-ter-change'a-ble-ness,** *n.*—**in-ter-change'a-bly,** *adv.* In an interchangeable manner; with interchange.—**interchangeably posed,** in *her.*, of charges, as fishes, swords, arrows, etc., so placed that the head of each appears between the tails or after ends of two others.—**in-ter-chan'ger** (-chān'jėr), *n.*

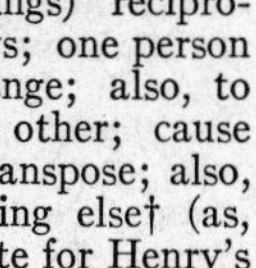
Interchangeably Posed.

in-ter-cit-y (in-tėr-sit'i), *a.* [See *inter-*.] Between cities, or representatives of different cities: as, an *intercity* contest or match.—**in-ter-civ'ic** (-siv'ik), *a.* Between citizens of the same place.—**in''ter-col-le'gi-ate** (-kọ-lē'ji-āt), *a.* Between colleges, or representatives of different colleges.—**in''ter-co-lo'ni-al** (-kō-lō'ni-ạl), *a.* Between colonies, as of one country: as, *intercolonial* commerce or trade; *intercolonial* relations.—**in''ter-co-lo'ni-al-ly,** *adv.*

in-ter-co-lum-nar (in''tėr-kō-lum'nạr), *a.* [See *inter-*.] Between columns.

in-ter-co-lum-ni-a-tion (in''tėr-kō-lum-ni-ā'shọn), *n.* [L. *intercolumnium*, space between columns, < *inter*, between, + *columna*, E. *column.*] In *arch.*, the space between two adjacent columns, usually the clear space between the lower parts of the shafts, but sometimes the distance from center to center; also, the system of spacing between columns.

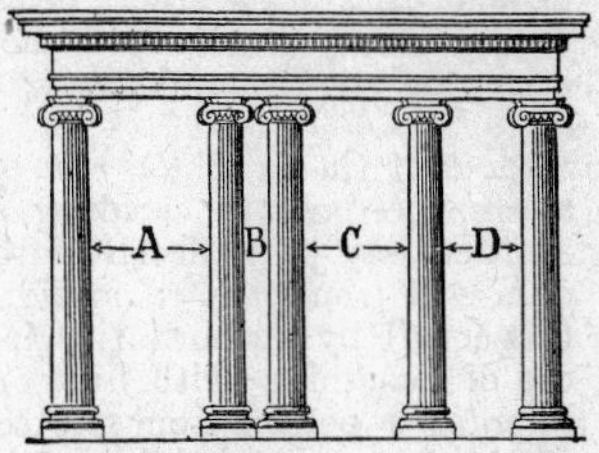

Intercolumniation. — *A*, of 3½ diameters; *C*, of 3 diameters; *D*, of 2¼ diameters; *B*, coupled columns.

in-ter-com-mon (in-tėr-kom'ọn), *v. i.* [OF. *entrecomuner*, < *entre-* (< L. *inter*, between) + *comuner*, share, E. *commune*[1].] To have intercourse with others or with each other†; also, to participate with others or mutually†; also, in *Eng. law*, to share in the use of the same common (as, "Common because of vicinage . . . is where the inhabitants of two townships, which lie contiguous to each other, have usually *intercommoned* with one another": Blackstone's "Commentaries," II. 33).—**in-ter-com'mon-age** (-ạj), *n.*

in-ter-com-mu-ni-cate (in''tėr-kọ-mū'ni-kāt), *v. t.* or *i.*; *-cated, -cating.* [ML. *intercommunicatus*, pp. of *intercommunicare*, < L. *inter*, between, + *communicare*, E. *communicate.*] To communicate reciprocally.—**in''ter-com-mu-ni-ca'tion** (-kā'shọn), *n.*—**in''ter-com-mu'ni-ca-tive** (-kạ-tiv), *a.*

in-ter-com-mu-nion (in''tėr-kọ-mū'nyọn), *n.* [See *inter-*.] Mutual communion, association, or intercourse.

in-ter-com-mu-ni-ty (in''tėr-kọ-mū'ni-ti), *n.* [See *inter-*.] Community between persons or parties; common ownership or use.

in-ter-com-pare (in''tėr-kọm-pãr'), *v. t.*; *-pared, -paring.* [See *inter-*.] To compare, one with another.—**in-ter-com'pa-ra-ble** (-kom'pạ-rạ-bl), *a.*—**in''ter-com-par'i-son** (-par'i-sọn), *n.*

in-ter-con-nect (in''tėr-kọ-nekt'), *v. t.* [See *inter-*.] To connect, one with another.—**in''ter-con-nec'tion** (-nek'shọn), *n.*

in-ter-con-ti-nen-tal (in''tėr-kon-ti-nen'tạl), *a.* [See *inter-*.] Between continents: as, an *intercontinental* railroad; *intercontinental* trade.

in-ter-con-ver-sion (in''tėr-kọn-vėr'shọn), *n.* [See *inter-*.] Reciprocal conversion; interchange of form or constitution.—**in''ter-con-vert'i-ble** (-vėr'ti-bl), *a.* Reciprocally convertible; interchangeable.—**in''ter-con-vert-i-bil'i-ty** (-bil'i-ti), *n.*—**in''ter-con-vert'i-bly,** *adv.*

in-ter-cos-tal (in-tėr-kos'tạl). [NL. *intercostalis*, < L. *inter*, between, + *costa*, rib.] **I.** *a.* Situated between the ribs; pertaining to muscles or parts between the ribs. **II.** *n.* An intercostal muscle or part.

in-ter-course (in'tėr-kōrs), *n.* [OF. *entrecors*, < L. *intercursus*, a running between, < *intercurrere*: see *intercurrent.*] A going to and fro between places in commercial or other dealings; dealings between the inhabitants of different places; also, dealings or communication between individuals; frequent or habitual meeting or contact between individuals, as in social life; interchange of thoughts, feelings, etc.; sometimes, sexual connection; also, continuous interchange or exchange (now rare: as, an *intercourse* of letters or of courtesies).

in-ter-cross (in-tėr-krôs'), *v.* [See *inter-*.] **I.** *tr.* To cross (things), one with another; also, to cross (each other), as streets do; also, to cross in interbreeding. **II.** *intr.* To cross each other; also, to interbreed.—**in'ter-cross,** *n.* An instance of intercrossing.

in-ter-cur-rent (in-tėr-kur′ent), *a.* [L. *intercurrens* (-*ent*-), ppr. of *intercurrere*, run between, intervene, < *inter*, between, + *currere*, run.] Running, coming, or situated between; intervening; in *pathol.*, of a disease, occurring while another disease is in progress.—**in-ter-cur′rence,** *n.*

in-ter-de-nom-i-na-tion-al (in″tėr-dē-nom-i-nā′shon-al), *a.* [See *inter*-.] Between (religious) denominations.

in-ter-den-tal (in-tėr-den′tal), *a.* [L. *inter*, between, + *dens* (*dent*-), tooth.] Between teeth; in *phonetics*, produced by placing the tip of the tongue between the upper and lower teeth.

in-ter-de-pend (in″tėr-dē-pend′), *v. i.* [See *inter*-.] To depend, each on the other; be mutually dependent.—**in″ter-de-pend′ent,** *a.* Mutually dependent.—**in″ter-de-pend′ence, in″ter-de-pend′en-cy,** *n.*—**in″ter-de-pend′ent-ly,** *adv.*

in-ter-dict (in-tėr-dikt′), *v. t.* [L. *interdictus*, pp. of *interdicere*, interpose by speaking, prohibit, < *inter*, between, + *dicere*, say.] To declare authoritatively against the doing or use of (something); forbid; prohibit; also, to restrain (a person) by authoritative injunction from the doing or use of something (with *from* or with double object: as, to *interdict* a person from proceeding, or from a place; to *interdict* a person indulgence in something, or to *interdict* him fire and water); *eccles.*, to cut off authoritatively from ecclesiastical functions and privileges; lay under an interdict.—**in′ter-dict,** *n.* [L. *interdictum*, orig. neut. of *interdictus*, pp.] An authoritative prohibition; a prohibitory order or decree; in the *Rom. Cath. Ch.*, a sentence debarring a place or person from ecclesiastical functions and privileges.—**in-ter-dic′tion** (-dik′shon), *n.* [L. *interdictio*(*n*-).] The act of interdicting; the state of being interdicted; also, an interdict.—**in-ter-dic′tive, in-ter-dic′to-ry** (-tō-ri), *a.* Interdicting; prohibitory.—**in-ter-dic′tor,** *n.*

in-ter-dig-i-tate (in-tėr-dij′i-tāt), *v. i.* or *t.*; *-tated, -tating.* [L. *inter*, between, + *digitus*, finger, E. *digit*.] To interlock like the fingers of the two hands.—**in-ter-dig-i-ta′tion** (-tā′shon), *n.*

in-ter-est (in′tėr-est), *n.* [For earlier *interess*, < ML. *interesse*, noun use of L. *interesse*, inf., be between, make a difference, concern, < *inter*, between, + *esse*, be.] The fact or relation of being concerned in or connected with a thing through having a right or title to it, a share in it, or some claim upon it; hence, a right to a share in something; a share or part (as, "A Persian . . . begg'd an *int'rest* in his frequent pray'rs": Cowper's "Conversation," 74); a share in the ownership of property, or in a commercial or financial undertaking or the like; any right of ownership in property, commercial undertakings, etc. (as, to sell one's *interests* and retire); also, the relation of being affected by something in respect of advantage or detriment (as, to choose an arbitrator having no *interest* in the outcome of a controversy); a relation of being affected advantageously by something (as, to have an *interest* in the success of a venture; what *interest* has he in misrepresenting the facts?); *sing.* or *pl.*, benefit or advantage (as, "Woe be to that man or woman who relied on her one inch beyond the point where it was her *interest* to be trustworthy," C. Brontë's "Villette," viii.; to have one's own *interest*, or *interests*, in mind); hence, *sing.*, regard for one's own advantage or profit (as, "*Interest* was the master-key of Madame's nature — the mainspring of her motives": C. Brontë's "Villette," viii.); self-interest; also, *sing.* or *pl.*, behalf, favor, or aid (as, he has been very active in your *interest*; to labor in the *interest*, or *interests*, of peace: see also phrase *in the interest of*, below); also, *sing.*, the feeling of one whose attention or curiosity is particularly engaged by something (as, to have little *interest* in a subject; a book which holds the *interest*); a particular feeling of this kind (as, a man of varied intellectual *interests*); hence, power of exciting such feeling, or interesting quality (as, questions of great *interest*; a book which lacks *interest*); sometimes, concernment, importance, or moment (as, a matter of primary, or of secondary, *interest*); also, something in which one has an interest, as of ownership, participation, advantage, engaged attention, etc.; a business, cause, or the like, in which a number of persons are interested; also, a number or group of persons, or a party, having a common interest (as, the banking *interest*; the labor *interest*); often, in *pl.*, the group of persons or organizations having extensive financial or business interests; also, *sing.*, influence, or power of influencing action (as, "Sir Anthony shall use his *interest* with Mrs. Malaprop," Sheridan's "Rivals," i. 2; to make *interest*, to bring one's influence to bear); also, money paid for the use of money borrowed (the *principal*) or for forbearance of a debt; the rate per cent per unit of time which this represents; fig., something added or thrown in above an exact equivalent (as, "You shall have your desires with *interest*": Shakspere's "1 Henry IV.," iv. 3. 49).—**compound interest,** interest paid, not only on the principal, but also on the interest after it has periodically become due and, remaining unpaid, been added to the principal: contrasted with *simple interest*, or interest paid only on the principal as lent.—**in the interest** (or **interests**) **of,** on the side of what is advantageous to (now rare: as, the party *in the interest*, or *interests, of* the king, or *of* the parliament); also, in behalf of (see def. above).—**in′ter-est,** *v. t.* [For earlier *interess, v.*, < *interess, n.*] To invest with a title to or a share in something, esp. a spiritual privilege (now rare); also, to cause or induce to take a share or part in an undertaking, scheme, etc.; engage in something; also, to concern (a person, etc.) in something, as through the bearing or effect upon personal or private interests (as, every citizen is *interested* in seeing that this bill shall become a law); involve; also, to engage or excite the attention or curiosity of (as, a subject which does not *interest* him; a story which *interested* him greatly); affect with a feeling of interest; also, to concern, relate to, or affect (obs. or rare: as, a matter which *interests* human welfare).—**in′ter-est-ed,** *p. a.* Invested with or having an interest in something; concerned in something through its bearing upon one's interests; hence, influenced by considerations of personal advantage; biased by personal or selfish motives; not disinterested; also, having the attention or curiosity engaged (as, an *interested* spectator); characterized by a feeling of interest (as, *interested* attention).—**in′ter-est-ed-ly,** *adv.*—**in′ter-est-ed-ness,** *n.*—**in′ter-est-ing,** *p. a.* That interests, or engages or excites the attention or curiosity (as, an *interesting* subject; an *interesting* book); having the quality of arousing a feeling of interest; also, that concerns, relates to, or affects†; important†.—**in′ter-est-ing-ly,** *adv.*—**in′ter-est-ing-ness,** *n.*

in-ter-face (in′tėr-fās), *n.* [See *inter*-.] A surface regarded as the common boundary of two bodies or spaces.—**in-ter-fa′cial** (-fā′shal), *a.* Included between two faces (as, an *interfacial* angle, one formed by the meeting of two planes); also, pertaining to an interface.

in-ter-fere (in-tėr-fēr′), *v. i.*; *-fered, -fering.* [OF. *entreferir*, refl., strike each other, < L. *inter*, between, + *ferire*, strike.] To strike one foot or leg against the opposite foot or leg in going, as a horse; also, of things, to strike against each other, or one against another, so as to hamper or hinder action; come into physical collision; specif., to act reciprocally, or one upon another, so as to modify the natural effect (said, in *physics*, of waves of light, sound, etc.); also, to come into non-physical collision, or clash in claims, tendencies, etc., as two things; come into opposition, as one thing with another, esp. with the effect of hampering action or procedure (as, he will come Saturday if nothing *interferes*; these interruptions *interfere* with the work); also, of persons, to use some opposing or hampering action with a person or thing or in a matter, esp. intrusively or without warrant (as, to *interfere* with a peaceable citizen in the exercise of his rights; to *interfere* with the carrying out of a plan); meddle; sometimes, to interpose or intervene for a particular purpose (as, the government *interfered* in the strike to prevent destruction of property or to protect the public); also, in football and other games, to obstruct the action of an opposing player in a way barred by the rules.—**in-ter-fer′ence** (-fēr′ens), *n.* The act or fact of interfering (in any sense); the striking together of opposite feet or legs, as of a horse; collision which hampers or hinders action; clashing of claims, etc.; opposing or hampering action; meddling; intervention; specif., in *physics*, the reciprocal action of waves (as of light, sound, etc.), as when meeting, by which they reinforce or neutralize each other.—**in″ter-fe-ren′tial** (-fē-ren′shal), *a.* In *physics*, of or pertaining to interference.—**in-ter-fer′er,** *n.*—**in-ter-fer′ing-ly,** *adv.*

—**in″ter-fe-rom′e-ter** (-rom′e-tėr), *n.* [See *-meter.*] An instrument for measuring small lengths or distances by means of the interference of two rays of light.

in-ter-flow (in-tėr-flō′), *v. i.* [See *inter-.*] To flow between; also, to flow into each other, or intermingle (as, "Good and evil *interflow*": Whittier's "Over-Heart").—**in′ter-flow,** *n.* An interflowing.

in-ter-flu-ent (in-tėr′flö̤-ent), *a.* [L. *interfluens* (*-ent-*), ppr. of *interfluere,* < *inter,* between, + *fluere,* flow.] Flowing between; also, flowing into each other; intermingling. Also **in-ter′flu-ous.**

in-ter-fold (in-tėr-fōld′), *v. t.* [See *inter-.*] To fold, one within another; fold together.

in-ter-fo-li-ate (in-tėr-fō′li-āt), *v. t.*; *-ated, -ating.* [L. *inter,* between, + *folium,* leaf.] To interleave (a book).

in-ter-fuse (in-tėr-fūz′), *v.*; *-fused, -fusing.* [L. *interfusus,* pp. of *interfundere,* pour between, < *inter,* between, + *fundere,* pour.] **I.** *tr.* To pour (something) between or through; diffuse throughout; also, to intersperse or intermingle with something (as, "floating vapors *interfused* with light": Longfellow's "Hanging of the Crane," ii.); also, to blend or fuse, one with another; also, to be diffused through; permeate. **II.** *intr.* To become blended or fused, one with another.—**in-ter-fu′sion** (-fū′zhon), *n.*

in-ter-gla-cial (in-tėr-glā′shial), *a.* [See *inter-.*] In *geol.,* occurring or formed between two periods of glacial action.

in-ter-grade (in-tėr-grād′), *v. i.*; *-graded, -grading.* [See *inter-.*] To pass gradually, one into another, as different species.—**in″ter-gra-da′tion** (-grā-dā′shon), *n.*—**in′ter-grade,** *n.* An intermediate grade.

in-ter-growth (in′tėr-grōth), *n.* [See *inter-.*] Growth or growing together, as of one thing with another.

in-ter-im (in′tėr-im), *n.* [L., in the meantime, < *inter,* between: see *inter-.*] An intervening time; the meantime; also, a temporary or provisional arrangement; [*cap.*] in *eccles. hist.,* any of three provisional arrangements for the settlement of religious differences between German Protestants and Roman Catholics during the Reformation.

in-te-ri-or (in-tē′ri-or). [L., inner, compar. adj. < *inter,* between: see *inter-.*] **I.** *a.* Inner (as, the *interior* side or surface of a thing); being inside of something, or pertaining to the inside; often, situated inside of and at a distance from the coast or border (as, the *interior* parts of a region or country); inland; pertaining to the inland or interior; also, internal or domestic, as opposed to *foreign*; sometimes, inner, private, or secret; also, of or pertaining to the mind, or soul; mental or spiritual. **II.** *n.* The interior or internal part; the inside; often, the inside of a building, room, etc., esp. with reference to artistic effect; also, a pictorial representation of the inside of a building, room, etc.; also, the interior or inland parts of a region, country, etc. (as, the *interior* of Africa, of Madagascar, or of Germany); also, the internal or domestic affairs of a country or state (as, the Department of the *Interior,* of the U. S.); also, the inner or inward nature or character of anything.—**in-te-ri-or′i-ty** (-or′i-ti), *n.*—**in-te′ri-or-ly,** *adv.*

in-ter-ja-cent (in-tėr-jā′sent), *a.* [L. *interjacens* (*-ent-*), ppr. of *interjacere,* < *inter,* between, + *jacere,* lie.] Lying between; intervening.—**in-ter-ja′cen-cy,** *n.*

in-ter-jac-u-late (in-tėr-jak′ū-lāt), *v. t.*; *-lated, -lating.* [L. *inter,* between, + *jaculari* (pp. *jaculatus*), throw, hurl: cf. *ejaculate.*] To interject as an ejaculation.—**in-ter-jac′u-la-to-ry** (-la-tō-ri), *a.*

in-ter-ject (in-tėr-jekt′), *v. t.* [L. *interjectus,* pp. of *interjacere, interjicere,* < *inter,* between, + *jacere,* throw.] To throw in between other things; interpolate; interpose, as a remark.—**in-ter-jec′tion** (-jek′shon), *n.* [L. *interjectio*(*n-*).] The act of interjecting, or something, as a remark, interjected; also, the utterance of ejaculations expressive of emotion; an ejaculation or exclamation; in *gram.,* an ejaculatory or exclamatory word, commonly without grammatical connection, regarded as a distinct part of speech, as *ah, alas, fie, hurrah, O, oh, pooh, pshaw, tut, whew,* etc.—**in-ter-jec′tion-al,** *a.* Pertaining to or of the nature of interjection or an interjection.—**in-ter-jec′tion-al-ly,** *adv.* In an interjectional manner; as an interjection.—**in-ter-jec′to-ry** (-tō-ri), *a.* Interjectional; interjected.—**in-ter-jec′to-ri-ly,** *adv.*

in-ter-knit (in-tėr-nit′), *v. t.* or *i.*; *-knitted* or *-knit, -knitting.* [See *inter-.*] To knit together, one with another; intertwine.

in-ter-lace (in-tėr-lās′), *v.*; *-laced, -lacing.* [OF. *entrelacier* (F. *entrelacer*), < *entre-* (< L. *inter,* between) + *lacier,* E. *lace, v.*] **I.** *tr.* To dispose (threads, strips, parts, branches, etc.) so as to intercross one another, passing alternately over and under (as, to *interlace* osiers in wickerwork; to *interlace* ribbons; to *interlace* the fingers); combine by interweaving or interlocking of parts; interweave; of parts, pieces, etc., to intercross as in an interwoven or interlocked whole (as, "The cane from India . . . sever'd into stripes That *interlac'd* each other": Cowper's "Task," i. 41); fig., to diversify as with threads woven in (as, meadows *interlaced* with streams); intersperse or intermingle with anything introduced. **II.** *intr.* To intercross, as threads, strips, etc., interwoven or interlocked; fig., to become intermingled.—**in-ter-lace′ment,** *n.* The act of interlacing, or the condition of being interlaced; also, the result or product of interlacing; something interlaced.

Heraldic Crescents Interlaced.

Interlacing Arches, Norwich Cathedral, England.

in-ter-lam-i-nate (in-tėr-lam′i-nāt), *v. t.*; *-nated, -nating.* [See *inter-.*] To interlay with or lay between laminæ; interstratify.—**in-ter-lam-i-na′tion** (-nā′shon), *n.*

in-ter-lap (in-tėr-lap′), *v. i.*; *-lapped, -lapping.* [See *inter-.*] To lap, one over another.

in-ter-lard (in-tėr-lärd′), *v. t.* [F. *entrelarder,* < *entre-* (< L. *inter,* between) + *larder,* E. *lard, v.*] To mix with alternate layers of fat†; lard (meat)†; also, to diversify with something intermixed or interjected (as, to *interlard* one's speech with oaths); intersperse (*with*); sometimes, of things, to be intermixed in (something: as, oaths *interlarded* his speech); also, to interpolate (as, "When a little trifle of new matter was *interlarded* [in a prayer], his ear detected it": Mark Twain's "Tom Sawyer," v.).—**in-ter-lard′ment,** *n.*

in-ter-lay (in-tėr-lā′), *v. t.*; *-laid, -laying.* [See *inter-.*] To lay between; interpose; also, to diversify with something laid between or inserted.

in-ter-leaf (in′tėr-lēf), *n.*; pl. *-leaves* (-lēvz). [See *inter-.*] A leaf inserted between other leaves, as a blank one for notes.—**in-ter-leave′** (-lēv′), *v. t.*; *-leaved, -leaving.* To furnish (a book) with interleaves; also, to insert (blank leaves, illustrations, etc.) between leaves.

in-ter-line[1] (in-tėr-līn′), *v. t.*; *-lined, -lining.* [See *inter-* and *line*[2].] To mark or inscribe (a document, book, etc.) with matter inserted between the lines; also, to write or insert (words, etc.) between the lines of writing or print (as, "These words were found *interlined* in Richard's grant": Stubbs's "Constitutional Hist. of Eng.," xviii. § 314); also, to write or print in alternate lines†.—**in′ter-line**[1], *n.* An intervening line.

in-ter-line[2] (in-tėr-līn′), *v. t.*; *-lined, -lining.* [See *inter-* and *line*[3].] To provide (a garment) with an inner lining inserted between the ordinary lining and the outer fabric.

in-ter-lin-e-ar (in-tėr-lin′ē-är), *a.* [ML. *interlinearis,* < L. *inter,* between, + *linea,* E. *line*[2].] Inserted between the lines; also, containing interpolated lines, as of translation.

in-ter-lin-e-ate (in-tėr-lin′ē-āt), *v. t.*; *-ated, -ating.* [ML. *interlineatus,* pp. of *interlineare,* < L. *inter,* between, + *linea,* E. *line*[2].] To mark (a document, etc.) with matter inserted between the lines; insert (matter) between lines, as of writing or print; interline.—**in-ter-lin-e-a′tion** (-ā′shon), *n.* The act of interlineating or interlining; insertion of matter between the lines of writing or print; also, the matter thus inserted.

in-ter-lin-ing[1] (in-tėr-lī′ning), *n.* [See *interline*[1].] Interlineation.

in-ter-lin-ing[2] (in′tėr-lī-ning), *n.* [See *inter-.*] An inner lining placed between the ordinary lining and the outer fabric of a garment.

in-ter-link (in-tėr-lingk′), *v. t.* [See *inter-*.] To link, one with another.—**in′ter-link,** *n.* A connecting link.

in-ter-lo-cate (in-tėr-lō′kāt), *v. t.*; *-cated, -cating.* [See *inter-*.] To place between other things; interlay.—**in″ter-lo-ca′tion** (-lọ-kā′shọn), *n.*

in-ter-lock (in-tėr-lok′), *v. t.* or *i.* [See *inter-*.] To lock or engage, one with another.—**in-ter-lock′er,** *n.*

in-ter-lo-cu-tion (in″tėr-lọ-kū′shọn), *n.* [L. *interlocutio(n-)*, < *interloqui*, speak between, < *inter*, between, + *loqui*, speak.] Interchange of speech; alternation in speaking; conversation; a dialogue or colloquy.—**in-ter-loc′u-tor** (-lok′ụ-tọr), *n.* One who takes part in a conversation or dialogue; one who enters into conversation with, or questions, another (as, "Your true rustic turns his back on his *interlocutor*": George Eliot's "Adam Bede," ii.); also, the man in the middle of the line of performers of a minstrel-troupe, who carries on conversation with the end-men; the middleman.—**in-ter-loc′u-to-ry** (-tọ-ri), *a.* Of the nature of, pertaining to, or occurring in conversation or dialogue; also, spoken intermediately (as, *interlocutory* observations); interjected into the main course of speech; in *law*, pronounced during the course of an action, as a decision or order; not finally decisive of a case; also, pertaining to a provisional decision.—**in-ter-loc′u-tress,** *n.* A female interlocutor. Also **in-ter-loc′u-trice** (-tris), **in-ter-loc′u-trix.**

in-ter-lope (in-tėr-lōp′), *v. i.*; *-loped, -loping.* [Origin uncertain: cf. *inter-* and *lope*, also D. *loopen*, run, and E. *landloper*.] To intrude into some region or field of trade without a proper license; hence, to thrust one's self into the domain or affair of others; intrude.—**in′ter-lop-er** (-lō-pėr), *n.* An intruding and unlicensed trader; hence, an intruder in any field or affair.

in-ter-lu-ca-tion (in″tėr-lụ-kā′shọn), *n.* [L. *interlucatio(n-)*, < *interlucare*, let light through (a tree) by thinning the branches, < *inter*, between, + *lux* (*luc-*), light.] The act of thinning a tree or a wood to let in light; specif., in *forestry*, the cutting of trees from a stand to let in light beyond the degree of severe thinning, so as to induce greater growth among the remaining trees.

in-ter-lude (in′tėr-lūd), *n.* [ML. *interludium*, < L. *inter*, between, + *ludere*, play.] An intermediate performance or entertainment, as between the acts of a play; specif., a kind of short dramatic piece, esp. of a light or farcical character, formerly introduced between the parts of miracle-plays and moralities or given as part of other entertainments; hence, one of the early English farces or comedies (such as those by John Heywood, 1497?–1580?) which grew out of such pieces; sometimes (now obs.), any play, esp. one of a popular character; also, an instrumental passage or a piece of music rendered between the parts of a song, church service, drama, etc.; also, an intervening episode, period, space, etc. (as, "He would look on the affair as no more than an *interlude* in the main business of his life": Hawthorne's "Twice-Told Tales," Wakefield).—**in′ter-lude,** *v.*; *-luded, -luding.* **I.** *intr.* To perform an interlude or play†; also, to occur as an interlude between other things; intervene. **II.** *tr.* To interrupt as with an interlude.—**in-ter-lu′di-al** (-lū′di-ạl), *a.* Pertaining to or of the nature of an interlude.

in-ter-lu-nar (in-tėr-lū′nạr), *a.* [See *inter-*.] Pertaining to the moon's monthly period of invisibility between the old moon and the new.—**in″ter-lu-na′tion** (-lụ-nā′shọn), *n.* The interlunar period; fig., any blank or dark interval.

in-ter-mar-ry (in-tėr-mar′i), *v. i.*; *-ried, -rying.* [See *inter-*.] To marry, one with another; also, to become connected by marriage, as two families, tribes, or castes; also, to marry within the limits of the family or of near relationship.—**in-ter-mar′riage** (-mar′ạj), *n.*

in-ter-med-dle (in-tėr-med′l), *v.*; *-dled, -dling.* [OF. *entremedler* (F. *entremêler*), < *entre-* (< L. *inter*, between) + *medler*, E. *meddle*.] **I.**† *tr.* To intermix; intermingle; also, to involve or concern (one's self) in a matter. **II.** *intr.* To take part in a matter, esp. officiously or impertinently; interfere; meddle.—**in-ter-med′dler,** *n.*

in-ter-me-di-a-cy (in-tėr-mē′di-ạ-si), *n.* The state of being intermediate; intermediate position, relation, or agency.

in-ter-me-di-al (in-tėr-mē′di-ạl), *a.* [L. *intermedius*, < *inter*, between, + *medius*, middle.] Being, occurring, or acting between; intermediate; intermediary.

in-ter-me-di-a-ry (in-tėr-mē′di-ạ-ri). [= F. *intermédiaire*, < L. *intermedius*: see *intermedial*.] **I.** *a.* Being between; intermediate; also, acting between persons, parties, etc.; serving as an intermediate agent or agency. **II.** *n.*; pl. *-ries* (-riz). An intermediate agent or agency; a go-between; a medium or means.

in-ter-me-di-ate (in-tėr-mē′di-ạt). [= F. *intermédiat*, < ML. *intermediatus*, < L. *intermedius*: see *intermedial*.] **I.** *a.* Being, situated, or occurring between two points, stages, things, etc.; also, acting between others; intervening. **II.** *n.* Something intermediate; also, an intermediary. —**in-ter-me′di-ate** (-āt), *v. i.*; *-ated, -ating.* To act as an intermediary; intervene; mediate.—**in-ter-me′di-ate-ly** (-ạt-li), *adv.*—**in-ter-me-di-a′tion** (-ā′shọn), *n.* The act of intermediating; intervention; mediation.—**in-ter-me′di-a-tor,** *n.*

in-ter-me-di-um (in-tėr-mē′di-um), *n.*; pl. *-dia* (-di-ạ). [L., neut. of *intermedius*: see *intermedial*.] Something intermediate; an interval of space or time†; an interlude†; esp., an intermediate agent or medium; an intermediary.

in-ter-ment (in-tėr′mẹnt), *n.* The act of interring; burial.

in-ter-mez-zo (in-tėr-med′zō), *n.*; pl. *-zi* (-zē). [It., < L. *intermedius*: see *intermedial*.] A short dramatic, musical, or other entertainment of light character introduced between the acts of a drama or opera; also, a short musical composition introduced between main divisions of an extended musical work; an independent musical composition of similar character.

in-ter-mi-gra-tion (in″tėr-mī-grā′shọn), *n.* [See *inter-*.] Reciprocal migration; interchange of country or habitat by migrating bodies.

in-ter-mi-na-ble (in-tėr′mi-nạ-bl), *a.* [LL. *interminabilis*, < L. *in-*, not, + *terminare*, E. *terminate*.] That cannot be terminated; unending; endless, or seemingly so (as, *interminable* talk).—**in-ter′mi-na-ble-ness,** *n.*—**in-ter′mi-na-bly,** *adv.*

in-ter-mi-nate (in-tėr′mi-nạt), *a.* [L. *interminatus*, < *in-*, not, + *terminatus*, bounded: see *terminate*.] Unbounded; unlimited; endless.

in-ter-min-gle (in-tėr-ming′gl), *v. t.* or *i.*; *-gled, -gling.* [See *inter-*.] To mingle, one with another; intermix: as, "It is a remarkable circumstance how our affairs appear to *intermingle*" (Stevenson's "David Balfour," xxv.).—**in-ter-min′gle-ment,** *n.*

in-ter-mis-sion (in-tėr-mish′ọn), *n.* [L. *intermissio(n-)*, < *intermittere*: see *intermit*.] The act or fact of intermitting (as, "I did laugh sans *intermission* An hour by his dial": Shakspere's "As You Like It," ii. 7. 32); temporary cessation; pause; also, a period during which action temporarily ceases; a space of time between periods of action or activity.—**in-ter-mis′sive** (-mis′iv), *a.* Characterized by intermission; intermittent.

in-ter-mit (in-tėr-mit′), *v.*; *-mitted, -mitting.* [L. *intermittere* (pp. *intermissus*), leave off, omit, leave an interval, < *inter*, between, + *mittere*, send.] **I.** *tr.* To discontinue temporarily; suspend: as, to *intermit* one's efforts. **II.** *intr.* To cease or stop, or break off operations, for a time (as, "The last application . . . had brought the fever to *intermit*," Fielding's "Tom Jones," v. 8; "Let me know the exact time when your Courts *intermit*," Johnson, in Boswell's "Johnson," July 5, 1773); stop or pause at intervals, or be intermittent.—**in-ter-mit′tent.** **I.** *a.* That intermits, or ceases for a time; alternately ceasing and beginning again (as, an *intermittent* fever); repeatedly interrupted (as, an *intermittent* current); coming at intervals. **II.** *n.* An intermittent fever.—**in-ter-mit′tence, in-ter-mit′ten-cy,** *n.*—**in-ter-mit′tent-ly, in-ter-mit′ting-ly,** *adv.*

in-ter-mix (in-tėr-miks′), *v. t.* or *i.* [L. *intermixtus*, pp. of *intermiscere*, < *inter*, between, + *miscere*, mix.] To mix, one with another; intermingle.—**in-ter-mix′ture** (-tụr), *n.* The act of intermixing; also, a mass of ingredients mixed together; also, something added by intermixing.

in-ter-mo-lec-u-lar (in″tėr-mọ-lek′ụ-lạr), *a.* [See *inter-*.] Between molecules.—**in-ter-mon′tane** (-mon′tān), *a.* Between mountains. Also **in-ter-moun′tain.**—**in-ter-mun′dane** (-mun′dān), *a.* Between worlds; between heavenly bodies.—**in-ter-mus′cu-lar** (-mus′kụ-lạr), *a.* Between muscles or muscular fibers.

in-tern (in-tėrn′). [F. *interne*, < L. *internus*, < *in*, in: cf. *extern*.] **I.** *a.* Internal. [Archaic.] **II.** *n.* (Also pron. in′tėrn.) An inmate; esp., a resident member of the medical staff of a hospital, commonly a recent medical graduate acting as assistant.—**in-tern′**, *v. t.* [F. *interner*, < *interne*.] To confine within the limits of a country or place; oblige to reside within prescribed limits under prohibition to leave them, as prisoners of war or enemy aliens, or as combatant troops who take refuge in a neutral country; hold within a country until the termination of a war, as a vessel of a belligerent which has put into a neutral port and remained beyond a limited period allowed.

in-ter-nal (in-tėr′nạl), *a.* [L. *internus*: see *intern*.] Of or pertaining to the inside or inner part; to be taken inwardly, as a remedy; also, situated or existing in the interior of something; interior; also, existing, occurring, or found within the limits or scope of something (as, the *internal* conditions or relations of a society; *internal* evidence of the date of a manuscript, such as a mention in the manuscript of particular events as contemporary); also, existing or occurring within a country, or domestic (as, *internal* affairs); pertaining to the domestic affairs of a country; also, being within or pertaining to the mind or soul; mental or spiritual; subjective.—**internal=combustion engine**, an engine of one or more working cylinders in which the pressure energy is produced by the explosion of gas or vapor inside the cylinder and against the piston-head: used in automobiles, motor-boats, etc.—**in-ter′nal-ist**, *n.* Same as *internist*.—**in-ter-nal′i-ty** (-nal′i-ti), *n.*; pl. *-ties* (-tiz). The state or quality of being internal; also, something internal.—**in-ter′nal-ize** (-nạl-īz), *v. t.*; *-ized*, *-izing*. To make internal or subjective.—**in-ter″nal-i-za′tion** (-i-zā′shọn), *n.* —**in-ter′nal-ly**, *adv.*

in-ter-nạ-tion-al (in-tėr-nash′ọn-ạl). [See *inter-*.] **I.** *a.* Between or among nations; of or pertaining to different nations or their citizens; pertaining to the relations between nations (as, *international* law); also [*cap.*], of or pertaining to any socialistic or other association known as an International. **II.** *n.* [*cap.*] A socialistic association (in full, 'International Working-Men's Association') intended to unite the working classes of all countries in promoting their own interests, and social and industrial reforms, by political means, formed in London in 1864, carried on largely under the influence of Karl Marx, and dissolved in Philadelphia in 1876 ('First International'); also, an international socialistic association formed in 1889, uniting socialistic groups or political parties of various countries, and holding international congresses from time to time ('Second International'); also, an ultraradical socialistic or communistic association formed in Moscow, under Bolshevist auspices, in 1919, uniting radical groups of various countries, and advocating the attainment of its ends by revolutionary or violent measures ('Third International'); also, any of certain other international associations. Also, a member or adherent of any of these associations.—**In-ter-na-tio-nale** (aṅ-ter-nȧ-syo-näl), *n.* [F.] An International (socialistic association); also, a French song ('*L'Internationale*') popular among French and other socialists.—**in-ter-na′tion-al-ism**, *n.* International character, relations, coöperation, or control; esp., the principle of coöperation among nations to promote their common good, sometimes as contrasted with *nationalism*, or devotion to the interests of a particular nation; also [*cap.*], the principles or methods advocated by any socialistic association known as an International.—**in-ter-na′tion-al-ist**, *n.* An advocate of internationalism; [*cap.*] a member or adherent of an International; also [*l. c.*], one versed in international law.—**in-ter-na-tion-al′i-ty** (-nash-ọ-nal′i-ti), *n.*—**in-ter-na′tion-al-ize** (-īz), *v. t.*; *-ized*, *-izing*. To make international; bring under international control, as a territory, etc.—**in-ter-na″tion-al-i-za′tion** (-i-zā′shọn), *n.*—**in-ter-na′tion-al-ly**, *adv.*

in-terne (in-tėrn′ or in′tėrn), *n.* [F.: see *intern*.] An intern (of the medical staff of a hospital).

in-ter-ne-cine (in-tėr-nē′sin or -sīn), *a.* [L. *internecinus*, < *internecio*, slaughter, destruction, < *internecare*, destroy, < *inter*, between, + *necare*, kill.] Characterized by great slaughter; murderous; deadly; destructive; now, usually, mutually destructive: applied esp. to war, strife, etc.

in-tern-ee (in-tėr-nē′), *n.* One who has been interned, as a prisoner of war.

in-tern-ist (in-tėr′nist), *n.* One who treats internal diseases, or those of the internal organs not amenable to operative measures; a physician, as distinguished from a surgeon.

in-tern-ment (in-tėrn′mẹnt), *n.* The act of interning, or the state of being interned.

in-ter-node (in′tėr-nōd), *n.* [L. *internodium*, < *inter*, between, + *nodus*, knot, E. *node*.] A part or space between two nodes, knots, or joints, as the portion of a plant stem between two nodes.—**in-ter-no′dal** (-nō′-dạl), *a.*

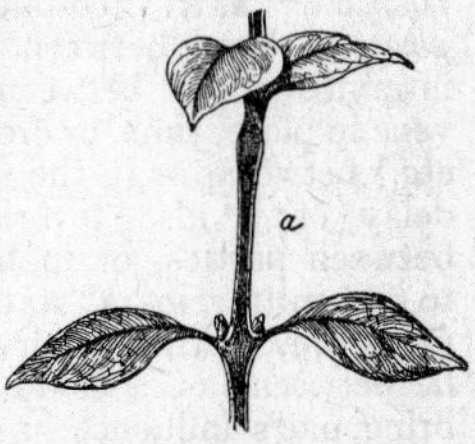

Part of Stem, showing (*a*) Internode.

in-ter-nun-ci-o (in-tėr-nun′shi-ō), *n.*; pl. *-os* (-ōz). [It., now *internunzio*, < L. *internuntius*, < *inter*, between, + *nuntius*, messenger.] A messenger between parties; also, a papal ambassador ranking next below a nuncio.

in-ter-nup-tial (in-tėr-nup′shạl), *a.* [See *inter-*.] Pertaining to intermarriage; also, occurring between two marriages of the same person.

in-ter-o-ce-an-ic (in″tėr-ō-shẹ̄-an′ik), *a.* [See *inter-*.] Between oceans: as, an *interoceanic* canal.

in-ter-os-cu-late (in-tėr-os′kụ̄-lāt), *v. i.*; *-lated*, *-lating*. [See *inter-* and *osculate*.] To connect, one with another; hence, to have points of contact or resemblance; also, to form a connecting link between objects, species, or the like. —**in-ter-os-cu-la′tion** (-lā′shọn), *n.*

in-ter-page (in-tėr-pāj′), *v. t.*; *-paged*, *-paging*. [See *inter-*.] To insert intermediate pages in; also, to insert on intermediate pages.

in-ter-pel-lant (in-tėr-pel′ạnt), *n.* [F.] One who interpellates.

in-ter-pel-late (in-tėr-pel′āt), *v. t.*; *-lated*, *-lating*. [L. *interpellatus*, pp. of *interpellare*, interrupt in speaking, < *inter*, between, + *-pellare*, akin to *pellere*, drive.] To interrupt†; also, in legislative proceedings (as in France), to call formally upon (a minister or member of the government) for an explanation of official action or government policy.—**in″ter-pel-la′tion** (-pe-lā′shọn), *n.*—**in″ter-pel-la′tor**, *n.*

in-ter-pen-e-trate (in-tėr-pen′ẹ̄-trāt), *v.*; *-trated*, *-trating*. [See *inter-*.] **I.** *tr.* To penetrate between the parts of; penetrate thoroughly; permeate; also, to penetrate reciprocally. **II.** *intr.* To penetrate between things or parts; also, to penetrate each other.—**in-ter-pen-e-tra′tion** (-trā′shọn), *n.*—**in-ter-pen′e-tra-tive** (-trạ-tiv), *a.*

in-ter-plane (in′tėr-plān), *a.* [See *inter-*.] Between planes: as, *interplane* struts of an aëroplane.

in-ter-plan-e-ta-ry (in-tėr-plan′e-tạ-ri), *a.* [See *inter-*.] In *astron.*, situated between or in the region of the planets; within the solar system, but not within the atmosphere of the sun or any planet.

in-ter-play (in′tėr-plā), *n.* [See *inter-*.] Reciprocal play, action, or influence; interaction.

in-ter-plead (in-tėr-plēd′), *v. i.* [AF. *enterpleder*, < OF. *entre-* (< L. *inter*, between) + *plaidier*, E. *plead*.] In *law*, to litigate with each other in order to determine which is the rightful claimant against a third party.—**in-ter-plead′er**, *n.* [AF. *enterpleder*.] In *law*, a proceeding by which two parties making the same claim against a third party determine judicially which is the rightful claimant.

in-ter-po-lar (in-tėr-pō′lạr), *a.* [See *inter-*.] Situated between or connecting the poles, as of a voltaic battery.

in-ter-po-late (in-tėr′pọ̄-lāt), *v.*; *-lated*, *-lating*. [L. *interpolatus*, pp. of *interpolare*, furbish, alter, falsify, < *inter*, between, + *-polare*, akin to *polire*, E. *polish*[2].] **I.** *tr.* To alter (a text, etc.) by the insertion of new matter, esp. deceptively or without authorization; also, to insert (new or spurious matter) thus; in general, to introduce (something additional or extraneous) between other things or parts; interject; interpose; intercalate; in *math.*, to insert or find intermediate terms in (a series); introduce (intermediate terms) in a series. **II.** *intr.* To make interpolations.—**in-ter-po-la′tion** (-lā′shọn), *n.* [L.

interpolatio(n-).] The act or an act of interpolating, or the fact of being interpolated; also, something interpolated, as a word or passage introduced into a text.—**in-ter′po-la-tor,** *n.*

in-ter-po-sal (in-tėr-pō′zal), *n.* The act of interposing; interposition; intervention.

in-ter-pose (in-tėr-pōz′), *v.*; *-posed, -posing.* [F. *interposer,* < L. *inter,* between, + F. *poser,* put (see *pose*[1]), but associated with derivatives of L. *interponere*: see *interposition.*] **I.** *tr.* To put (something) between (as, to *interpose* the hand between the eye and a light; to *interpose* intervals of rest between periods of work); cause to intervene in place, time, or order; esp., to put (a barrier, obstacle, etc.) between, or in the way; put or bring in (an objection, delay, etc.); also, to bring (influence, action, etc.) to bear between parties, or in behalf of a party or person; also, to put in (a remark, statement, etc.) in the midst of a conversation, discourse, or the like. **II.** *intr.* To come or lie between (as, a cloud *interposing* hid the sun); also, to bring one's influence or action to bear between parties at variance, or in behalf of a party or person; intervene as a mediator or intercessor; also, to interpose a remark or the like, as in the midst of a conversation.—**in-ter-pos′er** (-pō′-zėr), *n.*—**in-ter-pos′ing-ly,** *adv.*

in-ter-po-si-tion (in″tėr-pō-zish′on), *n.* [OF. F. *interposition,* < L. *interpositio(n-),* < *interponere,* put between, interpose, < *inter,* between, + *ponere,* place, put.] The act of putting between or interposing, or the state of being put between; interposal; fig., intervention, as between parties or in behalf of a person; also, something interposed (as, "A shelter, and a kind of shading cool *Interposition,* as a summer's cloud": Milton's "Paradise Regained," iii. 222).

in-ter-pret (in-tėr′pret), *v.* [L. *interpretari,* < *interpres* (*interpret-*), agent, broker, interpreter: cf. *inter-* and Skt. *prath-,* spread out.] **I.** *tr.* To set forth the meaning of (something not plain or clear: as, to *interpret* oracles or omens; to *interpret* an obscure passage or the writer); explain or elucidate; translate (as, "They shall call his name Emmanuel, which being *interpreted* is, God with us": Mat. i. 23); sometimes, to explain to one's self, or understand (as, to endeavor to *interpret* a person's expression); explain, construe, or understand in a particular way (as, to *interpret* a reply as favorable); also, to bring out the meaning of (a dramatic work or part, music, an artistic conception, etc.) by performance or execution; render or present in a revealing manner; also, of things, to express, indicate, or reveal (poetic: as, "Arms hanging idly down, hands clasp'd below, *Interpret* to the marking eye distress," Cowper's "Retirement," 287). **II.** *intr.* To give an explanation; esp., to translate what is said in a foreign language.—**in-ter′pret-a-ble,** *a.* Capable of being interpreted; explicable.—**in-ter-pre-ta′tion** (-pre-tā′shon), *n.* [L. *interpretatio(n-).*] The act of interpreting; explanation or elucidation; translation; the rendering of a dramatic part, music, etc., so as to bring out the meaning; also, a way of interpreting; an explanation given; a construction placed upon something; sometimes, the proper explanation or meaning.—**in-ter′pre-ta-tive** (-tā-tiv), *a.* Serving to interpret; explanatory; also, deduced by interpretation; constructive or inferential.—**in-ter′pre-ta-tive-ly,** *adv.*—**in-ter′pret-er,** *n.* One who interprets; esp., one whose function it is to interpret what is said in a foreign language, as for travelers or in the civil or military service of a government.—**in-ter′pret-er-ship,** *n.* The office or position of an interpreter.—**in-ter′pre-tive,** *a.* Same as *interpretative.*—**in-ter′pre-tress,** *n.* A female interpreter.

in-ter-pro-vin-cial (in″tėr-prō-vin′shal), *a.* [See *inter-.*] Between provinces: as, *interprovincial* relations or intercourse.

in-ter-punc-tion (in-tėr-pungk′shon), *n.* [L. *interpunctio(n-),* < *interpungere,* put points between, < *inter,* between, + *pungere,* prick.] The inserting of points or punctuation-marks between words, etc.; punctuation; also, a point or mark thus inserted.

in-ter-punc-tu-ate (in-tėr-pungk′tū-āt), *v. t.*; *-ated, -ating.* [See *inter-.*] To put punctuation-marks between; punctuate.—**in-ter-punc-tu-a′tion** (-ā′shon), *n.*

in-ter-reg-num (in-tėr-reg′num), *n.*; pl. *-nums,* L. *-na* (-nä). [L., < *inter,* between, + *regnum,* E. *reign.*] An interval of time between the close of a sovereign's reign and the accession of his normal or legitimate successor; any period during which a state has no ruler or only a temporary executive; hence, an intermission in any order of succession; an interval; a pause.—**in-ter-reg′nal,** *a.*

in-ter-re-late (in″tėr-rē-lāt′), *v. t.*; *-lated, -lating.* [See *inter-.*] To bring into reciprocal relation.—**in″ter-re-la′tion** (-lā′shon), *n.* Reciprocal relation.—**in″ter-re-la′tion-ship,** *n.*

in-ter-rer (in-tėr′ėr), *n.* One who inters or buries.

in-ter-rex (in′tėr-reks), *n.*; pl. *interreges* (in-tėr-rē′jēz). [L., < *inter,* between, + *rex,* king.] A person holding supreme authority in a state during an interregnum.

in-ter-ro-gate (in-ter′ō-gāt), *v.*; *-gated, -gating.* [L. *interrogatus,* pp. of *interrogare,* < *inter,* between, + *rogare,* ask.] **I.** *tr.* To ask a question or a series of questions of (a person); examine by questions; question. **II.** *intr.* To ask questions.—**in-ter-ro-ga′tion** (-gā′shon), *n.* [L. *interrogatio(n-).*] The act of interrogating; questioning, or a question; also, an interrogation-point.—**in-ter-ro-ga′tion-point,** *n.* A mark indicating a question: usually, as in English, the mark '?' placed after the question.—**in-ter-rog′a-tive** (-te-rog′a-tiv). [LL. *interrogativus.*] **I.** *a.* Pertaining to or conveying a question; questioning. **II.** *n.* An interrogation or question; in *gram.,* a word used in asking a question, as *who* or *why.*—**in-ter-rog′a-tive-ly,** *adv.*—**in-ter′ro-ga-tor,** *n.* [LL.] One who interrogates; a questioner.—**in-ter-rog′a-to-ry** (-tō-ri). [LL. *interrogatorius.*] **I.** *a.* Interrogative; questioning. **II.** *n.*; pl. *-ries* (-riz). A question or inquiry; in *law,* a formal or written question.—**in-ter-ro-ga′trix** (-gā′triks), *n.* A female interrogator.

in-ter-rupt (in-te-rupt′), *v.* [L. *interruptus,* pp. of *interrumpere,* < *inter,* between, + *rumpere,* break.] **I.** *tr.* To make a break in (an otherwise continuous extent, course, process, condition, etc.); break off or cause to cease, as in the midst or course (as, to *interrupt* one's view, work, speech, or rest; to *interrupt* the proceedings or a succession); hinder the continuation of, esp. temporarily; also, to stop (a person) in the midst of doing or saying something, esp. by some temporary interference, an interjected remark, or the like (as, "I don't want to be *interrupted* in my business," J. Conrad's "Victory," ii. 6; "neither *interrupt* men in the midst of their talk," Ecclus. xi. 8); also, sometimes, to say in interruption; also, to hinder† or prevent†. **II.** *intr.* To cause a break or discontinuance; interrupt action or speech.—**in-ter-rupt′ed-ly,** *adv.* In an interrupted manner; with interruptions; discontinuously.—**in-ter-rupt′er,** *n.* One who or that which interrupts; in *elect.,* a device for interrupting or periodically making and breaking a circuit.—**in-ter-rup′tion** (-rup′shon), *n.* [L. *interruptio(n-).*] The act of interrupting, or the state of being interrupted; a break in continuity or continuance; a stopping of action, speech, etc., esp. temporarily; an intermission or cessation; hindrance†.—**in-ter-rup′tive,** *a.* Tending to interrupt.—**in-ter-rup′tor,** *n.* [LL.] Same as *interrupter.*

in-ter-scap-u-lar (in-tėr-skap′ū-lär), *a.* [See *inter-.*] In *anat.* and *zoöl.,* between the scapulæ or shoulder-blades.

in-ter-scho-las-tic (in″tėr-skō-las′tik), *a.* [See *inter-.*] Between schools: as, *interscholastic* games.

in-ter-sect (in-tėr-sekt′), *v.* [L. *intersectus,* pp. of *intersecare,* < *inter,* between, + *secare,* cut.] **I.** *tr.* To cut or divide by passing through or lying across: as, one line or one road *intersects* another in crossing; "a bleak treeless region, *intersected* by lines of cold gray stone" (George Eliot's "Adam Bede," ii.). **II.** *intr.* To cross, as lines.—**in-ter-sec′tion** (-sek′shon), *n.* [L. *intersectio(n-).*] The act, fact, or place of intersecting.

in-ter-sep-tal (in-tėr-sep′tal), *a.* [See *inter-.*] Between septa or partitions.

in-ter-si-de-re-al (in″tėr-sī-dē′rē-al), *a.* [See *inter-.*] Between the stars; interstellar.

in-ter-space (in′tėr-spās), *n.* [See *inter-.*] A space between things (as, "The lucid *interspace* of world and world, Where never creeps a cloud": Tennyson's "Lucretius," 105); sometimes, an intervening space, or interval, of time.

—in-ter-space′, *v. t.*; *-spaced, -spacing.* To put a space between; also, to occupy or fill the space between.—**in-ter-spa′tial** (-spā′shạl), *a.* Of or pertaining to an interspace. —**in-ter-spa′tial-ly,** *adv.*

in-ter-sperse (in-tėr-spėrs′), *v. t.*; *-spersed, -spersing.* [L. *interspersus*, interspersed, < *inter*, between, + *spargere*, scatter.] To scatter here and there among other things (as, to *intersperse* shrubs among trees; verses *interspersed* among prose pieces); also, to diversify with something scattered or introduced here and there (as, lawns *interspersed* with beds of flowers; remarks *interspersed* with oaths); sometimes, of things, to be scattered here and there over (as, "A narrow brook . . . divides the field; Oaks *intersperse* it": Cowper's "Needless Alarm," 11).—**in-ter-sper′sion** (-spėr′shọn), **in-ter-sper′sal,** *n.* The act of interspersing, or the state of being interspersed.

in-ter-state (in′tėr-stāt), *a.* [See *inter-*.] Between states; esp., between, or jointly involving, States of the American Union: as, *interstate* commerce. Cf. *intrastate.*

in-ter-stel-lar (in-tėr-stel′ạ̈r), *a.* [See *inter-*.] Between the stars: as, *interstellar* space.

in-ter-stice (in′tėr-stis or in-tėr′-), *n.* [L. *interstitium*, < *intersistere*, stand between, < *inter*, between, + *sistere*, stand.] An intervening space, esp. a small or narrow space between things or parts; a small chink, crevice, or opening; also, an interval of time (archaic).—**in-ter-sti′tial** (-stish′ạl), *a.* Pertaining to, situated in, or forming interstices; specif., in *anat.*, situated between the cellular elements of a structure or part (as, *interstitial* tissue, fine connective tissue lying between the cells of other tissue; *interstitial* cells, specif., certain cells in the human and animal testis and ovary, supposed to have an endocrine function; an *interstitial* gland, a group of such interstitial cells).—**in-ter-sti′tial-ly,** *adv.*

in-ter-strat-i-fy (in-tėr-strat′i-fī), *v.*; *-fied, -fying.* [See *inter-*.] **I.** *tr.* To interlay with or interpose between other strata; arrange in alternate strata: used in the passive. **II.** *intr.* To lie in interposed or alternate strata.—**in-ter-strat″i-fi-ca′tion** (-fi-kā′shọn), *n.*

in-ter-tan-gle (in-tėr-tang′gl), *v. t.*; *-gled, -gling.* [See *inter-*.] To tangle, one with another.—**in-ter-tan′gle-ment,** *n.*

in-ter-tex-ture (in-tėr-teks′ṭūr), *n.* [L. *intertexere* (pp. *intertextus*), interweave, < *inter*, between, + *texere*, weave.] The act of interweaving; interwoven state; also, something formed by interweaving (as, "Lanes . . . skirted thick with *intertexture* firm Of thorny boughs": Cowper's "Task," i. 111).

in-ter-tri-bal (in-tėr-trī′bạl), *a.* [See *inter-*.] Between tribes: as, *intertribal* war or commerce.

in-ter-trop-i-cal (in-tėr-trop′i-kạl), *a.* [See *inter-*.] Between the tropics (of Cancer and Capricorn); tropical: as, *intertropical* islands; "I cannot refrain from lauding the very superior inducements which most *intertropical* countries afford" (H. Melville's "Omoo," lxvii.).

in-ter-twine (in-tėr-twīn′), *v. t.* or *i.*; *-twined, -twining.* [See *inter-*.] To twine, one with another.—**in-ter-twine′ment,** *n.*—**in-ter-twin′ing-ly** (-twī′ning-li), *adv.*

in-ter-twist (in-tėr-twist′), *v. t.* or *i.* [See *inter-*.] To twist, one with another.—**in′ter-twist,** *n.* An intertwisting; also, an intertwisted mass.—**in-ter-twist′ing-ly,** *adv.*

in-ter-urb-an (in-tėr-ėr′bạn), *a.* [L. *inter*, between, + *urbs*, city.] Between cities: as, an *interurban* railway.

in-ter-val (in′tėr-vạl), *n.* [OF. F. *intervalle*, < L. *intervallum*, interval, orig. space between palisades, < *inter*, between, + *vallum*, palisade, wall.] A space intervening between things, points, or limits (as, an *interval* of ten feet between columns); an open space; a gap; often, an intervening period of time (as, an *interval* of a week between letters; *intervals* between attacks of a disease); a period of cessation; a pause; in general, a separating space or extent of any kind (often fig.: as, "There seems to be no *interval* between greatness and meanness," Emerson's "Essays," Heroism); sometimes, an intervale (local, U. S. and Canada); in *music*, the difference in pitch between two tones (as, a harmonic *interval*, an interval between two tones sounded simultaneously; a melodic *interval*, an interval between two tones sounded successively).

in-ter-vale (in′tėr-vāl), *n.* [Var. of *interval*, associated with *vale*[1].] A low, level tract of land, esp. along a river: as, "From the lake that never fails, Falls the Saco in the green lap of Conway's *intervales*" (Whittier's "Mary Garvin"). [Local, U. S. and Canada.]

in-ter-vein (in-tėr-vān′), *v. t.* [See *inter-*.] To intersect with or as with veins: as, "Two rivers flow'd . . . and left between Fair champain with less rivers *intervein'd*" (Milton's "Paradise Regained," iii. 257).

in-ter-vene (in-tėr-vēn′), *v. i.*; *-vened, -vening.* [L. *intervenire* (pp. *interventus*), < *inter*, between, + *venire*, come.] To come or be between, as in place, time, or a series (as, mountains *intervene* between the two countries; a period of peace *intervening* between wars; two English sovereigns *intervened* between Henry VIII. and Elizabeth); also, to come between in action (as, to *intervene* between combatants); enter into an affair between parties, as for the purpose of adjusting differences or of interceding for or aiding one party; interpose; interfere; of things, to occur incidentally so as to modify a result.—**in-ter-ven′er** (-vē′nėr), *n.* —**in-ter-ve′nient** (-vē′nięnt), *a.* [L. *interveniens* (*-ent-*), ppr.] Intervening, as in place, time, order, or action; also, incidental (as, "Nature, *intervenient* till this time And secondary, now at length was sought For her own sake": Wordsworth's "Prelude," ii. 201).

in-ter-ven-tion (in-tėr-ven′shọn), *n.* [LL. *interventio*(*n-*).] The act or fact of intervening; esp., the interposition or interference of one state in the affairs of another, as to restore order or regulate matters (as, the *intervention* of the United States in Cuba in 1906).—**in-ter-ven′tion-ist,** *n.* One who favors intervention, as of one state in the affairs of another.

in-ter-view (in′tėr-vū), *n.* [F. *entrevue*, < *entrevoir*, refl., see (each other), < *entre-* (< L. *inter*, between) + *voir* (< L. *videre*), see.] A meeting of persons face to face, esp. for formal conference; specif., a meeting between a representative of the press and a person from whom information is sought for publication; the conversation at such a meeting, or the published report of it.—**in′ter-view,** *v. t.* To have an interview with, esp. to obtain information for publication.—**in′ter-view-er,** *n.*

in-ter-vi-tal (in-tėr-vī′tạl), *a.* [L. *inter*, between, + *vita*, life.] Between two lives, or stages of existence. See Tennyson's "In Memoriam," xliii.

in-ter-vo-cal-ic (in″tėr-vọ-kal′ik), *a.* [L. *inter*, between, + *vocalis*, E. *vowel*.] Between vowels: as, an *intervocalic* consonant.

in-ter-volve (in-tėr-volv′), *v. t.*; *-volved, -volving.* [L. *inter*, between, + *volvere* (pp. *volutus*), roll.] To roll, wind, or involve, one within another: as, "Mystical dance . . . mazes intricate, Eccentric, *intervolved*" (Milton's "Paradise Lost," v. 623).

in-ter-weave (in-tėr-wēv′), *v.*; pret. *-wove* (also *-weaved*), pp. *-woven* (also *-wove, -weaved*), ppr. *-weaving.* [See *inter-*.] **I.** *tr.* To weave together, one with another, as threads, strands, branches, roots, etc.; interlace or intertwine; fig., to intermingle or combine as if by weaving (as, to *interweave* truth with fiction). **II.** *intr.* To become woven together, interlaced, or intermingled.—**in-ter-weave′ment,** *n.*—**in-ter-weav′er,** *n.*

in-ter-wind (in-tėr-wīnd′), *v. t.* or *i.*; *-wound, -winding.* [See *inter-*.] To wind together, one with another; intertwine.

in-ter-work (in-tėr-wėrk′), *v.*; *-worked* or *-wrought, -working.* [See *inter-*.] **I.** *tr.* To work together or combine, one with another. **II.** *intr.* To work, one upon another; interact; also, to work or operate intermediately.

in-ter-wreathe (in-tėr-rēᴛʜ′), *v. t.*; *-wreathed, -wreathing.* [See *inter-*.] To wreathe together; intertwine.

in-tes-ta-ble (in-tes′tạ-bl), *a.* [L. *intestabilis*, < *in-*, not, + *testari*: see *intestate*.] Legally incompetent to make a will.

in-tes-ta-cy (in-tes′tạ-si), *n.* The state or fact of being intestate at death.

in-tes-tate (in-tes′tāt). [L. *intestatus*, < *in-*, not, + *testatus*, pp. of *testari*, bear witness, make a will, < *testis*, a witness.] **I.** *a.* Having made no will; also, not disposed of by will. **II.** *n.* One who dies intestate.

in-tes-ti-nal (in-tes′ti-nạl), *a.* Of or pertaining to the intestine; occurring or found in the intestine (as, *intestinal* worms); having an intestine.—**in-tes′ti-nal-ly,** *adv.*

in-tes-tine (in-tes′tin). [L. *intestinus*, < *intus*, within, < *in*, in.] **I.** *a.* Internal or inward; now, commonly, internal with respect to a country or community, as (usually) war, strife, foes, etc. **II.** *n.* In *anat.*, the lower part of the alimentary canal, extending from the pylorus to the anus, or a definite portion of this part (as, the small *intestine*, comprising the duodenum, jejunum, and ileum; the large *intestine*, comprising the cæcum, colon, and rectum); sometimes, the whole alimentary canal, as in animals having no stomach: in popular use commonly in *pl.*

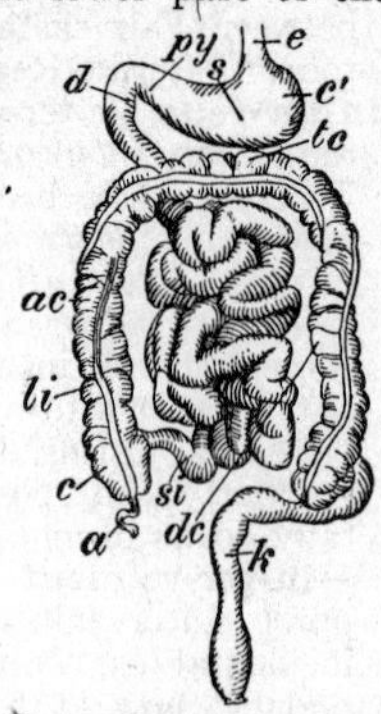

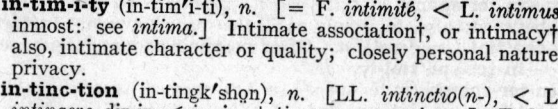

Human Stomach and Intestines.

a, vermiform appendix; *ac*, ascending colon; *c*, cæcum; *c′*, cardiac end of stomach; *d*, duodenum; *dc*, descending colon; *e*, termination of esophagus; *k*, rectum, ending at anus; *li*, large intestine, including *ac*, *tc*, *dc*; *py*, pyloric end of stomach, whence the coiled small intestine (duodenum, jejunum, and ileum) extends to *si*; *s*, stomach; *tc*, transverse colon.

in-ti-ma (in′ti-mạ̈), *n.*; pl. *-mæ* (-mē). [NL., prop. fem. of L. *intimus*, inmost, superl. of *interior*: see *interior*.] In *anat.*, the innermost membrane, coat, or lining of some organ or part, esp. that of an artery, vein, or lymphatic.

in-ti-ma-cy (in′ti-mạ-si), *n.*; pl. *-cies* (-siz). The state of being intimate; intimate association or intercourse; an intimate friendship; sometimes, illicit sexual relations between persons; an amour or liaison.

in-ti-mate[1] (in′ti-māt), *v. t.*; *-mated, -mating.* [LL. *intimatus*, pp. of *intimare*, put or press into, announce, < L. *intimus*, inmost: see *intima.*] To make known, esp. formally; announce; also, to make known indirectly; hint; suggest.

in-ti-mate[2] (in′ti-mạt). [In form < LL. *intimatus*, pp., but with sense of L. *intimus*: see *intimate*[1].] **I.** *a.* Inmost, or deep within (as, the *intimate*, or most *intimate*, recesses of the heart); hence, pertaining to the inmost or essential nature, or intrinsic (as, the *intimate* structure or constitution of a thing); also, pertaining to or existing in the inmost mind (as, *intimate* beliefs or convictions); also, peculiarly private, or closely personal (as, one's *intimate* affairs or experiences; "Winter . . . I crown thee king of *intimate* delights, Fire-side enjoyments, home-born happiness," Cowper's "Task," iv. 139); dealing with closely personal matters, as a narrative, description, etc.; also, associated in close personal relations and familiar intercourse (as, an *intimate* friend; to be *intimate* with a person; "The English colonists at Rome perforce become *intimate*, and in many cases friendly," Thackeray's "Newcomes," xxxix.); sometimes, maintaining illicit sexual relations; also, characterized by or involving personally close or familiar association, as relations, intercourse, etc.; also, of acquaintance, knowledge, etc., arising from close personal connection or familiar experience; also, characterized by close union or combination of particles or elements (as, an *intimate* mixture). **II.** *n.* An intimate friend or associate.—**in′ti-mate-ly,** *adv.*

in-ti-ma-tion (in-ti-mā′shọn), *n.* [LL. *intimatio(n-)*.] The act of intimating or announcing; an announcement; a formal notification; also, the act of intimating indirectly; a hint or suggestion (as in the title of Wordsworth's poem, "*Intimations* of Immortality from Recollections of Early Childhood").

in-tim-i-date (in-tim′i-dāt), *v. t.*; *-dated, -dating.* [ML. *intimidatus*, pp. of *intimidare*, < L. *in*, in, + *timidus*, E. *timid.*] To make timid, or inspire with fear (as, "He imagined that his power would *intimidate* all opponents": Lecky's "Hist. of Eng. in the 18th Century," i.); overawe; cow; esp., to make (a person) afraid, because of threats, hostile acts, etc., to do something, esp. to exercise some right or perform some duty (as, to *intimidate* a voter or a witness; to *intimidate* workers during a strike); force into or deter from some action by inducing fear.—**in-tim-i-da′tion** (-dā′shọn), *n.* The act of intimidating, or the state of being intimidated.—**in-tim′i-da-tor,** *n.*

in-tim-i-ty (in-tim′i-ti), *n.* [= F. *intimité*, < L. *intimus*, inmost: see *intima.*] Intimate association†, or intimacy†; also, intimate character or quality; closely personal nature; privacy.

in-tinc-tion (in-tingk′shọn), *n.* [LL. *intinctio(n-)*, < L. *intingere*, dip in, < *in*, in, + *tingere*, wet, moisten.] *Eccles.*, a dipping of the eucharistic bread in the wine in order to administer both together, as in the Oriental churches.

in-tine (in′tin or -tīn), *n.* [L. *intus*, within.] In *bot.*, a membrane forming the inner coat of a pollen-grain.

in-tit-ule (in-tit′ūl), *v. t.*; *-uled, -uling.* [OF. F. *intituler*, < LL. *intitulare*, < L. *in*, in, + *titulus*, E. *title.*] To give a title to; entitle. [Archaic.]—**in-tit-u-la′tion** (-ū-lā′shọn), *n.*

in-to (in′tö̜), *prep.* [Orig. two words, *in to.*] In to; in and to: expressing motion or direction toward the inner part of a place or thing, and hence entrance or inclusion within limits, or change to new circumstances, relations, condition, form, etc.

in-tol-er-a-ble (in-tol′ẹ-rạ-bl), *a.* [L. *intolerabilis.*] Not tolerable; unendurable; insufferable: as, *intolerable* agony; *intolerable* wrongs; an *intolerable* nuisance; "Something that has oppressed us all has become *intolerable* and has to be ended" (H. G. Wells's "Mr. Britling," i. 5. § 12).—**in-tol″er-a-bil′i-ty** (-bil′i-ti), **in-tol′er-a-ble-ness,** *n.*—**in-tol′er-a-bly,** *adv.*

in-tol-er-ant (in-tol′ẹ-rạnt), *a.* [L. *intolerans (-ant-).*] Not tolerant; unable or indisposed to tolerate or endure; esp., not tolerating contrary opinions, esp. in religious matters; bigoted.—**in-tol′er-ance,** *n.*—**in-tol′er-ant-ly,** *adv.*

in-tol-er-a-tion (in-tol-ẹ-rā′shọn), *n.* [See *in-*[2].] Want of toleration; intolerance.

in-to-nate (in′tö̜-nāt), *v. t.*; *-nated, -nating.* [ML. *intonatus*, pp. of *intonare*, < L. *in*, in, + *tonus*, E. *tone.*] To intone or chant; also, to utter with a particular tone or modulation of voice.—**in-to-na′tion** (-nā′shọn), *n.* The act of intonating or intoning; also, the utterance or production of musical tones; also, the manner of intonating in speaking; a modulation or inflection of voice (as, "I found the half-forgotten Southern *intonations* . . . as pleasing to my ear as they had formerly been": Mark Twain's "Life on the Mississippi," xliv.).

in-tone (in-tōn′), *v.*; *-toned, -toning.* [ML. *intonare*: see *intonate.*] **I.** *tr.* To utter in a singing voice, as in a liturgical service; chant; recite in monotone; also, to utter with a particular tone, or intonate. **II.** *intr.* To speak or recite in a singing voice, esp. in monotone; utter sonorous tones of musical quality.—**in-ton′er** (-tō′nėr), *n.*

in-tor′sion, *n.* See *intortion.*

in-tort (in-tôrt′), *v. t.* [L. *intortus*, pp. of *intorquere*, < *in*, in, + *torquere*, twist.] To twist inward, curl, or wind: as, "*intorted* horns" (Pope's tr. Homer's "Odyssey," iii.).—**in-tor′tion** (-tôr′shọn), *n.* [LL. *intortio(n-).*] A twisting or winding, as of the stem of a plant.

in-tox-i-cant (in-tok′si-kạnt). **I.** *a.* Intoxicating. **II.** *n.* An intoxicating agent, as alcoholic liquor or any of certain drugs.

in-tox-i-cate (in-tok′si-kāt), *v. t.*; *-cated, -cating.* [ML. *intoxicatus*, pp. of *intoxicare*, < L. *in*, in, + *toxicum*, poison: see *toxic.*] To poison†; also, to affect temporarily with loss of control over the physical and mental powers, by means of alcoholic liquor, a drug, or other substance, or as the liquor or substance does; excite, stupefy, or overcome by affecting thus; inebriate; make drunk; fig., to excite or transport mentally beyond self-control or reason (as, to be *intoxicated* with joy, vanity, or success).—**in-tox′i-cate** (-kāt), *a.* Intoxicated: as, "*intoxicate* with joy and pride" (Southey's "Thalaba," i. 34). [Archaic.]—**in-tox′i-cat-ing-ly** (-kā-ting-li), *adv.*—**in-tox-i-ca′tion** (-kā′shọn), *n.* The act of intoxicating, or the state of being intoxicated; poisoning (now only in *pathol.*: cf. *auto-intoxication*); inebriation; drunkenness; fig., overpowering action or effect upon the mind (as, "the sweet *intoxication* of young love": George Eliot's "Adam Bede," ix.).

intra-. [L. *intra-*, repr. *intra*, adv. and prep., within, akin to *interior*, inner, and *inter*, between: see *interior* and *inter-*, and cf. *intro-.*] A prefix of Latin origin, meaning 'within,' freely used as an English formative, esp. in scientific terms, sometimes in opposition to *extra-*.—**in-tra-ca-non-i-cal** (in″trạ̈-kạ-non′i-kạl), *a.* Included within the canon of Scripture.—**in-tra-cel′lu-lar** (-sel′ṳ̄-lạ̈r), *a.* Within a cell or cells.—**in-tra-cra′ni-al** (-krā′ni-ạl), *a.* Within the cranium or skull.

in-trac-ta-ble (in-trak′tạ-bl), *a.* [L. *intractabilis.*] Not tractable; hard to handle or manage; refractory; stubborn: as, "Fox, as the less proud and *intractable* of the refractory pair, was preferred" (Macaulay's "Essays," William Pitt, Earl of Chatham).—**in-trac-ta-bil′i-ty** (-bil′i-ti), **in-trac′-ta-ble-ness,** *n.*—**in-trac′ta-bly,** *adv.*

in-tra-dos (in-trā′dos), *n.* [F., < L. *intra*, within, + F. *dos*, < L. *dorsum*, back.] In *arch.*, the interior curve or surface of an arch or vault. Cf. *extrados.*

in-tra-lob-u-lar (in-trạ̈-lob′ṳ̄-lạ̈r), *a.* [See *intra-*.] Within a lobule, esp. of the liver.

in-tra-mar-gi-nal (in-trạ̈-mär′ji-nạl), *a.* [See *intra-*.] Within the margin, as of a leaf.

in-tra-mo-lec-u-lar (in″trạ̈-mọ̄-lek′ṳ̄-lạ̈r), *a.* [See *intra-*.] Within the molecule or molecules.

in-tra-mun-dane (in-trạ̈-mun′dān), *a.* [L. *intra*, within, + *mundus*, world.] Within the world or the material universe.

in-tra-mu-ral (in-trạ̈-mū′rạl), *a.* [L. *intra*, within, + *murus*, wall.] Within the walls or inclosing limits, as of a city or a building; in *anat.*, within the substance of a wall, as of an organ.

in-tran-si-geant (aṅ-träṅ-zē-zhäṅ), *a.* and *n.* [F.] Same as *intransigent.*—**in-tran-si-geance** (aṅ-träṅ-zē-zhäṅs), *n.*

in-tran-si-gent (in-tran′si-jẹnt). [= F. *intransigeant*, < Sp. *intransigente*, < L. *in-*, not, + *transigens* (*-ent-*), ppr. of *transigere*, settle, E. *transact.*] **I.** *a.* Uncompromising, esp. in politics; irreconcilable. **II.** *n.* One who is irreconcilable, esp. in politics.—**in-tran′si-gence, in-tran′si-gen-cy,** *n.*—**in-tran′si-gent-ism,** *n.*

in-tran-sit-a-ble (in-tran′sit-ạ-bl), *a.* [See *in-*[2].] Not transitable; not admitting of transit; impassable.

in-tran-si-tive (in-tran′si-tiv). [LL. *intransitivus.*] In *gram.*: **I.** *a.* Not transitive, as a verb; not taking a direct object. **II.** *n.* An intransitive verb.—**in-tran′si-tive-ly,** *adv.*

in-trant (in′trạnt), *n.* [L. *intrans* (*intrant-*), ppr. of *intrare*, E. *enter.*] One who enters (esp. a college, association, etc.); an entrant.

in-tra-spi-nal (in-trạ̈-spī′nạl), *a.* [See *intra-*.] Within the spinal column or spinal cord; pertaining to parts within the spinal column or spinal cord. Also **in-tra-spi′nous.**—**in-tra-spi′nal-ly, in-tra-spi′nous-ly,** *adv.*

in-tra-state (in′trạ̈-stāt), *a.* [See *intra-*.] Within a state; esp., within the boundaries of a State of the American Union: as, *intrastate* commerce or business. Cf. *interstate.*

in-tra-ve-nous (in-trạ̈-vē′nus), *a.* [L. *intra*, within, + *vena*, E. *vein.*] Within a vein or the veins; noting or pertaining to an injection into a vein.—**in-tra-ve′nous-ly,** *adv.*

in-treat (in-trēt′), etc. Obs. or archaic form of *entreat*, etc.

in-trench (in-trench′), *v.* [See *in-*[1].] **I.** *tr.* To surround with a trench; fortify with trenches or other defensive works; hence, fig., to establish in a strong position (as, to be safely *intrenched* behind undeniable facts); also, to furrow (as, "His face Deep scars of thunder had *intrench'd*": Milton's "Paradise Lost," i. 601). **II.** *intr.* To trench or encroach (*on* or *upon*: as, to *intrench* on the domain or rights of another); trespass; infringe; sometimes, to verge (*on* or *upon*: as, proceedings *intrenching* on impiety).—**in-trench′er,** *n.*—**in-trench′ment,** *n.* The act of intrenching; also, an intrenched position; in *fort.*, a defensive work consisting of a trench or ditch and a parapet.

in-trep-id (in-trep′id), *a.* [L. *intrepidus*: cf. *trepid.*] Fearless; dauntless: as, an *intrepid* adventurer; *intrepid* courage.—**in-tre-pid′i-ty** (-tre-pid′i-ti), *n.* The quality of being intrepid; fearless courage.—**in-trep′id-ly,** *adv.*

in-tri-ca-cy (in′tri-kạ̄-si), *n.*; pl. *-cies* (-siz). Intricate character or state; also, an intricate part, thing, proceeding, etc. (as, "the *intricacies* of political intrigue": Disraeli's "Coningsby," ii. 7).

in-tri-cate (in′tri-kạ̄t), *a.* [L. *intricatus*, pp. of *intricare*, entangle, perplex, < *in*, in, + *tricæ*, trifles, hindrances, perplexities.] Perplexingly entangled or involved, as a combination of paths or windings, a knot, or anything comprising various parts or proceedings; confusingly complex, or complicated, as a mechanism, design, plot, argument, etc. (as, "No one could soar into a more *intricate* labyrinth of refined phraseology": Trollope's "Warden," v.); hard to follow out or understand as a whole; obscure.—**in′tri-cate-ly,** *adv.*—**in′tri-cate-ness,** *n.*

in-tri-gant, in-tri-guant (in′trẹ-gạnt, F. aṅ-trē-gäṅ), *n.* [F. *intrigant*, < It. *intrigante*, ppr. of *intrigare*: see *intrigue, v.*] An intriguing person: as, "I knew him . . . as a bold *intriguant*" (Poe's "Purloined Letter").—**in-tri-gante, in-tri-guante** (in′trẹ-gȧnt, F. aṅ-trē-gäṅt), *n.* [F. *intrigante.*] Fem. of *intrigant, intriguant.*

in-trigue (in-trēg′), *v.*; *-trigued, -triguing.* [F. *intriguer*, < It. *intrigare*, < L. *intricare*, entangle, perplex: see *intricate.*] **I.** *tr.* To entangle, or involve in intricacies or complications (now chiefly as representing a French use: as, a highly *intrigued* drama); hence, to trick or cheat (obs. or rare); also, to bring or force by intrigue or underhand machinations (as, to *intrigue* a person into or out of office); also, recently (from French use), to puzzle; excite the curiosity or interest of by puzzling, novel, or otherwise arresting qualities (as, a mystery, subject, idea, or suggestion *intrigues* one); loosely, to take the fancy of (as, a picture or a hat *intrigues* one); sometimes, to beguile (*into*) by appeal to the curiosity, interest, or fancy (as, to be *intrigued* into reading a book). **II.** *intr.* To use underhand machinations, or seek to accomplish designs by plotting or crafty contrivance (as, "It was known or suspected that he was busily *intriguing* against his colleagues": Lecky's "Hist. of Eng. in the 18th Century," i.); also, to carry on a clandestine amour or illicit intimacy.—**in-trigue** (in-trēg′ or in′trēg), *n.* [F., < It. *intrigo*, < *intrigare.*] Intricacy†; also, the series of complications forming the plot of a play or the like (now chiefly as representing a French use); also, the use of underhand machinations to accomplish designs; a course of plotting or crafty dealings for some secret end (as, political or court *intrigues*); also, a clandestine amour or illicit intimacy.—**in-tri′guer** (-trē′gėr), *n.*—**in-tri′guing-ly,** *adv.*

in-trin-sic (in-trin′sik), *a.* [F. *intrinsèque*, < LL. *intrinsecus*, adj., inward, < L. *intrinsecus*, adv., inwardly, < *intra*, within, + *secus*, beside: see *extrinsic.*] Being inside of a thing, inward, or internal (now chiefly in *anat.* and *pathol.*); also, belonging to a thing by its very nature (as, *intrinsic* value or merit; the *intrinsic* meaning of a term); inherent; essential.—**in-trin′si-cal-ly,** *adv.*

intro-. [L. *intro-*, repr. *intro*, adv., inwardly, within, akin to *intra*, within: see *intra-*.] A prefix of Latin origin, meaning 'inwardly,' 'within,' occasionally used as an English formative.

in-tro-ac-tive (in-trọ̄-ak′tiv), *a.* [See *intro-*.] Acting within or upon itself.

in-tro-duce (in-trọ̄-dūs′), *v. t.*; *-duced, -ducing.* [L. *introducere* (pp. *introductus*), < *intro*, within, + *ducere*, lead.] To lead, bring, or put into a place, position, surroundings, relations, etc. (as, to *introduce* a person into a room, a figure into a design, or an anecdote into a discourse); insert (as, to *introduce* the hand into a cavity); also, to bring into notice, knowledge, use, vogue, etc. (as, to *introduce* a foreign article, or a doctrine, reform, custom, or fashion); also, to bring forward, usher in, or begin with something preliminary (as, "With preamble sweet Of charming symphony they *introduce* Their sacred song": Milton's "Paradise Lost," iii. 368); also, to bring (a person) into the acquaintance of another; make known, as one person to another, with mention of names, etc.; present formally, as to a person, an audience, or society; sometimes, to bring (a person) to the knowledge or experience of something (with *to*: as, to *introduce* a person to a new sport, or to city life); also, to bring forward for consideration, as a subject, a proposed measure, a legislative bill, etc.—**in-tro-du′cer** (-dū′-sėr), *n.*—**in-tro-du′ci-ble,** *a.* That may be introduced.

in-tro-duc-tion (in-trọ̄-duk′shọn), *n.* [L. *introductio(n-).*] The act of introducing, or bringing into a place, position, relations, notice, use, acquaintance, etc.; often, a formal presentation of one person to another or others; also, something introduced (as, the word is a recent *introduction*);

also, something that introduces; a preliminary part, as of a book, discourse, musical composition, or other work, leading up to the main part; often, a more or less elementary treatise designed to introduce the reader to some study or subject (as, an *introduction* to the study, or the science, of botany).—**in-tro-duc'tive,** *a.* Introductory.

in-tro-duc-tor (in-trǫ-duk'tǫr), *n.* [LL.] One who introduces. [Archaic.]—**in-tro-duc'to-ry** (-tǫ-ri), *a.* [LL. *introductorius.*] Serving to introduce; preliminary; prefatory. —**in-tro-duc'to-ri-ly,** *adv.*

in-tro-it (in-trō'it), *n.* [= F. *introït,* < L. *introitus,* entrance, < *introire,* enter, < *intro,* within, + *ire,* go.] *Eccles.,* an antiphon, psalm, or anthem sung as the priest approaches the altar to celebrate the mass or communion.

in-tro-mit (in-trǫ-mit'), *v.;* *-mitted, -mitting.* [L. *intromittere* (pp. *intromissus*), < *intro,* within, + *mittere,* send.] **I.** *tr.* To send, put, or let in; introduce; admit. **II.** *intr.* To interfere; meddle; concern one's self. [Sc.]—**in-tro-mis'sion** (-mish'ǫn), *n.*—**in-tro-mit'tent,** *a.*

in-trorse (in-trôrs'), *a.* [L. *introrsus,* toward the inside, < *intro,* within, + *versus,* toward.] In *bot.,* turned or facing inward, as anthers which open toward the gynœcium.—**in-trorse'ly,** *adv.*

in-tro-spect (in-trǫ-spekt'), *v.* [L. *introspectus,* pp. of *introspicere,* < *intro,* within, + *specere,* look at.] **I.** *tr.* To look into; examine. **II.** *intr.* To look within; practise introspection.—**in-tro-spec'tion** (-spek'shǫn), *n.* The act of looking within; esp., observation or examination of one's own mental states or processes.—**in-tro-spec'tive,** *a.* Looking within; given to or characterized by introspection.—**in-tro-spec'tive-ly,** *adv.*—**in-tro-spec'tive-ness,** *n.*

in-tro-ver-sion (in-trǫ-vėr'shǫn), *n.* The act of introverting; introverted state; in *psychol.,* interest directed inward or upon the self (cf. *extroversion*).

in-tro-vert (in-trǫ-vėrt'), *v. t.* [L. *intro,* within, + *vertere* (pp. *versus*), turn.] To turn inward; direct (the mind, etc.) inward or upon the self; in *zoöl.,* etc., to insheathe a part of within another part; invaginate.—**in'tro-vert,** *n.* In *zoöl.,* etc., a part that is or can be introverted; in *psychol.,* one characterized by introversion; a person concerned chiefly with his own thoughts (cf. *extrovert* and *ambivert*).—**in-tro-vert'ed,** *p. a.* In *psychol.,* characterized by introversion.

in-trude (in-tröd'), *v.;* *-truded, -truding.* [L. *intrudere* (pp. *intrusus*), < *in,* in, + *trudere,* thrust.] **I.** *tr.* To thrust or force in (as, rock *intruded* while molten into fissures or between strata); hence, to thrust or bring in without warrant, leave, or welcome (as, to *intrude* one's self into a place, or into a person's society; to *intrude* one's company or opinions on, or upon, others). **II.** *intr.* To thrust one's self in; come in without warrant or propriety; come uninvited or with unwelcome presence: as, to *intrude* into a place, or upon a person or his privacy.—**in-trud'er** (-trö'dėr), *n.*—**in-trud'ing-ly,** *adv.*

in-tru-sion (in-trö'zhǫn), *n.* [ML. *intrusio(n-).*] The act of intruding; a thrusting or forcing in; an unwarranted or unwelcome entrance (as, "Why this *intrusion?* Were not my orders that I would be private?" Addison's "Cato," v. 2); also, something intruded; in *law,* wrongful entry; usurpation; in *geol.,* the forcing of extraneous matter, as molten rock, into some other formation; the matter forced in.—**in-tru'sive** (-siv). **I.** *a.* Intruding; characterized by or involving intrusion; in *geol.,* of rocks, having been forced, while molten or plastic, into fissures or between layers of other rocks; in *philol.,* inserted without properly belonging, as a letter in a word. **II.** *n.* In *geol.,* an intrusive rock or mass of rock.—**in-tru'sive-ly,** *adv.*—**in-tru'sive-ness,** *n.*

in-trust, en-trust (in-trust', en-), *v. t.* [See *in-*[1] and *en-*.] To invest with a trust or responsibility; charge with a specified office of duty involving trust (as, "His wife was *intrusted* with the management of the privy purse": Lecky's "Hist. of Eng. in the 18th Century," i.); hence, to trust with anything confided or committed (as, to *intrust* a person with a secret, or with money); also, to commit (something) in trust (*to*); confide, as for care, use, or performance (as, to *intrust* money, powers, or work to another); hence, to commit as if with trust or confidence (as, to hesitate to *intrust* one's life to a frayed rope).

in-tu-bate (in'tū̦-bāt), *v. t.;* *-bated, -bating.* [L. *in,* in, + *tubus,* E. *tube.*] In *med.,* to insert a tube into; treat by inserting a tube, as into the larynx.—**in-tu-ba'tion** (-bā'shǫn), *n.*

in-tu-it (in'tū̦-it), *v. t.* or *i.;* *-ited, -iting.* [L. *intuitus,* pp. of *intueri,* look upon, regard, < *in,* in, on, + *tueri,* look at.] To know, or receive knowledge, by immediate perception.

in-tu-i-tion (in-tū̦-ish'ǫn), *n.* [ML. *intuitio(n-),* < L. *intueri:* see *intuit.*] Sight† or view†; hence, direct or immediate perception of truths, facts, etc., independently of any reasoning process (as, "mighty preacher, to whose blessed *intuition* it was given to know all human hearts": Kingsley's "Alton Locke," xxxvii.); instinctive knowledge; immediate apprehension or cognition; an act of immediate perception or apprehension (as, to regard a happy guess as an *intuition;* the *intuitions* of genius); also, something discerned by immediate perception; esp., a primary truth. —**in-tu-i'tion-al,** *a.* Pertaining to or of the nature of intuition; characterized by intuition; also, based on intuition as a principle, as a doctrine or school of philosophy or ethics.—**in-tu-i'tion-al-ism,** *n.* Intuitional doctrine, as in philosophy or ethics; the doctrine of the immediate perception of truths by intuition (intellectual or moral); specif., *metaph.,* the doctrine that the absolute is known by an immediate cognition of the understanding; also, intuitionism.—**in-tu-i'tion-al-ist,** *n.*—**in-tu-i'tion-al-ly,** *adv.* —**in-tu-i'tion-ism,** *n.* Intuitionalism; specif., in *metaph.,* the doctrine that in perception external objects are known immediately, without the intervention of a vicarious phenomenon.—**in-tu-i'tion-ist,** *n.*

in-tu-i-tive (in-tū'i-tiv), *a.* [ML. *intuitivus,* < L. *intueri:* see *intuit.*] Perceiving by intuition, as a person, the mind, etc.; concerned with or proceeding by intuition (as, the *intuitive* reason: opposed to *discursive*); of the nature of intuition (as, "Her perception of the right seemed almost *intuitive*": Cooper's "Deerslayer," iv.); also, perceived by, resulting from, or involving intuition (as, *intuitive* truths; *intuitive* knowledge or certainty).—**in-tu'i-tive-ly,** *adv.*—**in-tu'i-tive-ness,** *n.*—**in-tu'i-tiv-ism,** *n.* The doctrine that the fundamental principles of ethics are reached by intuition; ethical intuitionalism; also, intuitive perception; insight.—**in-tu'i-tiv-ist,** *n.*

in-tu-mesce (in-tū̦-mes'), *v. i.;* *-mesced, -mescing.* [L. *intumescere,* < *in,* in, on, + *tumescere,* begin to swell, < *tumere,* swell.] To swell up, as with heat; become tumid; bubble up.—**in-tu-mes'cence** (-mes'ẹns), *n.* A swelling up or bubbling up, as with heat; swollen state; also, a swollen mass or growth.—**in-tu-mes'cent,** *a.* Intumescing; becoming tumid.

in-turn (in'tėrn), *n.* A turning inward, as of the toes; an inward turn.

in-tus-sus-cept (in″tus-su-sept'), *v. t.* [L. *intus,* within, + *suscipere* (pp. *susceptus*), receive: see *susception.*] To take within, as one part of the intestine into an adjacent part; invaginate.—**in″tus-sus-cep'tion** (-sep'shǫn), *n.* [L. *intus* + *susceptio(n-),* E. *susception.*] A taking within; in *physiol.,* the taking in of foreign matter by a living organism, and its conversion into living tissue; in *pathol.,* the reception of one part within another, as when a part of the intestine is introduced into an adjacent part; invagination.—**in″tus-sus-cep'tive,** *a.*

in-twine (in-twīn'), etc. Same as *entwine,* etc.

in-twist (in-twist'), *v. t.* Same as *entwist.*

in-u-lase (in'ū̦-lās), *n.* [See *inulin* and *-ase.*] In *chem.,* an enzyme which converts inulin into levulose.

in-u-lin (in'ū̦-lin), *n.* [L. *inula,* elecampane.] A white starch-like substance obtained from the roots of certain plants, esp. elecampane, *Inula helenium.*

in-unc-tion (in-ungk'shǫn), *n.* [L. *inunctio(n-),* < *inunguere,* anoint: see *anoint,* and cf. *unction.*] The act of anointing; in *med.,* the rubbing in of an oil or ointment.

in-un-dant (in-un'dạnt), *a.* Inundating; overflowing.

in-un-date (in'un-dāt or in-un'-), *v. t.;* *-dated, -dating.* [L. *inundatus,* pp. of *inundare,* < *in,* in, on, + *undare,* rise in waves, overflow, < *unda,* a wave.] To overspread with a flood, or as a flood does; flood, deluge, or overflow; fig., to overspread as with or as in a flood (as, "The calm and the magical moonlight Seemed to *inundate* her soul with indefinable longings": Longfellow's "Evangeline," ii. 3); cover or fill with an overflowing abundance; overwhelm.—**in-un-da′tion** (-dā′shọn), *n.* [L. *inundatio(n-).*] The act of inundating, or the state of being inundated; an overflowing of water over the land (as, "heavy rains, which were causing *inundations* and much damage throughout the country": George Eliot's "Adam Bede," xxvii.); a flood; fig., an overspreading or overwhelming as if by flood; superabundance.

in-ur-bane (in-ėr-bān′), *a.* [L. *inurbanus.*] Not urbane; lacking in courtesy, politeness, or suavity; rude.—**in-ur-ban′i-ty** (-ban′i-ti), *n.*

in-ure (in-ūr′), *v.*; *-ured, -uring.* [Also *enure*; < *in-*[1], *en-*, + obs. *ure*, work, operation, use, < OF. *uevre* (F. *œuvre*), < L. *opera*, work.] **I.** *tr.* To put into operation†; exercise† or use†; also, to accustom by exercise or experience, as to something, or to do something, esp. a thing requiring discipline or endurance (as, to *inure* a person to military service, or to danger, hardship, or cold; to *inure* one's self to endure cold); habituate; harden. **II.** *intr.* To become operative or have effect (as, an agreement that *inures* to the especial benefit of one party); become serviceable *(to)*.—**in-ure′ment,** *n.*

in-urn (in-ėrn′), *v. t.* [See *in-*[1].] To put into an urn (esp. the ashes of the dead); hence, to entomb (as, "The sepulchre, Wherein we saw thee quietly *inurn'd*": Shakspere's "Hamlet," i. 4. 49).—**in-urn′ment,** *n.*

in-u-si-tate (in-ū′zi-tāt), *a.* [L. *inusitatus*, < *in-*, not, + *usitatus*, pp. of *usitari*, freq. of *uti*, use.] Not commonly used; unusual. [Now rare.]

in-u-tile (in-ū′til), *a.* [OF. F. *inutile*, < L. *inutilis*, < *in-*, not, + *utilis*, useful: see *utility.*] Useless; of no use or service; unprofitable.—**in-u-til′i-ty** (-ū-til′i-ti), *n.*; pl. *-ties* (-tiz). [L. *inutilitas.*] Uselessness (as, "The *inutility* of her best efforts . . . palsied the poor old gentlewoman": Hawthorne's "House of the Seven Gables," xv.); also, a useless thing or person.

in-ut-ter-a-ble (in-ut′ėr-ạ-bl), *a.* [See *in-*[2].] Unutterable; inexpressible: as, "*inutterable* unkindliness" (Tennyson's "Merlin and Vivien," 884).

in-vade (in-vād′), *v. t.*; *-vaded, -vading.* [L. *invadere* (pp. *invasus*), < *in*, in, + *vadere*, go.] To enter (a country, region, etc.) with armed force, as for conquest or spoliation; make a hostile incursion into; hence, fig., to enter like an enemy (as, locusts *invaded* the fields; disease *invades* the system); enter as if to take possession, overrun, or overspread (as, to *invade* a friend's quarters; tourists *invade* a city; night *invades* the sky); intrude upon (privacy, thoughts, etc.); intrench, encroach, or infringe upon (rights, etc.).—**in-vad′er** (-vā′dėr), *n.*

in-vag-i-nate (in-vaj′i-nāt), *v.*; *-nated, -nating.* [L. *in*, in, + *vagina*, sheath: cf. *evaginate.*] **I.** *tr.* To insert or receive as into a sheath; sheathe; specif., to fold or draw (a tubular organ, etc.) back within itself; introvert; intussuscept. **II.** *intr.* To become invaginated; undergo invagination.—**in-vag′i-nate,** *a.* Invaginated.—**in-vag-i-na′tion** (-nā′shọn), *n.* The act or process of invaginating, or the resulting state; also, an invaginated part; in *pathol.*, intussusception, as of a portion of the intestine; in *embryol.*, the drawing inward of a portion of the wall of a blastula in the formation of a gastrula.

in-val-id[1] (in-val′id), *a.* [L. *invalidus*, < *in-*, not, + *validus*, strong, powerful, effective, E. *valid.*] Not valid; having no force, weight, or cogency, as an argument; esp., without legal force, or void, as a contract.

in-va-lid[2] (in′vạ-lid, Brit. also in′vạ-lēd or in-vạ-lēd′). [F. *invalide*, < L. *invalidus*: see *invalid*[1].] **I.** *a.* Impaired in health; sick; infirm; also, of or for invalids. **II.** *n.* A person suffering from prolonged ill health or from some disabling injury; sometimes, one disabled for active service, as a soldier or a sailor.—**in′va-lid**[2], *v.* **I.** *tr.* To make an invalid of; also, to class or enroll, or remove from active service, as an invalid. **II.** *intr.* To become an invalid; also, of a soldier or a sailor, to cause one's self to be registered as an invalid, or retire from active service because of illness or injury (as, "He had been long suffering . . . and though repeatedly advised to *invalid*, he never would consent": Marryat's "Peter Simple," xxxvii.).

in-val-i-date (in-val′i-dāt), *v. t.*; *-dated, -dating.* [See *invalid*[1].] To render invalid, or of no force or effect; esp., to deprive of legal force or efficacy.—**in-val-i-da′tion** (-dā′shọn), *n.*—**in-val′i-da-tor,** *n.*

in-va-lid-ism (in′vạ-lid-izm), *n.* [See *invalid*[2].] The condition of an invalid; prolonged ill health.

in-va-lid-i-ty (in-vạ-lid′i-ti), *n.* [See *in-*[2].] Want of validity, cogency, or legal force.

in-val-u-a-ble (in-val′ụ̄-ạ-bl), *a.* [See *in-*[2] and *valuable.*] That cannot be valued or appraised; of inestimable value; priceless.—**in-val′u-a-ble-ness,** *n.*—**in-val′u-a-bly,** *adv.*

in-var (in-vär′), *n.* [Short for *invariable.*] An alloy of steel and nickel, having a coefficient of expansion which is virtually zero: used for making scientific instruments, etc.

in-va-ri-a-ble (in-vā′ri-ạ-bl). [See *in-*[2].] **I.** *a.* Not variable; unchangeable or unalterable; constant; uniform; always the same. **II.** *n.* In *math.*, a constant.—**in-va″ri-a-bil′i-ty** (-bil′i-ti), **in-va′ri-a-ble-ness,** *n.*—**in-va′ri-a-bly,** *adv.*

in-va-ri-ant (in-vā′ri-ạnt). [See *in-*[2].] **I.** *a.* Not variant; unvarying; invariable; constant. **II.** *n.* An invariable entity or quantity.—**in-va′ri-an-tive** (-ạn-tiv), *a.* Pertaining to an invariant.

in-va-sion (in-vā′zhọn), *n.* [LL. *invasio(n-)*, < L. *invadere*: see *invade.*] The act of invading; the entering of a country by an enemy force, as for conquest or spoliation; a hostile incursion; hence, the entrance or advent of anything troublesome or harmful, as disease; entrance as if to take possession or overrun (as, the peaceful *invasion* of Europe by tourists or foreign trade; the *invasion* of a region by plants from another region); infringement by intrusion (as, *invasion* of rights).—**in-va′sive** (-siv), *a.* Invading, or tending to invade; characterized by or involving invasion; offensive; intrusive.

in-vecked, in-vect-ed (in-vekt′, -vek′ted), *a.* [L. *invectus*, pp. of *invehere*, carry in: see *inveigh.*] Bordered by, or formed exteriorly of, small convex or outward curves or slightly projecting rounded lobes: chiefly in *her.*

Escutcheon with a Pale Invected.

in-vec-tive (in-vek′tiv). [LL. *invectivus*, < L. *invehere*: see *inveigh.*] **I.** *a.* Characterized by inveighing; vehemently denunciatory. **II.** *n.* An invective utterance; a vehement attack in words; also, invective language, or vehement denunciation (as, "He [the elder Pitt] far surpassed them all in the blasting fury of his *invective*": Lecky's "Hist. of Eng. in the 18th Century," viii.).—**in-vec′tive-ly,** *adv.*

in-veigh (in-vā′), *v. i.* [L. *invehere* (pp. *invectus*), carry in, refl. or pass. attack, assail, inveigh, < *in*, in, + *vehere*, carry.] To make a vehement attack in words; speak or write in vehement denunciation; rail: as, "He never fails to *inveigh* with hearty bitterness against democracy as the source of every species of crime" (Macaulay's "Essays," Mitford's Hist. of Greece).—**in-veigh′er,** *n.*

in-vei-gle (in-vē′gl), *v. t.*; *-gled, -gling.* [OF. *avugler* (F. *aveugler*), to blind, < *avugle*, blind, < L. *ab*, from, + *oculus*, eye.] To blind in mind or judgment†; beguile† or deceive†; also, to allure, win, or seduce by beguiling (as, "Yet have they many baits and guileful spells, To *inveigle* and invite the unwary sense Of them that pass": Milton's "Comus," 538); now, esp., to draw (*into*, sometimes *from, away*, etc.) by beguiling or artful inducements (as, to *inveigle* a person into a place, or into doing something; "Achilles hath *inveigled* his fool from him," Shakspere's "Troilus and Cressida," ii. 3. 99); entice.—**in-vei′gle-ment,** *n.* The act of inveigling; allurement; enticement; also, that which inveigles; a means of inveigling.—**in-vei′gler,** *n.*

in-vent (in-vent′), *v.* [L. *inventus*, pp. of *invenire*, come upon, find, < *in*, in, on, + *venire*, come.] **I.** *tr.* To come upon†, or find† (as, "And vowed never to returne againe, Till him alive or dead she did *invent*": Spenser's "Faerie Queene," iii. 5. 10); hence, to find out or hit upon with the mind; devise by thought or ingenuity, as something new or original (as, to *invent* a method or process, or a machine; to *invent* an alphabet or a name; "Who first *invented* work . . . ? Who but the being unblest . . . Sabbathless Satan!" Lamb's "Work"); originate as a product of one's own contrivance; also, to produce or create with the imagination (as, to *invent* a plot for a story); sometimes, to make up, or fabricate, as something merely fictitious or false (as, to *invent* a statement; to *invent* excuses or reasons). **II.** *intr.* To devise something new, as by thought or ingenuity; originate or create something by exercise of an inventive faculty: as, "Young men are fitter to *invent* than judge" (Bacon's "Essays," Of Youth and Age); "'They hunt old trails,' said Cyril, 'very well; But when did woman ever yet *invent?*'" (Tennyson's "Princess," ii. 369).—**in-vent'i-ble,** *a.* Capable of being invented.

in-ven-tion (in-ven'shọn), *n.* [L. *inventio(n-)*, < *invenire*: see *invent.*] The act of finding (obs. or archaic: cf. *Invention of the Cross,* below); also, the act of inventing or devising by thought or ingenuity (as, the *invention* of labor-saving processes or machinery; the *invention* of gunpowder); original contrivance, as of something new; something invented or devised, or a product of inventive ingenuity (as, to patent an *invention*; this plan was his *invention*); also, the act of producing or creating by exercise of the imagination; mental fabrication, or something fabricated, as a made-up story or a false statement; specif., the exercise of imaginative or creative power in literature or art; also, the power or faculty of inventing, devising, or originating; the creative faculty.—**Invention of the Cross,** a church festival, observed on May 3, in commemoration of the reputed finding of the cross of Christ by St. Helena, mother of Constantine the Great, at Jerusalem, A.D. 326.

in-ven-tive (in-ven'tiv), *a.* Apt at inventing, devising, or contriving, as a person, the mind, etc.; having the function of inventing (as, the *inventive* faculty); also, pertaining to, involving, or showing invention (as, *inventive* skill; *inventive* drawing).—**in-ven'tive-ly,** *adv.*—**in-ven'tive-ness,** *n.*

in-ven-tor (in-ven'tọr), *n.* [L.] One who invents; esp., one who devises some new process, appliance, machine, or article; one who makes inventions.

in-ven-to-ry (in'ven-tō̤-ri), *n.*; pl. *-ries* (-riz). [ML. *inventorium*, for LL. *inventarium*, < L. *invenire*: see *invent.*] A detailed list of articles, such as the items of property of an estate or the wares of a merchant, sometimes with a record of their nature or value; hence, a collection of articles which are or may be so listed.—**in-ven-to'ri-al** (-tō'ri-ạl), *a.*—**in-ven-to'ri-al-ly,** *adv.*—**in'ven-to-ry,** *v. t.*; *-ried, -rying.* To make an inventory of; enter in an inventory.

in-ven-tress (in-ven'tres), *n.* A female inventor.

in-ve-ra-cious (in-vē̤-rā'shus), *a.* [See *in-*[2].] Not veracious; untruthful.—**in-ve-ra'ci-ty** (-ras'i-ti), *n.*; pl. *-ties* (-tiz). Lack of veracity; untruthfulness; also, an untruth.

In-ver-ness (in-vėr-nes') **coat.** [From *Inverness*, in Scotland.] An overcoat with a long, removable cape (*Inverness cape*).

in-verse (in-vėrs'), *v. t.*; *-versed, -versing.* [L. *inversus*, pp. of *invertere*: see *invert.*] To invert; reverse. [Now rare.]—**in-verse** (in-vėrs' or in'vėrs). **I.** *a.* Inverted, or turned upside down (as, "I saw a tower builded on a lake, Mock'd by its *inverse* shadow": Hood's "Two Swans," 11); hence, in general, reversed in position, direction, or tendency (as, verify the addition by adding in *inverse* order); opposite in nature or effect, as a mathematical relation or operation (as, "The reigning taste was so bad, that the success of a writer was in *inverse* proportion to his labour, and to his desire of excellence": Macaulay's "Essays," John Dryden). **II.** *n.* That which is inverse; the direct opposite.—**in-verse'ly,** *adv.* In an inverse manner or order; in inverse proportion (as when one thing is greater in proportion as another is less, or less in proportion as the other is greater).

in-ver-sion (in-vėr'shọn), *n.* [L. *inversio(n-)*, < *invertere*: see *invert.*] The act of inverting, or an inverted state; reversal of position, direction, order, or relation; also, something inverted; in *rhet.*, reversal of the usual or natural order of words; anastrophe; in *chem.*, a hydrolysis of certain carbohydrates, as cane-sugar, which results in a reversal of direction of the rotatory power of the carbohydrate solution.—**in-ver'sive** (-siv), *a.* Characterized by inversion.

in-vert (in-vėrt'), *v. t.* [L. *invertere* (pp. *inversus*), < *in*, in, on, + *vertere*, turn.] To turn upside down (as, to *invert* a tumbler or bowl); hence, in general, to reverse in position, direction, or order (as, to *invert* the letters of a name or the parts of a sentence); turn or change to the opposite or contrary, as in nature, bearing, or effect; in *chem.*, to subject to inversion, as sugar.

in-vert-ase (in-vėr'tās), *n.* [From *invert* + *-ase.*] In *chem.*, an enzyme which causes the inversion of cane-sugar, thus changing it into invert-sugar: found in plants and in the digestive juices of animals.

in-ver-te-brate (in-vėr'tē̤-brāt). [NL. *invertebratus.*] **I.** *a.* Not vertebrate; without a backbone; of or pertaining to the *Invertebrata*, an obsolete zoölogical division (sometimes still used for convenience) including all the animals without a vertebral column; fig., without backbone, or strength of character. **II.** *n.* An invertebrate animal; fig., a person lacking strength of character.—**in-ver'te-bra-cy** (-brạ-si), **in-ver'te-brate-ness,** *n.*

in-vert-ed (in-vėr'ted), *p. a.* Turned upside down; reversed in position, direction, or order; turned or changed to the opposite.—**inverted arch,** in *arch.*, an arch set upside down, that is, with its intrados below the axis or springing-line: used in foundation construction, etc.—**in-vert'ed-ly,** *adv.*

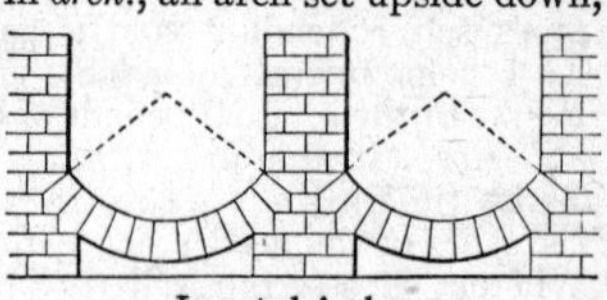

Inverted Arches.

in-vert-er (in-vėr'tėr), *n.* One who or that which inverts.

in-vert-i-ble (in-vėr'ti-bl), *a.* That may be inverted.

in-vert-or (in-vėr'tọr), *n.* An inverter; in *elect.*, a commutator.

in-vert=sug-ar (in'vėrt-shůg''ạ̈r), *n.* A mixture of dextroglucose and levulose formed naturally in fruits and produced artificially by the inversion of cane-sugar.

in-vest (in-vest'), *v.* [L. *investire* (pp. *investitus*), < *in*, in, + *vestire*, clothe, E. *vest*, *v.*] **I.** *tr.* To clothe in or with a garment or article of attire (as, "*Invest* me in my motley": Shakspere's "As You Like It," ii. 7. 58); cover or adorn as an article of attire does (as, a turban, or a diadem, *invested* his head); sometimes, to put on (a garment, etc.: obs. or rare); also, fig., to cover or surround as if with a garment, or like a garment (as, spring *invests* the trees with leaves; thick foliage *invested* the trees; darkness *invested* the earth); indue or endow (whether actually or by ascription) with a quality, attribute, or character (as, to *invest* a narrative with the charm of romance; to *invest* a friend with every virtue); belong to, as a quality or character does (as, the charm of romance *invested* the subject); also, to clothe in or with the insignia of office (as, "That, in the official marks *invested*, you Anon do meet the senate": Shakspere's "Coriolanus," ii. 3. 148); hence, to install in an office or position; furnish with power, authority, rank, a right, etc. (as, "He had twice been *invested* with the consular dignity": Gibbon's "Decline and Fall of the Roman Empire," xii.); sometimes, to settle or vest (a power, right, etc.), as in a person; also, to surround (a place) with military forces or works so as to prevent approach or escape; hem in, as in besieging; also, to put (money) to use, by purchase or expenditure, in something offering profitable returns, esp. interest or income (as, to *invest* one's capital in stocks, real estate, or goods for trade); loosely, to lay out or spend (as, to *invest* large sums in books; to *invest* a dollar in having one's fortune told). **II.** *intr.* To invest money; make an investment.

in-ves-ti-ga-ble (in-ves'ti-gạ-bl), *a.* [LL. *investigabilis.*] Capable of being investigated.

in-ves-ti-gate (in-ves'ti-gāt), *v.*; *-gated, -gating.* [L. *investigatus*, pp. of *investigare*, < *in*, in, + *vestigare*, track, trace out.] **I.** *tr.* To search or inquire into, in order to trace out or ascertain facts; make a searching inquiry into; examine in detail: as, to *investigate* natural phenomena, a crime, or a person's conduct or past. **II.** *intr.* To make inquiry, examination, or investigation.—**in-ves'ti-gat-ing-ly** (-gā-ting-li), *adv.*—**in-ves-ti-ga'tion** (-gā'shọn), *n.* [L. *investigatio(n-).*] The act or process of investigating; a searching inquiry in order to ascertain facts; a detailed or careful examination.—**in-ves'ti-ga-tive** (-gā-tiv), **in-ves'ti-ga-to-ry** (-tō̤-ri), *a.* Inclined or tending toward investigation; pertaining to investigation.—**in-ves'ti-ga-tor** (-gā-tọr), *n.*

in-ves-ti-tive (in-ves'ti-tiv), *a.* [L. *investire* (pp. *investitus*), E. *invest.*] Serving to invest; pertaining to investiture.

in-ves-ti-ture (in-ves′ti-ţūr), *n.* [ML. *investitura*, < L. *investire*, E. *invest.*] The act of investing, or the state of being invested, as with a garment, covering, quality, attribute, etc.; that which invests, as clothing or a covering (archaic or literary); specif., the formal investing of a person with the insignia of office, or with an office or dignity, power, a right, etc.

in-vest-ment (in-vest′mȩnt), *n.* The act of investing, or the state of being invested, with a garment or covering; a garment or vestment (archaic: as, "You, lord archbishop . . . Whose white *investments* figure innocence," Shakspere's "2 Henry IV.," iv. 1. 45); any covering, coating, outer layer, or integument, as of an animal or vegetable body; also, an investing with a quality, attribute, etc.; sometimes, investiture with an office, dignity, or right; also, the surrounding of a place with military forces or works, as in besieging; also, the investing of money or capital in order to secure profitable returns, esp. interest or income; a particular instance or mode of investing (as, a good income from judicious *investments*); a thing invested in (as, U. S. bonds are the safest *investment*); sometimes, a sum of money invested.

in-vest-or (in-ves′tọr), *n.* One who invests; esp., one who invests money, as in stocks, bonds, real estate, etc.

in-vet-er-ate (in-vet′ȩ-rāt), *a.* [L. *inveteratus*, pp. of *inveterare*, render old, < *in*, in, + *vetus* (*veter-*), old.] Old† (as, *inveterate* walls or trees); hence, firmly established by long continuance, as a disease or sore, a habit or practice (often bad), or a feeling (often hostile); chronic, settled, or fixed; also, confirmed in a habit, practice, feeling, or the like, as a person (as, an *inveterate* smoker; an *inveterate* gambler; "These savages are . . . the *inveterate* foe of the trappers," Irving's "Captain Bonneville," v.); also, embittered or virulent (obs. or rare).—**in-vet′er-a-cy** (-ȩ-rā-si), **in-vet′er-ate-ness,** *n.*—**in-vet′er-ate-ly,** *adv.*

in-vexed (in-vekst′), *a.* [From *in-*[1] + *-vex*, as in *convex*, + *-ed*[2].] In *her.*, curved inward or concavely.

Escutcheon with a Chief Invexed.

in-vid-i-ous (in-vid′i-us), *a.* [L. *invidiosus*, < *invidia*, ill-will, E. *envy.*] Full of ill-will†, grudging†, or envious†; also, regarded with ill-will†, hateful†, or odious† (as, "*invidious* crimes": Dryden's tr. Virgil's "Æneid," xi. 518); also, calculated to excite ill-will or resentment or give offense (as, *invidious* remarks; "He deprecated any *invidious* retrospect as to what had passed in former debates," Lecky's "Hist. of Eng. in the 18th Century," viii.); offensively or unfairly discriminating, as a distinction or comparison; such as to bring odium, unpopularity, or envious dislike (as, an *invidious* honor); also, enviable†.—**in-vid′i-ous-ly,** *adv.*—**in-vid′i-ous-ness,** *n.*

in-vig-i-late (in-vij′i-lāt), *v. i.*; *-lated, -lating.* [L. *invigilatus*, pp. of *invigilare*, < *in*, in, on, + *vigilare*, watch: see *vigilant.*] To keep watch; now, esp., to keep watch over students at an examination (Eng.).—**in-vig-i-la′tion** (-lā′shọn), *n.*—**in-vig′i-la-tor,** *n.*

in-vig-or-ant (in-vig′ọr-ạnt), *n.* An invigorating agent; a tonic.

in-vig-or-ate (in-vig′ọr-āt), *v. t.*; *-ated, -ating.* [For earlier *invigor*, < *in-*[1] + *vigor.*] To give vigor to; supply with healthy or active force; fill with life and energy: as, to *invigorate* the body or the mind; to *invigorate* the industries of a country.—**in-vig′or-at-ing-ly** (-ā-ting-li), *adv.*—**in-vig-or-a′tion** (-ā′shọn), *n.* The act of invigorating, or the state of being invigorated.—**in-vig′or-a-tive** (-ạ-tiv), *a.* Invigorating.—**in-vig′or-a-tor** (-ā-tọr), *n.*

in-vin-ci-ble (in-vin′si-bl), *a.* [L. *invincibilis*: cf. *vincible.*] That cannot be conquered or vanquished (as, an *invincible* foe, army, or fortress; the *Invincible* Armada, see *armada*); fig., not to be overcome (as, *invincible* difficulties; an *invincible* dislike; *invincible* courage; "I had an *invincible* impression upon my thoughts that my deliverance was at hand," Defoe's "Robinson Crusoe," i. 16); insuperable; insurmountable.—**in-vin-ci-bil′i-ty** (-bil′i-ti), **in-vin′ci-ble-ness,** *n.*—**in-vin′ci-bly,** *adv.*

in-vi-o-la-ble (in-vī′ọ-lạ-bl), *a.* [L. *inviolabilis*: cf. *violable.*] That cannot be violated, subjected to violence, or injured (as, "Jove, the *inviolable* king": Pope's tr. Homer's "Iliad," iii.); also, that must not be violated; that is to be kept free from violence or violation of any kind, or treated as if sacred (as, the person of the herald was *inviolable*; an *inviolable* sanctuary; *inviolable* faith or laws).—**in-vi″o-la-bil′i-ty** (-bil′i-ti), *n.*—**in-vi′o-la-bly,** *adv.*

in-vi-o-late (in-vī′ọ-lạt), *a.* [L. *inviolatus*, < *in-*, not, + *violatus*, pp., violated: see *violate.*] Not violated; free from violation, injury, desecration, or outrage (as, to keep a tomb or a sacred place *inviolate*; *inviolate* sanctity or purity); unbroken, as a law, agreement, or promise; not infringed, as rights; undisturbed, as privacy.—**in-vi′o-la-cy** (-lạ-si), **in-vi′o-late-ness,** *n.*—**in-vi′o-late-ly,** *adv.*

in-vis-i-ble (in-viz′i-bl), *a.* [L. *invisibilis.*] Not visible; not perceptible by the eye (as, *invisible* atoms; *invisible* vapor; *invisible* ink, sympathetic ink, see under *sympathetic*); withdrawn from or out of sight (as, to keep one's self *invisible*); not perceptible or discernible by the mind (as, differences or changes that are almost *invisible*); also, of colors, so dark as to be scarcely distinguishable from black (as, *invisible* green; *invisible* blue; "I saw about fifty girls exposed for sale, but all of them black or '*invisible*' brown," Kinglake's "Eothen," xviii.).—**Invisible Empire,** a title of the earlier 'Ku Klux Klan,' and of the later 'Knights of the Ku Klux Klan': as, "This proclamation [Feb. 20, 1869] . . . was followed by a proclamation from the 'Grand Wizard of the *Invisible Empire*' to his subjects" (Century Magazine, July, 1884, p. 410). See *Ku Klux.*—**in-vis′i-ble,** *n.* An invisible thing or being; with *the*, the unseen or spiritual world; [*cap.*] God.—**in-vis-i-bil′i-ty** (-bil′i-ti), **in-vis′i-ble-ness,** *n.*—**in-vis′i-bly,** *adv.*

in-vi-ta-tion (in-vi-tā′shọn), *n.* [L. *invitatio(n-)*, < *invitare*: see *invite.*] The act of inviting; a request to come to a place, gathering, or the like, or to do something; a form of words (often written, engraved, or printed) in which such a request is conveyed; sometimes, attraction or allurement (as, "She gives the leer of *invitation*": Shakspere's "Merry Wives of Windsor," i. 3. 50).

in-vi-ta-to-ry (in-vī′tạ-tō-ri). [LL. *invitatorius* (as n., ML. *invitatorium*), < L. *invitare*: see *invite.*] **I.** *a.* Serving to invite; conveying an invitation. **II.** *n.*; pl. *-ries* (-riz). An invitation; esp., some form of invitation in church service.

in-vite (in-vīt′), *v.*; *-vited, -viting.* [L. *invitare* (pp. *invitatus*); origin uncertain.] **I.** *tr.* To ask, in a kindly, courteous, or complimentary way, to come or go to some place, gathering, entertainment, etc., or to do something (as, to *invite* friends to dinner or to a wedding; to *invite* a person to join or to address a society); request politely or formally; also, to make request for (as, to *invite* a person's presence, attention, or opinion); fig., to act so as to bring on or render probable (as, "To resent his affronts was perilous; yet not to resent them was . . . to *invite* them": Macaulay's "Essays," Frederic the Great); give occasion for (as, this subject *invites* a few remarks); also, to attract, allure, or tempt (as, "I saw nothing in this country that could *invite* me to a longer continuance," Swift's "Gulliver's Travels," iii. 6: cf. *inviting*, *p. a.*). **II.** *intr.* To give invitation; offer attractions or allurements.—**in-vite** (in-vīt′ or in′vīt), *n.* An invitation. [Colloq.]—**in-vit′er** (-vī′tėr), *n.*—**in-vit′ing,** *p. a.* That invites; esp., attractive, alluring, or tempting (as, an *inviting* prospect; an *inviting* offer).—**in-vit′ing-ly,** *adv.*—**in-vit′ing-ness,** *n.*

in-vo-cate (in′vọ-kāt), *v. t.*; *-cated, -cating.* [L. *invocatus*, pp. of *invocare*: see *invoke.*] To invoke: as, "Be thou the tenth Muse, ten times more in worth Than those old nine which rhymers *invocate*" (Shakspere's "Sonnets," xxxviii.). [Now rare.]—**in-vo-ca′tion** (-kā′shọn), *n.* [L. *invocatio(n-)*.] The act or an act of invoking; a calling upon a deity, etc., as in prayer; a calling for aid or protection; a form of words used in invoking, esp. as part of a public religious service; a calling upon a spirit by incantation, or an incantation or magical formula used for such a purpose; in *law*, a judicial call or demand for something, as papers or evidence.—**in-voc-a-to-ry** (in-vok′ạ-tō-ri or in′vọ-kạ-), *a.* Pertaining to or of the nature of invocation.

in-voice (in′vois), *n.* [Appar. < F. *envois*, pl. of *envoi*, a sending, a thing sent: see *envoy*[1].] A list of items of merchandise shipped or sent to a purchaser, consignee, etc., with the value or prices, and charges; also, the merchandise or shipment itself; a shipment or consignment of invoiced goods.—**in'voice,** *v. t.*; *-voiced, -voicing.* To make an invoice of; enter in an invoice.

in-voke (in-vōk'), *v. t.*; *-voked, -voking.* [OF. F. *invoquer*, < L. *invocare* (pp. *invocatus*), < *in*, in, on, + *vocare*, call.] To call on (a divine being, etc.), as in prayer; appeal to, as for aid or protection; sometimes, to call on to come or to do something; also, to call forth or upon (a spirit) by incantation; conjure; also, to call for earnestly (as, to *invoke* mercy or assistance); make supplication for; in *law*, to call for judicially.—**in-vok'er** (-vō'kėr), *n.*

in-vol-u-cel (in-vol'ū-sel), *n.* [NL. *involucellum*, dim. of L. *involucrum*: see *involucre*.] In *bot.*, a secondary involucre, as in a compound cluster of flowers.—**in-vol-u-cel'late** (-sel'āt), *a.* Having involucels.

in-vo-lu-cral (in-vọ-lū'krạl), *a.* Of or pertaining to an involucre.

in-vo-lu-crate (in-vọ-lū'krāt), *a.* Having an involucre.

in-vo-lu-cre (in'vọ-lū-kėr), *n.* [F. *involucre*, < L. *involucrum*, wrapper, covering, < *involvere*: see *involve*.] A covering, esp. a membranous one; in *bot.*, a collection or rosette of bracts round a flower-cluster, umbel, or the like.—**in'-vo-lu-cred** (-kėrd), *a.* Having an involucre; involucrate.—**in-vo-lu'crum** (-krum), *n.*; pl. *-cra* (-krạ). [L.] An involucre.

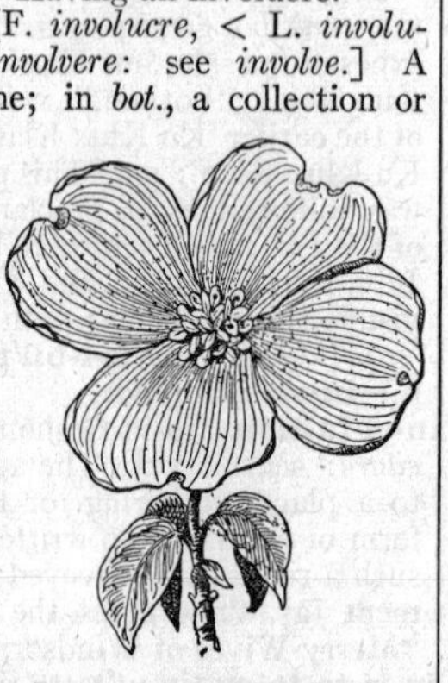

Involucre subtending the Cluster of Flowers of Flowering Dogwood (*Cornus florida*), forming the conspicuous part of the flower.

in-vol-un-ta-ry (in-vol'un-tạ-ri), *a.* [LL. *involuntarius*.] Not voluntary; acting, or done or made, without one's own volition, or otherwise than by one's own will or choice (as, an *involuntary* listener; an *involuntary* sigh; *involuntary* bankruptcy); done by accident, or unintentional (as, an *involuntary* affront); acting independently of, or done or occurring without exercise of, the will (as, *involuntary* muscles; *involuntary* movements).—**in-vol'un-ta-ri-ly,** *adv.*—**in-vol'un-ta-ri-ness,** *n.*

in-vo-lute (in'vọ-lūt). [L. *involutus*, pp. of *involvere*: see *involve*.] **I.** *a.* Rolled up on itself; curved spirally; also, involved or intricate (as, "the possible moves [in chess] being not only manifold, but *involute*": Poe's "Murders in the Rue Morgue"); specif., in *bot.*, rolled inward from the edge, as a leaf; in *conch.*, having the whorls closely wound, as certain shells. **II.** *n.* Something involved; in *geom.*, the curve traced by any point of a flexible and inextensible string when the latter is unwrapped, under tension, from a given curve (cf. *evolute*).—**in'vo-lut-ed** (-lū-ted), *a.* Involute.

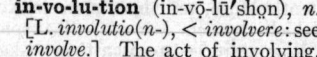

1, Branch of Poplar, showing Involute Leaves. 2, Outline of transverse section of an Involute Leaf.

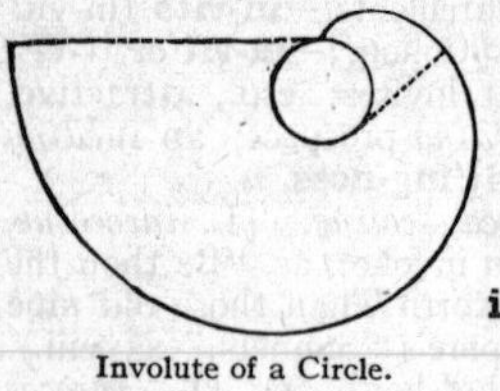

Involute of a Circle.

in-vo-lu-tion (in-vọ-lū'shọn), *n.* [L. *involutio(n-)*, < *involvere*: see *involve*.] The act of involving, or the state of being involved; a rolling up or folding in upon itself, or a part formed by this; entanglement or complication; complicated construction, as in the arrangement of words in a sentence; something complicated; inclusion, comprehension, or implication; in *physiol.*, etc., a retrograde change, as the return of an organ to its normal size after enlargement; in *biol.*, retrograde development; degeneration; in *math.*, the raising of a quantity or expression to any given power.

in-volve (in-volv'), *v. t.*; *-volved, -volving.* [L. *involvere* (pp. *involutus*), roll in or on, inwrap, involve, < *in*, in, on, + *volvere*, roll.] To roll, wrap, or shroud in something that surrounds or conceals (as, "She saw . . . Her sacred domes *involved* in rolling fire": Pope's "Windsor Forest," 324); envelop or infold, as the surrounding thing does (as, clouds *involved* the mountain); enshroud in mist, darkness, or obscurity (often fig.); also, to roll up on itself; wind spirally, coil, or wreathe (as, "Some of serpent kind . . . *involved* Their snaky folds": Milton's "Paradise Lost," vii. 483); also, to bring into an intricate or complicated form or condition (esp. in *involved, p. a.*); entangle; complicate; combine inextricably (*with*: as, "He knows His end with mine *involved*," Milton's "Paradise Lost," ii. 807); bring into difficulties (*with*: as, a plot to *involve* one government with another); cause to be inextricably associated or concerned, as in something embarrassing or unfavorable (as, "When they fell, they *involved* armies and provinces in their fall": Gibbon's "Decline and Fall of the Roman Empire," x.); implicate, as in guilt or crime, or in any matter or affair; also, to include, contain, or comprehend within itself or its scope (as, a combination *involving* various elements); include as a necessary circumstance, condition, or consequence; imply; entail; affect, as something within the scope of operation (as, changes *involving* the interests of the stockholders); also, to swallow up, engulf, or overwhelm (as, "The stormy fates descend: one death *involves* Tyrants and slaves": Thomson's "Seasons," Summer, 1022); in *math.*, to raise to a given power.—**in-volved',** *p. a.* Intricately formed or combined; complicated: as, an *involved* sentence or argument.—**in-volv'ed-ly** (-vol'ved-li), *adv.*—**in-volv'-ed-ness,** *n.*—**in-volve'ment,** *n.* The act of involving, or the state or fact of being involved.—**in-volv'er,** *n.*

in-vul-ner-a-ble (in-vul'nẹ-rạ-bl), *a.* [L. *invulnerabilis*.] Not vulnerable; incapable of being wounded or hurt; proof against attack (as, "*invulnerable* patience": Johnson's "Rasselas," xviii.).—**in-vul″ner-a-bil'i-ty** (-bil'i-ti), **in-vul'ner-a-ble-ness,** *n.*—**in-vul'ner-a-bly,** *adv.*

in-wall (in-wâl'), *v. t.* [See *in-*[1].] To wall in; inclose with or as with a wall.

in-ward (in'wạrd), *adv.* [AS. *inweard*, < *in*, in, + *-weard*: see *-ward*.] Toward the inside or interior, as of a place, a space, or a body; sometimes, in the inside or interior (as, "the Maple seeldom *inward* sound": Spenser's "Faerie Queene," i. 1. 9); fig., into the mind or soul (as, "Thou, celestial Light, Shine *inward*, and the mind through all her powers Irradiate": Milton's "Paradise Lost," iii. 52); in the mind or soul, or mentally or spiritually.—**in'ward.** [AS. *inweard*.] **I.** *a.* Proceeding or directed toward the inside or interior; also, situated within; interior; internal; pertaining to the inside or inner part; often, located within the body (as, the *inward* parts, commonly the organs within the trunk, esp. the stomach and intestines); pertaining to the inside of the body; hence, muffled or indistinct, as the voice (as, "The dog [in dreams] With *inward* yelp and restless forefoot plies His function of the woodland": Tennyson's "Lucretius," 45); also, inner, mental, or spiritual (as, "*Inward* security and peace . . . are the natural attendants of innocence and virtue": J. Butler's "Analogy of Religion," i. 3); sometimes, inland; sometimes, internal or domestic (obs. or rare: as, *inward* war); also, intrinsic, inherent, or essential (as, the *inward* nature of a thing); also, closely personal†; intimate† or familiar† (as, an *inward* friend); also, private† or secret† (as, "What is *inward* between us, let it pass": Shakspere's "Love's Labour's Lost," v. 1. 102). **II.** *n.* The inward or internal part; the inside; esp. (now only in *pl.*), the inward parts of the body, or the stomach and intestines (as, "ups and downs o' hills . . . to shake a body's victuals out of his *inwards*": Kingsley's "Alton Locke," xii.); also, an intimate acquaintance† (as, "Sir, I was an *inward* of his . . . I believe I know the cause of his withdrawing": Shakspere's "Measure for Measure," iii. 2. 138); also, *pl.*, imported articles, or dues on such articles (Eng.).—**in'ward-ly,** *adv.* Toward the inside or interior; also, in or on, or with reference to, the inside or inner part (as, "He had bled *inwardly*": Defoe's "Robinson Crusoe," i. 14); hence, in low tones, or not aloud, as in speaking to one's self (as, "Half *inwardly*, half audibly she spoke": Tennyson's "Marriage of Geraint," 109); also, in mind or thought; in spirit; privately; also, intrinsically; also, intimately† or closely†.—**in'ward-ness,** *n.* The state of being inward or internal; also, depth of thought or feeling; earnestness; also, occupation with what concerns man's inner nature; spirituality; also, the inward or intrinsic character of a thing; inward meaning; also, intimacy† or familiarity†.—**in'wards** (-wạrdz), *adv.* Inward.

in-weave (in-wēv'), *v. t.*; pret. *-wove* (also *-weaved*), pp. *-woven* (also *-wove, -weaved*), ppr. *-weaving.* [See *in-*¹.] To weave in or together; also, to introduce into or as into a fabric in weaving; also, to combine or diversify with something woven in.

in-wind (in-wīnd'), *v. t.* Same as *enwind.*

in-work (in-wėrk'), *v. t.*; *-worked* or *-wrought, -working.* [See *in-*¹.] To work into or with something, as by embroidering; also, to produce (something) within.

in-wrap (in-rap'), *v. t.*; *-wrapped, -wrapping.* [See *in-*¹.] To wrap or envelop in something; surround, as the enveloping thing does; hence, to enshroud in clouds, darkness, etc.; envelop, as the clouds, etc., do; fig., to wrap in slumber, etc.; absorb or engross in thought, etc.; also, to involve or imply.

in-wreathe (in-rēᴛʜ'), *v. t.*; *-wreathed, -wreathing.* [See *in-*¹.] To surround with or as with a wreath (as, "It was not at all a distressed blush, for it was *inwreathed* with smiles and dimples": George Eliot's "Adam Bede," vii.); encircle as a wreath does.

in-wrought (in-rôt' or in'rôt), *p. a.* Wrought or worked in, as a decorative pattern; also, wrought or worked with something by way of decoration (as, "Shirt of doeskin . . . All *inwrought* with beads of wampum": Longfellow's "Hiawatha," xi. 76).

in-ya-la (in-yä'lạ), *n.* [S. Afr.] A South African antelope, *Tragelaphus angasi.*

i-o (ī'ō). [L., = Gr. ἰώ.] **I.** *interj.* A Latin and Greek exclamation of joy, triumph, etc. **II.** *n.*; pl. *ios* (ī'ōz). A cry of 'io!'

i-o-date¹ (ī'ǭ-dāt), *n.* In *chem.*, a salt of iodic acid.

i-o-date² (ī'ǭ-dāt), *v. t.*; *-dated, -dating.* To combine, impregnate, or treat with iodine.—**i-o-da'tion** (-dā'shǫn), *n.*

i-od-ic (ī-od'ik), *a.* Of or containing iodine: as, *iodic* acid (an acid, HIO_3, formed by the action of oxidizing agents on iodine).

i-o-dide, i-o-did (ī'ǭ-dīd or -did, -did), *n.* In *chem.*, a compound of iodine with an element or radical; a salt of hydriodic acid.

i-o-dine, i-o-din (ī'ǭ-din or -dīn, -din), *n.* [Gr. ἰώδης, violet-like, < ἴον, violet, + εἶδος, form.] Chem. sym., I; at. wt., 126.92; sp. gr., 4.947. A non-metallic element occurring, at ordinary temperatures, as a grayish-black crystalline solid, which changes to a dense violet vapor when heated: used in medicine and the arts.—**i'o-dism,** *n.* In *pathol.*, a morbid condition due to the use of iodine or its compounds.—**i'o-dize,** *v. t.*; *-dized, -dizing.* To treat, impregnate, or affect with iodine.—**i-o-do-form** (ī-ō'dǭ-fôrm or ī-od'ǭ-), *n.* [From *iod(ine)* + *form(yl).*] In *chem.*, a yellowish crystalline compound, CHI_3, analogous to chloroform: used as an antiseptic.—**i'o-dol** (-dol or -dōl), *n.* In *chem.*, a crystalline compound containing iodine: used as a substitute for iodoform.

i-o-lite (ī'ǭ-līt), *n.* [Gr. ἴον, violet, + λίθος, stone.] A blue mineral consisting of a silicate of magnesium, aluminium, and iron.

i-on (ī'ǫn), *n.* [Gr. ἰόν, ppr. neut. of ἰέναι, go.] Either of the two substances into which a compound is decomposed by electrolysis; also, either of the two electrified atoms or groups of atoms into which the molecule of an electrolyte is separated by water, etc.; also, one of the electrically charged particles formed in a gas by the action of an electric current, etc.

-ion. [F. *-ion*, < L. *-io(n-)*, suffix forming nouns, esp. from verbs.] A suffix of nouns denoting action or process, state or condition, or sometimes things or persons, as in *alluvion, communion, flexion, fusion, legion, opinion, suspicion, union.* See *-tion* and *-ation.*

I-o-ni-an (ī-ō'ni-ạn). **I.** *a.* Pertaining to a branch of the Greek race named from Ion, the legendary founder; pertaining to ancient Ionia, a region on the western coast of Asia Minor, with adjacent islands, colonized by the Ionians; designating or pertaining to a group of Greek islands ('Ionian Islands') in the Mediterranean on the western coast of Greece proper, and a sea ('Ionian Sea') forming the part of the Mediterranean between Greece and southern Italy and Sicily (where the Ionians planted colonies). **II.** *n.* An Ionian Greek.

I-on-ic¹ (ī-on'ik). **I.** *a.* Pertaining to the Ionians; in *arch.*, noting or pertaining to one of the three Greek orders, distinguished by the volute (spiral scroll) of its capital; in *pros.*, noting or employing a foot consisting of two long syllables followed or preceded by two short. **II.** *n.* The Ionian dialect of ancient Greek, the form used by Homer, Hesiod, and Herodotus, and the source of the Attic dialect; in *pros.*, an Ionic foot, verse, or meter; in *printing* [also *l. c.*], a style of type (see *type*).

Ionic Architecture. — Temple of Wingless Victory, on the Acropolis of Athens.

i-on-ic² (ī-on'ik), *a.* Pertaining to ions.

i-o-ni-um (ī-ō'ni-um), *n.* [NL.: see *ion.*] In *chem.*, a radioactive element related to uranium.

i-on-ize (ī'ǫn-īz), *v. t.*; *-ized, -izing.* To separate into ions; produce ions in.—**i''on-i-za'tion** (-i-zā'shǫn), *n.*—**i'on-iz-er** (-ī-zėr), *n.* A device for ionizing a gas, etc.

i-on-o-sphere (ī-on'ǭ-sfēr), *n.* [See *ion* and *sphere.*] An ionized layer of the atmosphere about 65 miles up.

i-o-ta (ī-ō'tạ or ē-), *n.* [L., < Gr. ἰῶτα, the letter ι (the smallest in the Greek alphabet), a jot.] The ninth letter (I, ι, = English I, i) of the Greek alphabet (which is also the smallest letter); hence, a very small quantity; a jot.

I O U (ī' ō' ū'), *n.* [For *I owe you.*] An acknowledgment of debt, less formal than a promissory note, containing these three letters, the amount, and the signature of the debtor: as, "Mr. Micawber placed his *I. O. U.* in the hands of Traddles . . . this was quite the same to Mr. Micawber as paying the money" (Dickens's "David Copperfield," xxxvi.).

ip-e-cac (ip'ę-kak), *n.* Shortened form of *ipecacuanha.*

ip-e-cac-u-an-ha (ip-ę-kak-ų-an'ạ), *n.* [Pg.; from Brazilian name.] The dried root of a small, shrubby South American rubiaceous plant, *Cephaëlis ipecacuanha,* used as an emetic, purgative, etc.; a drug or extract prepared from it; the plant itself; also, any of various other plants with similar properties.

Ipecacuanha (*Cephaëlis ipecacuanha*).

ip-o-mœ-a (ip-ǭ-mē'ạ or ī-pǭ-), *n.* [NL., < Gr. ἴψ (ἰπ-), kind of worm, + ὅμοιος, like.] Any plant of the genus *Ipomœa,* of the morning-glory family, containing many species with ornamental flowers.

ip-se dix-it (ip'sē dik'sit). [L.] 'He himself has said (it)': an expression also used as a noun, meaning 'a mere dogmatic assertion,' as, "He took on him to decide dogmatically . . . as if it had been our duty to acquiesce in the *ipse dixit* of this new Pythagoras" (Smollett's "Humphry Clinker," June 2).

ir-¹, **ir-**². Forms of *in-*¹ and *in-*² used before *r.*

i-ra-cund (ī'rạ-kund), *a.* [L. *iracundus,* < *ira,* anger, E. *ire.*] Prone to anger; irascible.—**i-ra-cun'di-ty** (-kun'di-ti), *n.*

i-ra-de (ẹ-rä′dā), *n.* [Turk., < Ar. *irādah,* will, desire.] A decree of the Sultan of Turkey.

I-ra-ni-an (ī-rā′ni-ạn). [Pers. *Irān,* Persia.] **I.** *a.* Pertaining to Iran or Persia, or to that branch of the Aryan or Indo-European family of languages which includes the Old Persian and Avestan. **II.** *n.* An inhabitant of Iran; a Persian; specif., an Iranian Aryan.

i-ras-ci-ble (ī-ras′i-bl or i-), *a.* [F. *irascible,* < LL. *irascibilis,* < L. *irasci,* grow angry: see *irate.*] Easily provoked to anger, as a person; characterized by or showing proneness to anger, as the temper, disposition, actions, etc.; choleric; irritable.—**i-ras-ci-bil′i-ty** (-bil′i-ti), **i-ras′ci-ble-ness,** *n.*—**i-ras′ci-bly,** *adv.*

i-rate (ī-rāt′ or ī′rāt), *a.* [L. *iratus,* pp. of *irasci,* grow angry, < *ira,* anger, E. *ire.*] Excited to anger; incensed; enraged; angry.—**i-rate′ly,** *adv.*

ire (īr), *n.* [OF. *ire,* < L. *ira,* anger.] Anger; wrath.—**ire′ful,** *a.* Full of ire; wrathful; also, irascible.—**ire′ful-ly,** *adv.*—**ire′ful-ness,** *n.*

i-ren-ic, i-ren-i-cal (ī-ren′ik, -i-kạl), *a.* [Gr. εἰρηνικός, < εἰρήνη, peace.] Peaceful; pacific; tending to promote peace, esp. with reference to theological or ecclesiastical differences.—**i-ren′i-con** (-kon), *n.*; pl. *-ca* (-kạ̈). [Gr. εἰρηνικόν, neut. of εἰρηνικός.] A proposal for promoting peace, esp. in the church.—**i-ren′ics,** *n.* Irenical theology.

i-rid (ī′rid), *n.* [See *iris.*] The iris of the eye: as, "brown eyes, with a benignant light in their *irids*" (C. Brontë's "Jane Eyre," v.).

ir-i-da-ceous (ir-i-dā′shius or ī-ri-), *a.* [NL. *Iris* (*Irid-*), the iris genus: see *iris.*] Belonging to the *Iridaceæ,* or iris family of plants, which includes, besides various flags, the crocus, gladiolus, and freesia.

ir-i-dec-to-my (ir-i-dek′tọ-mi or ī-ri-), *n.* [Gr. ἶρις (ἰριδ-), iris, + ἐκ, out of, + -τομία, E. *-tomy.*] In *surg.,* the operation of cutting out a part of the iris.

ir-i-des-cence (ir-i-des′ẹns), *n.* The quality of being iridescent; intermingling or interchange of colors as in mother-of-pearl, etc.; a play of lustrous, changing colors.

ir-i-des-cent (ir-i-des′ẹnt), *a.* [L. *iris* (*irid-*), rainbow: see *-escent.*] Displaying colors like those of the rainbow; exhibiting a rainbow-like play of colors, as mother-of-pearl or shot silk.—**ir-i-des′cent-ly,** *adv.*

i-rid-i-um (ī-rid′i-um), *n.* [NL., < L. *iris* (*irid-*), rainbow: named from its iridescence in solution.] Chem. sym., Ir; at. wt., 193.1; sp. gr., 22.4. A rare metallic element resembling platinum: used in platinum alloys and for the points of gold pens.—**i-rid′ic,** *a.*

ir-i-dize (ir′i-dīz), *v. t.*; *-dized, -dizing.* [L. *iris* (*irid-*), rainbow.] To make iridescent.—**ir″i-di-za′tion** (-di-zā′shọn), *n.*

ir-i-dos-min, ir-i-dos-mi-um (ir-i-dos′min or -doz′min, -mi-um), *n.* [From *iridium* + *osmium.*] A native alloy of iridium and osmium, usually containing some rhodium, ruthenium, platinum, etc.: used for the points of gold pens and for other purposes.

ir-i-dot-o-my (ir-i-dot′ọ-mi or ī-ri-), *n.* [Gr. ἶρις (ἰριδ-), iris: see *-tomy.*] In *surg.,* incision into the iris.

i-ris (ī′ris), *n.*; pl. *irises,* L. *irides* (ī′ri-dēz). [L. *Iris,* the goddess Iris, *iris* (*irid-*), rainbow, kind of plant, < Gr. Ἶρις, Iris, ἶρις (ἰριδ-), rainbow, iris of the eye, iris plant.] [*cap.*] The goddess of the rainbow and messenger of the gods, in classical mythology; also [*l. c.*], a rainbow; hence, any appearance resembling a rainbow; a combination or play of colors; an iridescence; in *anat.,* the contractile circular diaphragm forming the colored portion of the eye and containing a circular opening (the *pupil*) in its center; in *bot.,* any plant of the genus *Iris,* including various perennial herbs with handsome flowers and sword-shaped leaves; the fleur-de-lis or flag; also, the flower of any such plant.—**i-ri-sat-ed** (ī′ri-sā-ted), *a.* Iridescent.—**i-ri-sa′tion** (-sā′shọn), *n.* Iridescent coloration.—**i′rised,** *a.* Rainbow-colored or iridescent (as, "Wrecked is the ship of pearl . . . Its *irised* ceiling rent": Holmes's "Chambered Nautilus"); also, of the eye, having an iris.

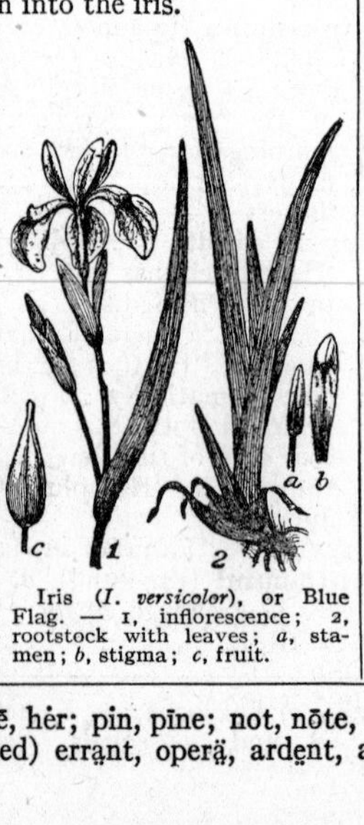

Iris (*I. versicolor*), or Blue Flag. — 1, inflorescence; 2, rootstock with leaves; *a,* stamen; *b,* stigma; *c,* fruit.

I-rish (ī′rish), *a.* [ME. *Irisc,* < AS. *Iras,* pl., the Irish: cf. OIr. *Eriu,* Erin, Ireland.] Of, pertaining to, or characteristic of Ireland or its people; also, designating, or belonging to, or spoken or written in, the Celtic language of the natives of Ireland.—**Irish bull.** See *bull*³.—**Irish moss,** carrageen.—**Irish potato,** the common white potato.—**Irish stew,** a stew made of mutton or beef, with potatoes, onions, etc.—**Irish terrier,** one of a breed of small, active, intelligent dogs with wiry hair usually of a reddish tinge.—**I′rish,** *n.* The inhabitants of Ireland and their immediate descendants elsewhere, esp. those of Celtic race; also, the Celtic language of the natives of Ireland; also, the dialect of English spoken by the Irish; also, temper (slang: as, to get one's *Irish* up).—**I′rish-ism,** *n.* An Irish peculiarity, as of speech.—**I′rish-man** (-mạn), *n.*; pl. *-men.*—**I′rish-ry** (-ri), *n.*; pl. *-ries* (-riz). The native Irish, as opposed to English settlers in Ireland; also, Irish character; an Irish trait.—**I′rish-wom″an,** *n.*; pl. *-women* (-wim″en).

i-ri-tis (ī-rī′tis), *n.* [NL.] In *pathol.,* inflammation of the iris of the eye.—**i-rit-ic** (ī-rit′ik), *a.*

irk (ėrk), *v.* [ME. *irken, yrken*: cf. MHG. *erken,* disgust.] **I.**† *intr.* To grow weary, as of something tedious or disagreeable; feel disgusted, annoyed, or troubled. **II.** *tr.* To find wearisome†, or regard with disgust†; also, to weary, annoy, or trouble (often used in the impersonal construction: as, "It *irked* him that he was forced to make one exception to this rule," C. Brontë's "Villette," xv.).—**irk′some** (-sum), *a.* Feeling weariness or disgust† (as, "He could not rest; but did his stout heart eat . . . *Yrkesome* of life": Spenser's "Faerie Queene," i. 2. 6); also, causing weariness, disgust, or annoyance (as, an *irksome* task; *irksome* restrictions; "Company was *irksome* to me," Mrs. Shelley's "Frankenstein," xix.); wearisome or tedious; annoying or vexatious; formerly, distressing†.—**irk′some-ly,** *adv.*—**irk′some-ness,** *n.*

i-ron (ī′ėrn), *n.* [AS. *īren, īsen, īsern,* = OS. and OHG. *īsarn* (G. *eisen*) = Icel. *īsarn* = Goth. *eisarn,* iron.] Chem. sym., Fe (see *ferrum*); at. wt., 55.84; sp. gr., about 7.9. A ductile, malleable, silver-white metallic element, scarcely known in a pure condition but abundantly used in its crude or impure forms (*pig-iron, cast-iron, steel,* and *wrought-iron*: see these entries) for making tools, implements, machinery, etc.; also, a form or variety of this metal, as wrought-iron or cast-iron, esp. as contrasted with steel; also, an instrument, utensil, weapon, etc., made of iron; a branding-iron; an iron implement used heated for smoothing or pressing cloth, etc.; a harpoon; an iron-headed golf-club intermediate between a cleek and a mashie (as, a driving *iron*; a lofting *iron*; a mid-*iron*); a sword (obs. or archaic), or swords and other weapons collectively; a pistol (slang); an iron shackle or fetter (chiefly in *pl.*); fig., something hard, strong, rigid, unyielding, or the like (in metaphorical expressions: as, "muscles and sinews of *iron,*" Longfellow's "Courtship of Miles Standish," i.; "hearts of *iron,*" Shakspere's "Henry VIII.," iii. 2. 424); in *med.,* a preparation of iron, or containing iron, used as a tonic, etc.—**in irons,** in shackles or fetters; *naut.,* of a sailing boat or vessel, with the head to the wind and not enough momentum to come around on either tack.—**i′ron,** *a.* Made of iron; also, pertaining to iron; also, resembling iron in appearance (as, "*iron* clouds": Dryden's tr. Virgil's "Georgics," i. 630); also, resembling iron in its characteristic qualities; hard or strong; extremely hardy or robust (as, an *iron* constitution); inflexible or unyielding (as, "*iron* virtues," Reade's "Christie Johnstone," ii.; "her *iron* will," Tennyson's "Princess," vi. 102); stern, harsh, or cruel; not to be broken, as sleep (a Latinism, with reference to death: see Dryden's tr. Virgil's "Æneid," xii. 467); also, pertaining to the iron age of mythology, or to any similar period (see *iron age,* below); degenerate, debased, or wicked (as, "these hard *iron* times": Dryden's tr. Virgil's "Pastorals," ix. 15).—**iron age,** the age in the history of mankind (subsequent to the stone and bronze ages) marked by the use of iron implements (see *ages in archæology*, under *age, n.*); also, the last and worst age of the world, or any age or period of degeneracy or wickedness (see *ages in mythology*, under *age, n.*)—**Iron Cross,** the badge of the Order of the Iron Cross (a Prussian order founded in 1813 and reorganized in 1870), conferred for services in war.—**iron hat,** a helmet of iron or steel shaped like a hat (with crown and brim), used during the middle ages and later.—**iron horse,** a locomotive; also, a bicycle or tricycle. [Colloq.]—**iron man,** a dollar. [Slang, U. S.]—**iron pyrites,** pyrite, or ordinary pyrites; also, marcasite ('white iron pyrites').—**iron ration,** a special ration of food carried by a soldier in his haversack, not to be used except at the commanding officer's order, as in an emergency. [Colloq.]—**i′ron,** *v.* **I.** *tr.* To furnish, cover, or arm with iron (as, "the gate that was *iron'd* within and without": Coleridge's "Christabel," i.); also, to shackle or fetter with irons; also, to smooth or press with a heated iron, as clothes, etc. **II.** *intr.* To press clothes, etc., with a heated iron: as, "Mrs. Nubbles *ironed* away in silence" (Dickens's "Old Curiosity Shop," x.).

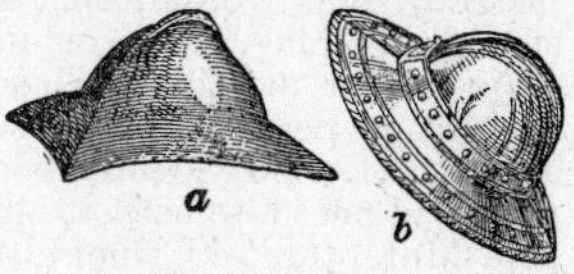

a, Iron Hat, 14th century. *b*, Iron Hat, time of Charles I. and Cromwell.

i-ron-bark (ī′ėrn-bärk), *n.* Any of various Australian eucalyptuses with a hard, solid bark, as *Eucalyptus resinifera*, a tall tree yielding a valuable timber.

Branch of Ironbark (*Eucalyptus resinifera*). — *a*, flower on larger scale.

i-ron=bound (ī′ėrn-bound), *a.* Bound with iron; hence, faced or surrounded with rocks (as, an *iron-bound* coast); fig., hard, rigid, or unyielding.

i-ron-clad (ī′ėrn-klad). **I.** *a.* Clad in iron; covered or protected with metal armor; fig., strengthened by special provisions, as an agreement. **II.** *n.* An ironclad naval vessel.

i-ron-er (ī′ėr-nėr), *n.* One who or that which irons.

i-ron=glance (ī′ėrn-glȧns), *n.* Specular iron ore. See under *specular*.

i-ron=gray (ī′ėrn-grā′), *a.* Of a gray like that of freshly broken iron: as, *iron-gray* hair.

i-ron=hand-ed (ī′ėrn-han′ded), *a.* Acting or ruling, or maintained or done, as if with an iron hand; severe; harsh; despotic: as, an *iron-handed* ruler; *iron-handed* rule.

i-ron=heart-ed (ī′ėrn-här′ted), *a.* Hard-hearted; unfeeling.

i-ron-ic, i-ron-i-cal (ī-ron′ik, -i-kal), *a.* [Gr. εἰρωνικός.] Pertaining to, of the nature of, or characterized by irony; using, or addicted to, irony.—**i-ron′i-cal-ly,** *adv.*—**i-ron′i-cal-ness,** *n.*

i-ron-mas-ter (ī′ėrn-mȧs″tėr), *n.* The master of iron-works; a manufacturer of iron.

i-ron-mong-er (ī′ėrn-mung″gėr), *n.* A dealer in ironware.—**i′ron-mong″er-y,** *n.* The goods, shop, or business of an ironmonger.

i-ron=rust (ī′ėrn-rust), *n.* The rust of iron. See *rust, n.*

i-ron-side, i-ron-sides (ī′ėrn-sīd, -sīdz), *n.* Epithets [often *cap.*] ascribing great strength, endurance, or power of resistance, applied to persons or ships: as, Edmund *Ironside* (Edmund II., king of the English, 1016); *Ironside*, or *Ironsides* (Oliver Cromwell); Oliver Cromwell's *Ironsides* (troopers); Old *Ironsides* (the old U. S. frigate Constitution).

i-ron-smith (ī′ėrn-smith), *n.* A worker in iron; a blacksmith.

i-ron-stone (ī′ėrn-stōn), *n.* Any ore of iron (commonly a carbonate of iron) with clayey or siliceous impurities.—**ironstone china,** a kind of hard, white, opaque pottery used esp. for table and toilet purposes.

i-ron-ware (ī′ėrn-wãr), *n.* Articles of iron, as pots, kettles, tools, etc.; hardware.

i-ron=weed (ī′ėrn-wēd), *n.* Any of certain North American plants of the asteraceous genus *Vernonia*, bearing tubular flowers, chiefly purple or red.

i-ron-wood (ī′ėrn-wůd), *n.* Any of various trees with hard, heavy wood, as *Carpinus caroliniana*, an American species of hornbeam, or *Lyonothamnus floribundus*, found on islands off the coast of southern California ('Santa Cruz ironwood'); also, the wood.

Santa Cruz Ironwood (*Lyonothamnus floribundus*). — *a*, flowering branch showing inflorescence and pinnate leaves; *b*, a simple leaf; *c*, a fruiting corymb.

i-ron-work (ī′ėrn-wėrk), *n.* Work in iron; parts or articles made of iron: as, "We got out a great deal of *ironwork*, as bolts, spikes, nails, &c." (Defoe's "Captain Singleton," iii.).—**i′ron-work″er,** *n.* A worker in iron; one employed in the manufacture of iron, or of articles of iron; one employed in the erection of steel structures, as bridges, etc.—**i′ron=works,** *n. pl.* or *sing.* An establishment where iron is smelted, or where it is cast or wrought into heavy work.

i-ron-y[1] (ī′ėr-ni), *a.* Consisting of, containing, or resembling iron.

i-ro-ny[2] (ī′rọ-ni), *n.*; pl. *-nies* (-niz). [L. *ironia*, < Gr. εἰρωνεία, < εἴρων, dissembling speaker, < εἴρειν, say, speak: cf. *rhetor*.] Dissimulation, esp. simulated ignorance in discussion ('Socratic irony'); also, a method of expression or a figure of speech in which the literal meaning of the words is the opposite of the thought in the speaker's mind and intended to be conveyed, and which is employed in ridicule or contempt or merely playfully; usually, agreeable or complimentary language intended to convey an opposite meaning (as, "A drayman in a passion calls out, 'You are a pretty fellow,' without suspecting that he is uttering *irony*": Macaulay's "Essays," Lord Bacon); also, an ironical utterance or expression; an ironical quality (as, "There was a staid *irony* in his tone": Kingsley's "Yeast," iii.); also, an outcome of events contrary to what was, or what might have been, expected (as, it was the *irony* of fate that made Joseph the ruler over the land of his captivity).

Ir-o-quoi-an (ir-ọ-kwoi′ạn), *a.* Belonging to or constituting a linguistic stock of North American Indians, of Canada and the eastern U. S., including the Iroquois confederacy (the Five Nations, comprising the Mohawks, Oneidas, Onondagas, Cayugas, and Senecas, with, later, the Tuscaroras) and the Cherokees, Wyandots or Hurons, and others.

ir-ra-di-ant (i-rā′di-ạnt), *a.* Irradiating; radiant; shining.—**ir-ra′di-ance, ir-ra′di-an-cy,** *n.*

ir-ra-di-ate (i-rā′di-āt), *v.*; *-ated, -ating.* [L. *irradiatus*, pp. of *irradiare*, < *in*, in, on, + *radiare*, beam: see *radiate*.] **I.** *tr.* To shed rays of light upon; illuminate; fig., to illumine intellectually or spiritually (as, "a sordid life . . . *irradiated* by no sublime principles, no romantic visions": George Eliot's "Mill on the Floss," iv. 1); brighten as if with light, as the countenance; also, to radiate (light, etc.). **II.** *intr.* To emit rays; shine; also, to become radiant.—**ir-ra′di-ate,** *a.* Irradiated; bright.—**ir-ra-di-a′tion** (-ā′shọn), *n.* The act of irradiating, or the state of being irradiated; an emitting of rays of light, or of other rays; sometimes, a ray of light; a beam; fig., intellectual or spiritual enlightenment; in *optics*, the apparent enlargement of a bright object when seen against a dark ground.—**ir-ra′di-a-tive** (-ạ-tiv), *a.* Serving to irradiate.

ir-ra-tion-al (i-rash′ọn-ạl), *a.* [L. *irrationalis*.] Not rational; without the faculty of, or not endowed with, reason (as, *irrational* animals); without, or deprived of, sound judgment; not in accordance with reason, or utterly illogical or absurd (as, "the *irrational* laws which bad critics have framed for the government of poets": Macaulay's "Essays," Moore's Byron); in *math.*, not capable of being exactly expressed by an integer or a vulgar fraction; surd.—**ir-ra′tion-al-ism,** *n.* Irrationality in thought or action.—**ir-ra-tion-al′i-ty** (-rash-ọ-nal′i-ti), *n.*; pl. *-ties* (-tiz). The quality of being irrational; also, an irrational, illogical, or absurd action, thought, etc. (as, "the confused *irrationalities* into which you all allow yourselves to fall": Kingsley's "Alton Locke," xvii.).—**ir-ra′tion-al-ize** (-īz), *v. t.*; *-ized, -izing.* To render irrational.—**ir-ra′tion-al-ly,** *adv.*

ir-re-cip-ro-cal (ir-ę-sip'rǫ-kạl), *a.* [See *ir-*[2].] Not reciprocal.—**ir-re-ci-pro-ci-ty** (i-res-i-pros'i-ti), *n.* Absence of reciprocity.

ir-re-claim-a-ble (ir-ę-klā'mạ-bl), *a.* [See *ir-*[2].] Not reclaimable; incapable of being reclaimed.—**ir-re-claim-a-bil'i-ty** (-bil'i-ti), **ir-re-claim'a-ble-ness,** *n.*—**ir-re-claim'a-bly,** *adv.*

ir-rec-og-ni-tion (i-rek-ǫg-nish'ǫn), *n.* [See *ir-*[2].] Absence of recognition.—**ir-rec'og-niz-a-ble** (-nī-zạ-bl), *a.* Not recognizable.

ir-rec-on-cil-a-ble (i-rek'ǫn-sī-lạ-bl or i-rek-ǫn-sī'-). [See *ir-*[2].] **I.** *a.* Not reconcilable; implacably opposed, as an enemy; that cannot be harmonized or adjusted, as a quarrel; that cannot be brought to acquiescence or content, as persons; incompatible, as statements or ideas. **II.** *n.* One who is irreconcilable; esp., one who remains implacably opposed to agreement or compromise, as in political matters.—**ir-rec''on-cil-a-bil'i-ty** (-bil'i-ti), **ir-rec'on-cil-a-ble-ness,** *n.*—**ir-rec'on-cil-a-bly,** *adv.*

ir-re-cov-er-a-ble (ir-ę-kuv'ėr-ạ-bl), *a.* [See *ir-*[2].] Not recoverable; that cannot be got back or regained (as, "If the path is . . . once lost, it is *irrecoverable*": Hardy's "Return of the Native," v. 8); that cannot be restored to health, as a person (archaic); incurable, as a disease (archaic); that cannot be remedied or rectified (as, *irrecoverable* sorrow).—**ir-re-cov'er-a-ble-ness,** *n.*—**ir-re-cov'er-a-bly,** *adv.*

ir-re-cu-sa-ble (ir-ę-kū'zạ-bl), *a.* [LL. *irrecusabilis*, < L. *in-*, not, + *recusare*, object to: see *recuse*.] Not to be objected to or rejected.—**ir-re-cu'sa-bly,** *adv.*

ir-re-deem-a-ble (ir-ę-dē'mạ-bl), *a.* [See *ir-*[2].] Not redeemable; incapable of being bought back or paid off (as, an *irredeemable* mortgage); not convertible into specie, as paper money; irremediable, irreparable, or hopeless (as, "a misfortune, but not an *irredeemable* one": Disraeli's "Lothair," liii.); beyond redemption, irreclaimable, or thoroughly depraved (as, an *irredeemable* criminal).—**ir-re-deem'a-bly,** *adv.*

ir-re-den-ta (ir-ę-den'tạ̈), *n.* [It.: see *irredentist*.] Any of certain regions situated near Italy, and having a considerable Italian population though politically subject to other governments, whose union to Italy was advocated by the Irredentists; hence, any region included politically in one country but claimed or desired by another as properly belonging to the latter by reason of racial or other ties.

ir-re-den-tist (ir-ę-den'tist). [It. *irredentista*, < (*Italia*) *irredenta*, (Italy) unredeemed, fem. of *irredento*, < L. *in-*, not, + *redemptus*, pp. of *redimere*, E. *redeem*.] **I.** *n.* [Usually *cap.*] A member of an Italian political party which became prominent in 1878, advocating the redemption, or the incorporation into Italy, of certain neighboring regions (*Italia irredenta*: see etym.) having an important part of their population Italian, but subject politically to other governments; hence [*l. c.*], a member of a party in any country advocating the taking over of some region, actually included in another country, but claimed as properly belonging to the former country by reason of racial or other ties. **II.** *a.* [*cap.* or *l. c.*] Of or pertaining to irredentists.—**ir-re-den'tism,** *n.*

ir-re-du-ci-ble (ir-ę-dū'si-bl), *a.* [See *ir-*[2].] Not reducible; incapable of being reduced.—**ir-re-du-ci-bil'i-ty** (-bil'i-ti), **ir-re-du'ci-ble-ness,** *n.*—**ir-re-du'ci-bly,** *adv.*

ir-re-flec-tion (ir-ę-flek'shǫn), *n.* [See *ir-*[2].] Want of reflection; thoughtlessness.—**ir-re-flec'tive,** *a.* Not reflective; unthinking; thoughtless.—**ir-re-flec'tive-ly,** *adv.*—**ir-re-flec'tive-ness,** *n.*

ir-re-form-a-ble (ir-ę-fôr'mạ-bl), *a.* [See *ir-*[2].] Not reformable; incapable of being reformed.

ir-ref-ra-ga-ble (i-ref'rạ-gạ-bl), *a.* [LL. *irrefragabilis*, < L. *in-*, not, + *refragari*, oppose, gainsay.] Not to be refuted; incontrovertible; undeniable: as, "*irrefragable* proofs that the account in the newspapers was correct" (Hardy's "Two on a Tower," xxxiii.).—**ir-ref''ra-ga-bil'i-ty** (-bil'i-ti), *n.*—**ir-ref'ra-ga-bly,** *adv.*

ir-re-fran-gi-ble (ir-ę-fran'ji-bl), *a.* [See *ir-*[2] and *refrangible*.] Not to be broken or violated; inviolable; also, not refrangible; incapable of being refracted.—**ir-re-fran'gi-bly,** *adv.*

ir-re-fut-a-ble (ir-ę-fū'tạ-bl or i-ref'ū̦-), *a.* [LL. *irrefutabilis*.] Not refutable; not to be disproved; incontrovertible.—**ir-re-fut-a-bil'i-ty** (-bil'i-ti), *n.*—**ir-re-fut'a-bly,** *adv.*

ir-reg-u-lar (i-reg'ū̦-lạ̈r). [ML. *irregularis*.] **I.** *a.* Not regular; not according to rule, or to the accepted principle, method, course, order, etc., as an action, proceeding, instance, or thing; not conformed or conforming to rules of justice or morality, as conduct, transactions, mode of life, etc., or persons (as, "Now that to steal by law is grown an art . . . And 'slightly *irregular*' dilutes the shame Of what had once a somewhat blunter name": Lowell's "Tempora Mutantur," 40); not characterized by any fixed principle, method, or rate (as, *irregular* movements; *irregular* intervals; *irregular* breathing); without symmetry, even shape, formal arrangement, etc. (as, an *irregular* figure; *irregular* features; an *irregular* pattern); specif., in *gram.*, not conforming to the normal or usual manner of inflection; *milit.*, of troops, not belonging to the regular army organization; in *bot.*, not uniform; of a flower, having the members of some or all of its floral circles or whorls differing from one another in size or shape, or extent of union. **II.** *n.* One who or that which is irregular; one who does not belong to the regular body, or who does something irregularly; *milit.*, a soldier not in the regular army.—**ir-reg-u-lar'i-ty** (-lar'i-ti), *n.*; pl. *-ties* (-tiz). The state or fact of being irregular; deviation from rule, principle, or method; want of conformity to rules of justice or morality; lack of any fixed principle, method, or rate; absence of symmetry, evenness, or formal arrangement; also, something irregular; a breach of rule; an act at variance with the rules of justice or morality; an irregular part, as of an outline; an uneven spot, as on a surface.—**ir-reg'u-lar-ly,** *adv.*

ir-re-lat-ed (ir-ę-lā'ted), *a.* [See *ir-*[2].] Not related.—**ir-re-la'tion** (-lā'shǫn), *n.* Absence of relation.—**ir-rel'a-tive** (-rel'ạ-tiv), *a.* Not relative; without relation; also, irrelevant.—**ir-rel'a-tive-ly,** *adv.*—**ir-rel'a-tive-ness,** *n.*

ir-rel-e-vant (i-rel'ę-vạnt), *a.* [See *ir-*[2].] Not relevant; not applicable or pertinent.—**ir-rel'e-vance, ir-rel'e-van-cy,** *n.*—**ir-rel'e-vant-ly,** *adv.*

ir-re-liev-a-ble (ir-ę-lē'vạ-bl), *a.* [See *ir-*[2].] Not relievable.

ir-re-li-gion (ir-ę-lij'ǫn), *n.* [L. *irreligio*(*n-*).] Lack of religion; hostility to or disregard of religion; impiety: as, "He denounced the pride and *irreligion* of the clergy" (H. G. Wells's "Outline of History," xxxiii. § 12).—**ir-re-li'gion-ist,** *n.*—**ir-re-li'gious** (-lij'us), *a.* [L. *irreligiosus*.] Not religious; without religious principles; hostile to religion; ungodly; also, showing disregard for or hostility to religion, as conduct, etc.—**ir-re-li'gious-ly,** *adv.*—**ir-re-li'gious-ness,** *n.*

ir-rem-e-a-ble (i-rem'ę-ạ-bl), *a.* [L. *irremeabilis*, < *in-*, not, + *remeare*, go back, < *re-*, back, + *meare*, go.] From which one cannot return; admitting of no return: as, "My three brave brothers in one mournful day All trod the dark, *irremeable* way" (Pope's tr. Homer's "Iliad," xix.). [Now poetic.]

ir-re-me-di-a-ble (ir-ę-mē'di-ạ-bl), *a.* [L. *irremediabilis*.] Not remediable; beyond remedy; irreparable: as, an *irremediable* disease; *irremediable* faults.—**ir-re-me'di-a-ble-ness,** *n.*—**ir-re-me'di-a-bly,** *adv.*

ir-re-mis-si-ble (ir-ę-mis'i-bl), *a.* [LL. *irremissibilis*.] Not remissible; unpardonable, as a sin; that cannot be remitted, as a duty.—**ir-re-mis-si-bil'i-ty** (-bil'i-ti), **ir-re-mis'si-ble-ness,** *n.*—**ir-re-mis'si-bly,** *adv.*

ir-re-mov-a-ble (ir-ę-mö'vạ-bl), *a.* [See *ir-*[2].] Not removable; not subject to removal; also, immovable†.—**ir-re-mov-a-bil'i-ty** (-bil'i-ti), *n.*—**ir-re-mov'a-bly,** *adv.*

ir-rep-a-ra-ble (i-rep'ạ-rạ-bl), *a.* [L. *irreparabilis*.] Not reparable; incapable of being rectified, remedied, or made good: as, an *irreparable* injury or loss.—**ir-rep'a-ra-ble-ness,** *n.*—**ir-rep'a-ra-bly,** *adv.*

ir-re-peal-a-ble (ir-ę-pē'lạ-bl), *a.* [See *ir-*[2].] Not repealable; irrevocable.

ir-re-place-a-ble (ir-ę-plā'sạ-bl), *a.* [See *ir-*[2].] Not replaceable; that cannot be replaced.

ir-re-plev-i-sa-ble, ir-re-plev-i-a-ble (ir-ę-plev'i-sạ-bl, -ạ-bl), *a.* [See *ir-*[2].] In *law*, not replevisable or repleviable; that cannot be replevied.

ir-re-press-i-ble (ir-ẹ̄-pres′i-bl), *a.* [See *ir-*[2].] Not repressible; irrestrainable; uncontrollable: as, "*irrepressible* wrath" (Browning's "Ring and the Book," iv.).—**ir-re-press-i-bil′i-ty** (-bil′i-ti), **ir-re-press′i-ble-ness,** *n.*—**ir-re-press′i-bly,** *adv.*

ir-re-proach-a-ble (ir-ẹ̄-prō′chạ-bl), *a.* [See *ir-*[2].] Not reproachable; free from blame; faultless: as, "an *irreproachable* repose of manner" (G. W. Curtis's "Prue and I," i.).—**ir-re-proach′a-ble-ness,** *n.*—**ir-re-proach′a-bly,** *adv.*

ir-re-sist-i-ble (ir-ẹ̄-zis′ti-bl), *a.* [See *ir-*[2].] Not resistible; that cannot be resisted or withstood: as, "an *irresistible* impulse" (Bulwer-Lytton's "Caxtons," x. 1).—**ir-re-sist-i-bil′i-ty** (-bil′i-ti), **ir-re-sist′i-ble-ness,** *n.*—**ir-re-sist′i-bly,** *adv.*

ir-res-o-lu-ble (i-rez′ọ̄-lụ̄-bl), *a.* [L. *irresolubilis.*] Not resoluble; indissoluble; insoluble.

ir-res-o-lute (i-rez′ọ̄-lūt), *a.* [See *ir-*[2].] Not resolute; doubtful or undecided; infirm of purpose, or vacillating.—**ir-res′o-lute-ly,** *adv.*—**ir-res′o-lute-ness,** *n.*—**ir-res-o-lu′tion** (-lū′shọn), *n.* Lack of resolution; indecision; vacillation: as, "His countenance betrayed *irresolution* and reluctance" (C. B. Brown's "Wieland," xvii.).

ir-re-solv-a-ble (ir-ẹ̄-zol′vạ-bl), *a.* [See *ir-*[2].] Not resolvable.

ir-re-spec-tive (ir-ẹ̄-spek′tiv), *a.* [See *ir-*[2].] Not respecting or regarding particular persons, circumstances, or conditions (obs. or rare: as, an *irrespective* decree); also, without respect or regard to something else, esp. something specified; independent (*of*: as, "No abstract intellectual plan of life Quite *irrespective* of life's plainest laws," Browning's "Bishop Blougram's Apology"); often, adverbially, irrespectively or independently (*of*).—**ir-re-spec′tive-ly,** *adv.* In a manner showing disregard of particular persons, circumstances, etc. (obs. or rare); also, with disregard of other things, esp. of something specified (as, to accept a proposed measure *irrespectively* of party relations).

ir-re-spir-a-ble (ir-ẹ̄-spīr′ạ-bl or i-res′pi-rạ-), *a.* [See *ir-*[2].] Not respirable; unfit for respiration.

ir-re-spon-si-ble (ir-ẹ̄-spon′si-bl). [See *ir-*[2].] **I.** *a.* Not responsible; not answerable, accountable, or subject to accounting (as, an *irresponsible* ruler; *irresponsible* commands); not capable of responsibility, or done without a sense of responsibility (as, to be mentally *irresponsible*; *irresponsible* actions). **II.** *n.* An irresponsible person.—**ir-re-spon-si-bil′i-ty** (-bil′i-ti), **ir-re-spon′si-ble-ness,** *n.*—**ir-re-spon′si-bly,** *adv.*

ir-re-spon-sive (ir-ẹ̄-spon′siv), *a.* [See *ir-*[2].] Not responsive; not responding, or not responding readily, as in speech, action, or feeling.—**ir-re-spon′sive-ness,** *n.*

ir-re-strain-a-ble (ir-ẹ̄-strā′nạ-bl), *a.* [See *ir-*[2].] Not restrainable; that cannot be restrained.—**ir-re-strain′a-bly,** *adv.*

ir-re-ten-tion (ir-ẹ̄-ten′shọn), *n.* [See *ir-*[2].] Lack of retention; inability to retain.—**ir-re-ten′tive,** *a.* Not retentive; lacking power to retain, esp. mentally.—**ir-re-ten′tive-ness,** *n.*

ir-re-trace-a-ble (ir-ẹ̄-trā′sạ-bl), *a.* [See *ir-*[2].] Not retraceable: that cannot be retraced.

ir-re-triev-a-ble (ir-ẹ̄-trē′vạ-bl), *a.* [See *ir-*[2].] Not retrievable; irrecoverable; irreparable: as, an *irretrievable* loss.—**ir-re-triev-a-bil′i-ty** (-bil′i-ti), **ir-re-triev′a-ble-ness,** *n.*—**ir-re-triev′a-bly,** *adv.*

ir-rev-er-ent (i-rev′ẹ-rẹnt), *a.* [L. *irreverens* (*-ent-*).] Not reverent; deficient in reverence or veneration: as, "a reckless and *irreverent* knight" (Tennyson's "Holy Grail," 853); an *irreverent* reply.—**ir-rev′er-ence,** *n.*—**ir-rev′er-ent-ly,** *adv.*

ir-re-vers-i-ble (ir-ẹ̄-vėr′si-bl), *a.* [See *ir-*[2].] Not reversible; that cannot be reversed: as, "*irreversible* laws" (George Eliot's "Mill on the Floss," iv. 3).—**ir-re-vers-i-bil′i-ty** (-bil′i-ti), **ir-re-vers′i-ble-ness,** *n.*—**ir-re-vers′i-bly,** *adv.*

ir-rev-o-ca-ble (i-rev′ọ̄-kạ-bl), *a.* [L. *irrevocabilis.*] Not revocable; that cannot be revoked, recalled, withdrawn, or annulled: as, "the *irrevocable* yesterday" (Kingsley's "Hereward," xii.); "Firm and *irrevocable* is my doom Which I have pass'd upon her" (Shakspere's "As You Like It," i. 3. 85).—**ir-rev″o-ca-bil′i-ty** (-bil′i-ti), **ir-rev′o-ca-ble-ness,** *n.*—**ir-rev′o-ca-bly,** *adv.*

ir-ri-ga-ble (ir′i-gạ-bl), *a.* That may be irrigated.

ir-ri-gate (ir′i-gāt), *v. t.*; *-gated, -gating.* [L. *irrigatus*, pp. of *irrigare*, < *in*, in, on, + *rigare*, moisten, water.] To moisten; wet; specif., to supply (land) with water by means of streams passing through it, esp. artificial streams provided to promote vegetation; water (land), as such streams do; in *med.*, to supply (a wound, etc.) with a constant flow of some liquid.—**ir-ri-ga′tion** (-gā′shọn), *n.* [L. *irrigatio*(*n-*).] The act of irrigating, or the state of being irrigated; specif., the supplying of land with water from artificial channels to promote vegetation (as, "Channels had been cut from the larger rills for the *irrigation* of the open land": J. H. Newman's "Callista," i.).—**ir-ri-ga′tion-al,** *a.*—**ir-ri-ga′tion-ist,** *n.* One who is interested or engaged in irrigation.—**ir′ri-ga-tive,** *a.* Serving for or pertaining to irrigation.—**ir′ri-ga-tor,** *n.*

ir-rig-u-ous (i-rig′ụ̄-us), *a.* [L. *irriguus*, < *in*, in, on, + *riguus*, watered, watering, < *rigare*: see *irrigate*.] Moist; wet; well-watered, as land (as, "The flowery lap Of some *irriguous* valley": Milton's "Paradise Lost," iv. 255); also, affording moisture; watering. [Now rare.]

ir-ri-sor (i-rī′sọr), *n.* [NL. use (with allusion to the cry) of L. *irrisor*, a derider, < *irridere*, laugh at, < *in*, in, on, + *ridere*, laugh.] Any bird of the African genus *Irrisor* or family *Irrisoridæ*, related to the hoopoes; a wood-hoopoe.

Irrisor (*I. erythrorhynchus*).

ir-ri-ta-ble (ir′i-tạ-bl), *a.* [L. *irritabilis.*] Easily irritated; readily excited to impatience or anger; also, responding readily to a stimulus; esp., morbidly excitable or sensitive, as a bodily organ or part; in *physiol.* and *biol.*, capable of being excited to a characteristic action or function by the application of some physical stimulus.—**ir″ri-ta-bil′i-ty** (-bil′i-ti), **ir′ri-ta-ble-ness,** *n.*—**ir′ri-ta-bly,** *adv.*

ir-ri-tant (ir′i-tạnt). [L. *irritans* (*-ant-*), ppr.] **I.** *a.* Irritating. **II.** *n.* Anything that irritates; in *pathol.* and *med.*, something, as a poison or a therapeutic agent, producing irritation.—**ir′ri-tan-cy,** *n.*

ir-ri-tate (ir′i-tāt), *v. t.*; *-tated, -tating.* [L. *irritatus*, pp. of *irritare*, excite, stimulate, provoke, irritate.] To excite or rouse, as to action†; give rise to, as action†; excite to greater intensity†, or stimulate† (as, "This exploit . . . served rather to *irritate* than to subdue the undaunted spirit of the northern invaders": Gibbon's "Decline and Fall of the Roman Empire," x.); also, to excite to impatience or anger (as, "Let me beg you, madam . . . not to *irritate* his worship": Fielding's "Tom Jones," xvi. 4); annoy; provoke; vex; specif., in *pathol.*, to bring (a bodily part, etc.) to an abnormally excited or sensitive condition; in *physiol.* and *biol.*, to excite (an organ) to some characteristic action or function.—**ir′ri-tat-ing-ly** (-tā-ting-li), *adv.*—**ir-ri-ta′tion** (-tā′shọn), *n.* [L. *irritatio*(*n-*).] The act of irritating, or the state of being irritated; esp., annoyance; vexation; in *pathol.*, the bringing of a bodily part or organ to an abnormally excited or sensitive condition; the condition itself.—**ir′ri-ta-tive** (-tạ-tiv), *a.* Serving or tending to irritate; causing mental irritation or annoyance; in *pathol.*, characterized or produced by irritation of some bodily part, etc. (as, an *irritative* fever); in *physiol.* and *biol.*, exciting to some characteristic action or function.—**ir′ri-ta-tor** (-tā-tọr), *n.*

ir-ro-ta-tion-al (ir-ọ̄-tā′shọn-ạl), *a.* [See *ir-*[2].] Not rotational; characterized by absence of rotation.—**ir-ro-ta′tion-al-ly,** *adv.*

ir-rupt (i-rupt′), *v. i.* [L. *irruptus*, pp. of *irrumpere*, < *in*, in, + *rumpere*, break.] To break in; burst or rush violently in.—**ir-rup-tion** (i-rup′shọn), *n.* [L. *irruptio*(*n-*).] A breaking or bursting in; a violent incursion or invasion; a sudden entry by a horde or multitude: as, "an inclosure of strong palisadoes, to guard against any sudden *irruption* of the savages" (Irving's "Knickerbocker's New York," ii. 8).—**ir-rup′tive,** *a.* Characterized by or pertaining to irruption.

Ir-ving-ite (ėr′ving-īt), *n.* A member of a religious denomination (the 'Catholic Apostolic Church') holding mystical doctrines and having a highly ritualistic service, which was founded in England on principles promulgated by Edward Irving (1792–1834).

is (iz). [AS. *is*, akin to G. *ist*, Goth. *ist*, L. *est*, Gr. ἐστί, Skt. *asti*, is: see *be*.] Third person singular, present indicative, of *be*.

is-a-bel (iz′a̤-bel), *n.* Same as *isabella*.

is-a-bel-la (iz-a̤-bel′ä̤), *n.* [From *Isabella*, woman's name.] A grayish-yellow color.—**is-a-bel′line** (-bel′in), *a.* Of the color called isabella.

i-sab-nor-mal (ī-sab-nôr′ma̤l). [See *iso-* and *abnormal*.] In *meteor.*: **I.** *a.* Noting or pertaining to an imaginary line on the earth's surface, or a corresponding line on a map or the like, connecting places which have the same deviation of the observed from the normal temperature, pressure, or the like. **II.** *n.* An isabnormal line.

i-sa-cous-tic (ī-sa̤-kös′tik), *a.* [See *iso-*.] Of or pertaining to equality or equal intensity of sound.

i-sa-go-ge (ī-sa̤-gō′jē), *n.* [L., < Gr. εἰσαγωγή, < εἰσάγειν, introduce, < εἰς, into, + ἄγειν, lead.] An introduction.—**i-sa-gog′ic** (-goj′ik), *a.* [L. *isagogicus*, < Gr. εἰσαγωγικός.] Introductory, esp. to the interpretation of the Bible.—**i-sa-gog′ics,** *n.* Introductory studies; esp., the department of theology which is introductory to exegesis or the interpretation of the Bible, and is concerned with the literary history of the books of the Bible.

I-sai-an, I-sai-an-ic (ī-zā′a̤n or ī-zī′-, ī-zā̤-an′ik or ī-zī-), *a.* Of or pertaining to the Hebrew prophet Isaiah, or the book of the Old Testament bearing his name.

i-sa-tin (ī′sa̤-tin), *n.* [NL. *Isatis*, genus of plants including woad, < Gr. ἰσάτις, woad.] In *chem.*, an orange-red compound, $C_8H_5O_2N$: a source of artificial indigo.

is-ba (iz-bä′ or iz′ba̤), *n.* [Russ. *izba*, peasant's cottage.] The dwelling of the Russian peasant; hence, an entertainment presenting scenes from Russian peasant life, with folk-songs, folk-dances, etc.

is-chi-ad-ic, is-chi-at-ic (is-ki-ad′ik, -at′ik), *a.* [L. *ischiadicus* (ML. *ischiaticus*), < Gr. ἰσχιαδικός, < ἰσχίον, hip-joint: see *ischium*, and cf. *sciatic*.] Pertaining to the ischium; sciatic. Also **is′chi-al.**

is-chi-um (is′ki-um), *n.*; pl. *ischia* (-ä̤). [NL., < Gr. ἰσχίον, hip-joint, haunch, ischium.] In *anat.*, the lowermost of the three parts composing either innominate bone; either of the bones on which the body rests when sitting.

-ise. See *-ize*.

-ish[1]. [AS. *-isc*: cf. *-esque*.] A suffix used to form adjectives (*a*) from nouns, with the sense of 'belonging to' (a people, country, etc.), as in *British, Danish, English, Spanish*, or 'after the manner of,' 'having characteristics of,' 'like,' as in *babyish, girlish, mulish, wolfish, womanish* (such words being now often depreciatory), or 'addicted to,' 'inclined or tending to,' as in *bookish, freakish, qualmish*, or (*b*) from other adjectives, with the sense of 'somewhat,' 'rather,' as in *baddish, latish, oldish, reddish, sweetish*.

-ish[2]. [OF. F. *-iss-*, in some parts of verbs with infinitive in *-ir*.] A termination (without assignable force) of many verbs from the French, as in *accomplish, blandish, cherish, embellish, finish, flourish, polish*.

Ish-ma-el (ish′mā̤-el), *n.* The son of Abraham and Hagar (see Gen. xvi. 11, 12), whose hand was to be "against every man, and every man's hand against him"; hence, one at war with society; an outcast.—**Ish′ma-el-ite″** (-īt″), *n.* A descendant of Ishmael (from whom the Arabs claim descent); hence, a wanderer; an outcast.—**Ish′ma-el-it″ish** (-ī″tish), *a.*

Ish-tar (ish′tär), *n.* [= *Astarte*.] The chief goddess of the Babylonians and Assyrians. Cf. *Astarte*.

I-si-ac (ī′si-ak), *a.* [L. *Isiacus*, < Gr. Ἰσιακός.] Of or pertaining to the Egyptian goddess Isis.

i-sin-glass (ī′zing-glȧs), *n.* [Appar. a corruption (simulating *glass*) of MD. *huysenblas* = G. *hausenblase*, isinglass, lit. 'sturgeon-bladder': cf. *hausen*.] A pure, transparent or translucent form of gelatin, esp. that derived from the air-bladders of certain fishes; also, mica.

I-sis (ī′sis), *n.* [L., < Gr. Ἶσις; from Egypt.] An Egyptian goddess, sister and wife of Osiris, usually distinguished by the solar disk and cow's horns on her head.

Isis. — Egyptian cavo-rilievo.

Is-lam (is′la̤m, iz′la̤m, or is-läm′), *n.* [Ar. *islām*, submission (to the will of God).] The religious system of Mohammed; Mohammedanism; also, the body of Mohammedans; the Mohammedan world.—**Is-lam′ic** (-lam′ik), *a.*—**Is′lam-ism,** *n.* Mohammedanism.—**Is′lam-ite** (-īt), *n.* A Mohammedan.—**Is-lam-it′ic** (-it′ik), *a.*—**Is′lam-ize** (-īz), *v. t.*; *-ized, -izing.* To Mohammedanize.

is-land (ī′la̤nd), *n.* [AS. *īland, īgland*, < *īg, īeg*, island, + *land*, land. The spelling *island* is due to association with *isle* (L. *insula*).] A tract of land completely surrounded by water; hence, something suggestive of this, in being detached or isolated; an isolated hill; a clump of woodland in a prairie; a platform in the middle of a street, at a crossing, for the safety of pedestrians; specif., in *anat.*, an isolated portion of tissue or aggregation of cells (as, the *island* of Reil, a central cluster of convolutions of each cerebral hemisphere; the *islands* of Langerhans, certain collections of cells in the interstitial tissue of the pancreas, thought to be independent ductless glands furnishing an internal secretion).—**Islands of the Blessed,** in *class. myth.*, certain islands in the remote western part of the ocean, where favored mortals, rescued by the gods from death, were supposed to live in everlasting joy.—**is′land,** *v. t.* To make into or as into an island (as, "A thousand streamlets . . . With labyrinthine channels *islanding* A thousand rocks": Southey's "Thalaba," vi. 10); place on or as on an island; also, to dot with or as with islands (as, "The waveless plain of Lombardy . . . *Islanded* by cities fair": Shelley's "Euganean Hills," 93).—**is′land-er,** *n.* A native or inhabitant of an island: as, "some surly *islander*, of manners rude" (Pope's tr. Homer's "Odyssey," xxiv.).

isle (īl), *n.* [OF. *isle, ile* (F. *île*), < L. *insula*, island.] An island; now, usually, a small island (except in certain established names, as 'the British Isles').—**Isles of the Blessed.** Same as *Islands of the Blessed*, under *island*.—**isle,** *v.*; *isled, isling.* **I.** *tr.* To make into or as into an isle; place on or as on an isle. **II.** *intr.* To dwell or remain on an isle: "Lion and stoat have *isled* together, knave, In time of flood" (Tennyson's "Gareth and Lynette," 871).—**isles-man** (īlz′ma̤n), *n.*; pl. *-men.* An islander: as, "The *Isles-men* carried at their backs The ancient Danish Battle-axe" (Scott's "Marmion," v. 5).

is-let (ī′let), *n.* [F. *islette* (now *îlette*).] A small island; hence, a small isolated tract or area, as of color; in *anat.*, an island, as of the pancreas.

ism (izm), *n.* [Noun use of *-ism*.] A distinctive doctrine, theory, system, or practice: as, "This is Abbot Samson's Catholicism of the Twelfth Century:—something like the *Ism* of all true men in all true centuries" (Carlyle's "Past and Present," ii. 15); a man interested in all the *isms* of the day. [Often in disparagement.]

-ism. [= F. *-isme*, < L. *-ismus, -isma*, < Gr. -ισμός, -ισμα, forming nouns from verbs with infinitive in -ίζειν, E. *-ize*.] A suffix of nouns denoting action or practice, state or condition, principles, doctrines, a usage or characteristic, etc., as in *baptism, barbarism, criticism, Darwinism, Latinism, plagiarism, realism, socialism, vandalism, westernism.* Cf. *-ist* and *-ize*.

iso-, is-. Forms of Gr. ἴσος, equal, used in combination: in *chem.*, sometimes prefixed to the name of one compound to denote another isomeric with it.

i-so-ab-nor-mal (ī″sō̤-ab-nôr′ma̤l), *a.* and *n.* Same as *isabnormal*.

i-so-bar (ī′sō̤-bär), *n.* [Gr. ἴσος, equal, + βάρος, weight.] In *meteor.*, etc., a line on a weather-map, etc., connecting places at which the barometric pressure (reduced to sea-level) is the same.—**i-so-bar′ic** (-bar′ik), *a.* Having or showing equal barometric pressure; of or pertaining to isobars.

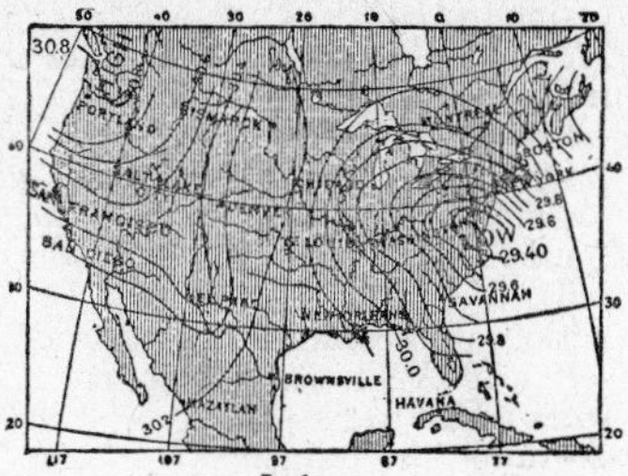

Isobars.

i-so-bath (ī′sọ-bath), *n.* [Gr. ἴσος, equal, + βάθος, depth.] In *phys. geog.*, a line connecting points that have the same depth below sea-level.—**i-so-bath′ic,** *a.*

i-so-bath-y-met-ric (ī″sọ-bath-i-met′rik), *a.* [Gr. ἴσος, equal, + βαθύς, deep, + μέτρον, measure.] Having the same depth below sea-level.

i-so-bath-y-therm (ī-sọ-bath′i-thėrm), *n.* [Gr. ἴσος, equal, + βαθύς, deep, + θέρμη, heat.] In *phys. geog.*, a line connecting points of equal temperature in a vertical section of a part of the ocean.—**i″so-bath-y-ther′mal, i″so-bath-y-ther′mic** (-thėr′mạl, -mik), *a.*

i-so-ceph-a-ly (ī-sọ-sef′ạ-li), *n.* [Gr. ἴσος, equal, + κεφαλή, head.] In *art*, a principle illustrated in ancient Greek friezes, etc., of representing the heads of the figures, whether seated or standing, at about the same level.—**i″so-ce-phal′ic** (-se-fal′ik), *a.*

Isocephaly. — Example from the frieze of the Parthenon.

i-so-chime, i-so-cheim (ī′sọ-kīm), *n.* [Gr. ἴσος, equal, + χεῖμα, winter.] In *phys. geog.*, a line on a map connecting places which have the same mean winter temperature.—**i-so-chi′mal, i-so-chei′mal** (-kī′mạl), *a.* and *n.*

i-so-chro-mat-ic (ī″sọ-krọ-mat′ik), *a.* [See *iso-*.] In *optics*, having the same color or tint; in *photog.*, orthochromatic.

i-soch-ro-nal, i-soch-ro-nous (ī-sok′rọ-nạl, -nus), *a.* [Gr. ἰσόχρονος, < ἴσος, equal, + χρόνος, time.] Equal or uniform in time; performed in equal times; characterized by motions or vibrations of equal duration.—**i-soch′ro-nism,** *n.* Isochronous character or action.—**i-soch′ro-nize,** *v. t.*; *-nized, -nizing.* To make isochronous.

i-soch-ro-ous (ī-sok′rọ-us), *a.* [Gr. ἴσος, equal, + χρόα, color.] Of the same color throughout.

i-so-cli-nal (ī-sọ-klī′nạl). [Gr. ἴσος, equal, + κλίνειν, incline.] **I.** *a.* Of or pertaining to equal inclination; inclining or dipping in the same direction; specif., noting or pertaining to a line on a map drawn through points at which the dip of the magnetic needle is the same; in *geol.*, noting or pertaining to a fold of strata which is of the nature of an isocline. **II.** *n.* An isoclinal line.—**i′so-cline** (-klīn), *n.* In *geol.*, a fold of strata so tightly compressed that the parts on each side of the axis dip in the same direction.—**i-so-clin′ic** (-klin′ik), *a.* and *n.* Same as *isoclinal*.

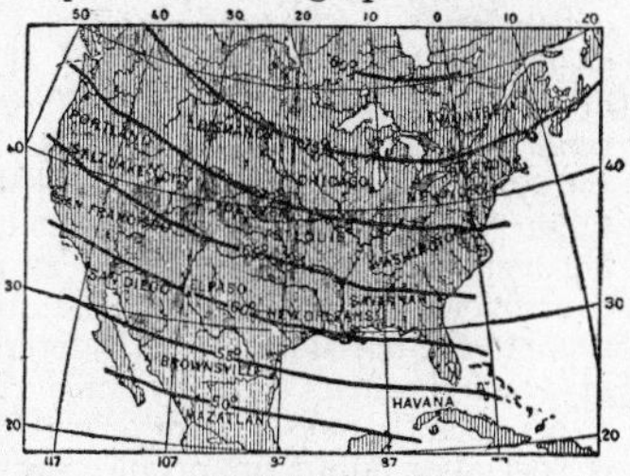

Isoclinal Lines.

i-soc-ra-cy (ī-sok′rạ-si), *n.* [Gr. ἰσοκρατία, < ἴσος, equal, + κρατεῖν, rule.] Equality of rule or power; a government in which all possess equal political power.—**i-so-crat** (ī′sọ-krat), *n.* An advocate of isocracy.—**i-so-crat′ic,** *a.*

i-so-cryme (ī′sọ-krīm), *n.* [Gr. ἴσος, equal, + κρυμός, cold.] In *phys. geog.*, a line on a map, etc., connecting points at which the temperature is the same during some specified coldest portion of the year.—**i-so-cry′mal** (-krī′mạl), *a.* and *n.*

i-so-di-a-met-ric (ī″sọ-dī-ạ-met′rik), *a.* [See *iso-*.] Having equal diameters or axes; in *bot.*, having the diameter similar throughout, as a cell. Also **i″so-di-a-met′ri-cal.**

i-so-di-mor-phism (ī″sọ-dī-môr′fizm), *n.* [See *iso-*.] In *crystal.*, isomorphism between the forms of two dimorphous substances.—**i″so-di-mor′phous** (-fus), *a.*

i-so-dy-nam-ic (ī″sọ-dī-nam′ik), *a.* [See *iso-*.] Pertaining to or characterized by equality of force, intensity, or the like; specif., noting or pertaining to an imaginary line on the earth's surface connecting points where the intensity of the magnetic force is the same. Also **i″so-dy-nam′i-cal.**

i-sog-a-mous (ī-sog′ạ-mus), *a.* [Gr. ἴσος, equal, + γάμος, marriage.] In *biol.*, having two similar gametes in which no differentiation of sex can be distinguished, or reproducing by the union of such gametes: opposed to *heterogamous*.—**i-sog′a-my,** *n.*

i-sog-e-nous (ī-soj′e-nus), *a.* [Gr. ἴσος, equal, + γεν-, bear, produce.] In *biol.*, of the same or a similar origin, as parts derived from the same or corresponding tissues of the embryo.—**i-sog′e-ny,** *n.*

i-so-ge-o-therm (ī-sọ-jē′ọ-thėrm), *n.* [Gr. ἴσος, equal, + γῆ, earth, + θέρμη, heat.] In *phys. geog.*, an imaginary line or surface passing through points in the interior of the earth which have the same mean temperature.—**i″so-ge-o-ther′mal, i″so-ge-o-ther′mic** (-thėr′mạl, -mik), *a.*

i-so-gon (ī′sọ-gon), *n.* [Gr. ἴσος, equal, + γωνία, angle.] In *geom.*, a figure whose angles are equal.—**i-sog-o-nal** (ī-sog′ọ-nạl), *a.* Equiangular; isogonic.—**i-so-gon′ic,** *a.* Having or pertaining to equal angles; specif., noting or pertaining to an imaginary line on the earth's surface connecting points at which the deviation of the magnetic needle from the true north is the same.

i-so-hy-e-tal (ī-sọ-hī′e-tạl), *a.* [Gr. ἴσος, equal, + ὑετός, rain.] Pertaining to or marking equality of rainfall: as, an *isohyetal* line (a line on a map connecting places having the same amount of annual or of seasonal rainfall).

is-o-la-ble (is′ọ-lạ-bl or ī′sọ-), *a.* Capable of being isolated.

is-o-late (is′ọ-lāt or ī′sọ-), *v. t.*; *-lated, -lating.* [First in *isolated*, p. a., < F. *isolé*, < It. *isolato*, pp. of *isolare*, isolate, < L. *insula*, island: cf. *insulate*.] To place or set apart; detach or separate so as to cause to be alone; cut off, as from contact, intercourse, or relations with others (as, "It became the maxim of Tory statesmen that England should . . . *isolate* herself from continental embarrassments": Lecky's "Hist. of Eng. in the 18th Century," i.); in *elect.*, to insulate; in *chem.*, to obtain (a substance) in an uncombined or pure state.—**is-o-la′tion** (-lā′shọn), *n.* The act of isolating, or the state of being isolated (as, "the *isolation* of Crusoe, depicted by Defoe's genius": W. Churchill's "Coniston," ii. 19); specif., the complete separation from others of persons suffering from contagious or infectious disease; also, the separation of a nation from other nations by a policy of non-participation in international affairs.—**is-o-la′tion-ist,** *n.* One who advocates isolation; esp., one who favors a national policy of political isolation, or non-participation in international affairs.—**is′o-la-tor,** *n.*

i-sol-o-gous (ī-sol′ọ-gus), *a.* [Gr. ἴσος, equal, + λόγος, relation.] In *chem.*, having similar relations: applied esp. to a series of hydrocarbons each member of which has two hydrogen atoms less than the one above it.

i-so-mag-net-ic (ī″sọ-mag-net′ik). [See *iso-*.] **I.** *a.* Noting or pertaining to an imaginary line on the earth's surface, or a corresponding line on a map or the like, connecting places which have the same magnetic elements. **II.** *n.* An isomagnetic line.

i-so-mer (ī′sọ-mėr), *n.* [Gr. ἴσος, equal, + μέρος, part.] In *chem.*, a compound isomeric with one or more other compounds.—**i′so-mere** (-mēr), *n.* In *zoöl.*, a homologous part or segment of a limb.—**i-so-mer′ic** (-mer′ik), *a.* In *chem.*, of compounds, composed of the same elements in the same proportions by weight, and (in the usual, restricted sense of the term) having the same molecular weight, but differing in one or more properties.—**i-som-er-ism** (ī-som′ẹ-rizm), *n.* The fact or condition of being isomeric.—**i-som′er-ous,** *a.* Having an equal number of parts, markings, etc.; in *bot.*, of a flower, having the same number of members in each whorl.

i-so-met-ric (ī-sọ-met′rik), *a.* [Gr. ἰσόμετρος, < ἴσος, equal, + μέτρον, measure.] Pertaining to or having equality of measure; in *crystal.*, noting or pertaining to that system of crystallization which is characterized by three equal axes at right angles to one another.—**isometric projection,** the projection of an object upon a plane equally inclined to the object's three principal axes, so that dimensions parallel to these are represented in their true proportions. Also **i-so-met′ri-cal.**—**i-so-met′ri-cal-ly,** *adv.*

i-so-me-tro-pi-a (ī″sǫ-me-trō′pi-ä), *n.* [NL., < Gr. ἴσος, equal, + μέτρον, measure, + ὤψ, eye.] A condition in which the refraction is the same in the two eyes.

i-so-morph (ī′sǫ-môrf), *n.* [Gr. ἴσος, equal, + μορφή, form.] An isomorphous substance; also, an organism isomorphic with another or others.—**i-so-mor′phic** (-môr′-fik), *a.* Isomorphous; in *biol.*, being of the same or of like form; different in ancestry, but alike in appearance.—**i-so-mor′phism,** *n.* The state or property of being isomorphous or isomorphic.—**i-so-mor′phous,** *a.* Crystallizing in the same or a related form: said esp. of substances of analogous chemical composition. Cf. *homœomorphous.*

i-son-o-my (ī-son′ǫ-mi), *n.* [Gr. ἰσονομία, < ἴσος, equal, + νόμος, law.] Equality of political rights, as among citizens of a state.—**i-so-nom-ic** (ī-sǫ-nom′ik), *a.*

i-so-pe-rim-e-ter (ī″sǫ-pe-rim′e-tėr), *n.* [Gr. ἰσοπερίμετρος, of equal perimeter: see *iso-* and *perimeter.*] In *geom.*, a figure equal in perimeter to another.—**i″so-per-i-met′ri-cal** (-per-i-met′ri-kạl), *a.*

i-so-pi-es-tic (ī″sǫ-pī-es′tik). [Gr. ἴσος, equal, + πιέζειν, press.] **I.** *a.* Pertaining to equal pressure: as, an *isopiestic* line (a curve showing the relation between volume and temperature in a body or system the pressure of which remains constant). **II.** *n.* An isopiestic line.

i-so-pod (ī′sǫ-pod), *n.* [NL. *Isopoda,* pl., < Gr. ἴσος, equal, + πούς (ποδ-), foot.] Any of the *Isopoda*, an order or suborder of crustaceans (fresh-water, marine, and terrestrial) with seven pairs of legs, which are usually similar.—**i-sop-o-dous** (ī-sop′ǫ-dus), *a.*

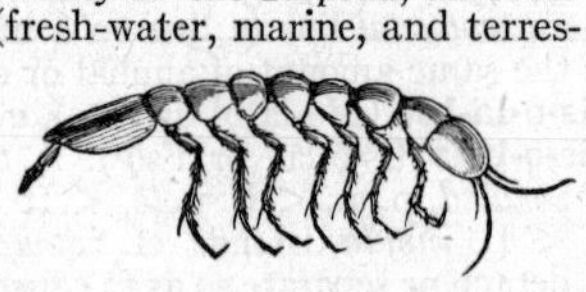

Blind Isopod (*Cæcidotea stygia*), Mammoth Cave, Kentucky.

i-so-pol-i-ty (ī-sǫ-pol′i-ti), *n.* [Gr. ἰσοπολιτεία, < ἰσοπολίτης, one having equal civil rights, < ἴσος, equal, + πολίτης, citizen: see *polity.*] Equality of rights of citizenship between different communities or states; mutual political rights.—**i″so-po-lit′i-cal** (-pǫ-lit′i-kạl), *a.*

i-so-prene (ī′sǫ-prēn), *n.* [See *iso-* and cf. *terpene.*] In *chem.*, a colorless liquid hydrocarbon, C_5H_8, of the terpene class, produced from caoutchouc or from oil of turpentine, and convertible into caoutchouc.

i-so-pyre (ī′sǫ-pīr), *n.* [Gr. ἴσος, equal, + πῦρ, fire.] An impure form of opal, sometimes used as a semiprecious stone.

i-sos-ce-les (ī-sos′ẹ-lēz), *a.* [LL., < Gr. ἰσοσκελής, < ἴσος, equal, + σκέλος, leg.] Of a triangle, having two sides equal.

Isosceles Triangle.

i-so-seis-mal (ī-sǫ-sīs′mạl or -sīz′mạl). [Gr. ἴσος, equal, + σεισμός, earthquake: see *seism.*] **I.** *a.* Pertaining to equal intensity of earthquake-shock; specif., noting or pertaining to an imaginary line on the earth's surface connecting points characterized by such intensity. **II.** *n.* An isoseismal line.—**i-so-seis′mic,** *a.* Isoseismal.

i-sos-ta-sy (ī-sos′tạ-si), *n.* [Gr. ἴσος, equal, + στάσις, a standing: see *stasis.*] Equilibrium when there is pressure from all sides; hydrostatic equilibrium; specif., the equilibrium of the earth's crust, a condition in which the forces tending to elevate balance those tending to depress.—**i-so-stat-ic** (ī-sǫ-stat′ik), *a.* Pertaining to or characterized by isostasy.

i-so-ste-mo-nous (ī-sǫ-stē′mǫ-nus or -stem′ǫ-nus), *a.* [Gr. ἴσος, equal, + στήμων, warp, thread.] In *bot.*, having the stamens equal in number to the sepals or petals.

i-so-there (ī′sǫ-thēr), *n.* [Gr. ἴσος, equal, + θέρος, summer.] In *phys. geog.*, an imaginary line connecting places on the earth's surface which have the same mean summer temperature.—**i-so-ther-al** (ī-sǫ-thēr′ạl or ī-soth′ẹ-rạl), *a.* and *n.*

i-so-therm (ī′sǫ-thėrm), *n.* [Gr. ἴσος, equal, + θέρμη, heat.] In *phys. geog.*, an imaginary line connecting points on the earth's surface having the same (mean) temperature.—**i-so-ther′mal** (-thėr′mạl). **I.** *a.* Pertaining to or indicating equality of temperature; pertaining to isotherms. **II.** *n.* An isotherm.—**i-so-ther′mal-ly,** *adv.*—**i-so-ther′-mic,** *a.* Isothermal.

i-so-ton-ic (ī-sǫ-ton′ik), *a.* [Gr. ἰσότονος, < ἴσος, equal, + τόνος, E. *tone.*] In *music*, pertaining to or characterized by equal tones; in *physiol.*, noting or pertaining to a contraction of a muscle when under a constant tension; in *physiol. chem.*, characterized by equal osmotic pressure; noting or pertaining to a solution containing just enough salt to prevent the destruction of the red blood-corpuscles when added to the blood.

i-so-tope (ī′sǫ-tōp), *n.* [Gr. ἴσος, equal, + τόπος, place.] In *chem.*, any of two or more chemical elements occupying the same place in the periodic table and apparently identical in properties, but differing slightly in atomic weight: as, certain of the common chemical elements are thought to be mixtures of *isotopes.*—**i-so-top′ic** (-top′ik), *a.* Pertaining to an isotope or isotopes; of the nature of an isotope.—**i-sot-o-py** (ī-sot′ǫ-pi), *n.* Isotopic character.

i-so-trop-ic (ī-sǫ-trop′ik), *a.* [Gr. ἴσος, equal, + τρόπος, turn, way.] In *physics*, having the same properties (as elasticity or conduction) in all directions. Also **i-sot-ro-pous** (ī-sot′rǫ-pus).—**i-sot′ro-py,** *n.*

Is-ra-el (iz′rā-el), *n.* [Heb. *Yisrāēl,* (appar.) 'he who striveth with God.'] A name given to Jacob after he had wrestled with the angel (see Gen. xxxii. 28); also, the people descended from Israel or Jacob; the Hebrew or Jewish people or nation; fig., God's chosen people; the elect; the Christian church.—**Is′ra-el-ite″** (-īt″). **I.** *n.* A descendant of Israel or Jacob; a Hebrew; a Jew; fig., one of God's chosen people. **II.** *a.* Pertaining to Israel; Jewish.—**Is′ra-el-it″ish** (-ī″tish), **Is″ra-el-it′ic** (-it′ik), *a.*

is-su-a-ble (ish′ö-ạ-bl), *a.* That may be issued or may issue; in *law*, that admits of issue being taken.—**is′su-a-bly,** *adv.*

is-su-ance (ish′ö-ạns), *n.* The act of issuing; issue.

is-su-ant (ish′ö-ạnt), *a.* Issuing; emerging: in *her.*, said of a beast of which only the upper half is seen.

Lion Issuant.

is-sue (ish′ö), *n.* [OF. *issue, eissue* (F. *issue*), < *issir, eissir,* < L. *exire,* go out, come forth, issue, < *ex,* out of, + *ire,* go.] A going, coming, passing, or flowing out; egress; outflow; hence, a place or means of egress; an outlet or vent; also, that which comes out, as an outflowing stream; also, offspring or progeny (now chiefly in legal use: as, to die without *issue*); a child or children; a descendant or descendants; also, the yield or profit from land or other property (now legal: as, the *issues*, rents, and profits of an estate); something proceeding from any source, as a product, effect, result, or consequence (as, "Many receipts he gave me; chiefly one . . . the dearest *issue* of his practice": Shakspere's "All's Well," ii. 1. 109); the ultimate result, event, or outcome of a proceeding, affair, etc. (as, to await the *issue* of a contest; the policy was vindicated in the *issue*); rarely, a proceeding† or action† (see Shakspere's "Julius Cæsar," iii. 1. 294); also, a point in question or dispute, as between contending parties in an action at law or in any controversy (as, to raise an *issue*; to try or decide an *issue*); a point the decision of which determines a matter; a point at which a matter is ready for decision (as, to bring or put a case to an *issue*); a point or matter the decision of which is of special or public importance (as, "Some awful moment to which Heaven has joined Great *issues*, good or bad for human kind," Wordsworth's "Character of the Happy Warrior," 50; to seek *issues* for a political campaign); also, the act of issuing, sending, or putting forth, or that which is issued; a quantity issued at one time (as, an *issue* of stamps, coins, or bonds; the daily *issues* of a newspaper); in *med.*, a discharge of blood, pus, or the like; also, an incision, ulcer, or the like emitting such a discharge, esp. one produced or maintained artificially to relieve morbid conditions in some other part.—**at issue,** in controversy; in question.—**to join issue,** to submit an issue jointly for legal decision; hence, to join in controversy; take issue.—**to take issue,** to join in controversy; take a contrary view; disagree, as with a speaker, statement, or conclusion.

—**is′sue,** *v.*; *-sued, -suing.* **I.** *intr.* To go, pass, or flow out; come forth; emerge; also, to proceed as offspring, or be born or descended (now chiefly legal); also, to come as a yield or profit, as from land (chiefly legal); come or proceed from any source; arise as a result or consequence; result, as from something; have the result or outcome as specified; result or end (*in*); also, to be sent or put forth authoritatively or publicly, as a writ, money, etc.; be published, as a book. **II.** *tr.* To send out, discharge, or emit (as, to *issue* water, smoke, or heat); esp., to put forth authoritatively, formally, or publicly (as, to *issue* an edict or a warrant; to *issue* invitations; to *issue* bonds); put into public circulation (as, to *issue* stamps or money); publish (a book, periodical, etc.); also, to give birth to†, or bear†.—**is′sue-less,** *a.* Without issue; childless; without result.—**is′sue=pea,** *n.* In *med.*, a pea or similar round body inserted in an issue or artificial ulcer in order to maintain the discharge of pus.—**is′su-er,** *n.*

-ist. [= F. *-iste*, < L. *-ista*, < Gr. *-ιστής*, forming agent-nouns from verbs with infinitive in *-ίζειν*, E. *-ize*.] A suffix of nouns, often accompanying verbs ending in *-ize* or nouns ending in *-ism*, denoting one who does, practises, or is concerned with something, or holds certain principles, doctrines, etc., as in *apologist, dramatist, machinist, plagiarist, realist, socialist, theorist.*

isth-mi-an (is′mi-ạn or ist′-). **I.** *a.* Of or pertaining to an isthmus, esp. [*cap.*] the Isthmus of Corinth, Greece (as, the *Isthmian* games, one of the great national festivals of ancient Greece, held every two years), or the Isthmus of Panama (as, the *Isthmian* Canal Zone, a strip of land, 10 miles wide, granted in 1904 to the United States in perpetuity by the Republic of Panama for use, occupation, and control in connection with the Panama Canal). **II.** *n.* A native or inhabitant of an isthmus.

isth-mi-tis (is-mī′tis or ist-), *n.* [NL., < L. *isthmus*: see *isthmus*.] In *pathol.*, inflammation of the isthmus of the fauces.

isth-mus (is′mus or ist′-), *n.* [L., < Gr. *ἰσθμός*, narrow passage, neck, isthmus, < *ἰέναι*, go.] A narrow strip of land, bordered on both sides by water, connecting two larger bodies of land; in *anat.*, etc., a connecting part, organ, or passage, esp. when narrow or joining structures or cavities larger than itself (as, the *isthmus* of the fauces, the contracted passage leading from the cavity of the mouth into that of the pharynx).

is-tle (is′tlē), *n.* [Mex. *ixtli.*] A fiber obtained from various tropical American plants, esp. *Bromelia sylvestris*, a kind of wild pineapple: used in making bagging, carpets, etc.

Is-tri-an (is′tri-ạn). **I.** *a.* Of or pertaining to Istria (a peninsula at the eastern side of the head of the Adriatic Sea) or its inhabitants. **II.** *n.* An inhabitant of Istria.

it (it), *pron.*; nom. *it*, poss. *its*, earlier *it* (obs. or prov.), *his*†, obj. *it*, pl. nom. *they*, poss. *their* or *theirs*, obj. *them.* [AS. *hit* (gen. *his*, dat. *him*, acc. *hit*), neut. of *hē*, he: see *he*.] A personal pronoun of the third person and neuter gender, corresponding to *he* and *she*: used (*a*) as a substitute for a neuter noun or a noun representing something possessing sex when sex is not particularized or considered; (*b*) to refer to some matter expressed or understood, or some thing or notion not definitely conceived; (*c*) to refer to the subject of inquiry or attention, whether impersonal or personal, in sentences asking or stating what or who this is (as, what was *it*? *it* is I; *it* is they who are at fault); (*d*) as the grammatical subject of a clause of which the logical subject is a phrase or clause, generally following, regarded as in apposition with *it* (as, *it* is hard to believe that; *it* is believed that he is dead; he is dead, *it* is generally believed); (*e*) in impersonal constructions (as, *it* snows); and (*f*) without definite force after an intransitive verb (as, to foot *it*, that is, to go on foot).

it-a-col-u-mite (it-ạ-kol′ū-mīt), *n.* [From *Itacolumi*, mountain in Brazil.] A rock consisting of interlocking quartz grains, talc, etc., found in Brazil, North Carolina, etc., and remarkable for its flexibility when in thin slabs.

I-tal-ian (i-tal′yạn), *a.* [L. *Italia*, < Gr. *Ἰταλία*, Italy.] Of or pertaining to Italy, its people, or their language.—**Italian architecture,** the architectural styles developed in and characteristic of Italy; specif., the architecture of the Italian Renaissance, developed through study of ancient Roman models by Brunelleschi and others in the 15th century.—**Italian millet.** See *foxtail millet*, under *foxtail*.—**I-tal′ian,** *n.* A native or inhabitant of Italy; also, the language of Italy, developed from Latin.—**I-tal′ian-ate,** (-āt), *v. t.*; *-ated, -ating.* To Italianize.—**I-tal′ian-ate,** *a.* Italianized; conformed to the Italian type or style: as, "the house most commodiously built in the French fashion, or perhaps *Italianate*" (Stevenson's "Master of Ballantrae," ii.).—**I-tal-ian-esque′** (-esk′), *a.* [See *-esque*.] In the Italian style.—**I-tal′ian-ism,** *n.* An Italian practice, trait, or idiom; also, Italian quality, spirit, or principles; attachment to Italian ideas or principles, or sympathy with Italy.—**I-tal′ian-ize** (-īz), *v. t.*; *-ized, -izing.* To render Italian.—**I-tal″ian-i-za′tion** (-i-zā′shọn), *n.*—**I-tal′ian-iz-er** (-ī-zėr), *n.*—**I-tal′ian-ly,** *adv.* In the Italian manner: as, to pronounce a word *Italianly*.

Italian Architecture.—Church of Santa Maria della Salute, Venice; constructed 1632.

I-tal-ic (i-tal′ik). [L. *Italicus*, < Gr. *Ἰταλικός*.] **I.** *a.* Of or pertaining to Italy, esp. ancient Italy or its tribes; specif., pertaining to parts of Italy other than Rome; also [*l. c.*], designating or pertaining to a style of printing-types (introduced by Aldus Manutius, of Venice, in 1501) in which the letters slope to the right (thus, *italic*), used for emphasis, etc. (cf. *Roman, a.*). **II.** *n.* [*l. c.*] Italic type or letters; also, an italic type, letter, or character (usually in *pl.*).—**I-tal′i-cism** (-i-sizm), *n.* An Italianism.—**i-tal′i-cize** (-sīz), *v.*; *-cized, -cizing.* **I.** *tr.* To print in italic type; also, to underscore (words, etc.) with a single line, as in indicating italics. **II.** *intr.* To use italics.—**i-tal″i-ci-za′tion** (-si-zā′shọn), *n.*

I-tal-i-ot, I-tal-i-ote (i-tal′i-ot, -ōt). [Gr. *Ἰταλιώτης*: see *-ot* and *-ote*.] **I.** *n.* A person of Greek birth or descent living in ancient Italy. **II.** *a.* Of or pertaining to the ancient Greek colonies in southern Italy.

It-a-lo- (it′ạ-lọ-). Form of L. *Italus*, Italian, used in combination, as in *Italo-American, Italo-Byzantine, Italo-Grecian.*—**It′a-lo-phil, It′a-lo-phile** (-fil). [+ *-phil, -phile.*] **I.** *a.* Friendly to Italy or the Italians; fond of Italian ways, institutions, etc. **II.** *n.* One who is friendly to Italy or the Italians.—**It′a-lo-phobe** (-fōb), *n.* [+ *-phobe.*] One who fears or hates Italy or the Italians.—**It″a-lo-pho′bi-a** (-fō′bi-ạ̈), *n.* [+ *-phobia.*] Fear or hatred of Italy or anything Italian.

itch (ich), *v.* [ME. *icchen*, < AS. *giccan* = D. *jeuken* = G. *jucken*, itch.] **I.** *intr.* To have or feel a peculiar irritation of the skin which causes a desire to scratch the part affected; fig., to have an uneasy desire, as after, for, or to do something (as, "I . . . after no field honours *itch*, Achiev'd by leaping hedge and ditch," M. Green's "The Spleen"; "Their hands had felt Queen Ino's gold, And *itched* for more," W. Morris's "Jason," ii. 408; to *itch* to ask questions). **II.** *tr.* To cause to itch: as, "There's been the devil's own fly *itching* my nose" (Synge's "Shadow of the Glen").—**itch,** *n.* The sensation of itching; fig., an uneasy or restless desire or longing (as, an *itch* for authorship; "The folk belonging to the cotton-mill . . . were afflicted with the *itch* of jacobinism," Galt's "Annals of the Parish," xliv.); in *pathol.*, any of various diseases of the skin accompanied by itching, esp. a contagious disease due to a small mite ('itch-mite,' *Sarcoptes scabiei*) which burrows under the skin.—**itch'y,** *a.* Having an itching sensation or the itch; of the nature of itching or the itch.—**itch'i-ness,** *n.*

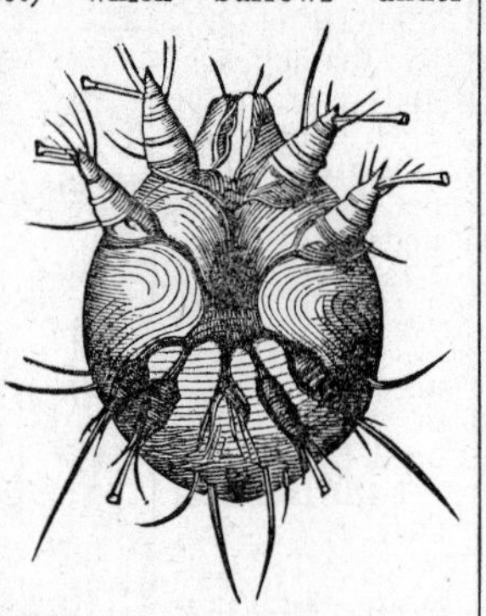
Under side of Itch-mite (*Sarcoptes scabiei*), highly magnified.

-ite. [= F. *-ite,* < L. *-ita, -ites,* < Gr. *-ίτης,* fem. *-ῖτις.*] A suffix of nouns denoting esp. (*a*) persons associated with a place, tribe, leader, doctrine, system, etc., as in *Campbellite, Carmelite, Israelite, Jacobite, laborite, sybarite,* (*b*) minerals and fossils, as in *ammonite, anthracite, dolomite,* (*c*) explosives, as in *cordite, dynamite, lyddite,* (*d*) chemical compounds, esp. salts of acids whose names end in *-ous,* as in *phosphite, sulphite,* and (*e*) pharmaceutical and commercial products, as in *glycerite, vulcanite.*

i-tem (ī'tem). [L., adv., from the stem of *is,* he, that.] **I.** *adv.* Likewise; also: used in introducing the separate articles or particulars of an enumeration (as, "Imprimis: She can milk . . . *Item:* She brews good ale . . . *Item:* She can sew": Shakspere's "Two Gentlemen of Verona," iii. 1. 304). **II.** *n.* A separate article or particular in an enumeration; a single particular or detail of any list or the like; also, a separate piece of information or news, as in a newspaper; also, a statement† or saying†; an admonition† or warning† (as, "He . . . has need of an *item,* to caution him to take heed every moment of the day": Bunyan's "Pilgrim's Progress," ii.); an intimation† or hint†.—**i'tem,** *v. t.* To set down or enter as an item, or by or in items.—**i'tem-ize** (-īz), *v. t.*; *-ized, -izing.* To set down by items; specify the items or particulars of (an account, etc.); also, to set down or enter as an item in an enumeration, bill, etc.—**i''tem-i-za'tion** (-i-zā'shọn), *n.*—**i'tem-iz-er** (-ī-zėr), *n.*

it-er-ant (it'ẹ-rạnt), *a.* [L. *iterans* (*-ant-*), ppr.] Iterating; repeating.—**it'er-ance, it'er-an-cy,** *n.*

it-er-ate (it'ẹ-rāt), *v. t.*; *-ated, -ating.* [L. *iteratus,* pp. of *iterare,* < *iterum,* again, from the stem of *is,* he, that.] To do (something) over again; perform or present a second time or repeatedly (as, to *iterate* an experiment; "the *iterated* nodes of a sea-shell," Emerson's "Essays," The Poet); now, usually, to utter again or repeatedly (as, "*iterating* and speaking again that which thou hast heard," Ecclus., xli. 23; to *iterate* a demand); repeat.—**it-er-a'tion** (-ẹ-rā'shọn), *n.* [L. *iteratio*(*n-*).] Repetition; repeated performance, occurrence, or utterance: as, "These . . . questions . . . pursued her in dreams with pitiless *iteration*" (Howells's "Chance Acquaintance," xii.).—**it'er-a-tive** (-ẹ-rā-tiv), *a.* [LL. *iterativus.*] Repeating; making repetition; in *gram.,* frequentative, as a verb.

ith-er (iᴛʜ'ėr), *a.* and *pron.* Scotch form of *other.*

ith-y-phal-lic (ith-i-fal'ik). [L. *ithyphallicus,* < Gr. *ἰθυφαλλικός,* < *ἰθύφαλλος,* < *ἰθύς,* straight, + *φαλλός,* E. *phallus.*] **I.** *a.* Pertaining to the phallus, as carried in ancient festivals of Bacchus; in *anc. pros.,* noting or pertaining to any of several meters employed in hymns sung in phallic processions. **II.** *n.* A poem in ithyphallic meter; also, a poem of indecent character.

i-tin-er-ant (ī-tin'ẹ-rạnt). [LL. *itinerans* (*-ant-*), ppr. of *itinerari*: see *itinerate.*] **I.** *a.* Itinerating; journeying; traveling from place to place, or on a circuit, in the performance of duty or business, as a preacher, a judge, or a peddler (as, "In 1739 arrived among us from Ireland the Reverend Mr. Whitefield, who had made himself remarkable there as an *itinerant* preacher": B. Franklin's "Autobiography," vii.). **II.** *n.* One who travels from place to place, esp. for duty or business.—**i-tin'er-an-cy,** *n.*—**i-tin'er-ant-ly,** *adv.*

i-tin-er-a-ry (ī-tin'ẹ-rā-ri). [LL. *itinerarius* (as n., *itinerarium*), < L. *iter* (*itiner-*), journey, way: see *itinerate.*] **I.** *a.* Pertaining to traveling or to routes of travel; also, itinerant (as, an *itinerary* judge). **II.** *n.*; pl. *-ries* (-riz). An account of a journey; a record of travel; also, a line of travel; a route; also, a book describing a route or routes of travel, with information for travelers; also, a plan of travel; a sketch of a proposed route; also, an itinerant (rare).

i-tin-er-ate (ī-tin'ẹ-rāt), *v. i.*; *-ated, -ating.* [LL. *itineratus,* pp. of *itinerari,* < L. *iter* (*itiner-*), a going, journey, way, road, < *ire,* go.] To travel; go from place to place, esp. in a regular circuit of duty or business, as to preach, hold court, or sell wares.—**i-tin-er-a'tion** (-ẹ-rā'shọn), *n.*

-itis. [L. *-itis,* < Gr. *-ῖτις,* fem. suffix: see *-ite.*] A noun suffix used in pathological terms denoting inflammation of some part or organ, as in *bronchitis, gastritis, neuritis.*

its (its). Possessive case of *it.*

it's (its). Contraction of *it is.*

it-self (it-self'), *pron.* Emphatic or reflexive form of *it.*

I-van I-van-o-vitch (ē-vän' ē-vän'ọ-vich). [Russ. *Ivan Ivanovich,* lit. 'Ivan (John) son of Ivan.'] The typical Russian; the Russian people.

I've (īv). Contraction of *I have.*

-ive. [L. *-ivus.*] A suffix of adjectives (and nouns of adjectival origin) expressing tendency, disposition, function, connection, etc., as in *active, corrective, destructive, detective, passive, sportive.* See *-ative.*

i-vied (ī'vid), *p. a.* Covered or overgrown with ivy: as, "Upon an *ivied* stone Reclined his languid head" (Shelley's "Alastor," 634).

i-vo-ried (ī'vọ-rid), *a.* Finished to resemble ivory.

i-vo-rist (ī'vọ-rist), *n.* A worker in ivory.

i-vo-ry (ī'vọ-ri), *n.*; pl. *-ries* (-riz). [OF. F. *ivoire,* < L. *eboreus,* made of ivory, < *ebur,* ivory.] The hard white substance, a variety of dentin, composing the main part of the tusks of the elephant, walrus, etc., used for carvings, billiard-balls, etc.; sometimes, dentin of any kind; also, some substance resembling ivory; the hard endosperm ('vegetable ivory') of the ivory-nut, used for ornamental purposes, buttons, etc.; also, an article made of ivory, as a carving or a billiard-ball; also, a tusk, as of an elephant; sometimes, a tooth, or the teeth (humorous); also, a creamy white color; the whiteness of the human skin.—**black ivory.** See under *black, a.*—**i'vo-ry,** *a.* Consisting or made of ivory (as, an *ivory* billiard-ball; an *ivory* box); also, resembling ivory; of a creamy white color.—**ivory tower.** Same as *tower of ivory,* under *tower²,* *n.*—**i'vo-ry-bill,** *n.* An American woodpecker, *Campephilus principalis,* with a hard white bill.—**i'vo-ry=billed,** *a.*—**i'vo-ry=black',** *n.* A fine black pigment made by calcining ivory.—**i'vo-ry=nut,** *n.* The seed of a low-growing South American palm, *Phytelephas macrocarpa,* forming the source of vegetable ivory; also, a similar seed obtained from other palms.—**i'vo-ry=palm,** *n.* The palm yielding the common ivory-nut.

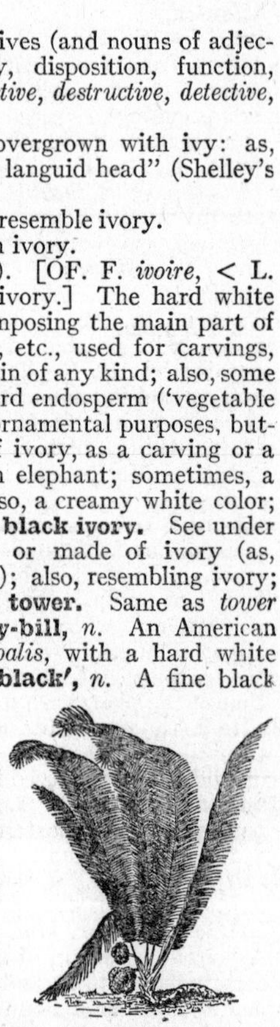
Fruiting Female Plant of Ivory-palm (*Phytelephas macrocarpa*).

i-vy (ī'vi), *n.*; pl. *ivies* (ī'viz). [AS. *īfig,* akin to G. *epheu,* ivy.] An araliaceous climbing plant, *Hedera helix,* with smooth, shiny evergreen leaves, yellowish inconspicuous flowers, and black berries ('English ivy'); any of various other climbing or trailing plants, as *Parthenocissus quinquefolia* ('American ivy': see *Virginia creeper*), *Glecoma hederacea* (see *ground-ivy*), *Parthenocissus tricuspidata* ('Japanese ivy,' a vine much used for ornament on walls, buildings, etc.), and *Cymbalaria cymbalaria* ('Kenilworth ivy,' a handsome trailing scrophulariaceous vine, often cultivated, and used in hanging baskets, etc.). Cf. *poison-ivy.*—**i'vy,** *v. t.*; *ivied, ivying.* To cover with or as with ivy: as, "Earth with her twining memories *ivies* o'er Their holy sepulchres" (Lowell's "Prometheus," 179).—**i'vy=bush,** *n.* A plant or bushy branch of ivy; also, this, or a representation of it, formerly placed outside a tavern as a sign that wine

Ivy (*Hedera helix*).—*a,* flower; *b,* fruit; *c,* leaf and aërial roots of young plant.

was sold there (ivy anciently having been sacred to Bacchus: cf. *bush*[1], *n.*).—**i'vy-tod** (-tod), *n.* [See *tod*[1].] An ivy-bush: as, "when the *ivy-tod* is heavy with snow" (Coleridge's "Ancient Mariner," vii.). [Archaic.]

i-wis, y-wis (i-wis'), *adv.* [ME., adv., < AS. *gewis*, adj. (= D. *gewis* = G. *gewiss*), certain, < *ge-*, a generalizing prefix, + *-wis*, akin to *witan*, know, E. *wit*, *v.*] Certainly; assuredly; indeed: in later use often erroneously taken as *I wis*, as if a form of *wit*, *v.* ('know'): as, "A well-bred horse he was *I wis*" (Hood's "Epping Hunt," 73); "*I wis*, in all the Senate, There was no heart so bold" (Macaulay's "Horatius," xviii.). [Archaic.]

I. W. W. See *Industrial Workers of the World*, under *industrial*, *a.*

ix-i-a (ik'si-ạ), *n.* [NL. (named with reference to the juice), < Gr. ἰξός, birdlime.] Any plant of the iridaceous genus *Ixia*, comprising South African plants with sword-shaped leaves and showy ornamental flowers.

ix-tle, ix-tli (iks'tlē), *n.* Same as *istle*.

I-yar (ē-yär'), *n.* [Heb.] In the Jewish calendar, the eighth month (29 days) of the civil year and the second of the ecclesiastical year, beginning in the latter part of April or the first part of May.

iz-ar (iz'ạr), *n.* [Ar. *izār*.] An outer garment worn by Moslem women, made of cotton and covering the whole person; also, a cloth girded round the waist, forming part of the ihram (pilgrim's dress).

iz-ard (iz'ạrd), *n.* [F. *isard*.] The chamois which inhabits the Pyrenees.

-ize. [Also *-ise*, < F. *-iser*, < L. *-izare*, < Gr. -ίζειν.] A suffix of verbs having the sense (*a*) intransitively, of following some line of action, practice, policy, etc., as in *Atticize*, *Bantingize*, *Judaize*, *apologize*, *economize*, *philosophize*, *theorize*, *tyrannize*, or of becoming (as indicated), as in *crystallize* and *oxidize* (*intr.*), and (*b*) transitively, of acting toward or upon, treating, or affecting in a particular way, as in *baptize*, *colonize*, *macadamize*, *patronize*, *plagiarize*, *stigmatize*, or of making or rendering (as indicated), as in *civilize*, *dramatize*, *legalize*, *mobilize*, *neutralize*, *realize*. Cf. *-ism* and *-ist*.

iz-zard (iz'ạrd), *n.* [Cf. *zed*.] A name for the letter Z. [Archaic or prov.]

J

J, j (jā); pl. *J's, j's* (jāz). A consonant, the 10th letter of the English alphabet.

jab (jab), *v.*; *jabbed*, *jabbing*. [Var. (orig. Sc.) of *job*[1].] **I.** *tr.* To strike (a person, etc.) with the end or point of something; also, to thrust (something) smartly or sharply into an object. [Colloq.] **II.** *intr.* To make a jab. [Colloq.]—**jab**, *n.* A stroke with the end or point of something; a smart or sharp thrust. [Colloq.]

jab-ber (jab'ėr), *v. i.* or *t.* [Appar. imit.: cf. *gab*[1], *gabble*, and *gibber*[1].] To talk or utter rapidly, indistinctly, or unintelligibly; chatter unintelligibly or senselessly: as, "Demons for fright *Jabber* and scream about him in the night" (W. B. Yeats's "Wanderings of Oisin," ii.).—**jab'ber**, *n.* Jabbering talk or utterance; chatter; gibberish.—**jab'ber-er**, *n.*—**jab'ber-ing-ly**, *adv.*

jab-ble (jab'l), *v.*; *-bled*, *-bling*. [Appar. a freq. form connected with *jaup*.] **I.** *tr.* To shake up (liquid matter); cause to splash. [Sc. and north. Eng.] **II.** *intr.* To splash, as water; break or dash in small waves. [Sc. and north. Eng.]—**jab'ble**, *n.* Agitation of a liquid; a splashing or dashing in small waves; fig., turmoil or confusion. [Sc. and north. Eng.]

American Jabiru (*Mycteria americana*).

jab-i-ru (jab'i-rö), *n.* [Brazilian.] A large wading bird, *Mycteria americana*, of the stork family, inhabiting the warmer parts of America; also, any of various similar birds of the Old World.

jab-o-ran-di (jab-ọ-ran'di), *n.* [Brazilian.] Any of certain South American shrubs of the rutaceous genus *Pilocarpus*; a drug yielded by their dried leaflets, used as a sudorific and sialagogue; also, any of various similar plants.

ja-bot (zhȧ-bō), *n.* [F., bird's crop, jabot.] A falling ruffle, cascade, or other arrangement of lace, embroidery, or the like, worn (formerly by men, now by women) for ornament at the throat or on the breast.

ja-cal (ʜä-käl'), *n.* [Mex. Sp.] A native Mexican house or hut whose walls consist of rows of thin vertical poles filled in and plastered with mud; also, this method of constructing walls and houses.

jac-a-mar (jak'ạ-mär), *n.* [Brazilian.] Any of the sharp-billed, usually brilliantly colored, insectivorous birds constituting the subfamily *Galbulinæ* (family *Galbulidæ*) of tropical America.

Kingfisher Jacamar (*Galbalcyrhynchus leucotis*).

jac-a-na (jak'ạ-nä), *n.* [Brazilian.] Any bird of the family *Jacanidæ*, which comprises aquatic birds resembling the plovers and usually having long, straight claws adapted for walking on the floating leaves of aquatic plants. See cut below.

jac-a-ran-da (jak-ạ-ran'dạ), *n.* [Brazilian.] Any of the tall tropical American trees constituting the bignoniaceous genus *Jacaranda*; the fragrant ornamental wood of such a tree; also, any of various related or similar trees, or the wood.

jac'co-net, *n.* See *jaconet*.

Mexican Jacana (*Jacana*, or *Parra*, *gymnostoma*).

ja-cinth (jā'sinth), *n.* [OF. *jacint*, *jacinte* (F. *jacinthe*), < L. *hyacinthus*: see *hyacinth*.] Among the ancients, a bluish gem; now, any of several gems, esp. a reddish-orange variety of zircon. Cf. *hyacinth*.

jack[1] (jak), *n.* [OF. *jaque*, *jaques*; origin uncertain.] A defensive coat, usually of leather, formerly worn by foot-soldiers and others. See cut on following page.

jack[2] (jak), *n.* [Pg. *jaca*; from E. Ind. name.] An East Indian moraceous tree, *Artocarpus integrifolia*, with a fruit resembling breadfruit; also, the fruit itself.

jack[3] (jak), *n.* [From *Jack*, in general use as a familiar equivalent of *John*, man's name, and possibly a var. of *John*, but commonly explained as < OF. *Jaques* (F. *Jacques*), < LL. *Jacobus*, Jacob, James: see *jacobus*.] [*cap.*] A nickname for the name *John*; hence, a popular name for a boy, lad, or man (as, "*Jack* shall have Jill," Shakspere's "Midsummer Night's Dream," iii. 2. 461: see *Gill*[4], *Jill*); [*cap.* or *l. c.*] a sailor (also *Jack Tar* and *Jacky*); a man or fellow (as, a *jack* of all trades: see below); [*l. c.*] a steeple-jack; any of the four knaves in playing-cards, orig. the knave of trumps; a figure, usually of a man, which strikes a bell attached to a clock; also, any of various mechanical contrivances or devices, as a contrivance for raising great weights small distances by a force exerted from below, a device for turning a spit, etc.; a bootjack; in the harpsichord, spinet, etc., an upright piece of wood at the inner end of a key, carrying a quill or spine by which the string is twanged; an analogous device in other instruments of this class; a wooden frame on which wood is sawed; a portable cresset used in hunting or fishing at night; a horizontal bar or crosstree of iron at the head of a topgallant-mast; also, a vessel for holding liquor, orig. one of waxed leather coated externally with tar (archaic: as, "a large black leathern *jack*, which contained two double flagons of strong ale," Scott's "Woodstock," ix.); also, a small bowl used as a mark for the players to aim at, in the game of bowls (see Shakspere's "Cymbeline," ii. 1. 2); also, a small union or ensign used by a ship or vessel as a signal, etc., and flown from the jack-staff as an indication of nationality; also, the male of certain animals; esp., the male ass, or jackass (as, "He leisurely untied From head and neck the halter of the *jack*": Longfellow's "Monk of Casal-Maggiore," 38); also, a jack-rabbit; also (pl. *jacks*, or, esp. collectively, *jack*), any of various fishes, as a pike or a pickerel.—**every man jack,** every one without exception: as, "Send them [children] all to bed — *every man jack* of them!" (Reade's "Peg Woffington," viii.). [Colloq.]—**jack in office,** a pretentious petty official.—**jack of all trades,** one who can turn his hand (after a fashion) to any kind of work or business: as, "a very handy, ingenious fellow, who was a cooper by trade . . . a good turner, and a good pot-maker . . . we called him our *Jack of all trades*" (Defoe's "Robinson Crusoe," ii. 1).—**jack**[3], *v.* **I.** *tr.* To lift or move with or as with a jack, or contrivance for raising (usually with *up*: often fig., in colloq. use, as in 'to jack up wages'); also, to throw up or abandon (with *up*: slang); also, to seek (game or fish) at night with a jack (portable cresset). **II.** *intr.* To hunt or fish with a jack.

Arbalister of the 14th century, wearing a Jack. See preceding page.

jack-a-dan-dy (jak-a-dan′di), *n.*; pl. *-dies* (-diz). [From *jack*[3] + *dandy*[3].] A foppish little fellow; a dandy.

jack-al (jak′âl), *n.* [Turk. *chakāl*, < Pers. *shaghāl*.] Any of several species of wild dog (genus *Canis*), of Asia and Africa, which hunt in packs at night, and which were formerly supposed to hunt prey for the lion; hence, one who does subordinate preliminary work or drudgery for another, or who meanly serves the purposes of another (as, "He's the man who has all your bills; Levy is only his *jackal*": Bulwer-Lytton's "My Novel," ix. 13).

Black-backed Jackal (*Canis mesomelas*).

Jack′-a-Lent′, *n.* See *Jack-o'-Lent*.

jack-a-napes (jak′a-nāps), *n.* [Earlier *Jack a Napes, Jack Napes*, perhaps meaning 'Jack of Naples.'] An ape or monkey (archaic: as, "a rebeck or a guitar at my back, and a *jackanapes* on my shoulder," Scott's "Fair Maid of Perth," xii.); hence, one who suggests an ape in behavior or airs; a pert, presuming fellow, or whipper-snapper (as, "Then there's her brother . . . a pert *jackanapes*, full of college petulance and self-conceit": Smollett's "Humphry Clinker," April 17).

jack-a-roo (jak-a-rö′), *n.*; pl. *-roos* (-röz′). [Said to be < *jack*[3] + (*kang*)*aroo*.] A new arrival gaining experience in the bush; an inexperienced colonist. [Colloq., Australia.]

jack-ass (jak′ås), *n.* A male ass; hence, a very stupid or foolish person (as, "I . . . began . . . to think I had borne myself something like a *jackass* in the matter": Scott's "Peveril of the Peak," vii.); also, a laughing-jackass (as, "A mob of *jackasses* were shouting and laughing uproariously": H. Kingsley's "Geoffry Hamlyn," xviii.).

jack-boot (jak′böt), *n.* A large, strong boot reaching above the knee, orig. one serving as armor.

Jack-boot, time of James II.

jack-daw (jak′dâ), *n.* A glossy-black European bird, *Corvus monedula*, of the crow family, frequenting church steeples, ruins, etc.

Jackdaw.

jack-er (jak′ėr), *n.* One who or that which jacks.

jack-et (jak′et), *n.* [OF. *jaquete* (F. *jaquette*), dim. of *jaque*, E. *jack*[1].] A short coat, in various forms, worn by both sexes; also, any of various outer coverings, as the coat of an animal, a casing round a steam-pipe, a paper cover for protecting the binding of a book, etc.—**jack′et,** *v. t.* To cover with a jacket; also, to beat or thrash (colloq.).—**jack′et-ing,** *n.* A jacket or covering, as of a steam-pipe; also, material for making jackets; also, a beating or thrashing (colloq.).

Jack Frost (jak frôst). Frost, or freezing cold, personified.

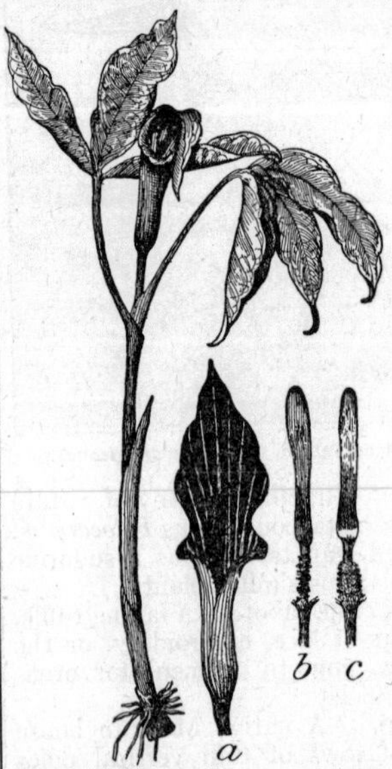

Jack-in-the-pulpit. — *a*, inflorescence, the spathe turned back; *b*, male, and *c*, female spadix.

jack-in-a-box (jak′in-a-boks″), *n.* A tropical tree, *Hernandia sonora*, which bears a large nut that rattles in its casing when shaken; also, a jack-in-the-box.

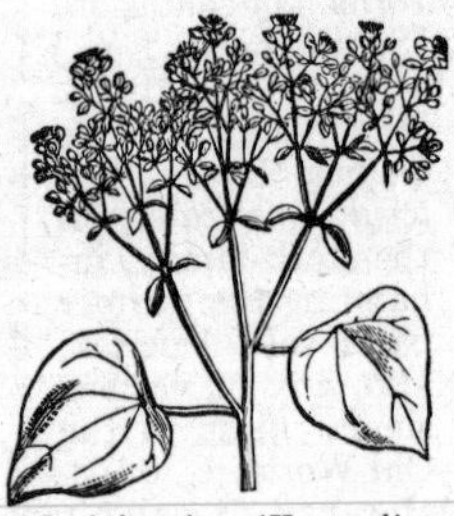

Jack-in-a-box (*Hernandia sonora*).

jack-in-the-box (jak′in-ᴛʜē-boks″), *n.* A toy consisting of a figure which is inclosed in a box and which springs up from the box when the lid is unfastened.

jack-in-the-pul-pit (jak′-in-ᴛʜē-pul′pit), *n.* An araceous herb, *Arisæma triphyllum*, of North America, having an upright spadix arched over by a spathe. Also called *Indian turnip.*

Jack Ketch (jak kech). [From an English executioner, *Jack* (or John) *Ketch* (died 1686).] A public executioner or hangman.

jack=knife (jak′nīf), *n.* A large, strong pocket-knife.

jack-leg (jak′leg), *n.* A lawyer or other professional man who employs questionable or dishonest practices. [Slang.]

jack=light (jak′līt), *n.* The light carried in a jack or cresset for hunting or fishing at night.—**jack′=light,** *v. i.* To hunt or fish with a jack-light.

jack=o′=lan-tern (jak′ọ-lan′tėrn), *n.* A man with a lantern†; also, an ignis fatuus or will-o'-the-wisp; also, a lantern made of a rind, as of a pumpkin, with holes cut to represent human eyes, nose, and mouth.

Jack=o′=Lent (jak′ọ-lent′), *n.* A figure of a man set up to be pelted during Lent; hence, a butt, as of scorn or ridicule; also, a puppet; an insignificant person. [Archaic.]

jack=pine (jak′pīn), *n.* A slender pine, *Pinus divaricata,* covering large tracts of barren land in Canada and the northern U. S.

jack=plane (jak′plān), *n.* A carpenter's plane used for rough work.

jack=pot (jak′pot), *n.* In *poker,* a pot or pool that must accumulate until one of the players can open the betting with a pair of jacks or better.

jack=pud-ding (jak′pu̇d′ing), *n.* A buffoon; a clown; a merry-andrew: as, "What make you in that fool's jacket and playing the pranks of a *jack-pudding?*" (Scott's "Woodstock," xxviii.). [Archaic.]

jack=rab-bit (jak′rab′it), *n.* Any of various large species of hare of western North America, noted for the length of their limbs and ears.

Jack-rabbit (*Lepus callotis*).

jack=screw (jak′skrö), *n.* A jack for raising weights, operated by a screw.

jack=snipe (jak′snīp), *n.* Any of several species of snipe, as *Gallinago delicata,* the common American snipe; also, the pectoral sandpiper.

Jack-so-ni-an (jak-sō′ni-ạn). **I.** *a.* Of or pertaining to some person named Jackson, as, in *U. S. hist.* and *politics,* Andrew Jackson, seventh President of the United States (1829–37) and long a prominent leader of the Democratic party. **II.** *n.* A follower of Andrew Jackson.

Jack Sprat (jak sprat). [Cf. *sprat.*] A dwarfish or insignificant-looking little fellow (prov. Eng.); also, a character in a familiar nursery rime who "could eat no fat," while "His wife could eat no lean; And so betwixt them both, you see, They licked the platter clean."

jack=staff (jak′ståf), *n.* *Naut.,* a short staff, set upon the bowsprit or at the bow of a ship or vessel, upon which the flag called the jack is hoisted: as, "a lantern hanging on the *jackstaff* of a double-hull ferryboat" (Mark Twain's "Huckleberry Finn," xiii.).

jack-stay (jak′stā), *n.* *Naut.,* a rope, rod, or the like, on a yard or gaff, for bending a sail to; also, a rod or rope running up and down on the forward side of a mast, for a yard to travel on.

jack-stone (jak′stōn), *n.* [For earlier *checkstone*: cf. *checker*[2].] A small round pebble or stone; esp., one of a set of pebbles or of shaped pieces of iron tossed up and caught and otherwise used in children's play; *pl.* (construed as *sing.*), a game played with these.

jack-straw (jak′strâ), *n.* A man of straw; a man of no substance or worth; an insignificant person; also, one of a set of straws, or strips of wood, bone, etc., used in a game in which they are thrown on a table in a confused pile and are to be picked up singly without disturbing the rest of the pile; *pl.* (construed as *sing.*), the game itself.

Jack Tar (jak tär). A sailor: as, "a jolly warm-hearted *Jack Tar*" (Lamb's "On Some of the Old Actors").

jack=tow-el (jak′tou″ẹl), *n.* A long towel with the ends sewed together, for hanging on a roller: as, "He . . . dipping his head into a bowl of water, had recourse to a *jack-towel* inside the closet door" (Dickens's "Barnaby Rudge," xxxi.).

Jack-y (jak′i), *n.*; pl. *-ies* (-iz). A diminutive of the name *Jack*; [*cap.* or *l. c.*] a sailor; also [*l. c.*], gin (prov. or slang, Eng.).

jack-yard (jak′yärd), *n.* *Naut.,* a light yard used to extend the head of a square-cut gaff-topsail; also, a spar to extend the foot of a gaff-topsail beyond the peak.—**jack′yard″er,** *n.* *Naut.,* a gaff-topsail extended by a jackyard.

jac-o-bæ-a (jak-ọ-bē′ä) **lil′y.** [NL. *jacobæa,* prop. fem. of *Jacobæus,* of James (here St. James): see *Jacobean.*] A red-flowered amaryllidaceous plant, *Sprekelia formosissima,* native in Mexico.

Jacobean Architecture.
Bramshill House, Hants, England.

Jac-o-be-an (jak-ọ-bē′ạn), *a.* [NL. *Jacobæus,* < LL. *Jacobus,* James: see *jacobus.*] Of or pertaining to some person named James; esp., of or pertaining to James I., king of England (1603–25), or his times (as, *Jacobean* architecture, late English Gothic architecture, subsequent to the Elizabethan, characterized by a large admixture of debased Italian forms).

Jac-o-bin (jak′ọ-bin). [OF. F. *Jacobin,* < ML. *Jacobinus,* < LL. *Jacobus,* James: see *jacobus.*] **I.** *n.* A Dominican friar, orig. a French Dominican (so called because the first convent of the order in Paris was established in a hospice for pilgrims going to the shrine of St. James of Compostella in Spain); also, a member of a famous club or society of French revolutionists organized in 1789, called Jacobins from the Jacobin or Dominican convent in Paris in which they met; hence, an extreme radical, esp. in politics; also [*l. c.*], one of a variety of domestic pigeons whose neck-feathers form a kind of hood. **II.** *a.* Of or belonging to the Jacobins or Dominican friars; also, pertaining to the revolutionary Jacobins; hence, in general, ultraradical, as in politics.—**Jac-o-bin′ic, Jac-o-bin′i-cal,** *a.* Of, pertaining to, or characteristic of the revolutionary Jacobins; hence, in general, ultraradical, as in politics.—**Jac-o-bin′i-cal-ly,** *adv.*—**Jac′o-bin-ism,** *n.* The principles of the revolutionary Jacobins; hence, extreme radicalism, esp. in politics.—**Jac′o-bin-ize,** *v. t.*; *-ized, -izing.* To render Jacobin; imbue with Jacobinism.

Jacobin Pigeon.

Jac-o-bite (jak′ọ-bīt), *n.* [LL. *Jacobus,* James: see *jacobus.*] A partizan or adherent of James II. of England, after his abdication (1688), or of his descendants; a supporter of the Stuarts or their claims after the English Revolution of 1688.—**Jac-o-bit′ic, Jac-o-bit′i-cal** (-bit′ik, -i-kạl), *a.*—**Jac′o-bit-ism** (-bīt-izm), *n.* The principles of the Jacobites; adherence to the Stuart cause.

Ja-cob's-lad-der (jā'ko̤bz-lad'ėr), *n.* [From the ladder seen by the patriarch Jacob in a dream: see Gen. xxviii. 12.] A common garden-plant, *Polemonium cæruleum*, whose leaves have a ladder-like arrangement; any of certain related species; also, *naut.*, a rope ladder with wooden or iron rungs.

ja-co-bus (ja̤-kō'bus), *n.* [LL. *Jacobus*, < Gr. Ἰάκωβος, Jacob, James, < Heb. *Ya'aqōb*, Jacob, lit. 'one who takes by the heel,' a supplanter: see Gen. xxv. 26, xxvii. 36.] An English gold coin struck in the reign of James I., worth orig. 20 shillings, later 24.

jac-o-net (jak'o̤-net), *n.* [From *Jagannath* (or Puri), in Orissa, India: cf. *Juggernaut.*] A soft, light cotton fabric, orig. from India.

Jac-quard (ja̤-kärd', F. zhȧ-kär) **loom.** A loom with an attachment invented by J. M. Jacquard (1752–1834), of Lyons, France, for weaving figured fabrics.

Jacque-mi-not (jak'mi-nō, F. zhȧk-mē-nō), *n.* [From J. F. *Jacqueminot* (1787–1865), French general.] A deep-red variety of the rose.

Jacob's-ladder (*Polemonium cæruleum*).
1, rootstock and lower part of stem; 2, upper part of stem with flowers; *a*, half of a flower, from within; *b*, fruit.

Jacque-rie (zhȧk-rē), *n.* [F. *Jacquerie*, OF. *Jaquerie*, < *Jaques* (see *jack*³), taken as a name for a peasant.] The revolt of the peasants of northern France against the nobles in 1358; hence [*l. c.*], any insurrection of peasants.

jac-tance (jak'ta̤ns), *n.* [OF. F. *jactance*, < L. *jactantia*, < *jactare*: see *jactation.*] Boasting; boastfulness. [Now rare.] Also **jac'tan-cy.**

jac-ta-tion (jak-tā'sho̤n), *n.* [L. *jactatio(n-)*, < *jactare*, throw, toss, agitate, discuss, boast, freq. of *jacere*, throw.] Agitation of the body, as for exercise; specif., a restless tossing of the body in disease; also, boasting, bragging, or ostentation.

jac-ti-ta-tion (jak-ti-tā'sho̤n), *n.* [ML. *jactitatio(n-)*, < L. *jactitare*, bring forward in public, utter, freq. of *jactare*: see *jactation.*] Public or open declaration, esp. of a boastful character; boasting or bragging; specif., in *law*, the assertion of a false claim, to the injury of another; in *pathol.*, a restless tossing of the body in disease.

jac-u-late (jak'ṳ̄-lāt), *v. t.* or *i.*; *-lated, -lating.* [L. *jaculatus*, pp. of *jaculari*, throw, hurl, < *jaculum*, a dart, < *jacere*, throw.] To hurl or dart. [Obs. or archaic.]—**jac-u-la'tion** (-lā'sho̤n), *n.*

jade¹ (jād), *n.* [F. *jade*, < Sp. (*piedra de*) *ijada*, '(stone of) colic,' so called from its supposed medicinal virtue (Sp. *ijada*, flank, pain in the side, colic, < L. *ilia*, flanks: see *ileum*).] The mineral nephrite, varying in color from whitish to dark green, anciently credited with medicinal virtues and long used for making implements and ornaments; also, the mineral jadeite, in similar colors, highly esteemed in the East and elsewhere as an ornamental stone for carvings, jewelry, etc.; also, any of various other stones of similar appearance and use; also, an object, carving, or the like, made from any variety of jade (as, a collection of *jades*).

jade² (jād), *n.* [ME.: cf. Icel. *jalda*, mare.] A horse, esp. one of inferior breed, or one that is worn-out or vicious; also, a woman (generally used opprobriously, sometimes playfully: as, "a light-minded, jilting *jade*," Cooper's "Deerslayer," i.; "some handsome young *jades*," Addison, in "Spectator," 130); rarely, a worthless man.—**jade**², *v.*; *jaded, jading.* **I.** *tr.* To make a jade of (a horse); exhaust by working hard; hence, in general, to weary or fatigue; tire; dull; also, to make a fool of† (as, "I do not now fool myself, to let imagination *jade* me": Shakspere's "Twelfth Night," ii. 5. 179). **II.** *intr.* To become weary or tired; grow dull.—**jad-ed** (jā'ded), *p. a.* Worn out or exhausted; fatigued; also, dulled from continual use, as the faculties; sated by continual indulgence, as the appetite.—**jad'ed-ly**, *adv.*—**jad'ed-ness**, *n.*

jade-ite (jād'īt), *n.* A mineral consisting essentially of a silicate of sodium and aluminium. See *jade*¹.

jade-stone (jād'stōn), *n.* Same as *jade*¹.

jad-ish (jā'dish), *a.* Like a jade; worthless; vicious.—**jad'ish-ly**, *adv.*—**jad'ish-ness**, *n.*

jad-y (jā'di), *a.* Like a jade; jadish.

jae-ger (yā'gėr), *n.* See *jäger.*

jag¹ (jag), *v. t.*; *jagged, jagging.* [ME. *jaggen*; origin uncertain.] To pierce, prick, or jab (now prov.); fig., to irritate, vex, or trouble (Sc. and prov. Eng.: as, "Easie Haggart *jagged* the minister sorely," Barrie's "Auld Licht Idylls," iii.); also, to cut or slash, esp. in points or pendants along the edge; make indentations in the edge or surface of; form notches, teeth, or ragged points in.—**jag**¹, *n.* [ME. *jagge.*] One of a series of points or pendants cut in the edge of a garment; also, a shred, as of cloth (now prov.); also, a sharp projection on an edge or surface; a tooth; also, a prick or jab with something sharp (Sc.).

jag² (jag), *n.* [Origin unknown.] A load, as of hay or wood (prov.); also (slang, U. S.), as much liquor as one can carry; a fit of intoxication.

Jag-an-nath (jug'u-nät), *n.* See *Juggernaut.*

jä-ger (yā'gėr), *n.* [G., hunter, < *jagen*, drive, chase, hunt.] A hunter; also, a member of any certain bodies of sharpshooters in the German or Austrian army; also, an attendant dressed like a huntsman (as, "our duke . . . supervised by his *jager*, who stood behind his chair": Disraeli's "Young Duke," ii. 8); also, any of the rapacious sea-birds constituting the subfamily *Stercorariinæ* or *Lestridinæ* of the gull family (*Laridæ*), which pursue weaker birds in order to make them disgorge their prey; a skua.

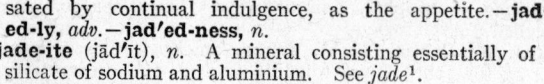

Parasitic Jäger (*Stercorarius parasiticus*).

jag-ged (jag'ed), *p. a.* Cut or formed into jags; notched; having the edge or surface formed into irregular indentations and projecting points; of plants, having jagged leaves or flowers.—**jag'ged-ly**, *adv.*—**jag'ged-ness**, *n.*

jag-ger (jag'ėr), *n.* One who or that which jags; a small wheel with a jagged or wavy edge and a handle, for cutting pastry; a toothed chisel.

jag-ger-y (jag'ėr-i), *n.* [Pg. *jágara*, < Skt. *çarkara*, Prakrit *sakkara*: see *sugar.*] Coarse sugar made in the East Indies from the sap of palm-trees.

jag-gy (jag'i), *a.* Jagged; notched.

ja-ghir, ja-ghire (jä-gēr'), *n.* [Hind. and Pers. *jāgīr.*] In the East Indies, an assignment of the government revenues of a district to a person or body of persons, either for private use or for the support of a public (esp. military) establishment; also, the district, or the revenues derived from it.

jag-u-ar (jag'wär or ja-gwär'), *n.* [Brazilian.] A large, ferocious, spotted feline mammal, *Felis onca*, of the

Jaguar.

warmer parts of America. Also called *American leopard*, and *panther*.

Jah-veh, Jah-ve (yä′vā), **Jah-vism** (yä′vizm), etc. Same as *Yahweh*, etc.

jail (jāl), *n.* [OF. *jaiole, gaiole* (F. *geôle*), < LL. *caveola*, dim. of L. *cavea*, cavity, inclosure, E. *cage*: cf. *gaol*.] A prison, esp. one for the detention of persons awaiting trial or convicted of minor offenses.—**jail,** *v. t.* To confine in or as in a jail; imprison.—**jail′bird,** *n.* One who is or has been confined in jail; a criminal.—**jail′=de-liv″er-y,** *n.* The act of clearing a jail of prisoners by bringing them to trial, as at the assizes in England; also, a deliverance of imprisoned persons, esp. by force.—**jail′er,** *n.* The keeper of a jail. —**jail′=fe″ver,** *n.* Typhus: formerly common in jails: as, "In most large prisons the *jail fever*, produced by squalor, overcrowding, bad drainage, insufficient nourishment, and insufficient exercise, made fearful ravages" (Lecky's "Hist. of Eng. in the 18th Century," iii.).

Jain (jīn or jān). [Skt. *jaina*, < *jina*, lit. 'conqueror' (applied to the sages or teachers of the sect).] **I.** *n.* A member of a non-Brahmanic sect of India, established about the 6th century B.C., the doctrinal system of which corresponds in many essential points with Buddhism. **II.** *a.* Of or pertaining to the Jains or their religion: as, *Jain* architecture (one of the chief styles of Indian architecture, at its best about the 11th century, seen in many temples and towers characterized notably by the predominance of horizontal courses). Also **Jai-na** (jī′nạ̈ or jā′nạ̈), *n.* and *a.*—**Jain′ism,** *n.* The religious system of the Jains.—**Jain′ist,** *n.*

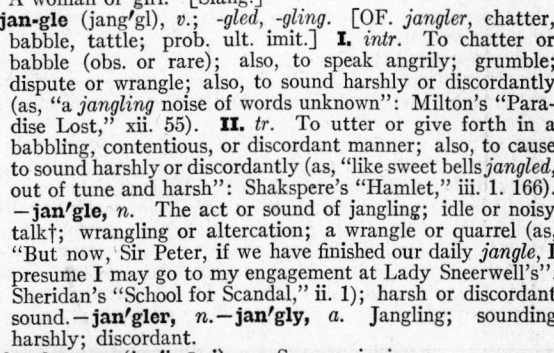

Jain Architecture.

jakes (jāks), *n.* [Origin uncertain.] A privy.

jal-ap (jal′ạp), *n.* [Sp. *jalapa*; so called from *Jalapa*, city in southeastern Mexico.] A purgative drug obtained from the tuberous roots of a convolvulaceous plant, *Exogonium purga*, of Mexico, or of any of various other convolvulaceous plants; also, any of these plants.—**ja-lap-ic** (jạ-lap′ik), *a.* —**jal′a-pin** (-ạ-pin), *n.* A resin which is one of the purgative principles of jalap.

ja-lop-py, ja-lop-y (jạ-lop′i), *n.*; pl. *-pies, -ies* (-iz). [Origin uncertain.] An old, decrepit, or unpretentious automobile; hence, anything regarded as having similar characteristics. [Colloq. or humorous.]

ja-louse (jạ-löz′), *v. t.*; *-loused, -lousing.* [F. *jalouser*, < *jaloux*, E. *jealous*.] To be suspicious about; suspect; also, to have a suspicion of; surmise. [Sc. and prov. Eng.]

jal-ou-sie (zhal′ọ̈-zē), *n.* [F., lit. 'jealousy': see *jealousy*.] A kind of blind or shutter made with slats.—**jal′ou-sied** (-zēd), *a.* Furnished with jalousies.

jam[1] (jam), *v.*; *jammed, jamming.* [Perhaps imit.: cf. *champ*.] **I.** *tr.* To press or squeeze tightly between bodies or surfaces, so that motion or extrication is made difficult or impossible; also, to bruise or crush by squeezing; also, to cause (a movable part) to become wedged, caught, or displaced, so that it cannot work; render (a machine, etc.) unworkable by such wedging, catching, or displacement; also, to press, push, or thrust violently, as into a confined space or against some object (as, "Everything was *jammed* into the tightest cases," Dickens's "Dombey and Son," iv.; "the steersman having *jammed* his helm hard down," Hughes's "Tom Brown at Oxford," ii.); press or squeeze (a number of objects) closely or tightly together (as, "drays and baggage-vans . . . getting blocked and *jammed* together": Mark Twain's "Life on the Mississippi," xvi.); also, to pull or draw tight or fast, as a noose; also, to fill or block up (a passageway, etc.) by crowding (as, "Crowds that in an hour Of civic tumult *jam* the doors, and bear The keepers down": Tennyson's "Lucretius," 169); also, in *wireless teleg.* and *teleph.*, to interfere with (signals, etc.) by sending out others of approximately the same wavelength; of signals, etc., to interfere with (other signals, etc.). **II.** *intr.* To become wedged or fixed; stick fast; also, of a machine, etc., to become unworkable as through the wedging or displacement of a part; also, to press or push violently, as into a confined space or against one another; also, of musicians, to enliven a musical score by impromptu variations and improvisations of a more or less unrestricted character.—**jam**[1], *n.* The act of jamming, or the state of being jammed; a condition of being pressed or crowded together so closely or tightly as to prevent or hinder motion, or the mass of objects so pressed or crowded together; a block or obstructed condition in a passageway.

jam[2] (jam), *n.* [Appar. < *jam*[1].] A preserve of fruit boiled to a pulp with sugar.

jam[3] (jäm), *n.* [E. Ind.] The title of certain native chiefs of northwestern India.

jamb (jam), *n.* [OF. *jambe*, leg, jamb (F. leg, supporting piece), < LL. *gamba*, hoof.] A jambe; also, in *arch.*, the side of an opening; a vertical piece forming the side of a doorway, window, or the like.

Church of St. Genest, Nevers, France; 12th century.—*J, J*, jambs.

jambe (jamb), *n.* [OF. *jambe*, leg: see *jamb*.] A piece of armor for the leg.

jam-bo-ree (jam-bọ-rē′), *n.* [Appar. a made word.] A carousal; a spree; any noisy merrymaking. [Slang, U. S.]

James-town (jāmz′-toun) **weed.** Same as *jimson-weed*.

jam-pan (jam′pan), *n.* [Hind. *jānpān*.] A kind of sedan-chair carried by four men, used in India.

jane (jān), *n.* [From *Jane*, woman's name.] A woman or girl. [Slang.]

jan-gle (jang′gl), *v.*; *-gled, -gling.* [OF. *jangler*, chatter, babble, tattle; prob. ult. imit.] **I.** *intr.* To chatter or babble (obs. or rare); also, to speak angrily; grumble; dispute or wrangle; also, to sound harshly or discordantly (as, "a *jangling* noise of words unknown": Milton's "Paradise Lost," xii. 55). **II.** *tr.* To utter or give forth in a babbling, contentious, or discordant manner; also, to cause to sound harshly or discordantly (as, "like sweet bells *jangled*, out of tune and harsh": Shakspere's "Hamlet," iii. 1. 166). —**jan′gle,** *n.* The act or sound of jangling; idle or noisy talk†; wrangling or altercation; a wrangle or quarrel (as, "But now, Sir Peter, if we have finished our daily *jangle*, I presume I may go to my engagement at Lady Sneerwell's": Sheridan's "School for Scandal," ii. 1); harsh or discordant sound.—**jan′gler,** *n.*—**jan′gly,** *a.* Jangling; sounding harshly; discordant.

jan-is-sa-ry (jan′i-sā-ri), *n.* Same as *janizary*.

jan-i-tor (jan′i-tọr), *n.* [L., < *janua*, door: cf. *Janus*.] A doorkeeper or porter; also, a person employed to take care of a building, offices, etc.—**jan-i-to′ri-al** (-tō′ri-ạl), *a.* —**jan′i-tor-ship,** *n.* The office or position of a janitor. —**jan′i-tress,** *n.* A female janitor.

jan-i-za-ry (jan′i-zā-ri), *n.*; pl. *-ries* (-riz). [= F. *janissaire*, < Turk. *yeñicheri*, 'new soldiery.'] [Also *cap.*] A member of a body of Turkish infantry constituting the Sultan's guard and the main part of the standing army of the Turks, in existence from the 14th century until 1826; also, any Turkish soldier; also, a West Indian labroid fish, *Clepticus parræ*.

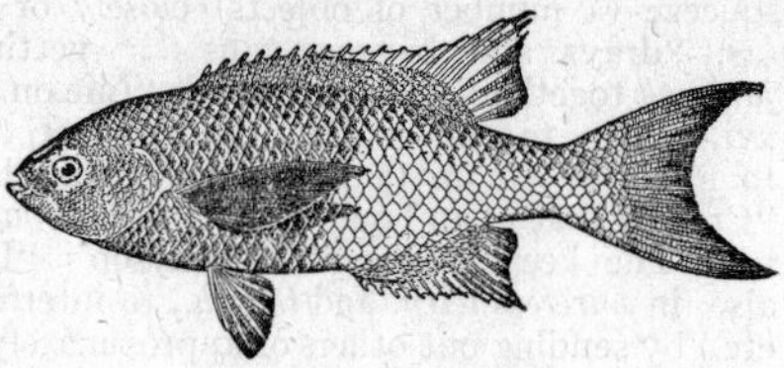

Janizary (*Clepticus parræ*).

jan-nock (jan′ọk), *n.* [Origin obscure.] A loaf of leavened oaten bread. [Prov. Eng.]

Jan-sen-ism (jan′sẹn-izm), *n.* The doctrinal system of Cornelis Jansen (1585–1638), Roman Catholic bishop of Ypres, and his followers, which maintained the perverseness and inability for good of the natural human will, and denied the possibility of resisting divine grace.—**Jan′sen-ist,** *n.* An adherent of Jansenism.—**Jan-sen-is′tic,** *a.*

Jan-u-a-ry (jan′ū-ā-ri), *n.* [L. *Januarius*, < *Janus*: see *Janus*.] The first month of the year, containing 31 days.

Ja-nus (jā′nus), *n.* [L.] An ancient Italian (perhaps solar) deity, regarded by the Romans as presiding over doors and gates and the beginning and ending of undertakings, and commonly represented with two faces looking in opposite directions.—**Ja′nus=faced,** *a.* Two-faced, like representations of the deity Janus; sometimes, double-dealing; deceitful.

Jap (jap), *a.* and *n.* Shortened form of *Japanese*. [Colloq.]

ja-pan (jạ-pan′), *n.* [From *Japan*, country in Asia.] Any of various hard, durable varnishes (orig. varnishes from Japan) used for coating wood, metal, etc.; a hard, glossy black varnish containing asphalt, used for coating tin, iron, etc.; a varnish-like liquid made of shellac, linseed-oil, and turpentine; also, Japanese work, esp. work varnished and figured in the Japanese manner.—**ja-pan′,** *v. t.*; *-panned, -panning*. To varnish with japan; lacquer; coat with any material which gives a hard, black gloss.

Jap-a-nese (jap-ạ-nēs′ or -nēz′). **I.** *a.* Of or pertaining to Japan, its people, or their language: as, *Japanese* porcelains or bronzes; *Japanese* art. **II.** *n.*; pl. *-nese*. A member of the native race of Japan; also, the Japanese language, an agglutinative tongue.

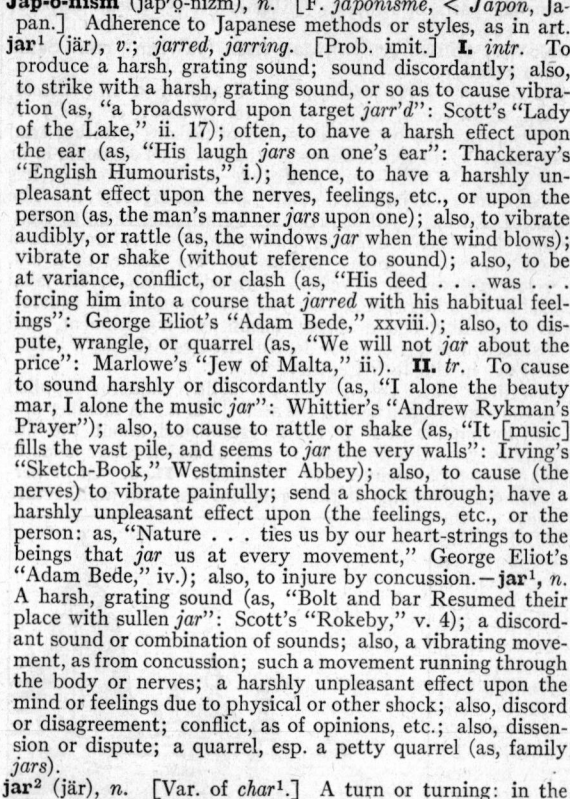

Japanese Art. — Example from a native Japanese book.

Jap-a-nesque (jap-ạ-nesk′), *a.* [See *-esque*.] In the Japanese style, as of art or decoration.—**Jap-a-nesque′ly,** *adv.*

Jap-a-nize (jap′ạ-nīz), *v. t.* To render Japanese; conform to Japanese usages or ideas.—**Jap″a-ni-za′tion** (-ni-zā′shọn), *n.*

jape (jāp), *v.*; *japed, japing*. [ME.: cf. OF. *japer*, yelp, and *gaber*, mock.] **I.** *tr.* To trick† or deceive†; also, to mock or deride (archaic). **II.** *intr.* To jest; joke; gibe: as, "I have no mind to jest and *jape*" (Swinburne's "Bothwell," i. 3). [Archaic.]—**jape,** *n.* A trick†; a deception† or fraud†; also (archaic), a jest or joke; a gibe.—**jap-er** (jā′pėr), *n.* One who japes; esp., a professional jester. [Archaic.]—**jap′er-y,** *n.*; pl. *-ies* (-iz). Trickery† or deception†; also (archaic), jesting or joking; raillery or mockery; a jest or gibe.

Ja-phet-ic (jā-fet′ik), *a.* Of or pertaining to Japheth, one of the sons of Noah; descended or supposed to be descended from Japheth: sometimes applied to the Indo-European peoples and languages.

Ja-pon-ic (jạ-pon′ik), *a.* [NL. *Japonicus*, < *Japonia*, Japan.] Of or pertaining to Japan; Japanese.—**Japonic earth.** See *terra Japonica*, under *terra*.

ja-pon-i-ca (jạ-pon′i-kạ̈), *n.* [NL. (see def.), fem. of *Japonicus*: see *Japonic*.] The camellia, *Thea japonica*; also, the Japanese quince, *Cydonia japonica*.

Jap-o-nism (jap′ọ-nizm), *n.* [F. *japonisme*, < *Japon*, Japan.] Adherence to Japanese methods or styles, as in art.

jar[1] (jär), *v.*; *jarred, jarring*. [Prob. imit.] **I.** *intr.* To produce a harsh, grating sound; sound discordantly; also, to strike with a harsh, grating sound, or so as to cause vibration (as, "a broadsword upon target *jarr'd*": Scott's "Lady of the Lake," ii. 17); often, to have a harsh effect upon the ear (as, "His laugh *jars* on one's ear": Thackeray's "English Humourists," i.); hence, to have a harshly unpleasant effect upon the nerves, feelings, etc., or upon the person (as, the man's manner *jars* upon one); also, to vibrate audibly, or rattle (as, the windows *jar* when the wind blows); vibrate or shake (without reference to sound); also, to be at variance, conflict, or clash (as, "His deed . . . was . . . forcing him into a course that *jarred* with his habitual feelings": George Eliot's "Adam Bede," xxviii.); also, to dispute, wrangle, or quarrel (as, "We will not *jar* about the price": Marlowe's "Jew of Malta," ii.). **II.** *tr.* To cause to sound harshly or discordantly (as, "I alone the beauty mar, I alone the music *jar*": Whittier's "Andrew Rykman's Prayer"); also, to cause to rattle or shake (as, "It [music] fills the vast pile, and seems to *jar* the very walls": Irving's "Sketch-Book," Westminster Abbey); also, to cause (the nerves) to vibrate painfully; send a shock through; have a harshly unpleasant effect upon (the feelings, etc., or the person: as, "Nature . . . ties us by our heart-strings to the beings that *jar* us at every movement," George Eliot's "Adam Bede," iv.); also, to injure by concussion.—**jar**[1], *n.* A harsh, grating sound (as, "Bolt and bar Resumed their place with sullen *jar*": Scott's "Rokeby," v. 4); a discordant sound or combination of sounds; also, a vibrating movement, as from concussion; such a movement running through the body or nerves; a harshly unpleasant effect upon the mind or feelings due to physical or other shock; also, discord or disagreement; conflict, as of opinions, etc.; also, dissension or dispute; a quarrel, esp. a petty quarrel (as, family *jars*).

jar[2] (jär), *n.* [Var. of *char*[1].] A turn or turning: in the phrase 'on the jar' (ajar): as, " 'I see Mrs. Bardell's street door *on the jar*.' 'On the what?' exclaimed the little judge. 'Partly open, my Lord,' said Serjeant Snubbin" (Dickens's "Pickwick Papers," xxxiv.).

jar[3] (jär), *n.* [F. *jarre*, < Sp. *jarra*, < Ar. *jarrah*, earthen vessel.] A broad-mouthed earthen or glass vessel, commonly cylindrical in form; also, the contents of such a vessel, or the quantity contained in it.

jar-di-nière (zhär-dē-nyãr), *n.* [F., < *jardin*, garden: see *garden*.] An ornamental receptacle or stand for holding plants, flowers, etc.

Drug-jar made at Kreussen, Bavaria, in 1657. — Pennsylvania Museum, Philadelphia.

jar-gon[1] (jär′gọn), *n.* [OF. F. *jargon*; origin uncertain.] The twittering or chattering of birds, or some similar sound (as, "With beast and bird the forest rings, Each in his *jargon* cries or sings": Longfellow's tr. Charles d'Orléans's "Return of Spring"); also, unintelligible or meaningless talk or writing; gibberish; in contempt, any talk or writing, or any speech or language, which one does not understand; also, a barbarous or rude language or dialect; esp., a hybrid speech resulting from a mixture of languages; often (with *the*), Yiddish; also, a kind of speech abounding in uncommon or unfamiliar words; a phraseology peculiar to a particular class, profession, trade, etc. (as, the *jargon* of the law).—**jar′gon**[1], *v. i.* To twitter or chatter as birds do, or give forth some similar sound (as, "They [little birds] seem'd to fill the sea and air With their sweet *jargoning*," Coleridge's "Ancient Mariner," v.; "the pensive *jargoning* of the crickets and grasshoppers," Howells's "Chance Acquaintance," x.); also, to utter or talk jargon or a jargon (as, "His ear was taken by the vibrant *jargoning* of the boatmen": Howells's "Foregone Conclusion," ii.).

jar-gon[2] (jär′gọn), *n.* [F. *jargon,* < It. *giargone*: cf. *zircon.*] A variety of the mineral zircon, from Ceylon. See *zircon.*

jar-go-nelle (jär-gọ-nel′), *n.* [F.] A variety of pear.

jar-gon-ize (jär′gọn-īz), *v.*; *-ized, -izing.* **I.** *intr.* To utter or talk jargon or a jargon. **II.** *tr.* To translate into jargon; also, to bring, put, etc., by means of jargon.

jar-goon (jär-gön′), *n.* Same as *jargon*[2].

jarl (yärl), *n.* [Icel.: see *earl.*] In *Scand. hist.*, a chieftain; an under-king or viceroy; an earl.

ja-ro-site (jạ-rō′sīt or jar′ọ-), *n.* [From Barranco *Jaroso*, in Almeria, southeastern Spain.] A yellowish or brownish mineral consisting of a hydrous sulphate of iron and potassium.

jar-rah (jar′ạ̈), *n.* [From native Australian name.] An Australian eucalyptus, *Eucalyptus marginata*, valued for its reddish, close-grained, durable wood; also, the wood itself.

jar-vey (jär′vi), *n.*; pl. *-veys* (-viz). [From *Jarvis* or *Jervis*, personal name.] The driver of a hackney coach; also, the driver of a jaunting-car; also, a hackney coach (as, "I . . . had despatched waiters in different directions for a *jarvey*": Lever's "Harry Lorrequer," xiv.). [Colloq.]

jas-bo (jas′bō), *n.* [Based on *jazz.*] Elements of low or vulgar comedy introduced into a play or the like. [Slang.]

ja-sey (jā′zi), *n.*; pl. *-seys* (-ziz). [Cf. *jersey.*] A wig, esp. one made of worsted.

jas-mine, jas-min (jas′min), *n.* [F. *jasmin*, < Ar. *yāsmīn*, < Pers. *yāsmīn.*] Any of the fragrant-flowered shrubs constituting the oleaceous genus *Jasminum*; also, any of various plants of other genera, as *Gelsemium sempervirens* ('yellow jasmine': see *gelsemium*), *Gardenia florida* ('Cape jasmine': see *gardenia*), *Tabernæmontana coronaria* ('crape jasmine,' a white-flowered shrub), and *Plumeria rubra* ('red jasmine,' the frangipani).

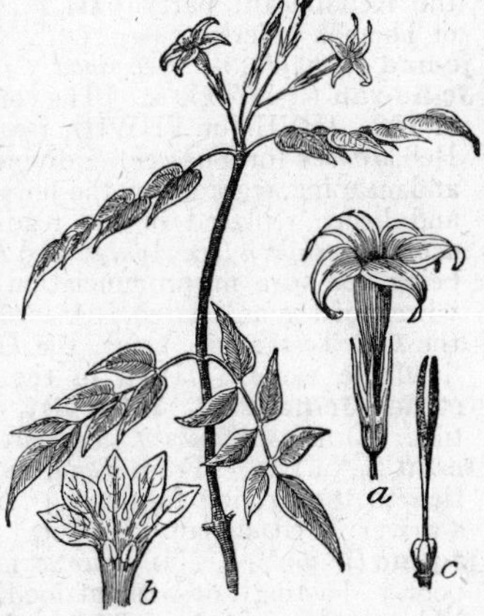

Flowering Branch of Jasmine (*Jasminum officinale*). — *a*, flower entire; *b*, flower opened to show the stamens; *c*, pistil.

jas-per[1] (jas′pėr), *n.* [Perhaps < *Jasper*, man's name.] A fellow; a man. [Slang.]

jas-per[2] (jas′pėr), *n.* [OF. *jaspre*, for *jaspe* (F. *jaspe*), < L. *iaspis* (*iaspid-*), < Gr. ἴασπις (ἰασπιδ-); of Eastern origin.] Among the ancients, a variety of chalcedony, apparently most commonly green, esteemed as a precious stone; now, a colored variety of quartz, usually red or brown. —**jas′per-ize**, *v. t.*; *-ized, -izing.* To convert into jasper or a jasper-like substance: as, *jasperized* wood.

jas-pid-e-ous (jas-pid′ẹ-us), *a.* [L. *iaspideus*, < *iaspis*: see *jasper*[2].] Of the nature of or resembling jasper.

jass (jas), etc. See *jazz*, etc.

jaun-dice (jân′dis or jän′-), *n.* [OF. F. *jaunisse*, < *jaune*, yellow, < L. *galbinus*, greenish-yellow, yellowish.] In *pathol.*, a morbid bodily condition due to the presence of bile-pigments in the blood, characterized by yellowness of the skin, the whites of the eyes, etc., by lassitude and loss of appetite, and in rare instances by yellow vision; hence, fig., a state of feeling in which views are colored or judgment is distorted (as, "jealousy, the *jaundice* of the soul": Dryden's "Hind and the Panther," iii. 73).—**jaun′dice**, *v. t.*; *-diced, -dicing.* To affect with jaundice; hence, fig., to affect with envy, jealousy, etc. (as, "The young man's handsome face and figure appeared to Courtier's *jaundiced* eye more obviously successful and complacent than ever": Galsworthy's "Patrician," ii. 6).

jaunt (jânt or jänt), *v. i.* [Origin obscure.] To trudge about† (as, "Sending me about, To catch my death with *jaunting* up and down": Shakspere's "Romeo and Juliet," ii. 5. 53); also, to make a short journey or excursion, esp. for pleasure.—**jaunt**, *n.* A fatiguing journey† (as, "Fie, how my bones ache! what a *jaunt* have I had!" Shakspere's "Romeo and Juliet," ii. 5. 26); also, a short journey or excursion, esp. for pleasure (as, "My uncle . . . talks of treating us with a *jaunt* to London": Smollett's "Humphry Clinker," May 6).—**jaunt′ing=car**, *n.* A light two-wheeled vehicle, popular in Ireland, having two seats, one on each side, set back to back or facing each other, and a perch in front for the driver.

jaun-ty (jân′ti or jän′-), *a.*; compar. *jauntier*, superl. *jauntiest.* [F. *gentil*: see *gentle* and *genteel.*] Genteel†; also, easy and sprightly in manner or bearing (as, "Light of step, as *jaunty*, gay As on some happy holiday They stepped with head high in the air": Joaquin Miller's "Walker in Nicaragua," ii. 11); airy; smart; smartly trim or effective in appearance, as articles of dress.—**jaun′ti-ly**, *adv.*—**jaun′ti-ness**, *n.*

jaup (jâp), *v.* [Appar. imit.: cf. *jabble.*] **I.** *intr.* To dash or splash, as water; make a splashing sound. [Sc. and north. Eng.] **II.** *tr.* To cause (water, etc.) to splash; also, to bespatter with water, mud, etc. [Sc. and north. Eng.]—**jaup**, *n.* The dashing or splashing of water, etc.; also, a splash or spot of water, mud, etc. [Sc. and north. Eng.]

Ja-va (jä′vạ̈), *n.* [From the Dutch East Indian island of *Java.*] A kind of coffee obtained from the Dutch East Indies.

Ja-va (jä′vạ̈) **man.** See *pithecanthropus.*

Jav-a-nese (jav-ạ-nēs′ or -nēz′). **I.** *a.* Of or pertaining to the island of Java, its people, or their language. **II.** *n.*; pl. *-nese.* A member of the native Malayan race of Java, esp. of that branch of it which occupies the central part of the island; also, the language of central Java, of the Malayan family.

Ja-va (jä′vạ̈) **spar′row.** A finch-like bird, *Munia oryzivora*, native in Java: a common cage-bird. Also called *rice-bird.*

Java Sparrow.

jave-lin (jav′lin or jav′ẹ-lin), *n.* [F. *javeline*; prob. from Celtic.] A spear to be thrown by the hand: as, "His figured shield, a shining orb, he takes, And in his hand a pointed *javelin* shakes" (Pope's tr. Homer's "Iliad," iii.).—**jave′lin**, *v. t.* To strike or pierce with or as with a javelin.

Ja-vel (zhȧ-vel) **wa′ter.** Same as *eau de Javel* (which see under *eau*).

jaw (jâ), *n.* [ME. *jawe, jowe*; prob. akin to E. *chew.*] One of the two bones or structures (upper and lower) which form the framework of the mouth; hence, the mouth-parts collectively, or the mouth (usually in *pl.*); also, either of the two sides of a narrow pass, gorge, or the like (as, "The guide . . . Led slowly through the pass's *jaws*": Scott's "Lady of the Lake," v. 3); also, one of two or more parts, as of a machine, which grasp or hold something; also, talk, esp. offensive talk (vulgar).—**jaw**, *v.* **I.** *intr.* To talk; gossip; often, to scold, find fault, or use abusive language (as, "Sambo's allers a *jawin'* at me, 'cause I doesn't pick faster": Mrs. Stowe's "Uncle Tom's Cabin," xxxii.). [Vulgar.] **II.** *tr.* To scold; address abusively: as, "I have been *jawed* for letting you go" (Marryat's "Peter Simple," xi.). [Vulgar.]—**jaw′=bone**, *n.* A bone of the jaws, esp. of the lower jaw: as, "He [Samson] found a new *jawbone* of an ass . . . and slew a thousand men therewith" (Judges, xv. 15).—**jaw′=break″er**, *n.* A word hard to pronounce. [Colloq.]—**jaw′=break″ing**, *a.*—**jawed**, *a.* Having a jaw or jaws.

jay (jā), *n.* [OF. *jai, gai* (F. *geai*); origin uncertain.] A noisy, arboreal European bird, *Garrulus glandarius*, with a crested head (see cut on following page); any of various birds of the same subfamily (*Garrulinæ*), as *Cyanocitta cristata*, an American bird with a bluish back ('blue jay'); hence, an impertinent chatterer; also, a flashy or loose woman†; also (slang), an absurdly dressed person; a guy; also (slang), a simple-minded or gullible person; a simpleton.

jay-hawk (jā′hâk), *v. t.* [Back-formation from *jayhawker.*] To harry as a jayhawker does; pillage; also, to carry off. [Slang, U. S.]

jay-hawk-er (jā′hâ″kėr), *n.* [Of disputed origin.] A plundering marauder; esp., one of a class of freebooting guerrillas in Kansas, Missouri, and other States before and during the Civil War; also, a native of Kansas (which is sometimes called 'the Jayhawker State').

European Jay (*Garrulus glandarius*).

jay-walk-er (jā′wâ″kėr), *n.* [Cf. *jay*, in sense of 'simpleton.'] One who crosses a street otherwise than by a regular crossing, as diagonally or at some point between crossings. [Colloq.]—**jay′walk″ing,** *n.*

jaz-e-rant (jaz′ẹ-rạnt), *n.* [OF. *jazerant, jaseran, jesseran*; prob. from Ar. (cf. Ar. *Al-Jezair*, Algiers).] A kind of mail composed of splints or small metal plates mounted on a lining of canvas or the like; also, a coat made of this.

jazz (jaz). [Origin obscure; said to have been long used by negroes of the southern U. S., esp. those of Louisiana, and to be of African origin.] **I.** *n.* A kind of noisy, discordant syncopated music (rag-time), such as is played by a jazz band (see phrase below); a piece of such music; also, dancing or a dance performed to such music, as with violent bodily motions and gestures; also, colloquially, in various fig. uses, violent or wild activity or animation; liveliness, spirit, dash, or 'go'; sometimes, lively comedy elements introduced into a play or the like. **II.** *a.* Of the nature of or pertaining to jazz (as, *jazz* music; a *jazz* band, see phrase below); also (colloq.), having some characteristic suggestive of jazz; violently active or lively; freakish; strikingly unusual.—**jazz band,** a band adapted for or devoted to the playing of jazz, which uses the cornet, trombone, saxophone, clarinet, piccolo, banjo, cymbals, drum, etc., producing peculiar effects by sliding from tone to tone, by various unusual manipulations or uses of the instruments, and by dissonances, independent tones, long-drawn wavering or wailing sounds, etc., and often accompanying the playing with singing, cries, and exaggerated gestures.—**jazz,** *v.* **I.** *intr.* To play the kind of music known as jazz; also, to dance to such music; also, to act or proceed with wild energy or great liveliness or dash (colloq.). **II.** *tr.* To play (music) in the manner of jazz; also (colloq.), to put jazz, liveliness, or 'go' into; stir or rouse by infusing jazz (often with *up*: as, to *jazz* up a dull play).—**jazz′er,** *n.*—**jazz′y,** *a.*; compar. *jazzier*, superl. *jazziest.* Pertaining to or suggestive of jazz music; wildly active or lively. [Colloq.]

jeal-ous (jel′us), *a.* [OF. *gelos* (F. *jaloux*), < ML. *zelosus*, < L. *zelus*, < Gr. ζῆλος, E. *zeal.*] Zealous, as in a cause†; also, solicitous or vigilant in maintaining or guarding something (as, a nation *jealous* of its liberties); anxiously or suspiciously watchful; wary or suspicious, as vigilance, attention, or care; also, inclined to or troubled by suspicions or fears of rivalry, as in love or aims (as, a *jealous* lover or husband; a *jealous* fellow-employee; a *jealous* disposition); resentfully fearful, as of a person regarded as a rival, or of his actions, etc. (with *of*); feeling envious resentment against a successful rival, or at success, advantages, etc., wherein another is thought to have surpassed one's self (with *of*: as, to be *jealous* of a victor, or of the victory or superiority of another); characterized by or proceeding from suspicious fears or envious resentment (as, *jealous* pride; *jealous* spite; *jealous* attacks or intrigues); also, in Biblical use, intolerant of unfaithfulness or rivalry (as, "Thou shalt worship no other god: for the Lord, whose name is *Jealous*, is a *jealous* God": Ex. xxxiv. 14); also, apprehensive or fearful, as of something evil†; also, doubtful† (as, "That you do love me, I am nothing *jealous*": Shakspere's "Julius Cæsar," i. 2. 162).—**jeal′ous-ly,** *adv.*—**jeal′ous-ness,** *n.*—**jeal′ous-y,** *n.*; pl. *-ies* (-iz). [OF. *gelosie* (F. *jalousie*).] The state or feeling of being jealous; anxious or suspicious vigilance; mental uneasiness from suspicion or fear of rivalry, as in love or aims; envious resentment against a successful rival or the possessor of any coveted advantage; an instance of jealous feeling (as, the petty *jealousies* of a small community).

Jeames (jēmz), *n.* [For *James*, man's name: cf. Thackeray's "Diary of C. *Jeames* de la Pluche, Esq."] A footman; a flunky. [Eng.]

jean (jān, commonly jēn), *n.* [Prob. < F. *Gênes*, Genoa.] A stout twilled cotton fabric; *pl.*, clothes of this material.

jee¹, jee². See *gee¹, gee².*

jeep (jēp), *n.* [Prob. imit.] A small army automobile.

jeer¹ (jēr), *n.* [Origin unknown.] *Naut.*, tackle for hoisting or lowering the lower yards: usually in *pl.*

jeer² (jēr), *v.* [Origin uncertain.] **I.** *intr.* To speak or shout derisively; direct derisive remarks at a person or thing; gibe or scoff rudely: as, "He was *jeered* at for his alacrity in retreating" (Irving's "Captain Bonneville," xxiv.); the mob *jeered* at his protestations of innocence. **II.** *tr.* To jeer at; assail with jeers or derisive utterances; drive (*out, off*, etc.) by jeers.—**jeer²,** *n.* A jeering utterance; a derisive or rude gibe.—**jeer′er,** *n.*—**jeer′ing-ly,** *adv.*

Jef-fer-so-ni-an (jef-ėr-sō′ni-ạn). **I.** *a.* Of or pertaining to some person named Jefferson, as, in *U. S. hist.* and *politics*, Thomas Jefferson, third President of the United States (1801–09), and the first great leader of the Democratic (then called the Republican) party. **II.** *n.* An adherent or follower of Thomas Jefferson.

je-had (jē-häd′), *n.* See *jihad.*

Je-ho-vah (jẹ-hō′vä), *n.* [The common European rendering of Heb. JHVH (or YHWH), representing, without vowels, Heb. *Jahveh* (or *Yahweh*), a divine name of uncertain origin and meaning, regarded by the Jews as too sacred for utterance and hence replaced in the reading of the Scriptures by *adōnāi* or *elōhīm* (see *Adonai* and *Elohim*); the form *Jehovah* being due to a mispronunciation of Heb. JHVH with the vowels of the associated Heb. *adōnāi.*] A name of God in the Old Testament, being the Christian rendering of the 'ineffable name,' JHVH, in the Hebrew Scriptures. See etym.—**Je-ho′vism, Je-ho′vist, Je-ho-vis-tic** (jē-hộ-vis′tik). Same as *Yahwism, Yahwist, Yahwistic.*

Je-hu (jē′hū), *n.* [From *Jehu*, in 2 Kings, ix. 20, with allusion to the driving furiously.] A fast driver; in general, a driver; a coachman. [Colloq.]

je-june (jẹ-jön′), *a.* [L. *jejunus*, fasting, empty, dry, barren, poor.] Fasting†, or without food†; also, deficient in nourishing or substantial qualities, as food or soil; fig., unsatisfying to the mind (as, *jejune* discourses, writings, or speculations; "Farce itself, most mournfully *jejune*, Calls for the kind assistance of a tune," Cowper's "Retirement," 711); without substance, pith, or solid merit; poor; bald; ineffective.—**je-june′ly,** *adv.*—**je-june′ness, je-ju′ni-ty** (-jö′ni-ti), *n.*

je-ju-num (jẹ-jö′num), *n.* [NL., prop. neut. of L. *jejunus*, fasting, empty (see *jejune*); so called because usually found empty after death.] In *anat.*, the middle portion of the small intestine, intervening between the duodenum and the ileum.

jell (jel), *v. i.* [Back-formation from *jelly.*] To assume the consistence of jelly. [Colloq.]

jel-li-fy (jel′i-fī), *v. t.* or *i.*; *-fied, -fying.* [See *-fy.*] To make or turn into jelly.—**jel″li-fi-ca′tion** (-fi-kā′shọn), *n.*

jel-ly (jel′i), *n.*; pl. *jellies* (-iz). [OF. *gelee* (F. *gelée*), frost, jelly, < L. *gelata*, pp. fem. of *gelare*, freeze, congeal.] A food preparation of a soft, elastic consistence due to the presence of gelatin; hence, any food preparation of similar consistence, as of fruit juice boiled down with sugar; also, in general, any gelatinous substance; anything of the consistence of jelly (as, "Mademoiselle was nearly crushed to a *jelly* in a hubbub at the theatre": C. Brontë's "Villette," xxiv.); also, a jellyfish (as, "When leagued about the 'wildered boat The rainbow *Jellies* fill and float": Kipling's "In the Matter of One Compass").—**jel′ly,** *v. t.* or *i.*; *-lied, -lying.* To bring or come to the consistence of jelly.—**jel′ly-fish,** *n.*; pl. *-fishes* or *-fish.* Any of various marine cœlenterates of a soft, gelatinous structure, esp. one with an umbrella-like body and long, trailing tentacles; a medusa.

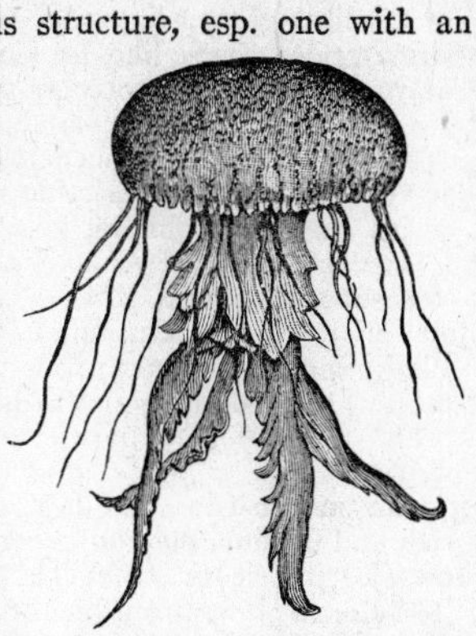
Jellyfish (*Dactylometra quinquecirra*).

jem-a-dar (jem′ạ-där), *n.* [Hind. and Pers. *jama'dār.*] In India, a native officer in a sepoy regiment, corresponding in rank to a lieutenant; also, any of various government officials, or the chief of a body of servants.

jem-my (jem′i), *n.* Same as *jimmy.*

jen-net (jen′et), *n.* [OF. F. *genet,* < Sp. *jinete,* mounted soldier, horse, prob. < Ar. *Zenāta,* name of a Berber tribe noted for its cavalry.] A small Spanish horse.

jen-net-ing (jen′et-ing), *n.* [Appar. from some dim. of F. *Jean,* John, with allusion to ripening by St. John's Day, June 24.] A kind of early apple: as, "the summer *jenneting*" (Tennyson's "Blackbird").

jen-ny (jen′i), *n.*; pl. *jennies* (-iz). [From *Jenny,* for *Jane,* woman's name.] The female of certain animals (used esp. attributively or in composition: as, *jenny*-ass; *jenny*-wren); also, a spinning-jenny.

jeop-ard (jep′ärd), *v. t.* [From *jeopardy.*] To jeopardize, risk, or imperil (as, "Zebulun and Naphtali . . . *jeoparded* their lives unto the death in the high places of the field": Judges, v. 18); also, to stake† or bet†.

jeop-ard-ize (jep′ạr-dīz), *v. t.*; *-ized, -izing.* To put in jeopardy; hazard; risk; imperil: as, "I dare not *jeopardize* my life for them" (Browning's "Ring and the Book," iv.).

jeop-ar-dy (jep′ạr-di), *n.* [OF. *jeu parti,* 'divided game,' even game or chance, < L. *jocus,* jest, sport, and *partitus,* pp. of *partire,* divide.] An evenly balanced situation, or even chance, as in a game†; chance†; hence, hazard or risk of loss or harm (as, "With the *jeopardy* of their lives they brought it [water]": 1 Chron. xi. 19); peril or danger (as, "For a moment his life was in *jeopardy*": Bret Harte's "Tennessee's Partner").

je-quir-i-ty (jē-kwir′i-ti), *n.* [Brazilian.] The Indian licorice plant, *Abrus abrus,* of India and Brazil, which bears a scarlet and black seed ('jequirity bean') used as a bead and in medicine; also, the seeds collectively.

jer-bo-a (jėr-bō′ạ or jėr′bō-ạ), *n.* [NL.; from Ar.] Any of various old-world mouse-like rodents (genus *Dipus,* etc.), with long hind legs used for jumping.

Jerboa (*Dipus ægypticus*).

je-reed, je-rid (jẹ-rēd′), *n.* [Ar. *jarīd.*] A blunt wooden javelin used in games by horsemen in Arabia, Persia, etc.: as, "The Bedoueen dashed off . . . in their game of throwing the *jereed* or lance, and so regaled us with Arabian sham fights" (G. W. Curtis's "Howadji in Syria," ii. 12).

jer-e-mi-ad (jer-ē-mī′ad), *n.* [F. *jérémiade,* < *Jérémie,* Jeremiah; with reference to the Biblical "Lamentations of Jeremiah."] A lamentation; a prolonged doleful utterance or effusion; a lugubrious complaint.

Jer-i-cho (jer′i-kō), *n.* [From *Jericho,* town in Palestine: see 2 Sam. x. 4, 5.] A place of retirement; an indefinitely remote place: used in colloquial phrases (as, to go to *Jericho*).

je-rid′, *n.* See *jereed.*

jerk[1] (jėrk), *v. t.* [Amer. Sp. *charquear,* < Peruvian *charqui,* jerked meat, charqui.] To cure (meat, esp. beef) by cutting into long, thin pieces and drying in the sun.—**jerk**[1], *n.* Jerked meat, esp. beef.

jerk[2] (jėrk), *v.* [Appar. imit.] **I.** *tr.* To strike with or as with a whip, switch, or the like†; also, to move with a quick, suddenly arrested motion (as, "He *jerked* his elbow in the direction of the . . . Board School": Arnold Bennett's "Helen with the High Hand," iv.); give a sudden thrust, pull, or twist to; sometimes, to throw with a quick, sharp motion; also, to utter abruptly. **II.** *intr.* To move with a quick, sharp motion; move spasmodically; give a jerk or jerks.—**jerk**[2], *n.* A stroke with a whip or the like†; also, a quick, suddenly arrested motion; a quick, sharp thrust, pull, throw, or the like; a sudden start; in *physiol.,* an involuntary spasmodic contraction of a muscle, due to reflex action resulting from a blow or other stimulus.—**jerk′er,** *n.*

jer-kin (jėr′kin), *n.* [Origin unknown.] A man's close-fitting jacket or short coat, as of leather, worn in the 16th and 17th centuries; also, some similar garment.

jer-kin=head (jėr′kin-hed), *n.* [Origin uncertain.] In *arch.,* the end of a roof when shaped like a gable but having the upper portion sloping backward or hipped.

Jerkin-head.

jerk-wa-ter (jėrk′wâ″tėr). **I.** *a.* Serving only to supply water to the engines of passing trains, as a place other than a regular station or stopping-place on a line of railroad; hence, of minor or slight importance (as, a *jerkwater* village; a *jerkwater* college). [Colloq.] **II.** *n.* A place on a railroad serving only to supply water to passing engines; hence, any place, institution, etc., of minor importance. [Colloq.]

jerk-y (jėr′ki), *a.*; compar. *jerkier,* superl. *jerkiest.* Characterized by jerks or sudden starts; spasmodic.—**jerk′i-ly,** *adv.*—**jerk′i-ness,** *n.*

jer-o-bo-am (jer-ọ-bō′ạm), *n.* [From *Jeroboam,* "a mighty man of valour" (1 Kings, xi. 28) "who made Israel to sin" (xiv. 16).] A large bowl, goblet, or bottle for spirituous beverages; also, the contents. [Eng. and Sc.]

jer-ry (jer′i), *a.* [Appar. < *Jerry,* for *Jeremiah* or *Jeremy,* man's name: perhaps first used in *jerry-built.*] Of poor construction or materials; flimsy; jerry-built.—**jer′ry=build,** *v. t.* To build cheaply and flimsily. See *jerry-built.*—**jer′ry=build″er,** *n.*—**jer′ry=built,** *a.* Built quickly, cheaply, and flimsily, of poor materials, as a house made to sell rather than to last.

jer-ry-man-der (jer′i-man-dėr), etc. Erroneous form of *gerrymander,* etc. [Eng.]

jer-sey (jėr′zi), *n.*; pl. *-seys* (-ziz). [From the island of *Jersey,* in the English Channel.] Worsted, orig. that from Jersey; also, wool combed but not spun into yarn†; also, a close-fitting knitted woolen jacket or shirt worn by seamen, athletes, and others; hence, a similar garment of machine-knitted or elastic material of wool, silk, etc., worn by women; also, jersey cloth (see phrase following); also [*cap.*], one of a celebrated breed of dairy cattle, smaller than the Guernsey, originating on the island of Jersey.—**jersey cloth,** a machine-knitted fabric of wool, silk, or other fiber, used for making garments, etc.—**jer′seyed,** *a.* Wearing a jersey.

Je-ru-sa-lem (jē-rö′sạ-lem) **ar′ti-choke.** See *artichoke.*

jess (jes), *n.* [OF. *ges, gies,* nom. (and pl.) of *get, giet,* orig. a throwing or casting: see *jet*[1], *n.*] A short strap of leather, silk, or other material, fastened round the leg of a hawk used in falconry, and serving as a means of attachment for the leash.—**jess,** *v. t.* To put jesses on (a hawk).

jes-sa-mine (jes′ạ-min), *n.* Same as *jasmine.*

jes-se-rant (jes′ẹ-rạnt), *n.* Same as *jazerant.*

jest (jest), *n.* [= *gest*[1].] A deed† or exploit† (cf. *gest*[1]); hence, a narrative of deeds or events†; a tale† or romance†; sometimes, an idle tale†; also, a derisive speech, or gibe; a piece of raillery or banter; also, something said in sport or to cause laughter (as, "With long-ear'd cap, and motley vest, The licensed fool retail'd his *jest*": Scott's "Marmion," v. 7); a witticism, joke, or pleasantry; sometimes, esp. formerly, a thing done to cause laughter; a playful action or trick; an amusing occurrence or circumstance; also, jesting, joking, or merry trifling (as, "a fellow of infinite *jest*, of most excellent fancy": Shakspere's "Hamlet," v. 1. 204); sport or fun; often, mere sport, as opposed to earnest (as, to speak half in *jest*, half in earnest); also, an object of derision or jesting (as, "Queens may die a *jest*," Pope's "Moral Essays," ii. 282; the attempt became a standing *jest*).—**jest,** *v.* **I.** *intr.* To utter derisive speeches, gibe, or scoff (as, "He *jests* at scars that never felt a wound": Shakspere's "Romeo and Juliet," ii. 2. 1); also, to speak in a playful, humorous, or facetious way; joke; also, to speak or act in mere sport, rather than in earnest; trifle. **II.** *tr.* To jest at; deride; banter.—**jest′er,** *n.* A reciter of tales or romances (archaic); also, a professed maker of amusement, using jests or witticisms, mimicry, buffoonery, etc., maintained by a prince or noble in the middle ages and later; a professional fool; also, one who jests or jokes. —**jest′ing-ly,** *adv.*

Jes-u-it (jez′ū-it), *n.* [NL. *Jesuita*, < L. *Jesus*, Jesus.] A member of a Roman Catholic religious order ('Society of Jesus') founded by Ignatius Loyola in 1534; also, a crafty, intriguing, or equivocating person (in allusion to the methods commonly ascribed to the order by its opponents).—**Jes-u-it′ic, Jes-u-it′i-cal,** *a.* Of or pertaining to the Jesuits; also [usually *l. c.*], of the character ascribed to the Jesuits by their opponents; crafty; intriguing; equivocating.—**jes-u-it′i-cal-ly,** *adv.*—**Jes′u-it-ism,** *n.* The system, principles, or practices of the Jesuits; also [usually *l. c.*], principles or practices such as are ascribed to the Jesuits; craft; subtle casuistry; sometimes, a quibble or equivocation. —**Jes′u-it-ize,** *v.*; *-ized, -izing.* **I.** *intr.* To be or become Jesuitical. **II.** *tr.* To make Jesuitical.—**Jes′u-it-ry,** *n.* Jesuitism; esp. [usually *l. c.*], craft; subtle casuistry; equivocation.

jet[1] (jet), *v.*; *jetted, jetting.* [F. *jeter*, OF. *jeter*, *geter*, < L. *jactare*, throw: see *jactation*.] **I.** *tr.* To throw (now prov. Eng.); also, to send forth in a stream, esp. from a small orifice; spout. **II.** *intr.* To shoot forth in a stream; spout; also, to jut† or project†; also, to encroach† (as, "Insulting tyranny begins to *jet* Upon the innocent and aweless throne": Shakspere's "Richard III.," ii. 4. 51); also, to strut† or swagger†.—**jet**[1], *n.* [F. *jet*, OF. *jet*, *get*, *giet*, < *jeter*, *geter*.] A shooting or spouting forth, as of water; also, a stream, as of water or gas, issuing forth, esp. from a small orifice (as, "Far off, the lofty *jet* of the whale might be seen": H. Melville's "Typee," ii.); also, a spout or nozzle for such a stream.

jet[2] (jet). [OF. *jaiet* (F. *jais*), < L. *gagates*, < Gr. γαγάτης, jet, < Γάγαι, town in Lycia, Asia Minor.] **I.** *n.* A black, inflammable fossil substance, susceptible of a high polish, found in beds of lignite and elsewhere, used for making beads, jewelry, buttons, etc.; also, some other mineral or substance of like appearance used as a substitute; also, the color of this substance, a deep, glossy black (as, "the pansy freak'd with *jet*": Milton's "Lycidas," 144). **II.** *a.* Consisting or made of jet (as, *jet* beads); also, of the color jet; black as jet.—**jet′=black′,** *a.*

jet-sam (jet′sạm), *n.* [= *jettison*.] Jettison†; also, goods thrown overboard to lighten a vessel in distress; esp., such goods when washed ashore. Also fig. Cf. *flotsam*.

jet-ted (jet′ed), *a.* Ornamented with jet.

jet-ti-son (jet′i-sọn), *n.* [OF. *getaison*, < L. *jactatio(n-)*, a throwing: see *jactation*.] The throwing overboard of goods, esp. to lighten a vessel in distress; also, jetsam.—**jet′ti-son,** *v. t.* To throw (cargo, etc.) overboard, esp. to lighten a vessel in distress.

jet-ton (jet′ọn), *n.* [F. *jeton*, < *jeter*, throw, cast, cast up (accounts, etc.): see *jet*[1].] A counter to reckon with; a token.

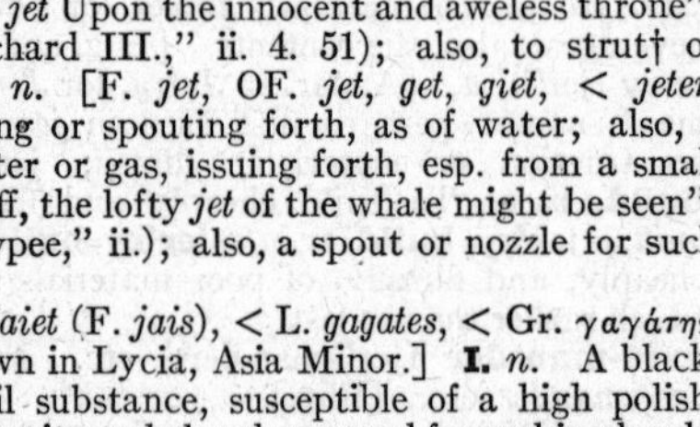

Obverse. Reverse.
Bronze Jetton of Louis XIV. — British Museum.

jet-ty[1] (jet′i), *n.*; pl. *jetties* (-iz). [OF. *jetee* (F. *jetée*), < *jeter*, throw: see *jet*[1].] A projecting and overhanging part of a building, as a bay-window; also, a pier or structure o stones, piles, or the like, projecting into the sea or other body of water so as to protect a harbor, influence the current etc.; also, a wharf or landing-pier.—**jet′ty**[1], *v. t.*; *-tied -tying.* To furnish with a jetty.

jet-ty[2] (jet′i), *a.* Consisting of jet; resembling jet; black as jet, or of the color jet (as, "The floods In which the full-formed maids of Afric lave Their *jetty* limbs": Thomson's "Seasons," Summer, 824).

jeu (zhė), *n.*; pl. *jeux* (zhė). [F., < L. *jocus*, jest, sport.] Play; sport; a game; also, gambling.—**jeu de mots** (dė mō). [F.] A play on words; a pun.—**jeu d'esprit** (des-prē). [F.] A play of wit; a witticism; a witty piece of writing.

jeu-nesse do-rée (zhė-nes dọ-rā). [F.] Gilded youth; rich and fashionable young people.

Jew (jö), *n.* [OF. *Juieu* (F. *Juif*), < L. *Judæus*, < Gr. Ἰουδαῖος, a Jew, prop. one of the tribe of Judah, < Heb. *Yehūdāh*, Judah.] Orig., a Hebrew of the tribe or kingdom of Judah; later, any one belonging to the Hebrew race or religion; a Hebrew; an Israelite; also, in opprobrious use (in allusion to practices popularly ascribed to the Jews), an extortionate money-lender, tricky dealer, or sharp bargainer.—**jew,** *v. t.* To overreach or cheat; also, to beat (*down*) in price. [Colloq.]—**Jew′=bait″er,** *n.* A person given to harrying or persecuting Jews.—**Jew′=bait″ing,** *n.* —**Jew′dom** (-dọm), *n.* The Jewish world; Jews collectively; the religion of the Jews.

jew-el (jö′ẹl), *n.* [OF. *jouel*, *joiel* (F. *joyau*), jewel; origin uncertain: cf. ML. *jocalia*, jewels, < L. *jocus* (F. *jeu*), jest, sport.] A costly article of personal adornment, now esp. one of gold or other precious metal set with a gem or gems; also, a gem or precious stone (as, a sword-hilt set with *jewels*); a precious stone (or some substitute) used as a bearing in a watch; a bit of glass, enamel, or other material, simulating a gem, used decoratively, as on costume; an ornamental boss of glass, sometimes cut with facets, in stained-glass work; also, fig., something resembling a gem in appearance, ornamental effect, etc., as a dewdrop, a star, a berry, etc.; a thing or person of great worth or rare excellence (as, "Oh! she is an inestimable *jewel*": Steele, in "Tatler," 95); a precious possession (as, "Good name in man and woman . . . Is the immediate *jewel* of their souls": Shakspere's "Othello," iii. 3. 156).—**jew′el,** *v. t.*; *-eled* or *-elled*, *-eling* or *-elling.* To set or adorn with jewels (as, "golden armour *jewell'd* everywhere": Tennyson's "Holy Grail," 412); furnish (a watch) with jewels for bearings; decorate with something simulating or suggesting jewels (as, *jeweled* porcelain or glass); fig., to adorn as if with jewels (as, "woods of birch all *jewelled* with the autumn yellow": Stevenson's "Travels with a Donkey," ii. 1).—**jew′el-er, jew′el-ler,** *n.* One who makes, or deals in, jewels or jewelry.—**jew′el-ly,** *a.* Jewel-like; brilliant; also, adorned with or as with jewels. —**jew′el-ry,** *n.* Jewelers' work; jewels; articles made of gold, silver, precious stones, enamel-work, or other materials, for personal adornment. Also **jew′el-ler-y.**—**jew′el=weed,** *n.* An American touch-me-not, as *Impatiens biflora*, with orange-yellow flowers spotted with brown, or *I. aurea*, with pale-yellow flowers.

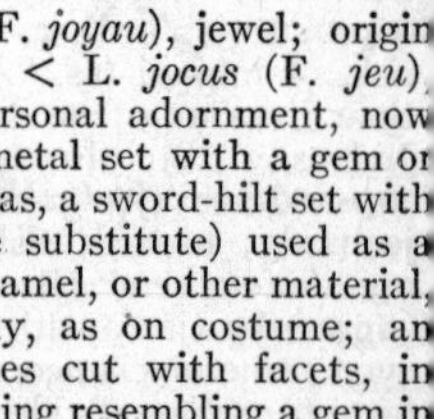
Jewel-weed (*Impatiens biflora*).

Jew-ess (jö′es), *n.* A Jewish girl or woman.

jew-fish (jö′fish), *n.* Any of various large marine fishes (chiefly of the family *Serranidæ*) frequenting southern waters, as *Promicrops itaiara* (or *guttatus*) of the southern and eastern coasts of the U. S., the West Indies, etc., which sometimes reaches a weight of several hundred pounds.

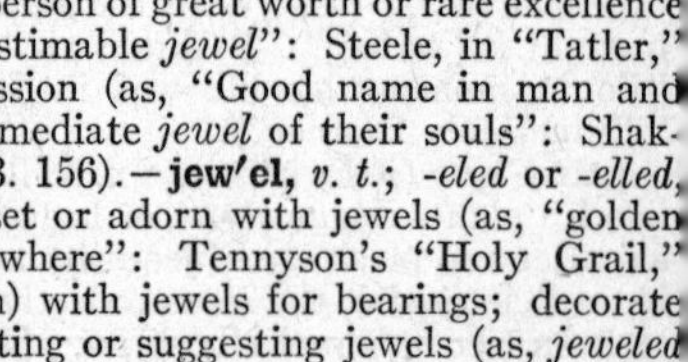
Jewfish (*Promicrops itaiara*).

Jew-ish (jö′ish), *a.* Of, pertaining to, or characteristic of the Jews; Hebrew; Israelitish.—**Jewish calendar,** the lunisolar calendar in use among the Jews, reckoning from the Creation (dated traditionally during the year 3761 B.C.), the year containing 12 or (in intercalary years) 13 months, of 29 or 30 days each, which, beginning during September or October, are as follows: Tishri, Heshvan, Kislev, Tebet, Shebat, Adar, Veadar (occurring only in intercalary years), Nisan, Iyar, Sivan, Tammuz, Ab, and Elul.

Jew-ry (jö′ri), *n.*; pl. *-ries* (-riz). [OF. *juierie* (F. *juiverie*).] Judea, in Palestine (obs. or archaic: as, "Jesus walked in Galilee: for he would not walk in *Jewry*, because the Jews sought to kill him," John, vii. 1); also, a district inhabited by Jews; a ghetto; also, the Jewish people.

jews'=harp (jöz′härp), *n.* A simple musical instrument consisting of a small lyre-shaped metal frame in which is fastened a flexible metal tongue with a projecting free end bent outward at a right angle, the instrument being played by holding it pressed against the teeth and striking the projecting free end with the finger, and variations of tone being produced by altering the shape and size of the mouth-cavity.

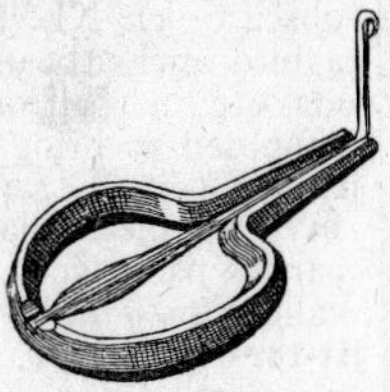

Jews'-harp.

je-zail (jẹ-zīl′ or -zāl′), *n.* [Pers. *jazā'il.*] A long, heavy Afghan musket.

Jez-e-bel (jez′ẹ-bel), *n.* [From *Jezebel*, wife of Ahab, king of Israel: see 1 Kings, xvi. 31, xxi. 25, 2 Kings, ix. 30-37.] A shameless, abandoned woman, esp. one who paints her face or uses meretricious adornments: as, "Mrs. Jenkins was . . . insulted with the opprobrious name of painted *Jezebel*" (Smollett's "Humphry Clinker," July 18).

jhil, jheel (jēl), *n.* [Hind. *jhīl.*] In India, a pool or lagoon remaining after an inundation.

JHVH. See *Jehovah*.

jib[1] (jib), *n.* [Origin uncertain: cf. *jib*[2], *jibe*[1].] *Naut.*, a triangular sail (or either of two triangular sails, 'inner jib' and 'outer jib') set in front of the forward (or single) mast, beyond the forestaysail if there is one; also (usually with a qualifying term), any of certain similar sails set beyond the jib proper, as a 'flying jib' (see under *flying*).

jib[2] (jib), *v. i.* or *t.* Same as *jibe*[1].

jib[3] (jib), *v. i.*; *jibbed, jibbing.* [Origin uncertain: cf. *jib*[2], *jibe*[1].] To move restively sidewise or backward instead of forward, as an animal in harness; refuse to go on; balk.—**jib**[3], *n.* A horse or other animal that jibs.

jib[4] (jib), *n.* [Cf. *gibbet.*] The projecting arm of a crane; the boom of a derrick.

jib-bah (jib′ạ̈), *n.* Same as *jubbah*.

jib=boom (jib′böm′), *n.* *Naut.*, a spar forming a continuation of a bowsprit.

jib=crane (jib′krān′), *n.* A crane which has a jib or projecting arm, esp. a horizontal arm which carries a trolley to which the hoisting tackle is attached.

jibe[1] (jīb), *v.*; *jibed, jibing.* [Cf. D. *gijpen*, Dan. *gibbe*, Sw. *gippa*, jibe.] *Naut.*: **I.** *intr.* To shift from one side to the other when running before the wind, as a fore-and-aft sail or its boom (as, "The boat capsized from the sail's '*jibing*'": H. Melville's "Omoo," xxv.); also, to alter the course so that the sail shifts in this manner. **II.** *tr.* To cause (a sail, etc.) to jibe.

jibe[2] (jīb), etc. See *gibe*, etc.

jibe[3] (jīb), *v. i.*; *jibed, jibing.* [Origin uncertain.] To agree; be in harmony or accord. [Colloq., U. S.]

jif-fy (jif′i), *n.*; pl. *jiffies* (-iz). [Origin obscure.] A very short space of time: as, "He was on his stool in a *jiffy*, driving away with his pen" (Dickens's "Christmas Carol," v.). [Colloq.]

jig (jig), *n.* [Appar. imit.] A rapid, lively, springy, irregular dance for one or more persons, usually in triple rhythm; also, a piece of music for, or in the rhythm of, such a dance (cf. *gigue*); also, a lively performance or entertainment given at the end or in an interval of a play†; also, a piece of sport, a prank, or a trick (now chiefly in the slang phrase 'the jig is up,' that is, the game is up, or there is no further chance); also, any of various mechanical contrivances or devices; an apparatus for separating ore from gangue, etc., by shaking in or treating with water; a device used in fishing, esp. a hook or collection of hooks loaded with metal or having a spoon-shaped piece of bone or other material attached, for drawing through the water.—**jig**, *v.*; *jigged, jigging.* **I.** *tr.* To dance (a jig or any lively dance); also, to sing or play in the time or rhythm of a jig; also, to move with a jerky or bobbing motion; jerk up and down or to and fro; also, to treat, cut, or produce in or with any of the mechanical contrivances called jigs; separate (ore) by shaking in a jig; catch (fish) with a jig. **II.** *intr.* To dance a jig; also, to play a jig; also, to move with a quick, jerky motion; hop; bob; also, to work with a jig (mechanical contrivance); fish with a jig.—**jig′ger**[1], *n.* One who or that which jigs; specif., any of various mechanical devices, many of which have a jerky or jolting motion; a kind of potters' wheel; a jig for separating ore or for fishing; in general, some contrivance, article, or part that one cannot name more precisely (colloq.: as, what is that little *jigger* on the pistol?); *naut.*, a light tackle used about the deck of a ship; also, a small sail set on a jigger-mast in the stern of a canoe, yawl, etc.; in *billiards*, a bridge; in *golf*, an iron-headed club, a cross between a mashie and a mid-iron, used in making an approach.

jig-ger[2] (jig′ėr), *n.* [Corruption of *chigo.*] A chigo; also, in the southern U. S., any of various harvest-ticks which fasten to the skin of human beings and cause great irritation.

jig-gered (jig′ėrd), *a.* [Origin obscure.] A word used in asseveration as a vague substitute for a profane word (as, "I'm *jiggered* if I don't see you home!" Dickens's "Great Expectations," xvii.); also, intoxicated; drunk. [Slang.]

jig-ger=mast (jig′ėr-mȧst), *n.* *Naut.*, a small mast for the jigger, in the stern of a canoe, yawl, etc.; also, the aftermost mast of a four-masted ship.

jig-get (jig′et), *v. i.*; *-geted, -geting.* [Freq. of *jig.*] To move or go in a jigging, hopping, or jerky way.

jig-gle (jig′l), *v. t.* or *i.*; *-gled, -gling.* [Freq. of *jig.*] To move up and down or to and fro with short, quick jerks.—**jig′gle,** *n.* A jiggling movement.

jig-gy (jig′i), *a.* Jig-like; suitable for a jig: as, "*jiggy* tunes" (Arnold Bennett's "Helen with the High Hand," xiv.).

jig=saw (jig′sâ), *n.* A narrow saw mounted vertically in a frame and operated with an up-and-down motion: used for cutting curves, etc.

ji-had (jẹ̄-häd′), *n.* [Ar. *jihād.*] A general religious war of Mohammedans against unbelievers in Islam; hence, a war or crusade, as against some belief or principle.

Jill (jil), *n.* Another spelling of *Gill*[4], esp. in connection with *Jack*: as, "Our wooing doth not end like an old play; Jack hath not *Jill*" (Shakspere's "Love's Labour's Lost," v. 2. 885).

jil-let (jil′et), *n.* [Dim. of *Jill.*] A giddy young woman; a jilt: as, "A *jillet* brak his heart at last" (Burns's "On a Scotch Bard, Gone to the West Indies"). [Sc. and north. Eng.]

jilt (jilt), *n.* [Origin uncertain: cf. *jillet.*] A wanton woman† (as, "When love was all an easy monarch's care . . . *Jilts* ruled the state": Pope's "Essay on Criticism," 538); also, a woman who casts off or jilts a lover after accepting or deliberately encouraging him; sometimes, a man who jilts a woman.—**jilt,** *v. t.* To cast off (a lover or sweetheart) as by a heartless breach of faith or a disappointing of justified expectations: as, "He had the mortification of being *jilted* by a little boarding-school girl" (Irving's "Tales of a Traveler," i. 2); "It is too ridiculous that such a girl . . . could so mortify us as to get *jilted* on the wedding-day" (Hardy's "Return of the Native," ii. 8).—**jilt′er,** *n.*

Jim Crow (jim krō). A negro. [U. S.]—**Jim Crow car,** a car, as on a railroad, set apart for the use of negroes; also, a car divided into two parts, one for whites and the other for negroes. [U. S.]

jim-jam (jim′jam), *n.* [Cf. *gimcrack.*] A gimcrack† or knickknack†; *pl.*, peculiarities or eccentricities (colloq.); also, delirium tremens (slang).

jim-my (jim′i), *n.*; pl. *jimmies* (-iz). [From *Jimmy*, for *James*, man's name.] A short crowbar used by burglars. —**jim′my,** *v. t.*; *-mied, -mying.* To use a jimmy on; force open by means of a jimmy, as a door or window.

jimp (jimp), *a.* [Origin obscure.] Slim or slender (as, "thy waist sae *jimp*": Burns's "O, Were I on Parnassus' Hill");

also, scanty; short. [Sc. and north. Eng.]—**jimp,** *adv.* Scarcely. [Sc. and north. Eng.]

jim-son=weed (jim′sọn-wēd), *n.* [Orig. *Jamestown weed;* from *Jamestown,* Va.] A species of datura, *Datura stramonium,* a coarse, ill-smelling weed with white flowers and poisonous, narcotic leaves.

Jimson-weed, with cross-section of seed-vessel.

jin′gal, *n.* See *jinjal.*

jin-gle (jing′gl), *v.*; *-gled, -gling.* [Imit.] **I.** *intr.* To make clinking or tinkling sounds, as coins, keys, etc., when struck together; move or proceed with such sounds; also, to sound in a manner suggestive of this, as verse or any sequence of words (as, "a *jingling* ballad": Macaulay's "Essays," Warren Hastings); also, to make rimes (as, "Whene'er my Muse does on me glance, I *jingle* at her": Burns's "Epistle to John Lapraik," 54). **II.** *tr.* To cause to jingle: as, "Dick *jingled* his spurs" (Bret Harte's "How Santa Claus Came to Simpson's Bar").—**jin′gle,** *n.* A clinking or tinkling sound, as of small bells or of small pieces of metal struck together (as, "a canvas bag, that gave forth, at a touch, the *jingle* of gold": Stevenson's "Treasure Island," iv.); also, something that makes such a sound, as a small bell or a metal pendant; also, a musical succession of like sounds, as in rime or alliteration, without particular regard for sense; jingling verse, or a piece of such verse; any catching sequence of words, whether in verse or in prose; also, a covered two-wheeled car (Ireland and Australia).—**jin′gler,** *n.* One who or that which jingles; a rimer.—**jin′glet,** *n.* A small, loose metal ball serving as the clapper for a globular sleigh-bell.—**jin′gling-ly,** *adv.*

jin-go (jing′gō). [Origin obscure; first in conjurers' jargon.] **I.** *n.*; pl. *-goes* (-gōz). A word used in vehement asseveration in the phrase 'by jingo!' or 'by the living jingo!' (colloq.: as, "She observed, that, *by the living jingo,* she was all of a muck of sweat," Goldsmith's "Vicar of Wakefield," ix.); also [*cap.*], a supporter of the aggressive policy of the Earl of Beaconsfield in sending a British fleet into Turkish waters to resist the advance of Russia in 1878; hence [*l. c.*], one who boasts of his country's preparedness for war, or who favors a bellicose or blustering foreign policy; a chauvinist. **II.** *a.* Of or pertaining to jingoes; characterized by jingoism.—**jin′go-ism,** *n.* The spirit, policy, or practices of jingoes.—**jin′go-ist,** *n.*—**jin-go-is′tic,** *a.*

jin-jal, jin-gal (jin′jâl, jing′gâl), *n.* [Hind. *janjāl.*] A large musket or piece fired from a rest, usually swiveled and sometimes mounted on a carriage: used by natives in India, China, etc.

jink (jingk), *v.* [Perhaps imit.] **I.** *intr.* To move nimbly; move in a jerky manner; dance; also, to make a quick, elusive turn; dodge. **II.** *tr.* To elude by dodging; dodge; also, to cheat; swindle. [Chiefly Sc.]—**jink,** *n.* A quick turn, as to elude a pursuer; also, a prank or frolic (as, "He was the star . . . of good company forty years ago. I remember him in the height of his *jinks,*" Hardy's "Laodicean," i. 5; high *jinks,* see phrase below). [Orig. Sc.]—**high jinks,** any of various frolics formerly indulged in at drinking-parties in Scotland (see Scott's "Guy Mannering," xxxvi.); hence, romping games or play, boisterous sport, or unrestrained merrymaking (colloq.: as, "All sorts of *high jinks* go on on the grass-plot," Hughes's "Tom Brown at Oxford," i.); sometimes, wild or unrestrained behavior in general (colloq.).

jinn (jin), *n. pl.* [Ar. *jinn,* pl. of *jinnī.*] In *Mohammedan myth.,* a class of spirits lower than the angels, made of fire, capable of appearing in human and animal forms, and exercising influence over mankind for good and evil; also, as *sing.* (with pl. *jinns*), a spirit of this class.—**jin-ni, jin-nee** (ji-nē′), *n.* [Ar. *jinnī.*] Singular of *jinn.*

jin-ny (jin′i), *n.*; pl. *jinnies* (-iz). [= *jenny.*] In *mining,* a stationary engine by means of which trucks are moved on an inclined plane; also, a jinny-road.—**jin′ny=road,** *n.* In *mining,* an inclined plane upon which descending loaded trucks are made to pull up empty trucks by an arrangement of cables, etc.

jin-rik-i-sha (jin-rik′i-shạ̈), *n.* [Jap., 'man power carriage.'] A small two-wheeled hooded vehicle drawn by one or more men, used in Japan and elsewhere. Also **jin-rik′sha.**

Jinrikisha.

jinx (jingks), *n.* [Origin obscure: cf. NL. *jynx,* L. *iynx,* < Gr. ἴυγξ, the wryneck a bird anciently used in magic rites against unfaithful lovers, etc., a spell or charm.] A person, thing, or influence supposed to bring bad luck; a hoodoo. [Colloq.]

jit-ney (jit′ni), *n.*; pl. *-neys* (-niz). [Origin obscure.] A five-cent piece (slang); also (colloq.), an automobile which carries passengers, orig., each for a fare of five cents (also called *jitney-bus*).—**jit′ney,** *v. i.* or *t.*

jit-ter (jit′ėr), *v.* [Origin uncertain.] **I.** *intr.* To be nervous; act nervously. [Slang.] **II.** *tr.* To utter nervously. [Slang.]—**jit-ter-bug** (jit′ėr-bug), *n.* A jive enthusiast. [Slang.]—**jit′ters,** *n. pl.* Nervousness; nerves. [Slang.]—**jit′ter-y,** *a.* Nervous; jumpy. [Slang.]

jiu=jit-su (jö-jit′sọ̈), *n.* See *jiu-jutsu.*

jiu=jut-su (jö-jüt′sọ̈), *n.* [Jap., 'soft (or pliant) art.'] A Japanese method of offense and defense without weapons in personal encounter, which employs the strength and weight of the opponent to his disadvantage or undoing, and which is used as a basis for physical training.

jive (jīv), *n.* Swing music, or dancing to swing music; the talk of swing enthusiasts. [Slang.]—**jive,** *v. i.*

jo, joe (jō), *n.*; pl. *joes* (jōz). [Origin uncertain: cf. Sc. *jo,* obs. form of *joy.*] A sweetheart; in address, dear. [Sc.]

Joan (jōn), *n.* See *Darby and Joan.*

job[1] (job), *v.*; *jobbed, jobbing.* [ME.; perhaps imit.: cf. *jab.*] **I.** *tr.* To punch or stab, as with something pointed; jab; also, to thrust (something pointed) into an object. **II.** *intr.* To thrust, as with something pointed; peck (*at*), as a bird does; penetrate (*into*).—**job**[1], *n.* A sharp thrust or stab; a jab.

job[2] (job). [Origin uncertain.] **I.** *n.* A piece of work; an individual piece of work done in the routine of one's occupation or trade; a piece of work of defined character undertaken for a fixed price; specif., a piece of printer's work of the miscellaneous class, as the printing of cards, circulars, posters, etc.; also, a theft or robbery, or any criminal deed (slang: as, "His comrades had plotted an orchard to rob, And ask'd him to go and assist in the *job,*" Cowper's "Pity for Poor Africans," 24); also, a piece of public or official business carried through with a view to improper private gain (as, "Who makes a trust of charity a *job,* And gets an act of parliament to rob": Pope's "Satires of Donne," iv. 142); also, anything one has to do (as, "It'll be a hard *job* for me to tell her aunt": George Eliot's "Adam Bede," xxxviii.); also, an affair, matter, occurrence, or state of affairs (colloq.: as, to make the best of a bad *job;* a put-up *job,* an affair arranged beforehand to impose upon or deceive some one); also, a situation, or post of employment (colloq.); also, a job lot (see below). **II.** *a.* Pertaining to, or hired or employed for, the job or particular piece of work; also, sold or bought together (as, a *job* lot, a quantity of goods, often of miscellaneous character, sizes, etc., sold or bought as a single lot for a lump sum and at a comparatively low price).—**job**[2], *v.*; *jobbed, jobbing.* **I.** *tr.* To let out (work) in separate portions, as among different contractors or workmen; also, to let out or hire (a horse, carriage, etc.) for a particular job or for a limited time (Eng.: as, "the liveryman from whom she *jobbed* her carriages," Thackeray's "Vanity Fair," xlviii.); also, to buy and sell (goods, etc.) as a broker or middleman; buy in large quantities, and sell to dealers in smaller lots, or to consumers; also, to deal with or manipulate corruptly for private gain. **II.** *intr.* To work at jobs or odd pieces of work; work by the piece; also, to buy and sell as a broker or middleman; do business as a jobber; also, to turn public business, etc., improperly to private gain.

jo-ba-tion (jō-bā'shon), *n.* [From obs. *job, jobe,* to lecture, reprove, < *Job,* the Biblical patriarch, in allusion to the reproofs he received from his friends.] A reproving harangue; a lecture; a lengthy, tedious reproof: as, "Don't be angry at my *jobation;* but write me a long answer" (Hughes's "Tom Brown at Oxford," xlii.). [Colloq.]

job-ber (job'ėr), *n.* One who jobs; specif., one employed by the job; also, one who lets out horses, etc., for hire (Eng.); also, a broker or middleman; one who buys goods, etc., in bulk from producers or importers, and sells them to retailers or to consumers; also, a stock-jobber, or stock-exchange operator who acts as intermediary between brokers (Eng.); also, one who perpetrates corrupt public or official jobs.

job-ber-nowl (job'ėr-nōl), *n.* [Appar. < ME. *jobard,* simpleton, + *nolle,* E. *noll.*] The head (used contemptuously: as, "And powdered th' inside of his skull, Instead of th' outward *jobbernol,*" Butler's "Hudibras," iii. 2); also, a stupid person; a blockhead. [Colloq. or prov., Eng.]

job-ber-y (job'ėr-i), *n.* The practice of turning public business, etc., improperly to private gain; the perpetration of corrupt public or official jobs.

job-less (job'les), *a.* Having no job, situation, or post of employment. [Colloq.]—**job'less-ness,** *n.*

jo-bo (jō'bō, Sp. hō'bō), *n.* [Sp.] An anacardiaceous tree, *Spondias lutea,* resembling the ash and native in tropical America, which has a soft wood used for making matches, etc., and bears an edible plum-like fruit.

job=press (job'pres), *n.* A small printing-press used for printing miscellaneous small jobs, as cards, circulars, etc.

job=print-er (job'prin'tėr), *n.* A printer who does job-work.—**job'=print'ing,** *n.*

Job's (jōbz) **com'fort-er.** [From *Job,* the Biblical patriarch.] A "miserable comforter" (see Job, xvi. 2); one whose ostensible efforts to comfort aggravate the distress of a sufferer; also, a boil (see Job, ii. 7).—**Job's news.** Bad news; tidings of disaster. See Job, i. 14–19.—**Job's post.** A bearer of bad news. See Job, i. 14–19.—**Job's'=tears',** *n. pl.* The hard, nearly globular involucres which surround the female flowers in a species of grass, *Coix lacryma-jobi,* and which when ripe are of a bluish-white color and are used as beads; also, as *sing.,* the grass itself, which is native in Asia but cultivated elsewhere.

job=work (job'wėrk), *n.* Work done by the job; in *printing,* miscellaneous work, as the printing of cards, circulars, posters, etc.

Jock (jok), *n.* [Sc. equivalent of *Jack,* for *John,* man's name.] A popular name for a Scotchman; also, a countryman or rustic (Sc.).

jock-ey (jok'i), *n.*; pl. *-eys* (-iz). [Orig. Sc., dim. of *Jock:* see *Jock.*] A fellow or lad (now prov. Eng.); also, a strolling minstrel or beggar† (as, "tribes of gipsies, *jockeys,* or cairds": Scott's "Guy Mannering," vii.); also, a horse-dealer (obs. or prov.); also, a crafty bargainer; a cheat; also, one who professionally rides horses in races.—**jock'ey,** *v.*; *-eyed, -eying.* **I.** *tr.* To trick or cheat; gain the advantage of by trickery; also, to manipulate trickily; also, to bring, put, etc., by trickery, or by skilful maneuvering (as, "His Majesty, Louis XIV., *jockeyed* his grandson on to the throne of Spain": Thackeray's "Newcomes," xxxiii.); also, to ride (a horse) as a jockey in a race. **II.** *intr.* To act trickily; seek an advantage by trickery; often, to aim at an advantage by skilful maneuvering (as, to *jockey* for position in a race).—**jock'ey-ship,** *n.*

jock-o (jok'ō), *n.*; pl. *-os* (-ōz). [F. *jocko;* from W. Afr. name.] Orig., the chimpanzee; now [*cap.*], a familiar name for any monkey.

jock-te-leg (jok'te-leg), *n.* [Origin uncertain.] A large clasp-knife. [Sc.]

jo-cose (jō-kōs'), *a.* [L. *jocosus,* < *jocus,* E. *joke.*] Given to or characterized by joking; jesting; humorous; playful: as, a *jocose* speaker or mood; *jocose* remarks.—**jo-cose'ly,** *adv.*—**jo-cose'ness,** *n.*

jo-co-se-ri-ous (jō-kō-sē'ri-us), *a.* [L. *jocus,* E. *joke,* + E. *serious.*] Partly jesting, partly serious: as, "Or drink a *joco-serious* cup With souls who've took their freedom up" (M. Green's "The Spleen").

jo-cos-i-ty (jō-kos'i-ti), *n.*; pl. *-ties* (-tiz). The state or quality of being jocose; also, joking or jesting; a joke or jest.

joc-u-lar (jok'ū-lär), *a.* [L. *jocularis,* < *joculus,* dim. of *jocus,* E. *joke.*] Given to, characterized by, intended for, or suited to joking or jesting; waggish; facetious: as, a *jocular* person; *jocular* talk or behavior; a *jocular* manner; a *jocular* wink.—**joc-u-lar'i-ty** (-lar'i-ti), *n.*; pl. *-ties* (-tiz). The state or quality of being jocular; also, jocular speech or behavior; a jocular remark or act.—**joc'u-lar-ly,** *adv.*

joc-und (jok'und), *a.* [LL. *jocundus,* for L. *jucundus,* pleasant, agreeable, < *juvare,* help, please.] Cheerful; merry; gay; blithe; glad. [Now literary.]—**jo-cun-di-ty** (jō-kun'di-ti), *n.*—**joc'und-ly,** *adv.*

jodh-purs (jōd'pörz, jod'pėrz), *n. pl.* [From *Jodhpur,* native state, also city, in northwestern India.] Riding-breeches reaching down to the ankle, and fitting closely from the knee to the ankle, worn also in sports, etc., and by both men and women.

joe, *n.* See *jo.*

Joe Mill-er (jō mil'ėr). [From *Joe* (or Joseph) *Miller* (1684–1738), an English comic actor whose name was attached to a popular jest-book published in 1739.] A jest-book; also, a jest or joke, esp. a stale joke, or 'chestnut.' [Colloq.]

joe-pye=weed (jō-pī'wēd), *n.* [Origin obscure.] A tall asteraceous weed, *Eupatorium purpureum,* of North America, with clusters of pinkish or purple flowers; also, another North American species, *E. maculatum,* with similar flowers, and stems that are often spotted with purple ('spotted joepye-weed').

Spotted Joepye-weed.

jo-ey (jō'i), *n.*; pl. *joeys* (-iz). [Native Australian.] A young kangaroo; any young animal; a young child. [Australia.]

jog[1] (jog), *n.* [Var. of *jag*[1].] An irregularity of line or surface; a jag; a projection; a notch; a recess. [Chiefly U. S.]

jog[2] (jog), *v.*; *jogged, jogging.* [Perhaps imit.: cf. *shog.*] **I.** *tr.* To move or shake with a push or jerk; also, to give a slight push to, as to arouse the attention; nudge; hence, to stir up by hint or reminder (as, to *jog* a person's memory). **II.** *intr.* To move with a jolt or jerk; move up and down or to and fro unsteadily (as, "Mr. Venus listened to these lamentations in silence, while Mr. Boffin *jogged* to and fro": Dickens's "Our Mutual Friend," iii. 14); also, to go or travel with a jolting pace or motion; move along in a heavy, labored, or plodding way; fig., to go (*on* or *along*) in a steady or humdrum fashion (as, "We *jogged* on together some time, till Alfred saw plainly that I was no planter": Mrs. Stowe's "Uncle Tom's Cabin," xix.); also, to move on or be off (as, "The door is open, sir; there lies your way; You may be *jogging*": Shakspere's "Taming of the Shrew," iii. 2. 213).—**jog**[2], *n.* The act or an act of jogging some thing or person; a shake; a slight push; a nudge; also, the act or an act of moving with a jolt, or with jolts or jerks; also, the act of going or traveling with a jolting pace or motion; a slow, steady walk, trot, etc.—**jog'ger,** *n.*

jog-gle[1] (jog'l), *n.* [Freq. of *jog*[1].] A projection on one of two joining surfaces, or a notch on the other, to prevent slipping; a key or dowel let in between two surfaces, as one for joining two blocks of masonry; a joint formed in either way.—**jog'gle**[1], *v. t.*; *-gled, -gling.* To join or fasten by a joggle or joggles.

jog-gle[2] (jog'l), *v. t.* or *i.*; *-gled, -gling.* [Freq. of *jog*[2].] To shake slightly; move to and fro as by repeated jerks.—**jog'gle**[2], *n.* The act or an act of joggling; a slight shake; a jolt; a moving with jolts or jerks.

jog=trot (jog'trot), *n.* A jogging trot; a slow, regular, jolting pace, as of a horse; fig., a routine or humdrum mode of procedure.

jo-han-nes, jo-an-nes (jō-han'ēz, jō-an'ēz), *n.* [ML. and LL.: see *John.*] A Portuguese gold coin formerly current, worth about $9, and named from King John (João) V. (who reigned 1706–50), by whom it was first issued. See cut on following page.

Jo-han-nine (jọ̄-han'in or -īn), *a.* [ML. *Johannes*, John: see *John.*] Of or pertaining to John, esp. the apostle John.

Obverse. Reverse.
Johannes of John V., King of Portugal, 1723. — British Museum.

Jo-han-nis-berg-er (jọ̄-han'is-bėr-gėr), *n.* [G., < *Johannisberg*, village on the Rhine, in Prussia.] A fine white Rhine wine.

John (jon), *n.* [ML. *Johannes*, LL. *Joannes*, < Gr. Ἰωάννης, < Heb. *Yōkhānān*, lit. 'Jehovah hath been gracious.'] A common masculine Christian name, often used for servants or others whose true name is unknown or unimportant: as, "Suddenly . . . her Majesty's own crimson footmen . . . came in. It was pitiable to see the other poor *Johns* slink off at this arrival!" (Thackeray's "Book of Snobs," ii.).—**John Bull,** the typical Englishman; the English people.—**John Company,** the English East India Company (which resigned its governing functions to the Crown in 1858).—**John Doe,** a fictitious personage in legal proceedings.—**John Hancock.** [From the first signer of the Declaration of Independence.] One's signature, as on a document. [Colloq.]—**John'=a=dreams'** (-ạ-drēmz'), *n.* A dreamy, unpractical fellow. See Shakspere's "Hamlet," ii. 2. 595.—**John'=do'ry** (-dō'ri), *n.* A kind of fish. See *dory*[1].

John-ny (jon'i), *n.*; pl. *Johnnies* (-iz). A familiar diminutive of *John*, often used as a nickname for men generally; [*cap.* or *l. c.*] a man, lad, or fellow; [*cap.*] a Confederate soldier in the U. S. Civil War (also called *Johnny Reb*); [*l. c.*] an idle young man of fashion, esp. a dangler about theaters. [Colloq.]—**Johnny Crapaud** (krȧ-pō). [F. *crapaud*, toad.] A Frenchman; the French people.—**Johnny Fresh.** Same as *Johnny Raw*. [Colloq.]—**Johnny Newcome,** a new-comer; a greenhorn. [Colloq.]—**Johnny on the spot,** one who is on hand to perform a duty, seize an opportunity, etc.; one who is always ready or on the alert. [Colloq.]—**Johnny Raw,** a raw or inexperienced person; a novice; a greenhorn. [Colloq.]—**Johnny Reb,** a Confederate soldier in the U. S. Civil War. [Colloq.]

john-ny=cake (jon'i-kāk), *n.* [Perhaps orig. *journey cake.*] A kind of cake or bread made of Indian meal, water or milk, and often eggs, etc. [U. S.]

John-ny=jump=up (jon-i-jump'up), *n.* Any of certain violets, esp. *Viola pedata*; also, the pansy, *Viola tricolor.* [U. S.]

John-son-ese (jon-sọn-ēs' or -ēz'), *n.* The language or literary style of Dr. Samuel Johnson (1709–84), characterized by pompous phraseology and the use of many words of Latin origin (as, "When he [Johnson] wrote for publication, he did his sentences out of English into *Johnsonese*": Macaulay's "Essays," Boswell's Johnson); in general, pompous or ponderously learned diction.

John-so-ni-an (jon-sō'ni-ạn), *a.* Of, pertaining to, or characteristic of Dr. Samuel Johnson, his writings, or his style: as, "delighting herself with the *Johnsonian* balance of the rhythmical sentences" (Mrs. Stowe's "Oldtown Folks," xxx.). See *Johnsonese.*—**John-so'ni-an-ism,** *n.* Johnsonian style; also, a Johnsonian word or expression.

join (join), *v.* [OF. F. *joindre*, < L. *jungere* (pp. *junctus*), join, yoke, akin to Gr. ζευγνύναι, Skt. *yuj-*, yoke: cf. *yoke.*] **I.** *tr.* To bring or put together in contact or connection (as, to *join* hands; to *join* planks end to end; to *join* islands by a bridge or words by a hyphen); connect; fig., to bring together in relation, purpose, action, coexistence, etc. (as, to *join* parties or forces; to *join* efforts or prayers for a common end; strength *joined* with beauty); unite, associate, combine, or conjoin; specif., to unite in marriage (as, "But were I *join'd* with her, Then might we live together as one life": Tennyson's "Coming of Arthur," 89); also to come into contact, connection, or union with (as, the broo *joins* the river; one floating mass *joins* another); adjoi (as, his land *joins* mine); come into the company of (as go now, and I will *join* you later); associate one's self wit (a person, party, etc.); become a member of (a society regiment, etc.); also, to enter into (company, relations, etc. now chiefly in 'to join company'); meet or engage in (battle conflict, etc.); also, to construct by putting parts togethe as furniture (obs. or rare: cf. *joiner*). **II.** *intr.* To com into or be in contact or connection, or form a junction; fig. to become united, associated, or combined; associate o ally one's self (*with*); take part with others (*in*, or to d something); also, to meet in battle or conflict (obs. o archaic).—**join,** *n.* A joining; also, a place or line o joining; a seam.

join-der (join'dėr), *n.* [F. *joindre*, inf., used as noun: se *join.*] The act of joining (as, "A contract of eternal bond of love, Confirm'd by mutual *joinder* of your hands": Shak spere's "Twelfth Night," v. 1. 160); in *law*, the joining o causes of action in a suit; also, the joining of parties in a suit; also, the acceptance by a party to an action of an issu tendered.

join-er (joi'nėr), *n.* One who or that which joins; esp., a craftsman who constructs things by joining pieces of wood usually, one who constructs the doors, windows, and othe fittings of houses, ships, etc.—**join'er-y,** *n.* The art o trade of a joiner; also, joiners' work.

joint (joint), *a.* [OF. F. *joint*, pp. of *joindre*, join: see *join.*] Joined or associated, as in relation, interest, or action (as, *joint* owners; *joint* tenants); sharing or acting in common; also, held, done, etc., by two or more in conjunction or in common (as, *joint* stock; *joint* ownership; *joint* action); shared by or common to two or more.—**joint,** *n.* [OF. F. *joint, jointe*, < *joindre.*] The place or part in which two things, or parts of one thing, are joined or united, either rigidly or so as to admit of motion; an articulation; in an animal body, a place or part where two bones or two segments join, or the hinge-like or other arrangement of such a part; in a plant, the part of a stem from which a branch or a leaf grows; a node; also, a portion, esp. of an animal or plant body, connected with another portion by an articulation, node, or the like, or a portion between two articulations, nodes, or the like; one of the portions into which a carcass is divided by a butcher (as, a *joint* of beef for roasting); also, a place of low resort, as for opium-smoking or for the illicit sale of liquor (colloq., U. S.); any resort or abode (slang, U. S.); in *geol.*, one of a series of planes (usually parallel and commonly occurring in two sets approximately at right angles to each other) along which a mass of rock fractures in directions transverse to the stratification.—**out of joint,** displaced from its position of articulation, as a bone; dislocated; fig., disordered, or out of order (as, "The time is *out of joint*: O cursed spite, That ever I was born to set it right!" Shakspere's "Hamlet," i. 5. 189).—**joint,** *v. t.* To unite by a joint or joints; also, to form or provide with a joint or joints; also, to prepare the edge or surface of (a board, etc.) for fitting in a joint; also, to divide at a joint, or separate into joints or pieces (as, to *joint* meat).—**joint'ed,** *a.* Having a joint or joints: as, a *jointed* doll; a loose-*jointed* frame.—**joint'er,** *n.* One who or that which joints; an implement or machine used in making joints.—**joint'less,** *a.* Without joints; hence, unbending; rigid.—**joint'ly,** *adv.* Together; in conjunction; in common.

join-tress (join'tres), *n.* A woman who has a jointure.

joint=stock (joint'stok'), *a.* Having stock or capital divided into a number of shares.—**joint=stock company,** a business partnership or association of individuals, of which the capital is represented by transferable shares of stock, and which resembles more or less closely a joint-stock corporation; sometimes, a joint-stock corporation (see *corporation*).

joint=stool (joint'stöl), *n.* [Orig. *joined stool.*] A stool made of parts skilfully joined or fitted together, as distinguished from one more roughly made.

join-ture (join'ţūr), *n.* [OF. F. *jointure*, < L. *junctura*, < *jungere*, join: see *join*, and cf. *juncture.*] Joining† or union†; also, a joint (now rare); also, an estate or property settled on a woman in consideration of marriage, and to be enjoyed by her after her husband's decease.—**join'ture,** *v. t.*; *-tured, -turing.* To settle a jointure upon (a woman).

oint-weed (joint'wēd), *n.* An American polygonaceous herb, *Polygonella articulata,* with many-jointed spike-like racemes of small white or rose-colored flowers.

oint=worm (joint'wėrm), *n.* The larva of any of certain hymenopterous insects (genus *Isosoma*), which is very injurious to grain, feeding near the joints of the stalk.

oist (joist), *n.* [OF. *giste* (F. *gîte*), lit. 'resting-place,' 'bed,' < *gesir,* lie, rest, < L. *jacere,* lie: cf. *gist.*] One of the parallel pieces of timber to which are fastened the boards of a floor, the laths of a ceiling, or the like.—**joist,** *v. t.* To furnish with or fix on joists.

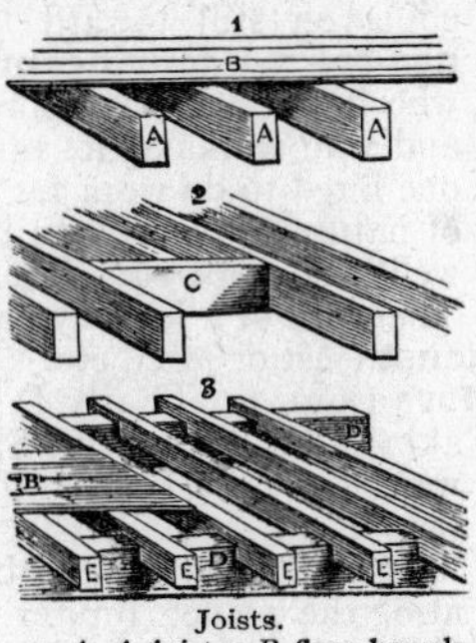

Joists.
1. *A, A,* joists; *B,* floor-boards. 2. *C,* trimming-joist. 3. *D, D,* binding-joists; *E, E,* bridging-joists: *B,* floor-boards.

oke (jōk), *n.* [L. *jocus,* jest, sport.] Something said or done to excite laughter or amusement; a jest; a playful or mischievous trick (as, a practical *joke*: see under *practical*); hence, an amusing or ridiculous circumstance (as, the *joke* of the matter was this; this was a good *joke* on me); also, joking or jesting (as, "He was full of *joke* and jest": Tennyson's "Death of the Old Year"); jest, as opposed to earnest (as, to speak in *joke*); also, an object of joking or jesting; a thing or person laughed at rather than taken seriously; a matter for joking about (as, the loss was no *joke,* that is, it was a serious matter).—**joke,** *v.*; *joked, joking.* **I.** *intr.* To speak or act in a playful or merry way; also, to say or do something in mere sport, rather than in earnest (as, "But court na anither, tho' *jokin'* ye be": Burns's "Whistle, and I'll Come to You"); jest. **II.** *tr.* To subject to jokes; banter, rally, or chaff: as, "He disliked any risk of being '*joked*' about Hetty" (George Eliot's "Adam Bede," xxiii.).—**jok-er** (jō'kėr), *n.* One who jokes; hence, a fellow or 'chap' (colloq.); also, an extra playing-card in a pack, used in some games, often counting as the highest card; also, any device or expedient for getting the better of or tricking another; esp., a clause or expression inserted in a legislative bill with the unavowed object of defeating the ostensible purpose of the bill if passed.—**joke'smith,** *n.* A maker or writer of jokes: as, a newspaper *jokesmith.*—**jok'ing-ly,** *adv.*

jole, joll (jōl). See *jowl*[1], *jowl*[2], *jowl*[3], *jowl*[4].

jol-li-fi-ca-tion (jol"i-fi-kā'shon), *n.* [See *-fication.*] Jolly merrymaking; a jolly festivity.

jol-li-fy (jol'i-fī), *v. t.* or *i.*; *-fied, -fying.* [See *-fy.*] To make or be jolly or merry.

jol-li-ly (jol'i-li), *adv.* In a jolly manner.—**jol'li-ness,** *n.*

jol-li-ty (jol'i-ti), *n.*; pl. *-ties* (-tiz). Jolly state, mood, or proceedings (as, "All now was turn'd to *jollity* and game": Milton's "Paradise Lost," xi. 714); *pl.,* jolly festivities (as, "As a beginning of our *jollities,* I must remind our leader that my aunt's board awaits him": Jane Porter's "Scottish Chiefs," xxiv.).

jol-ly (jol'i), *a.*; compar. *jollier,* superl. *jolliest.* [OF. *joli, jolif,* joyous, gay, gallant, fine (F. *joli,* pretty); origin uncertain.] Joyous, glad, or gay (archaic: as, "The *jolly* Hours lead on propitious May," Milton's "Sonnets," To the Nightingale); now, esp., cheerful or merry in an unaffected or sociable way (as, he is a *jolly* old soul; a *jolly* crowd; a *jolly* disposition; a *jolly* laugh); jovial; mirthful; cheerfully festive or convivial (as, "*jolly* supper-parties": Thackeray's "Newcomes," xviii.); sometimes, exhilarated by drink; also, gallant or brave, as a knight†; also, of fine appearance, buxom, or plump (now prov. Eng.: as, a *jolly* landlady); in general, fine or excellent, or pleasing or delightful (now colloq.: as, "I've got such a *jolly* pony," Thackeray's "Newcomes," i.); big or great (now colloq.: as, a *jolly* fool).—**Jolly Roger,** the pirates' flag, having a white skull and cross-bones on a black field: as, "The 'Hispaniola' still lay where she had anchored, but . . . there was the *Jolly Roger*—the black flag of piracy—flying from her peak" (Stevenson's "Treasure Island," xix.).—**jol'ly,** *n.*; pl. *jollies* (-iz). A British royal marine (as, "I'm a *Jolly*—'Er Majesty's *Jolly*—soldier an' sailor too!" Kipling's "Soldier an' Sailor Too"); also, a cheer, as for a person; also, a bit of agreeable talk or action intended to put or keep a person in good humor, often in order to secure some end. [Colloq.]—**jol'ly,** *adv.* Extremely; very: as, *jolly* well; *jolly* awkward; " 'Tis like you'll prove a *jolly* surly groom" (Shakspere's "Taming of the Shrew," iii. 2. 215). [Now colloq.]—**jol'ly,** *v.*; *-lied, -lying.* **I.** *tr.* To talk or act agreeably to (a person) in order to put or keep him in good humor; banter pleasantly. [Colloq.] **II.** *intr.* To make merry (obs. or rare); also, to jolly a person (colloq.).

jol-ly=boat (jol'i-bōt), *n.* [Cf. LG. and Dan. *jolle,* and E. *yawl*[2].] A clincher-built boat smaller than a cutter, usually hoisted at the stern of a ship.

jolt (jōlt), *v.* [Appar. for earlier *jot*[1], perhaps influenced by *jowl*[4].] **I.** *tr.* To jog† or nudge†; hence, to jar or shake as by a sudden rough thrust; shake up roughly, or transport with a rough shaking motion, as in passing over an uneven road. **II.** *intr.* To move with a shock or jerk, or a succession of shocks or jerks; travel or ride with a rough, jerky motion.—**jolt,** *n.* A jolting shock or movement.—**jolt-er** (jōl'tėr), *n.*

jolt-er-head, jolt-head (jōl'tėr-hed, jōlt'hed), *n.* [Cf. *jolt.*] A large, thick, or stupid head (as, "*jolterheads,* that have no more brains in them than a brick-bat": Scott's "Kenilworth," x.); also, a stupid person; a blockhead; a dolt. [Colloq. or prov.]—**jolt'er-head"ed, jolt'head"ed,** *a.*

Jo-nah (jō'nạ̈), *n.* [From *Jonah,* the Hebrew prophet, who was thrown overboard to allay a tempest at sea: see Jonah, i.] A person whose presence on shipboard or elsewhere is supposed to bring ill luck: as, "A *Jonah* must be cast overboard to save the ship" (J. H. Newman's "Callista," xvii.).

Jon-a-than (jon'ạ-thạn), *n.* See *Brother Jonathan.*

jon-gleur (zhôn-glėr), *n.* [F. *jongleur,* OF. *jogleor*: see *juggler.*] In medieval France and Norman England, an itinerant minstrel or entertainer who sang songs (sometimes of his own composition), told stories, and otherwise entertained people.

jon-quil (jong'kwil), *n.* [F. *jonquille,* < Sp. *junquillo,* jonquil, < *junco,* < L. *juncus,* a rush.] A species of narcissus, *Narcissus jonquilla,* with long, narrow, rush-like leaves and fragrant yellow or white flowers.

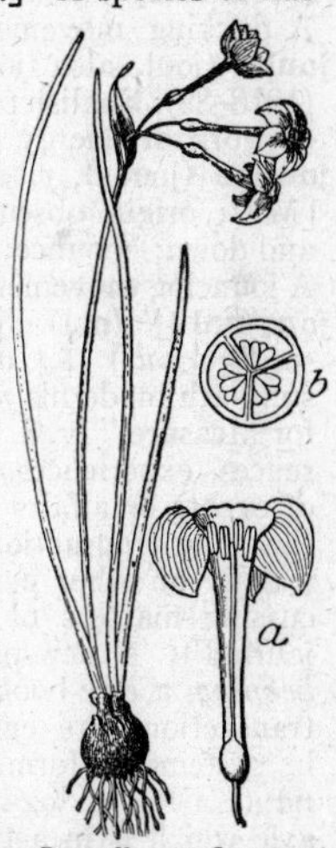

Jonquil.—*a,* flower cut longitudinally; *b,* fruit cut transversely.

jook (jŏk), *v.* and *n.* See *jouk*[2].

Jor-dan (jôr'dạn) **al'mond.** [Prob. < F. *jardin,* garden.] A choice variety of almond from Malaga.

jo-rum (jō'rum), *n.* [Said to be from *Joram,* who brought to David vessels of silver, gold, and brass: see 2 Sam. viii. 10.] A large bowl or vessel for holding drink, or its contents: as, a *jorum* of punch; "And here's to them that, like oursel, Can push about the *jorum!*" (Burns's "O May, Thy Morn").

jo-seph (jō'zẹf), *n.* [From *Joseph* (= It. *Giuseppe*), man's name: cf. Gen. xxxvii. 3, also xxxix. 12.] A long cloak with a cape, worn chiefly in the 18th century, esp. by women, as when riding (as, "Olivia would be drawn as an Amazon . . . dressed in a green *joseph,* richly laced with gold": Goldsmith's "Vicar of Wakefield," xvi.); also [*cap.*], a violin made by Giuseppe Guarneri (Joseph Guarnerius), 1683–1745, of Cremona, Italy.

josh (josh), *v. t.* [Origin uncertain.] To chaff; banter; rally in a teasing way. [Slang, U. S.]—**josh,** *n.* A chaffing remark; a piece of banter. [Slang, U. S.]—**josh'er,** *n.*

Josh-u-a=tree (josh'ụ-ạ̈-trē), *n.* A tree, *Yucca arborescens,* growing in arid or desert regions of the southwestern U. S. See *yucca.*

jos-kin (jos'kin), *n.* [Origin uncertain.] A raw or ignorant rustic; a country bumpkin; a yokel. [Prov. or slang, Eng. and Sc.]

joss (jos), *n.* [Pidgin-English corruption of Pg. *deos,* < L. *deus,* god.] A Chinese deity or idol, or any heathen deity or idol (as, "And one called out on a heathen *joss* and one on the Virgin's Name": Kipling's "Rhyme of the Three Sealers"); also, luck, fortune, or chance (colloq.).—**joss′=house,** *n.* A Chinese temple or place of idol-worship.—**joss′=stick,** *n.* A slender stick of a dried fragrant paste burned by the Chinese as incense or used for other purposes.

jos-tle (jos′l), *v.*; *-tled, -tling.* [Earlier *justle,* freq. of *just*[2].] **I.** *intr.* To contend in justing or tilting†; hence, to strive as with collisions, rough pushing, etc., for room, place, or any advantage; also, to collide (*with*) or strike or push (*against*) as in passing or in a crowd; push or elbow one's way rudely. **II.** *tr.* To strike or push roughly or rudely against; elbow roughly; hustle; also, to drive or force by or as by pushing or shoving.—**jos′tle,** *n.* A jostling; a collision, shock, or push, as in jostling.—**jos′tle-ment,** *n.*

jot[1] (jot), *v. t.* or *i.*; *jotted, jotting.* [Appar. imit.] To jog; bump; jar; jolt. [Now prov. Eng.]

jot[2] (jot), *n.* [L. *iota*: see *iota.*] An iota or least part or quantity of something, orig. of something written (as, "Till heaven and earth pass, one *jot* or one tittle shall in no wise pass from the law, till all be fulfilled": Mat. v. 18); indefinitely, a bit or whit (as, I do not care a *jot*; it does not matter one *jot*): commonly in negative expressions.—**jot**[2], *v. t.*; *jotted, jotting.* To write or mark down briefly; note, as for a memorandum: usually with *down.*—**jot′ter,** *n.*—**jot′ting,** *n.* The act of one who jots; also, something jotted down; a brief note or memorandum.

jo-tun, jö-tun (yō′tůn, yė′tůn), *n.* [Icel. *jötunn.*] One of a supernatural race of giants in Scandinavian mythology: as, "A great mist-*jotun* you will see Lifting himself up silently" (Lowell's "Pictures from Appledore," v.).

jougs (jögz), *n. pl.* [F. *joug,* a yoke, < L. *jugum*: see *yoke.*] An instrument of punishment formerly used in Scotland, consisting of a kind of iron collar made fast about an offender's neck, and attached by a chain to a wall, post, or the like.

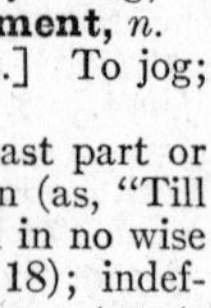
Jougs.

jouk[1] (jök), *v. i.* [OF. *joquier,* roost, rest: cf. *jug*[2].] To roost as a bird; settle down or lie at rest. [Obs. or prov. Eng.]

jouk[2] (jök), *v. i.* or *t.* [Cf. *duck*[1].] To duck, or elude by ducking; dodge. [Sc.]—**jouk,** *n.* A ducking movement; a dodge. [Sc.]

joule (joul, also jöl), *n.* [From J. P. *Joule* (1818–89), English physicist.] In *physics,* a unit of work or energy equal to 10,000,000 ergs.

jounce (jouns), *v. i.* or *t.*; *jounced, jouncing.* [ME.; origin obscure.] To move violently up and down; bounce; bump; jolt.—**jounce,** *n.* A jouncing movement; a bounce; a jolt.

jour-nal (jėr′nạl). [OF. F. *journal,* < LL. *diurnalis,* daily: see *diurnal.*] **I.**† *a.* Diurnal; daily: as, "ere twice the sun hath made his *journal* greeting" (Shakspere's "Measure for Measure," iv. 3. 92). **II.** *n.* A daily record, as of occurrences, experiences, or observations; a diary; any record of events or affairs from day to day; specif., a register of the daily transactions of a public or legislative body; also, a daily or other periodical publication giving news or discussing matters of current interest (often called 'public journal'); a newspaper, magazine, or the like; in *bookkeeping,* a day-book; in double entry, a book in which all transactions are entered (from the day-book or blotter), in systematic form, to facilitate posting into the ledger; *naut.,* a log or log-book; in *mach.,* that part of a shaft or axle which is in actual contact with a bearing.—**jour-nal-ese′** (-ēs′ or -ēz′), *n.* [See *-ese.*] The style of writing or expression (less precise and restrained than that of conventional literary work) supposed to be characteristic of newspapers: as, "It's a clumsy ending and vile *journalese*" (Kipling's "Light That Failed," iv.).—**jour′nal-ism,** *n.* The occupation or profession of writing for, editing, or conducting newspapers; also, newspapers collectively; the press.—**jour′nal-ist,** *n.* One who keeps a journal or diary; also, one engaged in journalism.—**jour-nal-is′tic,** *a.* Of, pertaining to, or characteristic of journalists or journalism.—**jour-nal-is′ti-cal-ly,** *adv.*—**jour′nal-ize,** *v.*; *-ized, -izing.* **I.** *tr.* To enter or record in a journal. **II.** *intr.* To keep, or make entries in, a journal; also, to engage in journalism.

jour-ney (jėr′ni), *n.*; pl. *-neys* (-niz). [OF. *jornee* (F. *journée*), a day's time, travel, or work, < L. *diurnus,* of the day, daily: see *diurnal,* and cf. *journal.*] A day's travel† (as, a place ten *journeys* from here); hence, a distance traveled, or suitable for traveling, in a specified time (as, a day's or a week's *journey*; a Sabbath-day's *journey,* see under *Sabbath, a.*); also, a course of travel from one place to another, esp. by land (cf. *voyage*); fig., the course or passage through life; also, a day's labor (obs. or prov. Eng.); also, a round of work, as in glass-making.—**jour′ney,** *v. i.* To make a journey; travel: as, "And Abram *journeyed,* going on still toward the south" (Gen. xii. 9).—**jour′ney-er,** *n.*—**jour′ney-man** (-mạn), *n.*; pl. *-men.* One who has served his apprenticeship at a trade or handicraft, and who works at it, as for day's wages, for another; fig., one hired to do work for another (as, "I have thought some of nature's *journeymen* had made men and not made them well": Shakspere's "Hamlet," iii. 2. 37).—**jour′ney=work,** *n.* The work of a journeyman.

joust (just or jöst), etc. See *just*[2], etc.

Jove (jōv), *n.* [Early L. *Jovis* (later only in oblique cases), akin to Gr. Ζεύς, Zeus, Skt. *dyaus,* heaven, AS. *Tīw,* god of war: see *deity,* and cf. *Jupiter.*] The Roman god Jupiter (as, "Keep in mind What *Jove* decrees," Dryden's tr. Virgil's "Æneid," iii. 328; the bird of *Jove,* the eagle; by *Jove!*); also, the planet Jupiter (poetic: as, "the moons of *Jove,*" Cowper's "Tirocinium," 634).—**Jo-vi-al** (jō′vi-ạl), *a.* [LL. *Jovialis.*] Of or pertaining to the god Jove or Jupiter; also, of or pertaining to the planet Jupiter; under the influence of, or having the characteristics imparted by, the planet Jupiter (which, in astrology, as a natal planet, was regarded as the source of joy and happiness); hence [*l. c.*], endowed with or characterized by a hearty, joyous humor or a spirit of good-fellowship (as, a *jovial* fellow or party; a *jovial* laugh); merry; jolly; convivial.—**jo-vi-al′i-ty** (-al′i-ti), **jo′vi-al-ness,** *n.*—**jo′vi-al-ly,** *adv.*—**Jo′vi-an,** *a.* Pertaining to the god Jove, or to the planet Jupiter.

jow (jou), *v.* [Prob. = *jowl*[4].] **I.** *tr.* To strike, knock, or bump (north. Eng.); also, to toll (a bell: Sc.). **II.** *intr.* To toll, as a bell does; also, to swing, rock, or roll to and fro (as, "when his coble is *jowing* awa in the Firth": Scott's "Antiquary," xxvi.). [Sc.]—**jow,** *n.* A stroke, as of a bell. [Sc.]

jowl[1] (joul or jōl), *n.* [ME. *chawl, chavel,* < AS. *ceafl,* jaw, akin to D. *kevel,* gum, G. *kiefer,* jaw, chap, Icel. *kjaptr,* mouth, jaw: cf. *chaft.*] A jaw, esp. the under jaw; also, the cheek.—**cheek by jowl.** See under *cheek.*

jowl[2] (joul or jōl), *n.* [ME. *cholle*: cf. AS. *ceole,* throat.] A fold of flesh hanging from the jaw, as of a fat person; also, the dewlap of cattle; also, the wattle of fowls.

jowl[3] (joul or jōl), *n.* [ME. *cholle, jolle*: cf. *jowl*[2].] The head of a man or beast (obs. or prov.); also, the head and adjacent parts of certain fish, as the salmon, sturgeon, etc., as for the table.

jowl[4] (joul or jōl), *v.* [ME. *cholle, joll*; perhaps < *jowl*[3].] **I.** *tr.* To strike, knock, bump, or dash (esp. the head: as, "That skull . . . how the knave *jowls* it to the ground," Shakspere's "Hamlet," v. 1. 84); also, to jolt or shake; also, to toll or ring (a bell). [Now prov. Eng. and Sc.] **II.** *intr.* To strike; knock; peck; also, to jolt along; also, to toll, as a bell does. [Now prov. Eng. and Sc.]—**jowl**[4], *n.* A knock; a bump; also, a stroke of a bell. [Now prov. Eng. and Sc.]

jowled (jould or jōld), *a.* [See *jowl*[1].] Having jowls or jaws (as specified): as, heavy-*jowled.*—**jowl′er,** *n.* A heavy-jawed dog, as a hound or beagle: now prov., except [*cap.*] as a name for such a dog.—**jowl′y,** *a.* Having large or prominent jowls.—**jowl′i-ness,** *n.*

joy (joi), *n.* [OF. F. *joie,* < L. *gaudia,* pl. of *gaudium,* joy, gladness, < *gaudere,* rejoice.] An emotion of keen or lively pleasure arising from present or expected good (as, "I caused the widow's heart to sing for *joy*": Job, xxix. 13); exultant satisfaction; great gladness; delight; also, the manifestation of glad feeling, or outward rejoicing (as, "The *joy* of Jerusalem was heard even afar off": Neh. xii. 43); festive gaiety (as, "On with the dance! let *joy* be unconfined": Byron's "Childe Harold," iii. 22); also, a source or cause of gladness or delight (as, "A thing of beauty is a *joy* for ever": Keats's "Endymion," i.); also, a state of happiness or felicity; esp., the bliss of heaven; also, glad praise or worship (archaic: as, "Glory and *joy* and honour to our Lord," Tennyson's "Holy Grail," 836).—**joy,** *v.* [OF. *joir* (F. *jouir*), < L. *gaudere.*] **I.** *intr.* To feel joy; be glad; rejoice: as, "those cruel potentates of the school, who *joy* in the smart of their subjects" (Irving's "Sketch-Book," Sleepy Hollow). [Archaic.] **II.** *tr.* To gladden or delight (archaic: as, a sight that *joys* the heart); also, to enjoy† (as, "I, Who might have lived, and *joy'd* immortal bliss": Milton's "Paradise Lost," ix. 1166); also, to felicitate†, compliment†, or welcome†.

joy-ance (joi'ạns), *n.* Joyous feeling, gladness, or delight (as, "With thy clear keen *joyance* Languor cannot be": Shelley's "To a Skylark," 76); also, enjoyment, merry-making, or festive gaiety (as, "His sports were faire, his *joyance* innocent": Spenser's "Astrophel," 25). [Archaic.]

joy-ful (joi'fůl), *a.* Full of joy, as a person, the heart, etc.; glad; delighted; showing or expressing joy, as looks, actions, speech, etc.; also, causing or bringing joy, as an event, a sight, news, etc.; highly pleasing; delightful.—**joy'ful-ly,** *adv.*—**joy'ful-ness,** *n.*

joy-less (joi'les), *a.* Destitute of joy or gladness (as, "With downcast looks the *joyless* victor sate": Dryden's "Alexander's Feast," iv.); also, causing no joy, cheerless, or dismal (as, a *joyless* prospect).—**joy'less-ly,** *adv.*—**joy'less-ness,** *n.*

joy-ous (joi'us), *a.* [OF. *joios* (F. *joyeux*).] Full of joy, gladness, or happy gaiety (as, a *joyous* person, heart, or mood; "a *joyous* city," Isa. xxii. 2); showing or expressing joy, as laughter, song, festivities, etc.; cheerful, blithe, or gay; also, delighted, pleased, or glad, as at something specified† (as, "Right *joyous* are we to behold your face": Shakspere's "Henry V.," v. 2. 9); also, causing joy or gladness (as, "No chastening for the present seemeth to be *joyous*, but grievous": Heb. xii. 11).—**joy'ous-ly,** *adv.*—**joy'ous-ness,** *n.*

joy=ride (joi'rīd), *n.* A pleasure-ride in an automobile, esp. when the car is driven recklessly or used without the owner's permission. [Colloq.]—**joy'=rid"er,** *n.*—**joy'=rid"-ing,** *n.* and *a.*

joy=stick (joi'stik), *n.* In *aëronautics*, a lever by means of which certain of the principal controls of an aëroplane are operated, as to regulate pitching and rolling. [Colloq.]

ju-ba (jö'bạ̈), *n.* [Negro word.] A characteristic dance of plantation negroes in the southern U. S., performed by one or more dancers, while the spectators clap hands, pat the knee or thigh, strike the ground with the foot, and sing a refrain in which the word *juba* is frequently repeated. The spectators in accompanying the dancers are said to 'pat juba': as, "They got out an old fiddle, and one played, and another *patted juba*, and the rest turned themselves loose on a . . . breakdown" (Mark Twain's "Life on the Mississippi," iii.).

jub-bah (jub'ạ̈), *n.* [Ar. *jubbah*: cf. *jupe.*] A kind of long outer garment with sleeves, worn in Mohammedan countries.

ju-be (jö'bē), *n.* [= F. *jubé*, < L. *jube*, 'bid thou,' the first word of a formula spoken from the gallery above the rood-screen.] In a church, a rood-loft, or the entire structure formed by the rood-loft and rood-screen.

ju-bi-lant (jö'bi-lạnt), *a.* [L. *jubilans* (*-ant-*), ppr.] Jubilating; rejoicing; exultant: as, "Great organs surged through arches dim Their *jubilant* floods in praise of him" (Lowell's "Parable").—**ju'bi-lance, ju'bi-lan-cy,** *n.*—**ju'bi-lant-ly,** *adv.*

ju-bi-late[1] (jö'bi-lāt), *v. i.*; *-lated, -lating.* [L. *jubilatus*, pp. of *jubilare*, shout, shout for joy, < *jubilum*, a wild cry, shout: cf. *jubilee.*] To shout for joy; hence, to manifest or feel great joy; rejoice; exult; sometimes, to celebrate a jubilee or joyful occasion.

Ju-bi-la-te[2] (jö-bi-lā'tē), *n.* [L. *jubilate*, 'shout ye': the first word of both psalms in the Vulgate.] The 100th Psalm (99th in the Vulgate), used as a canticle in the Anglican liturgy; a musical setting of this psalm; also, the third Sunday ('Jubilate Sunday') after Easter (when the 66th psalm, 65th in the Vulgate, is used as the introit).

ju-bi-la-tion (jö-bi-lā'shọn), *n.* [L. *jubilatio*(*n-*).] The act of jubilating; rejoicing; exultation; sometimes, a joyful or festive celebration.—**ju'bi-la-to-ry** (-lạ-tọ-ri), *a.*

ju-bi-le (jö'bi-lē), *n.* See *jubilee.*

ju-bi-lee (jö'bi-lē), *n.* [OF. *jubile* (F. *jubilé*), < LL. *jubilæus*, < Gr. ἰωβηλαῖος, < Heb. *yōbēl*, ram, ram's horn (used as a trumpet: cf. Lev. xxv. 9); not connected with *jubilate*[1].] Among the ancient Hebrews, a year to be observed every 50th year (see Lev. xxv.), and to be announced by the blowing of trumpets, during which the fields were to be left untilled, alienated lands to be restored, and Hebrew bondmen to be set free; hence, the completion of the 50th year of any continuous course or period, as of existence or activity, or its celebration; the celebration of any of certain anniversaries, as the 25th ('silver jubilee'), 50th ('golden jubilee'), or 60th or 75th ('diamond jubilee'); also, any season or occasion of rejoicing or festivity; also, rejoicing or jubilation (as, "They passed on . . . singing hymns of *jubilee*": Irving's "Conquest of Granada," c.); joyful shouting, or sounds of rejoicing (as, "All along the crowded way Was *jubilee* and loud huzza": Scott's "Lady of the Lake," v. 21); specif., in the *Rom. Cath. Ch.*, an appointed year (or other period), now ordinarily every 25th year, in which remission from the penal consequences of sin is granted upon repentance and the performance of certain religious acts.

Ju-dæ-o- (jọ-dē'ọ-). Form of L. *Judæus*, Jew, used in combination.—**Ju-dæ'o-phil, Ju-dæ'o-phile** (-fil). [+ *-phil, -phile.*] **I.** *a.* Friendly to the Jews. **II.** *n.* One who is friendly to the Jews.—**Ju-dæ'o-phobe** (-fōb), *n.* [+ *-phobe.*] One who fears or hates the Jews.—**Ju-dæ-o-pho'bi-a** (-fō'bi-ạ̈), *n.* [+ *-phobia.*] Fear or hatred of the Jews.

Ju-da-ic (jọ-dā'ik), *a.* [L. *Judaicus*, < Gr. Ἰουδαϊκός, < Ἰουδαῖος, E. *Jew.*] Of or pertaining to the Jews; Jewish. Also **Ju-da'i-cal.**—**Ju-da-ism** (jö'dạ-izm), *n.* [LL. *Judaismus*, < Gr. Ἰουδαϊσμός.] The religious system and polity of the Jews; also, conformity to or adoption of Jewish rites or practices.—**Ju'da-ist,** *n.* An adherent of Judaism; esp., a Jewish Christian in the early church who followed or advocated Jewish rites or practices.—**Ju-da-is'tic,** *a.*—**Ju'da-ize** (-īz), *v. i.* or *t.*; *-ized, -izing.* [LL. *Judaizare*, < Gr. Ἰουδαΐζειν.] To conform to Jewish usages or ideas.—**Ju"da-i-za'tion** (-i-zā'shọn), *n.*—**Ju'da-iz-er** (-ī-zėr), *n.*

Ju-das (jö'dạs), *n.* [From *Judas* Iscariot, the disciple who betrayed Jesus: see Mat. xxvi. 14–16, 47–49.] One treacherous enough to betray a friend (as, "Three *Judases*, each one thrice worse than Judas!" Shakspere's "Richard II.," iii. 2. 132); also [*l. c.*], an aperture or trap, as in a door, through which to look without being seen from the other side (also called *judas-hole* and *judas-trap*).—**Ju'das=col"-ored,** *a.* Of hair, red: from the medieval belief that Judas Iscariot had red hair.—**Ju'das=tree,** *n.* A purple-flowered cæsalpiniaceous European and Asiatic tree, *Cercis siliquastrum*, supposed to be of the same kind as that upon which Judas hanged himself; hence, any of various other trees of the same genus, as the redbud, *C. canadensis*, of America, or *C. occidentalis* ('California Judas-tree').

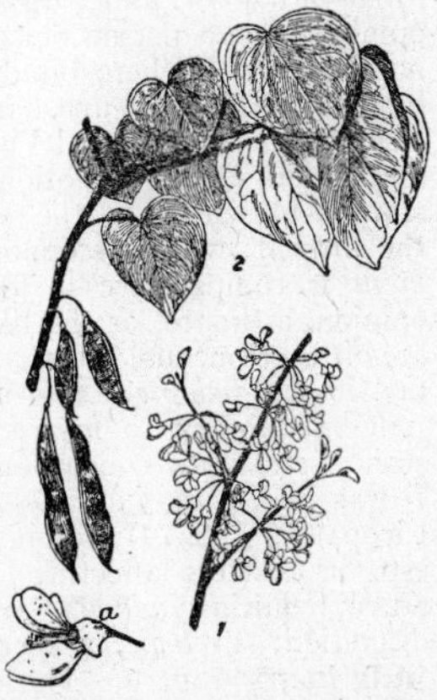

Judas-tree, or Redbud (*Cercis canadensis*). — 1, branch with flowers; 2, branch with leaves and fruit; *a*, flower.

judge (juj), *n.* [OF. F. *juge*, < L. *judex* (*judic-*), < *jus*, right, law, + *dicere*, say.] A public officer authorized to hear and determine causes in a court of law; a magistrate charged with the administering of justice; hence, in general, one who gives judgment or passes sentence (as, "God the *Judge* of all": Heb. xii. 23); one who gives decision in a dispute or contest, as an arbiter or umpire; one who judges or decides in any matter admitting of question or doubt (as, "sole *judge* of truth," Pope's "Essay on Man," ii. 17; to be the *judge* of the wisdom or propriety of one's conduct; you must let me be the *judge* of that); also, one qualified to pass a critical judgment (as, a *judge* of horses or of wines; a *judge* of character); also, an administrative officer at the head of the Hebrew nation in the period between Joshua and the kings; *pl.* [*cap.*], the seventh book of the Old Testament (called in full "The Book of Judges"), dealing with this period.—**judge,** *v.*; *judged, judging.* [OF. *jugier* (F. *juger*), < L. *judicare*, judge, decide, adjudge, < *judex*.] **I.** *tr.* To try (a person or a cause) as a judge does; pass sentence on or in; also, to decide or decree judicially or authoritatively (as, "touching such things as he *judged* to be referred to the king": 2 Mac. xi. 36); adjudge or award, as a prize; also, to pronounce an opinion (esp. unfavorable) upon (as, "Who art thou that *judgest* another?" James, iv. 12); criticize; condemn; also, to form an opinion or estimate of (as, to *judge* others by one's self; to *judge* a cause from its advocates); also, to infer, think, or hold in opinion (with a clause or complement: as, I *judged* that he had forgotten me; I *judged* it to be unintentional; "To-morrow, then, I *judge* a happy day," Shakspere's "Richard III.," iii. 4. 6); conclude, consider, or deem; also, of the Hebrew judges, to govern (as, "And Jephthah *judged* Israel six years": Judges, xii. 7). **II.** *intr.* To act as a judge; pass sentence; decide as an arbiter or umpire between parties; also, to form an opinion or estimate (as, to *judge* of the merits of a book; to *judge* of the probable consequences of a proposed measure); make a mental judgment.—**judge′=ad′vo-cate,** *n.* In military and naval use, the officer appointed to prosecute before a court-martial, and to act as its legal adviser.—**judge′ment,** etc. See *judgment*, etc.—**judg′er,** *n.*—**judge′ship,** *n.* The office, function, or period of incumbency of a judge.

judg-mat-ic, judg-mat-i-cal (juj-mat′ik, -i-kạl), *a.* [Irreg. < *judge* + *-matic* as in *dogmatic*.] Exercising or showing good judgment; judicious: as, "A *judgmatical* rap over the head stiffened the lying impostor for a time" (Cooper's "Last of the Mohicans," xxv.). [Colloq.]—**judg-mat′i-cal-ly,** *adv.*

judg-ment (juj′mẹnt), *n.* The act of judging or trying, as in a court of justice (as, a hall of *judgment*; "Be not fainthearted when thou sittest in *judgment*," Ecclus. iv. 9); hence, the final trial of all mankind, both the living and the dead, at the end of the world (often, 'Last Judgment'); also, the judicial decision of a cause in court; a decision, decree, or sentence given by a judge; hence, the obligation, esp. a debt, arising from a judicial decision; the certificate embodying such a decision; also, a divine decree or sentence (as, "I will utter my *judgments* against them . . . who have forsaken me": Jer. i. 16); hence, a misfortune regarded as inflicted by divine sentence, as for sin; also, justice or righteousness (archaic: as, "Learn to do well; seek *judgment*, relieve the oppressed," Isa. i. 17); also, the act of judging as an arbiter or umpire (as, the *judgment* of Paris, who awarded the golden apple to Aphrodite: see *apple of discord*, under *apple*); also, the pronouncing of an opinion upon a person or thing; criticism; an opinion pronounced (as, "Where blind and naked Ignorance Delivers brawling *judgments*, unashamed, On all things all day long": Tennyson's "Merlin and Vivien," 663); also, the forming of an opinion, estimate, notion, or conclusion, as from circumstances presented to the mind (as, "To judge rightly of the present, we must oppose it to the past; for all *judgment* is comparative": Johnson's "Rasselas," xxx.); an opinion, estimate, or the like, formed (as, hasty *judgments* are often erroneous); one's opinion, view, or way of thinking (as, in my *judgment* this is unwise); also, the faculty of judging; ability to form opinions, or to discern circumstances and draw conclusions (as, "My salad days, When I I was green in *judgement*": Shakspere's "Antony and Cleopatra," i. 5. 74); often, ability to judge justly or wisely, esp. in matters affecting action (as, men of *judgment*; a task requiring *judgment* rather than learning); good sense; discretion; in *logic*, a mental affirmation or assertion.—**judg′ment=day,** *n.* The day of God's final judgment of mankind at the end of the world; doomsday.

ju-di-ca-to-ry (jö′di-kạ-tō-ri). [LL. *judicatorius* (as n., *judicatorium*), < L. *judicare*, E. *judge*, *v.*] **I.** *a.* Of or pertaining to judgment or the administration of justice: as, *judicatory* power; a *judicatory* tribunal. **II.** *n.*; pl. *-ries* (-riz). A court of justice; a tribunal; also, the administration of justice.

ju-di-ca-ture (jö′di-kạ-tūr), *n.* [ML. *judicatura*, < L. *judicare*, E. *judge*, *v.*] The administration of justice, as by judges or courts; also, the office, function, or authority of a judge; also, the extent of jurisdiction of a judge or court; also, a body of judges; a judicatory.

ju-di-cial (jö-dish′ạl), *a.* [L. *judicialis*, < *judicium*, judgment, decision, opinion, court of justice, < *judex*, E. *judge*, *n.*] Pertaining to judgment in courts of justice or to the administration of justice (as, *judicial* proceedings; a *judicial* tribunal); pertaining to courts of law or to judges (as, *judicial* functions); decreed, sanctioned, or enforced by a court (as, a *judicial* sale; a *judicial* separation; *judicial* law, as opposed to moral law); also, inflicted by God as a judgment or punishment (as, "The government was under an infatuation such as, in a more simple age, would have been called *judicial*": Macaulay's "Hist. of Eng.," viii.); also, appropriate for or suggestive of a judge (as, a *judicial* mind; *judicial* gravity; a *judicial* attitude or manner); also, pertaining to judgment or decision in a dispute or contest (as, a *judicial* duel or combat, as in the middle ages); also, pertaining to judging of matters in doubt (as, *judicial* astrology, astrology as concerned with judging of the influence of the heavenly bodies on human affairs).—**ju-di′cial-ly,** *adv.*

ju-di-ci-a-ry (jö-dish′i-ā-ri). [L. *judiciarius*, < *judicium*: see *judicial*.] **I.** *a.* Pertaining to judgment in courts of justice, or to courts or judges; judicial. **II.** *n.*; pl. *-ries* (-riz). The judicial branch of government; the system of courts of justice in a country; the judges collectively.

ju-di-cious (jö-dish′us), *a.* [F. *judicieux*, < L. *judicium*: see *judicial*.] Having, exercising, or showing good judgment (as, a *judicious* historian; a *judicious* selection; "A tale should be *judicious*, clear, succinct," Cowper's "Conversation," 235); wise, sensible, or well-advised; esp., using or showing judgment as to action or practical expediency (as, "He did not answer immediately, for he had to be *judicious* and not truthful": George Eliot's "Adam Bede," xxviii.); discreet, prudent, or politic; also, judicial† (as, "His last offences to us Shall have *judicious* hearing": Shakspere's "Coriolanus," v. 6. 128).—**ju-di′cious-ly,** *adv.*—**ju-di′cious-ness,** *n.*

Ju-dy (jö′di), *n.* [For *Judith*.] The wife of Punch in the puppet-show called "Punch and Judy." See *Punch*[2].

jug[1] (jug), *n.* [Perhaps < *Jug*, for *Joan*, or *Joanna*, woman's name.] A vessel in various forms for holding liquids, commonly having a handle, often a spout or lip, and sometimes a lid; a pitcher; also, a deep vessel, usually of earthenware, with a handle and a narrow neck stopped by a cork (U. S.); also, the contents of any such vessel (as, "a *jug* of warm water": Dickens's "Dombey and Son," v.); also, a prison or jail (slang: as, "They sentenced me . . . to ten years in the *Jug*," Lowell's "Biglow Papers," ii. 1. 110).—**jug**[1], *v. t.*; *jugged, jugging.* To put into a jug; cook (a hare, etc.) in a jug or jar set in boiling water; also, to commit to jail, or imprison (slang: as, "He was the justice of the peace that *jugged* me for a vagrant," Mark Twain's "Tom Sawyer," xxix.).

Hound-handle Jug, of about 1850 (from Bennington, Vermont). — Pennsylvania Museum, Philadelphia.

jug[2] (jug), *v. i.*; *jugged, jugging.* [Prob. var. of *jouk*[1].] To nestle together, as partridges; collect in a covey.

jug[3] (jug), *n.* [Imit.] A sound uttered by the nightingale and some other birds.—**jug**[3], *v. i.*; *jugged, jugging.* To utter the sound 'jug.'

ju-gal (jö′gạl), *a.* [L. *jugalis*, < *jugum*, a yoke.] Of or pertaining to the bony arch of the cheek: as, the *jugal* bone (the cheek-bone, or principal bone of the cheek, in man; a corresponding bone in animals).

ju-gate (jö′gāt), *a.* [L. *jugatus*, pp. of *jugare*, join, < *jugum*, a yoke.] In *bot.*, having the leaflets in pairs, as a pinnate leaf.

jug-ful (jug′fůl), *n.*; pl. *-fuls.* A quantity sufficient to fill a jug.

Jug-ger-naut (jug′ėr-nât), *n.* [Hind. *Jagannāth*, < Skt. *Jagannātha*, 'lord of the world.'] A title of the Hindu deity Krishna, the eighth incarnation of Vishnu; also, an idol of this deity, at Puri in Orissa, India, annually drawn on an enormous car under whose wheels devotees are said to have thrown themselves to be crushed; hence, anything to which a person blindly devotes himself, or is cruelly sacrificed.

jug-gins (jug′inz), *n.* [Appar. < *Juggins*, proper name.] A simpleton; one easily imposed upon. [Slang, Eng.]

jug-gle (jug′l), *v.*; *-gled, -gling.* [OF. *jogler, jugler*, < L. *joculari*, to jest, joke, < *joculus*, dim. of *jocus*, E. *joke.*] **I.** *intr.* To act as a jester†; also, to perform tricks, as by sleight of hand; practise legerdemain; conjure; also, to perform feats of manual or bodily dexterity, such as tossing up and keeping in continuous motion a number of balls, plates, knives, etc.; also, to use artifice or trickery (as, "She never *juggles* or plays tricks with her understanding": Lamb's "Mackery End"). **II.** *tr.* To trick by or as by legerdemain or conjuring; also, to perform conjuring tricks with; perform juggling feats with (balls, knives, etc.); also, to manipulate by artifice or trickery (as, to *juggle* accounts).—**jug′gle,** *n.* An act of juggling; a trick; a deception: as, "Am I to be overawed By what I cannot but know Is a *juggle* born of the brain?" (Tennyson's "Maud," ii. 2. 5); "The Opposition . . . declared the whole transaction to be a mere *juggle*" (Lecky's "Hist. of Eng. in the 18th Century," xxxii.).—**jug′gler,** *n.* [OF. *jogleor* (F. *jongleur*), < L. *joculator*, jester, < *joculari*: cf. *jongleur.*] A jester† or buffoon†; also, a performer of legerdemain; a conjurer; also, one who performs juggling feats, as with balls, knives, etc.; also, one who deceives by trickery; a trickster.—**jug′gler-y,** *n.*; pl. *-ies* (-iz). [OF. *juglerie.*] The art or practice of a juggler; legerdemain; the performance of juggling feats; any trickery or deception.

ju-glan-da-ceous (jö-glan-dā′shius), *a.* [L. *juglans* (*jugland-*), walnut.] Belonging to the *Juglandaceæ*, or walnut family of trees.

Ju-go-slav (yö′gọ-släv or -slav). [Slav. *jug*, south.] **I.** *n.* A southern Slav; a member of the southern group of Slavic peoples (the Serbs, Croats, Slavonians, Slovenes, etc., with or without the Bulgars), as distinguished from the western group (the Poles, Czechs, Slovaks, etc.) and the eastern (the Russians, with the Ruthenians). **II.** *a.* Of or pertaining to the Jugoslavs.—**Ju-go-slav′ic,** *a.*

ju-gu-lar (jö′gū-lạ̈r or jug′ụ̄-). [NL. *jugularis*, < L. *jugulum*, collar-bone, throat, dim. of *jugum*, a yoke.] **I.** *a.* In *anat.*, of or pertaining to the throat or neck; esp., noting or pertaining to any of certain large veins of the neck, esp. one ('external jugular vein') collecting blood from the superficial parts of the head, or one ('internal jugular vein') receiving blood from within the skull; in *ichth.*, of a fish, having the ventral fins at the throat, in advance of the pectoral fins; also, noting a ventral fin so situated. **II.** *n.* In *anat.*, a jugular vein.

ju-gu-late (jö′gū-lāt or jug′ụ̄-), *v. t.*; *-lated, -lating.* [L. *jugulatus*, pp. of *jugulare*, < *jugulum*, throat: see *jugular.*] To cut the throat of; kill; fig., to check or suppress (disease, etc.) by extreme measures.—**ju-gu-la′tion** (-lā′shọn), *n.*

juice (jös), *n.* [OF. F. *jus*, < L. *jus*, broth, juice.] The liquid part of plant or animal substance; also, any of the liquid constituents of the body (often in *pl.*); also, any extracted liquid; also, electrical fluid (slang); also, gasoline (slang).—**juiced,** *a.* Having juice.—**juice′less,** *a.* Lacking juice; dry. Also fig.—**jui-cy** (jö′si), *a.*; compar. *juicier*, superl. *juiciest.* Full of juice; succulent. Also fig.—**jui′ci-ness,** *n.*

ju-ju (jö′jö), *n.*; pl. *jujus* (-jöz). [W. Afr.: cf. F. *joujou*, plaything.] Among native tribes of western Africa, some object venerated superstitiously and used as a fetish or amulet; the magical power attributed to such an object; a ban or interdiction effected by it; also, jujuism.

ju-jube (jö′jöb), *n.* [F. *jujube*, < L. *zizyphum*, < Gr. ζίζυφον.] The edible berry-like fruit of any of certain old-world trees of the genus *Zizyphus*; also, a gummy paste made of gum arabic or gelatin sweetened and flavored, orig. combined with the juice of the jujube fruit ('jujube paste'); a lozenge made of this paste; also, any of these trees.

ju-ju-ism (jö′jö-ism), *n.* The system of beliefs and observances connected with jujus.—**ju′ju-ist,** *n.*

ju=jut′su, *n.* See *jiu-jutsu.*

ju-lep (jö′lep), *n.* [OF. F. *julep*, < Ar. *julāb*, < Pers. *gulāb*, rose-water, julep.] A sweet drink, variously prepared and sometimes medicated; also, a beverage made of brandy or whisky, sugar, crushed ice, and sprigs of fresh mint ('mint julep').

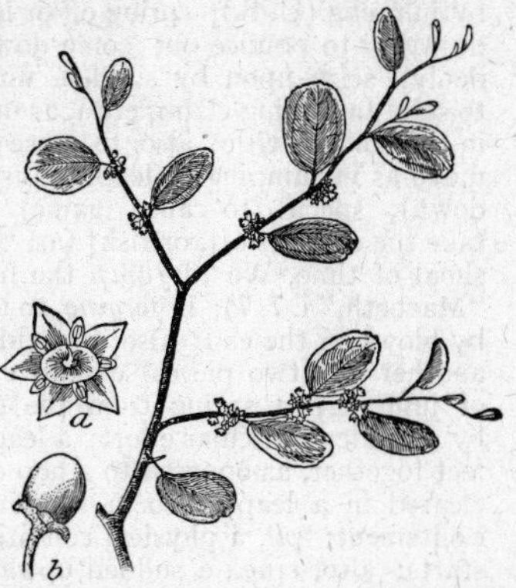

Flowering Branch of Jujube-tree (*Zizyphus jujuba*). — *a*, flower; *b*, fruit.

Ju-lian (jö′lyạn), *a.* Pertaining to or derived from Julius Cæsar: as, the *Julian* calendar (which fixed the average length of the year at 365¼ days: see *Old Style*, at *style*, *n.*, and cf. *Gregorian calendar*, under *Gregorian*).

ju-li-enne (jö-li-en′, F. zhü-lyen), *n.* [F., < *Jules*, or *Julien*, proper name.] A clear soup containing vegetables cut into thin strips or small pieces.

Ju-ly (jọ̈-lī′), *n.* [L. *Julius*; named from *Julius* Cæsar, who was born in this month.] The seventh month of the year, containing 31 days.

jum-ble (jum′bl), *v.*; *-bled, -bling.* [Perhaps imit.] **I.** *intr.* To move in a confused or disorderly way; flounder; stumble; also, to move or travel with jolting (as, "Trotting Nelly . . . *jumbled* off with her cart": Scott's "St. Ronan's Well," v.); also, to make a confused noise†. **II.** *tr.* To mix or throw together in confusion (as, "Things spiritual and things temporal are strangely *jumbled* together": Irving's "Knickerbocker's New York," v. 7); also, to shake up or jolt (as, "The coach *jumbled* us insensibly into some sort of familiarity": Steele, in "Spectator," 132); also, to muddle or confuse mentally.—**jum′ble,** *n.* A confused mixture; a medley; a state of confusion or disorder; also, a jolt or jolting; also, a small, flat, sweet cake, now commonly round, with a small hole in the middle.—**jum′ble-ment,** *n.*—**jum′bler,** *n.*

jum-bo (jum′bō), *n.*; pl. *-bos* (-bōz). [Cf. *mumbo-jumbo.*] A big, clumsy person, animal, or thing; something unusually large of its kind: in later use commonly with allusion to *Jumbo*, a large elephant exhibited 1882–85 by P. T. Barnum. —**jum′bo-ism,** *n.* Striving for bigness or mammoth proportions, as in productions or enterprises.

jump[1] (jump), *v.* [Appar. imit.] **I.** *intr.* To spring clear of the ground or other support by a sudden muscular effort; throw one's self in any direction, from the ground or other support; leap; specif., to leap with the feet together, as opposed to hopping on one foot; also, to move or go suddenly or abruptly, as with a leap (as, "I *jumped* hastily from my bed": Lever's "Harry Lorrequer," i.); also, to start, as from nervous excitement (as, "You made me *jump*, Charley": Dickens's "Our Mutual Friend," i. 6); also, to be thrown up or moved with a sudden jerk, as an inanimate object; also, fig., to rise suddenly in amount, price, etc.; pass abruptly as if by a leap (as, to *jump* to, or at, a conclusion); also, to agree, tally, or coincide (as, "For all men live and judge amiss, Whose talents *jump* not just with his": Butler's "Hudibras," i. 3); also, in the game of checkers, to jump an opponent's piece. **II.** *tr.* To pass over by a leap (as, to *jump* a stream); leap over; specif., in the game of checkers, to pass a man over (an opponent's piece) to a vacant square beyond it, thus capturing the piece; also, fig., to skip or pass over (as, "They *jumped* the Greek and Latin, and read law, medicine, or sermons, without it": Emerson's "New England Reformers"); abscond from, or evade by absconding (slang: as, to *jump* one's bail; to

(variable) ḍ as d or j, ș as s or sh, ț as t or ch, ẓ as z or zh; *o*, F. cloche; ü, F. menu; ċh, Sc. loch; ṅ, F. bonbon; ′, primary accent; ″, secondary accent; †, obsolete; <, from; +, and; =, equals. See also lists at beginning of book.

jump one's hotel bill); also, to get on or off (a train, etc.) by jumping (U. S.); spring off or leave (the track), as trains do; also, to pounce on; come down upon violently or suddenly; seize upon by sudden, unexpected action; specif., to seize (a mining claim, etc.), as on the ground of some flaw in the holder's title; also, to cause to jump or leap; cause to move as in jumping or leaping (as, to *jump* a child up and down); specif., to cause (game) to break cover; also, to take the chances of†, or risk† (as, "Here, upon this bank and shoal of time, We 'ld *jump* the life to come": Shakspere's "Macbeth," i. 7. 7); in *forging*, to upset or shape (a bar, etc.) by blows on the end; also, to weld (one piece) to the end of another, or (two pieces) end to end.—**jump[1]**, *n.* An act of jumping; a spring from the ground or other support by a sudden muscular effort; a leap; specif., a leap with the feet together, as opposed to a hop on one foot; also, a space cleared in a leap; also, a sudden start, as from nervous excitement; *pl.*, a physical condition characterized by such starts; also, *sing.*, a sudden upward or other movement of an inanimate object; also, fig., a sudden rise in amount, price, etc.; an abrupt change of level, as in building; a fault in a stratum or mineral vein; also, an abrupt transition from one point or thing to another, with omission of what intervenes (as, "Their nimble nonsense . . . gains remote conclusions at a *jump*": Cowper's "Conversation," 154); an interval or gap involving such a transition; also, a venture† or hazard† (as, "Our fortune lies Upon this *jump*": Shakspere's "Antony and Cleopatra," iii. 8. 6).—**jump[1]**†, *adv.* In exact agreement; exactly: as, "Thus twice before, and *jump* at this dead hour, With martial stalk hath he gone by our watch" (Shakspere's "Hamlet," i. 1. 65).

jump[2] (jump), *n.* [Perhaps var. of obs. *jup,* = *jupe.*] A kind of jacket worn by men; also, *pl.*, a kind of loose or easy stays worn by women. [Now prov. Eng. and Sc.]

jump-er[1] (jum'pėr), *n.* One who or that which jumps; a member of some sect practising leaping or dancing as a part of religious worship; an animal which progresses by jumping, as a maggot found in cheese; a tool or device working with a jumping motion; a kind of sled.

jump-er[2] (jum'pėr), *n.* [Cf. *jump[2]*.] A kind of loose outer jacket worn esp. by workmen and sailors (as, "clad in a loose duck '*jumper*' and trousers streaked and splashed with red soil": Bret Harte's "Tennessee's Partner"); also, a kind of sleeveless or short-sleeved overbodice worn by women.

jump-i-ness (jum'pi-nes), *n.* Jumpy condition.

jump-ing (jum'ping), *p. a.* That jumps; leaping.—**jump'-ing=bean,** *n.* The seed of any of certain Mexican euphorbiaceous plants (genus *Sebastiania*, etc.), which is inhabited by the larva of a small tortricid moth whose movements cause the seed to move about or jump.—**jump'-ing=hare,** *n.* A jerboa-like South African rodent, *Pedetes caffer*, having long, strong hind legs with which it can take long leaps (sometimes of 20 feet).—**jump'ing=jack,** *n.* A toy consisting of a jointed figure of a man which is made to jump, or go through various contortions, as by pulling a string attached to its limbs.—**jump'ing=mouse,** *n.* The deer-mouse, *Zapus hudsonius*.—**jump'ing=seed,** *n.* The jumping-bean.

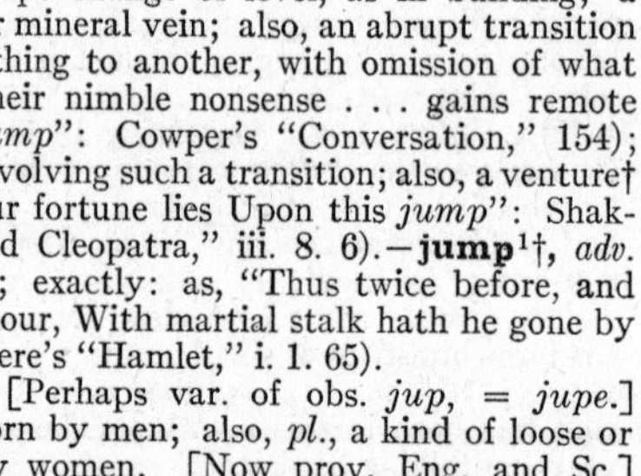

Jumping-hare.

Jumping-mouse, or Deer-mouse (*Zapus hudsonius*).

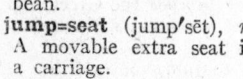

jump=seat (jump'sēt), *n.* A movable extra seat in a carriage.

jump=spark (jump'spärk), *n.* An electric spark which jumps a gap in a previously open circuit: frequently used for igniting the charge in an internal-combustion engine.

jump-y (jum'pi), *a.* Characterized by jumps or sudden, abrupt movements or transitions; also, characterized by or inclined to sudden, involuntary starts, as from nervousness (as, "You aren't at all well . . . You're as *jumpy* as a cat": Kipling's "Light That Failed," xi.); causing such starts.

jun-ca-ceous (jung-kā'shius), *a.* [L. *juncus*, a rush.] Belonging to the *Juncaceæ*, or rush family of plants.

jun-co (jung'kō), *n.*; pl. *-cos* (-kōz). [Sp. *junco*, a rush, < L. *juncus*, a rush.] The reed-bunting†; also, any finch of the North American genus *Junco*; a snowbird.

junc-tion (jungk'shọn), *n.* [L. *junctio(n-)*, < *jungere*, join: see *join.*] The act of joining, or the state of being joined; union; combination; also, a place of joining or meeting; specif., a place or station where railroad-lines meet or cross.—**junc'tion-al,** *a.* Pertaining to or of the nature of a junction.

junc-ture (jungk'ṭūr), *n.* [L. *junctura*, < *jungere*, join: see *join*, and cf. *jointure.*] The act of joining, or the state of being joined; junction; also, a point or line of junction; something by which two things are joined; also, a particular combination of circumstances or affairs; a conjuncture; esp., a critical state of affairs; a crisis; a critical moment.

June (jön), *n.* [L. *Junius*; named from the *Junius* gens of Rome.] The sixth month of the year, containing 30 days.—**June'=bee"tle,** *n.* The June-bug.—**June'=ber"ry,** *n.* The American service-berry.—**June'=bug,** *n.* In the northern U. S., any of various large brown beetles, esp. of the genus *Lachnosterna*, which appear about June; in the southern U. S., a large greenish beetle, *Allorhina nitida*.

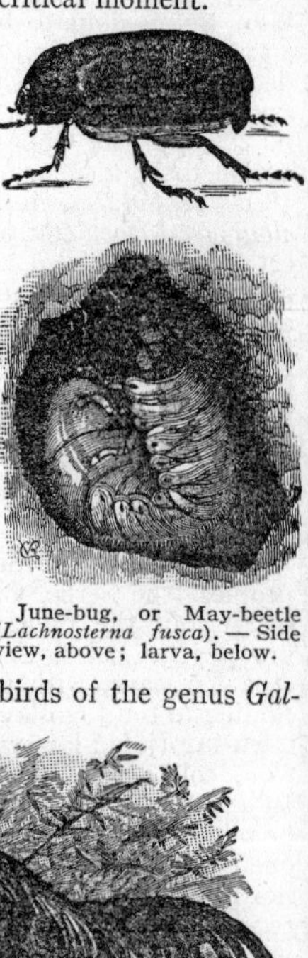

June-bug, or May-beetle (*Lachnosterna fusca*). — Side view, above; larva, below.

jun-gle (jung'gl), *n.* [Hind. *jangal*, < Skt. *jangala*, dry, desert.] Wild land overgrown with dense, rank vegetation, often nearly impenetrable, as in parts of India; a tract of such land; also, a dense growth of rank vegetation.—**jun'gled,** *a.* Covered with jungle or dense, rank vegetation.—**jun'gle=fowl,** *n.* Any of various East Indian gallinaceous birds of the genus *Gallus*, certain species of which are supposed to have given rise to the domestic fowl.—**jun'gly,** *a.* Characterized by jungle; jungle-like.

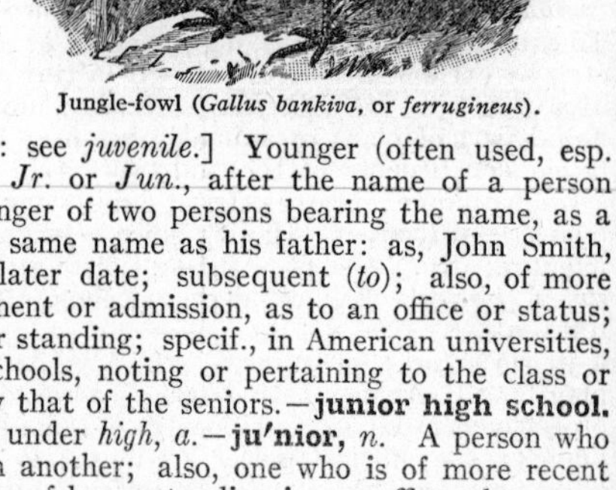

Jungle-fowl (*Gallus bankiva*, or *ferrugineus*).

ju-nior (jö'nyọr), *a.* [L. *junior*, contr. of *juvenior*, compar. of *juvenis*, young: see *juvenile.*] Younger (often used, esp. as abbreviated *Jr.* or *Jun.*, after the name of a person who is the younger of two persons bearing the name, as a son having the same name as his father: as, John Smith, *Jr.*); also, of later date; subsequent (*to*); also, of more recent appointment or admission, as to an office or status; of lower rank or standing; specif., in American universities, colleges, and schools, noting or pertaining to the class or year next below that of the seniors.—**junior high school.** See *high school*, under *high, a.*—**ju'nior,** *n.* A person who is younger than another; also, one who is of more recent entrance into, or of lower standing in, an office, class, profession, etc.; one employed as the subordinate of another; also, a member of the junior class in a university, college, or school.—**ju-nior-i-ty** (jö-nyor'i-ti), *n.* The state or fact of being junior; subsequence in birth; lesser age; later standing; lower rank.

ju-ni-per (jö'ni-pėr), *n.* [L. *juniperus*: cf. *geneva* and *gin*[3].] Any of the pinaceous evergreen shrubs or trees constituting the genus *Juniperus*, esp. *J. communis*, whose purple berries are used in making gin, or *J. virginiana*, a North American species (the 'red cedar': see *cedar*); also, any of various other trees, as the white cedar, *Chamæcyparis thyoides*; also, a tree mentioned in the Bible (see 1 Kings, xix. 4).

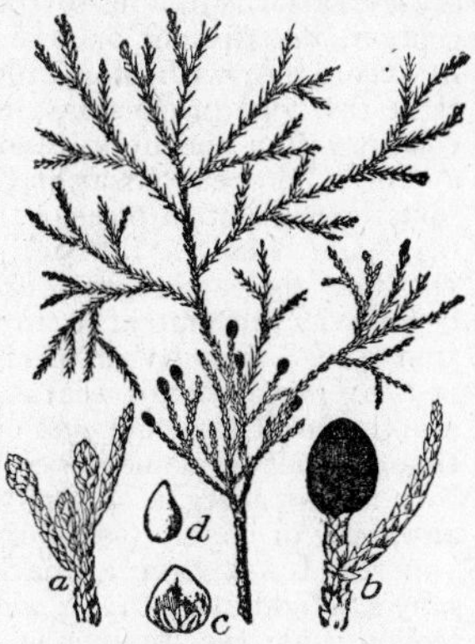

Juniper (*Junĭperus virginiana*). — *a*, branch with male flowers; *b*, branch with fruit; *c*, scale of male flower with two anthers; *d*, seed.

junk[1] (jungk), *n.* [Origin uncertain: cf. ME. *jonke*, < OF. *jonc*, < L. *juncus*, a rush.] Old cable or cordage used for making gaskets, swabs, oakum, etc. (as, "The owners of a vessel buy up incredible quantities of 'old *junk*,' which the sailors unlay": Dana's "Two Years before the Mast," iii.); also, any old or discarded material, as metal, paper, rags, etc.; hence, in general, anything that is regarded as worthless or mere trash (colloq.); also, hard salt meat used for food on shipboard.—**junk**[1], *v. t.* To cast aside as junk; hence, in general, to discard as no longer of use. [Colloq.]

junk[2] (jungk), *n.* [Pg. *junco*, < Malay *jong*.] A kind of large boat used in Chinese and other waters, having lug-sails, a high stern, and usually a flat bottom.

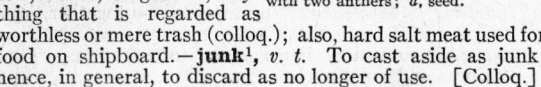

A Canton Trading-junk.

junk[3] (jungk), *n.* Same as *chunk*.

jun-ker (yùng'kėr), *n.* [G., < MHG. *junc herre*, young gentleman: cf. *younker*.] A young German noble; often, in disparagement, a narrow-minded, haughty, overbearing, esp. younger, member of the aristocracy of Prussia, etc.; specif. [*cap.*], a member of a reactionary aristocratic party in Prussia strongly devoted to maintaining the social and political privileges of their class.—**jun'ker-dom** (-dǫm), *n.* [Also *cap.*] The condition or character of a junker; the spirit or policy of the junkers; also, the body of junkers.—**jun'ker-ish,** *a.* [Also *cap.*] Pertaining to, characteristic of, or resembling the junkers.—**jun'ker-ism,** *n.* [Also *cap.*] The spirit or policy of the junkers.

jun-ket (jung'ket), *n.* [ME. *jonket*, basket made of rushes, *joncate*, curded food made in a vessel of rushes; ult. < L. *juncus*, a rush.] A basket, esp. for catching fish (now prov. Eng.); also, a food preparation of curded cream or milk; esp., a dish made of milk curdled with rennet or the like, and sweetened and flavored; also, any delicate, dainty, or sweet dish† (as, "With stories told of many a feat, How faery Mab the *junkets* eat": Milton's "L'Allegro," 102); also, a feast or merrymaking; a picnic; a pleasure excursion (in the U. S., often applied to a trip made ostensibly for official business, enjoyed at the public expense).—**jun'ket,** *v. i.* To feast; picnic; go on a junket or pleasure excursion.—**jun'ket-er,** *n.*

junk-man (jungk'mạn), *n.*; pl. *-men.* A dealer in junk, or old metal, paper, rags, etc.

junk=shop (jungk'shop), *n.* The shop or place of business of a junkman.

Ju-no (jö'nō), *n.*; pl. *-nos* (-nōz). [L.] An ancient Roman goddess, the wife of Jupiter, presiding over marriage and women (cf. *Hera*); also, a woman of imposing figure or appearance (as, "yon *Juno* of majestic size": Pope's "Dunciad," ii. 163).—**Ju-no-esque'** (-esk'), *a.* [See *-esque*.] Juno-like; stately or imposing (with reference to women).

Juno of Lanuvium. — Colossal statue in the Vatican Museum, Rome.

jun-ta (jun'tạ), *n.* [Sp., < L. *juncta*, fem. of *junctus*, pp. of *jungere*, join: see *join*.] A deliberative or administrative council, esp. in Spain; also, a junto (as, "There, then, were Madame Walravens, Madame Beck, Père Silas . . . the secret *junta*": C. Brontë's "Villette," xxxviii.).

jun-to (jun'tō), *n.*; pl. *-tos* (-tōz). [Erron. form of *junta*.] A self-appointed council or committee, esp. with political aims; a coterie of partizans or intriguers; a cabal or faction: as, "There was believed to be often a secret *junto* which really controlled the ministry" (Bryce's "American Commonwealth," xxv.); "At the corners are assembled *juntos* of village idlers and wise men" (Irving's "Sketch-Book," The Stage-Coach).

jupe (jöp, F. zhüp), *n.* [OF. F. *jupe*, < Ar. *jubbah*: see *jubbah*.] A kind of jacket or tunic worn by men†; a kind of jacket, bodice, or, *pl.*, loose stays, worn by women (obs. or Sc.); also, a woman's skirt (a modern use, from French: as, "a Norman nurse, with a high cap and a red *jupe*," Lever's "Harry Lorrequer," xlv.).

Ju-pi-ter (jö'pi-tėr), *n.* [L. *Jupiter*, *Juppiter*, for *Jovis pater*, 'Jove father,' 'father Jove': see *Jove*.] The supreme deity of the ancient Romans, the god of the heavens, known also as *Jove* (cf. *Zeus*); also, the largest of the major planets, being the fifth in order from the sun.

ju-pon (jö'pon or jǫ-pon'), *n.* [OF. *jupon*, *gippon*, < *jupe*: see *jupe*.] Orig., a close-fitting tunic or doublet for men, esp. one of heavy material, sometimes padded, worn under the hauberk; later, a surcoat worn over the armor.

ju-ral (jö'rạl), *a.* [L. *jus* (*jur-*), right, law.] Pertaining to law; legal; also, pertaining to rights and obligations.—**ju'ral-ly,** *adv.*

ju-ra-men-ta-do (hö"rä-men-tä'ᴛʜō), *n.*; pl. *-dos* (-ᴛʜōs). [Sp., pp. of *juramentar*, bind by oath, < *juramento*, < L. *juramentum*, oath, < *jurare*, swear: see *jurat*[1].] In the Philippines, a Moro or Mohammedan Malay who has taken an oath that he will die in killing enemies, esp. Christians.

ju-rant (jö'rạnt). [L. *jurans* (*jurant-*), ppr. of *jurare*, swear: see *jurat*[1].] **I.** *a.* Swearing; taking an oath. **II.** *n.* One who swears, or takes an oath.

Ju-ras-sic (jǫ-ras'ik). [F. *jurassique*; named from the *Jura* Mountains.] **I.** *a.* Noting or pertaining to a geological period or a system of rocks which precedes the Cretaceous and is characterized by the prevalence of a limestone common in the Jura Mountains. **II.** *n.* The Jurassic period or system.

ju-rat[1] (jö'rat, F. zhü-rä), *n.* [= F. *jurat*, < ML. *juratus*, lit. 'one sworn,' prop. pp. of L. *jurare*, swear, < *jus* (*jur-*), right, law.] One who has taken an oath (obs. or hist.); also, any of various public officials, as a municipal officer similar to an alderman in certain English towns, or one of a body of magistrates in the Channel Islands.

ju-rat[2] (jö'rat), *n.* [L. *juratum*, pp. neut. of *jurare*, swear: see *jurat*[1].] In *law*, a memorandum on an affidavit, showing when and before whom it was sworn to.

ju-rel (hǫ-rel'), *n.* [Sp.] Any of certain carangoid food-fishes of the genus *Carangus*, as *C. latus*, a species of the West Indies, etc.

ju-rid-ic, ju-rid-i-cal (jǫ-rid'ik, -i-kạl), *a.* [L. *juridicus*, <

jus (*jur-*), right, law, + *dicere*, say.] Of or pertaining to the administration of justice; also, of or pertaining to law or jurisprudence; legal.—**ju-rid′i-cal-ly,** *adv.*

ju-ris-con-sult (jö-ris-kon′sult or jö″ris-kọn-sult′), *n.* [L. *jurisconsultus*, < *juris*, gen. of *jus*, right, law, + *consultus*, skilled, pp. of *consulere*, take counsel: see *consult*.] One versed in law or jurisprudence; a jurist; esp., a master of the civil law.

ju-ris-dic-tion (jö-ris-dik′shọn), *n.* [L. *jurisdictio(n-)*, < *juris*, gen. of *jus*, right, law, + *dictio(n-)*, saying: see *diction*.] The right or power of administering law or justice; judicial authority; also, power or authority in general (as, "To live exempt From heaven's high *jurisdiction*": Milton's "Paradise Lost," ii. 319); rule; control; also, the extent or range of judicial or other authority; the territory over which authority is exercised; also, a judicial organization; a court, or system of courts, of justice (as, "By law the person of the king is sacred . . . no *jurisdiction* upon earth has power to try him in a criminal way": Blackstone's "Commentaries," I. 242).—**ju-ris-dic′tion-al,** *a.* Of or pertaining to jurisdiction.—**ju-ris-dic′tion-al-ly,** *adv.*

ju-ris-pru-dence (jö-ris-prö′dẹns), *n.* [L. *jurisprudentia*, < *juris*, gen. of *jus*, right, law, + *prudentia*, foreseeing, knowledge, E. *prudence*.] Knowledge of or skill in law; hence, the science or philosophy of law; also, a body or system of laws (as, Scottish *jurisprudence*); a department of law (as, medical *jurisprudence*: see under *medical*).—**ju-ris-pru′dent. I.** *a.* Versed in jurisprudence: as, "the eulogy of Cicero on Scævola, that he was the most *jurisprudent* of orators, and the most eloquent of lawyers" (Hallam's "Literature of Europe," i. 7. § 50). **II.** *n.* One versed in jurisprudence.—**ju″ris-pru-den′tial** (-prö-den′shạl), *a.* Pertaining to jurisprudence.

ju-rist (jö′rist), *n.* [OF. F. *juriste*, < ML. *jurista*, < L. *jus* (*jur-*), right, law.] One versed in law or jurisprudence, esp. in the civil law; a writer on law.—**ju-ris-tic** (jö-ris′tik), *a.* Of or pertaining to jurists or jurisprudence. Also **ju-ris′ti-cal.**—**ju-ris′ti-cal-ly,** *adv.*

ju-ror (jö′rọr), *n.* [AF. *jurour*, OF. *jureor*, < L. *jurator*, swearer, < *jurare*, swear: see *jurat*[1].] One of a body of persons sworn to deliver a verdict in a case submitted to them; a member of any jury; also, one of the panel from which a jury is selected; also, one who has taken an oath, or who has sworn allegiance (cf. *nonjuror*).

ju-ry (jö′ri), *n.*; pl. *-ries* (-riz). [AF. *juree*, jury (in OF. oath, judicial inquiry), < ML. *jurata*, orig. pp. fem. of L. *jurare*, swear: see *jurat*[1].] A body of persons sworn to render a verdict or true answer on a question or questions officially submitted to them; esp., such a body selected according to law and sworn to inquire into or determine the facts concerning a cause or an accusation submitted to them, and to render a verdict according to the evidence adduced; also, a body of persons chosen to adjudge prizes, etc., as in a competition.—**grand jury,** a jury of from 12 to 23 persons designated to inquire into alleged violations of law, in order to ascertain whether the evidence is sufficient to warrant trial by a petty jury.—**petty, petit,** or **trial jury,** a jury, usually of 12 persons, formed for the trial of an issue of fact in a civil or criminal action.—**ju′ry-man** (-mạn), *n.*; pl. *-men.* A member of a jury; a juror.

ju-ry=mast (jö′ri-màst), *n.* [With *jury-* of uncertain origin.] *Naut.*, a temporary mast replacing one that has been broken or carried away: as, "She [a vessel] had two *jury-masts* rigged, assistance having been sent from the other vessels" (Cooper's "Two Admirals," xxv.).—**ju′ry=rig,** *n.* *Naut.*, a temporary rig on a ship.—**ju′ry=rigged,** *a.*

ju-ry-wom-an (jö′ri-wům″ạn), *n.*; pl. *-women* (-wim″en). A female member of a jury.

jus-sive (jus′iv). [L. *jussus*, pp. of *jubere*, bid, command.] In *gram.*: **I.** *a.* Expressing a command. **II.** *n.* A jussive form or construction.

just[1] (just), *a.* [OF. F. *juste*, < L. *justus*, < *jus*, right, law.] Conforming or conformed to what is morally right, or righteous (esp. in Biblical use: as, "The *just* man walketh in his integrity," Prov. xx. 7; "Whatsoever things are *just*, whatsoever things are pure . . . think on these things," Phil. iv. 8); also, equitable or fair, as in dealing, action, or effect (as, to be *just* with others; a *just* apportionment; "O *just* but severe law!" Shakspere's "Measure for Measure," ii. 2. 41); deciding or decreeing rightly, as a judge; given or awarded rightly, or deserved, as a sentence, punishment, reward, etc.; also, based on right, rightful, or lawful (as, a *just* claim or title; "our *just* inheritance," Milton's "Paradise Lost," ii. 38); also, having good grounds, or well-founded (as, *just* pride; *just* complaints or fears; *just* cause); also, agreeable to truth or fact (as, a *just* conception, description, or statement); true or correct; also, in accordance with standards or requirements, proper, or right (as, *just* proportions; in *just* order; "When the ripe colours soften and unite, And sweetly melt into *just* shade and light," Pope's "Essay on Criticism," 489); due or fitting; sometimes, right in measure, weight, amount, etc., or exact (as, "*Just* balances, *just* weights . . . shall ye have": Lev. xix. 36); also, actual, real, or true (as, "Force not my drift beyond its *just* intent": Cowper's "Tirocinium," 505).—**just**[1], *adv.* Exactly or precisely (as, *just* here; *just* then; *just* so; *just* a pound; that is *just* the point); hence, almost exactly (as, I saw him *just* now); within a brief preceding time, or but a moment before (as, they have *just* gone); by a narrow margin, or barely (as, it *just* missed the mark); also, only or merely (as, he is *just* an ordinary man; "Well, you see, I *just* have a knack of foreseeing things," Dunsany's "Night at an Inn"); also, actually, truly, or positively (colloq.: as, the weather is *just* glorious; I *just* couldn't refuse).

just[2], **joust** (just, just or jöst), *v. i.* [OF. *juster*, *jouster* (F. *jouter*), < ML. *juxtare*, approach, come together, < L. *juxta*, near.] To join battle, esp. on horseback, as men-at-arms†; also, to contend in a just or tournament (as, "There are princes and knights come from all parts of the world to *just* and tourney for her love": Shakspere's "Pericles," ii. 1. 116); tilt.—**just**[2], **joust,** *n.* [OF. *juste*, *jouste* (F. *joute*).] A combat in which two armored knights or men-at-arms on horseback opposed each other with lances; esp., such a combat engaged in for exercise or sport, usually with blunted lances (as, "Nor cares For triumph in our mimic wars, the *jousts* — For if his own knight cast him down, he laughs": Tennyson's "Lancelot and Elaine," 311); a tilt; *pl.*, a tournament.—**just′er, joust′er,** *n.*

just-au-corps (zhüs-tō-kôr), *n.* [F., lit. 'close-fitting to the body.'] A close-fitting outer body-garment, esp. one reaching to the knees which was worn by men in the 17th and 18th centuries, or one worn by women in the 17th century.

jus-tice (jus′tis), *n.* [OF. F. *justice*, < L. *justitia*, < *justus*, E. *just*[1].] The quality of being just; righteousness, equitableness, or moral rightness (as, to question the *justice* of one's actions, dealings, or decisions; to uphold the *justice* of a cause); rightfulness or lawfulness, as of a claim or title; justness of ground or reason (as, to complain with *justice*); truth, correctness, or propriety (as, to admit the *justice* of a statement); also, the moral principle determining just conduct (as, to fulfil the requirements of *justice*; to have a sense of *justice*; "Wrath divine, when most severe, Makes *justice* still the guide of his career," Cowper's "Expostulation," 715); also, conformity to this principle as manifested in conduct (one of the cardinal virtues: see *virtue*); just conduct, dealing, or treatment (as, to explain in *justice* to the absent, or to one's self); also, the requital of desert, as by punishment or reward (as, "Revenge is a kind of wild *justice*," Bacon's "Essays," Of Revenge; "In the course of *justice*, none of us Should see salvation: we do pray for mercy," Shakspere's "Merchant of Venice," iv. 1. 199; poetic *justice*, see under *poetic*, *a.*); specif., judgment of persons or causes by judicial process (as, to administer *justice* in a community; to execute *justice* upon offenders); the administration of law, as by judicial and other proceedings (as, a court of *justice*; a governmental department of *justice*; the French minister of *justice*); also, a judicial officer; a judge or magistrate (as, the *justices* of the U. S. Supreme Court; *justice* of the peace, a local magistrate chosen to preserve the peace, try minor causes, etc.).—**high justice, low justice,** and **middle justice,** in feudal France, the three grades of justice administered by the seigneur or lord, the high justice involving the right of sentencing to death, mutilation, or other bodily punishment, the low justice being concerned with less grave cases, and the middle justice (of later origin than the others) dealing with cases of an intermediate character.—**to do justice to,** to render or concede what is due to (a person or thing, merits, good intentions, etc.); treat or judge fairly; sometimes, to exhibit (one's self) in a just light, as in doing something (as, the speaker hardly *did justice to* himself this evening; "He was too diffident to *do justice to* himself," Jane Austen's "Sense and Sensibility," iii.); also, to show just appreciation of by action (as, to *do justice to* a good dinner by eating heartily).

jus-ti-cer (jus′ti-sėr), *n.* [OF. F. *justicier.*] An administrator of justice; a judge or magistrate: as, "most learned *justicer*" (Shakspere's "King Lear," iii. 6. 23). [Archaic.]

jus-tice-ship (jus′tis-ship), *n.* The office, dignity, or function of a justice.

jus-ti-ci-a-ble (jus-tish′i-ạ-bl). [F. *justiciable.*] **I.** *a.* Subject to the action of a court of justice, as a person or an offense; subject to jurisdiction. **II.** *n.* One who is subject to the jurisdiction of another.—**jus-ti″ci-a-bil′i-ty** (-bil′i-ti), *n.*

jus-ti-cial (jus-tish′ạl), *a.* [ML. *justitialis.*] Of or pertaining to justice.

jus-ti-ci-ar (jus-tish′i-ä̤r), *n.* Same as *justiciary.*

jus-ti-ci-a-ry (jus-tish′i-ā̤-ri). [ML. *justitiarius.*] **I.** *a.* Of or pertaining to the administration of justice. **II.** *n.*; pl. *-ries* (-riz). An administrator of justice; in *Eng. hist.*, the chief administrator of justice and government from the time of William I. to that of Henry III. (called in full 'chief justiciary').

jus-ti-fi-a-ble (jus′ti-fī-ạ-bl), *a.* [F. *justifiable.*] Capable of being justified; that can be shown to be, or can be defended as being, just or right; defensible: as, *justifiable* homicide; *justifiable* resentment; "Just are the ways of God, And *justifiable* to men" (Milton's "Samson Agonistes," 294).—**jus″ti-fi-a-bil′i-ty** (-bil′i-ti), **jus′ti-fi-a-ble-ness,** *n.* —**jus′ti-fi-a-bly,** *adv.*

jus-ti-fi-ca-tion (jus″ti-fi-kā′shọn), *n.* [LL. *justificatio(n-).*] The act of justifying, or the state of being justified; also, something that justifies; a defensive plea; an excuse; a justifying fact or circumstance; in *theol.*, the act whereby man is made or accounted just, or freed from the guilt or penalty of sin.—**jus′ti-fi-ca-tive** (-kā̤-tiv), **jus′ti-fi-ca-to-ry** (-tọ̄-ri), *a.* Serving to justify; affording justification: as, "Those same *justificative* points you urge Might benefit . . . Count Guido Franceschini" (Browning's "Ring and the Book," xii.).

jus-ti-fi-er (jus′ti-fī-ėr), *n.* One who or that which justifies.

jus-ti-fy (jus′ti-fī), *v.*; *-fied, -fying.* [OF. F. *justifier,* < LL. *justificare,* < L. *justus,* just, + *facere,* do, make.] **I.** *tr.* To administer justice to†; also, to execute justice upon† (as, "Let them be *justified*: and leave exposed Their wavering relics in the place of judgment": Byron's "Marino Faliero," v. 1); also, to prove (a person) to be guiltless or blameless, or vindicate (as, "To *justify* this worthy nobleman, So vulgarly and personally accused, Her shall you hear disproved": Shakspere's "Measure for Measure," v. 1. 159); show (an act, claim, statement, etc.) to be just, right, or warranted (as, he failed to *justify* his conduct); furnish or afford a satisfactory reason or excuse for (as, the end *justifies* the means; necessity *justifies* the attempt); also, to declare guiltless, absolve, or acquit (as, "Woe unto them . . . Which *justify* the wicked for reward": Isa. v. 23); also, to defend or uphold as blameless, just, or right (as, "Or from a judge turn pleader, to persuade The choice we make, or *justify* it made": Pope's "Essay on Man," ii. 156); in *theol.*, to make, or accept as, just or righteous; free from the guilt or penalty of sin; in *printing*, to adjust exactly; make (lines) of the proper length by spacing. **II.** *intr.* In *law,* to show a satisfactory reason or excuse for something done; also, to qualify as bail or surety; in *printing*, to conform or fit exactly, as lines of type.

Jus-tin-i-an (jus-tin′i-ạn) **Code.** See *code.*

jus-tle (jus′l), *v.* and *n.* Earlier form of *jostle.*

just-ly (just′li), *adv.* In a just manner.—**just′ness,** *n.*

jut (jut), *v. i.*; *jutted, jutting.* [Var. of *jet*[1].] To extend beyond the main body or line; project; protrude: often with *out.*—**jut,** *n.* A jutting out; also, something that juts out; a projection or protruding point (as, "Tubal clambered by *jut* and scar And there he builded a town": Kipling's "Jubal and Tubal Cain").

jute[1] (jöt), *n.* [From Bengali name.] A strong fiber used for making fabrics, cordage, etc., obtained from two East Indian plants, *Corchorus capsularis* and *C. olitorius*; also, either of these plants, or any plant of the same genus.

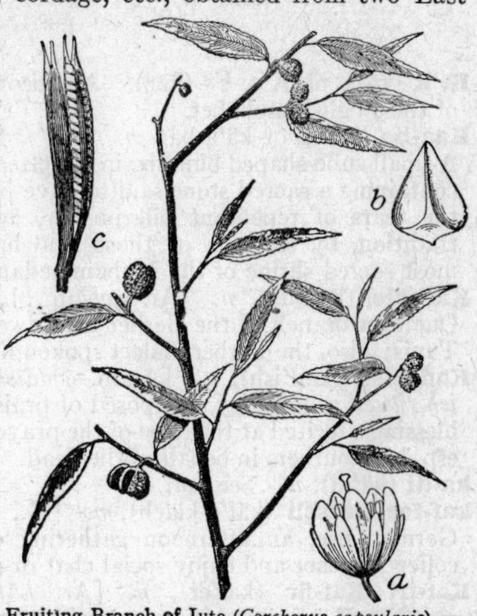

Fruiting Branch of Jute (*Corchorus capsularis*). — *a*, flower; *b*, seed; *c*, fruit of *C. siliquosus.*

Jute[2] (jöt), *n.* [AS. *Ēotas, Iōtas,* pl.] A member of a Low German tribe, said to have come from Jutland, Denmark, that invaded and settled in Britain in the 5th century.—**Jut-ish** (jö′tish), *a.*

jut-ty† (jut′i), *n.*; pl. *jutties* (-iz). [Var. of *jetty*[1].] A projecting part, as of a wall or building (as, "No *jutty,* frieze, Buttress, nor coign of vantage, but this bird Hath made his pendent bed": Shakspere's "Macbeth," i. 6. 6); also, a jetty, pier, or the like (as, "a curious harbour, formed by three stone *jutties*": Smollett's "Humphry Clinker," Sept. 6).—**jut′ty**†, *v. i.* or *t.*; *-tied, -tying.* To project, or project beyond. See Shakspere's "Henry V.," iii. 1. 13.

ju-ve-nal† (jö′vẹ-nạl). [L. *juvenalis,* < *juvenis*: see *juvenile.*] **I.** *a.* Juvenile. **II.** *n.* A youth: as, "the *juvenal,* the prince your master, whose chin is not yet fledged" (Shakspere's "2 Henry IV.," i. 2. 22).

ju-ve-nes-cent (jö-vẹ-nes′ẹnt), *a.* [L. *juvenescens* (*-ent-*), ppr. of *juvenescere,* reach the age of youth, grow young again, < *juvenis*: see *juvenile.*] Becoming youthful; growing young again; youthful.—**ju-ve-nes′cence,** *n.*

ju-ve-nile (jö′vẹ-nil or -nīl). [L. *juvenilis,* < *juvenis,* young, as n. a young person; akin to E. *young.*] **I.** *a.* Young or youthful (as, "He was a blessing to all the *juvenile* part of the neighbourhood": Jane Austen's "Sense and Sensibility," vii.); also, pertaining to, suitable for, or intended for young persons (as, *juvenile* books; a *juvenile* court). **II.** *n.* A young person, or a youth (as, "Tom Sawyer the Pirate looked around upon the envying *juveniles* about him": Mark Twain's "Tom Sawyer," xvii.); also, an actor who plays youthful parts; also, a book for young people. —**ju′ve-nile-ly,** *adv.*—**ju′ve-nile-ness,** *n.*—**ju-ve-nil′i-a** (-nil′i-ä̤), *n. pl.* [NL., prop. neut. pl. of L. *juvenilis.*] Works, esp. writings, produced in youth.—**ju-ve-nil′i-ty** (-nil′i-ti), *n.*; pl. *-ties* (-tiz). [L. *juvenilitas.*] Juvenile state, character, or manner, or youthfulness (as, "Cleopatra . . . in her *juvenility* was always playfully disposed," Dickens's "Dombey and Son," xxx.; "I forgave Miss Jessie . . . her *juvenility* of dress," Mrs. Gaskell's "Cranford," ii.); *pl.*, youthful qualities or performances; also, *sing.*, juveniles, or young persons, collectively.

jux-ta- (juks′tä̤-). [L. *juxta,* adv. and prep., near, near to, close to, akin to *jungere,* join: see *join.*] A prefix of Latin origin, meaning 'near,' 'close to,' 'beside,' sometimes used as an English formative, as in *juxta-articular* (near a joint), *juxtamarine* (beside the sea).

jux-ta-pose (juks-tä̤-pōz′), *v. t.*; *-posed, -posing.* [F. *juxtaposer,* < L. *juxta,* near, + F. *poser,* put: see *pose*[1].] To place in close proximity or side by side.—**jux″ta-po-si′tion** (-pọ̄-zish′ọn), *n.* [F. *juxtaposition,* < L. *juxta,* near, + *positio(n-),* a placing, E. *position.*] A placing or a being placed close together; position side by side.—**jux″ta-po-si′tion-al,** *a.*

jux-ta-ter-res-tri-al (juks″tä̤-te-res′tri-ạl), *a.* [See *juxta-* and *terrestrial.*] Near the land: as, the *juxtaterrestrial* parts of the ocean.

jynx (jingks), *n.* See *jinx.*

K

K, k (kā); pl. *K's, k's* (kāz). A consonant, the 11th letter of the English alphabet.

Kaa-ba (kä′bạ̈ or kä′ạ-bạ̈), *n.* [Ar. *ka'bah,* < *ka'b,* cube.] A small cube-shaped building in the Great Mosque at Mecca, containing a sacred stone said to have been turned black by the tears of repentant pilgrims or, according to another tradition, by the sins of those who have touched it: the most sacred shrine of the Mohammedans.

Ka-byle (kạ-bīl′), *n.* [Ar. *qabāil,* pl. of *qabīlah,* tribe.] One of a branch of the Berber race dwelling in Algeria and Tunis; also, the Berber dialect spoken by them.

Kad-dish (kad′ish), *n.* [Aram. *qaddīsh,* 'holy.'] In *Jewish ritual,* a doxology, composed of praise and invocation of blessings, recited at the close of the prayers in the synagogue, esp. by mourners in behalf of the dead.

ka-di (kä′di), *n.* See *cadi.*

kaf-fee-klatsch (käf′ā-kläch), *n.* [G., 'coffee gossip.'] In German use, an afternoon gathering of women to drink coffee together and enjoy social chat or gossip.

Kaf-ir, Kaf-fir (kaf′ėr), *n.* [Ar. *kāfir,* unbeliever.] A member of a South African negroid race inhabiting parts of the Cape of Good Hope, Natal, etc.; the language spoken by them; also, a member of a race, apparently of Aryan stock, inhabiting Kafiristan, in northeastern Afghanistan; also, *pl.,* South African mine shares (Eng.); also, *sing.* [*l. c.*], any of certain grain-sorghums (see *sorghum*), varieties of *Andropogon sorghum* with stout, short-jointed, leafy stalks, cultivated in South Africa and introduced into the U. S.—**Kaf′ir=corn,** *n.* A variety of sorghum grown in South Africa, much used by the Kafirs for making beer; in general, any sorghum of the kafir class (see above).

kaf-tan (kaf′tạn), *n.* See *caftan.*

ka-gu (kä′gö), *n.* [Native name.] A grallatorial bird, *Rhinochetus jubatus,* mostly gray, with a full pendent crest, peculiar to New Caledonia, but showing affinity to the sun-bittern and the rails.

Kagu.

kaif, kef (kīf, kef), *n.* [Ar.] Among the Arabs, easeful or dreamy quiescence as a form of enjoyment. Cf. *kief.*

kail (kāl), etc. See *kale,* etc.

kails (kālz), *n. pl.* [ME. *kayles, keyles*: cf. D. *kegel,* pin, skittle.] The game of skittles or ninepins. [Now prov. Eng.]

kaim (kām), *n.* See *kame.*

kai-nite (kī′nīt), *n.* [G. *kainit,* < Gr. καινός, new, recent.] A mineral substance, a combination of the sulphates of potassium and magnesium with chloride of magnesium, used as a fertilizer.

kai-ser (kī′zėr), *n.* [ME. *kaiser, caisere* (AS. *cāsere*), = G. *kaiser,* < L. *Cæsar,* Cæsar.] An emperor (as, "the old *kaisers* of Rome," Scott's "Quentin Durward," xxviii.; " 'What signifies 't,' continued she . . . 'to king, queen, or *keiser?*' " Scott's "Bride of Lammermoor," xxvi.); in later use [usually *cap.*], the Austrian or, esp., the German emperor. —**kai′ser-ism,** *n.* The rule of a kaiser; esp., autocratic rule or government, as of a kaiser (esp. with reference to William II. of Germany).—**kai′ser-ship,** *n.*

kaj-e-put (kaj′ẹ-put), *n.* See *cajuput.*

ka-ka (kä′kạ̈), *n.* [Maori.] Any of certain New Zealand parrots of the genus *Nestor,* esp. *N. meridionalis,* a species about the size of a crow with a mostly olive-brown coloration.

ka-ka-po (kä′kạ-pō), *n.*; pl. *-pos* (-pōz). [Maori.] A large nocturnal parrot, *Strigops habroptilus,* of New Zealand, which has well-developed wings but is practically flightless.

kak-e-mo-no (kak-ẹ-mō′nō), *n.*; pl. *-nos* (-nōz). [Jap.] A Japanese wall-picture, usually long and narrow, painted on silk, paper, or other material, and mounted on a roller.

kak-is-toc-ra-cy (kak-is-tok′rạ-si), *n.* [Gr. κάκιστος, superl. of κακός, bad: see *-cracy.*] Government by the worst citizens; a form of government in which the worst persons rule. Cf. *aristocracy.*

kako-, etc. See *caco-,* etc.

ka-la=a-zar (kä″lä-ä-zär′), *n.* [Hind. *kālā āzār,* 'black sickness.'] An infectious fever of India.

kale, kail (kāl), *n.* [Var. of *cole.*] A plant of the cabbage family, a variety of *Brassica oleracea* with curled leaves not forming a head; also, in Scotch use, cabbage or greens; cabbage soup; broth or soup made with various kinds of vegetables; dinner (as, "I will be back here to my *kail* against ane o'clock": Scott's "Black Dwarf," i.); also, in slang use, money.

ka-lei-do-scope (kạ-lī′dọ-skōp), *n.* [Gr. καλός, beautiful, + εἶδος, form: see *-scope.*] An optical instrument in which bits of colored glass, etc., in a rotating tube are shown by reflection in continually changing symmetrical forms.—**ka-lei-do-scop′ic** (-skop′ik), *a.* Of, pertaining to, or suggestive of the kaleidoscope or its changing combinations of forms and colors: as, "Maule's well . . . was throwing up a succession of *kaleidoscopic* pictures" (Hawthorne's "House of the Seven Gables," xxi.).—**ka-lei-do-scop′i-cal-ly,** *adv.*

kal-ends (kal′endz), *n. pl.* See *calends.*

kale-yard, kail-yard (kāl′yärd), *n.* A cabbage-garden; a kitchen-garden such as is attached to a small house. [Sc.] —**kailyard school,** a school of writers describing homely life in Scotland, with much use of Scottish dialect, in vogue toward the close of the 19th century, when books by J. M. Barrie, John Watson ("Ian Maclaren"), and others were appearing: named from the lines, "There grows a bonnie brier bush in our kail-yard, And white are the blossoms on 't in our kail-yard," quoted, from a Scottish song, by Watson in his "Beside the Bonnie Brier Bush" (1894), and used in the title of that book.

kal-i (kal′i or kā′li), *n.* [Ar. *qalī*: see *alkali.*] The plant *Salsola kali,* prickly glasswort or saltwort.

ka-li-um (kā′li-um), *n.* [NL., < Ar. *qalī*: see *kali.*] Potassium: in *chem.,* abbreviated K (without period).

kal-mi-a (kal′mi-ạ̈), *n.* [NL.; from P. *Kalm* (1715–79), Swedish botanist.] Any plant of the North American ericaceous genus *Kalmia,* comprising evergreen shrubs with showy flowers, as *K. latifolia,* the mountain-laurel.

Kal-muck (kal′muk), *n.* A member of any of a group of Buddhistic Mongol tribes of a region extending from western China to southeastern Russia; also, their language.

kal-pak (kal′pak), *n.* See *calpac.*

kal-pis (kal′pis), *n.* [Gr. κάλπις.] In *Gr. antiq.,* a vase or vessel for water, wine, etc., a form of the hydria in which the large handle, at the back, does not rise above the rim.

kal-so-mine (kal′sọ-mīn or -min), *n.* and *v.* Erroneous form of *calcimine.*

kam-a-la (kam′ạ-lạ̈), *n.* Same as *kamila.*

kame (kām), *n.* [Sc. var. of *comb*[1].] A comb for the hair (Sc.); also (orig. Sc. and north. Eng.), a ridge or mound of detrital material, esp. one left by a retreating ice-sheet; an eskar.

Kalpis. — Examples of Greek red-figured pottery.

ka-me-rad (kä-mė-rät′), *n.* [G.] Comrade; friend: esp. used by German soldiers in offering to surrender.

ka-mi-la (kạ-mē′lạ̈), *n.* [Hind. *kamīlā*.] A powder from the capsules of an East Indian euphorbiaceous tree, *Mallotus philippinensis*, used as a yellow dye and in medicine.

Kan-a-ka (kan′ạ-kạ̈ or kạ-nak′ạ̈), *n.* [Hawaiian, lit. 'man.'] A native Hawaiian; in general, a South Sea islander: as, "The long name of Sandwich Islanders is dropped, and they are called by the whites, all over the Pacific Ocean, '*Kanakas*,' from a word in their own language which they apply to themselves, and to all South Sea Islanders" (Dana's "Two Years before the Mast," xix.).

Kan-a-rese (kan-ạ-rēs′ or -rēz′), *n.* See *Canarese*.

kang (kang), *n.* [Chinese.] In China and Manchuria, a structure of brick or other material, with a place for a fire beneath, used to sleep on.

kan-ga-roo (kang-gạ-rö′), *n.*; pl. *kangaroos* or (esp. collectively) *kangaroo*. [Appar. native Australian.] A large marsupial mammal, *Macropus giganteus*, of the family *Macropodidæ* of Australia, etc., distinguished for the great development of its hinder parts and for its leaping powers; also, any animal of this family, as *Petrogale xanthopus* ('yellow-footed rock-kangaroo'), a species found in rocky districts.—**kan-ga-roo′,** *v. i.* To hunt the kangaroo; also, to leap like a kangaroo.—**kan-ga-roo′=bear,** *n.* The koala.—**kan-ga-roo′=rat,** *n.* A rat-kangaroo; also, any of various small jumping rodents of Mexico and the western U. S., of the family *Heteromyidæ*, as those of the genus *Dipodomys*.

Giant Kangaroo (*Macropus giganteus*).

Kangaroo-rat (*Dipodomys phillipsi*, or *ordi*).

ka-no-nen-fut-ter (kä-nō′nen-füt″ėr), *n.* [G., a rendering of Falstaff's "food for powder," in Shakspere's "1 Henry IV.," iv. 2. 71: see the quotation at *food*.] Cannon-fodder; common soldiers as the material used up in war.

kan-tar, can-tar (kan-tär′), *n.* [Ar. *qintār*: see *quintal*.] In Mohammedan countries, a unit of weight corresponding to the hundredweight, but varying in different localities.

Kant-i-an (kan′ti-ạn), *a.* Of or pertaining to the German philosopher Immanuel Kant (1724–1804), or his system of philosophy.—**Kant′i-an-ism,** *n.*

ka-o-lin (kā′ọ̄-lin), *n.* [F. *kaolin*, < Chinese *Kao-ling*, 'high ridge,' name of a hill in China which yielded the first kaolin sent to Europe.] A fine white clay used in the manufacture of porcelain.

ka-pel-le (kä-pel′ė), *n.* [G., chapel, chapel choir, orchestra.] A choir or orchestra such as was formerly maintained at German courts; any musical establishment, as an orchestra or band.—**ka-pell′meis″ter** (-mīs″tėr), *n.* [G.] The conductor or leader of a kapelle.

ka-pok (kä′pok), *n.* [Malay *kāpoq*.] The silky down which invests the seeds of a silk-cotton tree, *Ceiba pentandra*, of the East Indies, Africa, and tropical America: used for stuffing pillows, etc. See cut in next column.

kap-pa (kap′ạ̈), *n.* [Gr. κάππα.] The tenth letter (K, κ, = English K, k, or C, c) of the Greek alphabet.

kar-a-kul (kar′ạ-köl or -kul), *n.* See *caracul*.

kar-at (kar′ạt), *n.* See *carat*.

kar-ma (kär′mạ̈), *n.* [Skt., deed, action.] In *Buddhism* and *theosophy*, actions or activities in successive states of existence conceived as a determining or retributive force operating in subsequent states; the influence or effect of actions in the past in conditioning future existence.

Leaf and Seed-pod of *Ceiba pentandra*, yielding Kapok.

ka-roo, kar-roo (kạ-rö′). [From Hottentot name, meaning 'dry,' 'barren.'] **I.** *n.*; pl. *-roos* (-röz′). One of the barren tracts of clayey table-land in South Africa. **II.** *a.* [*cap.*] In *geol.*, noting or pertaining to a series of rocks of the Permian and Triassic systems of South Africa, consisting of shales, sandstones, etc.

ka-ross (kạ-ros′), *n.* [Appar. native name.] A garment made of skins with the hair left on, worn by Hottentots and other natives of South Africa.

karyo-. Form of Gr. κάρυον, nut, kernel, used in biological terms to denote the nucleus of a cell.—**kar-y-o-ki-ne-sis** (kar″i-ọ̄-ki-nē′sis), *n.* [NL. (Gr. κίνησις, movement).] In *biol.*, mitosis.—**kar″y-o-ki-net′ic** (-net′ik), *a.*—**kar-y-om′i-tome** (-om′i-tōm), *n.* [+ Gr. μίτος, a thread.] In *biol.*, the network or reticulum which extends through the nucleus of a cell before the process of mitosis begins.—**kar″y-o-mi-to′sis** (-mi-tō′sis), *n.* [NL.: see *mitosis*.] Same as *mitosis*.—**kar′y-o-plasm** (-plazm), *n.* [+ *-plasm*.] In *biol.*, the substance of the nucleus of a cell.—**kar″y-o-plas′mic** (-plaz′mik), *a.*—**kar′y-o-some** (-sōm), *n.* [+ *-some*³.] In *biol.*, any of certain irregular or spherical bodies observed in and supposed to be a portion of the net-like structure in the nucleus of a cell; also, the nucleus of a cell; also, a chromosome.

ka-tab′a-sis, ka-tab′o-lism, etc., **ka-thar′-sis, kath′ode,** etc., **kat′i-on.** See *catabasis*, *catabolism*, etc., *catharsis*, *cathode*, etc., *cation*.

ka-ty-did (kā′ti-did), *n.* [Imit. of the sound made.] Any of several large, usually green, arboreal orthopterous insects (family *Locustidæ*) of America, as *Cyrtophyllum concavum* ('broad-winged katydid'), which by stridulation produce a loud, shrill sound.

Broad-winged Katydid (*Cyrtophyllum concavum*).

kat-zen-jam-mer (kät′sen-yäm″ėr), *n.* [G., lit. 'cats' sickness.'] Indisposition following intoxication; crapulence.

kau-ri (kou′ri), *n.* [Maori.] A tall coniferous tree, *Dammara australis*, of New Zealand, yielding a valuable timber and a resin (*kauri-gum*); its wood; sometimes, any of various other trees of the same genus, or the wood.

ka-va (kä′vạ̈), *n.* [Polynesian.] A Polynesian shrub, *Piper methysticum*, of the pepper family; also, an intoxicating beverage prepared from its roots.

ka-yak (kä′yak), *n.* [Eskimo.] An Eskimo canoe made of sealskins stretched over a light wooden frame, with an opening in the middle for the navigator.

kayles (kālz), *n. pl.* See *kails*.

ke-a (kā′ạ̈), *n.* [Maori.] A large,

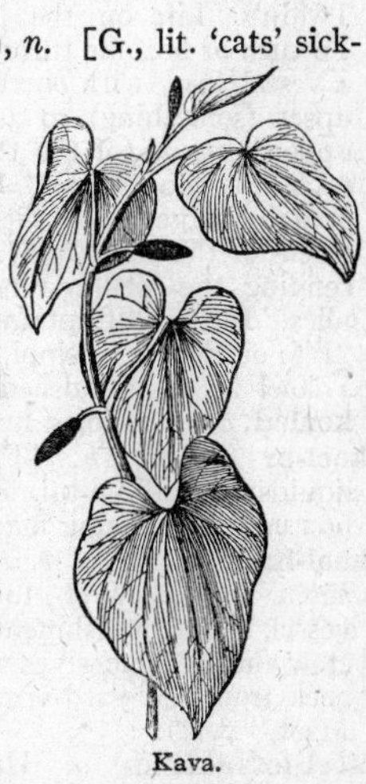

Kava.

greenish New Zealand parrot, *Nestor notabilis*, which kills sheep in order to feed upon their fat.

keb-bie (keb′i), *n.* [Origin uncertain.] A staff or stick with a hooked end: as, "Ane o' them was gaun to strike my mither . . . So I got up my *kebbie* at them" (Scott's "Old Mortality," xiv.). [Sc. and north. Eng.]

keb-buck (keb′uk), *n.* [Origin uncertain.] A cheese. See Scott's "Old Mortality," viii. [Sc., Ir., and north. Eng.]

keck (kek), *v. i.* [Imit.] To heave or retch; be affected with nausea; hence, to feel or manifest disgust or strong dislike.

keck-le[1] (kek′l), *v.* and *n.* Same as *cackle.*

keck-le[2] (kek′l), *v. t.*; *-led, -ling.* [Origin uncertain.] *Naut.*, to cover (a cable, etc.) by winding with something, as to prevent chafing.

keck-sy (kek′si), *n.* Same as *kex.* See Shakspere's "Henry V.," v. 2. 52. [Now prov.]

ked-dah (ked′ä), *n.* See *kheda.*

kedge (kej), *v.*; *kedged, kedging.* [Origin uncertain.] *Naut.*: **I.** *tr.* To warp or pull (a ship, etc.) along by means of a rope attached to an anchor. **II.** *intr.* To kedge a ship, etc.; of a ship, etc., to move by being warped with an anchor (as, "She went to windward as though she were *kedging*": Dana's "Two Years before the Mast," xxiv.).—**kedge, kedge′=an″chor,** *n.* A small anchor used in kedging and otherwise. Also **kedg′er.**

kedg-e-ree (kej′e-rē), *n.* [Hind. *khichrī.*] An East Indian dish of rice cooked with pulse, onions, eggs, etc.; also, a dish of flaked fish with rice, etc.

keek (kēk), *v. i.* [ME. *kiken* = D. *kijken* = LG. *kieken*, peep.] To peep; peek: as, "I *keeked* through a hole in the door" (Barrie's "Little Minister," vi.). [Now Sc. and north. Eng.]—**keek,** *n.* A peep: as, "Take a *keek* into Pate's letter before ye deliver it" (Scott's "Redgauntlet," ch. xii.). [Sc. and north. Eng.]

keel[1] (kēl), *n.* [ME. *keyle*; origin uncertain.] A red ocher used for marking sheep, timber, yarn, etc.; ruddle; also, a mark made with this.

keel[2] (kēl), *v. t.* [AS. *cēlan*, < *cōl*, E. *cool*, *a.*] To make cool; specif., to cool (a pot about to boil over), as by stirring (as, "while greasy Joan doth *keel* the pot": Shakspere's "Love's Labour's Lost," v. 2. 930). [Now prov.]

keel[3] (kēl), *n.* [Prob. partly from MD. *kiel* = AS. *cēol*, ship, boat, partly from Scand.: cf. Icel. *kjölr*, keel of a vessel.] A galley or ship (archaic); also, a barge or lighter (Eng.); also, a longitudinal timber, or combination of timbers, iron plates, or the like, extending along the middle of the bottom of a vessel from stem to stern and supporting the whole frame; hence, a corresponding part in some other structure, as in a dirigible balloon; in *bot.* and *zoöl.*, a longitudinal ridge, as on a leaf or bone; a carina. Also, a keel-boat: as, "The Mississippi receives . . . water from fifty-four subordinate rivers that are navigable by steamboats, and from some hundreds that are navigable by flats and *keels*" (Mark Twain's "Life on the Mississippi," i.).—**keel**[3], *v. t.* or *i.* To turn or become turned keel uppermost (with reference to a vessel: esp. with *over*); hence (esp. with *over*), to turn or upset (something) so as to bring the wrong side or part uppermost, or (of the thing) to move or fall so as to take such a position.—**keel′=boat,** *n.* A kind of shallow freight-boat or barge, built with a keel and decked over, used on rivers of the western U. S. (as, "Captain Sublette was ascending the Yellowstone with a *keel boat*, laden with supplies," Irving's "Captain Bonneville," xli.; see Mark Twain's "Life on the Mississippi," iii.); also, a yacht or the like with a keel as distinguished from one with a center-board.—**keeled,** *a.* Having a keel.

keel-er (kē′lėr), *n.* [From *keel*[2].] A vessel for cooling liquids; a shallow tub for various purposes; also, a shallow box used in dressing mackerel. [Chiefly prov.]

keel-haul (kēl′hâl), *v. t.* [D. *kielhalen*, < *kiel*, keel, + *halen*, haul.] *Naut.*, to haul (a person) under the keel of a vessel, as for punishment: as, "an effigy of Judas, which the crew amuse themselves with *keel-hauling* and hanging by the neck from the yard-arms" (Dana's "Two Years before the Mast," xvii.).

keel-less (kēl′les), *a.* Having no keel.

keel-son, kel-son (kel′sọn), *n.* [Appar. from Scand.: cf. Sw. *kölsvin*, Dan. *kjölsvin*, keelson.] *Naut.*, a strengthening line of timbers or iron plates in a ship, above and parallel with the keel.

keen[1] (kēn), *a.* [AS. *cēne* = D. *koen* = G. *kühn*, bold, = Icel. *kænn*, wise, skilful.] Bold† or brave†; also, fierce† or cruel†; also, animated by or showing strong feeling or desire (as, a *keen* fighter; *keen* competition); ardent; eager (often with *about, for*, etc., or an infinitive: as, "Never did I know A creature . . . So *keen* and greedy to confound a man," Shakspere's "Merchant of Venice," iii. 2. 278); intense, as feeling, desire, relish, etc.; also, sharp, or so shaped as to cut or pierce substances readily (as, a *keen* blade, edge, or point; "arrows *keen*," Milton's "Comus," 422); hence, acting on the senses or feelings like a sharp instrument; piercing in sound (poetic: as, "*keen* shrieks," Shelley's "Prometheus Unbound," ii. 4. 27); sharply bright (poetic: as, "yon starlight *keen*," Tennyson's "St. Agnes' Eve"); pungent, as odor or flavor (now rare); often, sharp, piercing, or biting, as wind, cold, etc.; acute, poignant, or sharply distressing, as pain, grief, remorse, etc.; cutting or stinging, as satire; incisive, trenchant, or sharply and clearly expressive, as language; also, characterized by strength and distinctness of perception, as the ear or hearing, the eye, sight, or glance, the smell or scent, etc.; acutely appreciative (as, "She had usually a *keen* sense of the ludicrous": Bret Harte's "Fool of Five Forks"); having or showing great mental penetration or acumen (as, a *keen* thinker or intellect; *keen* reasoning).

keen[2] (kēn), *v.* [From Ir.: cf. Ir. *caoinim*, I lament.] **I.** *intr.* To wail in lamentation for the dead (Ir.); in general, to wail or lament. **II.** *tr.* To mourn with wailing, as one dead: as, "Isn't it a bitter thing to think of him floating that way . . . and no one to *keen* him but the black hags that do be flying on the sea?" (Synge's "Riders to the Sea"). [Ir.]—**keen**[2], *n.* A wailing lament for the dead. [Ir.]—**keen′er,** *n.*

keen-ly (kēn′li), *adv.* In a keen manner.—**keen′ness,** *n.*

keep (kēp), *v. t.*; *kept, keeping.* [AS. *cēpan*, observe, heed, regard, await, take; origin and connections unknown.] To observe† or note†; hence, to observe in practice, or pay obedient regard to (a law, rule, promise, etc.); conform to, follow, or fulfil; also, to observe (a season, festival, etc.) with formalities or rites (as, to *keep* Lent or Christmas; "One feast, of holy days the crest, I, though no Churchman, love to *keep*," Lowell's "All-Saints"); also, to guard, protect, or preserve (as, "The Lord bless thee, and *keep* thee": Num. vi. 24); have the charge or custody of (as, to *keep* the stores of an establishment; to *keep* money or valuables for depositors); take care of, or tend (as, "Rachel came with her father's sheep: for she *kept* them": Gen. xxix. 9); maintain in condition or order, as by care and labor (as, "The Lord God took the man, and put him into the garden of Eden to dress it and to *keep* it," Gen. ii. 15; a neatly *kept* room; an ill-*kept* person); maintain or support (a person, etc.: as, he is not able to *keep* himself, much less a family); entertain or have as a guest, lodger, etc. (as, to *keep* a traveler overnight; to *keep* boarders); maintain in one's service or for one's use or enjoyment (as, to *keep* servants; to *keep* chickens; to *keep* a carriage); have habitually in stock or for sale (as, "The poor gentlewoman . . . gave her hot customer to understand that she did not *keep* the article": Hawthorne's "House of the Seven Gables," iii.); also, to maintain in active existence, or hold, as an assembly, council, court, fair, etc.; maintain or conduct the activities of (a school, shop, hotel, etc.); maintain by writing, entries, etc. (as, to *keep* a diary, record, or tally; to *keep* books, see *bookkeeping*); continue to make or do (often with *up*: as, to *keep* up a clamor); maintain in one's action or conduct (as, to *keep* watch, step, or silence); cause to continue in some place, position, state, course, or action specified (as, to *keep* a person at his desk or work, in office, or in suspense; to *keep* a light burning); also, to hold in custody or under guard, as a prisoner; detain, as in a place; prevent from coming or going (as, "'I wonder what *keeps* Eliza,' said Mrs. Shelby, after giving her bell repeated pulls, to no purpose": Mrs. Stowe's "Uncle Tom's Cabin," vi.); restrain, as from doing something; hold (*back, down, in, off, out*, etc.); also, to withhold from use, or reserve (as, to *keep* grain for seed); save, hold, or retain in possession (as, "*Keep* a thing, its use will come": Tennyson's "Epic," 42); continue to hold or have (as, to *keep* a thing in mind; to *keep* the interest of the public); withhold from the knowledge of others (as, to *keep* a secret; to *keep* one's own counsel, that is, to keep one's opinions or ideas to one's self); also, to continue to follow (a path, track, course, etc.); remain in (a place, etc.: as, to *keep* one's bed or room, as in sickness); maintain one's position in or on (as, to *keep* the field; to *keep* the saddle).—**to keep company,** to consort together; specif., to associate as sweethearts, or as a suitor or sweetheart (*with*) (colloq.).—**to keep house,** to maintain a household; also, to manage the affairs of a domestic establishment.—**to keep time,** to record time, as a watch or clock does; also, to perform rhythmic movements in unison; in *music*, to beat, mark, or observe the rhythmic accents.—**keep,** *v. i.* To dwell or live (now colloq.); remain or stay in a place (as, to *keep* indoors; "I will *keep* where there is wit stirring," Shakspere's "Troilus and Cressida," ii. 1. 129); continue in a position, state, etc. (as, to *keep* in sight or in touch; to *keep* in condition); remain, or continue to be, as specified (as, to *keep* cool; to *keep* strong and well); continue in an action, course, etc. (as, to *keep* at work; to *keep* on calling, or *keep* calling; to *keep* to the right or the north); also, to keep one's self or itself (*away, back, off, out,* etc.: as, to *keep* away from danger; to *keep* off the grass); restrain one's self (*from*: as, I could not *keep* from smiling); also, to continue unimpaired or without spoiling (as, the milk will *keep* on ice; those apples will *keep* all winter); last in good condition; fig., to admit of being reserved for a future occasion (as, "The dam was a subject of conversation that would *keep*": George Eliot's "Mill on the Floss," i. 3); also, to be in session, as school (colloq.).—**to keep in with,** to keep one's self in favor or friendly relations with (a person, etc.). [Now colloq.]—**to keep to,** to confine one's self to (as, to *keep to* one's bed; to *keep to* the society of one's friends); also, to adhere to (an agreement, plan, facts or truth, etc.).—**to keep to one's self,** to hold aloof from the society of others.—**to keep up,** to bear up, or continue without breaking down as under strain; also, to maintain an equal rate of speed, activity, or progress, as with another.—**keep,** *n.* Heed† or notice† (as, "Of nothing he takes *keepe*": Spenser's "Faerie Queene," i. 1. 40); also, charge or care (archaic: as, "In Baptista's *keep* my treasure is," Shakspere's "Taming of the Shrew," i. 2. 118); also, keeping, maintenance, or support, or the means of keeping (as, an allowance for the *keep* of a horse; work done in return for one's *keep*; not to be worth one's *keep*; "Long before they reached their teens they were earning their *keep* as herds," Barrie's "Auld Licht Idylls," iv.); condition as the result of keeping (chiefly prov. Eng.: as, horses in good or bad *keep*); also, the innermost and strongest structure or central tower of a medieval castle; a donjon.—**for keeps,** for keeping as one's own permanently (as, to play marbles *for keeps*, that is, with each player keeping what marbles he wins; to give one a thing *for keeps*); hence, permanently, for good, or altogether (as, I'm through with him *for keeps*). [Colloq.]

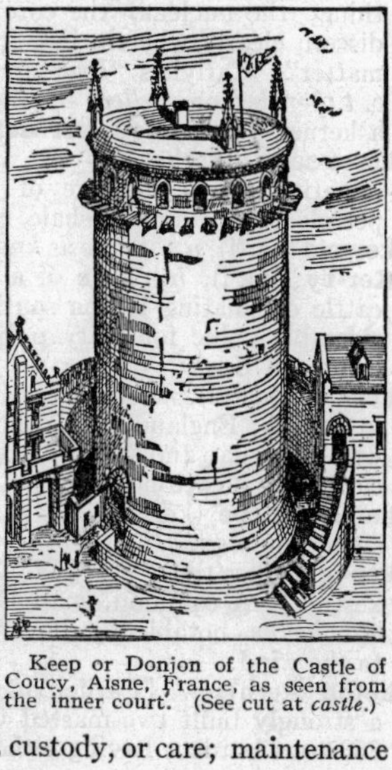

Keep or Donjon of the Castle of Coucy, Aisne, France, as seen from the inner court. (See cut at *castle.*)

keep-er (kē'pėr), *n.* One who keeps, or guards, watches, conducts, etc. (as, the *keeper* of a prison; a game*keeper*; a store*keeper*); also, something that keeps, or serves to guard, hold in place, retain, etc.; also, something that keeps or lasts well, as a fruit.—**keep'er-ship,** *n.* The office or position of a keeper.

keep-ing (kē'ping), *n.* The act of one who or that which keeps; observance; guarding, custody, or care; maintenance or keep; holding, reserving, or retaining; also, just conformity in things or elements associated together (orig. as maintained in a painting); agreement, congruity, or harmony (as, his deeds are not in *keeping* with his words).—**keep'ing-room,** *n.* A living-room or sitting-room: as, "In the family '*keeping-room*' . . . he will remember the staid, respectable old bookcase, with its glass doors" (Mrs. Stowe's "Uncle Tom's Cabin," xv.). [Local, Eng. and U. S.]

keep-sake (kēp'sāk), *n.* Anything kept, or given to be kept, for the sake of the giver.

keeve (kēv), *n.* [AS. *cȳf.*] A large tub or vat: used in bleaching, brewing, mining, etc.

kef (kef), *n.* See *kaif.*

kef-ir (kef'ėr), *n.* [Caucasian.] An effervescent, slightly alcoholic liquor, prepared from fermented cow's milk, orig. by the natives of the northern Caucasus: much used as a medicine or food for invalids.

keg (keg), *n.* [Earlier *cag*: cf. Icel. *kaggi*, keg, cask.] A small cask or barrel, usually holding from 5 to 10 gallons.

keir (kēr), *n.* See *kier.*

keit-lo-a (kīt'lọ-ạ), *n.* [S. Afr.] A two-horned black rhinoceros of South Africa.

kel-e-be (kel'ẹ-bē), *n.* [Gr. κελέβη.] In *Gr. antiq.*, a large, ovoid, wide-mouthed vase with a broad, flat rim, and two handles extending from the body to the rim but not above it.

Kelebe.—Greek red-figured pottery.

ke-loid (kē'loid), *n.* See *cheloid.*

kelp (kelp), *n.* [Origin unknown.] Large seaweeds of various kinds (chiefly of the families *Fucaceæ* and *Laminariaceæ*), such as are burned for the sake of the carbonate of soda, iodine, etc., that they contain; the ash of such seaweeds; also, a single species of such seaweeds, esp. *Macrocystis pyrifera*, a large, tough seaweed of the Pacific coast of America.

kel-pie, kel-py (kel'pi), *n.*; pl. *-pies* (-piz). [Origin unknown.] A fabled water-spirit, usually in the form of a horse, reputed to give warning of or to cause drowning: as, "The light diminished to a distant star that seemed to twinkle on the waters, like those which . . . the water-*kelpy* sends for the purpose of indicating the watery grave of his victims" (Scott's "Guy Mannering," xxvi.). [Sc.]

kel'son, *n.* See *keelson.*

Kelt (kelt), **Kel-tic** (kel'tik), etc. Same as *Celt*[2], *Celtic*, etc.

kel'ter, *n.* See *kilter.*

kemb (kem), *v. t.*; pp. *kembed* or *kempt.* [AS. *cemban*, < *camb*, E. *comb*[1], *n.*] To comb: now prov., except as in *kempt*, *p. a.*

kemp (kemp), *n.* [Cf. Icel. *kampr*, beard, whiskers of an animal.] A coarse hair occurring in wool or fur: esp. in *pl.*

kempt (kempt), *p. a.* [See *kemb.*] Combed, as the hair. Cf. *unkempt.* [Archaic.]

ken (ken), *v.*; *kenned, kenning.* [AS. *cennan* = Goth. *kannjan*, make known, = Icel. *kenna*, make known, know (cf. later E. senses), = G. *kennen*, know; orig. a causative of the verb represented by E. *can*[1].] **I.** *tr.* To make known†; also, to know; be acquainted with; recognize; descry or see; look at or scan. [Now archaic, Sc., or prov. Eng.] **II.** *intr.* To have knowledge of something; also, to see; look. [Archaic, Sc., or prov. Eng.]—**ken,** *n.* Knowledge or cognizance; mental perception; also, sight or view; look or gaze; esp., range of sight or vision (as, "Then felt I like some watcher of the skies When a new planet swims into his *ken*": Keats's "On First Looking into Chapman's Homer").

kench (kench), *n.* [Origin obscure.] A box or bin for use in salting fish or skins. [U. S.]

ken-dal (ken'dạl), *n.* [From *Kendal*, in Westmorland, England, where it was made.] A green woolen cloth formerly in use.—**Ken'dal green.** The cloth kendal (as, "A good archer thou as ever wore *Kendal green*": Scott's "Castle Dangerous," ii.); also, the green color of this cloth, produced by a process employing the plant woadwaxen.

Ken-il-worth (ken′il-wėrth) **i′vy.** See *ivy, n.*

ken-nel^{1} (ken′ẹl), *n.* [= F. *chenil,* < ML. *canile,* < L. *canis,* dog.] A house for a dog or dogs; an establishment where dogs are bred (often in *pl.*); hence, the lair of an animal; also, in contempt, a wretched abode (as, "He got us a room — we were in a *kennel* before": Dickens's "Pickwick Papers," xlv.); also, a pack of dogs or, sometimes, of other animals (as, "Hurt a dog, and the whole *kennel* will fall on him and worry him": Scott's "Woodstock," iv.).—**ken′-nel**^{1}, *v.*; *-neled* or *-nelled, -neling* or *-nelling.* **I.** *intr.* To take shelter or lodge in a kennel. **II.** *tr.* To put into or keep in a kennel.

ken-nel^{2} (ken′ẹl), *n.* [Earlier *cannel,* < OF. *canel,* also *chanel,* E. *channel*^{2}.] The gutter of a street: as, "Large pools of water had collected in the road: and the *kennels* were overflowing" (Dickens's "Oliver Twist," xxi.).

ken-ning (ken′ing), *n.* [Partly from *ken, v.,* partly from the related Icel. *kenning,* descriptive name, appellative.] The act of one who kens (archaic, Sc., or prov. Eng.); also, just enough to be recognized or perceived, a very small amount, or a little (Sc. and north. Eng.: as, "Tho' they may gang a *kennin* wrang, To step aside is human," Burns's "Address to the Unco Guid," 51); also, in Old Norse, Anglo-Saxon, and other early Teutonic poetry, a descriptive poetical name used for, or in addition to, the usual name of a person or thing, as 'the gannet's bath' for 'the sea,' or 'a wave-traveler' for 'a boat.'

ke-no (kē′nō), *n.* [Cf. F. *quine,* row of five numbers at lotto, < L. *quini,* five each, distributive of *quinque,* five.] A game of chance, adapted from lotto for gambling purposes.

ke-no-gen-e-sis (kē-nǫ-jen′e-sis or ken-ǫ-), etc. Same as *cenogenesis,* etc.

ke-no-sis (ke-nō′sis), *n.* [NL., < Gr. κένωσις, an emptying, < κενοῦν, make empty, < κενός, empty.] In *theol.,* an emptying; exinanition: used of Christ, "who, being in the form of God . . . *emptied himself,* taking the form of a servant, being made in the likeness of men" (Phil. ii. 6, 7, Revised Version), and referring to the renunciation of the divine nature or dignity in the incarnation.—**ke-not′ic** (-not′ik), *a.*

ken-o-tron (ken′ǫ-tron), *n.* [Gr. κενός, empty.] In *elect.,* a device for rectifying alternating currents, in which the chief feature is a vacuum-tube containing a hot metallic filament for a cathode. [Proprietary name.]

ken-speck-le (ken′spek-l), *a.* [Also earlier *kenspeck*: cf. Icel. *kennispeki,* the faculty of recognition, Sw. *kännspak,* quick at recognizing, also E. *conspicuous.*] Easily recognizable; of distinctive appearance; strongly marked; conspicuous. [Sc., Ir., and north. Eng.]

kent (kent), *n.* [Origin uncertain.] A long staff or pole used for leaping over ditches, etc.: as, "He bade me fling down my *kent,* and sae me and my mither yielded oursells prisoners" (Scott's "Old Mortality," xiv.). [Sc.]

Kent-ish (ken′tish), *a.* Of or pertaining to the English county of Kent or its inhabitants; also, of or pertaining to the former English kingdom of Kent, its inhabitants, or the dialect of Anglo-Saxon spoken by them.

kent-ledge (kent′lej), *n.* [Origin uncertain.] *Naut.,* pig-iron used as permanent ballast (as, "It [a dead body] was stitched up in one of the hammocks, some '*kentledge*' being placed at the feet instead of shot": H. Melville's "Omoo," xii.); also, *milit.,* in the British service, condemned shot, shell, etc.

kep-i (kep′i), *n.* [F. *képi,* < G. dial. *käppi,* dim. of G. *kappe,* cap.] A French military cap with a flat circular top and a horizontal vizor.

kept (kept). Preterit and past participle of *keep.*

ke-ram-ic (ke-ram′ik), etc. Same as *ceramic,* etc.

ker-a-tin (ker′ạ-tin), **ker-a-ti-tis** (ker-ạ-tī′tis), **kerato-,** etc. Same as *ceratin, ceratitis, cerato-,* etc.

ker-a-tol (ker′ạ-tōl), *n.* [Gr. κέρας (κερατ-), horn: see *-ol.*] An artificial substitute for leather, consisting of a strong cotton foundation with a pyroxylin coating containing oils and pigments and affording a durable, waterproof surface: used for upholstering furniture, automobiles, etc., for bookbinding, for making cases, handbags, and trunks, and for various other purposes. [Proprietary name.]

ke-rau-no-graph (ke-râ′nǫ-gråf), *n.* Same as *ceraunograph.*

kerb (kėrb), *n.* Occasional spelling of *curb*^{2} (stone border, edge of sidewalk). [Chiefly British.]—**kerb′stone,** *n.*

ker-chief (kėr′chif), *n.* [OF. *cuevrechief, couvrechief,* < *covrir,* E. *cover,* + *chief,* head, E. *chief.*] A cloth worn as a head-covering, esp. by women; also, a cloth worn or carried on the person, for some other purpose, as a neckerchief or a handkerchief.—**ker′chief,** *v. t.* To cover or attire with a kerchief.

kerf (kėrf), *n.* [AS. *cyrf,* a cutting, < *ceorfan,* cut, E. *carve.*] The act of cutting; a stroke with a cutting instrument; also, the cut or incision made by a saw or other cutting instrument; the place at which a tree or branch is or has been cut across; also, something which is or has been cut off; a cutting.

ke-rite (kē′rīt), *n.* [Gr. κηρός, wax.] A substitute for caoutchouc, made by combining asphalt or tar, animal or vegetable oil, and sulphur: used as an insulating material for electric wires, etc.

ker-mes (kėr′mēz), *n.* [Ar. and Pers. *qirmiz*: cf. *carmine* and *crimson.*] A red dyestuff consisting of the dried bodies of the females of a scale-insect, *Kermes* (or *Coccus*) *ilicis,* which lives on certain oaks (esp. *Quercus coccifera*) of Mediterranean regions; the insect itself; also, the small evergreen oak, *Quercus coccifera,* on which it is found. Cf. *cochineal.*

ker-mess, ker-mis (kėr′mes, -mis), *n.* [D. *kermis,* earlier *kermisse, kerkmisse,* 'church mass' (on the anniversary of the dedication of a church).] In the Low Countries and adjacent regions, an annual fair or festival attended with sports and merrymaking; in the U. S., an entertainment, usually for charitable purposes, in imitation of the European festival.

kern^{1} (kėrn), *n.* [F. *carne,* projecting angle, < L. *cardo,* hinge.] In *printing,* a part of the face of a type projecting beyond the body or shank, as in certain italic letters.—**kern**^{1}, *v. t.* To form or furnish with a kern, as a type or letter.

kern^{2}, *n.* See *kirn.*

kern^{3}, **kerne** (kėrn), *n.* [Ir. *ceithern,* band of foot-soldiers; akin to E. *cateran.*] A band of light-armed foot-soldiers of ancient Ireland; also, a soldier of this class (in Ireland or sometimes in the Scottish Highlands: as, "The outlawed king proposes to land near to Turnberry . . . with a number of stout *kernes* from Ireland," Scott's "Castle Dangerous," viii.); hence, an Irish peasant; also, any rustic or churl. [Archaic.]

ker-nel (kėr′nẹl), *n.* [AS. *cyrnel,* dim. of *corn,* E. *corn*^{1}.] A seed, as of an apple (obs. or prov.); also, the softer, usually edible, part contained in the shell of a nut or the stone of a fruit (as, "As brown in hue As hazel nuts and sweeter than the *kernels*": Shakspere's "Taming of the Shrew," ii. 1. 257); also, the body of a seed within its husk or integuments; a grain, as of wheat; also, the central part of anything; the nucleus; the core; fig., the gist (as, "He does discern clearly wherein lies, for him, the true *kernel* of the matter": Carlyle's "Past and Present," iv. 2).—**ker′nel,** *v. t.*; *-neled* or *-nelled, -neling* or *-nelling.* To inclose as a kernel.—**ker′neled, ker′nelled,** *a.* Having a kernel.

ker-o-sene (ker′ǫ-sēn), *n.* [Gr. κηρός, wax.] An illuminating oil, a mixture of hydrocarbons, distilled from petroleum, bituminous shale, etc.

ker-rie (ker′i), *n.* Same as *knobkerrie.*

Ker-ry (ker′i), *n.* One of a breed of small, active black cattle originating in the southwest of Ireland and of considerable value for dairy purposes: named from the Irish county of Kerry.

ker-sey (kėr′zi), *n.*; pl. *-seys* (-ziz). [Perhaps from *Kersey,* in Suffolk, England.] A compact, well-fulled woolen cloth with a fine nap and smooth face; also, a coarse twilled woolen cloth with a cotton warp.

ker-sey-mere (kėr′zi-mēr), *n.* A corruption of *cassimere,* simulating *kersey.*

kes-trel (kes′trẹl), *n.* [Cf. OF. *cresserele* (F. *crécerelle*), kestrel.] A common small European falcon, *Tinnunculus alaudarius,* notable for hovering in the air with its head to the wind.

ketch (kech), *n.* [Earlier *catch,* appar. < *catch, v.*] Orig., a strongly built two-masted vessel, usually of from 100 to 250 tons burden, having either square or fore-and-aft sails (cf. *bomb-ketch*); now, a fore-and-aft rigged vessel with two masts, a large mainmast (toward the bow) and a smaller mizzenmast (toward the stern, but in front of the rudder).

ketch-up (kech'up), *n.* See *catchup.*

ke-tene (kē'tēn), *n.* [See *ketone.*] In *chem.*, a gas, C_2H_2O, with a penetrating odor, derived from the anhydride of acetic acid; also, any of a class of related compounds.

ke-tone (kē'tōn), *n.* [G. *keton,* < *aceton,* acetone.] In *chem.*, any of a class of organic compounds, as acetone, each consisting of a group, CO, containing one atom of carbon and one of oxygen, united to one bivalent or two monovalent hydrocarbon radicals.—**ke-ton-ic** (kē-ton'ik), *a.*

ket-tle (ket'l), *n.* [AS. *cetel* = D. *ketel* = G. *kessel* = Icel. *ketill* = Goth. *katils,* kettle: cf. L. *catillus,* dim. of *catinus,* bowl, pot.] A metallic vessel for boiling liquids, cooking fruit, etc.; a pot; often, a tea-kettle; also, a kettledrum† (see Shakspere's "Hamlet," v. 2. 286); also, a kettle-hole or a pot-hole.—**kettle of fish,** a kettle of fish cooked in the open air at a picnic or the like, or the picnic itself (Sc. and north. Eng.: as, "The whole company go to the waterside to-day to eat a *kettle of fish,*" Scott's "St. Ronan's Well," xii.); also, a mess, muddle, or awkward state of things (often preceded ironically by *pretty, fine,* etc.: as, "Here's a pretty *kettle of fish* . . . you have brought upon us!" Fielding's "Joseph Andrews," i. 12).—**ket'tle-drum,** *n.* A kind of drum consisting of a hollow hemisphere of brass or copper with a head of parchment.—**ket'tle=hole,** *n.* A kettle-shaped cavity in rock or detrital material; esp., such a cavity in glacial drift, supposed to have been produced by the melting away of a mass of ice.

Kettledrums.

kev-el (kev'el), *n.* See *cavel.*

kex (keks), *n.* [ME. *kex, kyx;* origin uncertain.] The dry, hollow stalk of various umbelliferous or other plants; also, an umbelliferous plant with a hollow stalk, as the cowparsnip. [Now prov. Eng.]

key[1] (kē), *n.* Earlier form of *quay.*

key[2] (kē), *n.* [Var. of *cay.*] A reef or low island: as, the Florida *Keys.*

key[3] (kē). [AS. *cǣg* = OFries. *kei, kai,* key.] **I.** *n.* An instrument for fastening or opening a lock by moving its bolt; hence, something that secures or controls entrance to a place (as, Gibraltar is the *key* to the Mediterranean); also, a means of attaining, understanding, solving, etc. (as, a *key* to knowledge; a *key* to a cipher or a problem); a book or the like containing the solutions of mathematical or other problems proposed elsewhere as exercises; a translation of a book or the like in a foreign language; also, matter inserted in an advertisement in a magazine or the like, intended to enable the advertiser to identify replies to it; also, a pin, bolt, wedge, or other piece inserted in a hole or space to lock or hold parts of a mechanism or structure together; a cotter; sometimes, a keystone; also, a contrivance for grasping and turning a bolt, nut, etc. (as, a watch-*key*); also, one of a set of levers or parts pressed in operating a pianoforte, organ, flute, telegraph, typewriter, or other mechanism; also, *pl.* [*cap.*], a body of twenty-four representatives constituting the lower or elective branch of the legislature of the Isle of Man (called in full 'House of Keys'); also, *sing.* [*l. c.*], in *bot.*, a samara; also, in *music,* a scale or system of notes or tones based on a particular note (the 'key-note'); also, the sum of relations, melodic and harmonic, existing between the tones of such a system; tonality; hence, in general and fig. use, tone or pitch, as of voice (as, to speak in a high or low *key,* or a plaintive *key*); strain, or characteristic style, as of expression or thought; degree of intensity, as of feeling or action. **II.** *a.* Acting or operating like a key; controlling; of chief or critical importance; pivotal; fundamental: as, the *key* industries of a nation; *key* productions or materials.—**key**[3], *v. t.*; *keyed, keying.* To lock with or as with a key; also, to fasten, secure, or adjust with a key, wedge, or the like, as parts of a mechanism; insert the keystone in (an arch); also, to regulate the key or pitch of; hence, fig., to adjust (speech, etc.) as if to a particular key (as, a letter *keyed* to a tone of defiance); bring to a particular degree of intensity of feeling, excitement, energy, etc. (as, to *key,* or *key* up, the mind, or a person, to a high pitch of enthusiasm); also, to provide with a key or keys; insert a key in (an advertisement: see *key*[3], *n.*).

key-board (kē'bōrd), *n.* The row or set of keys in a pianoforte, organ, typewriter, etc.; any of two or more sets of keys, as in large organs.

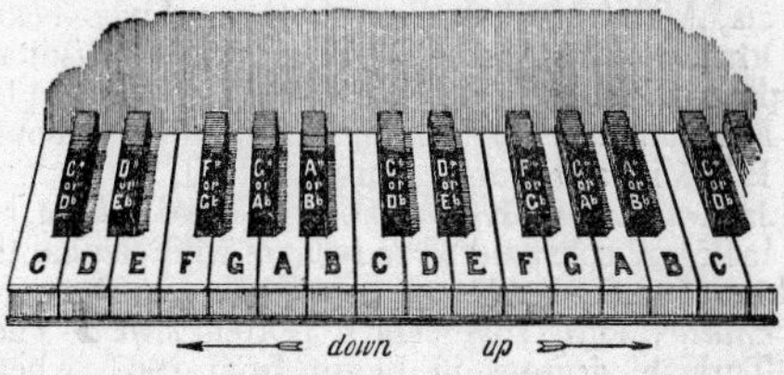

Keyboard of a Pianoforte, showing two octaves.

key=cold (kē'-kōld), *a.* Cold as a key; quite cold; esp., cold in death (as, "Poor *key-cold* figure of a holy king!" Shakspere's "Richard III.," i. 2. 5); fig., apathetic. [Archaic.]

keyed (kēd), *a.* Having a key or keys.

key=fruit (kē'fröt), *n.* In *bot.*, a samara.

key-hole (kē'hōl), *n.* A hole for admitting a key into a lock.

key-less (kē'les), *a.* Without a key or keys.

key-man (kē'man), *n.*; pl. *-men.* A telegraph-operator. [Colloq.]

key=note (kē'nōt), *n.* In *music,* the note or tone on which a key (system of tones) is founded; the tonic; hence, fig., the determining principle governing the tone, tenor, or spirit of speech, thought, action, etc.; specif., the line of policy to be followed by a party in a political (or other) campaign, as set forth authoritatively in advance in a public speech or other formal announcement; an introductory declaration of party principles, as by the temporary chairman of the national convention of a U. S. political party meeting to nominate candidates for President and Vice-President.—**key'=not''er** (-nō''tėr), *n.* One who gives the keynote, as of a political campaign. [Colloq.]

key=ring (kē'ring), *n.* A ring on which keys are kept together.

key-stone (kē'stōn), *n.* The wedge-shaped piece at the summit of an arch, regarded as holding the other pieces in place; fig., something occupying a central position, or something on which a number of associated things depend; the central or chief principle, as of a system (as, "The tenet of predestination was the *keystone* of his religion": Macaulay's "Hist. of Eng.," vii.).

key-way (kē'wā), *n.* An aperture for the reception of a key; a groove or slot cut in a shaft, etc., for the reception of a key.

kha-ki (kä'kē). [Hind. *khākī,* dusty, < *khāk,* dust.] **I.** *a.* Dust-colored; dull yellowish-brown; also, made of khaki. **II.** *n.*; pl. *-kis* (-kēz). A stout, twilled cotton cloth of a yellowish-brown, olive-brown, or other inconspicuous color, much used for military uniforms, orig. by British troops in India; a similar fabric of wool; also, clothing made of any such cloth or fabric; also, a soldier clothed in it.

kha-li-fa (ka-lē'fa), *n.* [Ar. *khalīfah.*] Same as *calif.*

kham-sin (kam'sin or kam-sēn'), *n.* [Ar. *khamsīn,* lit. 'fifty.'] A hot southerly wind (varying from southeast to southwest) that blows regularly in Egypt for about 50 days, commencing about the middle of March.

khan[1] (kän or kan), *n.* [Ar. and Turk. *khān.*] In Oriental coun-

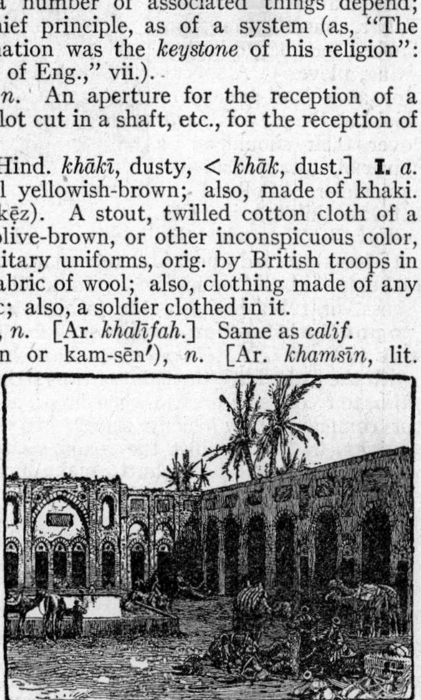
Interior of a Khan.

tries, an unfurnished inn for travelers; a caravansary: as, "I . . . took up my quarters at the caravanserai or '*Khan*,' as they call it in that part of Asia" (Kinglake's "Eothen," xvii.). See cut on preceding page.

khan² (kän or kan), *n.* [Orig. Tatar, whence Pers. and Ar. *khān*: cf. *cham.*] A Tatar title of a sovereign prince; a bearer of this title, as the supreme ruler of the Tatar tribes, as well as emperor of China, during the middle ages (the 'great khan'); also, a title of dignity or respect used in Persia, Afghanistan, India, etc., or one who bears this title.—**khan'ate** (-āt), *n.* The dominion or jurisdiction of a khan.

khan-sa-mah (kän'sa̤-mä or kän-sä'mä̤), *n.* [Hind. and Pers. *khānsāmān*, < *khān*, master, + *sāmān*, household goods.] In India, a butler or house-steward.

khed-a, ked-dah (ked'ä̤), *n.* [Hind. *khedā.*] In India, an inclosure constructed to insnare wild elephants.

khe-dive (ke̤-dēv'), *n.* [F. *khédive*, < Turk. *khidīw*, < Pers. *khidīw*, lord, sovereign.] [Often *cap.*] The title of the Turkish viceroys in Egypt from 1867, when assumed by Ismail Pasha, until 1914, when the country was made a British protectorate.—**khe-di'val, khe-di'vi-al** (-dē'va̤l, -vi-a̤l), *a.*—**khe-di'vi-ate** (-āt), *n.* The office, authority, or jurisdiction of the khedive.

khid-mut-gar, khit-mut-gar (kid'mut-gär, kit'-), *n.* [Hind. *khidmatgār.*] In India, a waiter or under-butler.

khud (kud), *n.* [Hind. *khad.*] A deep ravine; a precipitous cleft or chasm. [E. Ind.]

ki-a-boo-ca=wood (kī-a̤-bö'ka̤-wůd), *n.* [Malay *kayu-buku.*] An ornamental wood mottled in shades of yellowish red, from a Malaysian tree, *Pterocarpus indicus*: used in inlaying and for making small articles.

kiang (kyang), *n.* See *kyang.*

kib-ble (kib'l), *n.* [Cf. G. *kübel*, tub, bucket.] A large bucket for hoisting ore, etc., in the shaft of a mine.—**kib'-ble,** *v. t.* or *i.*; *-bled, -bling.* To hoist (ore, etc.) in a kibble.

kibe (kīb), *n.* [ME. *kybe*; perhaps from Welsh.] A chapped or ulcerated chilblain, esp. on the heel. See Shakspere's "Merry Wives of Windsor," i. 3. 35.—**kibed,** *a.* Affected with kibes: as, "a pair of *kibed* heels" (Lamb's "Praise of Chimney-Sweepers").

ki-bit-ka (ki-bit'ka̤), *n.* [Russ.; from Tatar.] A Tatar circular tent of collapsible latticework covered with felt; also, a Russian wagon or sledge with a rounded top or cover.

Kibitka, or Kirghiz Tent.

kib-itz-er (kib'it-sėr), *n.* [Yiddish, < G. *kiebitzen*, look on at cards, < *kiebitz*, *kibitz*, meddlesome onlooker, meddler, orig. lapwing, plover.] A spectator at a card-game who looks at the players' cards over their shoulders; a giver of unwanted advice; a meddler. [Colloq.]

kib-lah (kib'lä̤), *n.* [Ar. *qiblah*, lit. 'that which is opposite.'] The point (the Kaaba at Mecca) toward which Mohammedans turn at prayer.

ki-bosh (ki-bosh' or kī-), *n.* [Origin obscure.] Stuff, nonsense, or rubbish; also, the fashion or style. [Slang.]—**to put the kibosh on,** to dispose of finally; do for. [Slang.]

kick (kik), *v. i.* [ME. *kiken*; perhaps imit.] To strike out with the foot; have the habit of thus striking out, as a horse; also, to recoil, as a firearm when fired; also, to resist, object, or complain (now chiefly slang).—**to kick against the pricks,** to kick against the goads, as oxen; hence, to be refractory, to one's own hurt; make ineffectual and unwise resistance to superior force. See Acts, ix. 5.—**to kick off,** in *football*, to give the ball the first kick, which starts the play; in the American game, to make a kick-off (see *kick-off, n.*).—**kick,** *v. t.* To give a blow or thrust to with the foot; also, to strike smartly, as a gun does in the recoil; also, to drive, force, make, etc., by or as by kicks (as, "to *kick* the stool from under you," Fielding's "Tom Jones," i. 13; "Ball after ball flew over or fell short, or *kicked* up the sand in the enclosure," Stevenson's "Treasure Island," xviii.); in *football*, to win (a goal) by a kick.—**to kick the bucket,** to die: as, "Peter, I shall make my will, not that I am going to *kick the bucket* just yet" (Marryat's "Peter Simple," xxxvii.). [Slang.]—**kick,** *n.* An act of kicking; a blow or thrust with the foot; also, power or disposition to kick; also, a recoil, as of a gun (as, "The *kick* of the rifle disconcerts your aim": Cooper's "Last of the Mohicans," vii.); a jolt or jerk; also, vigor, energy, or vim (slang); a vigorous or lively quality in something (slang); often, a stimulating or intoxicating quality in alcoholic drink (slang); the alcoholic element of a beverage (slang); also, an objection or complaint (slang); also, one who kicks, esp. in football (as, "He's . . . the best *kick* . . . in Rugby": Hughes's "Tom Brown's School Days," i. 5); also, the indentation or inner protuberance in the bottom of some glass bottles; also, the projection on the front of the tang of a pocket-knife blade, by which the blade is prevented from striking the spring in closing; also, the style or fashion, or a thing in fashion (slang, Eng.); also, *pl.*, trousers (slang, orig. Eng.); also, *sing.*, a pocket (slang); also, *pl.*, shoes (slang).—**drop kick.** See *drop-kick, n.*—**free kick.** See under *free, a.*—**more kicks than halfpence,** more ill treatment than presents, favors, etc.; more harshness than kindness: as, "like monkey's allowance . . . *more kicks than halfpence*" (Scott's "St. Ronan's Well," xxxiv.).—**place kick.** See *place-kick, n.*—**kick'er,** *n.*—**kick'=off,** *n.* In *football*, the opening kick in a football match; in the American game, a place-kick down the field from the 40-yard line of the side kicking, as at the beginning of the first and third periods.

kick-shaw (kik'shâ), *n.* [F. *quelque chose*, something.] Any fancy dish in cookery (see Shakspere's "2 Henry IV.," v. 1. 29); also, any dainty, unsubstantial, or paltry trifle; a bit of trumpery; a gimcrack.

kid¹ (kid), *n.* [From Scand.: cf. Icel. *kidh*, Sw. and Dan. *kid*, and G. *kitze*, kid.] A young goat, or its flesh; also, the skin of a young goat, or leather made from it; *pl.*, gloves of this leather (colloq.: as, "His great hands . . . are encased in lemon-coloured *kids*," Thackeray's "Ravenswing," iv.); also, *sing.*, a child or young person (slang: as, "I started as a average *kid*, I finished as a thinkin' man," Kipling's "Return").—**kid¹,** *v. t.* or *i.*; *kidded, kidding.* Of a goat, to give birth to (young).

kid² (kid), *n.* [Cf. *kit¹.*] A small tub (prov. Eng.); also, a tub-like wooden vessel in which food is served to sailors (as, "Woe be unto him, if at meal-times he so much as look sideways at the beef-*kid* before the rest are helped": H. Melville's "Omoo," xiv.); also, a wooden pen on the deck of a fishing-vessel, to hold the fish caught.

kid³ (kid), *v.*; *kidded, kidding.* [Appar. < *kid¹, n.*] **I.** *tr.* To humbug or fool; hence, to chaff; banter. [Slang.] **II.** *intr.* To speak or act deceptively, in jest; jest. [Slang.]—**kid³,** *n.* Kidding; humbug; chaffing. [Slang.]—**kid'-der,** *n.*

Kid-der-min-ster (kid'ėr-min-stėr), *n.* [From *Kidderminster*, town in Worcestershire, England.] A kind of ingrain carpet.

kid-dle (kid'l), *n.* [OF. *quidel*, also *guidel* (F. *guideau*); origin uncertain.] A weir or barrier in a stream, fitted with nets, etc., for catching fish; also, an arrangement of stakes and network on a beach, for the same purpose.

kid-dy, kid-die (kid'i), *n.*; pl. *kiddies* (-iz). A little kid (young goat); also, a little child (slang or colloq.).

kid=glove (kid'gluv'), *a.* Wearing kid gloves; characterized by or suitable for the wearing of kid gloves; delicate, dainty, nice, or elegant (rather than rough or coarse): as, *kid-glove* reformers; *kid-glove* measures.—**kid=glove orange,** a mandarin or a tangerine (orange).

kid-let, kid-ling (kid'let, -ling), *n.* A little kid (young goat): as, "At yonder door Behold the favourite *kidling* bleats unheard" (Southey's "Roderick," xi. 95).

kid-nap (kid'nap), *v. t.*; *-napped, -napping.* [From *kid¹* + *nap³.*] To steal or abduct (a child or other person); carry off (a person) against his will by unlawful force or by fraud.—**kid'nap-per,** *n.*

kid-ney (kid'ni), *n.*; pl. *-neys* (-niz). [ME. *kidenei*; origin obscure.] In man, either of a pair of bean-shaped glandular organs (about 4 inches in length) in the back part of the abdominal cavity, which excrete urine (see cut at head of first column of following page); also, a corresponding organ in other vertebrate animals, or an organ of like function in invertebrate animals; also, fig., constitution or temperament (as, "a man of my *kidney* . . . that am as subject to heat as butter": Shakspere's "Merry Wives of Windsor," iii. 5. 116); hence, kind, sort, or class (as, "He paraded up and down the streets with a crew of hard swearers at his heels . . . heroes of his own *kidney*": Irving's "Knickerbocker's New York," vi. 5).—**floating kidney.** See under *floating*.—**kid′ney=bean,** *n.* The common bean, *Phaseolus vulgaris*, or its kidney-shaped seed; also, the scarlet runner, or its seed.—**kid′ney=shaped,** *a.* Having the general shape of a long oval indented at one side.—**kid′ney=vetch,** *n.* An old-world fabaceous herb, *Anthyllis vulneraria*, sometimes raised as fodder for sheep, and formerly used as a remedy for kidney diseases.

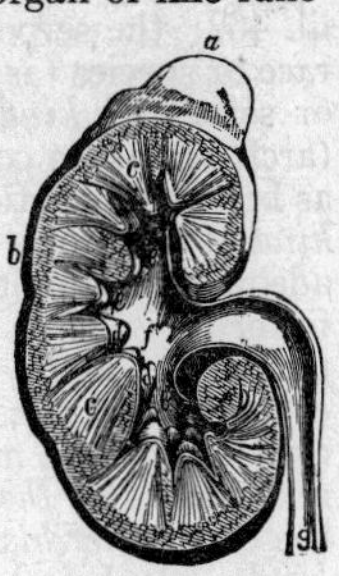

Section of Human Kidney. — *a*, suprarenal capsule; *b*, vascular or cortical portion of kidney; *c*, *c*, tubular portion, consisting of cones; *d*, *d*, two of the papillæ, projecting into their corresponding calyces; *e*, *e*, *e*, the three infundibula; *f*, pelvis; *g*, ureter.

Kidney-shaped Leaf.

kief (kēf or kē-ef′), *n.* [= *kaif.*] Among the Arabs, easeful or dreamy quiescence; a state of drowsy contentment, as from the use of a narcotic; also, a substance, esp. a smoking preparation of hemp leaves, used to produce this state.

kier (kēr), *n.* [Cf. Icel. *ker*, vessel, tub.] A large boiler or vat used in bleaching, etc.

kie-sel-guhr (kē′zel-gör), *n.* [G., < *kiesel*, flint, + *guhr*, earthy deposit.] A fine siliceous earth composed chiefly of diatomaceous remains: used as an absorbent for nitroglycerin in the manufacture of dynamite.

kike (kīk), *n.* [Origin obscure.] A Jew. [Slang.]

kik-u-mon (kik′ö-mon), *n.* [Jap. *kiku*, chrysanthemum, + *mon*, device, cognizance.] A device representing an open chrysanthemum of sixteen rays, often with the tips of sixteen others appearing between the ends of the first set, borne as the official cognizance or badge of the imperial family of Japan, as on the imperial standard. Cf. *kirimon* and *mon*.

Kikumon.

kil-[1] (kil-). [Ir. and Gael. *cill*, < L. *cella*, E. *cell.*] An element in Celtic place-names, meaning 'cell,' 'church, 'burial-place,' as in *Kilbride, Kildare, Kilkenny, Kilmarnock*.

kil-[2]. See *kilo-*.

kil-am-pere (kil′am-pãr″), *n.* Same as *kilo-ampere*.

kil-der-kin (kil′dėr-kin), *n.* [MD. *kindeken*; origin uncertain: cf. *firkin.*] A cask holding half a barrel; hence, a measure of capacity of this amount.

kil-erg (kil′ėrg), *n.* [See *kilo-* and *erg.*] In *physics*, a unit of work equal to 1,000 ergs.

kill[1] (kil), *v.* [ME. *cullen, kyllen*; origin uncertain.] **I.** *tr.* To strike† or smite†; hence, to deprive (any living creature or thing) of life in any manner (as, to *kill* a man or an animal; the blow or the drug *killed* him; the cold *killed* the vines); cause the death of; slay; fig., to destroy, do away with, or suppress (as, "As good almost kill a man as *kill* a good book": Milton's "Areopagitica"); put an end to, or extinguish (as, to *kill* sound or odor; to *kill* faith, hope, or joy; to *kill* one's prospects or chances); cancel (a word, paragraph, item, etc.); defeat or veto (a legislative bill, etc.); also, to destroy or neutralize the active qualities of (as, to *kill* land in farming; to *kill* grain by overheating in grinding; to *kill* wire by stretching so as to destroy ductility); spoil the effect of (as, one color may *kill* another near it; general laughter *killed* the speaker's lofty climax); also, to get rid of (time) by some method (usually easy or agreeable) of spending it (as, "The Knight of Kerry was walking along the Strand in London, *killing* an hour's time": Lever's "Harry Lorrequer," xxxix.); also, to overcome completely or with irresistible effect (as, "Vociferated logic *kills* me quite," Cowper's "Conversation," 113; "Surely that wad touch her heart, Wha *kills* me wi' disdaining," Burns's "To the Woodlark": cf. *killing, p. a.*). **II.** *intr.* To inflict or cause death (as, "The Lord *killeth*, and maketh alive": 1 Sam. ii. 6); specif., to commit murder (as, "Thou shalt not *kill*": Ex. xx. 13).—**kill**[1], *n.* The act of killing (game, etc.); also, an animal killed, as by sportsmen or a beast of prey (as, "If ye plunder his *Kill* from a weaker, devour not all in thy pride": Kipling's "Law of the Jungle").

kill[2] (kil), *n.* [D. *kil.*] A channel; a creek; a stream; a river: used esp. as an element in place-names (as *Catskill* and *Schuylkill*) in parts of the U. S. orig. settled by the Dutch.

kill-crop (kil′krop), *n.* [LG. *kilkrop*, G. *kielkropf*, changeling; origin uncertain.] In popular superstition, a fairy changeling endowed with an insatiable hunger.

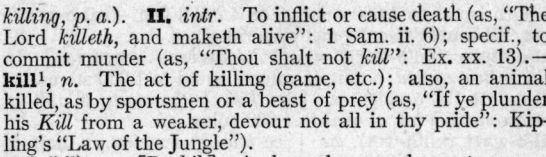

kill-deer, kill-dee (kil′dēr, kil′dē), *n.* [Imit. of its note.] A noisy American plover, *Ægialitis vociferus*.

Killdeer.

kill-er (kil′ėr), *n.* One who or that which kills; a person or an animal that is given to killing; specif., any of various ravenous, gregarious cetaceans of the dolphin family, esp. of the genus *Orca*, as *O. gladiator*, the common species of the northern Atlantic.

kil′lick, *n.* See *killock*.

kil-li-fish (kil′i-fish), *n.* [Appar. < *kill*[2].] Any of various fishes (genera *Fundulus, Hydrargyra*, etc.) of the family *Cyprinodontidæ*, which abound in shallow bays, channels, rivers, etc., of eastern North America, the species varying in length from less than an inch to about a foot.

kil-li-ki-nick (kil″i-ki-nik′), *n.* Same as *kinnikinick*.

kill-ing (kil′ing), *n.* The act of one who or that which kills; a slaying; fig., a stroke of deadly or extraordinary execution, as in a successful speculation in stocks (colloq.).—**kill′ing,** *p. a.* That kills; deadly; destructive, or fatal (as, "a *killing* frost": Shakspere's "Henry VIII.," iii. 2. 355); overpowering or exhausting (as, a *killing* pace); irresistibly captivating (colloq.); irresistibly funny (colloq.).—**kill′ing-ly,** *adv.*

kill=joy (kil′joi), *n.* A person or thing that spoils the joy or enjoyment of others.

kil-lock, kil-lick (kil′ok, kil′ik), *n.* [Origin obscure.] A small anchor or weight for mooring a boat, sometimes consisting of a stone secured by pieces of wood.

kiln (kil or kiln), *n.* [AS. *cyln, cyline*, < L. *culina*, kitchen.] A furnace or oven for burning, baking, or drying something, esp. one for calcining limestone or one for baking bricks.—**kiln,** *v. t.* To burn, bake, or treat in a kiln.—**kiln′=dry,** *v. t.* To dry in a kiln.

kilo-, kil-[2]. [F. *kilo-*, repr. Gr. χίλιοι, thousand.] A prefix meaning 'thousand,' used in the nomenclature of the metric system and of other scientific systems of measurement.

kil-o (kil′ō), *n.*; pl. *kilos* (-ōz). Shortened form of *kilogram*.

kil-o=am-pere (kil′ö-am-pãr″), *n.* [See *kilo-*.] In *elect.*, a unit equal to 1,000 amperes.

kil-o-cal-o-ry, kil-o-cal-o-rie (kil′ö-kal″ö-ri), *n.*; pl. *-ries* (-riz). [See *kilo-*.] In *physics*, a large calory. See *calory*.

kil-o-cy-cle (kil′ö-sī-kl), *n.* [See *kilo-*.] A unit equal to 1,000 cycles: used esp. in radio for measuring the frequency of electric waves (see *frequency*).

kil-o-dyne (kil′ö-dīn), *n.* [See *kilo-*.] In *physics*, a unit of force equal to 1,000 dynes.

kil-o-gram, kil-o-gramme (kil′ö-gram), *n.* [F. *kilogramme*: see *kilo-*.] In the *metric system*, a unit of weight equal to 1,000 grams, or 2.2046 pounds avoirdupois. See *gram*.—**kil′o-gram-me″ter, kil′o-gram-me″tre** (-mē″tėr), *n.* In *physics*, a unit used in measuring work, being that done in raising one kilogram a vertical distance of one meter.

kil-o-li-ter, kil-o-li-tre (kil′ö-lē-tėr), *n.* [F. *kilolitre*: see *kilo-*.] In the *metric system*, a unit of capacity equal to 1,000 liters (one cubic meter), 28.377 U. S. bushels, or 264.17 U. S. gallons.

kil-o-me-ter, kil-o-me-tre (kil′ö-mē-tėr), *n.* [F. *kilomètre*: see *kilo-*.] In the *metric system*, a measure of length equal to 1,000 meters, or 3,280.8 feet.—**kil-o-met′-ric, kil-o-met′ri-cal** (-met′rik, -ri-kạl), *a.*

kil-o-stere (kil′ọ-stēr), *n.* [F. *kilostère*: see *kilo-*.] In the *metric system*, a unit of volume equal to 1,000 steres.

kil-o-volt (kil′ọ-vōlt), *n.* [See *kilo-*.] In *elect.*, a unit of electromotive force equal to 1,000 volts.

kil-o-watt (kil′ọ-wot), *n.* [See *kilo-*.] In *elect.*, a unit of power equal to 1,000 watts.

kilt (kilt), *v. t.* [Prob. from Scand.: cf. Dan. *kilte*, tuck up.] To draw or tuck up (the skirt, etc.) about one (as, "The wives maun *kilt* their coats, and wade into the surf": Scott's "Antiquary," xxvi.); also, to pleat (cloth, a skirt, etc.) in deep vertical folds.—**kilt,** *n.* A sort of pleated skirt, reaching to the knees, worn by men in the Scottish Highlands; hence, any similar skirt worn elsewhere, by men, women, or children.—**kilt′ed,** *a.* Wearing a kilt; also, pleated like a kilt.

kil-ter, kel-ter (kil′tėr, kel′-), *n.* [Origin obscure.] Good condition; order: as, to be out of *kilter*, or *kelter*. [Colloq.]

kilt-ie, kilt-y (kil′ti), *n.*; pl. *kilties* (-tiz). One wearing a kilt; a Highland soldier, or a soldier in Highland dress.

kim-ber-lite (kim′bėr-līt), *n.* [From *Kimberley*, South Africa.] A diamond-bearing altered peridotite occurring in South Africa.

ki-mo-no (ki-mō′nō), *n.*; pl. *-nos* (-nōz). [Jap.] A long, loose outer garment held in place by a sash, worn by the Japanese of both sexes; hence, a woman's loose dressing-gown.

kin[1] (kin), *n.* [AS. *cynn* = OHG. *chunni* = Icel. *kyn* = Goth. *kuni*, kin; from a Teut. root equivalent to L. *gen-*, Gr. *γεν-*, Skt. *jan-*, beget, bear, produce: see *genius*, and cf. *kind*[1], *kind*[2], and *king*.] A group of persons descended from a common ancestor, or constituting a family, clan, tribe, or race (archaic); family, stock, or lineage (archaic or prov.: as, of good or noble *kin*); now, usually, one's relatives collectively, or kinsfolk (as, "Sir Torre . . . Past up the still rich city to his *kin*, His own far blood, which dwelt at Camelot," Tennyson's "Lancelot and Elaine," 797; one's kith and *kin*, see under *kith*); sometimes, a relative or kinsman (archaic: as, "Is he thy *kin*?" Shakspere's "Cymbeline," v. 5. 111); also, family relationship or kinship (as, "Within Prohibited degrees of *kin*": Butler's "Hudibras," iii. 1).—**next of kin.** See under *next, a.*—**of kin,** of the same family; related; akin: as, to be *of kin* to a person.—**kin**[1], *a.* Of kin; related; akin: as, "He is a Roman; no more *kin* to me Than I to your highness" (Shakspere's "Cymbeline," v. 5. 112). Also fig.

kin[2] (kin), *n.* See *kine*[2].

-kin. [D. and LG. *-ken* = G. *-chen*.] A noun suffix with a diminutive force, as in *catkin, manikin, minikin, pannikin, princekin.*

kin-æs-the-sia (kin-es-thē′ziạ̈ or kī-nes-), *n.* [NL., < Gr. *κινεῖν*, move, + *αἴσθησις*, perception.] The sense of muscular effort. Also **kin-æs-the′sis** (-sis).

kin-cob (king′kob), *n.* [Hind. *kimkhāb*.] A rich East Indian fabric of silk, or silk and cotton, with interwoven threads of gold or silver.

kind[1] (kīnd), *n.* [AS. *gecynd, gecynde*, < *ge-*, a generalizing prefix, + *-cynd, -cynde*, from the root of *cynn*, E. *kin*[1].] The nature, or natural disposition or character, of a person or thing (archaic: as, after one's or its *kind*, see phrase following; "The mother-bird is gone to sea, As she had chang'd her *kind*," Cowper's "Tale," 46); nature in general (archaic: as, the law of *kind*; "filthy lust, contrary unto *kinde*," Spenser's "Faerie Queene," iii. 2. 40); sometimes, sex†; also, manner, fashion, or way (archaic: as, "mirthful he, but in a stately *kind*," Tennyson's "Lancelot and Elaine," 320); also, nature or character as determining likeness or difference between things (as, things of like *kind*; things differing in degree rather than in *kind*; a work unique in *kind*); hence, a particular variety or sort as distinguished by nature or character (as, a rare *kind* of orchid; all *kinds* of merchandise; what *kind* of cloth is this?); a class or group of individuals of the same nature or character (as, this *kind* of shells is, or sometimes are, often found; irregularly, and now only colloquially, these, or those, *kind* of shells: cf. *sort*[2], *n.*, in similar uses); esp., a race of beings, or a natural group of animals or plants (as, "Middle spirits . . . Betwixt the angelical and human *kind*," Milton's "Paradise Lost," iii. 462; the serpent *kind*; the oak *kind*); one's or its own race or species (as, "France, beloved of every soul that loves or serves its *kind!*" Kipling's "France"); family or stock (archaic: as, to come of good *kind*); also, a person or thing as being of a particular character or class (as, he is a strange *kind* of hero for a romance); a more or less adequate or inadequate example, or a sort, of something (as, the vines formed a *kind* of roof; to take a *kind* of pleasure in one's troubles).—**after one's,** or **its, kind,** according to one's or its own nature; in the character or manner natural to him or it: as, "God made the beast of the earth *after his kind*, and cattle *after their kind*, and every thing that creepeth upon the earth *after his kind*" (Gen. i. 25); man will act *after his kind*. [Archaic.]—**in kind,** in the particular kind of thing, or in goods or natural produce, instead of money (as, to take tithes *in kind*; to make payment *in kind*); also, in something of the same kind (as, to return a favor *in kind*; to retaliate *in kind*).—**kind of** (used adverbially), after a fashion; to some extent; somewhat; rather: as, the room was *kind of* dark; this seemed *kind of* unfair; I *kind of* thought so; I liked it, *kind of*. [Colloq.]—**of a kind,** of the same kind, or alike (as, two *of a kind*); also, of a mediocre, indifferent, or makeshift kind (as, music *of a kind*; they make bread *of a kind* from roots); of sorts.

kind[2] (kīnd), *a.* [AS. *gecynde*, < *gecynd*: see *kind*[1].] Natural†, native†, or innate†; hence, proper† or fitting†; rightful† or lawful†; also, of a good stock, kind, or quality, or in good condition (now prov. Eng.); also, of a good or benevolent nature or disposition, as a person; having or showing, or proceeding from, a benevolent or good-natured readiness to benefit or please others (as, a *kind* master; a *kind* heart; *kind* words or acts); indulgent, considerate, merciful, or humane (often with *to*: as, "Be ye *kind* one to another, tenderhearted, forgiving one another," Eph. iv. 32; to be *kind* to animals); beneficent, helpful, or good (*to*); also, friendly or cordial (as, please give them my *kindest* regards); affectionate or loving (archaic or prov. Eng.: as, "Stiles where we stay'd to be *kind*, Meadows in which we met," Tennyson's "Window," 172); also, grateful or thankful (now prov. Eng.); also, pleasant, agreeable, or favorable, as weather (now prov. Eng.); also, soft, tender, or easily worked, as materials, soil, etc. (prov. or technical).

kin-der-gar-ten (kin′dėr-gär″tn), *n.* [G., 'children's garden.'] A school of a type originated by the German educational reformer Friedrich Fröbel (1782–1852), for furthering the mental, moral, and physical development of young children by means of games, occupations, etc., that make use of their natural tendency to express themselves in action.—**kin′der-gart″ner,** *n.* [G. *kindergärtner*.] A kindergarten teacher.

kind=heart-ed (kīnd′här′ted), *a.* Having or showing a kind heart; kindly.—**kind′=heart′ed-ness,** *n.*

kin-dle[1] (kin′dl), *v. t.* or *i.*; *-dled, -dling.* [ME. *kindlen*; akin to *kind*[1].] Of rabbits, etc., to bring forth (young). See Shakspere's "As You Like It," iii. 2. 358. [Now prov. Eng.]

kin-dle[2] (kin′dl), *v.*; *-dled, -dling.* [Prob. from Scand.: cf. Icel. *kynda*, kindle, *kyndill*, a candle, torch.] **I.** *tr.* To set fire to, or ignite (fuel or any combustible matter); light (a torch, etc.); more commonly, to set (a fire, flame, etc.) to burning or blazing; fig., to animate, rouse, or inflame (a person, the mind, etc.: as, "His talk, When wine and free companions *kindled* him, Was wont to glance and sparkle like a gem," Tennyson's "Geraint and Enid," 293); excite (a feeling, suspicion, etc.); stir up or set going (strife, war, etc.); also, to light up, illuminate, or make bright (as, "The fires expanding . . . *kindle* half the skies": Pope's tr. Homer's "Iliad," ii.); produce, as a glow of light or color. **II.** *intr.* To begin to burn, as combustible matter, a light, or a fire or flame; fig., to become roused, ardent, or inflamed (as, "The warrior spirit of the cavaliers *kindled* at the thoughts": Irving's "Conquest of Granada," ii.); spring or start up, as feelings, strife, etc.; also, to become lighted up, bright, or glowing, as the sky at dawn or the eyes with ardor.—**kin′dler,** *n.*

kind-li-ness (kīnd′li-nes), *n.* The state or quality of being kindly; kindly spirit; benevolence; also, a kindly deed.

kin-dling (kind′ling), *n.* The act of one who kindles; also, material for starting a fire (often in *pl.*).

kind-ly (kīnd′li), *a.*; compar. *kindlier*, superl. *kindliest.* [AS. *gecyndelīc*, < *gecynde*, E. *kind*[1], *n.*; in later senses associated with *kind*[2], *a.*] Natural†, native†, or innate† (as, "The earth shall sooner leave her *kindly* skil To bring forth fruit": Spenser's "Faerie Queene," i. 3. 28); hence, proper† or fitting†; hereditary†; rightful, lawful, or legitimate (obs. or archaic); also, of a good kind or quality, or in good condition (archaic or prov. Eng.); also, having, showing, or proceeding from, a benevolent disposition or spirit (as, a *kindly* people; *kindly* faces; *kindly* criticism); kind in feeling, spirit, manner, tone, etc.; kind-hearted; good-natured; sympathetic; also, pleasant, genial, or benign (as, "In soft silence shed the *kindly* shower": Pope's "Messiah," 14); gentle or mild, as rule or laws; favorable, as soil for crops.—**kind′ly,** *adv.* [AS. *gecyndelīce.*] Naturally†; hence, spontaneously or readily (now prov. or colloq.); also, in a kindly or kind manner; with sympathetic or helpful kindness; cordially or heartily (as, we thank you *kindly*); pleasantly, agreeably, or favorably; with pleasure or liking (as, to take *kindly* to an idea, or to a person).

kind-ness (kīnd′nes), *n.* The state or quality of being kind; also, kind action or treatment; a kind act, or favor; also, friendly feeling, or liking; a feeling of regard or affection (as, "I've a notion that there's a *kindness* between him and that nice modest girl, Mary Burge": George Eliot's "Adam Bede," ix.).

kin-dred (kin′dred). [ME. *kynrede*, *kynreden*, < AS. *cynn*, E. *kin*[1], + *rǣden*, condition.] **I.** *n.* Relationship by birth or descent, or sometimes (less correctly) by marriage; kinship; fig., natural relationship, or affinity (as, "Thy likeness to the wise below, Thy *kindred* with the great of old": Tennyson's "In Memoriam," lxxiv.); also, a body of persons related to one another, or a family, tribe, or race (as, "In thy seed shall all the *kindreds* of the earth be blessed": Acts, iii. 25); now, usually, one's relatives collectively, kinsfolk, or kin (as, "The queen's *kindred* are made gentlefolks": Shakspere's "Richard III.," i. 1. 95). **II.** *a.* Related by birth or descent, or having kinship (as, *kindred* tribes); belonging to kin or relatives (as, *kindred* blood); fig., associated by origin, nature, qualities, etc. (as, *kindred* languages; *kindred* souls; *kindred* phenomena); allied; cognate; of like character.

kine[1] (kin), *n.* Archaic plural of *cow*[1].

kine[2], **kin**[2] (kīn, kin), *n.* [Gr. κινεῖν, move.] In *physics*, the unit of velocity in the centimeter-gram-second system, being equivalent to a velocity of one centimeter per second.

kin-e-mat-ic (kin-ē-mat′ik or kī-nē-), *a.* [Gr. κίνημα (κινηματ-), motion, < κινεῖν, move.] Pertaining to pure motion or to kinematics.—**kinematic link.** See *link*[4], *n.*—**kinematic pair.** See *pair*, *n.*—**kin-e-mat′i-cal,** *a.* Kinematic.—**kin-e-mat′ics,** *n.* That branch of mechanics which treats of pure motion, without reference to mass or causes.

kin-e-mat-o-graph (kin-ē-mat′ō-gråf or kī-nē-), etc. Same as *cinematograph*, etc.

kin-es-the′sia, kin-es-the′sis. See *kinæsthesia*.

ki-net-ic (ki-net′ik or kī-), *a.* [Gr. κινητικός, < κινεῖν, move.] Of or pertaining to motion (as, *kinetic* energy, that due to motion); pertaining to kinetics. Also **ki-net′i-cal.** —**ki-net′ics,** *n.* That branch of mechanics which treats of the action of forces in producing or changing the motion of bodies.

kineto-. Form of Gr. κινητός, movable, used in combination.—**ki-net-o-graph** (ki-net′ō-gråf or ki-nē′tō-), *n.* [+ *-graph.*] A special camera for taking pictures for the kinetoscope; also, an apparatus for projecting such pictures on a screen.—**ki-net′o-phone** (-fōn), *n.* [+ *-phone.*] A kind of combination moving-picture machine and phonograph. [Proprietary name.]—**ki-net′o-scope** (-skōp), *n.* [+ *-scope.*] A device for presenting to the eye a series of photographs (taken in rapid succession) of moving objects, and thus giving a reproduction of a scene in actual movement, orig. such a device with an eyepiece or peep-hole for viewing the pictures directly, later one with an arrangement for projecting the pictures on a screen.—**ki-net-o-scop′ic** (-skop′ik), *a.*

king (king), *n.* [AS. *cyng*, *cynig*, *cyning*, = D. *koning* = G. *könig* = Icel. *konungr* = Sw. *konung* = Dan. *konge*, king; from the root of E. *kin*[1].] A male sovereign or monarch; a man who holds by life tenure (and usually by hereditary right) the chief authority over a country and people; hence [*cap.*], God or Christ (often in phrases, as 'King of kings,' 'King of heaven,' etc.: as, "Who is this *King* of glory? The Lord strong and mighty," Ps. xxiv. 8; "Yet ere thy craven spirit faints, Hear thine own *King*, the *King* of Saints," Keble's "Christian Year," xlix.); also [*l. c.* or *cap.*], a title given to any of certain persons holding supreme authority or functioning as the head or chief (as, a *king*-of-arms: see entry below); [*l. c.*] one who in a certain sphere or class has supremacy or preëminence over others (as, an oil-*king*, or a steel-*king*; "He's the *king* o' gude fellows," Burns's "Auld Rob Morris"); something preëminent in its class (as, the lion is the *king* of beasts; "He taught me a fisherman's bend, which he pronounced to be the *king* of all knots," Marryat's "Peter Simple," xiv.); also, the chief piece in the game of chess; a piece that has moved entirely across the board in the game of checkers or draughts; a playing-card bearing a picture of a king; also, *pl.* [*cap.*], certain books of the Bible which contain the history of the reigns of Jewish kings (the name being usually applied to the 11th and 12th books of the Old Testament, which are commonly called I. Kings and II. Kings, respectively, although these books are sometimes called III. Kings and IV. Kings, the two books of Samuel then being reckoned as I. Kings and II. Kings).—**King James Version** (of the Bible). See under *version*.—**king of terrors,** the chief of all terrors, death: as, "It shall bring him to the *king of terrors*" (Job, xviii. 14); "It surely is not worse to encounter the *king of terrors* in health" (Godwin's "Caleb Williams," xxiv.).—**king's English.** See under *English*, *n.*—**king's evidence.** See *evidence*, *n.* —**king's evil,** scrofula: orig. so called because it was supposed to be curable by the touch of the sovereign: as, "Young Johnson had the misfortune to be much afflicted with the scrophula, or *king's evil* . . . His mother . . . carried him to London, where he was actually touched by Queen Anne" (Boswell's "Johnson," 1712).—**king,** *v.* **I.** *intr.* To rule or act as a king. **II.** *tr.* To govern as king (see Shakspere's "Henry V.," ii. 4. 26); rule; also, to make (one) king (see Shakspere's "Richard II.," v. 5. 36).

Kingbird (*Tyrannus tyrannus*).

king=at=arms (king′at-ärmz′), *n.*; pl. *kings-*. Same as *king-of-arms*.

king-bird (king′bėrd), *n.* Any of various flycatchers of the family *Tyrannidæ*, esp. *Tyrannus tyrannus* (or *carolinensis*), a pugnacious crested bird of the eastern United States.

king=bolt (king′bōlt), *n.* A vertical bolt connecting the body of a vehicle with the fore axle, or the body of a car with a truck.

king=crab (king′krab), *n.* Any of various marine arthropods (esp. of the genus *Limulus*) with a carapace shaped somewhat like a horseshoe. Also called *horseshoe-crab*.

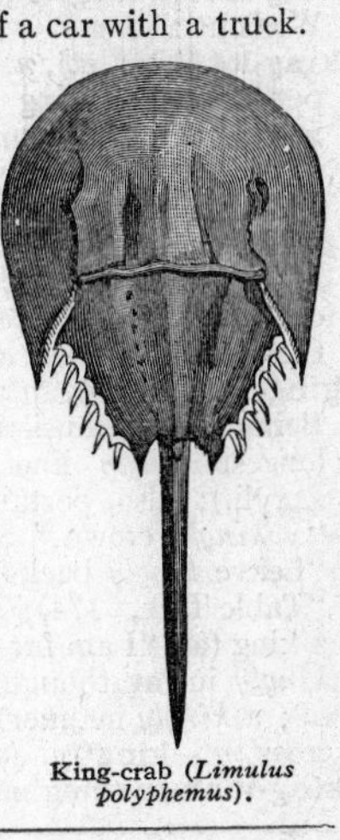
King-crab (*Limulus polyphemus*).

king-craft (king′kråft), *n.* The art of ruling as king; royal statesmanship; skill or craft in the exercise of royal functions: as, "James [I.] was always boasting of his skill in what he called *kingcraft*" (Macaulay's "Hist. of Eng.," i.).

king-cup (king′kup), *n.* Any of various common buttercups, as *Ranunculus bulbosus*; also, the marsh-marigold. [Chiefly Eng.]

king-dom (king′dọm), *n.* [AS. *cyningdōm.*] The power or authority of a king (archaic: as, "I must be married to my brother's daughter, Or else my *kingdom* stands on brittle glass," Shakspere's "Richard III.," iv. 2. 62); also, a state or government having a king or queen as its head; a country or territory subject to a king or queen; a realm; also, specif., the spiritual sovereignty of God or Christ, or the domain over which this extends, whether in heaven or on earth (as, "Jesus went about . . . preaching the gospel of the *kingdom*," Mat. iv. 23; "Jesus answered, My *kingdom* is not of this world," John, xviii. 36); also, fig., any sphere in which one is dominant (as, "The sick-chamber of the patient is the *kingdom* of the physician": Scott's "Talisman," vii.); any sphere or realm in which some condition, quality, or the like prevails (as, "the blest *kingdoms* meek of joy and love": Milton's "Lycidas," 177); anything conceived as constituting a realm or domain (as, the *kingdom* of thought); also, a realm or province of nature; esp., one of the three great divisions of natural objects (namely, the animal, vegetable, and mineral *kingdoms*).—**king′domed,** *a.* Constituted as or like a kingdom; also, divided into kingdoms.

king=duck (king′-duk), *n.* A handsome eider-duck, *Somateria spectabilis,* of the northerly coasts of Europe and America.

King-duck, male.

king-fish (king′-fish), *n.* Any of various fishes conspicuous for size or some other quality; esp., any of certain American fishes of the sciænoid genus *Menticirrus,* as *M. saxatilis,* a food-fish of the Atlantic coast; also, the pintado; also, the opah.

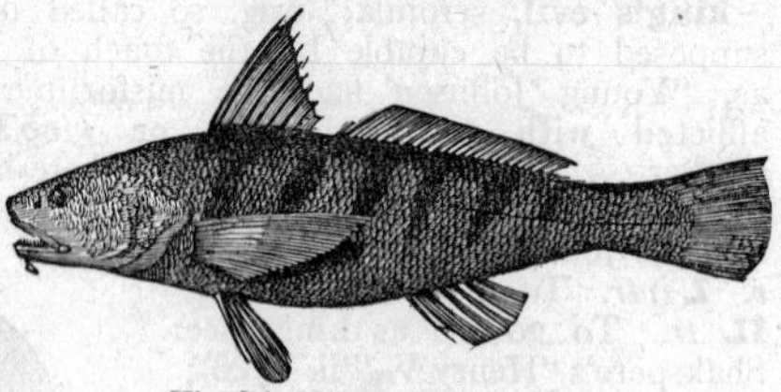
Kingfish (*Menticirrus saxatilis*).

king-fish-er (king′fish″ėr), *n.* Any bird of the family *Alcedinidæ,* the members of which are usually crested, stout-billed, and brilliantly colored, and are divided into two subfamilies, one feeding largely on insects, etc., and the other on fish, for which they plunge into the water.

Belted Kingfisher (*Ceryle alcyon*).

king-hood (king′hůd), *n.* Kingly character or rank; kingship.

king-less (king′les), *a.* Without a king.

king-let (king′let), *n.* A petty king; a king ruling over a small country or territory; also, any of the diminutive greenish birds constituting the genus *Regulus,* esp. *R. satrapa* of America (with a yellow or orange crest), *R. calendula* of America (with a red patch on the crown), and *R. cristatus,* the goldcrest of Europe.

king-ly (king′li), *a.*; compar. *kinglier,* superl. *kingliest.* Being a king, consisting of kings, or of royal rank (as, "the longest *kingly* line in Europe": Scott's "Woodstock," xxxvii.); also, pertaining or proper to a king or kings (as, "a *kingly* crown," Shakspere's "Julius Cæsar," iii. 2. 101; "Leave *kingly* backs to cope with *kingly* cares," Cowper's "Table Talk," 174); also, resembling, suggesting, or befitting a king (as, "I am far better born than is the king . . . more *kingly* in my thoughts," Shakspere's "2 Henry VI.," v. 1. 29; a *kingly* manner); king-like; regal; majestic.—**king′li-ness,** *n.*—**king′ly,** *adv.* In a kingly manner.

king-mak-er (king′mā″kėr), *n.* One who makes or sets up kings: applied specif. to Richard Neville (1428–71), Earl of Warwick, the principal agent in making Edward IV. king of England in place of Henry VI., and afterward in dethroning Edward and restoring Henry.

king=of=arms, king=at=arms (king′ov-ärmz′, king′at-), *n.*; pl. *kings-.* A chief heraldic officer. See *garter, Clarencieux,* and *Norroy.*

king=pin (king′pin), *n.* A king-bolt; also, in bowling games, the pin in the center when the pins are in place, or, esp., the pin at the front apex; also, the principal person in a company, enterprise, etc. (colloq.); the chief element of any system or the like (colloq.).

king=post (king′pōst), *n.* A vertical post between the apex of a triangular roof-truss and the tie-beam.

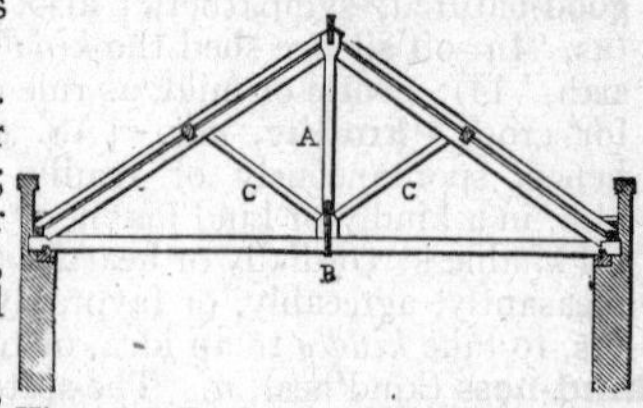

King-post Roof.—*A,* king-post; *B,* tie-beam; *C, C,* struts or braces.

king-ship (king′ship), *n.* Kingly state, office, or dignity; also, kingly rule; also, kingly nature or quality; also, sometimes, with *his,* etc., a title used in referring to a king.

king=snake (king′snāk), *n.* Any of certain large harmless American serpents, esp. *Ophibolus getulus,* which is supposed to kill rattlesnakes.

king=truss (king′trus), *n.* A truss framed with a king-post.

kink (kingk), *n.* [D. *kink* = Sw. and Dan. *kink.*] A twist or curl, as in a thread, rope, or hair, caused by its doubling or bending upon itself (as, "a *kink* in a cable": Marryat's "Peter Simple," xx.); also, a crick, as in the neck or back; also, fig., a mental twist, an odd notion, or a whim or crotchet (as, "when a woman gits a *kink* in her head agin a man": Mrs. Stowe's "Oldtown Fireside Stories," ii.); also, an original or ingenious idea, method, contrivance, etc. (colloq.).—**kink,** *v.* **I.** *intr.* To form a kink or kinks, as a rope. **II.** *tr.* To cause to kink; make kinks in.

kin-ka-jou (king′ka-jö), *n.* [Canadian F.; orig. the same word as *carcajou.*] A carnivorous, arboreal, prehensile-tailed quadruped, *Cercoleptes caudivolvulus,* of Central and South America, about the size of a cat, and related to the racoon.

Kinkajou of South America (*Cercoleptes caudivolvulus*).

kin-kle (king′-kl), *n.* A little kink.—**kin′kled,** *a.* Having kinkles; finely kinked or curled, as hair, etc.

kink-y (king′ki), *a.* Full of kinks: as, "*kinky* gray hair" (F. H. Smith's "Colonel Carter of Cartersville," iv.).

kin-less (kin′les), *a.* Without kin or relatives.

kin-ni-ki-nick, kin-ni-ki-nic (kin″i-ki-nik′), *n.* [N. Amer. Ind., lit. 'mixture.'] A material or mixture used by the North American Indians for smoking, commonly consisting of dried sumac leaves and the inner bark of a species of dogwood; also, any of various plants used for this purpose.

ki-no[1] (kē′nō), *n.* [Appar. W. Afr.] The reddish or black catechu-like inspissated juice or gum of certain tropical trees, esp. that obtained from *Pterocarpus marsupium,* a tall fabaceous tree of India and Ceylon: used in medicine, tanning, etc.

ki-no[2] (kē′nō), *n.* See *keno.*

kins-folk (kinz′fōk), *n.* Relatives or kindred: as, "And mark A country for him, *kinsfolk,* and a home" (M. Arnold's "Fragment of an 'Antigone' "). [Archaic or literary.]—**kins′folks,** *n. pl.* Same as *kinsfolk.* See Luke, xxi. 16. [Obs. or prov. Eng.]

kin-ship (kin′ship), *n.* The state or fact of being of kin; family relationship (as, to claim *kinship* with a person); fig., relationship by nature, qualities, etc.; affinity.

kins-man (kinz′man), *n.*; pl. *-men.* A man of one's own kin; a relative by birth, or sometimes (loosely) by marriage: as, "For I am of a numerous house, With many *kinsmen* gay" (Tennyson's "Will Waterproof's Lyrical Monologue," 90).—**kins′man-ship,** *n.* Kinship.—**kins′wom″an,** *n.*; pl. *-women* (-wim″en). A woman of one's own kin; a female relative.

ki-osk (ki-osk′), *n.* [= F. *kiosque,* < Turk. *kiūshk,* < Pers. *kūshk.*] A kind of open pavilion or summer-house common in Turkey and Persia and imitated elsewhere (as, "It was a small *kiosk,* built upon a projecting rock that looked down upon the Bosphorus and the city": Lever's "Harry Lorrequer," xlv.); hence, a similar structure used as a band-stand, or a news-stand, or for some other purpose; a small sheltering structure for the display of meteorological instruments, weather-maps, etc.; a structure covering a stairway leading to an underground railway or the like.

kip[1] (kip), *n.* [Origin uncertain.] The hide of a young or small beast; also, a bundle or set of such hides, containing a definite number.

kip[2] (kip), *n.* [Cf. Dan. *kippe,* brothel, low alehouse.] A brothel†; also, a cheap lodging-house; a bed in such a house; hence, any bed. [Slang.]

kip-per[1] (kip′ėr), *n.* [Origin uncertain.] The male salmon or sea-trout during the spawning season, or, according to some authorities, after the spawning season.

kip-per[2] (kip′ėr), *v. t.* [Cf. *kipper*[1].] To cure (herring, salmon, etc.) by cleaning, salting, etc., and drying in the air or in smoke.—**kip′per**[2], *n.* A kippered fish, esp. a herring.

Kir-ghiz (kir-gēz′), *n.*; pl. *Kirghiz.* [Said to be named from a legendary chief.] A member of a widespread people of Mongolian stock and Tatar speech, dwelling chiefly in west-central Asia.

ki-ri-mon (kē′ri-mon), *n.* [Jap. *kiri,* paulownia, + *mon,* device, cognizance.] A device representing three leaves of the paulownia-tree surmounted by three budding flower-stems, used as the unofficial or personal cognizance or badge of the imperial family of Japan, as on the harness of the emperor's horses. Cf. *kikumon* and *mon.*

Kirimon.

kirk (kėrk), *n.* Sc. and north. Eng. form of *church.*

kir′mess, *n.* See *kermess.*

kirn, kern[2] (kėrn), *n.* [Appar. connected with *corn*[1].] A feast held at the close of the harvest; a harvest-home; also, the last handful of grain cut down at the close of the harvest, or the cutting of this. [Sc. and north. Eng.]

ki-rom-bo, ki-rum-bo (ki-rom′bō, ki-rum′-), *n.* [Malagasy.] A bird, *Leptosomus discolor,* of Madagascar, allied to the rollers.

Kirombo.

kirsch (kirsh), *n.* Shortened form of *kirschwasser.*

kirsch-was-ser (kirsh′väs″ėr), *n.* [G., 'cherry water.'] A colorless cordial or liqueur distilled in Germany and Switzerland from wild cherries.

kir-tle (kėr′tl), *n.* [AS. *cyrtel* = Icel. *kyrtill,* tunic; perhaps dim. from L. *curtus,* cut short, E. *curt.*] A man's tunic or coat; also, a woman's gown or skirt. [Archaic or prov.]—**kir′tled,** *a.*

Kis-lev (kis′lev), *n.* [Heb.] In the Jewish calendar, the third month (29 or 30 days) of the civil year and the ninth of the ecclesiastical year, beginning in November or in the first part of December.

kis-met (kis′met), *n.* [Turk. *qismet,* < Ar. *qismah* (*qismat*), portion, lot, destiny, < *qasama,* divide.] Fate; destiny.

kiss (kis), *v.* [AS. *cyssan,* < *coss* = D. *kus* = G. *kuss* = Icel. *koss,* a kiss.] **I.** *tr.* To touch or press with the lips, while compressing and then separating them, in token of greeting, farewell, affection, reverence, etc.; salute or caress with the lips; give a kiss to; also, fig., to touch gently or lightly (as, "The sweet wind did gently *kiss* the trees": Shakspere's "Merchant of Venice," v. 1. 2); also, to put, bring, take, etc., by or as if by kissing (as, "Dews, that would have fall'n in tears, I *kiss'd* away," Tennyson's "Miller's Daughter," 152; "Every evening from thy feet Shall the cool wind *kiss* the heat," Whittier's "Barefoot Boy"). **II.** *intr.* To kiss some one or something, or each other (as, "*Kiss* and be friends!" Tennyson's "Princess," vi. 271); also, fig., to come into contact, or meet, with a light touch (as, "The secret boundary lines which mark Where soul and matter *kiss,*" Jean Ingelow's "Honours," ii.; two balls *kiss* in billiards).—**kiss,** *n.* An act of kissing; a salute or caress with the lips; fig., a slight touch or contact (as, "The pebble-paven shore Under the quick, faint *kisses* of the sea Trembles and sparkles": Shelley's "Epipsychidion," 547); also, a baked confection of egg-whites and powdered sugar; also, a lump or piece of confectionery containing nuts, cocoanut, or the like.—**kiss′a-ble,** *a.* That may be kissed; suitable for or inviting kisses.—**kiss′er,** *n.*—**kiss′ing=bug,** *n.* Any of various blood-sucking hemipterous insects of the family *Reduviidæ,* which sometimes bite persons upon the lip, etc.—**kiss′ing=crust,** *n.* A crust, as of a loaf, that has touched another crust in baking.

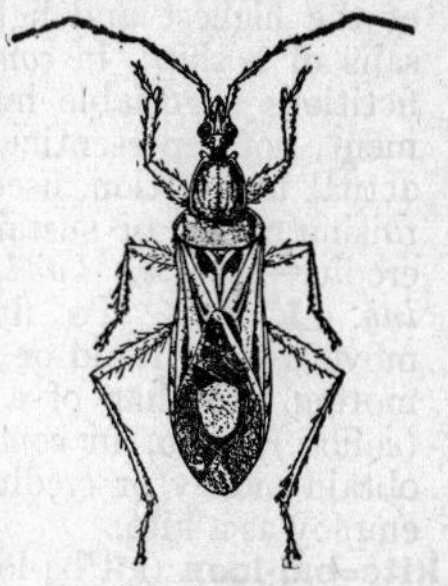

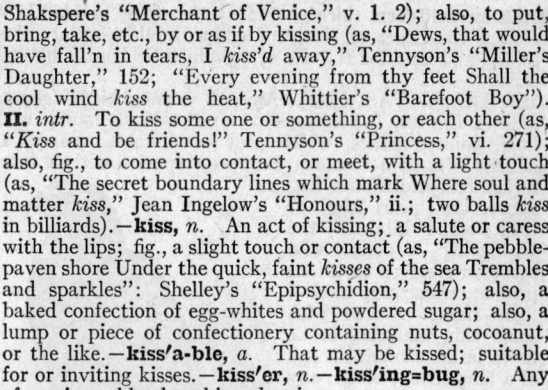

Kissing-bug (*Rasahus biguttatus*).

kist[1] (kist), *n.* Sc. and north. Eng. form of *chest.*

kist[2] (kist), **kist-vaen** (kist′vīn). See *cist*[2], *cistvaen.*

kit[1] (kit), *n.* [ME. *kyt, kitt:* cf. MD. *kitte,* vessel made of hooped staves.] A wooden vessel (small tub, pail, etc.), usually circular, of various sizes and for various purposes; also, a set or collection of tools, supplies, etc., for a special purpose (as, a shoemaker's, soldier's, or traveler's *kit*); the case containing these, or this with its contents; hence, in general, a set, lot, or collection of things or persons (often contemptuous: colloq.: as, "I'll show a better gentleman than the whole *kit* on you put together!" Dickens's "Great Expectations," xl.).—**kit**[1], *v. t.*; *kitted, kitting.* To put into kits, as fish for market.

kit[2] (kit), *n.* Shortened form of *kitten.*

kit[3] (kit), *n.* [Origin uncertain.] A kind of small violin.

kit=bag (kit′bag), *n.* A bag in which to carry a kit, as that of a soldier or a traveler.

kit=cat (kit′kat), *n.* [From the *Kit-Cat* Club, founded in London about 1703, and named from *Christopher Cat,* keeper of a pie-house at which the club first met.] A particular size of portrait (36 by 28 inches) which is less than half-length but may include the hands: said to have been so called from the size of the members' portraits in the meeting-room of the Kit-Cat Club at Barn Elms (the residence of the club's secretary, Jacob Tonson), which was too low for half-length pictures.

kitch-en (kich′ẹn), *n.* [AS. *cycene,* < L. *coquina,* kitchen, orig. fem. of *coquinus,* pertaining to cooks, < *coquus,* E. *cook, n.*: cf. *cuisine.*] A room or place equipped for or appropriated to cooking; also, the culinary department; cuisine; also, any kind of food (or drink) taken as a relish with bread, potatoes, etc. (chiefly Sc. and Ir.).—**kitchen police,** *milit.,* a form of duty comprising assistance of various kinds to the camp or army cooks; also, the men detailed for such duty: abbreviated *K.P.*—**kitch′en,** *v. t.* To entertain with the fare of the kitchen† (see Shakspere's "Comedy of Errors," v. 1. 415); also, to give a relish to (chiefly Sc.: as, "His wee drap parritch, or his bread, Thou *kitchens* fine," Burns's "Scotch Drink," 42).—**kitch′en-er,** *n.* One employed in or having charge of a kitchen (as, "two most important officers of the convent, the *kitchener* and refectioner": Scott's "Monastery," xv.); also, an elaborate kitchen stove with various useful appliances.

kitch-en-ette (kich-ẹn-et′), *n.* [Dim. of *kitchen*: see *-ette.*] A closet or small room fitted up as a kitchen.

kitch-en=gar-den (kich′ẹn-gär″dn), *n.* A garden in which vegetables and fruit for the table are grown; also, a school in which children are taught kitchen work and other household duties (U. S.).—**kitch′en=gar″den-er,** *n.*

kitch-en=mid-den (kich′ẹn-mid″n), *n.* [See *midden.*] A mound consisting of shells of edible mollusks and other refuse, and marking the site of a prehistoric human habitation.

kite (kīt), *n.* [AS. *cȳta.*] Any of various birds (genera *Milvus, Elanus, Elanoides,* etc.) of the hawk family with long, pointed wings, which prey on humble quarry, as *Milvus ictinus,* a common European species with a long, forked tail, and *Elanus leucurus,* the 'pearl kite' or 'white-tailed kite' of the U. S.; fig., a person who preys on others; a rapacious person; a sharper; also, a light frame covered with some thin material, to be flown in the wind at the end of a long string; *naut.,* any of the highest and lightest sails of a ship; in *com.,* a fictitious negotiable instrument, not representing any actual transaction, used for raising money or sustaining credit.—**kite,** *v.; kited, kiting.* **I.** *intr.* To fly or move with a rapid or easy motion like that of a kite (colloq.); also, in *com.,* to obtain money or credit through kites. **II.** *tr.* In *com.,* to employ as a kite.

Pearl Kite (*Elanus leucurus*).

kite=bal-loon (kīt′bạ-lön″), *n.* A balloon that can be flown in the manner of a kite; specif., a type of captive balloon used to elevate men for military observation, consisting essentially of a sausage-shaped gas-bag to which is attached a rudder-like air-bag, and acting more or less like a kite in retaining a fixed and steady position.

kit=fox (kit′foks′), *n.* [See *kit*[2].] A small fox, *Vulpes velox,* of the plains of the western U. S. and Canada, valued for its fur; also, the fur.

Kit-fox.

kith (kith), *n.* [AS. *cȳth, cȳththu,* knowledge, acquaintance, native land, < *cūth,* known, pp. of *cunnan,* E. *can*[1].] Knowledge† or acquaintance†; also, one's home country†, native land†, or home†; also, one's circle of acquaintance, or one's acquaintances or friends, or an acquaintance (as, no men of your *kith;* he is no *kith* of ours: now chiefly Sc. and prov. Eng., except in 'kith and kin,' etc., as below, and often confused in meaning with *kin*).—**kith and kin,** orig., home and kindred; later, acquaintances and kindred, or friends and relatives (as, "Lancelot's *kith and kin* so worship him That ill to him is ill to them": Tennyson's "Holy Grail," 648); sometimes, of a single person, a friend and relative (as, "My lady's white, my lady's red, And *kith and kin* o' Cassillis' blude": Burns's "My Lady's Gown"). Also, similarly, **kith or kin,** and **neither kith nor kin.**

kit′=kat, *n.* See *kit-cat.*

kit-ten (kit′n), *n.* [ME. *kitoun, kyton*: cf. OF. *chitoun,* for *chaton,* dim. of *chat,* cat.] A young cat; sometimes, a young animal of some other kind, as a young rabbit or beaver.—**kit′ten,** *v. i.* or *t.* To bring forth (kittens).—**kit′ten-ish,** *a.* Kitten-like; artlessly playful: as, "It was remarkable . . . how old and mature Helen could be when she chose, and how *kittenish* when she chose" (Arnold Bennett's "Helen with the High Hand," xviii.).—**kit′ten-ish-ly,** *adv.*—**kit′ten-ish-ness,** *n.*

kit-ti-wake (kit′i-wāk), *n.* [Imit. of its cry.] Any of various gulls of the genus *Rissa,* having the hind toe very short or rudimentary. See cut in next column.

kit-tle (kit′l), *v. t.; -tled, -tling.* [ME. *kytylle* = Icel. *kitla* = D. *kittelen* = G. *kitzeln,* tickle.] To tickle; also, to stimulate or rouse; esp., to stir or excite pleasurably (as, "Nobody amongst these brave English cooks can *kittle* up his Majesty's most sacred palate with our . . . Scottish dishes": Scott's "Fortunes of Nigel," xxvii.) [Now Sc. and prov. Eng.]—**kit′tle,** *a.* Ticklish; uncertain; risky: as, "Rob Roy . . . a *kittle* neighbour to the Low Country, and particularly obnoxious to his Grace" (Scott's "Rob Roy," xxxii.). [Sc. and prov. Eng.]

Kittiwake (*Rissa tridactyla*).

kit-ty[1] (kit′i), *n.*; pl. *kitties* (-iz). A kitten; also, a pet name for a cat.

kit-ty[2] (kit′i), *n.*; pl. *kitties* (-iz). [Origin uncertain.] A prison or jail (north. Eng. or slang); also, a pool into which each player in a card-game puts a certain amount of his winnings, for some special purpose, as to pay for refreshments, etc.; any similar pool.

ki-va (kē′vä), *n.* [N. Amer. Ind.] A large chamber, often wholly or partly underground, in a Pueblo Indian village, used for religious ceremonies and other purposes.

Ki-wa-nis (kẹ-wä′nis), *a.* [A made word.] Designating or pertaining to an organization, founded at Detroit in 1915, which comprises a great number of clubs located in various cities of the United States and Canada and chartered by a central international body. The membership of each club consists of representative business and professional men of its city, the number of members from each business or profession being limited; and the purpose of the organization is to provide a representative leadership for service and for the realization of higher ideals in business, industrial, and professional life.—**Ki-wa′ni-an** (-ni-ạn), *a.* and *n.*

ki-wi (kē′wẹ), *n.*; pl. *-wis* (-wẹz). [Maori.] An apteryx (flightless bird of New Zealand); also, among aviators, a man in an aviation service who does not make flights (colloq.). Also **ki′wi=ki′wi.**

Klan (klan), *n.* Short for *Ku Klux Klan.* See *Ku Klux.*—**Klans-man** (klanz′mạn), *n.*; pl. *-men.* A member of the Ku Klux Klan.

klee-ne-bok (klā′nẹ-bok), *n.* [S. Afr. D., 'little buck.'] A very small antelope, *Antilope perpusilla* (or *Cephalophus pygmæus*), of South Africa.

klepht (kleft), *n.* [NGr. κλέφτης, Gr. κλέπτης, thief, < κλέπτειν, steal.] A Greek or Albanian brigand.

klep-to-ma-ni-a (klep-tọ-mā′ni-ạ), *n.* [NL., < Gr. κλέπτειν, steal, + μανία, E. *mania.*] An irresistible propensity to steal.—**klep-to-ma′ni-ac** (-ak), *n.* One affected with kleptomania.

klip-spring-er (klip′spring″ėr), *n.* [S. Afr. D., 'cliff springer.'] A small, active African antelope, *Oreotragus saltator,* of mountainous regions from the Cape of Good Hope to Abyssinia.

Klipspringer.

kloof (klöf), *n.* [D., cleft: cf. *clove*[3].] A deep cleft in a mountain or between mountains; a ravine; a gorge. [South Africa.]

knack (nak), *v. t.* or *i.* [ME. *knacke*; imit.: cf. *knock.*] To strike, or strike together, with a sudden, sharp sound; crack; snap. [Now prov. Eng. and Sc.]—**knack,** *n.* A crack or snap (obs. or prov.); also, an adroit or smart trick or feat (obs. or prov.: as, "Some flying stroke alone [in painting] can hit them right: For how should equal colours do the *knack?*" Pope's "Moral Essays," ii. 155); also, a clever method or expedient, or 'dodge,' as for doing something (as, a *knack* of the trade); now, usually, a faculty or power of doing something with ease as from special or happy skill (as, to have a *knack* of making verses, or of managing men; "Diligence and attention soon gave him the *knack* of it [whistling]," Mark Twain's "Tom Sawyer," i.); aptitude or facility (as, this process requires *knack* as well as care); also, a habit or practice (as, "The lady . . . has only, with a very brisk air, a *knack* of saying the commonest things": Steele, in "Tatler," 31); also, an ingenious or pleasing trifle, or knickknack (obs. or archaic: see Shakspere's "Winter's Tale," iv. 4. 360).

knack-er (nak'ėr), *n.* [Origin uncertain.] One who buys and slaughters useless horses, or who buys and removes dead ones, for their hides, hoofs, etc. (as, "The *knackers* removed the slaughtered charger": Thackeray's "Newcomes," xxii); also, one who buys old houses, ships, etc., for the materials.

knap[1] (nap), *v.*; *knapped, knapping.* [ME. *knap*; imit.] **I.** *tr.* To strike with a short, sharp sound; also, to break with such a sound; break by a smart blow; shape (flints) by strokes of a hammer; also, to remove by such a blow (with *off*); also, to snap; bite. [Now prov.] **II.** *intr.* To strike against something with a short, sharp sound; also, to break with such a sound; also, to snap or bite. [Now prov.] —**knap**[1], *n.* A smart stroke or blow; also, a short, sharp noise. [Now prov.]

knap[2] (nap), *n.* [AS. *cnæp*: cf. Icel. *knappr*, knob, and E. *knop.*] The top of a hill; also, a hillock or knoll. [Now chiefly prov.]

knap-sack (nap'sak), *n.* [D. *knapzak*, < *knappen*, snap, catch, eat, + *zak*, sack, bag.] A soldier's leather or canvas case for clothes and the like, carried on the back, as when on the march; any similar receptacle used for a like purpose (as, "He had walked over France and Italy with a painter's *knapsack* on his back": H. James's "Europeans," v.).

knap-weed (nap'wēd), *n.* [Earlier *knopweed*: see *knop.*] A plant of the asteraceous genus *Centaurea*, esp. *C. nigra*, a perennial weed with rose-purple flowers set on a dark-colored knob-like involucre.

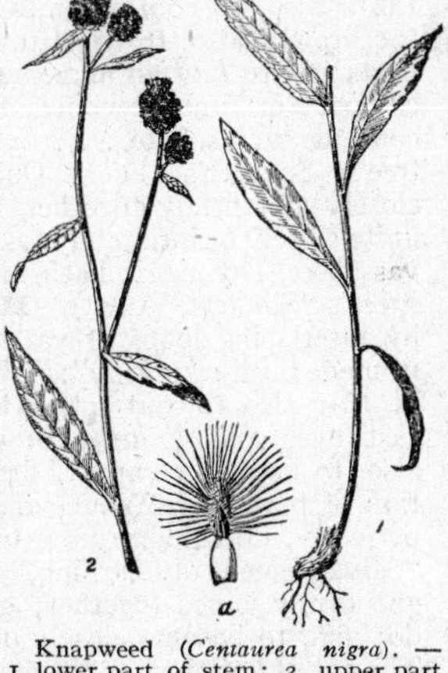
Knapweed (*Centaurea nigra*). — 1, lower part of stem; 2, upper part with flowers; *a*, scale of the involucre.

knar (när), *n.* [ME. *knarre* = LG. *knarre.*] A knot on a tree or in wood.

knarl (närl), *n.* [Appar. < *knar*: cf. *knurl* and *gnarl*[2].] A knot on a tree or in wood; a gnarl or knurl. [Obs. or prov.]

knarred (närd), *a.* Knotted; gnarled. Also **knar'ry.**

knave (nāv), *n.* [AS. *cnafa* = G. *knabe*, boy.] A boy†; also, a boy employed as a servant, or any male servant (archaic: as, "What nonsense would the fool thy master prate, When thou, his *knave*, canst talk at such a rate!" Dryden's tr. Virgil's "Pastorals," iii. 22); any man of humble position (archaic); also, an unprincipled or dishonest fellow, a rogue, or a rascal (as, "The honest dealer is always undone, and the *knave* gets the advantage," Swift's "Gulliver's Travels," i. 6; he is either a fool or a *knave*); also, a playing-card bearing a picture of a servant or a soldier; a jack.—**knav-er-y** (nā'vėr-i), *n.*; pl. *-ies* (-iz). Action or practice characteristic of a knave (as, "Why, this is flat *knavery*, to take upon you another man's name": Shakspere's "Taming of the Shrew," v. 1. 37); unprincipled or dishonest dealing; trickery; roguery; often, a knavish act or practice; also, roguishness† or mischievousness†; a roguish action†.—**knav'ish,** *a.* Like or befitting a knave; rascally; dishonest: as, "a low, *knavish* adventurer" (H. Melville's "Omoo," xxxii.); "a *knavish* piece of work" (Shakspere's "Hamlet," iii. 2. 250).—**knav'ish-ly,** *adv.*—**knav'ish-ness,** *n.*

knead (nēd), *v. t.* [AS. *cnedan* = D. *kneden* = G. *kneten*, knead.] To work (dough, etc.) into a homogeneous plastic mass, by pressing, squeezing, etc.; make (bread, etc.) in this way; also, to manipulate by similar movements, as the body in massage.—**knead'a-ble,** *a.* Capable of or fit for being kneaded.—**knead'er,** *n.*

knee (nē), *n.* [AS. *cnēow* = D. and G. *knie* = Icel. *knē* = Goth. *kniu*, knee; akin to L. *genu*, Gr. γόνυ, Skt. *jānu*, knee: cf. *kneel.*] The joint or region in man, between the thigh and the lower part of the leg; the corresponding or homologous joint or region of other vertebrates, as in the leg of a bird, the hind limb of a horse, etc.; a joint or region likened to this but not homologous with it, as the tarsal joint of a bird, or the carpal joint in the fore limb of the horse, cow, etc.; also, something resembling this joint, esp. when bent, as a piece of timber with an angular bend; also, the part of a garment covering the knee; also, a bending of the knee, as in reverence.—**knee,** *v.*; *kneed, kneeing.* **I.** *intr.* To bend the knee, as in reverence. **II.** *tr.* To kneel to, as in reverence; also, to make (one's way) on the knees (as, "Fall down, and *knee* The way into his mercy": Shakspere's "Coriolanus," v. 1. 5); also, to strike or touch with the knee; also, to cause to bulge at the knee by wearing, as trousers; in *building*, to fit with a knee or knees.—**knee'=boss,** *n.* A defensive cap for the knee, made of leather or other material, worn as armor in the middle ages.—**knee'=breech″es,** *n. pl.* Breeches reaching to or just below the knee.—**knee'=cap,** *n.* A protective covering for the knee; also, the patella, the flat movable bone at the front of the knee (in this sense often written *kneecap*).—**kneed,** *a.* Having knees (as, weak-*kneed*); also, having a knee-like joint or bend, as a plant-stem; geniculate.—**knee'=deep',** *a.* So deep as to reach the knees (as, the snow lay *knee-deep*); submerged or covered by something having such depth (as, the fields were *knee-deep* in water); sunk as far as the knees (as, to wade *knee-deep* in slush).—**knee'=high',** *a.* Reaching as high as the knees. —**knee'=jerk,** *n.* A sudden jerk of the knee, or involuntary kick, caused by a blow on the patellar tendon while the leg hangs loosely over the other knee: of importance in the diagnosis of certain diseases.

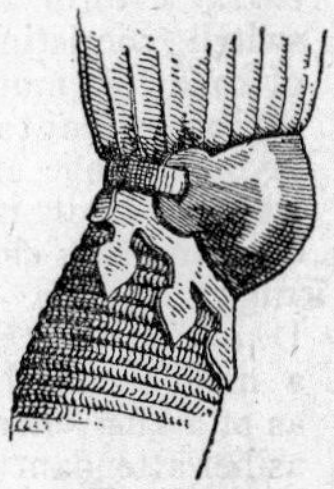
Knee-boss.

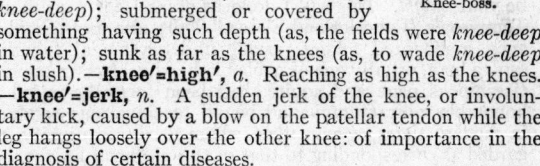

kneel (nēl), *v. i.*; *knelt* or *kneeled, kneeling.* [AS. *cnēowlian*, < *cnēow*, E. *knee.*] To fall or rest on the knees or a knee, as in supplication or homage: as, "I *kneeled* down, and gave God thanks aloud for my recovery from my sickness" (Defoe's "Robinson Crusoe," i. 6).—**kneel'er,** *n.*

knee-let (nē'let), *n.* A protective covering (armor or clothing) for the knee.

knee-pan (nē'pan), *n.* The knee-cap or patella.

knell (nel), *v.* [AS. *cnyllan*: cf. Icel. *knylla*, beat with a blunt weapon, G. *knallen*, clap, crack, give a report.] **I.** *tr.* To ring or toll (a bell)†; also, to announce or proclaim by or as by a knell (as, "Its [a city's] huge clocks had successively *knelled* three hours after midnight": Scott's "Quentin Durward," xxxvii.); summon by this means (as, "Each matin bell . . . *Knells* us back to a world of death": Coleridge's "Christabel," ii.). **II.** *intr.* To ring, as a bell; esp., to ring for a death or a funeral, or toll (as, "The sullen huge oracular bell, Which never *knells* but for a princely death": Byron's "Marino Faliero," iv. 2); hence, to give forth a mournful, ominous, or warning sound.—**knell,** *n.* The sound made by a bell when struck or rung; esp., the sound made by a bell rung slowly for a death or a funeral; hence, any sound announcing the death of a person or the passing away of a thing; anything serving as an intimation of extinction, failure, or the like (as, this announcement was a *knell* to his hopes); also, sometimes, any doleful sound.

knelt (nelt). Preterit and past participle of *kneel.*

knew (nū). Preterit of *know.*

Knick-er-bock-er (nik'ėr-bok″ėr), *n.* [From Diedrich *Knickerbocker*, pretended author of Washington Irving's "History of New York."] A descendant of the Dutch settlers of New York; hence, any New Yorker; also, *pl.* [*l. c.*], loosely fitting short breeches gathered in at the knee; a costume including these.

knick-ers (nik'ėrz), *n. pl.* Knickerbockers. [Colloq.]

knick-knack (nik'nak), *n.* [Varied redupl. of *knack.*] A petty trick†; also, a pleasing trifle; a trinket or gimcrack;

often, a bit of bric-à-brac; sometimes, a kickshaw or unsubstantial dainty.—**knick′knack″er-y,** *n.*; pl. *-ies* (-iz). Knickknacks collectively; also, a knickknack.

knife (nīf), *n.*; pl. *knives* (nīvz). [AS. *cnīf* = MLG. *knīf* = Icel. *knīfr* = Sw. *knif* = Dan. *kniv*, knife.] A cutting-instrument consisting essentially of a thin blade (usually of steel and with a sharp edge) attached to a handle; often, a knife-like weapon; a dagger; a short sword; also, a blade for cutting, as in a tool or machine.—**knife,** *v. t.*; *knifed, knifing.* To apply a knife to; cut, stab, etc., with a knife; also, fig. (slang, U. S.), to strike at secretly; try to defeat in an underhand way, as a candidate of one's own party.—**knife′=edge,** *n.* The edge of a knife; hence, anything very sharp; also, a wedge, as of steel, on the fine edge of which a scale-beam, pendulum, or the like, oscillates.—**knife′=edged,** *a.* Having a thin, sharp edge, like a knife.—**knife′=mon″ey,** *n.* An ancient Chinese currency consisting of bronze pieces shaped like a knife.—**knife′=switch,** *n.* In *elect.*, a form of switch consisting of one or more strips of metal pivoted at one end and arranged so that the other end (to which a handle is attached) can be pushed between metallic clips and thus close a circuit.

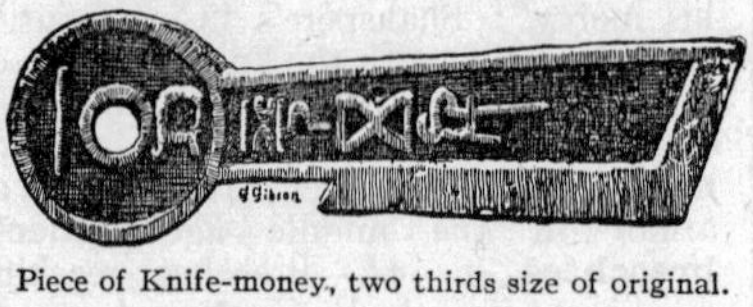

Piece of Knife-money, two thirds size of original.

knight (nīt), *n.* [AS. *cniht*, boy, man-servant, retainer, = D. and G. *knecht*, man-servant, workman.] A boy†; also, a male servant†; also, a military attendant or follower, as of a king; hence, a man devoted to the service of a lady as her attendant or champion (as, "In all your quarrels will I be your *knight*. This will I do, dear damsel, for your sake": Tennyson's "Lancelot and Elaine," 956); also, in the middle ages, a mounted soldier serving under a feudal superior; esp., a man, usually one of noble birth, who, after an apprenticeship as page and squire, had been formally raised to honorable military rank and bound to chivalrous conduct; in modern times, a man upon whom a certain dignity, regarded as corresponding to that of the medieval knight, has been conferred by a sovereign because of personal merit or as a reward for services rendered to the country (in the British Empire, holding a rank next below that of a baronet, and bearing the title *Sir* prefixed to the Christian name, as in 'Sir John Smith,' neither the dignity nor the title being transmissible to heirs as in the case of the baronet: see *baronet*); a member of a medieval or modern order or society of men raised to knighthood (as, *Knights* Hospitalers, see *hospitaler*; *Knights* Templars, see *Templar*; a *Knight* of the Garter, see *garter*); hence, a member of any order or association of men bearing the name of *Knights* (as, *Knights* of Pythias, or *Knights* of Columbus: see phrases below); sometimes, humorously, a member of some trade, profession, class, or the like, indicated (in phrases: as, a *knight* of the brush, a painter or artist; a *knight* of the pestle, an apothecary; a *knight* of the road, a highwayman or a vagabond); also, some person of a rank similar to that of the medieval knight; one of a particular class of citizens in ancient Greece or in ancient Rome; also, in *chess*, a certain piece having usually the figure of a horse's head.—**knight bachelor,** a knight of the lowest but most ancient order of knights; now, in the British Empire, one who has been raised to the dignity of knighthood without having been made a member of any specially named order, such as that of the Bath.—**knight banneret.** See *banneret*[1].—**Knights of Columbus,** a Roman Catholic fraternal organization, founded at New Haven, Conn., in 1882, operating in the U. S., Canada, and elsewhere, and aiming to associate men of the church for religious and civic usefulness.—**Knights of Pythias,** a secret fraternal order founded at Washington, D. C., in 1864.—**Knights of St. John of Jerusalem.** See *hospitaler*.—**knight,** *v. t.* To dub or create (one) a knight: as, "A soldier, by the honour-giving hand Of Cœur-de-lion *knighted* in the field" (Shakspere's "King John," i. 1. 54).

knight-age (nī′tāj), *n.* The body of knights collectively; also, a list or register of knights.

knight=er-rant (nīt′er′ant), *n.*; pl. *knights-errant.* A knight who traveled in search of adventures in which to exhibit military skill, bravery, and chivalry.—**knight′=er′rant-ry** (-ri), *n.*; pl. *-ries* (-riz). Conduct or a performance characteristic or suggestive of a knight-errant (as, "The Duke of Savoy . . . after so many years of *knight-errantry*, had regained his duchy": Motley's "Dutch Republic," i. 3); often, quixotic conduct or action.

knight=head (nīt′hed), *n.* *Naut.*, either of two timbers rising from the keel of a ship, one on each side, and supporting the inner end of the bowsprit.

knight-hood (nīt′hůd), *n.* The rank or dignity of a knight (as, "I would not take a *knighthood* for my fortune": Shakspere's "2 Henry IV.," v. 3. 133); also, the profession or vocation of a knight (as, "The champions, all of high degree, Who *knighthood* lov'd, and deeds of chivalry": Dryden's "Palamon and Arcite," iii. 10); also, knightly character or qualities; also, knights collectively (as, "Otho, reinforcing his German army by the *knighthood* of Flanders and Boulogne . . . invaded France": Green's "Short Hist. of the Eng. People," iii. 2).

knight-ly (nīt′li), *a.* Of, belonging to, or befitting a knight (as, a *knightly* sword; *knightly* deeds); also, being or resembling a knight; composed of knights.—**knight′li-ness,** *n.*—**knight′ly,** *adv.* In a manner befitting a knight: as, "Say . . . why thou comest thus *knightly* clad in arms" (Shakspere's "Richard II.," i. 3. 12).

knit (nit), *v.*; *knitted* or *knit*, *knitting.* [AS. *cnyttan*, tie, < *cnotta*, a knot: see *knot*[2].] **I.** *tr.* To tie or fasten by or as by knotting (archaic: as, "I *knit* my handkercher about your brows," Shakspere's "King John," iv. 1. 42); also, to form or make (stockings, a fabric, etc.) by interlacing loops of yarn or thread, as with needles; interlace loops of (yarn, etc.), as in making fabrics; sometimes, simply, to twine or plait together (as, "In twisted braids of lilies *knitting* The loose train of thy amber-dropping hair": Milton's "Comus," 862); interlock (as, "Come, *knit* hands": Milton's "Comus," 143); also, to contract into folds or wrinkles (as, to *knit* the brow); also, to constitute or establish as if by joining parts (as, to *knit* an agreement or a peace); also, to make compact or firm by contraction or consolidation of parts; concentrate (as, "He . . . *knitting* all his force, got one hand free": Spenser's "Faerie Queene," i. 1. 19); also, to join closely and firmly together, as members or parts; fig., to unite closely or intimately (as, "Lord of my love, to whom in vassalage Thy merit hath my duty strongly *knit*": Shakspere's "Sonnets," xxvi.). **II.** *intr.* To make a fabric, etc., by interlacing loops of yarn or thread (as, "a number of women, busily *knitting*": Dickens's "Tale of Two Cities," iii. 15); also, to contract, as the brow does (as, "with downcast eyes and *knitting* brow": Byron's "Parisina," x.); also, to become compact, firm, or strong by the consolidation of parts (as, "Young men, when they *knit* and shape perfectly, do seldom grow to a further stature": Bacon's "Advancement of Learning," i. 5. 4); also, to become closely and firmly joined together; grow together, as broken bones do; fig., to become closely or intimately united.—**knit,** *n.* The act of knitting, or the state or manner of being knitted; sometimes, a contraction into wrinkles, as of the brow.—**knit′ter,** *n.*—**knit′ting,** *n.* The act of a person or thing that knits; also, knitted work.

knives (nīvz), *n.* Plural of *knife*.

knob (nob), *n.* [ME. *knobbe* = MLG. *knobbe*, knob, protuberance: cf. D. *knobbel*, knob, and E. *knop*.] A rounded lump or protuberance on the surface or at the end of something, as a knot on a tree-trunk or a stick, a pimple or a wart on the skin, or a rounded ornamental part at the end of an umbrella-handle or the like; specif., a rounded (or otherwise shaped) projecting part forming the handle of a door, drawer, or the like; also, a rounded hill or mountain, esp. an isolated one (as, Pilot *Knob*, in Missouri); also, the head (slang: cf. *nob*[1]); in *arch.*, an ornamental boss, as of carved work.—**knobbed,** *a.* Having a knob or knobs.—**knob′by,** *a.* Abounding in knobs; also, knob-like.—**knob′bi-ness,** *n.*

knob-ker-rie (nob′ker″i), *n.* [S. Afr. D. *knopkiri*, < *knop*, knob, + Hottentot *kiri*, stick, club.] A short, heavy stick or club with a knob on one end, used as both a striking and a throwing weapon by natives of South Africa; hence, a similar weapon used elsewhere.

knock (nok), *v. i.* [AS. *cnocian*, *cnucian*, = Icel. *knoka*, knock, thump; imit.] To strike a sounding blow with the fist, knuckles, or anything hard, esp. on a door, gate, window, wall, or the like, as in seeking admittance, calling attention, giving a signal, etc. (as, "Who *knocks* so loud at door?" Shakspere's "2 Henry IV.," ii. 4. 381); rap, beat, or pound; also, to strike in collision (as, a drifting spar *knocked* against the vessel; his knees *knocked* together from fright); also, to make a noise as of striking or pounding, as machinery; also, fig., to make harsh or ill-natured criticisms (slang, U. S.).—**to knock about,** to go about or wander here and there in a haphazard or aimless way. [Colloq.]—**to knock off,** to leave off doing something; desist; stop; esp., to stop work (as, "Some of Rouncewell's hands have just *knocked off* for dinner time": Dickens's "Bleak House," lxiii.). [Now colloq.]—**to knock under** (formerly, *to knock under the table* or *under board*, as at a drinking-party), to succumb; yield; give in; acknowledge one's self beaten. [Colloq.]—**knock,** *v. t.* To give a sounding or forcible blow to; hit, strike, or beat; also, to drive, force, or render by a blow or blows (as, to *knock* a thing over; to *knock* a man senseless); also, to strike (a thing) against something else; bring into collision; dash; also, fig., to criticize harshly or ill-naturedly (slang, U. S.).—**to knock down,** to assign (a thing) as sold to a bidder at an auction, by or as by the bringing down of a hammer; also, to take to pieces, as a machine; also, of a car-conductor or other employee, to embezzle (money) from passengers' fares or other sums passing through his hands (colloq., U. S.).—**to knock off,** to dispose of, or get rid of (as, "The different men on the list were soon *knocked off* at prices which showed a pretty brisk demand in the market": Mrs. Stowe's "Uncle Tom's Cabin," xii.); also, to do or make quickly (as, to *knock off* a piece of work; to *knock off* verses); also, to deduct, as from a sum asked or due. [Colloq.]—**to knock out,** to defeat (an opponent) in a pugilistic contest by striking him down with a blow after which he does not rise within a prescribed time; hence, to disable, overcome, or defeat completely (colloq.).—**to knock up,** to arouse by knocking or rapping, as at a door; also, to construct, make, or arrange hastily (as, "I had had time, with the help of a carpenter, to *knock up* cabins . . . in the hold": Bulwer-Lytton's "Caxtons," xvi. 11); also, to exhaust with fatigue (colloq.: as, "The much-vaunted steed . . . was now nearly *knocked up* by travelling," Irving's "Captain Bonneville," xxxv.).—**knock,** *n.* The act or the sound of knocking; a rap, as at a door; a blow or thump; fig., an ill-natured criticism or comment (slang, U. S.).

knock-a-bout (nok′ạ-bout″). **I.** *a.* Characterized by knocking about; rough; boisterous; specif., using, consisting of, or marked by horse-play, as a theatrical performer or performance; also, suitable for rough use, as a garment; also, given to knocking about from place to place. **II.** *n.* A knockabout theatrical performer or performance; also, one who has knocked about from place to place, as a traveler; also, *naut.*, a small, easily handled yacht with a jib and mainsail but no bowsprit.

Knockabout.

knock=down (nok′-doun), *a.* Such as to knock something down; overwhelming; irresistible; also, pertaining to the knocking down of articles at an auction, or being a price below which an article will not be knocked down; also, constructed in separate parts, so as to be readily knocked down or taken apart, as a boat, a piece of furniture, etc.

knock-er (nok′ėr), *n.* One who or that which knocks; esp., a spirit or goblin supposed to dwell and work in mines, indicating by the sounds made the presence of ore; also, a hinged knob, bar, ring, or the like, fastened (esp. formerly) on a door, for use in knocking (as, "The front door . . . was ornamented with a gorgeous brass *knocker*, curiously wrought, sometimes in the device of a dog, and sometimes of a lion's head": Irving's "Knickerbocker's New York," iii. 3).

knock=knee (nok′nē), *n.* Inward curvature of the legs, causing the knees to knock together in walking; *pl.*, knees that knock together thus.—**knock′=kneed,** *a.*

knock=off (nok′ôf), *n.* The act of knocking off; also, a device for knocking something off; also, the point at which something is knocked off.

knock=out (nok′out). **I.** *a.* That knocks out: as, a *knock-out* blow (see *to knock out*, under *knock*, *v. t.*); *knock-out* drops (any powerful narcotic as used to stupefy an intended victim). **II.** *n.* The act of knocking out, or the state or fact of being knocked out; a knock-out blow.

knoll[1] (nōl), *v.* [ME. *knollen*; akin to *knell*.] **I.** *tr.* To ring or toll (a bell); also, to sound (a knell) by ringing or tolling (also fig.: as, "I would not wish them to a fairer death: And so, his knell is *knoll'd*," Shakspere's "Macbeth," v. 8. 50); hence, to ring a knell for; announce by strokes of a bell or the like (as, "All that night I heard The heavy clocks *knolling* the drowsy hours": Tennyson's "Gardener's Daughter," 180); summon by strokes of a bell, as to church. [Archaic or prov.] **II.** *intr.* To ring or toll, as a bell does; sound a knell; toll a summons, as to church. [Archaic or prov.]—**knoll**[1], *n.* A stroke of a bell in ringing or tolling, or the sound made. [Archaic or prov.]

knoll[2] (nōl), *n.* [AS. *cnoll*, hilltop, hill, = D. *knol* = G. *knollen*, knob, lump.] The top or crown of a hill (now prov.); hence, a small, rounded hill or eminence; a hillock.

knop (nop), *n.* [ME. *knoppe* = D. *knop* = G. *knopf*, knob: cf. *knob* and *knap*[2].] A small, rounded protuberance; a knob; a boss, stud, or the like, as for ornament; also, a bud, as of a flower (archaic: as, "The cedar of the house within was carved with *knops* and open flowers," 1 Kings, vi. 18).

knosp (nosp), *n.* [G. *knospe*, bud; akin to E. *knop*.] A bud-like ornament, as in architectural work; a knop, knob, or boss: as, "Ere from thy mural crown there fell The slightest *knosp*, or pinnacle" (Scott's "Marmion," v., Introd.).

knot[1] (not), *n.* [ME.; origin unknown.] A wading bird, *Tringa canutus*, of the snipe family.

Knot (*Tringa canutus*).

knot[2] (not), *n.* [AS. *cnotta* = D. *knot* = MHG. *knotze*, knot: cf. G. *knoten*, also L. *nodus*, knot.] An interlacement of parts of a cord, rope, or the like, drawn tight into a lump or knob, as for preventing slipping or for fastening the cord to something; a similar interlacement of two or more cords, etc., as for fastening them together; a tie in a cord, etc.; also, a tangle accidentally drawn tight; also, a piece of ribbon or similar material tied or folded upon itself and used or worn as an ornament; a bow, cockade, or the like; also, a figure formed of interlaced lines; also, a point of meeting or intersection of lines, nerves, etc.; also, fig., something involved or intricate; a difficulty; a knotty problem (as, "*Knots* worthy of solution, which alone A Deity could solve": Cowper's "Task," ii. 520); sometimes, the central point of anything involved or intricate; the main point of a problem; also, fig., a bond or tie (as, "O night, and shades! How are ye join'd with Hell in triple *knot!*" Milton's "Comus," 581); esp., the bond of wedlock; also, a knot-like mass; a lump, protuberance, or swelling; a boss or knob; a hill or summit, esp. a rocky one (prov. Eng.); a concretion, clot, or the like; specif., a protuberance in the tissue of a plant; an excrescence on a stem, branch, or root; a node or joint in a stem, esp. when of swollen form; the hard, cross-grained mass of wood at the place where a branch joins the trunk of a tree; also, any of various diseases of trees, characterized by the formation of excrescences; also, a group or cluster of persons or things (as, "A *knot* of boys . . . watched the arriving guests," Disraeli's "Coningsby," i. 11; "They had now arrived at the *knot* of palm-trees," Scott's "Talisman," ii.); also, *naut.*, one of a series of equal divisions on a log-line, marked off by strings knotted through the strands, and made of such a length that the number running out in a certain time will indicate the ship's speed in nautical miles per hour; hence, a unit of speed of one nautical mile an hour (as, "We sailed . . . with a light wind, the tide . . . carrying us at the rate of four or five *knots*," Dana's "Two Years before the Mast," xxvi.; a vessel with a speed of fifteen *knots*); loosely, a nautical mile (as, "Down she [a gunboat] came . . . running about three *knots* an hour": Marryat's "Mr. Midshipman Easy," xiii.).—**Gordian knot.** See *Gordian*.—**knot²**, *v.*; *knotted*, *knotting*. **I.** *tr.* To tie in a knot or knots; form a knot or knots in; also, to secure by a knot (as, "At his side a wretched scrip was hung, Wide-patch'd, and *knotted* to a twisted thong": Pope's tr. Homer's "Odyssey," xiii.); also, to form by making knots, as a fringe; also, fig., to combine or unite closely or intimately; entangle or complicate; also, to form protuberances, bosses, or knobs in; make knotty; knit (the brow: as, "Bradley Headstone *knotted* his brows," Dickens's "Our Mutual Friend," ii. 14). **II.** *intr.* To make a knot or knots; specif., to form or knit knots in making fringes, etc.; produce fancywork made by tying knots in cords; also, to become tied or tangled in a knot or knots; also, to gather in a knot or group† (see Shakspere's "Othello," iv. 2. 62).

knot=grass (not′grȧs), *n.* A common polygonaceous weed, *Polygonum aviculare*, with numerous nodes in its stems; also, any of certain other species of this genus, or any of various similar plants.

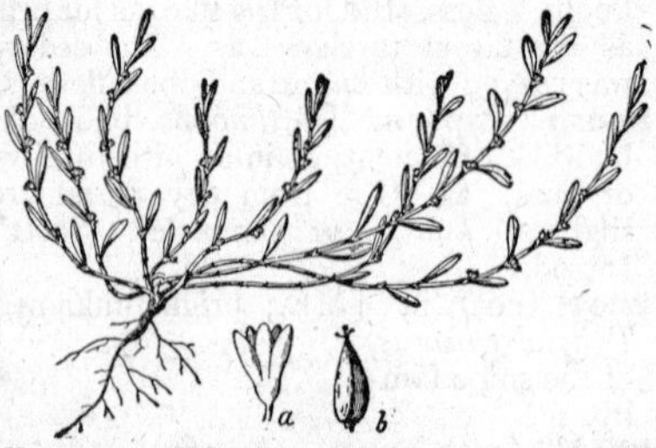

Knot-grass (*Polygonum aviculare*). — *a*, flower; *b*, fruit.

knot=hole (not′hōl), *n.* A hole in a board or plank formed by the falling out of a knot or a portion of a knot.

knot-ted (not′ed), *a.* Having a knot or knots; knotty.

knot-ter (not′ėr), *n.* One who or that which knots.

knot-ty (not′i), *a.*; compar. *knottier*, superl. *knottiest*. Full of knots, as a cord; tied or tangled in knots; hence, fig., involved, intricate, or difficult (as, "The Carrier . . . called Dot to . . . advise him on some *knotty* point": Dickens's "Cricket on the Hearth," ii.); also, characterized by knots, swellings, or rough protuberances; gnarled; containing knots, as a board or plank; also, of a hard or rough character; rugged.—**knot′ti-ness**, *n.*

knot-weed (not′wēd), *n.* Any of various knotty-stemmed plants of the polygonaceous genus *Polygonum*, as *P. maritimum* ('seaside knotweed'), a glaucous herb of sandy soils; also, any of certain species of knapweed, esp. *Centaurea nigra*.

knot-work (not′wėrk), *n.* Ornamental work consisting of or representing cords or the like knotted together, intertwined, or interlaced.

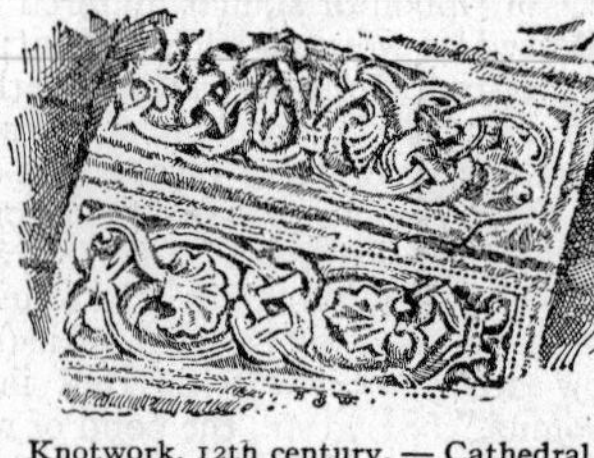

Knotwork, 12th century. — Cathedral of Angers, France.

knout (nout or nöt), *n.* [Russ. *knut.*] A kind of whip or scourge formerly used in Russia for flogging criminals.—**knout**, *v. t.* To flog with the knout.

know (nō), *v. t.*; pret. *knew*, pp. *known*, ppr. *knowing*. [AS. *cnāwan* (*gecnāwan*) = OHG. *-cnāan*, know, = Icel. *knā* (pres. ind.), know how, can; akin to L. *gnoscere*, *noscere*, Gr. *γιγνώσκειν*, Skt. *jñā-*, know; from the same root as E. *can*¹ and *ken*.] To perceive or understand as fact or truth, or apprehend with clearness and certainty (as, "things too wonderful for me, which I *knew* not," Job, xlii. 3; "What is it to be wise? 'Tis but to *know* how little can be *known*," Pope's "Essay on Man," iv. 261); also, to perceive the identity of, or recognize (as, you will *know* the house by the trees; you would hardly *know* him nowadays); be able to distinguish or tell, as one from another; also, to be cognizant or aware of (as, to *know* the cause of a thing; to *know* a person's name or wishes; do you *know* what he did?); also, to be acquainted with (a thing, place, person, etc.), as by sight, experience, or report; be familiar or conversant with (a subject, method, etc.); be versed in (an art, etc.); have fixed in the mind or memory (as, to *know* a lesson; to *know* a song, or a part in a play; to *know* a poem by heart); have experience of (trouble, hardship, defeat, etc.); often, to be personally or socially acquainted with (a person, etc.); also, to have sexual intercourse with (archaic).—**to know a hawk from a hand=saw.** See under *handsaw*.—**to know a thing or two,** to have practical or worldly knowledge; be knowing or shrewd. [Colloq.]—**to know one's own mind.** See under *mind*², *n.*—**to know the ropes,** to know the various ropes about a vessel, as a sailor does; hence (colloq.), to understand the details or methods of any business or the like; know the ways of a place.—**to know what's what,** to be well-informed; have competent knowledge; know what is proper or expedient: as, "He *knew what's what*, and that's as high As metaphysic wit can fly" (Butler's "Hudibras," i. 1); "I think ef there is anybody that *knows what's what* about funerals I'm the man" (Mrs. Stowe's "Oldtown Folks," iv.). [Colloq.]—**know**, *v. i.* To have knowledge, or clear and certain perception, as of fact or truth (as, "Thou, O Spirit . . . Instruct me, for thou *know'st*," Milton's "Paradise Lost," i. 19; "We have but faith: we cannot *know*, For knowledge is of things we see," Tennyson's "In Memoriam," Prologue); also, to be cognizant or aware, as of some fact, circumstance, or occurrence; have information, as about something; also, to be personally acquainted† (as, "Sir, we have *known* together in Orleans": Shakspere's "Cymbeline," i. 4. 36).—**know**, *n.* The fact of knowing; knowledge: now chiefly in the colloquial phrase 'in the know,' that is, in the circle of those who have private or inside knowledge of a case.

know-a-ble (nō′ạ-bl), *a.* That may be known.—**know′a-ble-ness**, *n.*

know-er (nō′ėr), *n.* One who knows.

know-ing (nō′ing), *p. a.* That knows; perceiving or understanding; having knowledge or information; intelligent, sagacious, or wise (as, "I have remarked that your *knowing* people, who are so much wiser than any body else, are eternally keeping society in a ferment": Irving's "Knickerbocker's New York," iii. 2); shrewd, sharp, or astute; often, affecting or suggesting shrewd or secret understanding of matters (as, he is always so *knowing*; a *knowing* glance; "laughing me down in a *knowing* way, as much as to say that he was not to be taken in by my professions of simplicity," Kingsley's "Alton Locke," xvi.); also, smart or stylish (colloq.).—**know′ing-ly**, *adv.* In a knowing manner; with knowledge, or consciously (as, to do a thing *knowingly*); intelligently; shrewdly.—**know′ing-ness**, *n.*

knowl-edge (nol′ej), *n.* [ME. *knaulage*, *knauleche*, *knowleche*, ult. < AS. *cnāwan*, know (perhaps through ME. *cnawlechen*, *knowlechen*, v., acknowledge, confess, recognize), with suffix of uncertain origin.] The fact or state of knowing; perception of fact or truth; clear and certain mental apprehension; also, recognition, cognizance, or notice (archaic: as, "Why have I found grace in thine eyes, that thou shouldest take *knowledge* of me?" Ruth, ii. 10); also, the state of being cognizant or aware, as of a fact or circumstance; cognizance of facts, or range of cognizance (as, this has happened twice within my *knowledge*); also, acquaintance with a thing, place, person, etc., as by sight, experience, or report; familiarity or conversance, as with a subject, language, branch of learning, etc.; acquaintance with facts, truths, or principles, as from study or investigation; practical understanding of an art, etc.; personal acquaintance†; sexual intercourse (now chiefly legal, in 'carnal knowledge'); also, that which is known, or may be known; the sum of what is known; the body of truths or facts accumulated by mankind in the course of time (sometimes personified: as, "But *Knowledge* to their eyes her ample page Rich with the spoils of time did ne'er unroll," Gray's "Elegy," xiii.); sometimes, a branch of learning (chiefly in *pl.*); also, information or intelligence given or received†; also, acknowledgment† or confession†.—**to one's knowledge,** according to one's certain knowledge, or as one actually knows (as, this was done twice, *to my knowledge*); with a negative, so far as one knows (as, I never saw him, *to my knowledge*). —**knowl′edge-a-ble,** *a.* Possessing knowledge or understanding; intelligent. [Colloq.]—**knowl′edge-less,** *a.* Destitute of knowledge.

known (nōn). Past participle of *know*.—**known,** *p. a.* Perceived or understood (as, death without a *known* cause); often, generally recognized, or familiar to all (as, a man of *known* integrity).—**known quantity,** in *math.*, a quantity whose value is given: in algebra, etc., usually represented by a letter from the first part of the alphabet, as *a*, *b*, or *c*.

know=noth-ing (nō′nuth″ing). **I.** *n.* An ignoramus; also, an agnostic; also [*cap.*], in *U. S. hist.*, a member of a political party (the 'American party': orig. a secret society whose members professed ignorance concerning it), prominent from 1853 to 1856, whose aim was to keep the control of the government in the hands of native citizens. **II.** *a.* Knowing nothing; grossly ignorant; also, denying the possibility of knowing; agnostic; also [*cap.*], in *U. S. hist.*, of or pertaining to the Know-nothings.

knub (nub), *n.* [= LG. *knubbe*, knob, protuberance: cf. *knob* and *nub*.] A protuberance; a small swelling; a small lump. [Now chiefly prov.]

knuck-le (nuk′l), *n.* [ME. *knokel* = D. *kneukel* = G. *knöchel*, knuckle; dim. of a form represented by D. *knok*, G. *knochen*, bone.] A joint of a finger, esp. one of the joints at the roots of the fingers; the rounded prominence of such a joint when the finger is bent; also, a joint of meat, consisting of the parts about the carpal or tarsal joint of a quadruped (as, "a *knuckle* of ham": Smollett's "Humphry Clinker," June 5); also, some thing or part shaped or protruding like a knuckle (as, "an old ragged wart of an edifice, standing on the *knuckle* of a hill": Irving's "Tales of a Traveler," i. 3); specif., a cylindrical projecting part on a hinge, through which an axis or pin passes; the joint of a hinge; also, a piece of metal, usually brass ('brass knuckle'), worn over the knuckles in order to protect them in striking a blow and to make the blow more effective (also called *knuckle-duster*). —**knuck′le,** *v.*; *-led, -ling.* **I.** *tr.* To strike, tap, or touch with the knuckles: as, "the . . . porter . . . *knuckling* his forehead as a sign of homage" (Dickens's "Hard Times," ii. 1). **II.** *intr.* To hold the knuckles close to the ground in playing marbles (often with *down*: as, "As happy as we once, to kneel and draw The chalky ring, and *knuckle down* at taw," Cowper's "Tirocinium," 307); also, to yield or submit (often with *down* or *under*: as, "Then followed a battle of looks between them; but the captain soon *knuckled under*," Stevenson's "Treasure Island," i.); also, to apply one's self vigorously or earnestly, as to a task (with *down*). —**knuck′le=bone,** *n.* In man, a bone forming a knuckle of a finger; the rounded end of a finger-bone at a joint; also, in quadrupeds, a leg-bone with a knobbed end, or the knobbed end itself; hence, a joint of meat including such a bone; also, a metacarpal or metatarsal bone of a sheep or the like; hence, *pl.*, a game in which such metacarpal or metatarsal bones are tossed up, caught, and otherwise used.—**knuck′le=dust″er,** *n.* See *knuckle*, *n.*—**knuck′le=joint,** *n.* A joint forming a knuckle; in *mach.*, a flexible joint formed by two abutting links; a kind of hinged joint.

knur, knurr (nėr), *n.* [Var. of *knar*.] A knot on a tree or in wood; a knotty lump or excrescence.

knurl (nėrl), *n.* [Appar. < *knur*: cf. *knarl*.] A knot, protuberance, or excrescence, as on a tree or one of its branches; a boss, knob, or nodule; also, a small ridge or the like, esp. one of a series, as on the edge of a milled coin.—**knurl,** *v. t.* To make knurls or ridges on; mill.—**knurled,** *a.* Having knurls or knots; gnarled; also, having small ridges on the edge or surface; milled.—**knurl′y,** *a.* Having knurls or knots; gnarled.

knut (nut), *n.* A nut, or idle young man of fashion. [Slang, Eng.]

Koala.

ko-a-la, koo-lah (kō′-ạ-lä, kö′lạ), *n.* [Native Australian.] A sluggish, furry, arboreal marsupial mammal, *Phascolarctos cinereus*, of Australia.

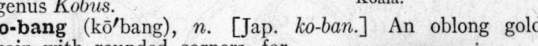

kob (kob), *n.* [W. Afr.] Any of various African antelopes of the genus *Kobus*.

ko-bang (kō′bang), *n.* [Jap. *ko-ban*.] An oblong gold coin with rounded corners, formerly current in Japan.

Kobang.

ko-bold (kō′bold or -bōld), *n.* [G. *kobold*, MHG. *kobolt*, perhaps < *kobe*, house: cf. *cobalt*.] In German folklore, a kind of spirit or goblin, often mischievous, that haunts houses; also, a kind of spirit that haunts mines or other underground places.

ko-dak (kō′dak), *n.* [Arbitrary word invented as a trade-mark.] A kind of portable photographic camera, esp. adapted for instantaneous work, employing a continuous roll of sensitized film upon which successive negatives are made; also, a photograph taken with it. [Proprietary name.]—**ko′dak,** *v. t.* or *i.*; *-daked, -daking.* To photograph with a kodak.—**ko′dak-er,** *n.*

koh=i=noor (kō′i-nör′), *n.* [From the famous *Koh-i-noor* or *Koh-i-nur* diamond (now 106 carats) among the British crown jewels: Pers. *kōh-i-nūr*, 'mountain of light.'] Any large and splendid diamond; fig., something rarely beautiful or precious; the most splendid or superb example of something.

kohl (kōl), *n.* [Ar. *koh'l*: cf. *alcohol*.] A powder, as finely powdered sulphide of antimony, used in the East to darken the eyelids, make eyebrows, etc.

kohl-ra-bi (kōl-rä′bi), *n.* [G., < It. *cavoli rape*, pl. of *cavolo rapa*, 'cabbage turnip': cf. *cole* and *rape*[4].] A kind of cabbage, a cultivated variety of *Brassica oleracea*, whose stem above ground swells into an edible bulb-like formation.

kok=sa-ghyz (kok′su′giz), *n.* [Russ.] A Russian plant related to our dandelion with roots that yield a milky juice from which a commercial rubber is made.

ko-la (kō′lạ), *n.* [W. Afr. *kola* (NL. *Cola*).] The kola-nut, or the tree producing it; an extract prepared from the kola-nut.—**ko′la=nut,** *n.* The bitter, brownish nut or seed of an African sterculiaceous tree, *Cola acuminata*, cultivated in the West Indies and Brazil, and used as a stimulant and tonic.

Koodoo.

ko-lin-sky (kọ-lin′-ski), *n.* [Russ. *Kolinski*, of Kola, in northern Russia.] Any of certain Asiatic animals of the mink kind, esp. *Puto-*

rius sibiricus (or *Mustela sibirica*), which has tawny fur and a long, bushy tail; also, the fur of such an animal: a furriers' name.

kom-mers (ko-mers′), *n.* [G., < L. *commercium*, trade, intercourse: see *commerce.*] In German use, a students' drinking-party.

koo-doo (kö′dö), *n.*; pl. *-doos* (-döz). [S. Afr.] A large, handsome African antelope, *Strepsiceros kudu.* See cut on preceding page.

koo′lah, *n.* See *koala.*

koor′bash, *n.* and *v.* See *kurbash.*

kop (kop), *n.* [D. *kop*, head: cf. *cop*¹.] A hill. [South Africa.]

ko-peck (kō′pek), *n.* [Russ. *kopeyka.*] A Russian monetary unit and copper coin, the hundredth part of a ruble, equivalent to about one half of a U. S. cent.

Obverse. Reverse.
Kopeck of Nicholas I. — British Museum.

kop-je (kop′i), *n.* [D., dim. of *kop*: see *kop.*] A small hill. [South Africa.]

Ko-ran (kǫ-rän′ or kō′rąn), *n.* [Ar. *qurān*, reading, recitation, < *qara'a*, read.] The sacred book of the Mohammedans, consisting of revelations delivered orally by Mohammed and taken down in writing.—**Ko-ran′ic** (-ran′ik), *a.*

kor-o-seal (kor′ǫ-sēl), *n.* [*koro* (from *corrosion*) + *seal.*] The trade-mark name for a rubber-like synthetic plastic.

ko-sher (kō′shėr). [Heb. *koshēr*, fit, proper, lawful.] **I.** *a.* Right, lawful, or clean, according to the Jewish law: used of food and vessels for food made ritually proper for use, esp. of meat slaughtered in accordance with the law of Moses. **II.** *n.* Kosher food; also, a shop where this is sold. —**ko′sher,** *v. t.* To prepare (food) in a kosher manner.

kos-mos (koz′mos), *n.* See *cosmos.*

ko-to (kō′tō), *n.* [Jap.] A Japanese musical instrument having thirteen strings, each five feet long and with a separate bridge, stretched over a sounding-box: played with both hands.

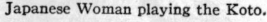

Japanese Woman playing the Koto.

ko-tow, kow-tow (kō-tou′), *n.* [Chinese *k'o-t'ou*, lit. 'knock-head.'] The Chinese ceremony of touching the forehead to the ground while kneeling, as an act of profound respect, humble submission, or worship (as, to perform the *kotow*); hence, an obsequious obeisance; a servile demonstration of respect.—**ko-tow′, kow-tow′,** *v. i.* To perform the kotow; hence, to bow or act in an obsequious manner; show servile deference.—**ko-tow′er, kow-tow′er,** *n.*

kou′miss, kou′myss, *n.* See *kumiss.*

kour′bash, *n.* and *v.* See *kurbash.*

kous-so (kůs′ō), *n.* See *cusso.*

kraal (kräl or krâl), *n.* [S. Afr. D., < Pg. *curral* = Sp. *corral*, inclosure: cf. *corral.*] A village of South African natives, usually surrounded by a stockade or the like and often having a central space for cattle, etc.; hence, the body of inhabitants; also, an inclosure for cattle, etc. [South Africa.]—**kraal,** *v. t.* To shut up in a kraal, as cattle. [South Africa.]

krait (krīt), *n.* [Hind. *karait.*] A small, extremely venomous snake, *Bungarus cæruleus*, of India, which causes a large number of deaths.

kra-ken (krä′kẹn or krā′-), *n.* [Norw.] A mythical sea-monster said to appear at times off the coast of Norway: as, "Then like a *kraken* huge and black, She crushed our ribs in her iron grasp!" (Longfellow's "The Cumberland"). See also Tennyson's poem, "The Kraken."

kran (krän), *n.* [Pers.] A Persian monetary unit and silver coin, equivalent to about 8 U. S. cents.

krans, krantz (kräns, kränts), *n.* [D. *krans*, wreath, crown, cornice: cf. *crants.*] A ring of rock or cliffs about a mountain summit; in general, a precipitous wall of rock; a cliff. [South Africa.]

krem-lin (krem′lin), *n.* [F. *kremlin*, < Russ. *kreml*, citadel.] The citadel of a Russian town or city; esp. [*cap.*], that of Moscow, including within its walls a palace, churches, an arsenal, etc.

kreut-zer, kreu-zer (kroit′sėr), *n.* [G. *kreuzer*, < *kreuz*, a cross (orig. the device on the coin).] A former German coin equivalent to about half a U. S. cent; also, an Austrian copper coin (no longer coined) and monetary unit, equal to one hundredth of a florin.

Obverse. Reverse.
Austrian Kreutzer.

krieg-spiel (krēg′-spēl), *n.* [G. *kriegsspiel*, 'war-game.'] A game designed to teach military science by means of blocks or the like, representing armies, guns, etc., moved about on maps or other surfaces.

krim-mer, crim-mer (krim′ėr), *n.* [G. *krimmer*, < *Krim*, Crimea.] A lambskin from the Crimean region, dressed as a fur, with wool in loose, soft curls and usually of a whitish or pale gray.

kris (krēs or kris), *n.* See *creese.*

kro-na (krō′ną), *n.*; pl. *kronor* (-nǫr). [Sw.: see *krone.*] The monetary unit and a silver coin of Sweden, equivalent to the krone of Denmark and Norway.

kro-ne (krō′nė), *n.*; pl. Dan. and Norw. *kroner* (-nėr), G. *kronen* (-nen). [Dan. and Norw. *krone* = Sw. *krona* = G. *krone* = E. *crown.*] The monetary unit and a silver coin of Denmark and of Norway (see also *krona*), equal to about 26.8 U. S. cents; also, a German gold coin equal to 10 marks, or about $2.38; also, the monetary unit and a silver coin of Austria, equal to 100 heller, or about 20.3 U. S. cents.

Obverse. Reverse.
Danish Krone.

Krupp-ize (krůp′īz), *v. t.*; *-ized, -izing.* [From the *Krupp* works at Essen, Prussia.] To subject (steel armor-plate) to the Krupp process, which gives it a hard face, leaving the interior and back ductile and slightly yielding.

kryp-ton (krip′ton), *n.* [NL., < Gr. κρυπτόν, neut. of κρυπτός, hidden: see *crypt.*] Chem. sym., Kr; at. wt., 82.92. An inert gaseous element present in very small amounts in the atmosphere.

Kshat-ri-ya (kshat′rẹ-yą), *n.* [Skt., < *kshatra*, rule, authority.] A member of the military caste among the Hindus.

ku-dos (kū′dos), *n.* [Gr. κῦδος.] Glory; renown: as, "Excepting Oliphant, who gained a little *kudos*, it is doubtful if Mundey's drama advanced any one professionally" (L. Merrick's "Actor-Manager," xv.). [Colloq., orig. Eng. university slang.]

ku-du (kö′dö), *n.* See *koodoo.*

Ku-fic (kū′fik), *a.* and *n.* See *Cufic.*

Ku Klux, Ku=Klux, Ku-klux (kū′kluks), *n.* [Said to be < Gr. κύκλος, circle.] A secret organization (also called 'Ku Klux Klan') in the southern U. S., active for several years after the Civil War, which aimed to protect the whites against the negroes (with their newly acquired powers) and against adventurers from the North, and was credited with many lawless and violent proceedings; a member of it;

also, a secret organization ('Knights of the Ku Klux Klan') inspired by the former, founded in 1915 and active in the southern and other parts of the U. S., making Americanism its professed object, and admitting to membership none but native-born, white, Gentile, Protestant Americans.

kuk-ri (kůk'rē), *n.* [Hindi.] A knife with a curved blade broadest toward the point and usually having the sharp edge on the concave side, used as a weapon and otherwise by the Gurkhas of India.

kul-tur (kůl-tör'), *n.* [G., < L. *cultura*, E. *culture.*] Culture; civilization: as, "assertions of the moral elevation and loveliness of Germany, of the insuperable excellencies of German *Kultur*" (H. G. Wells's "Italy, France, and Britain at War," i.).

Kul-tur-kampf (kůl-tör'kämpf''), *n.* [G., 'civilization struggle.'] The conflict between the German imperial government and the Roman Catholic Church from 1872 or 1873 until 1886, chiefly over the control of educational and ecclesiastical appointments.

ku-miss, ku-myss (kö'mis), *n.* [= F. *koumis* = G. *kumys*, < Russ. *kumys*; from Tatar.] Fermented mare's or camel's milk, used as a beverage by Asiatic nomads, etc.; an intoxicating liquor distilled from it; also, a similar drink prepared from other milk, esp. that of the cow, and used for dietetic and medicinal purposes.

küm-mel (küm'ęl), *n.* [G., cumin, kümmel.] A cordial or liqueur flavored with cumin, caraway-seeds, etc., made esp. in regions bordering on the eastern coast of the Baltic Sea.

kum-mer-bund (kum'ėr-bund), *n.* See *cummerbund.*

kum-quat (kum'kwot), *n.* See *cumquat.*

kunz-ite (könts'īt), *n.* [From G. F. *Kunz*, American expert in precious stones.] A transparent lilac variety of spodumene found in California, and used as a gem.

kur-bash (kör'bàsh), *n.* [Ar. *qurbāsh*, < Turk. *qirbāch.*] A whip made of hide, as of the hippopotamus or rhinoceros, used as an instrument of punishment in Turkey, Egypt, etc.: as, "The commander . . . disperses the rabble with his *kurbash*, or hippopotamus whip" (G. W. Curtis's "Howadji in Syria," i. 1).—**kur'bash,** *v. t.* To flog with the kurbash.

Kurd (körd), *n.* A member of a pastoral and predatory Aryan people speaking an Iranian language and dwelling chiefly in Kurdistan (a region east of Asia Minor and extending into western Persia).—**Kurd'ish,** *a.*

kur-gan (kör-gän'), *n.* [Russ.] A prehistoric burial-mound in Russia or Siberia.

kur-ra-jong (kur'ą-jông), *n.* [Native Australian.] Any of various malvaceous and sterculiaceous trees or shrubs of Australia, Tasmania, etc., which yield strong fibers used for making cordage, matting, etc., as *Plagianthus sidoides*, a malvaceous species.

kur-saal (kör'zäl), *n.* [G., 'cure hall.'] A public building or room for the use of visitors at a health resort in Germany or elsewhere.

kvass (kvàs), *n.* [Russ. *kvas.*] A Russian fermented drink, usually made from an infusion of rye flour or bread with malt.

ky-a-bu-ka=wood (kī-ą-bö'kä-wůd), *n.* See *kiabooca-wood.*

ky-ack (kī'ak), *n* See *kayak.*

kyang (kyang), *n.* [Tibetan.] A wild ass, *Equus kiang*, of Tibet.

ky-an-ize (kī'ąn-īz), *v. t.*; *-ized, -izing.* [From J. H. *Kyan*, the patentee (1832).] To treat (wood) with a solution of corrosive sublimate to prevent decay.—**ky''an-i-za'tion** (-i-zā'shǫn), *n.*

ky-bosh', *n.* See *kibosh.*

kye (kī), *n.* Obs. or prov. plural of *cow*[1].

ky-lix (kī'liks or kil'iks), *n.* Same as *cylix.*

ky-loe (kī'lō), *n.* [Origin uncertain.] One of a breed of cattle of the Hebrides and the Scottish Highlands.

ky-mo-graph (kī'mǫ-gràf), *n.* [Gr. κῦμα, wave: see *-graph.*] An instrument by which variations of fluid pressure, as the waves of the pulse, can be measured and graphically recorded.—**ky-mo-graph'ic** (-graf'ik), *a.*

Kym-ric (kim'rik), etc. See *Cymric*, etc.

Ky-ri-e e-le-ï-son (kē'ri-ā e-lā'i-son). [Gr. Κύριε ἐλέησον.] 'Lord, have mercy'—a brief petition used in various offices of the Eastern and Roman churches; also, a response or petition in the Anglican service, beginning with the words 'Lord, have mercy upon us'; also, a musical setting of either of these.

L

L[1], **l**[1] (el); pl. *L's, l's* (elz). A consonant, the 12th letter of the English alphabet.

L[2] (el), *n.*; pl. *L's* (elz). Something having, or contributing to form, a shape like that of the letter L, as a right-angled pipe-connection, or an extension to a building at right angles with the main part. See *ell*[2].

la[1] (lâ or lä), *interj.* [Cf. *lo.*] An exclamation, formerly of asseveration, now of wonder, surprise, etc.: as, "Truly, I will not go first; truly, *la!* I will not do you that wrong" (Shakspere's "Merry Wives of Windsor," i. 1. 322); "Oh *la!* my lady, what do you stay here for?" (Scott's "St. Ronan's Well," xxxi.). [Now prov. or vulgar.]

la[2] (lä), *n.* In *music*, the syllable used for the sixth tone of the scale (A, in the major scale of C), and sometimes for the tone A. See *sol-fa.*

laa-ger (lä'gėr), *n.* [S. Afr. D., = D. *leger*, camp: see *leaguer*[2].] A camp or encampment, esp. within an encircling line of wagons. [South Africa.]—**laa'ger,** *v. t.* or *i.* To arrange or encamp in a laager. [South Africa.]

lab-a-rum (lab'ą-rum), *n.*; pl. *-ra* (-rą). [LL., = LGr. λάβαρον; origin obscure.] The military standard of Constantine the Great and later Christian emperors of Rome, bearing Christian symbols (as, "The principal standard which displayed the triumph of the cross was styled the *Labarum*" : Gibbon's "Decline and Fall of the Roman Empire," xx.); also, an ecclesiastical standard or banner, as for carrying in processions (see cut in preceding column); hence, in general, any symbolic standard or banner (also fig.).

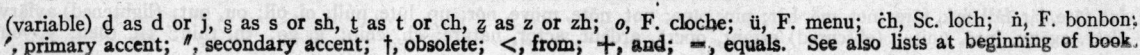

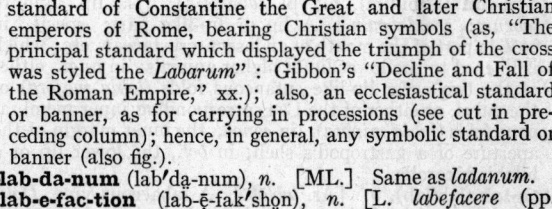

Ecclesiastical Labarum.

lab-da-num (lab'dą-num), *n.* [ML.] Same as *ladanum.*

lab-e-fac-tion (lab-ę-fak'shǫn), *n.* [L. *labefacere* (pp. *labefactus*), shake, weaken, < *labare*, totter, give way, + *facere*, do, make.] A shaking or weakening; overthrow; downfall.

la-bel (lā'bęl), *n.* [OF. *label, lambel*, pendent band or piece (F. *lambeau*, strip, shred); perhaps from Teut. and akin to E. *lap*[2].] A pendent band or strip, as one of those hanging down from a bishop's miter; also, a strip or narrow piece of anything†; also, a slip of paper or other material, suitably marked or inscribed, for affixing to something to indicate its nature, ownership, destination, etc.; in *her.*, a narrow band with pendants, used esp. to distinguish the oldest son during his father's life; in *arch.*, a molding or dripstone over a door or window, esp. one which extends horizontally across the top of the opening and vertically downward for a certain distance at the sides.—**la'bel,** *v. t.*; *-beled* or *-belled, -beling* or *-belling.* To affix a label to; mark or designate with or as with a label.—**la'bel-er, la'bel-ler,** *n.*

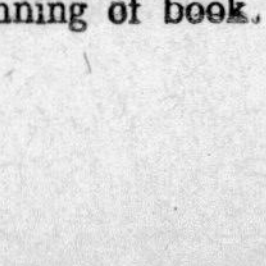
Heraldic Label.

la-bel-lum (lą-bel'um), *n.*; pl. *labella* (-ą). [L., dim. of *labrum*, lip: see *labrum*.] In *bot.*, that division of the corolla of an orchidaceous plant which differs more or less markedly from the other divisions, often forming the most conspicuous part, and which through a half-twist of the ovary occupies a position nearest the bract instead of its regular morphological one nearest the axis; also, a similar division in other corollas.

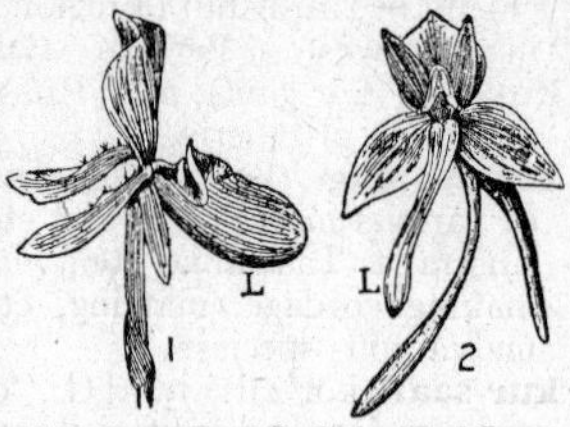

Labellum (*L*) of Orchid: (1) of *Cypripedium hirsutum*, (2) of *Habenaria orbiculata*.

la-bi-a (lā′bi-ạ̈), *n.* Plural of *labium*.

la-bi-al (lā′bi-ạl). [ML. *labialis*, < L. *labium*, lip: see *labium*.] **I.** *a.* Of or pertaining to the lips (as, "the *labial* melody with which the Typee girls carry on an ordinary conversation": H. Melville's "Typee," xxx.); in *zoöl.*, etc., pertaining to or of the nature of a labium; in *phonetics*, of speech-sounds, uttered with more or less complete closure of the lips, as *b*, *p*, *m*. **II.** *n.* In *phonetics*, a labial sound.—**la′bi-al-ism,** *n.* In *phonetics*, labial pronunciation; a tendency to labialize sounds.—**la′bi-al-ize** (-īz), *v. t.*; *-ized*, *-izing*. In *phonetics*, to give a labial character to (a sound); round (a vowel).—**la″bi-al-i-za′tion** (-i-zā′shọn), *n.*—**la′bi-al-ly,** *adv.*

la-bi-ate (lā′bi-āt). [NL. *labiatus*.] **I.** *a.* Having a labium or labia; lipped; in *bot.*, having one or more lip-like parts; specif., bilabiate; belonging to the *Labiatæ* (or *Menthaceæ*), or mint family of plants, most of whose members have bilabiate corollas. **II.** *n.* In *bot.*, a labiate plant.

Labiate (Bilabiate) Corolla of Self-heal (*Prunella vulgaris*).—*a*, seen from the side; *b*, laid open, front view.

la-bile (lā′bil or lab′il), *a.* [LL. *labilis*, < L. *labi*, fall, slide: cf. *lapse*.] Apt to lapse or change; unstable; in *med.*, noting or pertaining to a mode of application of electricity in which the active electrode is moved over the part to be acted upon (opposed to *stabile*).—**la-bil-i-ty** (lạ-bil′i-ti), *n.*

labio-. Form of L. *labium*, lip, used in combination.—**la-bi-o-den-tal** (lā″bi-ọ-den′tạl). In *phonetics*: **I.** *a.* Uttered with the coöperation of the lips and the teeth, as *f* and *v*. **II.** *n.* A labiodental sound.—**la″bi-o-na′sal** (-nā′zạl). In *phonetics*: **I.** *a.* Uttered with the coöperation of the lips and the nose, as *m*. **II.** *n.* A labionasal sound.

la-bi-um (lā′bi-um), *n.*; pl. *labia* (-ạ̈). [L., lip, akin to *labrum*: see *labrum*.] A lip or lip-like part; specif., in *zoöl.*, a part of the mouth of an insect, crustacean, etc., which is likened to the lower lip of higher animals; in *anat.*, either of the two outer lip-like cutaneous folds (*labia majora*) of the vulva, or either of the two corresponding inner membranous folds (*labia minora*); in *conch.*, the inner margin of the aperture of a gastropod's shell; in *bot.*, the lower lip of a bilabiate corolla.

lab-lab (lab′lab), *n.* [Ar. *lablāb*.] A fabaceous vine, *Dolichos lablab*, with edible seeds, native in India but widely cultivated in other warm countries; also, any of various related species.

la-bor (lā′bọr), *n.* [ME. *labour*, < OF. *labor*, *labour* (F. *labeur*), < L. *labor*, toil, trouble, distress.] Persistent exertion of body or mind for the accomplishment of an end; work, esp. of a hard or fatiguing kind; toil; specif., bodily toil for the sake of gain or economic production; hence, those engaged in such toil considered as a class (as, the claims or rights of *labor*); also, a work or task done or to be done (as, "My *labours*, of the body, at least, have been light enough": Bulwer-Lytton's "Rienzi," i. 1); also, the product or result of toil (archaic: as, "the waxen *labour* of the bees," Dryden's tr. Virgil's "Georgics," iii. 688); also, trouble or pains taken†; also, the pangs and efforts of childbirth; travail.—**Labor Day,** in the various States of the U. S., a legal holiday, commonly the first Monday in September, in honor of the laboring class.—**la′bor,** *v.* [OF. *laborer*, *labourer* (F. *labourer*), < L. *laborare*, < *labor*.] **I.** *intr.* To perform labor (as, "Six days shalt thou *labour*, and do all thy work": Ex. xx. 9); exert one's powers of body or mind; work; toil; also, to move as with effort or difficulty (as, "Let not all the people go up . . . and make not all the people to *labour* thither": Josh. vii. 3); roll or pitch heavily, as a ship (as, "The ship was *laboring* hard under her top-gallant-sails": Dana's "Two Years before the Mast," xxv.); also, to be burdened, troubled, or distressed; suffer under something burdensome, distressing, or disadvantageous (as, "We *labour* under two mighty evils," Swift's "Gulliver's Travels," i. 4; you are *laboring* under a misapprehension); also, to be in travail or childbirth. **II.** *tr.* To spend labor upon, work, or till (soil, etc.: archaic); also, to produce or accomplish by labor (archaic: as, "anvils *labour'd* by the Cyclops' hands," Dryden's tr. Virgil's "Æneid," vi. 858); also, to work out with effort; work out in detail; elaborate; also, to work or strive to bring about or achieve (archaic: as, to *labor* a person's reform); also, to cause to labor or work†; also, to belabor† (as, "Take shepherd, take a plant of stubborn oak, And *labour* him with many a sturdy stroke": Dryden's tr. Virgil's "Georgics," iii. 639).

lab-o-ra-to-ry (lab′ọ-rạ-tọ-ri), *n.*; pl. *-ries* (-riz). [ML. *laboratorium*, place to work in, < L. *laborare*, E. *labor*, *v.*] A building or part of a building fitted with apparatus for conducting scientific investigations, experiments, tests, etc., or for manufacturing chemicals, medicines, explosives, etc.—**lab″o-ra-to′ri-al** (-tō′ri-ạl), *a.*

la-bored (lā′bọrd), *p. a.* Made, done, or accomplished with labor; often, showing constrained or forced effort, or not easy, natural, or spontaneous (as, "a graceful and accomplished, if somewhat *laboured*, speaker," Lecky's "Hist. of Eng. in the 18th Century," iii.; "*labored* cordiality," Bret Harte's "Tennessee's Partner").

la-bor-er (lā′bọr-ėr), *n.* One who labors; esp., one engaged in work which requires bodily strength rather than skill or training.

la-bor-ing (lā′bọr-ing), *p. a.* That labors; working; toiling; engaged in manual or mechanical labor (as, the *laboring* class); struggling, as under difficulty, emotion, etc. (as, "an occasional sigh from the *laboring* heart of the Captain": Longfellow's "Courtship of Miles Standish," ii.); heaving, as the breast; rolling or pitching, as a ship.—**la′bor-ing-ly,** *adv.*

la-bo-ri-ous (lạ-bō′ri-us), *a.* [OF. *laborios* (F. *laborieux*), < L. *laboriosus*, < *labor*, E. *labor*, *n.*] Given to or diligent in labor, or industrious (as, "To drive The lazy drones from the *laborious* hive": Dryden's tr. Virgil's "Georgics," iv. 242); also, involving labor, or toilsome (as, "to scorn delights, and live *laborious* days": Milton's "Lycidas," 72); requiring labor in construction or execution (as, "*laborious* orient ivory sphere in sphere": Tennyson's "Princess," Prologue, 20).—**la-bo′ri-ous-ly,** *adv.*—**la-bo′ri-ous-ness,** *n.*

la-bor-ite (lā′bọr-īt), *n.* [See *labor*, *n.*] An advocate of the interests of labor; [*cap.*] a member of a party advocating labor interests, as in British politics.—**la′bor-less,** *a.* Free from labor; doing or requiring no labor.—**la′bor=mar″ket,** *n.* The available supply of labor considered with reference to the demand for it.—**la′bor=sav″ing,** *a.* Saving, or effecting economy in, labor: as, a *labor-saving* device; "The neat, *labor-saving* cook-stove had as yet no being" (Mrs. Stowe's "Oldtown Folks," vii.).—**la′bor-some** (-sum), *a.* Industrious†; also, laborious or toilsome (now rare or prov.: as, "He hath . . . wrung from me my slow leave By *laboursome* petition," Shakspere's "Hamlet," i. 2. 59).—**la′bor=u″nion,** *n.* A union or association of laboring people for the protection and furtherance of their interests. Cf. *trade-union*.

la′bour, la′boured, etc., **la′bour-ite,** etc. British preferred forms of *labor*, *labored*, etc., *laborite*, etc.

lab-ra-dor-ite (lab′rạ-dôr-īt), *n.* [From *Labrador*, in British America, where it was discovered.] A kind of feldspar, often characterized by a brilliant change of colors, used as an ornamental stone.

Lab-ra-dor (lab′rạ-dôr or lab-rạ-dôr′) **tea.** Any evergreen ericaceous shrub of the genus *Ledum*, of the colder parts of the northern hemisphere, which includes species whose leaves are used as a substitute for tea.

la-bret (lā′bret), *n.* [L. *labrum*, lip.] A lip-ornament worn by primitive tribes, in a hole pierced for the purpose.

la-broid (lā′broid). [NL. *Labrus*, the typical genus, L. *labrus*, *labros*, a kind of fish.] **I.** *a.* Belonging to or having the characteristics of the *Labridæ*, a family of acanthopterygian fishes which includes the tautog, wrasses, etc. **II.** *n.* A labroid fish.

la-brum (lā′brum), *n.*; pl. *labra* (-brạ̈). [L., lip; akin to E. *lip*: cf. *labellum* and *labium*.] A lip or lip-like part; specif., in *zoöl.*, a part of the mouth of an insect, crustacean, etc., which is likened to the upper lip of higher animals; in *conch.*, the outer margin of the aperture of a gastropod's shell.

la-bur-num (lạ-bėr′num), *n.* [L.] A small leguminous tree, *Laburnum laburnum*, having pendulous racemes of yellow flowers (as, "*Laburnum*, rich In streaming gold": Cowper's "Task," vi. 149); also, any of various allied or similar plants.

lab-y-rinth (lab′i-rinth), *n.* [L. *labyrinthus*, < Gr. λαβύρινθος.] A structure containing a number of intricate passages through which it is difficult to find one's way (as, the Cretan *labyrinth*, fabled to have been built by Dædalus for Minos, king of Crete, in which the Minotaur was confined); a maze; often, a maze of paths bordered by high hedges, as in a park or garden; hence, a complicated or tortuous arrangement, as of streets, buildings, etc. (as, "He was dragged into a *labyrinth* of dark narrow courts": Dickens's "Oliver Twist," xv.); fig., any confusingly intricate state of things, events, etc. (as, "No one could soar into a more intricate *labyrinth* of refined phraseology": Trollope's "Warden," v.); an entanglement; in *anat.*, the internal ear, a complex structure including a bony portion ('osseous labyrinth') and a membranous portion ('membranous labyrinth') contained in it.—**lab-y-rin′thi-an, lab-y-rin′thic,** *a.* Labyrinthine.—**lab-y-rin′thine** (-thin), *a.* Pertaining to, forming, or resembling a labyrinth; mazy; intricate: as, *labyrinthine* passages or windings.

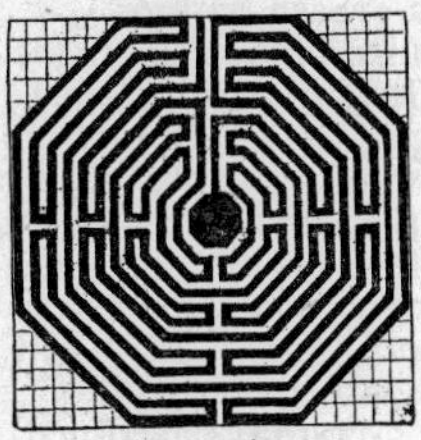
Labyrinth.

lab-y-rin-tho-don (lab-i-rin′thō-don), *n.* [NL., < Gr. λαβύρινθος, labyrinth, + ὀδούς (ὀδοντ-), tooth.] Any of certain large, extinct amphibians (genus *Labyrinthodon*) characterized by teeth with a labyrinth-like internal structure.—**lab-y-rin′-tho-dont** (-dont). **I.** *a.* Having teeth with a labyrinth-like internal structure; belonging or pertaining to the *Labyrinthodontidæ*, a family of large, sometimes huge, extinct amphibians typified by the genus *Labyrinthodon*. **II.** *n.* A labyrinthodont amphibian.

Labyrinthodon (restored).

lac[1] (lak), *n.* [Hind. *lākh* = Pers. *lāk*: cf. *lake*[1] and *lacquer*.] A resinous substance deposited on the twigs of various trees in southern Asia by a scale-insect, *Carteria lacca* ('lac-insect'): used in the manufacture of varnishes, sealing-wax, etc., and in the production of a red coloring matter. See *shellac*.

lac[2], **lakh** (lak), *n.* [Hind. *lākh*, < Skt. *laksha*, mark, hundred thousand.] The sum of 100,000, esp. of rupees; indefinitely, a great number. [India.]

lac-co-lite, lac-co-lith (lak′ō-līt, -lith), *n.* [Gr. λάκκος, pond, reservoir, + λίθος, stone.] In *geol.*, a mass of igneous rock or lava which when rising from below has not found its way to the surface, but has spread out laterally into a lenticular aggregate, thereby causing the overlying strata to bulge upward.—**lac-co-lit′ic, lac-co-lith′ic** (-lit′ik, -lith′ik), *a.*

lace (lās), *n.* [OF. *laz* (F. *lacs*), noose, string, < L. *laqueus*, noose, snare: cf. *lasso*.] A noose† or net†; also, a cord† or string†; now, a cord or string for holding or drawing together, as when passed through holes in opposite edges; also, ornamental cord or braid, as on uniforms (as, gold *lace*; silver *lace*); also, an ornamental openwork fabric made of threads netted or interwoven in a pattern, or of a ground-material wrought by thread-drawing or cutting, needlework, etc.; also, spirits added to coffee or the like (as, "He is forced . . . to drink his dish of coffee by itself, without the addition of the Spectator, that used to be better than *lace* to it": Addison, in "Spectator," 488).—**lace,** *v.*; *laced*, *lacing*. [OF. *lacier* (F. *lacer*).] **I.** *tr.* To fasten, draw together, or compress by means of a lace; also, to pass (a cord, etc.) as a lace, as through holes; also, to interlace or intertwine; also, to adorn or trim with lace; hence, to mark as with gold or silver lace; streak, as with color (as, "Here lay Duncan, His silver skin *laced* with his golden blood": Shakspere's "Macbeth," ii. 3. 118); also, to lash, beat, or thrash; also, to mix (coffee, etc.) with spirits (as, "Let's go drink a dish of *laced* coffee, and talk of the times": Wycherley's "Plain Dealer," iii.). **II.** *intr.* To be fastened with a lace.

Alençon Lace.

La-ce-dæ-mo-ni-an (las″ẹ-dẹ̄-mō′ni-ạn). **I.** *a.* Of or pertaining to Lacedæmon (Sparta, the capital of ancient Laconia, or sometimes the country itself) or its inhabitants. **II.** *n.* A native or inhabitant of Lacedæmon; a Spartan; a Laconian.

la-cer-a-ble (las′ẹ-rạ-bl), *a.* [LL. *lacerabilis*.] That may be lacerated; liable to laceration.

la-cer-ate (las′ẹ-rāt), *v. t.*; *-ated*, *-ating*. [L. *laceratus*, pp. of *lacerare*, < *lacer*, torn, mangled.] To tear roughly; mangle; fig., to harrow or distress (as, to *lacerate* a person's feelings).—**la′cer-ate,** *a.* Lacerated; jagged.—**la-cer-a-tion** (las-ẹ-rā′shọn), *n.* [L. *laceratio*(*n*-).] The act or process of lacerating; also, the result of lacerating; a rough or jagged tear.—**la-cer-a-tive** (las′ẹ-rạ̄-tiv), *a.* Tending to lacerate; lacerating.

la-cer-tian (lạ-sėr′shiạn). [L. *lacerta*, lizard.] **I.** *a.* Of or pertaining to the lizards; lizard-like. **II.** *n.* A lacertilian.

la-cer-til-i-an (las-ėr-til′i-ạn). [NL. *Lacertilia*, pl., < L. *lacerta*, *lacertus*, E. *lizard*.] **I.** *a.* Of or pertaining to the *Lacertilia*, an order of reptiles comprising the common lizards and their allies. **II.** *n.* A lacertilian reptile.

la-cer-tine (lạ-sėr′tin), *a.* [L. *lacerta*, lizard.] Lacertian; also, of decorative work, consisting of intertwined or curving lizard-like forms.

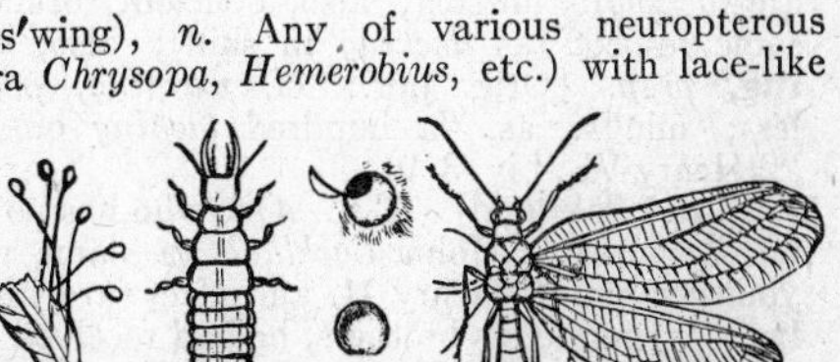
Lacertine Work, from a French manuscript of the 13th century.

lace-wing (lās′wing), *n.* Any of various neuropterous insects (genera *Chrysopa*, *Hemerobius*, etc.) with lace-like wings, whose larvæ prey on plant-lice. Also **lace′=winged fly.**

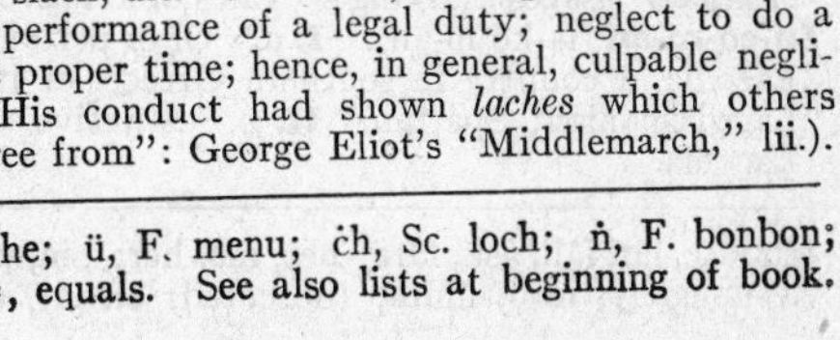

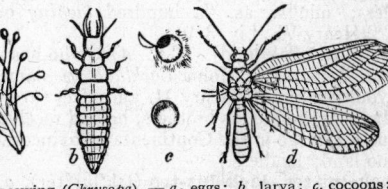

Lacewing (*Chrysopa*). — *a*, eggs; *b*, larva; *c*, cocoons; *d*, imago with left wings omitted.

lach-es (lach′ez), *n.* [OF. *laschesse*, < *lasche* (F. *lâche*), loose, slack, ult. < L. *laxus*, E. *lax*.] In *law*, remissness in the performance of a legal duty; neglect to do a thing at the proper time; hence, in general, culpable negligence (as, "His conduct had shown *laches* which others . . . were free from": George Eliot's "Middlemarch," lii.).

lach-ry-mal (lak′ri-mạl), etc. See *lacrymal*, etc.

la-cing (lā′sing), *n.* The act of one who or that which laces; often, a beating or thrashing; also, a laced fastening, or a lace for such use; also, a trimming of lace or braid; also, streaked coloration, as of flowers or plumage.

la-cin-i-ate (lạ-sin′i-āt), *a.* [NL. *laciniatus*, < L. *lacinia*, lappet.] In *bot.* and *zoöl.*, cut into narrow, irregular lobes; slashed; jagged. Also **la-cin′i-at-ed** (-ā-ted).—**la-cin-i-a′tion** (-ā′shọn), *n.* Laciniate formation; a lobe or projecting segment.

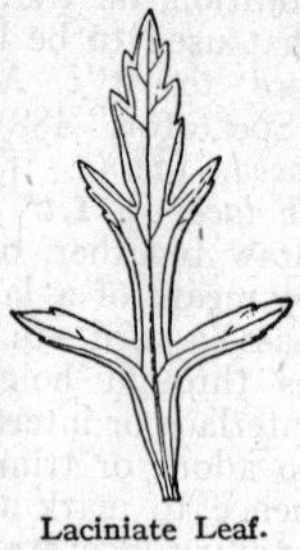
Laciniate Leaf.

lack (lak), *n.* [ME. *lac* = MLG. *lak*, defect, fault, blemish: cf. Icel. *lakr*, lacking, defective.] A defect†; a fault†; also, deficiency or absence of something requisite, desirable, or customary (as, *lack* of money, food, or sleep; *lack* of skill or sense; "Let his *lack* of years be no impediment," Shakspere's "Merchant of Venice," iv. 1. 162); want; specif., want of the means of subsistence, or need (obs. or archaic); also, something lacking or wanting (as, skilled labor was the chief *lack*).—**lack,** *v.* **I.** *intr.* To be absent or wanting, as something requisite or desirable (as, "Here *lacks* but your mother for to say amen": Shakspere's "Titus Andronicus," iv. 2. 44); also, to be deficient or fall short in something; be short (*of*); also, to be in want or need (obs. or archaic: as, "He that giveth unto the poor shall not *lack*," Prov. xxviii. 27). See *lacking, p. a.* **II.** *tr.* To be deficient in, destitute of, or without (as, to *lack* strength or courage; to *lack* materials for work); fall short in respect of (as, the vote *lacks* three of being a majority); also, to be in need of, or require (archaic or prov.: as, "strong-voiced apprentices, who kept up the cry of, 'What d'ye *lack?*' . . . accompanied with . . . recommendations of the articles in which they dealt," Scott's "Fortunes of Nigel," i.); also, to perceive or feel the absence of†, or miss†; also, to support the absence of†, or do without† (as, "Alas! dear love, I cannot *lack* thee two hours": Shakspere's "As You Like It," iv. 1. 182).

lack-a-dai-si-cal (lak-ạ-dā′zi-kạl), *a.* [From *lackaday.*] Sentimentally or affectedly languishing; weakly sentimental: as, "Mrs. Leyburn, poor *lackadaisical* thing! is no good whatever" (Mrs. H. Ward's "Robert Elsmere," ii.).—**lack-a-dai′si-cal-ly,** *adv.*—**lack-a-dai′si-cal-ness,** *n.*

lack-a-day (lak′ạ-dā), *interj.* [For *alackaday.*] An exclamation of sorrow or regret. [Archaic.]

lack′er, etc. See *lacquer*, etc.

lack-ey (lak′i), *n.*; pl. *-eys* (-iz). [F. *laquais*, < Sp. *lacayo*, orig. a kind of foot-soldier; origin uncertain.] A footman or liveried man-servant (as, "I saw a gay gilt chariot . . . the coachman with a new cockade, and the *lacqueys* with insolence and plenty in their countenances": Steele, in "Tatler," 44); hence, a servile follower; a toady.—**lack′ey,** *v.*; *-eyed, -eying.* **I.** *intr.* To act or serve as a lackey. [Now rare.] **II.** *tr.* To attend as a lackey does (as, "A thousand liveried angels *lacky* her": Milton's "Comus," 455); hence, to wait upon in a servile manner; be subservient to.

lack-ing (lak′ing), *p. a.* Wanting or absent (as, conveniences are *lacking*); missing; also, deficient, or falling short, in some respect (as, *lacking* in skill); also, needy†.—**lack′-ing,** *prep.* [Orig. ppr.: cf. *wanting, prep.*] Without; less; minus: as, "a hundred *lacking* one" (Shakspere's "2 Henry VI.," iv. 3. 9).

lack-land (lak′land). **I.** *n.* One who has no land or landed possessions: as, John *Lackland* (a name given to John, youngest son of Henry II. and afterward king of England, because, unlike his brothers, he had received from his father no appanage in the Continental provinces). **II.** *a.* Having no land; landless.

lack=lus-ter, lack=lus-tre (lak′lus″tėr), *a.* Lacking luster or brightness; dull: as, "looking on it with *lack-lustre* eye" (Shakspere's "As You Like It," ii. 7. 21); "pallid, leaden, *lackluster* visages" (Irving's "Tales of a Traveler," i. 9).

La-co-ni-an (lạ-kō′ni-ạn). **I.** *a.* Of or pertaining to ancient Laconia, a country in southern Greece, or its inhabitants; Lacedæmonian; Spartan. **II.** *n.* A native or inhabitant of Laconia.

La-con-ic (lạ-kon′ik), *a.* Laconian; Spartan; also [*l. c.*], brief in speech or expression, after the manner of the ancient Laconians (as, "Boccalini . . . indicts a *laconic* writer for speaking that in three words which he might have said in two": Steele, in "Tatler," 264); succinct; concise.—**la-con′i-cal-ly,** *adv.*—**la-con′i-cism** (-sizm), **lac-o-nism** (lak′ọ-nizm), *n.* Laconic brevity; also, a laconic utterance or sentence.

lac-quer (lak′ėr), *n.* [Obs. F. *lacre*, < Pg. *laca*, lac, < Hind. *lākh*, E. *lac*[1].] Lac†; also, a varnish consisting of shellac dissolved in alcohol, used for coating brass, etc.; also, any of various resinous varnishes, esp. a natural varnish obtained from a Japanese tree, *Rhus vernicifera*, used for producing a highly polished, lustrous surface on wood, etc.; hence, ware coated with any such varnish, and often inlaid.—**lac′-quer,** *v. t.* To coat with or as with lacquer.—**lac′quer-er,** *n.*

lac-quey (lak′i), *n.* and *v.* See *lackey*.

lac′ri-mal, etc. See *lacrymal*, etc.

la-crosse (lạ-krôs′), *n.* [F. *la crosse*, 'the crosse' (the racket used in the game): see *crosse.*] A game of ball, of American Indian origin, played by two parties of 12 players each, who strive to send a ball through a goal by means of long-handled rackets: much played in Canada.

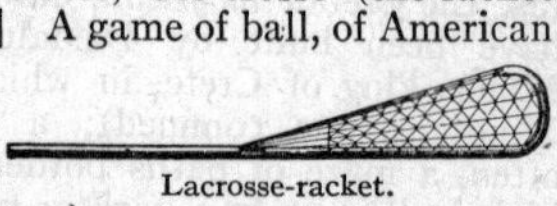
Lacrosse-racket.

lac-ry-ma Chris-ti (lak′ri-mạ̈ kris′tī). [NL., earlier *lacrymæ Christi*, 'tears of Christ.'] A strong, sweet red wine of southern Italy.

lac-ry-mal (lak′ri-mạl). [Also *lachrymal*, prop. *lacrimal*, < ML. *lacrimalis*, < L. *lacrima*, earlier *dacrima*, a tear, akin to Gr. δάκρυ, a tear, and E. *tear*[2].] **I.** *a.* Of or pertaining to tears; characterized by tears; indicative of weeping, as a person's countenance; intended to contain tears, as a vase (as, "collecting the drops of public sorrow into his volume, as into a *lachrymal* vase": Irving's "Knickerbocker's New York," v. 1); in *anat.*, etc., noting, pertaining to, or situated near the glands, ducts, or the like, concerned in the secretion or conveyance of tears. **II.** *n.* A lacrymatory; also, *pl.*, spells of weeping; also, the lacrymal organs; also, *sing.*, in *anat.*, etc., a lacrymal bone.

LG, Lacrymal Gland; *LD*, Lacrymal Duct.

lac-ry-ma-tion (lak-ri-mā′shọn), *n.* [L. *lacrimatio(n-)*, < *lacrimare*, shed tears, < *lacrima*: see *lacrymal.*] The shedding of tears.—**lac′-ry-ma-to-ry** (-mạ-tọ-ri). **I.** *a.* Of, pertaining to, or causing the shedding of tears: as, *lacrymatory* gas (same as *tear-gas*). **II.** *n.*; pl. *-ries* (-riz). One of a class of small, narrow-necked vases found in ancient Roman tombs: formerly thought to have been used for containing the tears of bereaved friends.

Lacrymatories. — Museum of Fine Arts, Boston.

lac-ry-mose (lak′ri-mōs), *a.* [L. *lacrimosus*, < *lacrima*: see *lacrymal.*] Given to shedding tears; tearful; also, suggestive of or tending to cause tears, or mournful (as, *lacrymose* verse).—**lac′ry-mose-ly,** *adv.*

lac-ta-ry (lak′tạ-ri), *a.* [L. *lactarius*, < *lac* (*lact-*), milk.] Of or pertaining to milk.

lac-tase (lak′tās), *n.* [L. *lac* (*lact-*), milk: see *-ase.*] In *chem.*, an enzyme capable of decomposing lactose, present in certain yeasts, etc.

lac-tate (lak′tāt), *n.* In *chem.*, a salt of lactic acid.

lac-ta-tion (lak-tā′shọn), *n.* [NL. *lactatio(n-)*, < L. *lactare*, give milk, < *lac* (*lact-*), milk.] The act or the period of giving suck to an infant; also, the secretion or formation of milk.

lac-te-al (lak′tẹ-ạl). [L. *lacteus*, < *lac* (*lact-*), milk, akin to Gr. γάλα (γαλακτ-), milk: cf. *galactic.*] **I.** *a.* Pertaining to, consisting of, or resembling milk; milky; in *anat.*, etc., conveying or containing chyle (as, the *lacteal* vessels). **II.** *n.* In *anat.*, any of the minute lymphatic vessels which convey chyle from the small intestine to the thoracic duct.—**lac′te-al-ly,** *adv.*

lac-te-ous (lak′tẹ-us), *a.* [L. *lacteus*: see *lacteal.*] Milky; of the color of milk.

lac-tes-cent (lak-tes′ẹnt), *a.* [L. *lactescens* (*-ent-*), ppr. of *lactescere*, become milky, < *lactere*, be milky, < *lac* (*lact-*), milk.] Becoming or being milky; also, producing milk; concerned with the secretion of milk; in *entom.*, secreting a milky fluid; in *bot.*, forming a milky juice.—**lac-tes′cence,** *n.*

lac-tic (lak′tik), *a.* [L. *lac* (*lact-*), milk.] Pertaining to or obtained from milk: as, *lactic* acid (an acid with three isomeric modifications, the most common one being found in sour milk).—**lac′tide** (-tīd or -tid), *n.* In *chem.*, a compound formed by heating lactic acid, and regarded as an anhydride of that acid; also, any of a class of similar compounds.

lac-tif-er-ous (lak-tif′ẹ-rus), *a.* [LL. *lactifer*, < L. *lac* (*lact-*), milk, + *ferre*, bear.] Producing or conveying milk or a milky fluid.

lac-to- (lak′tọ-). Form of L. *lac* (*lact-*), milk, used in combination, as in *lactoproteid* (any proteid existing in milk), *lactotoxin* (a toxin or poisonous principle found in milk).

lac-tom-e-ter (lak-tom′e-tėr), *n.* [See *lacto-* and *-meter.*] Any of various instruments for testing the purity or richness of milk.

lac-tone (lak′tōn), *n.* [From *lactic.*] In *chem.*, any of a class of anhydrides derived from hydroxy acids.—**lac-ton′ic** (-ton′ik), *a.*

lac-to-scope (lak′tọ-skōp), *n.* [See *lacto-* and *-scope.*] An instrument for testing the quality or richness of milk by its resistance to the passage of light.

lac-tose (lak′tōs), *n.* [L. *lac* (*lact-*), milk: see *-ose*[2].] In *chem.*, a crystalline sugar present in milk, used as a food and in medicine; sugar of milk.

la-cu-na (lạ-kū′nạ̈), *n.*; pl. *-nas* or *-næ* (-nē). [L., hole, cavity, gap, pool, pond, < *lacus*: see *lake*[3], and cf. *lagoon.*] A gap or hiatus, as in a manuscript; also, specif., a pit or cavity; an interstitial or intercellular space, as in plant or animal tissue; one of the numerous minute cavities in the substance of bone, supposed to contain nucleated cells.—**la-cu′nal, la-cu′nar** (-nạ̈r), *a.* Of or pertaining to a lacuna; having lacunæ.—**la-cu′nar,** *n.*; pl. *lacunars* or *lacunaria* (lak-ū-nā′ri-ạ̈). [L., < *lacuna.*] In *arch.*, a ceiling, or an under surface, as of a cornice, formed of sunken compartments; also, one of the compartments.—**lac-u-na-ry** (lak′ū-nā-ri or lạ-kū′nạ-ri), *a.* Lacunal; lacunar.—**la-cune″** (-kūn′), *n.* A lacuna.—**la-cu′nose** (-nōs), *a.* [L. *lacunosus.*] Full of or having lacunæ; pitted or furrowed.

Lacunars.—From vaulting of Basilica of Constantine, Rome.

la-cus-tri-an (lạ-kus′tri-ạn). **I.** *a.* Same as *lacustrine.* **II.** *n.* A lake-dweller.

la-cus-trine (lạ-kus′trin), *a.* [L. *lacus*, E. *lake*[3].] Of or pertaining to a lake; living or occurring on or in lakes, as various animals and plants; formed at the bottom of lakes, as geological strata.

la-cy (lā′si), *a.* Of or like lace; having a delicate, open texture or structure.

lad (lad), *n.* [ME. *ladde*; origin unknown.] A man-servant†; also, a boy or youth; often, familiarly, a male person of any age (as, "My *lads*, to-morrow morning, by four o'clock, early at Gadshill!" Shakspere's "1 Henry IV.," i. 2. 138; "How now, old *lad?*" Shakspere's "Taming of the Shrew," iv. 1. 113); also, a male sweetheart (Sc.: as, "Ye royal lasses dainty, Heav'n . . . gie you *lads* a-plenty," Burns's "Dream," 121).

lad-a-num (lad′ạ-num), *n.* [L., < Gr. λάδανον, λήδανον, < λῆδον, the shrub yielding ladanum: cf. *labdanum* and *laudanum.*] A resinous juice that exudes from various rock-roses of the genus *Cistus*: used in perfumery, fumigating substances, medicinal plasters, etc.

lad-der (lad′ėr), *n.* [AS. *hlǣder, hlǣdder*, = D. *ladder* = G. *leiter*, ladder; from the root of E. *lean*[1].] An appliance of wood, metal, or rope, commonly consisting of two side-pieces between which a series of bars or rungs are set at suitable distances, forming a means of ascent or descent; hence, something resembling or suggesting a ladder; a succession of cross threads in knitted work, resulting from dropped stitches; in fig. use, a means of rising, as to eminence.—**lad′dered,** *a.* Provided with a ladder or ladders.

lad-die (lad′i), *n.* A young lad; a boy; a male sweetheart. [Chiefly Sc.]

lade (lād), *v.*; pret. *laded*, pp. *laden* or *laded*, ppr. *lading.* [AS. *hladan*, load, take up (liquid), = D. and G. *laden* = Icel. *hladha* = Goth. *-hlathan*, load: cf. *ladle* and *last*[3].] **I.** *tr.* To load, as with a burden or cargo (as, "They *laded* their asses with the corn," Gen. xlii. 26; "He . . . help'd At *lading* and unlading the tall barks," Tennyson's "Enoch Arden," 812); charge or fill abundantly (chiefly in *pp.*: as, trees *laden* with fruit); load oppressively, or burden (chiefly in *pp.*: as, *laden* with responsibilities); also, to put (something) on or in as a burden, load, or cargo (as, to *lade* products on board vessels); take (something) on as a burden or cargo (as, a vessel *lading* wheat); also, to lift or throw (a liquid) out of or into something with a ladle, scoop, or the like. **II.** *intr.* To take on a load or cargo; load; also, to lade a liquid.—**lad-en** (lā′dn), *p. a.* Loaded; burdened.—**lad′en,** *v. t.* To load; lade.

La-din (lạ-dēn′), *n.* [Rhæto-Romanic, < L. *Latinus*, Latin.] A Rhæto-Romanic dialect spoken in parts of Switzerland and Tyrol; also, one of the people of these regions who speak it.

lad-ing (lā′ding), *n.* The act of one who or that which lades; also, that with which something, as a ship, is laden; load; freight; cargo.—**bill of lading.** See under *bill*[4], *n.*

La-di-no (lä-dē′nō), *n.*; pl. *-nos* (-nōz, Sp. -nōs). [Sp., < L. *Latinus*, Latin.] The ancient Spanish or Castilian language; also, a mixed Spanish and Hebrew dialect spoken by Jews of Spanish extraction now living in Turkey and elsewhere; also, in Spanish America, a Spanish-speaking half-breed; a mestizo.

la-dle (lā′dl), *n.* [AS. *hlædel*, < *hladan*, E. *lade.*] A long-handled utensil with a dish-shaped or cup-shaped bowl for dipping or conveying liquids.—**la′dle,** *v. t.*; *-dled*, *-dling.* To dip or convey with or as with a ladle.—**la′dle-ful** (-fůl), *n.*; pl. *-fuls.*

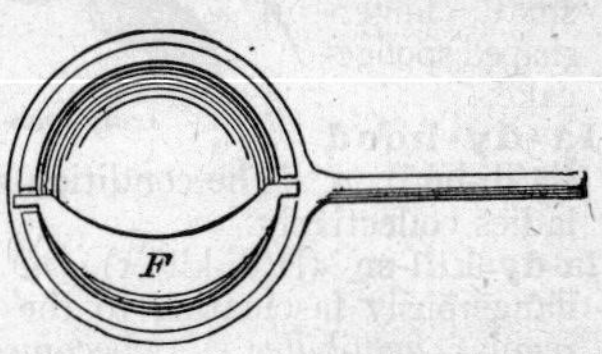

Foundry-ladle.—*F*, plate which serves to keep back impurities floating on the molten metal.

la-drone (lạ-drōn′), *n.* [Sp. *ladrón*, < L. *latro*(*n-*), mercenary, freebooter, robber.] A robber; a highwayman or brigand.—**la-dron′ism** (-drōn′izm), *n.*

la-dy (lā′di), *n.*; pl. *-dies* (-diz). [AS. *hlǣfdige*, perhaps orig. meaning 'loaf-kneader,' < *hlāf*, loaf, + *-dige*, akin to *dāh*, E. *dough*: cf. *lord.*] The mistress of a household; also, a woman who has proprietary rights or authority, as over a manor (correlative of *lord*); also, a woman who is the object of chivalrous devotion; a sweetheart or lady-love; also, a wife or consort (now regarded as inelegant: as, "By a former marriage, Mr. Henry Dashwood had one son; by his present *lady*, three daughters," Jane Austen's "Sense and Sensibility," i.); also [*cap.*], the Virgin Mary (usually, 'our Lady'); also [*l. c.*], a woman of good family or social position, or of good breeding, refinement, etc. (correlative of *gentleman*); a polite term for any woman (as a term of address, now chiefly in the *pl.*, as in addressing an audience, the ordinary term in the *sing.* being *madam*); also [*cap.*], a title of women of a certain rank, as, in British use, a prefixed title used as a less formal substitute for 'marchioness,' 'countess,' 'viscountess,' and 'baroness,' and used before the Christian name and surname of the daughters of dukes, marquises, and earls, and before the husband's Christian name and surname in the case of the wife of one who holds a courtesy title in which *Lord* precedes the Christian name, and before the surname of the wife of a baronet or knight; also [*l. c.*], the calcareous structure which triturates the food in a lobster's stomach.—**Ladies from Hell,** a nickname, said to have originated with the Germans, applied to the kilted Scottish troops during the World War.—**Lady chapel,** a chapel dedicated to the Virgin Mary, attached to a church, and generally placed behind the high altar, at the extremity of the apse.—**Lady Day,** one of various days celebrated in honor of the Virgin Mary, now only the feast of the Annunciation, March 25.—**lady in waiting,** a lady who is in attendance upon a queen or princess.—**Our Lady of the Snows,** a name applied to Canada: as, "'For we be also a people,' Said *our Lady of the Snows*" (Kipling's "Our Lady of the Snows," a poem referring to the Canadian preferential tariff of 1897). (R. L. Stevenson, in his "Travels with a Donkey," published in 1879, describes a visit to the Trappist monastery of "Our Lady of the Snows" in the Cévennes, in southern France.)

la-dy=ap-ple (lā'di-ap"l), *n.* A small, delicate, red, or red and yellow, variety of apple.

la-dy-bird (lā'di-bėrd), *n.* [With reference to 'our Lady' (the Virgin Mary).] Any of various small beetles (family *Coccinellidæ*) with rounded bodies, often brightly colored; also, a sweetheart.

Ladybird (*Epilachna borealis*), slightly enlarged.

la-dy-bug (lā'di-bug), *n.* The ladybird (beetle).

la-dy=chair (lā'di-chãr), *n.* A kind of seat for a third person, formed by two persons holding each other's hands crossed: as, "She insisted upon it that we should occasionally carry her in a *lady-chair* over to this island" (Mrs. Stowe's "Oldtown Folks," xxvi.).

la-dy=crab (lā'di-krab), *n.* Any of various handsome crabs, esp. of the family *Portunidæ*, as *Platyonychus ocellatus*, a species common on the Atlantic coast of the U. S.

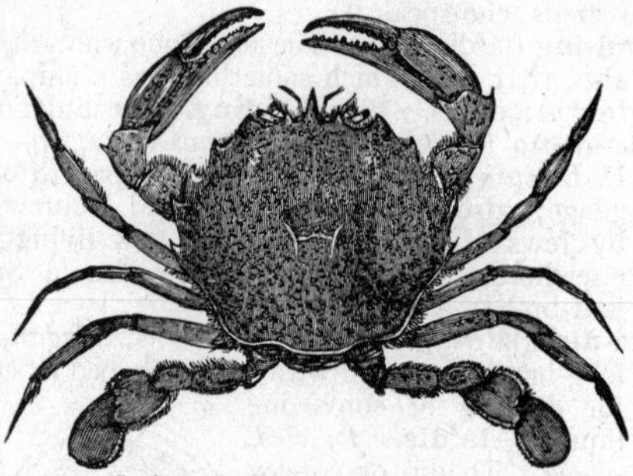

Lady-crab (*Platyonychus ocellatus*).

la-dy=fin-ger (lā'di-fing"gėr), *n.* A small, finger-shaped sponge-cake.

la-dy-hood (lā'di-hůd), *n.* The condition or character of a lady; also, ladies collectively.

la-dy=kill-er (lā'di-kil"ėr), *n.* A man supposed to be dangerously fascinating to the ladies: as, "I believe your regular *lady-killer* . . . becomes a very quiet animal by being occasionally jilted" (Lever's "Harry Lorrequer," xxii.).—**la'dy=kill"ing,** *n.* and *a.*

la-dy-kin (lā'di-kin), *n.* [See *-kin*.] A little lady.

la-dy-like (lā'di-līk), *a.* Like or befitting a lady (as, a *ladylike* young woman; a young woman with *ladylike* manners); also, effeminate (as, "fops at all corners, *ladylike* in mien": Cowper's "Tirocinium," 829).—**la'dy-like-ness,** *n.*

la-dy=love (lā'di-luv), *n.* A lady who is loved; a mistress or sweetheart: as, "With favour in his crest, or glove, Memorial of his *ladye-love*" (Scott's "Lay of the Last Minstrel," iv. 19).

la-dy's=bed-straw (lā'diz-bed'strâ), *n.* Our Lady's bedstraw. See *bedstraw*.

la-dy's=fin-ger (lā'diz-fing"gėr), *n.* Same as *lady-finger*.

la-dy-ship (lā'di-ship), *n.* The condition or rank of a lady; also [often *cap.*], with *her*, *your*, etc., the form used in speaking of or to a woman having the title of *Lady*.

la-dy's=maid (lā'diz-mād'), *n.* A maid who is a lady's personal attendant for services in the toilet, etc.

la-dy's=slip-per, la-dy=slip-per (lā'diz-slip"ėr, lā'di-), *n.* Any plant of the genus *Cypripedium*, comprising orchids whose flowers have a protruding labellum somewhat resembling a slipper.

la-dy's=smock, la-dy=smock (lā'diz-smok, lā'di-), *n.* A brassicaceous plant, *Cardamine pratensis*, with white or purple flowers (also called *cuckoo-flower*); also, any of certain related species.

Læs-try-go-ni-an (les-tri-gō'ni-ạn), *n.* [L. *Læstrygones*, < Gr. Λαιστρυγόνες, pl., the Læstrygonians.] One of a mythical race of cannibal giants who were encountered by Odysseus (Ulysses), the principal character in Homer's "Odyssey," in his wanderings, and by whom many of his companions were slain.

lævo-, etc. See *levo-*, etc.

la-fa-yette (lä-fạ-yet'), *n.* [From the French general *Lafayette*, during whose visit to America in 1824–25 the fish appeared in great numbers.] A small sciænoid food-fish, *Leiostomus xanthurus*, of the eastern coast of the U. S.; the spot.

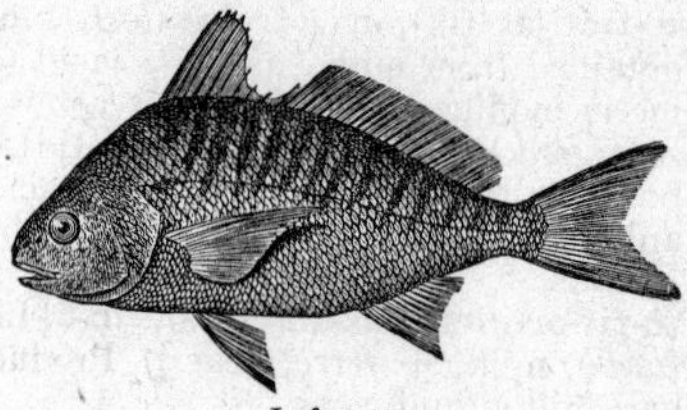

Lafayette.

lag[1] (lag). [Origin obscure.] **I.** *a.* Last or hindmost (as, "the *lag*-end of my life": Shakspere's "1 Henry IV.," v. 1. 24); also, behindhand or late; also, tardy or slow (as, "An' faith! thou's neither *lag* nor lame": Burns's "Address to the Deil," 17). [Now Sc. and prov. Eng.] **II.** *n.* The last or hindmost one (now rare: as, "What makes my ram the *lag* of all the flock?" Pope's tr. Homer's "Odyssey," ix.); also, the lowest class, as of people† (see Shakspere's "Timon of Athens," iii. 6. 90); also, a lagging or falling behind; retardation, as of a movement or a current.—**lag**[1], *v. i.*; *lagged*, *lagging*. To fall behind; hang back; loiter; linger: as, "When so she *lagged* . . . He with his speare . . . Would thumpe her forward" (Spenser's "Faerie Queene," vi. 2. 10).

lag[2] (lag), *n.* [Cf. Sw. *lagg*, stave of a cask.] One of the staves or strips which form the periphery of a wooden drum, the casing of a steam-cylinder, or the like.—**lag**[2], *v. t.*; *lagged, lagging*. To cover with lags or lagging.

lag[3] (lag), *v. t.*; *lagged, lagging*. [Origin obscure.] To transport as a convict (as, "He was *lagged* for coining": H. Kingsley's "Geoffry Hamlyn," xix.); send to penal servitude; also, to capture or catch. [Slang.]—**lag**[3], *n.* One who has been transported as a convict; one sent to penal servitude; a convict; also, a term of transportation or penal servitude. [Slang.]

lag-an (lag'ạn), *n.* [OF.; perhaps from Scand. or LG., from the root of E. *lie*[1].] In *law*, anything sunk in the sea, but attached to a buoy or the like in order that it may be recovered.

la-ger (lä'gėr), *n.* Same as *lager-beer*.

la-ger=beer (lä'gėr-bēr'), *n.* [G. *lagerbier*, < *lager*, bed, stand for casks, storehouse (see *lair*), + *bier*, beer.] A kind of beer which is kept in store from 6 weeks to 6 months before being used: orig. made in Germany.

lag-gard (lag'ạrd). [See *-ard*.] **I.** *a.* Lagging; backward; slow: as, "Then mend the horses' *laggard* pace!" (Kipling's "Heriot's Ford"). **II.** *n.* One who lags behind; a loiterer; a backward or dilatory person: as, "a *laggard* in love, and a dastard in war" (Scott's "Marmion," v. 12).—**lag'gard-ly,** *adv.*—**lag'gard-ness,** *n.*

lag-ger (lag'ėr), *n.* One who lags; a laggard.

lag-ging (lag'ing), *n.* [See *lag*[2].] The act of covering a boiler, etc., with lags, or with felt, asbestos, etc.; also, the covering formed, or the material used; in *arch.*, the narrow cross strips in the centering of an arch, etc.

la-gnappe, la-gniappe (lan-yap'), *n.* [Louisiana F., < Amer. Sp. *la ñapa*, 'the present.'] Something given with a purchase to a customer, by way of compliment or for good measure: as, "*Lagniappe* . . . is the equivalent of the thirteenth roll in a 'baker's dozen.' It is something thrown in, gratis, for good measure" (Mark Twain's "Life on the Mississippi," xliv.). Also fig. [Louisiana.]

la-goon (lạ-gön'), *n.* [It. and Sp. *laguna*, < L. *lacuna*, pool, pond: see *lacuna*.] An area of shallow water separated from the sea by low sand-banks (as, the *lagoons* of Venice); also, the expanse of water within an atoll (as, "These last [islands] are nothing more than narrow circles of land surrounding a smooth *lagoon*, connected by a single opening with the sea": H. Melville's "Omoo," xvii.); in general, any small, pond-like body of water, esp. one communicating with a larger body of water. Also **la-gune'** (-gön').

la-ic (lā'ik). [LL. *laicus*, < Gr. λαϊκός, < λαός, the people.] **I.** *a.* Of or pertaining to the people or laity, as distinguished from the clergy; lay; secular. **II.** *n.* A layman.—**la'i-cal,** *a.* Laic.—**la'i-cal-ly,** *adv.*—**la'i-cize** (-sīz), *v. t.*;

-cized, -cizing. To render lay; deprive of clerical character. —**la″i-ci-za′tion** (-si-zā′shọn), *n.*

laid (lād). Preterit and past participle of *lay*[1].—**laid,** *p. a.* Of paper, marked with close parallel lines or watermarks formed during the process of manufacture by pressure against fine wires. Cf. *wove, p. a.*

lain (lān). Past participle of *lie*[1].

lair (lãr), *n.* [AS. *leger* = D. *leger* = G. *lager* = Goth. *ligrs*, couch, bed; from the root of E. *lie*[1].] A place to lie in; a couch, bed, or resting-place (as, "Rising . . . he summoned his companions from their warm *lairs*": Cooper's "Prairie," xxiii.); now, commonly, the resting-place or den of a wild beast (as, to rouse the lion from his *lair*); also, a pen or shelter for cattle (Eng.); also, a grave or a burial-plot (obs. or Sc.).—**lair,** *v.* **I.** *intr.* To go to, lie in, or have a lair. **II.** *tr.* To place in a lair; also, to serve as a lair for. —**lair′age** (-ạj), *n.* The placing of cattle in lairs; also, space or a place for lairing cattle. [Eng.]

laird (lãrd), *n.* [Sc. form of *lord.*] A landed proprietor: as, "The *Laird* of St. Ronan's is nae landlord of mine" (Scott's "St. Ronan's Well," ii.). [Sc.]—**laird′ship,** *n.*

lais-ser=al-ler (lā′sā-al′ā, F. le-sā-à-lā), *n.* [F. *laisser-aller*, lit. 'to let go' (with F. *laisser*, infinitive): often given in English use as *laissez-aller* (with F. *laissez*, imperative), a form which, however, expresses an injunction to let go rather than the fact of doing so: cf. *laissez-faire.*] Absence of restraint, as in action, speech, manner, etc.; unconstraint; ease.

lais-sez=faire (lā′sā-fãr′, F. le-sā-fãr), *n.* [F. *laissez faire*, 'let do': an imperative phrase enjoining non-interference.] The principle of letting people do as they please; non-interference, as by a government with respect to trade, industrial affairs, etc.

laith (lāth), *a.* Scotch form of *loath.*

la-i-ty (lā′i-ti), *n.* The state of being a lay person; also, lay persons collectively, as distinguished from the clergy or from a professional class (as, "The *laity* nowadays take a pride in speaking evil of the clergy": Kingsley's "Alton Locke," xvii.).

lake[1] (lāk), *n.* [Var. of *lac*[1].] A red pigment prepared from lac or cochineal by combination with a metallic compound; hence, a red or crimson color; also, any of various pigments prepared from animal, vegetable, or coal-tar coloring matters by union (chemical or other) with metallic compounds; in *dyeing*, an insoluble colored compound formed in the fiber by the combination of an organic dyestuff with a metallic compound or mordant.

lake[2] (lāk), *v. i.*; *laked, laking.* [Cf. Icel. *leika*, move, play, = AS. *lācan*, move quickly, leap, = Goth. *laikan*, leap: cf. also *lark*[2].] To play; sport; trifle; idle. [Now north. Eng. and Sc.]—**lake**[2], *n.* Play; sport; fun; a game. [Now north. Eng. and Sc.]

lake[3] (lāk), *n.* [OF. F. *lac*, < L. *lacus*, basin, tank, pond, lake, pit: cf. *lacuna* and *lagoon.*] A body of water (fresh or salt) of considerable size, surrounded by land (as, the Great *Lakes*: see under *great*); hence, some similar body of water, as an artificial pond, a widened portion of a river, or a lagoon.—**Lake Country,** or **Lake District,** a picturesque mountainous region abounding in lakes, in the counties of Cumberland, Westmorland, and Lancashire, in northwestern England.—**Lake poets,** or **Lake school,** the poets Wordsworth, Coleridge, and Southey: from their residence in and association with the Lake Country of England.

lake=dwell-er (lāk′dwel″ėr), *n.* An inhabitant of a lake-dwelling.—**lake′=dwell″ing,** *n.* A dwelling, esp. of prehistoric times, built on piles or other support over the water of a lake: as, the prehistoric *lake-dwellings* of Switzerland. Cf. *crannog.*—**lake′=dwell″ing,** *a.*

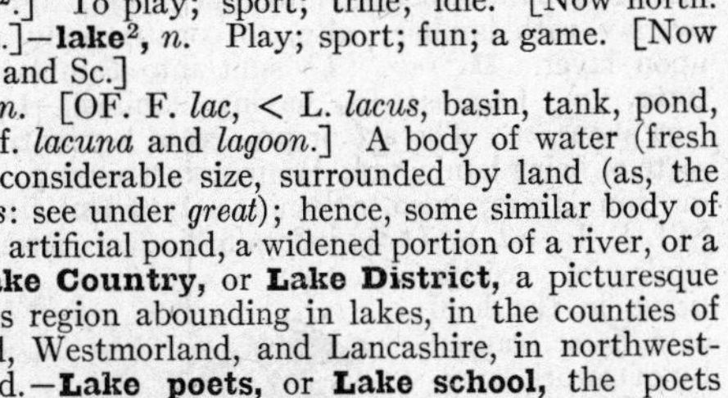

Lake-dwellings (restored).

lake=her-ring (lāk′her′ing), *n.* A cisco (whitefish), *Argyrosomus artedi*, of the Great Lakes, etc.

lake-let (lāk′let), *n.* A small lake.

lak-er (lā′kėr), *n.* One connected with lakes; [*cap.*] one of the Lake poets; also [*l. c.*], a fish of or taken from a lake, esp. a lake-trout; also, a vessel used or suited for lake navigation.

lake-side (lāk′sīd), *n.* The margin or shore of a lake.

lake=trout (lāk′trout), *n.* Any of various species of trout and salmon found in lakes and rivers, as *Salmo clarki*, a trout of western North America, and the namaycush, *Cristivomer namaycush*, a species common in the region of the Great Lakes and elsewhere.

Lake-trout (*Salmo clarki*).

lakh (lak), *n.* See *lac*[2].

la-kin† (lā′kin), *n.* Contraction of *ladykin*: used esp. in 'by our lakin' (by our Lady, that is, by the Virgin Mary: see Shakspere's "Tempest," iii. 3. 1).

lak-y[1] (lā′ki), *a.* Of or like lake, the red pigment; of the color of lake.

lak-y[2] (lā′ki), *a.* Of or pertaining to a lake, or body of water; lake-like: as, "By . . . flanking towers, and *laky* flood, Guarded . . . she stood" (Scott's "Marmion," v., Introd.).

Lal-lan (lal′ạn), *a.* and *n.* [Sc. form of *lowland.*] Lowland Scotch. [Sc.]

lal-la-tion (la-lā′shọn), *n.* [L. *lallare* (pp. *lallatus*), sing lullaby.] An imperfect pronunciation of the letter *r* whereby it is made to sound like *l.*

lam (lam), *v.*; *lammed, lamming.* [Cf. Icel. *lemja*, beat, thrash, lit. 'make lame'; akin to E. *lame.*] **I.** *tr.* To beat or thrash (as, "I bet you I'll *lam* Sid for that. I'll learn him!" Mark Twain's "Tom Sawyer," i.); strike or hit. [Now prov. or slang.] **II.** *intr.* To run quickly; run off or away. [Prov. or slang.]

la-ma[1] (lä′mạ), *n.* Same as *llama.*

la-ma[2] (lä′mạ), *n.* [Tibetan.] A priest or monk of a form of Buddhism prevailing in Tibet, Mongolia, etc., with a hierarchical system under two heads, the more important of which is known as the 'Dalai-lama' or 'Grand Lama.'—**La′ma-ism,** *n.* The religious system of the lamas.—**La′ma-ist,** *n.*

La-marck-i-an (lạ-märk′i-ạn). **I.** *a.* Of or pertaining to the French naturalist J. B. P. A. de M. de Lamarck (1744–1829), or his theory of organic evolution, esp. his principle of the inheritance of acquired characters. **II.** *n.* One who holds the Lamarckian theory.—**La-marck′ism,** *n.* The Lamarckian theory.

la-ma-se-ry (lä′mạ-se-ri), *n.*; pl. *-ries* (-riz). In Tibet, Mongolia, etc., a monastery of lamas.

lamb (lam), *n.* [AS. *lamb* = D. *lam* = G. *lamm* = Icel. and Goth. *lamb*, lamb.] A young sheep; fig., one who is like a lamb as being young, gentle, meek, innocent, etc. (as, "The widow she cried over me, and called me a poor lost *lamb*": Mark Twain's "Huckleberry Finn," i.); sometimes, one who is easily cheated, esp. an inexperienced speculator (slang); also, the flesh of the lamb used as food; also, lambskin.—**the Lamb of God,** or **the Lamb,** Christ (with allusion to the paschal lamb: see under *paschal*): as, "John seeth Jesus coming unto him, and saith, Behold *the Lamb of God*, which taketh away the sin of the world" (John, i. 29). —**lamb,** *v. t.* or *i.* To bring forth (a lamb).

lam-baste (lam-bāst′), *v. t.*; *-basted, -basting.* [Appar. < *lamb* + *baste*[1].] To beat or thrash. [Prov. or slang.]

lamb-da (lam′dạ), *n.* [Gr. λάμβδα.] The eleventh letter (Λ, λ, = English L, l) of the Greek alphabet.—**lamb′da-cism** (-dạ-sizm), *n.* [Gr. λαμβδακισμός.] A too frequent use of the letter *l* in speaking or writing; also, an imperfect pronunciation of *r*, making it sound like *l*; lallation.—**lamb′doid,** *a.* [Gr. λαμβδοειδής: see *-oid.*] Shaped like the Greek capital lambda (Λ): as, the *lambdoid* suture (that between the occipital bone and the parietal bones of the skull). Also **lamb-doi′dal** (-doi′dạl).

lam-bent (lam′bent), *a.* [L. *lambens* (*lambent-*), ppr. of *lambere*, lick, lap: see *lap*¹.] Licking (obs. or rare); hence, running or moving lightly over a surface, as a flame; playing lightly and brilliantly over a subject, as wit; also, softly bright (as, "Those [eyes] only are beautiful which, like the planets, have a steady, *lambent* light,—are luminous, but not sparkling": Longfellow's "Hyperion," iii. 4).—**lam′ben-cy,** *n.*—**lam′bent-ly,** *adv.*

lamb-kin (lam′kin), *n.* A little lamb; hence, any young and tender creature. Also **lamb′ling.**

lam-bre-quin (lam′brẹ-kin), *n.* [F.; from Flemish.] A kind of scarf or piece of stuff worn over the helmet in medieval times; also, a hanging or drapery covering the upper part of an opening, as a door or window, or suspended from a shelf.

lamb-skin (lam′skin), *n.* The skin of a lamb, esp. when dressed with the wool on; also, leather made from the skin of lambs; also, parchment made from the skin of lambs (as, "Dignified documents . . . are often of no more value than the *lambskin* on which they are engrossed": Motley's "Dutch Republic," ii. 3).

lamb's=wool (lamz′wůl), *n.* The wool of the lamb; a fabric made from this; also, hot ale mixed with the pulp of roasted apples and sweetened and spiced (as, "Lay a crab in the fire to roast for *lamb's wool*": Peele's "Old Wives' Tale").

lame (lām), *a.*; compar. *lamer,* superl. *lamest.* [AS. *lama* = D. *lam* = G. *lahm* = Icel. *lami,* lame.] Crippled or physically disabled, as a person or animal, esp. in the foot or leg so as to limp or walk with difficulty; impaired or disabled through defect or injury, as a limb (as, "tossing . . . from eight to ten thousand hides, until my wrists became so *lame* that I gave in": Dana's "Two Years before the Mast," xxix.); fig., halting, as verse or rime; imperfect, defective, or faulty (as, "The theory of comets . . . at present is very *lame* and defective," Swift's "Gulliver's Travels," iii. 3; "Santa Croce and the dome of St. Peter's are *lame* copies after a divine model," Emerson's "Essays," History).—**lame duck,** fig., a person or thing that is disabled or helpless, or is ineffective or inefficient; specif., one who is unable to meet his financial obligations; a bankrupt; a defaulter on the stock-exchange; also, a Congressman who has failed of reëlection and is serving at the last session of his term. [Colloq.]—**lame,** *v.*; *lamed, laming.* **I.** *tr.* To make lame; cripple; fig., to disable; render defective. **II.** *intr.* To become lame.

la-mel-la (lạ-mel′ạ̈), *n.*; pl. *lamellæ* (-ē) or *lamellas.* [L., dim. of *lamina*: see *lamina.*] A thin plate, scale, or layer, as of bone or tissue.—**lam-el-lar** (lam′ẹ-lạ̈r or lạ-mel′ạ̈r), *a.* Composed of, arranged in, or characterized by lamellæ.—**lam′el-late** (-lāt), *a.* Having lamellæ; lamellar. Also **lam′el-lat-ed** (-lā-ted).—**lam-el-la′tion** (-lā′shọn), *n.* Lamellate arrangement or structure.

la-mel-li-branch (lạ-mel′i-brangk), *n.* [NL. *Lamellibranchia,* pl., < L. *lamella,* thin plate, + Gr. βράγχια, gills.] Any of the *Lamellibranchiata,* a group or class of mollusks, including the oyster, clam, mussel, etc., having lamellate gills and a bivalved calcareous shell.—**la-mel-li-bran′chi-ate** (-brang′ki-āt), *a.* and *n.*

la-mel-li-corn (lạ-mel′i-kôrn). [NL. *lamellicornis,* < L. *lamella,* thin plate, + *cornu,* horn.] **I.** *a.* Having antennæ with a terminal segment of lamellar structure, as beetles of the group *Lamellicornia*; belonging to this group; also, of antennæ, having a terminal segment of lamellar structure. **II.** *n.* A lamellicorn beetle, as the scarab, cockchafer, etc.

lam-el-lose (lam′ẹ-lōs or lạ-mel′ōs), *a.* Lamellate; lamellar.

lame-ly (lām′li), *adv.* In a lame manner; with a limp; haltingly; imperfectly, defectively, or poorly (as, "We left . . . with the main purpose of my visit but *lamely* accomplished": Mark Twain's "Life on the Mississippi," li.).—**lame′ness,** *n.*

la-ment (lạ-ment′), *n.* [L. *lamentum,* a wailing, lamentation.] A mournful expression of grief or sorrow, as for the dead or for any loss or misfortune (as, "Good grandsire, leave these bitter deep *laments*": Shakspere's "Titus Andronicus," iii. 2. 46); an utterance of keen sorrow or sad regret; lamentation; also, a formal expression of sorrow or mourning, esp. in verse or song; an elegy or dirge; sometimes, an air or tune of mourning (as, "Soon as the dire *lament* was play'd, It waked the lurking ambuscade": Scott's "Lord of the Isles," v. 27).—**la-ment′,** *v.* [L. *lamentari* (pp. *lamentatus*), < *lamentum.*] **I.** *intr.* To utter laments; express grief or sorrow by words or cries (as, "In their wailing they shall take up a lamentation for thee, and *lament* over thee, saying . . . ": Ezek. xxvii. 32); wail; mourn audibly; also, to feel grief, sorrow, or sad regret. **II.** *tr.* To lament over, bewail, or bemoan (as, to *lament* the dead, or a person's death or sad fate; to *lament* one's misfortunes); mourn for or over; in a weaker sense, to express regret for (as, "We have been loudly *lamenting* your absence": H. Kingsley's "Geoffry Hamlyn," ix.); also, to feel sorrow or regret for, or regret (as, "I *lamented* my own folly and wilfulness in attempting a second voyage": Swift's "Gulliver's Travels," ii. 1).—**lam-en-ta-ble** (lam′en-tạ-bl), *a.* [L. *lamentabilis.*] That is to be lamented (as, a *lamentable* fate or occurrence; *lamentable* ignorance); giving cause for sorrow; deplorable; pitiable; also, mournful or doleful (archaic: as, a *lamentable* voice; "Cocytus' *lamentable* waters," Pope's tr. Homer's "Odyssey," x.).—**lam′en-ta-bly,** *adv.*—**lam-en-ta′tion** (-tā′shọn), *n.* [L. *lamentatio*(*n*-).] The act of lamenting, or the words, cries, or sounds uttered; a lament; *pl.* [*cap.*], a book of the Old Testament, called in full "The Lamentations of Jeremiah" and traditionally ascribed to the prophet Jeremiah, the subject of which is the destruction of Jerusalem by the Chaldeans.—**la-ment′ed,** *p. a.* Mourned for, as one who is dead (as, "his excellent, learned, and ever *lamented* friend the late Mr. Yorke": Burke's "American Taxation"); regretted; deplored.—**la-ment′er,** *n.*—**la-ment′ing-ly,** *adv.*

la-me-ter, la-mi-ter (lā′mẹ-tėr, lā′mi-), *n.* A lame person; a cripple: as, "You have now, no doubt, friends who will . . . not suffer you to devote yourself to a blind *lameter* like me" (C. Brontë's "Jane Eyre," xxxvii.). [Sc. and north. Eng.]

la-mi-a (lā′mi-ạ̈), *n.*; pl. *lamias* or *lamiæ* (-ē). [L., < Gr. λάμια.] One of a class of fabulous monsters of classical mythology, commonly represented with the head and breast of a woman and the body of a serpent, said to allure youths and children in order to suck their blood; hence, a vampire; a female demon. Cf. Keats's poem, "Lamia."

lam-i-na (lam′i-nạ̈), *n.*; pl. *-næ* (-nē) or *-nas.* [L., thin plate, leaf, layer: cf. *lamella.*] A thin plate, scale, or layer, as of metal, bone, etc.; in *bot.*, the limb of a leaf or petal.—**lam′i-na-ble,** *a.* Capable of being formed into a lamina or laminæ.—**lam′i-nar** (-nạ̈r), *a.* Composed of or arranged in laminæ.—**lam′i-nate** (-nāt), *v.*; *-nated, -nating.* **I.** *tr.* To form (metal) into a lamina, as by beating or rolling; also, to separate or split into thin layers; also, to cover or overlay with laminæ; also, to construct by placing layer upon layer. **II.** *intr.* To split into thin layers.—**lam′i-nate,** *a.* Laminated; having laminæ.—**lam-i-na′tion** (-nā′shọn), *n.* The act or process of laminating; also, the state of being laminated; laminated structure; arrangement in thin layers; also, a lamina.—**lam-i-ni′tis** (-nī′tis), *n.* [NL.] In *vet. science,* inflammation of certain plates or laminæ of sensitive tissue in the hoof of a horse, caused by overwork, overfeeding, etc.—**lam′i-nose** (-nōs), *a.* Laminate; laminar.

la′mi-ter, *n.* See *lameter.*

Lam-mas (lam′ạs), *n.* [AS. *hlāfmæsse,* 'loaf mass': see *-mas.*] Orig., a harvest festival formerly held in England on Aug. 1; hence, Aug. 1 ('Lammas Day').—**latter Lammas,** a day that

Lammergeier.

will never arrive (since there is no second Lammas in the year); as, "He is writing a treatise . . . which will be published, probably . . . in the season of *Latter Lammas* and the Greek Kalends" (Kingsley's "Two Years Ago," vii.).—**Lam′mas-tide** (-tīd), *n.* The season of Lammas: as, "How long is it now To *Lammas-tide?*" (Shakspere's "Romeo and Juliet," i. 3. 15).

lam-mer-gei-er, lam-mer-gey-er (lam′ėr-gī-ėr), *n.* [G. *lämmergeier*, lit. 'lambs' vulture' (from its preying on lambs).] The bearded vulture, *Gypaëtus barbatus*, the largest European bird of prey, ranging from the mountains of southern Europe to China. See cut on preceding page.

lamp (lamp), *n.* [OF. F. *lampe*, < L. *lampas*, < Gr. λαμπάς, torch, light, lamp, < λάμπειν, shine: cf. *lantern*.] A vessel for containing an inflammable liquid, as oil, which is burned at a wick as a means of illumination; hence, any of various devices for using an illuminant, as gas or electricity, or for heating, as by burning alcohol; also, a torch (poetic); also, a heavenly body, as the sun, the moon, or a star (as, "Yon clear *lamps* That measure and divide the weary years": Shelley's "Prometheus Unbound," i. 362); also, fig., a source of intellectual or spiritual light (as, "reason, that heav'n-lighted *lamp* in man": Young's "Night Thoughts," iii. 2); also, *pl.*, the eyes (see Shakspere's "Comedy of Errors," v. 1. 315: now slang).—**to smell of the lamp.** See under *smell, v. i.*—**lamp,** *v.* **I.** *intr.* To shine: as, "Fire—with smoke—All night went *lamping* on" (Browning's "Aristophanes' Apology"). **II.** *tr.* To supply with lamps; light as with a lamp (as, "Certain scattered lights *Lamping* the rush and roll of the abyss": Browning's "Ring and the Book," vi.); also, to look at or see (slang).

Ancient Roman Lamps. — Museum of Fine Arts, Boston.

lam-pas (lam′pạs), *n.* [F.; origin uncertain.] In *vet. science*, a congestion and swelling of the fleshy lining of the roof of a horse's mouth immediately behind the fore teeth.

lamp-black (lamp′blak), *n.* A fine black pigment consisting of almost pure carbon collected as soot from the smoke of burning oil, gas, etc.

lam-per=eel (lam′pėr-ēl′), *n.* A lamprey; also, the eelpout, *Zoarces anguillaris*.

lam-pi-on (lam′pi-ọn), *n.* [F., < It. *lampione*, < *lampa*, < L. *lampas*, E. *lamp*.] A kind of lamp, often of colored glass, used for illuminations.

lamp-light (lamp′līt), *n.* The light shed by a lamp.

lamp-light-er (lamp′lī″tėr), *n.* One who lights street-lamps; also, a contrivance for lighting lamps, as a torch or a spill.

lam-poon (lam-pön′), *n.* [F. *lampon*, said to be < *lampons*, 'let us drink' (used in songs or verses), impv. of *lamper*, drink, quaff, guzzle.] A malicious or virulent satire upon a person, in either prose or verse: as, "Pungent *lampoons*, impassioned invectives, and earnest remonstrances, were thrust into the hands of the Duchess" (Motley's "Dutch Republic," ii. 5).—**lam-poon′,** *v. t.* To assail in a lampoon.—**lam-poon′er,** *n.*

lamp=post (lamp′pōst), *n.* A post or pillar, usually of iron, used to support a lamp which lights a street, park, or the like.

lam-prey (lam′pri), *n.*; pl. *-preys* (-priz). [OF. *lampreie*, *lamproie* (F. *lamproie*), < ML. *lampreda*, LL. *lampetra*, lamprey; commonly explained as < L. *lambere*, lick, + *petra*, rock: cf. *limpet*.] Any of the eel-like marine and fresh-water cyclostomes constituting the group or order *Hyperoartia* (or *Petromyzontes*), most species of which have the habit of attaching themselves to fishes and rasping off the flesh with their horny teeth.

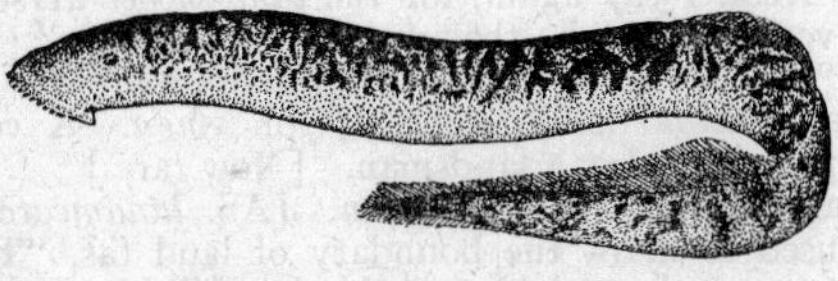
Sea-lamprey (*Petromyzon marinus*).

la-nate (lā′nāt), *a.* [L. *lanatus*, < *lana*, wool.] Woolly; covered with something resembling wool.

Lan-cas-te-ri-an (lang-kas-tē′ri-ạn), *a.* Of or pertaining to the English educator Joseph Lancaster (1778–1838), or the system of instruction employed by him, in which the younger pupils were taught by the more advanced pupils, who were called 'monitors.'

Lan-cas-tri-an (lang-kas′tri-ạn). **I.** *a.* In *Eng. hist.*, of or pertaining to the English royal house of Lancaster, descended from John of Gaunt (Duke of Lancaster), fourth son of Edward III., the reigning members of which were Henry IV., V., and VI., who reigned from 1399 to 1461. Cf. *Yorkist, a.*, also *Wars of the Roses* (under *rose*², *n.*). **II.** *n.* An adherent or member of the house of Lancaster, esp. in the Wars of the Roses.

lance (låns), *n.* [OF. F. *lance*, < L. *lancea*, lance.] A long spear-like weapon with a sharp iron or steel head, used by mounted soldiers in charging; also, a soldier armed with this weapon (as, "The count, at the head of an hundred *lances*, was gone towards the frontiers of Brabant": Scott's "Quentin Durward," xxvii.); one skilled in the use of it (as, "He was now in the ninetieth year of his age, yet . . . accounted the best *lance* in all Mauritania": Irving's "Conquest of Granada," x.); also, some similar weapon or implement, as a spear for killing a harpooned whale; also, a lancet.—**lance,** *v.*; *lanced, lancing.* [OF. *lancier* (F. *lancer*), < LL. *lanceare*, < L. *lancea*: cf. *launch*².] **I.** *tr.* To hurl or launch, as or like a weapon or missile (archaic: as, "The adder, in her haunts disturb'd, *Lanced* at the intruding staff her arrowy tongue," Southey's "Thalaba," v. 11); also, to pierce with or as with a lance (as, "They *lanced* his [Faithful's] flesh with knives": Bunyan's "Pilgrim's Progress," i.); in *surg.*, to make an incision in with a lancet. **II.** *intr.* To dart, rush, or bound along. [Now prov.]—**lance′=cor″po-ral,** *n.* *Milit.*, a private appointed to act temporarily as corporal, without increase in pay.

lance=knight (låns′nīt), *n.* [G. *lanzknecht* (*lanze*, lance), for *landsknecht*: see *lansquenet*.] A lansquenet (soldier): as, "a captain of pillagers . . . who slays priests and pilgrims as if they were so many *lance-knights* and men-at-arms" (Scott's "Quentin Durward," iv.). [Obs. or archaic.]

lance-let (låns′let), *n.* [Dim. of *lance, n.*] Any of various small, limbless, skull-less, fish-like marine animals (constituting the group or class *Acrania*, the lowest of existing vertebrates), found in the sand beneath shallow waters, and characterized by a thin, almost transparent body pointed at both ends.

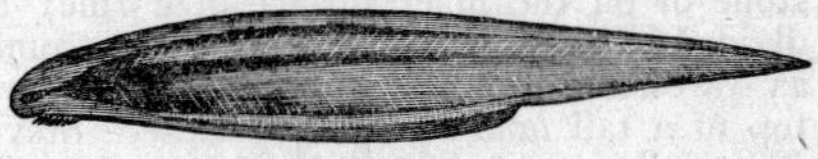
Lancelet.

lan-ce-o-late (lan′sẹ-ọ-lāt), *a.* [L. *lanceolatus*, < *lanceola*, dim. of *lancea*, E. *lance, n.*] Shaped like the head of a lance; of leaves, etc., narrow, and tapering toward the apex, or (sometimes) toward each end. Also **lan′ce-o-lat-ed** (-lā-ted).

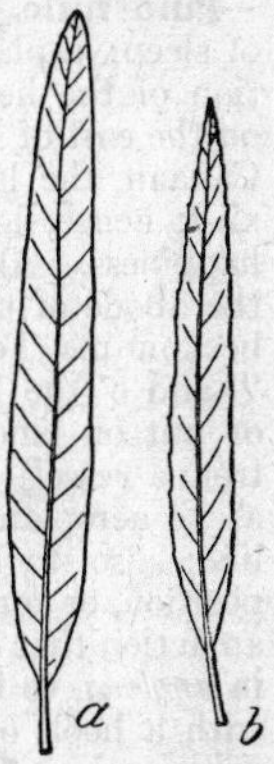

Lanceolate Leaves, of (*a*) *Quercus phellos* (willow-oak), and (*b*) *Salix fluviatilis* (sand-bar willow).

lan-cer (lån′sėr), *n.* [F. *lancier*, < *lance*, E. *lance, n.*] A mounted soldier armed with a lance; also, *pl.*, a form of quadrille (dance), or music for it.

lan-cet (lån′set), *n.* [OF. F. *lancette*, dim. of *lance*, E. *lance, n.*] A small surgical instrument, usually sharp-pointed and two-edged, for letting blood, opening abscesses, etc.; also, in *arch.*, a lancet-arch, or a lancet-window (as, "greenish glimmerings thro' the *lancets*": Tennyson's "Aylmer's Field," 622).—**lan′cet=arch′,** *n.* In *arch.*, an arch of which the head is acutely pointed.—**lan′cet-ed,** *a.* Having a lancet-arch or lancet-windows.—**lan′cet=win′dow,** *n.* In *arch.*, a high, narrow window terminating in a lancet-arch. See cut on following page.

lance-wood (låns′wůd), *n.* The tough, elastic wood of any of various trees (as *Aberemoa quitarensis*, of tropical America), used for carriage-shafts, cabinet-work, etc. (as, "He sent for *lancewood* to make the thills": Holmes's "Deacon's Masterpiece"); also, a tree which yields it.

Lancet-windows. — The Five Sisters, York Minster, England.

lan-ci-nate (lan′si-nāt), *v. t.*; *-nated*, *-nating*. [L. *lancinatus*, pp. of *lancinare*, tear, rend, lacerate.] To tear or rend; stab or pierce.—**lan′ci-nat-ing** (-nā-ting), *p. a.* Piercing; shooting: used esp. of pains, as in cancer.—**lan-ci-na′tion** (-nā′shon), *n.*

land (land), *n.* [AS. *land, lond*, = D., G., Icel., Sw., Dan., and Goth. *land*, land: cf. *lande* and *lawn*².] The solid substance of the earth's surface (as, dry *land*; submerged *land*); esp., the exposed part of the earth's surface, as distinguished from the submerged part (as, to travel by *land* and water); also, ground, esp. as considered with reference to quality, character, or use (as, poor *land*; arable *land*; forest *land*); also, a part of the earth's surface marked off by natural or political boundaries or the like; a region or country; hence, the people of a country (as, "These answers, in the silent night receiv'd, The king himself divulg'd, the *land* believ'd": Dryden's tr. Virgil's "Æneid," vii. 148); a nation; fig., a realm or domain (as, the *land* of the living, the present world or life; the *land* of nod, or the *land* of the leal, see phrases below); also, ground considered as a subject of possession, with its appurtenances, such as trees, water, etc., or buildings, fences, etc. (as, "a great buyer of *land*": Shakspere's "Hamlet," v. 1. 113); a piece of landed property (usually in *pl.*: as, "Thy *lands* and goods Are, by the laws of Venice, confiscate," Shakspere's "Merchant of Venice," iv. 1. 310); also, one of the strips into which a field is divided by plowing; also, a surface between furrows, as on a millstone or on the inner surface of a rifle; also, a building divided into separate tenements with a common entry (Sc.: as, "a certain frail old gentlewoman . . . who dwelt in the top of a tall *land* on a strait close," Stevenson's "David Balfour," xx.).—**how the land lies,** fig., what the state of affairs is: as, "Can you tell me *how the land lies*, with the rest of the company?" (Cooper's "Two Admirals," viii.).—**land mile.** See under *mile*.—**land of nod,** the realm of sleep: a play upon the word *nod* as meaning an inclination of the head from drowsiness, and "the land of *Nod*, on the east of Eden" (see Gen. iv. 16).—**Land of Promise,** Canaan, the land promised by God to Abraham (see Gen. xii.); hence, fig., heaven; [*l. c.*] any place or state of expected happiness. Also called *Promised Land*.—**land of the leal,** the abode of the blessed after death; heaven: as, "Angels beckon me To the *land o' the leal*" (Baroness Nairne's "Land o' the Leal"). [Sc.]—**land,** *v.* **I.** *tr.* To bring to or put on land or shore (as, to *land* passengers or goods from a vessel); also, to bring down upon the land or ground, as an aëroplane; set down from a train, a carriage, or the like; also, to bring into, or cause to arrive in, any place, position, or condition (as, to *land* a blow on a person's nose; an action that *landed* him in jail, or in bankruptcy); specif., in *angling*, to bring (a fish) to land, or into a boat, etc., as with a hook or a net; fig. (colloq.), to catch or capture; gain or win. **II.** *intr.* To come to land or shore, as a vessel; go or come ashore from a ship or boat; also, to come down upon the land or ground, as an aëroplane; alight upon the ground, as from an aëroplane or a train, or after a jump or the like; also, to come to rest or arrive in any place, position, or condition.

land-am-man, land-am-mann (länt′äm″än), *n.* [Swiss G., < *land*, land, + *amt*, office, + *mann*, man.] The title of the chief magistrate in some of the Swiss cantons.

lan-dau (lan′dâ), *n.* [From *Landau*, town in Germany.] A four-wheeled, two-seated vehicle with a top made in two parts, which may be let down or folded back.

lan-dau-let (lan-dâ-let′), *n.* A small landau; a coupé with a folding or collapsible top; also, an automobile having an inclosed portion (seating three or more) whose top can be partly let down or folded back, and a roofed seat for the driver in front.

lande (land, F. länd), *n.* [F. *lande*, OF. *lande, launde*; from Celtic, and cognate with E. *land*: cf. *lawn*².] An uncultivated or unfertile plain covered with heath, broom, ferns, etc., as in southwestern France.

land-ed (lan′ded), *a.* Owning land (as, "a *landed* squire": Shakspere's "King John," i. 1. 177); also, consisting of or pertaining to land (as, *landed* property; *landed* security).

land-er (lan′dėr), *n.* One who lands.

land-fall (land′fâl), *n.* *Naut.* and *aëronautics*, an approach to or sighting of land; also, the land sighted or reached.

land-grave (land′grāv), *n.* [G. *landgraf*, 'land count.'] In Germany, orig., a count having jurisdiction over a considerable territory; later, the title of certain German princes.—**land-gra′vi-ate** (-grā′vi-āt), *n.* The office, jurisdiction, or territory of a landgrave.—**land′gra-vine** (-gra-vēn), *n.* [G. *landgräfin*.] The wife of a landgrave; also, a woman of the rank of a landgrave.

land-hold-er (land′hōl″dėr), *n.* A holder, owner, or occupant of land.—**land′hold″ing,** *n.* and *a.*

land-ing (lan′ding), *n.* The act of one who or that which lands (as, the *landing* of the Pilgrims at Plymouth, Mass., Dec. 21, 1620); also, a place where persons or goods are landed, as from a ship; a platform at a railroad-station; any place to land at or on; specif., in *arch.*, the floor at the head or foot of a flight of stairs; a platform between flights of stairs.—**land′ing=gear,** *n.* In *aëronautics*, the under parts (wheels, skids, floats, etc.) of an aircraft, upon which it moves over the surface of the ground or water at the end or the beginning of a flight.—**land′ing=place,** *n.* A place for or of landing, as from a vessel, a vehicle, etc.; sometimes, a landing of a flight of stairs, or between flights of stairs.

land-la-dy (land′lā″di), *n.*; pl. *-dies* (-diz). [Cf. *landlord*.] A woman who owns and lets land, buildings, etc.; also, the mistress of an inn, lodging-house, or boarding-house; also, a hostess (Sc.).

land-less (land′les), *a.* [AS. *landlēas*.] Without land; having no landed property.

land-locked (land′lokt), *a.* Shut in more or less completely by land (as, "the best harbor on the coast, being completely *land-locked*," Dana's "Two Years before the Mast," xiv.; "the ship . . . lying *land-locked* far up the bay," H. Melville's "Omoo," lxxvi.); also, living in waters shut off from the sea, as fish.

land-lop-er, land-loup-er (land′lō″pėr, -lou″pėr), *n.* [Partly from *land* + *lope* or *loup*, for earlier *landleaper*, partly from the equivalent D. *landlooper*.] One who wanders about the country; a vagabond: as, "Bands of *land-loupers* had been employed . . . to set fire to villages and towns in every direction" (Motley's "Dutch Republic," iv. 3). [Archaic or prov.]—**land′lop″ing, land′loup″ing,** *a.*

land-lord (land′lôrd), *n.* A lord or owner of land; in ordinary use, one who owns and lets land, buildings, etc.; also, the master of an inn, lodging-house, or boarding-house; also, a host (Sc.).—**land′lord-ism,** *n.* The methods or practice of landlords; the system of renting from landlords; the principle of the supremacy of the landlord class.—**land′lord-ly,** *a.* Belonging or proper to a landlord.—**land′lord-ship,** *n.* The position or function of a landlord.

land′loup″er, etc. See *landloper*, etc.

land-lub-ber (land′lub″ėr), *n.* [See *lubber*.] A sailors' term of contempt for a landsman or a raw seaman: as, "Alas! I say again, for the *land-lubber* at sea. He is the veriest wretch the watery world over" (H. Melville's "Omoo," xiv.).—**land′lub″ber-ly,** *a.*

land-man (land′man), *n.*; pl. *-men*. A countryman or peasant; also, a landsman. [Now rare.]

land-mark (land′märk), *n.* [AS. *landmearc*.] Something used to mark the boundary of land (as, "Thou shalt not remove thy neighbour's *landmark*": Deut. xix. 14); also, a conspicuous object on land that serves as a guide, whether to persons on land or to vessels at sea (as, "Having no chart for the coast, nor any *landmark*, I did not know it [a place] when I saw it": Defoe's "Robinson Crusoe," ii. 2); any conspicuous object characterizing a locality; fig., a prominent or distinguishing feature, part, event, etc. (as, "the great achievements which are the *landmarks* of human action and human progress": Disraeli's "Coningsby," iv. 13).—**land′mark,** *v. t.* To mark or indicate by or as by a landmark.

land=meas-ure (land′mezh″ụr), *n.* Any denomination of measurement used in giving the area of land; also, a system of square measure used in measuring land (9 square feet = 1 square yard; 30¼ square yards = 1 square rod, or perch; 40 square rods = 1 rood; 4 roods or 160 square rods = 1 acre; 640 acres = 1 square mile).

land-oc-ra-cy (land-ok′rạ-si), *n.* [See *-cracy.*] A ruling or dominating landed class in a country.—**land′o-crat** (-ọ-krat), *n.* A member of a landocracy.

land=of-fice (land′of″is), *n.* A government office for the transaction of business relating to public lands.—**land=office business,** a rushing business: with allusion to the rush of applicants to a land-office when new lands are opened for settlement. [Colloq.]

land-own-er (land′ō″nėr), *n.* An owner or proprietor of land.—**land′own″er-ship,** *n.*—**land′own″ing,** *n.* and *a.*

land=poor (land′pör), *a.* Poor or in need of ready money while owning much unremunerative land; esp., poor because of taxes and other charges against such land.

land-scape (land′skāp), *n.* [D. *landschap*, < *land*, land, + *-schap*, akin to E. *-ship.*] A picture representing rural or natural inland scenery, as distinguished from a marine picture, a portrait, etc. (as, the *landscapes* of Claude Lorrain); also, a view or prospect, or a piece, of such scenery (as, "Now fades the glimmering *landscape* on the sight," Gray's "Elegy," ii.; "Through the open window behind, you see a quiet *landscape*—a hill, a tree, the glimpse of a river, and a few peaceful summer clouds," G. W. Curtis's "Prue and I," vi.); sometimes, such scenery, or its representation (as, "What a luxury of *landscape* meets My gaze!" Coleridge's "Brockley Coomb"; a painter specializing in *landscape*); also, a sketch† or outline†; a compendium† or epitome†.—**land′scape,** *v. t.*; *-scaped, -scaping.* To represent as a landscape; also, to furnish with a landscape.—**land′scape=ar″chi-tect,** *n.* One skilled in landscape-architecture.—**land′scape=ar″chi-tec-ture,** *n.* The art of arranging or modifying the features of a landscape, as in open country or parks, or of arranging the streets, open spaces, buildings, or other features of towns, so as to secure beautiful, artistic, or otherwise advantageous effects.—**land′scape=gar″den-er,** *n.* One skilled in landscape-gardening.—**land′scape=gar″den-ing,** *n.* The art of laying out grounds and arranging trees, shrubbery, paths, fountains, etc., so as to produce picturesque effects.—**land′scap-ist** (-skā-pist), *n.* A painter of landscapes.

land=side (land′sīd), *n.* The flat side of a plow, which presses against the unplowed land.

land-skip (land′skip), *n.* Old form of *landscape.*

land-slide (land′slīd), *n.* The sliding down of a mass of soil, detritus, or rock on a steep slope; also, the mass itself; also, in fig. use, the occurrence of a heavy or overwhelming mass or amount of something, esp., in political or other use, of votes for a particular candidate, party, or measure; an election in which a particular candidate or party receives an overwhelming mass or majority of votes (as, the election of 1920 was a Republican *landslide*); any overwhelming victory; also, a heavy or overwhelming mass or amount of something, as of votes. [Chiefly U. S.]

land-slip (land′slip), *n.* Same as *landslide* (esp. in literal sense). [Chiefly Eng.]

lands-man (landz′mạn), *n.*; pl. *-men.* One who lives, or engages in an occupation, on land (opposed to *seaman*); hence, in nautical use, a sailor on his first voyage; an inexperienced seaman, rated below an ordinary seaman; also, a fellow-countryman (rare: as, "Stand by me, countryman . . . for the love of Scotland and St. Andrew! I am innocent—I am your own native *landsman*," Scott's "Quentin Durward," vi.).

land-spout (land′spout), *n.* A cylindrical or funnel-shaped cloud resembling a waterspout but occurring on land, produced by any of certain severe whirling storms of small extent.

land-sturm (länt′shtụrm), *n.* [G., 'land storm.'] In Germany, Switzerland, etc., a general levy of the people in time of war; also, the force so called out or subject to such call, consisting of all men capable of bearing arms and not in the army, navy, or landwehr.

Land-tag (länt′täch), *n.* [G., 'land diet.'] In various German states, the diet or legislative body.

land=tied (land′tīd), *a.* Joined to the mainland or to other land by the growth of reefs or sand-spits, as islands.

A Land-tied Island near Genoa, Italy.

land-ward (land′wärd). **I.** *adv.* Toward the land. **II.** *a.* Lying, facing, or tending toward the land or away from the coast; being in the direction of the land (as, "All the *landward* noises died away . . . They heard no sound but washing of the seas": W. Morris's "Jason," iv. 91); also (Sc.), country; rural; rustic.—**land′wards** (-wärdz), *adv.* Landward.

land-wehr (länt′vār), *n.* [G., 'land defense.'] In Germany, Austria, etc., that part of the organized military forces of the nation which has completed a certain amount of compulsory training and of which continuous service is required only in time of war.

lane (lān), *n.* [AS. *lane* = D. *laan*, lane.] A narrow way or passage between hedges, fences, walls, or houses (as, "a parish all of fields, high hedges, and deep-rutted *lanes*": George Eliot's "Felix Holt," Introd.); hence, any narrow or well-defined passage, track, channel, or course; a navigable opening between fields of ice; a fixed route pursued by ocean steamers; in sprint-races, each of the spaces between the cords which mark the courses of the competitors.

lang (lang). Sc. and north. Eng. form of *long*[1].

lan-ga-ha (läng-gä′hä), *n.* [Malagasy.] A snake, *Xiphorhynchus* (or *Dryophis*) *langaha*, of Madagascar, having the snout prolonged into a sharp, flexible tip.

Langaha.

lan-grage (lang′grạj), *n.* [Origin unknown.] A kind of shot consisting of bolts, nails, etc., fastened together or inclosed in a case, formerly used for damaging sails and rigging in battles at sea.

lang syne (lang sīn). Long since; long ago. See *auld lang syne.* [Sc.]

lan-guage (lang′gwạj), *n.* [OF. F. *langage*, < L. *lingua*, tongue, speech, language.] The aggregate of words and of methods of combining them used by a particular nation, people, or race (as, the English *language*; the Semitic family of *languages*); a tongue; also, human speech, or words and the methods of combining them for the expression of thought, considered as a whole and without reference to differences depending on nationality or the like (as, "It is beyond all question . . . that the desire of communication was the only force directly impelling men to the production of *language*": Encyc. Brit., 11th ed., XXI. 415); in general, any means of expressing thought, feelings, etc., as by gestures or signs, or, on the part of the lower animals, by inarticulate sounds; also, the faculty or power of speech (now rare: as, "Oh that those lips had *language!*" Cowper's "My Mother's Picture," 1); also, the speech or phraseology peculiar to a class of persons, or to a profession, art, science, or the like (as, the *language* of the prize-ring; law *language*; "There is one *language* for the pulpit, and another for on board ship," Marryat's "Peter Simple," xiv.); also, form or manner of expression, as of individuals (as, "His pupil had permitted his escape, only because, in his own *language*, 'for such a bird he had no convenient cage' ": Motley's "Dutch Republic," i. 1); speech or expressions of a particular character (as, flowery *language*; strong or bad *language*); diction or style of written discourse or composition.—**lan′-guaged,** *a.* Having a language or languages (as, "many-*languaged* nations": Pope's tr. Homer's "Odyssey," iii.); also, versed in a language or languages, as a person; also, using speech† (as specified: as, fair-*languaged*; well-*languaged*).—**lan′guage-less,** *a.* Without language or speech.

langue d'oc (läṅg dok). [OF., 'language of *oc*' (Pr. *oc*, yes), that is, the language in which the Pr. affirmative *oc*, rather than the OF. *oïl* (F. *oui*), is used: see *langue d'oïl*.] The form of Romance spoken in southern France in the middle ages; hence, the modern Provençal.

langue d'oïl (läṅg dọ-ēl). [OF., 'language of *oïl*' (OF. *oïl*, F. *oui*, yes): see *langue d'oc*.] The form of Romance spoken in northern France in the middle ages; hence, the modern French. Also **langue d'oui** (dwē).

lan-guet, lan-guette (lang′get, lang-get′), *n.* [F. *languette*, dim. of *langue*, < L. *lingua*, tongue.] A little tongue; any of various small tongue-shaped parts, processes, or projections.

lan-guid (lang′gwid), *a.* [F. *languide*, < L. *languidus*, < *languere*: see *languish*.] Drooping or flagging from weakness or fatigue; weak or faint; hence, lacking in bodily energy; indisposed to activity or exertion; indolent; also, lacking in spirit, ardor, or interest (as, "Lord Ipsden relapsed into greater listlessness . . . He was too *languid* to go anywhere or do anything": Reade's "Christie Johnstone," i.); listless, apathetic, or indifferent; faint or slight, as interest or other feeling; also, lacking in vigor, briskness, or activity (as, a *languid* competition; a *languid* market); slack or dull; also, without force or effectiveness (as, a *languid* narrative; a *languid* style).—**lan′guid-ly,** *adv.*—**lan′-guid-ness,** *n.*

lan-guish (lang′gwish), *v. i.* [OF. F. *languir* (*languiss-*), < L. *languere*, be weak or faint, prob. akin to *laxus*, loose, slack, E. *lax*.] To become or be weak or feeble, or suffer with disease or pain, as a person or animal (as, "I still continued to *languish* under a complaint, the origin and nature of which were still a mystery": H. Melville's "Typee," xiii.); droop, wither, or fade, as a plant; pine or suffer under any unfavorable conditions (as, to *languish* in prison; "a man that *languishes* in your displeasure," Shakspere's "Othello," iii. 3. 43); sometimes, to pine with longing (as, "He began to *languish* for fresh air": Dickens's "Oliver Twist," x.); also, to assume the look or expression of one yielding to tender emotion (as, "When a visitor comes in, she smiles and *languishes*, you'd think that butter wouldn't melt in her mouth": Thackeray's "Pendennis," ii. 22); also, to fall off in vigor, activity, or force (as, "The execution of the system was never permitted to *languish*": Motley's "Dutch Republic," i. 1).—**lan′guish,** *n.* The act or state of languishing (as, "One desperate grief cures with another's *languish*": Shakspere's "Romeo and Juliet," i. 2. 49); also, a languishing look or expression (as, "the warm, dark *languish* of her eyes": Whittier's "Snow-Bound").—**lan′guish-er,** *n.*—**lan′guish-ing-ly,** *adv.*—**lan′-guish-ment,** *n.* The act or state of languishing; drooping; pining; sorrowful longing; also, languishing appearance or air; a languishing look or expression.

lan-guor (lang′gọr or -gwọr), *n.* [OF. *langour* (F. *langueur*), < L. *languor*, < *languere*: see *languish*.] Physical weakness or faintness, as from disease, wounds, fatigue, or other cause; languid physical condition; lassitude; formerly, sickness† or disease†; mental suffering†, or sorrow†; also, lassitude, quietude, or softness of mood under some emotional influence (as, "The silver light . . . Breathes also to the heart, and o'er it throws A loving *languor*, which is not repose": Byron's "Don Juan," i. 114); emotional softness or tenderness; also, lack of bodily energy; languidness of movement, bearing, etc.; indolence; also, lack of spirit, ardor, or vigorous activity (as, "But for the criminal . . . *languor* which characterized that commander's movements . . . the honor of France might still have been saved": Motley's "Dutch Republic," i. 2); also, soothing or oppressive quiet or stillness (as, "Only the rustle of the redescending birds and the boom of the distant surges disturbed the *languor* of the afternoon": Stevenson's "Treasure Island," xiv.).—**lan′guor-ous,** *a.* [OF. *langoureux*.] Characterized by or exhibiting languor; languid; languishing; also, inducing languor (as, *languorous* fragrance).—**lan′guor-ous-ly,** *adv.*

lan-gur (lung-gör′), *n.* [Hind. *langūr*.] Any of certain large, slender, long-limbed, long-tailed Asiatic monkeys of the genus *Semnopithecus* (or *Presbytis*), as the entellus.

lan-iard (lan′yạrd), *n.* See *lanyard*.

la-ni-a-ry (lā′ni-ā-ri or lan′i-), *a.* [= F. *laniaire*, < L. *laniare*, tear in pieces.] Fitted for lacerating or tearing: applied specif. to the canine teeth.

la-nif-er-ous, la-nig-er-ous (lā-nif′ẹ-rus, lā-nij′-), *a.* [L. *lanifer*, *laniger*, < *lana*, wool: see *-ferous* and *-gerous*.] Wool-bearing; woolly.

lank (langk), *a.* [AS. *hlanc*.] Meagerly thin or slim, or not filled out with the normal amount of flesh (as, "He was tall, but exceedingly *lank*, with narrow shoulders," Irving's "Sketch-Book," Sleepy Hollow; "her long, *lank* arm," Hawthorne's "House of the Seven Gables," ii.); lean; gaunt; fig., of a bag, purse, etc., not distended with contents, or only partially filled, or empty (as, "a long, *lank*, leathern purse": Irving's "Tales of a Traveler," iii. 2); also, spindling, or unduly long and slender, as plants, etc. (as, "Let not my land so large a promise boast, Lest the *lank* ears in length of stem be lost": Dryden's tr. Virgil's "Georgics," ii. 342); of hair, straight and flat (as, "His visage was meagre, his hair *lank* and thin": Swift's "Gulliver's Travels," iii. 8); also, drooping† or languid† (as, "Nereus . . . piteous of her woes, rear'd her *lank* head": Milton's "Comus," 836).—**lank′i-ness,** *n.* Lanky state or form.—**lank′ly,** *adv.*—**lank′ness,** *n.*—**lank′y,** *a.*; compar. *lankier*, superl. *lankiest*. Somewhat lank; ungracefully tall or long and thin.

lan-ner (lan′ẹr), *n.* [OF. F. *lanier*, appar. a noun use of OF. *lanier*, cowardly: cf. OF. *lanier*, wool-worker, L. *lanarius*, pertaining to wool, < *lana*, wool.] A falcon, *Falco lanarius* (or *feldeggi*), of southern Europe, northern Africa, and southern Asia; specif., in *falconry*, the female of this bird (cf. *lanneret*).—**lan′ner-et,** *n.* [OF. F. *laneret*.] In *falconry*, the male lanner, which is smaller than the female.

lan-o-lin, lan-o-line (lan′ọ-lin), *n.* [L. *lana*, wool, + *oleum*, oil.] A fatty substance, extracted from wool, used as a basis for ointments.

la-nose (lā′nōs), *a.* [L. *lanosus*, < *lana*, wool.] Woolly; lanate.

lans-downe (lanz′doun), *n.* [From the proper name.] A fine, soft dress-fabric of silk and wool.

Lanner (*Falco lanarius*).

lans-que-net (låns′kẹ-net), *n.* [F., < G. *landsknecht*, < *land*, land, country, + *knecht*, man-servant: see *knight*.] One of a class of mercenary foot-soldiers, commonly armed with a pike or lance, formerly employed in the German and other Continental armies; also, a game of cards, originating in Germany.

lan-ta-na (lan-tā′nạ̈ or -tan′ạ̈), *n.* [NL.] Any plant of the verbenaceous, mostly tropical genus *Lantana*, including species much cultivated for their aromatic yellow or orange flowers.

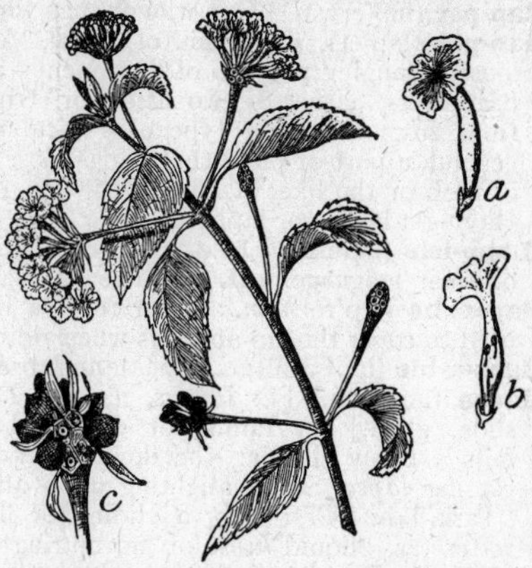

Lantana (*L. mutabilis*). — *a*, flower; *b*, flower cut longitudinally, showing pistil and two of the stamens; *c*, fruits.

lan-ter-loo† (lan′tėr-lö), *n.* [F. *lanturelu*, orig. the refrain of a popular song.] A game of cards, now called *loo*. See *loo*.

lan-tern (lan′tėrn), *n.* [OF. F. *lanterne*, < L. *lanterna*, < Gr. λαμπτήρ, a light, torch, lantern, < λάμπειν, shine: cf. *lamp*.] A case, generally transparent or translucent, for inclosing a light and protecting it from the wind, rain, etc., and either portable or fixed; sometimes, a magic lantern; also, the chamber at the top of a lighthouse, surrounding the light; also, a more or less open, upright structure erected on a roof, forming the upper part of a tower, or surmounting a dome, and serving for the admission of light, for ventilation, as a decorative feature, or for some other purpose; also, a lantern-wheel. —**Chinese lantern, dark lantern, magic lantern.** See under the adjectives.—**lan′tern,** *v. t.* To inclose as in a lantern; also, to furnish or light with a lantern.

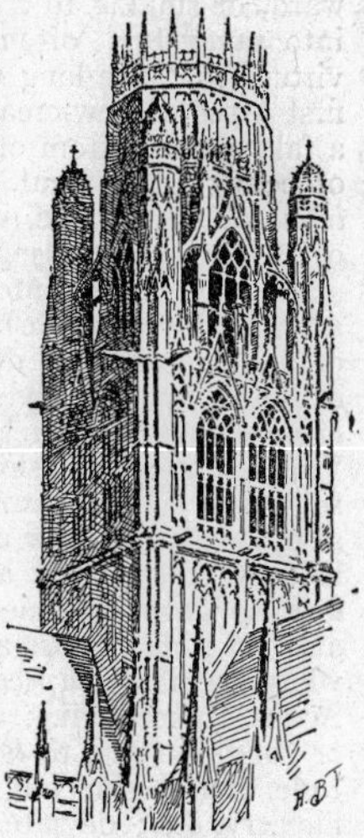

Lantern. — Church of St. Ouen, Rouen, France; 14th and 15th centuries.

lan-tern=fly (lan′tėrn-flī), *n.*; pl. *-flies* (-flīz). Any of various tropical hemipterous insects (genera *Fulgora*, *Laternaria*, etc.), formerly supposed to emit a light in the dark. See cut below.

lan-tern=jaws (lan′tėrn-jâz), *n. pl.* Long, thin jaws (with sunken or hollow cheeks).—**lan′tern=jawed,** *a.*

lan-tern=pin-ion (lan′tėrn-pin″yọn), *n.* A lantern-wheel.

lan-tern=wheel (lan′tėrn-hwēl), *n.* A wheel used like a pinion, consisting essentially of two parallel disks or heads whose peripheries are connected by a series of bars which engage with the teeth of another wheel. See cut opposite.

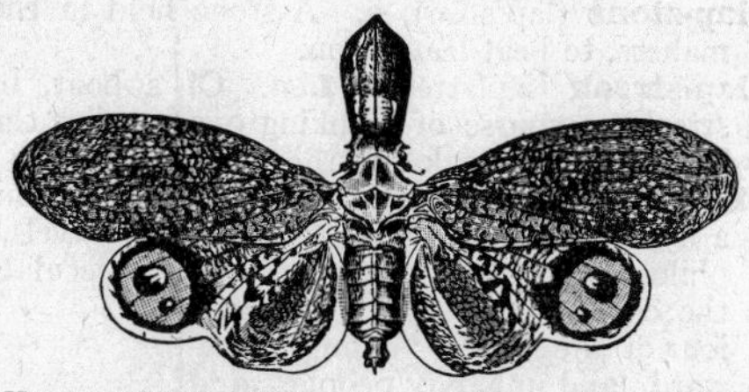

Honduras Lantern-fly (a species of *Laternaria*), reduced.

lan-tha-num (lan′thạ-num), *n.* [NL., < Gr. λανθάνειν, escape notice: see *latent*.] Chem. sym., La; at. wt., 139.0; sp. gr., 6.16. A rare metallic element, allied to aluminium, found in certain rare minerals, as cerite.

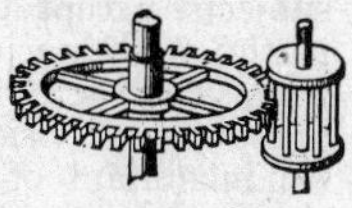

Lantern-wheel.

lant-horn (lant′hôrn or lan′tėrn), *n.* Old var. of *lantern*.

la-nu-gi-nose, la-nu-gi-nous (lạ-nū′ji-nōs, -nus), *a.* [L. *lanuginosus*.] Covered with lanugo, or soft, downy hairs; of the nature of down; downy.

la-nu-go (lạ-nū′gō), *n.* [L., < *lana*, wool.] A fine woolly or downy coating or growth, as on the surface of a leaf or fruit or on the body of an insect; in *anat.*, the coat of delicate downy hairs with which the human fetus or a new-born infant is covered.

lan-yard (lan′yạ̈rd), *n.* [For earlier *lanyer*, < OF. *lasniere* (F. *lanière*), thong, < *lasne*, thong: cf. L. *lacinia*, lappet, strip.] A thong†; *naut.*, a short rope or cord for securing or holding something (as, "Aboard ship he carried his crutch by a *lanyard* round his neck": Stevenson's "Treasure Island," x.); esp., a rope rove through deadeyes to secure and tighten rigging; *milit.*, a cord with a small hook at one end, used in firing certain kinds of cannon.

La-od-i-ce-an (lā̤-od-i-sē′ạn or lā″ọ̄-di-). **I.** *a.* Of or pertaining to Laodicea, an ancient city of Phrygia in Asia Minor, or its inhabitants; esp., lukewarm in religion, like the early Christians of Laodicea (see Rev. iii. 14–16); hence, in general, lukewarm; indifferent. **II.** *n.* An inhabitant of Laodicea; esp., a lukewarm Christian, like the early Christians of Laodicea; hence, in general, one who is lukewarm or indifferent.

lap[1] (lap), *v.*; *lapped, lapping.* [AS. *lapian* = MLG. *lapen* = OHG. *laffan*, lap; akin to L. *lambere*, Gr. λάπτειν, lick, lap: cf. *lambent*.] **I.** *intr.* To take up liquid with the tongue; lick up a liquid; also, of water, to wash with a sound as of licking up a liquid (as, "I heard the water *lapping* on the crag": Tennyson's "Passing of Arthur," 284). **II.** *tr.* To take up (liquid) with the tongue (as, "They'll take suggestion as a cat *laps* milk": Shakspere's "Tempest," ii. 1. 288); lick up; also, of water, to wash against or beat upon (something) with a lapping sound (as, "I . . . hear the water . . . *Lapping* the steps beneath my feet": Longfellow's "Cadenabbia").—**lap**[1], *n.* The act or an act of lapping liquid; also, the lapping of water against something, or the sound of this (as, "the *lap* and wash of undistinguishable waters": Bret Harte's "Princess Bob and Her Friends"); also, something lapped up; liquid food for dogs; hence (prov. or slang), liquid food in general; any weak beverage; liquor or drink.

lap[2] (lap), *n.* [AS. *læppa* = MLG. *lappe* = G. *lappen*, lap.] A flap or loosely hanging part, as of a garment; a part that hangs down at the bottom of a garment, as the skirt of a gown or coat; in general, a loose border or fold; also, the front part of a skirt, esp. as held up to contain something (as, "One . . . found a wild vine, and gathered thereof wild gourds his *lap* full": 2 Kings, iv. 39); the part of the clothing that lies on the front portion of the body from the waist to the knees when one sits; hence, this portion of the body with its covering garments as the place in or on which something is held or a child is nursed, cherished, etc.; hence, a lap-like or hollow place, as a hollow among hills (as, "The city of Malaga lies in the *lap* of a fertile valley, surrounded by mountains": Irving's "Conquest of Granada," lii.); in fig. use, that in which anything rests or reposes, or is nurtured or fostered (as, "Here rests his head upon the *lap* of earth," Gray's "Elegy," xxx.; "rear'd in luxury's *lap*," Byron's "Werner," ii. 2).

lap[3] (lap), *v.*; *lapped, lapping.* [ME. *lappen*; appar. < *lap*[2], and to some extent confused with *wrap*.] **I.** *tr.* To fold over or about something; wrap or wind round something; also, to infold or inwrap in something (as, "the soldier who, to keep himself from the cold, has *lapped* himself . . . in a tattered ensign": Scott's "Castle Dangerous," v.); wrap up; sometimes, to clothe; hence, to surround or envelop (as, "For peace her soul was yearning, And now peace *laps* her round": M. Arnold's "Requiescat"); also, to infold or hold in or as in the lap; nurse, fondle, or cherish; also, to lay (something) partly over something underneath; lay (things) together, one partly over another; also, to lie partly over (something underneath); come partly alongside of (something else); also, to get a lap or more ahead of (a competitor) in racing; also, to cut or polish (a gem, etc.) with a lap. **II.** *intr.* To be folded over; fold or wind round something; also, to lie partly over or alongside of something else; lie together, one partly over or beside another, as two things; also, to lie upon and extend beyond a thing; project beyond something else; fig., to extend beyond a limit (often with *over*: as, the reign of Elizabeth *lapped over* into the

17th century—she died in 1603).—**lap**³, *n.* The act of lapping; the folding or wrapping of a thing over or about something; the amount of a material required to go round a thing once; also, a single round or circuit of the course in racing (sometimes fig.); also, the act or state of overlapping, or of laying or lying partly over or alongside of, or extending beyond, something else; the point or place of overlapping; the extent or amount of overlapping; an overlapping part; also, a layer or sheet of cotton, wool, or flax (usually wound on a roller) in certain stages of manufacture; also, a rotating wheel or disk of lead, copper, wood, leather, or the like, holding an abrasive or polishing powder on its surface, and used for cutting gems, etc., or for polishing gems, cutlery, etc.

laparo-. Form of Gr. λαπάρα, flank, loin, used in combination.—**lap-a-ro-cele** (lap′ạ-rọ̄-sēl), *n.* [+ *-cele.*] In *pathol.*, hernia in the lumbar regions.—**lap-a-rot′o-my** (-rot′ọ̄-mi), *n.* [+ *-tomy.*] In *surg.*, incision into the abdominal cavity.

lap-board (lap′bōrd), *n.* A thin, flat board to be held on the lap for use as a table.

lap=dog (lap′dog), *n.* A small pet dog such as may be held in the lap.

la-pel (lạ-pel′), *n.* [Dim. of *lap*².] A part of a garment folded back on the breast, esp. a continuation of a coat-collar.—**la-pelled′**, *a.* Having a lapel or lapels; also, folded back in a lapel.

lap-ful (lap′fůl), *n.*; pl. *-fuls.* As much as the lap can hold.

lap-i-da-ry (lap′i-dā-ri). [L. *lapidarius*, < *lapis* (*lapid-*), a stone.] **I.** *a.* Of or pertaining to stones; also, pertaining to the cutting or engraving of stones, esp. precious stones, or gems (as, the *lapidary* art); engraved on stone, esp. monumental stones (as, "His grand principle is, that *lapidary* inscriptions . . . should be Historical rather than Lyrical": Carlyle's "Sartor Resartus," ii. 4); characteristic of or suitable for monumental inscriptions (as, the *lapidary* style of composition). **II.** *n.*; pl. *-ries* (-riz). An artificer who cuts, polishes, and engraves precious stones, or gems (as, "the shops of the goldsmiths and *lapidaries*": Motley's "Dutch Republic," vi. 6); also, a connoisseur of gems or precious stones, or of lapidary work (obs. or rare).

lap-i-date (lap′i-dāt), *v. t.*; *-dated, -dating.* [L. *lapidatus*, pp. of *lapidare*, < *lapis* (*lapid-*), a stone.] To pelt with stones; also, to stone to death.—**lap-i-da′tion** (-dā′shọn), *n.*

la-pid-i-fy (lạ-pid′i-fī), *v. t.* or *i.*; *-fied, -fying.* [F. *lapidifier*, < ML. *lapidificare*, < L. *lapis* (*lapid-*), a stone, + *facere*, make.] To turn into stone; petrify.—**la-pid″i-fi-ca′tion** (-fi-kā′shọn), *n.*

la-pil-li (lạ-pil′ī), *n. pl.* [L., pl. of *lapillus*, dim. of *lapis*, a stone.] Stony particles or fragments ejected from volcanoes.

la-pin (lȧ-pañ, E. lap′in), *n.* [F.] A rabbit; the fur of the rabbit.

la-pis laz-u-li (lā′pis, or lap′is, laz′ū-lī). [ML., < L. *lapis*, stone, + ML. *lazuli*, gen. of *lazulum*, lapis lazuli, from Ar. or Pers.: see *azure.*] A deep-blue stone containing sodium, aluminium, calcium, sulphur, and silicon, and consisting of a mixture of minerals, used chiefly for ornamental purposes and sometimes for preparing the pigment ultramarine; also, its color.

Lap-i-thæ (lap′i-thē), *n. pl.* [L., < Gr. Λαπίθαι, pl.] In *Gr. myth.*, a people of Thessaly who, upon the attempt of the centaurs, at the wedding of Pirithous, ruler of the Lapithæ, to carry off the bride and the other women, engaged with and defeated the centaurs in a bloody conflict.

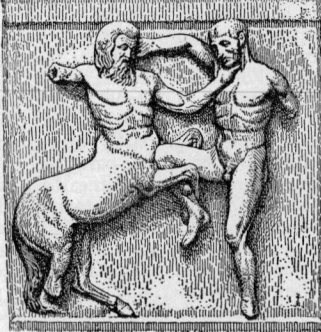

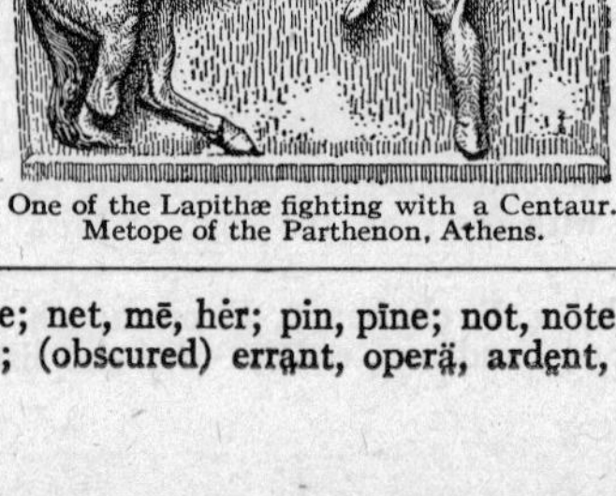
One of the Lapithæ fighting with a Centaur. Metope of the Parthenon, Athens.

lap=joint (lap′joint), *n.* A joint in which the edge of one board, plate, or the like, overlaps the edge of another.

Lapp (lap), *n.* One of a Finnic people of northern Norway, Sweden, and Finland, and adjacent regions, characterized by dwarfish stature and short, broad heads; also, the language of this people.

lap-per (lap′ėr), *n.* One who or that which laps.

lap-pet (lap′et), *n.* [Dim. of *lap*².] A small lap, flap, or loosely hanging part, as of a garment; a pendent part of a head-dress; either of two bands or strips hanging down in front from a certain type of clerical or other collar; in general, a part or piece that hangs loose; often, a loose fold of flesh or the like; a lobe of the ear, etc.—**lap′pet-ed**, *a.* Having a lappet or lappets.

Lapp-ish (lap′ish). **I.** *a.* Of or pertaining to the Lapps or their language. **II.** *n.* The language of the Lapps.

lap=robe (lap′rōb), *n.* A fur robe, a blanket, or the like, used to cover the lap and legs when riding in a carriage, etc.

laps-a-ble (lap′sạ-bl), *a.* Liable to lapse.

lapse (laps), *n.* [L. *lapsus*, n., < *labi* (pp. *lapsus*), fall, slide, glide.] A falling or gliding downward (as, "Fast falls a fleecy show'r: the downy flakes . . . with never-ceasing *lapse*, Softly alighting upon all below": Cowper's "Task," iv. 327); also, a gliding or flowing along, as of water (as, "liquid *lapse* of murmuring streams": Milton's "Paradise Lost," viii. 263); also, a gliding or passing away, as of time (as, "through the still *lapse* of ages": Bryant's "Thanatopsis"); hence, a period or interval elapsing (as, after a long *lapse* of time); also, fig., a falling, slipping downward, or sinking to a lower grade or condition (as, a *lapse* into savagery); often, a moral fall, as from rectitude or virtue (as, "The long strife with evil which began With the first *lapse* of new-created man": Whittier's "Panorama"); a falling away from one's faith; a deviation from principle or policy; in general, a slip, slight error, or mistake (as, a *lapse* of the tongue, or of grammar; a *lapse* of memory, or of judgment); also, a falling or passing into any specified state (as, a *lapse* into insensibility; a *lapse* into silence); also, a falling into disuse; in *law*, the termination of a right or privilege through neglect to exercise it or through failure of some contingency.—**lapse,** *v. i.*; *lapsed, lapsing.* [L. *lapsare*, freq. of *labi.*] To fall, slip, or glide downward (as, "to pick up an occasional dropper-off, as he *lapsed* from the seat of a jaunting car": Lever's "Harry Lorrequer," xl.); also, to glide or flow along, as water (sometimes associated in sense with *lap*¹: as, "The sound of streams . . . And *lapsing* waves on quiet shores," Whittier's "Snow-Bound"); also, to glide or pass away, as time (as, "two young people whose days now *lapsed* away together": Howells's "Chance Acquaintance," vii.); also, fig., to fall or sink to a lower grade or condition (as, to *lapse* into barbarism); fall from rectitude, or into sin; fall away from one's faith, or into heresy, idolatry, etc.; deviate from principles, accuracy, etc.; make a slip or error; also, to fall or pass into any specified state (as, to *lapse* into silence or reverie); also, to fall into disuse, cease, or disappear; in *law*, to become void, or to pass from one to another, by lapse.—**laps′er**, *n.*

lap-stone (lap′stōn), *n.* A stone held in the lap by shoemakers, to beat leather on.

lap-streak (lap′strēk). **I.** *a.* Of a boat, built with each streak or course of planking overlapping the one below it. **II.** *n.* A lapstreak boat.

La-pu-tan (lạ-pū′tạn). **I.** *a.* Of or pertaining to Laputa, a flying island in Swift's "Gulliver's Travels," inhabited by philosophers "taken up with intense speculations," who "in the common actions and behaviour of life" are a "clumsy, awkward, and unhandy people," and who are "slow and perplexed in their conceptions upon all other subjects, except those of mathematics and music" (see "Gulliver's Travels," iii. 2); hence, unpractical; visionary. **II.** *n.* An inhabitant of Laputa; a visionary.

lap-wing (lap′wing), *n.* [AS. *hlēapewince*, < *hlēapan*, leap, + *-wince*, akin to OHG. *winkan*, move aside, totter, and AS. *wincian*, E. *wink.*] An old-world

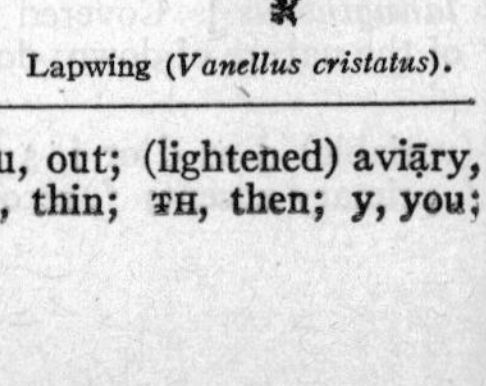
Lapwing (*Vanellus cristatus*).

crested plover, *Vanellus cristatus*, noted for its irregular flight and wailing cry (see cut on preceding page); also, any of various related or similar birds.

lar (lär), *n.*; pl. *lares* (lā′rēz) or *lars* (lärz). [L.] [Also *cap.*] Among the ancient Romans, one of a class of inferior deities presiding over particular localities, worshiped esp. as protectors of individual houses or households; a household god; fig., a cherished possession of a family or household: usually in *pl.* Cf. *penates*.

lar-board (lär′bōrd or -bọrd). [ME. *laddeborde*, < *ladde-* (of uncertain origin and meaning) + *borde*, side, E. *board*.] *Naut.*: **I.** *n.* The side of a ship to the left of a person looking from the stern toward the bow: opposed to *starboard*, and now supplanted by *port* or *left*. **II.** *a.* Pertaining to the larboard; being on the left or port side of a vessel: as, "our *larboard* bow" (Dana's "Two Years before the Mast," ii.).

lar-ce-ner (lär′sẹ-nėr), *n.* One who commits larceny. Also **lar′ce-nist.**

lar-cen-ic (lär-sen′ik), *a.* Larcenous: as, "Colley Cibber's version of 'Richard the Third' is impudent and slightly *larcenic*" (Reade's "Peg Woffington," i.).

lar-ce-nous (lär′sẹ-nus), *a.* Pertaining to or of the nature of larceny; characterized by larceny; guilty of larceny.—**lar′ce-nous-ly,** *adv.*

lar-ce-ny (lär′sẹ-ni), *n.*; pl. *-nies* (-niz). [OF. F. *larcin*, < L. *latrocinium*, robbery, < *latro*, robber.] In *law*, the wrongful taking and carrying away of the personal goods of another with intent to convert them to the taker's own use: sometimes distinguished as *grand larceny* and *petty* (or *petit*) *larceny*, according as the value of the property taken either equals or exceeds, or is less than, a fixed amount.

larch (lärch), *n.* [G. *lärche*, < L. *larix* (*laric-*), larch.] Any of the coniferous trees constituting the pinaceous genus *Larix*, characterized by a tough, durable wood; the wood of such a tree; also, any of various allied conifers.

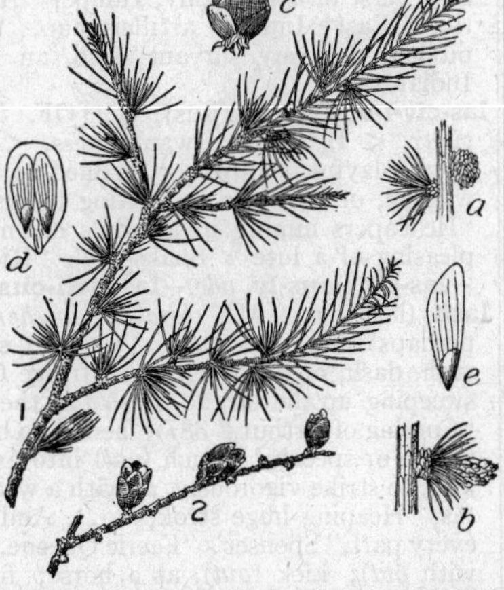

American Larch, or Tamarack (*Larix laricina*). — 1, branch with leaves; 2, branch with cones; *a*, branch with male flowers; *b*, branch with a young cone; *c*, cone; *d*, scale of cone with the two seeds; *e*, seed.

lard (lärd), *n.* [OF. F. *lard*, fat of pork, bacon, < L. *lardum*, *laridum*, fat of pork.] The fat of swine†; bacon† or pork†; now, the rendered fat of swine, esp. the internal fat of the abdomen.—**lard,** *v.t.* [OF. F. *larder*, < *lard*.] To prepare or enrich (lean meat, poultry, etc.) with pork or bacon, esp. with lardons or slender strips of fat drawn through; also, to fatten†; also, to strew, cover, or supply with something (obs. or rare); esp., to intersperse or garnish (speech, writing, etc.) with something (as, "An exact command, *Larded* with many several sorts of reasons," Shakspere's "Hamlet," v. 2. 20; to *lard* one's speech with oaths); interlard; also, to smear or cover with lard or grease.—**lar-da-ceous** (lär-dā′shius), *a.* [See *-aceous*.] Of the nature of or resembling lard; fatty; in *pathol.*, noting or pertaining to a form of degeneration in which a proteid substance (amyloid) is deposited in the tissues, esp. those of the abdominal organs.

lar-der (lär′dėr), *n.* [OF. *lardier*, < ML. *lardarium*, < L. *lardum*, E. *lard*, *n.*] A room or place where meat and other provisions are kept; a pantry; hence, the store of provisions in a house.

lar-don, lar-doon (lär′dọn, lär-dön′), *n.* [F. *lardon*, < *larder*, E. *lard*, *v.*] A piece of pork or bacon used in larding; esp., a slender strip of the fat drawn through the substance of meat, etc., with a kind of needle or pin.

lard-y (lär′di), *a.* Abounding in or resembling lard.

la-res (lā′rēz), *n.* Plural of *lar*.

large (lärj). [OF. F. *large*, < L. *largus*, abundant, plentiful, liberal.] **I.** *a.*; compar. *larger*, superl. *largest*. Abundant, copious, or ample (archaic: as, "We have yet *large* day; for scarce the sun Hath finish'd half his journey," Milton's "Paradise Lost," v. 558; "Forth they came and paced the shore . . . Drank the *large* air," Tennyson's "Sea Dreams," 34); also, liberal†, generous†, or lavish† (as, "The poor King Reignier, whose *large* style Agrees not with the leanness of his purse": Shakspere's "2 Henry VI.," i. 1. 111); also, being of more than common size, amount, or number (as, a *large* man, house, city, or field; a *large* sum; a *large* audience); great in dimensions (at least two dimensions), bulk, area, or quantity; big; also, of great scope or range, extensive, or broad (as, *large* powers; *large* experience; *large* sympathies); on a great scale (as, a *large* employer of labor; a *large* producer); extended or lengthy, as discourse or writing (archaic); grand or pompous (as, to talk in a *large* way); also, of great force, or heavy (as, "From Arac's arm, as from a giant's flail, The *large* blows rain'd": Tennyson's "Princess," v. 490); also, subject to few or no restrictions† (as, to be in *large* custody); free, or at liberty, as persons†; unrestrained by decorum, or improperly free, as the tongue, speech, jests, etc.†; lax† or indulgent†; also, *naut.*, of the wind, favorable in direction, as when on the beam or the quarter. **II.** *n.* Liberality†; also, liberty (obs. except as in the phrase 'at large': see below).—**at large,** at liberty, or free from restraint or confinement; also, at length, or to a considerable length (as, to discourse *at large* on a subject); also, as a whole, or in general (as, the country *at large*); also, in a general way, or without particularizing; also, representing the whole of a State, district, or body, and not merely one division or part of it (as, a Congressman *at large*).—**in large,** or **in the large,** on a large scale.—**large,** *adv.* Abundantly†, amply†, or liberally†; also, at length† or fully†; also, freely†; also, *naut.*, with a favorable wind, as on the beam or the quarter.

large=hand-ed (lärj′han′ded), *a.* Having large hands; fig., bountiful or generous; also, grasping† or rapacious† (as, "*large-handed* robbers": Shakspere's "Timon of Athens," iv. 1. 11).

large=heart-ed (lärj′här′ted), *a.* Having or showing a large heart or broad and generous sympathies; generous; magnanimous.—**large′=heart′ed-ness,** *n.*

large-ly (lärj′li), *adv.* In a large manner; amply or liberally (archaic); in great quantity, or much (as, "Elated with victory, they had drunk *largely*": Jane Porter's "Scottish Chiefs," liv.); on a large scale; now, esp., to a great extent, or in great part (as, the region consists *largely* of desert; the number is *largely* a matter of conjecture).

large=mind-ed (lärj′mīn′ded), *a.* Having or showing a large or broad mind; characterized by broad views or liberal ideas.—**large′=mind′ed-ness,** *n.*

lar-gen (lär′jn), *v.* **I.** *intr.* To become larger. **II.** *tr.* To make larger; enlarge: as, "Reddened, *largened*, The moon dips toward her mountain nest" (Lowell's "Pictures from Appledore," vi.).

large-ness (lärj′nes), *n.* The state or fact of being large; great size, extent, or scope; breadth, or freedom from narrowness.

lar-gess, lar-gesse (lär′jes), *n.* [OF. F. *largesse*, < L. *largus*, E. *large*.] Liberality† or munificence†; also, liberal bestowal of gifts, as formerly by a great personage on public occasions to attendants, the populace, etc., or the gifts or a gift (as of money) so bestowed (archaic: as, to cry *largess*, or cry a *largess*, to call for a largess or gift, or, sometimes, to shout in acknowledgment of one received); fig., generous or lavish bestowal, or something lavishly bestowed (poetic: as, "I could not bear to see those eyes On all with wasteful *largess* shine," Lowell's "Protest"; "shower'd *largess* of delight," Tennyson's "In Memoriam," xxix.).

lar-ghet-to (lär-get′tō). [It., dim. of *largo*: see *largo*.] In *music*: **I.** *a.* Somewhat slow; not so slow as largo, but usually slower than andante. **II.** *n.*; pl. *-tos* (-tōz). A larghetto movement.

lar-gish (lär′jish), *a.* Rather large: as, "The world's a *largish* place" (George Eliot's "Felix Holt," xi.).

lar-go (lär′gō). [It., < L. *largus*, E. *large*.] In *music*: **I.** *a.*

Slow, in a broad, dignified style. **II.** *n.*; pl. *-gos* (-gōz). A largo movement.

lar-i-at (lar′i-at), *n.* [Sp. *la reata*, 'the rope': see *reata*.] A rope or cord for picketing horses or mules while grazing; also, a long, noosed rope for catching horses, cattle, etc.; a lasso. [Western U. S.]—**lar′i-at,** *v. t.*; *-ated, -ating.* To picket or secure with a lariat or rope; also, to catch with a lariat or lasso. [Western U. S.]

lar-ine (lar′in), *a.* [NL. *Larinæ*, < LL. *larus*, < Gr. λάρος, kind of sea-bird.] In *zoöl.*, of or pertaining to the *Larinæ*, the subfamily of birds containing the gulls; of the nature of or resembling a gull.

lark[1] (lärk), *n.* [AS. *lāwerce* = D. *leeuwerik* = G. *lerche*, lark.] Any of various oscine singing birds, mostly of the Old World, of the family *Alaudidæ*, characterized by an unusually long hind claw, esp. the skylark, *Alauda arvensis*; also, any of various similar birds of other families.

lark[2] (lärk), *v.* [Perhaps a var. of *lake*[2]: cf. *skylark*, *v.*] **I.** *intr.* To frolic; play pranks; also, to ride in a frolicsome manner; ride across country. [Colloq.] **II.** *tr.* To make sport of, or tease (as, "a staid English maid . . . whom Georgy used to *'lark'* dreadfully with accounts of German robbers and ghosts": Thackeray's "Vanity Fair," lxvi.); also, to ride (a horse) across country. [Colloq.]—**lark**[2], *n.* A merry adventure; a frolic; a prank: as, "When you're well enough to go out for a ride—what *larks!*" (Dickens's "Great Expectations," lvii.). [Colloq.]

lark=bun-ting (lärk′bun′ting), *n.* A fringilline bird, *Calamospiza bicolor*, of the western U. S., the male of which is black with a white patch on the wing.

Lark-bunting.

lark-er (lär′kėr), *n.* One who larks. [Colloq.].

lark=heel (lärk′hēl), *n.* A long, projecting heel, occurring esp. in negroes.—**lark′=heeled,** *a.*

lark-spur (lärk′spėr), *n.* Any of the herbs constituting the ranunculaceous genus *Delphinium*, certain species of which are cultivated for their showy, irregular flowers: so called from the long spur of the calyx, which resembles the hind claw of a lark.

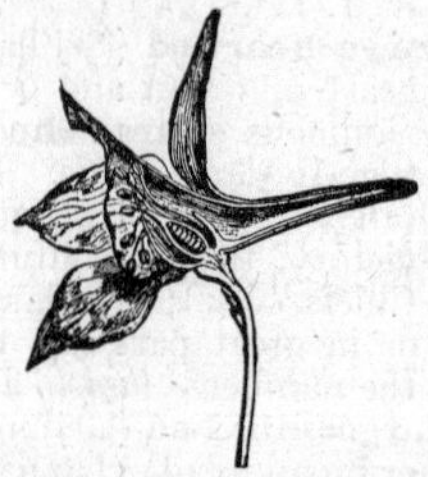

Flower of Larkspur (*Delphinium consolida*), cut longitudinally.

lar-moy-ant (lär-moi′ant, F. lär-mwo-yäṅ), *a.* [F., ppr. of *larmoyer*, be tearful, < *larme*, < L. *lacrima*, a tear.] Tearful; lacrymose.

lar-nax (lär′naks), *n.* [Gr. λάρναξ.] In *Gr. antiq.*, a box or coffer; esp., a box-like receptacle of clay or terra-cotta, often painted, found in early Greek or Mycenæan tombs.

Larnax. — Terra-cotta, from Crete.

lar-oid (lar′oid), *a.* [LL. *larus*: see *larine* and *-oid*.] Gull-like; belonging to the *Laridæ*, or gull family of birds.

lar-ri-kin (lar′i-kin), *n.* [Origin uncertain.] A street rowdy; a hoodlum. [Chiefly Australia.]

lar-rup (lar′up), *v. t.*; *-ruped, -ruping.* [Origin uncertain.] To beat; flog; thrash: as, "I . . . was *larruped* with the rope" (Dickens's "Hard Times," i. 5). [Colloq.]—**lar′rup-er,** *n.*

lar-um (lar′um, lăr′um, or lär′um), *n.* Shortened form of *alarum*, for *alarm*; as, "the first *larum* of the cock's shrill throat" (Cowper's "Task," iv. 569). [Archaic.]

lar-va (lär′vạ), *n.*; pl. *larvæ* (-vē). [NL. use of L. *larva*, ghost, specter, skeleton, mask.] In *zoöl.*, an insect undergoing metamorphosis, in the form which it has (as that of a caterpillar, grub, maggot, or the like) from the time it emerges from the egg until it becomes a pupa; also, any animal in an analogous immature form, as the tadpole, which develops into a frog, toad, or the like.—**lar′val,** *a.* Of, pertaining to, or in the form of a larva; also, in *pathol.*, of disease, masked, or not clearly defined.—**lar′vi-cide** (-vi-sīd), *n.* [See *-cide*.] An agent for killing larvæ, as of mosquitoes.—**lar-vip′a-rous** (-vip′ạ-rus), *a.* [See *-parous*.] Of certain insects, giving birth to young which have already passed from the egg to the larval stage.

la-ryn-ge-al (lạ-rin′jē-ạl), *a.* Of or pertaining to the larynx.

lar-yn-gi-tis (lar-in-jī′tis), *n.* [NL.] In *pathol.*, inflammation of the larynx.—**lar-yn-git′ic** (-jit′ik), *a.*

laryngo-. Form of Gr. λάρυγξ (λαρυγγ-), larynx, used in combination.—**lar-yn-gol-o-gy** (lar-ing-gol′ọ-ji), *n.* [+ *-logy*.] The science of the larynx and its diseases.—**la-ryn-go-log-i-cal** (lạ-ring-gọ-loj′i-kạl), *a.*—**lar-yn-gol′o-gist** (-jist), *n.*—**la-ryn′go-scope** (-skōp), *n.* [+ *-scope*.] An optical apparatus for examining the larynx.—**la-ryn-go-scop′ic** (-skop′ik), *a.*—**lar-yn-got′o-my** (-got′ọ-mi), *n.* [+ *-tomy*.] In *surg.*, the operation of cutting into the larynx.

lar-ynx (lar′ingks), *n.*; pl. *larynxes* or *larynges* (lạ-rin′jēz). [NL., < Gr. λάρυγξ (λαρυγγ-).] In *anat.*, the cavity at the upper end of the human trachea or windpipe, containing the vocal cords and acting as the organ of voice; a similar vocal organ in other mammals, etc., or a corresponding structure in other animals; in birds, either of two cavities, one at the top and one at the bottom of the trachea, the bottom one being the true vocal organ or syrinx.

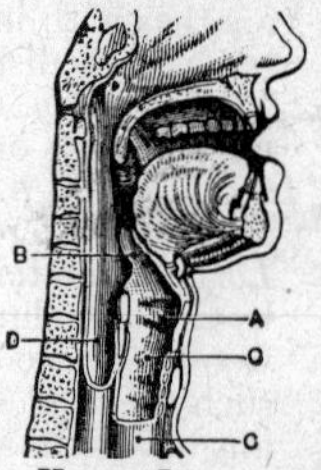

Human Larynx, as seen internally. — *A*, larynx; *B*, epiglottis; *C*, *C*, trachea; *D*, esophagus, or gullet.

las-car (las′kạ̈r or las-kär′), *n.* [Hind. and Pers. *lashkar*, army, camp.] A native East Indian artilleryman, tent-pitcher, or army servant; also, an East Indian sailor.

las-civ-i-ous (lạ-siv′i-us), *a.* [OF. *lascivieux*, < L. *lascivia*, wantonness, < *lascivus*, playful, wanton.] Inclined to lust, wanton, or lewd; also, inciting to lust or wantonness (as, "He capers nimbly in a lady's chamber To the *lascivious* pleasing of a lute": Shakspere's "Richard III.," i. 1. 13). —**las-civ′i-ous-ly,** *adv.*—**las-civ′i-ous-ness,** *n.*

lash (lash), *v.* [ME. *laschen*, *lasshen*, rush, dash, strike; perhaps imit.] **I.** *intr.* To move suddenly and swiftly, rush, dash, or flash (as, "The fringe Of that great breaker, sweeping up the strand, *Lash'd* at the wizard": Tennyson's "Coming of Arthur," 387); hence, to burst (*out*) into violent action or speech; launch (*out*) into excess or extravagance; also, to strike vigorously, as with a weapon, whip, or the like (as, "Heaping huge strokes . . . And *lashing* dreadfully at every part," Spenser's "Faerie Queene," iv. 6. 16: sometimes with *out*); kick (*out*), as a horse; fig., to direct a severe verbal attack, as by censure or satire (as, "to *lash* at vice": Dryden's tr. Persius's "Satires," v. 22). **II.** *tr.* To dash, fling, or toss suddenly and swiftly (as, "He falls, and, *lashing* up his heels, his rider throws": Dryden's tr. Ovid's "Metamorphoses," xii. 472); move or switch sharply through the air (as, a driver *lashes* his whip; "The oxen *lashed* their tails," Whittier's "Snow-Bound"); also (usually with *out*), to pour out vehemently, as words†, or spend extravagantly, as money†; also, to strike or beat, now usually with a whip or something slender and flexible; whip, flog, or scourge; drive by strokes of a whip or the like (as, "Yuba Bill . . . madly *lashed* his horses forward": Bret Harte's "Miggles"); beat violently or sharply against (as, the waves *lash* the shore; the rain *lashes* the window-panes); fig., to assail severely with words as by censure or satire (as, "Then wi' a rhyme or sang he *lasht* 'em": Burns's "Elegy on Ruisseaux"); castigate; also, to bind or fasten with a rope, cord, or the like (esp. *naut.*: as, to *lash* a person to the mast; to *lash* spars together to form a raft).—**lash,** *n.* A swift, dashing or sweeping movement, or switch (as, a *lash* of an animal's tail); also, a swift stroke or blow, now usually with a whip, thong, rope, or anything slender and flexible (specif. as a punishment: as, to be sentenced to fifty *lashes*); a violent beating or impact, as of waves, rain, etc., against something (as, "the *lashes* of a wintry storm": Cowper's "Hope," 185); fig., a sharp stroke given to the feelings, etc. (as, "How smart a *lash* that speech doth give my conscience!" Shakspere's "Hamlet," iii. 1. 50); a severe stroke of censure or satire; also, the flexible part of a whip, or the piece of cord or the like forming the extremity of a whip; anything slender and flexible used to whip with (as, "The Anglo-Saxons whipped prisoners with a three-corded knotted *lash*": Encyc. Brit., 11th ed., XXVIII. 590); a whip or scourge (also fig.); also, an eyelash (as, "Her large dark eyes hid a soft roguishness under their long *lashes*": George Eliot's "Adam Bede," vii.).—**lashed,** *a.* Having lashes, or eyelashes: as, long-*lashed* eyes.—**lash'er,** *n.* One who or that which lashes; specif., the water that lashes or rushes over an opening in a weir, or the pool formed by it (local, Eng.: as, "The stream was so strong, from the great fall of water from the *lasher* above, that Vere was exhausted," Disraeli's "Coningsby," i. 9).—**lash'ing,** *n.* The act of one who or that which lashes; a whipping or flogging; a binding or fastening with a rope or the like, or the rope or the like used; also, *pl.*, abundance or great plenty (prov.).—**lash'less,** *a.* Without lashes, or eyelashes, as eyes.

lass (las), *n.* [ME. *lasse, lasce*; origin uncertain.] A girl, or young woman (as, "A bonnie *lass*, I will confess, Is pleasant to the ee": Burns's "O, Once I Lov'd a Bonnie Lass"); also, a female sweetheart (as, "It was a lover and his *lass*": Shakspere's "As You Like It," v. 3. 17); also, a maid-servant (Sc. and north. Eng.).—**las'sie,** *n.* A young lass or girl: as, "My love she's but a *lassie* yet" (first line and title of a song by Burns). [Chiefly Sc.]

las-si-tude (las'i-tūd), *n.* [F. *lassitude*, < L. *lassitudo*, < *lassus*, faint, weary.] Weariness of body or mind; a state or feeling of weakened energies, as from physical or mental strain, oppressive climate, morbid conditions, etc.; languor: as, "His anger had evaporated; he felt nothing but utter *lassitude*" (Galsworthy's "Saint's Progress," ii. 9).

las-so (las'ō), *n.*; pl. *lassos* or *lassoes* (-ōz). [Sp. *lazo*, < L. *laqueus*, noose, snare: cf. *lace*.] A long rope or line of hide or other material, with a running noose at one end, used for catching horses, cattle, etc.: as, "The Californian horsemen seldom ride out without the *lasso* . . . a long coil of cord, with a slip noose" (Irving's "Captain Bonneville," xxxix.); "The swift long *lasso* twirl'd above is thrown From flying hand" (Joaquin Miller's "Vaquero").—**las'so,** *v. t.*; *-soed, -soing.* To catch with a lasso.—**las'so=cell,** *n.* In *zoöl.*, a nematocyst.—**las'so-er,** *n.*

las-sock (las'ọk), *n.* A little lass: as, "I mind, when I was a gilpy of a *lassock*, seeing the Duke" (Scott's "Old Mortality," v.). [Sc.]

last[1] (lâst), *n.* [AS. *lǣste*, last, *lāst*, footprint, track, = D. *leest*, G. *leisten*, last, = Icel. *leistr*, foot, sock, = Goth. *laists*, footprint, track: cf. *last*[2].] A model of the human foot, of wood or other material, on which boots or shoes are shaped, as in the making.—**last**[1], *v. t.* To shape on or fit to a last.

last[2] (lâst), *v.* [AS. *lǣstan*, follow, perform, continue, last, = OHG. *leisten*, follow, G. perform, = Goth. *laistjan*, follow, lit. 'track'; from the noun represented by E. *last*[1].] **I.**† *tr.* To follow; follow out; carry out; perform. **II.** *intr.* To go on, or continue in progress (as, the storm *lasted* three days); hence, to continue in existence or life, or endure (as, so long as the world *lasts*; the sick man cannot *last* till morning); continue without end or cessation (as, times or luck too good to *last*); hold out, or continue unexpended or unexhausted (as, while the money *lasts*; "The sooner all the wine was gone the better, as there would be nothing done while it *lasted*," Marryat's "Mr. Midshipman Easy," xiv.); continue in good condition or unimpaired (as, the cloth is too flimsy to *last*; colors that *last*); continue in force, vigor, effectiveness, etc. (as, to *last* in a race or contest; to *last* in popularity).—**last**[2], *n.* Continuance or duration (now rare); also, power of endurance, or staying power.

last[3] (lâst), *n.* [AS. *hlæst* = D. and G. *last*, load; from the root of E. *lade*.] A load†; also, a certain weight or measure, varying in amount in different localities and for different commodities, often equivalent to 4,000 pounds.

last[4] (lâst), *a.* [ME. *last, latst*, for *latest*, superl. of *lat, late*, E. *late*.] Occurring or coming latest, or after all others, as in time, order, or place (as, the *last* day of the year; the *last* man in the procession; the *last* line on the page); also, latest or next before the present or other particular time or instance (as, I saw him *last* week; the *last* two days had been stormy; this book is better than the *last* one); also, having no other or others following, or final (as, in his *last* hours; the *last* day, the judgment-day); final and conclusive (as, to say the *last* word on a subject); also, that remains or is reached after all others have disappeared or been exhausted (as, "'Tis the *last* rose of summer Left blooming alone," T. Moore's "'Tis the Last Rose of Summer"; his *last* dollar; "Patriotism is the *last* refuge of a scoundrel," Johnson, in Boswell's "Johnson," April 7, 1775); being the only remaining; also, coming after all others in importance or estimation (as, "If any man desire to be first, the same shall be *last* of all, and servant of all": Mark, ix. 35); coming after all others in suitability or likelihood, or least suitable or likely (as, he is the *last* person to be trifled with; the very *last* thing one would expect to find); also, utmost or extreme (as, to the *last* degree; "a certain document of the *last* importance," Poe's "Purloined Letter").—**Last Judgment.** See *judgment*.—**Last Supper,** the supper of Jesus and his apostles on the eve of his crucifixion, at which he instituted the sacrament of the Lord's Supper.—**last**[4], *n.* That which is last; the end or conclusion: as, at *last* (finally); to the *last* (until the end).—**last**[4], *adv.* After all others (as, to come *last* in time or order); also, on the occasion next before the present or some particular time (as, when did you *last* see him?); also, in the end, or finally; in conclusion; in the last place, or lastly.

last-er[1] (lâs'tėr), *n.* [See *last*[1].] One who fits the parts of boots or shoes to lasts; also, a tool used in stretching leather on a last.

last-er[2] (lâs'tėr), *n.* [See *last*[2].] One who or that which lasts or endures.

last-ing (lâs'ting), *n.* [See *last*[2].] Continuance or duration; endurance; permanence; also, a strong, durable, closely woven woolen fabric, used for the uppers of shoes, for covering buttons, etc.—**last'ing,** *p. a.* That lasts; enduring; permanent; durable.—**last'ing-ly,** *adv.*—**last'ing-ness,** *n.*

last-ly (lâst'li), *adv.* [See *last*[4], *a.*] In the end, or finally; now, esp., in enumerating facts, etc., in conclusion, or in the last place (as, "Sixth and *lastly*, they have belied a lady": Shakspere's "Much Ado about Nothing," v. i. 221).

lat (lät), *n.* [Hindi.] In India, an isolated pillar or column, esp. one of a class of Buddhist monumental pillars.

Lat.—Asoka's Pillar, Allahabad.

lat-a-ki-a (lat-ạ-kē'ạ̈), *n.* [From *Latakia* (anciently *Laodicea*), in Syria.] [Also *cap.*] A fine variety of Turkish tobacco: as, "The fragrant fumes of the *Latakiah* must have helped to keep me on my good behaviour" (Kinglake's "Eothen," viii.).

la-ta-ni-a (lạ-tā'ni-ạ̈), *n.* [NL.] Any of the fan-palms of the genus *Latania*, native in the Mascarene Islands but much cultivated in greenhouses. See cut on following page.

latch[1] (lach), *v. t.* [ME. *lacchen*, < AS. *læccan*, seize.] To seize; take; catch: as, "I have words That would be howl'd out in the desert air, Where hearing should not *latch* them" (Shakspere's "Macbeth," iv. 3. 195). [Now prov. Eng.]

latch[2] (lach), *n.* [ME. *lacche*, appar. < *lacchen*, E. *latch*[1].] A device for holding a door, gate, or the like closed or fastened without the operation of bolting or locking, consisting in its simple form of a movable bar falling or sliding into a catch (from which it is commonly released, on the other side of a door, by a string or a lever passed through the door), but occurring in other forms, now often one in which a movable piece of metal is shot by means of a spring into a cavity (from which it is often released, on the other side of a door, by a key).—**latch**[2], *v. t.* or *i.* To close or fasten with a latch.

Latania.

latch-et (lach′et), *n.* [OF. *lachet*, var. of *lacet*, dim. of *laz*, E. *lace*.] A strap or lace for fastening a shoe: as, "There cometh one . . . the *latchet* of whose shoes I am not worthy to stoop down and unloose" (Mark, i. 7). [Archaic.]

latch=key (lach′kē), *n.* A key for drawing back or releasing a latch, esp. a latch on the outer door of a house.

latch=string (lach′string), *n.* A string passed through a hole in a door, for raising the latch from the outside.

late (lāt), *a.*; compar. *later*, superl. *latest* (cf. *latter* and *last*[4]). [AS. *læt*, slow, tardy, late, = D. *laat* = G. *lass* = Icel. *latr* = Goth. *lats*, slothful; akin to E. *let*[1] and *let*[2].] Slow (obs. or prov. Eng.); hence, occurring, coming, or being after the usual or proper time (as, *late* frosts; *late* roses; to be *late*, or too *late*, for a train); behindhand, tardy, or delayed; backward, as a season, crop, etc.; also, continued until after the usual time or hour, or protracted (as, a *late* session; a *late* theatrical performance); also, far advanced in time (as, at a *late* hour in the day or evening; in the *later* years of one's life, or of the century); occurring at an advanced stage in life (as, "I have been told that *late* marriages are not eminently happy": Johnson's "Rasselas," xxix.); belonging to an advanced period or stage in the history or development of something (as, *Late* Greek, see *Greek*, *n.*; *Late* Latin, see *Latin*, *n.*); also, belonging to time just before the present, or recent (as, of *late* years; the *late* war; the *latest* fashions); having recently been (what is said: as, one's *late* employer; his *late* residence); recently deceased (as, "Of which disease Our *late* king, Richard, being infected, died": Shakspere's "2 Henry IV.," iv. 1. 58).—**of late**, during time shortly before the present; lately; recently: as, the practice has been losing ground *of late*.—**late,** *adv.* After the usual or proper time, or after delay (as, to come *late*); also, until after the usual time or hour (as, to work *late*); often, until a late hour at night (as, to sit up *late*); also, at or to an advanced time, period, or stage (as, this happened *late* in the afternoon; to marry *late* in life; this view lasted *late* in the century); also, recently, or of late (now poetic: as, "Thou art he, whom *late* our Arthur made Knight of his table," Tennyson's "Pelleas and Ettarre," 311); now, more commonly, recently but no longer (as, John Smith, *late* of Boston).

lat-ed (lā′ted), *a.* [From *late*, *a.*] Belated: as, "Now spurs the *lated* traveller apace To gain the timely inn" (Shakspere's "Macbeth," iii. 3. 6); "The *lated* peasant shunn'd the dell" (Scott's "Rokeby," ii. 10). [Poetic.]

la-teen (la-tēn′), *a.* [F. (*voile*) *latine*, 'Latin (sail).'] *Naut.*, noting a triangular sail extended by a long yard at an angle of about 45° to the mast, common on the Mediterranean, etc.; also, pertaining to or having such a sail or sails (as, a *lateen* yard, rig, or vessel).—**la-teen′=rigged,** *a.* Having a lateen sail or lateen sails.

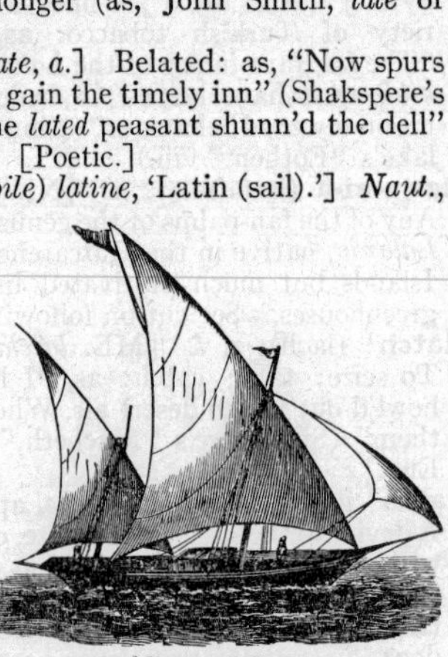
Lateen Sail.

late-ly (lāt′li), *adv.* Of late; recently; not long since.

lat-en (lā′tn), *v. i.* or *t.* To become or make late.

la-ten-cy (lā′tẹn-si), *n.* The state of being latent.

late-ness (lāt′nes), *n.* The state or fact of being late.

la-tent (lā′tẹnt), *a.* [L. *latens* (*latent-*), ppr. of *latere*, lie hid, akin to Gr. λανθάνειν, escape notice, λανθάνεσθαι, forget: see *lanthanum* and *Lethe*.] Hidden; concealed; present, but not visible or apparent: as, *latent* germs of disease; *latent* powers or ability.—**latent heat,** in *physics*, heat concerned in changing the state of a body but not its temperature, as the heat required to convert ice at 0° C. into water at 0° C.; the quantity of heat required to melt unit mass of a solid ('latent heat of fusion'); the quantity of heat required to vaporize unit mass of a liquid ('latent heat of vaporization').—**la′tent-ly,** *adv.*

lat-er (lā′tėr). [Compar. of *late*.] **I.** *a.* More late. **II.** *adv.* Late in a greater degree (as, to stay *later* than usual); also, at a later time or period, subsequently, or afterward (as, it can be done *later*, or *later* on; Prince Hal, *later* King Henry V. of England).

-later. [Gr. -λάτρης, < λατρεύειν, serve.] A noun termination meaning 'worshiper,' as in *idolater*, *physiolater*, *pyrolater*, and other words, corresponding usually to nouns ending in *-latry*.

lat-er-ad (lat′ẹ-rad), *adv.* [L. *latus* (*later-*), side: see *-ad*.] In *anat.*, toward the side.

lat-er-al (lat′ẹ-rąl). [L. *lateralis*, < *latus* (*later-*), side.] **I.** *a.* Of or pertaining to the side; situated at, proceeding from, or directed to a side. **II.** *n.* A lateral part or extension, as a branch or shoot.—**lat′er-al-ly,** *adv.*

Lat-er-an (lat′ẹ-rąn), *a.* Named from the ancient Roman family of the Laterani (early owners of the site): applied to a basilica in Rome, 'St. John Lateran,' ranking highest of all Roman Catholic churches, to an adjoining palace, which replaces an earlier palace once the residence of the popes, and hence to a number of general church councils held there.

lat-er-i-, lat-er-o- (lat′ẹ-ri-, -ẹ-rọ-). Forms of L. *latus* (*later-*), side, used in combination, as in *lateriflexion* (a bending to one side), *laterofrontal* (at one side, in front).

lat-er-ite (lat′ẹ-rīt), *n.* [L. *later*, a brick.] A reddish ferruginous soil formed in tropical regions by the decomposition of the underlying rocks, or, sometimes, a similar soil formed of materials transported by water; hence, any soil produced by the decomposition of the rocks beneath it.—**lat-er-it′ic** (-ẹ-rit′ik), *a.*

lat-er-i-tious (lat-ẹ-rish′us), *a.* [L. *lateritius*, *latericius*, < *later*, a brick.] Pertaining to or resembling bricks; of the red color characteristic of bricks.

lat′er-o-. See *lateri-*.

la-tes-cent (lą-tes′ẹnt), *a.* [L. *latescens* (*-ent-*), ppr. of *latescere*, hide one's self, < *latere*, lie hid: see *latent*.] Becoming latent, hidden, or obscure.—**la-tes′cence,** *n.*

lat-est (lā′test). [Superl. of *late*.] **I.** *a.* Most late; also, last (archaic: as, "He begs their flatt'ry with his *latest* breath," Cowper's "Truth," 315). **II.** *adv.* Late in the greatest degree, or after all others: as, the *latest*-born child.

la-tex (lā′teks), *n.* [L., a liquid.] In *bot.*, a milky liquid in certain plants, as milkweeds, euphorbias, poppies (see *opium*), the plants yielding india-rubber (see *india-rubber*), etc., which coagulates on exposure to the air.

lath (lȧth), *n.*; pl. *laths* (lȧᴛʜz). [ME. *laththe* (AS. *lætt*) = G. *latte*, lath.] A thin, narrow strip of wood used with others like it to form a groundwork for supporting the slates or other covering of a roof or the plastering of a wall or ceiling, to construct latticework, and for other purposes; also, such strips collectively, or work consisting of such strips (as, "a house built . . . with *lath* and plaster": Defoe's "Robinson Crusoe," ii. 14); also, wire cloth or the like used in place of laths, as in plastering; also, a thin, narrow, flat piece of wood used for any purpose; often, such a piece of wood carried or used by a performer (cf. *slapstick*, *n.*); wood in this form as the material of a counterfeit weapon, as that ('dagger of lath') carried by the Vice in the old morality plays (as, "Like to the old Vice . . . Who, with dagger of *lath*, In his rage and his wrath, Cries, ah, ha! to the devil," Shakspere's "Twelfth Night," iv. 2. 136; "He was equipped with a sword of *lath*, resembling that with which Harlequin operates his wonders upon the modern stage," Scott's "Ivanhoe," i.).—**lath,** *v. t.* To cover or line with laths.

lathe[1] (lāᴛʜ), *n.* [Prob. from Scand.: cf. Dan. *dreielad*, turning-lathe.] A machine for use in working wood, metal, etc., which holds the material and rotates it against a tool that shapes it; also, some similar machine on which articles are rotated in working, as one used in ironing, brushing, or otherwise treating hats; specif., a small form of potters' wheel.—**lathe**[1], *v. t.*; *lathed*, *lathing*. To cut, shape, or otherwise treat on a lathe.

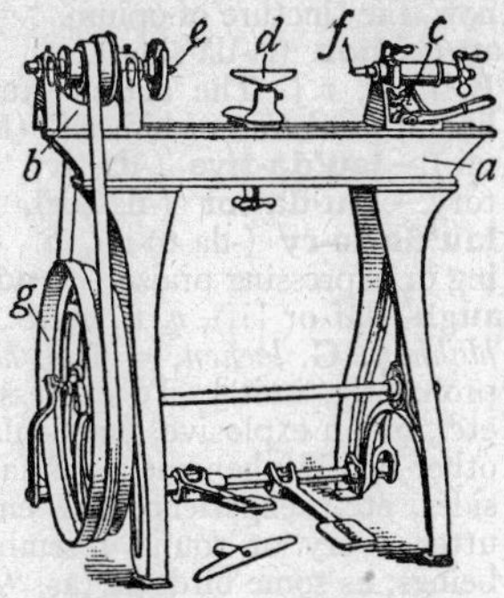

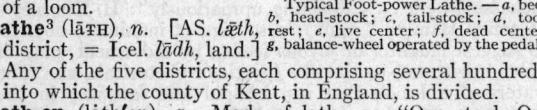

Typical Foot-power Lathe. —*a*, bed; *b*, head-stock; *c*, tail-stock; *d*, tool-rest; *e*, live center; *f*, dead center; *g*, balance-wheel operated by the pedals.

lathe[2] (lāᴛʜ), *n.* [= Sw. *lad* = G. *lade*, lathe of loom: cf. *lay*[6].] The movable frame which carries the reed of a loom.

lathe[3] (lāᴛʜ), *n.* [AS. *lǣth*, district, = Icel. *lādh*, land.] Any of the five districts, each comprising several hundreds, into which the county of Kent, in England, is divided.

lath-en (lȧth'ẹn), *a.* Made of lath: as, "One stool, One table and one *lathen* crucifix" (Browning's "Ring and the Book," i.). [Rare.]

lath-er[1] (lȧth'ėr), *n.* A workman who puts up laths, as for plastering.

lath-er[2] (laᴛʜ'ėr), *n.* [AS. *lēathor* = Icel. *laudhr*, washing-soda, foam.] Foam or froth made from soap moistened with water, as by a brush for shaving; also, foam or froth formed in profuse sweating, as of a horse.—**lath'er**[2], *v.* **I.** *tr.* To apply lather to; cover with lather; also, to beat or flog (colloq.). **II.** *intr.* To form a lather; also, to become covered with lather, as a horse.—**lath'er-er**, *n.*—**lath'er-y**, *a.* Consisting of or covered with lather.

lath-ing (lȧth'ing), *n.* The act or process of applying laths to a wall or the like; also, work consisting of laths; laths collectively.

lath-y (lȧth'i), *a.* Lath-like; long and slender; thin: as, "Phineas was tall and *lathy*" (Mrs. Stowe's "Uncle Tom's Cabin," xvii.).

lat-i-cif-er-ous (lat-i-sif'ẹ-rus), *a.* [L. *latex* (*latic-*), a liquid: see *-ferous*.] In *bot.*, bearing or containing latex.

lat-i-fo-li-ate (lat-i-fō'li-ạt), *a.* [L. *latus*, broad, + *folium*, leaf.] In *bot.*, having broad leaves.

lat-i-go (lat'i-gō), *n.*; pl. *-gos* (-gōz). [Sp. *látigo*.] A strong leather strap attached to a saddle, for tightening and fastening the cinch. [Western U. S. and Spanish America.]

Lat-in (lat'in), *a.* [L. *Latinus*, < *Latium*, Latium.] Of or pertaining to Latium (a country of ancient Italy in which Rome was situated) or its inhabitants (the Latins or Romans); also, pertaining to, composed in, or versed in the language of the ancient Romans or its later forms (as, *Latin* grammar; a *Latin* poem; a *Latin* scholar); also, noting or pertaining to the Western Church (which from early times down to the Reformation everywhere used Latin as its official language) or the Roman Catholic Church (as, the *Latin* Church; the *Latin* fathers); also, noting or pertaining to those races or peoples (the Italians, French, Spanish, etc.) using languages derived from that of ancient Rome.—**Latin cross**, an upright bar crossed near the top by a shorter transverse piece.—**Latin Empire**, the empire of Constantinople while under Latin emperors, from 1204 to 1261.—**Lat'in**, *n.* A native or inhabitant of ancient Latium; an ancient Roman; also, a member of any Latin race; also, a member of the Latin Church (now rare); also, esp., the language of the Latins or ancient Romans; the Latin language (divided for convenience into Old Latin; Latin, or classical Latin, extending to A.D. 200; Late Latin, from A.D. 200 to 600; Middle Latin, from A.D. 600 to 1500; and the subsequent New Latin).—**Low Latin**, the Latin language of times subsequent to the classical period, or to the fall of the Roman (Western) Empire, with a heavy admixture of foreign or barbarous elements; medieval Latin.—**Lat'in-ism**, *n.* Conformity to Latin models, or use of Latin forms; also, a Latin idiom or mode of expression.—**Lat'in-ist**, *n.* One skilled in Latin; a Latin scholar: as, "Church-ladders are not always mounted best By learned clerks and *Latinists* profess'd" (Cowper's "Tirocinium," 382).—**Lat-in-is'tic**, *a.*—**La-tin-i-ty** (lạ-tin'i-ti), *n.* [L. *latinitas*.] Use of the Latin language; method of speaking or writing Latin; Latin style or idiom: as, "Erasmus . . . will long be honored for his elegant *Latinity*" (Motley's "Dutch Republic," Introd., xii.).—**Lat'in-ize** (-īz), *v.*; *-ized*, *-izing*. **I.** *tr.* To translate into Latin; also, to make Latin in form or character; also, to cause to conform to the customs, etc., of the Latins or the Latin Church. **II.** *intr.* To use Latin words, idioms, etc.—**Lat"in-i-za'tion** (-i-zā'shọn), *n.*

lat-ish (lā'tish), *a.* and *adv.* Somewhat late.

lat-i-tude (lat'i-tūd), *n.* [L. *latitudo* (*latitudin-*), breadth, < *latus*, broad.] Breadth or width (now only humorous); also, extent, range, or scope (as, "This doctrine . . . hath a more ample *latitude* and extent than is perceived": Bacon's "Advancement of Learning," ii. 14. 7); esp., freedom from narrow restrictions; permitted freedom of action, opinion, etc. (as, "He gave a *latitude* to his friend's tongue, and desired him to speak plainly what he knew": Fielding's "Tom Jones," xv. 9); liberality in construction or interpretation (as, "Natural good is defined by Cumberland with more *latitude* than has been used by Paley": Hallam's "Literature of Europe," iv. 4. § 27); also, in *geog.*, angular distance measured on a meridian; esp., the angular distance north or south from the equator of a point on the earth's surface, measured on the meridian of the point; hence, a place or region as marked by its latitude (as, "I was something chilly, which I knew was not usual in that *latitude*": Defoe's "Robinson Crusoe," i. 6); also, in *astron.*, the angular distance of a heavenly body from the ecliptic ('celestial latitude').—**lat-i-tu'di-nal** (-tū'di-nạl), *a.* Pertaining to latitude.—**lat"i-tu-di-na'ri-an** (-nā'ri-ạn). **I.** *a.* Allowing, or characterized by, latitude in opinion or conduct; not insisting on or not marked by strict adherence to established principles or formulas, esp. in religious views. **II.** *n.* One who is latitudinarian in opinion or conduct, esp. in religious matters; specif., one of those divines of the Anglican Church in the 17th century who maintained the wisdom of the episcopal form of government and ritual, but denied their divine origin and authority; hence, one who regards with comparative indifference particular creeds, methods of church government, and forms of public worship.—**lat"i-tu-di-na'ri-an-ism**, *n.*

la-tri-a (lạ-trī'ạ), *n.* [LL., < Gr. λατρεία, service, worship, < λατρεύειν, serve.] In *Rom. Cath. theol.*, that supreme worship which may be offered to God only. Cf. *dulia* and *hyperdulia*.

la-trine (lạ-trēn'), *n.* [L. *latrina*, for *lavatrina*, bath, latrine, < *lavare*, wash.] A privy, esp. in a camp, barracks, a factory, or the like.

-latry. [Gr. λατρεία: see *latria*.] A noun termination meaning 'worship,' as in *anthropolatry*, *idolatry*, *necrolatry*, *physiolatry*. Cf. *-later*.

lat-ten (lat'ẹn), *n.* [OF. *laton* (F. *laiton*); perhaps from Teut. and akin to *lath*.] A brass-like alloy, commonly made in thin sheets, formerly much used for church utensils; also, iron plate tinned over; tin-plate; hence, any metal in thin sheets.

lat-ter (lat'ėr), *a.* [ME. *lattre*, *latere*, compar. of *lat*, *late*, E. *late*.] Occurring or coming later, or after some other thing, person, group, etc. (archaic: as, "I will give you the rain of your land in his due season, the first rain and the *latter* rain," Deut. xi. 14; "a *latter* Luther," Tennyson's "Sonnet to J. M. K."); also, being the second mentioned of two (opposed to *former*: as, I prefer the *latter* proposition to the former); also, more advanced in time, or later (as, in these *latter* days of human progress); also, nearer, or comparatively near, to the end or close (as, the *latter* part of the day; the *latter* years of one's life); concluding; being the concluding part of (poetic: as, "Then was *latter* April," Tennyson's "Coming of Arthur," 450); also, last† (as, "and in his bosom spend my *latter* gasp": Shakspere's "1 Henry VI.," ii. 5. 38).—**latter end**, the concluding part (as, the *latter end* of May); specif., the end of one's life, or one's death (as, "For some time it had been manifest to all who saw her, that her *latter end* was drawing nigh": Galt's

"Annals of the Parish," xl.).—**latter Lammas.** See under *Lammas.*—**lat'ter=day,** *a.* Of a latter or more advanced day or period, or modern (as, *latter-day* problems); also, of the concluding or final days of the world (cf. Job, xix. 25; 1 Thes. iii. 13; Jude, 14: as, "The Church of Jesus Christ of *Latter-day* Saints," the official title of the Mormon Church). —**lat'ter-ly,** *adv.* In the latter or concluding part of a period; also, of late, or lately (as, "Mr. Easy was a philosopher, and had *latterly* taken to craniology": Marryat's "Mr. Midshipman Easy," iii.).—**lat'ter-most,** *a. superl.* Latest; last.

lat-tice (lat'is), *n.* [OF. F. *lattis,* < *latte,* lath; from Teut., and akin to E. *lath.*] A structure of crossed wooden or metal strips with open spaces between, used as a screen, etc.; a window, gate, or the like, so constructed; specif., a window of latticework, usually painted red, used as the sign of an ale-house or inn†; also, latticework (as, "My good window of *lattice,* fare thee well": Shakspere's "All's Well," ii. 3. 225).—**lat'tice,** *v. t.*; *-ticed, -ticing.* To furnish with a lattice or latticework (as, "Each window was *latticed* with iron wire on the outside": Swift's "Gulliver's Travels," ii. 4); also, to form into or arrange like latticework; give the appearance of a lattice to. —**lat'tice=gird'er,** *n.* A built-up girder in which the central portion or web consists of diagonal pieces arranged like latticework.—**lat'tice-leaf,** *n.* Any of certain old-world monocotyledonous water-plants (genus *Aponogeton*) remarkable for their skeleton leaves, the cellular tissue between the veins being wanting, as *A. fenestralis,* of Madagascar. Also **lat'tice=plant.**—**lat'tice-work,** *n.* Work consisting of crossed strips with openings between; also, a lattice.—**lat-ti-cing** (lat'i-sing), *n.* The act or process of furnishing with or making a lattice or latticework; also, latticework.

Lattice-window.

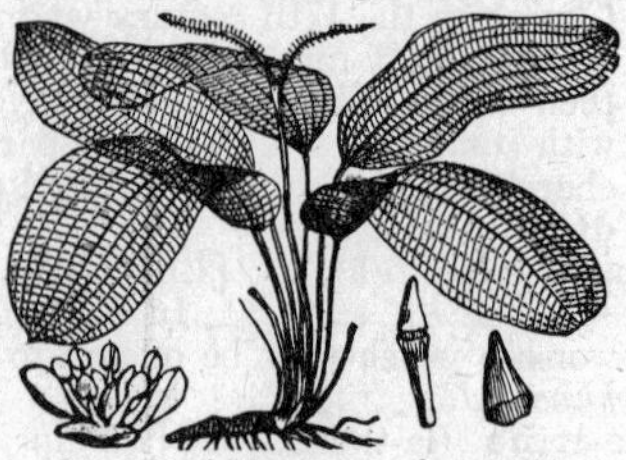

Latticeleaf (*Aponogeton fenestralis*).

Lat-vi-an (lat'vi-ạn). **I.** *a.* Of or pertaining to Latvia (the country of the Letts), on the eastern coast of the Baltic Sea, north of Lithuania and south of Esthonia. **II.** *n.* An inhabitant of Latvia.

laud (lâd), *n.* [OF. *laude,* < L. *laus* (*laud-*), praise.] Praise, or high commendation (now rare: as, "*Laud* be to God!" Shakspere's "2 Henry IV.," iv. 5. 236; "Great *laud* and praise were mine," Pope's tr. Homer's "Odyssey," xiv.); also, a song or ascription of praise, esp. to God (as, "She chanted snatches of old *lauds* [other versions, *tunes*]": Shakspere's "Hamlet," iv. 7. 178); also, *pl., eccles.,* a morning office or service, now usually recited with matins, characterized esp. by psalms of praise to God (Ps. cxlviii.–cl.). —**laud,** *v. t.* [L. *laudare,* < *laus.*] To praise; extol: as, "Praise the Lord, all ye Gentiles; and *laud* him, all ye people" (Rom. xv. 11); "aspirations which are *lauded* up to the skies" (Kingsley's "Alton Locke," v.).—**laud'a-ble,** *a.* [L. *laudabilis.*] Praiseworthy or commendable (as, "We all of us seemed to have come to Blithedale with the one thrifty and *laudable* idea of wearing out our old clothes": Hawthorne's "Blithedale Romance," viii.); also, in *med.,* healthy, wholesome, or not noxious (as, *laudable* pus).—**laud-a-bil'i-ty** (-bil'i-ti), **laud'a-ble-ness,** *n.*—**laud'a-bly,** *adv.*

lau-da-num (lâ'dạ-num), *n.* [NL. (used by Paracelsus), appar. a var. of L. *ladanum*: see *ladanum.*] Formerly, any preparation in which opium was the chief ingredient; now, the tincture of opium.

lau-da-tion (lâ-dā'shọn), *n.* [L. *laudatio(n-),* < *laudare,* E. *laud, v.*] The act of lauding; praise: as, "his very liberal *laudation* of himself" (Dickens's "Dombey and Son," vii.).—**lau'da-tive** (-dạ-tiv), *a.* [L. *laudativus.*] Laudatory.—**lau-da'tor** (-dā'tọr), *n.* [L.] One who lauds.—**lau'da-to-ry** (-dạ-tō-ri), *a.* [LL. *laudatorius.*] Containing or expressing praise.—**laud'er,** *n.*

laugh (läf or lâf), *v. i.* [AS. *hlehhan, hlæhhan,* = OHG. *hlahhan,* G. *lachen,* = Icel. *hlæja* = Goth. *hlahjan,* laugh; prob. orig. imit.] To express mirth, amusement, derision, etc., by an explosive, inarticulate sound of the voice and by other bodily phenomena, as facial distortion, shaking of the sides, etc.; experience the emotion so expressed; also, to utter a cry or sound resembling the laughing of human beings, as some birds do (as, "A mob of jackasses [laughing-jackasses] were . . . *laughing* uproariously": H. Kingsley's "Geoffry Hamlyn," xviii.); also, fig., of inanimate objects, to suggest laughter or joyous feeling by movement, play of light, brightness, or the like (poetic or rhetorical: as, "The waters of a brook that run Limpid and *laughing* in the summer sun," Longfellow's "Masque of Pandora," i.; "In the dazzling goblet *laughs* the wine," Pope's tr. Homer's "Odyssey," iii.; "The heavens *laugh* with you in your jubilee," Wordsworth's "Intimations of Immortality," iv.).—**to laugh at,** to indulge in laughter at; hence, to make fun of, deride, or ridicule (as, "I also will *laugh at* your calamity; I will mock when your fear cometh": Prov. i. 26). —**to laugh in one's sleeve,** to laugh inwardly at something; regard something with feelings of amusement while maintaining a serious countenance or demeanor: as, "His shrewd nephew was *laughing* at him *in his sleeve*" (Kingsley's "Yeast," xiv.).—**to laugh on the other side** (or **wrong side**) **of one's mouth** (or **face**), to do the reverse of laughing; display or feel vexation or sorrow: as, "You'll mayhap be making such a slip yourself some day; you'll *laugh o' th' other side o' your mouth* then" (George Eliot's "Adam Bede," i.).—**laugh,** *v. t.* To give utterance to (laughter or a laugh: as, "He *laugh'd* a laugh of merry scorn," Tennyson's "Lady Clare," 81); utter with laughter (as, "The large Achilles . . . From his deep chest *laughs* out a loud applause": Shakspere's "Troilus and Cressida," i. 3. 163); also, to drive, put, bring, etc., by or with laughter (as, "I shall *laugh* myself to death at this puppy-headed monster," Shakspere's "Tempest," ii. 2. 158; "I strove To *laugh* the thought away," Byron's "Marino Faliero," iv. 1).—**laugh,** *n.* The act or sound of laughing, or laughter (as, "a slap . . . which seemed only to knock out so much more *laugh* from the young ones": Mrs. Stowe's "Uncle Tom's Cabin," iv.); a characteristic manner of laughing; an expression of mirth, derision, etc., by laughing. —**laugh'a-ble,** *a.* Such as to excite laughter.—**laugh'a-ble-ness,** *n.*—**laugh'a-bly,** *adv.*—**laugh'er,** *n.*

laugh-ing (lä'fing or lâ'-), *n.* The act of one who or that which laughs; laughter.—**laugh'ing,** *p. a.* That laughs; giving vent to laughter, as persons; uttering sounds like the laughter of human beings, as some birds; fig., suggesting laughter or joyous feeling by movement, brightness, or the like, as water, etc.—**laugh'ing=gas,** *n.* Nitrous oxide, which when inhaled sometimes produces exhilarating effects: used as an anesthetic in dentistry, etc.—**laugh'ing=jack'ass,** *n.* A harsh-voiced Australian bird, *Dacelo gigas* (a kind of kingfisher), about the size of a crow. —**laugh'ing-ly,** *adv.*—**laugh'ing=stock,** *n.* A butt for laughter; an object of ridicule.

laugh-ter (läf'tėr or lâf'-), *n.* [AS. *hleahtor.*] The action or sound of laughing; sometimes, an experiencing of the emotion expressed by

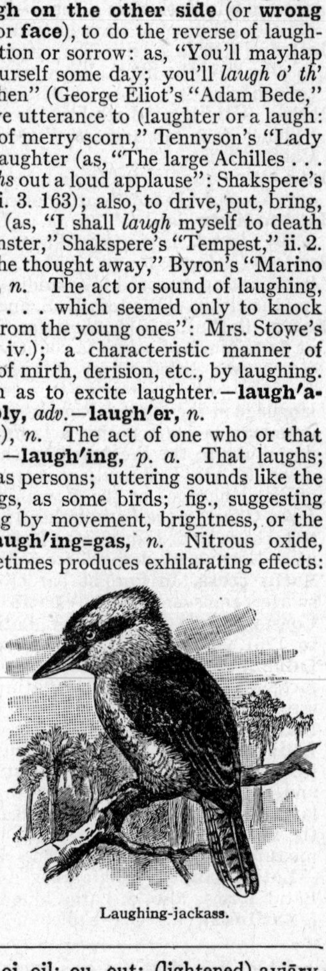

Laughing-jackass.

laughing (as, inward *laughter*); an expression or appearance of merriment or amusement, as in the countenance or eyes; also, a laugh†, or instance of laughing†; also, a subject or matter for laughing (as, "Hath Cassius lived To be but mirth and *laughter* to his Brutus?" Shakspere's "Julius Cæsar," iv. 3. 114).—**laugh'ter-ful,** *a.* Full of or given to laughter; mirthful.—**laugh'ter-less,** *a.* Without laughter.—**laugh'ter=lov"ing,** *a.* Fond of laughter, merriment, or mirth.

launch[1] (lânch or länch), *n.* [Sp. and Pg. *lancha.*] The largest boat carried by a man-of-war; also, a comparatively small boat or vessel, usually more or less open, propelled by steam, gasoline, electricity, or the like.

launch[2] (lânch or länch), *v.* [OF. *lanchier*, var. of *lancier*, E. *lance*, *v.*] **I.** *tr.* To throw or hurl, as a weapon or missile (as, "At him he *launch'd* his spear, and pierc'd his breast": Dryden's tr. Ovid's "Metamorphoses," xii. 161); in general, to cast or direct (as, "a threat *launched* especially at the Despensers": Stubbs's "Constitutional Hist. of Eng.," xvi. § 253); send forth; also, to send out (a boat) into the water (as, "A small fishing canoe, hauled up near by, was quickly *launched*": H. Melville's "Omoo," lvi.); cause (a newly built vessel) to move or slide from the stocks into the water; set afloat, or lower into the water (as, to *launch* a boat from a ship); also, fig., to start on a course, career, etc. (as, "citizens that were *launched* into the world with narrow fortunes": Addison, in "Spectator," 108); set going; also, to pierce†, cut†, or lance† (as, "A sharpe bore-speare, With which he wont to *launch* the salvage hart Of many a Lyon": Spenser's "Faerie Queene," vi. 2. 6). **II.** *intr.* To dart, rush, or bound along (now prov.); also, to start out or forth; push out or put forth on the water (as, "We *launched* for the main coast of Africa": Defoe's "Captain Singleton," iii.); also, fig., to enter on any course of action; burst out or plunge boldly into action, speech, etc.—**launch**[2], *n.* The act of launching; usually, the launching of a boat or vessel, esp. of a newly built vessel.—**launch'er,** *n.*

laun-der (lân'dėr or län'-), *n.* [Contr. of earlier *lavender*, < OF. *lavandier*, masc., *lavandiere* (F. *lavandière*), fem., < L. *lavandus*, gerundive of *lavare*, wash.] One who washes clothes†; also, a trough or channel for conveying water.—**laun'der,** *v. t.* To wash and iron (clothes, etc.).—**laun'der-er,** *n.*—**laun'dress,** *n.* A woman whose occupation is the washing and ironing of clothes, etc.—**laun'dry** (-dri), *n.*; pl. *-dries* (-driz). The act of washing†; also, a place or establishment where clothes, etc., are washed and ironed; also, articles sent to be washed (colloq.).—**laun'dry-man** (-mạn), *n.*; pl. *-men.* A man who works in or conducts a laundry.—**laun'dry-wom"an,** *n.*; pl. *-women* (-wim"en).

lau-ra (lâ'rạ̈), *n.*; pl. *lauras*, L. *lauræ* (-rē). [LL., < LGr. λαύρα, laura, Gr. alley, lane.] Among the early Christians in Palestine, Egypt, etc., a form of monastic community occupying a row or group of detached cells under the authority of a superior.

lau-ra-ceous (lâ-rā'shius), *a.* [L. *laurus*, laurel.] Belonging to the *Lauraceæ*, or laurel family of plants.

lau-re-ate (lâ'rē-ạ̄t). [L. *laureatus*, < *laurea*, laurel-tree, crown of laurel, < *laurus*, laurel.] **I.** *a.* Crowned or decked with laurel as a mark of honor or distinction (as, "The crown Which Petrarch's *laureate* brow supremely wore": Byron's "Childe Harold," iv. 57); hence, specially recognized or distinguished, or deserving of distinction, esp. for poetic achievement or merit (as, poet *laureate*: see under *poet*); also, of or pertaining to a poet, esp. a poet laureate; also, consisting of laurel, as a crown or wreath. **II.** *n.* One crowned with laurel; a poet laureate; also, a court panegyrist.—**lau're-ate** (-āt), *v. t.*; *-ated*, *-ating.* To crown with laurel, in token of honor (as, to *laureate* a victor); also, to confer a university degree upon; also, to appoint as poet laureate.—**lau're-ate-ship** (-ạ̄t-ship), *n.* The office of poet laureate.—**lau-re-a'tion** (-ā'shọn), *n.* The act of crowning with laurel; also, the conferring of a university degree; graduation; also, the appointment of a poet laureate.

lau-rel (lâ'rel or lor'el), *n.* [OF. F. *laurier*, < L. *laurus*, laurel.] A small lauraceous evergreen tree, *Laurus nobilis*, of southern Europe (the 'true laurel': also called *bay*, *bay-tree*, and *sweet-bay*); the foliage of this tree as an emblem of victory or distinction (as, "Their temples wreath'd with leafs, that still renew; For deathless *laurel* is the victor's due": Dryden's "Flower and the Leaf," 541); a branch or wreath of it (as, "The night . . . is a night of victory . . . horses, men, carriages, all are dressed in *laurels* and flowers": De Quincey's "English Mail-Coach," i.); hence, honor won, as by achievement (commonly in *pl.*: as, to win one's *laurels*; to rest on one's *laurels*, to rest in content and confidence on honors already won; to look to one's *laurels*, to guard one's honors against rivals); also, any tree of the same genus (*Laurus*); also, any of various trees or shrubs similar to the true laurel, as *Kalmia latifolia*, a large ericaceous shrub with glossy leaves and showy flowers (the 'American laurel,' or 'mountain-laurel'), or *Rhododendron maximum*, the great rhododendron (or 'great laurel').—**lau'rel,** *v. t.*; *-reled* or *-relled*, *-reling* or *-relling.* To adorn or wreathe with laurel; hence, to honor with marks of distinction.

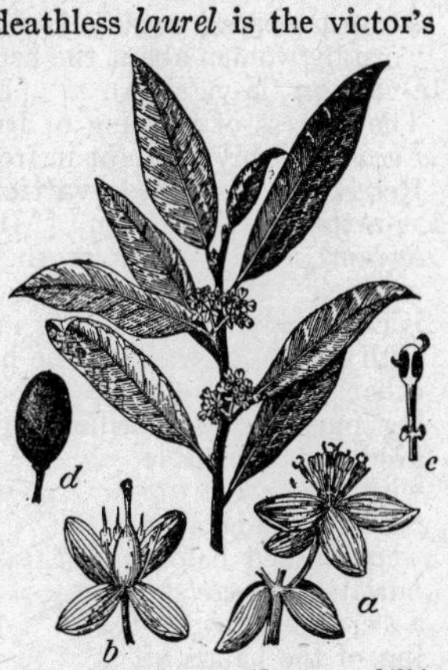

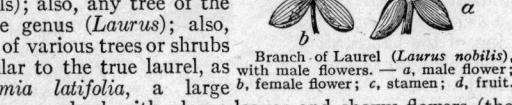

Branch of Laurel (*Laurus nobilis*), with male flowers. — *a*, male flower; *b*, female flower; *c*, stamen; *d*, fruit.

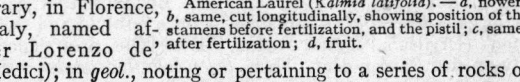

American Laurel (*Kalmia latifolia*). — *a*, flower; *b*, same, cut longitudinally, showing position of the stamens before fertilization, and the pistil; *c*, same, after fertilization; *d*, fruit.

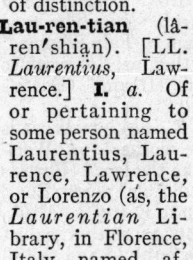

Lau-ren-tian (lâ-ren'shiạn). [LL. *Laurentius*, Lawrence.] **I.** *a.* Of or pertaining to some person named Laurentius, Laurence, Lawrence, or Lorenzo (as, the *Laurentian* Library, in Florence, Italy, named after Lorenzo de' Medici); in *geol.*, noting or pertaining to a series of rocks of the Archæan system, occurring in Canada near the St. Lawrence River and the Great Lakes. **II.** *n.* In *geol.*, the Laurentian series of rocks.

lau-rus-tine (lâ'rus-tīn), *n.* Same as *laurustinus*.

lau-rus-ti-nus (lâ-rus-tī'nus), *n.*; pl. *-tinuses.* [NL., < L. *laurus*, laurel, + *tinus*, kind of plant.] A caprifoliaceous evergreen garden-shrub, *Viburnum tinus*, native in southern Europe, with white or pinkish flowers.

lau-wine (lâ'win, G. lou-vē'nė), *n.* Same as *lawine*.

la-va (lä'vạ̈), *n.*; pl. *lavas.* [It., orig. 'stream,' < L. *lavare*, wash.] The molten or fluid rock which issues from a volcano or volcanic vent; also, the substance formed when this solidifies, occurring in many varieties differing greatly in structure and constitution; a variety of this substance (as, glassy and crystalline *lavas*).

la-va-bo (lạ-vā'bō), *n.* [L., 'I will wash.'] *Eccles.*, the ritual washing of the celebrant's hands after the offertory in the mass or eucharistic service, accompanied in the Roman rite by the recitation of Ps. xxvi. 6–12, or, in the Douay Version, Ps. xxv. 6–12 (so called from the first word of this passage in the Latin version); also, the passage recited; also, the small towel or the basin used in the washing.

lav-age (lav'ạ̄j, F. lȧ-väzh), *n.* [F., < *laver*, wash: see *lave*[2].] A laving or washing; in *med.*, the process of cleansing by injection or the like; specif., the washing out of the stomach.

la-val-lière (lä-vȧ-lyãr), *n.* [From the Duchesse de *La Vallière* (1644–1710), mistress of Louis XIV. of France.]

An ornamental, usually jeweled pendant on a small chain, worn by women about the neck.

la-va-tion (lạ-vā′shọn), *n.* [L. *lavatio(n-)*, < *lavare*, wash.] The process of washing or bathing: as, "appurtenances of *Lavation* richly wrought in frosted silver" (Carlyle's "Sartor Resartus," iii. 10).—**la-va′tion-al,** *a.*

lav-a-to-ry (lav′ạ-tọ̄-ri). [ML. *lavatorius* (as n., LL. *lavatorium*), < L. *lavare*, wash.] **I.** *a.* Of or pertaining to washing. **II.** *n.*; pl. *-ries* (-riz). A place where washing is done; specif., a room, as in a hotel or a school, fitted up with means for washing the hands and face, and often with other toilet conveniences; also, a vessel for washing or bathing purposes; in medieval monasteries, hospitals, etc., a kind of stone table with a concave top on which dead bodies were washed before burial; also, *eccles.*, a ceremonial washing of the hands of the celebrant of the eucharist.

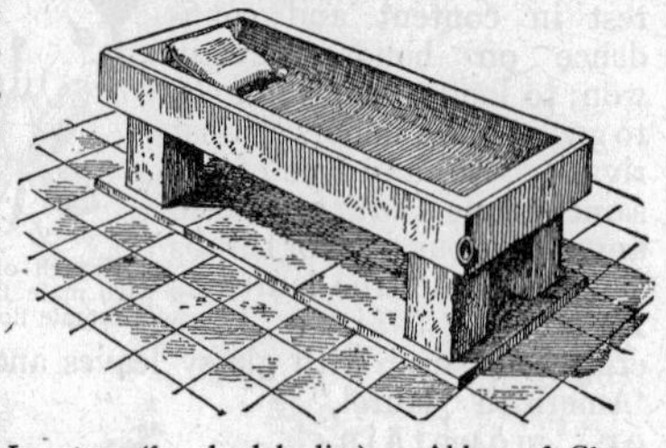

Lavatory (for dead bodies). — Abbey of Cluny, France.

lave[1] (lāv), *v. t.*; *laved, laving.* [AS. *lafian*: cf. *lave*[2].] To pour out (water, etc.); also, to lade, bail, or draw out (as, "employed in the unceasing toil of *laving* out the accumulating water": Jane Porter's "Scottish Chiefs," xxvii.). [Now prov. Eng. and Sc.]

lave[2] (lāv), *v.*; *laved, laving.* [OF. F. *laver*, < L. *lavare* (pp. *lavatus, lautus,* or *lotus*), wash: cf. *launder, lava,* and *lotion.*] **I.** *tr.* To wash or bathe (as, "basins and ewers to *lave* her dainty hands": Shakspere's "Taming of the Shrew," ii. 1. 350); fig., of a river, the sea, etc., to wash or flow against (as, "He tarries where the Rock of Spain Mediterranean waters *lave*": M. Arnold's "Stanzas from Carnac"); of light, to suffuse (as, "Where broad sunshine *laves* The lawn by some cathedral": Tennyson's "Dream of Fair Women," 189). [Now poetic.] **II.** *intr.* To bathe: as, "Ever since I heedlessly did *lave* In thy deceitful stream" (Keats's "Endymion," ii.). [Now poetic.]

lave[3] (lāv), *n.* [AS. *lāf*, akin to *lǣfan*, E. *leave*[1].] What is left; the remainder; the rest: as, "The mother . . . Weel-pleased to think her bairn's respected like the *lave*" (Burns's "Cotter's Saturday Night," 72). [Now Sc. and north. Eng.]

la-veer (lạ-vēr′), *v. i.* [D. *laveeren*; akin to E. *luff*.] *Naut.*, to sail to windward; beat; tack: as, "But those that 'gainst stiff gales *laveering* go, Must be at once resolv'd and skilful too" (Dryden's "Astræa Redux," 65). [Obs. or archaic.]

lav-en-der (lav′ẹn-dėr). [ML. *lavendula, lavandula*; origin uncertain; commonly referred to L. *lavare*, wash, from its use with freshly washed linen or in baths or toilet-water.] **I.** *n.* A plant of the menthaceous genus *Lavandula*, esp. *L. vera*, a small old-world shrub with spikes of fragrant pale-purple flowers, yielding an oil ('oil of lavender') used in medicine and perfumery; also, the dried flowers or other parts of this plant, used to place among linen, etc., for scent or as a preservative (as, "garments . . . carefully preserved between two layers of old newspapers, speckled with dried *lavender*": Dickens's "Oliver Twist," xxvii.); also, a pale, delicate purple color. **II.** *a.* Of the color called lavender. —**lav′en-der,** *v. t.* To scent with lavender; put lavender among.—**lav′en-der=wa″ter,** *n.* A toilet-water or perfume made with oil of lavender.

la-ver[1] (lā′vėr), *n.* [OF. *lavoir, laveoir*, < LL. *lavatorium*: see *lavatory*.] A basin, bowl, or cistern to wash in (see Ex. xxx. 18–21); any bowl or pan for water; fig., the font or the water of baptism; any spiritually cleansing agency.

la-ver[2] (lā′vėr), *n.* [L., kind of water-plant.] Any of several edible seaweeds, esp. of the genus *Porphyra*; also, such seaweed prepared as food.

lav-er-ock (lav′ėr-ọk), *n.* Sc. and prov. Eng. form of *lark*[1]: as, "Now *laverocks* wake the merry morn" (Burns's "Lament of Mary Queen of Scots," 9).

lav-ish (lav′ish), *a.* [ME. *lavas, lavage*, adj., lavish, *lavas*, n., extravagant outpouring: cf. OF. *lavasse, lavache*, deluge of rain, < L. *lavare*, wash.] Pouring out, using, expending, or bestowing in great abundance or without stint (often with *of*: as, to be *lavish* of words, or of one's tongue; to be *lavish* of color in a picture; *lavish* of time, labor, or money; "From that day Fortune was *lavish* of her favours upon him," Galt's "Annals of the Parish," xxix.); exceedingly liberal; profuse; prodigal; extravagant; also, characterized by or done with profusion or prodigality (as, *lavish* use of flattery; *lavish* expenditure of time or money; *lavish* spending or entertaining); also, expended, bestowed, or occurring in profusion (as, *lavish* sums; *lavish* gifts; "The *lavish* gold Of her loose hair," Lowell's "Legend of Brittany," ii. 24); unstinted; exceedingly bountiful or abundant; also, unbridled† or wild† (as, "curbing his *lavish* spirit": Shakspere's "Macbeth," i. 2. 57).—**lav′ish,** *v. t.* To pour out, expend, or bestow in great abundance or without stint (as, "They *lavish* gold out of the bag," Isa. xlvi. 6; to *lavish* gifts, favors, or abuse on a person); spend or give profusely or prodigally. —**lav′ish-er,** *n.*—**lav′ish-ly,** *adv.*—**lav′ish-ment,** *n.* The act of lavishing.—**lav′ish-ness,** *n.*

la-vol-ta (lạ-vol′tạ̈), *n.* [It., 'the turn.'] An old-time dance, in vogue in the 16th century and later: as, "They bid us to the English dancing-schools, And teach *lavoltas* high and swift corantos" (Shakspere's "Henry V.," iii. 5. 33).

law[1] (lâ), *interj.* [Cf. *la*[1].] An exclamation expressing wonder, surprise, etc. Also *laws.* [Now prov. or vulgar.]

law[2] (lâ), *n.* [= *low*[3].] A hill, esp. one of round or conical form. [Sc. and north. Eng., or in place-names.]

law[3] (lâ), *n.* [AS. *lagu*; from Scand.: cf. Icel. *lag*, layer, stratum, pl. *lög*, law, lit. 'that which is laid down,' from the root of E. *lay*[1] and *lie*[1].] The body of rules or principles, prescribed by authority or established by custom, which a state, community, society, or the like recognizes as binding on its members (as, the *law* of England); one of the individual rules belonging to such a body; also, the controlling influence of such rules, or the condition of society brought about by their observance (as, necessity knows no *law*; to maintain *law* and order); also, rules of this class collectively as an institution or authority in human life (as, courts of *law*; the domain of the *law*); the department of knowledge or study concerned with these rules, or jurisprudence; also, the body of such rules concerned with a particular subject (as, commercial *law*; the *law* of banking) or derived from a particular source (as, statute *law*; common *law*, see under *common, a.*); in British use, the ordinary (common and statute) law as distinguished from equity; also, the profession which deals with law and legal procedure (usually with *the*: as, a young man who is going into the *law*); the legal profession; also, legal action; judicial remedy; litigation; also, any rules or injunctions that must be obeyed (as, to lay down the *law*; his father's wishes were *law* to him); also, the rules or principles of conduct (or a single one of them) generally regarded as binding on mankind, viewed as expressions or revelations of the divine will or as derivable from conscience, reason, or nature; also [often *cap.*], a divinely appointed order or system (as, the old *law*, the Mosaic dispensation; the new *law*, the Christian dispensation); esp., with *the*, the Mosaic dispensation, or system of rules and ordinances ('the Mosaic law': often in contrast to *the gospel*); the books (the Pentateuch) containing this system and forming the first of the three Jewish divisions of the Old Testament (cf. *prophet* and *Hagiographa*); hence, the Old Testament; also [*l. c.*], one of the rules or principles by which any procedure, art, game, or the like is regulated (as, "the *laws* of hospitality," Swift's "Gulliver's Travels," i. 1; the *laws* of whist); a body or code of such rules (as, the *law* of arms); specif., in philosophical and scientific use, a statement of a relation or sequence of phenomena invariable under the same conditions; a mathematical rule on which something, as the construction of a curve, depends; also, in sports, an allowance in distance or time given to a weaker competitor in a race, an animal in the chase, etc. (as, "I trust your Grace will treat me as a beast of chase . . . and allow me fair *law?*" Scott's "Quentin Durward," xxxiii.); a start; hence, indulgence or mercy (as, "Merchant ships show but little *law* to pirates, if they get them in their power": Defoe's "Robinson Crusoe," ii. 11).—**law French,** a corrupt form of Norman French in legal use in England from the time of William the Conqueror to that of Edward

III. or later, and still surviving in some phrases and expressions.—**law Latin,** a corrupt form of Latin used since an early period in English legal proceedings and documents.—**law merchant,** the body of principles and rules, drawn chiefly from the customs of merchants, by which the rights and obligations arising in commercial transactions are determined; commercial law.—**law of nations,** in Roman use, the body of rules common to the law of all nations; in modern use, the body of rules which civilized nations recognize as binding them in their conduct toward one another (now usually called *international law*).—**the law of the Medes and Persians,** the typical law "which altereth not," or is unchangeable: see Dan. vi. 8, 12, 15.—**law**[3], *v.* **I.** *intr.* To go to law; litigate: as, "Your husband's . . . given to *lawing,* they say" (George Eliot's "Mill on the Floss," i. 9). [Colloq.] **II.** *tr.* To go to law with; prosecute; sue. [Colloq.]

law=a-bid-ing (lâ'ạ-bī″ding), *a.* Abiding by or keeping the law; obedient to law.

law-ful (lâ'fůl), *a.* Allowed or permitted by law (as, "Thy disciples do that which is not *lawful* to do upon the sabbath day": Mat. xii. 2); not contrary to law; also, recognized or sanctioned by law (as, *lawful* demands; *lawful* debts; *lawful* money; *lawful* game or prey); legally qualified or entitled (as, "great England's *lawful* king," Shakspere's "2 Henry VI.," v. 1. 4; the *lawful* heir).—**law'ful-ly,** *adv.*—**law'ful-ness,** *n.*

law-giv-er (lâ'giv″ėr), *n.* One who gives, or makes or promulgates, a law or a code of laws; a legislator.—**law'giv″-ing,** *n.* and *a.*

law=hand (lâ'hand), *n.* The style of handwriting customarily used in legal documents.

la-wine (lâ'win, G. lä-vē'ne), *n.* [G.] An avalanche.

lawk (lâk), *n.* and *interj.* A vulgar substitute for *Lord* in exclamatory uses: as, "*Lawk* help me" (Hood's "Lost Heir," 25).

law-less (lâ'les), *a.* Without law, or not regulated by law (as, a *lawless* wilderness); also, exempt from or being beyond the law; sometimes, deprived of the benefit or protection of the law†, or being in the position of an outlaw† (as, a *lawless* man); also, regardless of or contrary to law (as, to lead a *lawless* life; "*lawless* violence," Macaulay's "Hist. of Eng.," xiii.); uncontrolled by law, unbridled, or licentious (as, *lawless* passions); also, not submissive or obedient to law (as, "A valiant son-in-law thou shalt enjoy; One fit to bandy with thy *lawless* sons": Shakspere's "Titus Andronicus," i. 1. 312); fig., unruly (as, "Her *lawless* hair was caught in a net": Bret Harte's "Princess Bob and Her Friends").—**law'less-ly,** *adv.*—**law'less-ness,** *n.*

law-mak-er (lâ'mā″kėr), *n.* One who makes or enacts law; a legislator.

lawn[1] (lân), *n.* [ME. *laun, launde*; prob. from *Laon,* city in northern France.] A thin or sheer linen or cotton fabric, plain or printed; specif., this fabric as used for the sleeves of the dress of an Anglican bishop (as, "A saint in crape is twice a saint in *lawn*": Pope's "Moral Essays," i. 136).—**lawn sleeves,** the sleeves of lawn of an Anglican bishop; hence, the office or dignity of a bishop; also, a bishop or bishops.

lawn[2] (lân), *n.* [Earlier *laund,* < OF. *launde, lande*: see *lande.*] An open space in a forest (as, "Those long, rank, dark wood-walks drench'd in dew, Leading from *lawn* to *lawn*": Tennyson's "Dream of Fair Women," 76); a glade; also, a stretch of grass-covered land, esp. one kept closely mowed, as near a house or in a pleasure-ground; land kept in this condition.—**lawn**[2], *v. t.* To turn (land) into lawn.—**lawn'=ten'nis,** *n.* A modern adaptation of the old game of tennis, played, usually in the open air, on an uninclosed rectangular plot prepared and marked out on a lawn or other level surface, by two, three, or four persons. See *tennis.*

lawn-y[1] (lâ'ni), *a.* Of or like linen or cotton lawn; wearing lawn.

lawn-y[2] (lâ'ni), *a.* Containing lawns or glades; also, like a lawn, or covered with smooth turf (as, "the *lawny* slopes on which, when a child, I played": G. W. Curtis's "Prue and I," ii.).

laws (lâz), *interj.* Same as *law*[1].

law-suit (lâ'sūt), *n.* A suit at law; a prosecution of a claim in a court of justice.

law-yer (lâ'yėr), *n.* [ME. *lawyere, lawiere.*] One versed in the law; one whose profession it is to conduct suits in court or to give legal advice and aid; also, a long, thorny stem, as of a bramble (prov. Eng.).—**law'yer-ly,** *a.* Like or befitting a lawyer.

lax (laks), *a.* [L. *laxus,* loose, slack, prob. akin to *languere,* E. *languish,* and perhaps to E. *slack*[2].] Loose or slack (as, a *lax* cord); not tense, rigid, or firm; hence, lacking in tone or vigor (as, a *lax* constitution; *lax* mental powers); also, relaxed, as the limbs; also, open or not retentive, as the bowels; having the bowels unduly open, as a person; also, not close or tight, as an attachment or connection; also, of a loose texture (as, *lax* tissue; *lax* soil); loosely cohering; open or not compact, as a panicle of a plant; also, lacking in strictness or severity (as, *lax* discipline; *lax* morals; a *lax* disciplinarian); careless or negligent; also, not rigidly exact or precise (as, to have *lax* ideas of a subject); vague.

lax-a-tion (lak-sā'shǫn), *n.* [L. *laxatio(n-),* < *laxare,* loosen, relax, < *laxus,* E. *lax.*] A loosening or relaxing, or the state of being loosened or relaxed; also, a means of loosening or relaxing; specif., a laxative agent.

lax-a-tive (lak'sạ-tiv). [OF. F. *laxatif,* < L. *laxativus,* < *laxare*: see *laxation.*] **I.** *a.* Loosening or opening the bowels; mildly purgative; also, of the bowels, subject to looseness; also, of a disease, characterized by looseness of the bowels. **II.** *n.* A laxative medicine or agent.

lax-i-ty (lak'si-ti), *n.* [F. *laxité,* < L. *laxitas.*] The state or quality of being lax or loose; looseness; slackness.

lax-ly (laks'li), *adv.* In a lax manner.—**lax'ness,** *n.*

lay[1] (lā), *v. t.*; *laid, laying.* [AS. *lecgan* = D. *leggen* = G. *legen* = Icel. *leggja* = Goth. *lagjan,* lay; causative of the Teut. verb represented by E. *lie*[1].] To bring or throw down from an erect position (as, to *lay* a person low); hence, to cause to subside (as, to *lay* the dust); allay, appease, or suppress (as, to *lay* a person's doubts or anger); smooth down or make even (as, to *lay* the nap of cloth); also, to put or place in a position of rest or recumbency (as, to *lay* a book on a desk); bury (as, he was *laid* in a quiet churchyard); bring forth and deposit (an egg or eggs); also, to deposit as a pledge or pawn†; mortgage (lands)†; now, to deposit as a wager; stake; bet; hence, to make (a wager or bet); also, to place, set, or cause to be in a particular situation, state, or condition (as, to *lay* hands on a thing; to *lay* bare the land); place in contiguity, or apply (as, to *lay* a spark to a building); put (dogs) on a scent; place (something) before a person, or bring (something) to a person's notice or consideration; set (a snare, trap, etc.); set a guard in (a place)†; search (a place) for a person or thing†; post or station (soldiers, etc.)†; place or locate (a scene); also, to present, bring forward, or prefer, as a claim, charge, etc.; impute, attribute, or ascribe (as, the theft was *laid* to him); also, to impose (something) as a burden, duty, penalty, or the like; bring down (a stick, etc.), as on a person, in inflicting punishment; strike or beat (a person)†; also, to dispose or place in proper position or in an orderly fashion (as, to *lay* bricks); set (a table); form by twisting strands together, as a rope; place on or over a surface, as paint; cover or spread with something else (as, a brick wall *laid* with plaster); devise or arrange, as a plan.—**to lay by,** to put aside; also, to put away for future use; lay up in reserve; save (money).—**to lay hold of** or **on,** to grasp; seize; catch.—**to lay off,** to put aside; also, to discontinue; also, to dismiss, esp. temporarily, as a workman; also, to mark or plot off.—**to lay on the table,** in parliamentary use, to table, or postpone consideration of (a proposal, resolution, etc.).—**to lay out,** to extend at length; spread out to the sight, air, etc.; spread out in order; specif., to stretch out and prepare (a body) for burial; also (slang), to lay low; do for; thrash soundly; disable; defeat; reprimand or rebuke severely; also, to expend (money) for a particular purpose; also, to exert (one's self) to effect a purpose, produce a good effect, etc. (as, he *laid* himself *out* to be agreeable; they *laid* themselves *out* on that entertainment); also, to plot or plan out.—**to lay siege to,** to besiege.—**to lay up,** to put away in a place of safety, as for future use; store up; also, to cause to remain in bed or indoors through illness; also, *naut.,* to put (a ship, etc.)

in a dock or other place of safety.—**lay**[1], *v. i.* To lay eggs (as, "There shall the great owl make her nest, and *lay*, and hatch": Isa. xxxiv. 15); also, to wager or bet (as, to *lay* on a horse-race); also, to deal or aim blows (*on, at, about,* etc.: as, "*Lay* on, Macduff, And damn'd be him that first cries 'Hold, enough!' " Shakspere's "Macbeth," v. 8. 33; "The sword of him that *layeth* at him cannot hold," Job, xli. 26; to *lay* about one with a cane or one's fists); also, to apply one's self vigorously (as, to *lay* to one's oars); also, to lie in wait (*for*: now colloq.: as, to *lay* for a poacher or an enemy); also, to plan or scheme (sometimes with *out*: now prov. or colloq.: as, to *lay*, or *lay* out, to make a journey); also, *naut.*, to put or bring one's self into a specified position (as, "I obeyed the order to *lay* aloft": Dana's "Two Years before the Mast," iv.). Also used erroneously for *lie*[1], *v. i.*, as in 'there let him *lay*' (Byron's "Childe Harold," iv. 180), 'to *lay* down,' 'a book *laying* on the table,' etc.—**lay**[1], *n.* A wager†; also, a layer† or stratum†; also, a plan or line of activity (slang: as, "He's not to be found on his old *lay*," Dickens's "Bleak House," xxii.); also, a share of profits, as in a whaling voyage (as, "All hands, including the captain, received certain shares of the profits called *lays*": H. Melville's "Moby-Dick," xvi.); also, the way or position in which a thing is laid or lies (as, "The *lay* of the ground hindered my view towards the sea": Kinglake's "Eothen," iv.).

lay[2] (lā). Preterit of *lie*[1].

lay[3] (lā), *n.* [OF. F. *lai*; origin uncertain.] A short narrative or other poem, esp. one intended to be sung (as, "The only way to please a minstrel was to listen . . . to the *lays* which he liked best to sing": Scott's "Castle Dangerous," xviii.); a song; sometimes, the song of a bird.

lay[4] (lā), *a.* [OF. F. *lai*, < LL. *laicus*: see *laic*.] Belonging to, pertaining to, or performed by the people or laity, as distinguished from the clergy (as, a *lay* preacher; "with rev'rend tutor, clad in habit *lay*," Cowper's "Progress of Error," 371; a *lay* sermon); not clerical; also, not belonging to, connected with, or proceeding from a particular profession, esp. the law or medicine (as, a *lay* magistrate; a *lay* opinion on a medical matter); also, unlearned† or ignorant†.—**lay brother,** a man who has taken the vows and habit of a religious order, but is employed chiefly in manual labor and is exempt from the studies and special religious services of the other members.—**lay sister,** a woman who occupies a position in a female religious order analogous to that of a lay brother.

lay[5] (lā), *n.* Same as *lea*[3].

lay[6] (lā), *n.* Same as *lathe*[2].

lay=day (lā′dā), *n.* In *com.*, one of a certain number of days allowed by a charter-party for loading or unloading a vessel without demurrage.

lay-er (lā′ėr), *n.* One who or that which lays; also, something which is laid; a thickness of some material laid on or spread over a surface; a stratum; in *hort.*, a shoot or twig placed partly under ground while still attached to the living stock, for the purpose of propagation.—**lay′er,** *v. t.* In *hort.*, to propagate by layers; also, make a layer of.—**lay′ered,** *a.* Formed into or having layers.

Layer.

la-yette (lā-yet′), *n.* [F., box, drawer, layette, dim. of *laie*, chest, trough; from Flemish.] An outfit of clothing, toilet articles, etc., for a new-born child.

lay=fig-ure (lā′fig″ūr), *n.* [With *lay-* as in obs. *layman*, < D. *leeman*, lay-figure, < *led* (now *lid*), limb, joint, + *man*, man.] A jointed model of the human body used by artists to support draperies, etc.; a similar figure used in shops to display costumes; hence, a mere puppet or nonentity; a person of no importance.

lay-man (lā′mạn), *n.*; pl. *-men*. [See *lay*[4].] One of the laity; one not a clergyman or not a member of some particular profession.

lay=off (lā′ôf), *n.* The act of laying off; a dismissing of workmen temporarily from employment.

lay=out (lā′out), *n.* A laying or spreading out; an arrangement or plan; also, something laid or spread out; a display; a spread; the playing-cards or representations of them spread out on a table, on which the stakes are placed in the game of faro; a collection or set of tools, implements, or the like. [Chiefly colloq.]

lay-wom-an (lā′wụm″ạn), *n.*; pl. *-women* (-wim″en). A female member of the laity.

la-zar (lā′zạr), *n.* [= It. *lazzaro*, < ML. *lazarus*, < LL. *Lazarus*: see *Lazarus*.] A person, esp. a beggar or poor person, infected with a loathsome disease; a leper: as, "I marked a group of *lazars* in the marketplace—half-rag, half-sore—beggars" (Tennyson's "Becket," i. 4). [Archaic.]

laz-a-ret (laz-ạ-ret′), *n.* [F.] Same as *lazaretto*.

laz-a-ret-to (laz-ạ-ret′ō), *n.*; pl. *lazarettos* (-ōz). [It. *lazzaretto, lazzeretto*, < *lazzaro*, lazar, leper: see *lazar*.] A hospital for those affected with contagious or loathsome diseases; a pest-house; also, a building or a ship set apart for quarantine purposes; also, *naut.*, a place in some merchant ships, usually near the stern, in which provisions and stores are kept.

la-zar=house (lā′zạr-hous), *n.* A house or hospital for lazars or lepers, etc.; a pest-house.

Laz-a-rus (laz′ạ-rus), *n.* [LL., < Gr. Λάζαρος, < Heb. *El′āzār*, Eleazar.] The beggar, "full of sores," of the parable in Luke, xvi. 19–31; hence, any diseased beggar, esp. a leper.

laze (lāz), *v.*; *lazed, lazing.* [From *lazy*.] **I.** *intr.* To be lazy; idle or lounge lazily. **II.** *tr.* To pass (time, etc.) lazily (*away*).—**laze,** *n.* A process or period of lazing.

la-zi-ly (lā′zi-li), *adv.* In a lazy manner.—**la′zi-ness,** *n.*

laz-u-li (laz′ū-lī), *n.* Lapis lazuli.

laz-u-lite (laz′ū-līt), *n.* [ML. *lazulum*, lapis lazuli.] A native hydrous phosphate of aluminium, magnesium, and iron, of a blue color.

la-zy (lā′zi), *a.*; compar. *lazier*, superl. *laziest.* [Origin uncertain: cf. D. *leuzig*, MLG. *lasich, losich*, G. *lässig*, lazy.] Disinclined to exertion or work, indolent, or slothful (as, "All . . . combine to drive The *lazy* drones from the laborious hive": Dryden's tr. Virgil's "Georgics," iv. 242); characterized by, suggestive of, or conducive to such disinclination (as, a *lazy* mood; a *lazy* yawn; "Here they used to sit in the shade through a long, *lazy* summer's day . . . telling endless sleepy stories about nothing," Irving's "Sketch-Book," Rip Van Winkle); in general, having little activity or energy, languid, sluggish, or slow (as, a *lazy* wind; a *lazy* stream; to while away the *lazy* hours).—**lazy Susan,** a large, circular tray revolving on a base, used at table for holding articles of food, which, with the revolution of the tray, are passed to those around the table.—**la′zy,** *v. i.* and *t.*; *lazied, lazying.* To laze: as, "So we would put in the day, *lazying* around, listening to the stillness" (Mark Twain's "Huckleberry Finn," xix.).—**la′zy-bones, la′zy-boots,** *n.* A lazy person. [Colloq.]—**la′zy=tongs,** *n. pl.* or *sing.* A kind of extensible tongs for grasping objects at a distance, consisting of a series of pairs of crossing pieces, each pair pivoted together in the middle and connected with the next pair at the extremities; hence, a similar arrangement of crossing pieces used for other purposes.

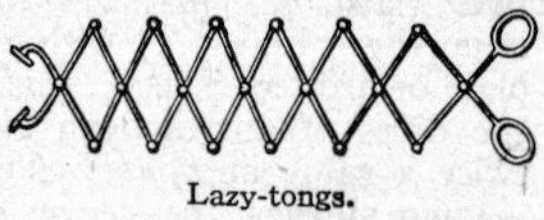

Lazy-tongs.

laz-za-ro-ne (laz-ạ-rō′nā, It. läd-zä-rō′nā), *n.*; pl. *-ni* (-nē). [It., < *lazzaro*: see *lazar*.] One of a class of very poor persons in Naples who frequent the streets and live by odd jobs or by begging: as, "picturesque *lazzaroni*" (George Eliot's "Adam Bede," xvii.).

-le. [AS. *-lian*.] A verb suffix with a frequentative or diminutive force, as in *crackle, dazzle, dribble, prattle, twinkle, wrestle.*

lea[1] (lē), *n.* [AS. *lēah*.] A tract of open ground, esp. grassland; a meadow or grassy field: as, "The lowing herd winds slowly o'er the *lea*" (Gray's "Elegy," i.). [Chiefly poetic.]

lea[2] (lē). [ME. *leye, laye*; from the root of E. *lie*[1].] **I.** *a.* Of land, fallow or untilled. [Now prov.] **II.** *n.* Fallow or untilled land, usually under grass. [Now prov.]

lea[3] (lē), *n.* [ME. *lee*; origin uncertain.] A measure of yarn of varying quantity, for wool usually 80 yards, cotton and silk 120 yards, linen 300 yards.

leach (lēch), *v.* [Cf. AS. *leccan*, moisten, wet, also E. *leak*.]

I. *tr.* To cause (water, etc.) to percolate through something; also, to remove soluble constituents from (ashes, etc.) by percolation; lixiviate; also, to remove (soluble constituents) by percolation. **II.** *intr.* To percolate, as water; also, of ashes, etc., to undergo the action of percolating water.—**leach,** *n.* A leaching; also, the material leached; also, a vessel for use in leaching.—**leach'y,** *a.* Such as to allow water to percolate through; porous.

lead[1] (lēd), *v. t.*; *led, leading.* [AS. *lǣdan* = D. *leiden* = G. *leiten* = Icel. *leidha*, lead; causative of the Teut. verb (AS. *līthan*, etc., go) whence also E. *lode.*] To take or bring (obs. or archaic: as, "So shall the king of Assyria *lead* away the Egyptians prisoners," Isa. xx. 4); also, to carry or convey, as in a cart (now prov. Eng. and Sc.); also, to take or conduct on the way, as a guide does; go before or with to show the way; often, to conduct by holding and guiding, as with the hand or by a rope, halter, or the like (as, to *lead* a blind man; to *lead* a horse); of signs, clues, light, sound, etc., to serve to guide; of a road, passage, course, etc., to serve to bring (a person, etc.) to a place, through a region, etc.; in general, to guide in direction, course, action, opinion, etc. (as, to go where the fancy *leads* one; "*Lead* us not into temptation," Mat. vi. 13; "Woman will have guidance. It is her delight and glory to be *led*," Kingsley's "Yeast," x.); influence or induce (as, to be too easily *led*; such actions have *led* us to distrust him); conduct or bring (water, steam, a rope or wire, etc.) in a particular channel or course; also, to go through or pass (life, etc.: as, to *lead* one's life in peace; to *lead* a dreary existence); also, to go at the head of or in advance of (a procession, list, body, etc.); be first in or go before; fig., to be at the head of, command, or direct (an army, party, organization, etc.); have the directing or principal part in (a movement, proceedings, etc.); act as leader of (an orchestra, chorus, etc.); begin or open, as a dance, discussion, etc. (often with *off*); in *card-playing*, to begin a round, etc., with (a card or suit specified).—**to lead the way,** to act as guide; go in advance of others; take the lead in any course of action.—**lead**[1], *v. i.* To act as a guide; show or lead the way; also, to afford passage to a place, etc., as a road, stairway, or the like does; fig., to be a means or cause of proceeding, as to some result or consequence (as, one word *led* to another; the frequent outbreaks *led* to civil war); also, to be led, or submit to being led, as an animal; also, to go first; be in advance; have the first place; fig., to take the directing or principal part; act as leader, as of an orchestra; take the initiative, or make a beginning (often with *off*); in *card-playing*, to make the first play.—**lead**[1], *n.* The act or function of leading; guidance; direction; precedence; also, the first or foremost place; position in advance of others, or the extent of advance; also, something that leads; an open channel through a field of ice; a conductor conveying electricity; a guiding indication; in *card-playing*, the act or right of playing first, as in a round; the card, suit, etc., so played; *naut.*, the course of a rope; in *mining*, a lode; also, an auriferous deposit in an old river-bed; in *theatrical use*, the principal part in a play, or the person who plays it.

lead[2] (led), *n.* [AS. *lēad* = D. *lood*, lead, = G. *lot*, plummet.] Chem. sym., Pb (see *plumbum*); at. wt., 207.20; sp. gr., 11.4. A heavy, comparatively soft, malleable bluish-gray metal, sometimes found native, but usually combined, as in galena; also, something made of this metal or of one of its alloys; a plummet or mass of lead suspended by a line, as for taking soundings; *pl.*, sheets or strips of lead used for covering roofs, or a roof-covering made of them (as, "The tempest crackles on the *leads*": Tennyson's "Sir Galahad," 53); frames of lead in which panes are fixed, as in windows of stained glass; *sing.*, a thin strip of type-metal or brass, less than type-high, for increasing the space between lines of printing-type; also, black-lead or graphite, or a small stick of it as used in pencils.—**red lead,** red oxide of lead, a heavy, granular powder used as a pigment, in making cement for the joints of pipes, and in the manufacture of glass; minium.—**white lead,** a white basic carbonate of lead, much used as a pigment.—**lead**[2], *v. t.* To cover, line, or weight with lead; fix (window-glass) in position with leads; glaze (pottery, etc.) with a glaze containing lead; in *printing*, to insert leads between the lines of.

lead=col-or (led'kul"or), *n.* A dull, dark bluish-gray color.—**lead'=col"ored,** *a.*

lead-ed (led'ed), *p. a.* Of printed matter, having extra space between the lines, due to the insertion of leads between the lines of type.

lead-en (led'n), *a.* [AS. *lēaden.*] Consisting or made of lead (as, a *leaden* coffin); also, resembling or suggesting lead in some respect; inertly heavy, or hard to lift or move, as weight, the limbs, etc.; oppressive, as the air; sluggish, as the pace; dull, spiritless, or gloomy, as the mood, thoughts, etc.; of a dull gray color, as the sky, the sea, etc.; sometimes, of a base or inferior nature (obs. or rare).—**lead'en=foot'ed,** *a.* Moving or passing slowly, as if with leaden feet: as, "*leaden-footed* hours" (Poe's "Mystery of Marie Rogêt").—**lead'en-ly,** *adv.*—**lead'en-ness,** *n.*

lead-er (lē'dėr), *n.* One who or that which leads; a guide or conductor; a guiding or directing head, as of an army, party, movement, etc. (as, "the *leaders* of scientific discovery in this wondrous age": Kingsley's "Alton Locke," xxvi.); one foremost or especially eminent in position, influence, etc. (as, *leaders* of society); one first in a line, procession, or the like; a horse harnessed at the front of a team (as, "The whips cracked, the *leaders* capered, and . . . away we rattled to Dover": Lever's "Harry Lorrequer," li.); a principal or important editorial article, as in a newspaper (as, "He only read one newspaper, innocent of *leaders*": George Eliot's "Adam Bede," lii.); a principal article of trade, esp. one offered at a low price to attract customers; a pipe for conveying water, etc.; a tendon; *pl.*, in *printing*, a row of dots or short lines to lead the eye across a space; *sing.*, in *fishing*, a length of silkworm gut or the like, to which the snell of a fly is attached; in *music*, a conductor or director, as of an orchestra, band, or chorus; also, the player at the head of the first violins in an orchestra, the principal cornetist in a band, or the principal soprano in a chorus.—**lead-er-ette'** (-et'), *n.* [See *-ette.*] A short leader or editorial paragraph, as in a newspaper. [Eng.]—**lead'er=gear,** *n.* A device for guiding ships over a fixed course, consisting essentially of an insulated cable laid on the bottom of the sea, the navigator being able to tell the position of and hence follow the cable, through which an alternating electric current passes, by means of delicate instruments installed on the ship: used esp. for guidance through mine-fields during the World War. Also called *leading-gear.*—**lead'er-less,** *a.* Without a leader.—**lead'er-ship,** *n.* The position, function, or guidance of a leader; also, ability to lead.

lead-ing[1] (lē'ding), *n.* The act of one who or that which leads; guidance; direction; lead.—**lead'ing**[1], *p. a.* That leads; guiding; directing; foremost, chief, or principal.—**leading article,** a principal editorial article in a newspaper; a leader.—**leading motive.** Same as *leitmotiv.*—**leading question,** a question so worded as to suggest the proper or desired answer.—**leading tone,** in *music*, the seventh tone of a scale, which (in ascending passages) leads to the tonic or key-note.

lead-ing[2] (led'ing), *n.* A covering or framing of lead; leads collectively.

lead-ing=gear (lē'ding-gēr), *n.* Same as *leader-gear.*

lead-ing=string (lē'ding-string), *n.* A string for leading an animal or any creature (as, "She . . . always held me fast by a *leading-string*": Swift's "Gulliver's Travels," ii. 2); esp., a string for leading and supporting a child when learning to walk (as, "one that still needs his *leading-string* and bib," Cowper's "Progress of Error," 531: more commonly in *pl.*); hence fig., *pl.*, guiding and regulating conditions, or restraining guidance (as, to be kept in *leading-strings*; to escape from *leading-strings*).

lead=pen-cil (led'pen"sil), *n.* An instrument for writing, drawing, etc., consisting of a slender cylinder or stick of graphite (black-lead) inclosed in a casing of wood or other material.

lead=plant (led'plant), *n.* A shrubby fabaceous plant, *Amorpha canescens*, of the western U. S., with canescent or hoary leaves: reputed to indicate the presence of lead ore.

lead=poi-son-ing (led'poi"zn-ing), *n.* In *pathol.*, a diseased condition due to the introduction of lead into the system; plumbism: common among workers in lead or its compounds.

leads-man (ledz′man), *n.*; pl. *-men.* *Naut.*, a man who heaves the lead in taking soundings: as, "The . . . cries of the *leadsmen* announced that there were no more than three feet of water under her keel" (J. Conrad's "Rescue," i. 4).
lead-wort (led′wėrt), *n.* Any plant of the genus *Plumbago*, or of the family *Plumbaginaceæ.* See *plumbago.*
lead-y (led′i), *a.* Like lead; leaden.
leaf (lēf), *n.*; pl. *leaves* (lēvz). [AS. *lēaf* = D. *loof* = G. *laub* = Icel. *lauf* = Goth. *laufs*, leaf: cf. *lodge* and *lobby.*] One of the expanded, usually green, organs borne by the stem of a plant ('foliage leaf'); sometimes, any similar or corresponding lateral outgrowth of a stem (as, a floral *leaf*: see under *floral*); often, popularly, a petal (as, a rose-*leaf*); also, foliage or leafage (as, the fall of the *leaf*; in *leaf*, covered with foliage or leaves); specif., the leaves of some plant, as tobacco or tea, as a commercial product; also, something resembling a foliage leaf, as in being broad and flat or in being a leaf-like attachment; a thin sheet of metal, etc.; a lamina or layer; a layer of fat, esp. that about the kidneys of a hog (see *leaf-lard*); a single thickness of paper, as in a folded sheet, a book, etc., containing two pages, one on the front and the other on the back; a sliding, hinged, or detachable flat part, as of a door, a shutter, or a table-top.—**to take a leaf out of,** or **from, the book of,** to take an idea from, as for conduct; follow the example of: as, "The Third Estate, *taking a leaf from the book of* the English House of Commons, then declared that it alone represented the nation" (H. G. Wells's "Outline of History," xxxvii. § 8).—**to turn over a new leaf.** See under *turn, v. t.*—**leaf,** *v. i.*; *leafed, leafing.* To put forth leaves; leave.

Foliage Leaf of Pansy, showing *B*, the blade, *P*, the petiole, and *S*, *S*, the two stipules.

leaf-age (lē′fāj), *n.* Leaves collectively; foliage: as, "I looked . . . through a frame of *leafage*, clustering round the high lattice" (C. Brontë's "Villette," xvi.).
leafed (lēft), *a.* Having a leaf or leaves; leaved.
leaf-en (lē′fen), *a.* Consisting or made of leaves: as, "Others were plying their fingers rapidly in weaving *leafen* baskets" (H. Melville's "Typee," xiii.).
leaf=hop-per (lēf′hop″ėr), *n.* Any of the small, leaping homopterous insects, feeding on plants, that constitute the family *Jassidæ.*

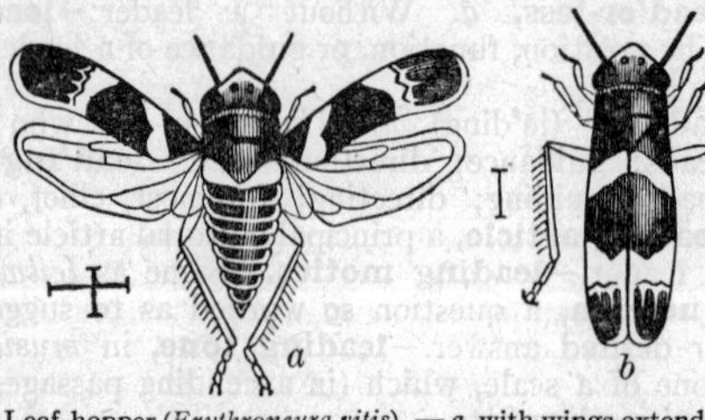

Leaf-hopper (*Erythroneura vitis*). — *a*, with wings extended; *b*, with wings closed. (Lines show natural sizes.)

leaf-i-ness (lē′fi-nes), *n.* Leafy state; leafage: as, "the *leafiness* of midsummer" (Galt's "Annals of the Parish," xxxv.).
leaf=in-sect (lēf′in″sekt), *n.* Any of the orthopterous insects constituting the genus *Phyllium* (family *Phasmidæ*), native in the East Indies, Australia, etc., remarkable for their resemblance in color and form to the green leaves on which they feed.
leaf=lard (lēf′lärd), *n.* Lard prepared from the leaf or internal fat of the hog.
leaf-less (lēf′les), *a.* Without leaves.—**leaf′less-ness,** *n.*
leaf-let (lēf′let), *n.* A small or young leaf; specif., one of the separate blades or divisions of a compound leaf; also, a small leaf-like part or structure; also, a small flat or folded sheet of printed matter, as for distribution.

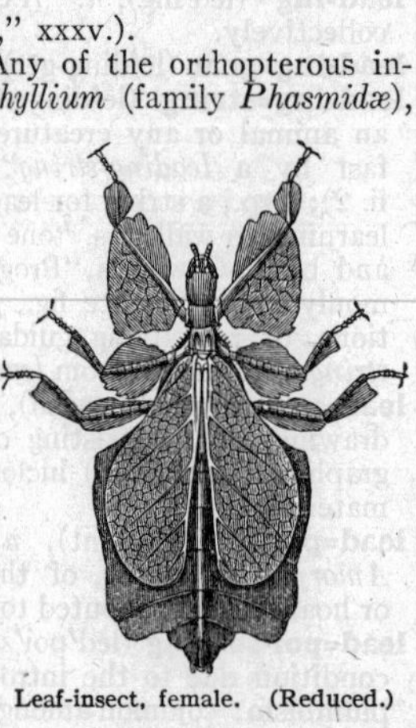
Leaf-insect, female. (Reduced.)

leaf-stalk (lēf′stâk), *n.* The stalk supporting a leaf; a petiole.
leaf-y (lē′fi), *a.*; compar. *leafier*, superl. *leafiest.* Abounding in, covered with, or consisting of leaves or foliage (as, "the *leafy* month of June," Coleridge's "Ancient Mariner," v.; "the *leafy* woods," Longfellow's "Hiawatha," v. 17; "My limb was now swathed in *leafy* bandages," H. Melville's "Typee," x.); also, leaf-like; laminate.
league[1] (lēg), *n.* [OF. F. *ligue*, < It. *liga*, *lega*, < L. *ligare*, bind.] A covenant or compact made between persons, parties, states, etc., for the maintenance or promotion of common interests or for mutual assistance or service; also, the aggregation of persons, parties, states, etc., associated in such a covenant; a confederacy; also, in general, any compact or alliance (as, "link'd in happy nuptial *league*": Milton's "Paradise Lost," iv. 339).—**Hanseatic League.** See *Hanseatic.*—**in league,** united by or having a compact or agreement; allied: as, "*in league* with the prince of darkness" (G. W. Curtis's "Prue and I," iv.).—**league of nations,** a league or covenant of the nations of the world for the purpose of promoting international coöperation and of achieving international peace and security; the nations associated in such a covenant; specif. [with two *caps.*], the covenant of this nature formulated at the Peace Conference at Paris in 1919, and incorporated in the treaty of peace terminating the World War; the nations associated in this covenant.—**league**[1], *v. t.* or *i.*; *leagued, leaguing.* To unite in a league; confederate; combine.
league[2] (lēg), *n.* [ME. *lege*, *leuge*, < LL. *leuga*, *leuca*; from Celtic.] A measure of distance, varying at different periods and in different countries, in English-speaking countries usually estimated roughly at 3 miles.—**marine league,** a measure of distance at sea, equal to 3 geographical or nautical miles.
lea-guer[1] (lē′gėr), *n.* A member of a league.
lea-guer[2] (lē′gėr), *n.* [D. *leger*, bed, camp: see *lair*, and cf. *laager.*] A military camp, esp. of a besieging army; a besieging force; also, a siege, or military investment (as, "the *leaguer* of Leyden": Motley's "Dutch Republic," iv. 1).—**lea′guer**[2], *v. t.* To besiege; beleaguer: as, "Two mighty hosts a *leaguer'd* town embrace" (Pope's tr. Homer's "Iliad," xviii.).
leak (lēk), *v.* [Prob. from Scand.: cf. Icel. *leka*, MLG. and G. *lecken*, D. *lekken*, leak.] **I.** *intr.* To let water, etc., enter or escape without design, as through a hole, crack, permeable material, or the like (as, the ship or the roof is *leaking*; the cellar *leaks*; a cask, boiler, or jar that *leaks*); also, to pass in or out in this manner, as water, etc. (as, the rain is *leaking* through the roof; gas *leaking* from a pipe); fig. (with *out*), to transpire, or become known undesignedly (as, "rumors . . . which had *leaked out* from the captain and mate": Dana's "Two Years before the Mast," xiv.). **II.** *tr.* To let (water, etc.) leak in or out: as, the roof *leaks* rain; a pipe that *leaks* gas.—**leak,** *n.* A hole, crack, or the like by which water, etc., enters or escapes without design (as, a *leak* in a ship or a roof; a *leak* in a cask or a pipe); also, the act or an act of leaking; also, in fig. use, any avenue or means of unintended entrance or escape, or the entrance or escape itself; often (colloq.), a means for the escape of a secret, or the escape itself; in *elect.*, a point where current escapes from a conductor, as because of poor insulation, or the escape itself.—**leak-age** (lē′kāj), *n.* The act of leaking; an entering or escape by a leak; also, in fig. use, any unintended entrance or escape; diminution or loss as if by leaking; the becoming known of something secret; also, that which leaks in or out (as, "the privilege of battening on . . . the *leakage* of the tap-room": Irving's "Sketch-Book," The Stage-Coach); also, in *com.*, an allowance for loss by leaking.—**leak′y,** *a.*; compar. *leakier*, superl. *leakiest.* Having a leak or leaks (as, "The ship was *leaky*, and very much disabled": Defoe's "Robinson Crusoe," i. 3); allowing water, etc., to leak in or out; fig., not retentive, as the memory; apt to disclose secrets, as a person.—**leak′i-ness,** *n.*
leal (lēl), *a.* [OF. *leial* (F. *loyal*): see *loyal.*] Loyal; faithful; true: as, "Yea, by the honour of the Table Round, I will be *leal* to thee and thy work" (Tennyson's "Pelleas and Ettarre," 335). [Archaic or Sc. and north. Eng.]—**land of the leal.** See under *land, n.*—**leal-ly** (lēl′li), *adv.*

lean[1] (lēn), *v.*; *leaned*, sometimes *leant* (lent), *leaning.* [AS. *hlinian, hleonian,* = D. *leunen* = G. *lehnen,* lean; akin to L. *-clinare,* Gr. κλίνειν, incline, Skt. *çri-,* lean: see *decline, incline, climate, climax,* and *ladder*.] **I.** *intr.* To recline, or lie down (obs. or Sc.); also, to rest against or on something for support (as, to *lean* against a wall; to *lean* on a person's arm); fig., to depend or rely, as for support or comfort (as, to *lean* on a person's friendship or promises); also, to incline or bend from a vertical position or in a particular direction (as, the *Leaning* Tower of Pisa; to *lean* down, back, or to one side); fig., to incline in feeling or opinion (as, to *lean* toward a particular candidate, policy, or doctrine); tend in action, effect, or character (as, "And he, who now to sense, now nonsense *leaning,* Means not, but blunders round about a meaning," Pope's "Prologue to the Satires," 185; "E'en his failings *lean'd* to virtue's side," Goldsmith's "Deserted Village," 164); also, to bow† or submit† (as, "'Twere good You *lean'd* unto his sentence": Shakspere's "Cymbeline," i. 1. 78). **II.** *tr.* To cause to lean or rest (*against, on, upon,* etc.: as, to *lean* the arm against or on a railing); also, to incline or bend (as, to *lean* the head forward).—**lean**[1], *n.* The act or state of leaning; inclination: as, "the cracked veranda with a tipsy *lean*" (Whittier's "Panorama").

lean[2] (lēn). [AS. *hlǣne.*] **I.** *a.* Scant of flesh, or not plump or fat (as, *lean* cattle; a *lean* body, arm, or face); thin; spare; of flesh or meat, containing little or no fat; fig., lacking in substantialness, richness, fullness, quantity, etc. (as, a *lean* diet; *lean* soil; "And left me gazing at a barren board, And a *lean* Order—scarce return'd a tithe," Tennyson's "Holy Grail," 890); meager; poor; unremunerative, as work; scantily supplied (as, a *lean* purse; a *lean* wardrobe); marked by scarcity (as, *lean* years). **II.** *n.* The lean part of anything; specif., that part of flesh which consists of muscle rather than fat.

lean-ing (lē'ning), *n.* Inclination; bias; tendency.

lean-ly (lēn'li), *adv.* In a lean manner.—**lean'ness,** *n.*

lean=to (lēn'tö). **I.** *a.* Having rafters or supports pitched against or leaning on an adjoining wall or building, as a roof. **II.** *n.*; pl. *-tos* (-töz). A structure with a lean-to roof.

leap (lēp), *v.*; *leaped* or *leapt* (lept), *leaping.* [AS. *hlēapan,* leap, run, = D. *loopen,* G. *laufen,* run, = Icel. *hlaupa,* leap, run, = Goth. *-hlaupan,* leap: cf. *lope* and *loup.*] **I.** *intr.* To run†; also, to spring through the air from one point or position to another (as, to *leap* over a ditch; to *leap* from a cliff; to *leap* upon a horse); jump, vault, or bound; skip, as in joy or sport; move or start quickly and lightly (as, to *leap* aside or back; to *leap* to one's feet); fly, shoot, or flash swiftly (as, the sword *leaps* from the scabbard; water, flame, or light *leaps* up); beat vigorously, as the heart; fig., to pass, come, rise, etc., as if with a leap or bound (as, to *leap* from one extreme to the other; the mind *leaps* to a conclusion; "A suspicion *leaped* to his brain," Bret Harte's "Outcasts of Poker Flat"). **II.** *tr.* To leap or jump over (as, to *leap* a ditch or a wall); fig., to pass over as if by a leap (as, the mind *leaps* an interval of time); also, to cause to leap (as, "They *leaped* their horses—over a trench where they could, into it . . . when they could not": De Quincey's "English Mail-Coach," i.).—**leap,** *n.* An act of leaping; a spring, jump, or bound; a light, springing movement; fig., a passing as if by leaping from one point or stage to another, as in progress or in reasoning (cf. *saltus*); an abrupt transition; also, a place leaped, or to be leaped, over or from (as, many a district has its Lover's *Leap*); also, the space cleared in a leap or jump.—**a leap in the dark,** fig., an act ventured upon in complete uncertainty as to the consequences; a blind venture.—**by leaps and bounds,** fig., by swift and great advances: as, the insurrection spread *by leaps and bounds.*—**leap'er,** *n.*

leap=frog (lēp'frog), *n.* A game in which one player leaps over another who is in a stooping posture.

leap=year (lēp'yēr), *n.* A year containing 366 days, or one day (Feb. 29) more than the ordinary year, to offset the difference in length between the ordinary year and the astronomical year (being, in practice, every year whose number is exactly divisible by 4, as 1928, except centenary years not exactly divisible by 400, as 1900); also, an intercalary year in any calendar.

lear (lēr), *a.* See *leer*[2].

learn (lėrn), *v.*; *learned* or *learnt, learning.* [AS. *leornian* = G. *lernen,* learn; akin to AS. *lǣran,* G. *lehren,* teach, and E. *lore*[1].] **I.** *tr.* To acquire knowledge of or skill in by study, instruction, or experience (as, to *learn* French; to *learn* piano-playing; to *learn* a trade); become versed or skilled in; come to know by study, memorizing, etc. (as, to *learn* a lesson; to *learn* a poem by heart; to *learn* a song); acquire (knowledge, skill, prudence, habits, etc.) by study or experience; also, to become informed of or acquainted with (as, to *learn* the truth, details, or news; to *learn* a man's name); hear or ascertain; also, to teach (now vulgar: as, "After supper she got out her book and *learned* me about Moses and the Bulrushers," Mark Twain's "Huckleberry Finn," i.). **II.** *intr.* To acquire knowledge or skill (as, to *learn* rapidly); profit by instruction or experience (as, to be too old or too stubborn to *learn*); also, to become informed, or hear (*of*: as, to *learn* of an occurrence).—**learn'a-ble,** *a.* That may be learned.—**learn'ed,** *p. a.* Possessed of learning or scholarly knowledge (as, a *learned* professor, jurist, or divine; a *learned* society); erudite; also, pertaining to or characterized by learning (as, *learned* pursuits; a *learned* treatise; "He had no inclination for any of the *learned* professions," Galt's "Annals of the Parish," xxxii.).—**learn'ed-ly,** *adv.*—**learn'ed-ness,** *n.*—**learn'er,** *n.*—**learn'ing,** *n.* The act or process of acquiring knowledge or skill; also, the possession of knowledge acquired by study, esp. by systematic and profound study (as, men of *learning*; "A pride there is of rank . . . A pride of *learning,*" Hood's "Ode to Rae Wilson," 315); scholarship: also, knowledge acquired by systematic study, in any field or fields of scholarly application (as, "A little *learning* is a dangerous thing," Pope's "Essay on Criticism," 215; "The lawyer . . . With . . . a wig full of *learning,*" Cowper's "Report of an Adjudged Case," 6); the knowledge acquired by the student or scholar, esp. that of an advanced or substantial kind; erudition; sometimes, the accumulated body of knowledge constituting the matter of scholarly study or attainment (as, the various branches or departments of *learning*; Greek *learning*; "whom they might teach the *learning* and the tongue of the Chaldeans," Dan. i. 4).—**New Learning.** See under *new, a.*

lear-y (lēr'i), *a.* See *leery*[1].

leas-a-ble (lē'sa-bl), *a.* That may be leased.

lease (lēs), *v. t.*; *leased, leasing.* [AF. *lesser,* lease, OF. *laissier* (F. *laisser*), let go, leave, let, < L. *laxare,* loosen: see *laxation.*] To grant the temporary possession or use of (lands, tenements, etc.) to another, usually for compensation at a fixed rate; grant or convey by lease; let; also, to take or hold by a lease, as lands.—**lease,** *n.* A contract conveying the possession of property to another for life, or for a definite term of years, or at will, usually in consideration of rent or other periodical compensation; also, the written instrument by which such a conveyance is made; also, the period of time for which it is made; hence, fig., an allotted period or term, esp. of life (as, "We miners have a short *lease* of life": Kingsley's "Yeast," xiii.).—**lease'hold** (-hōld). **I.** *n.* A tenure by lease; also, real estate held by lease. **II.** *a.* Held by lease.—**lease'hold"er,** *n.* A tenant under a lease.—**leas'er,** *n.*

leash (lēsh), *n.* [OF. F. *laisse,* < ML. *laxa,* leash, prop. fem. of L. *laxus,* loose, E. *lax.*] A thong or line for holding hounds, a hawk, or any dog or other animal in check (also fig.: as, to hold passion in a *leash*); also, among sportsmen, a brace and a half, as of hounds; hence, in general, a set of three (as, "I am sworn brother to a *leash* of drawers . . . Tom, Dick, and Francis": Shakspere's "1 Henry IV.," ii. 4. 7).—**leash,** *v. t.* To secure or hold in or as in a leash (as, "At his heels, *Leash'd* in like hounds, should famine, sword and fire Crouch for employment": Shakspere's "Henry V.," Prologue, 7); also, to associate or group together, esp. in a set of three.

leas-ing (lē'zing), *n.* [AS. *lēasung,* < *lēasian,* tell lies, < *lēas,* false: see *-less.*] Lying speech, or a lie: as, "Thou shalt destroy them that speak *leasing*" (Ps. v. 6); "all that fained is, as *leasings,* tales, and lies" (Spenser's "Faerie Queene," ii. 9. 51). [Archaic or Sc. and north. Eng.]

least (lēst). [AS. *lǣst,* superl. of *lǣssa,* E. *less.*] **I.** *a. superl.* Little beyond all others in size, amount, degree, etc. (as, not the *least* flake of snow; the *least* sum, distance, hope, sound, or light; the *least* depth or force); smallest; slightest; lowest in consideration or dignity (as, "He that is *least* among you all, the same shall be great": Luke, ix. 48): used as the superlative of *little*. **II.** *n.* That which is least; the least amount, quantity, degree, etc.—**at least,** at the least or lowest estimate (as, *at least* two hours); hence, at any rate, or in any case (as, "*At least* we'll die with harness on our back": Shakspere's "Macbeth," v. 5. 52).—**in the least,** in the smallest degree: as, a thing not *in the least* likely; it does not disturb me, not *in the least*.—**least,** *adv. superl.* To the least extent, amount, or degree: as, the *least* exacting of masters; I liked the last book *least* of all.—**least′ways,** *adv.* Same as *leastwise*. [Colloq. or prov.]—**least′wise,** *adv.* At least; at any rate.

leath-er (leᴛʜ′ėr), *n.* [AS. *lether* (in compounds) = D. and G. *leder* = Icel. *ledhr*, leather.] The skin of animals prepared for use by tanning or a similar process; also, some article or appliance made of this material; also, skin, esp. human skin (now slang).—**leath′er,** *v. t.* To cover or furnish with leather; also (colloq.), to beat with a leather thong; in general, to beat or thrash.

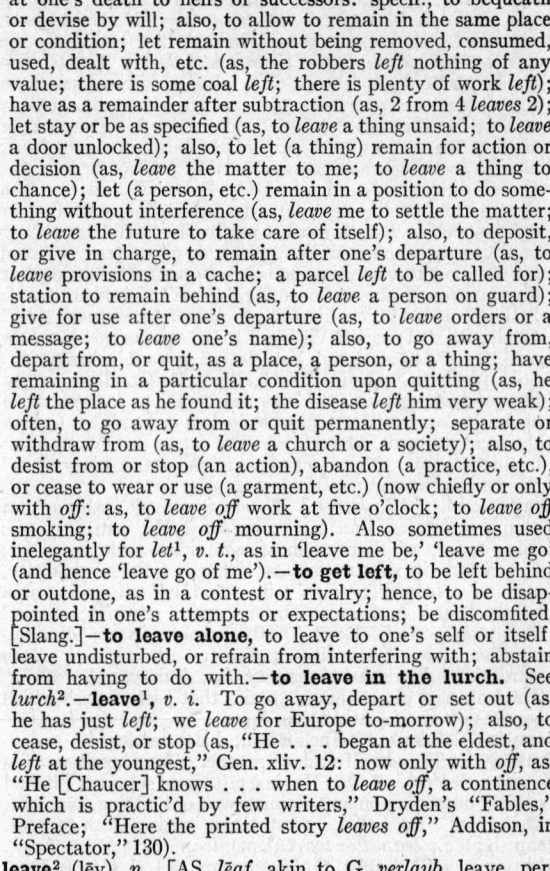

leath-er-back (leᴛʜ′ėr-bak), *n.* A large marine turtle, *Dermochelys coriacea*, with a longitudinally ridged flexible carapace formed of a mosaic of small bony plates embedded in a leathery skin.

Leatherback.

leath-er-coat (leᴛʜ′ėr-kōt), *n.* A russet apple. See Shakspere's "2 Henry IV.," v. 3. 44.

leath-er-ette (leᴛʜ-ėr-et′), *n.* [See *-ette*.] Imitation leather.

leath-er=head-ed (leᴛʜ′ėr-hed″ed), *a.* Thick-headed; stupid: as, "stupid and *leather-headed*" (Mark Twain's "Huckleberry Finn," xxv.).

leath-ern (leᴛʜ′ėrn), *a.* [AS. *letheren*.] Consisting or made of leather (as, "a *leathern* belt": Hawthorne's "House of the Seven Gables," xviii.); also, resembling leather (as, "The weak-eyed bat . . . flits by on *leathern* wing": Wm. Collins's "Ode to Evening," 10).

leath-er-neck (leᴛʜ′ėr-nek), *n.* A soldier or a marine. [Slang.]

leath-er-oid (leᴛʜ′ėr-oid), *n.* [See *-oid*.] A substitute for leather used in making bags, suitcases, etc., consisting mostly of vegetable fiber, as paper-stock, variously treated.

leath-er-wood (leᴛʜ′ėr-wůd), *n.* An American thymelæaceous shrub, *Dirca palustris*, with a tough bark.

leath-er-y (leᴛʜ′ėr-i), *a.* Like leather; tough and flexible.

leave[1] (lēv), *v. t.*; *left, leaving*. [AS. *lǣfan* = OHG. *leiben* = Icel. *leifa* = Goth. *-laibjan*, leave; a causative form from a root meaning in Teut. 'remain' (cf. AS. *belīfan* and G. *bleiben*, remain), Skt. *lip-*, smear, stick (cf. Gr. λιπαρός, oily, λιπαρής, persistent): cf. *lave*[3], *life*, and *live*[1].] To let remain, or have remaining, behind, after going, disappearing, ceasing, etc. (as, the acid *leaves* a stain in cloth; the wound *left* a scar); esp., to have remaining after death (as, he *leaves* a widow and two children; he *left* a large fortune; he *leaves* a great name behind him); hence, to transmit at one's death to heirs or successors: specif., to bequeath or devise by will; also, to allow to remain in the same place or condition; let remain without being removed, consumed, used, dealt with, etc. (as, the robbers *left* nothing of any value; there is some coal *left*; there is plenty of work *left*); have as a remainder after subtraction (as, 2 from 4 *leaves* 2); let stay or be as specified (as, to *leave* a thing unsaid; to *leave* a door unlocked); also, to let (a thing) remain for action or decision (as, *leave* the matter to me; to *leave* a thing to chance); let (a person, etc.) remain in a position to do something without interference (as, *leave* me to settle the matter; to *leave* the future to take care of itself); also, to deposit, or give in charge, to remain after one's departure (as, to *leave* provisions in a cache; a parcel *left* to be called for); station to remain behind (as, to *leave* a person on guard); give for use after one's departure (as, to *leave* orders or a message; to *leave* one's name); also, to go away from, depart from, or quit, as a place, a person, or a thing; have remaining in a particular condition upon quitting (as, he *left* the place as he found it; the disease *left* him very weak); often, to go away from or quit permanently; separate or withdraw from (as, to *leave* a church or a society); also, to desist from or stop (an action), abandon (a practice, etc.), or cease to wear or use (a garment, etc.) (now chiefly or only with *off*: as, to *leave off* work at five o'clock; to *leave off* smoking; to *leave off* mourning). Also sometimes used inelegantly for *let*[1], *v. t.*, as in 'leave me be,' 'leave me go' (and hence 'leave go of me').—**to get left,** to be left behind or outdone, as in a contest or rivalry; hence, to be disappointed in one's attempts or expectations; be discomfited. [Slang.]—**to leave alone,** to leave to one's self or itself; leave undisturbed, or refrain from interfering with; abstain from having to do with.—**to leave in the lurch.** See *lurch*[2].—**leave**[1], *v. i.* To go away, depart or set out (as, he has just *left*; we *leave* for Europe to-morrow); also, to cease, desist, or stop (as, "He . . . began at the eldest, and *left* at the youngest," Gen. xliv. 12: now only with *off*, as, "He [Chaucer] knows . . . when to *leave off*, a continence which is practic'd by few writers," Dryden's "Fables," Preface; "Here the printed story *leaves off*," Addison, in "Spectator," 130).

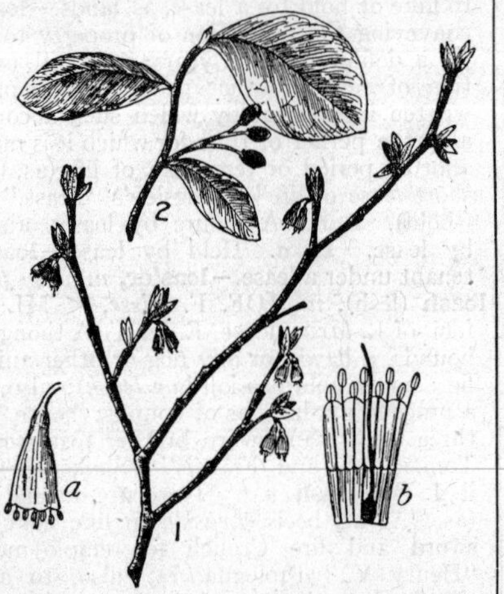

Leatherwood. — 1, branch with flowers; 2, branch with fruit and leaves; *a*, flower; *b*, flower laid open to show pistil and stamens.

leave[2] (lēv), *n.* [AS. *lēaf*, akin to G. *verlaub*, leave, permission; from the root of E. *lief* and *love*.] Permission to do something (as, "I desired *leave* of this prince to see the curiosities of the island": Swift's "Gulliver's Travels," iii. 3); specif., permission to be absent, as from duty (as, "He was going on *leave*, after some years of service, to see his kindred": Reade's "Cloister and the Hearth," xxxvii.); also, a farewell (chiefly in 'to take leave': as, "I took a solemn *leave* of his Majesty, and all my friends," Swift's "Gulliver's Travels," iii. 11).

leave[3] (lēv), *v. i.*; *leaved, leaving*. [From *leaf*.] To put forth leaves; leaf.—**leaved,** *a.* Having leaves; leafed: as, a four-*leaved* clover; "the great dining-room, whose two-*leaved* door stood open" (C. Brontë's "Jane Eyre," xii.).

leav-en (lev′n), *n.* [OF. F. *levain*, < L. *levamen*, that which raises, < *levare*, raise: see *lever*.] A substance used to produce fermentation in dough; specif., a mass of fermenting dough reserved for this purpose (cf. *sour-dough*); also, any substance which produces fermentation; a ferment; also, in fig. use (cf. Mat. xiii. 33, 1 Cor. v. 6), an agency which works in a thing to produce a gradual change or modification (as, the *leaven* of reform, or of discord, was working); a modifying element or admixture (as, to mix a *leaven* of charity in one's judgments; "He had a *leaven* of the old man in him which showed that he was his true-born son," Irving's "Tales of a Traveler," ii. 9); hence, character or sort (as, two men of the same *leaven*).—**the old leaven,** fig., an element, as of character, derived from an earlier and unregenerate or unenlightened stage or period (from the use in 1 Cor. v. 6–8): as, "A tinge of *the old leaven* is discernible, even unto this day, in their characters" (Irving's "Knickerbocker's New York," v. 8).—**leav′en,** *v. t.* To produce fermentation in (dough) by means of leaven (as, "Know ye not that a little leaven *leaveneth* the whole lump?" 1 Cor. v. 6); fig., to permeate with an altering or transforming influence; imbue with some modifying element.—**leav′en-ing,** *n.* The act of one who or something that leavens; also, that which leavens.

leav-er (lē′vėr), *n.* One who leaves.
leaves (lēvz), *n.* Plural of *leaf.*
leave=tak-ing (lēv′tā″king), *n.* The act of taking leave; the saying of farewell.
leav-ing (lē′ving), *n.* That which is left; residue; remains; refuse; usually in *pl.*
leav-y (lē′vi), *a.* Same as *leafy*: as, "the *leavy* beech" (Tennyson's "Margaret," v.). [Poetic.]
le-bes (lē′bēz), *n.* [L., < Gr. λέβης.] In *Gr. antiq.*, a basin-like or bowl-like vessel with rounded base, commonly of metal.

Lebes.

lech-er (lech′ėr), *n.* [OF. *lecheor*, gourmand, sensualist, < *lechier*, lick, live in gluttony or sensuality (F. *lécher*, lick); from Teut., and akin to E. *lick.*] A man immoderately given to sexual indulgence; a lewd or grossly unchaste man; a habitual libertine.—**lech′er**†, *v. i.* To play the lecher.—**lech′er-ous,** *a.* [OF. *lecheros*: cf. *lickerish.*] Given to or characterized by lechery; also, inciting to lechery.—**lech′er-ous-ly,** *adv.* —**lech′er-ous-ness,** *n.*—**lech′er-y,** *n.* [OF. *lecherie.*] Free indulgence of lust; lewdness.
le-ci-thin (les′i-thin), *n.* [Gr. λέκιθος, egg-yolk.] In *chem.*, any of various nitrogenous, phosphorus-containing substances found in animals and plants, esp. in leucocytes, in nerve-tissues, and in the yolk of eggs.
lec-tern (lek′tėrn), *n.* [OF. *letrun*, < ML. *lectrum*, < L. *legere*, read.] A reading-desk or singing-desk in a church, esp. that from which the lessons are read.
lec-tion (lek′shọn), *n.* [L. *lectio(n-)*, < *legere*, read: cf. *lesson.*] The act of reading†; also, a reading or version of a passage in a particular copy of a text; also, a lesson, or portion of sacred writing, read in divine service.—**lec′tion-a-ry** (-ā-ri), *n.*; pl. *-ries* (-riz). [ML. *lectionarium.*] A book, or a list, of lections or lessons for reading in divine service.
lec-tor (lek′tọr), *n.* [L., < *legere*, read.] A reader, as of lectures in a college or university or of scriptural lessons; specif., in the *Rom. Cath. Ch.*, one ordained to the next to the lowest of the four minor orders.—**lec′tor-ate** (-āt), *n.* The office of lector.—**lec′tress,** *n.* A female reader.—**lec′-trice** (-tris), *n.* [F., < L. *lectrix*, fem. of *lector.*] A woman employed to read aloud.
lec-ture (lek′ṭūr), *n.* [ML. *lectura*, < L. *legere*, read: see *legion.*] The act of reading, or something read (archaic: as, "That's he whose wondrous poem is become A *lecture* for the noble youth of Rome!" Dryden's tr. Persius's "Satires," i. 63); also, a discourse read or delivered before an audience, esp. for instruction or to set forth some subject (as, *lectures* on physics, art, or law; a *lecture* on Abraham Lincoln; *lectures* on travel); sometimes, a religious discourse less formal than. or other than, a regular sermon; also, an admonitory discourse, or speech of warning or reproof as to conduct (as, a mother's *lectures* to a thoughtless boy; a curtain-*lecture*; I'll give him a good *lecture*); a lengthy or tedious reprimand; also, fig., a lesson† or warning†.—**lec′-ture,** *v.*; *-tured, -turing.* **I.** *intr.* To deliver a lecture or lectures. **II.** *tr.* To deliver a lecture to or before; instruct by lectures; also, to address in admonition or rebuke; reprove or reprimand at some length.—**lec′tur-er,** *n.* One who lectures, esp. by way of instruction, as in a university or before the public; sometimes, an assistant to a professor in a university, or a person who performs professorial duties without having the professorial rank or title; in the *Ch. of Eng.*, one of a class of preachers chosen in some parishes to deliver lectures or religious discourses, but not holding the office of rector, vicar, or curate.—**lec′ture-ship,** *n.* The office of lecturer.
le-cy-thus (les′i-thus), *n.*; pl. *-thi* (-thī). [LL., < Gr. λήκυθος.] In *Gr. antiq.*, a relatively tall, slender, narrow-necked vase with a handle, for holding oil, unguents, etc.

Attic Lecythi.

led (led). Preterit and past participle of *lead*¹.—**led,** *p. a.* Under leading or control.—**led captain,** a hanger-on, henchman, or parasite: as, "Mr. Wagg, the celebrated wit, and a *led captain* and trencherman of my Lord Steyne" (Thackeray's "Vanity Fair," li.).
ledge (lej), *n.* [ME. *legge*, prob. < *leggen*, E. *lay*¹.] A transverse bar, timber, strip, etc. (now chiefly technical); hence, any relatively narrow, horizontal projecting part, or any part affording a horizontal shelf-like surface (as, a *ledge* above a fireplace; a window-*ledge*; to climb from *ledge* to *ledge* on the face of a building); often, a shelf-like projection on the side of a mountain, cliff, or the like (as, "He climbed up the side of the chasm to gain the *ledge* above": Marryat's "Mr. Midshipman Easy," xviii.); also, a more or less flat or low extent of rock in or under water; a reef, ridge, or line of rocks in the sea (as, "the Maldives, a famous *ledge* of islands," Defoe's "Captain Singleton," xiii.; a ship wrecked on an invisible *ledge*); also, a layer or mass of rock underground, as one struck in excavating; in *mining*, a lode or vein.—**ledged,** *a.* Having a ledge or ledges: as, a *ledged* wall or cliff.
ledg-er (lej′ėr). [ME. *legger* (book), prob. < *leggen*, E. *lay*¹ (cf. *ledge*); with later variant forms (early mod. E. *lidger*, *ligier*, etc.) and senses appar. due to the related E. *lie*¹ (ME. *liggen*).] **I.** *n.* A book kept permanently in a place, as a Bible, a breviary, or a register†; now, the principal book of accounts of a business concern, containing a record of all transactions, so entered as to exhibit the debits and credits of each account; also, a resident, esp. a resident agent or ambassador†; also, a fishing-bait fixed so as to remain in one place; also, a bar, beam, stone, or the like, that lies horizontally in a fixed position; a horizontal timber fastened to the vertical uprights of a scaffold, to support the putlogs; a flat slab of stone laid over a grave or tomb. **II.** *a.* Stationary or fixed (now only of bait, lines, tackle, etc., for fishing); also, resident†; also, in *music*, noting the short lines temporarily added above or below the staff to increase the range, or the spaces inclosed by these lines.—**ledg′er,** *v. i.* To use a ledger bait; fish with a bait fixed so as to remain in one place.
ledg-y (lej′i), *a.* Abounding in ledges; consisting of a ledge or ledges.
lee¹ (lē), *n.* [OF. F. *lie*, < ML. *lia*; perhaps from Celtic.] That which settles from a liquid, esp. from wine; sediment; dregs: usually in *pl.*, and often fig. (as, "I will drink Life to the *lees*": Tennyson's "Ulysses," 7).
lee² (lē). [AS. *hlēo*, shelter, = Icel. *hlē*, (naut.) lee.] **I.** *n.* Shelter; esp., the side or part that is sheltered or turned away from the wind (as, the *lee* of a ship; "Beneath the Castle's sheltering *lee*, They staid their course in quiet sea," Scott's "Lord of the Isles," i. 24); also, the quarter or region toward which the wind blows: chiefly *naut.* **II.** *a.* Of or pertaining to the lee, esp. of a ship (as, "She careened over so that her *lee* channels were under the water": Marryat's "Peter Simple," xv.); pertaining to, situated in, or moving toward the quarter or region toward which the wind blows (see phrases below): chiefly *naut.*, and opposed to *weather.*—**lee shore,** a shore toward which the wind blows. —**lee tide,** a tide running in the same direction in which the wind is blowing.
lee-an-gle (lē′ang″gl), *n.* [Native Australian.] A heavy club with a bent and pointed end, used by Australian aborigines.
lee=board (lē′bōrd), *n.* A flat board let down vertically into the water on the lee side of a ship or boat to prevent leeward motion.

Dutch Galiot, with Lee-board.

leech¹ (lēch), *n.* [AS. *lǣce* = OHG. *lāhhi* = Goth. *lēkeis*, physician.] A physician: as, "Thither came The King's own *leech* to look into his hurt" (Tennyson's "Geraint and Enid," 922). [Archaic.]—**leech**[1], *v. t.* To cure; heal: as, "Let those *leech* his wounds for whose sake he encountered them" (Scott's "Ivanhoe," xviii.). [Archaic.]

leech[2] (lēch), *n.* [AS. *lǣce, lȳce,* = MD. *lake, lieke,* leech.] Any of the blood-sucking or carnivorous, usually aquatic, worms constituting the order or class *Hirudinea,* certain fresh-water species of which were formerly much used by physicians for bloodletting; also, an instrument used for drawing blood; also, in fig. use, a person who clings to another with a view to gain (as, "The spendthrift, and the *leech* That sucks him": Cowper's "Task," iii. 817).—**leech**[2], *v. t.* To apply leeches to so as to bleed.

Leech (*Pontobdella muricata*), a species parasitic on skates and other fishes.

leech[3] (lēch), *n.* [Cf. Icel. *līk,* MLG. *līk,* D. *lijk,* G. *leik,* bolt-rope.] *Naut.,* either of the perpendicular or sloping edges of a square sail; the after edge of a fore-and-aft sail; sometimes, when qualified, either the after edge (*after leech*) or the forward edge (*forward* or *fore leech*) of a fore-and-aft sail.

leech-craft (lēch′kráft), *n.* [AS. *lǣcecræft.*] The art of the leech or physician; medical science, skill, or treatment: as, "Abbot Jerome, whose *leech-craft* is famous" (Scott's "Castle Dangerous," x.). [Archaic.]

leech-dom (lēch′dọm), *n.* [AS. *lǣcedōm.*] A medicine; a medicinal remedy. [Archaic.]

leek (lēk), *n.* [AS. *lēac* = D. *look* = G. *lauch* = Icel. *laukr,* leek.] A liliaceous plant, *Allium porrum,* allied to the onion but having a cylindrical bulb, and used in cookery (it is the national emblem of the Welsh); also, any of various allied species.—**leek′=green′,** *a.* Of the dull bluish-green color of the leek.

leer[1]† (lēr), *n.* [AS. *hlēor,* cheek, face.] The cheek; the face; hence, looks, personal appearance, or complexion (as, "He hath a Rosalind of a better *leer* than you": Shakspere's "As You Like It," iv. 1. 67).

leer[2], **lear** (lēr), *a.* [AS. *lǣr-* (in *lǣrnes,* emptiness) = G. *leer,* empty.] Empty; without contents, load, etc.; unoccupied; sometimes, hungry. [Now prov. Eng.]

leer[3] (lēr), *v.* [Perhaps < *leer*[1].] **I.** *intr.* To look obliquely, esp. with sly, suggestive, insulting, or malicious significance: as, "*leering* at his neighbour's wife" (Tennyson's "Vision of Sin," iv.). **II.** *tr.* To give an oblique glance with (the eye).—**leer**[3], *n.* A side glance, esp. of sly or insulting suggestion or malicious significance: as, "She gives the *leer* of invitation" (Shakspere's "Merry Wives of Windsor," i. 3. 50); "assent with civil *leer*" (Pope's "Prologue to the Satires," 201).—**leer′ing-ly,** *adv.*

leer-y[1], **lear-y** (lēr′i), *a.* [See *leer*[2].] Empty. [Prov. Eng.]

leer-y[2] (lēr′i), *a.* [See *leer*[3].] Knowing (as, "You're a very *leery* cove, by the look of you": Conan Doyle's "Exploits of Brigadier Gerard," iv.); also, wary; suspicious. [Slang.]

lees (lēz), *n. pl.* See *lee*[1].

leet (lēt), *n.* [AF. *lete* = AL. *leta*; origin uncertain.] A court-leet, its jurisdiction, or the district subject to it.

lee-ward (lē′wạrd, naut. lū′ạrd). **I.** *a.* On the lee, or the side turned away from the wind; pertaining to, situated in, or moving toward the quarter toward which the wind blows: opposed to *windward.* **II.** *n.* The lee side; the point or quarter toward which the wind blows: as, "She [a ship] sailed just like a hay-stack, one mile ahead and three to *leeward*" (Marryat's "Peter Simple," lvii.).—**lee′ward,** *adv.* Toward the lee.

lee-way (lē′wā), *n.* The lateral movement of a ship to leeward, or the resulting deviation from her true course; fig., loss of progress in general; also, convenient room or scope, as for action (colloq.).

left[1] (left). Preterit and past participle of *leave*[1].

left[2] (left). [AS. *left, lyft,* weak, = North Fries. *leeft,* MD. *luft, lucht,* MLG. *lucht,* left.] **I.** *a.* Belonging or pertaining to the side of a person or thing which is turned toward the west when the face is toward the north, or to that part of anything faced which appears on this side of the spectator (opposed to *right*): as, one's *left* hand or *left* glove; the *left* side of a deliberative assembly (that to the presiding officer's left); the *left* bank of a river (that on the left as one faces down the stream). **II.** *n.* The left side, or what is on the left side (as, to the *left,* toward the left side, also counter-clockwise); specif., the larboard or port of a ship; also [usually *cap.*], in continental Europe, that part of a legislative assembly which sits on the left side of the chamber as viewed by the president, a position customarily assigned to representatives holding liberal or democratic views; hence, a party holding such views.

left=hand (left′hand), *a.* Of, for, or with the left hand; also, on or to the left.—**left′=hand′ed,** *a.* Having the left hand or arm more serviceable than the right; preferably using the left hand; also, adapted to or performed by the left hand; also, situated on the side of the left hand; moving or rotating from right to left, or in a direction opposite to that of the hands of a clock (as, a *left-handed* screw, a screw which is advanced by turning from right to left, and whose thread runs upward from right to left when viewed from the side with the axis vertical; a *left-handed* helix or spiral, one that ascends or advances like the thread of a left-handed screw); also, in fig. use, clumsy or awkward (as, a *left-handed* method of proceeding; "It seems to me as if murder and massacre were but a very *left-handed* way of producing civilization and love," Godwin's "Caleb Williams," xiii.); ambiguous or doubtful (as, a *left-handed* compliment); also, morganatic, as a marriage (from the bridegroom's giving the bride his left hand instead of his right, as was customary at morganatic weddings).—**left′=hand′ed-ly,** *adv.*—**left′=hand′ed-ness,** *n.*—**left′=hand′er,** *n.* A left-handed person; also, a blow with the left hand.

left=o-ver (left′ō″vėr), *n.* Something left over or remaining; esp., a remnant of food, as from a meal.

left-ward (left′wạrd), *adv.* and *a.* Toward or on the left.—**left′wards,** *adv.* Leftward.

leg (leg), *n.* [From Scand.: cf. Icel. *leggr,* Sw. *lägg,* leg, Dan. *læg,* calf of the leg.] One of the members or limbs which support and move the human or animal body; specif., that part of the limb between the knee and the ankle; also, an obeisance made by drawing back one leg and bending the other (archaic: as, "He is one that cannot make a good *leg,*" Longfellow's "Hyperion," i. 7); also, that part of a garment, such as a stocking, trousers, or the like, which covers the leg; also, something resembling or suggesting a leg in use, position, or appearance; one of the supports of a piece of furniture; one of the sides of a pair of dividers or compasses; one of the sides of a triangle other than the base or, in a right-angled triangle, other than the hypotenuse; *naut.,* the course or run made by a sailing-vessel on one tack; one of the series of straight runs which make up the zigzag course of a sailing-vessel proceeding to windward; hence, fig., one of the distinct portions or stages of any course or journey (as, the last *leg* of a trip); also, in *cricket,* the part of the field to the left of and behind the batsman as he faces the bowler (or to the right of and behind him if he be left-handed); also, the fielder occupying this part of the field.—**leg,** *v. i.*; *legged, legging.* To walk or run: usually with indefinite *it*: as, "Then for Texas! We'll *leg* it together!" (Mark Twain's "Tom Sawyer," xxvi.). [Prov. or colloq.]

leg-a-cy (leg′ạ-si), *n.*; pl. *-cies* (-siz). [OF. *legacie,* legateship, < L. *legatus,* E. *legate*: cf. L. *legatum,* bequest, likewise from *legare,* send, depute, bequeath.] The office or function of a legate†; the mission or business committed to a legate†; a legation† or embassy†; also, a gift of property, esp. personal property, as money, by will; a bequest; hence, anything handed down by an ancestor or predecessor (as, "Books are the *legacies* that a great genius leaves to mankind": Addison, in "Spectator," 166).

le-gal (lē′gạl), *a.* [L. *legalis,* < *lex* (*leg-*), law.] Of or pertaining to law; connected with the law or its administration; sometimes, characteristic of the profession of the law (as, a *legal* mind); also, appointed, established, or authorized by law; deriving authority from law; sometimes, that is such in the view of the law (as, *legal* incapacity; a *legal* infant); specif., such as is recognized by law rather than by equity; also, permitted by law, or lawful (as, such acts are not *legal*); also, in *theol.,* of or pertaining to the Mosaic law; also, of or pertaining to the doctrine of salvation by good works rather than through free grace.—**legal tender.** See *tender*[3], *n.*—**le′gal-ism,** *n.* Strict adherence, or the principle of strict adherence, to law or prescription; in *theol.*, the doctrine of salvation by good works.—**le'gal-ist,** *n.* One who adheres strictly to law; also, an adherent of the theological doctrine of legalism; also, one versed in the law. —**le-gal-is'tic,** *a.*—**le-gal-i-ty** (lē-gal'i-ti), *n.* The state or quality of being legal or in conformity with the law; lawfulness; also, attachment to or observance of law; often, insistence on the letter of the law; in *theol.*, reliance on good works for salvation, rather than on free grace.—**le'gal-ize** (-īz), *v. t.*; *-ized, -izing.* To make legal; authorize; sanction.—**le"gal-i-za'tion** (-i-zā'shọn), *n.*—**le'gal-ly,** *adv.* In a legal manner; according to law.

leg-an-tine (leg'ạn-tin), *a.* Same as *legatine.*

leg-a-ta-ry (leg'ạ-tā-ri). [L. *legatarius*, < *legatum*, bequest: see *legacy.*] **I.** *a.* Of or pertaining to a bequest or legacy. **II.** *n.*; pl. *-ries* (-riz). A legatee.

leg-ate (leg'āt), *n.* [OF. *legat* (F. *légat*), < L. *legatus*, < *legare*, send, depute, appoint, bequeath, < *lex* (*leg-*), law.] A deputy, envoy, or ambassador (as, "the *legates* from Utrecht": Motley's "Dutch Republic," iii. 5); specif., an ecclesiastic delegated by the Pope as his representative (as, "The Lord Cardinal Pole, sent here as *legate* From our most Holy Father Julius, Pope": Tennyson's "Queen Mary," iii. 3. 71); in *Rom. hist.*, an envoy; also, a deputy or lieutenant of a general or of a governor of a province; also, under the emperors, a governor of a province.

leg-a-tee (leg-ạ-tē'), *n.* [L. *legatus*, pp. of *legare*, bequeath: see *legate.*] One to whom a legacy is bequeathed.

leg-ate-ship (leg'āt-ship), *n.* The office or position of a legate.

leg-a-tine (leg'ạ-tin), *a.* Of or pertaining to a legate; having the authority of a legate.

le-ga-tion (lē-gā'shọn), *n.* [L. *legatio*(*n-*), < *legare*, send, depute: see *legate.*] The act of sending a legate or deputy; a commissioning of one person to act at a distance for another; the fact of being so sent or commissioned; also, the commission or charge intrusted to a legate; also, the person or persons sent on a mission; an embassy; specif., a diplomatic minister and his suite when the minister is not of the highest (or ambassadorial) rank; also, the official residence or place of business of such a minister; also, the office or dignity of a legate.—**le-ga'tion-a-ry** (-ā-ri), *a.*

le-ga-to (lā-gä'tō), *a.* [It., pp. of *legare*, < L. *ligare*, bind, tie.] In *music*, smooth and connected, without breaks between the successive tones: opposed to *staccato.*

le-ga-tor (lē-gā'tọr), *n.* [L., < *legare*, bequeath: see *legate.*] One who bequeaths; a testator.—**leg-a-to-ri-al** (leg-ạ-tō'ri-ạl), *a.*

leg=bail (leg'bāl), *n.* Flight from custody or arrest: as, to give *leg-bail.* [Humorous.]

leg=bye (leg'bī), *n.* [See *by*, *bye*, *n.*] In *cricket*, a run made on a ball touching any part of the batsman's person except his hand.

leg-end (lej'ẹnd or lē'jẹnd), *n.* [OF. *legende* (F. *légende*), < ML. *legenda*, lit. 'something to be read,' orig. neut. pl. gerundive of L. *legere*, read: see *legion.*] A story of the life of a saint; a collection of such stories (as, the "Golden *Legend*," tr. ML. *Legenda Aurea*, written by Jacobus de Voragine, archbishop of Genoa, in the 13th century, the most popular of medieval works of this kind); a collection of stories of any admirable persons (obs. or archaic: as, Chaucer's "*Legend* of Good Women"); also, in general, a story†, history†, or account† (as, the *legend* of a person's life); now, commonly, a non-historical or unverifiable story handed down by tradition from earlier times and popularly accepted as historical (as, "A hoard of tales that dealt with knights Half-*legend*, half-historic," Tennyson's "Princess," Prologue, 30; "Listen to this Indian *Legend*, To this Song of Hiawatha!" Longfellow's "Hiawatha," Introd., 86); stories or matter of this kind (as, a hero of *legend*; a spot rich in *legend*); also, an inscription, esp. on a coin or medal, a coat of arms, or a monument, or accompanying a picture, book-illustration, or the like.—**leg'end,** *v. t.* To narrate or celebrate in legend (as, "Nor ladies wanton love, nor wandring knight, *Legend* I out in rimes all richly dight": J. Hall's "Satires," i. 1); also, to furnish with a legend or inscription.—**leg-en-da-ry** (lej'ẹn-dā-ri). [ML. *legendarius.*] **I.** *a.* Pertaining to or of the nature of a legend or legends (as, tales of a *legendary* character; "skill'd in *legendary* lore," Goldsmith's "Hermit"; "His *legendary* song . . . Of ancient deeds, so long forgot," Scott's "Lay of the Last Minstrel," iv., Conclusion); also, celebrated or described in legend (as, a *legendary* hero, exploit, or event); traditional; also, relating legends, as a writer. **II.** *n.*; pl. *-ries* (-riz). A collection or book of legends, esp. of the lives of saints; also, a relater or compiler of legends.—**leg'end-ry** (-ri), *n.* Legends collectively.

leg-er (lej'ėr), *a.* See *ledger*, *a.*

leg-er-de-main (lej"ėr-dē-mān'), *n.* [F. *léger de main*, 'light of hand.'] Sleight of hand; jugglery; conjuring tricks; fig., trickery or deception; also, a piece of sleight of hand; any artful trick.—**leg"er-de-main'ist,** *n.*

le-ger-i-ty (lẹ-jer'i-ti), *n.* [F. *légèreté*, < *léger*, < L. *levis*, light.] Lightness; nimbleness: as, "The organs . . . newly move, With casted slough and fresh *legerity*" (Shakspere's "Henry V.," iv. 1. 23). [Obs. or rare.]

legged (legd, in compounds often leg'ed), *a.* Having a leg or legs: as, one-*legged*; long-*legged.*

leg-gin (leg'in), *n.* Same as *legging.*

leg-ging (leg'ing), *n.* An extra outer covering for the leg, usually extending from the ankle to the knee but sometimes higher: usually in *pl.*

leg-gy (leg'i), *a.* Having long, esp. awkwardly long, legs: as, "Slapper's long-tailed *leggy* mare" (Thackeray's "Book of Snobs," x.).

Leg-horn (leg'hôrn). **I.** *a.* Of or pertaining to the seaport or the province of Leghorn, in Tuscany, Italy: applied esp. to a fine, smooth plaited straw and to hats, etc., made of it, also to a breed of the domestic fowl characterized by comparatively small size and by prolific laying. **II.** *n.* [*cap.* or *l. c.*] Leghorn straw, or a hat or bonnet of it; also, a Leghorn cock or hen.

leg-i-ble (lej'i-bl), *a.* [LL. *legibilis*, < L. *legere*, read.] That may be read or deciphered, esp. with ease, as writing or printing; fig., that may be discerned or distinguished (as, "the trouble *legible* in my countenance": Lamb's "Superannuated Man").—**leg-i-bil'i-ty** (-bil'i-ti), **leg'i-ble-ness,** *n.*—**leg'i-bly,** *adv.*

le-gion (lē'jọn), *n.* [OF. *legion* (F. *légion*), < L. *legio*(*n-*), < *legere*, gather, also read, akin to Gr. λέγειν, pick, gather, tell, speak: cf. *lecture*, *legend*, *legume*, and *Logos.*] A body of infantry in the army of ancient Rome, numbering from 3,000 to 6,000 men, and usually combined with from 300 to 700 cavalry; also, any of certain military bodies in other countries; sometimes, specif. [*cap.*], with *the*, the French Foreign Legion, or the American Legion; also, loosely [*l. c.*], any large body of armed men (as, "Nor knew great Hector how his *legions* yield": Pope's tr. Homer's "Iliad," xiii.); hence any great host or multitude, whether of persons or of things (as, "My name is *Legion*: for we are many," Mark, v. 9; "The *legions* Of horrid hell," Shakspere's "Macbeth," iv. 3. 55; "a cumbrous whale attacked on all sides by a *legion* of sword-fish," H. Melville's "Typee," xvii.).—**American Legion.** See under *American*, *a.*—**foreign legion.** See under *foreign.*—**Legion of Honor,** a French order of distinction, instituted in 1802 by Napoleon Bonaparte, membership in which is granted as a reward for meritorious civil or military services.—**le-gion-aire'** (-ãr'), *n.* [Also *legionnaire*; F. *légionnaire.*] A soldier or member of a legion; specif. [often *cap.*], a member of the American Legion.—**le'gion-a-ry** (-ā-ri). [L. *legionarius.*] **I.** *a.* Pertaining or belonging to a legion; constituting a legion or legions. **II.** *n.*; pl. *-ries* (-riz). A soldier of a legion; also, a member of the Legion of Honor.—**le'gioned,** *a.* Arrayed in legions.

leg-is-late (lej'is-lāt), *v.*; *-lated, -lating.* [Back-formation from *legislation* or *legislator.*] **I.** *intr.* To exercise the function of legislation; act as legislator; make or enact laws. **II.** *tr.* To effect, bring (*into*), put (*out*), etc., by legislation.

leg-is-la-tion (lej-is-lā'shọn), *n.* [LL. *legislatio*(*n-*), for L. *legis latio*(*n-*), 'bringing of a law': *legis*, gen. of *lex*, law; *latio*(*n-*), < *latus*, pp. of *ferre*, bear.] The act of making or enacting laws; also, a law or a body of laws enacted.— —**leg'is-la-tive** (-lā-tiv). **I.** *a.* Having the function of making laws (as, a *legislative* assembly or body); also, of or pertaining to legislation or the making of laws (as, *legislative* proceedings); ordained by legislation (as, a *legis-*

lative penalty); also, pertaining to a legislature (as, a *legislative* recess). **II.** *n.* The power of legislating†; also, the legislative branch of a government; the legislature.—**leg′is-la-tive-ly,** *adv.*

leg-is-la-tor (lej′is-lā-tọr), *n.* [L. *legis lator*, 'bringer of a law.'] One who gives or makes laws; a lawgiver; a member of a legislative body.—**leg″is-la-to′ri-al** (-lạ-tō′ri-ạl), *a.* Of or pertaining to legislators or legislation.—**leg″is-la-to′ri-al-ly,** *adv.*—**leg′is-la-tor-ship** (-lā-tọr-ship), *n.* The office or function of a legislator.—**leg′is-la-tress,** *n.* A female legislator. Also **leg-is-la′trix.**

leg-is-la-ture (lej′is-lā-ţụr), *n.* [= F. *législature.*] The legislative body of a country or state, esp., in the U. S., of a State.

le-gist (lē′jist), *n.* [OF. *legiste* (F. *légiste*), < ML. *legista*, < L. *lex* (*leg-*), law.] One versed in law.

le-git-i-ma-cy (lẹ-jit′i-mạ-si), *n.* The state or fact of being legitimate.

le-git-i-mate (lẹ-jit′i-māt), *v. t.*; *-mated, -mating.* [ML. *legitimatus*, pp. of *legitimare*, < L. *legitimus*, lawful, < *lex* (*leg-*), law.] To make or pronounce lawful; hence, to show or declare to be legitimate or proper (as, "Necessity *legitimates* my advice; for it is the only way to save our lives": Defoe's "Robinson Crusoe," i. 17); authorize; justify; specif., to establish as lawfully born; invest (a bastard) with the rights of one lawfully born.—**le-git′i-mate** (-mạt), *a.* According to law, or lawful; in accordance with established rules or principles, or proper; often, conforming to accepted standards (as, the *legitimate* drama, the body of Shaksperian and other standard dramas, or of plays of recognized literary or dramatic merit); of the normal or regular type or kind; specif., born in wedlock, or of parents legally married, as a child; hence, genuine, or not spurious, as a literary production; also, resting on or ruling by the principle of hereditary right (as, the *legitimate* title to a throne; a *legitimate* sovereign); also, in accordance with the laws of reasoning (as, a *legitimate* conclusion or inference); logically inferable; logical.—**le-git′i-mate-ly,** *adv.*—**le-git′i-mate-ness,** *n.*—**le-git-i-ma′tion** (-mā′shọn), *n.* [ML. *legitimatio*(*n-*).] The act or process of legitimating.—**le-git′i-ma-tize** (-mạ-tīz), *v. t.*; *-tized, -tizing.* To legitimate.

le-git-i-mist (lẹ-jit′i-mist), *n.* [F. *légitimiste*, < *légitime*, < L. *legitimus*, lawful: see *legitimate.*] A supporter of legitimate authority, esp. of a claim to a throne based on direct descent; [*cap.*] in France, a supporter of the claims to the crown of the elder branch of the Bourbons, deposed in 1830.—**le-git′i-mism,** *n.*—**le-git-i-mis′tic,** *a.*

le-git-i-mize (lẹ-jit′i-mīz), *v. t.*; *-mized, -mizing.* [L. *legitimus*, lawful: see *legitimate.*] To legitimate.—**le-git″i-mi-za′tion** (-mi-zā′shọn), *n.*

leg-less (leg′les), *a.* Without legs.

leg-let (leg′let), *n.* A little leg; also, an ornamental ring or band for the leg.

leg=of=mut-ton (leg′ọv-mut′n), *a.* Having the shape of a leg of mutton, as a kind of triangular sail (usually with a boom) often used as the only sail on a small boat, or as a full sleeve narrowing toward the wrist.

leg-ume (leg′ūm or lẹ-gūm′), *n.* [F. *légume*, < L. *legumen*, legume, pulse, lit. 'something gathered (or picked),' < *legere*, gather: see *legion.*] The edible part (seed, or seed and pod) of plants of the pea and bean kind (usually in *pl.*); also, the pod or seed-vessel of such a plant, which is usually dehiscent by both sutures, thus dividing into two parts or valves; also, a plant bearing such pods.

le-gu-min (lẹ-gū′min), *n.* [From *legume.*] In *chem.*, a proteid resembling casein, obtained from the seeds of leguminous and other plants.

le-gu-mi-nous (lẹ-gū′mi-nus), *a.* [NL. *leguminosus*, < L. *legumen*: see *legume.*] Pertaining to, of the nature of, or bearing legumes; specif., belonging or pertaining to the *Leguminosæ*, a group, order, or family regarded as comprising the legume-bearing plants, and sometimes subdivided into three families or subfamilies, the *Fabaceæ* (bean family), the *Cæsalpiniaceæ* (senna family), and the *Mimosaceæ* (mimosa family). Cf. *fabaceous, cæsalpiniaceous,* and *mimosaceous.*

lei (lāẹ), *n.* [Hawaiian.] In the Hawaiian Islands, a wreath of flowers, leaves, etc., for the neck or head.

lei-ot-ri-chous (lī-ot′ri-kus), *a.* See *liotrichous.*

lei-sure (lē′zhụr or lezh′ụr), *n.* [OF. *leisir* (F. *loisir*), noun use of *leisir*, inf., < L. *licere*, be permitted.] Freedom or opportunity to do something† (as, "Disguised . . . as a schoolmaster . . . That so I may . . . Have leave and *leisure* to make love to her": Shakspere's "Taming of the Shrew," i. 2. 136); now, opportunity or time afforded by freedom from pressing occupation, duty, etc. (as, "'Zounds! how has he the *leisure* to be sick In such a justling time?" Shakspere's "1 Henry IV.," iv. 1. 17); free or unoccupied time; also, the condition of having one's time free from the demands of work or duty (as, a gentleman of *leisure*; a life of *leisure*); ease.—**at leisure,** with free or unrestricted time (as, to proceed *at leisure*; we will speak more *at leisure* later); hence, without haste, or with deliberation (as, "Married in haste, we may repent *at leisure*": Congreve's "Old Bachelor," v. 3); also, unoccupied or disengaged (as, to be *at leisure*); often, having time (to do something: as, to be *at leisure* to see a caller).—**at one's leisure,** when one has leisure; at one's convenience: as, let me hear from you *at your leisure.*—**lei′sure,** *a.* Free or unoccupied (as, *leisure* hours; "A whole *leisure* Saturday afternoon was before him," Longfellow's "Kavanagh," xxiv.); also, having leisure, or leisured (as, the *leisure* class).—**lei′sured,** *a.* Having leisure, or not occupied with business (as, the *leisured* class of society); also, leisurely.—**lei′sure-less,** *a.* Without leisure.—**lei′sure-ly,** *a.* Acting, proceeding, or done at leisure or without haste (as, a *leisurely* person, speaker, or speech; *leisurely* movements; a *leisurely* performance); showing or suggesting ample leisure (as, a *leisurely* manner or air); unhurried; deliberate.—**lei′sure-li-ness,** *n.*—**lei′sure-ly,** *adv.* In a leisurely manner; without haste.

leit-mo-tiv (līt′mō-tēf″), *n.* [G., 'leading motive.'] In a music drama, a motif or theme associated throughout the work with a particular person, situation, or idea.

lem-an (lem′ạn or lē′mạn), *n.* [ME. *lemman, lefman, leofmon*, < AS. *lēof*, dear, E. *lief*, + *mann*, E. *man.*] A person beloved, or sweetheart (as, "He . . . offred kingdoms unto her in vew, To be his *Leman* and his Lady trew": Spenser's "Faerie Queene," iii. 8. 40); also, a paramour, or illicit lover (see Shakspere's "Merry Wives of Windsor," iv. 2. 172); in later use, esp., a mistress. [Archaic.]

lem-ma (lem′ạ), *n.*; pl. *lemmas* or *lemmata* (-ạ-tạ). [L., < Gr. λῆμμα, assumption, premise, thesis, theme, < λαμβάνειν, take.] A subsidiary proposition introduced in proving some other proposition, as in mathematics; also, an argument, theme, or subject.

lem-ming (lem′ing), *n.* [Norw.] Any of various small, mouse-like rodents of the genera *Lemmus* and *Dicrostonyx*, of far northern regions, as *L. lemmus*, of Norway, Sweden, etc., remarkable for periodic migration in great hordes from the highlands to the coast, swimming across streams and lakes, and finally plunging into the sea, to perish, when exhausted, beneath the waves; also, any of various small North American rodents of the genus *Synaptomys.*

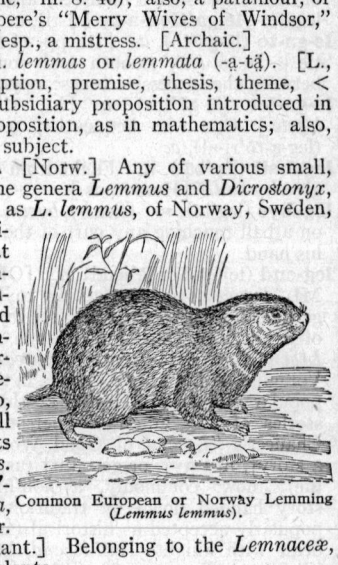

Common European or Norway Lemming (*Lemmus lemmus*).

lem-na-ceous (lem-nā′shius), *a.* [NL. *Lemna*, the typical genus, < Gr. λέμνα, kind of water-plant.] Belonging to the *Lemnaceæ*, or duckweed family of plants.

Lem-ni-an (lem′ni-ạn), *a.* Of or pertaining to the island of Lemnos, in the northern Ægean Sea.—**Lemnian earth** or **bole,** a soft, astringent, clayey substance found on the island of Lemnos, and formerly highly esteemed for medicinal purposes; terra sigillata; sphragide.

lem-on (lem′ọn). [OF. F. *limon*, < ML. *limo*(*n-*), < Ar. and Pers. *līmūn*, lemon.] **I.** *n.* The yellow acid fruit of a subtropical rutaceous tree, a variety of *Citrus medica* (see *citrus*, and cf. *citron* and *lime*[2]); the tree itself; also, lemon-color; also, in fig. use (slang), something 'sour,' distasteful, or disagreeable; something that proves disappointing or unpleasant. **II.** *a.* Lemon-colored.

lem-on-ade (lem-ọ-nād′), *n.* [F. *limonade*, < *limon*, E. *lemon*.] A beverage consisting of lemon-juice mixed with water and sweetened.

lem-on=col-or (lem′ọn-kul″ọr), *n.* A clear, pale yellow color.—**lem′on=col″ored,** *a.*

lem-on=ver-be-na (lem′ọn-vėr-bē′nạ̈), *n.* A verbenaceous garden shrub, *Lippia citriodora*, with long, slender leaves having a lemon-like fragrance.

lem-on-y (lem′ọn-i), *a.* Lemon-like, as in taste or smell.

le-mur (lē′mėr), *n.* [NL., < L. *lemures*, pl., ghosts, specters: cf. *lemures*.] Any of various small, arboreal, chiefly nocturnal mammals (esp. of the genus *Lemur*) allied to the monkeys, usually having a fox-like face and woolly fur, and found chiefly in Madagascar; also, any of certain animals resembling a lemur (see *flying-lemur*).

Varied Lemur (*Lemur varius*).

lem-u-res (lem′ū-rēz), *n. pl.* [L.: cf. *lemur*.] [Also *cap.*] Among the ancient Romans, the spirits of the departed: as, "The Lars and *Lemures* moan with midnight plaint" (Milton's "On the Morning of Christ's Nativity," 191).

lem-u-rine (lem′ū-rin), *a.* and *n.* Same as *lemuroid*.

lem-u-roid (lem′ū-roid). [See *-oid*.] **I.** *a.* Lemur-like; of the lemur kind. **II.** *n.* A lemur.

Le-nard (le-närt′) **rays.** [From P. *Lenard* (born 1862), German physicist.] The rays which penetrate a sheet of aluminium, etc., when cathode rays fall upon it, and which resemble cathode rays in all respects.—**Le-nard′ tube.** A special form of vacuum-tube containing a diaphragm or window of aluminium through which the Lenard rays penetrate.

lend (lend), *v. t.*; *lent*, *lending*. [AS. *lǣnan*, < *lǣn*, loan: see *loan*[2].] To grant the use of (something) with the understanding that it (or its equivalent in kind) shall be returned (as, to *lend* an umbrella; to *lend* a loaf of bread); also, to give the temporary use of (money, etc.) for a consideration (as, to *lend* money at interest; to *lend* sums on real estate, valuable articles, or other security); also, fig., to give or contribute obligingly or helpfully (as, to *lend* one's aid or influence to a cause; "I, that have *lent* my life to build up yours," Tennyson's "Princess," iv. 332); furnish or impart (as, "This sound of danger *lent* me wings," Stevenson's "Treasure Island," xiv.; "'Tis distance *lends* enchantment to the view," Campbell's "Pleasures of Hope," i. 7); give over or yield (*to*: as, "To *lend* our hearts and spirits wholly To the influence of mild-minded melancholy," Tennyson's "Choric Song," v.); accommodate or adapt (one's self or itself) to something (as, to *lend* one's self to the schemes of others; the subject *lends* itself admirably to dramatic treatment).—**to lend a (helping) hand,** to give help or assistance.—**to lend an ear** or **one's ears,** to give a hearing; listen; pay attention: as, "Friends, Romans, countrymen, *lend* me *your ears*" (Shakspere's "Julius Cæsar," iii. 2. 78).—**lend,** *v. i.* To make a loan or loans: as, "Unto a stranger thou mayest *lend* upon usury" (Deut. xxiii. 20).—**lend,** *n.* A loan: as, "He got the *lend* of my best suit of clothes" (Galt's "Annals of the Parish," viii.). [Prov. or colloq.]—**lend′a-ble,** *a.* That may be lent.—**lend′er,** *n.*—**lend′ing,** *n.* The act of one who or that which lends; also, something lent, borrowed, or not one's own.

Lend-Lease Act, an act (Mar. 11, 1941) enabling the **U. S.** government to furnish material aid to anti-Axis nations.

length (length), *n.* [AS. *length*, < *lang*, E. *long*[1].] The quality or fact of being long rather than short (as, a journey remarkable for its *length*; "to end a tale of *length*," Shakspere's "Troilus and Cressida," i. 3. 136); also, the linear magnitude of anything as measured from end to end (as, the *length* of a straight line, or of an arc of a circle; the *length* of a road, a river, or a rope); the magnitude of the greatest principal axis of a body or figure, or the greatest of its dimensions; hence, extent in time, or duration (as, the *length* of a day or a year; the *length* of a battle or a performance); extent from beginning to end of a series, enumeration, account, book, etc.; also, distance, or a distance (now chiefly Sc. or technical); the extent, or an extent, of going, proceeding, etc. (as, "He would go, at any time, any *lengths* for his party": Disraeli's "Coningsby," vii. 4); a distance determined by the length of something specified (as, to hold a thing at arm's *length*); specif., the measure from end to end of a horse, boat, etc., as a unit of distance in racing (as, a horse or a boat wins by two *lengths*); also, the body or form of something considered with reference to length or linear magnitude (as, "A needless Alexandrine . . . That, like a wounded snake, drags its slow *length* along," Pope's "Essay on Criticism," 357; "There is . . . The barn's brown *length*, and the cattle-yard," Whittier's "Telling the Bees"); also, a stretch or extent of something, esp. a long stretch (as, "to leap large *lengths* of miles," Shakspere's "Sonnets," xliv.; "From the bounded level of our mind, Short views we take, nor see the *lengths* behind," Pope's "Essay on Criticism," 222; "a *length* of rolling years," Dryden's tr. Virgil's "Georgics," iii. 717); a piece or portion of a certain or a known length (as, to cut a thing into short *lengths*; a *length* of rope); specif., a portion of a drama for acting, consisting of 42 lines (as, "I've got a part of twelve *lengths* here, which I must be up in to-morrow night": Dickens's "Nicholas Nickleby," xxiii.); also, in *pros.* and *phonetics*, of a vowel or syllable, quantity (whether long or short).—**at length,** to or in the full extent, or without curtailment (as, to read a document *at length*); also, after a time, or in the end (as, *at length* he reached his destination).

length-en (leng′thn), *v.* **I.** *tr.* To make greater in length: as, "The best of all ways To *lengthen* our days, Is to steal a few hours from the night" (T. Moore's "Young May Moon"). **II.** *intr.* To become greater in length: as, "the shadows *lengthening* as the vapours rise" (Dryden's "Absalom and Achitophel," i. 269).

length-i-ly (leng′thi-li), *adv.* In a lengthy manner.—**length′i-ness,** *n.*

length-ways, length-wise (length′wāz, -wīz), *adv.* and *a.* In the direction of the length.

length-y (leng′thi), *a.*; compar. *lengthier*, superl. *lengthiest*. Having length; usually, having, or being of, great length; esp., of discourses, writings, etc., extending to a great length; often, prolix; tedious.

le-nience, le-nien-cy (lē′niẹns, -niẹn-si), *n.* The quality of being lenient; lenient treatment: as, "When you have gone too far to recede, do not sue to me for *leniency*" (Dickens's "Oliver Twist," xlix.).

le-nient (lē′niẹnt), *a.* [L. *leniens* (*-ent-*), ppr. of *lenire*, soften, soothe, < *lenis*, soft, mild.] Softening, soothing, or alleviative, as remedies, agencies, influences, etc. (archaic: as, "Old Time . . . upon these wounds hath laid His *lenient* touches," Wordsworth's "Miscellaneous Sonnets," iii. 8; "Consolatories . . . *Lenient* of grief and anxious thought," Milton's "Samson Agonistes," 659); also, mild, clement, or merciful, as in treatment, spirit, or tendency (as, to be *lenient* to an offender; a *lenient* judgment or criticism); gentle; tolerant.—**le′nient-ly,** *adv.*

len-i-fy (len′i-fī), *v. t.*; *-fied*, *-fying*. [L. *lenis*, soft: see *-fy*.] To soften, soothe, or mitigate: as, "to *lenify* the pain" (Dryden's tr. Virgil's "Æneid," xii. 594). [Now rare.]

len-i-tive (len′i-tiv). [L. *lenire* (pp. *lenitus*), soften: see *lenient*.] **I.** *a.* Softening, soothing, or mitigating, as medicines or applications; sometimes, mildly laxative. **II.** *n.* A lenitive medicine or application; a mild laxative; also, anything that softens or soothes; a palliative.

len-i-ty (len′i-ti), *n.* [L. *lenitas*, < *lenis*, soft, mild.] The quality or fact of being mild or gentle, as toward others; clemency; mercifulness; lenience: as, "His Majesty gave many marks of his great *lenity*, often . . . endeavouring to extenuate your crimes" (Swift's "Gulliver's Travels," i. 7).

lens (lenz), *n.*; pl. *lenses* (len′zez). [L. *lens* (*lent-*), a lentil (which is shaped like a convexo-convex lens).] A piece of transparent substance, usually glass, having two (or two main) opposite surfaces, either both curved or one curved and one plane, used for changing the direction of light-rays, as in magnifying, or in correcting errors of vision; also, a combination of such pieces; also, some analogous device, as for affecting sound-waves; also, in *anat.*, a part of the eye, the 'crystalline lens' (see under *crystalline*).

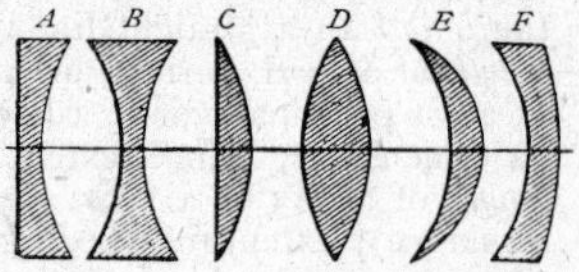

Lenses. — *A*, plano-concave; *B*, biconcave; *C*, plano-convex; *D*, biconvex; *E*, the meniscus; *F*, concavo-convex.

Lent[1] (lent), *n.* [Shortened form of *lenten.*] An annual season of fasting and penitence beginning on Ash Wednesday and including the forty week-days next before Easter, observed by the Roman Catholic, Anglican, and other churches in commemoration of Christ's fasting in the wilderness (see Mat. iv. 2); hence, any similar period of fasting.

lent[2] (lent). Preterit and past participle of *lend.*

len-ta-men-te (len-tä-men′tā), *adv.* [It., < *lento*: see *lento.*] In *music*, slowly.

len-tan-do (len-tän′dō), *a.* [It., gerund of *lentare*, slacken, < L. *lentus*, slow.] In *music*, slackening; becoming slower.

lent-en (len′tẹn). [AS. *lencten*, *lengten*, spring, Lent, prob. (as meaning the season of lengthening days) connected with *lang*, E. *long*[1].] **I.**† *n.* Spring; also, Lent. **II.** *a.* [*cap.* or *l. c.*] Of, pertaining to, or suitable for Lent; hence [*l. c.*], meager; plain; somber or dismal.

len-ti-cel (len′ti-sel), *n.* [F. *lenticelle*, dim. < L. *lens* (*lent-*), a lentil: see *lens.*] In *bot.*, a body of cells formed in the periderm of a stem, appearing on the surface of the plant as a lens-shaped spot, and serving as a pore.—**len-ti-cel′-late** (-sel′āt), *a.*

len-tic-u-lar (len-tik′ụ-lạ̈r), *a.* [L. *lenticularis*, < *lenticula*: see *lentil.*] Resembling a lentil (seed) in form; having the form of a convexo-convex lens; also, of or pertaining to a lens.—**len-tic′u-lar-ly**, *adv.*

len-ti-go (len-tī′gō), *n.*; pl. *lentigines* (-tij′i-nēz). [L., < *lens* (*lent-*), a lentil.] In *med.*, a freckle; also, a freckly condition.—**len-tig′i-nous** (-tij′i-nus), *a.*

len-til (len′til), *n.* [OF. F. *lentille*, < L. *lenticula*, dim. of *lens* (*lent-*), a lentil: see *lens.*] An annual fabaceous plant, *Lentilla lens*, widely cultivated in the Mediterranean region and the Orient, having flattened, convexo-convex seeds which constitute a food similar to peas and beans; also, the seed.

len-tis-cus (len-tis′kus), *n.* [L.] The mastic-tree, *Pistacia lentiscus.* Also **len′tisk** (-tisk).

len-to (len′tō), *a.* [It., < L. *lentus*, slow.] In *music*, slow.

len-toid (len′toid), *a.* [See *lens* and *-oid.*] Lens-shaped.

l'en-voi, l'en-voy (len′voi, F. loṅ-vwo), *n.* [OF. *l'envoy*, F. *l'envoi*, 'the envoy': see *envoy*[1].] The envoy of a poetical or prose composition. See Tennyson's "Day-Dream," L'Envoi, and Spenser's "Ruines of Time," L'Envoy.

Le-o (lē′ō), *n.* [L. *leo* (*leon-*), a lion, *Leo* (*Leon-*), the constellation, in LL. a man's name: see *lion.*] The Lion, a zodiacal constellation; also, the fifth sign of the zodiac. See *zodiac.*—**Leo Minor** (mī′nọr). [L., 'lesser lion.'] A northern constellation between Leo and Ursa Major.

Le-o-nid (lē′ọ-nid), *n.*; pl. *Leonids*, L. *Leonides* (lẹ-on′i-dēz). [See *Leo.*] In *astron.*, any of a shower of meteors occurring yearly about Nov. 15 (but with special profusion about once in 33 years), appearing to radiate from the constellation Leo.

le-o-nine[1] (lē′ọ-nīn or -nin), *a.* [L. *leoninus*, < *leo*, a lion: see *Leo.*] Of or pertaining to the lion; lion-like: as, a *leonine* aspect; "long-eared Neddies, giving themselves *leonine* airs" (Thackeray's "Newcomes," i.).—**leonine partnership**, a partnership in which one partner has all of the profits and none of the losses.

Le-o-nine[2] (lē′ọ-nīn or -nin). [LL. *Leoninus*, < *Leo*, man's name: see *Leo.*] **I.** *a.* Of or pertaining to some person named Leo, Leonius, or Leoninus: as, the *Leonine* City (a part of the city of Rome containing the Vatican, etc., first walled and fortified by Pope Leo IV., about 850); *Leonine* verse (a kind of Latin verse consisting of hexameters or alternate hexameters and pentameters, in which the last word of the line rimes with the word immediately preceding the middle cæsura: said to be so called from a medieval poet who bore one of the above names). **II.** *n. pl.* Leonine verse.

le-on-ti-a-sis (lē-on-tī′ạ-sis), *n.* [NL., < Gr. λεοντίασις, < λέων, E. *lion.*] In *pathol.*, a form of leprosy in which the face becomes bloated and wrinkled, thus appearing more or less leonine.

leop-ard (lep′ạ̈rd), *n.* [OF. *leopard*, *lepart* (F. *léopard*), < LL. *leopardus*, < Gr. λεόπαρδος, < λέων, lion, + πάρδος, pard.] A large, ferocious, spotted Asiatic or African mammal, *Felis pardus*, of the cat family, usually tawny with black markings; the old-world panther, or pard; also, any of various related animals, as the jaguar ('American leopard'), the chetah or hunting-leopard, and the ounce or snow-leopard.—**leop′ard-ess**, *n.* A female leopard.

Leopard (*Felis pardus*).

lep-er (lep′ėr), *n.* [OF. *lepre* (F. *lèpre*), leprosy, < L. *lepra*: see *lepra.*] Leprosy†; also, a person affected with leprosy (as, "a *leper* as white as snow": 2 Kings, v. 27); fig., one infected, or shunned as being infected, with moral evil (as, a moral *leper*).—**lep′er=house**, *n.* A hospital or asylum for lepers; a lazar-house.—**lep′er-ous**, *a.* Leprous. See Shakspere's "Hamlet," i. 5. 64. [Obs. or archaic.]

lep-i-do-lite (lep′i-dō-līt), *n.* [Gr. λεπίς (λεπιδ-), scale, + λίθος, stone.] A variety of mica containing lithium, commonly occurring in lilac, rose-colored, or grayish-white scaly masses.

lep-i-dop-ter (lep-i-dop′tėr), *n.* [NL. *Lepidoptera*, pl., < Gr. λεπίς (λεπιδ-), scale, + πτερόν, wing.] Any of the *Lepidoptera*, an order of insects, comprising the butterflies, moths, and skippers, which in the adult state have four membranous wings more or less covered with small scales. See *caterpillar.*—**lep-i-dop′ter-an**, *a.* and *n.*—**lep-i-dop′-ter-ist**, *n.* One versed in the study of lepidopters.—**lep-i-dop′ter-ous**, *a.* Having scaly wings; belonging or pertaining to the *Lepidoptera* (see *lepidopter*).

lep-i-do-si-ren (lep″i-dọ-sī′ren), *n.* [NL., < Gr. λεπίς (λεπιδ-), scale, + σειρήν, E. *siren.*] A scale-bearing dipnoous fish, *Lepidosiren paradoxa*, of the Amazon River, South America, having an eel-shaped body resembling that of the amphibian called the siren.

lep-i-dote (lep′i-dōt), *a.* [Gr. λεπιδωτός, < λεπίς (λεπιδ-), scale.] In *bot.*, covered with scurfy scales or scaly spots.

lep-o-rine (lep′ọ-rin or -rīn), *a.* [L. *leporinus*, < *lepus* (*lepor-*), hare.] Of or pertaining to the hare; hare-like.

lep-ra (lep′rạ̈), *n.* [L., < Gr. λέπρα, < λεπρός, scaly, < λέπος, scale, < λέπειν, peel.] In *pathol.*, leprosy.

lep-re-chaun (lep′rẹ-kân), *n.* [Ir.] In *Ir. folklore*, a pygmy sprite or goblin.

lep-ro-sa-ri-um (lep-rọ-sā′ri-um), *n.*; pl. *-riums* or *-ria* (-ri-ạ̈). [ML., < LL. *leprosus*: see *leprous.*] A hospital or asylum for lepers; a leper colony.

lep-rose (lep′rōs), *a.* [LL. *leprosus*: see *leprous.*] In *bot.*, scurf-like or scaly, as certain lichens.

lep-ro-se-ry (lep′rọ-se-ri), *n.*; pl. *-ries* (-riz). Same as *leprosarium.*

lep-ro-sy (lep′rọ-si), *n.* [See *leprous.*] Formerly, any of various loathsome cutaneous diseases; now, a loathsome, mildly infectious disease due to a micro-organism, *Bacillus lepræ*, and variously characterized by ulcerations, tubercular nodules, spots of pigmentary excess or deficit, loss of fingers and toes, anæsthesia in certain nerve-regions, etc.

lep-rous (lep'rus), *a.* [LL. *leprosus*, < L. *lepra*, leprosy: see *lepra*.] Affected or tainted with leprosy; of or like leprosy; sometimes, causing leprosy; also, scaly or scurfy; in *bot.*, leprose.—**lep'rous-ly,** *adv.*—**lep'rous-ness,** *n.*

Ler-næ-an (lėr-nē'an), *a.* [L. *Lernæus*, < Gr. Λερναῖος, < Λέρνα, Lerna.] Of Lerna, a marshy district near Argos, Greece, in Greek mythology the abode of the Hydra.

Les-bi-an (lez'bi-an). **I.** *a.* Of or pertaining to Lesbos (Mytilene), a Greek island in the Ægean Sea; also, erotic (from the reputed character of the ancient inhabitants and the tone of their poetry). **II.** *n.* An inhabitant of Lesbos; also, one addicted to Lesbianism.—**Les'bi-an-ism,** *n.* Unnatural sexual relations between women.

lese=maj-es-ty (lēz'maj'es-ti), *n.* [F. *lèse-majesté*, < ML. *læsa majestas*, 'injured majesty' (*læsa*, pp. fem. of L. *lædere*: see *lesion*).] In *law*, any crime or offense against the sovereign power in a state.

le-sion (lē'zhon), *n.* [OF. *lesion* (F. *lésion*), < L. *læsio(n-)*, < *lædere* (pp. *læsus*), hurt, injure.] Hurting or injury; a hurt; a wound; in *pathol.*, any morbid change (structural or functional) in an organ.

less (les). [AS. *læssa* = OFries. *lēssa*, less: a compar. form (positive lacking, superl. E. *least*) associated with the unrelated E. *little*.] **I.** *a. compar.* More little, or smaller in size, amount, degree, etc. (as, "Never be thy shadow *less*," Whittier's "To My Old Schoolmaster"; *less* money, time, or honor; *less* speed); not so large, great, or much; sometimes, fewer (now considered incorrect: as, *less* people; *less* words); lower in consideration, dignity, or importance (as, lords greater and *less*; no *less* a person than the manager); specif., lesser or minor (of two: now chiefly in 'St. James the Less': see Mark, xv. 40): used as the comparative of *little*. **II.** *n.* That which is less; a less or smaller amount or quantity.—**less,** *adv. compar.* [AS. *læs*.] To a less extent, amount, or degree: as, *less* exact; *less* known.—**less,** *prep.* Lacking; wanting; minus; without: as, a year *less* two days.

-less (-les). [AS. *-lēas*, repr. *lēas*, adj., free from, destitute of, without, also false, = Icel. *lauss*, loose, free: see *loose* and *leasing*.] A suffix meaning 'free from,' 'destitute of,' 'without,' freely used to form adjectives from nouns, as in *childless*, *endless*, *harmless*, *peerless*, and hence also, with a strongly negative force, from verbs, as in *fadeless*, *relentless*.

les-see (le-sē'), *n.* [AF., < *lesser*, E. *lease*, *v.*] One to whom a lease is granted.—**les-see'ship,** *n.*

less-en (les'n), *v.* **I.** *intr.* To become less; decrease; also, to come to appear less from increase of distance. **II.** *tr.* To make less; diminish; also, to represent as less, depreciate, or disparage (as, to *lessen* the achievements of a rival).

less-er (les'ėr), *a.* [Double compar. form for *less*.] Less; smaller, as in size, amount, importance, etc. (as, "I have seen the cuckoo chased by *lesser* fowl," Tennyson's "Coming of Arthur," 166; a *lesser* evil; *lesser* considerations); often, being the smaller or less important of two (see phrases following); minor: now always used attributively (or as if before a substantive understood).—**Lesser Asia,** Asia Minor. [Archaic.]—**Lesser Bear,** in *astron.*, the Little Bear, or Ursa Minor. See *bear*[2], *n.*—**lesser celandine.** See *celandine*.—**Lesser Dog,** in *astron.*, the Little Dog, or Canis Minor. See *dog*, *n.*—**lesser doxology.** See *doxology* and *Gloria*.—**Lesser Lion,** in *astron.*, the northern constellation Leo Minor. See *lion* and *Leo Minor*.

les-son (les'n), *n.* [OF. F. *leçon*, < L. *lectio(n-)*, a reading, E. *lection*.] A portion of Scripture or other sacred writing read, or appointed to be read, at divine service; also, a part of a book or the like assigned to a pupil for study; something to be learned or studied; a portion of instruction conveyed to a pupil or class, esp. at a set time (as, a music *lesson*); also, fig., something imparted or inculcated as if by teaching, or learned as if from a teacher (as, "On my heart Deeply hath sunk the *lesson* thou hast given," Bryant's "To a Waterfowl"; to learn a *lesson* from the example of others); often, a useful or salutary piece of practical wisdom imparted or learned (as, this experience taught me a *lesson*; I learned a *lesson* that time); also, something from which one learns or should learn, as an instructive or warning example (as, this experience was a *lesson* to me; his life is a *lesson* to his sons); sometimes, a reproof or punishment intended to teach one better ways.—**les'son,** *v. t.* To give a lesson to; teach or instruct (as, "Well hast thou *lesson'd* us; this shall we do": Shakspere's "Titus Andronicus," v. 2. 110); sometimes, to admonish or reprove.

les-sor (les'or), *n.* [AF., < *lesser*, E. *lease*, *v.*] One who grants a lease.

lest (lest), *conj.* [ME. *leste*, < AS. *thȳ læs the*, 'the less that,' lest.] For fear that, that . . . not, or so that . . . not (as, "Lord God of Hosts, be with us yet, *Lest* we forget—*lest* we forget!" Kipling's "Recessional"); also, after words expressing fear, danger, etc., that (as, "fearing *lest* they should fall into the quicksands," Acts, xxvii. 17; there was danger *lest* the plan should become known).

let[1] (let), *v. t.*; *let*, *letting*. [AS. *lǣtan* = D. *laten* = G. *lassen* = Icel. *lāta* = Goth. *lētan*, leave, let: cf. *late* and *let*[2].] To leave (now only in 'to let alone': see phrase below); also, to grant the occupancy or use of (land, buildings, rooms, space, etc., or movable property) for rent or hire (often with *out*: as, "His aunt *lets* lodgings," Thackeray's "Newcomes," xlii.; "You might think it for your interest to *let* your man to us on the terms proposed," Mrs. Stowe's "Uncle Tom's Cabin," ii.; to *let* out carriages or boats for hire); assign by contract for performance (as, to *let* work to a contractor: cf. *sublet*); also, to allow to escape (as, to *let* blood in surgery, by opening a vein; to *let* the water from a pond); allow to pass, go, or come (as, to *let* a person on board a ship; to *let* a person or thing in, out, through, off, down, etc.); also, to allow or permit (followed by an infinitive, now usually without *to*: as, "She plumes her feathers, and *lets* grow her wings," Milton's "Comus," 378; to *let* be, or to *let* go, see phrases below); also, to cause or make (now chiefly as in 'to let one know'); also, as an auxiliary, used to form the first and third persons of the imperative (as, *let* me see; *let* it be done).—**to let alone,** to leave alone; leave undisturbed, or refrain from interfering with; abstain from having to do with; also, to leave out of the question, or not to mention (chiefly in the imperative: as, one would not treat an animal so, *let alone* a man).—**to let be,** to let remain undisturbed; refrain from interfering with; abstain from having to do with; also, to cease, or leave off (as, *let be* this trifling). Cf. *leave*[1], *v. t.*, remark at end.—**to let go,** to allow to escape, or set at liberty; release one's hold of (as, *let* me *go*; to *let go* a rope or an anchor); relax (one's hold); hence, to give up; abandon; cease to regard or consider; also, to cease to restrain, or allow to follow a course unchecked (as, to *let* one's self *go*). Also sometimes followed by *of* preceding the object: as, *let go* of me; to *let go* of a rope or an anchor. Cf. *leave*[1], *v. t.*, remark at end.—**to let loose,** to allow to go free; liberate; release from restraint: as, to *let loose* a chained dog; to *let loose* wild passions.—**to let on,** to allow to be known, disclose one's knowledge of, or betray by word or look (followed by a clause expressed or understood: as, he did not *let on* that he saw me; he saw me, but he did not *let on*); also, to pretend (as, he *let on* that he did not see me; "It was bad work we did when we *let on* she was fine-looking, and not a wrinkled, wizened hag the way she is," Synge's "Well of the Saints," i.). [Colloq.]—**let**[1], *v. i.* To be rented or leased (as, the house *lets* for $100 a month).—**to let out,** to strike out; lash out; burst into violent speech; also, to be dismissed or concluded, as a school or a meeting. [Colloq.]—**to let up,** to cease: stop. [Colloq.]

let[2] (let), *v.*; *letted* or *let*, *letting*. [AS. *lettan*, < *læt*, slow, tardy, E. *late*: cf. *let*[1].] **I.** *tr.* To hinder; prevent; stand in the way of; often, to keep (*from*: as, "Mine ancient wound is hardly whole, And *lets* me from the saddle," Tennyson's "Lancelot and Elaine," 94). [Archaic or prov.] **II.**† *intr.* To forbear; refrain; also, to delay.—**let**[2], *n.* Hindrance or obstruction, or an impediment or obstacle (as, "That I may know the *let*, why gentle Peace Should not expel these inconveniences," Shakspere's "Henry V.," v. 2. 65: now chiefly in the tautological phrase 'without let or hindrance'); also, in certain games, as lawn-tennis, an interference with the course of the ball (of some kind specified in the rules) on account of which the stroke or point must be played over again.

-let. [OF. F. *-elet*, < *-el* (sometimes < L. *-ellus*, dim. suffix, sometimes < L. *-ale*, neut.: see *-al*[1]) + *-et*, dim. suffix, E. *-et*.] A noun suffix with a diminutive force (not perceptible in some words), as in *armlet, bracelet, frontlet, hamlet, kinglet, tartlet, verselet.*

letch[1] (lech), *n.* [Perhaps connected with *lecher.*] An inordinate fancy or desire, as for something; a passion; a craving. [Eng.]

letch[2] (lech), *v.* and *n.* Same as *leach.*

le-thal (lē′thạl), *a.* [L. *lethalis, letalis,* < *letum,* death.] Of, pertaining to, or such as to cause death; deadly: as, *lethal* weapons; a *lethal* dose of a drug.—**lethal chamber,** a chamber in which animals are put painlessly to death, as with deadly gases.

le-thar-gic (lẹ-thär′jik), *a.* [L. *lethargicus,* < Gr. ληθαργικός.] Pertaining to or affected with lethargy; unnaturally or morbidly drowsy; apathetic; sluggish; also, producing lethargy.—**lethargic encephalitis.** See under *encephalitis.*—**le-thar′gi-cal,** *a.* Lethargic.—**le-thar′gi-cal-ly,** *adv.*

leth-ar-gy (leth′ạr-ji), *n.*; pl. *-gies* (-jiz). [LL. *lethargia,* < Gr. ληθαργία, < λήθαργος, forgetful, < λήθη: see *Lethe.*] A state of drowsy dullness or suspension of the faculties and energies (as, "Oft I fall, Maybe for months, in such blind *lethargies* That Heaven, and Earth, and Time are choked": Tennyson's "St. Simeon Stylites," 101); fig., apathetic or sluggish inactivity (as, to rouse the nation from its *lethargy;* to sink into the *lethargy* of indifference); in *pathol.,* a morbid state or a disorder characterized by overpowering drowsiness or prolonged and profound sleep (cf. *sleeping-sickness,* also *encephalitis lethargica,* under *encephalitis*).

Le-the (lē′thē), *n.* [L., < Gr. λήθη, forgetfulness, oblivion, < λανθάνεσθαι, forget: see *latent.*] In *Gr. myth.,* a river in Hades, whose water caused forgetfulness of the past in those who drank of it; hence, in general, forgetfulness or oblivion (as, "Till that the conquering wine hath steep'd our sense In soft and delicate *Lethe*": Shakspere's "Antony and Cleopatra," ii. 7. 114).—**Le-the-an** (lẹ-thē′ạn), *a.* [L. *Lethæus.*] Pertaining to or resembling the river Lethe or its waters; inducing forgetfulness or oblivion: as, "daily labour's dull, *Lethæan* spring" (M. Arnold's "To a Gipsy Child").

le-thif-er-ous (lẹ-thif′ẹ-rus), *a.* [L. *lethifer, letifer,* < *letum,* death, + *ferre,* bear.] Death-bringing; deadly: as, *lethiferous* diseases.

Lett (let), *n.* One of a people living on and near the eastern coast of the Baltic Sea, south of Esthonia, and closely related to the Lithuanians; also, their language, the Lettish. Cf. *Latvian.*

let-ter[1] (let′ėr), *n.* [See *let*[1].] One who lets.

let-ter[2] (let′ėr), *n.* [OF. F. *lettre,* < L. *littera, litera,* alphabetic character, pl. epistle, writing, literature, learning: cf. *literal, literary, literate,* and *literature.*] One of the marks or signs conventionally used in writing and printing to represent speech-sounds; an alphabetic character; also, a printing-type bearing such a mark or character; such types collectively; a particular style of type; also, actual terms or wording, as distinct from *spirit,* or general meaning or intent (as, "Our sufficiency is of God; Who . . . hath made us able ministers of the new testament; not of the *letter,* but of the spirit: for the *letter* killeth, but the spirit giveth life," 2 Cor. iii. 6: see also phrase *to the letter,* below); also, anything written†; now, a missive communication in writing or printing addressed to a person or a number of persons; an epistle; specif., a telegram longer than an ordinary telegraphic message, sent at a reduced rate of charge because subject to the priority of regular messages (as, a day *letter;* a night *letter*: cf. *lettergram*); also, an official document granting some right or privilege (often in *pl.* in sense of *sing.*: as, *letters* patent, see *patent, a.*; *letters* of marque, see *marque*); also, *pl.,* literature in general; belles-lettres; hence, acquaintance with literature; polite learning; literary culture; sometimes, the profession of literature, or authorship (as, a man of *letters*).—**dead letter.** See under *dead, a.* —**letter of credit,** an order issued by a banker, allowing a person named to draw money to a specified amount from correspondents of the issuer ('traveler's letter of credit' or 'circular letter of credit'); an instrument issued by a banker, authorizing a person named to make drafts upon the issuer up to an amount specified ('commercial letter of credit').—**to the letter,** with close adherence to the actual wording or the literal meaning; hence, to the fullest extent: as, "He gave stringent and unequivocal instructions that these decrees . . . should be fulfilled *to the letter*" (Motley's "Dutch Republic," i. 3); "The trooper discharged his duty *to the letter*" (Cooper's "Spy," xxxiii.).—**let′ter**[2], *v.* **I.** *tr.* To mark with letters; also, to inscribe (a name, etc.) in letters. **II.** *intr.* To make letters.—**let′tered,** *a.* Educated or learned (as, "*lettered* coxcombs without good-breeding": Steele, in "Guardian," 94); also, pertaining to or characterized by polite learning or literary culture (as, "Forego thy dreams of *lettered* ease, Put thou the scholar's promise by": Whittier's "Sumner"); also, marked with or as with letters.—**let′ter-er,** *n.*

let-ter-gram (let′ėr-gram), *n.* [See *-gram.*] A telegram, usually of greater length than an ordinary message, sent at a reduced rate of charge because subject to the priority in transmission and delivery of regular telegrams: as, a night *lettergram.* Cf. *letter*[2], *n.*

let-ter=head (let′ėr-hed), *n.* A printed heading on letter-paper, esp. one giving the name and address of a business concern, an institution, etc.; also, a sheet of paper with such a heading.

let-ter-ing (let′ėr-ing), *n.* The act or process of inscribing with or making letters; also, the letters inscribed or made.

let-ter-less (let′ėr-les), *a.* Without letters; esp., unacquainted with letters or literature; illiterate.

let-tern (let′ėrn), *n.* Old form of *lectern.*

let-ter=per-fect (let′ėr-pėr′fekt), *a.* Knowing one's part, lesson, or the like, to the letter, or perfectly.

let-ter-press (let′ėr-pres), *n.* Matter printed from letters or types, rather than from engraved plates; printed text or reading matter, as distinguished from illustrations, etc.

let-ter=press (let′ėr-pres), *n.* A press for taking copies of letters by transfer; a copying-press.

Lett-ic (let′ik), *a.* Pertaining or related to the Letts; also, noting or pertaining to the group of peoples including the Letts, Lithuanians, and early Prussians, or the group of languages (closely related to the Slavic) including Lettish, Lithuanian, and Old Prussian.

Lett-ish (let′ish). **I.** *a.* Pertaining to the Letts or their language. **II.** *n.* The language of the Letts, belonging to the Lettic group.

lettre de ca-chet (letr dė kȧ-shā). [F., 'letter of seal.'] In *French hist.,* a letter under the seal of the sovereign, esp. one ordering imprisonment.

let-tuce (let′is), *n.* [ME. *letuse* = OF. F. *laitue* (pl. *laitues*), < L. *lactuca,* lettuce, so called from its milky juice, < *lac* (*lact-*), milk.] A cichoriaceous garden herb, *Lactuca sativa,* in many varieties, having large, succulent leaves (either forming a compact head, round or oblong, or spreading more or less loosely) which are much used for salad; also, any species of *Lactuca;* also, any of various plants resembling this genus.—**Cos lettuce.** See entry in vocabulary place.

let=up (let′up), *n.* A letting up; cessation; pause; intermission. [Colloq.]

leu-ce-mi-a, leu-cæ-mi-a (lụ-sē′mi-ạ), *n.* [NL., < Gr. λευκός, white, + αἷμα, blood.] In *pathol.,* a rare, usually fatal disease characterized by a large excess of the white corpuscles of the blood, with changes in the spleen, lymphatic glands, and bone-marrow.

leu-cin, leu-cine (lū′sin), *n.* [Gr. λευκός, white.] In *chem.,* a white, crystalline, nitrogenous compound formed in various ways, esp. by the pancreatic digestion of proteids in the body.

leu-cite (lū′sīt), *n.* [Gr. λευκός, white.] A whitish or grayish mineral consisting of a silicate of aluminium and potassium, found in certain volcanic rocks.—**leu-cit-ic** (lụ-sit′ik), *a.*

leuco-. Form of Gr. λευκός, white, used in combination. —**leu-co-cyte** (lū′kọ-sīt), *n.* [+ *-cyte.*] In *physiol.,* one of the white or colorless corpuscles of the blood, which are concerned in the destruction of disease-producing microorganisms, the clotting of blood, etc. (see *phagocyte,* and cf. *erythrocyte*); also, one of the lymph-corpuscles, which are supposed to be immature leucocytes of the blood.—**leu″co-**

cy-the′mi-a, leu″co-cy-thæ′mi-a (-sī-thē′mi-ạ̈), *n.* [NL. (Gr. κύτος, a hollow, αἷμα, blood).] In *pathol.*, leucemia.—**leu-co-cyt′ic** (-sit′ik), *a.* Pertaining to leucocytes; characterized by an excess of leucocytes.—**leu″co-cy-to′sis** (-tō′sis), *n.* [NL.] In *physiol.* and *pathol.*, the presence of an excessive number of leucocytes in the blood, esp. when merely the result of temporary causes and not of grave disease.—**leu″co-cy-tot′ic** (-tot′ik), *a.*—**leu-co-ma-ine** (lū-kō′mạ̈-in), *n.* [+ *-maine* as in *ptomaine.*] In *chem.*, any of a class of basic substances normally produced in a living animal body through metabolism.—**leu-co-plast** (lū′kọ-plast), *n.* [+ *-plast.*] In *bot.*, one of the colorless bodies found within the protoplasm of vegetable cells, and serving as points around which starch forms.—**leu-cor-rhe′a, leu-cor-rhœ′a** (-kọ-rē′ạ̈), *n.* [NL.: see *-rhea, -rhœa.*] In *pathol.*, a whitish mucous discharge from the female genital organs.

Le-vant[1] (lẹ-vant′). [F., prop. ppr. of *lever*, rise (with reference to the rising sun): see *lever.*] **I.** *n.* The East† or Orient†; also, the countries on the Mediterranean east of Italy; also [*l. c.*], a levanter (wind); also, a superior grade of morocco having a large and prominent grain, orig. made in the Levant. **II.** *a.* [*cap.* or *l. c.*] Of or from the Levant; also (pron. lev′ạnt), eastern or east (archaic: as, "Forth rush the *Levant* and the Ponent winds," Milton's "Paradise Lost," x. 704).

le-vant[2] (lẹ-vant′), *v. i.* [Cf. Sp. *levantar*, raise, break up (camp, house, etc.), < L. *levare*, raise: see *lever.*] To run away, decamp, or abscond; esp., to run away in order to avoid paying bets.

le-vant-er[1] (lẹ-van′tėr), *n.* [Also *cap.*] An easterly wind of the Mediterranean, from the direction of the Levant: as, "We were now soon in sight of the Moorish coast . . . A regular *Levanter* had now come on, and the vessel pitched and tossed" (Borrow's "Bible in Spain," li.).

le-vant-er[2] (lẹ-van′tėr), *n.* One who levants.

Le-van-tine (lẹ-van′tin or lev′ạn-tin). **I.** *a.* Of or pertaining to the Levant. **II.** *n.* A native or a vessel of the Levant; also [*l. c.*], a stout, double-faced, twilled silk fabric of which one face differs in color or shade from the other.

le-va-tor (lẹ-vā′tọr), *n.* [L., < *levare*, raise: see *lever.*] That which raises or elevates; in *anat.*, a muscle that raises some part of the body; in *surg.*, an instrument used to raise a depressed part of the skull.

lev-ee[1] (lev′ẹ̄ or le-vē′), *n.* [F. *levée*, < *lever*, raise: see *lever.*] An embankment for preventing the overflowing of a river; also, a landing-place for vessels; a quay. [U. S.]—**lev′ee**[1], *v. t.*; *leveed, leveeing.* To provide with levees. [U. S.]

le-vee[2] (le-vē′ or, chiefly Brit., lev′ẹ̄), *n.* [F. *levé*, also *lever*, a rising (from bed), reception of visitors by a great personage on rising, < *lever*, rise: see *lever.*] The act of rising, as from bed† (as, "Her hurried *levee* had not prevented her attending closely to all the mufflings and disguisings by which her pilgrim's dress was arranged": Scott's "Castle Dangerous," x.); hence, a reception of visitors held on rising from bed, as formerly by a royal or other personage (as, "The *levee* was exactly what the word imports. Some men of quality came every morning to stand round their master, to chat with him while his wig was combed and his cravat tied": Macaulay's "Hist. of Eng.," iii.); a morning reception held by a prince or great personage (as, "I think an English gentleman never appears to such disadvantage as at the *levee* of a minister": Smollett's "Humphry Clinker," June 2); in Great Britain, a public court assembly, held in the early afternoon, at which men only are received; in general, a reception (as, a presidential *levee* at the White House).

lev-el (lev′ẹl), *n.* [OF. *livel* (F. *niveau*), < L. *libella*, dim. of *libra*, a balance, level: see *libra.*] A device for determining, or adjusting something to, a line or plane perpendicular to the direction in which gravity acts; now, esp., such a device consisting of a glass tube containing alcohol or ether with a movable bubble which when in the center indicates horizontalness ('spirit-level'); also, a surveying instrument combining such a device with a mounted telescope; also, a measuring of differences in elevation with such an instrument; also, level position or condition; a horizontal condition (as, "a river whose course is more upon a *level*": Swift's "Gulliver's Travels," iii. 4); also, the horizontal line or plane in which anything is situated, with reference to its elevation (as, "To the *level* of his ear Leaning with parted lips, some words she spake," Keats's "Hyperion," i.; one thing or position on a *level* with another; two or more things on the same *level*, or on a *level*); hence, fig., a position or plane, high or low (as, "Foppish airs And histrionic mumm'ry, that let down The pulpit to the *level* of the stage," Cowper's "Task," ii. 564; "It was no little satisfaction to me, to view the mixed mass of all ages and dignities upon a *level*," Steele, in "Guardian," 174); also, a level or flat surface (as, "The vessel light along the *level* glides": Pope's tr. Homer's "Odyssey," xii.); a horizontal surface; esp., a level tract of land, or an extent of country approximately horizontal and unbroken by irregularities (as, "The lake overflowed its banks, and all the *level* of the valley was covered with the inundation," Johnson's "Rasselas," vii.; "In the far distance, across the vast *level*, something . . . is moving this way," G. W. Cable's "Bonaventure," i. 9); specif., a horizontal passage in a mine; also, aim, as of a weapon†; the line of fire†, or the range of a missile†.—**to find its,** or **one's, level,** to arrive at the natural or proper level or position, high or low: as, water always *finds its level*; a man sooner or later *finds his level* in the world.—**lev′el,** *a.* Having no part higher than another; having an even surface; also, being in a plane parallel to the plane of the horizon; horizontal; also, being in the same horizontal plane or, fig., on an equality, as one thing with another, or two or more things with one another (as, a crossing *level* with the street; a subject *level* with a writer's genius; a slope connecting two floors which are not *level*; writers whose abilities are *level*); also, even, equable, or uniform (as, "Their *level* life is but a mouldering fire," Goldsmith's "Traveller," 221; *level* coloring); also, mentally well-balanced (colloq.: as, a *level* head).—**one's level best,** one's very best; one's utmost: as, "an Indian chief who has taken off his last rag in order to appear at *his level best*" (Mark Twain's "Life on the Mississippi," ii.). [Colloq.]—**lev′el,** *v.*; *-eled* or *-elled*, *-eling* or *-elling*. **I.** *tr.* To make (a surface) level or even; remove or reduce inequalities of surface in; also, to bring into a plane parallel to the plane of the horizon; make horizontal; also, to raise or lower to a particular level, or horizontal plane, or, fig., to a particular position, high or low (as, to *level* a thing up or down; "You *level* your only son to the brute creation," Marryat's "Mr. Midshipman Easy," ii.); also, to bring (something) to the level of the ground; raze; knock down, as a person; also, to remove or reduce (inequalities, etc.: as, "The mercantile spirit *levels* all distinctions," Lamb's "Imperfect Sympathies"); also, to bring (two or more things) to a common level, or horizontal plane, or, fig., to an equality of status, condition, etc. (as, to *level* adjoining pieces of ground; to *level* ranks of society); also, to make even or uniform, as coloring; also, to aim or point at a mark, as a weapon, etc. (as, "One man . . . *levelled* his piece so true that the shot went through the fellow's head," Defoe's "Captain Singleton," xv.; "to guard all the passes to his valley with the point of his *levelled* spear," H. Melville's "Typee," xxvi.; "His spy-glass was *levelled* as we advanced," H. Melville's "Omoo," i.); turn (looks, etc.) in a particular direction (as, "The fair one . . . withdrew her eyes, and *levelled* them downwards": Fielding's "Tom Jones," ix. 5); fig., to aim or direct (as, "This fellow's writings . . . are *levelled* at the clergy": Fielding's "Joseph Andrews," i. 17); also, in *surv.*, to find the relative elevation of different points in (land), as with a surveyor's level. **II.** *intr.* To be on a level (*with*); hence, to accord† (as, "Such accommodation . . . As *levels* with her breeding": Shakspere's "Othello," i. 3. 240); also, to bring things or persons to a common level (as, "Your levellers wish to *level* down as far as themselves; but they cannot bear *levelling* up to themselves": Johnson, in Boswell's "Johnson," July 21, 1763); also, to aim a weapon, etc.; direct the mind,

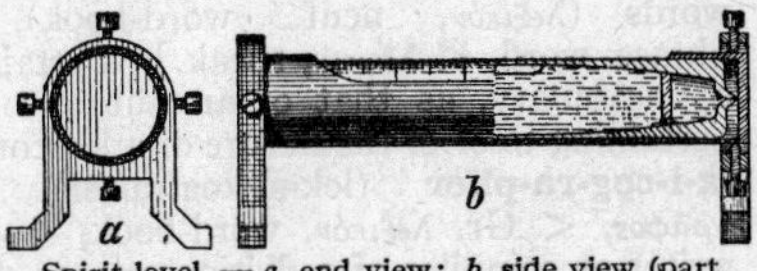

Spirit-level. — *a*, end view; *b*, side view (part shown in section).

purpose, etc., at something; guess (*at*)†; also, in *surv.*, to take levels; use a surveyor's level.

lev-el-er, lev-el-ler (lev'ẹl-ėr), *n.* One who or that which levels; esp., one who would bring all men to a common level, or abolish social or other distinctions.

lev-el-ing, lev-el-ling (lev'ẹl-ing), *n.* The act of one who or that which levels; specif., in *surv.*, the process or art of finding the relative elevation of points on the earth's surface, as with a surveyor's level and leveling-staff, or of determining horizontal lines, grades, etc., by such a method.—**lev'el-ing, lev'el-ling,** *p. a.* That levels; esp., bringing all to a common level, or abolishing social or other distinctions, or pertaining to levelers (as, "some *levelling* circumstance that puts down the overbearing, the strong, the rich, the fortunate, substantially on the same ground with all others," Emerson's "Essays," Compensation; "*levelling* doctrines," Galt's "Annals of the Parish," xxxii.).—**lev'el-ing-rod, lev'el-ing-staff,** *n.* A graduated rod or staff used for measuring heights in connection with a surveyor's level.

Leveling-staff.

lev-el-ly (lev'ẹl-li), *adv.* In a level manner or position.—**lev'el-ness,** *n.*

lev-en (lev'ẹn), *n.* See *levin.*

lev-er (lev'ėr or lē'vėr), *n.* [OF. F. *leveur*, lit. 'raiser,' < *lever*, raise, also rise, < L. *levare*, lighten, lift, raise, < *levis*, light.] A bar or rigid piece acted upon at different points by two forces, as a voluntarily applied force (the *power*) and a resisting force (the *weight*), which severally tend to rotate it in opposite directions about a fixed axis or support (the *fulcrum*); any of various mechanical devices operating on this principle, as a crowbar.—**lev'er,** *v. t.* or *i.* To move with or apply a lever.—**lev'er-age** (-āj), *n.* The action of a lever; also, the mechanical advantage or power gained by using a lever; fig., increased power of action.

lev-er-et (lev'ėr-et), *n.* [OF. *levrete*, dim. of *levre* (F. *lièvre*), < L. *lepus* (*lepor-*), hare.] A hare in its first year.

lev-i-a-ble (lev'i-ạ-bl), *a.* That may be levied; also, liable or subject to a levy.

le-vi-a-than (lẹ-vī'ạ-thạn), *n.* [LL., < Heb. *livyāthān.*] A sea-monster mentioned in the Old Testament (see Job, xli.); hence, any huge marine animal, as the whale; anything, esp. a ship, of huge size (as, "the oak *leviathans*": Byron's "Childe Harold," iv. 181); a man of vast power or wealth; as used by Thomas Hobbes (1588–1679), the commonwealth.

lev-i-er (lev'i-ėr), *n.* One who levies.

lev-i-ga-ble (lev'i-gạ-bl), *a.* That may be levigated.

lev-i-gate (lev'i-gāt), *v. t.*; *-gated, -gating.* [L. *levigatus*, pp. of *levigare*, < *levis*, smooth.] To make smooth†; polish†; also, to rub, grind, or reduce to a fine powder, as in a mortar, with or without the addition of a liquid.—**lev'i-gate,** *a.* Smooth, as if polished, as leaves or seeds.—**lev-i-ga'tion** (-gā'shọn), *n.* [L. *levigatio(n-)*.] The act or process of levigating.

lev-in (lev'in), *n.* [ME. *leven, levin*; origin unknown.] Lightning: as, "the flashing *Levin*" (Spenser's "Faerie Queene," v. 6. 40); "the lurid *levin*" (Longfellow's "Golden Legend," v. 426). [Archaic.]

lev-i-rate (lev'i-rāt or lē'vi-), *n.* [L. *levir*, husband's brother.] A custom, as among the ancient Hebrews, requiring a man under certain circumstances to marry the widow of his brother or nearest kinsman. See Deut. xxv. 5–10.—**lev-i-rat'ic** (-rat'ik), *a.*

lev-i-tate (lev'i-tāt), *v.*; *-tated, -tating.* [L. *levitas*, lightness, E. *levity*: cf. *gravitate.*] **I.** *intr.* To rise or float in the air by reason of lightness, or, now usually, as alleged, through some supernormal power that overcomes the force of gravity. **II.** *tr.* To cause to rise or float in the air.—**lev-i-ta'tion** (-tā'shọn), *n.* The act or phenomenon of levitating.—**lev'i-ta-tor,** *n.*

Le-vite (lē'vīt), *n.* [LL. *Levites*, < Gr. Λευίτης, < Heb. *Lēvī*, Levi.] In *Jewish hist.*, a descendant of Levi, one of the sons of Jacob; one of the tribe of Levi, esp. one of those who assisted the priests in the tabernacle and temple.

Le-vit-ic, Le-vit-i-cal (lẹ-vit'ik, -i-kạl), *a.* [LL. *Leviticus*, < Gr. Λευιτικός.] Of or pertaining to the Levites, the book of Leviticus, or the law ('Levitical law') contained in the book of Leviticus.—**Levitical degrees,** degrees of kindred named in Lev. xviii. 6–18, within which persons were forbidden to marry.—**Le-vit'i-cal-ly,** *adv.*

Le-vit-i-cus (lẹ-vit'i-kus), *n.* [LL.] The third book of the Old Testament, containing laws relating to the priests and Levites and to the forms of Jewish ceremonial observance.

lev-i-ty (lev'i-ti), *n.*; pl. *-ties* (-tiz). [L. *levitas*, < *levis*, light.] Lightness in weight (as, "He visited the work . . . and remarked many ingenious contrivances to facilitate motion, and unite *levity* with strength": Johnson's "Rasselas," vi.); hence, a hypothetical force opposed to gravity (obs. or hist.); also, fig., lightness of mind, character, or behavior (as, "Our graver business Frowns at this *levity*": Shakspere's "Antony and Cleopatra," ii. 7. 128); want of proper seriousness or earnestness; frivolity; volatility; fickleness; often, unseemly gaiety or mirth; also, an instance or exhibition of light or frivolous behavior.

levo-, lævo-. Forms of L. *lævus*, left, used in combination.—**le-vo-glu-cose, læ-vo-glu-cose** (lē-vọ-glö'kōs), *n.* The levorotatory form of glucose.—**le″vo-ro-ta'tion, læ″vo-ro-ta'tion** (-rọ-tā'shọn), *n.* Rotation toward the left; in *optics, chem.*, etc., the rotation of the plane of polarization of light to the left.—**le-vo-ro'ta-to-ry, læ-vo-ro'ta-to-ry** (-rō'tạ-tọ-ri), *a.* Turning or causing to turn toward the left; in *optics, chem.*, etc., turning the plane of polarization of light to the left, as certain crystals, etc.

lev-u-lin (lev'ų-lin), *n.* [See *levulose.*] In *chem.*, an amorphous substance from which levulose can be formed, occurring in the tubers of certain species of helianthus, etc.

lev-u-lose (lev'ų-lōs), *n.* [L. *lævus*, left: see *-ose*[2].] In *chem.*, a levorotatory sugar found in honey, fruits, etc.; fruit-sugar. Cf. *fructose.*

lev-y (lev'i), *n.*; pl. *levies* (-iz). [OF. *levee* (F. *levée*), < *lever*, raise: see *lever.*] A raising or collecting, as of money or troops, by authority or force (as, "She [Russia] increases her military *levies* upon our population every year": De Quincey's "Revolt of the Tartars"); also, that which is raised, as a tax or assessment or a body of troops.—**lev'y,** *v.*; *levied, levying.* **I.** *tr.* To make a levy of; collect (taxes, contributions, etc.); impose as an assessment (*on*: as, to *levy* a fixed amount on each citizen); often, to raise or enlist (troops, etc.) for service; hence, to set going, start, or make (war, etc.: as, "The Emperor . . . had peremptorily commanded him to refrain from *levying* war upon Alva," Motley's "Dutch Republic," iii. 4). **II.** *intr.* To make a levy.

lewd (lūd), *a.* [AS. *lǣwede*, lay; origin uncertain.] Lay† or non-clerical†; also, unlearned† or ignorant†; also, vulgar† or low†; also, base† or vile†; also, inclined to, characterized by, or inciting to lust or lechery; lascivious; unchaste; obscene or indecent, as language, songs, etc.—**lewd'ly,** *adv.*—**lewd'ness,** *n.*

lew-is (lū'is), *n.* [Origin uncertain.] A kind of tenon, in sections, fitted into a dovetail recess or mortise in a block of stone, and used to attach the block to a derrick or the like.

Lewis.

lew-is-ite (lū'is-īt), *n.* A heavy, oil-like liquid whose vapor is highly toxic both on inhalation and on direct contact with the skin, which was developed for the U. S. Government during the World War, for use in chemical warfare, under the direction of Winford Lee Lewis (born 1878), and which was being manufactured for use against the enemy when the armistice went into effect. It is prepared by passing acetylene through arsenic trichloride in the presence of aluminium trichloride as a catalyzer.

lew-is-son (lū'i-sọn), *n.* Same as *lewis.*

lex-ic, lex-i-cal (lek'sik, -si-kạl), *a.* [Gr. λεξικός, of or for words (λεξικόν, neut., word-book), < λέξις, speech, phrase, word, < λέγειν, speak.] Pertaining to words or to a vocabulary, as that of an author or a language; also, pertaining to or of the nature of a lexicon.—**lex'i-cal-ly,** *adv.*

lex-i-cog-ra-pher (lek-si-kog'rạ-fėr), *n.* [LGr. λεξικογράφος, < Gr. λεξικόν, word-book, + γράφειν, write.] A writer or compiler of a dictionary: as, "*Lexicographer* . . . A writer of dictionaries; a harmless drudge, that busies himself in tracing the original, and detailing the signification of words" (Johnson's "Dictionary").—**lex″i-co-graph′ic, lex″i-co-graph′i-cal** (-kō-graf′ik, -i-kạl), *a.* Of or pertaining to lexicography.—**lex″i-co-graph′i-cal-ly,** *adv.*—**lex-i-cog′ra-phist** (-fist), *n.* A lexicographer.—**lex-i-cog′ra-phy** (-fi), *n.* The writing or compiling of dictionaries.

lex-i-con (lek′si-kọn), *n.*; pl. *-cons.* [NL. (much used in Latin titles of dictionaries), < Gr. λεξικόν: see *lexic.*] A word-book or dictionary, esp. of Greek, Latin, or Hebrew; hence, the list or vocabulary of words belonging to a particular subject, field, or class (as, "In the *lexicon* of youth, which fate reserves For a bright manhood, there is no such word As—fail!" Bulwer-Lytton's "Richelieu," ii. 2).

Ley-den (lī′dẹn) **jar.** [From *Leyden* (*Leiden*), city in Holland.] In *elect.*, a device for accumulating frictional electricity, consisting essentially of a glass jar lined inside and outside, for about two thirds of its height, with tin-foil. See cut at *battery.*

leze′=maj′es-ty, *n.* See *lese-majesty.*

li (lē), *n.* [Chinese.] A Chinese linear measure equivalent to about one third of a mile.

li-a-bil-i-ty (lī-ạ-bil′i-ti), *n.*; pl. *-ties* (-tiz). The state or fact of being liable or under obligation (as, *liability* for debt; *liability* to jury duty); the extent to which one is liable, as for debt; an obligation, esp. for payment; *pl.*, debts or pecuniary obligations, as opposed to *assets*; also, *sing.*, the state of being liable or subject to something possible or probable (as, *liability* to disease; *liability* to error or to err).

li-a-ble (lī′ạ-bl), *a.* [Appar. < F. *lier*, < L. *ligare*, bind.] Bound or under obligation in law or equity (as, the surety is *liable* for the debt of his principal); responsible or answerable (*for*); under obligation, if called upon, to do something (as, *liable* to serve on a jury); subject, if required, to something obligatory (as, *liable* to jury duty); hence, subject, exposed, or open to something possible or likely, esp. something undesirable (as, land *liable* to inundation; to be *liable* to harm, loss, or error; methods *liable* to objection); subject to the possibility of doing or being as specified (with an infinitive: as, *liable* to go astray; *liable* to be mistaken); also, in subjection (*to*)†; also, suitable† or fit†.—**li′a-ble-ness,** *n.*

li-ai-son (lẹ-ā′zọn, F. lē-ā-zôn), *n.* [F., < L. *ligatio(n-)*, < *ligare*, bind.] An illicit intimacy between a man and a woman; also, in French pronunciation, the joining of a final consonant (usually silent) to a following word that begins with a vowel sound; also, *milit.*, etc., the connection or coöperative relation to be maintained between military units, officers and units, or various branches of the service, in order to ensure concerted action; hence, a similar connection or relation to be maintained between non-military units, bodies, etc.; also, in *cookery*, a thickening, as of beaten eggs, for sauces, etc.

li-an-a, li-ane (li-an′ạ̈ or -ä′nạ̈, li-än′), *n.* [F. *liane*, appar. < *lier*, < L. *ligare*, bind: cf. *lien.*] A climbing plant, esp. one of a kind that wind about and link together the trees of tropical forests.

li-ar (lī′ạ̈r), *n.* [AS. *lēogere.*] One who lies, or tells lies: as, "He's . . . an infinite and endless *liar*, an hourly promise-breaker" (Shakspere's "All's Well," iii. 6. 11); a *liar* should have a good memory (mentioned by the Roman rhetorician Quintilian as a common saying).

liard (lyär), *n.* [F.] A small copper coin formerly current in France, worth one fourth of a sou.

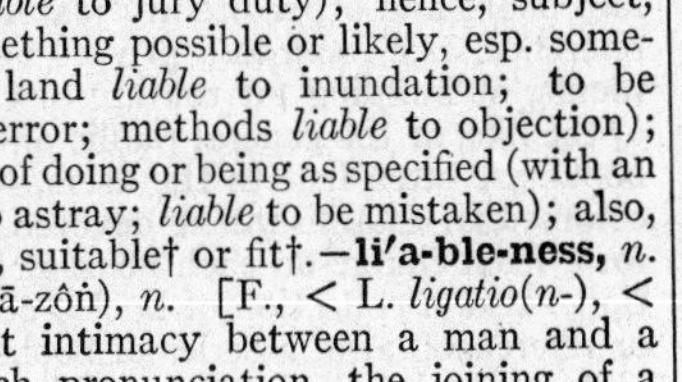

Obverse. Reverse.
Liard.

li-as (lī′ạs), *n.* [OF. *liois* (F. *liais*), a compact kind of limestone.] A blue limestone rock found in central and southwestern England; also [*cap.*], in *geol.*, the earlier division of the European Jurassic.—**Li-as-sic** (lī-as′ik), *a.* In *geol.*, of or pertaining to the Lias.

li-ba-tion (lī-bā′shọn), *n.* [L. *libatio(n-)*, < *libare*, pour out as a libation.] A pouring out of wine or other liquid in honor of a deity (a ceremonial practice esp. of the ancient Greeks and Romans); hence, the liquid poured out (as, "The goblet then she took . . . Sprinkling the first *libations* on the ground": Dryden's tr. Virgil's "Æneid," i. 1031); also, a pouring out of liquid for drinking, the liquid poured out, or a drinking or potation (humorous).—**li-ba-to-ry** (lī′bạ-tō-ri), *a.* Pertaining to libation.

lib-bard (lib′ạ̈rd), *n.* Old form of *leopard.* See Shakspere's "Love's Labour's Lost," v. 2. 551.

li-bec-cio (lē-bet′chō), *n.* [Also (erron.) *libecchio*; It., < L. *libs*, < Gr. λίψ, southwest wind.] The southwest wind. See Milton's "Paradise Lost," x. 706.

li-bel (lī′bẹl), *n.* [OF. *libel*, also *libelle* (F. *libelle*), < L. *libellus*, dim. of *liber*, book: see *liber.*] A little book†; a brief treatise or writing of any kind†; also, a formal written declaration or statement, as one containing the allegations of a plaintiff or the ground of a charge (now chiefly in *admiralty*, *eccles.*, and *Sc. law*); also, a publicly circulated or posted bill assailing a person; now, specif., in legal use, any malicious publication (expressed in printing or writing, or by pictures, etc.) tending to injure the reputation of a person assailed; also, the crime of publishing it (cf. *slander, n.*); hence, in general use, anything defamatory, or that maliciously or damagingly misrepresents (as, "His conversation is a perpetual *libel* on all his acquaintance," Sheridan's "School for Scandal," i. 1; "The parrot's mimicry . . . That odious *libel* on an human voice," Cowper's "Conversation," 450).—**li′bel,** *v. t.*; *-beled* or *-belled*, *-beling* or *-belling.* To set forth in a libel or formal legal statement; also, to institute suit against by means of a libel, as in an admiralty court; also, to publish a malicious libel against; in general, to misrepresent damagingly.—**li′bel-ant, li′bel-lant,** *n.* In *law*, one who libels, or institutes suit.—**li-bel-ee′, li-bel-lee′** (-bẹl-ē′), *n.* In *law*, one against whom a libel instituting a suit has been filed.—**li′bel-er, li′bel-ler,** *n.* One who libels; one who publishes a libel assailing another.—**li′bel-ous, li′bel-lous,** *a.* Containing, constituting, or involving a libel; maliciously defamatory.—**li′bel-ous-ly, li′bel-lous-ly,** *adv.*

li-ber (lī′bėr), *n.* [L., bark, paper, book: cf. *libel*, *library*, and *libretto.*] In *bot.*, the inner bark of exogens; phloëm.

lib-er-al (lib′ẹ-rạl). [OF. *liberal* (F. *libéral*), < L. *liberalis*, < *liber*, free.] **I.** *a.* Befitting a freeman, a gentleman, or a non-professional person (as, the *liberal* arts, see under *art*²; a *liberal* education); not narrowly utilitarian, professional, or technical; also, giving or given freely or in ample measure (as, a *liberal* donor; a *liberal* donation); generous or bountiful; ample or large; also, free from restraint†; free in speech or behavior†; sometimes, licentious†; also, not strict or rigorous (as, a *liberal* interpretation of a rule); also, free from prejudice or bigotry; broad-minded; catholic; tolerant; hence, favorable to progress or reform, as in religious or political affairs; [often *cap.*] noting or pertaining to a political party advocating measures of progressive political reform (as, the *Liberal* party in British politics). Cf. *conservative.* **II.** *n.* A person of liberal principles or views, esp. in religion or politics; [often *cap.*] a member of a liberal party in politics, esp. of the Liberal party in Great Britain.—**lib′er-al-ism,** *n.* Liberal principles, as in religion or politics; [sometimes *cap.*] the principles and practices of a liberal party in politics.—**lib′er-al-ist,** *n.* A liberal.—**lib″er-al-is′tic,** *a.*—**lib-er-al′i-ty** (-ẹ-ral′i-ti), *n.*; pl. *-ties* (-tiz). [L. *liberalitas.*] The quality of being liberal in giving; generosity; bounty; a liberal gift; also, breadth of mind; also, liberalism.—**lib″er-al-i-za′tion** (-i-zā′shọn), *n.* The act of liberalizing; liberalized state.—**lib′er-al-ize** (-īz), *v. t.* or *i.*; *-ized*, *-izing.* To make or become liberal.—**lib′er-al-iz-er** (-ī-zėr), *n.*—**lib′er-al-ly,** *adv.*—**lib′er-al-ness,** *n.*

lib-er-ate (lib′ẹ-rāt), *v. t.*; *-ated*, *-ating.* [L. *liberatus*, pp. of *liberare*, set free, < *liber*, free.] To set free, as from bondage; release; disengage; set free from combination, as a gas.—**lib-er-a′tion** (-ẹ-rā′shọn), *n.* [L. *liberatio(n-).*] The act of liberating; liberated state.—**lib′er-a-tor,** *n.* [L.] One who liberates; a deliverer.—**lib′er-a-tress,** *n.*

Liberator. A U. S. high-altitude, long-range heavy bomber (Consolidated Vultee).

Li-be-ri-an (lī-bē′ri-ạn). **I.** *a.* Of or pertaining to Liberia, a country on the western coast of Africa, colonized (beginning in 1822) with liberated American negroes sent by the American Colonization Society, and made a republic in 1847. **II.** *n.* A native or inhabitant of Liberia.

lib-er-ta-ri-an (lib-ėr-tā'ri-ạn), *n.* [See *liberty* and *-arian.*] One who maintains the doctrine of the freedom of the will (opposed to *necessitarian*); also, one who advocates liberty, esp. with regard to thought or conduct.—**lib-er-ta'ri-an-ism,** *n.*

li-ber-ti-cide (li-bėr'ti-sīd or lib'ėr-), *n.* [See *-cide.*] A destroyer of liberty; also, destruction of liberty.—**li-ber'ti-ci-dal** (-sī-dạl), *a.*

lib-er-tin-age (lib'ėr-tin-ā̤j), *n.* Libertinism.

lib-er-tine (lib'ėr-tin). [L. *libertinus*, < *libertus*, freedman, < *liber*, free.] **I.** *n.* A freedman of ancient Rome; also, one free from restraint or control (as, "When he speaks, The air, a charter'd *libertine*, is still": Shakspere's "Henry V.," i. 1. 48); specif., a freethinker; now, usually, one free from moral restraints; esp., a man of licentious life; a rake. **II.** *a.* Free or unrestrained (obs. or rare: as, "He is free and *libertine*, Pouring of his power the wine To every age, to every race," Emerson's "Woodnotes," ii.); also, freethinking; also, free from moral restraints, esp. with regard to the relations of the sexes; dissolute; licentious; characteristic of a libertine.—**lib'er-tin-ism,** *n.* Libertine principles, as in religious matters; freethinking; also, libertine practices or habits of life; licentiousness.

lib-er-ty (lib'ėr-ti), *n.*; pl. *-ties* (-tiz). [OF. *liberte* (F. *liberté*), < L. *libertas*, < *liber*, free.] The state of being free; freedom or release from bondage or slavery (as, to grant *liberty* to slaves); freedom from arbitrary or despotic government, or, often, from other rule or law than that of a self-governing community (as, "John . . . returned . . . to find the nobles . . . united in a definite claim of *liberty* and law," Green's "Short Hist. of the Eng. People," iii. 2; "My country . . . Sweet land of *liberty*," S. F. Smith's "America": often called 'civil liberty' or 'political liberty'); freedom from external or foreign rule, or independence (as, the Czecho-Slovaks won their *liberty* through the World War: often called 'political liberty'); freedom from captivity, confinement, or physical restraint (as, the prisoner soon regained his *liberty*: see *at liberty*, following); in general, freedom from control, interference, obligation, restriction, hampering conditions, etc.; power or right of doing, thinking, speaking, etc., according to choice (as, complete *liberty* of action, opinion, or speech; *liberty* of worship); power of free choice, or freedom in willing; also, power or opportunity to do or be as specified (as, "Give the water no passage; neither a wicked woman *liberty* to gad abroad": Ecclus. xxv. 25); hence, permission or leave; specif., leave granted to a sailor, esp. in the navy, to go ashore (as, "His *liberty*'s stopped for getting drunk": Marryat's "Peter Simple," iv.); also, the freedom of, or right of frequenting or using, a place, etc.; also, unwarranted or impertinent freedom in action or speech, or a form or instance of it (as, "He began to take *liberties* with me, calling me old governor": Galt's "Annals of the Parish," xvii.); an act, expression, or the like in disregard of ordinary civility or propriety; also, an immunity, privilege, or right enjoyed by grant or prescription (as, "He was in constant conflict with their ancient and dearly-bought political *liberties*": Motley's "Dutch Republic," i. 1); also, a place or district within which certain privileges may be, or once were, exercised (esp. in *pl.*: as, the Northern *Liberties* of Philadelphia; the *liberties* of a prison, districts outside a prison, as the Fleet in London, in which formerly prisoners were sometimes permitted to reside).—**at liberty,** free from bondage, captivity, confinement, or restraint (as, to set slaves or prisoners *at liberty*); also, unoccupied or disengaged (as, he will be *at liberty* very soon); also, free, permitted, or privileged to do or be as specified (as, "She is *at liberty* to be married to whom she will": 1 Cor. vii. 39).—**Liberty bond,** a bond belonging to any of the four issues of bonds known as the First, Second, Third, and Fourth Liberty Loans, put forth by the U. S. Government during 1917 and 1918, to provide funds for sustaining its part in the World War. Cf. *Victory note*, under *victory*.—**liberty cabbage,** sauerkraut: a name humorously used at the time of the World War.—**liberty hall.** See under *hall*.—**liberty of conscience,** freedom to follow the dictates of conscience in matters of religion, as in the profession of a creed or the manner of worship.—**liberty of the press,** the right (under ordinary conditions, as in time of peace) of printing and publishing whatever is desired, without governmental permission or censorship, although with liability to judicial punishment for any publication of an actionable or criminal nature.—**lib'er-ty=cap,** *n.* A Phrygian cap (which see, under *Phrygian*), used as a symbol of liberty: from the cap of this kind given to a freedman in ancient Rome at his manumission.—**lib'er-ty=pole,** *n.* A tall pole surmounted with the liberty-cap or other symbol of liberty, and commonly used as a flagstaff.—**lib'er-ty=tree,** *n.* Same as *tree of liberty* (see under *tree*, *n.*).

li-bid-i-nous (li-bid'i-nus), *a.* [L. *libidinosus*, < *libido*: see *libido.*] Full of lust; given to or characterized by lecherous indulgence; lustful; lecherous; lewd.—**li-bid'i-nous-ly,** *adv.*—**li-bid'i-nous-ness,** *n.*

li-bi-do (li-bī'dō or li-bē'-), *n.* [L. *libido*, pleasure, lust, < *libet*, it is pleasing; akin to E. *lief* and *love.*] In *physiol.* and *psychol.*, the sexual appetite or instinct; hence, instinct generally (in various manifestations); the innate actuating or impelling force in living beings; the vital impulse or 'urge.'

li-bra (lī'brạ), *n.*; pl. *-bræ* (-brē). [L. *libra*, pound, balance, level, *Libra*, the constellation: cf. *lira*, *livre*, and *liter.*] The ancient Roman pound (containing about 5,050 grains); also [*cap.*], in *astron.*, the Balance, a zodiacal constellation; also, the seventh sign of the zodiac (see *zodiac*).

li-bra-ri-an (lī-brā'ri-ạn), *n.* One in charge of a library or some department of a library, or trained in the methods employed in libraries.—**li-bra'ri-an-ship,** *n.*

li-bra-ry (lī'brā̤-ri), *n.*; pl. *-ries* (-riz). [OF. *librairie*, library (F. bookseller's shop), < ML. *libraria*, library, L. bookseller's shop, prop. fem. of L. *librarius*, pertaining to books, < *liber*, book: see *liber.*] A place set apart to contain books and other literary material for reading, study, or reference, as a room in a private house, or as a room, set of rooms, or building for the use of the members of a society or the like, or the general public or a part of it (in which case books are often lent to the users, to be taken out); also, a commercial establishment devoted to the lending of books for a fixed charge on each book or for a periodical subscription; also, a collection of books, etc., as for reading, study, or reference; also, a series of books of similar character, or alike in size, binding, etc., issued by a single publishing house.

li-brate (lī'brāt), *v.*; *-brated*, *-brating.* [L. *libratus*, pp. of *librare*, balance, poise, weigh, < *libra*, a balance: see *libra.*] **I.**† *tr.* To balance; poise; also, to weigh. **II.** *intr.* To be balanced or poised; sway or oscillate like the beam of a balance.—**li-bra'tion** (-brā'shọn), *n.* [L. *libratio(n-)*.] The act of librating; balanced state; in *astron.*, a real or apparent oscillatory motion.—**libration of the moon,** in *astron.*, an apparent irregularity of the moon's rotation, whereby those parts very near the border of the lunar disk become alternately visible and invisible, indicating, as it were, a sort of vibratory motion of the lunar globe.—**li'bra-to-ry** (-brạ-tọ̄-ri), *a.* Librating; oscillatory.

li-bret-tist (li-bret'ist), *n.* The writer of a libretto.

li-bret-to (li-bret'ō), *n.*; pl. *librettos* (-ōz). [It., dim. of *libro*, < L. *liber*, book.] The text or words of an opera or other extended musical composition; also, a book or booklet containing such a text.

li-bri-form (lī'bri-fôrm), *a.* [See *liber* and *-form.*] In *bot.*, having the form of or resembling liber.

Lib-yan (lib'ịạn). **I.** *a.* Of or pertaining to Libya, an ancient country of northern Africa, west of Egypt; also, noting or pertaining to a branch of the Hamitic family of languages spoken in this region. **II.** *n.* A native or inhabitant of Libya; also, the Libyan languages.

lice (līs), *n.* Plural of *louse*.

li'cence, *n.* and *v.* See *license*.

li-cens-a-ble (lī'sẹn-sạ-bl), *a.* That may be licensed.

li-cense, li-cence (lī'sẹns), *n.* [OF. F. *licence*, < L. *licentia*, < *licere*, be permitted.] Formal permission or authorization to do or forbear some act (as, "His Majesty . . . was pleased to give me his *licence* to depart": Swift's "Gulliver's Travels," iii. 11); esp., formal permission from a constituted authority to do something, as to marry, to carry on some business or profession, etc.; also, a certificate of such permission; an official permit; also, freedom of action, speech, thought, etc., permitted or conceded (as, "He . . . had obtained for himself a sort of *license* for the tongue," Cooper's "Two Admirals," xi.; "to have a degree of *licence* of judgment," Marryat's "Peter Simple," lxii.); often, excessive or undue freedom or liberty (as, "*License* they mean when they cry liberty": Milton's "Sonnets," vii.); disregard of legal or moral restraints; sometimes, licentiousness; also, intentional deviation from rule, convention, or fact, as for the sake of literary or artistic effect (as, poetic *license*).—**li′cense, li′cence,** *v. t.*; *-censed* or *-cenced*, *-censing* or *-cencing*. To give (a person, etc.) permission or license to do something (as, "They were *licensed* to make bold with any of his things": Bunyan's "Pilgrim's Progress," ii.); permit (a thing) to be done; esp., to grant (a person, etc.) authoritative permission or license to do something, as to practise some trade or profession; grant an official license to (a house, etc.), permitting it to be used for a specified purpose, as for the sale of alcoholic liquor; authorize (a thing) officially, as a book or a play; also, to allow freedom of action, etc., or free scope, to (as, "Imagination is a *licensed* trespasser": George Eliot's "Adam Bede," vi.); privilege, tolerate; also, to give leave to depart†, or dismiss† (as, "Thus *licensed*, the chief and Waverley left the presence-chamber": Scott's "Waverley," xl.).—**li-cens-ee′** (-sẹn-sē′), *n.* One to whom a license is granted.—**li′cens-er,** *n.*

li-cen-ti-ate (lī-sen′shi-āt), *n.* [ML. *licentiatus*, pp. of *licentiare*, to license, < L. *licentia*, E. *license*.] One who has received a license, as from a university, to practise an art or profession; also, the holder of a certain university degree intermediate between that of bachelor and that of doctor, now confined chiefly to certain continental European universities.—**li-cen′ti-ate-ship,** *n.*

li-cen-tious (lī-sen′shus), *a.* [L. *licentiosus*, < *licentia*, E. *license*.] Characterized by or using license; going beyond customary or proper bounds or limits; disregarding commonly accepted rules or principles, as in matters of literary style (as, "Latin verse . . . somewhat *licentious* in number of syllables": Hallam's "Literature of Europe," i. 1. § 34); esp., unrestrained by law or morality; lawless; immoral; now, usually, sensually unbridled; libertine; lewd.—**li-cen′tious-ly,** *adv.*—**li-cen′tious-ness,** *n.*

lich, lych (lich), *n.* [ME. *liche*, *lyche*, < AS. *līc* = D. *lijk* = G. *leiche* = Icel. *līk* = Goth. *leik*, body: see *like*¹.] The body†; also, a dead body, or corpse (archaic or prov. Eng. and Sc.). Cf. *lich-gate* and *likewake*.

li-chen (lī′kẹn), *n.* [L., < Gr. λειχήν, lichen.] Any of a group of compound plants (fungi in symbiotic union with algæ) having a thallus or body not differentiated into stem and leaf, and growing in greenish, gray, yellow, brown, or blackish crust-like patches or bush-like forms on rocks, trees, etc.; also, in *pathol.*, any of various eruptive skin-diseases.—**li′chen,** *v. t.* To cover with lichens.—**li-chen-a′ceous** (-ā′shius), *a.* Belonging to the lichens; lichen-like.—**li-chen-ol′o-gy** (-ol′ǭ-ji), *n.* [See *-logy*.] The branch of botany that treats of lichens.—**li′chen-ous,** *a.* Of, like, or abounding in lichens (plants); also, pertaining to lichen (disease).

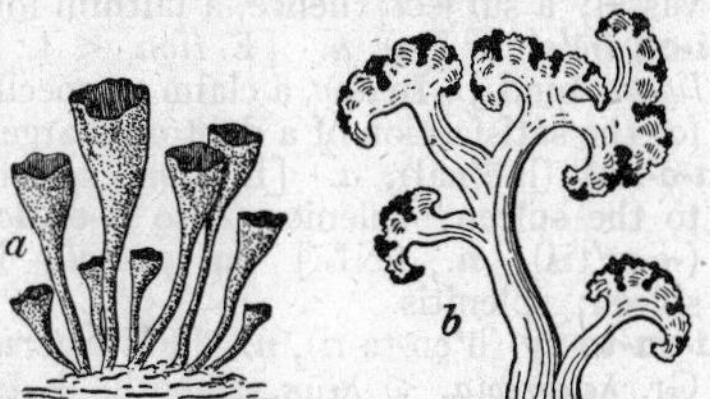

Lichens. — *a*, *Cladonia pyxidata*; *b*, *Cetraria cucullata*.

lich=gate, lych=gate (lich′gāt), *n.* [See *lich*.] In England and elsewhere, a roofed gate to a churchyard, under which a bier is set down to await the coming of the clergyman: as, "This patient couple walked . . . under the *lychgate*, past the dark yew that shadowed the peaceful graves" (H. Kingsley's "Geoffry Hamlyn," ii.).

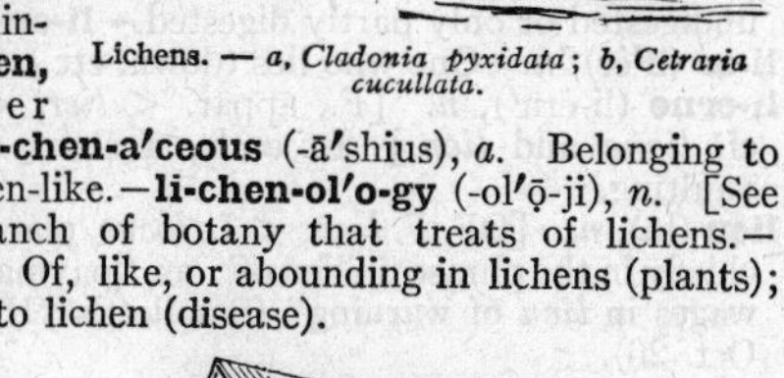

Lich-gate.

li-chi (lē-chē′), *n.* [Chinese *li-chi*.] The fruit of a Chinese sapindaceous tree, *Litchi chinensis*, consisting of a thin, brittle shell inclosing a sweet, jelly-like pulp and a single seed; also, the tree.

licht¹ (licht), **licht**², **licht**³. Sc. form of *light*¹, etc.

li-cit (lis′it), *a.* [L. *licitus*, pp. of *licere*, be permitted.] Permitted; allowable; lawful.—**li′cit-ly,** *adv.*—**li′cit-ness,** *n.*

lick (lik), *v. t.* [AS. *liccian* = D. *likken* = G. *lecken*, lick; akin to L. *lingere*, Gr. λείχειν, lick: cf. *electuary* and *lecher*.] To pass the tongue over the surface of (as, to *lick* a spoon; to *lick* one's fingers; to *lick* a postage-stamp; the cat *licks* its fur); take with the tongue (commonly with *up*, *off*, *from*, etc.: as, "The dogs *licked* up his blood," 1 Kings xxii. 38; the child *licked* the jam from its fingers); render or bring by strokes of the tongue (as, to *lick* the platter clean: see *to lick into shape*, below); also, fig., to pass or play lightly over, as waves or flames do; take (*up*, etc.) in passing over (as, "The fire . . . *licked* up the water that was in the trench": 1 Kings, xviii. 38); also (colloq.), to beat, thrash, or whip, as for punishment, or drive (*out*) by beating (as, to *lick* the deviltry out of a boy); overcome in a fight (colloq.: as, "I could *lick* you with one hand tied behind me, if I wanted to," Mark Twain's "Tom Sawyer," i.); defeat in a war or other struggle (colloq.: as, "We want such fellows as he to *lick* the French," George Eliot's "Adam Bede," ii.); outdo or surpass (colloq.).—**to lick into shape,** to bring into shape by licking (said esp. of the bear with its young: as, "A bear's a savage beast . . . Whelped without form, until the dam Has *licked* it *into shape* and frame": Butler's "Hudibras," i. 3); hence, fig., to bring (anything crude) into due form or condition (as, to *lick* a manuscript *into shape* for printing; to *lick* raw recruits *into shape* for service).—**to lick the dust,** lit., to eat the dust (an Old Testament expression implying utter abasement: see Micah, vii. 17, Gen. iii. 14); hence, fig., to grovel in abasement; lie prostrate in defeat; be slain, as in battle.—**lick,** *n.* An act of licking, as with the tongue; a stroke of the tongue over something; hence, a small quantity, such as might be taken up by the tongue; a smear, as of paint; also, a place to which wild animals resort to lick salt occurring naturally there ('salt-lick': U. S.: as, "shot down like deer standing at a *lick*," Cooper's "Deerslayer," iv.); also, a stroke or blow (colloq.: as, "That rascal of a boy gave me a devil of a *lick* on the shoulder," Marryat's "Mr. Midshipman Easy," xviii.); a brief or brisk stroke of activity or endeavor (colloq.: as, to take a *lick* at a piece of work; to give a thing a *lick* and a promise, to do some slight or hasty work upon it, as if with a promise of doing better later); a spurt, as in running or racing, and hence, also, speed (colloq.: as, to go at full *lick*).—**lick′er,** *n.*

lick-er-ish (lik′ėr-ish), *a.* [Also *liquorish*; earlier *lickerous*, from a var. of OF. *lecheros*, < *lecheor*, gourmand, sensualist: see *lecher*, and cf. *lecherous*.] Eager for choice food or dainty fare, as a person, the palate, etc.; also, choice, dainty, or tempting, as food or drink (as, "*lickerish* baits": Milton's "Comus," 700); also, in general, eagerly desirous; greedy; sometimes, lustful or lecherous. [Archaic or literary.]—**lick′er-ish-ly,** *adv.*—**lick′er-ish-ness,** *n.*

lick-ing (lik′ing), *n.* The act of one who or that which licks; a beating or thrashing (colloq.).

lick-spit-tle (lik′spit″l), *n.* An abject toady: as, "averring that they were a parcel of sneaks, a set of *lick-spittles*" (Thackeray's "Newcomes," xvii.).

lic-o-rice, li-quo-rice (lik′ǭ-ris), *n.* [OF. *licorece*, also *ricolice* (F. *réglisse*), < LL. *liquiritia*, corruption of L. *glycyrrhiza*, < Gr. γλυκύρριζα, licorice, < γλυκύς, sweet, + ῥίζα, root.] A fabaceous plant, *Glycyrrhiza glabra*, of Europe and Asia (see cut on following page); also, the sweet-tasting dried root of this plant, or an extract made from it, used in medicine, confectionery, etc.; also, any of various related or similar plants (as, the 'Indian licorice,' which see under *Indian*, *a.*).

lic-tor (lik′tọr), *n.* [L.] In ancient Rome, one of a body of attendants on a magistrate, charged with carrying the fasces before him, and with executing sentence on offenders.

lid (lid), *n.* [AS. *hlid* = D. and G. *lid*, lid.] A movable piece, whether separate or hinged, for closing the opening of a vessel, box, etc.; a movable cover; specif., an eyelid; also, one of the outer sidepieces of a book (colloq.); also, a hat (slang); also, fig., usually with *the*, means of repression or restraint (colloq.: as, to keep the *lid* on vice, gambling-houses, the circulation of news, etc.); in *bot.*, the upper section of a pyxidium; in mosses, the cover-like part on the theca.—**lid'ded,** *a.* Having a lid or lids: as, heavy-*lidded* eyes.—**lid'less,** *a.* Having no lid (as, a *lidless* box); of eyes, having no lids; hence, vigilant or watchful (poetic: as, "An eye like mine, A *lidless* watcher of the public weal," Tennyson's "Princess," iv. 306).

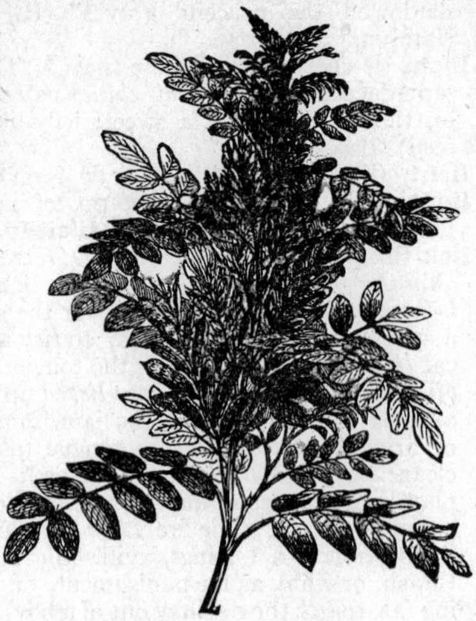

Licorice (*Glycyrrhiza glabra*).

lie[1] (lī), *v. i.*; pret. *lay*, pp. *lain*, ppr. *lying.* [AS. *licgan* = D. *liggen* = G. *liegen* = Icel. *liggja* = Goth. *ligan*, lie; akin to L. *lectus*, Gr. λέχος, bed: cf. *lay*[1], *lair*, *law*[3], *lea*[2], *litter*, and *low*[4].] To be in a recumbent or prostrate position, as on a bed or the ground, as a person or an animal; recline; assume such a position (as, to *lie* down on a couch, or on the ground); also, to rest in a horizontal or flat position, as an inanimate object (as, the log *lies* on the ground; a book *lying* on the table); be stretched out or extended; also, to be or remain in a position or state of inactivity, subjection, restraint, concealment, etc. (as, money *lying* in bank; a man *lies* in prison; to *lie* in ambush); continue or remain (as specified: as, ground *lying* fallow); also, to become quiet† or subside†; also, to pass the night, lodge, or sojourn (archaic: as, "He was to *lie* that night at a neighbour's," Goldsmith's "Vicar of Wakefield," vi.); also, to be placed or situated (as, land *lying* in Ohio, or along the coast); be in or have a specified direction, as a road or course (as, the trail from here *lies* to the west; "There *lies* your way," Shakspere's "Taming of the Shrew," iii. 2. 212); also, to be found, occur, or be (where specified: as, "The light that *lies* In woman's eyes," T. Moore's "The Time I've Lost in Wooing"; the fault *lies* here); also, to rest, press, or weigh (*on* or *upon*: as, "All the curses that are written in this book shall *lie* upon him," Deut. xxix. 20); depend (*on* or *upon*: as, "He persists As if his life *lay* on 't," Shakspere's "All's Well," iii. 7. 43); also, in *law*, to be sustainable or admissible, as an action or appeal.—**to lie in,** to be confined in childbed.—**to lie to,** *naut.*, of a vessel, to lie comparatively stationary, with the head as near the wind as possible: effected by arranging the sails and helm in a special manner, or by slowing down the engine.—**to lie with,** specif., to have sexual intercourse with.—**lie**[1], *n.* Manner of lying; the relative position or direction in which something lies; lay, as of land (as, "I was able from this position to get a very good idea of the general *lie* of the Italian eastern front": H. G. Wells's "Italy, France, and Britain at War," ii. 1); also, the place where a bird, beast, or fish is accustomed to lie or lurk.

lie[2] (lī), *v. i.*; *lied*, *lying.* [AS. *lēogan* = D. *liegen* = G. *lügen* = Icel. *ljūga* = Goth. *liugan*, lie.] To speak falsely or utter untruth knowingly, as with intent to deceive (as, "A faithful witness will not *lie*": Prov. xiv. 5); hence, in general, to express what is false, or convey a false impression (as, "That [chair], In which, or astronomy *lies*, Fair Cassiopeia sat," Cowper's "Gratitude," 15; a face that cannot *lie*); also, to get (*out*), as of a difficulty, by lies.—**to lie in one's throat** (or **teeth**), emphatic extension of *lie* used in contradicting, accusing, etc.: as, "He . . . indited a proud and lofty letter . . . declaring that whoever charged him with the plot . . . *lied in his throat*" (Irving's "Knickerbocker's New York," v. 5). [Archaic.]—**lie**[2], *v. t.* To bring, put, cast, etc., by lying: as, to *lie* one's self out of a difficulty; to *lie* an accused person's life away.—**lie**[2], *n.* [AS. *lyge.*] A false statement made with intent to deceive (as, "A *lie* which is half a truth is ever the blackest of *lies*": Tennyson's "Grandmother," viii.); an intentional untruth; a falsehood; hence, in general, something intended or serving to convey a false impression (as, "My life was all a *lie*": Godwin's "Caleb Williams," xxxiv.); also, the charge or accusation of lying, or a flat contradiction (as, the *lie* was passed, and blows followed).—**a lie made out of whole cloth,** a statement wholly fabricated, or without an element of truth; a tissue of falsehood.—**to give the lie (to),** to charge with lying, or contradict flatly (as, "to *give* each other *the lie* in a tavern brawl": Stevenson's "Travels with a Donkey," i. 1); hence, fig., to imply or show to be false, or belie (as, his actions *gave the lie to* his professions).—**white lie.** See under *white*, *a.*

lied (lēt), *n.*; pl. *lieder* (lē'dėr). [G.] A German song, lyric, or ballad.

lie-der-kranz (lē'dėr-kränts), *n.* [G., 'garland of songs.'] A German choral society or singing club, esp. of men.

lief (lēf), *a.* [AS. *lēof* = D. *lief* = G. *lieb* = Icel. *ljūfr* = Goth. *liufs*, dear; from the root of E. *love.*] Beloved or dear (as, "I charge thee, quickly go again, As thou art *lief* and dear": Tennyson's "Passing of Arthur," 248); also, pleasing or acceptable (as, "And now he deems his home-bred fare as *leefe* As his parcht brisket, or his barrel'd beefe": J. Hall's "Satires," iv. 6); also, glad or willing (as, "He up arose, however *liefe* or loth, And swore to him true fealtie for aye": Spenser's "Faerie Queene," vi. 1. 44). [Archaic.]—**lief,** *adv.* Gladly; willingly: now used only in such expressions as 'would as lief,' 'would liefer,' 'had as lief,' 'had liefer,' etc. See *had better*, under *had.*

liege (lēj). [OF. *lige*, liege, free, exempt, appar. < OHG. *ledig*, free.] **I.** *a.* Owing allegiance and service, as a feudal vassal to his lord (as, *liege* subjects; *liege* people); also, entitled to allegiance and service, as a feudal lord; also, pertaining to the relation between vassal and lord (as, *liege* homage); sometimes, loyal; faithful. **II.** *n.* A liegeman or vassal; a subject, as of a ruler; also, a liege lord (as, "And glory to our sovereign *liege*, King Henry of Navarre!" Macaulay's "Ivry").—**liege'man** (-man), *n.*; pl. *-men.* A vassal; a subject; hence, a faithful follower.

li-en (lē'en or lēn), *n.* [F. *lien*, < L. *ligamen*, band, tie, < *ligare*, bind.] In *law*, a claim on specific property of another for the satisfaction of a debt or charge.

li-e-nal (lī-ē'nal), *a.* [L. *lien*, spleen.] Of or pertaining to the spleen; splenic. Also **li-en'ic** (-en'ik).—**li-e-ni'tis** (-e-nī'tis), *n.* [NL.] In *pathol.*, inflammation of the spleen; splenitis.

li-en-te-ry (lī'en-te-ri), *n.* [F. *lienterie*, < ML. *lienteria*, < Gr. λειεντερία, < λεῖος, smooth, + ἔντερον, intestine.] In *pathol.*, a form of diarrhea in which the food is discharged undigested or only partly digested.—**li-en-ter'ic** (-ter'ik), *a.*

li-er (lī'ėr), *n.* One who lies (down, etc.).

li-erne (li-ėrn'), *n.* [F., appar. < *lier*, < L. *ligare*, bind: cf. *liane* and *lien.*] In *arch.*, a short connecting rib in vaulting.

lieu (lū), *n.* [OF. F. *lieu*, < L. *locus*, place.] Place; stead: chiefly in the phrase 'in lieu of': as, "paying to each a month's wages in *lieu* of warning" (Smollett's "Humphry Clinker," Oct. 26).

lieu-ten-an-cy (lū-ten'an-si, also, esp. Brit., lef-), *n.*; pl. *-cies* (-siz). The office, authority, incumbency, or jurisdiction of a lieutenant; also, lieutenants collectively.

lieu-ten-ant (lū-ten'ant, also, esp. Brit., lef-), *n.* [OF. F. *lieutenant*, < *lieu* (< L. *locus*), place, + *tenant*, ppr. of *tenir* (< L. *tenere*), hold: cf. *locum tenens.*] One who holds the place of another in the performance of a duty or function; a deputy or vicegerent; usually, one who holds an office, civil or military, in subordination to a superior, for whom he acts; specif., in the army, a commissioned officer ranking next below a captain (see *first lieutenant* and *second lieutenant*, below); in the navy, a commissioned officer ranking next below a lieutenant-commander (see also *lieutenant, junior grade,* below).—**first lieutenant,** in the U. S. army, a commissioned officer ranking next below a captain.—**lieutenant, junior grade,** in the U. S. navy, a commissioned officer ranking next below a lieutenant.—**second lieutenant,** in the U. S. army, the commissioned officer of the lowest rank, ranking next below a first lieutenant.—**lieu-ten′ant=colo′nel,** *n.*; pl. *-nels.* In the army, a commissioned officer ranking next below a colonel and next above a major.—**lieu-ten′ant=com-mand′er,** *n.*; pl. *-ers.* In the navy, an officer next in rank below a commander.—**lieu-ten′ant=gen′er-al,** *n.*; pl. *-als.* In the army, an officer ranking next below a general and next above a major-general, and usually in command of an army-corps.—**lieu-ten′ant=gov′er-nor,** *n.*; pl. *-nors.* A deputy governor; one serving as governor under a governor-general or other superior; in the U. S., a State officer next in rank to the governor, whose place he takes in case of the latter's absence, disability, or death.—**lieu-ten′ant-ship,** *n.* Lieutenancy.

lieve (lēv), *adv.* Same as *lief.*

life (līf), *n.*; pl. *lives* (līvz). [AS. *līf*, life, = D. *lijf*, life, body, = G. *leib*, body, = Icel. *līf*, life, body; from the root of E. *leave*[1]: cf. *live*[1].] That state of an animal or plant in which its organs are capable of performing their functions, or have not ceased permanently (as at death) from performing them (as, food enough to maintain *life*; while there's *life* there's hope; to restore the dead to *life*); animate existence as distinguishing living things from inanimate objects, or the principle of animate existence (as, a stone is without *life*; "The Lord God formed man of the dust of the ground, and breathed into his nostrils the breath of *life*; and man became a living soul," Gen. ii. 7); hence, a corresponding state, existence, or principle of existence conceived as belonging to the soul (as, the spiritual *life*; eternal *life*; "The law of the Spirit of *life* in Christ Jesus hath made me free from the law of sin and death," Rom. viii. 2); also, the animate existence, or the term of animate existence, of an individual (as, to risk one's *life*; to have a short *life* and a merry one); fig., the term of existence, activity, or effectiveness of something inanimate, as a machine or a lease; also, course or mode of existence (as, the hermit's *life*; married *life*; low *life*); existence in the world of affairs, society, etc. (as, young men on the threshold of *life*; to see *life*); also, animation, liveliness, vivacity, or spirit (as, a face, a speech, or a performance full of *life*; put more *life* into your work); pungency or strong, sharp flavor, as of substances when fresh or in good condition; effervescence or sparkle, as of liquors; also, that which makes or keeps alive, or the vivifying or quickening principle (lit. or fig.: as, "The blood is the *life*," Deut. xii. 23; "Definiteness is the *life* of preaching," J. H. Newman's "Idea of a University," ii. 6); a person or thing considered as necessary to one's remaining alive (as, "Let us have one bottle more, Deborah, my *life*," Goldsmith's "Vicar of Wakefield," xvii.; admiration was her *life*); one who or that which enlivens (as, "Ellery Davenport seemed to be the *life* of the table, and kept everybody laughing": Mrs. Stowe's "Oldtown Folks," xxv.); also, an embodied existence, or living being (as, "Were I join'd with her, Then might we live together as one *life*": Tennyson's "Coming of Arthur," 90); living things collectively, whether animals or plants (as, insect *life*; low forms of plant *life*; the possibility of *life* on the planet Mars): hence, the living form or model, as the subject of representation in art (as, a drawing from the *life*; as large as *life*); hence, the living reality (as, true to the *life*); also, a biography (as, a new *life* of Napoleon).

life=belt (līf′belt), *n.* A belt-like life-preserver.

life=blood (līf′blud), *n.* The blood necessary to life (as, "Ah! never shall the land forget How gushed the *life-blood* of her brave": Bryant's "Battle-Field"); fig., the element or agency that vivifies or animates anything.

life=boat (līf′bōt), *n.* A strong, buoyant boat specially constructed for saving life at sea or along a coast, as in case of shipwreck.

life=buoy (līf′boi), *n.* A buoyant device (in various forms) for throwing, as from a vessel, to persons in the water, to enable them to keep afloat until rescued.

life=cy-cle (līf′sī″kl), *n.* In *biol.*, the whole cycle or series of vital phenomena exhibited by an organism in its successive stages of development from the ovum.

life=ev-er-last-ing (līf′ev-ėr-lȧs′ting), *n.* Any of certain species of cudweed, genus *Gnaphalium*, etc., as *G. obtusifolium*, a fragrant herb common in the eastern U. S., or the related plant *Anaphalis margaritacea.*

life-ful (līf′fu̇l), *a.* Full of life; animated; also, life-giving. [Now rare.]—**life′ful-ly,** *adv.*—**life′ful-ness,** *n.*

life=giv-er (līf′giv″ėr), *n.* One who or that which gives life.—**life′=giv″ing,** *a.* Giving life; vivifying: as, "Nor on the virtue thought Of that *life-giving* plant" (Milton's "Paradise Lost," iv. 199).

life=guard (līf′gärd), *n.* A guard over the life of a person or persons; a body-guard of soldiers attending a prince or other person (*pl.* in same sense, esp. as the name of certain British cavalry regiments); also, a man employed on a bathing-beach to aid in case of danger or accident to bathers; a member of a life-saving service.

life-less (līf′les), *a.* [AS. *līflēas.*] Deprived of life, or dead (as, a battle-field strewn with *lifeless* bodies); hence, insensible, as one in a swoon (as, "I was *lifeless*, and did not recover my senses for a long, long time": Mrs. Shelley's "Frankenstein," v.); also, not endowed with life (as, a mere *lifeless* clod; *lifeless* matter); also, destitute of living things (as, a *lifeless* planet); also, without animation, liveliness, or spirit (as, a *lifeless* narrative or performance).—**life′less-ly,** *adv.*—**life′less-ness,** *n.*

life-like (līf′līk), *a.* Resembling or simulating life; giving the impression of real life: as, a *lifelike* picture or statue; a *lifelike* description.—**life′like-ness,** *n.*

life=line (līf′līn), *n.* A line or rope for saving life, as one attached to a life-boat.

life-long (līf′lông), *a.* Lasting or continuing through life: as, *lifelong* regret; "The youth . . . was destined to be the *life-long* companion of his toils and glories" (Motley's "Dutch Republic," iii. 1).

life=net (līf′net), *n.* A strong net or the like held by firemen or others to catch persons jumping from a burning building.

life=pre-serv-er (līf′prē-zėr″vėr), *n.* A buoyant jacket, belt, or other like device for saving persons in the water from sinking and drowning; also, a weapon, esp. a short stick with a loaded head, used for self-defense.

Life-preserver.

lif-er (lī′fėr), *n.* One sentenced to penal servitude for life (as, "They know what a clever lad he is; he'll be a *lifer*": Dickens's "Oliver Twist," xliii.); also, a sentence, as of penal servitude, for life. [Slang.]

life=sav-ing (līf′sā″ving), *a.* Saving or designed to save life, esp. from drowning, as along a seacoast: as, *life-saving* apparatus; a *life-saving* service.

life=size (līf′sīz′), *a.* Of the size of life or the living original: as, a *life-size* picture or statue.

life-time (līf′tīm), *n.* The time that one's life continues; one's term of life: as, reminiscences of a *lifetime*; that will not occur within my *lifetime.*

life=work (līf′wėrk′), *n.* The work, labor, or task of a lifetime.

lift[1] (lift), *n.* [AS. *lyft* = D. *lucht* = G. *luft* = Icel. *lopt* = Goth. *luftus*, the air: cf. *loft* and *lift*[2].] The air (above the earth); the sky: as, "when lightnings fire the stormy *lift*" (Burns's "Epistle to Robert Graham," 104). [Archaic or Sc. and north. Eng.]

lift[2] (lift), *v.* [Icel. *lypta*, lift, raise, orig. into the air; akin to Icel. *lopt*, AS. *lyft*, the air: see *loft* and *lift*[1].] **I.** *tr.* To move or bring (something) upward from the ground or other support into the air or to some higher position, as by the use of strength or power (as, to *lift* a weight or a table; to *lift* a child to one's shoulder; "Have you any levers to *lift* me up again, being down?" Shakspere's "1 Henry IV.," ii. 2. 36); heave or hoist; bear upward or aloft; in general, to raise to a higher position (as, to *lift* the hand, head, or eyes; "The floods *lift* up their waves," Ps. xciii. 3); hold up or display on high (as, "As through a night of storm, some tall, Strong lighthouse *lifts* its steady flame": Whittier's "Sumner"); bring above the horizon by approaching, as at sea (as, "That route is barred to steamers: you'll never *lift* again Our purple-painted headlands," Kipling's "Three-Decker": cf. *raise, v.*); also, fig., to raise in rank, dignity, condition, estimation, etc. (as, "Battle-fields, where thousands bleed To *lift* one hero into fame": Longfellow's "Hanging of the Crane," vi.); elevate or exalt; elate or uplift (usually with *up*); also, to send up audibly or loudly by utterance (as, to *lift*, or *lift* up, the voice or a cry; "May we *lift* a Deepsea Chantey such as seamen use at sea?" Kipling's "Last Chantey"); also, to pick or take up (Sc. or in *golf*: as, to *lift* a ball out of a hazard); collect (money, rents, etc.: now prov.); take away or remove (chiefly prov.); hence, to take dishonestly or steal (colloq.: as, to *lift* cattle; to *lift* articles from a shop); hence, to rob (a place: cf. *shoplifter*); also, to pay off (a mortgage, etc.: U. S.). **II.** *intr.* To move upward or rise; rise and disperse, as clouds, fog, etc.; rise to view above the horizon when approached, as land seen from the sea; also, to pull or strain in the effort to lift something (as, to *lift* at a heavy weight).—**lift²**, *n.* The act or an act of lifting, raising, or rising (as, the *lift* of a hand; a *lift* of the fog); a holding up of the head, etc.; the distance through which something is lifted; lifting or raising force; the weight or load lifted; also, fig., a helping upward or onward (as, to give a *lift* to one's fortunes); often, a ride in a vehicle, given to help along a traveler on foot (as, "perhaps getting a *lift* in a cart by the way": George Eliot's "Adam Bede," xxxviii.); exaltation or uplift, as in feeling (as, "without one thrill of inspiration, or one *lift* above the dust of earth": Mrs. Stowe's "Oldtown Folks," xxv.); also, a rise or elevation of ground; also, a device or apparatus for lifting; specif., an elevator, a dumb-waiter, or the like, in a building, or the shaft in which it moves (chiefly Eng.); also, one of the layers of leather forming the heel of a boot or shoe; also, *naut.*, a rope connecting an end of a yard with a masthead and serving to raise, support, square, or trim the yard.—**lift'a-ble,** *a.* That may be lifted.—**lift-age** (lif'tạj), *n.* Amount or capability of lifting: as, the lock *liftage* of a canal.

lift=bridge (lift'brij), *n.* A kind of drawbridge of which part may be lifted to permit of the passage of boats, etc.

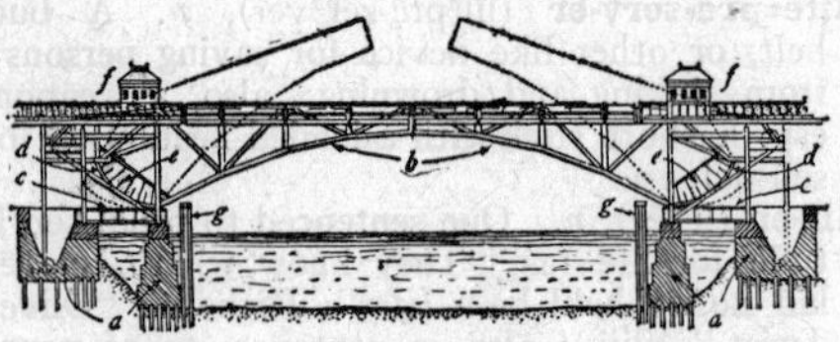

Rolling Lift-bridge.

a, foundation of concrete resting on piles; *b*, movable parts of bridge, closed; *c*, track on which movable part rolls in rising to open position; *d*, curved face that rolls on track; *e*, counterweights; *f*, house for motor and control; *g*, fender-piles. Dotted lines show movable parts of bridge rolling backward and upward and half open.

lift-er (lif'tėr), *n.* One who or that which lifts; an instrument or apparatus for lifting something.

lift=pump (lift'pump), *n.* Any pump which merely lifts or raises a liquid, and does not eject it forcibly under pressure: distinguished from *force-pump.*

lig-a-ment (lig'ạ-mẹnt), *n.* [L. *ligamentum*, < *ligare*: see *ligate.*] A connecting tie, or bond of union or attachment (as, "By such slight *ligaments* are we bound to prosperity or ruin": Mrs. Shelley's "Frankenstein," ii.); in *anat.*, a band of tissue, usually white and fibrous, serving to connect bones, hold organs in place, etc.—**lig-a-men'ta-ry** (-men'tạ-ri), *a.* Ligamentous.—**lig-a-men'tous,** *a.* Pertaining to, of the nature of, or forming a ligament.

li-gan (lī'gạn), *n.* Same as *lagan.*

li-gate (lī'gāt), *v. t.*; *-gated, -gating.* [L. *ligatus*, pp. of *ligare*, bind, tie.] To bind, as with a ligature; tie up, as a bleeding artery.—**li-ga'tion** (-gā'shọn), *n.* [L. *ligatio(n-).*] The act of ligating; a binding or tying up, esp. of an artery, etc.; also, something used to bind with; a band or tie; sometimes, the place of tying (as, "a bundle tied with tape, and sealed at each fold and *ligation* with black wax": Scott's "Guy Mannering," xxxviii.).

lig-a-ture (lig'ạ-ţūr), *n.* [LL. *ligatura*, < L. *ligare*: see *ligate.*] Anything that serves for binding or tying up, as a band, bandage, or cord (as, "I likewise felt several slender *ligatures* across my body, from my arm-pits to my thighs": Swift's "Gulliver's Travels," i. 1); fig., a tie or bond (as, *ligatures* of race and family); also, the act of binding or tying up; ligation; in *surg.*, a cord used for tying up bleeding arteries, etc., or for removing tumors by strangulation; in *music*, a slur; also, a group of notes connected by a slur; in *printing*, a character or type combining two or more letters, as *fi, ffl* (cf. *logotype*).—**lig'a-ture,** *v. t.*; *-tured, -turing.* To bind with a ligature; tie up; ligate.

light¹ (līt), *n.* [AS. *lēoht* = D. and G. *licht*, akin to Icel. *ljōs* and Goth. *liuhath*, light, also to L. *lux* and *lumen*, light, *lucere*, shine, *luna*, moon, Gr. λευκός, light, bright, white, ἀμφιλύκη, twilight, Skt. *ruc-*, shine.] That which makes things visible, or affords illumination (opposed to *darkness*); that form of radiant energy which, transmitted from a luminous body to the eye by undulations or waves in the luminiferous ether, acts on the organs of sight (as, *light* moves with a velocity of about 186,000 miles per second; to emit, transmit, reflect, or disperse *light*); the sensation thus produced; a similar form of radiant energy, as the ultra-violet rays, which does not affect the retina; also, a particular instance of light, or illuminating radiant energy, often with reference to intensity, quality, etc. (as, a *light* shot across the sky; a strong, bright, dim, soft, or pale *light*); measure or supply of light (as, the wall cuts off our *light*); illumination; the light, radiance, or illumination from a particular source (as, moon*light*; fire*light*; torch*light*; candle-*light*; electric *light*); specif., the illumination from the sun, or daylight; sometimes, daybreak or dawn (as, "The cock sung out an hour ere *light*": Tennyson's "Mariana," 27); fig., mental or spiritual illumination or enlightenment (as, to throw *light* on a mystery; to be guided by the *light* of nature; the *light* of religion); *pl.*, information, ideas, or mental capacities possessed (as, to act according to one's *lights*); also, *sing.*, the appearance or visible effect produced by light (as, a bar of *light* on the wall; a *light* on the waves); brightness or glow; a gleam or sparkle, as in the eyes (often as expressing animated feeling: as, to see the *light* of battle in one's eyes); specif., the effect of light falling on an object or scene as represented in a picture (as, "When the ripe colours soften and unite, And sweetly melt into just shade and *light*": Pope's "Essay on Criticism," 489); a lighter or brighter part of a picture; also, the state of being visible, exposed to view, or, fig., revealed to public notice or knowledge (esp. in 'to come to light,' or 'to bring to light'); also, a particular light or illumination in which an object seen takes on a certain appearance (as, "Walter stepped forward,—then back,—viewing Elinor's portrait in various *lights*": Hawthorne's "Twice-Told Tales," The Prophetic Pictures); hence, the aspect in which a thing appears or is regarded (as, "In this amiable *light* did Fayaway appear in my eyes": H. Melville's "Typee," xiii.); also, an illuminating agent or source, as the sun, a lamp, or a beacon (as, "Let there be *lights* in the firmament of the heaven," Gen. i. 14; "The *lights* burn blue. It is now dead midnight," Shakspere's "Richard III.," v. 3. 180); a lighthouse (as, the Sandy Hook *light*); fig., a source of mental or spiritual illumination (as, "The commandment is a lamp; and the law is *light*," Prov. vi. 23; "Then spake Jesus . . . saying, I am the *light* of the world," John, viii. 12); a person who is an illuminating or shining example (as, the *lights* of the legal profession); a luminary; a source of cheer or gladness (as, the child is the *light* of the house); sometimes, the spark or principle of life (as, "when Life her *light* withdraws": Tennyson's "Two Voices," 145); also, the eyesight (archaic); *pl.*, the eyes (now slang); also, *sing.*, a window, or a pane or compartment of a window (as, a fan*light*; a mullioned window of three *lights*); also, a means of igniting, as a spark, flame, match, or the like.—**Festival of Lights.** See *Hanukkah.*—**New Lights, Old Lights.** See under *new, a.*, and *old, a.*—**northern lights** or **southern lights,** the aurora borealis or the aurora australis: also called *polar lights.* See *aurora.*—**to see the light,** to be born; come into existence; also, to be made public, or published, as a book.—**to stand in one's own light,** to stand so as to cut off or lessen one's own light for seeing: hence, fig., to continue in a course opposed to one's own interest.—**light¹**, *a.* [AS. *lēoht* = D. and G. *licht*, light; from the same root as E. *light¹*, *n.*] Luminous, shining, or bright, as the sun, fire, etc.†; also, having light or illumination, rather than dark (as, the *lightest* room in the house;

"Even the night shall be *light* about me," Ps. cxxxix. 11); also, pale, whitish, or not deep or dark in color (as, a *light* red; *light* hair or complexion).—**light**[1], *v.*; *lighted* or *lit* (pp. also pseudo-archaic *litten*), *lighting*. [AS. *līhtan* = D. *lichten* = G. *leuchten* = Goth. *liuhtan*, shine.] **I.** *intr.* To give light†, or shine†; also, to become light†, or dawn† (as, "That shall be the day, whene'er it *lights*": Shakspere's "1 Henry IV.," iii. 2. 138); also, to take fire or become kindled; also, to become bright as with light or color (often with *up*: as, the sky *lights* up at sunset); often, to brighten with animation or joy, as the face, eyes, etc. (often with *up*). **II.** *tr.* To give light to, or illuminate (as, the sun *lights* the earth; the torches *lighted*, or *lighted* up, the street); furnish with light or illumination (as, to *light* a house with gas or electricity); conduct with a light (as, "To be to thee . . . a torch-bearer, And *light* thee on thy way to Mantua": Shakspere's "Romeo and Juliet," iii. 5. 15); also, to set burning (a candle, lamp, pipe for smoking, etc.); kindle (a fire); ignite (fuel, a match, etc.); also, to make bright as with light or color (usually with *up*); often, to brighten (the face, etc.: as, "A smile *lit* the eyes of the expiring Kentuck," Bret Harte's "Luck of Roaring Camp": often with *up*).

light[2] (līt). [AS. *lēoht*, *līht*, = D. *licht* = G. *leicht* = Icel. *lēttr* = Goth. *leihts*, light: cf. L. *levis*, light, Gr. ἐλαχύς, small, Skt. *laghu*, swift, light, also E. *lung*.] **I.** *a.* Of little weight, or not heavy or ponderous (as, a *light* load); of little weight in proportion to bulk, or of low specific gravity (as, a *light* metal; a *light* liquid or gas); of less than the usual or average weight (as, a *light* chain; *light* artillery; *light* clothing); weighing less than the proper or standard amount (as, to use *light* weights in trade; *light* coin); also, laden or encumbered but slightly or not at all (as, a ship sailing *light*); adapted by small weight or slight build for small loads or swift movement (as, a *light* carriage; "There issued from the port of Dieppe *light*, fast-sailing vessels," Besant's "Coligny," vii.); also, of little density (as, a *light* vapor or haze); porous or friable, as soil; spongy or well leavened, as bread; not heavy or strong, as wine, etc.; also, of small amount, force, intensity, etc. (as, a *light* vote; a *light* rain; a *light* touch or sound; *light* sleep); slight, gentle, or not violent; being such to but a small degree (as, a *light* drinker); also, easy to endure, deal with, or perform (as, *light* taxes or penalties; *light* duties); not especially burdensome, oppressive, or difficult; not very grievous or distressing (as, "our *light* affliction, which is but for a moment": 2 Cor. iv. 17); requiring little mental effort, or not profound, serious, or heavy (as, *light* reading; a *light* opera; a *light* comedy or comedian); easily digested, as food; also, of little moment or importance, trifling, or trivial (as, the loss was no *light* matter; to make *light* of threats or warnings, to treat or represent them as of little importance); also, slender or delicate in form or appearance (as, *light* spires or arches; a *light*, graceful figure); airy or buoyant in movement (as, "The leader of the herd . . . Steps with a tender foot, *light* as on air": Tennyson's "Princess," vi. 72); nimble or agile (as, *light* fingers or heels; a *light* leap); also, free from any burden of sorrow or care (as, to be *light* of heart; a *light* heart); buoyantly cheerful; gay, jesting, or cheerfully careless (as, a *light* retort; a *light* laugh); characterized by levity or want of proper seriousness, or frivolous (as, a *light* mind; *light* conduct); wanton or unchaste (as, a *light* woman); also, easily swayed or changing, facile, or volatile (as, to be *light* of belief, love, or purpose); also, affected with a sensation of unnatural lightness (as, his head is *light*; to be *light* of head); giddy or dizzy; flighty or slightly delirious; *milit.*, lightly armed or equipped (as, *light* cavalry; *light* marching order, the condition of soldiers equipped with arms, ammunition, canteen, and haversack, but without knapsack, etc.). **II.** *n. pl.* The lungs, esp. of sheep, pigs, etc.: so called from their lightness.—**light**[2], *adv.* [AS. *lēohte*.] Lightly: as, "The grass stoops not, she treads on it so *light*" (Shakspere's "Venus and Adonis," 1028).

light[3] (līt), *v. i.*; *lighted* or *lit*, *lighting*. [AS. *līhtan*, alight, orig. make light, relieve of a weight, < *līht*, E. *light*[2], *a.*] To get down or descend as from a horse or a vehicle; dismount or alight; also, to come to rest, as on a spot or thing (as, "A dove, sent forth . . . to spy Green tree or ground, whereon his foot may *light*": Milton's "Paradise Lost," xi. 858); land; also, to fall, as a stroke, weapon, vengeance, choice, etc., on a place or person (as, "I do prophesy the election *lights* On Fortinbras": Shakspere's "Hamlet," v. 2. 366); also, to come by chance, happen, or hit (*on* or *upon*: as, to *light* on a bargain or a purchaser; to *light* on a clue).—**to light out,** to leave a place, esp. suddenly or without notice; depart in haste; decamp: as, "When I couldn't stand it no longer I *lit out*" (Mark Twain's "Huckleberry Finn," i.). [Slang, U. S.]

light=armed (līt'ärmd), *a.* Equipped with light arms or armor, as troops.

light-en[1] (lī'tn), *v.* [From *light*[1], *a.*] **I.** *intr.* To shine, gleam, or be bright (as, "when her lamp *lightens* in the tower": Scott's "Rokeby," i. 29); specif., to emit a flash of lightning (as, "Too like the lightning, which doth cease to be Ere one can say 'It *lightens*'": Shakspere's "Romeo and Juliet," ii. 2. 120); flash as or like lightning; also, to become lighter or less dark; brighten. **II.** *tr.* To give light to, or illuminate (as, "The city had no need of the sun . . . for the glory of God did *lighten* it": Rev. xxi. 23); fig., to illuminate mentally or spiritually, or enlighten (as, "Now the Lord *lighten* thee! thou art a great fool": Shakspere's "2 Henry IV.," ii. 1. 208); also, to brighten (the face, eyes, etc.); also, to flash like lightning (as, "Now she *lightens* scorn At him that mars her plan": Tennyson's "Princess," v. 125).

light-en[2] (lī'tn), *v.* [From *light*[2], *a.*] **I.** *intr.* To become lighter; decrease in weight, amount, etc. (as, "As most of their luggage was our provision, it *lightened* every day": Defoe's "Captain Singleton," v.); become more cheerful, as the heart. **II.** *tr.* To make lighter; lessen the weight of (a load, etc.); reduce the load of (a ship, etc.); relieve or deprive (*of*: as, "I was *lightened* of my purse, in which was almost every farthing I had," Irving's "Tales of a Traveler," ii. 4); make less burdensome, oppressive, or distressing (as, to *lighten* taxes; to *lighten* cares); alleviate or mitigate; cheer or gladden (as, to *lighten* the heart).

light-en[3]† (lī'tn), *v. i.* [From *light*[3].] To light or alight; descend.

light-en-er[1] (lī'tn-ėr), *n.* One who or that which lightens or illuminates, or sends forth lightning.

light-en-er[2] (lī'tn-ėr), *n.* One who or that which lightens, makes less heavy, or alleviates.

light-er[1] (lī'tėr), *n.* One who or that which lights, illuminates, ignites, etc.

light-er[2] (lī'tėr), *n.* [Cf. D. *lichter*, lighter, < *lichten*, lighten, unload, < *licht*, light: see *light*[2].] A vessel, commonly a flat-bottomed barge, used in lightening or unloading and also in loading ships, or in transporting goods, etc., short distances.—**light'er**[2], *v. t.* To convey in or as in a lighter.—**light'er-age** (-ạ̄j), *n.* The process of or the charge for lightering goods, etc.—**light'er-man** (-mạn), *n.*; pl. *-men.* One who is employed on or manages a lighter.

light-er=than=air (lī'tėr-ᴛʜạn-ãr'), *a.* In *aëronautics*, of less specific gravity than the air, as aircraft (such as dirigible balloons); of or pertaining to such aircraft. Cf. *heavier-than-air.*

light=fin-gered (līt'fing'gėrd), *a.* Having light or nimble fingers; dexterous with the fingers, esp. in picking pockets or in other forms of petty theft (as, "There are many *light-fingered* gentry about": Marryat's "Mr. Midshipman Easy," xvii.); thievish.—**light'=fin'gered-ness,** *n.*

light=foot (līt'fůt), *a.* Light-footed: as, "*light-foot* Iris" (Tennyson's "Œnone," 81). [Poetic.]—**light'=foot'ed,** *a.* Light of foot; stepping lightly or nimbly.—**light'=foot'ed-ly,** *adv.*

light-ful (līt'fůl), *a.* Full of light; bright. [Now rare.] —**light'ful-ness,** *n.*

light=hand-ed (līt'han'ded), *a.* Having a light hand or touch; dexterous; also, having little in the hand; also, short-handed, as a factory.—**light'=hand'ed-ness,** *n.*

light=head-ed (līt'hed'ed), *a.* Having or showing a light head or a frivolous or volatile disposition (as, *light-headed* persons or actions); also, suffering from a light head; giddy or dizzy; flighty or delirious (as, "She is in a high fever; she is *light-headed*": Godwin's "Caleb Williams," x.).—**light'=head'ed-ly,** *adv.*—**light'=head'ed-ness,** *n.*

light=heart-ed (līt'här'ted), *a.* Having or showing a light heart; care-free; cheerful; gay: as, *light-hearted* lads; a *light-hearted* laugh.—**light′=heart′ed-ly,** *adv.*—**light′=heart′ed-ness,** *n.*

light=heeled (līt′hēld), *a.* Having light heels; light-footed; nimble: as, "The villain is much *lighter-heel'd* than I: I follow'd fast, but faster he did fly" (Shakspere's "Midsummer Night's Dream," iii. 2. 415).

light=horse-man (līt′hôrs′mạn), *n.*; pl. *-men.* A light-armed cavalry soldier.

light-house (līt′hous), *n.* A tower or other structure displaying a light or lights for the guidance of mariners.—**light′house-man** (-mạn), *n.*; pl. *-men.*

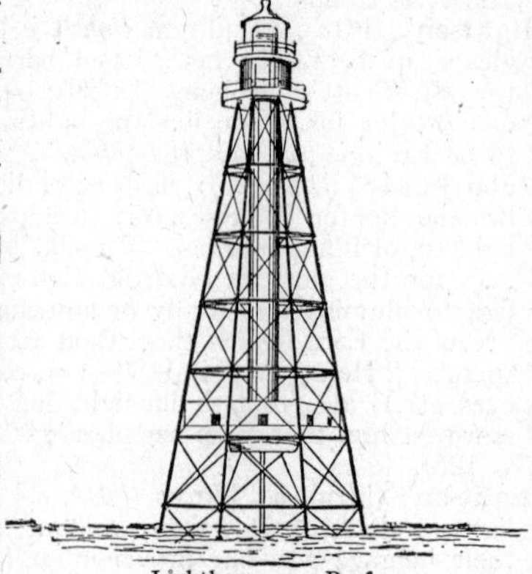

Lighthouse on a Reef.

light-ish (lī′tish), *a.* Rather light, as in color.

light-less (līt′les), *a.* [AS. *lēohtlēas.*] Without light; receiving no light; dark; also, giving no light.—**light′less-ness,** *n.*

light-ly (līt′li), *adv.* [AS. *lēohtlīce.*] In a light manner; with little weight, force, intensity, etc., or to but a small amount or degree (as, to rest or press *lightly* on a thing; *lightly* clad); slightly or gently; easily, or without trouble or effort (as, *lightly* come, *lightly* go — said proverbially of money); airily or buoyantly (as, flags floating *lightly*); nimbly (as, to leap *lightly* aside); cheerfully, or with cheerful unconcern (as, to take bad news *lightly*); indifferently or slightingly (as, to think *lightly* of one's achievements); with levity, or frivolously (as, to behave *lightly*); without due consideration or reason (often with a negative: as, an offer not *lightly* to be refused).—**light′ly,** *v. t.*; *-lied, -lying.* To regard or treat lightly; despise, disparage, or slight: as, "For laik [lack] o' gear ye *lightly* me" (Burns's "Tibbie"). [Sc. and north. Eng.]

light=mind-ed (līt′mīn′ded), *a.* Having or showing a light mind; characterized by levity; frivolous: as, "There would be a further most unedifying giggle and titter of *light-minded* young men and damsels" (Mrs. Stowe's "Oldtown Folks," v.).—**light′=mind′ed-ness,** *n.*

light-ness[1] (līt′nes), *n.* The state of being light, illuminated, or whitish.

light-ness[2] (līt′nes), *n.* The state or quality of being light as in weight, etc.

light-ning (līt′ning), *n.* [For *lightening,* < *lighten*[1].] A flashing of light or a sudden illumination of the heavens caused by the discharge of atmospheric electricity (as, chain-*lightning*; sheet-*lightning*; heat-*lightning*: cf. *fire-ball*); hence, in general, a flash of light (as, "The great brand Made *lightnings* in the splendour of the moon": Tennyson's "Passing of Arthur," 305); the flashing light or gleam of the eyes (as, "Zenobia's eyes darted *lightning*": Hawthorne's "Blithedale Romance," xix.).—**light′ning=bug,** *n.* A firefly.—**light′ning=rod,** *n.* A protective insulated metallic rod fixed on a house, vessel, etc., to conduct lightning or atmospheric electricity into the earth or water.

light=o'=love (līt′ọ-luv″), *n.* A woman inconstant in love; a wanton coquette; sometimes, a woman of loose life.

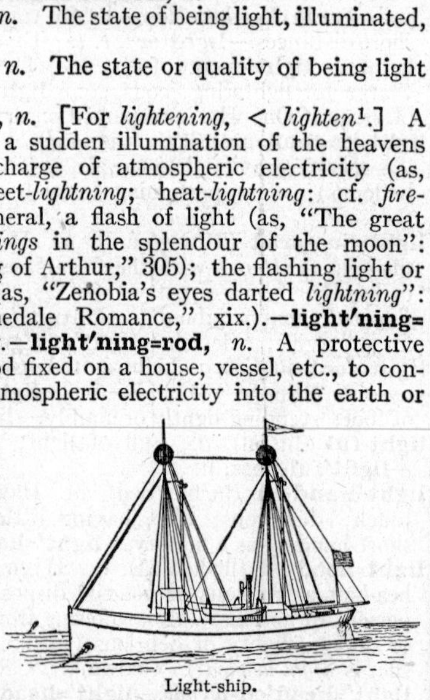

Light-ship.

lights (līts), *n. pl.* See *light*[2], *n.*

light=ship (līt′ship), *n.* An anchored ship displaying a light or lights for the guidance of mariners.

light-skirts (līt′skėrts), *n.* A light or wanton woman.

light-some[1] (līt′sum), *a.* Radiant with light, luminous, or bright, as the sun; also, well lighted or illuminated, as a room; also, clear to the mind (obs. or rare).—**light′some-ness**[1], *n.*

light-some[2] (līt′sum), *a.* Light, or not heavy, esp. in form, appearance, or movement; airy; buoyant; nimble; also, cheerful or gay (as, "when she sat at her piano trilling songs with a *lightsome* heart": Thackeray's "Vanity Fair," xxxvii.); also, frivolous or volatile.—**light′some-ly,** *adv.*—**light′some-ness**[2], *n.*

light=struck (līt′struk), *a.* In *photog.,* injured or fogged by accidental exposure to light, as a sensitized plate.

light=weight (līt′wāt), *n.* One of less than average weight; esp., a boxer or other contestant intermediate in weight between a middle-weight (or a welter-weight) and a feather-weight; fig., a person of little mental force or of slight influence or importance (colloq.).

light-wood (līt′wụ̇d), *n.* Wood used in lighting a fire; esp., in the southern U. S., resinous pine wood.

light=year (līt′yēr), *n.* In *astron.,* the distance traversed by light in one year (about 5,860,000,000,000 miles), being about 63,000 times the distance of the earth from the sun: used as a unit in measuring stellar distances.

lign-al-oes (līn-al′ōz), *n.* [OF. *lignaloes,* < L. *lignum aloës,* 'wood of aloes.'] Aloes wood; also, the drug aloes.

lig-ne-ous (lig′nē-us), *a.* [L. *ligneus,* < *lignum,* wood.] Of the nature of or resembling wood; woody.

ligni-. Form of L. *lignum,* wood, used in combination.—**lig-nic-o-lous** (lig-nik′ọ-lus), *a.* [+ *-colous.*] Living or growing on wood, as fungi; living in wood, as ship-worms.—**lig′ni-form** (-ni-fôrm), *a.* [+ *-form.*] Having the form of wood; resembling wood, as a variety of asbestos.—**lig′ni-fy** (-fī), *v. t.* or *i.*; *-fied, -fying.* [+ *-fy.*] To convert into or become wood.—**lig″ni-fi-ca′tion** (-fi-kā′shọn), *n.*

lig-nin (lig′nin), *n.* [L. *lignum,* wood.] In *bot.,* an organic substance which, with cellulose, forms the chief part of woody tissue.

lig-nite (lig′nīt), *n.* [F., < L. *lignum,* wood.] An imperfectly formed coal, usually dark-brown, and often having a distinctly seen woody texture. Also called *brown coal,* and sometimes *woodcoal.*—**lig-nit′ic** (-nit′ik), *a.* Of, pertaining to, or containing lignite.—**lig-ni-tif′er-ous** (-ni-tif′ẹ-rus), *a.* [See *-ferous.*] Bearing or containing lignite.—**lig′ni-tize** (-tīz), *v. t.*; *-tized, -tizing.* To convert into lignite.—**lig′ni-toid** (-toid), *a.* [See *-oid.*] Like lignite.

lig-niv-o-rous (lig-niv′ọ-rus), *a.* [L. *lignum,* wood, + *vorare,* devour.] Eating wood, as the larvæ of many insects; xylophagous.

lig-nose (lig′nōs), *n.* [L. *lignum,* wood.] One of the constituents of lignin; also, an explosive mixture consisting of wood-pulp saturated with nitroglycerin.

lig-num=vi-tæ (lig′num-vī′tē), *n.* [NL., 'wood of life.'] The hard, extremely heavy wood of either of two species of guaiacum, *Guaiacum officinale* and *G. sanctum,* used for making pulleys, rulers, etc., and formerly thought to have great medicinal powers; either tree; also, any of various other trees with a similar hard wood. See *guaiacum.*

lig-ro-in, lig-ro-ine (lig′rọ-in), *n.* [Origin obscure.] A volatile inflammable liquid (a petroleum distillate intermediate between naphtha and benzine) used as a solvent, etc.

lig-u-la (lig′ụ-lạ), *n.*; pl. *-læ* (-lē). [L., var. of *lingula,* dim. of *lingua,* tongue.] In *bot.* and *zoöl.,* a tongue-like or strap-shaped part or organ, as the blade formed by the gamopetalous corolla in the ray-flowers of numerous composite plants, or as the membranous appendage which projects from the summit of the leaf-sheath in many grasses.—**lig′u-lar** (-lạr), *a.* Of or like a ligula.—**lig′u-late** (-lāt), *a.* Having or forming a ligula. Also **lig′u-lat-ed** (-lā-ted).—**lig′ule** (-ūl), *n.* A ligula.

lig-ure (lig′ūr), *n.* [LL. *ligurius,* < Gr. λιγύριον (used to render Heb. *leshem*).] An unidentified precious stone mentioned in the Bible. See Ex. xxviii. 19.

Li-gu-ri-an (li-gū′ri-ạn). **I.** *a.* Of or pertaining to Liguria, an ancient district in northwestern Italy and southeastern France, or a territorial division of modern Italy including the province of Genoa. **II.** *n.* A native or inhabitant of Liguria; esp., one of a race represented by the ancient inhabitants of Liguria and their modern descendants.

lik-a-ble (lī'kạ-bl), *a.* Such as to be liked; pleasing.—**lik'a-ble-ness,** *n.*

like[1] (līk), *a.*; compar. *liker,* superl. *likest.* [ME. *lic, liche,* < AS. *gelīc* = D. *gelijk* = G. *gleich* = Icel. *glīkr* = Goth. *galeiks,* like, lit. 'of the same body, or form'; from a Teut. prefix (AS. *ge-,* together) and a noun meaning 'body': see *lich,* and cf. *alike.*] Of the same form, appearance, kind, character, amount, etc. (as, a *like* statue or scene; a *like* instance; a *like* sum or time); corresponding or agreeing in general or in some noticeable respect (as, drawing, painting, and other *like* arts; "These and a thousand other *like* questions beset her," Howells's "Chance Acquaintance," xii.); similar; analogous; bearing resemblance (as, "a portrait of Lady Jane, a full-length too, and wonderfully *like*": Lever's "Harry Lorrequer," iii.); often, resembling (followed formerly or in archaic use by *to* or *unto,* now commonly omitted, and a noun or pronoun: as, "The kingdom of heaven is *like* to a grain of mustard seed," Mat. xiii. 31; he is just *like* his father; I never saw anything *like* it); hence, characteristic of (as, it would be *like* him to come without notice); also, giving promise or indication of (as, it looks *like* rain; it feels *like* spring); also, disposed or inclined to (after *feel*: colloq.: as, to feel *like* going to bed); also, probable or likely (archaic or prov.: as, "'Tis *like* that they will know us," Shakspere's "1 Henry IV.," i. 2. 195); probably or apparently going, or likely (to do, be, etc.: archaic, prov., or colloq.: as, "He is *like* to die for hunger," Jer. xxxviii. 9); hence, about (to do, etc.: now prov. or colloq.: as, he seemed *like* to choke; he was *like,* or had *like,* to have been killed, see phrase following).—**had like** (for *was like*), was about or on the verge, or came near: with an infinitive (commonly the perfect infinitive): as, he *had like* to have been killed. [Now prov. or colloq.]—**like**[1], *n.* A like person or thing, or like persons or things (as, they and their *like*); a counterpart, match, or equal; with *the,* something of a similar nature; whatever is like what has been mentioned (as oranges, lemons, and the *like*).—**like**[1]. **I.** *adv.* In like manner (as, "*Like* as a father pitieth his children, so the Lord pitieth them that fear him": Ps. ciii. 13); also, to a like extent or degree, equally, or alike (archaic: as, "The enterprise . . . Shall be to you, as us, *like* glorious," Shakspere's "Henry V.," ii. 2. 183); also, as it were (prov. or vulgar: as, of a sudden *like*); also, likely or probably (now chiefly colloq.: as, *like* enough; very *like*; as *like* as not). **II.** *prep.* In like manner with; similarly to; in the manner characteristic of: as, striped *like* a zebra; to work *like* a beaver. **III.** *conj.* Like as, just as, or as (as, "*Like* goodly buildings left without a roof Soon fall to ruin," Shakspere's "Pericles," ii. 4. 36; "You talk exactly *like* the dad talks," Arnold Bennett's "Hilda Lessways," ii. 4: now prov. or colloq., and commonly condemned as vulgar); also, as if (prov. or vulgar: as, he acted *like* he was afraid).—**like**[1], *v.*; *liked, liking.* **I.**† *tr.* To liken or compare: as, "The prince broke thy head for *liking* his father to a singing-man of Windsor" (Shakspere's "2 Henry IV.," ii. 1. 97). **II.** *intr.* To come near: as, he *liked,* or had *liked,* to have choked. Cf. *had like,* under *like*[1], *a.* [Now prov. or colloq.]

like[2] (līk), *v.*; *liked, liking.* [AS. *līcian* = D. *lijken* = Icel. *līka* = Goth. *leikan,* please; appar. orig. meaning 'conform,' 'suit,' and from the same Teut. noun as E. *like*[1].] **I.** *intr.* To be pleasing, or suit the tastes or wishes (obs. or archaic: as, "The offer *likes* not," Shakspere's "Henry V.," iii., Prologue, 32); also, to be pleased (as, "They . . . looking *liked,* and *liking* loved": Scott's "Marmion," v., Introd.); approve (*of*: now prov. Eng.); feel inclined, or wish (as, come whenever you *like*); also, to get on well†, or thrive†. **II.** *tr.* To be pleasing to, please, or suit (orig. *intr.* with indirect object: archaic or prov.: as, "He shall dwell . . . where it *liketh* him best," Deut. xxiii. 16); also, to take pleasure in, or find agreeable or to one's taste (as, to *like* a place, a pastime, a book, a beverage, or to do something); regard with favor, or have a kindly or friendly feeling for (a person, etc.).—**like**[2], *n.* A liking, favorable feeling, or preference: chiefly in *pl.,* in 'likes and dislikes.'

-like. Suffixal use of *like*[1], *a.,* in the sense of 'resembling,' 'characteristic of,' 'befitting,' etc., used to form adjectives, esp. from nouns, as in *businesslike, childlike, godlike, lifelike,* and numerous other words: the older or more frequently used formations of this kind usually having no hyphen, and the less common (including many coined to answer a momentary need) being given with a hyphen, as in *bristle-like, carpet-like, hippopotamus-like, zither-like.*

like'a-ble, etc. See *likable,* etc.

like-li-hood (līk'li-hůd), *n.* Likeness† or similarity†; also, the state of being likely or probable; probability; a probability or chance of something (as, there is a strong *likelihood* of his succeeding); also, an indication or sign of something probable† (as, "Many *likelihoods* informed me of this before": Shakspere's "All's Well," i. 3. 128); also, promising character, or promise (obs. or archaic: as, "a fellow of no mark nor *likelihood,*" Shakspere's "1 Henry IV.," iii. 2. 45).

like-ly (līk'li), *a.*; compar. *likelier,* superl. *likeliest.* Like† or similar†; also, seeming like truth, fact, or certainty, or reasonably to be believed or expected (as, a *likely* story; it seems *likely* that he went, or will go; rain is *likely* before night); probable; also, probably or apparently going or destined (to do, be, etc.: as, *likely* to do well or be successful; not *likely* to happen); also, apparently suitable (as, a *likely* person or place for the purpose; a *likely* spot to build on); also, promising (as, "a fine *likely* boy": Mrs. Gaskell's "Cranford," vi.); also, good-looking or comely (now prov.).—**like'li-ness,** *n.*—**like'ly,** *adv.* Probably.

like=mind-ed (līk'mīn'ded), *a.* Having a like mind, opinion, or purpose; in agreement or accord.—**like'=mind'ed-ness,** *n.*

lik-en (lī'kn), *v. t.* To represent as like; compare: as, "The kingdom of heaven is *likened* unto a man which sowed good seed in his field" (Mat. xiii. 24).

like-ness (līk'nes), *n.* The state or fact of being like; similarity or resemblance (as, there is no *likeness* between them); also, the semblance or appearance of something (as, to assume the *likeness* of a swan; "What seem'd his head The *likeness* of a kingly crown had on," Milton's "Paradise Lost," ii. 673); also, the representation, picture, or image of something (as, "Take ye therefore good heed . . . Lest ye . . . make you a graven image, the similitude of any figure, the *likeness* of male or female": Deut. iv. 16); esp., a picture or portrait, as of a person; sometimes, a copy or reproduction (as, man is sometimes called God's *likeness*); a counterpart, match, or like (as, "Their *likeness* is not found on earth, in air, or sea!" Burns's "Brigs of Ayr," 141).

lik-er (lī'kėr), *n.* One who likes.

like-wake, lyke-wake (līk'wāk), *n.* [ME. *like,* var. of *liche,* body (see *lich*), + *wake,* watch, E. *wake*[2].] A watch kept at night over a dead body. [Archaic or Sc. and north. Eng.]

like-wise (līk'wīz), *adv.* In like manner; also, moreover; also; too.

li-kin (lē'kēn'), *n.* [Chinese.] A Chinese provincial duty imposed on articles of trade in transit.

lik-ing (lī'king), *n.* The state or feeling of one who likes; pleasure or taste (as, "James Binnie had found the Continental life pretty much to his *liking*": Thackeray's "Newcomes," lvi.); preference, inclination, or favor; kindly or friendly feeling.

li-lac (lī'lạk), *n.* [Sp. *lilac,* < Ar. *līlak,* < Pers. *līlak,* var. of *nīlak,* bluish, < *nīl,* blue, indigo, < Skt. *nīla,* dark-blue: cf. *anil.*] Any of the oleaceous shrubs constituting the genus *Syringa,* as *S. vulgaris* (the common garden lilac), with heart-shaped leaves and large clusters of fragrant purple or white flowers; also, a light-purple color.—**li-la'ceous** (-lā'shius), *a.* Of or approaching the color called lilac.

lil-i-a-ceous (lil-i-ā'shius), *a.* [LL. *liliaceus,* < L. *lilium,* E. *lily.*] Of or like the lily; belonging to the *Liliaceæ,* or lily family of plants.

lil-ied (lil'id), *a.* Abounding in lilies; also, lily-like; white.

lil-li-bul-le-ro (lil″i-bu-lē'rō), *n.* A part of the refrain to a song deriding the Irish Roman Catholics, popular in England during and after the Revolution of 1688; hence, the song, or the tune to which it was sung.

Lil-li-pu-tian (lil-i-pū'shạn). **I.** *a.* Of or pertaining to the imaginary country of Lilliput, or its pygmy inhabitants, described in Swift's "Gulliver's Travels," i.; hence, pygmy; tiny; diminutive. **II.** *n.* An inhabitant of Lilliput; hence, a pygmy; a tiny being; also, a person of small ideas, intellect, or importance.

lilt (lilt), *v.* [ME. *lulten*; origin obscure.] **I.** *tr.* To sound†; also, to strike up (a song, tune, etc.); sing or play in a light, tripping or rhythmic manner. **II.** *intr.* To lilt a song or tune (as, "Mak haste an' turn king David owre, An' *lilt* wi' holy clangor": Burns's "Ordination," 20); also, to dance to music (Sc.); also, to move in a light, springing manner.—**lilt,** *n.* A lilting song or tune; also, rhythmic swing or cadence; also, a springing movement or step.

lil-y (lil'i). [AS. *lilie*, < L. *lilium*, < Gr. λείριον, lily.] **I.** *n.*; pl. *lilies* (-iz). Any plant of the genus *Lilium*, comprising scaly-bulbed herbs with showy funnel-shaped or bell-shaped flowers of various colors, as *L. candidum*, a species often cultivated ('white lily' or 'Madonna lily,' also called 'Easter lily'), or *L. longiflorum eximium* (or *L. harrisii*), a large-flowered variety introduced from Bermuda (the common 'Easter lily'), or *L. philadelphicum*, a common wild species of the eastern U. S. with red or orange-red flowers ('red lily'); the flower or the bulb of such a plant; also, any of various related or similar plants or their flowers (as, the mariposa *lily*; the calla *lily*); also, a heraldic fleur-de-lis, as that of the royal arms of France, or the giglio of the arms of Florence, Italy ('Florentine lily'); also, fig., a woman or maiden delicately fair, lovely, or pure (as, "In the fragrant gloom Of foreign churches—I see her there, Bright English *lily*": Tennyson's "Maud," i. 19. 5). **II.** *a.* Like or suggestive of a (white) lily (as, "Elaine, the *lily* maid of Astolat," Tennyson's "Lancelot and Elaine," 2; a *lily* hand); white as a lily; delicately fair; pure or unsullied (as, "*lily* truth": Keats's "Endymion," iv.); sometimes, pale or bloodless.

Red Lily (*Lilium philadelphicum*).

lil-y=fin-gered (lil'i-fing"gėrd), *a.* Having white or delicate fingers; lily-handed: as, "Can't have no *lily-fingered* boys workin' for me" (Mrs. Stowe's "Oldtown Folks," ix.).

lil-y=hand-ed (lil'i-han"ded), *a.* Having white or delicate hands: as, "no little *lily-handed* baronet he" (Tennyson's "Princess," Conclusion, 84).

lil-y=liv-ered (lil'i-liv"ėrd), *a.* White-livered or cowardly: as, "thou *lily-liver'd* boy" (Shakspere's "Macbeth," v. 3. 15).

lil-y=of=the=val-ley (lil'i-ǫv-ᴛʜė-val'i), *n.*; pl. *lilies-*. A stemless convallariaceous herb, *Convallaria majalis*, with a raceme of drooping, bell-shaped, fragrant white flowers.

Lily-of-the-valley.

lil-y=pad (lil'i-pad), *n.* The large, floating leaf of a waterlily.

lil-y=white (lil'i-hwīt). **I.** *a.* White as a lily (as, *lily-white* hands); also [*cap.*], of or pertaining to the Lily-whites. **II.** *n.* [*cap.*] A member of a class or faction of Republicans in the southern U. S. who seek to exclude negroes from political affairs.—**lil'y=white"-ness,** *n.*

li-ma (lī'mạ̈), *n.* [NL., < L. *lima*, a file.] Any of the bivalve mollusks of the genus *Lima*, with obliquely oval shell, notable for their power of swimming by rapidly opening and closing the valves of the shell.

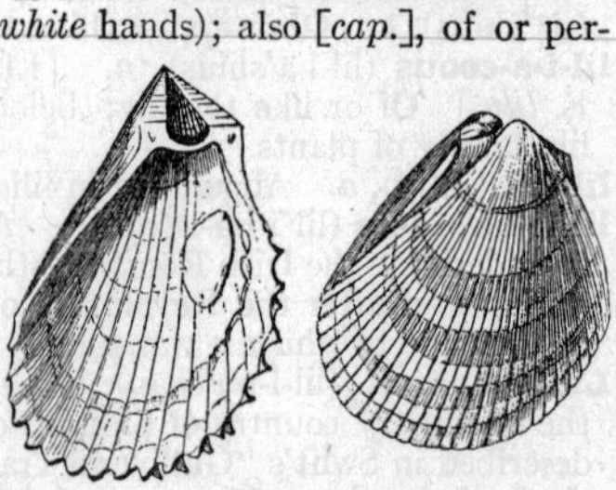

Species of Lima.

Li-ma (lī'mạ̈) **bean.** [From *Lima*, capital of Peru.] A kind of bean, a variety of *Phaseolus lunatus*, with a broad, flat edible seed; also, the seed, much used for food.

lim-a-cine (lim'ạ-sin or lī'mạ-), *a.* [L. *limax* (*limac-*), slug, snail.] In *zoöl.*, pertaining to, or having the characters of, the slugs.

limb[1] (lim), *n.* [AS. *lim* = Icel. *limr* = Sw. and Dan. *lem*, limb.] A part or member of an animal body distinct from the head and trunk, as a leg, arm, or wing; sometimes, specif., a leg (now chiefly in prudish use); also, a large or main branch of a tree; in general, a projecting part, section, or member (as, the four *limbs* of a cross; a *limb* or spur of a mountain); also, a person or thing regarded as a part, member, branch, offshoot, or scion of something (as, a *limb* of the law, humorously, a lawyer or legal functionary; "Bonaparte . . . was a perfect *limb* of Satan against our prosperity," Galt's "Annals of the Parish," xlix.); also, an imp, young scamp, or mischievous child (colloq.: as, "I always hated young uns, and this ere's a perfect little *limb*," Mrs. Stowe's "Oldtown Folks," xx.).—**limb**[1], *v. t.* To supply with limbs (obs. or archaic: see Milton's "Paradise Lost," vi. 352); also, to dismember.

limb[2] (lim), *n.* [L. *limbus*, border, edge: cf. *limbus* and *limbo*.] A border or edge, as the edge of the disk of the sun or moon, or the graduated edge of a quadrant or similar instrument; in *bot.*, the upper spreading part of a gamopetalous corolla; the expanded portion of a petal, sepal, or leaf.

lim-bate (lim'bāt), *a.* [LL. *limbatus*, bordered, < L. *limbus*, E. *limb*[2].] In *bot.* and *zoöl.*, bordered, as a flower in which one color is surrounded by an edging of another.

lim-beck (lim'bek), *n.* Same as *alembic*. [Archaic.]

limbed (limd), *a.* Having limbs: as, long-*limbed*.

lim-ber[1] (lim'bėr), *n.* [ME. *lymour*: cf. OF. F. *limon*, shaft.] The shaft of a cart or wagon (now prov. Eng. and Sc.); *milit.*, the detachable fore part of the carriage of a field-gun, consisting of two wheels, an axle, a pole, etc.—**lim'-ber**[1], *v. t.* or *i.* To attach the limber to (a gun), in preparation for moving away: usually with *up*.

Limber.

lim-ber[2] (lim'bėr), *n.* [Cf. F. *lumière*, light, opening, hole.] *Naut.*, one of a series of holes or channels for the passage of water to the pump-well.

lim-ber[3] (lim'bėr), *a.* [Origin obscure: cf. *limp*[1].] Bending readily, flexible, or pliant, as an oar, rod, plant-stalk, etc.; esp., bending readily at the joints, or characterized by ease in bending the body (as, "His fingers are very long and *limber*," Howells's "Rise of Silas Lapham," xi.; a *limber* fellow; *limber* movements); supple or lithe; fig., yielding readily to strain or influence (as, "You put me off with *limber* vows": Shakspere's "Winter's Tale," i. 2. 47).—**lim'ber**[3], *v.* **I.** *tr.* To render limber. **II.** *intr.* To make one's self limber: with *up*.—**lim'ber-ness,** *n.*

lim-bic (lim'bik), *a.* Pertaining to or of the nature of a limbus or border; marginal: as, a *limbic* lobe (in *anat.*, either of two lobes of the brain, one in each hemisphere).

limb-less (lim'les), *a.* Having no limbs; deprived of limbs or a limb.

limb-meal (lim'mēl), *adv.* [AS. *limmǣlum*, < *lim*, limb, + *mǣlum*, dat. pl. of *mǣl*, measure: see *meal*[2].] Limb by limb, or limb from limb; in pieces: as, "O, that I had her here, to tear her *limbmeal!*" (Shakspere's "Cymbeline," ii. 4. 147). [Archaic or prov. Eng.]

lim-bo (lim'bō), *n.* [L., abl. of *limbus*, border, edge, ML. a region on the border of hell: cf. *limb*[2] and *limbus*.] A supposed region on the border of hell, the abode after death of unbaptized infants ('limbo of infants'), or one serving as the temporary abode of the righteous who died before the coming of Christ ('limbo of the fathers' or 'limbo of the patriarchs'); hence, some similar region apart from this world (as, "A *limbo* large and broad, since call'd The Paradise of Fools": Milton's "Paradise Lost," iii. 495); also, a place to which persons or things are regarded as being relegated when cast aside, forgotten, past, or out of date (as, the *limbo* of petty poets; the *limbo* of discarded theories); a condition of neglect or oblivion; also, prison, jail, or confinement (as, "I should be better satisfied if you were in *limbo*, with a rope about your neck, and a comfortable bird's-eye prospect to the gallows": Godwin's "Caleb Williams," xli.).

Lim-burg-er (lim'bėr-gėr) **cheese.** [From *Limburg*, province of Belgium.] A soft variety of cheese of strong odor.

lim-bus (lim'bus), *n.*; pl. *-bi* (-bī). [L. and ML.: see *limbo*, and cf. *limb*².] Limbo; also, in scientific or technical use, a border, edge, or limb (see *limb*²).—**limbus infantium** or **infantum** (in-fan'ti-um or -tum). [ML.] The limbo of infants. See *limbo*.—**limbus patrum** (pā'trum). [ML.] The limbo of the fathers or patriarchs. See *limbo*.

lime¹ (līm), *n.* [Var. of obs. *line*, *lind*, < AS. *lind*: see *linden*.] The linden: as, "the broad ambrosial aisles of lofty *lime*" (Tennyson's "Princess," Prologue, 87).

lime² (līm), *n.* [F. *lime*, < Sp. *lima*, lime; from Ar., and akin to E. *lemon*.] A greenish-yellow acid fruit resembling the lemon but smaller and globose, borne by a tree, a variety of *Citrus medica*, allied to the lemon and citron; the tree itself; also, the acid drupaceous fruit of a species of tupelo, *Nyssa ogeche*, of the southern U. S., or the tree itself ('Ogeechee lime').

lime³ (līm), *n.* [AS. *līm* = D. *lijm* = G. *leim* = Icel. *līm*, lime, glue: cf. L. *limus*, slime, mud, *linere*, smear, and E. *loam*.] Birdlime; also, mortar or cement (obs. or Sc.); also, the oxide of calcium, CaO, a white caustic solid prepared by calcining limestone, etc., used in making mortar and cement (also called 'quicklime' and 'unslaked lime'; when treated with water it produces calcium hydroxide, or 'slaked lime': see *slake*, *v.*); also, calcium (in phrases, as 'carbonate of *lime*'); loosely, calcium carbonate.—**lime**³, *v. t.*; *limed*, *liming*. To smear (twigs, etc.) with birdlime; catch (birds) with birdlime (also fig.: as, "O *limed* soul, that struggling to be free, Art more engaged!" Shakspere's "Hamlet," iii. 3. 68); also, to cement (obs. or archaic: as, "I will not ruinate my father's house, Who gave his blood to *lime* the stones together," Shakspere's "3 Henry VI.," v. 1. 84); also, to treat with lime or calcium oxide; dress (land, etc.) with lime.—**lime'=burn''er**, *n.* One who makes lime by burning or calcining limestone, etc.

lime=juice (līm'jös), *n.* [See *lime*².] The juice of limes: much used in flavoring beverages, etc., and (by seamen, arctic explorers, etc.) as a preventive of scurvy.—**lime'=jui''cer** (-jö''sėr), *n.* A British sailor or ship: from the prescribed use of lime-juice against scurvy. [Colloq.]

lime=kiln (līm'kil or -kiln), *n.* A kiln or furnace for making lime by calcining limestone or shells.

lime-light (līm'līt), *n.* The calcium light or other similar light, esp. as thrown upon the stage of a theater to illuminate particular persons or objects; fig., the glare of public observation or of notoriety.

li-men (lī'men), *n.*; pl. *limens*, L. *limina* (lim'i-nä). [L., threshold.] In *psychol.*, the threshold. See *threshold*.

lim-er-ick (lim'ẹ-rik), *n.* [Said to be from *Limerick*, city in Ireland, as mentioned in extemporized nonsense verses.] A kind of nonsense verse of five lines, in which the first and second lines rime with the fifth line, and the third line rimes with the fourth.

lime-stone (līm'stōn), *n.* A rock consisting wholly or chiefly of calcium carbonate, originating principally from the calcareous remains of organisms, and when heated yielding lime.

lime=twig (līm'twig), *n.* A twig smeared with birdlime to catch birds; fig., a snare (as, "There are so many *lime-twigs* laid in his way, that I'll bet a cool hundred he swings before Christmas": Smollett's "Humphry Clinker," June 11).

lime=wa-ter (līm'wâ''tėr), *n.* An aqueous solution of slaked lime (calcium hydroxide), used medicinally and otherwise.

lim-ey (lī'mi), *n.* See *limy*².

li-mic-o-line (lī-mik'ọ-lin), *a.* [LL. *limicola*, a dweller in mud, < L. *limus*, mud, + *colere*, inhabit.] Of or pertaining to the *Limicolæ*, an order or group of birds which includes the plovers, snipes, sandpipers, and other shore-birds.

lim-i-nal (lim'i-nạl), *a.* [L. *limen* (*limin-*), threshold.] Of or pertaining to the threshold or entrance, or the limen: specif. in *psychol.* See *threshold*.

lim-it (lim'it), *n.* [OF. F. *limite*, < L. *limes* (*limit-*), boundary.] A boundary or bound, as of a country, tract, district, etc.; in general, a terminal line, mark, or point; the final or furthest bound or point as to extent, amount, continuance, procedure, etc. (as, the *limit* of vision; the *limit* of time or life; "Nature to all things fix'd the *limits* fit, And wisely curb'd proud man's pretending wit," Pope's "Essay on Criticism," 52); hence, with *the*, the utmost or worst possible (slang: as, that performance, or that book, is the *limit*; he's the *limit*); also, a tract or area within boundaries (as, "The archdeacon hath divided it [land] Into three *limits* very equally," Shakspere's "1 Henry IV.," iii. 1. 73; *limits* or lots of timber); *pl.*, territories or regions (as, "At length into the *limits* of the north They came": Milton's "Paradise Lost," v. 755); also, *sing.*, in *math.*, a fixed value or form which a variable quantity or form may approach indefinitely but can never reach.—**lim'it**, *v. t.* [OF. F. *limiter*, < L. *limitare*, < *limes*.] To set limits or bounds to (land, areas, etc.); serve as a limit or bound to (as, the mountains *limit* the plains on the west); in general, to confine or keep within limits (as, to *limit* powers, expenditures, scope, or number; to *limit* the duration or period of activity); restrict (*to*) by or as by fixing limits (as, to *limit* one to a certain space, income, diet, or time; "His own family . . . was *limited* to an only son and daughter," Scott's "Guy Mannering," xlii.); also, to fix or assign definitely or specifically (as, "Again, he *limiteth* a certain day," Heb. iv. 7: now chiefly or only in legal use).—**lim'it-a-ble**, *a.* That may be limited.—**lim'it-al**, *a.* Of or pertaining to a limit or boundary.

lim-i-ta-ry (lim'i-tạ-ri), *a.* [L. *limitaris*.] Of, pertaining to, or serving as a limit; also, subject to limits; limited.

lim-i-ta-tion (lim-i-tā'shọn), *n.* [L. *limitatio(n-)*.] The act of limiting, or the state of being limited (as, the *limitation* of armaments; *limitation* of immigration); confinement within limits; restriction; also, that which limits; a limit or bound (usually in *pl.*: as, to exceed the *limitations* assigned; within the *limitations* of thought); a limiting condition or circumstance, or restriction (as, a permission subject to various *limitations*); in *law*, the assignment, as by statute, of a period of time within which an action must be brought, or the period of time assigned (as, a statute of *limitations*).—**lim'i-ta-tive** (-tạ-tiv), *a.* Limiting; restrictive.

lim-it-ed (lim'i-ted), *p. a.* Confined within limits; restricted, circumscribed, or narrow (as, a *limited* space, amount, or time; *limited* resources); restricted with reference to governing powers by limitations prescribed in a constitution (as, a *limited* monarchy or monarch); restricted as to amount of liability (as, a *limited* company); of railroad-trains, specially restricted as to number of cars (weight), number or class of passengers, time occupied in transit, etc.—**lim'it-ed-ly**, *adv.* —**lim'it-ed-ness**, *n.*

lim-it-er (lim'i-tėr), *n.* One who or that which limits; formerly, a friar licensed to beg, preach, etc., within certain limits.

lim-it-less (lim'it-les), *a.* Without limit; boundless: as, the *limitless* expanse of space; *limitless* ambition.—**lim'it-less-ly**, *adv.*—**lim'it-less-ness**, *n.*

lim-mer (lim'ėr), *n.* [Origin uncertain.] A rogue or rascal; also, a worthless woman; a strumpet; in a milder sense, a minx or hussy (as, "Grizzel, ye *limmer*, gang to the door": Scott's "Guy Mannering," xi.). [Sc. and north. Eng.]

limn (lim), *v. t.* [ME. *lymne*, var. of *lumine*, illuminate, < OF. *luminer*, < L. *luminare*, light up: see *luminate*.] To illuminate (a manuscript, etc.)†; also, to paint (a picture); portray or depict (a subject) by painting; hence, to portray in any manner, esp. in words; describe vividly. [Now archaic or literary.]—**lim-ner** (lim'nėr), *n.* One who limns; esp., a portrait-painter. [Archaic or literary.]

lim-net-ic (lim-net'ik), *a.* [Gr. λιμνήτης, living in marshes, < λίμνη, marsh, pool, lake.] Living in fresh water; pertaining to fresh-water life or organisms.

limno-. Form of Gr. λίμνη, marsh, pool, lake, used in combination.—**lim-no-graph** (lim′nǫ-gráf), *n.* [+ *-graph.*] An apparatus for measuring and recording the variations of level in a body of water, esp. a lake; a recording limnometer. —**lim-nol′o-gy** (-nol′ǫ-ji), *n.* [+ *-logy.*] The scientific study of bodies of fresh water, as lakes and ponds, with reference to their physical, geographical, biological, and other features.—**lim-nom′e-ter** (-nom′e-tėr), *n.* [+ *-meter.*] An apparatus for measuring small variations of level in a body of water, esp. a lake.

lim-o-nene (lim′ǫ-nēn), *n.* [NL. *limonum*, lemon.] In *chem.*, a liquid terpene occurring in three optically different forms, the dextrorotatory one being present in the essential oils of lemon, orange, etc.

li-mo-ni-ad (lī-mō′ni-ad), *n.* [LL. *limoniades*, pl., < Gr. λειμωνιάδες, pl. of λειμωνιάς, < λειμών, meadow.] A meadow-nymph.

li-mo-nite (lī′mǫ-nīt), *n.* [Gr. λειμών, meadow.] An important iron ore, a hydrated ferric oxide, varying in color from dark brown to yellow: orig. only the kind (bog-ore) found in marshy places.—**li-mo-nit′ic** (-nit′ik), *a.*

lim-ou-sine (lim-ǫ-zēn′, F. lē-mö-zēn), *n.* [F., < *Limousin*, a former province in south-central France.] An automobile having a permanently inclosed compartment for from three to five persons, the roof of which projects forward over the driver's seat in front; the body of such an automobile.

limp[1] (limp), *a.* [Origin obscure: cf. *limp*[2] and *limber*[3].] Lacking stiffness or firmness, as of substance, fiber, structure, or bodily frame (as, *limp* garments; *limp* flowers; a *limp* body); drooping; flabby or flaccid, as flesh; without stiffening, or flexible, as book-covers; fig., without due firmness, force, energy, etc., as of character or mind.

limp[2] (limp), *v. i.* [Cf. AS. *lempheallt*, limping, lame, MHG. *limphen*, limp.] To walk with a labored, jerky movement, as when lame (as, "a white Pomeranian dog, evidently foot-sore . . . *limping* some yards in advance of his master": Bulwer-Lytton's "Kenelm Chillingly," i. 14); walk with a halting gait; fig., to proceed in a lame or faulty manner, as rime or verses.—**limp**[2], *n.* A limping movement or gait.—**limp′er**, *n.*

lim-pet (lim′pet), *n.* [AS. *lempedu*, < ML. *lampreda*, limpet, also lamprey: see *lamprey.*] Any of various marine gastropods with a low conical shell open beneath, found adhering to rocks, and used for bait and sometimes for food: as, "He . . . stuck like a *limpet* to a rock" (Scott's "St. Ronan's Well," xxxi.).

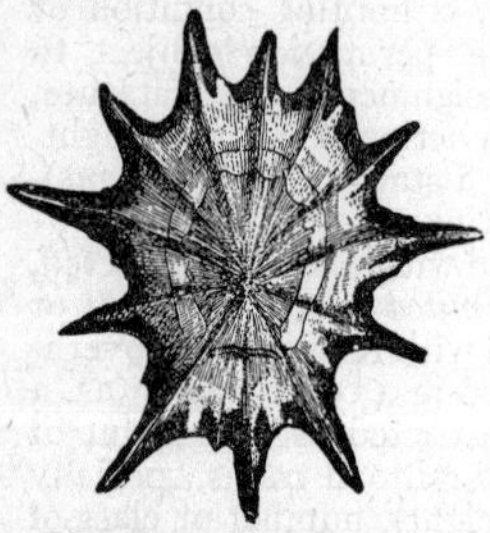

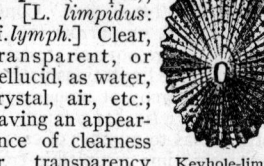

Rock-limpet (genus *Patella*).

Keyhole-limpet (genus *Fissurella*).

lim-pid (lim′pid), *a.* [L. *limpidus*: cf. *lymph.*] Clear, transparent, or pellucid, as water, crystal, air, etc.; having an appearance of clearness or transparency (as, "His look fell on those *limpid* blue eyes of my mother's": Bulwer-Lytton's "Caxtons," vii. 6); fig., free from obscurity, or lucid, as language, style, etc.—**lim-pid′i-ty, lim′pid-ness,** *n.*—**lim′pid-ly,** *adv.*

limp-ly (limp′li), *adv.* In a limp manner.—**limp′ness,** *n.*

limp-sy (limp′si), *a.* Limp: as, "She was all wore out, and looked sort o' *limpsy*, as if there wa'n't no starch left in her" (Mrs. Stowe's "Oldtown Folks," xlviii.). [Colloq. or prov.]

lim-u-lus (lim′ū-lus), *n.*; pl. *-li* (-lī). [NL. *Limulus*, < L. *limulus*, dim. of *limus*, sidelong.] A king-crab of the genus *Limulus.*—**lim′u-loid,** *a.* and *n.*

lim-y[1] (lī′mi), *a.* Smeared with birdlime; also, consisting of, containing, or resembling lime.

lim-y[2] (lī′mi), *n.*; pl. *limies* (lī′miz). Shortened form of *lime-juicer.* [Colloq.]

li-na-ceous (lī-nā′shius), *a.* [L. *linum*, flax.] Belonging to the *Linaceæ*, or flax family of plants.

lin-age (līn′āj), *n.* See *lineage*[2].

linch=pin (linch′pin), *n.* [AS. *lynis* = G. *lünse*, linch-pin.] A pin inserted through the end of an axletree to keep the wheel on.

lin-den (lin′dẹn), *n.* [Orig. adj., AS. *linden*, < *lind* = D. and G. *linde* = Icel., Sw., and Dan. *lind*, the linden: cf. *lime*[1].] Any of the trees of the genus *Tilia*, which have yellowish or cream-colored flowers and more or less heart-shaped leaves, as *T. europæa*, a common European species, and *T. americana*, a large American species often cultivated as a shade-tree. Cf. *basswood.*

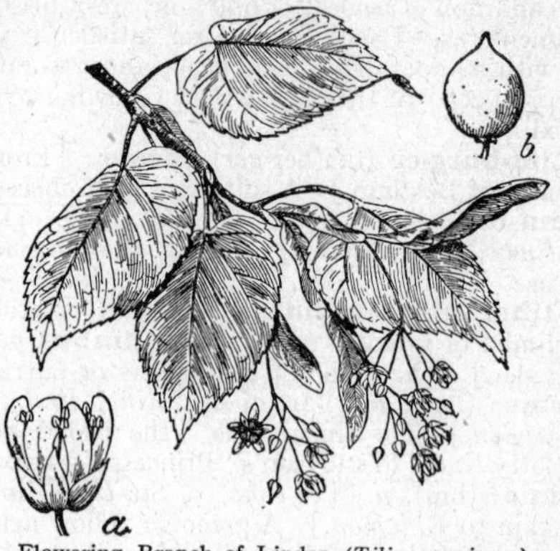

Flowering Branch of Linden (*Tilia americana*). *a*, flower; *b*, fruit.

line[1] (līn), *n.* [AS. *līn*, prob. < L. *linum* = Gr. λίνον, flax, linen.] Flax or linen (now chiefly prov.); in technical use, flax of fine, long staple, separated from the tow.

line[2] (līn), *n.* [In part, AS. *līne*, rope, line, row, prob. (if not < *līn*, E. *line*[1]) < L. *linea*, thread, string, stroke, line, prop. fem. of *lineus*, adj., of flax, linen, < *linum*, flax, E. *line*[1]; in part, OF. F. *ligne*, < L. *linea.*] A thread, string, cord, rope, or the like, esp. a strong cord or slender rope (as, a fishing-*line*; a clothes-*line*); specif., *pl.*, the reins used in driving (U. S. and prov. Eng.); *sing.*, a cord bearing a hook or hooks, used in fishing; a cord, wire, or the like, used for measuring or as a guide; hence, *pl.*, one's lot or portion (viewed as marked off by a measuring-line: cf. Ps. xvi. 6: now esp. in 'hard lines,' that is, hard or bad luck, as, "It is hard *lines* for me . . . to leave your honour in tribulation," Scott's "Redgauntlet," ch. iii.); *sing.*, a rule of life or conduct† (as, "Their *line* is gone out through all the earth, and their words to the end of the world": Ps. xix. 4); also, a mark or stroke long in proportion to its breadth, made with a pen, pencil, tool, etc., on a surface; specif., one of the straight, horizontal, parallel strokes of the musical staff, or placed above or below it; also, something resembling a traced line, as a band of color, a seam, a furrow, etc. (as, "Yon gray *lines* That fret the clouds are messengers of day," Shakspere's "Julius Cæsar," ii. 1. 103; *lines* of stratification in rock); specif., a furrow or wrinkle on the face, etc. (as, "He does smile his face into more *lines* than is in the new map": Shakspere's "Twelfth Night," iii. 2. 84); one of the furrows or marks on the palm of the hand supposed in palmistry to indicate one's fortune, character, etc. (as, the *line* of life, of the head, or of the heart); also (specif. in *math.*), a continuous extent of length, straight or curved, without breadth or thickness; the trace of a moving point; also, a circle of the terrestrial or of the celestial sphere (as, the equinoctial *line*); now, esp., with *the*, the equator (of either the earth or the celestial sphere: as, "We were in the latitude of 12 degrees 35 minutes south of the *line*," Defoe's "Captain Singleton," iv.; the sun crosses the *line* at the equinoxes); also, often, specif., a straight line, or extent of length (as, straight as a *line*); hence, fig., a position of uniformity or agreement (as, to bring an objector into *line*); also, with *the*, the line on a level with the spectator's eye on the wall of an exhibition of paintings or the like, where these may best be seen, and where the best pictures, etc., are usually placed; also, outline or contour (often in *pl.*: as, "She examined the *line* of my features," Kinglake's "Eothen," viii.; a ship of fine *lines*); *pl.*, fig., plan of construction, or of action or procedure (as, two books written on the same *lines*; to carry on a campaign on new *lines*); also, *sing.*, a line of demarcation, or a boundary or limit (lit. or fig.: as, Mason and Dixon's *line*, see entry in vocabulary place; to draw a *line* between right and wrong); also, a measure of length of varying magnitude, esp. one equal to the twelfth part of an inch, or one equal to a millimeter, or one equal to the fortieth part of an inch (as used in indicating the diameter of buttons); also, something arranged along a line, esp. a straight line; a row or series (as, a *line* of buildings or of trees); specif., a row of written or printed letters, words, etc. (as, a page of thirty *lines*; to read between the *lines*, to discover a meaning not explicitly expressed in a writing); *pl.*, a certificate of marriage ('marriage lines'); the spoken words of a drama, etc., or of an actor's part (as, the hero forgot his *lines*); often, *sing.*, a short written message (as, to receive a *line* from a friend); also, a verse of poetry (as, "*Lines* Written among the Euganean Hills," the title of a poem by Shelley); also, a continuous series of persons in chronological succession, esp. in family descent (as, the *line* of British poets laureate; a *line* of kings; "He From John of Gaunt doth bring his pedigree, Being but fourth of that heroic *line*," Shakspere's "1 Henry VI.," ii. 5. 78); hence, a family, stock, or race (as, "Shame not the *line* whence glorious you descend": Pope's tr. Homer's "Odyssey," xxiv.); also, a course of direction (as, the *line* of march); a route; also, a course of action, procedure, thought, etc. (as, a *line* of policy; "I desire to depart from the direct *line* of my subject and make a little excursion," Mark Twain's "Life on the Mississippi," lii.); also, a department of activity; a kind of occupation or business (as, a man in the hardware *line*); hence, one's field of experience, interest, or taste (as, a thing in, or out of, one's *line*; "This kind of writing is not much in my *line*," Thackeray's "Newcomes," liv.); also, a supply of commercial goods of the same general class; also, the wire or wires connecting points or stations in a telegraph or telephone system, or the system itself; a line of railroad-track, a railroad, or a railroad system; a system of public conveyances, as buses, steamers, etc., plying regularly between places; also, *milit.* and *naval*, a trench or rampart; a series of military field-works; a distribution of troops, sentries, etc., for the defense of a position (as, within the enemy's *lines*); a body of troops drawn up abreast (opposed to *column*); a disposition of ships at regular intervals, usually abreast; the line or arrangement of an army or of the ships of a fleet as drawn up ready for battle ('line of battle'); the regular forces of an army or navy; the combatant forces of an army, as distinguished from the supply departments, etc.; the officers in charge of the fighting operations and the operating of war-vessels in the U. S. navy.—**line of beauty,** in *art*, some kind of (curved or undulating) line held to be beautiful in itself and considered a necessary element of all beauty of form: differently represented by different persons, but commonly (as by Hogarth) as a curve resembling a slender, elongated letter S (see *Hogarthian*).—**to get (have,** etc.) **a line on,** fig., to get (have, etc.) information about: as, to *get a line on* business conditions or the popular attitude concerning a matter. [Colloq.]—**line²,** *v.*; *lined, lining.* **I.** *tr.* To tie with a line; also, to measure or test with a line; also, to trace by or as by a line or lines; sketch; delineate; also, to mark with a line or lines (as, paper *lined* for guidance in writing; "Selfish cares . . . had *lined* his narrow brow," Shelley's "Rosalind and Helen," 429); also, to track (wild bees) to their nests by following them in their line of flight (as, "Do you understand *lining* a bee from this open place into a wood, distant, perhaps, a dozen miles?" Cooper's "Prairie," x.); also, to bring into a line, or into line with others; also, to arrange a line along (as, to *line* a coast with colonies; "The thick hedges . . . were *lined* with musketeers," Macaulay's "Hist. of Eng.," v.); form a line along (as, "The rebels . . . *lined* the hedges leading to the town": Macaulay's "Hist. of Eng.," v.); also, to read out (a hymn, etc.), a line or two at a time, for repetition in singing (often with *out*: as, "The preacher was *lining* out a hymn. He *lined* out two lines, everybody sung it . . . and so on," Mark Twain's "Huckleberry Finn," xx.); 'deacon.' **II.** *intr.* To take a position in a line; form a line; range.

line³ (līn), *v. t.*; *lined, lining.* [ME.; < *line¹*.] To provide with a layer of material applied to the inner side (as, to *line* a coat with silk; to *line* a furnace with bricks); cover or fit on the inner side with something (as, "a great library, all *lined* with bookcases": Stevenson's "Treasure Island," vi.); be applied or disposed along the inner side of (as, the bricks that *line* a furnace); also, to furnish or fill with contents, or, of contents, to serve to fill (as, to *line* one's pockets with money; robbed of the gold that *lined* his purse; "Then the justice, In fair round belly with good capon *lined*," Shakspere's "As You Like It," ii. 7. 154); also, to cover on the outside, overlay, or face (obs. or archaic); also, to reinforce† or strengthen† (as, "Whether he . . . did *line* the rebel With hidden help and vantage . . . I know not": Shakspere's "Macbeth," i. 3. 112).

lin-e-age¹ (lin'ẹ-āj), *n.* [OF. F. *lignage*, < L. *linea*, E. *line²*.] Lineal descent from an ancestor, or ancestry or extraction (as, to be of ancient, Norman, or unknown *lineage*; pride of *lineage*; "Thy Levites, once a consecrated host, No longer Levites, and their *lineage* lost," Cowper's "Expostulation," 264); hence, the line of ancestors, or ancestral stock, from which one is descended (as, "She . . . by descent from Royall *lynage* came Of ancient Kinges and Queenes": Spenser's "Faerie Queene," i. 1. 5); also, the line of descendants of a particular ancestor (as, "He was of the house and *lineage* of David": Luke, ii. 4); in general, a family, stock, or race (as, "The Lords of Douglas . . . are second to no *lineage* in Scotland in the antiquity of their descent": Scott's "Castle Dangerous," iv.).

line-age² (līn'āj), *n.* Arrangement or position in a line; alinement; also, the quantity of printed or written matter estimated in lines (as, the *lineage* of the advertisements in a newspaper during a month, or a year); also, payment, or rate of payment, by the line.

lin-e-al (lin'ẹ-al), *a.* [LL. *linealis*, < L. *linea*, E. *line²*.] Of or pertaining to a line or lines; consisting of lines; extended in a line; involving the single measurement of length (as, *lineal* measure, long measure, which see under *long¹*, *a.*); linear; also, being in the direct line, as a descendant, ancestor, etc., or descent, ancestry, etc. (as, "*Lineal* consanguinity is that which subsists between persons, of whom one is descended in a direct line from the other," Blackstone's "Commentaries," II. 203: cf. *collateral*); pertaining to or transmitted by lineal descent (as, by *lineal* right).—**lin-e-al'i-ty** (-al'i-ti), *n.* Lineal state or form.—**lin'e-al-ly,** *adv.*

lin-e-a-ment (lin'ẹ-ạ-mẹnt), *n.* [F. *linéament*, < L. *lineamentum*, < *lineare*: see *lineate*.] A line†; also, an outline† or sketch†; also, a feature or detail of a body or figure, considered with respect to its outline or contour (as, "Man he seems In all his *lineaments*; though in his face The glimpses of his Father's glory shine": Milton's "Paradise Regained," i. 92); esp., a part of the face considered with respect to its outline (as, "He was pensively tracing in my countenance the early *lineaments* of my mother": Irving's "Tales of a Traveler," ii. 7); a feature; fig., a distinctive characteristic (as, "The style of Denman is more lofty, and impressed with stronger *lineaments* of sincerity": Galt's "Ayrshire Legatees," ix.).

lin-e-ar (lin'ẹ-ạr), *a.* [L. *linearis*, < *linea*, E. *line²*.] Of or pertaining to a line or lines (as, *linear* perspective: see under *perspective*, *n.*); consisting of or involving lines (as, *linear* design); extended in a line (as, a *linear* series); pertaining to length, or involving measurement in one direction only (as, *linear* measure, long measure, which see under *long¹*, *a.*); specif., of the first degree, as a mathematical equation; also, resembling a line or thread; narrow and elongated (as, a *linear* leaf).—**lin-e-ar'i-ty** (-ar'i-ti), *n.* Linear state or form.—**lin'e-ar-ize** (-ạr-īz), *v. t.*; *-ized, -izing.* To represent in linear form, or by means of lines.—**lin″e-ar-i-za'tion** (-i-zā'shọn), *n.*—**lin'e-ar-ly,** *adv.*

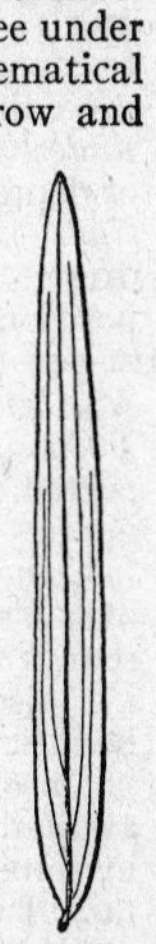

Linear Leaf.

lin-e-ate (lin'ẹ-āt), *a.* [L. *lineatus*, pp. of *lineare*, reduce to a straight line, mark with lines, < *linea*, E. *line²*.] Marked with lines, esp. longitudinal and more or less parallel lines. Also **lin'e-at-ed** (-ā-ted).—**lin-e-a'tion** (-ā'shọn), *n.* [L. *lineatio(n-)*.] A marking with or tracing by lines; also, a line; an outline; often, an arrangement or group of lines; also, a division into lines.

line=en-grav-ing (līn'en-grā'ving), *n.* A method of engraving in which lines are cut in a plate of copper, steel, or the like, from which an ink print is to be made (distinguished from the *dry-point* method in that in line-engraving a coarser tool is used, which cuts away the metal instead of leaving it as a burr); also, a plate so engraved, or a print or picture made from it.

line-man (līn'mạn), *n.*; pl. *-men.* One who carries the line in surveying, etc.; also, one employed to set up or keep in repair telegraph, telephone, or other wires; also, one employed to inspect the rails of a railroad.

lin-en (lin′en). [AS. *līnen*, < *līn*, E. *line*[1].] **I.** *a.* Made of flax, as thread or fabrics; made of linen, as a garment. **II.** *n.* Thread or yarn spun from flax fiber; also, cloth or a fabric woven from flax or some other fiber (as, butcher's *linen*, a coarse or heavy plain-woven flax fabric; ramie *linen*, a fabric woven of ramie fiber); also, clothes or other articles made of linen cloth or some substitute, as cotton (as, body-*linen*; bed-*linen*; table-*linen*).

lin-en=scroll (lin′en-skrōl), *n.* In *arch.*, a form of decorative ornament suggesting the convolutions of rolled or folded linen, used to fill panels, esp. during the Tudor period in England. Also called *linen pattern*.

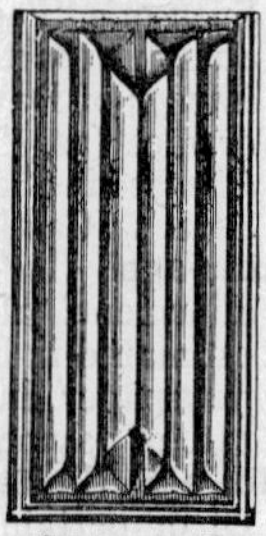

Linen-scroll.

lin-e-o-late (lin′ē-ǫ-lāt), *a.* [L. *lineola*, dim. of *linea*, E. *line*[2].] In *zoöl.* and *bot.*, marked with minute lines; finely lineate. Also **lin′-e-o-lat-ed** (-lā-ted).

lin-er[1] (lī′nėr), *n.* One who or that which lines, or traces by or marks with lines; also, one of a line of steamships; sometimes, a ship of the line (see under *ship*, *n.*: as, "a huge '*liner*' . . . looming dimly through the smoke, close on the enemy's quarter," G. A. Lawrence's "Sword and Gown," xvii.); in *baseball*, a ball batted or thrown, esp. batted, with much force nearly parallel to the ground.

lin-er[2] (lī′nėr), *n.* One who lines, or fits or provides linings; also, something serving as a lining.

lines-man (līnz′mạn), *n.*; pl. *-men.* A soldier of the line; also, a lineman, as on a telegraph or railroad line; also, in certain games, an official employed to watch the lines which mark out the field, etc.; in American football, an official who marks the distances gained and lost in the progress of the play and otherwise assists the referee and umpire; also, in football, one of the forwards.

line=up (līn′up), *n.* The formation of persons or things into line, or into position for action; also, a particular order or disposition of persons or things as lined up or drawn up for action; also, the persons or things themselves.

ling[1] (ling), *n.* [ME. *lenge* = D. and G. *leng* = Icel. *langa*, ling; akin to E. *long*[1].] An elongated marine gadoid food-fish, *Molva molva*, of Greenland and northern Europe; also, any of various other fishes.

Ling (*Molva molva*).

ling[2] (ling), *n.* [Icel. *lyng* = Dan. *lyng* = Sw. *ljung*, heather.] The common heather, *Calluna vulgaris*.

-ling[1]. [AS. *-ling*.] A noun suffix meaning 'one belonging to, or concerned with, or being' (what is indicated by the preceding part of the word), as in *darling*, *earthling*, *hireling*, *underling*, or having (as usually in modern use) a diminutive or depreciative force, as in *duckling*, *gosling*, *lordling*, *princeling*.

-ling[2]. [AS. *-ling*.] An adverbial suffix expressing direction, position, state, etc., as in *darkling*, *flatling*, *groveling*, *sideling*.

lin-ger (ling′gėr), *v.* [ME. *lenger*, freq. of *leng*, tarry, < AS. *lengan*, prolong, delay, < *lang*, E. *long*[1].] **I.** *intr.* To remain or stay on in a place longer than is usual or expected, as if from reluctance to leave it; tarry; loiter; hence, to dwell in contemplation, thought, or enjoyment (as, the eye *lingers* on a face or scene; the mind *lingers* over a subject; "This . . . he drank slowly, like a connoisseur, *lingering* on the taste," Stevenson's "Treasure Island," i.); also, to be tardy in action, delay, or dawdle (as, "He, be sure, Will not connive or *linger*, thus provoked": Milton's "Samson Agonistes," 466); be slow in coming, as something awaited; be protracted, as a process; also, to continue alive, in spite of weakness, sickness, or other adverse conditions (as, "I would not have thee *linger* in thy pain": Shakspere's "Othello," v. 2. 88); continue, remain, or persist, although tending to cease or disappear (as, hope *lingers*; traces *linger*); also, to long or hanker (usually with *after*: now prov. Eng.). **II.** *tr.* To delay by lingering or tardiness† (as, "How slow This old moon wanes! she *lingers* my desires": Shakspere's "Midsummer Night's Dream," i. 1. 4); also, to drag out or protract (now only with *out*: as, to *linger* out negotiations); also, to pass (time, life, etc.) in a leisurely or a tedious manner (with *away* or *out*: as, to *linger* away the hours in idleness; to *linger* out one's days in prison).—**lin′ger-er**, *n.*

linge-rie (lan̈zh-rē), *n.* [F., < *linger*, linen-draper, < *linge*, linen, < L. *linum*, E. *line*[1].] Underwear or other garments of linen, cotton, silk, lace, etc., worn by women.

lin-ger-ing (ling′gėr-ing), *p. a.* That lingers; loitering; delaying; slow to depart, cease, or disappear; protracted, as illness.—**lin′ger-ing-ly**, *adv.*

lin-go (ling′gō), *n.*; pl. *lingoes* (-gōz). [Cf. It. *lingua* (< L. *lingua*, tongue), also *lingua franca*.] A foreign language or speech, or any form of language or speech regarded as outlandish jargon: used contemptuously or humorously: as, "Bembo . . . gave him such a cursing in his broken *lingo* that it was enough to frighten one" (H. Melville's "Omoo," xxiii.); "Well, well, I shall understand your *lingo* one of these days, cousin; in the meanwhile I must answer in plain English" (Congreve's "Way of the World," iv.).

lin-got (ling′gọt), *n.* [F. *lingot*, for *l'ingot*, 'the ingot.'] An ingot, or mass of metal cast in a mold. [Archaic.]

lin-gua fran-ca (ling′gwạ frang′kạ). [It., 'Frankish tongue.'] A hybrid language, consisting largely of Italian, used by the Latin races in intercourse with the Arabs, Turks, Greeks, etc. (as, "A . . . voice . . . pronounced these words . . . in the *lingua franca*, mutually understood by Christians and Saracens": Scott's "Talisman," xiv.); hence, any hybrid language similarly used.

lin-gual (ling′gwạl). [ML. *lingualis*, < L. *lingua*, OL. *dingua*, tongue, speech, language: see *tongue*.] **I.** *a.* Of or pertaining to the tongue or some tongue-like part; also, pertaining to the tongue as the organ of speech, or to the use of the tongue in speaking; also, pertaining to languages; in *phonetics*, of speech-sounds, uttered with the aid of the tongue, as *d* and *t*. **II.** *n.* In *phonetics*, a lingual sound.—**lin′gual-ly**, *adv.*

lin-gui-form (ling′gwi-fôrm), *a.* [L. *lingua*, tongue: see *-form*.] Tongue-shaped.

lin-guist (ling′gwist), *n.* [L. *lingua*, tongue, language: see *lingual*.] One skilled in the use of languages; one who knows or can speak other languages besides his own; also, a philologist†.—**lin-guis-tic, lin-guis-ti-cal** (ling-gwis′tik, -ti-kạl), *a.* Of or pertaining to the knowledge or study of languages.—**lin-guis′ti-cal-ly**, *adv.*—**lin-guis′tics**, *n.* The science of languages; philology.

lin-gu-late (ling′gụ-lāt), *a.* [L. *lingulatus*, < *lingula*, dim. of *lingua*, tongue.] Formed or shaped like a tongue or strap; ligulate.

ling-y (ling′i), *a.* Abounding in ling or heather.

lin-i-ment (lin′i-mẹnt), *n.* [LL. *linimentum*, < L. *linire*, *linere*, smear: cf. *lime*[3].] In *med.*, a liquid preparation, usually oily, for rubbing on or applying to the skin, as for sprains, bruises, etc.

li-nin (lī′nin), *n.* [L. *linum*, flax, E. *line*[1].] In *chem.*, the crystallizable bitter principle of purging-flax; in *biol.*, the substance forming the net-like structure which incloses the chromatin in the nucleus of a cell.

lin-ing (lī′ning), *n.* [See *line*[3].] The act of one who or that which lines something; also, that with which something is lined; a layer of material on the inner side of something (as, a silk *lining* in a garment; a brick *lining* in a furnace); sometimes, contents, as of the pocket or purse.

link[1] (lingk), *v. i.* [Origin uncertain.] To go smartly; trip along: as, "The very bairns . . . gaed *linking* and louping in the steps of Mr. Macskipnish" (Galt's "Annals of the Parish," ii.). [Sc. and north. Eng.]

link[2] (lingk), *n.* [AS. *hlinc*, ridge, slope, hill, perhaps connected with *hlinian*, E. *lean*[1].] A ridge or bank (now prov. Eng.); also, *pl.*, flat or slightly undulating sandy ground near the sea (Sc.); also, *pl.*, the ground or course over which golf is played (sometimes construed as *sing.*).

link[3] (lingk), *n.* [Origin uncertain.] A torch of tow and pitch or the like: as, "The fog and darkness thickened so, that people ran about with flaring *links*" (Dickens's "Christmas Carol," i.).

link⁴ (lingk), *n.* [ME. *link, lenk*; from Scand.: cf. Icel. *hlekkr*, Sw. *länk*, link.] One of the rings or separate pieces of which a chain is composed; also, one of the 100 wire rods forming the divisions of a surveyor's chain, used as a unit of length (see *chain, n.*); also, one of the parts of any chain-like arrangement; one of a number of sausages in a chain (colloq. or prov.); sometimes, a ring, loop, or the like; also, anything serving to connect one part or thing with another; a member of a connected series; a bond or tie (as, "I had severed the *link* between myself and my former condition": Marryat's "Japhet," lvi.); specif., in machines, a rigid movable piece or rod connected with other parts by means of pivots or the like, for the purpose of transmitting motion; in steam-engines, the slotted piece or bar in a link-motion; in *mech.*, the structure or device formed when one of the two parts or halves of one kinematic pair is joined by a rigid piece to one of the two parts or halves of another kinematic pair ('kinematic link').—**missing link.** See under *missing*.—**link⁴**, *v. t.* or *i.* To join by or as by a link or links; unite.—**link-age** (ling′kạj), *n.* The act of linking; the state or manner of being linked; also, a system of links; in *mech.*, any of various mathematical or drawing devices consisting of a combination of bars or pieces pivoted together so as to turn about one another, usually in parallel planes.—**link′=belt**, *n.* In *mach.*, a belt composed of a series of detachable links, used to transmit motion.—**link′=belt″ing**, *n.*

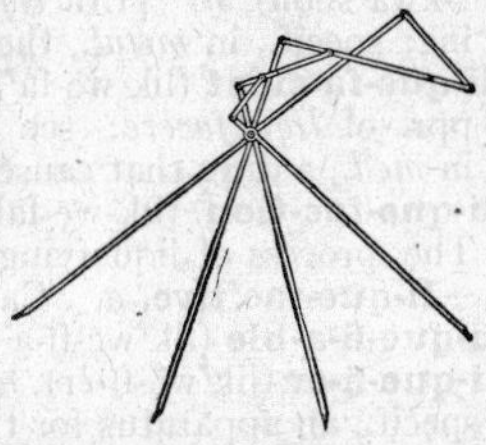
Linkage, for trisecting an angle.

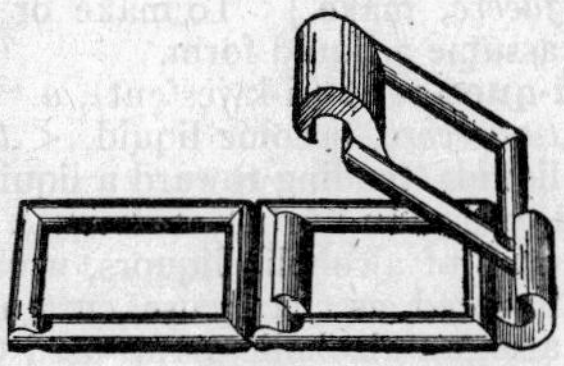
Link-belt.

link-boy (lingk′boi), *n.* A boy employed to carry a link or torch to light passengers in the streets: as, "*Link-boys* with their torches lighted the beaux over the mud" (Thackeray's "Newcomes," xvii.).—**link′man** (-mạn), *n.*; pl. *-men*.

link=mo-tion (lingk′mō″shọn), *n.* A mechanism for operating a valve in a steam-engine, one feature of which is a slotted bar (the *link*) in which slides a block (the *link-block*) which terminates the rod working the valve.

links (lingks), *n. pl.* See *link²*.—**links′man** (-mạn), *n.*; pl. *-men*. A golf-player.—**links′wo″man**, *n.*; pl. *-women* (-wim″en). A female golf-player.

link-work (lingk′wėrk), *n.* Work composed of links, as a chain; in *mech.*, mechanism or a device in which motion is transmitted by rods or links; also, a linkage.

linn (lin), *n.* [In part, AS. *hlynn*, torrent; in part, Gael. *linne* = Ir. *linn*, pool.] A waterfall; a pool, esp. one below a waterfall; a precipice; a steep ravine. [Chiefly Sc.]

Lin-ne-an, Lin-næ-an (li-nē′ạn), *a.* Of or pertaining to the Swedish botanist Carolus Linnæus (Karl von Linné, 1707–78), who established the binomial system of scientific nomenclature; specif., noting or pertaining to an artificial system of botanical classification introduced by him and formerly used, which was based mainly on the number and characteristics of the stamens.

lin-net (lin′et), *n.* [OF. *linette* (so called from its feeding on flaxseed), < *lin*, < L. *linum*, flax, E. *line¹*.] A small old-world song-bird, *Linota cannabina*; also, any of various related birds.

Linnet (*Linota cannabina*).

li-no-le-um (li-nō′lē-um), *n.* [L. *linum*, flax, + *oleum*, oil.] A kind of floor-cloth consisting of a mixture of oxidized linseed-oil with cork-cuttings, backed by canvas.

lin-on (lin′ọn, F. lē-nôṅ), *n.* [F., < *lin*, < L. *linum*, E. *line¹*.] The fabric lawn.

li-no-type (lī′nọ-tīp), *n.* [See *line²* and *type*.] A kind of type-setting machine, operated by pressing lettered keys, which casts solid lines of type. Cf. *monotype*.—**li′no-type**, *v. t.*; *-typed, -typing*. To set with a linotype.—**li′no-typ-er** (-tī-pėr), *n.*

lin-sang (lin′sang), *n.* [Javanese.] Any of the viverrine quadrupeds constituting the genus *Prionodon* (or *Linsang*) of the East Indies, and the related genus *Poina* of Africa. Cf. *delundung*.

lin-seed (lin′sēd), *n.* [AS. *līnsǣd*: see *line¹*.] Flaxseed.—**lin′seed=oil′**, *n.* The oil obtained by pressing linseed (flaxseed): used in making paints, printing-inks, linoleum, etc.

lin-sey (lin′zi), *n.* Same as *linsey-woolsey*: as, "a new suit of gray home-made *linsey*" (G. W. Cable's "Bonaventure," i. 3).

lin-sey=wool-sey (lin′zi-wůl′zi), *n.* [See *line¹* and *wool*.] A stout, coarse fabric with a warp of linen or cotton and a woof or filling of wool; also, fig., any poor or incongruous mixture.

lin-stock (lin′stok), *n.* [D. *lontstok*, < *lont*, match, + *stok*, stick.] A staff about 3 feet long with one end pointed to stick in the ground, etc., and the other forked to hold a lighted match, formerly used in firing cannon.

lint (lint), *n.* [ME. *lynt, lynnet*; appar. < *line¹*.] Flax (now chiefly Sc.: as, "From morning to night she sat at her wheel, spinning the finest *lint*," Galt's "Annals of the Parish," i.); also, a soft material for dressing wounds, etc., procured by scraping or otherwise treating linen cloth; charpie; also, fluff of any material.

lin-tel (lin′tẹl), *n.* [OF. *lintel* (F. *linteau*), < L. *limes*, boundary, E. *limit*.] In *arch.*, a horizontal timber or stone above a door or other opening, to support the structure above.

lint-ie (lin′ti), *n.* The linnet. [Sc.]

lint-white (lint′hwīt), *n.* [AS. *līnetwige*.] The linnet: as, "when *lintwhites* chant amang the buds" (Burns's "To William Simpson," 68). [Chiefly Sc.]

lint=white (lint′hwīt), *a.* White as lint or flax; flaxen: as, "Lassie wi' the *Lint-White* Locks" (the title of a poem by Burns). [Sc.]

lint-y (lin′ti), *a.* Full of or covered with lint; also, like lint.

lin-y (lī′ni), *a.* Full of or marked with lines; also, line-like.

li-on (lī′ọn), *n.* [OF. F. *lion*, < L. *leo* (*leon-*), < Gr. λέων, lion: cf. *Leo*.] A large, tawny, carnivorous animal, *Felis leo*, of the cat family, native in Africa and southern Asia, the male of which has a full, flowing mane (from its powerfulness and impressive appearance often called the 'king of beasts'); also, this animal as the national emblem of Great Britain, or, by transfer, the British nation itself (the 'British Lion'; hence, 'to twist the lion's tail,' see under *twist, v.t.*); also, a lion-like person; a man of great strength, courage, etc.; also, an object of interest or note, as of a town, etc. (as, "We took a coach, and went to see the *lions*, as he said": Galt's "Ayrshire Legatees," iv.); a person of note or celeb-

Head of Lion.

rity who is much sought after (as, "half a dozen *lions* from London . . . real authors, who had written whole books": Dickens's "Pickwick Papers," xv.); also [*cap.*], in *astron.*, the zodiacal constellation or sign Leo; also, the northern constellation Leo Minor ('Lesser Lion').—**lion's provider,** the jackal; hence, one who provides for another's requirements or occasions or meanly serves his purposes (as, "Old Lieschen . . . was his bed-maker and stove-lighter, his washer and wringer, cook, errand-maid, and general *lion's-provider*": Carlyle's "Sartor Resartus," i. 3).—**lion's share,** the largest or principal share or portion: from Æsop's fable of the lion who went hunting with other beasts, and in dividing the spoil assigned one third to himself as king, one third to himself individually, and one third to whoever should dare to take it.—**li′on-ess,** *n.* A female lion; also, a female celebrity, or a woman who is lionized (as, "Mr. Tupman was doing the honours of the lobster salad to several *lionesses*": Dickens's "Pickwick Papers," xv.).—**li′on-et,** *n.* A little or young lion.—**li′on=heart,** *n.* A person of great courage; esp. [*caps.*, rendering his French surname *Cœur de Lion*], Richard I., king of England.—**li′on=heart″ed,** *a.* Courageous; brave.—**li′on-ize** (-īz), *v.*; *-ized, -izing.* **I.** *tr.* To visit or exhibit the objects of interest of (a place); also, to exhibit such objects to (a person: as "He had *lionised* the distinguished visitors . . . over the University," Disraeli's "Lothair," xxiv.); also, to treat (a person) as a lion or celebrity (as, "Never, never have I been so *lionized!* I assure you, I was cock of the walk": H. James's "Europeans," iii.). **II.** *intr.* To visit the objects of interest of a place.—**li″on-i-za′tion** (-i-zā′shọn), *n.*

li-ot-ri-chous (lī-ot′ri-kus), *a.* [Gr. λεῖος, smooth, + θρίξ (τριχ-), hair.] Having smooth hair.

lip (lip), *n.* [AS. *lippa* = D. *lip* = G. *lippe*, lip; akin to L. *labium* and *labrum*, lip.] Either of the two fleshy parts or folds forming the margins of the mouth and performing an important function in speech; often, *pl.*, these parts as organs of speech, or speech as passing between them (as, "A wicked doer giveth heed to false *lips*": Prov. xvii. 4); hence, *sing.*, impudent talk (slang: as, " 'Don't you give me none o' your *lip*,' says he," Mark Twain's "Huckleberry Finn," v.); also, a lip-like part or structure; the edge of an opening or cavity; the margin or edge of a vessel, esp. a projecting edge as of a pitcher; any edge or rim; specif., in *bot.*, either of the two parts (upper and lower) into which the corolla or calyx of certain plants (esp. menthaceous plants) is divided; also, a labellum; in *conch.*, the outer or the inner margin of the aperture of a gastropod's shell.—**lip,** *v.*; *lipped, lipping.* **I.** *tr.* To touch with the lips (as, "after the final adjustment of the mouthpiece, *lipping* the instrument": Lover's "Handy Andy," xviii.); hence, to kiss (poetic: as, "A hand that kings Have *lipp'd*, and trembled kissing," Shakspere's "Antony and Cleopatra," ii. 5. 30); also, of water, to lap (rocks, etc.); also, to utter, esp. softly (as, "I heard my name Most fondly *lipp'd*": Keats's "Endymion," i.). **II.** *intr.* To use the lips in playing a musical wind-instrument.

lip-ase (lip′ās), *n.* [Gr. λίπος, fat: see *-ase.*] In *chem.*, an enzyme occurring in the pancreatic juice, certain seeds, etc., which is capable of resolving fats into fatty acids and glycerin.

lip-less (lip′les), *a.* Having no lips.

li-po-gram (lī′pọ-gram or lip′ọ-), *n.* [Gr. λιπογράμματος, wanting a letter, < λείπειν, leave, + γράμμα, letter, E. *gram*[2].] A written composition in which no word containing a particular letter or letters is used.—**li″po-gram-mat′ic** (-grạ-mat′ik), *a.*—**li-po-gram′ma-tism** (-gram′ạ-tizm), *n.* The writing of lipograms.—**li-po-gram′ma-tist,** *n.*

li-pol-y-sis (li-pol′i-sis), *n.* [Gr. λίπος, fat: see *-lysis.*] In *chem.*, the resolution of fats into fatty acids and glycerin, as by the action of lipase.—**lip-o-lyt-ic** (lip-ọ-lit′ik), *a.*

li-po-ma (li-pō′mạ), *n.*; pl. *-mas* or *-mata* (-mạ-tạ). [NL., < Gr. λίπος, fat: see *-oma.*] In *pathol.*, a fatty tumor.—**li-pom′a-tous** (-pom′ạ-tus), *a.*

lipped (lipt), *a.* Having lips or a lip; in *bot.*, labiate.

lip-pen (lip′n), *v. i.* or *t.* [ME. *lipnen*; origin obscure.] To trust or intrust. [Now Sc. and prov. Eng.]

lip-per (lip′ėr), *v. i.* [Cf. Icel. *hleypa*, cause to leap, run before a gale, akin to E. *leap.*] To break or flow in small waves; ripple. [Sc. and north. Eng.]—**lip′per,** *n.* A slight ruffling of the surface of water, esp. at sea; a ripple. [Prov. or naut.]

lip=read-ing (lip′rē″ding), *n.* The reading or understanding, as by a deaf person, of the movements of another's lips when forming words.

lip=ser-vice (lip′sėr″vis), *n.* Service with the lips or words only; insincere profession of devotion or good-will.

lip=stick (lip′stik), *n.* A stick or elongated piece of some cosmetic preparation for heightening the color of the lips.

li-quate (lī′kwāt), *v. t.*; *-quated, -quating.* [L. *liquatus*, pp. of *liquare*, make liquid, melt, < *liquere*, be liquid.] To liquefy; specif., in *metal.*, to subject (a metal, mixture of metals, or the like) to a degree of heat sufficient to melt the more fusible portion or portions and so separate a metal from impurities or from another metal; also, to separate by such a fusion (often with *out*); eliquate.—**li-qua′tion** (-kwā′shọn), *n.* [LL. *liquatio(n-).*] The process of liquating; specif., in *metal.*, the separation of metals by fusion.

li-que-fa-cient (lik-wẹ-fā′shẹnt), *n.* [L. *liquefaciens (-ent-)*, ppr. of *liquefacere*: see *liquefy.*] A liquefying agent, as, in *med.*, a drug that causes the liquefaction of solid deposits.

li-que-fac-tion (lik-wẹ-fak′shọn), *n.* [LL. *liquefactio(n-).*] The process of liquefying or making liquid; liquefied state.—**li-que-fac′tive,** *a.* Causing liquefaction.

li-que-fi-a-ble (lik′wẹ-fī-ạ-bl), *a.* Capable of being liquefied.

li-que-fi-er (lik′wẹ-fī-ėr), *n.* One who or that which liquefies; specif., an apparatus for the liquefaction of gases.

li-que-fy (lik′wẹ-fī), *v. t.* or *i.*; *-fied, -fying.* [F. *liquéfier*, < L. *liquefacere* (passive *liquefieri*), < *liquere*, be liquid, + *facere*, make.] To make or become liquid; reduce to or assume a liquid form.

li-ques-cent (li-kwes′ẹnt), *a.* [L. *liquescens (-ent-)*, ppr. of *liquescere*, become liquid, < *liquere*, be liquid.] Becoming liquid; tending toward a liquid state.—**li-ques′cence,** *n.*

li-queur (li-kūr′, F. lē-kėr), *n.* [F.: see *liquor.*] Any of a class of alcoholic liquors, usually strong, sweet, and highly flavored, as chartreuse, curaçao, maraschino, etc.; a cordial; also, an alcoholic syrup used to sweeten champagne, etc.—**li-queur′,** *v. t.* To treat or flavor with liqueur.—**li-queur′=glass,** *n.* A very small drinking-glass used for liqueurs.

li-quid (lik′wid), *a.* [OF. F. *liquide*, < L. *liquidus*, liquid, fluid, clear, < *liquere*, be liquid.] Such as to flow like water; composed of particles or molecules (as those of water, etc.) which move freely among themselves but do not tend to separate like those of gases; neither gaseous nor solid; also, clear, transparent, or bright (as, *liquid* light; *liquid* eyes); also, sounding smoothly or agreeably (as, "The Italian is the most *liquid* . . . language that can possibly be imagined": Hume's "Essays," Of National Characters); specif., of certain consonant sounds, flowing easily and smoothly (see *liquid, n.*); also, not fixed or stable; of movement, facile; also, of assets, securities, etc., in cash, or easily convertible into cash; also, plain or evident, as a proof or exposition†; in *civil* and *Sc. law*, clear or manifest, as a debt or claim; ascertained and constituted either by a written obligation or by the decree of a court. Also, of or pertaining to liquids: as, *liquid* measure (see below).—**liquid air,** the intensely cold, transparent, liquid product formed when air is greatly compressed and then cooled.—**liquid fire,** flaming petroleum or the like as employed against the enemy in warfare. See *flame-thrower.*—**liquid glass.** See *water-glass.*—**liquid measure,** the system of units of capacity ordinarily used in measuring liquid commodities, such as milk, oil, etc.: 4 gills = 1 pint; 2 pints = 1 quart; 4 quarts = 1 gallon (231 cubic inches in the old English wine-gallon or U. S. legal gallon, and approximately 277.274 cubic inches in the imperial, or British legal, gallon, the U. S. gallon being thus equivalent to about .833 British gallon); $31\frac{1}{2}$ gallons = 1 barrel; 2 barrels = 1 hogshead. In Great Britain, the liquid and dry measures are equivalent; in the U. S., the dry measures are about one sixth greater than the corresponding liquid measures; the British measures differ only a little from the corresponding U. S. dry measures.—**li′quid,** *n.* A liquid substance (distinguished from a gas by its slight compressibility, its definite volume, etc., and from a solid usually by its indefinite shape); also, in *phonetics*, a smoothly flowing consonant sound, as of *l*, *m*, *n*, and *r*.

li-quid-am-bar (lik′wid-am″bär), *n.* [NL., < L. *liquidus*, liquid, + ML. *ambar*, amber.] Any tree of the hamamelidaceous genus *Liquidambar*, as *L. styraciflua*, a large American tree having star-shaped leaves and, in warm regions, exuding a fragrant yellowish balsamic liquid used in medicine; also, this liquid. See *storax.*

Branch of Liquidambar (*L. styraciflua*).

li-qui-date (lik′wi-dāt), *v.*; *-dated, -dating.* [ML. *liquidatus*, pp. of *liquidare*, < L. *liquidus*, E. *liquid.*] **I.** *tr.* To clear up (a matter of doubt or disagreement)†; also, to reduce (accounts) to order; determine the amount of (indebtedness or damages); also, to settle or pay (a debt, etc.: as, to *liquidate* a claim); also, to settle the accounts and distribute the assets of (a firm, etc.) in winding up its affairs; hence, to do away with; murder (a person), esp. in cold blood. **II.** *intr.* To liquidate debts or accounts; go into liquidation.—**li-qui-da′tion** (-dā′shon), *n.* The act of liquidating; esp., the act or process of winding up the affairs of a firm, etc.; also, liquidated state.—**li′qui-da-tor,** *n.*

li-quid-i-ty (li-kwid′i-ti), *n.* Liquid state or quality.

li-quid-ize (lik′wi-dīz), *v. t.*; *-ized, -izing.* To make liquid.

li-quid-ly (lik′wid-li), *adv.* In a liquid manner; flowingly; smoothly; clearly.—**li′quid-ness,** *n.*

li-quor (lik′or), *n.* [OF. *licur* (F. *liqueur*), < L. *liquor*, liquid state, a liquid, < *liquere*, be liquid.] Any liquid substance; often, liquid for drinking; a beverage; specif., an alcoholic beverage, either distilled or fermented, esp. a distilled or spirituous beverage (as brandy or whisky) as distinguished from a fermented beverage (as wine or beer); also, a solution of a substance, esp. a concentrated one used in the industrial arts; in *phar.*, a solution of a medicinal substance in water.—**in liquor,** in a state of intoxication; drunk: as, "I shall overlook your being *in liquor*, this time; but take care" (Marryat's "King's Own," xli.).—**li′quor,** *v.* **I.** *tr.* To cover or treat with a liquor or liquid; also, to furnish with liquor or drink (often with *up*: slang). **II.** *intr.* To drink liquor: often with *up.* [Slang.]

li-quo-rice (lik′ō-ris), *n.* See *licorice.*

li-quor-ish (lik′or-ish), etc. See *lickerish*, etc.

li-ra (lē′rä), *n.*; pl. *liras*, It. *lire* (-rā). [It., < L. *libra*, pound: see *libra.*] The monetary unit and a silver coin of Italy, equal to 100 centesimi, and equivalent to one French franc, or to 19.3 U. S. cents; also, a monetary unit and a gold coin of Turkey, equal to 100 piasters, and equivalent to about $4.40.

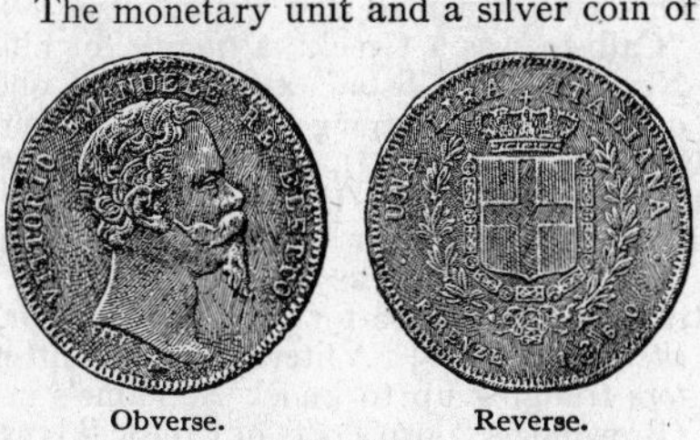

Obverse. Reverse.
Italian Lira.

lir-i-o-den-dron (lir″i-ō-den′dron), *n.*; pl. *-drons*, L. *-dra* (-drä). [NL., < Gr. λείριον, lily, + δένδρον, tree.] A tree of the magnoliaceous genus *Liriodendron*, of which the tulip-tree, *L. tulipifera*, is the only remaining representative. See *tulip-tree.*

lir-i-pipe, lir-i-poop (lir′i-pīp, -pöp), *n.* [ML. *liripipium*; origin unknown.] The tail or pendent part at the back of a hood, as in early academic costume, sometimes long enough, when the hood was drawn up, to wind about the head in the fashion of a turban.

lisle (līl), *n.* Same as *Lisle thread.*

Lisle (līl) **thread.** [Often *l. c.*] A fine, hard-twisted linen or cotton thread, orig. made in the city of Lille (formerly Lisle) in northern France: used for making hosiery, gloves, etc.

lisp (lisp), *v.* [ME. *lispen*, < AS. *wlisp*, lisping: cf. D. *lispen*, G. *lispeln*, lisp.] **I.** *intr.* To pronounce the sounds of *s* and *z* imperfectly in speaking, giving them the sound of *th* in *thin* or in *this*; hence, in general, to speak imperfectly, as in childhood; speak in a childish or affected manner. **II.** *tr.* To utter in a lisping manner: as, "When first his infant voice shall frame Imperfect words, and *lisp* his mother's name" (Pope's "Dryope," 81).—**lisp,** *n.* The act, habit, or sound of lisping.—**lisp′er,** *n.*—**lisp′ing-ly,** *adv.*

lis-some, lis-som (lis′um), *a.* [For *lithesome.*] Lithesome or lithe, esp. of body; limber or supple (as, "A daughter of our meadows . . . Straight, but as *lissome* as a hazel wand". Tennyson's "Brook," 70); agile or active.—**lis′some-ness, lis′som-ness,** *n.*

lis-sot-ri-chous (li-sot′ri-kus), *a.* [Gr. λισσός, smooth, + θρίξ (τριχ-), hair.] Having smooth hair.

list[1] (list), *v.* [AS. *hlystan*, < *hlyst*, hearing, = Icel. *hlust*, the ear; from the same root as E. *loud*: cf. *listen.*] **I.** *intr.* To listen; harken: as, "*List, list*; I hear Some far off halloo break the silent air" (Milton's "Comus," 480); "Go forth, under the open sky, and *list* To Nature's teachings" (Bryant's "Thanatopsis"). [Archaic or prov.] **II.** *tr.* To listen or harken to: as, "Elves, *list* your names" (Shakspere's "Merry Wives of Windsor," v. 5. 46). [Archaic or prov.]

list[2] (list), *v.* [AS. *lystan*, < *lust*, pleasure, desire, E. *lust.*] **I.** *tr.* To be pleasing to, or please (used impersonally, often with a dependent infinitive: as, permitted to come when him *listed*; "Me *lists* not at this tide declare The splendour of the spousal rite," Scott's "Lay of the Last Minstrel," vi. 4); also, to like or desire (as, "She takes all she can, not all she *listeth*": Shakspere's "Venus and Adonis," 564). [Archaic.] **II.** *intr.* To like; wish; choose: as, "The wind bloweth where it *listeth*" (John, iii. 8). [Archaic.]—**list**[2], *n.* Pleasure†; also, desire or inclination (archaic).

list[3] (list), *v.* [Origin uncertain: cf. *list*[2].] *Naut.*: **I.** *intr.* Of a ship, to careen, or incline to one side. **II.** *tr.* To cause (a ship) to lean to one side.—**list**[3], *n.* A careening, or leaning to one side, as of a ship.

list[4] (list). [AS. *līste* = D. *lijst* = OHG. *līsta*, G. *leiste*, border: cf. *list*[5], *list*[6], and *listel.*] **I.** *n.* A border or bordering strip of anything (now chiefly or only of cloth); a selvage, or selvages collectively; also, a strip of cloth or other material; also, a strip or band of any kind; a division of the hair or beard; a stripe of color; specif., one of the ridges of earth thrown up by a lister, or plow with a double mold-board; in *arch.*, a square molding; a fillet; in *carp.*, a strip, esp. of sap-wood, from the edge of a plank. **II.** *a.* Made of selvages or strips of cloth: as, *list* carpet; "her quiet tread muffled in a *list* slipper" (C. Brontë's "Jane Eyre," xvii.).—**list**[4], *v. t.* To border or edge; also, to arrange in strips, bands, or stripes; also, to apply list or strips of cloth to (as, to *list* a door at the edges against drafts); also, to produce furrows and ridges in (land) by means of a lister; in *cotton-culture*, to prepare (land) for the crop by making alternating beds and alleys; also, in *carp.*, to cut a strip, as of sap-wood, from the edge of (a plank, etc.); shape (a block, stave, etc.) roughly by chopping.

list[5] (list), *n.* [F. *liste*, list, roll, orig. border, band, strip, < OHG. *līsta*: see *list*[4].] A record consisting of a series of names, words, or the like; a number of names of persons or things set down one after another; a roll; a register; a catalogue.—**list**[5], *v.* **I.** *tr.* To set down together in a list, or make a list of; enter in a list with others; often, to set down or enter in a formal or official list or register; also, to enlist, as for military or naval service. **II.** *intr.* To enlist, as for military or naval service: as, "lads . . . that had *listed* to be soldiers" (Galt's "Annals of the Parish," xxv.).

list[6] (list), *n.* [ME. *liste*, bound, pl. lists of tournament; appar. the same word as *list*[4], but affected by OF. *lice*, barrier, lists (perhaps < OHG. *līsta*: see *list*[4]).] A bound† or limit†; also, an inclosure†; also, *pl.*, the barriers inclosing the field of combat at a tournament; the inclosed field; hence, any place or scene of combat.—**list**[6], *v. t.* To inclose, as for a tournament: as, "mortal combat on the *listed* plain" (Pope's tr. Homer's "Iliad," vii.).

list-a-ble (lis′ta-bl), *a.* That may be listed, or entered in a list.

list-ed (lis′ted), *p. a.* Set down or entered in a list; in the stock-exchange, of securities, entered in or admitted to the regular list of securities in which dealings are permitted. Cf. *unlisted.*

lis-tel (lis′tel), *n.* [F., < It. *listello*, dim. of *lista*, < OHG. *līsta*: see *list*[4].] In *arch.*, a narrow list or fillet.

lis-ten (lis′n), *v.* [AS. (Northumbrian) *lysna* = MHG. *lüsenen*, listen; akin to E. *list*[1].] **I.** *tr.* To give attention to with the ear; give ear to: as, "She *listen'd* my prayer" (Hood's "Lycus," 346). [Archaic.] **II.** *intr.* To give attention with the ear; attend closely for the purpose of hearing; give ear; hence, to give heed; yield to advice.—**to listen in,** to listen to talking carried on between others, esp. as an eavesdropper; specif., to listen to conversation carried on over a telephone, as by means of another connection with the circuit; also, to listen to radiophone talking, music, etc., by means of a receiving outfit.—**lis′ten-er,** *n.*—**lis′ten-ing=post,** *n. Milit.*, a post or position, as in advance of a defensive line, established for the purpose of listening to detect the enemy's movements; a post, as in a subterranean gallery, maintained for detecting mining operations of the enemy; a post established for the purpose of detecting the approach of aëroplanes; hence, in general use, any position maintained for the purpose of obtaining information.

list-er[1] (lis′tėr), *n.* [See *list*[4].] A plow with a double mold-board used to prepare the soil for planting by producing furrows and ridges, and often fitted with attachments for dropping and covering the seeds.

list-er[2] (lis′tėr), *n.* [See *list*[5].] One who makes a list, as of taxable property.

lis-ter-ine (lis′tėr-ēn), *n.* [From Lord *Lister*: see *Listerism.*] An antiseptic solution containing benzoic acid, boric acid, thymol, etc. [Proprietary name.]

Lis-ter-ism (lis′tėr-izm), *n.* An antiseptic method of operating introduced by the English surgeon Lord Lister (1827–1912), involving the spraying of the parts under operation with a carbolic acid solution.—**Lis′ter-ize,** *v. t.*; *-ized, -izing.* To treat according to Listerism.

list-less (list′les), *a.* [See *list*[2].] Having no desire or inclination for something specified† (as, "*listless* of their gain": Dryden's tr. Virgil's "Georgics," iv. 378); hence, feeling no inclination toward or interest in anything (as, "I found myself so *listless* and desponding, that I had not the heart to rise," Swift's "Gulliver's Travels," iii. 1; "I, *listless*, yet restless, Find every prospect vain," Burns's "Despondency," 27); apathetically indifferent in feeling or mood; characterized by or indicating such feeling (as, a *listless* mood; *listless* movements; "whetting his scythe with a *listless* hand," Whittier's "Wreck of Rivermouth"); in general, dull or sluggish (as, "From the *listless* repose of the place . . . this sequestered glen has long been known by the name of Sleepy Hollow": Irving's "Sketch-Book," Sleepy Hollow).—**list′-less-ly,** *adv.*—**list′less-ness,** *n.*

lists (lists), *n. pl.* See *list*[6].

lit (lit). Preterit and past participle of *light*[1] and *light*[3].

lit-a-ny (lit′ạ-ni), *n.*; pl. *-nies* (-niz). [OF. *letanie* (F. *litanie*), < LL. *litania*, < Gr. λιτανεία, litany, < λιτανεύειν, pray, < λίτεσθαι, λίσσεσθαι, beg, entreat.] A ceremonial or liturgical form of prayer consisting of a series of supplications with responses; [often *cap.*] with *the*, the "general supplication" of this form in the Book of Common Prayer; hence [*l. c.*], any similar form of supplication; also, any long enumeration or continuous repetition (as, a *litany* of curses; "Sing the Lovers' *Litany*:—'Love like ours can never die!'" Kipling's "Lovers' Litany").—**lit-a-neu′ti-cal** (-nū′ti-kạl), *a.*

li-tchi (lē-chē′), *n.* See *lichi.*

-lite. [F. *-lite* or *-lithe*, or G. *-lit* or *-lith*, < Gr. λίθος, stone; or directly < Gr. λίθος.] A noun termination in names of minerals, fossils, etc., as *aërolite, chrysolite, coprolite, dendrolite, laccolite, rhyolite, ripidolite.* Cf. *-lith.*

li-ter, li-tre (lē′tėr), *n.* [F. *litre*, < *litron*, old measure of capacity, < ML. *litra*, measure for liquids, < Gr. λίτρα (prob. < L. *libra*), pound.] In the *metric system*, a unit of capacity equal to the volume of one kilogram of water at its maximum density, or very nearly one cubic decimeter; hence, in practical use, a cubic decimeter: equivalent to 0.908 quart U. S. dry measure, or 1.0567 quarts U. S. liquid measure.

lit-er-a-cy (lit′ẹ-rạ-si), *n.* The state of being literate; possession of education.

lit-er-al (lit′ẹ-rạl), *a.* [OF. *literal* (F. *littéral*), < LL. *litteralis, literalis*, < L. *littera, litera*, E. *letter*[2].] Of or pertaining to the letters of the alphabet; of the nature of letters; expressed by letters; affecting a letter or letters (as, a *literal* error); also, following the letter, or exact words, of the original, as a translation; not free; also, in accordance with, involving, or being the natural or strict meaning of the words or word (as, the *literal* interpretation of Scripture; *literal* language; the *literal* sense of a passage or an expression); not figurative or metaphorical; sometimes, true to fact, or not exaggerated (as, a *literal* statement of conditions); also, being actually such, without metaphor, exaggeration, or inaccuracy (as, a *literal* downfall; the *literal* extermination of a race); also, of persons, tending to construe words in the strict sense or in an unimaginative way; matter-of-fact; prosaic.—**lit′er-al-ism,** *n.* Adherence to the exact letter or the literal sense, as in translation or interpretation; a peculiarity of expression resulting from this (as, a translator's *literalisms*); also, exact representation or protrayal, without idealization, as in art or literature.—**lit′er-al-ist,** *n.* One who adheres to the exact letter or the literal sense; also, one who represents or portrays without idealizing.—**lit″er-al-is′tic,** *a.*—**lit-er-al′i-ty** (-ẹ-ral′i-ti), *n.* The quality of being literal.—**lit′er-al-ize** (-īz), *v. t.*; *-ized, -izing.* To render literal; interpret literally.—**lit′er-al-iz-er** (-ī-zėr), *n.*—**lit′er-al-ly,** *adv.* In a literal manner; word for word (as, to translate *literally*; a speech reported *literally*); in the literal sense (as, to interpret a statement *literally*); actually, without metaphor, exaggeration, or the like (as, "My daily bread is *literally* implored": Dryden's "Hind and the Panther," iii. 107).—**lit′er-al-ness,** *n.*

lit-er-a-ry (lit′ẹ-rạ-ri), *a.* [L. *litterarius, literarius*, < *littera, litera*, E. *letter*[2].] Of or pertaining to letters or polite learning (as, *literary* culture); pertaining to or of the nature of books and writings, esp. those classed as literature (as, *literary* history; *literary* property, property in anything written or printed, or consisting in the right to control the reproduction and publication of this); pertaining to the writing of books, etc. (as, *literary* work); also, versed in or acquainted with literature; engaged in writing books, etc., or in literature as a profession (as, a *literary* man; "some gentlemen of the *literary* fraternity," Thackeray's "Newcomes," lxxiv.).—**lit′er-a-ri-ly,** *adv.*—**lit′er-a-ri-ness,** *n.*

lit-er-ate (lit′ẹ-rạt). [L. *litteratus, literatus*, lettered, educated, < *littera, litera*, E. *letter*[2].] **I.** *a.* Having a knowledge of letters; able to read and write; possessing education; educated; also, pertaining to literature; literary. **II.** *n.* One who can read and write; also, a learned person (as, "Callista was a Greek; a *literate*, or blue stocking": J. H. Newman's "Callista," xxviii.); also, one admitted to holy orders without having obtained a university degree (Eng.).

lit-er-a-ti (lit-ẹ-rā′tī), *n.* Plural of *literatus.*

lit-er-a-tim (lit-ẹ-rā′tim), *adv.* [ML., < L. *littera, litera*, E. *letter*[2].] Letter for letter; literally: as, to reproduce a text *literatim.*

lit-er-a-tor (lit′ẹ-rā-tọr), *n.* [L. *litterator, literator*, < *littera, litera*, E. *letter*[2].] A literary man; a littérateur: as, "*Literators* trudging up to knock At Fame's exalted temple-door" (Browning's "Two Poets of Croisic," lxxxi.).

lit-er-a-ture (lit′ẹ-rạ-ṭūr), *n.* [OF. *litterature* (F. *littérature*), < L. *litteratura, literatura*, grammar, philology, learning, < *littera, litera*, E. *letter*[2].] Polite learning or literary culture (now rare); also, literary work or production; the profession of a writer or author; also, literary productions collectively; esp., writings in which expression and form, in connection with ideas of permanent and universal interest, are characteristic or essential features, as poetry, romance, history, biography, essays, etc.; belles-lettres; also, the writings dealing with a particular subject (as, the *literature* of gems); also, printed matter of any kind, as circulars or advertising matter (colloq.).

lit-er-a-tus (lit-ẹ-rā′tus), *n.*; pl. *-ti* (-tī). [L., lettered, educated: see *literate.*] A man of learning or scholarship: chiefly in *pl.*: as, "the enlightened *literati*, who turn over the pages of history" (Irving's "Knickerbocker's New York," iii. 3).

-lith. Noun termination from Gr. λίθος, stone, as in *acrolith, coccolith, megalith, nephrolith, paleolith*: sometimes occurring in words, as *batholith, laccolith*, that are variants of forms in *-lite.* Cf. *-lite.*

li-thæ′mi-a, etc. See *lithemia*, etc.

lith-arge (lith′ärj), *n.* [OF. *litarge* (F. *litharge*), < L. *lithargyrus*, < Gr. λιθάργυρος, < λίθος, stone, + ἄργυρος, silver.] A yellowish-red oxide of lead, used for glazing earthenware and in making glass.

lithe (līᴛʜ), *a.*; compar. *lither*, superl. *lithest.* [AS. *līthe* = G. *lind*, soft, mild: cf. L. *lentus*, pliant, slow.] Soft, gentle, or mild (now Sc. and north. Eng.); also, bending readily, or pliant (as, "And bent or broke The *lithe* reluctant boughs to tear away Their tawny clusters": Tennyson's "Enoch Arden," 378); esp., bending readily at the joints, limber, or supple (as, to be *lithe* of body; *lithe* limbs); hence, agile or active (as, "I . . . engaged a *lithe*, active young Nazarene": Kinglake's "Eothen," xi.).—**lithe′ly,** *adv.*—**lithe′ness,** *n.*

li-the-mi-a, li-thæ-mi-a (li-thē′mi-ạ̈), *n.* [NL., < Gr. λίθος, stone (cf. *lithic*[1]), + αἷμα, blood.] In *pathol.*, a condition in which there is an excess of uric (lithic) acid in the blood.—**li-the′mic, li-thæ′mic,** *a.*

lith-er (liᴛʜ′ėr), *a.* [AS. *lȳthre*, bad: cf. G. *liederlich*, loose, dissolute, slovenly.] Bad† or wicked†; also, poor†, sorry†, or worthless†; withered†; also, lazy (now prov. Eng. and Sc.); also, pliant, supple, or yielding (now prov. Eng. and Sc.); active or nimble (prov. Eng.).—**lith′er-ly†,** *a.* Bad; mischievous; also, lazy.

lithe-some (līᴛʜ′sum), *a.* Lithe; lissome.

lith-i-a (lith′i-ạ̈), *n.* [NL., < Gr. λίθος, stone.] A white oxide of lithium, Li_2O.—**lithia water,** a mineral water, natural or artificial, containing lithium salts.

li-thi-a-sis (li-thī′ạ-sis), *n.* [NL., < Gr. λιθίασις, < λίθος, stone.] In *pathol.*, the formation of stony concretions in any part of the body, as in the bladder.

lith-ic[1] (lith′ik), *a.* [Gr. λιθικός, < λίθος, stone.] Pertaining to or consisting of stone; in *pathol.*, pertaining to stony concretions, or calculi, formed within the body, esp. in the bladder.—**lithic acid,** uric acid.

lith-ic[2] (lith′ik), *a.* Of, pertaining to, or containing lithium.

lith-i-um (lith′i-um), *n.* [NL., < Gr. λίθος, stone; so named because found in minerals.] Chem. sym., Li; at. wt., 6.94; sp. gr., 0.59. A soft, silver-white metallic element (the lightest of all metals) occurring combined in certain minerals.

litho-, lith-. Forms of Gr. λίθος, stone, used in combination.

li-tho-did (li-thō′did), *n.* [NL. *Lithodidæ*, pl., < *Lithodes*, the typical genus, < Gr. λιθώδης, stone-like, < λίθος, stone, + εἶδος, form.] Any of the crabs of the family *Lithodidæ*, with triangular carapace and the fifth pair of legs much reduced, as *Lithodes agassizi*, a deep-sea species.

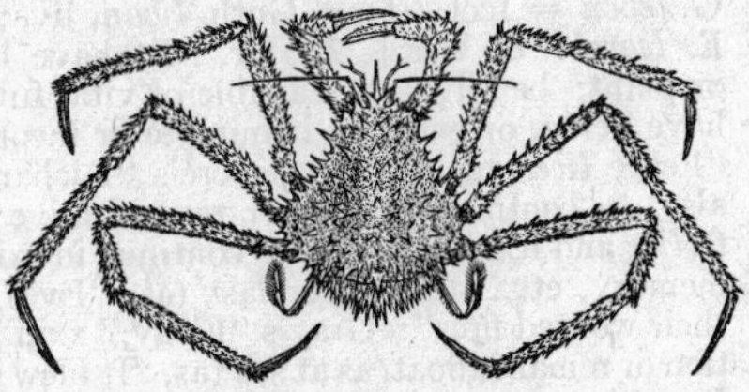
Lithodid (*Lithodes agassizi*).

lith-o-graph (lith′ọ-gráf), *n.* [See *litho-* and *-graph.*] A print produced by lithography.—**lith′o-graph,** *v. t.* To produce or copy by lithography.—**li-thog-ra-pher** (li-thog′rạ-fėr), *n.*—**lith-o-graph′ic** (-graf′ik), *a.* Of, pertaining to, or produced by lithography.—**lith-o-graph′i-cal-ly,** *adv.* —**li-thog′ra-phy** (-fi), *n.* [See *-graphy.*] The art or process of producing a picture, writing, or the like, on a flat, specially prepared stone, and of taking ink-impressions from this as in ordinary printing; a similar process in which a substance other than stone, as aluminium or zinc, is used.

lith-oid (lith′oid), *a.* [Gr. λιθοειδής: see *litho-* and *-oid.*] Stone-like; stony. Also **li-thoi-dal** (li-thoi′dạl).

li-thol-o-gy (li-thol′ọ-ji), *n.* [See *litho-* and *-logy.*] The science of rocks (now rare); esp., the science dealing with the minute mineral characters of rock specimens; also, in *med.*, the science treating of calculi in the human body.—**lith-o-log-ic, lith-o-log-i-cal** (lith-ọ-loj′ik, -i-kạl), *a.*

lith-o-man-cy (lith′ọ-man-si), *n.* [See *litho-* and *-mancy.*] Divination by means of stones.

lith-o-marge (lith′ọ-märj), *n.* [NL. *lithomarga*, < Gr. λίθος, stone, + L. *marga*, marl.] Any of several minerals, or mixtures of minerals, including kaolin, etc., which consist of a hydrous silicate of aluminium.

li-thoph-i-lous (li-thof′i-lus), *a.* [See *litho-* and *-philous.*] In *bot.*, growing on rocks; in *entom.*, living in stony places.

lith-o-phyl, lith-o-phyll (lith′ọ-fil), *n.* [See *litho-* and *-phyl.*] A fossil of a leaf, or a stone containing one.

lith-o-phyte (lith′ọ-fīt), *n.* [See *litho-* and *-phyte.*] In *zoöl.*, a polyp with a hard or stony structure, as a coral; in *bot.*, any plant growing on the surface of rocks.—**lith-o-phyt′ic** (-fit′ik), *a.*

lith-o-sphere (lith′ọ-sfēr), *n.* [See *litho-* and *sphere.*] The crust of the earth. Cf. *hydrosphere* and *atmosphere.*

li-thot-o-my (li-thot′ọ-mi), *n.* [LL. *lithotomia*, < Gr. λιθοτομία: see *litho-* and *-tomy.*] In *surg.*, the operation or art of cutting for stone in the bladder.—**lith-o-tom-ic** (lith-ọ-tom′ik), *a.*—**li-thot′o-mist,** *n.*

lith-o-trip-sy (lith′ọ-trip-si), *n.* [= NL. *lithotripsis*, < Gr. λίθος, stone, + τρῖψις, rubbing, < τρίβειν, rub.] Lithotrity.

lith-o-trite (lith′ọ-trīt), *n.* [From *lithotrity.*] An instrument for performing lithotrity.

li-thot-ri-ty (li-thot′ri-ti), *n.* [= F. *lithotritie*, < Gr. λίθος, stone, + L. *terere* (pp. *tritus*), rub.] In *surg.*, the operation of crushing stone in the bladder into particles that may be voided.—**li-thot′ri-tist,** *n.*

Lith-u-a-ni-an (lith-ū-ā′ni-ạn). **I.** *a.* Of or pertaining to Lithuania (to the east of the Baltic Sea, south of Latvia), its inhabitants, or their language. **II.** *n.* A native of Lithuania; also, the language of Lithuania, belonging to the Lettic group.

lith-y (lī′ᴛʜi or liᴛʜ′i), *a.* [Cf. *lithe.*] Flexible; supple; lithe. [Archaic or prov. Eng.]

lit-i-ga-ble (lit′i-gạ-bl), *a.* Subject to litigation.

lit-i-gant (lit′i-gạnt). **I.** *a.* Litigating. **II.** *n.* One engaged in a lawsuit.

lit-i-gate (lit′i-gāt), *v.*; *-gated, -gating.* [L. *litigatus*, pp. of *litigare*, < *lis* (*lit-*), dispute, lawsuit, + *agere*, drive.] **I.** *intr.* To carry on a lawsuit. **II.** *tr.* To make the subject of a lawsuit; contest at law; also, to dispute (a point, etc.). —**lit-i-ga′tion** (-gā′shọn), *n.* [LL. *litigatio(n-).*] The process of litigating, or carrying on a suit at law; sometimes, the practice of going to law; also, disputation (as, "The squire . . . was, after some *litigation*, obliged to consent to delay introducing Jones to Sophia": Fielding's "Tom Jones," xviii. 10).—**lit′i-ga-tor,** *n.*

li-ti-gious (li-tij′us), *a.* [L. *litigiosus*, < *litigium*, dispute, litigation, < *litigare*: see *litigate.*] Fond of litigation; inclined to go to law; also, in general, contentious; disputatious; also, subject to or involved in litigation; litigable; sometimes, in general, disputable; also, of or pertaining to litigation.—**li-ti′gious-ly,** *adv.*—**li-ti′gious-ness,** *n.*

lit-mus (lit′mus), *n.* [MD. *lijcmoes*, D. *lakmoes*, 'lac pulp.'] A blue coloring matter obtained from certain lichens, esp. *Roccella tinctoria.*—**lit′mus=pa″per,** *n.* Paper treated with litmus: used to indicate the presence of acids (which turn it red) or alkalis (which restore the blue color).

lit′o-ral, *a.* and *n.* See *littoral.*

lit-o-tes (lit′ọ-tēz or lī′tọ-), *n.* [NL., < Gr. λιτότης, < λιτός, plain, simple.] In *rhet.*, a figure in which an affirmative is expressed by the negative of its contrary, as in "a citizen of no mean city" (Acts, xxi. 39: meaning one of an illustrious city).

li′tre, *n.* See *liter.*

lit-ten (lit′n). Pseudo-archaic pp. of *light*[1].

lit-ter (lit′ėr), *n.* [OF. *litiere* (F. *litière*), < ML. *lectaria*, bedding, < L. *lectus*, bed: see *lie*[1].] Bedding† or a bed†; hence, a vehicle borne by men or animals, consisting of a bed or couch, usually covered and curtained, suspended between shafts (as, "Margaret travelled in a splendid

Ancient Roman Litter. — Capitoline Museum, Rome.

litter with gilt pillars, lined with scarlet velvet, and entirely enclosed in glass": Motley's "Dutch Republic," v. 3); also, a framework or stretcher for carrying a sick or wounded person; also, straw, hay, etc., used as bedding for animals, or as a protection for plants; also, things scattered about; scattered rubbish; hence, a condition of disorder or untidiness (as, the room was in a *litter*); also, number of young brought forth at one birth (as, "a *litter* of pigs," Galt's "Annals of the Parish," xiv.; "a *litter* of well-grown black puppies," Parkman's "Oregon Trail," ix.); also, in *forestry*, the rubbish of dead leaves and twigs scattered upon the floor of the forest. —**lit′ter,** *v.* **I.** *tr.* To supply (an animal) with litter for a bed; cover (a floor, etc.) with litter, or straw, hay, etc. (as, "We did our nightly chores . . . *Littered* the stalls": Whittier's "Snow-Bound"); use (straw, hay, etc.) for litter; also, to strew (a place) with scattered objects; be strewed about (a place) in disorder (as, "Armed ships allow nothing superfluous to *litter* up the deck": H. Melville's "Omoo," xxvii.); scatter (objects) in disorder (as, to *litter* things about a room; "*Littered* about were human bones," J. H. Newman's "Callista," xxiii.); also, to give birth to (young: said chiefly of animals). **II.** *intr.* To give birth to a litter: as, "a horrible desert . . . where the she wolf still *littered*" (Macaulay's "Hist. of Eng.," xii.).

lit-té-ra-teur (lē-tā-rȧ-tėr), *n.* [F., < L. *litterator*: see *literator*.] A literary man; a writer of literary works.—**lit-té-ra-trice** (-trēs), *n.* [F.] Fem. of *littérateur*.

lit-ter-y (lit′ėr-i), *a.* Consisting of or containing litter; covered or encumbered with litter; untidy.

lit-tle (lit′l), *a.*; compar. *less, lesser* (also *littler*), superl. *least* (also *littlest*). [AS. *lȳtel* = OS. *luttil* = D. *luttel* = G. dial. *lützel*, little.] Small in size (as, a *little* child; a *little* garden); not big or large; also, small in extent or duration (as, a *little* walk; a *little* while); short; brief; also, small in number (as, a *little* army); also, small in amount or degree (as, *little* money; *little* hope); not much; also, being such on a small scale (as, *little* farmers); also, small in force (as, a *little* voice); weak; also, small in consideration, dignity, consequence, etc. (as, to pay attention to *little* things; *little* discomforts); inconsiderable; insignificant; trivial; hence, mean, narrow, or illiberal (as, a *little* soul; a *little* mind).—**Little Bear.** See *bear*[2], *n.*—**Little Corporal** [tr. F. *petit caporal*], a popular nickname of Napoleon I. —**Little Dipper.** See *dipper*.—**Little Dog.** See *dog, n.* —**Little Englander,** in English politics, an opponent of the colonial extension or territorial aggrandizement of the empire.—**Little Entente,** an understanding or alliance entered into in 1920 by Czechoslovakia, Jugoslavia, and Rumania, primarily for defense against efforts on the part of Hungary to recover territories formerly Hungarian but awarded to the parties to this alliance after the World War; also, the parties to this alliance.—**Little Fox,** in *astron.*, the northern constellation Vulpecula.—**little go.** See *go, n.* —**Little Horse,** in *astron.*, the northern constellation Equuleus.—**Little Russian.** See under *Russian, n.*—**little theater,** a theater of small size for the production of plays whose effectiveness would be lost in larger houses, or plays of literary worth or other special interest that would not draw audiences sufficient to fill the ordinary theater, established in connection with a movement growing up in the early decades of the 20th century and identified with various experiments and innovations connected with the drama and its presentation.—**lit′tle,** *n.* That which is little; a small amount, quantity, or degree; a short distance (as, "to retire a *little* to the rear": De Quincey's "Revolt of the Tartars"); a short time (as, "Pray stay a *little*": Shakspere's "1 Henry IV.," ii. 4. 63).—**in little,** on a small scale; in miniature.—**to make little of,** to treat or represent as of little importance: as, "to *make little* . . . *of* the Elective Franchise" (Carlyle's "Sartor Resartus," iii. 7).—**lit′tle,** *adv.* In only a small amount or degree (as, "a zeal *little* tempered by humanity": Macaulay's "Hist. of Eng.," ii.); only slightly; not much; also, before a verb, not at all (as, he *little* knows what awaits him).

Lit-tle=end-i-an (lit″l-en′di-ạn), *n.* [Also *l. c.*] A designation for a member of the orthodox religious party in Lilliput, referred to in Swift's "Gulliver's Travels," i. 4, who maintained, in opposition to the Big-endians, that eggs should be broken at the little end; hence, a member of any set of disputers about trifles.

lit-tle=neck (lit′l-nek), *n.* The hard or round clam, *Venus mercenaria*, when young and of a size preferred for eating raw; hence, any of certain similar clams.

lit-tle-ness (lit′l-nes), *n.* The state of being little; smallness; triviality; meanness or pettiness; sometimes, a mean or petty quality or action.

lit-to-ral (lit′ọ̄-rạl). [L. *littoralis*, prop. *litoralis*, < *litus* (*litor-*), shore.] **I.** *a.* Of or pertaining to a shore, esp. that of the sea; existing or occurring on or near the shore. **II.** *n.* A littoral region: as, the Mediterranean *littoral* of France.

li-tur-gic, li-tur-gi-cal (li-tėr′jik, -ji-kạl), *a.* [Gr. λειτουργικός.] Of or pertaining to public worship; having to do with liturgies or forms of public worship; of or pertaining to the liturgy or eucharistic service; also, of or pertaining to liturgics.—**li-tur′gi-cal-ly,** *adv.*—**li-tur′gics,** *n.* The science or art of conducting public worship; also, the study of liturgies.

li-tur-gi-ol-o-gy (li-tėr-ji-ol′ọ̄-ji), *n.* [See *liturgy* and *-logy*.] The science or study of liturgies.—**li-tur″gi-o-log′i-cal** (-ọ̄-loj′i-kạl), *a.*—**li-tur-gi-ol′o-gist,** *n.*

lit-ur-gist (lit′ėr-jist), *n.* An authority on liturgies; a compiler of a liturgy or liturgies; also, one who uses, or favors the use of, a liturgy.

lit-ur-gy (lit′ėr-ji), *n.*; pl. *-gies* (-jiz). [Gr. λειτουργία, public duty, public worship, < λειτουργός, public servant, minister, priest, < λειτο- (akin to λαός, people) + -εργός, working, worker.] One of a class of public official duties or services in ancient Athens which were performed by the richer citizens at their own expense; hence, in Christian use, the public official services or rites of the church; a particular arrangement of these services; a form of public worship; a ritual; a collection of formularies for public worship; often, the Book of Common Prayer (usually with *the*); also, specif., the service of the eucharist, esp. in the Eastern Church (with *the*); a particular form or type of the eucharistic service.

liv-a-ble (liv′ạ-bl), *a.* Capable of being lived, as life; also, suitable for living in, or habitable, as a house or locality; also, that can be lived with, or companionable, as a person.—**liv′a-ble-ness,** *n.*

live[1] (liv), *v.*; *lived, living.* [AS. *lifian, libban,* = D. *leven* = G. *leben* = Icel. *lifa* = Goth. *liban*, live; from the root of E. *leave*[1]: cf. *life*.] **I.** *intr.* To have life, as an animal or plant; be alive; be capable of vital functions; hence, to have being, or exist, as inanimate or incorporeal things (as, "Peace *lives* again": Shakspere's "Richard III.," v. 5. 40); also, to continue in life, or remain alive (as, to *live* long; to *live* and learn); hence, to continue in existence, operation, memory, etc., survive, or last (as, "Ev'n in our ashes *live* their wonted fires": Gray's "Elegy," xxiii.); escape destruction or remain afloat, as at sea (as, "It blew so hard . . . that I could not suppose their boat could *live*, or that they ever reached to their own coast": Defoe's "Robinson Crusoe," i. 16); enjoy spiritual life (as, "Hear, and your soul shall *live*": Isa. lv. 3); also, to have or get means of subsistence (as, to *live* by toil, or by one's wits); maintain life, or rely for maintenance (as, to *live* on one's income, or on one's friends); feed or subsist (*on* or *upon*: as, to *live* on rice; animals that *live* upon insects); also, to pass life (as specified: as, to *live* content, or in content; to *live* happily or virtuously; to *live* as a vagrant); direct or regulate one's life, as by some rule or standard or for some object or purpose; experience or enjoy life to the full (as, "To-morrow do thy worst, for I have *liv'd* to-day": Dryden's tr. Horace's "Odes," iii. 29. 68); also, to dwell or reside (as, to *live* in a cottage, a city, or a desert; to *live* in Italy); also, to cohabit (*with* or *together*). **II.** *tr.* To pass (life: as, to *live* a life of ease); also, to carry out or exhibit in one's life (as, "He . . . *lived* himself the truth he taught": Whittier's "Sumner").—**to live down,** to live so as to cause (something) to lose force or be forgotten (as, to *live down* a calumny or a mistake); also, to outlive (a fancy, etc.).—**to live out,** to remain alive or hold out through: as, to *live out* a full century; to *live out* a war or a storm.

live[2] (līv), *a.* [Shortened form of *alive*, but (unlike *alive*) commonly used attributively.] Being in life, living, or alive (as, *live* animals; "A real *live* missionary was coming to take tea with us," Kingsley's "Alton Locke," i.); also, full of life, energy, or activity; alert, wide-awake, or up-to-date (colloq.); of present interest, as a question or issue (colloq.); burning or glowing, as a coal; vivid or bright, as color; flowing freely, as water (as, "a *live* fountain welling from the hill": Stevenson's "Travels with a Donkey," v. 4); fresh, as air; still in use, or to be used, as type set up or copy for printing; moving, or imparting motion or power (as, a *live* axle; the *live* center on a lathe); loaded or unexploded, as a cartridge or shell; charged with, or carrying a current of, electricity (as, a *live* wire: see below); also, in the native or pure state, as a mineral; not mined or quarried, as a rock; also, of or pertaining to life or living beings (as, *live* weight, the weight of an animal while living; *live* feathers, feathers taken from the living bird); also, characterized by or indicating the presence of living creatures (as, "all the *live* murmur of a summer's day": M. Arnold's "Scholar-Gipsy").—**live load.** See *load, n.*—**live steam,** steam fresh from the boiler and at full pressure; steam which has performed no work or only part of its work: distinguished from *dead steam* or *exhaust-steam.*—**live stock.** See *stock, n.*—**live wire,** a wire carrying a current of electricity; fig., an energetic, alert person (slang).

live-a-ble (liv′ạ-bl), etc. See *livable*, etc.

lived (līvd), *a.* Having life or a life (as specified): as, long-*lived.*

live=for-ev-er (liv′fọr-ev″ėr), *n.* The plant orpine.

live-li-hood[1] (līv′li-hůd), *n.* [AS. *līflād,* 'life way': see *life* and *lode.*] Course of life†, or way of living†; also, means of maintaining life (as, to gain a *livelihood*); maintenance.

live-li-hood[2]† (līv′li-hůd), *n.* [See *lively.*] Liveliness; lively color: as, "The tyranny of her sorrows takes all *livelihood* from her cheek" (Shakspere's "All's Well," i. 1. 58).

live-li-ly (līv′li-li), *adv.* In a lively manner.—**live′li-ness,** *n.* The state or quality of being lively; activity; animation; vivacity.

live-long (liv′lông), *a.* [ME. *lefe longe,* 'lief (dear) long,' an intensive expression later associated with *live*[1].] Long to the full extent (used of time: as, the *livelong* day or night; the *livelong* hours); in general, whole or entire (as, "So home we went, and all the *livelong* way . . . did Eustace banter me": Tennyson's "Gardener's Daughter," 163); also, lasting or enduring long† (as, "Thou . . . Hast built thyself a *live-long* monument": Milton's "Epitaph on Shakspeare," 8).

live-ly (līv′li). [AS. *līflīc,* < *līf,* E. *life.*] **I.** *a.*; compar. *livelier,* superl. *liveliest.* Living†; also, lifelike, as a picture or a description; also, full or suggestive of life or vital energy; active, vigorous, or brisk, as persons, efforts, discussion, imagination, etc.; animated, spirited, vivacious, or sprightly (as, a *lively* company; a *lively* tune or dance; *lively* sallies); eventful, stirring, or exciting (as, a *lively* time or experience; a *lively* scene); striking, telling, or effective, as an expression or instance; strong, keen, or distinct, as feelings, impressions, recollections, etc.; vivid or bright, as color or light; fresh, as air; brisk or sparkling, as liquors; riding the sea buoyantly, as a ship; rebounding quickly, as a baseball. **II.** *n.*; pl. *-lies* (-liz). A lively fellow: applied to sailors: as, "Speak the word, my *livelies,* and I'll pilot her in" (H. Melville's "Omoo," xx.).—**live′ly,** *adv.* [AS. *līflīce.*] In a lifelike manner (obs. or rare); also, with activity, vigor, or animation; briskly.

liv-en (lī′vn), *v.* [From *life*: cf. *enliven.*] **I.** *tr.* To put life into; rouse; cheer: often with *up.* **II.** *intr.* To become more lively; brighten: usually with *up.*—**liv′en-er,** *n.*

live=oak (līv′ōk′), *n.* An evergreen species of oak, *Quercus virginiana,* of the southern U. S., with a hard wood used in ship-building, etc.; also, any of various related trees.

liv-er[1] (liv′ėr), *n.* One who lives; a living being or creature; a dweller; also, one who has or leads a life (as specified: as, a long *liver*; evil *livers*).

liv-er[2] (liv′ėr), *n.* [AS. *lifer* = D. *lever* = G. *leber* = Icel. *lifr,* liver.] In man, a large, reddish-brown glandular organ (divided by fissures into five lobes) in the upper right-hand side of the abdominal cavity, secreting bile and performing various metabolic functions, and formerly supposed to be the seat of love, desire, courage, etc.; also, a similar or analogous organ in other animals; often, such an organ, or the flesh of one, used as food (as, chicken *livers*; calf's *liver*; a dish of *liver* and bacon).—**liv′er=col″or,** *n.* A dark reddish-brown color.—**liv′er=col″ored,** *a.*—**liv′ered,** *a.* Having a liver (as specified). Cf. *white-livered.*

liv-er-ied (liv′ėr-id), *p. a.* Clad in livery, as servants.

liv-er-leaf (liv′ėr-lēf), *n.* Any of the herbs of the ranunculaceous genus *Hepatica.* See *hepatica.*

liv-er-wort (liv′ėr-wėrt), *n.* Any of the cryptogamic plants, or bryophytes, which constitute the class *Hepaticæ,* comprising moss-like or thalloid plants which grow mostly on damp ground, tree-trunks, etc.; also, a hepatica (ranunculaceous herb), esp. *Hepatica hepatica.*

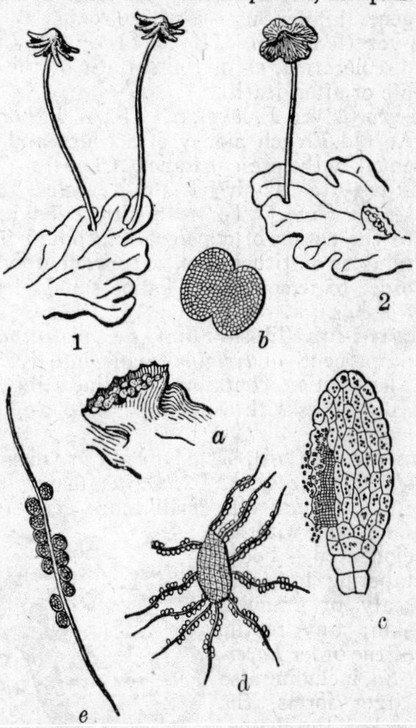

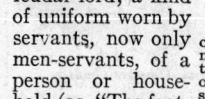

Common Liverwort (*Marchantia polymorpha,* class *Hepaticæ*). — 1, the female plant; 2, the male plant; *a,* a cupule with gemmæ; *b,* one of the gemmæ; *c,* the antheridium, opened; *d,* part of sporangium with the elaters, carrying the spores; *e,* elater with spores.

liv-er-y (liv′ėr-i), *n.*; pl. *-ies* (-iz). [OF. *livree* (F. *livrée*), < *livrer,* deliver, < L. *liberare,* E. *liberate.*] A delivering or dispensing of food, clothing, or other necessaries to retainers, servants, etc. (obs. or hist.); hence, an allowance of food or provisions so dispensed (obs. or hist.); also, a distinctive dress, badge, or cognizance provided for retainers, as of a feudal lord; a kind of uniform worn by servants, now only men-servants, of a person or household (as, "The footmen put on their newest canary-coloured *liveries*": Thackeray's "Vanity Fair," xi.); a distinctive dress worn by an official, a member of a company or gild, etc.; any characteristic dress, garb, or outward appearance (as, the green *livery* of summer; "Twilight gray Had in her sober *livery* all things clad," Milton's "Paradise Lost," iv. 599); also, liveried retainers or servants collectively (obs. or rare); also, the furnishing of provender, or an allowance of provender, for horses (obs. or hist.); hence, the keep, or feeding, stabling, etc., of horses for pay (as, to keep a horse at *livery*; a *livery*-stable); a livery-stable (U. S.); in *law,* the delivery of legal possession of property.—**liv′er-y,** *v. t.*; *-eried, -erying.* To clothe in or as in livery.—**liv′er-y-man** (-mạn), *n.*; pl. *-men.* A person in livery; specif., a freeman of the City of London belonging to a company or gild and entitled to wear its livery; also, a keeper of or an employee in a livery-stable.—**liv′er-y=sta″ble,** *n.* A stable where horses and vehicles are cared for or let out for pay.

lives (līvz), *n.* Plural of *life.*

liv-id (liv′id), *a.* [F. *livide,* < L. *lividus,* < *livere,* be livid.] Of a dull bluish or leaden color or tinge (as, a *livid* sea; "a sullen, old-fashioned building of cold grey stone, looking *livid* in the moonlight," Bulwer-Lytton's "Caxtons," xv. 1); esp., having the discolored bluish appearance due to a bruise, to congestion of blood-vessels, etc., as the flesh, face, hands, or nails. Cf. *livor.*—**li-vid-i-ty** (li-vid′i-ti), **liv′id-ness,** *n.*—**liv′id-ly,** *adv.*

liv-ing (liv′ing), *n.* The act or condition of one who or that which lives; also, lifetime†; also, manner or course of life (as, holy *living*); also, means of maintaining life, or livelihood (as, to earn one's *living*); also, property†, or an estate†; also, an ecclesiastical office or cure, as a rectory, with revenues attached (as, "The bishop . . . gave him . . . the *living* of Drumston, worth 350*l.* a-year": H. Kingsley's "Geoffry Hamlyn," ii.).—**liv′ing,** *p. a.* That lives; alive, or not dead; in actual existence or use (as, *living* languages); active, vigorous, or strong (as, a *living* faith); burning or glowing, as a coal; flowing freely, as water; furious or fierce, as a gale; existing in the original state and place, as rock; lifelike, as a picture; also, of or pertaining to living beings (as, within *living* memory); also, pertaining to or sufficient for living (as, *living* conditions; a *living* wage, a wage on which it is possible for a wage-earner to live).—**liv'ing-ly,** *adv.*—**liv'ing-ness,** *n.*—**liv'ing=room,** *n.* A room for general family use; a sitting-room.

li-vor (lī'vọr), *n.* [L., < *livere*: see *livid.*] Livid color or discoloration, as of the surface of the body (either during life or after death).

li-vre (lē'vėr, F. lēvr), *n.* [F., < L. *libra*, pound: see *libra.*] An old French money of account and coin, approximately equal to the present franc. Cf. *sol*².

lix-iv-i-ate (lik-siv'i-āt), *v. t.*; *-ated*, *-ating*. [L. *lixivium*: see *lixivium.*] To treat with a lixivium; also, to subject to the action of a percolating liquid in order to remove a soluble constituent (as, to *lixiviate* wood-ashes with water in order to remove the alkaline salts); leach.—**lix-iv-i-a'tion** (-ā'shọn), *n.*

lix-iv-i-um (lik-siv'i-um), *n.*; pl. *-iums* or *-ia* (-i-ạ). [L., prop. neut. of *lixivius*, made into lye, < *lix*, ashes, lye.] The solution, containing alkaline salts, obtained by leaching wood-ashes with water; lye; also, any solution obtained by leaching.

liz-ard (liz'ạrd), *n.* [OF. *laisart*, masc., *laisarde*, fem. (F. *lézard*, *lézarde*), < L. *lacertus*, masc., *lacerta*, fem., lizard.] Any of numerous small four-legged reptiles of the order *Lacertilia*, with an elongated body, tapering tail, and scaly or granular skin; any reptile of the order *Lacertilia*, including also larger forms, the geckos, the chameleons, and various allied limbless forms; also, any of certain similar reptiles, esp. of large size, as the crocodiles, dinosaurs, etc.; also, fig., an idler or lounger in places of social enjoyment, public resort, etc. (slang: as, a parlor *lizard*); also [*cap.*], in *astron.*, the northern constellation Lacerta.—**liz'ard=fish,** *n.* Any of various large-mouthed fishes (family *Synodontidæ*) with lizard-like heads, esp. *Synodus fœtens*, a species of the Atlantic Ocean.

Green Lizard of Europe (*Lacerta viridis*).

lla-ma (lä'mạ, Sp. lyä'mä), *n.* [Sp.; from Peruvian.] A woolly-haired South American ruminant animal of the genus *Lama* (or *Auchenia*), probably a domesticated variety of the guanaco, related to the camel but smaller and without a hump, and used as a beast of burden; also, any of certain allied animals, as the alpaca.

Common Llama.

lla-no (lä'nō, Sp. lyä'nō), *n.*; pl. *-nos* (-nōz, Sp. -nōs). [Sp., a plain, as adj. flat, level, < L. *planus*: see *plain*².] An extensive treeless plain. [Spanish America.]—**Llano Estacado** (es-tä-kä'dō). [Sp.] See *Staked Plain*, under *staked.*

lo¹ (lō), *interj.* [ME. *lo*, orig. < AS. *lā*, an exclamation of surprise, greeting, etc., but later appar. confused with ME. *loke*, impv. of *loken*, E. *look.*] Look! see! behold! as, "*Lo*, this is our God" (Isa. xxv. 9).

Lo² (lō), *n.* [From the expression in Pope's "Essay on Man," i. 99, "Lo, the poor Indian! whose untutor'd mind Sees God in clouds," *lo* here being merely the interjection: see *lo*¹.] A humorous name for the North American Indian.

loach (lōch), *n.* [OF. F. *loche*; origin unknown.] Any of various European fresh-water fishes of the carp kind, as *Nemachilus barbatulus*, a food-fish inhabiting small, clear streams.

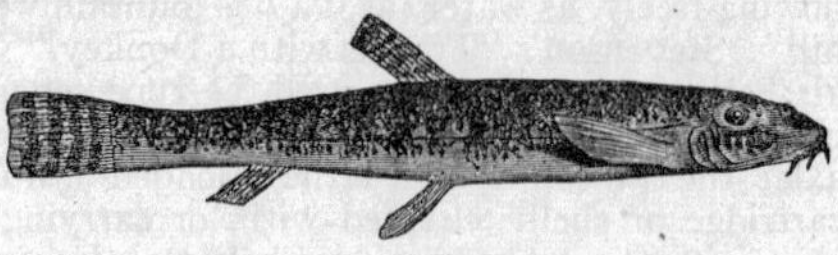
Common Loach (*Nemachilus barbatulus*).

load (lōd), *n.* [Orig. the same word as *lode* (AS. *lād*, way, course, carrying), but now differentiated in spelling and sense and associated with *lade.*] That which is laid on or placed in anything for conveyance; a burden; also, the quantity that can be or usually is carried, as in a cart, etc.; hence, this quantity taken as a unit of measure or weight; also, anything upborne or sustained (as, the *load* of fruit on a tree); fig., something that weighs down or oppresses like a burden (as, "I am compelled to drag for ever the intolerable *load* of existence," Godwin's "Caleb Williams," xii.; "My heart was now somewhat eased of the *load* of apprehension," C. B. Brown's "Wieland," x.); also, the charge of a firearm; also, a sufficient quantity of liquor drunk to intoxicate (slang); also, *pl.*, a great quantity or number (colloq.: as, *loads* of money; *loads* of people); also, *sing.*, in *mech.*, the weight supported by a structure or part (as, a live *load*, one that is temporary and extraneous, as the weight of a train passing over a bridge; a dead *load*, one that is permanent and fixed, as the weight of a bridge); also, the external resistance overcome by an engine, dynamo, or the like, under a given condition, measured by the power required.—**load,** *v.* **I.** *tr.* To put a load on or in (as, to *load* a beast of burden, a cart, or a vessel); hence, to charge as with a load or burden; esp., to supply abundantly or excessively with something (as, to *load* a person with gifts; "The climate is cold, and the air externally *loaded* with vapours," Smollett's "Humphry Clinker," July 4); fig., to weigh down, burden, or oppress (as, "over-great reverence of traditions, which cannot but *load* the Church": Bacon's "Essays," Of Superstition); overwhelm with abuse, etc. (as, "The Dutchman . . . *loaded* me with all the curses and injurious terms his language could afford": Swift's "Gulliver's Travels," iii. 1); also, to charge (a firearm); also, to add weight to, as with lead (as, to *load* a whip; to *load* dice, to make them heavier on one side than on the others by the fraudulent insertion of lead, so as to cause them to fall with a particular face upward); add to the weight of, often fraudulently (as, to *load* a thin wine to give it greater body); also, to place on or in something for conveyance (as, "We . . . fetched our luggage and *loaded* it . . . into the canoes": Defoe's "Captain Singleton," v.); hence, to heap or pile on something (as, "The more he sees I can do, the more he *loads* on": Mrs. Stowe's "Uncle Tom's Cabin," iii.); also, to take on as a load (as, a vessel *loading* coal). **II.** *intr.* To put on or take on a load; often, to load a firearm; sometimes, to become loaded, burdened, or weighted.—**load'er,** *n.*—**load'ing,** *n.* The act of one who or that which loads; also, that with which something is loaded; a load; a burden; a charge.

load'star, load'stone. See *lodestar*, *lodestone.*

loaf¹ (lōf), *n.*; pl. *loaves* (lōvz). [AS. *hlāf* = G. *laib* = Icel. *hleifr* = Goth. *hlaifs*, loaf, bread: cf. *Lammas*, *lady*, and *lord.*] A portion of bread or cake baked in a mass of definite form; hence, a shaped or molded mass of other food, as of sugar or of chopped meat, etc. (as, a *loaf* of jellied chicken; a veal *loaf*).

loaf² (lōf), *v.* [Origin obscure.] **I.** *intr.* To lounge or saunter lazily and idly (as, "I *loafe* and invite my Soul; I lean and *loafe* at my ease, observing a spear of summer grass," Whitman's "Walt Whitman," i.; to *loaf* about the streets); idle away time (as, to *loaf* over a piece of work; to *loaf* during a summer vacation). **II.** *tr.* To idle (*away*): as, "I haven't *loafed* my life away" (Howells's "Rise of Silas Lapham," ix.).—**loaf'er,** *n.* One who loafs; a lazy idler; esp., a habitual lounger about the streets.

loam (lōm), *n.* [AS. *lām* = D. *leem* = G. *lehm*, loam, clay; akin to E. *lime*³.] Clay†; also, earth (archaic); also, a loose soil composed of clay and sand, esp. a kind containing organic matter and of great fertility; also, a mixture of clay, sand, straw, etc., used in making molds for founding, and in plastering walls, stopping holes, etc.—**loam,** *v. t.* To cover or stop with loam.—**loam'y,** *a.* Pertaining to, of the nature of, or resembling loam.

loan¹ (lōn), *n.* [Var. of *lane.*] A lane; also, an open, uncultivated space near a farm-house or a village, in which cows are milked. [Now Sc. and north. Eng.]

loan² (lōn), *n.* [ME. *lane, lone*, from Scand.: cf. Icel. *lān* = AS. *lǣn*, loan, grant; akin to AS. *lēon*, G. *leihen*, Goth. *leihwan*, lend, L. *linquere*, Gr. λείπειν, Skt. *ric-*, leave.] The act of lending; a grant of the use of something temporarily (as, the *loan* of a book; "Tho' I ride unarm'd, I do not doubt To find . . . arms On *loan*, or else for pledge," Tennyson's "Marriage of Geraint," 220); esp., a furnishing or advance of money for use, for a consideration (as, *loans* made by a bank at the current interest; a government *loan*, a loan made to a government by the public in buying a particular issue of bonds; to float a *loan* for municipal or industrial purposes); also, something lent, or furnished on condition of being returned; esp., a sum of money lent at interest.—**loan**², *v.* **I.** *tr.* To make a loan of, or lend (as, "Not only did we have nothing to pay for hiring one [a canoe], but we could not expect to have it *loaned*": H. Melville's "Omoo," lxvi.); esp., to lend (money) at interest. [Chiefly U. S.] **II.** *intr.* To make a loan or loans. [Chiefly U. S.]—**loan'a-ble,** *a.* That may be loaned; available for loaning, as capital.—**loan'er,** *n.*

loan-ing (lō'ning), *n.* Same as *loan*¹. [Sc. and north. Eng.]

loan=of-fice (lōn'of″is), *n.* An office for making loans; specif., a pawnbroker's shop; also, a public office for receiving subscriptions to a government loan.

loan=shark (lōn'shärk), *n.* One who loans money at an excessive rate of interest. [Colloq.]

loan=word (lōn'wėrd), *n.* [Tr. G. *lehnwort.*] A word borrowed or adopted from another language.

loath, loth (lōth), *a.* [AS. *lāth*, hostile, hateful, = Icel. *leidhr*, loathed, = D. *leed* = G. *leid*, sorry.] Hateful† or odious†; also, feeling repugnance or reluctance (as, "Though *loath*, yet must I be content": Shakspere's "3 Henry VI.," iv. 6. 48); often, reluctant, averse, or unwilling (to do something: as, "I'm *loath* to think you'd speak false to me," George Eliot's "Adam Bede," xxviii.; "I was *loth* to risk any opportunity of throwing light on this business," Scott's "Guy Mannering," xlix.).

loathe (lōᴛʜ), *v.*; *loathed, loathing.* [AS. *lāthian*, be hateful, < *lāth*, E. *loath.*] **I.** *intr.* To be hateful†; also, to feel hatred, disgust, or intense aversion. **II.** *tr.* To be hateful to†; arouse disgust or intense aversion in†; also, to feel hatred, disgust, or intense aversion for, or abhor (as, "He knew the model boy very well though—and *loathed* him": Mark Twain's "Tom Sawyer," i.); sometimes, to feel a physical disgust for (food, etc.).—**loathe,** *n.* Loathing. [Obs. or archaic.]—**loath-er** (lō'ᴛʜėr), *n.*—**loath-ful** (lōᴛʜ'fůl), *a.* Hateful, odious, or loathsome (now rare: as, "a *lothfull* sight," Spenser's "Faerie Queene," iii. 4. 52); also, reluctant or bashful (now Sc.).—**loath'ing,** *n.* The feeling of one who loathes; strong dislike mingled with disgust; intense aversion; abhorrence; sometimes, physical disgust, as for food.—**loath'ing-ly,** *adv.*

loath-ly¹ (lōᴛʜ'li), *a.* [AS. *lāthlīc*, < *lāth*, E. *loath.*] Hateful; disgusting; loathsome: as, "a *loathly* toad" (Thomson's "Castle of Indolence," i. 61). [Now literary.]—**loath'li-ness,** *n.*

loath-ly² (lōth'li), *adv.* [From *loath.*] In the manner of one who is loath; reluctantly; unwillingly.—**loath'ness,** *n.*

loath-some (lōᴛʜ'sum), *a.* Such as to excite loathing; hateful, odious, or disgusting (as, "Your respectable nephew is about as *loathsome* a little villain as crawls on the earth": Thackeray's "Newcomes," liv.); often, physically disgusting, or sickening (as, a *loathsome* disease; a *loathsome* stench).—**loath'some-ly,** *adv.*—**loath'some-ness,** *n.*

loaves (lōvz), *n.* Plural of *loaf*¹.

lob (lob), *n.* [Prob. vaguely imit., as suggesting something thick and heavy.] Something thick and lumpish; a lump or large piece of something (chiefly prov.); a large sum of money (prov.); also, a lout or bumpkin (now prov.: as, "Farewell, thou *lob* of spirits [Puck]," Shakspere's "Midsummer Night's Dream," ii. 1. 16); also, in *cricket*, a slow underhand ball; in *lawn-tennis*, a ball struck high to the back of the opponent's court.—**lob,** *v.*; *lobbed, lobbing.* **I.** *intr.* To move heavily or clumsily; in *lawn-tennis*, to lob a ball. **II.** *tr.* To throw heavily or clumsily; in *cricket*, to bowl with a slow movement; in *lawn-tennis*, to strike (a ball) high into the air to the back of the opponent's court.

lo-bar (lō'bạ̈r), *a.* Of or pertaining to a lobe, as of the lungs: as, *lobar* pneumonia.

lo-bate (lō'bāt), *a.* [NL. *lobatus.*] Having a lobe or lobes; lobed; sometimes, having the form of a lobe; in *ornith.*, noting or pertaining to a foot in which the individual toes have membranous flaps or lobes along the sides. Also **lo'-bat-ed** (-bā-ted).—**lo'bate-ly,** *adv.*—**lo-ba-tion** (lọ-bā'-shọn), *n.* Lobate formation.

lob-by (lob'i), *n.*; pl. *lobbies* (-iz). [ML. *lobia, lobium*, covered walk; from Teut.: see *lodge.*] A corridor, vestibule, or entrance-hall, as in a public building, often serving as an anteroom; also, the persons who frequent the approaches to a legislative chamber, esp. to influence the members.—**lob'by,** *v.*; *-bied, -bying.* **I.** *intr.* To frequent the lobby of a legislative chamber to influence the members; solicit the votes of members of a legislative body in the lobby or elsewhere. **II.** *tr.* To influence (legislators), or urge or procure the passage of (a bill), by lobbying.—**lob'by-ism,** *n.* The system of lobbying; the practices of those who lobby.—**lob'by-ist,** *n.*

lobe (lōb), *n.* [F. *lobe*, < ML. *lobus*, < Gr. λοβός, lobe.] A roundish projection or division, as of an organ, a leaf, etc.; specif., the soft, pendulous lower part of the external ear.—**lobed,** *a.* Having a lobe or lobes; lobate; specif., in *bot.*, of a leaf, having lobes or divisions extending less than halfway to the middle or the base.—**lobe'let,** *n.* A little lobe; a lobule.

lo-be-lia (lọ-bē'liạ), *n.* [NL.; from M. de *Lobel* (1538–1616), French botanist, physician to James I., of England.] Any of the herbaceous plants constituting the genus *Lobelia*, comprising many species, both wild and cultivated, with blue, red, yellow, or white flowers.—**lo-be-li-a'-ceous** (-li-ā'-shius), *a.* Belonging to the *Lobeliaceæ*, or lobelia family of plants (also classed as belonging to the *Campanulaceæ*).

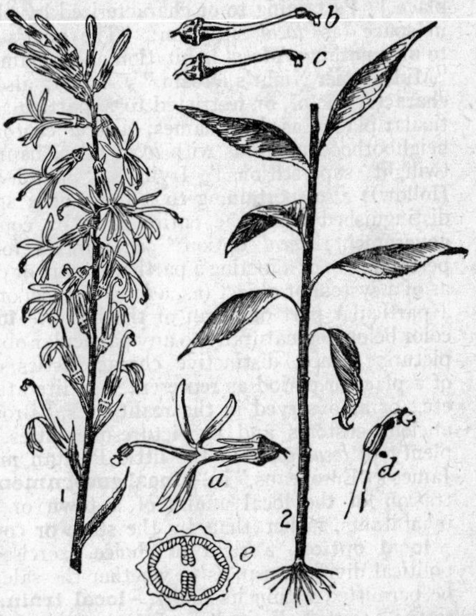

Lobelia (*L. cardinalis*, the Cardinal-flower). — *1*, inflorescence; *2*, lower part of stem; *a*, flower; *b*, stamen-tube inclosing pistil; *c*, pistil; *d*, upper part of pistil and stamen-tube; *e*, transverse section of fruit.

lob-lol-ly (lob'lol-i), *n.*; pl. *loblollies* (-iz). [Cf. *lob* and obs. prov. *lolly*, broth, boiled food.] Thick gruel or spoon-meat (now prov. Eng.); also, thick mud, swampy ground, or a swamp (southern U. S.); also, a bumpkin or lout (now prov. Eng.).—**lob'lol-ly=bay,** *n.* An ornamental white-flowered theaceous shrub or small tree, *Gordonia lasianthus*, of the southern U. S. See cut on following page.—**lob'lol-ly=pine,** *n.* A pine, *Pinus tæda*, of the southern U. S.

lob-scouse (lob'skous), *n.* [Origin obscure: cf. *loblolly.*] A kind of stew made of meat, potatoes, onions, etc., or (at sea) of salt meat, ship-biscuit, etc. [Prov. Eng. and nautical.]

Flower of Loblolly-bay.

Lob's (lobz) **pound.** [See *lob.*] Jail or prison (as, "Crowdero whom in irons bound, Thou basely threw'st into *Lob's pound*": Butler's "Hudibras," i. 3); hence, any situation of embarrassment or difficulty. [Now prov. Eng.]

lob-ster (lob'stėr), *n.* [AS. *loppestre*, < L. *locusta*, lobster, also locust.] Any of various large, edible, marine, stalk-eyed decapod crustaceans of the suborder *Macrura* and esp. of the genus *Homarus*, having two enormous claws and a long abdomen or so-called tail; any of various similar crustaceans, as certain craw-fishes; also, a British soldier (colloq.: orig. in allusion to the armor of cuirassiers, later, as also in 'boiled lobster,' to the characteristic red coat); also, a gullible, foolish, or stupid person (slang).—**lob'ster-ing,** *n.* The process or business of catching lobsters.

American Lobster (*Homarus americanus*).

lob-ule (lob'ūl), *n.* [NL. *lobulus*, dim. of ML. *lobus*, E. *lobe.*] A small lobe; a subdivision of a lobe.—**lob-u-lar** (lob'ū-lạ̈r), *a.*

lo-cal (lō'kạl), *a.* [F. *local*, < LL. *localis*, < L. *locus*, place.] Pertaining to or characterized by place, or position in space (as, *local* situation; "The poet's pen . . . gives to airy nothing A *local* habitation and a name," Shakspere's "Midsummer Night's Dream," v. 1. 17); also, pertaining to, characteristic of, or restricted to a particular place or particular places (as, *local* names; a *local* custom; "The whole neighborhood abounds with *local* tales, haunted spots, and twilight superstitions," Irving's "Sketch-Book," Sleepy Hollow); also, pertaining to a town or a small district as distinguished from the entire state or country (as, *local* government; *local* option: see phrases following); also, pertaining to or affecting a particular part or particular parts, as of a system or object (as, a *local* disease, one which affects a particular part or organ of the body).—**local color,** the color belonging naturally to any particular object or part in a picture; hence, distinctive characteristics or peculiarities of a place or period as represented in literature, the drama, etc., or as observed in the reality (as, "Brought up among ancient customs and in picturesque cities, he yet found plenty of *local color* in the little Puritan metropolis": H. James's "Europeans," i.).—**local government,** the administration of the local affairs of a town or district by its inhabitants, rather than by the state or country at large.—**local option,** a right of choice exercised by a minor political division, esp. as to whether the sale of liquor shall be permitted within its limits.—**local train,** a train which serves a certain limited district; an accommodation train.—**lo'cal,** *n.* One who or that which is local; one living or employed in a particular place or district; a newspaper item of local interest; a local train.

lo-cale (lọ-kál' or -käl'), *n.* [For F. *local*, noun use of *local*, adj.: see *local, a.*] A place or locality, esp. with reference to events or circumstances connected with it.

lo-cal-ism (lō'kạl-izm), *n.* Local character; attachment to a particular locality; provincialism; also, a local expression, custom, or the like.

lo-cal-i-ty (lọ-kal'i-ti), *n.*; pl. *-ties* (-tiz). [LL. *localitas.*] The state or fact of being local, or having place, or being in a place; also, the place in which a thing is or occurs, esp. the geographical place or situation (as, the *locality* of a mineral; the *locality* of a crime); a place, spot, or district, with or without reference to things or persons in it (as, "Feeling unsafe . . . in this *locality*, their colonels had led them into the new town": Motley's "Dutch Republic," v. 3); in *phren.*, the faculty of recognizing and remembering places and locations.

lo-cal-ize (lō'kạl-īz), *v. t.*; *-ized, -izing.* To make local; fix in, or assign or restrict to, a particular place or locality.—**lo'cal-iz-a-ble** (-ī-zạ-bl), *a.*—**lo''cal-i-za'tion** (-i-zā'shọn), *n.*

lo-cal-ly (lō'kạl-i), *adv.* In a local manner or respect; with regard to place (as, to be far separated *locally*); also, in a particular place, or in particular places (as, outbreaks of the disease occurred *locally*).

lo-cate (lō'kāt), *v.*; *-cated, -cating.* [L. *locatus*, pp. of *locare*, < *locus*, place.] **I.** *tr.* To set, fix, or establish in a place, situation, or locality (as, towns *located* along a river; to *locate* one's headquarters in New York); place; settle; also, to designate or determine the situation or limits of (chiefly U. S.: as, to *locate* a land-grant or a mining-claim); also, to discover the place or location of (as, "Udine keeps itself dark nowadays, and the Austrian sea-planes . . . find it easier to *locate* Venice," H. G. Wells's "Italy, France, and Britain at War," ii. 1; to *locate* a leak in a gas-pipe); also, to refer (something), as by opinion or statement, to a particular place (as, to *locate* the garden of Eden in Babylonia). **II.** *intr.* To establish one's self in a place; settle: as, "Beneath whatever roof they *locate*, they disturb the peace of mind and happiness of some confiding female" (Dickens's "Pickwick Papers," xviii.)—**lo-ca-tion** (lọ-kā'shọn), *n.* [L. *locatio(n-).*] The act of locating, or the state of being located; position, situation, or settlement in a place; hence, a place or situation occupied (as, a house in a fine *location*); a site (as, a *location* for a mill); a place of settlement or residence (as, a good *location* for a doctor); also, a tract of land located, or of designated situation or limits (as, a mining *location*); in South Africa, a portion of land set apart for the residence of the natives; specif, in the moving-picture industry, the finding and securing of places, outside of the studio, affording suitable environment for photographing particular plays, incidents, etc.; hence, a place suitable or used for the purpose.—**loc-a-tive** (lok'ạ-tiv). In *gram.*: **I.** *a.* Indicating place, or the place where or wherein: applied to a case in declension in Latin and some other languages, or to its forms or constructions. **II.** *n.* The locative case, or a word in that case.—**lo-ca-tor** (lō'kā-tọr), *n.*

loch (loch), *n.* [Gael.: cf. *lough.*] A lake (as, *Loch* Lomond); also, an arm of the sea, esp. when narrow or partially landlocked. [Sc.]

lo-chi-a (lō'ki-ạ̈ or lok'i-ạ̈), *n. pl.* [NL., < Gr. λόχια, neut. pl. of λόχιος, pertaining to childbirth, < λόχος, lying-in, childbirth.] In *med.*, the liquid discharge from the uterus after childbirth.—**lo'chi-al,** *a.*

lo-ci (lō'sī), *n.* Plural of *locus.*

lock[1] (lok), *n.* [AS. *locc* = D. *lok* = G. *locke* = Icel. *lokkr*, lock of hair.] A tress or portion of hair; *pl.*, the hair of the head; also, *sing.*, a flock or small portion of wool, cotton, flax, etc.; also, a quantity, esp. a small quantity, of anything (now Sc. and prov. Eng.: as, a *lock* of hay or straw; a *lock* of meal).

lock[2] (lok), *n.* [AS. *loc*, fastening; from the root of AS. *lūcan*, D. *luiken*, Icel. *lūka*, Goth. *galūkan*, shut, close.] A contrivance for fastening or securing something; specif., an appliance for securing a door, gate, lid, drawer, or the like, in position when closed, and consisting of a bolt or system of bolts propelled and withdrawn by a mechanism operated by a key or other device; also, a contrivance to keep a wheel from rotating, as in descending a hill; also, the mechanism in a firearm by means of which the charge is exploded; also, an inclosed portion of a canal, river, etc., with gates at each end, for raising or lowering vessels from one level to another; also, an air-tight chamber, or one of a series of such chambers, used in entering or leaving a compartment in which the air-pressure is above normal (cf. *air-lock*); also, a locking or fastening together; a state of being locked or fastened together; also, any of various grapples or holds in wrestling.—**lock**[2], *v.* **I.** *tr.* To fasten (a door, gate, etc.) by the operation of a lock; secure (a building, etc.) by so fastening its doors, gates, or the like (often with *up*); also, to shut in a place fastened by a lock or locks, as for security or restraint (with *up*, *in*, etc.: as, to *lock* up silver in a safe; to *lock* a prisoner in a cell); hence, to inclose, surround, or hem in (as, a vessel *locked* in ice; "With eddying whirl the waters *lock* Yon treeless mound forlorn," Holmes's "Agnes," ii.); render secure or inaccessible, as if in a locked receptacle (as, "She would never mention his name, but kept it *locked* in her bosom": Aldrich's "Story of a Bad Boy," v.); invest (money) in something not readily convertible into cash (often with *up*); hold fast in some condition (as, *locked* in sleep); also, to exclude by or as by a lock (usually with *out*: as, "Wherefore didst thou *lock* me forth to-day?" Shakspere's "Comedy of Errors," iv. 4. 98; "My heavy son . . . Shuts up his windows, *locks* fair daylight out," Shakspere's "Romeo and Juliet," i. 1. 145); hence, to subject (employees) to a lockout (with *out*); also, to make fast or immovable by or as by a lock (as, to *lock* a wheel); fasten or fix firmly, as by engaging parts (often with *up*); also, to join or unite firmly by interlinking or intertwining (as, to *lock* one's arm through another's arm; to *lock* hands together; two animals *lock* horns in combat); embrace closely (as, "*Lock'd* in each other's arms we stood": M. Arnold's "Switzerland," iii.); grapple in combat (as, "One glance . . . showed me Hands and his companion *locked* together in deadly wrestle": Stevenson's "Treasure Island," xxiii.); also, to move (a vessel) by means of a lock or locks, as in a canal; furnish with locks, as a canal. **II.** *intr.* To become locked (as, this door *locks* with a key, or will not *lock*); become fastened, fixed, or interlocked; also, to go or pass by means of a lock or locks, as a vessel.

lock-age (lok′ā̤j), *n.* The construction, use, or operation of locks, as in a canal or stream; the passing of a vessel through a lock or locks; also, works forming a lock, as in a canal or stream; locks collectively; also, the amount of elevation and descent effected by a lock or system of locks; also, toll paid for passage through a lock or locks.

lock-er (lok′ėr), *n.* One who or that which locks; also, a chest, drawer, compartment, closet, or the like, that may be locked; *naut.*, a chest or compartment in which to stow things.

lock-et (lok′et), *n.* [F. *loquet*, latch, catch, dim. of OF. *loc*, lock, from Teut., and akin to E. *lock*[2].] A catch or fastening for a necklace or other ornament†; also, a small case, as of gold, for holding a miniature portrait, a lock of hair, or other keepsake, and worn as an ornament, as on a necklace.

lock-fast (lok′fâst), *a.* Fastened or secured by a lock: as, "All the *lockfast* places had been broken open in quest of the chart" (Stevenson's "Treasure Island," xxv.). [Chiefly Sc.]

lock-jaw (lok′jâ), *n.* In *pathol.*, a form of tetanus in which the jaws become firmly locked together.

lock-less (lok′les), *a.* Having no lock (for fastening, etc.).

lock-out (lok′out), *n.* The act of locking out; the exclusion of persons from a place; esp., the refusal of an employer or employers to furnish work to employees, intended as a means of coercion.

lock-smith (lok′smith), *n.* One who makes or mends locks.

lock=step (lok′step), *n.* A mode of marching in very close file, in which the leg of each person moves with and closely behind the corresponding leg of the person ahead.

lock=stitch (lok′stich), *n.* A sewing-machine stitch in which two threads are locked together at small intervals.

lock-up (lok′up), *n.* The act of locking up, or the state of being locked up; also, a place for the temporary detention of persons under arrest; a jail.

lo-co (lō′kō), *a.* [Sp.] Insane; crazy. [Western U. S.]—**lo′co,** *n.* Loco-weed; also, loco-disease.—**lo′co,** *v. t.*; *-coed, -coing.* To poison with loco-weed; hence, to make crazy. [Western U. S.]—**lo′co=dis-ease′,** *n.* A disease affecting the brain of animals, caused by eating loco-weed.

lo-co-fo-co (lō-kọ-fō′kō), *n.*; pl. *-cos* (-kōz). [A made name for a self-lighting cigar or match, said to be < *loco-* in *locomotive* (erron. supposed to mean 'self-moving') + L. *focus*, hearth, fireplace.] A kind of self-lighting cigar†; also, a friction-match†; also [*cap.*], in *U. S. hist.*, a member of the radical (or 'equal rights') faction of the Democratic party in New York State about 1835; also, in disparagement, any Democrat of that period.

lo-co-mo-bile (lō-kọ-mō′bil), *a.* [L. *loco*, abl. of *locus*, place, + *mobilis*, E. *mobile.*] Having the power of moving from place to place; self-propelled.

lo-co-mo-tion (lō-kọ-mō′shọn), *n.* [L. *loco*, abl. of *locus*, place, + *motio(n-)*, E. *motion.*] The act or power of moving from place to place: as, "He began walking about the little room, as if such *locomotion* tended to bring him out of it" (J. H. Newman's "Callista," xxii.).

lo-co-mo-tive (lō-kọ-mō′tiv). [L. *loco*, abl. of *locus*, place, + ML. *motivus*, E. *motive.*] **I.** *a.* Of or pertaining to movement from place to place (as, the *locomotive* faculty; *locomotive* power); also, serving to produce such movement, or adapted for or used in locomotion (as, *locomotive* organs); also, having the power of locomotion; moving from place to place by its own powers of locomotion, as an animal; that is constantly traveling from place to place (as, "The Spanish troops . . . surrounded by their women, and constantly increasing swarms of children, constituted a *locomotive* city of considerable population": Motley's "Dutch Republic," iv. 1); specif., moving or traveling by means of its own mechanism, as a machine or vehicle, esp. a steam-engine adapted to draw or move cars on a railroad. **II.** *n.* A locomotive engine, motor, or vehicle; esp., a locomotive engine or motor (commonly a steam-engine) on wheels, used to draw or move cars on a railroad.

lo-co-mo-tor (lō-kọ-mō′tọr). [L. *loco*, abl. of *locus*, place, + *motor*, E. *motor.*] **I.** *n.* One who or that which has locomotive power. **II.** *a.* Of or pertaining to locomotion.—**locomotor ataxia,** in *pathol.*, a degenerative disease of the spinal cord, marked by loss of control over the muscular movements in walking and otherwise; tabes dorsalis.—**lo-co-mo′to-ry** (-tọ-ri), *a.* Pertaining to or having locomotive power.

lo-co=weed (lō′kọ-wēd), *n.* [See *loco.*] Any of various fabaceous plants of the genera *Astragalus*, *Aragallus*, etc., of the western U. S., producing loco-disease in sheep, horses, etc.

Loco-weed (*Aragallus*), with the fruit.

loc-u-lar (lok′ṳ̄-lä̤r), *a.* [See *loculus.*] Having one or more loculi, chambers, or cells: chiefly in composition, as in *bilocular*. Also **loc′u-late** (-lāt).

loc-ule (lok′ūl), *n.* A loculus.

loc-u-lose, loc-u-lous (lok′ṳ̄-lōs, -lus), *a.* [L. *loculosus.*] Divided into loculi or cells.

loc-u-lus (lok′ṳ̄-lus), *n.*; pl. *-li* (-lī). [L., dim. of *locus*, place.] In ancient tombs, a compartment or recess, as for a body or an urn; in *bot.*, *zoöl.*, and *anat.*, a small compartment or chamber; a cell.

lo-cum te-nens (lō′kum tē′nenz). [ML., '(one) holding place.'] One temporarily holding the place or office of another; a deputy or substitute.—**lo′cum=te′nen-cy,** *n.*

lo-cus (lō′kus), *n.*; pl. *loci* (-sī). [L., place.] A place; a locality; esp., a place or passage in a book or the like; the place in a text where a particular passage occurs, esp. as designated by part, chapter, volume, page, stanza, line, etc.; in *math.*, a curve or other figure considered as generated by a moving point, line, or surface; the place of all the points, and of only those points, which satisfy a given condition.

lo-cust (lō′kust), *n.* [L. *locusta*, locust, also lobster: cf. *lobster.*] Any of the grasshoppers with short antennæ which constitute the family *Acrididæ*, certain species of which migrate in large numbers, destroying vegetation, as *Pachytylus migratorius* and *P. cinerascens*, particularly destructive old-world species, and *Melanoplus* (or *Caloptenus*) *spretus*, which does great damage in western North America ('Rocky Mountain locust'); also, any of various cicadas, as *Cicada septendecim* ('seventeen-year locust': see *cicada*); also, a thorny-branched, white-flowered American

Migratory Locust (*Pachytylus migratorius*), natural size.

fabaceous tree, *Robinia pseudacacia*, or its durable wood; any of various other trees, as the carob and the honey-locust.

Locust (*Robinia pseudacacia*), with pod and flower.

lo-cus-ta (lō-kus′tą̈), *n.*; pl. *-tæ* (-tē). [NL. use of L. *locusta*, E. *locust.*] In *bot.*, the inflorescence or spikelet of grasses.

lo-cust=bean (lō′kust-bēn), *n.* The fruit of the carob.

lo-cu-tion (lō-kū′shǫn), *n.* [L. *locutio(n-)*, < *loqui*, speak.] Speaking† or utterance†; also, speech as expressing thought† (as, figures of *locution*); also, style of speech or verbal expression, or phraseology (as, to be accustomed to the rustic *locution*); also, a particular form of expression, or a phrase or expression (as, unfamiliar or striking *locutions*; foreign *locutions* are observable in some localities).

loc-u-to-ry (lok′ū-tō-ri), *n.*; pl. *-ries* (-riz). [ML. *locutorium*, < L. *locutor*, speaker, < *loqui*, speak.] A room or place in a monastery set apart for conversation.

lode (lōd), *n.* [AS. *lād*, way, course, carrying (see *load*), = OHG. *leita*, procession, = Icel. *leidh*, way, course; from a Teut. verb (AS. *līthan*, OHG. *līdan*, Icel. *līdha*, Goth. *-leithan*) meaning 'go,' whence also E. *lead*¹.] A way or road (now prov. Eng.); also, a watercourse (now prov. Eng.); in *mining*, a vein-like metalliferous deposit; any body of ore with more or less definite boundaries separating it from the surrounding rocks.—**lode′star, load′star,** *n.* A star that shows the way; esp., the pole-star; hence, fig., something that serves as a guide, or on which the attention is fixed (as, "Lady Isabelle, whose looks had been for so many days his *loadstar*": Scott's "Quentin Durward," xix.).—**lode′stone, load′stone,** *n.* A variety of magnetite which possesses magnetic polarity and attracts iron; a piece of this serving as a magnet; fig., something that attracts.

lodge (loj), *n.* [OF. F. *loge*, orig. 'leafy shelter'; from Teut. (cf. G. *laube*, arbor), and akin to E. *leaf* and *lobby*.] A small, slight or rude shelter or habitation, as of boughs, poles, skins, earth, rough boards, or the like (as, "So to the sylvan *lodge* They came, that like Pomona's arbour smiled," Milton's "Paradise Lost," v. 377; the *lodges* of the North American Indians); a booth, cabin, or hut; hence, a house used as a temporary abode, as in the hunting season; a house or cottage, as in a park or on an estate, occupied by a caretaker, gardener, or the like; in general, a place of abode or sojourn; the habitation of an animal, now esp. of a beaver or an otter; also, a workshop, esp. of masons or builders†; hence, the meeting-place of a branch of a secret society; the members composing the branch, or the meeting itself; a secret society as a whole.—**lodge,** *v.*; *lodged, lodging.* [OF. *logier* (F. *loger*), < *loge*.] **I.** *tr.* To furnish with a habitation or quarters, esp. temporarily (as, "The chief man . . . received us, and *lodged* us three days courteously": Acts, xxviii. 7); serve as a habitation or shelter for, as a house does; shelter; harbor; specif., to furnish with a room or rooms in one's house for payment, or have as a lodger; also, to put or deposit, as in a place, for storage or keeping (as, "I lay all night in the cave where I had *lodged* my provisions," Swift's "Gulliver's Travels," iii. 1; "The marriage certificate . . . had been found . . . and carefully *lodged* in the hands of Lady Lothrop," Mrs. Stowe's "Oldtown Folks," xxx.); fix or implant (as, "With such thoughts . . . *Lodged* in his breast": Milton's "Paradise Regained," i. 301); bring or send into a particular place or position (as, to *lodge* a bullet in one's heart); vest (power, etc.); lay (information, a complaint, etc.) before a court or the like; also, to beat down or lay flat, as vegetation in a storm (see Shakspere's "Macbeth," iv. 1. 55); also, to track (a deer) to its lair. **II.** *intr.* To have a habitation or quarters, esp. temporarily, as in a place or house; dwell, reside, or sojourn; specif., to live in hired quarters in another's house; also, to have the seat, or be fixed or implanted, in something (as, "Sure something holy *lodges* in that breast": Milton's "Comus," 246); come to rest, light, land, or be caught in a place or position (as, the kite *lodged* in a tree); also, of vegetation, to be beaten down or laid flat.—**lodge′a-ble,** *a.* Suitable for lodging or dwelling in: as, "The house is oldfashioned and irregular, but *lodgeable* and commodious" (Smollett's "Humphry Clinker," after Oct. 4).—**lodg′er,** *n.* One who or that which lodges; esp., one who lives in hired quarters in another's house.—**lodg′ing,** *n.* The act of one who or that which lodges; dwelling or abode; also, accommodation in a house, esp. in rooms for hire (as, to furnish board and *lodging*); also, a place of abode, esp. a temporary one; *pl.*, a room or rooms hired for residence in another's house.—**lodg′ing=house,** *n.* A house in which lodgings are let, esp. a house other than an inn or hotel.—**lodg′ment, lodge′ment,** *n.* The act of lodging, or the state of being lodged; also, a lodging-place; lodgings; also, something lodged or deposited; *milit.*, a position or foothold gained from an enemy, or an intrenchment made upon it.

lod-i-cule (lod′i-kūl), *n.* [L. *lodicula*, dim. of *lodix*, coverlet.] In *bot.*, one of the small scales outside of the stamens in the flower of grasses.

lo-ess (lō′es, G. lės), *n.* [G. *löss*.] A loamy deposit, usually yellowish and calcareous, common in the Mississippi valley and in Europe and Asia.

loft (lôft), *n.* [AS. *loft*, from Scand.: cf. Icel. *lopt*, the air, sky, an upper room, and E. *lift*¹ and *lift*².] The air† or sky† (cf. *aloft*); also, a floor or room above another, esp. that directly beneath the roof; an attic; the apartment over a stable, used for storing hay, straw, etc.; a gallery in a church, hall, etc.; any upper story of a warehouse or other mercantile building, or of a factory (U. S.); in *golf*, the slope of the face of a club backward from the vertical, tending to drive the ball upward; also, the act of lofting, or a lofting stroke.—**loft,** *v.* **I.** *tr.* To provide (a house, etc.) with a loft; in *golf*, to give loft to, as a club or its head; also, to hit (the ball) into the air or over an obstacle; also, to clear (an obstacle) thus. **II.** *intr.* In *golf*, to loft the ball.—**loft′er,** *n.* In *golf*, a lofting-iron.

loft-i-ly (lôf′ti-li), *adv.* In a lofty manner.—**loft′i-ness,** *n.*

loft-ing=i-ron (lôf′ting-ī″ėrn), *n.* In *golf*, an iron-headed club used in lofting the ball.

loft-y (lôf′ti), *a.*; compar. *loftier*, superl. *loftiest.* [From *loft.*] Extending high in the air, or of imposing height (as, *lofty* mountains; *lofty* towers); tall (as, "The men . . . are of *lofty* stature, scarcely ever less than six feet in height": H. Melville's "Typee," xxiv.); also, being high in the air, or at a great height (as, "Then from his *lofty* stand on that high tree Down he alights": Milton's "Paradise Lost," iv. 395); fig., exalted in rank, dignity, or character (as, "Thus saith the high and *lofty* One that inhabiteth eternity," Isa. lvii. 15; *lofty* station or fame; *lofty* aims); elevated in style or sentiment, as writings, language, etc.; also, haughty, proud, or affectedly superior (as, *lofty* looks; a *lofty* contempt for others; "He . . . treated them with *lofty* toleration," J. Conrad's "Rescue," i. 1).

log¹ (log). [ME. *logge*; prob. imit.: cf. *lob* and *clog*.] **I.** *n.* An unhewn portion or length of the trunk or a large limb of a felled tree; fig., something inert or heavy; a stolid, dull, or stupid person; also, *naut.*, a device for measuring the rate of a ship's progress, consisting orig. of a thin quadrant of wood ('log-chip') let out into the water at the end of a long line ('log-line') unwound from a reel, the number of divisions (knots) of the line let out in a certain time indicating the number of nautical miles the ship is sailing per hour; also, the official record of a ship's voyage; a log-book. **II.** *a.* Made or built of logs (as, a *log* cabin; a *log* house); made out of a log, as a canoe; also, of or pertaining to logs (as, a *log* boom, for confining floating logs or timber).—**log**¹, *v.*; *logged, logging.* **I.** *tr.* To cut (trees) into logs; cut down the trees or timber on (land); also, *naut.*, to enter in a

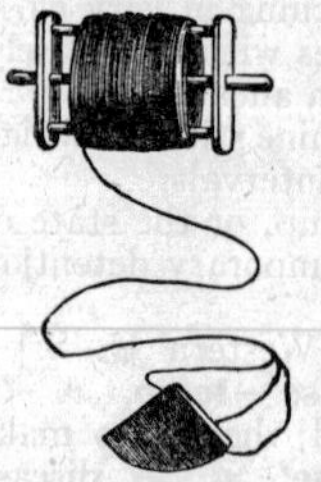

Log and Reel.

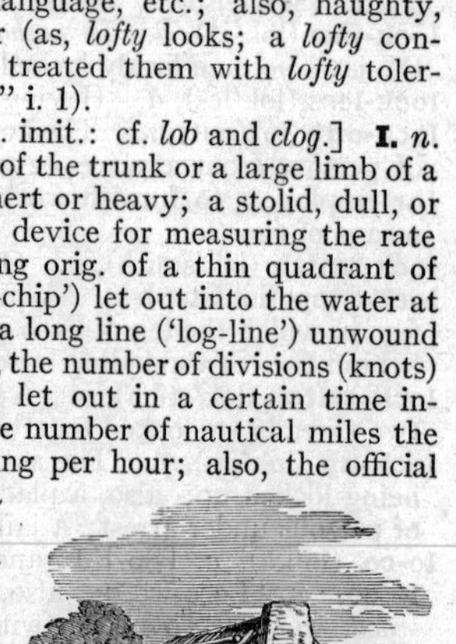

Log Cabin.

ship's log (or, in general, to set down or record); also, to enter the name of in the log as an offender, with a penalty attached, or to fine by such entry; also, to travel (a distance) according to the indication of the ship's log. **II.** *intr.* To cut down trees and get out logs from the forest for timber.

log² (log or lōg), *n.* [Heb.] A Hebrew liquid and dry measure, equal to the seventy-second part of the bath and the fourth part of the cab respectively.

log³ (log), *v. t.* or *i.*; *logged, logging.* [Perhaps imit.: cf. *logan-stone.*] To rock to and fro. [Prov. Eng.]

lo-gan-ber-ry (lō′gạn-ber″i), *n.*; pl. *-berries* (-iz). [From J. H. *Logan*, of California, the originator.] The large, dark-red fruit of a plant which is a hybrid between a variety of blackberry and a variety of raspberry; also, the plant.

lo-ga-ni-a-ceous (lọ-gā-ni-ā′shius), *a.* [NL. *Logania*, the typical genus; named from James *Logan* (1674–1751), of Philadelphia.] Belonging to the *Loganiaceæ*, a family of herbs, shrubs, and trees of tropical and subtropical regions, including the nux vomica tree and other plants with poisonous properties.

log-an=stone, log-gan=stone (log′ạn-stōn), *n.* [Cf. *log*³.] A rock so balanced on its base that it rocks to and fro readily, as under pressure of the hand or of the wind; a rocking-stone.

log-a-œ-dic (log-ạ-ē′dik). [LL. *logaœdicus*, < Gr. λογαοιδικός, < λόγος, speech, prose, + ἀοιδή, song.] In *anc. pros.*: **I.** *a.* Composed of dactyls and trochees or of anapæsts and iambi, producing a movement somewhat suggestive of prose: as, *logaœdic* verse. **II.** *n.* A logaœdic verse.

log-a-rithm (log′ạ-rithm or -riᴛʜm), *n.* [NL. *logarithmus*, < Gr. λόγος, proportion, + ἀριθμός, number.] In *math.*, the exponent of that power to which a fixed number (called the *base*) must be raised in order to produce a given number (called the *antilogarithm*); one of a tabulated series or system of such exponents, used for abridging computations. See *characteristic*, *n.*, and *mantissa.*—**log-a-rith′mic** (-rith′mik or -riᴛʜ′mik), *a.*—**log-a-rith′mi-cal-ly,** *adv.*

log=book (log′bůk), *n.* *Naut.*, a book in which are officially recorded the indications of the log, as well as the weather and other important particulars of a ship's voyage; the record itself; hence, in general, a journal of travel; a record of proceedings.

log=chip (log′chip), *n.* *Naut.*, the quadrant of wood attached to a log-line. See *log*¹, *n.*

loge (lōzh), *n.* [F.: see *lodge.*] A box in a theater or opera-house.

log′gan=stone, *n.* See *logan-stone.*

logged (logd), *p. a.* Cut into logs, as trees; cleared, as land by the cutting of timber; also, inert or unwieldy, like a log; water-logged, as a vessel; also, stagnant, as water.

log-ger (log′ėr), *n.* One engaged in logging, or cutting down trees and getting out logs from the forest; also, a machine for loading logs upon cars, etc.; also, a tractor employed in logging, as for skidding the logs to the loader, and hauling them loaded on sledges out of the forest.

Logger (for loading logs). — *a*, temporary base or bridge over track; *b*, hauling-boom; *c*, loading-boom; *d*, sluing-table; *e*, hauling-ropes; *f*, block for lifting and loading, with ropes and hook; *g*, engine-house; *h, h*, guy-ropes. About 35 feet high.

log-ger-head (log′ėr-hed), *n.* [Cf. *log*¹.] A large, thick head; hence, a thick-headed or stupid person; a blockhead; also, a ball or bulb of iron with a long handle, used, after being heated, to melt tar, heat liquids, etc.; also, a rounded post in the stern of a whale-boat, around which the harpoon-line is passed; also, a large-headed marine turtle, *Thalassochelys caretta*, of the Atlantic Ocean; also, a small American shrike, *Lanius ludovicianus* (see *butcher-bird*).—**at loggerheads,** contending over differences of opinion; engaged in dispute.

log-gia (loj′iạ, It. lôd′jä), *n.*; pl. *loggias*, It. *loggie* (lôd′jā). [It., = E. *lodge.*] A gallery or arcade open to the air on at least one side, esp. one contained within the body of a building at a height of one or more stories and serving as an open-air room.

Loggia, Ospedale Maggiore, Milan, Italy.

log-ging (log′-ing), *n.* The process, work, or business of cutting down trees and getting out logs from the forest for timber.

log-gy (log′i), *a.* [Cf. *log*¹ and *logy.*] Thick; also, heavy; sluggish. [Chiefly prov. Eng.]

log-ic (loj′ik), *n.* [OF. F. *logique*, < ML. *logica*, < Gr. λογική, prop. fem. of λογικός, pertaining to reason, < λόγος, reason: see *Logos.*] The science of reasoning; a particular exposition of this science, or a treatise upon it; also, the system or principles of reasoning applicable to a particular branch of knowledge or study; also, reasoning or argumentation, or an instance of it (as, "Vociferated *logic* kills me quite," Cowper's "Conversation," 113; "She could not cope with Lancelot's quaint *logic*," Kingsley's "Yeast," iii.); also, logical propriety, as in reasoning or arguments; hence, reason or sound sense, as in utterances or actions; also, a means of proving or convincing (as, "A certain Grand Monarch . . . writ upon his great guns—Ratio ultima Regum, The *Logic* of Kings": Addison, in "Spectator," 239); convincing force (as, the irresistible *logic* of facts).—**log′i-cal,** *a.* Of or pertaining to logic (as, *logical* terms; *logical* subtleties); according to the principles of logic (as, *logical* reasoning; a *logical* inference); hence, reasonable, or reasonably to be expected (as, war was the *logical* consequence of these conditions); also, reasoning in accordance with the principles of logic, or correctly, as a person, the mind, etc.—**log-i-cal′i-ty** (-kal′i-ti), **log′i-cal-ness,** *n.*—**log′i-cal-ly,** *adv.*—**lo-gi-cian** (lọ-jish′ạn), *n.* One skilled in logic.

log-i-on (log′i-on), *n.*; pl. *logia* (-ạ). [Gr. λόγιον, announcement, oracle, < λόγος, speech: see *Logos.*] A traditional saying or maxim, as of a religious teacher; esp. [often *cap.*], a saying of Jesus (used esp. with reference to sayings of Jesus contained in collections supposed to have been among the sources of the present Gospels, or to sayings ascribed to Jesus but not recorded in the Gospels).

lo-gis-tic (lọ-jis′tik), *a.* [Gr. λογιστικός, < λογίζεσθαι, reckon, calculate, < λόγος, account, reckoning: see *Logos.*] Pertaining to reckoning or calculation; also, pertaining to military logistics; in *math.*, logarithmic; also, sexagesimal. —**lo-gis′tics,** *n.* The art of arithmetical calculation; also, the branch of military science concerned with transportation and supply, arrangements for campaigning, etc.

log=line (log′līn), *n.* *Naut.*, the line of a log. See *log*¹, *n.*

logo-. Form of Gr. λόγος, word, speech, used in combination.

log-o-gram (log′ọ-gram), *n.* [See *logo-* and *-gram.*] A logograph; also, a single character, or a combination of characters regarded as a unit, representing a whole word, as in shorthand.—**log″o-gram-mat′ic** (-grạ-mat′ik), *a.*

log-o-graph (log′ọ-gråf), *n.* [See *logo-* and *-graph.*] A logograph; also, a logogram, as in shorthand; also, an instrument for recording spoken sounds.—**log-o-graph′ic** (-graf′ik), *a.* Of or pertaining to logography; also, consisting of characters or signs each representing a single word.—**lo-gog-ra-phy** (lọ-gog′rạ-fi), *n.* [See *-graphy.*] A method of printing employing types bearing words and syllables of frequent occurrence (cf. *logotype*); also, a method of reporting without stenography, each of several reporters in succession taking down a few words (in use in the French National Assembly, 1790–92).

log-o-griph (log′ọ̄-grif), *n.* [F. *logogriphe*, < Gr. λόγος, word, + γρῖφος, fishing-basket, riddle.] A puzzle in which a certain word, and other words formed from any or all of its letters, must be guessed from indications given in a set of verses; also, an anagram, or a puzzle involving anagrams.

lo-gom-a-chy (lọ̄-gom′ạ-ki), *n.*; pl. *-chies* (-kiz). [Gr. λογομαχία: see *logo-* and *-machy.*] Contention about words, or in words merely; also, a game played with cards, each bearing one letter, with which words are formed.

Log-os (log′os), *n.* [Gr. λόγος, word, speech, also reason, account, reckoning, proportion, < λέγειν, speak: see *legion.*] In *theol.*, Jesus Christ, the Divine Word (see John, i. 1, 14); the second person of the Trinity.

log-o-thete (log′ọ̄-thēt), *n.* [LGr. λογοθέτης, auditor of accounts, < Gr. λόγος, account, + τιθέναι, set.] Orig., an auditor of accounts; hence, any of various officers of the Byzantine Empire, as the head of an administrative department; also, a chancellor; in the *Gr. Ch.*, a lay officer acting as the representative of the patriarch of Constantinople at the Porte and elsewhere.

log-o-type (log′ọ̄-tīp), *n.* [See *logo-* and *type.*] In *printing*, a single type bearing two or more distinct (not combined) letters, or a syllable or word. Cf. *ligature.*—**log′o-ty-py** (-tī-pi), *n.*

log=roll (log′rōl), *v.* [Back-formation from *log-rolling.*] **I.** *tr.* To procure the passage of (a bill) by log-rolling. **II.** *intr.* To engage in political log-rolling.—**log′=roll″er,** *n.*

log=roll-ing (log′rō″ling), *n.* The action of rolling logs to a particular place; a joining of forces for the purpose of handling logs, as of a number of neighbors to assist one of them; hence, the combining of two or more persons to assist one of them, in consideration of like combined assistance in the interest of each of the others in return (used esp. with reference to legislators).

log-wood (log′wu̇d), *n.* The heavy, brownish-red heartwood of a West Indian and Central American cæsalpiniaceous tree, *Hæmatoxylon campechianum*, much used in dyeing and to some extent in medicine; also, the tree itself.

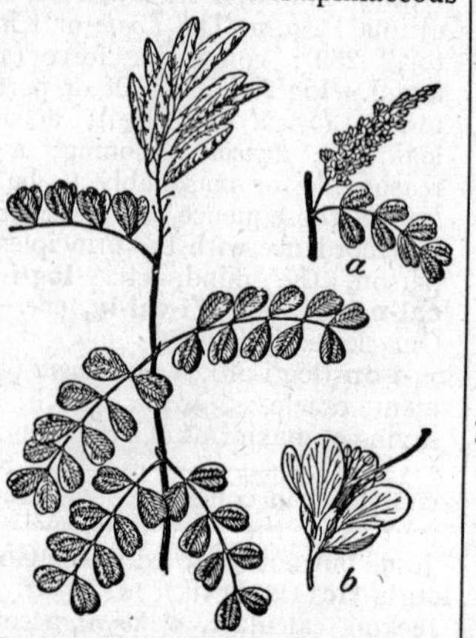

Branch with Fruits of Logwood. — *a*, inflorescence; *b*, flower.

lo-gy (lō′gi), *a.* [Cf. *loggy.*] Heavy; sluggish; dull. [U. S.]

-logy. [Gr. -λογία, < -λόγος, speaking, one speaking, < λέγειν, speak, also pick, gather, tell, recount: see *legion*, and cf. *Logos.*] A noun termination meaning 'a speaking,' 'discourse,' 'account,' 'doctrine,' 'science,' as in *astrology*, *eulogy*, *genealogy*, *physiology*, *tautology*, *teratology*, *theology*, and numerous other words, including many formed in English after this type. For other uses of *-logy*, of different meaning and history but all referable ultimately to Gr. λέγειν, see *analogy*, *anthology*, *martyrology*, *menology*, *micrology*, *misology*, *necrology*, *philology*, *trilogy*.

loin (loin), *n.* [OF. *loigne*, *longe* (F. *longe*), < L. *lumbus*, loin.] The part or parts of the body of man or of a quadruped animal on either side of the vertebral column, between the false ribs and the hip-bone (usually in *pl.*, often, esp. in Biblical and poetic use, as denoting the part of the body which should be clothed or girded, or which is regarded as the seat of physical strength and generative power); also, a cut of meat from this region of an animal, esp. a portion including the vertebræ of such parts.—**loin′=cloth,** *n.* A piece of cloth worn about the loins or hips, and often passing between the thighs, worn by natives of warm countries, commonly as the only garment.

loi-ter (loi′tėr), *v.* [ME., from Dutch: cf. mod. D. *leuteren*, wabble, trifle, loiter.] **I.** *intr.* To linger idly or aimlessly in or about a place or on one's way (as, "Upon leaving the house he *loitered* about the court-yard": Motley's "Dutch Republic," vi. 7); also, to move or go in a slow or lagging manner (as, to *loiter* along; "Two schoolboys . . . paused to look at him as they *loitered* down the pavement," Howells's "Chance Acquaintance," viii.); also, to waste time or dawdle over work, etc. (as, "Conscious how much the hand Of lubbard labour needs his watchful eye, Oft *loit'ring* lazily, if not o'erseen": Cowper's "Task," iii. 401). **II.** *tr.* To pass (time, etc.) in an idle or aimless manner: with *away*: as, to *loiter* away the hours.—**loi′ter-er,** *n.*—**loi′ter-ing-ly,** *adv.*

loll (lol), *v.* [ME.; prob. imit.: cf. *lull.*] **I.** *intr.* To recline or lean in a relaxed or indolent manner (as, to *loll* on a sofa or in an easy-chair; "Folding our hands within our arms, we both *loll'd* upon the counter," Sterne's "Sentimental Journey," The Gloves); lounge; also, to hang loosely or droopingly (as, a dog's tongue *lolls* out; "babies with their little round heads *lolling* forward," George Eliot's "Adam Bede," ii.). **II.** *tr.* To allow to loll, hang, or droop: as, a dog *lolls* out his tongue; "Gigantic sunflowers *lolled* their broad, jolly faces over the fences" (Irving's "Tales of a Traveler," iv. 4).—**loll,** *n.* The act or an act of lolling; also, one who or that which lolls.

Lol-lard (lol′ạ̈rd), *n.* [MD. *lollaerd*, mumbler, < *lollen*, mumble, hum.] One of the English or Scottish followers of John Wyclif (died 1384), regarded as heretics and at times persecuted, adherents of a widespread reform movement in the 14th and 15th centuries, partly religious and partly political and economic, and in some respects anticipating Protestantism and Puritanism.—**Lol′lard-ry, Lol′lard-y,** *n.* The principles of the Lollards, or adherence to them.

loll-er (lol′ėr), *n.* One who lolls; a lounger.

lol-li-pop, lol-ly-pop (lol′i-pop), *n.* [Origin obscure.] A kind of taffy or other candy, often a piece on the end of a stick.

lol-lop (lol′ọp), *v. i.* [Extended form of *loll.*] To loll or lounge indolently; also, to bob, toss, or go with clumsy movements, as of something heavy. [Colloq.]

Lom-bard (lom′bạ̈rd or lum′-). [OF. F. *Lombard*, < L. *Langobardi*, *Longobardi*, pl.; from Teut.] **I.** *n.* A member of a Germanic tribe which in the 6th century conquered the part of northern Italy thenceforth known as Lombardy; hence, one of the descendants of this tribe; a native or inhabitant of Lombardy; also, a banker† or money-lender† (from the Lombard bankers in London: cf. *Lombard Street*, following). **II.** *a.* Pertaining to the Lombards or to Lombardy.—**Lombard Street,** a street in London, orig. occupied by Lombard bankers, famous as a financial center; hence, the London money-market or the body of London financiers. —**Lom-bar′dic** (-bär′dik), *a.*

lo-ment (lō′ment), *n.* [L. *lomentum*, bean-meal, orig. as used in a cosmetic, < *lavare* (pp. *lotus*), wash.] In *bot.*, a legume which is contracted in the spaces between the seeds, and breaks at maturity into one-seeded indehiscent joints.—**lo-men-ta′ceous** (-men-tā′shius), *a.* In *bot.*, of the nature of a loment; loment-like; also, bearing loments.—**lo-men-tum** (lọ̄-men′tum), *n.*; pl. *-ta* (-tạ). [L.] In *bot.*, a loment.

Loment. — The fruits of *Meibomia canescens* (tick-trefoil).

Lon-don (lun′dọn) **smoke.** A dark, dull gray color.

lone (lōn), *a.* [For *alone.*] Being alone, unaccompanied, or solitary (as, a *lone* traveler; a *lone* survivor; the *lone* star of Texas, the single star used as a device upon the seal, etc., of that State, the 'Lone Star State'); also, unmarried or having lost the husband or wife (as, "a poor *lone* woman," Shakspere's "2 Henry IV.," ii. 1. 35: now chiefly prov. or humorous); also, standing apart, or isolated, as a house; lonely, as in situation (poetic: as, "Bokhara, and *lone* Khiva in the waste," M. Arnold's "Sohrab and Rustum"); also, lonesome, as in feeling.

lone-li-ly (lōn′li-li), *adv.* In a lonely manner.—**lone′li-ness,** *n.* The state or the feeling of being lonely.

lone-ly (lōn′li), *a.*; compar. *lonelier*, superl. *loneliest.* Lone, solitary, or without company (as, "I go alone, Like to a *lonely* dragon, that his fen Makes fear'd and talk'd of more than seen": Shakspere's "Coriolanus," iv. 1. 30); esp., destitute of sympathetic or friendly companionship, intercourse, or relationships (as, "Now a *lonely* man Wifeless and heirless," Tennyson's "Lancelot and Elaine," 1359; a *lonely* exile; a *lonely* old age); also, standing apart, or isolated (as, a *lonely* tower, peak, or tree); esp., remote from men or from places of human habitation or resort (as, a *lonely* spot; a *lonely* road; *lonely* seas); little frequented, or unfrequented, or desolate; also, affected with, characterized by, or causing a depressing feeling of being alone (as, to feel *lonely*; a *lonely* heart or mood; a *lonely* prospect); lonesome.

lone-ness (lōn′nes), *n.* Lone condition; loneliness.

lone-some (lōn′sum), *a.*; compar. *lonesomer*, superl. *lonesomest.* Lone or solitary; also, more commonly, lonely, esp. depressingly lonely, in situation (as, a *lonesome* road; "In November days, When vapours rolling down the valleys made A lonely scene more *lonesome*," Wordsworth's "Influence of Natural Objects," 18); also, lonely in feeling, or depressed by solitude or by a sense of being alone (as, to be or feel *lonesome*); attended with or causing such a state of feeling (as, a *lonesome* journey; *lonesome* surroundings).—**lone′some-ly,** *adv.*—**lone′some-ness,** *n.*

long[1] (lông), *a.* [AS. *lang*, *long*, = D. and G. *lang* = Icel. *langr* = Goth. *laggs*, long; akin to L. *longus*, long.] Having considerable or great extent from end to end (as, a *long* line; a *long* distance); not short; relatively much extended (as, a *long* arm); tall (now chiefly colloq. or humorous: as, "Like all lank men, my *long* friend had an appetite of his own," H. Melville's "Omoo," xxxiv.); having the greatest dimension unusually great in proportion; of the head or skull, of more than ordinary length from front to back (cf. *long-headed*); also, having considerable or great extent in duration (as, a *long* while); having considerable or great extension from beginning to end, as a series, enumeration, account, book, etc.; not brief; also, having a specified extension in space, duration, etc. (as, 5 feet *long*); also, continuing too long; lengthy; tedious; also, beyond the normal extension in space, duration, quantity, etc. (as, a *long* dozen, thirteen; a *long* ton, a ton of 2,240 pounds); also, extending to a great distance in space or time (as, a *long* sight; a *long* look forward; a *long* memory); having a long time to run, as a promissory note; also, distant or remote in time (as, a *long* date); also, in *pros.* and *phonetics*, occupying a relatively long time in utterance, as vowels or syllables (used commonly in English orthoëpy to note the sounds of a, e, i, o, u exemplified in the words *fate, me, pine, note, lute*); also, in *com.*, well supplied, as with some commodity or stock; hence, depending for profit on a rise in prices.—**in the long run,** after a long course of experience; in the final result.—**long measure,** the system of units ordinarily used in measuring length: 12 lines=1 inch; 12 inches=1 foot (30.48 centimeters); 3 feet=1 yard; 5½ yards=1 rod, pole, or perch; 40 rods=1 furlong; 8 furlongs=1 statute or land mile (5,280 feet or 1,609.3 meters); 3 miles=1 league.—**long primer.** See under *primer*[2].—**long**[1], *n.* Something that is long; a long time (as, before *long*; for *long*); in *pros.* and *phonetics*, a long sound or syllable.—**long**[1], *adv.* [AS. *lange*, *longe.*] For or through a great extent of space or, esp., time (as, a *long*-extended row; a reform *long* advocated); also, for or throughout a specified extent, esp. of time (as, how *long* did he stay?); also, in elliptical expressions, gone, occupying, delaying, etc., a long or a specified time (as, don't be *long*; how *long* will you be?); also, for emphasis, after nouns denoting a period of time, throughout the whole length (as, all summer *long*; the whole night *long*); also, at a point of time far distant from the time indicated (as, *long* before; *long* since).—**so** (or **as**) **long as,** provided that.

long[2] (lông), *v. i.* [AS. *langian*, grow long, have desire, appar. < *lang*, E. *long*[1].] To have a prolonged or unceasing desire, as for something not immediately (if ever) attainable (as, "Wherefore is . . . life [given] unto the bitter in soul; Which *long* for death, but it cometh not?" Job, iii. 21); in general, to have an earnest or strong desire (as, "I *long'd* so heartily then and there, To give him the grasp of fellowship": Tennyson's "Maud," i. 13. 2).

long[3] (lông), *adv.* Same as *along*[1]. [Archaic or prov.]

long[4] (lông), *v. i.* [ME. *longen*, *langen*, < AS. *gelang*, belonging, owing: cf. *along*[1] and *belong.*] To belong; pertain: commonly with *to* or *unto*: as, "He . . . bade his folk to bring Such feast as *'longed* unto a mighty king" (W. Morris's "Jason," v. 190). [Obs. or archaic; now usually taken as a shortened form of *belong*, and printed *'long.*]

lon-gæ-val, lon-gæ-vous (lon-jē′vạl, -vus), *a.* See *longeval.*

lon-gan (long′gạn), *n.* [Chinese *lung-yen*, 'dragon's eye.'] The lichi-like fruit of a sapindaceous tree, *Nephelium longanum*, cultivated in China and the East Indies; also, the tree itself.

lon-ga-nim-i-ty (long-gạ-nim′i-ti), *n.* [LL. *longanimitas*, < *longanimis*, long-suffering, patient, < L. *longus*, long, + *animus*, mind.] Long-suffering; forbearance; patience. [Now rare.]—**lon-gan-i-mous** (long-gan′i-mus), *a.* Long-suffering; patient. [Rare.]

long-beard (lông′bērd), *n.* A man with a long beard; also, a bellarmine; also, Florida moss.

long=boat (lông′bōt), *n.* *Naut.*, the largest and strongest boat belonging to a sailing-vessel: as, "The Captain called in at one or two ports, and sent in his *long-boat* for provisions" (Swift's "Gulliver's Travels," ii. 8).

long-bow (lông′bō), *n.* The bow drawn by hand and discharging a long feathered arrow: distinguished from *crossbow.*—**to draw the longbow,** fig., to tell exaggerated stories; make exaggerated statements: as, "At speaking truth perhaps they are less clever, But *draw the long bow* better now than ever" (Byron's "Don Juan," xvi. 1). [Colloq.]

long=cloth (lông′klôth), *n.* A fine, soft-finished cotton cloth.

long=drawn (lông′drân), *a.* Drawn out or prolonged to great length (as, a *long-drawn* sigh; a *long-drawn* narrative); hence, in general, long (as, "the *long-drawn* aisle": Gray's "Elegy," x.).

longe (lunj), *n.* and *v.* Same as *lunge*[2].

long=eared (lông′ērd), *a.* Having long ears or ear-like parts; fig., asinine.

lon-ge-ron (lon′jẹ-ron, F. lôṅ-zhė-rôṅ), *n.* [F.] In *aëronautics*, a main longitudinal brace or support on an aëroplane.

lon-ge-val, lon-ge-vous (lon-jē′vạl, -vus), *a.* [L. *longævus*, < *longus*, long, + *ævum*, age.] Long-lived; living to a great age.—**lon-gev′i-ty** (-jev′i-ti), *n.* [LL. *longævitas.*] Long life, or great duration of life (as, "a medicine that shall preserve him . . . until the utmost term of patriarchal *longevity*": Hawthorne's "House of the Seven Gables," xviii.); also, length or duration of life (as, the average *longevity* of human beings or of animals).

long-hand (lông′hand), *n.* Writing of the ordinary kind, in which the words are written out in full: distinguished from *shorthand.*

long=head-ed (lông′hed′ed), *a.* Having a long head; dolichocephalic; also, of great discernment or foresight, farseeing, or shrewd (as, "Mr. Kobbock, who was very *long-headed*, with more than a common man's portion of understanding": Galt's "Annals of the Parish," xxvii.).—**long′=head′ed-ness,** *n.*

long-horn (lông′hôrn), *n.* Any of various animals with long horns or horn-like appendages; esp., an animal of any of certain breeds of cattle with unusually long horns.

longi-. Form of L. *longus*, long, used in combination.

lon-gi-cau-date (lon-ji-kâ′dāt), *a.* [L. *longus*, long, + *cauda*, tail.] Having a long tail.

lon-gi-corn (lon′ji-kôrn). [NL. *longicornis*, < L. *longus*, long, + *cornu*, horn.] **I.** *a.* Having long antennæ, as beetles of the group *Longicornia*; belonging to this group. **II.** *n.* A longicorn beetle.

long-ing (lông′ing), *n.* The act or feeling of one who longs; prolonged, unceasing, or earnest desire, or an instance of it: as, "the restless, unsatisfied *longing*" (Longfellow's "Evangeline," ii. 5).—**long′ing,** *p. a.* That

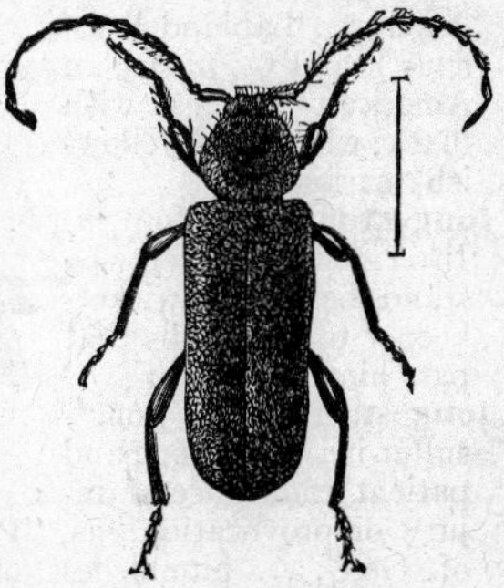

Longicorn Beetle (*Callidium antennatum*). (Vertical line shows natural size.)

longs; having a prolonged or earnest desire; also, characterized by or showing such desire (as, a *longing* look).—**long′ing-ly,** *adv.*

lon-gin-qui-ty (lon-jing′kwi-ti), *n.* [L. *longinquitas*, < *longinquus*, long, distant, remote, < *longus*, long.] Great length, extent, or duration; also, distance or remoteness. [Now rare.]

lon-gi-pen-nate (lon-ji-pen′āt), *a.* [L. *longus*, long, + *penna*, wing.] Having long wings.

lon-gi-ros-tral, lon-gi-ros-trate (lon-ji-ros′tral, -trāt), *a.* [L. *longus*, long, + *rostrum*, beak.] Having a long beak or bill.

long-ish (lông′ish), *a.* Somewhat long.

lon-gi-tude (lon′ji-tūd), *n.* [L. *longitudo* (*longitudin-*), length, < *longus*, long.] Length (now chiefly humorous: as, "a rusty sword of immense *longitude*," Hawthorne's "Twice-Told Tales," Howe's Masquerade); in *geog.*, distance east or west on the earth's surface, measured by the angle contained between the meridian of a particular place and some prime meridian, as that of Greenwich, England; in *astron.*, the arc of the ecliptic measured eastward from the vernal equinoctial point to the foot of the circle of latitude drawn through the object, as a star, whose position is in question ('celestial longitude').—**lon-gi-tu′di-nal** (-tū′di-nal), *a.* Of or pertaining to longitude or length (as, *longitudinal* distance; *longitudinal* measure); also, extending in the direction of the length of a thing (as, a flag with *longitudinal* stripes); running lengthwise; in *zoöl.*, pertaining to or extending along the long axis of the body, or the direction from front to back or head to tail; in *geog.* and *astron.*, pertaining to longitude.—**lon-gi-tu′di-nal-ly,** *adv.*

long=legged (lông′legd or -leg″ed), *a.* Having long legs.—**long′=legs,** *n.* A long-legged person or animal; specif., a daddy-long-legs.

long=lived (lông′līvd), *a.* Having a long life, or living a long time (as, *long-lived* animals or plants); also, lasting long (as, a *long-lived* soap-bubble; a *long-lived* scandal).

long-ly (lông′li), *adv.* At or to a great or considerable length (now rare); also, for a long time† (as, "You look'd so *longly* on the maid": Shakspere's "Taming of the Shrew," i. 1. 170).

long=moss (lông′môs), *n.* Same as *Florida moss.*

long-ness (lông′nes), *n.* Length.

Lon-go-bard (long′gō-bärd), *n.* and *a.* [L. *Longobardi*, pl.] Same as *Lombard.*—**Lon-go-bar′dic** (-bär′dik), *a.*

long-shanks (lông′shangks), *n.* A long-legged person; [*cap.*] a nickname given to Edward I., king of England (1272–1307), because of his long legs; also [*l. c.*], a stilt (bird).

long-shore (lông′shōr), *a.* [For *alongshore.*] Existing, found, or employed along the shore: as, *longshore* fisheries; *longshore* laborers.—**long′shore′man** (-man), *n.*; pl. *-men.* A man employed along the shore; esp., a man employed on the wharves of a port, as in loading and unloading vessels.

long=sight-ed (lông′sī′ted), *a.* Far-sighted; hypermetropic; also, having great foresight; foreseeing remote results.—**long′=sight′ed-ness,** *n.*

long-some (lông′sum), *a.* [AS. *langsum.*] Long; lengthy; tedious. [Archaic or prov. Eng. and Sc.]

long-spur (lông′spėr), *n.* Any of various fringilline birds of the genus *Calcarius*, inhabiting northerly regions and characterized by a long, spur-like hind claw, as *C. lapponicus*, of Europe, Asia, and America ('Lapland longspur'), and *C. pictus*, an American species with black, white, and yellowish markings.

Lapland Longspur.

long=stop (lông′stop), *n.* In *cricket*, a fielder who stands behind the wicket-keeper to stop balls that pass him.

long=suf-fer-ing (lông′-suf′ėr-ing), *n.* Long and patient endurance of injury or provocation: as, "Put on therefore, as the elect of God . . . humbleness of mind, meekness, *longsuffering*" (Col. iii. 12).—**long′=suf′fer-ing,** *a.* Enduring injury or provocation long and patiently: as, "Various were the excesses committed by the insubordinate troops . . . upon the *long-suffering* inhabitants" (Motley's "Dutch Republic," iii. 9).

long=tongued (lông′tungd), *a.* Having a long tongue; fig., talking much or too much, garrulous, or tattling (as, "a *long-tongued* babbling gossip": Shakspere's "Titus Andronicus," iv. 2. 150).

lon-gueur (lôṅ-gėr), *n.* [F., lit. 'length,' < *long*, < L. *longus*, long.] A long or tedious passage in a book, play, or the like: usually in *pl.*

long=waist-ed (lông′wās′ted), *a.* Comparatively long from neck to waist-line, as a person or a garment.

long-ways (lông′wāz), *adv.* Longwise; lengthwise.

long=wind-ed (lông′win′ded), *a.* Capable of long-continued exertion without being out of breath (as, "These horses are . . . remarkably stout and *long-winded*": Irving's "Captain Bonneville," xxxiv.); hence, talking or writing at tedious length, as persons; also, continued to a tedious length in speech or writing (as, a *long-winded* homily; "a *long-winded* epistle," Smollett's "Humphry Clinker," Sept. 30).—**long′=wind′ed-ly,** *adv.*—**long′=wind′ed-ness,** *n.*

long-wise (lông′wīz), *adv.* Lengthwise.

loo (lö), *n.* [Short for *lanterloo.*] A game at cards in which forfeits are paid into a pool; also, the forfeit or sum paid into the pool; also, the fact of being looed.—**loo,** *v. t.*; *looed, looing.* To subject to a forfeit at loo.

loo-by (lö′bi), *n.*; pl. *-bies* (-biz). [ME. *loby*: cf. *lob.*] An awkward, clownish fellow; a lout. [Now chiefly prov. Eng.]

loof[1] (löf), *n.* [From Scand.: cf. Icel. *lōfi*, also Goth. *lōfa*, palm of the hand.] The palm of the hand. [Sc. and north. Eng.]

loof[2] (löf), *n.* Same as *luff.*

loo-fah (lö′fä), *n.* [Ar. *lūfah.*] Any of the tropical cucurbitaceous plants constituting the genus *Luffa*; also, the fruit of such a plant, which contains a mass of coarse, strong fibers; also, this fibrous mass, used, when dried, as a sponge ('vegetable sponge').

look (lůk), *v. i.* [AS. *lōcian* = OS. *lōcon*, look: cf. G. *lugen*, look out, spy.] To fix the eyes upon something or in some direction in order to see (as, "I *looked*, and, lo, a Lamb stood on the mount Sion," Rev. xiv. 1; "He *looked* this way and that way," Ex. ii. 12); glance or gaze, often in a manner specified (as, to *look* questioningly or kindly at a person; "Latterly Sam Buckley and Cecil Mayford have been *looking* at one another like cat and dog," H. Kingsley's "Geoffry Hamlyn," xxxi.); use the sight in seeking, searching, examining, watching, etc. (as, to find a thing without *looking*; to *look* through or over papers: see *to look for* and *to look out*, following); fig., to direct the mental regard or attention (as, *look* at the facts; *look* into the matter carefully); direct the expectations or hopes (esp. with *for* or *to*: see *to look for* and *to look to*, following); also, to have a prospect or outlook, or afford a view (as, the room or the window *looks* upon the street); face or front (as, the house *looks* to the east); fig., to tend, as in bearing or significance (as, conditions *look* toward war; the latest reports *look* that way); also, to appear or seem (as specified) to the eye (as, to *look* pale; a tree *looking* like an elm); fig., to seem to the mind (as, the case *looks* promising; such proceedings will not *look* well; it *looks* as if he might succeed).—**to look after,** to follow with the eye, as a person or thing moving away; also, to look for or seek, as something desired; also, to keep an eye upon, watch, attend to, or take care of (as, to *look after* one's interests; to *look after* a child); also, to look forward to† or expect† (as, "*looking after* those things which are coming on the earth": Luke, xxi. 26).—**to look for,** to seek, or search for, as a person or thing; also, to look forward expectantly to, anticipate, or expect (as, to *look for* a coming Messiah; "Where all is given, much is *looked for* in return," Cooper's "Spy," viii.).—**to look in,** to take a look or glance into a place; hence, to come in for a brief call or visit.—**to look on,** to look or gaze as a mere spectator: as, to *look on* at a dance or a game of cards.—**to look out,** to look forth, as from a window or a place of observation; hence, to be on the watch, or on one's guard; watch vigilantly, as for something feared (as, to *look out* for squalls, or for trouble); also, to take watchful care (with *for*: as, to *look out* for one's self or one's own welfare).—**to look to,** to direct the glance or gaze to; also, to give attention to, attend to, or take care of (as, "A man who has the affairs of such a great bank as ours to *look to*, must be up with the lark": Thackeray's "Newcomes," lxvi.); give watchful heed to; also, to direct the expectations or hopes to, as for something desired (as, to *look to* a person for aid); also, to look forward expectantly to (as, "He *looks to* distant storms; He hears the thunder ere the tempest low'rs": Cowper's "Table Talk," 495).—**to look up,** to direct the eyes upward; also, to cheer up†; also, to rise in amount or value, advance, or improve (colloq.: as, "It was a nice sickly season . . . In commercial phrase, coffins were *looking up*," Dickens's "Oliver Twist," vi.).—**look,** *v. t.* To look at, view, inspect, or examine (now prov. Eng. and Sc., except in phrases: as, to *look* a person over, in the face, or up and down; to *look* a book through hastily); also, to look for, or seek (now prov. Eng., except as with *up* or *out*: as, to *look* a word up in the dictionary; to *look* up a friend at his home; "Let Pharaoh *look* out a man discreet and wise," Gen. xli. 33); also, to express or suggest by looks (as, "You need not *look* such impotent malice," Stevenson's "Master of Ballantrae," iv.; to *look* daggers at a person, to cast looks as of deadly hostility at him); also, to bring, put, etc., by looks (as, to *look* one out of countenance; "a pair of eyes which could have *looked* down the boldest mesmerist in three seconds," Kingsley's "Yeast," xv.).—**look,** *n.* The act or an act of looking; a glance or gaze (as, a *look* of inquiry); a visual search or examination (as, a careful *look* through a house or over documents); also, way of looking or appearing to the eye, or, fig., to the mind (as, the *look* of the sky; to have the *look* of an honest man; the affair has an unpleasant *look*); aspect; *pl.*, the ways collectively in which something appears, or the general aspect (as, to consider *looks* rather than enduring qualities; to like the *looks* of a place, or of a book); specif., personal appearance, as to comeliness, pleasingness, health, etc. (as, to be vain of one's *looks*; good *looks*; his *looks* are in his favor).

look-er (lůk′ėr), *n.* One who looks.—**look′er=on′,** *n.*; pl. *lookers-on.* One who looks on; a spectator.

look=in (lůk′in), *n.* A glance in; a hasty glance; hence, a brief visit; also, a chance of success, as in a horse-race (slang); a chance to participate, as in some venture (slang).

look-ing=glass (lůk′ing-glȧs), *n.* A mirror made of glass with a metallic or amalgam backing; also, such glass as a material.

look-out (lůk-out′ or lůk′out), *n.* The act of looking out; a watch kept, as for something that may come or happen (as, to keep a sharp *lookout*; to be on the *lookout* for an attack, signal, or opportunity); also, a person or party stationed or employed to keep such a watch (as, "There was nothing to do but steer the ship, and relieve the '*look-outs*' at the mast-heads": H. Melville's "Omoo," ix.); also, a station or place from which a watch is kept; also, view, prospect, or outlook; also, the proper object of one's watchful care or concern (colloq.: as, his risk is his own *lookout*; "Never you mind what I took her for; that's my *look-out*," Dickens's "Hard Times," iii. 3).

loom[1] (löm), *n.* [ME. *lome*, < AS. *gelōma*, tool, implement: cf. *heirloom*.] A tool or implement (now Sc. and north. Eng.); also, an open vessel, as a bucket (now Sc.); also, a machine or apparatus for weaving yarn or thread into a fabric; hence, the art or the process of weaving (as, "a splendid silk of foreign *loom*": Tennyson's "Geraint and Enid," 686); also, the part of an oar between the blade and the handle, or between the rowlock and the hand.—**loom**[1], *v. t.* To weave on a loom.

loom[2] (löm), *v. i.* [Origin uncertain.] To appear indistinctly, or come into view in indistinct and enlarged form (as, "We could just descry the ridge . . . *looming* dimly through the mists": H. Melville's "Typee," v.); hence, to rise before the vision with an appearance of great or portentous size (often fig.: as, "These measures were taken at a time when a danger of the greatest magnitude was *looming* on the horizon," Lecky's "Hist. of Eng. in the 18th Century," i.; trifles *loom* large to an anxious mind).—**loom**[2], *n.* A looming appearance, as of something seen indistinctly at a distance or through a fog: as, the *loom* of an iceberg in a ship's path.

loom[3] (löm), *n.* [From Scand.] A loon (bird); also, a guillemot.—**loom′er-y,** *n.*; pl. *-ies* (-iz). A breeding-place of looms or guillemots.

loon[1] (lön), *n.* [ME. *lowen, loun*; origin uncertain.] A worthless, sorry, lazy, or stupid fellow (used opprobriously, often without precise meaning: as, "thou cream-faced *loon!*" Shakspere's "Macbeth," v. 3. 11: now archaic, prov., or colloq.); also, a worthless or loose woman (Sc.); also, a peasant, or person of low condition (archaic or Sc.: as, "The lairds are as bad as the *loons*," Scott's "Rob Roy," xxvi.); in general, a man or fellow (chiefly Sc.); also, a boy or lad (chiefly Sc.).

loon[2] (lön), *n.* [Var. of *loom*[3].] Any of the large, fish-eating, web-footed diving birds of the northern hemisphere constituting the genus *Colymbus* (or *Urinator* or *Gavia*), as *C. torquatus* (or *imber* or *immer*), the great northern diver, which is noted for its loud, wild cry; sometimes, any of various other birds, as the crested grebe and the little grebe.

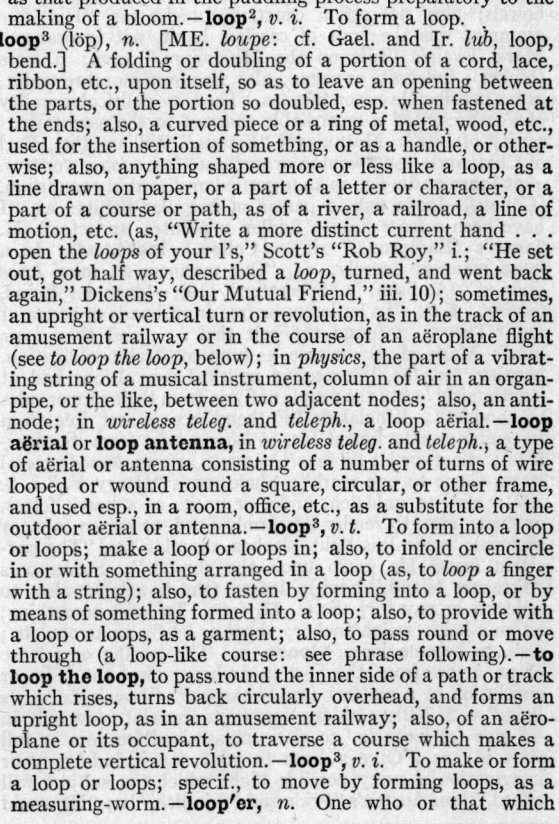

Loon, or Great Northern Diver (*Colymbus torquatus*).

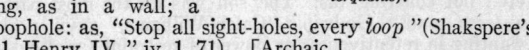

loo-ny (lö′ni). [For *luny*, < *lunatic*.] **I.** *a.* Lunatic; crazy; also, extremely or senselessly foolish. [Slang.] **II.** *n.*; pl. *-nies* (-niz). A lunatic. [Slang.]—**loo′ni-ness,** *n.*

loop[1] (löp), *n.* [ME. *loupe*: cf. D. *luip*, watch, ambush.] A small or narrow opening, as in a wall; a loophole: as, "Stop all sight-holes, every *loop*" (Shakspere's "1 Henry IV.," iv. 1. 71). [Archaic.]

loop[2] (löp), *n.* [F. *loupe*.] A ball-like pasty mass of iron, as that produced in the puddling process preparatory to the making of a bloom.—**loop**[2], *v. i.* To form a loop.

loop[3] (löp), *n.* [ME. *loupe*: cf. Gael. and Ir. *lub*, loop, bend.] A folding or doubling of a portion of a cord, lace, ribbon, etc., upon itself, so as to leave an opening between the parts, or the portion so doubled, esp. when fastened at the ends; also, a curved piece or a ring of metal, wood, etc., used for the insertion of something, or as a handle, or otherwise; also, anything shaped more or less like a loop, as a line drawn on paper, or a part of a letter or character, or a part of a course or path, as of a river, a railroad, a line of motion, etc. (as, "Write a more distinct current hand . . . open the *loops* of your l's," Scott's "Rob Roy," i.; "He set out, got half way, described a *loop*, turned, and went back again," Dickens's "Our Mutual Friend," iii. 10); sometimes, an upright or vertical turn or revolution, as in the track of an amusement railway or in the course of an aëroplane flight (see *to loop the loop*, below); in *physics*, the part of a vibrating string of a musical instrument, column of air in an organ-pipe, or the like, between two adjacent nodes; also, an anti-node; in *wireless teleg.* and *teleph.*, a loop aërial.—**loop aërial** or **loop antenna,** in *wireless teleg.* and *teleph.*, a type of aërial or antenna consisting of a number of turns of wire looped or wound round a square, circular, or other frame, and used esp., in a room, office, etc., as a substitute for the outdoor aërial or antenna.—**loop**[3], *v. t.* To form into a loop or loops; make a loop or loops in; also, to infold or encircle in or with something arranged in a loop (as, to *loop* a finger with a string); also, to fasten by forming into a loop, or by means of something formed into a loop; also, to provide with a loop or loops, as a garment; also, to pass round or move through (a loop-like course: see phrase following).—**to loop the loop,** to pass round the inner side of a path or track which rises, turns back circularly overhead, and forms an upright loop, as in an amusement railway; also, of an aëroplane or its occupant, to traverse a course which makes a complete vertical revolution.—**loop**[3], *v. i.* To make or form a loop or loops; specif., to move by forming loops, as a measuring-worm.—**loop′er,** *n.* One who or that which loops something or forms loops; specif., a measuring-worm.

loop-hole (löp′hōl), *n.* [See *loop*[1].] A small or narrow opening, as in a wall, for looking through, or for admitting light and air, or particularly, in a fortification, for the discharge of missiles against an enemy outside; in general, an opening or aperture; fig., an outlet, or means of escape or evasion (as, "Alva had been turning over the laws and regulations of the order, but could find no *loophole*": Motley's "Dutch Republic," iii. 2).—**loop′hole,** *v. t.*; *-holed, -holing.* To furnish with loopholes; as, "a stout log-house . . . *loopholed* for musketry on every side" (Stevenson's "Treasure Island," xvi.).

loop=stitch (löp′stich), *n.* In sewing, a kind of stitch forming a loop caught down at the point of doubling; chain-stitch; in crocheting, a kind of stitch in which projecting loops are formed on the surface of the work.

loop-worm (löp′wėrm), *n.* A looper or measuring-worm.

loop-y (lö′pi), *a.* [See *loop*[3].] Full of loops; fig., crafty or deceitful (Sc.).

loose (lös), *a.*; compar. *looser*, superl. *loosest.* [From Scand.; = Icel. *lauss*, loose, free, empty, = D. and G. *los*, loose, free, = AS. *lēas*, free from, without (see *-less*), = Goth. *laus*, empty, without; akin to E. *loss*.] Free from bonds, fetters, or restraint (as, to get one's hand *loose*; to set animals *loose*); free or released from fastening or attachment (as, a *loose* end; a few pages have come *loose*); uncombined, as a chemical element; not bound together, as papers or flowers; not put up in a package or other container (as, *loose* coffee; *loose* milk); unemployed or unappropriated (now colloq.: as, *loose* funds); also, not firmly or rigidly fixed in place (as, a *loose* tooth); also, not tightly drawn, as reins; lacking tension, slack, or relaxed; not fitting closely, as garments; also, not close or compact in structure or arrangement; having spaces between the parts, or open (as, a *loose* weave or texture); of earth, soil, etc., not cohering (as, "The soil was for the most part of a *loose* sand": Godwin's "Caleb Williams," xxvii.); also, wanting in retentiveness or power of restraint (as, "A kind of men so *loose* of soul, That in their sleeps will mutter their affairs": Shakspere's "Othello," iii. 3. 416); lax, as the bowels; also, not strict, exact, or precise (as, "His *loose* grammar was the fruit of careless habit, not ignorance," Mark Twain's "Life on the Mississippi," xxvi.; a *loose* thinker); indefinite or vague; also, free from moral restraint, or lax in principle or conduct (as, "The *loose* political morality of Fox presented a remarkable contrast to the ostentatious purity of Pitt": Macaulay's "Essays," William Pitt, Earl of Chatham); esp., wanton or unchaste (as, a *loose* woman).—**at loose ends,** fig., in an unsettled or disorderly condition. [Colloq.]—**loose fish,** a person of irregular habits: as, "I have been a *loose fish*—a fiddler, a painter, an actor" (H. James's "Europeans," xii.). [Colloq.]—**loose,** *adv.* In a loose manner; loosely: as, "Our manners sit more *loose* upon us" (Addison, in "Spectator," 119).—**loose,** *v.*; *loosed, loosing.* **I.** *tr.* To let loose, or free from bonds or restraint (as, "They . . . found the colt tied . . . and they *loose* him": Mark, xi. 4); release, as from constraint, obligation, penalty, etc. (as, "Successive political convulsions had at length fairly *loosed* the people of Syria from their former rules of conduct": Kinglake's "Eothen," xxv.); set free from fastening or attachment (as, to *loose* a boat from its moorings); shoot, or let fly (as, "As many arrows, *loosed* several ways, Come to one mark": Shakspere's "Henry V.," i. 2. 207); also, to unfasten, undo, or untie, as a bond, fetter, or knot; also, to render less firmly fixed, or loosen (obs. or archaic); make less tight, slacken, or relax (as, "The coxswain *loosed* his grasp upon the shrouds": Stevenson's "Treasure Island," xxvi.); loosen (the bowels)†; also, to redeem† or pay for† (Sc.). **II.** *intr.* To loose something; let go a hold; weigh anchor; shoot or let fly an arrow, etc.; also, to become loose.—**loose,** *n.* The loosing or release of an arrow from the bow in archery; also, the issue or conclusion of a matter† (see Shakspere's "Love's Labour's Lost," v. 2. 752); also, freedom from restraint (now only in 'to give (a) loose to,' to give unrestrained freedom or full vent to: as, "Give a *loose* to your fancy, indulge your imagination in every possible flight which the subject will afford," Jane Austen's "Pride and Prejudice," lx.; "He would not give *loose* to passion," George Eliot's "Adam Bede," xxvii.).

loose=coup-ler (lös′kup″lėr), *n.* In *wireless teleg.* and *teleph.*, a coupler (transformer) in which the primary coil and the secondary coil are associated without close inductive relation, as by being well separated from each other.

loose=joint-ed (lös′join′ted), *a.* Having loose joints; esp., loosely built or framed as to body (as, "a tall, shambling, *loose-jointed* man": Mrs. Stowe's "Oldtown Folks," iv.).

loose-ly (lös′li), *adv.* In a loose manner.

loos-en (lö′sn), *v.* **I.** *tr.* To let loose, or set free from bonds, restraint, or constraint; also, to unfasten or undo, as a bond or fetter; also, to render less firmly fixed in place (as, a blow which *loosens* a tooth); also, to render less tight, slacken, or relax (as, to *loosen* one's grasp); also, to render less close or compact in structure or arrangement; render less dense or coherent (as, to *loosen* the soil about the roots of a plant); also, to open, or relieve the costiveness of (the bowels); also, to relax in strictness or severity, as restraint or discipline. **II.** *intr.* To become loose or looser.—**loos′en-er,** *n.*

loose-ness (lös′nes), *n.* The state or quality of being loose.

loos-er (lö′sėr), *n.* One who or that which looses.

loose-strife (lös′strīf), *n.* [From *loose, v.,* + *strife*; intended as a translation of L. *lysimachia*, taken as < Gr. λύειν, loose, + μάχη, strife.] Any of various leafy-stemmed herbs of the primulaceous genus *Lysimachia*, as *L. vulgaris*, a common yellow-flowered species ('yellow loosestrife'), and *L. quadrifolia*, a species with leaves in whorls of four or five ('whorled loosestrife'); also, any of various herbaceous plants of the lythraceous genus *Lythrum*, as *L. salicaria*, a purple-flowered species ('purple loosestrife').

loose=tongued (lös′tungd), *a.* Talking too freely; blabbing: as, "He knew how *loose-tongued* is calumny" (Reade's "Peg Woffington," i.).

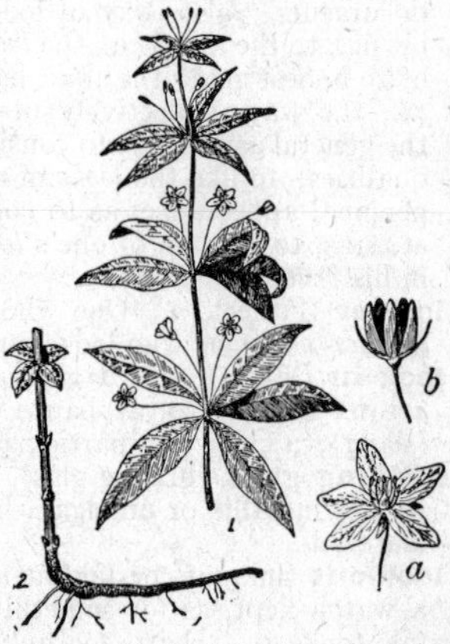

Loosestrife (*Lysimachia quadrifolia*). — 1, upper part of the stem with the flowers; 2, lower part, showing the rhizome; *a*, flower; *b*, fruit.

loot (löt), *n.* [Hind. *lūt.*] Spoils or plunder taken by pillaging, as in war; booty; hence, anything dishonestly and ruthlessly appropriated (as, a burglar's *loot*; the *loot* secured by a corrupt public official); also, the act of looting or plundering (as, the *loot* of a conquered city; the *loot* of the public treasury).—**loot,** *v.* **I.** *tr.* To despoil by taking loot; plunder or pillage (a city, house, etc.), as in war; rob, as by burglary, corrupt practice in public office, etc.; also, to take, or carry off, as loot. **II.** *intr.* To take loot; plunder.—**loot′er,** *n.*

lop[1] (lop), *v.*; *lopped, lopping.* [Cf. *lap*[2], also *lob.*] **I.** *intr.* To hang loosely or limply; droop; also, to sway, move, or go in a drooping or heavy, awkward way (as, to *lop* about in a saddle; "She . . . cried about it, she did, and *lopped* round, as if she'd lost every friend she had," Mrs. Stowe's "Uncle Tom's Cabin," viii.). **II.** *tr.* To let hang or droop.

lop[2] (lop), *v.*; *lopped, lopping.* [Cf. Norw. *loppa*, pluck, snatch, also D. *lubben*, castrate.] **I.** *tr.* To cut off the branches, twigs, etc., of (a tree or other plant); trim by cutting; hence, to cut off the head, limbs, etc., of (a person) or parts of (a thing); also, to cut off (branches, twigs, etc.) from a tree or other plant; hence, to cut off (the head, limbs, etc.) from a person; remove (parts) as by cutting (as, "Expunge the whole or *lop* the excrescent parts Of all our vices have created arts": Pope's "Essay on Man," ii. 49). **II.** *intr.* To cut off branches, twigs, etc., as of a tree; remove parts by or as by cutting.—**lop**[2], *n.* Parts or a part lopped off, esp. the smaller branches and twigs of trees; fagot-wood.

lope (lōp), *v.*; *loped, loping.* [Prob. orig. a var. of *loup* (see *loup*), with later use due in part to D. *loopen*, run: see *leap*, and cf. *interlope* and *landloper*.] **I.** *intr.* To leap or jump (obs. or prov. Eng.); also, to move or run with bounding steps, as a quadruped, or with a long, easy stride, as a person; specif., to canter leisurely with a rather long, easy stride, as a horse. **II.** *tr.* To cause to lope, as a horse: as, "I *loped* my cayuse full tilt by Mr. Snake" (Wister's "Virginian," xvi.).—**lope,** *n.* The act or the gait of loping; a long, easy stride: as, "Now and then a Shawanoe passed us, riding his little shaggy pony at a '*lope*'" (Parkman's "Oregon Trail," ii.).

lop=eared (lop′ērd), *a.* Having ears that lop or hang down: as, a *lop-eared* rabbit.

lo-pho-branch (lō′fǫ-brangk). [NL. *Lophobranchii,* pl., < Gr. λόφος, crest, + βράγχια, gills.] **I.** *n.* Any of the *Lophobranchii,* an order or group of teleostean fishes having gills arranged in tufts, as the sea-horses, pipe-fishes, etc. **II.** *a.* Belonging or pertaining to the *Lophobranchii* or lophobranchs.—**lo-pho-bran′chi-ate** (-brang′ki-āt), *a.* and *n.*

lop-per[1] (lop′ėr), *n.* One who lops (trees, etc.).

lop-per[2] (lop′ėr), *v. i.* or *t.* [Cf. Icel. *hlaup,* coagulation, curds.] To curdle, as milk. [Sc., prov. Eng., and U. S.]

lop-py (lop′i), *a.* Lopping; drooping; limp.

lop-sid-ed (lop′sī′ded), *a.* Lopping or inclining to one side; heavier, larger, or more developed on one side than on the other; unsymmetrical.—**lop′sid′ed-ly,** *adv.*—**lop′sid′ed-ness,** *n.*

lo-qua-cious (lǫ-kwā′shus), *a.* [L. *loquax* (*loquac-*), < *loqui,* speak.] Talking or disposed to talk much or freely (as, "Jack became *loquacious* on his favourite topic": Marryat's "Mr. Midshipman Easy," x.); talkative; characterized by or showing a disposition to talk much (as, a *loquacious* mood; "Mrs. Glibbans expressed, in very *loquacious* terms, her satisfaction," Galt's "Ayrshire Legatees," iv.); fig., making sounds as of much talking, as birds, frogs, water, etc.—**lo-qua′cious-ly,** *adv.*—**lo-qua′cious-ness,** *n.*—**lo-qua′ci-ty** (-kwas′i-ti), *n.* [L. *loquacitas.*] The state of being loquacious; loquacious flow of talk: as, "It was Ellery Davenport's delight to start Sam's *loquacity* and develop his conversational powers": Mrs. Stowe's "Oldtown Folks," xliii.).

lo-quat (lō′kwot), *n.* [From Chinese name meaning 'rush orange.'] A small, evergreen malaceous tree, *Eriobotrya japonica,* native in China and Japan, but often cultivated elsewhere for ornament and for its small, yellow, edible plum-like fruit; also, the fruit. Also called *Japanese medlar.*

lo-qui-tur (lok′wi-tėr). [L.] 'He (or she, or the person named) speaks': used in stage directions.

lo-ran-tha-ceous (lō-ran-thā′shius), *a.* [NL. *Loranthus,* the typical genus, < L. *lorum,* thong, + Gr. ἄνθος, flower.] Belonging to the *Loranthaceæ,* or mistletoe family of plants.

lor-cha (lôr′chạ̈), *n.* [Pg.: cf. Pg. *lancha,* E. *launch*[1].] A light Chinese sailing-vessel built somewhat after a European model, but rigged like a junk.

Lorcha.

lord (lôrd), *n.* [AS. *hlāford,* < *hlāf,* loaf, + *weard,* keeper: cf. *lady.*] The male head of a household†; also, one who has dominion over others; a master, chief, or ruler; also, one who exercises authority from property rights; an owner or possessor of land, houses, etc.; specif., a feudal superior; the proprietor of a manor; also, a husband (now chiefly humorous); also [*cap.*], the Supreme Being, Jehovah, or God (as, "Know ye that the *Lord* he is God: it is he that hath made us, and not we ourselves": Ps. c. 3); also, the Saviour, Jesus Christ (as, "Unto you is born this day . . . a Saviour, which is Christ the *Lord*": Luke, ii. 11); also [*l. c.*], a titled nobleman, or peer, or one whose ordinary appellation contains by courtesy the title *Lord* or some higher title; *pl.* [*cap.*], the temporal and spiritual peers constituting the upper of the two branches of the British Parliament ('House of Lords'); also, *sing.* [*cap.*], in British use, the title (in collocation with some other word or words) of certain high officials (as, *Lord* Chief Justice; First *Lord* of the Admiralty; *Lord* Mayor of London), and, in ceremonious use, of bishops (as, *Lord* Bishop of Durham); as a prefixed title, substituted in less formal use for 'marquis,' 'earl,' and 'viscount' (as in '*Lord* Salisbury' for 'the Marquis of Salisbury,' in '*Lord* Kitchener' for 'Earl Kitchener,' and in '*Lord* Bryce' for 'Viscount Bryce'), and used before the title of peerage of barons (as in '*Lord* Tennyson,' the Christian name, if mentioned, coming first, as in 'Alfred, *Lord* Tennyson'), and before the surname or territorial designation of justices of the Scottish Court of Session (as in '*Lord* Jeffrey,' and in 'James Burnett, *Lord* Monboddo'), and as a courtesy title before the Christian name and surname of the younger sons of dukes and marquises (as in '*Lord* Randolph Churchill'); also [*l. c.*], in *astrol.,* a planet having dominating influence (see *lord of the ascendant,* below).—**lord lieutenant** [usually with *caps.*], in British use, the title of various high officials holding authority deputed from the sovereign, as the chief executive officer in a county, or, formerly, the viceroy in Ireland; such an official himself.—**lord of misrule,** a person formerly chosen to direct revels and sports, as at Christmas.—**lord of the ascendant,** in *astrol.,* the planet dominating or ruling the ascendant or horoscope; fig., a person having dominating influence or power.—**Lord's Day,** Sunday.—**lords of creation,** mankind; esp., men as opposed to women.—**Lord's Prayer,** the prayer given by Jesus to his disciples (Mat. vi. 9–13; Luke, xi. 2–4).—**Lord's Supper,** the Last Supper; also, the sacrament in commemoration of this; the eucharist; the communion; the mass.—**lord,** *interj.* [Often *cap.*] The noun *Lord* (God) used as an exclamation of surprise, etc.: as, "O *Lord,* I must laugh!" (Shakspere's "Comedy of Errors," iii. 1. 50).—**lord,** *v.* **I.** *intr.* To play the lord; behave in a lordly manner; domineer: often with indefinite *it*: as, "the dominant dignity and absolute sway with which he [a schoolmaster] *lorded* it in his little empire, the school" (Irving's "Sketch-Book," Sleepy Hollow). **II.** *tr.* To rule or preside over as lord (rare); also, to raise to the rank of lord.

lord-ing (lôr′ding), *n.* A lord or master, or a gentleman (chiefly as a form of address: archaic); also, a lordling.

lord-less (lôrd′les), *a.* Having no lord; without a master or ruler.

lord-li-ly (lôrd′li-li), *adv.* In a lordly manner.—**lord′li-ness,** *n.*

lord-ling (lôrd′ling), *n.* A little or petty lord (often in contempt); sometimes, a lording.

lord-ly (lôrd′li), *a.*; compar. *lordlier,* superl. *lordliest.* [AS. *hlāfordlīc.*] Of or pertaining to a lord or lords; consisting of lords; also, having the character or attributes of a lord, as a person; befitting a lord, as actions; suitable for a lord, as things; hence, grand or magnificent (as, "He saw at a distance the *lordly* Hudson, far, far below him": Irving's "Sketch-Book," Rip Van Winkle); also, haughty, imperious, or insolent (as, *lordly* indifference or contempt).—**lord′ly,** *adv.* In the manner of a lord.

lor-do-sis (lôr-dō′sis), *n.* [NL., < Gr. λόρδωσις, < λορδοῦν, bend back, < λορδός, bent back.] In *pathol.,* abnormal curvature of the spine, with the convexity toward the front; also, any abnormal curvature of the bones.—**lor-dot′ic** (-dot′ik), *a.*

lord-ship (lôrd′ship), *n.* [AS. *hlāfordscipe.*] The state or dignity of a lord; [often *cap.*] with *his* or *your,* the form used in speaking of or to a man having the title of *Lord* (but not a duke or an archbishop: see *grace, n.*), or of or to a judge, as in British use; also [*l. c.*], the authority or power of a lord (as, "They which are accounted to rule over the Gentiles exercise *lordship* over them": Mark, x. 42); also, the domain of a lord (as, "From many a *lordship* forth they rode": W. Morris's "Jason," iii. 7).

lore[1] (lōr), *n.* [AS. *lār* = D. *leer* = G. *lehre,* teaching: cf. *learn.*] Teaching or instruction, or that which is taught (archaic: as, "The subtle fiend his *lore* Soon learn'd," Milton's "Paradise Lost," ii. 815); also, admonition or counsel (obs. or archaic): also, bidding† or command† (as, "If I vanquishe him, he shall obay My law, and ever to my *lore* be bound": Spenser's "Faerie Queene," v. 4. 49); also (now chiefly in literary use), learning, knowledge, or erudition (as, "cobwebs of scholastic *lore*": Whittier's "Bridal of Pennacook"); now, often, the body of knowledge, esp. of a traditional, anecdotal, or popular nature, on a particular subject (as, the *lore* of herbs; folk*lore*).

lore[2] (lōr), *n.* [L. *lorum*, thong.] In *zoöl.*, the space between the eye and the bill of a bird, or a corresponding space in other animals, as serpents.

lo-rette (lō-ret′), *n.* [F.; so called from living near the church of Notre Dame de *Lorette*, in Paris.] In French usage, a courtezan of the more elegant or pretentious class.

lor-gnette (lôr-nyet′), *n.* [F., < *lorgner*, look sidelong at, eye: cf. *lorgnon.*] An opera-glass; also, a pair of eye-glasses mounted on a long handle.

lor-gnon (lôr-nyôṅ), *n.* [F., < *lorgner*: see *lorgnette.*] An eye-glass, or a pair of eye-glasses; also, an opera-glass.

lo-ri-ca (lō-rī′kạ), *n.*; pl. *-cæ* (-sē). [L., < *lorum*, thong.] A cuirass or corselet, orig. of leather; in *zoöl.*, a hard protective case or sheath, as the protective covering secreted by certain infusorians, the carapace of a crustacean, etc. —**lor-i-cate, lor-i-cat-ed** (lor′i-kāt, -kā-ted), *a.* [L. *loricatus.*] Covered with a lorica.

lor-i-keet (lor′i-kēt), *n.* [From *lory* + *(parra)keet.*] Any of various small lories. See *lory.*

lo-ris (lō′ris), *n.* [F. and NL.; said to be < D. *loeris*, booby.] A small, slender, tailless, large-eyed, nocturnal lemur, *Loris gracilis*, a native of Ceylon; also, any of various lemurs of the related genus *Nycticebus.*

Loris (*L. gracilis*).

lorn (lôrn), *a.* [ME. *lorn*, < AS. *loren*, pp. of *lēosan*, lose (recorded in compounds): see *loss.*] Lost, ruined, or undone (archaic: as, "If thou readest, thou art *lorn!* Better hadst thou ne'er been born!" Scott's "Lay of the Last Minstrel," i. 23); also, forsaken, desolate, wretched, or forlorn (chiefly archaic or prov.: as, "*Lorn* stream, whose sullen tide No sedge-crown'd sisters now attend," Wm. Collins's "Ode on the Death of Thomson," 29; "I am a lone *lorn* creetur'," Dickens's "David Copperfield," iii.).

lor-ry (lor′i), *n.*; pl. *lorries* (-iz). [Cf. prov. Eng. *lurry*, pull, drag, lug.] A long, flat, horse-drawn wagon without sides, set on four low wheels, common in England; any of various other horse-drawn or self-propelled wagons or trucks, esp. for heavy work; also, a kind of traction-engine for hauling heavy loads over roads, etc.; also, any of various vehicles or cars running on rails, as for transporting material in a mine or factory; also, a movable wheeled platform running over the mouth of a shaft or pit of a mine.

lo-ry (lō′ri), *n.*; pl. *-ries* (-riz). [Malay *lūrī.*] Any of various parrots (subfamily *Loriinæ*) of the Malay Archipelago, Australia, etc., mostly bright-colored, brush-tongued, and of small size; also, any of certain other birds resembling the true lories.

Lory (*Lorius domicella*).

los-a-ble (lö′zạ-bl), *a.* That may be lost.

lose (löz), *v.*; *lost, losing.* [AS. *losian*, be lost, perish, also destrŏy, ruin, < *los*, E. *loss.*] **I.** *tr.* To bring to destruction or ruin (now chiefly in the passive: as, ship and crew were *lost*); also, to suffer the loss or deprivation of (as, to *lose* one's life, fortune, rank, or faculties; to *lose* an eye; to *lose* troops or supporters); be deprived or dispossessed of; be bereaved of by death (as, to *lose* a child); fail to keep, preserve, or maintain (as, to *lose* one's balance, hold, temper, or patience; to *lose* ground); cease to have (as, to *lose* all fear; the scene has *lost* its strangeness); also, to come to be without, by some chance, and not know the whereabouts of (as, to *lose* a purse or a ring; to *lose* an address); have slip from sight, hearing, attention, etc. (as, to *lose* a face in a crowd; to *lose* words here and there in a speech; to *lose* the thread of a narrative); become separated from and ignorant of (the way, etc.); leave far behind in a pursuit, race, etc.; also, to let pass without use or profit (as, to *lose* an opportunity; to *lose* time in waiting); use to no purpose, or waste (as, "You do but *lose* your labour," Shakspere's "Measure for Measure," v. 1. 433; the hint was not *lost* upon him); also, to fail to have, get, catch, etc., or miss (as, to *lose* a meal or a bargain; to *lose* a train); fail to win (a prize, stake, etc.); be defeated in (a game, lawsuit, battle, etc.); also, to cause the loss of (as, the delay *lost* the battle for them; "Find out this villain, Edmund; it shall *lose* thee nothing," Shakspere's "King Lear," i. 2. 125); also, to let (one's self) go astray, become bewildered, or, fig., become absorbed or engrossed in something to the exclusion of knowledge or consciousness of all else (as, to *lose* one's self in a labyrinth; "He seemed to *lose* himself in thought," J. Conrad's "Rescue," iv. 2; to be *lost* in a wood; to be *lost* in thought or wonder). **II.** *intr.* To suffer loss (as, to *lose* on a contract); also, to lose ground, fall behind, or fail to hold one's own, as in a race or other contest; also, to fail to win, as in a contest; be defeated.

lo-sel (lō′zẹl or loz′ẹl). [ME. *losel, lorel*; akin to E. *lorn.*] **I.** *n.* A worthless person; a rascal; a scamp: as, "A *losell* . . . One that to bountie never cast his mynd" (Spenser's "Faerie Queene," ii. 3. 4). [Archaic or prov.] **II.** *a.* Worthless; good-for-nothing: as, "those *losel* scouts" (Irving's "Knickerbocker's New York," iii. 1). [Archaic or prov.]

los-er (lö′zėr), *n.* One who loses. —**los-ing** (lö′zing), *p. a.* That loses; suffering loss; losing ground or failing to win (as, the *losing* side in a contest); attended with losing, or ill success (as, "King Henry was weary of the *losing* game which he had so long been playing": Motley's "Dutch Republic," i. 3). —**los′ing-ly,** *adv.*

loss (lôs), *n.* [AS. *los*, destruction, = Icel. *los*, breaking up; akin to AS. *lēosan*, lose (see *lorn*), E. *loose*, L. *luere*, Gr. λύειν, loose, Skt. *lū-*, cut.] Destruction or ruin (as, "Thou hast . . . quitted all to save A world from utter *loss*," Milton's "Paradise Lost," iii. 308; "Hard upon the cry of 'breakers' came The crash of ruin, and the *loss* of all But Enoch," Tennyson's "Enoch Arden," 545); also, a being deprived of or coming to be without something that one has had (as, *loss* of fortune, friends, or credit); a being bereaved by death, and hence death (as, to mourn the *loss* of a parent); failure to preserve or maintain (as, *loss* of speed); also, the accidental or inadvertent losing of something dropped, misplaced, or of unknown whereabouts (as, to discover the *loss* of a bracelet or of a document; to advertise a *loss* in the newspapers); also, failure to make good use of something, as time; waste; also, a losing by defeat, or failure to win (as, the *loss* of a bet, a game, a race, or a battle); also, detriment or disadvantage from failure to keep, have, or get (as, to bear the *loss* of a robbery; if he refuses, the *loss* is his; their *loss* is our gain); also, that which is lost (as, "The wager thou hast won; and I will add Unto their *losses* twenty thousand crowns": Shakspere's "Taming of the Shrew," v. 2. 113); a person or thing that when lost is seriously missed (as, the deceased is a great *loss* to the community); *milit.*, the losing of soldiers by death, capture, etc., or (often *pl.*) the number of soldiers so lost. —**at a loss,** in a state of bewilderment or uncertainty (orig. of hounds that had lost the scent); at a disadvantage for want of knowledge; more generally, in a state of embarrassment for want of something (as, to be *at a loss* for words).

löss (lės), *n.* See *loess.*

lost (lôst), *p. a.* [See *lose.*] Destroyed or ruined (as, *lost* ships; a *lost* soul); also, no longer possessed or retained (as, *lost* estates or powers; *lost* friends); also, no longer to be found (as, *lost* articles; animals *lost*, strayed, or stolen); missing; also, not used to good purpose, as opportunities, time, labor, etc.; wasted; also, that one has failed to win (as, a *lost* prize); attended with defeat (as, a *lost* battle); also, having gone astray or lost the way; bewildered as to place, direction, etc.—**lost cause,** a cause for which defeat has occurred or is inevitable: often used with reference to the cause of the Confederacy in the American Civil War.—**lost to,** no longer belonging to; also, no longer possible or open to (as, the opportunity was *lost to* him); also, insensible to (as, to be *lost to* all sense of duty; completely *lost to* reason or shame).

lot (lot), *n.* [AS. *hlot*, akin to G. *loos*, Icel. *hlutr*, Goth. *hlauts*, lot, and AS. *hlēotan*, cast lots, obtain by lot.] One of a set of objects, as pieces of wood or other material specially marked, or slips of paper of different lengths, used by casting all into a receptacle and then shaking or taking one out, or by drawing in turn and at random from the total number, to decide a question or choice by chance; hence, the casting or drawing of such objects as a method of deciding something (as, to choose a person by *lot* for a task); the decision or choice so made (as, "The *lot* fell upon Matthias": Acts, i. 26); also, something assigned by or as by the casting or drawing of lots, as a share of property (as, "This then was the *lot* of the tribe . . . of Judah . . . even to the border of Edom": Josh. xv. 1); allotted share or portion; fig., the portion in life assigned by fate or Providence, or one's fate, fortune, or destiny (as, "We will submit to whatever *lot* a wise Providence may send us," Hawthorne's "Twice-Told Tales," Edward Randolph's Portrait; to have a happy *lot*; happiness beyond the common *lot* of mankind); also, a tax or duty (cf. *scot and lot*, under *scot*¹); also, a prize in a lottery†; also, a distinct portion or piece of land; a distinct portion or parcel of anything, as of merchandise; hence, a number of things or persons collectively, or a collection, company, or set (colloq.: as, "They aint a bad *lot*,—them Blazin' Star boys," Bret Harte's "Fool of Five Forks"; "It's a wicked, thieving, lying, scheming *lot* you are," Synge's "Tinker's Wedding," ii.); sometimes, a person of a specified sort (colloq.: as, he is a bad, or a hard, *lot*); also, a great many or a great deal (colloq., and often in *pl.*: as, a *lot* of books, people, or courage; a *lot*, *lots*, or *lots* and *lots*, of money).—**lot,** *v.*; *lotted, lotting.* **I.** *tr.* To cast or draw lots for; divide or distribute by lot; also, to assign to one as his lot; allot; also, to divide into lots, as land. **II.** *intr.* To cast or draw lots.

lo-ta (lō'tạ̈), *n.* [Hindi.] A spheroidal pot, commonly of brass, used in the East Indies for holding water, etc.

lote (lōt), *n.* Same as *lotus.* [Archaic.]

loth (lōth), *a.* See *loath.*

Lo-tha-ri-o (lọ̄-thā'ri-ō), *n.*; pl. *-os* (-ōz). [From *Lothario*, a character in Rowe's play, "The Fair Penitent" (1703).] A jaunty libertine; a gay deceiver; a rake.

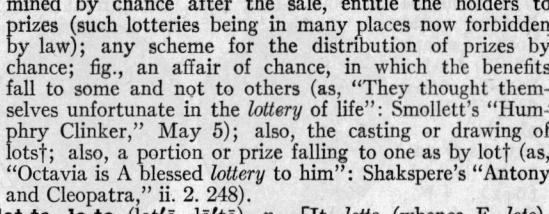

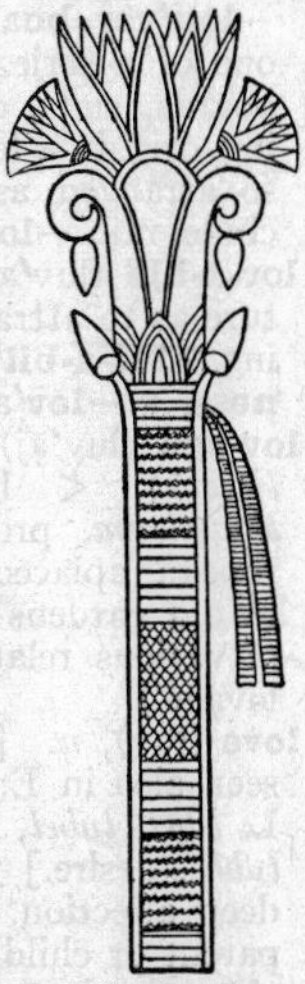
Egyptian Lotiform Decoration.

lo-ti-form (lō'ti-fôrm), *a.* [L. *lotus*, lotus, + *forma*, form.] Shaped like or resembling the lotus, as decorative forms, etc.

lo-tion (lō'shọn), *n.* [L. *lotio(n-)*, a washing, < *lavare* (pp. *lotus*), wash.] Washing† or ablution†; in *phar.*, etc., a liquid containing medicinal matter in solution, applied externally to relieve pain, heal, cleanse, etc., or to benefit the skin; a medicinal or cosmetic wash.

lo'to, *n.* See *lotto.*

Lo-toph-a-gi (lọ̄-tof'ạ-jī), *n. pl.* [L., < Gr. Λωτοφάγοι, < λωτός, lotus, + φαγεῖν, eat.] In Greek legend, esp. as in Homer's "Odyssey," ix., a people who ate the fruit of the lotus and lived in a state of dreamy forgetfulness induced by it; the lotus-eaters.—**lo-toph'a-gous** (-gus), *a.*

lo-tos (lō'tọs), *n.* Same as *lotus.*

lot-te-ry (lot'ẹ-ri), *n.*; pl. *-ries* (-riz). [It. *lotteria*, < *lotto*, lot; from Teut., and akin to E. *lot.*] A scheme or arrangement for raising money, as for some public, charitable, or private purpose, by the sale of a large number of tickets, certain among which, as determined by chance after the sale, entitle the holders to prizes (such lotteries being in many places now forbidden by law); any scheme for the distribution of prizes by chance; fig., an affair of chance, in which the benefits fall to some and not to others (as, "They thought themselves unfortunate in the *lottery* of life": Smollett's "Humphry Clinker," May 5); also, the casting or drawing of lots†; also, a portion or prize falling to one as by lot† (as, "Octavia is A blessed *lottery* to him": Shakspere's "Antony and Cleopatra," ii. 2. 248).

lot-to, lo-to (lot'ō, lō'tō), *n.* [It. *lotto* (whence F. *loto*), orig. lot: see *lottery.*] A game played by drawing numbered disks from a bag or the like and covering corresponding numbers on cards.

lo-tus (lō'tus), *n.*; pl. *lotuses.* [L. *lotus, lotos*, < Gr. λωτός, name of various plants.] A plant, commonly identified with a species of jujube or of nettle-tree (see *lotus-tree*), referred to in Greek legend as yielding a fruit which induced a state of dreamy and contented forgetfulness in those who ate it; the fruit itself; also, any of various nymphæaceous plants, as either of two Egyptian water-lilies, *Castalia lotus* and *C. cærulea*, or either of the two species of nelumbo, *Nelumbo nelumbo* ('sacred lotus' of India) and *N. lutea* (water-chinkapin); a representation of such a plant, common in Egyptian and Hindu decorative art; also, any of the shrubby herbs, with red, pink, or white flowers, constituting the fabaceous genus *Lotus*, certain of which are valued as pasture-plants.—**lo'tus=eat''er,** *n.* An eater of the fabled lotus-fruit of Greek legend (see *Lotophagi*, also Tennyson's "Lotos-Eaters" and "Choric Song"); hence, one who leads a life of dreamy, indolent ease, indifferent to the affairs or claims of the busy world.—**lo'tus=eat''ing,** *n.* and *a.*—**lo'tus=tree,** *n.* A species of jujube, *Zizyphus lotus*, of northern Africa and southern Europe, supposed by many to have produced the lotus-fruit of Greek legend; also, the old-world nettle-tree, *Celtis australis*, which has also been associated with this fruit.

loud (loud), *a.* [AS. *hlūd* = D. *luid* = G. *laut*, loud; orig. pp., lit. 'heard,' from a root represented also by L. *cluere*, Gr. κλύειν, Skt. *çru-*, hear: cf. *list*¹ and *client.*] Striking strongly upon the organs of hearing, as sound, noise, the voice, etc.; heard as strong, or of great volume, or carrying far; strongly audible; also, making, emitting, or uttering strongly audible sounds (as, *loud* knocking; *loud* winds; *loud* trumpets; a *loud* speaker); also, full of sound or noise, or resounding (as, "When all is gay with lamps, and *loud* With sport and song": Tennyson's "In Memoriam," xcviii.); also, clamorous, vociferous, or blatant (as, "Now see him . . . If lawyer, *loud* whatever cause he plead": Cowper's "Hope," 201); emphatic or insistent (as, to be *loud* in one's praises; *loud* in demands or objections); also, strong or offensive in smell (now colloq.); also, excessively striking to the eye, or offensively showy, as colors, dress or the wearer, etc.; vaguely ostentatious in appearance, manners, etc., as persons; obtrusively vulgar, as manners.—**loud,** *adv.* Loudly: as, to talk *loud* and long.

loud-en (lou'dn), *v. i.* or *t.* To become or make louder; increase in sound. Also fig.

loud-ish (lou'dish), *a.* Somewhat loud.

loud-ly (loud'li), *adv.* In a loud manner.

loud=mouthed (loud'mouᴛʜd'), *a.* Loud of voice or utterance; vociferous; blatant.

loud-ness (loud'nes), *n.* The state or quality of being loud.

loud=speak-er (loud'spē'kėr), *n.* Any of various devices for amplifying the sound of a speaker's voice, of music, etc.; specif., in *wireless teleph.*, any of certain devices by which speech, music, etc., received by a wireless telephone can be made audible throughout a room, hall, or the like, thus doing away with individual receivers.—**loud'=speak'ing. I.** *n.* The action or function of a loud-speaker, in amplifying sound. **II.** *a.* Acting as a loud-speaker; amplifying the sound of the voice, music, etc. (as, a *loud-speaking* device); pertaining to a loud-speaker (as, *loud-speaking* results).

loud=talk-er (loud'tâ'kėr), *n.* A loud-speaker.

lough (loċh), *n.* [Ir. *loch*: cf. *loch.*] A lake; also, an arm of the sea. [Ir.]

lou-is (lö'i, F. lö-ē), *n.*; pl. *louis* (lö'iz, F. lö-ē). [F.; from Louis XIII.] A French gold coin, issued 1640–1795, worth from about $4 to about $4.60; also, the current French 20-franc gold coin (worth $3.86). Also **lou-is d'or** (dôr) (F., 'louis of gold').

Obverse. Reverse.
Louis of Louis XIII., 1641.

Lou-is Qua-torze (lö-ē kä-tôrz). [F., 'Louis Fourteenth.'] Pertaining to the period of Louis XIV. of France (1643–1715) or to the styles of architecture, decoration, etc., then prevailing, characterized by a greater use of classical forms and details than in the Louis Treize period, and by great richness of ornamentation.—**Lou-is Quinze** (kañz). [F., 'Louis Fifteenth.'] Pertaining to the period of Louis XV. of France (1715–74) or to the styles of architecture, decoration, etc., then prevailing, characterized by a carrying to extremes of the peculiarities of the Louis Quatorze period, with disregard of symmetry, and with a profusion of ornament seen in its most debased form in the style termed 'rococo' (see *rococo*).—**Lou-is Seize** (sāz). [F., 'Louis Sixteenth.'] Pertaining to the period of Louis XVI. of France (1774–92) or to the styles of architecture, decoration, etc., then prevailing, characterized by a return to greater simplicity than in the Louis Quinze period, with recurrence to classical models.—**Lou-is Treize** (trāz). [F., 'Louis Thirteenth.'] Pertaining to the period of Louis XIII. of France (1610–43) or to the styles of architecture, decoration, etc., then prevailing, less light and elegant than those of the earlier Renaissance, and employing forms and features based on the classical.

lou-koum (lö-köm'), *n.* [Turk. *luqūm.*] Fig-paste.

loun-der (loun'dėr), *n.* [Origin obscure.] A heavy or violent blow. [Chiefly Sc.]—**loun'der,** *v. t.* To beat with heavy blows; thrash. [Chiefly Sc.]

lounge (lounj), *v.*; *lounged, lounging.* [Origin obscure.] **I.** *intr.* To move or go (*about, along, off,* etc.) in a leisurely, indolent manner (as, "The colonel *lounged* across the room": Kingsley's "Yeast," vi.); also, to recline indolently, or loll (as, "He has *lounged* long enough in the old chair": Hawthorne's "House of the Seven Gables," xviii.); also, to pass time idly and indolently; idle at one's ease. **II.** *tr.* To pass (time, etc.) in lounging: with *away* or *out.*—**lounge,** *n.* The act or a spell of lounging (as, "Every old tramper . . . sees the light of our kitchen fire, and comes in for a *lounge*": Mrs. Stowe's "Oldtown Folks," vi.); also, a lounging gait (as, "tall, raw-boned Kentuckians . . . with the easy *lounge* peculiar to the race": Mrs. Stowe's "Uncle Tom's Cabin," xi.); also, a place for lounging (as, "Po-Po's house was as pleasant a *lounge* as one could wish": H. Melville's "Omoo," lxxvii.); a place or resort for social or fashionable idlers (as, "Dublin . . . is, perhaps, the only city of its size . . . where there is no *lounge*—no promenade": Lever's "Harry Lorrequer," xii.); an apartment for lounging, as in a hotel; also, a kind of sofa for reclining on, with or without a back, and with a head-rest at one end.—**loun-ger** (loun'jėr), *n.*—**loun'ging-ly,** *adv.*

loup (loup), *v.* [From Scand.: cf. Icel. *hlaupa,* leap, run, and see *lope* and *leap.*] **I.** *intr.* To leap; spring; frisk or dance; also, to bound along; run; flee. [Sc. and north. Eng.] **II.** *tr.* To leap over or from; flee from. [Sc. and north. Eng.]—**loup,** *n.* A leap, spring, or bound: as, "The horses gave a sudden *loup*" (Galt's "Annals of the Parish," viii.). [Sc. and north. Eng.]

loup=cer-vier (lö-ser-vyā), *n.*; pl. *loups-cerviers* (lö-ser-vyā). [F., < L. *lupus cervarius,* wolf that hunts the deer (*cervus,* deer): cf. *lucivee.*] The Canada lynx, *Lynx canadensis.*

loupe (löp), *n.* See *loop*².

loup=ga-rou (lö-gȧ-rö), *n.*; pl. *loups-garous* (lö-gȧ-rö). [F., < *loup* (< L. *lupus*), wolf, + *garou* (from Teut.), = E. *werwolf.*] A werwolf.

lour (lour), **lour-ing** (lour'ing), etc. See *lower*¹, *lowering,* etc.

louse (lous), *n.*; pl. *lice* (līs). [AS. *lūs* (pl. *lȳs*) = D. *luis* = G. *laus* = Icel. *lūs,* louse.] Any of certain small, wingless, blood-sucking hemipterous insects of the genus *Pediculus,* as *P. capitis,* which infests the hair of the human head ('head-louse'), or *P. vestimenti,* which infests the human body and its clothing, causing great irritation ('body-louse'); any of the hemipterous group or order (*Parasitica*) to which these insects belong; also, any of various other insects parasitic on animals or plants, as those of the group or order *Mallophaga* ('bird-lice' or 'biting lice') or those of the homopterous family *Aphididæ* ('plant-lice' or aphids); also, any of various similar but non-parasitic insects; also, any of various parasitic or non-parasitic arachnids, crustaceans, etc. (cf. *wood-louse*).—**louse'wort** (-wėrt), *n.* Any of the scrophulariaceous herbs constituting the genus *Pedicularis,* as *P. sylvatica,* an English species formerly supposed to breed lice in sheep, and *P. canadensis,* wood-betony.—**lous-y** (lou'zi), *a.*; compar. *lousier,* superl. *lousiest.* Infested with lice; hence, dirty, mean, or contemptible (now vulgar).—**lous'i-ly,** *adv.*—**lous'i-ness,** *n.*

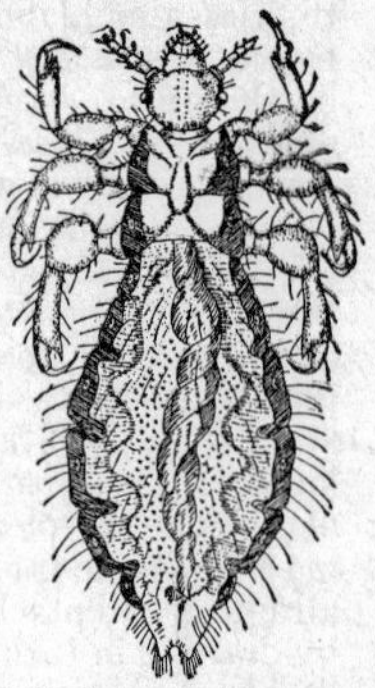

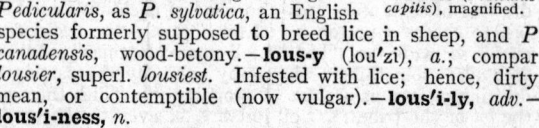

Head-louse (*Pediculus capitis*), magnified.

lout¹ (lout), *v. i.* [AS. *lūtan* = Icel. *lūta.*] To bow, bend, or stoop; esp., to bow in obeisance or salutation (as, "Lowly *louted* the boys, and lowly the maidens all courtesied": Longfellow's tr. Tegnér's "Children of the Lord's Supper," 76). [Archaic or Sc. and prov. Eng.]

lout² (lout), *n.* [Cf. *lout*¹, also Icel. *lūtr,* bowed, stooping.] An awkward, stupid fellow; a clown: as, "Grimes is a rough, rustic *lout*" (Godwin's "Caleb Williams," vii.).—**lout'ish,** *a.* Like or characteristic of a lout; clownish.—**lout'ish-ly,** *adv.*—**lout'ish-ness,** *n.*

lou-troph-o-ros (lö-trof'ọ-ros), *n.*; pl. *-roi* (-roi). [Gr. λουτροφόρος, < λουτρόν, bath, + φέρειν, bear.] In *Gr. antiq.,* a tall, long-necked vase for carrying water for a bath, esp. a ceremonial nuptial bath: hence often placed upon the tomb of a young person who died unmarried.

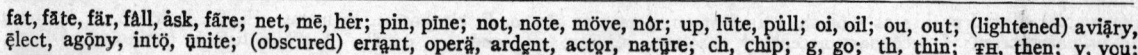

Funerary Loutrophoros.

lou-ver (lö'vėr), *n.* [OF. *lover, lovier*; origin obscure.] A turret or lantern on the roof of a medieval building, to supply ventilation or light; also, an arrangement of louver-boards or the like closing a window or other opening, or a single louver-board; also, one of a number of slit-like openings in the side of the hood of an automobile, for the escape of heated air from within. —**lou'ver=board,** *n.* In *arch.,* etc., one of a series of overlapping, sloping boards, slats, or the like, in an opening, orig. in a louver or medieval turret, so arranged as to admit air but exclude rain.—**lou'ver=board''ing,** *n.*

lov-a-ble (luv'ạ-bl), *a.* Of such a nature as to attract love; amiable; pleasing.—**lov-a-bil'i-ty** (-bil'i-ti), **lov'a-ble-ness,** *n.*—**lov'a-bly,** *adv.*

lov-age (luv'āj), *n.* [OF. *levesche* (F. *livêche*), < LL. *levisticum,* for L. *ligusticum,* prop. neut. of *Ligusticus,* Ligurian.] A European apiaceous herb, *Levisticum levisticum,* cultivated in old gardens and used as a domestic remedy; also, any of various related plants, as *Ligusticum scoticum* ('Scotch lovage').

love (luv), *n.* [AS. *lufu* = OHG. *luba,* love; from a root seen also in E. *lief* and *belief,* and further represented by L. *libet, lubet,* it is pleasing, Gr. λίπτεσθαι, be eager, Skt. *lubh-,* desire.] A feeling of warm personal attachment or deep affection, as for a friend (or between friends), for a parent or child, etc.; warm fondness or liking for another; also, the benevolent affection of God for his creatures, or the reverent affection due from them to God; also, the kindly affection proper for God's creatures toward one another; often, that strong or passionate affection for a person of the opposite sex which constitutes the emotional incentive to conjugal union; an instance or case of such affection (as, "The parents' harshness and the hapless *loves* . . . were widely murmur'd": Tennyson's "Aylmer's Field," 616); a love-affair; [*cap.*] a personification of sexual affection, as Eros or Cupid; [*l. c.*] a cupid, as in decoration; also, sexual passion or desire, or its gratification; also, strong predilection or liking for anything (as, *love* of books, truth, or ease); also, an object of love or affection; a sweetheart; something charming or delightful (colloq.); also, in certain games, as tennis, nothing, or no score.—**for love,** out of affection; hence, for nothing, or without compensation; also, without stakes (as, to play a game *for love*).—**for love or money,** for any consideration; by any means: as, things not to be had *for love or money*.—**for the love of,** for the sake of.—**in love,** in the condition of a person who loves, or is enamoured of, one of the opposite sex (as, to be deeply *in love*; to fall *in love* with a person); hence, greatly pleased, as with something (as, to be *in love* with a plan).—**no love lost,** formerly, no love lacking, as between persons who love each other† (as, "We grumble a little now and then . . . But there's *no love lost* between us": Goldsmith's "She Stoops to Conquer," iv.); now, no love wasted, as between persons who have little love for each other (as, "There was *no love lost* between the two ladies": Thackeray's "Newcomes," v.).—**to make love to,** to make professions or demonstrations of love to (one of the opposite sex); woo; hence, to devote one's self assiduously to (humorous: as, he is *making love to* the punch-bowl); also, to appropriate or take (humorous: as, somebody has *made love to* my pen).—**love,** *v.*; *loved, loving.* [AS. *lufian.*] **I.** *tr.* To have love or affection for; hold dear; often, to have a strong or passionate affection for (one of the opposite sex); be in love with; also, to have a strong liking for, or take great pleasure in (as, to *love* music or dancing: often used colloquially in extravagant assertions, as, "If there's any thing I just *love,* it's exposing a fraud!" G. W. Cable's "Bonaventure," ii. 10); hence, of animals and plants, to find (a climate, situation, etc.) agreeable or suited to needs; also, to caress (chiefly in childish use). **II.** *intr.* To have love or affection; esp., to be or fall in love with one of the opposite sex (as, "Who ever *lov'd,* that *lov'd* not at first sight?" Marlowe's "Hero and Leander," i.).

love′a-ble, etc. See *lovable,* etc.

love=af-fair (luv′ạ-fãr″), *n.* A particular experience of being in love.

love=ap-ple (luv′ap″l), *n.* An old name for the tomato.

love=bird (luv′bėrd), *n.* Any of various small parrots, esp. of the genera *Agapornis,* of Africa, and *Psittacula,* of South America, remarkable for the affection shown between mates.

Love-birds (*Agapornis cana*).

love=child (luv′chīld), *n.* An illegitimate child.

love=feast (luv′fēst), *n.* Among the early Christians, a meal eaten in token of brotherly love and charity; hence, an analogous service held by certain modern religious denominations, as the Methodists and Moravians; also, a banquet or other gathering of persons, as of members of a political party, to promote good feeling.

love=in=a=mist (luv′in-ạ-mist′), *n.* A ranunculaceous plant, *Nigella damascena,* a species of fennel-flower, with feathery dissected leaves and whitish or blue flowers: common in gardens. See cut in next column.

love=in=i-dle-ness (luv′in-ī′dl-nes), *n.* The wild pansy, *Viola tricolor.* See Shakspere's "Midsummer Night's Dream," ii. 1. 168.

love=knot (luv′not), *n.* An ornamental knot serving as a symbol of love (cf. *true-love knot,* under *true-love*); also, a knot of ribbon given or worn as a token of love.

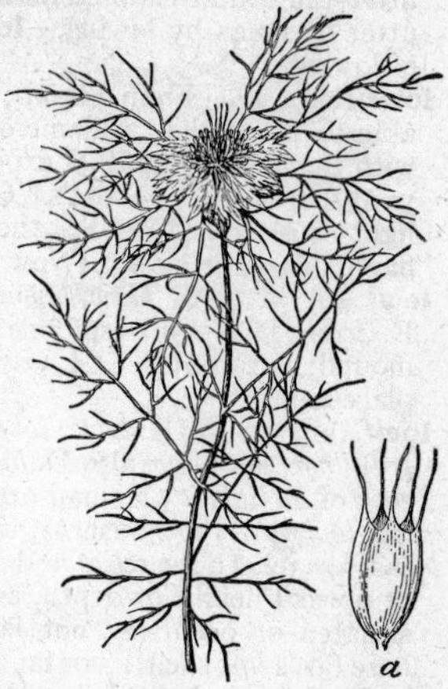
Flowering Branch of Love-in-a-mist. *a,* the fruit.

love-less (luv′les), *a.* Without love; feeling no love (as, a *loveless* heart); receiving or winning no love (as, a *loveless* child); devoid of or unattended with love (as, a *loveless* marriage).—**love′-less-ly,** *adv.*—**love′less-ness,** *n.*

love=let-ter (luv′let″ėr), *n.* A letter of love or amorous regard; a lover's letter; a billet-doux.

love=lies=bleed-ing (luv′līz-blē′ding), *n.* A plant, *Amarantus caudatus,* with spikes of crimson flowers; also, some other plant of the same genus. Cf. *amaranth.*

love-li-ly (luv′li-li), *adv.* In a lovely manner.—**love′li-ness,** *n.*

love=lock (luv′lok), *n.* Formerly, a long, flowing lock or curl, dressed separately from the rest of the hair, worn by courtiers; hence, any conspicuous lock of hair.

love=lorn (luv′lôrn), *a.* Forsaken by one's love; forlorn or pining from love: as, a *love-lorn* maiden; "the *love-lorn* nightingale" (Milton's "Comus," 234).—**love′=lorn″ness,** *n.*

love-ly (luv′li), *a.*; compar. *lovelier,* superl. *loveliest.* [AS. *luflīc.*] Loving†; also, lovable (now rare: as, "Affection may certainly exist independent of esteem; nay, the same object may be *lovely* in one respect and detestable in another," Smollett's "Humphry Clinker," Oct. 26); also, having a beauty that appeals to the heart as well as to the eye, as a person, a face, etc.; in general, charmingly or exquisitely beautiful (as, a *lovely* flower; a *lovely* scene; *lovely* moonlight); fig., of great moral or spiritual beauty (as, a *lovely* character; a *lovely* life); also, delightful, or highly pleasing (colloq.: as, we had a *lovely* time; "It's . . . very kind of you, Jack, to offer me this *lovely* holiday," G. B. Shaw's "Man and Superman," ii.).

love=match (luv′mach), *n.* A matrimonial match founded on love rather than on worldly considerations.

love=po-tion (luv′pō″shọn), *n.* A potion intended to induce love; a philter.

lov-er (luv′ėr), *n.* One who loves; a friend or well-wisher; specif., one who is enamoured of a person of the opposite sex (now used almost exclusively of the man, except when in the *pl.* and indicating two persons in love with each other); sometimes, a paramour; often, one who has a strong predilection or liking for something (as, a *lover* of music or of flowers).—**lov′er-ly,** *a.* Like or befitting a lover: as, *loverly* attentions.—**lov′er-li-ness,** *n.*—**lov′er-ly,** *adv.*

love=seat (luv′sēt), *n.* A double seat, for two persons.

love=sick (luv′sik), *a.* Sick or languishing with love; also, expressive of such languishing (as, *love-sick* sighs).—**love′=sick″ness,** *n.*

love-some (luv′sum), *a.* [AS. *lufsum.*] Lovable; also, lovely or beautiful (as, "One praised her ankles . . . One her dark hair and *lovesome* mien": Tennyson's "Beggar Maid"); also, loving, affectionate, or amorous (as, "shrubs that twined their arms together in *lovesome* tangles": Kinglake's "Eothen," vii.). [Archaic or Sc. and north. Eng.]—**love′some-ness,** *n.*

lov-ing (luv′ing), *n.* The act or the feeling of one who loves.—**lov′ing,** *p. a.* Feeling or showing love; affectionate; fond: as, *loving* hearts; *loving* glances.—**lov′ing=cup,** *n.* A large cup, as of silver, commonly with several handles, for passing from hand to hand among persons who drink from it in turn, as at the close of a banquet: as, "To-night the *loving-cup* we'll drain, To-morrow for the Spanish Main!" (H. Newbolt's "Laudabunt Alii").—**lov′ing=kind′ness,** *n.* Kindness arising from love: as, "How excellent is thy *lovingkindness,* O God!" (Ps. xxxvi. 7).—**lov′ing-ly,** *adv.*—**lov′ing-ness,** *n.*

low[1] (lō), *v.* [AS. *hlōwan* = D. *loeien*, low.] **I.** *intr.* To utter the sound characteristic of cattle; moo. **II.** *tr.* To utter by or as by lowing.—**low**[1], *n.* The act or the sound of lowing.

low[2] (lou), *n.* [From Scand.: cf. Icel. *logi*, Dan. *lue*, flame; akin to E. *light*[1].] A flame or blaze (as, "Ye would quarrel with these gipsies too! I expect every day to hear the barn-yard's in a *low*": Scott's "Guy Mannering," ix.); also, a light or glow. [Now Sc. and prov. Eng.]—**low**[2], *v. i.* To flame, blaze, or glow. [Now Sc. and prov. Eng.]

low[3] (lō), *n.* [AS. *hlāw*, *hlǣw*, hill, mound; from the root of E. *lean*[1].] A hill, esp. one of round or conical form; a mound; a tumulus. Cf. *law*[2]. [Archaic, prov. Eng., or in place-names.]

low[4] (lō), *a.* [ME. *lowe*, *lohe*, earlier *lah*, from Scand.: cf. Icel. *lāgr*, Dan. *lav*, also D. *laag*, G. dial. *läge*, low; from the root of E. *lie*[1].] Of small extent upward, or not high or tall (as, *low* walls; *low* bushes); rising but slightly from a surface (as, *low* relief: see *relief* and *bas-relief*); of less than average or normal height or depth, as a liquid, a stream, etc.; also, situated or occurring not far above the ground, floor, or base (as, a *low* shelf); not far above the horizon, as a heavenly body; lying or being below the general level (as, *low* ground); designating or pertaining to regions near the sea-level or the sea as opposed to highland or inland regions (as, the *Low* Germans: see under *German*[2], *n.*); prostrate or dead (as, to lay one *low*); profound or deep, as a bow; also, far down in the scale of rank or estimation, or humble (as, *low* birth or station; "Exalt him that is *low*, and abase him that is high," Ezek. xxi. 26); of inferior quality or character (as, a *low* type of mind); not advanced in civilization, organization, etc. (as, a *low* organism); lacking in dignity or elevation, as of thought or expression (as, "The Muse . . . no more attempts to rise, But in *low* numbers short excursions tries": Pope's "Essay on Criticism," 738); groveling or abject; mean or base (as, "*low* cunning," Wiseman's "Fabiola," i. 9; a *low* trick); coarse or vulgar (as, *low* company or tastes; a *low* word); dissolute or degraded (as, *low* women; *low* vices); also, lacking in strength or vigor, feeble, or weak (as, "The Master seemed extremely *low* . . . and lay much of the time insensible": Stevenson's "Master of Ballantrae," xi.); affording little strength or nourishment, as diet; also, small in amount, degree, force, etc., as a number, price, pressure, etc.; denoted by a low number (as, a *low* latitude, one near the equator); having a low price, or cheap; assigning or attributing no great amount, value, or excellence (as, a *low* estimate or opinion of something); also, produced by relatively slow vibrations, as sounds; grave in pitch; often, not loud (as, a *low* murmur); also, relatively late or recent, as a date; also, moderate or liberal in opinion or doctrine (cf. *Low-church*); also, depressed or dejected (as, to be *low* in one's mind; *low* spirits); also, lowly, humble, or meek (now rare).—**low area,** in *meteor.*, a region where the atmospheric or barometric pressure is lower than that of the surrounding regions: as, the *low area* in the central part of a cyclone.—**low=area storm,** in *meteor.*, a cyclone: so called from the region of low barometric pressure (low area) at its center.—**low comedy,** comedy of a broadly humorous kind, without the dignity of high comedy, and regularly employing characters of a less polite or refined type. Compare *high comedy*, under *high*, *a.*—**Low Countries,** the regions forming or corresponding to the former Netherlands, or Holland, Flanders (Belgium), etc.—**Low Latin.** See under *Latin*, *n.*—**low mass.** See under *mass*[1].—**Low Sunday,** the Sunday next after Easter.—**low tide,** the tide at low water; the time of low water; fig., the lowest point of decline.—**low water,** water at its lowest level, as in a river; the lowest state of the tide; the time when the lowest point of the tide is reached.—**low=water mark,** a mark showing the lowest level reached by a body of water; esp., the mark left or the limit reached by the tide at low water; fig., the lowest point reached, as in intensity, quality, quantity, etc.—**low**[4], *n.* That which is low; in *meteor.*, a low area (see phrase above).—**low**[4], *adv.* In or to a low position, point, degree, etc.; near the ground, floor, or base, or not aloft; humbly; meanly; cheaply; at or to a low pitch; in a low tone, softly, or quietly; far down in time, or late.

low=born (lō'bôrn), *a.* Of low station by birth; of humble birth.

low=boy (lō'boi), *n.* A low chest of drawers supported on short legs. Cf. *high-boy*.

low=bred (lō'bred), *a.* Of a low or inferior breed; also, characterized by or characteristic of low or vulgar breeding (as, a *low-bred* fellow; a *low-bred* air).

low-brow (lō'brou). **I.** *n.* A person of low intellectual caliber, or lacking in appreciation of intellectuality and culture: used humorously or disparagingly. Cf. *highbrow*. [Slang.] **II.** *a.* Being a lowbrow; pertaining or proper to lowbrows. [Slang.]

Low=church (lō'chėrch'), *a.* Laying little stress on church authority and usage, ritual, etc.; evangelical: used of a party in the Anglican Church, and opposed to *High-church*.—**Low'=church'man** (-man), *n.*; pl. *-men*.

low=down (lō'doun). **I.** *a.* Low, esp. in the social or moral scale; degraded; abject; mean: as, a *low-down* neighborhood. [Colloq.] **II.** *n.* With *the*, the actual, unadorned facts or truth on some subject. [Slang.]

lowe (lou), *n.* and *v.* See *low*[2].

low-er[1], **lour** (lou'ėr, lour), *v. i.* [ME. *louren*, frown, lurk: cf. MD. *loeren*, frown, lie in wait, D. lurk, spy, MLG. *lūren*, G. *lauern*, lurk, and E. *lurk*.] To frown, scowl, or look sullen; hence, to be dark and threatening, as the sky or the weather; also, to lurk, skulk, or crouch (now Sc.).—**low'er**[1], **lour,** *n.* A frown or scowl; hence, a dark, threatening appearance, as of the sky, weather, etc.

low-er[2] (lō'ėr), *a.* Comparative of *low*[4], *a.*: in *geol.*, noting an earlier division of a period, system, or the like (as, the *Lower* Devonian, *Lower* Cambrian, etc.).—**lower world,** the regions of the dead, conceived by the ancients as lying beneath the earth's surface; Hades; also, the earth, as distinguished from the heavenly bodies or from heaven.—**low'er**[2], *adv.* Comparative of *low*[4], *adv.*—**low'er**[2], *v.* **I.** *tr.* To cause to descend, or let down (as, to *lower* a flag; to *lower* a bucket into a well); also, to make lower in height or level (as, to *lower* the water in a canal); also, to bring down in rank or estimation, degrade, or humble; abase (one's self), as by some sacrifice of dignity; also, to reduce in amount, price, degree, force, etc.; make less loud, as the voice; in *music*, to make lower in pitch; flatten. **II.** *intr.* To descend; sink; also, to become lower or less.

low-er=case (lō'ėr-kās'), *a.* In *printing*, pertaining to or belonging in the lower case (see *case*[2], *n.*); of a letter, small (as opposed to *capital*).—**low'er=case',** *v. t.* To print or write with a lower-case letter or letters.

low-er-ing, lour-ing (lou'ėr-ing, lour'ing), *p. a.* [See *lower*[1].] Frowning or sullen, as the face, gaze, etc.; hence, dark and threatening, as the sky, clouds, weather, etc. (as, "a gloomy and *lowering* day": Parkman's "Oregon Trail," vi.); cloudy; gloomy.—**low'er-ing-ly, lour'ing-ly,** *adv.*

low-er-most (lō'ėr-mōst), *a. superl.* Lowest.

low-er-y, lour-y (lou'ėr-i, lou'ri), *a.* Lowering.

low=hung (lō'hung), *a.* Hung low; low in position or build; of a vehicle, having the body so attached to the axle as to be comparatively near the ground.

low-ing (lō'ing), *n.* [See *low*[1].] The act or the sound of cattle that low; a mooing sound.

low-land (lō'land). **I.** *n.* Land low with respect to neighboring country; *pl.* [usually *cap.*], a less mountainous region or part of a country (as, the *Lowlands* of Scotland, in the southern and eastern parts of the country). **II.** *a.* Of, pertaining to, or characteristic of lowland or lowlands, esp. [usually *cap.*] the Lowlands of Scotland.—**low'land-er,** *n.* An inhabitant of lowland or lowlands, esp. [*cap.*] a native of the Lowlands of Scotland.

low-li-head (lō'li-hed), *n.* Lowliness; humility: as, "The stately flower . . . Of perfect wifehood and pure *lowlihead*" (Tennyson's "Isabel"). [Archaic.]

low-li-ly (lō'li-li), *adv.* In a lowly manner; humbly.—**low'li-ness,** *n.* The state or quality of being lowly; lowly spirit; humility.

low=lived (lō'līvd), *a.* Belonging in or characteristic of a low order of life or society; vulgar; mean: as, "a *low-lived* Yankee, who had never known a gentleman in his life" (F. H. Smith's "Colonel Carter of Cartersville," i.); *low-lived* manners or performances.

ow-ly (lō′li), *a.*; compar. *lowlier*, superl. *lowliest.* Low in altitude or position (as, "Thy sun sets weeping in the *lowly* west": Shakspere's "Richard II.," ii. 4. 21); also, humble in station, condition, or character (as, a *lowly* shepherd; a *lowly* cottage); modest or unpretending; also, humble in spirit, or meek (as, "I am meek and *lowly* in heart": Mat. xi. 29).—**low′ly,** *adv.* In a low position, manner, or degree; also, in a lowly manner; humbly; modestly; meekly.

.ow=mind-ed (lō′mīn′ded), *a.* Having or showing a low, groveling, or abject mind; unaspiring; mean.

.own¹ (loun), *n.* Obs. or prov. form of *loon*¹. See Shakspere's "Othello," ii. 3. 95.

lown² (loun), *a.* [ME. *lowne*; from Scand.] Calm; quiet; still: as, "The night was *lown* and peaceful" (Galt's "Annals of the Parish," xxxvi.). [Sc. and north. Eng.]

low=necked (lō′nekt), *a.* Of a garment, cut low so as to leave the neck and shoulders exposed; décolleté.

low-ness (lō′nes), *n.* The state or quality of being low.

low=pres-sure (lō′presh′ųr), *a.* Having or involving a pressure (as of steam, water, etc.) which is low or below the normal.

low=spir-it-ed (lō′spir′i-ted), *a.* Having low spirits; depressed; dejected.—**low′=spir′it-ed-ness,** *n.*

lox-o-drom-ic (lok-sǫ-drom′ik), *a.* [Gr. λοξός, oblique, + δρόμος, a running, course.] Pertaining to oblique sailing, or sailing on rhumbs or loxodromic lines.—**loxodromic curve, line,** or **spiral,** a line on the surface of a sphere cutting all meridians at the same oblique angle, as that formed by the path of a ship when her course is constantly directed to the same point of the compass in a direction oblique to the equator.—**lox-o-drom′ics,** *n.* The art of oblique sailing.

loy-al (loi′ąl), *a.* [F. *loyal*, OF. *loial, leial*, < L. *legalis*, E. *legal*.] Faithful to one's oath, engagements, or obligations (as, to be *loyal* to a vow; "I will remain The *loyal'st* husband that did e'er plight troth," Shakspere's "Cymbeline," i. 1. 96); esp., faithful to one's allegiance, as to the sovereign, government, or state (as, a *loyal* subject or citizen); faithful to any leader, party, or cause, or to any person or thing conceived as imposing obligations (as, a *loyal* follower, servitor, or friend; *loyal* to a person's memory); also, characterized by or showing faithfulness to engagements, allegiance, obligations, etc. (as, *loyal* conduct or sentiments; *loyal* devotion).—**loy′al-ism,** *n.* The principles or actions of loyalists; adherence to the sovereign or the existing government.—**loy′al-ist,** *n.* One who is loyal; a supporter of the sovereign or the existing government, esp. in time of revolt; [sometimes *cap.*] in *Amer. hist.*, one who remained loyal to the British government during the Revolutionary period; a Tory.—**loy′al-ly,** *adv.*—**loy′al-ness,** *n.*—**loy′al-ty,** *n.* [OF. *loialte* (F. *loyauté*).] The state or quality of being loyal; faithfulness to engagements or obligations (as, "The Duke was more vehement than ever in his protestations of *loyalty* to his recent oaths": Motley's "Dutch Republic," vi. 6); faithful adherence to a sovereign or government, or to a leader, cause, or the like; loyal devotion; fidelity.

loz-enge (loz′ẹnj), *n.* [OF. *losenge* (F. *losange*); origin uncertain.] A plane figure with four equal sides, having two acute and two obtuse angles; a diamond (figure); hence, something shaped like such a figure, as a pane of glass in a window or the form of heraldic escutcheon appropriated to women; also, a small, flavored cake or confection of sugar, often medicated, orig. diamond-shaped; a small cake or tablet of some other substance, as concentrated meat extract.—**loz′enged,** *a.* Having the shape of a lozenge (as, "the *lozenged* panes of a very small latticed window": C. Brontë's "Jane Eyre," xxviii.); also, divided into or ornamented with lozenge-shaped figures, esp. of alternate colors.—**loz′en-ger** (-ẹn-jėr), *n.* A lozenge (confection or tablet). [Prov.]

Lozenge-molding.

lub-bard (lub′ärd). [For *lubber*.] **I.** *n.* A lubber; a stupid or lazy lout: as, "Here Lethargy . . . Stretched on his back a mighty *lubbard* lay" (Thomson's "Castle of Indolence," i. 74). [Archaic or Sc. and north. Eng.] **II.** *a.* Lubberly; loutish. [Obs. or archaic.]

lub-ber (lub′ėr), *n.* [ME. *lobre*: cf. *lob* and *looby*.] A big, clumsy, stupid fellow (as, "the rude tricks of an overgrown *lubber*": Godwin's "Caleb Williams," iii.); a stupid or lazy lout; among sailors, an awkward or unskilled seaman (cf. *landlubber*).—**lubber's hole,** *naut.*, an open space in the platform at the head of a lower mast, through which a sailor may mount and descend without going outside the rim of the platform.—**Lub′ber-land** (-land), *n.* An imaginary land, the paradise of lazy lubbers; [*l. c.*] any land or place of delightful idleness (as, "In *lubberlands* delectable—isles of palm And lotus . . . The shining, shifting Sovranties of Dream": Henley's "Arabian Nights' Entertainments").—**lub′ber-ly,** *a.* Like or characteristic of a lubber; loutish; clumsy, stupid, or lazy; awkwardly unseamanlike (as, "Such was Rope Yarn; of all land-lubbers, the most *lubberly* and most miserable": H. Melville's "Omoo," xiv.).—**lub′ber-ly,** *adv.* In a lubberly manner.

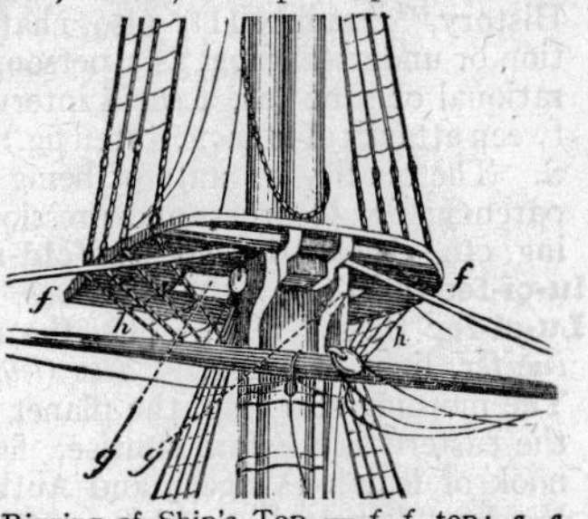

Rigging of Ship's Top.—*f, f,* top; *g, g,* lubber's holes; *h, h,* futtock-shrouds.

lu-bric, lu-bri-cal (lū′brik, -bri-kąl), *a.* Same as *lubricous*. [Obs. or archaic.]

lu-bri-cant (lū′bri-kąnt). **I.** *a.* Lubricating. **II.** *n.* A lubricating material, as oil.

lu-bri-cate (lū′bri-kāt), *v. t.*; *-cated, -cating.* [L. *lubricatus*, pp. of *lubricare*, < *lubricus*, slippery.] To make slippery or smooth; render smooth the action of, by the application of some fluid, etc.; esp., to apply some oily, greasy, or other substance to, in order to diminish friction; oil or grease, as parts of a mechanism.—**lu-bri-ca′tion** (-kā′shǫn), *n.* The act of lubricating, or the state of being lubricated.—**lu′bri-ca-tor,** *n.*

lu-bri-ci-ty (lų-bris′i-ti), *n.*; pl. *-ties* (-tiz). [LL. *lubricitas*, < L. *lubricus*: see *lubricous*.] Slipperiness or oily smoothness of surface (as, "this . . . *lubricity* of all objects, which lets them slip through our fingers then when we clutch hardest": Emerson's "Essays," Experience); fig., shiftiness, evasiveness, or elusiveness (as, "That learned jurisconsult, with characteristic *lubricity*, had evaded the dangerous honor": Motley's "Dutch Republic," iii. 1); also, wantonness, lasciviousness, or lewdness, or an instance of it.

lu-bri-cous (lū′bri-kus), *a.* [L. *lubricus*, slippery, uncertain, deceitful.] Slippery, as of surface; of an oily smoothness; fig., unstable or uncertain; shifty or elusive; also, wanton or lewd.

lu-carne (lų-kärn′), *n.* [F. *lucarne*, OF. *lucane*, appar. < L. *lux* (*luc-*), light.] A window in a roof or a spire; a dormer-window.

luce (lūs), *n.* [OF. *lus*, < LL. *lucius*, kind of fish.] The pike (fish), esp. when full-grown.

lu-cent (lū′sẹnt), *a.* [L. *lucens* (*lucent-*), ppr. of *lucere*, shine, be light or clear: see *light*¹, *n.*] Shining, bright, or luminous (as, "the sun's *lucent* orb": Milton's "Paradise Lost," iii. 589); also, clear, transparent, or translucent (as, "*lucent* syrops, tinct with cinnamon": Keats's "Eve of St. Agnes," xxx.). [Archaic or literary.]—**lu′cence, lu′cen-cy,** *n.*—**lu′cent-ly,** *adv.*

lu-cerne, lu-cern (lų-sėrn′), *n.* [F. *luzerne*, < Pr. *luzerno*; origin uncertain.] A European fabaceous forage-plant, *Medicago sativa*, with bluish-purple flowers, now much cultivated in the western U. S.; alfalfa.

lu-cid (lū′sid), *a.* [L. *lucidus*, < *lucere*: see *lucent*.] Shining or bright (as, "the *lucid* east": Tennyson's "In Memoriam," cv.); visible to the naked eye, as a star; also, clear or transparent (as, "*lucid* streams," Milton's "Paradise Lost," i. 469; "so *lucid* the air," Lowell's "Pictures from Apple-

Flowering Branch of Lucerne. *a*, flower; *b*, fruit.

dore," ii.); fig., clear to the mind, or easily understood (as, a *lucid* explanation; *lucid* language; "The tangled weights and measures of old France gave place to the simple and *lucid* decimal system," H. G. Wells's "Outline of History," xxxvii. § 11); also, characterized by clear perception or understanding, as a person, the mind, thoughts, etc.; rational or sane (as, a *lucid* interval, a period of sanity between attacks of lunacy: often fig.).—**lu-cid-i-ty** (lų-sid′i-ti), *n.* The quality or state of being lucid; brightness; transparency; fig., clearness of expression, perception, understanding, etc.—**lu′cid-ly,** *adv.*—**lu′cid-ness,** *n.*

lu-ci-fee (lö′si-fē), *n.* See *lucivee.*

Lu-ci-fer (lū′si-fėr), *n.* [L., the morning star, prop. adj., *lucifer*, light-bringing, < *lux* (*luc-*), light, + *ferre*, bear.] The morning star, esp. the planet Venus when appearing in the eastern sky before sunrise; fig., a name applied in the book of Isaiah (Vulgate and Authorized Version; Revised Version "day star") to a king of Babylon (as, "How art thou fallen from heaven, O *Lucifer*, son of the morning!" Isa. xiv. 12); hence (from an early Christian interpretation of the passage in Isaiah: cf. Luke, x. 18), a proud, rebellious archangel, identified with Satan, who fell from heaven (as, "*Lucifer* . . . brighter once amidst the host Of angels, than that star the stars among," Milton's "Paradise Lost," vii. 131; "When he falls, he falls like *Lucifer*, Never to hope again," Shakspere's "Henry VIII.," iii. 2. 371); also [*l. c.*], a friction-match (also called *lucifer match*).

lu-cif-er-ase (lų-sif′ẹ-rās), *n.* [L. *lucifer*, light-bringing: see *-ase.*] In *chem.*, a substance, probably an enzyme, which is present in the luminous organs of fireflies, etc., and which, acting with luciferin, is supposed to produce luminosity.

lu-cif-er-in (lų-sif′ẹ-rin), *n.* [L. *lucifer*, light-bringing: see *-in.*] In *chem.*, a substance in the blood of fireflies, etc., whose action on luciferase may be the cause of luminosity.

lu-cif-er-ous (lų-sif′ẹ-rus), *a.* [L. *lucifer*: see *Lucifer.*] Bringing or giving light. Also fig. [Now rare.]

lu-cif-ic (lų-sif′ik), *a.* [LL. *lucificus*, < L. *lux* (*luc-*), light, + *facere*, make.] Producing light.

lu-cif-u-gous (lų-sif′ų-gus), *a.* [L. *lucifugus*, < *lux* (*luc-*), light, + *fugere*, flee.] Shunning the light, as certain animals.

Lu-ci-na (lų-sī′nạ), *n.* [L., lit. 'she who brings to light,' < *lux* (*luc-*), light.] The Roman goddess of childbirth, sometimes identified with Juno or Diana; a midwife.

Lu-cite (lū′sīt), *n.* [From L. *lux*, light.] The trade-mark name for a plastic compound with unusual optical properties, used for reflectors, ornaments, etc.

lu-ci-vee (lö′si-vē), *n.* [Corruption of *loup-cervier.*] The Canada lynx, *Lynx canadensis.*

luck (luk), *n.* [ME. *lucke* = D. *luk*, *geluk*, = MLG. *lucke*, *gelucke*, = MHG. *gelücke*, G. *glück*, luck, fortune.] That which happens to a person, as if by chance, in the course of events (as, to have good, bad, hard, or indifferent *luck*; to try one's *luck*, to make a trial in order to see what one's luck will be); one's fortune or hap; esp., good fortune, or advantage or success considered as the result of chance (as, to wish one *luck*; to have *luck* in fishing; to be in *luck*, or out of *luck*); also, some object on which good fortune is supposed to depend (as, "The drinking-glass of crystal tall; They call it the *Luck* of Edenhall": Longfellow's tr. Uhland's "Luck of Edenhall").

luck′ie, *n.* See *lucky*².

luck-i-ly (luk′i-li), *adv.* In a lucky manner; by good luck; fortunately.—**luck′i-ness,** *n.*

luck-less (luk′les), *a.* Having no luck or good fortune (as, "dreary fates of *luckless* peers": J. Hall's "Satires," i. 5); unattended with good luck (as, a *luckless* venture); unfortunate; unlucky.—**luck′less-ly,** *adv.*—**luck′less-ness,** *n.*

luck=pen-ny (luk′pen″i), *n.*; pl. *-pennies* (-iz). A penny or other coin kept or given to bring good luck; also, a small sum given back for luck by the seller to the purchaser in a business transaction (Sc., Eng., and Ir.).

luck-y¹ (luk′i), *a.*; compar. *luckier*, superl. *luckiest.* Having luck or good fortune, as a person; attended with good luck, as a venture, a guess, etc.; favored by chance; fortunate; hence, felicitous, or happily apt (as, a *lucky* translation; "*Lucky* rhymes to him were scrip and share, And mellow metres more than cent for cent," Tennyson's "Brook," 4); also, of the nature of good luck, or happening fortunately (as, a *lucky* chance or accident; a *lucky* meeting); **also,** bringing or presaging good luck, or supposed to do so (as, one's *lucky* star; a *lucky* sixpence; "A fortunate event, too, was accepted as a *lucky* omen for the coming contest," Motley's "Dutch Republic," iii. 8); also, dependent on mere chance, or fortuitous (obs. or archaic).

luck-y², **luck-ie** (luk′i), *n.*; pl. *-ies* (-iz). [Prob. < *lucky*¹: cf. *goody*².] An elderly woman, esp. a grandmother (much used in familiar address or prefixed to a name: as, *Lucky* Maclaren); also, the mistress of an ale-house; a landlady; also, a witch. [Sc.]

lu-cra-tive (lū′krạ-tiv), *a.* [L. *lucrativus*, < *lucrari*, to gain, < *lucrum*, E. *lucre.*] Yielding lucre or gain; gainful; profitable; remunerative: as, a *lucrative* business or profession; a *lucrative* appointment.—**lu′cra-tive-ly,** *adv.*—**lu′cra-tive-ness,** *n.*

lu-cre (lū′kėr), *n.* [L. *lucrum*, gain.] Gain; profit; pecuniary advantage; esp., gain or money as the object of sordid desire (as, "not greedy of filthy *lucre*": 1 Tim. iii. 3); also, the gain or profit, or the acquisition, of something specified (obs. or archaic: as, "As for the *lucre* of gain, I renounce it," Smollett's "Humphry Clinker," after Oct. 4; "A Malabar, for the *lucre* of a knife, conducted them to a Dutch town," Defoe's "Captain Singleton," xviii.).

Lu-cre-tian (lų-krē′shiạn), *a.* Pertaining to Lucretius (about 96—about 55 B.C.), the Roman poet and Epicurean philosopher, or to his philosophical doctrines, set forth in a didactic poem, "De Rerum Natura" ("On the Nature of Things").

lu-cu-brate (lū′kų-brāt), *v. i.*; *-brated*, *-brating.* [L. *lucubratus*, pp. of *lucubrare*, work by lamplight, < *lux* (*luc-*), light.] To work by artificial light; pursue intellectual labors by night; write learnedly. [Now playful or humorous.]—**lu-cu-bra′tion** (-brā′shọn), *n.* [L. *lucubratio*(*n-*).] The act or a process of lucubrating (as, "the well-earned harvest of . . . many a midnight *lucubration*": Gibbon's "Decline and Fall of the Roman Empire," iii.); nocturnal intellectual labor; laborious study; also, a product of intellectual labor; a learned or carefully written production (as, "historical disquisition, citations from Solomon . . . with such *lucubrations* were reams of paper filled": Motley's "Dutch Republic," iv. 3); in general, a literary effort (as, "The writing of a book was considered . . . an enterprise of toil and difficulty, insomuch that the most trifling *lucubration* was denominated a 'work' ": Irving's "Tales of a Traveler," To the Reader). [Now playful or humorous.]—**lu′cu-bra-tor,** *n.*

lu-cule (lū′kūl), *n.* [NL. *lucula*, dim. of L. *lux* (*luc-*), light.] In *astron.*, any of certain small luminous spots on the sun's surface.

lu-cu-lent (lū′kų-lẹnt), *a.* [L. *luculentus*, < *lux* (*luc-*), light.] Full of light; bright; luminous; also, clear or lucid, as arguments, explanations, etc.; convincing.—**lu′cu-lent-ly,** *adv.*

Lu-cul-li-an (lų-kul′i-ạn), *a.* Pertaining to or worthy of Lucullus (about 110–57? B.C.), a wealthy Roman famous for luxury, esp. at the table: as, a *Lucullian* feast.

lu-cu-mo (lū′kų-mō), *n.*; pl. *lucumos*, L. *lucumones* (lū-kų-mō′nēz). [L.; from Etruscan.] Among the ancient Etruscans, a prince or ruling noble with priestly functions.—**lu′cu-mo-ny** (-mọ-ni), *n.*; pl. *-nies* (-niz). The district or state under the rule of a lucumo.

lud (lud), *n.* and *interj.* A minced or vulgar form of *lord*: as, "*Lud*, this news . . . puts me all in a flutter" (Goldsmith's "She Stoops to Conquer," i. 1).

Ludd-ite (lud′īt). [Said to have been named after a Ned *Ludd* or *Lud*, a weak-minded fellow of an earlier period who in anger broke two frames used in stocking manufacture.] **I.** *n.* A member of any of various bands of workmen in England (1811–16) organized to destroy manufacturing machinery, under the delusion that its use diminished employment. **II.** *a.* Of or pertaining to the Luddites: as, *Luddite* riots.

lu-di-crous (lū′di-krus), *a.* [L. *ludicrus*, < *ludus*, play, sport, jest, fun, < *ludere*, to play.] Playful† or sportive†; humorous† or witty†; derisive†; also, such as to cause laughter or derision (as, "A lucky joke, or any *ludicrous* incident, will set him a-laughing immoderately": Smollett's

"Humphry Clinker," April 30); ridiculous; amusingly absurd.—**lu′di-crous-ly,** *adv.*—**lu′di-crous-ness,** *n.*

lud-wig-i-a (lud-wij′i-ạ̈), *n.* [NL.; named from C. G. *Ludwig* (1709–73), German botanist.] Any plant of the onagraceous genus *Ludwigia*, comprising small herbs found in swamps, etc., of temperate and warm regions.

lu-es (lū′ēz), *n.* [L.] A plague or pestilence; a spreading disease, esp. syphilis.—**lu-et-ic** (lụ̄-et′ik), *a.* Pertaining to or affected with lues.—**lu-e-tin** (lū′e-tin), *n.* In *med.*, a preparation made from the dead micro-organisms of syphilis, used as a diagnostic test for syphilis.

luff (luf), *n.* [Cf. OF. *lof*, a contrivance for altering a ship's course, later, as also D. *loef*, the weather side.] *Naut.*, the part of a ship toward the wind†; also, the sailing of a ship closer to the wind; also, the forward edge of a fore-and-aft sail; also, the fullest and broadest part of a ship's bow.—**luff,** *v.* *Naut.*: **I.** *intr.* To bring a ship's head closer to the wind; come or sail nearer to the wind: as, "Now, my hearty, *luff!*" (Stevenson's "Treasure Island," xxvi.). **II.** *tr.* To bring the head of (a vessel) closer to the wind: as, the frigate was *luffed* handsomely to the wind.

luf-fa (luf′ạ̈), *n.* [NL.] Same as *loofah*.

luft-waf-fe (lůft′väf″fė), *n.* [G., *luft*, air, + *waffe*, weapon.] The German air force.

lug[1] (lug), *n.* [Origin obscure: cf. *lug*[3].] The ear (chiefly Sc. and prov. Eng.); hence, an object or part resembling the external human ear in form or position; a handle, as of a pitcher; a projecting piece by which anything is held or supported; specif., a leather loop dependent from a saddle, through which a shaft is passed for support.

lug[2] (lug), *n.* Same as *lug-sail*: as, "Up with the *lugs*" (Marryat's "King's Own," xiii.).

lug[3] (lug), *v.*; *lugged, lugging.* [ME. *luggen*: cf. Sw. *lugga*, pull by the hair.] **I.** *tr.* To pull (now chiefly prov.: as, "*Lug* him thrice by both ears," Swift's "Gulliver's Travels," iii. 6); also, to pull along with force or effort (as, "six starved horses . . . *lugging* along the hearse": "Guy Mannering," xxxvii.); carry (something heavy or burdensome); hence, fig., to bring (*in* or *into*) as by main force, or without appropriateness (colloq.: as, "an unfitness in the idea of marble fauns and satyrs . . . *lugged* in under the oaken roof . . . of an odd, old Norman hall," Kinglake's "Eothen," iv.; to *lug* an irrelevant matter into a discussion). **II.** *intr.* To pull; tug; also, to pull (*out*) something, esp. one's sword (archaic: "Their cause they to an easier issue put; They will be heard, or they *lug* out, and cut," Dryden's tr. Juvenal's "Satires," xvi. 78); also, to move heavily.—**lug**[3], *n.* An act of lugging; a forcible pull; a haul; also, *pl.*, affected or pretentious manners, or airs (slang: as, to put on *lugs*).

lug[4] (lug), *n.* [Cf. D. *log*, heavy, unwieldy.] A lugworm.

lug-gage (lug′ạ̄j), *n.* [From *lug*[3].] Something to be lugged, or carried with effort, as cumbersome baggage (obs. or archaic); also, a burden† or encumbrance†; also, in general, baggage, as of a traveler or an army (chiefly in British use: as, "I left my servant at the railway looking after the *luggage*," Dickens's "Hard Times," ii. 1).

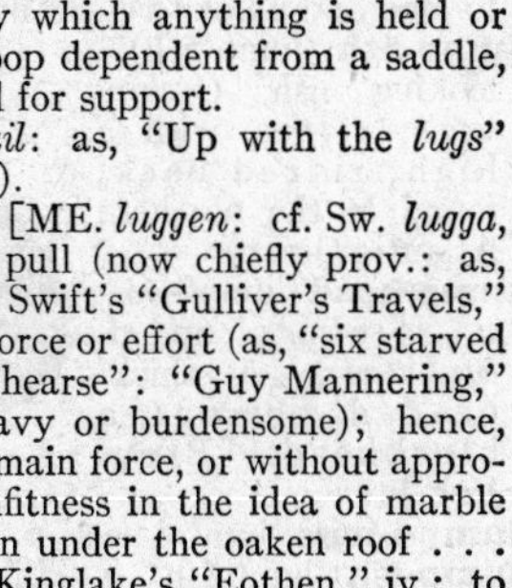

Lugger.

lug-ger (lug′ėr), *n.* [Cf. *lug-sail*.] A vessel with lug-sails.

lug-gie (lug′i), *n.* [From *lug*[1].] A small wooden vessel with a lug, ear, or handle: as, "They . . . drank it [tea] out of . . . *luggies*" (Galt's "Annals of the Parish," ii.). [Chiefly Sc.]

lug=sail (lug′sāl), *n.* [Origin uncertain: cf. *lug*[1] and *lug*[3].] *Naut.*, a quadrilateral sail bent upon a yard that crosses the mast obliquely. See cut in next column.

lu-gu-bri-ous (lụ̄-gū′bri-us), *a.* [L. *lugubris*, < *lugere*, mourn.] Characterized by, expressing, or suggestive of mourning (as, "Mannering . . . stood among this *lugubrious* company . . . composing his countenance to the decent solemnity of all": Scott's "Guy Mannering," xxxvii.); mournful, now usually in a particularly dismal way (as, a *lugubrious* face or tone; "A dog set up a long, *lugubrious* howl," Mark Twain's "Tom Sawyer," x.); doleful; dismal.—**lu-gu′bri-ous-ly,** *adv.*—**lu-gu′bri-ous-ness,** *n.*

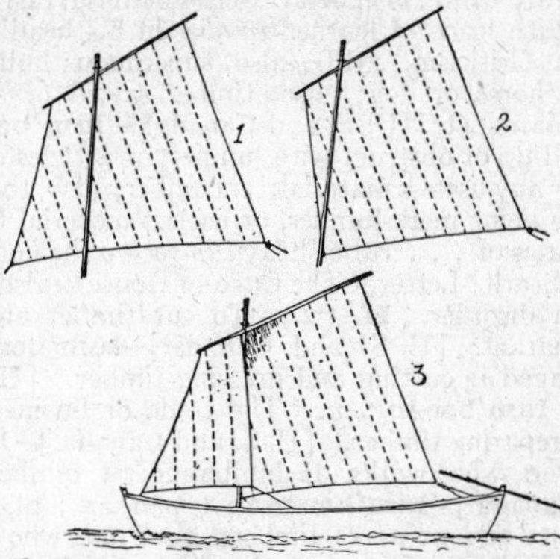

Lug-sails. — 1, dipping lug-sail; 2, standing lug-sail; 3, split lug-sail.

lug-worm (lug′wėrm), *n.* [See *lug*[4].] Any annelid of the genus *Arenicola*, comprising marine worms with tufted gills, which burrow in the sand of the seashore and are much used for bait.

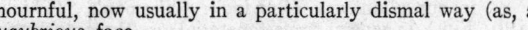

luke (lūk), *a.* [ME. *luke, lewk*: cf. AS. *hlēow, gehlēow*, warm.] Tepid; lukewarm: as, "Let me have nine penn'orth o' brandy and water *luke*" (Dickens's "Pickwick Papers," xxxiii.). [Now prov. Eng.]

luke-warm (lūk′wârm), *a.* [See *luke*.] Moderately warm; tepid; fig., having or showing little ardor or zeal (as, a *lukewarm* supporter; *lukewarm* obedience); indifferent.—**luke′warm″ly,** *adv.*—**luke′warm″ness,** *n.*

lull (lul), *v.* [ME. *lullen*; imit.: cf. Sw. *lulla*, Dan. *lulle*, G. *lullen*, lull, L. *lallare*, sing lullaby.] **I.** *tr.* To put to sleep or rest by soothing means (as, to *lull* a child by singing or rocking; "To bed they creep, By whispering winds soon *lull'd* asleep," Milton's "L'Allegro," 116); fig., to soothe to a quiet mental state (as, "I was . . . *lulled* in a certain degree to security," Godwin's "Caleb Williams," xviii.; "She *lulled* herself into patience," Mrs. Gaskell's "Cranford," ix.); quiet (feelings, suspicions, etc.); make peaceful or tranquil (as, "regions gladdened by plenty and *lulled* by peace": Johnson's "Rasselas," vi.); still (the sea, wind, a storm, etc.). **II.** *intr.* To become lulled, quieted, or stilled, as the wind, a storm, etc.—**lull,** *n.* Something that lulls; a soothing sound (as, the *lull* of falling waters); also, a lulled condition; a temporary quiet or stillness, or a period of lessened activity (as, a *lull* in a storm; a *lull* in strife).

lul-la-by (lul′ạ-bī). [Cf. *lull*.] **I.** *interj.* A lulling utterance used in putting a child to sleep. **II.** *n.*; pl. *-bies* (-bīz). The utterance 'lullaby,' or a song containing it; a cradle-song; hence, any lulling song (often fig.: as, soothed by the *lullaby* of the wind or the waves).—**lul′la-by,** *v. t.*; *-bied, -bying.* To lull with or as with a lullaby.

lum (lum), *n.* [Origin uncertain.] A chimney. [Sc. and north. Eng.]

lu-ma-chel-la (lū-mạ-kel′ạ̈), *n.* [It., lit. 'little snail,' < *lumaca*, < L. *limax* (*limac-*), snail.] A compact limestone or marble containing fossil shells, which are often iridescent, displaying a variety of brilliant colors. Also **lu′ma-chel** (-kel), **lu-ma-chelle′** (-kel′ or -shel′).

lum-ba-go (lum-bā′gō), *n.* [LL., < L. *lumbus*, loin.] In *pathol.*, myalgia in the lumbar region; pain in the muscles of the loins and the small of the back.

lum-bar (lum′bạ̈r). [L. *lumbus*, loin.] **I.** *a.* Of or pertaining to the loin or loins. **II.** *n.* A lumbar vertebra, artery, or the like.

lum-ber[1] (lum′bėr), *v. i.* [ME. *lomeren*: cf. Sw. dial. *lomra*, resound.] To move clumsily or heavily, esp. from great or ponderous bulk (as, "The great hippo . . . calmly *lumbered* along right underneath me," J. H. Patterson's "Man-Eaters of Tsavo," xii.; a heavy wagon *lumbers* along; "I . . . don't want you always *lumbering* after me with your advice," Mrs. Stowe's "Oldtown Folks," xxxvi.); also, to make a rumbling noise.

lum-ber[2] (lum′bėr), *n.* [Prob. < *lumber*[1].] Things more or less bulky or cumbersome that are not needed for present use, or that have been put away as in a lumber-room (as, "I have a quantity of useless plate at home—mere *lumber*

. . . in our plain way of living": Wiseman's "Fabiola," i. 9); hence, in general, useless material (as, "Ignorantly read, With loads of learned *lumber* in his head": Pope's "Essay on Criticism," 613); also, superfluous bulk or weight, as in a horse or dog; also, timber sawed or split into planks, boards, etc. (U. S. and Canada).—**lum'ber**², *v.* **I.** *tr.* To fill up or obstruct with lumber, or articles of no present use, or any useless material; encumber; also, to fill up or obstruct as being mere lumber, or useless material (as, "Large quantities of . . . rubbish lay *lumbering* the floor": Hawthorne's "Scarlet Letter," The Custom House); also, to heap together in disorder. **II.** *intr.* To cut timber and prepare it for market. [U. S. and Canada.]—**lum'ber-er,** *n.* One engaged in cutting and dressing timber. [U. S. and Canada.] —**lum'ber-ing,** *n.* The trade or business of cutting and preparing timber. [U. S. and Canada.]—**lum'ber-jack,** *n.* One who works at lumbering; a lumberer. [U. S. and Canada.]—**lum'ber-man** (-mạn), *n.*; pl. *-men.* One who cuts and prepares timber; also, one who deals in lumber. [U. S. and Canada.]—**lum'ber=port,** *n.* A port-hole or opening in the bow or stern of a vessel, for use in loading and unloading lumber.—**lum'ber=room,** *n.* A room for lumber, or articles not in use.—**lum'ber=yard,** *n.* A yard where lumber is stored for sale. [U. S. and Canada.]

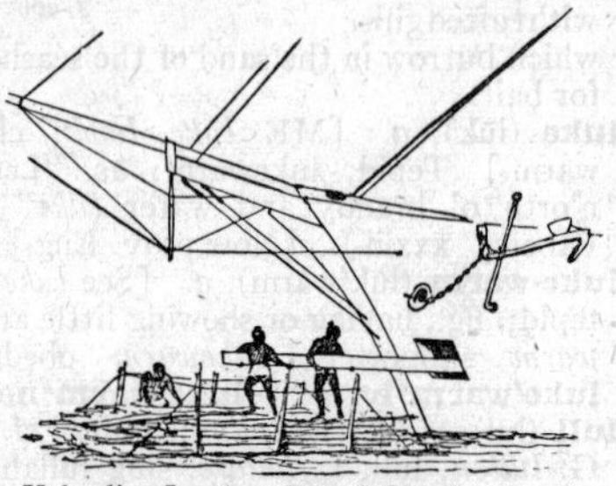

Unloading Lumber through Lumber-port in Bow of Vessel.

lu-men (lū'men), *n.*; pl. *lumina* (-mi-nạ̈). [L., light, window, opening: see *light*¹, *n.*] An opening or passageway; in *anat.*, the canal, duct, or cavity of a tubular organ.—**lu'mi-nal** (-mi-nạl), *a.*

lu-mi-nant (lū'mi-nạnt). [L. *luminans* (*-ant-*), ppr. of *luminare*: see *luminate.*] **I.** *a.* Illuminating; luminous. **II.** *n.* An illuminating agent; an illuminant.—**lu'mi-nance,** *n.*

lu-mi-na-ry (lū'mi-nā-ri), *n.*; pl. *-ries* (-riz). [OF. *luminarie* (F. *luminaire*), < LL. *luminare*, a light, lamp, heavenly body, L. window, < L. *lumen*, light.] A body or thing that gives light, esp. a celestial body, as the sun or moon; fig., a source of intellectual light; a person who enlightens mankind or makes some subject clear.

lu-mi-nate (lū'mi-nāt), *v. t.*; *-nated, -nating.* [L. *luminatus*, pp. of *luminare*, < *lumen*, light.] To light up; illuminate. [Obs. or archaic.]—**lu-mi-na'tion** (-nā'shọn), *n.*

lu-mi-nesce (lū-mi-nes'), *v. i.*; *-nesced, -nescing.* [See *luminescence.*] To exhibit luminescence.

lu-mi-nes-cence (lū-mi-nes'ẹns), *n.* [L. *lumen* (*lumin-*), light: see *-escence.*] An emission of light not due directly to incandescence and occurring at a temperature below that of incandescent bodies: a term including phosphorescence, fluorescence, etc.—**lu-mi-nes'cent,** *a.* Characterized by or pertaining to luminescence.

lu-mi-nif-er-ous (lū-mi-nif'ẹ-rus), *a.* [L. *lumen* (*lumin-*), light, + *ferre*, bear.] Producing or conveying light: as, the *luminiferous* ether (see *ether*).

lu-mi-nom-e-ter (lū-mi-nom'e-tėr), *n.* [L. *lumen* (*lumin-*), light: see *-meter.*] An instrument for measuring the intensity of illumination.

lu-mi-nos-i-ty (lū-mi-nos'i-ti), *n.*; pl. *-ties* (-tiz). The quality of being luminous; specif., the intensity of light in a color, measured photometrically; also, something luminous.

lu-mi-nous (lū'mi-nus), *a.* [L. *luminosus*, < *lumen*, light.] Radiating or reflecting light; shining; bright; also, lighted up or illuminated; well lighted (as, "The church of Ashbourne . . . is one of the . . . most *luminous* that I have seen": Boswell's "Johnson," Sept. 21, 1777); also, fig., brilliant intellectually; enlightening, as a writer or his writings; clear, or readily intelligible.—**lu'mi-nous-ly,** *adv.* —**lu'mi-nous-ness,** *n.*

lum-mox (lum'ọks), *n.* [Origin obscure.] A heavy or unwieldy, clumsy, stupid person. [Prov. or colloq.]

lump¹ (lump), *n.* [ME. *lumpe*: cf. D. *lomp*, lump, rag, Sw. *lump*, clod.] A piece or mass of solid matter without regular shape, or of no particular shape (as, "a great *lump* of beeswax . . . which weighed above half a hundred weight," Defoe's "Robinson Crusoe," i. 2; a *lump* of sugar); also, a protuberance or swelling (as, a *lump* on the head caused by a blow); also, an aggregation, collection, or mass (now chiefly in 'in the lump': see phrase below); also, a dull, stolid person (colloq.); also, a big, sturdy person (prov. or colloq.: as, "a brave *lump* of a boy," Lover's "Handy Andy," i.).—**in the lump,** in the mass; as a whole; in gross; wholesale. —**lump**¹, *a.* In the form of a lump or lumps; also, including all of a number of items taken together or in the lump (as, a *lump* sum).—**lump**¹, *v.* **I.** *tr.* To make into a lump or lumps; also, to raise into or cover with lumps; also, to unite into one aggregation, collection, or mass; deal with in the lump or mass. **II.** *intr.* To form a lump or lumps; also, to rise in a lump or lumps; also, to move heavily; also, to act as a lumper (laborer).

lump² (lump), *v.* [Cf. *glump.*] **I.** *intr.* To look sullen; sulk. [Obs. or prov.] **II.** *tr.* To regard or endure with displeasure; put up with as a disagreeable necessity: as, "That's what's the matter, and I've got to *lump* it" (Galsworthy's "Saint's Progress," iii. 12): often used in antithesis to *like* (as, if you don't like it, you may *lump* it). [Colloq.]

lump-er (lum'pėr), *n.* One who lumps things, or deals with things in the lump or mass; also, a laborer employed to load and unload vessels in port.

lump-fish (lump'fish), *n.* [Appar. < *lump*¹.] A clumsy-looking fish, *Cyclopterus lumpus*, with a high, ridged back, found in the northern Atlantic Ocean.

Lumpfish.

lump-head (lump'hed), *n.* [See *lump*¹, and cf. *lunkhead.*] A thick-headed person; a blockhead. [Prov. Eng.]

lump-i-ness (lum'pi-nes), *n.* Lumpy condition.

lump-ish (lum'pish), *a.* Like a lump; heavy and clumsy; dull or stupid; also, low-spirited† or melancholy† (as, "She is *lumpish*, heavy, melancholy": Shakspere's "Two Gentlemen of Verona," iii. 2. 62).—**lump'ish-ly,** *adv.*—**lump'ish-ness,** *n.*

lump-y (lum'pi), *a.*; compar. *lumpier*, superl. *lumpiest.* Full of lumps, as porridge or sugar; covered with lumps, as a surface; like a lump, as in being heavy or clumsy; of water, rough or choppy.—**lump'y=jaw,** *n.* In *pathol.*, actinomycosis of the jaw.

Lu-na (lū'nạ̈), *n.* [L. *luna*, moon, crescent, *Luna*, the goddess: see *light*¹, *n.*] The moon, personified by the Romans as a goddess; in *alchemy*, silver; in *her.*, argent (in the blazonry of sovereign princes).

lu-na-cy (lū'nạ-si), *n.*; pl. *-cies* (-siz). [Irreg. < *lunatic.*] Lunatic condition; intermittent insanity (as, "In one of these fits of *lunacy* or distraction . . . I fell down, and struck my face": Defoe's "Robinson Crusoe," ii. 8); hence, in general, any form of insanity (except, usually, idiocy); also, fig., extreme foolishness or folly, or an instance of it; specif., in *law*, unsoundness of mind sufficient to incapacitate one for civil transactions.

lu-na=moth (lū'nạ̈-môth'), *n.* [L. *luna*, moon, crescent: with reference to the spots on the wings.] A large American moth, *Tropæa luna*, with greenish wings (the hinder ones tailed), each of which contains a lunate spot surrounded by rings.

lu-nar (lū'nạ̈r), *a.* [L. *lunaris*, < *luna*, moon, crescent.] Of or pertaining to the moon (as, the *lunar* orbit; *lunar* observations); also, measured by the moon's revolutions (as, a *lunar* month; a *lunar* year: see *month* and *year*); also, resembling the moon; round; lunate or crescent-shaped; sometimes, marked with crescent-shaped spots; also, suggesting the moon rather than the sun; less brilliant; pale; also, in astrological use, subject to the influence of the moon, or having the character determined by the moon (cf. *solar*); also, of or pertaining to silver, of which the moon is the alchemical symbol (as, *lunar* caustic, silver nitrate).—**lu-na-ri-an** (lụ-nā'ri-ạn), *n.* A supposed inhabitant of the moon; also, a student of lunar phenomena; also, one who used or advocated a method of determining longitude at sea by means of lunar observations.

lu-nate (lū'nāt), *a.* [L. *lunatus*, < *luna*, moon, crescent.] Crescent-shaped. Also **lu'nat-ed** (-nā-ted).

lu-na-tic (lū'nạ-tik). [LL. *lunaticus*, < L. *luna*, moon.] **I.** *a.* Affected with intermittent insanity (formerly supposed to be dependent on the changes of the moon); hence, in general, insane or mad; crazy; also, indicating lunacy; characteristic of a lunatic; hence, fig., extremely or senselessly foolish (as, a *lunatic* policy); also, appropriated to insane persons (as, a *lunatic* asylum). **II.** *n.* A lunatic person; orig., one affected with intermittent insanity; now, any insane person (except, usually, an idiot); a madman; hence, fig., an extremely or senselessly foolish person.—**lu-nat-i-cal** (lụ-nat'i-kạl), *a.* Lunatic.—**lu-nat'i-cal-ly,** *adv.*

lu-na-tion (lụ-nā'shọn), *n.* [ML. *lunatio(n-)*, < L. *luna*, moon.] The time from one new moon to the next (about 29½ days); a lunar month.

lunch (lunch), *n.* [Perhaps an altered form of *lump*¹.] A lump or thick piece (now prov. Eng. and Sc.: as, "An' cheese an' bread . . . Was dealt about in *lunches*," Burns's "Holy Fair," 206); also, a portion of food for a light repast; also, a light repast, as between meals; a luncheon, or meal between breakfast and dinner (see *luncheon*).—**lunch,** *v.* **I.** *intr.* To take lunch: as, "She . . . made excursions to New York with them, and *lunched* in fashionable restaurants" (W. Churchill's "Modern Chronicle," ii. 3). **II.** *tr.* To provide lunch for.—**lunch'=coun''ter,** *n.* A counter or long elevated table, as in an eating-house, at which persons sit on stools or stand while taking a lunch.—**lunch'er,** *n.*

lun-cheon (lun'chọn), *n.* [Prob. an extended form of *lunch*.] A lump or thick piece, esp. of food (now prov. Eng. and Sc.: as, "Little Benjie . . . was cramming a huge *luncheon* of pie-crust into his mouth," Scott's "Redgauntlet," letter x.); also, a light repast; esp., a meal less substantial than dinner taken between breakfast and (evening) dinner (in this sense a more formal term than *lunch*).—**lun'cheon,** *v. i.* To take luncheon.

lune (lūn), *n.* [F. *lune*, < L. *luna*, moon, ML. a fit of lunacy.] Anything shaped like a crescent or a half-moon; specif., a crescent-shaped plane figure bounded by two arcs of circles; a figure formed on a sphere by two arcs of circles which inclose a space; also, *pl.*, fits of lunacy, or mad freaks or tantrums (archaic: as, "Why, woman, your husband is in his old *lunes* again," Shakspere's "Merry Wives of Windsor," iv. 2. 22).

lu-nette (lụ-net'), *n.* [F., dim. of *lune*: see *lune*.] Any of various objects of crescent-like or semicircular outline or section; a space of this shape in a vaulted ceiling, a wall, etc., as a space at the top of a wall intersected by a vault; a painting, etc., filling such a space; an arched or rounded aperture or window, as in a vault; in *fort.*, a work consisting of a salient angle with two flanks.

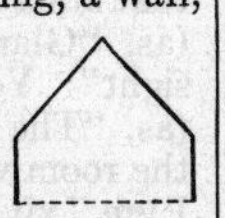

Lunette in Fortification.

lung (lung), *n.* [AS. *lungen* = D. *long* = G. *lunge* = Icel. *lunga*, lung; akin to E. *light*²: cf. *lights* in sense of 'lungs.'] An organ of respiration in an air-breathing vertebrate, esp. either of the two sac-like organs in the thorax of man and the higher vertebrates; also, an analogous organ in certain invertebrates, as arachnids, terrestrial gastropods, etc.

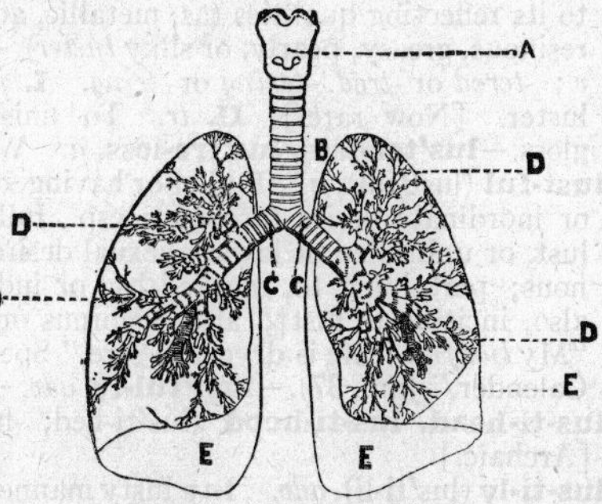

Structure of Lungs in Man.

A, larynx; *B*, trachea; *C*, *C*, bronchi, right and left; *D*, *D*, *D*, *D*, ramifications of bronchial tubes or air-passages in lungs; *E*, *E*, *E*, uncut smooth surface.

lunge¹ (lunj), *n.* [For obs. *allonge*, < F. *allonge*, < *allonger*, lengthen, extend, lunge, < *à* (< L. *ad*), to, + *long* (< L. *longus*), long.] A thrust, as in fencing; hence, any sudden forward movement (as, "At no time shall I be surprised to see a sudden *lunge* forward on that front": H. G. Wells's "Italy, France, and Britain at War," ii. 2); a plunge; a lurch.—**lunge**¹, *v.*; *lunged, lunging.* **I.** *intr.* To make a lunge or thrust; move with a lunge. **II.** *tr.* To thrust; cause to move with a lunge.

lunge² (lunj), *n.* [F. *longe*, halter, lunge, < L. *longus*, long.] A long rope used to guide a horse during training or exercise; also, a ring or circular track for such training or exercise.—**lunge**², *v. t.*; *lunged, lunging.* To train or exercise (a horse) by the use of a lunge or rope, or on a lunge or track.

lunged (lungd), *a.* Having lungs: as, weak-*lunged*.

lung-er¹ (lung'ėr), *n.* A person affected with pulmonary tuberculosis; a consumptive. [Slang.]

lun-ger² (lun'jėr), *n.* One who lunges.

lung-wort (lung'wėrt), *n.* A European blue-flowered boraginaceous plant, *Pulmonaria officinalis*, with spotted leaves fancied to resemble diseased lungs; also, an American blue-flowered plant, *Mertensia virginica*, of the same family.

luni-. Form of L. *luna*, moon, used in combination.—**lu-ni-form** (lū'ni-fôrm), *a.* [+ *-form*.] Resembling the moon in form; esp., lunate.—**lu-ni-so'lar** (-sō'lạ̈r), *a.* [+ L. *sol*, sun.] Pertaining to or depending upon the mutual relations or joint action of the moon and sun.—**lu-ni-ti'dal** (-tī'dạl), *a.* Pertaining to that part of the tidal movement dependent on the moon.

lunk-head (lungk'hed), *n.* [Var. of *lumphead*.] A thick-headed or stupid person; a blockhead. [Colloq., U. S.]

lunt (lunt), *n.* [D. *lont*, match: cf. *linstock*.] A match; a torch; a light; also, smoke; the smoke of a pipe. [Sc.]—**lunt,** *v.* **I.** *tr.* To kindle; light; also, to smoke (a pipe, etc.). [Sc.] **II.** *intr.* To take fire; flame; also, to emit smoke; also, to smoke a pipe. [Sc.]

lu-nu-la (lū'nụ-lạ̈), *n.*; pl. *-læ* (-lē). [L., dim. of *luna*, moon.] Something shaped like a narrow crescent, as the small white area at the base of the human finger-nail; in general, a lune.—**lu'nu-lar** (-lạ̈r), *a.* Pertaining to a lune or lunula; crescent-shaped.—**lu'nu-late, lu'nu-lat-ed** (-lāt, -lā-ted), *a.* Crescent-shaped; also, having lunular markings.—**lu'nule** (-nūl), *n.* A lunula.

lu-ny (lū'ni), etc. See *loony*, etc.

lu-pa-nar (lụ-pā'nạ̈r), *n.* [L., < *lupa*, prostitute, orig. she-wolf, fem. of *lupus*, wolf.] A brothel.

Lu-per-ca-li-a (lụ-pėr-kā'li-ạ̈), *n. pl.* [L., prop. neut. pl. of *Lupercalis*, adj. < *Lupercus* (see def.), appar. < *lupus*, wolf.] An ancient Roman festival celebrated annually on Feb. 15 in honor of Lupercus, a rustic deity identified with the Roman Faunus and the Greek Pan.

lu-pine¹ (lū'pin or -pīn), *a.* [L. *lupinus*, < *lupus*, wolf.] Pertaining or allied to the wolf; wolf-like; wolfish.

lu-pine² (lū'pin), *n.* [L. *lupinus, lupinum*: cf. *lupine*¹.] Any plant of the fabaceous genus *Lupinus*, as *L. albus* ('white lupine'), a European herb with edible seeds cultivated from ancient times, or *L. perennis*, a wild species with blue, pink, or white flowers common in sandy soil in the eastern U. S.; also, *pl.*, the seeds of this plant, esp. of *L. albus*.

lu-pu-lin (lū'pụ-lin), *n.* [NL. *lupulus*, dim. of L. *lupus*, hop.] A fine yellow powder with medicinal properties, consisting of small glandular bodies obtained from the strobiles of the hop; also, a crystalline substance regarded as the bitter principle of the hop.

lu-pus (lū'pus), *n.* [L., wolf: see *wolf*.] In *pathol.*, a cutaneous disease due to the tubercle bacillus.

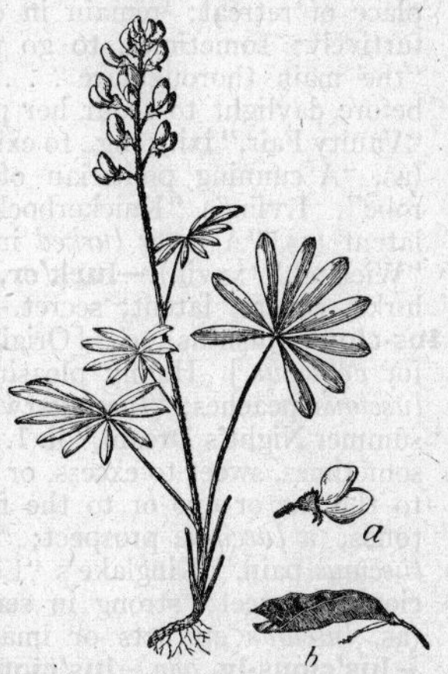

Flowering Plant of Lupine (*Lupinus perennis*). — *a*, flower; *b*, fruit, showing the dehiscence.

lurch[1] (lėrch), *n.* [Origin obscure; first in nautical use.] A sudden leaning or roll to one side, as of a ship, a carriage, or a staggering person (as, "A second *lurch* [of a boat] pitched me headlong into the sea": Lever's "Harry Lorrequer," xxxiii.); a sudden swaying or staggering movement; fig., a mental leaning or inclination (U. S.).—**lurch**[1], *v. i.* To make a lurch; move with lurches; stagger.

lurch[2] (lėrch), *n.* [F. *lourche*, an old-time game (see def.), as adj. discomfited; prob. from Teut.] An old game resembling backgammon†; also, a situation at the close of various kinds of games in which the loser scores nothing or is far behind his opponent; also, a game ending thus; also, fig., the position of one discomfited or in a helpless plight (now only in the phrase 'to leave in the lurch': as, "Dutton . . . a debauched fellow . . . leaving Win in the *lurch*, ran away with another man's bride," Smollett's "Humphry Clinker," Sept. 7).

lurch[3] (lėrch), *v.* [Appar. a var. of *lurk*.] **I.** *intr.* To lurk; prowl; sneak. [Now prov. Eng.] **II.** *tr.* To forestall, cheat, or rob (obs. or archaic); also, to pilfer† or steal†; also, to take (game) with a lurcher.—**lurch'er,** *n.* One who lurks or prowls; a petty thief; a poacher; also, a kind of cross-bred hunting-dog much used by poachers.

lur-dan, lur-dane (lėr'dạn). [OF. *lourdin*, < *lourd*, heavy, dull.] **I.** *n.* A sluggardly, stupid person; an idle rascal: as, "A fine thing it would be for me . . . to be afraid of a fat *lurdane*" (Scott's "Quentin Durward," xxviii.). [Archaic or prov.] **II.** *a.* Sluggardly; lazy; worthless: as, "*lurdane* knights" (Tennyson's "Pelleas and Ettarre," 421). [Archaic or prov.]

lure (lūr), *n.* [OF. *loire* (F. *leurre*); from Teut.] A feathered decoy, sometimes baited, on a long thong, used in falconry to recall the hawk; hence, any decoy; a bait, esp. an artificial bait, used in angling; anything that attracts, entices, or allures (as, "that grand *lure* in the eyes of the savage, a pocket mirror," Irving's "Captain Bonneville," xliii.; "monarchs, whom the *lure* of honour draws," Cowper's "Heroism," 41); an allurement or temptation.—**lure,** *v. t.*; *lured, luring.* To recall (a hawk) to the lure; hence, to draw as by a lure (as, "Pixies; don't go near 'em, child; they'll *lure* you on, Lord knows where": H. Kingsley's "Geoffry Hamlyn," xxx.); decoy; entice; allure.—**lur-er** (lūr'ėr), *n.*

lu-rid (lū'rid), *a.* [L. *luridus*, pale-yellow, wan, ghastly.] Wan, pallid, or ghastly in hue; also, lighted up or shining with an unnatural or wild (esp. red or fiery) glare (as, a *lurid* sky; *lurid* smoke, smoke lighted up by flames; *lurid* flashes of lightning); glaring in brightness or color (as, a *lurid* red; "a cheap *lurid* print," Aldrich's "Story of a Bad Boy," xx.); fig., glaringly vivid or sensational, as language, tales, etc.; conspicuous or terrible for fiery intensity, fierce passion, or wild unrestraint (as, a *lurid* episode in war; a *lurid* revenge; *lurid* crimes); in *bot.* and *zoöl.*, of a dirty-brown color.—**lu'rid-ly,** *adv.*—**lu'rid-ness,** *n.*

lurk (lėrk), *v. i.* [ME. *lurken*; prob. akin to E. *lower*[1].] To lie in concealment, as men in ambush or animals in a place of retreat; remain in or about a place secretly or furtively; sometimes, to go furtively, slink, or steal (as, "the main thoroughfare . . . by which cook *lurks* down before daylight to scour her pots and pans": Thackeray's "Vanity Fair," lxi.); fig., to exist unperceived or unsuspected (as, "A cunning politician often *lurks* under the clerical robe": Irving's "Knickerbocker's New York," v. 7); be latent (as, "A fever *lurked* in my veins": C. B. Brown's "Wieland," xxvii.).—**lurk'er,** *n.*—**lurk'ing,** *p. a.* That lurks; covert; latent; secret.—**lurk'ing-ly,** *adv.*

lus-cious (lush'us), *a.* [Origin uncertain: cf. obs. *licious* for *delicious*.] Highly pleasing to the taste or smell (as, *luscious* peaches; "*luscious* woodbine," Shakspere's "Midsummer Night's Dream," ii. 1. 251); richly sweet; delicious; sometimes, sweet to excess, or cloying; also, highly pleasing to the ear or eye or to the feelings or mind (as, *luscious* tones; a *luscious* prospect; "My chest . . . heaved with *luscious* pain," Kinglake's "Eothen," ix.); sensuously delicious or sweet; strong in sensuous or voluptuous appeal (as, *luscious* epithets or imagery; *luscious* descriptions).—**lus'cious-ly,** *adv.*—**lus'cious-ness,** *n.*

lush[1] (lush), *n.* [Origin obscure.] Intoxicating drink; liquor; also, a person under the influence of liquor. [Slang.]—**lush**[1], *v.* **I.** *intr.* To drink intoxicating liquor. [Slang.] **II.** *tr.* To drink (as, "some of the richest sort you ever *lushed!*" Dickens's "Oliver Twist," xxxix.); also, to supply with drink. [Slang.]

lush[2] (lush), *a.* [ME. *lusch*, prob. var. of *lasch*, < OF. *lasche*, loose, slack: see *laches*.] Lax†, flabby†, or soft†; also, tender and juicy, as plants or vegetation; succulent; luxuriant; characterized by luxuriant vegetation (as, "As the year Grows *lush* in juicy stalks": Keats's "Endymion," i.).—**lush'ly,** *adv.*—**lush'ness,** *n.*

Lu-si-ta-ni-an (lū-si-tā'ni-ạn). **I.** *a.* Of or pertaining to ancient Lusitania, a region, or a Roman province, almost equivalent to modern Portugal; hence, Portuguese. **II.** *n.* One of the people of Lusitania; hence, a Portuguese.

lust (lust), *n.* [AS. *lust* = D. and G. *lust*, pleasure, desire, = Goth. *lustus*, desire.] Pleasure† or delight† (as, "gazing upon the Greeks with little *lust*": Shakspere's "Lucrece," 1384); also, desire† or inclination† (as, "If you would consider your estate, you would have little *lust* to sing," Beaumont and Fletcher's "Knight of the Burning Pestle," i.; to live according to one's *lust*); specif., sensuous desire or appetite considered as sinful (as, "For all that is in the world, the *lust* of the flesh, and the *lust* of the eyes, and the pride of life, is not of the Father, but is of the world": 1 John, ii. 16); esp., sexual desire or appetite; now, commonly, unbridled or lawless sexual desire or appetite; hence, in general, passionate or overmastering desire (as, *lust* of power or gold; "that mere *lust* of fighting, common to man and animals," Kingsley's "Yeast," ix.); also, vigor†; fertility, as of the soil† (as, "a plant that cometh of the *lust* of the earth": Bacon's "Advancement of Learning," ii. 4. 5).—**lust,** *v. i.* To desire†, wish†, or choose†; also, to have a strong or inordinate desire (often with *for* or *after*: as, "The fruits that thy soul *lusted* after are departed from thee," Rev. xviii. 14); specif., to have strong sexual desire (see Mat. v. 28).—**lust'er**[1], *n.*

lus-ter[2], **lus-tre**[1] (lus'tėr), *n.* [L. *lustrum*.] A period of five years; a lustrum: as, "So it will be the turn of you young folks, come eight more *lustres*, and your heads will be bald like mine" (Thackeray's "Newcomes," xxxix.).

lus-ter[3], **lus-tre**[2] (lus'tėr), *n.* [F. *lustre*, < L. *lustrare*, illuminate, make bright, prob. akin to *lux*, light.] The state or quality of shining by reflecting light (as, the *luster* of gems or of satin; "beetles, glittering with metallic *luster*," Parkman's "Oregon Trail," vii.); glitter, glisten, sheen, or gloss; hence, some substance used to impart sheen or gloss; also, radiant or luminous brightness, or radiance, as of a light-giving body (as, "The sun's mild *lustre* warms the vital air": Pope's "Spring," 74); fig., radiance of beauty, or of aspect or countenance; shining excellence or merit, as of deeds; brilliant distinction, or glory (as, achievements that add *luster* to one's name); also, a shining body or object (as, "Glaring day Of these unnumber'd *lustres* robs our sight": Young's "Night Thoughts," v. 307); a chandelier (as, "The *lustre*, which had been lighted for dinner, filled the room with a festal breadth of light": C. Brontë's "Jane Eyre," xiv.); also, a fabric of wool and cotton, with a lustrous surface; in *ceram.*, a shiny, metallic, sometimes iridescent film produced on the surface of pottery or porcelain; in *mineral.*, the nature of the surface of a mineral with respect to its reflecting qualities (as, metallic, adamantine, vitreous, resinous, greasy, pearly, or silky *luster*).—**lus'ter**[3], **lus'tre**[2], *v.*; *-tered* or *-tred*, *-tering* or *-tring*. **I.** *intr.* To shine with luster. [Now rare.] **II.** *tr.* To finish with a luster or gloss.—**lus'ter-less, lus'tre-less,** *a.* Without luster.

lust-ful (lust'fůl), *a.* Full of or having, or marked by, strong or inordinate desire (archaic); esp., full of or imbued with lust, or unbridled or lawless sexual desire or appetite; libidinous; pertaining to, marked by, or indicating such desire; also, inciting to lust†; also, vigorous or lusty (archaic: as, "My *lustfull* leafe is drye and sere," Spenser's "Shepheardes Calender," Jan., 37).—**lust'ful-ly,** *adv.*—**lust'ful-ness,** *n.*

lus-ti-head, lus-ti-hood (lus'ti-hed, -hůd), *n.* Lustiness. [Archaic.]

lus-ti-ly (lus'ti-li), *adv.* In a lusty manner; now, vigorously; heartily.—**lus'ti-ness,** *n.* The state of being lusty; now, vigor; robustness.

lus-tra (lus'trạ), *n.* Latin plural of *lustrum*.

lus-tral (lus′tral), *a.* [L. *lustralis.*] Pertaining to a Roman lustrum or to lustration; also, occurring every five years.

lus-trate (lus′trāt), *v. t.*; *-trated, -trating.* [L. *lustratus*, pp. of *lustrare*, < *lustrum*: see *lustrum.*] To purify by a propitiatory offering; hence, to purify by any ceremonial method.—**lus-tra′tion** (-trā′shọn), *n.* [L. *lustratio(n-).*] The act of lustrating; ceremonial or religious purification by sacrifice, the use of water, or some other method (as, "The offender having ceased to exist, the *lustration* which the laws of knight-errantry prescribe was rendered impossible": Godwin's "Caleb Williams," xii.); also, washing (chiefly humorous).

lus′tre[1], **lus′tre**[2], etc. See *luster*[2], *luster*[3], etc.

lus-tring (lus′tring), *n.* [F. *lustrine*, < It. *lustrino*, < *lustro*, luster, gloss.] A glossy silk fabric much used for women's dresses in the 17th and 18th centuries.

lus-trous (lus′trus), *a.* Having luster; shining; glossy, as silk; bright, as eyes; fig., brilliant or splendid.—**lus′trous-ly,** *adv.*—**lus′trous-ness,** *n.*

lus-trum (lus′trum), *n.*; pl. *-trums*, L. *-tra* (-trạ). [L., < *luere*, loose, release, expiate.] A lustration or ceremonial purification of the ancient Roman people performed every five years, after the taking of the census; hence, a period of five years, or a luster (as, "Encompassed by the massy walls of this venerable academy, I passed . . . the years of the third *lustrum* of my life": Poe's "William Wilson").

lus-ty (lus′ti), *a.*; compar. *lustier*, superl. *lustiest.* [From *lust, n.*] Pleasant†, pleasing†, or delightful† (as, "some *lusty* grove": Marlowe's "Doctor Faustus," i.); beautiful† or handsome† (as, "her *lusty* mantle waving in the wind": Peele's "Arraignment of Paris," i. 1); also, joyful, merry, or cheerful (archaic or prov.: as, "with a *lusty* herte [heart]," Chaucer's "Knight's Tale," 655; "*lusty* banqueting," Scott's "Heart of Midlothian," iv.); also, full of lust, or sexual desire†; also, full of or characterized by healthy vigor (as, "The savage being a stout, *lusty* fellow, closing in with him, had thrown him down," Defoe's "Robinson Crusoe," i. 16; "the period of *lusty* youth," Disraeli's "Coningsby," iii. 1); healthy; robust; also, vigorous, as action, etc. (as, "the churches ringing out the *lustiest* peals he had ever heard": Dickens's "Christmas Carol," v.); hearty, as a meal or the like; often, massively or heavily built, as a person; sometimes, stout or fat; also, in general, large† or great†.

lu-ta-nist (lū′tạ-nist), *n.* [ML. *lutanista*, < *lutana*, lute.] A player on the lute: as, "I have heard Gog-Owza, the *lutanist*, playing his lute" (Dunsany's "Laughter of the Gods," ii.).

lute[1] (lūt), *n.* [OF. *lut, leut* (F. *luth*); from Ar.] A stringed musical instrument formerly much used, having a long, fretted neck and a hollow, resonant, typically pear-shaped body with a vaulted back, the strings being played with the fingers of one hand (or with a plectrum) and stopped on the frets with those of the other.—**lute**[1], *v.*; *luted, luting.* **I.** *intr.* To play on a lute; also, to sound like a lute (poetic: as, "Her new voice *luting* soft, Cried, 'Lycius!'" Keats's "Lamia," i.). **II.** *tr.* To express with or as with the music of a lute: as, "Knaves are men, That *lute* and flute fantastic tenderness" (Tennyson's "Princess," iv. 111). [Poetic.]

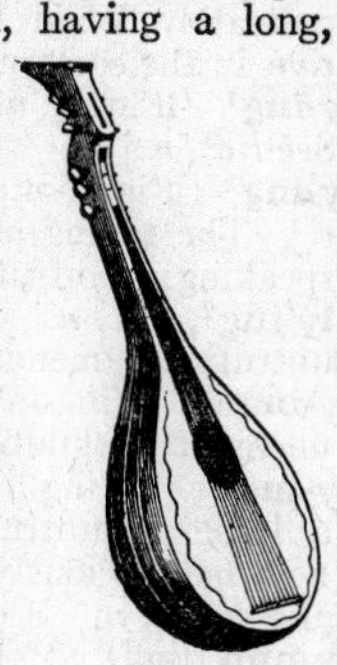

Lute.

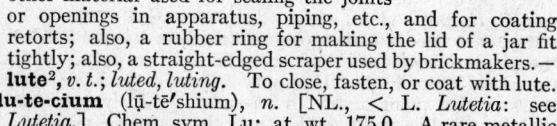

lute[2] (lūt), *n.* [OF. F. *lut*, < L. *lutum*, mud, clay.] A composition of clay or other material used for sealing the joints or openings in apparatus, piping, etc., and for coating retorts; also, a rubber ring for making the lid of a jar fit tightly; also, a straight-edged scraper used by brickmakers.—**lute**[2], *v. t.*; *luted, luting.* To close, fasten, or coat with lute.

lu-te-cium (lū-tē′shium), *n.* [NL., < L. *Lutetia*: see *Lutetia.*] Chem. sym., Lu; at. wt., 175.0. A rare metallic element.

lu-te-nist (lū′tẹ-nist), *n.* See *lutanist.*

lu-te-o- (lū′tẹ-ọ-). Form of L. *luteus*, luteous, yellow, used in combination, as in *luteofulvous* (both luteous and fulvous, tawny-yellow), *luteovirescent* (both luteous and virescent, greenish-yellow).

lu-te-o-lin (lū′tẹ-ọ-lin), *n.* [L. *luteolus*, yellowish, dim. of *luteus*, E. *luteous.*] In *chem.*, a yellow coloring matter obtained from the weld, *Reseda luteola*: used in dyeing silk, etc., and formerly in medicine.

lu-te-ous (lū′tẹ-us), *a.* [L. *luteus*, < *lutum*, a plant used in dyeing yellow, weld.] Of a golden-yellow or orange-yellow color.

lu-tes-cent (lū-tes′ẹnt), *a.* [L. *luteus*, luteous, yellow: see *-escent.*] Tending to yellow; yellowish.

lute-string (lūt′string), *n.* [Appar. a corruption of *lustring.*] Lustring; also, a plain, narrow, heavy ribbon used for attaching eye-glasses, etc.

Lu-te-tia (lū-tē′shiạ), *n.* [L.] An ancient town in Gaul on whose site Paris now stands; hence, Paris.—**Lu-te′tian,** *a.* Pertaining to ancient Lutetia or to Paris; Parisian.

Lu-ther-an (lū′thėr-ạn). **I.** *a.* Of or pertaining to Martin Luther (1483–1546), the German religious reformer; adhering to his doctrines, or belonging to the Protestant church which bears his name. **II.** *n.* A follower of Luther, or an adherent of his doctrines; a member of the Lutheran Church.—**Lu′ther-an-ism,** *n.*

lu-thern (lū′thėrn), *n.* [Cf. *lucarne.*] A dormer-window.

lut-ing (lū′ting), *n.* The act of sealing joints or openings with lute; also, lute.

lut-ist (lū′tist), *n.* A lute-player; also, a lute-maker.

lu-trine (lū′trin), *a.* [L. *lutra*, otter.] Pertaining to or resembling the otter; otter-like.

lux (luks), *n.* [L., light: see *light*[1], *n.*] A unit of illumination, being the illumination received by a surface at a distance of one meter from a light-source whose intensity is taken as unity.

lux-ate (luk′sāt), *v. t.*; *-ated, -ating.* [L. *luxatus*, pp. of *luxare*, < *luxus*, dislocated, < Gr. λοξός, oblique.] To put out of joint; dislocate.—**lux-a-tion** (luk-sā′shọn), *n.* [LL. *luxatio(n-).*] Dislocation, as of bones at a joint.

luxe (lüks), *n.* [F., < L. *luxus*, luxury.] Luxury; elegance. See *de luxe.*

lux-u-ri-ance (luk-sū′ri-ạns or lug-zū′-), *n.* The condition of being luxuriant; luxuriant growth or productiveness; rich abundance. Also **lux-u′ri-an-cy** (-ạn-si).

lux-u-ri-ant (luk-sū′ri-ạnt or lug-zū′-), *a.* [L. *luxurians* (*-ant-*), ppr. of *luxuriare*: see *luxuriate.*] Exuberant in growth, as vegetation or foliage; growing freely and abundantly, as hair; free and vigorous, as growth; sometimes, producing abundantly, as soil; fig., richly abundant or profuse, or superabundant, as if from exuberant production; florid, as imagery or ornamentation; of the fancy, invention, etc., exuberantly productive.—**lux-u′ri-ant-ly,** *adv.*

lux-u-ri-ate (luk-sū′ri-āt or lug-zū′-), *v. i.*; *-ated, -ating.* [L. *luxuriatus*, pp. of *luxuriare*, grow exuberantly, abound, indulge to excess, < *luxuria*: see *luxury.*] To grow exuberantly, as a plant (now rare); also, to indulge in luxury; revel; enjoy one's self without stint; hence, to take great delight (*in*: as, "You *luxuriate* in the contemplation of nature . . . I in my snuff-box," Marryat's "King's Own," xxxv.).—**lux-u-ri-a′tion** (-ā′shọn), *n.*

lux-u-ri-ous (luk-sū′ri-us or lug-zū′-), *a.* [L. *luxuriosus*, < *luxuria*: see *luxury.*] Luxuriant or exuberant, as vegetation (now rare); also, given or inclined to luxury or sumptuous living, pleasures, etc. (as, "She is too proud, too *luxurious*, to marry a beggar," Kingsley's "Yeast," xii.; a *luxurious* city or age; *luxurious* tastes); characterized by luxury (as, *luxurious* habits, pleasures, or living); ministering or conducing to luxury (as, a *luxurious* hotel; *luxurious* appointments); costly, elegant, or rich; delightfully comfortable (as, "a deep, *luxurious* arm-chair": Hawthorne's "Twice-Told Tales," Fancy's Show-Box); also, lascivious†.—**lux-u′ri-ous-ly,** *adv.*—**lux-u′ri-ous-ness,** *n.*

lux-u-ry (luk′sū-ri), *n.*; pl. *-ries* (-riz). [L. *luxuria*, luxuriance, profuseness, riotous living, < *luxus*, excess, luxury.] Luxuriance†; also, free indulgence in choice or costly means of gratifying the appetites or tastes; rich or sumptuous living or mode of life (as, "The world declined to support the lady in *luxury* for nothing": G. Meredith's "Ordeal of Richard Feverel," xxxviii.); use of choice or costly food, clothing, appointments, comforts, etc.; also, the means of luxurious enjoyment or sumptuous living (as, "He often sat before tables covered with *luxury*, and forgot to taste the dainties": Johnson's "Rasselas," ii.); an article or thing conducing to sumptuous living, or constituting a delicacy or an elegance or refinement of living rather than a necessary (as, table *luxuries*; toilet *luxuries*; "a table-cloth, a *luxury* unknown in the times of Horace," Wiseman's "Fabiola," i. 6); hence, something esteemed as desirable although not indispensable (as, "Nancy had treated herself to an expensive *luxury* in the shape of a husband": Mrs. Stowe's "Oldtown Folks," v.); also, any form or means of enjoyment or self-gratification (as, "Learn the *luxury* of doing good," Goldsmith's "Traveller," 22; "I had learned . . . not to indulge in the *luxury* of discontent," Godwin's "Caleb Williams," xxxi.); also, lasciviousness† or lust†.

LXX. The Roman numeral symbol for seventy, used to represent the Septuagint. See *Septuagint*.

-ly[1]. [AS. *-līc* = D. *-lijk* = G. *-lich* = Icel. *-ligr* = Goth. *-leiks*, all repr. a Teut. noun (AS. *līc*, etc.) meaning 'body': see *lich* and *like*[1].] An adjective suffix meaning 'having the form, appearance, or characteristics of,' 'like,' 'befitting,' 'proper to,' 'pertaining to,' as in *brotherly, ghostly, heavenly, kingly, manly, saintly, worldly*, and used also to form adjectives expressing relation to or recurrence with a period of time, as in *daily, hourly, monthly, nightly, yearly*.

-ly[2]. [AS. *-līce*, < *-līc*, E. *-ly*[1].] A suffix of adverbs indicating (*a*) manner, as in *gladly, quickly, safely*, (*b*) degree or extent, as in *extremely, moderately, slightly*, (*c*) place or direction, as in *externally, inwardly, northwardly*, (*d*) respect, as in '*financially* sound,' '*historically* correct,' and (*e*) time, as in *lately, recently, yearly*.

ly-can-thrope (lī'kan-thrōp), *n.* [Gr. λυκάνθρωπος, < λύκος, wolf, + ἄνθρωπος, man.] A werwolf or loup-garou; also, a person affected with lycanthropy.—**ly-can'thro-py** (-thrō-pi), *n.* [Gr. λυκανθρωπία.] The supposed or fabled assumption of the form of a wolf by a human being; also, a kind of insanity in which the patient imagines himself to be a wolf or other wild beast.—**ly-can-throp'ic** (-throp'ik), *a.*

ly-cée (lē-sā), *n.* [F., < L. *Lyceum*: see *lyceum*.] In France, a secondary school maintained by the state.

ly-ce-um (lī-sē'um). [L. *Lyceum*, < Gr. Λύκειον, the Lyceum at Athens, near a temple of Apollo, prop. neut. of Λύκειος, an epithet of Apollo, perhaps meaning 'wolf-slayer,' < λύκος, wolf.] **I.** *n.*; pl. *-ums*. [*cap.*] A public place with covered walks outside of ancient Athens, where Aristotle taught; hence, the Aristotelian or Peripatetic school of philosophy; also [*l. c.*], an institution or association, or a building, hall, or the like, devoted to instruction by lectures, a library, etc.; esp., in the U. S., an association for popular instruction by lectures and other means; hence, the field of instruction and entertainment through lectures, concerts, etc., usually given in a series at intervals and called a 'lyceum course' (cf. *Chautauqua, n.*); also, in France and elsewhere, a lycée or similar school. **II.** *a.* Of or pertaining to a lyceum or the lyceum (field): as, a *lyceum* assembly; a *lyceum* lecturer.

lych, lych'=gate. See *lich, lich-gate*.

lych-nis (lik'nis), *n.* [L., < Gr. λυχνίς, kind of plant with a red flower, akin to λύχνος, lamp.] Any of the showy-flowered plants constituting the silenaceous genus *Lychnis*, as *L. chalcedonica* ('scarlet lychnis'), a rather coarse herb cultivated for its flowers, which are usually scarlet, and *L. coronaria*, the rose-campion.

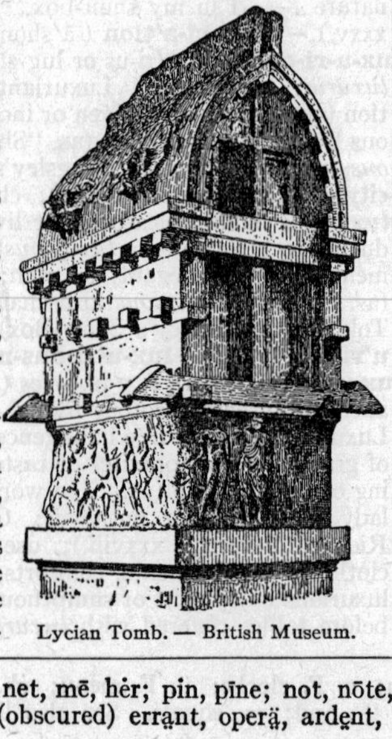
Lycian Tomb. — British Museum.

Ly-ci-an (lis'i-ạn). **I.** *a.* Of or pertaining to Lycia, an ancient district in southwestern Asia Minor, formerly inhabited by a distinct race which has left behind it notable monuments of architecture and sculpture. **II.** *n.* An inhabitant of ancient Lycia; also, the Lycian language.

ly-co-pod (lī'kō-pod), *n.* Any plant of the lycopodium family; a club-moss.

ly-co-po-di-a-ceous (lī"kō-pō-di-ā'shius), *a.* Belonging to the *Lycopodiaceæ*, or lycopodium family of plants.

ly-co-po-di-um (lī-kō-pō'di-um), *n.* [NL., < Gr. λύκος, wolf, + πούς (ποδ-), foot.] Any plant of the genus *Lycopodium*, which comprises erect or creeping, usually moss-like, evergreen-leaved plants, as *L. clavatum*, the common club-moss, and *L. obscurum*, the ground-pine, both much used in Christmas decorations; also, a fine, yellowish powder consisting of the spores of certain species of this genus, used for dusting on sores, etc., and on pills (to prevent stickiness), also (being highly inflammable) in making fireworks, producing stage lightning, and the like.

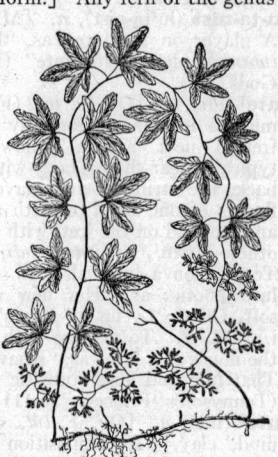

Lycopodium (*L. obscurum*).

lydd-ite (lid'īt), *n.* [From *Lydd*, in Kent, England.] A high explosive consisting chiefly of picric acid.

Lyd-i-an (lid'i-ạn). **I.** *a.* Of or pertaining to Lydia, an ancient district in western Asia Minor, famous for its wealth and luxury; also, designating a particular mode in ancient Greek music, or pertaining to or being in that mode; hence, of music, softly or sensuously sweet, or voluptuous (as, "Soft *Lydian* airs, Married to immortal verse," Milton's "L'Allegro," 136; "Softly sweet, in *Lydian* measures, Soon he sooth'd his soul to pleasures," Dryden's "Alexander's Feast," v.). **II.** *n.* An inhabitant of Lydia.

lye (lī), *n.* [AS. *lēag* = D. *loog* = G. *lauge*, lye.] The alkaline solution obtained by leaching wood-ashes, or any strong alkaline solution, as of potassium or sodium hydroxide, used chiefly in washing or cleaning, making soap, etc.; sometimes, any solution resulting from leaching, percolation, or other processes.—**lye**, *v. t.*; *lyed, lyeing*. To treat with lye.

ly-go-di-um (lī-gō'di-um), *n.* [NL., < Gr. λυγώδης, withe-like, < λύγος, withe, + εἶδος, form.] Any fern of the genus *Lygodium*, comprising widely distributed species notable for their twining or climbing habit, as *L. palmatum*, a delicate climbing plant with palmately lobed fronds, native in the eastern U. S.

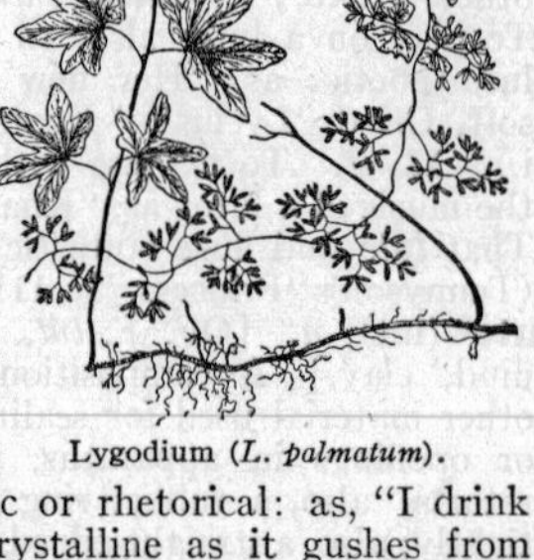
Lygodium (*L. palmatum*).

ly-ing[1] (lī'ing), *n.* and *ppr.* See *lie*[1], *v.*

ly-ing[2] (lī'ing), *n.* [See *lie*[2], *v.*] The telling of lies; false speaking; untruthfulness.—**ly'ing**[2], *p. a.* That lies; untruthful; mendacious.

ly-ing=in (lī'ing-in'), *n.* Confinement in childbed.

ly-ing-ly (lī'ing-li), *adv.* In a lying or untruthful manner; mendaciously.

lyke'wake, *n.* See *likewake*.

lymph (limf), *n.* [L. *lympha*, water, perhaps akin to *limpidus*, E. *limpid*.] Pure, clear water, or a stream of it (poetic or rhetorical: as, "I drink the virgin *lymph*, pure and crystalline as it gushes from the rock," Smollett's "Humphry Clinker," June 8); also, the sap of a plant†; also, in *physiol.*, a nearly colorless, slightly alkaline fluid (which may be regarded as dilute blood minus the red corpuscles) derived from the tissues of the body and conveyed to the blood-stream by the lymphatic vessels; in *pathol.*, a plastic material formed during the inflammation or healing of tissue; in *med.*, a serum or the like used for inoculation, vaccination, etc.

lym-phad (lim'fad), *n.* [Corruption of Gael. *longfhada*, 'long ship.'] A one-masted galley propelled by oars. [Sc., now hist. or in heraldry.]

lym-phan-gi-tis (lim-fan-jī′tis), *n.* [NL., < L. *lympha*, E. *lymph*, + Gr. ἀγγεῖον, vessel.] In *pathol.*, inflammation of the lymphatic vessels.

lym-phat-ic (lim-fat′ik). [NL. *lymphaticus.*] **I.** *a.* Pertaining to, containing, or conveying lymph (as, a *lymphatic* vessel, any of the small, more or less transparent vessels arising in the various tissues and organs of the body, which convey lymph; a *lymphatic* gland, any of the gland-like bodies occurring in the course of the lymphatic vessels, and supposed to be a source of leucocytes); also, noting, pertaining to, or having a temperament characterized by sluggishness of thought and action, formerly supposed to be due to an excess of lymph in the system. **II.** *n.* In *anat.*, a lymphatic vessel.

A Lymphatic Vessel laid open, showing valves. (Magnified.)

lymph=cor-pus-cle (limf′kôr″pus-l), *n.* In *physiol.*, one of the white or colorless corpuscles which occur in lymph, and which are supposed to become leucocytes when they enter the blood.

lym-pho-cyte (lim′fǫ-sīt), *n.* [L. *lympha*, E. *lymph*: see *-cyte.*] In lymph, a lymph-corpuscle; in blood, a special form of leucocyte.—**lym″pho-cy-to′sis** (-sī-tō′sis), *n.* [NL.] Increase, actual or relative, in the number of lymphocytes in the blood.

lym-phoid (lim′foid), *a.* [See *-oid.*] Resembling, of the nature of, or pertaining to, lymph; specif., noting or pertaining to a tissue ('lymphoid tissue') which forms the greater part of the lymphatic glands, etc.; also, noting or pertaining to a rounded cell ('lymphoid cell') which occurs in lymphoid tissue and which is supposed to become a lymph-corpuscle.

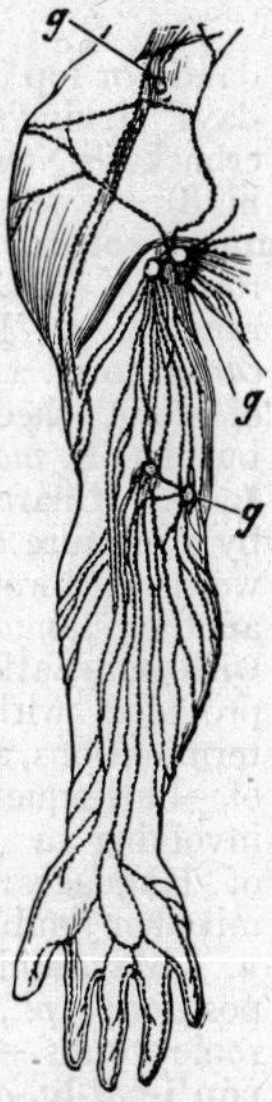

Lymphatics of Front of Right Arm. — *g, g, g,* three lymphatic glands.

lyn-ce-an (lin-sē′ạn), *a.* [L. *lynceus*, < Gr. λύγκειος, < λύγξ, E. *lynx.*] Lynx-like; lynx-eyed; sharp-sighted.

lynch (linch), *v. t.* To punish by lynch-law; specif., to put (a person) to death (by hanging, burning, or otherwise), by concerted action without authority or process of law, for some offense known or imputed. [Orig. U. S.]—**lynch′er**, *n.*

lynch=law (linch′lâ′), *n.* [Commonly said to be named from a 'Judge *Lynch*,' whose identity is disputed.] The administration of summary punishment, esp. death, upon an offender (actual or reputed) by private persons acting in concert without authority of law: as, "Had he exerted a little of the *Lynch law* of the wilderness, and hanged those dexterous horsemen in their own lassos, it would but have been a well-merited and salutary act of retributive justice" (Irving's "Captain Bonneville," xxxix.). [Orig. U. S.]

lynx (lingks), *n.* [L., < Gr. λύγξ, lynx.] Any of various wildcats (genus *Lynx*) with long limbs and short tail, and usually with tufted ears, as *L. rufus* ('bay lynx'), a common North American species, and *L. canadensis*, a large, shaggy species of Canada and the northern U. S.; also [*cap.*], in *astron.*, a northern constellation near Ursa Major. —**lynx′=eye**, *n.* A sharp eye or keen sight such as the lynx has long been fabled to have: as, "His *lynx eye* immediately perceives the paper" (Poe's "Purloined Letter").—**lynx′=eyed**, *a.* Having lynx-eyes; sharp-sighted: as, "a solitary *lynx-eyed* policeman" (Aldrich's "Story of a Bad Boy," xiii.).

Lynx (*L. canadensis*).

ly-on-naise (lī-ǫ-nāz′, F. lē-*o*-nāz), *a.* [F.] In the manner of the city of Lyons, in France: applied to food, esp. fried potatoes, cooked with pieces of onion.

ly-rate (lī′rāt), *a.* [NL. *lyratus.*] Lyre-shaped, as the tail of certain birds; of a leaf, divided transversely into several lobes, the smallest at the base. Also **ly′rat-ed** (-rā-ted).

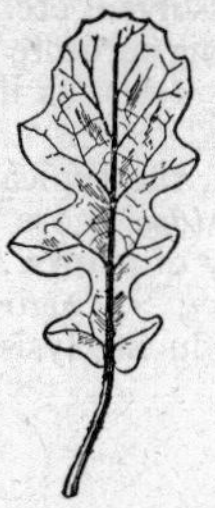

Lyrate Leaf.

lyre (līr), *n.* [OF. *lire* (F. *lyre*), < L. *lyra*, < Gr. λύρα, lyre.] An ancient musical instrument of the harp class, consisting typically of a hollow body with two curving arms connected near the top by a crosspiece from which strings are stretched to the body, much used by the Greeks for accompanying the voice in singing and recitation; hence, this instrument taken figuratively as the vehicle of the poet's expression (as, "Milton's golden *lyre*," Akenside's "Ode on a Sermon against Glory," ii.; "Here Poesy might wake her heav'n-taught *lyre*," Burns's "Written with a Pencil at Kenmore," 21); also [*cap.*], in *astron.*, the northern constellation Lyra.—**lyre′=bird**, *n.* An Australian passerine bird of the genus *Menura*, the male of which has a long tail which is lyrate when spread.

Ancient Greek Lyre. — From a cup in the Berlin Museum.

Lyre-bird (*Menura superba*).

lyr-ic (lir′ik). [F. *lyrique*, < L. *lyricus*, < Gr. λυρικός, < λύρα, E. *lyre.*] **I.** *a.* Pertaining, adapted, or sung to the lyre, or composing poems to be sung to the lyre (as, ancient Greek *lyric* odes or poets); hence, pertaining to, rendered by, or employing singing (as, the *lyric* drama or stage, the opera); also, of poetry, having the form and musical quality of a song, and esp. the character of a song-like outpouring of the poet's own thoughts and feelings (as distinguished from epic and dramatic poetry, with their more extended and set forms and their presentation of external subjects); pertaining to or writing such poetry (as, *lyric* meters; *lyric* composition; a *lyric* poet); hence, in general, characterized by or indulging in a spontaneous, ardent expression of feeling (as, a *lyric* outburst of joy; to become *lyric* in one's enthusiasm). **II.** *n.* A lyric poem; also, a verse of the kind commonly used in lyric poetry; also, a lyric poet.—**lyr′i-cal**, *a.* Lyric. —**lyr′i-cal-ly**, *adv.*—**lyr′i-cal-ness**, *n.*—**lyr′i-cism** (-sizm), *n.* Lyric character or style, as in poetry; a lyric form or expression; also, lyric outpouring of feeling; emotionally expressed enthusiasm.—**lyr′i-cist** (-sist), *n.* A lyric poet.

lyr-ism (lir′izm), *n.* [F. *lyrisme*, < *lyrique*, E. *lyric.*] Lyricism, esp. of expression; lyric enthusiasm; also, singing, or musical performance (rare: as, "The *lyrism* . . . had gradually assumed a rather deafening and complex character," George Eliot's "Adam Bede," liii.).

lyr-ist (līr′ist), *n.* [= F. *lyriste*, < L. *lyristes*, < Gr. λυριστής.] One who plays on the lyre; one who plays, and sings to, an accompaniment on the lyre; also (pron. lir′ist), a lyric poet.

ly-sin (lī′sin), *n.* [Gr. λύσις: see *lysis.*] In *physiol. chem.*, any of a class of substances which are developed in blood-serum, and which are capable of causing the dissolution or destruction of bacteria, blood-corpuscles, and other cellular elements.

ly-sis (lī′sis), *n.* [NL., < Gr. λύσις, a loosing, solution, dissolution, < λύειν, loose.] In *med.*, the gradual recession of a disease, as distinguished from the *crisis*, in which the change is more abrupt; in *physiol. chem.*, the dissolution or destruction of cells by lysins.

-lysis. [Gr. -λυσις or λύσις, < λύειν, loose: cf. *lysis.*] A noun termination meaning 'a loosing,' 'solution,' 'dissolution,' 'decomposition,' 'breaking down,' as in *analysis, catalysis, dialysis, electrolysis, hydrolysis, paralysis.* Cf. *-lyte, -lytic*, and *-lyze.*

ly-sol (lī′sol or -sōl), *n.* [Gr. λύσις, solution, + L. *oleum*, oil.] A clear, brown, oily liquid, a solution of cresols in soap: used as a disinfectant and antiseptic. [Proprietary name.]

lys-sa (lis′ạ̈), *n.* [NL., < Gr. λύσσα, λύττα, rage, rabies:

cf. *lytta.*] In *pathol.*, rabies.—**lys′sic,** *a.* Pertaining to lyssa.

-lyte. [Gr. -λυτος, that may be or is loosed, dissolved, etc.] A termination used to form nouns denoting a thing subjected to some process indicated by a noun ending in *-lysis*, as in *electrolyte, hydrolyte.*

lyth-ra-ceous (lith-rā′shius), *a.* [NL. *Lythrum*, the typical genus (having purple-flowered species), < Gr. λύθρον, gore.] Belonging to the *Lythraceæ*, or loosestrife family of plants.

lyt-ic (lit′ik), *a.* [Gr. λυτικός, able to loose, < λύειν, loose.] In *physiol. chem.*, pertaining to or producing lysis, or dissolution of cells by lysins.

-lytic. [Gr. -λυτικός.] A termination of adjectives corresponding to nouns ending in *-lysis*, as in *analytic, catalytic, paralytic.*

lyt-ta (lit′ạ), *n.* [L., < Gr. λύττα, λύσσα, rabies, also lytta (anciently supposed to induce rabies): cf. *lyssa.*] A long, worm-like cartilage in the tongue of a dog and other carnivorous animals.

-lyze. [F. *-lyser*, < *-lyse*, noun termination, = E. *-lysis.*] A termination used to form verbs signifying to act upon by or subject to some process or change indicated by a noun ending in *-lysis*, as in *analyze, hydrolyze, paralyze.*

M

M, m (em); pl. *M's, m's* (emz). A consonant, the 13th letter of the English alphabet.

ma (mä), *n.* Childish or colloquial form of *mamma*[1].

ma'am (mäm or mam), *n.* A contraction of *madam*: now used chiefly in respectful reply or address (esp. parenthetically or at the end of a sentence) by servants and others as to a superior, and regularly used in England in addressing the queen or a royal princess.

Mac-. Form of Gael. and Ir. *mac*, son, used as a prefix in Scotch and Irish family names. Also written *Mc-*, M^c-, and *M'*-.—**Mac** (mak), *n.* A person whose name begins with the prefix *Mac-* (or *Mc-*, or M^c-, or *M'*-): as, "Her *Macs* let Scotland boast" (Fielding's "Tom Thumb the Great," i. 3).

mac-a-baw (mak′ạ-bâ), *n.* Same as *maccoboy.*

ma-cabre (mạ-käbr′), *a.* [F., for OF. *Macabré* (in *danse Macabré*, as applied to the dance of death), appar. from a personal name.] Pertaining to or suggestive of the allegorical dance of death as represented in late medieval art, as by a skeleton Death dancing with all conditions of men (as, "Jörgenson . . . without being exactly *macabre*, behaved more like an indifferent but restless corpse": J. Conrad's "Rescue," v. 2); hence, gruesome.

ma-ca-co[1] (mạ-kā′kō), *n.*; pl. *-cos* (-kōz). [= F. *mococo*: cf. F. *maki*, lemur, < Malagasy *maka.*] Any of various species of lemur, esp. of the genus *Lemur*, as the ring-tailed lemur, *L. catta*, a species found in Madagascar.

ma-ca-co[2] (mạ-kā′kō), *n.* [Pg.] Same as *macaque.*

mac-ad-am (mạk-ad′ạm), *n.* [From J. L. *McAdam* (1756–1836), Sc. inventor.] Macadamized roadway, or the material used for making it.—**mac-ad′am-ize** (-īz), *v. t.*; *-ized, -izing.* To make or cover (a road) by the laying down and consolidation of layers of small broken stones.—**mac-ad″am-i-za′tion** (-i-zā′shọn), *n.*

ma-caque (mạ-käk′), *n.* [F., < Pg. *macaco*, said to be of African origin.] Any of various monkeys of the genus *Macacus*, found chiefly in Asia, as *M. sinicus*, of India and Ceylon, having a bonnet-like crest of hair on the head ('bonnet-macaque').

Bonnet-macaque (*Macacus sinicus*).

mac-a-ro-ni (mak-ạ-rō′ni), *n.*; pl. *-nis* or *-nies* (-niz). [It. *maccaroni*, now *maccheroni*, pl. of *maccarone*, now *maccherone*; origin uncertain: cf. *macaroon.*] A kind of paste of Italian origin, prepared from wheat flour, in the form of dried, hollow tubes, to be cooked for food (cf. *spaghetti* and *vermicelli*); also, one of a class of English exquisites or dandies of the 18th century who affected foreign ways (see cut in next column); hence, in general, a dandy or fop (as, "the pigmy *macaronies* of these degenerate days": Irving's "Knickerbocker's New York," iii. 3).

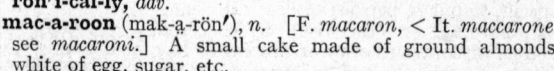

Macaroni and Lady, in dress of 1770–75.

mac-a-ron-ic (mak-ạ-ron′ik). [ML. *macaronicus*, < It. *maccaroni* (orig. a mixture of flour, cheese, and butter), E. *macaroni.*] **I.** *a.* Characterized by a mixture of Latin words with words from another language, or with non-Latin words provided with Latin terminations, as a kind of burlesque verse; involving a mixture of languages; hence, mixed or jumbled. **II.** *n.* Macaronic composition; *pl.*, macaronic verses.—**mac-a-ron′i-cal-ly,** *adv.*

mac-a-roon (mak-ạ-rön′), *n.* [F. *macaron*, < It. *maccarone*: see *macaroni.*] A small cake made of ground almonds, white of egg, sugar, etc.

Ma-cas-sar (mạ-kas′ạ̈r) **oil.** [From *Macassar*, district in Celebes, Dutch East Indies.] Orig., a hair-oil stated to be made from materials obtained from Macassar; hence, some similar oil or preparation for the hair. Cf. *antimacassar.*

ma-caw (mạ-kâ′), *n.* [Brazilian.] Any of various large, long-tailed parrots, chiefly of the genus *Ara*, inhabiting tropical and subtropical America, and notable for their brilliant plumage and harsh voice.

mac-co-boy, mac-ca-boy (mak′ọ-boi, -ạ-boi), *n.* [From *Macouba*, town in Martinique.] A kind of snuff, usually rose-scented.

mace[1] (mās), *n.* [OF. *mace* (F. *masse*): cf. L. *mateola*, mallet.] A medieval weapon of war consisting of a heavy staff or club, often with a spiked metal head; hence, any club-like weapon or implement (often fig.: as, "Hark! how the loud and ponderous *mace* of Time Knocks at the golden portals of the day!" Longfellow's "Spanish Student," i. 5); specif., a staff borne before or by certain officials as a symbol of office; hence, the bearer of such a staff; also, a light stick with a flat head, formerly used at times instead of a cue in playing billiards.

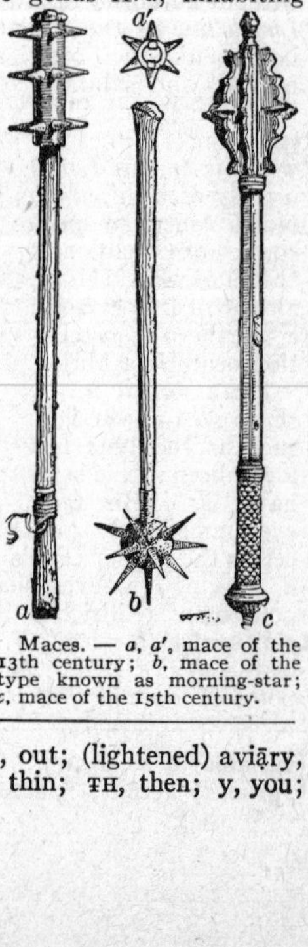

Maces. — *a*, *a′*, mace of the 13th century; *b*, mace of the type known as morning-star; *c*, mace of the 15th century.

mace[2] (mās), *n.* [OF. F. *macis*: cf. L. *macir*, Gr. *μάκερ*, an Indian spice.] A spice consisting of the dried outer covering of the nutmeg.

mace[3] (mās), *n.* [Origin obscure.] Swindling; also, a swindler. [Slang.]—**mace**[3], *v. t.* or *i.*; *maced, macing.* To swindle. [Slang.]

ma-cé-doine (mȧ-sā-dwȧn), *n.* [F., lit. 'Macedonia.'] A mixture of vegetables, served as a salad or otherwise; also, a jellied mixture of fruits; fig., a medley.

ma-cer[1] (mā'sėr), *n.* One who bears a mace (symbol of office); in Scotland, an officer who keeps order, calls the rolls, etc., in a court of law.

ma-cer[2] (mā'sėr), *n.* One who maces; a swindler. [Slang.]

ma-cer-ate (mas'ẹ-rāt), *v.*; *-ated, -ating.* [L. *maceratus*, pp. of *macerare*, soften, macerate.] **I.** *tr.* To soften, or separate the parts of (a substance) by steeping in a liquid, with or without heat; steep in order to extract soluble constituents (as, "extracting the odoriferous substances by *macerating* the flowers in hot oil or molten fat": Encyc. Brit., 11th ed., XX. 52); also, to soften or break up (food) by the digestive process; also, to cause to grow lean or waste away. **II.** *intr.* To undergo maceration.—**ma-cer-a-tion** (mas-ẹ-rā'shọn), *n.* [L. *maceratio(n-)*.] The process of macerating; steeping in order to soften, break up substance, or extract constituents; wasting of the body or flesh.—**ma'cer-a-tor,** *n.*

ma-chan (mạ-chän'), *n.* [Hind. *machān.*] An elevated platform; esp., a platform, built usually in a tree and concealed by the branches, from which a hunter watches for a tiger or other wild animal (as, "As there was no tree . . . close at hand, I had a staging erected . . . This *machan* was about twelve feet high and was composed of four poles stuck into the ground and inclined towards each other at the top, where a plank was lashed to serve as a seat": J. H. Patterson's "Man-Eaters of Tsavo," viii.).

ma-che-te (mä-chā'tā), *n.* [Sp.] A large, heavy knife used esp. in Spanish-American countries as both a tool and a weapon.

Mach-i-a-vel-li-an (mak″i-ạ-vel'i-ạn). **I.** *a.* Of, like, or befitting Niccolò Machiavelli (1469–1527), the Florentine statesman and writer; being or acting in accordance with Machiavelli's political doctrines, which placed expediency above political morality, and countenanced the use of craft and deceit in order to maintain the authority and effect the purposes of the ruler (as, "Educated in the *Machiavellian* . . . school of politics, she was versed in that 'dissimulation' to which liberal Anglo-Saxons give a shorter name": Motley's "Dutch Republic," ii. 1); hence, characterized by subtle or unscrupulous cunning; wily; astute. **II.** *n.* A follower of Machiavelli or his doctrines.—**Mach″i-a-vel'li-an-ism, Mach″i-a-vel'lism,** *n.*

ma-chic-o-late (mạ-chik'ọ-lāt), *v. t.*; *-lated, -lating.* [ML. *machicolatus*, pp. of *machicolare*, < OF. *machicouler, machecoller*, furnish with machicolations: cf. OF. *machecolis* (F. *mâchecoulis, mâchicoulis*), a machicolation; origin uncertain.] To furnish with machicolations, as a parapet or a tower.—**ma-chic-o-la'tion** (-lā'shọn), *n.* In *arch.*, an opening in the floor between the corbels of a projecting gallery or parapet, as on a wall or tower, or in the vault of a portal or passage, through which missiles, molten lead, hot liquids, etc., might be cast upon an enemy beneath (much used in medieval fortified structures); also, a projecting gallery or parapet with such openings.

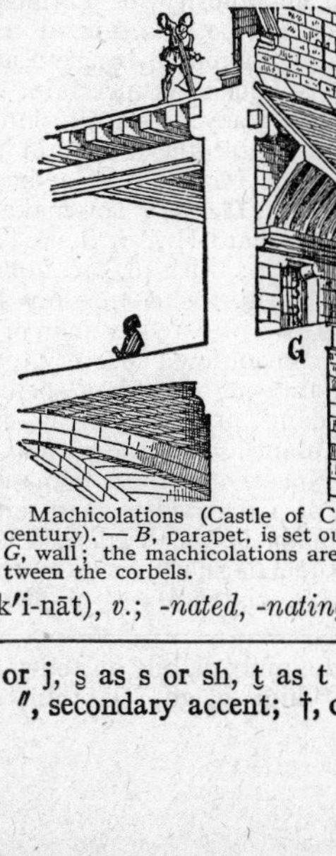

Machicolations (Castle of Coucy, France; 13th century). — *B*, parapet, is set out on corbels, beyond *G*, wall; the machicolations are the open spaces between the corbels.

mach-i-nate (mak'i-nāt), *v.*; *-nated, -nating.* [L. *machinatus*, pp. of *machinari*, contrive, < *machina*: see *machine*.] **I.** *tr.* To contrive or devise, esp. artfully or with evil purpose; plot. **II.** *intr.* To lay plots; intrigue.—**mach-i-na'tion** (-nā'shọn), *n.* [L. *machinatio(n-)*.] The act or process of machinating; artful or evil contrivance; also, a crafty scheme, evil design, or plot (commonly in *pl.*: as, "Was, then, the death of my father . . . the consequence of human *machinations?*" C. B. Brown's "Wieland," vii.).—**mach'i-na-tor,** *n.*

ma-chine (mạ-shēn'), *n.* [F. *machine*, < L. *machina*, < Gr. *μηχανή*, contrivance, machine, < *μῆχος*, means, expedient: cf. *mechanic*.] A structure or contrivance of any kind (now rare: as, "There was not a bed . . . except one oldfashioned *machine*, with a high-gilt tester," Smollett's "Humphry Clinker," Oct. 11); a conveyance or vehicle, as a coach, carriage, or cart, or formerly a ship or boat (now chiefly Sc.); a military engine (now rare); specif., an apparatus consisting of interrelated parts with separate functions, which is used in the performance of some kind of work (as, a sewing-*machine*; a reaping-*machine*; a riveting-*machine*); a mechanical apparatus or contrivance; a mechanism; something operated by a mechanical apparatus, as an automobile, a bicycle, or an aëroplane; also, a contrivance, esp. in the ancient theater, for producing stage effects (as, to introduce a god descending in a *machine*); hence, some agency, personage, incident, or other feature introduced for effect into a literary composition; also, the human or animal frame considered as a mere mechanical apparatus (as, to study the workings of the human *machine*); a person acting like a mere mechanical apparatus (as, "Public hacknies in the schooling trade . . . *Machines* themselves, and govern'd by a clock": Cowper's "Tirocinium," 625); any complex agency or operating system (as, the *machine* of government); the body of persons conducting and controlling the activities of a political party or other organization; also, in *mech.*, a device which transmits and modifies force (as, the simple *machines*, the six, sometimes more, elementary mechanisms, the lever, wedge, wheel and axle, pulley, screw, and inclined plane).—**ma-chine',** *v. t.*; *-chined, -chining.* To contrive†, plot†, or machinate†; also, to make, prepare, or finish with a machine or mechanical apparatus; also, to furnish with or develop by literary machinery, as a story.

ma-chine=gun (mạ-shēn'gun), *n.* A mounted gun operated by some form of mechanism, capable of delivering a rapid and continuous fire of projectiles.

ma-chine=made (mạ-shēn'mād'), *a.* Made by machine, rather than by hand.

ma-chin-er (mạ-shē'nėr), *n.* One who works or tends a machine.

ma-chin-er-y (mạ-shē'nėr-i), *n.*; pl. *-ies* (-iz). Machines or mechanical apparatus, or the parts of a machine, collectively (as, grain-milling *machinery*; the *machinery* of a watch); also, contrivances for producing stage effects (see *machine, n.*); hence, personages, incidents, etc., introduced into a literary composition, as in developing a story or plot; also, any combination or system of agencies by which action is maintained (as, the *machinery* of government; to set legal *machinery* in operation).

ma-chine=shop (mạ-shēn'shop), *n.* A workshop in which metal is cut, shaped, etc., by machine-tools, as in the manufacture and repair of machines.

ma-chine=tool (mạ-shēn'töl), *n.* A machine for cutting or shaping wood, metals, or the like, as a lathe, planer, etc.

ma-chin-ist (mạ-shē'nist), *n.* One versed in the principles and construction of machines; one who makes and repairs machines; one who operates machinery or machine-tools.

ma-chin-ize (mạ-shē'nīz), *v. t.*; *-ized, -izing.* To make into or make like a machine.—**ma-chin-i-za-tion** (mạ-shē-ni-zā'shọn), *n.*

-machy. [Gr. *-μαχία*, < *-μάχος*, fighting, < *μάχεσθαι*, fight.] A noun termination meaning 'a fighting,' 'combat,' 'war,' 'contention,' as in *aëromachy, centauromachy, gigantomachy, logomachy, tauromachy.*

ma-ci-lent (mas'i-lẹnt), *a.* [L. *macilentus*, < *macies*, leanness, < *macere*, be lean.] Lean; thin. [Now rare.]

mac'in-tosh, *n.* See *mackintosh.*

mack-er-el (mak'ẹ-rẹl), *n.*; pl. *mackerel*, occasionally (esp. with reference to different species) *mackerels.* [OF.

maquerel (F. *maquereau*); origin unknown.] An important scombroid food-fish, *Scomber scombrus*, of the northern Atlantic; also, any of various related fishes, as *Scomber colias* (the 'Spanish mackerel' of England) or *Scomberomorus maculatus* (the 'Spanish mackerel' of the U. S.).—**mack′-er-el=sky′,** *n.* A sky spotted with small white fleecy clouds.

Mackerel (*Scomber scombrus*).

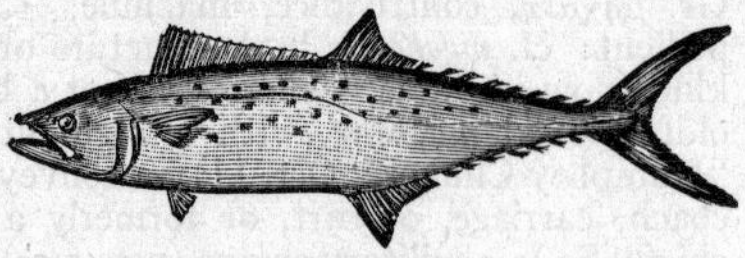

Spanish Mackerel of the U. S. (*Scomberomorus maculatus*).

mack-i-naw (mak′i-nâ), *n.* A Mackinaw blanket, boat, or coat; also, a coarse straw used for making hats.

Mack-i-naw (mak′i-nâ) **blan′ket.** [From *Mackinaw*, or *Mackinac*, name of an island, fort, city, and strait at the junction of Lakes Michigan and Huron.] A kind of thick blanket, often woven with bars of color, formerly much used in the northern and western U. S. by Indians, lumbermen, etc.—**Mack′i-naw boat.** A flat-bottomed boat with sharp prow and square stern, propelled by oars and sometimes sails, used on the upper Great Lakes, etc.—**Mack′i-naw coat.** A short coat of a thick, blanket-like, commonly plaid, woolen material.—**Mack′i-naw trout.** The namaycush.

mack-in-tosh (mak′in-tosh), *n.* [From Charles *Mackintosh* (1766–1843), the inventor.] An outer garment made of cloth rendered waterproof by means of india-rubber; loosely, any waterproof coat or cloak, as for use in wet weather; also, cloth made waterproof by means of india-rubber.

mack-le (mak′l), *n.* [F. *macule*, < L. *macula*, spot.] A blur in printing, as from a double impression.—**mack′le,** *v. t.* or *i.*; *-led, -ling.* To blur or become blurred, as from a double impression in printing.

mac-le (mak′l), *n.* [F. *macle*, < L. *macula*, spot.] A twin crystal; also, a dark spot in a mineral, as one due to the presence of a small mass of another mineral; also, chiastolite.

mac-ra-mé (mak-ra-mā′), *n.* [Said to be from Ar.] A kind of lace or ornamental work made by knotting thread or cord in patterns.

macro-. Form of Gr. μακρός, long, large, great, used in combination. Cf. *micro-*.

mac-ro-bi-ot-ic (mak″rō-bī-ot′ik), *a.* [Gr. μακρόβιοτος, < μακρός, long, + βίος, life.] Long-lived; also, pertaining or tending to the prolongation of life.

mac-ro-ce-phal-ic (mak″rō-se-fal′ik), *a.* [Gr. μακροκέφαλος, < μακρός, long, large, + κεφαλή, head.] Large-headed; having an abnormally large head or skull. Also **mac-ro-ceph′a-lous** (-sef′a-lus).—**mac-ro-ceph′a-ly** (-li), *n.*

mac-ro-chem-is-try (mak-rō-kem′is-tri), *n.* [See *macro-*.] Chemistry as concerned with substances or reactions observed by the unassisted eye, or without a microscope. Cf. *microchemistry.*—**mac-ro-chem′i-cal,** *a.*

mac-ro-cosm (mak′rō-kozm), *n.* [F. *macrocosme*, < ML. *macrocosmus*, < Gr. μακρός, long, large, + κόσμος, world.] The great world, or universe: opposed to *microcosm.* Also fig.—**mac-ro-cos′mic** (-koz′mik), *a.*

mac-ro-cys-tis (mak-rō-sis′tis), *n.* [NL., < Gr. μακρός, long, + κύστις, bladder.] A brown seaweed of the southern seas and the northern Pacific coasts, of the genus *Macrocystis* (with one species, *M. pyrifera*), remarkable as exhibiting the longest stems known in the vegetable kingdom, sometimes attaining a length of 700 feet.

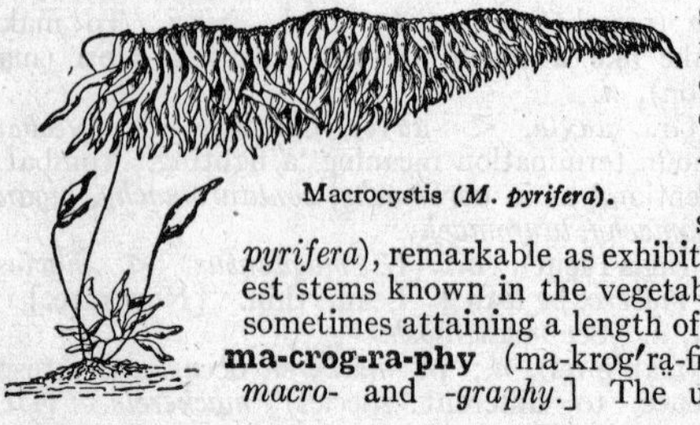

Macrocystis (*M. pyrifera*).

ma-crog-ra-phy (ma-krog′ra-fi), *n.* [See *macro-* and *-graphy.*] The use of very large characters in writing: sometimes an indication of nervous disorder.

ma-crom-e-ter (ma-krom′e-tėr), *n.* [See *macro-* and *-meter.*] An instrument for measuring the size and distance of remote or inaccessible objects.

mac-ron (mak′ron or mā′kron), *n.* [NL., < Gr. μακρόν, neut. of μακρός, long: see *meager.*] A short horizontal line placed over a vowel to show that it is long in quantity, as in the Latin *amāre, pendēre*, or to indicate the sound in pronunciation, as in (English) āle, ēve.

mac-ro-scop-ic (mak-rō-skop′ik), *a.* [See *macro-*, and cf. *microscopic.*] Visible to the naked eye: opposed to *microscopic.* Also **mac-ro-scop′i-cal.**—**mac-ro-scop′i-cal-ly,** *adv.*

mac-ro-spore (mak′rō-spōr), *n.* [See *macro-* and *spore.*] In *bot.*; a megaspore.

ma-cru-ran (ma-krö′ran). [NL. *Macrura*, pl., < Gr. μακρός, long, + οὐρά, tail.] **I.** *a.* Belonging or pertaining to the *Macrura*, a group of stalk-eyed decapod crustaceans with long tails, including the lobsters, prawns, shrimps, etc. **II.** *n.* A macruran crustacean.—**ma-cru′rous,** *a.* Long-tailed, as the lobster: opposed to *brachyurous.*

mac-ta-tion (mak-tā′shon), *n.* [LL. *mactatio(n-)*, < L. *mactare*, sacrifice, slay.] The slaying of a sacrificial victim.

mac-u-la (mak′ū-lä), *n.*; pl. *-læ* (-lē). [L., a spot.] A spot or stain; a spot on the sun, in a mineral, in the skin, or the like.—**mac′u-lar** (-lär), *a.*

mac-u-late (mak′ū-lāt), *v. t.*; *-lated, -lating.* [L. *maculatus*, pp. of *maculare*, < *macula*, a spot.] To mark with a spot or spots; stain; fig., to sully or pollute.—**mac′u-late,** *a.* Spotted; stained; fig., defiled or impure (see Shakspere's "Love's Labour's Lost," i. 2. 97).—**mac-u-la′tion** (-lā′shon), *n.* [L. *maculatio(n-)*.] A spotting, or a spotted condition; a marking of spots, as on an animal or a plant; a disfiguring spot or stain; fig., defilement.

mac-ule (mak′ūl), *n.* and *v.* Same as *mackle.*

mad (mad), *a.*; compar. *madder*, superl. *maddest.* [ME. *madd*, < AS. *gemǣdd, gemǣded*, pp. of a verb from *gemād*, mad; akin to Icel. *meidha*, hurt, maim, Goth. *maidjan*, change, corrupt.] Disordered in intellect, insane, or crazy (as, "Paul, thou art beside thyself; much learning doth make thee *mad*": Acts, xxvi. 24); esp., violently insane, or maniacal; also, senselessly foolish or imprudent (as, "the same trash *mad* mortals wish for here," Pope's "Essay on Man," iv. 174; "the *maddest* voyage, and the most unlikely to be performed, that ever was undertaken," Defoe's "Robinson Crusoe," i. 9); also, affected with or characterized by wild excitement, enthusiasm, passion, etc., as persons, the mood or feelings, actions, etc.; frenzied or frantic (as, *mad* cries; *mad* haste); wild with eagerness or desire (as, to be *mad* for revenge); furious with anger, enraged, or angry (now colloq.); wildly gay or merry (as, "To-morrow 'ill be of all the year the *maddest* merriest day": Tennyson's "May Queen," 43); also, of wind, storms, etc., furious in violence (as, "The *mad* tempest was riding the whitecaps in Berwick's Bay": G. W. Cable's "Bonaventure," iii. 3); also, of animals, abnormally furious (as, a *mad* bull); affected with rabies (as, a *mad* dog); rabid.—**like mad,** as if mad; frantically; furiously; with mad haste, impetuosity, or enthusiasm: as, to run, fight, work, or cheer *like mad.*—**mad as a hatter,** quite mad or crazy; also, thoroughly angry: a proverbial phrase of which the original allusion is uncertain.—**mad as a March hare,** quite mad or crazy: with allusion to the actions of the hare during the breeding season in March.—**mad,** *v.*; *madded, madding.* **I.** *intr.* To be or become mad; act as if mad. [Archaic.] **II.** *tr.* To make mad; madden. See Shakspere's "Richard II.," v. 5. 61. [Archaic.]

mad-am (mad′am), *n.*; with pl. *mesdames* (see *madame*²). [OF. F. *madame*, orig. *ma dame*, 'my lady': see *dame.*] A term of address used orig. to a woman of rank or authority, but now in mere conventional courtesy to any woman.

mad-ame¹ (mad′am), *n.* A variant spelling of *madam.*

ma-dame² (ma-dâm′ or mad′am, F. mà-dàm), *n.*; pl. *mesdames* (F. mā-dàm). [F.: see *madam.*] A conventional French title of respect, orig. for a woman of rank, used distinctively to or of a married woman, either separately or prefixed to the name: often used as a conventional prefix to the name of a female singer or other artiste (regardless of nationality). Abbreviated *Mme.*, pl. *Mmes.*

ma-dar, mu-dar (mu-där′), *n.* [Hind. *madār.*] An East Indian shrub of the asclepiadaceous genus *Calotropis*, esp. *C. gigantea*, yielding a drug highly esteemed in the East, also a latex used as a substitute for gutta-percha, and a fine, silky fiber.

Madar.

mad-cap (mad′kap). **I.** *n.* One who acts with mad or wild impulsiveness, esp. in pranks or frolics; now, often, a wildly impulsive, lively young woman. **II.** *a.* Being, or acting like, a madcap (as, a *madcap* girl); characteristic of or befitting a madcap (as, "Their going along was nothing more than a *madcap* frolic": H. Melville's "Omoo," lxxi.).

mad-den (mad′n), *v.* **I.** *intr.* To become mad; act as if mad; rage: as, "All Bedlam, or Parnassus, is let out . . . They rave, recite, and *madden* round the land" (Pope's "Prologue to the Satires," 6). **II.** *tr.* To make mad; render insane (as, "They . . . *maddened* by cold and hunger fed upon each other's flesh": Parkman's "Oregon Trail," x.); excite to frenzy; infuriate.—**mad′den-ing,** *p. a.* That maddens; raging or furious (as, "All the people rushed along with *maddening* eagerness to the anticipated solace": De Quincey's "Revolt of the Tartars"); driving to madness or frenzy (as, *maddening* pain); infuriating or exasperating (as, *maddening* delays).—**mad′den-ing-ly,** *adv.*

mad-der (mad′ėr), *n.* [AS. *mædere* = Icel. *madhra*, madder.] A plant of the rubiaceous genus *Rubia*, esp. *R. tinctorum*, a European herbaceous climbing plant with panicles of small yellowish flowers; the root of such a plant, esp. of *R. tinctorum*, used to some extent (esp. formerly) in medicine, and particularly for making dyes which give red and other colors; the dye or coloring matter itself; a color produced by such a dye (as, a crimson *madder*). Cf. *alizarin.*

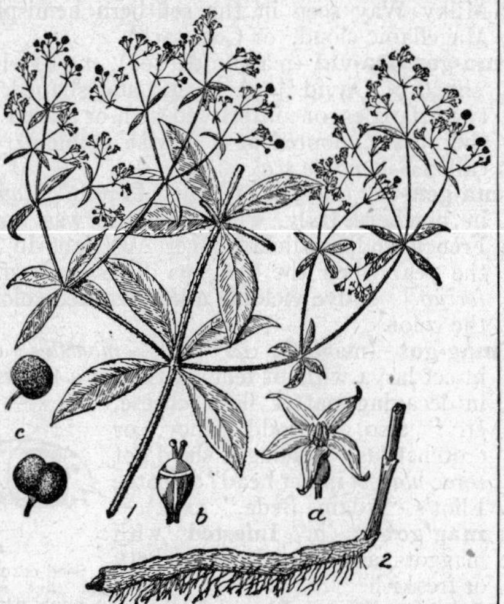

Madder (*Rubia tinctorum*). — 1, branch with flowers and fruits; 2, the rhizome; *a*, a flower; *b*, the pistil; *c*, two different fruits.

mad-ding (mad′ing), *p. a.* [See *mad, v.*] Being mad, or acting as if mad (as, "far from the *madding* crowd's ignoble strife": Gray's "Elegy," xix.); also, making mad (as, "in the distraction of this *madding* fever": Shakspere's "Sonnets," cxix.).

mad-dish (mad′ish), *a.* Somewhat mad.

made (mād). Preterit and past participle of *make.*—**made,** *p. a.* Produced by making, or fashioning, constructing, preparing, or some like process; artificially produced, rather than natural (as, *made* ground); invented or made-up (as, a *made* word); specially prepared or compounded (as, a *made* gravy; a *made* dish, a dish of food consisting of several articles combined, or of a single main article, prepared with a special seasoning, sauce, or garnish, or in a special form, as distinguished from a dish of food simply prepared or plainly cooked); also, assured of success or fortune (as, "You are a *made* man, Tom, if you get on the right side of that Rajah of yours": J. Conrad's "Rescue," ii. 3).

Ma-dei-ra (ma-dā′rä or -dē′rä), *n.* A fine wine resembling sherry, made on the island of Madeira.—**Ma-dei′ra=vine,** *n.* A basellaceous climbing plant, *Boussingaultia baselloides*, with bright-green leaves and long racemes of small, fragrant white flowers.

made-moi-selle (måd-mwo-zel), *n.*; pl. *mesdemoiselles* (mād-mwo-zel). [F., orig. *ma demoiselle*, 'my demoiselle': see *demoiselle* and *damsel.*] The conventional French title of respect for a girl or unmarried woman, either used separately or (like *Miss*) prefixed to the name. Abbreviated *Mlle.*, pl. *Mlles.*

made=up (mād′up′), *a.* Made by putting parts or things together; arranged in due form for printing, as pages of type; concocted, fabricated, or invented (as, a *made-up* story or name); also, complete† or consummate† (as, "He's a *made-up* villain": Shakspere's "Timon of Athens," v. 1. 101); also, prepared or embellished with artificial aids, as of dress or the toilet (as, "*Hastings.* You must allow her some beauty. *Tony.* Bandbox! She's all a *made up* thing": Goldsmith's "She Stoops to Conquer," ii.).

mad-house (mad′hous), *n.* An asylum for the insane.

mad-id (mad′id), *a.* [L. *madidus*, < *madere*, be wet.] Wet; moist; humid: as, "his large deep blue eye, *madid* and yet piercing" (Disraeli's "Coningsby," i. 3). [Now rare.]

mad-ly (mad′li), *adv.* In a mad manner.

mad-man (mad′man), *n.*; pl. *-men.* A man who is mad or insane; a lunatic; a maniac.

mad-ness (mad′nes), *n.* The state of being mad; insanity (as, "Great wits are sure to *madness* near allied": Dryden's "Absalom and Achitophel," i. 163); senseless folly, or a manifestation of it (as, "Be wise to-day; 'tis *madness* to defer": Young's "Night Thoughts," i. 390); wild enthusiasm; frenzy; fury or rage; sometimes, rabies ('canine madness').

ma-don-na (ma-don′ä), *n.* [It., 'my lady': see *donna.*] An Italian title of respect for a woman; [*cap.*] usually with *the*, an Italian designation of the Virgin Mary; also, a picture or statue representing the Virgin Mary.—**Madonna lily.** See *lily, n.*

ma-dras (ma-dräs′, popularly mad′ras), *n.* [From *Madras*, in southeastern India.] A light cotton fabric with cords set at intervals or with woven stripes or figures, often of another color: used for shirts, etc.

ma-dras-ah (ma-dras′ä), *n.* [Ar.] A Mohammedan school or college.

mad-re-po-ra-ri-an (mad″rē-pō-rā′ri-an). [NL. *Madreporaria*, pl., < *Madrepora*, the typical genus, < It. *madrepora*: see *madrepore.*] **I.** *a.* Belonging or pertaining to the *Madreporaria*, an order or group of actinozoans with a continuous calcareous skeleton, including most of the stony corals. **II.** *n.* A madreporarian actinozoan.

mad-re-pore (mad′rē-pōr), *n.* [F. *madrépore*, < It. *madrepora*, appar. < *madre* (< L. *mater*), mother, + L. *porus*, < Gr. πῶρος, kind of stone.] Formerly, any perforate coral; now, usually, any of various corals (madreporarians) of the genus *Madrepora*, noted for reef-building in tropical seas.—**mad-re-por′ic** (-por′ik), *a.*

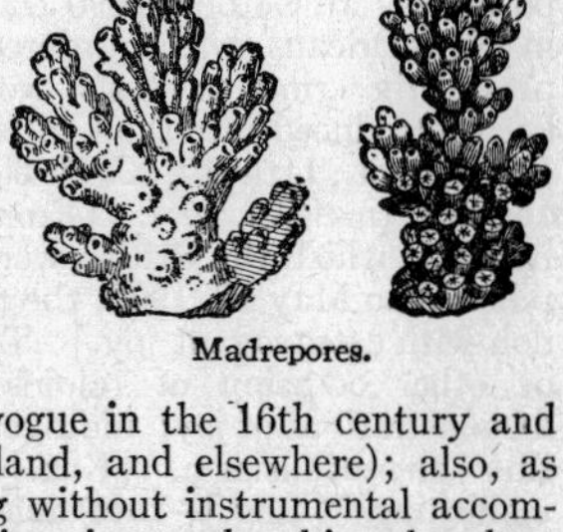

Madrepores.

mad-ri-gal (mad′ri-gal), *n.* [It. *madrigale*, earlier *madriale*, *mandriale*, appar. orig. a pastoral song, < *mandra*, < L. *mandra*, stall, herd, < Gr. μάνδρα, inclosed space, fold.] A lyric poem suitable for musical setting, usually short and often of amatory character (esp. in vogue in the 16th century and later in Italy, France, England, and elsewhere); also, as a form of music, a part-song without instrumental accompaniment, usually for five or six voices, and making abundant use of contrapuntal imitation; any part-song or glee; in general, a song (often fig.: as, "By shallow rivers, to whose falls Melodious birds sing *madrigals*," Marlowe's "Passionate Shepherd to His Love").—**mad′ri-gal-ist,** *n.* A composer or a singer of madrigals.

ma-dro-ña (ma-drō′nyä), *n.* Same as *madroño.*

ma-dro-ño (ma-drō′nyō), *n.*; pl. *-ños* (-nyōz). [Sp., the arbutus or strawberry-tree.] An ericaceous evergreen tree or shrub, *Arbutus menziesii*, of western North America, having a hard wood and a smooth bark, and bearing a yellow, scarcely edible berry; also, any of several related species, of the southwestern U. S. and northern Mexico.

Mad-u-ra (mad′ọ̈-rạ̈) **foot.** [From *Madura*, district in Madras, southeastern India.] In *pathol.*, a diseased condition of the feet and hands, occurring in India, etc., characterized by distortion, suppuration, softening of bones, etc., and due to a species of fungus; mycetoma.

mad-wom-an (mad′wům″ạn), *n.*; pl. *-women* (-wim″en). A woman who is mad or insane.

Mæ-ce-nas (mē̜-sē′nạs), *n.* [From *Mæcenas*, the Roman patron of letters, and friend of Virgil and Horace.] A generous patron, esp. of literature or art: as, "Are you not called . . . a mock *Mæcenas* to second-hand authors?" (Sheridan's "Critic," i. 1).

mael-strom (māl′strọm), *n.* [D. *maelstrom*, now *maalstroom*, < *malen*, grind, + *stroom*, stream; as a proper name prob. first used on Dutch maps.] [*cap.*] A famous whirlpool off the northwestern coast of Norway; hence [usually *l. c.*], any great or violent whirlpool; fig., a powerful or resistless vortex of affairs, influences, etc. (as, the *maelstrom* of dissipation; "The poor man lived always in the whirl of a perfect *Maelstrom* of promises and engagements," Mrs. Stowe's "Oldtown Folks," xvii.).

mæ-nad (mē′nad), *n.* [L. *Mænas* (*Mænad-*), < Gr. μαινάς (μαιναδ-), < μαίνεσθαι, rage, be mad.] A female attendant of Bacchus; a bacchante; hence, any frenzied or raging woman.—**mæ-nad′ic,** *a.*

Mænad. — From a Greek polychrome cup preserved at Munich.

ma-es-to-so (mä-es-tō′sō), *a.* [It.] In *music*, majestic.

ma-es-tro (mä-es′trō), *n.*; pl. *-tri* (-trē). [It.] A master; esp., an eminent musical composer, teacher, or conductor.

maf-fi-a, ma-fi-a (mäf′fē-ä, mä′-), *n.* [It. *maffia*, *mafia*; origin and original sense disputed.] In Sicily, a popular spirit of hostility to legal restraint, and to invoking the law for any purpose, often manifesting itself in criminal acts; also, those manifesting this spirit; specif. [*cap.*], a secret society of Sicilians or other Italians, at home or in foreign countries, for criminal purposes (as, "In October 1890 David Hennessy, chief of police in New Orleans, was murdered. Subsequent legal inquiry proved the crime to be the work of the *Mafia*, which had been introduced into the United States thirty years before": Encyc. Brit., 11th ed., XVII. 300).

maf-fick (maf′ik), *v. i.* [From *Mafeking*, town in South Africa in which the British were besieged by the Boers until relieved on May 18, 1900, the relief being celebrated in London with extravagant joy.] To celebrate a national victory or other occasion of rejoicing with extravagant public demonstrations of joy; indulge in a frenzy of popular exultation or enthusiasm. [Eng.]—**maf′fick,** *n.* An act of mafficking. [Eng.]—**maf′fick-er,** *n.*

mag-a-zine (mag-ạ-zēn′), *n.* [F. *magasin*, < It. *magazzino*, storehouse; from Ar.] A storehouse for goods, merchandise, etc.; a warehouse; a shop (as, "The lawyer afterwards compared his mind to the *magazine* of a pawnbroker, stowed with goods of every description": Scott's "Guy Mannering," xxxix.); also, a building or place for keeping military stores, as arms, ammunition, provisions, etc.; a room or place for keeping gunpowder and other explosives, as in a fort or on a war-ship; the chamber in a repeating gun or rifle from which the cartridges are automatically fed; also, a supply-chamber in a stove, a camera, etc.; in general, a repository or receptacle (lit. or fig.: as, "The mind of man in a long life will become a *magazine* of wisdom or folly," Steele, in "Tatler," 132); a place or region containing or yielding great abundance of something (as, the district is a *magazine* of mineral wealth); also, a store or stock of goods, supplies, or other material (as, "I had the biggest *magazine* of all kinds now that ever was laid up, I believe, for one man": Defoe's "Robinson Crusoe," i. 4); also, a periodical publication, usually with a paper cover, containing miscellaneous articles or pieces, in prose or verse, often with illustrations.—**mag-a-zine′,** *v. t.*; *-zined*, *-zining.* To store in or as in a magazine.—**mag-a-zine′=gun, mag-a-zine′=ri″fle,** *n.* A gun (cannon) or a rifle supplied with a magazine and firing a number of shots in quick succession without reloading.—**mag-a-zin′ism** (-zē′nizm), *n.* The occupation or profession of writing for, editing, or conducting magazines.—**mag-a-zin′-ist,** *n.* One engaged in magazinism, esp. writing for magazines.

mag-da-len, mag-da-lene (mag′dạ-len, -lēn), *n.* [From Mary *Magdalene*, Mary of Magdala (a town on the Sea of Galilee), mentioned in Luke, viii. 2, and traditionally identified with the repentant woman in Luke, vii. 37–50.] A reformed prostitute.

mage (māj), *n.* [See *Magus.*] A magician: as, "*mage* Merlin" (Tennyson's "Coming of Arthur," 279). [Archaic.]

Mag-el-lan-ic (maj-e-lan′ik or, chiefly Brit., mag-), *a.* Pertaining to or named after the Portuguese navigator Ferdinand Magellan (about 1480–1521).—**Magellanic cloud,** in *astron.*, either of two cloud-like tracts or patches of nebulous stars in the southern heavens; also, a dark space in the Milky Way seen in the southern hemisphere (the 'black Magellanic cloud,' or Coal-sack).

ma-gen=Da-vid (mä′gän-dä′vēd), *n.* [Heb. *magen Dawid*, 'shield of David.'] A mystic star-shaped figure formed of two triangles, one interlaced with or placed upon the other, adopted as a Jewish emblem. Also called *Solomon's seal.*

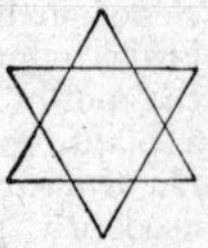

Magen-David.

ma-gen-ta (mạ-jen′tạ̈), *n.* [From *Magenta*, in northern Italy, where a battle was won by French and Sardinians over Austrians in 1859, the year when the dye was discovered: cf. *solferino.*] A dye yielding a purplish-red color; fuchsin; also, the color.

mag-got (mag′ọt), *n.* [ME. *magotte*: cf. *mawk.*] An insect larva without feet, as that of a fly, esp. a larva living in decaying matter, flesh, cheese, etc.; also, an odd fancy, or crotchet (as, "I thought she'd got some *maggot* in her head": George Eliot's "Adam Bede," xxxi.).—**mag′got-y,** *a.* Infested with maggots, as food; also, crotchety or freakish.

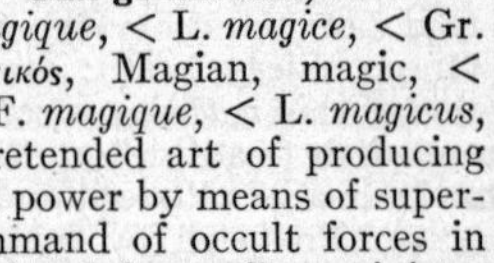

Seed-corn Maggot. — *a*, maggot (line shows natural size); *b*, pupa, natural size.

Ma-gi (mā′jī), *n.* Plural of *Magus.*

Ma-gi-an (mā′ji-ạn). **I.** *a.* Of or pertaining to the Magi or priestly caste of ancient Media and Persia; also [*l. c.*], magic (rare). **II.** *n.* One of the Magi.—**Ma′gi-an-ism,** *n.*

mag-ic (maj′ik). [As n., OF. *magique*, < L. *magice*, < Gr. μαγική, prop. fem. of adj. μαγικός, Magian, magic, < Μάγος, E. *Magus*; as adj., OF. F. *magique*, < L. *magicus*, < Gr. μαγικός.] **I.** *n.* The pretended art of producing effects beyond the natural human power by means of supernatural agencies or through command of occult forces in nature (as, black *magic*, magic involving evil or sinister methods, esp. invocation of evil spirits; white *magic*, innocent, harmless, or beneficent magic); the exercise of this art, or the effects produced (as, "All these appearances could be nothing else but necromancy and *magic*": Swift's "Gulliver's Travels," iv. 2); power or influence exerted through this art (as, "if she in chains of *magic* were not bound": Shakspere's "Othello," i. 2. 65); hence, any extraordinary or irresistible influence suggestive of magic power (as, the *magic* of love or of eloquence; "There is a *magic* in a great name," Lover's "Handy Andy," v.); also, legerdemain or conjuring. **II.** *a.* Of, pertaining to, or due to magic (as, the *magic* art; *magic* rites; "*magick* structures," Milton's "Comus," 798); employed in, or producing the effects of, magic (as, *magic* spells; "Gates of brass cannot withstand One touch of that *magic* wand," Longfellow's "Maidenhood"); also, operating like or suggestive of magic (as, "the painter's *magic* skill": Cowper's "Task," i. 422); marvelously potent. —**magic lantern,** an optical instrument for projecting on a screen or the like, in the dark, magnified images of transparent photographs, etc.—**mag′i-cal,** *a.* Magic.—**mag′i-cal-ly,** *adv.*—**ma-gi-cian** (mạ-jish′ạn), *n.* [OF. F. *magicien.*] One skilled in magic; a wizard; also, one who practises legerdemain; a conjurer.

ma-gilp (mạ-gilp′), *n.* [Origin unknown.] In *painting,* any of various jelly-like preparations, as a mixture of mastic varnish and linseed-oil, used by artists as a vehicle for oil-colors.

mag-is-te-ri-al (maj-is-tē′ri-ạl), *a.* [LL. *magisterius,* < L. *magister,* E. *master*².] Of, pertaining to, or befitting a master (as, a *magisterial* air; a *magisterial* pronouncement); authoritative; sometimes, imperious, domineering, or arrogant (as, "He paced up and down the room with a *magisterial* stride, and flashed an angry glance on every side": Godwin's "Caleb Williams," xi.); also, of, pertaining to, or befitting a magistrate or his office; of the rank of a magistrate.—**mag-is-te′ri-al-ly,** *adv.*—**mag-is-te′ri-al-ness,** *n.*

mag-is-te-ry (maj′is-te-ri), *n.*; pl. *-ries* (-riz). [L. *magisterium,* < *magister,* E. *master*².] In *alchemy, old med.,* etc., a master principle, agency, or agent, as for transmuting or healing; a substance, remedy, etc., of sovereign power; any of various extracts or preparations (as, the *magistery* of bismuth; the *magistery* of pearls).

mag-is-tra-cy (maj′is-trā-si), *n.*; pl. *-cies* (-siz). The office, dignity, or function of a magistrate; also, a body of magistrates (as, "He went from city to city, advising with the *magistracies*": Motley's "Dutch Republic," iii. 8); also, a district under a magistrate.

mag-is-tral (maj′is-trạl or mạ-jis′trạl), *a.* [L. *magistralis,* < *magister,* E. *master*².] Pertaining to or befitting a master (now rare); dogmatic (now rare); also, of sovereign virtue, as a remedy†; also, in *phar.,* prescribed or prepared for a particular occasion, as a remedy (opposed to *officinal*); also, in *fort.,* principal (as, a *magistral* line, the guiding line from which the position of the other lines or works is determined).

mag-is-trate (maj′is-trāt), *n.* [L. *magistratus,* < *magister,* E. *master*².] A civil officer charged with the administration of the law (as, the chief *magistrate,* the highest official of a government); specif., a minor judicial officer, as a justice of the peace or a police justice, having summary jurisdiction in certain cases.—**mag′is-trate-ship,** *n.* The office or dignity, or the term of office, of a magistrate.—**mag′is-tra-ture** (-trā-ţūr), *n.* The office, function, or term of office of a magistrate; also, the body of magistrates; the magistracy.

mag-ma (mag′mạ), *n.* [L., < Gr. μάγμα, < μάσσειν, knead.] Any crude mixture of mineral or organic matters in the form of a thin paste; in *geol.,* molten material beneath the solid crust of the earth, from which igneous rock is formed; also, the ground-mass of porphyritic igneous rocks, esp. when vitreous in character.—**mag-mat′ic** (-mat′ik), *a.*

Mag-na Char-ta, Mag-na Car-ta (mag′nạ kär′tạ). [ML., 'great charter.'] The great charter of the personal and political liberties of the people of England, obtained from King John by the English barons at Runnymede on June 15, 1215; hence, any fundamental constitution guaranteeing personal or other rights.

mag-na-nim-i-ty (mag-nạ-nim′i-ti), *n.*; pl. *-ties* (-tiz). The quality of being magnanimous (as, "*Magnanimity* in politicks is not seldom the truest wisdom": Burke's "Conciliation with the Colonies"); also, a display of magnanimous feeling; a magnanimous act.

mag-nan-i-mous (mag-nan′i-mus), *a.* [L. *magnanimus,* < *magnus,* great, + *animus,* mind.] Great of mind, heart, or soul, as persons, or proceeding from or showing such greatness, as actions, thoughts, feelings, etc.; esp., nobly brave, or heroic (now rare: as, "She is . . . A spur to valiant and *magnanimous* deeds," Shakspere's "Troilus and Cressida," ii. 2. 200); high-minded or noble (as, "To give a kingdom hath been thought Greater and nobler done, and to lay down Far more *magnanimous,* than to assume": Milton's "Paradise Regained," ii. 483); generous, or free from pettiness or meanness (as, "He spoke . . . with the *magnanimous* frankness of a man who had done great things, and who could well afford to acknowledge some deficiencies": Macaulay's "Hist. of Eng.," vii.); now, esp., generous under injury or insult, or free from petty resentment or vindictiveness.—**mag-nan′i-mous-ly,** *adv.*—**mag-nan′i-mous-ness,** *n.*

mag-nate (mag′nāt), *n.* [LL. *magnas* (*magnat-*), < L. *magnus,* great.] A great man or important person, as in a country, district, or community (as, "My grandfather, a well-to-do farmer, was one of the chief *magnates* of the village": Mrs. Stowe's "Oldtown Folks," iii.); a person of eminence or distinction in any field (as, literary *magnates*); often, a person of great or dominating influence in some field of industry or the like (as, a railroad *magnate*; a baseball *magnate*); also, a member of the upper house of certain European parliaments, as formerly in Hungary and Poland.

mag-na-vox (mag′nạ-voks), *n.* [L. *magna,* great, + *vox,* voice.] A telephonic device based on electrodynamic principles, used in large auditoriums, stadiums, etc., to project a speaker's voice or other sounds far beyond the natural range, and employed as a loud-speaking reproducer in connection with a radio receiving apparatus. [Proprietary name.]

mag-ne-sia (mag-nē′shiạ or -zhiạ), *n.* [ML. (in alchemy), NL. manganese oxide, also magnesium oxide (in this sense appar. associated with L. *magnes,* magnet); prop. fem. of L. *Magnesius,* pertaining to Magnesia (district in Thessaly).] A mineral said by alchemists to be an ingredient of the philosophers' stone†; also, manganese oxide†; also, magnesium oxide, a white tasteless substance used in medicine as an antacid and laxative; also, the hydrated basic carbonate of magnesium, similarly used; also, magnesium (in phrases, as 'carbonate of magnesia').—**mag-ne′sian,** *a.* Of, like, or containing magnesia.

mag-ne-sic (mag-nē′sik), *a.* Of or containing magnesium.

mag-ne-site (mag′nẹ-sīt), *n.* A mineral consisting of magnesium carbonate, usually occurring in compact white masses: used esp. in making fire-bricks for lining furnaces used in steel-making, etc.

mag-ne-sium (mag-nē′shium or -zhium), *n.* [NL., < *magnesia,* magnesium oxide.] Chem. sym., Mg; at. wt., 24.32; sp. gr., 1.75. A light, ductile, silver-white metallic element which burns with a dazzling white light.—**magnesium light,** the strongly actinic white light produced when magnesium (usually in the form of a ribbon or powder) is burned: used in photography, signaling, pyrotechny, etc.

mag-net (mag′net), *n.* [OF. *magnete,* < L. *magnes* (*magnet-*), lodestone, magnet, < Gr. Μάγνης (λίθος), '(stone) of Magnesia (in Thessaly),' lodestone: cf. *magnesia.*] Lodestone; also, a body (as a piece of iron or steel) which, like lodestone, possesses the property of attracting certain substances, esp. iron, and which, when freely suspended, tends to assume an approximately north and south position; fig., any thing or person that attracts or draws as by some inherent power or charm (as, the jewel was a *magnet* that attracted all eyes; he was the *magnet* that drew the great audiences).

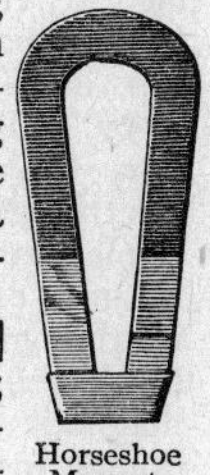

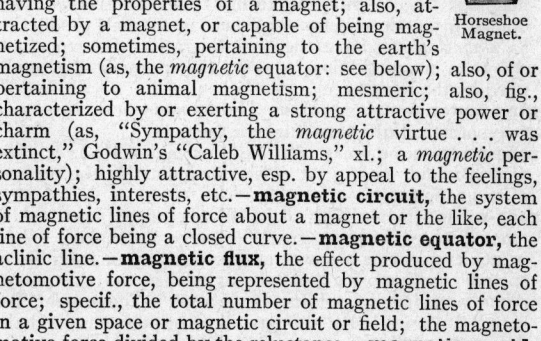

Horseshoe Magnet.

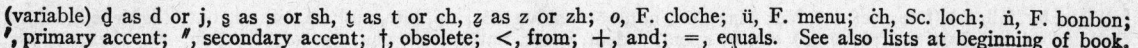

mag-net-ic (mag-net′ik), *a.* [LL. *magneticus.*] Of or pertaining to a magnet or magnetism; having the properties of a magnet; also, attracted by a magnet, or capable of being magnetized; sometimes, pertaining to the earth's magnetism (as, the *magnetic* equator: see below); also, of or pertaining to animal magnetism; mesmeric; also, fig., characterized by or exerting a strong attractive power or charm (as, "Sympathy, the *magnetic* virtue . . . was extinct," Godwin's "Caleb Williams," xl.; a *magnetic* personality); highly attractive, esp. by appeal to the feelings, sympathies, interests, etc.—**magnetic circuit,** the system of magnetic lines of force about a magnet or the like, each line of force being a closed curve.—**magnetic equator,** the aclinic line.—**magnetic flux,** the effect produced by magnetomotive force, being represented by magnetic lines of force; specif., the total number of magnetic lines of force in a given space or magnetic circuit or field; the magnetomotive force divided by the reluctance.—**magnetic merid-**

ian (of a place), a great circle the plane of which passes through a place and through the line of direction of the needle of a compass. The angle which the magnetic meridian makes with the true geographical meridian is different in different places and at different times. Cf. *magnetic needle* and *magnetic north*, below.—**magnetic needle,** a slender magnetized steel rod which, when adjusted to swing freely, as in a compass, indicates the direction of the earth's magnetism, or the approximate north and south. Cf. *dipping-needle* and *compass*.—**magnetic north,** the direction in which the needle of a compass points, differing in most places from the true north.—**magnetic pole,** a pole of a magnet; also, either of the two points on the earth's surface where the dipping-needle stands vertical, one in the arctic regions and the other in the antarctic.—**magnetic pyrites,** pyrrhotite.—**magnetic storm,** any of certain sudden and violent disturbances of the magnetic conditions of the earth, supposed to be connected in some way with the maximum development of sun-spots.—**mag-net′i-cal,** *a.* Magnetic. [Now rare.]—**mag-net′i-cal-ly,** *adv.*—**mag-net′ics,** *n.* The science of magnetism.

mag-net-ism (mag′net-izm), *n.* The characteristic properties possessed by the magnet; the manifestation of these properties; magnetic phenomena; the agency producing magnetic phenomena; the science dealing with magnetic phenomena; also, mesmerism ('animal magnetism'); fig., magnetic or attractive power or charm (as, the *magnetism* of eloquence; personal *magnetism*; "Suddenly the face softened, and shone with all its old *magnetism* on Elsmere," Mrs. H. Ward's "Robert Elsmere," xxv.); sympathetic attraction.

mag-net-ite (mag′net-īt), *n.* A black native oxide of iron which is strongly attracted by a magnet: an important iron ore. Cf. *lodestone*.

mag-net-ize (mag′net-īz), *v.*; *-ized, -izing.* **I.** *tr.* To communicate magnetic properties to; also, to mesmerize; fig., to exert an attracting or compelling influence upon (as, "His wife was a woman . . . who, coming under the dominion of a stronger nature, was perfectly *magnetized* by it": Mrs. Stowe's "Oldtown Folks," xxix.). **II.** *intr.* To acquire magnetic properties; become magnetic.—**mag″net-i-za′tion** (-i-zā′shọn), *n.*—**mag′net-iz-er** (-ī-zėr), *n.*

mag-ne-to- (mag-nē′tō-, mag-net′ō-, or mag′ne-tō-). Form of *magnet* or *magnetic* used in combination: often implying esp. *magneto-electric*.—**mag-ne′to,** *n.*; pl. *-tos* (-tōz). A magneto-electric machine; esp., a small electric generator used in connection with an internal-combustion engine, as on an automobile, to furnish the spark-producing current for igniting the gases.—**mag-ne′to=dy′na-mo,** *n.* A magneto-electric machine.—**mag-ne′to=e-lec′tric, mag-ne′to=e-lec′tri-cal,** *a.* Noting or pertaining to the induction of electric currents by means of magnets: as, a *magneto-electric* machine (an electric generator in which a magnet, esp. a permanent one, is used).—**mag-ne′to=e-lec-tri′ci-ty,** *n.* Electricity developed by the action of magnets; also, the science dealing with phenomena involving both electricity and magnetism.—**mag-ne′to=gen′er-a-tor,** *n.* A magneto-electric machine.—**mag-ne-to-graph** (mag-nē′tọ-gráf or mag-net′ọ-), *n.* [+ *-graph.*] A recording magnetometer, or its record.—**mag-ne-tom′e-ter** (-ne-tom′e-tėr), *n.* [+ *-meter.*] An instrument for measuring magnetic forces.—**mag-ne″to-mo′tive** (-mō′tiv), *a.* Producing magnetic effects, or pertaining to such production: as, *magnetomotive* force (the force which gives rise to magnetic effects or magnetic flux; specif., the magnetic flux multiplied by the reluctance).

mag-ne-ton (mag′ne-ton), *n.* [From *magnetic.*] In *physics*, a hypothetical ultimate magnetic particle.

mag-ne-to-scope (mag-nē′tọ-skōp or mag-net′ọ-), *n.* [See *magneto-* and *-scope.*] A device for indicating the presence of magnetic force.

mag-nif-ic (mag-nif′ik), *a.* [OF. F. *magnifique*, < L. *magnificus*, < *magnus*, great, + *facere*, do, make.] Great in achievement or renown, as persons†; also, magnificent, splendid, or imposing (archaic: as, "Then too the pillared dome *magnific* heaved Its ample roof," Thomson's "Seasons," Autumn, 134); also, grandiose or pompous (archaic). Also **mag-nif′i-cal.**—**mag-nif′i-cal-ly,** *adv.*

Mag-nif-i-cat (mag-nif′i-kat), *n.* [L., 'doth magnify': the first word of the hymn in the Vulgate.] The hymn of the Virgin Mary in Luke, i. 46–55, beginning "My soul doth magnify the Lord," used as a canticle at evensong or vespers; also, a musical setting of it.

mag-ni-fi-ca-tion (mag″ni-fi-kā′shọn), *n.* [LL. *magnificatio(n-).*] The act of magnifying, or the state of being magnified; also, a magnified reproduction.

mag-nif-i-cence (mag-nif′i-sẹns), *n.* [OF. F. *magnificence*, < L. *magnificentia.*] The quality or state of being magnificent; splendor; grandeur; impressiveness; sublimity.

mag-nif-i-cent (mag-nif′i-sẹnt), *a.* [OF. *magnificent*, < L. *magnificent-* (recorded in compar., superl., and other forms), for *magnificus*: see *magnific.*] Great in deeds or achievement, or illustrious (now only, with *the*, as a titular epithet: as, Lorenzo the *Magnificent*, Lorenzo de' Medici, about 1449–92, ruler of Florence); also, lavish or munificent (now rare); also, making a splendid appearance or show, as a person, a house, an equipage, furniture, dress, jewels, etc.; splendidly or richly imposing; sumptuous; grand; also, impressive, noble, or sublime (as, "Thy growth . . . into a state Of matchless grandeur, and declension thence Slow into such *magnificent* decay," Cowper's "Yardley Oak," 90; a *magnificent* poem or conception); fine in a way that commands admiration or awe; in general, extraordinarily fine, or superb (as, *magnificent* weather; a *magnificent* opportunity).—**mag-nif′i-cent-ly,** *adv.*

mag-nif-i-co (mag-nif′i-kō), *n.*; pl. *-coes* (-kōz). [It., < L. *magnificus*, E. *magnific.*] A Venetian grandee (as, "The duke himself, and the *magnificoes* Of greatest port": Shakspere's "Merchant of Venice," iii. 2. 282); hence, any grandee or great personage; also, a rector of a German university.

mag-ni-fi-er (mag′ni-fī-ėr), *n.* One who or that which magnifies; a magnifying device, as a lens or a combination of lenses.

mag-ni-fy (mag′ni-fī), *v.*; *-fied, -fying.* [OF. F. *magnifier*, < L. *magnificare*, < *magnus*, great, + *facere*, make.] **I.** *tr.* To glorify, extol, or praise (archaic: as, "My soul doth *magnify* the Lord," Luke, i. 46); also, to exalt in importance or dignity (archaic: as, "The Lord *magnified* Solomon exceedingly in the sight of all Israel," 1 Chron. xxix. 25); also, to represent as or cause to seem greater or more important than in reality (as, "My wife . . . used every art to *magnify* the merit of her daughter": Goldsmith's "Vicar of Wakefield," xvi.); also, to make greater in size, or enlarge (as, "Her head, adorn'd with lappets pinn'd aloft . . . And *magnified* beyond all human size": Cowper's "Task," iv. 542); now, esp., to increase the apparent size of (an object), as a lens or a combination of lenses does (see *magnifying-glass*, *microscope*, and *telescope*). **II.** *intr.* To increase the apparent size of an object, as a lens does.—**mag′ni-fy-ing=glass,** *n.* A lens, or a simple combination of lenses, used to magnify objects.

mag-nil-o-quent (mag-nil′ọ-kwẹnt), *a.* [L. *magnus*, great, + *loquens* (*loquent-*), ppr. of *loqui*, speak.] Speaking or expressed in a lofty or grandiose style; grandiloquent; also, talking pretentiously or boastfully (as, "She was a trifle more *magniloquent* than usual, and entertained us with stories of colonial governors and their ladies": Thackeray's "Newcomes," xxiii.).—**mag-nil′o-quence,** *n.*—**mag-nil′o-quent-ly,** *adv.*

mag-ni-tude (mag′ni-tūd), *n.* [L. *magnitudo*, < *magnus*, great; akin to Gr. *μέγας*, great, and E. *mickle* and *much*: cf. *major*, *maximum*, and *master*[2].] Greatness, or great size, amount, extent, importance, or the like (as, "The spinster did not forget to dwell on the *magnitude* of the pecuniary loss sustained," Cooper's "Spy," xi.; affairs of *magnitude*); also, size, amount, extent, or the like, without reference to greatness or smallness (as, to determine the *magnitude* of an object, or of an angle); the extended quantity of a line, surface, or solid; length, area, or volume; sometimes, continuous quantity which is comparable with extended quantity (as, the *magnitude* of a velocity, force, or the like); also, a particular quantity; a length, area, volume, weight, force, velocity, or the like; in *astron.*, the brightness of a star expressed according to the numerical system used by astronomers for that purpose (the brightest stars being of the first *magnitude*, and those less bright of the second, third, fourth, fifth, or other *magnitude*).

mag-no-lia (mag-nō′liạ), *n.* [NL.; named from P. *Magnol* (1638–1715), French botanist.] Any plant of the genus *Magnolia*, comprising shrubs and trees with large, usually fragrant flowers and an aromatic bark, much cultivated for ornament.—**mag-no-li-a′ceous** (-li-ā′-shius), *a.* Belonging to the *Magnoliaceæ*, or magnolia family of plants.

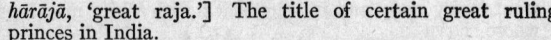

Flowering Branch of Magnolia (*M. fœtida*), with cone of ripe fruits.

mag-num (mag′num), *n.*; pl. *-nums* or (in *anat.*) *-na* (-nạ). [L., neut. of *magnus*, great.] A large bottle for wine or spirits, containing about two quarts, or the quantity of wine or spirits contained (as, "He . . . declared we must have wine, and sent for a *magnum* of the best": Stevenson's "Master of Ballantrae," iv.); also, in *anat.*, a bone of the carpus, at the base of the metacarpal bone of the second finger (next the index-finger).

mag-ot (mag′ọt, F. mȧ-gō), *n.* [F.] The Barbary ape (see *ape*, *n.*); also, a small, grotesque figure of porcelain, ivory, or the like, of a kind common in Chinese and Japanese art (as, "Her rooms were crowded with hideous China *magots*": Thackeray's "Barry Lyndon," xiii.).

Magot.

mag-ot=pie† (mag′ọt-pī), *n.* Same as *magpie*. See Shakspere's "Macbeth," iii. 4. 125.

mag-pie (mag′pī), *n.* [From *Mag*, for *Margaret*, woman's name, + *pie*[1].] Any of various noisy birds of the genus *Pica*, allied to the jays, and having a long, graduated tail, as *P. pica* (or *caudata*), a common European species with black and white plumage, noted for its mischievousness, and *P. hudsonica*, a species of western North America; also, any of various related or similar birds; fig., a chattering person.

Magpie (*Pica pica*).

ma-guey (mag′wā, Sp. mä-gā′ę̄), *n.* [Sp.; prob. from Haitian.] Any of various species of agave, as the century-plant, *Agave americana*.

Ma-gus (mā′gus), *n.*; pl. *Magi* (mā′jī). [L., < Gr. Μάγος; from Pers.] A member of the priestly caste in ancient Media and Persia, traditionally reputed to have practised supernatural arts; hence, in general [*cap.* or *l. c.*], a magician or sorcerer (as, "Thy *magus*, goddess! shall perform the rest": Pope's "Dunciad," iv. 516); also [*cap.* or *l. c.*], any of the three "wise men" who came "from the east" to Jerusalem to do homage to the infant Jesus, as narrated in Mat. ii. 1, 2 (later said to be three kings, and still later named as Kaspar, Melchior, and Balthasar: the "Adoration of the Magi" being the subject of many famous paintings).

Ma-gyar (mä′dyär). [Hung.] **I.** *n.* A member of the race, of the Finno-Ugrian stock, which forms the predominant element of the population of Hungary; also, the language of this race; Hungarian. **II.** *a.* Of or pertaining to the Magyars or their language; Hungarian.

ma-ha-ra-ja, ma-ha-ra-jah (mạ-hä-rä′jạ), *n.* [Skt. *mahārājā*, 'great raja.'] The title of certain great ruling princes in India.

ma-ha-ra-ni, ma-ha-ra-nee (mạ-hä-rä′nē), *n.* [Hind. *mahārānī*, 'great rani.'] The wife of a maharaja.

ma-hat-ma (mạ-hat′mạ), *n.* [Skt. *mahātman*, great-souled.] In *theosophy*, one of a class of reputed adepts with preternatural powers.

Mah-di (mä′dę̄), *n.*; pl. *-dis* (-dę̄z). [Ar. *mahdī*, lit. 'the guided or directed one.'] In Mohammedan use, the title of an expected spiritual and temporal ruler destined to establish a reign of righteousness throughout the world (cf. *Messiah*); also, any of various claimants of this title, esp. Mohammed Ahmed (died 1885), who set up in the Egyptian Sudan an independent government which lasted until 1898, when overthrown at the battle of Omdurman.—**Mah′-dism,** *n.* The doctrine of the coming of the Mahdi; also, adherence to or support of a claimant of this title.—**Mah′-dist,** *n.*

mah=jongg, mah=jong (mä′jong′ or -jung′), **ma=jung** (mä′jung′), *n.* [Corruption of Chinese *ma-ch'iao*, sparrow (lit. 'hemp-bird'): referring to the bird pictured on the first tiles of one of the suits.] A game of Chinese origin, played regularly by 4 persons (but sometimes 3, 2, or 5), with 136 (or sometimes 144) domino-like pieces, or 'tiles,' marked in suits, in connection with counters, and also dice, in which each player adds to and discards from the tiles originally drawn by him in order to form sets and sequences. Also called *pung-chow*. [Proprietary name, *mah-jongg*.]

mahl-stick, maul-stick (mäl′stik, mâl′-), *n.* [D. *maalstok*, < *malen*, paint, + *stok*, stick.] A painter's stick, held in one hand (usually the left) as a support for the other hand when holding the brush.

ma-hog-a-nize (mạ-hog′ạ-nīz), *v. t.*; *-nized*, *-nizing*. To stain or finish (wood) to resemble mahogany.

ma-hog-a-ny (mạ-hog′ạ-ni), *n.*; pl. *-nies* (-niz). [Prob. W. Ind.] A tropical American meliaceous tree, *Swietenia mahagoni*, yielding a hard, reddish-brown wood highly esteemed for making fine furniture, etc.; the wood itself; also, any of various related or similar trees, or the wood; also, a table, esp. a dinner-table (as, "I had hoped . . . to have seen you three gentlemen . . . with your legs under the *mahogany* in my humble parlour": Dickens's "Old Curiosity Shop," lxvi.); also, a reddish-brown color.

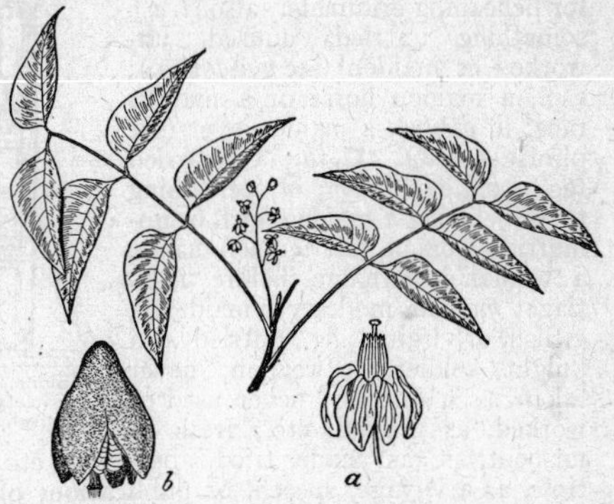

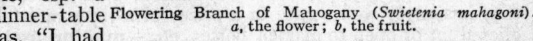

Flowering Branch of Mahogany (*Swietenia mahagoni*). *a*, the flower; *b*, the fruit.

Ma-hom-et-an (mạ-hom′e-tạn), etc. Same as *Mohammedan*, etc.

Ma-hound (mạ-hound′), *n.* [OF. *Mahun*, *Mahum*.] The Arabian prophet Mohammed, supposed by many during the middle ages to be worshiped as a deity (as, "Nor fright the reader with the pagan vaunt Of mightie *Mahound*, and great Termagaunt": J. Hall's "Satires," i. 1); hence, a false god, or idol; also, the devil (see Burns's "The De'il's Awa' wi' the Exciseman"). [Archaic.]

ma-hout (mạ-hout′), *n.* [Hind. *mahāut*, *mahāwat*.] In the East Indies, the keeper and driver of an elephant.

Mah-rat-ta (mạ-rat′ạ), *n.* A member of a Hindu people inhabiting central and western India.—**Mah-rat′ti** (-rat′i), *n.* The language of the Mahrattas.

mah-sir, mah-seer (mä′sēr), *n.* [Hind. *mahāsir*.] A large cyprinoid game-fish, *Barbus mosal*, of the fresh waters of India.

mai-a=moth (mā′ạ-môth), *n.* [NL. *maia* (specific name): cf. *maioid*.] An American moth, *Hemileuca maia*, with stout, hairy body and in color black with white markings, whose larva feeds on oak-leaves.

Maia-moth

maid (mād), *n.* [Shortened form of *maiden.*] A girl, or young unmarried woman (as, "Many a youth, and many a *maid*, Dancing in the chequer'd shade," Milton's "L'Allegro," 95: now chiefly archaic or prov.); hence, a virgin (archaic); a spinster (now usually in 'old maid,' an elderly or confirmed spinster); a female servant or attendant (as, a dairy*maid*; a lady's-*maid*; "With glittering train of *maid* and page, Advanced the castle's Queen," Scott's "Bridal of Triermain," i. 19).—**maid of all work,** a female servant who does all the work, or all kinds of work, for a household. —**maid of honor,** an unmarried woman, usually of noble birth, attached to a royal household as an attendant on the queen or a princess; also, at a wedding, the chief bridesmaid.

mai-dan (mī-dän'), *n.* [Pers. *maidān.*] In India, etc., a level, open space in or near a town; an esplanade.

maid-en (mā'dn). [AS. *mægden*, a dim. form akin to *mægeth*, Goth. *magaths*, G. *magd* maid, and AS *magu*, son, Goth. *magus*, boy.] **I.** *n.* A girl, or young unmarried woman (as, "Here's to the *maiden* of bashful fifteen," Sheridan's "School for Scandal," iii. 3: now chiefly literary); hence, a virgin (archaic); a spinster (archaic: as, "his sister, an agreeable old *maiden*," Smollett's "Humphry Clinker," Oct. 11); a female servant or attendant (archaic); also [sometimes *cap.*], with *the*, an instrument resembling the guillotine, formerly used in Edinburgh for beheading criminals; also [*l. c.*], something untried, unused, unworked, or 'maiden' (see *maiden, a.*); esp., a maiden horse or a maiden race; in *cricket*, a maiden over (see phrase below). **II.** *a.* Unmarried (as, a *maiden* lady); of, pertaining to, or befitting a maiden, girl, or unmarried woman (as, *maiden* name, a woman's surname before marriage; *maiden* modesty); maidenly, girlish, or virginal; fig., untried, as a knight, soldier, or weapon; never taken, as a fortress; never used or worked, as ground, etc.; fresh or unspent, as gas; made, tried, appearing, etc., for the first time, as a voyage, speech, or publication; of a horse, etc., that has never won a race or a prize; of a prize or a race, offered for or open to maiden horses, etc.—**maiden assize,** in Great Britain, formerly, an assize of a court at which no person was condemned to death; now, an assize at which no person is tried for crime.—**maiden over,** in *cricket*, an over in which no runs are made.

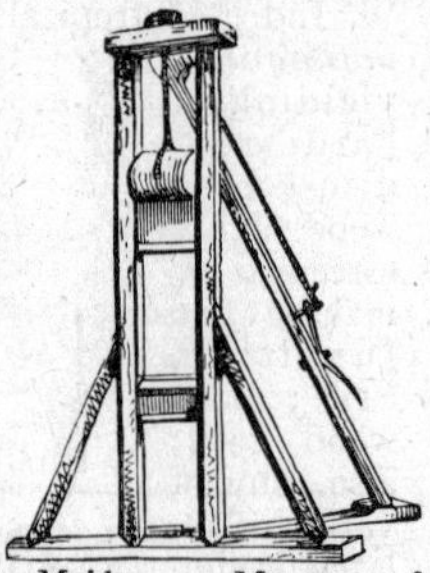
Maiden. — Museum of the Society of Antiquaries, Edinburgh.

maid-en-hair (mā'dn-hãr), *n.* Any of the ferns constituting the polypodiaceous genus *Adiantum*, with fine, dark, glossy stalks and delicate, finely divided fronds.

maid-en-head (mā'dn-hed), *n.* Maidenhood; virginity; also, the hymen, or vaginal membrane.

maid-en-hood (mā'dn-hu̇d), *n.* The state or time of being a maiden; virginity.

maid-en-ish (mā'dn-ish), *a.* Like or characteristic of a maiden: usually with a depreciatory force.

maid-en-ly (mā'dn-li), *a.* Pertaining to, characteristic of, or befitting a maiden (as, *maidenly* charms; *maidenly* behavior or reserve); having the qualities befitting a maiden, as modesty, gentleness, etc.; maiden-like; maidenish.—**maid'en-li-ness,** *n.*—**maid'en-ly,** *adv.* In the manner of a maiden.

maid-hood (mād'hu̇d), *n.* Maidenhood.

maid=ser-vant (mād'sėr"vạnt), *n.* A female servant.

mai-eu-tic (mạ-ū'tik), *a.* [Gr. μαιευτικός, < μαιεύεσθαι, act as midwife, < μαῖα, midwife.] Pertaining to midwifery: usually fig., as of the Socratic method of bringing out ideas latent in the mind (see *Socratic method,* under *Socratic, a.*).—**mai-eu'tics,** *n.* The maieutic art, esp. as practised by Socrates.

mai-gre (mā'gėr, F. mägr). [F.: see *meager.*] **I.** *a.* Containing neither flesh-meat nor its juices, as articles of diet permissible on days of religious abstinence (as, a *maigre* soup); hence, characterized by such abstinence in diet (as, a *maigre* day). **II.** *n.* A large food-fish, *Sciæna aquila*, common in the Mediterranean; any fish of the genus *Sciæna.*

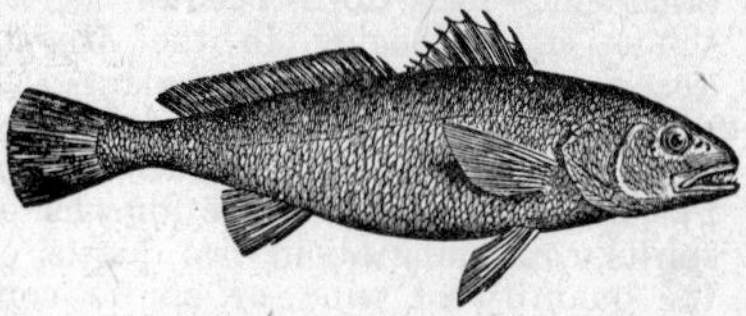
Maigre (*Sciæna aquila*).

mail[1] (māl), *n.* [OF. F. *maille*, < L. *macula*, spot, mesh of a net.] One of the metal rings interlinked in a flexible fabric formerly much used for defensive armor†; also, this fabric, or defensive armor composed of it; chain-mail; more generally, any defensive armor, as of metal plates (cf. *coat of mail,* under *coat, n.*); hence, the shell or hard protective covering of certain animals, as the tortoise or the lobster.—**mail**[1], *v. t.* To clothe or arm with or as with mail.

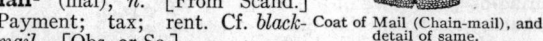

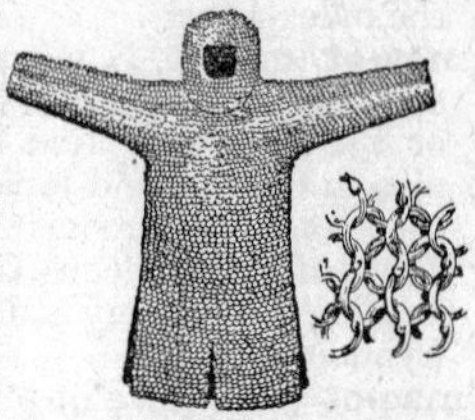
Coat of Mail (Chain-mail), and detail of same.

mail[2] (māl), *n.* [From Scand.] Payment; tax; rent. Cf. *blackmail.* [Obs. or Sc.]

mail[3] (māl), *n.* [OF. *male* (F. *malle*); from Teut.] A bag, or a piece of baggage, as of a traveler (obs. or Sc.: as, "Tell Gwyllim that she forgot to pack up my flannel and wide shoes in the trunk-*mail*," Smollett's "Humphry Clinker," April 17); also, the bag or bags of letters, papers, etc., conveyed from one post-office to another under governmental authority; letters, etc., arriving or sent by post; also, the person by whom or the conveyance, as a coach or a railroad-train, by which postal matter is carried (as, "Most of us disdained all coaches except his majesty's *mail*": De Quincey's "English Mail-Coach," i.); also, the system of transmission of letters, etc., by post.—**mail**[3], *v. t.* To place in a post-office or a letter-box for transmission; send by mail; post.—**mail'a-ble,** *a.* That may be mailed.—**mail-cert** (māl'sėrt), *n.* A certificate for facilitating the passage through British censorship of package mail to neutral countries.—**mail'=chute,** *n.* A chute for letters, etc.

mailed (māld), *a.* Clad or armed with mail (as, the *mailed* fist, fig., the force of arms or military power—an expression derived from one of the public utterances of William II. of Germany); in *zoöl.*, having a protective covering resembling a coat of mail.

mail-er (mā'lėr), *n.* One who mails letters, etc.; also, a boat that carries mail.

mail=or-der (māl'ôr"dėr), *n.* An order for goods, received or sent by mail.—**mail=order house,** a business house conducting a retail business by receiving orders and cash by mail and distributing the goods through the mail and otherwise.

mail-plane (māl'plān), *n.* An aëroplane for carrying mail.

maim (mām), *v. t.* [OF. *mahaignier* = ML. *mahanare*, *mahemiare*, maim; origin uncertain.] To deprive of the use of some bodily member; mutilate; cripple; fig., to impair seriously or render essentially defective (as, "You *maim'd* the jurisdiction of all bishops": Shakspere's "Henry VIII.," iii. 2. 312).—**maim,** *n.* [Cf. *mayhem.*] Deprivation or injury by maiming; a mutilation or crippling of the body; any serious hurt, injury, or defect. [Now rare.]—**maim,** *a.* Maimed. [Now rare.]—**maim-ed-ness** (mā'med-nes), *n.* —**maim'er,** *n.*

main[1] (mān), *n.* [Origin uncertain: cf. *main*[2], *a.*] In the game of hazard, a number called by the caster before throwing the dice (see *hazard, n.*); also, a throw, match, or stake at dice; also, a match at cock-fighting.

main[2] (mān), *n.* [AS. *mægen*, strength, power, = Icel. *megin*, strength, main part; akin to E. *may*[1] and *might*[2].

Later E. senses are from *main*², *a.*] Strength, force, or violent effort (now chiefly in the phrase 'with might and main': see under *might*²); also, the mainland (as, "They perceived that the land they saw from our island was not the *main*, but an island": Defoe's "Robinson Crusoe," ii. 4); also, the open ocean or high sea (now poetic: as, "Forced from their homes . . . To traverse climes beyond the western *main*," Goldsmith's "Traveller," 410); also, the chief, principal, or most important part or point (see phrase *in the main*, following); also, a principal duct, channel, pipe, or conductor for conveying water, sewage, gas, electricity, etc.—**in the main,** for the most part: as, "Milly . . . is an excellent girl *in the main*" (Cooper's "Two Admirals," viii.).—**Spanish Main.** See under *Spanish, a.*—**main**², *a.* [Appar. partly < AS. *mægen*, strength (see *main*², *n.*), and partly from Scand.: cf. Icel. *megn*, strong, also OF. *maine* (< L. *magnus*), great.] Strong† or mighty†; hence, exerted to the utmost, as strength, force, etc.; sheer; also, great in size, extent, degree, importance, etc. (now chiefly prov. Eng. and Sc.: as, a *main* crop of apples; "It were a *main* place for pirates once," Stevenson's "Treasure Island," xii.); also, chief in size, extent, importance, etc. (as, the *main* body of an army; the *main* branches of a river; "no more than an interlude in the *main* business of his life," Hawthorne's "Twice-Told Tales," Wakefield); principal; leading; also, general† (as, "Which is no further Than the *main* voice of Denmark goes withal": Shakspere's "Hamlet," i. 3. 28); *naut.*, pertaining to the mainmast or mainsail.—**the main chance,** the chief issue or contingency; esp., the chance or probability of greatest importance or advantage to one's self (as, "He knew that the ladies of the stage have an ear for flattery, and an eye to *the main chance*": Reade's "Peg Woffington," v.).—**main**², *adv.* Exceedingly; very: as, "I am *main* sorry to displease your worship" (Godwin's "Caleb Williams," ix.). [Now prov. Eng. and Sc.]

main=deck (mān'dek'), *n.* *Naut.*, the principal or upper deck of a vessel; the uppermost deck extending from stem to stern; specif., in certain war-vessels, the deck next below the spar-deck; in certain merchant vessels, that part of the upper, open deck between the forecastle and the poop.

main=de=fer (maṅ-dė-fãr), *n.* [F. *main de fer*, 'hand of iron.'] A defensive covering of iron for the hand, used in the old-time tournaments, etc.

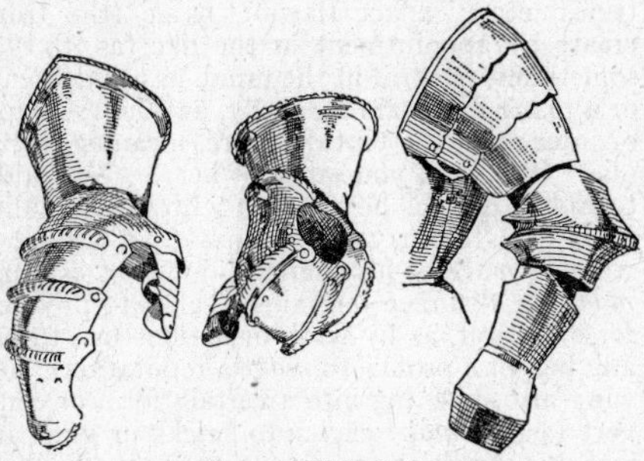

Forms of Main-de-fer.

main-land (mān'lạnd), *n.* The principal land, as distinguished from islands or peninsulas.—**main'land-er,** *n.*

main-ly (mān'li), *adv.* Mightily†; also, greatly†; also, chiefly or principally; for the most part.

main-mast (mān'mȧst), *n.* *Naut.*, the principal mast in a ship or other vessel; in a schooner, brig, brigantine, bark, barkantine, etc., the second mast from the bow (being thus the aftermost mast in a two-masted vessel, and the middle mast in a three-masted one); in a yawl or ketch, the mast nearer the bow.

main-sail (mān'sāl, naut. -sl), *n.* *Naut.*, in a square-rigged vessel, the sail bent to the main-yard; in a fore-and-aft rigged vessel, the large sail set on the after part of the mainmast.

main=sheet (mān'shēt), *n.* *Naut.*, a sheet of a mainsail.

main-spring (mān'spring), *n.* The principal spring in a mechanism, as in a watch; fig., the chief motive power; the impelling cause.

main-stay (mān'stā), *n.* *Naut.*, the stay which secures the head of the mainmast of a vessel forward; fig., a chief support.

main-tain (mạn-tān'), *v. t.* [OF. F. *maintenir*, < L. *manu tenere*, 'hold in the hand': *manu*, abl. of *manus*, hand; *tenere*, hold.] To keep up or carry on (as, to *maintain* an action or undertaking); persevere in; prosecute; also, to keep in existence or continuance (as, to *maintain* a state of affairs, an attitude, relations, etc.); preserve; retain; also, to keep in due condition, operation, or force (as, to *maintain* order, discipline, or public health; to *maintain* one's dignity or reputation); keep unimpaired; also, to keep or hold against attack (as, to *maintain* one's ground); also, to keep in a specified state, position, etc. (as, to *maintain* a tool in position for use); also, to sustain with the means of existence or subsistence; support, as by furnishing necessaries, defraying expenses, etc.; provide for; keep supplied, equipped, in repair, etc.; also, to support by aid, countenance, protection, championing, etc.; uphold; back; also, to support in speech or argument, as a statement, doctrine, etc.; affirm or assert (with a clause, or with an object and an infinitive).—**main-tain'a-ble,** *a.* That may be maintained.—**main-tain'er,** *n.*

main-te-nance (mān'tẹ-nạns), *n.* [OF. *maintenance*, < *maintenir*, E. *maintain*.] The act of maintaining, or the state of being maintained; a keeping up; preservation; sustentation; support; upholding; also, means or provision for maintaining; means of subsistence, or livelihood; in *law*, an officious intermeddling in a suit in which the meddler has no interest, by assisting either party with means to prosecute or defend it.—**cap of maintenance.** See under *cap, n.*

main-top (mān'top), *n.* *Naut.*, a platform at the head of the lower mainmast.

main-top-gal-lant-mast (mān-top-gal'ạnt-mȧst, naut. -tọ-gal'ạnt-mạst), *n.* *Naut.*, the mast next above the maintopmast.—**main-top-gal'lant=sail** (-sāl, naut. -sl), **main-top-gal'lant=yard,** *n.* *Naut.*, the sail or the yard belonging to the maintopgallantmast.

main-top-mast (mān-top'mȧst), *n.* *Naut.*, the mast next above the lower mainmast.

main-top-sail (mān-top'sāl, naut. -sl), *n.* *Naut.*, the sail set on the maintopmast.

main=yard (mān'yärd), *n.* *Naut.*, the lower yard on the mainmast.

mai-oid (mā'oid). [NL. *Maia*, the typical genus (< L. *maia*, < Gr. μαῖα, large kind of crab, orig. old woman, nurse, mother): see *-oid*.] **I.** *a.* Resembling the crabs (spider-crabs) of the genus *Maia*; belonging to the group *Maioidea*, containing the crabs of the genus *Maia*, with others of the same family (*Maiidæ*) and related families. **II.** *n.* Any crab of the group *Maioidea*; a spider-crab.

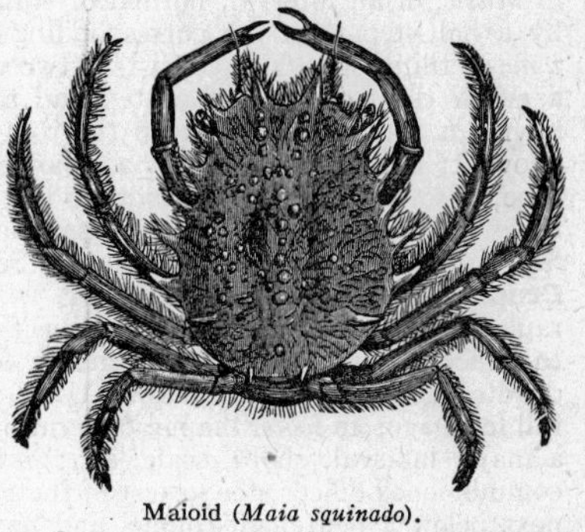

Maioid (*Maia squinado*).

ma-iol-i-ca (mạ-yol'i-kạ̈), *n.* See *majolica*.

mair, maist (mãr, māst). Scotch forms of *more, most*.

maître (mãtr), *n.* [F.: see *master*².] A master.—**maître d'hôtel** (dō-tel). [F., 'master of house.'] A steward or butler.—**à la maître d'hôtel** (ä lä mãtr dō-tel). [F.: see *à la*.] In *cookery*, with a sauce made of melted butter, minced parsley, and a little lemon-juice or vinegar.

Flowering Plant of Maize.

maize (māz), *n.* [Sp. *maíz*; from W. Ind.] A widely cultivated cereal plant, *Zea mays*, native in North America, bearing grain in large ears or spikes; also, the grain; also, corn-color. Cf. *Indian corn, corn*¹, and *mealie*.

Ear of Maize.

ma-jes-tic (mạ-jes'tik), *a.* Characterized by or possessing majesty; of lofty dignity or imposing aspect; stately; grand: as, "His face . . . *Majestic* though in ruin" (Milton's "Paradise Lost," ii. 305); "In more lengthen'd notes and slow, The deep, *majestic*, solemn organs blow" (Pope's "Ode on St. Cecilia's Day," i.). Also **ma-jes'ti-cal.**—**ma-jes'ti-cal-ly,** *adv.*

maj-es-ty (maj'es-ti), *n.*; pl. *-ties* (-tiz). [OF. *majeste* (F. *majesté*), < L. *majestas*, greatness, grandeur, majesty, akin to *major*, greater: see *major*.] Sovereign greatness, dignity, or authority (as, "His sceptre shows the force of temporal power, The attribute to awe and *majesty*": Shakspere's "Merchant of Venice," iv. 1. 191); sovereignty; hence [usually *cap.*], with *his, her, your*, etc., a title used when speaking of or to a sovereign; sometimes [*l. c.*], a royal personage, or royal personages collectively (as, to enjoy the favor of *majesty*); also, regal, lofty, or stately dignity, as of appearance, bearing, action, style, etc.; imposing character; grandeur.

ma-jol-i-ca, ma-iol-i-ca (mạ-jol'i-kạ̈, mạ-yol'-), *n.* [It. *maiolica*; said to be from an old form of the name of the island of Majorca.] A kind of Italian pottery coated with enamel and decorated, often in rich colors, made from the 15th century onward; hence, a more or less similar pottery made elsewhere.

Majolica. — Made at Pesaro, Italy, about 1510.

ma-jor (mā'jọr), *a.* [L. *major*, greater, larger, superior, older, compar. of *magnus*, great: see *magnitude*.] Greater, as in size, amount, extent, importance, rank, etc. (as, "His lordship . . . owned now the *major* part of the parish": Galt's "Annals of the Parish," xiv.); also, elder or senior (used after a name: as, Cato *Major*: cf. *minor, a.*); also, of full legal age; in *logic*, broader or more extensive (as, the *major* term of a syllogism, being the term that enters into the predicate of the conclusion; the *major* premise, that premise of a syllogism which contains the major term); in *music*, of an interval, normal or standard, being greater by a half-step than the corresponding minor interval (as, a *major* third, one which consists of two whole steps, whereas a minor third consists of a step and a half); of a chord, having a major third between the root and the note next above it; of a tone, distant by a major interval from a given tone; also, noting a scale, mode, or key whose third tone is major in relation to the fundamental tone.—**major orders.** See *order, n.*—**major planets.** See *planet.*—**Major Prophets.** See *prophet.*—**ma'jor,** *n.* One of superior rank in a specified class; also, a subject or a course of study to which a student, esp. a candidate for a degree, chiefly devotes his time and attention (U. S.); also, a person of full legal age; in *logic*, the major term or premise; in *music*, a major interval, chord, scale, etc.; *milit.*, in the army, a commissioned officer (the lowest of the field-officers) ranking next below a lieutenant-colonel and next above a captain, and usually in command of a battalion or squadron.—**ma'jor,** *v. i.* To act like a major; strut (as, "Mr. Waverley's wearied wi' *majoring* yonder afore the muckle pier-glass": Scott's "Waverley," xlii.); also, to pursue a major or principal subject or course of study (U. S.).

ma-jor-do-mo (mā''jọr-dō'mō), *n.*; pl. *-mos* (-mōz). [Sp. *mayordomo* or It. *maggiordomo*, < ML. *major domus*, 'chief officer of the house.'] A man in charge of a great household, as that of a sovereign; a chief steward; in general, a steward or butler.

ma-jor=gen-er-al (mā'jọr-jen'ẹ-rạl), *n.*; pl. *-als.* In the army, an officer ranking next below a lieutenant-general and next above a brigadier-general, and usually in command of a division.

ma-jor-i-ty (mạ-jor'i-ti), *n.*; pl. *-ties* (-tiz). [F. *majorité*, < ML. *majoritas*, < L. *major*: see *major*.] The state of being greater†; also, the state or time of being of full legal age (as, to attain one's *majority*); also, the greater part or number (as, the *majority* of mankind); specif., a number of voters or votes, jurors, or others in agreement, constituting the greater part or more than half of the total number (as, a *majority* of the jury favored acquittal); also, the excess whereby the greater number, as of votes, surpasses the remainder (as, to be elected by a *majority* of 1,000, that is, over one's single opponent, or over all opponents collectively: cf. *plurality*); also, the military rank or office of a major.—**the majority,** or **the great majority,** the dead.—**to go over to** (or **to join**) **the majority,** to die.

ma-jor-ship (mā'jọr-ship), *n.* The rank or office of a major.

ma=jung (mä'jung'), *n.* Same as *mah-jongg.*

ma-jus-cule (mạ-jus'kūl). [F., < L. *majusculus*, somewhat greater or larger, dim. of *major*: see *major*.] In *paleography*: **I.** *a.* Large, as letters (whether capital or uncial); also, written in such letters: opposed to *minuscule.* **II.** *n.* A majuscule letter (capital or uncial).—**ma-jus'cu-lar** (-kụ-lạ̈r), *a.*

mak-a-ble (mā'kạ-bl), *a.* Capable of being made.

make¹ (māk), *n.* [AS. *gemaca*, akin to *gemæcca*, mate, fellow (see *match²*), *gemæc*, well-matched, equal, Icel. *makr*, fit, suitable: cf. *make²*.] A match or equal; a mate or fellow; a consort; a companion or friend. [Now prov. Eng. and Sc.]

make² (māk), *v. t.*; *made, making.* [AS. *macian* = OFries. *makia* = OS. *macōn* = OHG. *mahhōn*, G. *machen*, make, OHG. also fit together; appar. from a Teut. adj. stem meaning 'fit, suitable,' involved also in E. *make¹*.] To bring (something) into existence by shaping a portion of matter or by combining parts or ingredients (as, to *make* an image, a boat, a wreath, a dress, or a medicine); form or fashion; frame or construct; manufacture or produce; prepare, as food; compose, as a poem; draw up, as a legal document; of constituent material or parts, to compose or constitute; be sufficient to constitute; serve for; become by development, or prove to be (as, the lawyer *makes* the best legislator); also, more generally, to bring into existence, bring about, or produce by any action or causative agency (as, to *make* a mark, a sound, or a light; to *make* a good appearance; to *make* trouble); give rise to, or cause; fix or establish (rules, etc.); enact (laws); name (the trump) at cards; create by appointment or the like (as, to *make* a knight); sometimes, to form in the mind, as a judgment, an estimate, or a plan; entertain mentally, as doubt, scruple, etc.; judge or infer as to the truth, nature, meaning, etc., of something (as, " 'What do you *make* of her . . . ?' said the first lieutenant to him, as he sat aloft with his glass directed towards the vessel," Marryat's "King's Own," xxx.; I don't know what to *make* of his silence); judge or estimate to be (as, I *made* the distance ten miles); also, to produce, earn, or get for one's self, as by work or actions (as, to *make* a fortune, a living, or a profit; to *make* a reputation); acquire, gain, or win; also, to bring into a certain form or condition, or convert (as, to *make* clay into bricks or grass into hay); put into due condition for use (as, to *make* a bed); train (a hawk, dog, etc.); assure the success or fortune of (a person, etc.: often as opposed to *mar* or *break*); also, to cause to be or become (as specified: as, to *make* a vessel air-tight; "a sight to *make* an old man young," Tennyson's "Gardener's Daughter," 140); render; constitute or appoint (as specified: as, "Who *made* thee a ruler and a judge over us?" Acts, vii. 27); also, to cause, constrain, or compel to do something (as, to *make* a horse go); also, to do, perform, execute, or effect (as, to *make* a movement; to *make* a bargain); put forth or deliver (as, to *make* a speech); accomplish by traveling, etc. (as, to *make* five miles an hour); also, to arrive at or reach (as, to *make* a port); in *elect.*, to complete (a circuit) and so allow the current to flow, or to cause (a current) to flow by so doing.—**to make a difference.** See under *difference, n.*—**to make a mission,** to follow the exercises or services of a religious mission.—**to make believe,** to pretend.—**to make good,** to make satisfactory; compensate for (a loss, deficiency, etc.); supply or restore; fulfil (promises, etc.); succeed in effecting (a purpose); prove (an assertion) to be valid or true.—**to make little of.** See under *little, n.*—**to make much of.** See under *much, n.*—**to make out,** to write out (a bill, a check, etc.); also, to discern, discover, or decipher (something not at first clear or intelligible); also, to establish by evidence or argument; prove; show or represent to be (as, to *make* one *out* a rogue); also, to manage (to do something: colloq.).—**to make over,** to make anew, as into a fresh or different form (as, to *make over* a dress); also, to transfer the title of (property); convey; hand over into the possession or charge of another.—**to make sail,** *naut.*, to expand or spread the sail or sails of a boat; hence, to set out on a voyage; also, to spread more sail.—**to make sport of.** See under *sport*, *n.* —**to make up,** to put together, construct, or compound; compose or compile (a list, etc.); concoct, fabricate, or invent (a story, etc.); of parts, to constitute, or contribute to the formation of; also, to complete; supply the deficiencies of; compensate for or make good (as, to *make up* a loss); also, to prepare, or put in order; prepare for a part, as on the stage, by appropriate dress, wig, cosmetics, etc.; beautify artificially, as the face; also, to adjust or balance, as accounts; also, to bring to a definite conclusion, as one's mind; also, to settle amicably, as differences; in *printing*, to arrange (set type, etc.) into columns or pages, or form (columns or pages) thus.—**to make water,** to urinate; *naut.*, to leak.—**to make way,** to give room for passing; give place; also, to advance.—**make²**, *v. i.* To make something; formerly, to compose verses†; also, to be of effect, or operate (usually with *for* or *against*); also, to cause one's self, or something understood, to be as specified (as, to *make* sure; to *make* ready; to *make* fast); show one's self in action or behavior (as, to *make* bold; to *make* merry); act or start (to do, or as if to do, something); also, to have to do with a person, matter, etc. (now prov.: as, "Meddle not and *make* not, and they'll do you nae harm," Scott's "Guy Mannering," xxiii.); also, to direct or pursue the course, or go (as, to *make* for home; "Leaving the bridge he *made* towards Barnes Common," Galsworthy's "Patrician," ii. 4); proceed, as tidal movement (as, "It's slack water; or, rather, the ebb is just beginning to *make*": Cooper's "Two Admirals," xi.); esp., to rise, as the tide, or as water in a ship, etc.; increase in depth, volume, etc.—**to make away with,** to kill or destroy; also, to remove; get rid of; dispose of.—**to make good,** to make satisfaction or compensation; also, to maintain one's promises, professions, pretensions, etc., by performance; prove to be a success.—**to make off,** to go off or depart suddenly or hastily; run off; decamp.—**to make out,** to get along; manage; succeed: as, "You *made out* well with that dinner" (Mrs. Stowe's "Uncle Tom's Cabin," iv.). [Colloq.]—**to make up,** to compensate, or make amends (*for*: as, "Though Barnes had come late he had drunk largely, *making up* for lost time," Thackeray's "Newcomes," xiii.); also, to make one's self up by appropriate dress, etc., as for a part; also, to become reconciled after a quarrel; also, to make advances or pay court (*to*: as, "If Lady Ellinor was a widow, I should certainly *make up* to her," Bulwer-Lytton's "Caxtons," xiv. 5).—**make²**, *n.* Style or manner of being made; form or build (as, "He was of a sturdy, raw-boned *make*": Irving's "Knickerbocker's New York," v. 1); structure; constitution; disposition, character, or nature (as, "To my natural *make* and my temper Painful the task is I do": Longfellow's "Evangeline," i. 4); also, the act or process of making; production with reference to the maker, the place or time of making, etc. (as, of our own *make*; of French *make*; of 18th century *make*); also, that which is made; yield or output; also, the making or seeking of gain or profit (used in the phrase 'on the make,' intent on gain or one's own advantage: slang); in *card-playing*, the act of naming the trump, or the suit named as trump; in *elect.*, the completing of a circuit; the passage of the current through a circuit.

make=and=break (māk'ạnd-brāk'), *n.* In *elect.*, a device for alternately making and breaking an electric circuit.

make-bate (māk'bāt), *n.* [Also erron. *make-bait*: see *bate³*, *n.*] One who or that which excites contention or discord: as, "It was ten to one if the gold, which was the *make-bait* of the world, did not . . . set us together by the ears" (Defoe's "Captain Singleton," vii.). [Archaic.]

make=be-lieve (māk'bẹ-lēv''). **I.** *n.* Pretense; feigning; sham. **II.** *a.* Pretended; feigned; sham: as, *make-believe* penitence; a *make-believe* reformer.

mak-er (mā'kėr), *n.* One who makes; a fashioner, framer, or constructor; a manufacturer; a poet (archaic); [*cap.*] often with *our*, *his*, *the*, etc., the Creator.

make=read-y (māk'red''i), *n.* In *printing*, the operation of making a form, etc., ready for printing; the result of this operation; the overlays, or the sheet on which the overlays are pasted, for the proper printing of a form, etc.

make-shift (māk'shift). **I.** *n.* A shifty person†; also, that with which one makes shift; a temporary expedient or substitute; also, the act of making shift. **II.** *a.* Serving as or of the nature of a makeshift (as, "drowsing in the scant shade of *make-shift* awnings": Mark Twain's "Life on the Mississippi," ii.); also, characterized by makeshifts (as, *makeshift* endeavors).

make=up (māk'up), *n.* The act of making up; also, the manner of being made up or put together; composition; constitution (physical or mental); also, the way in which an actor or other person dresses himself, paints his face, etc., for a part; the articles used for this purpose, esp. cosmetics, etc.; in *printing*, the arrangement of set type, illustrations, etc., into columns or pages; the matter so arranged.

make-weight (māk'wāt), *n.* Something put in a scale to complete a required weight; hence, anything added to supply a deficiency.

mak-ing (mā'king), *n.* The act of one who or that which makes; the process of being made; structure, constitution, or make-up; also, means or cause of success or advancement (as, this will be the *making* of him); also, material of which something may be made (often in *pl.*: as, the *makings* of a cigarette); fig., qualifications for becoming something (as, he has the *making* of a fine man in him); also, something which is or has been made; the quantity made at one time.

mal- (mal-). [OF. F. *mal-*, repr. *mal*, adv. (< L. *male*), badly, ill, or *mal*, adj. (< L. *malus*), bad.] A prefix meaning 'badly' or 'bad,' 'ill,' 'faulty,' occurring orig. in words from the French, and hence used also as an English formative, as in *maladaptation* (bad or faulty adaptation), *maladjustment*, *malconstruction*, *maldigestion*, *malexecution*, *malgrowth*, *malinfluence*.

Ma-lac-ca (mạ-lak'ạ̈) **cane.** [From *Malacca*, in the Malay Peninsula.] A cane or walking-stick made of the brown, often mottled or clouded stem of an East Indian ratan-palm, *Calamus scipionum*.

ma-la-ceous (mạ-lā'shius), *a.* [L. *malus*, apple-tree.] Belonging to the *Malaceæ*, or apple family of plants, which includes the apple, pear, quince, medlar, loquat, hawthorn, service-tree, mountain-ash, etc.

mal-a-chite (mal'ạ-kīt), *n.* [F. *malachite*, < L. *malache*, < Gr. μαλάχη, μολόχη, mallow (with reference to the color of the leaf).] A green mineral, a basic carbonate of copper, used for making ornamental articles.

mal-a-col-o-gy (mal-ạ-kol'ọ̄-ji), *n.* [Gr. μαλακός, soft (with reference to the soft body of the mollusks): see *-logy*.] The science that treats of mollusks.—**mal-a-col'o-gist,** *n.*

mal-a-cos-tra-can (mal-ạ-kos'trạ-kạn). [NL. *Malacostraca*, pl., < Gr. μαλακόστρακος, soft-shelled, < μαλακός, soft, + ὄστρακον, shell.] **I.** *a.* Belonging to the *Malacostraca*, a subclass of crustaceans which have a comparatively complex organization, including the lobsters, shrimps, crabs, etc. **II.** *n.* A malacostracan crustacean.

mal-ad-dress (mal-ạ-dres'), *n.* [= F. *maladresse*: see *mal-*.] Faulty address; clumsiness; awkwardness.

mal-ad-min-is-ter (mal-ad-min'is-tėr), *v. t.* [See *mal-*.] To administer (esp. public affairs) badly or inefficiently.—**mal''ad-min-is-tra'tion** (-trā'shọn), *n.* Bad or inefficient administration, esp. of public affairs: as, "The Whigs had repeatedly assailed the *maladministration* of the Prince" (Lecky's "Hist. of Eng. in the 18th Century," i.).—**mal-ad-min'is-tra-tor,** *n.*

mal-a-droit (mal-ạ-droit'), *a.* [F.: see *mal-* and *adroit*.] Lacking in adroitness or dexterity; unskilful; awkward.—**mal-a-droit'ly,** *adv.*—**mal-a-droit'ness,** *n.*

mal-a-dy (mal'ạ-di), *n.*; pl. *-dies* (-diz). [OF. F. *maladie*, < *malade*, sick, < L. *male habitus*: *male*, badly, ill; *habitus*, pp. of *habere*, have, hold, keep.] Any bodily disorder or disease, esp. one that is chronic or deep-seated; fig., any form of derangement of well-being (as, social *maladies*).

Mal-a-ga (mal'ạ-gä), *n.* Any of certain white wines produced in the province of Malaga, in Spain; also, any of the grapes grown in or exported from Malaga; esp., a kind of large, oval, firm white grape.

Mal-a-gas-y (mal-ạ-gas'i). **I.** *a.* Of or pertaining to Madagascar, its people, or their language. **II.** *n.*; pl. *-y* or *-ies* (-iz). A native of Madagascar; also, the language spoken there, belonging to the Malayo-Polynesian family.

ma-laise (ma-lāz'), *n.* [F.: see *mal-* and *ease.*] A condition of indefinite bodily uneasiness or discomfort, often preliminary to an attack of disease: as, "It was afflicting him with a general *malaise,* it was affecting his energy, his temper" (H. G. Wells's "Soul of a Bishop," i.).

ma-la-mute (mä'lạ-mūt), *n.* See *malemute.*

mal-an-ders (mal'ạn-dėrz), *n. pl.* [OF. F. *malandres,* < L. *malandria.*] A dry, scabby or scurfy eruption in horses, usually occurring on the fore legs back of the knee.

mal-a-pert (mal'ạ-pėrt). [OF. *malapert, malappert*: see *mal-* and *apert.*] **I.** *a.* Unbecomingly bold; forward; saucy; pert: as, "What! thou frontless dastard . . . must thou be *malapert?*" (Scott's "Quentin Durward," xxii.). [Archaic.] **II.** *n.* A malapert person. [Archaic.]

mal-ap-pro-pri-ate (mal-ạ-prō'pri-āt), *v. t.*; *-ated, -ating.* [See *mal-.*] To appropriate wrongly; misappropriate: as, "He had no idea that John Bold could really prove that the income of the hospital was *malappropriated*" (Trollope's "Warden," ii.).—**mal-ap-pro'pri-ate** (-ạt), *a.* Inappropriate.—**mal''ap-pro-pri-a'tion** (-ā'shọn), *n.* Misappropriation.

mal-a-prop (mal'ạ-prop). [From Mrs. *Malaprop* in Sheridan's play, "The Rivals" (1775), noted for her misuse of words: cf. *malapropos.*] **I.** *a.* Quaintly or ludicrously inappropriate, as words or their use. **II.** *n.* A malaprop expression; a ludicrous misuse of words.—**mal-a-prop'i-an,** *a.* —**mal'a-prop-ism,** *n.*

mal-ap-ro-pos (mal''ap-rọ-pō'). [F. *mal à propos,* 'ill to purpose': see *mal-* and *apropos.*] **I.** *adv.* Inappropriately; unseasonably. **II.** *a.* Inappropriate; unseasonable: as, a *malapropos* remark.

ma-lar (mā'lạ̈r). [NL. *malaris,* < L. *mala,* cheek-bone, cheek.] In *anat.*: **I.** *a.* Of or pertaining to the cheek-bone or cheek. **II.** *n.* The cheek-bone.

ma-la-ri-a (mạ-lā'ri-ạ̈), *n.* [It., for *mala aria,* 'bad air.'] Unwholesome or poisonous air, as the exhalations from a marsh; miasma; also, in *pathol.,* a febrile disease, usually intermittent or remittent, and characterized by attacks of chills, fever, and sweating, formerly supposed to be due to swamp exhalations, but now known to be caused by parasitic protozoans which are transferred to the human blood by mosquitoes (genus *Anopheles*) and which occupy and destroy the red blood-corpuscles.—**ma-la'ri-al,** *a.* Pertaining to, of the nature of, or infected with malaria. Also **ma-la'ri-an, ma-la'ri-ous.**—**ma-la'-ri-at-ed** (-ā-ted), *a.* Infected with malaria.

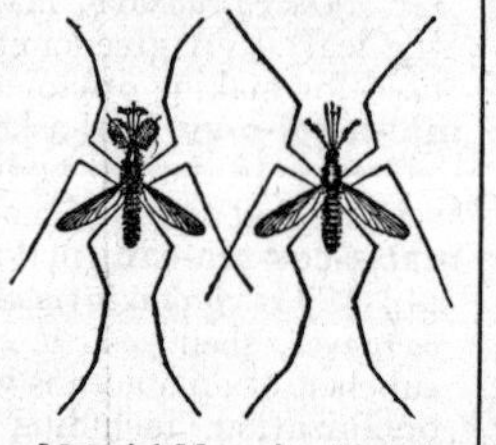

Malarial Mosquito (*Anopheles maculipennis*). — Male at left; female at right. (Enlarged.)

mal-as-sim-i-la-tion (mal''ạ-sim-i-lā'shọn), *n.* [See *mal-.*] In *pathol.,* imperfect assimilation or nutrition.

ma-late (mā'lāt), *n.* In *chem.,* a salt or ester of malic acid.

mal-ax-ate (mal'ak-sāt), *v. t.*; *-ated, -ating.* [L. *malaxatus,* pp. of *malaxare,* < Gr. μαλάσσειν, soften, < μαλακός, soft.] To soften by kneading, rubbing, mixing, making into a paste, or the like.—**mal-ax-a'tion** (-ak-sā'shọn), *n.*—**mal'ax-a-tor,** *n.* A malaxating or mixing machine.

Ma-lay (mạ-lā' or mā'lā). **I.** *n.* A member of the dominant people of the Malay Peninsula and adjacent islands; also, the language spoken by this people, belonging to the Malayo-Polynesian family of languages; also, a member of the Malay or brown race; also, one of a breed of domestic fowls. **II.** *a.* Of or pertaining to the Malays or their country or language; also, noting or pertaining to the so-called 'brown' race, characterized by short stature, brachycephalic skull, large mouth, prominent cheek-bones, and straight black hair (so named because the dominant people of the Malay Peninsula were considered typical).

Mal-a-ya-lam (mal-ạ-yä'lạm), *n.* A Dravidian language spoken in southwestern India.

Ma-lay-an (mạ-lā'ạn). **I.** *a.* Of or pertaining to the Malays or their country, language, etc.; Malay. **II.** *n.* A Malay; also, the Malay language.

Ma-lay-o- (mạ-lā'ọ-). Form of *Malay* used in combination, as in *Malayo-Chinese* (both Malay and Chinese).—**Ma-lay'o=Pol-y-ne'sian,** *a.* Both Malay and Polynesian; of or pertaining to both the Malays and the Polynesians: as, the *Malayo-Polynesian* family of languages.

Ma-lay-sian (mạ-lā'shiạn or -zhiạn). **I.** *a.* Of or pertaining to Malaysia, or the Malay Archipelago. **II.** *n.* A native of Malaysia.

mal-con-duct (mal-kon'dukt), *n.* [See *mal-.*] Bad or improper conduct, esp. in office.

mal-con-for-ma-tion (mal''kon-fôr-mā'shọn), *n.* [See *mal-.*] Imperfect or faulty conformation, as of parts.

mal-con-tent (mal'kọn-tent). [Also formerly *malecontent*; F. *malcontent*: see *mal-* and *content*², *a.*] **I.** *a.* Discontented or dissatisfied (as, "The neglect of the male sex rendered her *malecontent* and peevish": Smollett's "Humphry Clinker," Aug. 8); now, esp., dissatisfied with the existing administration or management of affairs (as, "A project was even formed by the *malcontent* troops to deliver Harlem into the hands of Orange": Motley's "Dutch Republic," iii. 9); disaffected; inclined to rebellion. **II.** *n.* A malcontent person: as, "He . . . granted a general pardon to all the *malecontents*" (Macaulay's "Hist. of Eng.," i.).

male (māl), *a.* [OF. *male, masle, mascle* (F. *mâle*), < L. *masculus,* male: see *masculine.*] Belonging to the sex which begets young, or any division or group corresponding to it; also, pertaining to or characteristic of this sex; masculine; hence, of superior vigor, strength, etc.; in *bot.,* designating or pertaining to any reproductive structure which produces or contains elements that bring about the fertilization of the female element; of seed-plants, staminate; in *mech.,* designating some part, etc., which fits into a corresponding part (as, a *male* screw: see *screw, n.*).—**male rime.** See *masculine rime,* under *masculine, a.*—**male,** *n.* A male human being; a man or boy; also, any animal of corresponding sex; in *bot.,* a staminate plant.

mal-e-dict (mal-ẹ-dikt'), *v. t.* [L. *maledictus,* pp. of *maledicere,* < *male,* ill, + *dicere,* say.] To speak evil of or to; esp., to curse.—**mal-e-dic'tion** (-dik'shọn), *n.* [L. *maledictio(n-).*] A speaking evil, as of or to a person; esp., the utterance of a curse; a curse or execration (as, "menaces and *maledictions* against king and nobles": Shakspere's "King Lear," i. 2. 160).—**mal-e-dic'to-ry** (-tọ-ri), *a.* Characterized by or of the nature of malediction.

mal-e-fac-tion (mal-ẹ-fak'shọn), *n.* [L. *malefactio(n-),* < *malefacere,* do evil, < *male,* ill, + *facere,* do.] Evil-doing; an evil deed; an offense; a crime.—**mal'e-fac-tor,** *n.* [L., < *malefacere.*] An evil-doer (as, "Rank and fortune were offered to any *malefactor* who would compass the murder": Motley's "Dutch Republic," vi. 7); an offender against the law; a criminal; sometimes, one who does evil to another (opposed to *benefactor*).—**mal'e-fac-tress,** *n.* A female malefactor.

ma-lef-ic (mạ-lef'ik), *a.* [L. *maleficus,* < *male,* ill, + *facere,* do.] Productive of evil; baleful; malign: specif. in *astrol.* Cf. *benefic.*

ma-lef-i-cence (mạ-lef'i-sẹns), *n.* [L. *maleficentia,* < *maleficent-,* for *maleficus*: see *malefic.*] The doing of evil or harm; also, maleficent or harmful character.—**ma-lef'i-cent,** *a.* Doing evil or harm; harmful; mischievous.

ma-le-mute (mä'lẹ-mūt), *n.* [Name of a native Alaskan tribe.] An Eskimo dog. [Alaska.]

male-ness (māl'nes), *n.* Male or masculine character.

ma-lev-o-lence (mạ-lev'ọ-lẹns), *n.* The state or feeling of being malevolent; the wish for evil to another or others; ill-will.

ma-lev-o-lent (mạ-lev'ọ-lẹnt), *a.* [L. *malevolens (-ent-),* < *male,* ill, + *volens,* ppr. of *velle,* wish.] Wishing evil to another or others, or characterized by or indicative of such a wish (as, *malevolent* persons, minds, feelings, or glances; "at the mercy of one whose purposes could not be other than *malevolent,*" Hawthorne's "Scarlet Letter," xvii.); feeling or showing ill-will; in *astrol.*, evil or malign in influence.—**ma-lev′o-lent-ly,** *adv.*

mal-fea-sance (mal-fē′zạns), *n.* [= F. *malfaisance*: see *mal-* and *feasance*, and cf. *misfeasance*.] Evil-doing; esp., official misconduct; violation of a public trust or obligation.—**mal-fea′sant. I.** *a.* Doing evil. **II.** *n.* An evil-doer; a malefactor.

mal-for-ma-tion (mal-fôr-mā′shọn), *n.* [See *mal-*.] Faulty or anomalous formation or structure, esp. in a living body. —**mal-formed′,** *a.* Faultily or badly formed; exhibiting malformation: as, "His bare head was curiously *malformed*, higher on one side than on the other" (Tarkington's "Gentleman from Indiana," iv.).

mal-gov-ern-ment (mal-guv′ėrn-mẹnt), *n.* [See *mal-*.] Bad government.

mal-gré (mâl-grā), *prep.* [F.: see *maugre*.] In spite of.

ma-lic (mā′lik), *a.* [L. *malum*, apple.] Pertaining to or derived from apples: as, *malic* acid (in *chem.*, a crystallizable acid occurring in apples and other fruits).

mal-ice (mal′is), *n.* [OF. F. *malice*, < L. *malitia*, badness, spite, malice, < *malus*, bad.] Badness† or wickedness†; also, harmful action or effect†; also, desire to inflict injury or suffering on another; active or vindictive ill-will (as, "I never bore *malice* to a brave enemy for having done me an injury": Scott's "Castle Dangerous," xix.); spite; sometimes, mischievous desire to tease; in *law*, evil intent on the part of one who commits a wrongful act injurious to others.

ma-li-cious (mạ-lish′us), *a.* [OF. *malicius* (F. *malicieux*), < L. *malitiosus*.] Full of, characterized by, or showing malice (as, "He cursed that blind and *malicious* power which delighted to cross his most deep-laid schemes": Godwin's "Caleb Williams," x.); proceeding from malice (as, *malicious* damage; *malicious* misstatements); malevolent; spiteful; sometimes, mischievous or teasing.—**ma-li′cious-ly,** *adv.*—**ma-li′cious-ness,** *n.*

ma-lif-er-ous (mạ-lif′ẹ-rus), *a.* [L. *malum*, an evil (prop. neut. of *malus*, bad): see *-ferous*.] Bringing evil; producing ill effects; unwholesome; unhealthful.

ma-lign (mạ-līn′), *a.* [OF. *maligne* (F. *malin*), < L. *malignus*, < *malus*, bad, + *-gnus*, akin to *genus*, kind: cf. *benign*.] Having or showing an evil disposition toward others (as, "The devil . . . with jealous leer *malign* Eyed them askance": Milton's "Paradise Lost," iv. 503); malevolent; malignant; also, evil in effect, pernicious, or baleful, as inanimate agencies, etc.; malignant, as a disease; in *astrol.*, having an evil influence.—**ma-lign′,** *v. t.* [OF. *malignier*, < LL. *malignare*, do or contrive maliciously, < L. *malignus*.] To regard with ill-will or envy†; also, to speak ill of, traduce, or slander (as, "Have not I taken your part when you were *maligned?*" Thackeray's "Newcomes," xlvii.).

ma-lig-nant (mạ-lig′nạnt). [LL. *malignans* (*-ant-*), ppr. of *malignare*: see *malign*, *v.*] **I.** *a.* Malign in disposition or spirit (as, "Events were fatally to prove . . . that there are natures too *malignant* to be trusted or to be tamed": Motley's "Dutch Republic," v. 5); intensely malevolent or malicious; also, evil in effect, pernicious, or baleful (as, "Unless the next word . . . Have some *malignant* power upon my life": Shakspere's "Two Gentlemen of Verona," iii. 1. 238); also, disaffected or malcontent (archaic or hist.); in *pathol.*, virulent, deadly, or tending to produce death, as a disease, a tumor, etc.; in *astrol.*, malign. **II.** *n.* A disaffected person, or malcontent (archaic or hist.); specif., in *Eng. hist.*, a supporter of the Stuarts against the Parliament during the civil wars (so called by opponents).—**ma-lig′nance, ma-lig′nan-cy,** *n.*—**ma-lig′nant-ly,** *adv.*

ma-lign-er (mạ-lī′nėr), *n.* One who maligns.

ma-lig-ni-ty (mạ-lig′ni-ti), *n.*; pl. *-ties* (-tiz). [OF. *malignite* (F. *malignité*), < L. *malignitas*.] The state or character of being malign; malevolence; malignant character, as of a disease; *pl.*, malignant feelings or actions.

ma-lign-ly (mạ-līn′li), *adv.* In a malign manner.

ma-lik (mä′lik), *n.* [Ar. *mālik*.] In parts of India and central Asia, the head-man of a village.

ma-lines (mạ-lēn′, F. mȧ-lēn), *n.* [From *Malines* (or Mechlin), city in Belgium.] Mechlin lace; also, a very fine, gauze-like silk net used for millinery, etc.

ma-lin-ger (mạ-ling′gėr), *v. i.* [F. *malingre*, sickly, ailing; origin obscure.] To feign sickness or injury, esp. in order to avoid duty, as soldiers, sailors, etc.: as, "Hastie examined him; and . . . knew not . . . whether the man was sick or *malingering*" (Stevenson's "Master of Ballantrae," xi.). —**ma-lin′ger-er,** *n.*

mal-i-son (mal′i-zọn or -sọn), *n.* [OF. *maleiçon*, < L. *maledictio*(*n-*), E. *malediction*.] A malediction; a curse: as, "I have no sorcerer's *malison* on me" (Tennyson's "Princess," ii. 388). [Archaic or prov.]

mal-kin, maw-kin (mâ′kin), *n.* [From *Malkin*, familiar dim. of *Matilda*, woman's name.] [*cap.*] A proper name formerly often used for a woman of the lower classes, and sometimes also for a female specter or demon, esp. one in the form of a cat (cf. *Graymalkin*, as a proper name, in Shakspere's "Macbeth," i. 1. 8); hence [*l. c.*], an untidy woman or maid-servant (archaic or prov. Eng.: as, "A draggled *mawkin*, thou, That tends her bristled grunters in the sludge," Tennyson's "Princess," v. 25); also, a scarecrow (now prov. Eng.); also, a mop (now prov. Eng.); also [*l. c.* or *cap.*], a cat (obs. or prov. Eng.), or, more commonly, a hare (chiefly Sc.).

mall (mâl), *n.* [OF. *mal*, *mail* (F. *mail*), < L. *malleus*, hammer.] A maul, or heavy hammer (see *maul*); also, the mallet used in the game of pall-mall; hence, the game, or the place or alley where it was played; also, a shaded walk; a public walk or promenade.

mal-lard (mal′ạrd), *n.* [OF. F. *malart*; origin uncertain.] The male of the common wild duck, *Anas boscas*, from which the domestic duck has descended; hence, any duck of this species.

Mallard (*Anas boscas*).

mal-le-a-ble (mal′ẹ-ạ-bl), *a.* [OF. *malleable* (F. *malléable*), < L. *malleare*, beat with a hammer, < *malleus*, hammer.] Capable of being extended or shaped by hammering or by pressure with rollers; fig., adaptable or tractable (as, "Human nature is often *malleable* . . . where religious interests are concerned": Motley's "Dutch Republic," iii. 5).—**malleable cast=iron,** cast-iron (in the form of castings) which has been decarburized after casting, and thus rendered more malleable and less brittle.—**malleable iron,** malleable cast-iron; also, wrought-iron.—**mal″le-a-bil′i-ty** (-bil′i-ti), **mal′le-a-ble-ness,** *n.*

mal-lee (mal′ẹ), *n.* [Australian.] Any of various dwarf Australian species of eucalyptus, as *Eucalyptus dumosa* and *E. oleosa*, which sometimes form large tracts of brushwood; also, such brushwood.

mal-le-muck (mal′ẹ-muk), *n.* [D. *mallemok*.] The fulmar, *Fulmarus glacialis*; also, any of various other oceanic birds, as the albatross.

mal-len-ders (mal′ẹn-dėrz), *n. pl.* See *malanders*.

mal-le-o-lus (ma-lē′ọ-lus), *n.*; pl. *-li* (-lī). [L., dim. of *malleus*, hammer.] In *anat.*, either of two bony protuberances, one on each side of the ankle, being situated in man at the lower end of the fibula and tibia respectively.—**mal-le-o-lar** (ma-lē′ọ-lạr or mal′ẹ-ọ-), *a.*

mal-let (mal′et), *n.* [OF. F. *maillet*, dim. of *mail*, E. *mall*.] A hammer, usually of wood, used chiefly for driving another tool, as a chisel; also, the wooden implement used to strike the balls in the game of croquet; also, the stick used to drive the ball in polo.—**mal′let,** *v. t.*; *-leted*, *-leting*. To strike or drive with or as with a mallet.

mal-le-us (mal′ẹ-us), *n.*; pl. *mallei* (-ī). [L., hammer.] In *anat.*, the outermost of three small bones in the middle ear of man and other mammals: so called from its hammer-like shape. See *incus* and *stapes*.

mal-low (mal′ō), *n.* [AS. *mealwe*, < L. *malva*, mallow: cf. *mauve*.] Any plant of the genus *Malva*, comprising herbs with leaves usually angularly lobed or dissected and purple, pink, or white flowers, as *M. sylvestris*, common in Europe, with reddish-purple flowers, and *M. rotundifolia* (the 'dwarf mallow'), with roundish serrate leaves and small pinkish-white flowers; also, any malvaceous plant (as, the marsh-*mallow*).

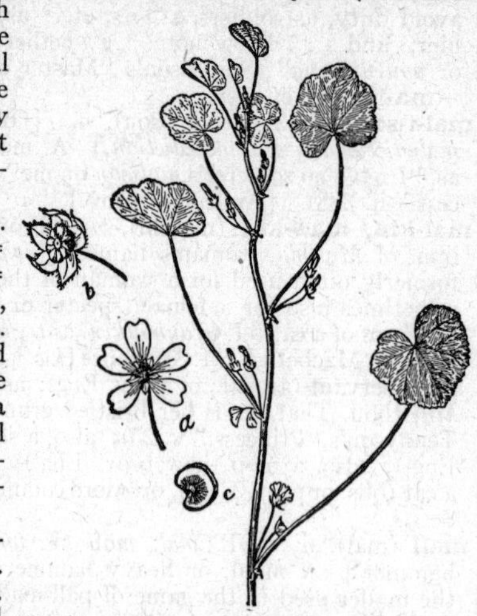

Branch of Mallow (*Malva rotundifolia*), with flowers and fruits.— *a*, a flower; *b*, the fruit; *c*, one of the carpels.

malm (mäm), *n.* [AS. *mealm* = Icel. *mālmr* = Goth. *malma*, sand; akin to E. *meal*[1].] A kind of soft, friable limestone; also, a chalk-bearing soil of the southeastern part of England.

malm-sey (mäm'-zi), *n.* [= F. *malvoisie* = It. *malvasia*; named from *Monemvasia*, or (Napoli di) *Malvasia*, a seaport of southeastern Greece.] A strong, sweet wine of a high flavor, orig. made in Greece.

mal-nour-ished (mal-nur'isht), *a.* [See *mal-*.] Poorly or insufficiently nourished: as, *malnourished* children.

mal-nu-tri-tion (mal-nū-trish'ọn), *n.* [See *mal-*.] Imperfect nutrition.

mal-oc-clu-sion (mal-o-klö'zhọn), *n.* [See *mal-*.] Faulty occlusion, closing, or meeting, as of opposing teeth in the upper and the lower jaw.

mal-o-dor (mal-ō'dọr), *n.* [See *mal-*.] A bad odor; a stench.—**mal-o'dor-ous,** *a.* Having a bad odor; ill-smelling; unsavory. Often fig.—**mal-o'dor-ous-ly,** *adv.* —**mal-o'dor-ous-ness,** *n.*

mal-o'dour, *n.* British preferred form of *malodor*.

mal-or-gan-i-za-tion (mal"ôr-gạn-i-zā'shọn), *n.* [See *mal-*.] Bad or faulty organization.—**mal-or'gan-ized** (-īzd), *a.* Badly organized.

mal-pigh-i-a-ceous (mal-pig-i-ā'shius), *a.* [NL. *Malpighia*, the typical genus; named from *Malpighi*: see *Malpighian*.] Belonging or pertaining to the *Malpighiaceæ*, a family of tropical herbs and shrubs, certain of which are cultivated for ornamental purposes.

Mal-pigh-i-an (mal-pig'i-ạn), *a.* Pertaining to, or discovered or investigated by, Marcello Malpighi (1628–94), an Italian anatomist and physiologist.—**Malpighian bodies** or **corpuscles,** in *anat.*, certain small round bodies occurring in the cortical substance of the kidney.—**Malpighian tubes** or **vessels,** in *zoöl.*, certain appendages of the alimentary canal of insects, generally regarded as representing the kidneys.

mal-posed (mal-pōzd'), *a.* [See *mal-*.] Badly placed.—**mal-po-si'tion** (-pọ-zish'ọn), *n.* Faulty or wrong position, esp. of a part or organ of the body or of a fetus in the uterus.

mal-prac-tice (mal-prak'tis), *n.* [See *mal-*.] Improper or wrong practice or conduct (as, "The sentence . . . stated that he [an official] had been guilty of much *malpractice*": Motley's "Dutch Republic," iii. 4); specif., improper professional action or treatment on the part of a physician, as from reprehensible ignorance or neglect or with criminal intent; often, the criminal inducing of abortion.—**mal-prac-ti'tion-er** (-tish'ọn-ėr), *n.*

malt (mâlt), *n.* [AS. *mealt* = D. *mout* = G. *malz* = Icel. *malt*, malt; from the root of E. *melt*.] Grain (usually barley) which has been partially germinated by steeping, heating, etc., used in brewing and distilling; also, liquor produced from malt by fermentation, as beer or ale.—**malt,** *v.* **I.** *tr.* To convert (grain) into malt; also, to make (liquor) with malt; also, to treat or mix with malt or a malt product. **II.** *intr.* To become malt; also, to produce malt from grain.

malt-ase (mâl'tās), *n.* [From *malt* + *-ase*.] In *chem.*, glucase.

Mal-tese (mâl-tēs' or -tēz'), *a.* Of or pertaining to Malta, an island in the Mediterranean south of Sicily, anciently colonized by the Phenicians; pertaining to the people or the language of Malta; also, of or pertaining to the religious and military order of the Knights of Malta, or Knights of St. John of Jerusalem (see *hospitaler*), who from 1530 to 1798 owned and occupied the island.—**Maltese cat,** a bluish-gray variety of the domestic cat.—**Maltese cross,** a cross having four equal arms that expand in width from the place of meeting outward and (in the typical form) are terminated at the end in a reëntrant angle: so called from its use as a device by the Knights of Malta.—**Maltese lace,** a pillow-lace of silk or linen of the guipure kind; also, a machine-made lace of coarse cotton thread.—**Mal-tese',** *n.*; pl. *-tese.* A native or inhabitant of Malta; also, the language of the natives of Malta, containing a considerable proportion of Arabic and Italian.

Maltese Lace (pillow-lace).

mal-tha (mal'-thạ), *n.* [L., < Gr. μάλθα, mixture of wax and pitch.] Any of various cements or mortars, bituminous or otherwise; also, any of various natural mixtures of hydrocarbons, as ozocerite; specif., any of certain black, viscid or semisolid bitumens, midway in consistence between asphalt and petroleum.

malt=horse† (mâlt'hôrs), *n.* A heavy horse used by maltsters: sometimes applied contemptuously to a person. See Shakspere's "Comedy of Errors," iii. 1. 32.

Mal-thu-sian (mal-thū'ziạn). **I.** *a.* Of or pertaining to T. R. Malthus (1766–1834), an English political economist who contended that population, tending to increase faster than the means of subsistence, should be checked by social and moral restraints. **II.** *n.* A follower of Malthus, or a believer in his doctrines.—**Mal-thu'sian-ism,** *n.*

malt-ose (mâl'tōs), *n.* [From *malt* + *-ose*[2].] In *chem.*, a white crystalline sugar formed by the action of diastase (as in malt) on starch.

mal-treat (mal-trēt'), *v. t.* [See *mal-*.] To treat ill; handle roughly or cruelly; ill-treat; abuse: as, "Many monasteries were robbed, many clerical persons maimed and *maltreated*" (Motley's "Dutch Republic," iii. 2).—**mal-treat'ment,** *n.*

malt-ster (mâlt'stėr), *n.* A maker of or dealer in malt.

malt=sug-ar (mâlt'shủg'ạr), *n.* Maltose.

malt-y (mâl'ti), *a.* Of, like, or containing malt; also (humorously), addicted to or affected by malt liquor; drunk.

mal-va-ceous (mal-vā'shius), *a.* [L. *malvaceus*, < *malva*, mallow.] Of or like the mallow; belonging to the *Malvaceæ*, or mallow family of plants, which includes the abutilon, althæa, hollyhock, okra, cotton-plant, etc.

mal-ver-sa-tion (mal-vėr-sā'shọn), *n.* [F., < *malverser*, < L. *male*, ill, + *versari*, occupy one's self: see *versed*[2].] Improper or corrupt behavior in an office or a position of trust; corrupt administration, as of justice or of funds.

mal-voi-sie (mal'voi-zi, F. mål-vwo-zē), *n.* [F.] Malmsey.

mam (mam), *n.* [Cf. *mamma*[1].] A childish word for *mother*.

ma-ma', *n.* See *mamma*[1].

mam-ba (mam'bạ), *n.* [S. Afr.] A long, slender, arboreal South African serpent, *Dendraspis angusticeps*, whose bite is almost certain death, and which has the habit of attacking without provocation. See cut on following page.

Mam-e-luke (mam'ẹ-lūk), *n.* [Ar. *mamlūk*, slave.] A member of a military body in Egypt, orig. recruited from slaves, which held the throne from about 1250 until 1517 and remained the ruling class until massacred or dispersed by Mehemet Ali in 1811; [*l. c.*] in Mohammedan countries, a slave.

ma-mey (ma-mā′ or -mē′), *n.* Same as *mammee.*

ma-mil′la, etc. See *mammilla,* etc.

mam-ma^{1}, ma-ma (mạ-mä′ or, esp. in U. S., mä′-mạ), *n.* [Redupl. of a syllable common in natural infantile utterance: cf. F. *maman,* L. *mamma,* Gr. *μάμμη,* Russ. and Lith. *mama.*] Mother: a word used esp. by children or young people: as, "entreating her to interpose with your *mamma* that you may be allowed to favour us with your company" (Smollett's "Humphry Clinker," Oct. 14).

Mamba.

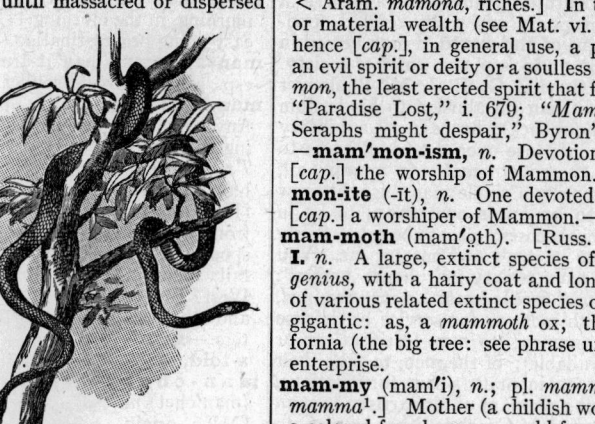

mam-ma^{2} (mam′ạ), *n.*; pl. *mammæ* (-ē). [L., breast, pap, teat.] In *anat.,* the organ, characteristic of mammals, which in the female secretes milk; a breast or udder.

mam-mal (mam′ạl), *n.* [NL. *Mammalia,* prop. neut. pl. of LL. *mammalis,* adj. < L. *mamma:* see *mamma^{2}.*] Any of the *Mammalia,* the highest class of vertebrate animals, comprising those which suckle their young; a mammiferous animal.—**mam-ma-lian** (ma-mā′li̤an). **I.** *a.* Belonging or pertaining to the *Mammalia* or mammals. **II.** *n.* An animal of the class *Mammalia;* a mammal.—**mam-mal-o-gy** (ma-mal′ọ̄-ji), *n.* [See *-logy.*] The science that treats of mammals.

mam-ma-ry (mam′ạ-ri), *a.* [NL. *mammarius,* < L. *mamma:* see *mamma^{2}.*] In *anat.,* etc., of or pertaining to the mamma or breast; mamma-like.

mam-mee (ma-mē′), *n.* [Haitian.] A tall, tropical American clusiaceous tree, *Mammea americana,* or its large, edible fruit (often called *mammee-apple*); also, the sapodilla; also, the marmalade-tree.

mam-mer (mam′ėr), *v.* [Prob. imit.] **I.** *intr.* To mutter; stammer; hesitate in speech or in thought: as, "I wonder . . . What you would ask me, that I should deny, Or stand so *mammering* on" (Shakspere's "Othello," iii. 3. 70). [Obs. or prov. Eng.] **II.** *tr.* To confuse; perplex. [Prov. Eng.]

mam-met (mam′et), etc. See *maumet,* etc.

mam-mi-fer (mam′i-fėr), *n.* [NL. *Mammifera,* pl., mammals, < L. *mamma,* breast, + *ferre,* bear.] An animal having mammæ; a mammal.—**mam-mif-er-ous** (ma-mif′ẹ-rus), *a.* Having mammæ; mammalian.

mam-mi-form (mam′i-fôrm), *a.* [See *mamma^{2}* and *-form.*] Having the form of a mamma or breast.

mam-mil-la (ma-mil′ạ), *n.*; pl. *mammillæ* (-ē). [L. *mammilla, mamilla,* dim. of *mamma,* E. *mamma^{2}.*] In *anat.,* the nipple of the mamma or breast; hence, in *entom., bot., mineral.,* etc., any nipple-like process or protuberance.—**mam-mil-lar** (mam′i-lạ̈r), *a.* Mammillary.—**mam′mil-la-ry** (-lạ̄-ri), *a.* Of, pertaining to, or resembling a mammilla; having mammillæ or rounded protuberances, as a mineral.—**mam′mil-late, mam′mil-lat-ed** (-lāt, -lā-ted), *a.* Having a mammilla or mammillæ; mammillary; mammilliform.—**mam-mil-li-form** (ma-mil′i-fôrm), *a.* [See *-form.*] Nipple-shaped; mammillary.

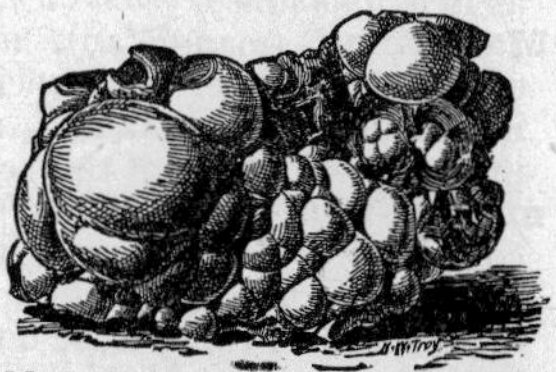
Mammillary Structure. — Malachite.

mam-mock (mam′ọk), *n.* [Origin obscure.] A broken or torn piece; a fragment; a shred. [Archaic or prov. Eng.] —**mam′mock,** *v. t.* To break, tear, or cut into pieces. See Shakspere's "Coriolanus," i. 3. 71. [Archaic or prov. Eng.]

mam-mon (mam′ọn), *n.* [L. *mammona,* < Gr. *μαμωνᾶς,* < Aram. *māmōnā,* riches.] In the New Testament, riches or material wealth (see Mat. vi. 24; Luke, xvi. 9, 11, 13); hence [*cap.*], in general use, a personification of riches as an evil spirit or deity or a soulless worldly agency (as, "*Mammon,* the least erected spirit that fell From heaven," Milton's "Paradise Lost," i. 679; "*Mammon* wins his way where Seraphs might despair," Byron's "Childe Harold," i. 9). —**mam′mon-ism,** *n.* Devotion to the pursuit of riches; [*cap.*] the worship of Mammon.—**mam′mon-ist, mam′-mon-ite** (-īt), *n.* One devoted to the pursuit of riches; [*cap.*] a worshiper of Mammon.—**mam-mon-is′tic,** *a.*

mam-moth (mam′ọth). [Russ. *mammot,* now *mamant.*] **I.** *n.* A large, extinct species of elephant, *Elephas primigenius,* with a hairy coat and long, curved tusks; also, any of various related extinct species of elephant. **II.** *a.* Huge; gigantic: as, a *mammoth* ox; the *mammoth* tree of California (the big tree: see phrase under *big^{1}, a.*); a *mammoth* enterprise.

mam-my (mam′i), *n.*; pl. *mammies* (-iz). [Cf. *mam* and *mamma^{1}.*] Mother (a childish word); in the southern U. S., a colored female nurse or old family servant.

mam-pa-lon (mam′pạ-lon), *n.* [Prob. native name.] A small, otter-like, viverrine animal, *Cynogale bennetti,* a native of Borneo, with webbed feet and semi-aquatic in habit.

Mampalon.

man (man), *n.*; pl. *men* (men). [AS. *mann, man* (pl. *menn, men*), = D. *man* = G. *mann* = Icel. *madhr* = Goth. *manna,* man; akin to Skt. *manu,* man.] The human creature or being, as representing the race or as distinguished from other beings, animals, or things (as, to fear neither God nor *man;* shelter for *man* and beast); the human race, or mankind; a human being, regardless of sex (as, "All *men* are created equal": U. S. Declaration of Independence); a person; also, the male human being (distinguished from *woman*); a male person, esp. of adult or full legal age (as, a little *man,* playfully, a little boy; a young *man;* "When I became a *man,* I put away childish things," 1 Cor. xiii. 11); a male follower, retainer, subordinate, or employee (as, Robin Hood and his merry *men;* the officers and *men* of the regiment; an agreement between employers and *men*); a liegeman or vassal (archaic); a male servant, often a valet; also, a husband (now chiefly prov., except in 'man and wife'); also, an adult male person possessing the qualities or virtues that befit one of his sex (as, "His life was gentle, and the elements So mix'd in him that Nature might stand up And say to all the world 'This was a *man!*' " Shakspere's "Julius Cæsar," v. 5. 75); also, manly character or courage (see Shakspere's "King Lear," ii. 4. 42); also, one of the pieces used in playing certain games, as chess or checkers; also, an image or figure of an adult male person; *naut.,* in compounds, a ship (as, a *man*-of-war; a merchant*man;* an India*man*).—**man about town,** a man of leisure who frequents places of public or social resort about the town; a fashionable idler.—**man Friday,** a devoted or servile follower; a factotum: in allusion to the man found by Robinson Crusoe on his deserted island, whom he speaks of as "my man Friday."—**man in the moon,** a fancied semblance of a man, or of a man's face, in the disk of the full moon: sometimes referred to as a type of an imaginary person.—**man in the street,** the common or ordinary man; the average citizen.—**man of affairs,** a man occupied in practical or business affairs; a man of large experience or wide interests in the field of business or public affairs.—**Man of Destiny,** Napoleon Bonaparte, who regarded himself as an instrument of fate.—**man of letters,** a literary man; an author.—**Man of Sorrows,** Jesus Christ: with allusion to Isa. liii. 3. —**man of straw,** a figure or effigy of a man, made of straw; hence, a man of no substance or worth; an irresponsible person put forward as a substitute or surety for another; a fictitious person, as an imaginary and easily refuted opponent in an argument.—**man of the world,** a man versed in the ways and usages of the world, esp. the world of society.—**Man on Horseback,** General G. E. J. M. Boulanger (1837–91), the French politician (in allusion to his custom of appearing in public on horseback); hence [*l. c.*], a military leader who acquires such influence over the populace as to threaten the existence of the government.—**to a man,** all, to the last man; not excepting a single man: as, the crew volunteered *to a man.*—**to be one's own man,** to be in command of one's faculties or senses; also, to be subject only to one's own wishes, or to be one's own master (as, "You shall not *be your own man* twenty-four hours longer": Godwin's "Caleb Williams," xxx.).—**man,** *v. t.*; *manned, manning.* To furnish with men, as for service or defense (as, to *man* a ship with seamen; to *man* fortifications or guns with all the force available); of the men, to take their places for service, or serve, on, in, or at (a ship, fortifications, guns, etc.: as, "He left but a remnant of his garrison to *man* its walls," Irving's "Conquest of Granada," xxx.); also, to make manly or courageous, or brace (as, "His pride and interest, like the fortitude of a North American Indian, *manned* him to sustain the tortures": Scott's "Guy Mannering," xli.); also, to accustom (a hawk) to the presence of men.

man-a-cle (man'ạ-kl), *n.* [OF. *manicle,* < L. *manicula,* dim. < *manus,* hand.] A shackle for the hand; a handcuff; fig., a restraint: usually in *pl.*—**man'a-cle,** *v. t.*; *-cled, -cling.* To handcuff or fetter (as, "*manacled* like a felon": Godwin's "Caleb Williams," Postscript); fig., to hamper or restrain in action (as, "The Assembly finally finding the proprietary obstinately persisted in *manacling* their deputies with instructions . . . resolved to petition the king against them": B. Franklin's "Autobiography," xiii.).

man-age (man'āj), *v.*; *-aged, -aging.* [= F. *manéger,* < It. *maneggiare,* manage, handle, < *mano,* < L. *manus,* hand; with sense affected by F. *ménager,* manage (a household, resources, etc.), husband, < *ménage*: see *ménage.*] **I.** *tr.* To handle or train (a horse) in the exercises of the manège; hence, in general, to handle, direct, or control in action or use; wield (a weapon, tool, etc.); conduct (an affair, undertaking, establishment, etc.); exercise the charge or care of; regulate or govern the action or course of; control; often, to dominate or influence (a person) by tact, address, or artifice (as, "He thoroughly understood the art of *managing* men, particularly his superiors": Motley's "Dutch Republic," ii. 1); also, to treat carefully, use sparingly, or husband (health, money, etc.: obs. or archaic); also, to bring about, or succeed in accomplishing; contrive (to do something). **II.** *intr.* To conduct affairs; also, to succeed in accomplishing a task; contrive to get along (as, "He *managed* a whole year upon the proceeds": Howells's "Foregone Conclusion," iii.).—**man'age,** *n.* [= F. *manège,* < It. *maneggio,* < *maneggiare.*] The manège; also, management. [Archaic.]

man-age-a-ble (man'āj-ạ-bl), *a.* That may be managed; wieldy; governable; tractable; contrivable.—**man''age-a-bil'i-ty** (-bil'i-ti), **man'age-a-ble-ness,** *n.*—**man'age-a-bly,** *adv.*

man-age-ment (man'āj-mẹnt), *n.* The act or manner of managing; handling; conduct, direction, or guidance; control; judicious use of means to accomplish anything; skilful or artful dealing; also, the person or body of persons managing an institution, business, etc.

man-ag-er (man'ā-jėr), *n.* One who manages; esp., one charged with the management or direction of an affair, or of the affairs of an institution, a business establishment, or the like; a managing official; a director; also, one who manages resources and expenditures, as of a household (as, "She was neat, industrious, honest, and a good *manager*": Cooper's "Spy," iii.).—**man'ag-er-ess,** *n.* A female manager.—**man-a-ge'ri-al** (-ā-jē'ri-ạl), *a.* Of or pertaining to a manager.—**man-a-ge'ri-al-ly,** *adv.*—**man'a-ger-ship,** *n.* The office, position, or control of a manager.

man-a-kin (man'ạ-kin), *n.* [See *manikin.*] A manikin; also, any of various songless passerine birds (family *Pipridæ*) of the warmer parts of America, mostly small and brilliantly colored.

ma-ña-na (mä-nyä'nä), *n.* and *adv.* [Sp., < L. *mane,* morning, in the morning.] To-morrow: often used to imply easy-going procrastination.

man=at=arms (man'ạt-ärmz'), *n.*; pl. *men-.* A soldier; esp., a heavy-armed soldier serving on horseback.

man-a-tee (man-ạ-tē'), *n.* [Sp. *manatí*; from Carib.] Any of various herbivorous, gregarious sirenians constituting the genus *Trichechus,* having two flippers in front and a spoon-shaped tail: found in West Indian and other waters.—**man'a-toid,** *a.*

American Manatee (*Trichechus manatus*).

man-chet (man'chet), *n.* [ME.; origin obscure.] A small loaf or roll of the finest white bread; bread made from the finest and whitest wheat flour. [Archaic or prov. Eng.]

man-chi-neel (man-chi-nēl'), *n.* [F. *mancenille,* < Sp. *manzanillo,* < *manzana,* apple, < L. (*mala*) *Matiana,* '(apples) of the Matius gens' (of Rome).] A tropical American euphorbiaceous tree, *Hippomane mancinella,* with a milky, highly caustic, poisonous sap and an acrid fruit.

Manchineel.

Man-chu (man-chö'). **I.** *n.*; pl. *-chus* (-chöz'). One of a Mongolian people inhabiting the region called from them Manchuria, who conquered China in the 17th century; also, their language, a Ural-Altaic tongue. **II.** *a.* Of or pertaining to the Manchus, their country, or their language.

Man-chu-ri-an (man-chö'ri-ạn). **I.** *a.* Of or pertaining to Manchuria, a region to the northeast of China, the home of the Manchus. **II.** *n.* A native or inhabitant of Manchuria.

man-ci-pa-tion (man-si-pā'shọn), *n.* [L. *mancipatio(n-),* < *mancipare,* transfer as property, < *manceps,* purchaser, < *manus,* hand, + *capere,* take.] A legal formality employed among the ancient Romans for certain transfers of property, for emancipating slaves and children, etc.; also, the act of enslaving, or the state of being enslaved.—**man'ci-pa-to-ry** (-pā-tọ-ri), *a.*

man-ci-ple (man'si-pl), *n.* [OF. *manciple,* slave, servant, < L. *mancipium,* purchase, possession, a slave, < *manceps*: see *mancipation.*] A steward or purveyor, esp. of an English college or inn of court, or other institution. See Chaucer's "Prologue to the Canterbury Tales," 567.

-mancy. A noun termination from Gr. μαντεία, divination, as in *capnomancy, geomancy, necromancy, oneiromancy.*

Man-dæ-an (man-dē'ạn), *n.* [Mandæan *mandā,* knowledge.] A member of an ancient Gnostic sect still surviving in southern Mesopotamia; also, the Aramaic dialect used in the sacred books of this sect.

man-da-mus (man-dā'mus), *n.*; pl. *-muses.* [L., 'we command.'] In *law,* a writ from a superior court to an inferior court, or to an officer, a corporation, etc., commanding a specified thing to be done.

man-da-rin (man'dạ-rin), *n.* [Pg. *mandarim,* through Malay and Hind. < Skt. *mantrin,* counselor, < *mantra,* thought, counsel: cf. *mantra.*] A member of any of the nine ranks of Chinese public officials, each distinguished by a particular kind of button worn on the cap; [*cap.*] the form of Chinese spoken by officials and educated people generally; the chief dialect of China; [*l. c.*] a small, flattish variety of orange of Chinese origin, of a characteristic sweet flavor, or the shrub or small tree producing it; also, any of certain coal-tar dyes producing yellow or orange colors.—**man′da-rin-ate** (-āt), *n.* The office or the jurisdiction of a mandarin; also, mandarins collectively; also, government by mandarins.—**man′da-rin=duck′**, *n.* A beautiful crested duck, *Aix galericulata*, with variegated plumage of purple, green, chestnut, and white, a native of China, where it is regarded as an emblem of conjugal affection.

Mandarin-duck.

man-da-ta-ry (man′dạ-tạ-ri), *n.*; pl. *-ries* (-riz). [LL. *mandatarius*, < L. *mandatum*, E. *mandate*.] One to whom a mandate is given.

man-date (man′dāt), *n.* [L. *mandatum*, prop. pp. neut. of *mandare*, commit, enjoin, command, < *manus*, hand, + *dare*, give.] A command, order, or injunction; specif., a command from a superior court or official to an inferior one; an order issued by the Pope, esp. one commanding the preferment of a certain person to a benefice; in *politics*, the instruction as to policy given or supposed to be given by the electors to a legislative body or to one or more of its members; in *civil law*, orig., a trust or commission by which one person requested another to act for him gratuitously, agreeing to indemnify him against losses, etc.; later, any contract of agency; in *international politics*, a commission given to one nation (the mandatary) by an associated group of nations to administer the government and affairs of a people or territory unable to maintain itself unaided.—**man′date**, *v. t.*; *-dated, -dating.* In *international politics*, to consign (a territory, etc.) to the charge of a particular nation under a mandate.—**man-da′tor** (-dā′tọr), *n.* [L.] One who gives a mandate.—**man-da-to′ri-al** (-dạ-tō′ri-ạl), *a.* Mandatory.—**man′da-to-ry** (-tọ-ri). [LL. *mandatorius*.] **I.** *a.* Pertaining to, of the nature of, or containing a mandate; obligatory by reason of a mandate, as actions; having received a mandate, as a nation commissioned to take charge of a dependent territory. **II.** *n.*; pl. *-ries* (-riz). A mandatary.

man=day (man′dā), *n.* A day of work by one man, used as a time-unit in specifying the duration of industrial activity or idleness. Cf. *man-hour*.

man-di-ble (man′di-bl), *n.* [LL. *mandibula, mandibulum*, jaw, < L. *mandere*, chew.] A jaw or jaw-bone, esp. the lower one; in birds, the upper or the lower part of the beak; in arthropods, either one of the anterior pair of buccal appendages used for biting, defense, etc.—**man-dib′u-lar** (-dib′ū-lạr), *a.* Pertaining to or of the nature of a mandible.—**man-dib′u-late** (-lāt), *a.* Having mandibles.

Man-din-go (man-ding′gō). **I.** *n.*; pl. *-gos* or *-goes* (-gōz). A member of any of a number of negro peoples forming an extensive linguistic group in western Africa; also, their language. **II.** *a.* Of or pertaining to the Mandingos or their language.

man-do-la (man-dō′lạ), *n.* [It., < LL. *pandura*: see *pandora*².] An older and larger variety of the mandolin.

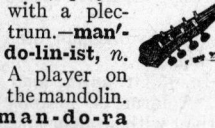

man-do-lin, man-do-line (man′dọ-lin), *n.* [F. *mandoline*, < It. *mandolino*, dim. of *mandola*: see *mandola*.] A musical instrument of the lute class, played with a plectrum.—**man′do-lin-ist**, *n.* A player on the mandolin.

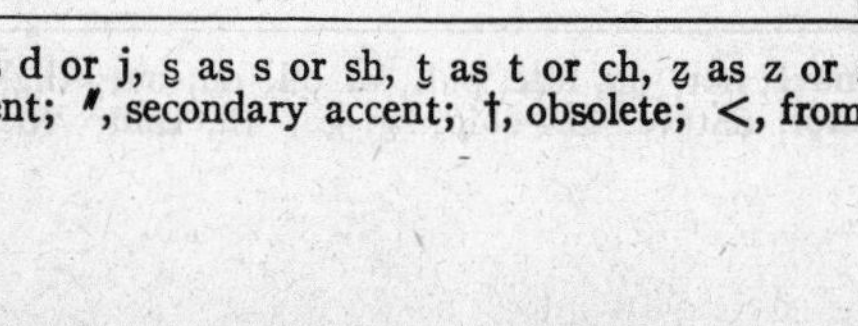
Mandolin.

man-do-ra (man-dō′rạ), *n.* Same as *mandola*. Also **man-dore′** (-dōr′).

man-dor-la (man-dôr′lạ), *n.*; pl. *-las* (-lạz), It. *-le* (-lā). [It., lit. 'almond.'] In *decorative art*, an almond-shaped or pointed oval panel, space, or piece.

Mandorla. — From Assumption of the Madonna, by Orcagna; Church of Or San Michele, Florence.

man-drag-o-ra (man-drag′ọ-rạ), *n.* [ML., < L. *mandragoras*, < Gr. μανδραγόρας.] The mandrake: in literary use commonly with allusion to its narcotic properties: as, "Not poppy, nor *mandragora*, Nor all the drowsy syrups of the world, Shall ever medicine thee to that sweet sleep" (Shakspere's "Othello," iii. 3. 330).

man-drake (man′drāk), *n.* [ME. *mandrake, mandragge*; short for *mandragora*.] A narcotic European solanaceous herb, *Mandragora officinarum*, with a very short stem and a fleshy, often forked root fancied to resemble the human form; any plant of the same genus; also, the May-apple.

man-drel, man-dril (man′drel, -dril), *n.* [Origin obscure: cf. F. *mandrin*.] A spindle, arbor, bar, or the like, to which an object is secured while being worked upon, as a slightly tapering round bar of steel which can be fitted into the bore of certain work in order to support it between the centers of a lathe; also, the live spindle of a lathe (see *spindle*); also, a rod or core around which metal or the like is cast or shaped.

man-drill (man′dril), *n.* [Perhaps native name: cf. *drill*².] A large, ferocious, gregarious baboon, *Papio* (or *Cynocephalus*) *maimon*, of western Africa, the male of which has the face marked with blue and scarlet.

Mandrill.

man-du-cate (man′dū-kāt), *v. t.*; *-cated, -cating.* [L. *manducatus*, pp. of *manducare*, < *mandere*, chew.] To chew; masticate; eat.—**man-du-ca′tion** (-kā′shọn), *n.* [LL. *manducatio(n-)*.] The act of manducating; chewing; eating.—**man′du-ca-to-ry** (-kạ-tọ-ri), *a.* Pertaining to or adapted for manducation.

mane (mān), *n.* [AS. *manu* = G. *mähne* = Icel. *mön*, mane; akin to L. *monile*, Gr. μάννος, necklace, Skt. *manyā*, nape of neck.] The long hair growing on the back of or about the neck and neighboring parts of some animals, as the horse and the lion; hence, a person's hair when long and abundant.

man=eat-er (man′ē″tėr), *n.* A cannibal; also, an animal that devours (or is reputed to devour) human beings, esp. a tiger, a lion, or a shark (as, "The *Man-Eaters* [lions] of Tsavo, and Other East African Adventures," the title of a book by J. H. Patterson, published in 1907); also, a horse given to biting.—**man′=eat″ing**, *a.* Eating or devouring human beings.

maned (mānd), *a.* Having a mane, as an animal.

ma-nège (mȧ-nāzh), *n.* [F.: see *manage*, *n.*] The art of training and riding horses; horsemanship; also, the action or movements of a trained horse; also, a school for training horses and teaching horsemanship.

ma-neh (mä′nạ), *n.* [Heb.: cf. *mina*¹.] A Hebrew unit of weight and value, equal to the sixtieth part of a talent.

mane-less (mān′les), *a.* Having no mane.

ma-nes (mā′nēz), *n. pl.* [L.] [Also *cap.*] Among the ancient Romans, the deified souls of the departed; the shades of the dead, as the object of reverence or awe; sometimes, the spirit or shade of a particular deceased person.

ma-neu-ver, ma-nœu-vre (mạ-nö′vėr or mạ-nū′-), *n.* [F. *manœuvre*, manipulation, management, maneuver, OF.

manuevre, hand-work, manual labor, < ML. *manuopera*, *manopera*, hand-work, < L. *manus*, hand, + *opera*, work.] In military and naval tactics, a planned and regulated movement or evolution of troops, war-vessels, etc.; a strategic movement or change of position; in general, an adroit move; an artful proceeding, measure, or expedient; an artifice; also, maneuvering; artful management.—**ma-neu′ver, ma-nœu′vre,** *v.*; *-vered, -vred, -vering, -vring.* [F. *manœuvrer*, manipulate, work, maneuver, OF. *manuvrer*, work by hand, < *manuevre*, hand-work: cf. *manure*, *v.*] **I.** *intr.* To perform a maneuver or maneuvers; also, to manage with address or art; scheme. **II.** *tr.* To cause to perform a maneuver or maneuvers; change the position of (troops, vessels, etc.) by a maneuver; in general, to manipulate with skill or adroitness; also, to bring, put, or drive by maneuvers (as, "He had *manœuvred* the one quite forth from the good graces of the other": Stevenson's "Master of Ballantrae," iv.); make by adroit movements (as, "He . . . *manœuvred* his way towards Lady Valleys": Galsworthy's "Patrician," ii. 6).—**ma-neu′ver-er, ma-nœu′vrer,** *n.*

man-ful (man′fůl), *a.* Having or showing the spirit of a man; manly; brave; resolute.—**man′ful-ly,** *adv.*—**man′ful-ness,** *n.*

'mang (mång), *prep.* Scotch form of *'mong* for *among.*

man-ga-nate (mang′gạ-nāt), *n.* In *chem.*, a salt of manganic acid.

man-ga-nese (mang-gạ-nēs′ or mang′gạ-nēz), *n.* [F. *manganèse*, < It. *manganese*, < ML. *magnesia*: see *magnesia.*] Chem. sym., Mn; at. wt., 54.93; sp. gr., 8.0. A hard, brittle, grayish-white metallic element, whose oxide (MnO_2) is a valuable oxidizing agent.—**man-gan-ic** (mang-gan′ik), *a.* Of or containing manganese. See *manganous.* —**manganic acid,** an acid, H_2MnO_4, not known in the free state.—**man-ga-nif′er-ous** (-nif′ẹ-rus), *a.* [See *-ferous.*] Containing or yielding manganese.—**man′ga-nite** (-nīt), *n.* A native hydrated oxide of manganese, used in certain industrial processes; in *chem.*, any of a class of salts derived from certain hydroxides of manganese.—**man′ga-nous,** *a.* Containing manganese (in larger proportion than a corresponding manganic compound).

mange (mānj), *n.* [OF. *manjue*, itch, < *mangier* (F. *manger*), eat, < L. *manducare*, chew, E. *manducate.*] Any of various skin-diseases (esp. diseases due to parasitic mites) affecting animals and sometimes man, and characterized by loss of hair and by scabby eruptions.

man-gel=wur-zel (mang′gl-wėr′zl), *n.* [G. *mangelwurzel*, for *mangoldwurzel*, 'beet-root.'] A coarse variety of the common beet, *Beta vulgaris*, extensively cultivated as food for cattle, etc.

man-ger (mān′jėr), *n.* [OF. F. *mangeoire*, < L. *manducare*: see *mange.*] A box or trough, as in a stable, from which horses or cattle eat; the receptacle of this kind in which the infant Jesus was laid (see Luke, ii. 7); *naut.*, a small space at the forward end of a deck, divided off by a bulkhead or board to shut off any water entering by the hawes-holes.—**dog in the manger.** See under *dog*, *n.*

man-gi-ly (mān′ji-li), *adv.* In a mangy manner.—**man′gi-ness,** *n.* Mangy condition.

man-gle[1] (mang′gl), *n.* [D. *mangel*; ult. akin to E. *mangonel.*] A machine for smoothing or pressing cloth, household linen, etc., by means of rollers.—**man′gle**[1], *v. t.*; *-gled, -gling.* To smooth with a mangle.—**man′gler**[1], *n.*

man-gle[2] (mang′gl), *v. t.*; *-gled, -gling.* [AF. *mangler*, perhaps freq. < OF. *mahaignier*, E. *maim.*] To injure or disfigure (a person or animal, the body, etc.) by hacking or crushing strokes, violent collision, etc. (as, a corpse *mangled* in battle; "There in the ghastly pit . . . a body was found . . . *Mangled*, and flatten'd, and crush'd, and dinted into the ground," Tennyson's "Maud," i. 1. 2); lacerate badly, or to the point of being unrecognizable; more generally, to mar (anything) by cutting, hacking, etc. (as, to *mangle* meat in carving; a bench *mangled* by school-boys' knives); fig., to mar or spoil by clumsy or improper treatment or performance (as, to *mangle* a text in editing, or a part in acting; to *mangle* words by faulty pronunciation).—**man′gler**[2], *n.*

man-go (mang′gō), *n.*; pl. *-goes* or *-gos* (-gōz). [Pg. *manga*; from Tamil.] The oblong, slightly acid, edible fruit of a tropical anacardiaceous tree, *Mangifera indica*, being eaten when ripe, or preserved or pickled when green; also, the tree itself; also, a pickled green melon or other fruit.

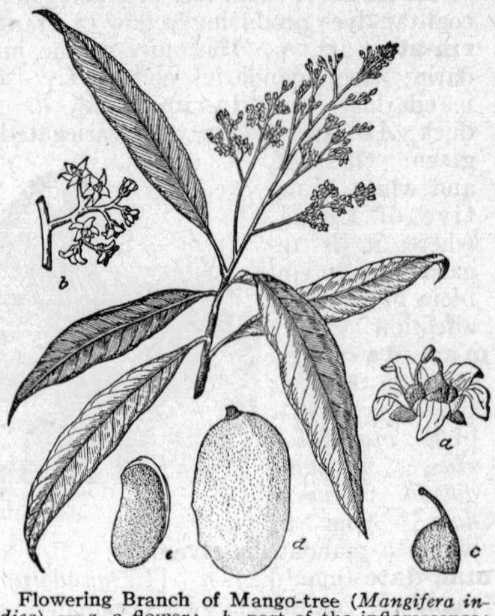

Flowering Branch of Mango-tree (*Mangifera indica*). — *a*, a flower; *b*, part of the inflorescence; *c*, the pistil; *d*, the fruit; *e*, the seed.

man-go-nel (mang′gō-nel), *n.* [OF. *mangonel* (F. *mangonneau*), dim. < ML. *manganum*, < Gr. μάγγανον, engine of war: cf. *mangle*[1].] A military engine formerly used for throwing stones, etc. See cut below.

man-go-steen (mang′gō-stēn), *n.* [Malay *mangustan.*] The juicy, edible fruit of an East Indian clusiaceous tree, *Garcinia mangostana*; also, the tree itself.

man-grove (mang′grōv), *n.* [Origin uncertain: cf. Sp. *mangle* and Malay *manggi-manggi*, mangrove.] Any tree or shrub of the tropical genus *Rhizophora*, the species of which are mostly low trees remarkable for a copious development of interlacing adventitious roots above the ground; also, any of various similar plants.

Mangonel.

man-gy (mān′ji), *a.*; compar. *mangier*, superl. *mangiest.* Having, due to, or resembling the mange; hence, squalid; shabby; also, contemptible or mean.

man-han-dle (man′han″dl), *v. t.*; *-dled, -dling.* To move by force of men, without mechanical appliances; also, to handle roughly (as, "If you worry me . . . I'll catch you and *manhandle* you, and you'll die": Kipling's "Light That Failed," iii.).

man=hat-er (man′hā″tėr), *n.* One who hates mankind; a misanthrope; sometimes, one who hates the male sex.

man-hole (man′hōl), *n.* A hole, usually with a cover, through which a man may enter a sewer, drain, steam-boiler, etc., as to make repairs.

man-hood (man′hůd), *n.* The state of being human; also, the state of being a man or adult male person; also, manly character (as, "Man . . . never deserves the name of *manhood* but in proportion as he is erect and independent": Godwin's "Caleb Williams," xxxi.); the possession of manly virtues; manliness; also, men collectively (as, the *manhood* of the nation).

man=hour (man′our), *n.* An hour of work by one man, used as an industrial time-unit. See *man-day.*

ma-ni-a (mā′ni-ạ̈), *n.*; pl. *manias.* [L., < Gr. μανία, madness, < μαίνεσθαι, rage, be mad.] A form of insanity characterized by great excitement, with or without delusions, and in its acute stage by great violence; hence, great excitement or enthusiasm; a vehement passion or desire; a rage or craze.—**ma′ni-ac** (-ak). [ML. *maniacus.*] **I.** *a.* Affected with mania; raving with madness; mad; frantic. **II.** *n.* A raving lunatic; a madman.—**ma-ni-a-cal** (mạ-nī'ạ-kạl), *a.* Of or pertaining to mania or a maniac; affected with mania.—**ma-ni'a-cal-ly,** *adv.*

Man-i-che-an, Man-i-chæ-an (man-i-kē'ạn). [LL. *Manichæus*, < LGr. Μανιχαῖος; from the name of the founder of the sect.] **I.** *a.* Of or pertaining to Mani or the Manicheans. See *Manichean, n.* **II.** *n.* An adherent of the religious system of the Persian teacher Mani or Manichæus (216?–276?), composed of Gnostic Christian, Buddhistic, Zoroastrian, and various other elements, the principal feature being a dualistic theology which represented a conflict between light and darkness and included belief in the inherent evil of matter.—**Man'i-chee** (-kē), *n.* A Manichean.—**Man'i-che-ism, Man'i-chæ-ism,** *n.* The doctrines of the Manicheans.

man-i-cure (man'i-kūr), *n.* [F. *manicure*, < L. *manus*, hand, + *curare*, care for: cf. *pedicure.*] One who makes a business of caring for the hands and finger-nails; also, professional care of the hands and finger-nails.—**man'i-cure,** *v. t.* or *i.*; *-cured, -curing.* To care for (the hands and finger-nails); perform the work of a manicure for (a person).—**man'i-cur-ist** (-kūr-ist), *n.* A manicure.

man-i-fest (man'i-fest), *a.* [L. *manifestus*, palpable, evident, plain.] Readily perceived by the eye or the understanding; evident; obvious; apparent; plain: as, "Neither is there any creature that is not *manifest* in his sight" (Heb. iv. 13); a *manifest* error or impossibility.—**man'i-fest,** *v. t.* [L. *manifestare*, < *manifestus.*] To make manifest to the eye or the understanding; show plainly, or reveal (as, "There is nothing hid, which shall not be *manifested*": Mark, iv. 22); evince or display (as, to *manifest* interest or ability); evidence, attest, or prove (as, "His dress . . . *manifested* the economy of its owner by the number and nature of its repairs": Cooper's "Spy," xxxv.); also, to record in a ship's manifest.—**man'i-fest,** *n.* [= F. *manifeste.*] A manifestation or indication (now rare); also, a manifesto†; also, a list of a ship's cargo, signed by the master, for the information and use of custom-house officers.

man-i-fes-tant (man-i-fes'tạnt), *n.* [= F. *manifestant.*] One who takes part in a public manifestation or demonstration.

man-i-fes-ta-tion (man″i-fes-tā'shọn), *n.* [= F. *manifestation*, < LL. *manifestatio(n-).*] The act of manifesting, or the state of being manifested; revelation; display; also, an instance or a means of manifesting; an indication or demonstration; specif., a public demonstration, as for political effect.

man-i-fest-ly (man'i-fest-li), *adv.* In a manifest manner; evidently.—**man'i-fest-ness,** *n.*

man-i-fes-to (man-i-fes'tō), *n.*; pl. *-toes* (-tōz). [It., = E. *manifest, n.*] A public declaration, as of a sovereign or government, or of any person or body of persons taking important action, making known intentions, objects, motives, etc.; a proclamation: as, "Orleans taken, the Huguenots proceeded to issue protestations and *manifestoes*" (Besant's "Coligny," viii.).

man-i-fold (man'i-fōld). [AS. *manigfeald*: see *many* and *-fold.*] **I.** *a.* Having many different parts, elements, features, forms, etc. (as, "the *manifold* wisdom of God," Eph. iii. 10; "a music strange and *manifold*," Tennyson's "Dying Swan," iii.); often (with a plural noun), of many kinds, numerous and varied, or multifarious (as, *manifold* duties; "attractions *manifold*," Wordsworth's "Excursion," i. 337); also, being such in many ways (archaic: as, a *manifold* traitor). **II.** *n.* That which is manifold; something having many different parts or features; a pipe with a number of inlets or outlets; also, a copy or facsimile, as of writing, such as is made by manifolding.—**man'i-fold,** *v. t.* To make manifold; multiply; esp., to make copies of (writing, etc.), as with carbon-paper.—**man'i-fold-er,** *n.* One who or that which manifolds; esp., a contrivance for making manifolds or copies, as of writing.—**man'i-fold-ly,** *adv.*—**man'i-fold-ness,** *n.*

man-i-hot (man'i-hot), *n.* [NL.; from Brazilian.] Any plant of the euphorbiaceous genus *Manihot*, comprising tall herbs and shrubs, native in tropical and subtropical America and cultivated elsewhere, as *M. manihot*, bitter cassava, and *M. glaziovii*, which yields a kind of caoutchouc. See *cassava.*

man-i-kin (man'i-kin), *n.* [MD. *manneken*, dim. of *man*, man: cf. *mannequin.*] A little man; a dwarf or pygmy; also, a model of the human body for teaching anatomy, demonstrating surgical operations, etc.; also, a lay-figure used by artists, tailors, etc. See also *manakin* and *mannequin.*

ma-nil-a, ma-nil-la (mạ-nil'ạ̈), *n.* [From *Manila*, capital of the Philippine Islands.] A fibrous material obtained from the leaves of *Musa textilis*, a Philippine plant of the banana genus: used for making ropes, fabrics, etc. Also called *Manila hemp.*—**manila paper,** a strong brown or buff paper made from manila; hence, a similar paper made from other material.

man-i-oc (man'i-ok), *n.* [= *manihot.*] Same as *cassava.*

man-i-ple (man'i-pl), *n.* [L. *manipulus*, handful, company of soldiers, < *manus*, hand, + *-pulus*, akin to *plere*, fill: see *full*¹.] A subdivision of the Roman legion, consisting of 120 or 60 men; *eccles.*, one of the eucharistic vestments, consisting of an ornamental band or strip worn on the left arm near the wrist.

ma-nip-u-lar (mạ-nip'ū-lạ̈r), *a.* [L. *manipularis*, < *manipulus*, E. *maniple.*] Of or pertaining to a Roman maniple of soldiers; also, less correctly, of or pertaining to manipulation or handling (as, "*manipular* operations": Bulwer-Lytton's "Caxtons," xi. 7).

ma-nip-u-late (mạ-nip'ū-lāt), *v. t.*; *-lated, -lating.* [Appar. < F. *manipuler*, manipulate (chemical or pharmaceutical substances, etc.), < *manipule*, handful, < L. *manipulus*: see *maniple.*] To treat or work (something) with the hands, as in order to bring it into a particular form or condition; operate upon by manual or mechanical means, as materials, etc.; in general, to handle, manage, or use, esp. with skill, in some process of treatment or performance (as, to *manipulate* the characters or incidents in a story; to *manipulate* resources to the best advantage); manage or influence by artful skill (as, to *manipulate* persons; to *manipulate* prices); adapt or change (accounts, figures, etc.) to suit one's purpose or advantage.—**ma-nip-u-la'tion** (-lā'shọn), *n.* [Cf. F. *manipulation.*] The act or art of manipulating; the state or fact of being manipulated; manual or mechanical treatment or operation; skilful or artful management; fraudulent adaptation, as to one's purpose or advantage.—**ma-nip'u-la-tive** (-lạ-tiv), *a.* Manipulatory.—**ma-nip'u-la-tor** (-lā-tọr), *n.*—**ma-nip'u-la-to-ry** (-lạ-tọ-ri), *a.* Of, pertaining to, or involving manipulation.

man-i-to, man-i-tou (man'i-tō, -tö), *n.* [Algonquian.] Among the Algonquian Indians, a good or evil spirit; a being or object of supernatural power. See Longfellow's "Hiawatha," xiv. 46, 52.

man-jak, man-jack (man'jak), *n.* [W. Ind.] A form of bitumen found in Barbados and elsewhere, used in the manufacture of varnish, for insulating electric cables, etc.

man-kind (man-kīnd'), *n.* The human race; human beings collectively; also (pron. man'kīnd), men, as distinguished from women (as, "Should all despair That have revolted wives, the tenth of *mankind* Would hang themselves": Shakspere's "Winter's Tale," i. 2. 199).

man-less (man'les), *a.* Having no man; without men; also, unmanly†; also, inhuman†.

man-like (man'līk), *a.* Resembling a man (as, "Under his forming hands a creature grew, *Man-like*, but different sex": Milton's "Paradise Lost," viii. 471); also, having qualities proper to a man as distinguished from a woman or child; also, belonging or proper to a man (as, *manlike* fortitude); manly.

man-ly (man'li), *a.*; compar. *manlier*, superl. *manliest.* Human†; also, possessing qualities proper to a man as distinguished from a woman or child; firm, strong, or independent in spirit; straightforward or honorable; of a woman, possessing qualities regarded as characteristic of a man (as, "My aunt was a lady of large frame, strong mind, and great resolution . . . a very *manly* woman": Irving's "Tales of a Traveler," i. 4); also, pertaining to or befitting a man (as, *manly* sports; *manly* resolution).—**man'li-ly,** *adv.*—**man'li-ness,** *n.*—**man'ly,** *adv.* In a manly manner. [Obs. or archaic.]

man-na (man′ạ), *n.* [L., < Gr. μάννα, < Heb. *mān*.] The food miraculously supplied the children of Israel in the wilderness (see Ex. xvi. 14–36); hence, divine or spiritual food; also, anything likened to the manna of the Israelites, as mental sustenance (as, "To some coffee-house I stray For news, the *manna* of a day": M. Green's "The Spleen"); in *phar.*, a sweetish exudation from a species of ash, *Fraxinus ornus*, of southern Europe, used as a mild laxative; also, a similar product obtained from other plants.

man-ne-quin (man′ẹ-kin, F. màn-kaṅ), *n.* [F.; from Dutch: cf. *manikin*.] A manikin or lay-figure; also, a young woman employed by a dressmaking establishment to put on gowns, etc., when shown to customers, or to wear them for exhibition in public places.

man-ner (man′ėr), *n.* [OF. *maniere* (F. *manière*), appar. orig. 'way of handling,' < L. *manuaria*, fem. of *manuarius*, of or for the hand, < *manus*, hand.] Way of doing, being done, or happening (as, to act or speak in a strange *manner*; the trouble arose in this *manner*); mode of action, procedure, or occurrence; fashion; often, characteristic or customary way of doing (as, houses built in the Mexican *manner*); usage or custom; *pl.*, prevailing customs, modes of living, etc., as of a people, a social class, or a period (as, "I . . . resolved to snatch this opportunity of seeing the *manners* of other nations," Johnson's "Rasselas," viii.; a study of contemporary *manners*; a comedy of *manners*); also, *sing.*, a person's way of acting or behaving, as in intercourse with others (as, "Her *manner* made me sensible that we stood upon no real terms of confidence": Hawthorne's "Blithedale Romance," xix.); outward bearing, or deportment; *pl.*, ways of behaving or deporting one's self, esp. with reference to polite standards (as, to have the *manners* of a tomboy; good or bad *manners*; courtly *manners*); esp., good or polite ways of behaving or deporting one's self (as, to leave a piece on the dish, for *manners*; have you no *manners?*); also, characteristic style in art, literature, or the like (as, drawings after the *manner* of Dürer; verses in the *manner* of Spenser); hence, mannered style, or mannerism; also, kind or sort (as, all *manner* of things; "What *manner* of man art thou?" Coleridge's "Ancient Mariner," vii.); also, nature, character, or guise (obs. or archaic).—**in a manner,** after a fashion; in one way or sense: as, "The bread is *in a manner* common" (1 Sam. xxi. 5).—**to make one's manners,** to show one's good manners by a bow, curtsy, or the like: as, "good children who . . . *made their manners* when they came into her house" (Mrs. Stowe's "Oldtown Folks," v.). [Prov.]—**to the manner born,** accustomed from birth to some way of doing, state of affairs, etc.: a Shaksperian expression: as, "Though I am native here And *to the manner born*" ("Hamlet," i. 4. 15).

män-ner-chor (men′ėr-kōr), *n.*; pl. *männerchöre* (-kė″rē). [G., 'chorus of men.'] A German male chorus or singing-society.

man-nered (man′ėrd), *a.* Having manners (as specified: as, ill-*mannered*); also, characterized by mannerism; affected.

man-ner-ism (man′ėr-izm), *n.* Marked or excessive adherence to a characteristic manner, as of acting, speaking, literary treatment, etc.; also, a habitual peculiarity of manner (as, "the same little dainty *mannerisms*, the same quick turns and movements": C. Brontë's "Villette," xxv.).—**man′ner-ist,** *n.* One addicted to mannerism.—**man-ner-is′tic,** *a.*

man-ner-less (man′ėr-les), *a.* Without (good) manners; unmannerly.

man-ner-ly (man′ėr-li), *a.* Having or showing (good) manners; courteous; polite: as, "Here is a *mannerly* forbearance" (Shakspere's "1 Henry VI.," ii. 4. 19).—**man′ner-li-ness,** *n.*—**man′ner-ly,** *adv.* With (good) manners; courteously; politely: as, "When we have supp'd, We'll *mannerly* demand thee of thy story" (Shakspere's "Cymbeline," iii. 6. 92).

man-nie (man′i), *n.* [Dim. of *man*.] Little man: often applied to a little boy. [Esp. Sc.]

man′ni-kin, *n.* See *manikin*.

man-nish (man′ish), *a.* Human†; also, characteristic of or natural to a man or adult male person (as, "A mob of boys, Childish in mischief only . . . Else of a *mannish* growth": Cowper's "Tirocinium," 208); also, resembling a man, as in appearance, dress, actions, etc. (as, a *mannish* woman); affecting or simulating manhood (as, a *mannish* youth); imitative or suggestive of what is proper to a man (as, *mannish* dress; a *mannish* stride); masculine.—**man′nish-ly,** *adv.*—**man′nish-ness,** *n.*

man-nite (man′īt), *n.* [See *manna*.] In *chem.*, a white, sweetish crystalline compound, of the alcohol class, occurring in three optically different forms, the common one being found in the manna of the ash *Fraxinus ornus*, and in other plants.—**man-nit-ic** (ma-nit′ik), *a.*—**man-ni-tol** (man′i-tol or -tōl), *n.* Mannite.—**man-nose** (man′ōs), *n.* In *chem.*, a sweetish compound of the sugar class, occurring in three optically different forms, and produced by the oxidation of mannite.

ma-nœu′ver, ma-nœu′vre, etc. See *maneuver*, etc.

man=of=the=earth (man′ọv-thẹ-ėrth′), *n.* The wild potato-vine, *Ipomœa pandurata*, of the eastern U. S.: named from the appearance often presented by the root.

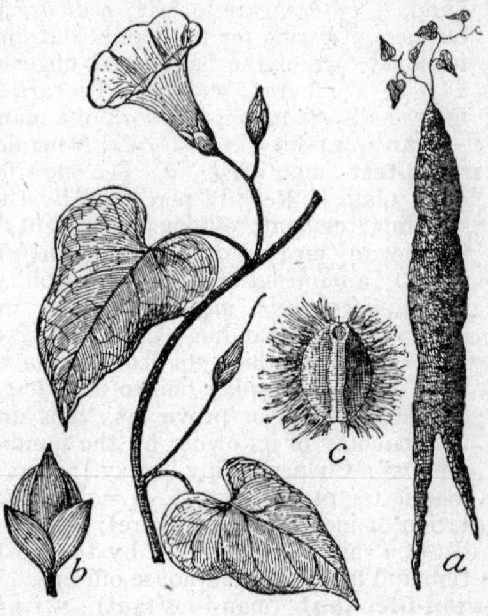

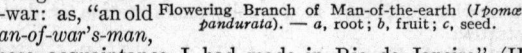

Flowering Branch of Man-of-the-earth (*Ipomœa pandurata*). — *a*, root; *b*, fruit; *c*, seed.

man=of=war (man′ọv-wâr′), *n.*; pl. *men-*. A ship equipped for war; an armed ship of a recognized navy.—**man=of=war bird,** a frigate-bird.—**Portuguese man=of=war.** See under *Portuguese*, *a.*—**man′=of=war's′=man** (-wârz′mạn), *n.*; pl. *-men*. A sailor serving on a man-of-war: as, "an old *man-of-war's-man*, whose acquaintance I had made in Rio de Janeiro" (H. Melville's "Omoo," i.).

ma-nom-e-ter (mạ-nom′e-tėr), *n.* [F. *manomètre*, < Gr. μανός, thin, rare, + μέτρον, measure.] An instrument for determining the pressure of gases or vapors; also, one for determining blood-pressure.—**man-o-met-ric, man-o-met-ri-cal** (man-ọ-met′rik, -ri-kạl), *a.* Pertaining to or obtained with the manometer; pertaining to the measurement of gaseous pressure.—**manometric flame,** an appearance produced by the reflection in a rotating mirror of a gas-flame which can be made to vary in size by the action of sound-waves.

man-or (man′ọr), *n.* [OF. *maneir* (F. *manoir*), noun use of *maneir*, inf., dwell, < L. *manere*, remain: cf. *mansion*.] A mansion†; also, the mansion of a lord with the land pertaining to it†; also, in England, a landed estate or territorial unit, orig. of the nature of a feudal lordship, consisting of a lord's demesne and of lands within which he has the right to exercise certain privileges and exact certain fees, etc.; in colonial America, a tract of land within which the proprietor had similar rights.—**man′or=house,** *n.* The house or mansion of the lord of a manor: as, "It was three stories high, of proportions not vast, though considerable; a gentleman's *manor-house*, not a nobleman's seat" (C. Brontë's "Jane Eyre," xi.).—**ma-no-ri-al** (mạ-nō′ri-ạl), *a.* Of, pertaining to, or constituting a manor: as, *manorial* rights; a *manorial* estate.—**man′or=place,** *n.* Same as *manor-house*.

man=pow-er (man′pou″ėr), *n.* The power of a man; specif., a unit assumed to be equal to the rate at which a man can do mechanical work, commonly taken as one tenth of a horse-power; also, rate or work in terms of this unit; also, a device for utilizing the force of a man, as in driving machinery; also, power in terms of men available or required (as, the *man-power* of an army).

man=rope (man′rōp), *n.* *Naut.*, a rope placed at the side of a gangway, ladder, or the like, to serve as a rail.

man-sard (man′särd), *n.* [F. *mansarde*; from François *Mansard* (or *Mansart*) (1598–1666), French architect.] A form of curb-roof the lower slope of which approaches the vertical and usually contains dormer-windows, while the upper slope is less inclined and commonly more or less flat (also called *mansard roof*); also, the story under such a roof; a garret.

Mansard Roof. — Château of Maisons-Laffitte, France, by François Mansart.

manse (mans), *n.* [ML. *mansa*, dwelling, orig. pp. fem. of L. *manere*, remain: cf. *mansion*.] The dwelling of a landholder with the land attached†; also, an ecclesiastical residence; now, esp., the house of the minister of a parish in Scotland; sometimes, a parsonage elsewhere.

man=ser-vant (man′sėr″vạnt), *n.*; pl. *men-servants*. A male servant.

man-sion (man′shọn), *n.* [OF. *mansion*, < L. *mansio(n-)*, a remaining, place of abode, dwelling, < *manere*, remain: cf. *manor* and *manse*.] The act of remaining†; stay† or abode†; also, a place of abode (archaic: as, "On whose [trees'] high branches . . . The birds of broadest wing their *mansions* form," Pope's tr. Homer's "Odyssey," v.); sometimes, a separate lodging or apartment, as in a house (often in *pl.*: archaic); also, a manor-house; now, esp., an imposing or stately residence (as, "country houses — not merely houses in the country, but *mansions*": W. Churchill's "Modern Chronicle," i. 6); also, any building or structure serving as a habitation† (as, "the village preacher's modest *mansion*": Goldsmith's "Deserted Village," 140); also, in Oriental and medieval astronomy, each of twenty-eight divisions of the ecliptic occupied by the moon on successive days ('lunar mansion'); in *astrol.*, a house (see *house*², *n.*). —**man′sion=house,** *n.* A dwelling-house†; also, a manor-house; hence, a mansion; a large, imposing house; also, an official residence, now esp. [*cap.*] that of the Lord Mayor of London.—**man′sion-ry** (-ri), *n.* Mansions. [Poetic.]

man-slaugh-ter (man′slâ″tėr), *n.* The killing of a human being by a human being; homicide; human slaughter; specif., in *law*, the killing of another person unlawfully but without malice.

man-slay-er (man′slā″ėr), *n.* One who kills a human being; a homicide.—**man′slay″ing,** *n.* and *a.*

man=stop-ping (man′stop″ing), *a.* *Milit.*, noting or pertaining to a bullet which, because of its force, expanding quality, or the like, will stop the advance of a soldier.

man-suete (man-swēt′), *a.* [L. *mansuetus*, pp. of *mansuescere*, make tame, < *manus*, hand, + *suescere*, accustom.] Tame; gentle; mild. [Archaic.]—**man′sue-tude** (-swẹ-tūd), *n.* [L. *mansuetudo*.] Tameness; gentleness; mildness: as, "our Lord Himself, made all of *mansuetude*" (Browning's "Ring and the Book," viii.). [Archaic.]

man-swear (man′swãr), *v. i.* or *t.*; pret. *-swore*, pp. *-sworn*, ppr. *-swearing*. [AS. *mānswerian*, < *mān*, wickedness, + *swerian*, swear.] To perjure (one's self): now chiefly in *mansworn*, *pp.* [Archaic or Sc. and north. Eng.]—**man′sworn** (-swôrn), *p. a.* Perjured; forsworn: as, "Defend yourself against the imputation . . . of being a *mansworn* disgrace to the rolls of chivalry!" (Scott's "Castle Dangerous," xx.). [Archaic or Sc. and north. Eng.]

man-ta (man′tạ̈), *n.* [Sp., < ML. *mantum*, cloak: cf. *mantle*.] In Spain and Spanish America, a cloak or wrap, esp., as in South America, a kind of wrap worn by women; *milit.*, a mantelet, or movable shelter formerly used to protect besiegers (as, "Seizing their *mantas*, or portable bulwarks, and their other defenses, they made a gallant assault": Irving's "Conquest of Granada," xxix.).

man-teau (man′tō, F. mäṅ-tō), *n.*; pl. *manteaus* (man′tōz), F. *manteaux* (mäṅ-tō). [F.: see *mantle*.] A mantle or cloak, esp. one worn by women; also, a kind of gown, open in front to show the petticoat, formerly worn by women.

man-tel (man′tl), *n.* [Var. of *mantle*.] The more or less ornamental structure above and about a fireplace, usually having a shelf or projecting ledge above the fireplace; also, the shelf.

man-tel-et (man′tẹ-let), *n.* [OF. F., dim. of OF. *mantel*, E. *mantle*.] A short mantle; *milit.*, a movable shelter formerly used to protect besiegers (as, "covering themselves . . . with bucklers and *mantelets*, to protect them from the deadly shower": Irving's "Conquest of Granada," v.); now, any of various bullet-proof shelters or screens, as to protect men working a gun.

man-tel-let-ta (man-tẹ-let′ạ̈), *n.* [It., dim. of *mantello*, < L. *mantellum*, E. *mantle*.] In the *Rom. Cath. Ch.*, a sleeveless vestment of silk or woolen stuff reaching to the knees, worn by cardinals, bishops, abbots, and other dignitaries.

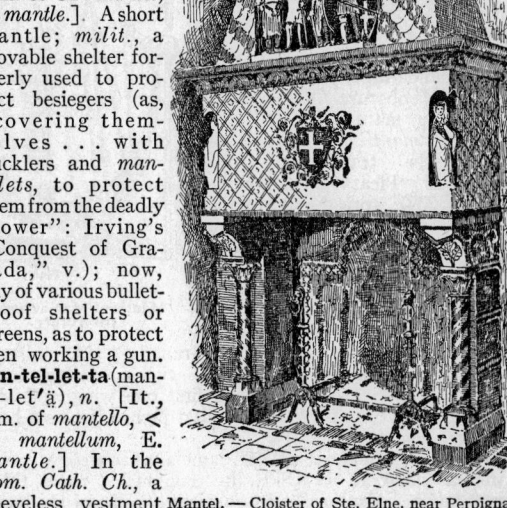

Mantel. — Cloister of Ste. Elne, near Perpignan, France; 13th century.

man-tel-piece (man′tl-pēs), *n.* [See *mantel*.] A mantel, above and about a fireplace; a chimneypiece; also, a mantel-shelf.—**man′tel-shelf,** *n.* The shelf of a mantel.—**man′tel-tree,** *n.* A beam, stone, or arch forming the lintel of a fireplace; also, a mantelpiece.

man-tic (man′tik), *a.* [Gr. μαντικός, < μάντις: see *mantis*.] Of or pertaining to divination; having the power of divination; divinatory; prophetic.—**man′ti-cal-ly,** *adv.*

man-til-la (man-til′ạ̈), *n.* [Sp., dim. of *manta*: see *manta*.] A short mantle or light cape; also, a veil or head-covering falling down over the shoulders, as worn by women in Spain, Mexico, etc.

man-tis (man′tis), *n.*; pl. *mantises*, L. *mantes* (-tēz). [NL., < Gr. μάντις, diviner, prophet, kind of insect, < μαίνεσθαι, rage, be mad, be moved by divine frenzy.] Any of the carnivorous orthopterous insects constituting the genus *Mantis* or the family *Mantidæ*, which have a long prothorax, with the fore legs peculiarly modified as grasping-organs for raptorial purposes, and which are remarkable for their ferocity, pugnacity, and tenacity of life, and for their manner of holding the fore legs doubled up as if in prayer, an attitude assumed for defense and aggression.

Mantis (*Mantis religiosa*), adult male; reduced one fourth.

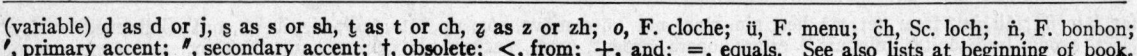

man-tis-sa (man-tis′ạ̈), *n.* [L., an addition, makeweight; from Etruscan.] In *math.*, the decimal part of a logarithm. Cf. *characteristic*, *n.*

man-tle (man′tl), *n.* [OF. *mantel* (F. *manteau*), < L. *mantellum*, *mantelum*, cloak, cloth, napkin (cf. *mantele*, *mantelium*, towel, napkin, table-cloth), appar. < *manus*, hand, + *tela*, web.] A loose, sleeveless cloak (see cut on following page); hence, something that covers, envelops, or conceals (as, "A thin *mantle* of snow made the woods gray": G. W. Cable's "John March, Southerner," xiv.); a covering;

Mantle of Man-at-arms, 15th century.

specif., a chemically prepared, incombustible network hood for a gas-jet, which, when the jet is lighted, becomes incandescent and gives a brilliant light; in *zoöl.*, the pallium of a mollusk or brachiopod; in *ornith.*, of a bird, the back and folded wings taken together.—**man′-tle,** *v.*; *-tled, -tling.* **I.** *tr.* To cover with or as with a mantle (as, "a small stagnant stream, *mantled* over with bright green mosses": Scott's "Guy Mannering," xxiii.); envelop; conceal or obscure. **II.** *intr.* To serve as a mantle (as, "O'er his shoulder, *mantling* to his knee, Flow'd the transparent robe": Akenside's "Pleasures of Imagination," ii. 232); spread like a mantle, as a blush over the face (as, "A crimson blush *mantled* in her cheek": Wiseman's "Fabiola," i. 5); hence, of the face, to flush (as, "Many a fair cheek was blanched with woe, which had lately *mantled* with secret admiration": Irving's "Conquest of Granada," xiii.); also, of a liquid, to be or become covered with a coating; foam; also, in *falconry*, to spread out first one wing and then the other over the corresponding outstretched leg, as a hawk does by way of relief.

mant-let (mant′let), *n.* *Milit.*, same as *mantelet.*

man-tra (man′trạ), *n.* [Skt., lit. 'thought,' < *man-*, think: see *mind²*.] [Also *cap.*] In *Sanskrit lit.*, one of the sacred texts or passages, chiefly metrical, of the nature of hymns, prayers, or (later) magical formulas, constituting the chief part of each of the four Vedas.

man-tu-a (man′ṭū-ạ), *n.* [Corruption of *manteau.*] A kind of loose gown formerly worn by women; also, a mantle. —**man′tu-a=mak″er,** *n.* A maker of mantuas, and hence a dressmaker: as, "in consultation with milliners and *mantua-makers*, preparing for the occasion, at which she made her appearance in a full suit of damask" (Smollett's "Humphry Clinker," Aug. 8). [Archaic.]

Man-tu-an (man′ṭū-ạn). **I.** *a.* Of or pertaining to the town or the province of Mantua, in northern Italy: as, the *Mantuan* swan (the Latin poet Virgil). **II.** *n.* A native or inhabitant of Mantua, as Virgil ('the Mantuan').

man-u-al (man′ū-ạl), *a.* [OF. F. *manuel*, < L. *manualis* (as n., ML. *manuale*), < *manus*, hand.] Of or pertaining to the hand or hands; performed, made, operated, or used by the hand or hands; also, of the nature of a manual, or handy book.—**manual training,** the training of pupils in the various manual crafts and arts by actual practice, as in a school; esp., the training of the hands of the young, as well as their minds, in the schools, by practice in various industrial crafts, domestic arts, etc., along with the usual literary and scientific instruction, as a method or system of education.—**man′u-al,** *n.* A small or handy book, esp. one designed as a textbook or for ready reference; also, an organ keyboard played with the hands; *milit.*, a prescribed exercise in the handling of a rifle, etc.—**man′u-al-ly,** *adv.*

man-u-duc-tion (man-ū-duk′shọn), *n.* [ML. *manuductio(n-)*, < L. *manu*, abl. of *manus*, hand, + *ducere*, lead.] A leading by or as by the hand; guidance. [Now rare.]—**man-u-duc′to-ry** (-tọ-ri), *a.*

man-u-fac-to-ry (man-ū-fak′tọ-ri), *n.*; pl. *-ries* (-riz). [See *manufacture.*] Something manufactured†; also, manufacturing†; also, a building or establishment in which goods are manufactured; a factory.

man-u-fac-ture (man-ū-fak′ṭūr), *n.* [F. *manufacture*, < L. *manu*, abl. of *manus*, hand, + *facere*, make.] The making of goods or wares by manual labor or by machinery, esp. on a large scale; also, a particular form of productive industry (as, the linen *manufacture*); also, any article or material manufactured; also, a manufacturing establishment† (as, "His linen *manufacture* was . . . in a prosperous way": Smollett's "Humphry Clinker," Sept. 6).—**man-u-fac′ture,** *v. t.*; *-tured, -turing.* To make or produce by hand or machinery, esp. on a large scale; also, to work up (material) into form for use; in fig. use (in disparagement), to produce as if by mere mechanical industry; produce artificially; invent fictitiously.—**man-u-fac′tur-er** (-ṭūr-ėr), *n.* One who manufactures; formerly, a factory operative† (as, "A shilling a day was the pay to which the English *manufacturer* then [in 1680] thought himself entitled": Macaulay's "Hist. of Eng.," iii.); now, one who maintains or conducts a manufacturing establishment.

man-u-mis-sion (man-ū-mish′ọn), *n.* [L. *manumissio(n-)*.] The act of manumitting, or the fact of being manumitted; formal release from slavery.

man-u-mit (man-ū-mit′), *v. t.*; *-mitted, -mitting.* [L. *manumittere*, < *manu*, abl. of *manus*, hand, + *mittere*, send.] To release from slavery or servitude; set free: as, "A former mistress of hers had become a Christian, and had *manumitted* all her other slaves" (Wiseman's "Fabiola," i. 12).—**man-u-mit′ter,** *n.*

ma-nure (mạ-nūr′), *v. t.*; *-nured, -nuring.* [OF. *manuvrer*, *manovrer*, work by hand (F. *manœuvrer*, manipulate, work, maneuver), < *manuevre*, hand-work, manual labor: see *maneuver, n.*, and cf. *maneuver, v.*] To cultivate or till (land)†; also, to treat (land) with fertilizing matter; apply manure to; also, to serve as a fertilizer or manure for.—**ma-nure′,** *n.* Any natural or artificial substance for fertilizing the soil, esp. dung or refuse of the stable, etc.—**ma-nu′ri-al** (-nū′ri-ạl), *a.* Of, pertaining to, or serving for manure.—**ma-nur′er** (-nūr′ėr), *n.*

ma-nus (mā′nus), *n.*; pl. *manus.* [L., hand.] In *anat.*, the distal segment of the fore limb of a vertebrate, including the carpus and the fore foot or hand.

man-u-script (man′ū-skript). [L. *manu*, abl. of *manus*, hand, + *scriptus*, pp. of *scribere*, write.] **I.** *a.* Written by hand (not printed). **II.** *n.* A book, document, etc., written by hand, esp. one so written before the introduction of printing; also, an author's copy of his work written by hand or typewritten; also, writing, as distinguished from print.—**man′u-script-al,** *a.*

man-ward (man′wạrd), *adv.* and *a.* Toward man.

Manx (mangks). **I.** *a.* Of or pertaining to the Isle of Man, in the Irish Sea, or its inhabitants or their language: as, the *Manx* cat (a tailless variety of the domestic cat). **II.** *n.* The inhabitants of the Isle of Man (construed as *pl.*); also, the native (Celtic) language of the inhabitants.—**Manx′man** (-mạn), *n.*; pl. *-men.*

man-y (men′i). [AS. *manig* = D. *menig* = G. *manch* = Goth. *manags*, many.] **I.** *a.*; compar. *more*, superl. *most.* Being one of a large number (now only with *a* or *an* following, or in certain archaic or colloquial expressions: as, *many* a day; *many*'s the day that); also, constituting a large number (as, *many* people; *many* years ago); numerous; also, sometimes, relatively numerous (after *as, so, too*, or *how*: as, two may be too *many*). **II.** *n.* A great or considerable number (often followed by a noun with *of* expressed or understood: as, "There were a vast *many* persons who . . . were heretics," J. H. Newman's "Callista," ii.); also, as a collective plural, many persons or things (as, "*Many* be called, but few chosen": Mat. xx. 16); often, many individuals of a body or class specified.—**the many,** the multitude.—**man′y=head′ed,** *a.* Having many heads: as, the *many-headed* beast or monster (fig., the people or populace).—**man′y-plies** (-plīz), *n. sing.* or *pl.* [See *ply, n.*] The omasum: so called from the many plies or folds of its membrane.—**man′y=sid′ed** (-sī′ded), *a.* Having many sides; fig., having many aspects, capabilities, etc. (as, a *many-sided* man).—**man′y=sid′ed-ness,** *n.*

man-za-ni-ta (man-zạ-nē′tạ), *n.* [Sp., dim. of *manzana*, apple: see *manchineel.*] Any of various shrubs of the ericaceous genus *Arctostaphylos*, of the western U. S.

Ma-o-ri (mä′ọ-ri or mou′ri), *n.*; pl. *-ris* or *-ri.* A member of the native brown race of New Zealand; also, its language.

map (map), *n.* [OF. *mappe*, < ML. *mappa* (*mundi*), map (of the world), L. *mappa*, napkin, cloth.] A representation, usually on a flat surface, of a part or the whole of the earth's surface, the heavens, or a heavenly body; hence, a map-like representation of anything.—**map,** *v. t.*; *mapped, mapping.* To represent or delineate in or as in a map; hence, to sketch or plan (often with *out*: as, "I set to work to *map* out a new career," Mark Twain's "Life on the Mississippi," v.).

ma-ple (mā′pl), *n.* [AS., in *mapeltrēow*, maple-tree.] Any tree of the genus *Acer*, of the north temperate zone, species of which are valued for shade or ornament, for their wood, or for their sap, from which a finely flavored syrup ('maple syrup') and a variety of sugar ('maple sugar') are obtained by evaporation; also, the wood of any such tree.—**ma′ple=leaf,** *n.* The leaf of the maple: used as the emblem of Canada.

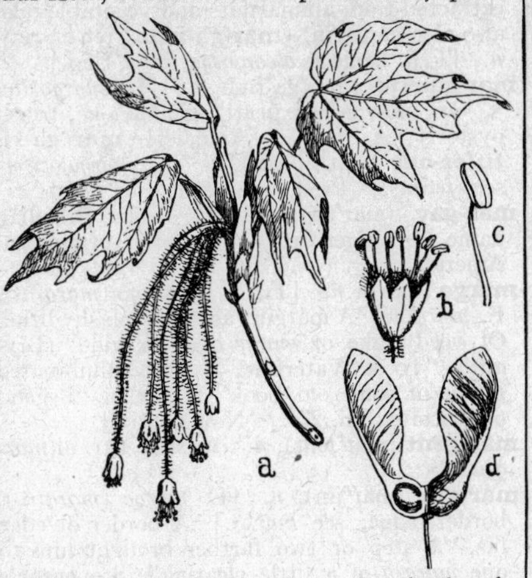

Sugar-maple (*Acer saccharum*). — *a*, flowering branch; *b*, sterile flower; *c*, stamen; *d*, fruit with one carpel cut open to show the seed.

map-per (map′ėr), *n.* [See *map*.] One who maps; a maker of maps.—**map′per-y,** *n.* The making of maps.—**map′-pist,** *n.* A maker of maps.—**map′py,** *a.* Map-like.

mar (mär), *v. t.*; *marred, marring.* [AS. *merran, mierran*, hinder, waste, = OHG. *marrjan*, hinder, = Icel. *merja*, bruise, crush, = Goth. *marzjan*, offend.] To hinder, or interfere with (obs. or prov.); also, to damage or impair; disfigure (as, "hideously *marred* about the face": H. Melville's "Moby-Dick," x.); deface; spoil or ruin (as, "Grant us felicity . . . nor let our sweet delight Be *marred* by aught": W. Morris's "Jason," ii. 310).—**mar,** *n.* Something that mars; a blemish; a drawback.

mar-a-bou (mar′ạ-bö), *n.* [F. *marabout*, orig. a Mohammedan marabout: see *marabout*[2].] Either of two large storks, *Leptoptilus crumenifer* of Africa, and *L. argala* (adjutant-bird) of the East Indies, having under the wings and tail soft, downy feathers that are used in millinery and for making a fur-like trimming or material; also, one of the feathers, or the trimming or material made of them; also, a peculiarly white kind of raw silk. Also **mar′a-bout**[1] (-bö).

mar-a-bout[2] (mar′ạ-böt), *n.* [F. *marabout*, < Pg. *marabuto*, < Ar. *murābit*, marabout: cf. *maravedi*.] In northern Africa, one of a class of Mohammedan holy men venerated as saints and exercising great influence in religious and secular affairs (as, "a little old Turk, poorly dressed like a *marabout* or santon of the desert," Scott's "Talisman," xx.: sometimes *cap.*); also, the tomb of such a holy man, serving as a shrine.

Ma-rah (mā′rạ or mãr′ạ̈), *n.* [From *Marah* (Heb. *mārāh*, bitter), place where the Israelites in their wanderings found only bitter water: see Ex. xv. 23.] A well or stream of bitter water; hence [*l. c.*], bitter water: in fig. uses: as, "The wasting famine of the heart they fed, And slaked its thirst with *marah* of their tears" (Longfellow's "Jewish Cemetery at Newport").

mar-a-na-tha (mar-ạ-nā′thạ̈). See *anathema*.

mar-an-ta-ceous (mar-an-tā′shius), *a.* [NL. *Maranta*, the typical genus; named from B. *Maranta* (16th century), Italian physician.] Belonging to the *Marantaceæ*, or arrowroot family of plants.

ma-ran-tic (mạ-ran′tik), *a.* [Gr. μαραντικός, < μαραίνειν, quench, waste.] In *pathol.*, pertaining to or associated with marasmus.

mar-as-chi-no (mar-ạs-kē′nō), *n.* [It., < *marasca, amarasca*, kind of cherry, < *amaro*, < L. *amarus*, bitter.] A cordial or liqueur distilled from a small black Dalmatian cherry.

ma-ras-mus (mạ-raz′mus), *n.* [NL., < Gr. μαρασμός, < μαραίνειν, quench, waste.] In *pathol.*, a wasting of the body; gradual loss of flesh and strength, as from malnutrition, old age, etc., rather than from actual disease.—**ma-ras′mic,** *a.*

Ma-ra-thi (mạ-rä′tẹ̄), *n.* Same as *Mahratti*.

mar-a-thon (mar′ạ-thọn), *n.* [From the feat of the Greek runner who in 490 B.C. bore the news of victory from *Marathon* to Athens, some 20 miles away.] A long-distance race, esp. a foot-race of about 26 miles.—**mar′a-thon-er,** *n.*

Mar-a-tho-ni-an (mar-ạ-thō′ni-ạn), *a.* Of or pertaining to Marathon, in Greece, or the battle fought there in 490 B.C., in which the Athenians overcame the Persians.

ma-raud (mạ-râd′), *v.* [F. *marauder*, < *maraud*, rogue, vagabond; origin uncertain.] **I.** *intr.* To rove in quest of plunder; make a raid for booty. **II.** *tr.* To rove over or raid for plunder: as, "The tract of country they intended to *maraud* was far in the Moorish territories" (Irving's "Conquest of Granada," xii.).—**ma-raud′,** *n.* The action of marauding; a marauding expedition, or raid for booty (as, "They were still liable to the *marauds* of the Blackfeet": Irving's "Captain Bonneville," xii.).—**ma-raud′er,** *n.* One who marauds, roves in quest of plunder, or makes raids for booty.

Marauder. A U. S. medium bomber (Martin).

mar-a-ve-di (mar-ạ-vā′di), *n.* [Sp. *maravedí*, < Ar. *Murābitīn*, the Moorish dynasty of the Almoravides (11th and 12th centuries), pl. of *murābit*, E. *marabout*[2].] A gold coin struck by the Moors in Spain; also, an obsolete Spanish copper coin worth about one third of a U. S. cent.

Obverse. Reverse.
Moorish Maravedi.

mar-ble (mär′bl). [OF. F. *marbre*, < L. *marmor*, < Gr. μάρμαρος, marble, akin to μαρμαίρειν, sparkle.] **I.** *n.* Limestone in a more or less crystalline state and capable of taking a polish, occurring in a wide range of colors and variegations, and much used in sculpture and architecture; a variety of this stone; hence, something resembling this stone in hardness, coldness, smoothness, etc.; also, a piece of this stone, esp. a sculptured or inscribed piece; a work of art in it; also, a little ball of stone, baked clay, glass, etc., used in a children's game; *pl.* (construed as *sing.*), the game itself; also, *sing.*, a marbled appearance or pattern; marbling. **II.** *a.* Consisting of marble; also, like marble, as being hard, cold, unfeeling, etc. (as, "that seeming *marble* heart": Byron's "Childe Harold," ii. 33); also, of variegated or mottled color; marbled.—**mar′ble,** *v. t.*; *-bled, -bling.* To color or stain like variegated marble: as, "the horizon bounded by a propitious sky, azure, *marbled* with pearly white" (C. Brontë's "Jane Eyre," xi.).—**mar′ble-ize,** *v. t.*; *-ized, -izing.* To marble.—**mar′bler,** *n.*—**mar′bling,** *n.* The act, process, or art of coloring or staining in imitation of variegated marble; also, an appearance like that of variegated marble.—**mar′bly,** *a.* Marble-like.

marc (märk), *n.* [F., < *marcher*, tread, press: see *march*[2].] The refuse which remains after pressing fruit, esp. grapes.

mar-ca-site (mär′kạ-sīt), *n.* [= F. *marcassite*, < ML. *marcasita*; said to be from Ar.] Formerly, any of the crystallized forms of iron pyrites, much used in the 18th century for ornaments; a specimen or ornament of this substance; in recent use, white iron pyrites, a native iron disulphide, FeS_2, similar to and of the same composition as pyrite or ordinary pyrites, but of lower specific gravity and crystallizing in the orthorhombic system.

mar-cel (mär-sel′), *v. t.*; *-celled, -celling.* [From *Marcel*, a French hair-dresser who introduced the process.] To wave (the hair) in a particular style by means of special irons, producing the effect of regular, continuous waves extending over the head.—**mar-cel′,** *n.* A marcelling or a marcelled condition of the hair.—**mar-cel′ler,** *n.*—**Mar-cel′ wave.** The wave produced in the hair by the process of marcelling.

mar-ces-cent (mär-ses′ẹnt), *a.* [L. *marcescens* (*-ent-*), ppr. of *marcescere*, wither, < *marcere*, wither, droop.] In *bot.*, withering but not falling off, as a part of a plant.—**mar-ces'cence,** *n.*

march[1] (märch), *n.* [OF. F. *marche*; from Teut., and akin to E. *mark*[2].] A boundary or border; esp., a border, or a tract of land along a border, of a country (as, "Those low and barren tracts were the outlying *marches* of the empire": Motley's "Dutch Republic," Introd., v.); a frontier; specif., *pl.*, the border districts between England and Scotland, or England and Wales.—**march**[1], *v. i.* To touch at the border; border: with *upon, with,* etc.

march[2] (märch), *v.* [F. *marcher*, walk, march, go, progress, earlier (OF. *marchier*), tread, trample; perhaps < L. *marcus*, hammer.] **I.** *intr.* To walk with regular and measured tread, as soldiers; advance in step in an organized body; also, to walk in a stately or deliberate manner (as, "Miss Ophelia *marched* straight to her own chamber": Mrs. Stowe's "Uncle Tom's Cabin," xxv.); hence, in general, to proceed; advance. **II.** *tr.* To cause (soldiers, etc.) to march; cause (a person) to go somewhere at one's command and under one's guidance; also, to traverse in marching.—**march**[2], *n.* [F. *marche.*] The action, or an act or course, of marching; in general, advance, forward movement, or progress (as, "We may resume The *march* of our existence," Byron's "Childe Harold," iii. 98; the *march* of time); also, the distance traversed in a single course of marching; also, a manner of marching, as in slow or quick time; also, a piece of music with a rhythm suited to accompany marching.—**to steal a march.** See under *steal, v. t.*

March[3] (märch), *n.* [OF. *marche* (F. *mars*), < L. *Martius*, lit. 'month of Mars,' < *Mars*, Mars.] The third month of the year, containing 31 days.

march-er[1] (mär'chėr), *n.* An inhabitant of, or an officer or lord having jurisdiction over, marches or border territory.

march-er[2] (mär'chėr), *n.* One who marches (on foot).

mar-che-sa (mär-kā'zä), *n.*; pl. *-se* (-zā). [It.] In Italian use, a marchioness.—**mar-che'se** (-zā), *n.*; pl. *-si* (-zē). [It.; see *marquis.*] In Italian use, a marquis.

mar-chion-ess (mär'shọn-es), *n.* [ML. *marchionissa*, fem. of *marchio(n-)*, officer of marches: see *marquis.*] The wife or widow of a marquis; a lady holding in her own right the rank equal to that of a marquis.

march-land (märch'lạnd), *n.* March or border territory; a frontier district.

march-man (märch'mạn), *n.*; pl. *-men.* An inhabitant of marches; a marcher.

march-pane (märch'pān), *n.* [Prob. < It. *marzapane*, whence also G. *marzipan*, F. *massepain*; origin obscure.] A confection made of almonds reduced to a paste with sugar, etc., and molded into various forms; marzipan.

mar-co-ni (mär-kō'ni), *v. t.* or *i.*; *-nied, -niing.* To telegraph by the wireless system perfected by Guglielmo Marconi (born 1874).—**mar-co'ni-gram** (-gram), *n.* [See *-gram.*] A marconied message.—**mar-co'ni-graph** (-gràf), *n.* [See *-graph.*] The apparatus used in sending marconigrams.

Mar-di gras (mär-dē grä). [F., 'fat Tuesday.'] Shrove Tuesday; the last day of carnival: celebrated in Paris, New Orleans, and other cities with special festivities.

mare (mãr), *n.* [AS. *mere, myre*, fem. of *mearh* = OHG. *marah* = Icel. *marr*, horse: cf. *marshal.*] The female of the horse kind; also, a trestle, as to support scaffolding (Sc.: as, "The three were seated aloft on a high stage, prepared on purpose, with two *mares* and scaffold-deals, borrowed from Mr. Trowel the mason," Galt's "Annals of the Parish," xxxvi.).—**mare's nest,** something imagined to be an extraordinary discovery but proving to be a delusion or a hoax.

ma-rem-ma (mạ-rem'ạ̈), *n.*; pl. *maremme* (-ā). [It., < L. *maritima*, fem. of *maritimus*, E. *maritime.*] A marshy, unhealthy region near the seashore, as in Italy; also, the miasma of such a region.

mar-e-schal (mar'ẹ-shạl), *n.* Obs. or archaic form of *marshal.*

mare's-tail (mãrz'tāl), *n.* An erect aquatic plant, *Hippuris vulgaris*, with crowded whorls of narrow, hair-like leaves (see cut in next column); sometimes, the horsetail (plant); also, a cirrus cloud resembling a horse's tail.

mar-gar-ic (mär-gar'ik), *a.* [F. *margarique*, < Gr. μάργαρον, pearl.] In *chem.*, noting or pertaining to a white fatty acid resembling stearic acid.—**mar'ga-rin** (-gạ-rin), *n.* [F. *margarine*, < *margarique.*] A fatty substance extracted from animal fats and vegetable oils; also, oleomargarin.—**mar'ga-rine** (-rēn or -rin), *n.* [F.] Same as *oleomargarin.* [Eng.]

mar-ga-rite (mär'gạ-rīt), *n.* [L. *margarita*, < Gr. μαργαρίτης, pearl, < μάργαρος, pearl-oyster.] A pearl. [Archaic.]—**mar''ga-ri-tif'er-ous** (-ri-tif'ẹ-rus), *a.* [L. *margaritifer*: see *-ferous.*] Producing or yielding pearls.

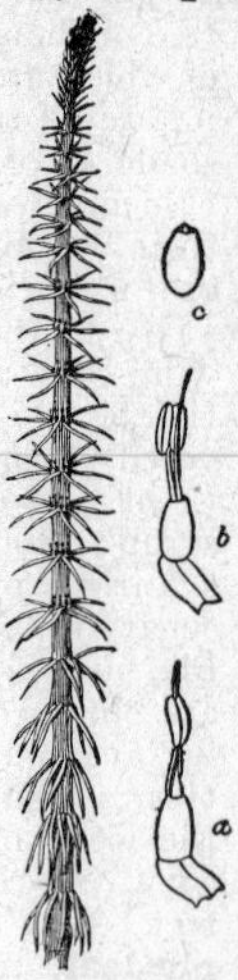

Flowering Branch of Mare's-tail (*Hippuris vulgaris*). — *a*, a flower before expansion; *b*, a flower after expansion; *c*, the fruit.

mar-gay (mär'gā), *n.* [F.; from Brazilian name.] A tiger-cat, *Felis tigrina*, of tropical America.

marge (märj), *n.* [F., < L. *margo* (*margin-*), E. *margin.*] A margin: as, "The plashy brink Of weedy lake, or *marge* of river wide" (Bryant's "To a Waterfowl"); "the illuminated *marge* of some old book" (Lowell's "Legend of Brittany," ii. 27). [Now poetic.]

mar-gent (mär'jẹnt), *n.* Archaic var. of *margin.*

mar-gin (mär'jin), *n.* [L. *margo* (*margin-*), border, edge: see *mark*[2].] A border or edge (as, "A step or two farther brought him to one *margin* of a little clearing": Stevenson's "Master of Ballantrae," xi.); also, the space surrounding the main body of writing or printing on a page; also, a limit, or a condition, etc., approximating a limit, beyond which something ceases to exist or be possible (as, the *margin* of consciousness); also, an amount allowed or available beyond what is actually necessary; in *com.*, the difference between the cost and the selling price; in *finance*, security, as a percentage in money, deposited with a broker as a provision against loss on transactions on behalf of his principal.—**mar'gin,** *v. t.* To provide with a margin or border (as, "The shore . . . was *margined* with foam": H. Melville's "Omoo," xvii.); also, to furnish with marginal notes, as a document; also, to enter in the margin, as of a book; in *finance*, to deposit a margin upon; secure by a margin.

mar-gi-nal (mär'ji-nạl), *a.* [NL. *marginalis.*] Pertaining to a margin; situated on the border or edge; written or printed in the margin of a page.—**mar-gi-na'li-a** (-nā'li-ạ̈), *n. pl.* [NL.] Marginal notes.—**mar'gi-nal-ly,** *adv.*

mar-gi-nate (mär'ji-nāt), *v. t.*; *-nated, -nating.* [L. *marginatus*, pp. of *marginare*, < *margo*, E. *margin.*] To furnish with a margin; border.—**mar'gi-nate,** *a.* Having a margin.—**mar-gi-na'tion** (-nā'shọn), *n.* Marginated condition or appearance.

mar-go-sa (mär-gō'sạ̈), *n.* [Pg. *amargosa*, fem. of *amargoso*, bitter.] An East Indian meliaceous tree, *Melia azadirachta*, whose oil and bitter bark are used in medicine.

mar-grave (mär'grāv), *n.* [G. *markgraf* = D. *markgraaf*, 'mark count.'] Orig., a German military governor of a mark, or border province; later, the hereditary title of the rulers of certain states.—**mar-gra'vi-ate** (-grā'vi-āt), *n.* The province of a margrave.—**mar'gra-vine** (-grạ-vēn), *n.* [G. *markgräfin.*] The wife of a margrave.

Marguerite (*Chrysanthemum frutescens*).

mar-gue-rite (mär'gẹ-rēt), *n.* [F., < L. *margarita*, pearl: see *margarite.*] Any of several flowers of the daisy kind, esp. *Chrysanthemum frutescens*, cultivated for its numerous white-rayed, yellow-centered flowers.

Ma-ri-an (mā'ri-ạn), *a.* [LL. *Maria*, Mary.] Of or pertaining to the Virgin Mary; also, of or pertaining to some other Mary, as Mary, queen of England (1553–58), or Mary Stuart.

Ma-rianne (må-ryån), *n.* [F.] A popular name for the French Republic personified.

mar-i-gold (mar′i-gōld), *n.* [From *Mary* (the Virgin) + *gold.*] Any of various chiefly golden-flowered plants, esp. of the asteraceous genus *Calendula,* as *C. officinalis,* a common garden plant of some use in dyeing and medicine, or of the asteraceous genus *Tagetes,* as *T. erecta,* with strong-scented foliage. See also *marsh-marigold.*

ma-ri-jua-na (mä-rē-hwä′nạ), *n.* Also *marihuana.* [Amer. Sp.; from Mex.] Any of certain plants with narcotic properties, as a shrubby species of tobacco, *Nicotiana glauca,* or, esp., the Indian hemp, *Cannabis indica* (see under *hemp*), whose dried leaves and flowers are smoked in cigarettes.

ma-rim-ba (mạ-rim′bạ), *n.* [W. Afr.] A musical instrument, originating in Africa but popularized and perfected in Central America, formed of a number of strips of wood of various sizes (often having resonators beneath to reinforce the sound) yielding different tones when struck by a hammer or stick, and usually played by a number of players.

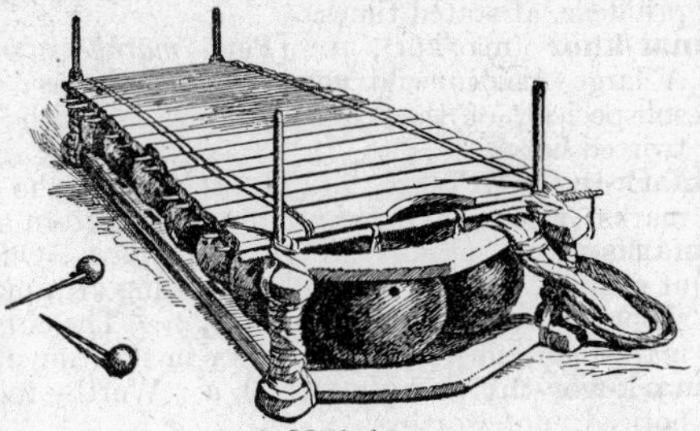

Marimba.

ma-rim-e-ter (mạ-rim′e-tėr), *n.* [L. *mare,* sea: see *-meter.*] *Naut.,* a device for taking soundings by determining the time required for a sound-wave to travel to the bottom of the ocean and be returned as an echo. [Proprietary name.]

mar-i-nade (mar-i-nād′), *n.* [F., < *mariner:* see *marinate.*] A pickle, usually of vinegar or wine seasoned with herbs, spices, etc., to steep meat or fish in before cooking; also, a dish of meat or fish thus steeped.—**mar′i-nade,** *v. t.*; *-naded, -nading.* To marinate.

mar-i-nate (mar′i-nāt), *v. t.*; *-nated, -nating.* [F. *mariner,* put in brine or pickle, < *marin,* E. *marine.*] To steep in a pickle or marinade.—**mar-i-na′tion** (-nā′shọn), *n.*

ma-rine (mạ-rēn′), *a.* [OF. F. *marin* (fem. *marine*), < L. *marinus,* < *mare,* sea: see *mere*[1].] Of or pertaining to the sea; existing in the sea; produced by the sea; also, pertaining to navigation or shipping; nautical; naval; maritime; also, serving on shipboard, as soldiers; also, adapted for use at sea (as, a *marine* barometer).—**Marine Corps,** a branch of the military service of the U. S., composed of officers, privates, etc., concerned with guard duty on board war-ships, the protection of American lives and interests abroad, the protection of naval property at home, etc.—**marine league.** See under *league*[2].—**ma-rine′,** *n.* Shipping in general; the maritime interest as represented by ships; sea-going vessels collectively, esp. with reference to nationality or class (as, the American *marine;* the mercantile *marine;* "the present war *marine* of Spain," Borrow's "Bible in Spain," xxxi.); also, naval affairs, or the department of a government (as in France) having to do with such affairs; also, one of a class of naval troops serving both on shipboard and on land; esp., a member of the U. S. Marine Corps; also, a picture with a marine subject.—**tell that to the marines, that will do for the marines,** etc., colloquial expressions of contemptuous disbelief, orig. implying an amount of credulity on the part of marines that would not be found in sailors: as, "*Tell that to the marines*—the sailors won't believe it" (Scott's "Redgauntlet," ch. xiii.).

mar-i-ner (mar′i-nėr), *n.* [OF. F. *marinier,* < ML. *marinarius,* < L. *marinus,* E. *marine.*] One who directs or assists in the navigation of a ship; a seaman; a sailor.

Mariner. A U. S. Navy patrol bomber (Martin).

Ma-ri-ol-a-try (mā-ri-ol′ạ-tri), *n.* [Gr. Μαρία, Mary, + λατρεία, worship.] The worship of the Virgin Mary.—**Ma-ri-ol′a-ter,** *n.*—**Ma-ri-ol′a-trous,** *a.*

mar-i-o-nette (mar″i-ọ-net′), *n.* [F. *marionnette,* < *Marion,* dim. of *Marie,* Mary.] A puppet moved by strings or the hands, as on a mimic stage.

mar-i-po-sa (mar-i-pō′sạ) **lil′y.** [Sp. *mariposa,* butterfly.] Any of the bulbous plants constituting the liliaceous genus *Calochortus,* of the western U. S. and Mexico, having tulip-like flowers of various colors.

mar-i-schal (mar′i-shạl), *n.* Obs. or Sc. form of *marshal.*

mar-ish (mar′ish). [OF. *maresch, mareis* (F. *marais*): see *morass.*] **I.** *n.* A marsh: as, "As long as sheep shall look from the side Of Oldtown Hill on *marishes* wide" (Whittier's "Prophecy of Samuel Sewall"). [Archaic or prov.] **II.** *a.* Marshy (as, "I . . . found, not the looked-for village, but another *marish* bottom": Stevenson's "Travels with a Donkey," ii. 1); also, such as is found in marshes (as, "a matted, *marish* vegetation": Stevenson's "Treasure Island," xxxi.). [Archaic or prov.]

Ma-rist (mā′rist). [F. *Mariste,* < LL. *Maria,* Mary.] **I.** *n.* A member of a Roman Catholic religious order which originated in 1816 at Lyons, France, devoted to missionary and educational work in a spirit of special devotion to the Virgin Mary. **II.** *a.* Belonging or pertaining to the Marists.

mar-i-tal (mar′i-tạl), *a.* [L. *maritalis,* < *maritus,* husband, as adj. married, pertaining to marriage: see *marry*[1].] Of or pertaining to a husband (as, a man's *marital* rights or responsibilities); also, of or pertaining to marriage (as, a *marital* relationship between two families); matrimonial; connubial.—**mar′i-tal-ly,** *adv.*

mar-i-time (mar′i-tim or -tīm), *a.* [L. *maritimus,* < *mare,* sea: see *mere*[1].] Bordering on the sea; living near the sea; also, of or pertaining to the sea; also, connected with the sea in relation to navigation, shipping, etc. (as, *maritime* law); also, characteristic of a seaman (as, "Solomon Gills . . . was far from having a *maritime* appearance": Dickens's "Dombey and Son," iv.); nautical.

mar-jo-ram (mär′jọ-rạm), *n.* [OF. *majorane* (F. *marjolaine*), < ML. *majorana;* origin obscure.] Any of the mints constituting the genus *Origanum,* esp. *O. majorana* ('sweet marjoram'), which is used for seasoning in cookery, or *O. vulgare,* a common wild species native in Europe and naturalized in North America ('wild marjoram').

Wild Marjoram (*Origanum vulgare*), with flowers. — *a,* a flower; *b,* the fruit.

mark[1] (märk), *n.* [AS. *marc* = G. *mark.*] A former European unit of weight, esp. for gold and silver, generally equal to 8 ounces; a former money of account, orig. of the value of this weight of silver; also, the monetary unit and a silver coin of Germany, normally equivalent to about 23.8 U. S. cents; also (Finnish *markka*), the monetary unit and a silver coin of Finland, equivalent to the franc (19.3 U. S. cents).

Obverse. Reverse.
German Mark.

mark[2] (märk), *n.* [AS. *mearc,* boundary, landmark, sign, = G. *mark,* boundary, march, = Goth. *marka,* boundary; akin to L. *margo,* border, E. *margin,* and to E. *march*[1].] A boundary or border, frontier, or border province (archaic); also, a tract of land held in common by a medieval community of freemen; also, a landmark†; also, an object aimed at, as a target (as, "Both balls had passed through the lungs—the true *mark* in shooting buffalo": Parkman's "Oregon Trail," vii.); an object of derision, scorn, hostile schemes, swindling, or the like (as, "So I was a *mark* for plunder at once, And lost my cash (can you wonder?) at once": Kipling's "Prodigal Son"); an object or end desired or striven for, as a goal; also, a sign, token, or indication (as, "They supplied me as fast as they could, showing a thousand *marks* of wonder and astonishment at my bulk and appetite": Swift's "Gulliver's Travels," i. 1); a distinctive property, character, or trait (as, a man having all the *marks* of a gentleman); also, an affixed or impressed device, symbol, inscription, etc., serving to give information, identify, indicate origin or ownership, attest to character or comparative merit, or the like (as, "I'll show you how to take the *marks* out of the handkerchiefs": Dickens's "Oliver Twist," ix.); a badge, brand, or other visible sign assumed or imposed; a sign, usually a cross, made by an illiterate person by way of signature; a symbol used in writing or printing (as, a punctuation-*mark*); often, a symbol used to denote a unit in recording conduct, proficiency, attainment, etc., as of pupils in a school; hence, a rating assigned for attainment, etc. (as, an examination *mark*); also, something serving as an indication of position (as, a book-*mark*); also, a recognized standard (as, to be below the *mark*); also, a visible trace or impression upon anything, as a line, cut, dent, stain, bruise, etc. (as, a birth-*mark*); also, note, importance, or distinction (as, "There was nothing of high *mark* in this," Dickens's "Christmas Carol," iii.; a man of *mark*); also, *naut.*, one of the points on a hand lead-line, at 2, 3, 5, 7, etc., fathoms, marked by pieces of leather, cloth, etc. (the unmarked fathoms 1, 4, 6, 8, etc., being called *deeps*).—**(God) save** (or **bless**) **the mark!** an exclamatory phrase of deprecation or apology, or of impatience or contempt.—**mark**[2], *v. t.* [AS. *mearcian.*] To put a mark or marks on; specif., to attach or affix to (something) figures or signs indicating price (as, to *mark* a thing down, or up, to attach a reduced price, or a higher price, to it); also, to trace or form by or as by marks (often with *out*); also, to indicate or designate by or as by marks; single out or destine (as, "Melancholy *mark'd* him for her own": Gray's "Elegy," xxx.); separate (*off*); also, to record, as a score; also, to make manifest (as, a glance *marking* displeasure); also, to be a mark on or of; be a distinguishing feature of (as, a day *marked* by rain); also, to notice or observe (as, "Full well I *mark'd* the features of his face": Pope's tr. Homer's "Odyssey," xvii.); give heed or attention to (as, "*Mark* my bidding, and be safe": C. B. Brown's "Wieland," vii.).—**to mark time,** *milit.*, to move the feet alternately as in marching, but without advancing; fig., to suspend advance or progress temporarily, as while awaiting developments.—**mark**[2], *v. i.* To take notice; give attention; consider: as, "*Mark*, I pray you, and see how this man seeketh mischief" (1 Kings, xx. 7).

marked (märkt), *p. a.* Furnished with a mark or marks; on which a mark has been made (as, a *marked* card); also, affixed or impressed as a mark (as, the *marked* price of goods); also, distinguished or singled out as if by a mark (as, a *marked* man, usually, one who is watched as an object for suspicion or vengeance); also, strikingly noticeable, plainly manifest, or conspicuous (as, in a *marked* degree; with *marked* success).—**mark'ed-ly,** *adv.* In a marked manner or degree; manifestly; conspicuously.—**mark'ed-ness,** *n.*

mark-er (mär'kėr), *n.* One who or that which marks; often, one who records a score, etc.; also, something used as a mark or indication (as, "Put a *marker* in that book . . . page seventy-four": Lover's "Handy Andy," xv.); a counter, as in a game; also, something worthy to be compared with something else (slang).

mar-ket (mär'ket), *n.* [AS. *market*, < L. *mercatus*, trading, traffic, market, < *mercari*, trade: see *merchant.*] A meeting of people for selling and buying; the assemblage of people at such a meeting; also, an open space or a covered building where such meetings are held, esp. for the sale of provisions, etc.; a store for the sale of provisions (as, a meat-*market*); also, trade or traffic, esp. as regards a particular commodity; a body of persons carrying on extensive transactions in a specified commodity (as, the cotton *market*); also, the field of trade or business (as, the best shoes in the *market*); also, opportunity for selling or buying (as, to lose one's *market*); also, demand for a commodity (as, an unprecedented *market* for leather); also, a region where anything is or may be sold (as, the foreign *market*); also, the rate of purchase and sale; current price or value (as, a rising or a falling *market*).—**mar'ket,** *v.* **I.** *intr.* To deal (buy or sell) in a market. **II.** *tr.* To carry or send to market for disposal; also, to dispose of in a market; sell.—**mar'ket-a-ble,** *a.* That may be marketed; salable; also, pertaining to selling or buying; of price, etc., current in the market.—**mar"ket-a-bil'i-ty** (-bil'i-ti), *n.*—**mar'ket-er,** *n.*—**mar'ket=house,** *n.* A building in which a market is held.—**mar'ket-ing,** *n.* Trading in a market; buying or selling; also, something bought or sold in a market.—**mar'ket-man** (-mạn), *n.*; pl. *-men.* A man who sells provisions, etc., in a market; also, one who buys in a market.—**mar'ket=place,** *n.* A place, esp. an open space in a town, where a market is held: as, "In open *market-place* produced they me, To be a public spectacle to all" (Shakspere's "1 Henry VI.," i. 4. 40).—**mar'ket=stead** (-sted), *n.* A market-place. See W. Morris's "Jason," ii. 286. [Archaic.]—**mar'ket=town,** *n.* A town in which markets are held, as in England, by privilege, at stated times.

mar-khor (mär'kôr), *n.* [Pers. *mārkhōr*, 'serpent-eater.'] A large Asiatic wild goat, *Capra falconeri* (with several subspecies), of the Himalaya regions, with long, spirally twisted horns.

mark-ing (mär'king), *n.* The act of one who or that which marks; also, a mark, or a number or pattern of marks.

marks-man (märks'mạn), *n.*; pl. *-men.* One who shoots at a mark, esp. one skilled in shooting at a mark; one who shoots well.—**marks'man-ship,** *n.* The art or skill of a marksman; degree of proficiency in shooting at a mark.

mark-wor-thy (märk'wėr"ᴛʜi), *a.* Worthy to be marked or noticed; noteworthy.

marl[1] (märl), *n.* [OF. *marle*, < ML. *margila*, dim. of L. *marga*, marl.] A soil or earthy deposit consisting of clay and calcium carbonate, used as a fertilizer; any of various other soft or crumbly deposits, as a mixture of green sand and clay also used as a fertilizer; also, earth (poetic: as, "to seize upon his foe flatt lying on the *marle*," Spenser's "Faerie Queene," ii. 11. 33).—**marl**[1], *v. t.* To fertilize with or as with marl.

marl[2] (märl), *v. t.* [D. *marlen*, appar. < *marren*, tie: cf. *marline.*] *Naut.*, to wind, cover, or fasten with marline, twine, or the like, each turn being secured by a hitch.

mar-la-ceous (mär-lā'shius), *a.* Of the nature of or resembling marl; marly.

mar-line (mär'lin), *n.* [D. *marlijn*, < *marren*, tie, + *lijn*, line; or perhaps, in part, D. *marling*, verbal noun < *marlen*, E. *marl*[2].] *Naut.*, small cord of two loosely twisted strands, used for seizing.

mar-line-spike, mar-lin-spike (mär'lin-spīk), *n.* [Prob. orig. *marling spike*: see *marl*[2].] *Naut.*, a pointed iron implement used in marling, separating the strands of rope in splicing, etc.

marl-ite (mär'līt), *n.* A variety of marl which resists the action of the air.—**marl-it-ic** (mär-lit'ik), *a.*

marl-y (mär'li), *a.* Of, like, or abounding in marl.

mar-ma-lade (mär'mạ-lād), *n.* [F. *marmelade*, < Pg *marmelada*, < *marmelo*, quince, < L. *melimelum*, < Gr. *μελίμηλον*, apple grafted on quince, < *μέλι*, honey, + *μῆλον*, apple.] A preserve of quinces, oranges, or other fruit boiled down with sugar to a thick consistence.—**mar'ma-lade=tree,** *n.* A sapotaceous tree, *Achras zapota*, of the West Indies, with a durable wood resembling mahogany and a fruit whose pulp resembles marmalade.

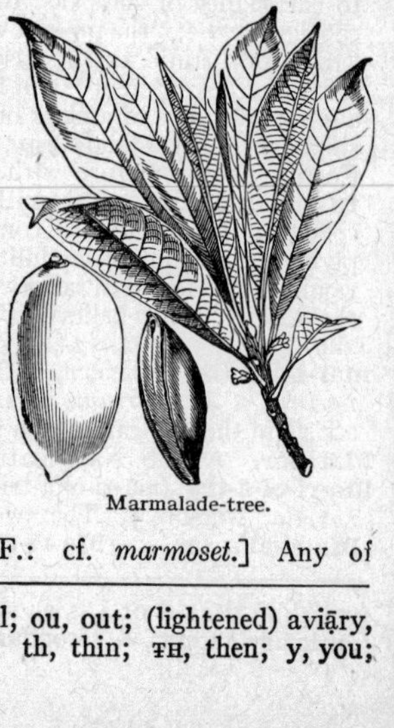

Marmalade-tree.

mar-mo-re-al (mär-mō'rẹ-ạl), *a.* [L. *marmoreus*, < *marmor*, E. *marble.*] Of or like marble. Also **mar-mo're-an.**

mar-mo-rize (mär'mọ-rīz), *v. t.*; *-rized*, *-rizing.* [= F. *marmoriser*, < L. *marmor*, E. *marble.*] In *geol.*, to convert (sedimentary limestone) into marble.—**mar"mo-ri-za'tion** (-ri-zā'shọn), *n.*

mar-mose (mär'mōs), *n.* [F.: cf. *marmoset.*] Any of

several small South American opossums, as *Didelphys dorsigera*, which carry the young on the back.

Marmose (*Didelphys dorsigera*).

mar-mo-set (mär′mō̤-zet), *n.* [OF. F. *marmouset*, grotesque little figure or creature; origin uncertain.] Any small monkey†; now, any of various small squirrel-like South and Central American monkeys (genera *Hapale* and *Midas*), with soft fur and a long, bushy non-prehensile tail.

mar-mot (mär′mọt), *n.* [F. *marmotte*, prob. < Rhæto-Romanic *murmont*, < L. *mus* (*mur-*), mouse, + *mons* (*mont-*), mountain.] Any of the bushy-tailed, thick-set rodents constituting the genus *Arctomys*, as the common woodchuck; also, any of certain related animals, as the prairie-dog (as, "Prairie dogs . . . they are no dogs at all, but little *marmots* rather smaller than a rabbit": Parkman's "Oregon Trail," xx.).

Common Marmoset (*Hapale jacchus*).

Mar-o-nite (mar′ō̤-nīt), *n.* [Said to be named from *Maro*, or *Maron*, a Syrian monk of the 4th century, or from a 7th century *Maro*.] One of a body of Syrian Christians in communion with the Roman Catholic Church.

ma-roon¹ (mạ-rön′). [F. *marron* = It. *marrone*, chestnut; origin unknown.] **I.** *n.* A very dark brownish-red or crimson color; also, a kind of small firework exploded to imitate the sound of a cannon. **II.** *a.* Of the color called maroon.

ma-roon² (mạ-rön′), *n.* [F. *marron*, < Sp. *cimarrón*, wild.] One of a class of negroes, orig. fugitive slaves, living in the wilder parts of the West Indies and Dutch Guiana; also, a person who is marooned (as, "Ben Gunn, the *maroon*": Stevenson's "Treasure Island," xxvii.).—**ma-roon′**², *v.* **I.** *tr.* To put ashore and leave on a desolate island or coast by way of punishment, as was done by buccaneers, etc. (as, "I was . . . condemned . . . to be *marooned* . . . on one of those little sandy, bushy islets, which are called in the West Indies, keys": Scott's "Pirate," xxii.); hence, to isolate as if on a desolate island. **II.** *intr.* To picnic or camp out for several days. [Southern U. S.]—**ma-roon′er,** *n.* One who maroons; also, one who is marooned; a maroon.

mar-plot (mär′plot), *n.* One who mars or defeats a plot, design, or project by officious interference; one who blunderingly hinders the success of any undertaking.

marque (märk), *n.* [OF. F. *marque*, < Pr. *marca*, < *marcar*, seize in reprisal.] Seizure by way of reprisal: in *letters* (or, sometimes, *letter*) *of marque* (*and reprisal*) (a license granted by a government authorizing the grantee to make reprisals on an enemy's goods and subjects, esp. at sea; a license to engage in privateering).

mar-quee (mär-kē′), *n.* [From *marquise*, taken as pl.] A large-sized tent, as an officer's field-tent or a tent put up for use during an outdoor entertainment: as, "the pretty striped *marquee* at the edge of the lawn" (George Eliot's "Adam Bede," xxii.).

mar-quess (mär′kwes), *n.* A form of *marquis* common in British use.

mar-quet-ry (mär′ket-ri), *n.*; pl. *-ries* (-riz). [F. *marqueterie*, < *marqueter*, mark, checker, inlay, < *marquer*, mark; from Teut., and akin to E. *mark*².] Inlaid work done with thin, shaped pieces of variously colored woods or other material, as metal, tortoise-shell, ivory, mother-of-pearl, etc., combined to form a design: used esp. in decorating furniture.

mar-quis (mär′kwis), *n.* [F. *marquis*, OF. *marchis*, = Sp. *marqués* = It. *marchese*, < ML. *marchensis* (also *marchio*), officer in charge of marches, < *marcha*, *marca*, march; from Teut., and akin to E. *march*¹ and *mark*².] Orig., an officer in charge of a march or frontier territory; now, a nobleman ranking next below a duke and above an earl or count.—**mar′quis-ate** (-āt), *n.* The dignity or rank of a marquis; also, the territory ruled by a marquis or a margrave.—**mar-quise′** (-kēz′), *n.* [F.] The wife or widow of a marquis, or a lady holding the rank equal to that of a marquis (a French use); also, a marquee (tent); also, a roof-like shelter, as of glass, projecting above an outer door.—**marquise ring,** a finger-ring set with a cluster of gems forming a pointed oval.

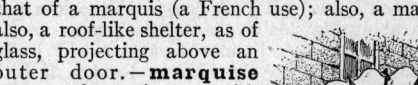

Coronet of a British Marquis.

Marquise.

mar-rer (mär′ėr), *n.* One who mars, spoils, or ruins.

mar-riage (mar′ạj), *n.* [OF. F. *mariage*, < *marier*, E. *marry*¹.] The state of being married, or of being a husband or wife; the relation between husband and wife; wedlock; also, the action or an act of marrying; the ceremony of marrying; a wedding; fig., any intimate union.—**mar′riage-a-ble,** *a.* Fit or proper for marriage: as, "two *marriageable* young creatures together beneath the same roof" (Howells's "Chance Acquaintance," iv.); to reach a *marriageable* age.—**mar″riage-a-bil′i-ty** (-bil′i-ti), **mar′riage-a-ble-ness,** *n.*

mar-ried (mar′id), *p. a.* United in wedlock; wedded; also, pertaining to marriage or married persons (as, *married* life).

mar-ri-er (mar′i-ėr), *n.* One who marries.

mar-ring-ly (mär′ing-li), *adv.* So as to mar or spoil.

mar-ron (mar′ọn, F. må-rôn̍), *n.* [F.: see *maroon*¹.] A chestnut: esp. as used in cookery, or candied (*glacé*) or preserved in a syrup.

mar-row¹ (mar′ō), *n.* [ME.; origin obscure.] A companion, partner, or associate; a mate; one of a pair; a match or equal. [Now Sc. and prov. Eng.]

mar-row² (mar′ō), *n.* [AS. *mearg*, *mearh*, = D. *merg* = G. *mark* = Icel. *mergr*, marrow.] A soft, fatty vascular tissue in the interior and cavities of bones (the marrow of some animals being eaten as a delicacy); hence, rich and nutritious food (cf. Ps. lxiii. 5); also, strength or vitality (as, "The *marrow* of the land was again in fair way of being thoroughly exhausted by its defenders and its foes": Motley's "Dutch Republic," vi. 6); also, the inmost or essential part (as, "We entered into the *marrow* of my case": Galt's "Annals of the Parish," xxxiii.).—**vegetable marrow.** See under *vegetable*, *a.*—**mar′row=bone,** *n.* A bone containing edible marrow; *pl.*, the knees (humorous: as, "I jest flopped down on my *marrow-bones*," John Hay's "Little Breeches"); also, cross-bones (as, "I . . . sailed under the black flag and *marrow-bones*": Scott's "Redgauntlet," ch. xiv.).—**mar′row-fat,** *n.* A tall variety of the pea with a large seed; also, the seed.—**mar′row-y,** *a.* Of, like, or full of marrow.

mar-ry¹ (mar′i), *v.*; *-ried*, *-rying*. [OF. F. *marier*, < L. *maritare*, < *maritus*, husband, as adj. married, pertaining to marriage, < *mas* (*mar-*), male, a male.] **I.** *tr.* To unite in wedlock; join as husband or wife to one of the opposite sex; also, to give in marriage; also, to take in marriage; fig., to unite intimately (as, "Soft Lydian airs, *Married* to immortal verse": Milton's "L'Allegro," 137); *naut.*, to join together, as two ropes, end to end without increasing the diameter. **II.** *intr.* To enter into the conjugal state; take a husband or wife.

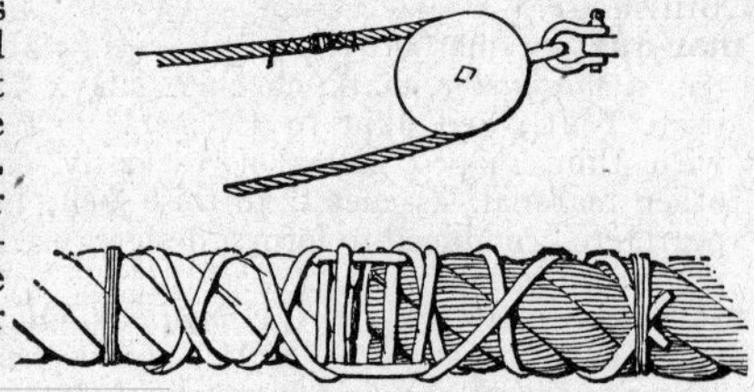

Ropes joined by Marrying.

mar-ry² (mar'-i), *interj.* [For *Mary* (the Virgin).] An exclamation of asseveration, surprise, etc.: as, "*Cal.* Wilt thou be pleased to hearken once again to the suit I made to thee? *Ste. Marry*, will I: kneel and repeat it" (Shakspere's "Tempest," iii. 2. 46). [Archaic or prov.]

Mars (märz), *n.* [L.] The ancient Roman god of war (cf. *Ares*); in *astron.*, the major planet next outside the earth, being the fourth in order from the sun.

Mar-sa-la (mär-sä'lä̦), *n.* [It.] A class of white wines made in Sicily, esp. about Marsala on the western coast.

Mar-seil-laise (mär-se-lāz', F. mär-se-yāz), *n.* [F.] The French national song, written in 1792 by Rouget de Lisle: so named from having been first sung in Paris by a band of patriots from Marseilles.

mar-seilles (mär-sālz'), *n.* [From *Marseilles*, city in France.] A thick cotton fabric woven in figures or stripes, with an embossed or quilted effect.

marsh (märsh), *n.* [AS. *mersc*, *merisc*, = MD. *mersche* = MLG. and G. *marsch*, marsh; from the source of E. *mere*¹: cf. *morass*.] A tract of low, wet land; a swamp; a fen.

mar-shal (mär'sha̦l), *n.* [OF. *mareschal* (F. *maréchal*) = ML. *marescalcus*, < OHG. *marahscalh*, 'horse servant,' < *marah*, horse (cf. *mare*), + *scalh*, servant (cf. G. *schalk*, knave, rogue).] A groom† or a farrier†; also, a high officer of a royal household or court, as the British earl marshal (see under *earl*); also, a general officer of high or the highest rank in various European (or other) armies (as, *marshal* of France, a French military dignitary of the highest rank); also, a person charged with the arrangement or regulation of ceremonies, etc.; also, any of various former or present law, police, or other officials, esp. an administrative officer of a U. S. judicial district who performs duties similar to those of a sheriff.—**mar'shal**, *v.*; *-shaled* or *-shalled*, *-shaling* or *-shalling*. **I.** *tr.* To arrange or place in due or proper order; array or draw up for battle, review, etc.; also, to usher or lead (as, "The abbot *marshalled* him to the door of Augustine's chamber": Scott's "Castle Dangerous," x.); in *her.*, to combine (two or more coats of arms) upon one shield so as to form a single composition; also, to associate (accessories) with a shield of arms so as to form a complete heraldic composition. **II.** *intr.* To take up positions in due or proper order, or as in military array: as, "no *marshaling* troop, no bivouac song" (Joaquin Miller's "Bravest Battle").—**mar'shal-cy** (-si), *n.*; pl. *-cies* (-siz). The office, rank, or position of a marshal.—**mar'shal-er, mar'shal-ler**, *n.*—**mar'shal-ship**, *n.*

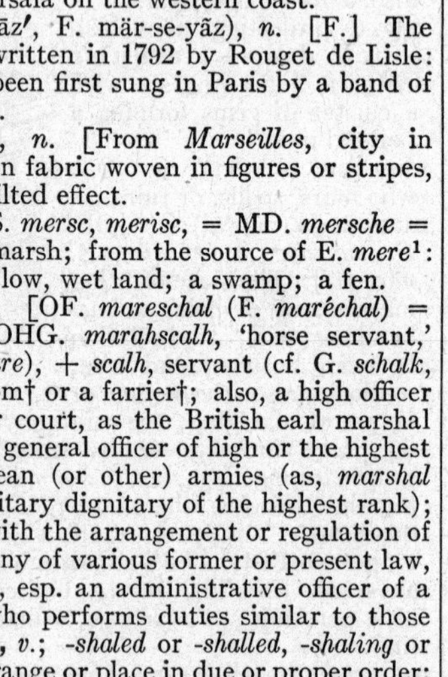

Heraldic Marshaling.—Escutcheon of Elizabeth, Queen of Henry VII.

marsh=el-der (märsh'el″dėr), *n.* The cranberry-tree or guelder-rose, *Viburnum opulus*; also, in the U. S., any of various plants of the genus *Iva*, of the ragweed family, as *I. fructescens*, which grows in salt-marshes.

marsh=gas (märsh'gas), *n.* Methane.

marsh=hawk (märsh'hâk), *n.* A hawk, *Circus hudsonius*, which frequents marshes and meadows, feeding on frogs, snakes, etc.

marsh=hen (märsh'hen), *n.* Any of various rails (birds) that frequent marshes.

marsh-i-ness (mär'shi-nes), *n.* Marshy state.

marsh-land (märsh'la̦nd), *n.* Marshy land.—**marsh'land-er**, *n.*

marsh=mal-low (märsh'mal″ō), *n.* A mallow, *Althæa officinalis*, with pink flowers, found in marshy places; also, a sweetened paste or confection made from the mucilaginous root of this plant, or a similar confection containing gum arabic or gelatin (usually written *marshmallow*).

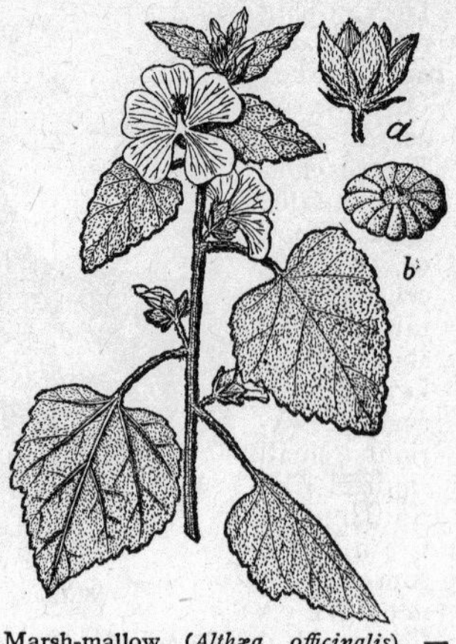

Marsh-mallow (*Althæa officinalis*).—*a*, involucre and calyx; *b*, the fruit.

marsh-man (märsh'ma̦n), *n.*; pl. *-men*. A dweller in a marsh or marshy region.

marsh=mar-i-gold (märsh'mar'i-gōld), *n.* A yellow-flowered ranunculaceous plant, *Caltha palustris*, growing in marshes and meadows. Also called *cowslip*.

marsh=wren (märsh'ren), *n.* Any of various wrens that breed in marshes, as *Cistothorus* (or *Telmatodytes*) *palustris*, of North America ('long-billed marsh-wren').

Long-billed Marsh-wren (*Cistothorus palustris*).

marsh-y (mär'shi), *a.*; compar. *marshier*, superl. *marshiest*. Pertaining to or of the nature of a marsh; consisting of or containing marshland; also, characteristic of marshland (as, *marshy* vegetation).

mar-si-po-branch (mär'si-pọ̄-brangk), *n.* [NL. *Marsipobranchii*, pl., < Gr. μάρσιπος, bag, pouch, + βράγχια, gills.] Any of the *Marsipobranchii* or *Cyclostomata*, a group or class of vertebrates comprising the cyclostomes (the lampreys and hags), characterized by pouch-like gills. See *cyclostome*.—**mar″si-po-bran'chi-ate** (-brang'ki-āt), *a.* and *n.*

mar-su-pi-al (mär-sū'pi-a̦l). [NL. *marsupialis*, < L. *marsupium*: see *marsupium*.] **I.** *a.* Pertaining to, resembling, or having a marsupium or pouch; of or pertaining to the marsupials. **II.** *n.* Any of the *Marsupialia*, an order of mammals which includes the kangaroo, opossum, etc., and of which most of the members have a marsupium or pouch on the abdomen of the female, containing the mammary glands and serving as a receptacle for the young. Also **mar-su'pi-ate** (-āt), *a.* and *n.*

mar-su-pi-um (mär-sū'pi-um), *n.*; pl. *-pia* (-pi-ä̦). [L., pouch, < Gr. μαρσύπιον, μαρσίπιον, dim. of μάρσιπος, bag, pouch.] The pouch or fold of skin on the abdomen of a female marsupial; also, a similar pouch in other animals, as certain fishes, crustaceans, etc.

mart (märt), *n.* [D. *markt*, < L. *mercatus*, E. *market*.] A market or fair (obs. or archaic); a market-place, market-house, or the like (now chiefly poetic or literary); now, esp., a city or locality where things are sold and bought (as, "Lisbon outshone Venice as a *mart* for oriental spices": H. G. Wells's "Outline of History," xxxvi. § 9); a seat of trade; an emporium; also, trade† or traffic†; a bargain† (as, "Now I play a merchant's part, And venture madly on a desperate *mart*": Shakspere's "Taming of the Shrew," ii. 1. 329).—**mart†**, *v.* **I.** *intr.* To traffic; bargain. **II.** *tr.* To traffic in.

mar-ta-gon (mär'ta̦-go̦n), *n.* [F. *martagon*, < Turk. *martagān*, kind of turban.] The Turk's-cap lily, *Lilium martagon*.

mar-tel (mär'tel), *n.* [OF. *martel* (F. *marteau*), < ML. *martellus*, for L. *martulus*, *marculus*, dim. of *marcus*, hammer.] A hammer, esp. one used as a weapon in war. [Archaic.]

mar-tel-lo (mär-tel'ō) **tow'er.** [From a tower on Cape *Mortella*, in Corsica.] A circular, tower-like fort with guns on the top.

mar-ten (mär'ten), *n.* [OF. *martrine*, prop. the fur, < *martrin*, adj. < *martre*, marten; from Teut. (cf. G. *marder*).] Any of various slender, fur-bearing carnivorous mammals of the genus *Mustela*, as *M. americana* ('American pine-marten') of the northern U. S. and Canada; also, the fur of such an animal.

American Pine-marten (*Mustela americana*).

mar-tial (mär'shạl), *a.* [L. *Martialis*, of Mars, < *Mars* (*Mart-*), Mars.] [*cap.*] Martian; also [*l. c.*], of, pertaining to, or appropriate for war (as, *martial* equipage; *martial* music); also, inclined or disposed to war; warlike; brave; also, characteristic of or befitting a warrior (as, a *martial* stride); also, pertaining to or connected with the army and navy (see *court-martial*).—**martial law,** the law imposed upon a district by the military power when it has superseded the civil authority, as in time of war.—**mar'tial-ism,** *n.* Martial or warlike character or spirit.—**mar'tial-ist,** *n.* A martial person; a warrior. —**mar'tial-ly,** *adv.*—**mar'tial-ness,** *n.*

Mar-tian (mär'shạn). [L. *Martius*, < *Mars* (*Mart-*), Mars.] **I.** *a.* Of or pertaining to the god or the planet Mars. **II.** *n.* An inhabitant of the planet Mars.

mar-tin (mär'tin), *n.* [From *Martin*, man's name.] Any of various swallows, as *Chelidon urbica*, the common European house-swallow or 'house-martin,' which builds its nest on the walls of houses, or *Progne subis*, one of the American 'purple martins,' one of the largest birds of the swallow family.

Purple Martin (*Progne subis*).

mar-ti-net (mär-ti-net'), *n.* [From Jean *Martinet* (died 1672), French inspector-general of infantry.] A rigid military or naval disciplinarian (as, "The commander-in-chief was a little of a *martinet*": Cooper's "Two Admirals," xi.); in general, a stickler for punctilious attention to all the forms or details of discipline.—**mar-ti-net'ism,** *n.*

mar-tin-gale (mär'ting-gāl or mär'tin-), *n.* [F.; origin uncertain.] A strap of a horse's harness passing from the bit or head-gear, between the fore legs, to the girth, for holding the head down; also, a short perpendicular spar under the end of a bowsprit, or a stay extending from such a spar to the jib-boom; also, a gambling system in which the stakes are doubled after each loss.

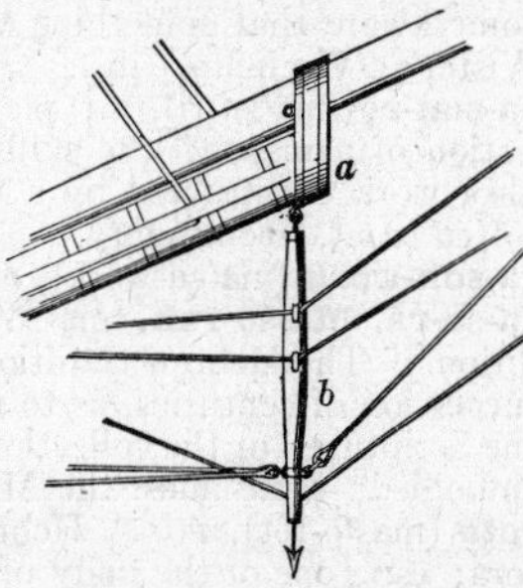

a, Bowsprit-cap; *b*, Martingale.

Mar-tin-mas (mär'tin-mạs), *n.* [See *-mas.*] A church festival in honor of St. Martin of Tours; also, Nov. 11, the day of this festival.

mart-let (märt'let), *n.* [Appar. for obs. *martinet*, < F. *martinet*, martin, < *Martin*, man's name.] A European martin; in *her.*, a bird represented without feet (see cut in next column).

mar-tyr (mär'tėr), *n.* [AS. *martyr*, < LL. *martyr*, < Gr. *μάρτυρ*, *μάρτυς*, witness, later martyr: see *memory*.] One who willingly suffers death rather than renounce his religion; hence, one who suffers death or grievous harm or loss on behalf of any belief, principle, or cause; also, one undergoing severe or constant suffering (as, a *martyr* to gout).—**mar'tyr,** *v. t.* To put to death as a martyr; make a martyr of; also, to torment or torture (as, "She was ever at my side . . . *martyring* me by the insufferable annoyance of her vulgar loquacity": Lever's "Harry Lorrequer," ix.).—**mar'tyr-dom** (-dọm), *n.* [AS. *martyrdōm.*] The condition, sufferings, or death of a martyr; also, torment; extreme suffering. —**mar'tyr-ize** (-īz), *v. t.*; *-ized*, *-izing.* To make a martyr of; also, to torment.—**mar"tyr-i-za'tion** (-i-zā'shọn), *n.*—**mar-tyr-ol'a-try** (-ol'ạ-tri), *n.* [See *-latry.*] Worship of martyrs.—**mar-tyr-ol'o-gy** (-ọ-ji), *n.*; pl. *-gies* (-jiz). [ML. *martyrologium*, < MGr. *μαρτυρολόγιον* (Gr. *λέγειν*, tell, recount).] A list or register of martyrs; an account or history of martyrs; also, such histories collectively; the branch of knowledge dealing with the lives of martyrs.—**mar"tyr-o-log'i-cal** (-ọ-loj'i-kạl), *a.*—**mar-tyr-ol'o-gist,** *n.*—**mar'tyr-y** (-i), *n.*; pl. *-ies* (-iz). [LL. *martyrium*, < LGr. *μαρτύριον*, martyr's shrine, earlier martyrdom, Gr. testimony.] A shrine, chapel, or the like, erected in honor of a martyr.

Heraldic Martlet.

mar-vel (mär'vẹl), *n.* [OF. F. *merveille*, < L. *mirabilia*, wonderful things, prop. neut. pl. of *mirabilis*, wonderful, < *mirari*, wonder at: cf. *miracle.*] A wonderful thing (as, "Before all thy people I will do *marvels*, such as have not been done in all the earth": Ex. xxxiv. 10); a wonder or prodigy; sometimes, a wonderful example (*of*: as, the book is a *marvel* of accuracy); also, the feeling of wonder, as at something surprising or extraordinary (archaic: as, "The vast acquirements of the new governor were the theme of *marvel* among the simple burghers," Irving's "Knickerbocker's New York," iv. 1).—**mar'vel,** *v.*; *-veled* or *-velled*, *-veling* or *-velling.* [OF. *merveillier.*] **I.** *intr.* To be affected with wonder, as at something surprising or extraordinary (as, "Lancelot *marvell'd* at the wordless man": Tennyson's "Lancelot and Elaine," 171); wonder. **II.** *tr.* To wonder at (now only with a clause as object: as, "The people . . . *marvelled* that he tarried so long in the temple," Luke, i. 21); also, to wonder or be curious about (with a clause: as, "I *marvel* what kin thou and thy daughters are," Shakspere's "King Lear," i. 4. 199).—**mar'vel=of=Pe-ru',** *n.* The four-o'clock (plant).—**mar'vel-ous, mar'vel-lous,** *a.* [OF. *merveillos* (F. *merveilleux*).] Such as to excite wonder; wonderful; surprising; extraordinary; sometimes, strange and surprising to the point of being improbable or incredible (often used absolutely in the phrase 'the marvelous': as, tales of *the marvelous*; an unreasoning fondness for *the marvelous*).—**mar'vel-ous-ly, mar'vel-lous-ly,** *adv.*—**mar'vel-ous-ness, mar'vel-lous-ness,** *n.*

Marx-i-an (märk'si-ạn), *a.* Of or pertaining to the German socialist Karl Marx (1818–83) or his theories.—**Marx'ist,** *n.*

mar-zi-pan (mär-tsẹ-pän'), *n.* [G.] Same as *marchpane.*

-mas. Noun termination from AS. *mæsse*, mass (see *mass*[1]), in the names of church festivals or feast-days, as *Candlemas*, *Christmas*, *Lammas*, *Michaelmas.*

mas'ca-longe, *n.* See *maskalonge.*

mas-ca-ron (mas'kạ-rọn), *n.* [F., < It. *mascherone*, aug. of *maschera*, mask: see *mask*[2].] A decorative ornament in the form of a more or less grotesque face or head.

Mascaron, handle of vase, French design of period of Louis XIV.

mas-cle (mas'kl), *n.* [Prob. for OF. *macle*, < L. *macula*, spot, mesh of a net: cf. *mail*[1].] A spot† or speck†; also, a small perforated steel plate, commonly lozenge-shaped, used with others like it in making medieval armor; in *her.*, a bearing in the form of a voided lozenge.

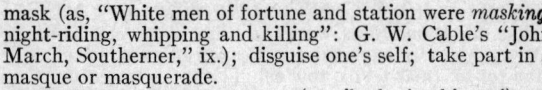

Heraldic Mascle.

mas-cot, mas-cotte (mas′kot), *n.* [F. *mascotte*, dim. < Pr. *masco*, witch.] A person or thing supposed to bring good luck: as, "She could and did believe in the efficacy of *mascots* against bullets and shrapnel and bayonets" (Arnold Bennett's "Pretty Lady," xxi.).

mas-cu-line (mas′kū̦-lin), *a.* [OF. F. *masculin*, < L. *masculinus*, < *masculus*, male, manly, dim. of *mas*, male, a male.] Belonging to the male sex (now somewhat rare); also, pertaining to or characteristic of a man or men (as, *masculine* attire); also, having manlike qualities: virile; strong; manly; of a woman, mannish; in *gram.*, noting or pertaining to the gender to which the words denoting males regularly belong.—**masculine rime,** in *pros.*, a rime of but a single (stressed) syllable, as *disdain*, *complain* ('single rime'). Cf. *feminine rime*, under *feminine*, *a.*—**mas′cu-line,** *n.* In *gram.*, the masculine gender; a masculine word or word-form.—**mas′cu-line-ly,** *adv.*—**mas′cu-line-ness, mas-cu-lin′i-ty** (-lin′i-ti), *n.*

mash (mash), *n.* [AS. *masc-*, *max-* (recorded in comp.), = G. *meisch*, mash.] Crushed malt or meal of grain mixed with hot water to form wort; also, a mess of boiled grain, bran, meal, etc., fed warm to horses and cattle; in general, a soft, pulpy mass (as, "One of his great toes was crushed into a *mash* between two stones": Smollett's "Humphry Clinker," July 13); also, a confused mixture; a muddle; also, pulpy state or condition; also, an overpowering sentimental admiration or attachment for a person (slang); a person who is the object of such an admiration or attachment (slang).—**mash,** *v. t.* To mix (crushed malt, etc.) with hot water to form wort; also, to reduce to a soft, pulpy mass, as by beating or pressure; in general, to crush; also, to inspire with a strong sentimental admiration or regard (slang: as, "Shan't I just *mash* the men!" Arnold Bennett's "Hilda Lessways," i. 12).—**mash′er,** *n.* One who or that which mashes; also, a man who frequents public places and tries to make advances to women (slang).

mash-ie, mash-y (mash′i), *n.* [Cf. F. *massue*, club.] In *golf*, a club having a short iron head with a greatly sloping face for making short lofting shots ('lofting mashie'), or with a less sloping face for longer, less lofted shots ('driving mashie').

mas-jid (mus′jid), *n.* [Ar.: see *mosque*.] A mosque.

mask[1] (måsk), *v. t.* [Var. of *mash*, *v.*] To mash (malt); also, to brew; also, to infuse (tea). [Sc. and north. Eng.]

mask[2] (måsk), *n.* [F. *masque*: cf. ML. *mascus*, *masca*, mask, specter, *masca*, witch, It. *maschera*, Sp. *máscara*, mask, all of uncertain origin and relations.] A covering for the face, worn for disguise, protection, etc.; a figure of a face or head worn by ancient Greek and Roman actors; a false face; also, a likeness of a person's face, as in marble, or as molded in plaster, wax, etc. (as, a death-*mask*); also, anything that disguises or conceals; a disguise; a pretense; a covering; also, a person wearing a mask (as, "A *mask*, in the character of an old woman, joined them": Fielding's "Tom Jones," xiii. 7); a masker; also, a masquerade or revel; also, a masque (entertainment or dramatic composition); in *arch.*, etc., a representation of a face or head, generally grotesque, used as an ornament; *milit.*, a screen, as of earth or brush, for concealing or protecting a battery or any military operation.—**mask**[2], *v.* [F. *masquer*.] **I.** *tr.* To cover with a mask; hence, to disguise or conceal (as, "This speech *masked* some secret design of personal ambition": Besant's "Coligny," vi.); specif., *milit.*, to conceal (a battery or any military operation) from the enemy; also, to hinder (an army, etc.) from conducting an operation, as by a superior force. **II.** *intr.* To put on a mask (as, "White men of fortune and station were *masking*, night-riding, whipping and killing": G. W. Cable's "John March, Southerner," ix.); disguise one's self; take part in a masque or masquerade.

Mask. — From cast of statue of Thalia, the Muse of comedy, in the Vatican Museum.

mas-ka-longe, mas-ki-nonge (mas′ką-lonj, -ki-nonj), *n.* [Algonquian *maskinonge*.] A large pike, *Esox masquinongy*, of the region of the Great Lakes of North America, attaining a length of from 4 to 6 feet.

mask=crab (måsk′krab), *n.* A crab having on its carapace markings suggestive of a mask; esp., *Corystes cassivelaunus*, a long-armed European species.

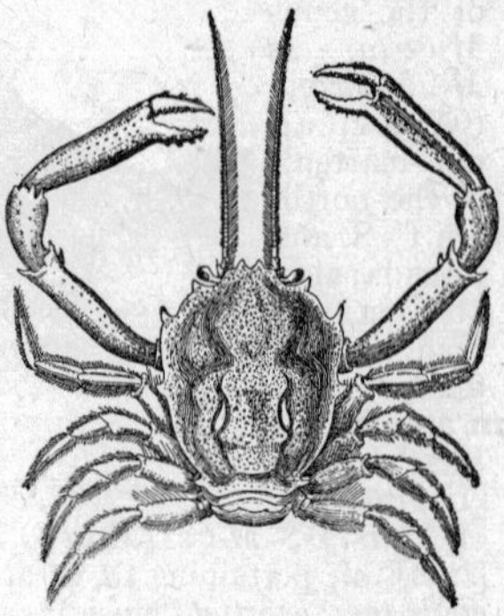
Mask-crab (*Corystes cassivelaunus*).

masked (måskt), *p. a.* Wearing, or provided with, a mask or masks; hence, disguised; concealed; specif., in *zoöl.*, marked on the face or head as if wearing a mask; also, having the wings, legs, etc., of the future imago indicated in outline beneath the integument, as certain insect pupæ; in *bot.*, personate.—**masked ball,** a ball at which the participants appear in masks.

mask-er (mås′kėr), *n.* One who masks; one who takes part in a masque or masquerade; a masquerader.

mas′ki-nonge, *n.* See *maskalonge.*

mas-lin[1] (maz′lin), *n.* [AS. *mæstling*: cf. G. *messing*, brass.] A kind of brass; also, a vessel made of it. [Chiefly prov.]

mas-lin[2] (maz′lin), *n.* [OF. *mesteillon*, < ML. *mistilio(n-)*, < L. *miscere*, mix.] A mixture of grains, esp. rye and wheat; bread made of it; fig., a mixture or medley. [Now prov.]

mas-och-ism (maz′ǫk-izm), *n.* [From Leopold von Sacher-*Masoch* (1836–95), Austrian novelist, who described it.] In *pathol.*, a form of sexual perversion in which the victim takes pleasure in physical abuse from a person of the other sex. Cf. *sadism.*—**mas-och-is′tic,** *a.*

ma-son (mā′sn), *n.* [OF. F. *maçon*, < ML. *macio(n-)*, *machio(n-)*, *mattio(n-)*; origin uncertain.] A builder and worker in stone; one who builds with brick, artificial stone, or the like; one who molds cement, concrete, etc., in imitation of stonework; also [often *cap.*], a freemason.—**ma′son,** *v. t.* To construct of or strengthen with masonry: as, "the *masoned* house" (Stevenson's "Master of Ballantrae," viii.).

Ma-son (mā′sn) **and Dix-on's** (dik′sǫnz) **line.** The boundary between Pennsylvania and Maryland, partly surveyed by Charles Mason and Jeremiah Dixon between 1763 and 1767, and celebrated before the extinction of slavery in the U. S. as a line of demarcation between the free and the slave States.

ma-son-ic (mą-son′ik), *a.* Pertaining to masons or masonry (rare); also [often *cap.*], pertaining to or characteristic of freemasons or freemasonry; [*l. c.*] suggestive of a spirit of freemasonry or a sympathetic understanding (as, "In some voiceless, *masonic* way, most people in that saloon had become aware that something was in process of happening": Wister's "Virginian," iii.).

ma-son-ry (mā′sn-ri), *n.*; pl. *-ries* (-riz). The art or occupation of a mason; the skill or workmanship of a mason; also, work constructed by a mason; esp., stonework; also [often *cap.*], freemasonry.

ma-son-work (mā′sn-wėrk), *n.* Masonry or stonework.

Ma-so-ra, Ma-so-rah (mą-sō′rą), *n.* [Heb. *māsōrāh*, tradition.] The Hebrew tradition, formed gradually through a succession of centuries, as to the correct form of the text of the Scriptures, or the collection of critical notes in which it is embodied; sometimes, the Masoretes collectively.—**Mas-o-rete** (mas′ǫ-rēt), *n.* A Hebrew scholar versed in the Masora; esp., one of the body of Jewish scholars who reduced the Masora to writing.—**Mas-o-ret′ic** (-ret′ik), *a.*

masque (måsk), *n.* [F.: see *mask*[2], *n.*] A masquerade; a revel; also, a form of amateur histrionic entertainment, commonly with elaborate costumes and scenery, in vogue at court and among the nobility in England in the 16th and 17th centuries, orig. consisting of dumb-show and dancing, but afterwards including dialogue and song; also, a dramatic composition for such an entertainment (as, the *masques* of Ben Jonson; Milton's *masque* of "Comus").

mas-quer-ade (mȧs-kẹ-rād′), *n.* [F. *mascarade,* < It. *mascherata* (= Sp. *mascarada*), < *maschera,* mask: see *mask*[2].] An assembly of persons wearing masks and other disguises, and often rich or fantastic dress, for dancing, etc.; also, disguise such as is worn at such an assembly; hence, in general, disguise, or false outward show (as, "And, after all, what is a lie? 'Tis but The truth in *masquerade*": Byron's "Don Juan," xi. 37); also, the act of masquerading; hence, a going about under false pretenses.—**mas-quer-ade′,** *v. i.*; *-aded, -ading.* To take part in a masquerade; disguise one's self; hence, to go about under false pretenses; assume a false character.—**mas-quer-ad′er** (-kẹ-rā′dėr), *n.*

mass[1] (mas), *n.* [AS. *mæsse,* < LL. *missa,* mass (the original application of the term being in dispute), < L. *mittere,* send.] [Also *cap.*] The celebration, or a celebration, of the eucharist; also, the sacrament of the eucharist, or Lord's Supper; also, the liturgy of the eucharist; also, a particular form of the eucharistic service or liturgy (see phrases below); also, a musical setting of certain parts of this service (as, Bach's "*Mass* in B Minor"): now used chiefly with reference to the eucharist as celebrated in the Roman Catholic Church.—**high mass,** mass accompanied with music, the celebrant usually being attended by a deacon and subdeacon.—**low mass,** the ordinary mass, said (not sung) by the priest.

mass[2] (mas), *n.* [OF. F. *masse,* < L. *massa,* mass, lump: cf. Gr. *μᾶζα,* barley-cake, *μάσσειν,* knead.] A body of coherent matter, usually of indefinite shape and often of considerable size (as, a *mass* of dough, flesh, or rock); also, an aggregation of incoherent particles, parts, or objects regarded as forming one body (as, a *mass* of sand, flowers, clouds, or buildings; a *mass* of troops); an agglomeration, congeries, or heap; in general, a considerable assemblage, number, or quantity (as, "I remember a *mass* of things, but nothing distinctly," Shakspere's "Othello," ii. 3. 289; a *mass* of debts, errors, information, or prejudice); a volume (of sound); an expanse, as of color, light, or shade in a painting; also, an object seen as of indefinite form or character (as, "Willy . . . observed a dark *mass* looming through the mist on the weather beam": Marryat's "King's Own," xiii.); also, the main body, bulk, or greater part of anything (as, the great *mass* of American products; the common *mass* of mankind); also, bulk, size, or massiveness (as, "Witness this army of such *mass* and charge," Shakspere's "Hamlet," iv. 4. 47; mountains notable for sheer *mass*); in *physics,* that property of a body, commonly defined as the measure of the quantity of matter in it, to which its inertia is ascribed; in *phar.*, a preparation of thick, pasty consistence from which pills are made (as, blue *mass*: see under *blue, a.*).—**in the mass,** as an aggregate whole, without distinction of parts or individuals: as, to consider mankind *in the mass.*—**the masses,** the great body of the common people; the working classes or lower social orders: often contrasted with 'the classes' (see under *class, n.*).—**mass**[2], *v.* **I.** *tr.* To gather into or dispose in a mass or masses; assemble: as, "The houses are *massed* in blocks" (Mark Twain's "Life on the Mississippi," xliv.); they are *massing* troops along the eastern border. **II.** *intr.* To come together in or form a mass or masses: as, the clouds are *massing* in the west.

mas-sa (mas′ạ), *n.* Negro corruption of *master*[2].

mas-sa-cre (mas′ạ-kėr), *n.* [F. *massacre,* massacre, OF. *maçacre, macecle,* butchery, shambles; origin unknown.] The unnecessary indiscriminate killing of a number of human beings, as in barbarous warfare or persecution, or for revenge or plunder (as, the *massacre* of St. Bartholomew, see *St. Bartholomew's Day,* under *saint, a.*; the *massacre* of the Innocents, see *innocent, n.*; the *massacre* of Glencoe, the treacherous slaying of the Macdonalds of Glencoe, Scotland, by their enemies the Campbells, under a warrant from William III., on Feb. 13, 1692); a general slaughter of human beings; hence, the wholesale killing of animals; sometimes, an atrocious murder.—**mas′sa-cre,** *v. t.*; *-cred, -cring.* [F. *massacrer.*] To kill indiscriminately, or in a massacre (as, "The savages had *massacred* many of the garrison after capitulation": B. Franklin's "Autobiography," xiv.); also, to murder atrociously, as a single human being.—**mas′-sa-crer** (-krėr), *n.*

mas-sage (mạ-säzh′, F. mȧ-säzh), *n.* [F., < *masser,* to massage: cf. Pg. *amassar,* knead, < *massa,* dough.] The act or art of treating the body by rubbing, kneading, or the like, to stimulate circulation, increase suppleness, etc.—**mas-sage′,** *v. t.*; *-saged, -saging.* To treat by massage.—**mas-sag′er, mas-sag′ist** (-sä′zhėr, -zhist), *n.*

mas-sé (ma-sā′ or mas′ā), *n.* [F., pp. of *masser,* strike by a massé, < *masse,* kind of cue, = E. *mace*[1].] In *billiards,* a stroke made by hitting the cue-ball with the cue held almost or quite perpendicularly.

mas-se-ter (ma-sē′tėr), *n.* [NL., < Gr. *μασητήρ,* < *μασᾶσθαι,* chew.] In *anat.*, an important masticatory muscle which serves to raise the lower jaw.—**mas-se-ter-ic** (mas-ẹ̄-ter′ik), *a.*

mas-seur (mȧ-sėr), *n.* [F.] A man who practises massage.—**mas-seuse** (mȧ-sėz), *n.* [F.] Fem. of *masseur.*

mas-si-cot (mas′i-kot), *n.* [F.; origin obscure.] Monoxide of lead, in the form of a yellow powder, used as a pigment and drier.

mas-sif (mas′if, F. mȧ-sēf), *n.* [F., noun use of *massif,* E. *massive.*] In *geol.*, a compact portion of a mountain-range, containing one summit or a number of summits, and surrounded more or less completely by depressions which give it the appearance of an independent whole; also, a band or zone of the earth's crust raised or depressed as a unit and bounded by faults.

mass-i-ness (mas′i-nes), *n.* The state of being massy.

mas-sive (mas′iv), *a.* [F. *massif,* < *masse,* E. *mass*[2].] Consisting of or forming a large mass; bulky and heavy; consisting of or marked by great masses, as a style of architecture; large, as the head or forehead (as, "my master's . . . square, *massive* brow": C. Brontë's "Jane Eyre," xvii.); also, solid, rather than hollow or plated, as gold or silver, plate, etc. (as, "a chain of *massive* gold": Scott's "Talisman," iv.); also, solid or substantial; great or imposing; broad in scope; of great magnitude, as a sensation; affecting a large continuous mass of bodily tissue, as a disease; specif., in *mineral.*, without crystalline form, although perhaps crystalline in structure; in *geol.*, homogeneous.—**mas′sive-ly,** *adv.*—**mas′sive-ness,** *n.*

mass=meet-ing (mas′mē″ting), *n.* A large or general assembly of the people to discuss or hear discussed some matter of common interest.

Mas-so′ra, etc. See *Masora,* etc.

mass-y (mas′i), *a.* Consisting of a large mass of heavy material, or massive (as, "We closed all the *massy* shutters of our old building": Poe's "Murders in the Rue Morgue"); characterized by great masses, as architecture; in general, of considerable bulk or volume; fig., great or impressive (as, "The darkness gathered on the rear and flanks in *massy* blackness": De Quincey's "English Mail-Coach," i.); also, solid and weighty, as metal; solid, rather than hollow or plated (as, "a great quantity of *massy* old plate": Sheridan's "School for Scandal," iii. 3). [Now chiefly archaic or literary.]

mast[1] (mȧst), *n.* [AS. *mæst* = G. *mast,* mast; akin to E. *meat.*] The fruit (acorns, chestnuts, etc.) of certain forest-trees, esp. as food for swine.

mast[2] (mȧst), *n.* [AS. *mæst* = D., G., Sw., and Dan. *mast,* mast.] A long pole or spar rising from the keel of a vessel to support the yards, sails, etc.; hence, any similar pole, as the upright pole of a derrick, or as a tall upright rod or spar on a flying-machine.—**before the mast.** See under *before, prep.*—**mast**[2], *v. t.* To provide with a mast or masts.

mas-ta-ba (mas′tạ-bạ̈), *n.* [Ar., 'bench.'] In Mohammedan countries, a bench or seat; also, an ancient Egyptian tomb, rectangular in plan, with sloping sides and a flat roof.

mast-ed (mȧs′ted), *a.* Having a mast or masts: as, a three-*masted* vessel.

mast-er[1] (mȧs′tėr), *n.* A vessel with (a specified number of) masts: as, a three-*master.*

mas-ter[2] (mȧs′tėr). [AS. *mægester*, also OF. *maistre* (F. *maître*), < L. *magister*, master, chief, head, akin to *magis*, in a greater degree, more, *magnus*, great: see *magnitude*.] **I.** *n.* A man who has authority or control, as a chief or leader, a presiding officer, the commander of a merchant vessel, the male head of a household, an employer of workmen or servants, an owner of a slave or a horse or dog, etc.; sometimes, in general, an owner or possessor (as, "those excellent qualities of the mind he was *master* of": Swift's "Gulliver's Travels," ii. 6); also, one who has the power of controlling, using, or disposing of something at pleasure (as, "He . . . was a perfect *master* of both languages," Swift's "Gulliver's Travels," iii. 9; "He is *master* of everything near him but himself," Cooper's "Deerslayer," v.); also, one who overcomes another; a victor; also, a male teacher, or schoolmaster (as, "The village *master* taught his little school": Goldsmith's "Deserted Village," 196); hence, a person whose teachings one accepts or follows; [*cap.*] with *the*, *our*, etc., Christ; also [*l. c.*], a person who has taken a certain advanced degree at a college or university, orig. conveying qualification to teach (as, *master* of arts; *master* of science); also, a workman qualified to teach apprentices and to carry on his trade independently; a workman of approved skill; also, a man eminently skilled in something, as an occupation, art, or science; an artist regarded as a model of excellence, or a work by such an artist (as, an old *master*); also, a title of respect for a man or a boy (now changed to *mister* in ordinary speech except when given to boys); hence, a youth or boy; a young gentleman; in Scotland, the title of the heir apparent of a viscount or a baron (as, the *Master* of Lovat, heir of Baron Lovat; "The *Master* of Ballantrae," the title of a novel by R. L. Stevenson). **II.** *a.* Being master, or exercising mastery; chief or principal; directing or controlling; dominating or predominant; also, being a master carrying on his trade independently, rather than a workman employed by another; also, being a master of some occupation, art, etc.; eminently or consummately skilled; also, belonging or pertaining to a master, esp. as contrasted with his servants (as, a house with 9 *master* bedrooms and 4 bedrooms for servants); also, characteristic of a master; showing mastery; exhibiting a high degree of skill.—**mas′ter**[2], *v. t.* To rule or direct as master; also, to become the master of; conquer or subdue; reduce to subjection; also, to make one's self master of; become an adept in.

mas-ter=at=arms (mȧs′tėr-ạt-ärmz′), *n.*; pl. *masters-*. A petty officer in the navy who has various duties, such as keeping order on the ship, taking charge of prisoners, etc.

mas-ter-dom (mȧs′tėr-dọm), *n.* Mastery; dominion.

mas-ter-er (mȧs′tėr-ėr), *n.* One who or that which masters.

mas-ter-ful (mȧs′tėr-fu̇l), *a.* Having or showing the qualities of a master; authoritative; imperious; domineering; also, showing mastery or skill; masterly.—**mas′ter-ful-ly,** *adv.*—**mas′ter-ful-ness,** *n.*

mas-ter-hood (mȧs′tėr-hu̇d), *n.* The condition or character of being a master.

mas-ter=key (mȧs′tėr-kē), *n.* A key that will open a number of locks whose proper keys are not interchangeable.

mas-ter-less (mȧs′tėr-les), *a.* Without a master (as, "Many a town must now be *masterless*, And women's voices rule": W. Morris's "Jason," iii. 9); uncontrolled or unprotected by a master (as, *masterless* men, formerly, vagabonds, or persons without reputable means of support).

mas-ter-ly (mȧs′tėr-li), *a.* Like or befitting a master, as in skill or art.—**mas′ter-li-ness,** *n.*—**mas′ter-ly,** *adv.* In a masterly manner.

mas-ter-piece (mȧs′tėr-pēs), *n.* One's most excellent production, as in an art (as, the *masterpiece* of a painter or sculptor; "A friend may well be reckoned the *masterpiece* of nature," Emerson's "Essays," Friendship); also, any production of masterly skill (as, a painter who has produced many *masterpieces*); a consummate example of skill or excellence of any kind (as, "This plan of setting our enemies to destroy one another seemed to us a *masterpiece* of policy": Parkman's "Oregon Trail," xxiii.).

mas-ter-ship (mȧs′tėr-ship), *n.* The office, function, or dignity of a master; the degree or status of a master, as at a university or in a craft (as, "Edinburgh College, where I had just received my *mastership* of arts": Stevenson's "Master of Ballantrae," ii.); also, the condition or authority of a master; dominion, rule, or control; also, ascendancy; victory; also, mastery, as of a subject; also, masterly skill or knowledge; also, with *your*, *his*, etc., the personality of a master† (as, "How now, Signior Launce! what news with your *mastership?*" Shakspere's "Two Gentlemen of Verona," iii. 1. 280).

mas-ter-sing-er (mȧs′tėr-sing″ėr), *n.* Same as *meistersinger*.

mas-ter=stroke (mȧs′tėr-strōk), *n.* A masterly action or achievement.

mas-ter-work (mȧs′tėr-wėrk), *n.* A chief or masterly performance or production; a masterpiece.

mas-ter-y (mȧs′tėr-i), *n.* [OF. *maistrie*.] The state of being master; power of command or control; dominion; also, ascendancy in strife or competition (as, "Four champions fierce, Strive here for *mastery*": Milton's "Paradise Lost," ii. 899); victory; also, command or grasp, as of a subject (as, "This consummate military leader . . . was distinguished by . . . a *mastery* of method rarely surpassed": Disraeli's "Lothair," lii.); the action of mastering a subject, etc.; also, expert skill or knowledge.

mast-head (mȧst′hed), *n.* *Naut.*, the top of a ship's mast, esp. of the lower mast.—**mast′head,** *v. t.* To send to the masthead as a punishment (as, "One of the midshipmen was *mastheaded* . . . for not waiting on deck until he was relieved": Marryat's "Peter Simple," xxix.); also, to raise to the masthead, as a flag.

mas-tic (mas′tik), *n.* [OF. F. *mastic*, < L. *mastiche*, < Gr. *μαστίχη*, mastic, perhaps (since it is used in the East as a chewing-gum) akin to *μασᾶσθαι*, chew.] An aromatic, astringent resin obtained from a small anacardiaceous evergreen tree, *Pistacia lentiscus*, native in the Mediterranean region; a similar resin yielded by other trees of the same genus, or a resin likened to it; also, a tree yielding a mastic, esp. *Pistacia lentiscus*; also, a sapotaceous tree, *Sideroxylon mastichodendron*, of Florida, etc., yielding a timber valued for boat-building; also, a distilled liquor flavored with the resin mastic; also, any of various cements or mortars.

mas-ti-ca-ble (mas′ti-kạ-bl), *a.* That may be masticated.

mas-ti-cate (mas′ti-kāt), *v. t.*; *-cated*, *-cating*. [LL. *masticatus*, pp. of *masticare*, chew: cf. *mastic*, also Gr. *μάσταξ*, jaw.] To grind with the teeth in preparation for swallowing; chew; also, to reduce to a pulp by crushing or kneading, as rubber.—**mas-ti-ca′tion** (-kā′shọn), *n.* [LL. *masticatio(n-)*.] The act or process of masticating.—**mas′ti-ca-tor,** *n.*—**mas′ti-ca-to-ry** (-kạ-tọ-ri). **I.** *a.* Of, pertaining to, or used in or for mastication. **II.** *n.* A substance that is chewed (not swallowed), as chewing-gum, betel-nut, tobacco, etc.; specif., a medicinal substance to be chewed, as to promote the secretion of saliva.

mas-tiff (mȧs′tif), *n.* [ME. *mastif*, appar. < OF. *mastin* (F. *mâtin*), mastiff, < L. *mansuetus*, tame: see *mansuete*.] One of a breed of powerful, stoutly built dogs with large head, drooping ears, and pendulous lips.

mas-ti-tis (mas-tī′tis), *n.* [NL., < Gr. *μαστός*, breast.] In *pathol.*, inflammation of the female breast.

mast-less (mȧst′les), *a.* Without a mast, as a vessel.

mas-to-don (mas′tọ-don), *n.* [NL., < Gr. *μαστός*, breast, + *ὀδούς* (*ὀδοντ-*), tooth.] Any of various species of large, extinct mammals (genus *Mastodon*, etc.) of the elephant kind, characterized by nipple-like excrescences on the molar teeth.—**mas-to-don′tic,** *a.*

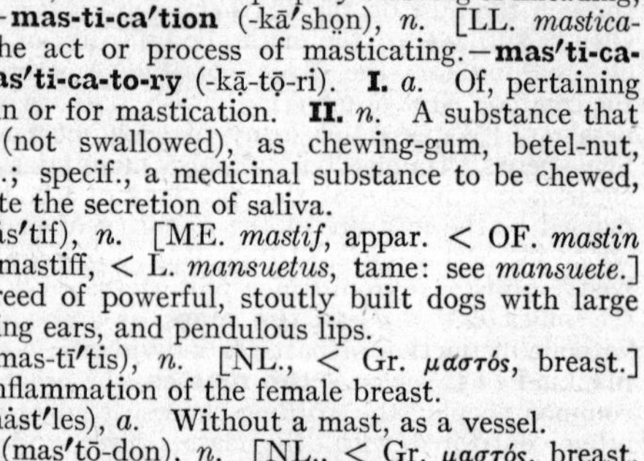

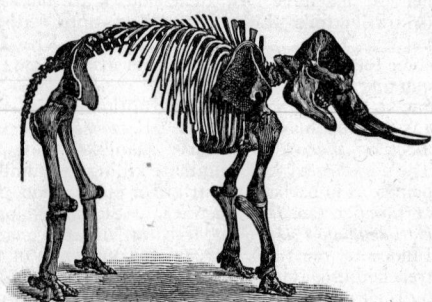

Mastodon (*Mastodon americanus*).—Skeleton discovered at Cohoes, New York, 1866; in the State Museum of Natural History, Albany.

mas-toid (mas′toid). [Gr. *μαστο-*

εἰδής, < μαστός, breast, + εἶδος, form.] **I.** *a.* Resembling a breast or nipple (applied esp. to a process of the temporal bone behind the ear); of or pertaining to the mastoid process. **II.** *n.* In *anat.*, the mastoid process.—**mas-toi-di′tis** (-toi-dī′tis), *n.* [NL.] In *pathol.*, inflammation in the mastoid process.

mas-tur-ba-tion (mas-tėr-bā′shọn), *n.* [L. *masturbatio(n-)*, < *masturbari*, practise masturbation.] Sexual self-abuse.

mat[1] (mat), *n.* [AS. *matt*, < L. *matta*, mat (of rushes).] A piece of fabric made of plaited or woven rushes, straw, hemp, coir, or other fiber, or a similar article made of some other material, used to lie or rest on, to cover a floor, to wipe the shoes on, or otherwise; also, a smaller piece of material, often ornamental, set upon a table or the like, as under a dish of food, a lamp, a vase, etc.; specif., a thick covering, as of padded canvas, laid on a floor on which wrestlers contend, in order to protect them (as, to go to the *mat* with a person, to meet him in a contest of wrestling, or, fig., in active contention as over a matter at issue); also, a sack made of matting, as for coffee or sugar; also, a thickly growing or thick and tangled mass, as of hair or weeds.—**mat**[1], *v.*; *matted, matting.* **I.** *tr.* To cover with or as with mats or matting; cover with an entangled mass (as, "This vine . . . has clothed and *matted* with its many branches the four walls": J. H. Newman's "Callista," xv.); also, to form into a mat, as by interweaving; entangle in a thick mass (as, "willow and cotton-wood trees, so closely interlocked and *matted* together, as to be nearly impassable": Irving's "Captain Bonneville," vi.). **II.** *intr.* To become entangled; form tangled masses.

mat[2] (mat). [F. *mat* = G. *matt*, dull: see *mate*[2].] **I.** *a.* Without luster; dull: as, *mat* gold. **II.** *n.* A mat surface or finish, as in metal; also, a tool for producing it.—**mat**[2], *v. t.*; *matted, matting.* To finish with a mat surface.

mat[3] (mat), *n.* [Origin uncertain: cf. *mat*[1], *n.*, and *mat*[2], *n.*] A more or less wide frame-like piece of pasteboard or other material (of gold, white, black, or any color) placed about a picture and extending to the outer frame.

mat-a-dor (mat-ạ-dôr′ or mat′ạ-dôr), *n.* [Sp., < L. *mactator*, slayer, < *mactare*, slay: cf. *mactation*.] The man appointed to kill the bull in bull-fights; also, one of the principal cards in certain games, as ombre and quadrille.

ma-ta-ma-ta (mä-tạ̈-mä′tạ̈), *n.* [S. Amer.] A fresh-water turtle, *Chelys matamata* (or *fimbriata*), of Guiana and Brazil, having a brown carapace covered with pyramidal eminences.

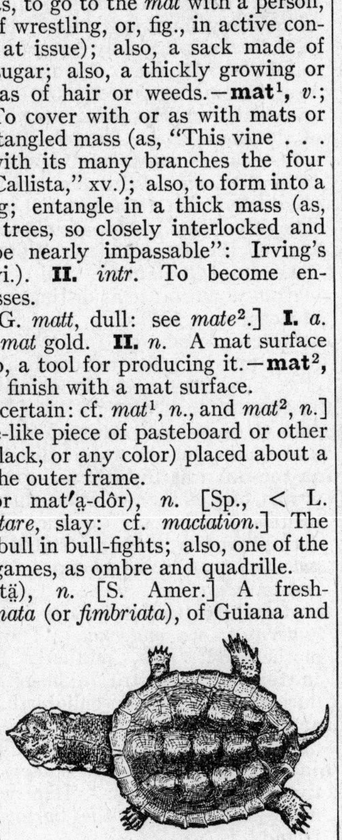

Matamata.

match[1] (mach), *n.* [OF. *meiche* (F. *mèche*); origin uncertain.] The wick of a candle or lamp†; now, a wick, cord, or the like, prepared to burn at a uniform rate, used to fire cannon, etc.; also, the material from which such matches are made; also, a splinter of wood or a piece of cord, cloth, paper, or the like, dipped in melted sulphur, so as to be readily ignited by the use of a tinder-box (now only hist.); a similar article burned for fumigation; also, a short, slender piece of wood or other material tipped with a chemical substance which produces fire when rubbed on a rough or chemically prepared surface, or, in the earlier forms, when brought into contact with a chemical reagent.

match[2] (mach), *n.* [AS. *gemæcca*, mate, fellow: see *make*[1].] A mate, as a husband or wife†; one's equal in age, station, etc.†; an opponent† or rival†; one able to cope with another as an equal (as, to meet one's *match*); a person or thing that equals another in some respect (as, "a period which . . . has not had its *match* in the history of the world": Galt's "Annals of the Parish," l.); a person or thing that is an exact counterpart of, or that corresponds to or closely resembles, another (as, a pair of horses that are good *matches*); also, a corresponding or suitably associated pair; also, an engagement for a contest or game; the contest or game itself; also, a matrimonial compact or alliance (as, "We had projected a *match* between him and a gentleman's daughter in the next county": Smollett's "Humphry Clinker," Oct. 11); hence, a person considered with regard to suitability as a partner in marriage (as, "the richest *match* in Rome": Wiseman's "Fabiola," i. 9); also, an agreement†, compact†, or bargain† (as, "A *match!* 'tis done": Shakspere's "Taming of the Shrew," v. 2. 74).—**match**[2], *v.* **I.** *tr.* To bring into association or coöperation†; mate† or couple†; also, to unite in marriage (esp. with reference to the fitness or unfitness of the union); procure a matrimonial alliance for (a son, daughter, etc.); also, to place in opposition or conflict; arrange a match or contest between or for; also, to compare with respect to superiority (as, "Chorus Hymeneal, Or triumphal chant, *Matched* with thine would be all But an empty vaunt": Shelley's "To a Skylark," 68); also, to pair as adversaries or competitors, or provide with an adversary or competitor, of equal power (as, the antagonists were well *matched*); also, to pair or assort (persons or things) with a view to equality or correspondence; arrange in a suitable pair or set; also, to adapt, or make to correspond (as, "To *match* our spirits to our day And make a joy of duty": Whittier's "Our River"); fit together, as two things; also, to furnish with a match; procure or produce an equal to (as, to *match* this scenery you must go a long distance); also, to obtain or supply a counterpart of or something similar to (a color, pattern, fabric, etc.); also, to encounter as an adversary with equal power; prove a match for (as, no one could *match* him as a swordsman); also, to equal, or be equal to (as, "The event does not . . . *match* the expectation": C. Brontë's "Villette," xxxvi.); also, to be the match or counterpart of (as, the color of the skirt does not *match* that of the coat); correspond to (as, "With mien to *match* the morning And gay delightful guise": A. E. Housman's "Shropshire Lad," xlii.). **II.** *intr.* To ally one's self in marriage; also, to be equal or suitable; correspond; be of corresponding size, shape, color, pattern, etc.

match-a-ble (mach′ạ-bl), *a.* That may be matched.

match=board (mach′bōrd), *n.* A board which has a tongue cut along one edge and a groove in the opposite edge: used in making floors, etc., the tongue of one such board fitting into the groove of the next.—**match′=board,** *v. t.* To cover or supply with match-boards.

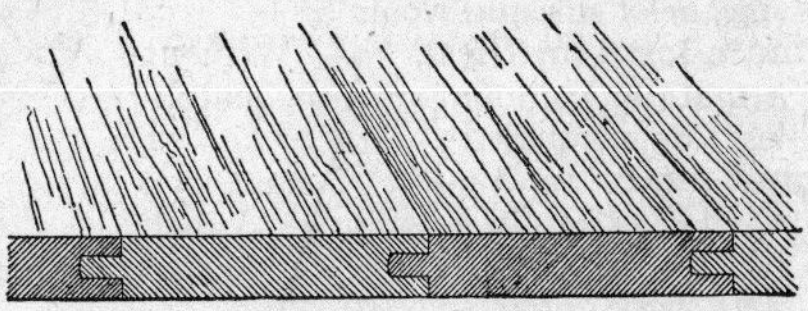

Match-boards.

match-er (mach′ėr), *n.* One who matches.

match-less (mach′les), *a.* Having no match or equal; peerless: as, "*matchless* courage" (De Quincey's "English Mail-Coach," i.); "the *matchless* symmetry of his form" (H. Melville's "Typee," xvii.).—**match′less-ly,** *adv.*

match-lock (mach′lok), *n.* An old form of gun-lock in which the priming was ignited by a slow-match; also, a musket with such a lock.

match=mak-er[1] (mach′mā″kėr), *n.* One who makes matches for burning.

match=mak-er[2] (mach′mā″kėr), *n.* One who makes, or seeks to bring about, matrimonial matches; also, one who makes or arranges matches for contests, etc.—**match′=mak″ing,** *n.* and *a.*

match=play (mach′plā), *n.* In *golf*, play in which the score is reckoned by counting the holes won by each side. Cf. *medal-play.*

match=safe (mach′sāf), *n.* A box made of incombustible material, for holding matches for use.

match=stick (mach′stik), *n.* A stick or slender piece of wood of which a match is made.

match=wood (mach′wụd), *n.* Touchwood†; also, wood suitable, or cut into pieces of the proper size, for matches; hence, splinters.

mate[1] (māt), *n.* [ME. *mate* = MLG. *mate* = D. *maat*, mate; appar. orig. meaning 'messmate,' and akin to E. *meat.*] A habitual associate; a comrade; a partner; also, a suitable associate, or an equal or match (archaic: as, "I know you proud to bear your name, Your pride is yet no *mate* for mine," Tennyson's "Lady Clara Vere de Vere"); also, husband or wife, esp. one who is a fitting or worthy partner; one of a pair of mated animals; hence, one joined with another in any pair; a counterpart; also, an officer of a merchant vessel who ranks next below the captain or master (called *first mate, second mate*, etc., when there are more than one on a ship); also, an assistant to a warrant-officer or other functionary on a ship; in the U. S. navy, one who ranks above a chief petty officer and below a warrant-officer, and who is regarded as occupying the status of both an officer and an enlisted man (also used with a qualifying term, as in *boatswain's mate, gunner's mate*, etc., as a title for certain petty officers).—**mate**[1], *v.*; *mated, mating.* **I.** *tr.* To join as a mate or as mates; match or marry; pair, as animals; also, to join suitably, as two things; sometimes, to treat as comparable, as one thing with another; also, to vie or cope with (obs. or rare: as, "In speed His galley *mates* the flying steed," Scott's "Lord of the Isles," i. 12). **II.** *intr.* To associate as a mate or as mates; marry (as, "She's above *mating* with such as I": Hardy's "Return of the Native," i. 2); pair; sometimes, to consort; keep company; also, to claim equality (*with*: archaic).

mate[2] (māt), *v. t.*; *mated, mating.* [OF. F. *mater*, < OF. *mat*, checkmated, overcome, exhausted (F. *mat*, dull: see *mat*[2]), < Pers. *māt*, helpless: see *checkmate.*] To defeat†; baffle†; daunt†; now, to checkmate.—**mate**[2], *n.* A checkmate.

ma-te[3], **ma-té** (mä'tā), *n.* [Sp. *mate*, prop. the vessel in which the beverage is made, < Peruvian *mati*, calabash.] A tea-like South American beverage made from the leaves of a species of holly, *Ilex paraguayensis*, native in Paraguay and Brazil; also, the leaves prepared for infusion; also, the plant itself.

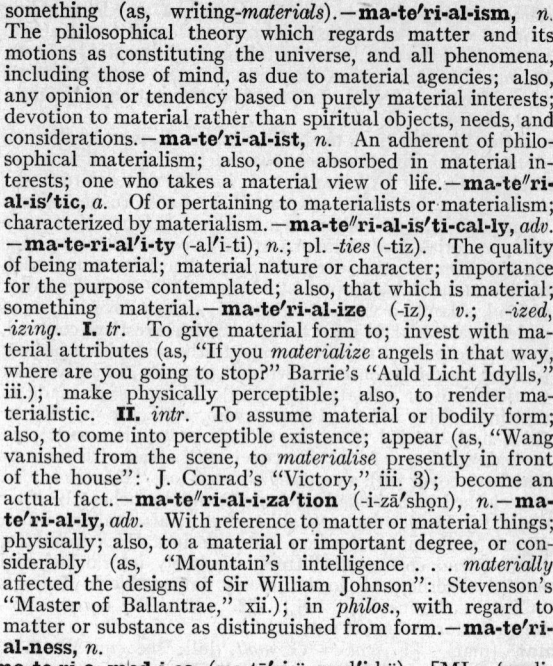

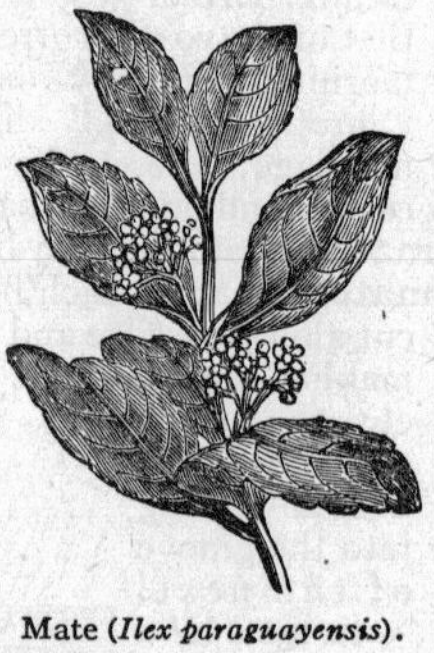
Mate (*Ilex paraguayensis*).

mate-las-sé (mȧt-lȧ-sā). [F., pp. of *matelasser*, to cushion, < *matelas*, mattress, cushion: see *mattress.*] **I.** *a.* Of fabrics, woven with a raised pattern, as if quilted. **II.** *n.* A matelassé fabric, as of silk, or of silk and wool.

mate-less (māt'les), *a.* Without a mate or companion; also, matchless† or unequaled†.

mat-e-lote (mat'ẹ-lōt, F. mȧt-lot), *n.* [F., < *matelot*, sailor.] A dish of fish (or meat) cut up and cooked with wine, onions, etc.

ma-ter (mā'tėr), *n.* [L.: see *mother*[2].] Mother: as, "'Hello, *mater!*' said the curly-headed Charlie" (Arnold Bennett's "Hilda Lessways," ii. 4).—**ma''ter-fa-mil'i-as** (-fạ-mil'i-as), *n.* [L.] The mother of a family.

ma-te-ri-al (mạ-tē'ri-ạl). [LL. *materialis*, < L. *materia*, E. *matter.*] **I.** *a.* Formed or consisting of matter (as, a *material* body; the *material* world); physical; corporeal; also, relating to, concerned with, or involving matter (as, *material* laws; *material* force); often, opprobriously, concerned or occupied unduly with corporeal things or interests (as, "his gross *material* soul": Dryden's "Cymon and Iphigenia," 135); also, pertaining to the physical rather than the spiritual or intellectual aspect of things (as, *material* civilization; the moral and *material* downfall of a people); pertaining to or affecting man's physical nature; also, of substantial import, of much consequence, or important (as, "I flatter myself that no *material* objection can be made to our request," Smollett's "Humphry Clinker," Oct. 14; it is *material* that we understand the facts); pertinent or essential (*to*: as, "I pass the rest, whose ev'ry race, and name, And kinds, are less *material* to my theme," Dryden's tr. Virgil's "Georgics," ii. 149); specif., of evidence, etc., of such significance as to be likely to influence the determination of a cause; also, full of matter or sound sense† (as, "A *material* fool!" Shakspere's "As You Like It," iii. 3. 32); in *philos.*, of or pertaining to matter as distinguished from form. **II.** *n.* The substance or substances of which a thing is made or composed; any constituent element of a thing; often, anything serving as crude or raw matter for working upon or developing (as, "the *materials* of seditions," Bacon's "Essays," Of Seditions and Troubles; the *materials* of a history or a drama); also, a textile fabric; also, *pl.*, articles of any kind requisite for making or doing something (as, writing-*materials*).—**ma-te'ri-al-ism,** *n.* The philosophical theory which regards matter and its motions as constituting the universe, and all phenomena, including those of mind, as due to material agencies; also, any opinion or tendency based on purely material interests; devotion to material rather than spiritual objects, needs, and considerations.—**ma-te'ri-al-ist,** *n.* An adherent of philosophical materialism; also, one absorbed in material interests; one who takes a material view of life.—**ma-te''ri-al-is'tic,** *a.* Of or pertaining to materialists or materialism; characterized by materialism.—**ma-te''ri-al-is'ti-cal-ly,** *adv.* —**ma-te-ri-al'i-ty** (-al'i-ti), *n.*; pl. *-ties* (-tiz). The quality of being material; material nature or character; importance for the purpose contemplated; also, that which is material; something material.—**ma-te'ri-al-ize** (-īz), *v.*; *-ized, -izing.* **I.** *tr.* To give material form to; invest with material attributes (as, "If you *materialize* angels in that way, where are you going to stop?" Barrie's "Auld Licht Idylls," iii.); make physically perceptible; also, to render materialistic. **II.** *intr.* To assume material or bodily form; also, to come into perceptible existence; appear (as, "Wang vanished from the scene, to *materialise* presently in front of the house": J. Conrad's "Victory," iii. 3); become an actual fact.—**ma-te''ri-al-i-za'tion** (-i-zā'shọn), *n.*—**ma-te'ri-al-ly,** *adv.* With reference to matter or material things; physically; also, to a material or important degree, or considerably (as, "Mountain's intelligence . . . *materially* affected the designs of Sir William Johnson": Stevenson's "Master of Ballantrae," xii.); in *philos.*, with regard to matter or substance as distinguished from form.—**ma-te'ri-al-ness,** *n.*

ma-te-ri-a med-i-ca (mạ-tē'ri-ạ med'i-kạ). [ML., 'medical material.'] The remedial substances employed in medicine; also, the branch of medical science treating of these.

ma-té-ri-el (mȧ-tā-rē-el), *n.* [F., 'material.'] The aggregate of things used or needed in carrying on any business, undertaking, or operation: distinguished from *personnel.*

ma-ter-nal (mạ-tėr'nạl), *a.* [OF. F. *maternel*, < L. *maternus*, of a mother, < *mater*, mother.] Of or pertaining to, befitting, having the qualities of, or being a mother; also, derived from a mother; related through a mother (as, "his *maternal* aunt": Thackeray's "Newcomes," v.).—**ma-ter'nal-ly,** *adv.*

ma-ter-ni-ty (mạ-tėr'ni-ti), *n.* [ML. *maternitas*, < L. *maternus*: see *maternal.*] The state of being a mother; motherhood; also, motherly character; motherliness.—**maternity hospital,** a hospital for the care of women during confinement in childbirth.

mate-ship (māt'ship), *n.* The condition or relation of a mate; companionship; fellowship.

mat-ey (mā'ti), *n.*; pl. *mateys* (-tiz). Familiar diminutive of *mate*[1], *n.*: as, "'Here you, *matey*,' he cried to the man who trundled the barrow" (Stevenson's "Treasure Island," i.).

math[1] (math), *n.* [AS. *mæth*, akin to *māwan*, E. *mow*[3].] A mowing, or what is gathered from mowing: obs. or prov. except in *aftermath*, etc.

math[2] (math), *n.* Shortened form of *mathematics.* [Colloq.]

math-e-mat-ic (math-ẹ-mat'ik). [L. *mathematicus* (as n., *mathematica*), < Gr. μαθηματικός (as n., μαθηματική), < μάθημα, learning, science, pl. esp. the mathematical sciences, < μανθάνειν, learn.] **I.** *a.* Mathematical. [Now rare.] **II.** *n.* Mathematics. [Now rare.]—**math-e-mat'i-cal,** *a.* Of, pertaining to, or of the nature of mathematics; employed in the operations of mathematics; also, having the exactness or precision of mathematics.—**math-e-mat'i-cal-ly,** *adv.* —**math''e-ma-ti'cian** (-mạ-tish'ạn), *n.* One versed in mathematics.—**math-e-mat'ics,** *n.* The science that treats of the measurement, properties, and relations of quantities, including arithmetic, geometry, algebra, etc.—**applied mathematics,** mathematics in its concrete applications, as in astronomy, the various branches of physics, the theory of probabilities, etc.—**higher mathematics,** the more scientifically treated or advanced portions of mathematics, embracing all beyond ordinary arithmetic, geometry, algebra, and trigonometry.—**pure mathematics,** mathematics as an abstract science, apart from its applications.

mat-in (mat′in). [OF. F. *matin*, morning, *matines*, fem. pl., matins, < L. *matutinus*, of or in the morning: see *matutinal*.] **I.** *n.* The morning† (as, "The glow-worm shows the *matin* to be near, And 'gins to pale his uneffectual fire": Shakspere's "Hamlet," i. 5. 89); *pl.*, the first of the seven canonical hours, or the service for it, properly beginning at midnight, sometimes at daybreak (cf. *nocturn* and *laud*); also, the order for public morning prayer in the Anglican Church; also, a morning song, esp. of a bird (in *pl.* or *sing.*: poetic: as, "Crowds of larks at their *matins* hang over," Jean Ingelow's "Divided," i.; "The sprightly lark's shrill *matin* wakes the morn," Young's "Night Thoughts," i. 438). **II.** *a.* Pertaining to the morning or to matins.—**mat′i-nal** (-i-nạl), *a.* [F., < *matin*.] Matutinal; morning; early; also, early-rising.

mat-i-née (mat-i-nā′, Brit. mat′i-nā), *n.* [F., < *matin*, morning: see *matin*.] An entertainment, esp. a dramatic or musical performance, held in the daytime, usually in the afternoon; also, a woman's house-dress for morning wear.

mat-ing (mā′ting), *n.* The act of one who or that which mates; a pairing, as of birds.—**mat′ing=time,** *n.*

mat-rass (mat′rạs), *n.* [F. *matras*; origin uncertain.] In *chem.*, a glass vessel with a roundish body and a long neck, used for distilling, evaporating, etc. (also called *bolt-head*); also, a small glass tube closed at one end, in which a substance to be tested is heated.

ma-tri-arch (mā′tri-ärk), *n.* [L. *mater*, mother, + E. *-arch* as in *patriarch*.] A woman holding a position analogous to that of a patriarch, as in a family or tribe.—**ma-tri-ar′chal** (-är′kạl), *a.* Of or pertaining to a matriarch; pertaining to or characterized by maternal rule or matriarchy.—**ma-tri-ar′chal-ism,** *n.*—**ma-tri-ar′chate** (-kāt), *n.* A matriarchal system or community.—**ma′tri-ar-chy** (-ki), *n.*; pl. *-chies* (-kiz). The matriarchal system; a form of social organization, as in certain primitive tribes, in which the mother (not the father) is head of the family, and in which descent is reckoned in the female line, the children belonging to the mother's clan.

mat-ri-cal (mat′ri-kạl), *a.* Pertaining to a matrix.

mat-ri-ca-ri-a (mat-ri-kā′ri-ạ), *n.* [ML. (named with reference to reputed medicinal virtues), < LL. *matrix*, womb, E. *matrix*.] The plant feverfew (now chiefly in 'matricaria camphor,' a camphor obtained from the oil of feverfew); also, any plant of the asteraceous genus *Matricaria* (orig. including feverfew), as *M. inodora*, native in Europe and naturalized in North America, or *M. chamomilla*, the German camomile; also, the dried flower-heads of *M. chamomilla*, used medicinally.

Flowering Plant of Matricaria (*M. inodora*). — *a*, ray-flower; *b*, disk-flower; *c*, achenium.

mat-ri-ces (mat′ri-sēz), *n.* Plural of *matrix*.

mat-ri-cide (mat′ri-sīd), *n.* [L. *matricida*, *matricidium*, < *mater*, mother: see *-cide*.] One who kills his mother; also, the act of killing one's mother.—**mat′ri-ci-dal** (-sī-dạl), *a.*

ma-tric-u-lant (mạ-trik′ū-lạnt), *n.* One who matriculates; a candidate for matriculation.

ma-tric-u-late (mạ-trik′ū-lāt), *v.*; *-lated*, *-lating*. [ML. *matriculatus*, pp. of *matriculare*, < LL. *matricula*, dim. of *matrix*, public register, list, roll: see *matrix*.] **I.** *tr.* To enroll, or admit to membership and privileges by enrolling, esp. in a college or university. **II.** *intr.* To be matriculated: as, "Tom Brown . . . went up to *matriculate* at St. Ambrose's College, Oxford" (Hughes's "Tom Brown at Oxford," Introd.).—**ma-tric′u-late,** *n.* One who has been matriculated.—**ma-tric-u-la′tion** (-lā′shọn), *n.* A matriculating, or a being matriculated; enrolment or admission as a member, esp. in a college or university.—**ma-tric′u-la-tor,** *n.*

mat-ri-mo-ni-al (mat-ri-mō′ni-ạl), *a.* [L. *matrimonialis*.] Of or pertaining to matrimony; nuptial; connubial.—**mat-ri-mo′ni-al-ly,** *adv.*

mat-ri-mo-ny (mat′ri-mọ-ni), *n.* [OF. *matrimonie*, *matrimoine*, < L. *matrimonium*, < *mater*, mother.] The rite or ceremony of marriage; also, the married state; wedlock; also, a game of cards, played by any number of persons; the combination of a king and a queen in this and certain other games.

ma-trix (mā′triks), *n.*; pl. *matrices* (mat′ri-sēz) or *matrixes*. [L., breeding animal, LL. womb, source, also public register, < L. *mater*, mother.] The womb; also, that which gives origin or form to a thing, or which serves to inclose it; specif., a mold for casting type-faces; also, the rock in which a crystallized mineral is embedded; in *anat.*, a formative part, as the corium beneath a nail; in *biol.*, the intercellular substance of a tissue.

ma-tron (mā′trọn), *n.* [OF. F. *matrone*, < L. *matrona*, married woman, < *mater*, mother.] A married woman, esp. one of ripe years and staid character or established position; also, a woman in charge of the feminine or domestic affairs of an institution or the like.—**matron of honor,** at a wedding, a married woman acting as the principal attendant of the bride.—**ma′tron-age** (-āj), *n.* The state of being a matron; also, guardianship by a matron; also, matrons collectively.—**ma′tron-al,** *a.* [L. *matronalis*.] Pertaining or proper to a matron; having matronly characteristics.—**ma′tron-ize,** *v. t.*; *-ized*, *-izing*. To render matronly; also, to chaperon.—**ma′tron-ly,** *a.* Like a matron, or having the characteristics of a matron (as, "Mrs. Dutton was a plain, *matronly* woman": Cooper's "Two Admirals," v.); also, characteristic of or suitable for a matron (as, "her . . . neat *matronly* attire": Hawthorne's "Twice-Told Tales," The Gentle Boy).—**ma′tron-li-ness,** *n.*—**ma′tron-ly,** *adv.*—**ma′tron-ship,** *n.* The condition or position of a matron.

mat-ro-nym-ic (mat-rọ-nim′ik), *a.* and *n.* Same as *metronymic*.

matt, *a.*, *n.*, and *v.* See *mat*².

matte (mat), *n.* [F.; origin uncertain.] In *metal.*, an unfinished metallic product of the smelting of certain sulphide ores, esp. those of copper; regulus.

mat-ted¹ (mat′ed), *p. a.* Covered with mats or matting (as, "Traversing the long and *matted* gallery, I descended the slippery steps of oak": C. Brontë's "Jane Eyre," xi.); covered with a dense growth or a tangled mass; also, formed into a mat; entangled in a thick mass (as, "a dense and *matted* thicket of willows," Irving's "Captain Bonneville," xxvii.; "*matted* sandy hair," Wiseman's "Fabiola," ii. 13); also, formed of mats, or of plaited or woven material.

mat-ted² (mat′ed), *p. a.* Having a mat or dull finish.

mat-ter (mat′ėr), *n.* [OF. *matere* (F. *matière*), < L. *materia*, stuff, material, matter, subject.] The substance or substances of which physical objects are composed; constituent substance or stuff; material; also, a particular kind of substance (as, coloring *matter*); specif., some substance excreted by a living body, esp. pus; also, physical or corporeal substance in general (whether solid, liquid, or gaseous), esp. as distinguished from incorporeal substance (as spirit or mind), or from qualities, actions, etc.; whatever occupies space; also, the material with which thought, discourse, etc., is concerned; the material or substance of a discourse, book, or the like, often as distinguished from the form in which it is presented; also, things or something of a specified kind or in a specified connection (as, *matter* of fact; *matter* of accident; *matter* of record); often, specif., things written or printed (as, typewritten *matter*; printed *matter*); among printers, etc., material for work; copy; also, type set up; in the postal service, mail; also, ground, reason, or cause (as, "Neither can he that mindeth but his own business find much *matter* for envy," Bacon's "Essays," Of Envy; *matter* of complaint); also, a thing, affair, or business (as, "They order, said I, this *matter* better in France," Sterne's "Sentimental Journey," opening line; to remedy the *matter*; a *matter* of life and death); also, an amount or extent reckoned approximately (as, a *matter* of ten miles; "the *matter* of a fortnight," Carlyle's "Past and Present," ii. 1); also, something of consequence (as, it is no *matter*); importance or significance (as, what *matter?*); in *philos.*, that out of which anything is made; that something which by receiving form becomes a substance or thing.—**the matter,** the trouble or difficulty: as, what is *the matter* with him? there is nothing *the matter.*—**mat'ter,** *v.* **I.** *intr.* To suppurate; also, to be of importance (as, "What they said *matters* little": Bret Harte's "Idyl of Red Gulch"); signify. **II.** *tr.* To be concerned about, or heed or mind (obs. or prov. Eng.: as, "When two squires lay their heads together, they do not much *matter* law," Godwin's "Caleb Williams," xxxi.); also, to care for or like (prov. Eng.).—**mat'ter-ful,** *a.* Full of matter, pith, or substance, as a book or a writer; pregnant. —**mat'ter-less,** *a.* Void of matter; immaterial; of no consequence.—**mat'ter=of=course',** *a.* Occurring or proceeding as if in the natural course of things; also, taking things as a matter of course.—**mat'ter=of=fact',** *a.* Adhering to actual facts; not imaginative or fanciful; prosaic; commonplace.—**mat'ter-y,** *a.* Purulent.

mat-ting (mat'ing), *n.* [See *mat*[1].] A coarse fabric of rushes, grass, straw, hemp, or the like, used for covering floors, as a material for wrapping articles, etc.; also, material for mats (as, "We saw a great deal of *matting* or bass there, that the natives make mats of": Defoe's "Captain Singleton," vi.).

mat-tock (mat'ọk), *n.* [AS. *mattuc.*] A kind of pick with an arm or blade like that of an adz, and commonly with another arm opposite either like a narrow ax-blade or terminating in a point: used for loosening the soil, etc.

mat-toid (mat'oid), *n.* [It. *mattoide,* < *matto,* mad, < L. *mattus,* intoxicated.] A person of abnormal mentality bordering on insanity.

mat-tress (mat'res), *n.* [OF. *materas* (F. *matelas*); from Ar.] A case filled with hair, straw, cotton, etc., usually quilted or fastened together at intervals, used as or on a bed; also, a framework over which is stretched a sheet of wire cloth or a combination of metal strips, etc., often resting on springs, used under such a case on a bed; also, a mat or mass of interwoven brushwood, poles, etc., used in building or protecting dikes and the like.

mat-u-rate (maṭ'ū-rāt), *v.*; *-rated, -rating.* [L. *maturatus,* pp. of *maturare,* ripen, E. *mature, v.*] **I.** *tr.* To mature or ripen; specif., to cause (a boil, etc.) to suppurate. **II.** *intr.* To mature; specif., to suppurate.—**mat-u-ra'tion** (-rā'shọn), *n.* [L. *maturatio(n-).*] The act or process of maturating; ripening; suppuration; in *biol.,* the final stages in the development of the ovum or the spermatozoön, characterized by a reduction in the number of chromosomes.—**mat'u-ra-tive** (-rạ-tiv), *a.* Tending to maturate; promoting suppuration; pertaining to or characterized by suppuration.

ma-ture (mạ-tūr'), *a.*; compar. *maturer,* superl. *maturest.* [L. *maturus,* ripe, timely, early: cf. *premature.*] Complete in natural growth or development, or fully grown, as plant and animal forms; ripe, as fruit; fully developed in body or mind, as a person; also, brought by time, treatment, etc., to the condition of full excellence, as wine, cheese, etc.; also, completed, perfected, or elaborated in full by the mind (as, *mature* deliberation; *mature* plans); also, pertaining to or characteristic of full development (as, *mature* years; a *mature* appearance); in *phys. geog.,* of topographical features, exhibiting the stage of maximum development, as in the process of erosion; in *com.,* having reached the limit of its time; having become payable or due, as a note.—**ma-ture',** *v.*; *-tured, -turing.* [L. *maturare,* ripen, < *maturus*: cf. *maturate.*] **I.** *tr.* To make mature; ripen, as fruits; bring to full development, as persons, the body or mind, etc.; bring to due condition, or age, as wine; complete or perfect (as, "She sat *maturing* this plan": Galsworthy's "Patrician," ii. 1). **II.** *intr.* To become mature; ripen; come to full development or due condition; in *com.,* to become due, as a note.—**ma-ture'ly,** *adv.*—**ma-ture'ness,** *n.*—**ma-tur'er** (-tūr'ėr), *n.*—**ma-tu'ri-ty** (-tū'ri-ti), *n.* [L. *maturitas.*] The state of being mature; ripeness; full development; perfected condition; in *com.,* the state of being due, or the time of becoming due, as of a note.

ma-tu-ti-nal (mạ-tū'ti-nạl or maṭ-ū-tī'nạl), *a.* [L. *matutinalis,* < *matutinus,* of or in the morning, < *Matuta,* ancient Italian goddess of dawn.] Pertaining to or occurring in the morning (as, "A thundering sound of cowhide boots on the stairs announced that Sol's *matutinal* toilet was complete": Mrs. Stowe's "Oldtown Folks," xiii.); early in the day; also, early-rising.—**ma-tu'ti-nal-ly,** *adv.*

mat-u-tine (maṭ'ū-tīn), *a.* Same as *matutinal.*

mat-zos (mät'sōs), *n. pl.* Same as *matzoth.*

mat-zoth (mät'sōth), *n. pl.* [Heb. *matstsōth,* pl. of *matstsāh,* cake of unleavened bread.] Cakes of unleavened bread, eaten by Jews at the Passover.

maud (mâd), *n.* [Origin uncertain.] A gray woolen plaid worn by shepherds and others in southern Scotland (as, "The huntsmen, though hardy . . . twitched their *mauds,* or Lowland plaids, close to their throats": Scott's "Castle Dangerous," vii.); also, a rug or wrap of like material, used in traveling.

maud-lin (mâd'lin), *a.* [From *Maudlin,* for *Magdalen* (Mary Magdalene), often represented in art as weeping: see *magdalen.*] Weeping or tearful (obs. or archaic); hence, tearfully or weakly emotional or sentimental (as, *maudlin* pathos; *maudlin* effusions; "Is this a time . . . for a *maudlin* universal sympathy?" Mrs. H. Ward's "Robert Elsmere," xii.); often, tearfully or emotionally silly from drink (as, the *maudlin* stage of drunkenness; "It is but yonder empty glass That makes me *maudlin*-moral," Tennyson's "Will Waterproof's Lyrical Monologue," 208). —**maud'lin-ly,** *adv.*—**maud'lin-ness,** *n.*

mau-gre (mâ'gėr), *prep.* [OF. *maugre* (F. *malgré*), orig. n., ill-will, spite, < *mal* (< L. *malus*), ill, + *gre,* E. *gree*[2].] In spite of; notwithstanding: as, "But, *maugre* all these hardships, they pursued their journey cheerily" (Irving's "Knickerbocker's New York," vii. 4). [Archaic.]

maul (mâl), *n.* [Another spelling of *mall.*] A heavy hammer or beetle, as for driving piles; also, a heavy club or mace (obs. or hist.).—**maul,** *v. t.* To beat with or as with a maul; split with a maul and a wedge, as a rail (U. S.); hence, to beat and bruise; handle or use roughly; injure by blows or other violence (as, "He seized the gunwale, but the knives of our rowers so *mauled* his wrists that he was forced to quit his hold": H. Melville's "Typee," xxxiii.); fig., to criticize severely or injuriously.—**maul'er,** *n.*

maul-stick (mâl'stik), *n.* See *mahlstick.*

mau-met, mam-met (mâ'met, mam'et), *n.* [OF. *mahumet,* idol, orig. Mahomet or Mohammed: cf. *Mahound.*] An idol†; also, an image, effigy, or puppet (now prov. Eng.). —**mau'met-ry, mam'met-ry,** *n.* Idolatry. [Obs. or archaic.]

maun (mân), *v. aux.* [= *mun.*] Must: as, "Folk *maun* do something for their bread" (Burns's "Death and Doctor Hornbook," 71). [Sc.]

maund[1] (mând), *n.* [AS. *mand* = D. *mand.*] A basket; a hamper: as, "A thousand favours from a *maund* she drew" (Shakspere's "Lover's Complaint," 36). [Now prov. Eng. and Sc.]

maund[2] (mând), *n.* [Hind. and Pers. *man.*] A unit of weight in India and other parts of Asia, varying greatly according to locality: in India, from about 25 to 82.286 pounds (the latter being the 'government maund').

maun-der (mân'dėr), *v. i.* [Origin obscure.] To grumble, mutter, or mumble (now prov. Eng. and Sc.); also, to talk in a rambling, foolish or imbecile way (as, "I don't see how you all can bear to listen to that man's *maundering!*" Mrs. Stowe's "Oldtown Folks," xliii.); also, to move, go, or act in an aimless, confused manner.—**maun'der-er,** *n.*

maun-dy (mân'di), *n.* [OF. *mande,* < L. *mandatum,* a command, mandate: see John, xiii. 5, 14, 34.] An old ceremony of washing the feet of a number of poor people, performed as a religious rite, as by a sovereign or an ecclesiastic, on the Thursday before Good Friday; also, alms distributed at the ceremony or on this day.—**Maundy Thursday,** the Thursday before Good Friday.

mau-so-le-um (mâ-sọ-lē'um), *n.*; pl. *-leums,* L. *-lea* (-lē'ạ). [L., < Gr. μαυσωλεῖον, < Μαύσωλος, Mausolus.] [*cap.*] A magnificent tomb erected at Halicarnassus, in Asia Minor, for Mausolus, king of Caria, by his queen, Artemisia, about 350 B.C. (ranking as one of the seven wonders of the world: see phrase under *wonder, n.*); hence [*l. c.*], any stately edifice erected as a burial-place, as for a person or for the members of a family; a magnificent tomb.—**mau-so-le'an,** *a.*

mauve (mōv), *n.* [F., orig. mallow, < L. *malva,* E. *mallow.*] A purple dye obtained from aniline; also, the color produced by it; a delicate, pale purple.

mav-er-ick (mav′ẹ-rik), *n.* [Said to be named from Samuel *Maverick*, a Texas cattle-raiser who neglected to brand his cattle.] In cattle-raising regions, an animal found without an owner's brand, esp. a calf separated from its dam. [U. S.]

ma-vis (mā′vis), *n.* [OF. F. *mauvis*; origin uncertain.] The European song-thrush, *Turdus musicus*: as, "Merry it is in the good greenwood, When the *mavis* and merle are singing" (Scott's "Lady of the Lake," iv. 12). [Now poetic or local.]

ma-vour-neen (mạ-vör′nēn), *n.* [Ir. *mo muirnín.*] My darling. [Ir.]

maw (mâ), *n.* [AS. *maga* = D. *maag* = G. *magen* = Icel. *magi*, maw.] The stomach; also, the mouth, throat, or gullet as concerned in devouring: now chiefly of animals or in figurative use.

mawk (mâk), *n.* [ME. *mawke*, maggot; from Scand.: cf. Icel. *madhkr.*] A maggot (now Sc. and north. Eng.); also, a whim or foolish fancy (north. Eng.); also, a squeamish or fastidious person (north. Eng.).

maw-kin (mâ′kin), *n.* See *malkin.*

mawk-ish (mâ′kish), *a.* [From *mawk.*] Slightly sick (now prov.); also, sickish or slightly nauseating (as, "If I would drink water, I must quaff the *mawkish* contents of an open aqueduct": Smollett's "Humphry Clinker," June 8); sickly; also, characterized by sickly sentimentality.—**mawk′ish-ly,** *adv.*—**mawk′ish-ness,** *n.*

maw-worm (mâ′wėrm), *n.* A worm infesting the maw or stomach; [*cap.*] (from a character so named in Bickerstaffe's play, "The Hypocrite," 1768) a hypocritical pretender to sanctity.

max-il-la (mak-sil′ạ), *n.*; pl. *maxillæ* (-ē). [L., a dim. form akin to *mala*, cheek-bone, jaw.] A jaw or jaw-bone, esp. a bone of the upper jaw; also, one of the paired appendages immediately behind the mandibles of insects and other arthropods, usually serving as accessory jaws.—**max-il-la-ry** (mak′si-lạ-ri). [L. *maxillaris.*] **I.** *a.* Of or pertaining to a jaw, jaw-bone, or maxilla. **II.** *n.*; pl. *-ries* (-riz). A maxilla or maxillary bone.

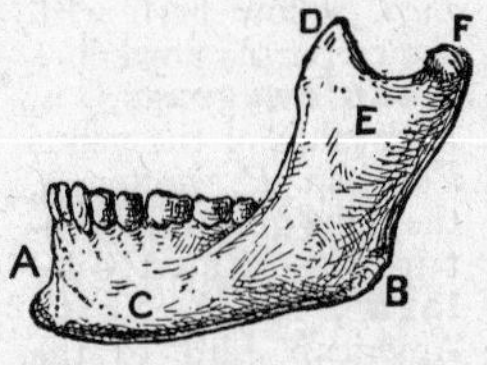

Inferior Maxillary or Lower Jaw-bone of Man. — *A*, symphysis of the lower jaw; *B*, angle of jaw; *C*, body, or horizontal ramus; *D*, coronoid process; *E*, ascending ramus; *F*, condyle. The concave line between *D* and *F* is the condyloid notch.

max-im (mak′sim), *n.* [ML. *maxima*, lit. 'greatest' (proposition or sentence), fem. of L. *maximus*: see *maximum.*] An axiom†, or self-evident proposition†; also, an expression, esp. an aphoristic or sententious one, of a general truth (as, "the trite *maxim* that every Englishman's house is his castle": Lecky's "Hist. of Eng. in the 18th Century," viii.); also, a sententious rule or precept as to conduct (as, "that *maxim* of the heathen, 'Enjoy the present, trust nothing to the future'": J. H. Newman's "Callista," xxix.); also, a principle of conduct (as, "My *maxim* is to obey orders": Cooper's "Two Admirals," xix.).

max-i-mal (mak′si-mạl), *a.* Pertaining to or being a maximum; greatest possible; highest.—**Max′i-mal-ism,** *n.* [Sometimes *l. c.*] The doctrines, methods, or procedure of Maximalists.—**Max′i-mal-ist,** *n.* [Sometimes *l. c.*] In Russian politics, a member of an extremist or more radical group or faction of socialists, as of a faction of the Social Revolutionary party, or of the Social Democratic party (in which case equivalent to *Bolshevik*) (see *Bolshevik, n.*); hence, a member of a similar group or faction elsewhere. Cf. *Minimalist.*—**max′i-mal-ly,** *adv.*

max-im-ist (mak′sim-ist), *n.* A maker or user of maxims.

max-im-ite (mak′sim-īt), *n.* [From Hudson *Maxim* (born 1853), American inventor.] A powerful explosive consisting largely of picric acid.

max-i-mize (mak′si-mīz), *v. t.*; *-mized, -mizing.* [L. *maximus*, greatest: see *maximum.*] To increase to the greatest possible amount or degree; also, to magnify to the utmost in estimation or representation.—**max″i-mi-za′tion** (-mi-zā′shọn), *n.*—**max′i-miz-er** (-mī-zėr), *n.*

max-i-mum (mak′si-mum). [L., neut. of *maximus*, greatest, superl. of *magnus*, great: see *magnitude.*] **I.** *n.*; pl. *-mums* or *-ma* (-mạ). The greatest quantity or amount possible, assignable, allowable, etc.; the highest amount, value, or degree attained or recorded: opposed to *minimum.* **II.** *a.* That is a maximum; greatest possible; highest; also, pertaining to a maximum or maximums.

may[1] (mā), *v.*; pres. 1 *may*, 2 *mayest* or *mayst*, 3 *may*, pl. *may*; pret. *might.* [AS. *mæg*, 1st and 3d pers. sing. pres. ind. (pret. *meahte, mihte*) of *magan* = OHG. *magan* (G. *mögen*) = Icel. *mega* = Goth. *magan*, be able: cf. *main*[2], *n.*, and *might*[2].] **A.**† *intr.* To be able; have power. **B.** *auxiliary.* Used to express (1) ability or power (more commonly *can*); (2) possibility, opportunity, or permission: as, you *may* enter; (3) wish or prayer: as, *may* you live long; (4) contingency, esp. in clauses expressing condition, concession, purpose, result, etc.

May[2] (mā), *n.* [OF. F. *mai*, < L. *Maius*, May; commonly associated with the goddess *Maia*, mother of Mercury.] The fifth month of the year, containing 31 days; fig., the early part or springtime, as of life (as, "the *May* of my years": Sidney's "Astrophel and Stella," xxi.); the prime; also, the festivities of May Day (as, "I'm to be Queen o' the *May*, mother": Tennyson's "May Queen," 4); also [*cap.* or *l. c.*], the hawthorn, or its blossoms (as, "blossoms red and white of fallen *May*": M. Arnold's "Thyrsis").—**May Day,** the first day of May, long celebrated with various festivities, as the crowning of the May-queen, dancing round the May-pole, etc., and in recent years often marked by socialist demonstrations in various countries.—**May**[2], *v. i.* [Also *l. c.*] To celebrate May Day; take part in the festivities of May Day or the pleasures of May: chiefly in *Maying, ppr.* Cf. *Maying, n.*

may[3] (mā), *n.* [AS. *mǣg*, akin to *mægden*, E. *maiden.*] A maiden: as "For ill beseems in a reverend friar, The love of a mortal *may*" (Peacock's "Nightmare Abbey," vi.). [Archaic or prov.]

ma-ya[1] (mä′yä), *n.* [Skt. *māyā.*] In *Hindu philos.*, illusion or deceptive appearance.

Ma-ya[2] (mä′yạ), *n.* A member of an aboriginal people of Yucatan which had attained a relatively high degree of civilization at the time of the discovery of America; also, the language of the Mayas.—**Ma-yan** (mä′yạn), *a.* and *n.*

May=ap-ple (mā′ap″l), *n.* An American perennial berberidaceous herb, *Podophyllum peltatum*, bearing an edible, yellowish, egg-shaped fruit; also, the fruit. Cf. *podophyllum.*

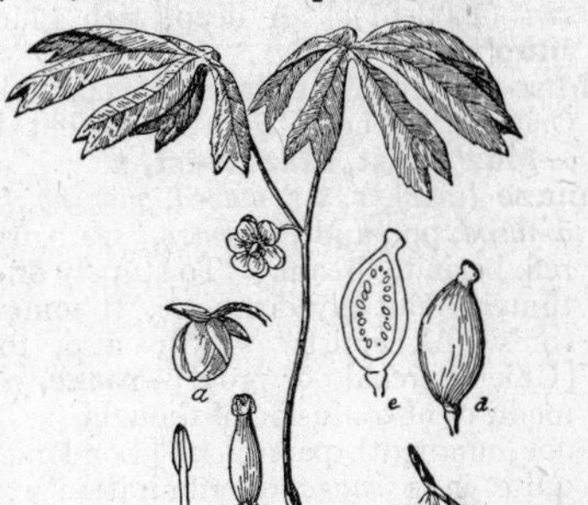

May-apple. — *a*, the flower-bud with the bractlets; *b*, a stamen; *c*, the pistil; *d*, the fruit; *e*, the fruit cut longitudinally.

May=bas-ket (mā′bås″ket), *n.* A basket of flowers, candy, or the like, hung on the outer knob of a house-door, or otherwise surreptitiously left for the recipient, as a May Day compliment or remembrance.

may-be (mā′bẹ), *adv.* It may be; perhaps: as, "Well, *maybe* it's right you are" (Synge's "Tinker's Wedding," ii.).

May=bee-tle (mā′bē″tl), *n.* A cockchafer; also, a June-bug (*Lachnosterna*).

May=bug (mā′bug), *n.* A May-beetle.

May=bush (mā′bush), *n.* The hawthorn.

May=day (mā′dā), *n.* See *May Day*, under *May*[2], *n.*

May=dew (mā′dū), *n.* The dew of May, or of May Day, popularly reputed to have extraordinary virtue for beautifying the complexion and for medicinal and bleaching purposes.

May-flow-er (mā′flou″ėr), *n.* Any of various plants whose flowers blossom in May: applied in England to the hawthorn, cowslip, etc., in the U. S. chiefly to the trailing arbutus.

May=fly (mā′flī), *n.*; pl. *-flies* (-flīz). An ephemerid; also, a caddis-fly.

may-hap (mā-hap′ or mā′hap), *adv.* [For *it may hap.*] Perhaps: as, "I'm going to the Hall Farm, but *mayhap* I may go to the school after" (George Eliot's "Adam Bede," xx.). Also **may-hap′pen.** [Archaic or prov.]

may-hem (mā′hem), *n.* [= *maim, n.*] In *law*, the crime of violently inflicting upon a person a bodily hurt such as renders him less able to defend himself or to annoy his adversary.

May-ing (mā′ing), *n.* [Also *l. c.*] The celebration of May Day; participation in May festivities or pleasures.

may-on-naise (mā-ọ-nāz′, F. mȧ-yo-nāz), *n.* [F.; origin uncertain.] A sauce composed of yolks of eggs beaten with olive-oil until thick, and seasoned with vinegar or lemon-juice, salt, pepper, etc.; also, a dish dressed with this sauce.

may-or (mā′ọr or mãr), *n.* [OF. F. *maire*, < L. *major*, greater: see *major*.] The principal officer of a municipality; the chief magistrate of a city or borough.—**may′or-al,** *a.* Of or pertaining to a mayor.—**may′or-al-ty** (-ạl-ti), *n.*; pl. *-ties* (-tiz). [OF. *mairalte*.] The office of a mayor, or the period of his service.—**may′or-ess,** *n.* The wife of a mayor. —**may′or-ship,** *n.*

May=pole (mā′pōl), *n.* [Also *l. c.*] A high pole, decorated with flowers or ribbons, for the merrymakers to dance round at May Day (or May) festivities; fig., a tall, slender person (as, "the daughter, a tall, trapesing, trolloping, talkative *maypole*": Goldsmith's "She Stoops to Conquer," i. 2).

may=pop (mā′pop), *n.* [Origin uncertain.] The edible fruit of a passion-flower, *Passiflora incarnata*, or the plant itself. [Southern U. S.]

May=queen (mā′kwēn′), *n.* A girl or young woman crowned with flowers and honored as queen in the sports of May Day (or May): as, "The *May Queen*" (the title of a poem by Tennyson).

may-thorn (mā′thôrn), *n.* The hawthorn.

May=time (mā′tīm), *n.* The season of May.

may-weed (mā′wēd), *n.* [Cf. AS. *mægtha*, mayweed.] An asteraceous plant, *Anthemis cotula*, native in Europe and Asia, and naturalized in America, having pungent, ill-scented foliage, and flower-heads with a yellow disk and white rays.

maz-ard (maz′ärd), *n.* [From *mazer*.] A mazer†; also, the head, or the face (archaic: as, "knocked about the *mazzard* with a sexton's spade," Shakspere's "Hamlet," v. 1. 97).

maz-a-rine (maz-ạ-rēn′), *n.* [Perhaps from Cardinal *Mazarin* (1602–61).] A deep, rich blue. Also **maz-a-rine′=blue′.**

Maz-da-ism, Maz-de-ism (maz′dạ-izm, maz′dẹ-), *n.* [Cf. *Ormazd*.] The religion of ancient Persia; Zoroastrianism. —**Maz′da-ist, Maz′de-ist,** *n.*

maze (māz), *v. t.*; *mazed, mazing.* [ME. *masen*: cf. AS. *āmasod*, pp., and E. *amaze*, also Norw. *masa*, be busy, pore, refl. begin to dream.] To stupefy or daze (as, "Finding This tumult 'bout my door . . . It somewhat *maz'd* me": Jonson's "Alchemist," v. 5); also, to bewilder or confuse. [Chiefly archaic or prov.]—**maze,** *n.* A state of bewilderment, or of confusion of thought (as, "I have not as yet seen one hundredth part of its [London's] curiosities, and I am quite in a *maze* of admiration": Smollett's "Humphry Clinker," May 31); also, a structure or place containing a confusing network of intercommunicating paths or passages, as of paths bordered by high hedges in a park or garden (as, the *maze* at Hampton Court in England); a labyrinth; hence, any complicated or tortuous assemblage or arrangement, as of streets, buildings, etc. (as, "Bath was then a *maze* of only four or five hundred houses": Macaulay's "Hist. of Eng.," iii.); a confusingly intricate state of things; also, *pl.*, the windings of a labyrinth or the like (as, "He turned short into one of the *mazes* of the wood": Scott's "Castle Dangerous," xv.); the intricacies of any complicated matter or state of things (as, the *mazes* of metaphysics, or of a tale of mystery); also, *sing.*, a winding movement, as in dancing (as, "Here would the good Peter . . . watch the *mazes* of the dance": Irving's "Knickerbocker's New York," vii. 2).—**maze′ment,** *n.*

ma-zer (mā′zėr), *n.* [OF. *masere, masre*, kind of wood, cup; from Teut.; cf. G. *maser*, knot or curl in wood, Icel. *mösurr*, maple.] A kind of ornamental wood, probably maple, used for making drinking-cups, etc.†; also, a drinking-cup or bowl, orig. one made of this wood, formerly in use.

maz-i-ly (mā′zi-li), *adv.* In a mazy manner; with intricate windings.—**maz′i-ness,** *n.*

ma-zu-ma (mạ-zö′mạ), *n.* [Origin obscure.] Money. [Slang.]

ma-zur-ka (mạ-zör′kạ or mạ-zėr′-), *n.* [Pol.] A lively Polish dance in moderately quick triple rhythm; also, a piece of music for, or in the rhythm of, this dance.

maz-y (mā′zi), *a.* Maze-like; full of intricate windings; intricate: as, "Five miles meandering with a *mazy* motion Through wood and dale the sacred river ran" (Coleridge's "Kubla Khan").

maz′zard, *n.* See *mazard*.

Mc-. See *Mac-*.

me (mē), *pron.* [AS. *mē*, dat. and acc.; from a pronominal stem seen also in D. *mij*, G. *mir, mich*, Icel. and Goth. *mik*, L. *me*, Gr. *μέ*, Skt. *mā*.] Objective case of the pronoun *I*. See *I*[2].

mea-cock† (mē′kok), *n.* [Origin uncertain.] An effeminate person; a weakling; a coward.

mead[1] (mēd), *n.* [AS. *meodu* = G. *met* = Icel. *mjödhr*, mead; akin to Gr. *μέθυ*, wine, Skt. *madhu*, honey.] An alcoholic liquor made by fermenting a mixture of honey and water; also, any of various non-alcoholic beverages.

mead[2] (mēd), *n.* [AS. *mǣd*: see *meadow*.] A meadow: as, "Downward sloped The path through yellow *meads*" (Lowell's "Parting of the Ways," 35). [Now chiefly poetic.]

mead-ow (med′ō), *n.* [AS. *mǣdw-*, in inflectional forms of *mǣd* (see *mead*[2]), akin to D. *mat*, G. *matte*, meadow; from the root of E. *mow*[3].] A piece of land kept under grass which is mowed for use as hay; any piece of grassland, whether used for the raising of hay or for pasture; a low, level tract of uncultivated ground, as along a river or in marshy regions near the sea, producing coarse grass; also, land used for or consisting of meadows.—**mead′ow=beau″ty,** *n.* Any plant of the genus *Rhexia*, esp. *R. virginica*, a low herb with showy purple flowers.—**mead′ow=grass,** *n.* Any grass of the genus *Poa*, esp. *P. pratensis*, the blue-grass of Kentucky.—**mead′ow=lark′,** *n.* A North American bird of the genus *Sturnella*, of the blackbird family (*Icteridæ*), esp. *S. magna*, which is about the size of a robin, brownish or grayish above, with a yellow breast marked with black.

Meadow-lark (*Sturnella magna*).

—**mead′ow=rue′,** *n.* Any plant of the ranunculaceous genus *Thalictrum*, having leaves resembling those of rue.—**mead′ow=sweet,** *n.* Any plant of the rosaceous genus *Spiræa*, esp. *S. salicifolia*, a low shrub with dense panicles of white or pink flowers; also, any plant of the closely related genus *Filipendula* (or *Ulmaria*).—**mead′-ow-y** (-ọ-i), *a.* Pertaining to, resembling, or consisting of meadow: as, "the *meadowy* land" (W. Morris's "Jason," vii. 47).

Flowering Branch of Male Plant of Meadow-rue (*Thalictrum polygamum*). —*a*, a male flower; *b*, a female flower with young fruit.

mea-ger, mea-gre (mē′gėr), *a.* [OF. F. *maigre*, < L. *macer* (*macr-*), lean; akin to AS. *mæger*, D. and G. *mager*, lean, and prob. to Gr. *μακρός*, long.] Having little flesh, lean, or thin (as, "a small, *meagre* man," Motley's "Dutch Republic," i. 1; "shaggy, *meager* little ponies," Parkman's "Oregon Trail," ii.); also, deficient in quantity or quality, or without fullness or richness (as, "The report that first reached us through the newspapers was *meagre* and contradictory," Aldrich's "Story of a Bad Boy," xx.; "the *meagre* waters of Turkey Creek," G. W. Cable's "John March, Southerner," iii.; *meager* fare); scanty; poor; sometimes, maigre (as, *meager* soup; "I called for supper, and, it being a *meagre* day, was fain to put up with eggs," Smollett's tr. Le Sage's "Gil Blas," i. 2).—**mea′ger-ly, mea′gre-ly,** *adv.*—**mea′ger-ness, mea′gre-ness,** *n.*

meal[1] (mēl), *n.* [AS. *melu* = D. *meel* = G. *mehl* = Icel. *mjöl*, meal; from a root meaning 'grind,' whence also L. *molere*: see *mill*[2].] The edible part of any grain (now usually excluding wheat) or pulse ground to a (coarse) powder and unbolted; specif., in Scotland and Ireland, oatmeal; in the U. S., corn-meal, or Indian meal; also, any ground or powdery substance resembling this.

meal[2] (mēl), *n.* [AS. *mǣl*, measure, fixed time, occasion, meal, = G. *mal*, time, *mahl*, meal, = Icel. *māl*, measure, time, meal, = Goth. *mēl*, time: cf. *limbmeal*.] One of the regular repasts of the day, as breakfast, dinner, or supper; in general, a repast; also, the food eaten or served for a repast.

meal-ie (mē′li), *n.* [S. Afr. D. *milje*, < Pg. *milho*, millet, maize, < L. *milium*, millet.] An ear of maize or Indian corn; *pl.*, maize. [South Africa.]

meal-i-ness (mē′li-nes), *n.* Mealy quality or state.

meal=time (mēl′tīm), *n.* The usual time for a meal.

meal=worm (mēl′wėrm), *n.* The larva of any of certain beetles, as *Tenebrio molitor*, infesting granaries, etc., and injurious to flour and meal.

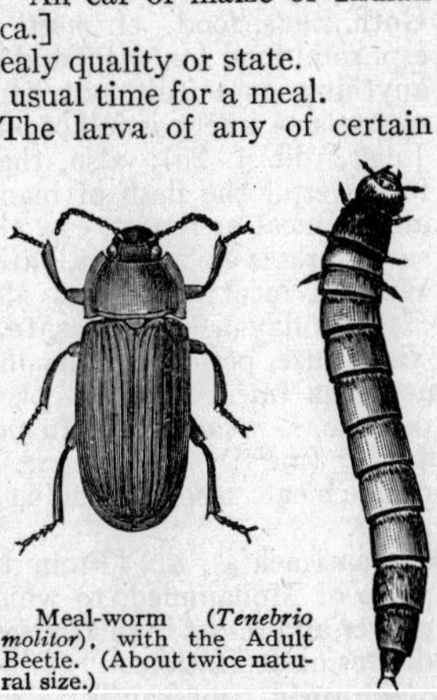

Meal-worm (*Tenebrio molitor*), with the Adult Beetle. (About twice natural size.)

meal-y (mē′li), *a.*; compar. *mealier*, superl. *mealiest*. Having the qualities of meal; powdery; often, soft, dry, and crumbly (as, *mealy* potatoes); also, of the nature of, or containing, meal (as, "the *mealy* treasures of the harvest bin": J. W. Riley's "A Child's Home—Long Ago"); farinaceous; also, covered with or as with meal or powder; flecked as if with meal, or spotty; pale, as the complexion; also, mealy-mouthed (as, "I didn't mince the matter with him. I'm never *mealy* with 'em": Dickens's "Hard Times," ii. 8).—**meal′y=mouthed** (-mouᴛʜd), *a.* Using soft words; esp., unduly soft-spoken; avoiding the use of plain terms, as from timidity, excessive delicacy, or hypocrisy.—**meal′y=mouthed″ness,** *n.*

mean[1] (mēn), *v.*; *meant, meaning.* [AS. *mǣnan* = D. *meenen* = G. *meinen*, mean; perhaps from the root of E. *mind*.] **I.** *tr.* To have in the mind as an intention or purpose (often with an infinitive as object: as, "It's no use waiting any longer, if you *mean* to go at all, to-day," Howells's "Chance Acquaintance," x.); purpose; also, to intend for a particular purpose, destination, etc.; also, to intend to express or indicate (as, say what you *mean*; whom do you *mean?*); also, of words, things, etc., to have as the signification; signify; import; denote. **II.** *intr.* To be minded or disposed; have intentions of some kind: as, he *means* well.

mean[2] (mēn), *a.* [AS. *gemǣne* = D. *gemeen* = G. *gemein* = Goth. *gamains*, common.] Common, or possessed jointly (obs. or prov.); also, low in station, rank, or dignity (as, "Kings have frequently . . . wished they had been placed in the middle of the two extremes, between the *mean* and the great," Defoe's "Robinson Crusoe," i. 1; "a groom of *mean* rank," Scott's "Castle Dangerous," iii.); inferior in grade, quality, or character (as, "He made it plain to the *meanest* capacity": Galt's "Annals of the Parish," xxxix.); of little importance or consequence (as, "the *meanest* floweret of the vale," Gray's "Ode on the Pleasure Arising from Vicissitude"; "Rightly viewed no *meanest* object is insignificant," Carlyle's "Sartor Resartus," i. 11); wanting in elevation or dignity, as literary style; unimposing or shabby (as, a *mean* abode; *mean* attire; a *mean* appearance); also, without moral dignity, small-minded, or ignoble (as, "the wisest, brightest, *meanest* of mankind," Pope's "Essay on Man," iv. 282; *mean* actions or motives); pettily offensive or unaccommodating (colloq.); small, humiliated, or ashamed (colloq.: as, to feel *mean* over some ungenerous action); troublesome or vicious, as a horse (colloq.); also, penurious, stingy, or miserly (as, a man who is *mean* about money); also, in poor physical condition (colloq.: as, I feel *mean* to-day).

mean[3] (mēn), *a.* [OF. *meien, moien* (F. *moyen*), < L. *medianus*, being in the middle: see *median*[2].] Occupying a middle position or an intermediate place; also, intermediate in kind, quality, etc.; intermediate in degree, middling, or moderate; also, intermediate in time, or intervening (cf. *meantime* and *meanwhile*); in *math.*, having a value intermediate between the values of other quantities; average. —**mean noon.** See under *noon, n.*—**mean solar time,** or **mean time.** See under *time, n.*—**mean sun.** See under *sun*[2], *n.*—**mean**[3], *n.* Something intermediate; that which is midway between two extremes; a medium; also, an agency, instrumentality, method, etc., used to attain an end (now usually in *pl.*: as, "There are no *means* that I will not resort to, to discover this infamous plot," Marryat's "Peter Simple," xli.; often with sense and construction of *sing.*, as, a *means* of communication is lacking); also, *pl.*, disposable resources, esp. pecuniary resources (as, to live beyond one's *means*); considerable pecuniary resources (as, a man of *means*); also, *sing.*, in *math.*, a quantity having a value intermediate between the values of other quantities, esp. the average ('arithmetical mean') obtained by adding several quantities together and dividing the sum by their number; also, either the second or third term of a proportion of four terms.—**by all means,** at any cost, or without fail (as, "I must *by all means* keep this feast": Acts, xviii. 21); also (in emphasis), certainly (as, go, *by all means*).—**by any means,** in any way; at all: as, "None of them can *by any means* redeem his brother" (Ps. xlix. 7).—**by no means,** in no way, or not at all (as, a thing *by no means* certain); also, on no account, or certainly not (as, a practice *by no means* to be recommended).

mean[4] (mēn), *v. t.* or *i.* [AS. *mǣnan*: see *moan*.] To moan or lament. [Now Sc. and north. Eng.]

me-an-der (mē-an′dėr), *n.* [L. *mæander*, < Gr. *μαίανδρος*, a winding, orig. the name of a winding river (the Mæander, now Mendere) in western Asia Minor, which flows into the Ægean Sea.] A turning or winding, or a winding path or course (usually in *pl.*); sometimes, a circuitous movement or journey (as, "Having performed a circuitous *meander*, we regained the stream": Bulwer-Lytton's "Caxtons," v. 1); also, an intricate variety of fret or fretwork.—**me-an′der,** *v. i.* To proceed by a winding course; also, to wander aimlessly (as, "He *meandered* to and fro in the hall, observing the manners and customs of Hillport society": Arnold Bennett's "Helen with the High Hand," xiv.).—**me-an′der-ing-ly,** *adv.*—**me-an′drous,** *a.* Meandering; winding.

Meander.

mean-ing (mē′ning), *n.* [See *mean*[1].] Intention or purpose (archaic: as, "I am no honest man if there be any good *meaning* towards you," Shakspere's "King Lear," i. 2. 190); also, that which is intended to be, or actually is, expressed or indicated; signification; import; sense; significance.—**mean′ing,** *p. a.* Intending; also, expressive or significant (as, "a *meaning* look": Dickens's "Nicholas Nickleby," ii.).—**mean′ing-ful,** *a.* Full of meaning; significant.—**mean′ing-less,** *a.* Without meaning or significance.—**mean′ing-less-ly,** *adv.*—**mean′ing-less-ness,** *n.*—**mean′ing-ly,** *adv.*—**mean′ing-ness,** *n.*

mean-ly (mēn′li), *adv.* In a mean manner; poorly; basely; stingily.—**mean′ness,** *n.* The state or quality of being mean; also, a mean act.

means (mēnz), *n. pl.* See *mean*[3], *n.*

meant (ment). Preterit and past participle of *mean*[1].

mean-time, mean-while (mēn′tīm, -hwīl), *n.* [For *mean time, mean while.*] The intervening time.—**mean′time, mean′while,** *adv.* In the intervening time; during the interval; at the same time.

mea-sle (mē′zl), *n.* [Sing. of *measles*.] One of the larvæ which produce the disease measles in swine and other animals. —**mea′sled,** *a.* Infected with measles, as pork; measly.

mea-sles (mē′zlz), *n.* [Orig. pl., ME. *mesels, maseles*, prop. the eruptive spots, akin to G. *masern*, pl., measles, *maser*, spot, OHG. *māsa*, spot; in the last sense, confused with obs. *mesel*, leprous, through F. < L. *misellus*, dim. of *miser*, wretched.] An acute infectious disease occurring mostly in children, characterized by catarrhal and febrile symptoms and an eruption of small red spots; rubeola; also, any of certain other eruptive diseases, as rubella ('German measles'); also, a disease in swine and other animals caused by the larvæ of certain tapeworms of the genus *Tænia*.—**mea'sly** (-zli), *a.* Pertaining to or resembling measles; also, infected with measles, as an animal or its flesh (as, "*measly* pork": Irving's "Knickerbocker's New York," iv. 3); also, wretchedly poor or unsatisfactory (slang).

meas-ur-a-ble (mezh'ūr-a-bl), *a.* That may be measured; also, moderate†.—**meas'ur-a-bly,** *adv.*

meas-ure (mezh'ūr), *n.* [OF. F. *mesure*, < L. *mensura*, < *metiri* (pp. *mensus*), measure: see *meter*³.] The act or process of ascertaining the extent, dimensions, quantity, etc., of something, esp. by comparison with a standard; also, size, dimensions, quantity, etc., as thus ascertained; also, an instrument, as a graduated rod or tape or a vessel of standard capacity, for measuring; also, a unit or standard of measurement; also, a definite or known quantity measured out (as, "Anon we'll drink a *measure* The table round": Shakspere's "Macbeth," iii. 4. 11); also, a system of measurement (as, dry *measure*, liquid *measure*, long *measure*, etc.: see under *dry*, *liquid*, *long*¹, etc.); also, any standard of comparison, estimation, or judgment (as, "Some . . . make themselves the *measure* of mankind": Pope's "Essay on Criticism," 453); also, a limit, or an extent or degree not to be exceeded (as, to know no *measure*); reasonable bounds or limits (as, beyond *measure*); also, moderation†; temperance†; also, a quantity, degree, or proportion (as, "Never was from Heaven imparted *Measure* of strength so great," Milton's "Samson Agonistes," 1439; "Objections against Christianity itself are, in a great *measure*, frivolous," J. Butler's "Analogy of Religion," ii. 3); also, treatment dealt out to a person (archaic: as, "I will not complain . . . of the *measure* that has been meted unto me," Galt's "Annals of the Parish," xviii.); also, rhythmical movement or arrangement, as in poetry or music; a particular kind of such arrangement; a metrical unit; a bar of music; also, an air or melody (poetic); also, a slow, stately dance or dance-movement (archaic: as, "'Now tread we a *measure*!' said young Lochinvar," Scott's "Marmion," v. 12); also, an action or procedure intended as a means to an end (as, "He . . . told what *measures* he had taken to avert suspicion": Mark Twain's "Life on the Mississippi," lv.); specif., a legislative bill or enactment; in *math.*, a quantity contained in another quantity some number of times without remainder; *pl.*, in *geol.*, beds; strata.—**meas'ure,** *v. t.*; *-ured, -uring.* [OF. F. *mesurer*, < L. *mensurare*, < *mensura*.] To ascertain the extent, dimensions, quantity, capacity, etc., of, esp. by comparison with a standard; also, to mark or lay off or out, or deal out, with reference to measure (often with *off* or *out*); also, to estimate the relative amount, value, etc., of, by comparison with some standard; judge of or appraise by comparison with something else (as, "Fabiola had *measured* his character; had caught, with her penetrating eye, the affectation of his manner, and the cunning of his looks": Wiseman's "Fabiola," i. 8); also, to serve as the measure of (as, "the now almost effaced sun-dials . . . seeming coevals with that Time which they *measured*": Lamb's "Old Benchers of the Inner Temple"); also, to adjust or proportion (as, "Bertram carefully *measured* his own conduct by that of his host": Scott's "Guy Mannering," li.); also, to bring into comparison or competition (as, to *measure* one's abilities with those of another); also, to travel over or traverse (as, "At each stride a mile he *measured*," Longfellow's "Hiawatha," iv. 25; "She turned back into the room and *measured* its length with a restless step," H. James's "Europeans," i.).—**to measure one's length,** to fall or be thrown down, or lay one's self, or lie, at full length.—**to measure swords,** to ascertain that swords are of equal length, as adversaries in a duel; hence, to fight with swords; fig., to contend in battle, debate, etc.—**meas'ure,** *v. i.* To take measurements; also, to admit of measurement; also, to be of a specified measure.—**meas'ured,** *p. a.* Ascertained or apportioned by measure; hence, accurately regulated or proportioned; often, regular or uniform, as in movement, or rhythmical (as, "She hears the *measured* beating of our horses' hoofs": De Quincey's "English Mail-Coach," i.); in the form of meter or verse, or metrical (as, "For the unquiet heart and brain, A use in *measured* language lies": Tennyson's "In Memoriam," v.); also, deliberate and restrained (as, "He was a master of *measured* speech": Ian Maclaren's "Beside the Bonnie Brier Bush," v.).—**meas'ured-ly,** *adv.* —**meas'ure-less,** *a.* Without measure or bounds; unlimited; immeasurable: as, "the *measureless* prairie" (Longfellow's "Evangeline," ii. 3).—**meas'ure-less-ly,** *adv.*—**meas'ure-less-ness,** *n.*—**meas'ure-ment,** *n.* The act of measuring; also, an ascertained dimension; extent, size, etc., ascertained by measuring; also, a system of measuring or of measures.—**meas'ur-er,** *n.*—**meas'ur-ing=worm,** *n.* The larva of any geometrid moth: so called because it moves by bringing the rear end of the body forward, thus forming a loop, and then advancing the front end.

meat (mēt), *n.* [AS. *mete* = OHG. *maz* = Icel. *matr* = Goth. *mats*, food: cf. *mast*¹ and *mate*¹.] Food in general, esp. solid food (as, *meat* and drink); also, the edible part of anything, as a fruit, nut, etc. (as, "Thy head is as full of quarrels as an egg is full of *meat*": Shakspere's "Romeo and Juliet," iii. 1. 25); also, the flesh of animals as used for food; esp., the flesh of mammals so used; butcher-meat; also, a meal or repast, esp. the principal meal (now only in such phrases as 'at meat,' 'after meat,' etc.).—**meat'less,** *a.* Without meat; foodless; also, without butcher-meat (as, *meatless* days).—**meat'=safe,** *n.* A cupboard with walls of wire gauze, perforated zinc, or the like, for keeping food in.

me-a-tus (mē-ā'tus), *n.*; pl. *-tuses*, L. *-tus.* [L., a going, passage, < *meare*, go.] In *anat.*, a passage, duct, or opening.

meat-y (mē'ti), *a.*; compar. *meatier*, superl. *meatiest.* Of or like meat; also, abounding in meat; fig., full of substance; pithy.

Mec-ca (mek'ạ), *n.* [From *Mecca*, the Arabian city, birthplace of Mohammed, to which the Mohammedans turn in prayer and resort in pilgrimage.] The goal of one's supreme desires or aspirations.

me-chan-ic (mē-kan'ik). [L. *mechanicus*, < Gr. μηχανικός, < μηχανή, E. *machine*.] **I.** *a.* Mechanical. **II.** *n.* One employed in a manual occupation or art; a handicraftsman; an artisan; esp., a skilled worker with tools or machines.—**me-chan'i-cal,** *a.* Pertaining to or concerned with manual labor or skill; esp., pertaining to or concerned with the use of tools and the like, or the contrivance and construction of machines or mechanism; having to do with machinery; also, exhibiting skill in the use of tools and the like, or in the contrivance of machines, etc. (as, a *mechanical* genius); also, belonging to the artisan class (now rare); sometimes, mean† or vulgar†; also, of the nature of a device or contrivance for controlling or utilizing material forces, or of a mechanism or machine; acting or operated by means of such a contrivance, or of a mechanism or machine; produced by such means; also, acting or performed as if by machinery; without spontaneity, spirit, individuality, etc. (as, a *mechanical* writer or painter; "some tedious and *mechanical* ceremony of devotion," Irving's "Tales of a Traveler," i. 9); also, of or pertaining to the material forces of nature acting on bodies or masses; belonging or pertaining to the subject-matter of mechanics; in accordance with the laws of mechanics; often, pertaining to, or controlled or effected by, physical forces that are not chemical; physical, as opposed to *chemical* (as, a *mechanical* mixture: see phrase below); also, explaining phenomena as due to mechanical action or the material forces of the universe, as philosophical theories or their advocates; subordinating what is spiritual to what is material; materialistic; also, involving material objects or physical conditions (as, to be hindered by *mechanical* difficulties).—**mechanical drawing,** drawing, as of machinery or structures, done with the aid of rulers, scales, compasses, etc.—**mechanical mixture,** a mixture in which the several ingredients have not entered into chemical combination, but still retain their identity and can be separated by mechanical means.—**mechanical powers,** the six (sometimes more) simple machines. See *machine*, *n.*—**me-chan'i-cal-ize,** *v. t.*; *-ized, -izing.* To render mechanical.—**me-chan'i-cal-ly,**

adv.—**me-chan′i-cal-ness,** *n.*—**mech-a-ni-cian** (mek-ạ-nish′ạn), *n.* A mechanic or artisan (now rare); a skilled workman who accompanies the driver of an automobile (as during a race) or who attends upon an aëroplane, in order to care for or repair the engine, etc.; one versed in the principles of machines or skilled in mechanical construction.—**me-chan′ics,** *n.* The branch of knowledge concerned (both theoretically and practically) with machinery or mechanical appliances; also, the science dealing with the action of forces on bodies and with motion, and comprising kinetics, statics, and kinematics.

mech-a-nism (mek′ạ-nizm), *n.* [Gr. μηχανή: see *machine.*] The structure, or arrangement of parts, of a machine or similar device, or of anything analogous; also, such parts collectively; a piece of machinery; the machinery, or the agencies or means, by which a particular effect is produced or a purpose is accomplished; also, machinery or mechanical appliances in general; also, mechanical execution, as in painting or music; technique; also, the theory that everything in the universe is produced by mechanical or material forces.—**mech′a-nist,** *n.* An artisan†; a machinist; a mechanician.—**mech-a-nis′tic,** *a.* Pertaining to mechanists or mechanism, or to mechanics, or to mechanical theories in philosophy, etc.

mech-a-nize (mek′ạ-nīz), *v. t.*; *-nized, -nizing.* To render mechanical; turn into a machine or something suggesting a machine; operate or perform by or as if by machinery; introduce machinery into (an industry, etc.).—**mech″a-ni-za′tion** (-ni-zā′shọn), *n.*

mechano-. Form of Gr. μηχανή, machine, used in combination.—**mech-a-no-ther-a-peu-tics** (mek″ạ-nọ-ther-ạ-pū′tiks), *n.* That branch of therapeutics which deals with the curative use of mechanical means.—**mech″a-no-ther-a-peu′tic,** *a.*—**mech″a-no-ther′a-py** (-ther′ạ-pi), *n.* Curative treatment by mechanical means.—**mech″a-no-ther′a-pist,** *n.*

mé-chant (mā-shäṅ), *a.* [F.] Malicious; mischievous; naughty; bad.—**mé-chante** (mā-shäṅt), *a.* [F.] Fem. of *méchant.*

Mech-lin (mek′lin) **lace.** [From *Mechlin* (Malines), city in Belgium: cf. *malines.*] A fine pillow-lace having the pattern outlined by a distinct thread.

Mechlin Lace.

me-con-ic (mẹ-kon′ik), *a.* [Gr. μηκωνικός, < μήκων, poppy.] Pertaining to or derived from the poppy: as, *meconic* acid (a crystalline acid obtained from opium).

med-al (med′ạl), *n.* [F. *médaille,* < It. *medaglia,* medal, < L. *metallum,* E. *metal.*] A flat piece of metal, usually circular in form, bearing an inscription, device, etc., issued to commemorate a person, action, or event, or given to serve as a reward for bravery, merit, or the like.—**Medal of Honor,** a medal awarded by Congress, or by the President (or a commanding officer representing him) in the name of Congress, to soldiers, sailors, and marines of the U. S. who, in action involving actual conflict with an enemy, distinguish themselves conspicuously by gallantry and intrepidity at the risk of life above and beyond the call of duty. Cf. *Distinguished Service Cross* and *Distinguished Service Medal.*—**med′al,** *v. t.*; *-aled* or *-alled, -aling* or *-alling.* To decorate or honor with a medal.—**med′al=cup,** *n.* A drinking-vessel, usually of silver, in which medals or coins are set as part of the decoration.—**med′al-ist, med′al-list,** *n.* One versed in medals; also, a designer, engraver, or maker of medals; also, one to whom a medal has been awarded.—**me-dal-lic** (mẹ-dal′ik), *a.* Pertaining to medals; of the nature of a medal.

Medal-cup.

me-dal-lion (mẹ-dal′yọn), *n.* [F. *médaillon,* < It. *medaglione,* aug. of *medaglia,* E. *medal.*] A large medal; also, something resembling this, as a circular or other tablet or panel bearing objects or figures in relief, a decorative design in a carpet or on a book-cover, or a separate ornament of lace, etc.—**me-dal′lioned,** *a.* Ornamented with a medallion or medallions; formed into a medallion.—**me-dal′lion-ist,** *n.* A maker of medallions.

med-al=play (med′ạl-plā), *n.* In *golf,* play in which the score is reckoned by counting the total number of strokes taken to complete the round. Cf. *match-play.*

med-dle (med′l), *v.*; *-dled, -dling.* [OF. *medler, mesler* (F. *mêler*), < ML. *misculare,* < L. *miscere,* mix.] **I.**† *tr.* To mix; mingle. **II.** *intr.* To mingle in combination, union, company, etc.†; also, to join or engage in combat†; also, to have to do, or concern one's self (now rare: as, "What measures they took . . . is too long a story to *meddle* with here," Defoe's "Captain Singleton," xiii.); now, usually, to concern or busy one's self with or in something without warrant or necessity (as, "I will teach them . . . what it is to *meddle* with another man's concerns," Cooper's "Spy," xii.; "wholly unacquainted with the world in which they are so fond of *meddling,*" Burke's "Revolution in France," 14); interfere.—**med′dler,** *n.*—**med′dle-some** (-sum), *a.* Given to meddling.—**med′dle-some-ly,** *adv.*—**med′dle-some-ness,** *n.*

Mede (mēd), *n.* A native or inhabitant of Media, an ancient kingdom of Asia, south of the Caspian Sea.—**the law of the Medes and Persians.** See under *law*³, *n.*

me-di-a (mē′di-ä), *n.* Plural of *medium.*

me-di-a-cy (mē′di-ạ-si), *n.* The state of being mediate.

me-di-æ-val (mē-di-ē′vạl), etc. See *medieval,* etc.

me-di-al (mē′di-ạl). [LL. *medialis,* < L. *medius,* middle: see *medium.*] **I.** *a.* Situated in or pertaining to the middle; median; intermediate; often, of letters, situated in the middle of, or within, a word; also, pertaining to a mean or average; average; hence, ordinary. **II.** *n.* A medial letter; also, a form of a letter used in the middle of a word; also, in *gram.,* any of the three Greek voiced mutes, γ, δ, β, or any of their equivalents, as *g, d, b,* in other languages (as intermediate in sound between the tenues and the aspirates).—**me′di-al-ly,** *adv.*

Me-di-an¹ (mē′di-ạn). **I.** *a.* Of or pertaining to Media or the Medes. **II.** *n.* A Mede.

me-di-an² (mē′di-ạn), *a.* [L. *medianus,* < *medius,* middle: see *medium,* and cf. *mean*³.] Situated in or pertaining to the middle; medial; specif., noting or pertaining to a plane dividing something into two equal parts, esp. one dividing an animal into right and left halves; also, noting or pertaining to the middle number, value, or the like, in a given series (as, 4 is the *median* number in the series 1, 3, 4, 8, 9, while 5 is the average; *median* age, that age in a given population, which constitutes a point such that the total number of persons beyond it and the total number falling short of it are equal).—**me′di-an-ly,** *adv.*

me-di-ant (mē′di-ạnt), *n.* [It. *mediante,* < LL. *medians* (*-ant-*), ppr. of *mediare*: see *mediate.*] In *music,* the third tone of a scale.

me-di-as-ti-num (mē″di-as-tī′num), *n.*; pl. *-na* (-nä). [NL., prop. neut. of ML. *mediastinus,* in the middle, < L. *medius,* middle: see *medium.*] In *anat.,* a median septum or partition between two parts of an organ, or between two paired cavities of the body; esp., the membranous partition separating the right and left thoracic cavities, formed of the two inner pleural walls, and, in man, in whom these do not meet, including also the space between them, which contains all the viscera of the thorax except the lungs.—**me″di-as-ti′nal,** *a.*

me-di-ate (mē′di-āt), *v.*; *-ated, -ating.* [LL. *mediatus,* pp. of *mediare,* divide or be in the middle, < L. *medius,* middle: see *medium.*] **I.** *intr.* To occupy an intermediate place or position; esp., to form a connecting link or a transitional stage between other things; also, to act between parties in order to effect an agreement, compromise, or reconciliation (as, "Bacon attempted to *mediate* between his friend and the Queen": Macaulay's "Essays," Lord Bacon). **II.** *tr.* To effect (a result), convey (a gift), communicate (knowledge), etc., as or by an intermediary or medium; also, to bring about (an agreement, peace, etc.) between parties by acting as mediator; also, to settle (disputes, etc.) by mediation; reconcile.—**me′di-ate** (-ạt), *a.* Intermediate (now rare); also, acting through, dependent on, or involving an intermediate agent or agency; not direct or immediate.—**me′di-ate-ly,** *adv.*—**me′di-ate-ness,** *n.*—**me-di-a′tion** (-ā′shọn), *n.* [LL. *mediatio(n-).*] Action or relation as an intermediary or medium (as, "The visible government which God exercises over the world, is by the instrumentality and *mediation* of others": J. Butler's "Analogy of Religion," ii. 5); instrumentality; also, action in mediating between parties, as to effect an agreement or reconciliation.—**me′di-a-tive** (-ạ-tiv), *a.* Mediating; mediatory.

me-di-a-tize (mē′di-ạ-tīz), *v. t.*; *-tized, -tizing.* [F. *médiatiser*, or G. *mediatisieren*, < LL. *mediatus*, pp.: see *mediate.*] Orig., under the Holy Roman Empire, to reduce (a prince, principality, etc.) from a position of immediate vassalage to the empire to one of mediate vassalage; in later times, to annex (a principality) to another state (while allowing certain rights to its former sovereign).—**me″di-a-ti-za′tion** (-ti-zā′shọn), *n.*

me-di-a-tor (mē′di-ā-tọr), *n.* [LL.] One who mediates; esp., one who mediates between parties at variance; sometimes [*cap.*], with *the*, Jesus Christ as mediating between God and men (cf. 1 Tim. ii. 5).—**me″di-a-to′ri-al** (-ạ-tō′ri-ạl), *a.*—**me′di-a-tor-ship,** *n.* The office or function of a mediator.—**me′di-a-to-ry** (-ạ-tọ-ri), *a.* Pertaining to mediation; having the function of mediating.—**me′di-a-tress** (-ā-tres), *n.* A female mediator. Also **me′di-a-trice** (-tris), **me-di-a′trix.**

med-ic[1] (med′ik). [L. *medicus*, pertaining to healing, medical, as n. a physician, < *mederi*, heal, cure: see *meditate*, and cf. *remedy.*] **I.** *a.* Medical. [Poetic.] **II.** *n.* A medical practitioner; also, a medical student. [Now colloq.]

med-ic[2] (med′ik or mē′dik), *n.* [L. *medica*, < Gr. (*πόα*) *Μηδική*, 'Median (grass).'] Any plant of the fabaceous genus *Medicago*, as *M. sativa* ('purple medic,' or lucerne), and *M. lupulina* ('black medic'), a yellow-flowered herb with black pods.

med-i-ca-ble (med′i-kạ-bl), *a.* [L. *medicabilis*, < *medicare*: see *medicate.*] Susceptible of medical treatment; curable.

med-i-cal (med′i-kạl), *a.* [ML. *medicalis*, < L. *medicus*: see *medic*[1].] Of or pertaining to the science or practice of medicine.—**medical jurisprudence,** the science which treats of the application of medical knowledge to certain questions of civil and criminal law. More properly called *forensic* (or *legal*) *medicine.*—**med′i-cal-ly,** *adv.*

med-i-ca-ment (med′i-kạ-mẹnt or mẹ-dik′ạ-), *n.* [L. *medicamentum*, < *medicare*: see *medicate.*] Any curative or healing substance.—**med″i-ca-men′tal** (-men′tạl), **med″i-ca-men′ta-ry** (-tạ-ri), *a.*

med-i-cas-ter (med′i-kas-tėr), *n.* [= It. *medicastro*, < L. *medicus*: see *medic*[1].] A pretender to medical skill; a quack.

med-i-cate (med′i-kāt), *v. t.*; *-cated, -cating.* [L. *medicatus*, pp. of *medicare, medicari*, < *medicus*: see *medic*[1].] To treat with medicine or medicaments; cure or heal; also, to impregnate with a medicinal substance.—**med-i-ca′tion** (-kā′shọn), *n.*—**med′i-ca-tive** (-kạ-tiv), *a.* Medicinal; remedial.

Med-i-ce-an (med-i-sē′ạn), *a.* Of or pertaining to the Medici, an illustrious Florentine family of great power and wealth which flourished in the 15th and 16th centuries.

me-di-ci-na-ble (mẹ-dis′i-nạ-bl, formerly med′i-si-), *a.* [OF. *medicinable.*] Medicinal; curative: as, "Some griefs are *med'cinable*; that is one of them, For it doth physic love" (Shakspere's "Cymbeline," iii. 2. 33). [Archaic.]

me-di-ci-nal (mẹ-dis′i-nạl), *a.* [L. *medicinalis.*] Pertaining to, or having the properties of, a medicine; curative; remedial: as, *medicinal* properties; *medicinal* substances; "*medicinal* springs" (H. Melville's "Typee," xx.).—**me-di′ci-nal-ly,** *adv.*

med-i-cine (med′i-sin), *n.* [OF. *medicine* (F. *médecine*), < L. *medicina*, < *medicus*: see *medic*[1].] The art or science of restoring or preserving health or due physical condition, as by means of drugs, surgical operations or appliances, manipulations, etc. (often divided into medicine proper, surgery, and obstetrics); esp., the art or science of treating disease with drugs or curative substances (medicine proper, as distinguished from surgery and obstetrics); sometimes, the medical profession; also, any substance or substances used in treating disease; a medicament; a remedy; now, commonly, a medicament or medicaments taken internally; also, a drug or the like used for other than remedial purposes, as a love-potion or a poison† (as, "If the rascal have not given me *medicines* to make me love him, I'll be hanged": Shakspere's "1 Henry IV.," ii. 2. 19); also, any object or practice regarded by savages as of magical efficacy (as, "They [Indian tribe] are firm believers . . . in the power and efficacy of charms and amulets, or *medicines*, as they term them": Irving's "Captain Bonneville," x.); sometimes, a medicine-man (as, "When they come to learn that you are a great *medicine*, they will adopt you in the tribe": Cooper's "Prairie," xxi.).—**forensic medicine.** Same as *medical jurisprudence.*—**med′i-cine,** *v. t.*; *-cined, -cining.* [OF. *mediciner* (F. *médeciner*).] To administer medicine to; work upon or affect by or as if by medicine.—**med′i-cine=ball,** *n.* A large, solid leather-covered ball, of considerable weight, thrown from one person to another for exercise.—**med′i-cine=man** (-man), *n.*; pl. *-men.* Among savages, a man who professes to cure disease and exercise various magical or supernatural powers by the aid of 'medicine.'—**med′i-cin-er** (-si-nėr), *n.* A physician: as, "It is unbecoming a *mediciner* of thine eminence to interfere with the practice of another" (Scott's "Talisman," xviii.). [Obs. or archaic.]

med′ick, *n.* See *medic*[2].

med-i-co (med′i-kō), *n.*; pl. *-cos* (-kōz). [It. and Sp., < L. *medicus*: see *medic*[1].] A medical practitioner (as, "The *medico* held my chin in the usual way, and examined my throat": Kinglake's "Eothen," xviii.); also, a medical student. [Now colloq.]

medico-. Form of L. *medicus*, medical, used in combination.—**med-i-co-chi-rur-gi-cal** (med″i-kọ-kī-rėr′ji-kạl), *a.* Medical and chirurgical; pertaining to both medicine and surgery.—**med″i-co-le′gal** (-lē′gạl), *a.* Pertaining to medical jurisprudence, or to the legal aspects of medical affairs.

me-di-e-val, me-di-æ-val (mē-di-ē′vạl). [L. *medius*, middle, + *ævum*, age.] **I.** *a.* Of or pertaining to, characteristic of, or in the style of, the middle ages: as, *medieval* architecture (the most important branch of medieval art, comprising a number of styles, including all those grouped under the collective terms Romanesque and Gothic, and representing a continuous development from the classical Roman to the modifications wrought by the Renaissance, and exemplified esp. by many famous European churches). **II.** *n.* One who lived in the middle ages.—**me-di-e′val-ism, me-di-æ′val-ism,** *n.* The spirit, practices, or methods of the middle ages; devotion to or adoption of medieval ideals or practices; also, a medieval belief, prac-

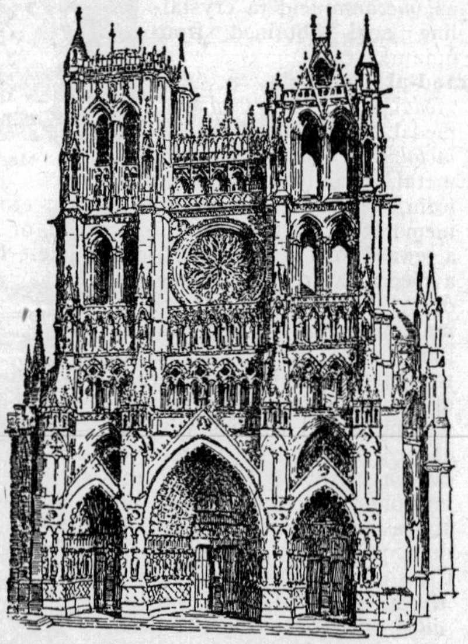

Medieval Architecture, of the best period. — West front of Amiens Cathedral, France; 13th century.

tice, or the like.—**me-di-e′val-ist, me-di-æ′val-ist,** *n.* One versed in medieval history and affairs; one in sympathy with the spirit and methods of the middle ages; also, a medieval.—**me-di-e′val-ize, me-di-æ′val-ize,** *v. t.*; *-ized, -izing.* To render medieval; conform to medieval types, ideas, etc.—**me-di-e′val-ly, me-di-æ′val-ly,** *adv.*

me-di-o- (mē′di-ǫ-). Form of L. *medius,* middle, used in combination, as in *mediofrontal* (in the middle of the frontal region, or forehead), *medio-occipital, medioposterior, medioventral.*

me-di-o-cre (mē′di-ō-kėr), *a.* [F. *médiocre,* < L. *mediocris,* < *medius,* middle: see *medium.*] Of middling quality; of only moderate excellence; neither good nor bad; indifferent; ordinary: as, "a gentleman of *mediocre* station and character" (Motley's "Dutch Republic," ii. 2); "a person of *mediocre* abilities" (Motley's "Dutch Republic," iii. 2).—**me-di-oc′ri-ty** (-ok′ri-ti), *n.*; pl. *-ties* (-tiz). [L. *mediocritas.*] The state or quality of being mediocre; mediocre ability or accomplishment; also, a person of but moderate ability (as, "A *Mediocrity* . . . was induced to withdraw, and the great name of Wellington supplied his place in council": Disraeli's "Coningsby," ii. 1).

med-i-tant (med′i-tạnt). [L. *meditans* (*-ant-*), ppr.] **I.** *a.* Meditating; engaged in meditation. **II.** *n.* One who meditates, or gives himself up to meditation.

med-i-tate (med′i-tāt), *v.*; *-tated, -tating.* [L. *meditatus,* pp. of *meditari,* meditate; akin to Gr. *μέδεσθαι,* care for, think of, *μήδεσθαι,* intend, devise, and L. *mederi,* heal, cure: see *medic*[1].] **I.** *tr.* To reflect upon, or consider (now rare: as, "Alberti had deeply *meditated* the remains of Roman antiquity," Hallam's "Literature of Europe," i. 3. § 111); also, to observe intently (now rare: as, "The ready spaniel . . . *meditates* the prey," Pope's "Windsor Forest," 102); also, to consider in the mind as something to be done or effected (as, "The King struck the blow he had for some time *meditated*": Lecky's "Hist. of Eng. in the 18th Century," viii.); hence, to intend or purpose (as, "He, too, *meditated* a visit to the Captain": H. Kingsley's "Geoffry Hamlyn," xxviii.). **II.** *intr.* To engage in thought or contemplation; reflect: as, "He quitted her presence to *meditate* upon revenge" (Marryat's "King's Own," xlvii.).—**med-i-ta′tion** (-tā′shǫn), *n.* [L. *meditatio(n-)*.] The act of meditating; continued thought; reflection; specif., religious contemplation; also, a written or spoken discourse of a contemplative character.—**med′i-ta-tive** (-tā-tiv), *a.* [LL. *meditativus.*] Given to, characterized by, or indicative of meditation.—**med′i-ta-tive-ly,** *adv.*—**med′i-ta-tive-ness,** *n.*

med-i-ter-ra-ne-an (med″i-tẹ-rā′nẹ-ạn), *a.* [L. *mediterraneus,* midland, inland, < *medius,* middle, + *terra,* land.] In the midst of an expanse of land; inland; also, surrounded by land (as, the *Mediterranean* Sea); [*cap.*] of or pertaining to the Mediterranean Sea (as, the *Mediterranean* ports; the *Mediterranean* region or races).

me-di-um (mē′di-um). [L., neut. of *medius,* middle, intermediate, middling: see *mid*[2].] **I.** *n.*; pl. *mediums* or *media* (-ạ̈). Something intermediate in nature or degree; a middle state or condition; a mean; also, an intervening substance, as air, ether, etc., through which a force acts or an effect is produced; hence, a pervading or enveloping substance; the element in which an organism has its natural habitat; fig., one's environment; surrounding things, conditions, or influences; also, an agency, means, or instrument (as, a newspaper much used as an advertising *medium;* the *medium* of exchange, or circulating *medium,* of a country, as coins, bank-notes, etc.); hence, instrumentality (as, "A negotiation was opened through the *medium* of the ambassador, Sam": C. Brontë's "Jane Eyre," xviii.); specif., a person serving, or conceived as serving, as an instrument for the manifestation of another personality or of some alleged supernatural agency (as, a spiritualistic *medium*); in *bact.,* the nutritive substance in or upon which micro-organisms are grown for study; in *painting,* a liquid with which pigments are mixed for application. **II.** *a.* Intermediate in degree, quality, etc.; middling: as, a man of *medium* size.—**me″di-um-is′tic,** *a.* Pertaining to a spiritualistic medium.—**me′di-um-ship,** *n.*

med-lar (med′lạ̈r), *n.* [OF. *medler, meslier,* the tree (medlar), < *mesle,* the fruit, < L. *mespilum,* < Gr. *μέσπιλον,* tree and fruit.] A small malaceous tree, *Mespilus germanica,* the fruit of which resembles a crab-apple and is not edible until in the early stages of decay; also, its fruit; also, any of certain other malaceous trees, as the loquat ('Japanese medlar') or the azarole ('Neapolitan medlar'); also, the fruit of such a tree.

Leaves and Fruit of Medlar (*Mespilus germanica*).

med-ley (med′li). [OF. *medlee, meslee* (F. *mêlée*), < *medler, mesler:* see *meddle.*] **I.** *n.*; pl. *-leys* (-liz). Conflict, esp. hand-to-hand fighting (archaic); also, a mixture, esp. of heterogeneous elements; a jumble; also, a piece of music combining airs or passages from various sources. **II.** *a.* Mixed; mingled; motley: as, "A *medley* air Of cunning and of impudence" (Wordsworth's "Peter Bell," i.).—**med′ley,** *v. t.*; *-leyed, -leying.* To mix as in a medley.

Mé-doc (mā-dok′ or mā′dok, F. mā-dok), *n.* [From *Médoc,* region in the Gironde department.] A class of French red wines, including the finest varieties of red Bordeaux (claret).

me-dul-la (mẹ-dul′ạ̈), *n.* [L., marrow, pith, < *medius,* middle.] In *anat.,* the marrow of bones; the spinal cord; the mẹdulla oblongata; the deep or inner substance of an organ or part, as of a kidney; in *bot.,* the pith of plants.—**me-dul′la ob-lon-ga-ta** (ob-long-gā′tạ̈). [NL., 'prolonged medulla.'] In *anat.,* the lowest or hindmost part of the brain, continuous with the spinal cord.—**med-ul-la-ry** (med′u-lạ̄-ri or mẹ-dul′ạ-ri), *a.* [LL. *medullaris.*] Pertaining to, consisting of, or resembling the medulla or the medulla oblongata.—**medullary ray,** in *bot.,* in the stems of exogenous plants, one of the vertical bands or plates of parenchymatous tissue which radiate between the pith and the bark.

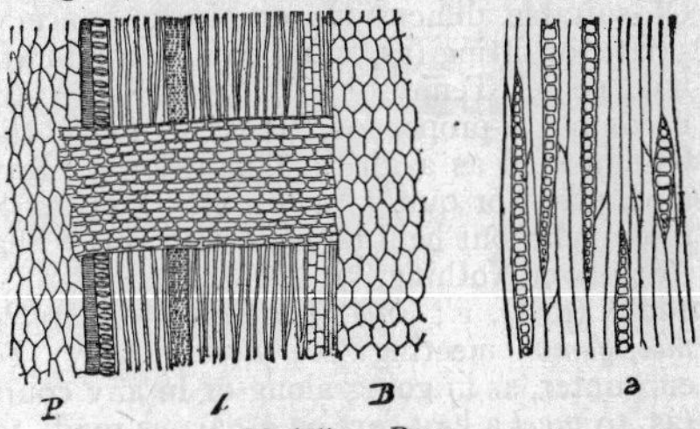

P　1　B　2

Medullary Rays.

1. Longitudinal radial section through the wood of a branch of maple one year old: *P,* pith; *B,* bark. 2. Longitudinal tangential section of the same wood, showing the ends of the medullary rays.

Me-du-sa (mẹ-dū′sạ̈), *n.*; pl. *-sas* or *-sæ* (-sē). [L., < Gr. Μέδουσα.] That one of the three Gorgons of Grecian legend who was slain by Perseus and whose head was afterward borne on the ægis or shield of Athene; also [*l. c.*], any of various soft, gelatinous, free-swimming cœlenterates, produced in some cases directly from the egg, and in other cases, through alternation of generations, by budding off from the hydroid form of a hydrozoan (also called *jellyfish*); hence, such a free-swimming form ('medusa form') of a hydrozoan, as distinguished from the hydroid form, which is colonial and usually fixed.—**me-du′san. I.** *a.* Pertaining to a medusa or jellyfish. **II.** *n.* A medusa or jellyfish.

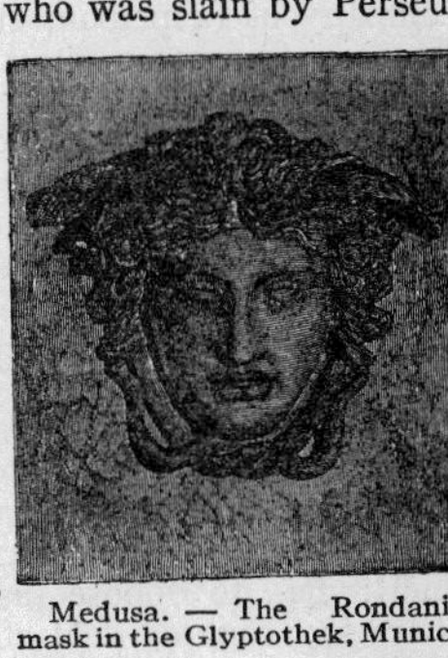

Medusa. — The Rondanini mask in the Glyptothek, Munich.

meed (mēd), *n.* [AS. *mēd,* reward, = G. *miete,* hire; akin to Goth. *mizdō,* reward, and Gr. *μισθός,* pay.] A reward or recompense for service or desert (good or bad); now, usually, a reward, esp. of praise, honor, or the like, for meritorious achievement or good desert (poetic or literary: as, "The youthful commander-in-chief obtained more than his full *meed* of glory," Motley's "Dutch Republic," v. 1); sometimes, formerly, a bribe†; also, merit† (as, "My *meed* hath got me fame": Shakspere's "3 Henry VI.," iv. 8. 38).

meek (mēk), *a.* [ME. *meke, meoc;* from Scand.: cf. Icel. *mjūkr,* soft, mild, meek, Sw. *mjuk,* Dan. *myg,* soft.]

Gentle, mild, or kind, as to others†; also, humbly patient or submissive, as under provocation from others (as, "Even the man Moses, the *meekest* of men, was wrathful sometimes": George Eliot's "Adam Bede," l.); sometimes, unduly patient or submissive; spiritless; tame.—**meek′en,** *v. t.* or *i.* To make or become meek.—**meek′ly,** *adv.*—**meek′ness,** *n.*

meer-kat (mēr′kat), *n.* [D.; origin uncertain.] A small South African carnivorous animal, *Cynictis penicillata*, allied to the ichneumon; also, the suricate.

Meerkat (*Cynictis penicillata*).

meer-schaum (mēr′shâm or -shum), *n.* [G., 'sea-foam.'] A native hydrous silicate of magnesium, occurring in white, soft, clay-like masses light enough when dry to float on water; also, a tobacco-pipe the bowl of which is made of this substance (as, "a German student . . . with a beard, a blouse, and a *meerschaum*": Lever's "Harry Lorrequer," xlv.).

meet[1] (mēt), *a.* [ME. *mete*, < AS. *gemǣte*, of suitable dimensions, = G. *gemäss*, conformable; akin to E. *mete*[2].] Of suitable dimensions or size†; hence, suitable, appropriate, or fitting (as, "And pay *Meet* adoration to my household gods," Tennyson's "Ulysses," 42: see also *helpmeet*); becoming or proper (as, "It was not *meet* that his son should be educated as a girl": Longfellow's "Kavanagh," xviii.); also, even† or quits† (*with*: as, "You tax Signior Benedick too much; but he'll be *meet* with you," Shakspere's "Much Ado about Nothing," i. 1. 47).

meet[2] (mēt), *v.*; *met*, *meeting*. [AS. *mētan*, *gemētan*, < *mōt*, *gemōt*, meeting: see *moot*.] **I.** *tr.* To come upon or encounter, as in going along or in any course of proceeding (as, to *meet* a hay-cart on a narrow road; to *meet* a passage in reading); come face to face with or into the presence of (as, to turn aside to avoid *meeting* a person); go to the place of arrival of, as to welcome, speak with, or accompany, or for some other purpose (as, to *meet* travelers at a railroad station; to *meet* a train or a steamship); come into the company of (a person, etc.) in intercourse, dealings, conference, etc.; come into personal acquaintance with, as by formal presentation (as, "I had the good fortune to *meet* Lady Bareacres at the Duchess of Richmond's ball": Thackeray's "Vanity Fair," xlix.); also, to come into contact, junction, or connection with (as, when hand *meets* hand; one line *meets* another; "The broad seas swell'd to *meet* the keel," Tennyson's "Voyage," ii.); also, to come before or to (the eye, gaze, ear, etc.: as, "I could not but be entertained by the . . . sight which now *met* my view," H. Melville's "Typee," xiii.); sometimes, to face (the eye, etc.) directly or without avoidance (as, "He *meets* her glance with so frank a look": Wiseman's "Fabiola," i. 2); also, to encounter in opposition or conflict (as, to *meet* a person in a duel); fig., to oppose (as, to *meet* charges with countercharges); cope or deal effectively with (an objection, difficulty, etc.); satisfy (needs, obligations, demands, etc.); come into conformity with (wishes, expectations, views, etc.); also, to encounter in experience (as, to *meet* one's fate; to *meet* open hostility or derision); receive (as, to *meet* one's deserts; "such cruelties, as surely cannot *meet* the approbation of Heaven," Scott's "Castle Dangerous," v.). **II.** *intr.* To come together, face to face, or into company (as, we *met* on the street); assemble, as for action or conference, as a committee, a legislature, a society, etc.; become personally acquainted; also, to come into contact or form a junction, as lines, planes, areas, etc.; fig., to be conjoined or united (as, qualities that seldom *meet* in one person); concur or agree (as, "We *meet* at last in one sincere desire": Cowper's "Retirement," 389); also, to come together in opposition or conflict, as adversaries, hostile forces, etc.—**to meet with,** to come upon or encounter, as in going along or proceeding; come across; light upon; also, to encounter in experience (as, to *meet with* strong opposition); experience or undergo; receive (praise, blame, etc.).—**meet**[2], *n.* A meeting, as of huntsmen for a hunt, of cyclists for a ride, etc.; also, those assembled at such a meeting, or the place of meeting.—**meet′ing,** *n.* A coming together; an assembling, as of a number of persons for some common purpose; an assembly or gathering held, or the persons present; often, an assembly for religious worship (used specif. with reference to the Friends or Quakers, or, in England, to dissenters: cf. *meeting-house*); also, a coming into or being in contact, as of things; junction or union; confluence, as of rivers; also, a hostile encounter; a duel.—**meet′ing=house,** *n.* A house or building for religious worship: applied specif. to the houses of worship of Friends, or in England (esp. disparagingly) to those of dissenters, but used in the U. S. of any house of worship, or church (as, "In the front gallery of the *meeting-house*, opposite the pulpit, was seated the choir of the church," Mrs. Stowe's "Oldtown Folks," v.: now somewhat archaic or prov.).

meet-ly (mēt′li), *adv.* In a meet manner; suitably; fittingly; properly.—**meet′ness,** *n.*

meg- (meg-), **meg-a-** (meg′ạ-), **meg-a-lo-** (meg′ạ-lō-). Forms of Gr. μέγας (μεγαλ-), large, great, used in combination: in *physics*, used to mean 'million,' as in *megadyne* (a million dynes), *megaerg* or *megerg* (a million ergs), *megafarad* (a million farads), *megampere*, *megavolt*, *megawatt*, *megohm*, etc. Cf. *micro-*.

meg-a-ce-phal-ic (meg″ạ-se-fal′ik), *a.* [Gr. μέγας, large, + κεφαλή, head.] Large-headed; in *craniom.*, having a skull with a large cranial capacity or one exceeding the mean (cf. *mesocephalic* and *microcephalic*). Also **meg-a-ceph′a-lous** (-sef′ạ-lus).

meg-a-dyne (meg′ạ-dīn), *n.* See *meg-*, *mega-*.

meg-a-erg (meg′ạ-ėrg), *n.* See *meg-*, *mega-*.

meg-a-far-ad (meg′ạ-far″ad), *n.* See *meg-*, *mega-*.

meg-a-lith (meg′ạ-lith), *n.* [See *mega-* and *-lith*.] A stone of great size, esp. in ancient constructive work (as the Cyclopean masonry) or in primitive monumental remains (as menhirs, dolmens, cromlechs, alinements, etc.). Cf. *monolith*.—**meg-a-lith′ic,** *a.* Pertaining to, consisting of, or characterized by megaliths.

meg′a-lo-. See *meg-*.

meg-a-lo-ce-phal-ic (meg″ạ-lō-se-fal′ik), **meg-a-lo-ceph-a-lous** (meg″ạ-lō-sef′ạ-lus), *a.* Same as *megacephalic*.

meg-a-lo-ma-ni-a (meg″ạ-lō-mā′ni-ạ̈), *n.* [NL.: see *meg-*, *megalo-*, and *mania*.] A form of mental alienation marked by delusions of greatness, wealth, etc.; also, a mania for big or great things.—**meg″a-lo-ma′ni-ac** (-ak), *a.* and *n.*

meg-a-lo-mar-tyr (meg″ạ-lō-mär′tėr), *n.* [LGr. μεγαλόμαρτυρ: see *meg-*, *megalo-*, and *martyr*.] A great or eminent martyr.

meg-a-lo-saur (meg′ạ-lō-sâr), *n.* [NL. *megalosaurus*: see *meg-*, *megalo-*, and *-saur*.] Any of the gigantic carnivorous dinosaurs which constitute the extinct genus *Megalosaurus*. Also **meg″a-lo-sau′rus** (-sâ′rus).

Megalosaur. — 1, animal restored; 2, tooth; 3, part of jaw.

meg-am-pere (meg′am-pãr″), *n.* See *meg-*.

meg-a-phone (meg′ạ-fōn), *n.* [See *mega-* and *-phone*.] A device for magnifying sound, or for directing it in increased volume, as a large funnel-shaped instrument used in addressing a large audience out of doors or in calling to a distance.—**meg′a-phone,** *v. t.* or *i.*; *-phoned*, *-phoning*. To magnify or direct (sound) by means of a megaphone.—**meg-a-phon′ic** (-fon′ik), *a.*

meg-a-pod, meg-a-pode (meg′ạ-pod, -pōd), *n.* [NL. *Megapodius*, the typical genus, < Gr. μέγας, large, + πούς (ποδ-), foot.] Any of the *Megapodiidæ*, a family of large-footed gallinaceous birds of the Australian region, notable for their habit of scratching up heaps of soil, etc., in which their eggs are buried and left to be hatched.

Megapod, or Mound-bird (*Megapodius tumulus*).

meg-a-scope (meg′ạ-skōp), *n.* [See *mega-* and *-scope.*] A kind of magic lantern by which enlarged images of opaque objects are thrown upon a screen.—**meg-a-scop′ic** (-skop′ik), *a.* Pertaining to the megascope; also, enlarged or magnified; also, macroscopic.

meg-a-seism (meg′ạ-sīsm or -sīzm), *n.* [See *mega-* and *seism.*] A great or severe earthquake.—**meg-a-seis′mic** (-sīs′mik or -sīz′mik), *a.*

meg-a-spo-ran-gi-um (meg″ạ-spọ̄-ran′ji-um), *n.*; pl. *-gia* (-ji-ạ̈). [NL.: see *mega-* and *sporangium.*] In *bot.*, a sporangium containing megaspores.

meg-a-spore (meg′ạ-spōr), *n.* [See *mega-* and *spore.*] In *bot.*, one of the larger of the two kinds of reproductive bodies or spores produced asexually by certain plants, as the embryo-sac of a seed-bearing plant.

meg-a-there (meg′ạ-thēr), *n.* [NL. *megatherium*: see *mega-* and *-there.*] Any of the huge sloth-like animals constituting the extinct genus *Megatherium.* Also **meg-a-the′ri-um** (-thē′ri-um).

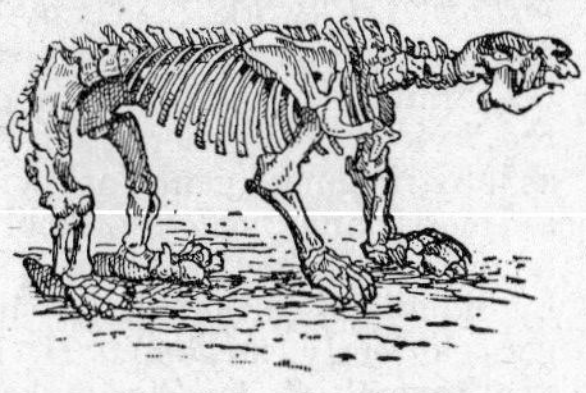

Skeleton of Megathere.

meg-a-volt (meg′ạ-vōlt), *n.* See *meg-*, *mega-*.

meg-a-watt (meg′ạ-wot), *n.* See *meg-*, *mega-*.

meg-erg (meg′ėrg), *n.* See *meg-*.

me-gilp (mẹ̄-gilp′), *n.* See *magilp.*

meg-ohm (meg′ōm), *n.* See *meg-*.

me-grim (mē′grim), *n.* [OF. F. *migraine*, < LL. *hemicrania*: see *hemicrania.*] Hemicrania or migraine; also, a whim, fancy, or caprice (archaic or prov.: as, "It was a pity she should take such *megrims* into her head," George Eliot's "Adam Bede," xviii.); also, *pl.*, morbid low spirits; vapors; also, in animals, the staggers.

mei-nie, mei-ny (mā′ni or mē′ni), *n.* [OF. *mesnie, maisnie*, < L. *mansio(n-)*: see *mansion*, and cf. *menial.*] A household or family; also, a body of retainers or followers (as, "They summon'd up their *meiny*, straight took horse": Shakspere's "King Lear," ii. 4. 35); a retinue or train; also, more generally, a company or assemblage; a multitude; an army. [Obs. or archaic.]

Mei-o-cene (mī′ọ̄-sēn), *a.* and *n.* See *Miocene.*

meis-ter-sing-er (mīs′tėr-sing″ėr, G. mīs′tėr-zing″ėr), *n.* [G., 'mastersinger.'] A member of one of the gilds, chiefly of working-men, established during the 14th, 15th, and 16th centuries in the principal cities of Germany, for the cultivation of poetry and music.

mel-an-cho-li-a (mel-ạn-kō′li-ạ̈), *n.* [LL.: see *melancholy.*] A form of mental disease characterized by great depression of spirits with gloomy forebodings.—**mel-an-cho′li-ac** (-ak). **I.** *a.* Affected with melancholia. **II.** *n.* One affected with melancholia.

mel-an-chol-ic (mel-ạn-kol′ik), *a.* [L. *melancholicus*, < Gr. μελαγχολικός, < μελαγχολία: see *melancholy.*] Pertaining to, affected by, or producing black bile†; atrabiliar†; also, disposed to or affected with melancholy; characterized by or showing melancholy (as, "*melancholic* notions": Johnson's "Rasselas," xlvi.); gloomy; melancholy; also, pertaining to or affected with melancholia.—**mel-an-chol′i-cal-ly,** *adv.*

mel-an-chol-i-ly (mel′ạn-kol-i-li), *adv.* In a melancholy manner.—**mel′an-chol-i-ness,** *n.*

mel-an-cho-li-ous (mel-ạn-kō′li-us), *a.* Melancholy; gloomy. [Archaic.]

mel-an-chol-y (mel′ạn-kol-i). [OF. *melancolie* (F. *mélancolie*), < LL. *melancholia*, < Gr. μελαγχολία, atrabiliousness, < μέλας (μελαν-), black, + χολή, bile.] **I.** *n.*; pl. *-ies* (-iz). The condition of having too much black bile†, or black bile itself† (see under *bile*); hence, melancholia; also, a gloomy state of mind, esp. when habitual or prolonged; depression, or a fit of depression; sadness; sometimes, sober thoughtfulness, or pensiveness (as, "I . . . began, Wrapp'd in a pleasing fit of *melancholy*, To meditate my rural minstrelsy": Milton's "Comus," 546). **II.** *a.* Pertaining to or affected with melancholia†; also, affected with, characterized by, or showing melancholy, depression, or sadness, as persons or the mood, feelings, thoughts, aspect, tone, etc.; attended with or inducing melancholy or sadness (as, a *melancholy* duty, occasion, or fact); gloomy, dreary, or somber in appearance or character (as, "old Ocean's gray and *melancholy* waste": Bryant's "Thanatopsis"); sometimes, soberly thoughtful, or pensive (as, "the pensive *melancholy* mind": Thomson's "Castle of Indolence," i. 40).

Mel-a-ne-sian (mel-ạ-nē′shiạn or -zhiạn). [From *Melanesia*, < Gr. μέλας (μελαν-), black, + νῆσος, island.] **I.** *a.* Of or pertaining to Melanesia (a group of islands in the western Pacific, including New Caledonia, the Fiji Islands, the Solomon Islands, etc.), its inhabitants, or their languages. **II.** *n.* A member of any of the dark-skinned peoples inhabiting Melanesia; also, any of the languages or dialects spoken there.

mé-lange (mā-läṅzh), *n.* [F., < *mêler*, mix: see *meddle.*] A mixture; a medley.

me-lan-ic (me-lan′ik), *a.* [Gr. μέλας (μελαν-), black.] Having black hair and a dark complexion; characterized by or pertaining to melanism; also, characterized by or pertaining to melanosis.—**mel-a-nin** (mel′ạ-nin), *n.* Any of various dark pigments in the body of man and certain animals, as that occurring in the hair, epidermis, etc., of colored races, or one produced in certain diseases.—**mel′a-nism,** *n.* An abnormal development of black or dark pigment in the skin, hair, and eyes of a human being, or in the skin, coat, plumage, etc., of an animal.—**mel-a-nis′tic** (-nis′tik), *a.* Characterized by melanism.—**mel′a-nize,** *v. t.*; *-nized, -nizing.* To produce melanism in.

melano-. Form of Gr. μέλας (μελαν-), black, used in combination.—**mel-a-no-ce-tus** (mel″ạ-nọ̄-sē′tus), *n.* [NL. (Gr. κῆτος, whale).] A deep-sea fish of the genus *Melanocetus* (family *Ceratiidæ*), black in color, with a mouth suggesting that of a whale, and an enormously distensible belly.—**mel″a-no-chro′ic** (-krō′ik), *a.* [Gr. μελανόχροος, having a black skin (χρόα, skin, complexion).] Dark-colored; belonging or pertaining to the dark-complexioned or dark-haired peoples of the white race. Cf. *xanthochroic.*—**mel″a-no-sar-co′ma** (-sär-kō′mạ̈), *n.*; pl. *-mas* or *-mata* (-mạ-tạ̈). [NL.] In *pathol.*, a highly malignant form of sarcoma characterized by the presence of dark pigment.

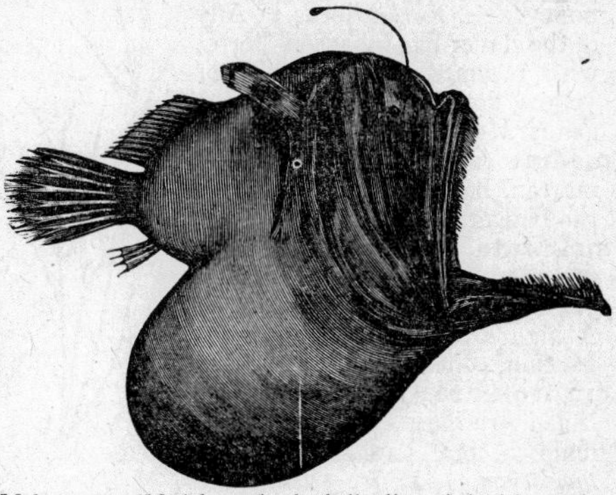

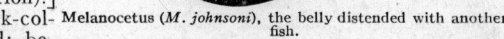

Melanocetus (*M. johnsoni*), the belly distended with another fish.

mel-a-no-sis (mel-ạ-nō′sis), *n.*; pl. *-noses* (-nō′sēz). [NL., < Gr. μελάνωσις, a becoming black, < μέλας (μελαν-), black.] In *pathol.*, morbid deposition or development of black or dark pigment in the tissues, sometimes leading to the production of malignant pigmented tumors; also, a discoloration caused by this.—**mel-a-not′ic** (-not′ik), *a.* Characterized by or pertaining to melanosis; also, melanistic.

mel-a-nous (mel′ạ-nus), *a.* [Gr. μέλας (μελαν-), black.] Black-haired and dark-complexioned; melanic.

me-lan-thi-a-ceous (me-lan-thi-ā′shius), *a.* [NL. *Melanthium*, the typical genus, < Gr. μέλας (μελαν-), black, + ἄνθος, flower.] Belonging to the *Melanthiaceæ*, a family of monocotyledonous bulbless plants related to the lily family, including the bellwort (genus *Uvularia*), white hellebore (genus *Veratrum*), etc.

mel-a-phyre (mel′ạ-fīr), *n.* [F. *mélaphyre*, < Gr. μέλας, black, + F. (*por*)*phyre*, porphyry.] Any of various dark-colored igneous rocks of porphyritic texture.

Mel-chite (mel′kīt), *n.* [MGr. Μελχῖται, pl., 'royalists' (as adhering to the creed supported by the Byzantine emperor); from Syriac.] Formerly, in Syria, Palestine, and Egypt, an orthodox Eastern Christian, orig. as distinguished from a Monophysite or a Nestorian; now, one of the Uniat Christians of these countries.

meld (meld), *v. t.* or *i.* [G. *melden*, announce.] In *pinochle*, to announce and display (a counting combination of cards in the hand) for a score.—**meld,** *n.* In *pinochle*, an act of melding; also, any counting combination of cards to be melded.

mel-der (mel′dėr), *n.* [Cf. Icel. *meldr*, akin to E. *meal*[1].] A quantity of meal ground at one time. [Chiefly Sc.]

mel-e (mel′e), *n.* [Native name.] A native Hawaiian song or melody.

mê-lée (mā′lā, F. mā-lā), *n.* [F.: see *medley*.] A confused combat; a hand-to-hand fight among a number of combatants; a fray: as, "Placing himself at the head of his handful of cavalry, he dashed into the *mêlée*" (Motley's "Dutch Republic," iii. 2).

me-li-a-ceous (mē-li-ā′shius), *a.* [NL. *Melia*, the typical genus, < Gr. μελία, ash-tree.] Belonging to the *Meliaceæ*, a family of trees and shrubs including the azedarach, margosa, mahogany, Spanish cedar, etc.

mel-ic (mel′ik), *a.* [Gr. μελικός, < μέλος, song.] Pertaining to song; intended to be sung; specif., noting or pertaining to the more elaborate form of Greek lyric poetry, as distinguished from iambic and elegiac poetry.

mel-ic=grass (mel′ik-gras), *n.* [NL. *Melica*.] Any grass of the genus *Melica*, comprising species widely distributed in temperate regions but of no great agricultural value.

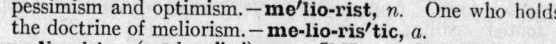

Melic-grass (*Melica mutica*).—1, flowering plant; 2, the panicle; *a*, a spikelet; *b*, the empty glumes; *c*, a flowering glume, side view; *d*, the same, back view.

mel-i-lot (mel′i-lot), *n.* [OF. *melilot* (F. *mélilot*), < L. *melilotos*, < Gr. μελίλωτος, < μέλι, honey, + λωτός, lotus.] Any of the clover-like fabaceous herbs, with racemes of small white or yellow flowers, constituting the genus *Melilotus*.

me-line (mē′lin), *a.* [L. *meles*, marten, badger.] Pertaining to the badger; badger-like.

mel-i-nite (mel′i-nīt), *n.* [F. *mélinite*, < Gr. μήλινος, quince-yellow, < μῆλον, apple, quince.] A high explosive, of French invention, containing picric acid.

me-lio-rate (mē′lyọ-rāt), *v.*; *-rated, -rating.* [LL. *meliorare*, make better, < L. *melior*: see *meliorism*.] **I.** *tr.* To make better; improve; ameliorate: as, "My position is every hour *meliorated*" (Emerson's "Essays," Character). **II.** *intr.* To become better; improve.—**me-lio-ra′tion** (-rā′shọn), *n.* [LL. *melioratio*(*n*-).] A making or becoming better; improvement; an instance or form of improvement.—**me′lio-ra-tive** (-rạ-tiv), *a.* Serving to make better.—**me′lio-ra-tor** (-rā-tọr), *n.*

me-lio-rism (mē′lyọ-rizm), *n.* [L. *melior*, better (compar. of *bonus*, good); akin to Gr. μάλα, very much, μᾶλλον, more, rather.] The doctrine that the world tends to become better, or may be made better by human effort: a mean between pessimism and optimism.—**me′lio-rist,** *n.* One who holds the doctrine of meliorism.—**me-lio-ris′tic,** *a.*

me-lior-i-ty (mē-lyor′i-ti), *n.* [ML. *melioritas*, < L. *melior*: see *meliorism*.] The quality or state of being better; superiority.

mell (mel), *v.* [OF. *meller*, var. of *medler*, mix: see *meddle*.] **I.** *tr.* To mix; mingle. [Archaic or prov.] **II.** *intr.* To mingle; also, to join or engage in combat (as, "They are too many to *mell* with in the open field": Scott's "Quentin Durward," xxxvii.); also, to have to do, as with a person or thing; concern one's self; meddle or interfere. [Archaic or prov.]

mel-lay (mel′ā), *n.* Same as *mêlée*: as, "My hat had been struck from my head in the *mellay*" (Stevenson's "Master of Ballantrae," vii.). [Archaic.]

mel-lif-er-ous (me-lif′ẹ-rus), *a.* [L. *mellifer*, < *mel* (*mell*-), honey, + *ferre*, bear.] Yielding or producing honey.

mel-lif-lu-ent (me-lif′lọ̈-ẹnt), *a.* [LL. *mellifluens* (*-ent-*): see *mellifluous*.] Mellifluous.—**mel-lif′lu-ence,** *n.*

mel-lif-lu-ous (me-lif′lọ̈-us), *a.* [LL. *mellifluus*, < L. *mel* (*mell*-), honey, + *fluere*, flow.] Flowing with honey; sweetened with or as with honey; fig., sweetly or smoothly flowing as sound, speech, etc. (as, "*mellifluous* tones": Lever's "Harry Lorrequer," ix.); of persons, speaking, singing, or writing in a sweetly flowing manner.—**mel-lif′lu-ous-ly,** *adv.*—**mel-lif′lu-ous-ness,** *n.*

mel-liv-o-rous (me-liv′ọ̄-rus), *a.* [L. *mel* (*mell*-), honey, + *vorare*, devour.] Feeding on honey.

mel-low (mel′ō), *a.* [ME. *melwe*: cf. AS. *melu* (*melw*-), meal, also *mearu*, tender.] Soft and full-flavored from ripeness, as fruit; hence, well-matured, as wines; friable or loamy, as soil; soft or flexible, as hides, leather, etc.; soft and rich, as color, light, etc.; often, softened in color or appearance by time (as, "A Tudor-chimney'd bulk Of *mellow* brickwork": Tennyson's "Edwin Morris," 12); soft and full, as sound, tones, etc., or giving forth such sound (as, "flutes so musical and *mellow*": Longfellow's "Hiawatha," vi. 32); in general, softened, toned down, or improved as if by ripening; genial or jovial (as, "The Baronet was . . . as merry and *mellow* an old bachelor as ever followed a hound": Irving's "Tales of a Traveler," i. 2); also, affected by liquor or drinking, or slightly tipsy (as, "The party got gloriously *mellow*": H. Melville's "Omoo," lxxx.).—**mel′low,** *v.* **I.** *tr.* To make mellow; soften by or as by ripening (as, to *mellow* fruit; age *mellows* the disposition); make pleasingly soft, as color, light, sound, etc.; bring under the influence of liquor. **II.** *intr.* To become mellow; soften; become toned down.—**mel′low-ly,** *adv.*—**mel′low-ness,** *n.*

me-lo-de-on (me-lō′dē-ọn), *n.* [LL. *melodia*, E. *melody*.] A small reed-organ or American organ; also, a kind of accordion.

me-lod-ic (me-lod′ik), *a.* [LL. *melodicus*, < Gr. μελῳδικός.] Pertaining to or characterized by melody; melodious; also, pertaining to melody as distinguished from harmony and rhythm.—**me-lod′i-cal-ly,** *adv.*

me-lo-di-ous (me-lō′di-us), *a.* [OF. *melodieus* (F. *mélodieux*).] Of the nature of or characterized by melody (as, "The sound Of instruments, that made *melodious* chime, Was heard, of harp and organ": Milton's "Paradise Lost," xi. 559); tuneful; musically sweet; also, producing melody or sweet sound (as, "*melodious* birds": Cowper's "Task," iv. 574).—**me-lo′di-ous-ly,** *adv.*—**me-lo′di-ous-ness,** *n.*

mel-o-dist (mel′ọ̄-dist), *n.* A composer or a singer of melodies.

mel-o-dize (mel′ọ̄-dīz), *v.*; *-dized, -dizing.* **I.** *intr.* To make melody; also, to blend melodiously (as, "Such a strain . . . Might *melodize* with each tumultuous sound": Scott's "Vision of Don Roderick," Introd., ii.). **II.** *tr.* To make melodious.—**mel′o-diz-er** (-dī-zėr), *n.*

mel-o-dra-ma (mel′ọ̄-drä-mạ̈ or mel-ọ̄-drä′mạ̈), *n.* [F. *mélodrame*, < Gr. μέλος, song, music, + δρᾶμα, E. *drama*.] In the late 18th and early 19th centuries, a romantic dramatic composition with music interspersed; now, a drama with startling or sensational incidents, exaggerated appeals to the emotions, and typically a happy ending (as, "It is the custom on the stage, in all good murderous *melodramas*, to present the tragic and the comic scenes, in . . . regular alternation": Dickens's "Oliver Twist," xvii.); also, the species of composition represented by such dramas; hence, any narrative or performance, or writing, speech, or action, suggestive of a stage melodrama.—**mel″o-dra-mat′ic** (-dra̤-mat′ik), *a.* Of, like, or befitting melodrama: as, "His soldiers, who, save for a few rare *melodramatic* encounters, saw nothing of him, idolized their 'Little Corporal' " (H. G. Wells's "Outline of History," xxxviii. § 6).—**mel″o-dra-mat′i-cal-ly,** *adv.*—**mel-o-dram′a-tist** (-dram′a̤-tist), *n.* A writer of melodrama.—**mel-o-dram′a-tize** (-tīz), *v. t.*; *-tized, -tizing.* To make into a melodrama; also, to render melodramatic.

mel-o-dy (mel′ọ̄-di), *n.*; pl. *-dies* (-diz). [OF. *melodie* (F. *mélodie*), < LL. *melodia,* < Gr. μελῳδία, singing, choral song, < μέλος, song, music, + ἀείδειν, sing.] Musical sounds in agreeable succession or arrangement, or music (as, "Take an harp . . . make sweet *melody,* sing many songs," Isa. xxiii. 16; "The birds chant *melody* on every bush," Shakspere's "Titus Andronicus," ii. 3. 12); sweet sound; also, musical quality (as, the *melody* of a voice; the *melody* of verse); also, a poem suitable for singing (as, Thomas Moore's "Irish *Melodies*"; Byron's "Hebrew *Melodies*"); in *music,* the succession of single tones in musical compositions, as distinguished from harmony and rhythm; also, a rhythmical succession of single tones producing a distinct musical phrase or idea; more commonly, a pleasing rhythmical succession of musical sounds forming an air or tune; also, the principal part in a harmonic composition; the air.

mel-o-ma-ni-a (mel-ọ̄-mā′ni-ä̤), *n.* [F. *mélomanie,* < Gr. μέλος, song, music, + μανία, E. *mania.*] A mania or inordinate passion for music.—**mel-o-ma′ni-ac** (-ak), *n.*

mel-on (mel′ọn), *n.* [OF. F. *melon,* < LL. *melo(n-),* for L. *melopepo,* < Gr. μηλοπέπων, apple-shaped melon, < μῆλον, apple, + πέπων: see *pepo.*] The fruit of any of various cucurbitaceous plants (as, the musk*melon;* the water*melon*); the plant itself; also (colloq.), an accumulation of profits, exceeding ordinary dividends, for distribution among the stockholders of a company (esp. in the phrase 'to cut a melon,' to distribute such profits).—**mel′on=shaped,** *a.* Oval, esp. with depressed lines running at intervals from end to end.—**mel′on=shell,** *n.* The shell of a marine gastropod of the genus *Melo,* family *Volutidæ* (see *volute, n.*): so called from the shape and markings.

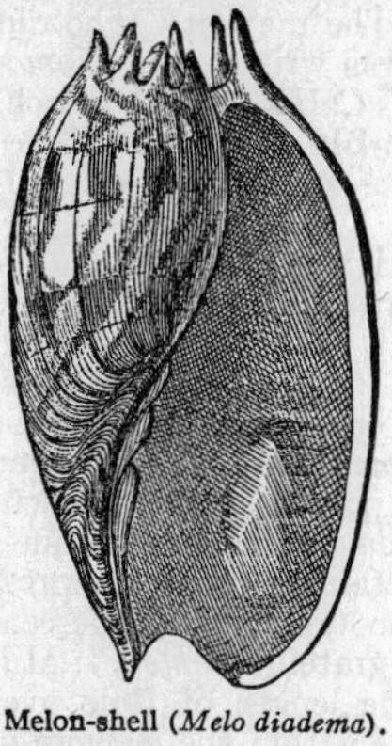

Melon-shell (*Melo diadema*).

Statue of Melpomene, in the Louvre, Paris.

Mel-pom-e-ne (mel-pom′-e-nē), *n.* [L., < Gr. Μελπομένη, prop. ppr. fem. of μέλπεσθαι, sing.] The Muse of tragedy.

melt (melt), *v.*; pret. *melted,* pp. *melted* or *molten,* ppr. *melting.* [AS. *meltan,* intr., *mieltan,* tr.; akin to Icel. *melta,* to malt, digest, Goth. *gamalteins,* dissolution, Gr. μέλδειν, to melt, and E. *malt,* and perhaps ult. to E. *smelt*[2].] **I.** *intr.* To become liquefied by heat, as ice, snow, butter, metal, etc.; hence, to become dissolved, as solid matter in a liquid; become disintegrated, dispersed, or dissipated (as, "They *melt* like mist, the solid lands," Tennyson's "In Memoriam," cxxiii.; a vision *melts* before the eyes); pass, dwindle, or fade gradually (*away*: as, the crowd *melted* away; money *melts* away; "The usual reserve of their manner . . . has on this night *melted* away," De Quincey's "English Mail-Coach," i.); pass, change, or blend gradually (*into*: as, one color *melts* into another; mountain summits *melting* into the clouds); also, to fail or faint, as the heart or soul, from fear, grief, etc. (obs. or archaic: see Josh. ii. 11); also, to become softened in feeling by pity, sympathy, love, or the like (as, "I had a good deal *melted* towards our enemy": Stevenson's "Master of Ballantrae," xi.); sometimes, to break down (into or in tears). **II.** *tr.* To reduce to a liquid state, or liquefy, by heat; fuse; hence, to dissolve, as in a liquid; disperse or dissipate; cause to pass or fade (*away*); spend or squander (money) or cash (a check, etc.) (chiefly slang); cause to pass or blend gradually (*into*: as, distance *melts* the varied colors or sounds into one); also, to weaken†, or cause to degenerate†; also, to soften in feeling, as a person, the heart, etc.; move, as to pity or tenderness, or to tears.—**melt,** *n.* The act or process of melting, or the state of being melted; also, that which is melted; a quantity melted at one time.—**melt′a-ble,** *a.* That may be melted.—**melt-a-bil′i-ty** (-bil′i-ti), *n.*—**melt′er,** *n.*—**melt′ing,** *p. a.* That melts; liquefying; softening; tender, feeling, or tearful (as, "One whose subdued eyes, Albeit unused to the *melting* mood, Drop tears": Shakspere's "Othello," v. 2. 349); also, of a liquid softness (as, *melting* eyes; *melting* tones); softly yielding or flowing, as the form, outlines, etc.—**melt′ing-ly,** *adv.*—**melt′ing=point,** *n.* The point or degree of temperature at which a solid substance melts or fuses.—**melt′ing=pot,** *n.* A pot in which metals or other substances are melted or fused. Also fig., esp. of a country in which immigrants of various races are united in citizenship: as, "America is the New World, where there are no races and nations any more; she is the *Melting Pot,* from which we will cast the better state" (H. G. Wells's "Mr. Britling," iii. 1. § 13).

mel-ton (mel′tọn), *n.* [From *Melton* Mowbray, town in Leicestershire, central England.] A smooth, heavy, well-fulled woolen cloth, used for overcoats, etc.

mem-ber (mem′bėr), *n.* [OF. F. *membre,* < L. *membrum,* limb, part.] A part or organ of an animal body, esp. a limb, as a leg, arm, or wing; hence, a constituent part of any structural or composite whole, as a subordinate architectural feature of a building or the like, a clause of a sentence, either side of an algebraic equation, etc.; also, each of the persons composing a society, party, community, or other body; specif., each of the persons included in the membership of a legislative body, as the British Parliament (chiefly with reference to the House of Commons) or the U. S. Congress (chiefly with reference to the House of Representatives).—**mem′bered,** *a.* Having members: as, many-*membered.*—**mem′ber-less,** *a.* Without a member or members.—**mem′ber-ship,** *n.* The state of being a member, as of a society or other body; the status of a member; also, the total number of members belonging to a body (as, a church with a large *membership*; to increase the *membership* of a club).

mem-bral (mem′bra̤l), *a.* [L. *membrum,* E. *member.*] Of or pertaining to a member, esp. a member or limb as distinguished from the body proper.

mem-bra-na-ceous (mem-bra̤-nā′shius), *a.* [L. *membranaceus.*] Membrane-like; membranous; specif., in *bot.,* thin, soft, and more or less translucent, as certain leaves.

mem-brane (mem′brān), *n.* [L. *membrana,* < *membrum,* E. *member.*] A thin, pliable sheet or layer of animal or vegetable tissue, serving to line an organ, connect parts, etc.—**mem′brane=bone,** *n.* A bone which originates in membranous tissue, instead of being developed or preformed in cartilage: distinguished from *cartilage-bone.*—**mem′brane-less,** *a.* Without a membrane.

mem-bra-nous (mem′bra̤-nus), *a.* [F. *membraneux.*] Consisting of, of the nature of, or resembling membrane; membranaceous; also, characterized by the formation of a membrane (as, *membranous* croup).

me-men-to (mẹ̄-men′tō), *n.*; pl. *-tos* or *-toes* (-tōz). [L., impv. of *meminisse*, remember: see *mind*².] [*cap.*] In the canon of the mass, either of two prayers beginning with the word *Memento*, the first for persons living, and the second for persons deceased; [*l. c.*] an injunction or warning to remember something (obs. or rare: as, "These speak a loud *memento*," Cowpẹr's "Task," i. 482); hence, anything serving as a reminder or warning (as, "I have been . . . a *memento* to those who are touched with the general plague of mankind": Defoe's "Robinson Crusoe," i. 14); also, something that serves as a reminder of what is past or gone (as, a *memento* of a lost friend; "I shall soon be gone, but I want to leave with you some *memento* of my love for you," G. W. Curtis's "Prue and I," iv.); a souvenir, as of an event or occasion (as, "offering for sale all sorts of *mementoes* of the fight, crosses, and epaulets, and shattered cuirasses": Thackeray's "Vanity Fair," xxxv.).—**me-men′to mo-ri** (mō′rī). [L., 'remember to die' (that thou must die).] A warning to be mindful of death (as, "The hand of time was very legible on all; I seemed to read in their changed faces a *memento mori*": Stevenson's "Master of Ballantrae," viii.); also, an object, as a skull or the like, serving as a reminder of death.

mem-oir (mem′wor or mē′mwor), *n.* [F. *mémoire*, masc., memorandum, memorial, memoir, < *mémoire*, fem., memory: see *memory*.] A memorandum, esp. a record or written statement of something for official or historical purposes (as, "Pierre Arsens . . . addressed an elaborate *memoir* to the Duke of Alva, criticising the case according to the rules of law," Motley's "Dutch Republic," iii. 2; "During his captivity, the Admiral had . . . the leisure . . . to write a *memoir* of the siege of St. Quentin," Besant's "Coligny," v.); *pl.*, records of facts or events in connection with a particular subject, historical period, etc., as known to the writer or gathered from special sources; also, records of one's own life and experiences (as, "Published *Memoirs* indicate the end of a man's activity, and that he acknowledges the end": G. Meredith's "Lord Ormont and His Aminta," iii.); *sing.*, a biography; a biographical notice; also, an essay or dissertation on some learned subject; *pl.*, a collection of reports made to a scientific or other learned society. —**mem′oir-ist,** *n.* A writer of memoirs or a memoir.

mem-o-ra-bil-i-a (mem″ọ-rạ-bil′i-ạ̈), *n. pl.* [L., pl. of *memorabile*, a memorable thing, prop. neut. of *memorabilis*, E. *memorable*.] Memorable things; matters or events worthy to be remembered: as, "a full disclosure of the *memorabilia* of my life" (Lever's "Harry Lorrequer," x.).

mem-o-ra-ble (mem′ọ-rạ-bl). [L. *memorabilis*, < *memorare*, bring to remembrance, < *memor*, mindful: see *memory*.] **I.** *a.* Worthy to be remembered, or notable (as, a *memorable* occasion; a *memorable* speech, deed, or event); also, easy to be remembered. **II.** *n.* A memorable or notable thing: usually in *pl.*: as, "when I take up my pen to record the *memorables* of this Ann. Dom." (Galt's "Annals of the Parish," ix.).—**mem″o-ra-bil′i-ty** (-bil′i-ti), **mem′o-ra-ble-ness,** *n.*—**mem′o-ra-bly,** *adv.*

mem-o-ran-dum (mem-ọ-ran′dum). [L., neut. of *memorandus*, that is to be remembered, gerundive of *memorare*: see *memorable*.] **I.** 'To be remembered': a word, often abbreviated *mem.*, used to introduce a note of something to be borne in mind or to be done. **II.** *n.*; pl. *-dums* or *-da* (-dạ̈). A note made of something to be remembered, as in future action (as, "I desire these gentlemen will bear witness to this my intention, of which I have a *memorandum* in my pocketbook": Smollett's "Humphry Clinker," after Oct. 4); also, a record or written statement of something (as, "I contented myself . . . to write down only the most remarkable events of my life, without continuing a daily *memorandum* of other things": Defoe's "Robinson Crusoe," i. 7); also, a reminder† or warning† (as, "I was obliged to let it [canoe] lie where it was, as a *memorandum* to teach me to be wiser next time": Defoe's "Robinson Crusoe," i. 9); in *law*, a writing containing the terms of a transaction; in *diplomacy*, a summary of the state of a question, the reasons for a decision agreed on, or the like.

me-mo-ri-al (mẹ-mō′ri-ạl), *a.* [L. *memorialis*, < *memoria*, E. *memory*.] Of or pertaining to the memory; also, preserving the memory of a person or thing, or commemorative (as, a *memorial* tablet, window, or arch; *memorial* services); also, of which the memory is preserved (obs. or rare: as, "I seem'd to move in old *memorial* tilts," Tennyson's "Princess," v. 468).—**Memorial Day,** a day, May 30, set apart in most of the States of the U. S. for observances in memory of dead soldiers and sailors (orig. those who fell in the Civil War), esp. for the decoration of their graves with flowers and flags; Decoration Day; also, some day ('Confederate Memorial Day') similarly observed in various Southern States.—**me-mo′ri-al,** *n.* [LL. *memoriale*, prop. neut. of L. *memorialis*, adj.] Memory† or remembrance†; also, an act of commemoration; also, something designed or adapted to preserve the memory of a person, an event, or anything belonging to past time, as a monument, a tablet or inscription, a periodical observance, etc. (as, "These stones shall be for a *memorial* unto the children of Israel for ever": Josh. iv. 7); also, a record (as, "Though of their names in heavenly records now Be no *memorial*," Milton's "Paradise Lost," i. 362; "*Memorials* of a Quiet Life," title of a biographical book by A. J. C. Hare); a written statement (as, "Should he . . . desire to make a *memorial* of the debts which he would wish paid, he was to be allowed that liberty": Motley's "Dutch Republic," iii. 5); specif., a written statement of facts presented to a sovereign, a legislative body, or the like, as the ground of, or expressed in the form of, a petition or remonstrance; in *diplomacy*, any of various informal state papers.—**me-mo′ri-al-ist,** *n.* A writer of memorials; also, one who presents a memorial.—**me-mo′ri-al-ize** (-īz), *v. t.*; *-ized, -izing.* To commemorate; also, to present a memorial to.—**me-mo″ri-al-i-za′tion** (-i-zā′shọn), *n.*—**me-mo′ri-al-iz-er** (-ī-zėr), *n.*—**me-mo′ri-al-ly,** *adv.*

me-mo-ri-a tech-ni-ca (mẹ-mō′ri-ạ̈ tek′ni-kạ̈). [NL., 'artificial memory.'] A method of assisting the memory by special contrivances; a form of words or other device for assisting the memory; a system of mnemonics.

mem-o-ried (mem′ọ-rid), *a.* Having a memory (as, long-*memoried*); also, fraught or associated with memories.

me-mor-i-ter (mẹ-mor′i-tėr), *adv.* [L.] From memory: used with reference to reciting, speaking, etc.

mem-o-rize (mem′ọ-rīz), *v. t.*; *-rized, -rizing.* To preserve the memory or remembrance of (now rare); also, to commit to memory, or learn by heart (as, "The majority, who did not know every line of the sermon was written and *memorized*, marvelled at its facility": G. W. Cable's "John March, Southerner," xxiii.).—**mem′o-riz-a-ble** (-rī-zạ-bl), *a.*—**mem″o-ri-za′tion** (-ri-zā′shọn), *n.*—**mem′o-riz-er** (-rī-zėr), *n.*

mem-o-ry (mem′ọ-ri), *n.*; pl. *-ries* (-riz). [OF. *memorie* (F. *mémoire*), < L. *memoria*, memory, period of remembrance, historical account, record, memorial, < *memor*, mindful, remembering; akin to Gr. μέριμνα, care, μάρτυρ, witness, martyr, Skt. *smar-*, remember.] The mental capacity or faculty of retaining and reviving impressions, or of recalling previous experiences; this faculty as possessed by a particular individual (as, to have a good *memory*; to refresh one's *memory*); also, the act or fact of retaining mental impressions, or remembrance or recollection (as, "Thy condescension . . . shall be honour'd ever With grateful *memory*": Milton's "Paradise Lost," viii. 650); the length of time over which recollection extends (as, a time within the *memory* of men still living); also, a mental impression retained, or a recollection (as, "My earliest *memories* were connected with the South," Aldrich's "Story of a Bad Boy," ii.; "*Memories* and Portraits," title of a book by R. L. Stevenson); a person or thing remembered (as, "The idol of my youth . . . and, alas! Now the most blessed *memory* of mine age": Tennyson's "Gardener's Daughter," 273); also, the state or fact of being remembered (as, to remain in perpetual *memory*); the repute of a person or thing among those remembering, or reputation left behind, esp. after death (as, "The truth is a debt I owe my lord's *memory*," Stevenson's "Master of Ballantrae," i.; "Their fragrant *mem'ry* will out-last their tomb," Cowper's "Conversation," 631); also, commemorative remembrance, or commemoration (as, a monument erected in *memory* of a person or an event); an act or service of commemoration (obs. or hist.); also, a memorial† or memento† (as, "O my sweet master! O you *memory* Of old Sir Rowland!" Shakspere's "As You Like It," ii. 3. 3).

Mem-phi-an (mem′fi-ạn), *a.* Of or pertaining to Memphis, an ancient city of Egypt; hence, Egyptian (as, "Monitors . . . Like skulls at *Memphian* banquets": Byron's "Don Juan," iii. 65).
Mem-phite (mem′fīt), *n.* A native or inhabitant of ancient Memphis in Egypt; also, the Coptic dialect spoken in the neighborhood of ancient Memphis, or, formerly, that spoken in the neighborhood of Alexandria.—**Mem-phit′ic** (-fit′ik), *a.*
mem=sa-hib (mem′sä″ib), *n.* [= *ma'am sahib*: see *sahib.*] In India, a natives' term of respect for a European lady: as, "an English *mem-sahib*" (Kipling's "Kim," iii.).
men (men), *n.* Plural of *man.*
men-ace (men′ạs), *n.* [OF. F. *menace,* < L. *minaciæ,* pl., threats, < *minax,* threatening, < *minari,* jut out, threaten: cf. *eminent.*] A declaration or indication of a hostile intention, or of a probable evil to come (as, "*menaces* and maledictions against king and nobles": Shakspere's "King Lear," i. 2. 159); a threat; threatening or menacing (as, "the figures of fiends in aspects of *menace*": Poe's "Pit and the Pendulum"); also, something that threatens, or has the effect of threatening, to cause evil or harm (as, the fortress was a standing *menace* to the citizens; open sewers are a *menace* to the public health).—**men′ace,** *v.*; *-aced, -acing.* [OF. *menacier* (F. *menacer*).] **I.** *tr.* To utter or direct a menace or threat against; assail with menaces; serve as a menace, or probable cause of evil, to (as, conditions that *menace* our well-being); also, to give a menace or threat of as intended or impending (as, "Crowds streamed . . . into the Forum, curious to read the tremendous edict so long *menaced*": Wiseman's "Fabiola," ii. 15); serve as a menace of. **II.** *intr.* To utter or give a menace; threaten evil; be threatening.—**men′ace-ment,** *n.* Menacing; menace.—**men′a-cer** (-ạ-sėr), *n.*—**men′a-cing-ly,** *adv.*
me-nad (mē′nad), etc. See *mænad,* etc.
mé-nage (mā-näzh), *n.* [F., < ML. *mansionaticum,* < L. *mansio(n-),* E. *mansion.*] Housekeeping; also, a household; a domestic establishment.
me-nag-e-rie (mẹ-naj′ẹ-ri or mẹ-nazh′-), *n.* [F. *ménagerie,* management of a household or farm, also menagerie, < *ménager,* manage (a household, etc.), < *ménage*: see *ménage.*] A collection of wild or strange animals, esp. for exhibition, or a place where they are kept or exhibited; fig., a curious collection or assortment of persons (as, "An old quack doctor named Levett . . . completed this strange *menagerie*": Macaulay's "Essays," Samuel Johnson).
mend (mend), *v. t.* [For *amend.*] To remove or correct faults in (a person, the heart, life, or, now esp., the ways or manners); remove or correct defects or errors in (a thing, esp. a law, text, etc.); remove or correct (a fault, defect, etc.); now, commonly, to make whole or sound by repairing, as something broken, worn, or otherwise damaged (as, to *mend* broken china; to *mend* shoes or clothes; to *mend* a fence or a road); repair (a break, tear, hole, etc.); restore to due condition by any suitable action (as, to *mend* a fire by adding fuel; to *mend* a worn quill pen by trimming the point; to *mend* sails by adjusting them properly); set right (as, to *mend* matters); make amends for (now chiefly in 'least said soonest mended'); cure or heal (archaic); in general, to make better, improve, or advance (as, "He . . . *mended* his worldly prospects by a matrimonial union with a widow lady of large property": Mrs. Stowe's "Oldtown Folks," i.); enhance in attractiveness, force, etc. (as, "Truths divine came *mended* from that tongue": Pope's "Eloisa to Abelard," 66); quicken (as, "Our horses . . . pricked up their ears and *mended* their pace": Parkman's "Oregon Trail," xxvii.); also, to improve on or surpass (now colloq.).—**to mend one's fences,** fig., to look after one's political interests at home, as in preparation for renomination or the next campaign: said of a political office-holder. [Colloq., U. S.]—**mend,** *v. i.* To become better or improve (as, "The man seems to *mend* on further acquaintance," Smollett's "Humphry Clinker," Oct. 26; "with no prospect of matters *mending,*" H. Melville's "Typee," iii.); often, to progress toward recovery, as a sick person (as, "Roland still continued to *mend,* as the surgeon phrased it": Bulwer-Lytton's "Caxtons," viii. 3); also, to mend or repair something.—**mend,** *n.* The act or fact of mending; improvement; the way to recovery (as, to be on the *mend*); also, a repair, or a mended place; also, *pl.,* amends†.—**mend′a-ble,** *a.* That may be mended.
men-da-cious (men-dā′shus), *a.* [L. *mendax* (*mendac-*), akin to *mentiri,* lie.] Lying or untruthful (as, "*mendacious* rogues": Hawthorne's "Blithedale Romance," viii.); also, false or untrue (as, *mendacious* assertions; a *mendacious* report).—**men-da′cious-ly,** *adv.*—**men-da′cious-ness,** *n.*—**men-da′ci-ty** (-das′i-ti), *n.*; pl. *-ties* (-tiz̧). [LL. *mendacitas.*] The quality of being mendacious; also, a falsehood; a lie.
Men-de-li-an (men-dē′li-ạn), *a.* Pertaining to Gregor Johann Mendel (1822–84), an Austrian monk and scientific investigator, or to Mendelism.—**Men-del-ism** (men′delizm), *n.* A theory or doctrine of heredity based upon Mendel's experiments with peas: it involves a principle or law (*Mendel's law*) governing the inheritance of many characters in animals and plants, according to which there occurs, in the second and later generations of hybrids, every possible combination of the characters of the original parent animals or plants, each combination in a definite proportion of individuals. See *dominant character,* under *dominant,* and *recessive character,* under *recessive.*
mend-er (men′dėr), *n.* One who mends.
men-di-cant (men′di-kạnt). [L. *mendicans* (*-ant-*), ppr. of *mendicare,* beg, < *mendicus,* beggarly, needy.] **I.** *a.* Begging, practising begging, or living on alms (as, a *mendicant* friar); also, pertaining to or characteristic of a beggar (as, the *mendicant* life). **II.** *n.* One who lives by begging; a beggar; sometimes, a mendicant friar; also, one who begs for something specified (as, "He was still a shameless *mendicant* of pecuniary favors and lucrative offices": Motley's "Dutch Republic," ii. 1).—**men′di-can-cy,** *n.*
men-di-ci-ty (men-dis′i-ti), *n.* [L. *mendicitas,* < *mendicus*: see *mendicant.*] The condition or life of a beggar; the practice of begging.
men-ha-den (men-hā′dn), *n.* [N. Amer. Ind.] A marine clupeoid fish, *Brevoortia tyrannus,* having the appearance of a shad but with a more compressed body, common along the eastern coast of the U. S., and used for making oil and fertilizer.

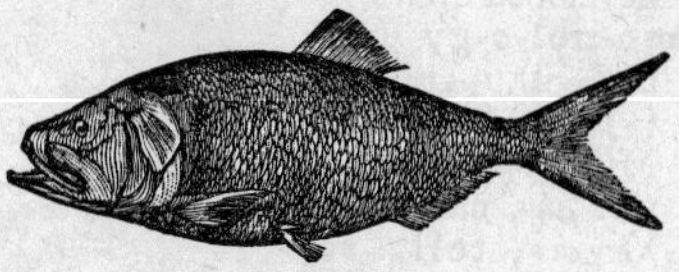
Menhaden.

men-hir (men′hēr), *n.* [Breton *men hir,* 'long stone.'] In *archæol.,* an upright monumental stone, standing either alone or with others, as in a cromlech or an alinement.

Group of Menhirs at Carnac, Brittany.

me-nial (mē′niạl). [AF. *menial, meignal,* < OF. *mesnie,* E. *meinie.*] **I.** *a.* Belonging to the household, as domestic servants; also, pertaining or proper to domestic servants (as, "Her ladyship was of humble, I have heard even *menial,* station originally," Thackeray's "Newcomes," viii.; *menial* service or duties: now used contemptuously); hence, servile or mean (as, "Freebooters, sprung from low castes, and accustomed to *menial* employments, became mighty Rajahs": Macaulay's "Essays," Warren Hastings). **II.** *n.* A domestic servant (now contemptuous); a flunky.—**me′nial-ly,** *adv.*
Mé-niè-re's (mā-nyãrz) **dis-ease′.** [From *Ménière,* French physician, who first described it.] In *pathol.,* a disease characterized by vertigo and more or less complete deafness, usually due to or associated with a morbid condition of the labyrinth of the ear.
me-nin-ges (mẹ-nin′jēz), *n. pl.* [NL., pl. of *meninx,* < Gr. μῆνιγξ, membrane, esp. of the brain.] In *anat.,* the three membranes (dura mater, arachnoid, and pia mater) investing the brain and spinal cord.—**me-nin′ge-al** (-jẹ-ạl), *a.*
men-in-gi-tis (men-in-jī′tis), *n.* [NL.] In *pathol.,* inflammation of the meninges.—**epidemic cerebrospinal men-**

ingitis. See under *cerebrospinal.*—**men-in-git′ic** (-jit′-ik), *a.*

me-nis-cus (mẹ-nis′kus), *n.*; pl. *meniscuses* or *menisci* (-nis′ī). [NL., < Gr. μηνίσκος, crescent, dim. of μήνη, moon.] A crescent or crescent-shaped body; specif., a lens with a crescent-shaped section; also, the convex or concave upper surface of a column of liquid, caused by capillarity.—**me-nis′coid,** *a.*

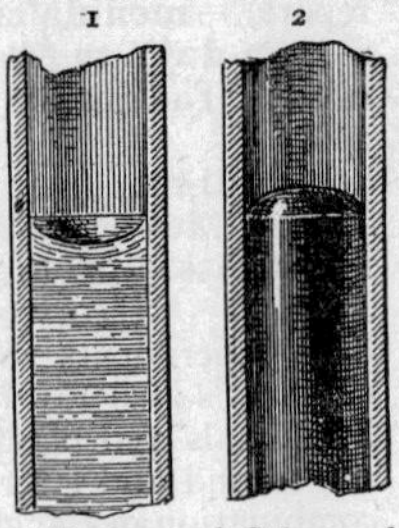

Meniscus of Column of Liquid.—1, concave; 2, convex.

men-i-sper-ma-ceous (men″i-spėr-mā′shius), *a.* [NL. *Menispermum*, the typical genus, moonseed, < Gr. μήνη, moon, + σπέρμα, seed.] Belonging to the *Menispermaceæ*, a family of dicotyledonous plants, mostly woody climbers, having small, usually three-parted, diœcious flowers, and possessing narcotic properties. See *moonseed.*

Men-non-ist (men′ọn-ist), *n.* Same as *Mennonite.*

Men-non-ite (men′ọn-īt), *n.* A member of a Christian denomination (named after Menno Simons, 1492–1559, of Friesland, one of its leaders) opposed to infant baptism, the taking of oaths, the holding of public office, and military service.

men-o-branch (men′ọ-brangk), *n.* [NL. *Menobranchus*, < Gr. μένειν, remain, + βράγχια, gills.] Any of the tailed amphibians constituting the North American genus *Menobranchus* (or *Necturus*), characterized by persistent gills forming external tufts, and by four limbs each having four well-developed digits.

Menobranch (*M. maculatus*).

me-nol-o-gy (mẹ-nol′ọ-ji), *n.*; pl. *-gies* (-jiz). [ML., < MGr. μηνολόγιον, < Gr. μήν, month, + λέγειν, tell, recount.] A calendar of the months; specif., the calendar of the Greek Church, with lives of the saints in the order of their festivals; hence, in general, a record or account, as of saints, arranged in the order of a calendar.

men-o-pause (men′ọ-pâz), *n.* [Gr. μήν, month, + παῦσις, cessation, E. *pause.*] In *physiol.*, the final cessation of the menses, occurring normally between the ages of 45 and 50.

men-o-pome (men′ọ-pōm), *n.* [NL. *Menopoma*, < Gr. μένειν, remain, + πῶμα, lid.] Any of the amphibians constituting the genus *Menopoma*, as the hellbender: so called from the persistence of the branchial apertures.

me-no-rah (me-nō′rạ), *n.* [Heb.] In Jewish use, a candlestick, esp. the seven-branched candlestick of the synagogue. Cf. Ex. xxv. 31–37.

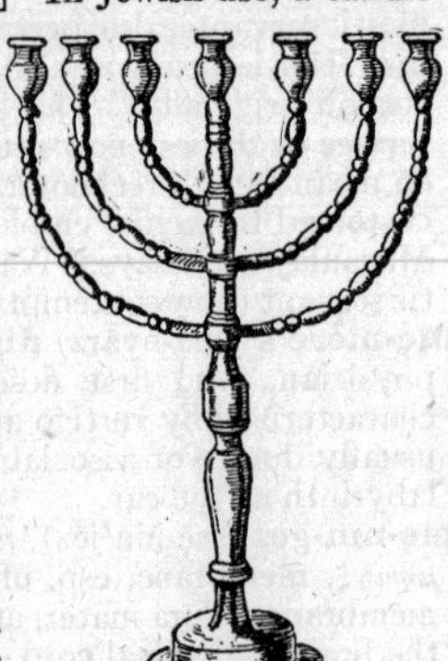
Menorah.

men-or-rha-gi-a (men-ọ-rā′ji-ạ), *n.* [NL., < Gr. μήν, month, + -ραγία, < ῥηγνύναι, break, burst forth.] In *pathol.*, excessive menstrual discharge.

men-sal¹ (men′sạl), *a.* [LL. *mensalis*, < L. *mensa*, table.] Of, pertaining to, or used at the table.

men-sal² (men′sạl), *a.* [L. *mensis*, month.] Monthly.

men-ses (men′sēz), *n. pl.* [L., pl. of *mensis*, month.] In *physiol.*, the monthly discharge of blood from the uterus, occurring in women.

Men-she-vik (men′she-vēk, Russ. men-she-vēk′). [Russ., < *menshe*, less: with allusion to the minority (Russ. *menshinstvo*) or smaller faction of the party.] **I.** *n.*; pl. *Mensheviki* (men-she-vē′kẹ, Russ. men-she-vē-kē′) or *-viks* (-vēks). In Russian politics, orig. (from 1903), a member of the less radical faction (the Mensheviki) of the Social Democratic party (see *Bolshevik*, *n.*); later, after the taking over of governmental control by the Bolshevik group through the revolution of Nov. 7, 1917, a member of a less radical socialistic party or group succeeding the earlier Menshevik faction and forming one of the parties opposed to that supporting the Bolshevik government. **II.** *a.* Of or pertaining to the Mensheviki or their doctrines.—**Men′she-vism,** *n.* The doctrines or principles of the Mensheviki.—**Men′she-vist. I.** *n.* A Menshevik. **II.** *a.* Pertaining to or characteristic of the Mensheviki or Menshevism.

men-stru-al (men′strọ-ạl), *a.* [L. *menstrualis*, < *menstruus*, monthly, < *mensis*, month.] Monthly; in *physiol.*, of or pertaining to the menses.

men-stru-ate (men′strọ-āt), *v. i.*; *-ated*, *-ating.* [LL. *menstruatus*, pp. of *menstruare*, < L. *menstruus*, monthly: see *menstrual.*] To discharge the menses.—**men-stru-a′tion** (-ā′shọn), *n.*

men-stru-um (men′strọ-um), *n.*; pl. *-struums* or *-strua* (-strọ-ạ). [ML., prop. neut. of L. *menstruus*, monthly: see *menstrual.*] Any liquid substance which dissolves a solid; a solvent. Also fig.

men-su-al (men′shụ-ạl), *a.* [LL. *mensualis*, < L. *mensis*, month.] Monthly.

men-su-ra-ble (men′shụ-rạ-bl), *a.* [LL. *mensurabilis*, < L. *mensurare*, E. *measure*, *v.*] Capable of being measured; measurable.—**men″su-ra-bil′i-ty** (-bil′i-ti), *n.*

men-su-ral (men′shụ-rạl), *a.* [LL. *mensuralis*, < L. *mensura*, E. *measure*, *n.*] Pertaining to measure.

men-su-rate (men′shụ-rāt), *v. t.*; *-rated*, *-rating.* [L. *mensuratus*, pp. of *mensurare*, E. *measure*, *v.*] To measure.—**men-su-ra′tion** (-rā′shọn), *n.* [LL. *mensuratio(n-).*] The act, art, or process of measuring; specif., that branch of mathematics which deals with the determination of length, area, and volume.—**men′su-ra-tive** (-rạ-tiv), *a.* Adapted for or concerned with measuring.

-ment. [F. *-ment*, < L. *-mentum*, suffix forming nouns from verbs.] A suffix of nouns denoting the means or instrument of some action, as in *aliment*, *monument*, *ornament*, the product or result, as in *fragment*, *segment*, or an action or process, or a state resulting from action, as in *abridgment*, *bewilderment*, *internment*, *management*, *postponement*, *refreshment.*

men-tal¹ (men′tạl), *a.* [L. *mentum*, chin.] Of or pertaining to the chin.

men-tal² (men′tạl), *a.* [LL. *mentalis*, < L. *mens* (*ment-*), mind: see *mind².*] Of or pertaining to the mind (as, *mental* faculties); esp., pertaining to the intellect, or intellectual (as, *mental* exertion; "a *mental* chaos," Peacock's "Nightmare Abbey," xi.); also, performed by or existing in the mind (as, *mental* arithmetic, in which the operations are performed in the mind, without the use of written figures, etc.; a *mental* reservation, an unexpressed qualification, as to a statement); also, concerned with the mind and its phenomena (as, *mental* science).—**mental age,** in *psychol.*, the degree of mental development or intelligence of an individual, as considered in relation to the average degrees of intelligence of normal children at different ages up to the normal or average limit of the growth of intelligence: determined by a series of tests, in the form of tasks and questions, graded to suit the respective degrees of intelligence of average children of different ages, such tests being prepared so as to show natural intelligence rather than the result of education: as, a child of 10 years having a *mental age* of 12 years; a moron has a *mental age* of from 8 to 12 years.—**men-tal′i-ty** (-tal′i-ti), *n.*; pl. *-ties* (-tiz). Mental capacity or endowment; intellectuality; mind.—**men′tal-ly,** *adv.*

men-ta-tion (men-tā′shọn), *n.* [L. *mens* (*ment-*), mind.] Mental action.

men-tha-ceous (men-thā′shius), *a.* [L. *mentha*, E. *mint².*] Belonging to the *Menthaceæ*, or mint family of plants, including the horsemint, peppermint, pennyroyal, savory, etc.

men-thene (men′thēn), *n.* [L. *mentha*, E. *mint².*] In *chem.*, a liquid hydrocarbon derived from oil of peppermint and from menthol.

men-thol (men′thol or -thōl), *n.* [G., < L. *mentha*, E. *mint*[2].] In *chem.*, a white crystalline compound obtained from oil of peppermint: used in medicine, esp. externally.

men-ti-cul-ture (men′ti-kul-tūr), *n.* [L. *mens* (*ment-*), mind, + *cultura*, culture.] The cultivation of the mind.—**men-ti-cul′tur-al,** *a.*

men-tion (men′shon), *n.* [OF. F. *mention*, < L. *mentio(n-)*, a calling to mind, mention, akin to *meminisse*, remember: see *mind*[2].] An incidental introduction of the name of a person or thing in the course of speech or writing; an express or direct reference by naming or specifying; a speaking of or mentioning.—**men′tion,** *v. t.* [F. *mentionner.*] To make mention of; refer to by name incidentally; name, specify, or speak of; also, to say incidentally (with a clause).—**men′tion-a-ble,** *a.* That may be, or is worthy to be, mentioned.—**men′tion-er,** *n.*

men-ton-nière (men-to-nyār′, F. moṅ-to-nyār), *n.* [F., < *menton*, < L. *mentum*, chin.] A piece of armor for protecting the chin or lower part of the face and neck, used only on occasions of special danger.

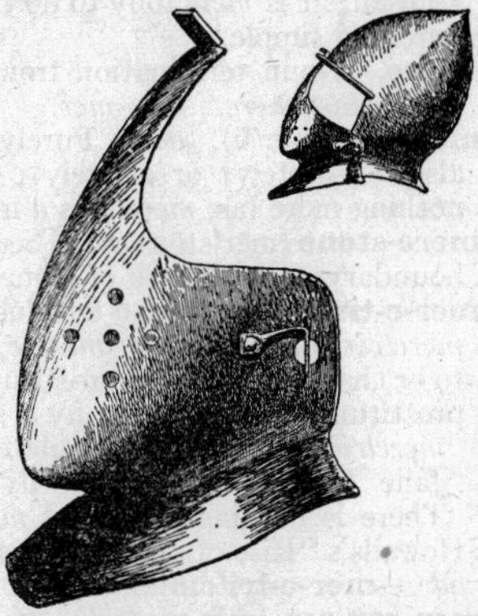

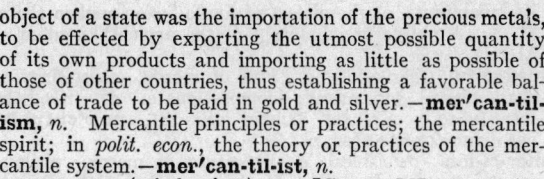

Mentonnière (close of 15th century).

men-tor (men′tor), *n.* [Gr. Μέντωρ, Mentor, the friend to whom Odysseus, when departing for Troy, intrusted the education of his son Telemachus.] A wise and trusted monitor or counselor.—**men′tor-ship,** *n.* The office of mentor.

men-u (men′ū, F. me-nü), *n.* [F., minute detail, detailed list, menu, orig. adj., small, < L. *minutus*, E. *minute*[1].] A list of the dishes served at a meal; a bill of fare (as, "An obsequious waiter handed Honora a *menu* in a silver frame, with a handle": W. Churchill's "Modern Chronicle," i. 6); also, the dishes served.

Meph-is-toph-e-les (mef-is-tof′e-lēz), *n.* A powerful evil spirit of German legend, represented in Goethe's "Faust" as a crafty, sardonic, scoffing fiend.—**Meph″is-toph-e-le′an** (-lē′an), **Meph″is-to-phe′lian** (-tō-fē′lian), *a.*

me-phit-ic (mē-fit′ik), *a.* [LL. *mephiticus.*] Of or pertaining to mephitis; offensive to the smell; noxious; pestilential; poisonous.—**me-phit′i-cal-ly,** *adv.*

me-phi-tis (mē-fī′tis), *n.* [L.] A noxious or pestilential exhalation, esp. from the earth; a noisome or poisonous stench.

-mer. Noun termination from Gr. μέρος, part, as in *isomer*, *metamer*. Cf. *-mere.*

mer-can-tile (mėr′kan-til or -tīl), *a.* [F. *mercantile*, < It. *mercantile*, < L. *mercans* (*mercant-*), ppr. of *mercari*, trade: see *merchant.*] Of or pertaining to merchants, or trade or commerce; commercial; engaged in trade or commerce (as, a *mercantile* house; the *mercantile* marine); in *polit. econ.*, of or pertaining to the mercantile system (see phrase below).—**mercantile agency,** the position or office of any mercantile agent; also, an establishment which supplies to its patrons or subscribers information regarding the commercial and financial standing, etc., of individuals, firms, and corporations engaged in mercantile, financial, and industrial enterprises, and also publishes reports on the state of, and on transactions in, the commercial and financial world in general.—**mercantile law.** Same as *law merchant.* See under *law*[3], *n.*—**mercantile paper,** commercial paper consisting of promissory notes given by merchants for merchandise purchased and of drafts drawn against purchasers of merchandise.—**mercantile system,** in *polit. econ.*, a system of political and economic policy, coincident in its evolution with the modern national state, which sought through minute regulation of commerce and industry to secure the political supremacy of a state in its rivalry with other states. According to this system, money alone constituted wealth, and the great object of a state was the importation of the precious metals, to be effected by exporting the utmost possible quantity of its own products and importing as little as possible of those of other countries, thus establishing a favorable balance of trade to be paid in gold and silver.—**mer′can-til-ism,** *n.* Mercantile principles or practices; the mercantile spirit; in *polit. econ.*, the theory or practices of the mercantile system.—**mer′can-til-ist,** *n.*

mer-cap-tan (mėr-kap′tan), *n.* [G., < ML. *mercurius*, mercury, + L. *captans* (*captant-*), ppr. of *captare*, strive to take: see *catch.*] In *chem.*, any of a class of sulphur-containing compounds (mostly ill-smelling liquids) analogous to the alcohols and combining readily with mercury; esp., the most important member of this class, C_2H_5SH ('ethyl mercaptan'), a colorless liquid, with an offensive, garlic-like odor.

Mer-ca-tor's (mėr-kā′torz) **chart.** [From Gerardus *Mercator* (Gerhard Kremer, 1512–94), Flemish cartographer.] A chart made according to Mercator's projection.—**Mer-ca′tor's pro-jec′tion.** A method of map-making in which the whole or a part of the globe is represented as a rectangular plane surface, the meridians being equidistant parallel straight lines, and the parallels of latitude being parallel straight lines the distance between which increases from the equator toward the pole.

mer-ce-na-ry (mėr′se-nā-ri). [L. *mercenarius*, < *merces*, pay, reward: see *mercy.*] **I.** *a.* Working or acting merely for gain; having gain alone for a motive; venal; sordid; also, hired (now only of soldiers serving in a foreign army). **II.** *n.*; pl. *-ries* (-riz). One who works merely for pay; a hireling; also, any one who receives pay for his services, esp. (now only) a professional soldier serving in a foreign army.—**mer′ce-na-ri-ly,** *adv.*—**mer′ce-na-ri-ness,** *n.*

mer-cer (mėr′sėr), *n.* [OF. F. *mercier*, < L. *merx* (*merc-*), goods, wares: cf. *merchant.*] A dealer in textile fabrics, esp. silks, etc. [Eng.]

mer-cer-ize (mėr′sėr-īz), *v. t.*; *-ized, -izing.* [From J. *Mercer*, English calico-printer, the patentee (1850) of the process.] To treat (cotton fiber or fabric) with lye or a caustic solution, in order to cause it to receive the dye better, or to give it a silky luster.—**mer″cer-i-za′tion** (-i-zā′shon), *n.*

mer-cer-y (mėr′sėr-i), *n.*; pl. *-ies* (-iz). [OF. F. *mercerie.*] Mercers' wares (also in *pl.*: as, "He left outlandish *merceries* stored up With many a brazen bowl and silver cup," W. Morris's "Jason," iii. 223); also, a mercer's shop. [Eng.]

mer-chan-dise (mėr′chan-dīz), *n.* [OF. F. *marchandise*, < *marchand*, E. *merchant.*] Trade or commerce (archaic); also, the commodities of commerce; wares; goods.—**mer′chan-dize, mer′chan-dise** (-dīz), *v. i.* or *t.*; *-dized, -dised, -dizing, -dising.* To traffic, or traffic in. [Archaic.]—**mer′chan-diz-er, mer′chan-dis-er** (-dī-zėr), *n.*

mer-chant (mėr′chant). [OF. *marcheant*, later (also F.) *marchand*, < ML. *mercatare*, freq. of L. *mercari*, trade, deal, buy, < *merx* (*merc-*), goods, wares.] **I.** *n.* One who buys and sells marketable commodities for profit (in England applied only to wholesale dealers, but in the U. S. and Scotland applied also to retail dealers, as shopkeepers, peddlers, etc.); also, a trading vessel† (as, "the masters of some *merchant*": Shakspere's "Tempest," ii. 1. 5). **II.** *a.* Pertaining to trade or commerce (as, law *merchant*: see under *law*[3], *n.*); engaged or employed in trade or commerce (as, "The Lord hath given a commandment against the *merchant* city, to destroy the strong holds thereof," Isa. xxiii. 11; a *merchant* ship; the *merchant*, or mercantile, marine); pertaining to the mercantile marine (as, the *merchant* service).—**merchant adventurer,** a person, esp. a member of a commercial company, engaged in the sending out of trading expeditions to foreign parts and the establishment there of factories and trading stations.—**merchant tailor,** a tailor who furnishes the cloth for the garments which he fits and makes to order.—**mer′chant-a-ble,** *a.* Suitable for trade or sale; marketable.—**mer′chant-man** (-man), *n.*; pl. *-men.* A merchant (archaic); also, a trading vessel (as, "a stout *merchantman* of 350 tons": Swift's "Gulliver's Travels," iv. 1).—**mer′chant-ry,** *n.* The business of a merchant; trade; also, merchants collectively.

Mer-cian (mėr′shian). **I.** *a.* Of or pertaining to the ancient Anglian kingdom of Mercia in the central part of England, its inhabitants, or the dialect of Anglo-Saxon spoken there. **II.** *n.* A native or inhabitant of the ancient kingdom of Mercia.

mer-ci-ful (mėr′si-fu̇l), *a.* Full of mercy; exercising, or characterized by, mercy; compassionate: as, "God be *merciful* to me a sinner" (Luke, xviii. 13).—**mer′ci-ful-ly,** *adv.*—**mer′ci-ful-ness,** *n.*

mer-ci-less (mėr′si-les), *a.* Destitute of mercy; pitiless: as, "a *merciless* foe" (Ian Maclaren's "Beside the Bonnie Brier Bush," vii. 3); "the most *merciless* flaying" (Mark Twain's "Tom Sawyer," xx.).—**mer′ci-less-ly,** *adv.*—**mer′-ci-less-ness,** *n.*

mer-cu-ri-al (mėr-kū′ri-ạl). [L. *Mercurialis.*] **I.** *a.* [*cap.*] Of or pertaining to the god Mercury or the planet Mercury; [*l. c.*] of or pertaining to, consisting of or containing, or caused by, the metal mercury; also [*l. c.*], having qualities ascribed to the god Mercury, supposed to belong to persons born under the planet Mercury, or resembling the properties of the metal mercury; esp., sprightly, volatile, flighty, or fickle (as, "I was ardent in my temperament; quick, *mercurial*, impetuous": Irving's "Tales of a Traveler," i. 9). **II.** *n.* A preparation of mercury used as a drug.—**mer-cu′ri-al-ism,** *n.* In *pathol.*, a morbid condition caused by mercury.—**mer-cu′ri-al-ize** (-īz), *v. t.*; *-ized*, *-izing*. To make mercurial; also, to treat or impregnate with mercury or one of its compounds; in *med.*, to affect with, or subject to the action of, mercury.—**mer-cu″ri-al-i-za′tion** (-i-zā′shọn), *n.*—**mer-cu′ri-al-ly,** *adv.*

mer-cu-ric (mėr-kū′rik), *a.* [See *Mercury.*] Of or containing mercury. See *mercurous.*—**mer-cu-rous** (mėr′kụ̄-rus or mėr-kū′rus), *a.* Containing mercury (in larger proportion than a corresponding mercuric compound).

Mer-cu-ry (mėr′kụ̄-ri), *n.*; pl. *-ries* (-riz). [L. *Mercurius*, the god, also the planet, ML. *mercurius*, metallic mercury, prob. < L. *merx* (*merc-*), goods, wares: cf. *merchant.*] A Roman deity, messenger of the gods, and god of commerce, dexterity, and eloquence (cf. *Hermes*); hence [*l. c.* or *cap.*], a statue or image of Mercury, specif. a herma; also, a messenger, or carrier of news (sometimes used as the name of a newspaper or periodical); also [*cap.*], the major planet nearest to the sun; also [*l. c.*], a heavy, silver-white metallic element (chem. sym., Hg—see *hydrargyrum*; at. wt., 200.6; sp. gr., 13.6), remarkable for its fluidity at ordinary temperatures; quicksilver; also, a preparation of this metal used in medicine; also, the column of it in a thermometer or barometer, esp. with reference to the temperature or the state of the atmosphere shown by it; also, any herb of the euphorbiaceous genus *Mercurialis*, as *M. perennis* ('dog's-mercury'), a poisonous weed; also, the poison-ivy.

Mercury.—Statue in the British Museum, London.

mer-cy (mėr′si), *n.*; pl. *-cies* (-siz). [OF. F. *merci*, fem., favor, mercy, masc. thanks, < L. *merces*, pay, reward, ML. mercy: cf. *amerce*, *gramercy*, and *mercenary.*] Compassionate or kindly forbearance shown toward an offender, an enemy, or other person in one's power; clemency; leniency; also, compassion, pity, or benevolence (as, a work of *mercy*); sometimes, disposition to be merciful (as, an adversary wholly without *mercy*); also, an act of forbearance, compassion, or favor, esp. of God toward his creatures; a blessing, or fortunate or providential circumstance (as, "What a *mercy* master was not burned in his bed!" C. Brontë's "Jane Eyre," xvi.); also, discretionary power as to clemency or severity, pardon or punishment, or the like (as, to be at the *mercy* of a conqueror or a tribunal); in general, power to deal with or treat at will (as, "The poor lunatic . . . was at the *mercy* of his servants, who robbed, laughed at, and neglected him": Marryat's "Mr. Midshipman Easy," xxxvi.).—**mer′cy=seat,** *n.* The gold covering on the ark of the covenant, regarded as the resting-place of God (see Ex. xxv. 17–22); hence, the throne of God.

mere[1] (mēr), *n.* [AS. *mere*, lake, sea, = G. *meer* = Icel. *marr*, sea; akin to L. *mare*, sea.] A lake; a pond. [Now chiefly poetic or prov.]

mere[2] (mēr), *n.* [AS. *mǣre*, *gemǣre.*] A boundary. [Archaic or prov.]

mere[3] (mēr), *a.*; superl. *merest.* [L. *merus*, pure, unmixed, mere.] Pure† or unmixed† (as, *mere* wine; "This fellow was himself a *mere* Tartar, and perfectly spoke their language," Defoe's "Robinson Crusoe," ii. 15); also, belonging or pertaining to a single individual or group, or sole (chiefly legal: as, "The whole country was my own *mere* property, so that I had an undoubted right of dominion," Defoe's "Robinson Crusoe," i. 16; of one's *mere* motion); also, absolute† or unqualified† (as, "Certain tidings now arrived, importing the *mere* perdition of the Turkish fleet": Shakspere's "Othello," ii. 2. 3); also, being nothing more or better than what is specified (as, "Even when a *mere* child I began my travels," Irving's "Sketch-Book," Author's Account of Himself; it is *mere* folly to do this; this is the *merest* trash); pure and simple.

-mere. Noun termination from Gr. μέρος, part, as in *antimere*, *blastomere*. Cf. *-mer.*

mere-ly (mēr′li), *adv.* Purely†, or without admixture†; also, absolutely† or entirely†; also, only as specified, and nothing more (as, *merely* as a matter of form); simply.

mere-stone (mēr′stōn), *n.* [See *mere*[2].] A stone marking a boundary; a landmark of stone. [Archaic or prov.]

mer-e-tri-cious (mer-ḗ-trish′us), *a.* [L. *meretricius*, < *meretrix*, prostitute, < *merere*, deserve, earn.] Pertaining to or characteristic of a prostitute; having the character of a prostitute; also, alluring by a show of false attractions (as, "*meretricious* arts and calculated manœuvres": C. Brontë's "Jane Eyre," xviii.); showily attractive, or tawdry (as, "There is nothing showy or *meretricious* about the man": Howells's "Rise of Silas Lapham," i.).—**mer-e-tri′cious-ly,** *adv.*—**mer-e-tri′cious-ness,** *n.*

mer-gan-ser (mėr-gan′sėr), *n.* [NL., < L. *mergus*, diver (bird), + *anser*, goose.] Any of the swimming birds, resembling the common duck, which constitute the subfamily *Merginæ* (family *Anatidæ*), as *Mergus merganser*, a European species the male of which has a crested head, or *Lophodytes cucullatus*, a small North American species with an erect semicircular crest on the male's head ('hooded merganser').

Hooded Merganser (*Lophodytes cucullatus*).

merge (mėrj), *v.*; *merged*, *merging*. [L. *mergere* (pp. *mersus*), dip, plunge, sink.] **I.** *tr.* To cause to be swallowed up or absorbed; sink the identity of by combination: often with *in* or *into*: as, "*merging* night in day" (C. Brontë's "Jane Eyre," xxxvii.); "the same forces which *merged* the Dane in the Englishman" (Green's "Short Hist. of the Eng. People," ii. 3). **II.** *intr.* To become swallowed up or absorbed in something else; lose identity by absorption: often with *in* or *into.*—**mer-gence** (mėr′jẹns), *n.* A merging or becoming merged.—**mer′ger**[1], *n.* One who or that which merges.—**mer′ger**[2], *n.* [OF., inf. (< L. *mergere*), used as n.] A merging or being merged; specif., the absorption of one estate, title, etc., in another; also, a combination of the interests and control of two or more corporations by the issue of stock of a controlling corporation in exchange for a majority of the stock of the corporations to be controlled.

me-rid-i-an (mḗ-rid′i-ạn). [OF. *meridien* (F. *méridien*), < L. *meridianus*, < *meridies*, midday, the south, < *medius*, middle, + *dies*, day.] **I.** *a.* Of or pertaining to midday or noon (as, the *meridian* hour); also, pertaining to or situated at the position reached by the sun at midday, when it is highest, or the highest point reached by any heavenly body during its daily course (as, the sun's *meridian* beams; "The *meridian* moon shone full into the hovel," Jane Porter's "Scottish Chiefs," lxxix.); fig., pertaining to a period of greatest elevation, prosperity, splendor, etc. (as, Athens reached its *meridian* glory in the age of Pericles); culminating; also, of or pertaining to a meridian; also, southern or meridional (rare). **II.** *n.* Midday (obs. or rare); also, the highest point reached by the sun or some other heavenly body; fig., a point or period of highest development, greatest prosperity, or the like (as, "I imagined my fortune had passed its *meridian*, and must now decline": C. Brontë's "Jane Eyre," xxv.); the middle period of a person's life, when his powers are at their full (as, "They were men who had attained the *meridian* of life": Cooper's "Spy," xxvi.); in *astron.*, the great circle of the celestial sphere which passes through its poles and the observer's zenith; in *geog.*, a great circle of the earth passing through the poles and any given point on the earth's surface, or the half of such a circle included between the poles; hence, in fig. use, particular locality, situation, condition, or circumstances (as, governmental methods suited to the *meridian* of Asia; persons belonging to the same social *meridian*).—**magnetic meridian.** See under *magnetic*.

me-rid-i-o-nal (mē̤-rid′i-ọ-nạl). [OF. *meridional* (F. *méridional*), < LL. *meridionalis*, < L. *meridies*: see *meridian*.] **I.** *a.* Southern; southerly; also, characteristic of the south or people inhabiting the south, as of Europe, esp. of France (as, "Foremost among the Spanish Grandees . . . stood the famous favorite, Ruy Gomez . . . a man of *meridional* aspect, with coal-black hair and beard": Motley's "Dutch Republic," i. 1); also, of, pertaining to, or resembling a meridian. **II.** *n.* An inhabitant of the south, esp. the south of France.—**me-rid′i-o-nal-ly,** *adv.* In the direction of the meridian; north and south.

me-ringue (mẹ-rang′), *n.* [F.; origin unknown.] A mixture of sugar and beaten whites of eggs formed into small cakes and baked, or spread over pastry, puddings, etc.; also, a dish made with it.

me-ri-no (mẹ-rē′nō). [Sp.] **I.** *a.* Noting or pertaining to a variety of sheep which originated in Spain, valued for its fine wool; also, made of merino. **II.** *n.*; pl. *-nos* (-nōz). A merino sheep; also, merino wool; also, a thin twilled fabric made of merino wool or some substitute; also, a knitted underwear and hosiery fabric made of wool and cotton.

Head of Merino Ram, before and after shearing.

mer-i-spore (mer′i-spōr), *n.* [Gr. μερίς, part, + σπορά, E. *spore*.] In *biol.*, one of the individual cells or secondary spores of a multicellular or compound spore.

mer-i-stem (mer′i-stem), *n.* [Irreg. < Gr. μεριστός, divided, < μερίζειν, divide, < μέρος, part.] In *bot.*, embryonic tissue; undifferentiated, growing, actively dividing cells.—**mer″i-ste-mat′ic** (-stē̤-mat′ik), *a.*

mer-it (mer′it), *n.* [OF. *merite* (F. *mérite*), < L. *meritum*, prop. pp. neut. of *merere*, *mereri*, deserve, earn.] That which is deserved, whether good or bad† (as, "A dearer *merit*, not so deep a maim . . . Have I deserved at your highness' hands": Shakspere's "Richard II.," i. 3. 156); also, the state or fact of deserving, or desert (also in *pl.* in same sense: as, to treat a person according to his *merits*); *pl.*, the right and wrong of a case, orig. at law, as distinguished from extraneous points concerning it, or the intrinsic excellences or defects of any matter (as, the *merits* of a case; to consider a proposition on its *merits*); also, *sing.*, the state or fact of deserving well, or good desert (as, "Reputation is . . . oft got without *merit*, and lost without deserving": Shakspere's "Othello," ii. 3. 270); sometimes, the credit due for bringing about something favorable (as, the *merit* of our success belongs to him); also, in general, claim to commendation, or excellence or worth (as, "To him the wit of Greece and Rome was known, And every author's *merit* but his own," Pope's "Essay on Criticism," 728; a book or a play without *merit*); also, something that entitles to reward or commendation (as, "What a *merit* were it in death to take this poor maid from the world!" Shakspere's "Measure for Measure," iii. 1. 240); often, a commendable quality (as, the *merits* of a book or a play).—**to make a merit of,** to represent (some action, circumstance, or quality) as meritorious: as, "the party felon whose unblushing face . . . coolly *makes a merit of* disgrace" (Whittier's "Panorama").—**mer′it,** *v.* [OF. *meriter* (F. *mériter*).] **I.** *tr.* To be worthy of, or deserve (as, "Those best can bear reproof who *merit* praise," Pope's "Essay on Criticism," 583; "Nor had I ever done anything that *merited* the name of dishonest or fraudulent, much less thievish," Defoe's "Robinson Crusoe," ii. 11); also, to earn by commendable action (esp. in *theol.*). **II.** *intr.* To deserve (as, "a simple, religious fanatic, who felt sure that . . . he was *meriting* well of God and his King": Motley's "Dutch Republic," vi. 7); also, to acquire merit (esp. in *theol.*).—**mer′it-ed,** *p. a.* Deserved.—**mer′it-ed-ly,** *adv.* —**mer′it-less,** *a.* Without merit; undeserving; without excellence or commendable qualities.

mer-i-to-ri-ous (mer-i-tō′ri-us), *a.* [ML. *meritorius*, meritorious, L. serving to earn money, < *merere*: see *merit*.] Deserving of reward or commendation; possessing merit; now, specif., deserving of moderate but not high commendation; also, of actions, serving to earn reward (esp. in *theol.*). —**mer-i-to′ri-ous-ly,** *adv.*—**mer-i-to′ri-ous-ness,** *n.*

Merle, or European Blackbird.

merle (mėrl), *n.* [OF. F. *merle*, < L. *merula*, *merulus*.] The common European blackbird, *Merula vulgaris*: as, "The *merle*, in his noontide bow'r, Makes woodland echoes ring" (Burns's "Lament of Mary Queen of Scots," 11). [Chiefly Sc. and poetic.]

mer-lin (mėr′lin), *n.* [OF. *esmerillon* (F. *émerillon*), < *esmeril*, merlin.] Any of various small falcons of the genus *Falco*, esp. a species, *F. æsalon*, one of the smallest European birds of prey, and one of the boldest, which does not hesitate to attack birds of twice its own size, or a North

Merlin (*Falco æsalon*).

American species, *F. columbarius*, the common pigeon-hawk.
mer-lon (mėr′lǫn), *n.* [F. *merlon*, < It. *merlone*, aug. of *merlo*, merlon.] In a battlement, the solid part between two embrasures or crenels.
mer-maid (mėr′mād), *n.* [See *mere*1.] An imaginary female marine creature, typically having the head and trunk of a woman and the tail of a fish (as, "A *mermaid* fair, Singing alone, Combing her hair Under the sea": Tennyson's "Mermaid," i.); hence, a woman who is at home in the water. Also **mer′maid″en.**
mer-man (mėr′mạn or -man), *n.*; pl. *-men.* [See *mere*1.] An imaginary man of the sea, corresponding to a mermaid (see Tennyson's poem, "The Merman"); a Triton (as, "Did they with ocean's hidden sovereigns dwell, And sound with *mermen* the fantastic shell?" Byron's "Island," iv. 5); hence, a man who is at home in the water.
mero-. Form of Gr. μέρος, part, used in combination.—**mer-o-blast** (mer′ǫ-blast), *n.* [+ *-blast.*] In *biol.*, an ovum the contents of which consist of considerable nutritive as well as formative or germinal matter: opposed to *holoblast.*—**mer-o-blas′tic** (-blas′tik), *a.*—**mer-o-crys′tal-line** (-kris′tạ-lin), *a.* Partially crystalline.—**mer-o-sym′me-try** (-sim′e-tri), *n.* In *crystal.*, partial symmetry.—**mer″o-sym-met′ri-cal** (-si-met′ri-kạl), *a.*
-merous. Adjective termination from Gr. μέρος, part, as in *heteromerous, pentamerous.*
Mer-o-vin-gi-an (mer-ǫ-vin′ji-ạn), *a.* [ML. *Merovingi*, pl., the Merovingian dynasty, < *Merovæus*, Merovech, Merowig, or Merwig, a 5th century king of the Salian Franks.] Designating or pertaining to the Frankish dynasty which reigned in Gaul, or France, from about 500 to 751. Cf. *Carolingian.*
mer-ri-ly (mer′i-li), *adv.* In a merry manner.
mer-ri-ment (mer′i-mẹnt), *n.* Merrymaking† or festivity†; also, merry gaiety (as, "your flashes of *merriment*, that were wont to set the table on a roar": Shakspere's "Hamlet," v. 1. 210); mirth; hilarity; laughter.
mer-ri-ness (mer′i-nes), *n.* The quality or state of being merry.
mer-ry (mer′i), *a.*; compar. *merrier*, superl. *merriest.* [AS. *myrige, myrge*, pleasant, delightful: cf. *mirth.*] Pleasant or delightful (archaic: as, the *merry* month of May; *merry* England); also, amusing (archaic: as, a *merry* jest); also, full of cheer or gaiety, gladsome, or festive (as, *merry* Christmas; *merry* bells; "The wood-nymphs . . . Their *merry* wakes and pastimes keep," Milton's "Comus," 121); joyous in disposition or spirit (as, the *Merry* Monarch, Charles II. of England); moved to or showing gaiety of mood or animated enjoyment (as, "I am never *merry* when I hear sweet music," Shakspere's "Merchant of Venice," v. 1. 69; "Take thine ease, eat, drink, and be *merry*," Luke, xii. 19; *merry* talk or laughter); laughingly gay; mirthful; hilarious; sometimes, hilarious from drink, or slightly tipsy; also, jesting or facetious (archaic: as, "His lordship is but *merry* with me," Shakspere's "Timon of Athens," iii. 2. 42).—**merry dancers.** See *dancer.*—**to make merry,** to indulge in merry pleasures; hold festivities; also, to indulge in laughter or jesting, as over a matter.—**mer″ry=an′drew,** *n.* One whose business it is to make sport for others by antics, jokes, etc., esp. formerly as a mountebank's assistant (as, "propagating the report that I had a quarrel with a mountebank's *merry-andrew* at Gloucester": Smollett's "Humphry Clinker," April 18); a buffoon; a clown.—**mer′ry=go=round″,** *n.* A revolving machine, as a circular platform fitted with hobby-horses, etc., on which persons, esp. children, ride for amusement; fig., any whirl or rapid round.—**mer′ry-make,** *v. i.*; *-made, -making.* To make merry; hold festivities: as, "young inseparables . . . who . . . pawn each other's watches and *merrymake* together on the proceeds" (Du Maurier's "Trilby," iii.).—**mer′ry-mak″er** (-mā″kėr), *n.*—**mer′ry-mak″ing,** *n.* The act of making merry; an instance or occasion of making merry; a merry festivity; a gay social or convivial entertainment; a revel.—**mer′ry-thought,** *n.* The wishbone or furcula of a bird.
me-sa (mā′sạ̈), *n.* [Sp., < L. *mensa*, table.] A comparatively small, high table-land or plateau with the sides or a side descending steeply, of a type common in the southwestern U. S.: as, "A conspicuous feature of the New Mexican landscape is the *mesa*, a flat-topped hill created by differential erosion and projecting above the surrounding country like a table" (Encyc. Brit., 11th ed., XIX. 521).
mé-sal-liance (mā-zȧ-lyäṅs), *n.* [F.] A misalliance; a marriage with a social inferior.
mes-cal (mes-kal′), *n.* [Sp. *mezcal*; from Mex.] An intoxicating spirit distilled from the fermented juice of certain species of agave; any agave yielding this spirit; also, either of two species of cactus, *Lophophora williamsii* and *L. lewinii*, of Texas and northern Mexico, whose button-like tops ('mescal-buttons') are dried and used as a stimulant, esp. by the Indians.

Mescal-button (*Lophophora williamsii*). — One third natural size.

mes-dames (mā-dȧm), *n.* Pl. of *madame*2, also of *madam.*
mesde-moi-selles (mād-mwo-zel), *n.* Pl. of *mademoiselle.*
me-seems (mẹ-sēmz′), *v. impers.*; pret. *meseemed.* It seems to me: as, "They talk'd, *Meseem'd*, of what they knew not" (Tennyson's "Lancelot and Elaine," 671). [Archaic.]
mes-en-ceph-a-lon (mes-en-sef′ạ-lon), *n.*; pl. *-la* (-lạ̈). [NL.: see *meso-* and *encephalon.*] In *anat.*, the middle segment of the brain; the midbrain.—**mes″en-ce-phal′ic** (-se-fal′ik), *a.*
mes-en-chy-ma (mes-eng′ki-mạ̈), *n.* [NL., < Gr. μέσος, middle, + *-enchyma* as in *parenchyma.*] In *embryol.*, that portion of the mesoderm which is not mesothelial in character.—**mes-en′chy-mal, mes-en-chym′a-tous** (-eng-kim′ạ-tus), *a.*
mes-en-ter-ic (mes-ẹn-ter′ik), *a.* Of or pertaining to a mesentery.
mes-en-te-ron (mes-en′tẹ-ron), *n.* [NL.: see *meso-* and *enteron.*] In *embryol.*, a primitive intestinal cavity bounded by endoderm.
mes-en-ter-y (mes′ẹn-ter-i), *n.*; pl. *-ies* (-iz). [NL. *mesenterium*, < Gr. μεσεντέριον, < μέσος, middle, + ἔντερον, intestine.] In *anat.*, a fold or duplicature of peritoneum investing, and attaching to the posterior wall of the abdomen, a part or parts of the intestine or other abdominal viscus; in *zoöl.*, one of the membranous partitions which divide the digestive cavity in actinozoans.
mesh (mesh), *n.* [Cf. MD. *masche, maesche*, D. *maas*, G. *masche*, Icel. *möskvi*, mesh, AS. *max*, net.] One of the open spaces of network or a net; *pl.*, the threads that bound such spaces; any interlinked or interlaced strands or parts (as, the *meshes* of tangled hair; "Fountains . . . showering down In *meshes* of the jasmine and the rose," Tennyson's "Princess," i. 216); fig., means of catching or holding fast (as, caught in the *meshes* of the law); also, *sing.*, netted or net-like work (as, "Her beds were . . . covered with the white *mesh* of her own crochet-needle": G. W. Cable's "Bonaventure," i. 10); a network or net (esp. fig.: as, "Here in her hairs The painter plays the spider and hath woven A golden *mesh* to entrap the hearts of men," Shakspere's "Merchant of Venice," iii. 2. 122); in *mach.*, the engagement of gear-teeth.—**mesh,** *v.* **I.** *tr.* To catch or entangle in or as in the meshes of a net; enmesh; also, to form with meshes, as a net; in *mach.*, to engage, as gear-teeth. **II.** *intr.* To become enmeshed; in *mach.*, to become engaged, as the teeth of one wheel with those of another.—**meshed,** *a.* Having meshes; reticulated.—**mesh′work,** *n.* Meshed work; network.—**mesh′y,** *a.* Formed with meshes; meshed; reticulated.
mes-i-al (mes′i-ạl or mē′zi-ạl), *a.* [Gr. μέσος, middle: see *mid*2.] Middle; median; pertaining to or situated in a median line or plane.—**mes′i-al-ly,** *adv.*
mes-mer-ic (mez-mer′ik), *a.* Pertaining to, characteristic of, or produced by mesmerism.—**mes-mer′i-cal-ly,** *adv.*
mes-mer-ism (mez′mėr-izm), *n.* [From F. A. *Mesmer* (1733–1815), German physician, who propounded the doctrine.] The doctrine of the induction of a hypnotic

state through an influence or emanation transmitted from the operator to the subject; the induction, influence, or state concerned; in general, hypnotism.—**mes′mer-ist,** *n.* One who practises mesmerism.—**mes′mer-ize** (-īz), *v. t.*; *-ized, -izing.* To subject to mesmeric influence.—**mes″mer-i-za′tion** (-i-zā′shọn), *n.*—**mes′mer-iz-er** (-ī-zėr), *n.*

mesn-al-ty (mē′nąl-ti), *n.* In *law*, the estate of a mesne lord; the condition of a mesne lord.

mesne (mēn), *a.* [Archaic spelling of *mean*³.] In *law*, middle, intermediate, or intervening: as, a *mesne* lord (a feudal lord who held land of a superior).

meso-, mes-. Forms of Gr. μέσος, middle, used in combination, chiefly in scientific terms.—**mes-o-blast** (mes′ọ-blast), *n.* [+ *-blast.*] In *embryol.*, the mesoderm.—**mes-o-blas′tic** (-blas′tik), *a.*—**mes′o-carp** (-kärp), *n.* [+ *-carp.*] In *bot.*, the middle layer of pericarp, as the fleshy part of certain fruits. See cut at *endocarp.*—**mes″o-ce-phal′ic** (-se-fal′ik), *a.* [+ Gr. κεφαλή, head.] In *craniom.*, having a skull of medium cranial capacity (used as an intermediate term between *megacephalic* and *microcephalic*); also, having a skull of medium proportion (used as an intermediate term between *brachycephalic* and *dolichocephalic*); in *anat.*, of or pertaining to the mesencephalon.—**mes′o-derm** (-dėrm), *n.* [+ *-derm.*] In *embryol.*, the middle primary layer of cells in the embryo of a metazoan.—**mes-o-der′mal, mes-o-der′mic,** *a.*—**mes-o-gas′tri-um** (-gas′tri-um), *n.* [NL. (Gr. γαστήρ, belly).] In *anat.*, the umbilical region of the abdomen, situated above the hypogastrium and below the epigastrium; also, the mesentery of the stomach. —**mes-o-gas′tric,** *a.*—**mes-o-neph′ros** (-nef′ros), *n.* [NL. (Gr. νεφρός, kidney).] In *embryol.*, the central or intermediate part of the primitive renal organ or kidney of a vertebrate embryo, situated between the pronephros and the metanephros.—**mes-o-neph′ric,** *a.*—**mes′o-phyl, mes′o-phyll** (-fil), *n.* [+ *-phyl, -phyll.*] In *bot.*, the green parenchyma which forms the interior parts of a leaf.—**mes′o-phyte** (-fīt), *n.* [+ *-phyte.*] A plant growing under conditions of medium moisture and dryness. Cf. *hydrophyte* and *xerophyte.*—**mes-o-phyt′ic** (-fit′ik), *a.* —**mes′o-plast** (-plast), *n.* [+ *-plast.*] In *biol.*, the nucleus of a cell; nuclear protoplasm.—**mes-o-plas′tic** (-plas′tik), *a.*—**mes-o-the′li-um** (-thē′li-um), *n.*; pl. *-liums* or *-lia* (-li-ä). [NL. (with *-thelium* as in *epithelium*).] In *embryol.*, *anat.*, etc., that portion of the mesoderm which lines the primitive cœlom of the embryo; epithelium of mesodermic origin.—**mes-o-the′li-al,** *a.*—**mes-o-tho′rax** (-thō′raks), *n.* [NL.] The middle one of the three divisions of an insect's thorax, bearing the second pair of legs and the first pair of wings.—**mes″o-tho-ra′cic** (-thọ-ras′ik), *a.*

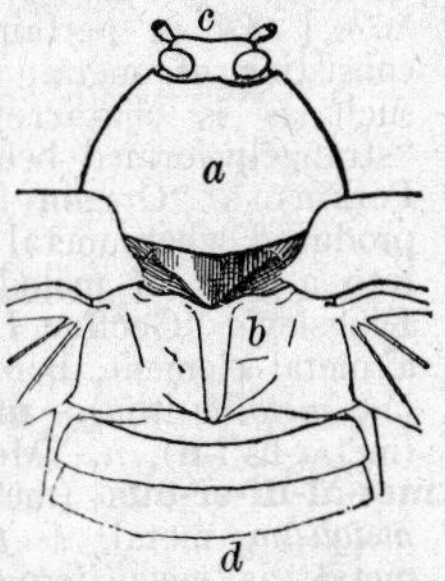

Mesothorax, shaded, between prothorax (*a*) and metathorax (*b*); *c*, head; *d*, two abdominal segments.

mes-o-tho-ri-um (mes-ọ-thō′ri-um), *n.* [NL.: see *meso-* and *thorium.*] In *chem.*, a disintegration product of thorium.

Mes-o-zo-ic (mes-ọ-zō′ik). [Gr. μέσος, middle, + ζωή, life.] **I.** *a.* Noting or pertaining to a geological era or a group of rocks whose fossils represent forms of life between those of relatively ancient (Paleozoic) and those of recent (Cenozoic) geological times. Cf. *Paleozoic, Cenozoic.* **II.** *n.* The Mesozoic era or group.

mes-quit (mes-kēt′ or mes′kēt), *n.* Same as *mesquite.*

mes-quite (mes-kēt′ or mes′kēt), *n.* [Sp. *mezquite*; from Mex.] A mimosaceous tree or shrub, *Prosopis glandulosa*, of the southwestern U. S., Mexico, etc., whose bean-like pods are rich in sugar and form a valuable fodder; also, any species of *Prosopis*, as the screw-bean. See cut in preceding column.

Branch of Mesquite, with Flowers and Leaves.—*a*, a flower; *b*, a pod.

mess (mes), *n.* [OF. *mes* (F. *mets*), lit. 'something put' (on the table), < L. *missum*, pp. neut. of *mittere*, send, later put.] A service or dish of food at table or for a meal (archaic); hence, a quantity of meat, vegetables, or other food sufficient for a dish or a single occasion, or a quantity of food of indefinite amount (now colloq. or prov.: as, a *mess* of peas for dinner; a *mess* of trout; "barrels of pink-hued salt-pork . . . or immense *messes* of sausage-meat," Mrs. Stowe's "Oldtown Folks," xiii.); also, a dish or quantity of soft, semiliquid, or liquid food (as, a *mess* of porridge; a *mess* of pottage, an expression used in older versions of the Bible, and hence, often fig., with reference to the pottage for which Esau sold his birthright to his brother Jacob, as narrated in Gen. xxv. 29–34); hence, a sloppy or unappetizing preparation of food (as, "The first edge of hunger blunted, I perceived I had got in hand a nauseous *mess*": C. Brontë's "Jane Eyre," v.); a quantity of any matter or things in a dirty or untidy mass, litter, or jumble (as, a *mess* of fallen plaster; a *mess* of papers); a dirty or untidy condition (as, the room was in a *mess*); a state of embarrassing confusion (as, his affairs are in a *mess*); an unpleasant muddle, scrape, or affair (as, to make a *mess* of an undertaking; to get into a *mess*; "Then maybe he would a locked her up, and this awful *mess* wouldn't ever happened," Mark Twain's "Huckleberry Finn," xviii.); also, a number of persons (formerly often four) eating together at table, now a company regularly taking meals together as in the army or navy (as, "A man admitted to his *mess* [at a tavern] is always sure of eating delicate victuals," Smollett's "Humphry Clinker," May 6; "Each *mess* had its fire, where the men cooked, ate, gossiped, and slept," Irving's "Captain Bonneville," ii.); the meal so taken; also, a company or set of four† (as, "You three fools lack'd me fool to make up the *mess*": Shakspere's "Love's Labour's Lost," iv. 3. 207). —**mess,** *v.* **I.** *tr.* To serve up or dish out (food), as for a meal (now prov. Eng.); also, to supply with meals, as soldiers, etc.; also, to get into a dirty, untidy, or disorderly mess (often with *up*: as, to *mess* up one's clothes, or a room); make a mess of, or muddle (affairs, etc.). **II.** *intr.* To eat in company, esp. as a member of a mess (as, "We turned in to bunk and *mess* with the crew forward": Dana's "Two Years before the Mast," viii.); also, to make a dirty or untidy mess; dabble in water, mud, etc.; busy one's self in an untidy or confused way.

mes-sage (mes′ąj), *n.* [OF. F. *message*, < ML. *missaticum*, < L. *mittere* (pp. *missus*), send.] A communication, as of information, advice, direction, or the like, transmitted through a messenger or other agency (as, an oral or a written *message*; a wireless *message*; a *message* of acceptance or of congratulation); specif., an official communication, as from a chief executive to a legislative body (as, the President's *message* to Congress); sometimes, an inspired or momentous communication to be delivered to the world (as, the *message* of a prophet; to come forward as the bearer of a *message* to mankind); also, the business, errand, or mission of a messenger (as, "On some *message* high they guess'd him bound": Milton's "Paradise Lost," v. 290).—**mes′sage=shell,** *n.* *Milit.*, a projectile in the interior of which messages may be placed to be propelled to a distance.

mes-sa-line (mes′ą-lēn), *n.* [F.] A thin, soft silk fabric with a twilled or a satin weave, used for women's dresses, etc.

mes-san, mes-sin (mes′ąn, mes′in), *n.* [Cf. Gael. *measan.*] A small dog; a cur. [Sc.]

mes-sen-ger (mes′ẹn-jėr), *n.* [OF. F. *messager*, < *message*, E. *message.*] One who bears a message or goes on an errand; one whose duty or business it is to bear messages or go on errands; one employed to convey official despatches or to go on other official or special errands (as, a bank-*messenger*); fig., anything regarded as sent on an errand (as, "His steady eye was enabled to look directly into their [guns'] muzzles . . . in anticipation of the fatal *messenger* that was to issue from each": Cooper's "Deerslayer," xxix.); a herald or harbinger (as, "Down to short repose they lay; Till radiant rose the *messenger* of day": Pope's tr. Homer's "Odyssey," xv.).—**mes'sen-ger-ship,** *n.* The office of a messenger.

Messerschmitt. A German fighter plane.

Mes-si-ah (me-sī'ä), *n.* [For LL. *Messias,* < Gr. Μεσσίας, < Heb. *māshīakh,* anointed.] 'The Anointed,' the title applied to an expected deliverer of the Jewish people, and hence to Jesus (cf. John, iv. 25, 26); hence, in general, an expected deliverer.—**Mes-si'ah-ship,** *n.* The character or office of a Messiah.—**Mes-si-an-ic** (mes-i-an'ik), *a.* Of or pertaining to the Messiah or a Messiah.—**Mes-si-a-nism** (me-sī'ạ-nizm), *n.* Belief in a coming Messiah.—**Mes-si'as** (-ạs), *n.* [LL.] Same as *Messiah.*

Mes-si-dor (mes-ē-dôr), *n.* [F. *messidor,* < L. *messis,* harvest, + Gr. δῶρον, gift.] In the calendar of the first French republic, the tenth month of the year, extending from June 19 to July 18.

mes-sieurs (mā-syė, E. often mes'yėrz), *n.* Plural of *monsieur.* See *Messrs.*

mes'sin, *n.* See *messan.*

mes-sire (me-sēr), *n.* [OF., 'my lord': see *sire.*] A French title of honor and form of address formerly applied to high nobles, and also to men of quality and members of the learned professions.

mess-mate (mes'māt), *n.* An associate in a mess, now esp. in a ship's mess: as, "I found myself one of ten *messmates* seated at table" (Smollett's "Humphry Clinker," June 10); "He would be more comfortable on board a ship in which he had many old *messmates* and friends" (Marryat's "King's Own," xli.).

Messrs. (F. mā-syė, E. commonly mes'ėrz). Abbreviated form of *messieurs,* used before personal names as if a plural of E. *Mr.*

mes-suage (mes'wāj), *n.* [OF. *mesuage,* ult. < L. *manere* (pp. *mansus*), remain: cf. *manse* and *mansion.*] In *law,* a dwelling-house with its adjacent buildings and the lands appropriated to the use of the household.

mess-y (mes'i), *a.* Of the nature of a mess (as, a *messy* concoction); being in a mess (as, a *messy* table); attended with or making a mess (as, *messy* work); dirty; untidy.

mes-tee (mes-tē'), *n.* [Cf. *mestizo.*] The offspring of a white person and a quadroon. [West Indian.]

mes-ti-za (mes-tē'zä), *n.* [Sp.] Fem. of *mestizo.*

mes-ti-zo (mes-tē'zō), *n.*; pl. *-zos* (-zōz). [Sp., = F. *mêtis,* < LL. *misticius, mixticius,* of mixed race, < L. *miscere,* mix.] In Spanish America, etc., a person of mixed blood, esp. of Spanish and American Indian blood.

met (met). Preterit and past participle of *meet*².

meta-. [Gr. μετα-, repr. μετά, prep.] A prefix of Greek origin, meaning 'among,' 'between,' 'with,' 'after,' 'behind,' and often denoting change, sometimes used as a modern formative, chiefly in scientific words.

me-tab-a-sis (me-tab'ạ-sis), *n.*; pl. *-ases* (-ạ-sēz). [NL., < Gr. μετάβασις, < μεταβαίνειν, pass over, < μετα- (denoting change) + βαίνειν, go.] Transition, as from one subject to another.

me-tab-o-lism (me-tab'ō-lizm), *n.* [Gr. μεταβολή, a change, < μεταβάλλειν, to change, < μετα- (denoting change) + βάλλειν, throw.] In *biol.,* the sum of the processes or chemical changes in an organism or a single cell by which food is built up (*anabolism*) into living protoplasm and by which protoplasm is broken down (*catabolism*) into simpler compounds with the liberation of energy.—**met-a-bol-ic** (met-ạ-bol'ik), *a.*—**me-tab'o-lize,** *v. t.*; *-lized, -lizing.* To subject to metabolism.

met-a-car-pal (met-ạ-kär'pạl). **I.** *a.* Of or pertaining to the metacarpus. **II.** *n.* A metacarpal bone.

met-a-car-pus (met-ạ-kär'pus), *n.*; pl. *-pi* (-pī). [NL.: see *meta-* and *carpus.*] In *anat.,* the part of a hand or fore limb (esp. of its bony structure) included between the wrist or carpus and the fingers or phalanges.

met-a-cen-ter, met-a-cen-tre (met'ạ-sen-tėr), *n.* [F. *mêtacentre,* < Gr. μετά, after, + κέντρον, E. *center*².] The point where the vertical line passing through the center of buoyancy of a ship or other floating body when in equilibrium, or in its normal upright position, meets the vertical line passing through the new center of buoyancy when the floating body is in a slightly inclined position, the equilibrium of the floating body being stable or unstable according as this point is above or below the center of gravity of the body.—**met-a-cen'tric,** *a.*

met-a-chro-ma-tism (met-ạ-krō'mạ-tizm), *n.* [See *meta-.*] Change of color, esp. that due to variation in the temperature of a body.—**met"a-chro-mat'ic** (-krō-mat'ik), *a.*—**met'a-chrome** (-krōm), *n.* A body or substance that changes color.

met-age (mē'tāj), *n.* [From *mete*².] The official measurement of contents or weight; also, the charge for it.

met-a-gen-e-sis (met-ạ-jen'e-sis), *n.* [See *meta-.*] In *biol.,* reproduction characterized by the alternation of a sexual generation and a generation which reproduces asexually by budding.—**met"a-ge-net'ic** (-jē-net'ik), *a.*

me-tag-na-thous (me-tag'nạ-thus), *a.* [Gr. μετά, with, + γνάθος, jaw.] In *ornith.,* having the tips of the mandibles crossed, as the crossbills.—**me-tag'na-thism,** *n.*

mé-tai-rie (mā-tā-rē), *n.* [F., < *métayer*: see *métayer.*] A farm or piece of land cultivated by a métayer.

met-al (met'ạl), *n.* [OF. *metal* (F. *métal*), < L. *metallum,* mine, mineral, metal, < Gr. μέταλλον, mine.] Any of a class of elementary substances, as gold, silver, copper, etc., many of which are characterized by opacity, ductility, conductivity, and a peculiar luster; also, an alloy or mixture composed wholly or partly of such substances; also, the constituent material of such substances or alloys without regard to kind; also, an object made of such material, as one of the rails of a railroad (as, "He had fallen from an engine, And been dragged along the *metals*": Henley's "In Hospital," xiii.); also, the aggregate number, mass, or power of the guns on a war-ship; also, any material, matter, or substance; often, formative material (as, "I am made Of the self-same *metal* that my sister is": Shakspere's "King Lear," i. 1. 71); that of which anything is composed (cf. *mettle*); specif., material for roads, as broken stone; also, the material of glass, etc., in a state of fusion; in *printing,* etc., type-metal; in *her.,* either of the tinctures or (gold) and argent (silver).—**met'al,** *v. t.*; *-aled* or *-alled, -aling* or *-alling.* To furnish with metal; also, to cover (a road) with metal, or broken stone.

me-tal-lic (me-tal'ik), *a.* [L. *metallicus,* < Gr. μεταλλικός.] Of or pertaining to metal; of the nature of, or consisting of, metal; containing metal; resembling metal; such as is characteristic of metal, as color, etc. (as, "strangely formed beetles, glittering with *metallic* luster": Parkman's "Oregon Trail," vii.); resembling the sound produced when metal is struck (as, "The bird . . . broke into a gush of melody . . . rich, full, and *metallic*": H. Kingsley's "Geoffry Hamlyn," xxvii.); in specific use, of a metal element, being in the free or uncombined state (as, *metallic* iron).—**me-tal'li-cal-ly,** *adv.*—**met-al-li-ci-ty** (met-ạ-lis'i-ti), *n.* Metallic nature or character.

met-al-lif-er-ous (met-ạ-lif'ẹ-rus), *a.* [L. *metallifer,* < *metallum,* metal, + *ferre,* bear.] Containing or yielding metal: as, *metalliferous* mines.

met-al-line (met'ạ-lin or -līn), *a.* [= F. *métallin.*] Metallic; metal-like; specif., containing one or more metals or metallic salts.

met-al-list (met'ạl-ist), *n.* A worker in metals, or one skilled in the knowledge of metals.

met-al-lize (met'ạl-īz), *v. t.*; *-lized, -lizing.* To render metallic; give the appearance or other characteristics of metal to.—**met"al-li-za'tion** (-ạl-i-zā'shọn), *n.*

metallo-. Form of L. *metallum,* metal, used in combination.—**met-al-lo-ge-net-ic** (met"ạ-lō-jē-net'ik), *a.* Producing metals.—**met-al-log'ra-phy** (-ạ-log'rạ-fi), *n.* [+ *-graphy.*] The microscopic study of the structure of metals and alloys; also, an art or process allied to lithography, in which metallic plates are substituted for stones.—**met'al-loid.** [See *-oid.*] **I.** *a.* Resembling metal; in *chem.,* pertaining to or of the nature of a metalloid. **II.** *n.* In *chem.,* a non-metallic element; sometimes, an element, as arsenic, with both metallic and non-metallic properties.

met-al-lur-gic, met-al-lur-gi-cal (met-ạ-lėr'jik, -ji-kạl), *a.* Of or pertaining to metallurgy.—**met-al-lur'gi-cal-ly,** *adv.*

met-al-lur-gist (met'ạ-lėr-jist), *n.* One versed in metallurgy.

met-al-lur-gy (met'ạ-lėr-ji), *n.* [NL. *metallurgia,* < Gr. μεταλλουργός, mine-worker, < μέταλλον, mine, + -εργός,

working, worker.] The art or science of separating metals from their ores.
met-al-work (met′ąl-wėrk), *n.* Work, esp. artistic work, in metal.
met-a-mer (met′ą-mėr), *n.* [Gr. μετά, with, after, + μέρος, part.] In *chem.*, a compound which is metameric with another.—**met′a-mere** (-mēr), *n.* In *zoöl.*, one of the longitudinal series of more or less similar parts or segments composing the body of the earthworm and other animals. —**met-a-mer′ic** (-mer′ik), *a.* In *chem.*, of compounds, having the same molecular weight and the same elements combined in the same proportion, but differing in structure and chemical properties; in *zoöl.*, of or pertaining to a metamere or metameres; segmental.—**me-tam-er-ism** (me-tam′ę-rizm), *n.* In *chem.*, the state of being metameric; in *zoöl.*, the condition of consisting of metameres.
met-a-mor-phic (met-ą-môr′fik), *a.* [Gr. μετα- (denoting change) + μορφή, form.] Pertaining to or characterized by change of form, or metamorphosis; in *geol.*, pertaining to or exhibiting structural change, or metamorphism.—**met-a-mor′phism,** *n.* Change of form; metamorphosis; in *geol.*, a change in the structure or constitution of a rock, due to natural agencies, as pressure and heat, esp. when the rock becomes harder and more crystalline; also, metamorphic state.
met-a-mor-phose (met-ą-môr′fōz or -fōs), *v. t.*; *-phosed*, *-phosing.* To subject to a metamorphosis; transform; specif., to subject to metamorphosis or metamorphism (in scientific applications).
met-a-mor-pho-sis (met-ą-môr′fǫ-sis), *n.*; pl. *-phoses* (-fǫ-sēz). [L., < Gr. μεταμόρφωσις, < μεταμορφοῦν, transform, < μετα- (denoting change) + μορφή, form.] Change of form, structure, or substance; specif., transformation by magic or witchcraft; in general, any complete change in appearance, character, circumstances, etc. (as, "His visage . . . changed as from a mask to a face . . . I know not that I have ever seen in any other human face an equal *metamorphosis*": C. Brontë's "Villette," xxvii.); also, a form resulting from any such change (as, "an amount of fat on the nape of her neck, which made her look like the *metamorphosis* of a white sucking-pig": George Eliot's "Adam Bede," vi.); specif., in *zoöl.*, a marked change in the form, and usually the habits, of an animal in its development after the embryonic stage, as the transformation of a tadpole into a frog, or of the pupa of an insect into an imago; in *bot.*, the structural or functional modification of a plant organ or structure during the course of its development; in *physiol.*, metabolism.
met-a-neph-ros (met-ą-nef′ros), *n.* [NL., < Gr. μετά, after, + νεφρός, kidney.]. In *embryol.*, the most posterior part of the primitive renal organ or kidney of a vertebrate embryo. Cf. *mesonephros.*—**met-a-neph′ric,** *a.*
met-a-phor (met′ą-fǫr), *n.* [F. *métaphore*, < L. *metaphora*, < Gr. μεταφορά, < μεταφέρειν, transfer, < μετα- (denoting change) + φέρειν, bear.] A figure of speech in which a term or phrase is applied to something to which it is not literally applicable, in order to suggest a resemblance, as in "A mighty fortress is our God"; also, a verbal expression of this figure; a metaphorical expression.—**mixed metaphor,** a figurative expression in which two or more metaphors are employed, producing an incongruous assemblage of ideas, as in "He embarked early on the sea of public life, where he climbed at last to the very summit of success."—**met-a-phor′ic, met-a-phor′i-cal** (-for′ik, -i-kąl), *a.* [Gr. μεταφορικός.] Pertaining to, of the nature of, or involving metaphor; figurative.—**met-a-phor′i-cal-ly,** *adv.*—**met′a-phor-ist,** *n.* One who coins or uses metaphors.
met-a-phrase (met′ą-frāz), *n.* [NL. *metaphrasis*, < Gr. μετάφρασις, < μεταφράζειν, express in another form, < μετα- (denoting change) + φράζειν, tell.] A translation, esp. a literal translation.—**met′a-phrase,** *v. t.*; *-phrased*, *-phrasing.* To translate, esp. literally; also, to change the phrasing or literary form of.—**met′a-phrast** (-frast), *n.* [Gr. μεταφράστης.] One who metaphrases.—**met-a-phras′tic** (-fras′tik), *a.*
met-a-phys-ic (met-ą-fiz′ik). [ML. *metaphysica*, n. pl., < Gr. μετά, after, + φυσικά, things pertaining to nature (neut. pl. of φυσικός: see *physic*); orig. with reference to writings of Aristotle that in the accepted arrangement came after his physical treatises.] **I.** *n.* Metaphysics. **II.** *a.* Metaphysical: as, "He knew what's what, and that's as high As *metaphysic* wit can fly" (Butler's "Hudibras," i. 1). [Now rare.]—**met-a-phys′i-cal,** *a.* Pertaining to or of the nature of metaphysics; such as is recognized in metaphysics; hence, highly abstract or abstruse; apart from ordinary or practical modes of thought; loosely, philosophical or theoretical (as, "wars . . . waged for points of *metaphysical* right": Scott's "Woodstock," vi.); also, concerned with abstract thought or subjects, as a person, the mind, etc.; also, preternatural or supernatural (obs. or archaic: as, "*metaphysical* aid," Shakspere's "Macbeth," i. 5. 30); immaterial or supersensible (as, *metaphysical* substance); fanciful or imaginary (obs. or archaic); also, designating or pertaining to a group of 17th century English poets, including Donne, Cowley, and others, whose work is characterized by abstruse conceits, extravagances of imagery, etc.—**met-a-phys′i-cal-ly,** *adv.*—**met″a-phy-si′cian** (-fi-zish′ąn), *n.* One versed in metaphysics. —**met-a-phys′ics,** *n.* That branch of philosophy which treats of first principles, including both the science of being (ontology) and the science or theory of knowledge (epistemology), but sometimes restricted to either alone; in general, philosophy, esp. in its more abstruse branches.
met-a-pla-sia (met-ą-plā′ziä), *n.* [NL., < Gr. μεταπλάσσειν, form differently, < μετα- (denoting change) + πλάσσειν, form, mold.] In *physiol.*, transformation of one kind of adult tissue into another kind.
met-a-plasm (met′ą-plazm), *n.* [See *meta-* and *-plasm.*] In *biol.*, the lifeless matter or inclusions (as starch, pigment, etc.) in the protoplasm of a cell.—**met-a-plas′mic** (-plaz′mik), *a.*
met-a-po-di-us (met-ą-pō′di-us), *n.*; pl. *-dii* (-di-ī). [NL., < Gr. μετά, after, + πούς (ποδ-), foot.] A large American heteropterous insect, *Metapodius femoratus* ('thick-thighed metapodius'), of the family *Coreidæ*: abundant in the southern U. S., and an important enemy of the cottonworm and the army-worm.

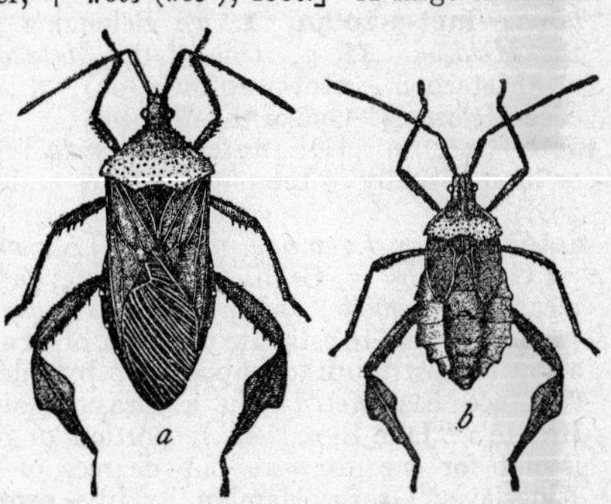

Metapodius (*M. femoratus*). — *a*, adult; *b*, nymph. (Enlarged one fourth.)

met-a-so-ma-tism (met-ą-sō′mą-tizm), *n.* [Gr. μετα- (denoting change) + σῶμα (σωματ-), body.] In *geol.*, the process whereby the chemical constitution of a rock is changed.—**met″a-so-mat′ic** (-sǫ-mat′ik), *a.*—**met″a-so-ma-to′sis** (-sō-mą-tō′sis), *n.* [NL.] Same as *metasomatism.*
me-tas-ta-sis (me-tas′tą-sis), *n.*; pl. *-tases* (-tą-sēz). [LL., < Gr. μετάστασις, < μεθιστάναι, remove, change, < μετα- (denoting change) + ἱστάναι, cause to stand.] A rapid transition, as from one subject to another; also, a transformation; in *physiol.* and *pathol.*, a transference of a fluid, disease, or the like, from one part of the body to another; in *biol.*, metabolism.—**met-a-stat-ic** (met-ą-stat′ik), *a.*
met-a-tar-sal (met-ą-tär′sąl). **I.** *a.* Of or pertaining to the metatarsus. **II.** *n.* A metatarsal bone.
met-a-tar-sus (met-ą-tär′sus), *n.*; pl. *-si* (-sī). [NL.: see *meta-* and *tarsus.*] In *anat.* and *zoöl.*, the part of a foot or hind limb (esp. of its bony structure) included between the tarsus and the toes or phalanges; in birds, a bone composed of both tarsal and metatarsal elements, extending from the tibia to the phalanges.
me-ta-te (mā-tä′tā), *n.* [Sp.; from Mex.] A stone with a flat or concave upper surface, and sometimes with legs beneath, on which corn or

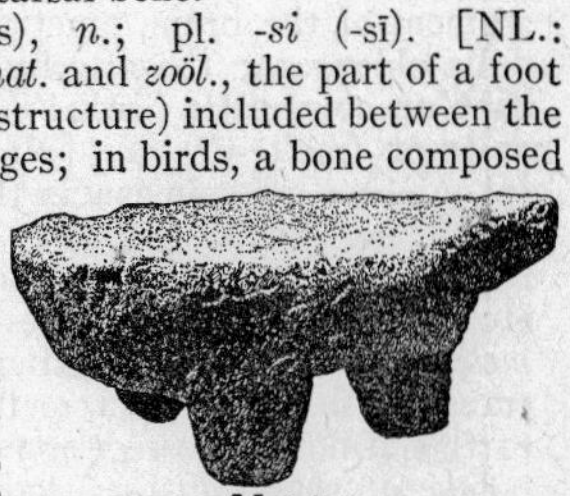

Metate.

the like is ground by hand by means of a smaller stone: used in Mexico and the southwestern U. S.

me-tath-e-sis (me-tath′e-sis), *n.*; pl. *-eses* (-e-sēz). [LL., < Gr. μετάθεσις, < μετατιθέναι, transpose, < μετα- (denoting change) + τιθέναι, set.] Transposition; reversal or change of conditions; specif., in *gram.*, transposition of letters, syllables, or sounds in a word; in *pathol.*, the transference of a morbid substance from one part to another where it will be less harmful; in *chem.*, a double decomposition, as when two compounds react with each other to form two other compounds.—**met-a-thet-ic, met-a-thet-i-cal** (met-ạ-thet′ik, -i-kạl), *a.*

met-a-tho-rax (met-ạ-thō′raks), *n.* [NL.: see *meta-* and *thorax.*] The posterior division of an insect's thorax, bearing the third pair of legs and the second pair of wings.—**met″a-tho-ra′cic** (-thō-ras′ik), *a.*

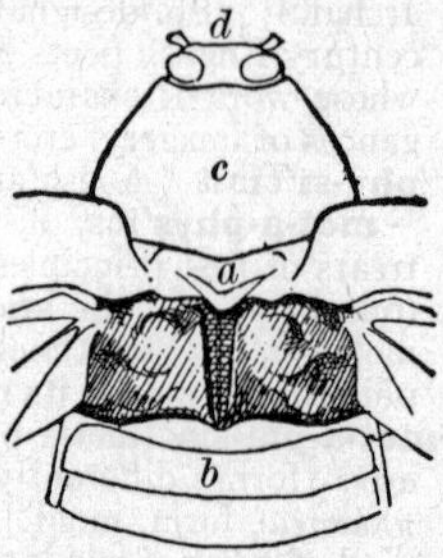

Metathorax, shaded, between mesothorax (*a*) and abdomen (*b*); *c*, prothorax; *d*, head.

mé-tay-age (me-tā′yạj, F. mā-tā-yäzh), *n.* [F.] The métayer system of agriculture.

mé-tay-er (me-tā′yėr, F. mā-tā-yā), *n.* [F., < ML. *medietarius*, < LL. *medietas*, half: see *moiety.*] One who cultivates land for a share of the produce, usually a half, the owner commonly supplying stock, tools, etc.

Met-a-zo-a (met-ạ-zō′ạ̈), *n. pl.* [NL., pl. of *metazoön*, < Gr. μετά, after, + ζῷον, animal.] A large zoölogical division comprising all the animals above the protozoans, or, in other words, those organisms which, although originating from a single cell or ovum, are composed of many cells. Cf. *Protozoa.*—**met-a-zo′an. I.** *a.* Belonging or pertaining to the *Metazoa.* **II.** *n.* One of the *Metazoa.*—**met-a-zo′ic,** *a.* Metazoan.—**met-a-zo′ön** (-on), *n.*; pl. *-zoa* (-zō′ạ̈). [See *Metazoa.*] One of the *Metazoa.*

mete[1] (mēt), *n.* [OF. *mete*, < L. *meta.*] A limiting mark, or limit (usually in the phrase 'metes and bounds'); also, a goal†.

mete[2] (mēt), *v. t.*; *meted, meting.* [AS. *metan* = D. *meten* = G. *messen* = Goth. *mitan*, mete; akin to L. *modus*, measure, E. *mode*, and perhaps to *meter*[3].] To measure (archaic); also, to estimate the value of, or appraise (archaic); also, to distribute or apportion by measure; allot (as, "Chance has *meted* you a measure of happiness": C. Brontë's "Jane Eyre," xix.); portion or deal (*out*: as, "It is not for me to *mete* out degrees of punishment," H. Kingsley's "Geoffry Hamlyn," xvi.).—**mete**[2], *n.* Measure. [Archaic.]

met-em-pir-ic (met-em-pir′ik), *n.* [See *meta-* and *empiric.*] Metempirics; also, a supporter of the metempirical philosophy.—**met-em-pir′i-cal,** *a.* Beyond, or outside of, the field of experience; also, of or pertaining to metempirics.—**met-em-pir′ics,** *n.* The philosophy dealing with things outside of the field of experience.

me-temp-sy-cho-sis (me-temp-si-kō′sis), *n.*; pl. *-choses* (-kō′sēz). [L., < Gr. μετεμψύχωσις, < μετεμψυχοῦν, cause the soul to pass into another body, < μετα- (denoting change) + ἐν, in, + ψυχή, soul.] The passage of the soul from one body to another; usually, the passage or transmigration of the soul at death into another (living) body, either that of a human being or that of an animal.

met-en-ceph-a-lon (met-en-sef′ạ-lon), *n.*; pl. *-la* (-lạ̈). [NL.: see *meta-* and *encephalon.*] In *anat.*, the posterior segment of the brain, practically coextensive with the medulla oblongata; the afterbrain; also, the epencephalon.—**met″en-ce-phal′ic** (-se-fal′ik), *a.*

me-te-or (mē′tẹ-ọr), *n.* [NL. *meteorum*, < Gr. μετέωρον, (pl. μετέωρα, phenomena in the heavens), neut. of μετέωρος, raised, high in air, < μετα- (denoting change) + ἀείρειν, raise.] Any atmospheric phenomenon, as hail, a typhoon, etc. (as, "In starry flake, and pellicle, All day the hoary *meteor* [snow] fell": Whittier's "Snow-Bound"); specif., a transient fiery body (a meteoroid which has entered the earth's atmosphere) seen moving through the sky or air; a bolide or shooting-star; loosely, any meteoroid.—**me-te-or′ic** (-or′ik), *a.* Atmospheric; meteorologic; also, pertaining to or of the nature of a meteor (shooting-star); consisting of meteors (as, a *meteoric* shower); hence, fig., flashing like a meteor; transiently brilliant, or brilliant, swift, and soon ended (as, a *meteoric* statesman; "the *meteoric* course of Charles the Bold," Motley's "Dutch Republic," Introd., vii.); swift or rapid.—**me-te-or′i-cal-ly,** *adv.*

me-te-or-ite (mē′tẹ-ọr-īt), *n.* [From *meteor.*] A mass of stone or metal that has reached the earth from outer space; a fallen meteor; loosely, a meteor or a meteoroid.—**me″te-or-it′ic** (-it′ik), *a.*

Meteorite (Iron).

me-te-or-o-graph (mē′tẹ-ọ-rọ-gráf), *n.* [See *meteor* and *-graph.*] An instrument for automatically recording various meteorological conditions, as of barometric pressure, temperature, etc., at the same time.

me-te-or-oid (mē′tẹ-ọ-roid), *n.* [See *meteor* and *-oid.*] Any of the many small bodies which travel through space and which, when encountering the earth's atmosphere, are heated to luminosity, thus becoming meteors or shooting-stars.

me-te-or-o-lite (mē′tẹ-ọ-rọ-līt), *n.* Same as *meteorite.*

me-te-or-o-log-ic, me-te-or-o-log-i-cal (mē″tẹ-ọ-rọ-loj′ik, -i-kạl), *a.* Pertaining to meteorology, or to phenomena of the atmosphere or weather.—**me″te-or-o-log′i-cal-ly,** *adv.*

me-te-or-ol-o-gist (mē″tẹ-ọ-rol′ọ-jist), *n.* One versed in meteorology.

me-te-or-ol-o-gy (mē″tẹ-ọ-rol′ọ-ji), *n.* [Gr. μετεωρολογία: see *meteor* and *-logy.*] The science dealing with the atmosphere and its phenomena, esp. as relating to weather.

me-te-or-ous (mē′tẹ-ọr-us), *a.* Meteoric: as, "a *meteorous* refulgence" (C. B. Brown's "Wieland," xvi.). [Now rare.]

me-ter[1] (mē′tėr), *n.* [See *mete*[2].] One who metes or measures; also, an instrument that measures, esp. one that automatically measures and records the quantity of gas, water, electricity, or the like, passing through it or actuating it.—**me′ter**[1], *v. t.* To measure by means of a meter.

me-ter[2], **me-tre**[1] (mē′tėr), *n.* [F. *mètre*, < Gr. μέτρον, measure: see *meter*[3].] In the *metric system*, the fundamental unit of length, intended to be, and being very nearly, equal to one ten-millionth of the distance from the equator to the pole measured on a meridian, but actually being equal to the distance between two lines on a platinum-iridium bar preserved at the International Bureau of Weights and Measures, near Paris: equivalent to 39.37 inches.

me-ter[3], **me-tre**[2] (mē′tėr), *n.* [OF. *metre* (F. *mètre*), < L. *metrum*, poetic meter, verse, < Gr. μέτρον, measure, due measure, meter, verse; akin to L. *metiri*, Skt. *mā-*, measure, and perhaps ult. to E. *mete*[2].] Poetic measure; arrangement of words in measured or rhythmic lines or verses; also, a particular form of such arrangement, depending on the kind and number of feet constituting the verse (as, Alcaic *meter*; elegiac *meter*); also, verse or poetry (as, "Those luckless brains, That . . . Indite much *metre* with much pains, And little or no meaning": Cowper's "Ode to Apollo," 3); also, in *music*, the rhythmic element as measured by division into parts of equal time-value.

-meter. [Gr. μέτρον, measure: see *meter*[3].] A noun termination used to form names of instruments for measuring, or ascertaining or recording quantity, extent, degree, etc., as in *altimeter, barometer, chronometer, hodometer, planimeter, rotameter.* Cf. *-metry.*

mete-wand, mete-yard (mēt′wond, -yärd), *n.* [See *mete*[2].] A measuring-stick or yardstick: now chiefly fig. [Archaic.]

meth-ane (meth′ān), *n.* [From *methyl.*] In *chem.*, a colorless, odorless, inflammable gas, CH_4, occurring in the emanations from marshes, petroleum-wells, and volcanoes, and esp. in the fire-damp of coal-mines: the first member of a homologous series of hydrocarbons.—**meth′a-nol** (-ạ-nol or -ạ-nōl), *n.* [See *-ol.*] In *chem.*, methyl alcohol, or wood-alcohol.

me-theg-lin (mẹ-theg′lin), *n.* [W. *meddyglyn.*] A variety of mead (liquor), orig. made in Wales.

met-hem-o-glo-bin, met-hæm-o-glo-bin (met-hem-ọ-glō′-bin or met-hē-mọ-), *n.* [See *meta-.*] In *physiol. chem.*, a brownish compound, a combination of oxygen and hemoglobin, formed in the blood, as by the use of certain drugs.

meth-er (meᴛʜ′ėr), *n.* [Ir. *meadar.*] A square wooden drinking-vessel, formerly in common use in Ireland.

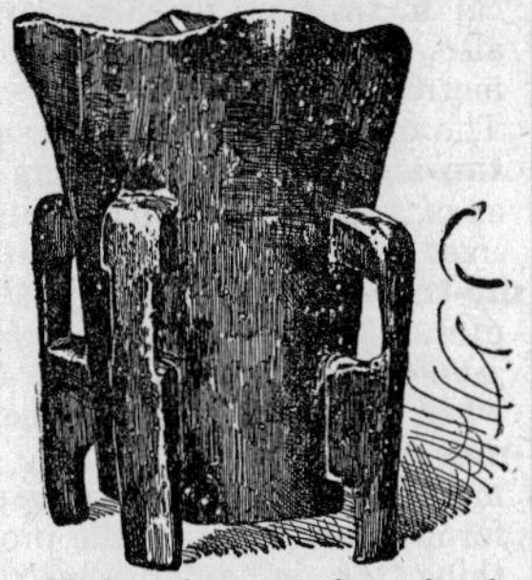

Mether, from specimen in the Museum of the Royal Irish Academy, Dublin, Ireland.

me-thinks (mẹ-thingks′), *v. impers.*; pret. *methought.* [See *think*[1].] It seems to me: as, "The lady doth protest too much, *methinks*" (Shakspere's "Hamlet," iii. 2. 240); "*Methought* I heard a voice cry 'Sleep no more!' " (Shakspere's "Macbeth," ii. 2. 35). [Archaic.]

meth-od (meth′ọd), *n.* [L. *methodus,* mode of procedure, method, < Gr. μέθοδος, a following after, pursuit, method, system, < μετά, after, + ὁδός, way.] A mode of procedure, esp. an orderly or systematic mode (as, a *method* of instruction, of exposition, or of investigation); a way of doing something, esp. in accordance with a definite plan; also, order or system in doing anything (as, to work with *method*); orderly or systematic arrangement (as, "You must not expect either *method* or coherence in what I am going to relate": Smollett's "Humphry Clinker," Oct. 14); plan or design.—**me-thod-ic** (me-thod′ik), *a.* [LL. *methodicus,* < Gr. μεθοδικός.] Methodical.—**me-thod′i-cal,** *a.* Characterized by method; performed, disposed, or acting in a systematic way; systematic; orderly: as, *methodical* procedure; a *methodical* discourse; a *methodical* man.—**me-thod′i-cal-ly,** *adv.*—**me-thod′i-cal-ness,** *n.*

meth-od-ism (meth′ọd-izm), *n.* Adherence or devotion to fixed methods; also [*cap.*], the doctrines, polity, and worship of the Methodist Church.—**meth′od-ist. I.** *n.* One who adheres to or favors fixed methods; one versed in method; also [*cap.*], a member of a Christian denomination which originated in a religious society founded in 1729 by John Wesley (1703–91) and others at Oxford University. **II.** *a.* [*cap.*] Of or pertaining to the Methodists or Methodism.—**Meth-od-is′tic, Meth-od-is′ti-cal,** *a.* Of, like, or suggestive of the Methodists.

meth-od-ize (meth′ọd-īz), *v. t.*; *-ized, -izing.* To reduce to method; arrange with method: as, "I . . . had endeavoured to arrange and *methodise* my ideas upon the subject" (Godwin's "Caleb Williams," xxxi.).—**meth′od-iz-er** (-ī-zėr), *n.*

meth-od-less (meth′ọd-les), *a.* Without method; not methodical or systematic.

meth-od-ol-o-gy (meth-ọ-dol′ọ-ji), *n.*; pl. *-gies* (-jiz). [See *method* and *-logy.*] The science of method; specif., a branch of logic dealing with the application of the principles of that science in the production of knowledge; also, a treatise on method, as in a particular science.

me-thought (mẹ-thôt′). Preterit of *methinks.*

Me-thu-se-lah (me-thū′zẹ-lạ), *n.* [From the Biblical patriarch who lived 969 years: see Gen. v. 27.] One who lives to an extraordinarily great age.

meth-yl (meth′il), *n.* [Gr. μέθυ, wine, + ὕλη, wood.] In *chem.*, a monovalent hydrocarbon radical, CH_3, occurring in methyl alcohol (wood-alcohol), etc.—**methyl alcohol,** in *chem.*, a colorless, inflammable, poisonous liquid compound, CH_3OH, of the alcohol class, obtained by the distillation of wood: used as a fuel, solvent, etc. Also called *wood-alcohol.*—**meth′yl-al** (-i-lal), *n.* In *chem.*, a liquid compound with a pleasant odor, obtained by the oxidation of methyl alcohol: used in medicine.—**meth-yl-am′ine** (-am′in), *n.* In *chem.*, a compound regarded as ammonia in which one or more hydrogen atoms have been replaced by one or more methyl radicals; esp., the compound (a gas with a fishy ammonia-like odor) in which only one hydrogen atom has been so replaced.—**meth′yl-ate** (-i-lāt), *n.* In *chem.*, a methyl alcohol derivative in which the hydrogen of the hydroxyl group has been replaced by a metal.—**meth′yl-ate,** *v. t.*; *-ated, -ating.* To combine with methyl; mix with methyl alcohol (as, *methylated* spirit, ordinary alcohol denatured with methyl alcohol).—**meth′yl-ene** (-i-lēn), *n.* In *chem.*, a bivalent hydrocarbon radical, CH_2, occurring in many compounds.—**me-thyl-ic** (me-thil′ik), *a.* Pertain ing to or containing the radical methyl.

meth-y-lo-sis (meth-i-lō′sis), *n.* [NL., < Gr. μετα- (denoting change) + ὕλη, wood, matter.] In *geol.*, that variety of metamorphism which involves change of chemical substance.

me-tic-u-lous (mẹ-tik′ụ-lus), *a.* [L. *meticulosus,* fearful, < *metus,* fear.] Fearful† or timid†; also, solicitous about minute details, or minutely or finically careful (as, "He had throughout been almost worryingly *meticulous* in his business formalities": Arnold Bennett's "Hilda Lessways," iii. 4).—**me-tic-u-los′i-ty** (-los′i-ti), *n.*—**me-tic′u-lous-ly,** *adv.*

mé-tier (mā-tyā), *n.* [F., < L. *ministerium,* E. *ministry.*] Trade; profession; line of work or activity.

mé-tis (mā-tēs), *n.* [F.: see *mestizo.*] In Canada, a half-breed of white, esp. French, and Indian parentage.—**mé-tisse** (mā-tēs), *n.* [F.] Fem. of *métis.*

me-tœ-cious (me-tē′shus), *a.* [Gr. μετα- (denoting change) + οἶκος, house.] In *bot.*, heterœcious.—**me-tœ′cism** (-sizm), *n.*

met-ol (met′ol or -ōl), *n.* [G.] In *photog.*, a soluble white powder, a cresol derivative, used as a developer.

Me-ton-ic (mẹ-ton′ik), *a.* Of or pertaining to Meton, an Athenian astronomer of the 5th century B.C.: as, the *Metonic* cycle (a cycle of 19 years, after which the new moon recurs on the same day of the year as at the beginning of the cycle).

met-o-nym (met′ọ-nim), *n.* A word used by metonymy.

me-ton-y-my (me-ton′i-mi), *n.* [LL. *metonymia,* < Gr. μετωνυμία, < μετα- (denoting change) + ὄνυμα, name.] In *rhet.*, the use of the name of one thing for that of another which it naturally suggests, as of *scepter* for *sovereignty,* or of *the bottle* for *strong drink.*—**met-o-nym-ic, met-o-nym-i-cal** (met-ọ-nim′ik, -i-kạl), *a.*—**met-o-nym′i-cal-ly,** *adv.*

met-o-pe (met′ọ-pē), *n.* [Gr. μετόπη, < μετά, between, + ὀπή, opening, hole.] In *arch.*, one of the square spaces, either decorated or plain, between triglyphs in the Doric frieze.

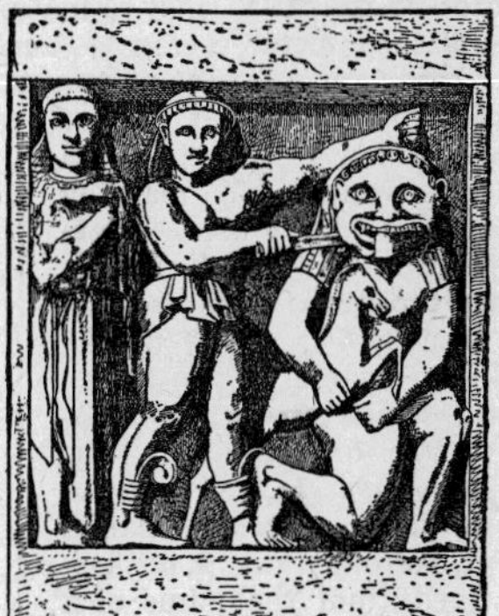

Metope, from Selinus, Sicily (Perseus beheading Medusa).—Museum of Palermo, Sicily.

me-top-ic (me-top′ik), *a.* [Gr. μέτωπον, forehead, < μετά, between, + ὤψ (ὠπ-), eye.] In *anat.*, of or pertaining to the forehead; frontal.

me-tral-gia (mẹ-tral′jiạ), *n.* [NL., < Gr. μήτρα, uterus, + ἄλγος, pain.] In *pathol.*, pain in the uterus.

me-tre[1], **me-tre**[2] (mē′tėr). See *meter*[2], *meter*[3].

met-ric[1] (met′rik), *a.* [F. *métrique,* < *mètre,* E. *meter*[2].] Pertaining to the meter (metre), or to the system of measures and weights based upon it.—**metric system,** a decimal system of measures and weights, of which the meter is the fundamental unit: adopted first in France, but now in general use, esp. for scientific purposes. *For measuring lengths:* 10 millimeters = 1 centimeter; 10 centimeters = 1 decimeter; 10 decimeters = 1 meter (39.37 inches); 10 meters = 1 decameter; 10 decameters = 1 hectometer; 10 hectometers = 1 kilometer; 10 kilometers = 1 myriameter. *For measuring surfaces:* 100 square millimeters = 1 square centimeter; 100 square centimeters = 1 square decimeter; 100 square decimeters = 1 square meter or 1 centiare; 100 square meters, or centiares = 1 square decameter or 1 are (119.6 square yards); 100 square decameters, or ares = 1 square hectometer or 1 hectare; 100 square hectometers, or hectares = 1 square kilometer or 1 myriare; 100 square kilometers, or myriares = 1 square myriameter. *For measuring volumes:* 1000 cubic millimeters = 1 cubic centimeter; 1000 cubic centimeters = 1 cubic decimeter or 1 millistere; 1000 cubic decimeters, or millisteres = 1 cubic meter or 1 stere (35.315 cubic feet); 1000 cubic meters, or steres = 1 cubic decameter or 1 kilostere; 1000 cubic decameters, or kilosteres = 1 cubic hectometer; 1000 cubic hectometers = 1 cubic kilometer; 1000 cubic kilometers = 1 cubic myriameter. (Other measures for volumes are the centistere, or one hundredth of a stere; the decistere, or one tenth of a stere; the decastere, or 10 steres; and the hectostere, or 100 steres.) *For measuring capacities*: 10 milliliters = 1 centiliter; 10 centiliters = 1 deciliter; 10 deciliters = 1 liter (0.908 quart U. S. dry measure, or 1.0567 quarts U. S. liquid measure); 10 liters = 1 decaliter; 10 decaliters = 1 hectoliter; 10 hectoliters = 1 kiloliter; 10 kiloliters = 1 myrialiter. *For measuring weights*: 10 milligrams = 1 centigram; 10 centigrams = 1 decigram; 10 decigrams = 1 gram (15.432 grains); 10 grams = 1 decagram; 10 decagrams = 1 hectogram; 10 hectograms = 1 kilogram; 10 kilograms = 1 myriagram; 10 myriagrams = 1 quintal; 10 quintals = 1 millier, tonneau, or metric ton. For further details and equivalents, see *meter*², *are*², *stere, liter, gram*², and the various other units.—**metric ton,** in the *metric system*, a millier.

met-ric² (met′rik), *a.* [L. *metricus*, < Gr. μετρικός, < μέτρον, E. *meter*³.] Same as *metrical*.—**met′ri-cal,** *a.* Pertaining to measurement; also, pertaining to meter (see *meter*³) or poetic measure; composed in meter or verse. —**met′ri-cal-ly,** *adv.*—**me-tri-cian** (mę-trish′ạn), *n.* One versed in the subject of poetic meters.—**met′rics,** *n.* The science of meter; the art of metrical composition.

met-ri-fy (met′ri-fī), *v. t.*; *-fied, -fying.* [OF. *metrifier*, < ML. *metrificare*, < L. *metrum*, meter, verse, + *facere*, make.] To put into meter; render or compose in verse.—**met″ri-fi-ca′tion** (-fi-kā′shǫn), *n.*—**met′ri-fi-er** (-fī-ėr), *n.*

me-trist (mē′trist or met′rist), *n.* [ML. *metrista*, < L. *metrum*, E. *meter*³.] One versed in the use of poetic meters.

me-tri-tis (mę-trī′tis), *n.* [NL., < Gr. μήτρα, uterus.] In *pathol.*, inflammation of the uterus.

me-trol-o-gy (me-trol′ǫ-ji), *n.*; pl. *-gies* (-jiz). [Gr. μέτρον, measure: see *-logy*.] The science of measures and weights; also, a system of measures.—**met-ro-log-i-cal** (met-rǫ-loj′i-kạl), *n.*

met-ro-ma-ni-a (met-rǫ-mā′ni-ạ̈), *n.* [NL., < Gr. μέτρον, measure, meter, verse, + μανία, E. *mania*.] A mania for writing verse.—**met-ro-ma′ni-ac** (-ak), *n.*

met-ro-nome (met′rǫ-nōm), *n.* [Gr. μέτρον, measure, + νόμος, law.] A mechanical contrivance for marking time, as for music.—**met-ro-nom′ic** (-nom′ik), *a.*

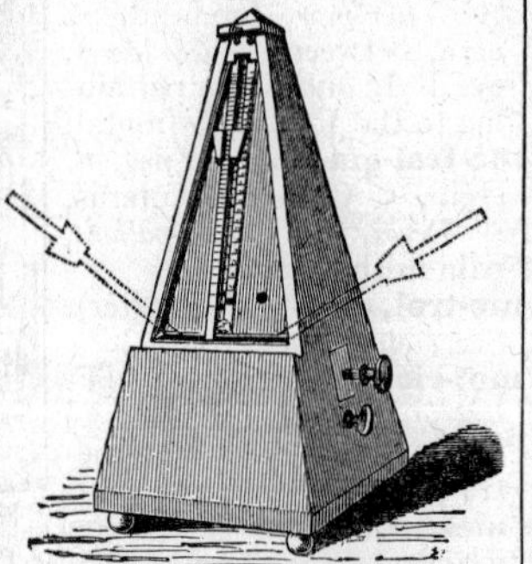

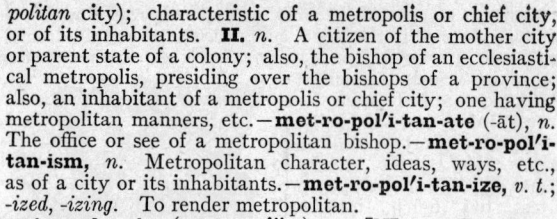

Maelzel's Metronome.
(The dotted lines show the extent of vibration of the pendulum.)

me-tro-nym (mē′trǫ-nim or met′rǫ-), *n.* A metronymic name.

me-tro-nym-ic (mē-trǫ-nim′ik or met-rǫ-). [Gr. μητρωνυμικός, < μήτηρ, mother, + ὄνυμα, name: cf. *patronymic*.] **I.** *a.* Derived from the name of a mother or other female ancestor: as, a *metronymic* name. **II.** *n.* A metronymic name.

met-ro-pole (met′rǫ-pōl), *n.* [F. *métropole*.] A metropolis, now esp. an ecclesiastical metropolis.

me-trop-o-lis (mę-trop′ǫ-lis), *n.*; pl. *-lises.* [LL., < Gr. μητρόπολις, < μήτηρ, mother, + πόλις, city.] The mother city or parent state of an ancient Greek (or other) colony; also, the chief see of an ecclesiastical province; also, the chief city (not necessarily the capital) of a country, state, or region (as, "He had fled northward to the New England *metropolis* [Boston]": Hawthorne's "Blithedale Romance," xxii.); hence, a central or principal point, as of some form of activity (as, a commercial *metropolis*; a *metropolis* of art or music).

met-ro-pol-i-tan (met-rǫ-pol′i-tạn). [LL. *metropolitanus*.] **I.** *a.* Pertaining to or constituting a mother-country (as, "the political connection between the people of the *metropolitan* country and their colonies": Cooper's "Two Admirals," iii.); also, pertaining to an ecclesiastical metropolis (as, a *metropolitan* bishop); also, pertaining to or constituting a metropolis or chief city (as, *metropolitan* police; a *metropolitan* city); characteristic of a metropolis or chief city, or of its inhabitants. **II.** *n.* A citizen of the mother city or parent state of a colony; also, the bishop of an ecclesiastical metropolis, presiding over the bishops of a province; also, an inhabitant of a metropolis or chief city; one having metropolitan manners, etc.—**met-ro-pol′i-tan-ate** (-āt), *n.* The office or see of a metropolitan bishop.—**met-ro-pol′i-tan-ism,** *n.* Metropolitan character, ideas, ways, etc., as of a city or its inhabitants.—**met-ro-pol′i-tan-ize,** *v. t.*; *-ized, -izing.* To render metropolitan.

me-tror-rha-gi-a (mē-trǫ-rā′ji-ạ̈), *n.* [NL., < Gr. μήτρα, uterus, + -ραγία, < ῥηγνύναι, break, burst forth.] In *pathol.*, excessive discharge of blood from the uterus, esp. when not menstrual; uterine hemorrhage.

-metry. [Gr. -μετρία, < -μέτρης, measurer, or -μετρος, measuring, < μέτρον, measure.] A termination used to form nouns denoting the process or art of measuring something, as in *anthropometry, chronometry, nephelometry, planimetry*, sometimes in connection with words in *-meter*.

met-tle (met′l), *n.* [Variant spelling of *metal*.] Metal†; also, the 'material' or 'stuff' of which one is supposed to be made as determining the animating spirit; characteristic disposition or temper (as, to try a man's *mettle*); hence, spirited temper, spirit, or courage (as, "They . . . tell me flatly I am . . . a lad of *mettle*": Shakspere's "1 Henry IV," ii. 4. 13).—**to put one on** (or **upon,** or **to**) **his mettle,** to put one to a test of his mettle, spirit, or courage: as, "A whiff of Celtic hostility in the atmosphere *put him on his mettle*" (G. Meredith's "Diana of the Crossways," ii.).—**met′tled,** *a.* Having mettle; spirited.—**met′tle-some** (-sum), *a.* Full of mettle; spirited.

me-um (mē′um), *pron.* [L.] Mine: used in the phrase 'meum and tuum' (L. *meum et tuum*, mine and thine) as implying rights of property.

mew¹ (mū), *n.* [AS. *mǣw*.] A gull; esp., the common European gull, *Larus canus*; the sea-mew.

mew² (mū), *v. i.* [Imit.] To cry as a cat: as, "Thrice the brinded cat hath *mew'd*" (Shakspere's "Macbeth," iv. 1. 1). —**mew**², *interj.* and *n.* A word representing or imitating the cry of a cat.

mew³ (mū), *v. t.* or *i.* [OF. F. *muer*, < L. *mutare*, change: cf. *molt*.] To shed (feathers); molt. [Archaic.]

mew⁴ (mū), *n.* [OF. F. *mue*, < *muer*, E. *mew*³.] A cage for hawks, esp. while molting; also, a place where fowls were confined for fattening†; also, a place of retirement or concealment.—**mew**⁴, *v. t.* To shut up in or as in a mew; confine; conceal: often with *up*: as, "to *mew* us up here until our lives' end" (Scott's "Quentin Durward," xi.); "The bush . . . In which vaine Braggadocchio was *mewd*" (Spenser's "Faerie Queene," ii. 3. 34).

mewl (mūl), *v. i.* [Imit.] To cry as a young child: as, "The infant, *Mewling* and puking in the nurse's arms" (Shakspere's "As You Like It," ii. 7. 144).

mews (mūz), *n.* [Orig. pl. of *mew*⁴, the royal stables in London being built on the site of mews for hawks.] A set of stables about a court or alley.

Mex-i-can (mek′si-kạn). **I.** *a.* Of or pertaining to Mexico: as, the *Mexican* War (between the United States and Mexico, during 1846–48). **II.** *n.* A native or inhabitant of Mexico.

Me-zen-tian (mę-zen′shiạn), *a.* Pertaining to or suggestive of Mezentius, a legendary Etruscan king who is said to have had living men bound face to face with corpses and then left to die.

me-ze-re-on (mę-zē′rę-ǫn), *n.* [NL.; from Ar.] An old-world thymelæaceous shrub, *Daphne mezereum*, cultivated for its fragrant purplish or pink flowers, which appear in early spring before the foliage; also, mezereum (drug).

me-ze-re-um (mę-zē′rę-um), *n.* [NL.: cf. *mezereon*.] The plant mezereon; in *phar.*, the acrid dried bark of mezereon, used in liniments, and internally as a diuretic, diaphoretic, and alterative.

me-zu-zah (me-zö′zạ̈), *n.*; pl. *-zoth* (-zōth). [Heb., door-post (see Deut. vi. 9, xi. 20).] Among the Jews, a piece of parchment inscribed on one side with the passages Deut. vi. 4–9 and xi. 13–21, and on the other with the word

Flowering Branch of Mezereon.

"Shaddai" (a name applied to God), and so placed in a case that the divine name is visible from the outside, the case being attached to the door-post of a house in fulfilment of the injunction in each of the passages.

mez-za (med′zä), *a.* [It.] Fem. of *mezzo.*

mez-za-nine (mez′ą-nin or -nēn), *n.* [F., < It. *mezzanino*, dim. of *mezzano*, middle, < L. *medianus*, E. *median*².] A low story between two higher stories; an entresol.

mez-zo (mez′ō, It. med′zō), *a.* [It., < L. *medius*, middle.] Middle; medium; half.

mez-zo=ri-lie-vo (med″zō-rē-lyā′vō), *n.*; pl. *-vos* (-vōz). [It.] Middle relief, intermediate between alto-rilievo and bas-relief.

mez-zo=so-pra-no (med″zō-sō-prä′nō), *n.*; pl. *-nos* (-nōz). [It.] In *music*, a voice or voice-part intermediate in compass between soprano and contralto; also, a person having such a voice.

mez-zo-tint (mez′ǫ-tint or med′zǫ-), *n.* [It. *mezzotinto*, half-tint.] A method of engraving on copper or steel by burnishing or scraping away a uniformly roughened surface; also, a print produced by this method.—**mez′zo-tint,** *v. t.* To engrave in mezzotint.—**mez′zo-tint-er,** *n.*—**mez-zo-tin-to** (med-zō-tin′tō), *n.* [It.] Mezzotint.

mho (mō), *n.* [Reversed spelling of *ohm.*] In *elect.*, a unit of conductivity, equal to the conductivity of a body whose resistance is one ohm.

mi (mē), *n.* In *music*, the syllable used for the third tone of the scale (E, in the major scale of C), and sometimes for the tone E. See *sol-fa.*

mi-aow (mi-ou′), *v. i.* [Imit.: cf. *mew*².] To utter the cry of a cat; miaul; mew.—**mi-aow′,** *interj.* and *n.*

mi-asm (mī′azm), *n.* Same as *miasma.*

mi-as-ma (mī-az′mą), *n.*; pl. *-mas* or *-mata* (-mą-tą). [NL., < Gr. μίασμα, pollution, < μιαίνειν, stain, pollute.] Noxious exhalations from putrescent organic matter; poisonous effluvia or germs infecting the atmosphere.—**mi-as′mal, mi-as-mat′ic** (-mat′ik), **mi-as′mic,** *a.*

mi-aul (mi-âl′), *v. i.* [F. *miauler*; imit.] To miaow: as, "a *miauling* kitten" (Scott's "Kenilworth," xxxiii.).

mi-ca (mī′ką), *n.*; pl. *-cas.* [NL. use of L. *mica*, crumb, grain, little bit, prob. with supposition of a connection with L. *micare*, sparkle.] Any of a group of minerals, silicates of aluminium with other bases, that separate readily into thin, tough, often transparent, and usually elastic laminæ.—**mi-ca′ceous** (-kā′shius), *a.* Consisting of, containing, or resembling mica; of or pertaining to mica.

Mi=Ca-rême (mē-kȧ-rãm), *n.* [F. *mi-carême.*] Mid-Lent.

mice (mīs), *n.* Plural of *mouse.*

Mich-ael-mas (mik′ęl-mąs), *n.* [See *-mas.*] A festival celebrated on Sept. 29, in honor of the archangel Michael; hence, Sept. 29 ('Michaelmas Day').—**Michaelmas daisy.** See under *daisy.*

miche (mich), *v.*; *miched, miching.* [ME. *michen, mychen*, pilfer: cf. OF. *muchier, mucier*, hide, skulk.] **I.** *tr.* To pilfer. [Obs. or prov.] **II.** *intr.* To lurk; skulk; sneak; also, to play truant. [Now prov.]—**mich′er,** *n.* A petty thief; also, a sneak; also, a truant (as, "How like a *micher* he stands, as though he had truanted from honesty!" Lyly's "Mother Bombie," i. 3). [Now prov.]

mick (mik), *n.* [From *Mick*, for *Michael*, man's name.] An Irishman. [Slang.]

mick-le (mik′l). [AS. *micel* = OHG. *mihhil* = Icel. *mikill* = Goth. *mikils*, great, much; akin to L. *magnus*, Gr. μέγας, great: cf. *much.*] **I.** *a.* Great; large; much. [Archaic or prov. Eng. and Sc.] **II.** *n.* Size or bigness (now prov. Eng.); also, a large amount (archaic or prov.: as, many a little makes a *mickle*).—**mick′le,** *adv.* Greatly; much. [Now prov.]

mi-cri-fy (mī′kri-fī), *v. t.*; *-fied, -fying.* [Gr. μικρός, small, + E. *-fy* as in *magnify.*] To make small or insignificant.

mi-cro- (mī′krǫ-), **micr-.** Forms of Gr. μικρός, small, used in combination, often in the sense of 'minute,' 'microscopic': in *physics*, etc., used to mean 'one millionth,' as in *microampere* (one millionth of an ampere), *microcoulomb* (one millionth of a coulomb), *microcurie* (one millionth of a curie), *microdyne* (one millionth of a dyne), *microfarad, microgram, microhm, microvolt*, etc. Cf. *macro-* and *meg-.*—**mi′cro=am-pere″** (-am-pãr″), *n.* See *micro-.*—**mi″cro=a-nal′y-sis** (-ą-nal′i-sis), *n.* Analysis by means of the microscope.—**mi-cro-bal′ance** (-bal′ąns), *n.* A delicate balance for weighing one milligram or less.—**mi-cro-bar′o-graph** (-bar′ǫ-gráf), *n.* A barograph for recording minute fluctuations of atmospheric pressure.

mi-crobe (mī′krōb), *n.* [F., < Gr. μικρός, small, + βίος, life.] A microscopic organism, usually one of vegetable nature; a germ; often, a bacterium, esp. one causing disease.—**mi-cro′bi-al** (-krō′bi-ąl), **mi-cro′bic,** *a.* Of, pertaining to, or caused by microbes.—**mi-cro′bi-cide** (-sīd), *n.* [See *-cide.*] An agent that kills microbes.—**mi-cro′bi-ci-dal** (-sī-dąl), *a.*—**mi-cro-bi-ol′o-gy** (-bi-ol′ǫ-ji), *n.* [See *-logy.*] The science which deals with microbes or micro-organisms; bacteriology.—**mi-cro′bi-on** (-on), *n.*; pl. *-bia* (-bi-ä). [NL.] A microbe.

mi-cro-ce-phal-ic (mī″krǫ-se-fal′ik), *a.* [Gr. μικροκέφαλος, < μικρός, small, + κεφαλή, head.] Small-headed; in *craniom.*, having a skull with a small cranial capacity (cf. *mesocephalic* and *megacephalic*); in *pathol.*, having an abnormally small head or skull, as certain idiots. Also **mi-cro-ceph′a-lous** (-sef′ą-lus).—**mi-cro-ceph′a-ly** (-li), *n.*

mi-cro-chem-is-try (mī-krǫ-kem′is-tri), *n.* [See *micro-.*] Chemistry as concerned with minute or microscopic objects or quantities.—**mi-cro-chem′i-cal,** *a.*

mi-cro-cline (mī′krǫ-klīn), *n.* [G. *mikroklin*, < Gr. μικρός, small, + κλίνειν, incline.] A kind of feldspar with the same composition as orthoclase, but belonging to the triclinic system.

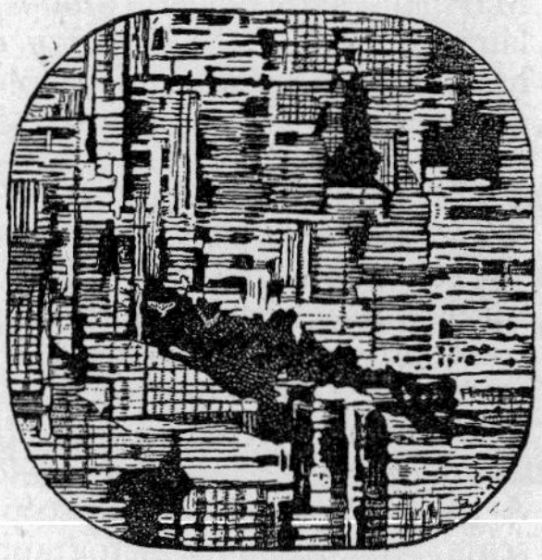

Section of Microcline as seen in polarized light.

mi-cro-coc-cus (mī-krǫ-kok′us), *n.*; pl. *-cocci* (-kok′sī). [NL., < Gr. μικρός, small, + NL. *coccus*: see *coccus.*] Any member of the genus *Micrococcus*, comprising globular or oval bacterial organisms of which certain species cause disease, and others produce fermentation, coloration, etc.

mi-cro-cosm (mī′krǫ-kozm), *n.* [F. *microcosme*, < ML. *microcosmus*, < Gr. μικρός, small, + κόσμος, world.] A little world; anything regarded as a world in miniature; often, man viewed as an epitome of the great world, or universe: opposed to *macrocosm.*—**mi-cro-cos′mic** (-koz′mik), *a.* Of or pertaining to, or of the nature of, a microcosm.—**microcosmic salt,** in *chem.*, a phosphate of sodium and ammonium, orig. obtained from human urine, much used as a blowpipe flux in testing metallic oxides.

mi-cro-cou-lomb (mī′krǫ-kö-lom″), *n.* See *micro-.*

mi-cro-crys-tal (mī-krǫ-kris′tąl), *n.* [See *micro-.*] A minute or microscopic crystal.—**mi-cro-crys′tal-line** (-tą-lin), *a.* Minutely crystalline; composed of microscopic crystals.

mi-cro-cu-rie (mī′krǫ-kū″rē), *n.* See *micro-.*

mi-cro-cyte (mī′krǫ-sīt), *n.* [See *micro-* and *-cyte.*] A minute cell or corpuscle; esp., in *pathol.*, one of the dwarfed or abnormally small red corpuscles of the blood occurring in certain forms of anemia.

mi-cro-dont (mī′krǫ-dont), *a.* [See *micro-* and *-odont.*] Having small or short teeth.

mi-cro-dyne (mī′krǫ-dīn), *n.* See *micro-.*

mi-cro=e-lec-tric (mī″krǫ-ę-lek′trik), *a.* [See *micro-.*] Having electric properties in a very small degree; pertaining to minute electric quantities.

mi-cro-far-ad (mī′krǫ-far″ad), *n.* See *micro-.*

mi-cro-gram, mi-cro-gramme (mī′krǫ-gram), *n.* See *micro-.*

mi-cro-graph (mī′krǫ-gráf), *n.* [See *micro-* and *-graph.*] An instrument for executing extremely minute writing or engraving; also, a photograph or a drawing of an object as seen through a microscope.—**mi-cro-graph′ic** (-graf′ik), *a.* Of or pertaining to micrography, or the writing of very small characters; minutely written; also, pertaining to micrography, or the delineation of microscopic objects.—**mi-crog′ra-phy** (-krog′rą-fi), *n.* [See *-graphy.*] The art or practice of writing in very small characters; also, the description or delineation of microscopic objects; examination or study with the microscope.

mi-crohm (mī′krōm), *n.* See *micro-*.

mi-crol-o-gy (mī-krol′ǫ-ji), *n.* [Gr. μικρολογία, < μικρός, small, + λέγειν, pick, gather.] Attention to small or trifling matters; excessive care for petty details or distinctions.—**mi-cro-log′i-cal** (-krǫ-loj′i-kạl), *a.*

mi-crom-e-ter (mī-krom′e-tėr), *n.* [See *micro-* and *-meter.*] Any of various devices for measuring minute distances, angles, etc., as in connection with a telescope or a microscope.—**mi-crom′e-ter=screw,** *n.* A screw with a very fine thread and a graduated head, used in micrometers, etc. —**mi-cro-met′ric, mi-cro-met′ri-cal** (-krǫ-met′rik, -ri-kạl), *a.* Of, pertaining to, or made with the micrometer. —**mi-cro-met′ri-cal-ly,** *adv.*—**mi-crom′e-try,** *n.* [See *-metry.*] The method or art of measuring with a micrometer.

mi-cro-mil-li-me-ter, mi-cro-mil-li-me-tre (mī-krǫ-mil′i-mē-tėr), *n.* [See *micro-.*] The millionth part of a millimeter; also, sometimes, a micron.

mi-cron (mī′kron), *n.* [NL., < Gr. μικρόν, neut. of μικρός, small.] The millionth part of a meter. Symbol *μ.*

Mi-cro-ne-sian (mī-krǫ-nē′shiạn or -zhiạn). [From *Micronesia,* < Gr. μικρός, small, + νῆσος, island.] **I.** *a.* Of or pertaining to Micronesia (a collection of small islands in the western Pacific, including the Caroline, Mariana or Ladrone, Marshall, and Gilbert groups), its inhabitants, or their languages. **II.** *n.* A native of Micronesia, which is inhabited by a mixture of peoples, chiefly Polynesian; also, any of the (Malayo-Polynesian) languages or dialects spoken there.

mi-cro=or-gan-ism (mī-krǫ-ôr′gạn-izm), *n.* [See *micro-.*] A microscopic (animal or vegetable) organism.

mi-cro-phone (mī′krǫ-fōn), *n.* [See *micro-* and *-phone.*] An instrument or device for augmenting small sounds or for transmitting sounds; a transmitter, as of a radiobroadcasting apparatus.—**mi-cro-phon′ic** (-fon′ik), *a.* Pertaining to a microphone; serving to intensify small sounds.

mi-cro-pho-to-graph (mī-krǫ-fō′tǫ-grȧf), *n.* [See *micro-.*] A photograph of a macroscopic object on a microscopic scale; also, a photomicrograph.—**mi″cro-pho-tog′ra-phy** (-fǫ-tog′rạ-fi), *n.*

mi-cro-phys-ics (mī-krǫ-fiz′iks), *n.* [See *micro-.*] Physics as concerned with minute masses or the ultimate particles and structure of matter.—**mi-cro-phys′i-cal,** *a.*

mi-cro-phyte (mī′krǫ-fīt), *n.* [See *micro-* and *-phyte.*] A microscopic plant, esp. a bacterium.—**mi-cro-phyt′ic** (-fit′ik), *a.*

mi-crop-ter-ous (mī-krop′tẹ-rus), *a.* [Gr. μικρόπτερος, < μικρός, small, + πτερόν, wing.] In *zoöl.*, having small wings or fins.—**mi-crop′ter-ism,** *n.*

mi-cro-pyle (mī′krǫ-pīl), *n.* [F., < Gr. μικρός, small, + πύλη, gate, orifice.] In *bot.*, the minute orifice or opening in the integuments of an ovule; in *zoöl.*, any minute opening in the coverings of an ovum, through which spermatozoa may gain access to the interior.—**mi′cro-py-lar** (-pī-lạ̈r), *a.*

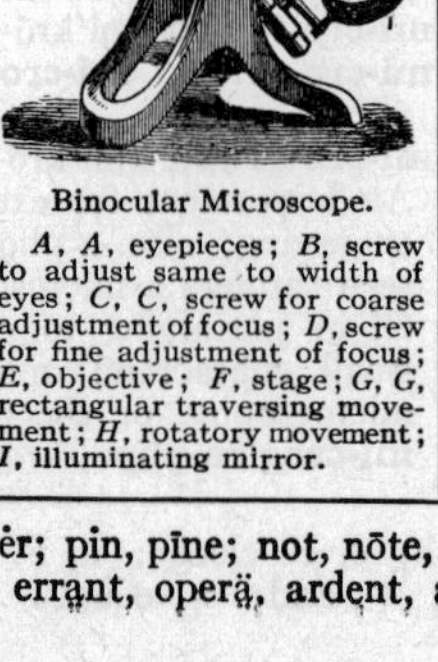

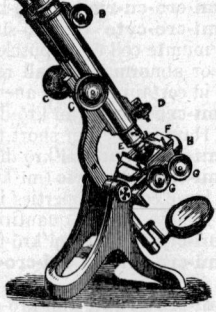

Binocular Microscope.

A, A, eyepieces; *B,* screw to adjust same to width of eyes; *C, C,* screw for coarse adjustment of focus; *D,* screw for fine adjustment of focus; *E,* objective; *F,* stage; *G, G,* rectangular traversing movement; *H,* rotatory movement; *I,* illuminating mirror.

mi-cro-scope (mī′krǫ-skōp), *n.* [NL. *microscopium,* < Gr. μικρός, small, + σκοπεῖν, view.] An optical instrument having a lens or a combination of lenses for magnifying for inspection objects too small to be seen, or to be seen distinctly and in detail, by the naked eye.—**mi′cro-scope,** *v. t.*; *-scoped, -scoping.* To examine with or as with a microscope; magnify.—**mi-cro-scop′ic** (-skop′ik), *a.* Of or pertaining to the microscope or its use; fig., suggestive of the use of the microscope (as, *microscopic* inquiry; *microscopic* exactness); also, performing the work of a microscope (often fig.: as, "Wilhelmus Kieft . . . was a great legislator on a small scale, and had a *microscopic* eye in public affairs," Irving's "Knickerbocker's New York," iv. 8); also, so small as to be invisible or indistinct without the use of the microscope; minute; in general, very small; tiny. Also **mi-cro-scop′i-cal.**—**mi-cro-scop′i-cal-ly,** *adv.*—**mi-cros′co-pist** (-kros′kǫ-pist), *n.* One versed in microscopy.—**mi-cros′co-py,** *n.* The use of the microscope; microscopic investigation.

mi-cro-seism (mī′krǫ-sīsm or -sīzm), *n.* [Gr. μικρός, small, + σεισμός, earthquake.] A very slight earthquake-tremor. —**mi-cro-seis′mic** (-sīs′mik or -sīz′mik), *a.*—**mi-cro-seis′mo-graph** (-mǫ-grȧf), *n.* [See *-graph.*] An instrument for recording very slight earthquake-tremors.

mi-cro-some (mī′krǫ-sōm), *n.* [NL. *microsoma,* < Gr. μικρός, small, + σῶμα, body.] In *biol.*, one of the minute granules in the protoplasm of animal and plant cells.

mi-cro-spec-tro-scope (mī-krǫ-spek′trǫ-skōp), *n.* [See *micro-.*] A combination of the microscope and the spectroscope, for the examination of minute traces of substances. —**mi″cro-spec-tro-scop′ic** (-skop′ik), *a.*

mi-cro-spo-ran-gi-um (mī″krǫ-spǫ-ran′ji-um), *n.*; pl. *-gia* (-ji-ạ̈). [NL.: see *micro-* and *sporangium.*] In *bot.*, a sporangium containing microspores.

mi-cro-spore (mī′krǫ-spōr), *n.* [See *micro-* and *spore.*] In *bot.*, one of the smaller of the two kinds of reproductive bodies or spores produced asexually by certain plants, as a single pollen-grain of a seed-bearing plant.

mi-cro-spo-ro-phyl, mi-cro-spo-ro-phyll (mī-krǫ-spō′rǫ-fil), *n.* [See *micro-* and *sporophyl.*] In *bot.*, a sporophyl bearing microsporangia.

mi-cro-struc-ture (mī′krǫ-struk-ṭūr), *n.* [See *micro-.*] Microscopic structure.

mi-cro-ther-mom-e-ter (mī″krǫ-thėr-mom′e-tėr), *n.* [See *micro-.*] A thermometer for measuring minute variations of temperature.

mi-cro-tome (mī′krǫ-tōm), *n.* [See *micro-* and *-tome.*] An instrument for cutting very thin sections, as of organic tissue, for microscopic examination.—**mi-cro-tom′ic, mi-cro-tom′i-cal** (-tom′ik, -i-kạl), *a.* Pertaining to the microtome or to microtomy.—**mi-crot′o-my** (-krot′ǫ-mi), *n.* [See *-tomy.*] The cutting of very thin sections, as with the microtome.—**mi-crot′o-mist,** *n.*

mi-cro-volt (mī′krǫ-vōlt), *n.* See *micro-*.

mi-cro-wave (mī′krǫ-wāv), *n.* [See *micro-.*] An extremely short electric wave.

mi-cro-zo-ön (mī-krǫ-zō′on), *n.*; pl. *-zoa* (-zō′ạ̈). [NL., < Gr. μικρός, small, + ζῷον, animal.] A microscopic animal, esp. a protozoan.—**mi-cro-zo′an,** *a.* and *n.*

mi-cro-zyme (mī′krǫ-zīm), *n.* [NL. *microzyma,* < Gr. μικρός, small, + ζύμη, leaven.] Any micro-organism supposed to act like a ferment in producing disease. [Rare.]

mic-tu-rate (mik′ṭū-rāt), *v. i.*; *-rated, -rating.* [Irreg. < L. *micturire,* desiderative of *mingere,* urinate.] To pass urine; urinate.—**mic-tu-ri′tion** (-rish′ǫn), *n.* The desire to urinate; morbidly frequent urination; also (but incorrectly), the act of passing urine.

mid[1], **'mid** (mid), *prep.* Amid: as, "*'mid* pleasures and palaces though we may roam" (J. H. Payne's "Home, Sweet Home"). [Poetic.]

mid[2] (mid). [AS. *midd* = OHG. *mitti* = Icel. *midhr* = Goth. *midjis,* middle; akin to L. *medius,* Gr. μέσος, Skt. *madhya,* middle.] **I.** *a.* At or near its middle point (as, "the *mid* sea," Milton's "Paradise Lost," vii. 403; "in *mid* air," Cowper's "Hope," 353; in *mid*-channel; at *mid*night); also, occupying a middle place or position (as, "the *mid* days of autumn," Keats's "Isabella," xxxii.; in the *mid*-nineties of the last century; the *mid*rib of a leaf): now usually joined to its noun with a hyphen, or written with it, without a hyphen, in certain established compounds, and sometimes combined with an adjective (as in *mid-monthly* and *mid-Victorian*). **II.** *n.* The middle: as, "the *mid* of night" (Shakspere's "Richard III.," v. 3. 77). [Archaic or prov.]

Mi-das (mī′dạs), *n.* [From *Midas,* mythical king of Phrygia, whose touch turned everything to gold, but who was given ass's ears by Apollo for deciding against Apollo in a musical contest with Pan.] A man of great wealth or great money-making ability: often implying want of esthetic perception or appreciation.

mid-brain (mid′brān), *n.* The mesencephalon.

mid-day (mid′dā), *n.* The middle of the day; noon.

mid-den (mid′n), *n.* [From Scand.] A dunghill or refuse-heap (archaic or prov.); also, a kitchen-midden.

mid-dle (mid′l), *a.* [AS. *middel* = D. *middel* = G. *mittel*, middle; from the adj. represented by E. *mid*².] Equally distant from extremes or limits (as, the *middle* point of a line); hence, intervening or intermediate (as, the *middle* distance: see phrase below); also, medium (as, a man of *middle* size); also, at or near its middle (now rare: as, "the holy cloud of incense . . . which had risen into the *middle* dome," Hawthorne's "Marble Faun," xxxix.; *middle* summer); also, specif., of a period in the history of a language, intermediate between periods classified respectively as old (or late) and as new or modern (as, *Middle* English, *Middle* French, *Middle* High German, *Middle* Low German, *Middle* Greek, and *Middle* Latin: see *English, French, German, Greek,* and *Latin*); in *gram.*, intermediate between active and passive, as a voice of Greek verbs which represents the subject as acting on or for itself; in *geol.*, noting the intermediate principal division (that between the upper and lower divisions) of a period, system, or the like (as, the *Middle* Devonian, *Middle* Cambrian, etc.).—**middle age,** the period of life between youth, or the earlier period of adult life, and old age: as, "He was past youth, but had not reached *middle age*; perhaps he might be thirty-five" (C. Brontë's "Jane Eyre," xii.). See *middle-aged.*—**middle ages.** See *ages in history*, under *age, n.*—**middle class,** an intermediate class; esp., the class of the people intermediate between the classes of higher and lower social rank or standing; in Great Britain, the class socially and conventionally intermediate between the aristocratic class and the laboring class.—**middle distance,** in *painting*, etc., the space intermediate between the foreground and the background or distance. Also called *middle ground.*—**middle ear,** in *anat.*, the tympanum.—**middle passage,** the passage across the Atlantic Ocean formerly made by ships carrying slaves from the west coast of Africa to the West Indies or America: as, "the horrors of the *Middle Passage*, and the terrible mortality that attended it" (Lecky's "Hist. of Eng. in the 18th Century," xxiii.); "The term *Middle Passage* arose from the fact that each slaving voyage was made up of three passages—the passage from the home port to the slave coast, the passage from the slave coast to the market, and the passage from that market back to the home port—say, Newport or Liverpool. It was during the middle of the three passages that the slaves were on board" (J. R. Spears's "American Slave-Trade," vi.).—**middle term,** in *logic*, that term of a categorical syllogism with which the two other terms are separately compared, and by means of which they are brought together in the conclusion; that term of a syllogism which appears twice in the premises, but is eliminated from the conclusion.—**mid′dle,** *n.* The point, part, etc., equidistant from extremes or limits; specif., the waist, or middle part of the human body (as, "a long wig that reaches down to his *middle*": Addison, in "Spectator," 407); also, something intermediate; a mean; in *journalism*, an extended article on some social, literary, or other subject, such as in certain English journals occupies a position between the leading articles and the reviews (a British use).

mid-dle=aged (mid′l-ājd′), *a.* Intermediate in age between youth, or the earlier period of adult life, and old age; commonly, from about 40 to about 50 years old; also, characteristic of or suitable for middle-aged people (as, "I bought her a pretty, neat, *middle-aged* cap": Mrs. Gaskell's "Cranford," ix.).

mid-dle=class (mid′l-klås′), *a.* Belonging or pertaining to or characteristic of a middle class, esp., the social middle class; bourgeois: as, "She was the most obnoxious variety of snob: the *middle-class* woman who has married into the fringe of society" (L. Merrick's "Conrad in Quest of His Youth," iii.).

mid-dle-man (mid′l-man), *n.*; pl. *-men.* One who acts as an intermediary between others; esp., a trader intermediate between the producer and the consumer.

mid-dle=man (mid′l-man), *n.* A man in the middle of a row or line; esp., in a minstrel-troupe, the interlocutor.

mid-dle-most (mid′l-mōst), *a. superl.* Being in the very middle; midmost; middle.

mid-dle=weight (mid′l-wāt), *n.* One of average weight; esp., a boxer or other contestant intermediate in weight between a heavy-weight and a light-weight (or a welter-weight).

mid-dling (mid′ling). **I.** *a.* Medium in size, quality, grade, rank, etc.; moderately large, good, etc.; sometimes, in fairly good health, or not in good health yet not very ill (colloq. or prov.: as, "The children's *middlin'*, — Doctor Merrill ses he thinks they've got past the wust on 't," Mrs. Stowe's "Oldtown Folks," xliii.). **II.** *n. Pl.*, any of various products or commodities of intermediate quality, grade, etc., as the coarser particles of ground wheat mingled with bran.—**mid′dling,** *adv.* Moderately; fairly: as, "a *middling* good anvil" (Defoe's "Robinson Crusoe," ii. 5); "She worked me *middling* hard" (Mark Twain's "Huckleberry Finn," i.). [Colloq. or prov.]—**mid′dling-ly,** *adv.*

mid-dy (mid′i), *n.*; pl. *middies* (-iz). A midshipman. [Colloq.]—**middy blouse,** a loose blouse with a sailor collar, and often extending below the waist-line to terminate in a broad band or fold, worn by children, young girls, etc.

midge (mij), *n.* [AS. *mycg* = D. *mug* = G. *mücke*, midge.] Any of numerous small or minute dipterous insects, esp. species of the family *Chironomidæ*, certain of which are extremely troublesome on account of their bites; a gnat; fig., a small or diminutive person (as, "that *midge* of a governess": C. Brontë's "Jane Eyre," xxxvi.).

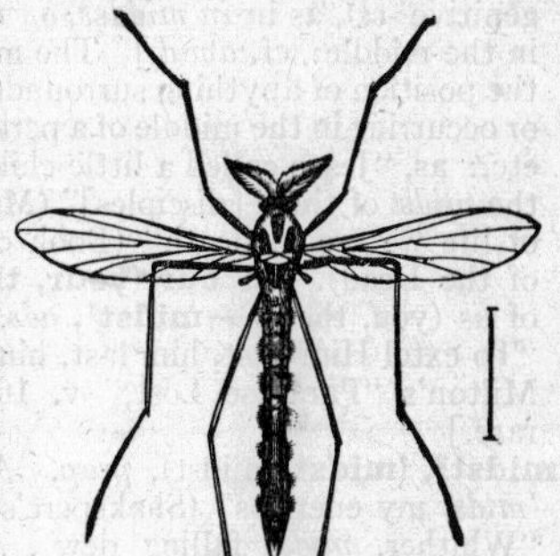

Midge (*Chironomus plumosus*). (Vertical line shows natural size.)

midg-et (mij′et), *n.* [Dim. of *midge.*] Something very small of its kind; esp., a very small person (as, "Parson Kendall's a little *midget* of a man": Mrs. Stowe's "Oldtown Folks," xvi.).

mid=gut (mid′gut), *n.* The middle part of the alimentary canal; specif., the mesenteron.

mid=heav-en (mid′hev′n), *n.* The middle of the sky; the midst of heaven; in *astron.*, the meridian of a place.

Mi-di (mē-dē), *n.* [F. *midi*, midday, noon, the south, < L. *medius*, middle, + *dies*, day.] The south; esp., the south of France.

mi-di-nette (mē-dē-net), *n.* [F., < *midi*, noon: see *Midi.*] One of the class of working-girls seen coming out at noon (the lunch-hour) from the business establishments of Paris.

mid=i-ron (mid′ī″ėrn), *n.* In *golf*, an iron whose face has a medium degree of slope. See *iron, n.*

mid-land (mid′land). **I.** *n.* The middle or interior part of a country; *pl.*, inland regions. **II.** *a.* In or of the midland; inland; also, surrounded by land, or mediterranean (as, the *Midland* Sea, the Mediterranean Sea).

Mid=Lent (mid′lent′), *n.* The middle of Lent.

mid-most (mid′mōst), *a. superl.* Being in the very middle; middlemost; middle; also, at or near its middle point (chiefly poetic).—**mid′most. I.** *adv.* In the midmost part; in the midst. **II.** *prep.* In the midst of: as, "*midmost* the hall" (W. Morris's "Jason," vi. 489).

mid-night (mid′nīt). [AS. *midniht.*] **I.** *n.* The middle of the night; 12 o'clock at night. **II.** *a.* Of or pertaining to midnight; also, resembling midnight, as in darkness.—**midnight oil,** oil burned in a lamp at midnight: used chiefly in the phrase 'to burn the midnight oil' (to study or work at midnight or far into the night).—**midnight sun,** the sun visible at midnight in arctic and antarctic regions.—**mid′night-ly. I.** *a.* Occurring at midnight or every midnight. **II.** *adv.* At midnight; every midnight.

mid=noon (mid′nön′), *n.* Midday; noon: as, "the deep *midnoon*" (Tennyson's "Œnone," 90).

mid=o-cean (mid′ō′shạn), *n.* The middle of the ocean.

mid-rash (mid′rash), *n.*; pl. *midrashim* (mid-rash′im). [Heb.] In *Jewish lit.*, an exposition of the Scriptures or a part of them; esp. [*cap.*], the whole body of traditional

Scriptural exegesis, partly of a legal nature ('Midrash Halakah'), but mostly of a homiletic character ('Midrash Haggadah'). Cf. *halakah* and *haggadah*.

mid-rib (mid'rib), *n.* In *bot.*, the central or middle rib of a leaf.

mid-riff (mid'rif), *n.* [AS. *midhrif*, < *midd*, mid, + *hrif*, belly.] The diaphragm (in the body).

mid-ship (mid'ship), *a.* In or belonging to the middle part of a ship.

mid-ship-man (mid'ship-man), *n.*; pl. *-men.* [So called from his place of duty aboard ship in former times.] Formerly, in the British navy, one of a class of boys or young men (usually of good family) who had various duties, such as carrying messages between officers, and who formed material from which officers were made; now, in the British navy, an officer of the rank held by young men on leaving the government naval schools; in the U. S. navy, one of the rank held by young men while attending, and before graduation from, the Naval Academy at Annapolis (the rank after graduation being that of *ensign*).

mid-ships (mid'ships), *adv.* Amidships.

midst[1] (midst), *n.* [ME. *middest*, for *middes* (with adverbial genitive *-es*), as in *in middes, on middes*, for AS. *on middan*, in the middle: cf. *amid.*] The middle point, part, or stage; the position of anything surrounded by other things or parts, or occurring in the middle of a period of time, course of action, etc.: as, "Jesus called a little child unto him, and set him in the *midst* of them [disciples]" (Mat. xviii. 2); "In the *midst* of life we are in death" (Book of Common Prayer, Burial of the Dead).—**in our (your, their) midst,** in the midst of us (you, them).—**midst**[1], *adv.* In the middle place (as, "To extol Him first, him last, him *midst*, and without end": Milton's "Paradise Lost," v. 165); in the midst. [Now rare.]

midst[2], **'midst** (midst), *prep.* Amidst: as, "They left me *'midst* my enemies" (Shakspere's "1 Henry VI.," i. 2. 24); "Whither, *midst* falling dew . . . dost thou pursue Thy solitary way?" (Bryant's "To a Waterfowl"). [Poetic.]

mid-stream (mid'strēm'), *n.* The middle of the stream.

mid-sum-mer (mid'sum''ėr or mid'sum'ėr), *n.* The middle of summer; in British usage, the period of the summer solstice, about June 21.—**Midsummer Day,** in England, June 24, one of the quarter-days.—**midsummer madness,** the height of madness: as, "Why, this is very *midsummer madness*" (Shakspere's "Twelfth Night," iii. 4. 61).

mid=Vic-to-ri-an (mid-vik-tō'ri-an). **I.** *a.* Of, pertaining to, or characteristic of the middle portion of the reign or period of Queen Victoria (reigned 1837–1901) in England: as, *mid-Victorian* writers, literature, art, or ideas; "The lawn . . . was . . . of a pretty *mid-Victorian* irregularity as regards shape" (Arnold Bennett's "Helen with the High Hand," xiv.). **II.** *n.* A person, as a writer, belonging to the mid-Victorian time; also, a person of mid-Victorian ideas, tastes, etc.

mid-way (mid'wā). **I.** *n.* The middle of the way or distance† (as, "an inn in the *midway* between Mile-end and Wapping": Godwin's "Caleb Williams," xxxiv.); also, a medium, or a middle course (now rare: as, "No *midway* 'Twixt these extremes at all," Shakspere's "Antony and Cleopatra," iii. 4. 19); also, a place or part situated midway (as, the *Midway*, or, in full, Midway Plaisance, a part of the exhibition park at the World's Fair at Chicago, in 1893, devoted to amusements of various kinds); hence, a place for side-shows and other amusements at any fair or the like. **II.** *a.* Situated in the middle of the way or distance; occupying a middle place or position: as, "a *midway* position" (George Eliot's "Adam Bede," xviii.); "the *midway* region" (J. H. Newman's "Callista," xxix.).—**mid-way** (mid'wā or mid-wā'), *adv.* In or to the middle of the way or distance; half-way: as, "*Midway* between the hill . . . and the city lay the ravine" (J. H. Newman's "Callista," xx.).

mid-week (mid'wēk). **I.** *n.* The middle of the week; [*cap.*] among the Quakers, Wednesday. **II.** *a.* Occurring in the middle of the week.

mid-wife (mid'wīf), *n.*; pl. *-wives* (-wīvz). [ME., prob. < AS. *mid*, with, + *wīf*, woman.] A woman who assists women in childbirth; an accoucheuse; fig., one who helps to bring anything into existence or to light (as, "So, Green, thou art the *midwife* to my woe," Shakspere's "Richard II.," ii. 2. 62: cf. *maieutic*).—**mid'wife''ry** (-wīf''ri or -wif-ri), *n.* The art or practice of assisting women in childbirth; obstetrics. Also fig.

mid-win-ter (mid'win''tėr or mid'win'tėr), *n.* The middle of winter; in British usage, the period of the winter solstice, about Dec. 22.

mid-year (mid'yēr), *n.* The middle of the year.

mien (mēn), *n.* [Cf. obs. *demean*, demeanor, and F. *mine*, aspect, look, air.] Air, bearing, or aspect, as showing character, feeling, etc.: as, a man of noble *mien*; "His *mien* was firm and erect" (Marryat's "King's Own," liii.); "Vice is a monster of so frightful *mien*, As, to be hated, needs but to be seen" (Pope's "Essay on Man," ii. 217).

miff (mif), *n.* [Origin obscure: cf. G. *muff*, sullenness.] A fit of petulant displeasure (as, "At the stare of the vulgar she took a *miff*": Hood's "Miss Kilmansegg," 1637); also, a petty quarrel (as, "when a little quarrel, or *miff*, as it is vulgarly called, arose between them": Fielding's "Tom Jones," iii. 6). [Colloq.]—**miff,** *v.* **I.** *intr.* To take offense; have a petty quarrel. [Colloq.] **II.** *tr.* To give offense to; offend. [Colloq.]—**miff'y,** *a.* Quick to take offense; touchy. [Colloq.]

might[1] (mīt). Preterit of *may*[1].

might[2] (mīt), *n.* [AS. *miht, meaht*, = D. and G. *macht* = Goth. *mahts*, might; from the root of E. *may*[1].] Power to do or accomplish, or ability (as, to work, run, or shout with all one's *might*; "To the measure of his *might* Each fashions his desires," Wordsworth's "Rob Roy's Grave," 47); effective power or force of any kind (as, the *might* of intellect, or of public opinion; "the *might* of gravitation," Pope's "Dunciad," ii. 318); efficacy, virtue, or potency, as of remedies, spells, oaths, etc. (archaic); bodily strength (as, "Samson, with *might* endued Above the sons of men": Milton's "Samson Agonistes," 1293); also, great or extraordinary power or strength (as, "men of *might*," 1 Chron. xii. 8; "Praise the Lord of *might*," Tobit, xiii. 6); powerful influence, agencies, resources, etc. (as, "The *might* of the Gentile, unsmote by the sword, Hath melted like snow in the glance of the Lord!" Byron's "Destruction of Sennacherib," vi.); also, superior power or strength serving for compulsion or control (often opposed to *right*: as, the doctrine that *might* makes right). —**with might and main,** with all the power or strength possessed; with great force or vigor: as, "They fell to work and belabored each other *with might and main*" (Irving's "Captain Bonneville," vii.).—**might'i-ly,** *adv.* In a mighty manner; powerfully; vigorously; also, to a great extent or degree, or very much (as, to be *mightily* pleased).—**might'i-ness,** *n.* The state of being mighty; also [usually *cap.*], with *your*, *his*, etc., and often preceded by *high*, a title of dignity (now rare or ironical).—**might'less,** *a.* Without might; powerless; impotent.—**might'y.** [AS. *mihtig.*] **I.** *a.*; compar. *mightier*, superl. *mightiest.* Possessing, characterized by, or showing might or power (as, *mighty* rulers or forces; *mighty* works); potent or strong, as remedies, liquors, spells, etc.; having, showing, or requiring great bodily strength, as persons, the arm, blows, efforts, etc.; also, of great size, or huge (as, a *mighty* rock; a *mighty* bowl); great in amount, extent, degree, or importance (as, a *mighty* concourse of people; "a *mighty* famine," Luke, xv. 14; "What was her *mighty* need of blessing or forgiveness?" Howells's "Chance Acquaintance," v.: now chiefly colloq.). **II.** *n.*; pl. *-ies* (-iz). A mighty or powerful person: as, "Eleazar . . . who was one of the three *mighties*" (1 Chron. xi. 12). [Archaic.]—**might'y,** *adv.* To a great extent or degree; exceedingly; very: as, a *mighty* long time; "a *mighty* good sort of a woman" (Smollett's "Humphry Clinker," Oct. 26). [Now colloq.]

mi-gnon (mē-nyôn). [F.; origin uncertain: cf. *minion.*] **I.** *a.* Small and pretty; delicately pretty. **II.** *n.* A darling (often used of a child, young girl, or woman); also, a favorite, as of a prince (as, "These worthless *mignons* applauded their weak master to the echo": Motley's "Dutch Republic," vi. 6).

mi-gnon-ette (min-yon-et'), *n.* [F. *mignonnette*, dim. of *mignon*: see *mignon.*] A plant, *Reseda odorata*, common in gardens, having racemes of small, fragrant, greenish-white flowers with prominent reddish-yellow or brownish anthers;

any species of *Reseda*; also, a soft grayish-green color; reseda.

mi-gnonne (mē-nyon), *a.* and *n.* [F.] Fem. of *mignon.*

mi-graine (mi-grān′, F. mē-grăn), *n.* [F.: see *megrim.*] Same as *hemicrania.*

mi-grant (mī′grant). **I.** *a.* Migrating; migratory. **II.** *n.* One who or that which migrates, as a migratory bird.

mi-grate (mī′grāt), *v. i.*; *-grated, -grating.* [L. *migratus,* pp. of *migrare,* migrate.] To move from one place to another, travel, or go (as, "those truly homebred and genuine sons of the soil who have never *migrated* beyond the sound of Bow-bells": Irving's "Sketch-Book," John Bull); esp., to go from one country, region, or place of abode to settle in another, as bodies of persons, or sometimes individuals; go to a new habitat, as animals; specif., to pass periodically from one region to another, as certain birds and fishes.—**mi-gra′tion** (-grā′shon), *n.* [L. *migratio(n-)*.] The act of migrating; a migratory movement (as, "those almighty instincts that propel the *migrations* of the swallow and the lemming": De Quincey's "Revolt of the Tartars"); also, a number or body of persons or animals migrating together.—**migration of ions,** in *physical chem.*, the movement of ions toward one or the other of the electrodes during electrolysis.—**mi′gra-tor** (-grā-tor), *n.*—**mi′gra-to-ry** (-gra-tō-ri), *a.* Migrating; hence, roving or nomad; also, pertaining to a migration.

mi-ka-do (mi-kä′dō), *n.*; pl. *-dos* (-dōz). [Jap., lit. 'exalted gate.'] [Often *cap.*] A title of the emperor of Japan.

mike (mīk), *n.* In *radio,* short for *microphone.* [Colloq.]

mi′kron, *n.* See *micron.*

mil (mil), *n.* [L. *mille,* thousand.] A unit of length equal to .001 of an inch, used in measuring the diameter of wires; also, in *phar.*, a milliliter (.001 of a liter), or cubic centimeter.

mi-la-di, mi-la-dy (mi-lā′di). A Continental rendering of the English *my lady,* used in speaking to or of an English lady. Cf. *milord.*

mil′age, *n.* See *mileage.*

milch (milch), *a.* [ME. *milche, mielch;* akin to E. *milk.*] Giving milk: said of cows, goats, etc.—**milch′er,** *n.* A milch animal, as a cow.

mild (mīld), *a.* [AS. *milde* = D. and G. *mild* = Icel. *mildr* = Goth. *-milds,* mild.] Kind or gracious (archaic: as, "*Mild* Heaven . . . disapproves that care . . . That with superfluous burden loads the day," Milton's "Sonnets," To Cyriack Skinner, 11); also, amiably gentle or temperate in feeling or behavior toward others (as, "The stern were *mild* when thou wert by," Tennyson's "In Memoriam," cx.; "a *mild,* inoffensive man," Bret Harte's "Tennessee's Partner"); characterized by or showing such gentleness, as manners, aspect, speech, etc.; not harsh, fierce, or stern; also, gentle or moderate in force or effect (as, *mild* penalties or measures; *mild* remedies or doses); softly shining, as light, a luminary, etc.; not cold, severe, or extreme, as air, weather, climate, etc.; not acute, as disease, etc.; not sharp, pungent, or strong (as, *mild* flavor or perfume; a *mild* beverage; *mild* tobacco); in general, moderate in intensity, degree, or character (as, *mild* heat; *mild* efforts; *mild* pleasure or regret); also, easily worked, as soil, stone, wood, etc. (prov. Eng.).—**mild steel,** a form of steel, containing a low percentage of carbon, of great toughness but without the hardening power of ordinary steel.—**mild′en,** *v. t.* or *i.* To make or become mild.

mil-dew (mil′dū), *n.* [AS. *mildēaw, meledēaw,* < *mil-, mele-,* honey, + *dēaw,* E. *dew.*] Honey-dew†; also, any of numerous minute parasitic fungi producing a whitish coating or a discoloration on plants; the coating or discoloration, or the disease or diseased condition, produced by such fungi; also, any similar discoloration due to fungi, as on cotton and linen fabrics, paper, leather, etc., when exposed to damp.—**mil′dew,** *v. t.* or *i.* To affect or become affected with mildew.—**mil′dew-y,** *a.* Of, like, or affected with mildew.

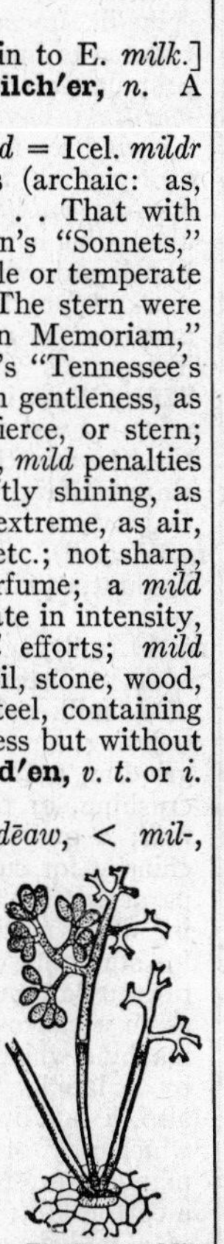

The Downy Mildew of the Grape (*Plasmopara viticola*), magnified.

mild-ly (mīld′li), *adv.* In a mild manner or degree.—**mild′ness,** *n.*

mile (mīl), *n.* [AS. *mīl,* < L. *milia, millia,* pl. of *mille,* thousand (as of paces or steps).] A unit of linear measure, of varying length at different periods and in different countries, but now in the U. S. and Great Britain legally equivalent to 5,280 feet.—**geographical** or **nautical mile,** a unit of linear measure equivalent to one minute of a great circle of the earth: officially fixed in the U. S. at 6,080.27 feet, and in Great Britain at 6,080 feet.—**statute** or **land mile,** the common or ordinary mile (5,280 feet).—**mile′age** (-āj), *n.* Length, extent, or distance in miles (as, the track *mileage* of a railroad); the aggregate number of miles made or traveled over in a given time (as, car *mileage;* passenger *mileage*); also, an allowance for traveling expenses at a fixed rate per mile, esp. to a public official; also, a fixed charge per mile, as for railroad transportation (hence *mileage ticket,* a book or ticket of coupons good for a certain number of miles of transportation at a fixed rate per mile); colloquially, a mileage ticket, or its detachable coupons collectively.—**mile′=post,** *n.* A post set up to mark distance by miles, as along a highway.

Mi-le-sian (mi-lē′shian or -zhian). [From *Milesius,* a fabulous king of Spain whose sons are said to have conquered Ireland.] **I.** *a.* Irish: as, "a racy *Milesian* brogue" (H. Melville's "Omoo," xxxvii.). **II.** *n.* A native of Ireland.

mile-stone (mīl′stōn), *n.* A stone set up to mark distance by miles, as along a highway or other line of travel. Also fig., as of a birthday or some event regarded as marking a stage in the journey of life.—**mile′stone,** *v. t.*; *-stoned, -stoning.* To mark as with a milestone: as, "a path whose every stage was *milestoned* with a mutilated corpse" (Stevenson's "Master of Ballantrae," xi.).

mil-foil (mil′foil), *n.* [OF. *milfoil,* < L. *milifolium, millefolium,* < *mille,* thousand, + *folium,* leaf.] The plant yarrow, *Achillea millefolium.*

mil-i-a-ri-a (mil-i-ā′ri-ä), *n.* [NL., prop. fem. of L. *miliarius,* E. *miliary.*] In *pathol.*, an inflammatory disease of the skin, located about the sweat-glands, marked by the formation of vesicles or papules resembling millet-seeds; miliary fever.

mil-i-a-ry (mil′i-ā-ri), *a.* [L. *miliarius,* < *milium,* millet.] Resembling a millet-seed or millet-seeds; in *pathol.*, accompanied by spots or vesicles resembling millet-seeds (as, *miliary* fever, miliaria).

mi-lieu (mē-lyė), *n.* [F., < *mi* (< L. *medius*), middle, + *lieu* (< L. *locus*), place.] Medium or environment: as, "He [man] takes the *milieu* in which he finds himself for granted" (H. G. Wells's "Outline of History," xxxvi. § 6).

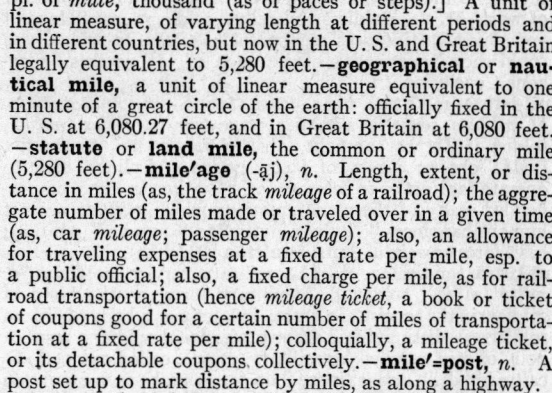

mil-i-o-lite (mil′i-ō-līt), *n.* [NL. *Miliola,* dim. < L. *milium,* millet.] A fossil foraminifer of the genus *Miliola,* the minute shells of which, occurring in immense numbers in some strata, are the chief constituent of certain limestones.

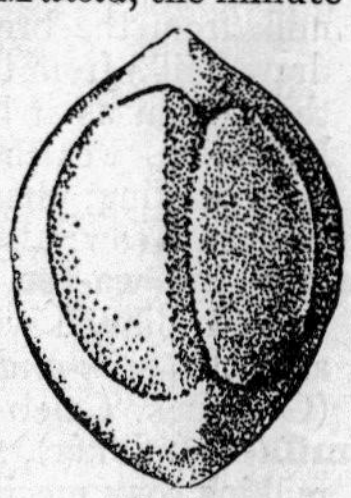

Miliolite.

mil-i-tant (mil′i-tant). [L. *militans* (*-ant-*), ppr. of *militare:* see *militate.*] **I.** *a.* Engaged in warfare; warring; also, combative (as, a *militant* nature). **II.** *n.* One engaged in warfare or strife; esp., formerly, one of a group using vigorous or violent methods in the effort to obtain the suffrage for women.—**mil′i-tan-cy,** *n.*—**mil′i-tant-ly,** *adv.*

mil-i-ta-ri-ly (mil′i-tā-ri-li), *adv.* In a military manner or respect.—**mil′i-ta-ri-ness,** *n.*

mil-i-ta-rism (mil′i-tā-rizm), *n.* Military spirit or policy: the principle of maintaining a large military establishment; now, esp., the tendency to regard military efficiency as the supreme ideal of the state, and to subordinate all other interests to those of the military organization.—**mil′i-ta-rist,** *n.* One who is proficient in the art of war; also, one who is imbued with militarism.—**mil″i-ta-ris′tic,** *a.* Of or pertaining to militarists or militarism; characterized by militarism.—**mil′i-ta-rize** (-rīz), *v. t.*; *-rized, -rizing.* To render military; imbue with militarism: as, "In Germany the nation was *militarised*" (H. G. Wells's "Mr. Britling," ii. 2. § 3).—**mil″i-ta-ri-za′tion** (-ri-zā′shon), *n.*

mil-i-ta-ry (mil′i-tā-ri). [L. *militaris,* < *miles* (*milit-*), soldier.] **I.** *a.* Of or pertaining to soldiers; befitting a soldier; following the life of a soldier; having the characteristics of a soldier; soldierly; more generally, of or pertaining to the army, armed forces, affairs of war, or a state of war. **II.** *n.* Soldiers generally; soldiery: as, "Haven't you any acquaintances among the *military*, to whom you could show your model [of a cannon]?" (Howells's "Foregone Conclusion," i.).

mil-i-tate (mil′i-tāt), *v. i.*; *-tated, -tating.* [L. *militatus*, pp. of *militare*, serve as a soldier, wage war, < *miles* (*milit-*), soldier.] To war or fight (obs. or rare); fig., to conflict (*with*: obs. or rare); of facts, evidence, feelings, etc., to operate (*against* or *in favor of*: as, "Passion, in him, comprehended many of the worst emotions which *militate* against human happiness," Bulwer-Lytton's "Caxtons," viii. 3); have force or weight.—**mil-i-ta′tion** (-tā′shọn), *n.*

mi-li-tia (mi-lish′ạ̈), *n.* [L., military service, soldiery, < *miles* (*milit-*), soldier.] A military force, as the body of soldiers in the service of a state; in later use, a body of citizen soldiers as distinguished from professional soldiers; esp., a body of men enrolled for military service, called out periodically for drill and exercise but for actual service only in emergencies; specif., in the U. S., all able-bodied male citizens, and all able-bodied males who have declared their intention to become citizens, who are more than 18 and not more than 45 years of age (divided into (1) the *organized militia*, made up of the *National Guard*, see under *national, a.*, and the *naval militia*, an organized body of militia trained for naval service, and (2) the *unorganized* or *reserve militia*, made up of that portion of the militia not belonging to the National Guard or the naval militia). —**mi-li′tia-man** (-mạn), *n.*; pl. *-men.*

mil-i-um (mil′i-um), *n.*; pl. *milia* (-ạ̈). [L., millet.] In *pathol.*, a small white or yellowish nodule resembling a millet-seed, produced in the skin by the retention of a sebaceous secretion.

milk (milk), *n.* [AS. *milc, meolc,* = D. *melk* = G. *milch* = Icel. *mjōlk* = Goth. *miluks*, milk; akin to L. *mulgere*, Gr. ἀμέλγειν, to milk.] An opaque white or bluish-white liquid secreted by the mammary glands of female mammals, serving for the nourishment of their young, and, in the case of the cow and some other animals, used for food or as a source of dairy products; also, any liquid resembling this, as the liquid within a cocoanut, the juice or sap (latex) of certain plants (see *milkweed*), or various pharmaceutical preparations.—**milk,** *v.* [AS. *milcian, meolcian,* < *milc, meolc.*] **I.** *tr.* To press or draw milk from the breast or udder of (a cow, etc.); extract or draw (milk) from the breast or udder; fig., to extract something from as if by milking; drain contents, strength, information, wealth, etc., from; exploit; also, to extract as if by milking; draw (*out*); elicit. **II.** *intr.* To draw milk, as from a cow; also, to yield milk, as a cow.

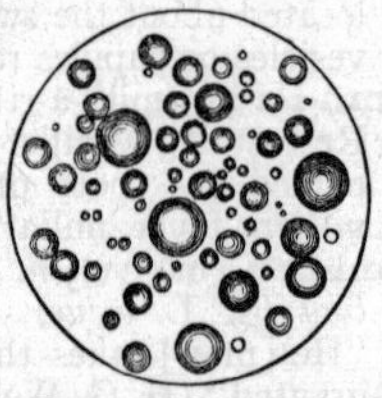
Drop of Milk, showing fat-globules (highly magnified).

milk=and=wa-ter (milk′ạnd-wâ′tėr), *a.* Weak or insipid, as milk diluted with water; wishy-washy; foolishly weak: as, "the *milk-and-water* softness of your former master" (Godwin's "Caleb Williams," xli.).

milk-er (mil′kėr), *n.* One who milks; also, an apparatus for milking cows mechanically; also, a cow or other animal that gives milk (colloq.).

milk=fe-ver (milk′fē′vėr), *n.* In *pathol.*, a slight fever sometimes occurring in women about the beginning of lactation; also, a similar but serious disease in cows.

milk-i-ly (mil′ki-li), *adv.* In a milky manner; with a milky appearance.—**milk′i-ness,** *n.*

milk-ing=stool (mil′king-stöl), *n.* A stool (in various forms) for sitting on while milking a cow or other animal.

milk=leg (milk′leg), *n.* In *pathol.*, a painful swelling of the leg, due to thrombosis of the large veins, occurring most frequently in connection with parturition.

milk-less (milk′les), *a.* Without milk; not secreting milk.

Swiss Milking-stool, Canton of Bern.

milk=liv-ered (milk′liv″ėrd), *a.* White-livered; cowardly: as, "*Milk-liver'd* man! That bear'st a cheek for blows" (Shakspere's "King Lear," iv. 2. 50).

milk-maid (milk′mād), *n.* A woman who milks cows or is employed in a dairy.

milk-man (milk′mạn or -man), *n.*; pl. *-men.* A man who sells or delivers milk.

milk=room (milk′röm), *n.* A cool room in which milk and other food or stores of a household are kept: as, "Her sensibilities were almost paralyzed, on opening her *milk-room* door, to find there, with creamy whiskers . . . her own model cat" (Mrs. Stowe's "Oldtown Folks," xi.).

milk=sick-ness (milk′sik″nes), *n.* A malignant disease, formerly common in the western U. S., affecting farm stock and communicable to man.

milk-sop (milk′sop), *n.* A piece of bread soaked in milk†; fig., a soft, unmanly fellow; an effeminate man or youth.—**milk′sop-ism,** *n.*

milk=sug-ar (milk′shụg′ạ̈r), *n.* Lactose.

milk=tooth (milk′töth), *n.*; pl. *-teeth* (-tēth). One of the temporary teeth of a mammal which are replaced by the permanent teeth.

milk=vetch (milk′vech), *n.* [So called from an old belief that these plants increased the secretion of milk in goats feeding on them.] Any of various plants of the fabaceous genus *Astragalus*, or of certain allied genera.

milk-weed (milk′wēd), *n.* Any of various plants with a milky juice, as certain spurges; specif., any of various plants (mostly with milky juice) of the family *Asclepiadaceæ*, esp. those of the genus *Asclepias*, as *A. syriaca* (the common milkweed), an herb with downy stems and leaves.

milk=white (milk′hwīt′), *a.* [AS. *meolchwīt.*] White as milk: as, a *milk-white* steed; "black crags tinctured with *milk-white* mists" (Parkman's "Oregon Trail," xiii.).

milk-wort (milk′wėrt), *n.* Any of the herbs and shrubs constituting the genus *Polygala*, having (mostly) spikes or spike-like racemes of variously colored flowers, and formerly reputed to increase the secretion of milk in women; also, a primulaceous seaside plant, *Glaux maritima*, having small purplish-white flowers ('sea-milkwort').

milk-y (mil′ki), *a.*; compar. *milkier*, superl. *milkiest.* Of or like milk; abounding in or yielding milk or a milk-like liquid; white as milk; fig., mild, meek, tame, or spiritless (as, "the soft and *milky* rabble of womankind": Tennyson's "Princess," vi. 290).—**Milky Way,** in *astron.*, the faintly luminous band or tract stretching across the heavens, composed of innumerable stars too faint for unassisted vision; the Galaxy.

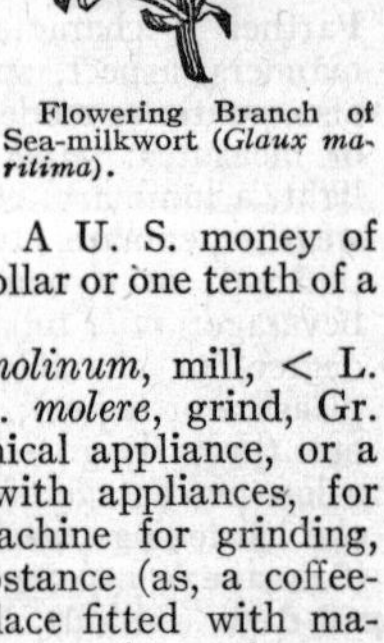
Flowering Branch of Sea-milkwort (*Glaux maritima*).

mill[1] (mil), *n.* [L. *mille*, thousand.] A U. S. money of account, equal to one thousandth of a dollar or one tenth of a cent.

mill[2] (mil), *n.* [AS. *mylen*, < LL. *molinum*, mill, < L. *mola*, millstone, pl. mill; akin to L. *molere*, grind, Gr. μύλη, mill, and E. *meal*[1].] A mechanical appliance, or a building or establishment equipped with appliances, for grinding grain into flour; also, a machine for grinding, crushing, or pulverizing any solid substance (as, a coffee-*mill*; a quartz-*mill*); a building or place fitted with machinery for such a purpose; also, any of various other apparatuses for working materials into due form or performing other mechanical operations; a machine formerly used for stamping coins; a steel roller for receiving under great pressure an impressed design and transferring it by pressure, as to a calico-printing cylinder or a note-printing plate; a machine which does its work by rotary motion, as one used by a lapidary for cutting and polishing precious stones; also, a building or establishment fitted with machinery, in which any of various mechanical operations or forms of manufacture is carried on (as, a planing-*mill*; a rolling-*mill*; a cotton-*mill*; a silk-*mill*); also, the notched or ridged edge of a milled coin, etc.; also, a pugilistic encounter (slang). —**mill**[2], *v.* **I.** *tr.* To grind, work, treat, or shape in or with a mill; also, to finish the edge of (a coin, etc.) with a series of fine notches or transverse grooves; also, to beat or stir, as to a froth (as, to *mill* chocolate); also, to beat or strike, or fight, or overcome (slang). **II.** *intr.* To move confusedly in a circle, as a herd of cattle; also, to fight or box (slang).

mill-board (mil′bōrd), *n.* A stout kind of pasteboard used in bookbinding, etc.

mill=cake (mil′kāk), *n.* The cake or mass resulting from the incorporation of the ingredients of gunpowder, preliminary to granulation.

mill=dam (mil′dam), *n.* A dam built in a stream to furnish a head of water for turning a mill-wheel; also, a mill-pond.

mil-le-fi-o-ri (mil″ẹ-fi-ō′ri), *n.* [It. *millefiori*, 'thousand flowers.'] Ornamental glasswork made by fusing together glass tubes or rods of various colors and cutting the fused mass into sections, which are then embedded in clear glass or otherwise treated.

mille-fleurs (mēl-flėr), *n.* [F. *mille-fleurs*, 'thousand flowers.'] A perfume containing extracts from a variety of flowers.

mil-le-na-ri-an (mil-e-nā′ri-ạn). [LL. *millenarius*: see *millenary*.] **I.** *a.* Of or pertaining to a thousand, esp. the thousand years of the prophesied millennium. **II.** *n.* A believer in the millennium; a chiliast.—**mil-le-na′ri-an-ism,** *n.* The doctrine of or belief in the millennium.

mil-le-na-ry (mil′e-nạ-ri). [LL. *millenarius*, of or containing a thousand, < *milleni*, a thousand each, < L. *mille*, thousand.] **I.** *a.* Consisting of or pertaining to a thousand, esp. a thousand years; hence, pertaining to the millennium. **II.** *n.*; pl. *-ries* (-riz). An aggregate of a thousand; esp., a period of a thousand years (as, "We danced through three nights, dancing the old *millenary* out, dancing the new *millenary* in": J. H. Newman's "Callista," v.); a millennium; also, a millenarian.

mil-len-ni-al (mi-len′i-ạl), *a.* Of or pertaining to a millennium or the millennium; worthy or suggestive of the millennium (as, "There was to be a *millennial* abundance of new gates . . . and returns of ten per cent.": George Eliot's "Adam Bede," vii.).—**mil-len′ni-al-ly,** *adv.*

mil-len-ni-um (mi-len′i-um), *n.*; pl. *-niums* or *-nia* (-ạ). [NL., < L. *mille*, thousand, + *annus*, year.] A period of a thousand years (as, "*millenniums* hence": Tennyson's "Two Voices," 89); sometimes, a thousandth anniversary; specif., the period of "a thousand years" (a phrase variously interpreted) during which Christ is to reign on earth, according to the prophetic statement in Rev. xx. 1–7; hence, a period of general righteousness and happiness, esp. in the indefinite future.

mil-le-pede, mil-le-ped (mil′ẹ-pēd, -ped), *n.* [L. *millepeda*, < *mille*, thousand, + *pes* (*ped-*), foot.] A myriapod of the order or group *Chilognatha* or *Diplopoda*, characterized by two pairs of legs apiece for most of the segments of the body. Cf. *centipede.*

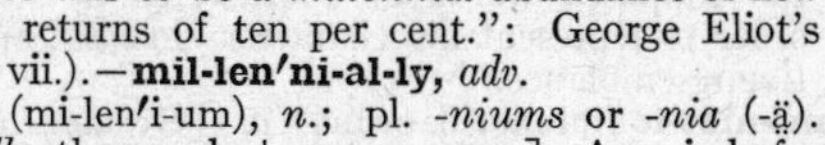

Millepede (*Cambala annulata*). (Line shows natural size.)

mil-le-pore (mil′ẹ-pōr), *n.* [NL. *Millepora*, < L. *mille*, thousand, + *porus*, E. *pore*².] A coralline hydrozoan of the genus *Millepora*, having a smooth calcareous surface with many perforations.—**mil′le-po-rine** (-pọ-rin), *a.*

Millepore (*M. alcicornis*).

mill-er (mil′ėr), *n.* One who keeps or operates a mill, esp. a grain-mill; also, a milling-machine; also, any of various moths which appear as if powdered with flour.

Mill-er-ite¹ (mil′ėr-īt), *n.* A disciple of William Miller (1782–1849), an American preacher, who taught that the second advent of Christ and the beginning of the millennium were to occur in the immediate future (at first, about 1843).

mill-er-ite² (mil′ėr-īt), *n.* [From W. H. *Miller* (1801–80), British crystallographer.] Native nickel sulphide, a mineral with a bronze color and a metallic luster.

mill-er's=thumb (mil′ėrz-thum′), *n.* Any of various small, spiny-finned fresh-water fishes, esp. of the genus *Cottus.*

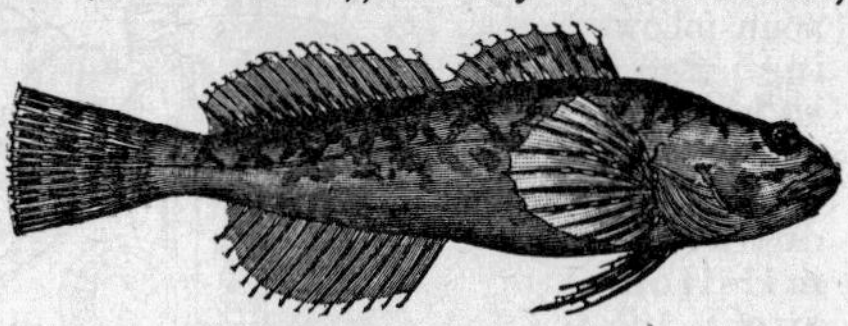

Miller's-thumb (*Cottus gobio*).

mil-les-i-mal (mi-les′i-mạl). [L. *millesimus*, < *mille*, thousand.] **I.** *a.* Thousandth; consisting of thousandth parts. **II.** *n.* A thousandth part.

mil-let (mil′et), *n.* [F. *millet*, dim. of *mil*, < L. *milium*, millet.] A cereal grass, *Panicum miliaceum*, extensively cultivated in the East and in southern Europe for its small seed or grain (used as a food for man and for fowls), but in the U. S. grown chiefly for fodder; any of various related or similar grasses cultivated as grain-plants or forage-plants (as, Indian *millet*, durra; Italian or foxtail *millet*, see under *foxtail*); also, the grain of any of these grasses.

mil-li- (mil′i-). Form of L. *mille*, thousand, used in combination, esp., in the sense of 'one thousandth,' in the names of units of measurement, as in *milliampere* (one thousandth of an ampere), *millicurie* (one thousandth of a curie), *millimeter*, *millimicron*, etc.

mil-li-am-pere (mil′i-am-pãr″), *n.* See *milli-*.

mil-liard (mil′iärd), *n.* [F., < L. *mille*, thousand.] A thousand millions.

mil-li-a-ry (mil′i-ạ-ri). [L. *milliarius*, containing a thousand (as n., *milliarium*), < *mille*, thousand.] **I.** *a.* Pertaining to the ancient Roman mile of a thousand paces; marking a mile. **II.** *n.*; pl. *-ries* (-riz). A milestone.

mil-li-cu-rie (mil′i-kū″rẹ), *n.* See *milli-*.

mil-lier (mē-lyā), *n.* [F., < L. *mille*, thousand.] In the *metric system*, a unit of weight equal to 1,000,000 grams, or 2,204.6 pounds avoirdupois; a metric ton.

mil-li-gram, mil-li-gramme (mil′i-gram), *n.* [F. *milligramme*: see *milli-*.] In the *metric system*, a unit of weight equal to one thousandth of a gram, or 0.0154 grain.

mil-li-li-ter, mil-li-li-tre (mil′i-lē-tėr), *n.* [F. *millilitre*: see *milli-*.] In the *metric system*, a unit of capacity equal to one thousandth of a liter (one cubic centimeter), 0.061 cubic inch, or 0.27 U. S. fluid dram.

mil-li-me-ter, mil-li-me-tre (mil′i-mē-tėr), *n.* [F. *millimètre*: see *milli-*.] In the *metric system*, a measure of length equal to one thousandth of a meter, or 0.03937 inch.

mil-li-mi-cron (mil′i-mī″kron), *n.* [See *milli-*.] A unit of length, the thousandth part of a micron. Symbol $\mu\mu$.

mil-li-ner (mil′i-nėr), *n.* [From obs. *Milaner*, an inhabitant of Milan, a dealer in articles from Milan.] A dealer in fancy wares, miscellaneous articles of dress, etc., orig. such as came from Milan in Italy†; in modern use, one who makes or sells hats, bonnets, and other head-gear (and sometimes other articles of dress) for women (as, "a jade of a *milliner*, who made and dressed caps for the girls at the boarding-school": Smollett's "Humphry Clinker," April 17).—**mil′li-ner-y** (-nėr-i or -ner-i), *n.* Articles made or sold by milliners (as, "Little Rosey bloomed in *millinery*": Thackeray's "Newcomes," lxiii.); also, the business or trade of a milliner.

mill-ing (mil′ing), *n.* The act of subjecting something to the operation of a mill; also, the process of finishing the edge of a coin, etc., with fine notches or transverse grooves; the notches or grooves themselves; also, a thrashing (slang).—**mill′ing=ma-chine″,** *n.* Any of a class of machines used for shaping metal surfaces, cutting slots, etc., as in the machining of large castings. See cut on following page.

mil-lion (mil′yọn), *n.*; pl. *millions* or (as after a numeral) *million.* [OF. F. *million*, < L. *mille*, thousand.] The number of ten hundred thousand, or a thousand thousand; often, the amount of a thousand thousand units of money, as pounds, dollars, or francs (as, to be worth a *million*; "*Millions* would not bribe her to wrong him," Marryat's "Peter Simple," lxiv.); indefinitely, a very great number; with *the*, the multitude, or the mass of the common people (as, "The play . . . pleased not *the million*": Shakspere's

"Hamlet," ii. 2. 457). Also used as a quasi-adjective, by omission of *of* before a noun following: as, a *million* (of) men; ten *million* (of) dollars.—**mil-lion-aire′** (-ãr′), *n.* [F. *millionnaire.*] A person worth a million or millions, as of pounds, dollars, or francs.—**mil-lion-air′ess,** *n.* A female millionaire.—**mil′lion-a-ry** (-ā̤-ri). **I.** *a.* Possessing millions, as of money: as, "these *millionary* people" (Kipling's "Captains Courageous," ix.). **II.** *n.*; pl. *-ries* (-riz). A millionaire.—**mil′lioned,** *a.* Numbered by the million; also, possessed of millions, as of money.—**mil′lionth. I.** *a.* Coming last in a series of a million; also, being one of a million equal parts. **II.** *n.* The millionth member of a series; also, a millionth part.

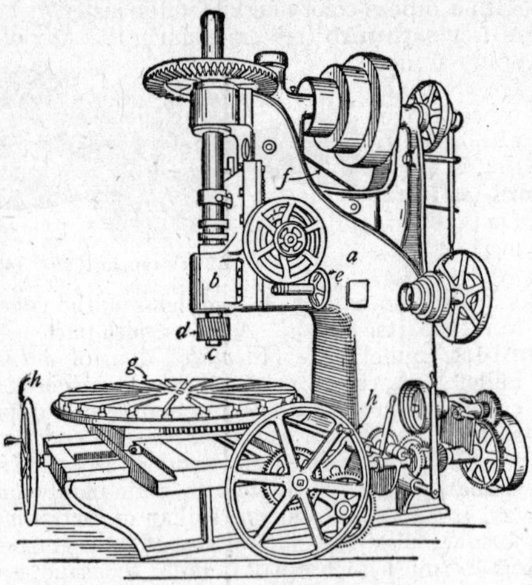

Large Vertical Milling-machine.
a, frame supporting spindle; *b*, vertical sliding support for spindle; *c*, spindle; *d*, milling-cutter; *e*, control of sliding support to adjust cutter to work; *f*, cable to counterweight for sliding support, counterweight inside the frame; *g*, table for work with rotary, cross, and longitudinal feed having hand or power control; *h*, *h*, control of feed.

mil-li-pede, mil-li-ped (mil′i-pēd, -ped), *n.* See *millepede.*

mil-li-stere (mil′i-stēr), *n.* [F. *millistère*: see *milli-.*] In the *metric system*, a unit of volume equal to one thousandth of a stere, or one cubic decimeter.

mil-lo (mil′ō) **maize.** [Sp. *millo*, *mijo*, < L. *milium*, millet.] A variety of sorghum of the grain-sorghum group, resembling durra. See *milo.*

mill=pond (mil′pond), *n.* A pond for supplying water to drive a mill-wheel.

mill=race (mil′rās), *n.* The current of water that drives a mill-wheel; also, the channel in which it flows to the mill.

mill-stone (mil′stōn), *n.* Either of a pair of circular stones between which grain or other substance is ground, as in a mill; stone for making these; fig., something that grinds or crushes; also, a heavy burden (in allusion to Mat. xviii. 6).

mill=wheel (mil′hwēl), *n.* A wheel, esp. a water-wheel, used to drive a mill.

mill-wright (mil′rīt), *n.* One who designs, builds, or sets up mills or mill-machinery.

mi-lo (mī′lō, also mil′ō), *n.*; pl. *-los* (-lōz). [See *millo maize.*] Any of several grain-sorghums (see *sorghum*), varieties of *Andropogon sorghum* with slender, pithy stalks, introduced into the U. S. soon after 1880, and cultivated for grain and forage.

mi-lord (mi-lôrd′). A Continental rendering of the English *my lord*, used in speaking to or of an English lord or gentleman. Cf. *miladi.*

mil-reis (mil′rās), *n.*; pl. *milreis.* [Pg., 'a thousand reis.'] A Portuguese gold coin and former monetary unit (superseded in 1911 by the escudo), equal to 1,000 reis, or $1.08; also, a Brazilian silver coin and monetary unit, equal to 1,000 reis, or about 54.6 U. S. cents.

Obverse. Reverse.
Milreis of Portugal.

milt[1] (milt), *n.* [AS. *milte* = G. *milz.*] The spleen.

milt[2] (milt), *n.* [Appar. for *milk*, as formerly used in this sense: cf. G. *milch*, milk, also milt.] The male generative organ of fishes when filled with secretion, or the secretion itself.—**milt**[2], *v. t.* To impregnate (roe of female fish) with milt.—**milt′er,** *n.* A male fish in breeding-time.

Mil-to-ni-an (mil-tō′ni-a̤n), *a.* Miltonic.

Mil-ton-ic (mil-ton′ik), *a.* Of or pertaining to the English poet John Milton (1608–74), or resembling his style: as, "*Miltonic* images" (De Quincey's "Revolt of the Tartars").

mil-vine (mil′vin), *a.* [L. *milvus*, kite.] Pertaining to or resembling the kites (birds), esp. those of the genus *Milvus.*

mim (mim), *a.* [Imit.: cf. *mum*[1].] Primly silent, quiet, or restrained; affectedly modest; prim; demure. [Sc. and prov. Eng.]

mim-bar, min-bar (mim′bä̤r, min′-), *n.* [Ar. *minbar.*] In Mohammedan countries, the pulpit in a mosque.

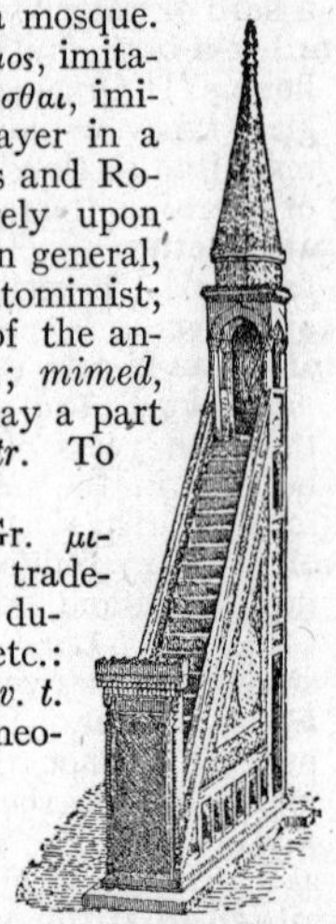
Mimbar in Mosque of Sultan Selim, Adrianople.

mime (mīm), *n.* [L. *mimus*, < Gr. μῖμος, imitator, actor, mime or farce, akin to μιμεῖσθαι, imitate: cf. *mimesis* and *mimetic.*] A player in a kind of farce among the ancient Greeks and Romans which depended for effect largely upon ludicrous actions, gestures, etc.; hence, in general, a comedian or buffoon; an actor; a pantomimist; any mimic or imitator; also, a farce of the ancient kind above described.—**mime,** *v.*; *mimed, miming.* **I.** *intr.* To act as a mime; play a part by mimicry, esp. without words. **II.** *tr.* To represent by acting; also, to mimic.

Mim-e-o-graph (mim′ē̤-ō̤-gråf), *n.* [Gr. μιμεῖσθαι, imitate, + γράφειν, write.] A trade-mark name for a stencil device for duplicating letters, circulars, drawings, etc.: sometimes used *l. c.*—**mim′e-o-graph,** *v. t.* To copy or make by means of a Mimeograph.

mim-er (mī′mėr), *n.* One who mimes; a mime.

mi-me-sis (mi-mē′sis or mī-), *n.* [NL., < Gr. μίμησις, < μιμεῖσθαι, imitate.] In *rhet.*, imitation or reproduction of the supposed words of another, as in order to represent his character; in *zoöl.*, mimicry; simulative resemblance.

mi-met-ic (mi-met′ik or mī-), *a.* [Gr. μιμητικός, < μιμεῖσθαι, imitate: cf. *mime.*] Pertaining to or concerned with imitation or mimicry (as, the *mimetic* faculty); also, characterized by or of the nature of mimicry (as, *mimetic* gestures); also, mimic or make-believe; in *zoöl.*, pertaining to or exhibiting mimicry.—**mi-met′i-cal-ly,** *adv.*

mim-ic (mim′ik). [L. *mimicus*, < Gr. μιμικός, < μῖμος, E. *mime.*] **I.** *a.* Pertaining to or acting as a mime†; hence, apt at or given to imitating in action, speech, etc. (as, "the *mimic* bird": Cowper's tr. V. Bourne's "The Parrot," 14); also, characterized by or of the nature of such imitation (as, *mimic* gestures or expression); imitative; simulative; also, being merely an imitation or reproduction of the true thing, often on a smaller scale (as, a *mimic* battle; a *mimic* railroad; "He soon grew impatient . . . of the quiet and inaction of his *mimic* kingdom," Irving's "Conquest of Granada," lxxxv.); having merely the semblance of the reality; make-believe. **II.** *n.* A mime, comedian, or actor (obs. or archaic); hence, one apt at imitating or mimicking; also, one who or that which imitates or mimics (as, "Cunning is only the *mimic* of discretion": Addison, in "Spectator," 225); an imitator or ape; a thing that has the semblance or appearance of something else.—**mim′ic,** *v. t.*; *-icked, -icking.* To act in imitation of; imitate or copy in action, speech, etc., often playfully or derisively; sometimes, to imitate unintelligently or servilely; ape; also, to produce an imitation of, as by drawing, painting, or other processes; reproduce or represent imitatively; also, of things, to be an imitation of, or simulate (as, "Fresh carved cedar, *mimicking* a glade Of palm and plantain": Keats's "Lamia," ii.); have the semblance or appearance of (specif. in *zoöl.*: see *mimicry*).—**mim′ick-er,** *n.*—**mim′ic-ry** (-ri), *n.*; pl. *-ries* (-riz). The act, practice, or art of mimicking (as, "By the talent of *mimicry* . . . I could copy their pronunciation of the English language": Godwin's "Caleb Williams," xxxiv.); an instance, performance, or result of mimicking; an imitation produced; in *zoöl.*, the close external resemblance, as if from imitation or simulation, of an animal to some different animal or to environing objects, esp. as serving for protection or concealment.

mi-mo-sa (mi-mō'sạ or -zạ), *n.* [NL., < L. *mimus*, E. *mime*: so called from the seeming mimicry of animal life by the sensitive-plant.] Any plant of the genus *Mimosa*, native in tropical or warm regions, and comprising trees, shrubs, and plants having usually bipinnate and often sensitive leaves, and small flowers in globular heads or cylindrical spikes; esp., the sensitive-plant, *M. pudica*.—**mim-o-sa-ceous** (mim-ọ-sā'shius), *a.* Belonging to the *Mimosaceæ*, or mimosa family of plants.

mi-na[1] (mī'nạ), *n.*; pl. *minas*, L. *minæ* (-nē). [L., < Gr. μνᾶ; from Semitic: cf. *maneh*.] An ancient unit of weight and value, equal to the sixtieth part of a talent.

mi-na[2] (mī'nạ), *n.* [Hind. *mainā*.] Any of various Asiatic birds of the starling family (*Sturnidæ*), esp. those of the genus *Acridotheres*, or those of the genus *Eulabes* (see *hill-mina*).

min-a-ble (mī'nạ-bl), *a.* Capable of being mined: as, *minable* deposits; *minable* ores.

mi-na-cious (mi-nā'shus), *a.* [L. *minax* (*minac-*): see *menace*.] Menacing; threatening; minatory.—**mi-na'cious-ly,** *adv.*—**mi-na'cious-ness, mi-na'ci-ty** (-nas'i-ti), *n.*

mi-nar (mi-när'), *n.* [Ar. *manār*, akin to *nār*, fire.] In Mohammedan countries, a lighthouse; a tower; a minaret.

min-a-ret (min'ạ-ret), *n.* [F. *minaret*, < Ar. *manārah* (*manārat*), < *manār*, E. *minar*.] A slender, lofty tower or turret attached to a Mohammedan mosque, surrounded by one or more projecting balconies, from which the muezzin calls the people to prayer: as, "The *minarets* [of Damascus] peered out from the midst of shade into the glowing sky" (Kinglake's "Eothen," xxvii.).

Minaret. — Mosque of Ahmed, Constantinople.

min-a-to-ry (min'ạ-tọ-ri), *a.* [LL. *minatorius*, < L. *minari*, threaten: see *menace*.] Menacing; threatening: as, "A *minatory* inscription on one side of the gate intimated 'prosecution according to law' . . . to all who should be found trespassing" (Scott's "Guy Mannering," vii.).—**min'a-to-ri-ly** (-ri-li), *adv.*

min'bar, *n.* See *mimbar*.

mince (mins), *v.*; *minced*, *mincing*. [OF. *mincier* (F. *mincer*), prob. var. of *menuisier*, make small, reduce to small pieces: see *minish*.] **I.** *tr.* To cut or chop (meat or other food substance) into very small pieces; cut (anything) into bits (as, "*mincing* with his sword her husband's limbs": Shakspere's "Hamlet," ii. 2. 537); subdivide minutely, as land, a subject or discourse, etc.; also, to minimize in representation (as, "You have either omitted some material circumstances, or *minced* or changed them": Swift's "Gulliver's Travels," Letter from Captain Gulliver); extenuate (faults); speak of (matters) in polite or euphemistic terms; also, to soften or moderate (one's words, etc.), as in stating unpleasant facts; modify or alter (an oath, profane word, etc.) to a milder or less obvious form (see *minced*); also, to perform or utter in an affectedly nice or elegant manner. **II.** *intr.* To walk or move with short, affectedly dainty steps (as, "The daughters of Zion are haughty, and walk with stretched forth necks . . . *mincing* as they go": Isa. iii. 16); act or behave in an affectedly nice or elegant manner (as, "Vanity, vanity! . . . the same sentiment that sets a lassie *mincing* to her glass!" Stevenson's "Master of Ballantrae," ix.); speak with affected niceness or elegance.—**mince,** *n.* Minced meat or other food; a dish of minced meat or the like (as, a *mince* of chicken); specif., mince-meat, as for pies (as, "'We children' were employed in chopping *mince* for pies to a most wearisome fineness": Mrs. Stowe's "Oldtown Folks," xxvii.).—**minced,** *p. a.* Of food, cut or chopped into very small pieces; of oaths, etc., altered to a milder or less obvious form (cf. *drat*, *gad*[1], *golly*, *gosh*, *lud*, *od*[2], *zounds*).—**mince'=meat,** *n.* Minced meat; anything cut up very small; specif., a mixture composed of minced apples, suet (and sometimes meat), candied citron, etc., with raisins, currants, and other ingredients, for filling pies.—**mince'=pie',** *n.* A pie filled with mince-meat.—**min-cer** (min'sėr), *n.*—**min'cing,** *p. a.* That minces; esp., walking, acting, or speaking in an affectedly nice or elegant manner; hence, affectedly nice or elegant, as the gait, behavior, air, speech, etc.—**min'cing-ly,** *adv.*—**min'cing-ness,** *n.*

mind[1] (mīnd), *n.* [Ir.] In *archæol.*, a diadem or crescent-shaped ornament found in Ireland.

mind[2] (mīnd), *n.* [AS. *gemynd*, memory, remembrance, thought, = Goth. *gamunds*, memory; akin to L. *meminisse*, Gr. μνᾶσθαι, remember, L. *monere*, remind, Skt. *man-*, think, L. *mens*, mind, Gr. μένος, spirit, disposition: cf. *amnesty*, *Eumenides*, *mantra*, *memento*, *mental*[2], *mention*, *monition*, and *mint*[3].] The faculty of memory†; also, remembrance or recollection (as, to bear or keep in *mind*; to bring to *mind*; time out of *mind*, or beyond remembrance); also, commemoration (now chiefly in 'month's mind': see under *month*); also, mention† (as, to make *mind* of a thing); also, thought, consideration, or inward contemplation (as, the point I have in *mind* is this); also, that which thinks, feels, and wills, as in a human or other conscious being (as, the powers or processes of the *mind*); the subject of consciousness; the soul; a particular instance of this (as, "Not of Tydeus' kind, Whose little body lodged a mighty *mind*," Pope's tr. Homer's "Iliad," v.; to exert power over the *minds* of men); less precisely, a conscious or intelligent agency or being (as, the doctrine of a *mind* creating or pervading the universe); sometimes, psychical or spiritual being, as opposed to matter; also, the intellect or understanding, as distinguished from the faculties of feeling and willing; the intelligence; a particular instance of the intellect or intelligence, as in a person (as, "A *mind* for ever Voyaging through strange seas of Thought, alone": Wordsworth's "Prelude," iii. 62); the intellectual powers or capacities of a body of persons (as, explanations adapted to the popular *mind*); intellectual power or ability (as, men of *mind*); a person considered with reference to intellectual power (as, the greatest *minds* of the time); also, reason, sanity, or sound mental condition (as, to lose one's *mind*; to be out of one's *mind*); also, the thinking and feeling faculty with reference to condition (as, an uncertain or anxious state of *mind*; peace of *mind*); way of thinking and feeling, disposition, or temper (as, to be brought to a better *mind*; many men, many *minds*); opinion or sentiments (as, "Wherever he should find Barnes, Thomas Newcome was determined to tell him his *mind*": Thackeray's "Newcomes," liii.); inclination or desire (as, "William . . . had a great *mind* one day to go on shore," Defoe's "Captain Singleton," xiii.; "Joe Stedman . . . asserted his democratic right to do just as he had a *mind* to," Mrs. Stowe's "Oldtown Folks," v.); purpose, intention, or will (as, "Since it is my father's *mind* That I repair to Rome, I am content": Shakspere's "Titus Andronicus," v. 3. 1); also, attention, thought, or mental effort (as, to keep one's *mind* on a subject or object; to give one's *mind* to doing something).—**a piece of one's mind.** See under *piece*, *n.*—**to be of one mind,** to agree in opinion, desire, or purpose: as, "Why should we quarrel . . . when we *are* both *of one mind?*" (Marryat's "King's Own," xxv.).—**to change one's mind,** to change one's way of thinking or feeling, or one's plans or purposes.—**to have a mind of one's own,** to have definite or decided opinions, inclinations, or purposes.—**to have half a mind** (to do something), to be half inclined, or have a fairly strong inclination (to do as stated): as, I *have half a mind* to go.—**to know one's own mind,** to know what one really thinks, wishes, or intends: as, "They are both very young, and may not *know their own minds*" (H. Kingsley's "Geoffry Hamlyn," xxix.).—**to put in mind,** to remind, as of something, or to do something.—**mind**[2], *v. t.* To remind (archaic or prov.); also, to remember (archaic or prov.: as, "I *mind* being there when I was a lad—dear, it comes over me like an old song!" Stevenson's "Master of Ballantrae," xi.); also, to perceive or notice (now prov.: as, "*Martin Doul.* Will he *mind* the way we are, and not tidied or washed cleanly at all? *Molly Byrne.* He'll not see what way you are," Synge's "Well of the Saints," i.); also, to pay attention to, heed, or obey (a person, advice, instructions, etc.); also, to apply one's self or attend to (as, "bidding him be a good child and *mind* his book," Addison, in "Spectator," 383; "*Mind* your own business and let other people *mind* theirs," Kipling's "Light That Failed," xiv.); look after, take care of, or tend (as, to *mind* the baby; to *mind* the furnace); look out for or take watchful care of (as, "*Mind* yourself: lest, when the roof falls, you too should be crushed under the ruins": Stevenson's "Master of Ballantrae," x.); be careful, cautious, or wary concerning (as, *mind* what you say; *mind* that dog!); also, to care about or feel concern at (as, "You know I do *mind* parting with you": George Eliot's "Adam Bede," l.); esp., in negative and interrogative expressions, to feel disturbed or inconvenienced by, or object to (as, "He and I walked, and rode, and hunted . . . without *minding* the vicissitudes of the weather," Smollett's "Humphry Clinker," Oct. 11; would you *mind* handing me that book?); regard as concerning one's self or as mattering (as, never *mind* what he does); also, to intend†, purpose†, or plan†.—**to mind one's p's and q's,** to be careful or particular about what one says or does: as, "Even the cleverest must *mind their p's and q's* with such a lady" (Arnold Bennett's "Hilda Lessways," i. 6).—**mind²,** *v. i.* To remember (now prov.); also, to take notice, observe, or understand (chiefly in the imperative: as, "Now *mind*, I don't tell you these are my idees," Cooper's "Deerslayer," xxv.); also, to obey (as, "The servants know they must *mind*": Mrs. Stowe's "Uncle Tom's Cabin," xvi.); also, to be careful or wary (as, if you don't *mind*, you'll get hurt); also, to care, feel concern, or object (often in negative and interrogative expressions: as, all right, I don't *mind*; do you *mind* if I go?); regard a thing as concerning one's self or as mattering (as, never *mind* about them).

mind=cure (mīnd′kūr), *n.* The curing of disease by influence exerted upon the mind of the patient.

mind-ed (mīn′ded), *a.* Having a mind (as, high-*minded*); also, inclined or disposed (as, "I was several times *minded* to argue the question out with my mother": Kingsley's "Alton Locke," v.).

mind-er (mīn′dėr), *n.* One who minds.

mind-ful (mīnd′fůl), *a.* Having remembrance or thought (as, "What is man, that thou art *mindful* of him?" Ps. viii. 4); regardful; heedful; careful (to do something).—**mind′ful-ly,** *adv.*—**mind′ful-ness,** *n.*

mind-less (mīnd′les), *a.* Without mind or intelligence (as, "the shrieking of the *mindless* wind": Whittier's "Snow-Bound"); senseless or stupid; also, unmindful, regardless, or heedless (as, "Cursed Athens, *mindless* of thy worth, Forgetting thy great deeds": Shakspere's "Timon of Athens," iv. 3. 93).—**mind′less-ly,** *adv.*—**mind′less-ness,** *n.*

mind=read-er (mīnd′rē″dėr), *n.* One who practises mind-reading.—**mind′=read″ing,** *n.* Reading or discerning of the thoughts in the minds of others, esp. by some supernormal power.

mine¹ (mīn), *pron.* [AS. *mīn*, possessive adj. from the stem of *mē*, E. *me*, used also as the genitive of *mē*.] The possessive form of *me* regularly used predicatively or without a noun following, or, archaically, either before a noun beginning with a vowel or *h* (as, *mine* host) or after a noun in the vocative (as, sister *mine*). Cf. *my, pron.*

mine² (mīn), *n.* [OF. F. *mine*; origin uncertain.] An excavation made in the earth for the purpose of getting out ores, precious stones, coal, etc.; a place where such minerals may be obtained, either by excavation or by washing the soil (cf. *placer²*); a deposit of such minerals, either under the ground or at its surface; fig., an abounding source or store of anything (as, "Her memory was a *mine*," Byron's "Don Juan," i. 11; this book is a *mine* of information); *milit.*, a subterranean passage made to extend under the enemy's works or position, as for the purpose of securing access or of depositing explosives for blowing up the position; the explosives so used; also, a large charge of explosive in a water-tight casing placed beneath or on the water, as for blowing up the enemy's vessels.—**mine²,** *v.*; *mined, mining.* [OF. F. *miner*.] **I.** *intr.* To dig in the earth for the purpose of extracting ores, coal, etc.; make a mine; work in a mine; extract ores, etc., from mines; also, in general, to make subterranean passages; specif., to dig or lay mines, as in military operations. **II.** *tr.* To dig in (earth, etc.) in order to obtain ores, coal, etc.; extract (ores, coal, etc.) from a mine; also, in general, to make subterranean passages in; burrow; make (passages, etc.) by digging or burrowing; also, to form subterranean passages under; dig away or remove the foundations of; hence, fig., to attack, ruin, or destroy by secret or slow methods; undermine; also, to dig or lay military mines under; lay military mines in (water).

mine′a-ble, *a.* See *minable*.

mine=field (mīn′fēld), *n.* *Milit.*, an area on land or water throughout which mines have been laid; also, the mines in such an area.

min-er (mī′nėr), *n.* One who mines; one who works in a mine; one who digs or lays military mines.

min-er-al (min′ẹ-rạl), *a.* [F. *minéral*, < ML. *mineralis*, < *minera*, < OF. *miniere*, mine, < *mine*, E. *mine²*.] Pertaining to mines or mining†; also, obtained from mines; of the nature of a mineral; pertaining to minerals; also, impregnated with a mineral or minerals (as, *mineral* water); also, neither animal nor vegetable (as, the *mineral* kingdom); inorganic.—**mineral oil,** any of a class of oils of mineral origin, as petroleum and its derivatives, consisting of mixtures of hydrocarbons, and used as illuminants, fuels, etc., and in medicine.—**mineral pitch,** asphalt (bituminous substance).—**mineral tallow,** hatchettin.—**mineral tar,** bitumen of the consistence of tar; maltha.—**mineral wax,** ozocerite.—**min′er-al,** *n.* A substance obtained by mining; specif., any of a class of substances occurring in nature, usually comprising inorganic substances (as quartz, feldspar, etc.) of definite chemical composition, but sometimes including aggregations of these substances (more correctly called *rocks*), and also certain natural products of organic origin, as asphalt, coal, etc.; in mining use, ore; also, sometimes, any substance neither animal nor vegetable.

min-er-al-ize (min′ẹ-rạl-īz), *v.*; *-ized, -izing.* **I.** *tr.* To convert into a mineral substance (as, "We had fairly unearthed an oblong chest of wood, which, from its perfect preservation and wonderful hardness, had plainly been subjected to some *mineralizing* process": Poe's "Gold-Bug"); specif., to transform (a metal) into an ore; also, to impregnate or supply with mineral substances. **II.** *intr.* To search for or study minerals.—**min″er-al-i-za′tion** (-i-zā′shọn), *n.*—**min′er-al-iz-er** (-ī-zėr), *n.* That which mineralizes; specif., a substance which combines with a metal to form an ore.

min-er-a-log-i-cal (min″ẹ-rạ-loj′i-kạl), *a.* Of or pertaining to mineralogy.—**min″er-a-log′i-cal-ly,** *adv.*

min-er-al-o-gist (min-ẹ-ral′ọ-jist), *n.* One versed in mineralogy.

min-er-al-o-gy (min-ẹ-ral′ọ-ji), *n.*; pl. *-gies* (-jiz). [See *mineral* and *-logy*.] The science which treats of minerals; also, a treatise on this science.

Mi-ner-va (mi-nėr′vạ), *n.* [L.] The Roman goddess of wisdom, the arts, and war; hence, a woman of great wisdom or learning. Cf. *Athene*.

mi-ne-stro-ne (mē-ne-strō′nā), *n.* [It., aug. < *minestra*, soup, < L. *ministrare*, E. *minister*, *v.*] A favorite Italian soup containing vegetables, herbs, etc., in a broth of chicken or meat.

mine=sweep-er (mīn′swē″pėr), *n.* *Milit.*, a vessel or ship used for dragging a body of water in order to remove mines laid by an enemy.—**mine′=sweep″ing,** *n.*

min-gle (ming′gl), *v.*; *-gled, -gling.* [ME. *mengel*, freq. < AS. *mengan*, mix.] **I.** *tr.* To mix or combine (liquids or substances, or one liquid or substance with another); put together in a mixture; blend; put in as an added element (as, "The physicians . . . had *mingled* a sleepy potion in the hogshead of wine": Swift's "Gulliver's Travels," i. 1); form by mixing, compound, or concoct (as, "men of strength to *mingle* strong drink": Isa. v. 22); also, to unite, join, or conjoin (as, to *mingle* voices in song; to *mingle* truth and error; joy *mingled* with pain); connected by some relation (as, "I was intimately *mingled* with the last years and history of the house": Stevenson's "Master of Ballantrae," i.); associate in company or intercourse (as, "They *mingled* not themselves with the Gentiles": 2 Mac. xiv. 38). **II.** *intr.* To become mixed, blended, or united (as, "The blood of all nations is *mingling* with our own": Longfellow's "Kavanagh," xx.); also, to associate or mix in company or intercourse (as, "His companions *mingled* freely and joyously with the natives": Irving's "Captain Bonneville," xliii.); take part with others, or participate (*in*: as, to *mingle* in strife).—**min′gle-ment,** *n.* The act of mingling, or the result; a mixture.—**min′gler,** *n.*

min-i-ate (min′i-āt), *v. t.*; *-ated, -ating.* [L. *miniatus*, pp. of *miniare*, color with minium, < *minium*: see *minium.*] To color or paint with minium; rubricate or illuminate (a manuscript, etc.).—**min′i-ate,** *a.* Of the color of minium; orange-red.—**min′i-a-tor** (-ā-tọr), *n.*

min-i-a-ture (min′i-ạ-ṭūr or min′i-ṭūr). [It. *miniatura*, < L. *miniare*: see *miniate, v.*] **I.** *n.* Illumination, as of manuscripts†; also, illuminated work, or an illumination; a picture in an illuminated manuscript; hence, a very small painting, esp. a portrait, on ivory, vellum, or the like; the art of executing such paintings; also, a representation or image of anything on a very small scale (as, "Tragedy is the *miniature* of human life": Dryden's Dedication, in tr. Virgil's "Æneid"); greatly reduced or abridged form (as, "I run over the whole history of my life in *miniature*, or by abridgement, as I may call it": Defoe's "Robinson Crusoe," i. 14). **II.** *a.* On a very small scale; in a greatly reduced form: as, a *miniature* city; "She constructed a *miniature* canoe from the pasteboard covers of her primer" (Bret Harte's "Princess Bob and Her Friends").—**min′i-a-ture,** *v. t.*; *-tured, -turing.* To represent or present in miniature: as, "Still shine the words that *miniature* his deeds" (S. Lanier's "Dying Words of Stonewall Jackson").—**min′i-a-tur-ist** (-ṭūr-ist), *n.* A painter of miniatures.

Min-i-é (min′i-ā, often min′i) **ball** or **bul′let.** [From C. E. *Minié* (1804–79), the (French) inventor.] A conical bullet with a hollow base, expanding, when fired, to fit the rifling. —**Min′i-é ri′fle.** A rifle for firing the Minié ball.

min-i-fy (min′i-fī), *v. t.*; *-fied, -fying.* [Irreg. < L. *minor*, less, + E. *-fy* as in *magnify.*] To make less; also, to represent as less than in reality.—**min″i-fi-ca′tion** (-fi-kā′-shọn), *n.*

min-i-kin (min′i-kin). [MD. *minneken*, dim. of *minne*, love.] **I.** *n.* An endearing term for a girl†; also, anything delicate or diminutive; a small kind of pin. **II.** *a.* Delicate; dainty; mincing; also, diminutive; also, of the voice, shrill†.

min-im (min′im). [L. *minimus*, least, smallest, superl. of *minor*: see *minor.*] **I.** *a.* Smallest; very small. **II.** *n.* Something very small or insignificant (as, "Not all *Minims* of nature; some of serpent kind, Wondrous in length and corpulence": Milton's "Paradise Lost," vii. 482); also, the least quantity, or a jot, of anything; specif., the smallest liquid measure, the sixtieth part of a fluid dram, or about a drop; in *music*, a note, formerly the shortest in use, but now equivalent in time-value to one half of a semibreve; a half-note; [*cap.*] *eccles.*, a member of a mendicant religious order founded in the 15th century by St. Francis of Paula (1416–1507).

min-i-mal (min′i-mạl), *a.* Pertaining to or being a minimum; least possible; smallest; very small.—**Min′i-mal-ism,** *n.* [Sometimes *l. c.*] The doctrines, methods, or procedure of Minimalists.—**Min′i-mal-ist,** *n.* [Sometimes *l. c.*] In Russian politics, a member of a less radical group or faction of socialists, as of a faction of the Social Revolutionary party, or of the Social Democratic party (in which case equivalent to *Menshevik*) (see *Bolshevik, n.*); hence, a member of a similar group or faction elsewhere. Cf. *Maximalist.*

min-i-mi-za-tion (min″i-mi-zā′shọn), *n.* The act or process of minimizing.

min-i-mize (min′i-mīz), *v. t.*; *-mized, -mizing.* [L. *minimus*, least, smallest: see *minim.*] To reduce to the smallest possible amount or degree; also, to represent at the lowest possible estimate (as, "The Genteel Whig struggles persistently to *minimise* the German outrage upon civilisation and to find excuses for Germany": H. G. Wells's "Italy, France, and Britain at War," iv. 2).—**min′i-miz-er** (-mī-zėr), *n.*

min-i-mum (min′i-mum). [L., neut. of *minimus*: see *minim.*] **I.** *n.*; pl. *-mums* or *-ma* (-mạ̈). The least quantity or amount possible, assignable, allowable, etc. (as, "Admiral Bluewater devoted the *minimum* of time to sleep": Cooper's "Two Admirals," xi.); the lowest amount, value, or degree attained or recorded: opposed to *maximum.* **II.** *a.* That is a minimum; least possible (as, "I was only a poor devil of a painter with a *minimum* knowledge of such matters": F. H. Smith's "Colonel Carter of Cartersville," iv.); lowest (as, a *minimum* rate; a *minimum* temperature); also, pertaining to a minimum or minimums.

min-i-mus (min′i-mus), *n.*; pl. *-mi* (-mī). [L., least, smallest: see *minim.*] A very small or insignificant creature: as, "Get you gone, you dwarf, You *minimus*" (Shakspere's "Midsummer Night's Dream," iii. 2. 329).

min-ing (mī′ning), *n.* The act or work of one who mines; esp., the action, process, or industry of extracting ores, etc., from mines.

min-ion (min′yọn). [F. *mignon*: see *mignon.*] **I.** *a.* Dainty; elegant; trim; pretty; also, darling; favorite. [Now rare.] **II.** *n.* A lover or a mistress (chiefly in an opprobrious sense: now rare); a darling or favorite (as, "A son . . . Who is sweet Fortune's *minion* and her pride," Shakspere's "1 Henry IV.," i. 1. 83: now only in contempt); esp., a servile or base favorite of a prince or any patron; also, a minx or hussy (obs. or archaic: as, "If I once get that proud *minion* into my grasp, she shall be mine as I will," Jane Porter's "Scottish Chiefs," x.); also, a printing-type (7 point) of a size between nonpareil and brevier (see *type*).

min-ish (min′ish), *v.* [OF. *menuisier* (F. *menuiser*), make small, < L. *minutus*, E. *minute*[1].] **I.** *tr.* To diminish, lessen, or reduce; also, to depreciate or belittle; also, to take away or deduct (as, "Ye shall not *minish* ought from your bricks of your daily task": Ex. v. 19). [Archaic.] **II.** *intr.* To become less; decrease. [Archaic.]

min-is-ter (min′is-tėr), *n.* [OF. F. *ministre*, < L. *minister*, servant, attendant, inferior officer, akin to *minor*, less: see *minor*, and cf. *master*[2] (L. *magister*, akin to *magis*, more).] A servant or attendant (archaic); also, one acting as the agent or instrument of another (as, "The angry Victor hath recall'd His *ministers* of vengeance and pursuit": Milton's "Paradise Lost," i. 170); specif., one appointed by (or under the authority of) the sovereign or executive head of a government to some high office of state, esp. to that of head of an administrative department (as, the prime *minister*, see under *prime*[1], *a.*; the French *minister* of justice); also, a diplomatic representative accredited by one government to another; specif., an envoy, or diplomatic agent of the second class ('envoy extraordinary and minister plenipotentiary': see *envoy*[2]); also, one authorized to conduct religious worship; a clergyman; a pastor (as, "Preaching is the smallest portion of the duties of a faithful *minister*": Galt's "Annals of the Parish," Introd.).—**min′is-ter,** *v.* [OF. *ministrer*, < L. *ministrare* (pp. *ministratus*), < *minister.*] **I.** *tr.* To serve (food, etc.)†; also, to furnish, supply, or afford (archaic: as, "I will endeavour most faithfully not to *minister* any occasion of strife," Scott's "Castle Dangerous," xix.); also, to administer† or apply†. **II.** *intr.* To give service, care, or aid (as, "When saw we thee an hungred, or athirst, or a stranger, or naked, or sick, or in prison, and did not *minister* unto thee?" Mat. xxv. 44); attend, as to wants, necessities, etc.; contribute, as to comfort, happiness, etc.; conduce, or tend to add (as, "My lord's clearness of mind . . . had not ceased to *minister* to my amazement": Stevenson's "Master of Ballantrae," v.); also, to officiate in religious worship.

min-is-te-ri-al (min-is-tē′ri-ạl), *a.* [LL. *ministerialis*, < L. *ministerium*, E. *ministry.*] Of or pertaining to ministry or service; ministering; subservient or subsidiary; instrumental; also, pertaining to or invested with delegated executive authority (as, a *ministerial* act, an act, as one arising from official duty, performed under given circumstances in a prescribed manner, without dependence on the exercise of judgment as to its propriety); also, pertaining to a ministry or minister of state; pertaining to the ministry of state in office; also, pertaining to the ministry of religion, or to a minister or clergyman.—**min-is-te′ri-al-ist,** *n.* In *politics*, a supporter of the ministry in office.—**min-is-te′ri-al-ly,** *adv.*

min-is-ter-ship (min′is-tėr-ship), *n.* The office of a minister.

min-is-trant (min′is-trạnt). [L. *ministrans* (*-ant-*), ppr. of *ministrare*, E. *minister, v.*] **I.** *a.* Ministering: as, "angels *ministrant*" (Milton's "Paradise Regained," ii. 385). **II.** *n.* One who ministers.

min-is-tra-tion (min-is-trā′shọn), *n.* [L. *ministratio(n-).*] The act of ministering; furnishing, supplying, or giving; ministering service, care, or aid, or an instance of it (as, "in sore extremity, when she most needed the *ministration* of her own sex," Bret Harte's "Luck of Roaring Camp"; kindly *ministrations*); religious ministering or service, or an instance of it (as, the *ministration*, or *ministrations*, of a priest).—**min'is-tra-tive** (-trā-tiv), *a.* Ministering; rendering service.

min-is-tress (min'is-tres), *n.* A female minister.

min-is-try (min'is-tri), *n.*; pl. *-tries* (-triz). [L. *ministerium*, < *minister*, E. *minister*, *n.*] The act of ministering; ministration; service; agency; specif., the service, function, or office of a minister of state; the body of ministers of state, or head of administrative departments, in a country (as, the French *ministry*: in the U. S. the corresponding body is called the *cabinet*); any of the administrative departments of a country; also, the service, functions, or profession of a minister of religion; the body or class of ministers of religion; the clergy.

min-i-um (min'i-um), *n.* [L., native cinnabar, also red lead.] Vermilion; also, red lead (see under *lead*², *n.*).

min-i-ver (min'i-vėr), *n.* [OF. *menu vair*, 'small vair': see *menu* and *vair*.] A kind of fur formerly much used for lining and trimming garments, variously described, as a finely spotted white and gray fur, or a white fur symmetrically adorned with pieces of a dark fur, or a plain white fur; also, an ermine in its white winter coat (prov. Eng.).

mink (mingk), *n.* [Cf. Sw. *mänk*.] A semiaquatic weasel-like animal of the genus *Putorius*, esp. the North American *P. vison*; also, its fur, of a chestnut-brown color.

North American Mink (*Putorius vison*).

min-ne-sing-er (min'ė-sing"ėr, G. min'ė-zing"ėr), *n.* [G., 'love singer.'] One of a class of German lyric poets and singers of the 12th, 13th, and 14th centuries: so called because love was the chief theme of their songs.

min-nie (min'i), *n.* [Cf. *mammy*.] A childish word for *mother*. [Sc. and north. Eng.]

min-now (min'ō), *n.* [ME. *menow*, appar. < AS. *myne*, kind of fish.] A small European cyprinoid fish, *Phoxinus phoxinus*; also, as in the U. S., any of various other small fishes, esp. cyprinoids.

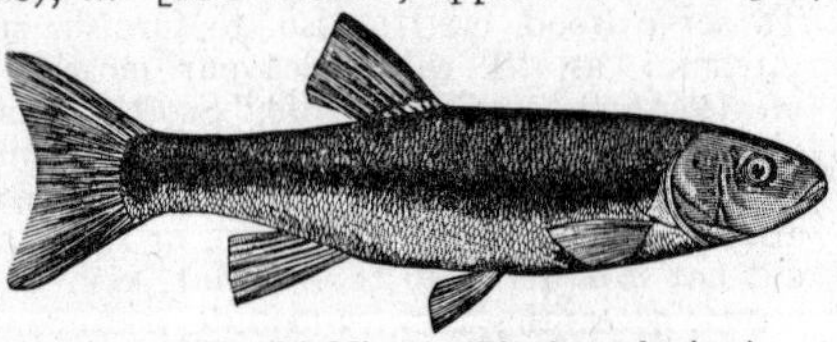

Common English Minnow (*Phoxinus phoxinus*).

mi-no (mē'nō), *n.*; pl. *-nos* (-nōz). [Jap.] A kind of cloak or outer covering made of long grass, rushes, or the like, worn by laborers, etc., in Japan.

Mino.

mi-nor (mī'nọr), *a.* [L. *minor* (neut. *minus*), less, smaller, inferior, younger, a compar. form (with superl. *minimus*: see *minim*) associated with *parvus*, little: cf. *minute*¹ and *minister*.] Lesser, as in size, extent, or importance, or being the lesser of two (as, Asia *Minor*; the *minor* group in a divided deliberative body); of a less important or not especially important class or kind (as, *minor* officials; *minor* poets; *minor* faults or considerations); also, younger or junior (used after a name, in contradistinction to *major*: see *major*, *a.*); also, under legal age; in *logic*, less broad or extensive (as, the *minor* term of a syllogism, being the term that appears as the subject of the conclusion; the *minor* premise, that premise of a syllogism which contains the minor term); in *music*, of an interval, smaller by a half-step than the corresponding major interval (see *major*, *a.*); of a chord, having a minor third between the root and the second note; of a tone, distant by a minor interval from a given tone; also, noting a scale, mode, or key whose third tone is minor in relation to the fundamental tone.—**Friars Minor.** See under *friar*.—**minor orders.** See *order*, *n.*—**minor planets.** See *planet*.—**Minor Prophets.** See *prophet*. —**mi'nor,** *n.* One of inferior rank or importance in a specified class; also, a subject or a course of study pursued by a student, esp. a candidate for a degree, subordinately or supplementarily to a major or principal subject or course (U. S.); also, a person under legal age; also [*cap.*], a Minorite or Franciscan friar; [*l. c.*] in *logic*, the minor term or premise; in *music*, a minor interval, chord, scale, etc.—**mi'nor,** *v. i.* To pursue a minor subject or course of study. [U. S.]

Mi-nor-ca (mi-nôr'kạ̈), *n.* [From the island of *Minorca*.] One of a breed of domestic fowls of moderate size, notable for prolific laying.

Mi-nor-ite (mī'nọr-īt), *n.* [See *minor*.] One of the Friars Minor; a Franciscan friar.

mi-nor-i-ty (mi-nor'i-ti or mī-), *n.*; pl. *-ties* (-tiz). [F. *minorité*, < ML. *minoritas*, < L. *minor*: see *minor*.] The state of being less, smaller, or less important†; also, the state or period of being a minor or under legal age (as, "the long *minority* of Henry the Sixth, who was a boy nine months old at his father's death": Green's "Short Hist. of the Eng. People," vi. 1); also, the smaller part or number, or a number forming less than half of the whole (as, such cases represent only a *minority* of the total number); specif., a smaller party or group opposed to a majority, as in voting or other action (sometimes used attributively: as, a *minority* opinion or report).

Min-o-taur (min'ọ-târ), *n.* [L. *Minotaurus*, < Gr. Μινώταυρος, < Μίνως, Minos (king of Crete, for whom the labyrinth was built), + ταῦρος, bull.] A fabulous monster of Greek mythology, half bull and half man, confined in the Cretan labyrinth and fed with human flesh; hence, any devouring or destroying agency.

min-ster (min'stėr), *n.* [AS. *mynster*, < LL. *monasterium*, E. *monastery*.] A monastery†; also, a church actually or originally connected with a monastic establishment; hence, any large or important church, as a cathedral.

min-strel (min'strẹl), *n.* [OF. *menestrel* (F. *ménestrel*), minstrel, orig. servant, attendant, < LL. *ministerialis*, of or for service, E. *ministerial*.] A professional entertainer†; specif., one of a class of medieval musicians who sang or recited to the accompaniment of instruments (as, "Here to the harp did *minstrels* sing": Scott's "Marmion," v. 7); hence, any musician, singer, or poet (poetic); also, one of a troupe of comedians, usually white men made up as negroes, presenting negro songs, jokes, etc. (also *negro minstrel*). — **min'strel-sy** (-si), *n.*; pl. *-sies* (-siz). [OF. *menestralsie*.] The art or practice of a minstrel; also, minstrels' songs, ballads, etc. (as, Scott's "*Minstrelsy* of the Scottish Border"); also, a body of minstrels (as, "Nodding their heads before her goes The merry *minstrelsy*": Coleridge's "Ancient Mariner," i.).

Minstrel. — From the Maison des Musiciens, Rheims, France; 13th century.

mint¹ (mint), *v.* [AS. *myntan*.] **I.** *tr.* To intend; attempt; aim; also, to hint at; insinuate. [Now Sc. and prov.

Eng.] **II.** *intr.* To make an attempt; aim (*at*); also, to hint. [Now Sc. and prov. Eng.]

mint[2] (mint), *n.* [AS. *minte*, < L. *menta*, *mentha*, < Gr. *μίνθα*, mint.] Any plant of the genus *Mentha*, comprising aromatic herbs with opposite leaves and small verticillate flowers, as the spearmint, the peppermint, and the horsemint; also, any menthaceous plant.

mint[3] (mint), *n.* [AS. *mynet*, coin, < L. *moneta*, mint, money, < *Moneta*, lit. 'adviser,' surname of Juno, in whose temple at Rome money was coined, < *monere*, remind, advise: see *mind*[2], and cf. *money*.] A coin†; coined money†; money†; also, a place where money is coined by public authority; fig., a place where anything is made or fabricated (as, "A man . . . That hath a *mint* of phrases in his brain": Shakspere's "Love's Labour's Lost," i. 1. 166); also, a vast amount (of money); a very great amount or number (of anything: as, to give one a *mint* of trouble; "He has a *mint* of reasons; ask," Tennyson's "The Epic," 33).—**mint**[3], *v. t.* To make (coins) by stamping metal; coin (money); fig., to make or fabricate as if by coining (as, to *mint* words or phrases); give a form or character to as by stamping (as, "when scandal has new *minted* an old lie": Cowper's "Charity," 513).—**mint-age** (min'tāj), *n.* The act or process of minting; coinage; fabrication; also, the product or result of minting; the output of a mint; a word, phrase, or the like minted or coined; a stamp or character impressed (as, "Pleasing poison . . . unmoulding reason's *mintage* Character'd in the face": Milton's "Comus," 529); also, the charge for or cost of minting or coining.—**mint'er,** *n.* —**mint'=mark,** *n.* A private mark put upon coins by mint authorities, as to indicate the place of coinage.

min-u-end (min'ū-end), *n.* [L. *minuendus*, gerundive of *minuere*, make smaller: see *minute*[1].] In *math.*, the number or quantity from which another (the *subtrahend*) is to be deducted in the operation of subtraction.

min-u-et (min-ū-et'), *n.* [F. *menuet*, orig. adj., very small (with reference to the small steps taken in the dance), dim. of *menu*, small: see *menu*.] A slow, stately dance of French origin; also, a piece of music for such a dance or in its rhythm (sometimes forming a movement in the suite).

mi-nus (mī'nus). [L., adj., neut. of *minor*: see *minor*.] **I.** *a.* Less (by a certain amount: a quasi-prepositional use: see *minus*, *prep.*); also, involving or denoting subtraction (as, a *minus* quantity; the *minus* sign, −); negative; also, lacking (colloq.: as, the profits were *minus*). **II.** *n.* The minus sign; also, a minus quantity; also, a deficiency or loss.—**mi'nus,** *prep.* Less by the subtraction of, or decreased by (as, 10 *minus* 3; gross earnings *minus* costs); hence, wanting or without (as, a book *minus* its title-page; to escape *minus* hat and coat; "We went away a complete carcass; we come back *minus* a leg, an arm, an eye," W. De Morgan's "Alice-for-Short," xxix.).

mi-nus-cule (mi-nus'kūl). [F., < L. *minusculus*, rather small, dim. of *minor*: see *minor*.] In *paleography*: **I.** *a.* Small, as letters not capital or uncial; also, written in such letters: opposed to *majuscule*. Hence fig., or in general use, very small. **II.** *n.* A minuscule letter as distinguished from a capital or an uncial; also, the small cursive script developed in the 7th century from the uncial, which it afterward superseded.—**mi-nus'cu-lar** (-kū-lär), *a.*

mi-nute[1] (mi-nūt' or mī-), *a.*; compar. *minuter*, superl. *minutest*. [L. *minutus*, pp. of *minuere*, make smaller, akin to *minor*, less, smaller: see *minor*.] Extremely small, as in size, amount, extent, or degree (as, *minute* animals; *minute* portions, differences, or variations); of very small scope or individual importance (as, to detail the *minutest* particulars of a case); sometimes, petty or trifling; also, attentive to or concerned with even very small details or particulars (as, a *minute* observer; *minute* inquiries; "after the *minutest* consideration I was able to bestow upon this question," Godwin's "Caleb Williams," xxxiv.); detailing even very small or trifling particulars, as an account or report.

min-ute[2] (min'it), *n.* [OF. F. *minute*, < ML. *minuta*, small part or division, prop. fem. of L. *minutus*, E. *minute*[1].] The sixtieth part of an hour, or sixty seconds; hence, an indefinitely short space of time (as, wait a *minute*); also, a point of time, or an instant or moment (as, come here this *minute*; we expect him at any *minute*); also, a rough draft, as of a document; a written summary, as of a transaction; a note or memorandum (as, "Glossin had made careful *minutes* of the information derived from these examinations": Scott's "Guy Mannering," xxxiii.); specif., *pl.*, the official record of the proceedings at a meeting of a society, board, committee, council, or other body; also, *sing.*, in *geom.*, etc., the sixtieth part of a degree, or sixty seconds (often represented by the sign ′: as, 12° 10′, that is, twelve degrees and ten minutes). —**min'ute**[2], *v. t.*; *-uted*, *-uting*. To time exactly, as movements, speed, etc.; also, to make a draft of (a document, etc.); record (something) in a memorandum; note (*down*: as, "I . . . told them the story . . . just as I have since *minuted* it down," Defoe's "Robinson Crusoe," ii. 16; "'Clerk,' said Pleydell, '*minute* down that reply,'" Scott's "Guy Mannering," lvi.); enter in the minutes of a society or other body.—**min'ute=gun,** *n.* A gun which is being fired at intervals of a minute, as in token of mourning or of distress.—**min'ute=hand,** *n.* The hand that indicates the minutes on a clock or watch. Cf. *hour-hand*.

mi-nute-ly[1] (mi-nūt'li or mī-), *adv.* In a minute manner, form, or degree; in minute detail.

min-ute-ly[2] (min'it-li). **I.** *a.* Occurring every minute: as, "Now *minutely* revolts upbraid his faith-breach" (Shakspere's "Macbeth," v. 2. 18). **II.** *adv.* Every minute; minute by minute.

min-ute=man (min'it-man), *n.*; pl. *-men*. One of a class of American militiamen just before and during the Revolutionary War who held themselves in readiness for instant military service.

mi-nute-ness (mi-nūt'nes or mī-), *n.* The state or quality of being minute; extreme smallness; attention to minute details; minute particularity.

mi-nu-ti-a (mi-nū'shi-ä), *n.*; pl. *-tiæ* (-shi-ē). [L., < *minutus*, E. *minute*[1].] A small or trivial detail; a trifling circumstance or matter: usually in *pl.*: as, "They waited . . . for the exchange of pass-words, the delivery of keys, and all the slow *minutiæ* attendant upon the movements of a garrison in a well-guarded fortress" (Scott's "Castle Dangerous," viii.).—**mi-nu'ti-ose** (-shi-ōs), *a.* Attentive to or concerned with minutiæ. Also **mi-nu'tious** (-shus).

minx (mingks), *n.* [Origin uncertain.] A pet dog†; also, a pert girl, or hussy (as, "She liked the notion of humbling the haughty *minx*," J. H. Newman's "Callista," vii.: often used playfully); also, a lewd woman†.

Mi-o-cene (mī'ō-sēn). [Gr. *μείων*, less, + *καινός*, new.] In *geol.*: **I.** *a.* Noting or pertaining to a division of the Tertiary period or system preceding the Pliocene. **II.** *n.* The Miocene division of the Tertiary.

mir (mēr), *n.* [Russ.] A Russian commune or peasant community.

mir-a-cle (mir'a-kl), *n.* [OF. F. *miracle*, < L. *miraculum*, a wonderful thing, < *mirari*, wonder at: cf. *marvel*.] Something that excites wonder or astonishment; a wonderful thing; a marvel; often, a wonderful or surpassing example of some quality (as, "representing him as a perfect *miracle* of goodness and generosity," Smollett's "Humphry Clinker," after Oct. 4; "They deemed the young clergyman a *miracle* of holiness," Hawthorne's "Scarlet Letter," xi.); esp., an effect in the physical world which surpasses all known human or natural powers and is therefore ascribed to supernatural agency (as, "A *miracle* may be accurately defined, a transgression of a law of nature by a particular volition of the Deity, or by the interposition of some invisible agent": Hume's "Essays," Of Miracles, i., note); also, a miracle-play. —**mir'a-cle=man** (-man), *n.*; pl. *-men*. A man who performs miracles; a wonder-worker; sometimes (colloq.), a man who accomplishes something of unusual difficulty or previously thought impossible.—**mir'a-cle=play,** *n.* A medieval dramatic representation or composition based on Biblical events or the legends of the saints, or (as sometimes restricted) on the latter alone. Cf. *mystery*[1].

mi-rac-u-lous (mi-rak'ū-lus), *a.* [F. *miraculeux*, < ML. *miraculosus*, < L. *miraculum*, E. *miracle*.] Of the nature of a miracle; marvelous or extraordinary (as, "By some *miraculous* accident, Hawkins was passing by": Godwin's "Caleb Williams," xviii.); esp., performed by or involving a power beyond the ordinary agency of natural laws (as, *miraculous* cures at the shrine of a saint); supernatural;

also, having power to work miracles; wonder-working.—**mi-rac′u-lous-ly,** *adv.*—**mi-rac′u-lous-ness,** *n.*

mi-rage (mi-räzh′), *n.* [F., < *mirer*, look at (one's self) in a mirror, see reflected, < ML. *mirare*: see *mirror*.] An optical illusion, due to atmospheric conditions, by which reflected images of distant objects are seen, often inverted.

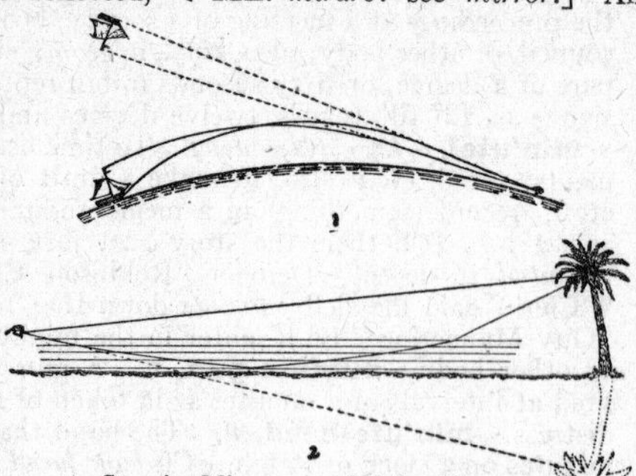

1. Superior Mirage. 2. Inferior Mirage.

mire (mīr), *n.* [ME. *myre*; from Scand.: cf. Icel. *mȳrr* = Sw. and Dan. *myr*, bog, swamp: see *moss*.] A piece of wet, swampy ground (as, "As when a wandering fire . . . Misleads the amaz'd night-wanderer from his way To bogs and *mires*": Milton's "Paradise Lost," ix. 641); also, ground of this kind; wet, slimy soil of some depth, or deep mud (as, "I sink in deep *mire*, where there is no standing": Ps. lxix. 2); muddy or wet matter, or dirt (as, "like the troubled sea . . . whose waters cast up *mire* and dirt": Isa. lvii. 20).—**mire,** *v.*; *mired, miring.* **I.** *tr.* To plunge and fix in mire; cause to stick fast in mire; fig., to involve in difficulties; also, to soil with mire or filth; bespatter with mire. **II.** *intr.* To sink in mire; stick in the mud: as, "a path . . . that is so muddy that one *mires* afore he sets out" (Cooper's "Deerslayer," ii.).

mi-rif-ic (mī-rif′ik), *a.* [OF. F. *mirifique*, < L. *mirificus*, < *mirus*, wonderful, + *facere*, make.] Causing wonder; wonderful; marvelous. [Now rare.]

mir-i-ness (mīr′i-nes), *n.* Miry condition.

mirk (mėrk), etc. See *murk*, etc.

mir-ror (mir′ǫr), *n.* [OF. *mireor* (F. *miroir*), < ML. *mirare*, look at, < L. *mirari*, wonder at, admire: cf. *mirage*.] A piece of some reflecting substance, orig. polished metal, now usually glass with a metallic or amalgam backing, used esp. to reflect the face or person as an aid in making the toilet; a looking-glass; specif. (in *optics*), a surface (plane, concave, or convex) for reflecting rays of light; a speculum; also, a glass, crystal, or the like used by magicians, etc. (as, "With a single drop of ink for a *mirror*, the Egyptian sorcerer undertakes to reveal . . . visions of the past": George Eliot's "Adam Bede," i.); also, any of certain objects suggesting a mirror, as a small oval architectural ornament, or a speculum on the wing of a bird; also, in fig. use, something that gives a faithful reflection or true picture of something else (as, "those *mirrors* of life, plays and novels": Bulwer-Lytton's "Caxtons," ix. 2); a pattern for imitation, or exemplar (as, "Sir Philip Sidney, the *mirror* of chivalry": Motley's "Dutch Republic," vi. 5); a model of excellence† (as, "the *mirror* of all Christian kings": Shakspere's "Henry V.," ii., Prologue, 6).—**mir′ror,** *v. t.* To reflect in or as in a mirror, or as a mirror does: as, "Where Lisbon *mirrors* in the stream Her belt of ancient towers" (Holmes's "Agnes," iv.).—**mir′ror=writ″ing,** *n.* Writing reversed from the usual order, as if seen reflected in a mirror: sometimes indicative of aphasia or nervous disease.

mirth (mėrth), *n.* [AS. *myrgth, myrigth*, < *myrige*, E. *merry*.] Joy† or delight†; also, rejoicing, joyous gaiety, or festive jollity (as, "I commended *mirth*, because a man hath no better thing under the sun, than to eat, and to drink, and to be merry": Eccl. viii. 15); merriment or hilarity; often, humorous amusement, as at something ludicrous, or laughter excited by it (as, to listen with inward *mirth*; a ripple of *mirth* passed over the audience; "Again the young friends gave way to their *mirth*," Longfellow's "Kavanagh," xvii.); also, a cause or source of merriment†.—**mirth′ful,** *a.* Full of mirth; joyous; jolly; merry; laughingly gay or amused; also, affording mirth, or amusing.—**mirth′ful-ly,** *adv.*—**mirth′ful-ness,** *n.*—**mirth′less,** *a.* Without mirth; joyless; gloomy.—**mirth′less-ly,** *adv.*—**mirth′less-ness,** *n.*

mir-y (mīr′i), *a.* Of the nature of mire (as, *miry* ground); swampy; also, abounding in mire (as, "the *miry* defiles of the mountains": Irving's "Conquest of Granada," lxx.); muddy; also, covered or bespattered with mire; also, fig., dirty; filthy.

mir-za (mēr′zä), *n.* [Pers. *mīrzā*, < *mīr*, prince (< Ar. *amīr*: see *amir*), + *zād*, born.] In Persia, a royal prince (as a title, placed after the name); also, a Persian title of honor for men, prefixed to the name.

mis-. [Partly < AS. *mis-* = D. *mis-* = G. *miss-* = Icel. *mis-* = Goth. *missa-*, amiss, wrongly or wrong, ill, repr. an old participial form whence also E. *miss*[1] (see *miss*[1]); partly < OF. *mes-*, F. *més-*, *mes-*, *mé-*, amiss, ill, not, < L. *minus*, adv., less, not (cf. *minus*).] A prefix of twofold origin, first in words from the Anglo-Saxon and later in others from the French, meaning 'amiss,' 'wrongly' or 'wrong,' 'ill,' 'perversely' or 'perverse,' or expressing negation of something good or desirable, much used as an English formative prefixed to verbs (including participles) and nouns, as in *misapply, misbehave, miscall, miscopy, misdeem, misfaith, mismove, mistrial*, and occasionally to adjectives, as in *miscontent, misproud*.

mis-ad-dress (mis-ą-dres′), *v. t.* [See *mis-*.] To address wrongly, improperly, or incorrectly.

mis-ad-ven-ture (mis-ąd-ven′tụ̄r), *n.* [OF. *mesaventure* (F. *mésaventure*): see *mis-* and *adventure*.] Ill fortune; also, a piece of ill fortune; a mishap.—**mis-ad-ven′tur-ous,** *a.* Unfortunate; unlucky.

mis-ad-vice (mis-ąd-vīs′), *n.* [See *mis-*.] Bad advice.

mis-ad-vise (mis-ąd-vīz′), *v. t.*; *-vised, -vising.* [See *mis-*.] To advise wrongly.

mis-al-li-ance (mis-ą-lī′ąns), *n.* [See *mis-*, and cf. *mésalliance*.] An improper alliance or association, esp. in marriage; a mésalliance.—**mis-al-ly′** (-ą-lī′), *v. t.*; *-lied, -lying.* To ally improperly or unsuitably.

mis-an-thrope (mis′ąn-thrōp), *n.* [Gr. μισάνθρωπος, hating mankind, < μισεῖν, hate, + ἄνθρωπος, man.] A hater of mankind; one who harbors dislike or distrust of human character or motives in general.—**mis-an-throp′ic, mis-an-throp′i-cal** (-throp′ik, -i-kąl), *a.* Of, pertaining to, or characteristic of a misanthrope (as, "scowling on all the world from his *misanthropic* seclusion": Parkman's "Oregon Trail," xxvi.); having the character of, or resembling, a misanthrope (as, "a *misanthropic* recluse": Jane Porter's "Scottish Chiefs," xxxv.).—**mis-an-throp′i-cal-ly,** *adv.*—**mis-an′thro-pist** (-an′thrǭ-pist), *n.* A misanthrope.—**mis-an′thro-pize** (-pīz), *v.*; *-pized, -pizing.* **I.** *intr.* To play the misanthrope; hate mankind. **II.** *tr.* To render misanthropic.—**mis-an′thro-py** (-pi), *n.* [Gr. μισανθρωπία.] Hatred, dislike, or distrust of mankind: as, "My *misanthropy* increases every day. The longer I live, I find the folly and the fraud of mankind grow more and more intolerable" (Smollett's "Humphry Clinker," April 28).

mis-ap-ply (mis-ą-plī′), *v. t.*; *-plied, -plying.* [See *mis-*.] To apply wrongly; make a wrong application or use of.—**mis-ap-pli-ca′tion** (-ap-li-kā′shǫn), *n.*

mis-ap-pre-ci-ate (mis-ą-prē′shi-āt), *v. t.*; *-ated, -ating.* [See *mis-*.] To appreciate ill; estimate or value wrongly.—**mis-ap-pre-ci-a′tion** (-ṣi-ā′shǫn), *n.* Wrong appreciation or estimation.—**mis-ap-pre′ci-a-tive** (-shi-ą-tiv), *a.* Misappreciating.

mis-ap-pre-hend (mis-ap-rę̄-hend′), *v. t.* or *i.* [See *mis-*.] To apprehend wrongly; misunderstand.—**mis-ap-pre-hen′sion** (-hen′shǫn), *n.* Wrong apprehension; misunderstanding, as of meaning; misconception.—**mis-ap-pre-hen′sive** (-siv), *a.* Misapprehending; apt to misapprehend.—**mis-ap-pre-hen′sive-ly,** *adv.*

mis-ap-pro-pri-ate (mis-ą-prō′pri-āt), *v. t.*; *-ated, -ating.* [See *mis-*.] To appropriate wrongly; put to a wrong use; esp., to apply wrongfully or dishonestly to one's own use, as funds intrusted to one.—**mis-ap-pro′pri-ate** (-ąt), *a.* Inappropriate.—**mis-ap-pro-pri-a′tion** (-ā′shǫn), *n.* Appropriation to a wrong use.

mis-ar-range (mis-ą-rānj′), *v. t.*; *-ranged, -ranging.* [See *mis-*.] To arrange wrongly.—**mis-ar-range′ment,** *n.*

mis-be-come (mis-bę̄-kum′), *v. t.*; pret. *-came*, pp. *-come*, ppr. *-coming.* [See *mis-*.] To become or befit ill; be unsuitable or unseemly for: as, "Secundra Dass . . . wore a decent plain black suit, which *misbecame* him strangely" (Stevenson's "Master of Ballantrae," viii.).

mis-be-get (mis-bē-get′), *v. t.* [See *mis-*.] To beget unlawfully.—**mis-be-got′ten** (-got′n), **mis-be-got′**, *p. a.* Unlawfully or irregularly begotten; illegitimate.

mis-be-have (mis-bē-hāv′), *v. t.* or *i.*; *-haved, -having.* [See *mis-*.] To behave badly: as, "She was not the woman to *misbehave* towards her betters" (George Eliot's "Adam Bede," xxxii.).—**mis-be-hav′ior, mis-be-hav′iour** (-hāv′-yọr), *n.*

mis-be-lief (mis-bē-lēf′), *n.* [See *mis-*.] Wrong or erroneous belief; false opinion; esp., erroneous or unorthodox religious belief.—**mis-be-lieve′**, *v.*; *-lieved, -lieving.* **I.** *intr.* To believe wrongly; hold an erroneous or false belief. **II.** *tr.* To disbelieve; doubt. [Now prov.]—**mis-be-liev′er**, *n.*

mis-be-stow (mis-bē-stō′), *v. t.* [See *mis-*.] To bestow improperly.—**mis-be-stow′al**, *n.*

mis-cal-cu-late (mis-kal′kū-lāt), *v. t.* or *i.*; *-lated, -lating.* [See *mis-*.] To calculate wrongly.—**mis-cal-cu-la′tion** (-lā′shọn), *n.* Wrong calculation.—**mis-cal′cu-la-tor**, *n.*

mis-call (mis-kâl′), *v. t.* [See *mis-*.] To call by a wrong name; misname; sometimes, to mispronounce (prov.: as, "I did not . . . understand the half of what I read, and *miscalled* the words to myself," Mrs. Stowe's "Oldtown Folks," xvii.); also, to revile (now prov.: as, "You would begin some of your tantrums, and *miscall* her," H. Kingsley's "Geoffry Hamlyn," vi.).

mis-car-riage (mis-kar′ạj), *n.* [See *miscarry*.] The act of miscarrying; misbehavior†; mischance†; failure to attain the right end or the purposed or desired result (as, a *miscarriage* of justice; "With infinite difficulty and repeated *miscarriages* I at length effected my purpose," Godwin's "Caleb Williams," Postscript); failure of a letter, etc., to reach its destination; also, premature expulsion of a fetus from the uterus, esp. before it is viable.

mis-car-ry (mis-kar′i), *v. i.*; *-ried, -rying.* [Appar. orig. < OF. *meskarier*, go from the right path, < *mes-* (see *mis-*) + *karier*, *carier*, E. *carry*; later associated rather with E. *mis-* and *carry*.] To do wrong†, or misbehave†; suffer harm or destruction†; fail to attain the right end (as, justice sometimes *miscarries*); fail in one's purpose or object, or be unsuccessful (as, "I would never *miscarry* in this project through any neglect of mine": Godwin's "Caleb Williams," xxx.); prove abortive or a failure, as a project or undertaking (as, "Some of his schemes *miscarried*": Smollett's "Humphry Clinker," Sept. 6); go astray or be lost in transit, as a letter; also, to bring forth a fetus prematurely, esp. before it is viable; have a miscarriage.

mis-ce-ge-na-tion (mis″ē-je-nā′shọn), *n.* [L. *miscere*, mix, + *genus*, race.] Mixture of races by sexual union; interbreeding between different races, as the white and the black.

mis-cel-la-ne-a (mis-ẹ-lā′nē-ạ), *n. pl.* [L., neut. pl. of *miscellaneus*, E. *miscellaneous*.] A miscellaneous collection, esp. of literary compositions.

mis-cel-la-ne-ous (mis-ẹ-lā′nē-us), *a.* [L. *miscellaneus*, < *miscellus*, mixed, < *miscere*, mix.] Consisting of members or elements of different kinds (as, *miscellaneous* volumes); of mixed character (as, "My reading . . . had been extremely *miscellaneous*": Godwin's "Caleb Williams," xxv.); also, having various qualities or aspects; dealing with various subjects; many-sided (as, "The Baron of Hohenfels was rather a *miscellaneous* youth, rather a universal genius": Longfellow's "Hyperion," i. 6).—**mis-cel-la′ne-ous-ly**, *adv.*—**mis-cel-la′ne-ous-ness**, *n.*

mis-cel-la-nist (mis′ẹ-lạ-nist), *n.* A writer of miscellanies.

mis-cel-la-ny (mis′ẹ-lạ-ni), *n.*; pl. *-nies* (-niz). [L. *miscellanea*: see *miscellanea*.] A miscellaneous collection, esp. of literary compositions; *pl.*, miscellaneous writings assembled in a volume or book.

mis-chance (mis-chȧns′), *n.* [OF. *mescheance*: see *mis-* and *chance*.] Ill luck; a mishap or misfortune.—**mis-chance′ful**, *a.* Unlucky; unfortunate. [Archaic.]

mis-charge (mis-chärj′), *v. t.*; *-charged, -charging.* [See *mis-*.] To charge wrongly, as an item in an account.—**mis-charge′**, *n.* An erroneous charge.

mis-chief (mis′chif), *n.* [OF. *meschief* (F. *méchef*), < *meschever*, succeed ill, < *mes-* (see *mis-*) + *chever*, come to an end, < *chef*, head, end: see *chief*.] Ill fortune†; also, harm or trouble, esp. as due to an agent or cause (as, "Who can tell the *mischief* which the very virtuous do?" Thackeray's "Newcomes," xx.; to make *mischief*, to make trouble or create discord, as by talebearing); an injury caused by a person or other agent, or an evil due to some cause (as, "Thy tongue deviseth *mischiefs*," Ps. lii. 2; "Cut along . . . before I do you a *mischief*," H. Kingsley's "Geoffry Hamlyn," xiii.); also, the vexatious or unfortunate thing or circumstance about some matter (as, the *mischief* of it is that we cannot prove anything); also, a cause or source of harm or evil, or of annoyance (as, "The sacred implement I now employ Might prove a *mischief*, or at best a toy": Cowper's "Progress of Error," 302); also, vexatious or annoying action; a tendency or disposition to vex or annoy; sometimes, conduct such as to cause petty annoyance by way of sport; a roguish disposition to tease; also, with *the*, the devil (colloq.: as, what the *mischief* do you mean?).—**mis′chief=mak″er**, *n.* One who makes mischief; one who stirs up discord, as by talebearing.—**mis′chief=mak″ing**, *n.* and *a.*—**mis′chie-vous** (-chi-vus), *a.* [AF. *meschevous*.] Unfortunate†; also, harmful or injurious (as, "vicious actions . . . *mischievous* to society": J. Butler's "Analogy of Religion," i. 3); also, maliciously or playfully annoying, as persons, actions, etc.; fond of mischief, as children; roguishly or archly teasing, as speeches, glances, etc.—**mis′chie-vous-ly**, *adv.*—**mis′chie-vous-ness**, *n.*

mis-choice (mis-chois′), *n.* [See *mis-*.] A wrong choice.

mis-choose (mis-chöz′), *v. t.* or *i.*; pret. *-chose*, pp. *-chosen*, ppr. *-choosing.* [See *mis-*.] To choose wrongly or ill.

mis-ci-ble (mis′i-bl), *a.* [= F. *miscible*, < L. *miscere*, mix.] Capable of being mixed.—**mis-ci-bil′i-ty** (-bil′i-ti), *n.*

mis-cite (mis-sīt′), *v. t.*; *-cited, -citing.* [See *mis-*.] To cite erroneously; misquote.—**mis-ci-ta′tion** (-sī-tā′shọn), *n.*

mis-col-or (mis-kul′ọr), *v. t.* [See *mis-*.] To give a wrong color to; fig., to misrepresent.

mis-com-pre-hend (mis-kom-prē-hend′), *v. t.* [See *mis-*.] To misunderstand.—**mis-com-pre-hen′sion** (-hen′shọn), *n.*

mis-con-ceive (mis-kọn-sēv′), *v. t.* or *i.*; *-ceived, -ceiving.* [See *mis-*.] To conceive wrongly; misapprehend or misunderstand.—**mis-con-cep′tion** (-sep′shọn), *n.* Erroneous conception; a mistaken notion.

mis-con-duct (mis-kon′dukt), *n.* [See *mis-*.] Mismanagement, often on the part of an official in regard to his office; also, improper conduct (as, "a long remonstrance against the *misconduct* of the soldiery": Motley's "Dutch Republic," iv. 3); wrong behavior.—**mis-con-duct′** (-kọn-dukt′), *v. t.* To mismanage; also, to misbehave (one's self).

mis-con-struc-tion (mis-kọn-struk′shọn), *n.* The act of misconstruing; wrong construction; misinterpretation.

mis-con-strue (mis-kon′strö or -kọn-strö′), *v. t.*; *-strued, -struing.* [See *mis-*.] To construe wrongly; take in a wrong sense; misinterpret; misunderstand: as, "I felt a pang at the idea she should . . . *misconstrue* what she had seen" (C. Brontë's "Jane Eyre," xxiii.).

mis-con-tent (mis-kọn-tent′), *a.* [See *mis-*, and cf. F. *mécontent*.] Ill content; discontented. [Archaic or prov.]

mis-cook (mis-kůk′), *v. t.* [See *mis-*.] To cook badly (as, "For unnumbered years Mrs. Butt had *miscooked* his meals": Arnold Bennett's "Helen with the High Hand," vii.); fig., to bungle; mismanage. [Chiefly Sc.]

mis-cop-y (mis-kop′i), *v. t.*; *-copied, -copying.* [See *mis-*.] To copy wrongly or incorrectly.—**mis-cop′y**, *n.*; pl. *-ies* (-iz). An incorrect copy; an error in copying.

mis-coun-sel (mis-koun′sel), *v. t.*; *-seled* or *-selled, -seling* or *-selling.* [See *mis-*, and cf. OF. *mesconseillier*.] To counsel wrongly; misadvise.—**mis-coun′sel**, *n.* Wrong counsel.

mis-count (mis-kount′), *v. t.* or *i.* [See *mis-*, and cf. OF. *mesconter*.] To count erroneously; miscalculate.—**mis-count′**, *n.* An erroneous counting; a miscalculation.

mis-cre-ance (mis′krē-ạns), *n.* [OF. *mescreance*, < *mescreant*: see *miscreant*.] Wrong belief; misbelief; false religious faith. [Archaic.]

mis-cre-ant (mis′krē-ạnt). [OF. *mescreant* (F. *mécréant*), < *mes-* (see *mis-*) + *creant*, ppr. of *creire* (F. *croire*), < L. *credere*, believe.] **I.** *a.* Misbelieving, or holding a false religious belief (archaic); also, depraved, villainous, or base (as, "the *miscreant* race of human kind": Pope's tr. Homer's "Odyssey," xvii.). **II.** *n.* A misbelieving person, as a heretic or an infidel (archaic: as, "The emperor's generosity to the *miscreants* was interpreted as treason to the Christian cause," Gibbon's "Decline and Fall of the Roman Empire," lviii.); also, a vile wretch, or villain (as, "The voyagers were notorious . . . for desperate, bloody-minded *miscreants*": Stevenson's "Master of Ballantrae," xi.).—**mis'cre-an-cy** (-ạn-si), *n.*

mis-cre-ate (mis-krē̦-āt'), *v. t.*; *-ated, -ating.* [See *mis-*.] To create amiss; misform.—**mis-cre-ate',** *a.* Miscreated. [Archaic.]—**mis-cre-at'ed** (-ā'ted), *p. a.* Wrongly created; misshapen; monstrous.—**mis-cre-a'tion** (-ā'shọn), *n.* The act of miscreating; also, something miscreated.

mis-cue (mis-kū'), *n.* [See *mis-*.] In *billiards*, etc., a slip of the cue, causing it to strike the ball improperly; a false stroke with the cue.—**mis-cue',** *v. i.*; *-cued, -cuing.* In *billiards*, etc., to make a miscue.

mis-date (mis-dāt'), *v. t.*; *-dated, -dating.* [See *mis-*.] To date wrongly; assign or affix a wrong date to.—**mis-date',** *n.* A wrong date.

mis-deal (mis-dēl'), *v. t.* or *i.*; *-dealt, -dealing.* [See *mis-*.] To deal wrongly, esp. at cards.—**mis-deal',** *n.* A wrong deal.

mis-deed (mis-dēd'), *n.* [AS. *misdǣd*: see *mis-* and *deed*.] An ill deed; a reprehensible or wicked action.

mis-deem (mis-dēm'), *v. i.* or *t.* [See *mis-*.] To deem or judge wrongly. [Archaic.]

mis-de-mean (mis-dē̦-mēn'), *v. t.* [See *mis-*.] To demean (one's self) improperly; misconduct.—**mis-de-mean'ant,** *n.* One guilty of misbehavior; in *law*, one convicted of a misdemeanor.—**mis-de-mean'or, mis-de-mean'our,** *n.* Misbehavior; a misdeed; in *law*, any indictable offense not amounting to a felony.

mis-de-rive (mis-dē̦-rīv'), *v. t.*; *-rived, -riving.* [See *mis-*.] To derive wrongly; assign a wrong derivation to.—**mis-der-i-va'tion** (-der-i-vā'shọn), *n.*

mis-de-scribe (mis-dē̦-skrīb'), *v. t.*; *-scribed, -scribing.* [See *mis-*.] To describe incorrectly or falsely.—**mis-de-scrip'tion** (-skrip'shọn), *n.*

mis-di-rect (mis-di-rekt'), *v. t.* [See *mis-*.] To direct wrongly.

mis-di-vide (mis-di-vīd'), *v. t.*; *-vided, -viding.* [See *mis-*.] To divide wrongly.—**mis-di-vi'sion** (-vizh'ọn), *n.*

mis-do (mis-dö'), *v. t.* or *i.*; pret. *-did*, pp. *-done*, ppr. *-doing.* [AS. *misdōn*: see *mis-* and *do*[1].] To do amiss.—**mis-do'er,** *n.*—**mis-do'ing,** *n.* Wrong-doing; also, a misdeed.

mis-doubt (mis-dout'), *v. t.* or *i.* [See *mis-*.] To doubt, suspect, or mistrust; also, to fear. [Now chiefly colloq. or prov.]—**mis-doubt',** *n.* Doubt; suspicion; mistrust. [Archaic or prov.]

mis-draw (mis-drâ'), *v. t.*; pret. *-drew*, pp. *-drawn*, ppr. *-drawing.* [See *mis-*.] To draw, draft, or depict wrongly or badly.

mise (mēz or mīz), *n.* [OF. F. *mise*, < *mettre*, put, set, < L. *mittere*, send.] Outlay† or expenses†; also, a grant, payment, or tribute made to secure a liberty or immunity; also, a settlement or agreement, esp. either of two agreements made between Henry III. of England and his rebellious barons, the first ('mise of Amiens') in Jan., 1264, and the second ('mise of Lewes') in May, 1264.

mis-ease (mis-ēz'), *n.* [OF. *mesaise* (F. *mésaise*): see *mis-* and *ease*.] Discomfort; distress; suffering; uneasiness. [Archaic.]

mis-ed-u-cate (mis-ed'ū̦-kāt), *v. t.*; *-cated, -cating.* [See *mis-*.] To educate improperly.—**mis-ed-u-ca'tion** (-kā'shọn), *n.*

mis-em-ploy (mis-em-ploi'), *v. t.* [See *mis-*.] To employ wrongly or improperly.—**mis-em-ploy'ment,** *n.*

mi-ser[1] (mī'zėr), *n.* [L. *miser*, wretched, unhappy, sick, bad.] A wretched or unhappy person†; a wretch†, or contemptible person†; now, one who lives in wretched circumstances in order to save and hoard money; a meanly penurious hoarder of wealth; a niggardly, avaricious person.

mi-ser[2] (mī'zėr), *n.* [Origin uncertain.] A boring tool, as for sinking wells, which forces upward the material drilled out.

mis-er-a-ble (miz'ė̦-rạ-bl). [OF. *miserable* (F. *misérable*), < L. *miserabilis*, pitiable, < *miserari*, pity, < *miser*, wretched.] **I.** *a.* Being in a state of misery, or in wretched circumstances (as, "O *miserable* mankind, to what fall Degraded, to what wretched state reserved!" Milton's "Paradise Lost," xi. 500); often, wretchedly poor; needy; esp., wretchedly unhappy; wretchedly uneasy or uncomfortable (as, "Nothing makes mankind so completely *miserable* as . . . being in constant fear": Defoe's "Robinson Crusoe," ii. 12); being in poor health, or ailing (colloq.); also, attended with or causing misery (as, a *miserable* existence); manifesting misery; also, pitiable or deplorable (as, a *miserable* failure); hence, of wretched character or quality; contemptible; sorry; wretchedly bad; wretchedly inadequate (as, "a *miserable* dole of twopence": Trollope's "Warden," ii.); also, miserly (now prov. Eng.). **II.** *n.* A miserable person; one who is in misery: as, "many *miserables* . . . driven out of their own proper class into the very verge of another" (Sterne's "Sentimental Journey," The Dwarf).—**mis'er-a-ble-ness,** *n.*—**mis'er-a-bly,** *adv.*

Mis-e-re-re (miz-ė̦-rē'rē), *n.* [L., 'have pity,' 'have mercy': the first word of the psalm in the Vulgate.] The 51st psalm (50th in the Vulgate), being one of the penitential psalms; a musical setting for it; also [*l. c.*], a prayer or expression asking for mercy; also, the misericord of a church stall.

Miserere, or Misericord, from All Souls College, Oxford, England. — *a*, with seat turned back, showing carving; *b*, with seat let down.

mis-er-i-cord (miz"ė̦-ri-kôrd' or mi-zer'i-kôrd), *n.* [OF. *misericorde* (F. *miséricorde*), < L. *misericordia*, < *misericors*, compassionate, < *misereri*, to have pity, + *cor*, heart.] Compassion or mercy (archaic); also, a relaxation of a monastic rule, or a room in a monastery where such relaxations were permitted; also, a small projection on the under side of a hinged seat of a church stall, which, when the seat was thrown back, gave support to a person standing in the stall and leaning against it; also, a kind of medieval dagger used to give the death-blow to a fallen adversary.

mi-ser-ly (mī'zėr-li), *a.* Of, like, or befitting a miser; penurious; niggardly: as, *miserly* habits; a *miserly* wretch.—**mi'ser-li-ness,** *n.*

mis-er-y (miz'ė̦-ri), *n.*; pl. *miseries* (-riz). [OF. *miserie* (F. *misère*), L. *miseria*, < *miser*, wretched.] Wretchedness of condition or circumstances; often, wretchedness or distress caused by privation or poverty; also, great distress of mind; extreme unhappiness; also, extreme bodily discomfort; bodily pain, or a pain (prov.: as, "He had got the worst '*misery* in his back' he had ever suffered," G. W. Cable's "John March, Southerner," vi.); also, a cause or source of wretchedness (as, "Weep and howl for your *miseries* that shall come upon you": Jas. v. 1); also, miserliness†.

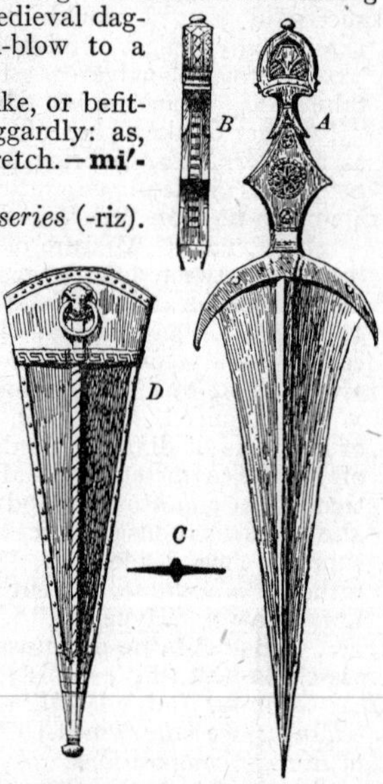

Misericord, 15th century. — *A*, the dagger; *B*, profile of hilt; *C*, section of blade; *D*, scabbard.

mis-es-teem (mis-es-tēm'), *v. t.* [See *mis-*.] To esteem wrongly; fail to esteem or respect properly.—**mis-es-teem',** *n.* Want of esteem or respect; disesteem.

mis-es-ti-mate (mis-es'ti-māt), *v. t.*; *-mated, -mating.* [See *mis-*.] To estimate wrongly or incorrectly.—**mis-es-ti-ma'tion** (-mā'shọn), *n.*

mis-faith (mis-fāth'), *n.* [See *mis-*.] Want of faith; mistrust.

mis-fea-sance (mis-fē′zans), *n.* [= OF. *mesfaisance*: see *mis-* and *feasance*, and cf. *malfeasance*.] In *law*, a wrong done; specif., the wrongful performance of a lawful act, or the wrongful and injurious exercise of lawful authority.—**mis-fea′sor** (-zor), *n.* In *law*, one guilty of misfeasance.

mis-fea-ture (mis-fē′tūr),, *n.* [See *mis-*.] Ill feature or aspect; also, a bad feature or trait.—**mis-fea′ture,** *v. t.*; *-tured, -turing.* To distort the features of.

mis-fire (mis-fīr′), *v. i.*; *-fired, -firing.* [See *mis-*.] To fail to be fired or exploded.—**mis-fire′,** *n.*

mis-fit (mis-fit′), *v. t.* or *i.*; *-fitted, -fitting.* [See *mis-*.] To fit badly.—**mis-fit′,** *n.* A bad fit; an ill-fitting garment, etc.

mis-form (mis-fôrm′), *v. t.* [See *mis-*.] To form amiss; misshape.—**mis-for-ma′tion** (-fôr-mā′shon), *n.*

mis-for-tune (mis-fôr′tūn), *n.* [See *mis-*.] Ill or adverse fortune; ill luck; also, an instance of this; a mischance or mishap (as, "The good man then began to complain of his *misfortunes*": Defoe's "Robinson Crusoe," i. 19).

mis-give (mis-giv′), *v.*; *-gave, -giving.* [See *mis-*.] **I.** *tr.* To give doubt or apprehension to (one); cause to be apprehensive: said of one's mind, heart, etc.: as, "His mind now *misgave* him; he began to doubt whether both he and the world around him were not bewitched" (Irving's "Sketch-Book," Rip Van Winkle). **II.** *intr.* To be apprehensive; also, to fail (chiefly Sc.).—**mis-giv′ing,** *n.* A feeling of doubt, distrust, or apprehension: as, "I had a strong *misgiving* that his nightly absence was for no good purpose" (Dickens's "Old Curiosity Shop," i.).

mis-gov-ern (mis-guv′ėrn), *v. t.* [See *mis-*.] To govern or manage (something) badly.—**mis-gov′ern-ment,** *n.*—**mis-gov′er-nor,** *n.*

mis-guide (mis-gīd′), *v. t.*; *-guided, -guiding.* [See *mis-*.] To guide wrongly; mislead; also (chiefly Sc.), to mismanage; ill-use.—**mis-guid′ance** (-gī′dans), *n.*—**mis-guid′ed,** *p. a.* Misled; misdirected; erring.—**mis-guid′ed-ly,** *adv.*

mis-han-dle (mis-han′dl), *v. t.*; *-dled, -dling.* [See *mis-*.] To handle badly; maltreat: as, "It is a shame to see how they have *mishandled* the old man among them" (Scott's "Quentin Durward," xxi.).

mis-hap (mis-hap′), *n.* [See *mis-*.] Ill hap; mischance; bad luck; also, an unfortunate accident (as, "secure from worldly chances and *mishaps*": Shakspere's "Titus Andronicus," i. 1. 152).

mis-hear (mis-hēr′), *v. t.* or *i.*; *-heard* (-hėrd), *-hearing.* [See *mis-*.] To hear incorrectly or imperfectly.

mish-mash (mish′mash), *n.* [Varied redupl. of *mash*.] A hodgepodge; a jumble.

mish-nah (mish′nä), *n.*; pl. *mishnoth* (-nōth). [Heb. *mishnāh*, instruction.] In *Jewish lit.*, instruction in the traditional or oral doctrine of the Jews; [*cap.*] the doctrine itself as contained in halakoth down to the beginning of the 3d century A.D.; any collection of this doctrine; esp., the collection of halakoth made by Judah ha-Nasi (about 135–about 220), which forms the basis of the Talmud; also [*l. c.*], a single tenet of the Jewish traditional doctrine; a paragraph of the Mishnah.—**Mish-na′ic** (-nā′ik), **Mish′nic,** *a.*

mis-in-form (mis-in-fôrm′), *v. t.* [See *mis-*.] To inform wrongly; give false or misleading information to.—**mis-in-form′ant, mis-in-form′er,** *n.* One who misinforms.—**mis-in-for-ma′tion** (-fôr-mā′shon), *n.* The act of misinforming, or the state of being misinformed; incorrect information.

mis-in-ter-pret (mis-in-tėr′pret), *v. t.* [See *mis-*.] To interpret wrongly; explain or understand incorrectly; misconstrue.—**mis-in-ter-pre-ta′tion** (-pre-tā′shon), *n.* Wrong interpretation.—**mis-in-ter′pret-er,** *n.*

mis-join (mis-join′), *v. t.* [See *mis-*.] To join wrongly or improperly.—**mis-join′der** (-dėr), *n.* In *law*, a joining in one suit or action of causes or of parties that ought not to be so joined.

mis-judge (mis-juj′), *v. t.* or *i.*; *-judged, -judging.* [See *mis-*.] To judge wrongly or unjustly.—**mis-judg′ment, mis-judge′ment,** *n.*

mis-kal (mis-käl′), *n.* [Ar. *mithqāl*.] An Eastern unit of weight varying from 71 grains, as in Persia, to 74 grains, as in Smyrna.

mis-ken (mis-ken′), *v. t.*; *-kenned, -kenning.* [See *mis-* and *ken*.] To fail to know, recognize, or perceive; ignore; mistake; misunderstand. [Sc. and prov. Eng.]

mis-know (mis-nō′), *v. t.*; pret. *-knew*, pp. *-known*, ppr. *-knowing.* [See *mis-*.] To know badly; fail to know rightly; misapprehend; also, to fail to recognize (Sc.).—**mis-knowl′edge** (-nol′ej), *n.* Faulty knowledge; misapprehension of truth or fact.

mis-lay (mis-lā′), *v. t.*; *-laid, -laying.* [See *mis-*.] To lay or place wrongly; misplace; also, to put in a place afterward forgotten (as, "Was ever anything so provoking—to *mislay* my own jewels, and force me to wear her trumpery": Goldsmith's "She Stoops to Conquer," iii.).

mis-lead (mis-lēd′), *v. t.*; *-led, -leading.* [AS. *mislǣdan*: see *mis-* and *lead*¹.] To lead or guide wrongly, or lead astray (as, "As when a wandering fire . . . *Misleads* the amaz'd night-wanderer from his way To bogs and mires": Milton's "Paradise Lost," ix. 640); fig., to lead into error of conduct or thought; often, to cause to think or judge wrongly or form a mistaken opinion.—**mis-lead′er,** *n.*—**mis-lead′ing,** *p. a.* That misleads; tending to lead astray; deceptive.—**mis-lead′ing-ly,** *adv.*—**mis-lead′ing-ness,** *n.*

mis-like (mis-līk′), *v. t.*; *-liked, -liking.* [AS. *mislīcian*: see *mis-* and *like*².] To displease (archaic: as, "Dost thou . . . see About me somewhat that *misliketh* thee?" W. Morris's "Jason," vii. 206); also, to dislike (archaic or prov.: as, "*Mislike* me not for my complexion," Shakspere's "Merchant of Venice," ii. 1. 1).—**mis-like′,** *n.* Dislike; aversion; distaste. [Now rare.]—**mis-lik′er** (-lī′kėr), *n.*—**mis-lik′ing,** *n.*

mis-make (mis-māk′), *v. t.*; *-made, -making.* [See *mis-*.] To make badly. [Now Sc.]

mis-man-age (mis-man′āj), *v. t.* or *i.*; *-aged, -aging.* [See *mis-*.] To manage badly: as, "This property had been greatly *mismanaged*" (Godwin's "Caleb Williams," xl.).—**mis-man′age-ment,** *n.*—**mis-man′ag-er,** *n.*

mis-match (mis-mach′), *v. t.* [See *mis-*.] To match badly or unsuitably.—**mis-match′,** *n.* A bad or unsatisfactory match.

mis-mate (mis-māt′), *v. t.*; *-mated, -mating.* [See *mis-*.] To mate amiss or unsuitably.

mis-move (mis-möv′), *n.* [See *mis-*.] A wrong move, as in a game or any course of procedure.

mis-name (mis-nām′), *v. t.*; *-named, -naming.* [See *mis-*.] To call by a wrong name.

mis-no-mer (mis-nō′mėr), *n.* [OF. *mesnommer*, < *mes-* (see *mis-*) + *nommer*, name, < L. *nominare*: see *nominate*.] An error in naming a person or thing; also, a misapplied name or designation (as, "She [a vessel] was called the 'Alert,' and certainly a more unfortunate *misnomer* could scarcely be conceived": Lever's "Harry Lorrequer," ix.).—**mis-no′mer,** *v. t.* To call by a misnomer; misname.

mi-sog-a-mist (mi-sog′a-mist or mī-), *n.* [Gr. μισεῖν, hate, + γάμος, marriage.] A hater of marriage.—**mi-sog′a-my,** *n.* Hatred of marriage.

mi-sog-y-nist (mi-soj′i-nist or mī-), *n.* [Gr. μισογύνης, < μισεῖν, hate, + γυνή, woman.] A hater of women.—**mi-sog′y-nous,** *a.* Hating women.—**mi-sog′y-ny,** *n.* Hatred of women.

mi-sol-o-gy (mi-sol′ō-ji or mī-), *n.* [Gr. μισολογία, < μισεῖν, hate, + λόγος, reason: see *Logos*.] Hatred of reason or reasoning.—**mi-sol′o-gist,** *n.*

mis-o-ne-ism (mis-ō-nē′izm or mī-sō-), *n.* [It. *misoneismo*, < Gr. μισεῖν, hate, + νέος, new.] Hatred or dislike of what is new.—**mis-o-ne′ist,** *n.* A hater of what is new.—**mis″o-ne-is′tic** (-nē-is′tik), *a.*

mis-per-form (mis-pėr-fôrm′), *v. t.* [See *mis-*.] To perform badly or improperly.—**mis-per-form′ance,** *n.*

mis-pick-el (mis′pik-el), *n.* [G.] Arsenopyrite.

mis-place (mis-plās′), *v. t.*; *-placed, -placing.* [See *mis-*.] To put in a wrong place (as, to *misplace* a book); also, to place or bestow improperly or unsuitably (as, "a *misplaced* lenity towards a wretch unworthy to live": Marryat's "Mr. Midshipman Easy," xviii.).—**mis-place′ment,** *n.*

mis-play (mis-plā′), *n.* [See *mis-*.] A wrong play.

mis-print (mis-print′), *v. t.* [See *mis-*.] To print incorrectly.—**mis-print′,** *n.* A mistake in printing.

mis-prise′¹†, **mis-prise′**². See *misprize*¹, *misprize*².

mis-pri-sion[1] (mis-prizh′on), *n.* [OF. *mesprision, mesprison,* < *mesprendre,* mistake, do wrong, < *mes-* (see *mis-*) + *prendre,* < L. *prehendere,* take.] A wrongful action or omission, esp. of a public official (as, *misprision* of treason or of felony, orig., a grave offense or misdemeanor bordering on treason or felony; later, neglect to give notice of an act of treason or felony); also (archaic), the mistaking of one thing for another; misunderstanding; a misapprehension; a mistake.

mis-pri-sion[2] (mis-prizh′on), *n.* [See *misprize*[2].] A misprizing, despising, or undervaluing; contempt: as, "those unhappy persons, who . . . have their hearts barred against conviction by prejudice and *misprision*" (Scott's "Guy Mannering," iii.). [Archaic.]

mis-prize[1]† (mis-prīz′), *v. t.*; *-prized, -prizing.* [OF. *mespris,* pp. of *mesprendre*: see *misprision*[1].] To mistake; misapprehend.

mis-prize[2] (mis-prīz′), *v. t.*; *-prized, -prizing.* [OF. *mesprisier* (F. *mépriser*), < *mes-* (see *mis-*) + *prisier,* E. *prize*[2].] To despise; undervalue; slight. [Archaic.]

mis-pro-nounce (mis-prō-nouns′), *v. t.* or *i.*; *-nounced, -nouncing.* [See *mis-*.] To pronounce incorrectly.—**mis-pro-nun-ci-a′tion** (-nun-si-ā′shon), *n.*

mis-proud (mis-proud′), *a.* [See *mis-*.] Unduly proud; arrogant: as, "thy *mis-proud* ambitious clan" (Scott's "Lady of the Lake," v. 26). [Archaic.]

mis-punc-tu-ate (mis-pungk′tū-āt), *v. t.*; *-ated, -ating.* [See *mis-*.] To punctuate wrongly.—**mis-punc-tu-a′tion** (-ā′shon), *n.*

mis-quote (mis-kwōt′), *v. t.* or *i.*; *-quoted, -quoting.* [See *mis-*.] To quote incorrectly.—**mis-quo-ta′tion** (-kwō-tā′shon), *n.*

mis-read (mis-rēd′), *v. t.*; *-read* (-red), *-reading.* [See *mis-*.] To read wrongly; misinterpret.

mis-reck-on (mis-rek′n), *v. t.* or *i.* [See *mis-*.] To reckon incorrectly; miscalculate.

mis-re-mem-ber (mis-rē-mem′bėr), *v. t.* or *i.* [See *mis-*.] To remember incorrectly; also (colloq.), to fail to remember.

mis-ren-der (mis-ren′dėr), *v. t.* [See *mis-*.] To render or interpret wrongly.

mis-re-port (mis-rē-pōrt′), *v. t.* [See *mis-*.] To report incorrectly or falsely.—**mis-re-port′,** *n.* An incorrect or false report.—**mis-re-port′er,** *n.*

mis-rep-re-sent (mis-rep-rē-zent′), *v. t.* [See *mis-*.] To represent incorrectly, improperly, or falsely.—**mis-rep″re-sen-ta′tion** (-zen-tā′shon), *n.* A misrepresenting; an incorrect, improper, or false representation.—**mis-rep-re-sen′ta-tive** (-ta-tiv), *a.* That misrepresents or is not properly representative.—**mis-rep-re-sent′er,** *n.*

mis-rule (mis-röl′), *n.* [See *mis-*.] Bad or unwise rule; misgovernment; hence, disorder or lawless tumult (as, "Catherine . . . regarded the little cottage on the hill as a spot of *misrule* in the general order of the parish": Mrs. H. Ward's "Robert Elsmere," xi.).—**lord** (also **master,** etc.) **of misrule.** See under *lord, n.*—**mis-rule′,** *v. t.*; *-ruled, -ruling.* To rule badly; misgovern.—**mis-rul′er** (-rö′lėr), *n.*

miss[1] (mis), *v. t.* [AS. *missan* = D. and G. *missen* = Icel. *missa,* miss; from an old participial form prob. from the root of AS. *mīthan,* conceal, OHG. *mīdan,* G. *meiden,* shun: cf. *mis-*.] To fail to hit, light upon, meet, receive, obtain, attain, accomplish, see, hear, etc. (as, to *miss* a mark, a plank on which one would step, one's road, a person with whom a meeting was desired or possible, a ball thrown to one, a reward desired, an end sought, an exhibition, a speech, etc.); also, to let slip (an opportunity, etc.); fail to catch (a train, boat, etc.); also, to fail to perceive or apprehend intellectually (as, to *miss* the point of a remark); also, to escape or avoid (as, he just *missed* being caught); also, to leave out or omit (as, "I never heard him *miss* one of the responses [in church] in my life": Scott's "Old Mortality," xii.); fail to perform, attend to, be present at, etc. (as, to *miss* attendance, an appointment, a meal, church or school, etc.); also, to be without†, or lack†; do without† (as, "We cannot *miss* him: he does make our fire, Fetch in our wood": Shakspere's "Tempest," i. 2. 311); also, to perceive the absence or loss of (as, the guard did not *miss* the prisoner until the next day); hence, to perceive the absence or loss of with regret, or feel the want of (as, "Thee I have *miss'd,* and thought it long, deprived Thy presence": Milton's "Paradise Lost," ix. 857).—**to miss fire,** to fail to go off, as a firearm; fig., to fail in any action, or prove unsuccessful (as, "He got up half way about three times, and *missed fire* and fell every time": Mark Twain's "Huckleberry Finn," xxxiv.).—**miss**[1], *v. i.* To miss something, or fail to hit, light upon, receive, or attain it; fail of effect or success, or be unsuccessful (as, "If thy scheme *miss,* then . . . We are enow to storm the hold": Scott's "Rokeby," iii. 26); also, to make a mistake†, or err† (as, "Art may err, but nature cannot *miss*": Dryden's "Cock and the Fox," 452); also, to be lacking or wanting (now only in *missing, p. a.*).—**to miss of,** to fail to hit, meet, obtain, or attain (something); miss: as, "Time hath a quiver full of purposes Which *miss* not *of* their aim" (Lowell's "Ode for the Fourth of July, 1876," ii. 3). [Archaic or prov.]—**miss**[1], *n.* A failure to hit, meet, obtain, or accomplish something (as, a *miss* is as good as a mile, that is, in missing, a slight failure or error is just as effective as a great one); sometimes, an omission; also, wrong-doing†; an error† or mistake†; also, loss or lack, or regret caused by loss or lack (now prov.: as, "Aged people feel the *miss* of children," George Eliot's "Silas Marner," xvii.).

miss[2] (mis), *n.* [Shortened form of *mistress.*] [*cap.*] The conventional title of respect for an unmarried woman, prefixed to the name (as, *Miss* Smith, in restricted use often meaning the eldest daughter of the name as distinguished from her younger sisters, as, for example, *Miss* Mary Smith and *Miss* Jane Smith; the *Misses* Smith, or, with less formality, the *Miss* Smiths); [*l. c.*] without the name, a term of address to an unmarried woman (not now in conventional or elegant use); also, a young unmarried woman, or a girl (as, "an arch little *miss* . . . to whom we strove to make ourselves particularly agreeable": H. Melville's "Omoo," lxxxi.); in trade use, a girl not fully grown (as, women's, *misses',* and children's sizes); also, a kept mistress†; a prostitute†.

mis-sal (mis′al), *n.* [ML. *missale,* < LL. *missa,* E. *mass*[1].] The book containing the service for celebrating the mass throughout the year.

mis-say (mis-sā′), *v.*; *-said* (-sed′), *-saying.* [See *mis-*.] **I.** *tr.* To say or speak ill of; abuse; slander; also, to say wrongly. [Archaic.] **II.** *intr.* To speak wrongly. [Archaic.]

mis-see (mis-sē′), *v. t.* or *i.*; pret. *-saw,* pp. *-seen,* ppr. *-seeing.* [See *mis-*.] To see wrongly.

mis-sel (mis′l), *n.* Same as *missel-thrush.*

mis-sel=thrush (mis′l-thrush), *n.* [AS. *mistel,* mistletoe.] A large European thrush, *Turdus viscivorus,* which is fond of the berries of the mistletoe.

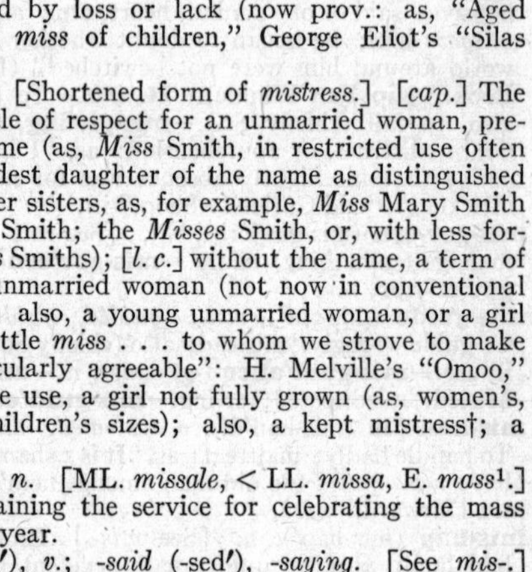
Missel-thrush.

mis-send (mis-send′), *v. t.*; *-sent, -sending.* [See *mis-*.] To send amiss; send to a wrong place or person.

mis-shape (mis-shāp′), *v. t.*; pret. *-shaped,* pp. *-shaped* or *-shapen,* ppr. *-shaping.* [See *mis-*.] To shape ill; misform; deform.—**mis-shap′en** (-shā′pn), *p. a.* Badly shaped; deformed; distorted.—**mis-shap′en-ly,** *adv.*—**mis-shap′en-ness,** *n.*

mis-sile (mis′il). [L. *missilis,* adj. (*missile,* n., a missile), < *mittere,* send.] **I.** *a.* Capable of being thrown, hurled, or shot, as from the hand or from an instrument or machine (as, "We . . . bend the bow, or wing the *missile* dart":

Pope's tr. Homer's "Odyssey," ix.); also, that discharges missiles (as, "long-bows, slings, and other *missile* weapons": Scott's "Ivanhoe," xxix.). **II.** *n.* A missile object or weapon, as a stone, a bullet, a lance, or an arrow.

miss-ing (mis'ing), *p. a.* [See *miss*[1].] Lacking; wanting; absent; not found; gone.—**missing link,** something lacking for the completion of a series or sequence of any kind; esp., a hypothetical form of animal assumed to have constituted a connecting link between the anthropoid apes and man. See *pithecanthropus.*

mis-sion (mish'ǫn), *n.* [L. *missio(n-)*, < *mittere,* send.] A sending or being sent for some duty or purpose; also, those sent; specif., a body of persons sent to a foreign country to conduct negotiations, establish relations, or the like; also, a body of persons sent into a foreign land for religious work among a heathen people, or into any region for the spiritual betterment of the inhabitants; an establishment of missionaries in a foreign land, or a missionary post or station; a similar establishment in any region, designed for the spiritual betterment of its people; sometimes, the district assigned to a missionary priest; also, missionary duty or work; esp., *pl.*, organized missionary work or activities in any country, region, or field (as, foreign *missions;* home *missions*); *sing.*, an organization for carrying on missionary work; also, a series of special religious services for quickening piety and converting unbelievers (as, to preach a *mission*); also, the business with which an agent, envoy, etc., is charged (as, "Hast thou perform'd my *mission* which I gave?" Tennyson's "Passing of Arthur," 235); hence, a duty or function for which a person is conceived to be delegated or destined; a self-imposed duty; an operation, by one or more aircraft, against the enemy.—**mission furniture,** a dark furniture characterized by great plainness, solidity, and straight lines: said to have been patterned after some chairs from one of the Spanish missions in California. —**mis'sion,** *v. t.* To send on or intrust with a mission.— **mis'sion-a-ry** (-ā-ri). [NL. *missionarius.*] **I.** *a.* Pertaining to or connected with religious missions; characteristic of or proper to one employed in such a mission; engaged in such a mission, or devoted to work connected with missions; hence, pertaining to any propaganda; characteristic of a propagandist. **II.** *n.*; pl. *-ries* (-riz). One sent on a mission; now, esp., a person sent to labor for the propagation of his religious faith in a heathen land or a newly settled district, or for the spiritual or moral betterment of the poor or of particular classes of persons; hence, any propagandist. —**mis'sion-er,** *n.* A missionary; also, one who conducts a mission (series of religious services), or is devoted to the holding of missions.

mis-sis, mis-sus (mis'iz, -uz), *n.* [For *mistress.*] A contracted form of *mistress,* used in speaking of the mistress of a household by servants and others (as, "*Missis* and the young ladies and Master John are going out to tea this afternoon": C. Brontë's "Jane Eyre," iv.); also, a man's wife. [Vulgar.]

miss-ish (mis'ish), *a.* Like, characteristic of, or befitting a miss; prim; affected; prudish: as, "You are not going to be *missish,* I hope, and pretend to be affronted at an idle report" (Jane Austen's "Pride and Prejudice," lvii.).— **miss'ish-ness,** *n.*

Mis-sis-sip-pi-an (mis-i-sip'i-ąn). **I.** *a.* Of or pertaining to the State of Mississippi or the river Mississippi; in *geol.*, noting or pertaining to a geological period or a system of rocks which comprises the lower or earlier portion of the Carboniferous period or system in North America. **II.** *n.* A native or inhabitant of Mississippi; in *geol.*, the Mississippian period or system.

mis-sive (mis'iv). [= F. *missive* (fem.), < ML. *missivus,* < L. *mittere,* send.] **I.** *a.* Sent; esp., sent from an authoritative or official source (as, a letter *missive*); also, missile. **II.** *n.* A written message; a letter; also, a messenger† (as, "You . . . with taunts Did gibe my *missive* out of audience": Shakspere's "Antony and Cleopatra," ii. 2. 74).

mis-speak (mis-spēk'), *v. t.*; pret. *-spoke,* pp. *-spoken,* ppr. *-speaking.* [See *mis-.*] To speak, utter, or pronounce wrongly or incorrectly.

mis-speech (mis-spēch'), *n.* [See *mis-.*] Faulty or incorrect speech.

mis-spell (mis-spel'), *v. t.*; *-spelled* or *-spelt, -spelling.* [See *mis-.*] To spell incorrectly.—**mis-spell'ing,** *n.* Wrong spelling; a wrongly spelled form of a word.

mis-spend (mis-spend'), *v. t.*; *-spent, -spending.* [See *mis-.*] To spend improperly; squander; waste.—**mis-spent'** (-spent'), *p. a.* Badly spent; wasted: as, "a *misspent,* ruined life" (H. Kingsley's "Geoffry Hamlyn," xliii.).

mis-state (mis-stāt'), *v. t.*; *-stated, -stating.* [See *mis-.*] To state wrongly.—**mis-state'ment,** *n.* A wrong or erroneous statement: as, "In justice both to Mr. Garrick and Dr. Johnson, I think it necessary to rectify this *misstatement*" (Boswell's "Johnson," 1764).

mis-step (mis-step'), *n.* [See *mis-.*] A wrong step (as, "A *mis-step* to the right or left was fatal": Motley's "Dutch Republic," iv. 3); fig., an error or slip in conduct.

mis-sus (mis'uz), *n.* See *missis.*

miss-y (mis'i), *n.*; pl. *missies* (-iz). A little or young miss. [Colloq.]—**miss'y,** *a.* Missish.

mist (mist), *n.* [AS. *mist* = D., LG., and Sw. *mist* = Icel. *mistr,* mist: cf. Gr. ὀμίχλη, Skt. *mih,* mist.] A cloud-like aggregation of minute globules of water suspended in the atmosphere at or near the earth's surface; fog or haze; also, precipitation consisting of extremely fine droplets of water, smaller and more closely aggregated than in rain; hence, a cloud of particles resembling a mist (as, "The rustling straw sends up a frequent *mist* Of atoms": Cowper's "Task," i. 360); a haze or haziness, as that produced by distance, or, fig., that due to remoteness in time; something conceived as obscuring mental vision by enveloping the mind or veiling the character of a thing (as, "the *mists* of prejudice," Carlyle's "Sartor Resartus," i. 2; "things view'd at distance through the *mist* of fear," Southey's "Thalaba," iv. 9); also, a hazy appearance before the eyes, as due to tears or to bodily disorders.—**Scotch mist.** See under *Scotch*[3], *a.*—**mist,** *v.* [AS. *mistian.*] **I.** *intr.* To become misty; also, to rain in very fine drops; drizzle. **II.** *tr.* To make misty.

mis-tak-a-ble (mis-tā'ką-bl), *a.* That may be mistaken, misapprehended, or misunderstood.

mis-take (mis-tāk'), *v. t.*; pret. *-took,* pp. *-taken,* ppr. *-taking.* [ME. *mistaken:* see *mis-* and *take,* and cf. Icel. *mistaka,* take by mistake.] To take wrongly or in error†; also, to choose amiss (obs. or archaic: as, "There were some few who *mistook* their profession," Marryat's "King's Own," xli.); also, to take or regard as something or somebody else (as, to *mistake* a fixed star for a planet; "He had often been *mistaken* for an Englishman," Howells's "Chance Acquaintance," i.; there is no *mistaking* the fact, or the man); also, to conceive of or understand wrongly (as, to *mistake* a person's meaning, or the person himself); misapprehend; misunderstand.—**to be mistaken,** to make a mistake; be in error: as, "I *was* . . . quite *mistaken* In what I thought would have succeeded best" (Milton's "Samson Agonistes," 907). See *mistaken, p. a.*—**mis-take',** *v. i.* To err in opinion or judgment; be in error: as, "He . . . told me . . . that I *mistook* in my guesses" (Defoe's "Robinson Crusoe," ii. 7). —**mis-take',** *n.* A mistaking†, or taking amiss† (as, "Previously to the time that I . . . was aware of the *mistake* of the road, the sky had become black and lowering": Godwin's "Caleb Williams," xxxiii.); hence, an error in action, opinion, or judgment; a slip or blunder; a misconception or misapprehension.—**and no mistake,** without any mistake; assuredly.—**mis-tak'en** (-tā'kn), *p. a.* Having made a mistake, or being in error (as, *mistaken* persons); also, wrongly conceived, entertained, or done (as, "a *mistaken* notion," Galt's "Annals of the Parish," xlvi.; *mistaken* pity; a *mistaken* choice); erroneous; wrong.—**mis-tak'en-ly,** *adv.*— **mis-tak'en-ness,** *n.*—**mis-tak'er,** *n.*

mis-teach (mis-tēch'), *v. t.*; *-taught, -teaching.* [See *mis-.*] To teach wrongly or badly.

mis-ter (mis'tėr), *n.* [Var. of *master*[2].] [*cap.*] The conventional title of respect for a man, prefixed to the name and to certain official designations (usually written *Mr.*: as, *Mr.* Jones; *Mr.* President); [*l. c.*] in address, without the name, sir (now vulgar: as, "'Good morning, *mister,*' said Dominicus," Hawthorne's "Twice-Told Tales," Mr. Higginbotham's Catastrophe).—**mis'ter,** *v. t.* To address or speak of as 'mister' or 'Mr.' [Colloq.]

mis-term (mis-tėrm′), *v. t.* [See *mis-*.] To term wrongly.

mist=flow-er (mist′flou″ėr), *n.* A North American asteraceous plant, *Eupatorium* (or *Conoclinium*) *cœlestinum*, with cymose heads of blue flowers.

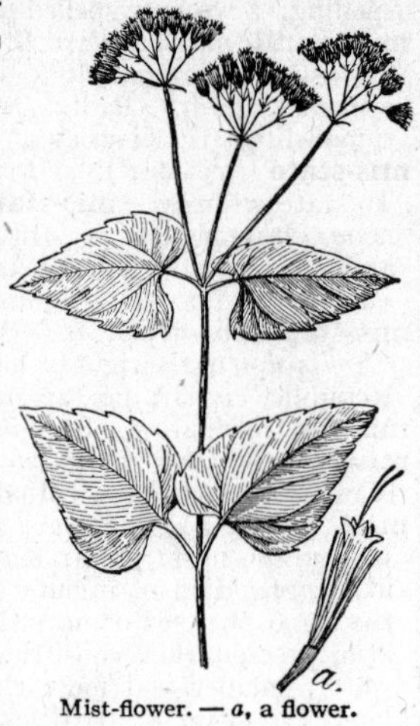

Mist-flower. — *a*, a flower.

mist-ful (mist′fụl), *a.* Abounding in mist; misty.

mis-think (mis-thingk′), *v.*; *-thought*, *-thinking*. [See *mis-*.] **I.** *intr.* To think mistakenly; also, to think unfavorably (obs. or archaic). **II.** *tr.* To think ill or unfavorably of. [Obs. or archaic.]

mist-i-ly (mis′ti-li), *adv.* In a misty manner.

mis-time (mis-tīm′), *v. t.*; *-timed*, *-timing*. [See *mis-*.] To time wrongly; perform, say, etc., at a wrong time (as, to *mistime* a move or a remark); miscalculate or misstate the time of (an action, etc.).

mist-i-ness (mis′ti-nes), *n.* Misty condition.

mist-less (mist′les), *a.* Free from mist.

mis-tle-thrush (mis′l-thrush), *n.* See *missel-thrush*.

mis-tle-toe (mis′l-tō or miz′-), *n.* [AS. *misteltān*, < *mistel*, mistletoe, + *tān*, twig.] A European plant, *Viscum album* (family *Loranthaceæ*), with yellowish flowers and white berries, growing parasitically on various trees (held in veneration by the Druids, esp. when found growing on the oak, and much used in Christmas decorations: as, "The *mistletoe* is still hung up in farm-houses and kitchens at Christmas; and the young men have the privilege of kissing the girls under it," Irving's "Sketch-Book," Christmas Eve, note); also, any of various other plants of the same family, as *Phoradendron flavescens* of the U. S. (also used in Christmas decorations).

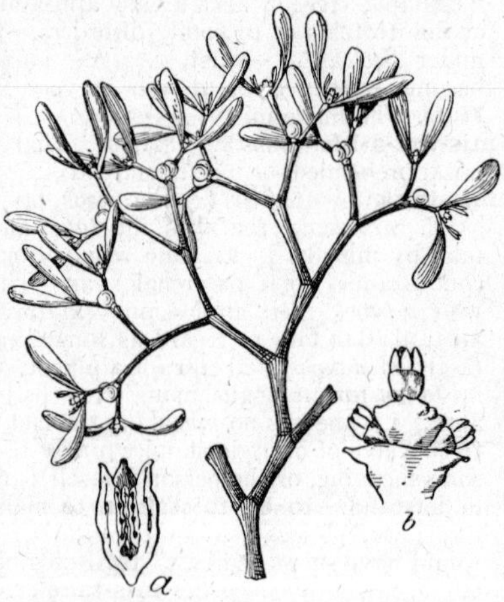

Branch of Mistletoe (*Viscum album*), with fruits. — *a*, longitudinal section through the male flower; *b*, the female inflorescence.

mis-took (mis-tụk′). Preterit of *mistake*.

mis-tral (mis′tr̤al or mis-träl′), *n.* [F., < Pr. *mistral*, 'master-wind,' < L. *magistralis*, E. *magistral*.] A cold, dry northerly wind common in southern France and neighboring regions.

mis-trans-late (mis-trans-lāt′), *v. t.*; *-lated*, *-lating*. [See *mis-*.] To translate incorrectly.—**mis-trans-la′tion** (-lā′-sh̤on), *n.*

mis-treat (mis-trēt′), *v. t.* [See *mis-*.] To ill-treat; maltreat.

mis-tress (mis′tres), *n.* [OF. *maistresse* (F. *maîtresse*), fem. of *maistre*, E. *master*².] A woman who has authority or control; the female head of a household or some other establishment; a woman employing, or in authority over, servants or attendants; a female owner of a slave, or a horse, dog, etc.; hence, in general, a female owner or possessor (as, "I show more mirth than I am *mistress* of": Shakspere's "As You Like It," i. 2. 4); also, a woman who has the power of controlling or disposing of something at pleasure (as, to be *mistress* of vast powers or resources); also, fig., something regarded as feminine which has control or supremacy (as, ancient Rome, the *mistress* of the world); also, a female teacher; a schoolmistress; a woman who teaches some subject (as, a drawing-*mistress*); also, a woman who has mastered some art, branch of study, or the like (as, "If she can spin, and is *mistress* of plain work, so much the better": Smollett's "Humphry Clinker," Nov. 20); sometimes, a woman who has taken a certain degree in a particular subject or field of study, as at a college; also, a woman who has command over a man's heart, a woman beloved and courted, or a sweetheart (now chiefly poetic or archaic); esp., a woman who illicitly occupies the place of a wife; also, [*cap.*] a title of respect, prefixed to the name, or [*l. c.*] a term of address, for a woman (now archaic or prov.: cf. *Mrs.* and *miss*²).—**mis′tress-hood** (-hụd), **mis′tress=ship**, *n.*

mis-tri-al (mis-trī′a̤l), *n.* [See *mis-*.] In *law*, a trial vitiated by some error; loosely, an inconclusive trial, as where the jury cannot agree.

mis-trust (mis-trust′), *n.* [See *mis-*.] Lack of trust or confidence; distrust: as, "a curling of the upper lip, which inspired a feeling of *mistrust*" (Wiseman's "Fabiola," i. 6).—**mis-trust′**, *v.* **I.** *tr.* To regard with mistrust; distrust; also, to suspect or surmise (now rare: as, "This is an accident of hourly proof, Which I *mistrusted* not," Shakspere's "Much Ado about Nothing," ii. 1. 189). **II.** *intr.* To be distrustful.—**mis-trust′er**, *n.*—**mis-trust′ful**, *a.* Full of mistrust; suspicious.—**mis-trust′ful-ly**, *adv.*—**mis-trust′-ful-ness**, *n.*—**mis-trust′less**, *a.* Without mistrust; unsuspicious.

mist-y (mis′ti), *a.*; compar. *mistier*, superl. *mistiest*. [AS. *mistig*.] Abounding in or clouded by mist; of the nature of or consisting of mist; also, appearing as if seen through mist; indistinct in form or outline; also, fig., obscure; vague; indistinct; hazy.

mis-un-der-stand (mis-un-dėr-stand′), *v. t.* or *i.*; *-stood*, *-standing*. [See *mis-*.] To understand wrongly, or misapprehend; take (words, statements, etc.) in a wrong sense; misinterpret the words or actions of (a person).—**mis-un-der-stand′ing**, *n.* Failure to understand; mistake as to meaning; also, disagreement or dissension; a disagreement.

mis-us-age (mis-ū′zā̤j or -ū′sā̤j), *n.* [See *mis-*.] Wrong or improper usage, as of words; also, ill usage; bad treatment.—**mis-use′** (-ūs′), *n.* Wrong or improper use; misapplication; also, ill usage.—**mis-use′** (-ūz′), *v. t.*; *-used*, *-using*. To use wrongly or improperly; misapply; also, to ill-use; maltreat.—**mis-us′er**¹ (-ū′zėr), *n.* One who misuses.—**mis-us′er**², *n.* [OF. *mesuser*, prop. inf.: cf. *user*².] In *law*, abuse of a liberty or benefit.

mis-val-ue (mis-val′ṳ̄), *v. t.*; *-ued*, *-uing*. [See *mis-*.] To value wrongly.—**mis-val-u-a′tion** (-ā′sh̤on), *n.*

mis-ven-ture (mis-ven′t̤ṳ̄r), *n.* [See *mis-*.] An unfortunate venture; a misadventure; a mischance. [Archaic.]

mis-word (mis-wėrd′), *v. t.* [See *mis-*.] To word wrongly.

mis-wor-ship (mis-wėr′ship), *n.* [See *mis-*.] Wrong or improper worship.—**mis-wor′ship**, *v. t.*; *-shiped* or *-shipped*, *-shiping* or *-shipping*. To worship wrongly.

mis-write (mis-rīt′), *v. t.*; pret. *-wrote*, pp. *-written*, ppr. *-writing*. [See *mis-*.] To write incorrectly.

Mitchell. A U. S. long-range medium bomber (North American Aviation).

mite¹ (mīt), *n.* [AS. *mīte* = D. *mijt*.] Any of various small arachnids (order *Acarida*) with a sac-like body, many of which are parasitic on plants and animals, others living in cheese, flour, unrefined sugar, etc.

mite² (mīt), *n.* [MD. *mite*, D. *mijt*; prob. = *mite*¹.] A coin of very small value; a very small sum of money; also, a small contribution, as to some public or charitable object, but all that one can afford to give (in allusion to Mark, xii. 42–44); any very small contribution, but the best one can offer; also, a small amount or portion (now colloq.); a jot or bit (now colloq.: as, "Never suspected a *mite*, did he?" W. Churchill's "Coniston," i. 15); also, a very small object; a very small creature (as, "a *mite* of a boy," Dickens's "Bleak House," xv.; "a wretched little heavy-eyed *mite* sitting on the edge of a chair," S. Butler's "Way of All Flesh," xxviii.).

mi-ter, mi-tre (mī′tėr), *n.* [OF. F. *mitre*, < L. *mitra*, < Gr. *μίτρα*, belt, girdle, head-band, head-dress.] An ancient head-band or fillet for women; also, a kind of head-dress formerly worn by Asiatics; also, the official head-dress of the ancient Jewish high priest; also, the official head-dress of a bishop in the Western Church, in its modern form a tall cap with a top deeply cleft crosswise, the outline of the front and back resembling that of a pointed arch; also, a miter-joint, or the abutting surface or bevel on either of the pieces joined.—**mi′ter, mi′tre,** *v.*; *-tered, -tred, -tering, -tring.* **I.** *tr.* To bestow a miter upon, or raise to a rank entitled to it; also, to join with a miter-joint; make a miter-joint in; cut to a miter. **II.** *intr.* To meet in a miter-joint.—**mi′ter=box, mi′tre=box,** *n.* A box or apparatus for use in cutting miters; esp., a narrow box or trough the two opposite sides of which have vertical kerfs for guiding a saw at the proper angle to cut for miter-joints pieces placed in the box.—**mi′tered, mi′tred,** *p. a.* Wearing, or entitled or privileged to wear, a miter (as, a *mitered* abbot, an abbot who has the privilege of using the miter and other insignia, and exercising certain of the functions, of a bishop); ruled by a mitered abbot (as, a *mitered* abbey); also, shaped like a bishop's miter, or having a miter-shaped apex; also, joined with a miter-joint; cut to a miter.—**mi′ter=joint, mi′tre=joint,** *n.* A joint in which the plane of the abutting surfaces bisects the angle (properly 90°) formed by the abutting pieces.—**mi′ter=shell, mi′tre=shell,** *n.* The fusiform shell of any gastropod of the genus *Mitra* or the family *Mitridæ*, mostly of warm seas: so called from the shape of the spire.—**mi′ter-wort, mi′tre-wort** (-wėrt), *n.* Any of the low herbs which constitute the saxifragaceous genus *Mitella*: so called from the capsule, which resembles a bishop's miter.

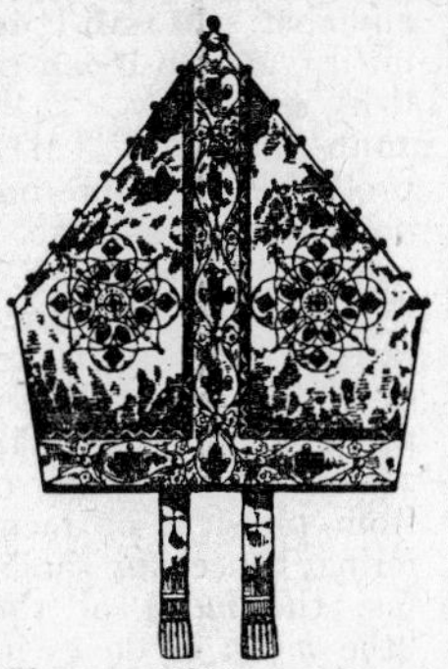

Bishop's Miter. — French type of the 14th century.

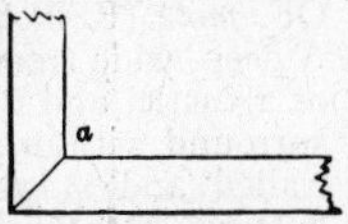

a, Miter-joint.

mith-ri-date (mith′ri-dāt), *n.* [ML. *mithridatum*, < L. *Mithridates*, name of a king of Pontus who is said to have invented a universal antidote, and to have rendered himself immune to poisons by the method called 'mithridatism.'] In *old phar.*, an electuary of many ingredients, supposed to serve as a universal antidote or preservative against poison.—**mith-ri-dat′ic** (-dat′ik), *a.*—**mith′ri-dat-ism** (-dā-tizm), *n.* The production of immunity against the action of a poison by taking the poison in gradually increased doses; the immunity thus acquired.

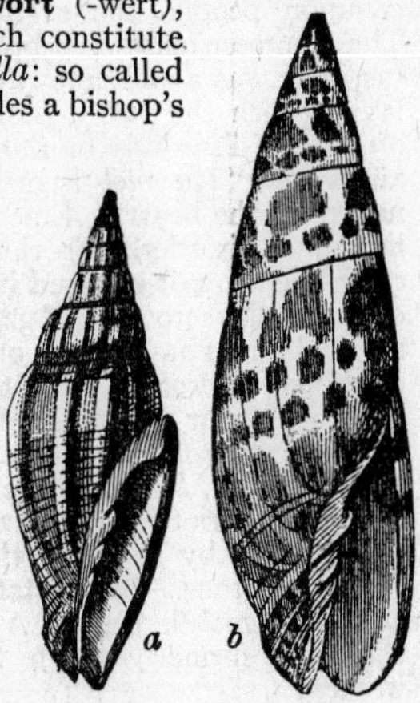

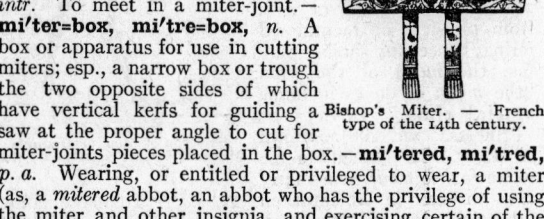

Miter-shells. — *a*, *Mitra vulpecula*; *b*, *Mitra episcopalis.*

mit-i-ga-ble (mit′i-gạ-bl), *a.* That may be mitigated.

mit-i-gate (mit′i-gāt), *v.*; *-gated, -gating.* [L. *mitigatus*, pp. of *mitigare*, < *mitis*, mild, + *agere*, drive, do.] **I.** *tr.* To make milder or more gentle, soften, or mollify (a person, the mind, etc.: now rare); also, to lessen in force or intensity (wrath, harshness, severity, etc.); assuage (pain or grief); moderate the severity of (anything distressing: as, "I . . . prayed to the Lord to *mitigate* a calamity which seemed to me past the capacity of man to remedy," Galt's "Annals of the Parish," xlix.); make more bearable; temper; moderate; sometimes, to lessen the gravity of (an offense). **II.** *intr.* To become milder; moderate in severity.—**mit-i-ga′tion** (-gā′shọn), *n.* [L. *mitigatio(n-)*.] The act of mitigating, or the state of being mitigated; also, something that mitigates, or lessens severity.—**mit′i-ga-tive** (-gā-tiv), **mit′i-ga-to-ry** (-tọ-ri), *a.* Tending to mitigate.—**mit′i-ga-tor** (-gā-tọr), *n.*

mi-tis (mī′tis), *a.* and *n.* [L. *mitis*, mild.] A name applied to a malleable iron ('mitis metal,' or 'mitis') produced by fusing wrought-iron with a small amount of aluminium, the aluminium rendering the product fluid enough to cast.

mi-to-sis (mi-tō′sis), *n.* [NL., < Gr. μίτος, a thread.] In *biol.*, the usual (indirect) method of cell-division, characterized typically by the resolving of the chromatin of the nucleus into a thread-like form, which separates into segments or chromosomes, each of which in turn separates longitudinally into two parts, one part of each chromosome being retained in each of two new cells resulting from the original cell. Cf. *amitosis*.—**mi-tot′ic** (-tot′ik), *a.* Pertaining to or characterized by mitosis.—**mi-tot′i-cal-ly,** *adv.*

mi-traille (mē-trä-y′), *n.* [F., < OF. *mitaille*, < *mite*, small coin.] Small missiles or projectiles, as pieces of iron, fired in masses from a cannon, etc.—**mi-trail-leur** (-trä-yėr), *n.* [F., masc.] A mitrailleuse, or a man who operates one.—**mi-trail-leuse** (-trä-yėz), *n.* [F., fem.] A breech-loading machine-gun for firing small projectiles with great rapidity; esp., a gun of this type with a number of barrels fitted together, introduced into the French army about 1868.

mi-tral (mī′trạl), *a.* Of, pertaining to, or resembling a miter; in *anat.*, noting or pertaining to a valve in the heart which prevents the blood in the left ventricle from returning to the left auricle.

mi-tre (mī′tėr), etc. See *miter*, etc.

mitt (mit), *n.* [Short for *mitten.*] A mitten; also, a kind of long glove extending only to, or slightly over, the fingers, worn by women; in *baseball*, a kind of glove having the side next the palm of the hand protected by a large, thick mitten-like pad.

mit-ten (mit′n), *n.* [OF. F. *mitaine*; origin uncertain.] A kind of hand-covering inclosing the four fingers together and the thumb separately; also, a mitt (kind of long glove); also, *pl.*, boxing-gloves (slang).—**to get** (or **give**) **the mitten,** to be rejected (or reject), as a lover.—**mit′tened,** *a.* Covered with or wearing mittens: as, "men, furred and *mittened*" (Jack London's "Call of the Wild," vi.).

mit-ti-mus (mit′i-mus), *n.* [L., 'we send.'] In *law*, a warrant of commitment to prison; also, a writ for removing a suit or a record from one court to another.

mit-y (mī′ti), *a.* Containing mites, as cheese.

mix (miks), *v.* [First in *mixed*, pp., for older *mixt*, < L. *mixtus*, pp. of *miscere*, mix; akin to Gr. μιγνύναι, Skt. *miç-*, mix.] **I.** *tr.* To put together (substances or things, or one substance or thing with another) in one mass or assemblage with more or less thorough diffusion of the constituent elements among one another (as, to *mix* wine and water, or water with wine; to *mix* the ingredients for a cake); put in as an added element or ingredient (as, *mix* a little soda into the flour); form by combining ingredients (as, to *mix* bread; to *mix* mortar); also, in general, to combine, unite, or join (as, to *mix* business and pleasure; "You *mix* your sadness with some fear," Shakspere's "2 Henry IV.," v. 2. 46); associate, as in company, intercourse, or relations (as, "The holy seed is *mixed* with the strange people of the land": 1 Esdras, viii. 70); often, to put together indiscriminately or confusedly, jumble, or confuse (often with *up*). **II.** *intr.* To become mixed (as, oil and water will not *mix*); also, to associate, as in company or intercourse (as, "It would be very disagreeable to me to *mix* in the sort of company this place affords": Scott's "Guy Mannering," xliv.).—**mix,** *n.* A mixing, or a mixed condition; esp., a muddle or mess (colloq.).—**mix′a-ble,** *a.* Capable of being mixed.—**mixed,** *p. a.* Put together or formed by mixing; composed of different constituents or elements (as, a *mixed* tea; a *mixed* chorus, of both male and female voices; a *mixed* character); of different kinds combined (as, *mixed* candies; *mixed* emotions); comprising persons of different classes, status, character, opinions, etc. (as, *mixed* society; a *mixed* company); mentally confused (colloq.).—**mixed metaphor.** See under *metaphor*.—**mixed number,** a number consisting of a whole number and a fraction, as $4\frac{1}{2}$.—**mixed′ly,** *adv.*—**mixed′ness,** *n.*

mix-en (mik′sn), *n.* [AS. *mixen*, < *meox*, dung.] A dunghill; a heap of refuse. [Archaic or prov. Eng.]

mix-er (mik′sėr), *n.* One who or that which mixes; also, a person with reference to capacity for entering sociably into intercourse with others (slang: as, a good *mixer*).

mix-o-bar-bar-ic (mik″sọ̄-bär-bar′ik), *a.* [Gr. μιξοβάρβαρος, < μιξο-, repr. μιγνύναι, mix, + βάρβαρος, barbarous.] Partly barbaric; barbaric with an admixture of characteristics due to civilized (esp. Greek) influences.

mix-ti-lin-e-ar (miks-ti-lin′ẹ̄-ạ̈r), *a.* [L. *mixtus*, mixed, + *linea*, line.] Consisting of both straight and curved lines.

mix-ture (miks′ṭūr), *n.* [L. *mixtura*, < *miscere*: see *mix*.] The act of mixing, or the state of being mixed; also, a product of mixing; an assemblage of ingredients mixed together but not chemically combined; a fabric woven of yarns combining various colors (as, a heather *mixture*: see under *heather*); any combination of differing elements, kinds, qualities, etc. (as, "He showed a curious *mixture* of eagerness and terror": Parkman's "Oregon Trail," vii.); also, an added element or ingredient; an admixture.

mix=up (miks′up), *n.* A confused state of things; a muddle; a tangle; also, a fight. [Colloq.]

miz-en (miz′n), etc. See *mizzen*, etc.

mi-zer (mī′zėr), *n.* See *miser*[2].

Miz-pah (miz′pạ̈). [From *Mizpah* (Heb., lit. 'watch-tower'), a name given to the heap of stones bearing witness to the covenant of Jacob and Laban.] A word used allusively, as when inscribed on a ring given to a friend, to recall the words of Laban in making a covenant with Jacob: "The Lord watch between me and thee, when we are absent one from another" (Gen. xxxi. 49).

miz-zen (miz′n), *n.* [F. *misaine*, < It. *mezzana*, prop. fem. of *mezzano*, middle, < L. *medianus*, E. *median*[2].] *Naut.*, the aftermost fore-and-aft sail of a three-masted vessel, set abaft the mizzenmast; the sail on the mizzenmast of a ketch, yawl, or the like; also, a mizzenmast.—**miz′zen-mast** (-måst), *n.* *Naut.*, the aftermost mast of a three-masted vessel; in a ketch, yawl, or the like, the mast nearest the stern.—**miz′zen-top** (-top), *n.* *Naut.*, a platform at the head of the lower mizzenmast.—**miz″zen-top-gal′lant-mast** (-top-gal′ạnt-måst, naut. -tọ-gal′ạnt-mạst), *n.* *Naut.*, the mast next above the mizzentopmast.—**miz-zen-top′-mast** (-top′måst), *n.* *Naut.*, the mast next above the lower mizzenmast.

miz-zle[1] (miz′l), *v. i.*; *-zled, -zling.* [Origin obscure.] To disappear suddenly; run off; decamp: as, "Bealby had not '*mizzled*,' although he was conspicuously not in evidence about the camp" (H. G. Wells's "Bealby," iv.). [Slang.]

miz-zle[2] (miz′l), *v. i.*; *-zled, -zling.* [Late ME. *miselle* = LG. *miseln*.] To rain in very fine drops; drizzle. [Now prov. or colloq.]—**miz′zle**[2], *n.* A fine rain; a drizzle; a thick mist. [Now prov. or colloq.]—**miz′zly,** *a.* Drizzly; misty. [Now prov. or colloq.]

mne-mon-ic (nẹ̄-mon′ik), *a.* [Gr. μνημονικός, < μνήμων, mindful, < μνᾶσθαι, remember: see *mind*[2].] Assisting, or intended to assist, the memory; also, pertaining to mnemonics or to memory.—**mne-mon′ics,** *n.* The art of improving or developing the memory; also, a system of precepts and rules to assist or improve the memory.—**mne-mo-nist** (nē′mọ̄-nist), *n.* One versed in mnemonics.

mne-mo-tech-ny (nē′mọ̄-tek-ni), *n.* [Gr. μνήμη, memory, + τέχνη, art.] The art of improving or developing the memory; mnemonics.—**mne-mo-tech′nic,** *a.*

mo (mō), *adv.*, *n.*, and *a.* [AS. *mā*, akin to *māra*, E. *more*.] More. [Obs. or prov.]

-mo (-mō). [L. *-mo*, abl. of *-mus*, termination of ordinal numerals.] The final syllable of certain terms of Latin origin, as *duodecimo*, *sextodecimo*, denoting the number of leaves into which a sheet of paper is folded in book-making, sometimes appended to an English numeral or to the Arabic figures, as in *twelvemo* or 12*mo* (also 12°), *sixteenmo* or 16*mo* (also 16°).

mo-a (mō′ạ̈), *n.* [Maori.] Any of various extinct, flightless, chiefly large birds of New Zealand, constituting the family *Dinornithidæ*, allied to the apteryx but resembling an ostrich in general appearance. See cut in next column.

Mo-ab-ite (mō′ạ-bīt). [Said to be descended and named from *Moab*, one of the sons of Lot: see Gen. xix. 37.] **I.** *n.* A member of a people of ancient Palestine inhabiting a district called (like the people themselves) Moab, east of the Dead Sea and the river Jordan. **II.** *a.* Of or pertaining to the Moabites.—**Moabite stone,** a slab of black basalt bearing an inscription in Hebrew-Phenician characters, which records the victories of Mesha, king of Moab, over the Israelites. It was discovered in 1868, and is the oldest known monument (9th century B.C.) of the Semitic alphabet.—**Mo-ab-it-ic** (mō-ạ-bit′ik), **Mo-ab-it-ish** (mō′ạ-bī-tish), *a.*

Skeleton of Moa, or Dinornis.—Museum of Natural History, New York.

moan (mōn), *n.* [ME. *mone*, prob. from an unrecorded AS. noun whence also AS. *mǣnan*, complain of, lament, E. *mean*[4].] Complaint or lamentation (archaic: as, to make *moan*, or make one's *moan*); also, a prolonged, low, inarticulate sound uttered from or as if from physical or mental suffering; hence, any similar sound (as, the *moan* of the wind; "the *moan* of doves in immemorial elms," Tennyson's "Princess," vii. 206).—**moan,** *v.* **I.** *tr.* To lament or bemoan (as, to *moan* one's fate); also, to utter in lamentation. **II.** *intr.* To make lament (archaic); also, to utter moans, as of pain or grief; make any sound suggestive of such moans (said of the wind, sea, trees, etc.).—**moan′ing-ly,** *adv.*

moat (mōt), *n.* [ME. *mote*, moat, also earlier mound, < OF. *mote* (F. *motte*), mound, eminence; prob. from Teut.] A deep, wide trench surrounding a fortified place, as a town or a castle, and usually filled with water.—**moat,** *v. t.* To surround with or as with a moat: as, "The faubourg, being walled and *moated*, could be taken only by escalade or battery" (Motley's "Dutch Republic," vi. 4).

mob[1] (mob), *n.* [Origin uncertain.] A mob-cap.

mob[2] (mob), *n.* [Short for L. *mobile vulgus*, the movable common people, the excitable or changeable multitude.] The common mass of people, or the populace or multitude (as, "He was a well-known character in town, and much in favour with the *mob*": Lever's "Harry Lorrequer," xlvi.); often, the disorderly or riotous rabble, as in public disturbances (as, "The *mob* is man voluntarily descending to the nature of the beast": Emerson's "Essays," Compensation); hence, a disorderly or riotous assemblage of persons; a crowd bent on or engaged in lawless violence; any tumultuous or noisy crowd; in general (and often disparagingly), a promiscuous assemblage or aggregation of persons, animals, or things; a crowd; a multitude; also, a gang of thieves or pickpockets, or a member of one (slang, Eng.).—**mob**[2], *v. t.*; *mobbed, mobbing.* To beset as a mob does; crowd round tumultuously, as from rude curiosity or with hostile intent; attack with riotous violence; also, to drive or force (*from*, *into*, etc.) by such action.—**mob′bish,** *a.* Mob-like; vulgar; riotous.—**mob′bist,** *n.* A member of a mob.

mob=cap (mob′kap), *n.* A large, full cap fitting down over the ears, formerly much worn indoors by women.

Mob-cap, 18th century.

mo-bile (mō′bil), *a.* [OF. F. *mobile*, < L. *mobilis*, < *movere*, E. *move*.] Movable, or moving readily; capable of easy and rapid movement, as a military force; flowing freely, as a liquid; changing easily in expression, as features; fig., quickly responding to impulses, emotions, etc., as the mind; facile; versatile.—**mo-bil-i-ty** (mọ̄-bil′i-ti), *n.* [F. *mobilité*, < L. *mobilitas*.] The quality of being mobile; ability or readiness to move or change.—**mo-bi-liz-a-ble** (mō′bi-lī-zạ-bl), *a.* Capable of being mobilized.—**mo″bi-li-za′tion** (-li-zā′shọn), *n.* [F. *mobilisation*.] The process of mobilizing, or the state of being mobilized; specif., the putting of troops, war-vessels, etc., into readiness for active service.—**mo′bi-lize** (-līz), *v.*; *-lized, -lizing.* [F. *mobiliser*, < *mobile*.] **I.** *tr.* To render mobile; put into motion, circulation, or active use (as, to *mobilize* the wealth of a country); specif., to put (troops, war-vessels, etc.) into readiness for active service; assemble and prepare for action in war;

sometimes, to organize or adapt (industries, etc.) for service to the government in time of war. **II.** *intr.* To undergo mobilization.

mob-le (mob′l), *v. t.*; *-led, -ling.* [Cf. *mob*¹.] To muffle, as in a hood or shawl. See Shakspere's "Hamlet," ii. 2. 525. [Obs. or prov. Eng.]

mob-oc-ra-cy (mob-ok′rạ-si), *n.*; pl. *-cies* (-siz). [See *-cracy.*] Rule by the mob; political control by a mob; also, the mob as a ruling class.—**mob′o-crat** (-ǫ-krat), *n.* [See *-crat.*] One who advocates mobocracy; also, a leader of the mob; a demagogue.—**mob-o-crat′ic, mob-o-crat′i-cal,** *a.*

mobs-man (mobz′mạn), *n.*; pl. *-men.* One of a mob or crowd; also, a stylishly dressed pickpocket, usually one of a gang (slang, Eng.).

Moccasin.

moc-ca-sin (mok′ạ-sin), *n.* [N. Amer. Ind.] A shoe made entirely of soft leather, as deerskin, worn by the American Indians and hence by others; also, a venomous snake, *Ancistrodon piscivorus*, of the southern U. S., found in or near water ('water-moccasin'); a similar snake, *A. atrofuscus*, found on dry land.—**moc′ca-sined,** *a.* Shod with moccasins.—**moc′ca-sin=flow″er,** *n.* A cypripedium or lady's-slipper.

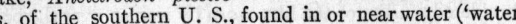

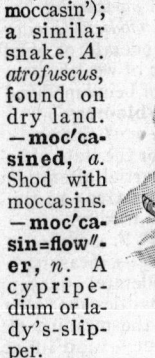

Water-moccasin (*Ancistrodon piscivorus*).

Mo-cha (mō′kạ), *n.* [From *Mocha* (Mokha), seaport of Arabia near the mouth of the Red Sea.] [Also *l. c.*] A choice variety of coffee, originally coming from Mocha, Arabia.

mock (mok), *v.* [OF. F. *moquer*; origin uncertain.] **I.** *tr.* To assail or treat with ridicule or derision (as, "Little children . . . *mocked* him, and said . . . Go up, thou bald head": 2 Kings, ii. 23); deride; now, commonly, to ridicule by mimicry of action or speech; mimic derisively; sometimes, merely, to mimic, imitate, or counterfeit (chiefly poetic: as, "Prepare To see the life as lively *mock'd* as ever Still sleep *mock'd* death," Shakspere's "Winter's Tale," v. 3. 19); also, to defy, or set at naught (chiefly fig.: as, "health that *mocks* the doctor's rules," Whittier's "Barefoot Boy"); also, to deceive, delude, or disappoint (as, "Mind is a light which the Gods *mock* us with, To lead those false who trust it": M. Arnold's "Empedocles on Etna," i. 2). **II.** *intr.* To use ridicule or derision; scoff; jeer: often with *at.*—**mock. I.** *n.* A mocking or derisive action or speech; mockery or derision; also, something mocked or derided; an object of derision; also, imitation, or an imitation or counterfeit. **II.** *a.* Being an imitation or having merely the semblance of something; counterfeit; sham; false: as, a *mock* battle; *mock* modesty. —**mock moon.** Same as *paraselene.*—**mock sun.** Same as *parhelion.*—**mock turtle,** a dish made of calf's head with sauce and seasoning to resemble turtle; also, a soup made, usually of calf's head, in imitation of turtle soup ('mock turtle soup').

mock-a-ble (mok′ạ-bl), *a.* That may be mocked; subject to mockery.

mock-er (mok′ėr), *n.* One who or that which mocks; specif., a mocking-bird.

mock-er-y (mok′ėr-i), *n.*; pl. *-ies* (-iz). Ridicule or derision; a derisive action or speech; a subject or occasion of derision; also, imitation, or an imitation, esp. of a ridiculous or unsatisfactory kind (as, "disdaining to be pleased with the provincial *mockery* of a court festival": Hawthorne's "Twice-Told Tales," Lady Eleanore's Mantle); a mere travesty, or mocking pretense (as, "The result of the trial . . . was another of those *mockeries* of justice which made the Roman law-courts the jest of mankind": Froude's "Cæsar," xviii.); hence, something absurdly or offensively inadequate or unfitting.

mock=he-ro-ic (mok′hẹ-rō′ik). **I.** *a.* Imitating or burlesquing what is heroic, as in style, character, or action: as, a *mock-heroic* poem; *mock-heroic* dignity. **II.** *n.* An imitation or burlesque of what is heroic: as, "We all found it impossible to withstand the ludicrous *mock-heroic* of his face and tone" (Lever's "Harry Lorrequer," xxvii.).—**mock′=he-ro′i-cal-ly,** *adv.*

mock-ing (mok′ing), *p. a.* That mocks; deriding; mimicking or imitating; deluding.—**mock′ing=bird,** *n.* A song-bird, *Mimus polyglottus*, of the southern U. S., remarkable for its imitative vocal powers; also, any of various allied or similar birds.—**mock′ing-ly,** *adv.*

Mocking-bird (*Mimus polyglottus*).

mock=or-ange (mok′or″ạnj), *n.* Any of the shrubs constituting the genus *Philadelphus*, esp. *P. coronarius*, the common cultivated syringa. See *syringa.*

mo-dal (mō′dạl), *a.* [ML. *modalis.*] Of or pertaining to mode, manner, or form; often, pertaining to mode or form as distinguished from substance or matter; specif., pertaining to mode in grammar, logic, or music.—**mo-dal-i-ty** (mǫ-dal′i-ti), *n.*; pl. *-ties* (-tiz). [ML. *modalitas.*] The state of being modal; modal quality or relation; also, a modal attribute or circumstance.—**mo′dal-ly,** *adv.*

mode (mōd), *n.* [OF. F. *mode*, manner, way, usage, later vogue, fashion, < L. *modus*, measure, due measure, manner, form: see *mete*², and cf. *mood*¹.] Manner of acting or doing; a method; a way; also, the manner or state of existence of a thing; a form; also, customary or conventional usage in manners, dress, etc., esp. as observed by persons of fashion; a prevailing style or fashion; in *gram.*, distinctive form of a verb indicating whether the act or state predicated is conceived as a certainty, a contingency, a command, or the like; any of the groups of forms of a verb serving to indicate this (as, the indicative, subjunctive, or imperative *mode*: also *mood*); in *logic*, the form of a proposition with reference to the necessity, contingency, possibility, or impossibility of its content; also, any of the various forms of valid syllogisms (see *mood*¹); in *music*, any of various arrangements of the diatonic tones of an octave, differing from one another in the order of the whole steps and half-steps.

mod-el (mod′ẹl). [F. *modèle*, < It. *modello*, dim. < L. *modus*, E. *mode.*] **I.** *n.* A standard for imitation or comparison; a pattern; an exemplar; also, a set of plans for a building†; also, a representation, generally in miniature, to show the construction or serve as a copy of something; fig., an exact likeness (as, "I had my father's signet in my purse, Which was the *model* of that Danish seal," Shakspere's "Hamlet," v. 2. 50: now colloq. or prov.); also, an image in clay, wax, or the like, to be reproduced in more durable material; also, a person or thing that serves as an artist's pattern for a work of painting, etc. (as, "Nearly every individual of their number might have been taken for a sculptor's *model*": H. Melville's "Typee," xxiv.); a person who poses for artists and art-students; hence, one employed to put on articles of apparel to display them to customers; also, mode of structure or formation (as, "The ship was of a *model* such as I had never seen": G. W. Curtis's "Prue and I," v.); a typical form or style. **II.** *a.* Serving as a model; also, worthy to serve as a model; exemplary.—**mod′el,** *v.*; *-eled* or *-elled, -eling* or *-elling.* **I.** *tr.* To form or plan according to a model; also, to give shape or form to; fashion; esp., to fashion in clay, wax, or the like; also, to make a model or representation of. **II.** *intr.* To make models; esp., to produce designs in some plastic material; also, to assume a typical or natural appearance, or an appearance of natural relief, as the parts of a drawing in progress.—**mod′el-er, mod′el-ler,** *n.*—**mod′el-ing, mod′el-ling,** *n.* The act or art of one who models; the production of designs in some plastic material, as for reproduction in a more durable material; the representation of solid form, as in sculpture; the bringing of surfaces into proper relief, as in carving; the rendering of the appearance of relief, as in painting.

mod-er-ate (mod′ẹ-rāt), *v.*; *-ated, -ating.* [L. *moderatus,* pp. of *moderari, moderare,* keep within bounds, regulate, < *modus,* measure, E. *mode.*] **I.** *tr.* To reduce the excessiveness of (as, "He . . . did what he could to *moderate* the grief of his friend": Trollope's "Warden," iii.); render less violent, severe, intense, or rigorous; also, to preside over or at, as a deliberative body or a public meeting; also, to decide as an arbitrator†. **II.** *intr.* To become less violent, severe, intense, or rigorous (as, "The storm *moderated*": Parkman's "Oregon Trail," v.); also, to act as moderator; preside; also, to mediate between parties†.—**mod′er-ate** (-ẹ-rāt). **I.** *a.* Kept or keeping within due bounds; not extreme, excessive, or intense; restrained; temperate; also, of medium quantity, extent, etc. (as, "He took a *moderate* profit on what he sold": Galt's "Annals of the Parish," xxxix.); hence, mediocre; also, of or pertaining to moderates, as in politics or religion. **II.** *n.* One who is moderate in opinion or action, or opposed to extreme views and courses, esp. in politics or religion.—**mod′er-ate-ly,** *adv.*—**mod′er-ate-ness,** *n.*—**mod-er-a′tion** (-ẹ-rā′shọn), *n.* [L. *moderatio(n-).*] The act of moderating; also, the state or quality of being moderate; due restraint; avoidance of extremes; freedom from excess; temperance.—**mod′er-at-ism** (-ẹ-rạ-tizm), *n.* The principles or practices of a moderate party; adherence to these.—**mod′er-at-ist,** *n.*

mod-e-ra-to (mod-e-rä′tō), *a.* [It.] In *music,* moderate; in moderate time.

mod-er-a-tor (mod′ẹ-rā-tọr), *n.* [L.] One who or that which moderates; esp., a presiding officer, as over an ecclesiastical body in the Presbyterian Church; also, an arbitrator; a mediator.—**mod′er-a-tor-ship,** *n.*

mod-ern (mod′ėrn). [F. *moderne,* < LL. *modernus,* < L. *modo,* just now, just, only, orig. abl. of *modus,* measure, E. *mode.*] **I.** *a.* Of or pertaining to present and recent time; not ancient or remote in time; also, characteristic of present and recent time; not antiquated or obsolete; also, familiar†, commonplace†, or trite† (as, "The justice . . . Full of wise saws and *modern* instances": Shakspere's "As You Like It," ii. 7. 156). **II.** *n.* A person of modern times; also, one whose views and tastes are modern.—**mod′ern-ism,** *n.* A modern usage or characteristic; also, modern character; modern tendencies; sympathy with what is modern; specif., a tendency or movement in modern thought characterized by the use of independent critical methods in dealing with theological questions, and having as its object the harmonizing of the teachings of Christianity with modern intellectual requirements, which attracted attention in the Roman Catholic Church in the early years of the 20th century, and was condemned by Pope Pius X. in 1907, and which has since attained importance in Protestant churches in conflict with fundamentalism.—**mod′ern-ist. I.** *n.* One who follows or favors modern ways, tendencies, etc.; specif., one who advocates the study of modern subjects in preference to the ancient classics; also, an adherent of modernism in theological questions. **II.** *a.* Pertaining to modernists or modernism.—**mod-ern-is′tic,** *a.*—**mo-der-ni-ty** (mọ-dėr′ni-ti), *n.*; pl. *-ties* (-tiz). The quality of being modern; also, something modern.—**mod′ern-ize** (-īz), *v.*; *-ized, -izing.* **I.** *tr.* To render modern; give a modern character or appearance to. **II.** *intr.* To become modern; adopt modern ways, views, etc.; specif., to hold modernist views in theology.—**mod″ern-i-za′tion** (-i-zā′shọn), *n.*—**mod′ern-ly,** *adv.*—**mod′ern-ness,** *n.*

mod-est (mod′est), *a.* [F. *modeste,* < L. *modestus,* keeping due measure, moderate, unassuming, modest, < *modus,* measure, E. *mode.*] Having or showing a moderate or humble estimate of one's merits, importance, achievements, etc. (as, "a *modest* unpretending young man," Scott's "Guy Mannering," xxi.; a *modest* account of one's exploits); pleasingly free from vanity, egotism, boastfulness, or great pretensions; also, having or showing a nice regard for the decencies of behavior, speech, dress, etc.; delicate or decent; pure in thought and conduct; also, free from ostentation or showy extravagance (as, a *modest* dwelling or equipage; "Those who visited me in a *modest* way, I received," Smollett's "Humphry Clinker," Oct. 11); simple or unpretentious; also, moderate, or not extreme, excessive, or exaggerated (as, a *modest* estimate or statement).—**mod′est-ly,** *adv.*—**mod′es-ty** (-es-ti), *n.*; pl. *-ties* (-tiz). [F. *modestie,* < L. *modestia.*] The quality of being modest; freedom from vanity, boastfulness, etc. (as, "Few 'letters home' of successful men or women display the graces of *modesty* and self-forgetfulness": H. G. Wells's "Outline of History," xxxviii. § 3); nice regard for decency of behavior, speech, dress, etc.; purity of thought and conduct; unostentatiousness or simplicity; moderation; also, a modesty-piece.—**mod′es-ty=piece,** *n.* A piece or article of lace, net, embroidered muslin, or the like, worn by women over the bosom with a low-cut or open bodice. Also called *modesty-bit.*

mod-i-cum (mod′i-kum), *n.* [L., neut. of *modicus,* moderate, < *modus,* measure, E. *mode.*] A moderate or small quantity; a limited amount: as, a *modicum* of wealth.

mod-i-fi-a-ble (mod′i-fī-ạ-bl), *a.* Capable of being modified.—**mod″i-fi-a-bil′i-ty** (-bil′i-ti), **mod′i-fi-a-ble-ness,** *n.*

mod-i-fi-ca-tion (mod″i-fi-kā′shọn), *n.* [F. *modification,* < L. *modificatio(n-).*] The act of modifying, or the state of being modified; limitation or qualification; partial alteration; also, a modified form; a variety.—**mod′i-fi-ca-tive** (-kā-tiv), **mod′i-fi-ca-to-ry** (-kā-tọ-ri), *a.* Serving to modify.

mod-i-fy (mod′i-fī), *v. t.*; *-fied, -fying.* [OF. F. *modifier,* < L. *modificare, modificari,* set limits to, < *modus,* measure, + *facere,* make.] To reduce in degree; moderate; qualify; also, to change somewhat the form or qualities of; alter somewhat; in *gram.,* to limit or qualify the meaning of; in *philol.,* to change (a vowel) by umlaut.—**mod′i-fi-er** (-fī-ėr), *n.*

mo-dil-lion (mọ-dil′yọn), *n.* [It. *modiglione*: cf. L. *mutulus,* E. *mutule.*] In *arch.,* one of a series of ornamental blocks or brackets placed under the corona of a cornice in the Corinthian and other orders, or similarly used in medieval and modern styles.

Romanesque Modillion.

mo-di-o-lus (mọ-dī′ọ-lus), *n.*; pl. *-li* (-lī). [NL., < L. *modiolus,* dim. of *modius,* measure for grain, < *modus,* measure, E. *mode.*] In *anat.,* the central conical axis round which the cochlea of the ear winds.—**mo-di′o-lar** (-lạr), *a.*

mod-ish (mō′dish), *a.* In accordance with the mode or prevailing fashion; fashionable; stylish: as, "a nurse, in a *modish* Paris cap" (Hood's "Miss Kilmansegg," 221).—**mod′ish-ly,** *adv.*—**mod′ish-ness,** *n.*

mo-diste (mō-dēst), *n.* [F., < *mode,* fashion: see *mode.*] A maker of or dealer in articles of fashionable attire, esp. women's gowns, millinery, etc.

mo-di-us (mō′di-us), *n.*; pl. *-dii* (-di-ī). [L., < *modus,* measure, E. *mode.*] An ancient Roman dry measure, equal to about a peck; hence, a tall cylindrical head-dress worn by certain divinities as represented in ancient art. See cut on following page.

mod-u-lar (mod′ū-lạr), *a.* Of or pertaining to a module or a modulus.

mod-u-late (mod′ū-lāt), *v.*; *-lated, -lating.* [L. *modulatus,* pp. of *modulari,* measure, regulate, modulate, < *modulus*: see *module.*] **I.** *tr.* To regulate by or adjust to a certain measure or proportion; vary conformably; temper; soften; tone down; specif., to attune to a certain pitch or key; vary or inflect in tone; alter or adapt (the voice) fittingly in utterance (as, "He had a really noble voice, which he could *modulate* with great skill": Kinglake's "Eothen," xviii.); also, to sing or intone (a song, etc.); specif., in *wireless teleph.*, to cause the amplitude or intensity of (the continuous oscillations or high-frequency current in a radio sending apparatus) to vary in accordance with the sound-waves produced by the voice or the like, the effect of one sound-wave being spread over a considerable number of the oscillations, and the process being accomplished directly or indirectly by means of a telephone transmitter or microphone; cause (electric waves) to vary by producing them from such oscillations. **II.** *intr.* In *music*, to pass from one key to another in the course of a piece. —**mod-u-la'tion** (-lā'shọn), *n.* [OF. F. *modulation*, < L. *modulatio(n-)*.] The act of modulating, or the state of being modulated; specif., in *music*, transition from one key to another in the course of a piece.—**frequency modulation,** the modulation of the frequency of a radio wave in order to produce static-free reception.—**mod'u-la-tive** (-lā-tiv), **mod'u-la-to-ry** (-tọ-ri), *a.* Serving to modulate. —**mod'u-la-tor** (-lā-tọr), *n.* One who or that which modulates; in *radio*, a device for altering frequency.

Modius. — Head of statuette of Proserpine, found at Cnidus.

mod-ule (mod'ūl), *n.* [L. *modulus*, dim. of *modus*, measure, E. *mode.*] Measure†; also, a representation, image, or model on a small scale†; also, a mere image†; also, a standard or unit for measuring; in *arch.*, the size of some part, as the semidiameter of a column at the base of the shaft, taken as a unit of measure.

mod-u-lus (mod'ū-lus), *n.*; pl. *-li* (-lī). [L.: see *module.*] In *physics*, etc., a quantity expressing the measure of some function, property, or the like, esp. under conditions whose measure is unity.

mo-dus (mō'dus), *n.* [L.: see *mode.*] Mode; manner or method of procedure.—**modus operandi** (op-ẹ-ran'dī). [L.] Mode of operating or working.—**modus vivendi** (vi-ven'dī). [L.] Mode of living; way of getting along; a temporary arrangement between persons or parties pending a settlement of matters in debate.

moe (mō), *adv.*, *n.*, and *a.* See *mo.*

Mœ-ra (mē'rạ), *n.*; pl. *Mœræ* (-rē). [L., < Gr. Μοῖρα, personification of μοῖρα, part, lot, fate.] In *Gr. myth.*, the goddess of fate; *pl.*, the Fates.

Mœ-so-goth (mē'sọ-goth), *n.* One of a Gothic tribe which settled in Mœsia, an ancient Roman province corresponding nearly to modern Bulgaria and Serbia.—**Mœ-so-goth'ic,** *a.*

mo-fette (mọ-fet'), *n.* [F., < It. *mofetta*, < L. *mephitis*, noxious exhalation.] A noxious emanation, consisting chiefly of carbon dioxide, escaping from the earth in regions of nearly extinct volcanic activity; also, one of the openings or fissures from which this emanation issues.

mo-fus-sil (mọ-fus'il), *n.* [Ar. *mufaççal*, < *façcala*, divide, separate.] In India, the rural or provincial localities of a district as distinguished from the chief station; the country.

mog (mog), *v.*; *mogged*, *mogging.* [Origin obscure.] **I.** *intr.* To move on; depart; decamp; also, to move along slowly but steadily; jog. [Prov.] **II.** *tr.* To cause to move; remove. [Prov.]

Mo-gul (mọ-gul'), *n.* [Ar. and Pers. *Mughal*, Mongol.] A Mongol or Mongolian; esp., one of the Mongol conquerors of Hindustan in the 16th century, or of their descendants; also [*l. c.*], a type of locomotive for hauling heavy trains.—**the Great** (or **Grand**) **Mogul,** or **the Mogul,** the emperor of the Mongol empire of Hindustan, or empire of Delhi, which at one time included most of Hindustan (the last nominal emperor having been deposed in 1857); fig. [also *l. c.*], any great or pretentious personage.—**Mo-gul',** *a.* Of or pertaining to the Moguls, or the Mongol empire of Hindustan: as, *Mogul* architecture (the style of Mohammedan architecture evolved and carried out by the Mogul emperors in India, from the 16th to the 19th century: see cut at *taj*).

mo-hair (mō'hãr), *n.* [Ar. *mukhayyar.*] A lustrous fabric made of the hair of the Angora goat, or (partly or wholly) of some substitute for it; also, the hair, or yarn made from it.

Mo-ham-med-an (mọ-ham'e-dạn). **I.** *a.* Of or pertaining to the Arabian prophet Mohammed (570?–632), or the religious system founded by him. **II.** *n.* A follower of Mohammed; a believer in his religion.—**Mo-ham'med-an-ism,** *n.* The Mohammedan religion; Islam.—**Mo-ham'-med-an-ize,** *v. t.*; *-ized*, *-izing.* To make Mohammedan; convert or conform to Mohammedanism.

Mo-har-ram (mọ-hur'um), *n.* See *Muharram.*

mo-ho (mō'hō), *n.* [Hawaiian.] Any bird of the genus *Moho*, comprising honey-eaters peculiar to the Hawaiian Islands, having a blackish plumage with yellow pectoral tufts which were formerly used to adorn the cloaks of the native chiefs.

Moho (*M. nobilis*).

Mo-hock (mō'hok), *n.* [= *Mohawk*, Indian of the tribe so called, of N. Y., etc.] One of a class of ruffians, often aristocrats, who infested the streets of London at night early in the 18th century.

mo-hur (mō'hėr), *n.* [Pers. *muhr*, seal, gold coin.] A gold coin of British India, no longer coined, worth about $7.00: usually called *gold mohur.*

moi-der, moi-ther (moi'dėr, moi'ᴛʜėr), *v. t.* [Origin obscure.] To confuse; bother or worry; fatigue. [Prov. Eng., Ir. and Sc.]

moi-dore (moi'dōr), *n.* [Pg. *moeda d'ouro*, 'coin of gold.'] A former gold coin of Portugal, which was current in England in the 18th century, and was equivalent to about $6.50.

Obverse. Reverse.
Moidore.

moi-e-ty (moi'ẹ-ti), *n.*; pl. *-ties* (-tiz). [OF. *moitie*, *meitie* (F. *moitié*), < LL. *medietas*, half, L. middle point, < L. *medius*, middle.] A half (as, "War, pestilence, and famine, had consumed . . . the *moiety* of the human species": Gibbon's "Decline and Fall of the Roman Empire," x.); also, an indefinite portion (as, "I have seen what but a small *moiety* of the world . . . has seen": H. Kingsley's "Geoffry Hamlyn," xxv.).

moil (moil), *v.* [OF. *moillier* (F. *mouiller*), wet, moisten, < L. *mollis*, soft.] **I.** *tr.* To wet; soil; daub; also, to fatigue; weary. [Archaic or prov.] **II.** *intr.* To work hard; toil; drudge; sometimes, to work in wet and mire. [Archaic or prov.]—**moil,** *n.* Mud; mire; defilement; a spot; also, toil or drudgery (as, "These feet . . . Made to tread the mills of toil, Up and down in ceaseless *moil*": Whittier's "Barefoot Boy"); also, confusion, turmoil, or trouble. [Archaic or prov.]—**moil′er,** *n.*

moire (mwor), *n.* [F., < E. *mohair.*] A watered fabric, as of silk or wool; also, a watered or wave-like pattern or finish, as on silk or metal.—**moire antique,** silk watered in a large pattern.—**moi-ré** (mwo-rā). [F.] **I.** *a.* Watered, as silk; having a wave-like pattern. **II.** *n.* Same as *moire.*

moist (moist), *a.* [OF. *moiste, muste* (F. *moite*), moist, OF. also moldy, prob. < L. *mucidus,* moldy, musty: see *mucid,* and cf. *musty.*] Moderately or slightly wet; damp; humid; of the eyes, tearful; also, accompanied by or connected with liquid or moisture.—**moist-en** (moi′sn), *v.* **I.** *tr.* To make moist. **II.** *intr.* To become moist: as, "Trilby's eyes *moistened* with tender pleasure at such a pretty compliment" (Du Maurier's "Trilby," viii.).—**moist′en-er,** *n.*—**moist′ly,** *adv.*—**moist′ness,** *n.*—**mois-ture** (mois′ṭūr), *n.* [OF. *moistour* (F. *moiteur*).] The state or quality of being moist†, or moistness†; also, water or other liquid rendering anything moist.—**mois′ture-less,** *a.* Without moisture.—**moist′y,** *a.* Moist; damp.

·**moi′ther,** *v. t.* See *moider.*

moke (mōk), *n.* [Origin unknown.] A donkey; also, a negro (U. S.). [Slang.]

mol, mole^{5} (mōl), *n.* [G. *mol,* < *molekül,* molecule.] In *chem.,* the molecular weight of a substance expressed in grams; gram-molecule.—**mo-lal** (mō′lạl), **mo′lar^{1}** (lặr), *a.*

mo-lar^{2} (mō′lặr). [L. *molaris,* < *mola,* millstone: see *mill^{2}.*] **I.** *a.* Adapted for grinding, as teeth, esp. those in man, with a broad biting surface, situated behind the bicuspids; pertaining to such teeth. **II.** *n.* A molar tooth.

mo-lar^{3} (mō′lặr), *a.* [L. *moles,* mass: cf. *mole^{3}.*] Pertaining to mass, or to a body as a whole: often contrasted with *molecular.*—**mo-lar-i-ty** (mọ-lar′i-ti), *n.*

mo-las-ses (mọ-las′ez), *n.* [Pg. *melaço* or Sp. *melaza,* < L. *mel,* honey.] The thick, dark-colored syrup drained off from sugar during the process of manufacture; any of various similar syrups, as that produced during the refining of sugar, or that produced from sorghum. Cf. *treacle.*

mold^{1}, mould^{1} (mōld), *n.* [AS. *molde* = OHG. *molta* = Icel. *mold* = Goth. *mulda,* mold, dust; akin to E. *meal^{1}.*] Loose, friable earth, esp. such as is rich in organic matter and favorable to the growth of plants; also, the ground or earth, esp. as used for a grave, or the grave itself (archaic or prov.); also, earth considered as the material of the human body (archaic: as, a man of *mold,* a mortal man; "whether spirits or men of *mould,*" Carlyle's "Past and Present," ii. 17).

mold^{2}, mould^{2} (mōld), *n.* [ME. *mowlde,* appar. < *mowled, mouled,* pp. of *moulen,* earlier *muwlen,* grow moldy, akin to Icel. *mygla,* Sw. *mögla,* Dan. *mugne,* grow moldy.] A growth of minute fungi forming on vegetable or animal matter, commonly as a downy or furry coating, and associated with decay; also, any of the fungi that produce such a growth.—**mold^{2}, mould^{2},** *v. i.* or *t.* To become or make moldy.

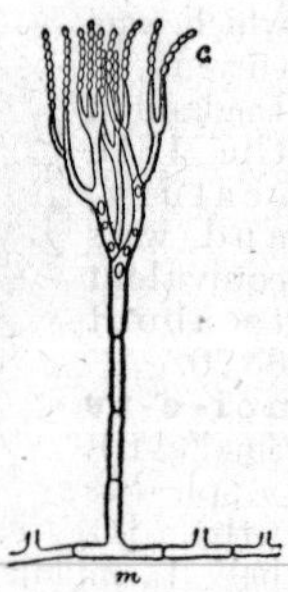

Mold (*Penicillium crustaceum*), magnified.—*m,* the mycelium; *c,* the conidia.

mold^{3}, mould^{3} (mōld), *n.* [OF. *modle, molle* (F. *moule*), < L. *modulus,* E. *module.*] A pattern, commonly a thin plate, as of cardboard or metal, used as a gage in shaping a piece of work; a templet; also, a hollow form or matrix for giving a particular shape to something in a molten or plastic state; also, that on or about which something is formed or made; also, the shape imparted to a thing by a mold; hence, in general, shape or form (as, "a human figure, but of singular *mould* and of unusual deformity": Cooper's "Spy," xxv.); sometimes, the body with reference to form or shape (poetic: as, "What doth she look on? . . . His vital presence? his corporeal *mould?*" Wordsworth's "Laodamia," 16); also, fig., distinctive nature, or native character (as, "Her mind was wholly of a different *mould* from my own," Bulwer-Lytton's "Pelham," v.; "Condé, more ambitious and of more generous *mould,*" Besant's "Coligny," vii.); also, something formed in or on a mold; a dish of food shaped in a mold (as, a *mold* of jelly); something molded; in *arch.,* a group of moldings.—**mold^{3}, mould^{3},** *v. t.* To shape or form in or on a mold; also, to work into a required shape or form; shape; fig., to fashion; model the style or character of (as, "The strong will prevail, subduing and *moulding* the gentler": Longfellow's "Courtship of Miles Standish," ii.); also, to produce by or as if by molding or shaping material; form; also, to ornament with moldings; in *founding,* to cast in a mold; also, to form a mold of or from, in order to make a casting.—**mold′a-ble, mould′a-ble,** *a.* Capable of being molded.

mold=board (mōld′bōrd), *n.* [See *mold^{1}.*] The curved board or metal plate in a plow, which turns over the earth from the furrow.

mol-der^{1}, moul-der^{1} (mōl′dėr), *v.* [Appar. < *mold^{1}.*] **I.** *intr.* To turn to dust by natural decay; crumble; waste away: as, "She now lies *mouldering* in the grave" (Godwin's "Caleb Williams," xi.); "Her glory *mouldered* and did cease From immemorial Nineveh" (Rossetti's "Burden of Nineveh"). **II.** *tr.* To cause to molder, crumble, or waste away.

mold-er^{2}, mould-er^{2} (mōl′dėr), *n.* [See *mold^{3}.*] One who molds; a maker of molds; specif., one who makes molds for castings in a foundry; also, in *printing,* one of a set of electrotyped plates used only for making duplicate electrotypes.

mold-i-ness, mould-i-ness (mōl′di-nes), *n.* The state of being moldy.

mold-ing, mould-ing (mōl′ding), *n.* The act or process of one who or that which molds; also, something molded; specif., in *arch.,* etc., a decorative variety of contour or outline given to cornices, jambs, strips of woodwork, etc.; a shaped member introduced into a structure to afford such variety or decoration; also, shaped material in the form of a strip, used for supporting pictures, covering electric wires, etc.

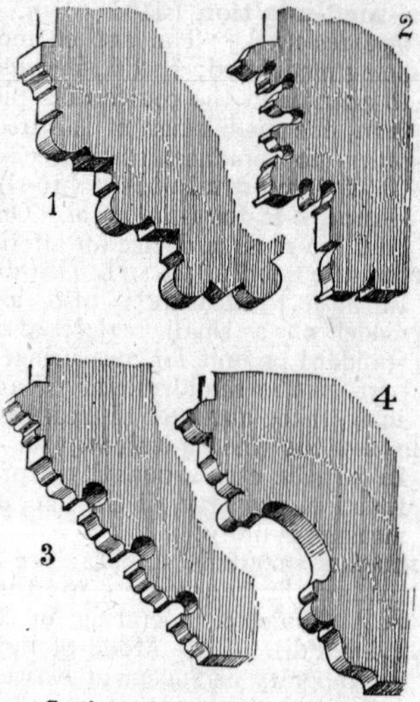

Sections of Medieval Moldings.
1, Norman style; 2, early English style; 3, decorated style; 4, perpendicular style.

mold=loft (mōld′lôft), *n.* A large room (usually a loft) in a shipyard, on the floor of which the lines of a ship are drawn in full size, in plan and elevation, from the designer's drawings.

mold-warp, mould-warp (mōld′wârp), *n.* [ME. *moldewarpe,* 'earth-thrower': see *mold^{1}* and *warp.*] A mole. See *mole^{2}.* [Now Sc. and prov. Eng.]

mold-y, mould-y (mōl′di), *a.*; compar. *moldier, mouldier,* superl. *moldiest, mouldiest.* Overgrown or covered with mold (as, "a bit of bread, *mouldy* and black": Godwin's "Caleb Williams," xxvi.); musty, as from decay or age (as, "A *mouldy* odour of aristocracy lingered about the place": Mrs. Gaskell's "Cranford," ix.); moldering or moldered (as, "*mouldy* walls": Cowper's "Task," v. 418); stale (as, a *moldy* joke); also, of or like mold.

mole^{1} (mōl), *n.* [AS. *māl* = OHG. *meil* = Goth. *mail,* spot.] A spot† or stain†; now, a small permanent spot or blemish on the human skin, usually of a dark color and slightly elevated, and often hairy (as, "Upon one cheek he had a *mole,* not unbecoming": Stevenson's "Master of Ballantrae," iv.).

mole^{2} (mōl), *n.* [ME. *molle* = MLG. *mol, mul,* mole; appar. connected with E. *mold^{1}*: cf. *moldwarp.*] Any of various small mammals, esp. of the family *Talpidæ,* living chiefly underground, and having velvety fur, very small eyes, and strong, fossorial fore feet; also, the fur; moleskin. See cut on following page.

mole^{3} (mōl), *n.* [F. *môle,* < L. *moles,* mass, massive structure, mole.] A massive structure, esp. of stone, set up in the water, as for a breakwater or a pier (as, "As I entered the harbor between the *moles* which embrace it . . . I felt at once its title to the appellation of 'Genoa the Superb'": Irving's "Tales of a Traveler," i. 9); hence, an anchorage or harbor protected by such a structure.

Common European Mole (*Talpa europæa*).

mole[4] (mōl), *n.* [F. *môle*, < L. *mola*, mole, lit. 'millstone': see *mill*[2].] In *pathol.*, a mass of fleshy matter occurring in the uterus as the result of an abortive conception, etc.

mole[5], *n.* See *mol.*

mole=cast (mōl'kȧst), *n.* A mole-hill.

Mo-lech (mō'lek), *n.* Same as *Moloch.*

mole=crick-et (mōl'krik"et), *n.* Any of various crickets, esp. those constituting the genus *Gryllotalpa*, having large fossorial fore legs adapted for burrowing in the ground, as *G. vulgaris*, the common European species, or *G. borealis*, of North America.

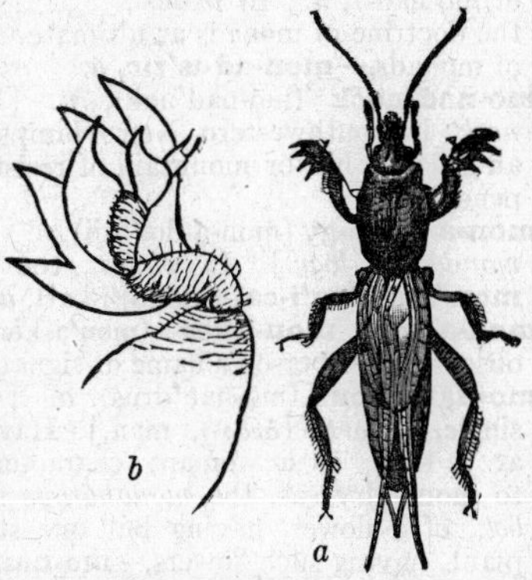

Mole-cricket (*Gryllotalpa borealis*). — *a*, adult, somewhat enlarged; *b*, anterior tarsus or fore foot, greatly enlarged.

mo-lec-u-lar (mō-lek'ū-lär), *a.* Pertaining to, caused by, or consisting of molecules. —**molecular weight,** in *chem.*, the relative weight of the molecule of an element or compound according to a certain system, usually one in which the atomic weight of oxygen is 16; the sum of the atomic weights of all the atoms in a molecule.—**mo-lec'u-lar-ly,** *adv.*

mol-e-cule (mol'e-kūl or mō'le-), *n.* [F. *molécule*, < NL. *molecula*, dim. of L. *moles*, mass: cf. *mole*[3].] In *chem.* and *physics*, the smallest particle of an element or compound that is capable of existing separately without loss of chemical identity; hence, in general, any very small particle.

mole=hill (mōl'hil), *n.* A small mound or ridge of earth raised up by moles burrowing under the ground; also, something insignificant, esp. an obstacle or difficulty, to which great importance is attributed (in allusion to the phrase 'to make a mountain out of a mole-hill').

mole=rat (mōl'rat), *n.* Any of the mole-like rodents of the old-world family *Spalacidæ*, which live under ground and burrow extensively.

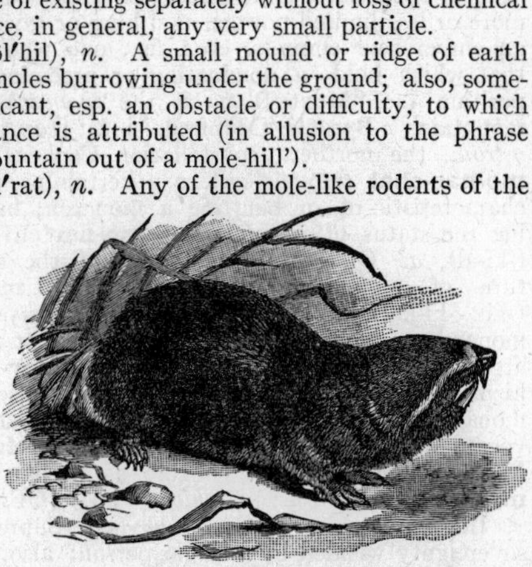

Mole-rat (*Spalax typhlus*).

mole-skin (mōl'skin), *n.* The skin of the mole, used as a fur; also, a stout twilled cotton fabric used for sportsmen's and laborers' clothing; *pl.*, garments, esp. trousers, of this fabric.

mo-lest (mō-lest'), *v. t.* [OF. F. *molester*, < L. *molestare*, < *molestus*, troublesome, appar. < *moles*, mass, also difficulty, labor, trouble: see *mole*[3].] To trouble†; afflict†; now, to interfere or meddle with annoyingly, injuriously, or with hostile intent (chiefly with a negative: as, "They had not been much *molested* by the savages," Defoe's "Robinson Crusoe," ii. 9).—**mo-les-ta-tion** (mol-es-tā'shọn or mō-les-), *n.* The act of molesting, or the state of being molested; annoying or hostile interference: as, "We were all allowed to disembark without the least *molestation*" (Kinglake's "Eothen," xxix.).—**mo-lest'er,** *n.*

moll (mol), *n.* [From *Moll*, for *Mary*, woman's name: cf. *molly.*] [Also *cap.*] A prostitute; also, the unmarried female companion of a thief or vagrant; also, a molly. [Slang.]

mol-lah (mol'ä), *n.* Same as *mullah.*

mol-li-fi-ca-tion (mol"i-fi-kā'shọn), *n.* The act of mollifying, or the state of being mollified.

mol-li-fy (mol'i-fī), *v. t.*; *-fied*, *-fying.* [OF. F. *mollifier*, < L. *mollificare*, < *mollis*, soft, + *facere*, make.] To make soft, supple, or tender, as in substance (now rare); fig., to soften in feeling or temper, as a person, the heart or mind, etc.; mitigate or appease, as rage; lessen the harshness or severity of, as demands, laws, etc. (now rare); make less grave or serious (now rare: as, "The transgression was certainly *mollified* by the nature of the performance," Galt's "Ayrshire Legatees," vi.).—**mol'li-fi-er** (-fī-ėr), *n.*

mol-li-tious (mo-lish'us), *a.* [L. *mollities*, softness, < *mollis*, soft.] Luxurious; voluptuous: as, "*mollitious* alcoves gilt" (Browning's "Sordello," iii.). [Rare.]

mol-lusc (mol'usk), *n.* See *mollusk.*

mol-lus-can (mo-lus'kạn). **I.** *a.* Of or pertaining to the *Mollusca* or mollusks. **II.** *n.* A mollusk.

mol-lus-coid (mo-lus'koid). [See *-oid.*] **I.** *a.* Resembling a mollusk. **II.** *n.* A molluscoid animal.

mol-lus-cous (mo-lus'kus), *a.* Belonging to or resembling the mollusks; fig., spineless; flabby; soft; weak.

mol-lusk, mol-lusc (mol'usk), *n.* [F. *mollusque*, < NL. *mollusca*, pl., < L. *molluscus*, soft (applied to a thin-shelled nut), < *mollis*, soft.] Any of the *Mollusca*, a large phylum of animals having soft, unsegmented bodies commonly covered with a hard shell of one, two, or more pieces, and including the snails, mussels, oysters, clams, etc.

mol-ly (mol'i), *n.*; pl. *mollies* (-iz). [From *Molly*, for *Mary*, woman's name: cf. *moll.*] [Also *cap.*] An effeminate man or boy; a mollycoddle. [Colloq.]

mol-ly-cod-dle (mol'i-kod-l), *n.* [See *molly.*] A man or boy who is used to being coddled; a milksop; an effeminate fellow: as, "You have been bred up as a *molly-coddle*, Pen, and spoilt by the women" (Thackeray's "Pendennis," i. 31). —**mol'ly-cod-dle,** *v. t.*; *-dled*, *-dling.* To make a mollycoddle of; coddle unfittingly.

Mo-loch (mō'lok), *n.* [Also *Molech*; LL. *Moloch*, < Gr. Μολόχ, < Heb. *Molek*, prob. for *melek*, king.] The title or name of a Semitic deity, mentioned in the Bible, whose worship was marked by the sacrifice by burning of children offered by their own parents (see Lev. xviii. 21; Amos, v. 26); hence, fig., anything conceived as requiring frightful sacrifice (as, the *Moloch* of war); also [*l. c.*], a spiny Australian lizard, *Moloch horridus.*

molt, moult (mōlt), *v.* [ME. *mouten*, < L. *mutare*, change: cf. *mew*[3].] **I.** *intr.* Of birds, reptiles, etc., to cast or shed the feathers, skin, or the like, to be succeeded by a new growth. **II.** *tr.* To cast or shed (feathers, etc.) in the process of renewal.—**molt, moult,** *n.* The act or process of molting.

molt-en (mōl'tn), *p. a.* [See *melt.*] Liquefied by heat; in a state of fusion; also, produced by melting and casting (as, a *molten* image).—**molten sea.** See *brazen sea*, under *brazen, a.*—**molt'en-ly,** *adv.*

mo-ly (mō'li), *n.* [L., < Gr. *μῶλυ.*] A fabulous herb with a milk-white flower and a black root, said by Homer to have been given by Hermes to Odysseus to counteract the spells of Circe (see Pope's tr. Homer's "Odyssey," x.); also, the wild garlic, *Allium moly.*

mo-lyb-date (mọ-lib'dāt), *n.* In *chem.*, a salt of molybdic acid.

mo-lyb-de-nite (mọ-lib'dẹ-nīt), *n.* A soft, graphite-like native sulphide of molybdenum: a valuable ore.

mol-yb-de-num (mol-ib-dē'num or mọ-lib'dẹ-), *n.* [NL., < L. *molybdæna*, < Gr. *μολύβδαινα*, galena, < *μόλυβδος*, lead.] Chem. sym., Mo; at. wt., 96; sp. gr., 9.01. A silver-white, almost infusible metallic element.—**mo-lyb-**

dic (mō-lib′dik), *a.* Of or containing molybdenum. See *molybdous.*—**molybdic acid,** any of certain acids containing molybdenum.—**mo-lyb′dous,** *a.* Containing molybdenum (in larger proportion than a corresponding molybdic compound).

mome (mōm), *n.* [Origin uncertain: cf. *mum*[1].] A blockhead or dolt. See Shakspere's "Comedy of Errors," iii. 1. 32. [Obs. or archaic.]

mo-ment (mō′mẹnt), *n.* [OF. F. *moment,* < L. *momentum,* movement, moment of time, weight, influence, importance, < *movere,* E. *move.*] An indefinitely short space of time (as, wait a *moment;* in a *moment* all was changed); an instant; any one of the passing instants of time (as, "Do not delay; the golden *moments* fly!" Longfellow's "Masque of Pandora," vii.); also, the present or other particular instant, or point of time (as, I cannot, or could not, recall his name at the *moment;* to act on the spur of the *moment,* see *spur, n.*); the precise instant of opportunity (as, to improve the *moment*); the present or current brief space of time (as, supplies sufficient for the *moment*); also, a definite stage, as in a course of events; also, weight, importance, or consequence (as, "To some she gave To weigh the *moment* of eternal things," Akenside's "Pleasures of Imagination," i. 89: now only in such phrases as 'of moment,' 'of great, little, or no moment,' etc.); also, moving cause† or determining influence†; in *philos.,* an essential or constituent element, or factor; a momentum; in *mech.,* tendency to produce motion, esp. about an axis.—**psychological moment.** See under *psychological.*—**mo-men-ta′ne-ous**† (-mẹn-tā′nẹ-us), **mo′men-ta-ny**† (-tạ-ni), *a.* [LL. *momentaneus.*] Momentary.—**mo′men-ta-ri-ly** (-tạ-ri-li), *adv.* For a moment (as, to hesitate *momentarily*); also, every moment, or from moment to moment (as, danger *momentarily* increasing); also, at any moment (as, *momentarily* liable to occur).—**mo′men-ta-ri-ness,** *n.*—**mo′men-ta-ry,** *a.* [L. *momentarius.*] Lasting but a moment (as, a *momentary* glimpse; a *momentary* impulse); of very short duration; very brief; short-lived or ephemeral, as a living creature (archaic); also, occurring or present every moment (as, *momentary* interruptions); constant; also, occurring at any moment (as, to live in fear of *momentary* exposure).—**mo′ment-ly,** *adv.* Every moment, or from moment to moment (as, "The throng *momently* increased": Poe's "Man of the Crowd"); also, at any moment; also, for a moment; momentarily.—**mo-men-tous** (mō-men′tus), *a.* Of great moment, importance, or consequence; now, esp., fraught with serious or far-reaching consequences, as events, issues, decisions, etc.—**mo-men′tous-ly,** *adv.*—**mo-men′tous-ness,** *n.*

mo-men-tum (mō-men′tum), *n.;* pl. *-tums* or *-ta* (-tạ). [L.: see *moment.*] Impetus, as of a moving body; in *mech.,* the quantity of motion of a moving body, being equivalent to the product of its mass and velocity; in *philos.,* an essential or constituent element; a moment.

Tokugawa Mon — that is, the mon of the Tokugawa family.

Mo-mus (mō′mus), *n.* [Gr. Μῶμος, lit. 'blame,' 'ridicule.'] The Greek god of censure and ridicule; hence [*cap.* or *l. c.*], a faultfinder; a carping critic.

mon (mon), *n.* [Jap.] In Japanese use, a personal or family device or cognizance.

mon-. See *mono-.*

mo-na (mō′nạ), *n.* [NL., < Sp. and Pg. *mona,* fem. of *mono,* monkey.] A small, long-tailed African monkey, *Cercopithecus mona,* of docile disposition and often kept in captivity. See cut in next column.

mon-a-chal (mon′ạ-kạl), *a.* [ML. *monachalis,* < LL. *monachus,* E. *monk.*] Of, pertaining to, or characteristic of monks or monastic life; monastic.—**mon′a-chism** (-kizm), *n.* Monasticism.—**mon′a-chize** (-kīz), *v.; -chized, -chizing.* **I.** *intr.* To become a monk; live a monastic life. **II.** *tr.* To make (a person) a monk.—**mon″a-chi-za′tion** (-ki-zā′shọn), *n.*

mon-a-cid (mon-as′id), *a.* [See *mono-.*] In *chem.,* capable of combining with one molecule of a monobasic acid.

mon-ad (mon′ad or mō′nad), *n.* [LL. *monas* (*monad-*), < Gr. μονάς (μοναδ-), < μόνος, alone, single.] Unity; a unit; in *philos.,* an absolutely simple entity, conceived as the ultimate unit of being; in *biol.,* any simple, single-celled organism; in *chem.,* an element, atom, or radical having a valence of one.

mon-a-del-phous (mon-ạ-del′fus), *a.* [Gr. μόνος, single, + ἀδελφός, brother.] In *bot.,* of stamens, united into one bundle or set by their filaments; of a plant or flower, having the stamens so united.

Monadelphous Flower.

Mona.

mo-nad-ic (mō-nad′ik), *a.* [Gr. μοναδικός.] Pertaining to or composed of monads; of the nature of a monad. Also **mo-nad′i-cal.**—**mo-nad′i-cal-ly,** *adv.*

mon-ad-ism (mon′ad-izm or mō′nad-), *n.* In *philos.,* the doctrine of monads as ultimate units of being; a theory of monads.—**mon-ad-is′tic,** *a.*

mo-nad-nock (mō-nad′nok), *n.* [From Mount *Monadnock,* in southwestern New Hampshire.] In *phys. geog.,* an isolated hill or mountain of resistant rock standing in a peneplain.

mon-a-dol-o-gy (mon-ạ-dol′ọ-ji), *n.* [F. *monadologie:* = E. *monad* + *-logy.*] In *philos.,* the doctrine of monads.—**mon″a-do-log′i-cal** (-dọ-loj′i-kạl), *a.*

mon-a-ker, mon-i-ker (mon′ạ-kėr, -i-kėr), *n.* [Origin obscure.] A person's name or signature. [Slang.]

mo-nan-drous (mō-nan′drus), *a.* [Gr. μόνανδρος, < μόνος, single, + ἀνήρ (ἀνδρ-), man.] Having but one husband at a time, as a woman; characterized by or pertaining to monandry (as, the *monandrous* system or custom); in *bot.,* of a flower, having but one stamen; of a plant, having such flowers.—**mo-nan′dry** (-dri), *n.* The practice or the condition of having but one husband at a time.

Monandrous Flower of Mare's-tail (*Hippuris vulgaris*), in the axil of the leaf.

mo-nan-thous (mō-nan′thus), *a.* [Gr. μόνος, single, + ἄνθος, flower.] In *bot.,* one-flowered.

mon-arch (mon′ärk), *n.* [LL. *monarcha,* < Gr. μονάρχης, μόναρχος, < μόνος, alone, + ἄρχειν, lead, rule.] Orig., a sole and absolute ruler of a state; commonly, a hereditary sovereign with more or less limited powers, as a king or queen, an emperor or empress, etc.; fig., one who or that which holds a dominating or preëminent position (as, "Mont Blanc is the *monarch* of mountains": Byron's "Manfred," i. 1); [*cap.*] in *astron.,* the northern constellation Cepheus.—**mo-nar-chal** (mō-när′kạl), *a.* Pertaining to, characteristic of, or befitting a monarch; having the status of a monarch.—**mo-nar′chi-al** (-ki-ạl), *a.* Of, pertaining to, or of the nature of a monarchy.—**mo-nar′chic, mo-nar′chi-cal** (-kik, -ki-kạl), *a.* [Gr. μοναρχικός.] Of or pertaining to a monarch or monarchy; characterized by or favoring monarchy.—**mo-nar′chi-cal-ly,** *adv.*—**mon′ar-chism** (-är-kizm), *n.* The principles of monarchy; also, advocacy of monarchical principles.—**mon′ar-chist** (-kist), *n.* An advocate or adherent of monarchy.—**mon′ar-chize** (-kīz), *v. i.* or *t.; -chized, -chizing.* To rule as or like a monarch.—**mon′ar-chy** (-ki), *n.;* pl. *-chies* (-kiz). [OF. F. *monarchie,* < LL. *monarchia,* < Gr. μοναρχία.] Supreme power or sovereignty wielded by a single person; also, a government or state in which the supreme power is actually or nominally lodged in a monarch (being known as an *absolute* or *despotic monarchy* when the monarch's authority is not limited by the laws or a constitution of the realm, and as a *limited* or *constitutional monarchy* when the monarch's authority is so limited); also, the monarchical system of government.

mon-as (mon′as or mō′nas), *n.;* pl. *monades* (mon′ạ-dēz). [LL.] Same as *monad.*

mon-as-te-ry (mon′ạs-te-ri or -tẹ-ri), *n.*; pl. *-ries* (-riz). [LL. *monasterium*, < LGr. *μοναστήριον*, < *μοναστής*, a solitary, a monk: see *monastic.*] A house or place of residence occupied by a community of persons, esp. monks, living in seclusion from the world under religious vows; also, the community of persons living in such a place.—**mon-as-te′ri-al** (-tē′ri-ạl), *a.*

mo-nas-tic (mō-nas′tik). [ML. *monasticus*, < LGr. *μοναστικός*, < *μοναστής*, a solitary, a monk, < Gr. *μονάζειν*, be or live alone, < *μόνος*, alone.] **I.** *a.* Of, pertaining to, or characteristic of monks, or other persons living in seclusion from the world under religious vows (as, *monastic* vows, vows of poverty, chastity, and obedience, imposed under monastic rule); also, of or pertaining to monasteries (as, *monastic* architecture; "He had visited . . . some *monastic* ruins in the county of Dumfries," Scott's "Guy Mannering," i.). **II.** *n.* A member of a monastic community or order; a monk: as, "*monastics* . . . who have retired to the sacred sites of Palestine" (Kinglake's "Eothen," x.).—**mo-nas′ti-cal,** *a.* Monastic.—**mo-nas′ti-cal-ly,** *adv.*—**mo-nas′ti-cism** (-sizm), *n.* The monastic system, condition, or mode of life.—**mo-nas′ti-cize** (-sīz), *v. t.*; *-cized, -cizing.* To make monastic.

mon-a-tom-ic (mon-ạ-tom′ik), *a.* [See *mono-.*] In *chem.*, having one atom in the molecule; also, containing one replaceable atom or group.

mo-naul (mọ-nâl′), *n.* [Hind. *munāl.*] Any of several East Indian pheasants of the genus *Lophophorus*, esp. *L. impeyanus* (see *Impeyan pheasant*); sometimes, any of certain other East Indian pheasants.

mon-ax-i-al (mon-ak′si-ạl), *a.* [See *mono-.*] Having but one axis; in *bot.*, uniaxial.

mon-a-zite (mon′ạ-zīt), *n.* [G. *monazit*, < Gr. *μονάζειν*, be alone: see *monastic.*] A rare mineral consisting essentially of a phosphate of cerium and related metals.

mon-daine (môṅ-dān), *n.* [F.: cf. *monde.*] A woman of the fashionable world or of society.

Mon-day (mun′dā), *n.* [AS. *mōndæg, mōnandæg*, 'moon's day,' used to render LL. *lunæ dies.*] The second day of the week, following Sunday.

monde (môṅd), *n.* [F., < L. *mundus*, world.] The world; esp., the world of fashion, or society (cf. *beau monde*); also, a particular social sphere or circle.

mo-ne-cious (mō-nē′shus), *a.* See *monœcious.*

mo-nel (mō-nel′) **met′al.** [From Ambrose *Monell* (died 1921), of New York City.] A non-rusting, silvery-white alloy with the strength of steel, containing about 67 per cent nickel, 28 per cent copper, and 5 per cent other metals, which is produced from the nickeliferous ores of the Sudbury district in Canada, and used for a great number of purposes. [Proprietary name.]

mon-e-ta-ry (mon′e-tā-ri or mun′-), *a.* [L. *monetarius*, < *moneta*: see *money.*] Of or pertaining to the coinage or currency of a country (as, the *monetary* unit, the unit of currency, as the dollar in the U. S., the pound in the British Empire, and the franc in France); also, of or pertaining to money, or pecuniary (as, *monetary* consideration; one's *monetary* affairs).

mon-e-tize (mon′e-tīz or mun′-), *v. t.*; *-tized, -tizing.* [= F. *monétiser*, < L. *moneta*: see *money*, and cf. *demonetize.*] To give the character of money to; legalize as money; coin into money: as, to *monetize* gold or silver.—**mon″e-ti-za′tion** (-ti-zā′shọn), *n.*

mon-ey (mun′i), *n.*; pl. *-eys* (-iz). [OF. *moneie* (F. *monnaie*), < L. *moneta*, mint, money: see *mint*³.] Gold, silver, or other metal in pieces of convenient form stamped by public authority and issued as a medium of exchange and measure of value; current coin; coin, or certificates (as bank-notes, etc.) representing it and currently accepted as an equivalent; also, any articles or substance similarly used (see *hook-money, knife-money, cowry, wampum*); also, a particular form or denomination of currency; a money of account (see below); also, property considered with reference to its pecuniary value; wealth; *pl.*, pecuniary sums (as, "Importune him for my *moneys*," Shakspere's "Timon of Athens," ii. 1. 16: now archaic or legal); also, *sing.*, pecuniary profit (as, there is *money* in this contract, or in these goods); a source of pecuniary profit (as, these goods were easy *money*, or good or bad *money*).—**for love or money.** See under *love, n.*—**for my money,** for my choice (as if in spending money); for me: as, "The wars *for my money*" (Shakspere's "Coriolanus," iv. 5. 248).—**money of account,** a monetary denomination used in reckoning, esp. one not issued as a coin, as the U. S. mill.—**mon′ey,** *v.* **I.** *tr.* To coin or mint, as money; also, to supply with money†; also, with *out*, to set forth at a given price or sum, as articles in a bill, or as an estimate (Great Britain). **II.** *intr.* To come or turn (*out*) as to money value or profit: as, "Let them see how this making haste to get rich *moneys out* in actual practice" (S. Butler's "Way of All Flesh," lxxviii.). [Great Britain.]

mon-ey=bag (mun′i-bag), *n.* A bag for money; *pl.*, wealth; *pl.* (construed as *sing.*), a wealthy person.

mon-ey=chan-ger (mun′i-chān″jėr), *n.* One whose business it is to change money at a fixed or authorized rate. See Mat. xxi. 12.

mon-ey=cow-ry (mun′i-kou″ri), *n.*; pl. *-ries* (-riz). The shell of a marine gastropod, *Cypræa moneta*, used as money in parts of Asia and Africa. See *cowry.*

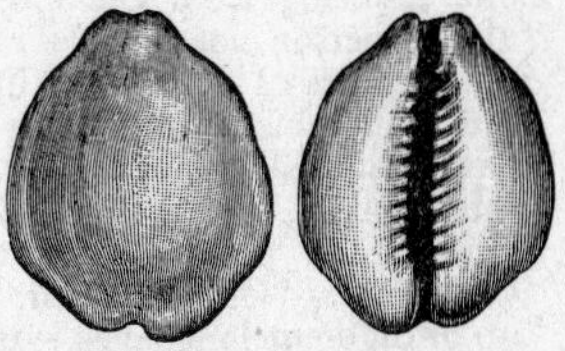

Money-cowry.

mon-eyed (mun′id), *a.* Having money, or wealthy (as, "the not too gracious bounty of *moneyed* relatives": Carlyle's "Sartor Resartus," ii. 5); also, consisting of or representing money (as, *moneyed* capital or resources).

mon-ey-er (mun′i-ėr), *n.* One who coins or mints money; also, a banker or capitalist (obs. or archaic: as, "F. B. moves among *moneyers* and City nobs," Thackeray's "Newcomes," lxiv.).

mon-ey=grub-ber (mun′i-grub″ėr), *n.* One sordidly devoted to making money or gaining wealth.

mon-ey=lend-er (mun′i-len″dėr), *n.* One whose business it is to lend money at interest.

mon-ey-less (mun′i-les), *a.* Without money; impecunious.

mon-ey=mak-er (mun′i-mā″kėr), *n.* One who makes or mints money†; also, one engaged in or successful at the gaining of money; also, something that yields pecuniary profit.—**mon′ey=mak″ing,** *n.* and *a.*

mon-ey=mar-ket (mun′i-mär″ket), *n.* The market or field for the investment or employment of money; the district or sphere within which financial operations are carried on; also, the body of persons carrying on such operations. See *Lombard Street* and *Wall Street.*

mon-ey=mong-er (mun′i-mung″gėr), *n.* A dealer in money; a money-lender.—**mon′ey=mong″er-ing,** *n.* and *a.*

mon-ey=or-der (mun′i-ôr″dėr), *n.* An order for the payment of money, specif. one issued by one post-office and payable at another.

mon-ey-wort (mun′i-wėrt), *n.* A creeping primulaceous herb, *Lysimachia nummularia*, with roundish leaves and yellow flowers; also, any of various other plants.

'mong (mung), *prep.* Among. [Poetic.]

mong-er (mung′gėr), *n.* [AS. *mangere*, < *mangian*, traffic, trade.] A dealer in some commodity (as, a cheese*monger*; a fish*monger*); fig., in a depreciatory sense, one who exploits, or busies himself with, something in a sordid or petty way (as, a scandal-*monger*; a fashion-*monger*): now used only as the second element in compounds.—**mong′er-ing, mong′ing,** *n.* and *a.*

Mon-gol (mong′gol). **I.** *n.* One of an Asiatic race now chiefly resident in Mongolia, a vast region north of China proper and south of Siberia; also, a member of the Mongolian race. **II.** *a.* Mongolian.—**Mon-go-li-an** (mong-gō′li-ạn). **I.** *a.* Pertaining or related to, or characteristic of, the Mongols or their languages (which form a branch of the Ural-Altaic family of languages); pertaining to Mongolia; also, noting or pertaining to the so-called 'yellow' race, characterized chiefly by yellowish complexion, prominent cheek-bones, almond-shaped eyes, short broad nose, and straight black hair, and embracing the Mongols, Chinese, Tatars, Eskimos, etc. **II.** *n.* A Mongol; also, a member of the Mongolian race; also, the language, or group of languages, of the Mongols, of the Ural-Altaic family.

—**Mon-gol-ic** (mong-gol′ik). **I.** *a.* Of or pertaining to the Mongols; Mongolian. **II.** *n.* Mongolian (language).—**Mon-go-loid** (mong′gō̤-loid). **I.** *a.* Resembling the Mongols; having characteristics of the Mongolian race. **II.** *n.* A person of a Mongoloid race.

mon-goos, mon-goose (mong′gös), *n.*; pl. *-gooses.* [E. Ind.] A slender carnivorous mammal, *Herpestes griseus* (or *mungo*), of India, of the same genus as the common ichneumon of Egypt, and resembling the ferret in form and habits, used for destroying rats, etc., and noted for its ability to kill venomous snakes without being harmed; also, any animal of the same genus or of related genera; an ichneumon.

mon-grel (mung′grẹl). [ME. *mengrell*, prob. < AS. *mengan*, mix: cf. *mingle.*] **I.** *n.* The offspring resulting from the crossing of different breeds of dogs; now, a dog of no definable breed, the product of various crossings; also, any animal or plant resulting from the crossing of different breeds or kinds (in scientific use sometimes restricted to one resulting from the crossing of varieties: cf. *hybrid*); also, a person not of pure race; the offspring of parents of different races or nationalities; also, any cross between different things; something intermediate in character between different things. **II.** *a.* That is a mongrel; being of mixed breed, race, origin, nature, etc.: as, a *mongrel* pup; "groups of squaws . . . with their *mongrel* progeny" (Parkman's "Oregon Trail," x.); a *mongrel* dialect made up of different languages.—**mon′grel-ism,** *n.*

'mongst (mungst), *prep.* Amongst. [Poetic.]

mon′i-ker, *n.* See *monaker.*

mo-nil-i-form (mō̤-nil′i-fôrm), *a.* [L. *monile*, necklace: see *-form.*] Resembling a string of beads; in *bot.* and *zoöl.*, consisting of or characterized by a series of bead-like swellings alternating with contractions, as certain roots, stems, etc.

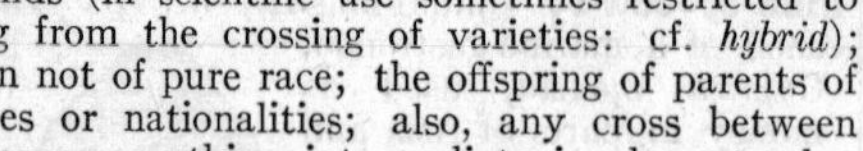

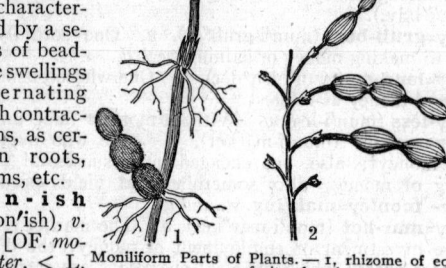

Moniliform Parts of Plants.—1, rhizome of equisetum; 2, fruits of sophora.

mon-ish (mon′ish), *v. t.* [OF. *monester*, < L. *monere*, remind.] To admonish. [Archaic.]

mon-ism (mon′izm or mō′nizm), *n.* [Gr. μόνος, single.] In *philos.*, the doctrine of one ultimate substance or principle, as mind (idealism) or matter (materialism), or something that is neither mind nor matter but the substantial ground of both. Cf. *dualism* and *pluralism.*—**mon′ist,** *n.* An adherent of the doctrine of monism.—**mo-nis-tic** (mō̤-nis′tik), *a.* Of, pertaining to, or characterized by monism.—**mo-nis′ti-cal-ly,** *adv.*

mo-ni-tion (mō̤-nish′ọn), *n.* [OF. F. *monition*, < L. *monitio(n-)*, < *monere*, remind, advise: see *mind*[2].] Admonition; an admonition or warning (as, "the *monitions* of Christianity": H. Melville's "Omoo," xlv.); also, an intimation or indication; also, an official or legal notice; specif., a formal notice from a bishop requiring the amendment of some ecclesiastical offense.

mon-i-tor (mon′i-tọr), *n.* [L., < *monere*: see *monition.*] One who admonishes, or gives advice or warning with reference to conduct (sometimes fig., as of something personified: as, "Conscience has been described as a most importunate *monitor*, paying no respect to persons, and making cowards of us all," Marryat's "King's Own," l.); also, a pupil or student appointed for some duty of assistance in the conduct of a school, as to assist in teaching the younger pupils (cf. *Lancasterian*), to keep order, or to keep a record of attendance; also, something that serves to remind or give warning; also, any of the large lizards constituting the genus *Varanus* and family *Varanidæ*, of Africa, southern Asia, and Australia (so called because fabled to give warning of the presence of crocodiles); also, an ironclad war-vessel with a low free-board and one or more revolving turrets, each containing one or more great guns (so called from the name given to the first vessel of this type by its inventor, John Ericsson, during the American Civil War).—**mon-i-to′ri-al** (-tō′ri-ạl), *a.* Of or pertaining to a monitor; esp., pertaining to, connected with, or performed by monitors in schools (as, a *monitorial* system of education; *monitorial* duties); also, serving to admonish or warn; monitory.—**mon′i-tor-ship,** *n.* The position, office, or period of service of a monitor.—**mon′i-to-ry** (-tō̤-ri). [L. *monitorius.*] **I.** *a.* Giving monition; serving to admonish or warn; admonitory: as, "The mottoes of their families are *monitory* proverbs" (Emerson's "English Traits," vii.). **II.** *n.* An admonition†; also, a letter, as one from a bishop, containing an admonition.—**mon′i-tress,** *n.* A female monitor.

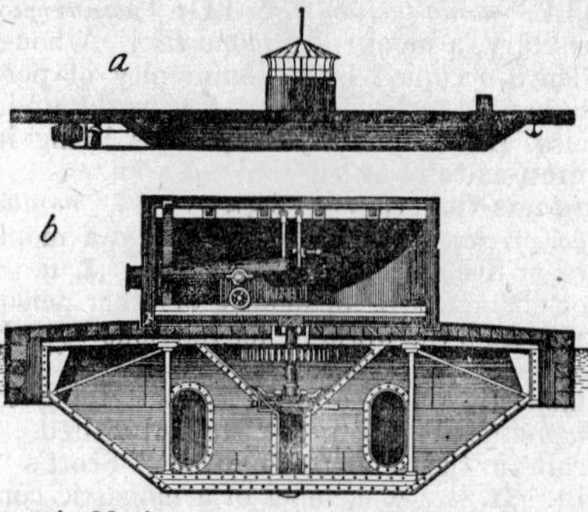

Ericsson's Monitor.—*a*, side elevation; *b*, transverse section through the center of the turret.

monk (mungk), *n.* [AS. *munuc*, < LL. *monachus*, < LGr. μοναχός, a monk, noun use of Gr. μοναχός, solitary, < μόνος, alone, single.] A man who has withdrawn from the world from religious motives, either as an eremite or, esp., as a member of an order of cenobites living under vows of poverty, chastity, and obedience, according to a rule: as, "the anchorite *monk* of the desert" (Longfellow's "Evangeline," ii. 4); a cloistered *monk.*—**monk′er-y,** *n.*; pl. *-ies* (-iz). The condition, life, or practices of monks; monasticism; *pl.*, monastic practices, appurtenances, etc.; also, *sing.*, a monastery; monks collectively: usually depreciatory.

mon-key (mung′ki), *n.*; pl. *-keys* (-kiz). [Origin uncertain: cf. F. (obs.) *monne*, It. *monna*, Sp. *mona*, female monkey.] Broadly, any member, except man and (usually) the lemurs, of the highest order of mammals (*Primates*), as the apes, baboons, marmosets, etc.; in a restricted sense, any of various smaller, long-tailed forms, as the capuchins, guenons, etc.; also, a person likened to such an animal, as a mischievous child, a mimic, etc.; also, any of various mechanical devices, as the ram of a pile-driving apparatus.—**mon′key,** *v.*; *-keyed, -keying.* **I.** *tr.* To imitate as a monkey does; ape; mimic; also, to mock. **II.** *intr.* To play or trifle idly; fool: often with *with.* [Colloq.]—**mon′key=bread,** *n.* The gourd-like fruit of the baobab, eaten by monkeys; also, the tree itself.—**mon′key=cup,** *n.* Any pitcher-plant of the genus *Nepenthes*, chiefly natives of the Malay Archipelago.—**mon′key=en″gine,** *n.* A form of pile-driver having a ram or monkey working in a wooden frame; the engine which lifts such a ram or monkey.—**mon′key=flow″er,** *n.* Any plant of the scrophulariaceous genus *Mimulus*, which includes species cultivated in gar-

Common Green Monkey (Guenon) (*Cercopithecus sabæus*).

dens and greenhouses, as *M. luteus*, having yellow flowers spotted with brown, and *M. moschatus*, the musk-plant.—**mon'key-ish,** *a.* Like, or characteristic of, a monkey: as, "He drinks and smokes, in a *monkeyish* way" (Dickens's "Bleak House," xx.).—**mon'key-ism,** *n.* Monkey-like character or behavior.—**mon'key=jack"et,** *n.* A short, close-fitting jacket or coat, much worn by sailors.—**mon'key=pot,** *n.* The woody, operculate seed-vessel of any of certain large South American trees of the genus *Lecythis*; also, the tree bearing it.—**mon'key=puz"zle,** *n.* A South American pinaceous tree, *Araucaria imbricata*, with twisted branches and edible nuts.—**mon'key=shine,** *n.* A monkeyish trick or prank. [Slang, U. S.]—**mon'key=wrench,** *n.* A wrench with an adjustable jaw, for turning nuts, etc.

monk-hood (mungk'hůd), *n.* The condition or profession of a monk; also, monks collectively.

monk-ish (mung'kish), *a.* Of or pertaining to, characteristic of, or resembling a monk; monastic: often depreciatory.—**monk'ish-ness,** *n.*

monk's=hood (mungks'hůd), *n.* A plant of the genus *Aconitum* (see *aconite*), esp. *A. napellus*: so called from the hooded flowers.

mon-ni-ker (mon'i-kėr), *n.* See *monaker*.

mono-, mon-. [Gr. μονο-, μον-, repr. μόνος, alone, single.] A combining-form or prefix, meaning 'alone,' 'single,' 'one,' first occurring in words from the Greek, but now used freely as a general formative, esp. in scientific words, and often in correlation with *di-*[1] or *bi-* ('two'), *tri-* ('three'), *tetra-* ('four'), *penta-* ('five'), etc., or *poly-* ('many'), as in *monatomic, monobasic, monocotyledon, monometallic, monopetalous, monophase, monovalent, monoxide*.—**mon-o-ba-sic** (mon-ǫ-bā'sik), *a.* In *chem.*, of an acid, having but one atom of hydrogen replaceable by a basic atom or radical.—**mon'o-carp** (-kärp), *n.* [+ *-carp*.] In *bot.*, a plant that dies after having once borne fruit.—**mon-o-car'pel-la-ry** (-kär'pe-lą-ri), *a.* In *bot.*, consisting of a single carpel.—**mon-o-car'pic,** *a.* In *bot.*, producing fruit but once and then dying; of the nature of a monocarp.—**mon-o-car'-pous,** *a.* In *bot.*, having a gynœcium which forms only a single ovary; also, monocarpic.—**mon-o-cha'si-um** (-kā'zi-um), *n.*; pl. *-sia* (-zi-ą). [NL. (Gr. χάσις, separation).] In *bot.*, a form of cymose inflorescence in which the main axis produces only a single branch.—**mon-o-cha'si-al,** *a.*—**mon"o-chla-myd'e-ous** (-klą-mid'ẹ-us), *a.* [+ Gr. χλαμύς (χλαμυδ-), mantle.] In *bot.*, having a single instead of a double perianth, as certain flowers.

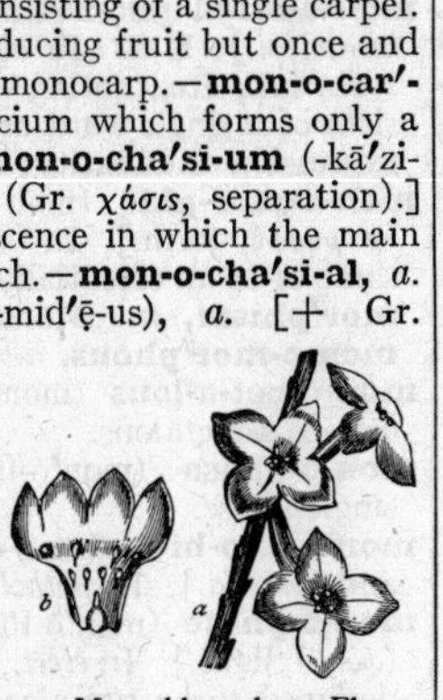

a, Monochlamydeous Flower (Mezereon); *b*, Perianth cut open, showing the single envelop.

mon-o-chord (mon'ǫ-kôrd), *n.* [Gr. μονόχορδον, < μόνος, single, + χορδή, string.] An acoustical instrument, of ancient invention, consisting of a sounding-board with a single string, used for the mathematical determination of musical intervals; also, a harmonious combination of sounds; fig., harmony or agreement.

mon-o-chro-ic (mon-ǫ-krō'ik), *a.* [Gr. μονόχροος, < μόνος, single, + χρόα, color.] Of one color.

mon-o-chro-mat-ic (mon"ǫ-krǫ-mat'ik), *a.* [See *mono-* and *chromatic*.] Of or pertaining to one color only; specif., consisting of light of but one wave-length, and in that sense of one color only; producing such light.—**mon"o-chro-mat'i-cal-ly,** *adv.*

mon-o-chrome (mon'ǫ-krōm). [Gr. μονόχρωμος, of one color, < μόνος, single, + χρῶμα, color.] **I.** *n.* Representation, or a painting or drawing, in a single color or in different shades of a single color; also, a tract or expanse of one color (as, "A profile was visible against the dull *monochrome* of cloud around her": Hardy's "Return of the Native," i. 6). **II.** *a.* Of or in one color.—**mon-o-chro'-mic** (-krō'mik), *a.*—**mon'o-chro-mist,** *n.* One who paints or draws in monochrome.

mon-o-cle (mon'ǫ-kl), *n.* [F. *monocle*, < LL. *monoculus*, one-eyed: see *monocular*.] A single eye-glass.—**mon'o-cled,** *a.* Wearing a monocle.

mon-o-cli-nal (mon-ǫ-klī'nąl). [Gr. μόνος, single, + κλίνειν, incline.] In *geol.*: **I.** *a.* Dipping in one direction, as strata; pertaining to strata which dip in the same direction. **II.** *n.* A monocline.—**mon-o-cli'nal-ly,** *adv.*—**mon'-o-cline** (-klīn), *n.* In *geol.*, a monoclinal structure or fold, as the oblique portion of a belt of strata at the place where it changes from one horizontal position to another of different level.

mon-o-clin-ic (mon-ǫ-klin'ik), *a.* [Gr. μόνος, single, + κλίνειν, incline.] In *crystal.*, noting or pertaining to that system of crystallization in which the crystals have three unequal axes, with one oblique intersection.

mon-o-cli-nous (mon-ǫ-klī'nus), *a.* [Gr. μόνος, single, + κλίνη, bed.] In *bot.*, of a plant species, etc., having both the andrœcium and the gynœcium in the same flower; of a flower, having both stamens and pistils; bisexual. Cf. *diclinous*.

mon-o-cot-y-le-don (mon"ǫ-kot-i-lē'dǫn), *n.* [See *mono-*.] In *bot.*, a plant with only one cotyledon; a member of the group *Monocotyledones*, one of the two subclasses of angiospermous plants, characterized by producing seeds with a single cotyledon or seed-leaf, and by an endogenous mode of growth. Cf. *endogen*, also *dicotyledon*.—**mon"o-cot-y-le'don-ous,** *a.* In *bot.*, having only one cotyledon; belonging or pertaining to the *Monocotyledones* (see *monocotyledon*).

mo-noc-ra-cy (mǫ-nok'rą-si), *n.*; pl. *-cies* (-siz). [LGr. μονοκρατία, < Gr. μόνος, alone, + κρατεῖν, rule.] Government by a single person; autocracy.—**mon-o-crat-ic** (mon-ǫ-krat'ik), *a.*

mon-o-crot-ic (mon-ǫ-krot'ik), *a.* [Gr. μόνος, single, + κρότος, beat.] Having only one arterial beat for each heartbeat, as the pulse in health; pertaining to such a pulse.—**mo-noc-ro-tism** (mǫ-nok'rǫ-tizm), *n.* Monocrotic condition.

mo-noc-u-lar (mǫ-nok'ų-lär), *a.* [LL. *monoculus*, one-eyed, < Gr. μόνος, single, + L. *oculus*, eye.] Having only one eye; also, pertaining to or intended for one eye only.

mon-o-cy-cle (mon'ǫ-sī-kl), *n.* [See *mono-* and *cycle*.] A kind of velocipede having only one wheel.

mon-o-dac-tyl (mon-ǫ-dak'til), *a.* [Gr. μονοδάκτυλος, < μόνος, single, + δάκτυλος, finger or toe.] In *zoöl.*, having only one digit or claw. Also **mon-o-dac'ty-lous** (-ti-lus).

mo-nod-ic (mǫ-nod'ik), *a.* [Gr. μονῳδικός.] Of, pertaining to, or of the nature of a monody; in *music*, pertaining to or of the nature of monody.—**mo-nod'i-cal-ly,** *adv.*

mon-o-dist (mon'ǫ-dist), *n.* One who composes or sings a monody.

mon-o-dra-ma (mon'ǫ-drä-mą), *n.* [See *mono-*.] A dramatic piece for a single performer.—**mon"o-dra-mat'ic** (-drą-mat'ik), *a.*

mon-o-dy (mon'ǫ-di), *n.*; pl. *-dies* (-diz). [LL. *monodia*, < Gr. μονῳδία, < μόνος, alone, + ἀείδειν, sing.] A Greek ode sung by a single voice, as in a tragedy; hence, a mournful song or dirge; also, a poem in which one person laments another's death (as, "Thyrsis: A *Monody*, to commemorate the author's friend, Arthur Hugh Clough, who died at Florence, 1861," the title of a poem by Matthew Arnold); also, monotonous sound (as, "Hear the tolling of the bells—Iron bells! What a world of solemn thought their *monody* compels!" Poe's "Bells," iv.); in *music*, a style of composition in which one part or melody predominates; homophony, as distinguished from polyphony; also, a piece written in this style.

Branch of Monœcious Tree (Alder). — *a*, male catkins; *b*, female catkins; *c*, fruit.

mo-nœ-cious, mo-ne-cious (mǫ-nē'-shus), *a.* [Gr. μόνος, single, + οἶκος, house.] In *biol.*, having both male and female organs in the same individual; hermaphroditic; specif., in *bot.*, of a plant species, etc., having the andrœcium and the gynœcium in separate flowers on the same plant (cf. *diœcious*).

mo-nog-a-mist (mǫ-nog'ą-mist), *n.* One who practises or advocates monogamy.—**mo-nog'a-mist, mo-nog-a-mis'tic,** *a.*

mo-nog-a-mous (mọ̄-nog′ạ-mus), *a.* [LL. *monogamus*, < Gr. μονόγαμος, < μόνος, single, + γάμος, marriage.] Practising or advocating monogamy; also, pertaining to monogamy.—**mo-nog′a-my,** *n.* [LL. *monogamia*, < Gr. μονογαμία.] The practice of marrying only once during life (opposed to *digamy*); now, esp., the practice or condition of being married to only one person at a time (opposed to *bigamy* or *polygamy*); in *zoöl.*, the habit of having only one mate.

mon-o-gen-e-sis (mon-ọ̄-jen′e-sis), *n.* [See *mono-* and *genesis.*] The theoretical descent of all living things from a single cell; also, the theoretical descent of the whole human race from a single pair; also, asexual reproduction.—**mon″o-ge-net′ic** (-jẹ̄-net′ik), *a.* Of or pertaining to monogenesis or monogenism; in *geol.*, resulting from one genetic process.

mon-o-gen-ic (mon-ọ̄-jen′ik), *a.* [See *mono-* and *-genic.*] Of or pertaining to monogenesis or monogenism.—**mo-nog-e-nism** (mọ̄-noj′e-nizm), *n.* The theory that the whole human race has descended from a single pair; monogeny.—**mo-nog′e-nist,** *n.* One who maintains any doctrine of monogenesis; esp., a believer in monogenism.—**mo-nog′e-ny,** *n.* [See *-geny.*] The theoretical descent of the whole human race from a single pair; monogenism; also, asexual reproduction.

mon-o-glot (mon′ọ̄-glot). [Gr. μονόγλωττος, < μόνος, single, + γλῶττα, γλῶσσα, tongue.] **I.** *a.* Using or understanding only one language; also, written in only one language. **II.** *n.* One who knows only one language.

mon-o-gram (mon′ọ̄-gram), *n.* [LL. *monogramma*, < Gr. μόνος, single, + γράμμα, character, letter, < γράφειν, write.] A character consisting of two or more letters combined or interlaced, commonly letters which are the initials of a person's name: often cut on a seal, stamped on note-paper, embroidered on clothing, etc.—**mon″o-gram-mat′ic** (-grạ-mat′ik), *a.* Pertaining to or having the form of a monogram.—**mon′o-grammed,** *a.* Bearing a monogram.

mon-o-graph (mon′ọ̄-gräf), *n.* [See *mono-* and *-graph.*] An account or description of a single thing or class of things, as of a species or genus of animals or plants; a treatise on a particular subject (as, "He . . . returned home laden with guide-books to Quebec, and *monographs* upon episodes of local history": Howells's "Chance Acquaintance," v.); occasionally, a monogram.—**mon′o-graph,** *v. t.* To write a monograph on; treat in a monograph.—**mo-nog-ra-pher** (mọ̄-nog′rạ-fėr), *n.* The writer of a monograph.—**mon-o-graph′ic** (-graf′ik), *a.* Pertaining to or of the nature of a monograph; also, monogrammatic.—**mon-o-graph′i-cal-ly,** *adv.*

mo-nog-y-nous (mọ̄-noj′i-nus), *a.* [Gr. μόνος, single, + γυνή, woman.] Having but one wife at a time, as a man; characterized by or pertaining to monogyny (as, a *monogynous* condition); in *bot.*, of a flower, having only one pistil or style; of a plant, having such flowers.—**mo-nog′y-ny,** *n.* The practice or the condition of having but one wife at a time.

mo-nol-a-try (mọ̄-nol′ạ-tri), *n.* [Gr. μόνος, single, + λατρεία, worship.] The worship of but one god, esp. when other gods are recognized as existing.—**mo-nol′a-trous,** *a.*

mon-o-lith (mon′ọ̄-lith). [F. *monolithe*, < LL. *monolithus*, < Gr. μονόλιθος, < μόνος, single, + λίθος, stone.] **I.** *a.* Consisting or formed of a single block of stone. **II.** *n.* A single block or piece of stone of considerable size, esp. one forming a monument or used for architectural or sculptural purposes; an obelisk, column, statue, or other object or work formed of a single large block of stone. Cf. *megalith.*—**mon-o-lith′ic,** *a.*

mon-o-log-ic, mon-o-log-i-cal (mon-ọ̄-loj′ik, -i-kạl), *a.* [See *monologue.*] Pertaining to, characterized by, or of the nature of monologue.—**mo-nol-o-gist** (mọ̄-nol′ọ̄-jist), *n.* One who talks or acts in monologue, or delivers monologues; also, one who monopolizes conversation.—**mo-nol′o-gize** (-jīz), *v. i.*; *-gized, -gizing.* To talk in monologue; deliver a monologue.

mon-o-logue (mon′ọ̄-log), *n.* [F. *monologue*, < Gr. μονόλογος, speaking alone, < μόνος, alone, + λέγειν, speak.] A part of a drama in which a single actor speaks alone; a dramatic composition for a single actor; a kind of dramatic entertainment by a single speaker; also, this form of dramatic composition or entertainment; also, any composition, as a poem, in which a single person speaks alone; also, any long speech or harangue delivered by one person while in company or conversation with others (as, "Mrs. Ellison's *monologue* ran on with scarcely a break from Kitty": Howells's "Chance Acquaintance," ii.); prolonged talk or discourse by a single speaker.—**mon′o-lo-guist** (-log-ist), *n.* A monologist.—**mon′o-lo-guize** (-log-īz), *v. i.*; *-guized, -guizing.* To monologize.

mo-nom-a-chy (mọ̄-nom′ạ-ki), *n.*; pl. *-chies* (-kiz). [LL. *monomachia*, < Gr. μονομαχία, < μόνος, single, + μάχεσθαι, fight.] Single combat; a contest between single combatants.—**mo-nom′a-chist** (-kist), *n.*

mon-o-ma-ni-a (mon-ọ̄-mā′ni-ạ̈), *n.* [NL., < Gr. μόνος, single, + μανία, E. *mania.*] Insanity in which the patient is irrational on one subject only; also, an exaggerated zeal for or interest in some one thing, or a craze (as, "Frederic was . . . anxious . . . about the efficiency of his army. But this anxiety never degenerated into a *monomania*, like that which led his father to pay fancy prices for giants": Macaulay's "Essays," Frederic the Great).—**mon-o-ma′ni-ac** (-ak), *n.* One affected with monomania; also, one who has a mania or craze for some one thing.—**mon″o-ma-ni′a-cal** (-mạ-nī′ạ-kạl), *a.*

mo-nom-er-ous (mọ̄-nom′ẹ-rus), *a.* [Gr. μονομερής, < μόνος, single, + μέρος, part.] In *bot.*, of flowers, having one member in each whorl.

mon-o-me-tal-lic (mon″ọ̄-me-tal′ik), *a.* [See *mono-.*] Pertaining to or using one metal; pertaining to monometallism.—**mon-o-met′al-lism** (-met′ạl-izm), *n.* The use of one metal only (as gold or silver) as the standard of money values.—**mon-o-met′al-list,** *n.* An advocate of monometallism.

mon-o-met-ric (mon-ọ̄-met′rik), *a.* [Gr. μόνος, single, + μέτρον, measure.] In *crystal.*, isometric.

mo-no-mi-al (mọ̄-nō′mi-ạl). [From *mono-* + *-mial* as in *binomial.*] **I.** *a.* In *alg.*, consisting of one term only; in *zoöl.*, *bot.*, etc., noting or pertaining to a name which consists of a single word or term. **II.** *n.* In *alg.*, a monomial expression or quantity; in *zoöl.*, *bot.*, etc., a monomial name.

mon-o-mor-phic (mon-ọ̄-môr′fik), *a.* [Gr. μόνος, single, + μορφή, form.] In *biol.*, having only one form; of the same or of an essentially similar type of structure.—**mon-o-mor′phism,** *n.* Monomorphic condition or character.—**mon-o-mor′phous,** *a.* Monomorphic.

mon-o-pet-a-lous (mon-ọ̄-pet′ạ-lus), *a.* [See *mono-.*] In *bot.*, gamopetalous.

mon-o-phase (mon′ọ̄-fāz), *a.* [See *mono-.*] In *elect.*, single-phase.

mon-o-pho-bi-a (mon-ọ̄-fō′bi-ạ̈), *n.* [NL.: see *mono-* and *-phobia.*] In *pathol.*, morbid dread of being alone.

mon-o-phote (mon′ọ̄-fōt), *a.* [Gr. μόνος, single, + φῶς (φωτ-), light.] In *elect.*, noting or pertaining to an arc-lamp designed to be run alone on its own circuit, and not to be used in series with other lamps.

mon-oph-thong (mon′of-thông), *n.* [Gr. μονόφθογγος, with one sound, < μόνος, single, + φθόγγος, sound.] A single, simple vowel sound; also, a combination of two written vowels pronounced as one; a vowel digraph.—**mon-oph-thon′gal** (-thông′gạl), *a.*—**mon′oph-thong-ize** (-īz), *v. t.*; *-ized, -izing.* To convert into a monophthong.

mon-o-phy-let-ic (mon″ọ̄-fī-let′ik), *a.* [Gr. μόνος, single, + φυλή, tribe.] Of or pertaining to a single tribe or stock; developed from a single ancestral type, as a group of animals.

mon-o-phyl-lous (mon-ọ̄-fil′us), *a.* [Gr. μονόφυλλος, < μόνος, single, + φύλλον, leaf.] In *bot.*, consisting of one leaf, as a calyx; having only one leaf.

mon-o-phy-o-dont (mon-ọ̄-fī′ọ̄-dont). [Gr. μονοφυής, single, + ὀδούς (ὀδοντ-), tooth.] **I.** *a.* Having only one set of teeth. Cf. *diphyodont.* **II.** *n.* A monophyodont animal.

Mo-noph-y-site (mọ̄-nof′i-sīt), *n.* [LGr. μονοφυσίτης, < Gr. μόνος, single, + φύσις, nature.] One holding that there is in Christ but a single nature, or one composite nature, partly divine and partly human, as the members of the Coptic Church of Egypt: used esp. with reference to the Christological controversies of the 5th and 6th centuries.—**Mo-noph′y-sit-ism** (-sīt-izm), *n.*

mon-o-plane (mon′ǭ-plān), *n.* [See *mono-*.] A flying-machine or aëroplane with a single sustaining plane or with all its sustaining planes in practically the same geometric plane.

mon-o-ple-gi-a (mon-ǭ-plē′ji-ạ̈), *n.* [NL., < Gr. μόνος, single, + -πληγία as in παραπληγία, E. *paraplegia.*] In *pathol.*, paralysis affecting only one limb or part of the body. —**mon-o-pleg′ic** (-plej′ik or -plē′jik), *a.*

mon-o-pode (mon′ǭ-pōd). [= F. *monopode*, < Gr. μονόπους (μονοποδ-), < μόνος, single, + πούς (ποδ-), foot.] **I.** *a.* Having but one foot. **II.** *n.* A creature having but one foot; esp., one of a fabled race of men having but one leg; in *bot.*, a monopodium.

mon-o-po-di-um (mon-ǭ-pō′di-um), *n.*; pl. *-dia* (-di-ạ̈). [NL., < Gr. μόνος, single, + πούς (ποδ-), foot.] In *bot.*, a single main axis which continues to extend at the apex in the original line of growth, giving off lateral branches beneath in acropetal succession. —**mon-o-po′di-al,** *a.*

mo-nop-o-lism (mǭ-nop′ǭ-lizm), *n.* The existence or prevalence of monopolies. —**mo-nop′o-list,** *n.* One who has a monopoly (as, "to raise the value of the possessions in the hands of the great private *monopolists*": Burke's "Conciliation with the Colonies"); an advocate of monopoly. —**mo-nop-o-lis′tic,** *a.*

mo-nop-o-lize (mǭ-nop′ǭ-līz), *v. t.*; *-lized, -lizing.* To acquire, have, or exercise a monopoly of; engross; hence, to obtain exclusive possession of (as, "The few tolerable rooms are *monopolized* by the friends and favourites of the house": Smollett's "Humphry Clinker," June 26); keep entirely to one's self. —**mo-nop″o-li-za′tion** (-li-zā′shǫn), *n.* —**mo-nop′o-liz-er** (-lī-zėr), *n.*

mo-nop-o-ly (mǭ-nop′ǭ-li), *n.*; pl. *-lies* (-liz). [L. *monopolium*, < Gr. μονοπώλιον, < μόνος, alone, single, + πωλεῖν, sell.] Exclusive control of a commodity or service in a particular market, or a control that makes possible the manipulation of prices (as, "You have, in this kingdom, an advantage in lead, that amounts to a *monopoly*": Burke's "American Taxation"); also, an exclusive privilege to carry on a traffic or service, granted by a sovereign, state, etc. (as, "Raleigh held a *monopoly* of cards, Essex a *monopoly* of sweet wines": Macaulay's "Essays," Lord Bacon); hence, in general, the exclusive possession or control of something (as, "It is not easy indeed to make a *monopoly* of theorems and corollaries": Burke's "Conciliation with the Colonies"); also, something which is the subject of a monopoly; a commodity, service, etc., which is exclusively controlled; also, a company or the like having a monopoly (as, "The pilots' association was now the compactest *monopoly* in the world": Mark Twain's "Life on the Mississippi," xv.).

mon-o-pol-y-logue (mon-ǭ-pol′i-log), *n.* [Gr. μόνος, single, + πολύς, much, + -λογος, < λέγειν, speak.] An entertainment in which a single actor sustains many characters. —**mon″o-po-lyl′o-gist** (-pǭ-lil′ǭ-jist), *n.*

mo-nop-ter-al (mǭ-nop′tę-rąl), *a.* [Gr. μονόπτερος, < μόνος, single, + πτερόν, wing, row of columns.] In *arch.*, of a temple, etc., having a single row of columns arranged in a circle, either about a cella or, often, without a cella.

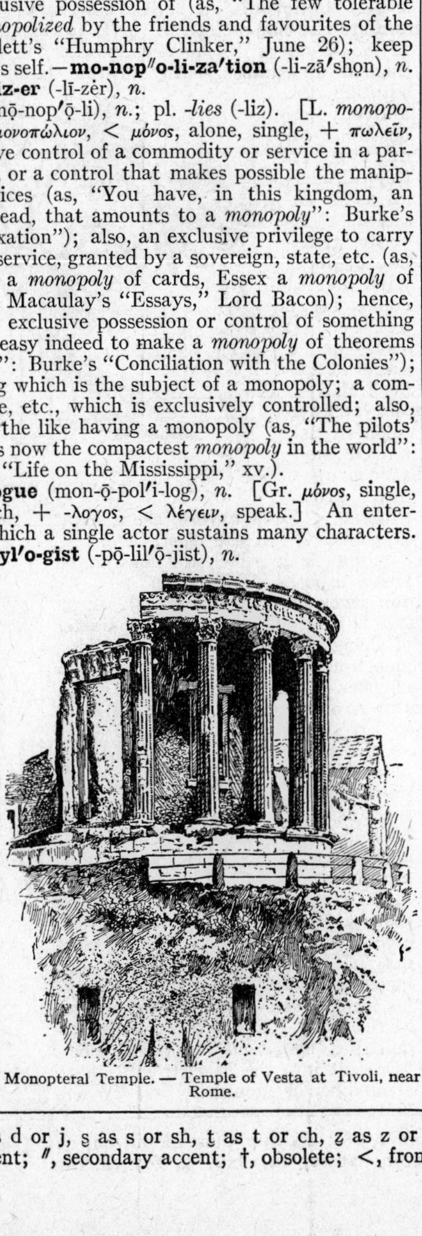

Monopteral Temple. — Temple of Vesta at Tivoli, near Rome.

mon-o-rail (mon′ǭ-rāl), *n.* [See *mono-*.] A single rail serving as a complete track; a railway in which the cars run on a single rail, either suspended from it, or balanced upon it (cf. *gyro-car*).

mon-o-rime, mon-o-rhyme (mon′ǭ-rīm), *n.* [See *mono-*.] Verse or a poetical composition in which all the lines end in the same rime; also, *pl.*, lines of such verse.

mon-o-sep-a-lous (mon-ǭ-sep′ą-lus), *a.* [See *mono-*.] In *bot.*, gamosepalous.

mon-o-sper-mous (mon-ǭ-spėr′mus), *a.* [See *mono-* and *-spermous.*] In *bot.*, one-seeded.

mon-o-stich (mon′ǭ-stik), *n.* [LL. *monostichum*, < Gr. μονόστιχον, neut. of μονόστιχος, consisting of one line, < μόνος, single, + στίχος, row, line.] A poem or epigram consisting of a single metrical line.

mo-nos-ti-chous (mǭ-nos′ti-kus), *a.* [Gr. μονόστιχος: see *monostich.*] In *bot.*, arranged in a single vertical row on one side of an axis, as flowers.

mon-o-stroph-ic (mon-ǭ-strof′ik), *a.* [Gr. μονοστροφικός, < μόνος, single, + στροφή, E. *strophe.*] Noting or pertaining to verse in which all the strophes or stanzas are of the same metrical form.

mon-o-style (mon′ǭ-stīl), *a.* [Gr. μόνος, single, + στῦλος, pillar, column.] In *arch.*, having or consisting of a single shaft, as a pier or pillar.

mon-o-sul-phide (mon-ǭ-sul′fīd or -fid), *n.* [See *mono-*.] In *chem.*, a sulphide in which one atom of sulphur is combined with the other element or radical.

mon-o-syl-lab-ic (mon″ǭ-si-lab′ik), *a.* [See *monosyllable.*] Consisting of one syllable, as a word; consisting of a monosyllable or monosyllables (as, "The curate answered only in *monosyllabic* compliance": Marryat's "King's Own," xlviii.); specif., of languages, as the Chinese, having a vocabulary composed exclusively of monosyllables; also, using or uttering monosyllables (as, "Lothair . . . was . . . somewhat *monosyllabic* and absent": Disraeli's "Lothair," viii.). —**mon″o-syl-lab′i-cal-ly,** *adv.* —**mon-o-syl′la-bism** (-sil′ą-bizm), *n.* Monosyllabic character, as of speech or language; use of monosyllables.

mon-o-syl-la-ble (mon-ǭ-sil′ą-bl), *n.* [LL. *monosyllabus*, < Gr. μονοσύλλαβος, of one syllable, < μόνος, single, + συλλαβή: see *syllable.*] A word of one syllable, as *yes* and *no.*

mon-o-the-ism (mon′ǭ-thē-izm), *n.* [Gr. μόνος, single, + θεός, god.] The doctrine or belief that there is but one God. —**mon′o-the-ist,** *n.* One who believes that there is only one God. —**mon″o-the-is′tic,** *a.* —**mon″o-the-is′ti-cal-ly,** *adv.*

mon-o-tint (mon′ǭ-tint), *n.* [See *mono-*.] A single tint or color; also, a picture in one color.

mon-o-tone (mon′ǭ-tōn). [= F. *monotone*, < LGr. μονότονος, of one tone, < Gr. μόνος, single, + τόνος, E. *tone.*] **I.** *a.* Continuing in one tone, as utterance; monotonous; also, of one tone or color. **II.** *n.* A continuance of the same tone, as in utterance; utterance unvaried in pitch; any unvaried sound or repetition of sounds (as, "Tolling, tolling, tolling, In that muffled *monotone*," Poe's "Bells," iv.; "a tall black clock . . . that kept its invariable *monotone* of tick-tack," Mrs. Stowe's "Oldtown Folks," viii.); also, sameness of style, as in composition or writing; something characterized by such sameness; hence, a monotonous continuance of anything; also, a single tone or color; a picture or print in one tone or color. —**mon′o-tone,** *v. t.* or *i.*; *-toned, -toning.* To recite in monotone. —**mon-o-ton′ic** (-ton′ik), *a.* Pertaining to or uttered in a monotone. —**mo-not-o-nous** (mǭ-not′ǭ-nus), *a.* [LGr. μονότονος.] Uttered or continuing in the same tone, or on one note (as, "the *monotonous* . . . chant of a Gaelic song," Scott's "Waverley," xvii.; "A voice, *Monotonous* and hollow," Tennyson's "Guinevere," 417); hence, unvarying in any respect, lacking in variety, or tiresomely uniform (as, "a *monotonous* labor wholly void of stimulus," C. Brontë's "Jane Eyre," xxx.; "We crept slowly . . . along the *monotonous* banks of the Arkansas," Parkman's "Oregon Trail," xxiii.). —**mo-not′o-nous-ly,** *adv.* —**mo-not′o-nous-ness,** *n.* —**mo-not′o-ny,** *n.* [LGr. μονοτονία.] Sameness of tone or pitch, as in utterance; the continuance of an unvarying sound; monotone; hence, in general, want of variety, or wearisome uniformity, as in occupation, scenery, etc. (as, "They repined at the tedious *monotony* . . . of their fortified camp," Irving's "Conquest of Granada," lxxiv.;

"An occasional clump of wood . . . relieved the *monotony* of the waste," Parkman's "Oregon Trail," vi.).

mon-o-treme (mon'ọ-trēm), *n.* [Gr. μόνος, single, + τρῆμα, hole, < τετραίνειν, bore, perforate.] Any of the *Monotremata*, the lowest order of mammals, comprising the duckbill and the echidnas, oviparous animals in which the genital, urinary, and digestive organs have a common opening.—**mon-o-trem'a-tous** (-trem'ạ-tus), *a.*

mon-o-tri-glyph (mon-ọ-trī'glif), *a.* [See *mono-* and *triglyph.*] In *arch.*, having only one triglyph in the portion of the frieze over the space between two columns, as usually in the Doric order. Also **mon''-o-tri-glyph'ic.**

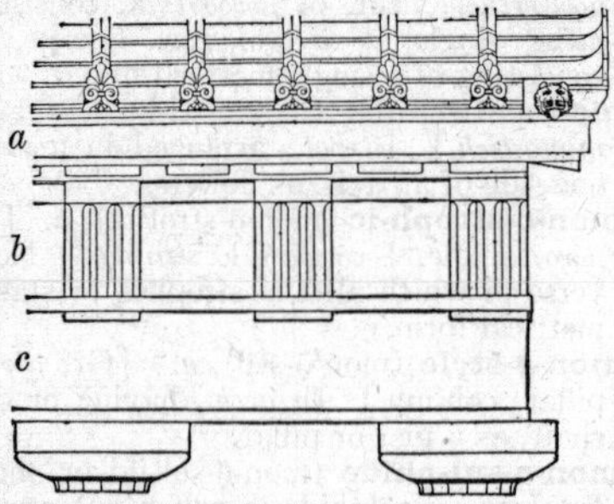

Monotriglyph Intercolumniation. — *a*, cornice; *b*, frieze composed of alternating triglyphs and metopes; *c*, architrave.

mon-o-type (mon'-ọ-tīp), *n.* [See *mono-* and *type.*] The only or sole type of its group, as a single species constituting a genus; also, a print from a metal plate on which a picture is painted, as in oil-color or printing-ink; the method of producing such a print; also, a device for casting and setting type, consisting of two distinct machines, the first having a keyboard with keys corresponding to the type characters, which when pressed produce perforations in a paper ribbon, and the second comprising the casting mechanism, etc., by means of which separate types are cast and set according to the perforations in the ribbon (cf. *linotype*).—**mon'o-type,** *v. t.*; *-typed, -typing.* To set with a monotype.—**mon'o-typ-er** (-tī-pėr), *n.*—**mon-o-typ'ic** (-tip'ik), *a.* Having only one type; of the nature of a monotype.

mon-o-va-lent (mon-ọ-vā'lẹnt or mọ-nov'ạ-), *a.* [See *mono-* and *-valent.*] In *chem.*, univalent.—**mon-o-va'lence,** *n.*

mon-ox-ide (mon-ok'sīd or -sid), *n.* [See *mono-.*] In *chem.*, an oxide containing one oxygen atom to the molecule.

mo-nox-y-lon (mọ-nok'si-lon), *n.*; pl. *-la* (-lạ̈). [Gr. μονόξυλον, neut. of μονόξυλος, made of one piece of timber, < μόνος, single, + ξύλον, wood.] A boat made out of a single piece of timber; a dugout.—**mon-ox-yl-ic** (mon-ok-sil'ik), **mo-nox'y-lous,** *a.*

Mon-roe (mun-rō') **doc'trine.** The doctrine, based upon statements contained in the message to Congress, Dec. 2, 1823, of President Monroe of the U. S., that the interposition of any European power to control the destiny of a Spanish-American state should be looked upon as a manifestation of unfriendly disposition toward the U. S., and that the American continents should no longer be subjects for any new European colonial settlement.

mon-sei-gneur (môṅ-se-nyėr), *n.*; pl. *messeigneurs* (mā-se-nyėr). [F., 'my lord': see *seigneur.*] A French title of honor given to princes, bishops, and other persons of eminence; a person bearing this title.

mon-sieur (mė-syė, m'syė), *n.*; pl. *messieurs* (mā-syė, E. often mes'yėrz). [F., 'my lord' (orig. applied to men of high station): see *sieur.*] The conventional French title of respect and term of address for a man, corresponding to *Mr.* (abbreviated *M.*; pl. *MM.*) and to *sir*; also, formerly, a title given distinctively to the next younger brother of the king of France; also, a Frenchman (now rare).

mon-si-gnor, mon-si-gno-re (mon-sē'nyọr or It. mon-sē-nyôr', It. mon-sē-nyō'rā), *n.*; It. pl. *-gnori* (-nyō'rē). [It., < F. *monseigneur*: see *monseigneur*, and cf. *signor.*] In the *Rom. Cath. Ch.*, a title conferred upon certain dignitaries; a person bearing this title (as, "It seemed that the whole court of Rome was there; *monsignori* and prelates without end": Disraeli's "Lothair," lxvi.).

mon-soon (mon-sön'), *n.* [Pg. *monção*, < Ar. *mausim*, time, season.] A seasonal wind of the Indian Ocean and southern Asia, blowing from the southwest from April to October and from the northeast during the rest of the year; also, the season during which this wind blows from the southwest, commonly marked by heavy rains; also, any wind whose direction is reversed periodically.—**mon-soon'al,** *a.*

mon-ster (mon'stėr). [OF. F. *monstre*, < L. *monstrum*, omen, portent, prodigy, monster, < *monere*, remind: see *mind²*.] **I.** *n.* A prodigy† or marvel†; hence, something unnatural; specif., an animal or a plant of abnormal form or structure, as from marked malformation, the presence of parts or organs not proper to the species or sex, or the absence of certain parts or organs (cf. *teratology*); also, a fabulous animal compounded of brute and human shape or of the shapes of various brutes, as a centaur, a griffin, or a sphinx; any frightful, terrifying, or hideous creature, imaginary or real (as, "His imagination transformed shadows into *monsters*," C. B. Brown's "Wieland," xi.; the Gila *monster*, see the entry); also, a person that excites horror, as by wickedness, cruelty, or any revolting qualities or actions (as, "I was a *monster* with whom the very earth groaned!" Godwin's "Caleb Williams," xxxiii.); a horrible or monstrous example (*of*: as, a *monster* of wickedness; a *monster* of ingratitude); also, any animal or thing of huge size; anything enormous of its kind. **II.** *a.* Being a monster, as in size; huge; enormous; monstrous.—**mon'ster,** *v. t.* To make monstrous (as, "Her offence Must be of such unnatural degree, That *monsters* it": Shakspere's "King Lear," i. 1. 223); also, to represent or exhibit as something prodigious or marvelous (as, "to hear my nothings *monster'd*": Shakspere's "Coriolanus," ii. 2. 81). [Archaic.]

mon-ste-ra (mon-stē'rạ̈), *n.* [NL. (F. *monstère*), appar. < L. *monstrum* or F. *monstre*, monster, in allusion to the singular appearance.] Any of the climbing shrubs constituting the araceous genus *Monstera*, native in tropical America, as *M. deliciosa*, a favorite greenhouse plant with aërial roots, large perforated leaves, and a succulent edible fruit.

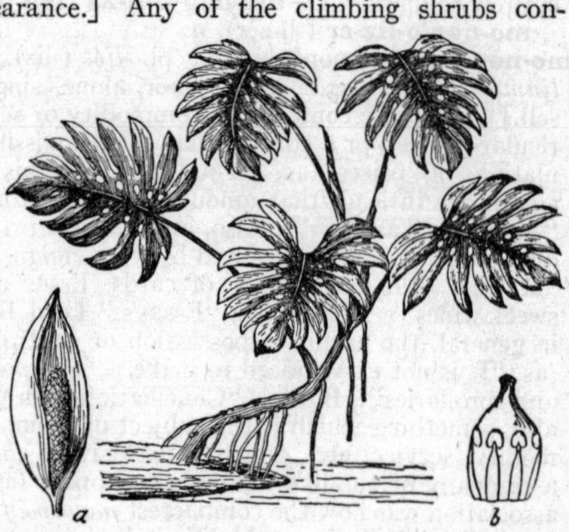

Monstera (*M. deliciosa*). — *a*, the spadix within the spathe; *b*, the flower.

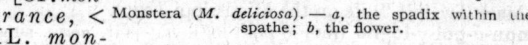

mon-strance (mon'strạns), *n.* [OF. *monstrance*, < ML. *monstrantia*, < L. *monstrare*, show, akin to *monstrum*, omen, E. *monster.*] In the *Rom. Cath. Ch.*, a receptacle in which the consecrated host is exposed for adoration.

mon-stros-i-ty (mon-stros'i-ti), *n.*; pl. *-ties* (-tiz). The state or character of being monstrous; also, something monstrous, esp. in form or growth; a monster.

mon-strous (mon'strus), *a.* [OF. *monstreux*, < L. *monstrosus*, *monstruosus*, < *monstrum*, E. *monster.*] Of the nature of a monster; deviating greatly from the natural or normal form or type (as, a *monstrous* birth; *monstrous* plant-growths); having the nature or appearance of a fabulous monster; frightful or hideous; revolting, shocking, or outrageous (as, a *monstrous* proposal or situation; "There was no excess too *monstrous* for them to commit," Wiseman's "Fabiola," ii. 13); huge, enormous, or prodigiously great (as, a *monstrous* wolf; a *monstrous* sum; "Even while I gazed, this current acquired a *monstrous* velocity," Poe's "Descent into the Maelström"); also, abounding in monsters† (as, "Where

Monstrance. — French work of end of 14th century.

thou, perhaps, under the whelming tide, Visit'st the bottom of the *monstrous* world": Milton's "Lycidas," 158). —**mon'strous,** *adv.* Exceedingly; extremely: as, "You shall see a *monstrous* pretty girl" (Jane Austen's "Sense and Sensibility," xix.). [Now colloq.]—**mon'strous-ly,** *adv.*—**mon'strous-ness,** *n.*

mons Ven-er-is (monz ven'ẹ-ris). [L., 'mount of Venus.'] In *anat.*, a rounded eminence of fatty tissue over the pubic symphysis of the human female.

mon-tane (mon'tān), *a.* [L. *montanus*, < *mons* (*mont-*), E. *mount*[1].] Of or pertaining to mountains; inhabiting mountainous country.

mont=de=pié-té (môṅ-dė-pyā-tā), *n.*; pl. *monts-* (môṅ-). [F., < It. *monte di pietà*, lit. 'mountain (heap, fund) of pity.'] A public pawnbroking establishment for lending money on reasonable terms, esp. to the poor.

mon-te (mon'tẹ), *n.* [Sp., mountain, heap (of cards), < L. *mons* (*mont-*), E. *mount*[1].] A Spanish and Spanish-American gambling-game at cards.—**three=card monte,** a gambling-game of Mexican origin, played with three cards.

mon-teith (mon-tēth'), *n.* [From a personal name.] A kind of large bowl, originating about 1683, commonly of silver, with a notched, often movable rim from which drinking-glasses were hung by the foot so as to cool in water within the bowl: also used (sometimes with the rim removed) as a punch-bowl.

Monteith.

Mon-te-ne-grin (mon-tẹ-nē'grin). **I.** *a.* Of or pertaining to Montenegro or its inhabitants. **II.** *n.* A native or inhabitant of Montenegro.

Mon-tes-so-ri (mon-tes-sō'rē) **sys'tem.** A system for training and instructing young children, of which the fundamental aim is self-education by the children themselves, and which lays special emphasis on the training of the senses: so called from its originator, Maria Montessori (born 1870), an Italian physician and educationist.

mont-gol-fi-er (mont-gol'fi-ėr, F. môṅ-gol-fyā), *n.* [From the French brothers *Montgolfier*, who in 1783 sent up the first balloon.] A balloon raised by heated air from a fire in the lower part.

month (munth), *n.* [AS. *mōnath* = G. *monat* = Icel. *mānudhr* = Goth. *mēnōths*, month; akin to E. *moon.*] The period ('lunar month') of a complete revolution of the moon with regard to some point, usually the interval from one new moon to the next (called 'synodical month,' and equivalent to 29 days, 12 hours, 44 minutes, and 2.7 seconds); also, the twelfth part of a tropical or solar year ('solar month'); also, any one of the twelve parts (January, February, etc.) into which the calendar year is divided ('calendar month'); also, the time from any day of one calendar month to the corresponding day of the next; sometimes, a period of four weeks, or of thirty days.—**month of Sundays,** an indefinitely long time.—**month's mind,** in the *Rom. Cath. Ch.*, the commemoration of a deceased person, esp. by a requiem mass, a month after death. Also (now prov. Eng.), a mind, inclination, or fancy: as, "Clinker . . . has a *month's mind* to play the fool . . . with Mrs. Winifred Jenkins" (Smollett's "Humphry Clinker," Oct. 14).—**month'ly. I.** *a.* Pertaining to a month, or to each month; also, done, happening, appearing, etc., once a month, or every month; also, continuing or lasting for a month. **II.** *n.*; pl. *-lies* (-liz). A periodical published once a month. **III.** *adv.* Once a month; by the month.

mon-ti-cle (mon'ti-kl), *n.* Same as *monticule.*

mon-ti-cule (mon'ti-kūl), *n.* [F. *monticule*, < LL. *monticulus*, dim. of L. *mons* (*mont-*), E. *mount*[1].] A small mountain, hill, or mound; a little elevation: as, "Seen from this *monticule*, everything [in a town] looks tranquil and happy" (Besant's "Coligny," i.).

mon-u-ment (mon'ụ-mẹnt), *n.* [OF. F. *monument*, < L. *monumentum*, monument, memorial, sepulcher, < *monere*, remind: see *mind*[2].] Something erected, in some public or appropriate place, in memory of a person, a number of persons, an event, or the like, as a column, pillar, or other structure, often a statue or other sculptural work (as, the Washington *Monument*; the equestrian *monument* of Colleoni in Venice; the many *monuments* of the World War); a memorial in stone, marble, or other enduring material, often of striking appearance or great artistic merit; specif., a memorial erection marking the grave of a dead person; formerly, a tomb†, sepulcher†, or burial vault† (as, "Her body sleeps in Capel's *monument*": Shakspere's "Romeo and Juliet," v. 1. 18); also, any building, structure, megalith, or the like surviving from a past age, and regarded (in some countries, specially preserved) as of historical or archæological importance; any work, writing, or the like by a person, regarded as a memorial of him after his death (as, "Except some unpublished despatches . . . and a few detached sayings, he has left no *monument* behind him": Lecky's "Hist. of Eng. in the 18th Century," iii.); any enduring evidence or example of something (as, "This letter, one of the most striking *monuments* of Philip's cold-blooded perfidy, was dated the 26th of March": Motley's "Dutch Republic," ii. 10); a notable instance (as, "Here are a great many living *monuments* of longevity": Smollett's "Humphry Clinker," Sept. 6); a record, document, or legal instrument; any object fixed in the soil and serving to indicate location or fix a boundary; an indication, sign, or token (obs. or archaic); a portent†; also, a statue†.—**mon-u-men'tal** (-men'tạl), *a.* [LL. *monumentalis.*] Of or pertaining to a monument or monuments; of the nature of or serving as a monument; also, resembling a monument; massive or imposing, as a structure, an oak, etc.; substantial and important, as a literary work; historically prominent (as, a *monumental* figure or event; "This year well deserved the name of the *monumental* year in our parish," Galt's "Annals of the Parish," v.); also, conspicuously great or gross (colloq.: as, a *monumental* fraud or lie; *monumental* stupidity). —**mon-u-men'tal-ize** (-īz), *v. t.*; *-ized, -izing.* To establish an enduring memorial or record of.—**mon-u-men"tal-i-za'tion** (-i-zā'shọn), *n.*—**mon-u-men'tal-ly,** *adv.*

Roman Sepulchral Monument. — British Museum.

mon-y (mon'i), *a.* and *n.* Sc. and prov. Eng. form of *many.*

mon-zo-nite (mon'zọ-nīt), *n.* [From *Monzoni*, in Tyrol.] Any of a group of igneous rocks intermediate in composition between syenite and diorite.—**mon-zo-nit'ic** (-nit'ik), *a.*

moo (mö), *v. i.*; *mooed, mooing.* [Imit.] To utter the characteristic cry of a cow; low.—**moo,** *n.*; pl. *moos* (möz). A mooing sound.

mooch (möch), *v.* [Also *mouch*: cf. *miche.*] **I.** *intr.* To skulk or sneak (as, "They sort of *mouched* after me, and I tells a policeman": Dunsany's "Night at an Inn"); also, to hang or rove about, esp. with the idea of picking up what one can. [Now prov. or slang.] **II.** *tr.* To appropriate surreptitiously; pilfer. [Prov. or slang.]—**mooch'er,** *n.*

mood[1] (möd), *n.* [Var. of *mode.*] In *gram.*, same as *mode*; in *logic*, any of the various forms of valid syllogisms, depending on the quantity and quality of their constituent propositions.

mood[2] (möd), *n.* [AS. *mōd*, mind, spirit, mood, = D. *moed*, G. *mut*, spirit, courage, = Icel. *mōdhr*, Goth. *mōths*, wrath.] Mind† or heart†; also, frame of mind, or state of feeling, as at a particular time (as, a peaceful, angry, or uncertain *mood*; "I was in no *mood* to laugh and talk with strangers," Mrs. Shelley's "Frankenstein," xix.); humor or temper; *pl.*, fits of uncertain, gloomy, or sullen humor (as, "Then turn'd Sir Torre, and being in his *moods* Left them": Tennyson's "Lancelot and Elaine," 794); also, *sing.*, anger†.—**mood'y,** *a.*; compar. *moodier*, superl. *moodiest.* [AS. *mōdig*.]

Spirited†, brave†, or proud†; also, dominated by a gloomy or sullen mood (as, "George was *moody* and captious all day": H. Kingsley's "Geoffry Hamlyn," vi.); proceeding from or showing such a mood (as, a *moody* silence; a *moody* face); gloomy; sullen; ill-humored; also, angry†.—**mood'i-ly,** *adv.*—**mood'i-ness,** *n.*

moon (mön), *n.* [AS. *mōna* = D. *maan* = OHG. *māno* = Icel. *māni* = Goth. *mēna*, moon; akin to Gr. *μήνη*, moon, *μήν*, month, L. *mensis*, month, Skt. *mās*, moon, month: cf. *month.*] A heavenly body which revolves around the earth monthly, accompanying it in its annual revolution about the sun; this heavenly body during a particular lunar month, or during a certain period of time, or at a certain point of time, regarded as a distinct object or entity (as, the harvest-*moon*, see *harvest-moon*; new *moon*, the moon when in conjunction with the sun and hence invisible, or the phase so represented, or the moon soon afterward when visible as a slender crescent; half-*moon*, the moon when half its disk is illuminated, occurring when at either quadrature, or quarter; full *moon*, the moon when the whole of its disk is illuminated, occurring when in opposition to the sun, or the phase so represented; old *moon*, the waning moon; waxing *moon*, the moon at any time before it is full, so called because its illuminated area is increasing daily; waning *moon*, the moon at any time after it has been full, so called because its illuminated area is decreasing daily: cf. *phase*² and *quarter*, *n.*); the moon as visible at a given time or place (as, there was a *moon* that evening); also, a lunar month, or, in general, a month (as, "a young and tender suckling—under a *moon* old": Lamb's "Dissertation upon Roast Pig"); also, moonlight (as, "By the *moon* the reaper weary, Piling sheaves in uplands airy": Tennyson's "Lady of Shalott," i. 33); also, something shaped like an orb or a crescent; also, any planetary satellite.—**moon,** *v.* **I.** *tr.* To expose to the moon's rays; also, to spend (time) idly. **II.** *intr.* To shine as a moon; also, to wander about or gaze idly or listlessly, as if moonstruck (colloq.: as, "to go *mooning* about the house and stables," Aldrich's "Story of a Bad Boy," vi.; "If you *moon* at me in that stupid way . . . I shall certainly end in an insane asylum," Howells's "Chance Acquaintance," v.).

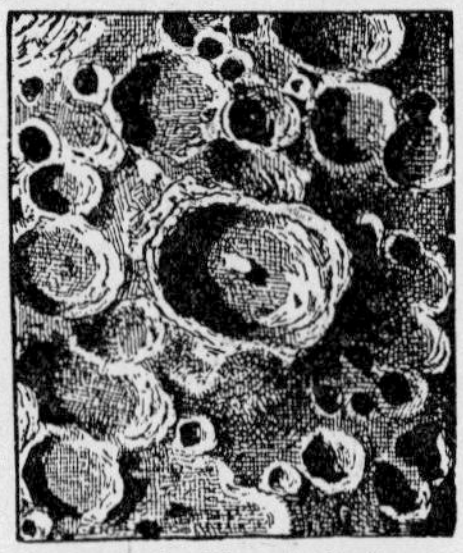

Part of the Moon's Surface.

moon-beam (mön'bēm), *n.* A ray of moonlight.

moon=blind (mön'blīnd), *a.* Of horses, afflicted with the disease moon-eye; also, of persons, suffering from temporary night-blindness erroneously ascribed to sleeping in the moonlight (as, "It would be well . . . to request the officer of the watch not to permit the men to sleep on the upper-deck. We shall have many of them *moon-blind*": Marryat's "King's Own," xxii.).—**moon'=blind"ness,** *n.*

moon=calf (mön'käf), *n.* A misshapen creature, or monstrosity; also, a congenital idiot; a fool or dolt (as, " 'Now you see, you *moon-calf*,' says Ballantrae": Stevenson's "Master of Ballantrae," iii.).

moon=creep-er (mön'krē"pėr), *n.* The moon-flower, *Calonyction bona-nox.*

moon=dai-sy (mön'dā"zi), *n.* The oxeye daisy, *Chrysanthemum leucanthemum.*

mooned (mönd), *a.* Shaped like a moon or crescent; ornamented with moons or crescents; also, identified with the moon.

moon-er (mö'nėr), *n.* One who moons about.

moon=eye (mön'ī), *n.* In *vet. science*, an eye affected with an intermittent inflammation (formerly attributed to the moon's influence) usually resulting in complete blindness; also, the disease itself.—**moon'=eyed,** *a.* Of horses, affected with the disease moon-eye; moon-blind; also, of persons, having round, wide-open eyes, as from terror.

moon=faced (mön'fāst), *a.* Having a round face like a full moon: as, "the long *moon-faced* clock in the corner" (F. H. Smith's "Colonel Carter of Cartersville," xi.).

moon-fish (mön'fish), *n.* Any of various fishes resembling or suggestive of the moon; esp., any of certain fishes having a deep, compressed, silvery or yellowish body, as of the carangoid genera *Selene* and *Vomer*, as *S. vomer* or *V. setipinnis* of the southern coasts of North America.

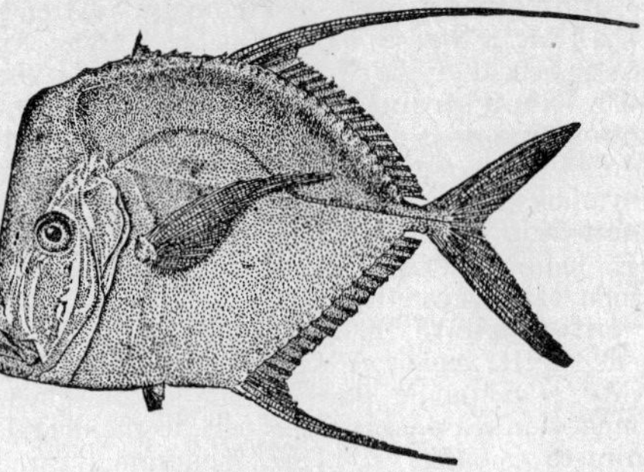

Moonfish (*Selene vomer*).

moon=flow-er (mön'flou"ėr), *n.* A night-blooming convolvulaceous plant, *Calonyction bona-nox*, with fragrant white flowers; any of several allied plants; also, the oxeye daisy, *Chrysanthemum leucanthemum.*

moon-ish (mö'nish), *a.* Like or characteristic of the moon; influenced by or due to the moon (as, " 'Tis *moonish* madness!" Sir H. Taylor's "Philip van Artevelde," ii. 4. 2); changeable as the moon, or fickle.

moon-less (mön'les), *a.* Without a moon or moonlight: as, "The *moonless* night and dark was come" (W. Morris's "Jason," i. 103).

moon-let (mön'let), *n.* A little moon.

moon-light (mön'līt). **I.** *n.* The light of the moon. **II.** *a.* Pertaining to moonlight; illuminated by moonlight (as, "the *moonlight* woods": Mrs. Shelley's "Frankenstein," xiii.); occurring by moonlight, or by night (as, "a *moonlight* flitting": Galt's "Annals of the Parish," xxxi.).—**moon'lit** (-lit), *a.* Lighted or illuminated by the moon: as, "*moonlit* groves" (Disraeli's "Lothair," xv.).—**moon'lit"ten** (-lit"n), *a.* Moonlit. [Poetic.]

moon-rise (mön'rīz), *n.* The rising of the moon (as, "watching a chilly autumnal *moonrise* over the stubbles of the corn-field": Mrs. H. Ward's "Robert Elsmere," xix.); also, the time when the moon rises (as, "At *moonrise* the cautious coolies got under way": Kipling's "Kim," xiv.).

moon-seed (mön'sēd), *n.* Any of the climbing herbs constituting the genus *Menispermum* (family *Menispermaceæ*), as *M. canadense*, with panicles of greenish-white flowers: so called from the crescent-shaped seeds.

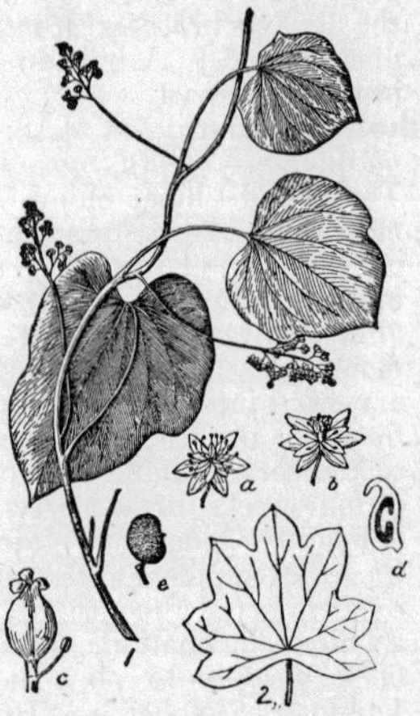

Moonseed (*Menispermum canadense*).—1, flowering branch; 2, a deeply lobed leaf; *a*, male flower; *b*, female flower; *c*, the pistils and a stamen; *d*, vertical section through one of the pistils; *e*, the fruit.

moon-set (mön'set), *n.* The setting of the moon.

moon-shine (mön'shīn), *n.* The light of the moon (as, "a night's journey by *moonshine*": Scott's "Quentin Durward," xxiv.); also, show without substance or reality; empty show; foolish talk, ideas, etc.; nonsense; also, smuggled or illicitly distilled liquor (colloq.).—**moon'shin"er** (-shī"nėr), *n.* One who pursues an illegal trade at night; esp., in the U. S., an illicit distiller (as, "vast cliffs from whose bushy brows the armed *moonshiner* watched the bridle-path below": G. W. Cable's "John March, Southerner," viii.). [Colloq.]—**moon'shin"y,** *a.* Like moonlight; sometimes, unreal; also, illuminated by moonlight.

moon-stone (mön'stōn), *n.* A translucent variety of feldspar with a pearly luster, used as a gem.

moon-strick-en (mön'strik"n), *a.* Moonstruck.

moon-struck (mön'struk), *a.* Injuriously affected in mind (or otherwise), supposedly by the influence of the moon; dazed; crazed.

moon-wort (mön′wėrt), *n.* Any fern of the genus *Botrychium*, esp. *B. lunaria* whose fronds have crescent-shaped pinnæ; also, the plant honesty.

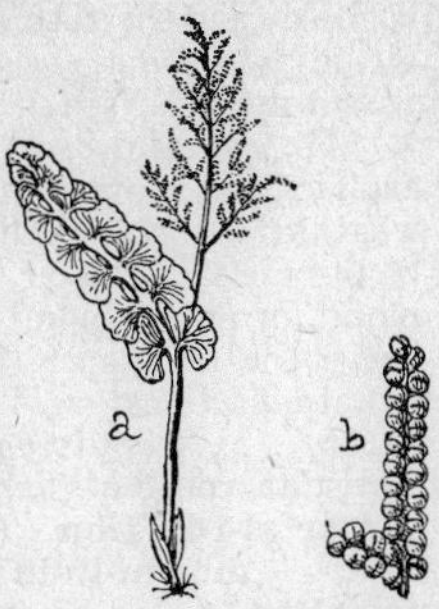

Moonwort (*Botrychium lunaria*). — *a*, entire plant; *b*, branch of the fertile frond, showing sporangia.

moon-y (mö′ni), *a.* Pertaining to or characteristic of the moon; also, resembling the moon; round; crescent-shaped; also, illuminated by moonlight; resembling moonlight; also, mooning, listless, or silly (colloq.: as, "*moony* dreamings over inscrutable beautiful eyes," G. Meredith's "Lord Ormont and His Aminta," v.).

Moor[1] (mör), *n.* [OF. F. *More*, *Maure*, < L. *Maurus*, < Gr. Μαῦρος.] Orig., one of the ancient inhabitants of a region of northwestern Africa corresponding to parts of the modern Morocco and Algeria; later, a Mohammedan of the mixed Berber and Arab race inhabiting this region; specif., one belonging to that group of this race which in the 8th century invaded and conquered Spain.

moor[2] (mör), *n.* [AS. *mōr*, moor, = MLG. *mōr*, G. *moor*, marsh.] A tract of open waste land, often overgrown with heath; a heath; also, a tract of land preserved for game-shooting; also, a marsh (now prov. Eng.).

moor[3] (mör), *v.* [Late ME. *more*: cf. D. *marren*, tie, moor.] **I.** *tr.* To secure (a ship, etc.) in a particular place, as by cables and anchors (esp. two or more) or by lines; hence, in general, to secure, or fix firmly. **II.** *intr.* To moor a ship, etc.; also, to take up a position or be made secure by means of anchors or the like, as a ship.—**moor′age** (-āj), *n.* The act of mooring, or the state of being moored; also, a place for mooring; also, a charge or payment for the use of moorings.

moor-ber-ry (mör′ber″i), *n.*; pl. *-berries* (-iz). [See *moor*[2].] The bilberry; also, the small cranberry, *Oxycoccus oxycoccus*.

moor=cock (mör′kok), *n.* [See *moor*[2].] The male moor-fowl.—**moor′=fowl,** *n.* The red grouse. See *grouse*[1].—**moor′=game,** *n.* The moor-fowl.—**moor′=hen,** *n.* The female moor-fowl; also, a common European gallinule, *Gallinula chloropus*.

moor-ing (mör′ing), *n.* The act of one who or that which moors; also, something by which a ship or the like is moored, as a cable, line, etc. (usually in *pl.*); also, *pl.*, the place where a vessel is or may be moored.

Moor-ish[1] (mör′ish), *a.* Of or pertaining to the Moors; in the style of the Moors, as architecture, decoration, etc.

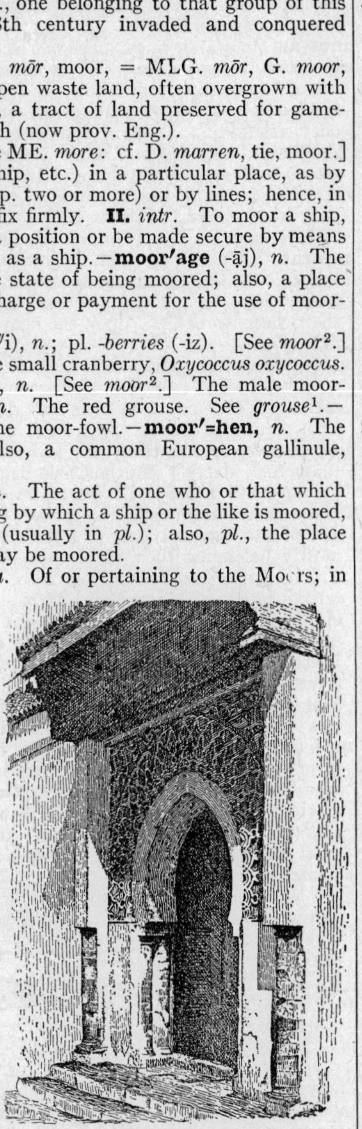
Moorish Art. — Doorway of mosque, Tangier, Morocco.

moor-ish[2] (mör′ish), *a.* Of, pertaining to, or of the nature of a moor or heath; abounding in or covered with moors (as, "*moorish* hills, where was no sound but the crying of moor-fowl in the wet heather": Stevenson's "Master of Ballantrae," ix.); also, marshy (obs. or archaic: as, *moorish* fens; "a low *moorish* ground near the sea," Defoe's "Robinson Crusoe," i. 4).

moor-land (mör′land). **I.** *n.* Land consisting of a moor or moors; a moor. **II.** *a.* Of the nature of or pertaining to moorland; situated, dwelling, or found on moorland.—**moor′land-er,** *n.*

moor-y (mör′i), *a.* Same as *moorish*[2].

moose (mös), *n.*; pl. *moose.* [Algonquian.] A large animal, *Alces americanus*, of the deer family, inhabiting Canada and the northern U. S., the male of which has enormous antlers, long legs, and a large, unshapely head; also, a similar species, *Alces gigas*, found in Alaska; also, the European elk, *Alces machlis* (see *elk*); also [*cap.*], in *U. S. politics*, a member of the Progressive party; a Bull Moose.

moot (möt). [AS. *mōt*, *gemōt*, meeting, assembly; akin to Icel. *mōt*, MLG. *mōte*, *gemōte*, D. *gemoet*, meeting: cf. *meet*[2].] **I.** *n.* An early English assembly of the people, exercising political, administrative, and judicial powers; also, an argument or discussion, esp. of a hypothetical legal case for practice. **II.** *a.* Pertaining to a moot; also, subject to argument or discussion, debatable, or doubtful (as, a *moot* point).—**moot court,** a mock court for the conduct of hypothetical legal cases, as for practice for students of law.—**moot,** *v.* **I.** *intr.* To dispute or argue, esp. in a hypothetical legal case. **II.** *tr.* To argue (a case, etc.), esp. in a mock court; in general, to bring forward (any point, subject, project, etc.) for discussion.—**moot′er,** *n.*

mop[1] (mop), *v. i.* [Cf. D. *moppen*, pout.] To make a wry face; grimace. [Archaic.]—**mop**[1], *n.* A grimace: as, "with *mop* and mow" (Shakspere's "Tempest," iv. 1. 47). [Archaic.]

mop[2] (mop), *n.* [ME. *mappe*: cf. L. *mappa*, napkin, cloth, E. *map*.] A bundle of coarse yarn, a piece of cloth, or the like, fastened at the end of a stick or handle, used for washing floors, etc.; any similar implement; also, a thick mass, as of hair (as, "a *mop* of hair not a little resembling the shag of a Newfoundland dog": Irving's "Knickerbocker's New York," v. 9).—**mop**[2], *v. t.*; *mopped*, *mopping.* To rub, wipe, clean, or remove with a mop; hence, in general, to wipe (as, to *mop* the face with a handkerchief; "*Mop* your eyes," Kipling's "Light That Failed," xiv.); dry or clean as by wiping.—**to mop up,** to clean up (a place, surface, etc.) or take up (liquid, etc.) with or as with a mop; hence, in military slang, to clear (ground, trenches, etc.) of scattered or remaining enemy combatants, as in connection with an attack, or to dispose of (combatants) thus.—**mop′-board,** *n.* A baseboard (around the walls of a room).

mope (mōp), *v.*; *moped*, *moping.* [Origin uncertain.] **I.** *intr.* To go about abstractedly or aimlessly (now prov.); also, to act in a listless, dispirited way, or give way to low spirits (as, "I began to ail and *mope*": Bulwer-Lytton's "Caxtons," i. 5); be sunk in listless apathy or dull dejection. **II.** *tr.* To cause to mope; render listless and dispirited.—**mope,** *n.* A mopish person (as, "no meagre, muse-rid *mope*, adust and thin": Pope's "Dunciad," ii. 37); *pl.*, low spirits.—**mop-er** (mō′pėr), *n.*—**mop′ing-ly,** *adv.*—**mop′ish,** *a.* Given to moping; listless and dispirited; dejected.—**mop′ish-ly,** *adv.*—**mop′ish-ness,** *n.*

Mop-lah (mop′lạ̈). [Malayalam *māppila*.] **I.** *n.* One of a class of Mohammedan inhabitants of southwestern India, esp. Malabar, descended from Arab settlers and native women, and notable for their fiercely fanatical spirit. **II.** *a.* Of or pertaining to the Moplahs.

mo-poke, more-pork (mō-pōk′, mōr-pōrk′), *n.* [Imit. of its note.] Any of several birds of the Australian region, esp. a kind of goatsucker, *Podargus cuvieri*, or a small owl, *Ninox boobook*.

Mopoke (*Podargus cuvieri*).

mop-per (mop′ėr), *n.* One who mops.

mop-pet (mop′et), *n.* [Dim. < ME. *moppe*, fool, doll, baby.] A familiar term for a child or a young girl. [Archaic or prov.]

mop-py (mop′i), *a.* Like a mop, as hair.

mop-y (mō′pi), *a.* Mopish: as, "Taffy and the Laird grew quite sad and *mopy*" (Du Maurier's "Trilby," v.).

mo-quette (mọ-ket′), *n.* [F.] A kind of carpet with a thick velvety pile.

mo-ra (mō′rạ̈), *n.*; pl. *moræ* (-rē). [L., delay.] In *pros.*, the unit of time, equivalent to the ordinary or normal short sound or syllable.

mo-ra-ceous (mọ-rā′shius), *a.* [L. *morus*, mulberry-tree.] Belonging to the *Moraceæ*, or mulberry family of plants, which includes the mulberry, breadfruit, fig, hemp, hop, Osage orange, etc.

mo-raine (mọ-rān′), *n.* [F.; origin uncertain.] An accumulation of rocks, detrital material, etc., carried down with or deposited by a glacier: known as a *lateral moraine* when at the side of a glacier, a *terminal moraine* when at the extremity of a glacier, or a *medial moraine* when between two uniting glaciers.—**mo-rain′al, mo-rain′ic,** *a.*

mor-al (mor′ạl). [OF. F. *moral*, < L. *moralis*, < *mos* (*mor-*), manner, custom, practice.] **I.** *a.* Pertaining to or concerned with right conduct, or the distinction between right and wrong (as, the *moral* sense; *moral* considerations; the *moral* aspect of an action); concerned with the principles or rules of right conduct (as, *moral* philosophy); ethical; also, expressing or conveying truths or counsel as to right conduct, as a speaker or writer, a literary work, etc. (as, Pope's "*Moral* Essays"; Maria Edgeworth's "*Moral* Tales"); moralizing; also, founded on the fundamental principles of right conduct, rather than on enactment or custom (as, the *moral* law; *moral* rights or obligations); amenable or subject to the rules of right conduct (as, man is a *moral* agent; *moral* actions); also, conforming to the rules of right conduct (opposed to *immoral*); virtuous; good; esp., sexually virtuous; also, pertaining to or affecting the character as shown in conduct (as, the *moral* nature; *moral* courage; favorable *moral* conditions; *moral* discipline: often opposed to *physical* or *intellectual*); also, being virtually or practically such through the effect on the mind or feelings or on results generally (as, a *moral* victory or defeat; *moral* support); also, depending upon what is observed of human nature and actions or of things generally, rather than upon demonstration (as, *moral* evidence); resting upon convincing grounds of probability (as, a *moral* certainty). **II.** *n.* The moral teaching or practical lesson contained in a fable, tale, experience, etc.; hence, import† or meaning†; also, a symbolic figure† (as, "Fortune is painted blind . . . also with a wheel . . . Fortune is an excellent *moral*": Shakspere's "Henry V.," iii. 6. 40); hence, the embodiment or type of something (as, "She is the very *moral* of old-fashioned prejudice": Hawthorne's "Twice-Told Tales," Old Esther Dudley); the image or counterpart of a person or thing (colloq.: as, "They said I was the very *moral* of Lady Rickmanstone, but not so pale," Smollett's "Humphry Clinker," Nov. 20); also, *pl.*, principles or habits with respect to right or wrong conduct (as, "Her *morals* had been greatly neglected in her youth": Galt's "Annals of the Parish," xii.); also, *pl.* (usually construed as *sing.*), moral philosophy; ethics; also (F., pron. mo-ràl), *sing.*, morale.—**mor′al,** *v. i.*; *-aled* or *-alled, -aling* or *-alling.* To moralize: as, "When I did hear The motley fool thus *moral* on the time" (Shakspere's "As You Like It," ii. 7. 29). [Archaic.]

mo-rale (mọ-ràl′ or -räl′), *n.* [For F. *moral*: see *moral.*] Moral or mental condition, as with respect to courage, confidence, zeal, etc.: as, the *morale* of troops.

mor-aled, mor-alled (mor′ạld), *a.* Having morals (as specified): as, high-*moraled*; loose-*moraled.*

mor-al-ism (mor′ạl-izm), *n.* The habit of moralizing; moral counsel; also, the practice of morality, as distinct from religion.

mor-al-ist (mor′ạl-ist), *n.* One who teaches or inculcates morals or morality; also, one who practises morality.—**mor-al-is′tic,** *a.*

mo-ral-i-ty (mọ-ral′i-ti), *n.*; pl. *-ties* (-tiz). [OF. *moralite* (F. *moralité*), < LL. *moralitas.*] Moral quality or character; the quality of an action, purpose, or the like, as conforming to or deviating from the principles of right conduct; also, conformity to the rules of right conduct; moral or virtuous conduct; sometimes, the practice of moral duties quite apart from the influence of religion; sometimes, sexual virtue; also, morals or ethics; *pl.*, moral principles or rules; also, *sing.*, moral instruction; a moral lesson or precept; a moralizing discourse or utterance (as, "A genial optimist, who daily drew From what he saw his quaint *moralities*": Bryant's "Old Man's Counsel"); also, a kind of allegorical drama in vogue during the 16th century, employing personifications of virtues, vices, etc.

mor-al-ize (mor′ạl-īz), *v.*; *-ized, -izing.* [OF. F. *moraliser*, < ML. *moralizare*, < L. *moralis*: see *moral.*] **I.** *tr.* To explain in a moral sense, or draw a moral from (as, "But what said Jaques? Did he not *moralize* this spectacle?" Shakspere's "As You Like It," ii. 1. 44); also, to render moral, or give a moral quality or character to; also, to improve the morals of (cf. *demoralize*). **II.** *intr.* To make moral reflections: as, "I found this islander a philosopher of nature . . . *moralizing* upon the vices and follies of the Christian court of Tahiti" (H. Melville's "Omoo," lxxxi.).—**mor″al-i-za′tion** (-i-zā′shọn), *n.*—**mor′al-iz-er** (-ī-zėr), *n.*—**mor′al-iz-ing-ly,** *adv.*

mor′alled, *a.* See *moraled.*

mor-al-ly (mor′ạl-i), *adv.* In a moral manner or respect; from a moral point of view, or ethically (as, things *morally* considered; *morally* good); virtuously (as, to live *morally*); virtually or practically (as, "Murder has been done, to which you were *morally* if not really a party": Dickens's "Oliver Twist," xlix.); with moral certainty (as, *morally* sure; *morally* impossible).

mor-als (mor′ạlz), *n. pl.* See *moral, n.*

mo-rass (mọ-ras′), *n.* [D. *moeras*, < OF. *mareis* (F. *marais*), marsh; from Teut., and akin to E. *marsh.*] A tract of low, soft, wet ground (as, "a wide *morass*, in which oozy islands . . . were interspersed among lagoons and shallows": Motley's "Dutch Republic," Introd., i.); a marsh or bog; marshy ground (as, miles of *morass*); any stretch of troublesomely muddy ground (as, "The towing path was a *morass* of sticky brown mud": Arnold Bennett's "Clayhanger," i. 1). [Now chiefly literary.]—**mo-rass′y,** *a.*

mo-rat (mō′rat), *n.* [ML. *moratum*, < L. *morum*, mulberry.] An old-time beverage made of honey flavored with mulberries: as, "Place the best mead, the mightiest ale, the richest *morat* . . . upon the board" (Scott's "Ivanhoe," iii.).

mor-a-to-ri-um (mor-ạ-tō′ri-um), *n.*; pl. *-ria* (-ri-ạ̈). [NL., prop. neut. of LL. *moratorius*, E. *moratory.*] A legal authorization to delay payment of money due, as in an emergency; also, the period during which such authorization is in effect.

mor-a-to-ry (mor′ạ-tọ-ri), *a.* [LL. *moratorius*, delaying, < L. *morari*, delay.] Authorizing delay of payment: as, a *moratory* bill or law. Cf. *moratorium.*

Mo-ra-vi-an (mọ-rā′vi-ạn). **I.** *a.* Pertaining to Moravia, a region to the southeast of Bohemia, or to its inhabitants, mostly belonging to a Slavic people closely related to the Czechs proper, or Bohemians; also, of or pertaining to the religious body of Moravians. **II.** *n.* A native or inhabitant of Moravia; also, a member of a Christian denomination entitled the 'Unitas Fratrum' (Unity of Brethren) or 'United Brethren,' and known also as 'Moravian Brethren,' which traces its origin to John Huss, and which after expulsion from Moravia and Bohemia in the early part of the 17th century was revived in Saxony in the early part of the 18th century.

mo-ray (mō′rā or mọ-rā′), *n.* [Cf. Pg. *moreia*, < L. *muræna.*] Any of numerous eels constituting the family *Murænidæ*, esp. those of the genus *Muræna*, as *M. helena*, a species common in the Mediterranean and valued as a food-fish (the *muræna* of the ancient Romans, esteemed as a great delicacy and preserved in ponds and tanks), or *Gymnothorax moringa*, a species common in West Indian waters ('spotted moray').

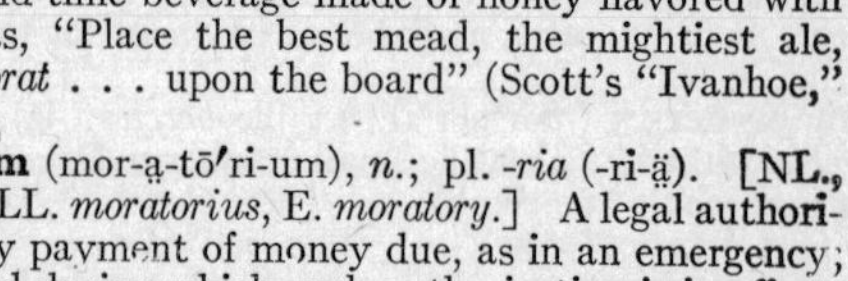

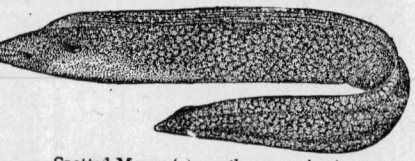

Spotted Moray (*Gymnothorax moringa*).

mor-bid (môr′bid), *a.* [L. *morbidus*, < *morbus*, disease.] Affected by, proceeding from, or characteristic of disease (as, *morbid* tissues; *morbid* states; *morbid* discharges or symptoms); also, pertaining to diseased parts (as, *morbid* anatomy); also, being in, showing, or suggesting an unhealthy mental state (as, a *morbid* dreamer; *morbid* fancies; a *morbid* book); unhealthy, as the mental state; unwholesomely gloomy, sensitive, extreme, etc.; unwholesome.

mor-bi-dez-za (môr-bē-det′sä), *n.* [It., < *morbido*, delicate, < L. *morbidus*, E. *morbid.*] The soft delicacy of living flesh as represented in painting or other forms of art.

mor-bid-i-ty (môr-bid′i-ti), *n.* Morbid state or quality; also, the proportion of sickness in a district.

mor-bid-ly (môr′bid-li), *adv.* In a morbid manner.—**mor′bid-ness,** *n.*

mor-bif-ic (môr-bif′ik), *a.* [F. *morbifique*, < L. *morbus*, disease, + *facere*, make.] Causing disease: as, *morbific* agents.—**mor-bif′i-cal-ly,** *adv.*

mor-bil-li (môr-bil′ī), *n. pl.* [ML., pl. of *morbillus*, dim. < L. *morbus*, disease.] In *pathol.*, the eruptive spots of measles; hence, measles.—**mor-bil′li-form** (-bil′i-fôrm), *a.* Resembling measles.—**mor-bil′lous,** *a.* Of or pertaining to measles.

mor-ceau (môr-sō), *n.*; pl. *-ceaux* (-sōz, F. -sō). [F.: see *morsel.*] A bit or piece; esp., a short literary or musical piece, whether belonging to a larger work or not.

mor-cel-late (môr′sẹ-lāt), *v. t.*; *-lated*, *-lating.* [F. *morceler*, divide into pieces, < *morceau*: see *morceau* and *morsel.*] To divide into many pieces; break up.—**mor-cel-la′tion** (-sẹ-lā′shọn), *n.* Division into many pieces; in *surg.*, the removal of a tumor, fetus, or the like piecemeal, instead of by excision in a mass.

mor-celle-ment (môr-sel-moṅ), *n.* [F., < *morceler*: see *morcellate.*] Division into many pieces; a dividing, as of land, into small portions; in *surg.*, morcellation.

mor-da-cious (môr-dā′shus), *a.* [L. *mordax* (*mordac-*), < *mordere*, bite: cf. *mordant.*] Biting; given to biting; fig., caustic; mordant. [Now rare.]—**mor-da′cious-ly,** *adv.*—**mor-da′ci-ty** (-das′i-ti), *n.*

mor-dan-cy (môr′dạn-si), *n.* Mordant or biting quality.

mor-dant (môr′dạnt). [OF. F. *mordant*, ppr. of *mordre*, < L. *mordere*, bite: see *smart*, *v.*] **I.** *a.* Biting, as with the teeth (rare); hence, pungent, acrid, or corrosive, as substances; sharp, as pain; caustic, sarcastic, or cutting, as speech or speakers, wit, etc. (as, "restraining his tongue from *mordant* allusions to that 'prancing, red-haired fellow'": Galsworthy's "Patrician," ii. 5); also, having the property of fixing colors, as in dyeing. **II.** *n.* A substance used in dyeing to fix the coloring matter, esp. a metallic compound, as an oxide or hydroxide, which combines with the organic dyestuff and forms an insoluble colored compound or lake in the fiber; also, an adhesive substance for attaching gold-leaf to something; also, an acid or other corrosive substance used in etching to eat out the lines, etc.—**mor′dant,** *v. t.* To impregnate or treat with a mordant.—**mor′dant-ly,** *adv.*

mor-dent (môr′dẹnt), *n.* [It. *mordente*, prop. ppr. of *mordere*, < L. *mordere*, bite.] In *music*, a melodic embellishment consisting of a rapid alternation of a principal tone with a supplementary tone a half-step below it, called *single* or *short* when the supplementary tone occurs but once, and *double* or *long* when this occurs twice or oftener; also, the pralltriller ('inverted mordent').

more (mōr). [AS. *māra* = OHG. *mēro* = Icel. *meiri* = Goth. *maiza*, more, greater: see *most.*] **I.** *a. compar.* Greater, as in size or extent (now chiefly in the archaic phrase 'the more part'); also, in greater quantity, amount, measure, degree, or number (as, *more* money; *more* help; *more* haste; *more* men: used as the comparative of *much* and *many*, with the superlative *most*); also, additional or further (as, do not lose any *more* time; without *more* words he departed). **II.** *n.* A greater quantity, amount, or degree; also, something of greater importance (as, "Kind hearts are *more* than coronets": Tennyson's "Lady Clara Vere de Vere"); also, a greater number of a class specified, or the greater number of persons (construed as *pl.*); also, an additional quantity, amount, or number.—**more,** *adv. compar.* In or to a greater extent or degree (in this sense much used before adjectives and adverbs, and regularly before those of more than two syllables, to form comparative phrases having the same force and effect as the comparative degree formed by the termination *-er*: as, *more* rapid, *more* curious, *more* wisely, *more* fittingly: cf. *most*, *adv.*); also, in addition; further; longer; again.

mo-reen (mọ-rēn′), *n.* [Cf. *moire.*] A heavy fabric of wool, or wool and cotton, commonly watered, used for curtains, petticoats, etc.

more′ish, *a.* See *morish.*

mo-rel (mọ-rel′ or mor′el), *n.* [F. *morille*; from Teut. (cf. G. *morchel*).] An edible mushroom of the genus *Morchella*, esp. *M. esculenta.*

mo-rel-lo (mọ-rel′ō), *n.*; pl. *morellos* (-ōz). [Cf. It. *morello*, dark-colored.] A kind of cherry with a dark-colored skin.

more-o-ver (mōr-ō′vėr), *adv.* Beyond what has been said; further; besides.

more-pork′, *n.* See *mopoke.*

mo-res (mō′rēz), *n. pl.* [L.] Customs; manners; ways; specif., customs prevailing among a people or a social group which are accepted as right and obligatory.

Mo-resque (mọ-resk′), *a.* [F.] Moorish; in the Moorish style, as architecture, decoration, etc.

Mor-gan (môr′gạn), *n.* One of a superior breed of American trotting-horses descended from a horse owned by Justin Morgan of Vermont.

mor-ga-nat-ic (môr-gạ-nat′ik), *a.* [ML. (*matrimonium ad*) *morganaticam*, '(marriage with) morning-gift' (in lieu of a share in the husband's possessions), < OHG. *morgan*, morning: cf. *morning-gift.*] Designating or pertaining to a form of marriage in which a man of high rank takes to wife a woman of lower station with the stipulation that neither she nor the issue (if any) shall have any claim to his rank or property.—**mor-ga-nat′i-cal-ly,** *adv.*

mor-gen (môr′gen), *n.* [D. and G.] A land-measure equal to about two acres, formerly in use in Holland and the Dutch colonies and still used in South Africa; also, a land-measure equal to about two thirds of an acre, formerly used in Prussia, Norway, and Denmark.

morgue[1] (môrg), *n.* [F.; origin unknown.] Haughty demeanor or air; haughty superiority.

morgue[2] (môrg), *n.* [F., a morgue, earlier a seat or place in a prison in which a prisoner was placed for inspection by the keepers: cf. *morgue*[1].] A place in which the bodies of persons found dead are exposed for identification.

mor-i-bund (mor′i-bund). [L. *moribundus*, < *mori*, die.] **I.** *a.* In a dying state; fig., on the verge of extinction or termination (as, a *moribund* political party; a *moribund* enterprise). **II.** *n.* A dying person.—**mor-i-bun′di-ty** (-bun′di-ti), *n.* Moribund condition.

mo-rin (mō′rin), *n.* [NL. *Morus*, genus formerly including the fustic-tree, < L. *morus*, mulberry.] A yellow coloring matter obtained from the fustic-tree, *Chlorophora tinctoria.*

mor-i-on[1] (mor′i-ọn), *n.* [F. *morion*, < Sp. *morrión*, < *morra*, crown of the head.] A kind of helmet without beaver or vizor, worn during the 16th and 17th centuries.

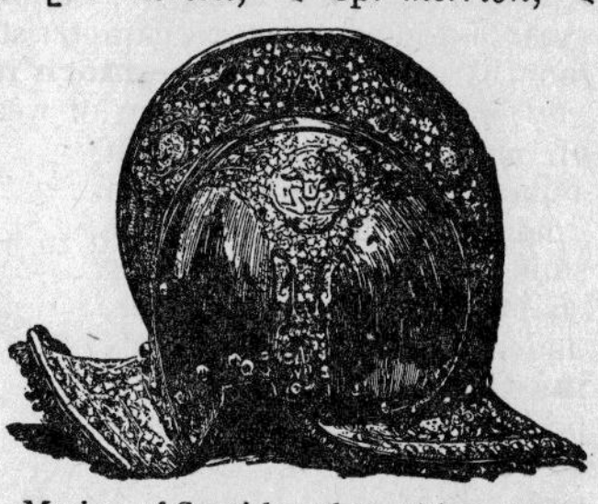

Morion, of Spanish make; 16th century.

mo-ri-on[2] (mō′ri-ọn), *n.* [For L. *mormorion.*] A variety of smoky quartz of a dark-brown or nearly black color.

Mo-ris-co (mọ-ris′kō). [Sp.] **I.** *a.* Moorish. **II.** *n.*; pl. *-cos* or *-coes* (-kōz). A Moor, esp. one of the Moors of Spain; also, a morris-dance†, or a person dancing it† (as, "I have seen Him caper upright like a wild *Morisco*, Shaking the bloody darts as he his bells": Shakspere's "2 Henry VI.," iii. 1. 365).

mor-ish (mōr′ish), *a.* Such that more is desired, as food or drink. [Colloq.]

Mor-mon (môr′mọn). [From *Mormon*, a character in the "Book of Mormon," one of the authoritative writings of the Mormon Church.] **I.** *n.* A member of a religious body in the U. S., founded in 1830 by Joseph Smith and calling itself "The Church of Jesus Christ of Latter-day Saints," formerly notable for the practice of polygamy (officially discountenanced since 1890). **II.** *a.* Of or pertaining to the Mormons or their religious system.—**Mor′mon-ism,** *n.*

morn (môrn), *n.* [ME. *morn*, *morwen*, < AS. *morgen* = D. and G. *morgen* = Icel. *morgunn* = Goth. *maurgins*, morning.] Morning (now poetic or prov.: as, "the golden light of *morn*," Hood's "Ruth"); also, the morrow, or next day (now chiefly Sc.).—**the morn's morning** (or **morn**), to-morrow morning; the next morning: as, "He would have to come for the postage *the morn's morning*" (Galt's "Ayrshire Legatees," vi.). [Chiefly Sc.]

morne (môrn), *a.* [F.; from Teut.: cf. *mourn.*] Mournful; dreary; somber; gloomy: as, "The chaunt was *morne* and doleful" (Kinglake's "Eothen," xvi.).

morn-ing (môr′ning). [ME. *morning, morwening,* < *morn, morwen:* see *morn.*] **I.** *n.* The beginning of day, or the dawn (often personified: as, "Lucifer, son of the *morning*," Isa. xiv. 12); hence, the first part or period of the day, extending from dawn, or from midnight, to noon (as, at 10 o'clock in the *morning*; the small hours of the *morning*, see *small hours*, under *small, a.*); sometimes, the part of the day before a late dinner-time (cf. *matinée*); fig., the first or early period of anything (as, the *morning* of life; "A king lived long ago, In the *morning* of the world," Browning's "Pippa Passes," iii.); also, the first part of the morrow or next day (as, wait until *morning*; I'll come in the *morning*). **II.** *a.* Of or pertaining to morning (as, the *morning* hours); occurring, appearing, coming, used, etc., in the morning (as, a *morning* walk; *morning* clouds; the *morning* papers; *morning* dress); fig., of or pertaining to the first or early period of life or existence (as, "Young he appear'd, for on his cheek there shone The *morning* glow of health": Southey's "Thalaba," i. 14).—**morning star,** a bright planet, esp. Venus (Lucifer), seen in the east before sunrise. See also *morning-star*, below.—**morn′ing=gift,** *n.* [Cf. AS. *morgengifu*, G. *morgengabe*, also E. *morganatic.*] A gift made to a woman by her husband the morning after marriage: a practice formerly common in Europe.—**morn′ing=glo″ry,** *n.*; pl. *-ries* (-riz). Any of various convolvulaceous plants, esp. of the genera *Ipomœa* and *Convolvulus*, as *I. purpurea*, a twining plant with cordate leaves and funnel-shaped flowers of various colors, common in cultivation.—**morn′ing=gown,** *n.* A dressing-gown: as, "Mr. Justice was led into the parlour, in his nightcap and loose *morning-gown*" (Smollett's "Humphry Clinker," Oct. 3).—**morn′ing=land,** *n.* [= G. *morgenland.*] The Orient; the East: as, "Where through the sand of *morning-land* The camel bears the spice" (Macaulay's "Prophecy of Capys," xxxi.).—**morn′ing-less,** *a.* Without a morning: as, "the *morningless* and unawakening sleep" (M. Arnold's "Thyrsis").—**morn′ing=room,** *n.* A room used as a sitting-room during the early part of the day, or before dinner.—**morn′ing=sick″ness,** *n.* Nausea occurring in the early part of the day, as a characteristic symptom in the first months of pregnancy.—**morn′ing=star′,** *n.* [Cf. G. *morgenstern.*] An old form of weapon consisting of a ball of metal, usually set with spikes, either mounted upon a long handle or staff or slung to one by a thong or chain. See also *morning star*, under *morning, a.*—**morn′ing-tide,** *n.* Morning. [Now poetic.]

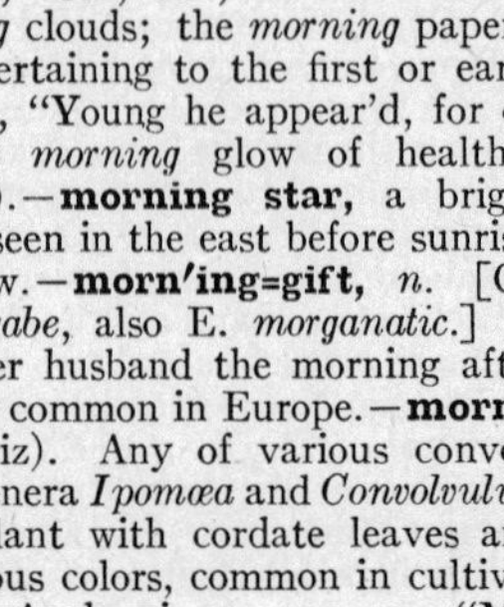
Morning-star; beginning of 15th century.

Mo-ro (mō′rō), *n.*; pl. *-ros* (-rōz). [Sp., a Moor.] A member of any of various tribes of Mohammedan Malays in the southern Philippine Islands; also, the language of these people.

mo-roc-co (mǫ-rok′ō), *n.*; pl. *moroccos* (-ōz). [From *Morocco*, country and city in northwestern Africa.] A fine leather made from goatskins tanned with sumac, orig. in Morocco; hence, any leather made in imitation of this.

mor-o-graph (môr′ǫ-gráf), *n.* [L. *mors*, death: see *-graph.*] A device invented by Sir Jagadis Chandra Bose (born 1858), of India, for observing and recording the death-movements of plants and thus establishing the instant of death, by greatly magnifying the actual movements. Cf. *crescograph.*

mo-ron (mō′ron), *n.* [Gr. μωρός, dull, foolish.] A person of arrested intellectual development whose mentality corresponds to that of a normal child from 8 to 12 years of age.—**mo-ron-i-ty** (mǫ-ron′i-ti), *n.* The condition of being a moron.

mo-rose (mǫ-rōs′), *a.* [L. *morosus*, < *mos* (*mor-*), manner: cf. *moral.*] Gloomily or sullenly ill-humored, as persons, the disposition or mood, aspect, etc. (as, "A *morose*, almost a malignant, scowl blackened his features": C. Brontë's "Jane Eyre," xv.); also, harsh, as doctrines.—**mo-rose′ly,** *adv.*—**mo-rose′ness, mo-ros′i-ty** (-ros′i-ti), *n.*

-morph. Noun termination from Gr. μορφή, form, as in *allomorph, isomorph, pseudomorph.*

Mor-pheus (môr′fūs, commonly môr′fē-us), *n.* [L. (first in Ovid), < Gr. μορφή, form, in allusion to the forms seen in dreams.] The god of dreams.—**Mor′phe-an** (-fē-ạn), *a.*

mor-phi-a (môr′fi-ä), *n.* Same as *morphine.*

mor-phic (môr′fik), *a.* [Gr. μορφή, form.] In *biol.*, of or pertaining to form.

-morphic. Adjective termination from Gr. μορφή, form, as in *automorphic, metamorphic.*

mor-phine (môr′fin or -fēn), *n.* [F. *morphine*, < L. *Morpheus:* see *Morpheus.*] A bitter crystalline alkaloid, the most important narcotic principle of opium, used in medicine (usually in the form of a sulphate or other salt) to dull pain, induce sleep, etc.—**mor′phin-ism,** *n.* In *pathol.*, a morbid condition induced by the habitual use of morphine; also, the habit inducing it.—**mor″phi-no-ma′ni-a** (-fi-nǫ-mā′ni-ä), *n.* In *pathol.*, uncontrollable craving for morphine.—**mor″phi-no-ma′ni-ac** (-ak), *n.*

mor-pho-log-ic, mor-pho-log-i-cal (môr-fǫ-loj′ik, -i-kạl), *a.* Of or pertaining to morphology; relating to form; structural.—**mor-pho-log′i-cal-ly,** *adv.*

mor-phol-o-gy (môr-fol′ǫ-ji), *n.* [G. *morphologie*, < Gr. μορφή, form, + -λογία, < λέγειν, speak.] The science of form; specif., that branch of biology which deals with the form and structure of animals and plants, without regard to functions; also, that branch of the study of language which deals with the form of words as affected by inflection, derivation, etc.—**mor-phol′o-gist,** *n.*

mor-phon (môr′fon), *n.* [G., < Gr. μορφή, form.] In *biol.*, a unit or individual which is morphologically or structurally independent, as contrasted with one (a *bion*) which is only functionally or physiologically independent: a term embracing forms ranging from the plastid to the compound organism.

-morphous. [Gr. -μορφος, < μορφή, form.] A termination of adjectives having reference to form, as *anthropomorphous, homœomorphous, rhizomorphous.*

mor-rhu-ol (mor′ǫ-ol or -ōl), *n.* [NL. *Morrhua*, the cod genus of fishes, + L. *oleum*, oil.] A pungent, partly crystalline oily principle extracted from cod-liver oil, containing phosphorus, iodine, and bromine.

mor′rice, mor′rice=dance, etc. See *morris*[1], etc.

mor-ris[1] (mor′is), *n.* Same as *morris-dance.*

mor-ris[2] (mor′is), *n.* [Corruption of *merels*, < OF. *merel* (F. *méreau*), counter, token, quoit.] An old game played between two persons, each having an equal number of pins or counters, often nine ('nine men's morris' or 'ninepenny morris'), which were placed at the angles of a certain figure traced on a board or on the ground, and moved alternately as at checkers; also, the board or ground on which the game was played.

Mor-ris (mor′is) **chair.** [Said to have been devised by William *Morris* (1834–96).] A kind of arm-chair with an adjustable back.

mor-ris=dance (mor′is-dàns), *n.* [= *Moorish dance.*] A picturesque dance performed by persons in costume, often representing personages of the Robin Hood legend, as Maid Marian and Friar Tuck, formerly common in England, esp. in the May Day festivities.—**mor′ris=dan″cer,** *n.*

mor-ris=pike (mor′is-pīk), *n.* [Appar. = *Moorish pike.*] A kind of pike (weapon) formerly in use.

mor-ro (mor′ō), *n.* [Sp., something round.] A round hill, hillock, or promontory.

mor-row (mor′ō), *n.* [ME. *morwe*, for *morwen*, E. *morn.*] Morning, as the beginning or first part of the day (archaic: as, to bid one good *morrow*); also, the day next after this or after some other particular day or night (as, "Ye know not what shall be on the *morrow*," Jas. iv. 14; "The flight and carnage . . . went on through the night and the *morrow*," Green's "Short Hist. of the Eng. People," vi. 2: cf. *to-morrow*); hence, the time immediately following a particular event, etc. (as, on the *morrow* of a disastrous war).

morse[1] (môrs), *n.* [OF. *mors,* < L. *morsus,* bite, catch (of a buckle, etc.), < *mordere,* bite.] The clasp or fastening of a cope or the like, often made of gold or silver and set with jewels.

morse[2] (môrs), *n.* [Prob. from Lapp.] The walrus.

Morse[3] (môrs), *n.* The Morse alphabet, or telegraphy or a telegram by means of it, or the apparatus used.—**Morse**[3], *v. t.* or *i.*; *Morsed, Morsing.* To transmit or communicate by means of the Morse alphabet.

Morse (môrs) **al'pha-bet.** [From S. F. B. *Morse* (1791–1872), American inventor.] A system of dots, dashes, and spaces, or the corresponding sounds or the like, used in telegraphy and signaling to represent the letters of the alphabet, numerals, etc.

mor-sel (môr'sl), *n.* [OF. *morsel* (F. *morceau*), dim. of *mors,* a bite, < L. *morsum,* pp. neut. of *mordere,* bite.] A bite, mouthful, or small portion of food or the like (as, "having not eaten a *morsel* for some hours," Swift's "Gulliver's Travels," i. 1; "Take a *morsel* of our bread and cheese," Hawthorne's "Blithedale Romance," x.); a bit or dish of food of specified character (as, a dainty *morsel;* "On these herbs . . . Feed first; on each beast next . . . No homely *morsels,*" Milton's "Paradise Lost," x. 605); fig., something to be enjoyed, disposed of, or endured (as, "I was A *morsel* for a monarch," Shakspere's "Antony and Cleopatra," i. 5. 31; to find a person a tough *morsel;* this decision was a bitter *morsel*); also, a small piece, quantity, or amount of anything (as, a *morsel* of chalk or of land; a tiny *morsel* of humanity; not a *morsel* of conscience or pity); a scrap; a bit.

mort[1] (môrt), *n.* [OF. F. *mort,* death, < L. *mors* (*mort-*): see *mortal.*] Death†; hence, in *hunting,* a note sounded on the horn at the death of the deer.

mort[2] (môrt), *n.* [Origin uncertain.] A great quantity or number: as, a *mort* of money or of trouble; a *mort* of folks. [Prov. Eng.]

mort[3] (môrt), *n.* [Origin unknown.] A woman or girl; also, a prostitute. [Beggars' and thieves' slang.]

mor-tal (môr'tạl). [OF. F. *mortel,* < L. *mortalis,* < *mors* (*mort-*), death, < *mori,* die; akin to Gr. *μορτός,* mortal, Skt. *mar-,* die, and E. *murder.*] **I.** *a.* Liable or subject to death (as, all *mortal* creatures); hence, of or pertaining to man as subject to death (as, this *mortal* life; *mortal* powers); human (as, "past all *mortal* aid": Marryat's "King's Own," xvii.); belonging to this world (as, "The Bard . . . gazed upon the object of his fear as if he had looked upon something not *mortal*": Scott's "Castle Dangerous," v.); also, pertaining to death (as, *mortal* throes; the *mortal* hour); involving spiritual death (opposed to *venial:* as, a *mortal* sin); also, causing death, or fatal (as, a *mortal* disease, wound, or blow); to the death (as, *mortal* combat); deadly or implacable (as, a *mortal* enemy; *mortal* hatred); dire, grievous, or bitter (as, in *mortal* fear; to give *mortal* offense); hence, long and wearisome (colloq.: as, three *mortal* hours); extreme, or very great (colloq.: as, in a *mortal* hurry); also, possible or conceivable (colloq.: as, of no *mortal* use); also, drunk (for *mortal drunk,* dead drunk: Sc. and prov. Eng.). **II.** *n.* A being subject to death; a human being: as, "What fools these *mortals* be!" (Shakspere's "Midsummer Night's Dream," iii. 2. 115).—**mor'tal,** *adv.* Extremely; exceedingly: as, *mortal* hard; *mortal* angry. [Prov. or colloq.] —**mor-tal'i-ty** (-tal'i-ti), *n.* [OF. *mortalite* (F. *mortalité*), < L. *mortalitas.*] The condition of being mortal, or subject to death; mortal character, nature, or existence; also, mortal beings collectively; humanity (as, "Young Sir Harry is about as puny and feeble a little bit of *mortality* as I ever saw": Mrs. Stowe's "Oldtown Folks," xxxviii.); also, death (as, "How gladly would I meet *Mortality* my sentence": Milton's "Paradise Lost," x. 776); now, usually, death or destruction on a large scale, or great extent or frequency of death, as from war, plague, famine, earthquake, etc.; also, relative frequency of death, or death-rate, as in a district or community (as, statistics of *mortality;* a place or a year of low *mortality*).—**mor'tal-ly,** *adv.* In a mortal manner; so as to cause death (as, *mortally* wounded); implacably (as, *mortally* hostile); grievously or bitterly (as, *mortally* offended); extremely or exceedingly (colloq.: as, *mortally* ugly).

mor-tar[1] (môr'tạr), *n.* [AS. *mortere* (vessel) and OF. F. *mortier* (vessel, cannon), < L. *mortarium,* vessel in which substances are pounded, or one in which mortar (see *mortar*[2]) is made.] A vessel of hard material, having a bowl-shaped cavity, in which drugs, etc., are reduced to powder with a pestle; hence, any of various mechanical appliances in which substances are pounded or ground; also, a cannon short in proportion to its bore, for throwing shells at high angles; hence, some similar contrivance, as for throwing pyrotechnic bombs or a life-line.

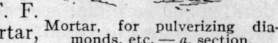

Mortar, for pulverizing diamonds, etc. — *a,* section.

mor-tar[2] (môr'tạr), *n.* [OF. F. *mortier,* < L. *mortarium,* mortar, also a vessel in which it is made: see *mortar*[1].] A material used for binding together stones or the like into a compact mass; esp., a mixture of quicklime, sand, and water (ordinary mortar, or 'lime mortar') which hardens in the air and is used for binding bricks, etc., together, or a mixture of cement, sand or the like, and water ('cement mortar').—**mor'tar**[2], *v. t.* To plaster or fix with mortar.—**mor'tar=board,** *n.* A board, commonly square, used by masons to hold mortar; also, a kind of academic cap with a close-fitting crown surmounted by a stiff, flat, cloth-covered square piece (colloq.).

mort-cloth (môrt'klôth), *n.* [See *mort*[1].] A funeral pall. [Chiefly Sc.]

mort-gage (môr'gạj), *n.* [OF. *morgage* (F. *mort-gage*), < *mort,* dead, + *gage,* pledge, E. *gage*[1].] In *law,* a conditional conveyance of property to a creditor as security, as for the repayment of money; also, the deed by which such a transaction is effected; also, the rights conferred by it, or the state of the property conveyed. Also fig.—**mort'gage,** *v. t.;* *-gaged, -gaging.* To convey or place (property, esp. houses or land) under a mortgage; fig., to pledge (as, to *mortgage* one's future for a present advantage; "He would not *mortgage* an inch of his independence by asking a favour from a minister," Bulwer-Lytton's "Caxtons," vii. 2).—**mort-ga-gee'** (-gạ-jē'), *n.* One to whom property is mortgaged. —**mort'ga-ger** (-gạ-jėr), *n.* One who mortgages property. Also **mort'ga-gor** (-gạ-jọr), **mort'ga-geor** (-gạ-jọr).

mor'tice, *n.* and *v.* See *mortise.*

mor-ti-cian (môr-tish'ạn), *n.* [L. *mors* (*mort-*), death, with termination as in E. *physician.*] An undertaker.

mor-tif-er-ous (môr-tif'ẹ-rus), *a.* [L. *mortiferus, mortifer,* < *mors* (*mort-*), death, + *ferre,* bear.] Death-bringing; deadly.

mor-ti-fi-ca-tion (môr"ti-fi-kā'shọn), *n.* [OF. F. *mortification,* < LL. *mortificatio(n-).*] The act of mortifying, or the resulting state; subjection of the passions, etc., by abstinence or other discipline; humiliation in feeling, as by some wound to pride; also, a cause or source of such humiliation; in *pathol.,* the death of one part of an animal body while the rest is alive; gangrene; necrosis.

mor-ti-fy (môr'ti-fī), *v.;* *-fied, -fying.* [OF. F. *mortifier,* < LL. *mortificare,* < *mortificus,* causing death, < L. *mors* (*mort-*), death, + *facere,* make.] **I.** *tr.* To kill† (a person, plant, etc.); deaden†, or render insensible†; also, to bring (the body, passions, etc.) into subjection by abstinence, ascetic discipline, or rigorous austerities (as, "*Mortify* therefore your members which are upon the earth," Col. iii. 5; "*Mortify* Your flesh . . . with scourges and with thorns," Tennyson's "St. Simeon Stylites," 176); also, to humiliate in feeling, as by a severe wound to the pride or self-complacency (as, "He was not a little *mortified* to find his present returned": Smollett's "Humphry Clinker," June 12); wound (the pride, etc.) in a humiliating way; in *pathol.,* to affect with gangrene or necrosis. **II.** *intr.* To practise mortification or disciplinary austerities; in *pathol.,* to undergo mortification, or become gangrened or necrosed (as, "We had . . . their fingers and toes to thaw, and take care of, lest they should *mortify* and fall off": Defoe's "Robinson Crusoe," ii. 16).—**mor'ti-fi-er** (-fī-ėr), *n.*—**mor'ti-fy-ing-ly,** *adv.*

mor-tise (môr'tis), *n.* [OF. F. *mortaise;* origin unknown.] A cavity in one piece of wood, etc., for receiving a corresponding projection (*tenon*) on another piece, so as to form a joint.—**mor'tise,** *v. t.*; *-tised, -tising.* To fasten by or as by a mortise; fig., to join securely; also, to cut a mortise in.

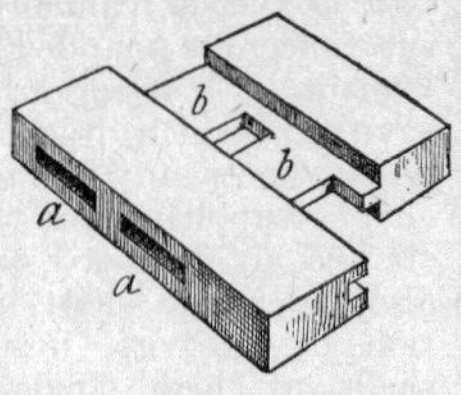

Mortise-joint.—*a, a,* mortises; *b, b,* tenons.

mort-main (môrt'mān), *n.* [OF. *mortemain* (F. *mainmorte*), 'dead hand,' < L. *mortua*, fem. of *mortuus*, dead, + *manus*, hand.] In *law*, the condition of lands or tenements held without right of alienation, as by an ecclesiastical corporation; inalienable possession.

mor-tu-a-ry (môr'tū-ā-ri). [L. *mortuarius*, < *mortuus*, dead, pp. of *mori*, die: see *mortal.*] **I.** *a.* Of or pertaining to the burial of the dead; also, pertaining to or connected with death. **II.** *n.*; pl. *-ries* (-riz). A customary gift formerly claimed by and due to the incumbent of a parish in England from the estate of a deceased parishioner; also, a place for the temporary reception of the dead; a dead-house.

mor-u-la (mor'ö-lą), *n.*; pl. *-læ* (-lē). [NL., dim. of L. *morum*, mulberry.] In *embryol.*, the spherical mass of cells forming the embryo of a metazoan just after the segmentation of the ovum and before the formation of a blastula.—**mor'u-lar** (-lär), *a.*—**mor-u-la'tion** (-lā'shon), *n.* The formation of a morula.

mo-sa-ic[1] (mō-zā'ik), *a.* [F. *mosaïque*, < ML. *mosaicus*, *musaicus* (LL. *musivus*), lit. 'of the Muses,' artistic, < Gr. Μοῦσα, E. *Muse*[1].] Made of small pieces of stone, glass, etc., of different colors, inlaid to form a design; pertaining to work so made; also, resembling such work; composed of diverse elements combined.—**mosaic gold,** stannic sulphide, a yellowish compound used in making gilding preparations; also, ormolu.—**mosaic map,** a map made by piecing together topographical photographs taken from an aircraft.—**mo-sa'ic**[1], *n.* Mosaic work; the process of producing it; also, a piece of mosaic work; also, something resembling such work in composition; something composed of diverse elements combined; sometimes, a mosaic map.—**mo-sa'ic**[1], *v.t.*; *-icked, -icking.* To combine as in mosaic; also, to form like mosaic; also, to decorate with mosaics.

Mosaic.—Detail from apse of the Basilica of Torcello, near Venice; 12th century.

Mo-sa-ic[2] (mō-zā'ik), *a.* Of or pertaining to Moses, the Hebrew lawgiver, or the writings and institutions attributed to him.—**Mosaic law,** the ancient law of the Hebrews, attributed to Moses and contained chiefly in the Pentateuch; also, the part of the Scripture containing this law.

mo-sa-i-cist (mō-zā'i-sist), *n.* A maker of or a dealer in mosaics.

mo-sa-saur (mō'sa-sâr), *n.* [NL. *mosasaurus*, < L. *Mosa*, the river Meuse (where, near Maastricht, the first mosasaur was found), + Gr. σαῦρος, lizard.] Any of the large marine reptiles constituting the extinct genus *Mosasaurus*. Also **mo-sa-sau'rus** (-sâ'rus).

mos-cha-tel (mos-ka-tel'), *n.* [F. *moscatelle*, < It. *moscatella*, < *moscato*, < ML. *muscatus*, musky: see *muscat.*] A small, inconspicuous plant, *Adoxa moschatellina*, having greenish or yellowish flowers with a musky odor.

Mo-selle (mō-zel'), *n.* A white wine produced along the river Moselle, a left-bank tributary of the Rhine.

mo-sey (mō'zi), *v. i.*; *-seyed, -seying.* [Cf. *vamose.*] To move or go along or away; make off; decamp: as, "I'll *mosey* along now" (Mark Twain's "Huckleberry Finn," xxxv.). [Slang, U. S.]

mosk, *n.* See *mosque.*

Mos-lem (moz'lem or mos'-). [Ar. *muslim*, 'one professing submission' (Ar. *islām*): see *Islam.*] **I.** *n.*; pl. *Moslems*, sometimes *Moslem.* A follower of Mohammed; an orthodox Mohammedan. **II.** *a.* Mohammedan.—**Mos-lem'ic,** *a.*—**Mos'lem-ism,** *n.* Mohammedanism.—**Mos'lem-ize,** *v. t.*; *-ized, -izing.* To Mohammedanize.

mosque (mosk), *n.* [F. *mosquée*, < It. *moschea*, < Ar. *masjid*, mosque, < *sajada*, prostrate one's self, worship.] A Mohammedan temple or place of worship: as, "A Mohammedan *mosque* is as much a place of rest and refuge as of prayer . . . the houseless Arab may take shelter there by night or day" (Amelia B. Edwards's "Thousand Miles up the Nile," ii.).

Mosque of Mehemet Ali, Cairo.

mos-qui-to (mos-kē'tō), *n.*; pl. *-toes* or *-tos* (-tōz). [Sp., dim. of *mosca*, < L. *musca*, a fly.] Any of various dipterous insects of the family *Culicidæ* (genera *Culex*, *Anopheles*, etc.), the females of which have a long proboscis by means of which they puncture the skin of animals (including man) and draw blood, some species transmitting certain diseases, as malaria and yellow fever; also, any of the boats or vessels comprising a mosquito fleet.—**mosquito fleet,** a fleet composed of comparatively small craft; esp., an assemblage of speedy armed motor-boats, etc., used to chase and destroy submarines, do scout duty, etc.—**mos-qui'to=bar,** *n.* A mosquito-net.—**mos-qui'to=net,** *n.* A screen, curtain, or canopy of net, gauze, or the like, for keeping out mosquitoes.—**mos-qui'to=net"ting,** *n.* A fabric for mosquito-nets.

Mosquito. A British swift medium bomber (De Havilland).

moss (môs), *n.* [AS. *mos*, bog, = D. *mos*, moss, = G. *moos*, bog, moss; akin to L. *muscus*, moss, F. *mousse* (see *mousse*), and E. *mire.*] A swamp or bog, esp. a peat-bog (chiefly Sc. and north. Eng.: as, "With anxious eye he wander'd o'er Mountain and meadow, *moss* and moor," Scott's "Lady of the Lake," i. 5); also, any of the small, herbaceous cryptogamous plants, or bryophytes, of the class *Musci*, with leafy, often tufted stems, growing in matted masses in bogs, on stones or trees, etc.; a growth of such plants; also, any of various similar plants, as certain lichens (see *Iceland moss*), the lycopods (see *club-moss*), etc.—**Florida moss.** See entry in alphabetical place.—**Irish moss,** carrageen.—**moss,** *v. t.* To cover with a growth of moss: as, "an oak, whose boughs were *moss'd* with age" (Shakspere's "As You Like It," iv. 3. 105).—**moss'=ag'ate,** *n.* A kind of agate containing brown or black moss-like dendritic markings.—**moss'back,** *n.* A person attached to antiquated notions; an extreme conservative: as, "He says Major Garnet means well, only he's a *moss-back*" (G. W. Cable's "John March, Southerner," xx.). [Slang, U. S.]

moss-bunk-er (môs'bung"kėr), *n.* [D. *marsbanker.*] The menhaden (fish).

moss=grown (môs'grōn), *a.* Overgrown with moss: as, "*moss-grown* towers" (Shakspere's "1 Henry IV.," iii. 1. 33).

moss=hag (môs′hag), *n.* [See *hag*[3].] A hollow or pit in a bog; a hole or pit from which peat has been dug: as, "The Men of the *Moss-Hags*" (the title of a novel by S. R. Crockett). [Sc.]

moss-i-ness (môs′i-nes), *n.* Mossy state.

moss=pink (môs′pingk′), *n.* A species of phlox, *Phlox subulata*, of the eastern U. S., with showy pink to purple flowers.

moss=rose (môs′rōz′), *n.* A cultivated variety of rose with a moss-like growth on the calyx and stem.

moss=troop-er (môs′trö″pėr), *n.* One of a class of marauders who infested the mosses or bogs of the border between England and Scotland during the 17th century; hence, any marauder, raider, or brigand (as, "The result . . . was augmented audacity on the part of the *moss-troopers* of Connecticut": Irving's "Knickerbocker's New York," v. 3).—**moss′=troop″ing,** *a.*

moss-y (môs′i), *a.*; compar. *mossier*, superl. *mossiest.* Marshy (Sc. and prov. Eng.); also, overgrown with or abounding in moss (as, "a wood of *mossy* distorted trees": Parkman's "Oregon Trail," xvii.); hence, covered with a moss-like growth; appearing as if covered with moss; also, resembling moss.

most (mōst). [AS. *mǣst* = G. *meist* = Icel. *mestr* = Goth. *maists*, most, greatest; superl. from the same stem as E. *more*.] **I.** *a. superl.* Greatest, as in size or extent (now chiefly in the phrase 'the most part'); also, in the greatest quantity, amount, measure, degree, or number (as, *most*, or the *most*, money; of *most* advantage or use; *most* intensity; *most* votes: used as the superlative of *much* and *many*, with the comparative *more*); often, in the majority of instances (as, *most* exercise is beneficial; *most* men would say so). **II.** *n.* The greatest quantity, amount, or degree; the utmost; also, the greatest number or the majority of a class specified, or the greatest number or the majority of persons (construed as *pl.*).—**most,** *adv. superl.* In or to the greatest extent or degree (in this sense much used before adjectives and adverbs, and regularly before those of more than two syllables, to form superlative phrases having the same force and effect as the superlative degree formed by the termination *-est*: as, *most* rapid, *most* curious, *most* wisely, *most* fittingly: cf. *more, adv.*); also, almost or nearly (colloq.: as, "I felt so lonesome I *most* wished I was dead," Mark Twain's "Huckleberry Finn," i.).

-most. [Orig. < AS. *-mest*, a double superl. suffix, < *-ma* + *-est*, both forming superlatives; later associated with E. *most*.] A suffix serving to form superlatives of adjectives and adverbs, as in *foremost, inmost, utmost.*

most-ly (mōst′li), *adv.* For the most part; chiefly; in the main: as, the work is *mostly* done; many persons, *mostly* men; "All afternoon we sat together, *mostly* in silence" (Stevenson's "Master of Ballantrae," x.).

mot[1] (mot), *n.* [OF. F. *mot*, word, saying, note of a horn, etc., = It. *motto* (see *motto*), < L. *muttum*, a mutter, grunt.] A word†; also, a motto†; also, a note on a horn, bugle, or the like (obs. or archaic: as, "Three *mots* on this bugle will . . . bring round, at our need, a jolly band of yonder honest yeomen," Scott's "Ivanhoe," xl.).

mot[2] (mō), *n.* [F.: see *mot*[1].] A saying; a pithy or witty remark.

mote[1] (mōt), *n.* Obs. or archaic form of *moot.*

mote[2] (mōt), *v.* [AS. *mōt*, pres.: see *must*[1].] May or might (archaic: as, "Was never knight on ground *mote* be with him compared," Thomson's "Castle of Indolence," ii. 9); also, must† (as, "At last their wayes so fell, that they *mote* part": Spenser's "Faerie Queene," iii. 3. 62).

mote[3] (mōt), *n.* [AS. *mot.*] A particle or speck of dust (as, "thikke as *motes* in the sonne-beem," Chaucer's "Tale of the Wyf of Bathe," 12; to have a *mote* in one's eye, see Mat. vii. 3–5); hence, any small piece of extraneous matter; any very small thing.—**mot-ed** (mō′ted), *a.* Full of motes: as, "the *moted* sunlight" (Whittier's "Witch's Daughter").—**mote′less,** *a.* Free from motes.

mo-tet (mọ-tet′), *n.* [OF. F. *motet*, dim. of *mot*, word: see *mot*[1].] In *music*, a vocal composition in polyphonic style, on a Biblical or similar prose text, intended for use in a church service.

moth (môth), *n.*; pl. *moths* (môᴛʜz). [AS. *moththe* = D. *mot* = G. *motte* = Icel. *motti*, moth.] Any of certain small lepidopterous insects of the genus *Tinea*, whose larvæ feed on clothes, fur, etc. ('clothes-moth'); any insect destructive to woolens, etc.; in *entom.*, any of the group (sometimes classed as the suborder *Heterocera*) of lepidopters to which the clothes-moths belong, its members being distinguished from the butterflies by being (mainly) nocturnal or crepuscular, and by usually not having their antennæ clubbed.—**moth′=eat″en,** *a.* Eaten or damaged by or as by moths.

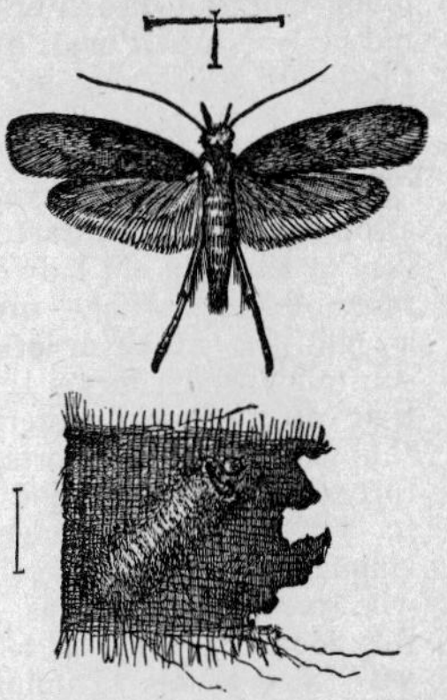
Clothes-moth (*Tinea pellionella*), with piece of cloth attacked by larva. (Cross and line show natural sizes.)

moth-er[1] (muᴛʜ′ėr), *n.* [= MD. *moeder* (D. *moer*) = G. *mutter*; perhaps the same word as *mother*[2].] Dregs†; scum†; now, a stringy, mucilaginous substance formed on the surface of a liquid undergoing acetous fermentation (as wine changing to vinegar), and consisting of the various bacteria which cause such fermentation ('mother of vinegar').

moth-er[2] (muᴛʜ′ėr), *n.* [AS. *mōdor* = D. *moeder* = G. *mutter* = Icel. *mōdhir*, mother; akin to L. *mater*, Gr. *μήτηρ*, Skt. *mātar-*, mother.] She who gives birth to a child; a female parent; one's nearest female ancestor; also, any female ancestor (now rare); also, a mother-in-law, stepmother, or adoptive mother (colloq.); fig., something that gives rise to, or exercises protecting care over, something else (as, "Necessity, *mother* of invention!" Wycherley's "Love in a Wood," iii. 3; "France, the *mother* of ideas," Besant's "Coligny," ii.; *Mother* Nature; *Mother* Church); also, a woman looked upon as a mother, or exercising control or authority like that of a mother; the head or superior of a female religious community; also, a term of familiar address for an old or elderly woman; also, the qualities characteristic of a mother, or maternal affection (as, "Straight all the *mother* in her soul awakes": Pope's tr. Homer's "Odyssey," xi.); also, the womb†; also, hysteria (obs. or archaic: as, "She is . . . much subject to fits of the *mother*," Smollett's "Humphry Clinker," July 18).—**Mother of God,** a designation of the Virgin Mary.—**Mother's Day,** a day for acts of grateful affection by each person toward his mother, or for loving remembrance of her, designed to deepen and perpetuate all family ties: observed annually on the second Sunday in May (in schools, on the Friday preceding).—**moth′er**[2], *a.* That is a mother (as, a *mother* bird); also, bearing a relation like that of a mother, as in giving origin or rise, or in exercising protective care (as, a *mother* plant or cell; the *mother* city, or metropolis, of an ancient Greek colony); also, pertaining to or characteristic of a mother (as, *mother* love); derived from one's mother, or native (cf. *mother-tongue, mother-wit*).—**moth′er**[2], *v. t.* To be the mother of; give origin or rise to; also, to care for or protect as a mother does; also, to acknowledge one's self the mother of; acknowledge one's self the author of, or assume as one's own; also, to provide with a mother; also, to attribute the maternity of (a child) to a woman; fig., to ascribe the authorship of or responsibility for (with *on* or *upon*).—**Moth′er Ca-rey's** (kā′riz) **chick′en.** Any of various small petrels, esp. the stormy petrel.—**moth′er=coun′try,** *n.* A country in relation to its colonies or its natives.—**moth′er-craft,** *n.* The art of fulfilling the duties of a mother, as in the household; the knowledge and skill proper to a mother with reference to her children and home.—**moth′er-hood** (-hůd), *n.* The state of being a mother; maternity; also, the qualities or spirit of a mother.—**Moth′er Hub-bard** (hub′ạrd). [From the old woman in a familiar nursery rime.] A kind of full, loose gown worn by women.—**moth′er=in=law″,** *n.*; pl. *mothers-*. The mother of one's husband or wife; also, a stepmother (colloq., Eng.: as, " 'Wy, Sammy,' said the father, 'I han't seen you for two year and better.' 'Nor more you have, old codger,' replied the son. 'How's *mother-in-law?*' " Dickens's "Pickwick Papers," xx.).—**moth′er-land** (-land), *n.* One's

(variable) ḑ as d or j, ş as s or sh, ţ as t or ch, ẓ as z or zh; *o*, F. cloche; ü, F. menu; ċh, Sc. loch; ṅ, F. bonbon; **′**, primary accent; **″**, secondary accent; †, obsolete; <, from; +, and; =, equals. See also lists at beginning of book.

native country, or the land of one's ancestors; fatherland. —**moth'er-less,** *a.* Having no mother; destitute of a living mother.—**moth'er-li-ness,** *n.* The quality of being motherly.—**moth'er=li'quor,** *n.* In *chem.* and *phar.*, the liquid which remains after the removal of crystallizing substances from a solution.—**moth'er-ly,** *a.* Pertaining to, characteristic of, or befitting a mother (as, *motherly* affection; "the Church's *motherly* care," Wiseman's "Fabiola," ii. 18); also, having the character, appearance, etc., of a mother (as, "a *motherly* old lady": Dickens's "Oliver Twist," xii.); resembling a mother.—**moth'er-ly,** *adv.* In the manner of a mother.—**moth'er=of=pearl',** *n.* A hard, iridescent substance which forms the inner layer of certain shells, as that of the pearl-oyster; nacre.—**moth'er=ship,** *n.* A ship which guards, escorts, or acts as a base for, one or more torpedo-boats, submarines, or the like.—**moth'er=tongue',** *n.* One's native language; also, a language to which other languages owe their origin.—**moth'er=wit',** *n.* Native wit; common sense: as, "*Kath.* Where did you study all this goodly speech? *Pet.* It is extempore, from my *mother-wit*" (Shakspere's "Taming of the Shrew," ii. 1. 265).

moth-er-y (muᴛʜ'ėr-i), *a.* [See *mother*[1].] Containing, consisting of, or resembling mother, as of vinegar.

moth-y (môth'i), *a.* Containing moths; moth-eaten.

mo-tif (mō̤-tēf', F. mo-tēf), *n.* [F.: see *motive.*] A subject or theme for development or treatment, as in art, literature, or music; a dominant idea or feature; also, a distinctive figure in a design, as of lace; a separate ornament of lace, embroidery, or other trimming.

mo-tile (mō'til). [L. *movere* (pp. *motus*), E. *move.*] **I.** *a.* In *biol.*, moving, or capable of moving, spontaneously: as, *motile* cells or spores. **II.** *n.* In *psychol.*, one in whose mind motor images are predominant or especially distinct. —**mo-til-i-ty** (mō̤-til'i-ti), *n.*

mo-tion (mō'sho̤n), *n.* [OF. F. *motion*, < L. *motio(n-)*, < *movere*, E. *move.*] The process of moving, or changing place or position; manner of moving; a movement; also, power of movement, as of the body; often, the act or manner of moving the body in walking, etc. (as, grace of *motion*); gait; also, a bodily movement, or change of posture; a gesture; also, commotion or agitation; an irregular movement; also, in general, action, activity, or active operation (as, to set an enterprise in *motion*); also, *pl.*, movements, actions, or activities, as of a person, or of an army in the field (now rare: as, "Mr. Glossin was well aware that such a hint was of power sufficient to decide the *motions* of his . . . colleague," Scott's "Guy Mannering," xliii.); also, *sing.*, a suggestion or proposal; now, chiefly or only, a proposal formally made to a deliberative assembly (as, to make a *motion* to adjourn); also, an inward prompting or impulse, or an inclination (now chiefly in 'of one's own motion,' that is, of one's own accord); also, a puppet-show† (see Shakspere's "Winter's Tale," iv. 3. 103); a puppet† (see Shakspere's "Two Gentlemen of Verona," ii. 1. 100); in *music*, melodic progression, as the change of a voice-part from one pitch to another; in *law*, an application made to a court or judge for an order, ruling, or the like; in *mech.*, a piece of mechanism with a particular action or function.—**mo'tion,** *v.* **I.** *tr.* To direct by a significant motion, or gesture, as with the hand (as, to *motion* a person to a seat); also, to propose†. **II.** *intr.* To make a significant motion, or gesture, as with the hand, for the purpose of directing or guiding (as, to *motion* to a person); also, to make a proposal†.—**mo'tion-al,** *a.* Of or pertaining to motion; characterized by particular motions, as certain diseases.—**mo'tion-less,** *a.* Without, or incapable of, motion: as, "Some sat on horseback, *motionless* as equestrian statues" (Parkman's "Oregon Trail," xi.).—**mo'tion-less-ness,** *n.*—**mo'tion=pic'ture,** *n. Pl.*, moving pictures; *sing.*, a moving picture; a photoplay.

mo-ti-vate (mō'ti-vāt), *v. t.*; *-vated, -vating.* [Cf. F. *motiver.*] To provide with a motive or motives.—**mo-ti-va'tion** (-vā'sho̤n), *n.*

mo-tive (mō'tiv), *a.* [OF. *motif*, adj. (as n., OF. F. *motif*), < ML. *motivus*, < L. *movere*, E. *move.*] Causing, or tending to cause, motion; having the power of initiating motion; pertaining to motion; also, prompting to action; constituting a motive or motives.—**motive power,** any power used to impart motion; a source of mechanical energy; a device for imparting motion, as a motor or a locomotive; in *railroading*, the locomotives of a road collectively (as, superintendent of *motive power*).—**mo'tive,** *n.* Something that prompts a person to act in a certain way or that determines volition (as, "The unjust punishment which he had received had been the *motive* of his desertion," Marryat's "King's Own," i.; "The poor savages . . . had merely gathered together through *motives* of curiosity," Irving's "Captain Bonneville," xxxviii.); a moving consideration or reason; an incentive; often, the object one has in any action (as, his *motive* was the good of all); sometimes, a person who prompts or induces† (as, "Nor are they living Who were the *motives* that you first went out": Shakspere's "Timon of Athens," v. 4. 27); also, in art, literature, and music, a motif. —**mo'tive,** *v. t.*; *-tived, -tiving.* To provide with a motive; supply a motive for.—**mo'tive-less,** *a.* Without motive; objectless.—**mo-tiv-i-ty** (mō̤-tiv'i-ti), *n.* The power of initiating or producing motion.

mot-ley (mot'li). [ME. *motteley*; origin uncertain.] **I.** *a.* Being of different colors combined, or party-colored (as, "dressed in the *motley* garb that jesters wear": Longfellow's "King Robert of Sicily," 113); wearing a party-colored dress (as, "a *motley* fool": Shakspere's "As You Like It," ii. 7. 13); fig., exhibiting great diversity of elements, or heterogeneous (as, "A *motley* mixture! in long wigs, in bags, In silks, in crapes, in garters, and in rags": Pope's "Dunciad," ii. 21). **II.** *n.*; pl. *-leys* (-liz). Cloth of a mixed color†; also, a combination of different colors; a party-colored effect of color; fig., a heterogeneous assemblage; a medley; also, the motley or party-colored dress of the old-time professional fool or jester (as, "A worthy fool! *Motley*'s the only wear": Shakspere's "As You Like It," ii. 7. 34); hence, a fool or jester (obs. or archaic).—**mot'ley-ness,** *n.*

mot-mot (mot'mot), *n.* [Appar. imit. of the bird's note.] Any of the tropical and subtropical American birds constituting the family *Momotidæ*, the sawbills, related to the kingfishers, and having a serrate bill and chiefly greenish and bluish plumage.

Motmot (*Momotus cæruleiceps*).

mo-to-cy-cle (mō'tō̤-sī-kl), *n.* Same as *motor-cycle.*

mo-tom-e-ter (mō̤-tom'e-tėr), *n.* [L. *motus*, motion: see *-meter.*] A device for indicating the number of revolutions made by a shaft or the like.

mo-tor (mō'to̤r). [L., < *movere*, E. *move.*] **I.** *n.* One who or that which imparts motion; esp., a contrivance (as a steam-engine) which receives and modifies energy from some natural source in order to utilize it in driving machinery, etc.; a prime mover; specif., a machine for converting electric energy into mechanical energy, similar in construction to a dynamo, but working in a different manner, the entering current being made to produce a rotation of the armature or the field ('electric motor'); a comparatively small and powerful engine, esp. an internal-combustion engine in an automobile, motor-boat, or the like; also, a motor-car. **II.** *a.* Causing or imparting motion; also, pertaining to or operated by a motor; in *physiol.*, conveying an impulse that results or tends to result in motion, as a nerve; of or pertaining to such nerves; in *psychol.*, pertaining to or involving consciousness of action (as, *motor* images).—**mo'tor,** *v.* **I.** *intr.* To ride or travel in an automobile: as, "The two spent their time . . . *motoring* and walking on the Downs" (Galsworthy's "Patrician," ii. 12). **II.** *tr.* To convey in an automobile.—**mo'tor=boat,** *n.* A boat propelled by a motor on board, usually by a gasoline engine.—**mo′tor=boat″-ing,** *n.*—**mo′tor=bus,** *n.* A self-propelled bus, with a gasoline engine or the like.—**mo′tor-cade** (-kād), *n.* [+ *-cade* from *cavalcade.*] A procession or parade of motor-cars.—**mo′tor=car,** *n.* A car carrying its own source of motive power; esp., an automobile.—**mo′tor=cy″cle,** *n.* A bicycle, tricycle, or the like, propelled by a motor carried.—**mo′tor-drome** (-drōm), *n.* [+ *-drome.*] A rounded course or track, often rising at an angle or in a curve toward its outer edge, upon which automobile and motor-cycle races are run.—**mo′tor=gen′er-a-tor,** *n.* In *elect.*, an apparatus consisting of a combination of motor and dynamo, used to lower voltage, etc.—**mo-to-ri-al** (mō-tō′ri-al), *a.* Of or pertaining to motion or a motor nerve.—**mo′tor-ist,** *n.* One who uses an automobile, esp. habitually.—**mo′tor-ize** (-īz), *v. t.*; *-ized, -izing.* To furnish with a motor or motors, as vehicles; also, to supply with motor-driven vehicles in the place of horses and horse-drawn vehicles.—**mo″tor-i-za′tion** (-i-zā′shon), *n.*—**mo′tor-less,** *a.* Having no motor; without a motor: as, a *motorless* aircraft (see *gliding-machine*); *motorless* aviation.—**mo′tor-man** (-man), *n.*; pl. *-men.* One who operates a motor; esp., one who operates the motor of an electric car or electric locomotive on a railway.—**mo′to-ry** (-tō-ri), *a.* [LL. *motorius.*] Motor.

mot-tet-to (mot-tet′tō), *n.*; pl. *-ti* (-tē). [It.] A motet.

mot-tle (mot′l), *v. t.*; *-tled, -tling.* [From *motley.*] To diversify with spots or blotches of a different color or shade: as, "the gray stone parapet, *mottled* with the green and gold of innumerable mosses" (Mrs. H. Ward's "Robert Elsmere," vii.).—**mot′tle,** *n.* A diversifying spot or blotch of color; also, mottled coloring or pattern.—**mot′tled,** *p. a.* Spotted or blotched in coloring.—**mot′tling,** *n.* Mottled coloring.

mot-to (mot′ō), *n.*; pl. *mottoes* (-ōz). [It.: see *mot*[1].] A sentence, phrase, or word attached to or inscribed on anything as indicative of or appropriate to its purpose or character (as, the *motto* appended to a coat of arms); also, a maxim adopted as expressing one's guiding idea or principle; also, a short passage, usually a quotation, prefixed to a literary work or one of its parts as suggestive of the contents.—**mot′toed,** *a.* Inscribed with or bearing a motto.

mouch (möch), etc. See *mooch,* etc.

mou-chard (mö-shär), *n.* [F., < *mouche,* a fly, spy.] A police spy; an informer: as, "I think the fellow's a cursed *mouchard*—some Government spy" (Kingsley's "Alton Locke," xxxiii.).

mou-choir (mö-shwor), *n.* [F., < *moucher,* wipe the nose of, < L. *mucus,* E. *mucus.*] A handkerchief.

moue (mö), *n.* [F.: see *mow*[1].] A pouting grimace: as, "She pouted. The doctor could not help laughing at the sort of '*moue*' she made" (C. Brontë's "Villette," xiii.).

mouf-lon, mouf-flon (möf′lon), *n.* [F. *mouflon*; said to be from Sardinian name.] A wild sheep, *Ovis musimon,* inhabiting the mountainous regions of Sardinia, Corsica, etc., the male of which has large curving horns; also, any of various similar wild sheep.

mought (mout). Obs. or prov. preterit of *may*[1].

mouil-lé (mö-yā), *a.* [F., pp. of *mouiller,* wet, moisten: see *moil.*] Pronounced with a following *y* sound, as *l* (*ll, gl*) and *n* (*gn, ñ*) in Spanish *llama,* Italian *imbroglio,* English *million, minion,* French *mignon,* Spanish *cañon,* etc.: also applied to *l* and *ll* in certain positions in modern French pronunciation, where only the *y* sound now remains, as in *bouillon.*

mou-jik (mö-zhik′ or mö′zhik), *n.* See *muzhik.*

mould[1], **mould**[2], **mould**[3], **moul′der**[1], etc. See *mold*[1], etc.

mou-lin (mö-laṅ), *n.* [F., < LL. *molinum,* mill: see *mill*[2].] A nearly vertical shaft or cavity worn in a glacier by surface water falling through a crack in the ice.

moult, *v.* and *n.* See *molt.*

Mound.

mound[1] (mound), *n.* [OF. F. *monde,* < L. *mundus,* world.] The world†; also, a globe of gold or other precious material, taken as an emblem of sovereignty, often surmounting a crown or otherwise included among regalia; an orb.

mound[2] (mound), *n.* [Cf. AS. *mund,* hand, guardianship, protection, also E. *mount*[1].] A hedge or fence, as about a field (now prov. Eng.); also, an artificial elevation of earth, long, round, or of other form, as for a defensive work, or a dam or barrier, or for any other purpose; an embankment; often, an elevation of earth upon a grave; specif., a tumulus or other raised work of earth dating from a prehistoric or long-past period (as, the Indian *mounds* of the Mississippi valley and States eastward, comprising burial-mounds, mounds having the form of animals, platforms, and inclosures: cf. *mound-builder*); also, a natural elevation of earth; a hillock or knoll; an elevation formed of earth or sand, debris, etc., overlying ruins (as, "Mesopotamia . . . is covered with countless *mounds* (tells), each of which marks the site of a town": Encyc. Brit., 11th ed., XVIII. 181); in general, a heap or raised mass (as, a *mound* of hay or of refuse; "Heapt in *mounds* and ridges all the sea Drove like a cataract," Tennyson's "Holy Grail," 795); in *baseball,* the slightly elevated ground from which the pitcher delivers the ball and which slopes gradually from the pitcher's box to the base-lines.—**mound**[2], *v. t.* To inclose or separate by a hedge or fence (now prov. Eng.); also, to furnish with a mound of earth, as for a defense or barrier; form a mound about or along (as, "A sand-built ridge Of heaped hills that *mound* the sea": Tennyson's "Ode to Memory," v.); also, to form into a mound; heap up.—**mound′=bird,** *n.* Any bird of the family *Megapodiidæ,* esp. one of the genus *Megapodius.* See *megapod.*—**mound′=build″er,** *n.* One of the race or people (of uncertain or varying antiquity) that constructed the 'Indian mounds' of the U. S. (see *mound*[2], *n.*); also, a mound-bird.

Serpent Mound, Adams County, Ohio.

mount[1] (mount), *n.* [AS. *munt* = OF. F. *mont* = Sp., Pg., and It. *monte,* < L. *mons* (*mont-*), mountain, hill, heap.] A mountain or hill (now chiefly poetic, except in proper names, as *Mount* Etna); also, a mound, as for military purposes†; in *palmistry,* any of the fleshy prominences in the palm of the hand, supposed to indicate by their development the degree of influence exercised by certain planets (as, the *mount* of Venus, at the base of the thumb).

mount[2] (mount), *v.* [OF. F. *monter,* < L. *mons* (*mont-*), E. *mount*[1].] **I.** *intr.* To rise or go from a lower to a higher position, level, etc. (as, "They shall *mount* up with wings as eagles," Isa. xl. 31; the water *mounted* in the ship's hold; a flush *mounts* to the brow); move or proceed upward; ascend; often, to get up on something, as a platform; get up on the back of a horse, etc., for riding; also, to rise in amount (often with *up*: as, the costs are steadily *mounting,* or *mounting up*); increase in extent, degree, intensity, etc. (as, with *mounting* hope or fear; "The rage of each had *mounted* to delirium," Marryat's "King's Own," lvi.). **II.** *tr.* To go up or ascend (as, to *mount* stairs, a ladder, or a hill; "It was our design to *mount* the head-waters of the Hudson, to the neighbourhood of Crown Point," Stevenson's "Master of Ballantrae," iii.); get up on (a platform, a horse, etc.); ascend to a position or seat upon; also, to cause to ascend or rise†; elevate†; also, to set or place at an elevation (as, to be *mounted* on stilts); set on horseback; furnish with a horse or other mount for riding; raise or put into position for use, as a gun; hence, to have or carry (guns) in position for use, as a fortress or a vessel does; also, to fix on or in a support, backing, setting, etc. (as, to *mount* a tablet on a wall; to *mount* a photograph; to *mount* precious stones); prepare with accessories, ornamentation, etc. (as, "a case of pistols curiously *mounted* with silver": Smollett's "Humphry Clinker," Nov. 8); provide (a play, etc.) with scenery, costumes, and other appurtenances for production; also, to put on (as, "He found Dick *mounting* a large top-coat, and muffling up," Lover's "Handy Andy," xxi.; "It was then that I *mounted* the turban," H. Melville's "Omoo," lxi.); also, to go on (guard), as a sentry or watch does.—**mount**[2], *n.* The act or manner of mounting; an act or occasion of riding a horse, esp. in a race; also, a horse or other animal (or sometimes a bicycle) used, provided, or available for riding (as, "There was not another *mount* in the stable": George Eliot's "Adam Bede," xii.); also, a support, backing, setting, or the like, on or in which something is, or is to be, mounted or fixed.—**mount'a-ble,** *a.* That may be mounted.

moun-tain (moun'tān). [OF. *montaigne* (F. *montagne*), < ML. *montania, montanea,* for L. *montana,* fem. sing. or neut. pl. of *montanus,* pertaining to mountains, mountainous, < *mons* (*mont-*), E. *mount*[1].] **I.** *n.* A natural elevation of the earth's surface rising more or less abruptly to a summit, and attaining an altitude greater than that of a hill; also, something resembling this, as in size (as, a *mountain* of ice, an iceberg; a *mountain* of rubbish; a great *mountain* of a man); fig., a huge amount (as, a *mountain* of debt); also [*cap.*], with *the,* in *Fr. hist.,* a popular name for the extreme revolutionary party (led by Danton and Robespierre) in the legislatures of the French Revolution, whose members occupied the highest seats (cf. *plain*[2], *n.*). **II.** *a.* Of or pertaining to mountains (as, *mountain* air or scenery; a *mountain* lake); living, growing, or found on mountains (as, *mountain* people; *mountain* animals or plants); also, resembling or suggesting a mountain, as in size (as, *mountain* waves).—**mountain time.** See *standard time,* under *standard, a.*—**moun'tain=ash',** *n.* Any of various small ash-like trees of the malaceous genus *Sorbus,* as the European rowan-tree, *S. aucuparia,* and the American *S. americana,* both having pinnate leaves and bearing small white corymbose flowers succeeded by bright-red berries; also, any of certain other trees, as several Australian species of eucalyptus.—**moun'tain=chain,** *n.* A connected series of mountains; two or more mountain-ranges of close geographical relation.—**moun'tain=dam'son,** *n.* Any of certain tropical American trees of the genus *Simaruba* (family *Simarubaceæ*), the bark of whose root is used in medicine as a tonic and astringent, esp. *S. amara,* chiefly of the West Indies.—**moun'tain=dew',** *n.* Scotch whisky; hence, any whisky, esp. such as has been illicitly distilled.—**moun'tained,** *a.* Set on or as on a mountain (as, "Like old Deucalion *mountain'd* o'er the flood": Keats's "Endymion," ii.); also, covered with mountains; mountainous. [Poetic.]—**moun-tain-eer'** (-ēr'), *n.* An inhabitant of a mountainous district; also, a climber of mountains (as, "Fitzpatrick was a hardy and experienced *mountaineer,* and knew all the passes and defiles": Irving's "Captain Bonneville," vi.).—**moun-tain-eer',** *v. i.* To climb mountains: usually in *mountaineering, ppr.* and *n.*—**moun'tain=goat',** *n.* The Rocky Mountain goat, *Oreamnos montanus.* See *goat.*—**moun'tain=lau'rel,** *n.* The American laurel, *Kalmia latifolia.* See *laurel.*—**moun'tain=li'on,** *n.* The cougar.—**moun'tain=meal',** *n.* Bergmehl.—**moun'tain-ous,** *a.* Abounding in mountains; also, of the nature of a mountain (as, a *mountainous* rise of land); also, resembling a mountain or mountains (as, *mountainous* waves); large and high; huge.—**moun'tain=range,** *n.* A series of more or less connected mountains ranged in a line; a series of mountains, or of more or less parallel ridges of mountains, closely related in origin, etc.—**moun'tain=sheep',** *n.* Any of various wild sheep inhabiting mountains, esp. the bighorn *Ovis montana* (or *canadensis*), of the Rocky Mountains.—**moun'tain=sick''ness,** *n.* In *pathol.,* a morbid condition characterized by difficulty of breathing, with headache, nausea, etc., due to the rarefaction of the air at high altitudes.—**moun'tain-side,** *n.* The side or slope of a mountain.—**moun'tain=to-bac'co,** *n.* An asteraceous plant, *Arnica montana,* the source of the medicinal arnica. See *arnica.* See also cut in next column.—**moun'tain-top,** *n.* The top or summit of a mountain.—**moun'tain-ward** (-wạrd), *adv.* and *a.* Toward the mountain or mountains.—**moun'tain-wards,** *adv.*

moun-te-bank (moun'tẹ-bangk), *n.* [It. *montambanco,* lit. 'mount-on-bench.'] One who sells quack medicines from a platform in public places, appealing to his audience by tricks, story-telling, etc.; hence, any buffoonish charlatan or pretender.—**moun'te-bank,** *v.* **I.**† *tr.* To work upon (persons, feelings, etc.) in the manner of a mountebank. **II.** *intr.* To play the mountebank.—**moun'te-bank-er-y,** *n.*; pl. *-ies* (-iz). The action or practice of a mountebank; a performance characteristic of or suited to a mountebank.

Mountain-tobacco.

mount-ed (moun'ted), *p. a.* [See *mount*[2], *v.*] Raised up or elevated; also, seated or riding on a horse or the like; serving on horseback, or on some special mount, as soldiers, police, etc.; performed on horseback, or on some mount, as evolutions; also, put into position for use, as guns; also, fixed on or in a support, backing, setting, or the like (as, a *mounted* skeleton; a *mounted* photograph; *mounted* gems).

mount-er (moun'tẽr), *n.* One who or that which mounts.

mount-ing (moun'ting), *n.* The act of one who or that which mounts; also, something that serves as a mount, support, setting, or the like.

mourn (mōrn), *v.* [AS. *murnan,* mourn, = OHG. *mornēn,* Goth. *maurnan,* be anxious, = Icel. *morna,* pine: cf. *morne.*] **I.** *intr.* To feel or express sorrow or grief (as, "I left them to *mourn* over my folly, and now I am left to *mourn* under the consequences of it": Defoe's "Robinson Crusoe," i. 6); grieve; esp., to grieve or lament for the dead; hence, to display the conventional tokens of sorrow after a person's death (see *mourning, n.*). **II.** *tr.* To feel or express sorrow or grief over (misfortune, loss, or anything regretted); deplore; esp., to grieve or lament over (the dead: as, "But she must die . . . and all the world shall *mourn* her," Shakspere's "Henry VIII.," v. 5. 63); also, to utter in a sorrowful manner (chiefly poetic: as, "Where the love-lorn nightingale Nightly to thee her sad song *mourneth* well," Milton's "Comus," 235).—**mourn'er,** *n.* One who mourns; esp., one who attends a funeral as a mourning friend or relative of the deceased; at religious revival meetings, one who professes penitence for sin, with desire for salvation.—**mourners' bench,** at religious revival meetings, a bench or seat at the front of the church or room, set apart for mourners or penitent sinners seeking salvation.—**mourn'ful,** *a.* Full of, expressing, or showing sorrow or grief, as persons, the feelings, mood, tone, words, aspect, etc.; sorrowful; sad; sometimes, expressing, or used in, mourning for the dead (as, "No *mournful* bell shall ring her burial," Shakspere's "Titus Andronicus," v. 3. 197; "The busy heralds hang the sable scene With *mournful* 'scutcheons, and dim lamps between," Cowper's "Hope," 265); also, causing, or attended with, sorrow or mourning (as, "his *mournful* death," Shakspere's "1 Henry VI.," ii. 2. 16; a *mournful* occasion); deplorable or regrettable, as an occurrence, circumstance, or fact; also, gloomy, somber, or dreary, as in appearance or character (as, *mournful* shadows; a *mournful* prospect; the *mournful* howling of the wind).—**mourn'ful-ly,** *adv.*—**mourn'ful-ness,** *n.*—**mourn'ing. I.** *n.* The act of one who mourns; sorrowing or lamentation; specif., the conventional manifestation of sorrow for a person's death, as by the wearing of black (or some other color), the draping of buildings, the hanging of flags at half-mast, etc.; also, the outward tokens of such sorrow, as black garments, bands, draperies, etc. **II.** *a.* Of, pertaining to, or used in mourning: as, *mourning* garments or jewelry; *mourning* note-paper (with a black border).—**mourn'ing=dove',** *n.* A wild dove, *Zenaidura carolinensis* (or *macrura*), of North America: so called from its plaintive note. See *dove*². — **mourn′ing-ly,** *adv.*

mouse (mous), *n.*; pl. *mice* (mīs). [AS. *mūs* (pl. *m̄ys*) = D. *muis* = G. *maus* = Icel. *mūs*, mouse; akin to L. *mus*, Gr. *μῦς*, Skt. *mūsh*, mouse (cf. Skt. *mush-*, steal).] Any of various small rodents of the family *Muridæ* and esp. of the genus *Mus*, as *M. musculus*, which infests houses (cf. *rat*); also, any similar animal of some other family; also, a playful epithet or term of endearment for a person, now usually for a child or young girl (cf. Shakspere's "Hamlet," iii. 4. 183); *naut.*, several turns of small rope or the like uniting the shank and the point of a hook; also, a knot formed on a rope with yarn or the like. — **mouse** (mouz), *v.*; *moused, mousing.* **I.** *intr.* To hunt for or catch mice; hence, to seek or search stealthily or watchfully, as if for prey (often fig.: as, to *mouse* for faults); prowl (*about*, etc.), as if seeking something. **II.** *tr.* To hunt out, as a cat hunts out mice; also, to handle or treat as a cat does a mouse† (as, "Now he [Death] feasts, *mousing* the flesh of men": Shakspere's "King John," ii. 1. 354). — **mouse=bird** (mous′bėrd), *n.* A colie: probably so called from the manner in which it creeps about on trees. — **mouse′=col″or,** *n.* A soft, dark, dull gray. — **mouse′=col″ored,** *a.* — **mouse′=ear,** *n.* Any of various plants with small hairy leaves, as the hawkweed, *Hieracium pilosella*, the forget-me-not, *Myosotis palustris*, etc. — **mouse′=le′mur,** *n.* Any of the small lemurs constituting the genus *Chirogaleus*, of Madagascar. — **mous-er** (mou′zėr), *n.* An animal that catches mice, or with reference to its ability to catch mice (as, "A scalded cat may prove a good *mouser*": Smollett's "Humphry Clinker," June 3), also, one who mouses, or seeks or prowls as if for prey. — **mouse-tail** (mous′tāl), *n.* Any plant of the ranunculaceous genus *Myosurus*, esp. *M. minimus*, the flowers of which have a tail-like torus. — **mouse′=trap,** *n.* A trap for catching mice. Also fig. — **mous-ie** (mou′si), *n.* A diminutive of *mouse*: used playfully or kindly. See Burns's "To a Mouse." [First recorded in Scotch use.] — **mous-ing** (mou′zing), *n.* *Naut.*, a mouse.

Mouse (*Mus musculus*).

Brown Mouse-lemur (*Chirogaleus milii*).

mous-que-taire (mös-kė-tãr), *n.* [F.] A musketeer; esp., a member of either of two bodies of mounted musketeers belonging to the French royal household troops in the 17th and 18th centuries, and famous as dandies. — **mousquetaire glove,** a long glove closed, or having only a short opening, at the wrist.

mousse (mös), *n.* [F., moss, froth; from Teut., and akin to E. *moss*.] Any of various preparations of whipped cream, beaten eggs, etc., sweetened and flavored and often frozen.

mousse-line (mös-lēn), *n.* [F.: see *muslin*.] Muslin. — **mousseline de laine** (dė lān). [F., 'muslin of wool.'] A thin woolen fabric, often having a printed pattern. — **mousseline de soie** (swo). [F., 'muslin of silk.'] A thin muslin-like silk fabric.

mous-tache (mus-tåsh′), etc. See *mustache*, etc.

mous-y (mou′si), *a.* Resembling or suggesting a mouse, as in color, odor, etc.; quiet as a mouse; also, infested with mice; smelling of mice.

mouth (mouth), *n.*; pl. *mouths* (mouᴛʜz). [AS. *mūth* = D. *mond* = G. *mund* = Icel. *munnr* = Goth. *munths*, mouth.] The opening through which an animal takes in food, or the cavity containing or the parts inclosing the masticating apparatus; the oral opening, cavity, or parts; hence, a person or other animal as requiring food (as, "The Lord never sends a *mouth* into the world without providing meat for it": Galt's "Annals of the Parish," iii.); also, the oral opening or cavity considered as the source of vocal utterance (as, "All . . . wondered at the gracious words which proceeded out of his *mouth*": Luke, iv. 22); hence, utterance or expression (as, to give *mouth* to one's thoughts); cry or bay, as of hounds (as, "My hounds are . . . match'd in *mouth* like bells": Shakspere's "Midsummer Night's Dream," iv. 1. 128); also, a spokesman for another or others (obs. or rare); also, a grimace made with the lips (as, "Penelope made a droll *mouth*": Howells's "Rise of Silas Lapham," vii.); also, an opening leading out of or into any cavity or hollow place or thing (as, the *mouth* of a cave, tunnel, well, or volcano; the *mouth* of a bag, bottle, or pitcher; the cannon's *mouth*); a place of exit from or entrance into a valley, harbor, or other inclosed area; a part of a river or the like where its waters are discharged into some other body of water (as, the *mouths* of the Nile; the *mouth* of the Ohio River; the *mouth* of Lake Ontario); also, the opening between the jaws of a vise or the like. — **from hand to mouth.** See under *hand*, *n.* — **mouth** (mouᴛʜ), *v.* **I.** *tr.* To utter (archaic); now, more commonly, to utter in a sonorous, oratorical or pompous manner, or with unnecessarily noticeable use of the mouth-parts (as, "She *mouthed* her words in speaking; her voice was deep, its inflections very pompous": C. Brontë's "Jane Eyre," xvii.); also, to put or take into the mouth, as food; seize with the mouth or jaws; also, to press, rub, or mumble with the mouth or lips (as, "Psyche . . . hugg'd . . . And in her hunger *mouth'd* and mumbled it [babe]": Tennyson's "Princess," vi. 196); also, to accustom (a horse) to the use of the bit and bridle. **II.** *intr.* To speak or declaim sonorously and oratorically, or with mouthing of the words (as, "I'll bellow out for Rome and for my country, And *mouth* at Cæsar till I shake the senate": Addison's "Cato," i. 3); also, to join mouths, as in kissing†; also, to make a mouth, or grimace with the lips. — **mouthed** (mouᴛʜd), *a.* Having a mouth or mouths (as, "a *mouthed* shell," Keats's "Hyperion," ii.; a many-*mouthed* monster); often, having the mouth or mouths as specified (as, open-*mouthed*; wide-*mouthed*). — **mouth-er** (mou′ᴛʜėr), *n.* — **mouth-ful** (mouth′fůl), *n.*; pl. *-fuls.* As much as a mouth can hold; as much as is taken into the mouth at one time; hence, a small quantity. — **mouth′less,** *a.* Having no mouth. — **mouth′=or″gan,** *n.* Pan's pipes (see under *Pan*²); also, a harmonica; in *zoöl.*, one of the parts or appendages of the mouth of an insect, crustacean, etc. — **mouth′-piece,** *n.* A piece placed at or forming the mouth, as of a receptacle, tube, or the like; also, a piece or part, as of an instrument, to which the mouth is applied or which is held in the mouth (as, the *mouthpiece* of a trumpet, or of a tobacco-pipe); the part of a bit or bridle, as for a horse, that passes through the animal's mouth; also, a person, or a newspaper or the like, that voices or communicates the words, sentiments, decisions, etc., of another or others

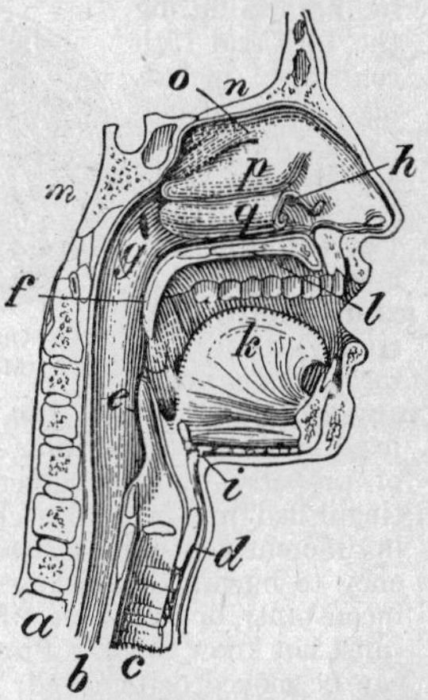

Longitudinal Vertical Section of Mouth, Nose, etc., taken a little to the left of the middle line. — *a*, cervical vertebræ; *b*, gullet or esophagus; *c*, windpipe or trachea; *d*, larynx; *e*, epiglottis; *f*, uvula; *g*, opening of left Eustachian tube; *h*, opening of left lacrymal duct in the nose; *i*, hyoid bone; *k*, tongue; *l*, hard palate; *m*, *n*, base of cranial cavity; *o*, *p*, *q*, superior, middle, and inferior turbinate bones.

(as, "They fancied him the *mouth-piece* of Heaven's messages of wisdom, and rebuke, and love": Hawthorne's "Scarlet Letter," xi.); a spokesman.—**mouth-y** (mou'thi or -ᴛʜi), *a.* Loud-mouthed; ranting; bombastic.

mou-ton (mö'ton), *n.* [OF.: see *mutton.*] Any of several gold coins bearing the figure of a lamb (Agnus Dei), current in France during the 14th and 15th centuries: including coins struck by Edward III. and Henry V. of England for their French dominions.

Obverse. Reverse.
Mouton of Henry V. of England.

mou-ton-née (mö-to-nā), *a.* See *roche moutonnée.*

mov-a-ble (mö'va-bl). **I.** *a.* Capable of being moved; not fixed in one place, position, or posture; specif., in legal use, of property, not permanent in place; personal, as distinguished from real; also, changing from one date to another in different years (as, a *movable* feast); also, having a tendency to move†, or quick in movement†; fig., changeable†, inconstant†, or fickle† (as, "Her ways are *moveable,* that thou canst not know them": Prov. v. 6). **II.** *n.* Anything that can be moved or removed; an article of furniture which is not fixed in place (as, "The apartment . . . was destitute of all *moveables* save a broken arm-chair, and an old couch or sofa": Dickens's "Oliver Twist," xxvi.); in legal use, a piece of personal property: usually in *pl.*—**mov-a-bil'i-ty** (-bil'i-ti), **mov'a-ble-ness,** *n.*—**mov'a-bly,** *adv.*

move (möv), *v.*; *moved, moving.* [OF. *moveir* (F. *mouvoir*), < L. *movere* (pp. *motus*), move.] **I.** *tr.* To change the place or position of; take from one place or situation to another; shift; sometimes, to dislodge (a thing fixed in place); specif., in games, as chess and checkers, to change the position of (a piece) in the course of play (as, "My liege, I *move* my bishop": Tennyson's "Becket," Prologue, 15); in commercial use, to dispose of (goods in stock) to purchasers; also, to set or keep in motion; stir or shake (as, the wind *moves* the trees); often, to set or keep in a regular or recurrent motion, as an implement or a machine; also, to change the position or posture of (the body or a bodily part: as, to *move* one's head, hand, or foot; "She *moved* her lips . . . but could not speak," Hardy's "Return of the Native," iv. 7); also, to cause (the bowels) to act or operate; also, to prompt, actuate, or impel to some action (as, what *moved* you to do this?); also, to urge or exhort to do something† (as, "I . . . begged him . . . that he would *move* the Captains to take some pity on us": Swift's "Gulliver's Travels," iii. 1); apply to, as for something† (as, "The Florentine will *move* us For speedy aid": Shakspere's "All's Well," i. 2. 6); also, to submit a formal request or proposal to (a sovereign, a court, etc.); also, to suggest, propose, or urge (something: obs. or archaic: as, "My mother refused to *move* it [a proposition] to my father," Defoe's "Robinson Crusoe," i. 1; "My lord *moved* that Mr. Henry should be present," Stevenson's "Master of Ballantrae," i.); now, to propose formally, as to a court or judge, or for consideration by a deliberative assembly; also, to rouse or excite the feelings or passions of; affect with emotion; excite (*to*: as, "an ardent and impetuous race, easily *moved* to tears or to laughter, to fury or to love," Macaulay's "Hist. of Eng.," i.); specif., to affect with tender or compassionate emotion; touch; also, to stir up or excite (an emotion, etc.: as, "All the prejudices, all the exaggerations, of both the great parties in the state *moved* his scorn," Macaulay's "Hist. of Eng.," ii.). **II.** *intr.* To change place or position; pass from one place or situation to another; sometimes, to become dislodged or displaced, as a thing fixed in place; often, to go forward, or march, as a body of persons; also, to change one's abode; go from one place of residence to another; specif., in games, as chess and checkers, of a piece, to be transferred from one position to another; of a player, to make a move; in commercial use, to be disposed of to purchasers, as goods in stock; also, to advance, progress, or make progress (as, "Then the tale Shall *move* on soberly": Keats's "Isabella," xx.); also, to start off, or depart (now colloq.: as, it's time to be *moving*); also, to be in motion, be stirred, or shake (as, "Then *move* the trees, the copses nod": Tennyson's "Sir Galahad," 77); often, to have a regular motion, as an implement or a machine; turn; revolve; also, to change position or posture, as a living creature or a bodily part (as, "He heareth not, he stirreth not, he *moveth* not": Shakspere's "Romeo and Juliet," ii. 1. 15); carry the body in walking, etc. (as, "Not one woman in a thousand could *move* so admirably as Zenobia": Hawthorne's "Blithedale Romance," xviii.); also, of living creatures, to exist or live; sometimes, to be active in a particular sphere (as, to *move* in society); also, to take action, or act, as in an affair (as, "God *moves* in a mysterious way, His wonders to perform," Cowper's "Light Shining out of Darkness"; "Had the city *moved* sooner . . . there would have been no rising, no riot," J. H. Newman's "Callista," xxvii.); also, of the bowels, to operate; also, to make a formal request, application, or proposal (*for*: as, to *move* for a new trial).—**move,** *n.* The act or an act of moving; a movement (as, "an impatient *move* of her head": Hardy's "Return of the Native," iv. 7); a beginning to move or depart; a change of abode or residence; specif., in games, as chess and checkers, a changing of the position of a piece in the course of play; the right or turn to move (as, "It is your *move*": Tennyson's "Becket," Prologue, 8); fig., an action toward an end; a step.—**on the move,** in the process of moving from place to place; constantly moving: as, "a wandering people . . . continually *on the move*" (Irving's "Captain Bonneville," xli.).

move'a-ble, etc. See *movable,* etc.

move-less (möv'les), *a.* Without movement or motion; motionless; immovable: as, "His limbs were *moveless* in an exasperating and obstinate calm" (Arnold Bennett's "Hilda Lessways," iii. 2).—**move'less-ly,** *adv.*—**move'less-ness,** *n.*

move-ment (möv'ment), *n.* The act or process of moving; a particular manner of moving; an act of moving, as in going from place to place, or in changing posture; also, an action or activity, as of a person or a body of persons (chiefly in *pl.*: as, to be guided by the *movements* of others); also, an inward impulse, as of the mind (now rare); also, the progress of events, as in narrative or drama; rapid progress of events, or abundance of events or incidents; also, the suggestion of action, as in a painting or the like; also, a series of actions or activities directed or tending toward a particular end (as, the antislavery *movement*; the Oxford *movement,* see entry in alphabetical place); also, the course of tendency, or trend, of affairs in a particular field; also, the activity in the market with reference to some commodity; also, an evacuation of the bowels; also, the works, or a distinct portion of the works, of a mechanism, as a watch (as, "Men are like Geneva watches with crystal faces which expose the whole *movement*": Emerson's "Conduct of Life," v.); *milit.* and *naval,* a change of position in tactical or strategical evolutions; in *music,* motion; rhythm; time; tempo; also, a principal division or section of a sonata, symphony, or the like; in *pros.,* rhythmical structure or character.

mov-er (mö'vėr), *n.* One who or that which moves.—**prime mover.** See under *prime*[1], *a.*

mov-ie (mö'vi), *n.* In *pl.* (*movies*), moving pictures; in *sing.* (*movie*), a moving picture; a photoplay. [Colloq.]

mov-ing (mö'ving), *p. a.* That moves; causing or producing motion; having motion; fig., actuating, instigating, or impelling (as, the *moving* cause of a dispute; he is the *moving* spirit of the enterprise); also, that excites the feelings, or affects with emotion; esp., touching or pathetic (as, "A decayed widow . . . has laid her case of destitution before him in a very *moving* letter": Hawthorne's "House of the Seven Gables," xviii.).—**moving picture.** See entry below.—**moving platform** or **sidewalk,** a platform or sidewalk constructed on the principle of an endless belt and moving at a regular speed, for carrying along objects or persons.—**moving staircase** or **stairway,** a stairway constructed and operated like a moving sidewalk. See *escalator.*—**mov'ing-ly,** *adv.*—**mov'ing-ness,** *n.*

mov-ing pic-ture (mö'ving pik'tūr). In *pl.* (*moving pictures*), consecutive pictures or photographs of objects in motion presented to the eye (esp. by being thrown on a screen by a cinematograph) so rapidly as to give the illusion that the objects are moving as they did in the original scenes; in *sing.* (*moving picture*), a number of such pictures or photographs representing an event, play, or the like; a photoplay. —**moving=picture camera,** a camera for taking moving pictures.—**moving=picture machine,** an apparatus for presenting moving pictures, as by projection on a screen.

mow[1] (mou or mō), *n.* [OF. *moe* (F. *moue*), a pouting grimace, earlier mouth, lip; origin uncertain.] A wry mouth, or grimace, as of a person or an ape; often, a derisive grimace (as, "that devil that . . . made *mows* and mockery at his insufferable tortures": Godwin's "Caleb Williams," x.).—**mow**[1], *v. i.* To make mows, mouths, or grimaces: as, "like apes that *mow* and chatter at me" (Shakspere's "Tempest," ii. 2. 9).

mow[2] (mou), *n.* [AS. *mūga, mūha*, mow, = Icel. *mūgi*, swath.] A heap or pile of hay or of sheaves of grain in a barn; also, the place in a barn where hay, sheaves of grain, etc., are stored (as, "Littered the stalls, and from the *mows* Raked down the herd's-grass for the cows": Whittier's "Snow-Bound").—**mow**[2], *v. t.* To put in a mow, as hay.

mow[3] (mō), *v.*; pret. *mowed*, pp. *mowed* or *mown*, ppr. *mowing*. [AS. *māwan* = D. *maaien* = G. *mähen*, mow; akin to Gr. ἀμᾶν and L. *metere*, reap, and E. *math*[1] and *meadow*.] **I.** *tr.* To cut down (grass, grain, etc.) with a scythe or a machine; hence, to cut down, destroy, or kill indiscriminately or in great numbers, as men in battle; also, to cut the grass, etc., from (land); also, to make (a passage, etc.) by mowing. **II.** *intr.* To cut down grass, grain, etc.; hence, to sweep down men in battle.—**mow′er,** *n.*—**mow′-ing=ma-chine″,** *n.* A machine for mowing or cutting down standing grass, etc.

mox-a (mok′sạ), *n.* [Jap. *mokusa.*] A soft, downy substance prepared from the leaves of a Chinese species of wormwood, *Artemisia moxa*, used as a cautery or counter-irritant by igniting on the skin; also, the plant itself; also, any similar cauterizing substance or device.

Moz-ar-ab (mō-zar′ạb), *n.* [Sp. *Mozárabe*, < Ar. *musta'rib*, lit. 'one Arabized.'] One of a class of Spanish Christians who submitted to the domination of the Moors and were permitted to retain their own religion.—**Moz-ar′a-bic** (-ạ-bik), *a.* Of or pertaining to the Mozarabs; also, designating or pertaining to the ancient Christian liturgy of Spain, a modified form of which is still used in certain Spanish chapels (probably so called as having been retained by the Mozarabs after its use was discontinued by the other Christians of Spain).

mo-zet-ta (mọ-zet′ä), *n.* Same as *mozzetta*.

moz-zet-ta (mot-set′tä), *n.*; pl. *-te* (-tā). [It.: cf. *amice*[2] and *mutch*.] In the *Rom. Cath. Ch.*, a short cape which covers the shoulders and can be buttoned over the breast, and to which a hood is attached, worn by the Pope and by cardinals, bishops, abbots, and other dignitaries.

Mr. (mis′tėr); with pl. *Messrs.* (see *Messrs.*). Abbreviated written form of *mister* as prefixed to a man's name.—**Mrs.** (mis′iz); occasionally with pl. *Mesdames* (see *madame*[2]). Abbreviated written form of the title (orig. *mistress*) conventionally prefixed to the name of a woman, now distinctively to that of a married woman.

M=roof (em′röf′), *n.* A roof formed by the junction of two gable-roofs with a valley between, so as in transverse section to resemble somewhat the letter M.

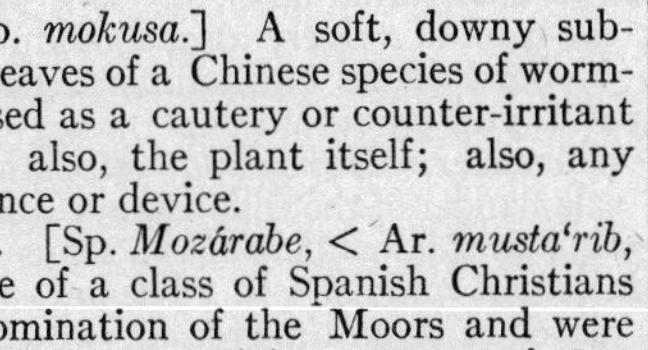

M-roof.

mu (mū), *n.* [Gr. μῦ.] The twelfth letter (M, μ, = English M, m) of the Greek alphabet.

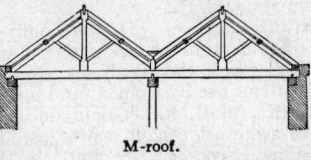

much (much). [ME. *muche, moche*, for *muchel, mochel*, var. of *michel*, < AS. *micel*, great, much: see *mickle*.] **I.** *a.*; compar. *more*, superl. *most*. Great in size†, or big†; also, in great quantity, amount, measure, or degree (as, *much* money; *much* work; *much* pleasure, zeal, or haste); also, many in number†, or a great number of† (as, "Edom came out against him with *much* people": Num. xx. 20). **II.** *n.* A great quantity or amount, or a great deal (as, we searched without finding *much*; *much* of this is true); also, a great, important, or notable thing or matter (as, the house is not *much* to look at; the rain did not amount to *much*, it is *much* to have won him over).—**to make much of,** to treat, represent, or consider as of great importance (as, "Young folks don't *make* so *much of* dinner as old ones": H. Kingsley's "Geoffry Hamlyn," xxxiii.); often, to treat (a person) with great, flattering, or fond consideration (as, to be *made much of* in society; to spoil a child by *making* too *much of* it).—**much,** *adv.* To a great extent or degree, greatly, or far (as, *much* enlarged; *much* pleased; *much* higher or better); also, nearly, approximately, or about (as, this is *much* the same as the others; to find a place *much* what one had expected it to be; *much* of a muchness, see under *muchness*).—**much′ness,** *n.* Greatness, as in quantity, measure, or degree.—**much of a muchness,** much the same; much alike: as, "*much of a muchness*—no better, and perhaps no worse" (H. Kingsley's "Geoffry Hamlyn," xxviii.).

mu-cic (mū′sik), *a.* [L. *mucus*, mucus.] In *chem.*, noting or pertaining to a dibasic crystalline acid obtained by oxidizing certain gums, milk-sugar, etc.

mu-cid (mū′sid), *a.* [L. *mucidus*, < *mucere*: see *mucilage*.] Moldy; musty.

mu-cif-er-ous (mū-sif′ẹ-rus), *a.* [L. *mucus*, mucus, + *ferre*, bear.] Conveying or secreting mucus.

mu-cig-e-nous (mū-sij′e-nus), *a.* [L. *mucus*, mucus: see *-genous*.] Secreting mucus; muciparous.

mu-ci-lage (mū′si-lạj), *n.* [F. *mucilage*, < LL. *mucilago*, a musty juice, < L. *mucere*, be moldy or musty.] Any of various gummy secretions or gelatinous substances present in plants; also, any of various preparations of gum, glue, or the like, for causing adhesion.—**mu-ci-lag′i-nous** (-laj′i-nus), *a.* [F. *mucilagineux*.] Of the nature of or resembling mucilage; moist, soft, and viscid; also, of, pertaining to, or secreting mucilage.

mu-cin (mū′sin), *n.* [L. *mucus*, mucus.] In *physiol. chem.*, any of a group of nitrogenous substances found in mucous secretions, etc., and varying in composition according to their source.—**mu′cin-ous,** *a.*

mu-cip-a-rous (mū-sip′ạ-rus), *a.* [L. *mucus*, mucus, + *parere*, bring forth.] Producing or secreting mucus, as glands.

muck (muk), *n.* [Prob. from Scand.: cf. Icel. *myki*, dung.] Farmyard dung, decaying vegetable matter, etc., in a moist state; manure; hence, filth; dirt; anything foul or disgusting; fig., lucre† or money† (in contempt); also, a dirty or disgusting state, or mess (prov. or colloq.: as, "a *muck* of sweat," Goldsmith's "Vicar of Wakefield," ix.); in *mining*, etc., earth, rock, or other useless matter to be removed in order to get out the mineral or other substance sought.—**muck,** *v.* **I.** *tr.* To manure; also, to dirty or soil (prov. or colloq.: as, "You can't touch pitch and not be *mucked*, lad," Stevenson's "Treasure Island," x.); also, to remove muck from. **II.** *intr.* To drudge or toil (prov. Eng.); also, to potter or go aimlessly (*about*: slang, Eng.).—**muck′er,** *n.* A heavy fall, as into muck (slang); also, a vulgar, ill-bred person (slang, U. S.); in *mining*, etc., one who removes muck.

muck-le (muk′l), *a.*, *n.*, and *adv.* Same as *mickle*. [Sc. and north. Eng.]

muck-luck (muk′luk), *n.* See *mukluk*.

muck=rake (muk′rāk), *n.* A rake for use on muck or filth. Often fig., as in Bunyan's "man . . . with a muck-rake" (seeking for worldly gain: see "Pilgrim's Progress," ii.), or with reference to any search, from whatever motives, into what is unsavory or vile.—**muck′=rake,** *v. i.*; *-raked*, *-raking*. To exploit, esp. in print, political or other corruption, real or alleged. [Colloq.]—**muck′=rak″er** (-rā″kėr), *n.*

muck-worm (muk′wėrm), *n.* A worm or grub living in muck or manure; also, a miser.

muck-y (muk′i), *a.* Consisting of or resembling muck; defiled with or as with muck; filthy; dirty.

mu-co- (mū′kọ-). Form of *mucus* used in combination, as in *mucopurulent* (both mucous and purulent), *mucoserous* (both mucous and serous).

mu-coid[1] (mū′koid), *a.* [From *mucus* + *-oid*.] Resembling mucus.

mu-coid[2] (mū′koid), *n.* [From *mucin* + *-oid*.] In *physiol. chem.*, any of a group of substances resembling the mucins, occurring in connective tissue, etc.

mu-cor (mū′kọr), *n.* [L., mold, < *mucere*, be moldy.] Any of the minute fungi constituting the genus *Mucor* (family *Mucoraceæ*), characterized by the formation of zygospores, and including some of the commonest molds.—**mu-co-ra′ceous** (-kọ-rā′shius), *a.*

mu-co-sa (mụ-kō′sạ̈), *n.*; pl. *-sæ* (-sē). [NL., fem. of L. *mucosus*, E. *mucous*.] In *anat.*, a mucous membrane.

mu-cous (mū′kus), *a.* [L. *mucosus*, < *mucus*, E. *mucus*.] Pertaining to, consisting of, or resembling mucus; also, containing or secreting mucus (as, the *mucous* membrane, in *anat.*, the lining membrane of the respiratory passages, the alimentary canal, etc.).—**mu-cos-i-ty** (mụ-kos′i-ti), *n.*

mu-cro (mū′krō), *n.*; pl. *mucros* (-krōz) or *mucrones* (mụ-krō′nēz). [L.] A sharp point or tip; a spine-like part; in *bot.*, a short point projecting abruptly, as at the end of a leaf.—**mu′cro-nate, mu′cro-nat-ed** (-krọ-nāt, -nā-ted), *a.* [L. *mucronatus*.] Having a mucro, or spine-like or abruptly projecting point, as a shell, a feather, a leaf, etc.; also, having the form of a mucro, as a process.—**mu′cro-nate-ly,** *adv.*—**mu-cro-na′tion** (-nā′shọn), *n.* Mucronate condition or form; also, a mucronate process.—**mu-cron-u-late** (mụ-kron′ụ-lāt), *a.* Having a small mucro or abruptly projecting point, as a leaf.

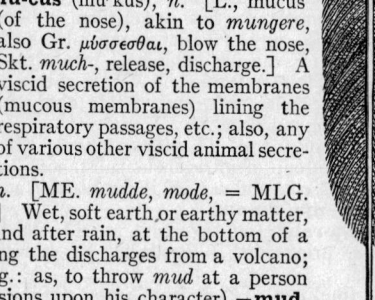

Mucronulate Leaflet of Vetch (*Vicia sativa*). — *a*, the mucro.

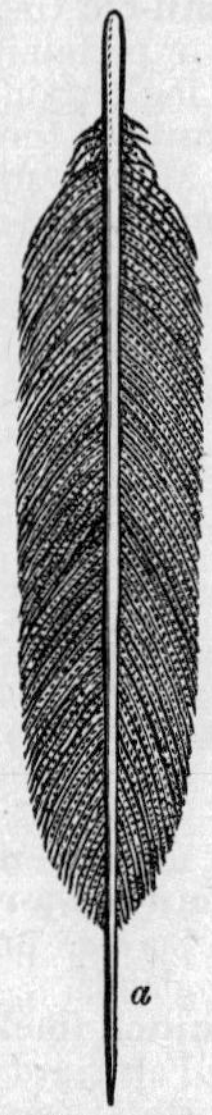

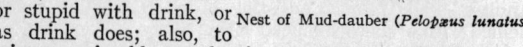

Mucronate Tail-feather of Chimney-swift.—*a*, the mucro.

mu-cus (mū′kus), *n.* [L., mucus (of the nose), akin to *mungere*, also Gr. *μύσσεσθαι*, blow the nose, Skt. *much-*, release, discharge.] A viscid secretion of the membranes (mucous membranes) lining the respiratory passages, etc.; also, any of various other viscid animal secretions.

mud (mud), *n.* [ME. *mudde*, *mode*, = MLG. *mudde*, mud.] Wet, soft earth or earthy matter, as on the ground after rain, at the bottom of a pond, or among the discharges from a volcano; mire. Also fig.: as, to throw *mud* at a person (to cast aspersions upon his character).—**mud,** *v. t.*; *mudded*, *mudding*. To cover or bedaub with mud; also, to bury in mud (as, "I wish Myself were *mudded* in that oozy bed Where my son lies": Shakspere's "Tempest," v. 1. 151); also, to make (water, etc.) turbid, as by stirring up mud or sediment at the bottom (as, "The wolf *Mudded* the brook": Tennyson's "Harold," v. 1. 2). [Now rare.]

mu-dar (mu-där′), *n.* See *madar*.

mud=bath (mud′bȧth), *n.* A bath in which the body or part of it is immersed in mud charged with saline or other medicinal agents, esp. as a remedy for rheumatism, gout, etc.

mud=daub-er (mud′dâ″bėr), *n.* Any of numerous wasps of the family *Sphegidæ*, which construct nests of mud, as *Pelopæus* (or *Sceliphron*) *lunatus*, a common North American species.

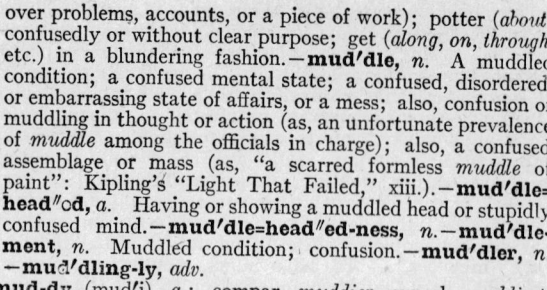

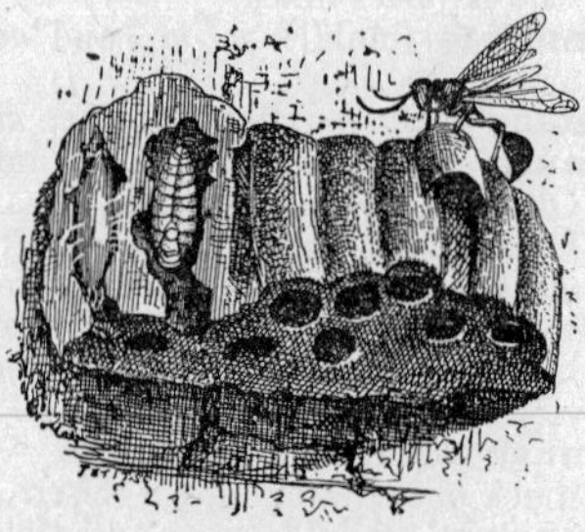
Nest of Mud-dauber (*Pelopæus lunatus*).

mud-di-ly (mud′i-li), *adv.* In a muddy manner; turbidly.—**mud′di-ness,** *n.*

mud-dle (mud′l), *v.*; *-dled*, *-dling*. [Freq. < *mud*.] **I.** *tr.* To make muddy or turbid, as water; fig., to render confused mentally, or unable to think clearly; often, to render confused or stupid with drink, or as drink does; also, to mix up or jumble together in a confused or bungling way; bring (things, affairs, etc.) into a muddle or mess (sometimes with *up*: as, "Do you want to . . . get things all *muddled* up?" Mark Twain's "Huckleberry Finn," ii.); also, to fritter (*away*), as time, money, etc., in a stupid or unthinking manner; also, to mix or stir (chocolate, etc.). **II.** *intr.* To dabble or wallow in mud (archaic); also, to think or act in a confused, ineffective way (as, to *muddle* over problems, accounts, or a piece of work); potter (*about*) confusedly or without clear purpose; get (*along*, *on*, *through*, etc.) in a blundering fashion.—**mud′dle,** *n.* A muddled condition; a confused mental state; a confused, disordered, or embarrassing state of affairs, or a mess; also, confusion or muddling in thought or action (as, an unfortunate prevalence of *muddle* among the officials in charge); also, a confused assemblage or mass (as, "a scarred formless *muddle* of paint": Kipling's "Light That Failed," xiii.).—**mud′dle=head″ed,** *a.* Having or showing a muddled head or stupidly confused mind.—**mud′dle=head″ed-ness,** *n.*—**mud′dle-ment,** *n.* Muddled condition; confusion.—**mud′dler,** *n.*—**mud′dling-ly,** *adv.*

mud-dy (mud′i), *a.*; compar. *muddier*, superl. *muddiest*. Abounding in or covered with mud; consisting of or resembling mud; turbid with or as with mud, as water, coffee, wine, etc.; hence, not clear or pure, as color; dull, as the complexion; fig., not clear mentally (as, *muddy* brains); obscure or vague, as thought, expression, literary style, etc.; also, morally impure or unclean (now rare).—**mud′dy,** *v.*; *-died*, *-dying*. **I.** *tr.* To make muddy; soil with mud; make turbid; render confused or obscure. **II.** *intr.* To become muddy.

mud-fish (mud′fish), *n.* Any of various fishes that live in muddy water or burrow in the mud, as the bowfin, the lepidosiren, etc.

mud=guard (mud′gärd), *n.* A guard or shield so placed as to protect riders or passengers from mud thrown by the wheel of a bicycle, automobile, or the like.

mu-dir (mṳ-dēr′), *n.* [Ar. *mudīr*.] In Egypt, Turkey, etc., a local administrator; a governor.

mud=lark (mud′lärk), *n.* One who works in mud, as along the bank of a river; also, a gamin or street Arab (as, "a mere *mud-lark* of the Paris slums": Du Maurier's "Trilby," ii.).

mud=pup-py (mud′pup″i), *n.*; pl. *-puppies* (-iz). The hellbender, *Menopoma alleghaniensis*, a large aquatic salamander of the Ohio valley; also, any of various American aquatic salamanders of the genus *Amblystoma*.

mud-sill (mud′sil), *n.* The lowest sill of a structure, usually placed in or on the ground; fig., the class of persons, or one of the class of persons, forming the lowest stratum of society (U. S.).

mud=sling-ing (mud′sling″ing), *n.* The making of injurious charges or imputations, esp. of an unseemly kind, as against a candidate in a political campaign. [Slang.]

mud-stone (mud′stōn), *n.* A clayey rock of nearly uniform texture throughout, with little or no lamination.

mud=tur-tle (mud′tur′tl), *n.* Any of various fresh-water turtles of the U. S., as *Cinosternum pennsylvanicum*, a small turtle found in many parts of the country.

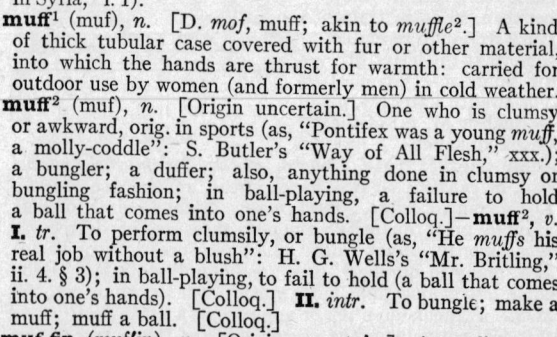

Mud-turtle (*Cinosternum pennsylvanicum*).

mu-ez-zin (mụ-ez′in), *n.* [Ar. *mu'adhdhin*.] In Mohammedan countries, a crier who, from the minaret or other part of a mosque, at stated hours gives the call (*azan*) summoning the people to prayer: as, "the musical pathos of the *muezzin's* cry" (G. W. Curtis's "Howadji in Syria," i. 1).

muff[1] (muf), *n.* [D. *mof*, muff; akin to *muffle*[2].] A kind of thick tubular case covered with fur or other material, into which the hands are thrust for warmth: carried for outdoor use by women (and formerly men) in cold weather.

muff[2] (muf), *n.* [Origin uncertain.] One who is clumsy or awkward, orig. in sports (as, "Pontifex was a young *muff*, a molly-coddle": S. Butler's "Way of All Flesh," xxx.); a bungler; a duffer; also, anything done in clumsy or bungling fashion; in ball-playing, a failure to hold a ball that comes into one's hands. [Colloq.]—**muff**[2], *v.* **I.** *tr.* To perform clumsily, or bungle (as, "He *muffs* his real job without a blush": H. G. Wells's "Mr. Britling," ii. 4. § 3); in ball-playing, to fail to hold (a ball that comes into one's hands). [Colloq.] **II.** *intr.* To bungle; make a muff; muff a ball. [Colloq.]

muf-fin (muf′in), *n.* [Origin uncertain.] A small, round cake made with wheat flour, corn-meal, or the like, eaten with butter and usually served hot.—**muf-fin-eer′** (-ēr′), *n.* A small vessel with a perforated top for sprinkling sugar, salt, or the like over muffins.

Muffineers.

muf-fle[1] (muf′l), *n.* [F. *mufle*; origin unknown.] The thick, bare part of the upper lip and nose of ruminants and rodents.

muf-fle[2] (muf′l), *n.* [F. *moufle*, mitten, OF. *moufle, mouffle*, < ML. *muffula*, mitten, thick glove; from Teut.] A mitten (Sc.); also, a boxing-glove (as, "Just like a black eye in a recent scuffle (For sometimes we must box without the *muffle*)": Byron's "Don Juan," ii. 92).

muf-fle[3] (muf′l), *n.* [F. *moufle*, appar. another use of *moufle*, mitten, E. *muffle*[2].] An oven or arched chamber in a furnace or kiln, used for heating substances without direct contact with the fire; also, a furnace containing such a chamber.

muf-fle[4] (muf′l), *v.*; *-fled, -fling.* [ME. *muflen*, appar. < OF. *moufle*, mitten, glove, E. *muffle*[2]: cf. OF. *enmouflé*, mittened, gloved, wrapped up.] **I.** *tr.* To wrap or envelop in a cloak, shawl, scarf, or the like disposed about the person, esp. about the face and neck (as, "He was so *muffled* in a multiplicity of clothing, that he was scarcely to be recognized," Motley's "Dutch Republic," iii. 1: often with *up*); formerly, sometimes, to blindfold†; also, to wrap with something to deaden or prevent sound (as, to *muffle* oars, drums, bells, or a canary-bird's cage; "I vish you could *muffle* that 'ere Stiggins, and take him vith you," Dickens's "Pickwick Papers," xxvii.); deaden (sound) by wrappings or other means (as, "I heard voices, too, speaking with a hollow sound, and as if *muffled* by a rush of wind or water": C. Brontë's "Jane Eyre," iii.); also, to dim (light: as, "through the dim length of the apartment, where crimson curtains *muffled* the glare of sunshine," Hawthorne's "Twice-Told Tales," Fancy's Show-Box). **II.** *intr.* To muffle one's self (*up*), as in garments or other wrappings.—**muf′fle**[4], *n.* Something that muffles; esp., something that deadens sound; also, muffled sound.—**muf′fler,** *n.* Anything used for muffling; esp., a scarf or wrapping, usually of wool or silk, worn about the neck or throat for warmth; also, any of various devices for deadening sound, as the sound of the escaping gases of an internal-combustion engine.

muf-ti[1] (muf′ti), *n.*; pl. *-tis* (-tiz). [Ar. *muftī.*] An official expounder of the Mohammedan law; in Turkey, the official head of the state religion or one of his deputies.

muf-ti[2] (muf′ti), *n.* [Orig. Anglo-Ind.; perhaps for *mufti dress*: see *mufti*[1].] Civilian dress as opposed to military or other uniform, or as worn by one who usually wears a uniform: as, "Who was that person on deck in *mufti*?" (Marryat's "Mr. Midshipman Easy," xxv.); "some officer in *mufti*" (Marryat's "Peter Simple," ii.).

mug[1] (mug), *n.* [Cf. Sw. *mugg*, Norw. *mugge*, mug.] A drinking-vessel, usually cylindrical and commonly with a handle; also, such a vessel with its contents (as, "He had a large *mug* of cider between his hands": Mrs. Stowe's "Oldtown Folks," xvii.); the quantity it holds.

Beer-mug. — German pottery with pewter mountings; 18th century.

mug[2] (mug), *n.* [Origin obscure.] The face; also, the mouth; also, a grimace. [Slang.]—**mug**[2], *v.*; *mugged, mugging.* **I.** *tr.* To take a photograph of (a person), esp. in compliance with an official or legal requirement; also, of a thug, etc., to assault (a victim, etc.) from the rear by locking the forearm around the neck and throttling. [Slang.] **II.** *intr.* To grimace. [Slang.]

mug[3] (mug), *n.* [Origin obscure.] A fool; a simpleton; a dupe. [Slang, Eng.]

mug[4] (mug), *n.* [Cf. Icel. *mugga*, soft drizzling mist.] A mist; a drizzle; a damp, gloomy state of the atmosphere. [Prov. Eng. and Sc.]

mug-ful (mug′fu̇l), *n.*; pl. *-fuls.* A quantity sufficient to fill a mug: as, "Many a *mugful* [of cider] did I draw" (Mrs. Stowe's "Oldtown Folks," xxvii.).

mug-ger (mug′ėr), *n.* [Hindi *magar.*] A man-eating crocodile, *Crocodilus palustris*, of India, etc., growing to about 12 feet in length.

mug-gi-ness (mug′i-nes), *n.* Muggy condition.

mug-gins (mug′inz), *n.* [Appar. < *Muggins*, proper name: cf. *juggins.*] A simpleton (slang, Eng.); also, a game of dominoes in which any player, if he can make the sum of the two ends of the line equal five or a multiple of five, adds the number so made to his score; also, any of several simple games at cards in which the object of each player is to get rid of his cards according to certain rules; the exclamation used in exacting a penalty in such a game; the player penalized.

mug-gy (mug′i), *a.* [See *mug*[4].] Of the atmosphere, weather, etc., damp and close; humid and oppressive.

mug-wump (mug′wump), *n.* [Algonquian *mugquomp*, leader.] A great man; one who affects superiority, esp. in political principles: hence applied in the presidential campaign of 1884 to Republicans who refused to support the party nominee (J. G. Blaine), and later to any political independent. [U. S.]—**mug′wump″er-y, mug′wump-ism,** *n.* The principles or practice of mugwumps.

Mu-ham-mad-an (mọ̈-ham′ạ-dạn), etc. See *Mohammedan*, etc.

Mu-har-ram (mọ̈-hur′um), *n.* [Ar., lit. 'forbidden,' 'sacred.'] The first month of the Mohammedan year; also, an annual Mohammedan religious celebration held during this month.

mu-jik (mö-zhik′ or mö′zhik), *n.* See *muzhik.*

muk-luk (muk′luk), *n.* [Eskimo.] In Alaska, a seal; also, sealskin; also, a kind of boot made of sealskin.

mu-lat-to (mụ̄-lat′ō), *n.*; pl. *mulattoes* (-ōz). [Sp. and Pg. *mulato*, mulatto (so called from the hybrid origin), < *mulo*, < L. *mulus*, E. *mule*[2].] The offspring of parents of whom one is white and the other a negro.

mul-ber-ry (mul′ber″i), *n.*; pl. *-berries* (-iz). [Cf. OHG. *mūlberi* (G. *maulbeere*), for *mūrberi*, < L. *morum*, mulberry, + OHG. *beri*, berry.] The edible, berry-like collective fruit of any tree of the genus *Morus*; a tree of this genus, as *M. rubra* ('red mulberry'), with dark-purple fruit, *M. nigra* ('black mulberry'), with dark-colored fruit, and *M. alba* ('white mulberry'), with fruit nearly white and with leaves especially valued as food for silkworms; also, a dull, dark purplish-red color. —**mul′ber-ry=col″ored,** *a.*

Black Mulberry (*Morus nigra*).

mulch (mulch or mulsh), *n.* [Cf. ME. *molsh*, soft (as soil), also G. *molsch*, soft, overripe (as fruit).] In *gardening*, straw, leaves, loose earth, etc., spread on the ground to protect the roots of newly planted trees, etc.—**mulch,** *v. t.* To cover with mulch.

mulct (mulkt), *n.* [L. *mulcta, multa.*] A fine; a penalty. —**mulct,** *v. t.* [L. *mulctare, multare*, < *mulcta, multa.*] To punish (a person, or, formerly, an offense) by fine or forfeiture (as, "Some [apostates] . . . were again received into the Christian fold, after being severely *mulcted*": Irving's "Conquest of Granada," lxvii.); deprive of something as a penalty (as, "The Prince . . . remitted two-thirds of the sum in which they had been *mulcted*," Motley's "Dutch Republic," iv. 1; to *mulct* one of his pay); hence, in general, to deprive or divest of something.

mule[1] (mūl), *n.* [F.] A kind of slipper which leaves the heel exposed.

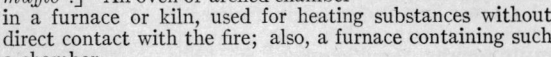

mule[2] (mūl), *n.* [OF. *mul*, masc., *mule* (F. *mule*), fem., < L. *mulus*, masc., *mula*, fem., mule.] The offspring of a male ass and a mare, a valuable product of artificial selection, characterized by long ears and by a tail destitute of hair at the root, but of the general form and the size of the horse, and possessing the patience and sure-footedness of the ass and the vigor and strength of the horse, and superior to the latter as a beast of burden; sometimes, a hinny; also, any hybrid; also, a stupid or stubborn person (colloq.: as, "'Now don't be a young *mule*,' said Good Mrs. Brown," Dickens's "Dombey and Son," vi.); also, a coin which, owing to mistake or caprice, has the same design on both sides or any improper association of designs; also, a machine which spins cotton, etc., into yarn and winds it on spindles.—**mule'=deer,** *n.* A deer, *Odocoileus hemionus*, with large ears, common in western North America.—**mu-le-teer** (mū-lẹ-tēr'), *n.* [F. *muletier*, < *mulet*, dim. of OF. *mul*.] A driver of mules: as, "*muleteers* hurrying forward their burdened animals" (Irving's "Conquest of Granada," lxx.).

Mule-deer.

mul-ey (mụl'i). [Cf. Ir. *maol*, bald.] **I.** *a.* Of cattle, hornless; polled. **II.** *n.* A muley animal; also, any cow.

mu-li-eb-ri-ty (mū-li-eb'ri-ti), *n.* [LL. *muliebritas*, < L. *muliebris*, womanly, < *mulier*, woman.] Womanly nature or qualities; womanhood.

mul-ish (mū'lish), *a.* Like a mule; characteristic of a mule; stubborn, obstinate, or intractable.—**mul'ish-ly,** *adv.*—**mul'ish-ness,** *n.*

mull[1] (mul), *n.* [Cf. Icel. *mūli*, a jutting crag, promontory.] A promontory. [Sc.]

mull[2] (mul), *v. t.* [Origin uncertain.] To heat, sweeten, and spice for drinking, as ale, wine, etc.: as, "*mulled* port" (Lever's "Harry Lorrequer," xiv.); "*mulled* cider" (Irving's "Knickerbocker's New York," vii. 2).

mull[3] (mul), *n.* [Earlier *mulmul*, < Hind. *malmal*.] A soft, thin kind of muslin.

mull[4] (mul), *v.* [Cf. *muddle* and *moil*.] **I.** *tr.* To confuse mentally†, or stupefy† (as, "Peace is a very apoplexy, lethargy; *mulled*, deaf, sleepy, insensible": Shakspere's "Coriolanus," iv. 5. 239); also, to make a mess or failure of (colloq.). **II.** *intr.* To work or think in a confused or ineffective way; study or ruminate (*over*). [Colloq., U. S.]—**mull**[4], *n.* A mess, muddle, or failure: as, to make a *mull* of anything attempted. [Colloq.]

mull[5] (mul), *n.* [Sc. form of *mill*[2].] A snuff-box: as, "Hendry once offered Mr. Dishart a snuff from his *mull*" (Barrie's "Auld Licht Idylls," iii.). [Sc.]

mul-lah (mụl'ä or mul'ä), *n.* [Turk., Pers., and Hind. *mullā*, < Ar. *maulā*.] In Mohammedan countries, a title of respect for one who is learned in or teaches or expounds the sacred law: as, "He made Kim learn whole chapters of the Koran by heart, till he could deliver them with the very roll and cadence of a *mullah*" (Kipling's "Kim," x.).

mul-len, mul-lein (mul'ẹn), *n.* [AF. *moleine*, perhaps < OF. *mol*, < L. *mollis*, soft.] A stout scrophulariaceous weed, *Verbascum thapsus*, with coarse woolly leaves and dense spikes of yellow flowers; any plant of the same genus, or any of various similar plants.

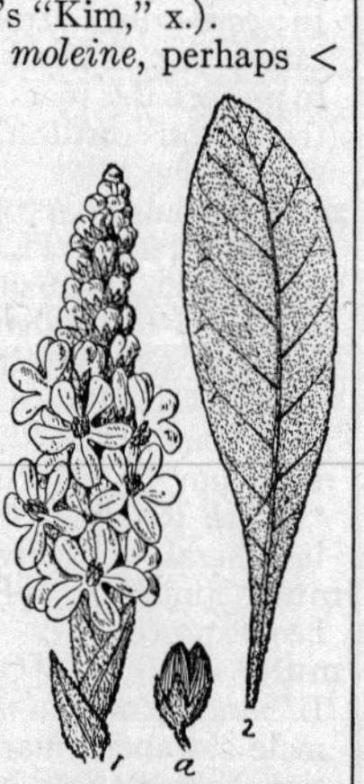
Mullen (*Verbascum thapsus*). — 1, the inflorescence; 2, the leaf; *a*, the fruit.

mul-ler (mul'ėr), *n.* [ME. *molour*, prob. < OF. *moldre* (F. *moudre*), < L. *molere*, grind.] An implement of stone or other substance with a flat base for grinding paints, powders, etc., on a slab of stone or the like; also, any of various mechanical devices for grinding.

mul-let[1] (mul'et), *n.* [OF. F. *mulet*, dim. < L. *mullus*, red mullet.] Any of the fishes of the genus *Mullus* or the family *Mullidæ*, having two long barbels at the mouth and a mostly red coloration, and including European species highly esteemed as a delicacy by the ancient Romans (the 'red mullets,' or 'surmullets'); also, any fish of the genus *Mugil* or of the family *Mugilidæ*, which includes various marine and fresh-water species with a nearly cylindrical body and a generally gray coloration (the 'gray mullets'); also, any of various other fishes.

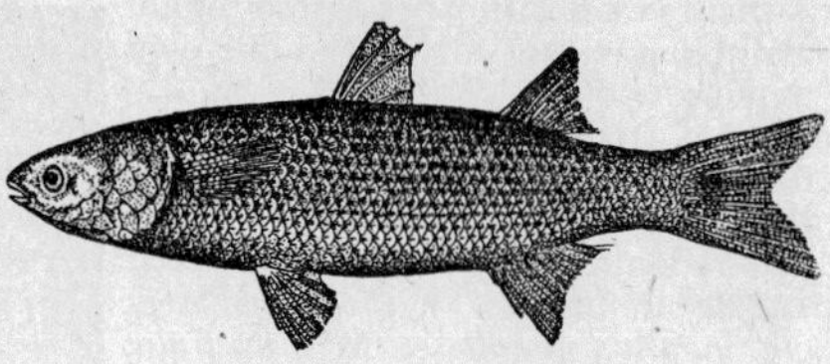
Gray Mullet (*Mugil cephalus*).

mul-let[2] (mul'et), *n.* [OF. F. *molette*, rowel, mullet, dim. < L. *mola*, millstone.] In *her.*, a star-shaped figure, usually with five straight or regular points. Cf. *estoile*.

Arms with Three Mullets.

mul-ley (mụl'i), *a.* and *n.* See *muley*.

mul-li-ga-taw-ny (mul"i-gạ-tâ'ni), *n.* [Tamil *milagu-tannīr*, 'pepper-water.'] A soup of East Indian origin, flavored with curry.

mul-li-grubs (mul'i-grubz), *n.* [A humorous made word.] Low spirits; the sulks; also, stomach-ache. [Slang.]

mul-lion (mul'yọn), *n.* [Prob. a corruption of *munnion* for earlier *moniel*, *monial*: cf. OF. *meigneaul* (F. *meneau*), mullion.] In *arch.*, a vertical member, as of stone or wood, between the lights of a window, the panels in wainscoting, or the like (as, "On the one side ran a range of windows lofty and large, divided by carved *mullions* of stone": Scott's "Guy Mannering," iv.); also, one of the radiating bars of a rose-window or the like.—**mul'lioned,** *a.* Having mullions: as, *mullioned* windows.

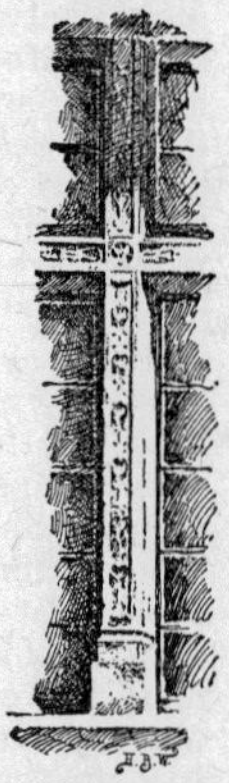
Renaissance Mullion.—Hôtel de Ville, Beaugency, France.

mulsh (mulsh), *n.* and *v.* See *mulch*.

mul-tan-gu-lar (mul-tang'gū-lär), *a.* [See *multi-*.] Having many angles.

mul-te-i-ty (mul-tē'i-ti), *n.* [L. *multus*, much, many.] The quality of being ma y; manifoldness.

multi-, mult-. Forms of L. *mul us*, much, many, used in combination.—**mul-ti-ax-i-al** (mul-ti-ak'si-ạl), *a.* Having many or several axes.—**mul-ti-cel'lu-lar** (-sel'ū-lär), *a.* Having many or several cells.—**mul'ti-coil** (-koil), *a.* Having more than one coil, as an electrical device.—**mul'ti-col-ored** (-kul-ọrd), *a.* Of many colors.—**mul-ti-cos'tate** (-kos'tāt), *a.* Having many costæ, ribs, or ridges.—**mul-ti-den'tate** (-den'tāt), *a.* Having many teeth or tooth-like pro cesses.

mul-ti-fa-ri-ous (mul-ti-fā'ri-us), *a.* [L. *multifarius*: see *multi-* and *-farious*.] Having many different parts, elements, forms, etc. (as, a *multifarious* whole; "the *multifarious* growth of gardens," Hawthorne's "House of the Seven Gables," xix.); often (with a plural noun), of many kinds, or numerous and varied (as, *multifarious* activities or interests); manifold; also, arranged in many rows.—**mul-ti-fa'ri-ous-ly,** *adv.*—**mul-ti-fa'ri-ous-ness,** *n.*

mul-ti-fid (mul'ti-fid), *a.* [L. *multifidus*, < *multus*, much, many, + *fid-*, stem of *findere*, cleave.] Cleft into many parts, divisions, or lobes. Also **mul-tif'i-dous** (-tif'i-dus).

mul-ti-flo-rous (mul-ti-flō'rus), *a.* [LL. *multiflorus*, < L. *multus*, much, many, + *flos* (*flor-*), flower.] In *bot.*, bearing many flowers, as a peduncle.

mul-ti-foil (mul'ti-foil), *n.* [See *multi-* and *foil*[1].] In *arch.*, an ornament or

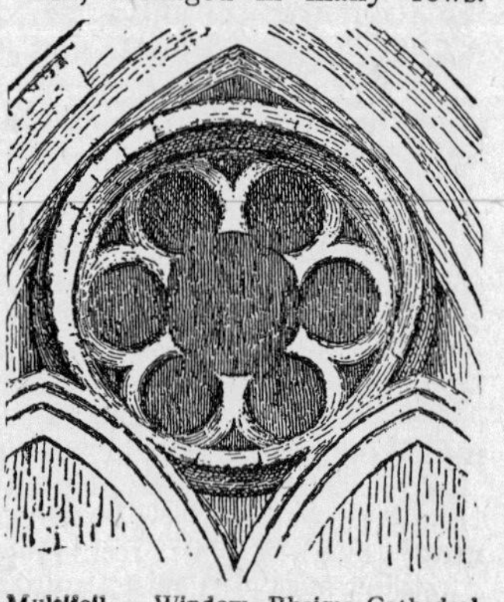
Multifoil. — Window, Rheims Cathedral, France; 13th century.

decorative feature having many foils or lobes, esp. more than five (see *cinquefoil*).

mul-ti-fold (mul′ti-fōld), *a.* [See *multi-*.] Manifold.

mul-ti-fo-li-ate (mul-ti-fō′li-ạ̄t), *a.* [NL. *multifoliatus*, < L. *multus*, much, many, + *folium*, leaf.] In *bot.*, having many leaves or leaflets.

mul-ti-form (mul′ti-fôrm), *a.* [L. *multiformis*, < *multus*, much, many, + *forma*, form.] Having many forms; of many different forms or kinds: as, "The shifts and turns, Th' expedients and inventions, *multiform*, To which the mind resorts" (Cowper's "Task," ii. 287).—**mul-ti-for′mi-ty** (-fôr′mi-ti), *n.*

mul-ti-graph (mul′ti-gräf), *n.* [L. *multus*, much, many, + Gr. γράφειν, write.] A kind of type-setting and printing machine, as for office use, for printing circulars, imitation typewritten letters, etc. [Proprietary name.]—**mul′ti-graph,** *v. t.* To copy or make by means of a multigraph.

mul-ti-lam-i-nate (mul-ti-lam′i-nāt), *a.* [See *multi-*.] Having many laminæ or layers.—**mul-ti-lat′er-al** (-lat′ẹ-rạl), *a.* Having many sides; many-sided.—**mul-ti-lin′e-al, mul-ti-lin′e-ar** (-lin′ē-ạl, -ạ̈r), *a.* Having many lines.—**mul-ti-lo′bate** (-lō′bāt), *a.* Having many lobes.—**mul-ti-lob′u-lar** (-lob′ụ̄-lạ̈r), *a.* Having many lobules.—**mul-ti-loc′u-lar** (-lok′ụ̄-lạ̈r), *a.* Having many loculi, chambers, or cells.

mul-til-o-quent (mul-til′ọ̄-kwẹnt), *a.* [L. *multus*, much, + *loquens* (*loquent-*), ppr. of *loqui*, speak.] Speaking much; talkative; verbose.—**mul-til′o-quence,** *n.*

mul-ti-mil-lion-aire (mul″ti-mil-yọn-ãr′), *n.* [See *multi-*.] One with property worth several millions, as of dollars.

mul-ti-mo-tored, *a.* With a number of motors or engines.

mul-ti-no-mi-al (mul-ti-nō′mi-ạl), *a.* and *n.* [From *multi-* + *-nomial* as in *binomial*.] Same as *polynomial*.

mul-ti-nom-i-nal (mul-ti-nom′i-nạl), *a.* [L. *multinominis*, < *multus*, much, many, + *nomen*, name.] Having many names.

mul-ti-nu-cle-ar (mul-ti-nū′klẹ̄-ạ̈r), *a.* [See *multi-*.] Having many or several nuclei, as a cell. Also **mul-ti-nu′cle-ate, mul-ti-nu′cle-at-ed** (-āt, -ā-ted).

mul-tip-a-ra (mul-tip′ạ-rạ̈), *n.*; pl. *-ræ* (-rē). [NL., < L. *multus*, much, many, + *parere*, bring forth.] In *obstet.*, a woman who has borne two or more children, or who is parturient the second time.—**mul-tip′a-rous,** *a.* [NL. *multiparus*.] Producing many, or more than one, at a birth; in *bot.*, of a cyme, having many lateral axes.

mul-ti-par-tite (mul-ti-pär′tīt), *a.* [L. *multipartitus*, < *multus*, much, many, + *partitus*, pp. of *partire*, divide.] Divided into many parts; having many divisions.

mul-ti-ped, mul-ti-pede (mul′ti-ped, -pēd). [L. *multipes* (*multiped-*), adj. and n. (as n., also *multipeda*), < *multus*, much, many, + *pes* (*ped-*), foot.] **I.** *a.* Having many feet. **II.** *n.* A multiped animal.

mul-ti-phase (mul′ti-fāz), *a.* [See *multi-*.] Having many phases; in *elect.*, polyphase.

mul-ti-plane (mul′ti-plān), *n.* [See *multi-*.] A flying-machine or aëroplane with several sustaining planes.

mul-ti-ple (mul′ti-pl). [ML. *multiplus*, < L. *multus*, much, many, + *-plus*: see *double*.] **I.** *a.* Consisting of, having, or involving many individuals, parts, elements, relations, etc.; manifold; in *bot.*, of a fruit, collective. **II.** *n.* In *math.*, a number which contains another number some number of times without a remainder: as, 12 is a *multiple* of 3; a common *multiple* of two or more numbers (a number that can be divided by each of them without a remainder).—**in multiple,** in *elect.*, in parallel.

mul-ti-plex (mul′ti-pleks), *a.* [L. *multiplex*, < *multus*, much, many, + *-plex*: see *duplex*.] Manifold; multiple: as, *multiplex* telegraphy (a system for sending several messages, esp. more than two in each direction, simultaneously over the same wire).—**mul′ti-plex-ly,** *adv.*

mul-ti-pli-a-ble (mul′ti-plī-ạ-bl), *a.* That may be multiplied. Also **mul′ti-pli-ca-ble** (-pli-kạ-bl).

mul-ti-pli-cand (mul″ti-pli-kand′ or mul′ti-pli-kand), *n.* [L. *multiplicandus*, gerundive of *multiplicare*, E. *multiply*¹.] In *math.*, the number to be multiplied by another.

mul-ti-pli-cate (mul′ti-pli-kāt), *a.* [L. *multiplicatus*, pp. of *multiplicare*, E. *multiply*¹.] Multiple; manifold.

mul-ti-pli-ca-tion (mul″ti-pli-kā′shọn), *n.* [L. *multiplicatio*(*n-*).] The act or process of multiplying, or the state of being multiplied (as, the *multiplication* of books; "I fairly cowered down . . . under this *multiplication* of hardships," H. Melville's "Typee," viii.); in *math.*, the process of finding the quantity (the *product*) resulting from the addition of a given quantity (the *multiplicand*) taken as many times as there are units in another given quantity (the *multiplier*).—**mul″ti-pli-ca′tion-al,** *a.*

mul-ti-pli-ca-tive (mul′ti-pli-kā-tiv), *a.* Tending to multiply or increase; having the power of multiplying.—**mul′ti-pli-ca-tive-ly,** *adv.*

mul-ti-pli-ca-tor (mul′ti-pli-kā-tọr), *n.* [LL.] A multiplier: chiefly in *math.*

mul-ti-pli-ci-ty (mul-ti-plis′i-ti), *n.*; pl. *-ties* (-tiz). [LL. *multiplicitas*, < L. *multiplex*: see *multiplex*.] The state of being multiplex or manifold (as, "the *multiplicity* of his benevolence": Hawthorne's "House of the Seven Gables," xviii.); manifold variety; also, a multitude or great number (as, "A strange *multiplicity* of sensations seized me": Mrs. Shelley's "Frankenstein," xi.).

mul-ti-pli-er (mul′ti-plī-ėr), *n.* One who or that which multiplies; in *math.*, the number by which another is to be multiplied.

mul-ti-ply¹ (mul′ti-plī), *v.*; *-plied*, *-plying*. [OF. F. *multiplier*, < L. *multiplicare* (pp. *multiplicatus*), multiply, < *multiplex*: see *multiplex*.] **I.** *tr.* To make many or manifold; increase the number, quantity, etc., of (as, "May thy days be *multiplied!*" Scott's "Talisman," xviii.); sometimes, to increase by procreation (as, "that all creatures might be tempted to *multiply* their kind, and fill the world with inhabitants": Addison, in "Spectator," 413); propagate; hence, to produce (animals or plants) by propagation; in *math.*, to take by addition a given number of times; find the product of by multiplication. **II.** *intr.* To grow in number, quantity, etc.; increase; sometimes, to increase in number by procreation or natural generation (as, "Be fruitful, and *multiply*," Gen. i. 22; "As for my cats, they *multiplied*," Defoe's "Robinson Crusoe," i. 13); in *math.*, to perform the process of multiplication.

mul-ti-ply² (mul′ti-pli), *adv.* [From *multiple*.] In a multiple or manifold way; in the manner of a multiple.

mul-ti-po-lar (mul-ti-pō′lạ̈r), *a.* [See *multi-*.] Having many poles.

mul-tip-o-tent (mul-tip′ọ̄-tẹnt), *a.* [L. *multipotens* (*-ent-*), < *multus*, much, + *potens*, E. *potent*.] Having much power; very powerful: as, "by Jove *multipotent*" (Shakspere's "Troilus and Cressida," iv. 5. 129).

mul-ti-tude (mul′ti-tūd), *n.* [OF. F. *multitude*, < L. *multitudo* (*multitudin-*), < *multus*, much, many.] The state or character of being many, or numerousness (as, "Ye are this day as the stars of heaven for *multitude*": Deut. i. 10); also, a great number, or host (as, a *multitude* of friends; a *multitude* of words, reasons, or faults); also, a great number of persons gathered together, or a crowd or throng (as, "Great *multitudes* followed him, and he healed them all": Mat. xii. 15).—**the multitude,** the great mass of people; the many; the common people; the populace: as, a play that appeals to *the multitude*; the fickle favor of *the multitude*.—**mul-ti-tu′di-nous** (-tū′di-nus), *a.* Forming a multitude or great number, or existing, occurring, or present in great numbers (as, a *multitudinous* race or sect; *multitudinous* followers; "*Multitudinous* echoes awoke and died in the distance," Longfellow's "Evangeline," ii. 2); very numerous; comprising many items, parts, or elements (as, "his *multitudinous* correspondence with the public bodies," Motley's "Dutch Republic," iv. 4; "I heard again the *multitudinous* murmur of the city," G. W. Curtis's "Prue and I," iii.); also, crowded or thronged (poetic: as, "the *multitudinous* streets," Shelley's "Revolt of Islam," xii. 1); also, of or pertaining to the multitude† (as, "Pluck out The *multitudinous* tongue; let them not lick The sweet which is their poison": Shakspere's "Coriolanus," iii. 1. 156).—**mul-ti-tu′di-nous-ly,** *adv.*—**mul-ti-tu′di-nous-ness,** *n.*

mul-ti-va-lent (mul-ti-vā′lẹnt or mul-tiv′ạ-), *a.* [See *multi-* and *-valent*.] In *chem.*, having a valence of more than one; also, having more than one degree of valence.—**mul-ti-va′lence,** *n.*

mul-ti-valve (mul′ti-valv). [See *multi-*.] **I.** *a.* Having many valves, as a shell. **II.** *n.* A multivalve shell, or an animal having one.—**mul-ti-val'vu-lar** (-val'vū-lär), *a.* Multivalve.

mul-tiv-o-cal (mul-tiv'ǫ-kal), *a.* [L. *multus*, much, many + *vox* (*voc-*), voice, speech.] Admitting of many meanings; equivocal; ambiguous.

mul-toc-u-lar (mul-tok'ū-lär), *a.* [L. *multus*, much, many, + *oculus*, eye.]. Having many, or more than two, eyes.

mum[1] (mum). [Imit.] **I.** *a.* Silent; not saying a word: as, to keep *mum*; "The company being otherwise rather *mum* and silent, my uncle told . . . anecdotes" (Thackeray's "Newcomes," xlix.). **II.** *interj.* Silence! as, "*Mum*, then, and no more" (Shakspere's "Tempest," iii. 2. 59).

mum[2] (mum), *v. i.*; *mummed, mumming.* [OF. *momer* mask one's self, masquerade; from Teut.] To mask, as for sport; go about making diversion in masquerade dress, as a mummer does; act as a mummer: as, "Christmas was the grand season for *mumming* in England. Some were disguised as bears, others as unicorns, or wore deer's hide and antlers" (Encyc. Brit., 11th ed., XVIII. 966).

mum[3] (mum), *n.* [G. *mumme.*] A strong ale or beer (orig. from Brunswick) popular in England during the 17th and 18th centuries.

mum-ble (mum'bl), *v.*; *-bled, -bling.* [ME. *momelen* = D. *mommelen* = G. *mummeln* = Sw. *mumla* = Dan. *mumle*, mumble; orig. imit.] **I.** *intr.* To speak indistinctly or unintelligibly, as with partly closed lips or from imperfect use of the mouth-parts (as, "She appeared as if she wanted to say something, and kept making signs . . . and *mumbling*": C. Brontë's "Jane Eyre," xxi.); mutter low, indistinct words; also, to chew ineffectively, as from loss of teeth (as, to *mumble* on a crust); work upon food, etc., with toothless gums. **II.** *tr.* To utter indistinctly, as with partly closed lips or imperfect use of the mouth-parts (as, "He affirmed that we *mumbled* our speech with our lips and teeth, and ran the words together without pause or distinction": Smollett's "Humphry Clinker," July 13); also, to chew, or try to eat, with difficulty, as from loss of teeth; work upon (food, etc.) with toothless gums; also, to press, rub, or caress with the mouth or lips.—**mum'ble,** *n.* A low, indistinct utterance or sound.—**mum'bler,** *n.*—**mum'bling-ly,** *adv.*

mum-bo=jum-bo (mum'bō-jum'bō), *n.*; pl. *-bos* (-bōz). [From *Mumbo Jumbo*, an idol or bugbear of west African tribes.] An object of superstitious awe or reverence.

mum-mer (mum'ėr), *n.* [OF. *momeur*, < *momer*, E. *mum*[2].] One who wears a mask, fantastic disguise, or any masquerade dress, for sport or in making diversion for others, esp. as formerly and still locally at Christmas, New Year's, and other festive seasons (cf. *guiser*); specif., an actor in one of the rural plays long given, as at Christmas, in England and elsewhere (as, "The play was hastily rehearsed, whereupon the other *mummers* were delighted with the new knight": Hardy's "Return of the Native," ii. 5); hence, in general, a stage-player or actor (playful or disparaging).—**mum'mer-y,** *n.*; pl. *-ies* (-iz). [OF. F. *momerie.*] The performance of mummers; a performance or show given by mummers; hence, any mere theatrical performance or ceremony or empty spectacular pretense, or what is regarded as such (as, "Archbishop Grindal long hesitated about accepting a mitre from dislike of what he regarded as the *mummery* of consecration," Macaulay's "Hist. of Eng.," i.; "I wished to see what sort of *mummery* my magician would practise," Kinglake's "Eothen," xviii.).

mum-mi-fi-ca-tion (mum''i-fi-kā'shǫn), *n.* The process of mummifying, or the state of being mummified.

mum-mi-fy (mum'i-fī), *v. t.*; *-fied, -fying.* [See *-fy.*] To make (a dead body) into a mummy, as by embalming and drying; hence, to make like a mummy; dry or shrivel up.

Head of Mummy of Seti I., father of Rameses II.

mum-my (mum'i), *n.*; pl. *mummies* (-iz). [OF. F. *momie*, < ML *mumia*, < Ar. *mūmiyā*, embalmed body, < *mūm*, wax.] The dead body of a human being or animal preserved by the ancient Egyptian (or some similar) method of embalming; hence, a dead body dried and preserved by the agencies of nature; also, a withered or shrunken living being; also, the bituminous or other embalming matter found about Egyptian mummies, or, later, the substance of mummies or of dead bodies, formerly used as a medicine; a bituminous drug obtained from the East†; a brown bituminous pigment; also, a pulpy mass (colloq. or prov.: as, beaten or mashed to a *mummy*; "battering the warriors' faces into *mummy* by terrible yerks from their hinder hoofs," Swift's "Gulliver's Travels," iv. 12).—**mum'my,** *v. t.*; *-mied, -mying.* To make into or like a mummy; mummify.—**mum'my=case,** *n.* A case of wood or other material in which a mummy, wrapped in cloth, was inclosed before being placed in an outer receptacle: the case being shaped to conform to the body, and carved and painted to represent the dead person.—**mum'my=cloth,** *n.* Cloth in which mummies are found enveloped; also, a modern fabric, as of linen, with a slightly irregular weave, used esp. as a foundation for embroidery.

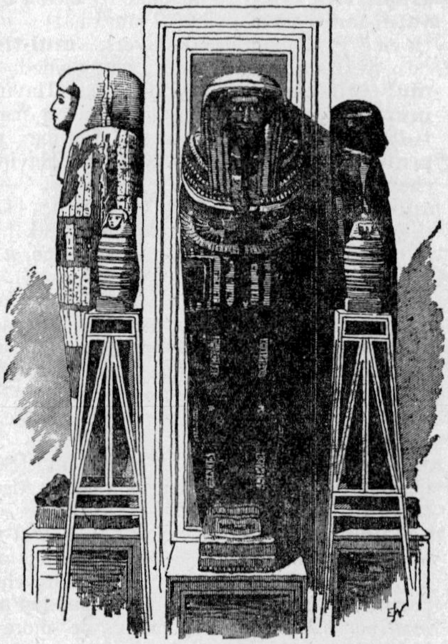

Mummy-cases, Cairo, Egypt.

mump (mump), *v.* [Imit.: cf. *mumble* and *mum*[1].] **I.** *tr.* To mumble or mutter; also, to munch or chew; also, to beg; also, to overreach or cheat. [Now chiefly prov.] **II.** *intr.* To mumble or mutter; also, to mope; sulk; also, to make mouths; grimace; grin; also, to munch or chew; also, to beg; sponge on others. [Now chiefly prov.]—**mump,** *n.* A grimace†; *pl.*, the sulks (now prov. Eng.). See *mumps.*—**mumps,** *n.* In *pathol.*, a specific infectious disease characterized by inflammatory swelling of the parotid and (usually) other salivary glands, and sometimes by inflammation of the testicles, ovaries, etc.

mump-si-mus (mump'si-mus), *n.* [From the old story of the illiterate priest who, on being told of an error in his reading of the (Latin) mass, replied, "I will not change my old *mumpsimus* for your new *sumpsimus.*"] One who clings obstinately to old errors or disproved ideas†; also, an error obstinately clung to, regardless of right or reason.

mun (mun), *v. aux.* [From Scand.: cf. Icel. *mon, mun* (inf. *munu*), will, shall.] Must: as, "Poor folk *mun* get on as they can" (C. Brontë's "Jane Eyre," xxviii.). [Sc. and prov. Eng.]

munch (munch), *v.* [ME. *monchen*; appar. imit.] **I.** *tr.* To chew with steady or vigorous working of the jaws, and often audibly: as, "He *munches* his dry toast" (Thackeray's "Newcomes," xiv.); "The horses went on *munching* the contents of their leathern head-bags" (Howells's "Chance Acquaintance," v.). **II.** *intr.* To chew steadily or vigorously, and often audibly (as, "A sailor's wife had chestnuts in her lap, And *munch'd*, and *munch'd*, and *munch'd*": Shakspere's "Macbeth," i. 3. 5); also, to work the jaws as in chewing.

Mun-chau-sen-ism (mun-châ'zen-izm), *n.* A disposition to indulge in extravagant romance and wild exaggeration, in the manner of Baron Munchausen, the hero (based upon

Karl Friedrich Hieronymus, Freiherr von Münchhausen, 1720–97) and pretended author of a book of incredible adventures originally written (in English) by Rudolf Erich Raspe (1737–94) and published in 1785, but afterward much expanded by others; hence, a grossly extravagant story or statement; an incredible tale.

munch-er (mun′chėr), *n.* A person or animal that munches.

mun-dane (mun′dān), *a.* [LL. *mundanus*, < L. *mundus*, world, universe, also toilet articles, < *mundus*, clean, neat, fine, elegant: cf. *cosmos*.] Of or pertaining to the world, universe, or earth; also, of or pertaining to this world or earth as contrasted with heaven (as, *mundane* affairs; *mundane* glory); worldly; earthly.—**mun′dane-ly,** *adv.*—**mun′dane-ness, mun-dan′i-ty** (-dan′i-ti), *n.*

mun-go (mung′gō), *n.* [Origin uncertain.] A fibrous material obtained by pulling to pieces woolen rags and remnants, or a fabric made of it: similar but superior to shoddy.

mun-goos, mun-goose (mung′gös), *n.* See *mongoos.*

mu-ni-ci-pal (mū-nis′i-pal), *a.* [L. *municipalis*, < *municeps*, citizen of a privileged (sometimes self-governing) town standing in a certain relation to Rome, < *munus*, duty, gift, + *capere*, take.] Of or pertaining to the local self-government or corporate government of a city or town (as, a *municipal* charter; *municipal* officers; a *municipal* election; *municipal* railways or waterworks); also, having local self-government (as, a *municipal* borough); also, pertaining to the internal affairs of a state or nation (as, *municipal* law, the law of a particular state, as distinguished from international law or the law of nations).—**mu-ni-ci-pal′i-ty** (-pal′i-ti), *n.*; pl. *-ties* (-tiz). A city, town, or other district possessed of corporate privileges of local self-government; a community under municipal jurisdiction; also, the governing body of such a district or community.—**mu-ni′ci-pal-ize** (-īz), *v. t.*; *-ized, -izing.* To endow with municipal institutions; make a municipality of; also, to bring under municipal ownership or control (as, to *municipalize* street-railways).—**mu-ni″ci-pal-i-za′tion** (-i-zā′shon), *n.*—**mu-ni′ci-pal-ly,** *adv.*

mu-nif-i-cence (mū-nif′i-sens), *n.* [L. *munificentia*, < *munificent-*, for *munificus*, bountiful, munificent, < *munus*, gift, + *facere*, make.] Great liberality in giving (as, "a scene which the *munificence* of nature had adorned with unrivalled beauties": C. B. Brown's "Wieland," xxiii.); also, ample measure, or bountifulness (as, the *munificence* of a gift).—**mu-nif′i-cent,** *a.* Extremely liberal in giving or bestowing (as, a *munificent* benefactor; "My father gave me ten shillings and my mother five for pocket money and I thought them *munificent*," S. Butler's "Way of All Flesh," vi.); very generous; also, characterized by great generosity, as giving; given in ample measure or bountifully, as a gift.—**mu-nif′i-cent-ly,** *adv.*

mu-ni-ment (mū′ni-ment), *n.* [OF. *muniment*, < L. *munimentum*, fortification, defense, < *munire*: see *munition*.] A defense or protection (now rare: as, "We cannot spare the coarsest *muniment* of virtue," Emerson's "Conduct of Life," vi.); also, *pl.*, equipments† or furnishings†; also, *sing.*, in *law*, a document, as a title-deed or a charter, by which rights or privileges are defended or maintained (chiefly in *pl.*: as, "The privileges of London were recognized [in 1066] by a royal writ which still remains, the most venerable of its *muniments*, among the city's archives," Green's "Conquest of Eng.," xi.).

mu-ni-tion (mū-nish′on), *n.* [F. *munition*, < L. *munitio(n-)*, fortifying, a fortification, defense, < *munire*, wall, fortify, strengthen, < *mœnia*, walls.] **I.** *n.* Fortification†, or a fortification†; also, *sing.* or (now usually) *pl.*, materials used in war for defense or attack; military stores or supplies, esp. ammunition, weapons, etc. (as, "to bring up reinforcements and supplies of military *munition*," Scott's "Talisman," xx.; "two thousand men, with seven field-pieces, and many wagon-loads of *munitions*," Motley's "Dutch Republic," iii. 8); in general, material or equipment for carrying on any undertaking. **II.** *a.* Pertaining to or having to do with munitions: as, a *munition* ship (for carrying munitions); a *munition* plant (for manufacturing munitions).—**mu-ni′tion,** *v. t.* To provide with munitions.—**mu-ni′tion-ment,** *n.*

mun-nion (mun′yon), *n.* Same as *mullion.*

munt-jac (munt′jak), *n.* [Javanese.] Any of various small deer constituting the genus *Cervulus*, of southern and eastern Asia and the adjacent islands, esp. *C. muntjac*, of Java, India, etc.; also, any of the small deer of the related genus *Elaphodus*, of China and Tibet.

A Chinese Muntjac (*Elaphodus michianus*).

mu-ræ-na, mu-re-na (mū-rē′nạ), *n.* [L., < Gr. *μύραινα*, sea-eel.] A moray or eel of the genus *Muræna*, esp. *M. helena.* See *moray.*

mu-ral (mū′ral), *a.* [F. *mural*, < L. *muralis*, < *murus*, wall.] Of or pertaining to a wall (as, "Disburden'd heaven rejoiced, and soon repair'd Her *mural* breach": Milton's "Paradise Lost," vi. 879); also, resembling a wall; perpendicular or steep, as a precipice; also, placed or executed on a wall (as, a *mural* painting, a painting executed, esp. in distemper, upon the wall of a building); also, executing mural paintings (as, a *mural* painter).—**mural crown,** a golden crown formed with indentations to resemble a battlement, bestowed among the ancient Romans on the soldier who first mounted the wall of a besieged place and there lodged a standard.—**mu′ral-ly,** *adv.*

Mu-ra-to-ri-an (mū-ra-tō′ri-an), *a.* Of or pertaining to L. A. Muratori (1672–1750), an Italian scholar.—**Muratorian fragment,** a fragment of early Christian literature, written probably toward the end of the 2d century, containing a list or canon (*Muratorian canon*) of New Testament writings: so called because discovered and first edited by Muratori.

mur-der (mėr′dėr), *n.* [AS. *morthor* = Goth. *maurthr* = F. *meurtre* (from Teut.), murder; akin to L. *mors*, death: see *mortal*.] The unlawful killing of a human being with malice aforethought.—**murder will out,** the crime of murder is not to be hidden; a thing that one wishes to keep secret is sure to come out or become known.—**mur′der,** *v.* **I.** *tr.* To kill (a human being) unlawfully with malice aforethought: hence, to kill or slaughter inhumanly or barbarously; fig., to put an end to, or destroy; also, to spoil or mar by bad execution, representation, pronunciation, etc. (as, to *murder* a piece of music; "to have *murdered* Shakespeare," Marryat's "King's Own," xlv.; to *murder* the king's English); also, to spend (time) unprofitably (as, "Their evenings they *murder* in private parties": Smollett's "Humphry Clinker," May 5). **II.** *intr.* To commit murder.—**mur′der-er,** *n.* One who commits murder.—**mur′der-ess,** *n.* A woman who commits murder.—**mur′der-ous,** *a.* Guilty of, bent on, or capable of murder (as, "Enforced to fly Thence into Egypt, till the *murderous* king Were dead, who sought his life": Milton's "Paradise Regained," ii. 76); also, of the nature of or involving murder (as, "a *murderous* deed," Shakspere's "2 Henry VI.," v. 1. 185; a *murderous* assault); intentionally deadly.—**mur′der-ous-ly,** *adv.*—**mur′der-ous-ness,** *n.*

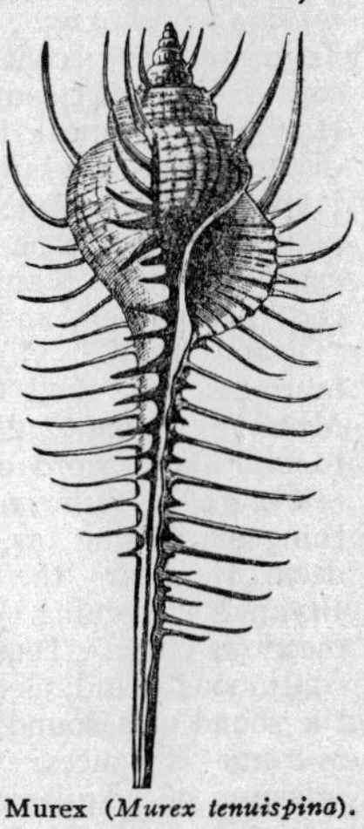

Murex (*Murex tenuispina*).

mure† (mūr), *n.* [OF. F. *mur*, < L. *murus*.] A wall.—**mure,** *v. t.*; *mured, muring.* [OF. F. *murer*, < LL. *murare*, < L. *murus*.] To provide or surround with a wall or walls, as a building or a town; block up with a wall, as a doorway; shut up or inclose within walls, immure, or imprison, as a person.

mu-re′na, *n.* See *murænа.*

mu-rex (mū′reks), *n.*; pl. *murexes,* L. *murices* (-ri-sēz). [L.] Any of the marine gastropods, common in tropical seas, constituting the genus *Murex* or the family *Muricidæ,* certain species of which yielded the celebrated purple dye of the ancients (see cut on preceding page); also, a shell used as a trumpet, as in representations of Tritons in art.

Triton with Murex.

mu-ri-ate (mū′ri-āt), *n.* [L. *muria,* brine.] Same as *chloride.* [Now chiefly in commercial use.]—**mu′ri-at-ed** (-ā-ted), *a.* Charged with or containing a chloride or chlorides, as mineral waters. —**mu-ri-at′ic** (-at′ik), *a.* [L. *muriaticus,* pickled, < *muria.*] Pertaining to or obtained from brine or salt: now only in 'muriatic acid,' the commercial name for hydrochloric acid.

mu-ri-form (mū′ri-fôrm), *a.* [L. *murus,* wall: see *-form.*] In *bot.,* resembling or suggesting a wall composed of bricks arranged in courses: as, *muriform* cellular tissue.

Muriform Epidermis of the Superior Face of a Grass-leaf.

mu-rine (mū′rin). [L. *murinus,* < *mus* (*mur-*), mouse.] **I.** *a.* Pertaining to or resembling a mouse or rat; belonging or pertaining to the *Muridæ,* the family of rodents containing the mice and rats, or to the *Murinæ,* the subfamily including the domestic species. **II.** *n.* A murine rodent.

murk (mėrk). [Also *mirk;* AS. *mirce* = OS. *mirki* = Icel. *myrkr* = Sw. and Dan. *mörk,* dark.] **I.** *a.* Dark, or with little light, as night, places, etc.; obscured with mist or the like, as the air, etc.; dim; obscure; also, darkening or obscuring the air (as, "sea-mists *mirk*": Lowell's "Black Preacher," 38); also, dark in color; fig., gloomy or cheerless. [Now chiefly prov. or poetic.] **II.** *n.* Darkness (as, "Ere twice in *murk* and occidental damp Moist Hesperus hath quench'd his sleepy lamp": Shakspere's "All's Well," ii. 1. 166); also, air obscured with mist or the like. [Now chiefly prov. or poetic.]—**murk′y,** *a.*; compar. *murkier,* superl. *murkiest.* Dark, esp. intensely or utterly (as, "through the *murky* blackness of the night," Lever's "Harry Lorrequer," xlvii.; "Soon that *murky* prison was radiant with the brightness of the Spirit," J. H. Newman's "Callista," xxxiii.); obscured or thick with mist, haze, or the like, as the air, etc.; also, obscuring the air, as mist, etc. (as, "The great metropolis lay . . . buried under a homemade cloud of *murky* smoke": Irving's "Tales of a Traveler," ii. 4); also, dark in color; fig., gloomy; cheerless; sullen.—**murk′i-ly,** *adv.*—**murk′i-ness,** *n.*

mur-mur (mėr′mėr), *v.* [OF. F. *murmurer,* < L. *murmurare,* < *murmur,* a murmuring sound; imit.] **I.** *intr.* To make a low, continuous sound, or a succession of low, soft, or indistinct sounds, as bees, a brook, the wind, trees, etc.; also, to speak in a low tone, or indistinctly as from distance (as, "We saw the lights and heard The voices *murmuring*": Tennyson's "Princess," iv. 537); also, to complain in a low tone, or without open, public, or formal expression (as, "Many were *murmuring* against the leader they had chosen, and wished to depose him": Parkman's "Oregon Trail," vi.); grumble. **II.** *tr.* To sound by murmurs (as, "Fell Charybdis *murmur'd* soft applause": Milton's "Comus," 259); also, to utter in a low tone (as, to *murmur* a word of caution).—**mur′mur,** *n.* [OF. F. *murmure,* < *murmurer.*] The sound or a sound of something murmuring (as, "Listening to thy *murmur,* he shall deem He hears the rustling leaf and running stream," Bryant's "Evening Wind"; "Faint *murmurs* from the meadows come," Tennyson's "Day-Dream," 26); any low, continuous sound, as of a brook, the wind, trees, etc.; also, the sound or a sound of low or indistinct speaking (as, the *murmur* of voices; "The visitor made a grateful little *murmur* of acquiescence," Hawthorne's "Blithedale Romance," x.); hence, a whispered report, or rumor (archaic: as, "There was a *murmur* . . . that he possesses other sciences, now lost to the world," Scott's "Guy Mannering," xvii.); also, an expression of discontent in a low voice, privately, or without public or formal protest (as, "In the City of London, lately so turbulent, scarcely a *murmur* was heard": Macaulay's "Hist. of Eng.," iv.); in *med.,* any of various normal or pathological sounds heard in auscultation of the heart, lungs, etc.—**mur′mur-er,** *n.*—**mur′mur-ing-ly,** *adv.*—**mur′mur-less,** *a.* Without murmur: as, "a *murmurless* vision of cataract" (Lowell's "Pictures from Appledore," iii.).—**mur′mur-ous,** *a.* Abounding in or characterized by murmurs; murmuring: as, *murmurous* waters; "There was a slight *murmurous* sound in the room, as of wind long pent up in many lungs suddenly exhaled" (W. H. Hudson's "Green Mansions," i.).—**mur′mur-ous-ly,** *adv.*—**mur′mur-ous-ness,** *n.*

mur-phy (mėr′fi), *n.*; pl. *-phies* (-fiz). [From *Murphy,* Irish surname.] An Irish or white potato; also, occasionally, a sweet potato (as, "The rich, tawny soil seemed specially adapted to the crop; the great yellow *murphies* rolling out of the hills like eggs from a nest": H. Melville's "Omoo," lix.). [Colloq.]

mur-ra (mur′ạ), *n.* [L.] See *murrine.*

mur-rain (mur′ẹn), *n.* [OF. *morine,* < L. *mori,* die: see *mortal.*] A plague or pestilence (archaic or prov., and much used in imprecations, etc.: as, "A *murrain* on your monster!" Shakspere's "Tempest," iii. 2. 88); also, any of various diseases of cattle, as anthrax, foot-and-mouth disease, and Texas fever.

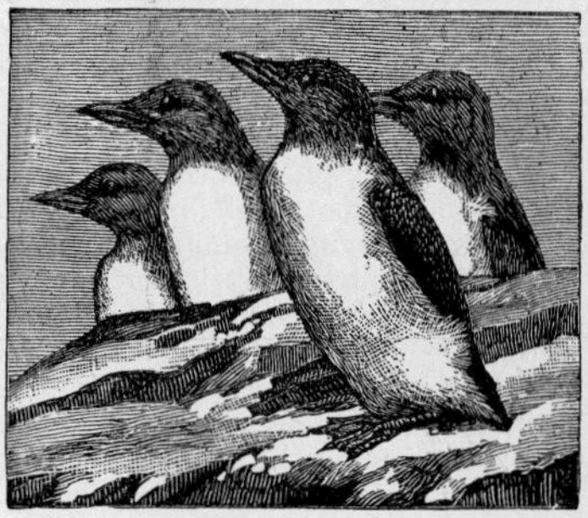

Murre, or Foolish Guillemot (*Uria troile*).

murre (mėr), *n.* [Origin obscure.] Any guillemot of the genus *Uria;* also, the razor-billed auk.

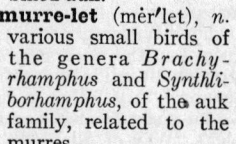

murre-let (mėr′let), *n.* [From *murre* + *-let.*] Any of various small birds of the genera *Brachyrhamphus* and *Synthliborhamphus,* of the auk family, related to the murres.

Black-throated Murrelet (*Synthliborhamphus antiquus*).

mur-rey (mur′i). [OF. *more,* < ML. *moratus,* < L. *morum,* mulberry.] **I.** *a.* Of the color called mulberry; of a dull, dark purplish red. [Archaic.] **II.** *n.* Murrey color. [Archaic.]

mur-rine, mur-rhine (mur′in), *a.* [L. *murrinus,* also *murrhinus,* < *murra,* less properly *murrha.*] Made of or pertaining to a substance (L. *murra,* commonly explained as a stone, perhaps fluor-spar or agate, but also conjectured to be porcelain) highly esteemed by the Romans as a material for vases, cups, etc.—**murrine** (or **murrhine**) **glass,** any of certain kinds of glassware supposed to resemble the Roman murrine ware; esp., a ware composed of glass in which metals, precious stones, or the like are embedded.

mur-ther (mėr′ᴛʜėr), etc. Obs. or prov. form of *murder,* etc.

mu-sa-ceous (mū̦-zā′shius), *a.* [NL. *Musa,* the typical genus; from Ar.] Belonging to the *Musaceæ,* or banana family of plants.

mu-sang (mū̦-sang′), *n.* [Malay *mūsang.*] An East Indian palm-cat or palm-civet, *Paradoxurus hermaphroditus* (or *musanga*); hence, any of various related or similar animals. See cut on following page.

mus-ca-del (mus-kạ-del′), *n.* Same as *muscatel.*

mus-ca-din (müs-kȧ-daṅ), *n.* [F. musk-flavored sweetmeat, also dandy, < It. *moscardino*, < ML. *moscus*, LL. *muscus*, E. *musk*.] A dandy; an exquisite: specif. applied during the French Revolution to members of a party of men of fashion or of the better class socially (about 1794–96) who held moderate or reactionary opinions.

Musang (*Paradoxurus hermaphroditus*).

mus-ca-dine (mus′kạ-din or -dīn), *n.* Same as *muscatel*.

mus-cæ vol-i-tan-tes (mus′sē vol-i-tan′tēz). [NL., 'flies flying about.'] Specks that seem to dance in the air before the eyes, due to defects in the vitreous humor of the eye or to other causes.

mus-cat (mus′kat), *n.* [F., < Pr. *muscat*, < ML. *muscatus*, having the flavor of musk, musky, < LL. *muscus*, E. *musk*.] Any of several varieties of grape, usually of light color and having the flavor or odor of musk; also, muscatel wine.

mus-ca-tel (mus-kạ-tel′), *n.* [OF. *muscatel*, *muscadel*, dim. < Pr. *muscat*: see *muscat*.] A strong, sweet wine made from muscat grapes; also, the muscat grape.

mus-cid (mus′id). [NL. *Muscidæ*, pl., < L. *musca*, a fly.] **I.** *n.* Any of the *Muscidæ*, a family of dipterous insects including the common house-fly. **II.** *a.* Belonging or pertaining to the *Muscidæ*.

mus-cle (mus′l), *n.* [F. *muscle*, < L. *musculus*, muscle, lit. 'little mouse' (from the appearance of certain muscles), dim. of *mus*, mouse: see *mouse*, and cf. *mussel*.] An organ or part, composed of contractile tissue, whose function is to produce movement in the animal body; the tissue composing such organs; also, muscular strength, or brawn (as, a man of *muscle*); also, a mussel.—**mus′cle=bound,** *a.* Having muscles enlarged and inelastic, as from excessive athletic training.—**mus-cled** (mus′ld), *a.* Supplied with muscles.—**mus-cly** (mus′li), *a.* Muscular.

mus-coid (mus′koid), *a.* [L. *muscus*, moss: see *-oid*.] Moss-like.

mus-col-o-gy (mus-kol′ọ-ji), *n.* [L. *muscus*, moss: see *-logy*.] The branch of botany that treats of mosses; bryology.—**mus-col′o-gist,** *n.*

mus-co-va-do (mus-kō-vā′dō), *n.* [Sp. (*azúcar*) *mascabado*, Pg. (*açucar*) *mascavado*, (sugar) of inferior quality.] Raw or unrefined sugar, obtained from the juice of the sugar-cane by evaporation and draining off the molasses.

Mus-co-vite (mus′kọ-vīt). **I.** *n.* A native or inhabitant of Muscovy (the former principality of Moscow, or, by extension, Russia generally); a Russian; also [*l. c.*], the common light-colored variety of mica. **II.** *a.* Of or pertaining to Muscovy or its inhabitants; pertaining to Russia generally; Russian.

mus-co-vy (mus′kọ-vi) **duck.** [Erron. for *musk-duck*.] The American musk-duck.

mus-cu-lar (mus′kū-lạ̈r), *a.* [L. *musculus*, E. *muscle*.] Of or pertaining to muscle or the muscles (as, *muscular* contractions; *muscular* rheumatism); dependent on or effected by the muscles (as, *muscular* strength; *muscular* labor); also, of the nature of or consisting of muscle (as, *muscular* tissue); also, having well-developed muscles, brawny, or strong (as, "spreading shoulders, *muscular* and broad," Thomson's "Liberty," iv. 146; "His figure was short, fleshy, and enormously *muscular*," Lever's "Harry Lorrequer," vi.).—**muscular Christianity,** a type of Christianity that recognizes the value of sound physical powers, maintained by wholesome exercise and enjoyments, in fulfilling the duties of life; popularly, a type of Christianity that employs muscular as well as spiritual powers in the service of religion: orig. (about 1857) a playful expression for a conception derived from the writings of Charles Kingsley, although the phrase itself was expressly objected to by him.—**mus-cu-lar′i-ty** (-lar′i-ti), *n.* The state of being muscular; muscular development; muscular strength.—**mus′cu-lar-ly,** *adv.*

mus-cu-la-tion (mus-kū-lā′shọn), *n.* [= F. *musculation*, < L. *musculus*, E. *muscle*.] The action or the disposition of the muscles.

mus-cu-la-ture (mus′kū-lạ-ṭūr), *n.* [= F. *musculature*, < L. *musculus*, E. *muscle*.] The system of muscles.

mus-cu-lo- (mus′kū-lọ-). Form of L. *musculus*, muscle, used in combination, as in *musculocutaneous* (both muscular and cutaneous), *musculotendinous* (both muscular and tendinous).

Muse[1] (mūz), *n.* [OF. F. *Muse*, < L. *Musa*, < Gr. Μοῦσα, Muse.] Any of the nine sister goddesses of classical mythology, daughters of Zeus and Mnemosyne ('Memory'), presiding over poetry and song, the drama, dancing, astronomy, etc. (see *Calliope*, *Clio*, *Erato*, *Euterpe*, *Melpomene*, *Polyhymnia*, *Terpsichore*, *Thalia*, *Urania*); hence, some other goddess supposed to preside over a particular field, or some person considered supreme in some field, as of literary accomplishment (see phrases following); also [*cap.* or *l. c.*], the goddess or the power conceived to inspire a poet (as, "Fool, said my *Muse* to me, look in thy heart and write": Sidney's "Astrophel and Stella," i.); hence [*l. c.*], a poet's characteristic genius, bent, or powers (as, a theme suited to one's *muse*); sometimes, a poet (chiefly poetic).—**Attic Muse,** Xenophon, the Greek historian and miscellaneous writer: so called from the elegance of his Attic Greek.—**tenth Muse,** a tenth goddess, presiding over a particular field, added to the nine classical Muses (as, "the *tenth Muse* who now governs the periodical press": Trollope's "Warden," xiv.); also, an admiring appellation for a woman deemed worthy, for her poetic or literary powers, to be ranked with the nine classical Muses (applied to women of various countries and periods, ancient and modern).

muse[2] (mūz), *v.*; *mused*, *musing*. [OF. *muser*, muse, ponder, also (OF. and F.) dawdle, loiter, trifle (cf. *amuse*); origin uncertain.] **I.** *intr.* To pursue one's thoughts with complete absorption, often as in a reverie (as, "The Vicar sat *musing* before the fire in his study": H. Kingsley's "Geoffry Hamlyn," ix.); reflect or meditate in silence, as on some subject; ponder, as with a view to forming an opinion or reaching a decision (as, "The King *Mused* for a little on his plea, but, last, Allowing it": Tennyson's "Marriage of Geraint," 42); also, to wonder (archaic: as, "Do not *muse* at me, my most worthy friends," Shakspere's "Macbeth," iii. 4. 85); also, to gaze meditatively or wonderingly (archaic: as, "For some time Rip lay *musing* on this scene," Irving's "Sketch-Book," Rip Van Winkle). **II.** *tr.* To muse or meditate on (archaic: as, "Come then, expressive Silence, *muse* his praise," Thomson's "Hymn on the Seasons," 118); also, to wonder (with a clause: archaic: as, "I *muse* what this young fox may mean!" M. Arnold's "Sohrab and Rustum").—**muse**[2], *n.* A fit of musing (archaic: as, "He would fall into a deep *muse* over our accounts, staring at the page or out of the window," Stevenson's "Master of Ballantrae," ii.); also, wonder† (as, "He . . . was fill'd With admiration and deep *muse*, to hear Of things so high and strange": Milton's "Paradise Lost," vii. 52).—**muse′ful,** *a.* Deeply thoughtful.

mu-se-ol-o-gy (mū-zẹ-ol′ọ-ji), *n.* [See *museum* and *-logy*.] The science of arranging and managing museums.—**mu-se-ol′o-gist,** *n.*

mus-er (mū′zėr), *n.* One who muses.

mu-sette (mū-zet′), *n.* [F., dim. of OF. *muse*, bagpipe: cf. *Muse*[1] and *music*.] A kind of bagpipe; also, a soft pastoral melody appropriate to this instrument or imitating a bagpipe air; a dance to such a tune.

mu-se-um (mū-zē′um), *n.*; pl. *-ums*. [L., < Gr. μουσεῖον, seat of the Muses, place of study, library, < Μοῦσα, E. *Muse*[1].] A building or place for the keeping and exhibition of a collection of objects of interest or curiosity, works of art, scientific specimens, or the like; commonly, the building or place together with the collection of objects.

mush[1] (mush), *n.* [Prob. var. of *mash*.] Meal, esp. Indian meal, boiled in water or milk until it forms a thick, soft mass (cf. *hasty-pudding*); hence, any thick, soft matter or mass (as, soil reduced to *mush* by rain; a *mush* of mud);

fig., anything unpleasantly lacking in firmness, force, dignity, etc. (as, "I hate, where I looked for . . . at least a manly resistance, to find a *mush* of concession," Emerson's "Essays," Friendship; a *mush* of words or of flattery); specif., weak or maudlin sentiment or sentimental language (colloq.).

mush² (mush), *v.* [Prob. < F. *marcher*, walk: see *march²*.] **I.** *intr.* To go or travel on foot, esp. over the snow with a dog-team. [Northwestern America.] **II.** *tr.* To make (one's way) by mushing. [Northwestern America.]—**mush²**, *n.* A march on foot, esp. over the snow with a dog-team. [Northwestern America.]—**mush′er,** *n.*

mush-room (mush′röm). [OF. *mosseron* (F. *mousseron*), < *mosse* (F. *mousse*), moss: see *mousse*.] **I.** *n.* Any of various fleshy fungi, usually of very rapid growth, including the toadstools, puffballs, etc.; esp., any of certain edible species belonging to the family *Agaricaceæ*, characterized by a stalk with an umbrella-like cap (cf. *toadstool*); hence, anything of similar shape, or of correspondingly rapid growth; often, a person, family, or thing that has suddenly sprung into prominence (as, "Here is now a *mushroom* of opulence, who pays a cook seventy guineas a week for furnishing him with one meal a day": Smollett's "Humphry Clinker," May 5). **II.** *a.* Of, pertaining to, or made of mushrooms (as, a *mushroom* sauce); also, resembling or suggesting a mushroom in shape, as one form of anchor, a piece of a mechanism, or a woman's hat with the brim turning more or less markedly downward toward the edge; often, having sprung up like a mushroom, with great rapidity (as, a *mushroom* city; a *mushroom* aristocracy); sometimes, of rapid growth and brief duration, or ephemeral (as, a *mushroom* fame).—**mush′room,** *v. i.* To gather mushrooms; also, to have or assume the shape of a mushroom; expand at the end like a mushroom, as a bullet when striking an object.

Common Edible Mushroom (*Agaricus campestris*).

mush-y (mush′i), *a.* Mush-like (as, "Buck's feet sank into a white *mushy* something very like mud": Jack London's "Call of the Wild," i.); pulpy; fig., weakly sentimental (colloq.).

mu-sic (mū′zik), *n.* [OF. F. *musique*, < L. *musica*, < Gr. μουσική, any art over which the Muses presided, esp. lyric poetry sung to music, music, prop. fem. of μουσικός, adj. < Μοῦσα, E. *Muse¹*.] The art of combining tones or sounds, as of the singing voice or of special instruments (whether by audible execution or by composing and noting), with sweet or agreeable effect to the ear, emotional effectiveness, etc., or the science concerned with this subject and the principles of melody, harmony, rhythm, etc., involved in it (as, to teach *music*; the history of *music*); also, tones or sounds so combined, produced by the voice or by instruments (as, "*Music*, when soft voices die, Vibrates in the memory," Shelley's "To ——"; "How martial *music* every bosom warms!" Pope's "Ode on St. Cecilia's Day," iii.); hence, any sweet, pleasing, or harmoniously effective sounds or sound (as, the *music* of birds, of the wind, or of the waves; the *music* of the storm: also fig.); something delightful to hear (as, the words were *music* to our ears); musical, pleasing, or harmoniously effective quality in something heard (as, the *music* in a voice; "There is . . . *music* in its [the sea's] roar," Byron's "Childe Harold," iv. 178: also fig.); also, tones or sounds suitably combined or arranged, and usually indicated by a special notation, for being rendered by singing or by musical instruments (as, to set words to *music*); musical work or compositions for singing or playing (as, a piece of *music*; to compose *music*; the *music* of Wagner; Italian operatic *music*); the written or printed score of a musical composition, or such scores collectively; also, appreciation of or responsiveness to musical sounds or harmonies (as, "The man that hath no *music* in himself, Nor is not moved with concord of sweet sounds, Is fit for treasons, stratagems and spoils": Shakspere's "Merchant of Venice," v. i. 83); also, a company of musicians, as a band (as, "*Page.* The *music* is come, sir. *Fal.* Let them play. Play, sirs": Shakspere's "2 Henry IV.," ii. 4. 245).—**music drama,** an opera in which the musical form is specially adapted to dramatic requirements: applied orig. and specif. to the dramatic type of opera developed by Richard Wagner. See *Wagnerism*.—**music of the spheres,** a music, imperceptible to human ears, formerly supposed to be produced by the movements of the spheres or heavenly bodies (in accordance with the Pythagorean doctrine of the 'harmony of the spheres'), or of the spheres or concentric transparent spherical shells revolving round the earth, in which the older astronomers believed the heavenly bodies to be set (cf. "And after shewed he him the nyne speres, And after that the melodye herde he That cometh of thilke speres thryes three": Chaucer's "Parlement of Foules," 59–61).

mu-si-cal (mū′zi-kạl), *a.* [OF. F. *musical*, < ML. *musicalis*.] Of, pertaining to, or producing music; also, of the nature of or resembling music; melodious; harmonious; sweet or pleasing to the ear; also, set to or accompanied by music (as, a *musical* comedy); also, fond of or skilled in music.—**mu-si-cale** (mū-zi-kȧl′), *n.* [F., fem. of *musical*.] A social entertainment of a musical character.—**mu′si-cal-ly,** *adv.*—**mu′si-cal-ness,** *n.*

mu-sic=box (mū′zik-boks), *n.* A box or case containing an apparatus for producing music mechanically, as by means of a comb-like steel plate with tuned teeth sounded by small pegs or pins in the surface of a revolving cylinder or disk.

mu-sic=hall (mū′zik-hâl), *n.* A hall for musical entertainments; esp., a hall or theater for vaudeville, etc.

mu-si-cian (mū-zish′ạn), *n.* [OF. F. *musicien*.] One skilled in music (as, "The Scots are all *musicians*. Every man you meet plays on the flute, the violin, or violoncello": Smollett's "Humphry Clinker," Aug. 8); also, one who makes music a profession, esp. as a performer on an instrument.—**mu-si′cian-er,** *n.* A musician: as, "The '*musicianers*' amused the retainers . . . with a tune on the clarionet, fife, or trumpet" (Lover's "Handy Andy," xviii.). [Archaic or prov.]—**mu-si′cian-ly,** *a.* Of or befitting a musician; showing the skill and taste of a good musician.—**mu-si′cian-ship,** *n.* Musicianly skill.

mu-sic-less (mū′zik-les), *a.* Without music (as, a *musicless* entertainment); also, unmusical, or harsh or discordant in sound; also, ignorant of music.

musico-. Form of L. *musicus*, pertaining to music, musical, used in combination.—**mu-si-co-dra-mat-ic** (mū″zi-kǫ-drạ-mat′ik), *a.* Pertaining to or combining both music and the drama; musical and dramatic.—**mu-si-cog′ra-phy** (-kog′rạ-fi), *n.* [+ *-graphy*.] The art of writing down music in suitable characters; musical notation.—**mu-si-col′o-gy** (-kol′ǫ-ji), *n.* [+ *-logy*.] Systematic study or knowledge of the subject of music, its history, forms, methods, principles, etc.—**mu″si-co-log′i-cal** (-loj′i-kạl), *a.*—**mu-si-col′o-gist,** *n.*—**mu″si-co-ma′ni-a** (-mā′ni-ạ̈), *n.* A mania for music; musical monomania.—**mu″si-co-pho′bi-a** (-fō′bi-ạ̈), *n.* [+ *-phobia*.] A morbid dread or dislike of music.

mu-sic=room (mū′zik-röm), *n.* A room, as in a house, set apart or fitted up for use in performing music.

mu-sic=shell (mū′zik-shel), *n.* The shell of any of several marine gastropods of the family *Volutidæ* (the volutes), having markings that resemble written music; esp., the shell of *Voluta musica*, a species inhabiting the Caribbean Sea.

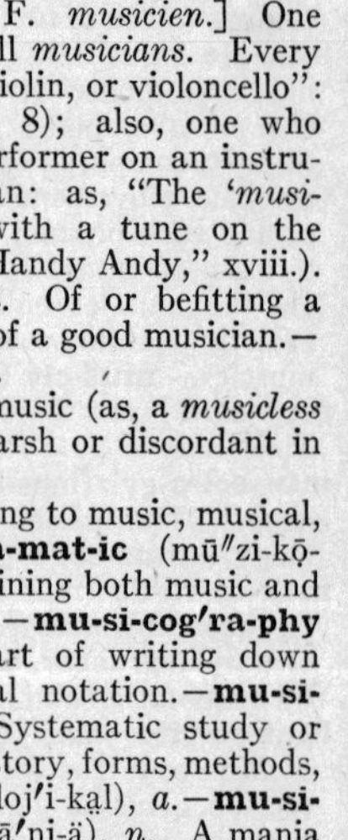

Music-shell (*Voluta musica*).

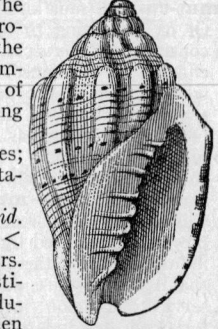

mus-ing (mū′zing), *p. a.* That muses; absorbed in thought; dreamy; meditative.—**mus′ing-ly,** *adv.*

mus-jid (mus′jid), *n.* Same as *masjid*.

musk (musk), *n.* [OF. F. *musc*, < LL. *muscus*, < LGr. μόσχος, < Pers. *mushk*, musk: cf. Skt. *mushka*, testicle.] A substance secreted in a glandular sac under the skin of the abdomen of the male musk-deer, having a strong, lasting odor, and much used in perfumery; a similar secretion of other animals; also, an artificial imitation of the substance; also, the odor, or some similar odor; also, the musk-deer. —**musk,** *v. t.* To perfume with musk.—**musk′=deer,** *n.* A small, hornless animal of the deer kind, *Moschus moschiferus,* of central Asia, the male of which secretes musk. —**musk′=duck,** *n.* A large, widely domesticated duck, *Cairina moschata,* orig. native in the American tropics; also, an Australian duck, *Biziura lobata.*

mus-keg (mus′keg), *n.* [N. Amer. Ind.] A bog or marsh; wet, boggy land. [Canadian.]

mus-kel-lunge (mus′kẹ-lunj), *n.* Same as *maskalonge.*

mus-ket (mus′ket), *n.* [F. *mousquet,* < It. *moschetto,* musket, orig. a kind of hawk, prob. a dim. < L. *musca,* a fly: cf. *mosquito.*] A hand-gun for infantry soldiers, introduced in the 16th century: the predecessor of the modern rifle.—**mus-ket-eer′** (-ke-tēr′), *n.* [Cf. F. *mousquetaire.*] A soldier armed with a musket.—**mus′ket-ry,** *n.* Muskets collectively (as, "The storming parties were assailed with cannon, with *musketry,* with pistols": Motley's "Dutch Republic," iii. 9); also, the fire of muskets; also, the art of firing small arms; also, troops armed with muskets.

Mus-kho-ge-an (mus-kō′gē-ạn), *a.* Belonging to or constituting a linguistic stock of North American Indians of the southeastern U. S., including the Choctaw, Creek, Seminole, Yazoo, and other tribes.

musk-mel-on (musk′mel″ọn), *n.* A kind of melon, of many varieties, a globular or oblong fruit with a juicy, often aromatically sweet, edible flesh (yellow, white, or green); also, the plant, *Cucumis melo,* bearing this fruit. See *cantaloup, Casaba melon,* and *nutmeg melon* (under *nutmeg*).

musk=ox (musk′oks), *n.* A bovine ruminant, *Ovibos moschatus,* intermediate between the ox and the sheep in size and other respects, now confined to arctic America: named from its musky odor.

Musk-ox.

musk=plant (musk′plant), *n.* A North American scrophulariaceous herb, *Mimulus moschatus,* cultivated for its yellow flowers and musk-scented foliage.

musk-rat (musk′rat), *n.* A large aquatic North American rodent, *Fiber zibethicus,* with a musky odor; the musquash; also, the fur of this animal, important commercially, and much used, when suitably dressed and dyed, as a substitute for sealskin (see *seal*², *n.*); also, any of various other more or less rat-like animals with a musky odor.

Muskrat (*Fiber zibethicus*).

musk=rose (musk′rōz′), *n.* A species of rose, *Rosa moschata,* having fragrant white flowers.

musk-y (mus′ki), *a.* Of or like musk, as odors; also, scented with musk; having an odor like that of musk.

Mus-lim (muz′lim or mus′-), *n.* and *a.* Same as *Moslem.*

mus-lin (muz′lin), *n.* [F. *mousseline,* < It. *mussolina,* muslin, < *Mussolo,* Mosul, town in Mesopotamia.] A thin cotton fabric made in various degrees of sheerness or fineness, and often printed, woven, or embroidered in patterns; also, heavier cotton cloth, bleached or unbleached, used for sheets, undergarments, etc.; also, sails or canvas, as of a ship (sailors' slang: as, "They staggered out of the bay . . . with a strong breeze, and under all the '*muslin*' they could carry," H. Melville's "Omoo," lxxvii.); also, womankind or femininity (slang, Eng.: as, "That was a pretty bit of *muslin* hanging on your arm — who was she?" Thackeray's "Pendennis," ii. 12).—**mus′lin=de=laine′** (-dē-lān′), *n.* Same as *mousseline de laine.* See under *mousseline.*—**mus′lined,** *a.* Hung with or dressed in muslin.

mus-quash (mus′kwosh), *n.* [Algonquian.] The muskrat.

mus-qui-to (mus-kē′tō), etc. See *mosquito,* etc.

muss (mus), *n.* [Origin uncertain; in later use associated with *mess.*] A scramble, as for something thrown (obs. or prov.: as, "When I cried 'Ho!' Like boys unto a *muss,* kings would start forth," Shakspere's "Antony and Cleopatra," iii. 13. 91); hence, a disorderly struggle, fracas, or row (colloq.); also, a state of disorder, or an untidy or dirty mess (colloq.).—**muss,** *v. t.* To put into disorder; make untidy or messy; rumple. [Colloq.]

mus-sel (mus′l), *n.* [AS. *muscle,* < L. *musculus,* muscle, also mussel: see *muscle.*] Any of the bivalve mollusks, mostly marine, constituting the family *Mytilidæ,* esp. any of those of the genera *Mytilus* and *Modiola,* as the common edible species, *Mytilus edulis;* also, any of the fresh-water bivalve mollusks constituting the family *Unionidæ.*

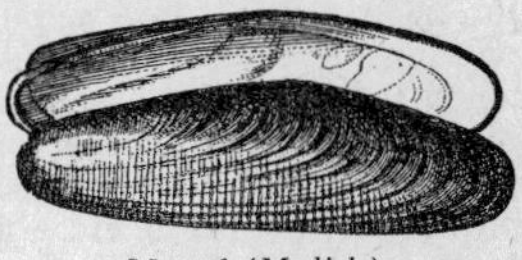

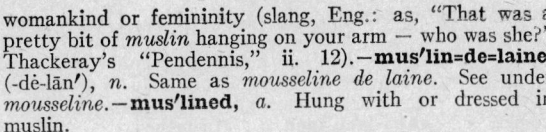

Mussel (*Modiola*).

Mus-sul-man (mus′ul-mạn), *n.*; pl. *-mans.* [Pers. *musulmān,* < Ar. *muslim:* see *Moslem.*] A Mohammedan: as, "I assembled a group of grave and worthy *Mussulmans* in the courtyard of the Khan" (Kinglake's "Eothen," xxiii.).

muss-y (mus′i), *a.* [From *muss.*] Untidy; messy; rumpled. [Colloq.]

must¹ (must), *v. aux.*; pret. *must.* [AS. *mōste,* pret. (pres. *mōt*), akin to D. *moeten,* G. *müssen,* inf., be obliged, Goth. *gamōtan,* find room, have place: cf. *mote*².] Am (is, are, etc.) obliged or compelled to, as by some constraining force or necessity (as, I *must* yield to my fate; man *must* eat to live); am bound by some imperative requirement to (as, I *must* keep my word; elliptically, "When Duty whispers low, Thou *must,* The youth replies, I can," Emerson's "Voluntaries," iii.); less strongly or definitely, have to, ought to, or should, for some reason (as, I *must* go soon; we *must* talk the matter over; you *must* read that article); also, am inevitably certain to (as, I *must* seem unpardonably careless; "What *must* be my feelings?" Godwin's "Caleb Williams," xii.); may reasonably be supposed to (as, you *must* have seen him many a time; it *must* be a large sum now); am expected to, or am to (as, "You *must* know he is a great writer": Smollett's "Humphry Clinker," April 26). *Must* is sometimes used (now archaically) with ellipsis of *go, get,* or some similar verb readily understood from the context: as, we *must* away; we *must* to horse at once.

must² (must), *n.* [AS. *must,* < L. *mustum,* prop. neut. of *mustus,* new, fresh.] New wine; the unfermented juice as pressed from the grape or other fruit.

must³ (must). [Hind. *mast:* cf. Skt. *matta,* intoxicated.] **I.** *a.* In a state of strong nervous excitement and dangerous irritability, as a male elephant or camel. **II.** *n.* The condition of being must.

must⁴ (must), *v. i.* or *t.* [Appar. < *musty.*] To become or make musty or moldy.—**must**⁴, *n.* Musty state, odor, or flavor; mold.

mus-tache, mous-tache (mus-tȧsh′), *n.* [F. *moustache,* < It. *mostaccio,* < Gr. μύσταξ, upper lip, mustache: cf. μάσταξ, mouth, < μασᾶσθαι, chew.] The hair growing on the upper lip, or on either half of the upper lip, of men (as, "a lofty, lordly kind of man . . . with a meagre face, furnished with huge *moustaches*": Irving's "Knickerbocker's New York," iii. 5); also, hairs or bristles growing near the mouth of an animal; also, a stripe of color suggestive of a mustache on the head or neck of a bird.—**old mustache.** See under *old, a.*—**mus-tache′=cup,** *n.* A man's drinking-cup having over the top at one side a piece with an opening to drink through, the mustache being kept out of the liquid. —**mus-tached′, mous-tached′,** *a.* Having a mustache: as, "The tall, slim, white-*moustached* man . . . was everything that was offensively aristocratic" (Howells's "Rise of Silas Lapham," vii.).

mus-tach-io (mus-tȧsh′iō), *n.*; pl. *-ios* (-iōz). [It. *mostaccio* or Sp. *mostacho*.] A mustache, usually of a man: as, "His face . . . was more than half hidden by whisker and *mustachio*" (Poe's "Murders in the Rue Morgue"); "a gentleman with . . . long black *mustachios*" (Thackeray's "Newcomes," i.).—**mus-tach′ioed,** *a.* Mustached.

mus-tang (mus′tang), *n.* [Sp. *mestengo, mestenco,* old var. of *mostrenco,* stray, ownerless.] The small, wild or half-wild horse of the American plains, descended from Spanish stock (as, "She [Indian woman] was mounted on a *mustang,* or half-wild horse": Irving's "Captain Bonneville," xix.); also, a grape, *Vitis candicans,* having light-colored fruit with an acrid taste, found in Texas (called in full *mustang grape*).

mus-tard (mus′tạrd), *n.* [OF. *moustarde* (F. *moutarde*), orig. a condiment of powdered mustard-seed mixed with must, < L. *mustum,* E. *must*².] Any of various brassicaceous plants, esp. *Brassica* (or *Sinapis*) *nigra* ('black mustard') and *Sinapis* (or *Brassica*) *alba* ('white mustard'), cultivated for their seed; also, a pungent powder prepared from the seed, much used as a food-seasoning or condiment (often in the form of a moist paste), also medicinally in plasters, poultices, etc.—**mus′tard=col″ored,** *a.* Of the color of ordinary ground mustard, a dull yellow with a tinge of green.—**mus′tard=gas,** *n.* A gas producing burns, blindness, and death, introduced by the Germans in the World War: being an organic compound containing sulphur and chlorine, and in its first state a liquid, subsequently gasified by the explosion of a shell containing it, and lingering for days in trenches, clothing impregnated, etc.—**mus′tard=oil,** *n.* Oil expressed from the seed of mustard.—**mus′tard=seed,** *n.* The seed of mustard: as, "The kingdom of heaven is like to a grain of *mustard seed* . . . Which indeed is the least of all seeds" (Mat. xiii. 31).

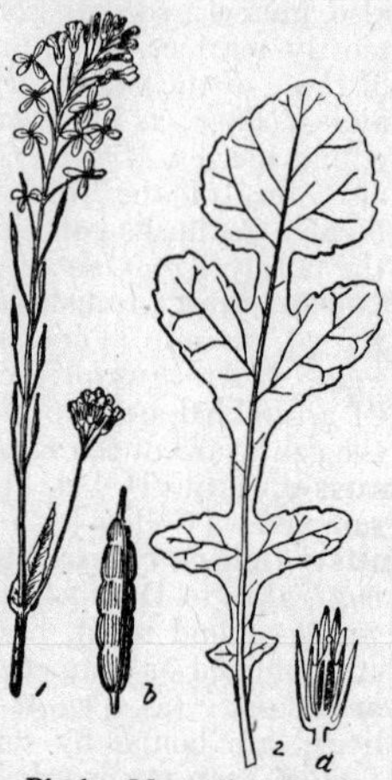

Black Mustard (*Brassica nigra*).—1, part of the inflorescence; 2, a leaf; *a,* flower cut longitudinally, the petals removed; *b,* a pod.

mus-tee (mus-tē′), *n.* Same as *mestee.*

mus-te-line (mus′tẹ-lin), *a.* [L. *mustelinus,* < *mustela,* weasel.] Weasel-like; tawny or brown, like a weasel in summer; also, belonging or pertaining to the subfamily *Mustelinæ* or to the family *Mustelidæ,* including the martens, sables, minks, weasels, badgers, otters, etc.

mus-ter (mus′tėr), *v. t.* [OF. *mostrer, monstrer* (F. *montrer*), < L. *monstrare,* show: see *monstrance.*] To show† or display†; also, to assemble (troops, a ship's crew, etc.), as for display, inspection, orders, discharge, etc. (as, "The garrison of Douglas was *mustered,* and . . . small parties . . . were sent out," Scott's "Castle Dangerous," xiv.; "The starboard watch were *mustered* upon the quarter-deck, and our worthy captain . . . harangued us," H. Melville's "Typee," v.); gather (forces, men, etc.) for service; enlist or enroll; call the roll of (now chiefly *naut.*); also, in general, to bring or get together (persons or things) for any purpose (as, bring all the good players you can *muster*; they could *muster* only a few dollars between them); fig., to gather or summon (strength, energy, spirit, courage, etc.: often with *up*); also, of an assembled force, etc., to number or comprise (as, "The whole garrison *mustered* but six or eight men": Irving's "Captain Bonneville," xxxiv.).—**to muster in,** or **to muster into service,** to enlist or enroll as recruits.—**to muster out,** or **to muster out of service,** to bring together, as soldiers, in order to discharge from service; discharge, as soldiers or a soldier, from service.—**mus′ter,** *v. i.* To show† or appear†; also, to assemble for inspection, service, etc., as troops or forces (as, "I see them *muster* in a gleaming row": Lowell's "Commemoration Ode," viii.); in general, to come together, collect, or gather (as, clouds were *mustering* in the sky; "Why does my blood thus *muster* to my heart?" Shakspere's "Measure for Measure," ii. 4. 20).—**mus′ter,** *n.* [OF. *mostre* (F. *montre*).] Exhibition† or display†; also, a pattern, specimen, or sample (now only in *com.*); also, the act or an act of mustering; specif., an assembling of troops or men for inspection or other purposes (as, "a fall training, or general *muster* of the militia": Longfellow's "Kavanagh," x.); also, a force or number mustered (as, "Our present *musters* grow upon the file To five and twenty thousand men of choice": Shakspere's "2 Henry IV.," i. 3. 10); an assemblage or collection; also, a muster-roll.—**to pass muster.** See under *pass, v. t.*—**mus′ter=roll,** *n.* An official roll or list, as of officers and men in a military body or a ship's company; also, the roll-call.

mus-ty (mus′ti), *a.*; compar. *mustier,* superl. *mustiest.* [Cf. OF. *muste, moiste,* moldy, moist, also E. *moist* and *moisty.*] Moldy, or in bad condition from dampness, want of airing, etc.; having an odor or flavor suggestive of mold, as old buildings, long-closed rooms, food or wine, etc.; unpleasantly affected, as odor or flavor; stale; fig., staled by time, or antiquated (as, *musty* laws; "dry, *musty* arts," Burns's "To William Simpson," 20); of antiquated ideas, as persons.—**mus′ti-ly,** *adv.*—**mus′ti-ness,** *n.*

mu-ta-ble (mū′tạ-bl), *a.* [L. *mutabilis,* < *mutare,* change.] Liable or subject to change or alteration (as, "His will though free, Yet *mutable*": Milton's "Paradise Lost," v. 237); also, given to changing, or ever changing (as, "Nature is a *mutable* cloud, which is always and never the same": Emerson's "Essays," History); of persons, the mind, etc., fickle or inconstant (as, "the *mutable,* rank-scented many": Shakspere's "Coriolanus," iii. 1. 66).—**mu-ta-bil′i-ty** (-bil′i-ti), **mu′ta-ble-ness,** *n.*—**mu′ta-bly,** *adv.*

mu-tate (mū′tāt), *v.*; *-tated, -tating.* [L. *mutatus,* pp. of *mutare,* change.] **I.** *tr.* To change; alter; in *phonetics,* to change by mutation or umlaut. **II.** *intr.* To change; undergo mutation.—**mu-ta-tion** (mụ-tā′shọn), *n.* [L. *mutatio(n-)*.] The act or process of changing (as, "The past is exempt from *mutation*": C. B. Brown's "Wieland," i.); a change or alteration, as in form, qualities, or nature; in *phonetics,* umlaut, esp. through the influence of an *i* in the following syllable; in *biol.,* a sudden departure from the parent type, as when an individual differs from its parents in one or more inheritable characteristics; also, an individual, species, or the like, resulting from such a departure.—**mu-ta′tion-al,** *a.*—**mu′ta-tive** (-tạ-tiv), *a.* Of or pertaining to mutation or change; marked by change.

mutch (much), *n.* [MD. *mutse,* D. *muts,* = G. *mütze,* cap, prob. < ML. *almucia*: see *amice*².] A cap worn by women and young children: as, "an old granny in a woollen *mutch*" (Stevenson's "Master of Ballantrae," ix.). [Sc. and prov. Eng.]

mutch-kin (much′kin), *n.* [MD. *mudseken.*] A Scotch liquid measure equal to a little less than a U. S. legal pint.

mute (mūt). [L. *mutus,* silent, dumb.] **I.** *a.* Silent, or refraining from speech or utterance (as, "*Mute* did the minstrels stand To hear my story": Longfellow's "Skeleton in Armor," 79); hence, not emitting or having sound of any kind (as, "*Mute* was the room — *mute* the house": C. Brontë's "Shirley," x.); also, incapable of speech; dumb; sometimes, temporarily bereft of speech (as, *mute* with astonishment); also, unaccompanied by speech or sound (as, "a *mute* refusal of our offer," Lever's "Harry Lorrequer," xlv.; "*mute* astonishment," Marryat's "Mr. Midshipman Easy," iv.); in *law,* making no response when arraigned, as a prisoner (in 'to stand mute'); in *phonetics,* silent; not pronounced; also, involving a complete closure of the voice-organs in utterance, as the consonants *t, p, k, d, b, g.* **II.** *n.* A person destitute of the power of speech; also, a hired attendant at a funeral (as, "I saw the coffin, and the *mutes,* and the mourners": Galt's "Ayrshire Legatees," v.); also, in some Eastern countries, a dumb servant, usually one who has been deprived of the power of speech; also, an actor whose part is confined to dumb-show; in *law,* a person who makes no response when arraigned; in *phonetics,* a silent letter; also, a consonant uttered with complete closure of the voice-organs (see *mute, a.*); in *music,* a device to deaden or muffle the sound of an instrument.—**mute,** *v. t.*; *muted, muting.* To deaden or muffle the sound of (a musical instrument, etc.).—**mute′ly,** *adv.*—**mute′ness,** *n.*

mu-ti-late (mū′ti-lāt), *v. t.*; *-lated, -lating.* [L. *mutilatus*, pp. of *mutilare*, mutilate, < *mutilus*, maimed.] To deprive (a person or animal, the body, etc.) of a limb or other important part or parts (as, to *mutilate* prisoners or malefactors; to *mutilate* dead bodies; "'On this arm, I have neither hand nor nails,' he said, drawing the *mutilated* limb from his breast," C. Brontë's "Jane Eyre," xxxvii.); hence, to injure or disfigure (anything) by removing or irreparably damaging parts (as, to *mutilate* a statue, a picture, or a tree); make (a record, text, etc.) imperfect by removing or destroying parts; cut or abridge (literary work) so as to spoil the effect.—**mu′ti-late,** *a.* Mutilated (now only poetic); in *biol.*, destitute of some organ or part, or having it only in rudimentary or modified form.—**mu-ti-la′tion** (-lā′shọn), *n.* [LL. *mutilatio(n-)*.] The act of mutilating, or a being mutilated; deprivation of a limb, member, or any important part: as, "Many [in 1685] . . . were also sentenced to *mutilation* . . . the hangman of Edinburgh cut off the ears of thirty-five prisoners" (Macaulay's "Hist. of Eng.," v.).—**mu′ti-la-tor,** *n.*

mu-tine† (mū′tin). [F. *mutin*, rebellious (as n., rebel, also formerly rebellion), < OF. *muete*, *mute*, rising, insurrection, < L. *movere*, E. *move*.] **I.** *a.* Rebellious; mutinous. **II.** *n.* A mutinous person, or mutineer (as, "Methought I lay Worse than the *mutines* in the bilboes": Shakspere's "Hamlet," v. 2. 6); also, a mutiny.—**mu′tine†,** *v. i.* [F. *mutiner*, < *mutin*.] To rebel; mutiny. See Shakspere's "Hamlet," iii. 4. 83.

mu-ti-neer (mū-ti-nēr′), *n.* [Obs. F. *mutinier*, < *mutin*: see *mutine*.] One guilty of mutiny.—**mu-ti-neer′,** *v. i.* To mutiny.

mu-ti-nous (mū′ti-nus), *a.* [From *mutine*.] Disposed to, engaged in, or involving revolt against constituted authority (as, "The men became *mutinous* and insubordinate," Besant's "Coligny," vii.; *mutinous* actions or language); guilty of or characterized by mutiny; rebellious (often fig.: as, *mutinous* passions); often (in a milder or playful use), petulantly unsubmissive or discontented (as, a *mutinous* toss of the head; a *mutinous* air).—**mu′ti-nous-ly,** *adv.*—**mu′ti-nous-ness,** *n.*

mu-ti-ny (mū′ti-ni), *n.*; pl. *-nies* (-niz). [From *mutine*.] Revolt, or a revolt or rebellion, against constituted authority, esp. by soldiers or seamen; also, discord† or strife† (as, "A man . . . whom right and wrong Have chose as umpire of their *mutiny*": Shakspere's "Love's Labour's Lost," i. 1. 170).—**mu′ti-ny,** *v. i.*; *-nied, -nying.* To commit the offense of mutiny, or revolt against constituted authority (as, "His troops, who had received no wages for a long time, had *mutinied*": Motley's "Dutch Republic," iii. 2); also, to quarrel†.

mut-ism (mū′tizm), *n.* The state of being mute: as, "Paulina was awed by the savants, but not quite to *mutism*" (C. Brontë's "Villette," xxvii.).

mu-to-graph (mū′tọ-grȧf), *n.* [L. *mutare*, change: see *-graph*.] A camera designed for taking a series of photographs of moving objects, as for the mutoscope.

mu-to-scope (mū′tọ-skōp), *n.* [L. *mutare*, change: see *-scope*.] A device in which photographs of moving objects (as those produced in a mutograph) are mounted around the periphery of a wheel and viewed through an eyepiece or aperture as they are brought rapidly into sight one after another, thus giving the optical effect known as a moving picture.

mutt (mut), *n.* [Origin obscure.] A dog (used disparagingly or humorously); also, a simpleton; a stupid person. [Slang.]

mut-ter (mut′ėr), *v.* [ME. *moteren*: cf. G. dial. *muttern*, also L. *mutire*, *muttire*, mutter; ult. imit.] **I.** *intr.* To utter words in a low tone with lips nearly closed, often in talking to one's self or in making obscure complaints, threats, etc. (as, "He *mutters* of vengeance as he walks": Dunsany's "Laughter of the Gods," iii.); murmur; grumble; also, to make a low, rumbling sound (as, "We heard thunder *muttering*; a storm was coming on": Parkman's "Oregon Trail," xiii.). **II.** *tr.* To utter in a low or half-suppressed tone, often in talking to one's self or in sullen anger or discontent: as, "He *muttered* curses as he went" (Godwin's "Caleb Williams," iii.); "The surgeon *muttered* his dissatisfaction" (Cooper's "Spy," ix.).—**mut′ter,** *n.* The act or utterance of one that mutters: as, "his ungracious *mutters*" (J. Conrad's "Rescue," v. 2).—**mut′ter-er,** *n.*—**mut′ter-ing-ly,** *adv.*

mut-ton (mut′n), *n.* [OF. *mouton*, *multun*, ram (F. *mouton*, sheep), < ML. *multo(n-)*, ram; perhaps from Celtic.] A sheep (now only humorous); also, the flesh of sheep, used as food; specif., the flesh of the well-grown or more mature sheep, as distinguished from lamb.—**mut′ton=chop′,** *n.* A rib-piece of mutton having the bone chopped off at the small end, or some similar piece, for broiling or frying; also, *pl.*, side-whiskers shaped like a mutton-chop, narrow at the top, and broad and trimmed short at the bottom, the chin being shaved both in front and beneath. —**mut′ton-head** (-hed), *n.* A dull or stupid person. [Colloq.]—**mut′ton=head″ed,** *a.*—**mut′ton-y,** *a.* Having the qualities of mutton.

mu-tu-al (mū′ṭụ-ạl), *a.* [OF. F. *mutuel*, < L. *mutuus*, exchanged, reciprocal, borrowed or lent, akin to *mutare*, change.] Involving an interchange between persons or things; possessed, experienced, performed, etc., by each of two or more with respect to the other or others (as, *mutual* love or admiration; "The recognition was *mutual*," Marryat's "Peter Simple," lxiv.; *mutual* aid; *mutual* insurance, see phrase below); reciprocal; also, having the same relation each toward the other or others (as, *mutual* foes); also, of or pertaining to each of two or more, or common (now commonly regarded as incorrect, although still often used in such expressions as 'mutual friend' and 'mutual acquaintance': as, "*mutual* happiness," Shakspere's "Two Gentlemen of Verona," v. 4. 173; "Our *Mutual* Friend," the title of a novel by Charles Dickens; "Ethel and Lady Ann and my lord talked . . . about their *mutual* acquaintance," Thackeray's "Newcomes," xlii.); also, pertaining to mutual insurance (as, a *mutual* company).—**mutual insurance,** insurance in which those insured become members of a company who reciprocally engage, by payment of certain amounts into a common fund, to indemnify one another against loss.—**mu-tu-al′i-ty** (-al′i-ti), *n.*—**mu′tu-al-ly,** *adv.*

mu-tule (mū′ṭūl), *n.* [F. *mutule*, < L. *mutulus*.] In *arch.*, a projecting flat block under the corona of the Doric cornice, corresponding to the modillion of other orders.

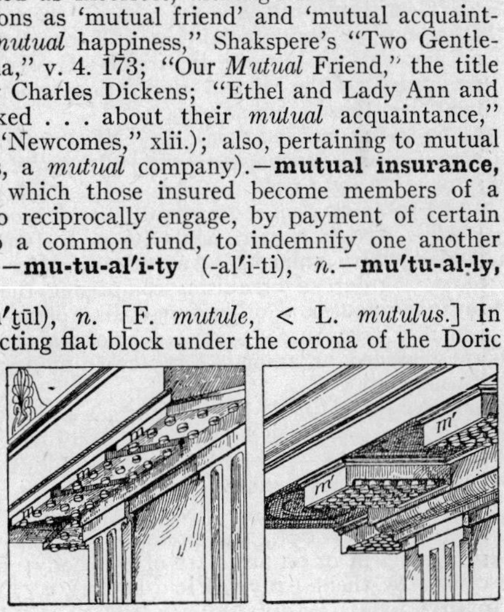

1. *m, m, m,* Greek Mutules. 2. *m′, m′,* Roman Mutules.

mu-zhik (mö-zhik′ or mö′zhik), *n.* [Russ.] A Russian peasant.

muz-zle (muz′l), *n.* [OF. *musel* (F. *museau*), < ML. *musellus*, dim. of *musus*, muzzle; origin uncertain.] The projecting part of the head of an animal, including jaws, mouth, and nose (as, "His nose turned up, and the corners of his mouth turned down, pretty much like the *muzzle* of an irritable pug-dog," Irving's "Knickerbocker's New York," iv. 1; "The antler'd deer . . . thrust his *muzzle* in the air," Joaquin Miller's "Tale of the Tall Alcalde"); also, the mouth, or end for discharge, of a gun, pistol, etc. (as, "Friday . . . clapped the *muzzle* of his piece into his ear, and shot him dead as a stone": Defoe's "Robinson Crusoe," i. 20); also, a device, usually an arrangement of straps or wires, placed over an animal's mouth to prevent the animal from biting, eating, etc.; also, an ornamental piece of armor formerly used to cover a horse's nose.—**muz′zle,** *v. t.*; *-zled, -zling.* To put a muzzle on (an animal or its mouth)

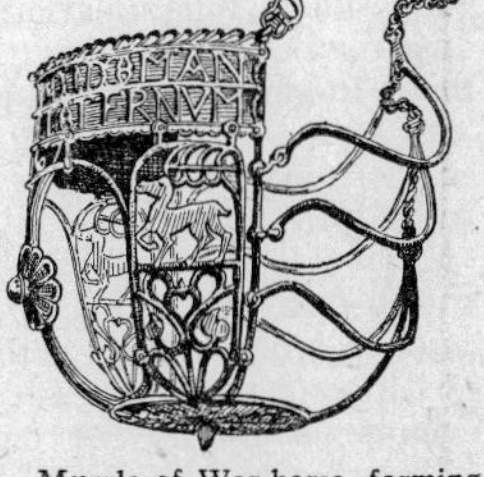

Muzzle of War-horse, forming part of the bards or defensive armor; 16th century.

so as to prevent biting, eating, etc.; also, fig., to restrain from speech or the expression of opinion.—**muz′zle=load″er**, *n.* A firearm which is loaded through the muzzle. Cf. *breech-loader.*—**muz′zle=load″ing**, *a.* Of a firearm, receiving the charge or load through the muzzle.

muz-zy (muz′i), *a.* [Origin obscure.] Dull or gloomy, as places, occasions, etc.; also, misty or hazy, as weather; blurred or indistinct, as things seen; also, hazy or confused as to perception, esp. from drinking (as, "The whole company stared at me with a whimsical, *muzzy* look, like men whose senses were a little obfuscated by beer": Irving's "Tales of a Traveler," ii. 9); muddled with drink. [Colloq.]

my (mī), *pron.* [ME. *mi*, reduced form of *min*, < AS. *mīn*, E. *mine*[1].] The possessive form corresponding to *I* and *me*, used before a noun. Cf. *mine*[1].—**my**, *interj.* [Short for some exclamatory phrase, as 'my God,' 'my Lord.'] An exclamation of surprise: often in the expression 'oh, my!'—as, "*Oh, my!* A nice example to servants!" (Arnold Bennett's "Hilda Lessways," ii. 1). [Colloq.]

my-al-gia (mī-al′jiạ̈), *n.* [NL., < Gr. μῦς, muscle, + ἄλγος, pain.] In *pathol.*, pain in the muscles; muscular rheumatism.—**my-al′gic**, *a.*

my-as-the-ni-a (mī-ạs-thē′ni-ạ̈), *n.* [NL., < Gr. μῦς, muscle, + ἀσθένεια, weakness: see *asthenia.*] In *pathol.*, muscular debility.—**my-as-then′ic** (-then′ik), *a.*

my-ce-li-um (mī-sē′li-um), *n.* [NL., < Gr. μύκης, fungus.] In *bot.*, the vegetative part of the thallus of fungi, composed of one or more filamentous elements, or hyphæ.—**my-ce′li-al**, *a.*—**my-ce′li-oid**, *a.*

My-ce-næ-an (mī-sẹ-nē′ạn), *a.* Of or pertaining to the ancient city of Mycenæ in Argolis (Greece), or noting or pertaining to the Ægean civilization which flourished there. See *Ægean, a.*

my-ce-to-ma (mī-sẹ-tō′mạ̈), *n.* [NL., < Gr. μύκης (μυκητ-), fungus: see *-oma.*] In *pathol.*, same as *Madura foot.*

my-ce-to-zo-ön (mī-sē-tọ-zō′on), *n.*; pl. *-zoa* (-zō′ạ̈). [NL., < Gr. μύκης (μυκητ-), fungus, + ζῷον, animal.] Any of the *Mycetozoa*, a group of organisms comprising the myxomycetous and other fungus-like organisms: a term used when such organisms are regarded as animals.—**my-ce-to-zo′an**, *a.* and *n.*

my-col-o-gy (mī-kol′ọ-ji), *n.* [Gr. μύκης, fungus: see *-logy.*] The branch of botany that treats of fungi.—**my-co-log′i-cal** (-kọ-loj′i-kạl), *a.*—**my-col′o-gist**, *n.*

Mycenæan Art. —Figure from vase, about 1200 B.C.

my-co-sis (mī-kō′sis), *n.* [NL., < Gr. μύκης, fungus.] In *pathol.*, the presence of parasitic fungi in or on any part of the body; also, a disease caused by them.—**my-cot′ic** (-kot′ik), *a.*

my-dri-a-sis (mi-drī′ạ-sis), *n.* [L., < Gr. μυδρίασις.] Excessive dilatation of the pupil of the eye, as the result of disease, drugs, or the like.—**myd-ri-at-ic** (mid-ri-at′ik). **I.** *a.* Pertaining to or producing mydriasis. **II.** *n.* A mydriatic drug.

my-e-len-ceph-a-lon (mī″ẹ-len-sef′ạ-lon), *n.* [NL., < Gr. μυελός, marrow, + NL. *encephalon*: see *encephalon.*] In *anat.*, the brain and spinal cord taken together and considered as a whole; also, the medulla oblongata.

my-e-lin (mī′ẹ-lin), *n.* [G., < Gr. μυελός, marrow.] In *anat.*, a soft, white, fatty substance incasing the axis-cylinder of certain nerve-fibers.

my-e-li-tis (mī-ẹ-lī′tis), *n.* [NL., < Gr. μυελός, marrow.] In *pathol.*, inflammation of the spinal cord or the bone-marrow.

my-e-lo-gen-ic (mī″ẹ-lọ-jen′ik), *a.* [Gr. μυελός, marrow: see *-genic.*] Originating or produced in the bone-marrow, as certain tumors. Also **my-e-log′e-nous** (-loj′e-nus).

my-e-loid (mī′ẹ-loid), *a.* [Gr. μυελός, marrow: see *-oid.*] Marrow-like; pertaining to marrow.

my-lo-don (mī′lọ-don), *n.* [NL., < Gr. μύλη, mill, millstone, + ὀδούς (ὀδοντ-), tooth.] Any of the gigantic sloths, with teeth more or less cylindrical, constituting the extinct genus *Mylodon.* See cut in next column.—**my′lo-dont** (-dont), *a.* and *n.*

my-na (mī′nạ̈), *n.* See *mina*[2].

myn-heer (mīn-hār′), *n.* [D. *mijnheer*, < *mijn*, my, + *heer*, lord, gentleman.] The Dutch term of address and title of respect corresponding to *sir* and *Mr.*; hence, a Dutchman (colloq.).

Skeleton of Mylodon.

myo-, my-. Forms of Gr. μῦς, muscle, used in combination.—

my-o-car-di-tis (mī″ọ-kär-dī′tis), *n.* [NL.] In *pathol.*, inflammation of the myocardium.—**my-o-car′di-um** (-kär′di-um), *n.* [NL. (Gr. καρδία, heart).] In *anat.*, the muscular substance of the heart.—**my′o-graph** (-gråf), *n.* [+ *-graph.*] An instrument for taking tracings of muscular contractions and relaxations.—**my′oid** (-oid), *a.* [+ *-oid.*] Resembling, or pertaining to, muscle.—**my-ol′o-gy** (-ol′ọ-ji), *n.* [+ *-logy.*] The science of muscles; the branch of anatomy that treats of muscles.—**my-ol′o-gist**, *n.*

my-o-ma (mī-ō′mạ̈), *n.*; pl. *-mas* or *-mata* (-mạ-tạ̈). [NL., < Gr. μῦς, muscle: see *-oma.*] In *pathol.*, a tumor composed of muscular tissue.—**my-om′a-tous** (-om′ạ-tus), *a.*

my-op-a-thy (mī-op′ạ-thi), *n.* [NL. *myopathia*, < Gr. μῦς, muscle, + παθεῖν, suffer.] In *pathol.*, disease of the muscles.—**my-o-path′ic** (-ọ-path′ik), *a.*

my-ope (mī′ōp), *n.* [F. *myope*, < LL. *myops* (*myop-*), < Gr. μύωψ (μυωπ-), short-sighted, < μύειν, shut, close, + ὤψ, eye.] A near-sighted or myopic person.—**my-o′pi-a** (-ō′pi-ạ̈), *n.* [NL.] In *pathol.*, a condition of the eye in which parallel rays are focused in front of the retina, objects being seen distinctly only when near to the eye; near-sightedness: opposed to *hypermetropia.*—**my-op′ic** (-op′ik), *a.* Pertaining to or affected with myopia; near-sighted.—**my′o-py** (-ọ-pi), *n.* Same as *myopia.*

my-o-scope (mī′ọ-skōp), *n.* [See *myo-* and *-scope.*] An apparatus or instrument for observing muscular contraction.

my-o-sin (mī′ọ-sin), *n.* [Gr. μῦς, muscle.] In *physiol. chem.*, a globulin which separates from muscle-plasma on coagulation, as after death.

my-o-sis (mī-ō′sis), *n.* [NL., < Gr. μύειν, close (the eyes).] Excessive contraction of the pupil of the eye, as the result of disease, drugs, or the like.

my-o-so-tis (mī-ọ-sō′tis), *n.* [L., < Gr. μυοσωτίς, < μυός, gen. of μῦς, mouse, + οὖς (ὠτ-), ear.] Any plant of the boraginaceous genus *Myosotis*, as the common forget-me-not.

my-ot-ic (mī-ot′ik). **I.** *a.* Pertaining to or producing myosis. **II.** *n.* A myotic drug.

myria-, myri-. Forms of Gr. μυριάς (μυριαδ-), myriad, ten thousand, an indefinitely great number, used in combination, as in *myriagram, myriare.*

myr-i-ad (mir′i-ạd). [Gr. μυριάς (μυριαδ-), < μυρίος, numberless, pl. μύριοι, ten thousand.] **I.** *n.* The number of ten thousand; ten thousand persons or things (as, the Greek army numbered three *myriads*); hence, an indefinitely great number (as, a *myriad* of stars; "The grove bloomed with *myriads* of wild roses," Parkman's "Oregon Trail," x.); a very great number, or host, of persons or things (as, "This is he that . . . Against the *myriads* of Assaye Clash'd with his fiery few and won": Tennyson's "Ode on the Death of the Duke of Wellington," vi.). **II.** *a.* Of an indefinitely great number, or innumerable (as, "the City's moonlit spires and *myriad* lamps," Shelley's "Revolt of Islam," v. 1; a *myriad* host); having innumerable phases, aspects, etc. (as, the *myriad* mind of Shakspere).—**myr′i-ad-fold** (-fōld), *a.* and *n.*

myr-i-a-gram, myr-i-a-gramme (mir′i-ạ-gram), *n.* [F. *myriagramme*: see *myria-.*] In the *metric system*, a unit of weight equal to 10,000 grams, or 22.046 pounds avoirdupois.

myr-i-a-li-ter, myr-i-a-li-tre (mir′i-ạ-lē″tėr), *n.* [F. *myrialitre*: see *myria-.*] In the *metric system*, a unit of capacity equal to 10,000 liters, 283.774 U. S. bushels, or 2,642 U. S. gallons.

myr-i-a-me-ter, myr-i-a-me-tre (mir′i-ạ-mē″tėr), *n.* [F. *myriamètre*: see *myria-*.] In the *metric system*, a measure of length equal to 10,000 meters, or 6.2137 miles.

myr-i-a-pod (mir′i-ạ-pod). [NL. *Myriapoda*, pl., < Gr. μυριάς, myriad, + πούς (ποδ-), foot.] **I.** *n.* Any of the *Myriapoda*, a class or group of arthropods including the centipedes and millepedes, the members of which have elongated worm-like bodies, composed (usually) of a large number of similar segments, nearly all of which bear true articulated legs. **II.** *a.* Having very numerous legs; specif., belonging or pertaining to the *Myriapoda*, or myriapods.—**myr-i-ap′o-dous** (-ap′ǫ-dus), *a.*

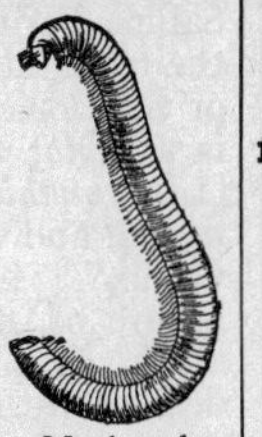

Myriapod or Millepede (*Julus flavozonatus*).

myr-i-are (mir′i-ãr), *n.* [F. *myriare*: see *myria-*.] In the *metric system*, a surface measure equal to 10,000 ares, 1,000,000 square meters, or 247.1 acres.

myr-i-o-ra-ma (mir″i-ǫ-rä′mạ̈), *n.* [Gr. μυρίος, numberless, + ὅραμα, view.] A picture made up of interchangeable parts which can be harmoniously arranged to form a great variety of picturesque scenes.

my-ris-tic (mī-ris′tik or mi-), *a.* [NL. *Myristica*: see *myristicaceous*.] Pertaining to or derived from the nutmeg: as, *myristic* acid (an organic acid found in oil of nutmeg, spermaceti, etc.).

my-ris-ti-ca-ceous (mī-ris-ti-kā′shius or mi-), *a.* [NL. *Myristica*, genus of plants including the nutmeg-tree, < Gr. μυρίζειν, anoint, < μύρον, unguent.] Belonging to the *Myristicaceæ*, or nutmeg family of trees and shrubs.

myrmeco-. Form of Gr. μύρμηξ (μυρμηκ-), ant, used in combination.—**myr-me-col-o-gy** (mėr-mẹ-kol′ǫ-ji), *n.* [+ *-logy*.] The branch of entomology that treats of ants.—**myr″me-co-log′i-cal** (-kǫ-loj′i-kạl), *a.*—**myr-me-col′o-gist**, *n.*—**myr-me-coph′a-gous** (-kof′ạ-gus), *a.* [+ *-phagous*.] Feeding on ants, as the ant-eaters.—**myr-me-coph′i-lous** (-i-lus), *a.* [+ *-philous*.] Fond of ants, as insects that live in ant-hills; also, benefited by ants, as plants that are cross-fertilized by them.

Myr-mi-don (mėr′mi-dǫn), *n.* [L. *Myrmidones*, pl., < Gr. Μυρμιδόνες, the Myrmidons.] One of a warlike people of ancient Thessaly who, according to legend, accompanied Achilles, their king, to the Trojan War; hence [*l. c.*], an obedient and unquestioning follower (as, "No man could now be safe, when men like him [Egmont] were in the power of Alva and his *myrmidons*": Motley's "Dutch Republic," iii. 1); one who executes without scruple his master's commands; often, in contempt, a bailiff, policeman, or other inferior administrative officer of the law (as, "the justice and his *myrmidons*," Smollett's "Humphry Clinker," June 11; *myrmidons* of the law).

my-rob-a-lan (mī-rob′ạ-lạn or mi-), *n.* [F. *myrobolan*, < L. *myrobalanum*, < Gr. μυροβάλανος, kind of fruit or nut, < μύρον, unguent, + βάλανος, acorn.] The dried plum-like fruit of certain tropical trees of the combretaceous genus *Terminalia*: used in dyeing and ink-making, and formerly in medicine.

My-ron-ic (mī-ron′ik), *a.* Of or pertaining to the Greek sculptor Myron, of the 5th century B.C., who worked chiefly in bronze, and was especially noted for his representations of athletes; in the style of Myron.

my-ro-sin (mī′rǫ-sin), *n.* [Gr. μύρον, unguent.] In *chem.*, an enzyme occurring in the seeds of the mustard and of various other brassicaceous and allied plants.

Myronic Style in Sculpture.—Discobolus of the Lancellotti Palace, Rome.

myrrh (mėr), *n.* [AS. *myrre*, < L. *myrrha*, *murra*, < Gr. μύρρα: cf. Ar. *murr*, bitter, also myrrh.] An aromatic resinous exudation from certain plants of the genus *Balsamea*, esp. *B. myrrha*, a spiny shrub: used for incense, perfume, etc.—**myrrh′y**, *a.* Abounding with myrrh; fragrant with or as with myrrh: as, "the *myrrhy* lands" (Browning's "Waring," i. 6).

myr-ta-ceous (mėr-tā′shius), *a.* [L. *myrtaceus*, < *myrtus*, myrtle: see *myrtle*.] Of, pertaining to, or resembling the myrtle; belonging to the *Myrtaceæ*, or myrtle family of plants, which includes the myrtle, the clove and allspice trees, the guava, the eucalyptus, etc.

myr-tle (mėr′tl), *n.* [OF. *mirtile*, myrtle-berry (F. *myrtille*, bilberry), dim. < L. *myrtus*, < Gr. μύρτος, myrtle.] Any plant of the genus *Myrtus*, esp. *M. communis*, a shrub of southern Europe with evergreen leaves, fragrant white flowers, and aromatic berries (this plant is used as an emblem of love and was anciently held sacred to Venus); any of various other myrtaceous plants; also, any of certain plants of other families, as the common periwinkle, *Vinca minor*; also, myrtle-green.—**myr′tle=bird, myr′tle=war′bler**, *n.* A North American warbler, *Dendrœca* (or *Dendroica*) *coronata*, having distinct yellow marks on the crown, the rump, and each side of the breast.—**myr′tle=green′**, *n.* A dark green with a bluish tinge: from the color of myrtle leaves.

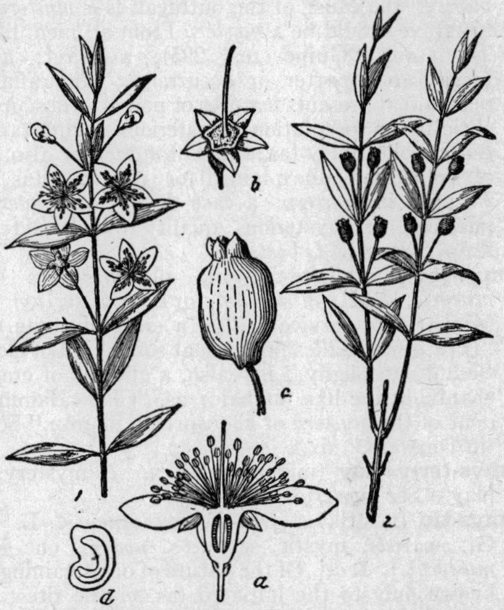

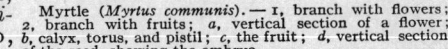

Myrtle (*Myrtus communis*).—1, branch with flowers; 2, branch with fruits; *a*, vertical section of a flower; *b*, calyx, torus, and pistil; *c*, the fruit; *d*, vertical section of the seed, showing the embryo.

myr-tol (mėr′tol or -tōl), *n.* [L. *myrtus*, myrtle, + *oleum*, oil.] An oil obtained from the leaves of the common myrtle, *Myrtus communis*: used as an antiseptic, stimulant, etc.

my-self (mī-self′), *pron.* An emphatic form of *me* or *I* (as, this was an injury to *myself*; I *myself* will go; "Which way I fly is hell; *myself* am hell," Milton's "Paradise Lost," iv. 75); also, a reflexive form of *me* (as, I betook *myself* to the place).

mys-ta-gogue (mis′tạ-gog), *n.* [L. *mystagogus*, < Gr. μυσταγωγός, < μύστης, one initiated (see *mystery*¹), + ἀγωγός, leading, < ἄγειν, lead.] One who initiates persons into, or interprets, mysteries, esp. religious mysteries; a hierophant.—**mys-ta-gog′ic, mys-ta-gog′i-cal** (-goj′ik, -i-kạl), *a.*—**mys′ta-go-gy** (-gō-ji), *n.* [Gr. μυσταγωγία, < μυσταγωγός.] The work or teaching of a mystagogue; initiation into or interpretation of mysteries.

mys-te-ri-al (mis-tē′ri-ạl), *a.* Characterized by mystery; mysterious. [Now rare.]

mys-te-ri-ous (mis-tē′ri-us), *a.* [F. *mystérieux*, < L. *mysterium*, E. *mystery*¹.] Full of, characterized by, or involving mystery (as, *mysterious* rites; *mysterious* symbols, lights, fires, or deaths; a *mysterious* case); of obscure nature, meaning, origin, etc.; puzzling; inexplicable; also, implying or suggesting a mystery (as, a *mysterious* air or smile); having an air of mystery (as, "Why are you all so *mysterious*, so reserved in your communications?" J. H. Newman's "Callista," xix.).—**mys-te′ri-ous-ly**, *adv.*—**mys-te′ri-ous-ness**, *n.*

mys-ter-y¹ (mis′tẹ-ri), *n.*; pl. *mysteries* (-riz). [L. *mysterium*, < Gr. μυστήριον, mystery, < μύστης, one initiated, < μυεῖν, initiate into mysteries, < μύειν, close (the lips).]

Pl., in ancient pagan religions, certain rites to which only the initiated were admitted (as, the Eleusinian *mysteries*); hence, in later and general use, rites or secrets known only to those specially initiated (as, the *mysteries* of freemasonry); *sing.*, in the Christian religion, a sacramental rite; specif., the eucharist, and hence, esp. *pl.*, the eucharistic elements; any truth unknowable except by divine revelation; an incident or scene in connection with the life of Christ, regarded as of special significance (as, the *mysteries* of the Passion); also, a miracle-play (sometimes restricted to one based on Biblical subjects, as events in the life of Christ); also, in general, anything that is kept secret or remains unexplained or unknown (as, to investigate the *mysteries* of nature; the cause of the outbreak is a *mystery*; "And that his grave should be a *mystery* From all men, like his birth," Tennyson's "Guinevere," 295); a secret; a puzzling or inexplicable matter or occurrence; any affair, thing, or person that presents features or points so obscure as to arouse curiosity or speculation; mysterious circumstances or occurrences collectively (as, a tale of *mystery*); also, obscurity, as of something unexplained or puzzling (as, proceedings wrapped in *mystery*; a case devoid of *mystery*); obscure, puzzling, or mysterious quality or character.—**mystery ship.** Same as *Q boat*.

mys-ter-y[2] (mis'tẹ-ri), *n.*; pl. *mysteries* (-riz). [ME. *misterie*, < ML. *misterium*, for L. *ministerium*, E. *ministry*.] Ministry† or service†; also, a craft or trade (archaic: as, "It [a town] makes pretence at some kind of cloth *mystery*," Besant's "Coligny," i.); also, a gild, as of craftsmen, merchants, or the like (archaic: as, "Claus Hammerlein, president of the *mystery* of the workers in iron," Scott's "Quentin Durward," xix.).

mys-ter-y=play (mis'tẹ-ri-plā), *n.* A mystery, or miracle-play. See *mystery*[1].

mys-tic (mis'tik). [OF. F. *mystique*, < L. *mysticus*, < Gr. μυστικός, mystic, secret, < μύστης, one initiated: see *mystery*[1].] **I.** *a.* Of the nature of or pertaining to mysteries known only to the initiated (as, *mystic* rites; *mystic* arts; "*mystic* implements of magic might," Scott's "Lay of the Last Minstrel," vi. 17); of occult character, power, or significance (as, a *mystic* formula, number, or circle); often, spiritually significant or symbolic (as, the *mystic* dove used in religious art to symbolize the Holy Ghost, see Luke, iii. 22; the *mystic* marriage of the Lamb, see Rev. xix. 7); in general, of obscure or mysterious character or significance (as, "To him all nature is instinct with *mystic* influence," Parkman's "Oregon Trail," xviii.; "*Mystic* gleams, Like glimpses of forgotten dreams," Tennyson's "Two Voices," 380); also, of or pertaining to mystics or mysticism. **II.** *n.* One initiated into mysteries; also, one who claims to attain, or believes in the possibility of attaining, insight into mysteries transcending ordinary human knowledge, as by immediate intuition in a state of spiritual ecstasy.—**mys'ti-cal,** *a.* Mystic; occult; spiritually symbolic; mysterious; often, of or pertaining to mystics or mysticism (as, *mystical* contemplation; *mystical* doctrines).—**mys'ti-cal-ly,** *adv.*—**mys'ti-cal-ness,** *n.*—**mys'ti-cism** (-sizm), *n.* The beliefs, ideas, or mode of thought of mystics; the doctrine of an immediate spiritual intuition of truths believed to transcend ordinary understanding, or of a direct, intimate union of the soul with the Divinity through contemplation and love.—**mys-ti'ci-ty** (-tis'i-ti), *n.* Mystic quality or character.—**mys'ti-cize** (-sīz), *v. t.* To render mystical; attribute a mystical character or meaning to.

mys-ti-fi-ca-tion (mis"ti-fi-kā'shọn), *n.* [F. *mystification.*] The act of mystifying, or the state of being mystified; bewilderment or perplexity; also, something designed to mystify; a hoax.

mys-ti-fi-ca-tor (mis'ti-fi-kā-tọr), *n.* [F. *mystificateur.*] One who mystifies; a mystifier.—**mys'ti-fi-ca-to-ry** (-tọ-ri), *a.* Causing mystification; mystifying.

mys-ti-fy (mis'ti-fī), *v. t.*; *-fied, -fying.* [F. *mystifier*, appar. < *mystère*, mystery, + *-fier*, E. *-fy*.] To impose upon (a person) by playing upon his credulity; bewilder purposely; in general, to perplex or puzzle; also, to involve (a subject, etc.) in mystery or obscurity.—**mys'ti-fi-er** (-fī-ėr), *n.*

myth (mith), *n.* [LL. *mythos*, NL. *mythus*, < Gr. μῦθος, word, speech, tale, legend, myth.] A traditional or legendary story, usually concerning some superhuman being or some alleged person or event, whether without or with a determinable basis of fact or a natural explanation (as, the Greek and Roman *myths* of the divinities of heaven; the *myth* of the sun-god Helios; the Greek *myths* of the Creation; "Curious *Myths* of the Middle Ages," the title of a work by Sabine Baring-Gould); stories or matter of this kind (as, in the realm of *myth*); also, any invented story; an imaginary or fictitious thing or person (as, his journey through Asia is a *myth*; his wealthy uncle was a *myth*).—**myth'ic,** *a.* [LL. *mythicus*, < Gr. μυθικός.] Mythical: as, "some *mythic* and allegorical being" (Mrs. Stowe's "Uncle Tom's Cabin," xiv.).—**myth'i-cal,** *a.* Pertaining to, of the nature of, or involving a myth or myths; dealt with in myth, as a period; existing only in myth, as a person; dealing with myths, as a writer; explaining narratives of supernatural events as myths, as theories; also, having no foundation in fact (as, "Her influence is *mythical*": Disraeli's "Lothair," xxxii.); imaginary; fictitious.—**myth'i-cal-ly,** *adv.*—**myth'i-cize** (-sīz), *v. t.*; *-cized, -cizing.* To turn into, or treat or explain as, a myth.

my-thog-ra-pher (mi-thog'rạ-fėr), *n.* [Gr. μυθογράφος, < μῦθος, myth, + γράφειν, write.] A writer or narrator of myths.—**my-thog'ra-phy,** *n.* [Gr. μυθογραφία.] Descriptive mythology; also, the representation of myths in graphic or plastic art.

myth-o-log-ic, myth-o-log-i-cal (mith-ọ-loj'ik, -i-kạl), *a.* [LL. *mythologicus*, < Gr. μυθολογικός.] Of or pertaining to mythology.—**myth-o-log'i-cal-ly,** *adv.*

my-thol-o-gist (mi-thol'ọ-jist), *n.* A writer of myths; also, one versed in mythology.

my-thol-o-gize (mi-thol'ọ-jīz), *v.*; *-gized, -gizing.* **I.** *intr.* To construct myths; relate myths; explain myths. **II.** *tr.* To interpret in relation to mythology; also, to make into or explain as a myth; render mythical.—**my-thol'o-giz-er** (-jī-zėr), *n.*

my-thol-o-gy (mi-thol'ọ-ji), *n.*; pl. *-gies* (-jiz). [LL. *mythologia*, < Gr. μυθολογία, < μῦθος, myth, + λέγειν, speak.] The science of myths; also, myths collectively; a myth (obs. or rare); often, a body of myths, as that of a particular people, or that relating to a particular person (as, Greek *mythology*; Teutonic *mythology*; "the tender and delicious *mythology* of Arthur," Emerson's "English Traits," iv.).

myth-o-pe-ic, myth-o-pœ-ic (mith-ọ-pē'ik), *a.* [Gr. μυθοποιός, making myths, < μῦθος, myth, + ποιεῖν, make.] Myth-making; pertaining to the making of myths.—**myth-o-pe'ism, myth-o-pœ'ism,** *n.* The making of myths.—**myth-o-pe'ist, myth-o-pœ'ist,** *n.* A myth-maker.

myx-a-mœ-ba (mik-sạ-mē'bạ), *n.*; pl. *-bæ* (-bē) or *-bas.* [NL., < Gr. μύξα, mucus, slime, + NL. *amœba*: see *amœba.*] In *bot.*, a myxomycetous individual when in the form of a cell which has a creeping motion like that of an amœba.

myx-e-de-ma, myx-œ-de-ma (mik-sẹ-dē'mạ), *n.* [NL., < Gr. μύξα, mucus, + NL. *edema*, *œdema*: see *edema.*] In *pathol.*, a disease characterized by thickening of the skin, blunting of the senses and intellect, labored speech, etc., associated with diminished functional activity of the thyroid gland.—**myx-e-dem'a-tous, myx-œ-dem'a-tous** (-dem'ạ-tus or -dē'mạ-tus), *a.*

myx-o-ma (mik-sō'mạ), *n.*; pl. *-mas* or *-mata* (-mạ-tạ). [NL., < Gr. μύξα, mucus: see *-oma.*] In *pathol.*, a tumor consisting of mucous tissue.

myx-o-my-ce-tous (mik"sọ-mī-sē'tus), *a.* [NL. *Myxomycetes*, pl., < Gr. μύξα, mucus, slime, + μύκης (μυκητ-), fungus.] Belonging or pertaining to the *Myxomycetes*, or slime-molds, a group or class of low, fungus-like vegetable organisms (sometimes regarded as a distinct phylum, *Myxophyta*, and sometimes as a class of thallophytes) having characteristics of both animals and plants, and occurring in slimy masses on decaying logs, etc.

myx-o-phyte (mik'sọ-fīt), *n.* [NL. *Myxophyta*, pl., < Gr. μύξα, mucus, slime, + φυτόν, plant.] Any of the myxomycetous vegetable organisms, which are sometimes regarded as constituting a distinct phylum (the *Myxophyta*), and sometimes included among the thallophytes.

N

N, n (en); pl. *N's*, *n's* (enz). A consonant, the 14th letter of the English alphabet.

nab (nab), *v. t.*; *nabbed*, *nabbing*. [Origin obscure.] To catch or seize, esp. suddenly; capture or arrest. [Colloq.]

na-bob (nā′bob), *n.* [Hind. *nawwāb*: see *nawab*, and cf. F. *nabab*.] A nawab; hence, a person who has come home from India with a fortune acquired there (as, "Major Gilchrist, a *nabob* from India": Galt's "Annals of the Parish," iii.); any wealthy and luxurious person.—**na′bob-ess,** *n.* A female nabob; the wife of a nabob.—**na′bob-ish,** *a.* Like or befitting a nabob.

nac-a-rat (nak′ạ-rat), *n.* [F.] A bright red with a tinge of orange.

na-celle (nȧ-sel′), *n.* [F., < LL. *navicella*, dim. of L. *navis*, ship.] The car of a balloon; also, the part of an airship or dirigible which contains the machinery, etc., and in which the passengers are carried; also, the inclosed part of a flying-machine or aëroplane, in which passengers, etc., are carried.

na-cre (nā′kėr), *n.* [F., = It. *nacchera*; prob. from Pers.] Mother-of-pearl.—**na-cré** (nȧ-krā), *a.* [F.] Having a nacreous iridescence.—**na-cre-ous** (nā′krę-us), *a.* Of, like, or containing nacre; iridescent; pearly. Also **na′crous.**

na-dir (nā′dėr), *n.* [OF. F. *nadir*, < Ar. *nazīr*, corresponding, opposite (that is, to the zenith).] The point of the celestial sphere vertically beneath any place or observer, and diametrically opposite to the zenith; hence, the lowest point, as of adversity.

nae[1], **nae**[2] (nā). Scotch form of *no*[1], *no*[2].

nae-thing (nā′thing), *n.* and *adv.* Scotch form of *nothing*.

næ-vus (nē′vus), *n.*; pl. *-vi* (-vī). [L.] In *pathol.*, a discolored or pigmented spot on the skin, usually congenital; a birth-mark; an angioma of the skin; often, a mole.—**næ′void,** *a.*

nag[1] (nag), *n.* [ME. *nagge* = D. *negge*.] A small horse, or pony, esp. for riding (as, "My Ralph, whom I left training his little Galloway *nag* . . . may one day attain thy years": Scott's "Talisman," xv.); hence, in general, a horse (colloq.: as, "Bringing his *nags* up to the inn door in very pretty style, he gave the reins to his servant," Lever's "Harry Lorrequer," ii.); also, a worthless person†.

nag[2] (nag), *v.*; *nagged*, *nagging*. [Prob. from Scand.: cf. Sw. *nagga*, nibble, peck, nag, also E. *gnaw*.] **I.** *tr.* To gnaw (prov. Eng.); hence, fig., to torment by persistent faultfinding, complaints, or importunities; worry by peevish, irritating speeches. **II.** *intr.* To gnaw (prov. Eng.); fig., to keep up an irritating or wearisome faultfinding, complaining, or the like (often with *at*).

na-ga-na (nạ-gä′nạ), *n.* [S. Afr.] The tsetse-fly disease. See under *tsetse*.

nag-ger (nag′ėr), *n.* One who nags.

na-gor (nā′gôr), *n.* [Coined by Buffon.] An antelope, *Cervicapra redunca*, of western Africa, having the horns curved forward.

Nagor.

na-iad (nā′yạd or nī′ạd), *n.* [L. *Naias* (pl. *Naiades*), < Gr. Ναϊάς (pl. Ναϊάδες), akin to νάειν, flow.] [Also *cap.*] In *class. myth.*, one of a class of water-nymphs fabled to dwell in and preside over streams and springs: as, "The *Naiad* 'mid her reeds Press'd her cold finger closer to her lips" (Keats's "Hyperion," i.).

na-ïf (nä-ēf), *a.* [F., masc.: see *naïve*.] Naïve.

nail (nāl), *n.* [AS. *nægel* = D. and G. *nagel* = Icel. *nagl*, nail.] A thin, horny plate, consisting of modified epidermis, growing on the upper side of the end of a finger or toe; also, something resembling it, as the horny part at the end of the bill of a duck, etc.; also, a slender piece of metal, usually with one end pointed and the other enlarged, for driving into or through wood, etc., as to hold separate pieces together (as, a fourpenny *nail*: see *penny*); also, a measure of length for cloth, equal to $2\frac{1}{4}$ inches.—**a nail in one's coffin,** fig., something that helps to put one in his coffin or hasten his death: as, "Every minute he lies here is *a nail in his coffin*" (Scott's "Redgauntlet," ch. xv.). Often applied humorously to a drink of liquor, a cigarette, etc.—**on the nail,** on the spot, there and then, or at once (chiefly with reference to paying money: as, "One hundred and fifty thousand crowns were offered *on the nail*," Motley's "Dutch Republic," v. 3); also, of present interest, or under discussion, as a subject. [Colloq.]—**nail,** *v. t.* [AS. *næglian*.] To fix or fasten with a nail or nails (as, to *nail* the cover on a box; to *nail* a notice to a door; to *nail* a door fast); shut (*up*) within something by driving nails in (as, to *nail* goods up in a box); also, to pierce with a nail (obs. or rare: as, "Jael, who . . . Smote Sisera sleeping, through the temples *nail'd*," Milton's "Samson Agonistes," 990); also, to stud with or as with nails driven in; also, in fig. use, to make fast or keep firmly in one place or position, or rivet (as, surprise *nailed* him to the spot; his eyes were *nailed* on the approaching figure); pin (*down*), as to something from which there is no escape; settle decisively, or clinch, as a bargain; secure by prompt action, catch, or seize (colloq.: as, "lubbers as couldn't keep what they got, and want to *nail* what is another's," Stevenson's "Treasure Island," iii.); catch (a person) in some difficulty, a lie, etc., or detect and expose (a lie, etc.) (colloq.).—**nail′er,** *n.* One who nails anything; also, a maker of or dealer in nails.—**nail′er-y,** *n.*; pl. *-ies* (-iz). An establishment in which nails are made.—**nail′=head,** *n.* The head or enlarged end of a nail; hence, an ornament (usually one of a number) resembling the head of a nail driven in, as a square, round, or otherwise shaped piece of metal, jet, or the like used on dress, etc., or a small projection in architectural work.—**nail′=head″ed,** *a.* Having a head like that of a nail; cuneiform, as written characters; also, formed of or with nail-heads, as an architectural molding.

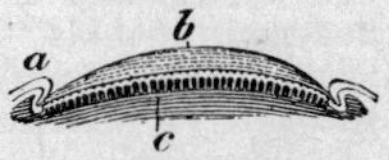

Cross-section of Human Nail, enlarged. — *a*, lateral fold of skin; *b*, the nail; *c*, bed of the nail, with its ridges.

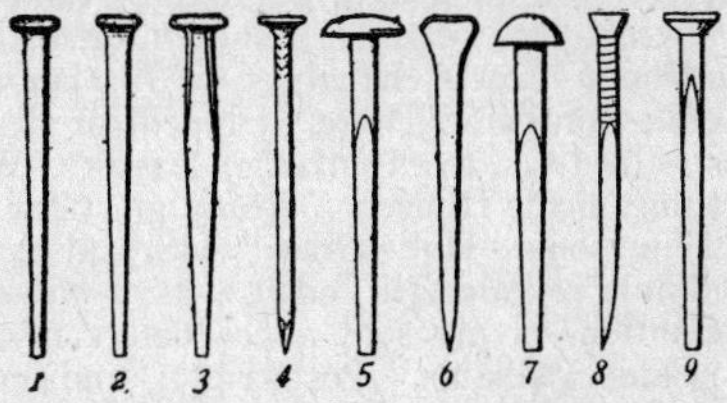

Nails. — 1, cut-nail; 2, finishing-nail; 3, shingle-nail; 4, wire nail; 5, saddle-nail; 6, horseshoe-nail; 7, hame-nail; 8, clinching-nail; 9, countersunk boat-nail.

nain-sook (nān′sůk or nan′-), *n.* [Hind. *nainsukh*, lit. 'eye pleasure.'] A fine, soft-finished cotton fabric, woven plain or with stripes, checks, etc.

na-ïve (nä-ēv′), *a.* [F. *naïve*, fem. of *naïf*, < L. *nativus*, native, natural: see *native*.] Having or showing the simplicity of nature; artless; ingenuous: as, "this *naïve* simple creature, with his straightforward and friendly eyes so eager to believe appearances" (Arnold Bennett's "Clay-

Nail-headed Molding. — Ducal Palace, Venice.

hanger," i. 1); a *naïve* reply.—**na-ïve'ly,** *adv.*—**na-ïve-té** (nä-ēv-tā), *n.*; pl. *-tés* (-tāz, F. -tā). [F.] The quality of being naïve, artless simplicity, or ingenuousness (as, "Mrs. M'Catchley was amused and pleased with his freshness and *naïveté*": Bulwer-Lytton's "My Novel," v. 8); also, a naïve action, remark, etc.

na-ked (nā'ked), *a.* [AS. *nacod* = D. *naakt* = G. *nackt* = Icel. *nökvidhr* = Goth. *naqaths*, naked; all being orig. pp., and akin to L. *nudus*, E. *nude*.] Bare of clothing or covering, or nude, as a person, the body, or parts of the body ordinarily clothed (as, "They were both *naked* . . . and were not ashamed": Gen. ii. 25); sometimes, stripped to an undergarment† (as, "Most of them were *naked* to the smock": Smollett's "Humphry Clinker," July 4); also, destitute of adequate or sufficient clothing (as, "Poor *naked* wretches . . . How shall . . . Your loop'd and window'd raggedness, defend you From seasons such as these?" Shakspere's "King Lear," iii. 4. 28); also, without armor or weapons†; hence, defenseless or unprotected; exposed, as to attack or harm; in general, bare of any covering, overlying matter, vegetation, foliage, or the like (as, *naked* rock; *naked* fields; *naked* trees); without a sheath, or unsheathed, as a sword; without carpets, hangings, or furnishings, as rooms, walls, etc.; sometimes, bare, stripped, or destitute of something specified (as, trees *naked* of leaves; "When the Lord of all things made Himself *Naked* of glory for His mortal change," Tennyson's "Holy Grail," 448); also, exposed to view, or plainly revealed (lit. or fig.: as, a *naked* nerve; "to lay the emotions of my soul *naked* before my hearers," Godwin's "Caleb Williams," Postscript); undisguised, unadorned, or plain, as facts, truth, etc.; plain-spoken or blunt (as, "the *naked* word shame": Stevenson's "Master of Ballantrae," v.); also, not accompanied or supplemented by anything else, bare, or mere (as, a *naked* outline of facts; "To speak the truth, I rate your chance Almost at *naked* nothing," Tennyson's "Princess," i. 160); of the eye, sight, etc., unassisted by a microscope, telescope, or other instrument; in *bot.*, of seeds, not inclosed in an ovary (cf. *gymnosperm*); of flowers, without a calyx or perianth; of stalks, etc., without leaves; also, of stalks, leaves, etc., without hairs or pubescence; in *law*, unsupported, as by authority or consideration (as, a *naked* promise).—**na'ked-ly,** *adv.*—**na'ked-ness,** *n.*

na-ker (nā'kėr), *n.* [OF. *nacre*, *nacaire*; from Ar.] A kettledrum: as, "the deep and hollow clang of the *nakers*" (Scott's "Ivanhoe," xxix.). [Archaic.]

nam-a-ble (nā'ma-bl), *a.* That may be named.

nam-ay-cush (nam'ā-kush), *n.* [N. Amer. Ind.] A large trout, *Cristivomer namaycush*, found in the lakes of the northern U. S. and Canada.

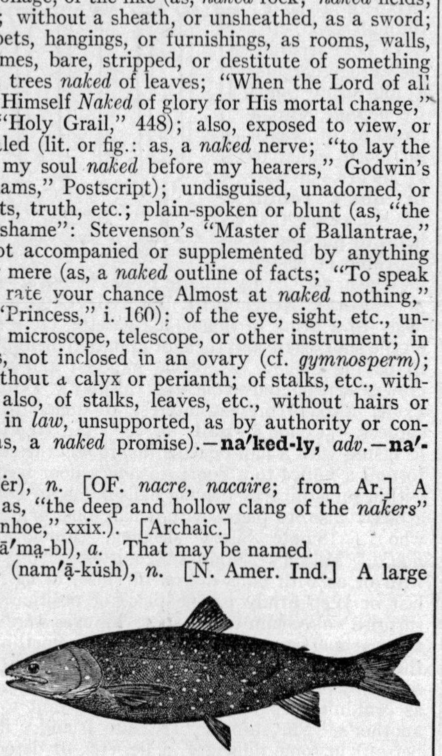

Namaycush.

nam-by=pam-by (nam'bi-pam'bi). [Orig. a nickname, *Namby Pamby*, for *Ambrose* Philips (1675?-1749), English poet, first used by Henry Carey in a burlesque poem, "Namby Pamby" (1726), ridiculing Philips's verses addressed to babies.] **I.** *a.* Weakly simple or sentimental, as verse, etc., or the writer; insipid, as sentiment; in general, insipidly simple, mild, amiable, or nice, as ideas, utterances, persons, etc.; milk-and-water. **II.** *n.*; pl. *-bies* (-biz). Namby-pamby verse or prose, or a piece of it; also, namby-pamby sentiment, as in writing or speech (as, "*Namby-pamby* in these days is not thrown away if it be introduced in the proper quarters": Trollope's "Warden," xv.); also, a namby-pamby person.—**nam'by=pam'bi-ness,** *n.*

name (nām), *n.* [AS. *nama* = D. *naam* = G. *name* = Goth. *namō*, name; akin to L. *nomen*, Gr. ὄνομα, Skt. *nāman*, name.] A word or a combination of words by which a person, place, or thing, a body or class, or any object of thought, is designated or known (as, the *name* of John, or of John Paul Jones; the *name* of the United States; *names* of plants, animals, books, churches, tribes, processes, emotions, or diseases; a proper or a common *name*, see *proper* and *common*, *a.*, as used in *gram.*); also, a word or a combination of words applied, as to a person or thing, descriptively, in honor or abuse, or otherwise (as, the *name* of friend, or of world's champion; the *name* of lion's provider, given to the jackal; "Walter hail'd a score of *names* upon her, And 'petty Ogress,' and 'ungrateful Puss,'" Tennyson's "Princess," Prologue, 155); an appellation, title, or epithet; also, a term of designation apart from or without a corresponding reality (as, "What is friendship but a *name?*" Goldsmith's "Hermit"); mere designation as distinguished from fact (as, king in *name* only); also, a personal or family name (in first sense) as exercising influence or bringing distinction (as, to bow to the authority of the author's *name*; to marry for the *name*); a distinguished or famous name, or great reputation (as, "He is likely to make a *name* for himself": Cooper's "Two Admirals," v.); great repute, or fame (as, to seek *name* and fortune; "men of *name*," Shakspere's "Richard III.," iv. 5. 8); sometimes, a widely known or famous person (as, "I am become a *name*": Tennyson's "Ulysses," 11); also, a repute or reputation of a particular kind given by common report (as, "The people . . . have a bad *name* as cannibals," H. Melville's "Omoo," xvii.; "They always hated anybody who had the *name* of being careless," Mark Twain's "Life on the Mississippi," viii.); also, a person as represented by his name (as, "Tullus Aufidius, The second *name* of men, obeys his points As if he were his officer": Shakspere's "Coriolanus," iv. 6. 125); a body of persons grouped under one name, as a family or race (as, "Let Egypt's plagues . . . proclaim The favours pour'd upon the Jewish *name*": Cowper's "Expostulation," 170).—**Christian name,** or **given name.** See under *Christian*, *a.*—**in the name of,** with appeal to the name of (much used in invocation, adjuration, or emphatic expressions: as, *in the name of* God, have mercy! what *in the name of* common sense is this?); also, as the representative of, or on behalf of (as, to write or act *in the name of* others); by the authority of; also, under the name of (one specified as owning or responsible: as, money deposited or debts incurred *in the name of* a person); also, under the designation of, or in the character of (as, a contribution exacted *in the name of* a benevolence).—**name,** *v. t.*; *named*, *naming*. [AS. *namian*.] To give a name to (as, to *name* a baby, a street, or a strange plant); call or designate by a specified name (as, to *name* a child John; Milton's poem *named* "Paradise Lost"); denominate, entitle, or style; also, to tell the name of (as, "Behold! there came A thing which Adam had been posed to *name*": Pope's "Satires of Donne," iv. 25); specify or mention by name (as, three persons were *named* in the report); hence, in general, to mention, speak of, or state (as, "I did not add to Miss Matty's anxieties by *naming* my suspicions": Mrs. Gaskell's "Cranford," iii.); specify or fix (as, to *name* a price; to *name* the day, commonly, of a woman, to fix the day for her marriage); also, to designate for some duty or office (as, "I have taken the freedom to *name* you for one of my executors": Stevenson's "Master of Ballantrae," vi.); nominate or appoint.—**name'a-ble,** *a.* See *namable*.—**name'=day,** *n.* The day sacred to a saint whose name a person bears: observed (like a birthday) on the Continent of Europe with congratulations, festivities, etc.—**name'less,** *a.* Having or bearing no name (as, a *nameless* star; a *nameless* grave); having no legitimate paternal name, as a child born out of wedlock; having no distinguished name, or unknown to fame, as a person; obscure or undistinguished, as the life, name, etc.; also, left unnamed (as, a certain person who shall be *nameless*); also, of unknown name; anonymous, as a writer or, formerly, a letter, etc.; also, that cannot be named, specified, or defined, or indefinable (as, "dreading a thousand *nameless* evils," Mrs. Shelley's "Frankenstein," vii.; a *nameless* longing; a *nameless* charm); also, too shocking or vile to be named or specified, as vices or crimes.—**name'less-ly,** *adv.*—**name'less-ness,** *n.*—**name'ly,** *adv.* With specific or definite mention or statement; that is to say; to wit: used to introduce words of specification or explanation: as, two cities, *namely*, Paris and London; a new contention, *namely* that the plan is impracticable.—**nam-er** (nā'mėr), *n.*—**name'sake,** *n.* [See *sake*[1].] One having the same name as another; esp.,

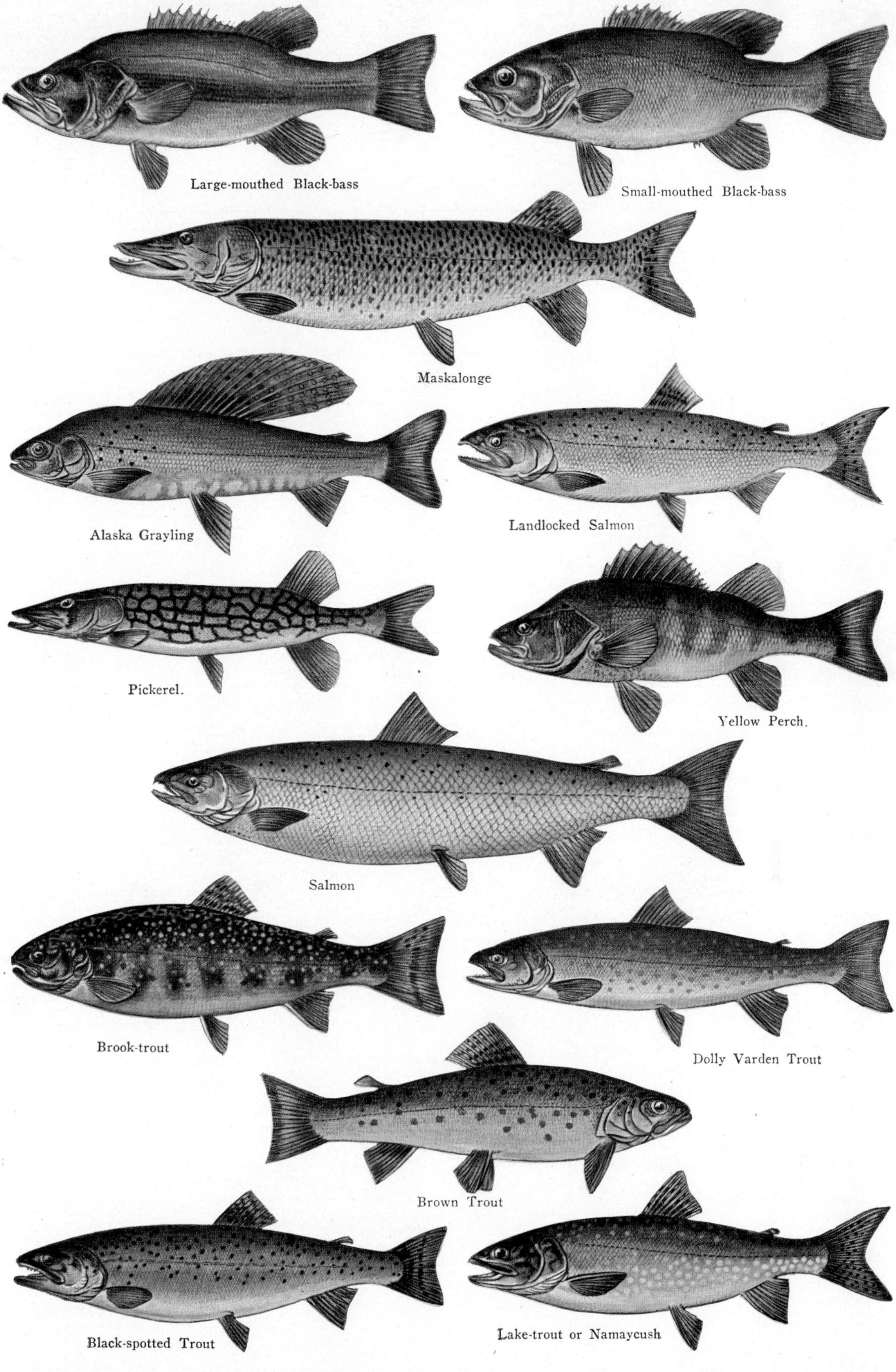

GAME-FISHES OF NORTH AMERICAN LAKES AND STREAMS

one named after another (as, "Lamoral Egmont, younger son and *namesake* of the great general [Lamoral, Count of Egmont]": Motley's "Dutch Republic," vi. 6).

nan-dine (nan′din), *n.* [From native name.] A spotted, ring-tailed viverrine animal of the African genus *Nandinia*, closely related to the Asiatic palm-cats.

Nandine (*Nandinia binotata*).

nan-du (nan′-dö), *n.* [Brazilian.] A rhea, or American ostrich, esp. *Rhea americana.*

nane (nān), *a.*, *pron.*, and *adv.* Sc. form of *none.*

na-nism (nā′nizm), *n.* [F. *nanisme*, < L. *nanus*, < Gr. νᾶνος, a dwarf.] In animals and plants, abnormally small size or stature; dwarfishness.

nan-keen (nan-kēn′), *n.* [From *Nankin*, or *Nanking*, city in China.] A firm, durable yellow or buff fabric, made orig. from a natural-colored Chinese cotton but now from other cotton and dyed (as, "His nether garment was of yellow *nankeen*": Cooper's "Last of the Mohicans," i.); *pl.*, trousers or breeches made of it (as, "humanity in *nankeens*": Bulwer-Lytton's "My Novel," i. 2); also, *sing.*, a yellow or buff color. Also **nan-kin′** (-kēn′).

nan-ny=goat (nan′i-gōt), *n.* [From *Nanny*, for *Ann*, woman's name.] A she-goat. Cf. *billy-goat.* [Colloq.]

na-os (nā′os), *n.* [Gr. ναός, temple, < ναίειν, dwell.] A temple; in *arch.*, the central chamber, or cella, of an ancient temple.

nap[1] (nap), *v. i.*; *napped, napping.* [AS. *hnappian.*] To have a short sleep; doze; fig., to be off one's guard (as, "I took thee *napping*, unprepared": Butler's "Hudibras," i. 3).—**nap**[1], *n.* A short sleep; a doze.

nap[2] (nap), *n.* [ME. *noppe* = MD. and MLG. *noppe.*] A coating of woolly or hairy substance on the surface of cloth; pile; also, any downy coating, as on plants.—**nap**[2], *v. t.*; *napped, napping.* To raise a nap on.

nap[3] (nap), *v. t.*; *napped, napping.* [Cf. *nab*, also *kidnap.*] To seize; catch; nab; steal. [Slang or prov., Eng.]

nap[4] (nap), *n.* Shortened form of *napoleon* (gold coin, card-game, and bid in that game).

nape (nāp), *n.* [ME. *nape*; origin uncertain.] The back of the neck: usually in the phrase 'nape of the neck.'

na-per-y (nā′pėr-i), *n.* [OF. *naperie*, < *nape*, table-cloth: see *napkin.*] Linen for household use, esp. table-linen; table-cloths, table-napkins, etc.: as, "Three tables were spread with *napery*, not so fine as substantial" (Lamb's "Praise of Chimney-Sweepers").

naph-tha (naf′thạ̈), *n.* [L., < Gr. νάφθα.] Orig., a variety of petroleum; now, a colorless, volatile liquid, a petroleum distillate (esp. a product intermediate between gasoline and benzine), used as a solvent, fuel, etc.; any of various similar liquids distilled from other products.—**naph′tha-lene** (-lēn), *n.* In *chem.*, a white crystalline hydrocarbon, $C_{10}H_8$, usually prepared from coal-tar: used in making dyes, etc. Also **naph′tha-line** (-lin).—**naph′thol** (-thol or -thōl), *n.* In *chem.*, either of two hydroxy derivatives of naphthalene, having the formula $C_{10}H_7OH$, and occurring in coal-tar.

Na-pier-i-an (nạ-pē′ri-ạn), *a.* Of or pertaining to John Napier (1550–1617), Scotch mathematician, the inventor of logarithms.

na-pi-form (nā′pi-fôrm), *a.* [L. *napus*, turnip: see *-form.*] Turnip-shaped; large and round above and slender below, as a root.

nap-kin (nap′kin), *n.* [ME. *napekyn*, dim. < OF. *nape* (F. *nappe*), table-cloth, cloth, < L. *mappa*, napkin, cloth: cf. *map.*] A square piece of linen used at meals to wipe the lips and hands, to protect the clothes, or otherwise; also, a square or oblong linen or cotton cloth for some other purpose; a towel; esp., a handkerchief (now Sc.).—**nap′kined,** *a.* Furnished with, covered with, or served on a napkin.—**nap′kin=ring,** *n.* A ring, often of silver, for holding a table-napkin, folded and rolled up, when not in use.

nap-less (nap′les), *a.* Having no nap; also, threadbare.

Na-po-le-on (nạ-pō′lẹ-ọn), *n.* [From *Napoleon* I., of France.] A man of commanding and constructive genius in the military or some other field (as, "We live in a world full of would-be *Napoleons* of finance, of the press, of the turf": H. G. Wells's "Outline of History," xxxviii. § 6); [*l. c.*] a French gold coin of the value of 20 francs, or about $3.86; also, a game at cards in which the players bid for the privilege of naming the trump, stating the number of tricks they propose to win; a bid in this game to take all five tricks of a hand; also, a piece of pastry consisting of puff-paste in layers with a cream filling.—**Na-po″le-on-a′na** (-ā′nạ̈), *n. pl.* [NL.: see *-ana.*] Writings, articles, etc., associated with Napoleon I., of France; Napoleonic relics, esp. such as are of interest to collectors.—**Na-po-le-on′ic** (-on′ik), *a.* Pertaining to, resembling, or suggestive of Napoleon I., or, less often, Napoleon III.—**Na-po-le-on′i-cal-ly,** *adv.*

Obverse. Reverse.
Napoleon.

napped (napt), *a.* Having a nap, as cloth.

nap-per (nap′ėr), *n.* One who raises a nap on cloth; a machine for putting a nap on cloth.

nap′pie, *n.* See *nappy*[3].

nap-py[1] (nap′i), *a.* Napped; downy.—**nap′pi-ness,** *n.*

nap-py[2] (nap′i). [Origin uncertain: cf. *nappy*[1].] **I.** *a.* Heady or strong, as ale; also, tipsy (chiefly Sc.). **II.** *n.* Liquor, esp. ale. [Chiefly Sc.]

nap-py[3] (nap′i), *n.*; pl. *nappies* (-iz). [Origin obscure.] A small dish, usually round and often of glass, with a flat bottom and sloping sides, for holding food, etc.

na-pu (nä′pö), *n.* [Malay.] Any of several species of chevrotain, esp. *Tragulus napu* of Sumatra.

nar-ce-ine (när′sẹ-in), *n.* [L. *narce*, < Gr. νάρκη, numbness, torpor.] In *chem.*, a bitter, white, crystalline alkaloid contained in opium, sometimes used in medicine as a substitute for morphine.

nar-cis-sus (när-sis′us), *n.*; pl. *-cissuses*, L. *-cissi* (-sis′ī). [L., < Gr. νάρκισσος (named from its narcotic properties), < νάρκη, numbness, torpor.] Any plant of the amaryllidaceous genus *Narcissus*, which comprises bulbous plants bearing showy flowers with a cup-shaped corona, and includes the jonquil and the daffodil; also [*cap.*], in *class. myth.*, a beautiful youth who, not responding to the love of the mountain-nymph Echo, was caused by Nemesis to fall in love with his own image reflected in a fountain, and who, unable to grasp this image, pined away and was changed into the flower narcissus.

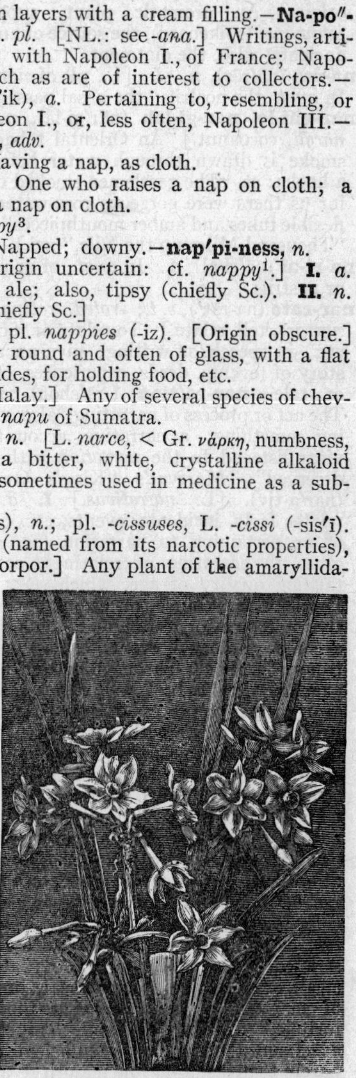

Narcissus (*N. tazetta*).

nar-co-ma-ni-a (när-kọ̄-mā′ni-ạ̈), *n.* [NL., < Gr. νάρκη, numbness, + μανία, E. *mania.*] In *pathol.*, a morbid craving for a narcotic drug.—**nar-co-ma′ni-ac** (-ak), *n.*

nar-co-sis (när-kō′sis), *n.* [NL., < Gr. νάρκωσις, < ναρκοῦν, benumb, < νάρκη, numbness, torpor.] The production of stupor or insensibility; the action of a narcotic; also, a state of stupefaction or insensibility.

nar-cot-ic (när-kot′ik). [Gr. ναρκωτικός, < ναρκοῦν, benumb: see *narcosis*.] **I.** *a.* Having the power to produce stupor or insensibility, as a drug; hence, in general, producing sleep or dullness (as, "He . . . habitually fell asleep at that horrible council-board . . . while the other murderers had found their work less *narcotic*": Motley's "Dutch Republic," v. 4); also, pertaining to or of the nature of narcosis. **II.** *n.* Any of a class of substances that blunt the senses, relieving pain, etc., and inducing sleep, and in large quantities producing complete insensibility: often used habitually to satisfy morbid appetite.—**nar-cot′i-cal-ly,** *adv.*—**nar′co-tine** (-kọ-tin), *n.* In *chem.*, a crystalline alkaloid present in opium: formerly (erroneously) supposed to be a narcotic.—**nar′co-tism,** *n.* The action or influence of narcotics, or the effects or condition produced by their use; narcosis; hence, any influence likened to that of a narcotic; also, an abnormal inclination to sleep.—**nar′co-tize** (-tīz), *v. t.*; *-tized, -tizing.* To subject to the influence of a narcotic; stupefy.—**nar″co-ti-za′tion** (-ti-zā′shọn), *n.*

nard (närd), *n.* [L. *nardus*, < Gr. νάρδος; of Eastern origin.] An aromatic plant, supposedly *Nardostachys jatamansi* (spikenard), the source of an ointment used by the ancients; also, the ointment.

na-res (nā′rēz), *n. pl.* [L., pl. of *naris*, nostril: see *nose*.] In *anat.*, the nostrils; the nasal passages or openings.

nar-ghi-le, nar-gi-leh (när′gi-lạ̄), *n.* [Pers. *nārgīleh*, < *nārgīl*, cocoanut.] An Oriental tobacco-pipe in which the smoke is drawn through water before reaching the lips; a hooka: as, "The gentlemen smoked chibouques . . . while for us there were gorgeous rose-water *narghilehs* with long flexible tubes and amber mouthpieces" (Amelia B. Edwards's "Thousand Miles up the Nile," xxi.).

na-ri-al (nā′ri-ạl), *a.* In *anat.*, of or pertaining to the nares or nostrils.

nar-rate (na-rāt′), *v. t.*; *-rated, -rating.* [L. *narratus*, pp. of *narrare*, tell, relate.] To relate or recount (facts, incidents, etc.) in speech or writing; give an account of or tell the story of (events, deeds, experiences, etc.); recite, as a story or tale.—**nar-ra′tion** (-rā′shọn), *n.* [L. *narratio(n-)*.] The act or process of narrating; also, words or matter narrating something; a narrative, account, or story (as, "The vicar listened to the *narration* with the interest which it deserved": Marryat's "King's Own," l.).—**nar-ra-tive** (nar′ạ-tiv). [L. *narrativus*.] **I.** *a.* That narrates, or relates facts, incidents, events, etc. (as, a *narrative* poem); of or pertaining to narration (as, *narrative* skill); also, given to narrating or relating†, or garrulous† (as, "the tattling quality of age, which . . . is always *narrative*": Dryden's "Discourse concerning Satire"). **II.** *n.* A narrative statement or recital, as of facts or incidents; a relation, account, or story of events, experiences, or the like, whether true or fictitious; narrative matter, as in literary work (as, pages of *narrative* broken by occasional descriptive passages); also, the act or process of narrating, or narration (as, "The path of *narrative* with care pursue, Still making probability your clue": Cowper's "Conversation," 217).—**nar′ra-tive-ly,** *adv.*—**nar-ra-tor** (na-rā′tọr), *n.*

nar-row (nar′ō). [AS. *nearu* = OS. *naru*, narrow.] **I.** *a.* Of little breadth or width, or not broad or wide (as, a *narrow* path or passage); of less than a specified, understood, or usual width (as, *narrow* cloths; *narrow* gage, see *gage*³, *n.*); also, limited in extent or space, or affording little room (as, *narrow* quarters; the *narrow* house, the grave; *narrow* compass or bounds); fig., limited in range or scope (as, *narrow* powers or opportunities; a *narrow* lot in life); restricted, as the range, scope, etc.; also, limited in amount, small, or meager (as, *narrow* means or resources; "the charge of maintaining me . . . being too great for a *narrow* fortune," Swift's "Gulliver's Travels," i. 1); straitened, as circumstances; barely sufficient or adequate, or being barely that (as, a *narrow* majority; a *narrow* escape); also, lacking breadth of view or sympathy, as persons, the mind, ideas, etc.; illiberal or narrow-minded; also, close, parsimonious, or stingy (now prov. Eng. and Sc.: as, "The chancellor's long robe . . . was not so good as my own gown; but he is said to be a very *narrow* man," Galt's "Ayrshire Legatees," viii.); also, close, careful, or minute, as a scrutiny, search, or inquiry; looking closely, or with narrowed space between the upper and the lower lid, as the eye, etc.; in *phonetics*, uttered with a relatively narrow opening of the vocal organs; not wide. **II.** *n.* A narrow part, place, or thing; *pl.*, a narrow part of a strait, river, sound, or the like (as, the *Narrows* at the entrance of New York Harbor); a narrow part of an ocean current (as, the *narrows* of the Gulf Stream at the south point of Florida); a narrow part of a valley, of a passage between mountains, or of any road.—**nar′row,** *v.* **I.** *tr.* To make narrower; reduce in breadth, extent, scope, etc.; limit or restrict; make illiberal or narrow-minded. **II.** *intr.* To become narrower; decrease in breadth, extent, etc.: as, "The cave . . . was about fifty feet long, *narrowing* to a mere hole at the extremity" (W. H. Hudson's "Green Mansions," xvi.).—**nar′row-ly,** *adv.*—**nar′row=mind′ed,** *a.* Having or showing a narrow mind, as persons, opinions, utterances, etc.; devoid of breadth of view or sympathy; illiberal; narrow.—**nar′row=mind′ed-ly,** *adv.*—**nar′row=mind′ed-ness,** *n.*—**nar′row-ness,** *n.*

nar-thex (när′theks), *n.* [Gr. νάρθηξ, kind of plant, casket, later narthex.] In *arch.*, a kind of portico or vestibule forming the entrance of early Christian churches.

nar-whal (när′hwạl), *n.* [Sw. and Dan. *narhval* = Icel. *nāhvalr*.] An arctic cetacean, *Monodon monoceros*, the male of which has a long, straight, spirally twisted tusk extending forward from the upper jaw.

Narwhal.

nar-y (nãr′i), *a.* [Corruption of *ne'er a*, never a.] Never a; not a; no: as, "three dozen steamboats and *nary* barge or raft" (Mark Twain's "Life on the Mississippi," xxviii.). [Prov. or vulgar.]

na-sal (nā′zạl). [NL. *nasalis*, < L. *nasus*, nose: see *nose*.] **I.** *a.* Of or pertaining to the nose; also, uttered with or characterized by resonance in the nose (as, a *nasal* consonant; a *nasal* twang). **II.** *n.* A part of a helmet, protecting the nose and adjacent parts of the face; in *phonetics*, a nasal speech-sound, as *m*, *n*, or *ng*; in *anat.*, a nasal bone.—**na-sal-i-ty** (nạ-zal′i-ti), *n.* Nasal quality.—**na-sal-ize** (nā′zạl-īz), *v. t.* or *i.*; *-ized, -izing.* To utter or speak with a nasal sound.—**na″sal-i-za′tion** (-i-zā′shọn), *n.*—**na′sal-ly,** *adv.*

Nasals (adjustable); 13th century.

nas-cent (nas′ẹnt), *a.* [L. *nascens* (*nascent-*), ppr. of *nasci* (pp. *natus*), be born, grow: see *native*.] In process of coming into being (as, "the *nascent* republic," Motley's "Dutch Republic," v. 5; a *nascent* sense of right and wrong); beginning to exist, grow, or develop; incipient; in *chem.*, noting the state or condition of an element at the instant it is set free from a combination; of an element, being in that state.—**nas′cence, nas′cen-cy,** *n.*

na-so- (nā′zọ̄-). Form of L. *nasus*, nose, used in combination, esp. in anatomical terms, as in *nasolabial* (of both nose and upper lip), *nasopalatine* (of both nose and palate), *nasopharyngeal* (of both nose and pharynx).

na-sol-o-gy (nạ-zol′ọ̄-ji), *n.* [See *naso-* and *-logy*.] The study of the nose or of noses.—**na-sol′o-gist,** *n.*

nas-ti-ly (nȧs′ti-li), *adv.* In a nasty manner; filthily; offensively.—**nas′ti-ness,** *n.* The quality or state of being nasty; also, that which is nasty; filth or dirt; often, moral filth; obscenity.

nas-tur-tium (nạs-tėr′shium), *n.* [L., kind of cress, < *nasus*, nose, + *torquere*, twist (from its pungency).] Any of the pungent-flavored plants constituting the genus *Roripa*, as the water-cress; now, more commonly, any of the garden plants constituting the genus *Tropæolum*, much cultivated for their showy flowers of yellow, red, and other colors, and for their fruit, which is pickled and used like capers.

nas-ty (nȧs′ti), *a.*; compar. *nastier*, superl. *nastiest.* [ME. *nasty*; origin obscure.] Physically filthy, or disgustingly dirty, foul, or unclean, as matter, places, persons, the condition, etc.; hence, morally filthy, or vile, indecent, or obscene, as persons, the mind, language, stories, etc.; also, offensive to taste or smell, or nauseous; also, very unpleasant, as weather, etc.; in general, offensive, obnoxious, or objectionable (as, "He [Napoleon] was . . . no longer the embodied spirit of a world reborn; he was just a new and *nastier* sort of autocrat": H. G. Wells's "Outline of History," xxxviii. § 4); often, in vague disparagement or as a mere expression of personal dislike, odious, wretched, or abominable (as, "I had . . . money . . . Alas! there the *nasty*, sorry, useless stuff lay," Defoe's "Robinson Crusoe," i. 9; "The jugs are bewitched . . . It's them *nasty* glazed handles – they slip o'er the finger like a snail," George Eliot's "Adam Bede," xx.); also, bad to deal with, encounter, undergo, etc. (as, a *nasty* customer in a fight; a *nasty* cut or fall); also, ill-natured, vicious, spiteful, or 'ugly,' as persons, the temper, speech, actions, etc. [In the general and other later senses, commonly regarded in the U. S. as colloquial.]

na-sute (nạ-sūt′ or nā′sūt), *a.* [L. *nasutus*, having a large nose, < *nasus*, nose.] Having a large or long nose or nose-like process (as, the *nasute* termites: see *nasutus*); also, keen-scented†; discerning†; sagacious†.

na-su-tus (nạ-sū′tus), *n.*; pl. *-ti* (-tī). [NL., < L. *nasutus*: see *nasute*.] One of a class of termites, or white ants, having the head prolonged in a nose-like process, from which a fluid is discharged which serves as a cement in nest-building.

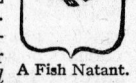

Nasutus. — Two and one half times natural size.

na-tal (nā′tạl), *a.* [L. *natalis*, < *natus*, birth, < *nasci*, be born: see *native*.] Of or pertaining to one's birth (as, one's *natal* hour or day); presiding over or affecting one at birth (as, *natal* stars or influences); of places, native (chiefly poetic).—**na-tal-i-ty** (nạ-tal′i-ti), *n.* Birth; also, birth-rate.

na-tant (nā′tạnt), *a.* [L. *natans* (*natant-*), ppr. of *natare*, swim, float, freq. of *nare*, swim.] Swimming; floating; in *her.*, represented as swimming, or horizontally, as a fish; in *bot.*, floating on water, as a leaf of an aquatic plant.—**na-ta-tion** (nạ-tā′shọn), *n.* [L. *natatio*(*n-*), < *natare*.] The act or art of swimming.—**na-ta′tor**, *n.* [L.] A swimmer.—**na-ta-to-ri-al** (nā-tạ-tō′ri-ạl), *a.* Pertaining to, adapted for, or characterized by swimming: as, *natatorial* powers or organs; *natatorial* birds.—**na-ta-to′ri-um** (-um), *n.*; pl. *-riums* or *-ria* (-ri-ạ). [LL.] An establishment having a pool or tank for the use of persons learning or practising swimming.—**na′ta-to-ry** (-tọ-ri), *a.* [LL. *natatorius*.] Natatorial.

A Fish Natant.

nathe-less, nath-less (nāth′les, nath′les). [AS. *nā the lǣs*, not the less.] **I.** *adv.* Nevertheless: as, "The torrid clime Smote on him sore . . . *Nathless* he so endured" (Milton's "Paradise Lost," i. 299). [Archaic.] **II.** *prep.* Notwithstanding. [Archaic.]

nat-i-ca (nat′i-kạ), *n.*; pl. *-cas*, L. *-cæ* (-sē). [NL.: cf. ML. *naticæ*, buttocks, < L. *natis*, buttock.] Any of the sea-snails of the widespread genus *Natica*, all active, predatory, and carnivorous, having a globose shell with a flattened spire, and including species common on the Atlantic coast of the U. S.

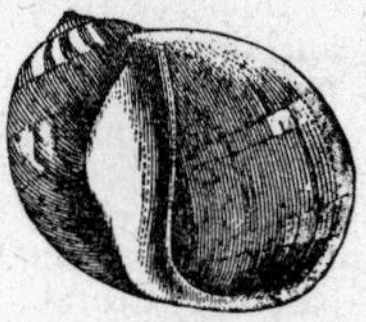

Natica.

na-tion (nā′shọn), *n.* [OF. *nacion* (F. *nation*), < L. *natio*(*n-*), race, people, nation, orig. birth, < *nasci*, be born: see *native*.] An aggregation of people having a common origin, language, or history (as, the Jewish *nation*; "All *nations* . . . shall come and worship before thee, O Lord," Ps. lxxxvi. 9); a people, race, or tribe; also, a body of people occupying a country and united under one general government as an independent political unit, or state (as, "If we accept this Constitution, we shall be a *nation*," Mrs. Stowe's "Oldtown Folks," vi.; "the Plymouth Rock . . . the corner-stone of a *nation*!" Longfellow's "Courtship of Miles Standish," v.); also, in medieval universities, and still in certain Scottish universities, a division of students grouped together according to their place of birth or origin (as, the four *nations* of the faculty of arts of the University of Paris; "The governing body [of the University of Glasgow] includes . . . the lord rector elected triennially by the students voting in '*nations*' according to their birthplace," Encyc. Brit., 11th ed., XII. 82); also, any set, class, or tribe, as of persons or animals†; also, a multitude, or great number (obs. or archaic: as, "The French had such a *nation* of hedges, and copses, and ditches," Sterne's "Tristram Shandy," v. 21).—**Five Nations.** See under *five*, *a.*—**the nations,** in Biblical use, the heathen nations, or Gentiles (as, "All the gods of *the nations* are idols": Ps. xcvi. 5); in general use, the peoples of the earth collectively.

na-tion-al (nash′ọn-ạl), *a.* [F. *national*, < *nation*: see *nation*.] Of, pertaining to, or characteristic of a nation or people (as, a *national* language or literature; *national* traits, customs, or dress); also, of, pertaining to, or maintained by a nation as an organized whole or independent political unit (as, *national* affairs, finances, or politics; a *national* holiday; the *national* government; a *national* church); also, devoted to one's own nation, its interests, etc., or patriotic.—**national bank,** a bank associated with the finances of a nation; in the U. S., a bank chartered by the national government and authorized to issue notes that serve as money.—**National Guard,** in the U. S., the organized militia armed, equipped, and trained for military service. See *militia*.—**na′tion-al,** *n.* In diplomatic use, a citizen or subject of a particular nation.—**na′tion-al-ism,** *n.* National spirit or aspirations; devotion to the interests of one's own nation; desire for national advancement or independence; also, a form of socialism which advocates the nationalizing of all industries.—**na′tion-al-ist,** *n.* One inspired with nationalism; an advocate of national independence; specif. [*cap.*], in Irish politics, a member of a political party advocating the more or less complete political separation of Ireland from Great Britain; also [*l. c.*], a believer in socialistic nationalism.—**na″tion-al-is′tic,** *a.* —**na-tion-al-i-ty** (nash-ọ-nal′i-ti), *n.*; pl. *-ties* (-tiz). National quality or character; also, the fact or relation of belonging to a particular nation or country, or origin with respect to nation (as, to claim French *nationality*; to learn the *nationality* of an immigrant or of a ship; men of several *nationalities*); also, devotion to one's own nation; nationalism; also, existence as a distinct nation; national integrity or independence; also, a nation or people (as, the various *nationalities* of the Balkan Peninsula).—**na′tion-al-ize** (-īz), *v.*; *-ized*, *-izing*. **I.** *tr.* To make national; esp., to bring under the control or ownership of a nation, as industries, land, etc.; also, to admit or establish as part of a nation, as persons; naturalize; also, to make into a nation, as a colony. **II.** *intr.* To become naturalized.—**na″tion-al-i-za′tion** (-i-zā′shọn), *n.*—**na′tion-al-iz-er** (-ī-zėr), *n.* One who nationalizes; also, an advocate of the nationalizing of all industries, etc.—**na′tion-al-ly,** *adv.*—**na′tion-al-ness,** *n.*

na-tion=wide (nā′shọn-wīd′), *a.* Extending throughout the nation: as, a *nation-wide* inquiry or campaign.

na-tive (nā′tiv). [OF. F. *natif*, < L. *nativus*, native, innate, natural, < *nasci* (pp. *natus*), be born, grow, orig. *gnasci*, < *gen-*, beget, produce: see *genius*, and cf. *naïve*.] **I.** *a.* Belonging to a person or thing by birth or nature; inborn; inherent; natural (often with *to*); also, remaining in a natural state or as formed by nature (as, *native* beauty or simplicity); unadorned; simple; untouched by art; also, being the place or environment in which one was born (as, one's *native* land, woods, or air: also fig., with reference to things); hence, forming the source or origin of a person or thing (as, "Heaps of broken stone That mingled slowly with their *native* earth": Shelley's "Queen Mab," ix. 121); also, belonging or pertaining to one by reason of his country or nationality (as, one's *native* language); also, belonging to one as a possession by virtue of his birth (as, "his just and *native* rights": Cowper's "Task," v. 436); also, closely related, as by birth (now rare: as, "The head is not more *native* to the heart . . . Than is the throne of Denmark to thy father," Shakspere's "Hamlet," i. 2. 47); also, occurring in nature pure or uncombined, as metals, etc. (as, *native* copper); found in nature rather than produced artificially, as a mineral substance; also, born in a particular place or country (as, *native* American citizens); originating naturally in a particular country or region, as animals or plants; of indigenous origin, growth, or production; indigenous (*to*);

also, pertaining to the natives of a place; in specif. use, belonging by birth to a people regarded as 'natives,' or outside of the general body of superior, esp. white peoples (as, "*native* policemen [in India]," Kipling's "Kim," ii.; *native* African tribes); of, pertaining to, or characteristic of natives (as, a *native* uprising; *native* dress or customs in India or Java; the *native* name of an animal of Madagascar); occupied by natives (as, the *native* quarter of Algiers or Shanghai); under the rule of natives (as, the *native* states of India). **II.** *n.* One born in a particular place or country (as, Daniel Defoe was a *native* of London; George Washington was a *native* of Virginia; Andrew Carnegie was a *native* of Scotland who emigrated to the U. S. when a boy); also, one of the original inhabitants of a place or country, as distinguished from strangers or foreigners; specif., one of the original inhabitants of a place or country beyond the limits of European or modern civilization, who are regarded as outside the general body of superior, esp. white peoples (as, the *natives* of India or Arabia, or of Borneo or the Congo); also, an animal or plant indigenous to a particular region; also, one's native place or country (now prov. Eng. and Sc.: as, "She was wearying the very heart out of her to be home again to Lauder, which she said was her *native*," Moir's "Mansie Wauch," vi.); in *astrol.*, one born under a particular planet (as, "Mars having dignity in the cusp of the twelfth house, threatened captivity, or sudden and violent death, to the *native*": Scott's "Guy Mannering," iv.).—**na′tive-born,** *a.* Born in a place or country indicated.—**na′tive-ly,** *adv.*—**na′tive-ness,** *n.*—**na′tiv-ism,** *n.* The policy of protecting the interests of native inhabitants against those of immigrants; the policy or practice of favoring natives above naturalized citizens, as in elections or in appointments to political office; in *philos.*, the doctrine of innate ideas.—**na′tiv-ist,** *n.*—**na-tiv-i-ty** (nā-tiv′i-ti), *n.*; pl. *-ties* (-tiz). [OF. *nativite* (F. *nativité*), < LL. *nativitas*.] Birth (as, "I have served him from the hour of my *nativity* to this instant": Shakspere's "Comedy of Errors," iv. 4. 32); often, birth with reference to place or attendant circumstances (as, to be of Scotch or Irish *nativity*); specif. [*cap.*], the birth of Christ; the church festival (Christmas) commemorating the birth of Christ; a representation of the birth of Christ, as in art; also [*l. c.*], in *astrol.*, a horoscope (as, "He . . . proceeded to calculate the *nativity* of the young heir of Ellangowan": Scott's "Guy Mannering," iv.).

na-tri-um (nā′tri-um), *n.* [NL., < Ar. *natrūn*: see *natron*.] Sodium: in *chem.*, abbreviated *Na* (without period).

nat-ro-lite (nat′rō-līt or nā′trō-), *n.* [From *natron* + *-lite*.] A mineral, a hydrous silicate of sodium and aluminium, occurring usually in white or colorless, often acicular crystals.

na-tron (nā′tron), *n.* [F. *natron*, < Sp. *natrón*, < Ar. *natrūn*, *nitrūn*, < Gr. *νίτρον*, natron: see *niter*.] Native sodium carbonate.

nat-ter-jack (nat′ėr-jak), *n.* [Origin uncertain.] A European toad, *Bufo calamita*, having a clouded yellowish or brownish coloration with a bright-yellow stripe down the middle of the back, and progressing with a motion that resembles running.

Natterjack.

nat-ty (nat′i), *a.* [Cf. *neat*[2] and *net*[2].] Neatly smart in dress or appearance, spruce, or trim (as, a *natty* young officer; a *natty* uniform; "He wore . . . *natty* round-toed boots," Thackeray's "Newcomes," vi.); also, deft, skilful, or clever (prov. Eng.).—**nat′ti-ly,** *adv.*—**nat′ti-ness,** *n.*

nat-u-ral (nat′ū-ral), *a.* [OF. *natural*, *naturel* (F. *naturel*), < L. *naturalis*, < *natura*: see *nature*.] Of, pertaining to, or proper to the nature or essential constitution (as, *natural* ability; *natural* delicacy); innate or inherent; consonant with the nature or character; often, essentially pertaining, or coming easily or spontaneously (*to*: as, he acted in a manner *natural* to one in his position); also, being such by nature; born such (as, a *natural* fool); also, by birth merely, and not legally recognized; illegitimate (as, "Margaret of Parma . . . was the *natural* daughter of Charles the Fifth, and his eldest-born child": Motley's "Dutch Republic," ii. 1); also, having or showing the nature, disposition, feelings, etc., befitting a person (as, "a noble . . . brother, in his love toward her ever most kind and *natural*," Shakspere's "Measure for Measure," iii. 1. 229: now rare: cf. *unnatural*); also, in accordance with the nature of things (as, it is *natural* that so prominent a man should make enemies); proper to the circumstances of the case; also, of or pertaining to nature or the created universe (as, *natural* history, *natural* science, *natural* philosophy: see phrases below); physical; occupied with the study of natural science (as, a *natural* philosopher, a physicist); also, constituted by nature (as, the *natural* divisions of the earth; the *natural* day); based on the state of things in nature; also, in conformity with the ordinary course of nature; happening in the ordinary course of things, without the intervention of accident, violence, etc. (as, a *natural* death); in general, normal; not unusual or exceptional; also, existing in or formed by nature; not artificial; often, growing spontaneously, as vegetation; also, true to nature, or closely imitating nature (as, "How *natural* these paintings, which seem to contend with life!" Scott's "Kenilworth," vi.); also, free from affectation or constraint (as, "When Kavanagh was present, Alice was happy, but embarrassed; Cecilia, joyous and *natural*," Longfellow's "Kavanagh," xxiii.; a *natural* manner); not affected or strained; also, in a state of nature; uncultivated, as land; unenlightened or unregenerate (as, the *natural* man); also, based on what is learned from nature, rather than on revelation (as, *natural* religion; *natural* theology); also, having a real or physical existence, as opposed to one that is spiritual, intellectual, fictitious, etc. (as, "Which is the *natural* man, And which the spirit?" Shakspere's "Comedy of Errors," v. 1. 333; a corporation is an artificial person created by law from a group or succession of *natural* persons); also, based upon the innate moral feeling of mankind (as, *natural* law or justice); in *music*, neither sharp nor flat; without sharps or flats; also, produced by the voice (distinguished from *instrumental*).—**natural gas,** combustible gas formed naturally in the earth, as in petroleum regions, and consisting typically of methane with certain amounts of hydrogen and other gases: used as a fuel, etc.—**natural history,** the science or study dealing with all objects in nature, now esp. animals and sometimes also plants; also, the aggregate of knowledge connected with such objects; also, a work dealing with such objects.—**natural philosophy,** physics.—**natural science,** science or knowledge dealing with objects in nature, as distinguished from mental or moral science, abstract mathematics, etc.—**natural selection.** See *selection*.—**natural sine, tangent,** or the like, a sine, tangent, or the like, which is not expressed as a logarithm, but as the actual value of a ratio in which the radius of the circle or the hypotenuse of the triangle is taken as the measuring unit.—**nat′u-ral,** *n.* That which is natural, or in accordance with the ordinary course of things (with *the*); also, one naturally deficient in intellect; an idiot; also, a thing or a person that is naturally or by nature notably satisfactory or a success (colloq.); in *music*, a natural tone or note; also, the sign ♮ used to cancel the effect of a preceding sharp or flat; also, a white key on the pianoforte, etc.

nat-u-ral-ism (nat′ū-ral-izm), *n.* Action arising from or based on natural instincts and desires alone; also, adherence or attachment to what is natural; in art and literature, close adherence to nature or reality; realism; specif., the principles or methods of a group of 19th century French and other realistic writers, including esp. Zola, who aimed to present a photographic picture of modern life, without suppression of details usually suppressed, and sometimes with extremely repulsive effect; in *philos.*, the view of the world which takes account only of natural elements and forces, excluding the supernatural or spiritual; in *theol.*, the doctrine that all religious truth is derived from a study of nature, and not from revelation.

nat-u-ral-ist (nat′ū-ral-ist), *n.* One versed in natural history or natural science; now, esp., one who makes a study of animals or (sometimes) plants; also, an adherent of naturalism.—**nat″u-ral-is′tic,** *a.* Pertaining to naturalists or natural history; also, pertaining to naturalism (in any sense), esp. naturalism in art and literature; also, pertaining to or in accordance with nature.—**nat″u-ral-is′ti-cal-ly,** *adv.*

nat-u-ral-ize (naṭ′ū̦-ra̤l-īz), *v.*; *-ized, -izing.* **I.** *tr.* To make natural; bring into conformity with nature; free from conventional characteristics; also, to regard or explain as natural rather than supernatural (as, to *naturalize* miracles); also, to invest (an alien) with the rights and privileges of a native subject or citizen (as, "a measure carried in 1709 for *naturalising* all foreign Protestants who settled in England": Lecky's "Hist. of Eng. in the 18th Century," i.); confer the rights and privileges of citizenship upon; also, to introduce or adopt (foreign practices, words, etc.) into a country or into general use (as, "She must be foudroyant and pyramidal, — if these French adjectives may be *naturalized* for this one particular emergency": Holmes's "Elsie Venner," xxi.); also, to introduce (animals or plants) into a region and cause to flourish as if native (as, "Senhouse stayed out the winter at Land's End, engaged in . . . *naturalising* Alpine plants upon the faces of rock there": M. Hewlett's "Open Country," xiv.); also, in general, to adapt or accustom to a place or to new surroundings (as, "I was now in my twenty-third year of residence . . . and was . . . *naturalized* to the place, and to the manner of living": Defoe's "Robinson Crusoe," i. 13). **II.** *intr.* To become naturalized, or as if native; also, to be occupied with natural history.—**nat″u-ral-i-za′tion** (-i-zā′sho̤n), *n.*—**nat′u-ral-iz-er** (-ī-zėr), *n.*

nat-u-ral-ly (naṭ′ū̦-ra̤l-i), *adv.* In a natural manner; by nature; spontaneously, or without the aid of art or cultivation; as a natural consequence, or as might be expected; in accordance with natural laws; in a lifelike or realistic manner; without affectation.—**nat′u-ral-ness,** *n.*

na-ture (nā′ṭū̦r), *n.* [OF. F. *nature,* < L. *natura,* birth, natural constitution or character, nature, < *nasci,* be born: see *native.*] The particular combination of qualities belonging to a person or thing by birth or constitution; native or inherent character or disposition (as, "To weep was not in Lady Kew's *nature,*" Thackeray's "Newcomes," xlvi.; "It is my habit, — I hope I may say, my *nature,* — to believe the best of people," G. W. Curtis's "Prue and I," iv.); in general, character, kind, or sort (as, a thing impossible from the very *nature* of the case; a book of the same *nature*); also, a person of a particular character or disposition (as, "It was a gentle *nature's* dream of a passion": Howells's "Foregone Conclusion," xviii.); also, the physical being (as, "In swinish sleep Their drenched *natures* lie as in a death": Shakspere's "Macbeth," i. 7. 68); the vital powers (as, food sufficient to sustain *nature*); also, the inherent principle sustaining the physical and mental activities (as, "*Nature,* crescent, does not grow alone In thews and bulk": Shakspere's "Hamlet," i. 3. 11); the instincts or inherent tendencies directing conduct (as, "He thought *nature* and reason were sufficient guides for a reasonable animal": Swift's "Gulliver's Travels," iv. 5); also, the sum total of the forces at work throughout the universe, considered collectively as a single operative principle and often personified as feminine (usually *cap.*: as, "Who can paint Like *Nature?* Can imagination boast . . . hues like hers?" Thomson's "Seasons," Spring, 469; "Go forth, under the open sky, and list To *Nature's* teachings," Bryant's "Thanatopsis"); also, the universe, with all its phenomena; the material world, esp. as surrounding man and existing independently of his activities; also, reality, as distinguished from any effect of art (as, true to *nature*); also, a primitive, wild condition; an uncultivated state; the moral state as unaffected by grace.—**na′-tured,** *a.* Having a nature (as specified): as, good-*natured.*

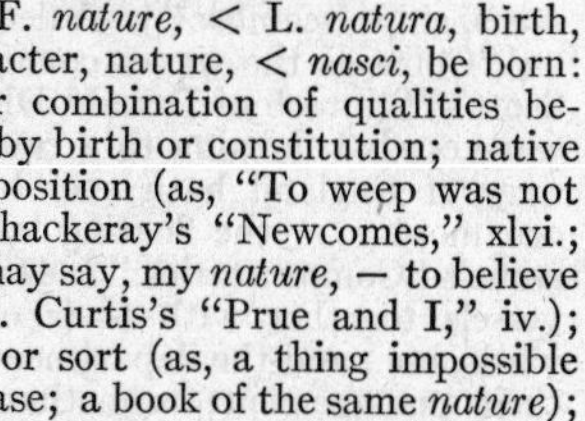

Naucratite Pottery, 7th or 8th century B.C.

Nau-cra-tite (nâ′kra̤-tīt), *a.* Of or pertaining to Naucratis, an ancient Greek colony in the Nile delta, Egypt, the site of which has yielded important archæological remains, notably pottery.

naught (nât), *n.* [Also *nought*; AS. *nāwiht, nōwiht,* < *ne,* not, + *āwiht, ōwiht,* E. *aught*¹, *ought*¹.] Nothing (now archaic or literary: as, to ask *naught* for one's self); also, a cipher (0).—**to bring to naught,** to bring to destruction, ruin, or complete failure, as armies, kingdoms, plans, etc [Archaic.]—**to come to naught,** to come to destruction or ruin; fail, or prove of no effect. [Archaic.]—**to set at naught,** to regard or treat as of no importance; despise, disregard, or defy: as, "virtue, talent, everything *set at naught* —intrinsic value despised" (Marryat's "Peter Simple," xl.). [Archaic.]—**naught,** *a.* Of no value, worthless, or useless (obs. or archaic); also, bad or poor in quality, as food†; also, morally bad†, or wicked†; also, lost† or ruined† (as, "Away! All will be *naught* else": Shakspere's "Coriolanus," iii. 1. 231).—**naught,** *adv.* In no respect or degree; not at all: as, "The trial hath . . . Me *naught* advantaged, missing what I aim'd" (Milton's "Paradise Regained," iv. 208). [Obs. or archaic.]

naught-y (nâ′ti), *a.*; compar. *naughtier,* superl. *naughtiest.* [From *naught.*] Having nothing†, or poor†; also, worthless†, of little value†, or poor in quality† (as, "The other basket had very *naughty* figs, which could not be eaten, they were so bad": Jer. xxiv. 2); also, disagreeable, as weather, odors, etc.†; also, morally bad†, wicked†, or evil† (as, "*naughty* persons, lewdly bent," Shakspere's "2 Henry VI.," ii. 1. 167; "a *naughty* world," Shakspere's "Merchant of Venice," v. 1. 91); now, an equivalent of *bad* used in speaking to children, or with reference to children, their behavior, etc., or playfully with reference to older persons or to things generally (as, "You *naughty* little thing! . . . Why don't you come when you are called?" C. Brontë's "Jane Eyre," iv.; a *naughty* man; a *naughty* word; a *naughty* book).—**naught′i-ly,** *adv.*—**naught′i-ness,** *n.*

nau-ma-chi-a (nâ-mā′ki-ä), *n.*; pl. *-chiæ* (-ki-ē). [L., < Gr. ναυμαχία, < ναῦς, ship, + μάχεσθαι, fight.] A mock sea-fight, given as a spectacle among the ancient Romans; also, a place for presenting such spectacles. Also **nau′ma-chy** (-ma̤-ki); pl. *-chies* (-kiz).

nau-pli-us (nâ′pli-us), *n.*; pl. *nauplii* (-ī). [L., kind of shell-fish.] In *zoöl.*, in many crustaceans, a larval form with an unsegmented body, three pairs of appendages, and a single median eye, occurring (usually) as the first stage of development after leaving the egg.—**nau′pli-al,** *a.*

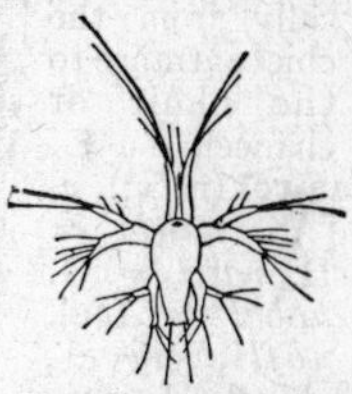

Nauplius of a Prawn (*Penæus*).

nau-se-a (nâ′s̤ē-ä), *n.* [L. *nausea, nausia,* < Gr. ναυσία, seasickness, nausea, < ναῦς, ship.] Seasickness; sickness at the stomach; a sensation of impending vomiting; fig., extreme disgust; loathing.

nau-se-ate (nâ′s̤ē-āt), *v.*; *-ated, -ating.* [L. *nauseatus,* pp. of *nauseare,* < *nausea*: see *nausea.*] **I.** *intr.* To become affected with nausea. **II.** *tr.* To have a sensation of nausea at (as, "Putting a little [salt] into his own mouth, he seemed to *nauseate* it": Defoe's "Robinson Crusoe," i. 15); fig., to feel extreme disgust at, or loathe; also, to affect with nausea; sicken; fig., to cause to feel loathing.—**nau′se-at-ing-ly,** *adv.*—**nau-se-a′tion** (-ā′sho̤n), *n.* The act of nauseating, or the condition of being nauseated.

nau-se-ous (nâ′s̤ē-us), *a.* [L. *nauseosus.*] Causing nausea, or sickening (as, "a kind of slimy stuff . . . of a most *nauseous,* odious smell": Defoe's "Captain Singleton," iv.); fig., disgusting or loathsome (as, "The theme by amplification became *nauseous*": Godwin's "Caleb Williams," vi.).—**nau′se-ous-ly,** *adv.*—**nau′se-ous-ness,** *n.*

nautch (nâch), *n.* [Hind. *nāch.*] An East Indian exhibition of dancing by professional dancing-girls ('nautch-girls'): as, "We like to sit and look on at a wedding *nautch*" (F. M. Crawford's "Mr. Isaacs," i.).

nau-tic (nâ′tik), *a.* [L. *nauticus,* < Gr. ναυτικός, < ναύτης, sailor, or ναῦς, ship: see *nave*².] Nautical. [Obs. or poetic.]—**nau′ti-cal,** *a.* Of or pertaining to seamen, ships, or navigation: as, *nautical* terms.—**nautical mile.** See under *mile.*—**nau′ti-cal-ly,** *adv.*

nau-ti-lus (nâ′ti-lus), *n.*; pl. *-luses* or *-li* (-lī). [L., < Gr. *ναυτίλος*, lit. 'sailor,' < *ναῦς*, ship.] The argonaut ('paper-nautilus'), which was formerly believed to use its webbed arms as sails; also, any of the tetrabranchiate cephalopods constituting the genus *Nautilus*, which have a spiral, chambered shell with pearly septa ('pearly nautilus').

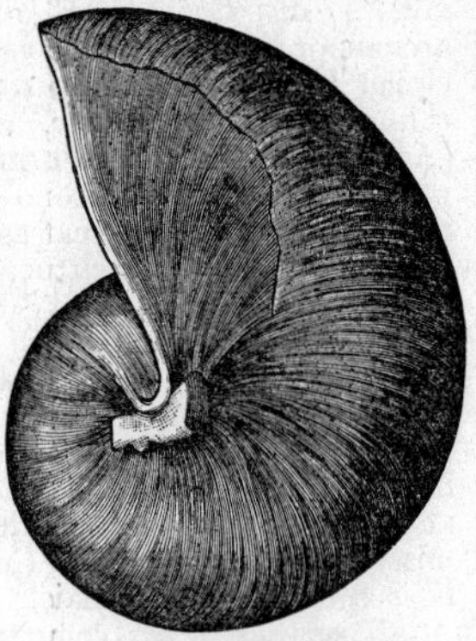

Pearly Nautilus.

na-val (nā′vạl), *a.* [L. *navalis*, < *navis*, ship: see *nave*².] Of or pertaining to ships, esp., and now only, ships of war (as, *naval* architecture; a *naval* battle); hence, belonging or pertaining to, or connected with, a navy (as, *naval* vessels, officers, guns, or stores; a *naval* hospital; *naval* affairs); possessing a navy (as, the great *naval* powers).—**naval auxiliary.** See *auxiliary, n.*—**naval holiday,** a period of cessation or reduction of naval activities, among nations not actually at war, by limitation of armaments and construction, etc., in the interest of international peace, decreased taxation, and general well-being.—**naval militia.** See *militia.*—**na′val-ism,** *n.* The principle or policy of building up or maintaining a strong naval establishment for a country. Cf. *militarism.*—**na′val-ist,** *n.* An advocate of navalism.—**na′val-ly,** *adv.*

nave¹ (nāv), *n.* [AS. *nafu* = D. *naaf* = G. *nabe* = Icel. *nöf*, nave; akin to Skt. *nābhi*, nave, navel: cf. *navel.*] The central part or piece of a wheel; the hub; also, the navel†.

nave² (nāv), *n.* [ML. *navis*, nave of a church, L. ship; akin to Gr. *ναῦς*, Skt. *nāu*, ship.] The main body, or middle part, lengthwise, of a church, flanked by the aisles, or lateral divisions, and extending typically from the chief entrance to the choir or chancel.

Nave. — Rheims Cathedral, France; 13th century.

na-vel (nā′vl), *n.* [AS. *nafela* = D. *navel* = G. *nabel* = Icel. *nafli*, navel; akin to L. *umbilicus*, Gr. *ὀμφαλός*, navel, Skt. *nābhi*, nave, navel: see *nave*¹.] A pit or depression in the middle of the surface of the belly; the umbilicus (see *umbilicus*); hence, a similar depression on anything; also, the central point or middle of any thing or place (as, "Within the *navel* of this hideous wood . . . a sorcerer dwells": Milton's "Comus," 520); in *her.*, same as *nombril.*—**navel orange,** a variety of orange having at the apex a navel-like formation containing a small secondary fruit.—**na′vel-wort** (-wėrt), *n.* A crassulaceous plant, *Cotyledon umbilicus*, having round, succulent, peltate leaves with a central navel-like depression (also called *pennywort*); also, any plant of the boraginaceous genus *Omphalodes.*

na-vew (nā′vū), *n.* [F. *naveau*, dim. < L. *napus*, turnip.] The wild turnip.

nav-i-cert (nav′i-sėrt), *n.* A British consulate certificate specifying the character of a ship's cargo, etc.

na-vic-u-lar (nạ-vik′ū-lạ̈r), *a.* [LL. *navicularis*, < L. *navicula*, dim. of *navis*, ship.] Of or pertaining to a boat†; also, boat-shaped (used in *anat.*, of certain bones, etc.).

nav-i-ga-ble (nav′i-gạ-bl), *a.* [L. *navigabilis.*] That may be navigated, as waters, or vessels or aircraft.—**nav″i-ga-bil′i-ty** (-bil′i-ti), **nav′i-ga-ble-ness,** *n.*—**nav′i-ga-bly,** *adv.*

nav-i-gate (nav′i-gāt), *v.*; *-gated, -gating.* [L. *navigatus*, pp. of *navigare*, < *navis*, ship, + *agere*, drive.] **I.** *intr.* To travel by using a ship or boat, as over the water; sail; sometimes, to pass over the water, as a vessel does; also, to direct or manage a vessel or an aircraft on its course. **II.** *tr.* To traverse (the sea, a river, etc.) in a vessel, or (the air) in an aircraft; sometimes, to pass over (the sea, etc.), as a vessel does; also, to direct or manage (a vessel or an aircraft) on its course (as, "If the captain died, the mate was in duty bound to *navigate* the ship to the nearest civilized port": H. Melville's "Omoo," xiii.).—**nav-i-ga′tion** (-gā′shọn), *n.* [L. *navigatio(n-).*] The act or process of navigating; also, the art or science of directing the course of vessels; seamanship; also, the art of directing aircraft ('aërial navigation'); also, a voyage (now rare); also, ships or shipping (now rare).—**nav-i-ga′tion-al,** *a.*—**nav′i-ga-tor,** *n.* [L.] One who navigates; one who practises, or is skilled in, navigation, whether of vessels or of aircraft; sometimes, one who conducts explorations by sea (as, Columbus, Magellan, and other great *navigators*); also, a navvy or laborer (Eng.).

nav-vy (nav′i), *n.*; pl. *navvies* (-iz). [Abbr. of *navigator.*] A laborer employed in making canals, embankments, railways, etc. (Eng.); also, a machine for excavating earth.

na-vy (nā′vi), *n.*; pl. *navies* (-viz). [OF. *navie*, < L. *navis*, ship: see *nave*².] A fleet of ships (now chiefly poetic: as, "Come as the waves come, when *Navies* are stranded," Scott's "Pibroch of Donald Dhu"); also, the whole body of war-vessels belonging to a country or ruler (as, "The royal *navy* of England hath ever been its greatest defence and ornament . . . the floating bulwark of the island": Blackstone's "Commentaries," I. 418); hence, such a body of war-vessels together with their officers and men, equipment, yards, etc., and the department of government charged with their management; sometimes, the fighting aircraft of a nation ('air navy' or 'aërial navy').—**navy bean,** the common white bean, dried for use.—**navy blue,** a dark blue.—**na′vy=yard,** *n.* A government dockyard where naval vessels are built, repaired, and fitted out, and naval stores and munitions of war are laid up.

na-wab (nạ-wâb′), *n.* [Hind. *nawwāb*, < Ar. *nawwāb*, pl. of *nā'ib*, deputy, viceroy.] A viceroy or deputy governor under the former Mogul empire in India; also, an honorary title conferred upon Mohammedans of distinction in India (cf. *raja*); also, a nabob, or possessor of wealth brought from India.

nay (nā), *adv.* [ME. *nai, nei*, from Scand.: cf. Icel. and Dan. *nei*, Sw. *nej*, nay, no, and E. *no*¹.] No (used in dissent, denial, or refusal: as, "By what law? of works? *Nay*: but by the law of faith," Rom. iii. 27); also, and not only so, but (as, "There were many good, *nay*, noble points in her character": H. Kingsley's "Geoffry Hamlyn," xxxviii.); indeed. [Chiefly archaic.]—**nay,** *n.* An utterance of the word 'nay'; a denial or refusal; specif., a negative vote or voter.—**nay′=say,** *n.* An utterance of 'nay'; a denial or refusal: as, "like a maiden too soon taken at her first *nay-say*" (Scott's "Castle Dangerous," xiii.). [Archaic or prov.]

nay-word (nā′wėrd), *n.* [Origin uncertain.] A watchword (as, "We have a *nay-word* how to know one another: I . . . cry 'mum'; she cries 'budget' ": Shakspere's "Merry Wives of Windsor," v. 2. 5); also, a byword. [Now chiefly prov. Eng.]

Naz-a-rene (naz-ạ-rēn′), *n.* [LL. *Nazarenus*, < Gr. Ναζαρηνός, < Ναζαρέτ, Nazareth.] A native or inhabitant of Nazareth, in Palestine, as Jesus Christ ('the Nazarene'); hence, a Christian (so called by the Jews, Mohammedans, etc.: as, "We have found this man [Paul] . . . a ringleader of the sect of the *Nazarenes*," Acts, xxiv. 5); also, one of a

sect of early Jewish Christians who retained the Mosaic ritual.
Naz-a-rite (naz′a̤-rīt), *n.* [LL. *Nazaræus*, < Gr. Ναζαραῖος, < Heb. *nāzar*, consecrate.] Among the ancient Hebrews, a religious devotee who had taken certain vows. See Num. vi.
Na-zi (nät′sē̤). [G., short for *Nationalsozialist*, National Socialist.] **I.** *n.*; pl. *-zis* (-sē̤z). A member of the National Socialist party of Germany, which in 1933, under Adolf Hitler, obtained political control of the country, suppressing all opposition and establishing a dictatorship. **II.** *a.* Of or pertaining to the Nazis.—**Na′zism** (nät′sizm), **Na′zi-ism,** *n.* [Also *l. c.*] The principles or methods of the Nazis.
ne (nē). [AS. *ne* = OHG. *ni, ne,* = Icel. *ne* = Goth. *ni,* not; akin to L. *ne*, Gr. νη-, Skt. *na*, not.] **I.** *adv.* Not. [Obs. or archaic.] **II.** *conj.* Nor. [Obs. or archaic.]
neaf (nēf), *n.* Same as *nieve.* [Obs. or prov.]
Ne-an-der-thal-oid (nā-än′dėr-täl-oid), *a.* Resembling a skull ('Neanderthal skull') of very low type found in the Neanderthal, a valley near Düsseldorf, believed to be that of a member of a dolichocephalic race ('Neanderthal race') widespread in Europe in the paleolithic period; pertaining to this type of skull or to the race it is believed to represent.
neap[1] (nēp). [AS., in *nēpflōd*, 'neap flood.'] **I.** *a.* Designating those tides, midway between spring-tides, which attain the least height. **II.** *n.* A neap tide.
neap[2] (nēp), *n.* [Origin uncertain.] The pole or tongue of a wagon, etc. [U. S.]
Ne-a-pol-i-tan (nē-a̤-pol′i-ta̤n), *a.* [L. *Neapolitanus*, < *Neapolis*, < Gr. Νεάπολις, Naples, < νέος, new, + πόλις, city.] Of or pertaining to Naples, in Italy.—**Neapolitan ice=cream,** ice-cream in layers of different flavors and colors.
near (nēr). [AS. *nēar*, compar. of *nēah*, E. *nigh.*] **I.** *adv.* Nigher or closer, as in space, time, or relation†; also, nigh; at, within, or to a short distance (as, to stand or be *near*; to come *near*); close (as, *near* by); also, close at hand in time (as, "when their deaths be *near*": Shakspere's "Sonnets," cxl.); also, close in relation; closely with respect to connection, similarity, etc. (as, *near* allied); also, all but, almost, or nearly (now chiefly colloq. or prov.: as, "I had *near* screamed with terror," Stevenson's "Master of Ballantrae," v.; a period of *near* thirty years); also, *naut.*, close to the wind. **II.** *prep.* [Strictly the adverb with *to* understood: cf. the corresponding quasi-prepositional uses of *nearer* and *nearest.*] At, within, or to a short distance, or no great distance, from (as, regions *near* the equator; to come *near* a place); also, close upon in time (as, *near* the beginning of the year); also, close upon (a condition, etc.: as, a task *near* completion); close to (doing something: as, this action came *near* spoiling his chances); close to in similarity, resemblance, etc. (as, a case which comes *near* this one); in recent use, approximating or resembling closely (used in compounds denoting things intended for imitations or substitutes: as, *near*-silk; *near*-beer).—**near,** *a.* Being close by (as, "the *near* meadows": Keats's "Ode to a Nightingale"); not distant; less distant (as, the *near* side); also, close in time (as, the *near* future); also, closely related or connected; closely allied by blood or kinship (as, "This man was our *nearest* relation": C. B. Brown's "Wieland," xviii.); intimate or familiar (as, a *near* friend); also, closely affecting one's interests or feelings (as, a matter of *near* consequence to one); also, close to an original (as, a *near* translation); also, narrow (as, a *near* escape); also, with reference to animals or vehicles, left (as opposed to *off*, or right: as, the *near* horse of a pair; a horse's *near* fore leg); also, short or direct, as a road; also, parsimonious or niggardly (as, a *near* man; "He lived in a *near* manner," Steele, in "Spectator," 402).—**Near East.** See under *east, n.*—**near,** *v.* **I.** *intr.* To come or draw near; approach: as, "A speck, a mist, a shape, I wist! And still it *near'd* and *near'd*" (Coleridge's "Ancient Mariner," iii.). **II.** *tr.* To come or draw near to; approach: as, "a little vessel . . . *nearing* the shore" (G. W. Curtis's "Prue and I," iv.); a task *nearing* completion.—**near′=by′,** *a.* Close at hand; not far off; adjacent; neighboring: as, a *near-by* village. [Chiefly U. S.]
Ne-arc-tic (nē̤-ärk′tik), *a.* [Gr. νέος, new, + ἀρκτικός, E. *arctic.*] In *zoögeog.*, belonging to the northern division of the New World (temperate and arctic North America, with Greenland).
near=hand (nēr′hand), *adv.* Near at hand; also, nearly or almost (as, "His race is *near-hand* run": Scott's "Rob Roy," xxix.). [Now prov. Eng. and Sc.]
near-ly (nēr′li), *adv.* In a near manner or degree; closely; with close inspection, or carefully (now rare: as, "I implore the Douglas to look *nearly* to the safety of the ladies," Scott's "Castle Dangerous," xx.); with close kinship, relationship, or connection; intimately; with close relation to one's interest (as, "I have something to tell you, that very *nearly* concerns you": Defoe's "Robinson Crusoe," ii. 11); with close agreement or resemblance (as, a case *nearly* approaching this one); with close approximation (as, "to live more *nearly* as we pray": Keble's "Christian Year," i.); all but, or almost (as, *nearly* dead with cold; *nearly* a hundred: often with a negative, as in 'not nearly,' that is, not by a great deal, or nothing like); with parsimony or niggardliness.—**near′ness,** *n.*
near=sight-ed (nēr′sī′ted), *a.* Seeing distinctly at a short distance only; myopic.—**near′=sight′ed-ly,** *adv.*—**near′=sight′ed-ness,** *n.*
neat[1] (nēt), *n.* [AS. *nēat* = Icel. *naut*: see *nowt.*] Cattle of the ox kind (as, "The herdsmen drave Full oft to Chiron woolly sheep, and *neat,*" W. Morris's "Jason," i. 241: often called *neat cattle*); also, a single bovine animal (now rare).
neat[2] (nēt), *a.* [F. *net*, clean, clear, < L. *nitidus*, bright, fine, handsome, neat: see *nitid*, and cf. *net*[2].] Clean†; clear† or bright†; unadulterated or undiluted, as liquors (as, "hogsheads of *neat* port," Steele, in "Spectator," 264; a glass of brandy *neat*); also, clear of or free from deductions (as, *neat* profits; *neat* weight: now usually *net*); also, pleasingly free from unnecessary and detrimental features; of a simple, pleasing appearance (as, a *neat* cottage or carriage; a *neat* foot or figure; *neat* styles of dress; a *neat* bookbinding); nicely or cleverly effective in character or execution (as, a *neat* contrivance or scheme; a *neat* trick); simply and pleasingly expressive (as, a *neat* characterization; "He had quite an apt wit of his own, and a *neat* way of saying things," Howells's "Chance Acquaintance," iii.); sometimes, of persons, etc., clever, dexterous, or apt, as in performance or expression; also, in a pleasingly orderly condition (as, to keep a room *neat*; *neat* piles of papers; *neat* hair and dress); tidy; often, habitually orderly or nice in appearance, habits, etc., as persons.
neath, 'neath (nēth), *prep.* Beneath. [Poetic or Sc.]
neat=hand-ed (nēt′han′ded), *a.* Neat or dexterous in the use of the hands; deft: as, "Their savoury dinner . . . Of herbs, and other country messes, Which the *neat-handed* Phillis dresses" (Milton's "L'Allegro," 86).
neat-herd (nēt′hėrd), *n.* A cowherd.
neat-ly (nēt′li), *adv.* In a neat manner.—**neat′ness,** *n.*
neb (neb), *n.* [AS. *nebb.*] A bill or beak, as of a bird; hence, a person's mouth; also, the nose; an animal's snout; also, the tip or pointed end of anything; the nib of a pen. [Now chiefly prov. Eng. and Sc.]
neb-u-la (neb′ṳ̄-lä̤), *n.*; pl. *-læ* (-lē). [L., mist, vapor, cloud; akin to Gr. νεφέλη, cloud, Icel. *nifl*, G. *nebel*, mist, fog.] An indistinct, cloud-like luminous mass of supposed gaseous matter far beyond the limits of the solar system, or a very distant star-cluster resembling this (as, the great *nebula* in Orion); in *pathol.*, a cloud-like spot on the cornea.—**neb′u-lar** (-lä̤r), *a.* Pertaining to, of the nature of, or resembling a nebula or nebulæ: as, the *nebular* hypothesis (the theory that the solar system has been evolved from a mass of nebulous matter).—**ne-bu-li-um** (ne-bū′li-um), *n.* [NL.] A supposed chemical element to which certain green lines in the spectra of nebulæ are attributed.—**neb′u-lize** (-līz), *v. t.*; *-lized, -lizing.* To reduce to fine spray; atomize.—**neb′u-liz-er** (-lī-zėr), *n.* An apparatus for reducing a liquid to fine spray, for medicinal or other purposes; an atomizer.—**neb′u-lose** (-lōs), *a.* [L. *nebulosus.*] Nebulous; cloud-like; fig., hazy or indistinct; also, clouded; having cloud-like markings.—**neb-u-los′i-ty** (-los′i-ti), *n.*; pl. *-ties* (-tiz). Nebulous state; cloud-like character; also, nebulous or nebular matter; also, a nebulous or nebular mass or appearance; a nebula.—**neb′u-lous,** *a.* [L. *nebulosus.*] Cloudy or cloud-like; fig., hazy, vague, indistinct, or confused (as, "*nebulous* disquisitions on Religion":

Carlyle's "Sartor Resartus," ii. 9); also, nebular.—**neb′u-lous-ly,** *adv.*—**neb′u-lous-ness,** *n.*

ne-ces-sa-ri-an (nes-e-sā′ri-ạn). **I.** *n.* A necessitarian. **II.** *a.* Pertaining to necessitarians or necessitarianism.—**ne-ces-sa′ri-an-ism,** *n.*

ne-ces-sa-ri-ly (nes′e-sạ-ri-li), *adv.* In a necessary manner; by or of necessity; as a necessary result or consequence.—**ne′ces-sa-ri-ness,** *n.*

ne-ces-sa-ry (nes′e-sạ-ri). [L. *necessarius*, < *necesse*, unavoidable, indispensable.] **I.** *a.* Such as must be (as, "Death, a *necessary* end, Will come when it will come": Shakspere's "Julius Cæsar," ii. 2. 36); happening or existing by necessity; inevitable; also, acting or proceeding from compulsion or necessity (as, a *necessary* agent); not free; involuntary; also, that cannot be dispensed with; indispensable; essential; requisite; needful; also, rendering indispensable or useful services (archaic). **II.** *n.*; pl. *-ries* (-riz). Something necessary, indispensable, or requisite (as, "bread and gunpowder (the two great *necessaries* of martial life)," Kinglake's "Eothen," xxviii.; the *necessaries* of life); a requisite; also, a privy or water-closet.

ne-ces-si-ta-ri-an (nẹ-ses-i-tā′ri-ạn). **I.** *n.* One who maintains that the action of the will is a necessary effect of antecedent causes: opposed to *libertarian.* **II.** *a.* Pertaining to necessitarians or necessitarianism.—**ne-ces-si-ta′ri-an-ism,** *n.* The doctrine of the inevitable determination of the will by antecedent causes, as opposed to that of the freedom of the will.

ne-ces-si-tate (nẹ-ses′i-tāt), *v. t.*; *-tated, -tating.* [ML. *necessitatus*, pp. of *necessitare*, < L. *necessitas*, E. *necessity.*] To render necessary (as, "There was little or nothing in the place . . . to *necessitate* the interference of the magistrate": J. H. Newman's "Callista," vii.); also, to compel, oblige, or force (as, "I was *necessitated* to fight with an imaginary enemy": H. Melville's "Typee," xxx.).—**ne-ces-si-ta′tion** (-tā′shọn), *n.*

ne-ces-si-tous (nẹ-ses′i-tus), *a.* Being in or involving necessity or want; needy; indigent: as, "He . . . grew *necessitous* . . . and wanted bread" (B. Franklin's "Autobiography," iv.); to be in *necessitous* circumstances.—**ne-ces′si-tous-ly,** *adv.*—**ne-ces′si-tous-ness,** *n.*

ne-ces-si-ty (nẹ-ses′i-ti), *n.*; pl. *-ties* (-tiz). [OF. *necessite* (F. *nécessité*), < L. *necessitas*, < *necesse*: see *necessary.*] The state or fact of being necessary or inevitable; also, constraint or compulsion proceeding from the natural constitution of things; esp., such constraint viewed as a principle of universal causation, determining even the action of the will; also, the constraining power of circumstances (as, a course justified by *necessity*; "Of *necessity* he must release one unto them at the feast," Luke, xxiii. 17); a state of things compelling a certain course of action; also, an unavoidable compulsion of doing something (as, "We . . . were under a *necessity* of steering westward": Swift's "Gulliver's Travels," iii. 9); an imperative requirement or need for something (as, there is no *necessity* for a decision at this time); also, the fact of being necessary or indispensable; indispensableness; also, something necessary or indispensable (as, the *necessities* of life); something requisite or urgently needed (as, "The rehabilitation of the cabin became a *necessity*": Bret Harte's "Luck of Roaring Camp"); also, the state of being in difficulty or straits, as for lack of something; commonly, a state of want or need; indigence; poverty; also, a case or instance of want or need (usually in *pl.*: as, "This money was loudly called for by my lord's *necessities*," Stevenson's "Master of Ballantrae," i.).

neck (nek), *n.* [AS. *hnecca* = Icel. *hnakki*, nape of the neck, = D. *nek*, G. *nacken*, nape, neck.] The part of the body connecting the head and the trunk; the part of a garment covering it or extending about it; also, the length of the neck of a horse or other animal as a measure in racing (as, "The ladies being mounted on thoroughbreds, got a full *neck* before me," Lever's "Harry Lorrequer," ii.; a horse wins by a *neck*); also, any narrow connecting or projecting part suggesting the neck of an animal; a narrow strip of land, as an isthmus or a cape; a strait, or narrow body of water connecting two larger bodies; the slender part of a bottle, retort, or any similarly shaped object; the long, slender part of a violin or the like, extending from the body to the head; in *printing*, the part of a type between the face and the shoulder; the beard; in *arch.*, the lowest part of the capital of a column, immediately above the astragal at the head of the shaft; in *anat.*, a constricted part of a bone, organ, or the like; also, the part of a tooth between the crown and the root.—**neck and neck,** abreast, or side by side, as horses in a race; hence, fig., equally advanced in any competition or the like.—**neck or nothing,** venturing everything; taking all risks or chances. Hence, as an adjective (*neck-or-nothing*), headlong; reckless.

neck=band (nek′band), *n.* A band worn round the neck; esp., a band of cloth at the neck of a garment.

neck=cloth (nek′klôth), *n.* A cloth worn round the neck, esp. by men; a cravat.

necked (nekt), *a.* Having a neck (esp. as specified): as, long-*necked.*

neck-er-chief (nek′ėr-chif), *n.* [For *neck kerchief.*] A cloth worn round the neck by women or men.

neck-ing (nek′ing), *n.* In *arch.*, a molding or group of moldings between the projecting part of a capital of a column and the shaft; a gorgerin. Cf. *neck.*

neck-lace (nek′lạs), *n.* [From *neck* + *lace* ('string').] An ornament of precious stones, beads, or the like, worn round the neck.

neck-let (nek′let), *n.* An ornament to be worn about the neck; a necklace: as, "These Indians wore *necklets* . . . one . . . possessed a *necklet* . . . made of thirteen gold plates . . . linked together with fibres" (W. H. Hudson's "Green Mansions," i.).

neck=rest (nek′rest), *n.* A support for the neck in resting or sleeping, used in China, Japan, Africa, etc.

Wooden Neck-rest of a South African Tribe.

neck-tie (nek′tī), *n.* A narrow band, as of silk or satin, worn round the neck, commonly under or about a collar, and tied in front; any band, scarf, or tie fastened at the front of the neck; also, fig., a hangman's rope (slang).

neck=verse (nek′vėrs), *n.* A Latin verse printed in black-letter, usually Ps. li. 1, formerly set before an accused person claiming benefit of clergy, in order to test his ability to read: if he could read it, he was released, thus saving his neck: as, "Letter nor line know I never a one, Wer't my *neck-verse* at Hairibee" (Scott's "Lay of the Last Minstrel," i. 24).

neck-wear (nek′wãr), *n.* Articles of dress worn round or at the neck.

neck=yoke (nek′yōk), *n.* A bar, usually of wood, which is connected with the collars of a harness and from which the end of the tongue of a vehicle is suspended.

necro-. Form of Gr. νεκρός, dead body, dead, used in combination.—**nec-ro-gen-ic** (nek-rọ-jen′ik), *a.* [+ *-genic.*] In *pathol.*, produced or caused by dead bodies or dead animal matter.—**ne-crog-ra-pher** (ne-krog′rạ-fėr), *n.* [+ *-grapher* as in *biographer.*] A writer of obituary notices.

ne-crol-a-try (ne-krol′ạ-tri), *n.* [Gr. νεκρολατρεία: see *necro-* and *-latry.*] Worship of the dead.

ne-crol-o-gy (ne-krol′ọ-ji), *n.*; pl. *-gies* (-jiz). [ML. *necrologium*, < Gr. νεκρός, dead body, + -λόγιον, < λέγειν, tell, recount.] A register formerly kept by ecclesiastical institutions, containing entries of the deaths of persons to be prayed for, as benefactors or members; also, a list of persons who have died within a certain time; also, an obituary notice.—**nec-ro-log-i-cal** (nek-rọ-loj′i-kạl), *a.*—**ne-crol′o-gist,** *n.*

nec-ro-man-cer (nek′rọ-man-sėr), *n.* One who practises necromancy.

nec-ro-man-cy (nek′rọ-man-si), *n.* [L. *necromantia* (ML. corruptly *nigromantia*, by association with L. *niger*, black), < Gr. νεκρομαντεία, < νεκρός, dead body, + μαντεία, divination.] The pretended art of divination through communication with the dead; the black art; hence, magic in general; enchantment; conjuration.—**nec-ro-man′tic,** *a.* Pertaining to necromancy (as, "old Merlin's *necromantic* spells": Hood's "Midsummer Fairies," cxvi.); given to the practice of necromancy (as, "a *necromantic* dwarf": Scott's "Pirate," xx.).

ne-croph-a-gous (ne-krof′ạ-gus), *a.* [Gr. νεκροφάγος: see *necro-* and *-phagous.*] Feeding on dead bodies or carrion.

ne-crop-o-lis (ne-krop′ọ-lis), *n.* [NL., < Gr. νεκρόπολις, lit. 'city of the dead,' < νεκρός, dead body, + πόλις, city.] A cemetery, often one of large size in or near a city or town (as, the *Necropolis* in Glasgow, Scotland, adjoining the Cathedral); an old or prehistoric burying-ground, as of an ancient people (as, "Hill and hill-slope were the *necropolis* of a vanished race": Green's "Short Hist. of the Eng. People," i. 2).

nec-rop-sy (nek′rop-si), *n.*; pl. *-sies* (-siz). [From *necro-* + *-opsy* as in *autopsy.*] The examination of a body after death; a post-mortem examination, or autopsy.

ne-cros-co-py (ne-kros′kọ-pi), *n.* [See *necro-* and *-scopy.*] The examination of bodies after death; post-mortem examination.—**nec-ro-scop-ic, nec-ro-scop-i-cal** (nek-rọ-skop′ik, -i-kạl), *a.*

ne-crose (ne-krōs′), *v. t.* or *i.*; *-crosed, -crosing.* To affect or be affected with necrosis.

ne-cro-sis (ne-krō′sis), *n.* [NL., < Gr. νέκρωσις, < νεκροῦν, make dead, mortify, < νεκρός, dead body.] In *pathol.*, death of a circumscribed piece of tissue; esp., mortification of bone in mass; in *bot.*, a disease which causes the tissue of plants to turn black and decay.—**ne-crot′ic** (-krot′ik), *a.*

nec-tar (nek′tạr), *n.* [L., < Gr. νέκταρ.] The drink, or, less properly, the food, of the gods of classical mythology; hence, any delicious drink; in *bot.*, the saccharine secretion of a plant, serving to attract the insects or birds which pollinate the flower, and collected by bees, in whose body it is elaborated into honey.—**nec-ta′re-an** (-tā′rẹ-ạn), *a.* Nectareous.—**nec′tared,** *a.* Filled or flavored with or as with nectar; delicious: as, "a perpetual feast of *nectar'd* sweets" (Milton's "Comus," 479).—**nec-ta′re-ous,** *a.* [L. *nectareus.*] Of the nature of or resembling nectar; delicious; sweet: as, "a certain kind of beer, *nectareous* to the palate" (Hawthorne's "House of the Seven Gables," v.).—**nec′tar-ine** (-in), *a.* Nectar-like; delicious.—**nec′-tar-ine** (-in or -ēn), *n.* A variety of the common peach, having a skin destitute of down.—**nec′tar-ous,** *a.* Nectareous.—**nec′ta-ry** (-tạ-ri), *n.*; pl. *-ries* (-riz). [NL. *nectarium.*] In *bot.*, an organ or part that secretes nectar.

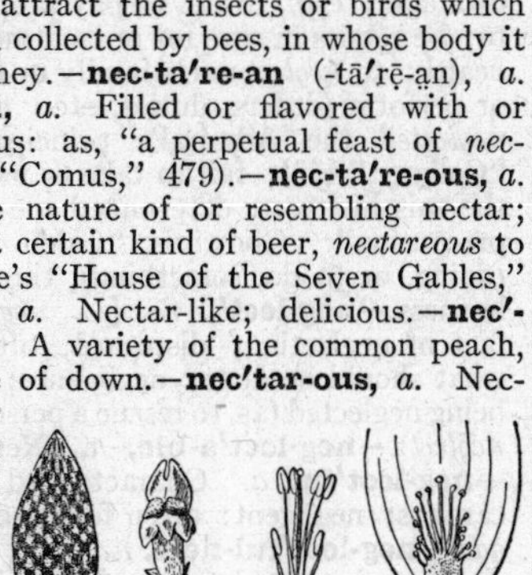

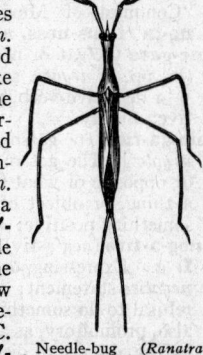

Nectaries of Plants of Various Genera: — (*a*) *Fritillaria*; (*b*) *Linaria*; (*c*) *Barbarea*; (*d*) *Parnassia*; (*e*) *Staphylea*; (*f*) *Aquilegia*; (*g*) *Lilium.*

ned-dy (ned′i), *n.*; pl. *neddies* (-iz). [Dim. of *Ned*, for *Edward*, man's name.] [Also *cap.*] A donkey: as, "long-eared *Neddies*, giving themselves leonine airs" (Thackeray's "Newcomes," i.).

née (nā), *a.* [F., fem. of *né*, pp. of *naître*, < L. *nasci* (pp. fem. *nata*), be born.] Born: placed after the name of a married woman to introduce her maiden name: as, Madame de Staël, *née* Necker.

need (nēd), *n.* [AS. *nīed, nēd, nēad, nēod,* = D. *nood* = G. *not* = Icel. *naudh* = Goth. *nauths*, need.] Necessity arising from the circumstances of a case (as, I will come if *need* be; there is no *need* to worry; "We shall have *need* To employ you against this Roman," Shakspere's "Cymbeline," ii. 3. 67; one had *need* (to) be very careful, that is, one ought to be very careful); also, urgent want, as of something requisite (as, "Nature hath *need* of what she asks," Milton's "Paradise Regained," ii. 253; "He has no *need* of your kindness," Thackeray's "Newcomes," xlii.); also, a situation or time of difficulty due to urgent requirements (as, "When each To other speedy aid might lend at *need,*" Milton's "Paradise Lost," ix. 260; a friend in *need* is a friend indeed); exigency; esp., a condition marked by the lack of something requisite (as, "We have . . . our evening and our morn . . . for change delectable, not *need*": Milton's "Paradise Lost," v. 629); commonly, a condition of want or destitution; extreme indigence or poverty; also, a case or instance in which some necessity or want exists (as, to meet the *needs* of the occasion; one's daily *needs*); a requirement.—**need,** *v.* [AS. *nēodian*, be necessary.] **I.** *intr.* To be necessary (as, there *needs* no apology; "It *needs* not to enlarge on the joy of the meeting which followed," J. H. Newman's "Callista," xxx.); also, to be under a necessity (with infinitive, in certain cases without *to*: as, I *need* not go; *need* I go? — the 3d pers. sing. in such cases being *need*, not *needs*: as, he *need* not go; *need* he go?); also, to be in need or want. **II.** *tr.* To have need of; want; require: as, to *need* care, rest, supplies, or money; "He passes to his rest from a place that *needs* him not" (Bryant's "Waiting by the Gate").—**need′er,** *n.*

need-fire (nēd′fīr), *n.* [From *need* + *fire*: cf. G. *notfeuer.*] Fire produced from dry wood by means of friction, formerly credited with peculiar virtues, as that of curing disease among cattle; also, a beacon-fire or bonfire (as, "The ready page, with hurried hand, Awaked the *need-fire's* slumbering brand": Scott's "Lay of the Last Minstrel," iii. 29). [Sc. and north. Eng.]

need-ful (nēd′fụl), *a.* Needy or necessitous (now rare); also, necessary or requisite (as, "For man's well-being, Faith is properly the one thing *needful,*" Carlyle's "Sartor Resartus," ii. 7: see Luke, x. 42).—**the needful,** what is necessary or requisite; esp., money (colloq.: as, "I must live, and to live I must have what you call *'the needful,'* which I can only get by working," C. Brontë's "Professor," vi.).—**need′ful-ly,** *adv.*—**need′ful-ness,** *n.*

need-i-ness (nē′di-nes), *n.* Needy state; want; indigence.

nee-dle (nē′dl), *n.* [AS. *nǣdl* = OHG. *nādela*, G. *nadel*, = Icel. *nāl* = Goth. *nēthla*, needle.] A small, slender, pointed instrument, now usually of polished steel, with an eye or hole for thread, used in sewing; also, a slender, rod-like implement for use in knitting, or one hooked at the end for use in crocheting, etc.; also, any of various objects resembling or suggesting a needle; a magnetic needle (see under *magnetic*); a pointed instrument used in engraving, etc.; the slender steel pin used in firing a needle-gun; the sharply pointed end of a syringe, as for hypodermic injections; a post, beam, or the like, of wood or metal, used for various purposes in building, etc.; a sharp-pointed mass or pinnacle of rock; an obelisk, or tapering, four-sided shaft of stone (as, the Cleopatra's *Needle* in Central Park, New York City, or that on the Thames Embankment, in London, two ancient Egyptian monoliths which formerly stood together in Alexandria, Egypt, and were originally erected at Heliopolis, Egypt, about 1500 B.C.); in *chem.* and *mineral.*, a needle-like crystal; in *zoöl.*, a slender, sharp spicule; in *bot.*, a needle-shaped leaf, as of a conifer (as, a pine-*needle*).—**nee′dle,** *v.*; *-dled, -dling.* **I.** *tr.* To sew or pierce with or as with a needle. **II.** *intr.* To work with a needle; also, to form needles in crystallization.—**nee′dle=bath,** *n.* A bath in which the water is forced against the body in fine needle-like jets.—**nee′dle=bug,** *n.* Any of the slender-bodied, long-legged hemipterous insects of the genus *Ranatra*, found in fresh-water ponds, as *R. fusca*, common in the U. S.—**nee′dle=fish,** *n.* A garfish (family *Belonidæ*); also, a pipe-fish (family *Syngnathidæ*).—**nee′dle-ful** (-fụl), *n.*; pl. *-fuls.* A suitable length of thread for using at one time with a needle: as, "She took a new *needleful* of thread, waxed it carefully, threaded her needle" (C. Brontë's "Jane Eyre," xvi.).—**nee′dle=gun,** *n.* A breech-loading rifle in which the charge is exploded by the impact of a

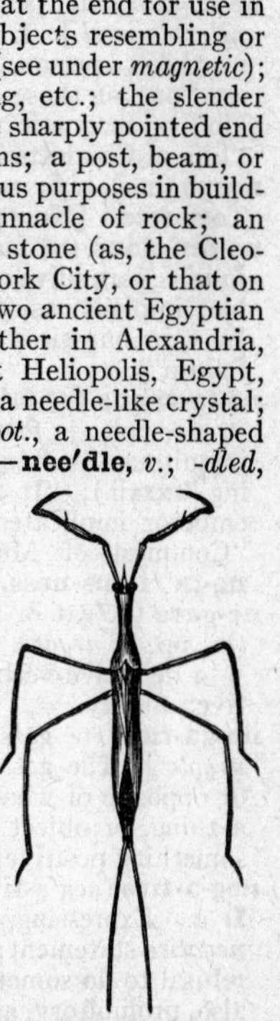
Needle-bug (*Ranatra fusca*), two thirds natural size.

needle or slender steel pin: used by the Prussian army in 1866 and 1870.—**nee'dle=point,** *n.* The point of a needle; also, point-lace.

need-less (nēd'les), *a.* Not in need or want†; also, not needed or wanted; unnecessary.—**need'less-ly,** *adv.*—**need'less-ness,** *n.*

nee-dle=valve (nē'dl-valv), *n.* In *mach.*, *engin.*, etc., a valve with a needle-like part, a fine adjustment, or a small opening; esp., a valve in which the opening is controlled by a needle-like or conical point which fits into a conical seat.

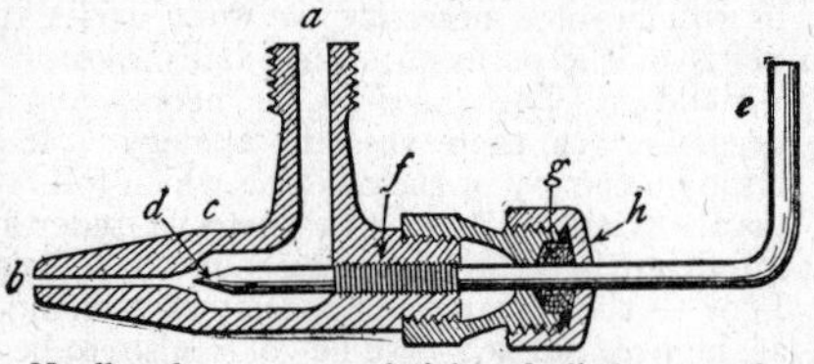

Needle-valve. — *a*, supply inlet; *b*, discharge outlet; *c*, body of valve; *d*, needle-valve; *e*, lever or handle; *f*, screw on spindle; *g*, packing in stuffing-box; *h*, stuffing-box gland.

nee-dle-wom-an (nē'dl-wu̇m"ạn), *n.*; pl. *-women* (-wim"en). A woman who works with a needle, as in sewing or embroidery.

nee-dle-work (nē'dl-wėrk), *n.* The process or the product of working with a needle as in sewing or embroidering.

need-ments (nēd'mẹnts), *n. pl.* Things needed; necessaries; requisites: as, "collecting from her household stores such *needments* as could be arranged in the smallest compass" (Mrs. Stowe's "Uncle Tom's Cabin," xvii.).

needs (nēdz), *adv.* [AS. *nēdes*, orig. genitive of *nēd*, *nīed*, E. *need.*] Of necessity; necessarily: generally with *must*: as, "You must *needs* be a stranger in this region . . . else you would surely have heard of Mistress Hester Prynne" (Hawthorne's "Scarlet Letter," iii.); "*Needs* must thou on thy way" (W. Morris's "Jason," ii. 40).

need-y (nē'di), *a.*; compar. *needier*, superl. *neediest.* In, or characterized by, need or want; very poor; indigent; necessitous: as, a *needy* family; to be in *needy* circumstances.

neep (nēp), *n.* [AS. *nǣp*, < L. *napus.*] A turnip. [Now Sc. and prov. Eng.]

ne'er (nãr), *adv.* Contraction of *never.* [Chiefly poetic.]

ne'er=do=well (nãr'dọ̈-wel). [Also Sc. and north. Eng. *ne'er-do-weel.*] **I.** *n.* One who will never do well; a worthless person. **II.** *a.* Worthless; good-for-nothing: as, "one of those *ne'er-do-weel* lads who seem to have a kind of magnetic power for misfortunes" (Mrs. Gaskell's "Life of Charlotte Brontë," ii.).

neeze (nēz), *v. i.*; *neezed, neezing.* [ME. *nesen*: cf. *sneeze.*] To sneeze. [Now prov. Eng. and Sc.]

ne-fan-dous (nẹ̄-fan'dus), *a.* [L. *nefandus*, < *ne*, not, + *fandus*, gerundive of *fari*, speak.] Unmentionable; abominable; impious: as, "The press restrain'd! *nefandous* thought! In vain our sires have nobly fought" (M. Green's "The Spleen").

ne-fa-ri-ous (nẹ̄-fā'ri-us), *a.* [L. *nefarius*, < *nefas*, wrong, < *ne*, not, + *fas*, divine law, right.] Extremely wicked; iniquitous: as, "*nefarious* practices" (Scott's "Guy Mannering," xxxii.); "It grieved him much, he added, to find the emperor implicated in so *nefarious* a scheme" (Prescott's "Conquest of Mexico," iii. 6).—**ne-fa'ri-ous-ly,** *adv.*—**ne-fa'ri-ous-ness,** *n.*

ne-gate (nē'gāt or nẹ̄-gāt'), *v. t.*; *-gated, -gating.* [L. *negatus*, pp. of *negare*, say no, deny, < *neg-*, *nec-* (for *ne*), not, + a defective verb, pres. ind. *aio*, I say.] To deny; negative; nullify.

ne-ga-tion (nẹ̄-gā'shọn), *n.* [L. *negatio(n-)*, < *negare*: see *negate.*] The act of denying; a denial; also, the absence or opposite of what is actual, positive, or affirmative; also, a thing, or object of thought, consisting in the absence of something positive; a negative thing; a nonentity.

neg-a-tive (neg'ạ-tiv). [L. *negativus*, < *negare*: see *negate.*] **I.** *a.* Expressing or containing negation or denial (as, a *negative* statement; a *negative* proposition); also, expressing refusal to do something; refusing consent, as to a proposal; also, prohibitory, as a command or order; also, characterized by the absence of distinguishing or marked qualities or features (as, a *negative* attitude; a *negative* character or person); lacking positive attributes; in specif. use, involving or denoting subtraction (as, a *negative* quantity; the *negative* or minus sign); minus; also, measured or proceeding in the opposite direction to that which is considered as positive; in *elect.*, noting or pertaining to the kind of electricity developed on resin, amber, etc., when rubbed with flannel, or the kind of electricity present at that pole ('negative pole') connected with the zinc or most attacked plate of a voltaic cell; noting the carbon or least attacked plate or element of a voltaic cell; in *chem.*, of an element or radical, non-metallic or acid; in *photog.*, showing light and shade, and right and left, reversed from the conditions in nature. **II.** *n.* A negative statement or proposition, answer or reply, or term or word (opposed to *affirmative*); also, a refusal of assent, a veto; also, the negative form of statement (opposed to *affirmative*); also, that side of a question which denies what the opposite side affirms (opposed to *affirmative*); also, a negative (rather than positive) quality or characteristic; also, specif., a negative quantity or symbol; in *elect.*, the negative plate or element in a voltaic cell; in *photog.*, a negative picture, as on a glass plate, used chiefly for printing positive pictures.—**neg'a-tive,** *v. t.*; *-tived, -tiving.* To deny, as a statement or proposition; contradict; also, to prove the contrary of; disprove; also, to refuse assent or consent to; pronounce against; veto; also, to neutralize or counteract.—**neg'a-tive-ly,** *adv.*—**neg'a-tive-ness, neg-a-tiv'i-ty** (-tiv'i-ti), *n.*

ne-ga-tor (nẹ̄-gā'tọr), *n.* [LL., < L. *negare*: see *negate.*] One who denies.—**neg-a-to-ry** (neg'ạ-tọ̄-ri), *a.* Denying; negative.

neg-lect (neg-lekt'), *v. t.* [L. *neglectus*, pp. of *neglegere*, *negligere*, < *neg-*, *nec-* (for *ne*), not, + *legere*, gather, pick up.] To pay no attention to, disregard, or treat with indifference (as, to *neglect* worldly ends; a poet *neglected* in his own age); esp., to fail to pay proper or becoming attention to; be remiss in care for or treatment of (as, to *neglect* one's health; to *neglect* one's family or friends); fail to carry out or perform (orders, duties, etc.: as, "Laudonnière had not *neglected* the Admiral's principal injunction," Besant's "Coligny," vii.); fail to take or use (as, "The magnitude of the mischief . . . determined me to *neglect* no imaginable precaution": Godwin's "Caleb Williams," xxx.); omit (doing, or to do, something), through indifference or carelessness.—**neg-lect',** *n.* [L. *neglectus*, n.] The act or fact of neglecting; disregard; often, want of attention to what should be done; negligence; also, the fact or state of being neglected (as, to rescue a person's name or memory from *neglect*).—**neg-lect'a-ble,** *a.* Negligible.—**neg-lect'er,** *n.*—**neg-lect'ful,** *a.* Characterized by neglect; disregardful; careless; negligent: often followed by *of.*—**neg-lect'ful-ly,** *adv.*—**neg-lect'ful-ness,** *n.*

né-gli-gé (nā-glē-zhā), *n.* [F., orig. pp. of *négliger*, < L. *negligere*: see *neglect.*] Easy, informal attire; undress.

neg-li-gée (neg-li-zhā' or neg'li-zhā). [Appar. for *négligé.*] **I.** *n.* A form of loose gown worn by women in the 18th century (as, "silk and satin *negligées* which her ladyship had worn at the French court": Galt's "Annals of the Parish," xvi.); also, a woman's loose house-gown. **II.** *a.* Of a loose, easy kind, as dress or garments; for informal wear.

neg-li-gence (neg'li-jẹns), *n.* The state or fact of being negligent; neglect; culpable carelessness; often, careless disregard of ceremony or conventional usage; easy informality, as of manner or style (as, "Horace still charms with graceful *negligence*": Pope's "Essay on Criticism," 653); also, an instance of being negligent; a defect due to carelessness.

neg-li-gent (neg'li-jẹnt), *a.* [OF. *negligent* (F. *négligent*), < L. *negligens* (-*ent-*), ppr. of *negligere*: see *neglect.*] Guilty of or characterized by neglect, as of duty (as, *negligent* officials; "O, *negligent* and heedless discipline!" Shakspere's "1 Henry VI.," iv. 2. 44); neglectful; culpably remiss or careless; often, in a milder sense, careless with respect to ceremony or conventional formality, as a person, the manner or air, gestures, etc.; carelessly easy or informal; of dress, negligée; sometimes, in careless disorder (as, "All loose her *negligent* attire, All loose her golden hair": Scott's "Lay of the Last Minstrel," i. 10).—**neg'li-gent-ly,** *adv.*

neg-li-gi-ble (neg'li-ji-bl), *a.* [L. *negligere*: see *neglect.*] That may be neglected or disregarded.—**neg'li-gi-bly,** *adv.*

ne-go-tia-ble (nē-gō′shia̤-bl), *a.* Capable of being negotiated; esp., of bills, etc., transferable by delivery, with or without indorsement, according to the circumstances, the title passing to the transferee.—**ne-go-tia-bil′i-ty** (-bil′-i-ti), *n.*

ne-go-ti-ant (nē-gō′shi-a̤nt), *n.* One who negotiates; a negotiator.

ne-go-ti-ate (nē-gō′shi-āt), *v.*; *-ated, -ating.* [L. *negotiatus*, pp. of *negotiari*, < *negotium*, business, < *neg-, nec-* (for *ne*), not, + *otium*, leisure.] **I.** *intr.* To carry on business†; hence, to deal or treat, one with another, in order to reach an agreement. **II.** *tr.* To arrange for or bring about by discussion and settlement of terms (as, to *negotiate* a loan or a treaty; "A satisfactory arrangement was *negotiated* between Vitelli and the rebellious garrison," Motley's "Dutch Republic," iv. 1); also, to conduct or manage (an affair, etc.); also, to transfer (a bill, etc.) by assignment or delivery; obtain or give money in exchange for (bills, checks, etc.); also, to clear or pass (an obstacle, difficult place, etc.), orig. in hunting (as, to *negotiate* a fence; "when he had *negotiated* the corner safely [in driving an automobile]," H. G. Wells's "Mr. Britling," i. 5. § 14).—**ne-go-ti-a′tion** (-ā′sho̤n), *n.* [L. *negotiatio(n-)*.] The act of negotiating; a process of treating carried on between parties in order to reach an agreement (often in *pl.*).—**ne-go′ti-a-tor,** *n.*

ne-gress (nē′gres), *n.* A female negro.

Ne-gril-lo (nē-gril′ō), *n.*; pl. *Negrillos* (-ōz). [Sp., dim. of *negro*, E. *negro*.] A Negrito, esp. of the African division.

ne-grit-ic (nē-grit′ik), *a.* Of or pertaining to negroes or [*cap.*] the Negritos.

Ne-gri-to (nē-grē′tō), *n.*; pl. *-tos* (-tōz). [Sp., dim. of *negro*, E. *negro*.] A member of any of certain dwarfish negroid peoples of southeastern Asia and of Africa, esp. of the Philippine Islands and the East Indies.

Ne-gro (nē′grō). [Sp. and Pg. *negro*, black, as n. a black person, Negro, < L. *niger*, black.] **I.** *n.*; pl. *Negroes* (-grōz). [also *l. c.*] A member of a black-skinned people; [also *l. c.*] a person having more or less Negro blood; specif. [sometimes *l. c.*], a member of the Negro or black race (see below). **II.** *a.* [also *l. c.*] Belonging to a black-skinned people (as, "The first *negro* slaves were brought to Jamestown in Virginia by a Dutch ship as early as 1620": H. G. Wells's "Outline of History," xxxvii. § 2); [also *l. c.*] of, pertaining to, or characteristic of Negroes (as, *Negro* blood; *Negro* melodies); [also *l. c.*] inhabited by Negroes; specif. [sometimes *l. c.*], noting or pertaining to the so-called 'black' race, characterized chiefly by a black complexion, short, broad, and flat nose, projecting jaws, thick lips, and crisp or woolly hair, and generally regarded as embracing the native inhabitants of the Sudan, Senegambia, and the region southward to the vicinity of the equator, and their descendants elsewhere, but sometimes considered to include also many other African tribes further south.—**negro minstrel.** See *minstrel.*

ne-groid (nē′groid). [See *-oid.*] **I.** *a.* Resembling, or akin to, the Negro race; of a Negro type. **II.** *n.* A person of a negroid race.—**ne-groi′dal,** *a.*

ne-gro-phil, ne-gro-phile (nē′gro̤-fil), *n.* [See *-phil.*] One who is friendly to the Negroes.—**ne-groph-i-lism** (nē-grof′i-lizm), *n.*

ne-gro-phobe (nē′gro̤-fōb), *n.* [See *-phobe.*] One who fears, or has a strong antipathy to, Negroes.—**ne-gro-pho′bi-a** (-fō′bi-a̤), *n.* [See *-phobia.*] Fear of, or strong antipathy to, Negroes.

ne-gus[1] (nē′gus), *n.* [From Colonel Francis *Negus* (died 1732), its reputed inventor.] A beverage made of wine (usually port or sherry) and hot water, with sugar, nutmeg, and lemon: as, "Leah, make a little hot *negus*, and cut a sandwich or two" (C. Brontë's "Jane Eyre," xi.).

Ne-gus[2] (nē′gus), *n.* [Native name.] [Also *l. c.*] The title of the sovereign of Abyssinia.

neigh (nā), *v. i.* [AS. *hnǣgan.*] To utter the cry of a horse; whinny.—**neigh,** *n.* The cry of a horse; a whinny.

neigh-bor (nā′bo̤r). [AS. *nēahgebūr*, < *nēah*, nigh, + *gebūr*, dweller, countryman.] **I.** *n.* One who lives near another (as, "I call him my *neighbour*, because his plantation lay next to mine": Defoe's "Robinson Crusoe," i. 3); also, a person or thing that is near another, as in an assemblage or group (as, "My *neighbour* chokes in the clutch of chloral": Henley's "In Hospital," iii.); also, any person brought into contact, intercourse, or relations with another, esp. as a fellow-being subject to the obligations of humanity (from the passage in Luke, x. 25–37). **II.** *a.* Living or situated near to another; neighboring: as, "two *neighbour* villages" (Tennyson's "Circumstance").—**neigh′bor,** *v.* **I.** *intr.* To live or be situated near (as, "a copse that *neighbours* by": Shakspere's "Venus and Adonis," 259); also, to associate on the terms of neighbors; be neighborly or friendly (*with*). **II.** *tr.* To live or be situated near to; adjoin; border on; also, to place or bring near (as, "So *neighbour'd* to him, and yet so unseen, She stood": Keats's "Lamia," i.).—**neigh′-bor-hood** (-hu̇d), *n.* The relationship or relations between neighbors (as, "I . . . made them promise me to live in love and good *neighbourhood* with one another": Defoe's "Robinson Crusoe," ii. 7); neighborly feeling or conduct; also, presence or situation near, nearness, or proximity (as, "a large brindled cat . . . kept back from its prey by our unwelcome *neighbourhood*": Bulwer-Lytton's "Caxtons," xvi. 1); also, the region near or about some place or thing, or the vicinity (as, "The immediate *neighbourhood* of the city was occupied by gardens, vineyards . . . and meadows": J. H. Newman's "Callista," i.); also, a district or locality, often with reference to its character or inhabitants (as, all the houses in this *neighborhood*; an unhealthy or a fashionable *neighborhood*); also, a number of persons living near one another or in a particular locality (as, "The whole *neighbourhood* came out to meet their minister": Goldsmith's "Vicar of Wakefield," iv.).—**neigh′bor-ing,** *p. a.* Living or situated near; adjacent.—**neigh′bor-less,** *a.* Without neighbors.—**neigh′bor-ly,** *a.* Befitting, or acting as befits, a neighbor; kindly; friendly; sociable.—**neigh′bor-li-ness,** *n.*—**neigh′bor-ly,** *adv.* In the manner of a neighbor.

neigh′bour, etc. British preferred form of *neighbor*, etc.

nei-ther (nē′ᴛʜėr or nī′ᴛʜėr), *a.* and *pron.* [ME. *neither*, var. of *nauther*, < AS. *nāhwæther*, < *ne*, not, + *āhwæther*, either, < *ā*, ever, + *hwæther*, E. *whether*.] Not either; not the one or the other: as, *neither* statement is true; *neither* of us was present; *neither* man, or *neither*, will consent.—**nei′ther,** *conj.* Not either (a disjunctive connective preceding a series of two or more alternative words, etc., connected by the correlative *nor*: as, *neither* you nor I nor anybody else knows that); also, nor yet (as, "Ye shall not eat of it, *neither* shall ye touch it": Gen. iii. 3).

nek-ton (nek′ton), *n.* [G., < Gr. νηκτόν, neut. of νηκτός, swimming, < νήχειν, swim.] The aggregate of actively swimming organisms at the surface of the sea. Cf. *plankton* and *benthos.*—**nek-ton′ic,** *a.*

ne-lum-bo (nē-lum′bō), *n.* [Singhalese.] Either of the two water-lilies constituting the genus *Nelumbo*, the sacred lotus (*N. nelumbo*) or the water-chinkapin (*N. lutea*).

nem-a-thel-minth (nem-a̤-thel′minth), *n.* [NL. *Nemathelminthes*, pl., < Gr. νῆμα (νηματ-), thread, + ἕλμινς (ἑλμινθ-), worm.] Any of the *Nemathelminthes*, a phylum or group of worms, including the nematodes, etc., characterized by an elongated, unsegmented cylindrical body.

nem-a-to-cyst (nem′a̤-to̤-sist), *n.* [Gr. νῆμα (νηματ-), thread, + κύστις, bladder.] In *zoöl.*, an organ of offense and defense peculiar to cœlenterates, consisting of a cell-like

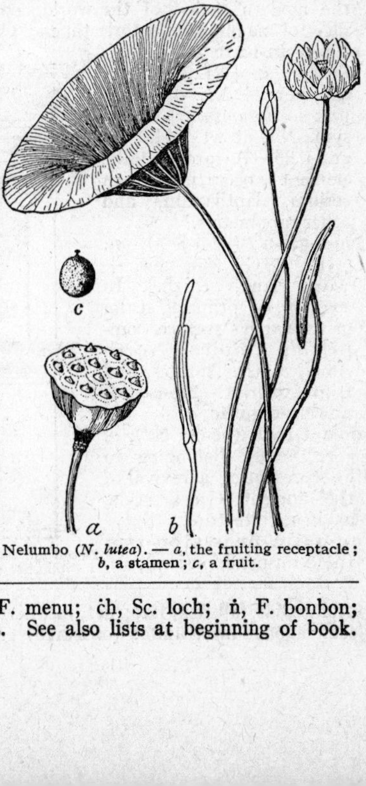

Nelumbo (*N. lutea*).— *a*, the fruiting receptacle; *b*, a stamen; *c*, a fruit.

structure which contains a thread capable of being ejected and of causing a sting.

nem-a-tode (nem′ạ-tōd). [NL. *Nematoda*, pl., < Gr. νηματώδης, thread-like, < νῆμα (νηματ-), thread, + εἶδος, form.] **I.** *a.* Belonging to the *Nematoda*, a class or group of nemathelminths, including the trichina and many other thread-like worms. **II.** *n.* A nematode nemathelminth.

nem-a-toid (nem′ạ-toid). [NL. *Nematoidea*, pl., < Gr. νῆμα (νηματ-), thread, + εἶδος, form.] **I.** *a.* Thread-like; belonging to the *Nematoidea*, an order containing the typical nematodes, or sometimes all the nematodes. **II.** *n.* A nematoid worm.

nem-a-tol-o-gy (nem-ạ-tol′ǫ-ji), *n.* [See *nematode* and *-logy.*] The branch of zoölogy that treats of nematodes.

Ne-me-an (nẹ-mē′ạn or nē′mẹ-ạn), *a.* Of or pertaining to Nemea, a valley in Argolis, Greece: as, the *Nemean* lion (a lion said to have been killed by Hercules); the *Nemean* games (one of the great festivals of the ancient Greeks, held every two years).

ne-mer-te-an (nẹ-mėr′tẹ-ạn). [NL. *Nemertea*, pl., < Gr. Νημερτής, name of a Nereid.] **I.** *n.* Any of the *Nemertea*, or *Nemertinea*, a class or group of worms with cylindrical or depressed, unsegmented bodies, mostly living in the sea, and often brilliantly colored. **II.** *a.* Belonging or pertaining to the nemerteans.

Nem-e-sis (nem′e-sis), *n.* [L., < Gr. Νέμεσις, < νέμειν, deal out, distribute.] The goddess of retribution or vengeance; hence [sometimes *l. c.*], in general, an agent of retribution or punishment (as, "That woman is the *Nemesis* of our life": Thackeray's "Newcomes," lxxiv.); also, retributive justice, or punishment (as, "the inward suffering which is the worst form of *Nemesis*": George Eliot's "Adam Bede," xvi.).

nem-o-ral (nem′ǫ-rạl), *a.* [L. *nemoralis*, < *nemus* (*nemor-*), wood, grove.] Of or pertaining to a wood or grove; inhabiting or frequenting woods, as animals.

nen-u-phar (nen′ū-fär), *n.* [ML., < Ar. and Pers. *nīnūfar*, *nīlūfar*.] A water-lily, esp. the European water-lily *Castalia alba.*

ne-o- (nē′ǫ-). Form of Gr. νέος, new, recent, used in combination, as in *Neo-Darwinism* (a new or modified form of Darwinism), *neo-Gothic* (Gothic after a new or modern style), *neo-Hebraic* (Hebraic of the modern period), *neo-Hellenic*, *neo-Latin*, *neo-Persian.*

Ne-o-cene (nē′ǫ-sēn). [Gr. νέος, new, recent, + καινός, new.] In *geol.*: **I.** *a.* Noting or pertaining to a division of the Tertiary period or system including the Miocene and the Pliocene. **II.** *n.* The Neocene division of the Tertiary.

ne-o-clas-sic (nē-ǫ-klas′ik), *a.* [See *neo-.*] Belonging or pertaining to a revival of classic style, as in art or literature.

ne-o-cos-mic (nē-ǫ-koz′mik), *a.* [See *neo-.*] Belonging to the modern period of the world: specif., applied to the races of mankind in historic times. Cf. *paleocosmic.*

ne-o-dym-i-um (nē-ǫ-dim′i-um), *n.* [NL., < Gr. νέος, new, + NL. (*di*)*dymium*: see *didymium.*] Chem. sym., Nd; at. wt., 144.3; sp. gr., 6.96. A rare metallic element occurring with cerium, lanthanum, and other rare metals.

Detail in Neo-Greek Architecture. — Bibliothèque Ste. Geneviève, Paris.

Ne-o-gæ-a (nē-ǫ-jē′ạ), *n.* [NL., < Gr. νέος, new, + γαῖα, land, earth.] In *zoögeog.*, a primary realm of the earth's surface, comprising tropical North America, the Antilles, and South America.—**Ne-o-gæ′-an, Ne-o-gæ′ic,** *a.*

ne-o=Greek (nē-ǫ-grēk′), *a.* [See *neo-.*] Belonging to or representing a revival of the ancient Greek style, as in architecture.

ne-o=im-pres-sion-ism (nē″ǫ-im-presh′ǫn-izm), *n.* [See *neo-.*] The theory and methods of certain of the later impressionistic painters (from about 1886), characterized by an attempt to render the impressionistic method strictly scientific and by employment of the pointillistic technique.—**ne″o=im-pres′sion-ist,** *n.*

ne-o-lith (nē′ǫ-lith), *n.* [Gr. νέος, new, + λίθος, stone.] A neolithic stone implement; also, a person belonging to the neolithic period.—**ne-o-lith′ic,** *a.* Noting or pertaining to the later part of the stone age, characterized by the use of highly finished or polished stone implements.

ne-o-lo-gian (nē-ǫ-lō′jiạn). **I.** *a.* Given to or characterized by neology, as in views on religious subjects. **II.** *n.* A neologist, as on religious subjects: as, "Dean Alford's notes on the Greek Testament . . . made him feel how shallow and impotent were the conclusions arrived at by German *neologians*" (S. Butler's "Way of All Flesh," xlix.).

ne-o-log-i-cal (nē-ǫ-loj′i-kạl), *a.* Of, pertaining to, or characterized by neology or neologism.—**ne-o-log′i-cal-ly,** *adv.*

ne-ol-o-gism (nē-ol′ǫ-jizm), *n.* [F. *néologisme*, < Gr. νέος, new, + λόγος, word, speech.] The introduction or use of new words, or new senses of words, in speech or writing; a new word, or a new sense of a word; also, the introduction or adoption of new views or doctrines, esp. on religious subjects.—**ne-ol′o-gist,** *n.* One who introduces or uses neologisms in language; also, one given to neologism in views, esp. on religious subjects.—**ne-ol′o-gize,** *v. i.*; *-gized, -gizing.* To introduce or use neologisms in language; also, to introduce or adopt new views, esp. on religious subjects.—**ne-ol′o-gy,** *n.*; pl. *-gies* (-jiz). [F. *néologie.*] Neologism in language; a neologism, or new word or new sense of a word; also, neologism in views, esp. on religious subjects (as, "He had been taught to scent German *neology* in everything, as some folks are taught to scent Jesuitry": Kingsley's "Yeast," vi.).

ne-on (nē′on), *n.* [NL., < Gr. νέον, neut. of νέος, new: see *new.*] Chem. sym., Ne; at. wt., 20.2. A gaseous element occurring in the earth's atmosphere.

ne-o-phyte (nē′ǫ-fīt), *n.* [LL. *neophytus*, < Gr. νεόφυτος, newly planted, < νέος, new, + φυτός, verbal adj. of φύειν, produce.] A new convert; one newly admitted to a religious body; hence, in general, a beginner, novice, or tyro (as, "Mr. Rossiter . . . looked complacently upon him as a hopeful young *neophyte*": Mrs. Stowe's "Oldtown Folks," xxxviii.).

ne-o-plasm (nē′ǫ-plazm), *n.* [Gr. νέος, new, + πλάσμα, something formed, < πλάσσειν, form, mold.] In *pathol.*, a new growth of different or abnormal tissue; a tumor.

ne-o-plas-ty (nē′ǫ-plas-ti), *n.* [Gr. νεόπλαστος, newly formed, < νέος, new, + πλάσσειν, form, mold.] In *surg.*, the repairing or restoration of a part by a plastic operation.

Ne-o-pla-to-nism (nē-ǫ-plā′tǫ-nizm), *n.* [See *neo-.*] A philosophical and religious system composed chiefly of elements of Platonism and Oriental mysticism, later influenced by Christianity, which originated at Alexandria in the 3d century: also applied to later similar schools of thought.—**Ne″o-pla-ton′ic** (-plạ-ton′ik), *a.*—**Ne-o-pla′to-nist,** *n.*

ne-o-prene (nē′ǫ-prēn), *n.* [*neo-* + (*chloro*)*prene.*] A synthetic rubber formed by polymerization of chloroprene: superior to natural rubber in oil resistance, etc.

ne-o=Ro-man (nē-ǫ-rō′mạn), *a.* [See *neo-.*] Belonging to or representing a revival of the ancient Roman style, as in architecture.

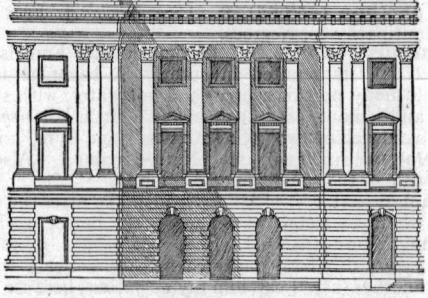

Neo-Roman Architecture. — From the Capitol at Washington.

ne-o-sal-var-san (nē-ǫ-sal′vạr-san), *n.* [See *neo* and *salvarsan.*] A soluble modification or improved form of salvarsan. [Proprietary name.]

ne-o-ter-ic (nē-ǫ-ter′ik). [LL. *neotericus*, < Gr. *νεωτερικός*, < *νεώτερος*, compar. of *νέος*, new.] **I.** *a.* New; recent; modern. **II.** *n.* A modern; a writer, thinker, or other person of modern times.

ne-ot-er-ism (nē-ot′ę-rizm), *n.* [Gr. *νεωτερισμός*, < *νεωτερίζειν*, make innovations, < *νεώτερος*: see *neoteric.*] Innovation, esp. in language; a new word or expression; a neologism.—**ne-ot′er-ist,** *n.*

Ne-o-trop-i-cal (nē-ǫ-trop′i-kąl), *a.* [See *neo-*.] In *zoögeog.*, belonging to that part of the New World extending from the tropic of Cancer southward.

ne-pen-the (nę̄-pen′thę̄), *n.* [L. *nepenthes*, < Gr. *νηπενθές*, neut. of *νηπενθής*, banishing sorrow, < *νη-*, not, + *πένθος*, sorrow.] A drug or draft (or the plant yielding it) mentioned by ancient writers as capable of bringing forgetfulness of sorrow or trouble; hence, anything inducing easeful forgetfulness (as, "This western wind hath Lethean powers, Yon noonday cloud *nepenthe* showers": Whittier's "Summer by the Lakeside," i.).

ne-pen-thes (nę̄-pen′thēz), *n.* [L.: see *nepenthe.*] Nepenthe; also, any of the pitcher-plants of the genus *Nepenthes*, native chiefly in the East Indies, and cultivated also in hothouses.

Nepenthes.— *a, N. distillatoria*; *b,* pitcher of *N. rafflesiana.*

neph-a-lism (nef′ą-lizm), *n.* [Gr. *νηφαλισμός*, < *νηφάλιος*, sober, < *νήφειν*, be sober.] Total abstinence from intoxicating drink.—**neph′a-list,** *n.*

ne-phe-li-ad (ne-fē′li-ad), *n.* [Gr. *νεφέλη*, cloud: cf. *limoniad* and *naiad.*] A cloud-nymph.

neph-e-line (nef′e-lin), *n.* [F. *néphéline*, < Gr. *νεφέλη*, cloud: see *nebula.*] A mineral, a silicate of aluminium, sodium, and potassium, occurring in various volcanic rocks.—**neph-e-lin′ic** (-lin′ik), *a.*—**neph′e-lin-ite** (-īt), *n.* In *petrog.*, a heavy, dark-colored rock of volcanic origin, essentially a basalt containing nepheline but no feldspar and little or no olivine.—**neph′e-lite** (-līt), *n.* Same as *nepheline.*

neph-e-lom-e-try (nef-e-lom′e-tri), *n.* [Gr. *νεφέλη*, cloud: see *-metry.*] The measurement of the amount of cloudiness in the sky.

neph-ew (nef′ū or nev′ū), *n.* [OF. F. *neveu*, < L. *nepos* (*nepot-*), grandson, nephew; akin to Gr. *νέποδες*, offspring, Skt. *napāt*, grandson, AS. *nefa*, nephew: cf. *niece.*] A grandson†, or a male descendant of more remote degree†; also, a son of one's brother or sister, or (loosely) of one's husband's or wife's brother or sister; also, in euphemistic use, an illegitimate son of an ecclesiastic.

nepho-. Form of Gr. *νέφος*, cloud, used in combination.—**neph-o-gram** (nef′ǫ-gram), *n.* [+ *-gram.*] A photograph of a cloud or clouds.—**neph′o-graph** (-gråf), *n.* [+ *-graph.*] An instrument for photographing clouds.—**ne-phol-o-gy** (ne-fol′ǫ-ji), *n.* [+ *-logy.*] The branch of meteorology that treats of clouds.—**neph-o-log′i-cal** (-loj′i-kąl), *a.*—**neph′o-scope** (-skōp), *n.* [+ *-scope.*] An instrument for determining the altitude of clouds and the velocity and direction of their motion.—**neph-o-scop′ic** (-skop′ik), *a.*

ne-phral-gia (ne-fral′jiạ̈), *n.* [NL., < Gr. *νεφρός*, kidney, + *ἄλγος*, pain.] In *pathol.*, pain in the kidneys; renal neuralgia.

ne-phrec-to-my (ne-frek′tǫ-mi), *n.* [Gr. *νεφρός*, kidney, + *ἐκ*, out of, + *-τομία*, E. *-tomy.*] In *surg.*, excision of a kidney.

ne-phrid-i-um (ne-frid′i-um), *n.*; pl. *-ia* (-i-ạ̈). [NL., dim. < Gr. *νεφρός*, kidney.] In *zoöl.*, a primitive excretory organ in annelids, brachiopods, mollusks, etc., analogous in function to the kidney, and in some cases serving also in reproduction.—**ne-phrid′i-al,** *a.*

neph-rite (nef′rīt), *n.* [G. *nephrit*, < Gr. *νεφρός*, kidney; named with reference to an old belief in its efficacy against disease of the kidneys.] A mineral, a compact or finely fibrous variety of amphibole, varying in color from whitish to dark green. See *jade*[1].

ne-phrit-ic (ne-frit′ik), *a.* [LL. *nephriticus*, < Gr. *νεφριτικός*, < *νεφρῖτις*, E. *nephritis.*] Of, pertaining to, or affected with nephritis, or kidney disease; efficacious against kidney disease (as, *nephritic* stone, nephrite; *nephritic* wood, a kind of wood, variously identified, formerly credited with medicinal properties).

ne-phri-tis (ne-frī′tis), *n.* [LL., < Gr. *νεφρῖτις*, < *νεφρός*, kidney.] In *pathol.*, inflammation of the kidneys; esp., Bright's disease.

nephro-. Form of Gr. *νεφρός*, kidney, used in combination.—**neph-ro-lith** (nef′rǫ-lith), *n.* [+ *-lith.*] In *pathol.*, a renal calculus.—**neph-ro-pex′i-a** (-pek′si-ạ̈), **neph′ro-pex-y,** *n.* [NL. *nephropexia* (Gr. *πῆξις*, a making fast).] In *surg.*, fixation of a floating kidney.—**ne-phrot-o-my** (ne-frot′ǫ-mi), *n.* [+ *-tomy.*] In *surg.*, incision into the kidney, as for the removal of a calculus.

nep-o-tism (nep′ǫ-tizm), *n.* [L. *nepos* (*nepot-*), grandson, nephew: see *nephew.*] Favoritism, as in conferring offices, shown by popes or other ecclesiastics to nephews or other relatives; hence, in general, patronage bestowed in consideration of family relationship and not of merit.—**nep′o-tist,** *n.* One given to nepotism.—**nep-o-tis′ti-cal,** *a.*

Nep-tune (nep′tūn), *n.* [L. *Neptunus.*] The Roman god of the sea (cf. *Poseidon*); hence, the sea or ocean (as, "Ye that on the sands . . . Do chase the ebbing *Neptune*": Shakspere's "Tempest," v. 1. 35); also, a major planet, the eighth from the sun (see *Pluto*), being invisible to the naked eye.—**Nep-tu′ni-an** (-tū′ni-ąn), *a.* Pertaining to Neptune, the god of the sea, or to the sea or ocean itself; also, pertaining to the planet Neptune; [also *l. c.*] in *geol.*, formed by the action of water; specif., noting or pertaining to an old, untenable theory that many rocks now known to be volcanic or plutonic were deposited by water.—**Nep′tun-ist** (-tų̄n-ist), *n.* In *geol.*, an advocate of the Neptunian theory.

Ne-re-id (nē′rę̄-id), *n.* [L. *Nereis* (pl. *Nereides*), < Gr. *Νηρηίς* (pl. *Νηρηίδες*).] In *class. myth.*, any one of the fifty daughters of the ancient sea-god Nereus; a sea-nymph.

ner-ka (nėr′kạ̈), *n.* [Appar. native name.] An important salmon, *Oncorhynchus nerka*, of Alaska, Kamchatka, etc.; the blueback.

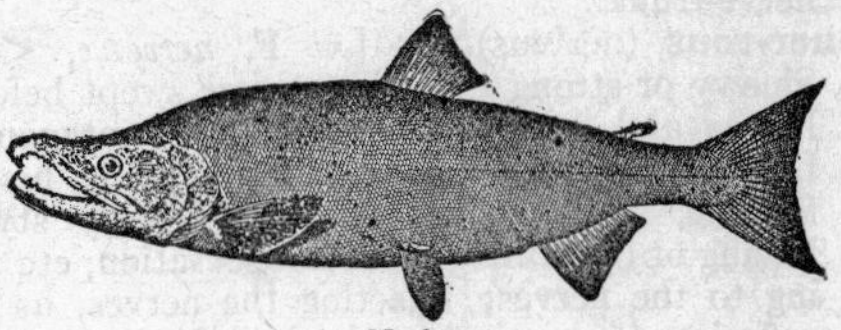
Nerka.

Nernst (nernst) **lamp.** [From Walter *Nernst* (born 1864), German physicist, who invented it.] An incandescent electric lamp in which the filament of the ordinary type of lamp is replaced by a rod made of a mixture of magnesia and other metallic oxides and not inclosed in a vacuum.

ner-o-li (ner′ǫ-li or nē′rǫ-li), *n.* [From an Italian Princess *Neroli.*] An essential oil extracted from orange-flowers, used in perfumes, etc. Also called *oil of neroli.*

Ne-ro-ni-an (nę̄-rō′ni-ąn), *a.* Of, pertaining to, or suggestive of the Roman emperor Nero (reigned A.D. 54–68), noted for his profligacy, cruelty, and tyranny.

ner-vate (nėr′vāt), *a.* [L. *nervus*, E. *nerve.*] In *bot.*, of leaves, having nerves or veins; nerved. Also **ner′vat-ed** (-vā-ted).—**ner-va′tion** (-vā′shǫn), *n.* The arrangement of nerves, as in a leaf or in an insect's wing. Also **ner′va-ture** (-vạ-tų̄r).

nerve (nėrv), *n.* [L. *nervus*, akin to Gr. *νεῦρον*, sinew, tendon, nerve.] A sinew or tendon (now chiefly in the phrase 'to strain every nerve,' expressing intense exertion, and often fig.); fig., that which supplies the strength or sustains the activities of anything (as, "Agamemnon, Thou great commander, *nerve* and bone of Greece," Shakspere's "Troilus and Cressida," i. 3. 55; the *nerves* of war, the sinews of war, or money, see *sinew, n.*); hence, strength, vigor, or energy (as, "He led me on to mightiest deeds, Above the *nerve* of mortal arm": Milton's "Samson Agonistes," 639); also, a fiber, or one or more bundles of fibers, forming part of a system which conveys impulses of sensation, motion, etc., between the brain or spinal cord and other parts of the body; hence, *pl.*, organs or capacities of feeling, with reference to their condition or to their action under strain (as, sound *nerves*; "The action . . . shook the *nerves* of the Englishman," Cooper's "Spy," xxxiii.); often, weak or disordered organs of feeling, or nervousness (as, to suffer from *nerves*; a fit of *nerves*); also, *sing.*, firmness or courage under trying circumstances (as, a position requiring *nerve*; "It was really an affair of no small *nerve* to look her in the face," Hawthorne's "Twice-Told Tales," Old Esther Dudley); impertinent assurance (slang); also, a line or one of a system of lines traversing something (as, railroads are *nerves* of communication throughout the country); in *bot.*, a vein, as in a leaf; in *entom.*, a nervure, as in an insect's wing; in *arch.*, a rib or projecting molding in vaulted work.—**nerve,** *v. t.*; *nerved, nerving.* To give strength or vigor to, or strengthen (as, "Were I a man . . . justice . . . would *nerve* my arm with the strength of a host": Jane Porter's "Scottish Chiefs," viii.); also, to give courage to (as, "The kind eyes Soothing yet *nerving* you": Henley's "In Hospital," xi.); bring by inspiring or summoning courage (as, "Yet *nerve* thy spirit to the proof," Bryant's "Battle-Field"; to *nerve* one's self to resist).—**nerve′=cell,** *n.* Any of the cells constituting the cellular element of nervous tissue; esp., one of the essential cells of a nerve-center.—**nerve′=cen″ter,** *n.* A group of nerve-cells closely connected with one another and acting together in the performance of some function.—**nerved,** *a.* Having nerves (as, strong-*nerved*); in *bot.*, nervate; in *entom.*, having nervures.—**nerve′=fi″ber,** *n.* One of the minute fibers or cords which, either singly or in numbers, constitute the chief part of nerves.—**nerve′less,** *a.* Destitute of nerve, strength, or vigor (as, "Joe's pipe dropped from his *nerveless* fingers": Mark Twain's "Tom Sawyer," xvi.); feeble; weak; also, lacking firmness or courage; spiritless or pusillanimous; in *anat.*, *bot.*, etc., without nerves.—**nerve′less-ly,** *adv.*—**nerve′less-ness,** *n.*

ner-vine (nėr′vin, -vīn, or -vēn). [= F. *nervin*, < LL. *nervinus.*] **I.** *a.* Of or pertaining to the nerves; acting on, or relieving disorders of, the nerves; strengthening or soothing the nerves. **II.** *n.* A nervine medicine.

nerv-ing (nėr′ving), *n.* In *vet. surg.*, the excision of part of a nerve-trunk.

ner-vous (nėr′vus), *a.* [= F. *nerveux*, < L. *nervosus.*] Sinewy or strong (as, "They were swept before the mettled horses and *nervous* arms of their antagonists like chaff before the wind": Cooper's "Spy," vii.); hence, vigorous or forcible, as language, writings, literary style, etc.; also, having or containing nerves of sensation, etc.; of or pertaining to the nerves; affecting the nerves, as diseases; also, suffering from, characterized by, or proceeding from disordered nerves (as, a *nervous* patient; a *nervous* condition; a *nervous* twitching); highly excitable; unnaturally or acutely uneasy or apprehensive; characterized by or attended with acute uneasiness or apprehension (as, "A time of *nervous* suspense it was both to Cæcilius and the youth who befriended him": J. H. Newman's "Callista," xx.).—**nervous system,** in *anat.* and *zoöl.*, the system of nerves and nerve-centers in an animal, or a particular part of this system: as, the central or cerebrospinal *nervous system* (the brain and spinal cord); the peripheral *nervous system* (the system of nerves and ganglia derived from the central system, comprising the cranial nerves, the spinal nerves, the various sense-organs, etc.); the sympathetic *nervous system* (the system of nerves and ganglia which supply the walls of the vascular system and the various viscera and glands).—**ner′vous-ly,** *adv.*—**ner′vous-ness,** *n.*

ner-vure (nėr′vūr), *n.* [F., < L. *nervus*, E. *nerve.*] In *bot.*, a nerve or vein of a leaf; in *entom.*, one of the tubes or tubular thickenings which ramify in an insect's wing (see cut in next column).

nerv-y (nėr′vi), *a.* Sinewy, strong, or vigorous; also, having or showing nerve or courage; requiring nerve (as, a *nervy* undertaking); also, audacious or impudently bold (slang); also, nervous, highly excitable, or acutely uneasy or apprehensive (colloq.).

nes-cient (nesh′ient), *a.* [L. *nesciens* (*nescient-*), ppr. of *nescire*, not to know, < *ne*, not, + *scire*, know.] Not knowing; ignorant.—**nes′cience,** *n.*

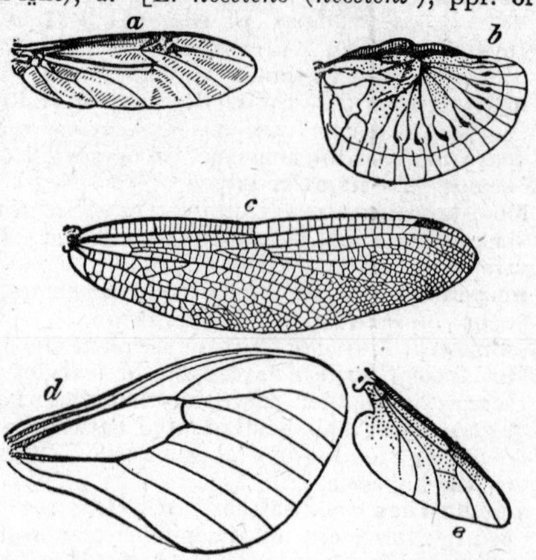

Nervures of Wings in Insects. — *a*, cockchafer; *b*, earwig; *c*, dragon-fly; *d*, butterfly; *e*, fly (dipter).

nesh (nesh), *a.* [AS. *hnesce.*] Soft, tender, or succulent; also, delicate or weakly; also, poor-spirited; effeminate; also, dainty or squeamish. [Now prov.]

ness (nes), *n.* [AS. *næs* = Icel. *nes*, headland; akin to E. *nose.*] A headland; a promontory; a cape: as, "Over headland, *ness*, and voe — The Coastwise Lights of England watch the ships of England go!" (Kipling's "Coastwise Lights"). [Archaic, prov., or in place-names.]

-ness. [AS. *-nes, -ness, -nis, -nys.*] A suffix used to form, from adjectives and participles, nouns denoting quality or state, also often, by extension, something exemplifying a quality or state, as in *darkness, goodness, kindness, obligingness, preparedness.*

nest (nest), *n.* [AS. *nest* = D. and G. *nest*, nest; akin to L. *nidus*, nest, Skt. *nīda*, resting-place, nest.] A structure formed or a place used by a bird for incubation and the rearing of its young; a place used by insects, fishes, turtles, rabbits, or the like, for depositing their eggs or young; in general, a place of habitation or retirement; esp., a snug abode, retreat, or resting-place (as, "Labourers' homes . . . At random scatter'd, each a *nest* in bloom," Tennyson's "Aylmer's Field," 150; to make a *nest* of pillows); an abode or haunt of evil or obnoxious persons (as, a robbers' *nest*); a place where something bad is fostered or flourishes (as, a *nest* of vice or crime); also, the occupants or frequenters of a nest; a number of birds or other animals inhabiting one nest; a number of persons, esp. evil or obnoxious persons, dwelling or consorting together (as, "when we observe with our own eyes such a *nest* of traitors here assembled": Scott's "Castle Dangerous," viii.); also, an assemblage of things lying or set close together (as, a *nest* of bushes; a *nest* of little streets); also, a set or series of boxes, baskets, bowls, trays, or other articles, of such size and shape that the smaller fit within the larger; a number of hollow articles arranged to rest one within another, as to save space (as, a *nest* of paper drinking cups); in *geol.*, an isolated mass of ore or mineral in a rock.—**nest,** *v.* **I.** *intr.* To build or have a nest; settle or lodge in or as in a nest; also, to search for nests (as, "This is dull work for a bairn. Let's go *nesting*": Stevenson's "Master of Ballantrae," vi.). **II.** *tr.* To settle or place in or as in a nest; provide with a nest; also, to fit or place, one within another, to form a nest, as boxes, cups, or other articles.—**nest′=egg,** *n.* An egg (natural or artificial) left in a nest to induce a hen to continue laying eggs there; fig., something laid up as the beginning of a fund or accumulation or as a reserve.—**nest′er,** *n.*

nes-tle (nes′l), *v.*; *-tled, -tling.* [AS. *nestlian*, < *nest*, E. *nest.*] **I.** *intr.* To make or have a nest; also, to lie close and snug, like a bird in a nest; snuggle or cuddle; lie in a sheltered or pleasant situation (as, "Even now . . . *nestles* the little city in the angle of the two rivers": Motley's "Dutch Republic," v. 3). **II.** *tr.* To provide with or settle in a nest, as birds; also, to settle or ensconce snugly (as, "a litter of well-grown black puppies, comfortably *nestled* among some buffalo robes": Parkman's "Oregon Trail," ix.); put or press confidingly or affectionately (as, to *nestle* one's hand into that of another; to *nestle* one's head against a person's breast).—**nes′tler,** *n.*

nest-ling (nest′ling), *n.* A young bird in the nest; hence, a young child.

Nes-tor (nes′tọr), *n.* [From *Nestor*, king of Pylus, oldest counselor of the Greeks before Troy.] The oldest and wisest man of a company or body; a wise old man: as, "We were summoned to the lodge of an old man, in good truth the *Nestor* of his tribe" (Parkman's "Oregon Trail," xi.).

Nes-to-ri-an (nes-tō′ri-ạn), *n.* One of a sect of Christians, followers of Nestorius, patriarch of Constantinople (428–431), who denied the hypostatic union and maintained the existence of two distinct persons in Christ; also, one of a modern remnant of this sect in northwestern Persia and adjoining regions.—**Nes-to′ri-an-ism,** *n.*

net[1] (net), *n.* [AS. *net* = D. *net* = G. *netz* = Icel. *net* = Goth. *nati*, net.] A bag or other contrivance of strong thread or cord wrought into an open, meshed fabric, for catching fish, birds, or other animals; fig., anything serving to catch or insnare (as, "I find more bitter than death the woman, whose heart is snares and *nets*": Eccl. vii. 26); also, a piece of meshed fabric for any purpose (as, a mosquito-*net*; a tennis-*net*; a hair-*net*); also, a lace-like fabric or material with uniform meshes, used for garments, millinery, trimming, etc., or forming the ground of many kinds of lace; also, any network or reticulated system of filaments, lines, veins, or the like.—**net**[1], *v.*; *netted, netting.* **I.** *tr.* To take with a net (as, to *net* fish, birds, or butterflies); fig., to catch or insnare; also, to set or use nets in (a river, etc.), as for fish; also, to cover, screen, or inclose with a net or netting; cover with a network of lines, veins, or the like; also, to make with meshes in the manner of network (as, "She now produced . . . some little wooden instruments . . . and proceeded to knit, or *net*, an article which ultimately took the shape of a silk purse": Hawthorne's "Blithedale Romance," v.). **II.** *intr.* To make network or netted articles.

net[2] (net). [F. *net*, clean, clear: see *neat*[2].] **I.** *a.* Clean†; hence, pure or unadulterated (now rare); also, exclusive of deductions made, as for charges, expenses, loss, discount, etc., or not subject to deductions (as, *net* profits; *net* prices: cf. *gross*); sold at net prices (as, a *net* book). **II.** *n.* Net income, profits, or the like.—**net**[2], *v. t.*; *netted, netting.* To gain or yield as clear profit: as, to *net* a thousand dollars by a sale; the sale *netted* him a thousand dollars.

neth-er (neᴛʜ′ėr), *a.* [AS. *nithera*, *neothera* (= D. *neder* = G. *nieder*), < *nither*, adv., downward, down, a compar. form akin to *neothan*, below (see *beneath*), also to Skt. *ni*, down.] Lower or under, as in position (opposed to *upper*: as, "His *nether* lip quivered," Smollett's "Humphry Clinker," July 10; "He . . . wore . . . dark cotton stockings on his *nether* limbs," Dickens's "Oliver Twist," xxxvii.); of places, situated at a lower level, or nearer the sea-level (as, "*Nether* Germany was entitled to the same privileges as Upper Germany": Motley's "Dutch Republic," iii. 4); also, lying, or conceived as lying, beneath the earth's surface (as, the *nether* world, the lower world of the ancients, see under *lower*[2], *a.*); infernal (as, the *nether* regions); also, lying beneath the heavens, or sometimes, as conceived, beneath the celestial heaven (as, this *nether* world or sphere, the earth); earthly, or done on earth (as, "This shows you are above, You justicers, that these our *nether* crimes So speedily can venge!" Shakspere's "King Lear," iv. 2. 79).—**nether millstone,** the lower of a pair of millstones in a mill for grinding grain, etc.: often taken as a type of great hardness, in expressions (such as 'a heart as hard as the nether millstone') based on the Biblical use, "His heart is as firm as a stone; yea, as hard as a piece of the nether millstone" (Job, xli. 24).

Neth-er-land-er (neᴛʜ′ėr-lạn-dėr), *n.* [D. *Nederlander*: cf. *nether*.] A native or inhabitant of the Netherlands (now Holland, but formerly including Flanders also).

neth-er-more (neᴛʜ′ėr-mōr), *a. compar.* Lower. [Now rare.]—**neth′er-most,** *a. superl.* Lowest: as, "the *nethermost* abyss" (Milton's "Paradise Lost," ii. 956).

neth-er=stock (neᴛʜ′ėr-stok), *n.* A stocking. [Archaic.]

neth-er-ward, neth-er-wards (neᴛʜ′ėr-wạ̈rd, -wạ̈rdz), *adv.* Downward.

net-su-ke (net′sö-kā), *n.* [Jap.] In Japanese use, a small knob or button, usually ornamental, with holes for the cord of a tobacco-pouch or other article worn suspended from the girdle.

net-ted (net′ed), *p. a.* Caught in a net; also, covered or screened with a net (as, a *netted* window); covered with a network of lines, veins, or the like (as, the *netted* wings of a dragon-fly); reticulate; also, made with meshes in the manner of network (as, *netted* fabrics; a *netted* purse).

net-ter (net′ėr), *n.* One who nets; esp., one who uses a net.

net-ting (net′ing), *n.* The act of one who nets; also, a net or netted fabric; any of various netted, meshed, or open-textured materials (as, mosquito-*netting*; wire *netting*).

net-tle (net′l), *n.* [AS. *netele* = D. *netel* = G. *nessel*, nettle.] Any plant of the genus *Urtica*, comprising widely distributed herbs armed with stinging hairs; also, any of various allied or similar plants.—**net′tle,** *v. t.*; *-tled, -tling.* To subject to the stinging of nettles; sting as a nettle does; fig., to irritate, provoke, or vex (as, "Not a little *nettled* at this arrogant remark, I told her . . . ": Smollett's "Humphry Clinker," June 26).—**net′tle=rash,** *n.* Urticaria.—**net′tle-some** (-sum), *a.* Easily nettled or irritated.—**net′tle=tree,** *n.* An ulmaceous tree, *Celtis australis*, of Europe and Asia, bearing a sweet, cherry-like fruit (also called *lotus-tree*); also, some allied species, as *C. occidentalis*, the American hackberry; also, any of certain Australian trees of the urticaceous genus *Urticastrum*.

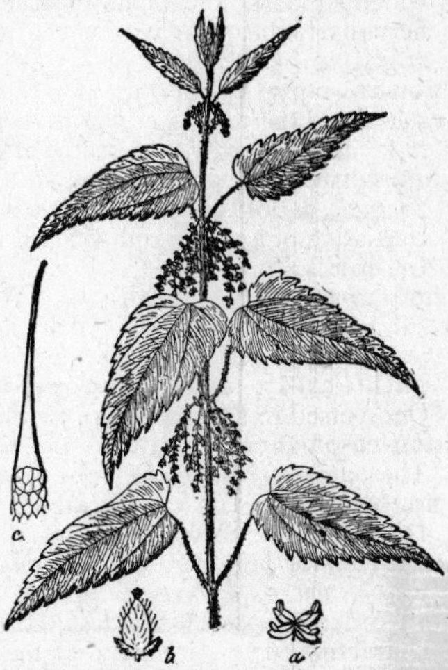

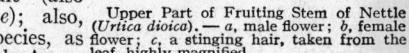

Upper Part of Fruiting Stem of Nettle (*Urtica dioica*). — *a*, male flower; *b*, female flower; *c*, a stinging hair, taken from the leaf, highly magnified.

net-work (net′wėrk), *n.* Work or a piece of work having the texture of a net (as, "a grate of *network* of brass," Ex. xxvii. 4; a *network* of ropes); a netting or net; any net-like combination of filaments, lines, veins, passages, or the like (as, a *network* of fibers; a *network* of vines; "a complete labyrinth, or *net-work*, of subterranean corridors," Wiseman's "Fabiola," ii. 2); a reticulated system of parts; fig., a tissue (as, a *network* of reasoning; "Their law is a *network* of fictions," Emerson's "English Traits," v.).

Neuf-châ-tel (nė-shä-tel) **cheese.** [From *Neufchâtel*-en-Bray, town in northern France.] A soft, white variety of cheese made from milk with or without the cream.

neu-ral (nū′rạl), *a.* [Gr. νεῦρον, sinew, tendon, nerve: see *nerve*.] Of or pertaining to a nerve or the nervous system; also, noting, pertaining to, or situated on that side of the body on which the brain and spinal cord lie (cf. *hemal*); dorsal.—**neural arch,** in *anat.*, the arch on the dorsal side of a vertebra.—**neural canal,** in *anat.*, the canal formed by the vertebral foramina, inclosing and protecting the spinal cord.—**neural spine,** in *anat.*, a process on the dorsal side of a vertebra.

neu-ral-gia (nụ-ral′jiạ̈), *n.* [NL., < Gr. νεῦρον, nerve, + ἄλγος, pain.] In *pathol.*, pain, usually sharp and paroxysmal, along the course of a nerve.—**neu-ral′gic,** *a.*

neu-ras-the-ni-a (nū-rạs-thē′ni-ạ̈), *n.* [NL., < Gr. νεῦρον, nerve, + ἀσθένεια, weakness: see *asthenia*.] In *pathol.*, nervous debility or exhaustion, as from overwork or prolonged mental strain.—**neu-ras-then′ic** (-then′ik). **I.** *a.* Pertaining to or suffering from neurasthenia. **II.** *n.* A person suffering from neurasthenia.—**neu-ras-then′i-cal-ly,** *adv.*

neu-ra-tion (nụ-rā′shọn), *n.* [Gr. νεῦρον, nerve.] Nervation.

neu-rec-to-my (nụ-rek′tọ-mi), *n.* [Gr. νεῦρον, nerve, + ἐκ, out of, + -τομία, E. *-tomy*.] In *surg.*, the excision of a nerve or part of a nerve.

neu-ri-lem-ma (nū-ri-lem′ạ̈), *n.* [NL., < Gr. νεῦρον, nerve, + λέμμα, husk, skin.] In *anat.*, the delicate membranous sheath of a nerve-fiber.

neu-ril-i-ty (nū-ril′i-ti), *n.* [= F. *neurilité*, < Gr. νεῦρον, nerve.] The characteristic property of nerves, of conducting stimuli.

neu-ri-tis (nū-rī′tis), *n.* [NL., < Gr. νεῦρον, nerve.] In *pathol.*, inflammation of a nerve or nerves.—**neu-rit′ic** (-rit′ik), *a.*

neuro-. Form of Gr. νεῦρον, sinew, tendon, nerve, used in combination.

neu-ro-blast (nū′rō-blast), *n.* [See *neuro-* and *-blast.*] In *embryol.*, one of the cells in the embryonic brain and spinal cord of vertebrates, which are said to give rise to nerve-cells.

neu-rog-li-a (nū-rog′li-ạ), *n.* [NL., < Gr. νεῦρον, nerve, + γλία, glue.] In *anat.*, the delicate connective tissue which supports and binds together the essential elements of nervous tissue, esp. in the central nervous system.—**neu-rog′li-ar** (-ạr), *a.*

neu-rol-o-gy (nū-rol′ō-ji), *n.* [See *neuro-* and *-logy.*] The science of the nerves or the nervous system.—**neu-ro-log-i-cal** (nū-rō-loj′i-kạl), *a.*—**neu-rol′o-gist,** *n.*

neu-rone, neu-ron (nū′rōn, -ron), *n.* [Gr. νεῦρον, nerve.] In *anat.*, one of the structural elements of the nervous system, consisting of a nerve-cell with all its processes.—**neu-ron-ic** (nū-ron′ik), *a.*

neu-ro-path (nū′rō-path), *n.* [See *neuropathy.*] A person subject to or affected with nervous disease.—**neu-ro-path′ic,** *a.* Of or pertaining to neuropathy.—**neu-ro-path′i-cal-ly,** *adv.*—**neu-rop-a-thist** (nū-rop′ạ-thist), *n.* One versed in the subject of neuropathy.

neu-ro-pa-thol-o-gy (nū″rō-pạ-thol′ō-ji), *n.* [See *neuro-*.] The pathology of the nervous system.

neu-rop-a-thy (nū-rop′ạ-thi), *n.* [See *neuro-* and *-pathy.*] Disease of the nervous system.

neu-rop-ter (nū-rop′tėr), *n.* [NL. *Neuroptera*, pl., < Gr. νεῦρον, nerve, + πτερόν, wing.] Any of the *Neuroptera*, an order of insects, including the ant-lions and lacewings, characterized by two pairs of membranous wings with net-like nervation.—**neu-rop′ter-an,** *a.* and *n.*—**neu-rop′ter-ous,** *a.* Belonging to the *Neuroptera*.

neu-ro-sis (nū-rō′sis), *n.*; pl. *-roses* (-rō′sēz). [NL., < Gr. νεῦρον, nerve.] In *pathol.*, a nervous affection or disease, esp. one without apparent organic change; in *psychol.*, the action of a nerve, esp. as corresponding to a mental process, or psychosis.—**neu-rot′ic** (-rot′ik). **I.** *a.* Pertaining to the nerves or to nervous disease; also, suffering from or subject to neurosis. **II.** *n.* A drug which acts upon the nerves; also, a neurotic person.—**neu-rot′i-cism** (-i-sizm), *n.*

neu-rot-o-my (nū-rot′ō-mi), *n.* [See *neuro-* and *-tomy.*] Surgical cutting of a nerve, as to relieve neuralgia.—**neu-rot′o-mist,** *n.*

Neus-tri-an (nūs′tri-ạn), *a.* [LL. *Neustria*; from Teut.] Of or pertaining to Neustria, the western kingdom of the Franks. Cf. *Austrasian.*

neu-ter (nū′tėr). [L. *neuter*, < *ne*, not, + *uter*, either.] **I.** *a.* Being neither the one thing nor the other (as, things good, bad, and *neuter*); also, taking no part with either side, or neutral; in *gram.*, neither masculine nor feminine (as, the *neuter* gender; the *neuter* pronoun 'it'); also, neither active (transitive) nor passive, as a verb; intransitive; in *bot.*, having neither stamens nor pistils; asexual; in *entom.*, having imperfectly developed sexual organs, as the workers among bees and ants. **II.** *n.* A neutral; in *gram.*, the neuter gender, or a word or word-form of that gender; also, a neuter verb; in *entom.*, a neuter insect.—**neu′ter-pas′sive.** In *gram.*: **I.** *a.* Having both a neuter (intransitive) and a passive character: applied to certain verbs or verb-forms in foreign languages, and also to such uses of verbs in English as are exemplified in *cuts* in 'the bread cuts easily,' that is, is cut, or admits of being cut, easily, and in *sell* in 'these goods sell at higher prices.' **II.** *n.* A neuter-passive verb, verb-form, or use.

neu-tral (nū′trạl). [L. *neutralis*, < *neuter*: see *neuter.*] **I.** *a.* Neuter in character or relations; of neither of two specified or implied kinds, classes, etc.; also, taking no part with either side in a controversy or war, or belonging to a party or nation that refrains from taking part; also, of no particular kind, color, characteristics, etc.; indefinite; in *bot.* and *entom.*, neuter; in *chem.*, neither acid nor alkaline (or basic); in *elect.*, neither positive nor negative. **II.** *n.* A person or a nation that remains neutral; a citizen or a vessel of a neutral nation.—**neu′tral-ism,** *n.* The maintaining or the advocating of a neutral attitude or policy.—**neu′tral-ist,** *n.*—**neu-tral-i-ty** (nū-tral′i-ti), *n.* The state of being neutral; esp., the state or fact of taking no part with either side in a controversy; the attitude or policy of a nation which does not take part directly or indirectly in a war between other nations; neutral character or status, as of a place, during a war (as, the *neutrality* of a port).—**neu′tral-ize** (-īz), *v. t.*; *-ized, -izing.* To make neutral; declare neutral, as in time of war, or invest with neutrality; render ineffective, or counteract; in *chem.*, to render neutral; render inert the peculiar properties of; in *elect.*, to render electrically inert.—**neu″tral-i-za′tion** (-i-zā′shọn), *n.*—**neu′tral-iz-er** (-ī-zėr), *n.*—**neu′tral-ly,** *adv.*

neu-tro-dyne (nū′trō-dīn), *n.* [L. *neuter*, neither, + Gr. δύναμις, power.] A type of radio amplifying or receiving apparatus in which regeneration, due to the coupling capacity of the vacuum-tubes or other coupling capacity, is eliminated by neutralization of this coupling capacity with auxiliary or added capacity: a term applied esp. to tuned radio-frequency amplifiers or receivers. [Proprietary name.]

né-vé (nā-vā), *n.* [F., < L. *nix* (*niv-*), snow.] Granular snow accumulated on high mountains and subsequently compacted into glacial ice; firn; also, a field of such snow.

nev-er (nev′ėr), *adv.* [AS. *nǣfre*, < *ne*, not, + *ǣfre*, E. *ever.*] Not ever, or at no time (as, better late than *never*; a *never*-failing solace); also, in no case, or under no circumstances (as, "He would *never* else cross me thus": Shakspere's "Merry Wives of Windsor," v. 5. 40); hence (with emphatic force, in various idiomatic expressions), not at all, absolutely not, or not even (as, *never* mind what they say; he said *never* a word; *never* a man returned); to no extent or degree (followed by *the* with a comparative: as, for all our efforts, success is *never* the nearer; *never* the wiser: cf. *nevertheless*).—**never so,** not even so (*much*, etc.); also, never to such an extent or degree, or no matter how (as, "which will not hearken to the voice of charmers, charming *never so* wisely": Ps. lviii. 5).

nev-er-more (nev′ėr-mōr′), *adv.* Never again; never at any future time.

nev-er-the-less (nev′ėr-ᴛʜē-les′), *adv.* or *conj.* None the less; notwithstanding; however: as, you will find this to be true, *nevertheless*; "Lazarus is dead . . . *nevertheless* let us go unto him" (John, xi. 15).

new (nū), *a.* [AS. *nīwe*, *nēowe*, = D. *nieuw* = G. *neu* = Icel. *nýr* = Goth. *niujis*, new; akin to L. *novus*, Gr. νέος, Skt. *nava*, new.] Of recent origin or production, or having but lately come or been brought into being (as, a *new* bud or shoot; *new* potatoes; a *new* book, photograph, coat, or building; a *new* theory or invention); only lately arisen, produced, made, or devised; not long or not before existent; also, of a kind now existing or appearing for the first time (as, a story whose plot is decidedly *new*; "There is no *new* thing under the sun. Is there any thing whereof it may be said, See, this is *new?* it hath been already of old time," Eccl. i. 9, 10); different in character from anything preceding; novel; also, having but lately or but now come into knowledge (as, a *new* chemical element; a *new* species of animal; a *new* anecdote of Lincoln); only lately or only now seen, encountered, experienced, or used for the first time (as, *new* scenes; a *new* sensation; a *new* path, method, or recipe); unfamiliar or strange (*to*: as, ideas or ways *new* to us); also, having but lately come to a place or position or to notice or prominence (as, a *new* minister or president; a *new* favorite; a *new* popular hero); having but recently come, and hence not yet accustomed (*to*: as, men *new* to such work); also, coming or occurring afresh, or further or additional (as, *new* gains or successes; *new* efforts; *new* resistance); also, fresh or unused (as, take a *new* sheet of paper; a *new* copy of a book); unimpaired by, or free from the effects of, use, time, decay, etc. (as, "This plumage . . . wears a splendour ever *new*": Cowper's "On Mrs. Montagu's Feather-Hangings," 19); different and better, physically or morally, through some process of change (as, the voyage made a *new* man of him; under the wholesome discipline he became a *new* man; to vow to lead a *new* life); also, other than the former or old (as, to republish a story under a *new* name; to enter upon a *new* era; "The old order changeth, yielding place to *new*," Tennyson's "Passing of Arthur," 408); often, being the later or latest of two or more things of the same kind, or of two or more stages of a thing (as, the *New* Testament, see *testament*; the *New* World, see *world*; *New* England, *New* York, *New* Jersey, *New* Orleans; *New* Greek, *New* Latin, see the nouns).—**New Church.** Same as *New Jerusalem Church* (see below).—**New Jerusalem,** the heavenly city; the abode of God and his saints: with allusion to Rev. xxi. 2.—**New Jerusalem Church,** or **Church of the New Jerusalem,** the church or denomination composed of the followers of Emanuel Swedenborg. See *Swedenborgian.*—**New Learning,** the studies, esp. the study of the Greek language and literature, introduced into England in the 16th century, being the development in England of the Italian Renaissance; also, the doctrines of the English Reformation.—**New Lights,** *eccles.*, the members of any of various parties adhering to new doctrines, or forming bodies separate from others with which they were formerly associated, because of adherence to some new view of doctrine or duty. Cf. *Old Lights*, under *old, a.*—**New Red Sandstone.** See under *sandstone.*—**New Style.** See *style, n.*—**New Thought,** an optimistic system of doctrine and practice based on the general theory that through new thought, or the suggestion of favorable and beneficial ideas, all the circumstances of life, both physical and mental, may be regulated and controlled.—**new year, New Year's Day.** See entry below.—**new,** *adv.* [AS. *nīwe.*] Newly; recently or lately; freshly; anew or afresh: now chiefly in composition, as in *new-born*, *new-create*, *new-found*, *new-furnished*, *new-laid*, *new-risen*, and other similar words, mostly self-explanatory.

new=born (nū′bôrn), *a.* Recently or only just born (as, "Many a childing mother then, And *new-born* baby died": Southey's "Battle of Blenheim," viii.); also, born anew, or reborn.

new=come (nū′kum). **I.** *a.* Newly or lately come or arrived: as, *new-come* settlers. **II.** *n.* A new-comer. [Now rare.]—**new′=com′er** (-kum′ėr), *n.* One who has newly come; a new arrival.

new=cre-ate (nū′krē̜-āt′), *v. t.*; *-ated, -ating.* To create anew: as, "The landscape Lay as if *new-created* in all the freshness of childhood" (Longfellow's "Evangeline," i. 2).

new-el (nū′e̜l), *n.* [OF. *noel*, *noiel* (F. *noyau*), fruit-stone, kernel, newel, < LL. *nucale*, neut. of *nucalis*, of or like a nut, < L. *nux* (*nuc-*), nut.] A central pillar or upright from which the steps of a winding stair radiate; sometimes, a central open space within a winding stair ('open newel,' or 'hollow newel'); also, a post at the head or foot of a stair, supporting the hand-rail (also called *newel-post*).

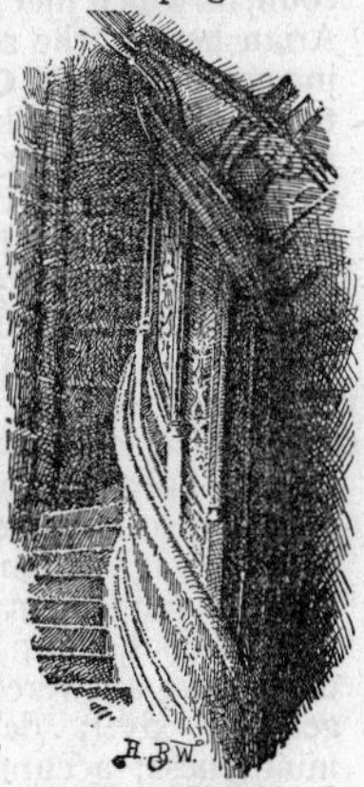
Newel. — Château of Blois, France.

new-fan-gle (nū′fang′gl or nū′fang″gl). [ME. *newefangel*, < *newe*, new, + *-fangel*, < AS. *fōn* (pp. *fangen*), take.] **I.** *a.* Newfangled. [Now prov.] **II.** *n.* A new thing or fashion; a novelty. [Now prov.]—**new′fan′gled,** *a.* [For *newfangle.*] Disposed to take up new things; fond of novelty; also, new-fashioned, or of a new kind (used depreciatingly or humorously: as, "the *newfangled* doctrine of utility," Galt's "Annals of the Parish," xxxv.; "these *new-fangled* things they call lucifer matches," Mark Twain's "Tom Sawyer," xxxiii.).—**new′fan′gled-ness,** *n.*

new=fash-ioned (nū′fash′o̜nd), *a.* Of a new fashion; lately come into fashion.

new=form (nū′fôrm′), *v. t.* To form anew; change to a new form.

New-found-land (nū̜-found′la̜nd or nū′fund-la̜nd), *n.* [For *Newfoundland dog.*] One of a breed of large, shaggy dogs, orig. from the island of Newfoundland, noted for their sagacity, docility, swimming powers, etc.: as, "whistling to the lumbering *Newfoundland*, who came pitching tumultuously toward them" (Mrs. Stowe's "Uncle Tom's Cabin," vii.).

new-ish (nū′ish), *a.* Rather new.

new=laid (nū′lād′), *a.* Newly laid, as eggs; fresh.

new-ly (nū′li), *adv.* Recently, lately, or at a time only just past (as, a *newly* discovered star; a *newly* wedded couple; "The Duke of York is *newly* come from Ireland," Shakspere's "2 Henry VI.," iv. 9. 24); freshly, or only just (as, a *newly* torn garment); also, anew or afresh (as, a *newly* repeated slander); also, in a new manner or form (as, "That sweet passion . . . the refyned mynd doth *newly* fashion Unto a fairer forme": Spenser's "Hymne in Honour of Love," 192).

new=made (nū′mād′), *a.* Newly, recently, or freshly made (as, a *new-made* peer; a *new-made* grave); also, made anew, or remade.

new-mar-ket (nū′mär″ket), *n.* [From *Newmarket*, town in England.] A kind of card-game; also (orig. *Newmarket coat*), a man's long, close-fitting outdoor coat, or a similar coat for women.

new=mod-el (nū′mod′e̜l), *v. t.*; *-eled* or *-elled*, *-eling* or *-elling.* To model anew; remodel; give a new form to: as, to *new-model* a house, an army, or a government; "To *new-model* opinion would be to *new-model* society" (Peacock's "Nightmare Abbey," ii.).

new=mold, new=mould (nū′mōld′), *v. t.* To mold anew; remold.

new=mown (nū′mōn′), *a.* Newly or freshly mown: as, "Rarely smells the *new-mown* hay" (Tennyson's "The Owl").

new-ness (nū′nes), *n.* The state or fact of being new.

news (nūz), *n.* [Orig. pl., < *new, a.*] As *pl.*, new things†; as *sing.*, a new thing†; also, as *sing.* (earlier *pl.*), tidings or intelligence of new or hitherto unknown things (as, "As cold waters to a thirsty soul, so is good *news* from a far country": Prov. xxv. 25); often, intelligence of recent events as published in the newspapers; also, the newspapers, or a newspaper (now prov.).—**news′boy,** *n.* A boy who sells or delivers newspapers.—**news′=deal″er,** *n.* A dealer in newspapers and often magazines, etc.—**news′=let″ter,** *n.* A letter circulated, orig. in manuscript, to communicate the news of the day: especially in vogue in the 17th and 18th centuries, and being the precursor of the newspaper.—**news′mong″er** (-mung″gėr), *n.* One who gathers and retails news: as, "a knot of anxious *newsmongers*, each of whom departed . . . to carry the story home to his family" (Irving's "Knickerbocker's New York," iv. 11); "Every rancorous knave . . . may skulk behind the press of a *newsmonger*" (Smollett's "Humphry Clinker," June 2).—**news′pa″per,** *n.* A printed publication issued at regular intervals, usually daily or weekly, containing news, other matter of interest, advertisements, etc.—**news′print.** **I.** *a.* Used or made to print newspapers on, as a particular kind or class of paper; also, of or pertaining to such paper (as, a *newsprint* shortage; *newsprint* prices). **II.** *n.* Newsprint paper.—**news′=stand,** *n.* A stand at which newspapers and often magazines, etc., are sold.—**news′y[1],** *a.* Full of news, as on various subjects. [Colloq.]—**news′y[2],** *n.*; pl. *newsies* (-iz). A newsboy. [Colloq.]

newt (nūt), *n.* [ME. *newte*, for *ewte* (*an ewte* being taken as *a newte*), < AS. *efete*, E. *eft*[1].] Any of various small, tailed amphibians; an aquatic salamander; a triton.

Crested Newt (*Triton cristatus*).

New-to-ni-an (nū̜-tō′ni-a̜n), *a.* Of, pertaining to, or discovered or devised by Sir Isaac Newton (1642–1727), the English natural philosopher: as, the *Newtonian* law of gravitation; the *Newtonian* telescope.

new=world (nū′wėrld′), *a.* Of or pertaining to the new or modern world (as, "This *new-world* lore that takes account Of tangled star-dust": Jean Ingelow's "Honours," i.); also, of or pertaining to the New World or western hemisphere. Cf. *old-world.*

new year (nū yēr). The year approaching or newly begun; also [*caps.*], the first day or days of a year (also commonly *New Year's*).—**New Year's Day,** the first day of the year; Jan. 1.

next (nekst). [AS. *nēahst, nēhst, nīehst,* superl. of *nēah,* E. *nigh.*] **I.** *adv.* In the place or position nearest or adjoining (as, the building standing *next;* to sit *next* to a person); in the time immediately following or preceding (as, in the month *next* after, or *next* before); in the place in order, succession, rank, importance, etc., immediately after or (when expressly specified) before (as, in the chapter *next* following, or *next* preceding; Pennsylvania comes *next* to New York in population); often, in the next place in time or order, or immediately afterward (as, what shall we do *next?* who plays *next?*); also, on the first subsequent occasion (as, "when *next* we meet": Milton's "Paradise Lost," vi. 439). **II.** *prep.* Next or nearest to (as, the house *next* the church); next after (as, the grade *next* the highest or best; "one *next* himself in power," Milton's "Paradise Lost," i. 79).—**next,** *a.* [AS. *nēahsta, nēhsta, nexta.*] Nearest in place or position (as, the *next* town; the *next* room); also, nearest in relationship or kinship (as, "Their friends attend the hearse; the *next* relations mourn," Dryden's tr. Virgil's "Georgics," iv. 374; *next* of kin, see phrase below); closest, or most intimate (in 'next friend': see phrase below); also, immediately following in time (as, the *next* day; *next* month); coming directly after another of the same kind in time, or coming afterward and without any other intervening (as, the *next* time you come; his *next* visit; in your *next* letter; a story to be continued in the *next* number of a magazine); immediately succeeding or (when expressly specified) preceding in order, succession, rank, importance, etc. (as, the *next* chapter; the *next* person in authority; the *next* page before); also, shortest or most direct, as a way or road†.—**next door to,** in or at the house next to; hence, fig., very close to or all but (as, this is *next door to* a crime; a thing *next door to* impossible).—**next friend,** nearest friend or relative; specif., in *law,* a person who, as the nearest friend, acts, as in a suit at law, for the benefit of an infant or other person under legal disability.—**next of kin,** closest of kin; a person's nearest blood-relative or blood-relatives; the blood-relatives of an intestate entitled to share in his estate.—**next′ness,** *n.*

nex-us (nek′sus), *n.*; pl. *nexus.* [L., < *nectere,* bind.] A tie or link; a means of connection; also, a connected series.

ni-a-cin (nī′ạ-sin), *n.* Nicotinic acid.

Ni-ag-a-ra (nī-ag′ạ-rạ̈), *n.* [From *Niagara* Falls.] A cataract; a deluge: often fig.

niaise-rie (nyāz-rē), *n.* [F., < *niais,* simple, foolish, orig. being a nestling: see *eyas.*] Ignorant or stupid simplicity; foolishness; silliness; an instance or example of silliness.

nib[1] (nib), *n.* [Var. of *neb.*] A bill or beak, as of a bird; also, the point of a pen, or either of its divisions; a pen, for insertion into a penholder; also, the point of anything; any pointed extremity; also, either of the two short projecting handles on the long shaft of a scythe.—**nib**[1], *v. t.*; *nibbed, nibbing.* To furnish with a nib or point; mend or trim the nib of: as, to *nib* a quill pen; "The lawyer *nibbed* his pen, spread out his paper, and prepared to write" (Irving's "Tales of a Traveler," iv. 5).

nib[2] (nib), *n.* [Cf. prov. Eng. *nib,* a bit, lump, or small piece or quantity, also E. *nub* and *nubbin.*] *Pl.,* the roasted and crushed seeds of the cacao; also, *sing.,* a coffee-bean.

nib-ble (nib′l), *v.*; *-bled, -bling.* [= LG. *nibbeln, knibbeln.*] **I.** *tr.* To bite off small bits of (a thing); eat by biting off small pieces; also, to bite (*off,* etc.) in small pieces. **II.** *intr.* To bite off small bits; eat or feed by biting off small pieces; bite slightly or gently (*at:* as, fishes *nibble* at bait); also, fig., to carp (*at:* as, "I saw the critics prepared to *nibble* at my letter," Steele, in "Tatler," 87); make trifling objections; find fault.—**nib′ble,** *n.* The act or an instance of nibbling; also, a small morsel or bit.—**nib′bler,** *n.*—**nib′bling-ly,** *adv.*

nib-lick (nib′lik), *n.* [Origin obscure.] In *golf,* a club with a short, rounded, flat iron head whose face slopes greatly from the vertical, used to get the ball out of a bad lie.

nibs (nibz), *n.* [Cf. *nob*[2].] With a possessive pronoun, a jocular title of respect for a person, as if in recognition of importance: as, how is *his nibs,* or *his* royal *nibs?* [Slang.]

nic-co-lite (nik′ǫ-līt), *n.* [NL. *niccolum,* nickel.] A mineral of a pale copper-red color and metallic luster, consisting essentially of nickel arsenide, and usually occurring massive. Also called *copper-nickel.*

nice (nīs), *a.*; compar. *nicer,* superl. *nicest.* [OF. *nice,* ignorant, simple, foolish, < L. *nescius,* not knowing, < *ne,* not, + *scire,* know.] Foolish†; also, wanton†; also, coy†, shy†, or reluctant† (as, "We'll not be *nice:* take hands": Shakspere's "Love's Labour's Lost," v. 2. 219); also, exacting in requirements of taste, particular, or fastidious; dainty as to food (as, "This supposed alligator was very *nice* in his eating": Marryat's "King's Own," xlii.); carefully neat as to dress, habits, etc.; refined as to manners, language, etc.; also, scrupulous as to principle, honor, or the moral aspect of things (as, "too *nice* for a statesman": Goldsmith's "Retaliation," 38); also, having or showing delicate and accurate perception or discrimination (as, a *nice* observer; a *nice* ear for music; a *nice* sense of color; *nice* analysis or criticism); minute, fine, or subtle, as a distinction; sometimes, trivial†; also, showing minute differences, or minutely accurate, as instruments; characterized by or requiring great accuracy or precision (as, *nice* workmanship or adjustment; a *nice* test or experiment); precise or exact; also, delicately skilful in manipulation or execution (as, a *nice* hand or touch); fig., delicately tactful (as, *nice* handling of a difficult matter); requiring tact or care, or delicate (as, "It's a *nice* point to speak about . . . and I'm afraid o' being wrong": George Eliot's "Adam Bede," li.); also, dainty or delicious, as food; hence, in general, pleasing, agreeable, or delightful (as, a *nice* face; a *nice* girl; a *nice* house, book, breeze, visit, or nap; "How *nice* it must be to be able to do such things!" Howells's "Chance Acquaintance," i.); amiably pleasant, or kind (as, they are always *nice* to strangers; he was very *nice* about our mistake); pleasingly suitable or proper (as, "It wasn't a *nice* song — for a parlor, anyway": Mark Twain's "Life on the Mississippi," iii.).—**nice′ly,** *adv.*

Ni-cene (nī′sēn or nī-sēn′), *a.* [LL. *Nicænus.*] Of or pertaining to Nicæa, or Nice, an ancient city in Bithynia, Asia Minor.—**Nicene Council,** either of two general ecclesiastical councils which met at Nicæa, the first in 325 to deal with the Arian heresy, the second in 787 to consider the question of images.—**Nicene Creed,** a formal statement of the chief tenets of Christian belief, adopted by the first Nicene Council; now, usually, a later creed of closely similar form referred to the Council of Constantinople (in 381) and hence sometimes known as the 'Nicæno-Constantinopolitan Creed,' received universally in the Eastern Church, and, with an addition introduced in the 6th century, accepted generally throughout western Christendom.

nice-ness (nīs′nes), *n.* The quality of being nice.

ni-ce-ty (nī′sẹ-ti), *n.*; pl. *-ties* (-tiz). [OF. *nicete,* < *nice,* E. *nice.*] Folly†, or a foolish action†; foolish or wanton conduct†; also, coyness† or shyness†; also, the quality of being nice (in various modern senses); fastidiousness, as of taste; delicate refinement, as of manners, etc.; scrupulosity (as, "For their honour, their *nicety* of honour, I could in other days have answered with my own": Scott's "Castle Dangerous," xiv.); delicacy of perception or discrimination; minuteness; accuracy or precision; delicate skill in manipulation, handling, management, etc.; delicacy of character, as of something requiring care or tact (as, a matter of considerable *nicety*); also, something nice; a refinement or elegance, as of manners or living (often in *pl.*); a delicate or fine point (as, "I had no leisure to heed the *niceties* of punctilio": C. B. Brown's "Wieland," xii.); a finedrawn distinction, or subtlety (as, "*niceties* in doctrines": Defoe's "Robinson Crusoe," i. 15); a dainty or delicacy for eating (obs. or archaic).—**to a nicety,** to precisely the point or degree required; to perfection; to a turn: as, "The champagne was iced *to a nicety*" (Thackeray's "Newcomes," xxiii.).

niche (nich), *n.* [F. *niche,* < It. *nicchia.*] A recess or hollow, as in a wall; esp., an ornamental recess in a wall, etc., as for a statue or other decorative object (as, "Just over the grave, in a *niche* of the wall, is a bust of Shakspeare": Irving's "Sketch-Book," Stratford-on-Avon); fig., a place or position suitable or appropriate for a person or thing.—**niche,** *v. t.*; *niched, niching.* To place in a niche.

Niche. — Great western portal, Amiens Cathedral, France; 13th century.

nick[1] (nik), *n.* [Origin uncertain.] A notch, groove, or the like, cut into or existing in a thing (as, "It would be easy enough, by the aid of the *nicks* in the stone pillars, to climb over the brick wall": George Eliot's "Adam Bede," vi.); specif., a small groove on one side of the shank of a printing-type, serving as a guide in setting or to distinguish different types; also, a notch cut as a means of keeping a score or account (as, "That's another *nick* in the score": Kipling's "Light That Failed," iii.); hence, reckoning† or account† (as, "He loved her out of all *nick*": Shakspere's "Two Gentlemen of Verona," iv. 2. 76); also, a hollow place produced in an edge or surface, as of a dish, by breaking; also, a gap, as between hills; also, the act or an act of nicking or cutting into a thing; also, the precise moment or time of some occurrence (as, "In the *nick* of being surprised, the lovers . . . escape at a trap-door": Steele, in "Guardian," 82); the exact moment or point of time which accords with the necessities of the case, or the critical moment (as, "I never could have found him in a sweeter temper for my purpose . . . I'm just come in the *nick!*" Sheridan's "Rivals," iv. 3; "in the very *nick* of time," Smollett's "Humphry Clinker," April 30); a critical moment or point (as, "Here was a man in an interesting *nick* of life": Stevenson's "Travels with a Donkey," iii. 3); also, the exact point or mark aimed at†; also, in the game of hazard, a winning throw following the calling of a main, being the same as the main, or 11 if the main is 7, or 12 if the main is 6 or 8.—**nick**[1], *v. t.* To make a nick or nicks in; notch; also, to record by means of a notch or notches; also, to cut into or through; cut short or abridge; mark out by cutting; also, to make an incision at the root of (a horse's tail) to cause him to carry it higher; cut (a horse) thus; also, to hit, guess, catch, etc., exactly; capture or arrest (slang, Eng.: as, "He has come to get off his accomplice, and now we've just *nicked* them both," Marryat's "Japhet," lvii.); also, in the game of hazard, to throw a nick of (the main); also, to trick, cheat, or defraud (obs. or rare: as, "the . . . adventurer, who *nicked* you out of your money," Scott's "Rob Roy," iii.).

Nick[2] (nik), *n.* [Appar. for *Nicholas,* proper name.] The devil: usually *old Nick.*

nick-el (nik'ẹl), *n.* [Sw. *nickel,* abbr. of *kopparnickel,* G. *kupfernickel,* niccolite, said to mean 'copper demon,' as looking like copper but yielding none.] Chem. sym., Ni; at. wt., 58.68; sp. gr., 8.9. A hard, silvery-white, ductile and malleable metallic element, allied to iron and cobalt, not readily oxidized, and much used in the arts, in making alloys, etc.; also, a coin composed of or containing nickel, now a five-cent piece (colloq., U. S.).—**nick'el,** *v. t.*; *-eled* or *-elled, -eling* or *-elling.* To cover or coat with nickel.—**nick-el-ic** (nik'ẹl-ik or ni-kel'ik), *a.* Of or containing nickel. See *nickelous.*—**nick-el-if'er-ous** (-ẹ-lif'ẹ-rus), *a.* [See *-ferous.*] Containing or yielding nickel.—**nick-el-o'de-on** (-ẹ-lō'dẹ-ọn), *n.* [Cf. *odeum.*] A place of amusement with moving-picture exhibitions or the like, to which the price of admission is a nickel, or five cents. [U. S.]—**nick'el-ous,** *a.* Containing nickel (in larger proportion than a corresponding nickelic compound).

nick-er[1] (nik'ėr), *n.* One who or that which nicks.

nick-er[2] (nik'ėr), *v. i.* [Imit.] To neigh (as, "mounted on nags that *nicker* at the clash of the sword": Scott's "Monastery," xxxiii.); also, to laugh; snicker. [Chiefly prov.]—**nick'er**[2], *n.* A neigh; also, a laugh; a snicker. [Prov.]

nick-er[3], **nick-er=tree** (nik'ėr, -trē), *n.* [Origin uncertain.] The bonduc.—**nick'er=nut,** *n.* The seed of the bonduc. See *bonduc.*

nick-nack (nik'nak), etc. See *knickknack,* etc.

nick-name (nik'nām), *n.* [ME. *nekename,* for *ekename* (*an ekename* being taken as *a nekename*): cf. *eke*[1].] A name added to or substituted for the proper name of a person, place, etc., as in ridicule or familiarity (as, "As he [a doctor] wanted that deep magisterial voice which gives authority to a prescription . . . he . . . got the *nick-name* of the Squeaking Doctor": Steele, in "Tatler," 226); also, a familiar form of a proper name, as *Jim* for *James.*—**nick'name,** *v. t.*; *-named, -naming.* To call by an incorrect or improper name, or misname (as, "with no great care for what is *nicknamed* glory": Byron's "Don Juan," xv. 19); also, to give a nickname to, or call by a specified nickname (as, the Duke of Wellington was *nicknamed* 'Old Nosey').

ni-co-tian (ni-kō'shiạn). [From J. *Nicot,* French ambassador to Portugal, who sent tobacco to France about 1560.] **I.** *n.* Tobacco†; also, a tobacco-smoker (rare: as, "It isn't for me to throw stones . . . who have been a *Nicotian* a good deal more than half my days," Holmes's "Poet at the Breakfast-Table," v.). **II.** *a.* Pertaining to tobacco or smoking.

nic-o-tine (nik'ọ-tin or -tēn), *n.* [F., < *Nicot*: see *nicotian.*] A poisonous alkaloid, the active principle of tobacco, obtained as a colorless, or nearly colorless, oily, acrid liquid.—**nic-o-tin-ic** (nik-ọ-tin'ik), *a.* Noting an acid with pellagra-preventing action and belonging to the vitamin B complex.—**nic-o-tin-ism** (nik'ọ-tin-izm), *n.* A condition due to excessive use of tobacco.—**nic'o-tin-ize,** *v. t.*; *-ized, -izing.* To affect with nicotine.

nic-tate (nik'tāt), *v. i.*; *-tated, -tating.* [L. *nictatus,* pp. of *nictare,* wink.] To wink; nictitate.—**nic-ta'tion** (-tā'shọn), *n.*

nic-ti-tate (nik'ti-tāt), *v. i.*; *-tated, -tating.* [ML. *nictitatus,* pp. of *nictitare,* freq. of L. *nictare*: see *nictate.*] To wink.—**nictitating membrane,** in *zoöl.*, a thin membrane, or inner or third eyelid, present in many animals, capable of being drawn across the eyeball, as for protection.—**nic-ti-ta'tion** (-tā'shọn), *n.*

nid-a-men-tal (nid-ạ-men'tạl), *a.* [L. *nidamentum,* materials for a nest, nest, < *nidus,* nest.] In *zoöl.*, pertaining to or forming a covering or protection for an egg or eggs.

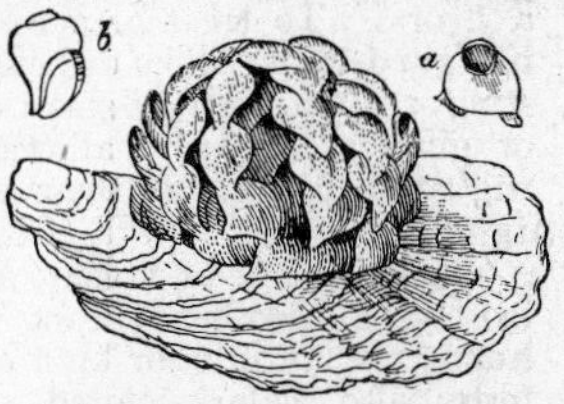

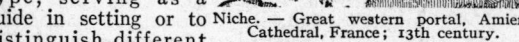

Nidamental Capsule of the Common Whelk (*Buccinum undatum*), on an oyster-shell. — *a, b,* young whelks.

nide (nīd), *n.* [L. *nidus,* nest.] A nest or brood, esp. of pheasants. [Archaic or prov. Eng.]

nid-er-ing, nid-der-ing (nid'ėr-ing). [Erron. form of *nithing.*] **I.** *n.* A cowardly or base person. [Archaic.] **II.** *a.* Cowardly; base. [Archaic.]

nidge (nij), *v. t.*; *nidged, nidging.* Same as *nig.*

nid-i-fi-cate (nid'i-fi-kāt), *v. i.*; *-cated, -cating.* [L. *nidificatus,* pp. of *nidificare,* < *nidus,* nest, + *facere,* make.] To build a nest.—**nid"i-fi-ca'tion** (-kā'shọn), *n.* The process or the manner of building a nest.

nid-i-fy (nid'i-fī), *v. i.*; *-fied, -fying.* [F. *nidifier,* < L. *nidificare*: see *nidificate.*] To build a nest; nidificate.

nid-nod (nid'nod), *v. i.* or *t.*; *-nodded, -nodding.* [Varied redupl. of *nod.*] To nod repeatedly; keep nodding: as, "Lady K. *nid-nodded* her head" (Hood's "Miss Kilmansegg," 1108).

nid-u-lant (nid'ū-lạnt), *a.* [L. *nidulans* (*-ant-*), ppr. of *nidulari,* build a nest, < *nidus,* nest.] In *bot.*, lying free, or partially embedded, in a nest-like receptacle, as sporangia; also, lying loose in a pulp, as seeds.

ni-dus (nī′dus), *n.*; pl. *niduses* or *nidi* (-dī). [L.: see *nest.*] A nest, esp. one in which insects, etc., deposit their eggs; hence, a place or source of origin or development.

niece (nēs), *n.* [OF. *niece* (F. *nièce*), < ML. *neptia*, for L. *neptis*, granddaughter, niece, akin to *nepos*, grandson, nephew: see *nephew.*] A granddaughter†, or a more remote female descendant†; also, a daughter of one's brother or sister, or (loosely) of one's husband's or wife's brother or sister; also, in euphemistic use, an illegitimate daughter of an ecclesiastic.

ni-el-list (ni-el′ist), *n.* A worker in niello.

ni-el-lo (ni-el′ō), *n.*; pl. *niellos* (-ōz), It. *nielli* (-ē). [It., < L. *nigellus*, blackish, dim. of *niger*, black.] A black metallic composition, consisting of silver, copper, lead, and sulphur, with which an incised design or ground on metal is filled in to produce an ornamental effect; ornamental work so produced; a specimen of such work.

Niello, from top of snuff-box.

nieve (nēv), *n.* [ME. *neve*, *nefe*, from Scand.: cf. Icel. *hnefi*, fist.] A closed hand; a fist: as, "The cudgel in my *nieve* did shake" (Burns's "Address to the Deil," 43). [Archaic or Sc. and prov. Eng.]

nif-ty (nif′ti). [Origin obscure.] **I.** *a.* Smart; stylish; fine. [Slang, U. S.] **II.** *n.* A smart or clever remark. [Slang, orig. theatrical, U. S.]

nig (nig), *v. t.*; *nigged*, *nigging*. [Cf. *nick*[1].] To dress (stone) with a sharp-pointed hammer.

nig-gard (nig′ärd). [ME. *nygard*, *negarde*; origin obscure.] **I.** *n.* One excessively reluctant to give or spend; a parsimonious or stingy person: as, "Little *niggard!* . . . refusing me a pecuniary request!" (C. Brontë's "Jane Eyre," xxi.). **II.** *a.* Niggardly; stingy: as, "lands which a *niggard* nature had apparently condemned to perpetual poverty" (Motley's "Dutch Republic," Introd., vi.).—**nig′gard**†, *v. t.* or *i.* To treat or act in the manner of a niggard.—**nig′gard-ly**, *a.* Like or befitting a niggard; parsimonious; stingy; often, meanly small or scanty (as, a *niggardly* sum or gift; a niggardly allowance).—**nig′gard-li-ness**, *n.*—**nig′gard-ly**, *adv.* In the manner of a niggard; stingily.

nig-ger (nig′ėr), *n.* [F. *nègre*, < Sp. *negro*, E. *negro.*] A negro (colloq. or vulgar, and commonly contemptuous); loosely, a member of any dark-skinned race.—**nig′ger-head**, *n.* An inferior kind of tobacco pressed in a twisted form; also, a dark-colored, rounded rock or boulder; also, tête-de-nègre (cloth or color).

nig-gle (nig′l), *v. i.*; *-gled*, *-gling*. [Appar. from Scand.] To trifle; work ineffectively; work with excessive care for minor or petty details.—**nig′gler**, *n.*—**nig′gling**, *p. a.* Trifling; petty; also, finical; excessively elaborate.

nigh (nī). [AS. *nēah*, *nēh*, = D. *na* = G. *nahe* = Icel. *nā* = Goth. *nehw*, nigh: cf. *near* and *next.*] **I.** *adv.* Near in space, time, or relation; also, nearly or almost (as, "*nigh* dead with feare," Spenser's "Faerie Queene," i. 3. 13; "I've been about horses *nigh* fifty year," Whyte-Melville's "Katerfelto," x.). [Chiefly archaic or prov.] **II.** *prep.* [Cf. note at *near*, *prep.*] Near to; near: as, "a bay *nigh* the northern termination of the lake" (Cooper's "Last of the Mohicans," xx.). [Chiefly archaic or prov.]—**nigh**, *a.* [AS. *nēah.*] Being near; not distant; near in relationship; also, with reference to animals or vehicles, left or near; also, short or direct (as, "I kept the left bank, as being both the *nigher* and the safer road to Liege": Scott's "Quentin Durward," xxxii.); also, parsimonious. [Chiefly archaic or prov.]—**nigh**, *v. i.* or *t.* To draw nigh (to); approach. [Archaic.]—**nigh′=hand**, *adv.* [Cf. *near-hand.*] Near at hand (as, "The shock made . . . woods and mountains all *nigh hand* resound": Fairfax's tr. Tasso's "Jerusalem Delivered," vi. 41); also, almost or nearly (as, "to *nighhand* kill one o' my horses": Lover's "Handy Andy," ix.). [Archaic or prov.]

night (nīt), *n.* [AS. *niht*, *neaht*, = D. and G. *nacht* = Icel. *nātt*, *nōtt*, = Goth. *nahts*, night; akin to L. *nox*, Gr. *νύξ*, Skt. *nakta*, night.] The interval of darkness between day and day; the time between sunset and sunrise; also, a particular interval of this kind as a point or unit of time, or on which something occurs, or which is assigned to a particular purpose, observance, etc. (as, the *night* before last; to travel three days and *nights*; the first *night* of a new play; a servant's *night* out); also, the darkness of night (as, to go out into the *night*); the dark; also, fig., a state or time of obscurity, ignorance, misfortune, depression, old age, death, etc. (as, the *night* of the dark ages; "The *night* of sorrow now is turn'd to day," Shakspere's "Venus and Adonis," 481; "Dido . . . clos'd her lids at last in endless *night*," Dryden's tr. Virgil's "Æneid," iv. 992); also, the time when darkness comes on, or nightfall (as, "the hour of *night*": Milton's "Paradise Regained," ii. 260).—**night letter.** See *letter*[2], *n.*—**night′=blind″ness**, *n.* Nyctalopia.—**night′=bloom″ing ce′re-us.** See *cereus.*—**night′cap**, *n.* A cap for the head, intended primarily to be worn in bed; also, an alcoholic drink taken before going to bed (colloq.).—**night′capped**, *a.* Wearing a nightcap.—**night′=club**, *n.* A night-resort furnishing food, drink, and entertainment, and operating as if a social club.—**night′=dress**, *n.* Dress or clothing for wearing in bed; commonly, a nightgown.—**night′ed**, *a.* Made dark as night (obs. or archaic: as, "*nighted* colour," Shakspere's "Hamlet," i. 2. 68); also, overtaken by night, or benighted (poetic).—**night′-fall**, *n.* The coming of night; the time when darkness of night falls upon the earth.—**night′=glass**, *n.* A telescope (usually binocular) constructed so as to concentrate as much light as possible, and thus adapted for use at night.—**night′-gown**, *n.* A man's or woman's dressing-gown†; also, a loose gown, commonly of cotton, worn in bed by women or children; sometimes, a man's nightshirt.—**night′gowned**, *a.* Wearing a nightgown.—**night′=hawk**, *n.* The European goatsucker or night-jar, *Caprimulgus europæus*; also, an allied American bird of the genus *Chordeiles*, as *C. virginianus*, flying chiefly by night; fig., one who is habitually up or prowling about at night (colloq.); specif., a night cabman.—**night′=her″on**, *n.* Any of certain herons of crepuscular or somewhat nocturnal habits, of the genus *Nycticorax* and allied genera, as *Nycticorax nycticorax*, the common old-world species, or *N. nycticorax nævius*, a common variety of the U. S.

Night-hawk (*Chordeiles virginianus*).

night-in-gale[1] (nī′ting-gāl or nī′tin-), *n.* [AS. *nihtegale* = D. *nachtegaal* = G. *nachtigall*, lit. 'night singer' (cf. AS. *galan*, sing).] A small old-world migratory bird of the genus *Daulias*, esp. *D. luscinia*, of Europe, noted for the melodious song of the male heard chiefly

Night-heron (*Nycticorax nycticorax*).

at night during the breeding season (and commonly attributed by poets to the female bird: as, "The solemn *nightingale* . . . all night tuned her soft lays," Milton's "Paradise Lost," vii. 435; "All about us peal'd the *nightingale*, Rapt in her song," Tennyson's "Princess," i. 217); hence, any of various other birds that sing sweetly; also, a person who sings or speaks with a melodious voice (as, the Swedish *nightingale*, Jenny Lind, the famous Swedish singer).

Nightingale (*Daulias luscinia*).

night-in-gale² (nī′ting-gāl or nī′tin-), *n.* [From Florence *Nightingale* (1820–1910), famous English nurse.] A kind of cape or wrap with sleeve-pieces, for a person confined to bed.
night=jar (nīt′jär), *n.* The European goatsucker, *Caprimulgus europæus*; hence, any goatsucker.
night=lamp (nīt′lamp), *n.* A lamp for burning during the night, as in a bedroom or a sick-room.
night=latch (nīt′lach), *n.* A spring-latch for a house-door or the like, which when adjusted for use, as at night, prevents the door from being opened from without except by a key.
night-less (nīt′les), *a.* Being without night: as, the *nightless* period in arctic regions.—**night′less-ness**, *n.*
night=light (nīt′līt), *n.* The faint light perceptible during the night; also, an artificial light, esp. a short, thick candle with a small wick, for burning during the night, as in a bedroom or a sick-room.
night=long (nīt′lông). **I.** *a.* Lasting all night: as, "Sleep . . . thou hast forged . . . A *night-long* Present of the Past" (Tennyson's "In Memoriam," lxxi.). **II.** *adv.* Throughout the whole night.
night-ly (nīt′li), *a.* [AS. *nihtlīc.*] Of, pertaining to, or characteristic of night (as, the *nightly* darkness or coolness; the *nightly* skies); coming, occurring, appearing, or active at night (as, a *nightly* visitor; *nightly* revels; *nightly* dews; "to expose themselves to the *nightly* beasts," J. H. Newman's "Callista," xxxv.); nocturnal; also, coming or occurring each night (as, *nightly* alarms or attacks; *nightly* recurrences of the disorders); also, resembling night, or dark as night (obs. or rare).—**night′ly**, *adv.* At or by night (as, "the clamorous owl that *nightly* hoots": Shakspere's "Midsummer Night's Dream," ii. 2. 6); also, every night (as, performances given *nightly* except on Sunday).
night-mare (nīt′mãr), *n.* [ME. *nightemare* (AS. *mare*, incubus).] A monster or evil spirit formerly supposed to oppress persons during sleep (as, "King Arthur panted hard, Like one that feels a *nightmare* on his bed": Tennyson's "Passing of Arthur," 345); hence, a condition during sleep, or a dream, marked by a feeling of suffocation or distress, with acute fear, anxiety, or other painful emotion (as, "I would find myself plunged . . . in some foul and ominous *nightmare*, from the which I would awaken strangling": Stevenson's "Master of Ballantrae," ix.); fig., a condition, situation, or experience suggestive of a nightmare in sleep (as, "Life is a practical *nightmare* — Hideous asleep or awake," Henley's "In Hospital," vii.; the journey was one long *nightmare*); a horrible thought or fear oppressing one; also, a sight, object, or person such as might be seen in some evil dream (as, "What could have made so handsome a young man lend his arm to assist such a *nightmare* as Sister Ursula?" Scott's "Castle Dangerous," xii.).—**night′mare**, *v. t.*; *-mared*, *-maring.* To oppress with or as with a nightmare, or as a nightmare does.
night=owl (nīt′oul), *n.* An owl of notably or exclusively nocturnal habits; fig., a person given to staying up late at night (colloq.).
night-rail (nīt′rāl), *n.* [See *rail²*.] A woman's dressing-gown or nightgown. [Archaic or prov.]
night=ra-ven (nīt′rā″vn), *n.* A bird that cries in the night; esp., a night-heron. [Now poetic.]
night=ride (nīt′rīd), *v. i.* To ride by night for lawless purposes, as a night-rider does: as, "White men of fortune and station were masking, *night-riding*, whipping and killing" (G. W. Cable's "John March, Southerner," ix.). [Southern U. S.]—**night′=rid″er** (-rī″dėr), *n.* One of a band of mounted men committing deeds of violence at night, as for purposes of intimidation or vengeance. [Southern U. S.]—**night′=rid″ing**, *n.*
nights (nīts), *adv.* During the night; at night. [Now colloq. or prov.]
night=school (nīt′sköl), *n.* A school held at night, esp. for those who cannot attend a day-school.
night-shade (nīt′shād), *n.* [AS. *nihtscada.*] Any of various plants of the genus *Solanum*, esp. *S. nigrum* ('black nightshade'), having white flowers and black poisonous berries, or *S. dulcamara* ('woody nightshade,' or bittersweet); also, any of various other solanaceous plants, as *Atropa belladonna* ('deadly nightshade,' or belladonna) or *Hyoscyamus niger* ('stinking nightshade,' or henbane).
night-shirt (nīt′shėrt), *n.* A long shirt or loose garment worn in bed by men or boys.
night=soil (nīt′soil), *n.* The contents of privies, etc., removed at night and used as manure.
night=stick (nīt′stik), *n.* A heavy stick or long club carried by a policeman at night, and sometimes in the daytime.
night=sweat (nīt′swet), *n.* In *pathol.*, a profuse sweating occurring during the night, as in certain diseases.
night=tide (nīt′tīd), *n.* Night-time. [Poetic.]
night=time (nīt′tīm), *n.* The time between evening and morning: as, "In the *night-time* once did Jason wake" (W. Morris's "Jason," i. 267).
night=walk-er (nīt′wâ″kėr), *n.* One who walks or roves about in the night, as a thief, a prostitute, etc.; also, any of various animals that move about by night, as a large earthworm.
night=watch (nīt′woch′), *n.* A watch or guard kept during the night; also, the person or persons keeping such a watch; also, a period or division of the night (usually in *pl.*: as, "when I . . . meditate on thee in the *night watches*," Ps. lxiii. 6).—**night′=watch′man** (-mạn), *n.*; pl. *-men.*
night-y (nī′ti), *n.*; pl. *nighties* (-tiz). A nightgown or nightshirt. [Colloq.]
ni-gres-cent (nī-gres′ẹnt), *a.* [L. *nigrescens* (*-ent-*), ppr. of *nigrescere*, become black, < *niger*, black.] Blackish; somewhat black.—**ni-gres′cence**, *n.*
nig-ri-fy (nig′ri-fī), *v. t.*; *-fied*, *-fying.* [LL. *nigrificare*, < L. *niger*, black, + *facere*, make.] To blacken.
Ni-gri-tian (ni-grish′ạn). **I.** *a.* Of or pertaining to Nigritia, a region in central Africa, nearly equivalent to the Sudan, and the home of the most pronounced types of the negro race; hence, of or pertaining to the negro race. **II.** *n.* An inhabitant of Nigritia; hence, a negro.
Ni-grit-ic (ni-grit′ik), *a.* Of, pertaining to, or resembling the Nigritians.
nig-ri-tude (nig′ri-tūd), *n.* [L. *nigritudo*, < *niger*, black.] The state of being black; blackness, or black color (as, "I like to meet a sweep . . . one of those tender novices. blooming through their first *nigritude*": Lamb's "Praise of Chimney-Sweepers"); also, something black.
ni-hil (nī′hil), *n.* [L. *nihil*, contr. *nil*, nothing, < *ne*, not, + *hilum*, a little thing, a whit: cf. *nil.*] Nothing; a thing of no value.
ni-hil-ism (nī′hil-izm, commonly nī′il-), *n.* [= F. *nihilisme*, < L. *nihil*, nothing.] An extreme form of skepticism, denying all real existence; also, nothingness or nonexistence; also, total disbelief in religion or moral principles and obligations, or in established laws and institutions; specif. [*l. c.* or *cap.*], the principles of a Russian revolutionary party, active in the latter half of the 19th century, holding that existing social and political institutions must be destroyed in order to clear the way for a new state of society, and in its extreme measures employing terrorism, assassination, etc. (as in the assassination of the Czar Alexander II. with bombs, in 1881).—**ni′hil-ist**, *n.* One who believes in or advocates some form of nihilism; specif. [*l. c.* or *cap.*], one of the party advocating, or seeking to enforce, the principles of Russian nihilism.—**ni-hil-is′tic**, *a.* Of or pertaining to nihilists or nihilism.

ni-hil-i-ty (nī-hil′i-ti), *n.* [L. *nihil*, nothing.] Nothingness; also, a mere nothing; a nullity.

nil (nil), *n.* [L., contr. of *nihil.*] Nothing.

Nile (nīl) **blue.** [From the river *Nile*, in Egypt.] A pale greenish-blue color.—**Nile green.** A pale green with a tinge of blue.

nil-gau, nil-gai (nil′gâ, -gī), *n.* [Pers. *nīlgāu*, Hind. *nīlgāī*, 'blue ox.'] A large East Indian antelope, *Boselaphus tragocamelus*, of a bluish-gray color.

Nilgau.

nill (nil), *v. t.* or *i.* [AS. *nyllan*, *nellan*, for *ne willan*, 'not will.'] Not to will, wish, or like; oppose or be unwilling: now only in certain archaic phrases, in opposition to *will*: as, will he, *nill* he (whether he will or not: cf. *willy-nilly*); "Will you, *nill* you, I will marry you" (Shakspere's "Taming of the Shrew," ii. 1. 273).

Ni-lom-e-ter (nī-lom′e-tėr), *n.* [Gr. Νειλομέτριον, < Νεῖλος, the Nile, + μέτρον, measure.] A graduated column or the like used to measure the height of the floods of the Nile; hence [*l. c.*], any instrument for making a continuous and automatic register of river-heights.

Ni-lot-ic (nī-lot′ik), *a.* [L. *Niloticus*, < Gr. Νειλωτικός.] Of or pertaining to the river Nile or the inhabitants of the Nile region.

nim (nim), *v. t.*; *nimmed*, *nimming.* [AS. *niman* = D. *nemen* = G. *nehmen* = Icel. *nema* = Goth. *niman*, take: cf. *nimble* and *numb.*] To take; seize; hence, to steal (as, "They'll question Mars, and, by his look, Detect who 'twas that *nimmed* a cloak": Butler's "Hudibras," i. 1). [Archaic.]

nim-ble (nim′bl), *a.*; compar. *nimbler*, superl. *nimblest.* [ME. *nymel*, < AS. *numol*, quick at taking, < *niman*, take: see *nim.*] Quick and light in movement, or moving with celerity and ease (as, *nimble* feet or fingers; "He had stripped off his coat, that he might be more *nimble* in his motions," Smollett's "Humphry Clinker," April 24); agile, active, or rapid; hence, circulating briskly, as money; also, quick in apprehending, devising, etc. (as, *nimble* wits; a *nimble* fancy; a mind or a person *nimble* in debate). —**nim′ble-ness**, *n.*—**nim′bly**, *adv.*

nim-bus (nim′bus), *n.*; pl. *-buses* or *-bi* (-bī). [L., rainstorm, cloud.] A bright cloud anciently conceived to surround a deity of the classical mythology when appearing on earth; hence, a cloud or atmosphere of some kind surrounding a person or thing; in *art*, a disk or otherwise shaped figure representing a radiance about the head of a divine or sacred personage, a medieval sovereign, etc.; in *meteor.*, the type of cloud or cloud-mass, dense, with ragged edges, which yields rain or snow; a rain-cloud.

The Nimbus as variously represented.—1, God the Father; 2 and 3, Christ; 4, Charlemagne; 5, Emperor Henry II.

ni-mi-e-ty (ni-mī′ẹ-ti), *n.* [L. *nimietas*, < *nimius*, excessive, < *nimis*, too much.] Excess; redundancy.

nim-i-ny=pim-i-ny (nim′i-ni-pim′i-ni), *a.* [Imit. of a mincing utterance.] Mincing; affectedly nice, refined, or delicate: as, a *niminy-piminy* creature; a *niminy-piminy* lisp or manner.

Nim-rod (nim′rod), *n.* [From *Nimrod*, described in Gen. x. 9 as "a mighty hunter before the Lord."] A 'mighty hunter'; one expert in or devoted to hunting: as, "The Baronet . . . took to fox hunting like a perfect *Nimrod*" (Irving's "Tales of a Traveler," i. 2); "A tiger-hunting party would not be the thing without some seasoned *Nimrod* to advise and direct us" (F. M. Crawford's "Mr. Isaacs," vi.).

nin-com-poop (nin′kọm-pöp), *n.* [Prob. a made word.] A fool, simpleton, or blockhead: as, "I was hectored and lectured in my own greenroom, and made an absolute *nincompoop* on my own stage" (Irving's "Tales of a Traveler," ii. 10).

nine (nīn). [AS. *nigon* = D. *negen* = G. *neun* = Icel. *nīu* = Goth. *niun*, nine; akin to L. *novem*, Gr. ἐννέα, Skt. *nava*, nine.] **I.** *a.* One more than eight. **II.** *n.* A number composed of nine units, or a symbol, as 9 or ix, representing it; a set of nine persons or things, as a team of baseball players; a playing-card with nine pips.—**the Nine**, the nine Muses.—**nine′bark**, *n.* An American rosaceous shrub, *Opulaster opulifolius*, with alternate lobed leaves and corymbose white flowers, and a bark that peels off in numerous thin layers.—**nine′fold** (-fōld). **I.** *a.* Comprising nine parts or members; nine times as great or as much. **II.** *n.* A ninefold amount or number. **III.** *adv.* In ninefold measure.—**nine′pence** (-pẹns), *n.* The sum of nine English pennies, or about 18 U. S. cents; also, a coin of this value.—**nine′-pins** (-pinz), *n.* A game played with nine wooden pins at which a ball is bowled to knock them down (construed as *sing.*); also, the pins used in this game (construed as *pl.*).

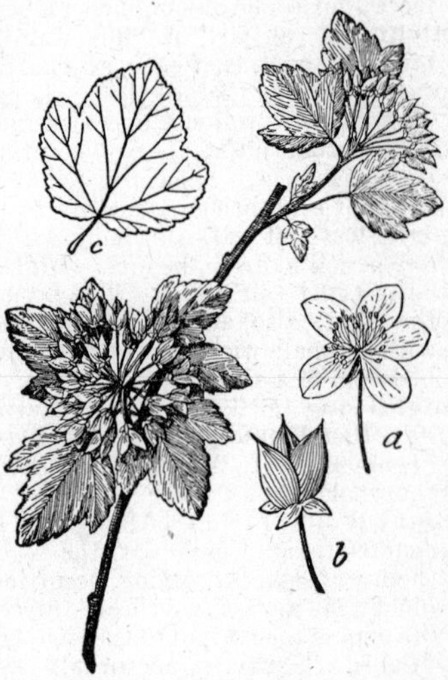

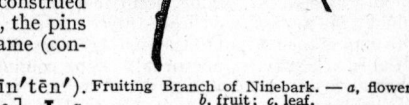

Fruiting Branch of Ninebark.—*a*, flower; *b*, fruit; *c*, leaf.

nine-teen (nīn′tēn′). [AS. *nigontȳne.*] **I.** *a.* Nine more than ten. **II.** *n.* A number composed of nineteen units, or a symbol, as 19 or xix, representing it.—**nine′teenth′**, *a.* Next after the eighteenth; also, being one of nineteen equal parts.—**nineteenth hole**, humorously, a stage in the course of a golf-player, after the eighteenth (and last) hole, at which he resorts to liquid refreshments.—**nine′teenth′**, *n.* The nineteenth member of a series; also, a nineteenth part.

nine-ti-eth (nīn′ti-eth). **I.** *a.* Next after the eighty-ninth; also, being one of ninety equal parts. **II.** *n.* The ninetieth member of a series; also, a ninetieth part.

nine-ty (nīn′ti). [AS. *nigontig.*] **I.** *a.* Nine times ten. **II.** *n.*; pl. *-ties* (-tiz). A number composed of ninety units, or a symbol, as 90 or xc, representing it.

nin-ny (nin′i), *n.*; pl. *ninnies* (-iz). [Origin uncertain.] A fool; a simpleton: as, "What a pied *ninny*'s this!" (Shakspere's "Tempest," iii. 2. 71); "Prince Adolf, between ourselves, is a *ninny*" (H. James's "Europeans," ii.).

nin-ny-ham-mer (nin′i-ham″ėr), *n.* Same as *ninny.*

ninth (nīnth). **I.** *a.* Next after the eighth; also, being one of nine equal parts. **II.** *n.* The ninth member of a series; also, a ninth part; in *music*, a tone distant from another tone by an interval of an octave and a second; the interval between such tones; the harmonic combination of such tones. —**ninth′ly**, *adv.*

Ni-o-be (nī′ọ-bē), *n.* [From *Niobe*, daughter of Tantalus, of Greek legend, who, even after being turned to stone, wept for her children, slain because of her boasting of them.] A woman who weeps unrestrainedly or incessantly; also, an inconsolable bereaved mother (sometimes fig.: as, "The *Niobe* of nations! there she [Rome] stands, Childless and crownless, in her voiceless woe," Byron's "Childe Harold," iv. 79).—**Ni-o-be′an,** *a.*

ni-o-bi-um (nī-ō′bi-um), *n.* [NL.; named from *Niobe,* daughter of Tantalus, because found associated with tantalum, named from Tantalus.] In *chem.*, same as *columbium*: abbreviated *Nb* (no period).—**ni-o′bic,** *a.*

nip[1] (nip), *v.*; *nipped, nipping.* [ME. *nyppen*: cf. D. *knippen,* clip, snip, snap, catch.] **I.** *tr.* To compress sharply between two surfaces or points; pinch; bite suddenly, as an animal does; also, to take off by pinching, biting, or snipping (commonly with *off*: as, to *nip* off buds or shoots from a plant); hence, fig., to check in growth or development as if by taking off buds (now chiefly in 'to nip in the bud,' to check or stop at the very beginning); also, to affect sharply and painfully or injuriously, as cold does (as, "A chill wind was blowing that *nipped* him sharply," Jack London's "Call of the Wild," ii.; plants *nipped* by frost); irritate or vex keenly, or sting, as unpleasant circumstances, speeches, etc., do; also, to snatch or take suddenly or quickly (*away, up,* etc.: prov. or colloq.: as, "She . . . *nipped* up her petticoats, when she came out, as quick and sharp as ever I see," Mrs. Gaskell's "Cranford," viii.); purloin or steal (slang: as, "Now you get hold of all the door-keys you can find, and I'll *nip* all of auntie's," Mark Twain's "Tom Sawyer," xxvii.). **II.** *intr.* To move or go suddenly or quickly, or slip (*away, off, up,* etc.). [Prov. or colloq.] —**nip**[1], *n.* The act of nipping; a pinch (as, "I gave Mrs. Nugent a kindly *nip* on her sonsy arm": Galt's "Annals of the Parish," xxxvii.); the painful or injurious action of sharp cold, or a sharp touch of frost (as, "So have I seen some tender slip, Sav'd with care from winter's *nip*": Milton's "Epitaph on the Marchioness of Winchester," 36); a biting quality, as in cold or frosty air; a sharp or biting remark; also, a small bit or quantity of anything.—**nip and tuck** (cf. *tuck*[1], *n.*), in a race or other contest, with one competitor equaling the speed or efforts of the other: as, "So they had it, *nip and tuck,* for five miles or more" (Mark Twain's "Huckleberry Finn," xviii.). [U. S.]

nip[2] (nip), *n.* [Origin uncertain.] A small quantity or draft of spirits or the like.

ni-pa (nē′pä or nī′pä), *n.* [Malay *nīpah.*] A palm, *Nypa fruticans,* of the East Indies, the Philippines, etc., whose foliage is much used for thatching, mat-making, etc.; also, the foliage.

nip-per (nip′ėr), *n.* One who or that which nips; *sing.* or (usually) *pl.*, a device for nipping, as pincers or forceps; *pl.*, handcuffs; *sing.*, one of the great claws of a crustacean; one of the incisors of a horse; also, a small boy (colloq.).

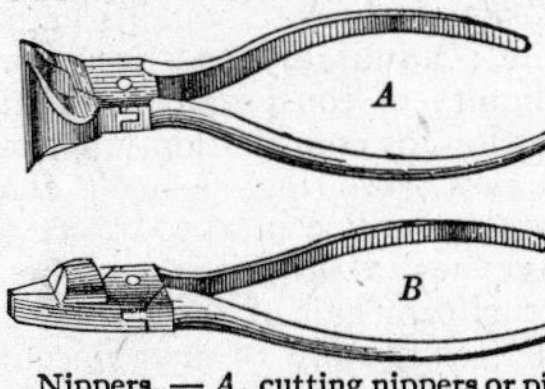

Nippers. — *A,* cutting nippers or pincers; *B,* combined cutting nippers and ordinary pliers.

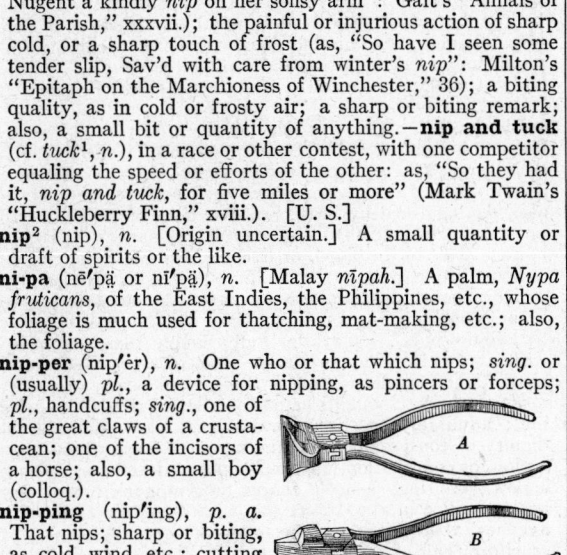

nip-ping (nip′ing), *p. a.* That nips; sharp or biting, as cold, wind, etc.; cutting or sarcastic (as, *nipping* speeches; "'My opinion is,' said Aunt Lois, in her most *nipping* tones, 'that if folks don't mind their own business . . . the Millennium won't come at all,'" Mrs. Stowe's "Oldtown Folks," iv.).—**nip′ping-ly,** *adv.*

nip-ple (nip′l), *n.* [Formerly also *nibble* and *neble*; origin uncertain.] A protuberance of the mamma or breast where, in the female, the milk-ducts discharge; a teat; hence, something resembling it, as the mouthpiece of a nursing-bottle; also, a short piece of pipe used as a coupling.

Nip-pon-ese (nip-on-ēs′ or -ēz′). **I.** *a.* Of or pertaining to Nippon, or Japan; Japanese. **II.** *n.*; pl. *-ese.* A Japanese.

nip-py (nip′i), *a.* Apt to nip; sharp; biting; also, keen, smart, or active (slang, Eng.); also, smart in appearance, or stylish (slang, orig. Eng.); also, grasping, avaricious, or stingy (Sc. and prov. Eng.).

nir-va-na (nir-vä′nạ), *n.* [Skt., a blowing out (as of a light), extinction.] [Also *cap.*] In Buddhism, the extinction of the individual soul by absorption into the universal; the attainment of perfect happiness by the annihilation of all desire, passion, unrest, etc.

Ni-san (nī′san), *n.* [Heb.] In the Jewish calendar, the seventh month (30 days) of the civil year and the first of the ecclesiastical year, beginning in the latter part of March or the first part of April.

ni-si (nī′sī), *conj.* [L.] Unless: a term used esp. in law, as after *decree, order,* etc., to specify or suggest some contingency.

ni-sus (nī′sus), *n.* [L., < *niti,* strive.] Effort; endeavor; impulse; esp., an instinctive or natural impulse toward some action or condition.

nit (nit), *n.* [AS. *hnitu* = G. *niss.*] The egg of a louse or similar insect; also, the insect itself while young.

ni-ter, ni-tre (nī′tėr), *n.* [OF. F. *nitre,* < L. *nitrum,* < Gr. *νίτρον,* natron, native sodium carbonate: cf. *natron.*] Native carbonate of sodium†, or natron†; also, nitrate of potassium, KNO_3, a white salt used in making gunpowder, etc.; saltpeter; also, nitrate of sodium, or Chile saltpeter. —**sweet spirit of niter,** an alcoholic solution of ethyl nitrite, $C_2H_5NO_2$, employed medicinally as a diaphoretic, diuretic, and antispasmodic.

ni-thing (nī′ᴛʜing), *n.* [AS. *nīthing* = Icel. *nīdhingr*: cf. *nidering.*] A cowardly or despicable person; a base wretch. [Obs. or archaic.]

nit-id (nit′id), *a.* [L. *nitidus,* < *nitere,* shine: cf. *neat*[2].] Bright; shining; lustrous; glossy. [Now rare.]

ni-to (nē′tō), *n.* [Philippine.] In the Philippine Islands, a climbing fern, *Lygodium scandens,* the glossy, wiry stems of which are woven into hats and other articles. See *lygodium.*

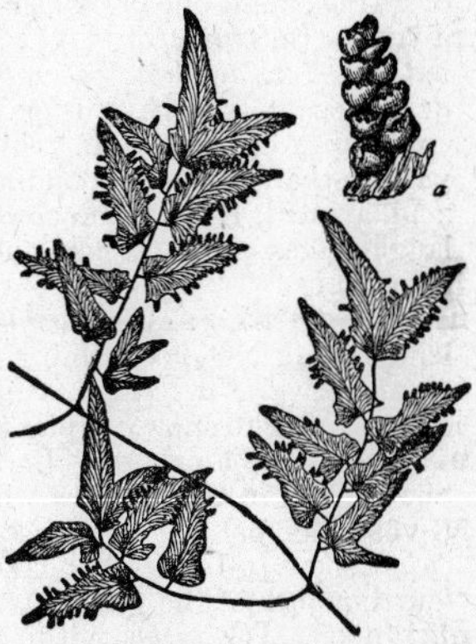

Nito. — *a,* group of sporangia, enlarged.

ni-ton (nī′ton), *n.* [NL., < L. *nitere,* shine.] Chem. sym., Nt; at. wt., 222.4. A gas, the radium emanation, now regarded as an element.

ni-trate (nī′trāt), *n.* In *chem.*, a salt of nitric acid; in *agric.*, potassium nitrate or sodium nitrate, employed as a fertilizer.—**ni′trate,** *v. t.*; *-trated, -trating.* To treat with nitric acid or a nitrate; convert into a nitrate.

ni′tre, *n.* See *niter.*

ni-tric (nī′trik), *a.* Of or pertaining to niter or nitrogen; specif., noting or pertaining to a nitrogen-containing compound in which the nitrogen has a higher valence than in a corresponding nitrous compound (as, *nitric* acid, a corrosive liquid, HNO_3, with powerful oxidizing properties; *nitric* oxide, a colorless gaseous compound of nitrogen and oxygen, NO, formed when copper is treated with dilute nitric acid).

ni-tride (nī′trīd or -trid), *n.* In *chem.*, a compound of nitrogen with a more electropositive element or radical, as phosphorus, boron, or a metal.

ni-tri-fy (nī′tri-fī), *v. t.*; *-fied, -fying.* [See *niter* and *-fy.*] To convert into niter; oxidize (ammonia compounds, etc.) to nitrites or nitrates, esp. by bacterial action; impregnate (soil, etc.) with nitrates.—**ni″tri-fi-ca′tion** (-fi-kā′shọn), *n.* —**ni′tri-fi-er** (-fī-ėr), *n.*

ni-trile (nī′tril), *n.* [From *nitrogen.*] In *organic chem.*, any of a class of compounds which are regarded as cyanides of hydrocarbon radicals or as compounds derived from ammonia by replacing its three hydrogen atoms by a single carbon atom to which is united a monovalent hydrocarbon radical.

ni-trite (nī′trīt), *n.* In *chem.*, a salt of nitrous acid.

nitro-. Form of L. *nitrum,* Gr. *νίτρον,* native sodium carbonate, used in combination to represent E. *niter* (in its modern sense, potassium nitrate), and sometimes implying *nitric* or *nitrogen* or indicating the presence of the radical nitryl, NO_2 (in this last sense, also as adj., *nitro*).—**ni-tro-bac-te-ri-a** (nī″trō-bak-tē′ri-ạ), *n. pl.* Certain bacteria of the soil, concerned in nitrifying processes.—**ni-tro-ben′zene** (-ben′zēn), *n.* A yellowish liquid, $C_6H_5NO_2$, a derivative of benzene, with an odor like that of oil of bitter almonds: used in the manufacture of aniline, and in perfumery and candy. Also **ni-tro-ben′zol** (-zol or -zōl).—**ni-tro-cel′lu-lose** (-sel′ū-lōs), *n.* A common name for cellulose nitrate. See *cellulose nitrate*, under *cellulose*[1], and cf. *guncotton*.—**ni-tro-gel′a-tin** (-jel′ạ-tin), *n.* An explosive of jelly-like consistence, containing nitroglycerin, guncotton, and camphor.

ni-tro-gen (nī′trọ-jen), *n.* [F. *nitrogène*, < *nitre*, niter, + Gr. γεν-, bear, produce.] Chem. sym., N; at. wt., 14.01. A colorless, odorless gaseous element which forms about four fifths of the volume of the air and is present (combined) in animal and vegetable tissue.—**ni′tro-gen=fix″ing**, *a.* Causing atmospheric nitrogen to combine with elements in the soil: said of certain bacteria, and of certain plants whose roots serve as hosts for bacteria.—**ni-trog-e-nize** (nī-troj′e-nīz), *v. t.*; *-nized*, *-nizing*. To combine or impregnate with nitrogen.—**ni-trog′e-nous**, *a.* Containing nitrogen.

ni-tro-gly-cer-in (nī-trọ-glis′ẹ-rin), *n.* [See *nitro-*.] An oily, explosive liquid made by treating glycerin with nitric and sulphuric acids: used in blasting, etc., and in making dynamite.

ni-trom-e-ter (nī-trom′e-tėr), *n.* [See *nitro-* and *-meter*.] An apparatus for determining the amount of nitrogen, nitrates, or the like, in a substance or compound.

ni-tro-so- (nī-trō′sọ-). Form of NL. *nitrosus*, nitrous, used in combination to indicate the presence of nitrosyl.

ni-tro-syl (nī′trọ-sil), *n.* [NL. *nitrosus*, nitrous: see *-yl*.] In *chem.*, a univalent radical, NO, composed of one atom of nitrogen and one of oxygen.—**ni-tro-syl′ic**, *a.*

ni-trous (nī′trus), *a.* [NL. *nitrosus*, nitrous, L. full of natron, < L. *nitrum*: see *niter*.] Of or pertaining to niter or nitrogen; specif., noting or pertaining to a nitrogen-containing compound in which the nitrogen has a lower valence than in a corresponding nitric compound (as, *nitrous* acid, an acid, HNO_2, known only in solution; *nitrous* oxide, laughing-gas, N_2O, a gaseous compound of nitrogen and oxygen).

ni-tryl (nī′tril), *n.* [See *nitro-* and *-yl*.] In *chem.*, a univalent radical, NO_2, containing nitrogen and oxygen.

ni-val (nī′vạl), *a.* [L. *nivalis*, < *nix* (*niv-*), snow.] Of or pertaining to snow; of plants, growing in or near the snow.

niv-e-ous (niv′ẹ̄-us), *a.* [L. *niveus*, < *nix* (*niv-*), snow.] Snowy, esp. in color; snow-white.

Ni-vôse (nē-vōz), *n.* [F. *nivôse*, < L. *nivosus*, snowy, < *nix* (*niv-*), snow.] In the calendar of the first French republic, the fourth month of the year, extending from Dec. 21 to Jan. 19.

nix[1] (niks). [G. *nichts*, nothing.] **I.** *n.* Nothing. [Slang.] **II.** *adv.* No. [Slang.]

nix[2] (niks), *n.* [G. *nix*, masc.] In *Teut. myth.*, a water-spirit, usually small, and either good or bad.—**nix-ie** (nik′si), *n.* [G. *nixe*, fem.] In *Teut. myth.*, a female water-spirit: as, "She who sits by haunted well, Is subject to the *Nixie's* spell" (Scott's "Pirate," xxviii.).

Ni-zam (ni-zäm′), *n.* [Hind. and Turk. *nizām*, < Ar. *nazama*, arrange, govern.] The hereditary title of the native rulers of Hyderabad, India; also [*l. c.*], the soldiers, or one of the soldiers, of the Turkish regular army.

no[1] (nō), *adv.* [AS. *nā*, *nō* (= Icel. *nei*), < *ne*, not, + *ā*, *ō*, ever: see *ne* and *ay*[1], and cf. *nay*.] Not (now only Sc. and prov. Eng., or in phrases like 'whether or no'); also, not in any degree, or not at all (used with a comparative: as, he is *no* better); also, a word used to express dissent, denial, or refusal, as in response (as, 'Will you come?' '*No.*'), or to emphasize a previous negative or qualify a previous statement (as, it is not fair, *no*, it is unjust; I must, *no*, I do believe it) (opposed to *yes*).—**no**[1], *n.*; pl. *noes* (nōz). An utterance of the word 'no'; a denial or refusal; specif., a negative vote or voter.

no[2] (nō), *a.* [ME. *no*, reduced form of *non*, E. *none*.] Not any (as, *no* money or friends; he and *no* other; of *no* use; by *no* means); also, not at all, or very far from being, or not at all a (as, this was *no* harmless trifling; he is *no* genius; "Turnbull . . . caught hold of her with *no* very gentle grasp," Scott's "Castle Dangerous," xvii.).—**no one**, no person; nobody.

No-a-chi-an (nọ-ā′ki-ạn), *a.* Of or pertaining to the patriarch Noah or his time (as, the *Noachian* deluge); fig., extremely ancient or old-fashioned. Also **No-a′chic** (-kik).

nob[1] (nob), *n.* [Prob. = *knob*.] The head (slang); in *cribbage*, the knave of the same suit as the card turned up, counting one to the holder.

nob[2] (nob), *n.* [Origin uncertain.] A person of wealth or social distinction (as, "His ship was full of '*nobs*,' as they term it in the British navy, or the sons and relatives of nobles": Cooper's "Two Admirals," xx.); also, *pl.*, with a possessive pronoun (esp. *his*), a facetious title of respect, as if for an important personage (cf. *nibs*). [Slang.]

nob-ble (nob′l), *v. t.*; *-bled*, *-bling*. [Origin uncertain.] To tamper with (a horse), as by drugging it, in order to destroy its chance of winning a race; also, to win over (a person, etc.) by illicit or underhand means; get or take (money, etc.) dishonestly; swindle (as, "I don't know out of how much the reverend party has *nobbled* his poor old sister": Thackeray's "Newcomes," xxv.); also, to seize, catch, or capture. [Slang, Eng.]

nob-by (nob′i), *a.* [From *nob*[2].] Smart, fashionable, or elegant, as persons, the appearance, clothes, etc.; also, capital or first-rate (as, "We'll play Robin Hood — it's *nobby* fun": Mark Twain's "Tom Sawyer," xxvi.). [Slang.]

no-bil-i-a-ry (nọ-bil′i-ạ-ri), *a.* [F. *nobiliaire*, < L. *nobilis*, E. *noble*.] Of or pertaining to the nobility: as, *nobiliary* rank; a *nobiliary* particle (a preposition such as the French *de* or the German *von* used distinctively in the titles or names of persons belonging to the nobility).

no-bil-i-ty (nọ-bil′i-ti), *n.*; pl. *-ties* (-tiz). [OF. *nobilite*, < L. *nobilitas*.] The state or quality of being noble; noble birth or rank; special hereditary preëminence in virtue of birth or of authoritative grant (as, "No title of *nobility* shall be granted by the United States": Constitution of the United States, i. 9. 8); exalted moral excellence, as of personal character; admirable dignity, as of conception; imposingness, as of appearance; also, the noble class, or the body of nobles, in a country or state; in Great Britain and Ireland, the peerage.

no-ble (nō′bl). [OF. F. *noble*, < L. *nobilis*, well-known, famous, high-born, noble, from the stem of *noscere*, know: see *know*.] **I.** *a.*; compar. *nobler*, superl. *noblest*. Famous, illustrious, or great, as persons or their achievements, etc.†; also, distinguished by birth, rank, or title, or pertaining to persons so distinguished (as, a *noble* personage, family, or house; *noble* birth, blood, or lineage); specif., belonging to or constituting a class (the nobility) possessing a hereditary social or political preëminence in a country or state (as, to become *noble* by royal patent; "My children will be *noble* by two descents," Marryat's "Peter Simple," lx.; a country without a *noble* order or class); also, of an exalted moral character or excellence (as, a *noble* man, heart, or spirit; *noble* qualities, thoughts, aims, words, or deeds; a *noble* life); admirably fine in a moral aspect; also, admirable in dignity of conception, or in the manner of expression, execution, or composition (as, a *noble* poem, drama, or oration; a *noble* painting; a *noble* chorus or symphony); also, imposing or fine in appearance (as, a *noble* prospect; a *noble* avenue; a *noble* arch, dome, mansion, or monument; "a cruciform hall of *noble* dimensions," Wiseman's "Fabiola," ii. 20); stately or magnificent; also, of an admirably high quality, type, or class (as, *noble* wines or vintages; a *noble* feast; a *noble* prize; a *noble* animal; "skill of *noblest* architects," Milton's "Paradise Regained," iv. 52); fine, choice, notably superior, or superexcellent; of metals, minerals, etc., precious or valuable. **II.** *n.* A person of noble birth or rank; a nobleman; in Great Britain and Ireland, a peer;

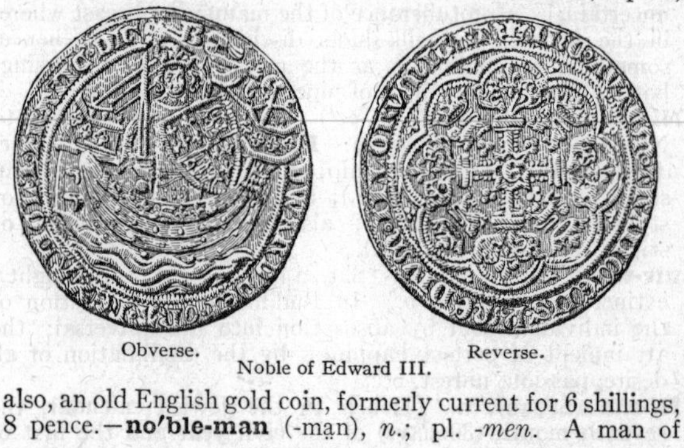

Obverse. Reverse.
Noble of Edward III.

also, an old English gold coin, formerly current for 6 shillings, 8 pence.—**no′ble-man** (-mạn), *n.*; pl. *-men*. A man of noble birth or rank; a noble; hence, one of some other specially favored or superior class (as, "The warrior, from the excellence of his physical proportions, might certainly have been regarded as one of nature's *noblemen*," H. Melville's "Typee," x.; "I will go with Paul Tregarva, whom I honour and esteem as one of God's own *noblemen*," Kingsley's "Yeast," xi.).—**no′ble=mind′ed,** *a.* Having or showing a noble mind; magnanimous.—**no′ble=mind′ed-ness,** *n.*—**no′ble-ness,** *n.*

no-blesse (nō-bles′, F. no-bles), *n.* [F., < *noble*, E. *noble*.] Noble birth or condition; also, persons of noble rank collectively; the nobility.

no-ble-wom-an (nō′bl-wům″ạn), *n.*; pl. *-women* (-wim″en). A woman of noble birth or rank.

no-bly (nō′bli), *adv.* In a noble manner.

no-bod-y (nō′bọd-i or nō′bod-i), *n.*; pl. *-ies* (-iz). No person, or no one (as, "Ill blows the wind that profits *nobody*": Shakspere's '3 Henry VI.," ii. 5. 55); also, no one of importance (as, don't mind him — he is *nobody*); a person of no importance, esp. socially (as, to marry a *nobody*; a host of *nobodies* were present).

no-cent (nō′sẹnt), *a.* [L. *nocens* (*nocent-*), ppr. of *nocere*, harm, hurt: cf. *innocent*.] Hurtful, harmful, or injurious; also, guilty or criminal. [Now rare.]

nock (nok), *n.* [ME. *nocke*, bow tip: cf. D. *nok* (naut.).] A tip of horn at either end of a bow, with a notch for holding the string†; also, a piece at the butt-end of an arrow, with a notch for the bowstring; hence, the notch itself, of either a bow or an arrow; *naut.*, the forward upper corner of a sail set to a boom or of a staysail cut with a square tack.—**nock,** *v. t.* To furnish (a bow or an arrow) with a nock; also, to adjust (the arrow) to the bowstring, in readiness to shoot.

noct-, nocti-. Forms of L. *nox* (*noct-*), night, used in combination.

noc-tam-bu-lism (nok-tam′bū-lizm), *n.* [L. *nox* (*noct-*), night, + *ambulare*, walk.] Somnambulism.—**noc-tam′bu-list,** *n.* A somnambulist.

noc-ti-flo-rous (nok-ti-flō′rus), *a.* [See *nocti-* and *-florous*.] In *bot.*, flowering at night.

noc-ti-lu-ca (nok-ti-lū′kạ), *n.*; pl. *-cæ* (-sē). [L., something that shines by night, < *nox* (*noct-*), night, + *lucere*, shine.] A pelagic flagellate protozoan (genus *Noctiluca*), notable for its phosphorescence.

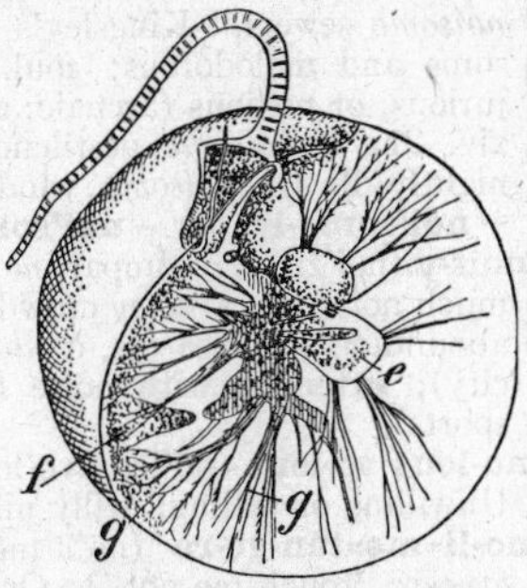

Noctiluca (*N. miliaris*).—*e*, gastric vacuole; *f*, anal aperture; *g*, *g*, radiating filaments. (Magnified.)

noc-ti-lu-cent (nok-ti-lū′sẹnt), *a.* [L. *nox* (*noct-*), night, + *lucens* (*lucent-*), ppr. of *lucere*, shine.] Shining or luminous at night.—**noc-ti-lu′cence,** *n.*

noc-tiv-a-gant (nok-tiv′ạ-gạnt), *a.* [L. *nox* (*noct-*), night, + *vagans* (*vagant-*), ppr. of *vagari*, wander.] Wandering by night.

noc-tu-id (nok′tū-id). [NL. *Noctuidæ*, pl., < L. *noctua*, night-owl, < *nox* (*noct-*), night.] **I.** *n.* Any of the *Noctuidæ*, or owlet-moths, a large family of (mostly) medium-sized and dull-colored nocturnal moths, having usually naked larvæ many of which are highly injurious to vegetation and crops. See *army-worm*, *boll-worm*, *cotton-worm*, and *cutworm*. **II.** *a.* Belonging or pertaining to the *Noctuidæ*.

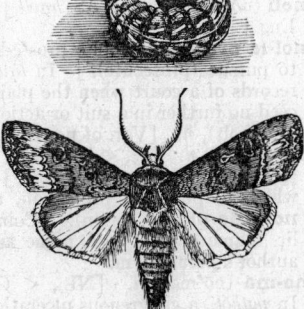

Noctuid. — Above, a larva (cutworm); below, a moth.

noc-turn (nok′tėrn), *n.* [OF. F. *nocturne*, < L. *nocturnus*: see *nocturnal*.] An ecclesiastical office forming a part of matins.

noc-tur-nal (nok-tėr′nạl), *a.* [LL. *nocturnalis*, < L. *nocturnus*, of or in the night, < *nox* (*noct-*), night: see *night*.] Of or pertaining to the night; done, occurring, or coming by night; active by night, as certain animals; opening by night and closing by day, as certain flowers.—**noc-tur′nal-ly,** *adv.*

noc-turne (nok′tėrn or nok-tėrn′), *n.* [F.: see *nocturn*.] In *music*, a piece appropriate to the night or evening, esp. an instrumental composition of a dreamy or pensive character; in *painting*, a night scene.

nod (nod), *v.*; *nodded*, *nodding*. [ME. *nodden*; origin uncertain.] **I.** *intr.* To make a slight, quick inclination of the head, as in assent, salutation, beckoning, or command, or with other significance (as, "He *nods* at us, as who should say, I'll be even with you": Shakspere's "2 Henry VI.," iv. 7. 99); also, to let the head fall or slip forward with a sudden, involuntary movement when drowsy or sleepy (as, "The sentinel . . . began to *nod* at his post": Irving's "Captain Bonneville," xxiv.); hence, fig., to be guilty of a lapse or inadvertence, or grow careless or dull, as if yielding to drowsiness (as, Homer sometimes *nods* — a saying derived from Horace's "Ars Poetica," 359); also, of trees, branches, flowers, plumes, etc., to droop, bend, or incline with a swaying motion (as, "Or columbines, in purple dressed, *Nod* o'er the ground-bird's hidden nest": Bryant's "To the Fringed Gentian"); of structures, etc., to sway or totter, as if about to fall. **II.** *tr.* To incline (the head) in a short, quick movement, as of assent, salutation, or the like; express or signify by such a movement of the head (as, to *nod* assent); summon, bring, or send by a nod of the head (as, "Cleopatra Hath *nodded* him to her," Shakspere's "Antony and Cleopatra," iii. 6. 66; to *nod* a person away); also, in general, to incline, or cause to lean or sway (as, "when the whale-boats . . . *nodded* their slender masts at each other, and the dories pitched and tossed in the surf": Hawthorne's "Twice-Told Tales," The Village Uncle).—**nod,** *n.* A short, quick inclination of the head, as in assent, salutation, or command (as, "With mute obeisance, grave and slow, Repaid by *nod* polite": Holmes's "Agnes," i.); also, a sudden, involuntary inclination or movement of the head from drowsiness; hence, a short sleep, or nap; also, in general, a bending or swaying movement of anything.—**land of nod.** See under *land*, *n.*

no-dal (nō′dạl), *a.* Pertaining to or of the nature of a node.

nod-der (nod′ėr), *n.* One who nods.

nod-ding (nod′ing), *p. a.* That nods; in *bot.*, bent downward, or cernuous, as the flowers of the cyclamen.—**nod′ding=cap,** *n.* An orchidaceous plant, *Triphora trianthophora*, of eastern North America, with nodding purple flowers.—**nod′ding-ly,** *adv.*

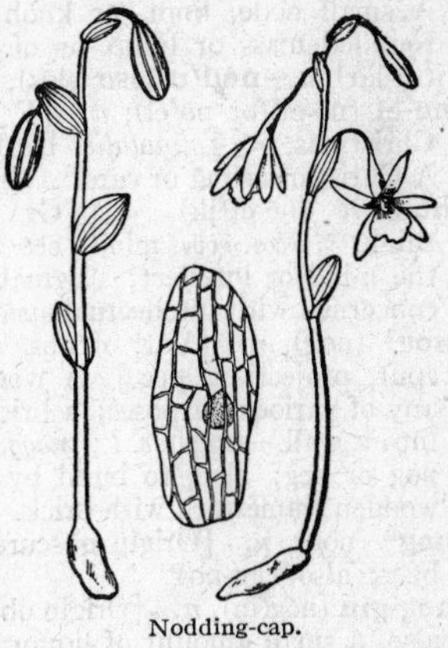
Nodding-cap.

nod-dle (nod′l), *n.* [ME. *nodel*, *nodul*; origin obscure.] The head: as, "Just now I've taen the fit o' rhyme, My barmie *noddle*'s working prime" (Burns's "To James Smith," 20). [Colloq.]—**nod′dled,** *a.* Having a noddle or head (as specified): as, "idle, empty-*noddled* boarders" (Arnold Bennett's "Hilda Lessways," vi. 6). [Colloq.]

nod-dy (nod′i), *n.*; pl. *noddies* (-iz). [Perhaps < *nod*.] A fool or simpleton (as, "an arrant *noddy*": Beaumont and Fletcher's "Knight of the Burning Pestle," ii.); also, any of various terns of warm seacoasts, usually of a sooty-brown color, as *Anoüs stolidus*, common on the southeastern coast of the U. S. (so called because so fearless of man as to seem stupid).

Noddy (*Anous stolidus*).

node (nōd), *n.* [L. *nodus*, knot: cf. *knot*[2].] A knot, complication, or difficulty (as, "There are characters which are continually creating collisions and *nodes* for themselves in dramas which nobody is prepared to act with them": George Eliot's "Middlemarch," xix.); also, a knot, protuberance, or knob; in *bot.*, a joint in a stem; a part of a stem which normally bears a leaf, a whorl of leaves, or foliar organs; in *pathol.*, a swelling or concretion, as on a bone; in *physics*, a point, line, or plane in a vibrating body at which there is comparatively no vibration; in *astron.*, either of the two points at which two great circles of the celestial sphere intersect each other; either of the two points at which the orbit of a heavenly body cuts the plane of the ecliptic (that passed as the body goes to the north of the ecliptic being called the *ascending node*, and that passed as it goes to the south being called the *descending node*); in *geom.*, a point on a curve or surface, at which there can be more than one tangent line or plane.

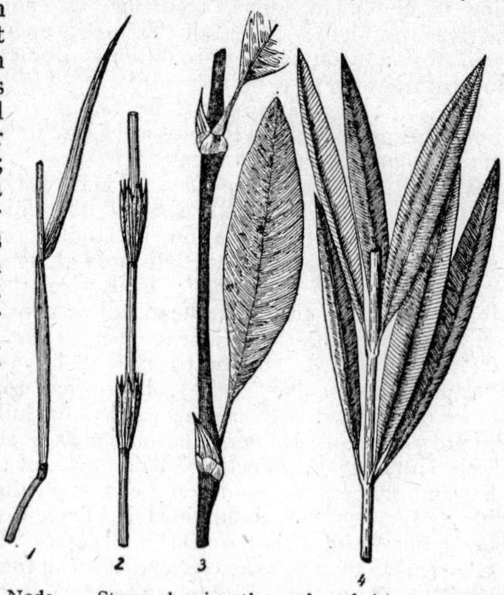

Node. — Stems showing the nodes of (1) rye-grass; (2) horsetail; (3) polygonum; (4) oleander.

No-don (no-dôṅ) **valve.** [From Albert *Nodon*, French physicist.] In *elect.*, a device for transforming alternating currents into direct currents, consisting typically of an electrolytic cell or electrolytic cells containing a solution of ammonium phosphate and electrodes of iron and aluminium.

no-dose (nō'dōs or nǫ-dōs'), *a.* [L. *nodosus*, knotty, < *nodus*, E. *node.*] Knotty; knobbed; having nodes.—**no-dos-i-ty** (nǫ-dos'i-ti), *n.*; pl. *-ties* (-tiz). The state of being nodose; also, a knot; a knob; a knotty swelling or protuberance.

nod-ule (nod'ūl), *n.* [L. *nodulus*, dim. of *nodus*, E. *node.*] A small node, knot, or knob; a tubercle; also, a small rounded mass or lump, as of mineral matter.—**nod'u-lar** (-ū-lär), *a.*—**nod'u-lose** (-lōs), *a.* Having nodules.

no-ël (nō-el' or nō'el), *n.* [F. *noël*, Christmas carol, *Noël*, Christmas, < L. *natalis*, birthday, orig. adj.: see *natal.*] A Christmas song or carol. Cf. *nowel.*

no-ët-ic (nǫ-et'ik), *a.* [Gr. νοητικός, < νοεῖν, perceive, think, < νόος, νοῦς, mind: see *nous.*] Of or pertaining to the mind or intellect; originating or existing in the mind; concerned with intellectual speculation.

nog[1] (nog), *n.* [Var. of obs. or prov. *knag*, ME. *knagge*, spur, projection, peg.] A wooden peg, pin, or block, for any of various purposes; a brick-shaped piece of wood built into a wall.—**nog**[1], *v. t.*; *nogged, nogging.* To secure by a nog or peg; also, to build by filling the open spaces in a wooden framework with brick.

nog[2] (nog), *n.* [Origin obscure.] A kind of strong ale or beer; also, egg-nog.

nog-gin (nog'in), *n.* [Origin obscure.] A small cup or mug; also, a small amount of liquor, usually a gill (as, "Many a *noggin* of whiskey is here quaffed": Hawthorne's "Our Old Home," viii.).

nog-ging (nog'ing), *n.* [See *nog*[1], *v.*] Brickwork serving to fill the interstices in a wooden frame.

no-how (nō'hou), *adv.* In no manner; not in any way; not at all; also, in no particular manner; with no distinctive appearance or character. [Chiefly colloq.]

noil (noil), *n.* [Origin uncertain.] A short fiber or a knot of wool or cotton, such as is separated from the long fiber in combing, or a similar piece of waste silk; also, such waste collectively.

noise (noiz), *n.* [OF. *noise*, noise, uproar, F. quarrel; of disputed origin.] Loud shouting, outcry, or clamor, or a din made by loud shouting, talking, etc. (as, "Whose *noise* is this that cries on murder?" Shakspere's "Othello," v. 1. 48); hence, public talk, or an outburst of public talk, as over some matter of interest or wonder (as, the letter made considerable *noise*; "The first [ballad] sold wonderfully, the event being recent, having made a great *noise*," B. Franklin's "Autobiography," i.); also, report, bruit, or rumor (archaic: as, "So grateful is the *noise* of noble deeds To noble hearts," Tennyson's "Marriage of Geraint," 437); also, sound, or a sound, of a loud, harsh, or confused kind, however caused (as, the *noise* of a cataract, of thunder, or of artillery or machinery; deafening *noises*); a din; also, a sound of any kind (as, the little *noises* of the meadows; "the reapers' rustling *noise*," Burns's "Vision," 224); also, music, or a sound of music (obs. or archaic: as, "Thus all Israel brought up the ark . . . making a *noise* with psalteries and harps," 1 Chron. xv. 28); hence, a company of musicians†.—**to make a noise in the world,** to arouse public talk, or make a public sensation: as, "It was pronounced . . . the greatest poem of the age, and all anticipated the *noise* it would *make in the* great *world*" (Irving's "Tales of a Traveler," ii. 4).—**noise,** *v.*; *noised, noising.* **I.** *intr.* To make a noise, outcry, or clamor (as, "*Noising* loud And threatening nigh": Milton's "Paradise Regained," iv. 488); also, to talk much or publicly (*of*). **II.** *tr.* To spread the report or rumor of (as, "All these sayings were *noised* abroad": Luke, i. 65); spread (a report, rumor, etc.); report, bruit, or rumor (as, "It is *noised* he hath a mass of treasure": Shakspere's "Timon of Athens," iv. 3. 404).—**noise'ful,** *a.* Noisy.—**noise'less,** *a.* Making, or attended with, no noise; silent; quiet: as, a *noiseless* step; a *noiseless* gesture; "I stood and watched by the window The *noiseless* work of the sky" (Lowell's "First Snow-Fall").—**noise'less-ly,** *adv.*—**noise'less-ness,** *n.*

noi-sette (noi-zet', F. nwo-zet), *n.* [From a personal name.] Any of several fine varieties of rose descended from a hybrid of the musk-rose and the China rose.

nois-i-ly (noi'zi-li), *adv.* In a noisy manner.—**nois'i-ness,** *n.*

noi-some (noi'sum), *a.* [From obs. or prov. *noy*, for *annoy.*] Annoying, unpleasant, or objectionable (now rare); also, offensive or disgusting as to physical conditions, and often as to odor (as, a *noisome* dungeon; "kitchens and areas with *noisome* sewers," Kingsley's "Alton Locke," i.); unwholesome and malodorous; foul, as odors; also, harmful, injurious, or noxious (archaic: as, "the *noisome* beast," Ezek. xiv. 21; a *noisome* pestilence; "My plants I save from nightly ill Of *noisome* winds," Milton's "Arcades," 49).—**noi'some-ly,** *adv.*—**noi'some-ness,** *n.*

nois-y (noi'zi), *a.*; compar. *noisier*, superl. *noisiest.* Making much noise (as, a *noisy* crowd; a *noisy* boy; a *noisy* clock); abounding in noise (as, a *noisy* house or street; the *noisy* city); attended with noise (as, a *noisy* argument; *noisy* sports).

no-lens vo-lens (nō'lenz vō'lenz). [L., 'unwilling willing.'] Unwilling or willing; willy-nilly.

no-li=me=tan-ge-re (nō'lī-mē-tan'ję-rē), *n.* [L. *noli me tangere*, 'touch me not.'] One who or that which must not be touched or interfered with; also, a picture representing Christ appearing to Mary Magdalene after his resurrection (see John, xx. 17); in *pathol.*, any of various ulcerous cutaneous diseases of the face, esp. lupus of the nose; in *bot.*, the touch-me-not.

noll (nōl or nol), *n.* [AS. *hnoll.*] The head. [Obs. or prov. Eng.]

nol-le pros-e-qui (nol'ę pros'ę-kwī). [L., 'to be unwilling to pursue (prosecute).'] In *law*, an entry made upon the records of a court when the plaintiff or prosecutor will proceed no further in a suit or action.

nolt (nōlt), *n.* [Var. of *nowt.*] Cattle; neat. [Sc.]

nom (nôṅ), *n.* [F., < L. *nomen.*] Name.—**nom de guerre** (dė gãr). [F., 'name of war.'] An assumed name under which to pursue a profession, undertaking, or the like.—**nom de plume** (plüm). [Coined in Eng. from F. words: lit. 'name of pen.'] A name assumed to write under; an author's pseudonym.

no-ma (nō'mą), *n.* [NL., < Gr. νομή, a corroding sore.] In *pathol.*, a gangrenous ulceration of the mouth and cheeks (and sometimes other parts), occurring mainly in debilitated children.

nom-ad (nom′ad or nō′mad). [L. *nomas* (*nomad-*), < Gr. νομάς (νομαδ-), < νέμειν, deal out, pasture, graze.] **I.** *n.* One of a race or tribe without fixed abode, but moving about from place to place according to the state of the pasturage; hence, one who leads a roving life; a wanderer. **II.** *a.* Nomadic.—**no-mad-ic** (nọ-mad′ik), *a.* [Gr. νομαδικός.] Of, pertaining to, or characteristic of nomads (as, "The geography of Asia and of Africa necessitated a *nomadic* life": Emerson's "Essays," History); also, leading the life of a nomad or nomads (as, "The Mongols of the great realm of Kipchak remained *nomadic*": H. G. Wells's "Outline of History," xxxiv. § 5c); leading a roving life.—**no-mad′i-cal-ly,** *adv.*—**nom′ad-ism,** *n.* The mode of life of nomads: as, "*Nomadism* cuts men off from fixed temples and intense local associations" (H. G. Wells's "Outline of History," xix. § 1).

no=man's=land (nō′manz-land), *n.* A tract of land to which no one can lay recognized or established claim; a tract of land which is the subject of dispute between two parties, as one between opposing lines of trenches in war: as, "They were now pushing forward saps into *No Man's Land* . . . creeping nearer to the enemy" (H. G. Wells's "Italy, France, and Britain at War," i.).

nom-arch (nom′ärk), *n.* [Gr. νομάρχης, < νομός, nome, + ἄρχειν, lead, rule.] The governor of a nome or a nomarchy.—**nom′ar-chy** (-ạ̈r-ki), *n.*; pl. *-chies* (-kiz). [Gr. νομαρχία.] One of the provinces into which modern Greece is divided for administrative purposes.

nom-bril (nom′bril), *n.* [F., < L. *umbilicus*, navel.] In *her.*, the point in an escutcheon midway between the middle base-point and the fesse-point.

E, Fesse-point; *F*, Nombril; *G*, Middle Base-point.

nome (nōm), *n.* [Gr. νομός, territorial division, < νέμειν, deal out; akin to L. *numerus*, E. *number*, *n.*: cf. *nomistic.*] One of the provinces of ancient Egypt; also, a nomarchy.

no-men (nō′men), *n.*; pl. *nomina* (nom′i-nạ̈). [L.: see *name.*] A name; specif., the second name (in order) of a Roman citizen, indicating his gens or clan, as in 'Caius *Julius* Cæsar.' Cf. *prænomen, cognomen, agnomen.*

no-men-cla-tor (nō′mẹn-klā-tọr), *n.* [L., < *nomen*, name, + *calare*, call.] One who calls things or persons by their names; an announcer of names; also, one who assigns names, as in scientific classification; also, a word-book†. —**no″men-cla-to′ri-al** (-klạ-tō′ri-ạl), **no′men-cla-to-ry** (-tọ-ri), *a.* Pertaining to naming or nomenclature.

no-men-cla-ture (nō′mẹn-klā-ṭūr), *n.* [L. *nomenclatura*, < *nomen*, name, + *calare*, call.] A name or appellation (now rare); also, a list of names; a catalogue; also, a set or system of names or terms, as those used in a particular science or art, or those employed by an individual or community; also, names or terms forming a set or system.—**no-men-cla′tur-al,** *a.*—**no-men-cla′tur-ist,** *n.* One who devises a nomenclature.

nom-i-nal (nom′i-nạl), *a.* [L. *nominalis*, < *nomen* (*nomin-*), name.] Of, pertaining to, or consisting in a name or names; also, containing or bearing a name or names; assigned to a person by name (as, *nominal* shares of stock); also, pertaining to or of the nature of a noun or nouns; also, being such in name only, or so-called (as, "A state of *nominal* peace existed between Spain, France, and England," Motley's "Dutch Republic," vi. 5; "an office . . . with merely *nominal* duties," Hawthorne's "Twice-Told Tales," Old Esther Dudley); of a price, consideration, etc., named as a mere matter of form, being trifling in comparison with the actual value; also, nominalistic.—**nom′i-nal-ism,** *n.* The philosophical doctrine that universals are mere names without real, objective existence corresponding to them. Cf. *realism* and *conceptualism.*—**nom′i-nal-ist,** *n.* A believer in nominalism.—**nom″i-nal-is′tic,** *a.* Of, pertaining to, or characteristic of nominalists or nominalism.—**nom′i-nal-ly,** *adv.*

nom-i-nate (nom′i-nāt), *v. t.*; *-nated, -nating.* [L. *nominatus*, pp. of *nominare*, < *nomen* (*nomin-*), name.] To call by a particular name, entitle, or designate (now rare); also, to mention by name (now rare); also, to fix, appoint, or specify (now rare: as, "Let the forfeit Be *nominated* for an equal pound Of your fair flesh," Shakspere's "Merchant of Venice," i. 3. 150); also, to appoint by name for a duty or office; also, to propose as a proper person for appointment or election to an office; specif., to name formally as a candidate for an elective office.—**nom′i-nate,** *a.* Having a particular name; also, mentioning a particular name; also, nominated, as to an office.—**nom-i-na′tion** (-nā′-shọn), *n.* [L. *nominatio*(*n-*).] The act of nominating, or the state of being nominated; specif., formal selection as a candidate for an elective office.—**nom″i-na-ti′val** (-nạ-tī′vạl), *a.* Of or pertaining to the nominative case.—**nom′i-na-tive** (-tiv). [L. *nominativus.*] **I.** *a.* Nominated; appointed by nomination; also, assigned to a person by name, as shares of stock; in *gram.*, indicating the subject, as the case in declension that is appropriated to the subject of a verb and to words in agreement with the subject; being in or pertaining to this case. **II.** *n.* In *gram.*, the nominative case, or a word in that case.—**nom′i-na-tor** (-nā-tọr), *n.*

nom-i-nee (nom-i-nē′), *n.* [From *nomin*(*ate*) + *-ee.*] One named or nominated, as to fill an office or to stand for election to office.

no-mis-tic (nọ-mis′tik), *a.* [Gr. νόμος, law, < νέμειν, deal out: see *nome.*] Founded on or acknowledging law or a system of laws, esp. as embodied in a sacred book.

nomo-. Form of Gr. νόμος, law, used in combination.—**no-moc-ra-cy** (nọ-mok′rạ-si), *n.* [+ *-cracy.*] Government, or a government, established and carried out in accordance with a code of laws.—**no-mog′ra-phy** (-mog′rạ-fi), *n.* [+ *-graphy.*] The process or art of drawing up laws.—**no-mol′o-gy** (-mol′ọ-ji), *n.* [+ *-logy.*] The science of law or laws; also, the science of the laws of the mind.

nom-o-pel-mous (nom-ọ-pel′mus), *a.* [Gr. νόμος, usage, custom, law, + πέλμα, sole of the foot.] In *ornith.*, having the normal arrangement of the two deep flexor tendons of the toes, that is, having one going to the first digit (or hallux) only, and the other entirely separate and dividing and going to the remaining three digits.

nom-o-thet-ic, nom-o-thet-i-cal (nom-ọ-thet′ik, -i-kạl), *a.* [Gr. νομοθετικός, < νόμος, law, + τιθέναι, set.] Lawgiving; legislative; also, founded on law or a system of laws; nomistic.

-nomy. [Gr. -νομία, < -νόμος, -νομος, < νέμειν, deal out, distribute, manage; less often, Gr. νόμος, law, < νέμειν.] A noun termination meaning 'distribution,' 'arrangement,' 'management,' or having reference to laws or government, as in *astronomy, autonomy, bionomy, economy, isonomy, taxonomy.*

non- (non-). [L. *non*, not, = *ne unum*, not one: cf. *none.*] A prefix of Latin origin, meaning 'not,' freely used as an English formative, usually with a simple negative force as implying mere negation or absence of something (rather than the opposite or reverse of it, as often expressed by *un-*[1]), as in *non-adherence, non-concurrence, non-episcopal, non-execution, non-fulfilment, non-interference, non-observance, non-payment, non-performance, non-professional* (cf. *unprofessional*), and many other words, mostly self-explanatory, and formed at will to meet the needs: commonly with a hyphen (which serves to set off distinctly the positive form on which the negative is based, as in *non-attendance* and *non-ego*, which plainly suggest *attendance* and *ego*), except in certain well-established formations (of which the positive is usually less definitely implied, as in *nonentity, nonjuror*, and *nonsense*, which do not so readily suggest *entity, juror*, and *sense*).

non=ac-cept-ance (non-ak-sep′tạns), *n.* [See *non-.*] Failure to accept; a refraining from acceptance: as, "Fifteen articles . . . were to be proposed forthwith to the insurgents, and in case of *non-acceptance* to be enforced" (Motley's "Dutch Republic," ii. 9).

non-age (non′ạ̄j or nō′nạ̄j), *n.* [AF. *nonage*, OF. *nonaage*, < *non*, not, + *aage*, age.] The period of legal infancy (see *infancy*); minority; hence, fig., the period of immaturity of anything (as, the *nonage* of the world).

non-a-ge-na-ri-an (non″ạ-je-nā′ri-ạ̈n). [L. *nonagenarius*, < *nonageni*, ninety each, distributive of *nonaginta*, ninety, related to *novem*, nine.] **I.** *a.* Of the age of 90 years, or between 90 and 100 years old. **II.** *n.* A nonagenarian person.

non-a-gon (non′ą-gon), *n.* [Irreg. < L. *nonus*, ninth, + Gr. *γωνία*, angle.] A plane figure having nine angles and nine sides; an enneagon.

non=ap-pear-ance (non-ą-pēr′ąns), *n.* [See *non-*.] Failure or neglect to appear, as in a court.

nonce (nons), *n.* [In ME. *for the nones*, prop. *for then ones*, lit. 'for the once' (ME. *then*, < AS. *tham*, dat. of *the*, E. *the*[1]).] The one or particular occasion or purpose: chiefly, and now only, in the phrase 'for the nonce': as, "I'll have prepared him A chalice *for the nonce*" (Shakspere's "Hamlet," iv. 7. 161); "We must compare the Marquis of Farintosh to a lamb *for the nonce*" (Thackeray's "Newcomes," xlvi.). [Archaic or literary.]—**nonce′=word,** *n.* A word coined and used only for the particular occasion.

non-cha-lance (non′shą-ląns, F. nôṅ-shȧ-läṅs), *n.* [F.] The quality of being nonchalant; cool unconcern or indifference: as, "A certain superciliousness of look, coolness of manner, *nonchalance* of tone, express fully their sentiments . . . without committing them by any positive rudeness" (C. Brontë's "Jane Eyre," xxi.).

non-cha-lant (non′shą-ląnt, F. nôṅ-shȧ-läṅ), *a.* [F., ppr. of *nonchaloir*, have no concern for, < L. *non*, not, + *calere*, be hot.] Coolly unconcerned or indifferent; carelessly calm; cool: as, a *nonchalant* manner, demeanor, or reply; "I rose with a *nonchalant* yawn of ennui" (Bulwer-Lytton's "Pelham," lxi.).—**non′cha-lant-ly,** *adv.*

non=col-le-gi-ate (non-kǫ-lē′ji-ąt), *a.* [See *non-*.] Not belonging to a college; belonging to the body of students in a university not attached to any particular college or hall; of a university, not composed of colleges.

non=com (non′kom′), *n.* A non-commissioned officer. [Colloq.]

non=com-bat-ant (non-kom′bą-tąnt). [See *non-*.] **I.** *n.* One who is not a combatant; a civilian in time of war; specif., one connected with a military or naval force in some capacity other than that of a fighter, as a surgeon, a chaplain, etc. **II.** *a.* Belonging or pertaining to non-combatants; having the status of a non-combatant.

non=com-mis-sioned (non-kǫ-mish′ǫnd), *a.* [See *non-*.] Not commissioned: applied esp. to military officers, as sergeants and corporals, ranking below second lieutenant.

non=com-mit-tal (non-kǫ-mit′ąl). [See *non-*.] **I.** *n.* Absence of committal; a refraining from committing one's self, as to a particular view or course. **II.** *a.* Not committing one's self, or not involving committal, to a particular view, course, or the like: as, on this point he remained *non-committal*; a *non-committal* answer.—**non=com-mit′tal-ly,** *adv.*

non=com-mu-ni-cant (non-kǫ-mū′ni-kąnt), *n.* [See *non-*.] One who is not a communicant; one who does not communicate, as at a particular service.

non=com-pli-ance (non-kǫm-plī′ąns), *n.* [See *non-*.] Failure or refusal to comply.—**non=com-pli′ant,** *n.* One who fails or refuses to comply.

non com-pos men-tis (non kom′pos men′tis). [L., not having control of one's mind.] Not of sound mind; not capable, mentally, of managing one's own affairs.

non=con-duct-ing (non-kǫn-duk′ting), *a.* [See *non-*.] Not conducting or transmitting; of the nature of a non-conductor.—**non=con-duc′tor,** *n.* A substance which does not conduct or transmit (or conducts with difficulty) a particular form of energy, as heat or electricity.

non-con-form-ing (non-kǫn-fôr′ming), *a.* [See *non-*.] Failing or refusing to conform, as to an established church. —**non-con-form′ism,** *n.* The practice or system of nonconformists.—**non-con-form′ist,** *n.* One who refuses to conform, as to an established church; esp. [often *cap.*], one who refuses to conform to the Church of England; a Protestant dissenter from the Church of England.—**non-con-for′mi-ty** (-fôr′mi-ti), *n.* Lack of conformity or agreement; also, failure or refusal to conform, as to an established church; esp. [often *cap.*], refusal to conform to the Church of England; the principles or practice of Nonconformists; also, the body of Nonconformists.

non=con-tent (non′kǫn-tent″), *n.* [See *non-*.] In the British House of Lords, a negative vote or voter.

non=co-öp-er-a-tion (non″kō-op-ę-rā′shǫn), *n.* [See *non-*.] Failure or refusal to coöperate; specif., the practice or policy, for political or revolutionary ends, of refraining from coöperating in activities instituted or maintained by the government (as, the movement of *non-coöperation* conducted by Gandhi and his followers in India in 1919 and years following).—**non=co-öp′er-a-tor,** *n.* One who refuses to coöperate; specif., a member of a group or party maintaining political non-coöperation.

non-de-script (non′dē-skript). [L. *non*, not, + *descriptus*, pp. of *describere*, E. *describe*.] **I.** *a.* Not hitherto described, as a species of animal or plant†; hence, of no recognized, definite, or particular type or kind (as, a *nondescript* garment or vehicle; "a multitude of *nondescript* articles, indispensable on the prairies," Parkman's "Oregon Trail," i.). **II.** *n.* A species not hitherto described†; hence, a person or a thing not conforming to any particular type (as, "one of those originals and *nondescripts*, more frequent in German Universities than elsewhere," Carlyle's "Sartor Resartus," i. 3; "the old-fashioned wheeled *nondescript* belonging to the captain," Hardy's "Return of the Native," iii. 8).

none (nun). [ME. *non*, < AS. *nān*, < *ne*, not, + *ān*, one: see *ne* and *one*, and cf. *no*[2] and *non-*.] **I.** *a.* Not any; no: in later use only before a vowel or *h*: as, "Thou shalt have *none* other gods before me" (Deut. v. 7); "He maketh the devices of the people of *none* effect" (Ps. xxxiii. 10). [Archaic.] **II.** *pron.* No one, or not one (as, "There is *none* to help," Ps. xxii. 11; *none* of these is a typical case); not any, as of something indicated (as, we have *none* of that paper left; as for pride, he had little or *none*; that matter is *none* of our business); no part, or nothing (*of*: as, "He had *none* of the appearance of a man who sailed before the mast," Stevenson's "Treasure Island," i.); often, as *pl.*, no, or not any, persons or things (as, "*None* come to the solemn feasts," Lam. i. 4; "I hear a voice, but *none* are there," Tennyson's "Sir Galahad," 30).—**none,** *adv.* To no extent; in no way; not at all: as, the supply is *none* too great; "Oh, our world is *none* the safer Now Great-Heart hath died!" (Kipling's "Great-Heart: Theodore Roosevelt in 1919").

non=ef-fec-tive (non-e-fek′tiv). [See *non-*.] **I.** *a.* Not effective; not fit for duty or active service, as a soldier or sailor. **II.** *n.* A non-effective person; a soldier or sailor not fit for duty or active service.

non=e-go (non-ē′gō or -eg′ō), *n.* [See *non-*.] In *metaph.*, all that is not the ego or conscious self; the object as opposed to the subject.

non-en-ti-ty (non-en′ti-ti), *n.*; pl. *-ties* (-tiz). [See *non-* and *entity*.] Non-existence; also, something which does not exist, or which exists only in the imagination (as, "Mermaids do not exist: why speak of them as if they did? How can you find interest in speaking of a *nonentity*?" C. Brontë's "Shirley," xiii.); also, a person or thing of no importance (as, to be a mere *nonentity* in one's own family).

nones (nōnz), *n. pl.* [L. *nonæ*, orig. fem. pl. of *nonus*, ninth, < *novem*, nine: cf. *noon*.] In the ancient Roman calendar, the ninth day before the ides, both days included, thus being the 7th of March, May, July, and October, and the 5th of the other months; *eccles.*, the fifth of the seven canonical hours, or the service for it, orig. fixed for the ninth hour of the day (or 3 P.M.) (as, "From noon till *nones* The brethren sate; and when the quire was done, Renew'd their converse till the vesper bell": Southey's "Madoc," i. 13. 164).

non=es-sen-tial (non-e-sen′shąl). [See *non-*.] **I.** *a.* Not essential; not necessary. **II.** *n.* A non-essential thing or person.

none-such (nun′such), *n.* A person or thing without equal or parallel; a paragon; in *bot.*, the black medic.

non=Eu-cli-de-an (non″ū-kli-dē′ąn or non-ū-klid′ę-ąn), *a.* [See *non-*.] Not included in, or not in conformity with, the system of geometry established by Euclid.

non=ex-ist-ence (non-eg-zis′tęns), *n.* [See *non-*.] Absence of existence; also, a thing that has no existence.—**non=ex-ist′ent,** *a.* Not existent; having no existence.

non=ex-por-ta-tion (non″eks-pǫr-tā′shǫn), *n.* [See *non-*.] Failure or refusal to export.

non-fea-sance (non-fē′ząns), *n.* [See *non-* and *feasance*.] In *law*, the omission of some act which ought to have been performed.

no-nil-lion (nō-nil′yǫn), *n.* [F. *nonillion*, < L. *nonus*, ninth, + F. (*m*)*illion*, million.] In Great Britain, the ninth power of a million, represented by 1 followed by 54 ciphers; in France and the U. S., a thousand octillions, represented by 1 followed by 30 ciphers.—**no-nil′lionth,** *a.* and *n.*

non=im-por-ta-tion (non″im-pǭr-tā′shǫn), *n.* [See *non-*.] Failure or refusal to import.

non=in-ter-ven-tion (non″in-tėr-ven′shǫn), *n.* [See *non-*.] Failure or refusal to intervene; systematic non-interference by a nation in the affairs of other nations or of its own states, etc.

non=join-der (non-join′dėr), *n.* [See *non-*.] In *law*, omission to join, as of one who should have been a party to an action.

non-ju-ror (non-jö′rǫr), *n.* [See *non-* and *juror*.] One who refuses to take a required oath, as of allegiance; esp., one of those clergymen of the Church of England who in 1689 refused to swear allegiance to William and Mary.—**non-ju′rant,** *a.* and *n.*—**non-ju′ring,** *a.*

non=le-gal (non-lē′gạl), *a.* [See *non-*.] Not (definitely) legal; having no legal aspect: distinguished from *illegal*.

non=met-al (non-met′ạl), *n.* [See *non-*.] In *chem.*, an element not having the character of a metal, as carbon, nitrogen, etc.—**non=me-tal′lic** (-me-tal′ik), *a.*

non=mor-al (non-mor′ạl), *a.* [See *non-*.] Having no relation to morality; having no moral aspect; neither moral nor immoral.—**non=mo-ral′i-ty** (-mō-ral′i-ti), *n.*

non-pa-reil (non-pạ-rel′). [F., < *non* (< L. *non*), not, + *pareil*, equal, < ML. *pariculus*, dim. of L. *par*, equal.] **I.** *a.* Having no equal; peerless. **II.** *n.* A person or thing having no equal (as, "Though you were crown'd The *nonpareil* of beauty": Shakspere's "Twelfth Night," i. 5. 273); something unique; also, a beautifully colored finch, *Cyanospiza ciris*, of the southern U. S.; also, a printing-type (6 point) of a size between agate and minion (see *type*).

non=par-ti-zan, non=par-ti-san (non-pär′ti-zạn), *a.* [See *non-*.] Not partizan; not supporting any of the established or regular parties.—**Non=Partisan League,** in *U. S. politics*, an organization with socialistic tendencies, devoted to the interests of the farmer, which was organized in North Dakota in 1915, gaining political control of that State in 1916, and extending its influence into Minnesota, South Dakota, Montana, and other States.

non-plus (non′plus′), *n.* [L. *non plus*, not more, no further.] A state in which no more can be said or done; a state of utter perplexity: as, "Certain freebooting Swedes had become very troublesome . . . in . . . the reign of William the Testy . . . putting his admiral . . . to a perfect *nonplus*" (Irving's "Knickerbocker's New York," v. 9).—**non′plus′,** *v. t.*; *-plussed*, *-plussing*. To bring to a nonplus; render at a loss from perplexity as to what to say, do, or think; puzzle completely: as, "He had been *nonplussed* on a sudden by Mr. Dry's desiring him to tell the company what it was that he endeavoured to prove" (Addison, in "Spectator," 476).

non pro-se-qui-tur (non prō-sek′wi-tėr). [L., 'he does not pursue (prosecute).'] In *law*, a judgment entered against the plaintiff in a suit when he does not appear to prosecute it.

non=res-i-dence (non-rez′i-dẹns), *n.* [See *non-*.] The fact of not residing in a particular place; esp., failure to reside where official duties require one to reside.—**non=res′i-dent. I.** *a.* Not resident in a particular place; esp., not residing where official duties require one to reside. **II.** *n.* One who is non-resident.

non=re-sist-ance (non-rē-zis′tạns), *n.* [See *non-*.] A refraining from resistance; esp., the practice or principle of submitting to authority, even when unjustly exercised.—**non=re-sist′ant. I.** *a.* Not resistant; passively obedient. **II.** *n.* One who does not resist authority or force; one who maintains that violence should never be resisted by force.

non=re-straint (non-rē-strānt′), *n.* [See *non-*.] Absence of restraint; in *med.*, the treatment of the insane without mechanical means of restraint.

non=rig-id (non-rij′id), *a.* [See *non-*.] Not rigid; specif., designating a type of airship having a flexible gas-container without a supporting structure and held in shape only by the pressure of the gas within.

non-sense (non′sens or -sẹns), *n.* [See *non-*.] That which makes no sense or is lacking in sense; words without sense or conveying absurd ideas (as, "He says we must wait with patience, and trust to Providence, and such *nonsense*," Smollett's "Humphry Clinker," Oct. 14; "You are talking the greatest *nonsense*; and you know it," G. B. Shaw's "Man and Superman," ii.); also, senseless or absurd action; foolish conduct, notions, etc. (as, to stand no *nonsense* from a person; a man with no *nonsense* about him); also, absurdity (as, the *nonsense* of an idea or an action); also, stuff, trash, or anything useless.—**non-sen′si-cal** (-sen′si-kạl), *a.* Of the nature of nonsense; devoid of sense; absurd; foolish; of persons, given to or indulging in nonsense (as, a *nonsensical* fellow; "Come, now, Marie . . . Don't be *nonsensical*," Mrs. Stowe's "Uncle Tom's Cabin," xv.).—**non-sen′si-cal-ly,** *adv.*—**non-sen′si-cal-ness,** *n.*

non se-qui-tur (non sek′wi-tėr). [L., 'it does not follow.'] An inference or a conclusion which does not follow from the premises.

non=stri-at-ed (non-strī′ā-ted), *a.* [See *non-*.] Not striated; unstriped, as muscular tissue.

non-such (non′such), *n.* Same as *nonesuch*.

non-suit (non′sūt), *n.* [AF. *nounsute*, < OF. *non*, not, + *sieute*, E. *suit*, *n.*] In *law*, a judgment given against a plaintiff who neglects to prosecute, or who fails to show a legal cause of action or to bring sufficient evidence.—**non′-suit,** *v. t.* In *law*, to subject to a nonsuit.

no-nu (nō′nö), *n.* [Samoan.] A rubiaceous tree, *Morinda citrifolia*, of the East Indies, the Pacific islands, etc., with a fleshy composite fruit full of seeds, and a bark that yields a valuable dye.

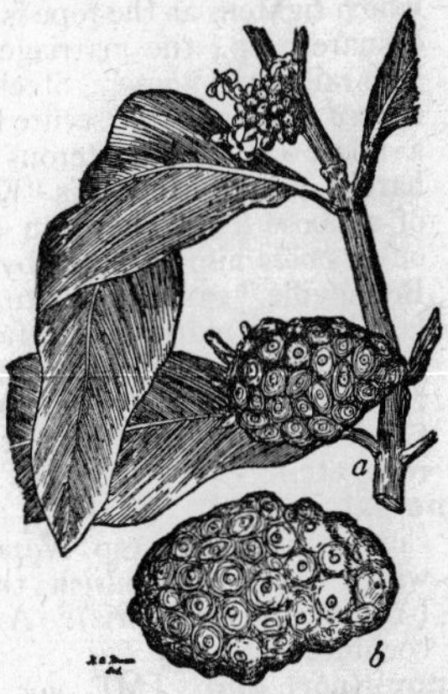

Nonu. — *a*, branch with flowers and young fruit, one fourth natural size; *b*, mature fruit, one fourth natural size.

non=u-nion (non-ū′nyǫn), *a.* [See *non-*.] Not belonging to, or not in accordance with the rules of, a trade-union; not recognizing or favoring trade-unions.—**non=u′nion-ism,** *n.* Disregard of or opposition to trade-unions.—**non=u′nion-ist,** *n.*

non=us-er (non-ū′zėr), *n.* [See *non-*.] In *law*, failure to use a right or privilege.

noo-dle[1] (nö′dl), *n.* [Origin obscure.] A simpleton.

noo-dle[2] (nö′dl), *n.* [G. *nudel*.] A strip or lump of a dough or paste resembling macaroni, served in soups, etc.

nook (nůk), *n.* [ME. *noke*, *nok*; origin obscure.] A corner or external angle of a thing (now rare except prov.); a piece at a corner or broken from a corner, or any piece or part (obs. or prov.); a projecting piece of land, as one running into the sea (obs. or prov.); also, an interior angle, formed by the meeting of two walls or the like; a corner, as in a room (as, an ingle-*nook*); also, any retired or obscure corner (as, "The shades of twilight still hide themselves among the *nooks* of the adjacent buildings": Hawthorne's "Twice-Told Tales," Sunday at Home); any small recess; a secluded or sheltered place (as, "a shady *nook*," Milton's "Paradise Lost," ix. 277; "The wily quarry . . . In the deep Trosachs' wildest *nook* His solitary refuge took," Scott's "Lady of the Lake," i. 8); hence, a remote spot (as, "That rare *nook* Yet untroubled by the tourist": Browning's "La Saisiaz").—**nook′=shot″ten** (-shot″n), *a.* Running out into corners or angles: as, "that *nook-shotten* isle of Albion" (Shakspere's "Henry V.," iii. 5. 14). [Archaic or prov. Eng.]—**nook′y,** *a.* Full of nooks; also, nook-like.

no-öl-o-gy (nō-ol′ǭ-ji), *n.* [Gr. νόος, mind: see *-logy*.] The science of the understanding.

noon (nön), *n.* [AS. *nōn*, < L. *nona*, ninth hour, orig. fem. of *nonus*, ninth: see *nones*.] The ninth hour of the day, reckoned from sunrise according to the Roman method, or about 3 o'clock in the afternoon†; also, the ecclesiastical hour or service of nones†; also, midday; 12 o'clock in the daytime; also, the middle point of night, or midnight (poetic:

as, "at *noon* of night," Dryden's tr. Virgil's "Æneid," iv. 744; "Night was at the *noon*," Jean Ingelow's "Dreams That Came True"); also, the middle and brightest or finest point or part of any period (as, "the *noon* of a life illustrated by many brilliant actions": Motley's "Dutch Republic," iii. 2); also, the highest point (poetic: as, "To behold the wandering moon Riding near her highest *noon*," Milton's "Il Penseroso," 68).—**apparent noon,** the moment when the sun's center crosses the meridian.—**mean noon,** the moment when the mean sun's center crosses the meridian.—**noon,** *v. i.* To halt for or take a noonday rest or meal, as during a journey: as, "We traveled six or seven miles farther, and '*nooned*' near a brook" (Parkman's "Oregon Trail," iv.). [U. S. and prov. Eng.]—**noon'day. I.** *n.* Midday; noon. **II.** *a.* Of or at noonday.—**noon'ing,** *n.* Noontime; also, an interval at noon for rest or food (as, "She had said she would look at pictures all through the *nooning* [at school]": Mark Twain's "Tom Sawyer," xviii.); a rest at noon; a noonday meal. [Now U. S. and prov. Eng.]—**noon'tide.** [AS. *nōntīd.*] **I.** *n.* The time of noon; midday; also, the middle point of night, or midnight (chiefly poetic); also, the middle and best point or part (as, "the *noontide* of your prosperity": Lamb's "Poor Relations"); also, the highest point (poetic: as, "the *noontide* of the moon," Byron's "Don Juan," xiii. 63). **II.** *a.* Of or at noontide: as, "their *noontide* slumbers" (H. Melville's "Typee," xxiii.).—**noon'time,** *n.* The time of noon.

noose (nös), *n.* [Ult. < L. *nodus*, knot.] A loop with a running knot, as in a snare, lasso, hangman's halter, etc., which tightens as the rope is pulled; in fig. use, a tie or bond; a snare; esp., the marriage tie (as, "your marriage-haters, who rail at the *noose*": Steele, in "Tatler," 77).—**noose,** *v. t.*; *noosed, noosing.* To secure by or as by a noose; insnare with a noose (as, "as dexterous a gipsy as ever . . . *noosed* a hare": Whyte-Melville's "Katerfelto," xii.); catch by means of a noose (as, "They run out, and with the lasso, dexterously *noose* him [a bear] by either leg": Irving's "Captain Bonneville," xxxix.); put to death by hanging; fig., to make fast by the marriage tie (as, "His . . . rival . . . set out with the lady for Coldstream . . . where there was a parson . . . and there they were *noosed*": Smollett's "Humphry Clinker," July 18); also, to make a noose with or in (a rope, etc.).

no-pal (nō'pal), *n.* [Sp.; from Mex.] Any of several cactaceous plants, esp. *Nopalea* (or *Opuntia*) *coccinellifera*, which serve to nourish the cochineal-insect.—**no'pal-ry** (-ri), *n.*; pl. *-ries* (-riz). A plantation of nopals for raising cochineal-insects.

nor[1] (nôr), *conj.* [ME. *nor*, contr. of *nother*, var. of *neither*, E. *neither.*] A negative conjunction used (1) as the correlative to a preceding *neither* (as, neither he *nor* I was there; he could neither read *nor* write); (2) with a preceding *neither* omitted, its negative force being understood (archaic or poetic: as, "Great brother, thou *nor* I have made the world," Tennyson's "Last Tournament," 203); (3) instead of *neither*, as correlative to a following *nor* (now chiefly poetic: as, "Drake *nor* devil nor Spaniard feared," H. Newbolt's "Admirals All"); (4) to continue the force of a negative, as *not, no, never*, etc., occurring in a preceding clause (as, "Eye hath not seen, *nor* ear heard," 1 Cor. ii. 9; "Have you no wit, manners, *nor* honesty?" Shakspere's "Twelfth Night," ii. 3. 94); (5) after an affirmative clause, or as a continuative, in the sense of 'and . . . not' (as, "The tale is long, *nor* have I heard it out": Addison's "Cato," iv. 3).

nor[2] (nôr), *conj.* [Origin uncertain: cf. *nor*[1].] Than: as, "Hev a dog, Miss! — they're better friends *nor* any Christian" (George Eliot's "Mill on the Floss," iv. 3); "Mighty small specimen . . . Ain't bigger *nor* a derringer" (Bret Harte's "Luck of Roaring Camp"). [Prov. or vulgar.]

Nord (nôrd), *n.* In *ethnol.*, a member of the Nordic race.

Nord-hau-sen (nôrt'hou"zen) **a'cid.** [From *Nordhausen*, town in Prussian Saxony, where it was first manufactured.] A fuming liquid obtained when sulphur trioxide is dissolved in sulphuric acid.

Nor-dic (nôr'dik). [F. *nordique*, < *nord*, north; from Teut., and akin to E. *north.*] In *ethnol.*: **I.** *a.* Designating, or belonging or pertaining to, a race of men or a racial type characterized by tall stature, blond hair, blue eyes, and elongated head, exemplified by the Scandinavians and other Teutonic peoples: as, "The *Nordic* peoples came into Italy and Greece under leader kings" (H. G. Wells's "Outline of History," xxxv. § 1). **II.** *n.* A member of the Nordic race.

Nor-folk (nôr'fok) **jack'et.** [From *Norfolk*, county in eastern England.] A loosely belted jacket or coat with box-plaits on both front and back.

no-ri-a (nō'ri-ä), *n.* [Sp.; from Ar.] A device consisting essentially of a series of buckets or pitchers traveling with or over a wheel, used in Spain and the Orient for raising water.

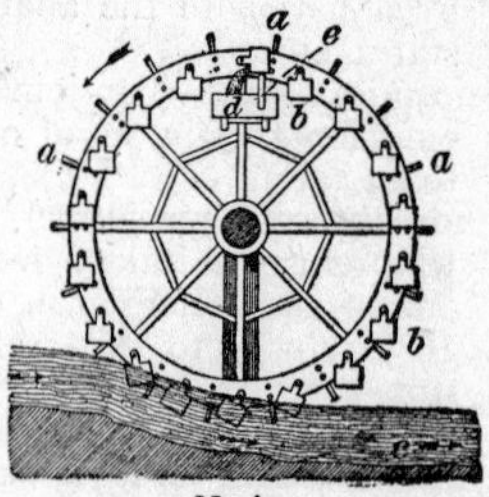

Noria.

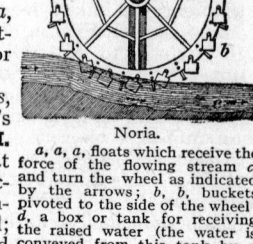

a, a, a, floats which receive the force of the flowing stream *c*, and turn the wheel as indicated by the arrows; *b, b,* buckets pivoted to the side of the wheel; *d*, a box or tank for receiving the raised water (the water is conveyed from this tank by a pipe or chute, not shown, to the point of delivery); *e*, upright attached rigidly to the tank, which, acting in conjunction with the motion of the wheel, successively empties the buckets into the tank.

nor-land (nôr'land), *n.* Same as *northland.* [Chiefly poetic.]

norm (nôrm), *n.* [L. *norma*, carpenter's square, rule, pattern.] A standard, model, or pattern.

nor-mal (nôr'mal). [L. *normalis*, made according to a carpenter's square, < *norma*: see *norm.*] **I.** *a.* Right-angled; also, being at right angles, as a line; perpendicular; of the nature of or pertaining to a mathematical normal; also, conforming to the standard or the common type; regular, usual, natural, or not abnormal (as, the *normal* mode of procedure; the *normal* condition of affairs); also, serving to fix a standard (as, a *normal* school, a school for the training of teachers); in *chem.*, noting a solution of a salt, acid, or the like, which contains in one liter the reactive equivalent of one gram of hydrogen; also, noting that one of two or more isomeric hydrocarbons, whose structural formula is made up of a single unbranched chain of carbon atoms, no carbon atom being joined directly to more than two other carbon atoms. **II.** *n.* The standard or type; the normal form or state; the average or mean; in *math.*, a perpendicular line or plane, esp. one perpendicular to a tangent of a curve or surface at the point of contact.—**nor'mal-cy** (-si), *n.* The character or state of being normal (as, "those . . . who, having . . . accepted the ideas of the older school of economists as to the relationships of labour, capital, and the state, have obtained therefrom a false sense of the continued *normalcy* and rigidity of these relationships": B. Kidd's "Social Evolution," viii.); the normal condition, as of affairs (as, "back to *normalcy*," Warren G. Harding, in Address at Marion, Ohio, July 5, 1920; "We must . . . strive for *normalcy*," Warren G. Harding, in Speech accepting the Republican nomination for President, July 22, 1920); in *math.*, the state or fact of being normal or a normal (as, the point of *normalcy*).—**nor-mal'i-ty** (-mal'i-ti), *n.* The character or state of being normal.—**nor'mal-ize** (-iz), *v. t.*; *-ized, -izing.* To render normal.—**nor"mal-i-za'tion** (-i-zā'shon), *n.*—**nor'mal-ly,** *adv.*

Nor-man (nôr'man). [OF. *Normant* (F. *Normand*), lit. 'Northman'; from Scand.] **I.** *n.*; pl. *-mans.* A native or inhabitant of Normandy, a former province of northern France bordering on the English Channel; a member of that branch of the Northmen or Scandinavians who in the 10th century conquered Normandy (named after them), or one of the mixed Scandinavian and French (Norman French) race later inhabiting this region, which conquered England in 1066; also, Norman French. **II.** *a.* Of or pertaining to the Normans; in *arch.*, noting or pertaining to a style of medieval architecture, a variety of the Romanesque, characterized by simplicity, massiveness, and the use of the rounded arch, which was introduced from Normandy into Great Britain before the Norman Conquest (see cut on following page).—**Norman Conquest,** the conquest of England by the Normans, under William the Conqueror, in 1066.—**Norman French,** the form of French spoken by the Normans, or a later form of it used in England in legal procedure.

Nor-man-esque (nôr-mạn-esk′), *a.* [See *-esque.*] After the Norman style, as of architecture.

Norn (nôrn), *n.* [Icel.] In *Scand. myth.*, any one of the goddesses of fate, commonly represented as three in number, whose decrees were irrevocable: as, "Skuld, the younger *Norn*, Who watches over birth and death" (Whittier's "Dole of Jarl Thorkell").

Norman Architecture. — Porch and stairway in the close of Canterbury Cathedral, England.

Nor-roy (nor′-oi), *n.* [AF., lit. 'north king.'] The title of the third English king-of-arms, ranking after Clarencieux.

Norse (nôrs). [Cf. Norw., Sw., and Dan. *Norsk*, Norwegian, Norse, < *nord*, north.] **I.** *a.* Belonging or pertaining to Norway, esp. ancient Norway with its colonies (as in Iceland), or to ancient Scandinavia generally; pertaining to the language of Norway, or to that of the Northmen or ancient Scandinavians. **II.** *n.* As *pl.*, the Norwegians, esp. the ancient Norwegians; the Northmen or ancient Scandinavians generally; as *sing.*, the language of Norway, esp. of ancient Norway with its colonies (as, Old *Norse*, exemplified by Old Norwegian and Old Icelandic: see *Icelandic, n.*); the language of the Northmen or ancient Scandinavians.—**Norse′man** (-mạn), *n.*; pl. *-men.* A man of the Norse people; a Norwegian, esp. an ancient Norwegian or (as in literary use) a modern Norwegian regarded as exhibiting the characteristics of the ancient race; a Northman or ancient Scandinavian.

north (nôrth), *adv.* [AS. *north* = D. *noord* = G. *nord* = Icel. *nordhr* = Norw., Sw., and Dan. *nord*, north.] In the direction which is to the right of a person facing the setting sun or west; toward or in the north; also, from the north (as with reference to wind).—**north,** *n.* A cardinal point of the compass lying in the plane of the meridian and to the right of a person facing the setting sun or west; the direction in which this point lies; also [*l. c.* or *cap.*], a quarter or territory situated in this direction; [*cap.*] that part of the U. S. which in general lies north of Maryland, the Ohio River, and Missouri; also [*l. c.*], the north wind (chiefly poetic: as, "The *north* breathes steadily Beneath the stars, they tremble with the cold!" Shelley's "Revolt of Islam," viii. 1).—**magnetic north.** See under *magnetic.*—**north,** *a.* Lying toward or situated in the north; directed or proceeding toward the north; also, coming from the north, as a wind; *eccles.*, designating, situated in, or lying toward that side of a church to the left of one facing the altar or high altar.—**North Britain,** Scotland.—**North Briton,** a Scot.—**north star,** the pole-star.

north-east (nôrth′ēst′). [AS. *northēast.*] **I.** *adv.* In the direction of a point midway between north and east; also, from this direction. **II.** *n.* The point or direction midway between north and east; also, a region in this direction. **III.** *a.* Lying toward or situated in the northeast; directed or proceeding toward the northeast; also, coming from the northeast, as a wind.—**northeast passage,** a passage for ships along the northern coast of Europe and Asia as a possible course for navigation between the Atlantic Ocean and the Pacific Ocean: as, "In April 1566 he [Sir Humphrey Gilbert] had already joined with Antony Jenkinson in a petition to Elizabeth for the discovery of the *North-East Passage*" (Encyc. Brit., 11th ed., XII. 7).—**north′east′er,** *n.* A wind or gale from the northeast.—**north′east′er-ly,** *a.* and *adv.* Toward or from the northeast.—**north′-east′ern,** *a.* Situated or going toward the northeast; also, coming from the northeast, as a wind; also, of or pertaining to the northeast.—**north′east′ward** (-wạrd). **I.** *adv.* and *a.* Toward the northeast. **II.** *n.* The northeast.—**north′east′ward-ly,** *adv.* and *a.*

north-er (nôr′ᴛʜėr), *n.* A wind or storm from the north.

north-er-ly (nôr′ᴛʜėr-li). **I.** *a.* Moving, directed, or situated toward the north; also, coming from the north, as a wind. **II.** *adv.* Toward the north; also, from the north.

north-ern (nôr′ᴛʜėrn), *a.* [AS. *northerne.*] Lying toward or situated in the north; directed or proceeding northward; also, coming from the north, as a wind; also, of or pertaining to the north, esp. [*cap.*] the North of the U. S.; in *astron.*, north of the celestial equator or of the zodiac (as, the *northern* signs of the zodiac; a *northern* constellation).—**Northern Car,** in *astron.*, Charles's Wain, or the Dipper.—**Northern Crown,** in *astron.*, the northern constellation Corona Borealis.—**northern lights,** the aurora borealis. See *aurora.*—**northern spy,** an American winter apple marked with red and yellow stripes.—**northern star,** the north star.—**north′ern,** *n.* One living in a northern region or country.—**north′ern-er,** *n.* A native or inhabitant of the north, esp. [*cap.*] of the northern U. S.—**north′ern-most,** *a.* *superl.* Furthest north.

north-ing (nôr′ᴛʜing or -thing), *n.* Movement or deviation toward the north; also, distance due north; the distance due north made by a ship on any course tending northward; also, in *astron.*, north declination.

north-land (nôrth′lạnd), *n.* [AS. *northland.*] The land or region in the north; the northern part of a country; [*cap.*] the northern regions of the world, esp. the land or lands of the Northmen or Scandinavians (as, "I am the God Thor . . . Here in my *Northland* . . . Reign I forever!" Longfellow's "Saga of King Olaf," i.).—**north′land-er,** *n.*

North-man (nôrth′mạn), *n.*; pl. *-men.* [AS. *Northman.*] A member of the Scandinavian race, or group of peoples, of northern Europe, notable for their adventurous daring upon the sea, which from about the 8th to the 11th century made many raids and settlements both on Great Britain, Ireland, and other islands, and on the mainland of Europe. See *Norman, n.*, and cf. *viking.*

north-most (nôrth′mōst), *a.* *superl.* Northernmost: as, "the *northmost* part of the coast of Mozambique" (Defoe's "Captain Singleton," v.).

North-um-bri-an (nôr-thum′bri-ạn). **I.** *a.* Of or pertaining to Northumbria, an Anglian kingdom which extended north of the Humber to the Forth, or Northumberland, the northernmost county of modern England, or the inhabitants or dialect of either. **II.** *n.* A native or inhabitant of Northumbria or Northumberland; also, the dialect of Anglo-Saxon spoken in Northumbria; also, the modern English dialect of Northumberland.

north-ward (nôrth′wạrd). [AS. *northweard.*] **I.** *adv.* Toward the north; north. **II.** *a.* Moving, bearing, facing, or situated toward the north. **III.** *n.* The northward part, direction, or point.—**north′ward-ly. I.** *a.* Having a northward direction or situation; also, coming from the north, as a wind. **II.** *adv.* Toward the north; also, from the north.—**north′wards,** *adv.* Northward.

north-west (nôrth′west′). [AS. *northwest.*] **I.** *adv.* In the direction of a point midway between north and west; also, from this direction. **II.** *n.* The point or direction midway between north and west; also, a region in this direction. **III.** *a.* Lying toward or situated in the northwest; directed or proceeding toward the northwest; also, coming from the northwest, as a wind.—**northwest passage,** a passage for ships along the northern coast of North America as a possible course for navigation between the Atlantic Ocean and the Pacific Ocean: as, "From 1573 to 1578 he [Sir Humphrey Gilbert] lived in retirement at Limehouse, devoting himself especially to the advocacy of a *North-West Passage*" (Encyc. Brit., 11th ed., XII. 7).—**north′-west′er,** *n.* A wind or gale from the northwest.—**north′-west′er-ly,** *a.* and *adv.* Toward or from the northwest.—

north′west′ern, *a.* Situated or going toward the northwest; also, coming from the northwest, as a wind; also, of or pertaining to the northwest.—**north′west′ward** (-wąrd). **I.** *adv.* and *a.* Toward the northwest. **II.** *n.* The northwest.—**north′west′ward-ly,** *adv.* and *a.*

Nor-we-gian (nôr-wē′jiąn). [From *Norway*, after ML. *Norvegia*, Norway.] **I.** *a.* Of or pertaining to Norway, its inhabitants, or their language. **II.** *n.* A native or inhabitant of Norway; also, the language of Norway, belonging to the Scandinavian group.

nose (nōz), *n.* [AS. *nosu*, akin to *nasu*, G. *nase*, Icel. *nös*, nose, also to L. *nasus*, nose, *nares*, nostrils, Skt. *nas*, nose, *nāsā*, nostrils, nose.] The part (usually prominent) of the face or head which contains the nostrils, affording passage for air in respiration, also for the discharge of secretions from the head, and serving to modify the sound of the voice (as, an aquiline *nose*; a pug-*nose*; the *nose* of a monkey or a dog; to wipe or blow the *nose*; to talk through the *nose*); specif., this part as the organ of smell (as, savory odors greeted the *nose*; "The *nose* of Memory . . . dilates with pleasure over the rich perfume of Miss Abigail's forty mince-pies," Aldrich's "Story of a Bad Boy," xii.); hence, the sense of smell, faculty of smelling, or scent (as, a dog with a good *nose*); fig., a faculty of perceiving or detecting (as, to have a *nose* for news or for scandal); also, something regarded as resembling the nose of a person or animal, as a spout or nozzle, the beak of a still, the prow of a ship, the forward end of an aircraft, or a projecting part of anything.—**nose of wax,** fig., a thing or person that may be easily bent or turned to any purposes: as, "They pretend it was because I let David . . . manage the business his ain gait, as if I had been a *nose o' wax*" (Scott's "Guy Mannering," v.). [Now chiefly Sc. and prov. Eng.]—**to count** or **tell noses,** to count the persons in a group or party. [Colloq.]—**to cut off one's nose to spite one's face.** See *spite, v.*—**to follow one's nose,** to go straight ahead; also, to be guided by one's sense of smell, or by instinct.—**to lead by the nose,** fig., to lead like some tame, unintelligent animal, or in an ignominious way: as, "Seven-eighths of the town are *led by the nose* by this or that periodical work, having wholly lost sight of the fact, that reviews are far from being gospel" (Marryat's "King's Own," xxviii.).—**to pay through the nose.** See under *pay*[2], *v. i.*—**to put one's nose out of joint,** to displace one in the favor of others, in a mortifying way. With corresponding expressions, *to have one's nose out of joint, his nose is out of joint*, etc.—**under** or **beneath one's nose,** immediately before one, so as to be seen if one will but look; within one's immediate range of observation: as, "Things are done *under our* very *noses*, and we know nothing of the matter" (Godwin's "Caleb Williams," xxvi.); "A wagon-load of valuable merchandise had been smuggled ashore . . . directly *beneath their* unsuspicious *noses*" (Hawthorne's "Scarlet Letter," The Custom House).—**nose,** *v.*; *nosed, nosing.* **I.** *tr.* To perceive by or as by the nose or the sense of smell (as, "Tears of rage started into his eyes, as though he *nosed* the very offence in question [onions]": Irving's "Knickerbocker's New York," iv. 2); smell (*out*); seek or find as if by following a scent (as, "A dozen times, Perrault, *nosing* the way, broke through the ice bridges": Jack London's "Call of the Wild," iii.); also, to touch or rub with the nose, or nuzzle (as, "The two horses had been . . . *nosing* each other's muzzles": G. W. Cable's "John March, Southerner," iv.); approach the nose to, as in smelling or examining, or smell or sniff (as, "Ingram *nosed* his port, then sipped it": M. Hewlett's "Open Country," xiii.); make (one's way) by pushing with the nose or forward end; also, to lead (*about*) by the nose (as, "I presume as long as you live you'll have to be *nosed* about like a perfect — I don't know what!" Howells's "Rise of Silas Lapham," xi.); also, to face, confront, or oppose boldly or insolently (obs. or archaic); also, to furnish with a nosing. **II.** *intr.* To smell or sniff; seek as if by smelling or scent (*after, for,* etc.); pry (*about, into,* etc.); also, to push with the nose or forward end (as, the boat *nosed* in toward the shore; an aircraft is said to *nose* down or up).

nose=band (nōz′band), *n.* That part of a bridle or halter which passes over the animal's nose.

nose-bleed (nōz′blēd), *n.* Bleeding from the nose; epistaxis.

nosed (nōzd), *a.* Having a nose: as, long-*nosed*.

nose=dive (nōz′dīv), *n.* A dive or plunge of an aëroplane with the nose or fore part of the craft downward.—**nose′=dive,** *v. i.*; *-dived, -diving.* To execute a nose-dive.

nose-gay (nōz′gā), *n.* [From *nose* + (obs.) *gay*, *n.*, something gay, a toy.] A bunch of flowers; a bouquet; a posy: as, "a garden in which I had in childhood gathered so many a *nosegay*" (S. Butler's "Way of All Flesh," xxxvi.).

nose-less (nōz′les), *a.* Destitute or deprived of a nose.—**nose′less-ness,** *n.*

nose=ring (nōz′ring), *n.* A ring fixed in an animal's nose; also, a ring-like ornament worn in the nose, as by savages.

nos-ey (nō′zi), *a.* and *n.* See *nosy*.

nos-ing (nō′zing), *n.* A projecting edge, as the part of the tread of a step extending beyond the riser, or a projecting part of a buttress.

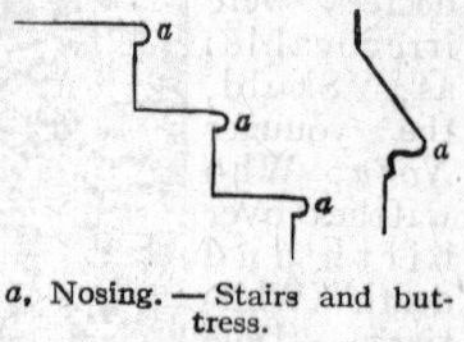
a, Nosing. — Stairs and buttress.

noso-. Form of Gr. νόσος, disease, used in combination.

nos-o-co-mi-al (nos-ǫ-kō′mi-ąl), *a.* [LL. *nosocomium*, < Gr. νοσοκομεῖον, hospital, < νόσος, disease, + κομεῖν, take care of.] Of or pertaining to a hospital.

no-sog-ra-phy (nǫ-sog′rą-fi), *n.* [See *noso-* and *-graphy.*] The systematic description of diseases.—**no-sog′ra-pher,** *n.*—**nos-o-graph-ic** (nos-ǫ-graf′ik), *a.*

no-sol-o-gy (nǫ-sol′ǫ-ji), *n.*; pl. *-gies* (-jiz). [See *noso-* and *-logy.*] The systematic classification of diseases, or the branch of medical science that deals with this; also, a systematic classification or arrangement of diseases.—**nos-o-log-i-cal** (nos-ǫ-loj′i-kąl), *a.*—**no-sol′o-gist,** *n.*

nos-tal-gia (nos-tal′jią), *n.* [NL., < Gr. νόστος, a return home, + ἄλγος, pain.] Homesickness; esp., homesickness in its severe forms, producing derangement of mental and physical functions.—**nos-tal′gic,** *a.*

nos-toc (nos′tok), *n.* [NL.; coined by Paracelsus.] Any of the fresh-water algæ constituting the genus *Nostoc*: often found in jelly-like colonies in moist places.

nos-tol-o-gy (nos-tol′ǫ-ji), *n.* [Gr. νόστος, a return home: see *-logy.*] The science that treats of senile decline in organisms.—**nos-to-log′ic** (-tǫ-loj′ik), *a.*

nos-tril (nos′tril), *n.* [AS. *nosthyrl*, < *nosu*, nose, + *thyrel*, hole, E. *thirl*[1], *n.*] An external opening of the nose.—**nos′triled, nos′trilled,** *a.* Having nostrils.

nos-trum (nos′trum), *n.* [L., neut. of *noster*, our, ours, < *nos*, we.] A medicine made by the person who recommends it; hence, a patent medicine; often, a quack medicine; also, fig., a special means recommended for accomplishing something (as, "infallible *nostrums* for procuring universal disesteem and hatred": Fielding's "Tom Jones," x. 4, chapter heading); a pet scheme or device for effecting some purpose.

nos-y, nos-ey (nō′zi). **I.** *a.* Having a large or prominent nose; also, prying; inquisitive. [Colloq.] **II.** *n.* A person with a large or prominent nose: as, Old *Nosey* (a nickname of the first Duke of Wellington).

not (not), *adv.* [ME. *not*, reduced form of *noht*, *nouht*, E. *nought.*] A word expressing negation, denial, refusal, or prohibition: as, "they toil *not*" (Mat. vi. 28), or (as now commonly) they do *not* toil; it matters *not*, or (more commonly) it does *not* matter; *not* that it matters; *not* to reply would be wiser; *not* many; a reward, *not* a punishment; *not* far from here; *not* very good; that is *not* true; I will *not* answer; you must *not* do that.—**not at all,** not in any degree or respect.

no-ta be-ne (nō′tą bē′nē). [L.] Note well; take notice: abbreviated *N. B.*

no-ta-bil-i-ty (nō-tą-bil′i-ti), *n.*; pl. *-ties* (-tiz). The quality of being notable; notable character; distinction; also, a notable thing, feature, or circumstance (now rare); also, a notable person, or a person of note or distinction (as, "The first auto-da-fé had been consummated . . . in the presence of the royal family and the principal *notabilities*, civil, ecclesiastical, and military": Motley's "Dutch Republic," i. 3).

no-ta-ble (nō′tą-bl). [OF. F. *notable*, < L. *notabilis*, < *notare*, E. *note*, *v.*] **I.** *a.* Worthy of note or notice (as, a *notable* deed, event, or occasion; *notable* excellence;

"What is truly *notable*: he said not a word to any one of the duel," Stevenson's "Master of Ballantrae," v.); noteworthy, signal, or remarkable; prominent, important, or distinguished, as persons; in an unfavorable sense, egregious or notorious (obs. or archaic: as, "He's a most *notable* coward," Shakspere's "All's Well," iii. 6. 10; "They had then a *notable* prisoner, called Barabbas," Mat. xxvii. 16); also, capable of being noted or perceived, perceptible, or appreciable, as a quantity of some constituent; also (commonly, esp. formerly, pron. not′ạ-bl), capable, thrifty, and industrious as a housewife, or pertaining to housewifely arts or activities (now chiefly prov. or literary: as, "His *notable* little wife, too, had enough to do to attend to her housekeeping," Irving's "Sketch-Book," Sleepy Hollow). **II.** *n.* A notable thing; also, a notable person, or a person of note or distinction (as, "He found my lord . . . with the governor upon one hand and various *notables* upon the other": Stevenson's "Master of Ballantrae," x.); a prominent or important citizen; [often *cap.*] in *Fr. hist.*, one of a number of prominent men from the three estates, convoked by the king on extraordinary occasions.—**no′ta-ble-ness,** *n.* —**no′ta-bly,** *adv.*

no-tan-dum (nọ̄-tan′dum), *n.*; pl. *-dums* or *-da* (-dạ̈). [L., gerundive of *notare*, E. *note, v.*] A thing to be noted; also, a record of something to be noted; a memorandum.

no-ta-ri-al (nọ̄-tā′ri-ạl), *a.* Of or pertaining to, or drawn up or executed by, a notary.—**no-ta′ri-al-ly,** *adv.*

no-ta-rize (nō′tạ-rīz), *v. t.* To notary (a contract, etc.).

no-ta-ry (nō′tạ-ri), *n.*; pl. *-ries* (-riz). [L. *notarius*, shorthand writer, clerk, secretary, < *nota*, E. *note, n.*] A clerk† or secretary†; also, a public officer authorized to authenticate deeds and contracts, take affidavits, protest bills of exchange, etc. (usually called *notary public*).—**no′ta-ry,** *v. t.*; *-ried, -rying.* To execute or attest (a contract, statement, etc.) as a notary does.

no-ta-tion (nọ̄-tā′shọn), *n.* [L. *notatio(n-)*, < *notare*, E. *note, v.*] The act of noting, marking, or setting down in writing, or a record or jotting (as, "I should not, in my *notations*, forget to mark a new luxury that got in . . . at this time": Galt's "Annals of the Parish," xxviii.); specif., the process of noting or setting down by means of a special system of signs or symbols, or the particular method or the system of signs used (as, the Arabic system of arithmetical *notation*, employing the figures 1, 2, 3, etc., or the Roman system, employing the letters I, V, X, etc., see *Roman numeral*, under *Roman, a.*; algebraic *notation*; chemical *notation*; musical *notation*).—**no-ta′tion-al,** *a.*

notch (noch), *n.* [Prob. (with *n* belonging to a preceding article *an*) < OF. *oche* (F. *hoche*), notch.] A more or less angular cut, indentation, or hollow in a narrow object or surface or an edge (as, a pole with *notches* for aid in climbing; the *notch* at each end of a bow, for holding the string; the *notches* between the teeth of a saw; "I had three large axes . . . but with much chopping and cutting knotty hard wood, they were all full of *notches*," Defoe's "Robinson Crusoe," i. 5); a nick; specif., a cut or nick made in a stick or other object for record, as in keeping a score; hence, a point in a score, as of a game; also, a step, degree, or grade (colloq.: as, the top *notch* of fashion or elegance); also, the nock or notched piece at the butt-end of an arrow (as, "drawing out an arrow, which, with the exception of the *notch* at the end, had entirely disappeared in the animal": Parkman's "Oregon Trail," xv.); also, a deep, narrow opening or pass between mountains (U. S.); in *anat.*, an indentation or depression in a bone, organ, or part.—**notch,** *v. t.* To cut or make a notch or notches in; indent; nick; often, to make notches in by way of record (as, "Many days had passed . . . how many may not be known, since I *notched* no stick": W. H. Hudson's "Green Mansions," xxi.); also, to record by a notch or notches, as on a stick; hence, to score, as in a game; also, to fix or secure by inserting in notches, as timbers; also, to nock or adjust (an arrow) to the bowstring.—**notch′er,** *n.*

note (nōt), *n.* [OF. F. *note*, < L. *nota*, a mark, sign, note, < *noscere* (pp. *notus*), know: see *know*.] A mark, token, or indication of something, or from which something may be inferred (as, "It is a *note* Of upstart greatness, to observe and watch For these poor trifles": Jonson's "Sejanus," v. 8); a characteristic or distinguishing feature; also, a stigma (now rare: as, "My posterity, shamed with the *note*, Shall curse my bones," Shakspere's "Lucrece," 208); also, a mark or sign, as of punctuation, used in writing or printing (as, a *note* of exclamation, or of interrogation); also, a brief record of something set down to assist the memory, or for reference or development (as, "When found, make a *note* of," Dickens's "Dombey and Son," xv.; "A chield's amang you taking *notes*," Burns's "Captain Grose's Peregrinations," 5; to speak from *notes*); often, *pl.*, a record of a speech, statement, testimony, etc., or of one's impressions of something; also, *sing.*, a brief written or printed statement giving particulars or information; sometimes, an account† or bill† (as, "Here is now the smith's *note* for shoeing and plough-irons": Shakspere's "2 Henry IV.," v. 1. 19); also, an explanatory or critical comment, or a reference to authority quoted, appended to a passage in a book or the like; an annotation; also, a short informal letter (as, "Not a *note*, not a line, did I receive in the meantime": Jane Austen's "Pride and Prejudice," xxvi.); a formal diplomatic or official communication in writing; also, a paper acknowledging a debt and promising payment (also called *note of hand*); also, a certificate, as of a government or a bank, passing current as money; a piece of paper money; also, a sign or character used in music to represent a tone, its position and form indicating the pitch and duration of the tone (see paragraph following); a key, as of a pianoforte; a musical sound or tone (as, "First, rehearse your song by rote, To each word a warbling *note*," Shakspere's "Midsummer Night's Dream," v. 1. 405; "the brazen *notes* of the orchestra," Thackeray's "Newcomes," xxxiii.); a melody, tune, or song (poetic: as, "Through the long-drawn aisle and fretted vault The pealing anthem swells the *note* of praise," Gray's "Elegy," x.); often, a sound of musical quality uttered by a bird (as, "the nightingale's complaining *notes*": Shakspere's "Two Gentlemen of Verona," v. 4. 5); the musical song or call of a bird (as, "The wakeful bird . . . Tunes her nocturnal *note*": Milton's "Paradise Lost," iii. 40); sometimes, any call, cry, or sound of a bird, fowl, etc. (as, "a raven's *note*," Shakspere's "2 Henry VI.," iii. 2. 40; "fowls of many sorts, making a confused screaming, and crying every one according to his usual *note*," Defoe's "Robinson Crusoe," i. 4); also, a tone sounded on a trumpet or other musical instrument as a signal, and hence, in fig. use, a signal, announcement, or intimation (as, to sound the *note* of war, or a *note* of warning; "The armourers . . . With busy hammers closing rivets up, Give dreadful *note* of preparation," Shakspere's "Henry V.," iv., Prologue, 14); also, a new or unexpected element in a situation (slang: as, this is a pretty *note!*); also, fig., way of speaking or thinking (in 'to change one's note'); also, eminence or distinction (as, a man of *note*); importance or consequence (as, "There was no other thing of *note* in this year": Galt's "Annals of the Parish," iii.); also, notice, observation, or heed (as, "Small matters win great commendation, because they are continually in use and in *note*," Bacon's "Essays," Of Ceremonies and Respects; "What if thou withdraw In silence from the living, and no friend Take *note* of thy departure?" Bryant's "Thanatopsis"); also, information or intelligence (obs. or rare: as, "Rouse him and give him *note* of our approach," Shakspere's "Troilus and Cressida," iv. 1. 43).

⁂ The system of musical notes now in use includes the following: the *breve*, 𝅜; the *semibreve* or *whole-note*, 𝅝; the *minim* or *half-note*, 𝅗𝅥 𝅗𝅥; the *crotchet* or *quarter-note*, ♩ ♩; the *quaver* or *eighth-note*, ♪ ♪ ♫; the *semiquaver* or *sixteenth-note*, 𝅘𝅥𝅯 𝅘𝅥𝅯 𝅘𝅥𝅯𝅘𝅥𝅯; the *demisemiquaver* or *thirty-second-note*, 𝅘𝅥𝅰 𝅘𝅥𝅰 𝅘𝅥𝅰𝅘𝅥𝅰; and the *hemidemisemiquaver* or *sixty-fourth-note*, 𝅘𝅥𝅱 𝅘𝅥𝅱 𝅘𝅥𝅱𝅘𝅥𝅱.

—**note,** *v. t.*; *noted, noting.* [OF. F. *noter*, < L. *notare*, mark, write, denote, observe, < *nota*.] To mark, as with some sign or written character†; also, to brand† or stigmatize†; also, to mark down, as in writing (as, "Write it before them in a table, and *note* it in a book," Isa. xxx. 8; "*Noting* down The features of the last degen'rate times," Cowper's "Task," vi. 899); make a memorandum of; make particular mention of in a writing; also, of a notary, to make a memorandum or record upon (a bill of exchange, etc.) to the effect that it has been dishonored; also, to furnish with notes or annotations; annotate; also, to set down in or furnish with musical notes; also, to indicate or designate; signify or denote; also, to observe carefully; give attention or heed to (as, your letter is received and the contents are *noted*); take notice of; perceive (as, we have not *noted* any difference between them).

note=book (nōt′bu̇k), *n.* A book for notes or memorandums; also, a book in which notes of hand are registered.

not-ed (nō′ted), *p. a.* Specially observed or noticed; conspicuous; celebrated; famous: as, "the butler, who was *noted* for round shoulders, and a Roman nose" (Addison and Steele, in "Tatler," 75); a man *noted* for his size, strength, or bravery; a *noted* criminal; "a *noted* story in Don Quixote" (Hume's "Essays," Of the Standard of Taste); a *noted* traveler, orator, or general.—**not′ed-ly,** *adv.* Conspicuously; markedly; particularly.—**not′ed-ness,** *n.*

note-less (nōt′les), *a.* Of no note; undistinguished; unnoticed; also, unmusical or voiceless.

note-let (nōt′let), *n.* A short note.

note=pa-per (nōt′pā″pėr), *n.* Paper of various sizes and qualities used for correspondence.

not-er (nō′tėr), *n.* One who notes.

note-wor-thy (nōt′wėr″ᴛʜi), *a.* Worthy of note or notice; notable.—**note′wor″thi-ly,** *adv.*—**note′wor″thi-ness,** *n.*

noth-ing (nuth′ing). [Orig. two words, *no thing.*] **I.** *n.* No thing, not anything, or naught (as, to see, do, or say *nothing*; "I opened wide the door: Darkness there, and *nothing* more!" Poe's "Raven"); no part, share, or trace (*of*: as, the place shows *nothing* of its former magnificence; there is *nothing* of his father about him); also, that which is non-existent (as, to create a world out of *nothing*; to reduce something to *nothing*, as by a process of extinction or annihilation); also, something of no importance or significance (as, "Gratiano speaks an infinite deal of *nothing*," Shakspere's "Merchant of Venice," i. 1. 114; "The defeat itself was *nothing* . . . but the death of the Prince was a blow," Besant's "Coligny," ix.); a trifling action, matter, circumstance, or thing; a trivial remark (as, "In pompous *nothings* on his side, and civil assents on that of his cousins, their time passed": Jane Austen's "Pride and Prejudice," xv.); a person of no importance, or a nobody or nonentity; in *arith.*, that which is without quantity or magnitude; also, a cipher or naught (0). **II.** *adv.* In no respect or degree; not at all: as, it was *nothing* like what we expected; we were *nothing* loath to go; "Maud to him is *nothing* akin" (Tennyson's "Maud," i. 13. 3).—**noth′ing-ness,** *n.* The state of being nothing; non-existence, or that which is non-existent (as, "such beings of cloudy fantasy [pictured ghosts], so near akin to *nothingness*": Hawthorne's "Twice-Told Tales," Fancy's Show-Box); also, the state of that which has ceased to exist (as, "A thing of beauty is a joy for ever . . . it will never Pass into *nothingness*": Keats's "Endymion," i.); sometimes, unconsciousness; also, utter insignificance, emptiness, or worthlessness (as, "the vanity and *nothingness* of the things of time in comparison to those of eternity": Scott's "Talisman," xxii.); triviality, as of speech or writing; also, something insignificant or trivial, or a mere nothing.

noth-o-fa-gus (noth-ọ-fā′gus), *n.* [NL., < Gr. νόθος, bastard, + L. *fagus*, beech.] Any tree or shrub of the fagaceous genus *Nothofagus*, of southern South America, Australia, and New Zealand, closely related to the beech (*Fagus*), but having usually much smaller leaves.

Nothofagus (*N. antarctica*). — *a*, cupule with nuts; *b*, a nut.

no-tice (nō′tis), *n.* [OF. F. *notice*, < L. *notitia*, < *notus*, pp. of *noscere*, know: see *know*.] Information or intelligence, or intimation or warning (as, to give or have *notice* of a thing; at short *notice*); sometimes, a single intimation or warning (as, "The will is the tool of the understanding, which must fashion its conclusions on the *notices* of sense," C. B. Brown's "Wieland," iv.; "His Epistles and Satires are full of proper *notices* for the conduct of life in a court," Steele, in "Tatler," 173); often, formal intimation or warning (as, "The people had *notice* by proclamation of my design to visit the town": Swift's "Gulliver's Travels," i. 4); an intimation or notification of the termination, at a specified time, of an agreement, as for renting or employment, given by one of the parties to the agreement (as, "All I've come about, is . . . to give my governor's *notice*," Dickens's "Pickwick Papers," xxvi.; "The . . . servant gave *notice*," Arnold Bennett's "Helen with the High Hand," xvi.); also, a note, placard, or the like conveying information or warning; also, observation, attention, or heed (as, take *notice*; not worthy of *notice*); a noting, remarking, or perceiving (as, to come forth to *notice*; to escape *notice*); often, interested or favorable attention (as, "They court the *notice* of a future age": Cowper's "On the Biographia Britannica," 4); sometimes, a single observation or perception (as, "See what it is to trust to imperfect memory, and the erring *notices* of childhood!" Lamb's "Old Benchers of the Inner Temple"); also, a brief written mention or account, as of a newly published book.—**no′tice,** *v. t.*; *-ticed*, *-ticing.* To give information or intimation of†; also, to make mention of or refer to (as, to *notice* a matter in a speech or book); mention or point out, as to a person (as, "After church, Miss Thornton *noticed* it to her": H. Kingsley's "Geoffry Hamlyn," xi.); also, to give intimation or notice to, or serve with a notice (as, "Their attorneys have *noticed* us that they have withdrawn the suit": Trollope's "Warden," xvii.); also, to take notice of or pay attention to (as, "The wretch that works and weeps without relief, Has one that *notices* his silent grief": Cowper's "Charity," 207); perceive (as, did you *notice* what he was doing?); often, to treat with attention, politeness, or favor (as, "If you *notice* her so much she will be vain": Mrs. Stowe's "Oldtown Folks," xxiv.); acknowledge acquaintance with (as, to refuse to *notice* a person).—**no′tice-a-ble,** *a.* That may be noticed or perceived; such as to attract notice (as, "His long, feminine eyelashes were very *noticeable*": J. Conrad's "Victory," ii. 4).—**no′tice-a-ble-ness,** *n.*—**no′tice-a-bly,** *adv.*

no-ti-fi-ca-tion (nō″ti-fi-kā′shọn), *n.* [OF. F. *notification*, < ML. *notificatio(n-)*.] The act of notifying, making known, or giving notice; notice given; a notice; specif., a formal notifying or informing (as, the *notification* of a presidential nominee of his nomination).

no-ti-fy (nō′ti-fī), *v. t.*; *-fied*, *-fying.* [OF. F. *notifier*, < L. *notificare*, < *notus*, pp. of *noscere*, know, + *facere*, make.] To make known, or give information or notice of (as, "The Khan had . . . *notified* his intention to pass the summer heats on the banks of the Torgau": De Quincey's "Revolt of the Tartars"); also, to give notice to, or inform, of something; also, to take note of†, or observe†.—**no′ti-fi-er** (-fī-ėr), *n.*

no-tion (nō′shọn), *n.* [L. *notio(n-)*, a becoming acquainted, conception, notion, < *noscere*, know: see *know*.] A general concept under which a particular thing is classed; also, a conception or idea (as, "A blind man can form no *notion* of colours": Hume's "Inquiry concerning Human Understanding," ii.); often, a more or less general, vague, or imperfect conception or idea of something (as, crude *notions* of beauty; "She certainly has some *notion* of drawing," Kipling's "Light That Failed," vi.); also, an opinion, view, or belief (as, "They are for holding their *notions*, though all other men be against them": Bunyan's "Pilgrim's Progress," i.); also, an inclination or fancy (as, I have a *notion* to try it); a whim (as, "She's got this *notion* o' being a lady's-maid wi' going among them servants": George Eliot's "Adam Bede," xxxi.); a fanciful or foolish idea (as, a girl with a head full of *notions*); sometimes, a fancy or affection for one of the opposite sex (Sc. and prov. Eng.: as, "During this visit, he took a *notion* of Effie Malcolm, and the lassie of him," Galt's "Annals of the Parish," xvii.); also, the mind† or intellect† (as, "His *notion* weakens, his discernings Are lethargied": Shakspere's "King Lear," i. 4. 248); also, a device, contrivance, or ingenious article; *pl.*, small useful wares, esp. pins, needles, thread, tapes, etc. (as, a dealer in dry-goods and *notions*); also, miscellaneous articles or wares forming a cargo (as, "Her cargo consisted of what the Americans called *notions*; that is, in English, an assorted cargo," Marryat's "Peter Simple," xliii.; "a cargo of fresh provisions, mules, tin bake-pans, and other *notions*," Dana's "Two Years before the Mast," xxxv.).—**no′tion-al,** *a.* Pertaining to or expressing a notion or idea; of the nature of a notion; abstract or speculative, as knowledge; ideal or imaginary, as things; also, given to or full of notions, as a person; fanciful.—**no′tion-al-ly,** *adv.*—**no′tion-ate** (-āt), *a.* Full of notions or fancies; also, possessed with a notion; opinionated. [Colloq. or prov.]

no-to-chord (nō′tọ-kôrd), *n.* [Gr. νῶτον, back, + χορδή, string.] In *biol.*, a rod-like embryonic structure which is the primitive backbone of the higher vertebrates, but which persists throughout life in certain of the lower forms.

no-to-don-tid (nō-tọ-don′tid). [NL. *Notodontidæ*, pl., < *Notodonta*, the typical genus, < Gr. νῶτον, back, + ὀδούς (ὀδοντ-), tooth.] **I.** *n.* Any moth of the family *Notodontidæ*, as *Notodonta concinna*, a common North American species whose larva eats the leaves of the apple, plum, etc. **II.** *a.* Belonging or pertaining to the *Notodontidæ*.

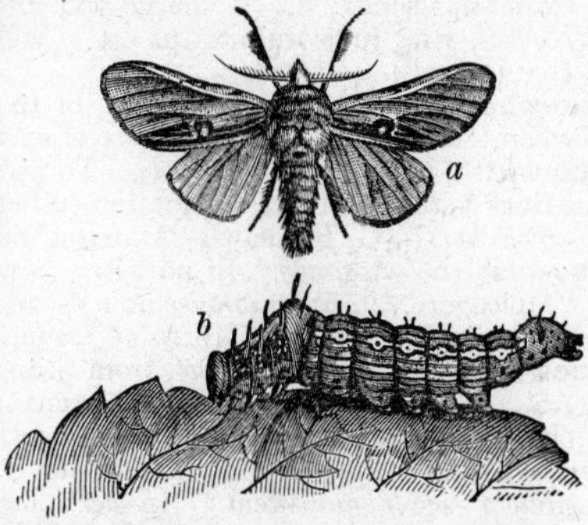

Notodontid (*Notodonta concinna*). — *a*, imago; *b*, larva.

No-to-gæ-a (nō-tọ-jē′ạ̈), *n.* [NL., < Gr. νότος, the south, + γαῖα, land, earth.] In *zoögeog.*, a primary realm of the earth's surface, comprising Australia, New Zealand, etc., and sometimes South America and tropical North America.—**No-to-gæ′an, No-to-gæ′ic,** *a.*

no-to-ri-e-ty (nō-tọ-rī′ẹ-ti), *n.*; pl. *-ties* (-tiz). [ML. *notorietas*.] The state or character of being notorious, or publicly or widely known (as, a man of considerable *notoriety*; a craze for *notoriety*); also, a widely known or well-known person (as, "There were all the Dublin *notorieties*; swarming in barouches": Lever's "Harry Lorrequer," xlvi.).

no-to-ri-ous (nọ-tō′ri-us), *a.* [ML. *notorius*, < L. *noscere*, know: see *know*.] Publicly or generally known (as, "It was *notorious* that he commanded only the wreck of an army": Motley's "Dutch Republic," i. 2); often, of objectionable things, evil persons, etc., publicly or widely known as such, flagrant, or arrant (as, a *notorious* nuisance; *notorious* crimes; a *notorious* thief); hence, widely but unfavorably known (as, a *notorious* resort; a *notorious* woman; his practices were *notorious*).—**no-to′ri-ous-ly,** *adv.*—**no-to′ri-ous-ness,** *n.*

no-tor-nis (nọ-tôr′nis), *n.* [NL., < Gr. νότος, the south, + ὄρνις, bird.] Any of the extinct or rare flightless birds constituting the genus *Notornis*, chiefly of New Zealand, allied to the gallinules.

not-with-stand-ing (not-wiᴛʜ-stan′ding). **I.** *negative ppr.* Not withstanding or preventing; not availing to the contrary: used after a substantive in absolute constructions: as, he persisted, remonstrances *notwithstanding*. **II.** *prep.* Without being withstood or prevented by; in spite of: as, he persisted *notwithstanding* remonstrances. **III.** *conj.* In spite of the fact that; although: as, *notwithstanding* there were remonstrances, he persisted. **IV.** *adv.* Nevertheless; yet: as, there were remonstrances, but he persisted *notwithstanding*.

nou-gat (nö′gạt or nö′gạ̈, F. nö-gä), *n.* [F., < Pr. *nougat*, < L. *nux* (*nuc-*), nut.] A paste-like sweetmeat containing almonds or other nuts.

nought (nôt), *n.*, *a.*, and *adv.* [AS. *nōwiht*: see *naught*.] Same as *naught*.

nou-me-non (nö′me-non or nou′-), *n.*; pl. *-na* (-nạ̈). [Gr. νοούμενον, neut. ppr. pass. of νοεῖν, perceive, < νόος, mind: see *nous*.] In the *Kantian philos.*, that which can be the object only of a purely intellectual (non-sensuous) intuition; the real or transcendental object to which a phenomenon is referred as to the basis or cause; a thing in itself, as distinguished from a phenomenon, or thing as it appears to us.—**nou′me-nal,** *a.*—**nou′me-nal-ly,** *adv.*

noun (noun), *n.* [AF. *noun*, OF. *non*, *nom* (F. *nom*), < L. *nomen*, name: see *name*.] In *gram.*, a word used as the name of a person or thing, as *man*, *dog*, *tree*, *health*, *John*, *France*, etc.—**common noun.** See *common*, *a.*—**proper noun.** See *proper*.—**noun′al,** *a.* Of, pertaining to, or of the nature of a noun.—**noun′al-ly,** *adv.*

nour-ish (nur′ish), *v. t.* [OF. *norir* (*noriss-*) (F. *nourrir*), < L. *nutrire* (pp. *nutritus*), suckle, feed, foster, maintain.] To suckle (a child or young animal)†; also, to sustain (a living or organized body, animal or vegetable) with food or nutriment; supply with what is necessary for maintaining life (as, "Thou shalt dwell in the land of Goshen . . . And there will I *nourish* thee": Gen. xlv. 11); in general, to supply with what is needed to promote growth or keep in due condition or in existence (as, a river *nourished* by many small streams); maintain; fig., to foster or promote (a feeling, etc.: as, "I could find nothing to *nourish* my suspicion," Defoe's "Robinson Crusoe," i. 15); cherish in one's heart or mind (as, "Clodius . . . *nourishing* an implacable hate against Cicero": Froude's "Cæsar," xv.); also, to bring up†, rear†, or nurture†.—**nour′ish-er,** *n.*—**nour′ish-ing-ly,** *adv.*—**nour′ish-ment,** *n.* The act of nourishing, or the state of being nourished; also, that which nourishes; food, nutriment, or sustenance (as, "Their *nourishment* consisted entirely of the vegetables of their garden, and the milk of one cow": Mrs. Shelley's "Frankenstein," xii.).

nous (nös or nous), *n.* [Gr. νοῦς, contr. of νόος, mind, prob. akin to γιγνώσκειν, know, and E. *know*.] In *Gr. philos.*, mind or intellect; also, in colloquial use, common sense, or gumption.

nou-veau riche (nö-vō rēsh); pl. *nouveaux riches* (nö-vō rēsh). [F. (fem. *nouvelle riche*), 'new rich.'] One who has newly become rich; a wealthy parvenu: as, "the . . . modern mansion of a *nouveau riche*" (Bulwer-Lytton's "Pelham," xxiii.).

no-va (nō′vạ̈), *n.*; pl. *-væ* (-vē) or *-vas* (-vạ̈z). [NL., prop. fem. of L. *novus*, new: see *new*.] In *astron.*, a new star which makes its appearance suddenly and then gradually grows fainter, becoming telescopic or disappearing entirely.

no-vac-u-lite (nọ-vak′ụ̄-līt), *n.* [L. *novacula*, sharp knife, razor, < *novare*, renew: see *novate*.] In *petrog.*, a very hard, compact, siliceous rock, probably sedimentary in origin, used for hones, etc.

no-vate (nō′vāt or nọ-vāt′), *v. t.*; *-vated*, *-vating*. [L. *novatus*, pp. of *novare*, make new, renew, < *novus*, new.] To replace by something new; in *law*, to replace by a new obligation, debt, etc.

No-va-tian (nọ-vā′shiạn), *n.* One of a sect founded in the middle of the 3d century by Novatianus, or Novatian, a Roman schismatic bishop, who denied that the church had power to restore to communion those guilty of idolatry after Christian baptism, and whose followers appear to have refused the grant of forgiveness to all grave sin committed after baptism.—**No-va′tian-ism,** *n.*

no-va-tion (nọ-vā′shọn), *n.* [L. *novatio(n-)*, < *novare*: see *novate*.] The introduction of something new; an innovation; esp., in *law*, the substitution of a new obligation for an old one, usually by the substitution of a new debtor or of a new creditor.

nov-el (nov′ẹl). [As adj., OF. *novel* (F. *nouveau*), < L. *novellus*, dim. of *novus*, new; as n., OF. *novele*, something new, news, F. *nouvelle* and It. *novella*, story, also LL. *novella* (in Rom. law), all < L. *novella*, fem. of *novellus*, adj.] **I.** *a.* New as to origin or production†, or newly arisen or made†; also, of a new kind, or different from anything seen or known before (as, a *novel* scene; a *novel* experience; "The Spaniards were astonished at these *novel* manœuvres [by musketeers on skates] upon the ice," Motley's "Dutch Republic," iii. 8); unusual or strange, esp. in a noticeable or interesting way. **II.** *n.* Something new†, or a novelty†; also, a piece of news†, or (in *pl.*) news†; also, formerly, a short story, as a novella; now, a fictitious prose narrative of considerable length, portraying characters, actions, and scenes representative of real life in a plot of more or less intricacy; also, a new or supplementary decree or constitution of the Roman law; *pl.* [*cap.*], those made by Justinian (emperor 527–65).—**nov-el-ette′** (-et′), *n.* [See *-ette.*] A short novel.—**nov′el-ist,** *n.* One who introduces novelties or innovations†; also, a newsmonger†; also, a writer of novels.—**nov-el-is′tic,** *a.* Of, pertaining to, or characteristic of novels.—**nov-el-is′ti-cal-ly,** *adv.*—**nov′el-ize** (-īz), *v. t.*; *-ized, -izing.* To put into the form of a novel: as, to *novelize* history; to *novelize* a play.—**nov″el-i-za′tion** (-i-zā′shọn), *n.*

no-vel-la (nō-vel′lä), *n.*; pl. *-le* (-lā). [It.: see *novel.*] A tale or short story of the type of those contained in the "Decameron" of Boccaccio, the "Heptameron" of Margaret of Navarre, etc.

nov-el-ly (nov′ẹl-li), *adv.* In a novel manner.

nov-el-ty (nov′ẹl-ti), *n.*; pl. *-ties* (-tiz). [OF. *novelte* (F. *nouveauté*), < LL. *novellitas*, < L. *novellus*, E. *novel.*] Novel character, newness, or strangeness (as, "Every day brings something new; but we lose the sense of *novelty*": Galt's "Ayrshire Legatees," viii.); also, something novel or new; a novel thing, experience, or proceeding; an innovation; specif., a new or novel article of trade; a variety of goods differing from the staple or ordinary kinds.

No-vem-ber (nọ-vem′bėr), *n.* [L. *November*, the ninth month of the Roman year, < *novem*, nine.] The eleventh month of the year, containing 30 days.

no-ve-na (nọ-vē′nạ̈), *n.* [ML., prop. fem. of L. *novenus*, nine each, < *novem*, nine.] In the *Rom. Cath. Ch.*, a devotion consisting of prayers or services on nine consecutive days, sometimes nine corresponding days in consecutive months (as, a *novena* of nine first Fridays).

no-ven-ni-al (nọ-ven′i-ạl), *a.* [LL. *novennis*, < L. *novem*, nine, + *annus*, year.] Occurring every nine years.

no-ver-cal (nọ-vėr′kạl), *a.* [L. *novercalis*, < *noverca*, stepmother.] Of, like, or befitting a stepmother.

nov-ice (nov′is), *n.* [OF. F. *novice*, < L. *novicius*, later *novitius*, new, < *novus*, new.] One who has been received into a religious order or congregation for a period of probation before taking vows; hence, in general, a beginner in some calling, art, work, or the like (as, a *novice* in carpentry, cookery, or politics); one who is new to the circumstances in which he is placed; a tyro.—**nov′ice-ship,** *n.* The state or period of being a novice; novitiate.

no-vi-ti-ate, no-vi-ci-ate (nọ-vish′i-āt), *n.* [ML. *novitiatus.*] The state or period of being a novice of a religious order or congregation; hence, the state or period of being a beginner in anything; also, a novice, specif. of a religious order or congregation; also, the house or quarters occupied by religious novices during their period of probation.

no-vo-ca-ine, no-vo-ca-in (nō-vọ-kā′in, -kān′), *n.* [L. *novus*, new, + E. (*co*)*caine.*] A non-irritant local anesthetic, a synthetic and much less toxic substitute for cocaine. [Proprietary name *novocain.*]

now (nou), *adv.* [AS. *nū* = D. and G. *nu* = Icel. *nū* = Goth. *nu*, now; akin to L. *nunc*, Gr. *νυ*, *νῦν*, Skt. *nu*, *nūnam*, now.] At the present time or moment (as, he is here *now*; the clock is *now* striking one); more emphatically, immediately or at once (as, do it *now*; *now* or never); also, at the time or moment only just past (now chiefly in 'just now': as, I saw him just *now* on the street; the book was here only just *now*); also, at this time or juncture in some period under consideration or in some course of proceedings described (as, night was *now* approaching; the people *now* rose in revolt; the case *now* passes to the jury; the committee having reported the bill, the assembly will *now* take action); also, in these present times, or nowadays (as, a bird *now* rarely seen; practices *now* disused or prohibited); also, under the present or existing circumstances, or as matters stand (as, I could believe almost anything *now*; "What cares he *now* for curb or pricking spur?" Shakspere's "Venus and Adonis," 285); also, often used as a preliminary word before some statement, question, or the like (as, *now*, the charge was a false one; *now*, what does he mean?), or to strengthen a command, entreaty, or the like (as, come, *now*, stop that! *now*, please don't!).—**now and again,** at one time and again at another; now and then.—**now and then,** at one time and another; occasionally.—**now . . . now,** at one time . . . at another time: as, "like a stormy day, *now* wind, *now* rain" (Shakspere's "Venus and Adonis," 965).—**now that,** since it is the case now that; seeing that: as, *now that* you are here, you can help us; *now that* the trouble is over, why dwell upon it?—**now,** *conj.* Now that, since, or seeing that: as, *now* you are here, why not stay?—**now,** *n.* The present time or moment: as, "It seemed an age since that morning, as if a chasm ran between the *now* and the then" (J. H. Newman's "Callista," xxxv.).—**now,** *a.* Being, or being such, now; present: as, the *now* king. [Now rare.]

now-a-days (nou′ạ-dāz). [See *a*[2].] **I.** *adv.* At the present day; in these times: as, "People are getting so cursedly in earnest *now-a-days*" (Kingsley's "Yeast," vi.). **II.** *n.* The present day; these days: as, the sports of *nowadays.*

no-way (nō′wā), *adv.* In no way, respect, or degree; not at all. Also **no′ways.**

now-el, now-ell (nō-el′ or nō′el), *n.* and *interj.* [= *noël.*] An exclamation of joy over the birth of the Saviour, used in Christmas songs: as, "I charge you, brothers, sing *Nowell, Nowell*, Rex Judæorum natus est" (Masefield's "Christmas Eve at Sea"). Cf. *noël.*

no-where (nō′hwãr), *adv.* In, at, or to no place; not anywhere: as, a plant found *nowhere* else; to go *nowhere.*

no-whith-er (nō′hwiᴛʜ″ėr), *adv.* To no place; nowhere: as, "Does a ship sail to its destination no better than a log drifts *nowhither?*" (G. B. Shaw's "Man and Superman," iii.).

no-wise (nō′wīz), *adv.* In no wise; noway; not at all: as, "Meleager . . . Who *nowise* now dreaded the proffered cup Of life and death" (W. Morris's "Jason," iii. 394).

nowt (nout), *n.* [ME. *nowt*, from Scand.: cf. Icel. *naut* = AS. *nēat*, E. *neat*[1].] Cattle or oxen; also, an ox; fig., a clumsy or stupid person. [Sc. and north. Eng.]

now-y (nou′i or nō′i), *a.* [F. *noué*, lit. 'knotted,' pp. of *nouer*: see *dénouement.*] In *her.*, having a small semicircular projection at or near the middle, as a line or fesse; of a cross, having a projection in each angle between the arms (the projection being rounded in case of a 'cross nowy,' and angular in case of a 'cross nowy quadrant': see cut at *cross, n.*).

nox-al (nok′sạl), *a.* [L. *noxalis*, < *noxa*: see *noxious.*] In *Rom. law*, relating to wrongful injury: as, a *noxal* action.

nox-ious (nok′shus), *a.* [L. *noxius*, < *noxa*, harm, injury, < *nocere*, to harm, hurt.] Harmful or injurious to health or physical well-being (as, *noxious* vapors; "He began . . . to rail at tobacco, as a *noxious*, nauseous weed," Irving's "Knickerbocker's New York," iv. 8); deleterious; unwholesome; also, morally harmful, or pernicious (as, *noxious* teachings; "an unjust and *noxious* tyranny," Macaulay's "Hist. of Eng.," i.).—**nox′ious-ly,** *adv.*—**nox′ious-ness,** *n.*

noy-ade (nwo-yäd), *n.* [F., < *noyer*, drown, < L. *necare*, kill.] Destruction or execution by drowning, esp. as practised at Nantes, France, by the Revolutionary agent Carrier in 1793–94.

noy-au (nwo-yō), *n.* [F., lit. 'kernel': see *newel.*] A cordial or liqueur flavored with the kernels of peaches, cherries, or other fruit, or with some substitute.

noz-zle (noz′l), *n.* [Dim. of *nose.*] A projecting spout, terminal discharging pipe, or the like, as of a bellows or a hose; hence, any projecting part or end; the nose (slang: as, "His whole face was overshadowed by this tremendous *nozzle*," Smollett's "Humphry Clinker," April 18); also, the socket of a candlestick.

nu (nū), *n.* [Gr. *νῦ.*] The thirteenth letter (Ν, *ν*, = English N, n) of the Greek alphabet.

nu-ance (nū-äns′ or nū′äns, F. nü-äṅs), *n.* [F., < *nuer*, to shade, < *nue*, < L. *nubes*, a cloud.] A shade of color, or, fig., of expression, meaning, feeling, etc.: as, "He was well read in Greek, Italian, and English literature, and exceedingly sensitive to *nuances* of style" (M. Hewlett's "Open Country," v.).—**nu-anced** (nū-änst′ or nū′änst), *a.* Marked by or exhibiting nuances.

nub (nub), *n.* [= *knub.*] A knob or protuberance; a lump or small piece; also, the point or gist of anything (colloq., U. S.).

nub-bin (nub′in), *n.* [Cf. *nub.*] A small lump or piece; also, a small or imperfect ear of maize, or an undeveloped fruit (U. S.).

nub-ble (nub′l), *n.* [Dim. of *nub.*] A small knob or protuberance (as, "He was lying on a piece of dingy ticking full of lumps and *nubbles*": Kipling's "Captains Courageous," i.); a small lump or piece.—**nub′bly,** *a.* Full of small protuberances; also, in the form of small lumps (as, "Quick, some coal, some *nubbly* pieces": Hood's "Steam Service," ii.).

nu-bi-a (nū′bi-ạ), *n.* [L. *nubes,* cloud.] A woman's light knitted woolen scarf for the head or neck.

Nu-bi-an (nū′bi-ạn). **I.** *a.* Of or pertaining to Nubia, a region of Africa south of Egypt and bordering on the Red Sea. **II.** *n.* One of a negroid people, of mixed descent, inhabiting Nubia; the negro language spoken by this people; also, a Nubian or negro slave; also, a Nubian horse.

nu-bile (nū′bil), *a.* [L. *nubilis,* < *nubere,* marry.] Marriageable, esp. as to age or physical development, as a girl; suitable for marriage, as the age.—**nu-bil-i-ty** (nū-bil′i-ti), *n.*

nu-bi-lous (nū′bi-lus), *a.* [LL. *nubilosus,* or L. *nubilus,* cloudy, < *nubes,* cloud.] Cloudy or foggy; fig., obscure; indefinite.

nu-cel-lus (nū-sel′us), *n.*; pl. *nucelli* (-ī). [NL., dim. of L. *nux* (*nuc-*), nut.] In *bot.,* the central cellular mass of the body of the ovule, containing the embryo-sac.—**nu-cel′lar** (-sel′ạr), *a.*

nu-cha (nū′kạ), *n.*; pl. *nuchæ* (-kē). [ML.; from Ar.] The nape of the neck.—**nu′chal,** *a.* Pertaining to the nape of the neck; in *entom.,* situated on the thorax just behind the head, as certain markings.

nu-civ-o-rous (nū-siv′ọ-rus), *a.* [L. *nux* (*nuc-*), nut, + *vorare,* devour.] Nut-eating; feeding on nuts.

nu-cle-ar (nū′klē-ạr), *a.* Of, pertaining to, or forming a nucleus. Also **nu′cle-a-ry** (-ạ-ri).

nu-cle-ate, nu-cle-at-ed (nū′klē-āt, -ā-ted), *a.* [L. *nucleatus,* having a kernel or stone, < *nucleus*: see *nucleus.*] Having a nucleus.—**nu′cle-ate,** *v.*; *-ated, -ating.* **I.** *tr.* To form into a nucleus. **II.** *intr.* To form, or gather round, a nucleus.—**nu-cle-a′tion** (-ā′shọn), *n.*

nu-cle-i (nū′klē-ī). Plural of *nucleus.*

nu-cle-in (nū′klē-in), *n.* [From *nucleus.*] In *physiol. chem.,* any of a class of phosphorus-containing proteid substances occurring in cell-nuclei.—**nu-cle-in′ic, nu-cle-ic** (nū-klē′ik), *a.*

nu-cle-o-lus (nū-klē′ọ-lus), *n.*; pl. *-li* (-lī). [L., little nut, dim. of *nucleus*: see *nucleus.*] In *biol.,* a body, rounded structure, or granule within the nucleus of a cell.—**nu-cle′o-lar** (-lạr), *a.*—**nu-cle-o-late, nu-cle-o-lat-ed** (nū′klē-ọ-lāt, -lā-ted), *a.*

nu-cle-o-plasm (nū′klē-ọ-plazm), *n.* [See *nucleus* and *-plasm.*] In *biol.,* same as *karyoplasm.*

nu-cle-us (nū′klē-us), *n.*; pl. *nucleuses* or *nuclei* (-ī). [L., nut, kernel, fruit-stone, dim. < *nux* (*nuc-*), nut.] A central part or thing about which other parts or things are grouped; anything constituting a central part, foundation, or beginning (as, "Here Ribaut resolved on leaving the *nucleus* of a settlement," Besant's "Coligny," vii.; "a very strange old gentleman, whose eccentricity had become the *nucleus* for a thousand fantastic stories," Hawthorne's "Twice-Told Tales," Dr. Heidegger's Experiment); in *biol.,* a differentiated mass (usually rounded) of protoplasm present in the interior of nearly all living cells and forming an essential element in their growth and reproduction; in *anat.,* a mass of gray matter in the brain or spinal cord, having special functions; in *astron.,* the more condensed portion of the head of a comet.

nu-cule (nū′kūl), *n.* [L. *nucula,* dim. of *nux* (*nuc-*), nut.] In *bot.,* a nutlet.

nude (nūd). [L. *nudus*: see *naked.*] **I.** *a.* Naked or unclothed, as a person, the body, etc.; destitute of drapery or covering, as a human figure represented in art; in general, destitute of the usual coverings, overlying matter, furnishings, etc.; bare; also, being such and no more, or mere; in *law,* unsupported or naked (as, a *nude* pact, one made without a consideration). **II.** *n.* A nude figure as represented in art; with *the,* the undraped human figure, or the condition of being undraped.—**nude′ly,** *adv.*—**nude′ness,** *n.*

nudge (nuj), *v.*; *nudged, nudging.* [Origin obscure.] **I.** *tr.* To push slightly or jog, esp. with the elbow, as in calling attention or giving a hint or with sly meaning: as, "His next neighbours *nudged* him" (Dickens's "Oliver Twist," ii.). **II.** *intr.* To give a nudge or slight push.—**nudge,** *n.* A slight push or jog, as with the elbow.

nu-di-cau-lous (nū-di-kâ′lus), *a.* [L. *nudus,* naked, + *caulis,* stem.] In *bot.,* having leafless stems.

nud-ism (nū′dizm), *n.* The practice of going nude or naked as a measure of healthful living, as by a company of persons. —**nud′ist,** *n.* One who practises nudism.

nu-di-ty (nū′di-ti), *n.*; pl. *-ties* (-tiz). The state or fact of being nude; nakedness; also, something nude or naked; a nude figure, esp. as represented in art.

nug (nug), *n.* [Cf. *nog*[1].] A lump or mass of something; also, a knot or protuberance. [Prov. Eng.]

nu-ga-to-ry (nū′gạ-tọ-ri), *a.* [L. *nugatorius,* < *nugari,* to jest, trifle, < *nugæ,* jests, trifles, nonsense.] Trifling, of no real value, or worthless (as, "Descartes was perhaps the first who saw that definitions of words, already as clear as they can be made, are *nugatory* or impracticable": Hallam's "Literature of Europe," iii. 3. § 101); also, of no force or effect, futile, or vain (as, "The numerous codicils of some wills . . . to a certain degree make the will *nugatory*": Marryat's "Mr. Midshipman Easy," xii.).

nug-gar (nug′ạr), *n.* [Egyptian.] A large, broad boat used on the Nile for the transportation of cargo, troops, etc.

nug-get (nug′et), *n.* [Appar. a dim. of *nug.*] A lump of something; esp., a lump of native gold.—**nug′get-y,** *a.*

nui-sance (nū′sạns), *n.* [OF. *nuisance,* < *nuire,* < L. *nocere,* harm, hurt.] Injury, trouble, or annoyance (now rare: as, without *nuisance* to others); also, something offensive or annoying to individuals or to the community, to the prejudice of their legal rights (as, "The ringing of bells, building operations, vibration of machinery, fireworks, bands . . . have been held under certain circumstances to constitute *nuisances* . . . and have been restrained by injunction": Encyc. Brit., 11th ed., XIX. 733); hence, in general, any cause of trouble or annoyance (as, "The quartering of soldiers upon the colonists was a great *nuisance,*" H. G. Wells's "Outline of History," xxxvii. § 3; "He had had no idea how great a *nuisance* a baby was," S. Butler's "Way of All Flesh," xx.); a highly obnoxious thing or person.

null (nul), *a.* [F. *nul,* < L. *nullus,* not any, no, none, < *ne,* not, + *ullus,* any, dim. < *unus,* one.] Being none, wanting, or non-existent (as, the effect was small or *null*); also, of no legal or binding force (as, "The King's grant and letters . . . were legally *null* and void": Green's "Short Hist. of the Eng. People," v. 4); invalid; void; also, of no effect, consequence, or significance (as, "Here the principle of contribution . . . is reprobated as *null,* and destructive to equality": Burke's "Revolution in France," 259); also, lacking distinctive character or individuality (as, "His personality during his residence was *null*": Motley's "Dutch Republic," vi. 4); expressionless (as, "A cold and clear-cut face . . . All that I saw . . . Faultily faultless, icily regular, splendidly *null*": Tennyson's "Maud," i. 2).

nul-lah (nul′ạ), *n.* [Hind. *nālā.*] In the East Indies, a watercourse; often, the bed of a stream, whether with water or dry; a ravine.

nul-li-fi-ca-tion (nul″i-fi-kā′shọn), *n.* [LL. *nullificatio(n-).*] The act of nullifying, or the state of being nullified; in *U. S. hist.,* the action of a State in declaring a federal law inoperative within its limits, under the assumption of absolute State sovereignty (as, "The conflict of these views [as to State sovereignty], which became acute in 1830 when South Carolina claimed the right of *nullification,* produced Secession and the war of 1861–65": Bryce's "American Commonwealth," xxxvi.).—**nul″li-fi-ca′tion-ist,** *n.*

nul-li-fid-i-an (nul-i-fid′i-ạn), *n.* [L. *nullus,* not any, + *fides,* faith.] One who has no faith or religion; a skeptic; an unbeliever.

nul-li-fy (nul′i-fī), *v. t.*; *-fied, -fying.* [LL. *nullificare,* < L. *nullus,* E. *null,* + *facere,* make.] To make null; render or declare legally void or inoperative (as, to *nullify* a contract or a law); make ineffective, futile, or of no consequence (as, to *nullify* efforts or influence; a defect that *nullifies* the advantages of a plan).—**nul′li-fi-er** (-fī-ėr), *n.*

nul-lip-a-ra (nu-lip′ạ-rä̤), *n.*; pl. *-ræ* (-rē). [NL., < L. *nullus*, not any, + *parere*, bring forth.] In *obstet.*, a woman who has never borne a child.—**nul-lip′a-rous,** *a.* Having never borne a child, as a woman.—**nul-li-par-i-ty** (nul-i-par′i-ti), *n.*

nul-li-pen-nate (nul-i-pen′āt), *a.* [L. *nullus*, not any, + *penna*, feather.] Having no flight-feathers, as the penguin.

nul-li-pore (nul′i-pōr), *n.* [L. *nullus*, not any, + *porus*, E. *pore*[2].] Any of various marine algæ having the power of secreting lime, as a coralline: as, "Some marine plants, like the calcareous *nullipores*, afford protection to shore rocks by covering them with a hard incrustation" (Encyc. Brit., 11th ed., XI. 663).

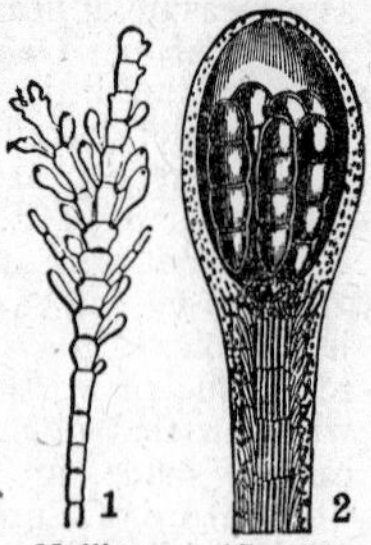

Nullipore (*Corallina officinalis*). — 1, portion of a frond, about one half natural size; 2, tip of a branch, bearing a conceptacle and cut longitudinally.

nul-li-ty (nul′i-ti), *n.*; pl. *-ties* (-tiz). The state or fact of being null; nothingness; invalidity; want of effect, or futility (as, "Mr. Falkland had experienced the *nullity* of all expostulation with Mr. Tyrrel": Godwin's "Caleb Williams," ix.); also, something null; a mere nothing; a nonentity (as, "Reduced almost to a *nullity* by the Prince of Orange, it was time for him to make a stand": Motley's "Dutch Republic," v. 3); something of no legal force or validity (as, "The Declaration was, in the eye of the law, a *nullity*": Macaulay's "Hist. of Eng.," vii.).

numb (num), *a.* [ME. *nome*, pp., lit. 'taken,' 'seized,' for *nomen, numen*, < AS. *numen*, pp. of *niman*, take: see *nim*.] Deprived of or deficient in the power of sensation and movement (as, fingers *numb* with cold); benumbed; also, of the nature of numbness (as, a *numb* sensation); also, causing numbness† (as, "the *numb* cold night": Shakspere's "Richard III.," ii. 1. 117).—**numb,** *v. t.* To make numb: as, "arms and ankles . . . *numbed* and stiff with . . . binding" (Defoe's "Robinson Crusoe," i. 16); "Phryxus . . . dizzy with the murmuring sea, *Numbed* by the cold wind" (W. Morris's "Jason," ii. 695).

num-ber (num′bėr), *n.* [OF. F. *nombre*, < L. *numerus*, number, aggregate, class, musical measure, verse; akin to Gr. *νέμειν*, deal out: see *nome*.] The sum, total, or aggregate of a collection of units (as, the *number* of eggs in a nest, or of soldiers in an army; the greatest *number* of books ever collected together); *pl.* [*cap.*], the fourth book of the Old Testament, containing a census of the Israelites; also, *sing.* [*l. c.*], a word or symbol, or a combination of words or symbols, used in counting or to denote a total; a numeral; *pl.*, arithmetic; also, *sing.*, the particular numeral assigned to anything in order to fix its place in a series (as, the *number* of a house on a street; the license-*number* of an automobile; a policeman's *number*); also, one of a series of things distinguished by numerals; a single part of a book published in parts (as, "I consider it vulgar, and below the dignity of literature, to publish in *numbers*": Mrs. Gaskell's "Cranford," i.); a single issue of a periodical (as, the April *number* of a magazine); any of a collection of poems or songs (as, "There was a *number* in the hawker's collection . . . which may rank among the most dissuasive war-lyrics on record": Stevenson's "Inland Voyage," xii.); a distinct part of an extended musical work; a single part of a program made up of a number of parts; also, the full count of a collection or company (as, "Here is two more called than your *number*; you must have but four here, sir": Shakspere's "2 Henry IV.," iii. 2. 201); a collection or company (as, "The head One of our *number*": Milton's "Paradise Lost," v. 843); a quantity (large or small) of individuals (as, "an innumerable *number* of fowls of many sorts," Defoe's "Robinson Crusoe," i. 4; a small *number* of persons); a certain collection, company, or quantity not precisely reckoned, but usually considerable or large (as, to have a *number* of hats; doubtful for a *number* of reasons; a *number* of complaints were made); *pl.*, considerable collections or quantities (as, "A lazar-house . . . wherein were laid *Numbers* of all diseased": Milton's "Paradise Lost," xi. 480); *sing.*, numerical strength or superiority (as, "*Number* itself in armies importeth not much, where the people are of weak courage": Bacon's "Essays," Of the True Greatness of Kingdoms and Estates); also, quantity as composed of units (as, the difference between 'many' and 'few' is a matter of *number*); also, conformity in music or verse to regular beat or measure (as, "Instrumental sounds, In full harmonic *number* join'd": Milton's "Paradise Lost," iv. 687); rhythm; *pl.*, musical periods, measures, or groups of notes (as, "Harp of the North! that . . . down the fitful breeze thy *numbers* flung": Scott's "Lady of the Lake," i., Introd.); metrical feet, or verse (as, "I lisp'd in *numbers*, for the *numbers* came," Pope's "Prologue to the Satires," 128; "Tell me not, in mournful *numbers*, Life is but an empty dream!" Longfellow's "Psalm of Life"); also, *sing.*, in *gram.*, the property of words which serves to indicate whether they refer to one, or more than one, person or thing; the form of a word, or a group of forms, indicating this (as, the singular *number*, the plural *number*, or the dual *number*: see the adjectives); in *phren.*, the faculty of calculating.—**golden number.** See under *golden, a.*—**mixed number.** See under *mixed*.—**number one,** one's self, with reference to one's own interests: as, to look out for *number one*; "Almost every person . . . is occupied about *Number One*" (Thackeray's "Pendennis," ii. 18).—**without number,** of which the number is unknown or too great to be counted: as, times *without number*.—**num′ber,** *v.* [OF. F. *nombrer*, < L. *numerare*, < *numerus*: cf. *numerate*.] **I.** *tr.* To ascertain the number of (as, "prodigious multitudes of people, which no man could *number*": Addison, in "Tatler," 81); reckon (*up*); count over one by one (as, "To wear out time in *numb'ring* to and fro The studs that thick emboss his iron door": Cowper's "Task," v. 425); mention one by one, or enumerate (as, "But hear me, while I *number* o'er The proffer'd presents, an exhaustless store": Pope's tr. Homer's "Iliad," ix.); also, to fix the number of, limit in number, or make few in number (as, "The minutes of his earthly career were *numbered*": De Quincey's "English Mail-Coach," ii.); also, to collect, up to a certain number† (as, "*Number* thee an army, like the army that thou hast lost": 1 Kings, xx. 25); also, to reckon or include in a number (as, "That . . . family afterwards *numbered* the Netherland Nassaus among its most staunch . . . adherents": Motley's "Dutch Republic," ii. 1); also, to mark with or distinguish by a number or numbers (as, to *number* a book belonging to a collection; "The houses were not *numbered*," Macaulay's "Hist. of Eng.," iii.); also, to apportion (archaic: as, "So teach us to *number* our days, that we may apply our hearts unto wisdom," Ps. xc. 12); also, to appoint† or allot† (as, "Therefore will I *number* you to the sword": Isa. lxv. 12); also, to live or have lived (so many years: as, "The brave soldier had already *numbered*, nearly or quite, his threescore years and ten," Hawthorne's "Scarlet Letter," The Custom House; "My birth (Since which I *number* three-score winters past)," Cowper's "Yardley Oak," 3); also, to have or comprise in number (as, a country that *numbers* a million men under arms; a city that *numbers* a million inhabitants); amount to in number (as, a crew *numbering* fifty men). **II.** *intr.* To make enumeration; count; also, to be numbered or included (poetic: as, "Thou *numberest* with the followers Of One who cried, 'Leave all and follow me,'" Tennyson's "Aylmer's Field," 663); also, to be equal in number (poetic: as, "A wife . . . Whose troubles *number* with his days," Tennyson's "Two Voices," 330).—**num′ber-er,** *n.*—**num′ber-less,** *a.* Innumerable; countless.

numb=fish (num′fish), *n.* An electric ray (fish): so called from its power of numbing its prey by means of electric shocks.

num-bles (num′blz), *n. pl.* [OF. *nombles*, prob. ult. < L. *lumbus*, loin.] Certain of the inward parts of an animal, esp. of a deer, used as food. [Archaic.]

numb-ly (num′li), *adv.* In a numb manner.—**numb′ness,** *n.*

nu-mer-a-ble (nū′mẹ-ra-bl), *a.* [L. *numerabilis*.] That may be numbered or counted.

nu-mer-al (nū′mẹ-ral). [LL. *numeralis*, < L. *numerus*, E. *number, n.*] **I.** *a.* Of or pertaining to number; pertaining to or consisting of numbers; also, expressing or denoting number (as, a *numeral* word or adjective; a *numeral* letter or character). **II.** *n.* A word or words expressing a number; a letter or figure, or a group of letters or figures, denoting a number (as, the Roman *numerals*, see under *Roman*, *a.*; the Arabic *numerals*, see *Arabic*, *a.*).—**nu′mer-al-ly,** *adv.*

nu-mer-a-ry (nū′mẹ-rạ̄-ri), *a.* [ML. *numerarius*, < L. *numerus*, E. *number*, *n.*] Of or pertaining to a number or numbers.

nu-mer-ate (nū′mẹ-rāt), *v. t.*; *-ated*, *-ating.* [L. *numeratus*, pp. of *numerare*, E. *number*, *v.*] To number; count; enumerate; specif., to read (an expression in numbers).—**nu-mer-a′tion** (-mẹ-rā′shọn), *n.* [L. *numeratio(n-)*.] The act, process, or result of numbering or counting; the process or a method of reckoning or calculating; specif., the act or art, or a method, of reading numbers expressed in numerals or figures.—**nu′mer-a-tor,** *n.* [LL.] One who or that which numbers; in *math.*, that term (usually written above the line) of a fraction which shows how many parts of a unit are taken (cf. *denominator*).

nū-mer-i-cal (nụ-mer′i-kạl), *a.* [NL. *numericus*, < L. *numerus*, E. *number*, *n.*] Of or pertaining to number; of the nature of number; denoting number or a number; bearing, or designated by, a number; specif., expressed by a number or figure, or by figures, and not by a letter or letters (as, 10 is a *numerical* quantity, *ab* a literal or algebraic quantity); denoting value or magnitude irrespective of sign (as, the *numerical* value of −10 is greater than that of −5, though its algebraic value is less).—**nu-mer′i-cal-ly,** *adv.*

nu-mer-ous (nū′mẹ-rus), *a.* [L. *numerosus*, < *numerus*, E. *number*, *n.*] Consisting of or comprising a great number of units or individuals (as, "a *numerous* acquaintance among the best sort of people," Steele, in "Spectator," 88; "a *numerous* body of people," Johnson, in Boswell's "Johnson," April 10, 1778); also, very many, or forming a great number (as, "life . . . with its *numerous* woes," Cowper's "Hope," 546; "*numerous* talented men," Carlyle's "Sartor Resartus," ii. 8); also, measured or rhythmical (obs. or rare: as, "in prose or *numerous* verse," Milton's "Paradise Lost," v. 150; "blank verse . . . falling occasionally almost into *numerous* prose," Hallam's "Literature of Europe," ii. 6. § 28).—**nu-mer-os′i-ty** (-mẹ-ros′i-ti), **nu′mer-ous-ness,** *n.* —**nu′mer-ous-ly,** *adv.*

Nu-mid-i-an (nụ-mid′i-ạn), *a.* Of or pertaining to Numidia, an ancient country of northern Africa, corresponding generally to the modern Algeria.—**Numidian crane,** the demoiselle, *Anthropoides virgo.*—**Nu-mid′i-an,** *n.* A native or inhabitant of Numidia; also, the language of ancient Numidia, belonging to the Hamitic group.

nu-mis-mat-ic (nū-miz-mat′ik), *a.* [F. *numismatique*, < L. *numisma*, *nomisma*, coin, medal, < Gr. *νόμισμα*, current coin, < *νομίζειν*, use customarily, < *νόμος*, custom, law.] Of or pertaining to, or consisting of, coins and medals; pertaining to numismatics.—**nu-mis-mat′i-cal-ly,** *adv.*—**nu-mis-ma-ti-cian** (nụ-miz-mạ-tish′ạn), *n.* A numismatist.—**nu-mis-mat′ics,** *n.* The science of coins and medals. —**nu-mis-ma-tist** (nụ-miz′mạ-tist), *n.* One versed in numismatics.—**nu-mis-ma-tol′o-gy** (-tol′ọ̄-ji), *n.* [See *-logy.*] Numismatics.

num-ma-ry (num′ạ-ri), *a.* [L. *nummarius*, < *nummus*, coin.] Of or pertaining to coins or money; occupied with coins or money.

num-mu-lar (num′ụ̄-lạ̈r), *a.* [L. *nummulus*, dim. of *nummus*, coin.] Coin-shaped.—**num′mu-la-ry** (-lạ̄-ri), *a.* Pertaining to coins or money; nummary.—**num′mu-lat-ed** (-lā-ted), *a.* Coin-shaped; nummular.—**num-mu-la′tion** (-lā′shọn), *n.* In *physiol.*, the arrangement, like that of piles of coins, assumed by red blood-corpuscles in freshly drawn blood.

num-mu-lite (num′ụ̄-līt), *n.* [NL. *nummulites*, < L. *nummulus*, dim. of *nummus*, coin.] Any of the foraminifers (mostly fossil) constituting the family *Nummulitidæ*: so called from the coin-like shell.—**num-mu-lit′ic** (-lit′ik), *a.*

num-skull (num′skul), *n.* [From *numb* + *skull*².] A dull-witted person; a dunce; a dolt: as, "You *numskulls!* and so while . . . you are quarrelling for places, the guests must be starved" (Goldsmith's "She Stoops to Conquer," ii.).

nun (nun), *n.* [AS. *nunne*, < LL. *nonna*, fem. of *nonnus*, monk.] A woman devoted to a religious life under vows, esp. one living in a convent under vows of poverty, chastity, and obedience; also, any of various birds, as the European blue titmouse, *Parus cæruleus*, the smew, *Mergus albellus* (often 'white nun'), the nun-bird, or a variety of domestic pigeon with a veil-like crest.

nu-na-tak (nö′nạ-tak), *n.* [Eskimo.] A crest or ridge of rock appearing above the surface of the inland ice in Greenland.

nun=bird (nun′bėrd), *n.* Any of the South American puff-birds of the genus *Monasa* (or *Monacha*): so called from their dark plumage relieved by white on the head.

Nun-bird (*Monasa peruana*).

Nunc Di-mit-tis (nungk di-mit′is). [L., 'now thou lettest depart' (the first words as given in the Vulgate).] The canticle of Simeon (Luke, ii. 29–32), beginning "Lord, now lettest thou thy servant depart in peace"; hence [*l. c.*], permission to depart; dismissal; departure.

nun-cheon (nun′chọn), *n.* [ME. *nonechenche*, < AS. *nōn*, noon, + *scenc*, draft.] A light refreshment taken between meals; a luncheon: as, "I left London this morning . . . and the only ten minutes I have spent out of my chaise . . . procured me a *nuncheon* at Marlborough" (Jane Austen's "Sense and Sensibility," xliv.). [Now prov. Eng.]

nun-ci-a-ture (nun′shi-ạ̄-ṭụ̄r), *n.* The office or the term of service of a papal nuncio.

nun-ci-o (nun′shi-ō), *n.*; pl. *-os* (-ōz). [It. *nuncio*, now *nunzio*, < L. *nuntius*, messenger.] A messenger (obs. or archaic: see Shakspere's "Twelfth Night," i. 4. 28); also, a permanent diplomatic representative of the Pope at a foreign court or capital.

nun-cle (nung′kl), *n.* Uncle. [Now prov. Eng.]

nun-cu-pa-tive (nung′kụ̄-pạ̄-tiv or nung-kū′pạ-), *a.* [LL. *nuncupativus*, < L. *nuncupare*, call by name, declare, < *nomen*, name, + *capere*, take.] Of wills, etc., oral, rather than written: as, "He left me a small legacy in a *nuncupative* will, as a token of his kindness for me" (B. Franklin's "Autobiography," iv.).

nun-dine (nun′dīn), *n.* [L. *nundinæ*, pl., < *novem*, nine, + *dies*, day.] Among the ancient Romans, a periodical market-day, being the ninth day as reckoned from the preceding market-day taken as the first, or, as expressed in modern reckoning, occurring every eighth day.—**nun′di-nal** (-di-nạl), *a.*

nun=moth (nun′môth), *n.* A European moth, *Lymantria monacha*, whose larva does great damage to forest-trees.

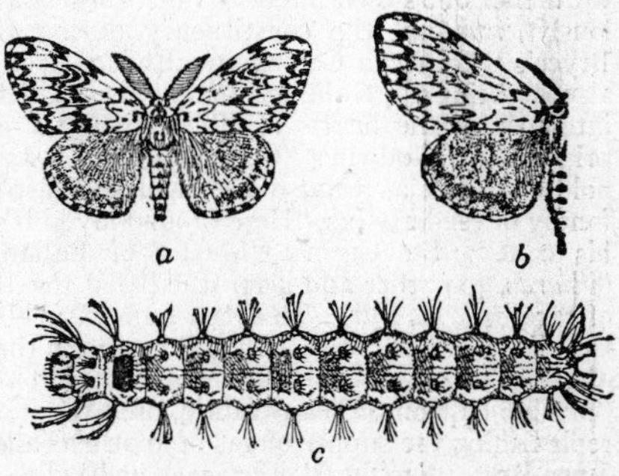

Nun-moth.—*a*, male moth; *b*, female; *c*, full-grown caterpillar: all reduced about one third.

nun-na-tion (nu-nā′shọn), *n.* [Ar. *nūn*, the letter *n*.] The addition of a final *n* in the declension of Arabic nouns; also, a similar addition of *n* in Middle English.

nun-ner-y (nun′ėr-i), *n.*; pl. *-ies* (-iz). A religious house for nuns; a convent: as, "I shall take up my abode in a religious house, near Lisle — a *nunnery*, you would call it" (C. Brontë's "Jane Eyre," xxii.).

nun's=cot-ton (nunz′kot″n), *n.* Fine cotton embroidery thread: so called from its use by nuns.

nun's=veil-ing (nunz′vā′ling), *n.* A thin, plain-woven woolen fabric, used for women's veils, dresses, etc.

nu-phar (nū′fär), *n.* [NL., < Ar. and Pers. *nūfar*, for *nīnūfar*, E. *nenuphar*.] The yellow water-lily (genus *Nymphæa*).

nup-tial (nup′shal). [L. *nuptialis*, < *nuptiæ*, a marriage, < *nubere* (pp. *nuptus*), marry.] **I.** *a.* Of or pertaining to marriage or the marriage ceremony: as, the *nuptial* day, a *nuptial* song; *nuptial* festivities. **II.** *n.* Marriage; wedding: now usually in *pl.*, and commonly implying some degree of state or elegance: as, "a feast . . . rich as for the *nuptials* of a king" (Tennyson's "Lover's Tale," iv. 211). —**nup′tial-ly,** *adv.*

nu-ra-ghe (nö-rä′gā), *n.*; pl. *-ghi* (-gē). [Sardinian.] A tower-like structure of ancient date, of a kind peculiar to Sardinia.

Nu-rem-berg (nū′rem-bėrg) **coun′ter.** One of a class of circular pieces of brass or other material bearing various devices and inscriptions, made in Nuremberg, Germany, esp. in the 16th and 17th centuries, chiefly for use in casting up accounts.

Nuremberg Counter (obverse).

nurse (nėrs), *n.* [OF. *nurice* (F. *nourrice*), < LL. *nutricia*, nurse, prop. fem. of *nutricius*, that nourishes: see *nutritious*.] A woman employed to suckle an infant (often called *wet-nurse*: cf. *dry-nurse*); a woman who has the general care of a child or children; also, a person (woman or man) who has the care of the sick or infirm (as, a hospital *nurse*; a trained *nurse*); also, fig., one who looks after, tutors, or guides another, as in a period of inexperience; a country or place that nourishes or fosters (as, "Fertile Egypt . . . The *nurse* of Gods and wonder-working men": W. Morris's "Jason," iii. 29); any fostering agency or influence (as, "Gentle sleep, Nature's soft *nurse*": Shakspere's "2 Henry IV.," iii. 1. 6); in *billiards*, the act of nursing the balls.—**at nurse,** in the care of a nurse, as an infant.—**to put (out) to nurse,** to put (out) into the care of a nurse, as an infant.—**nurse,** *v.*; *nursed*, *nursing*. [Orig. a var. of *nourish*, later associated with *nurse*, *n.*] **I.** *tr.* To suckle (an infant); feed and tend in infancy; also, to tend in sickness or infirmity; bring by such tending (as, to *nurse* a person back to health); seek to cure (a cold, etc.) by taking care of one's self; also, fig., to look after carefully so as to promote growth, development, favorable condition, etc. (as, to *nurse* an art or industry; "He *nursed* what property was yet left to him," Scott's "Guy Mannering," ii.); foster; cherish (a feeling, etc.: as, "Life appears to me too short to be spent in *nursing* animosity," C. Brontë's "Jane Eyre," vi.; "I will *nurse* my grievance," Arnold Bennett's "Hilda Lessways," i. 2); sometimes, to treat or handle with adroit care in order to further one's own interests (as, to *nurse* a client; "sedulously '*nursing*' the constituency during the vacations," Bryce's "American Commonwealth," xix.; to *nurse* a job); also, to bring up, train, or nurture (as, "The law . . . turns into marble the hearts of all those that are *nursed* in its principles": Godwin's "Caleb Williams," xxxvii.); also, to hold or dandle as a nurse does a child; clasp or handle as if fondly or tenderly (as, "Here I found my lord seated, *nursing* his cane": Stevenson's "Master of Ballantrae," x.); in *billiards*, to gather and keep (the balls) together for a series of caroms. **II.** *intr.* To act as nurse; suckle a child; tend the sick or infirm; also, of a child, to take the breast.

nurse=bal-loon (nėrs′ba-lön″), *n.* In *aëronautics*, a small portable balloon of heavy fabric, used for storing gas, as for replenishing the supply of gas of another balloon.

nurse-ling (nėrs′ling), *n.* See *nursling*.

nurse=maid (nėrs′mād), *n.* A maid-servant employed to take care of children.

nurs-er (nėr′sėr), *n.* One who or that which nurses; a nurse; a fosterer.

nurs-er-y (nėr′sėr-i), *n.*; pl. *-ies* (-iz). The service or care of a nurse† (see Shakspere's "King Lear," i. 1. 126); also, a room or place set apart for young children (as, "What I should like best . . . would be to go to the *nursery*, and see your dear little children," Thackeray's "Vanity Fair," xli.: cf. *day-nursery*); hence, a place where young trees or other plants are raised for transplanting or with a view to sale; a place in which young fish or other animals are reared; any place in which something is bred, nourished, or fostered (as, "those ever-swarming *nurseries* of mercenary warriors, the smaller German states," Motley's "Dutch Republic," iv. 1; "Those little seminaries are among the best *nurseries* of talent and virtue in the land," Irving's "Tales of a Traveler," ii. 7); any situation, condition, circumstances, practice, etc., serving to foster something (as, poverty is a *nursery* of ambition; "This keeping of cowes is of it selfe a verye idle life, and a fitt *nurserye* of a theefe," Spenser's "State of Ireland").—**nurs′er-y-man** (-man), *n.*; pl. *-men*. One who owns or conducts a nursery for plants.

nurs-ling, nurse-ling (nėrs′ling), *n.* [See *-ling*[1].] An infant or child under a nurse's care; hence, any person or thing under fostering care, influences, or conditions (as, *nurslings* of our alma mater; "this *nurseling* of another sky," Tennyson's "Daisy," 98).

nur-ture (nėr′tūr), *n.* [OF. *nurture* (F. *nourriture*), < LL. *nutritura*, < L. *nutrire*: see *nourish*.] The feeding and care of the young through the stages of growth; rearing; fig., fostering care; also, upbringing or training as to mind, manners, etc. (as, "children . . . disporting themselves in such grim fashion as the Puritanic *nurture* would permit": Hawthorne's "Scarlet Letter," vi.); education; breeding; also, nourishment or food.—**nur′ture,** *v. t.*; *-tured*, *-turing*. To feed, nourish, or support during the stages of growth, as children or young; rear; fig., to foster (as, "an inheritance of affections *nurtured* by a simple family life": George Eliot's "Adam Bede," xix.); cherish (as, "The hopes which this fond forgiving creature had *nurtured* . . . were destined to be disappointed": Thackeray's "Newcomes," xlviii.); also, to bring up, train, or educate (as, "Persons who are *nurtured* in office do admirably well as long as things go on in their common order": Burke's "American Taxation"). —**nur′tur-er,** *n.*

nut (nut), *n.* [AS. *hnutu* = D. *noot* = G. *nuss* = Icel. *hnot* = Sw. *nöt* = Dan. *nöd*, nut.] A fruit consisting of an edible kernel inclosed in a woody or leathery shell; the kernel itself; in botanical use, a hard, indehiscent, one-seeded fruit, as the chestnut or the acorn; also, something suggesting a nut that is hard to crack, as a difficult question, problem, or undertaking; also, the head (slang: as, a crack on the *nut*; off one's *nut*, out of one's mind, or crazy); a witless or crazy person (slang); a person or fellow (in disparagement: slang); an idle young man of fashion (slang, Eng.); also, *pl.*, something especially enjoyable or delightful (slang: as, "This was *nuts* to us; for we liked to have a Spaniard wet with salt water," Dana's "Two Years before the Mast," xxv.; "Tom had his store clothes on, and an audience — and that was always *nuts* for Tom Sawyer," Mark Twain's "Huckleberry Finn," xxxiii.); also, *sing.*, any of various devices or parts supposed in some way to resemble a nut; a perforated block (usually of metal) with an internal thread or female screw, used to screw on the end of a bolt, etc.; in musical instruments of the violin type, the piece, as of ebony, at the upper end of the neck, over which the strings pass; the movable piece at the lower end of the bow for such instruments, by means of which the hairs may be slackened or tightened.—**to be nuts on,** to be enthusiastically devoted to, pleased with, or bent on. [Slang.]—**nut,** *v. i.*; *nutted*, *nutting*. To seek for or gather nuts.

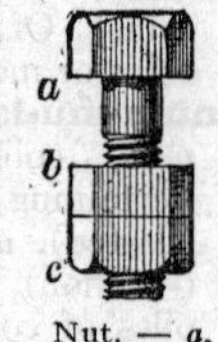

Nut. — *a*, bolt; *b*, principal nut; *c*, nut screwed upon *b* to prevent it from turning.

nu-tant (nū′tant), *a.* [L. *nutans* (*nutant-*), ppr. of *nutare*, freq. of *-nuere*, nod (see *innuendo*), akin to Gr. νεύειν, nod, incline.] In *bot.*, drooping; nodding; in *entom.*, sloping.

nu-ta-tion (nū-tā′shon), *n.* [L. *nutatio(n-)*, < *nutare*, nod: see *nutant*.] A nodding; in *astron.*, a slight oscillation of the earth's axis; in *bot.*, a side-to-side movement of a part during growth.

nut=brown (nut′broun), *a.* Brown as a ripe nut: as, "spicy *nut-brown* ale" (Milton's "L'Allegro," 100); "The *Nut-browne* Maide" (the title of a famous English ballad, recorded as early as 1502).

nut-crack-er (nut′krak″ėr), *n.* An instrument for cracking nuts (often in *pl.* in same sense); also, any of several birds (genus *Nucifraga*) of the crow family, which feed on nuts.

European Nutcracker (*Nucifraga caryocatactes*).

nut-gall (nut′gâl), *n.* A nut-like gall or excrescence, esp. one formed on an oak.

nut-hatch (nut′-hach), *n.* [ME. *notehache, nuthage, nuthake*: cf. *hack*[1].] Any of numerous small sharp-beaked birds constituting the widely distributed family *Sittidæ*, which creep on trees and feed on small nuts and insects.

nut-let (nut′let), *n.* A small nut; a small nut-like fruit or seed; also, the stone of a drupe.

nut-meg (nut′meg), *n.* [ME. *notemuge*, < *note*, nut, + OF. *muge, mugue*, musk.] The hard, aromatic seed of the fruit of an East Indian tree, *Myristica fragrans*, used as a spice (cf. *mace*[2]); the tree itself; also, the similar product of certain other trees of the same genus or other genera, or the tree; also, a nutmeg melon. —**nutmeg melon,** a variety of muskmelon having a rather soft rind with a netted surface, and a sweet, green flesh.—**wooden nutmeg,** an imitation nutmeg made of wood, an alleged article of manufacture in Connecticut for export, according to an old story (whence Connecticut is called the 'Nutmeg State'); hence, in general, something fraudulent; a fraud; a trick.

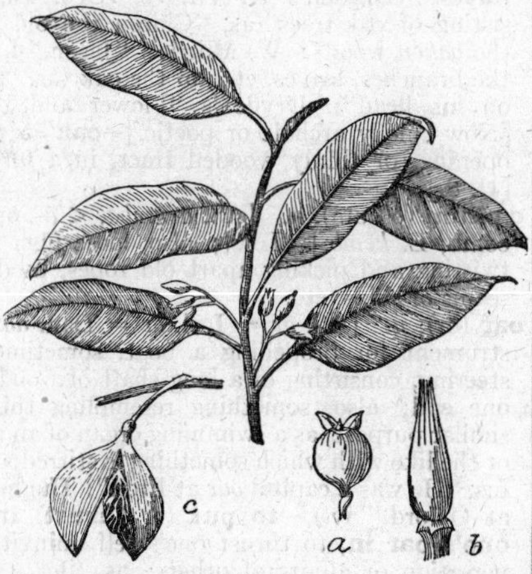

Branch of Nutmeg (*Myristica fragrans*), with male flowers.—*a*, the female flower; *b*, the stamens of the male flower; *c*, the fruit.

nu-tri-a (nū′tri-ạ̈), *n.* [Sp., otter, < L. *lutra*, otter.] The coypu; also, its fur.

nu-tri-ent (nū′tri-ẹnt). [L. *nutriens* (*-ent-*), ppr. of *nutrire*: see *nourish.*] **I.** *a.* Nourishing, or affording nutriment, as matter or substances; also, conveying nutriment, as vessels of the body. **II.** *n.* A nutrient substance.

nu-tri-ment (nū′tri-mẹnt), *n.* [L. *nutrimentum*, < *nutrire*: see *nourish.*] That which nourishes; nourishment, food, or aliment; any matter that, taken into a living organism (animal or vegetable), serves to sustain it in its existence, promoting growth and repairing waste. Also fig.—**nu-tri-men′tal** (-men′tạl), *a.*

nu-tri-tion (nū̦-trish′ọn), *n.* [= F. *nutrition*, < L. *nutrire*: see *nourish.*] The act or process of nourishing or of being nourished; specif., the process by which the food material taken into an organism (animal or vegetable) is converted into living tissue, etc.; also, food; nutriment.—**nu-tri′tion-al,** *a.*—**nu-tri′tion-al-ly,** *adv.*

nu-tri-tious (nū̦-trish′us), *a.* [L. *nutricius, nutritius*, that nourishes, < *nutrix* (*nutric-*), a nurse, < *nutrire*: see *nourish*, and cf. *nurse.*] Such as to nourish; nourishing, esp. in a high degree; affording or containing much nutriment: as, *nutritious* matter; *nutritious* fruits; *nutritious* food.—**nu-tri′tious-ly,** *adv.*—**nu-tri′tious-ness,** *n.*

nu-tri-tive (nū′tri-tiv), *a.* [ML. *nutritivus*, < L. *nutrire*: see *nourish.*] Serving to nourish; affording nutriment; also, of, pertaining to, or concerned in nutrition.—**nu′tri-tive-ly,** *adv.*—**nu′tri-tive-ness,** *n.*

nut-shell (nut′shel), *n.* The shell of a nut: much used in phrases as a type of small size, content, scope, etc.—**in a nutshell,** in very brief form; in a few words: as, "You have my history *in a nutshell*" (Browning's "Ned Bratts").

nut-ter (nut′ėr), *n.* One who gathers nuts.—**nut′ting,** *n.* The act of seeking or gathering nuts.

nut-ty (nut′i), *a.* Abounding in or producing nuts (as, "*nutty* hedgerows": George Eliot's "Silas Marner," i.); also, nut-like, esp. in taste (as, "the *nutty* Spanish ale": Masefield's "Trade Winds"); hence, full of flavor or zest; also, witless or crazy (slang).—**nut′ti-ness,** *n.*

nux vom-i-ca (nuks vom′i-kạ̈). [NL., 'vomiting nut': L. *nux*, nut; NL. *vomica*, < L. *vomere*, vomit.] The strychnine-containing seed (used in medicine) of the orange-like fruit borne by an East Indian loganiaceous tree, *Strychnos nux-vomica*; also, the tree itself.

Nux Vomica.—*a*, the fruit cut transversely; *b*, a seed; *c*, a seed cut longitudinally.

nuz-zle (nuz′l), *v.*; *-zled, -zling.* [Freq. of *nose*; to some extent confused with *nestle.*] **I.** *intr.* To burrow or root with the nose, as an animal does; thrust the nose (*at, against, in*, etc.: as, "*Nuzzling* in his flank, the loving swine Sheathed unaware the tusk in his soft groin," Shakspere's "Venus and Adonis," 1115); also, to nestle, snuggle, or cuddle. **II.** *tr.* To root up with the nose; touch or rub with the nose; thrust the nose against or into (sometimes fig., of boats: as, "Some twenty whale-boats were *nuzzling* a sand-bank," Kipling's "Light That Failed," ii.); thrust (the nose or head), as into something; also, to cuddle (a child, etc.).

nyck-el-har-pa (nik′ẹl-här″pạ̈), *n.* [Sw., lit. 'key harp.'] An old-time Swedish stringed musical instrument, similar to the hurdy-gurdy but sounded with a bow instead of a wheel.

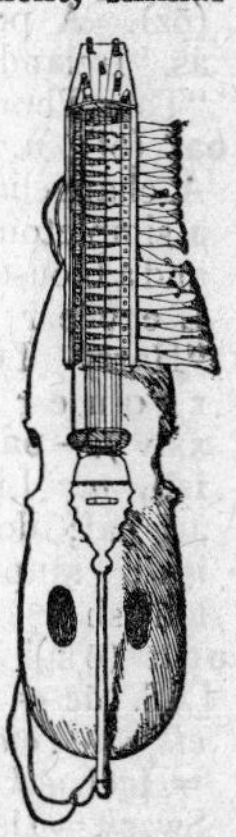

Nyckelharpa.

nyc-tag-i-na-ceous (nik-taj-i-nā′shius), *a.* [NL. *Nyctago*, former name for genus *Mirabilis*, < Gr. νύξ (νυκτ-), night.] Belonging to the *Nyctaginaceæ*, or four-o'clock family of plants. Also **nyc-ta-gin-i-a′ceous** (-tạ-jin-i-ā′shius).

nyc-ta-lo-pi-a (nik-tạ-lō′pi-ạ̈), *n.* [LL., < Gr. νυκτάλωψ, blind by night, < νύξ (νυκτ-), night, + ἀλαός, blind, + ὤψ, eye.] A condition of the eyes in which sight is normal in the day or in a strong light, but is abnormally poor or wholly gone at night or in a dim light; night-blindness; also, hemeralopia, a visual condition exactly opposite; day-blindness.

nyc-ti-trop-ic (nik-ti-trop′ik), *a.* [Gr. νύξ (νυκτ-), night, + E. *-tropic.*] In *bot.*, tending to assume at or just before nightfall positions unlike those maintained during the day, as the leaves of certain plants. Cf. *sleep, v. i.* —**nyc-tit′ro-pism** (-tit′rọ-pizm), *n.*

nyl-ghau (nil′gâ), *n.* See *nilgau.*

ny-lon (nī′lon), *n.* [Coined name.] A synthetic organic chemical substance formable into fibers, sheets, etc., of extreme toughness, strength, and elasticity: used as yarn (as for hosiery), for bristles (as for brushes), etc.

nymph (nimf), *n.* [OF. *nimphe* (F. *nymphe*), < L. *nympha*, < Gr. νύμφη, bride, nymph, pupa.] One of a numerous class of inferior divinities of mythology, conceived as beautiful maidens inhabiting the sea, rivers, woods, trees, mountains, meadows, etc., and frequently mentioned as attending a superior deity; hence, a beautiful or graceful young woman, or, in general, a maiden (chiefly poetic or playful); in *entom.*, an insect in an intermediate stage of development, between a larva and an imago; esp., an immature insect of the class that undergo only an incomplete metamorphosis, in a form in which the external wing-rudiments have become apparent.

nym-pha (nim′fä), *n.*; pl. *-phæ* (-fē). [L.] In *entom.*, a nymph; *pl.*, in *anat.*, the labia minora (see *labium*).

nym-phæ-a-ceous (nim-fē-ā′shius), *a.* [L. *nymphæa*, < Gr. νυμφαία, water-lily, prop. fem. of νυμφαῖος, sacred to the nymphs, < νύμφη, E. *nymph.*] Belonging to the *Nymphæaceæ*, or water-lily family of plants.

nym-phal (nim′fal), *a.* Of or pertaining to a nymph or nymphs. Also **nym-phe′an** (-fē′an), **nym′phic** (-fik).

nym-pho-lep-sy (nim′fō-lep-si), *n.* [Gr. νύμφη, nymph, + -ληψία, seizure, < λαμβάνειν, take: cf. *epilepsy.*] An ecstasy supposed to be inspired by nymphs; hence, a frenzy of emotion, as for something unattainable.—**nym′pho-lept**, *n.* [Gr. νυμφόληπτος, seized by nymphs.] One seized with nympholepsy.—**nym-pho-lep′tic**, *a.*

nym-pho-ma-ni-a (nim-fō-mā′ni-ä), *n.* [NL., < Gr. νύμφη, nymph, + μανία, E. *mania.*] In *pathol.*, morbid and uncontrollable sexual desire in women. Cf. *satyriasis.* —**nym-pho-ma′ni-ac** (-ak), *a.* and *n.*

nys-tag-mus (nis-tag′mus), *n.* [NL., < Gr. νυσταγμός, < νυστάζειν, nod in sleep, akin to νεύειν, nod: see *nutant.*] In *pathol.*, an involuntary oscillation of the eyeball, usually lateral but sometimes rotatory or vertical: occurring esp. among miners and human albinos, and in certain diseases. —**nys-tag′mic**, *a.*

O

O[1], **o**[1] (ō); pl. *O's, o's* (ōz). A vowel, the 15th letter of the English alphabet.—**O**[1], **o**[1], *n.*; pl. *O's, o's* (ōz). Something resembling the letter O in its round or rounded shape (as, "May we cram Within this wooden *O* [theater] the very casques That did affright the air at Agincourt?" Shakspere's "Henry V.," Prologue, 13); esp., the Arabic cipher, or naught (0); hence, a mere nothing.

O[2] (ō), *interj.* A word used before the name in address, esp., as in solemn or poetic language, to lend earnestness to an appeal (as, "Praise the Lord, *O* Jerusalem," Ps. cxlvii. 12; "Break, break, break, On thy cold gray stones, *O* Sea!" Tennyson's "Break, Break, Break"); also, an expression of surprise, pain, longing, gladness, etc. (as, "*O* for the touch of a vanish'd hand!" Tennyson's "Break, Break, Break": in prose now commonly written *oh*).—**O**[2], *n.*; pl. *O's* (ōz). The exclamation 'O': as, "*O's* of admiration" (Thackeray's "Pendennis," i. 37); "Why should you fall into so deep an *O*?" (Shakspere's "Romeo and Juliet," iii. 3. 90).

o' (o), *prep.* An abbreviated form of *of*, now chiefly prov. or colloq., except as in *o'clock, will-o'-the-wisp*, etc.

O'-. Form of Ir. *ō*, descendant, used as a prefix in Irish family names, as in *O'Brien, O'Connor.*—**O**[3] (ō), *n.*; pl. *O's* (ōz). A person whose name begins with the prefix *O'-*: as, "Ireland her *O's*, her Macs let Scotland boast" (Fielding's "Tom Thumb the Great," i. 3).

oaf (ōf), *n.* [From Scand.: cf. Icel. *ālfr*, elf, and E. *elf.*] A changeling; hence, a deformed or idiotic child; an idiot; a simpleton or blockhead (as, "a great *oaf*, in wooden shoes and a blouse": Lever's "Harry Lorrequer," xxiv.).—**oaf′ish**, *a.* Like an oaf; doltish; stupid; loutish.

oak (ōk), *n.* [AS. *āc* = D. *eik* = G. *eiche* = Icel. *eik* = Sw. *ek* = Dan. *eg*, oak.] Any tree or shrub of the fagaceous genus *Quercus*, including many large forest-trees with hard, durable wood, and bearing as fruit the acorn; any of certain other trees or shrubs resembling these in some respect; also, the wood of an oak-tree; hence, a door made of this or, by extension, of other wood (chiefly in 'to sport one's oak': see *sport, v. t.*); also, the leaves of the oak-tree, esp. as worn in a chaplet (as, "To a cruel war I sent him; from whence he returned, his brows bound with *oak*": Shakspere's "Coriolanus," i. 3. 16). —**oak′=ap″ple**, *n.* Any of various roundish galls produced on oaks.—**oak′en**, *a.* Made of oak (as, an *oaken* chest; "The Old *Oaken* Bucket," the title of a poem by Samuel Woodworth); of or pertaining to the oak (as, "*oaken* leaves": Dryden's tr. Virgil's "Georgics," i. 200); consisting of oak-trees (as, "Chiron the old roamed through the *oaken* wood": W. Morris's "Jason," i. 121); formed of the branches, leaves, etc., of the oak (as, "an *oaken* chaplet on his head": Dryden's "Flower and the Leaf," 253). [Now chiefly archaic or poetic.]—**oak′=o″pen-ing**, *n.* An opening, or thinly wooded tract, in a forest of oak-trees. [U. S.]

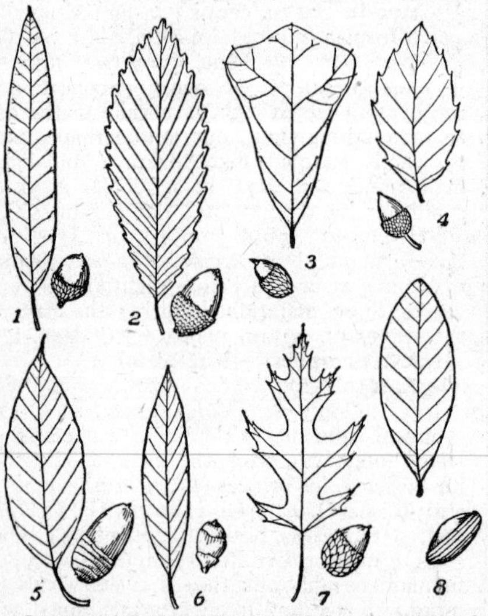

Leaves and Acorns of Species of Oak. — 1, willow-oak of North America (*Quercus phellos*); 2, chestnut-oak of North America (*Q. prinus*); 3, black-jack of North America (*Q. marilandica*); 4, holm-oak of Europe (*Q. ilex*); 5, *Q. acuta*, of Japan; 6, *Q. lanceæfolia*, of the Malay Peninsula; 7, scarlet oak of North America (*Q. coccinea*); 8, *Q. lucida*, of the Malay Peninsula.

oa-kum (ō′kum), *n.* [AS. *ācumba*, < *ā-*, out, + *cemban*, to comb, E. *kemb.*] Tow†; also, loose fiber obtained by untwisting and picking apart old ropes, used for calking the seams of ships, etc.

oar (ōr), *n.* [AS. *ār* = Icel. *ār* = Dan. *aare*, oar.] An instrument for propelling a boat, sometimes used also for steering, consisting of a long shaft of wood with a blade at one end; also, something resembling this or used for a similar purpose, as a swimming organ of an animal; a paddle or the like with which something is stirred; also, an oarsman (as, "He was a capital *oar* at Eton": Hughes's "Tom Brown at Oxford," iv.).—**to put** (or **thrust**) **in one's oar,** or **one's oar in,** to thrust one's self uninvited into the conversation or affairs of others: as, "I . . . *put in my oar* whenever I thought I could say a good thing" (Malkin's tr. Le Sage's "Gil Blas," i. 7); "What I don't like to see is a young girl *thrusting her oar in* in that way" (H. Kingsley's "Geoffry Hamlyn," xxix.).—**to rest** (or **lie**) **on one's oars,** to rest on the handles of one's oars in suspending rowing; fig., to suspend one's efforts; rest for a time after effort or labor.—**oar**, *v.* **I.** *tr.* To propel with or as with oars; row; also, to traverse (the sea, etc.), or make (one's way), by or as if by rowing; also, to move or use (an arm, hand, etc.) as an oar. **II.** *intr.* To row; move or advance as if by rowing.—**oar′age** (-āj), *n.* The use of oars; rowing; also, rowing apparatus.—**oared**, *a.* Furnished with oars.—**oar′=fish**, *n.* Any of the deep-sea fishes constituting the genus *Regalecus*, characterized by a compressed, tape-like body from 12 to over 20 feet long.—**oar′less**, *a.* Without oars, as a boat; also, undisturbed by oars, as water (as,

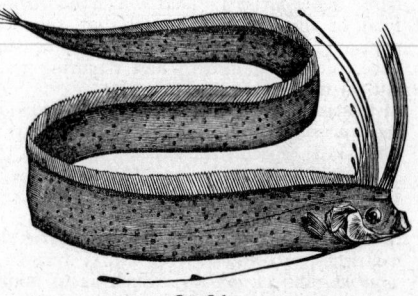

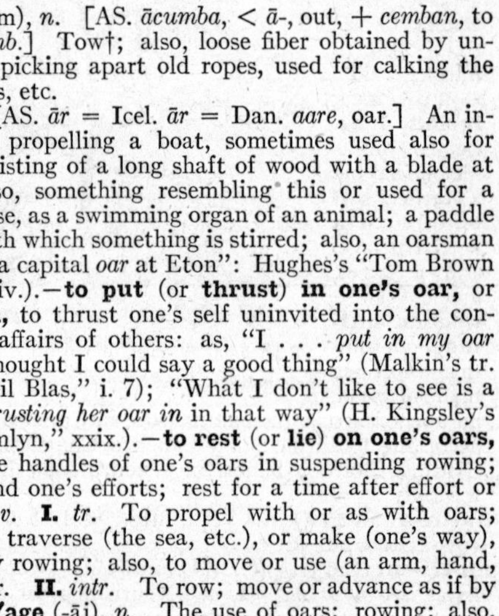
Oar-fish.

"the . . . *oarless* sea": Tennyson's "To Virgil," v.).—**oar′lock,** *n.* [AS. *ārloc.*] A rowlock.—**oars′man** (-man), *n.*; pl. *-men.* One skilled in the use of oars; a rower; often, one who rows for exercise or sport.—**oars′man-ship,** *n.*—**oar′y,** *a.* Oar-like; also, oared, or furnished with oars. [Chiefly poetic.]

o-a-sis (ō-ā′sis or ō′a-sis), *n.*; pl. *oases* (-sēz). [L., < Gr. ὄασις; prob. of Egyptian origin.] A fertile spot in a desert (as, "a tiny *oasis* where there were camels, and a well . . . and a patch of emerald-green barley": Amelia B. Edwards's "Thousand Miles up the Nile," x.); hence, any place or spot, or any scene or part of one's experience, that is refreshingly different from others.—**o-a′sal** (-sal), **o-a-sit-ic** (ō-a-sit′ik), *a.*

oast (ōst), *n.* [AS. *āst* = D. *eest.*] A kiln for drying hops or malt.

oat (ōt), *n.* [AS. *āte* (pl. *ātan*).] A cereal grass, *Avena sativa*, cultivated for its edible seed, which is used in making oatmeal and as a food for horses, etc. (usually in *pl.*); *pl.*, the seeds (as, "*Oats* . . . A grain, which in England is generally given to horses, but in Scotland supports the people": Johnson's "Dictionary"); also, *sing.* or *pl.*, any species of the same genus, as *A. fatua*, the common wild oat, a grass or weed resembling the cultivated oat, which is perhaps derived from it (see phrase below); also, *sing.*, a musical pipe made of an oat-straw (poetic: as, "That strain I heard was of a higher mood: But now my *oat* proceeds," Milton's "Lycidas," 88).—**to feel one's oats.** See under *feel*, *v. t.*—**to sow one's wild oats,** to indulge in excesses or follies such as are common to youth, esp. to young men; practise the dissipations of youth before settling down to sedate maturity: with allusion to the sowing of wild oats rather than good grain.—**oat′=cake,** *n.* A cake, usually thin and brittle, made of oatmeal.—**oat′en,** *a.* Made of oats or of oatmeal (as, "an *oaten* cake": Cooper's "Two Admirals," iii.); also, made of an oat-straw (as, "his *oaten* pype": Spenser's "Shepheardes Calender," Jan., 72); also, of or pertaining to the oat (as, "*oaten* straws": Shakspere's "Love's Labour's Lost," v. 2. 913).—**oat′=grass,** *n.* Any wild species of oat; also, any of certain oat-like grasses.

Panicle of Oat (*Avena sativa*).—*a*, a spikelet; *b*, the lower flowering glume with awn; *c*, the upper flowering glume; *d*, a neutral flower; *e*, grain inclosed by the flowering glumes and the palet, the awn detached.

oath (ōth), *n.*; pl. *oaths* (ōᴛʜz). [AS. *āth* = D. *eed* = G. *eid* = Icel. *eidhr* = Goth. *aiths*, oath.] A solemn appeal to God, or to some revered person or thing, in attestation of the truth of a statement or the binding character of a promise (as, to testify upon *oath*; to take an *oath* upon the Bible; to make *oath*); a statement or promise strengthened by such an appeal, or, loosely, a formally affirmed statement or promise accepted as an equivalent; the form of words in which such a statement or promise is made (as, the President's *oath* of office, as set forth in the U. S. Constitution, ii. 1. 8; the Hippocratic *oath*, see under *Hippocratic*); also, a light or blasphemous use of the name of God or anything sacred, as in asseveration, imprecation, or ejaculation (as, "a terrible *oath*, with a swaggering accent sharply twanged off," Shakspere's "Twelfth Night," iii. 4. 197; talk interlarded with *oaths*; a minced *oath*, see *minced*); any profane expression or expletive; a curse; sometimes, a mild or harmless expression used in asseveration or ejaculation (as, "She . . . laugh'd, and blush'd, and oft did say Her pretty *oath*, by Yea, and Nay, She could not, would not, durst not play!" Scott's "Marmion," v. 11).

oat-meal (ōt′mēl), *n.* Meal made from oats; also, porridge of this.

ob-. [L. *ob-* (also, by assimilation to a following consonant, *oc-*, *of-*, *og-*, *op-*), repr. *ob*, prep., toward, to, about, before, on, over, against.] A prefix meaning 'toward,' 'to,' 'on,' 'over,' 'against,' orig. occurring in words from the Latin, but now used also, with the sense of 'reversely' or 'inversely,' to form New Latin and English scientific terms.

ob-bli-ga-to (ob-blē-gä′tō). [It., 'obliged.'] In *music*: **I.** *a.* Obligatory or indispensable; so important that it cannot be omitted. **II.** *n.*; pl. *-tos* (-tōz), It. *-ti* (-tē). An obbligato part or accompaniment; esp., an accompanying instrumental solo of more or less distinct character and independent value.

ob-con-ic, ob-con-i-cal (ob-kon′ik, -i-kal), *a.* [See *ob-*.] In *bot.*, etc., inversely conical; conical, with the base upward or outward.

ob-cor-date (ob-kôr′dāt), *a.* [NL. *obcordatus*: see *ob-* and *cordate.*] In *bot.*, inversely cordate; heart-shaped, with the attachment at the pointed end, as a leaf.

Obcordate Leaflets.

ob-du-rate (ob′dū-rāt), *a.* [L. *obduratus*, pp. of *obdurare*, harden, < *ob* (see *ob-*) + *durare*, harden, < *durus*, hard.] Hardened against moral influence, or persistently impenitent (as, an *obdurate* sinner); also, hardened against persuasions or tender feelings (as, "Be . . . *obdurate*, do not hear him plead," Shakspere's "Richard III.," i. 3. 347; "He would manfully sally forth with pipe in mouth to besiege some fair damsel's *obdurate* heart," Irving's "Knickerbocker's New York," iii. 4); hard-hearted; unfeelingly firm or stubborn; inexorable.—**ob′du-ra-cy** (-rā-si), **ob′du-rate-ness,** *n.*—**ob′du-rate-ly,** *adv.*

o-be-ah (ō′bē-ä), *n.* Same as *obi*[1].

o-be-di-ence (ō-bē′di-ens), *n.* The state or fact of being obedient; the act or practice of obeying; dutiful or submissive compliance (with *to*: as, "I went on board in *obedience* to my orders," Marryat's "Peter Simple," lx.); also, authority or rule, esp. ecclesiastical, as over those who should obey; a sphere of authority, or a body of persons, etc., subject to some particular authority, esp. ecclesiastical (as, the churches of the Roman *obedience*); also, an obeisance, bow, or curtsy (archaic or prov.: as, to make one's *obedience*).

o-be-di-ent (ō-bē′di-ent), *a.* [OF. *obedient*, < L. *obœdiens* (*-ent-*), ppr. of *obœdire*, E. *obey.*] Obeying, or willing to obey; submissive to authority or constraint; dutiful; compliant: as, "Servants, be *obedient* to them that are your masters" (Eph. vi. 5); "The *obedient* colonies in this scheme are heavily taxed; the refractory remain unburthened" (Burke's "Conciliation with the Colonies").—**o-be′di-ent-ly,** *adv.*

o-bei-sance (ō-bā′sans or ō-bē′-), *n.* [OF. *obeissance* (F. *obéissance*), obedience, < *obeir*, E. *obey.*] Obedience†; also, a movement of the body expressing deep respect or deferential courtesy, as before a superior (as, "After three profound *obeisances* . . . we were permitted to sit on three stools near . . . his Highness's throne": Swift's "Gulliver's Travels," iii. 7); a bow or curtsy; also, deference or homage (as, to pay or do *obeisance* to a person; "He . . . made the usual humiliating acts of *obeisance*," Prescott's "Conquest of Mexico," iv. 3).

ob-e-lis-cal (ob-e-lis′kal), *a.* Pertaining to or having the form of an obelisk: as, *obeliscal* stones.

ob-e-lisk (ob′e-lisk), *n.* [L. *obeliscus*, < Gr. ὀβελίσκος, dim. of ὀβελός: see *obelus.*] A tapering, four-sided shaft of stone, usually monolithic and having a pyramidal apex (see cut on following page), of which notable examples are seen among the monuments of ancient Egypt (as, "The *obelisk* is of red, highly polished, and covered on all four sides with superb hieroglyphs . . The true height of this wonderful monolith is over seventy feet," Amelia B. Edwards's "Thousand Miles up the Nile," viii.: see *needle*); hence, something resembling such a shaft (as, an *obelisk* of rock in mountain scenery; "Fluted cypresses rear'd up Their living *obelisks*," Southey's "Thalaba," vi. 20); also, a mark, the obelus, used in ancient manuscripts (see *obelus*); in *printing*, the dagger (†), used to make reference to an accompanying note, to indicate a doubtful passage in a text (as in the Globe Edition of Shakspere), to mark an obsolete word or sense (as in dictionaries), and for other purposes.—**double obelisk,** in *printing*, the double dagger (‡), used for references, etc.

Obelisks. — Karnak (Thebes), Egypt.

ob-e-lize (ob′e-līz), *v. t.*; *-lized, -lizing.* To mark (a word or passage) with an obelus; condemn as spurious, corrupt, or doubtful.

ob-e-lus (ob′e-lus), *n.*; pl. *-li* (-lī). [LL., < Gr. ὀβελός, spit, pointed pillar, obelus.] A mark (— or ÷) used in ancient manuscripts to point out spurious, corrupt, doubtful, or superfluous words or passages; later, the obelisk or dagger (†).

o-ber-land (ō′bėr-länt), *n.* [G., 'upper land.'] High land; highlands: as, the Bernese *Oberland* (in the canton of Bern, Switzerland).

o-bese (ọ-bēs′), *a.* [L. *obesus*, having eaten itself fat, pp. of *obedere*, < *ob*, to, + *edere*, eat: see *eat.*] Excessively fat or fleshy, as a person or animal, the body, etc.; corpulent to the point of being gross or unwieldy: as, "a woman of robust frame . . . though stout, not *obese*" (C. Brontë's "Jane Eyre," iv.); "operations which should transform the plethoric, *obese* inhabitants of the sty into barrels of pink-hued salt-pork" (Mrs. Stowe's "Oldtown Folks," xiii.).—**o-bese′ly,** *adv.*—**o-bese′ness, o-bes-i-ty** (ọ-bes′i-ti), *n.*

o-bey (ọ-bā′), *v.* [OF. *obeir* (F. *obéir*), < L. *obœdire*, give ear, harken, obey, < *ob*, to, + *audire*, hear.] **I.** *tr.* To comply with or fulfil the commands or instructions of (as, "Children, *obey* your parents in all things," Col. iii. 20; "He commandeth even the winds and water, and they *obey* him," Luke, viii. 25); do as bidden by; sometimes, to submit to the authority of, or serve obediently, as a ruler or superior (as, "thou, great Anna! whom three realms *obey*": Pope's "Rape of the Lock," iii. 7); also, to comply with or fulfil (a command, etc.); fig., to submit or conform one's self in action to (some guiding principle, etc.: as, to *obey* reason; "unto them that . . . do not *obey* the truth, but *obey* unrighteousness," Rom. ii. 8); yield to or follow (an impulse, etc.); of things, to respond conformably in action to (as, a ship *obeys* her helm; "The rising waves *obey* th' increasing blast," Cowper's "Retirement," 532). **II.** *intr.* To obey commands or instructions; do as bidden; be obedient.—**o-bey′er,** *n.*—**o-bey′ing-ly,** *adv.*

ob-fus-cate (ob-fus′kāt), *v. t.*; *-cated, -cating.* [LL. *obfuscatus*, pp. of *obfuscare*, < L. *ob* (see *ob-*) + *fuscare*, darken, < *fuscus*, E. *fuscous.*] To darken or obscure; esp., fig., to obscure or confuse (the mind, etc.: as, "The whole company stared . . . like men whose senses were a little *obfuscated* by beer," Irving's "Tales of a Traveler," ii. 9); confuse in mind, as a person; bemuse; stupefy.—**ob-fus-ca′tion** (-kā′shọn), *n.* [LL. *obfuscatio(n-).*] The act of obfuscating, or the state of being obfuscated; also, something that obfuscates.

o-bi[1] (ō′bi), *n.* [Of African origin.] A kind of sorcery practised by the negroes of Africa, the West Indies, etc.; also, a fetish or charm used in it.

o-bi[2] (ō′bi), *n.*; pl. *obis.* [Jap.] A long, broad sash worn by Japanese women and children.

Obispo.

ob-i-it (ob′-i-it). [L.] '(The person named) died': followed by the date of death. Abbreviated *ob.*

o-bis-po (ọ-bis′pō), *n.* [Sp., lit. 'bishop.'] A four-horned sheep of Bolivia, Peru, etc.

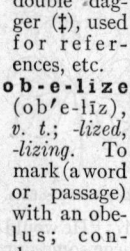

o-bit (ō′bit or ob′it), *n.* [L. *obitus*, < *obire*, go to, go down, die, < *ob*, to, + *ire*, go.] Death; the date of a person's death; an obituary notice; a funeral service; a memorial service for one deceased. [Obs. or rare.]

ob-i-ter (ob′i-tėr), *adv.* [L., < *ob*, on, + *iter*, way.] By the way; in passing; incidentally.—**obiter dictum** (dik′tum); pl. *-ta* (-tạ̈). [L., something said by the way.] An incidental opinion of a judge, not part of his judicial decision, and not binding; hence, in general, an incidental opinion; a passing remark.

o-bit-u-a-rist (ọ-bit′ū-ạ̄-rist), *n.* A writer of an obituary notice.

o-bit-u-a-ry (ọ-bit′ū-ạ̄-ri). [ML. *obituarius*, < L. *obitus*, death, E. *obit.*] **I.** *a.* Pertaining to or recording a death: as, an *obituary* notice. **II.** *n.*; pl. *-ries* (-riz). A list of deaths, or of anniversary days when service is performed for the dead; also, a notice of the death of a person, often with a brief biographical sketch, as in a newspaper.

ob-ject (ọb-jekt′), *v.* [L. *objectus*, pp. of *objicere*, throw before, present, expose, oppose, reproach with, < *ob*, to, before, + *jacere*, throw.] **I.** *tr.* To throw or place in the way† (as, "Pallas to their eyes The mist *objected*": Pope's tr. Homer's "Odyssey," vii.); also, to present† or bring forward†; also, to bring forward or adduce in opposition; urge as an objection (as, "if it be *objected*, that good actions . . . are often punished": J. Butler's "Analogy of Religion," i. 3); also, to bring as a charge; attribute as a fault (as, "I have heard it *objected* against that piece, that its instructions are not of general use": Steele, in "Spectator," 95). **II.** *intr.* To offer a reason or argument in opposition; express disapproval; feel disapproval, have an objection, or be averse (as, do you *object* to my going now? I will go now, if you do not *object*).—**ob-ject** (ob′jekt), *n.* [ML. *objectum*, prop. neut. of L. *objectus*, pp.] Something that may be perceived by the senses, esp. by sight or touch, or a visible or tangible thing (as, "Children, from their very birth, are daily growing acquainted with the *objects* about them": J. Butler's "Analogy of Religion," i. 5); a material thing; also, anything that may be presented to the mind (as, *objects* of thought); also, a thing with reference to the impression it makes on the mind (as, "No other allegorist [besides Bunyan] has ever been able to touch the heart, and to make abstractions *objects* of terror, pity, and of love": Macaulay's "Hist. of Eng.," vii.); sometimes, a person or thing which arouses feelings of pity (as, "Doctor, canst thou do nothing for this poor *object?*" Smollett's "Humphry Clinker," Oct. 3); often, a person or thing of pitiable or ridiculous aspect, or a 'sight' (as, "Every old tramper and queer *object* sees the light of our kitchen fire, and comes in for a lounge and a drink," Mrs. Stowe's "Oldtown Folks," vi.; what an *object* the old house has become!); also, a thing or person to which attention or action is directed (as, an *object* of study; a worthy *object* of charity); also, the end toward which effort is directed (as, "The chief *object* of the English was to establish . . . a great empire on the Continent": Macaulay's "Hist. of Eng.," i.); in *metaph.*, that toward which a cognitive act is directed; the non-ego as distinguished from the ego; in *gram.*, a noun or its equivalent dependent upon or governed by a verb or a preposition (as, the direct *object* of a verb, one on which the action is directly exerted, as *book* in 'give [to] him the book'; the indirect *object* of a verb, one indirectly affected, as *him* in the same example).

ob-ject=ball (ob'jekt-bâl), *n.* In *billiards*, etc., the ball which the striker aims to hit with the cue-ball; any ball except the striker's.

ob-ject=glass (ob'jekt-glås), *n.* In a telescope, microscope, etc., the lens or combination of lenses which first receives the rays from the object and forms the image viewed through the eyepiece.

ob-jec-ti-fy (ǫb-jek'ti-fī), *v. t.*; *-fied, -fying.* [ML. *objectum*, an object: see *-fy.*] To present as an object, esp. of sense; render objective; externalize.—**ob-jec"ti-fi-ca'tion** (-fi-kā'-shǫn), *n.*

ob-jec-tion (ǫb-jek'shǫn), *n.* [LL. *objectio(n-)*.] The act of objecting; also, something adduced, urged, or said in objecting; an adverse reason or argument; an expression of disagreement or disapproval; often, a feeling of disapproval or dislike; also, a ground or cause of objecting (as, "It was his obesity that was the great *objection* to him": Marryat's "Mr. Midshipman Easy," xxxvii.).—**ob-jec'tion-a-ble,** *a.* That may be objected to; exciting disapproval; disagreeable: as, "This was highly *objectionable* to Jael" (Miss Mulock's "John Halifax," ii.).—**ob-jec'tion-a-ble-ness,** *n.*—**ob-jec'-tion-a-bly,** *adv.*

ob-jec-ti-vate (ǫb-jek'ti-vāt), *v. t.*; *-vated, -vating.* [From *objective.*] To render objective; objectify.

ob-jec-tive (ǫb-jek'tiv). [ML. *objectivus.*] **I.** *a.* As presented to or perceived by the mind, rather than as in its own nature† (as, the *objective* being or nature of a thing); also, being the object of perception or thought; belonging to the object of thought rather than to the thinking subject (opposed to *subjective*); also, intent upon or dealing with things external to the mind rather than thoughts or feelings, as a person, a book, etc.; also, being the object of one's endeavors or actions (as, an *objective* point); in *perspective*, being, or pertaining to, the object whose perspective delineation is required (as, an *objective* plane); in *gram.*, noting the case in declension in English that indicates the grammatical object; being in or pertaining to this case (cf. *accusative, a.*). **II.** *n.* An object-glass; also, an end toward which efforts are directed; something aimed at; an objective point; in *gram.*, the objective case, or a word in that case.—**ob-jec'-tive-ly,** *adv.*—**ob-jec'tive-ness,** *n.*—**ob-jec'tiv-ism,** *n.* A tendency to lay stress on the objective or external elements of cognition; a doctrine characterized by this tendency; also, the tendency to deal with things external to the mind rather than thoughts or feelings, as in a writer or his writings.—**ob-jec'tiv-ist,** *n.*—**ob-jec-tiv-i-ty** (ob-jek-tiv'i-ti), *n.* The state or quality of being objective; external reality; intentness on objects external to the mind.

ob-ject-less (ob'jekt-les), *a.* Having no object; destitute of visible objects (as, "As we were obliged to keep the glasses up, our drive . . . was *objectless* and dreary": Galt's "Ayrshire Legatees," i.); not directed toward any object (as, "His eyes . . . Fix'd lifelessly, or *objectless* they roll'd": Southey's "Madoc," i. 3. 229); having no object or end in view, purposeless, or aimless (as, "Strangers would wonder what I am doing, lingering here at the sign-post, evidently *objectless* and lost": C. Brontë's "Jane Eyre," xxviii.).

ob-ject=les-son (ob'jekt-les"n), *n.* A lesson in which instruction is conveyed by means of a material object; fig., a practical illustration of a principle.

ob-jec-tor (ǫb-jek'tǫr), *n.* One who objects.—**conscientious objector.** See under *conscientious.*

ob-jur-gate (ǫb-jėr'gāt or ob'jėr-), *v. t.*; *-gated, -gating.* [L. *objurgatus*, pp. of *objurgare*, < *ob* (see *ob-*) + *jurgare*, scold, chide.] To reproach vehemently or roundly; upbraid violently; berate.—**ob-jur-ga-tion** (ob-jėr-gā'shǫn), *n.* [L. *objurgatio(n-)*.] The act of objurgating; a vehement upbraiding.—**ob-jur'ga-to-ry** (-gą-tō-ri), *a.*

ob-lan-ce-o-late (ob-lan'sē-ǭ-lāt), *a.* [See *ob-*.] In *bot.*, inversely lanceolate, as a leaf; shaped like the head of a lance, but with the tapering end at the base.

ob-late[1] (ob'lāt or ob-lāt'), *n.* [ML. *oblatus*, noun use of L. *oblatus*, pp. of *offerre*, E. *offer.*] Orig., a person offered to the service of a monastery, but not under monastic vows; later, a member of any of various congregations or societies (of men or women) of the Roman Catholic Church, devoted to special religious work.

ob-late[2] (ob'lāt or ob-lāt'), *a.* [From *ob-* + *-late* as in *prolate.*] Flattened at the poles, as a spheroid generated by the revolution of an ellipse about its shorter axis: opposed to *prolate.*—**ob'late-ly,** *adv.*—**ob'late-ness,** *n.*

ob-la-tion (ob-lā'shǫn), *n.* [LL. *oblatio(n-)*, < L. *oblatus*, pp. of *offerre*, E. *offer.*] The act of making an offering, now esp. to God or a deity; specif., the offering or presenting to God of the elements of bread and wine in the eucharist; hence, the whole office of the eucharist; also, something offered, now esp. to God or a deity (as, "to make choice of some *oblation*, which might . . . refer to the propriety and excellency of your individual person," Bacon's "Advancement of Learning," i., To the King; "He . . . shall bring his *oblation* unto the Lord," Lev. vii. 29); a sacrificial offering; a donation made to God for the services of the church or for other pious uses; a gift or bequest of property made to God or the church.—**ob-la'tion-al, ob'la-to-ry** (-lą-tō-ri), *a.*

ob-li-ga-ble (ob'li-gą-bl), *a.* Capable of being bound by an obligation: as, "One man can come under obligations on which you can rely, — is *obligable*; and another is not" (Emerson's "Conduct of Life," vii.).

ob-li-gate (ob'li-gāt), *v. t.*; *-gated, -gating.* [L. *obligatus*, pp. of *obligare*: see *oblige.*] To oblige, bind, or render bound, morally or legally (as, to *obligate* one's self to fulfil certain conditions; his office *obligated* him to the prosecution of the offenders); hence, to constrain or compel (archaic or prov.: as, "I was *obligated* to postpone the purchase," Galt's "Annals of the Parish," ii.); also, to render indebted or obliged, as for a benefit or favor (archaic or prov.).—**ob'li-gate,** *a.* Obligated, bound, or constrained; in *biol.*, having of necessity a particular character, or restricted to a particular condition of life, as certain parasites (opposed to *facultative*).

ob-li-ga-tion (ob-li-gā'shǫn), *n.* [L. *obligatio(n-)*, < *obligare*: see *oblige* and *obligate.*] The act of binding one's self by a promise, engagement, or contract, or a binding promise or the like made; also, the binding operation or force of a promise or engagement, or of anything imposing a moral or legal duty (as, to be under *obligation* to complete a work; to be released from all *obligation* in a case; to incur *obligation*); a binding requirement as to action, or a duty imposed or resting upon one (as, to fulfil every *obligation* of a post, of good citizenship, or of a father; rank imposes *obligations*; "Man's *obligations* infinite, of course His life should prove that he perceives their force," Cowper's "Truth," 197); a thing that one is bound to do (as, " 'The cultivation of the soil,' we are told, 'is an *obligation* imposed by nature on mankind' ": Irving's "Knickerbocker's New York," i. 5); also, the state or fact of being indebted for a benefit, favor, or service, or a debt of gratitude (as, to express one's sense of *obligation* for a kindness; "a person to whom . . . this country owes very great *obligations*," Burke's "American Taxation"); a benefit, favor, or service, for which gratitude is due (as, "When a kindly face greets us . . . we should feel it as an *obligation*": Lamb's "Valentine's Day"); in *law*, an agreement enforceable by law, or a document containing such an agreement; a bond containing a penalty, with a condition annexed, for payment of money, performance of covenants, or the like; any bond, note, bill, certificate, or the like, as of a government or a corporation, serving as security for payment of indebtedness.—**days** (or **holy days**) **of obligation,** *eccles.*, days on which every one is required to abstain from work and to attend divine service.—**ob-li-ga'tion-al,** *a.*

ob-li-ga-tive (ob'li-gā-tiv), *a.* Imposing or implying obligation.—**ob'li-ga-tive-ness,** *n.*

ob-li-ga-to (ob-li-gä'tō), *a.* and *n.* See *obbligato.*

ob-li-ga-to-ry (ob'li-gą-tō-ri or ǫb-lig'ą-), *a.* [LL. *obligatorius.*] Imposing obligation, or binding, morally or legally (as, an *obligatory* promise; *obligatory* force); also, required as a matter of obligation (as, a reply is expected but not *obligatory*; a fixed period of residence is *obligatory* before naturalization); incumbent or compulsory (*on* or *upon*: as, duties *obligatory* on all); in *law*, creating or recording an obligation, as a writing.—**ob'li-ga-to-ri-ly,** *adv.*—**ob'li-ga-to-ri-ness,** *n.*

o-blige (ǫ-blīj′), *v. t.*; *obliged, obliging.* [OF. *obligier* (F. *obliger*), < L. *obligare* (pp. *obligatus*), < *ob*, to, + *ligare*, bind: cf. *obligate.*] To bind (a person, etc.) by a promise, engagement, or contract (as, to *oblige* one's self to perform some service; "My father had *obliged* me to the improvement of my stock, not by a promise . . . but by a penalty which I was at liberty to incur," Johnson's "Rasselas," viii.); render (a person, etc.) morally or legally bound, as a promise, contract, or the like does; hence, in general, to require or constrain, as the law, a command, duty, or necessity does; place under some binding requirement as to action; compel or force (to do something, or to a particular course of action); also, to render (an action, course, etc.) incumbent or obligatory (as, "Had he done all that nobility *obliged?*" Howells's "Chance Acquaintance," iv.); also, to render indebted, or place under an obligation of gratitude, for some benefit, favor, or service (much used in polite requests and conventional expressions of gratitude: as, kindly *oblige* me by closing the door; "We are very much *obliged* for your kind offer," Dunsany's "If," i. 2); favor or accommodate (*with*: as, he consented to *oblige* the company with a song).—**ob-li-gee** (ob-li-jē′), *n.* In *law*, one to whom another is bound by contract; the person to whom a bond is given; also, in general language, one who is under obligation or indebted to another for a benefit or favor received.—**o-bli-ger** (ǫ-blī′-jėr), *n.* One who obliges.—**o-bli′ging,** *p. a.* That obliges; disposed to oblige, or do favors or services; accommodating; complaisant.—**o-bli′ging-ly,** *adv.*—**o-bli′ging-ness,** *n.*—**ob-li-gor** (ob′li-gôr), *n.* In *law*, one who binds himself to another by contract; the person who gives a bond.

ob-lique (ǫb-lēk′ or ǫb-līk′), *a.* [L. *obliquus.*] Neither perpendicular to nor parallel with a given line or surface; slanting; sloping; often, diverging from a given straight line or course; not straight or direct, as a course, etc. (as, "This terrace or garden . . . took in an *oblique* view of the open sea": Peacock's "Nightmare Abbey," i.); in specif. use, of an angle, either obtuse or acute, rather than right; of a solid, as a cone or a cylinder, not having the axis perpendicular to the plane of the base; also, in fig. use, not going straight to the point; indirectly stated or expressed (as, "She . . . indulged herself in certain *oblique* hints calculated to strengthen his suspicions," Godwin's "Caleb Williams," ii.; an *oblique* reproach); also, indirectly aimed at or reached, as ends, results, etc.; also, being awry or wrong; mentally perverse, as views; morally wrong, or not upright, as conduct or dealings; in *gram.*, noting or pertaining to any case except the nominative and vocative, or sometimes except the nominative, vocative, and accusative; also, of speech, etc., not narrated directly, but put into a reported form (see *indirect discourse*, under *discourse*, *n.*); in *bot.*, having unequal sides, as a leaf.—**oblique sailing.** See under *sailing.*—**ob-lique′,** *v. i.*; *-liqued, -liquing.* To have or take an oblique direction; slant; advance obliquely; *milit.*, to advance obliquely by turning 45° to the right or left and marching in the new direction.—**ob-lique′ly,** *adv.*—**ob-lique′ness,** *n.*—**ob-li′qui-tous** (-lik′wi-tus), *a.* Exhibiting intellectual or moral obliquity.—**ob-li′qui-ty,** *n.*; pl. *-ties* (-tiz). The state of being oblique; inclination, or degree of inclination; indirectness, as in conduct or speech, or an instance of it; mental perversity, as of opinions, or an instance of it; divergence from moral rectitude, or a moral delinquency (as, "a moral *obliquity* which grated very harshly against Ilbrahim's instinctive rectitude": Hawthorne's "Twice-Told Tales," The Gentle Boy).

ob-lit-er-ate (ǫb-lit′ẹ-rāt), *v. t.*; *-ated, -ating.* [L. *obliteratus*, pp. of *obliterare*, better *oblitterare*, < *ob* (see *ob-*) + *littera*, E. *letter*[2].] To blot out or render undecipherable (writing, marks, etc.); cancel; efface; in general, to remove all traces of, do away with, or destroy (as, "They resumed the attack of Pityus; and by the destruction of that city, *obliterated* the memory of their former disgrace": Gibbon's "Decline and Fall of the Roman Empire," x.).—**ob-lit-er-a′tion** (-ẹ-rā′shǫn), *n.* [L. *obliteratio*(*n-*).] The act of obliterating, or the state of being obliterated; effacement.—**ob-lit′er-a-tive** (-ẹ-rạ-tiv), *a.* Tending to obliterate.

ob-liv-i-on (ǫb-liv′i-ǫn), *n.* [OF. *oblivion*, < L. *oblivio*(*n-*), akin to *oblivisci*, forget.] The forgetting, or forgetfulness, of something in particular or of the past or present generally (as, "Gabriel . . . Sought in the Western wilds *oblivion* of self and of sorrow," Longfellow's "Evangeline," ii. 2; "Oh, what would he have given for one five minutes of *oblivion*, of slumber, of relief from the burning thirst!" J. H. Newman's "Callista," xxiv.); hence, disregard or overlooking (as, *oblivion* of political offenses; "He [William III.] expressed his hope that a bill of general pardon and *oblivion* would be . . . presented for his sanction," Macaulay's "Hist. of Eng.," xiv.); also, the state of being forgotten, as by the world (as, "Pompeii and Herculaneum might have passed into *oblivion*, with a herd of their contemporaries, had they not been fortunately overwhelmed by a volcano": Irving's "Knickerbocker's New York," vii. 6).—**ob-liv′i-ous,** *a.* [L. *obliviosus*, < *oblivio*(*n-*).] Forgetful, or without remembrance (as, "I became so *oblivious* of my former failure as again to tempt fortune": Lever's "Harry Lorrequer," xxxiv.); unmindful; loosely, unconscious (with *of* or *to*: as, "She could hardly have been *oblivious* of Yuba Bill's adoration," Bret Harte's "Miggles"); also, inducing forgetfulness (as, "some sweet *oblivious* antidote": Shakspere's "Macbeth," v. 3. 43); also, forgotten†, or of or for forgotten things† (as, "consigned to the *oblivious* lumber-room": Lamb's "My Relations").—**ob-liv′i-ous-ly,** *adv.*—**ob-liv′i-ous-ness,** *n.*

ob-li-vis-cence (ob-li-vis′ẹns), *n.* [L. *obliviscens* (*-ent-*), ppr. of *oblivisci*, forget.] Forgetting; forgetfulness.

ob-long (ob′lông). [L. *oblongus*, rather long, oblong, < *ob* (see *ob-*) + *longus*, long.] **I.** *a.* Elongated, usually from the square or circular form (as, an *oblong* card; an *oblong* leaf); esp., in the form of a rectangle of greater length than breadth. **II.** *n.* An oblong figure, esp. an elongated rectangle.

Oblong Leaf.

ob-lo-quy (ob′lǭ-kwi), *n.*; pl. *-quies* (-kwiz). [LL. *obloquium*, < L. *obloqui*, speak against, blame, abuse, < *ob*, against, + *loqui*, speak.] Censorious or abusive language aimed at a person, etc., esp. by numbers of persons or by the public generally (as, "Was he not himself the mark of *obloquy* among the Reformers, because of his leniency to Catholics?" Motley's "Dutch Republic," v. 2; "He was . . . exposed to a storm of mendacious *obloquy*," Lecky's "Hist. of Eng. in the 18th Century," i.); public blame or revilement; vilification; calumny; also, the discredit or disgrace resulting from public blame or revilement (as, "his long public life, so singularly chequered with good and evil, with glory and *obloquy*": Macaulay's "Essays," Warren Hastings); reproach; also, a cause of reproach† (as, "The jewel of our house . . . Which were the greatest *obloquy* i' the world In me to lose": Shakspere's "All's Well," iv. 2. 48).

ob-nounce (ob-nouns′), *v. i.*; *-nounced, -nouncing.* [L. *obnuntiare*, < *ob*, against, + *nuntiare*, announce, < *nuntius*, messenger.] In *Rom. antiq.*, to announce an unfavorable omen with reference to a proposed public action (thus opposing the proceeding).

ob-nox-ious (ǫb-nok′shus), *a.* [L. *obnoxius*, < *ob*, to, + *noxa*, harm, injury: cf. *noxious.*] Exposed or liable (to harm, evil, or anything objectionable: as, "Made hereby *obnoxious* more To all the miseries of life," Milton's "Samson Agonistes," 106; "that punishment to which we were *obnoxious*," J. Butler's "Analogy of Religion," ii. 5: now archaic); also, liable to punishment or censure†, or reprehensible†; also, harmful† or injurious†; now, usually, objectionable, offensive, or odious (as, *obnoxious* practices or laws; "Persons *obnoxious* to the government were frequently imprisoned without any other authority than a royal order," Macaulay's "Hist. of Eng.," i.).—**ob-nox′ious-ly,** *adv.*—**ob-nox′ious-ness,** *n.*

o-boe (ō′bō, It. ō′bǭ-ā), *n.* [It., < F. *hautbois*: see *hautboy.*] A wooden wind-instrument in the form of a slender tapering

Oboe.

tube, in which the tone is produced by a double reed. Cf. *English horn* (under *horn*, *n.*), *heckelphone*, and *bassoon.*—**o-bo-ist** (ō′bǭ-ist), *n.* A player on the oboe.

ob-ol (ob′ǫl), *n.* Same as *obolus.*

ob-o-lus (ob′ǫ-lus), *n.*; pl. *-li* (-lī). [L., < Gr. ὀβολός.] An ancient Greek silver coin and weight, the sixth part of a drachma; also, any of various coins, mostly of small value, formerly current in Europe.

Obverse. Reverse.
Obolus of Athens.

ob-o-vate (ob-ō′vāt), *a.* [See *ob-*.] Inversely ovate; ovate with the narrow end at the base, as a leaf (see cut below).—**ob-o′void,** *a.* Inversely ovoid; ovoid with the narrow end at the base, as certain fruits.

Obovate Leaf.

ob-py-ram-i-dal (ob-pi-ram′i-dąl), *a.* [See *ob-*.] In *bot.*, inversely pyramidal; having the form of an inverted pyramid.

ob-scene (ǫb-sēn′), *a.*; compar. *obscener*, superl. *obscenest.* [L. *obscenus, obscænus,* of evil omen, offensive, disgusting.] Ill-boding or ominous (a Latinism: as, "The boding bird . . . Which . . . beats about the tombs with nightly wings, Where songs *obscene* on sepulchers she sings," Dryden's tr. Virgil's "Æneid," xii. 1250); also, abominable, foul, disgusting, loathsome, or repulsive (as, "so heinous, black, *obscene* a deed," Shakspere's "Richard II.," iv. 1. 131; "It is that *obscene* idol . . . come from India," Dunsany's "Night at an Inn": now archaic and literary); now, usually, offensive to modesty or decency, indecent, or lewd (as, *obscene* language, books, or pictures; an *obscene* dance).—**ob-scene′ly,** *adv.*—**ob-scene′ness,** *n.*—**ob-scen′i-ty** (-sen′i-ti), *n.*; pl. *-ties* (-tiz). Obscene quality or character; indecency; also, something obscene; esp., obscene language; an obscene remark, expression, etc.

ob-scur-ant (ǫb-skūr′ąnt). [L. *obscurans* (*-ant-*), ppr. of *obscurare*, E. *obscure*, *v.*] **I.** *n.* One who obscures; one who strives to prevent inquiry and enlightenment. **II.** *a.* Pertaining to or characteristic of obscurants.—**ob-scur′ant-ism,** *n.* The principles or practice of obscurants; opposition to inquiry and enlightenment.—**ob-scur′ant-ist,** *n.* and *a.*

ob-scu-ra-tion (ob-skū-rā′shǫn), *n.* [L. *obscuratio*(*n-*).] The act of obscuring, or the state of being obscured.

ob-scure (ǫb-skūr′). [OF. F. *obscur*, < L. *obscurus*, dark, dim, indistinct, unknown, ignoble: cf. Skt. *sku-*, cover.] **I.** *a.*; compar. *obscurer*, superl. *obscurest.* Dark, as from want of light or illumination (as, "*Obscurest* night involv'd the sky," Cowper's "Castaway," 1; the *obscure* recesses of a cave); murky; dim; also, enveloped in, concealed by, or frequenting darkness (as, "Thus wrapp'd in mist Of midnight vapour glide *obscure*," Milton's "Paradise Lost," ix. 159; "The *obscure* bird Clamour'd the livelong night," Shakspere's "Macbeth," ii. 3. 64); also, dark, dull, or not bright or lustrous, as color or appearance; also, indistinct to the sight, or to some other sense, esp. hearing (as, *obscure* details in a picture; an *obscure* syllable in pronunciation; the *obscure* sound of *a* in *formula*); also, not readily seen, or remote from observation, or retired, as a place; also, not such as to attract notice; inconspicuous or unnoticeable (as, the *obscure* beginnings of a great movement); of no prominence, note, or distinction (as, a host of *obscure* writers; "the pleasure of seeing . . . *obscure* villages become the seats of kings," Swift's "Gulliver's Travels," iii. 10); unknown to fame; sometimes, of no social prominence, or humble (as, "this *obscure* family of ours," B. Franklin's "Autobiography," i.; *obscure* birth or condition); also, unclear to the mind or understanding; imperfectly known or understood, or uncertain (as, the cause of the trouble is *obscure*; an *obscure* malady; *obscure* features of a case); of meaning, not clear or plain, or not clearly expressed; of language, statements, style, etc., or a speaker or writer, not expressing the meaning clearly or plainly (as, "This *obscure* saying baffled him": Arnold Bennett's "Helen with the High Hand," xiv.); not perspicuous; blind. **II.** *n.* Darkness or obscurity: as, "Who shall tempt with wandering feet The dark . . . abyss, And through the palpable *obscure* find out His uncouth way?" (Milton's "Paradise Lost," ii. 406).—**ob-scure′,** *v. t.*; *-scured, -scuring.* [L. *obscurare*, < *obscurus.*] To make obscure; darken or dim (as, "Gloomy clouds *obscure* the cheerful day": Pope's "Winter," 30); envelop or cover so as to conceal (as, mountains *obscured* by mists); hide; render indistinct to sight; make obscure in sound, as a vowel in pronunciation; render unclear to the mind or understanding (as, to *obscure* a subject by unnecessary details or ambiguous language).—**ob-scure′ly,** *adv.*—**ob-scure′ment,** *n.* Obscuration.—**ob-scure′ness,** *n.*—**ob-scur′er** (-skūr′ėr), *n.*—**ob-scu′ri-ty** (-skū′ri-ti), *n.*; pl. *-ties* (-tiz). The state or quality of being obscure; darkness; dimness; indistinctness; inconspicuous or obscure condition or situation, or a person who is obscure or of no note; uncertainty, as of something not clear to the mind; often, uncertainty of meaning or expression, or a point or passage of uncertain meaning, as in a discourse or writing.

ob-se-crate (ob′sę-krāt), *v. t.*; *-crated, -crating.* [L. *obsecratus*, pp. of *obsecrare*, < *ob*, to, + *sacrare*, make or declare sacred: see *sacre.*] To entreat (a person, etc.) solemnly, as in the name of something sacred; beseech; supplicate; implore; also, to make supplication for (a thing: as, "Andrew Fairservice employed his lungs in *obsecrating* a share of Dougal's protection," Scott's "Rob Roy," xxxi.).—**ob-se-cra′tion** (-krā′shǫn), *n.*

ob′se-quies, *n. pl.* See *obsequy.*

ob-se-qui-ous (ǫb-sē′kwi-us), *a.* [L. *obsequiosus*, < *obsequium*, compliance, < *obsequi*, comply with, < *ob*, to, + *sequi*, follow. Formerly sometimes associated with *obsequy.*] Compliant, obedient, or dutiful (now rare); also, servilely compliant, complaisant, or deferential (as, *obsequious* servants or courtiers; "The court was *obsequious* to the Proconsul, afraid of Rome," J. H. Newman's "Callista," xxvii.); characterized by or showing servile complaisance or deference (as, *obsequious* compliance or courtesies; an *obsequious* bow); also, dutiful or proper in the observance of funeral rites or in mourning for the dead† (as, "The survivor bound In filial obligation for some term To do *obsequious* sorrow": Shakspere's "Hamlet," i. 2. 92).—**ob-se′qui-ous-ly,** *adv.*—**ob-se′qui-ous-ness,** *n.*

ob-se-quy (ob′sę-kwi), *n.*; pl. *-quies* (-kwiz). [LL. *obsequiæ*, pl., for L. *exsequiæ, exequiæ*, funeral rites: see *exequy.*] A funeral rite or ceremony: now only in *pl.*, and often implying state or pomp: as, "His funeral *obsequies* were celebrated with the utmost grandeur and solemnity" (Irving's "Knickerbocker's New York," vii. 12); "Buried . . . with gorgeous *obsequies*, And mass, and rolling music, like a queen" (Tennyson's "Lancelot and Elaine," 1324).

ob-serv-a-ble (ǫb-zėr′vą-bl), *a.* [L. *observabilis.*] That may be or is to be observed or noticed; noticeable; noteworthy; also, that may be or is to be observed, followed, or kept.—**ob-serv′a-ble-ness,** *n.*—**ob-serv′a-bly,** *adv.*

ob-ser-vance (ǫb-zėr′vąns), *n.* [OF. F. *observance*, < L. *observantia.*] The action of observing, regarding attentively, or noticing; observation; also, the action of observing, conforming to, following, or keeping (as, *observance* of laws, rules, customs, or methods); a rule or custom to be observed (as, "There are other strict *observances*; As, not to see a woman": Shakspere's "Love's Labour's Lost," i. 1. 36); the rule of a religious order, esp. that of the Observants; also, observing, keeping, or celebration by appropriate procedure, ceremonies, etc. (as, "Our Sundays, at Blithedale, were not ordinarily kept with such rigid *observance* as might have befitted the descendants of the Pilgrims": Hawthorne's "Blithedale Romance," xiv.); a procedure, ceremony, or rite, as for a particular occasion or use (as, patriotic *observances*; pious or religious *observances*; to honor the memory of the dead with public *observances*); also, respectful attention or service, or, *pl.*, attentions or assiduities (archaic: as, "I have long loved her . . . followed her with a doting *observance*," Shakspere's "Merry Wives of Windsor," ii. 2. 203; "He compass'd her with sweet *observances* And worship," Tennyson's "Marriage of Geraint," 48).

ob-ser-vant (ǫb-zėr′vąnt). [L. *observans* (*-ant-*), ppr.] **I.** *a.* Observing or regarding attentively, or watchful (as, "Wandering from clime to clime, *observant* stray'd, Their manners noted, and their states survey'd": Pope's tr. Homer's "Odyssey," i.); also, quick to notice or perceive (as, "He was *observant* and thoughtful, and given to asking sagacious questions": Galt's "Annals of the Parish," xlii.); also, careful in the observing of a law, rule, custom, policy, or the like (with *of*); also, given to formal or ceremonial observance (*of*: as, "No man . . . could have been more *observant* of religious rites," Motley's "Dutch Republic," i. 1); also, respectfully attentive or regardful†. **II.** *n.* An observer of law or rule; [*cap.*] a member of a branch of the Franciscan order which in the 15th century became separated from the Conventuals, and which observes strictly the rule of St. Francis (also called *Friar Minor*); also [*l. c.*], an obsequious attendant†.

Ob-ser-vant-ine (ọb-zėr′vạn-tin), *n.* [F. *observantin.*] An Observant (Franciscan friar). Also **Ob-ser′vant-ist.**

ob-ser-vant-ly (ọb-zėr′vạnt-li), *adv.* In an observant manner.

ob-ser-va-tion (ob-zėr-vā′shọn), *n.* [L. *observatio(n-).*] The act of observing, regarding attentively, or watching; often, the act or an act of observing, viewing, or noting something, without or with the aid of instruments, for some scientific or other special purpose, or the information or record secured thereby; specif., an observing or ascertaining of the altitude of the sun or other heavenly body in order to determine the latitude and longitude of a position, as at sea, or the result obtained (as, "I had no instruments to take an *observation* to know what latitude we were in": Defoe's "Robinson Crusoe," i. 2); also, the act of noticing or perceiving, or notice (as, a case which lately came under my *observation*; to escape a person's *observation*; "He had almost gone by, before Hester Prynne could gather voice enough to attract his *observation*," Hawthorne's "Scarlet Letter," xvii.); the faculty or habit of observing or noticing (as, a man of great *observation*); also, that which is learned by observing, or an observed truth or fact (now rare); also, an utterance by way of remark or comment (as, "He spoke in the most casual way. He made the thing seem the most incidental of *observations*": H. G. Wells's "Soul of a Bishop," iv.); also, observance, as of law, rule, custom, or the like, or of a holy day (obs. or rare); a ceremony† or rite†.—**ob-ser-va′tion-al,** *a.* Of, pertaining to, or founded on observation, esp. as contrasted with experiment.—**ob-ser-va′tion-al-ly,** *adv.*—**ob-ser-va′tion=car,** *n.* A railroad-car designed for purposes of observation; esp., a car with an open platform at the rear, commonly attached at the end of a train, for enabling passengers to view the scenery.

ob-ser-va-to-ry (ọb-zėr′vạ-tọ̄-ri), *n.*; pl. *-ries* (-riz). [= F. *observatoire*, < NL. *observatorium.*] A place or building set apart and fitted up for making observations of astronomical, meteorological, or other natural phenomena; also, a place or structure for affording an extensive view (as, "I never knew of a ship sailing . . . but I went up to the State House cupola or to the *observatory* on some friend's house . . . and there watched the departure": G. W. Curtis's "Prue and I," iii.).—**ob-ser-va-to′ri-al** (-tō′ri-ạl), *a.*

ob-serve (ọb-zėrv′), *v.*; *-served, -serving.* [OF. F. *observer*, < L. *observare* (pp. *observatus*), watch, note, heed, comply with, observe, < *ob*, to, + *servare*, keep, watch, observe.] **I.** *tr.* To regard with attention, so as to see or learn something (as, "*Observe* each face, how sober and demure!" Cowper's "Progress of Error," 135; "Look to your wife; *observe* her well with Cassio," Shakspere's "Othello," iii. 3. 197); watch; often, to watch, view, or note for some scientific, official, or other special purpose (as, to *observe* an eclipse; to *observe* meteorological indications; to *observe* military movements, effect of gun-fire, etc.); make or take an observation of; also, to become aware of by seeing, or notice or remark (as, he did not *observe* the approaching visitor; I *observed* several new books on the table; "I saw the pots . . . red-hot . . . and *observed* that they did not crack at all," Defoe's "Robinson Crusoe," i. 9); see; perceive; also, to say by way of remark or comment, or remark (as, "He *observed* in apology, that it [z] was a letter you never wanted hardly," George Eliot's "Adam Bede," xxi.; "'It's a rare lot of money,' he *observed*," Arnold Bennett's "Helen with the High Hand," xviii.); also, to give obedient heed to, comply with, or conform to (as, to *observe* a law, rule, agreement, conditions, etc.); adhere to or follow in practice (as, to *observe* a custom, policy, method, etc.); keep or maintain in one's action, conduct, etc. (as, to *observe* moderation, patience, silence, etc.; "Hush . . . You must *observe* quiet," Cooper's "Spy," xii.); also, to show regard for by some appropriate procedure, ceremonies, etc. (as, to *observe* a holiday or anniversary; to *observe* the Sabbath, Lent, or Christmas); keep or celebrate; perform duly, or solemnize (ceremonies, rites, etc.); also, to treat (a person) with respect, deference, or consideration† (as, "He is gracious, if he be *observed*": Shakspere's "2 Henry IV.," iv. 4. 30). **II.** *intr.* To take note or notice; also, to remark or comment (commonly with *on* or *upon*).—**ob-serve′,** *n.* An observation or remark: as, "Thomas said he had not heard a mair sound *observe* for some time" (Galt's "Annals of the Parish," i.). [Sc.]—**ob-serv′er,** *n.*—**ob-serv′ing,** *p. a.* That observes; observant.—**ob-serv′ing-ly,** *adv.*

ob-sess (ob-ses′), *v. t.* [L. *obsessus*, pp. of *obsidere*, besiege, beset, < *ob*, to, before, + *sedere*, sit.] To besiege†; fig., of an evil spirit, to beset, or dominate from without, as a person; hence, of a feeling, idea, etc., to beset, trouble, or dominate, after the manner of an evil spirit (as, "This thought had been *obsessing* Hilda all the afternoon and evening": Arnold Bennett's "Hilda Lessways," iii. 4).—**ob-ses′sion** (-sesh′ọn), *n.* [L. *obsessio(n-).*] The act of obsessing, or the state of being obsessed; besetment, or domination from without, by an evil spirit (cf. *possession*); the besetting or dominating action or influence of a persistent feeling, idea, or the like, which the person cannot escape; hence, the feeling or idea itself; a 'fixed idea.'

ob-sid-i-an (ob-sid′i-ạn), *n.* [L. *Obsidianus*, erron. for *Obsianus*, pertaining to Obsius, reputed discoverer of a similar mineral.] A glassy form of lava, usually of a very dark color.

ob-sid-i-o-nal (ob-sid′i-ọ-nạl), *a.* [L. *obsidionalis*, < *obsidio(n-)*, siege, < *obsidere*: see *obsess.*] Of or pertaining to a siege: as, an *obsidional* crown (a crown or wreath, as of grass, conferred upon an ancient Roman general who delivered a besieged place); *obsidional* coins (coins struck in besieged places, as a substitute for current money). Also **ob-sid′i-o-na-ry** (-nā-ri).

ob-so-les-cent (ob-sọ̄-les′ẹnt), *a.* [L. *obsolescens* (*-ent-*), ppr. of *obsolescere*: see *obsolete.*] Becoming obsolete; passing out of use, as a word; tending to become out of date, or being no longer of the most modern type or kind, as machinery, etc.; in *biol.*, gradually disappearing, or imperfectly developed or visible, as organs, marks, etc.—**ob-so-les′cence,** *n.*—**ob-so-les′cent-ly,** *adv.*

ob-so-lete (ob′sọ̄-lēt), *a.* [L. *obsoletus*, pp. of *obsolescere*, fall into disuse, appar. < *ob* (see *ob-*) + *solere*, be accustomed.] Fallen into disuse, or no longer in use (as, an *obsolete* custom; an *obsolete* word; "*obsolete* methods of study," Hallam's "Literature of Europe," iii. 3. § 32); of a discarded type (as, an *obsolete* battle-ship); out of date; also, effaced by wearing down or away (as, an *obsolete* inscription); also, in *biol.*, imperfectly developed; indistinct, esp. in comparison with the corresponding character in other individuals, as of the opposite sex or of a related species.—**ob′so-lete-ly,** *adv.*—**ob′so-lete-ness,** *n.*—**ob′so-let-ism** (-lēt-izm), *n.* An obsolete custom, expression, word, or the like; also, the condition of being obsolete.

ob-sta-cle (ob′stạ-kl), *n.* [OF. F. *obstacle*, < L. *obstaculum*, < *obstare*, stand before, < *ob*, before, + *stare*, stand.] Something that stands in the way or obstructs progress; an obstruction; a hindrance: as, an *obstacle* to passage, or to a measure; an *obstacle* to a proposed marriage.

ob-stet-ric, ob-stet-ri-cal (ọb-stet′rik, -ri-kạl), *a.* [NL. *obstetricus*, for L. *obstetricius*, < *obstetrix* (*obstetric-*), midwife, < *obstare*: see *obstacle.*] Pertaining to the care and treatment of women in childbirth and during the period before and after delivery; of or pertaining to obstetrics.—**ob-ste-tri-cian** (ob-ste-trish′ạn), *n.* One skilled in obstetrics.—**ob-stet′rics,** *n.* The branch of medical art or science concerned with caring for and treating women in, before, and after childbirth; midwifery.

ob-sti-na-cy (ob′sti-nā-si), *n.*; pl. *-cies* (-siz). The quality or state of being obstinate; obstinate adherence to purpose, opinion, etc. (as, "that inexplicable, hateful *obstinacy*, which will neither yield to reason, common sense, expediency, or fear": J. H. Newman's "Callista," xxvii.); stubborn persistence (as, "The battle continued with incredible *obstinacy*": Irving's "Conquest of Granada," xxxix.); unyielding nature, as of a disease; also, an instance of being obstinate, or an obstinate action (as, "rebuke for their pedantries and *obstinacies*": Carlyle's "On Heroes," vi.).

ob-sti-nate (ob′sti-nạ̄t), *a.* [L. *obstinatus*, pp. of *obstinare*, set one's mind firmly on, < *ob*, to, + *-stinare*, akin to *stare*, stand: cf. *destine*.] Firmly and often perversely adhering to purpose, opinion, etc. (as, "The Englishers are sae *obstinate* in their own way, that I can get them to do nothing like Christians": Galt's "Ayrshire Legatees," vi.); not yielding to argument, persuasion, or entreaty (as, "Mr. Quincy labored hard with the governor to obtain his assent, but he was *obstinate*": B. Franklin's "Autobiography," xi.); stubborn; headstrong; also, inflexibly persisted in or carried out (as, "The Moors defended their posts with *obstinate* valor," Irving's "Conquest of Granada," liii.; to make *obstinate* resistance); pertinaciously or stubbornly fought out (as, "The sides . . . played a long, *obstinate*, even game": H. G. Wells's "Mr. Britling," i. 3. § 4); also, not easily controlled (as, "the stiff, *obstinate* growth of the endless wild-sage bushes": Parkman's "Oregon Trail," xv.); not yielding readily to treatment, as a disease.—**ob′sti-nate-ly,** *adv.*—**ob′sti-nate-ness,** *n.*

ob-strep-er-ous (ǫb-strep′ẹ-rus), *a.* [L. *obstreperus*, clamorous, < *obstrepere*, clamor at, < *ob*, to, + *strepere*, make a noise.] Making, or characterized by, great noise or outcry (as, "the *obstreperous* peals of broad-mouthed laughter of the Dutch negroes at Communipaw": Irving's "Knickerbocker's New York," ii. 2); boisterous; often, noisy or clamorous in opposition; also, resisting control or guidance in a noisy manner; unruly; disorderly; turbulent.—**ob-strep′er-ous-ly,** *adv.*—**ob-strep′er-ous-ness,** *n.*

ob-struct (ǫb-strukt′), *v. t.* [L. *obstructus*, pp. of *obstruere*, build before, block up, obstruct, < *ob*, before, + *struere*, pile up, build.] To block or close up, or make difficult of passage, with obstacles, as a way, road, channel, or the like (as, "All the streets are *obstructed* with building material": Mark Twain's "Life on the Mississippi," lx.); also, to interrupt or make difficult the passage or progress of (a person or thing in motion); impede or retard in motion; block or hinder (passage); hence, to oppose, hinder, or retard the course of (proceedings, or a person or thing in some proceeding: as, "to *obstruct* the union of man and wife," Goldsmith's "Vicar of Wakefield," xxviii.; to *obstruct* an officer in the discharge of his duty); also, to interrupt, or come in the way of (a view, etc.); cut off the view of (an object: rare).—**ob-struct′er,** *n.*—**ob-struc′tion** (-struk′shǫn), *n.* [L. *obstructio(n-)*.] The act of obstructing, or the state of being obstructed; often, persistent or systematic effort directed to stopping or retarding the progress of business in a legislative assembly or the like; also, something that obstructs; an obstacle or hindrance (as, *obstructions* to navigation; *obstructions* to progress).—**ob-struc′tion-ism,** *n.* The practice of obstruction, as in a legislative assembly.—**ob-struc′tion-ist,** *n.*—**ob-struc′tive. I.** *a.* Tending or serving to obstruct. **II.** *n.* Something that obstructs; one given to obstruction.—**ob-struc′tive-ly,** *adv.*—**ob-struc′tor,** *n.*

ob-stru-ent (ob′strọ̈-ẹnt). [L. *obstruens* (*obstruent-*), ppr. of *obstruere*: see *obstruct*.] **I.** *a.* Obstructing. **II.** *n.* Something that obstructs; specif., a medicine that closes the natural passages of the body.

ob-tain (ǫb-tān′), *v.* [OF. F. *obtenir*, < L. *obtinere*, take hold of, hold, get, intr. prevail, continue, < *ob*, to, + *tenere*, hold.] **I.** *tr.* To come into possession of, or procure, as by effort or request (as, "Under all these disadvantages, he *obtained* a competent knowledge of Greek and Latin," Scott's "Guy Mannering," ii.; to *obtain* leave of absence); in general, to get or acquire (as, an idea that has lately *obtained* currency); also, to win (a battle or other contest)†; also, to attain or reach (obs. or archaic); also, to hold† or possess† (as, "His mother then is mortal, but his Sire He who *obtains* the monarchy of Heaven": Milton's "Paradise Regained," i. 87). **II.** *intr.* To procure what is desired (as, "The simple heart, that freely asks In love, *obtains*": Whittier's "Hermit of the Thebaid"); also, to prevail or succeed (obs. or archaic); also, to attain (*to*)† (as, "if a man cannot *obtain* to that judgment": Bacon's "Essays," Of Simulation and Dissimulation); also, to be prevalent, customary, or in vogue (as, "the low standard of civilization that *obtained* at Logport in the year 1860": Bret Harte's "Princess Bob and Her Friends").—**ob-tain′a-ble,** *a.* That may be obtained.—**ob-tain′er,** *n.*—**ob-tain′ment,** *n.* The act of obtaining.

ob-ten-tion (ǫb-ten′shǫn), *n.* [F. *obtention*, < L. *obtinere*: see *obtain*, and cf. *detention*.] The act of obtaining; obtainment.

ob-test (ob-test′), *v.* [L. *obtestari*, < *ob*, to, + *testari*, call to witness, < *testis*, a witness.] **I.** *tr.* To invoke (the Deity, etc.) as witness; hence, to make a solemn appeal to; supplicate earnestly; beseech. **II.** *intr.* To protest; also, to make earnest supplication.—**ob-tes-ta′tion** (-tes-tā′shǫn), *n.*

ob-trude (ǫb-tröd′), *v.*; *-truded, -truding.* [L. *obtrudere* (pp. *obtrusus*), < *ob*, to, + *trudere*, thrust.] **I.** *tr.* To thrust forth; push out; also, to thrust forward or upon a person, esp. without warrant or invitation (as, "He would *obtrude* his assistance, if it were declined," Motley's "Dutch Republic," v. 5; to *obtrude* one's opinions upon others). **II.** *intr.* To thrust one's self or itself forward, esp. unduly or in an unwelcome manner; intrude: as, "The remembrance that our poor captain was lying dead in the cabin was constantly *obtruding*" (Marryat's "Peter Simple," xxx.); "imagination . . . that forward delusive faculty, ever *obtruding* beyond its sphere" (J. Butler's "Analogy of Religion," i. 1).—**ob-trud′er** (-trö′dėr), *n.*

ob-trun-cate (ob-trung′kāt), *v. t.*; *-cated, -cating.* [L. *obtruncatus*, pp. of *obtruncare*, < *ob* (see *ob-*) + *truncare*: see *truncate*.] To cut or lop off the head or top from: as, "the stumps of *obtruncated* trees" (Hawthorne's "Our Old Home," ii.).

ob-tru-sion (ǫb-trö′zhǫn), *n.* [LL. *obtrusio(n-)*.] The act of obtruding; also, something obtruded.

ob-tru-sive (ǫb-trö′siv), *a.* Having or showing a disposition to obtrude (as, "What matters if you are considered *obtrusive*, provided that you obtrude?" Thackeray's "Newcomes," viii.); forward; of a thing, obtruding itself unduly upon the notice (as, "Drumtochty . . . held that *obtrusive* prosperity was an irresistible provocation to the higher powers": Ian Maclaren's "Beside the Bonnie Brier Bush," i. 3).—**ob-tru′sive-ly,** *adv.*—**ob-tru′sive-ness,** *n.*

ob-tund (ob-tund′), *v. t.* [L. *obtundere* (pp. *obtusus*), < *ob*, to, against, + *tundere*, beat.] To blunt; dull; deaden.—**ob-tund′ent.** [L. *obtundens* (*-ent-*), ppr.] **I.** *a.* Dulling sensibility, as of nerves. **II.** *n.* An obtundent agent; an anesthetic application for the nerves of teeth.

ob-tu-rate (ob′tụ̄-rāt), *v. t.*; *-rated, -rating.* [L. *obturatus*, pp. of *obturare*, stop up.] To stop up; close; specif., in *gun.*, to close (a hole, joint, or cavity) so as to prevent the flow of gas through it.—**ob-tu-ra′tion** (-rā′shǫn), *n.*—**ob′tu-ra-tor,** *n.* Something that closes an opening, as the shutter of a photographic camera, a surgical plate for closing an abnormal opening, or a device for preventing the backward escape of gas from a breech-loading gun in firing.

ob-tuse (ǫb-tūs′), *a.*; compar. *obtuser*, superl. *obtusest.* [L. *obtusus*, pp. of *obtundere*: see *obtund*.] Blunt in form; not sharp or acute; specif., of a leaf, petal, etc., rounded at the extremity; also, of an angle, exceeding 90° (or a right angle) but less than 180°; in fig. use, indistinctly felt or perceived, as pain, sound, etc.; also, dull in perception, feeling, or intellect (as, "a person . . . *obtuse* in sensibility and unimaginative in temperament": Mrs. Stowe's "Oldtown Folks," xi.); not sensitive or observant; stupid; exhibiting dullness or stupidity.—**ob-tuse′=an″gled,** *a.* Having an obtuse angle.—**ob-tuse′ly,** *adv.*—**ob-tuse′ness, ob-tu′si-ty** (-tū′si-ti), *n.*

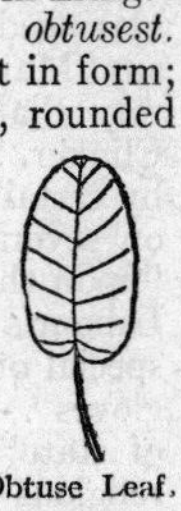

Obtuse Leaf.

o-bus (ō-büz), *n.*; pl. *obus.* [F.] *Milit.*, a shell.

ob-verse (ob-vėrs′ or ob′vėrs), *a.* [L. *obversus*, pp. of *obvertere*: see *obvert*.] Turned toward or facing one; also, corresponding to something else as a counterpart; also, having the base narrower than the top, as a leaf.—**ob′verse,** *n.* That side of a coin, medal, etc., which bears the principal design (opposed to *reverse*); also, the front or principal face of anything; also, a counterpart.—**ob-verse′ly,** *adv.*

ob-ver-sion (ob-vėr′shǫn), *n.* [See *obvert*.] In *logic*, a form of immediate inference in which a negative proposition is inferred from an affirmative or an affirmative from a negative: as, 'all men are mortal' becomes by *obversion* 'no men are immortal.'

ob-vert (ob-vėrt′), *v. t.* [L. *obvertere* (pp. *obversus*), < *ob*, toward, + *vertere*, turn.] To turn (something) toward an object; in *logic*, to change (a proposition) by obversion.

ob-vi-ate (ob′vi-āt), *v. t.*; *-ated*, *-ating*. [LL. *obviatus*, pp. of *obviare*, meet, oppose, prevent, < L. *ob*, before, + *via*, way.] To meet†; also, to oppose†; also, to meet and dispose of (difficulties, objections, etc.) by effective measures (as, "the objections against Christianity . . . having . . . been *obviated* in the preceding chapter": J. Butler's "Analogy of Religion," ii. 4); preclude or prevent by anticipatory measures (as, to take steps to *obviate* further trouble).—**ob-vi-a′tion** (-ā′shọn), *n.*

ob-vi-ous (ob′vi-us), *a.* [L. *obvius*, < *ob*, before, + *via*, way.] Being or standing in the way†; also, exposed or open (*to*)† (as, "The pedant is . . . *obvious* to ridicule": Steele, in "Tatler," 244); also, coming in one's way†, or frequently met with†; also, open to view or knowledge (as, "The rough tones . . . were heard before his figure was *obvious* to her eye," Scott's "Castle Dangerous," xvii.; an *obvious* advantage, duty, or necessity); manifest; evident; patent; palpable.—**ob′vi-ous-ly,** *adv.*—**ob′vi-ous-ness,** *n.*

ob-vo-lute (ob′vọ-lūt), *a.* [L. *obvolutus*, pp. of *obvolvere*, wrap up, < *ob*, to, + *volvere*, roll.] In *bot.*, noting or pertaining to a kind of vernation in which two leaves are folded together in the bud so that one half of each is exterior and the other interior. Also **ob′vo-lu-tive** (-lū-tiv).

oc-a-ri-na (ok-ạ-rē′nạ̈), *n.* [Prob. dim. of It. *oca*, goose, with reference to the shape.] A simple musical instrument of terra-cotta, shaped somewhat like an elongated egg, with finger-holes and a whistle-like mouthpiece.

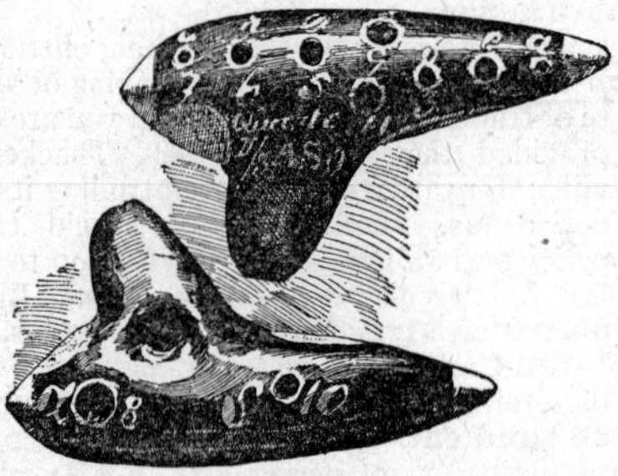

Ocarinas.

oc-ca-sion (ọ-kā′zhọn), *n.* [L. *occasio(n-)*, < *occidere* (pp. *occasus*), fall: see *occident*.] A convenient or favorable juncture or time; an opportunity; also, the ground, reason, or incidental cause of some action or result (as, to avoid giving *occasion* of offense; the woman who was the *occasion* of the trouble); also, a pretext† or excuse† (as, "Delay . . . Whose manner was all passengers to stay And entertaine with her *occasions* sly": Spenser's "Faerie Queene," iv. 10. 13); also, need or necessity (as, "They have no longer *occasion* for me": Lamb's "Superannuated Man"); a particular need or requirement (obs. or archaic, and chiefly in *pl.*: as, "Martin . . . could not supply his *occasions* any other way than by taking to the road," Smollett's "Humphry Clinker," June 11); also, a particular time, esp. as marked by certain circumstances or occurrences (as, he has said this on several *occasions*; poems written on various *occasions*; "upon the next *occasion* that we meet," Shakspere's "Love's Labour's Lost," v. 2. 143); also, an occurrence†; also, a special or important time, event, or function (as, "a pair of gloves . . . which were to be worn on some great *occasion* of state": Hawthorne's "Scarlet Letter," vii.); specif., a religious function, esp. a communion service or periodical sacramental season (chiefly Sc.: as, "They should see about getting him [a minister] to help at the summer *Occasion*," Galt's "Ayrshire Legatees," i.); sometimes, in recent use, a bargain sale.—**on occasion,** as occasion or opportunity arises; now and then; occasionally.—**oc-ca′sion,** *v. t.* To give occasion or cause for; be the occasion of; bring about: as, "I said nothing: I was afraid of *occasioning* some shock by declaring my identity" (C. Brontë's "Jane Eyre," xxi.).—**oc-ca′sion-al,** *a.* Pertaining to, arising out of, or intended for the occasion (as, "The ruin of the ancient democracies was, that they ruled . . . by *occasional* decrees": Burke's "Revolution in France," 301); produced on or for a special occasion, as a speech, a poem, etc. (as, "two quarto volumes . . . of his own poetry, consisting of little *occasional* pieces addressed to his friends and relations": B. Franklin's "Autobiography," i.); delivering or writing such compositions (as, an *occasional* speaker; an *occasional* poet); intended for use whenever needed (as, "Upon a little *occasional* table, was a tray with breakfast things": H. G. Wells's "Soul of a Bishop," vii.); acting or serving for the occasion or on particular occasions (as, "The *occasional* soldier is no match for the professional soldier": Macaulay's "Hist. of Eng.," xxiii.); also, occurring or appearing on one occasion or another or now and then (as, "Mr. Rainscourt made *occasional* visits to the Hall," Marryat's "King's Own," xlvii.; an *occasional* visitor at a place); also, serving as the occasion or incidental cause.—**oc-ca′sion-al-ism,** *n.* In *philos.*, the doctrine that the interaction of mind and matter is to be explained by the supposition that God takes an act of the will as the occasion of producing a corresponding movement of the body, and a state of the body as the occasion of producing a corresponding mental state.—**oc-ca′sion-al-ist,** *n.*—**oc-ca′sion-al-ly,** *adv.* As occasion arises; at times; now and then.

oc-ci-dent (ok′si-dẹnt), *n.* [OF. F. *occident*, < L. *occidens* (*occident-*), the west (where the sun sets), prop. ppr. of *occidere*, fall, go down, set, < *ob*, to, + *cadere*, fall.] The west; the western regions; [*cap.*] the western countries; western Europe; Europe, as opposed to Asia or the Orient; also, the western hemisphere.—**oc-ci-den′tal** (-den′tạl). [OF. F. *occidental*, < L. *occidentalis*.] **I.** *a.* Of the occident or west; western; [usually *cap.*] of, pertaining to, or characteristic of the Occident; also [*l. c.*], of gems, not oriental or orient; of inferior quality. **II.** *n.* [Usually *cap.*] A native or inhabitant of the Occident.—**oc-ci-den′tal-ism,** *n.* [Usually *cap.*] Occidental character or characteristics.—**oc-ci-den′tal-ist,** *n.* [Usually *cap.*] A student or an advocate of Occidental institutions, etc.—**oc-ci-den′tal-ize,** *v. t.*; *-ized*, *-izing*. To render Occidental.—**oc-ci-den′tal-ly,** *adv.*

oc-cip-i-tal (ok-sip′i-tạl). [ML. *occipitalis*.] In *anat.*: **I.** *a.* Of or pertaining to the occiput: as, the *occipital* bone (a compound bone which forms the posterior part of the skull). **II.** *n.* The occipital bone.—**oc-cip′i-tal-ly,** *adv.*

oc-cip-i-to- (ok-sip′i-tọ-). Form of L. *occiput* (*occipit-*), occiput, used in combination, as in *occipitofrontal* (pertaining to both occiput and forehead), *occipitohyoid* (pertaining to both the occipital and the hyoid bone), *occipitoparietal*, *occipitosphenoid*.

oc-ci-put (ok′si-put), *n.* [L., < *ob*, against, + *caput*, head.] In *anat.*, the back part of the head or skull. Cf. *sinciput*.

oc-clude (o-klöd′), *v.*; *-cluded*, *-cluding*. [L. *occludere* (pp. *occlusus*), < *ob*, to, + *cludere*, *claudere*, shut, close.] **I.** *tr.* To close, shut, or stop up (a passage, etc.); also, to shut in, out, or off (as, "the lights alternately *occluded* and revealed": Stevenson's "Travels with a Donkey," iii. 2); specif., in *chem.*, of certain metals and other solids, to absorb and retain (gases). **II.** *intr.* In *dentistry*, to meet closely or fit into each other, as opposing teeth in the upper and the lower jaw.—**oc-clu-sion** (o-klö′zhọn), *n.* The act of occluding, or the state of being occluded; in *chem.*, the retention of gases in the pores of a metal, etc.; also, in *dentistry*, the meeting closely of opposing teeth in the upper and the lower jaw.

oc-cult[1] (ọ-kult′), *a.* [L. *occultus*, pp. of *occulere*, cover over, conceal, < *ob*, before, + *-culere*, prob. akin to *celare*, hide: see *conceal*.] Hidden from view (obs. or rare: as, "We two will stand beside that shrine, *Occult*, withheld, untrod," Rossetti's "Blessed Damozel"); also, not disclosed; kept secret; communicated only to the initiated; also, beyond the bounds of ordinary or natural knowledge; mysterious; transcendental; also, in early science, not apparent on mere inspection but discoverable by experimentation, or of a nature not understood, as physical qualities; dealing with such qualities, or experimental (as, *occult* science); also, of the nature of or pertaining to certain reputed sciences, as magic, astrology, etc., involving the alleged knowledge or employment of secret or mysterious agencies; having to do with such sciences (as, an *occult* philosopher).

oc-cult[2] (ọ-kult′), *v.* [L. *occultare* (pp. *occultatus*), freq. of *occulere*: see *occult*[1].] **I.** *tr.* To hide; shut off (an object) from view, as by interposing something between the object and the eye; specif., in *astron.*, to eclipse (a heavenly body); hide by occultation. **II.** *intr.* To become hidden or shut off from view, as an intermittent beam of light from a lighthouse.—**oc-cul-ta-tion** (ok-ul-tā'shọn), *n.* [L. *occultatio(n-)*.] The act of occulting, or the resulting state; in *astron.*, the hiding of one heavenly body by another passing between it and the observer; esp., the eclipse of a star or planet by the moon or of a satellite by its primary planet; in fig. use, disappearance from view or notice.—**oc-cult'er,** *n.* One who or that which occults, or shuts off from view, as a mechanism in a lighthouse which periodically interrupts the beam of light.

oc-cult-ism (ọ-kul'tizm), *n.* [See *occult*¹.] The doctrine or study of the occult.—**oc-cult'ist,** *n.* One who believes or is versed in occultism.—**oc-cult'ly,** *adv.* In an occult manner.—**oc-cult'ness,** *n.*

oc-cu-pant (ok'ū-pạnt), *n.* [L. *occupans* (*-ant-*), ppr.] One who occupies; one in actual possession of a house, estate, office, etc.—**oc'cu-pan-cy,** *n.*

oc-cu-pa-tion (ok-ū-pā'shọn), *n.* [OF. F. *occupation*, < L. *occupatio(n-)*.] The act of occupying, or the state of being occupied; seizure, as by invasion; possession, as of a place or house; tenure, as of an office; employment with or in something; also, that in which one is engaged or employed; esp., one's habitual or stated employment; a business, trade, or calling.—**Occupation Day.** Same as *Capitulation Day.* —**oc-cu-pa'tion-al,** *a.* Of or pertaining to occupation; esp., of or pertaining to an occupation, trade, or calling (as, tables of *occupational* mortality; an *occupational* disease).—**occupational therapy,** in *med.*, a method of treatment for convalescents, esp. wounded soldiers, consisting of some kind of light work, such as basket-making, carpentry, etc., which takes the mind of the patient off himself, and frequently serves to exercise an affected part or to give vocational training.

oc-cu-py (ok'ū-pī), *v.*; *-pied, -pying.* [OF. F. *occuper*, < L. *occupare* (pp. *occupatus*), take possession of, take up, employ, < *ob*, to, + *capere*, take.] **I.** *tr.* To take possession of (a place), as by invasion (as, "The . . . commanders . . . descended upon Rhode Island, and *occupied* it without resistance": Lecky's "Hist. of Eng. in the 18th Century," xiv.); also, to hold (a position, house, office, etc.) in possession and use; be resident or established in; also, to take up (space, time, etc.); also, to engage or employ (the mind, attention, etc., or the person); also, to practise or follow as an employment†; also, to use† (as, "new ropes that never were *occupied*": Judges, xvi. 11). **II.** *intr.* To take or hold possession; also, to trade† or traffic† (as, "He called his ten servants, and delivered them ten pounds, and said unto them, *Occupy* till I come": Luke, xix. 13).—**oc'cu-pi-er** (-pī-ėr), *n.*

oc-cur (ọ-kėr'), *v. i.*; *-curred, -curring.* [L. *occurrere*, < *ob*, to, + *currere*, run.] To run up, as to a person or place†; meet† or encounter†; also, to be met with or found (as, this plant *occurs* chiefly in mountain regions; silver often *occurs* native; the name *occurs* twice in the letter); present itself, or appear; also, to come to pass, take place, or happen, as an event, accident, or the like (as, his death *occurred* in June; outbreaks *occurred* in many cities; changes are liable to *occur*); also, to suggest itself in thought (commonly with *to*: as, an idea *occurs* to a person, or to his mind; the name does not *occur* to me at the moment; "There *occurred* to me no mode of accounting for Priscilla's behavior," Hawthorne's "Blithedale Romance," v.).—**oc-cur-rence** (ọ-kur'ẹns), *n.* The act or fact of occurring (as, the *occurrence* of gold in a region; the *occurrence* of an earthquake; the *occurrence* of a happy idea to the mind); also, something that occurs; an event, happening, or incident (as, an important or mysterious *occurrence*; newspapers record the chief *occurrences* of the day).—**oc-cur'rent. I.** *a.* Occurring; happening; incidental. [Obs. or rare.] **II.** *n.* An occurrence: as, "He has my dying voice; So tell him, with the *occurrents*, more and less" (Shakspere's "Hamlet," v. 2. 368). [Obs. or rare.]

o-cean (ō'shạn). [OF. *occean* (F. *océan*), < L. *oceanus*, < Gr. ὠκεανός, the ocean, orig. the great stream supposed to encompass the earth, and personified as a god, Oceanus.] **I.** *n.* The vast body of salt water which covers almost three fourths of the earth's surface (as, "The deck it was their field of fame, And *Ocean* was their grave": Campbell's "Ye Mariners of England," ii.); also, any of the geographical divisions of this body (commonly given as five—the Atlantic, Pacific, Indian, Arctic, and Antarctic oceans); in fig. use, a vast expanse or quantity (as, "I turned and looked back over the undulating *ocean* of grass," Parkman's "Oregon Trail," xxiii.; *oceans* of trouble). **II.** *a.* Of or pertaining to the ocean.

O-ce-an-i-an (ō-shẹ-an'i-ạn), *a.* Same as *Oceanican.*

o-ce-an-ic (ō-shẹ-an'ik), *a.* [NL. *oceanicus.*] Of or belonging to the ocean; pelagic; also, ocean-like; vast.

O-ce-an-i-can (ō-shẹ-an'i-kạn), *a.* Of or pertaining to Oceanica or Oceania, a geographical division comprising the islands of the central and western Pacific (including Australia).

O-ce-a-nid (ọ-sē'ạ-nid), *n.* [Gr. Ὠκεανίς (pl. Ὠκεανίδες).] In *Gr. myth.*, a daughter of Oceanus, the ocean-god; an ocean-nymph.

o-cean-og-ra-phy (ō-shạn-og'rạ-fi), *n.* [See *-graphy.*] The branch of physical geography dealing with the ocean.—**o-cean-og'ra-pher,** *n.*—**o″cean-o-graph'ic, o″cean-o-graph'i-cal** (-ọ-graf'ik, -i-kạl), *a.*

o-cean-ward, o-cean-wards (ō'shạn-wạrd, -wạrdz), *adv.* Toward the ocean.

o-cel-late, o-cel-lat-ed (os'e-lāt, -lā-ted), *a.* Having ocelli, or eye-like spots; also, of a spot or marking, eye-like.—**o-cel-la-tion** (os-e-lā'shọn), *n.* An eye-like spot or marking.

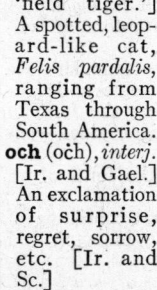

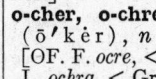

Ocellate or Ocellated Markings. — 1, feather of peacock; 2, feather of argus-pheasant; 3, blenny; 4, butterfly; 5, mariposa lily.

o-cel-lus (ọ-sel'us), *n.*; pl. *ocelli* (-ī). [L., dim. of *oculus*, eye.] A little eye; specif., one of the single-lens eyes, usually three in number, situated between the compound eyes of an insect, etc.; also, one of the small eyes or elements composing a compound eye (rare); also, in certain of the lower invertebrates, a kind of rudimentary eye consisting of a patch of cells sensitive to light; also, an eye-like spot, as on a peacock-feather.

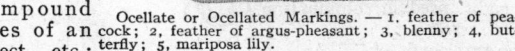

o-ce-lot (ō'se-lot), *n.* [F.; from Mex. name, meaning 'field tiger.'] A spotted, leopard-like cat, *Felis pardalis*, ranging from Texas through South America.

Ocelot.

och (ọ̈ch), *interj.* [Ir. and Gael.] An exclamation of surprise, regret, sorrow, etc. [Ir. and Sc.]

o-cher, o-chre (ō'kėr), *n.* [OF. F. *ocre*, < L. *ochra*, < Gr.

ὤχρα, yellow ocher, < ὠχρός, pale, pale-yellow.] Any of a class of natural earths, mixtures of hydrated oxide of iron with various earthy materials, ranging in color from pale yellow to orange, brown, and red, and used as pigments; also, money, esp. gold coin (in allusion to the color: slang: as, "Pay your *ochre* at the doors," Dickens's "Hard Times," i. 6).—**o′cher, o′chre,** *v. t.*; *ochered, ochred, ochering, ochring.* To color or mark with ocher.—**o-cher-ous, o-chre-ous** (ō′kėr-us, ō′krē-us), *a.* Of the nature of or containing ocher; also, resembling ocher in color; specif., brownish-yellow.—**o′cher-y, o′chry** (-kri), *a.*

och-loc-ra-cy (ok-lok′rạ-si), *n.*; pl. *-cies* (-siz). [F. *ochlocratie*, < Gr. ὀχλοκρατία, < ὄχλος, crowd, mob, + κρατεῖν, rule.] Government by the mob; mobocracy; mob-rule: as, "The commonest of the old charges against democracy was that it passed into *ochlocracy*" (Bryce's "American Commonwealth," xcv.).—**och′lo-crat** (-lọ-krat), *n.* An upholder of ochlocracy.—**och-lo-crat′ic,** *a.*

och-one, o-hone (oċh-ōn′, ō-hōn′), *interj.* [Ir. and Gael.: cf. *och.*] An exclamation used in lamentation. [Ir. and Sc.]

o′chre, etc. See *ocher*, etc.

o-chroid (ō′kroid), *a.* [Gr. ὠχροειδής, < ὠχρός, pale, pale-yellow, + εἶδος, form.] Of a pale-yellow color; yellowish.

-ock. [AS. *-oc, -uc.*] A noun suffix having a diminutive force, as in *bittock, bullock, hillock, lassock.*

o′clock (ọ-klok′). Of or by the clock: used in specifying or inquiring the hour of the day: as, one *o'clock*; what *o'clock* is it?

o-co-til-lo (ō-kọ-tēl′yō), *n.* [Mex. Sp., dim. of *ocote*, kind of pine.] A shrub, *Fouquieria splendens*, a candlewood of arid parts of Mexico and the southwestern U. S., with resinous spiny stems terminating in slender panicles of bright scarlet flowers; also, any of several related species.

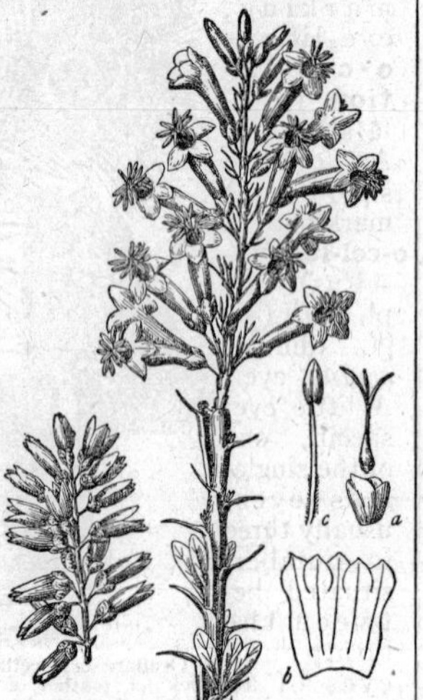
Ocotillo (*Fouquieria splendens*). — *a*, calyx and pistil; *b*, corolla; *c*, stamen.

oc-re-a (ok′rē-ạ̈), *n.*; pl. *ocreæ* (-ē). [L., greave, legging.] In *bot.* and *zoöl.*, a sheathing part, as a pair of stipules united about a stem.—**oc′re-ate** (-āt), *a.* [L. *ocreatus.*] Having an ocrea or ocreæ; sheathed.

Ocrea.

oct-. Form of *octa-* and *octo-* used before a vowel.

octa-. A form of Gr. ὀκτώ, eight, used in combination. Cf. *octo-*.

oc-ta-chord (ok′tạ-kôrd), *n.* [Gr. ὀκτάχορδος, eight-stringed: see *octa-* and *chord*[1].] In *music*, an instrument with eight strings; also, a diatonic series of eight tones.

oc-tad (ok′tad), *n.* [LL. *octas* (*octad-*), < Gr. ὀκτάς (ὀκταδ-), < ὀκτώ, eight; akin to L. *octo*, eight, and E. *eight.*] A group or series of eight; in *chem.*, an element, atom, or radical having a valence of eight.—**oc-tad′ic,** *a.*

oc-ta-gon (ok′tạ-gon), *n.* [Gr. ὀκτάγωνος, octangular: see *octa-* and *-gon.*] A plane figure having eight angles and eight sides.—**oc-tag′o-nal** (-tag′ọ-nạl), *a.* Having the form of an octagon; having eight angles and eight sides.—**oc-tag′o-nal-ly,** *adv.*

oc-ta-he-dral (ok-tạ-hē′drạl), *a.* Having the form of an octahedron.

oc-ta-he-drite (ok-tạ-hē′drīt), *n.* A mineral consisting of titanium dioxide, and commonly occurring in octahedral crystals.

oc-ta-he-dron (ok-tạ-hē′drọn), *n.*; pl. *-drons* or *-dra* (-drạ̈). [Gr. ὀκτάεδρον: see *octa-* and *-hedron.*] A solid figure having eight plane faces. See cut in next column.

oc-tam-er-ous (ok-tam′ẹ-rus), *a.* [Gr. ὀκταμερής: see *octa-* and *-merous.*] Consisting of or divided into eight parts; in *bot.*, of flowers, having eight members in each whorl.

oc-tam-e-ter (ok-tam′e-tėr). [LL. *octameter*, < Gr. ὀκτάμετρος, < ὀκτώ, eight, + μέτρον, measure.] In *pros.*: **I.** *a.* Consisting of eight measures or feet. **II.** *n.* An octameter verse.

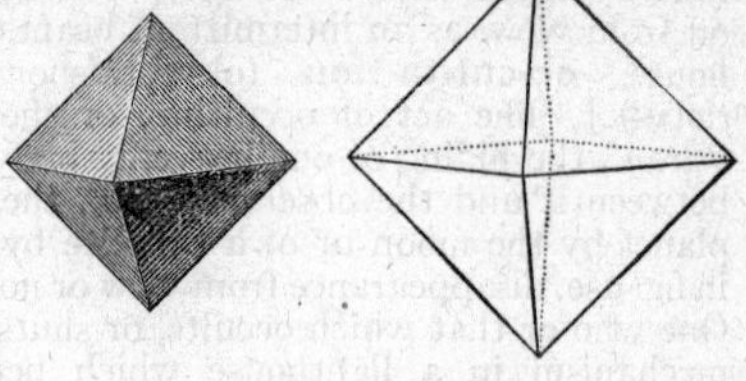
Regular Octahedron.

oc-tan (ok′tạn), *a.* [L. *octo*, eight.] Characterized by paroxysms which recur every eighth day, both days of consecutive occurrence being counted, as a fever.

oc-tane (ok′tān), *n.* [Gr. ὀκτώ, eight (with reference to the atoms of carbon): cf. *heptane, hexane.*] In *chem.*, a hydrocarbon, C_8H_{18}, of the methane series; also, a fuel value (**octane number**) that increases with anti-knock tendency.

oc-tan-gu-lar (ok-tang′gū-lär), *a.* [L. *octangulus*, < *octo*, eight, + *angulus*, E. *angle*[3].] Having eight angles.

oc-tant (ok′tạnt), *n.* [L. *octans* (*octant-*), < *octo*, eight.] The eighth part of a circle; also, the position of one heavenly body when 45° distant from another; also, an instrument having an arc of 45°, used by seamen for measuring angles.

oc-tar-chy (ok′tär-ki), *n.*; pl. *-chies* (-kiz). [Gr. ὀκτώ, eight: see *-archy.*] A government by eight persons; also, a group of eight states or kingdoms, each under its own ruler.

oc-ta-stich (ok′tạ-stik), *n.* [Gr. ὀκτάστιχος, of eight lines, < ὀκτώ, eight, + στίχος, row, line.] In *pros.*, a strophe, stanza, or poem consisting of eight lines or verses.

oc-ta-style (ok′tạ-stīl). [L. *octastylos*, < Gr. ὀκτάστυλος, < ὀκτώ, eight, + στῦλος, pillar, column.] **I.** *a.* Having eight columns in front, as a temple or a portico. **II.** *n.* An octastyle structure.

Octastyle Portico of the Pantheon, Rome.

Oc-ta-teuch (ok′tạ-tūk), *n.* [LL. *octateuchus*, < Gr. ὀκτάτευχος, consisting of eight books, < ὀκτώ, eight, + τεῦχος, book.] The first eight books of the Old Testament.

oc-ta-val (ok-tā′vạl or ok′tā-), *a.* Of or pertaining to an octave, or group of eight; proceeding by eights.

oc-ta-va-lent (ok-tạ-vā′lẹnt or ok-tav′ạ-), *a.* [See *octa-* and *-valent.*] In *chem.*, having a valence of eight.

oc-tave (ok′tāv). [OF. F. *octave*, < L. *octava*, fem. of *octavus*, eighth, < *octo*, eight: see *octad.*] **I.** *n.* The eighth of a series, or a series or group of eight; *eccles.*, the eighth day from a feast-day (counted as the first); the period of eight days beginning with a feast-day; in *music*, a tone on the eighth degree from a given tone (counted as the first); the interval between such tones; the harmonic combination of such tones; a series of tones, or of keys of an instrument, extending through this interval; in a scale, the eighth tone from the bottom, with which the repetition of the scale begins; in organ-building, a stop whose pipes give tones an octave above the normal pitch of the keys used; in *fencing*, the eighth in a series of eight parries; in *pros.*, a group or a stanza of eight lines, as the first eight lines of a sonnet. **II.** *a.* Consisting of eight (lines, etc.).

oc-ta-vo (ok-tā′vō or ok-tä′-). [NL. *in octavo*, 'in eighth.'] **I.** *n.*; pl. *-vos* (-vōz). The page size of a book in which each leaf is one eighth of a whole sheet of paper; a volume of this size. Abbreviated 8*vo* or 8°. **II.** *a.* In octavo.

oc-ten-ni-al (ok-ten′i-ạl), *a.* [LL. *octennis*, < L. *octo*, eight, + *annus*, year.] Of or for eight years; also, occurring every eight years.

oc-tet, oc-tette (ok-tet′), *n.* [L. *octo*, eight.] A musical composition for eight voices or instruments; also, a company of eight singers or players; also, any group of eight; in *pros.*, a group of eight lines of verse, esp. the first eight lines (octave) of a sonnet.

oc-til-lion (ok-til′yọn), *n.* [F. *octillion*, < L. *octo*, eight, + F. (*m*)*illion*, million.] In Great Britain, the eighth power of a million, represented by 1 followed by 48 ciphers; in France and the U. S., a thousand septillions, represented by 1 followed by 27 ciphers.—**oc-til′lionth,** *a.* and *n.*

octo-. Form of L. *octo* and Gr. ὀκτώ, eight, used in combination. Cf. *octa-* (from Gr.).

Oc-to-ber (ok-tō′bėr), *n.* [L. *October*, the eighth month of the Roman year, < *octo*, eight.] The tenth month of the year, containing 31 days; also, ale brewed in this month (as, "a bumper of *October*": Smollett's "Humphry Clinker," June 26).

oc-to-de-ci-mo (ok-tọ-des′i-mō). [NL. *in octodecimo*, 'in eighteenth.'] **I.** *n.*; pl. *-mos* (-mōz). The page size of a book in which each leaf is one eighteenth of a whole sheet of paper; a volume of this size. Abbreviated 18*mo* or 18°. **II.** *a.* In octodecimo.

oc-to-ge-na-ri-an (ok″tọ-je-nā′ri-ạn). [L. *octogenarius*, < *octogeni*, eighty each, distributive of *octaginta*, eighty, < *octo*, eight.] **I.** *a.* Of the age of 80 years, or between 80 and 90 years old. **II.** *n.* An octogenarian person. Also **oc-tog′e-na-ry** (-toj′e-nạ-ri), *a.* and *n.*

oc-to-nal (ok′tọ-nạl), *a.* [L. *octoni*, eight each, < *octo*, eight.] Based on the number eight, as a system of reckoning; octonary.

oc-to-na-ry (ok′tọ-nạ-ri). [L. *octonarius*, < *octoni*: see *octonal.*] **I.** *a.* Pertaining to the number eight; consisting of eight; proceeding by eights; noting or pertaining to a system of reckoning based on the number eight. **II.** *n.*; pl. *-ries* (-riz). A group of eight; an ogdoad.

oc-to-pod (ok′tọ-pod). [NL. *Octopoda*, pl., < Gr. ὀκτώπους (ὀκτωποδ-), eight-footed, < ὀκτώ, eight, + πούς (ποδ-), foot.] **I.** *n.* Any of the *Octopoda*, an order of eight-armed dibranchiate cephalopods which includes the octopus and the paper-nautilus. **II.** *a.* Having eight feet or arms; belonging to the *Octopoda*.—**oc-top′o-dous** (-top′ọ-dus), *a.*

oc-to-pus (ok′tọ-pus, L. ok-tō′pus), *n.*; pl. *-puses*, L. *-pi* (-pī). [NL., < Gr. ὀκτώπους, eight-footed: see *octopod.*] Any animal of the genus *Octopus*, comprising octopods with a soft oval body and eight sucker-bearing arms, and living mostly on the sea-bottom; hence, any octopod; fig., a far-reaching and grasping or devouring agency.

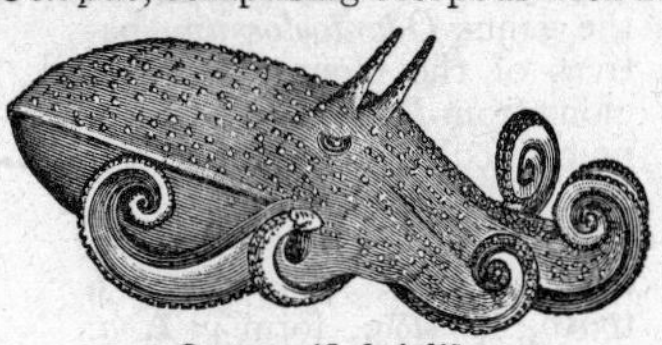

Octopus (*O. bairdii*).

oc-to-roon (ok-tọ-rön′), *n.* [From *octo-* + *-roon* as in *quadroon.*] A person having one eighth negro blood; the offspring of a quadroon and a white.

oc-to-style (ok′tọ-stīl), *a.* and *n.* Same as *octastyle.*

oc-to-syl-la-ble (ok-tọ-sil′ạ-bl), *n.* [LL. *octosyllabus*, < Gr. ὀκτώ, eight, + συλλαβή: see *syllable.*] A word or a line of verse of eight syllables.—**oc″to-syl-lab′ic** (-si-lab′ik), *a.* and *n.*

oc-troi (ok-trwo), *n.* [F., < *octroyer*, grant, < ML. *auctorizare*, E. *authorize.*] In France and elsewhere, a local tax levied on certain articles on their admission into a city; the barrier or place at which the tax is collected; the officials charged with collecting it (as, "This is the criminal Saint-Rambertese Who smuggled in tobacco, half-a-pound! The *Octroi* found it out and fined the wretch": Browning's "Red Cotton Night-Cap Country," i.).

oc-tu-ple (ok′tụ-pl), *a.* [L. *octuplus*, < *octo*, eight, + *-plus*: see *double.*] Eightfold; having eight effective units or elements; eight times as great.—**oc′tu-ple,** *v. t.*; *-pled*, *-pling.* To make eight times as great.—**oc′tu-ply** (-pli), *adv.*

oc-u-lar (ok′ụ-lạr). [LL. *ocularis*, < L. *oculus*, eye: cf. *eye*, also *optic.*] **I.** *a.* Of or pertaining to the eye (as, *ocular* movements); of the nature of an eye (as, an *ocular* organ); performed by the eye or eyesight (as, *ocular* inspection); perceived by the eye or eyesight (as, *ocular* demonstration); derived from actual sight (as, *ocular* proof); actually seeing (as, an *ocular* witness). **II.** *n.* The eyepiece of an optical instrument.—**oc′u-lar-ly,** *adv.*

oc-u-list (ok′ụ-list), *n.* [L. *oculus*, eye.] One skilled in the examination and treatment of the eye; an ophthalmologist.

oc-u-lo-mo-tor (ok″ụ-lọ-mō′tọr). [L. *oculus*, eye, + *motor*, E. *motor.*] In *anat.*: **I.** *a.* Moving the eyeball: as, an *oculomotor* nerve (either of the pair of cranial nerves which supply most of the muscles moving the eyeball). **II.** *n.* An oculomotor nerve.

od[1] (od or ōd), *n.* [Arbitrary name, given by Baron Karl von Reichenbach (1788–1869).] A hypothetical force formerly held to pervade all nature and to manifest itself in magnetism, mesmerism, chemical action, etc.

od[2], **'od** (od), *n.* [Also *odd.*] Reduced form of *God*, used interjectionally and in minced oaths: as, "*Od*, ye are a clever birkie!" (Scott's "Redgauntlet," letter x.); *od* rot 'em! *od's* vengeance! *od's* wounds! [Archaic or prov.]

o-da-lisque, o-da-lisk (ō′dạ-lisk), *n.* [F. *odalisque*, < Turk. *ōdalik*, < *ōdah*, chamber.] A female slave in an Eastern harem, esp. in that of the Sultan of Turkey.

odd (od), *a.* [ME. *odde*, from Scand.: cf. Icel. *odda-* (as in *odda-madhr*, odd man), < *oddi*, point, triangle, odd number.] Remaining over after a division into pairs, or into equal numbers or parts; also, leaving a remainder of 1 when divided by 2, as a number (opposed to *even*); also, additional to a whole mentioned in round numbers (as, fifty and *odd* men; the men numbered fifty *odd*, that is, fifty and more; "Eighty *odd* years of sorrow have I seen," Shakspere's "Richard III.," iv. 1. 96); being a surplus over a definite quantity or sum, esp. a small surplus of a lower denomination (as, full weight with several *odd* ounces; two dollars and some *odd* cents, or, elliptically, two dollars *odd*); hence, additional to what is taken into account, or not forming part of any particular group, set, or class (as, the outfit includes various *odd* articles for possible use; to employ an *odd* man for casual jobs; *odd* bits of information); occasional or casual (as, reading done at *odd* times; *odd* jobs); also, being part of a pair, set, or series of which the rest is wanting (as, an *odd* glove; an *odd* saucer; an *odd* number of a magazine); also, out-of-the-way, or secluded (as, "in an *odd* angle of the isle," Shakspere's "Tempest," i. 2. 223; "from some *odd* corner of the brain," Tennyson's "Miller's Daughter," 68); also, differing in character from what is ordinary or usual, or singular, peculiar, or strange (as, an *odd* shape, sound, name, or pastime; an *odd* choice or remark; an *odd* affair); often, singular or peculiar in a freakish or eccentric way, as persons or their appearance, manners, actions, etc.; queer; fantastic or bizarre, as things (as, "The presence seems, with things so richly *odd*, The mosque of Mahound, or some queer pagod": Pope's "Satires of Donne," iv. 238).—**odd fish,** an odd or singular person: as, "He was an *odd fish*; ignorant of common life, fond of rudely opposing received opinions, slovenly to extreme dirtiness, enthusiastic in some points of religion, and a little knavish withal" (B. Franklin's "Autobiography," iv.). [Colloq.]—**odd lot,** a lot or quantity of goods or securities smaller than some amount common in business transactions, as a lot of stocks numbering less than 100 shares, or a lot of bonds representing less than $10,000.—**odd,** *n.* That which is odd; *pl.*, odd things, bits, or scraps (in 'odds and ends,' miscellaneous things, bits, or remnants: as, "If there's ever a bit o' *odds an' ends* as nobody else 'ud eat, you're sure to pick it out," George Eliot's "Adam Bede," xlix.); *sing.*, in *golf*, a stroke more than the opponent has played. See *odds.*

Odd-fel-low, Odd Fel-low (od′fel″ō), *n.* [A fanciful name (as if implying odd or whimsical ways) orig. assumed by the members of various social clubs in England.] A member of a secret social and benevolent society ('Independent Order of Oddfellows') which originated in various clubs formed in England in the 18th century and mostly united early in the 19th century, and which has spread into other countries, including the United States and Canada (in which countries there now exists a separate organization, with branches elsewhere), and which is made up of local lodges distributed throughout these countries.

odd-i-ty (od′i-ti), *n.*; pl. *-ties* (-tiz). The quality of being odd; singularity or strangeness (as, "Lady Johnson (that was Peggy Heath's name now, and we can't get over the *oddity* of it)": W. De Morgan's "Alice-for-Short," xxix.); also, an odd characteristic, or peculiarity (as, "By a hundred whimsical *oddities*, my long friend became a great favorite with these people": H. Melville's "Omoo," lxviii.); also, an odd person or thing (as, "Here is a strange, fantastical *oddity* . . . who harangues every day in the pump-room," Smollett's "Humphry Clinker," April 20; literary *oddities*).

odd-ly (od'li), *adv.* In an odd manner.

odd-ment (od'mȩnt), *n.* An odd article, bit, remnant, or the like, or an article belonging to a broken or incomplete set; *pl.*, odds and ends: as, "a wreck of *oddments* that began with felt-covered water-bottles, belts, and regimental badges, and ended with a small bale of second-hand uniforms and a stand of mixed arms" (Kipling's "Light That Failed," iv.); "*oddments* of furniture, including a desk" (Arnold Bennett's "Hilda Lessways," iii. 4).

odd-ness (od'nes), *n.* The state, character, or quality of being odd; also, something odd.

odd=pin-nate (od'pin'āt), *a.* In *bot.*, pinnate with an odd terminal leaflet; imparipinnate.

odds (odz), *n. pl.* or *sing.* [See *odd.*] Things that are odd, uneven, or unequal (only as *pl.*: as, "Yet death we fear, That makes these *odds* all even," Shakspere's "Measure for Measure," iii. 1. 41); hence, inequality or difference, esp. in favor of one as against another, or the amount of difference (as, "Together both . . . one stroke they aim'd . . . nor *odds* appear'd In might or swift prevention," Milton's "Paradise Lost," vi. 319; there is no great *odds* between them); difference in the way of benefit or detriment (as, what's the *odds*, or what *odds* does it make, whether we go or not?); advantage or superiority on the side of one of two contending parties (as, to strive against *odds*; "How can man die better Than facing fearful *odds*, For the ashes of his fathers, And the temples of his Gods?" Macaulay's "Horatius," xxvii.); an equalizing allowance, as that given to a weaker side in a game or contest; the amount or proportion by which the bet of one party to a wager exceeds that of the other; also, balance of probability in favor of something occurring or being the case (as, "The *odds* are, that she has a thousand faults, at least": Maria Edgeworth's "Belinda," ix.); also, disagreement, variance, or strife (chiefly in 'at odds': as, "Pity 'tis you lived *at odds* so long," Shakspere's "Romeo and Juliet," i. 2. 5). See *odd*, *n.*

ode (ōd), *n.* [F. *ode*, < LL. *ode*, *oda*, < Gr. ᾠδή, contr. of ἀοιδή, song, < ἀείδειν, sing.] Orig., a poem intended to be sung; in modern use, a lyric poȩm typically of elaborate or irregular metrical form and expressive of exalted or enthusiastic emotion, such as Dryden's "Alexander's Feast," Wordsworth's "Intimations of Immortality," Tennyson's "Ode on the Death of the Duke of Wellington," and Lowell's "Commemoration Ode."

-ode[1]. [Gr. -οδος, < ὁδός, way.] A noun termination meaning 'way,' as in *anode*, *cathode*, *electrode*.

-ode[2]. [Gr. -ώδης, like, contr. of -οειδής, E. *-oid.*] A suffix of nouns denoting something having some resemblance to what is indicated by the preceding part of the word, as in *arillode*, *cladode*, *geode*, *phyllode*.

o-de-um (ō-dē'um), *n.*; pl. *odea* (-ạ̈). [L., < Gr. ᾠδεῖον, music-hall, < ᾠδή, song: see *ode.*] In ancient Greece and Rome, a roofed building for musical performances; in modern use, a hall or structure devoted to musical or dramatic performances.

Ruins of Odeum of Regilla, Athens.

od-ic[1] (ō'dik), *a.* Of or pertaining to an ode.

od-ic[2] (od'ik or ō'dik), *a.* Of or pertaining to the hypothetical force od.—**od'i-cal-ly**, *adv.*

O-din (ō'din), *n.* [Cf. Icel. *Odhinn* = AS. *Wōden*: see *Woden.*] The chief deity of the Scandinavian mythology, being the god of wisdom, culture, war, and the dead. Cf. *Woden.*

o-di-ous (ō'di-us), *a.* [OF. *odieus* (F. *odieux*), < L. *odiosus*, < *odium*: see *odium.*] Deserving of or exciting hatred, hateful, or detestable (as, "I am myself the basest and most *odious* of mankind!" Godwin's "Caleb Williams," Postscript; "whom thou hatedst for doing most *odious* works of witchcrafts, and wicked sacrifices," Wisdom of Solomon, xii. 4); hence, in general, highly displeasing or offensive (as, an *odious* thought or experience; "consequences *odious* to those you govern," Burke's "American Taxation"); disgusting (as, "a kind of slimy stuff . . . of a most nauseous, *odious* smell": Defoe's "Captain Singleton," iv.); often, in expression of strong personal feeling, highly objectionable or obnoxious (as, "Tell me what could take you to that *odious* Mrs. Luttridge's": Maria Edgeworth's "Belinda," i.).—**o'di-ous-ly**, *adv.*—**o'di-ous-ness**, *n.*

od-ist (ō'dist), *n.* The composer of an ode.

o-di-um (ō'di-um), *n.* [L., < *odi*, I hate.] Hatred, esp. general or public hatred, directed against or incurred by a person or other object (as, "It was his lot to taste the bitterness of popular *odium*": Hawthorne's "Twice-Told Tales," Edward Randolph's Portrait); also, the reproach, discredit, or opprobrium attaching to something hated or odious (as, to bear or to escape the *odium* of an unpopular measure or an unsuccessful war).

o-dom-e-ter (ọ-dom'e-tėr), *n.* Same as *hodometer.*

-odont. A termination from Gr. ὀδούς (ὀδοντ-), tooth, serving to form adjectives and nouns, as *conodont*, *diphyodont*, *microdont*, *pleurodont*.

odont-, odonto-. Forms of Gr. ὀδούς (ὀδοντ-), tooth, used in combination.—**o-don-tal-gia** (ō-don-tal'jiạ̈), *n.* [NL., < Gr. ὀδονταλγία (ἄλγος, pain).] In *pathol.*, toothache. —**o-don-tal'gic. I.** *a.* Of or pertaining to odontalgia or toothache. **II.** *n.* A remedy for toothache.—**o-don-to-blast** (ọ-don'tọ-blast), *n.* [+ *-blast.*] In *anat.*, one of a layer of cells which, in the development of a tooth, give rise to the dentin.—**o-don-to-blas'tic**, *a.*

o-don-to-glos-sum (ọ-don-tọ-glos'um), *n.* [NL., < Gr. ὀδούς (ὀδοντ-), tooth, + γλῶσσα, tongue.] Any of the epiphytic orchids constituting the genus *Odontoglossum*, natives of the mountainous regions from Bolivia to Mexico, much cultivated for their showy flowers.

Odontoglossum (*O. cordatum*).

o-don-toid (ọ-don'toid). [Gr. ὀδοντοειδής, < ὀδούς (ὀδοντ-), tooth, + εἶδος, form.] **I.** *a.* Resembling a tooth; specif., noting or pertaining to a prominent tooth-like process of the axis, or second cervical vertebra, upon which the atlas rotates. **II.** *n.* In *anat.*, the odontoid process.

o-don-tol-o-gy (ō-don-tol'ọ-ji), *n.* [See *odonto-* and *-logy.*] The branch of anatomy that treats of the teeth.—**o-don-to-log-i-cal** (ọ-don-tọ-loj'i-kạl), *a.*—**o-don-tol'o-gist**, *n.*

o-don-to-phore (ọ-don'tọ-fōr), *n.* [Gr. ὀδοντοφόρος, bearing teeth, < ὀδούς (ὀδοντ-), tooth, + φέρειν, bear.] In *zoöl.*, a structure in the mouth of most mollusks, over which the radula is drawn backward and forward in the process of breaking up food.—**o-don-toph-o-rous** (ō-don-tof'ọ-rus), *a.*

o-don-tor-nith-ic (ọ-don-tôr-nith'ik), *a.* [NL. *Odontornithes*, pl., < Gr. ὀδούς (ὀδοντ-), tooth, + ὄρνις (ὀρνιθ-), bird.] Of or belonging to the *Odontornithes*, a group of extinct birds of the Mesozoic era, which had true teeth.

o-don-to-scope (ọ-don'tọ-skōp), *n.* [See *odonto-* and *-scope.*] A small mirror with a long slender handle, for examining the teeth.

o-do-phone (ō'dọ-fōn), *n.* [L. *odor*, odor, + Gr. *φωνή*, sound; from the analogy to the musical scale.] A scale of odors or scents, as for the use of perfumers: as, "Septimus Piesse endeavoured to show that a certain scale or gamut existed amongst odours as amongst sounds . . . Thus on his *odophone*, santal, geranium, acacia, orange-flower, camphor . . . constitute the bouquet of chord C" (Encyc. Brit., 11th ed., XXI. 142).

o-dor (ō'dọr), *n.* [OF. *odor*, *odour* (F. *odeur*), < L. *odor*, odor, scent; akin to Gr. *ὄζειν*, smell.] That property of a substance which affects the sense of smell (as, a gas without *odor*; the *odor* of a plant, animal, drug, or burning substance; savory, pungent, or rank *odors*); smell or scent; sometimes, agreeable scent, or fragrance; also, a fragrant substance, flower, or plant (obs. or archaic: as, "Through groves of myrrh, And flowering *odours*, cassia, nard, and balm," Milton's "Paradise Lost," v. 293); also, fig., savor characteristic or suggestive of something (as, there is no *odor* of impropriety about the case); also, repute or estimation (good or bad: as, "These Sydney gentry . . . are in excessively bad *odor*," H. Melville's "Omoo," lxxxii.).—**odor of sanctity,** a sweet odor said to have been exhaled from the bodies of certain saints at death or on disinterment, and held to be evidence of their sanctity; fig., established reputation for sanctity or holiness.—**o'dored,** *a.* Having an odor; scented.—**o-dor-if-er-ous** (ō-dọ-rif'ẹ-rus), *a.* [L. *odorifer*: see *-ferous.*] Yielding or diffusing an odor (as, "warehouses, ships, and smell of tar, and other *odoriferous* circumstances of fishery and the sea": Galt's "Ayrshire Legatees," i.); commonly, yielding an agreeable odor, fragrant, or aromatic (as, *odoriferous* flowers or herbs).—**o-dor-if'er-ous-ly,** *adv.* —**o-dor-if'er-ous-ness,** *n.*—**o'dor-less,** *a.* Without odor or smell: as, an *odorless* gas.—**o'dor-ous,** *a.* Having or diffusing an odor, esp. a fragrant odor: as, "the *odorous* breath of morn" (Milton's "Arcades," 56).—**o'dor-ous-ly,** *adv.*—**o'dor-ous-ness,** *n.*

o'dour, o'doured, o'dour-less. British preferred forms of *odor*, etc.

od-yl, od-yle (od'il or ō'dil), *n.* [See *-yl.*] Same as *od*[1].

Od-ys-sey (od'i-si), *n.*; pl. *-seys* (-siz). [L. *Odyssea*, < Gr. Ὀδύσσεια, < Ὀδυσσεύς, Odysseus, Ulysses.] A Greek epic poem, attributed to Homer, describing the ten years of wandering of Odysseus (Ulysses) in returning to Ithaca after the Trojan War; hence [*cap.* or *l. c.*], any long series of wanderings or varied experiences (as, "gradually beginning to be interested in the *odyssey* of Mr. Seven Sachs": Arnold Bennett's "The Old Adam," v.).—**Od-ys-se'an** (-i-sē'ạn), *a.*

œ-col-o-gy (ẹ-kol'ọ-ji), etc., **œc-u-men-ic** (ek-ū-men'ik), etc., **œ-de-ma** (ẹ-dē'mạ), etc. See *ecology*, etc., *ecumenic*, etc., *edema*, etc.

œil=de=bœuf (ė-y'-dė-bėf), *n.*; pl. *œils-de-bœuf* (ė-y'-). [F., 'eye of ox,' bull's-eye.] In *arch.*, a comparatively small round or oval window, as in a frieze.

œil-lade (ė-yäd), *n.* [F., < *œil*, < L. *oculus*, eye.] A glance of the eye, esp. an amorous glance, or ogle: as, "She gave strange *œillades* and most speaking looks To noble Edmund" (Shakspere's "King Lear," iv. 5. 25).

œ-nan-thic (ẹ-nan'thik), *a.* [Gr. *οἰνάνθη*, vine-blossom, vine, < *οἴνη*, vine, + *ἄνθη*, blossom.] Having or imparting the odor of wine: as, *œnanthic* acid (a mixture of acids obtained from œnanthic ether); *œnanthic* ether (an oily liquid, a mixture of organic esters, with a wine-like odor, obtained from wine by distillation).

œno-. Form of Gr. *οἶνος*, wine, used in combination.

œ-noch-o-ë (ẹ-nok'ọ-ē), *n.* Same as *oinochoë.*

œ-nol-o-gy (ẹ-nol'ọ-ji), *n.* [See *œno-* and *-logy.*] The science of wines.—**œ-no-log-i-cal** (ē-nọ-loj'i-kạl), *a.*—**œ-nol'o-gist,** *n.*

œ-no-ma-ni-a (ē-nọ-mā'ni-ạ̈), *n.* [NL.: see *œno-* and *mania.*] In *pathol.*, an insatiable craving for wine or other intoxicating drink; also, mania or delirium resulting from intoxication; delirium tremens.

œ-no-mel (ē'nọ-mel), *n.* [LL. *œnomeli*, < Gr. *οἰνόμελι*, < *οἶνος*, wine, + *μέλι*, honey.] A drink made of wine mixed with honey; fig., something combining strength with sweetness.

œ-noph-i-list (ẹ-nof'i-list), *n.* [Gr. *οἶνος*, wine, + *φίλος*, loving.] A lover of wine.

œ-no-pli-a (ẹ-nō'pli-ạ̈), *n.* [NL.] Any of the plants, mostly climbing shrubs, of the rhamnaceous genus *Œnoplia* (or *Berchemia*), species of which are used for covering trellis-work.

œ-no-the-ra (ē-nọ-thē'rạ), *n.* [L., < Gr. *οἰνοθήρας*, kind of plant.] Any plant of the onagraceous genus *Œnothera* or of certain allied genera, esp. the common evening primrose, *Onagra* (formerly *Œnothera*) *biennis.*

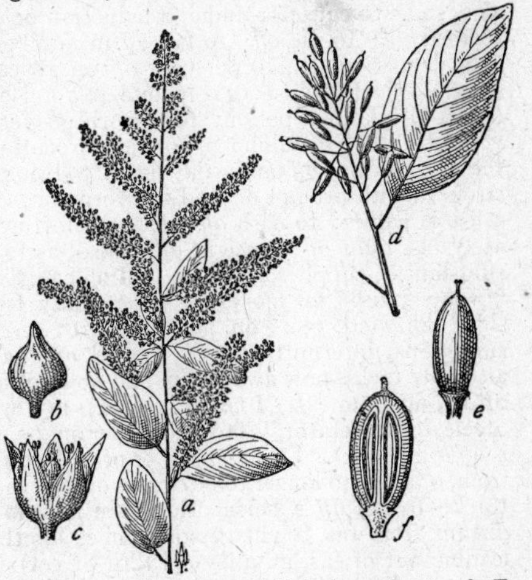

Œnoplia.—*a*, *Œ. racemosa*; *b*, bud; *c*, flower; *d*, *Œ. scandens*; *e*, a fruit; *f*, section of a fruit.

o'er (ōr), *prep.* and *adv.* Contraction of *over.* [Poetic or prov.]

oer-sted (ėr'sted), *n.* [From H. C. *Oersted* (1777–1851), Danish physicist.] In *elect.*, the unit of magnetic reluctance, equal to the reluctance of a centimeter cube of air or vacuum between parallel surfaces.

œ-soph-a-gus (ẹ-sof'ạ-gus), etc. See *esophagus*, etc.

œs-trus (es'trus or ēs'-), *n.* [L., < Gr. *οἶστρος*, gadfly, sting, frenzy.] A gadfly; hence, a stimulus; passion or passionate impulse; specif., the rut of animals.

of (ov or ọv), *prep.* [AS. *of*, prep. and adv. (see *off*), = D. *af* = G. *ab* = Icel., Sw., and Dan. *af* = Goth *af*: see *ab-* and *apo-*.] A particle expressing primarily literal departure from a place (now obs.), and hence used in a great variety of figurative and derived applications: in particular, used in expressions indicating (1) distance or direction, separation, deprivation, riddance, etc.: as, within a mile *of*; east *of*; to rob, rid, or cure *of*; (2) derivation, origin, or source: as, *of* good family; to beg or buy *of*; nothing came *of* it; (3) cause, occasion, or reason: as, *of* necessity; *of* one's own accord; (4) material or substance, and hence a relation of identity: as, a rod *of* iron; a pound *of* sugar; the city *of* Paris; (5) belonging or possession, connection, or association: as, the property *of* all; all the owners *of* the property; members *of* a club; a man *of* his time; (6) inclusion in a number, class, or whole: as, one *of* us; part *of* it; (7) objective relation: as, the ringing *of* bells; betrayal *of* secrets; (8) reference or respect: as, think *of* it; swift *of* foot; what *of* that? (9) qualities or attributes: as, a man *of* tact; news *of* importance; (10) the agent by whom something is done (chiefly archaic): as, beloved *of* all; (11) time: as, *of* late; *of* an evening.—**of his, of hers, of mine, of ours, of his father's, of her mother's,** etc., idiomatic phrases in which the possessive has virtually the value of an objective case, 'a friend of his' meaning 'a friend of him' (or 'one of his friends'), and 'a friend of his father's' meaning 'a friend of his father' (or 'one of his father's friends').

off (ôf), *adv.* [ME. *off*, *of*, < AS. *of*: see *of.*] To or at a distance from, or away from, a place (as, to run *off*; to stand *off*; far *off*); hence, on one's way or journey, as from a place (as, "The whip cracked, and we were *off!*" Bret Harte's "Miggles"; to see a friend *off* on a journey, by attending him to or at the place of departure); also, away from a position occupied, or from contact, connection, or attachment (as, to take *off* one's hat, the cover of a box, or the rind of an orange; to break, cut, shake, fall, or flake *off*; to mark *off* a space or tract); away from or out of association or relation (as, to cast *off* a son); away from employment or service (as, to lay *off* workmen; to have two weeks *off* in summer); sometimes, wide of the truth or fact, or in error (now colloq.: as, you are *off*, or away *off*, on that point); also, so as to interrupt continuity or cause discontinuance (as, to turn *off* the gas; to break *off* negotiations or relations); out of operation or effective existence, or no longer in contemplation (as, the agreement is *off*; the match is *off*, at least for the present); also, so as to cause or undergo reduction or diminution (as, to wear *off*; to die *off*; to fall *off* in number or intensity); as a deduction (as, 10 per cent *off* on all cash purchases); so as to exhaust, finish, or complete, to a finish, or completely (as, to drink *off* a potion; to smooth *off* verses; to kill *off* vermin); also, to fulfilment, or into execution or effect (as, the contest came *off* on the day fixed; to bring *off* a successful stroke); with prompt or ready performance (as, to rattle *off* a list of names; to dash *off* a letter); forthwith or immediately (as, right *off*; straight *off*); also, as to condition, circumstances, supplies, etc. (as, well or badly *off*; better *off*; how are you *off* for money?); *naut.*, away from the land, a ship, the wind, etc.—**off and on,** with cessations and resumptions; intermittently (as, to work *off and on*); *naut.*, on alternate tacks, now away from and now toward the land.—**off of,** off from (as, "I could not keep my eyes *off of* her": Steele, in "Spectator," 306); no longer on (as, when the cover is *off of* the box). [Now colloq. or prov.]—**off,** *prep.* Away from, or so as no longer to be or rest on (as, to wander *off* the track; to fall *off* a horse; that care is now *off* his mind); distant from (as, a village some miles *off* the main road); leading out of (as, an alley *off* 12th Street); also, away or disengaged from (duty, work, etc.); deviating from (something normal or usual: as, *off* the pitch or key, in music; *off* color, see phrase below; *off* one's balance); also, from by subtraction or deduction (as, to take 5 *off* the total number; 25 per cent *off* the marked price); also, from, indicating source (colloq. or vulgar: as, I bought it *off* him); indicating material (as, to make a meal *off* fish); *naut.*, to seaward of.—**off color,** defective in color, as a gem; fig., below the standard; out of condition; of doubtful reputation or propriety: sometimes used, with a hyphen, as an adjective (as, an *off-color* gem; an *off-color* story).—**off side,** away from one's own or the proper side, or being on the wrong side, as of the ball or the like, or of a player who last played or touched it, in football, hockey, etc. (a position subject to restrictions or penalties in particular cases): also used, with a hyphen, as an adjective (as, an *off-side* play).—**off. I.** *a.* More distant, or farther (as, the *off* side of a wall); with reference to animals or vehicles, right (as opposed to *near*, or left: as, "He always used to drive the bay on the near side, and the sorrel on the *off*," Tarkington's "Gentleman from Indiana," xix.); also, lying off from or leading out of a main part, street, or the like (as, an *off* thoroughfare); of a chance, remote, or not immediate (as, "Are you staying here on the *off* chance of another row?" Kipling's "Light That Failed," iii.); also, of time, on which work is suspended (as, pastime for one's *off* hours; "It was with a team of these very horses [used for plowing, etc.], on an *off*-day, that Miss Sharp was brought to the Hall," Thackeray's "Vanity Fair," ix.); of less than the ordinary activity, liveliness, or lively interest (as, an *off* season in the woolen trade; an *off* year in politics); not so good or satisfactory as usual (as, an *off* year for apples; we all have our *off* days, physically, intellectually, or otherwise); *naut.*, farther from the shore; in *cricket*, noting that side of the wicket or of the field opposite to that on which the batsman stands. **II.** *n.* The state or fact of being off; in *cricket*, the off side (as, "Johnson the young bowler is getting wild, and bowls a ball almost wide to the *off*": Hughes's "Tom Brown's School Days," ii. 8).—**off,** *interj.* Be off! stand off! away!

of-fal (of′al), *n.* [ME. *offal*, < *of*, off, + *fal*, fall.] That which falls off, or is allowed to fall off as of little value (now chiefly technical); esp., the waste parts of a butchered animal; specif., those inedible portions of food animals, fowl, and fish used as raw material for manufacture into inedible products; also, putrid flesh; carrion; also, refuse in general; garbage; fig., dregs or scum (as, "on the testimony of wretches . . . whom everybody now believes to have been . . . liars and murderers, the *offal* of gaols and brothels": Macaulay's "Essays," Hallam).

off-cast (ôf′kȧst). **I.** *a.* Cast off; rejected. **II.** *n.* One who or that which is cast off or rejected.

off=col-or (ôf′kul′or), *a.* See *off color*, under *off*, *prep.*

of-fence′, etc. See *offense*, etc.

of-fend (o-fend′), *v.* [OF. *offendre*, < L. *offendere*, strike against, displease, offend, commit an offense, < *ob*, against, + *-fendere*, strike: cf. *defend*.] **I.** *tr.* To attack† or assail†; also, to injure†, harm†, or hurt†; give physical pain to†; also, to irritate in mind or feelings, or cause resentful displeasure in (as, "He often *offended* men who might have been useful friends": Motley's "Dutch Republic," i. 1); wound (one's pride, etc.); affect (the sense, ear, eye, etc.) disagreeably (as, "Far voices, sudden loud, *offend* my ear": Henley's "In Hospital," vi.); be repugnant to (the moral sense, good taste, etc.); also, to sin against, as a person†; violate or transgress, as a law†; also, in Biblical use, to cause to stumble or sin† (as, "If thy right eye *offend* thee, pluck it out": Mat. v. 29). **II.** *intr.* To act on the offensive (obs. or rare: as, "the stroke and parry of two swords, *offending* on the one side and keeping the defensive on the other," Scott's "Castle Dangerous," xx.); also, to give offense or cause displeasure; also, to strike the foot against something†, or stumble†; hence, fig., to err in conduct, or commit a sin, crime, or fault (as, "We have *offended* against thy holy laws": Book of Common Prayer, General Confession).—**of-fend′er,** *n.* One who offends; one who commits an offense.—**of-fend′ress,** *n.* A female offender.

of-fense, of-fence (o-fens′), *n.* [OF. F. *offense*, < L. *offensa*, a striking against, offense, < *offendere*: see *offend*.] The act of attacking or assailing; attack or assault (as, weapons or arms of *offense*; "He drew his sword, and with a deliberate and prepared attitude of *offence*, moved slowly to the encounter," Scott's "Castle Dangerous," xvii.); also, injury†, harm†, or hurt† (as, "So shall he waste his means, weary his soldiers, Doing himself *offence*": Shakspere's "Julius Cæsar," iv. 3. 201); pain†; also, the act of offending or displeasing, or the feeling of resentful displeasure caused (as, to give *offense*, to offend or displease; to take *offense*, to be offended, or take umbrage; without *offense*, without giving or taking offense); offensive or disagreeable effect†, or offensiveness†; something that offends; a cause of resentful displeasure, or of annoyance or disgust; also, stumbling† (as, "He shall be . . . for a stone of stumbling and for a rock of *offence* to both the houses of Israel": Isa. viii. 14); a stumbling-block (obs. or archaic); also, a breach of duty, propriety, etc.; a sin; a transgression; a wrong; a fault; often, a transgression of law; a crime or misdemeanor; sometimes, specif., a transgression of law which is not indictable, but is punishable summarily or by the forfeiture of a penalty.—**of-fense′less, of-fence′less,** *a.* Without offense; incapable of offense or attack; unoffending, or giving no offense; inoffensive, or not objectionable.—**of-fense′less-ly, of-fence′less-ly,** *adv.*

of-fen-sive (o-fen′siv). [ML. *offensivus*.] **I.** *a.* Serving for offense or attack (as, *offensive* arms); consisting in or characterized by attack (as, an *offensive* war); pertaining to offense or attack (as, an *offensive* attitude); also, injurious† or harmful†; also, causing offense or displeasure; irritating; highly annoying; often, disagreeable to the senses or the organs of sense (as, an *offensive* odor; a combination of sounds *offensive* to the ear); repugnant to or jarring upon the moral sense, good taste, or the like; objectionable; disgusting. **II.** *n.* An offensive movement, as of an attacking party (as, "on the very eve of the big Russian *offensive*": H. G. Wells's "Italy, France, and Britain at War," ii. 2); also, with *the*, the position or attitude of offense or attack.—**of-fen′sive-ly,** *adv.*—**of-fen′sive-ness,** *n.*

of-fer (of′ėr), *v.* [AS. *offrian*, < L. *offerre*, bring before, present, offer, < *ob*, before, + *ferre*, bear.] **I.** *tr.* To present for acceptance or rejection, make a tender of, or proffer (as, "I *offer* thee three things; choose thee one of them," 2 Sam. xxiv. 12; "Bets were freely *offered* and taken regarding the result," Bret Harte's "Luck of Roaring Camp"); proffer (one's self) for marriage (as, "Mr. Arbuton has *offered* himself to Kitty": Howells's "Chance Acquaintance," xi.); tender or bid as a price (as, to *offer* ten dollars for a thing); present for sale; also, to propose or volunteer (to do something: as, "Shaw *offered* to accompany him," Parkman's

"Oregon Trail," x.); also, to present solemnly as an act of worship or devotion, as to God, a deity, a saint, etc.; sacrifice; give in worship; also, to present or render (homage, thanks, etc.); in general, to present, or put forward (as, "I can give you no assistance, neither will I *offer* you any obstacle," Trollope's "Warden," iii.; "Little conversation was *offered*," G. W. Cable's "Bonaventure," ii. 3; "She *offered* no response," Arnold Bennett's "Pretty Lady," xxxv.); present to sight or notice (as, "the scene . . . *offered* to his view": Cooper's "Two Admirals," xxi.); put forward for consideration (as, to *offer* a suggestion); also, to attempt to inflict, do, or make, and hence actually to do or make (violence, resistance, etc.: as, "He was not afraid of their *offering* him any harm," H. Melville's "Typee," Sequel); attempt or try (to do something: as, "ready to shoot me if I should *offer* to stir," Swift's "Gulliver's Travels," i. 1); make a show of intention (to do something: as, "When they *offered* to depart he entreated their stay," Johnson's "Rasselas," xx.). **II.** *intr.* To make an offer, proffer, or tender; sometimes, to make an offer of marriage, or propose (as, "Miss Pole had a cousin . . . who had *offered* to Miss Matty long ago": Mrs. Gaskell's "Cranford," iii.); also, to make an offering as an act of worship or devotion; sacrifice; also, to present itself, or occur (as, "on every occasion that *offered*": Scott's "Guy Mannering," xii.); also, to make an attempt (*at*: obs. or rare).—**of′fer,** *n.* An act of offering or tendering something (as, an *offer* of assistance); sometimes, a proposal of marriage (as, "the modern way of girls, who count their lovers and *offers* as an Indian does his scalps": Mrs. Stowe's "Oldtown Folks," xxxvi.); often, a proposal to give or accept something as a price or equivalent for something else, or a bid (as, an *offer* of ten thousand dollars for a house; to make an *offer* for the building of a bridge); the condition of being offered (as, on *offer*, that is, for sale); also, something offered; also, an attempt or endeavor, or a show of intention (as, "He had no sooner spoke these words, but he made an *offer* of throwing himself into the water": Steele, in "Spectator," 118).—**of′fer-er,** *n.*—**of′fer-ing,** *n.* The act of one who offers; a proffer or tender, as for acceptance or for sale, or something proffered; esp., the presenting of something as an act of worship or devotion, as to God, a deity, etc.; oblation; sacrifice; also, something offered in worship or devotion, as to God, a deity, etc.; an oblation; a sacrifice; a contribution given to or through the church for a particular purpose, as at a service; sometimes, more generally, a present or gift, esp. as a tribute of honor or esteem.

of-fer-to-ry (of′ėr-tō-ri), *n.*; pl. *-ries* (-riz). [LL. *offertorium*, place to which offerings were brought, also offering, oblation, < L. *offerre*: see *offer*.] *Eccles.*, the verses, anthem, or music said, sung, or played while the offerings of the people are received at a religious service; that part of a service at which offerings are made; the offerings themselves; also, in the *Rom. Cath. Ch.*, the oblation of the unconsecrated elements made by the celebrant at this part of the eucharistic service.—**of-fer-to′ri-al** (-tō′ri-al), *a.*

off-hand (ôf′hand′), *adv.* At once; forthwith; without previous thought or preparation; extempore: as, to decide *offhand*; to make a speech *offhand*.—**off′hand,** *a.* Done or made offhand, or extemporaneous (as, an *offhand* remark or speech); unstudied, easy, or without effort or ceremony (as, "He had gone about next day with his usual cool, *off-hand* manner": Galsworthy's "Patrician," ii. 5); also, doing or saying things offhand (as, "She tried to make herself light and *offhand*": H. G. Wells's "Mr. Britling," i. 5. § 8); sometimes, cavalier, curt, or brusque.—**off′hand′ed,** *a.* Offhand.—**off′hand′ed-ly,** *adv.*—**off′hand′ed-ness,** *n.*

of-fice (of′is), *n.* [OF. F. *office*, < L. *officium*, service, duty, function, ceremony, appar. a contr. of *opificium*, a working, work, < *opus*, work, + *facere*, do.] Something (good, or occasionally bad) done for another, or a service (as, "He will be favoured, and good *offices* will be done him from regard to his character": J. Butler's "Analogy of Religion," i. 3); also, a service or task to be performed (as, "He was deft and neat-handed as a girl about any little *offices* of a domestic nature": Mrs. Stowe's "Oldtown Folks," xxi.); also, the duty, function, or part of a particular person or agency (as, to perform the *office* of adviser or of nurse; "It has been the *office* of art to educate the perception of beauty," Emerson's "Essays," Art); also, a position of duty, trust, or authority, esp. in the public service, or in some corporation, society, or the like; official employment or position (as, to be in, or out of, *office*; to seek *office*; "Men too much conversant with *office* are rarely minds of remarkable enlargement," Burke's "American Taxation"); also, a ceremony or rite, esp. for the dead; any prescribed service, or form of service, for the church or for devotional use (as, the communion *office*; the confirmation *office*; the *office* of lauds); also, a room or place for the transaction of business, the discharge of professional duties, or the like (as, a broker's *office*; a ticket-*office*; a lawyer's *office*; an editorial *office*); the room or rooms in which the clerical work of an industrial or other establishment is done; a building or a set of rooms devoted to the business of a branch of a governmental organization (as, the foreign *office*; the patent *office*; the post-*office*); also, the staff or body of persons carrying on work in a business or other office; the officials or the administrative department occupying a governmental office; also, *pl.*, the parts of a house, as the kitchen, pantry, laundry, etc., devoted to household work, often also the stables and other outbuildings, or the barns, cow-houses, etc., of a farm; also, *sing.*, with *the*, the hint or signal, or private intimation of something (slang: as, to give one the *office*).—**of′fice†,** *v. t.* To perform in the way of office or service (see Shakspere's "All's Well," iii. 2. 129); also, to place in office (see Shakspere's "Winter's Tale," i. 2. 172); also, to drive by official authority (see Shakspere's "Coriolanus," v. 2. 68).—**of′fice=boy,** *n.* A boy employed in an office, as of a business house.—**of′fice=hold″er,** *n.*

of-fi-cer (of′i-sėr), *n.* [OF. F. *officier*, < ML. *officiarius*, < L. *officium*: see *office*.] An agent† or minister† (as, "slavish *officers* of vengeance": Milton's "Comus," 218); also, one who holds an office or position of duty, trust, or authority; a functionary of a royal or other great household; a person appointed or elected to some position of responsibility and authority in the public service, or in some corporation, society, or the like; a policeman or constable; one who holds a position of rank or authority in the army, navy, or any similar organization, esp. one who holds a commission in the army or navy; the master or captain of a merchant vessel or pleasure vessel, or any of his chief assistants; in some honorary orders, a member of higher rank than the lowest, as, in the French Legion of Honor, one of the degree next higher than that of chevalier.—**officer of the day,** *milit.*, an officer who has charge, for the time being, of the guard, prisoners, and police of a military force or camp, and who inspects the guard, messes, barracks, corrals, etc.—**of′fi-cer,** *v. t.* To furnish with officers; also, to command or direct as an officer does (as, "Most of the cavalry regiments . . . were led and *officered* by gentlemen from the south": Cooper's "Spy," vii.); hence, in general, to direct, conduct, or manage.—**of′fi-cer-less,** *a.* Without officers.—**of′fi-cer-ship,** *n.* The position or rank of an officer; also, a body of officers.

of-fice=seek-er (of′is-sē″kėr), *n.* One who seeks public office: as, "Don John . . . was soon surrounded by courtiers, time-servers, noble *office-seekers*" (Motley's "Dutch Republic," v. 1).—**of′fice=seek″ing,** *n.* and *a.*

of-fi-cial (o-fish′al). [LL. *officialis*, < L. *officium*: see *office*.] **I.** *a.* Of or pertaining to an office or position of duty, trust, or authority (as, *official* labors, powers, or dignity; *official* dress); also, holding office, or appointed or authorized to act in a special capacity (as, *official* personages; an *official* body; an *official* representative or observer); also, authorized or issued by governmental or other authorities (as, "Since the previous August [1792] the guillotine had been in use as the *official* instrument in French executions," H. G. Wells's "Outline of History," xxxvii. § 10; an *official* statement or report); also, having or suggesting the manner of persons in office; formal or ceremonious; in *phar.*, authorized by the pharmacopœia. **II.** *n.* One who holds an office or is charged with some form of official duty: as, a government *official*; police *officials*; railroad *officials*.—**of-fi′cial-dom** (-dom), *n.* The position or domain of officials; also, the official class.—**of-fi′cial-ism,** *n.* Official methods or system; excessive attention to official routine; also, officials collectively.—**of-fi′cial-ize,** *v. t.*; *-ized, -izing.* To render official in character.—**of-fi′cial-ly,** *adv.*

of-fi-ci-ant (o̤-fish′i-a̤nt), *n.* [ML. *officians* (*-ant-*), ppr. of *officiare*: see *officiate*.] One who officiates at a religious service or ceremony.

of-fi-ci-a-ry (o̤-fish′i-ā̤-ri). [ML. *officiarius*, < L. *officium*: see *office*.] **I.** *a.* Pertaining to or derived from an office, as a title; also, having a title or rank derived from an office, as a dignitary. **II.** *n.*; pl. *-ries* (-riz). An officer or official; also, officers collectively.

of-fi-ci-ate (o̤-fish′i-āt), *v.*; *-ated*, *-ating.* [ML. *officiatus*, pp. of *officiare*, < L. *officium*: see *office*.] **I.** *intr.* To perform the office of a priest or minister, as at divine worship or on any ceremonial occasion (as, "the Bishop of Glasgow, *officiating* at a high festival in the church of Douglas": Scott's "Castle Dangerous," xix.); hence, to perform the duties of any office or position; serve or act (*as*: as, "The apothecary occasionally *officiated* as a barber," Godwin's "Caleb Williams," xxxix.; "Joshua Rann *officiated* as head sexton as well as clerk," George Eliot's "Adam Bede," xviii.). **II.**† *tr.* To perform (a religious service, etc.); hence, to perform (duties, work, etc.); serve in (another's place); also, to minister or supply (as, "Stars, that seem to roll Spaces incomprehensible . . . merely to *officiate* light Round this opacous earth": Milton's "Paradise Lost," viii. 22).—**of-fi-ci-a′tion** (-ā′-sho̤n), *n.*—**of-fi′ci-a-tor,** *n.*

of-fi-ci-nal (o̤-fis′i-na̤l), *a.* [ML. *officinalis*, < L. *officina*, workshop, laboratory, contr. of *opificina*, < *opifex*, workman, < *opus*, work, + *facere*, do, make.] Kept in stock by apothecaries, as a drug (cf. *magistral*); hence, recognized by the pharmacopœia; also, pertaining to a shop.—**of-fi′ci-nal-ly,** *adv.*

of-fi-cious (o̤-fish′us), *a.* [= F. *officieux*, < L. *officiosus*, < *officium*: see *office*.] Ready to serve†, or obliging†; dutiful†; also, forward in tendering or obtruding one's services upon others (as, "being, as boys usually are, very *officious* to help . . . and sometimes lending a hand," Defoe's "Robinson Crusoe," i. 7; "You are too *officious* In her behalf that scorns your services," Shakspere's "Midsummer Night's Dream," iii. 2. 330); marked by or proceeding from such forwardness (as, *officious* zeal; *officious* interference); in *diplomacy*, proceeding unofficially from an official source (as, an *officious* communication); of an unofficial character.—**of-fi′cious-ly,** *adv.*—**of-fi′cious-ness,** *n.*

off-ing (ôf′ing), *n.* The more distant part of the sea as seen from the shore, beyond the anchoring-ground; also, position at a distance from the shore (as, "We were obliged to keep to the northward, keeping as good an *offing* as we could with respect to the coast of China": Defoe's "Captain Singleton," xiv.).

off-ish (ôf′ish), *a.* Inclined to keep aloof; distant in manner. [Colloq.]—**off′ish-ness,** *n.*

off-print (ôf′print), *n.* A reprint in separate form of an article which originally appeared as part of a larger publication.—**off-print′,** *v. t.* To reprint separately, as an article from a larger publication.

off-sad-dle (ôf′sad″l), *v. t.* or *i.*; *-dled*, *-dling.* To take the saddle off (a horse), as at a halt in a journey. [South Africa.]

off-scour-ing (ôf′skour″ing), *n.* That which is scoured off; filth; refuse: commonly in *pl.*, and often fig., of persons: as, "We are made as the filth of the world, and are the *offscouring* of all things" (1 Cor. iv. 13); "Here the very *offscourings* of the frontier were congregated, to be marshaled for the expedition" (Parkman's "Oregon Trail," iii.).

off-scum (ôf′skum), *n.* That which is skimmed off; scum; refuse.

off-set (ôf-set′ or ôf′set), *v.*; *-set*, *-setting.* **I.** *tr.* To set off as an equivalent (as, to *offset* one thing against another); also, to balance by something else as an equivalent (as, to *offset* one thing by another); often, to counterbalance as an equivalent does (as, the gains more than *offset* the losses); compensate for, or countervail; in *mech.*, to bend in an offset, as a pipe; in *arch.*, to build with an offset or set-off, as a wall; in *printing*, to make an offset of. **II.** *intr.* To project as an offset or branch; in *printing*, to make an offset.—**off′set,** *n.* A setting off or starting; the start or outset; also, a short lateral shoot by which certain plants are propagated; any offshoot; a branch; a spur of a mountain-range; an offshoot from a family or race; also, something that offsets or counterbalances; a compensating equivalent; in *mech.*, a more or less abrupt bend in a pipe, bar, rod, or the like, to serve some particular purpose; in *arch.*, a set-off; in *surv.*, a short distance measured perpendicularly from a main line, as in determining the area of an irregular section; in *printing*, a faulty transfer of superabundant or undried ink on a printed sheet to any opposed surface, as the opposite page; in *lithog.*, an impression from an inked design or the like on a lithographic stone or plate, made on another surface, as a sheet of rubber, and then transferred to paper, instead of being made directly on the paper.

off-shoot (ôf′shöt), *n.* A shoot from a main stem, as of a plant; a lateral shoot; hence, anything conceived as springing or proceeding from a main stock (as, an *offshoot* of a mountain-range, a railroad, a society, or a school of art); sometimes, a branch, or a descendant or scion, of a family or race.

off-shore (ôf′shōr′), *adv.* Off or away from the shore (as, a wind blowing *offshore*); also, at a distance from the shore (as, vessels lying *offshore*).—**off′shore,** *a.* Moving or tending away from the shore (as, an *offshore* wind); also, being or operating at a distance from the shore (as, *offshore* fisheries or fishermen).

off-side (ôf′sīd′), *a.* See *off side*, under *off*, *prep.*

off-spring (ôf′spring), *n.* [AS. *ofspring*.] Children or young sprung from a particular parent or progenitor (as, "His fair *offspring* . . . Are coming to attend their father's state," Milton's "Comus," 34; the mother of a numerous *offspring*; the hen gathers her *offspring* about her); progeny; descendants collectively; often, a child or an animal in relation to its parent or parents (as, "the son endeavouring to appear the worthy *offspring* of such a father," Steele, in "Spectator," 263; the mule is the *offspring* of a male ass and a mare); a descendant (as, "Thou *offspring* of the house of Lancaster . . . Good angels guard thy battle!" Shakspere's "Richard III.," v. 3. 136); fig., the product, result, or effect of something (as, "He appeared to consider it [an assertion] as the *offspring* of delirium": Mrs. Shelley's "Frankenstein," xxii.).

of-fus-cate (o-fus′kāt), etc. Same as *obfuscate*, etc.

oft (ôft). [AS. *oft* = OHG. *ofto*, G. *oft*, = Icel. *oft*, *opt*, = Goth. *ufta*, often.] **I.** *adv.* Often; frequently: as, "*Oft* I talk'd with him apart" (Tennyson's "Talking Oak," 17). [Now archaic, poetic, or prov.] **II.** *a.* Frequent: as, "warn'd by *oft* experience" (Milton's "Samson Agonistes," 382). [Obs. or Sc.]

of-ten (ôf′n). [Extended form of *oft*.] **I.** *adv.* Many times; frequently; in many cases. **II.** *a.* Frequent: as, "Use a little wine for . . . thine *often* infirmities" (1 Tim. v. 23). [Archaic.]—**of′ten-times,** *adv.* Often; frequently.

oft-times (ôft′tīmz), *adv.* Oftentimes; often. [Archaic.]

og-do-ad (og′dō-ad), *n.* [LL. *ogdoas* (*ogdoad-*), < Gr. ὀγδοάς (ὀγδοαδ-), < ὀκτώ, eight.] The number eight; also, a group of eight.

o-gee (ō-jē′ or ō′jē), *n.* [Appar. < F. *ogive*: see *ogive*.] A double curve (like the letter S) formed by the union of a concave and a convex line; also, in *arch.*, etc., a molding with such a curve for a profile; a cyma.—

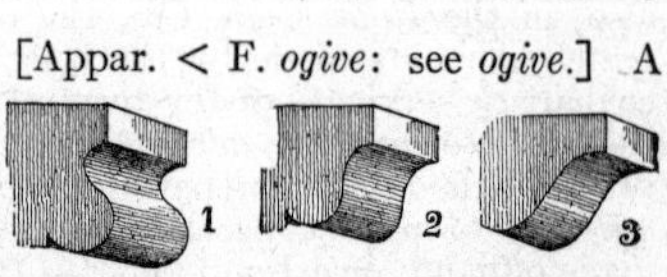

Ogee Moldings. — 1. Early English period. 2. Decorated period. 3. Perpendicular period.

ogee arch, in *arch.*, a form of pointed arch, each side of which has the curve of an ogee.

og-ham, og-am (og′a̤m), *n.* [Ir. *ogham*, OIr. *ogam*.] An alphabet of twenty characters used by the ancient Irish and British; an inscription in such characters; any of the characters. See cut on following page.—**og-ham-ic, og-am-ic** (og′a̤m-ik or o-gam′ik), *a.* Of or pertaining to the ogham (alphabet); consisting of oghams (characters).

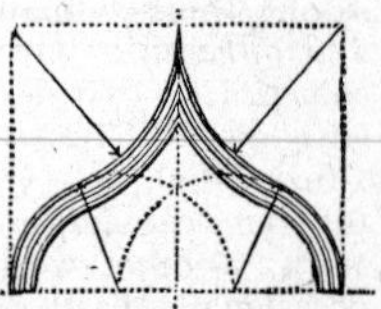
Ogee Arch.

o-give (ō′jīv or ō-jīv′), *n.* [F. *ogive*, also formerly *augive*; origin uncertain.] In *arch.*, a diagonal groin or rib of a vault; also, a pointed arch.—**o-gi-val** (ō-jī′va̤l), *a.*

o-gle (ō′gl), *v.*; *ogled*, *ogling.* [Appar. from a freq. form (= LG. *oegeln* = G. *äugeln*) of D. *oogen*, to eye, < *oog*, the eye: see *eye*.] **I.** *intr.* To cast amorous, ingratiating, or impertinently familiar glances: as, "He sighs, and *ogles*, and languishes at this amiable object" (Smollett's "Humphry Clinker," Nov. 8); "She *ogled*, and nodded, and kissed her hands quite affectionately to Kew" (Thackeray's "Newcomes," xxxiv.). **II.** *tr.* To eye with amorous, ingratiating, or impertinently familiar glances (as, "He *ogled* the ladies with an air of supreme satisfaction," H. Melville's "Omoo," xlvi.; "In his insane conceit he *ogled* the girls as they waved their handkerchiefs to me," Conan Doyle's "Exploits of Brigadier Gerard," vii.); also, in general, to eye; look at.—**o'gle,** *n.* An ogling glance: as, "Miss Brindle-mew . . . gave him two or three *ogles*" (Peacock's "Headlong Hall," xiii.).—**o'gler,** *n.*

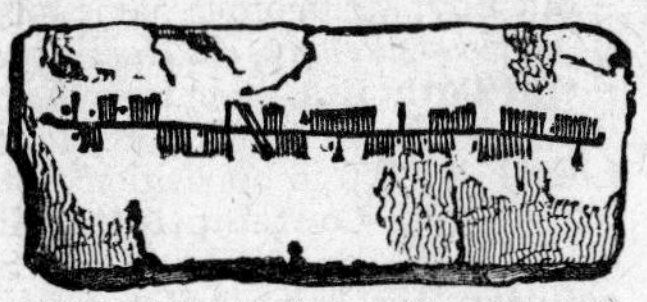
Ogham Inscription, from a stone found near Ennis, Ireland.

og-mic (og'mik), *a.* Same as *oghamic.*

Og-pu (og'pö), *n.* [From the initials of the Russian name.] The secret service of Soviet Russia.

o-gre (ō'gėr), *n.* [F.; origin uncertain.] A monster, commonly represented as a hideous giant, of fairy-tales and popular legends, supposed to live on human flesh; hence, a person likened to such a monster, as in appearance or character (as, "If those robber-barons were somewhat grim and drunken *ogres*, they had a certain grandeur of the wild beast in them": George Eliot's "Mill on the Floss," iv. 1).—**o-gre-ish, o-grish** (ō'gėr-ish, ō'grish), *a.* Resembling, or characteristic of, an ogre.—**o'gress,** *n.* A female ogre.

O-gyg-i-an (ǫ-jij'i-ạn), *a.* Of or pertaining to Ogyges, a legendary ruler in ancient Greece (in Bœotia or Attica); of or in the time of Ogyges (as, the *Ogygian* deluge); hence, of obscure antiquity; very ancient.

oh (ō), *interj.* A form of *O*², esp. as an expression of surprise, pain, disapprobation, etc., more common in prose or ordinary language.—**oh,** *n.* The exclamation 'oh.'

ohm (ōm), *n.* [From G. S. *Ohm* (1787–1854), German physicist.] In *elect.*, the unit of resistance; the resistance of a conductor in which one volt, the unit difference of potential, produces a current of one ampere.—**ohm-age** (ō'mạ̄j), *n.* Electrical resistance expressed in ohms.—**ohm'ic,** *a.* Of or pertaining to the ohm; measured in ohms.—**ohm-me-ter** (ōm'mē''tėr), *n.* An instrument for measuring in ohms electrical resistance.

o-ho (ǫ-hō'), *interj.* An exclamation expressing surprise, taunting, exultation, etc.

o-hone (ō-hōn'), *interj.* See *ochone.*

-oid. [Gr. -οειδής, < -ο-, stem-vowel belonging to preceding word-element (as in κωνο-ειδής, E. *conoid*), + -ειδής, having the form of, like, < εἶδος, form: cf. *-ode*².] A termination used to form adjectives meaning 'like' or 'resembling,' and nouns meaning 'something resembling,' what is indicated by the preceding part of the word (and often implying an incomplete or imperfect resemblance), as in *alkaloid, anthropoid, cardioid, cuboid, lithoid, ovoid, planetoid.*

oil (oil), *n.* [OF. *oile* (F. *huile*), < L. *oleum*, oil, olive-oil; akin to Gr. ἔλαιον, olive-oil, ἐλαία (L. *olea*), olive-tree.] Any of a large class of substances typically unctuous, viscous, combustible, liquid at ordinary temperatures, and soluble in ether or alcohol but not in water, used for anointing, perfuming, lubricating, illuminating, heating, smoothing waves at sea in a storm, and many other purposes (as, a fatty or fixed *oil*, see under *fixed*; an essential or volatile *oil*, see under *essential*, *a.*; a mineral *oil*, see under *mineral*, *a.*); also, some substance of similar consistence (as, *oil* of vitriol, sulphuric acid); also, an oil-color (as, to paint in *oils*); sometimes, an oil-painting; also, an oilskin garment (as, dressed in *oils*).—**oil,** *v.* **I.** *tr.* To apply oil to; anoint with oil; moisten, smear, or lubricate with oil; also, to supply with oil; also, to convert (butter, etc.) into oil by melting; also, in fig. use, to bribe; make oily or smooth, as in speech (as, to *oil* the tongue). **II.** *intr.* To become oil by melting, as butter does.—**oil'=bird,** *n.* The guacharo.—**oil'=bug,** *n.* Same as *synura.*—**oil'=burn''er,** *n.* Any apparatus, machine, or conveyance which burns oil as fuel (for heat or as a source of power); esp., a vessel or ship which does this.—**oil'=cake,** *n.* A cake or mass of linseed, cotton-seed, etc., from which the oil has been expressed, used as a food for cattle or sheep, or as manure.—**oil'=can,** *n.* A can to hold oil.—**oil'cloth,** *n.* Cloth made waterproof with oil, or a piece of it (as, "a hat covered with an *oil-cloth*": Hawthorne's "Twice-Told Tales," Wakefield); oilskin; also, any of various fabrics coated or prepared with paint or the like, for use as table-cloths, floor-cloths, etc. (as, "a table with a very shining black *oil-cloth*," Mrs. Stowe's "Uncle Tom's Cabin," viii.; "The thresholds and doorsteps were covered with the neatest and brightest *oil-cloth*," Howells's "Chance Acquaintance," viii.).—**oil'=col''or,** *n.* A color or paint made by grinding a pigment in oil; also, a painting executed in such colors.—**oil'er,** *n.* One who oils; a workman employed to oil machinery; also, any contrivance for lubricating with oil; a can with a long spout, used for oiling machinery; also, an oilskin coat (colloq.).—**oil'i-ly,** *adv.* In an oily manner.—**oil'i-ness,** *n.*—**oil'=nut,** *n.* Any of various nuts and seeds yielding oil, as the buffalo-nut, the North American butternut, or the castor-bean; also, any of the plants producing them.—**oil'=paint'ing,** *n.* The art of painting with oil-colors; also, a picture in oil-colors.—**oil'skin,** *n.* Cloth made waterproof by treatment with oil; a piece of this, or a garment made of it.—**oil'=slick,** *n.* A slick, or smooth place, on the surface of water, due to the presence of oil; an oil-covered area on the ocean.—**oil'stone,** *n.* A fine-grained whetstone, whose rubbing-surface is lubricated with oil.—**oil'=well,** *n.* A well sunk to obtain petroleum.—**oil'y,** *a.*; compar. *oilier*, superl. *oiliest.* Pertaining to oil; of the nature of or consisting of oil; resembling oil; full of or containing oil; smeared or covered with oil, or greasy; in fig. use, smooth, as in manner or speech, or as manner or speech (as, an *oily* knave or hypocrite; an *oily* tongue; "*oily* eloquence," Cowper's "Task," iv. 64); bland; unctuous.

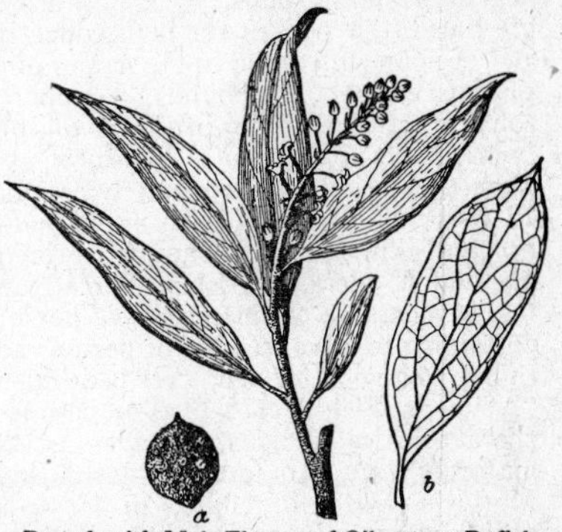

Branch with Male Flowers of Oil-nut, or Buffalo-nut (*Pyrularia pubera*).—*a*, the fruit; *b*, a leaf, showing the nervation.

oi-no- (oi-nǫ-), etc. Same as *œno-*, etc.

oi-noch-o-ë (oi-nok'ǫ-ē), *n.* [Gr. οἰνοχόη, < οἶνος, wine, + χεῖν, pour.] In *Gr. antiq.*, a pitcher-like vessel with a three-lobed rim, for dipping wine from the crater or bowl and pouring it into the drinking-cups.

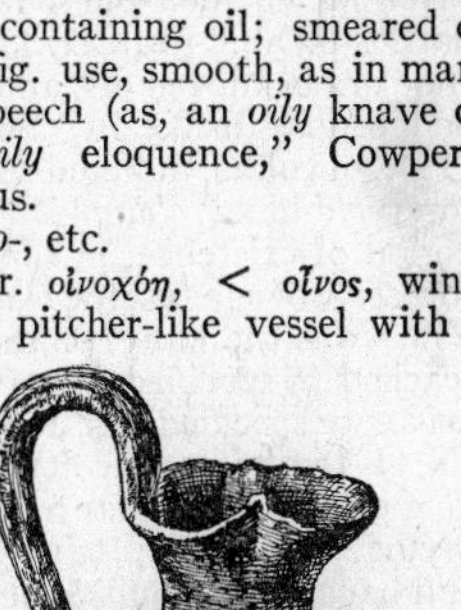
Oinochoë.

oint-ment (oint'mẹnt), *n.* [OF. *oignement*, < *oindre*, < L. *unguere*, smear, anoint.] A soft, unctuous preparation, often medicated, for application to the skin, esp. one which has a butter-like consistence and melts when in contact with the body; an unguent.

Oi-reach-tas (ǫ-rä̇ch'thạs), *n.* [Ir. *oireachtas*, assembly, conference, council.] A national assembly or festival held annually in Ireland for the encouragement of the Irish language as a spoken and literary medium; also, the National Parliament of the State of Ireland (established Dec. 29, 1937), consisting of the President of the State of Ireland, the Dail Eireann (House of Representatives), and the Seanad Eireann (Senate).

O. K. (ō'kā'). [Origin variously explained; said to be from Choctaw Indian *okeh*, 'it is so.'] All right; correct: often written by way of indorsement on a bill or the like. [Colloq.] —**O. K.,** *v. t.*; *O. K.'d, O. K.'ing.* To put 'O. K.' on (a bill, etc.); indorse; approve. [Colloq.]

o-ka-pi (ō-kä′pi), *n.*; pl. *okapis* or *okapi.* [African.] An African mammal, *Okapia johnstoni*, closely related to the giraffe, but smaller and with a much shorter neck.

Okapi.

o-kra (ō′krą or ok′rą), *n.*; pl. *okras.* [African.] A tall malvaceous plant, *Abelmoschus* (or *Hibiscus*) *esculentus*, native in Africa, and cultivated in the East and West Indies and the southern U. S. for its edible mucilaginous pods, which are used as a vegetable and in soups, etc.; also, the pod, or the pods collectively.

-ol. A noun suffix used in the names of chemical derivatives, pharmaceutical compounds, commercial products, etc.: sometimes representing (*a*) L. *oleum*, oil, as in *caffeol*, *eucalyptol*, *lysol*, *myrtol*, or (*b*) E. *alcohol*, as in *glycerol*, *naphthol*, *phenol*, or being of less definitely assignable origin.

old (ōld), *a.* [AS. *ald*, *eald*, = D. *oud* = G. *alt*, old; orig. pp., and akin to Icel. *ala*, nourish, bring up, Goth. *alan*, grow up, and L. *alere*, nourish.] Far advanced in years or life (as, a venerable *old* man; an *old* horse; an *old* oak); of or pertaining to advanced life or persons advanced in years (as, to live to a good *old* age; "*old* bedridden palsy," Tennyson's "Aylmer's Field," 178); also, having the appearance or characteristics of advanced age (as, "He had grown prematurely *old*. At forty-six years his hair was white": Motley's "Dutch Republic," iii. 1); sedate, sensible, or wise, as if from age or mature years (as, a little girl *old* in her ways; to have an *old* head on young shoulders); of long experience (as, an *old* hand at the game; to be *old* in sin or crime); also, having existed long, or made long ago (as, an *old* garden, well, wall, or tomb; *old* jewelry or lace; *old* wine); hence, deteriorated through age or long use (as, *old* clothes; an *old* pen; "Neither do men put new wine into *old* bottles: else the bottles break," Mat. ix. 17); worn, decayed, or dilapidated; stale or hackneyed (as, an *old* joke; "Your fooling grows *old*, and people dislike it," Shakspere's "Twelfth Night," i. 5. 119); of colors, dull and soft in hue, as if from fading (as, *old* rose; *old* blue; *old* gold); also, advanced in years, or in the period of existence, in comparison with others or relatively to a scale of age (as, the *oldest* boy; the *older* horse of the two; how *old* is the baby, or the picture, or the house?); having reached a specified age (with *old* following the length of existence specified: as, a man thirty years *old*; trees centuries *old*; a two-year-*old* colt); also, having originated or arisen long ago, or dating far back into the past (as, an *old* custom, saying, or legend); having had a long history (as, "an *old* and haughty nation," Milton's "Comus," 33; an *old* family); of long standing, or having long been such (as, an *old* friend); long known or in use, or familiar (as, flowers, drugs, patterns, or methods new and *old*; the same *old* excuse); as an expression of familiarity, used in affectionate mention of a place, institution, or the like (as, *old* England; *old* Yale; *Old* Glory, see phrase below), or in speaking to or of a person, as if implying long acquaintance or friendly feeling (as, *old* man; good *old* Henry: much used in colloquial or slang phrases, as 'old dear,' or 'old thing,' see phrase below); also, carried to great lengths, or great (as, "We shall have *old* swearing," Shakspere's "Merchant of Venice," iv. 2. 15: now chiefly in colloquial expressions such as 'a rare old fight,' 'a high old time,' etc.); also, former, past, or ancient, as time, days, etc.; belonging to a past time or age (as, *old* scenes, battles, or kingdoms; the *old* Italian painters; the *old* Greek drama); proper to or characteristic of a past time or age, archaic, or antique (as, *old* words; *old* lettering or script); also, being the earlier or earliest of two or more things of the same kind, or stages of a thing (as, the *Old* Testament, see *testament*; the *Old* World, see *world*; *Old* English, *Old* French, *Old* Latin, *Old* Norse, etc., see the nouns); in *phys. geog.*, of topographical features, far advanced in reduction by erosion, etc. —**old boy,** a humorous name for the devil. Also called *old Bogy*, *old gentleman*, *old Harry*, *old Nick*, *old one*, *old Scratch*. —**Old Catholics,** an independent ecclesiastical organization which developed from a party formed in the Roman Catholic Church in 1870 in opposition to the dogma of papal infallibility. —**Old Contemptibles,** the British 'Contemptibles' of 1914 in the World War. See *contemptible*, *n.* —**old country,** the home country from which emigrants come: often referring to Great Britain or Ireland. —**Old Dominion,** a popular name for the State of Virginia. —**old English,** in *printing*, the form of black-letter used by English printers of the 16th century. —**old folks,** old or aged people; also, those of an older generation in a family, as the parents (as, "The *old folks* encouraged me by continual invitations to supper, and by leaving us together": B. Franklin's "Autobiography," v.). [Colloq.] —**Old Glory,** the flag of the United States. [Colloq.] —**Old Hundred,** properly **Old Hundredth,** a celebrated tune set about the middle of the 16th century to the 100th psalm in the metrical version of William Kethe (died 1608?), and marked "Old Hundredth" in Tate and Brady's new version in 1696, as being retained from the old version. —**old leaven.** See under *leaven*, *n.* —**Old Lights,** *eccles.*, the members of any of various parties adhering to old doctrines. See *New Lights*, under *new*, *a.* —**old maid,** an elderly or confirmed spinster; also, a game of cards in which the players draw from one another, and match and discard pairs, until but one card, an odd queen, remains, the holder of which is dubbed the *old maid* (or *old bachelor*). —**old mustache** [tr. F. *vieille moustache*], an old soldier. —**old Nick.** See *Nick*[2], also *old boy*, above. —**Old Pretender.** See *pretender*. —**Old Probabilities.** See *probability*. —**Old Red Sandstone.** See under *sandstone*. —**old school.** See *school*[2], *n.* —**old Scratch.** See *scratch*[1], also *old boy*, above. —**old sledge,** the card-game of seven-up. —**old story,** a story long told or often repeated; hence, something that has lost all its novelty (as, aëroplanes are an *old story* to them; you must find the trip quite an *old story*); also, the statement, excuse, complaint, or the like that is repeatedly heard, or the thing that is repeatedly encountered (as, "The judges looked at each other, as much as to say, 'It is the *old story*; it is that inexplicable, hateful obstinacy'": J. H. Newman's "Callista," xxvii.). —**Old Style.** See *style*, *n.* —**old thing, old top,** familiar forms of address used to a person: as, "By-bye, *old thing*" (Arnold Bennett's "Pretty Lady," xix.). [Slang, Eng.] —**old wife,** an old woman (archaic or prov.: as, *old wives'* tales or fables, stories such as old women tell); also, the oldwife (sea-duck). —**old,** *n.* Old or former time, often time long past: used in *of old*. —**of old,** of or in a former time or former days (as, the friends or the hopes *of old*; "The reverend walls In which *of old* I wore the gown," Tennyson's "In Memoriam," lxxxvii.); often, of or in a period or age long past (as, the knights *of old*; legends of the days *of old*; "*Of old* hast thou laid the foundation of the earth," Ps. cii. 25).

old-en[1] (ōl′dn), *v.* **I.** *intr.* To grow old; age, as in appearance or character: as, "In six weeks he *oldened* more than he had done for fifteen years before" (Thackeray's "Vanity Fair," xviii.). **II.** *tr.* To cause to grow or appear old.

old-en[2] (ōl′dn), *a.* Old, or of old; former, past, or ancient (as, *olden* days; "I' the *olden* time, Ere humane statute purged the gentle weal," Shakspere's "Macbeth," iii. 4. 75); of former days (as, "Within her *Olden* memories rose," Longfellow's "Evangeline," ii. 3; "Their lips will laugh with the *olden* evening voices," Dunsany's "Tents of the Arabs," ii.); of a former period or age (as, "islands which the *olden* voyagers had so glowingly described": H. Melville's "Typee," i.). [Archaic.]

old-fan-gled (ōld′fang′gld), *a.* [Formed to correspond to *newfangled*.] Old-fashioned: as, "his vesture so *old-fangled*" (Browning's "Pied Piper of Hamelin," vi.).

old=fash-ioned (ōld′fash′ǫnd), *a.* Of an old fashion or a style or type formerly in vogue (as, *old-fashioned* dress or furniture; "The writing was *old-fashioned* and rather uncertain, like that of an elderly lady," C. Brontë's "Jane Eyre," x.); often, disparagingly, out of fashion, or antiquated (as, "I must wear gloves, by Jove I must, and my coat is *old-fashioned*, as Binnie says": Thackeray's "Newcomes," xv.); in general, favored or prevalent in a former period (as, *old-fashioned* flowers; *old-fashioned* ways or ideas); of persons, having the ways, ideas, or tastes of a former period; hence, old or mature in ways, thoughts, etc., as a child (as, "'Oh! the *old-fashioned* little soul!' cried Mrs. Blimber": Dickens's "Dombey and Son," xiv.); intelligent or knowing, as children or animals (prov. Eng.).

old-ish (ōl′dish), *a.* Somewhat old: as, "I'm getting an *oldish* man" (Arnold Bennett's "Helen with the High Hand," ix.).

old=maid-ish (ōld′mā′dish), *a.* Like, suggesting, or befitting an old maid or elderly spinster; prim: as, "The little kettle with her odd, *old-maidish* looks sat humming away" (Kinglake's "Eothen," xvii.).

old-ness (ōld′nes), *n.* The state or fact of being old.

old=squaw (ōld′skwâ′), *n.* The oldwife (sea-duck).

old-ster (ōld′stėr), *n.* [Formed to correspond to *youngster*.] An old or older person (colloq.: as, "The discreet and sober conversation of the *oldsters* was much disturbed by the loud laughter of the younger folks," H. Kingsley's "Geoffry Hamlyn," xxxiv.); also, in the British navy, a midshipman of four years' standing.

old=time (ōld′tīm′), *a.* Belonging to or characteristic of old or former times: as, a revival of the *old-time* spirit; the *old-time* glory of Athens.—**old′=tim′er** (-tī′mėr), *n.* One whose residence, membership, or experience dates from old times; also, one who adheres to old-time ideas or ways. [Colloq.]

old-wife (ōld′wīf), *n.*; pl. *-wives* (-wīvz). A lively, voluble sea-duck, *Harelda glacialis*, of northern regions, the male of which has long tail-feathers in the breeding season; also, any of various fishes, as the alewife or the menhaden.

Male Oldwife (*Harelda glacialis*). — Left-hand figure shows summer plumage, and right-hand figure winter plumage.

old=world (ōld′wėrld′), *a.* Of or pertaining to the old or ancient world (as, "an *old-world* mammoth": Tennyson's "Princess," v. 142); also, belonging to or characteristic of a former period or age (as, an *old-world* grace or charm; "*Old-world* trains, upheld at court By Cupid-boys of blooming hue," Tennyson's "Day-Dream," 277; "*Old-World* Idylls," the title of a collection of poems on 18th century subjects, by Austin Dobson, published in 1883); also, of or pertaining to the Old World or eastern hemisphere. Cf. *new-world.*

o-le-a-ceous (ō-lē̦-ā′shius), *a.* [L. *olea*, olive.] Belonging to the *Oleaceæ*, or olive family of plants, which includes the ash, jasmine, etc.

o-le-ag-i-nous (ō-lē̦-aj′i-nus), *a.* [F. *oléagineux*, oily, < L. *oleaginus*, of the olive, < *olea*, olive.] Having the nature or qualities of oil; containing oil; producing oil; fig., oily or unctuous.—**o-le-ag′i-nous-ness**, *n.*

o-le-an-der (ō-lē̦-an′dėr), *n.* [F. *oléandre*, < ML. *oleander*; origin uncertain.] Any plant of the apocynaceous genus *Nerium*, esp. *N. oleander*, a poisonous evergreen shrub with leathery lanceolate leaves and handsome rose-colored or white flowers, native in the Mediterranean region but widely cultivated, or *N. odorum*, a species from India with fragrant flowers.

o-le-as-ter (ō-lē̦-as′tėr), *n.* [L., < *olea*, olive.] The wild variety of the olive (the true wild olive); also, a shrub or small tree, *Elæagnus angustifolia*, of southern Europe and western Asia, with fragrant yellow flowers and an olive-like fruit (also called *wild olive*: see cut in next column).

o-le-ate (ō′lē̦-āt), *n.* In *chem.*, a salt of oleic acid.

o-le-fi-ant (ō′lē̦-fī-ąnt), *a.* [F. *oléfiant*, < L. *oleum*, oil, + *facere*, make.] Forming oil: as, *olefiant* gas (ethylene, which forms with chlorine an oily compound).

o-le-fine (ō′lē̦-fin), *n.* [From *olefiant*.] In *chem.*, any of a series of hydrocarbons homologous with ethylene, which form with bromine and chlorine oily compounds.—**o-le-fin′ic,** *a.*

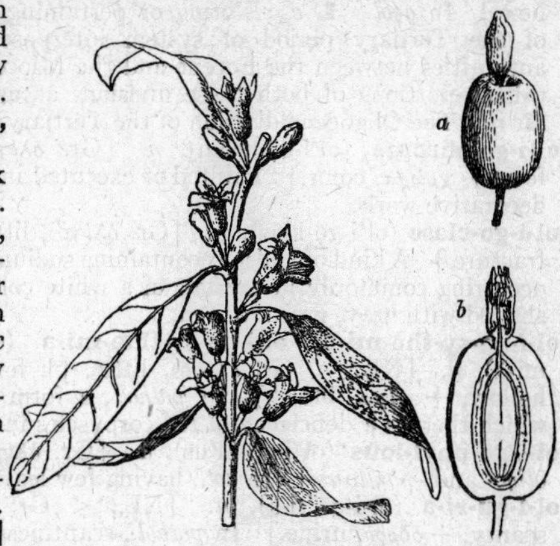

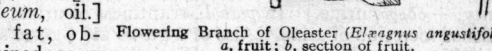

Flowering Branch of Oleaster (*Elæagnus angustifolia*). *a*, fruit; *b*, section of fruit.

o-le-ic (ō-lē′ik or ō′lē̦-ik), *a.* [L. *oleum*, oil.] Pertaining to or derived from oil: as, *oleic* acid (an oily liquid obtained from fats).

o-le-in (ō′lē̦-in), *n.* [L. *oleum*, oil.] A fat, obtained as a colorless oily liquid, occurring abundantly in animal and vegetable tissue.

o-lent (ō′lḙnt), *a.* [L. *olens* (*olent-*), ppr. of *olere*, emit a smell.] Odorous; scented. [Obs. or rare.]

oleo-. Form of L. *oleum*, oil, used in combination.

o-le-o (ō′lē̦-ō), *n.* Shortened form of *oleomargarin.*

o-le-o-graph (ō′lē̦-ō̦-gråf), *n.* [See *oleo-* and *-graph.*] A kind of chromolithograph printed in oil-colors.—**o″le-o-graph′ic** (-graf′ik), *a.*—**o-le-og′ra-phy** (-og′rą-fi), *n.*

o-le-o-mar-ga-rin, o-le-o-mar-ga-rine (ō″lē̦-ō̦-mär′gą-rin, -rēn or -rin), *n.* [See *oleo-* and *margarin.*] Oleo-oil; also, a substitute for butter made from this by admixture of refined lard and milk, and sometimes vegetable oil and pure butter.

o-le-om-e-ter (ō-lē̦-om′e-tėr), *n.* [See *oleo-* and *-meter.*] A hydrometer for testing the purity of an oil by means of its density.

o-le-o=oil (ō′lē̦-ō̦-oil′), *n.* [See *oleo.*] A product obtained from beef-fat, consisting mainly of a mixture of olein and palmitin: used for making butter substitutes.

o-le-o-res-in (ō″lē̦-ō̦-rez′in), *n.* [See *oleo-*.] A natural mixture of an essential oil and a resin; in *phar.*, an oil holding resin in solution, extracted from a substance (as ginger) by means of alcohol, ether, or acetone.

ol-er-a-ceous (ol-ḙ-rā′shius), *a.* [L. *oleraceus*, < *olus* (*oler-*), better *holus*, pot-herb.] Of the nature of a pot-herb or kitchen vegetable.

ol-er-i-cul-ture (ol′ḙ-ri-kul″ţūr), *n.* [L. *olus* (*oler-*), pot-herb (see *oleraceous*), + *cultura*, culture.] The cultivation of pot-herbs or other esculent plants.—**ol″er-i-cul′tur-al-ly,** *adv.*

ol-fac-tion (ol-fak′shọn), *n.* [L. *olfacere* (pp. *olfactus*), smell, < *olere*, emit a smell, + *facere*, make.] The act of smelling; the sense of smell.—**ol-fac′tive,** *a.* Olfactory.—**ol-fac-tom′e-ter** (-tom′e-tėr), *n.* [See *-meter.*] An instrument for measuring the acuteness of the sense of smell.—**ol-fac′-to-ry** (-tō̦-ri). **I.** *a.* Of or pertaining to the sense of smell: as, *olfactory* organs; "holding a book in close contiguity to her nose, as if with the hope of gaining an *olfactory* acquaintance with its contents" (Hawthorne's "House of the Seven Gables," vii.). **II.** *n.*; pl. *-ries* (-riz). An olfactory organ: usually in *pl.*

o-lib-a-num (ō̦-lib′ą-num), *n.* [ML., < Gr. λίβανος.] Frankincense.

ol-i-garch (ol′i-gärk), *n.* [Gr. ὀλιγάρχης, < ὀλίγος, little, pl. few, + ἄρχειν, lead, rule.] One of a small number of persons holding the ruling power in a state; one of the rulers in an oligarchy.—**ol-i-gar′chic, ol-i-gar′chi-cal** (-gär′kik, -ki-kąl), *a.* [Gr. ὀλιγαρχικός.] Of, pertaining to, or having the form of an oligarchy.—**ol-i-gar′chi-cal-ly,** *adv.*—**ol′i-gar-chy** (-ki), *n.*; pl. *-chies* (-kiz). [Gr. ὀλιγαρχία.] A form of government in which the power is vested in a few; also, a state so governed; also, the ruling few collectively.

oligo-. Form of Gr. ὀλίγος, little, small, scanty, *pl.* few, used in combination.

Ol-i-go-cene (ol′i-gō-sēn). [Gr. ὀλίγος, little, + καινός, new.] In *geol.*: **I.** *a.* Noting or pertaining to a division of the Tertiary period or system interposed by certain authorities between the Eocene and the Miocene, and comprising portions of both these divisions as usually known. **II.** *n.* The Oligocene division of the Tertiary.
ol-i-go-chrome (ol′i-gō-krōm), *n.* [Gr. ὀλίγος, little, pl. few, + χρῶμα, color.] Painted or executed in few colors, as decorative work.
ol-i-go-clase (ol′i-gō-klās), *n.* [Gr. ὀλίγος, little, + κλάσις, fracture.] A kind of feldspar containing sodium and calcium, occurring commonly in crystals of a white color, sometimes shaded with gray, green, or red.
ol-i-go-cy-the-mi-a, ol-i-go-cy-thæ-mi-a (ol″i-gō-sī-thē′-mi-ạ̈), *n.* [NL., < Gr. ὀλίγος, little, pl. few, + κύτος, a hollow, + αἷμα, blood.] In *pathol.*, a form of anemia in which there is a deficiency of red corpuscles in the blood.
ol-i-go-phyl-lous (ol″i-gō-fil′us), *a.* [Gr. ὀλιγόφυλλος: see *oligo-* and *-phyllous.*] In *bot.*, having few leaves.
ol-i-gu-ri-a (ol-i-gū′ri-ạ̈), *n.* [NL., < Gr. ὀλίγος, little, scanty, + οὖρον, urine.] In *pathol.*, scantiness of urine; diminished secretion of urine. Also **ol″i-gu-re′sis** (-gū-rē′sis).
o-lio (ō′liō), *n.*; pl. *olios* (ō′liōz). [Sp. *olla*, pot, stew: see *olla.*] A dish of many ingredients; hence, any mixture of heterogeneous elements; a medley or potpourri (musical, literary, or the like); a miscellany; specif., the vaudeville portion of a minstrel or burlesque show.
ol-i-to-ry (ol′i-tō-ri), *a.* [L. *olitorius*, < *olitor*, kitchen-gardener, < *olus, holus*, pot-herb: cf. *oleraceous.*] Of, pertaining to, or producing pot-herbs or kitchen vegetables.
ol-i-va-ceous (ol-i-vā′shius), *a.* [NL. *olivaceus.*] Of an olive hue or tint.
ol-i-va-ry (ol′i-vā-ri), *a.* [L. *olivarius.*] Shaped like an olive; in *anat.*, noting or pertaining to either of two oval bodies or prominences, one on each side of the anterior surface of the medulla oblongata.
ol-ive (ol′iv). [OF. F. *olive*, < L. *oliva*, akin to Gr. ἐλαία, olive-tree, olive.] **I.** *n.* An evergreen tree, *Olea europæa*, of Mediterranean and other warm regions, cultivated chiefly for its fruit, but yielding also a wood valued for ornamental work; also, the fruit, a small oval drupe, esteemed as a relish (pickled in brine when either green or ripe), and valuable as a source of oil; also, any of various related or similar trees; also, the foliage of the olive-tree (*Olea*), or a wreath of it, or an olive-branch (an emblem of peace: as, "I hold the *olive* in my hand; my words are as full of peace as matter," Shakspere's "Twelfth Night," i. 5. 226); also, an olive color, tint, or tinge; also, any of the gastropod mollusks of the family *Olividæ*, with elongated oval shell, numerous in tropical seas (see *olive-shell*). **II.** *a.* Of the dull, yellowish-green color of the unripe olive (fruit); tinged with this color (as, an *olive* complexion); also, of the dull ashen or silvery green of the foliage of the olive (tree).—**ol′ive=branch,** *n.* A branch of the olive-tree (an emblem of peace); hence, anything offered in token of peace; also (in allusion to Ps. cxxviii. 3), a child (usually in *pl.*: as, "The lodgers . . . were the wife and *olive branches* of one Mr. Kenwigs," Dickens's "Nicholas Nickleby," xiv.).—**ol′ive=brown′,** *n.* and *a.* Brown with a greenish tinge.—**ol′ive=green′,** *n.* and *a.* Green with a yellowish or brownish tinge.

Olive (*Olea europæa*). — 1, branch with fruits; 2, branch with flowers; *a*, a flower.

o-liv-en-ite (ō-liv′ẹn-īt), *n.* [For G. *olivenerz*, 'olive ore.'] A mineral consisting of arsenate of copper, occurring in crystals and in masses, usually olive-green in color.
ol-ive=oil (ol′iv-oil′), *n.* An oil expressed from the pulp of olives, much used with food, in medicine, and for various other purposes; sweet-oil.
Ol-i-ver (ol′i-vėr), *n.* See *Roland.*
ol-ive=shell (ol′iv-shel), *n.* The shell of an olive, or gastropod mollusk of the family *Olividæ*, of an elongated oval form, with a fine polish and often handsomely colored and marked; also, a mollusk of this family.

Olive-shell (*Oliva porphyria*).

ol-i-vette (ol-i-vet′), *n.* [F. *olivette*, OF. *olivete*, also *olivet*, < L. *olivetum*, < *oliva*, E. *olive.*] A piece of ground planted with olive-trees; an olive-grove: as, "In France the *olivettes* suffer occasionally from frost" (Encyc. Brit., 11th ed., XX. 86).
ol-i-vine (ol′i-vin or -vēn), *n.* [L. *oliva*, olive.] Chrysolite, esp. when of a greenish color.
ol-la (ol′ạ̈, Sp. ōl′yä), *n.* [Sp., pot, stew, < L. *olla*, pot, jar.] In Spanish-speaking countries, an earthen pot or jar for holding water or for cooking, etc.; also, a dish of meat and vegetables cooked in such a pot; an olio.—**olla podrida** (pō-drē′dạ̈). [Sp., 'rotten pot.'] A favorite Spanish stew of various kinds of meat and vegetables; hence, any incongruous mixture or miscellaneous collection.
ol-o-gy (ol′ō-ji), *n.*; pl. *-gies* (-jiz). [Noun use of *-ology* as in *biology, geology*, etc., the first *o* properly belonging to the first element in the combination and the suffix being *-logy* (that is, *bio-logy*, not *bi-ology*): see *-logy.*] Any science or branch of knowledge. [Colloq.]
ol-pe (ol′pē), *n.* [Gr. ὄλπη.] In *Gr. antiq.*, a leathern oil-flask, used esp. in the palestra; also, a small pitcher-like vessel resembling an oinochoë but having a more slender body.

Olpe (in 2d sense).

O-lym-pi-ad (ō-lim′pi-ad), *n.* [Gr. Ὀλυμπιάς (-αδ-).] A period of four years reckoned from one celebration of the Olympic games to the next, by which the Greeks computed time from 776 B.C.; also, a celebration of the modern Olympic games.
O-lym-pi-an (ō-lim′pi-ạn). **I.** *a.* Pertaining to Olympia in Elis (see *Olympic*); also, pertaining to or dwelling on Mount Olympus (see *Olympus*), as the greater gods of Greece. **II.** *n.* A contender in the Olympic games; also, an Olympian deity.
O-lym-pic (ō-lim′pik), *a.* Pertaining to Mount Olympus (see *Olympus*); Olympian; also, pertaining to Olympia, a plain in ancient Elis, Greece (see phrase following); pertaining to the Olympic games.—**Olympic games,** the greatest of the games or festivals of ancient Greece, held every four years in the plain of Olympia in Elis, in honor of Zeus; also, a modern revival of these games, consisting of international competitions in running, jumping, swimming, shooting, etc., held every four years, each time in a different country. —**O-lym′pic,** *n.* An Olympic game; *pl.*, with *the*, the Olympic games.
O-lym-pus (ō-lim′pus), *n.* [L., < Gr. Ὄλυμπος.] A mountain of Greece, on the borders of Thessaly and Macedonia, anciently fabled to be the abode of the greater Grecian gods; hence, heaven; the sky.
-oma. [Gr. -ωμα, suffix forming nouns from verbs with infinitive in -όειν, -οῦν.] A suffix of nouns denoting a morbid condition or growth (tumor), as in *carcinoma, glaucoma, sarcoma.*
om-a-dhaun (om′ạ-dân or -ᴛʜân), *n.* [Ir. *amadan.*] A fool; a simpleton: as, "I'd knock your brains out if you had any, you *omadhaun!*" (Lover's "Handy Andy," iii.). [Ir.]
o-ma-sum (ō-mā′sum), *n.*; pl. *-sa* (-sạ̈). [NL., < L. *omasum*, bullock's tripe.] The third stomach of a ruminant, between the reticulum and the abomasum; the manyplies.
om-bre, om-ber (om′bėr), *n.* [F. *ombre, hombre*, < Sp. *hombre*, lit. 'man,' < L. *homo*, man.] A game at cards, fashionable in the 17th and 18th centuries, played, usually

by three persons, with forty cards, the eights, nines, and tens being thrown out; also, the player who undertakes to win the pool in this game.

o-me-ga (ō-mē′gạ̈, ō-meg′ạ̈, or ō′mẹ-gạ̈), *n.* [LGr. ὦ μέγα, 'great o.'] The last letter (Ω, ω, = English long O, o) of the Greek alphabet; hence, the last of any series; the end. —**alpha and omega.** See under *alpha.*

om-e-let (om′ẹ-let or om′let), *n.* [F. *omelette,* prob. ult. < L. *lamella,* thin plate: see *lamella.*] A dish consisting of eggs beaten up with milk and fried or baked: often made with other ingredients also, as chopped ham, or with a filling, as of oysters, cheese, vegetables, or jelly.—**Spanish omelet.** See under *Spanish, a.*

o-men (ō′men), *n.* [L. *omen* (*omin-*), omen, perhaps connected with *audire,* hear.] Anything perceived or happening that is regarded as portending good or evil or giving some indication as to the future (as, the Roman augurs were charged with interpreting *omens* for guidance in public affairs; the rainbow was hailed as a good *omen*; "Scarce landed, the first *omens* I beheld Were four white steeds . . . 'War, war is threaten'd . . . ' My father cried, 'where warlike steeds are found,' " Dryden's tr. Virgil's "Æneid," iii. 708); a prophetic sign; a prognostic; also, prophetic significance, or presage (as, a bird of ill *omen*).—**o′men,** *v. t.* To be an omen of; portend; also, to divine, as if from omens (as, "the yet unknown verdict, of which, however, all *omened* the tragical contents": Scott's "Heart of Midlothian," xxiv.). —**o′mened,** *a.* Preceded by or attended with omens; containing an omen: chiefly in composition: as, ill-*omened.*

o-men-tum (ō-men′tum), *n.*; pl. *-ta* (-tạ̈). [L.] In *anat.,* a fold or duplication of the peritoneum passing between certain of the viscera: as, the great *omentum,* or epiploön (attached to and hanging down from the stomach and the transverse colon); the lesser *omentum* (between the stomach and the liver).—**o-men′tal,** *a.*

o-mer (ō′mėr), *n.* [Heb. *'ōmer.*] A Hebrew measure, the tenth part of an ephah.

om-i-cron (om′i-kron), *n.* [LGr. ὂ μικρόν, 'small o.'] The fifteenth letter (O, *o,* = English short O, o) of the Greek alphabet.

om-i-nous (om′i-nus), *a.* [L. *ominosus,* < *omen,* E. *omen.*] Having the significance of an omen (good or bad); affording an omen; prophetically indicative (*of*: as, "I feel a thousand fears Which are not *ominous* of right," Byron's "Heaven and Earth," i.); now, usually, of ill omen, or portending evil (as, "thou *ominous* and fearful owl of death": Shakspere's "1 Henry VI.," iv. 2. 15); suggestive of impending evil, causing forebodings, or vaguely disquieting (as, "a dull, *ominous* rumble," Bret Harte's "Fool of Five Forks"; "Why was my mind absorbed in thoughts *ominous* and dreary?" C. B. Brown's "Wieland," vi.).—**om′i-nous-ly,** *adv.*—**om′i-nous-ness,** *n.*

o-mis-si-ble (ō-mis′i-bl), *a.* That may be omitted.

o-mis-sion (ō-mish′ọn), *n.* [LL. *omissio(n-).*] The act of omitting, or the state of being omitted; a forbearing or failing to include or to do something; also, something omitted.

o-mit (ō-mit′), *v. t.*; *omitted, omitting.* [L. *omittere* (pp. *omissus*), let go, neglect, omit, < *ob,* to, + *mittere,* send.] To let go† or lay aside† (as, "Tempests themselves . . . As having sense of beauty, do *omit* Their mortal natures, letting go safely by The divine Desdemona": Shakspere's "Othello," ii. 1. 71); also, to let slip, or neglect (an opportunity, means, etc.: see Shakspere's "Julius Cæsar," iv. 3. 220); also, to leave out, or forbear or fail to include (as, to *omit* passages of a text; to *omit* a letter from a word; to *omit* an ingredient in cookery; the card was accidentally *omitted* from the package); also, to forbear or fail to mention (as, please *omit* names; "I must not *omit* that Sir Roger is a justice of the quorum," Steele, in "Spectator," 2); also, to forbear or fail to do, make, or perform (as, to *omit* an act, service, or greeting; to *omit* reference to a subject); leave undone; forbear or neglect (to do something: as, he *omitted* to state his reasons); refrain from sending, giving, etc. (as, to *omit* flowers; to *omit* gifts); refrain from using (as, to *omit* ceremony).—**o-mit′tance,** *n.* Omission. See Shakspere's "As You Like It," iii. 5. 133. [Obs. or archaic.]—**o-mit′ter,** *n.*

om-ma-te-um (om-ạ-tē′um), *n.*; pl. *-tea* (-tē′ạ̈). [NL., < Gr. ὄμμα (ὀμματ-), eye, < ὀπ-, see: see *optic.*] In *zoöl.,* a compound eye, as in insects and crustaceans.—**om-ma-te′al,** *a.*

om-ma-tid-i-um (om-ạ-tid′i-um), *n.*; pl. *-ia* (-i-ạ̈). [NL., dim. < Gr. ὄμμα (ὀμματ-), eye: see *ommateum.*] In *zoöl.,* one of the radial elements or segments which make up the compound eye (ommateum) of insects, crustaceans, etc.—**om-ma-tid′i-al,** *a.*

om-mat-o-phore (o-mat′ō-fōr), *n.* [NL. *ommatophorus,* < Gr. ὄμμα (ὀμματ-), eye, + -φόρος, < φέρειν, bear.] In *zoöl.,* a tentacle or movable stalk bearing an eye, as in certain snails.—**om-ma-toph-o-rous** (om-ạ-tof′ō-rus), *a.*

om-ni- (om′ni-). Form of L. *omnis,* all, used in combination, as in *omniactive* (all-active, active everywhere), *omnibenevolent, omnicompetent, omnicredulous, omniprevalent,* and various other words, mostly of obvious meaning.

om-ni-bus (om′ni-bus). [L., 'for all,' dat. pl. of *omnis,* all.] **I.** *a.* Pertaining to or covering numerous distinct objects or items at once: as, an *omnibus* bill or resolution. **II.** *n.*; pl. *-buses* (-bus-ez). A long-bodied, four-wheeled public vehicle with seats inside and sometimes also on the roof, used for carrying passengers, usually between fixed stations, orig. having the seats extending lengthwise along the sides and the entrance at the rear, but now often otherwise arranged; a bus; also, a large box in a theater or the like, to hold a number of persons (also called *omnibus-box*); also, a waiter's assistant in a hotel or restaurant.

om-ni-fa-ri-ous (om-ni-fā′ri-us), *a.* [L. *omnifarius*: see *omni-* and *-farious.*] Of all forms, varieties, or kinds.—**om-ni-fa′ri-ous-ness,** *n.*

om-nif-ic (om-nif′ik), *a.* [L. *omnis,* all, + *-ficus,* < *facere,* make.] Creating all things: as, "Silence, ye troubled waves, and thou deep, peace, Said then the *omnific* Word" (Milton's "Paradise Lost," vii. 217).

om-ni-form (om′ni-fôrm), *a.* [L. *omniformis,* < *omnis,* all, + *forma,* form.] Of all forms or shapes; taking any or every form or shape: as, the *omniform* sea.—**om-ni-for′mi-ty** (-fôr′mi-ti), *n.*

om-nig-e-nous (om-nij′e-nus), *a.* [L. *omnigenus,* < *omnis,* all, + *genus,* kind.] Of all kinds: as, "a vast and *omnigenous* mass of information" (J. H. Newman's "Idea of a University," ii. 7).

om-nip-o-tence (om-nip′ō-tẹns), *n.* The quality of being omnipotent; almighty or unlimited power; esp., infinite power as an attribute of deity; hence [*cap.*], God.

om-nip-o-tent (om-nip′ō-tẹnt). [L. *omnipotens* (*-ent-*), < *omnis,* all, + *potens,* E. *potent.*] **I.** *a.* Almighty, or infinite in power, as God or a deity, or attributes of deity (as, "The Lord God *omnipotent* reigneth," Rev. xix. 6; the *omnipotent* will of God); hence, in general, having absolute power, or unlimited or very great authority or influence (as, "The Senate was . . . made *omnipotent* and irresponsible": Froude's "Cæsar," viii.); sometimes, capable of anything, arrant, or utter (humorous: as, "The most *omnipotent* villain that ever cried 'Stand' to a true man," Shakspere's "1 Henry IV.," i. 2. 121). **II.** *n.* An omnipotent being; esp. [*cap.*], with *the,* the Almighty, or God (as, "Boasting I could subdue The *Omnipotent*": Milton's "Paradise Lost," iv. 86).—**om-nip′o-tent-ly,** *adv.*

om-ni-pres-ent (om-ni-prez′ẹnt), *a.* [ML. *omnipræsens* (*-ent-*), < L. *omnis,* all, + *præsens,* E. *present*[1].] Present everywhere at the same time (as, "the *omnipresent* God": Godwin's "Caleb Williams," xix.); also, present or found everywhere (as, "the *omnipresent* Times newspaper": Kinglake's "Eothen," xviii.).—**om-ni-pres′ence,** *n.*—**om-ni-pres′ent-ly,** *adv.*

om-nis-cience (om-nish′ẹns), *n.* The quality of being omniscient; infinite or very extensive knowledge; hence [*cap.*], God (as, "the eye of *Omniscience,* pursuing the guilty sinner": Godwin's "Caleb Williams," xl.).

om-nis-cient (om-nish′ẹnt). [L. *omnis,* all, + *sciens* (*scient-*), ppr. of *scire,* know.] **I.** *a.* Knowing all things, or having infinite knowledge (as, "What can 'scape the eye Of God all-seeing, or deceive his heart *Omniscient*?" Milton's "Paradise Lost," x. 7); sometimes, having very extensive knowledge. **II.** *n.* An omniscient being; esp. [*cap.*], with *the,* God.—**om-nis′cient-ly,** *adv.*

om-ni-tude (om′ni-tūd), *n.* [L. *omnis*, all: see *-tude*.] The state or fact of being or comprising all; universality.

om-ni-um=gath-er-um (om′ni-um-gaᴛʜ′ẹ-rum), *n.* [L. *omnium*, 'of all,' + *gatherum*, a formation simulating Latin, < E. *gather*.] A miscellaneous collection; a confused mixture or medley. [Colloq.]

om-ni-vore (om′ni-vōr), *n.* An omnivorous animal.

om-niv-o-rous (om-niv′ọ-rus), *a.* [L. *omnivorus*, < *omnis*, all, + *vorare*, devour.] Devouring or eating everything; of animals, eating all kinds of food indiscriminately; fig., devouring or taking in everything, as with the mind; often, reading everything, or books, etc., of all sorts (as, "Miss Mehitable . . . was an *omnivorous* reader": Mrs. Stowe's "Oldtown Folks," vi.).—**om-niv′o-rous-ly**, *adv.*—**om-niv′o-rous-ness**, *n.*

o-mo-pha-gi-a (ō-mọ-fā′ji-ạ̈), *n.* [LL., < Gr. ὠμοφαγία, < ὠμός, raw, + φαγεῖν, eat.] The eating of raw flesh or raw food.—**o-mo-phag′ic** (-faj′ik), **o-moph-a-gous** (ọ-mof′ạ-gus), *a.*

o-mo-plate (ō′mọ-plāt), *n.* [F. *omoplate*, < Gr. ὠμοπλάτη, < ὦμος, shoulder, + πλάτη, flat surface.] The shoulder-blade or scapula.

om-pha-los (om′fạ-los), *n.* [LL., < Gr. ὀμφαλός: see *navel*.] The navel; fig., the central point; in *Gr. antiq.*, a rounded or conical stone in the temple of Apollo at Delphi, reputed to mark the center of the earth.—**om-phal′ic**(-fal′ik), *a.*

The Delphic Apollo, seated on the Omphalos ornamented with Fillets. (From a Greek vase.)

on (on), *prep.* [AS. *on*, *an*, on, in, to, = D. *aan* = G. *an* = Icel. *ā* = Goth. *ana*; akin to Gr. ἀνά, up, upon: see *ana-*.] A particle expressing primarily (1) position above and in contact with a supporting surface: as, *on* the table; and hence (2) immediate proximity: as, Bingen *on* the Rhine; to border *on* absurdity; (3) situation, place, etc.: as, a scar *on* the face; *on* the map; *on* a jury; (4) support, suspension, dependence, or reliance: as, *on* wheels or *on* foot; hanging *on* a nail; to live *on* one's family; *on* my honor; (5) state, condition, course, process, etc.: as, *on* fire; *on* the march; *on* strike; (6) ground or basis: as, *on* this account; *on* purpose; a duty *on* silk; profit *on* sales; (7) risk or liability; as, *on* pain of death; (8) time or occasion: as, *on* Sunday; *on* our arrival; (9) direction or end of motion: as, to go *on* one's way; to march *on* the capital; (10) encounter: as, to happen *on* a person or thing; (11) object or end of action, thought, desire, etc.: as, to gaze *on* a scene; to seize *on* an excuse; bent *on* mischief; to tell *on* one; (12) subject, reference, or respect: as, a poem *on* spring; views *on* public matters.—**on side**, on one's own or the proper side, as of the ball, etc., in football, hockey, etc.; not off side: also used, with a hyphen, as an adjective. Cf. *off side*, under *off*, *prep.* —**on**, *adv.* On a thing, place, or person (as, put the coffee *on*; put coal *on*); on one's self or itself (as, to put one's coat *on*; to take *on* polish or color); fast to a thing, as for support (as, to catch or hold *on*); also, toward a place, point, or object (as, to look *on*; broadside *on*); also, forward, onward, or along, as in any course or process (as, come *on*; to get *on* in the world; further *on*); with continuous procedure (as, to work *on*); also, into or in active operation or performance (as, turn *on* the gas; war is *on*; the watchman is *on* from 6 to 6).—**to be on to**, to be fully aware of or alive to (an attempt, scheme, situation, etc.); be aware of the activities, plans, or purposes of (a person, etc.). [Slang.]—**on.** **I.** *a.* Situated nearer; near; in *cricket*, noting that side of the wicket, or of the field, on which the batsman stands. **II.** *n.* The state or fact of being on; in *cricket*, the on side.

on-a-ger (on′ạ-jėr), *n.* [L. *onager*, *onagrus*, < Gr. ὄναγρος, < ὄνος, ass, + ἀγρός, field.] A wild ass, *Equus onager* (or *hemippus*), of southwestern Asia; also, an ancient and medieval engine of war for throwing stones.

Onager.

on-a-gra-ceous(on-ạ-grā′shius), *a.* [NL. *Onagra*, the typical genus, < Gr. ὀνάγρα, kind of plant.] Belonging to the *Onagraceæ*, or evening primrose family of plants.

o-nan-ism (ō′nạn-izm), *n.* [From *Onan*, son of Judah: see Gen. xxxviii. 9.] Sexual self-abuse; masturbation.—**o′nan-ist**, *n.*

once (wuns), *adv.* [ME. *ones*, *anes*, adv. (orig. genitive), < *on*, *an*, E. *one*.] A single time (as, *once* a day; "God speaketh *once*, yea twice," Job, xxxiii. 14; "A man can die but *once*," Shakspere's "2 Henry IV.," iii. 2. 251); also, even a single time, at any time, or ever (as, *once* seen, never forgotten; if the facts *once* become known; "Who may stand in thy sight when *once* thou art angry?" Ps. lxxvi. 7); also, at one time in the past, or formerly (as, a *once* powerful nation; "This world was *once* a fluid haze of light," Tennyson's "Princess," ii. 101); also, at some future time (as, "meditating that she must die *once*," Shakspere's "Julius Cæsar," iv. 3. 191: now rare).—**once and again**, more than once; repeatedly; now and again: as, "That good woman would open the door *once and again* in the morning, and put her head through" (Mrs. H. Ward's "Robert Elsmere," viii.).—**once for all**, once, for all time; once, finally and decisively: as, to settle a matter *once for all*; to refuse, *once for all*.—**once in a while**, now and then; occasionally: as, we see him *once in a while*.—**once or twice**, a few times: as, "So the merchants . . . lodged without Jerusalem *once or twice*" (Neh. xiii. 20).—**once over**, a single time over, or over once (as, to look a thing *once over*); hence, substantively, the action of looking over something once, or a single or brief glance of inspection (slang: as, to give a thing the, or a, *once over*).—**once upon**, or **on, a time**, once, in a former time or long ago: a favorite beginning of a legendary tale, children's story, or the like: as, "*Once on a time* (so runs the fable) A country mouse . . . Received a town mouse at his board" (Pope's "Imitations of Horace," Satires, ii. 6. 157).—**once**, *conj.* [For *if once* or *when once*: see *once*, *adv.*] If or when at any time; if ever; whenever: as, *once* suspicion arises, nothing can be done; *once* you reach the river, the way is plain.—**once**, *n.* One time, as of doing or occurring; a single occasion: as, only this *once*; *once* is enough.—**all at once**, all or wholly at one time (rather than gradually); suddenly: as, the end came *all at once*; *all at once* a light shone out.—**at once**, at one or the same time (as, do not all speak *at once*; *at once* a soldier and a poet); also, immediately, or without delay (as, come *at once*).—**for once**, for one time; on one occasion, at least or at any rate: as, try it *for once*. —**once**, *a.* That once was; former: as, a *once* friend.

on-cid-i-um (on-sid′i-um), *n.* [NL., dim. < Gr. ὄγκος, barb of an arrow; from the shape of the labellum.] Any of the tropical American epiphytic orchids constituting the genus *Oncidium*, some species of which, as *O. papilio*, have flowers resembling butterflies.

Oncidium (*O. papilio*).

on-col-o-gy (ong-kol'ǫ-ji), *n.* [Gr. ὄγκος, bulk, mass: see *-logy*.] The part of medical science that treats of tumors.—**on-co-log-i-cal** (ong-kǫ-loj'i-kạl), *a.*

on-com-ing (on'kum''ing), *n.* The coming on or approaching of something; approach: as, the *oncoming* of winter; "the *oncoming* of numbness" (George Eliot's "Middlemarch," xx.).—**on'com''ing,** *a.* Coming on; approaching.

on dit (ôṅ dē). [F.] 'One says'; they say; hence, substantively, a report; an item of gossip.

on-do-graph (on'dǫ-gràf), *n.* [F. *onde* (< L. *unda*), wave, + Gr. γράφειν, write.] In *elect.*, an instrument for recording oscillatory variations, as in alternating currents.

on-dom-e-ter (on-dom'e-tėr), *n.* [F. *onde* (< L. *unda*), wave, + Gr. μέτρον, measure.] In *elect.*, an instrument for measuring Hertzian waves.

one (wun), *a.* [ME. *one, on, an,* < AS. *ān* = D. *een* = G. *ein* = Icel. *einn* = Goth. *ains*, one; akin to L. *unus*, one, Gr. οἴνη, ace on dice: cf. *an*[1].] Being a single unit or individual (rather than two or more: as, *one* apple; *one* cent; *one* piece, *one* half, or *one* third; *one* man against many); a single; also, being a person, thing, or individual instance of a number or kind indicated (as, *one* member of the party; *one* end of a plank; not to know *one* color from another); also, a certain (often used in naming a person otherwise unknown or undescribed: as, *one* John Smith was chosen as leader; "*one* Miss Willis, who had been her intimate companion at the boarding-school," Smollett's "Humphry Clinker," Oct. 26); a particular (day, night, time, etc., in the past: as, I saw him *one* evening last week; "Thus it chanced *one* morn," Tennyson's "Guinevere," 21); some (day, etc., in the future: as, "You will see both of them on the canvas *one* day," Thackeray's "Newcomes," xxxv.); also, single through union or combination (as, "They two shall be *one* flesh," Eph. v. 31; "All the people answered with *one* voice," Ex. xxiv. 3); single through agreement or harmony (as, all were of *one* mind or opinion; to assent with *one* accord); of a single kind, nature, or character, or the same (as, graphite and the diamond are chemically *one* substance; "Lo, all our pomp of yesterday Is *one* with Nineveh and Tyre!" Kipling's "Recessional").—**all one** (used predicatively), all the same, as in character, meaning, consequence, etc.: as, art, science, and literature are *all one* to him; these statements were *all one* to us; now or later, it is *all one* as far as we are concerned.—**one,** *n.* The first and lowest whole number, or a symbol, as 1 or i, representing it; unity; a unit; a single person or thing (as, to come *one* at a time, or by *ones* and twos; there is only *one* left).—**at one,** in a state of unity, agreement, or accord: as, hearts *at one*; we are *at one* on that point; "He shewed himself unto them as they strove, and would have set them *at one* again" (Acts, vii. 26). Cf. *atone*.—**number one.** See under *number*, *n.*—**one and all,** every one, individually and collectively.—**one by one,** one after another; singly and in succession: as, to file *one by one* past a point; "He together calls, Or several *one by one*, the regent powers" (Milton's "Paradise Lost," v. 697).—**to make one,** to form or be one of a number, assembly, or party, as on some occasion: as, "I *made one* upon that winter's journey of which so many tales have gone abroad" (Stevenson's "Master of Ballantrae," i.).—**one,** *pron.* A person or thing of a number or kind indicated or understood (as, *one* of the poets or the poems; *one* of the best reasons given; such a *one* as you describe; this *one*; each *one*); often (to avoid repetition), a person or thing of the kind just mentioned (as, "The only way to have a friend is to be *one*," Emerson's "Essays," Friendship; the portraits are fine *ones*); in certain pronominal combinations, a person (unless definitely specified otherwise: as, any *one*; every *one*; no *one*; some *one*); with a defining clause or other qualifying words, a person or a personified being or agency (as, consult *one* who knows; *one* experienced in the law; *one* of ripe judgment; the evil *one*; "I have commanded my sanctified *ones*, I have also called my mighty *ones*," Isa. xiii. 3); also, a certain person or being (archaic: as, "Hence I go, and *one* will crown me king Far in the spiritual city," Tennyson's "Holy Grail," 482); also, some person indefinitely, or some one (archaic: as, "Oh that *one* would give me drink of the water of the well of Beth-lehem!" 2 Sam. xxiii. 15); also, a person indefinitely, or any one of us all (as, to give *one* a thrashing; "a good cause as *one* would desire," Shakspere's "As You Like It," iii. 4. 5; "Familiar to *one* from the days of early childhood are the forms of the Egyptian Pyramids," Kinglake's "Eothen," xix.); often, a person of the speaker's kind, or such as the speaker himself (as, *one* cannot do a thing like that; *one* does not like to press *one's* own claims at such a time).—**one another,** a collocation of *one*, orig. in the nominative, with *another*, in an oblique case (as, they struck *one another*, that is, they struck, *one* striking *another*), later taken, in oblique cases, as a compound reciprocal pronoun (as, they struck at *one another*; to be in *one another's* way). See *each other*, under *each*, *pron.*—**one of these days,** some day or some time before long: as, you will hear from me *one of these days*.—**one's self,** a person's self, rather than another (as, to give a few facts about *one's self*): often used for emphasis (as, one must do it *one's self*) or reflexively (as, one hurts *one's self* by such methods). Cf. *oneself*.

-one. [Gr. -ωνη, in fem. patronymics.] A noun suffix used in the names of chemical derivatives, esp. ketones.

one-eyed (wun'īd), *a.* Having but one eye; also, having but one eye capable of seeing.

one-fold (wun'fōld), *a.* Consisting of but one; single; simple.

one-hand-ed (wun'han''ded), *a.* Having but one hand; also, having but one hand capable of use; also, used or performed with one hand.

one-horse (wun'hôrs), *a.* Drawn or worked by a single horse (as, "a little *one-horse* sleigh": Mrs. Stowe's "Oldtown Folks," xxxvii.); using or having only a single horse (as, a *one-horse* farmer); hence, limited in scope, capacity, or importance, minor, or petty (colloq.: as, a *one-horse* concern; a *one-horse* town; "some *one-horse* junction near the Dutch frontier that I can't even learn the name of," H. G. Wells's "Mr. Britling," ii. 1. § 14).

o-nei-ro-crit-ic (ǫ-nī-rǫ-krit'ik), *n.* [Gr. ὀνειροκριτικός, pertaining to the interpretation of dreams, < ὀνειροκρίτης, interpreter of dreams, < ὄνειρος, dream, + κρίνειν, distinguish, judge.] An interpreter of dreams; also, oneirocriticism.—**o-nei-ro-crit'i-cal,** *a.* Pertaining to or practising the interpretation of dreams.—**o-nei-ro-crit'i-cism** (-sizm), *n.* The art of interpreting dreams. Also **o-nei-ro-crit'ics.**

o-nei-ro-man-cy (ǫ-nī'rǫ-man-si), *n.* [Gr. ὄνειρος, dream, + μαντεία, divination.] Divination through dreams.—**o-nei'ro-man-cer,** *n.*

one-legged (wun'legd or -leg''ed), *a.* Having but one leg; fig., having but half of what is proper; one-sided.

one-ness (wun'nes), *n.* The quality of being one; singleness; unity; sameness.

on-er (wun'ėr), *n.* [From *one*.] A person or thing of a unique or remarkable kind (slang); often, a person expert at or much addicted to something (slang: as, "Miss Sally's such a *one-er* for that," Dickens's "Old Curiosity Shop," lviii.); also, something denoted by or in some way connected with the number one (colloq.).

on-er-ous (on'ẹ-rus), *a.* [OF. *onereus* (F. *onéreux*), < L. *onerosus*, < *onus* (*oner-*), load: cf. *onus*.] Burdensome, oppressive, or troublesome (as, *onerous* duties or responsibilities); specif., in *law*, of the nature of or imposing a legal burden or obligation.—**on'er-ous-ly,** *adv.*—**on'er-ous-ness,** *n.*

one-self (wun-self'), *pron.* A contracted form of *one's self* (see under *one*, *pron.*), common in recent use.

one-sid-ed (wun'sī'ded), *a.* Having but one side, or but one developed or finished side; having one side larger or more developed than the other; having the parts all on one side, as an inflorescence; turned or leaning to one side; also, existing or occurring on one side only; also, in fig. use, concerned with or considering but one side of a matter or question; partial, unjust, or unfair (as, a *one-sided* judgment); in *law*, unilateral, as a contract.—**one'-sid'ed-ly,** *adv.*—**one'-sid'ed-ness,** *n.*

one-step (wun'step), *n.* A kind of round dance, danced by couples to rag-time.

one-time (wun'tīm), *a.* Having been (as specified) at one time; former; quondam: as, the *one-time* possessor of a large fortune; his *one-time* partner.

on-fall (on′fâl), *n.* An onset; an attack: as, "I was all strung up to meet and to resist an *onfall*" (Stevenson's "David Balfour," x.).

on-flow (on′flō), *n.* An onward flow.

on-ion (un′yọn), *n.* [OF. F. *oignon*, < L. *unio*(*n*-), large pearl, onion: see *union*.] A widely cultivated liliaceous plant, *Allium cepa*, having an edible succulent bulb of pungent taste and smell; also, the bulb; also, any of certain similar plants, as *A. fistulosum* ('Welsh onion,' or cibol).—**on′ion=fly,** *n.* A dipterous insect whose larva feeds underground on the onion; esp., *Phorbia* (or *Anthomyia*) *ceparum* of Europe, now widely distributed in the U. S., and a serious pest.—**on′ion=mag″got,** *n.* The larva of an onion-fly.—**on′ion=skin,** *n.* A thin, translucent, glossy kind of paper.—**on′ion-y,** *a.* Onion-like; having the taste or smell of onions.

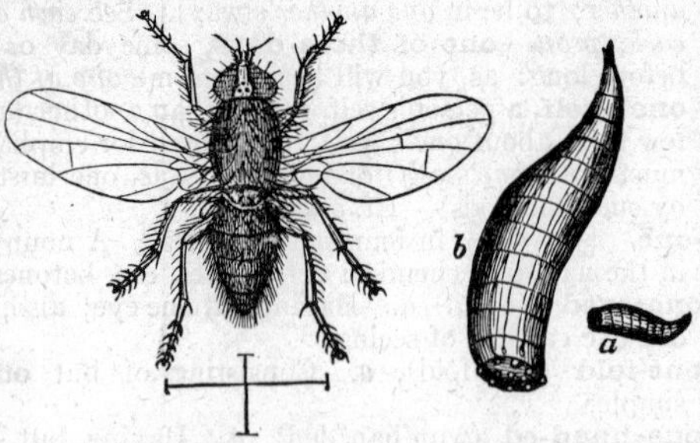

Onion-fly (*Phorbia ceparum*). (Cross shows natural size.) — *a*, larva, natural size; *b*, larva, enlarged.

on-look-er (on′lu̇k″ėr), *n.* One who looks on; a spectator.

on-ly (ōn′li), *a.* [AS. *ānlīc*, *ǣnlīc*, < *ān*, E. *one*.] Being the single one or the relatively few of the kind, or sole (as, an *only* son; the *only* children in the colony; the *only* time we met; the *only* one or ones found); being one or ones of which there are no more; also, solitary or lonely (now prov. Eng.); also, single in superiority or distinction (as, "He is the *only* man of Italy, Always excepted my dear Claudio": Shakspere's "Much Ado about Nothing," iii. 1. 92); also, singular, extraordinary, or odd (prov. Eng.).—**on′ly. I.** *adv.* Without others or anything further, alone, solely, or exclusively (as, he *only*, or *only* he, remained; not from friendship *only*; not *only* these but many others; the property of this company *only*); also, no more than, merely, but, or just (as, he is *only*, or *only* just, alive; if you would *only* consent; he *only* thought he saw her; *only* last night); also, singly, or as the only one (as, "the *only* begotten Son of God": John, iii. 18); also, above all others†, or preëminently†. **II.** *conj.* But (introducing a single restriction, restraining circumstance, or the like: as, "Pharaoh said, I will let you go . . . *only* ye shall not go very far away," Ex. viii. 28; I would have gone, *only* you objected); except that; sometimes, but or except (*for*: as, *only for* him you would not be here: now colloq.). **III.** *prep.* But; except: as, there are none *only* this. [Prov. or colloq.]

on-o-mas-tic (on-ọ-mas′tik), *a.* [Gr. ὀνομαστικός, pertaining to naming, < ὀνομάζειν, to name, < ὄνομα, name.] Of, pertaining to, or connected with a name or names, or the naming of something; consisting of names; in *law*, noting the signature of an instrument the body of which is in the handwriting of another person.

on-o-mas-ti-con (on-ọ-mas′ti-kon), *n.* [Gr. ὀνομαστικόν, prop. neut. of ὀνομαστικός: see *onomastic*.] A vocabulary of names, now of proper names, esp. of persons, arranged in alphabetical or other regular order.

on-o-mat-o-pœ-ia (on-ọ-mat-ọ-pē′ịạ), *n.* [LL., < Gr. ὀνοματοποιία, < ὄνομα (ὀνοματ-), name, + ποιεῖν, make.] The formation of a name or word by imitating sound associated with the thing designated (as, the words 'buzz,' 'hum,' 'cuckoo,' and 'whippoorwill' are due to *onomatopœia*); the imitative principle in word-formation; also, a word so formed; in *rhet.*, the use of imitative and naturally suggestive words for rhetorical effect. Also **on-o-mat″o-po-ē′sis** (-pọ-ē′sis).—**on-o-mat-o-pœ′ic** (-pē′ik), **on-o-mat″o-po-et′ic** (-pọ-et′ik), *a.* Pertaining to or characterized by onomatopœia; imitative in sound; echoic.—**on-o-mat″o-po-et′i-cal-ly,** *adv.*

on-rush (on′rush), *n.* A rush onward: as, "the tremendous *onrush* and check of the German attack in the west that opened the great war" (H. G. Wells's "Mr. Britling," ii. 1. § 12).—**on′rush″ing,** *a.*

on-set (on′set), *n.* A setting or rushing upon; an assault or attack (as, "A violent *onset* was made upon the gate by the whole Spanish force": Motley's "Dutch Republic," iii. 6); also, a beginning or start (as, "There is surely no greater wisdom than well to time the beginnings and *onsets* of things": Bacon's "Essays," Of Delays).—**on′set″ter,** *n.*—**on′set″ting,** *a.*

on=side (on′sīd′), *a.* See *on side*, under *on*, *prep.*

on-slaught (on′slât), *n.* [Cf. D. *aanslag*, stroke, attempt, MLG. *anslach*, attack, onslaught.] An onset, assault, or attack, esp. a vigorous or furious one.

on-sweep (on′swēp), *n.* A sweeping onward; onward sweep: as, "the *onsweep* of our van" (Kipling's "General Joubert").

on-to (on′tọ), *prep.* [A combination of *on* and *to* (after the analogy of *into*) sometimes used in the sense defined as expressing more than is conveyed by the words *on to* separately. The combination *onto* is more common in spoken (colloquial) than in literary use, being avoided by most writers, and is condemned as objectionable in any case where the separate words equally well convey the meaning intended.] To a place or position on; upon; on: as, to throw a ball *onto* the roof; to get *onto* a horse; a boat driven *onto* the rocks; "I wormed your address from him and threw myself *onto* the boat rejoicing" (L. Merrick's "Conrad in Quest of His Youth," x.). See etym.

onto-. Form of Gr. ὤν (ὀντ-), being, used in combination.—**on-to-gen-e-sis** (on-tọ-jen′e-sis), *n.* Ontogeny.—**on″to-ge-net′ic** (-jẹ-net′ik), *a.*—**on-tog′e-ny** (-toj′e-ni), *n.* [+ *-geny*.] In *biol.*, the development or evolution of an individual organism. Cf. *phylogeny*.—**on-to-gen′ic** (-jen′ik), *a.*—**on-tog′e-nist,** *n.*—**on-tol′o-gy** (-tol′ọ-ji), *n.* [+ *-logy*.] The science of being; the branch of metaphysics that investigates the nature of being and of the essence of things.—**on-to-log′i-cal** (-loj′i-kạl), *a.*—**on-tol′o-gist,** *n.*

o-nus (ō′nus), *n.* [L., load, burden: cf. *onerous* and *exonerate*.] A burden; a responsibility: as, "to guard against any mischance, of which the *onus* may fall upon myself" (Marryat's "Peter Simple," liv.); "The *onus* of proving that it was not right lay with those who disputed its being so" (S. Butler's "Way of All Flesh," xxxi.).

on-ward (on′wạrd). **I.** *adv.* Toward a point ahead or in front; forward, as in space or time; also, at a position or point in advance (as, "My grief lies *onward* and my joy behind": Shakspere's "Sonnets," l.). **II.** *a.* Directed or moving onward or forward; forward; also, situated in advance (rare); also, advanced, or being in a condition of advancement (rare).—**on′wards,** *adv.* Onward.

on-y-cha (on′i-kạ), *n.* [LL., < Gr. ὄνυχα, acc. of ὄνυξ, kind of aromatic substance (see def.), orig. nail, claw: see *onyx*.] An ingredient of the incense used in the Mosaic ritual: supposed to be the operculum of a marine gastropod. See Ex. xxx. 34.

-onym. Noun termination from Gr. ὄνυμα, name, as in *allonym*, *antonym*, *cryptonym*, *toponym*.

on-yx (on′iks), *n.* [L., < Gr. ὄνυξ, nail, claw, veined gem, thickening in the cornea; akin to L. *unguis*, nail, claw.] A variety of quartz consisting of layers or bands which differ in color, used for ornamental purposes; also, in *pathol.*, a collection of pus in the cornea, resembling a finger-nail.

Onyx.

oö-. Form of Gr. ᾠόν, egg, used in combination.—**o-ö-blast** (ō′ọ-blast), *n.* [+ *-blast*.] In *biol.*, a primitive or formative ovum not yet developed into a true ovum.—**o′ö-cyte** (-sīt), *n.* [+ *-cyte*.] In *biol.*, an ovum in the stage which precedes maturation.

oo-dle (ö′dl), *n.* [Prov. (Ir.) form of *huddle*.] A heap; a large quantity: usually in *pl.*: as, "You haven't got much plumbago . . . but you've got dead *oodles* of silica" (G. W. Cable's "John March, Southerner," xxiv.); *oodles* of money. [Slang.]

oof (öf), *n.* [Said to be for earlier *ooftish,* Yiddish for G. *auf tische,* 'on (the) table' (as 'cash down').] Cash; money. [Slang, Eng.]—**oof′=bird,** *n.* The (imaginary) bird that produces oof; hence, a person from whom money may be obtained. [Slang, Eng.]—**oof′y,** *a.* Rich; wealthy. [Slang, Eng.]

o-ög-a-mous (ọ-og′ạ-mus), *a.* [See *oö-* and *-gamous.*] In *biol.*, heterogamous.—**o-ög′a-my,** *n.*

o-ö-gen-e-sis (ō-ọ-jen′e-sis), *n.* [See *oö-* and *genesis.*] In *biol.*, the genesis or origin and development of the ovum. Also **o-ög-e-ny** (ọ-oj′e-ni).—**o″ö-ge-net′ic** (-jẹ-net′ik), *a.*

o-ö-go-ni-um (ō-ọ-gō′ni-um), *n.*; pl. *-nia* (-ni-ạ̈). [NL., < Gr. ᾠόν, egg, + *-gonium* as in *archegonium.*] In *bot.*, the female reproductive organ in certain thallophytic plants, usually a more or less spherical sac containing one or more oöspheres; in *biol.*, one of the primitive germ-cells which undergo division and give rise to the oöcytes.—**o-ö-go′ni-al,** *a.*

oo-la-kan, oo-la-chan (ö′lạ-kạn), *n.* [Native name.] The candle-fish, *Thaleichthys pacificus,* of the northwestern coast of America.

o-ö-lite (ō′ọ-līt), *n.* [F. *oolithe,* < Gr. ᾠόν, egg, + λίθος, stone.] A rock (usually limestone) composed of rounded concretions resembling the roe of a fish; [*cap.*] in *geol.*, the later division of the European Jurassic, which contains such limestone.—**o-ö-lit′ic** (-lit′ik), *a.*

o-öl-o-gy (ọ-ol′ọ-ji), *n.* [See *oö-* and *-logy.*] The part of ornithology that treats of birds' eggs.—**o-ö-log-i-cal** (ō-ọ-loj′i-kạl), *a.*—**o-öl′o-gist,** *n.*

oo-long (ö′long), *n.* [Chinese *wu,* black, + *lung,* dragon.] A variety of black tea.

oom (ōm), *n.* [D.] In Dutch use, uncle: often prefixed, affectionately or familiarly, to the name of an elderly man (as, *Oom* Paul, popular name of Stephanus Johannes Paulus Kruger, 1825–1904, president of the South African Republic).

oo-mi-ak (ö′mi-ak), *n.* See *umiak.*

o-ö-phore (ō′ọ-fōr), *n.* [Gr. ᾠοφόρος, bearing eggs, < ᾠόν, egg, + φέρειν, bear.] In *bot.*, that stage or form in certain plants, as ferns, mosses, etc., which, in the alternation of generations, bears sexual organs.—**o-ö-phor′ic** (-for′ik), *a.*

o-ö-pho-rec-to-my (ō″ọ-fọ-rek′tọ-mi), *n.* [NL. *oophoron,* ovary, + Gr. ἐκ, out of, + -τομία, E. *-tomy.*] In *surg.*, excision of an ovary.—**o″ö-pho-rec′to-mist,** *n.*

o-ö-pho-ri-tis (ō″ọ-fọ-rī′tis), *n.* [NL., < *oophoron,* ovary, < Gr. ᾠοφόρον, neut. of ᾠοφόρος, bearing eggs: see *oöphore.*] In *pathol.*, inflammation of an ovary; ovaritis.

o-ö-phyte (ō′ọ-fīt), *n.* [See *oö-* and *-phyte.*] Same as *oöphore.*—**o-ö-phyt′ic** (-fit′ik), *a.*

oo-ri-al (ö′ri-ạl), *n.* [Native name.] A wild sheep, *Ovis cycloceros,* of Asia.

oo-rie, ou-rie (ö′ri), *a.* [Cf. Icel. *ūrigr,* wet, < *ūr,* drizzling rain.] Cold or chill; chilly or shivering; weakly or drooping; dreary or dismal; dull or dingy. [Sc.]

o-ö-sperm (ō′ọ-spėrm), *n.* [Gr. ᾠόν, egg, + σπέρμα, seed.] In *zoöl.*, a fertilized ovum; in *bot.*, an oöspore.

o-ö-sphere (ō′ọ-sfēr), *n.* [See *oö-* and *sphere.*] In *bot.*, a female reproductive cell which after fertilization develops into an oöspore.

o-ö-spore (ō′ọ-spōr), *n.* [See *oö-* and *spore.*] In *bot.*, the cell or spore resulting from the fertilization of an oösphere, which possesses the power of germination and growth after a period of rest.—**o-ö-spor′ic** (-spor′ik), **o-ös-po-rous** (ọ-os′pọ-rus), *a.*

o-ö-the-ca (ō-ọ-thē′kạ̈), *n.*; pl. *-cæ* (-sē). [NL., < Gr. ᾠόν, egg, + θήκη, case.] In *zoöl.*, a case or capsule containing eggs, as that of certain gastropods and insects.—**o-ö-the′-cal,** *a.*

ooze (öz), *n.* [In part < AS. *wōs,* juice, moisture, in part < AS. *wāse,* mud, with confusion between the derivatives of the two forms.] Juice†; specif., an infusion of oak-bark, sumac, etc., used in tanning; also, soft mud, or slime; a marsh or bog; specif., a calcareous mud (chiefly the shells of small organisms) covering parts of the ocean-bottom; also, the act of oozing; exudation; gentle flow; also, that which oozes; an oozing stream.—**ooze,** *v.*; *oozed, oozing.* **I.** *intr.* Of moisture, etc., to percolate or exude, as through pores or small openings (as, "The mineral waters . . . *ooze* forth from the crevices of a rock": H. Melville's "Typee," xx.); hence, of air, etc., to pass slowly or gradually as if through pores or small openings (as, "She ascribed these sounds to the wind *oozing* through the rat holes of the old mansion": Irving's "Tales of a Traveler," i. 4); fig., of information, courage, etc., to leak or pass (*out,* etc.) slowly or imperceptibly (as, "Something of this nature *oozed* out when he was last in Durrisdeer," Stevenson's "Master of Ballantrae," viii.; "I own my courage '*oozed* out' a little at this sight," Maria Edgeworth's "Belinda," iv.); also, of a substance, to exude moisture, etc. **II.** *tr.* To make by oozing (as, "a scarcely perceptible creek, *oozing* its way through a wilderness of reeds and slime": Poe's "Gold-Bug"); also, to exude (moisture, etc.).—**ooze′=leath″er,** *n.* Leather prepared from calfskin or other skin so as to have a soft, velvety finish on the flesh side.—**ooz′y,** *a.* Containing ooze or mud (as, an *oozy* pool); composed of or resembling ooze, soft mud, or slime (as, "a low *oozy* meadow," Parkman's "Oregon Trail," ii.; "the shore on that side being a soft *oozy* sand," Defoe's "Robinson Crusoe," i. 17); also, exuding moisture; damp with moisture.—**ooz′i-ly,** *adv.*—**ooz′i-ness,** *n.*

o-pa-ci-ty (ọ-pas′i-ti), *n.*; pl. *-ties* (-tiz). [F. *opacité,* < L. *opacitas,* < *opacus,* E. *opaque.*] The state of being opaque; darkness; imperviousness to light; imperviousness to sound, etc.; obscurity of meaning; denseness or stupidity; also, something opaque; an opaque object, part, or spot.

o-pa-cous (ọ-pā′kus), *a.* Same as *opaque.* [Archaic.]

o-pah (ō′pạ̈), *n.* [W. Afr.] A large, brilliantly colored deep-sea fish, *Lampris luna.*

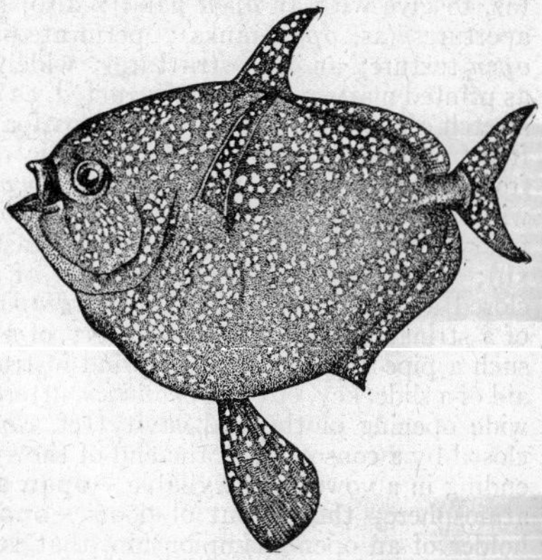

Opah.

o-pal (ō′pạl). [L. *opalus,* < Gr. ὀπάλλιος, opal: cf. Skt. *upala,* stone.] **I.** *n.* A mineral, an amorphous form of silica, found in many varieties and colors (often a milky white), certain of which have a peculiar iridescence and are valued as gems. See *cacholong, geyserite, girasol* (fire-opal), *hyalite, hydrophane, wood-opal.* **II.** *a.* Pertaining to or resembling the opal; opalescent: as, an *opal* appearance; "the *opal* murmuring sea" (Jean Ingelow's "Honours," i.).—**o-pal-esce** (ō-pạ-les′), *v. i.*; *-esced, -escing.* [See *-esce.*] To exhibit a play of colors like that of the opal.—**o-pal-es-cent** (ō-pạ-les′ẹnt), *a.* Exhibiting a play of colors like that of the opal; having a milky iridescence.—**o-pal-es′cence,** *n.*—**o-pal-esque** (ō-pạ-lesk′), *a.* [See *-esque.*] Opal-like; opalescent.—**o′pal-ine** (-in), *a.* Of or like opal; opalescent.—**o′pal-ize,** *v. t.*; *-ized, -izing.* To convert into opal; render opaline or opalescent.

o-paque (ọ-pāk′). [= F. *opaque,* < L. *opacus,* shady, darkened.] **I.** *a.* Being in shadow†; not illuminated†; also, not shining or bright; dark; dull; also, impermeable to light, or not transparent (as, "It was so dark that . . . he could scarcely distinguish the transparent window from the *opaque* walls of his chamber," Dickens's "Christmas Carol," ii.; "The water is so charged with mud and sand that it is perfectly *opaque,*" Parkman's "Oregon Trail," i.); sometimes, impenetrable to sight; also, not transmitting or conducting sound, heat, electricity, etc.; in fig. use, hard to understand; not clear or lucid; obscure; also, unintelligent; dense; stupid. **II.** *n.* Something opaque; something through which light cannot pass.—**o-paque′,** *v. t.*; *opaqued, opaquing.* To render opaque: as, "his ray, *opaqued* with intermittent mist" (S. Lanier's "Crystal").—**o-paque′ly,** *adv.*—**o-paque′ness,** *n.*

ope (ōp), *a.* and *v.* Reduced form of *open.* [Archaic.]

o-pen (ō′pn), *a.* [AS. *open* = D. *open* = G. *offen* = Icel. *opinn,* open; prob. from the root of E. *up.*] Not shut, as a door, gate, etc.; also, not closed, covered, or shut up, as a

(variable) ḑ as d or j, ș as s or sh, ţ as t or ch, ẓ as z or zh; *o,* F. cloche; ü, F. menu; ċh, Sc. loch; ṅ, F. bonbon; ′, primary accent; ″, secondary accent; †, obsolete; <, from; +, and; =, equals. See also lists at beginning of book.

house, box, drawer, etc.; also, not inclosed as by barriers, as a space; hence, that may be entered, used, shared, competed for, etc., by all (as, an *open* session; an *open* market; an *open* championship); accessible or available (often with *to*: as, the only course still *open*; a privilege *open* to a certain class of persons, or to all); accessible to appeals, ideas, offers, etc. (often with *to*: as, to be *open* to conviction, impressions, or proposals); without prohibition as to hunting or fishing, as a season; without legal restrictions, or not enforcing legal restrictions, as to saloons, gambling-places, etc., as a town or the like (colloq.); unfilled, as a position; disengaged, as time; undecided, as a question; not yet balanced or adjusted, as an account; also, having no cover, roof, etc., as a boat or a carriage; also, not covered or protected, or being exposed or bare (as, to lay *open* internal parts with a knife); hence, liable or subject (*to*: as, *open* to temptation; a matter *open* to question); also, exposed to general view or knowledge, or existing, carried on, etc., without concealment (as, to do a thing in an *open* manner; *open* disregard of rules); public; acting without concealment or publicly, as a person; also, unreserved, candid, or frank, as persons or their speech, aspect, etc. (as, "I will be *open* and sincere with you," Addison, in "Tatler," 97; "a face so *open* and frank that it attracted our notice at once," Parkman's "Oregon Trail," ii.); also, expanded, extended, or spread out (as, an *open* flower; the *open* hand; an *open* newspaper); also, generous, liberal, or bounteous (as, to give with an *open* hand); also, having openings or apertures (as, *open* ranks); perforated or porous (as, an *open* texture; an *open* structure); widely spaced or leaded, as printed matter; also, unobstructed, as a passage, country, stretch of water, view, etc.; not constipated, as the bowels; free from ice (as, *open* water in arctic regions); free from frost, or being mild or moderate (as, *open* weather; an *open* winter; "The days were in the beginning *open*, but the nights frosty from the first," Stevenson's "Master of Ballantrae," xi.); *naut.*, free from fog; in *music*, of an organ-pipe, not closed at the upper end (cf. *open diapason*, at *diapason*); of a string, not stopped by a finger; of a note, produced by such a pipe or string or, on a wind-instrument, without the aid of a slide, key, etc.; in *phonetics*, uttered with a relatively wide opening of the oral cavity (cf. *close*², *a.*); also, not closed by a consonant at the end of the syllable, as a vowel; ending in a vowel, as a syllable.—**open air,** the unconfined atmosphere; the air out of doors.—**open champion,** the holder of an open championship, that is, one that may be competed for by all, without restrictions.—**open door,** fig., free admission or access; admission to all upon equal terms; specif., the policy of the admission of all nations to a country upon equal terms, esp. for purposes of trade.—**open forum,** a forum or assembly for the discussion of questions of public interest, open to all who wish to take part.—**open house,** a house hospitably thrown open to all friends who may wish to visit it or enjoy its entertainment: as, "I keep *open house*, and receive all comers, for the honour of old England" (Smollett's "Humphry Clinker," June 26).—**open shop.** See under *shop*, *n.*—**o′pen,** *n.* An open or clear space; also, an opening or aperture; also, an opening or opportunity.—**in open**†, in public; openly. See Shakspere's "Henry VIII.," iii. 2. 404.—**the open,** the open, uninclosed, or unobstructed country; the open water, as of the sea; the open air; in fig. use, the situation of one who does not use or seek concealment (as, to come out into *the open* with one's plans or endeavors).—**o′pen,** *v.* [AS. *openian.*] **I.** *tr.* To move (a door, gate, etc.) from a shut or closed position so as to admit of passage; also, to make (a house, box, drawer, etc.) open; also, to render (any inclosed space) open to passage or access; hence, in general, to give access to; make accessible or available, as for use; establish for the entrance or use of the public, customers, etc. (as, to *open* an office or a shop); also, to render accessible to knowledge, enlightenment, sympathy, etc. (as, "Then *opened* he their understanding, that they might understand the scriptures," Luke, xxiv. 45; "He must travel to *open* his mind, to enlarge his views," Steele, in "Guardian," 34); also, to make an incision or opening in (as, "Who stooping, *open'd* my left side, and took From thence a rib": Milton's "Paradise Lost," viii. 465); cut or break into; also, to uncover, lay bare, or expose to view (as, "Herbs . . . that sudden flower'd, *Opening* their various colours": Milton's "Paradise Lost," vii. 318); disclose, reveal, or divulge (as, to *open* one's mind, feelings, or plans to a person; "He had *opened* a dangerous secret to an entire stranger," Motley's "Dutch Republic," v. 4); expound, explain, or interpret (obs. or archaic: as, "while he *opened* to us the scriptures," Luke, xxiv. 32); also, to expand, extend, or spread out (as, to *open* one's hand, a fan, or a map); also, to make less compact, less close together, or the like (as, to *open* ranks); also, to clear of obstructions, as a passage, etc.; make (bodily passages) clear; also, to make or produce (an opening of some kind) by cutting or breaking, or by pushing aside or removing obstructions (as, "Soon had his crew *Open'd* into the hill a spacious wound," Milton's "Paradise Lost," i. 689; to *open* a breach in the enemy's walls; to *open* a way through a crowd); also, to set in action, begin, start, or commence (as, to *open* a session of Congress; to *open* a campaign; to *open* a ball; to *open* fire; to *open* an account); in *law*, to make the first statement of (a case) to the court or jury; also, to recall or revoke, as a judgment or decree, for the purpose of allowing further contest or delay; *naut.*, to come in sight of, or get a view of, as by passing some intervening object (as, "keeping a yellow warehouse on our starboard hand till we *opened* a white church to the larboard": H. Melville's "Moby-Dick," xv.). **II.** *intr.* To open a door, building, etc. (as, "I *opened* to my beloved: but my beloved . . . was gone": Cant. v. 6); also, to open a book, etc. (as, *open* at page 32); also, to disclose or reveal one's knowledge, thoughts, feelings, etc. (as, "He did not *open* on the subject of Seraphina, nor did we attempt to draw him out": Malkin's tr. Le Sage's "Gil Blas," xii. 13); also, to become open, as a door, building, box, inclosure, etc.; come apart or asunder, or burst open, so as to admit of passage or display the interior (as, "The earth *opened* and swallowed up Dathan," Ps. cvi. 17; "The clouds methought would *open* and show riches Ready to drop upon me," Shakspere's "Tempest," iii. 2. 150); also, to afford access (*into*, *to*, etc.: as, "He . . . unbolted a door that *opened* into a garden; and . . . another door that *opened* to the street," H. Brooke's "Fool of Quality," xviii.); have an opening, passage, or outlet (*into*, *upon*, etc.: as, a room that *opens* into a corridor; "The track . . . *opened* at both ends upon the water," Stevenson's "Master of Ballantrae," iii.); have its opening or outlet (*toward*, *to*, etc.: as, "a large upper chamber, whose window *opened* toward the sunrising," Bunyan's "Pilgrim's Progress," i.); also, to become receptive to knowledge, sympathy, etc., as the mind; also, to come into view, or become more visible or plain, as on nearer approach or with change of position; become disclosed or revealed; also, to spread out or expand, as the hand or a fan; also, to become less compact, less close together, or the like (as, ranks *open*); also, to begin, start, or commence; start operations; begin a session or term, as a school; begin a season or tour, as a theatrical company; in *hunting*, of hounds, to begin to bark, as on scent of game.—**open sesame.** See entry below.

o-pen-a-ble (ō′pn-ạ-bl), *a.* Capable of being opened.

o-pen=air (ō′pn-ãr′), *a.* Existing in, taking place in, or characteristic of the open air; outdoor.

o-pen-bill (ō′pn-bil), *n.* One of the storks of the genus *Anastomus*, with species in Africa and southern Asia, characterized by a bill with mandibles separated by an interval before meeting at the tip.

East Indian Openbill (*Anastomus oscitans*).

o-pen-er (ō′pn-ėr), *n.* One who or that which opens.

o-pen=eyed (ō′pn-īd′), *a.* Having the eyes open; hence, watchful or vigilant; observant of or alive to what is before one or passing, occurring, etc.; often, having the eyes wide open as in wonder (as, "We saw him now, dumb with fear and astonishment, staring *open-eyed* at the Emperor": Conan Doyle's "Exploits of Brigadier Gerard," viii.); also, done or experienced with the eyes open.

o-pen=faced (ō′pn-fāst′), *a.* Having the face uncovered; of a watch, having the dial covered only by the crystal; also, having a frank or ingenuous face.

o-pen=hand-ed (o′pn-han′ded), *a.* Generous; liberal: as, "Mr. Harding was an *open-handed* . . . man, and . . . he had . . . declared his intention of adding twopence a day to each man's pittance" (Trollope's "Warden," i.).—**o′pen=hand′ed-ly,** *adv.*—**o′pen=hand′ed-ness,** *n.*

o-pen=heart-ed (ō′pn-här′ted), *a.* Unreserved, candid, or frank (as, "a good, honest, *open-hearted*, and positive naval officer of the old school": Kinglake's "Eothen," viii.); also, accessible to noble emotions; kindly.—**o′pen=heart′ed-ly,** *adv.*—**o′pen=heart′ed-ness,** *n.*

o-pen=hearth (ō′pn-härth′), *a.* Noting a reverberatory furnace with an open hearth, used in making steel; designating or pertaining to the process by which steel is made in such a furnace.

o-pen-ing (ō′pn-ing or ōp′ning), *n.* The act of one who or that which opens (in any sense); a making or becoming open; often, the act of beginning, starting, or commencing; the first part or initial stage of anything; specif., a formal beginning of a season's sale of goods (as, a millinery *opening*; spring *openings*); also, an open space in solid matter; a gap, hole, or aperture; an open or clear space affording entrance or passage; an unobstructed or unoccupied space or place; a tract of land thinly wooded as compared with adjoining forest tracts (U. S.); also, a vacancy, or vacant position, that admits of being occupied; hence, an opportunity or chance; in *law*, the statement of the case made by counsel to the court or jury preliminary to adducing evidence; in *chess*, a mode of beginning a game; specif., one of the many series of consecutive moves made at starting which are frequently played (cf. *gambit*).

o-pen-ly (ō′pn-li), *adv.* In an open manner; without concealment; publicly; unreservedly or frankly.

o-pen=mind-ed (ō′pn-mīn′ded), *a.* Having or showing a mind open or accessible to new arguments or ideas: as, "The Committee sit *open-minded*, listening with laudable impartiality" (W. Churchill's "Coniston," ii. 17).—**o′pen=mind′ed-ly,** *adv.*—**o′pen=mind′ed-ness,** *n.*

o-pen=mouthed (ō′pn-mouᴛʜd′), *a.* Having the mouth open; gaping with surprise or astonishment (as, "Countless men . . . stared *open-mouthed* at the news": H. G. Wells's "Mr. Britling," ii. 1. § 11); greedy, ravenous, or rapacious; clamoring at the sight of game or prey, as hounds; vociferous or clamorous (as, "*open-mouthed* abuse of a man": Motley's "Dutch Republic," vi. 2); also, having a wide mouth, as a vessel.

o-pen-ness (ō′pn-nes), *n.* The state or quality of being open (in any sense); often, absence of concealment or reserve, or candor or frankness (as, "I will answer him as clearly as I am able, and with great *openness*": Burke's "American Taxation").

o-pen ses-a-me (ō′pn ses′ạ-mẹ). [See *sesame.*] A password or charm at which doors or barriers fly open: from the use of these words to open the door of the robbers' den in the tale of "Ali Baba and the Forty Thieves," in the "Arabian Nights' Entertainments." Also as *n.*, *open-sesame.*

o-pen-work (ō′pn-wėrk), *n.* Any kind of work, esp. ornamental, as of metal, stone, wood, embroidery, lace, etc., showing openings through its substance.

op-er-a[1] (op′ẹ-rạ̈), *n.* Plural of *opus.*

op-er-a[2] (op′ẹ-rạ̈), *n.* [It., < L. *opera*, service, work, a work, < *opus* (*oper-*), work: cf. *opus.*] An extended dramatic composition in which music is an essential and predominant factor, consisting of recitatives, arias, choruses, etc., with orchestral accompaniment, scenery, and acting, and sometimes dancing; a musical drama; also, the form or branch of musical and dramatic art represented by such compositions (as, the history of the *opera*, or of *opera*; Italian or German *opera*; to sing in *opera*); also, the score or the words of a musical drama; also, a performance of one; also, a theater in which such performances are given; an opera-house.—**grand opera,** an elaborate musical drama, without spoken dialogue.

op-er-a-ble (op′ẹ-rạ-bl), *a.* [F. *opérable*, < L. *operari*: see *operate.*] Admitting of a surgical operation. Cf. *inoperable.*

o-pé-ra bouffe (o-pā-rä böf). [F.] A comic opera, esp. of farcical character. Also (It.) **o-pe-ra buf-fa** (ō′pe-rä böf′fä).

o-pé-ra co-mique (o-pā-rä ko-mēk). [F.] A light opera of the nature of a comedy, usually consisting partly of spoken dialogue.

op-er-a=glass (op′ẹ-rạ̈-glås), *n.* A small binocular telescope for use in theaters, etc. Also called *opera-glasses.*

op-er-a=hat (op′ẹ-rạ̈-hat), *n.* A man's collapsible tall hat, held open or in shape by springs.

op-er-a=house (op′ẹ-rạ̈-hous), *n.* A theater devoted chiefly or largely to the performance of operas.

op-er-am-e-ter (op-ẹ-ram′e-tėr), *n.* [L. *opera*, work, + Gr. μέτρον, measure.] An instrument for indicating the number of movements made by a part of a machine or the like, as the turns made by a shaft.

op-er-and (op′ẹ-rand), *n.* [L. *operandum*, neut. gerundive of *operari*: see *operate.*] In *math.*, the quantity or expression which is to be subjected to a mathematical operation.

op-er-ant (op′ẹ-rạnt). **I.** *a.* Operating; producing effects. **II.** *n.* One who or that which operates.

op-er-at-a-ble (op′ẹ-rā-tạ-bl), *a.* That may be operated; also, admitting of a surgical operation; operable.

op-er-ate (op′ẹ-rāt), *v.*; *-ated, -ating.* [L. *operatus*, pp. of *operari*, do work, labor, have effect, < *opus* (*oper-*), work.] **I.** *intr.* To be working, act effectively, or exert force or influence (as, the same causes are *operating* to-day; a new spirit was *operating* among them; "No fear of thee *operates* in my mind to render this a peaceful meeting," Scott's "Castle Dangerous," xvii.); act (*on* or *upon*: as, "These tidings *operated* upon me like magic," H. Melville's "Typee," xiii.); often, of medicines, etc., to produce the effect intended; also, to perform some process of work or treatment upon raw material, an article being made, or the like; work or use a machine, apparatus, or the like; work or run, as a machine does (as, so long as the machinery was *operating*); also, to carry on transactions in stocks, etc., or some commodity, esp. speculatively or on a large scale; in *surg.*, to perform some manual act or series of acts upon the body of a patient, usually with instruments, to remedy deformity, injury, or disease; *milit.* and *naval*, to carry on operations in war. **II.** *tr.* To bring about, effect, or produce, as by action or the exertion of force or influence (as, "We admitted that the Book . . . had even *operated* changes in our way of thought": Carlyle's "Sartor Resartus," i. 4); also, to keep (a machine, apparatus, factory, industrial system, etc.) working or in operation; manage or use (a machine, etc.) at work (as, to *operate* a sewing-machine, a telegraphic apparatus, or a switchboard).

op-er-at-ic (op-ẹ-rat′ik), *a.* Of or pertaining to opera: as, *operatic* music.—**op-er-at′i-cal-ly,** *adv.*

op-er-a-tion (op-ẹ-rā′shọn), *n.* [L. *operatio(n-)*.] The act, process, or manner of operating (as, "Each works its end . . . And to their proper *operation* still, Ascribe all good; to their improper, ill": Pope's "Essay on Man," ii. 57); exertion of force or influence; agency; also, the state of being operative (as, a rule no longer in *operation*); also, the power of operating, or efficacy, influence, or virtue; also, a particular course or mode of activity, or a process (as, mental *operations*); a process of a practical or mechanical nature in some form of work or production (as, the various *operations* in the making of bread, leather, paper, or photographs; a delicate *operation* in gem-cutting); a course of productive or industrial activity (as, building *operations*); a business transaction, esp. one of a speculative nature or on a large scale (as, *operations* in stocks, or in wheat, sugar, or oil); in *surg.*, a process or method of operating on the body of a patient, as with instruments, to remedy injury, etc.; *milit.* and *naval*, a course of warlike proceedings; in *math.*, the action of working upon a quantity so as to change its value or form (as in addition, subtraction, etc.), to derive some other quantity from it (as in extracting the cube root), or to arrive at some other result.

op-er-a-tive (op′ẹ-rạ̄-tiv). [LL. *operativus.*] **I.** *a.* Operating, or exerting force or influence (as, "the *operative* motives, hidden or avowed": De Quincey's "Revolt of the Tartars"); having force, or being in effect or operation (as, laws *operative* in a community); effective or efficacious (as, "Our foster-nurse of nature is repose . . . that to provoke . . . Are many simples *operative*": Shakspere's "King Lear," iv. 4. 14); also, engaged in, concerned with, or pertaining to work or productive activity (as, the *operative* employees or departments of a manufacturing establishment); also, concerned with, involving, or pertaining to remedial operations (as, *operative* surgery; a tumor requiring *operative* measures; *operative* dentistry, which is concerned with preserving the teeth, as distinguished from prosthetic dentistry, by which artificial substitutes are supplied). **II.** *n.* A worker; one engaged, employed, or skilled in some branch of work, esp. productive or industrial work; a workman, artisan, or factory-hand; sometimes, a detective.—**op′er-a-tive-ly,** *adv.*—**op′er-a-tive-ness,** *n.*

op-er-a-tize (op′ẹ-rạ-tīz), *v. t.*; *-tized, -tizing.* To put (a play, etc.) into the form of an opera.

op-er-a-tor (op′ẹ-rā-tọr), *n.* [LL.] One who operates; a worker; one employed or skilled in operating a machine, apparatus, or the like (as, a monotype *operator*; a telegraph *operator*; a telephone *operator*); one who conducts some working or industrial establishment, enterprise, or system (as, the *operators* of a mine or a railroad); one who operates in stocks, etc., or a commodity, esp. speculatively or on a large scale; one who performs a surgical operation.

o-per-cu-lar (ọ-pėr′kū-lạ̈r), *a.* [See *operculum.*] Of, pertaining to, or of the nature of an operculum.—**o-per′cu-late, o-per′cu-lat-ed** (-lāt, -lā-ted), *a.* Having an operculum.—**o-per′cu-li-form,** *a.* Having the form of an operculum; lid-like.

o-per-cu-lum (ọ-pėr′kụ-lum), *n.*; pl. *-lums* or *-la* (-lạ̈). [L., a cover, lid, < *operire*, cover: see *overt.*] In *bot.*, *zoöl.*, etc., a part or organ serving as a lid or cover, as a covering flap on a seed-vessel, or, in many gastropods, a horny plate which closes the opening of the shell when the animal is retracted.

Operculum of Capsule of Moss.

op-er-et-ta (op-ẹ-ret′ạ̈), *n.* [It., dim. of *opera*: see *opera*[2].] A short opera, commonly of a light character.

op-er-ose (op′ẹ-rōs), *a.* [L. *operosus*, < *opera*, work, pains: see *opera*[2].] Laborious or industrious, as a person; also, done with or involving much labor (as, "What an *operose* method! What a train of means to secure a little conversation!" Emerson's "Essays," Nature); elaborate.—**op′er-ose-ly,** *adv.*—**op′er-ose-ness,** *n.*

oph-i-cleide (of′i-klīd), *n.* [F. *ophicléide*, < Gr. ὄφις, serpent, + κλείς (κλειδ-), key.] A musical wind-instrument, a development of the old wooden serpent, consisting of a conical metal tube bent double, and usually having eleven keys.

Ophicleide.

o-phid-i-an (ọ-fid′i-ạn). [NL. *Ophidia*, pl., < Gr. ὄφις, serpent.] **I.** *a.* Belonging to the *Ophidia*, an order of reptiles consisting of the snakes or serpents; pertaining to or suggestive of a snake (as, "the tremendous *ophidian* head . . . with glistening scales and symmetrical markings": W. H. Hudson's "Green Mansions," xxii.). **II.** *n.* An ophidian reptile; a snake.

o-phid-i-a-ri-um (ọ-fid-i-ā′ri-um), *n.*; pl. *-riums* or *-ria* (-ri-ạ̈). [NL., < *Ophidia*: see *ophidian.*] A place where snakes are kept in confinement, for exhibition or for other purposes.

oph-i-dism (of′i-dizm), *n.* [NL. *ophidismus*, < *Ophidia*: see *ophidian.*] Poisoning by snake-venom. Also **oph-i-dis′mus** (-diz′mus).

ophio-. Form of Gr. ὄφις, serpent, used in combination.—**oph-i-ol-a-try** (of-i-ol′ạ-tri), *n.* [+ *-latry.*] Serpent-worship.—**oph-i-ol′o-gy** (-ọ-ji), *n.* [+ *-logy.*] The part of zoölogy that treats of serpents.—**oph-i-oph′a-gous** (-of′ạ-gus), *a.* [+ *-phagous.*] Feeding on serpents.

oph-ite (of′īt), *n.* [L. *ophites*, < Gr. ὀφίτης, serpent-like, serpentine, < ὄφις, serpent.] Orig., a variety of serpentine spotted like a serpent; now, a greenish altered diabase.—**o-phit-ic** (ọ-fit′ik), *a.* Noting or pertaining to a rock texture exhibited by certain ophites (diabases), in which feldspar crystals are embedded in a matrix.

oph-i-u-ran (of-i-ū′rạn). [NL. *Ophiura*, < Gr. ὀφίουρος, serpent-tailed, < ὄφις, serpent, + οὐρά, tail.] **I.** *a.* Belonging or pertaining to the genus *Ophiura*, or to the *Ophiuroidea*, a class or group of echinoderms more or less resembling the starfishes (asteroids) but having slender arms which are sharply marked off from the central disk. **II.** *n.* An ophiuroid echinoderm.

oph-i-u-roid (of-i-ū′roid). **I.** *a.* Belonging or pertaining to the *Ophiuroidea*. See *ophiuran, a.* **II.** *n.* One of the *Ophiuroidea*; an ophiuran.

oph-thal-mi-a (of-thal′mi-ạ̈), *n.* [LL., < Gr. ὀφθαλμία, < ὀφθαλμός, eye.] In *pathol.*, inflammation of the eye, esp. of its membranes or external structures. Cf. *ophthalmitis.*

oph-thal-mic (of-thal′mik), *a.* [Gr. ὀφθαλμικός, < ὀφθαλμός, eye, < ὀπ-, see: see *optic.*] Of or pertaining to the eye; ocular; also, pertaining to or affected with ophthalmia.

oph-thal-mi-tis (of-thal-mī′tis), *n.* [NL.] In *pathol.*, inflammation of the eye, esp. of the eyeball in both its external and its internal structures. Cf. *ophthalmia.*—**oph-thal-mit′ic** (-mit′ik), *a.*

ophthalmo-. Form of Gr. ὀφθαλμός, eye, used in combination.—**oph-thal-mol-o-gy** (of-thal-mol′ọ-ji), *n.* [+ *-logy.*] The science that deals with the anatomy, functions, and diseases of the eye.—**oph-thal-mo-log′i-cal** (-mọ-loj′i-kạl), *a.*—**oph-thal-mol′o-gist,** *n.*—**oph-thal-mom′e-ter** (-mom′e-tėr), *n.* [+ *-meter*] An instrument for determining the curvature of the cornea of the eye.—**oph-thal-mo-ple′gi-a** (-plē′ji-ạ̈), *n.* [NL.: cf. *paraplegia.*] In *pathol.*, paralysis of one or more of the muscles of the eye.—**oph-thal′mo-scope** (-skōp), *n.* [+ *-scope.*] An instrument for viewing the interior of the eye or examining the retina.—**oph-thal-mo-scop′ic, oph-thal-mo-scop′i-cal** (-skop′ik, -i-kạl), *a.*—**oph-thal-mos′co-py** (-mos′kọ-pi), *n.*

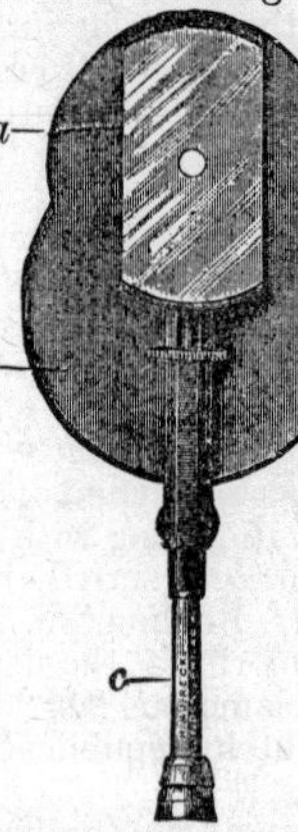

Ophthalmoscope. — *a*, concave mirror for throwing light into eye, and having hole through which observer examines eye; *b*, body; *c*, shank, into which handle (not shown) is screwed.

-opia. [Gr. -ωπία, < ὤψ, eye.] A termination of nouns denoting a condition of sight or of the visual organs, as in *amblyopia, diplopia, emmetropia, hemeralopia, myopia.*

o-pi-ate (ō′pi-ạt). [ML. *opiatus*, < L. *opium*, E. *opium.*] **I.** *a.* Mixed or prepared with opium; hence, inducing sleep; soporific; narcotic; fig., causing dullness or inaction. **II.** *n.* A medicine that contains opium and hence has the quality of inducing sleep; a narcotic; fig., anything that causes dullness or inaction, or that quiets the feelings (as, "The thought . . . was by no means an *opiate* to reflection," Godwin's "Caleb Williams," Postscript; "*opiates* to grief," C. B. Brown's "Wieland," xvii.).—**o′pi-ate** (-āt), *v. t.*; *-ated, -ating.* To subject to the influence of an opiate; stupefy; fig., to dull or deaden.—**o-pi-at′ic** (-at′ik), *a.* Of, pertaining to, or caused by an opiate.

o-pine (ọ-pīn′), *v. i.* or *t.*; *opined, opining.* [L. *opinari* (pp. *opinatus*), think, deem.] To think; deem; hold or express an opinion, or as one's opinion: often followed by a clause: as, "He *opined* that the rich should pay" (Thackeray's "Newcomes," lxvii.); "Edwin had *opined* to his father that the frost was breaking" (Arnold Bennett's "Clayhanger," i. 16).—**o-pin-er** (ọ-pī′nėr), *n.*

o-pin-i-a-tive (ọ-pin′i-ạ̄-tiv), *a.* [Obs. F. *opiniatif.*] Same as *opinionative.*—**o-pin′i-a-tive-ly,** *adv.*—**o-pin′i-a-tive-ness,** *n.*

o-pin-ion (ọ-pin′yọn), *n.* [OF. F. *opinion*, < L. *opinio(n-)*, < *opinari*, E. *opine.*] What is thought, or the way of thinking, on any matter or subject, or judgment or belief resting on grounds insufficient to produce certainty (as, personal or public *opinion*; a matter of *opinion*; to concur in *opinion*); a particular judgment or belief of this kind, or a view or notion (held or expressed: as, to have or give an *opinion* on a subject; "After all, the idea of purgatory as a fire is only an *opinion*, not a dogma of the church," Kingsley's "Yeast," viii.; "Trixton Brent's *opinions* were usually worth listening to," W. Churchill's "Modern Chronicle," ii. 9); also, a formal or professional judgment expressed, as on a case submitted for examination or coming under official consideration (as, a medical *opinion*; expert *opinions* on public problems; a judicial *opinion* on the facts in a case, or on some question involved); also, a judgment or estimate (favorable or unfavorable) of a person or thing with respect to character, merit, etc. (as, to have a high, low, good, or poor *opinion* of a man or of his abilities or work; "I have bought Golden *opinions* from all sorts of people," Shakspere's "Macbeth," i. 7. 33); a favorable estimate, or esteem (chiefly with a negative: as, "She is a selfish, hypocritical woman, and I have no *opinion* of her," Jane Austen's "Pride and Prejudice," ii.); hence, self-esteem† or self-conceit† (as, "audacious without impudency, learned without *opinion*": Shakspere's "Love's Labour's Lost," v. 1. 6); also, reputation† or credit† (as, "Thou hast redeem'd thy lost *opinion*": Shakspere's "1 Henry IV.," v. 4. 48).—**o-pin'ion-al,** *a.* Pertaining to or of the nature of opinion.—**o-pin'ion-at-ed** (-ā-ted), *a.* Obstinate or conceited with regard to one's opinions; conceitedly dogmatic.—**o-pin'ion-at-ed-ness,** *n.* —**o-pin'ion-a-tive** (-ạ-tiv), *a.* Disposed to or characterized by obstinacy or conceit in opinion (as, "Young men are too *opinionative* and volatile to be guided by the sober dictates of their seniors": Swift's "Gulliver's Travels," iii. 10); opinionated; also, of, pertaining to, or of the nature of opinion or belief.—**o-pin'ion-a-tive-ly,** *adv.*—**o-pin'-ion-a-tive-ness,** *n.*—**o-pin'ioned,** *a.* Having an opinion (as specified: as, to be otherwise *opinioned*); also, opinionated.

opio-. Form of Gr. ὄπιον, opium, used in combination.—**o-pi-o-cap-nism** (ō″pi-ọ-kap'nizm), *n.* [+ Gr. καπνός, smoke.] Opium-smoking.—**o-pi-ol'o-gy** (-ol'ọ-ji), *n.* [+ *-logy.*] The study of the nature and properties of opium. —**o″pi-o-ma'ni-a** (-mā'ni-ạ), *n.* Uncontrollable craving for opium.—**o″pi-o-ma'ni-ac** (-ak), *n.*—**o-pi-oph'a-gy** (-of'ạ-ji), *n.* [+ *-phagy.*] Opium-eating.

op-is-thog-na-thous (op-is-thog'nạ-thus), *a.* [Gr. ὄπισθεν, behind, + γνάθος, jaw.] Of a skull or a person, having retreating jaws; of a jaw, retreating.

o-pi-um (ō'pi-um), *n.* [L., < Gr. ὄπιον, poppy-juice, opium, dim. of ὀπός, juice.] The inspissated juice of a poppy, *Papaver somniferum*, containing morphine and other alkaloids: a stimulant narcotic (in sufficient quantities a powerful narcotic poison) of great value in medicine to relieve pain, induce sleep, etc., but in habitual use exceedingly difficult to forgo and leading to disastrous results. See *codeine, heroin, morphine, narceine, narcotine, thebaine,* also *opium-eating* and *opium-smoking.*—**o'pi-um=eat″er,** *n.* One addicted to opium-eating.—**o'pi-um=eat″ing,** *n.* The habitual use of opium in some form by eating or swallowing, as for its soothing and stimulating effects.—**o'pi-um-ism,** *n.* In *pathol.*, a morbid condition induced by the habitual use of opium.—**o'pi-um=smok″er,** *n.* One addicted to opium-smoking.—**o'pi-um=smok″ing,** *n.* The practice or habit of smoking opium as a stimulant or intoxicant. See *chandoo.*

op-o-del-doc (op-ọ-del'dok), *n.* [NL. *oppodeltoch*, name applied by Paracelsus to certain medicinal plasters.] Any of various liniments containing soap, camphor, alcohol, etc.

Common Opossum (*Didelphys virginiana*).

o-pop-a-nax (ọ-pop'ạ-naks), *n.* [L., < Gr. ὀποπάναξ, < ὀπός, juice, + πάναξ, kind of plant.] A gum-resin formerly much esteemed in medicine, obtained from the root of *Opopanax opopanax*, an apiaceous plant of southern Europe; also, the plant itself; also, a myrrh-like gum-resin used in perfumery, obtained from an African tree, *Balsamea kataf.*

o-pos-sum (ọ-pos'um), *n.* [N. Amer. Ind.] Any of the marsupials constituting the American family *Didelphyidæ*; esp., *Didelphys virginiana* (see cut in preceding column), a prehensile-tailed, pouched animal about the size of a large cat, common in the southern U. S., which when caught feigns death (see *to play possum*, under *possum*).—**o-pos'sum=shrew,** *n.* A solenodon.—**o-pos'sum=shrimp,** *n.* Any of the small, shrimplike, schizopod crustaceans constituting the family *Mysidæ*, the females of which carry their eggs in a pouch between the legs.

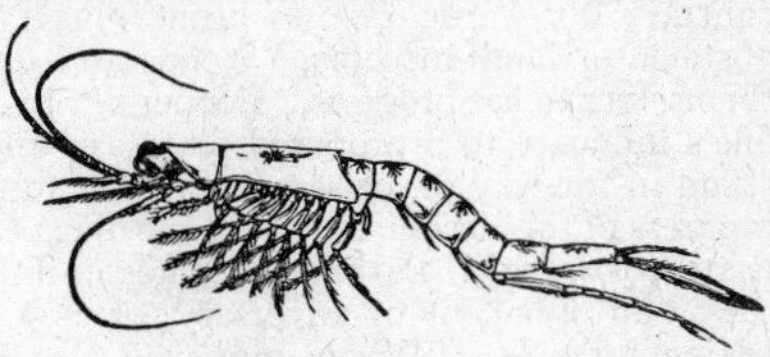

Opossum-shrimp (*Mysis mixta*).

op-o-ther-a-py (op-ọ-ther'ạ-pi), *n.* [Gr. ὀπός, juice: see *therapy.*] Treatment of disease by means of extracts made from the organs of animals; organotherapy.

op-pi-dan (op'i-dạn). [L. *oppidanus*, < *oppidum*, town.] **I.** *a.* Of or pertaining to a town; urban. **II.** *n.* A townsman; at Eton College, England, a student not on the foundation, but boarding in the town (cf. *colleger*).

op-pi-late (op'i-lāt), *v. t.*; *-lated, -lating.* [L. *oppilatus*, pp. of *oppilare*, < *ob*, against, + *pilare*, ram down.] To stop up; fill with obstructing matter; obstruct.—**op-pi-la'tion** (-lā'shọn), *n.*

op-po-nent (ọ-pō'nẹnt). [L. *opponens* (*-ent-*), ppr. of *opponere*: see *opposite* and *oppose.*] **I.** *a.* Being opposite, as in position; also, opposing; antagonistic; adverse; contrary. **II.** *n.* One who opposes, or makes opposition (as, the *opponents* of a proposed measure; "two men, one . . . a zealous supporter and the other a zealous *opponent* of the system pursued," Macaulay's "Essays," Gladstone on Church and State); often, one who is on the opposite side in a contest, controversy, or the like; an antagonist; an adversary.

op-por-tune (op-ọr-tūn' or op'ọr-tūn), *a.* [OF. F. *opportun*, < L. *opportunus*, fit, convenient, timely, < *ob*, before, + *portus*, entrance, harbor, E. *port*[1]: cf. *importune, a.*] Fit or appropriate for the purpose (as, "the most *opportune* place," Shakspere's "Tempest," iv. 1. 26; "Satan . . . Consider'd every creature, which of all Most *opportune* might serve his wiles," Milton's "Paradise Lost," ix. 85); now, usually, appropriate or favorable, as a time, moment, etc.; occurring or coming at an appropriate or favorable time, seasonable, or timely (as, an *opportune* event, arrival, or warning; an *opportune* visitor).—**op-por-tune'ly,** *adv.*—**op-por-tune'ness,** *n.*—**op-por-tun'ism** (-tū'nizm), *n.* The policy or practice, in politics or otherwise, of adapting actions, etc., to expediency or circumstances (often with implication of sacrifice of principle); also, an action or proceeding due to this policy.—**op-por-tun'ist,** *n.* One who adheres to the policy of opportunism; also [*cap.*], one who at the Vatican Council in 1870 held that the time was opportune for the publication of the dogma of papal infallibility.—**op-por-tun-is'tic,** *a.*—**op-por-tu'ni-ty** (-tū'ni-ti), *n.*; pl. *-ties* (-tiz). The quality or fact of being opportune, or opportuneness (now rare); also, time or circumstances appropriate or favorable for the purpose (as, "A wise man will hold his tongue till he see *opportunity*," Ecclus. xx. 7; "He would . . . trust to time and *opportunity* for the gratification of his revenge," Marryat's "King's Own," xlvii.); an appropriate or favorable time or occasion (as, to make use of an *opportunity*; an *opportunity* to secure a bargain; "The blind have many *opportunities* for thinking," Kipling's "Light That Failed," xi.); also, erroneously, importunity† (see Shakspere's "Merry Wives of Windsor," iii. 4. 20).

op-pos-a-ble (ọ-pō'zạ-bl), *a.* That may be opposed (in any sense); esp., capable of being placed opposite to something else (as, the thumb is *opposable* to the other fingers).—**op-pos-a-bil'i-ty** (-bil'i-ti), *n.*

op-pose (ọ-pōz'), *v.*; *-posed, -posing.* [OF. F. *opposer*, < *op-* (< L. *ob*, before, against) + *poser*, put (see *pose*[1]), but associated with derivatives of L. *opponere*: see *opposite* and *opponent.*] **I.** *tr.* To set (something) over against something else in place, or so as to face or be opposite (as,

"*Oppose* thy steadfast-gazing eyes to mine, See if thou canst outface me with thy looks": Shakspere's "2 Henry VI.," iv. 10. 48); of a thing, place, etc., to face, or be opposite to (now rare); also, to set against in some relation, as of offsetting, antithesis, or contrast (as, to *oppose* the advantages to the disadvantages; to *oppose* one phrase or clause in a sentence to another); use or take as being opposite or contrary (as, words *opposed* in meaning); also, to set as an obstacle or hindrance (as, "Woods and rocks . . . *opposed* themselves to her progress," Cooper's "Spy," xxx.; to *oppose* one's influence to a proposed plan); of an obstacle, etc., to stand in the way of, or serve to hinder (as, "a record of the progress of this design . . . and the unexpected impediments that *opposed* it": Parkman's "Oregon Trail," x.); also, to set as an opponent or adversary, or as a resisting or combating force (as, "Whom may you else *oppose*, That can from Hector bring his honour off, If not Achilles?" Shakspere's "Troilus and Cressida," i. 3. 333; to *oppose* an army-corps to the enemy in a given area); of a person, a force, etc., to act or contend in opposition to; strive against, resist, or combat; endeavor to withstand or defeat; be hostile or adverse to, as in opinion. **II.** *intr.* To be or act in opposition; make opposition or resistance.—**op-posed′,** *p. a.* Placed opposite; also, opposite or contrary; also, hostile or adverse (*to*).—**op-pose′less,** *a.* Not to be opposed; resistless: as, "your great *opposeless* wills" (Shakspere's "King Lear," iv. 6. 38).—**op-pos-er** (ǫ-pō′zėr), *n.*—**op-pos′ing-ly,** *adv.*

op-po-site (op′ǭ-zit). [OF. F. *opposite*, < L. *oppositus*, pp. of *opponere*, put before or against, oppose, < *ob*, before, against, + *ponere*, place, put: see *oppose* and *opponent.*] **I.** *a.* Placed or lying over against something else or each other, or in a corresponding position from an intervening line, space, or thing (as, the house *opposite* to ours; the person *opposite* to me at the table; *opposite* sides or ends of a room); also, tending or going the other way, or counter to another or each other (as, the *opposite* direction or way; they started in *opposite* directions); also, contrary or diametrically different, as in nature, qualities, result, or significance (as, "It is said that *opposite* characters make a union happiest," Reade's "Christie Johnstone," ii.; to have an effect *opposite* to that intended; words of *opposite* meaning); also, opposed in feeling or action†, adverse†, or inimical† (as, "a design of strengthening a party *opposite* to the public interest": Swift's "Gulliver's Travels," ii. 6); in *bot.*, situated on diametrically opposed sides of an axis, as leaves when there are two on one node. **II.** *n.* One who or that which is opposite or contrary; also, an opponent or adversary (obs. or rare: as, "By the law of arms thou wast not bound to answer An unknown *opposite*," Shakspere's "King Lear," v. 3. 153).—**op′po-site-ly,** *adv.*—**op′po-site-ness,** *n.*

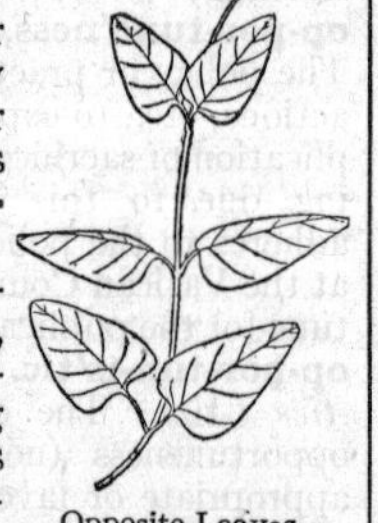
Opposite Leaves.

op-po-si-tion (op-ǭ-zish′ǫn), *n.* [L. *oppositio(n-)*, < *opponere*: see *opposite*, and cf. *oppose.*] The act of placing opposite, or the state or position of being placed opposite (as, "Before mine eyes in *opposition* sits Grim Death": Milton's "Paradise Lost," ii. 803); also, the act of opposing or the state of being opposed by way of offset, antithesis, or contrast; antithesis or contrast; contradistinction; oppositeness, or radical difference (as, "Between him and Darcy there was a very steady friendship, in spite of great *opposition* of character": Jane Austen's "Pride and Prejudice," iv.); also, the action of opposing, resisting, or combating; proceedings or efforts intended to check, thwart, or defeat; antagonism or hostility; also, an opposing party or body, esp. the political party opposed to the party in power; in *astron.*, the situation of two heavenly bodies when their longitudes differ by 180°; in *logic*, the relation between two propositions which have the same subject and predicate, but which differ in quantity or quality, or in both.—**op-po-si′tion-al,** *a.*—**op-po-si′tion-ist,** *n.* One who practises opposition; a member of the opposition, as in politics.

op-pos-i-tive (ǫ-poz′i-tiv), *a.* Characterized by or expressing opposition; adversative.

op-press (ǫ-pres′), *v. t.* [OF. F. *oppresser*, < ML. *oppressare*, freq. of L. *opprimere* (pp. *oppressus*), press against, bear down, subdue, < *ob*, against, + *premere*, press.] To press against† or press down†; bear down by force, as in battle†; put down†, subdue†, or suppress†; also, to weigh down, as sleep or weariness does; affect with a distressing sense of pressure or of overpowering physical influences (as, "His body felt feverish and *oppressed*. This was chiefly owing to the close and confined air of the small apartment": Scott's "Guy Mannering," xlviii.); lie heavily upon (the mind, a person, etc.), as care, sorrow, or any disturbing thought does; in a milder sense, to affect uncomfortably by being too great, pretentious, elaborate, or the like (as, his position or surroundings *oppressed* him; to be *oppressed* by grandeur or ceremony); also, to subject to a burdensome or harsh exercise of authority or power (as, "My princes shall no more *oppress* my people," Ezek. xlv. 8; "*Oppress* not the widow, nor the fatherless . . . nor the poor," Zech. vii. 10); burden with cruel or unjust impositions or restraints; also, to molest or harass, as an enemy does† (see Num. x. 9).

op-pres-sion (ǫ-presh′ǫn), *n.* [OF. F. *oppression*, < L. *oppressio(n-)*, < *opprimere*: see *oppress.*] The act of oppressing, or the state of being oppressed; the feeling of being oppressed by something weighing down the bodily powers or depressing the mind; the exercise of authority or power in a burdensome, cruel, or unjust manner.

op-pres-sive (ǫ-pres′iv), *a.* [ML. *oppressivus.*] That oppresses; weighing down the bodily powers, or overpowering (as, *oppressive* heat or weather; *oppressive* odors); distressing or grievous, as sorrows; causing discomfort, or uncomfortably great (as, *oppressive* formalities or compliments; "an *oppressive* modesty that found vent in endless apologies," Mrs. Gaskell's "Cranford," vii.); oppressing by burdensome or unjust impositions or restraints, as a ruler; burdensome, unjustly harsh, or tyrannical, as taxes, measures, etc.—**op-pres′sive-ly,** *adv.*—**op-pres′sive-ness,** *n.*

op-pres-sor (ǫ-pres′ǫr), *n.* [L.] One who oppresses.

op-pro-bri-ous (ǫ-prō′bri-us), *a.* [LL. *opprobriosus.*] Conveying or expressing opprobrium, as language, epithets, a speaker, etc. (as, "feelings of anger which found vent in the most *opprobrious* invectives against his rival": Prescott's "Conquest of Mexico," iv. 6); imputing disgrace or shame; contumelious; abusive; also, disgraceful or shameful (obs. or archaic: as, "this dark *opprobrious* den of shame," Milton's "Paradise Lost," ii. 58).—**op-pro′bri-ous-ly,** *adv.*—**op-pro′bri-ous-ness,** *n.*

op-pro-bri-um (ǫ-prō′bri-um), *n.* [L., < *ob*, against, + *probrum*, disgraceful act, disgrace.] The disgrace or the reproach incurred by conduct considered shameful (as, "Because I had turned against him . . . I was loaded with general *opprobrium*," C. Brontë's "Jane Eyre," ii.; "The name of Muley . . . was . . . a by-word of scorn and *opprobrium* throughout the city," Irving's "Conquest of Granada," l.); infamy; contumelious reproach; also, a cause or object of such reproach.

op-pugn (ǫ-pūn′), *v. t.* [L. *oppugnare*, < *ob*, against, + *pugnare*, fight.] To attack in fight or war†; hence, fig., to assail by criticism, argument, or action (as, "I justify myself On every point where cavillers like this *Oppugn* my life": Browning's "Bishop Blougram's Apology"); esp., to call in question (rights, merits, judgment, etc.); dispute (statements, etc.).—**op-pug-nant** (ǫ-pug′nąnt), *a.* Oppugning, assailing, or opposing; hence, antagonistic or contrary; repugnant.—**op-pug′nance, op-pug′nan-cy,** *n.*—**op-pug-na-tion** (op-ug-nā′shǫn), *n.* [L. *oppugnatio(n-)*.] The act of oppugning; opposition. [Now rare.]—**op-pugn-er** (ǫ-pū′nėr), *n.*

op-si-math (op′si-math), *n.* [Gr. ὀψιμαθής, late in learning, < ὀψέ, late, + μανθάνειν, learn.] One who begins to learn or study late in life.—**op-sim′a-thy** (-sim′ą-thi), *n.*; pl. *-thies* (-thiz). [Gr. ὀψιμαθία.] Learning or education late in life; something learned late.

op-son-ic (op-son′ik), *a.* In *bact.*, of, pertaining to, or influenced by opsonin: as, the *opsonic* index (the ratio between the number of bacteria taken up by phagocytes in the blood-serum of a patient and the number taken up in normal blood-serum).

op-so-nin (op′sǫ-nin), *n.* [Gr. ὄψον, cooked meat.] In *bact.*, a constituent of blood-serum which causes invading bacteria to become more susceptible to the destructive action of the phagocytes.

opt (opt), *v. i.* [F. *opter*, < L. *optare* (pp. *optatus*), choose, wish.] To make a choice; choose. Also **op-tate** (op′tāt).

op-ta-tive (op′tạ-tiv). [LL. *optativus*, < L. *optare*: see *opt.*] **I.** *a.* Expressing desire or wish: as, the *optative* mode of a verb (in Greek, etc.). **II.** *n.* Something to be desired†; in *gram.*, the optative mode, or a verb-form belonging to it.—**op′ta-tive-ly,** *adv.*

op-tic (op′tik), *a.* [F. *optique*, < ML. *opticus*, < Gr. ὀπτικός, < ὀπ-, see, whence also ὄψις, sight, appearance, ὤψ, ὀφθαλμός, and ὄμμα, eye: cf. L. *oculus*, eye.] Pertaining to sight, or visual (now rare); more commonly, pertaining to or connected with the eye as the organ of sight, or sight as a function of the brain; also, constructed to assist the sight; acting by means of sight or light; optical; also, pertaining to optics.—**optic axis,** in *crystal.*, a line or direction in a crystal exhibiting double refraction, along which this phenomenon does not occur.—**optic nerve,** the nerve of sight, connecting the eye with the brain.—**optic thalamus.** See *thalamus.*—**op′tic,** *n.* The eye: chiefly in *pl.*: as, "I concluded that, by the position of their *optics*, their sight was so directed downward, that they did not readily see objects that were above them" (Defoe's "Robinson Crusoe," i. 4).—**op′ti-cal,** *a.* Pertaining to sight, or visual (as, an *optical* illusion: see cut at *illusion*); also, constructed to assist the sight, as devices; acting by means of sight or light, as instruments; also, pertaining to optics; dealing with or skilled in optics (as, "his [Descartes's] mathematical and *optical* writings," Hallam's "Literature of Europe," iii. 3. § 109; *optical* writers).—**op′ti-cal-ly,** *adv.*—**op-ti′cian** (-tish′ạn), *n.* One skilled in optics (now rare); also, a maker or seller of optical glasses and instruments; one who makes glasses for remedying defects of vision, in accordance with the prescriptions of oculists.—**op′tics,** *n.* The branch of physical science that deals with the properties and phenomena of light (the medium of sight) and with vision.

op-ti-mal (op′ti-mạl), *a.* Of or pertaining to the optimum; most favorable; best.

op-ti-mate (op′ti-māt), *n.* [L. *optimas* (pl. *optimates*), < *optimus*, best: see *optimum.*] One of the nobility; an aristocrat.

op-ti-me (op′ti-mē), *n.* [L., adv., best, very well, < *optimus*: see *optimum.*] At Cambridge University, England, one of those in the second or third grade of honors in mathematics ('senior optimes' or 'junior optimes'), the wranglers constituting the first rank.

op-ti-mism (op′ti-mizm), *n.* [F. *optimisme*, < L. *optimus*, best: see *optimum.*] The doctrine that the existing world is the best of all possible worlds; also, the belief that good will ultimately predominate over evil in the world; also, disposition to hope for the best; tendency to look on the bright side of things. Cf. *pessimism.*—**op′ti-mist,** *n.* An adherent of optimism; also, one given to practical optimism; one disposed to look on the bright side of things.—**op-ti-mis′tic,** *a.* Of or pertaining to optimism; disposed to take a favorable view of things.—**op-ti-mis′ti-cal-ly,** *adv.*—**op′ti-mize** (-mīz), *v.*; *-mized, -mizing.* **I.** *intr.* To hold or express optimistic views. **II.** *tr.* To make the best of.—**op″ti-mi-za′tion** (-mi-zā′shǫn), *n.*

op-ti-mum (op′ti-mum), *n.* [L., prop. neut. of *optimus*, best (superl. of *bonus*, good), akin to *ops*, power, means, wealth.] The best or most favorable point, degree, amount, etc., for the purpose, as of temperature, light, moisture, etc., for the growth or reproduction of an organism.

op-tion (op′shǫn), *n.* [F. *option*, < L. *optio(n-)*, akin to *optare*, choose.] The act of choosing; choice; also, power or liberty of choosing; right or freedom of choice; also, something which may be or is chosen; also, a privilege acquired, as by the payment of a premium or consideration, of demanding, within a specified time, the carrying out of a commercial transaction upon stipulated terms.—**local option.** See under *local*, *a.*—**op′tion,** *v. t.* To obtain, or to grant, an option in reference to or upon.—**op′tion-al. I.** *a.* Left to one's option or choice (as, attendance is *optional*); also, leaving something to choice (as, an *optional* writ, in *law*, a writ which commands the defendant to do the thing required, or show the reason why he has not done it). **II.** *n.* An optional study; an elective.—**op′tion-al-ly,** *adv.*

op-tom-e-ter (op-tom′e-tėr), *n.* [Gr. ὀπτικός, E. *optic*, + μέτρον, measure.] Any of various instruments for testing the vision.—**op-tom′e-trist,** *n.* One skilled in optometry; specif., one who is skilled in testing the eyes and fitting them with glasses, and is legally authorized to carry on such work, although not an oculist or physician.—**op-tom′e-try,** *n.* The measurement of the visual powers, as by the optometer; specif., the practice or art of testing the eyes by means of suitable instruments or appliances (usually without the use of drugs), for defects of vision, in order to fit them with glasses.

op-to-phone (op′tǫ-fōn), *n.* [Gr. ὀπτικός, E. *optic*, + φωνή, sound.] An apparatus for converting optical effects into acoustic effects; esp., a telephonic device for enabling the blind to read books, etc., the light effects peculiar to each printed letter being made to give rise to a characteristic sound.

op-u-lence (op′ụ̄-lẹns), *n.* The state of being opulent; wealth, riches, or affluence; fig., abundance, as of resources, etc. (as, "He has that *opulence* which furnishes, at every turn, the precise weapon he needs": Emerson's "Representative Men," ii.).

op-u-lent (op′ụ̄-lẹnt), *a.* [L. *opulens (-ent-)*, *opulentus*, < *ops*, power, means, wealth.] Wealthy, rich, or affluent, as persons or places (as, "Very few, even of the most *opulent* citizens of London, kept any equipage," Smollett's "Humphry Clinker," May 29; "the magnificence of that *opulent* metropolis of the muslin manufacturers," Galt's "Ayrshire Legatees," iv.); characterized by or showing wealth (as, "The arrangements of the house, and the general air of the housekeeping, indicated easy and even *opulent* circumstances": Mrs. Stowe's "Uncle Tom's Cabin," i.); bringing or yielding wealth (as, "the seat of *opulent* commerce": Irving's "Conquest of Granada," xlvii.); fig., rich in some respect, or richly or abundantly supplied with something (as, "Beauty *opulent* in charms": Bret Harte's "How Santa Claus Came to Simpson's Bar"); also, abundant or plentiful (as, *opulent* sunshine); often, of flowers or their fragrance, etc., rich, splendid, or fine (as, "beast or bird or fish, or *opulent* flower": Tennyson's "Lucretius," 248).—**op′u-lent-ly,** *adv.*

o-pun-ti-a (ǫ-pun′shi-ạ̈), *n.* [NL., < L. *Opuntius*, pertaining to Opus, a town in Locris, Greece.] Any plant of the cactaceous genus *Opuntia*, comprising fleshy herbs, shrubby plants, and sometimes trees, with branches usually composed of flattened or globose joints, and with (usually) yellow flowers and pear-shaped or ovoid, often edible fruit; a prickly-pear.

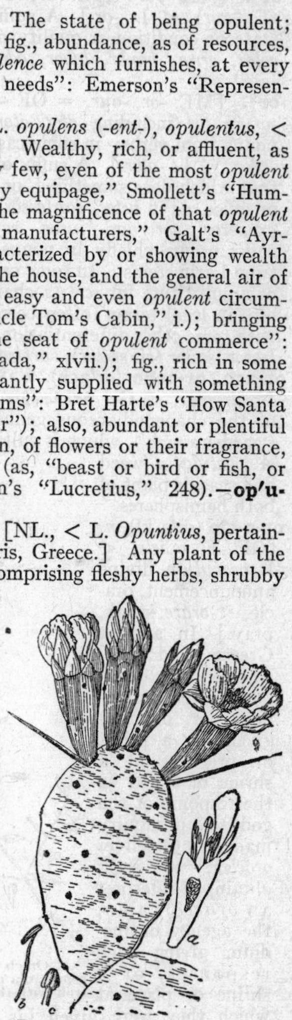

Flowering Branch of Opuntia (*O. vulgaris*). — *a*, longitudinal section of flower; *b*, a stamen; *c*, the stigma.

o-pus (ō′pus), *n.*; pl. *opera* (op′ẹ-rạ̈). [L., work, labor, a work: cf. Skt. *apas*, work, also E. *opera.*] A work or composition; esp., a musical composition, often one of the compositions of a particular composer as numbered in sequence according to date of publication.

o-pus-cule (ǫ-pus′kūl), *n.* [L. *opusculum*, dim. of *opus*: see *opus.*] A small work; esp., a literary or musical work of small size.

o-quas-sa (ǫ-kwas′ạ̈), *n.* [Said to be named from one of the Rangeley Lakes, in Maine.] A small trout, *Salvelinus oquassa*, with dark-blue coloration, found in the Rangeley Lakes, Maine.

or[1] (ôr), *conj.* [ME. *or*, contr. of *other*, < AS. *oththe* = OHG. *eddo*, *odo* (G. *oder*), = Goth. *aiththau*, or.] A particle used to connect words, phrases, or clauses representing alternatives (as, this road *or* that), or to connect alternative terms (as, the Hawaiian *or* Sandwich Islands): often used in correlation, as in *either . . . or, or . . . or* (archaic or poetic), and *whether . . . or*.

or² (ôr). [ME. *or, ar*, var. (due in part to Icel. *ār*, early) of *er*, < AS. *ǣr*, E. *ere*.] **I.** *prep.* Before; ere: as, "I'll be there long *or* that" (Stevenson's "David Balfour," xii.). [Archaic or prov.] **II.** *conj.* Before or ere (as, "Scarcely the knife was redden'd with his gore, *Or* the black poison stain'd the sandy floor": Dryden's tr. Virgil's "Georgics," iii. 742); also, sooner than or rather than (as, "I think He'll grant the tribute . . . *Or* look upon our Romans": Shakspere's "Cymbeline," ii. 4. 14). [Archaic or prov.]—**or ever,** or **or e'er** (sometimes written *or ere*), before ever; before: as, "We, *or ever* he come near, are ready to kill him" (Acts, xxiii. 15); "This heart Shall break . . . *Or ere* I'll weep" (Shakspere's "King Lear," ii. 4. 289). [Archaic or prov.]

or³ (ôr), *n.* [F. *or*, < L. *aurum*, gold.] In *her.*, the tincture gold, or yellow.

-or¹. [Also *-our*: ME. *-or, -our, -ur*, < OF. *-or, -our, -ur* (F. *-eur*), < L. *-or*.] A suffix of nouns denoting action, state or condition, a quality or property, etc., as in *ardor, color, error, honor, labor, odor, tremor, valor, vigor*. See *-our¹*.

-or². [ME. *-or, -our*, = OF. *-or, -our, -ur* (F. *-eur*), < L. *-or*, in *-tor* (including *-ator, -itor, -utor*), *-sor*, forming agent-nouns from verbs; in some cases, OF. *-eor* (F. *-eur*), earlier *-edor*, < L. *-ator*.] A suffix of nouns denoting one who or that which does something, or has some particular function or office, as in *actor, confessor, creditor, distributor, elevator, emperor, governor, juror, refractor, tailor, traitor*. This suffix occurs chiefly in nouns originally Latin, or formed from Latin stems. In some cases it is used as an alternative or a substitute for *-er¹* (a characteristically English suffix), esp. in legal terms (often correlative with forms in *-ee*) or with some other differentiation of use, as in *assignor, grantor, lessor, sailor* (cf. *sailer*), *survivor, vendor*. Cf. *-er¹* and *-ee*.

or-ach, or-ache (or'ạch), *n.* [OF. *arache* (F. *arroche*), < L. *atriplex*, < Gr. *ἀτράφαξυς*, orach.] Any of the plants of the chenopodiaceous genus *Atriplex*, esp. *A. hortensis* ('garden orach'), which is cultivated for use like spinach, or *A. patula*, a weed and seaside plant of both hemispheres.

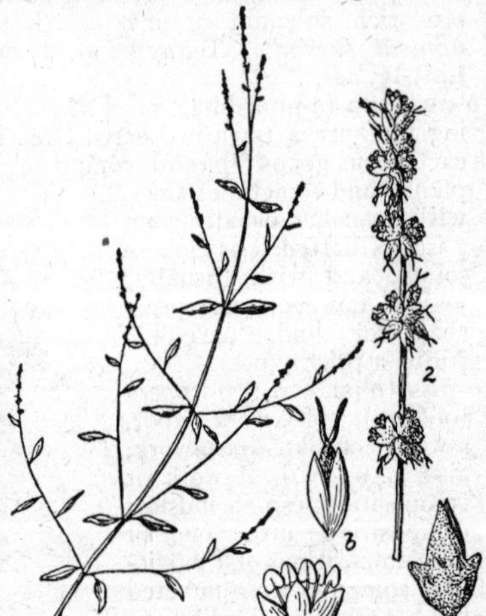

1, Orach (*Atriplex patula*); 2, the inflorescence; *a*, a male flower; *b*, a female flower; *c*, the fruit with the calyx.

or-a-cle (or'ạ-kl), *n.* [OF. F. *oracle*, < L. *oraculum*, divine announcement, oracle, < *orare*, speak, pray.] In ancient Greece and elsewhere, an utterance (often ambiguous or obscure) given by a priest or priestess at a shrine of a god as the response of the god to an inquiry made (as, to deliver *oracles*; to seek, obtain, or interpret an *oracle*); also, the agency or medium giving such responses, or a shrine or place at which they were given (as, the *oracle* of Zeus at Dodona; the *oracle* of Apollo at Delphi); in general use, a divine communication or revelation (as, "Unto them [the Jews] were committed the *oracles* of God": Rom. iii. 2); any utterance made or received as authoritative and infallible; an oracular response or pronouncement; also, any person or thing serving as an agency of divine communication (as, "God hath now sent his living *oracle* Into the world to teach his final will," Milton's "Paradise Regained," i. 460; "Man's conscience is the *oracle* of God," Byron's "Island," i. 6); a person who delivers authoritative or highly regarded pronouncements, or who speaks as with authority on some subject (as, "I am Sir *Oracle*, And when I ope my lips let no dog bark!" Shakspere's "Merchant of Venice," i. 1. 93; "Under the instructions of these political *oracles* the good people . . . became exceedingly enlightened," Irving's "Knickerbocker's New York," iv. 7); something regarded as an infallible guide or indicator, as a compass or a watch; also, the holy of holies in the Jewish temple (see 1 Kings, vi. 16, 19–23).—**or'a-cle,** *v. t.* or *i.*; *-cled, -cling.* To declare or speak as an oracle. [Obs. or rare.]—**o-rac-u-lar** (ǫ-rak'ū-lạ̈r), *a.* Of the nature of, resembling, or suggesting an oracle or divinely inspired utterance (as, an *oracular* response); uttered or delivered as if divinely inspired or infallible; sententious; sometimes, ambiguous or obscure; portentous; also, delivering oracles (as, "Oh couldst thou speak, As in Dodona once thy kindred trees *Oracular*": Cowper's "Yardley Oak," 42); giving forth utterances or decisions as if by special inspiration or authority (as, "They referred to each other as *oracular* sources of wisdom and good taste": Arnold Bennett's "Old Wives' Tale," i. 7); also, communicating (supposedly) through oracles, as a deity; also, resorted to for oracles, as a shrine or place.—**o-rac'u-lar-ly,** *adv.*—**o-rac'u-lar-ness,** *n.*

o-ra-gious (ǫ-rā'jus), *a.* [F. *orageux*, < *orage*, storm, < L. *aura*, breeze.] Stormy or tempestuous (lit. or fig.): as, "M. d'Ivry, whose early life may have been rather *oragious*" (Thackeray's "Newcomes," xxxi.).

o-ral (ō'rạl), *a.* [L. *os* (*or-*), mouth.] Of or pertaining to the mouth (as, the *oral* cavity); also, done, taken, or administered by the mouth (as, *oral* communion; an *oral* dose of morphine); often, uttered by the mouth, or spoken (as, *oral* testimony); also, employing speech, as teachers or methods of teaching.—**o'ral-ly,** *adv.* In an oral manner; by the mouth; by spoken (not written) words.

-orama. Noun termination from Gr. *ὅραμα*, view, as in *cyclorama, diorama, myriorama, panorama*.

o-rang (ǫ-rang'), *n.* Shortened form of *orang-utan*.

or-ange (or'ạnj). [OF. *orenge* (F. *orange*), < Ar. *nāranj*, < Pers. *nārang*, orange.] **I.** *n.* The globose, reddish-yellow edible fruit of *Citrus aurantium*, a white-flowered evergreen rutaceous tree cultivated in warm countries; the tree itself, occurring in several varieties, as *Citrus aurantium sinensis* (common sweet orange) and *C. aurantium amara* ('bitter orange' or 'Seville orange'); any of several other citrous trees, as *C. trifoliata* ('trifoliate orange'), a hardy Japanese species cultivated widely in the U. S., largely for hedges, the fruit being inferior; the fruit of such trees; also, any of certain trees of other genera, as *Toxylon pomiferum* (see *Osage orange*), or the fruit; also, a reddish-yellow color. **II.** *a.* Of or pertaining to the orange; esp., of a reddish-yellow color.—**or-ange-ade'** (-ād'), *n.* A drink made of orange-juice and water sweetened.—**o-ran-geat** (o-räṅ-zhä), *n.* [F.] Candied orange-peel.—**or'ange=blos"som,** *n.* The flower of the orange: much worn in wreaths, etc., by brides at the marriage ceremony.

Or-ange-ism, Or-an-gism (or'ạnj-izm), *n.* The principles and practices of the Orangemen.—**Or'ange-ist, Or'an-gist,** *n.*

Or-ange-man (or'ạnj-mạn), *n.*; pl. *-men.* [From William of *Orange* (William III. of England).] A member of a secret society formed in the north of Ireland in 1795, having for its object the maintenance of the Protestant religion and ascendancy.

or-ange-ry (or'ạnj-ri), *n.*; pl. *-ries* (-riz). [F. *orangerie*.] A place, as a glass-house, in which orange-trees are cultivated: as, "The *Orangery* (built in 1685 by Mansart) is the finest piece of architecture at Versailles; the central gallery is 508 ft. long" (Encyc. Brit., 11th ed., XXVII. 1040).

o-rang=u-tan, o-rang=ou-tang (ǫ-rang'ǫ-tan", -tang"), *n.* [Malay *ōrang ūtan*, 'man of the woods.'] A large, long-armed anthropoid ape, *Simia satyrus*, of arboreal habits, found in Borneo and Sumatra. See cut on following page.

o-rate (ǫ-rāt' or ō'rāt), *v. i.*; *orated, orating.* [Back-formation from *oration*.] To make an oration; hold forth; speechify. [Chiefly humorous or contemptuous.]

o-ra-tion (ǫ-rā'shǫn), *n.* [L. *oratio*(*n-*), speech, discourse, oration, prayer, < *orare*, speak, plead, pray, < *os* (*or-*), mouth.] A formal speech or discourse, as by an orator (as, the *orations* of Demosthenes or of Cicero); now, esp., a formal discourse delivered on a special occasion, as on an anniversary or at a funeral, or at academic exercises; also, a prayer (obs. or hist.).

Orang-utan.

or-a-tor (or′ą-tọr), *n.* [AF. *oratour*, OF. F. *orateur*, < L. *orator*, speaker, orator, suppliant, < *orare*: see *oration*.] One who delivers an oration or formal discourse; a public speaker, esp. one of great eloquence (as, "I come not, friends, to steal away your hearts: I am no *orator*, as Brutus is": Shakspere's "Julius Cæsar," iii. 2. 221); also, a spokesman†; a messenger† or envoy†; an advocate†; also, a petitioner† or suppliant†.—**or-a-to′ri-al** (-tō′ri-ąl), *a.* Of, pertaining to, or befitting an orator; also, of or pertaining to an oratorio.—**or-a-to′ri-al-ly,** *adv.*

Or-a-to-ri-an (or-ą-tō′ri-ąn). In the *Rom. Cath. Ch.*: **I.** *a.* Of or pertaining to an Oratory. **II.** *n.* A member of an Oratory.

or-a-tor-ic (or-ą-tor′ik), *a.* Oratorical.

or-a-tor-i-cal (or-ą-tor′i-kąl), *a.* Of, pertaining to, or characteristic of an orator or oratory; given to oratory.—**or-a-tor′i-cal-ly,** *adv.*

or-a-to-ri-o (or-ą-tō′ri-ō), *n.*; pl. *-os* (-ōz). [It., < LL. *oratorium*, E. *oratory*²; so named from the musical services in the church of the Oratory of St. Philip Neri, in Rome.] An extended musical composition, with a text more or less dramatic in character and usually based upon a religious theme, for solo voices, chorus, and orchestra, and performed without action, costume, or scenery: as, the *oratorios* of Bach or of Handel.

or-a-tor-ize (or′ą-tọr-īz), *v. i.*; *-ized, -izing.* To play the orator; 'orate': as, "They reached the magistrate's house . . . Mr. Pickwick *oratorising*, and the crowd shouting" (Dickens's "Pickwick Papers," xxiv.).

or-a-to-ry¹ (or′ą-tọ-ri), *n.* [L. *oratoria*, prop. fem. of *oratorius*, pertaining to an orator or to praying, < *orator*: see *orator*.] The art of an orator; the art of public speaking; also, the exercise of eloquence; eloquent speaking or language.

or-a-to-ry² (or′ą-tọ-ri), *n.*; pl. *-ries* (-riz). [LL. *oratorium*, place of prayer, prop. neut. of L. *oratorius*: see *oratory*¹.] A place of prayer, as a small chapel or a room for private devotions; also [*cap.*], any of certain religious societies of the Roman Catholic Church, esp. one ('Oratory of St. Philip Neri') composed of secular priests, not bound by vows, devoted to simple and familiar preaching; a local branch or house of this society.

or-a-tress (or′ą-tres), *n.* A female orator: as, "Tabby's eloquence . . . would have shamed the first-rate *oratress* of Billingsgate" (Smollett's "Humphry Clinker," May 24).

orb (ôrb), *n.* [L. *orbis*, circle, disk, orb.] A circle, or anything circular (now rare); the orbit of a heavenly body† (as, "Instruct the planets in what *orbs* to run": Pope's "Essay on Man," ii. 21); a cyclic period†; also, a sphere or globe (as, "What a hell of witchcraft lies In the small *orb* of one particular tear!" Shakspere's "Lover's Complaint," 289); any of the heavenly bodies (chiefly poetic or rhetorical: as, the *orb* of day, the sun; the *orb* of night, the moon); the earth† (see Shakspere's "Twelfth Night," iii. 1. 43); the eyeball or eye (chiefly poetic or rhetorical: as, "His eyelids heavily closed over their *orbs*," Irving's "Knickerbocker's New York," ii. 5); the mound, or emblem of sovereignty; any of the concentric hollow spheres of the old astronomy, conceived as surrounding and revolving round the earth and as carrying the heavenly bodies with them (see *sphere, n.*); in *astrol.*, the space within which the influence of a planet, etc., is supposed to act.—**orb,** *v.* **I.** *tr.* To encircle; inclose; also, to form into a circle or a sphere. **II.** *intr.* To move in an orbit; also, to assume the shape of an orb.—**orbed,** *p. a.* Formed into an orb; circular; spherical; rounded.

or-bic-u-lar (ôr-bik′ū-lạr), *a.* [LL. *orbicularis*, < L. *orbiculus*, dim. of *orbis*, E. *orb*.] Like an orb; circular; ringlike; spherical; rounded; in *bot.*, approximately circular, as a leaf.—**or-bic-u-lar′i-ty** (-lar′i-ti), *n.*—**or-bic′u-lar-ly,** *adv.*

Orbicular Leaf.

or-bic-u-late (ôr-bik′ū-lāt), *a.* [L. *orbiculatus*, < *orbiculus*: see *orbicular*.] Orbicular; rounded.—**or-bic′u-late-ly,** *adv.*

or-bit (ôr′bit), *n.* [L. *orbita*, wheel-track, course, circuit, < *orbis*, E. *orb*.] The course of a heavenly body; the elliptical or curved path described by a planet, etc., about another body, as the sun; fig., a course regularly pursued, as in life (as, "They knew each other by sight, but their *orbits* did not touch": Arnold Bennett's "Helen with the High Hand," v.); also, the bony cavity of the skull which contains the eye; also, the part surrounding the eye of a bird or insect; also, an orb or sphere; the eye.—**or′bi-tal** (-bi-tąl), *a.*—**or″bi-to-na′sal** (-tọ-nā′ząl), *a.* Pertaining to the orbit of the eye and to the nose.—**or″bi-to-sphe′noid** (-sfē′noid). In *anat.*: **I.** *a.* Pertaining to the orbit of the eye and to the sphenoid bone: as, the *orbitosphenoid* bone (a section of the sphenoid bone forming a part of the bony orbit of the eye). **II.** *n.* The orbitosphenoid bone.

orb-y (ôr′bi), *a.* Orb-like; pertaining to an orb. [Poetic.]

orc (ôrk), *n.* [L. *orca*, kind of whale.] Any of various marine mammals, as the grampus or killer: as, "the haunt of seals, and *orcs*, and sea-mews' clang" (Milton's "Paradise Lost," xi. 835).

Or-ca-di-an (ôr-kā′di-ąn). [L. *Orcades*, the Orkney Islands.] **I.** *a.* Of or pertaining to the Orkney Islands, north of Scotland. **II.** *n.* A native or inhabitant of the Orkney Islands.

or-ce-in (ôr′sẹ-in), *n.* [From *orcin*.] In *chem.*, a red dyestuff obtained by oxidizing an ammoniacal solution of orcin, and forming the principal coloring matter of cudbear and orchil.

or-chard (ôr′chạrd), *n.* [AS. *ortgeard*, appar. < L. *hortus*, garden, + AS. *geard*, E. *yard*¹: cf. Goth. *aurtigards*, Icel. *jurtagardhr*, garden.] A garden†; also, a piece of ground, usually inclosed, devoted to the cultivation of fruit-trees; a collection of such trees.—**or′chard-ist,** *n.* One who cultivates an orchard. Also **or′chard-man** (-mąn); pl. *-men.*

or-ches-tic (ôr-kes′tik), *a.* [Gr. ὀρχηστικός, < ὀρχεῖσθαι, dance.] Of or pertaining to dancing.

or-ches-tra (ôr′kes-trä), *n.* [L., < Gr. ὀρχήστρα, < ὀρχεῖσθαι, dance.] In the ancient Greek theater, the circular space in front of the stage, allotted to the chorus; in the Roman theater, a similar space reserved for the seats of senators and other persons of distinction; also, in a modern theater, etc., the space reserved for the musicians, usually the front part of the main floor; hence, by extension, the parquet, or often the entire main floor space for spectators; also, a company of performers on various musical instruments, including esp. stringed instruments of the viol class, also clarinets and flutes, cornets and trombones, drums, cymbals, etc., for playing concerted music, as symphonies, operas, and other compositions; the set of instruments played by such a company.—**or-ches-tral** (ôr-kes′trąl or ôr′kes-), *a.* Of or pertaining to an orchestra; composed for or performed by an orchestra.—**or-ches′tral-ly,** *adv.*

or-ches-trate (ôr′kes-trāt), *v. t.*; *-trated, -trating.* [Cf. F. *orchestrer*.] To compose or arrange (music) for performance by an orchestra.—**or-ches-tra′tion** (-trā′shọn), *n.* The act, art, or result of orchestrating.

or-ches-tri-on (ôr-kes′tri-on), *n.* [From *orchestra.*] A mechanical musical instrument, resembling a barrel-organ but more elaborate, for producing the effect of an orchestra.

or-chid (ôr′kid), *n.* [NL. *Orchideæ* (later *Orchidaceæ*), pl., irreg. < L. *orchis* (stem *orchi-*, not *orchid-*): see *orchis.*] Any plant of the family *Orchidaceæ*, comprising terrestrial and epiphytic perennial herbs of temperate and tropical regions, with flowers which are usually beautiful and often singular in form, many species being highly valued in cultivation. **—or-chi-da′ceous** (-ki-dā′shius), *a.* Belonging to the *Orchidaceæ*, or orchid family of plants.—**or′chid-ist,** *n.* One who cultivates orchids. **—or-chid-ol′o-gy** (-ki-dol′ō-ji), *n.* [See *-logy.*] The branch of botany or of horticulture that deals with orchids.—**or-chid-ol′o-gist,** *n.*

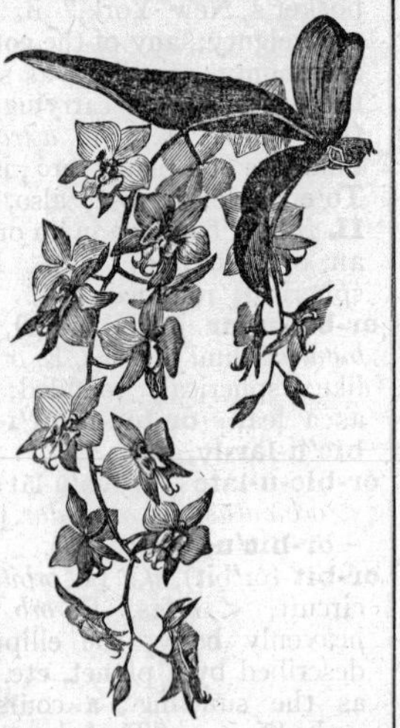

Orchid (*Phalænopsis schilleriana*).

or-chil (ôr′kil or ôr′chil), *n.* [ME. *orchell*: cf. It. *orcello, oricello*, Sp. *orchilla*, F. *orseille*, OF. *orsolle.*] A violet coloring matter obtained from certain lichens, chiefly species of *Roccella*; also, any such lichen. Cf. *litmus.*

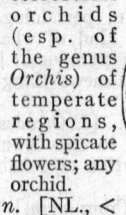

Orchil (*Roccella tinctoria*).

or-chis (ôr′kis), *n.* [L., < Gr. ὄρχις, orchis (named from the shape of the root), orig. testicle.] Any of various terrestrial orchids (esp. of the genus *Orchis*) of temperate regions, with spicate flowers; any orchid.

Flowering Plant of Showy Orchis (*Orchis spectabilis*).

or-chi-tis (ôr-kī′tis), *n.* [NL., < Gr. ὄρχις, testicle.] In *pathol.*, inflammation of the testicle.—**or-chit′ic** (-kit′ik), *a.*

or-cin (ôr′sin), *n.* [Related to *orchil.*] In *chem.*, a colorless crystalline compound found in many lichens, and also prepared synthetically. Also **or′cin-ol** (-si-nol or -nōl).

or-dain (ôr-dān′), *v.* [OF. *ordener* (F. *ordonner*), < L. *ordinare* (pp. *ordinatus*), order, arrange, appoint, < *ordo* (*ordin-*): see *order.*] **I.** *tr.* To set in order†, arrange†, or prepare†; also, to institute, establish, or found (archaic); also, to appoint authoritatively; decree; give orders for (as, "It was mainly to acquire gold for himself that he *ordained* all this carnage": Motley's "Dutch Republic," iii. 7); of God, fate, etc., to destine or predestine; *eccles.*, to invest with ministerial or sacerdotal functions; confer holy orders upon; admit to the Christian ministry. **II.** *intr.* To decree; order; command.—**or-dain′er,** *n.*—**or-dain′ment,** *n.*

or-de-al (ôr′dē-al), *n.* [AS. *ordāl, ordēl*, ordeal, = D. *oordeel* = G. *urteil*, judgment.] A primitive form of trial to determine guilt or innocence, as by the effect of fire, poison, or water upon the accused, the result being regarded as a divine or preterhuman judgment; hence, any severe test or trial; a trying experience (as, "She wondered how he, and how she, would comport themselves in the *ordeal* of adieu": Arnold Bennett's "Hilda Lessways," v. 2).—**ordeal bean,** the poisonous Calabar bean, of Africa: used by the natives in a form of ordeal.

or-der (ôr′dėr), *n.* [OF. F. *ordre*, < L. *ordo* (*ordin-*), row, series, rank, class, regular arrangement, order.] A row or series (now rare); also, a rank, grade, or class of the community (as, "He had found, in general, the lower *orders* debased; the superior immersed in sordid pursuits": Disraeli's "Coningsby," iv. 10); a body of persons of the same profession, occupation, or pursuits (as, "The spirit of the whole clerical *order* rose against this injustice": Macaulay's "Hist. of Eng.," vi.); any class, kind, or sort, as of persons or things, having a particular rank in a scale, or distinguished from others by nature or character (as, talents of a high *order*; an institution, or a publication, of a different *order*); specif., any of the nine grades of angels in medieval angelology (see *angel*); also, the rank or status of an ordained Christian minister (now usually in *pl.*: as, to take *orders*, or holy *orders*, that is, to enter the Christian ministry); any of the degrees or grades of the clerical office (the number of which varies in different churches, the Roman Catholic Church, for example, having the 'major orders' of bishop, priest, deacon, and subdeacon, and the 'minor orders' of acolyte, exorcist, lector, and ostiary, while the Anglican Church recognizes only the three grades of bishop, priest, and deacon); the rite or sacrament of ordination (usually in *pl.*); also, a body or society of persons living by common consent under the same religious, moral, or social regulations; a monastic society or fraternity (as, an *order* of monks or friars; the Benedictine *order*; the Franciscan *order*); a society or fraternity of knights, of combined military and monastic character, as in the middle ages (as, the Teutonic *Order*: see under *Teutonic, a.*); an institution, partly an imitation of the medieval orders of military monks, having as its purpose the rewarding of meritorious service by the conferring of a dignity (as, the *Order* of the Golden Fleece: see phrase below); the badge or insignia of such an institution; a modern organization or society more or less resembling the knightly orders (as, fraternal *orders*; the Independent *Order* of Oddfellows); also, a column (base, shaft, and capital) with its entablature, viewed as the characteristic element of a particular architectural style; any one of the typical styles (Doric, Ionic, Corinthian, Tuscan, and Composite) of classical architecture; also, a zoölogical or botanical group or category ranking below the class and above the family; also, degree, as in algebra; also, the disposition of things following one after another, as in space, time, etc. (as, "pageants on pageants, in long *order* drawn," Pope's "Satires and Epistles of Horace Imitated," Epistles, ii. 1. 316; the *order* of the days of the week, or the months of the year); succession or sequence; course or method of occurrence; also, formal disposition or array (as, "I hear their drums: let's set our men in *order*": Shakspere's "3 Henry VI.," i. 2. 70); methodical or harmonious arrangement; hence, a condition in which everything is in its proper place with reference to other things and to its purpose (as, "At his second bidding darkness fled, Light shone, and order from disorder sprung": Milton's "Paradise Lost," iii. 713);

Doric Order. — Temple of Castor and Pollux (so called), Girgenti, Sicily. — *a*, entablature, consisting of cornice, frieze, and architrave; *b*, capital and shaft; *c*, stylobate, which in the Doric order performs the function of a base.

also, state or condition generally (as, affairs are in good *order*, or bad *order*; "The venison proved in high *order*, the claret excellent," Scott's "Guy Mannering," xxxix.); proper or satisfactory condition (as, to put one's affairs in *order*; my watch is out of *order*); also, suitable action in relation to some particular result or end (obs. or archaic: as, "Provide me soldiers, lords, Whiles I take *order* for mine own affairs," Shakspere's "2 Henry VI.," iii. 1. 320); also, customary mode of procedure, or established usage, or conformity to this; specif., the customary or prescribed mode of proceeding in debates or the like, or in the conduct of deliberative or legislative bodies, public meetings, etc., or conformity to this (as, the *order* of business; the motion is not in *order*); also, a prevailing course of things, or an established system or régime (as, the *order* of nature; "The old *order* changeth, yielding place to new," Tennyson's "Passing of Arthur," 408); also, conformity to law or established authority; absence of revolt, disturbance, turbulence, unruliness, etc.; also, a prescribed form of divine service, or of administration of a rite or ceremony, or the service itself; also, the position of a rifle in a military drill when the butt is brought to the ground and the weapon held vertically against the right side; also, an authoritative direction, injunction, or mandate; an instruction; a command; specif., a direction of a court or judge, made or entered in writing and not included in a judgment; a written direction to pay money or deliver property, given by a person legally entitled to dispose of it; a direction or commission to make, provide, or furnish something (as, shoes made to *order*; an *order* for groceries); a pass for admission to a theater, museum, or the like; *pl.*, commands or notices issued by a military commander to the troops under him.—**holy order, holy orders.** See *holy order*, under *holy*, *a.*—**in order that,** to the end that: as, he came *in order that* he might see for himself.—**in order to,** as a means to; with a view to: as, "I determined . . . to direct my course this way, *in order to* my return to Europe" (Swift's "Gulliver's Travels," iii. 7); "I shall next week come down . . . *in order to* take my seat at the board" (Steele, in "Spectator," 48).—**order in council,** in Great Britain, a special order issued by the sovereign with the advice of the privy council under the authorization of a general act of Parliament, and having the full force of law.—**Order of the Bath, of the Garter, of the Golden Fleece, of the Holy Ghost, of the Thistle.** See *bath*[1], *garter*, *golden*, *holy*, and *thistle*.—**to put one's house in order.** See under *house*[2], *n.*—**or′der,** *v.* **I.** *tr.* To arrange in order, or in a particular order; arrange methodically or suitably; specif., in military use, to bring (a rifle) to the position called order (chiefly in the command 'order arms'); also, to regulate, conduct, or manage (as, "They *order*, said I, this matter better in France," Sterne's "Sentimental Journey," opening line; "I had to *order* my life methodically," J. Conrad's "Rescue," v. 5); sometimes, to ordain, as God or fate does; also, to give an order, direction, or command to; instruct authoritatively or imperatively to do something; sometimes, by ellipsis, to direct or command to go or come (as specified: as, to *order* a person out of one's house, or into one's presence); also, to give an order for; direct or command to be done, etc. (as, "He *ordered* my companions to be handcuffed": Malkin's tr. Le Sage's "Gil Blas," ii. 5); prescribe (as, a doctor *orders* a medicine, or rest, for a patient); direct to be made, supplied, or furnished (as, "Alva immediately *ordered* seven thousand pairs of skates," Motley's "Dutch Republic," iii. 8; to *order* one's dinner); also, *eccles.*, to invest with clerical rank or authority. **II.** *intr.* To issue orders, instructions, or commands; also, to give an order or commission.

or-der-er (ôr′dėr-ėr), *n.* One who orders.

or-der-less (ôr′dėr-les), *a.* Without order, arrangement, method, or regularity; disorderly.

or-der-li-ness (ôr′dėr-li-nes), *n.* Orderly state or character; orderly manner of behavior.

or-der-ly (ôr′dėr-li). **I.** *a.* Arranged or disposed in order; characterized by regular sequence or arrangement; exhibiting system or method; regular; also, observant of order, system, or method, as persons, the mind, etc.; also, characterized by or observant of order, rule, or discipline (as, "The behaviour of these animals [horses] was . . . *orderly* and rational," Swift's "Gulliver's Travels," iv. 1; "an *orderly* citizen," Mrs. Stowe's "Oldtown Folks," v.); not tumultuous, unruly, or disorderly; also, *milit.*, pertaining to orders or commands, or the issuing of them; charged with the communication or execution of orders; being on duty. **II.** *n.*; pl. *-lies* (-liz). A private soldier or a non-commissioned officer attending on a superior officer to carry orders, etc.; also, an attendant in a hospital, charged with the maintenance of order, cleanliness, etc.; also, a street-cleaner (Eng.).—**or′der-ly,** *adv.* In order; in regular sequence; with proper arrangement; methodically; also, according to established order or rule; in conformity with good order or discipline.

or-di-nal (ôr′di-nạl). [LL. *ordinalis* (as n., in eccles. use, ML. *ordinale*), < L. *ordo* (*ordin-*): see *order*.] **I.** *a.* Indicating order or succession, or position in a series (as, the *ordinal* numbers or numerals, *first*, *second*, *third*, etc., as opposed to the *cardinal*); also, pertaining to an order, as of animals or plants. **II.** *n.* An ordinal number or numeral; also, a directory of ecclesiastical services; also, a book containing the forms for the ordination of priests, consecration of bishops, etc.—**or′di-nal-ly,** *adv.*

or-di-nance (ôr′di-nạns), *n.* [OF. *ordenance* (F. *ordonnance*), < ML. *ordinantia*, < L. *ordinans*, ppr.: see *ordinant*.] Orderly arrangement or disposition; also, preparation† or provision†; hence, something prepared or provided†; apparatus† or equipment†; military equipment†; ordnance†; also, regulation, direction, or management (archaic); also, an authoritative direction; a decree or command; an established rule or law; a public injunction or regulation; also, a prescribed practice or usage; *eccles.*, an established rite or ceremony.

or-di-nand (ôr′di-nand), *n.* [L. *ordinandus*, gerundive of *ordinare*: see *ordain*.] *Eccles.*, one about to be ordained, or to receive holy orders.

or-di-nant (ôr′di-nạnt). [L. *ordinans* (*-ant-*), ppr. of *ordinare*: see *ordain*.] **I.** *a.* Ordering; directing; ordaining: as, "Why, even in that was heaven *ordinant*" (Shakspere's "Hamlet," v. 2. 48). **II.** *n.* *Eccles.*, one who ordains, or confers holy orders.

or-di-na-ri-ly (ôr′di-nā̤-ri-li), *adv.* In the ordinary way; as is customary or usual; also, in ordinary cases; usually; also, in an ordinary degree; to the usual extent.—**or′di-na-ri-ness,** *n.*

or-di-na-ry (ôr′di-nā̤-ri). [L. *ordinarius*, < *ordo* (*ordin-*): see *order*.] **I.** *a.* Of the customary or established order, or regular; specif., of a judge, etc., having jurisdiction by virtue of office and not by special delegation; of jurisdiction, etc., immediate, as contrasted with that which is delegated; of officials, etc., belonging to the regular staff or the fully recognized class (as, an *ordinary* professor in a German university: cf. *extraordinary*); in general, customary, usual, or normal (as, for all *ordinary* purposes; in *ordinary* practice; his *ordinary* frame of mind); also, such as is commonly met with; of the usual kind; not distinguished in any way from others; often, not above, or rather below, the average level of quality; commonplace; somewhat inferior. Cf. *ornery*. **II.** *n.*; pl. *-ries* (-riz). One having ordinary or immediate jurisdiction, as a bishop in his diocese; in some of the States of the U. S., a judge of a court of probate; formerly, in England, a clergyman appointed to prepare condemned prisoners for death; also, an order or form for divine service, esp. that for saying mass; the service of the mass exclusive of the canon; also, something regular, customary, or usual; a high bicycle of the earlier type, with one large and one small wheel; often, a meal regularly served at a fixed price in an eating-house or inn (as, "a great inn, crowded with travellers, who dine at the landlord's *ordinary*": Smollett's "Humphry Clinker," June 26); a table d'hôte; a place where such meals are served, as an eating-house or inn, or its dining-room; also, in heraldic use, any of the simplest and commonest heraldic charges or bearings, usually bounded by straight lines; any of the more important of these ('honorable ordinaries'), as distinguished from the subordinaries; also, the ordinary condition, degree, run, or the like (as, out of the *ordinary*).—**in ordinary,** of officials, etc., ordinary or regular, or in regular service: as, a physician *in ordinary* to a king. See *ordinary*, *a.*, and cf. *extraordinary*.

or-di-nate (ôr′di-nạt). [L. *ordinatus*, pp. of *ordinare*: see *ordain*.] **I.** *a.* Orderly†; regular†; in *entom.*, arranged in a row or rows. **II.** *n.* Any of a set of parallel chords of a conic section, drawn at right angles to the axis and bisected by it; either half of such a chord. See also *coördinate*, *n.*
or-di-na-tion (ôr-di-nā′shọn), *n.* [L. *ordinatio(n-)*, < *ordinare*: see *ordain*.] The act of ordering or arranging, or the resulting state; also, an ordaining or decreeing; *eccles.*, the act or ceremony of ordaining, or admitting to the Christian ministry; the fact of being ordained.
or-di-nee (ôr-di-nē′), *n.* One who receives ordination.
ord-nance (ôrd′nạns), *n.* [Var. of *ordinance*.] Military weapons of all kinds with their equipments, ammunition, etc.; esp., cannon or artillery.—**Ordnance Survey,** the government survey of Great Britain and Ireland, orig. carried out under the direction of the ordnance department.
or-don-nance (ôr′dọ-nạns, F. ôr-do-näṅs), *n.* [F.: see *ordinance*.] Arrangement or disposition of parts, as of a building, a picture, or a literary composition; also, an ordinance, decree, or law.
Or-do-vi-cian (ôr-dọ-vish′ịạn). [L. *Ordovices*, pl., an ancient British tribe in northern Wales.] In *geol.*: **I.** *a.* Noting or pertaining to a geological period or a system of rocks recognized by certain authorities, and commonly taken as comprising the earlier or older portions of what is usually known as the Silurian. **II.** *n.* The Ordovician period or system.
or-dure (ôr′dụr), *n.* [OF. F. *ordure*, < *ord*, filthy, < L. *horridus*, E. *horrid*.] Filth; dung; excrement. Also fig.
ore (ōr), *n.* [AS. *ōra* (= D. *oer*), ore; with mod. form prob. due to association with AS. *ār*, brass.] A metal-bearing mineral or rock, or a native metal, esp. when valuable enough to be mined; also, a mineral or natural product serving as a source of some non-metallic substance, as sulphur; also, metal, esp. precious metal (archaic).
ö-re (ė′re), *n.*; pl. *öre*. [Dan., Norw., and Sw.] A bronze coin and money of account of Denmark, Norway, and Sweden, equal to one hundredth of a krone or krona, or about one fourth of a U. S. cent.

Obverse. Reverse.
Swedish Öre.

o-re-ad (ō′rẹ-ad), *n.* [L. *Oreas* (pl. *Oreades*), < Gr. Ὀρειάς (pl. Ὀρειάδες), < ὄρος, mountain.] In *class. myth.*, a mountain-nymph: as, "Lovelier than whatever *Oread* haunt The knolls of Ida" (Tennyson's "Œnone," 72).
o-rec-tic (ọ-rek′tik), *a.* [Gr. ὀρεκτικός, < ὀρέγειν: see *orexis*.] Of or pertaining to appetite or desire; appetitive.
Or-e-gon (or′ẹ-gon) **pine.** Same as *Douglas spruce.*
o-rex-is (ọ-rek′sis), *n.* [L., < Gr. ὄρεξις, < ὀρέγειν, reach out, desire.] Appetite; desire.
or-gan (ôr′gạn), *n.* [L. *organum*, < Gr. ὄργανον, instrument, tool, bodily organ, musical instrument, < ἐργ-, do work: see *work*, *n.*] An instrument or means, as of performance (as, "His be the praise . . . Who made my hand the *organ* of his might": Spenser's "Faerie Queene," ii. 1. 33); now, esp., a means or medium of communicating thoughts, opinions, etc. (as, "He was . . . the sole *organ* of communication with foreign powers," Macaulay's "Hist. of Eng.," i.; "There was no efficient *organ* of financial criticism," Lecky's "Hist. of Eng. in the 18th Century," iii.); often, a newspaper serving as the mouthpiece of a political party; also, in an animal or a plant, a part or member, as the heart, having some specific function; any part of the human brain held by phrenologists to be the seat of a particular faculty or aptitude; also, any of various musical instruments, esp. wind-instruments (as, "Praise him with stringed instruments and *organs*," Ps. cl. 4: now only as in the specific senses following); a musical instrument ('pipe-organ') consisting of one or more sets of pipes sounded by means of compressed air, played by means of keys arranged in one or more key-boards (in its full modern development the largest, most complicated, and noblest of musical instruments, and particularly suited to ecclesiastical and other stately music); one of the independent sets of pipes of which such an instrument is made up ('partial organ'); a reed-organ, harmonium, or American organ (see *reed-organ*); a barrel-organ or hand-organ (cf. *organ-grinder*).—**or′gan=build″er,** *n.* One who builds or constructs organs, esp. pipe-organs.—**or′gan=build″ing,** *n.*
or-gan-die, or-gan-dy (ôr′gạn-di), *n.* [F. *organdi*.] A fine, translucent, stiff-finished muslin, often printed with flowered or other patterns, used for women's dresses, etc.
or-gan=grind-er (ôr′gạn-grīn″dėr), *n.* A street musician who plays a hand-organ by turning the crank.—**or′gan=grind″ing,** *n.* and *a.*
or-gan-ic (ôr-gan′ik), *a.* [L. *organicus*, < Gr. ὀργανικός, < ὄργανον, E. *organ*.] Serving as an instrument or means, or instrumental (now rare); also, of or pertaining to an organ or the organs of an animal or a plant (as, *organic* functions; an *organic* disease, see phrase below); also, having organs, or exhibiting the functional parts or complex structure characteristic of living bodies or matter (animal or vegetable); characteristic of, pertaining to, or derived from living organisms (as, *organic* structure; substances of *organic* origin; *organic* remains found in rocks); specif., noting or pertaining to a class of chemical compounds which formerly comprised only those existing in or derived from living organisms (animal or plant), but which now includes these and all other compounds of carbon (cf. *inorganic*); also, of or pertaining to the constitution or structure of a thing; innate; constitutional; structural; also, characterized by the systematic arrangement of parts into a whole; organized; systematic; also, of or like a (musical) organ.—**organic disease,** a disease in which there is a structural alteration in the organ involved: opposed to *functional disease*.—**or-gan′i-cal-ly,** *adv.*
or-gan-ism (ôr′gạn-izm), *n.* Organic structure; organization; also, a body exhibiting organization and organic life; an individual composed of a number of mutually dependent parts constituted for subserving vital processes; any form of animal or plant life (often used of minute, obscure, or not readily classified forms: as, microscopic *organisms*; low *organisms*); hence, any organized body or system analogous to a living being (as, "the British social *organism*": H. G. Wells's "Tono-Bungay," i. 1. § 1).—**or-gan-is′mal** (-iz′mạl), *a.*
or-gan-ist (ôr′gạn-ist), *n.* A player on an organ, esp. a pipe-organ.
or-gan-iz-a-ble (ôr′gạn-ī-zạ-bl), *a.* Capable of being organized; in *biol.*, capable of being converted into living tissue.—**or″gan-iz-a-bil′i-ty** (-bil′i-ti), *n.*
or-gan-i-za-tion (ôr″gạn-i-zā′shọn), *n.* The act or process of organizing; the state or the manner of being organized; organic structure; also, that which is organized; an organism; any organized whole; often, a body of persons organized for some end or work.—**or″gan-i-za′tion-al,** *a.*—**or″gan-i-za′tion-ist,** *n.* One who advocates, or is skilled in, organization, as for united action or work.
or-gan-ize (ôr′gạn-īz), *v.*; *-ized, -izing.* [= F. *organiser*, < ML. *organizare*, < Gr. ὀργανίζειν, organize, < ὄργανον, E. *organ*.] **I.** *tr.* To form or constitute of different organs or parts adapted for subserving vital processes, or give organic structure or character to (usually in *organized*, *pp.*: as, *organized* bodies or matter); hence, in general, to form as or into a whole consisting of interdependent or coördinated parts, esp. for harmonious or united action (as, to *organize* a party, or *organize* men into a party; "A fresh army had . . . been collected . . . and was already *organized* at Pierrepoint," Motley's "Dutch Republic," i. 3; to *organize* the industries of a country for service in time of war); arrange in a systematic whole, or systematize (as, to *organize* knowledge or facts; to *organize* work or efforts); prepare by arranging for various factors or details involved (as, to *organize* an expedition, conspiracy, or revolt). **II.** *intr.* To assume organic structure; become living tissue; also, to combine in an organized company, party, or the like.—**or′gan-iz-er** (-ī-zėr), *n.*
organo-. Form of Gr. ὄργανον, instrument, organ, used in combination.—**or-ga-no-gen-e-sis** (ôr″gạ-nọ-jen′e-sis), *n.* In *biol.*, the origin or development of the organs of living bodies. Also **or-ga-nog′e-ny** (-noj′e-ni).—**or-ga-nog′ra-phy** (-nog′rạ-fi), *n.* [+ *-graphy*.] The description of the organs of animals or plants; descriptive organology.—**or-ga-nol′o-gy** (-nol′ọ-ji), *n.* [+ *-logy*.] The branch of biology

that deals with the structure and functions of the organs of animals or plants; also, phrenology.

or-ga-non (ôr′gạ-non), *n.*; pl. *-na* (-nạ̈). [Gr. ὄργανον: see *organ.*] A bodily organ†; also, an instrument of thought or knowledge; esp., a system of rules or principles of demonstration or investigation; specif. [*cap.*], the title of the logical writings of Aristotle. Cf. *organum.*

or-ga-no-ther-a-peu-tics (ôr″gạ-nō-ther-ạ-pū′tiks), *n.* [See *organo-.*] That branch of therapeutics which deals with the use of remedies prepared from the organs of animals (as the thyroid gland, the pancreas, the suprarenal bodies, etc.).—**or″ga-no-ther-a-peu′tic,** *a.*—**or″ga-no-ther′a-py** (-ther′ạ-pi), *n.* Treatment of disease by administering preparations made from the organs of animals; opotherapy.

or-gan=pipe (ôr′gạn-pīp), *n.* One of the pipes of a pipe-organ; hence, something resembling such a pipe.—**organ=pipe coral,** any coral of the family *Tubiporidæ*, characterized by tubular corallites united in masses.

Organ-pipe Coral (*Tubipora musica*).

or-gan=point (ôr′gạn-point), *n.* In *music*, same as *pedal-point.*

or-ga-num (ôr′gạ-num), *n.*; pl. *-na* (-nạ̈). [L.: see *organ.*] A bodily organ†; also, an organon, or instrument of thought or knowledge (esp. in the title of Bacon's "Novum Organum," that is, New Instrument, with allusion to Aristotle's "Organon").

or-gan-zine (ôr′gạn-zēn), *n.* [F. *organsin*, < It. *organzino.*] Silk thread made of several single threads twisted together: used for the warp in weaving.

or-gasm (ôr′gazm), *n.* [F. *orgasme*, < Gr. ὀργᾶν, swell, be excited.] Immoderate excitement; in *physiol.*, excitement and turgescence in an organ; specif., the height of venereal excitement.—**or-gas′tic** (-gas′tik), *a.*

or-geat (ôr′zhat, F. ôr-zhä), *n.* [F., < *orge*, < L. *hordeum*, barley.] A syrup or drink made from almonds (orig. from barley), sugar, and a water prepared from orange-flowers.

Org-esch (ôr′gesh), *n.* [G., < *org*(*anisation*), organization, + *Esch*(*erich*), name of the founder.] A semi-secret political and military organization in Bavaria and other parts of Germany, active after the close of the World War, being reactionary in principles and opposed to socialism and communism, and favorable to a return to monarchy.

or-gi-ac, or-gic (ôr′ji-ak, -jik), *a.* Pertaining to orgies; orgiastic.

or-gi-as-tic (ôr-ji-as′tik), *a.* [Gr. ὀργιαστικός, < ὀργιάζειν, celebrate orgies, < ὄργια: see *orgy.*] Of, pertaining to, or of the nature of orgies; characterized by orgies: as, "an *orgiastic* carnival, gross in all its manifestations of joy" (Arnold Bennett's "Old Wives' Tale," i. 4).—**or-gi-as′ti-cal-ly,** *adv.*

or′gic, *a.* See *orgiac.*

or-gu-lous, or-gil-lous (ôr′gụ̄-lus, -gi-lus), *a.* [OF. *orguillus* (F. *orgueilleux*), < *orguil*, pride; prob. from Teut.] Proud; haughty: as, "From isles of Greece The princes *orgulous*, their high blood chafed, Have to the port of Athens sent their ships" (Shakspere's "Troilus and Cressida," Prologue, 2). [Archaic.]

or-gy (ôr′ji), *n.*; pl. *-gies* (-jiz). [F. *orgie*, < L. *orgia*, pl., < Gr. ὄργια, pl., secret rites, any rites of worship, prob. < ἐργ-, do work: cf. *organ.*] *Pl.*, secret rites or ceremonies connected with the worship of certain deities of classical mythology, esp. the rites in honor of Dionysus or Bacchus, which were celebrated with wild dancing and singing, drinking, etc. (rarely in *sing.*); hence, in general, ceremonies of worship, commemoration, or the like; also, wild, drunken, or licentious festivities or revelry; *sing.*, a wild carouse; an unbridled or licentious revel; any course of proceedings marked by unbridled indulgence of passions (as, an *orgy* of massacre or blood).

or-i-chalc (or′i-kalk), *n.* [L. *orichalcum*, < Gr. ὀρείχαλκος, < ὄρος, mountain, + χαλκός, copper.] A yellow metal or metallic alloy, perhaps brass, highly prized by the ancients.

o-ri-el (ō′ri-ẹl), *n.* [OF. *oriol*, porch, passage, gallery, < ML. *oriolum*, porch, hall; origin unknown.] A recess with a window, or a recessed window, usually having a semi-polygonal plan, projecting from the outer face of a wall, esp. in an upper story: as, "All in an *oriel* on the summer side, Vine-clad, of Arthur's palace toward the stream, They met" (Tennyson's "Lancelot and Elaine," 1170). Cf. *bay-window.*—**o′ri-el=win′dow,** *n.*

Oriel. — Castle of Heidelberg, Baden.

o-ri-ent (ō′ri-ẹnt). [As adj., L. *oriens* (*orient-*), ppr. of *oriri*, rise; as n., OF. F. *orient*, < L. *oriens*, the east (where the sun rises), noun use of *oriens*, ppr.] **I.** *a.* Rising, or appearing as from beneath the horizon (as, "the *orient* sun," Milton's "Paradise Lost," v. 175; "the roseate breath of *orient* day," Thomson's "Castle of Indolence," ii. 10); also, eastern or oriental (now poetic: as, "Now morning from her *orient* chamber came," Keats's "Imitation of Spenser"); also, fine or precious, as gems, esp. pearls (orig. with reference to gems coming from the East: cf. *occidental, a.*); hence, brilliant, shining, or bright (archaic: as, "Ten thousand banners . . . With *orient* colours waving," Milton's "Paradise Lost," i. 546). **II.** *n.* The east; the eastern regions; [*cap.*] the countries to the east (and southeast) of the Mediterranean; also, the countries of Asia generally; [*l. c.*] an orient pearl (as, "a very Sea of Thought . . . wherein the toughest pearl-diver may dive . . . and return . . . with true *orients*": Carlyle's "Sartor Resartus," i. 2); the peculiar luster or coloring of a pearl; also, shining brightness, or radiance (poetic: as, "In every nobler mood We feel the *orient* of their spirit glow," Lowell's "Commemoration Ode," viii.).—**o′ri-ent** (-ent), *v.* [F. *orienter*, < *orient*, the east.] **I.** *tr.* To place so as to face the east; build (a church) with the chief altar to the east and the chief entrance to the west; bury (a corpse) with the feet to the east; also, to place in any definite position with reference to the points of the compass or other points (as, to *orient* a building north and south); fig., to direct to a particular object (as, "What is the good of *orienting* one's devotion to a firm, or to class solidarity?" H. G. Wells's "Italy, France, and Britain at War," iv. 5); adjust with relation to, or bring into due relation to, surroundings, circumstances, facts, etc. (as, to *orient* one's self, or one's mind, ideas, etc.); also, to ascertain the position of with reference to the points of the compass or other points; find the bearings of (also fig., esp. reflexively: as, to *orient* one's self, to find out one's actual situation, so as to know what course to follow). **II.** *intr.* To turn toward the east, or in any specified direction.

o-ri-en-tal (ō-ri-en′tạl). [OF. F. *oriental*, < L. *orientalis*, < *oriens*, the east: see *orient.*] **I.** *a.* Of the orient or east; eastern; [usually *cap.*] of, pertaining to, or characteristic of the Orient or East; also [*l. c.*], of gems, orient; [*cap.*] in *zoögeog.*, belonging to a division comprising southern Asia and the Malay Archipelago as far as and including the Philippines, Borneo, and Java. **II.** *n.* [Usually *cap.*] A native or inhabitant of the Orient or East, esp. one belonging to a native race; an Asiatic.—**o-ri-en′tal-ism,** *n.* [Usually *cap.*] Oriental character or characteristics; an

Oriental peculiarity; also, knowledge of Oriental languages, literature, etc.—**o-ri-en′tal-ist,** *n.* [Usually *cap.*] An Oriental†; also, one versed in Oriental languages, literature, etc.—**o-ri-en′tal-ize,** *v. t.*; *-ized, -izing.* To render Oriental. —**o-ri-en′tal-ly,** *adv.*

o-ri-en-tate (ō′ri-en-tāt or ō-ri-en′tāt), *v.*; *-tated, -tating.* [F. *orienter*: see *orient, v.*] **I.** *tr.* To orient. **II.** *intr.* To face or turn toward the east, or in any specified direction; be oriented, as a church.—**o″ri-en-ta′tion** (-tā′shọn), *n.* The act or process of orienting or orientating, or the state of being oriented; in *zoöl.*, the faculty by which homing pigeons, migratory birds, etc., return to a given place.

or-i-fice (or′i-fis), *n.* [F. *orifice,* < L. *orificium,* < *os* (*or-*), mouth, + *facere,* make.] A mouth or aperture, as of a tube or pipe; a mouth-like opening or hole; a vent.—**or-i-fi′cial** (-fish′ạl), *a.*

or-i-flamme (or′i-flam), *n.* [F. *oriflamme,* OF. *oriflambe,* < L. *aurum,* gold, + *flamma,* E. *flame.*] The red banner of the abbey of St. Denis, near Paris, carried before the early kings of France as a military ensign; hence, any ensign or standard (lit. or fig.: as, "Press where ye see my white plume shine . . . And be your *oriflamme* to-day the helmet of Navarre," Macaulay's "Ivry").

or-i-gan (or′i-gạn), *n.* [OF. F. *origan,* < L. *origanum,* < Gr. ὀρίγανον.] Marjoram, esp. the wild marjoram, *Origanum vulgare*; also, the pennyroyal, *Mentha pulegium.*

or-i-gin (or′i-jin), *n.* [F. *origine,* < L. *origo* (*origin-*), < *oriri,* rise.] The rise into being, or the beginning of existence, of anything (as, the date or place of *origin* of a sect; the rumor took its *origin* from a casual remark; "The *origin* and commencement of his grief Sprung from neglected love," Shakspere's "Hamlet," iii. 1. 185); hence, the first stage of existence, or the beginning (as, "Some say that, in the *origin* of things, When all creation started into birth, The infant elements receiv'd a law": Cowper's "Task," vi. 198); also, rise or derivation from a particular source (as, these and other reports of like *origin*; a theory of twofold *origin*); often, birth, parentage, or extraction (as, a man of humble *origin*; "He came . . . of mixed French and Scottish *origin*," C. Brontë's "Villette," i.); also, that from which anything arises or is derived, or the source (as, to follow a stream to its *origin*; the *origins* of a nation; this refusal was the *origin* of the whole trouble).

o-rig-i-nal (ọ-rij′i-nạl), *a.* [OF. F. *original,* < L. *originalis,* < *origo* (*origin-*): see *origin.*] Belonging or pertaining to the origin or beginning of something, or to a thing at its beginning (as, the *original* state of man; the *original* binding of a book; the *original* price of an article); initial, earliest, pristine, or first; also, being that from which a copy, a translation, or the like is made (as, compare the copy with the *original* portrait; the *original* document is at Washington; a literal rendering of the *original* Greek); also, arising or proceeding from a thing itself, or independently of anything else; esp., proceeding from a person as the inventor, maker, composer, or author (as, an *original* device, plan, or poem; a method *original* with the introducer); first-hand; hence, new, fresh, or novel (as, "This story . . . was not particularly *original,* for Sir Gervaise himself had told it at least a dozen times before," Cooper's "Two Admirals," xx.; an *original* way of advertising); of persons, the mind, etc., capable of or given to thinking or acting independently in self-suggested and individual ways (as, an *original* thinker or writer; to be highly *original* in one's methods; "Her mind was young, healthy, somewhat *original,* full of fire and faith," Reade's "Christie Johnstone," i.).—**original sin,** in *theol.*, a depravity, or tendency to evil, held to be innate in mankind and transmitted from Adam to the race in consequence of his sin; as otherwise defined (and esp. in Roman Catholic theology), the privation of sanctifying grace in consequence of Adam's sin.—**o-rig′i-nal,** *n.* Origin, rise, or beginning (archaic); also, birth or extraction (archaic: as, "She is really a good sort of a woman, in spite of her low *original,*" Smollett's "Humphry Clinker," June 26); also, a source of being, or author or originator (archaic); *pl.*, original elements, as of nature† (see Milton's "Paradise Lost," vi. 511); *sing.*, a primary form or type from which varieties are derived; also, that from which a copy, a translation, or the like is made; a picture, writing, text, or the like in its relation to a reproduction or translation of it; the person or thing represented by a picture or other work of art; sometimes, the person on whom a literary portrait or character is based; also, an original work, writing, or the like as opposed to any copy or imitation; also, one who is original in his ways of thinking or acting, esp. a singular or eccentric person, or oddity (as, "Teufelsdröckh passed . . . as one of those *originals* and nondescripts, more frequent in German Universities than elsewhere": Carlyle's "Sartor Resartus," i. 3).—**o-rig-i-nal′i-ty** (-nal′i-ti), *n.*; pl. *-ties* (-tiz). The state or quality of being original; first-hand and authentic character, as of a work of art; freshness or novelty, as of an idea, method, or performance; ability to think or act in an independent, individual manner (as, "He seems to want life, *originality* . . . He knows nothing but what he has picked up ready-made from books": Kingsley's "Yeast," vii.); also, an original idea, remark, or the like.—**o-rig′i-nal-ly,** *adv.* With respect to origin, or by origin (as, a plant *originally* African); hence, at the origin, in the beginning, or at first (as, a house *originally* small; a club which consisted *originally* of fifteen members); in the first place, or primarily (as, a word *originally* denoting quality); sometimes, from the beginning, or from the first; also, in an original, novel, or distinctively individual manner. —**o-rig′i-nal-ness,** *n.*

o-rig-i-nant (ọ-rij′i-nạnt), *a.* Originating; giving origin.

o-rig-i-nate (ọ-rij′i-nāt), *v.*; *-nated, -nating.* [L. *origo* (*origin-*): see *origin.*] **I.** *tr.* To give origin or rise to; initiate; invent. **II.** *intr.* To take its origin or rise; come into existence; arise; spring: as, "The proposal ought to *originate* from us" (Burke's "Conciliation with the Colonies"). —**o-rig-i-na′tion** (-nā′shọn), *n.* The act or process of originating; a giving or taking origin; also, a place of origin, or a starting-point, as of a muscle or nerve.—**o-rig′i-na-tive** (-nạ-tiv), *a.* Having, or characterized by, the power of originating; inventive; creative.—**o-rig′i-na-tor** (-nā-tọr), *n.*

Golden Oriole (*Oriolus galbula*).

o-ri-ole (ō′ri-ōl), *n.* [Obs. F. *oriol,* or NL. *oriolus,* < L. *aureolus,* golden: see *aureola.*] Any bird of the family *Oriolidæ,* esp. *Oriolus galbula,* a European bird with yellow and black plumage ('golden oriole'); also, any of various American birds of the family *Icteridæ,* as *Icterus galbula,* which has yellow or orange and black plumage ('Baltimore oriole').

Baltimore Oriole (*Icterus galbula*).

O-ri-on (ọ-rī′ọn), *n.* [L., < Gr. Ὠρίων, the hunter Orion slain by Artemis, also the constellation.] In *astron.*, a constellation, south of Gemini and Taurus, containing the bright stars Betelgeuse and Rigel, as well as several other conspicuous stars, as the three situated in a straight line and forming the *Belt* (or *Girdle*) *of Orion,* and also containing a remarkable nebula.—**O-ri′on-id** (-id), *n.* In *astron.*, any of a shower of meteors occurring in October and appearing to radiate from the constellation Orion.

or-i-son (or′i-zọn or -sọn), *n.* [OF. *orison* (F. *oraison*), < L. *oratio(n-)*, prayer: see *oration.*] A prayer (as, "Nymph, in thy *orisons* Be all my sins remember'd": Shakspere's "Hamlet," iii. 1. 89); also, praying. [Archaic.]

-orium. [L., prop. neut. of *-orius*: see *-ory*[1] and *-ory*[2].] A suffix of nouns denoting esp. a place or an instrument or apparatus for some purpose, as in *auditorium, crematorium, sanatorium, sensorium, haustorium.*

ork, *n.* See *orc.*

orle (ôrl), *n.* [F. *orle,* dim. < L. *ora,* border.] In *her.*, a bearing resembling a border but not reaching the edge of the escutcheon, so that the field is seen outside of it as well as within.

Orle.

Or-le-an-ist (ôr′lẹ̄-ạn-ist), *n.* [F. *Orléaniste.*] In *French politics,* an adherent of the Orleans family, which is descended from a younger brother of Louis XIV. (reigned 1643–1715) and has furnished one sovereign, Louis Philippe (reigned 1830–48).

or-lop (ôr′lop), *n.* [D. *overloop,* < *overloopen,* overrun, spread over; from its covering the ship's hold.] The lowest deck of a ship: also called *orlop deck*: as, "like great cables and hawsers coiled away in the subterranean *orlop-deck* of a line-of-battle-ship" (H. Melville's "Moby-Dick," civ.).

Or-mazd (ôr′mazd), *n.* [Pers.] In the Zoroastrian religion, the spirit or principle of good, in ceaseless conflict with Ahriman, the spirit of evil.

or-mer (ôr′mėr), *n.* [For F. *ormier,* or *oreille-de-mer,* or ML. *auris maris,* 'sea-ear.'] A sea-ear, or ear-shell, *Haliotis tuberculata,* a gastropod mollusk abundant in the Channel Islands, where it is found clinging to rocks and is gathered for food; hence, any mollusk of the genus *Haliotis* or the family *Haliotidæ.*

or-mo-lu (ôr′mọ̄-lö), *n.* [F. *or moulu,* 'ground gold': *or,* < L. *aurum,* gold; *moulu,* pp. of *moudre,* < L. *molere,* grind.] Orig., gold prepared for use in gilding; hence, gilded metal; now, an alloy of copper and zinc, used to imitate gold.

or-na-ment (ôr′nạ-mẹnt), *n.* [OF. F. *ornement,* < L. *ornamentum,* < *ornare,* equip, deck, adorn.] Any accessory, adjunct, or equipment (now only in ecclesiastical use); also, an accessory, article, or detail used to beautify, or to enrich or improve the appearance or general effect (as, personal *ornaments,* as of jewelry or dress; mantel *ornaments*; architectural *ornaments*; rhetorical *ornaments*); an adornment, decoration, or embellishment; fig., anything that lends beauty or renders more pleasing or attractive (as, "the *ornament* of a meek and quiet spirit": 1 Peter, iii. 4); a person who adds luster, as to surroundings, society, or a class, profession, place, or time (as, "He was tacitly felt to be an *ornament* to his circle": H. James's "Europeans," vi.); also, the act of adorning, or the state of being adorned; adornment, or means of adornment (as, "Loveliness Needs not the foreign aid of *ornament*": Thomson's "Seasons," Autumn, 205); sometimes, mere ornament, or outward display (as, "The world is still deceived with *ornament*": Shakspere's "Merchant of Venice," iii. 2. 74).—**or′na-ment** (-ment), *v. t.* To furnish with ornaments or something ornamental (as, "Her fat neck was *ornamented* with jewels," Thackeray's "Newcomes," xlix.; walls *ornamented* with sculpture); adorn, decorate, or embellish; also, to be an ornament to; serve to adorn.—**or-na-men′tal** (-men′tạl). **I.** *a.* Of the nature of an ornament or of ornamentation (as, *ornamental* vases; *ornamental* work); decorative; also, such as to ornament or adorn, or lend beauty or attractiveness (as, a highly *ornamental* lamp; to be neither useful nor *ornamental*); also, used for purposes of ornament (as, *ornamental* plants; *ornamental* woods or stones); of or pertaining to ornament (as, *ornamental* purposes or considerations). **II.** *n.* Something ornamental; specif., a plant cultivated for ornamental or decorative purposes.—**or-na-men′tal-ly,** *adv.*—**or-na-men′tal-ness,** *n.*—**or″na-men-ta′tion** (-tā′shọn), *n.* The act of ornamenting, or the state of being ornamented; also, that with which a thing is ornamented; objects or work used to ornament something (as, "The chapel . . . is bare and rude inside, with only the commonest *ornamentation* about the altar": Howells's "Chance Acquaintance," xiii.).—**or′na-ment-er,** *n.*

or-nate (ôr-nāt′ or ôr′nāt), *a.* [L. *ornatus,* pp. of *ornare*: see *ornament.*] Elaborately adorned (as, "But who is this . . . ? Female of sex it seems, That so bedeck'd, *ornate,* and gay, Comes this way sailing Like a stately ship," Milton's "Samson Agonistes," 712; an *ornate* façade; an *ornate* binding of a book); often, of discourse, writing, literary style, etc., embellished with fine rhetoric; also, in a more general sense, sumptuously or showily splendid or fine (as, "*ornate* onyx pilasters": Arnold Bennett's "Pretty Lady," xiii.).—**or-nate′ly,** *adv.*—**or-nate′ness,** *n.*

or-ner-y (ôr′nẹ-ri), *a.* [Corruption of *ordinary.*] Ordinary; common; hence, as a general term of depreciation, inferior or poor, as in quality; plain or homely, as in appearance; ugly in disposition or temper; mean or contemptible; low or vile; lewd. [Prov. or vulgar.]

or-nis (ôr′nis), *n.* [G., < Gr. ὄρνις, bird.] The avifauna of a region.

or-nith-ic (ôr-nith′ik), *a.* [Gr. ὀρνιθικός, < ὄρνις (ὀρνιθ-), bird.] Of or pertaining to birds.

ornitho-. Form of Gr. ὄρνις (ὀρνιθ-), bird, used in combination.

or-nith-o-lite (ôr-nith′ọ̄-līt), *n.* [See *ornitho-* and *-lite.*] The fossilized remains of a bird.

or-ni-thol-o-gy (ôr-ni-thol′ọ̄-ji), *n.* [See *ornitho-* and *-logy.*] That branch of zoölogy that deals with birds; also, a treatise on this subject.—**or″ni-tho-log′i-cal** (-thọ̄-loj′i-kạl), *a.*—**or-ni-thol′o-gist,** *n.*

or-ni-tho-man-cy (ôr′ni-thọ̄-man″si), *n.* [Gr. ὀρνιθομαντεία: see *ornitho-* and *-mancy.*] Divination from birds.

or-ni-tho-pod (ôr′ni-thọ̄-pod). [NL. *Ornithopoda,* pl., < Gr. ὄρνις (ὀρνιθ-), bird, + πούς (ποδ-), foot.] **I.** *n.* Any of the *Ornithopoda,* a group of dinosaurs with hind feet closely resembling those of birds in structure and function. **II.** *a.* Belonging or pertaining to the *Ornithopoda.*

or-ni-thop-ter (ôr-ni-thop′tėr), *n.* [Gr. ὄρνις (ὀρνιθ-), bird, + πτερόν, wing.] A flying-machine sustained in and propelled through the air by upward and downward (flapping) movements of parts analogous to the wings of a bird.

or-ni-tho-rhyn-chus (ôr″ni-thọ̄-ring′kus), *n.* [NL., < Gr. ὄρνις (ὀρνιθ-), bird, + ῥύγχος, snout, beak.] A duckbill.

or-o-ban-cha-ceous (or″ọ̄-bang-kā′shius), *a.* [L. *orobanche,* < Gr. ὀροβάγχη, broom-rape.] Belonging to the *Orobanchaceæ,* or broom-rape family of parasitic plants.

o-rog-e-ny (ọ̄-roj′e-ni), *n.* [Gr. ὄρος, mountain: see *-geny.*] In *geol.*, the process of mountain-making or upheaval.—**or-o-gen-ic** (or-ọ̄-jen′ik), *a.*

o-rog-ra-phy (ọ̄-rog′rạ-fi), *n.* [Gr. ὄρος, mountain: see *-graphy.*] That branch of physical geography that deals with mountains.—**or-o-graph-ic, or-o-graph-i-cal** (or-ọ̄-graf′ik, -i-kạl), *a.*

o-ro-ide (ō′rọ̄-īd or -id), *n.* [F. *or* (< L. *aurum*), gold, + Gr. εἶδος, form.] An alloy containing copper, tin, etc., used to imitate gold.

o-rol-o-gy (ọ̄-rol′ọ̄-ji), *n.* [Gr. ὄρος, mountain: see *-logy.*] The science of mountains.—**or-o-log-i-cal** (or-ọ̄-loj′i-kạl), *a.*—**o-rol′o-gist,** *n.*

o-rom-e-ter (ọ̄-rom′e-tėr), *n.* [Gr. ὄρος, mountain: see *-meter.*] An aneroid barometer with a scale giving elevations above sea-level: used to determine altitudes of mountains, etc.—**o-rom′e-try,** *n.* [See *-metry.*] The measurement of mountains.—**or-o-met-ric** (or-ọ̄-met′rik), *a.*

o-ro-tund (ō′rọ̄-tund), *a.* [L. *ore rotundo,* 'with round mouth,' with well-rounded speech, abl. of *os,* mouth, and *rotundus,* E. *rotund.*] Of the voice or utterance, characterized by strength, fullness, richness, and clearness; also, contemptuously, of a style of utterance, pompous or bombastic.—**o-ro-tun′di-ty** (-tun′di-ti), *n.*

or-phan (ôr′fạn). [LL. *orphanus,* < Gr. ὀρφανός, without parents, bereaved.] **I.** *a.* Bereaved by death of both parents, or, less commonly, of one parent (also fig.); also, of or for orphans (as, an *orphan* asylum). **II.** *n.* An orphan child. Also fig.—**or′phan,** *v. t.* To bereave of parents or a parent.—**or′phan-age** (-ạ̄j), *n.* The state of being an orphan; also, orphans collectively; also, an institution or home for orphans.—**or′phan-hood** (-hůd), *n.* The condition of an orphan.

Or-phe-an (ôr-fē′ạn), *a.* [L. *Orpheus,* < Gr. Ὀρφεύς.] Of or pertaining to Orpheus, a legendary poet and musician of ancient Thrace, who had the power of charming animate and inanimate objects with his lyre (as, "the *Orphean* lyre": Milton's "Paradise Lost," iii. 17); hence, melodious; entrancing.

Or-phic (ôr′fik), *a.* [L. *Orphicus*, < Gr. Ὀρφικός.] Of or pertaining to Orpheus; Orphean; also, attributed to or associated with Orpheus; pertaining to a religious or philosophical school maintaining a form of the cult of Dionysus or Bacchus, ascribed to Orpheus as founder (as, *Orphic* mysteries); hence [*cap.* or *l. c.*], mystic; oracular (as, " 'No summer ever came back . . .' said I, with a degree of *Orphic* wisdom that astonished myself": Hawthorne's "Blithedale Romance," xvi.).—**Or′phism** (-fizm), *n.* The religious or philosophical system of the Orphic school.

or-phrey (ôr′fri), *n.*; pl. *-phreys* (-friz). [OF. *orfreis* (F. *orfroi*), < ML. *aurifrigium*, < L. *aurum*, gold, + *Phrygius*, Phrygian.] Gold embroidery; rich embroidery of any sort; a piece of richly embroidered stuff; now, usually, an ornamental band or border, esp. on an ecclesiastical vestment.

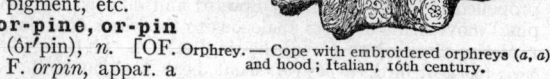

Orphrey. — Cope with embroidered orphreys (*a, a*) and hood; Italian, 16th century.

or-pi-ment (ôr′pi-mẹnt), *n.* [OF. F. *orpiment*, < L. *auripigmentum*, < *aurum*, gold, + *pigmentum*, E. *pigment*.] Arsenic trisulphide, As_2S_3, found native as a yellow mineral and also prepared artificially: used as a pigment, etc.

or-pine, or-pin (ôr′pin), *n.* [OF. F. *orpin*, appar. a shortened form of *orpiment*: see *orpiment*.] Orpiment†; also, a crassulaceous herb, *Sedum telephium*, bearing purple flowers.

Or-ping-ton (ôr′ping-tọn), *n.* [From *Orpington*, town in Kent, southeastern England.] One of a modern breed of large domestic fowls originated at Orpington, England.

or-ra (or′ạ̈), *a.* [Origin obscure.] Odd; left over; extra; superfluous; occasional or casual; idle, vagabond, or worthless. [Sc.]

or-re-ry (or′ẹ-ri), *n.*; pl. *-ries* (-riz). [From the Earl of *Orrery* (1676–1731), for whom such an apparatus was made.] An apparatus for representing the motions and phases of the planets, etc., in the solar system.

or-ris (or′is), *n.* [Appar. a corruption of *iris*.] Any of certain species of iris, as *Iris florentina*, with a fragrant rootstock; the rootstock itself, used as a perfume, etc.

Or-son (ôr′sọn), *n.* [From *Orson*, one of the twin brothers, born in a forest, in the old romance of "Valentine and Orson"; Orson, carried off by a bear, became rough and uncouth, while his brother grew up a courtier.] A rough or uncouth fellow: as, "a great, tall, bristling *Orson* of a fellow" (Mrs. Stowe's "Uncle Tom's Cabin," ix.); "a stupid, sullen, commercial *Orson*" (G. A. Lawrence's "Guy Livingstone," xxv.).

ort (ôrt), *n.* [= MLG. *ort* = MD. *ooraete, oorete*, what is left after eating.] A fragment of food left at a meal; a scrap; a piece of refuse: usually in *pl.*: as, "a beggar's *orts* to crave" (Shakspere's "Lucrece," 985); "Their feasting caused a multiplication of *orts*, which were the heirlooms of the poor" (George Eliot's "Silas Marner," iii.).

ortho-, orth-. Forms of Gr. ὀρθός, straight, upright, right, correct, used in combination: specif. in *chem.*, in the names of certain benzene derivatives and of certain acids in series.—**or-tho-cen-ter** (ôr′thō-sen-tėr), *n.* In *geom.*, the common intersection point of the straight lines through the three vertexes of a triangle perpendicular to the opposite sides.—**or″tho-ce-phal′ic** (-se-fal′ik), *a.* [+ Gr. κεφαλή, head.] Having the relation between the height of the skull and the breadth or the length medium or intermediate; also, intermediate between brachycephalic and dolichocephalic. Also **or-tho-ceph′a-lous** (-sef′ạ-lus).—**or-tho-ceph′a-ly,** *n.*—**or″tho-chro-mat′ic** (-krō-mat′ik), *a.* In *photog.*, pertaining to, producing, or representing the correct relations of colors or the normal gradations of light and shade, as in nature.—**or-tho-chro′ma-tism** (-krō′mạ-tizm), *n.*—**or′tho-clase** (-klās), *n.* [+ Gr. κλάσις, fracture.] A kind of feldspar containing potassium, which belongs to the monoclinic system, and which has two cleavages, at right angles to each other.—**or-tho-clas′tic** (-klas′tik), *a.* [See *clastic*.] In *mineral.*, characterized by cleavages at right angles to each other, as certain feldspars, esp. orthoclase.

or-tho-don-ti-a (ôr-thō-don′shi-ạ̈), *n.* [NL., < Gr. ὀρθός, straight, + ὀδούς (ὀδοντ-), tooth.] The branch of dentistry that is concerned with the straightening of irregular teeth.—**or-tho-don′tist** (-tist), *n.*

or-tho-dox (ôr′thō-doks), *a.* [LL. *orthodoxus*, < Gr. ὀρθόδοξος, < ὀρθός, right, + δόξα, opinion.] Sound or correct in opinion or doctrine, esp. theological or religious doctrine (as, "a great *orthodox* divine," Galt's "Ayrshire Legatees," i.; *orthodox* views); conforming to the Christian faith as represented in the primitive ecumenical creeds; hence, in general, approved; conventional; also [*cap.*], the common epithet of the Eastern or Greek Church; of or pertaining to the Greek Church.—**or′tho-dox-ly,** *adv.*—**or′tho-dox-y** (-dok-si), *n.*; pl. *-doxies* (-dok-siz). [Gr. ὀρθοδοξία.] Orthodox character; orthodox belief or practice.

or-tho-ë-py (ôr′thō-e-pi or ôr-thō′ẹ-pi), *n.* [Gr. ὀρθοέπεια, < ὀρθός, right, + ἔπος, word.] The art of uttering words correctly; correct pronunciation; also, that part of grammar which treats of pronunciation; phonology.—**or-tho-ëp′ic, or-tho-ëp′i-cal** (-ep′ik, -i-kạl), *a.*—**or-tho-ë-pist** (ôr′thō-e-pist or ôr-thō′ẹ-), *n.*

or-tho-gen-e-sis (ôr-thō-jen′e-sis), *n.* [See *ortho-* and *genesis*.] In *biol.*, the direct origin of species, according to the opinion that it takes place by the growth of one species into another in a definite line which is predetermined by the constitution which outward circumstances have given to each organism.—**or″tho-ge-net′ic** (-jẹ-net′ik), *a.*

or-thog-na-thous (ôr-thog′nạ-thus), *a.* [Gr. ὀρθός, straight, + γνάθος, jaw.] Straight-jawed; having the profile of the face vertical or nearly so.

or-tho-gon (ôr′thō-gon), *n.* [L. *orthogonius*, < Gr. ὀρθογώνιος, right-angled, < ὀρθός, right, + γωνία, angle.] A rectangular figure.—**or-thog′o-nal** (-thog′ō-nạl), *a.* Rectangular; pertaining to or involving right angles.—**or-thog′o-nal-ly,** *adv.*

or-thog-ra-pher (ôr-thog′rạ-fėr), *n.* One versed in orthography or spelling; one who spells correctly.

or-tho-graph-ic, or-tho-graph-i-cal (ôr-thō-graf′ik, -i-kạl), *a.* Pertaining to orthography or correct spelling, or to spelling in general (as, "some little *orthographical* mistakes": Addison, in "Spectator," 499); also, in *geom.*, etc., pertaining to right lines or angles; noting or pertaining to a kind of projection in which an object is projected on a plane by lines perpendicular to the plane.—**or-tho-graph′i-cal-ly,** *adv.*

or-thog-ra-phist (ôr-thog′rạ-fist), *n.* One versed in orthography or spelling.

or-thog-ra-phy (ôr-thog′rạ-fi), *n.* [OF. *ortographie* (F. *orthographe*), < L. *orthographia*, < Gr. ὀρθογραφία, < ὀρθός, straight, upright, right, + γράφειν, mark, draw, write.] The art of writing words with the proper letters, according to accepted usage; correct spelling; also, that part of grammar which treats of letters and spelling; also, orthographic projection, or an elevation drawn by means of it.

or-tho-pæ-di-a, or-tho-pe-di-a (ôr-thō-pē′di-ạ̈), *n.* [NL., < Gr. ὀρθός, straight, right, + παῖς (παιδ-), child.] The correction or cure of deformities of the spine, limbs, or other parts of the body in children or in persons of any age; orthopædic surgery.—**or-tho-pæ′dic, or-tho-pe′dic** (-pē′dik or -ped′ik), *a.* Pertaining to the correction or cure of deformities in children and others.—**or-tho-pæ′dics, or-tho-pe′dics,** *n.* Orthopædic surgery; orthopædia.—**or-tho-pæ′dist, or-tho-pe′dist,** *n.* One skilled in orthopædics.

or-tho-phyre (ôr′thō-fīr), *n.* [F. *orthophyre*, < *orthose*, orthoclase, + (*por*)*phyre*, porphyry.] Porphyry in which the embedded crystals consist chiefly of orthoclase.

or-thop-nœ-a (ôr-thop-nē′ạ̈), *n.* [L., < Gr. ὀρθόπνοια, < ὀρθός, straight, upright, + πνεῖν, blow, breathe.] In *pathol.*, a condition in which breathing can take place only when one is in an erect position.

or-thop-ter (ôr-thop′tėr), *n.* [NL. *Orthoptera*, pl., < Gr. ὀρθός, straight, + πτερόν, wing.] Any of the *Orthoptera*, an order of insects including the crickets, grasshoppers, cockroaches, etc., characterized usually by longitudinally folded, membranous hind wings; also, a flying-machine operated by the moving or flapping of wings.—**or-thop′ter-an,** *a.* and *n.*—**or-thop′ter-ous,** *a.* Belonging to the *Orthoptera*.

or-thop-tic (ôr-thop′tik), *a.* [See *ortho-* and *optic.*] Pertaining to or producing normal binocular vision: as, *orthoptic* exercises or training (a method of exercising the muscles of the eye in order to cure strabismus, etc.).

or-tho-rhom-bic (ôr-thọ̄-rom′bik), *a.* [See *ortho-* and *rhomb.*] In *crystal.*, noting or pertaining to a system of crystallization characterized by three unequal axes intersecting at right angles.

or-tho-scop-ic (ôr-thọ̄-skop′ik), *a.* [Gr. ὀρθός, straight, right, + σκοπεῖν, view.] Pertaining to, characterized by, or produced by normal vision; presenting objects correctly to the eye (as, an *orthoscopic* eyepiece).

or-those (ôr′thōs), *n.* [F., < Gr. ὀρθός, straight, right.] Orthoclase.

or-thos-ti-chy (ôr-thos′ti-ki), *n.*; pl. *-chies* (-kiz). [Gr. ὀρθός, straight, upright, + στίχος, row.] In *bot.*, a vertical rank or row; an arrangement of members, as leaves, at different heights on an axis so that their median planes coincide.—**or-thos′ti-chous** (-kus), *a.*

or-tho-tone (ôr′thọ̄-tōn). [Gr. ὀρθότονος, having the right accent, < ὀρθός, right, + τόνος, E. *tone.*] **I.** *a.* Having an accent, as a word; esp., acquiring an accent, as from position, though not ordinarily accented. **II.** *n.* An orthotone word.

or-tho-trop-ic (ôr-thọ̄-trop′ik), *a.* [Gr. ὀρθός, straight, upright, + -τροπος, < τρέπειν, turn.] In *bot.*, noting, pertaining to, or exhibiting a mode of growth which is more or less vertical, either upward or downward.—**or-thot′ro-pism** (-thot′rọ̄-pizm), *n.* In *bot.*, orthotropic tendency or growth. —**or-thot′ro-pous,** *a.* In *bot.*, of an ovule, straight and symmetrical, with the chalaza at the evident base and the micropyle at the opposite extremity.—**or-thot′ro-py,** *n.* In *bot.*, orthotropous condition.

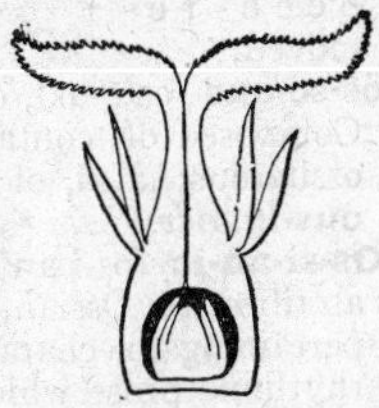

Orthotropous Ovule.
Flower of *Juglans nigra* (black walnut) cut longitudinally and showing the ovule.

or-to-lan (ôr′tọ̄-lạn), *n.* [F., < Pr. *ortolan*, lit. 'gardener' (from its frequenting gardens), < L. *hortulanus*, < *hortus*, garden.] An old-world bunting, *Emberiza hortulana*, esteemed as a table delicacy; hence, any of various American birds eaten as a delicacy, as the reed-bird.

Ortolan (*Emberiza hortulana*).

-ory[1]. [L. *-orius* (neut. *-orium*: see *-orium* and *-ory*[2]), suffix of adjectives associated esp. with agent-nouns in *-or*: see *-or*[2].] A suffix of adjectives meaning 'having the function or effect of,' 'serving for,' or 'pertaining to' (what is indicated by the rest of the word, usually some action), as in *compulsory, contributory, declaratory, hortatory, illusory.*

-ory[2]. [L. *-orium*: see *-orium* and *-ory*[1].] A suffix of nouns denoting esp. a place or an instrument or thing for some purpose, as in *ambulatory, directory, dormitory, laboratory, purgatory.*

or-yx (or′iks), *n.*; pl. *oryxes* or (esp. collectively) *oryx.* [L., < Gr. ὄρυξ, pickax, oryx, < ὀρύσσειν, dig.] Any of various African antelopes (genus *Oryx*), with long, nearly straight horns.

Oryx (*O. beisa*).

os[1] (os), *n.*; pl. *ossa* (os′ạ̈). [L. *os* (*oss-*); akin to Gr. ὀστέον and Skt. *asthan*, bone.] In *anat.* and *zoöl.*, a bone: occurring in the Latin names of certain bones, as *os innominatum* (the innominate bone) or *os pubis* (the pubis).

os[2] (os), *n.*; pl. *ora* (ō′rạ̈). [L. *os* (*or-*), mouth: cf. *oral.*] In *anat.*, a mouth; an opening or entrance: occurring in the Latin names of certain orifices of the body, as *os uteri* (the orifice of the uterus).

os[3] (ōs), *n.*; pl. *osar* (ō′sär). [Sw. *ås* (pl. *åsar*), ridge.] In *geol.*, an eskar, esp. when of great length, as in Sweden.

O-sage (ō′sāj) **or′ange.** [From the *Osage* Indians.] An ornamental moraceous tree, *Toxylon pomiferum*, native in Arkansas and adjacent regions, used for hedges; also, its fruit, which resembles a warty orange.

o-sar (ō′sär), *n.* Plural of *os*[3]: sometimes used as singular, with plural *osars.*

Os-can (os′kạn), *n.* [L. *Osci*, pl.] A member of a race inhabiting southern Italy in ancient times; also, their language, akin to the Latin.

os-cil-late (os′i-lāt), *v.*; *-lated, -lating.* [L. *oscillatus*, pp. of *oscillare*, to swing, < *oscillum*, a swing.] **I.** *intr.* To swing to and fro, as a pendulum does; move to and fro between two points; vibrate; fig., to fluctuate between states, opinions, purposes, etc. (as, "a king . . . *oscillating* between fear of Rome and desire of independence": Besant's "Coligny," viii.); vary between states, etc., reached alternately; waver; in *elect.*, to have, or to produce or generate, oscillations (as, a vacuum-tube *oscillates*, that is, generates the undamped oscillations, or high-frequency alternating current, used in radio transmitting apparatus). **II.** *tr.* To cause to swing or move to and fro.—**os-cil-la′tion** (-lā′shọn), *n.* [L. *oscillatio(n-).*] The act or fact of oscillating; swinging or other movement to and fro; a vibration in which a body or the like swings or moves to and fro; a single swing, or movement in one direction, of such a body, etc.; specif., a rapid change in electromotive force; a single backward or forward surging of the charge in an oscillatory discharge of a Leyden jar or the like; a single flow of electricity in either direction in an alternating current, esp. one of high frequency; sometimes, loosely, an electric wave; also, in fig. use, fluctuation, or a swaying, between states, opinions, etc. —**os′cil-la-tor,** *n.* One who or that which oscillates; a device or machine producing or concerned with oscillations; in *wireless teleg.* and *teleph.*, a device producing the oscillations which give rise to electric waves, as the vacuum-tube of a radio transmitting apparatus.—**os′cil-la-to-ry** (-lạ-tọ̄-ri), *a.* Characterized by or involving oscillation.—**oscillatory discharge,** the electric discharge characteristic of a Leyden jar, which is a backward and forward surging of the charge, with a continual decrease in magnitude; any analogous electric discharge.

oscillo-. Form used to represent L. *oscillare*, to swing, in combination.—**os-cil-lo-gram** (os′i-lọ̄-gram), *n.* [+ *-gram.*] The tracing or record made by an oscillograph.—**os′cil-lo-graph** (-gräf), *n.* [+ *-graph.*] An instrument for recording oscillations, esp. electric oscillations; specif., a device for recording the wave-forms of alternating currents.

—**os″cil-lo-graph′ic** (-graf′ik), *a.*—**os-cil-lo-scope** (o-sil′ọ-skōp), *n.* [+ *-scope.*] An optical device by which a rapidly moving object, as a revolving gear, can be made to appear as if moving slowly or at rest, the illusion being due to a series of carefully timed flashes of light during which the object is seen only in definite positions in its path of motion: used for detecting defects in the working of machinery.

os-cine (os′in), *a.* [L. *oscen* (*oscin-*), a singing bird from which auguries were taken, < *ob*, before, + *canere*, sing.] Of or pertaining to the *Oscines*, a large group of passerine birds, containing those with the most highly developed vocal organs.

os-ci-tant (os′i-tạnt), *a.* [L. *oscitans* (*-ant-*), ppr. of *oscitare*, gape, yawn, < *os*, mouth, + *ciere*, move.] Gaping; yawning; hence, drowsy; inattentive; negligent.—**os′ci-tan-cy,** *n.*

os-ci-ta-tion (os-i-tā′shọn), *n.* [L. *oscitatio*(*n-*), < *oscitare*, gape, yawn: see *oscitant.*] The act of gaping or yawning; hence, drowsiness; inattention.

os-cu-lant (os′kū-lạnt), *a.* [L. *osculans* (*-ant-*), ppr. of *osculari*, kiss: see *osculate.*] In *biol.*, intermediate; connecting two or more groups; also, united by certain common characters; in *zoöl.*, adhering closely; embracing.

os-cu-lar (os′kū-lạ̈r), *a.* [L. *osculum*, little mouth, kiss: see *osculum.*] Pertaining to the mouth or to kissing; also, pertaining to an osculum.

os-cu-late (os′kū-lāt), *v.*; *-lated, -lating.* [L. *osculatus*, pp. of *osculari*, kiss, < *osculum*, little mouth, kiss: see *osculum.*] **I.** *tr.* To kiss; also, to bring into close contact or union; in *geom.*, to touch so as to have three or more consecutive points in common at the point of contact. **II.** *intr.* To kiss each other; also, to come into close contact or union; in *biol.*, to have contact through an intermediate species or group; be osculant or intermediate; in *geom.*, to osculate each other, as two curves.—**os-cu-la′tion** (-lā′shọn), *n.* [L. *osculatio*(*n-*).] The act of osculating; kissing, or a kiss (as, "If *osculation* is a mark of love, surely Mrs. Mack is the best of mothers": Thackeray's "Newcomes," xxiii.); close contact; in *geom.*, the contact between two osculating curves or the like.—**os′cu-la-to-ry** (-lạ-tọ-ri), *a.* Pertaining to osculation.

os-cule (os′kūl), *n.* Same as *osculum.*

os-cu-lum (os′kū-lum), *n.*; pl. *-la* (-lạ̈). [L., dim. of *os*, mouth.] A small mouth-like aperture, as of a sponge or a tapeworm.

-ose[1]. [L. *-osus*: cf. *-ous.*] An adjective suffix meaning 'full of,' 'abounding in,' 'given to,' 'like,' as in *frondose, globose, jocose, otiose, verbose.*

-ose[2]. [F. *-ose*, in *glucose*: see *glucose.*] A noun termination used to form chemical terms, esp. names of sugars and other carbohydrates, as *amylose, fructose, hexose, lactose*, and of proteid derivatives, as *proteose.*

o-sier (ō′zhėr). [OF. F. *osier*; origin uncertain.] **I.** *n.* Any of various willows, as *Salix viminalis* (the common basket-osier) and *Salix purpurea* ('red osier'), with tough, flexible twigs or branches which are used for wickerwork; a twig from such a willow; also, any of certain American dogwoods, as *Cornus stolonifera* ('red osier'). **II.** *a.* Pertaining to or made of osiers.—**o′siered,** *a.* Abounding in osiers; consisting of osiers.

O-si-ris (ọ-sī′ris), *n.* [L., < Gr. Ὄσιρις; from Egyptian.] One of the principal Egyptian gods, brother and husband of Isis, usually represented as a mummy wearing the crown of Upper Egypt.

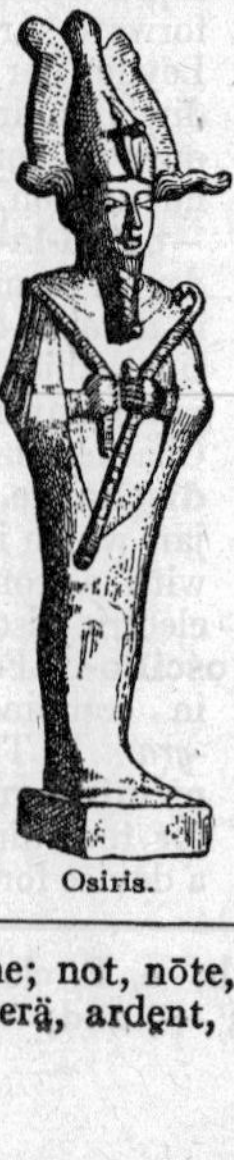

Osiris.

-osis. [L. *-osis*, < Gr. -ωσις, suffix forming nouns from verbs with infinitive in -όειν, -οῦν.] A noun suffix denoting action, process, state, condition, etc., as in *apotheosis, metamorphosis*, and in many pathological terms, as *necrosis, neurosis, sclerosis, tuberculosis.*

Os-man-li (os-man′li). [Turk.: cf. *Ottoman*[1].] **I.** *a.* Ottoman. **II.** *n.*; pl. *-lis* (-liz). An Ottoman; also, the language of the Ottoman Turks.

os-mi-um (os′mi-um or oz′-), *n.* [NL., < Gr. ὀσμή, smell, odor; named from the penetrating odor of one of its oxides.] Chem. sym., Os; at. wt., 190.9; sp. gr., 22.48. A hard, heavy metallic element, used for electric-light filaments, etc.—**os′mic,** *a.*—**os′mi-ous,** *a.*

os-mo-sis, os-mose (os-mō′sis or oz-, os′mōs or oz′-), *n.* [NL. *osmosis*, < Gr. ὠσμός, a thrusting, < ὠθεῖν, thrust.] The tendency of two fluids separated from each other by a porous membrane to pass through the membrane and become mixed, thus equalizing the conditions; the diffusion of fluids through membranes or porous partitions. Cf. *endosmosis* and *exosmosis.*—**os-mot′ic** (-mot′ik), *a.*—**os-mot′i-cal-ly,** *adv.*

Osmund Royal.

os-mund (os′mund or oz′-), *n.* [OF. F. *osmonde*, < ML. *osmunda*; origin uncertain.] Any fern of the genus *Osmunda*, which comprises species with tall, upright fronds growing in clumps, esp. *O. regalis* ('osmund royal').

os-prey (os′prạ̄ or -pri), *n.*; pl. *-preys* (-prạ̄z or -priz). [ME. *ospray* = F. *orfraie*, < L. *ossifraga*, lit. 'bone-breaker': see *ossifrage.*] A large hawk, *Pandion haliaëtus*, which feeds on fish. Also called *fish-hawk.*

Osprey.

os-se-in (os′ẹ-in), *n.* [L. *osseus*: see *osseous.*] In *physiol. chem.*, the organic basis of bone, which remains after the mineral matter has been removed.

os-se-ous (os′ẹ-us), *a.* [L. *osseus*, bony, < *os* (*oss-*), bone.] Composed of, containing, or resembling bone; bony; also, ossiferous; also, of a fish, having a bony skeleton.—**os′se-ous-ly,** *adv.*

Os-si-an-ic (os-i-an′ik or osh-i-), *a.* Of, pertaining to, or ascribed to Ossian, a legendary 3d century Gaelic bard; pertaining to, characteristic of, or resembling the poetry or rhythmic prose which was published by James Macpherson in 1762–63 as a translation of the poems of Ossian, and which, though possessing romantic charm, is marked by grandiloquence and monotony; hence, grandiloquent; bombastic.

os-si-cle (os′i-kl), *n.* [L. *ossiculum*, dim. of *os* (*oss-*), bone.] A little bone; a small bony or bone-like part.—**os-sic-u-lar** (o-sik′ū-lạ̈r), *a.*

os-sif-er-ous (o-sif′ẹ-rus), *a.* [L. *os* (*oss-*), bone, + *ferre*, bear.] Containing bones, as a deposit.

os-sif-ic (o-sif′ik), *a.* [L. *os* (*oss-*), bone, + *facere*, make.] Making or forming bone; ossifying.

os-si-fi-ca-tion (os″i-fi-kā′shọn), *n.* The act or process of ossifying, or the resulting state; also, that which is ossified.

os-si-frage (os′i-frạ̄j), *n.* [L. *ossifragus*, masc., *ossifraga*, fem., lit. 'bone-breaker,' < *os* (*oss-*), bone, + *frangere*, break: cf. *osprey.*] The lammergeier; also, the osprey.

os-si-fy (os′i-fī), *v.*; *-fied, -fying.* [F. *ossifier*, < L. *os* (*oss-*), bone, + *facere*, make.] **I.** *tr.* To convert into bone; harden like bone. **II.** *intr.* To become bone; become hard like bone.

os-su-a-ry (os̱′ū-ạ̄-ri), *n.*; pl. *-ries* (-riz). [LL. *ossuarium*, < L. *os* (*oss-*), bone.] A place or receptacle for the bones of the dead.

os-te-al (os′tẹ-ạl), *a.* [Gr. ὀστέον, bone: see *os*[1].] Of or pertaining to bone; osseous.—**os′te-in,** *n.* Same as *ossein.*—**os-te-i′tis** (-ī′tis), *n.* [NL.] In *pathol.*, inflammation of the substance of bone.—**os-te-it′ic** (-it′ik), *a.*

os-ten-si-ble (os-ten′si-bl), *a.* [F. *ostensible*, < L. *ostendere* (pp. *ostentus*, also *ostensus*), show, display, < *ob*, before, + *tendere*, stretch, E. *tend*[1].] That may be, or is intended to be, shown† (as, an *ostensible* letter); also, open to view, visible, or apparent (as, "My lord continued his stay in Albany, where he had no *ostensible* affairs": Stevenson's "Master of Ballantrae," xi.); also, given out or outwardly appearing as such, professed, or pretended (as, "My *ostensible* errand . . . was to get measured for a pair of shoes; so I discharged that business first," C. Brontë's "Jane Eyre," x.; the *ostensible* reason for an action, which may be quite different from the actual reason).—**os-ten′si-bly**, *adv.* In an ostensible manner; professedly or apparently (often as opposed to *actually* or *really*).

os-ten-sive (os-ten′siv), *a.* [LL. *ostensivus*, < L. *ostendere*, show: see *ostensible*.] Manifestly demonstrative; of a logical demonstration, setting forth a general principle manifestly including the proposition to be proved; also, ostensible.—**os-ten′sive-ly**, *adv.*

os-ten-so-ri-um (os-ten-sō′ri-um), *n.*; pl. *-ria* (-ri-ạ̈). [ML., < L. *ostendere*, show: see *ostensible*.] In the *Rom. Cath. Ch.*, a monstrance. Also **os-ten′so-ry** (-sọ-ri); pl. *-ries* (-riz).

os-tent (os-tent′), *n.* [L. *ostentus*, a showing, display, and *ostentum*, prop. pp. neut., something shown, a portent, both < *ostendere*: see *ostensible*.] The act of showing; a show or display (as, "fair *ostents* of love": Shakspere's "Merchant of Venice," ii. 8. 44); ostentatious display; also, a sign, portent, or prodigy (as, "Latinus, frighted with this dire *ostent*, For counsel to his father Faunus went": Dryden's tr. Virgil's "Æneid," vii. 121). [Archaic.]

os-ten-ta-tion (os-ten-tā′shọn), *n.* [L. *ostentatio(n-)*, < *ostentare*, show, show off, freq. of *ostendere*, show: see *ostensible*.] The act of showing, or a show or display of something, esp. publicly or conspicuously (archaic: as, "to hide the distress and danger . . . under an *ostentation* of festivity," Hawthorne's "Twice-Told Tales," Howe's Masquerade; "this *ostentation* of ingratitude," Stevenson's "Master of Ballantrae," x.); also, a show† or spectacle† (see Shakspere's "Love's Labour's Lost," v. 1. 118); now, usually, pretentious show; display intended to impress others; parade.—**os-ten-ta′tious** (-shus), *a.* Characterized by or given to ostentation or pretentious show (as, an *ostentatious* display of wealth or learning; "My father was *ostentatious* beyond his means," Irving's "Tales of a Traveler," i. 9); pretentious; of actions, manner, qualities exhibited, etc., intended to attract notice (as, *ostentatious* avoidance or indifference; "Glossin took . . . a pair of . . . pistols, which he loaded with *ostentatious* care," Scott's "Guy Mannering," xxxiii.).—**os-ten-ta′tious-ly**, *adv.*—**os-ten-ta′tious-ness**, *n.*

osteo-, oste-. Forms of Gr. ὀστέον, bone, used in combination.—**os-te-o-blast** (os′tē-ọ-blast), *n.* [+ *-blast*.] In *anat.*, a bone-forming cell.—**os-te-oc′la-sis** (-ok′lạ-sis), *n.* [NL. (Gr. κλάσις, fracture).] In *anat.*, the breaking down or absorption of osseous tissue; in *surg.*, the fracturing of a bone to correct deformity.—**os′te-o-clast** (-klast), *n.* [+ Gr. κλαστός, broken.] In *anat.*, one of the large multinuclear cells found in growing bone, which are concerned in the absorption of osseous tissue, as in the formation of canals, etc.; in *surg.*, an instrument for effecting osteoclasis.—**os″te-o-gen′e-sis** (-jen′e-sis), *n.* The formation or growth of bone.—**os″te-o-ge-net′ic** (-jẹ-net′ik), *a.*—**os′te-oid,** *a.* [+ *-oid*.] Bone-like; bony.—**os-te-ol′o-gy** (-ol′ọ-ji), *n.* [+ *-logy*.] The branch of anatomy that treats of bones.—**os″te-o-log′i-cal** (-loj′i-kạl), *a.*—**os-te-ol′o-gist,** *n.*

os-te-o-ma (os-tē-ō′mạ̈), *n.*; pl. *-mas* or *-mata* (-mạ-tạ̈). [NL., < Gr. ὀστέον, bone: see *-oma*.] In *pathol.*, a tumor composed of osseous tissue.

os-te-o-ma-la-cia (os″tē-ọ-mạ-lā′siạ̈), *n.* [NL., < Gr. ὀστέον, bone, + μαλακία, softness, < μαλακός, soft.] In *pathol.*, softening of the bones, due to the gradual disappearance of earthy salts.—**os″te-o-ma-la′cic** (-las′ik), *a.*

os-te-o-path (os′tē-ọ-path), *n.* [See *osteopathy*.] An osteopathist.—**os″te-o-path′ic,** *a.* Pertaining to osteopathy.—**os″te-o-path′i-cal-ly,** *adv.*—**os-te-op′a-thist** (-op′ạ-thist), *n.* One who practises or favors osteopathy.

os-te-op-a-thy (os-tē-op′ạ-thi), *n.* [Gr. ὀστέον, bone, + παθεῖν, suffer.] A theory of disease and a method of treatment resting upon the supposition that most diseases are due to deformation of some part of the body and can be cured by some kind of manipulation.

os-te-o-phyte (os′tē-ọ-fīt), *n.* [Gr. ὀστέον, bone, + φυτόν, a growth.] In *pathol.*, a small osseous excrescence or outgrowth.—**os″te-o-phyt′ic** (-fit′ik), *a.*

os-te-o-plas-ty (os′tē-ọ-plas″ti), *n.* [See *osteo-* and *-plasty*.] In *surg.*, the transplanting or inserting of bone to supply a defect or loss.—**os″te-o-plas′tic,** *a.*

os-te-o-tome (os′tē-ọ-tōm), *n.* [See *osteo-* and *-tome*.] In *surg.*, an instrument for cutting or dividing bone.—**os-te-ot′o-my** (-ot′ọ-mi), *n.* [See *-tomy*.] In *surg.*, the dividing of a bone, or the excision of part of it.

os-ti-a-ry (os′ti-ā-ri), *n.*; pl. *-ries* (-riz). [L. *ostiarius*, doorkeeper, < *ostium*, door: cf. *usher*.] A doorkeeper, as of a church; esp., in the *Rom. Cath. Ch.*, one ordained to the lowest of the four minor orders.

os-ti-ole (os′ti-ōl), *n.* [L. *ostiolum*, dim. of *ostium*, door.] A small opening or orifice.—**os-ti-o-lar** (os′ti-ọ-lạ̈r or os-tī′-), *a.*

os-tler (os′lėr), *n.* [Var. of *hostler*.] A hostler; a groom: as, "a lame old *ostler*, clattering about his stable-yard in wooden clogs" (Whyte-Melville's "Katerfelto," x.).

os-to-the-ca (os-tọ-thē′kạ̈), *n.*; pl. *-cæ* (-sē). [NL., < Gr. ὀστοθήκη, < ὀστέον, bone, + θήκη, case, box.] In *Gr. antiq.*, a receptacle for the bones of the dead.

Ostotheca.

os-tra-cism (os′trạ-sizm), *n.* [Gr. ὀστρακισμός, < ὀστρακίζειν, E. *ostracize*.] The act of ostracizing, or the fact or state of being ostracized.

os-tra-cize (os′trạ-sīz), *v. t.*; *-cized*, *-cizing*. [Gr. ὀστρακίζειν, < ὄστρακον, earthen vessel, potsherd, voting tablet, shell.] Among the ancient Greeks, to banish (a citizen) temporarily by public vote with ballots consisting of tablets of earthenware; hence, in general, to banish (a person) from his native country; expatriate; fig., to exclude by general consent from society, intercourse, etc. (as, "A pattern morality could regard the woman as *ostracized*": G. Meredith's "Diana of the Crossways," xxiii.).—**os′tra-ciz-a-ble** (-sī-zạ-bl), *a.*—**os′tra-ciz-er** (-sī-zėr), *n.*

os-tre-i-cul-ture (os′trē-i-kul″t̤ūr), *n.* [L. *ostrea*, oyster, + *cultura*, culture.] The artificial breeding and cultivation of oysters.—**os″tre-i-cul′tur-al** (-t̤ūr-ạl), *a.*—**os″tre-i-cul′tur-ist,** *n.*

os-trich (os′trich), *n.* [OF. *ostruce* (F. *autruche*), < L. *avis*, bird, + LL. *struthio*, < Gr. στρουθίων, ostrich: see *struthious*.] Any of the large two-toed, swift-footed, flightless birds of the ratite genus *Struthio*; esp., the species *S. camelus*, the largest of existing birds, a native of northern Africa and Arabia, now extensively reared for the plumage; also, a rhea (more fully, 'American ostrich').

A Male Ostrich (*Struthio camelus*).

Os-tro-goth (os'trǫ-goth), *n.* [LL. *Ostrogothi*, pl.; from Teut.: cf. *Austrasian.*] A member of the easterly division of the Goths, which maintained a monarchy in Italy from 493 to 555.—**Os-tro-goth'ic,** *a.*

Os-we-go (os-wē'gō) **tea.** [From *Oswego*, N. Y.] An American menthaceous plant, *Monarda didyma*, bearing showy, bright-red flowers.

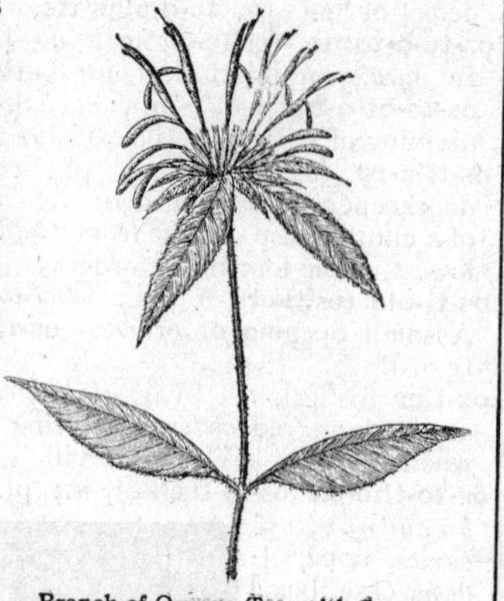
Branch of Oswego Tea, with flowers.

-ot. [Gr. -ωτης.] A suffix of nouns denoting persons of a particular place or country, class, or character, as in *Candiot*, *Cypriot*, *Helot*, *Italiot*, *Phanariot*, *idiot*, *patriot*, *zealot*. Cf. *-ote.*

o-tal-gia (ǫ-tal'jiạ), *n.* [NL., < Gr. ὠταλγία, < οὖς (ὠτ-), ear, + ἄλγος, pain.] In *pathol.*, earache.—**o-tal'gic,** *a.*

o-ta-ry (ō'tạ-ri), *n.*; pl. *-ries* (-riz). [NL. *Otaria*, the typical genus, < Gr. οὖς (ὠτ-), ear.] Any of the eared seals. See *seal*[2], *n.*—**o'ta-rine** (-rin), *a.*

-ote. Same as *-ot*, in nouns denoting persons of a particular place or country, as in *Candiote*, *Corfiote*, *Cypriote*, *Italiote*.

oth-er (uᴛʜ'ėr), *a.* [AS. *ōther* = OHG. G. *ander* = Icel. *annarr* = Goth. *anthar*, other; all compar. forms akin to Skt. *antara*, other, and perhaps to L. *alter* and Gr. ἕτερος, other.] Being the remaining one of two or more (as, the *other* hand; the *other* party; the *other* third); with plural nouns, being the remaining ones of a number (as, the *other* men; the *other* books); also, additional or further (as, he and one *other* person; "There are also many *other* things which Jesus did," John, xxi. 25); also, different or distinct from the one or ones mentioned or implied (as, in this or some *other* city; "There is none *other* name under heaven . . . whereby we must be saved," Acts, iv. 12); also, different in nature or kind (as, "I would not have him in one jot or tittle *other* than he is": Lamb's "My Relations"); also, former (as, "strange, antique portraits of the men and women of *other* days": C. Brontë's "Jane Eyre," xxix.).—**every other,** every second, or every alternate: as, this occurs *every other* day; a meeting *every other* week.—**the other day (night,** etc.), orig., the following or the preceding day (night, etc.)†; now, a day (night, etc.) or two ago.—**the other world,** the world of the dead; the world to come.—**oth'er,** *pron.*; pl. *others*, archaic *other*. The other one (as, you will find the *other* more satisfactory; each praises the *other*); also, another person or thing (as, there are *others* to be considered; there is no *other* in existence).—**of all others,** above or beyond all others: as, the man *of all others* for the place; the thing *of all others* to be feared.—**or other,** or some person or thing else: a phrase added to increase the indefiniteness of words: as, some man *or other* says so; I'll do it some time *or other*; "a vague desire to be doing something *or other*" (J. H. Newman's "Callista," xvi.).—**oth'er,** *adv.* Otherwise; differently.

oth-er-gates (uᴛʜ'ėr-gāts). [See *gate*[2].] **I.** *adv.* In another manner; differently; otherwise. [Now prov. Eng.] **II.** *a.* Of another or different kind. Cf. *another-gates.* [Obs. or prov. Eng.]

oth-er-guess (uᴛʜ'ėr-ges). [Corruption of *othergates.*] **I.** *adv.* Otherwise. [Prov. Eng.] **II.** *a.* Of another kind. [Archaic or prov. Eng.]

oth-er-ness (uᴛʜ'ėr-nes), *n.* The state or fact of being other.

oth-er-where, oth-er-wheres (uᴛʜ'ėr-hwãr, -hwãrz), *adv.* Elsewhere: as, "His chair desires him here in vain, However they may crown him *otherwhere*" (Tennyson's "Holy Grail," 898). [Archaic or prov.]

oth-er-while, oth-er-whiles (uᴛʜ'ėr-hwīl, -hwīlz), *adv.* At another time or other times; also, sometimes. [Archaic or prov.]

oth-er-wise (uᴛʜ'ėr-wīz). **I.** *adv.* In another manner, or differently (as, to think *otherwise*; the island of Crete, *otherwise* called Candia); also, in other respects (as, a statement *otherwise* correct; an *otherwise* happy life); also, under other circumstances (as, he reminded me of what I should *otherwise* have forgotten). **II.** *conj.* Under any other circumstances; in any other case; if not; or else: as, "Hear my conditions: promise (*otherwise* You perish) as you came, to slip away" (Tennyson's "Princess," ii. 275). **III.** *a.* Other or different, or of another nature or kind (as, the result could not have been *otherwise*; "His features . . . were rather handsome than *otherwise*," Scott's "Guy Mannering," ii.); also, that would otherwise be or exist (as, the *otherwise* certainty of success).

oth-er-world-ly (uᴛʜ'ėr-wėrld"li), *a.* Of, pertaining to, or devoted to another world, as the world of mind or imagination, or the world to come.—**oth'er-world"li-ness,** *n.*

Oth-man (oth'mạn), *a.* and *n.* Same as *Ottoman*[1].

o-tic (ō'tik), *a.* [Gr. ὠτικός, < οὖς (ὠτ-), ear.] In *anat.*, etc., of or pertaining to the ear; auricular.

o-ti-ose (ō'shi-ōs), *a.* [L. *otiosus*, < *otium*, leisure, ease.] Being at leisure or ease; idle; indolent; lazy; hence, ineffective or futile; superfluous or useless.—**o'ti-ose-ly,** *adv.*—**o'ti-ose-ness, o-ti-os'i-ty** (-os'i-ti), *n.*

o-ti-tis (ǫ-tī'tis), *n.* [NL., < Gr. οὖς (ὠτ-), ear.] In *pathol.*, inflammation of the ear.

oto-. Form of Gr. οὖς (ὠτ-), ear, used in combination.

o-to-cyst (ō'tǫ-sist), *n.* [See *oto-* and *cyst.*] In *zoöl.*, one of the supposed organs of hearing in many invertebrates, which probably serve chiefly as organs of the sense of direction and equilibrium.

o-to-lith (ō'tǫ-lith), *n.* [See *oto-* and *-lith.*] In *anat.* and *zoöl.*, a calcareous concretion in the internal ear of vertebrates and some invertebrates.

o-tol-o-gy (ǫ-tol'ǫ-ji), *n.* [See *oto-* and *-logy.*] The science of the ear and its diseases.—**o-to-log-i-cal** (ō-tǫ-loj'i-kạl), *a.*—**o-tol'o-gist,** *n.*

o-to-scope (ō'tǫ-skōp), *n.* [See *oto-* and *-scope.*] An instrument for examining internal parts of the ear; also, an instrument for auscultation of sounds in the ear.—**o-to-scop'ic** (-skop'ik), *a.*—**o-tos-co-py** (ǫ-tos'kǫ-pi), *n.*

ot-tar (ot'ạr), *n.* Same as *attar.*

ot-ta-va ri-ma (ot-tä'vä rē'mä). [It., 'octave rime.'] In *pros.*, an Italian stanza of eight lines, each of eleven syllables (or, in the English adaptation, of ten or eleven syllables), the first six lines riming alternately and the last two forming a couplet with a different rime. It is employed in English in Keats's "Isabella" and Byron's "Don Juan" and "Beppo."

ot-ter[1] (ot'ėr), *n.* [AS. *oter*, *otor*, = D. and G. *otter* = Icel. *otr*, otter; akin to Skt. *udra*, otter, Gr. ὕδρα, water serpent, hydra, ὕδωρ, water: see *water.*] Any of various aquatic, fur-bearing, carnivorous musteline mammals of the genus *Lutra* and allied genera, with webbed feet, adapted for swimming, and a long tail slightly flattened horizontally, acting as a rudder and enabling the animal to change its course in the water with great ease and rapidity, as *L. vulgaris*, of Europe, which in Great Britain is much hunted with dogs, or *L. canadensis*, of the U. S. and Canada, or the sea-otter (which see); also, its skin or fur; also, a kind of tackle with float, line, and hooks, used in fresh-water fishing; a kind of gear used in deep-sea trawling; also, a paravane; also, the larva of a moth, *Epialus humuli*, very destructive to hop-vines.

Canada Otter (*Lutra canadensis*).

ot-ter[2], **ot-to** (ot'ėr, ot'ō), *n.* Same as *attar.*

ot-ter=gear (ot'ėr-gēr), *n.* A kind of gear used in trawling (see *otter*[1]); also, a paravane.

Ot-to (ot'ō) **cy'cle.** [From Dr. Nikolaus *Otto* (1832–91), German inventor.] The common four-cycle of internal-combustion engines. See *four-cycle.*

Ot-to-man[1] (ot′ọ-mạn). [F. *ottoman*; from the name of the founder of the empire.] **I.** *a.* Of or pertaining to the Turkish dynasty or empire founded about 1300 by Othman (or Osman) I.; Turkish of the dominions of the Sultan. **II.** *n.*; pl. *-mans.* A Turk of the family or tribe of Othman; a Turkish subject of the Sultan.

ot-to-man[2] (ot′ọ-mạn), *n.*; pl. *-mans.* [F. *ottomane*, prop. fem. of *ottoman*, E. *Ottoman*[1].] A divan or sofa; a low cushioned seat without back or arms; a cushioned footstool; also, a corded silk fabric with a large transverse cord.

oua-na-niche (wä-nạ-nēsh′), *n.* [Canadian F.; of Indian origin.] A fresh-water salmon, *Salmo salar ouananiche*, of the Saguenay River, Quebec, and neighboring waters.

ou-bli-ette (ö-bli-et′), *n.* [F., < *oublier*, forget, < L. *oblivisci*, forget.] A secret dungeon with an opening only at the top, as in certain old castles, often having a pit below, into which a prisoner could be precipitated (as, "The deep-down *oubliette*, Down thirty feet below the smiling day": Tennyson's "Harold," ii. 2. 234); sometimes, the pit itself. —**ou-bli-ette′**, *v. t.*; *-etted, -etting.* To shut up in or as in an oubliette. See Tennyson's "Becket," iv. 2. 92.

ouch[1] (ouch), *n.* [ME. *ouche*, for *nouche* (*a nouche* being taken as *an ouche*), < OF. *nouche, nusche*; from Teut.] A clasp, buckle, or brooch, as for holding together the parts of a garment; a clasped ornament for the person; a buckle or brooch worn for ornament; also, the setting of a precious stone (as, "onyx stones inclosed in *ouches* of gold": Ex. xxxix. 6).—**ouch**[1], *v. t.* To adorn with or as with ouches. [Now poetic.]

ouch[2] (ouch), *interj.* An exclamation expressing sudden pain.

ought[1] (ôt), *n.* and *adv.* [AS. *ōwiht.*] Same as *aught*[1].

ought[2] (ôt), *v. aux.* [Orig. pret. of *owe.*] Was (were) or am (is, are) bound in duty or moral obligation (as, "To help King Edward in his time of storm, As every loyal subject *ought* to do," Shakspere's "3 Henry VI.," iv. 7. 44; "We *ought* to obey God rather than men," Acts, v. 29); hence, in general, was or am bound or required on any ground, as of justice, propriety, expediency, fitness, or the like (as, he *ought* to have been punished; we *ought* not to miss such an opportunity; "You *ought* to go on the stage," Arnold Bennett's "Hilda Lessways," ii. 4): followed by an infinitive with *to* (or sometimes archaically without *to*), or having the infinitive omitted but understood (as, have you done as you *ought?*).—**ought**[2], *n.* Duty or obligation, or a particular obligation: as, "Do you think that anything is strong enough to impose *oughts* on a passion except a stronger passion still?" (G. B. Shaw's "Man and Superman," i.).

ought[3] (ôt), *n.* Same as *aught*[2].

oui-ja (wē′jạ), *n.* [F. *oui*, yes, + G. *ja*, yes.] A device consisting of a small heart-shaped or other board supported on legs, which rests on a larger board marked with words, the letters of the alphabet, and other characters, and which, by moving over the larger board and touching the words, letters, etc., while the fingers of persons, as mediums, rest lightly upon it, is employed to give answers, messages, etc. Cf. *planchette.*

ounce[1] (ouns), *n.* [OF. *unce* (F. *once*), < L. *uncia*, twelfth part, inch, ounce: cf. *inch.*] A unit of weight; esp., the sixteenth of a pound (437½ grains) in avoirdupois weight, or the twelfth of a pound (480 grains) in troy and apothecaries' weight; also, a fluid ounce (see under *fluid, a.*); also, in loose and fig. use, a small quantity or portion.

ounce[2] (ouns), *n.* [OF. F. *once*, OF. also *lonce* (prob. taken as *l'once*, 'the ounce'), perhaps < L. *lynx* (*lync-*), E. *lynx.*] A lynx (obs. or local); sometimes, a jaguar; commonly, the snow-leopard, a leopard-like feline mammal, *Felis uncia*, inhabiting the mountain-ranges of central Asia.

Ounce, or Snow-leopard (*Felis uncia*).

ouphe (öf), *n.* [= *oaf.*] An elf, sprite, or goblin (see Shakspere's "Merry Wives of Windsor," iv. 4. 49, and v. 5. 61); also, an oaf, simpleton, or blockhead.

our (our), *pron.* [AS. *ūre*, gen. pl.: see *us.*] The possessive form corresponding to *we* and *us*, used before a noun. Cf. *ours.*—**Our Lady of the Snows.** See under *lady.*

-our[1]. [ME. *-our.*] An early spelling of *-or*[1] preferred in British use for certain words, as *ardour, colour, honour, labour, odour, valour.*

-our[2]. [ME. *-our.*] A former spelling of *-or*[2], still seen in certain instances, as in *saviour* (beside *savior*).

ou-rang=ou-tang (ọ-rang′ọ-tang″), *n.* See *orang-outang.*

ou-ra-nog-ra-phy (ö-rạ-nog′rạ-fi), etc. See *uranography*, etc.

ou-ra-ri (ö-rä′rē), *n.* Same as *curare.*

ou-rie (ö′ri), *a.* See *oorie.*

ours (ourz), *pron.* Form of *our* used predicatively or without a noun following.

our-self (our-self′), *pron.* A form corresponding to *ourselves*, used of a single person, esp. (like *we* for *I*) in the regal or formal style: as, "*Ourself* will grace, with early morn, The Bridal of the Maid of Lorn" (Scott's "Lord of the Isles," vi. 37).—**our-selves′**, *pron. pl.* An emphatic form of *we* or *us*; also, a reflexive form of *us.*

-ous. [OF. *-os, -us, -ous, -eus*, F. *-eux*, < L. *-osus* (cf. *-ose*[1]); sometimes, L. *-us* or Gr. *-os.* The suffix *-ous* is used freely as an English formative, being attached to stems of either Latin or non-Latin origin.] An adjective suffix meaning 'full of,' 'abounding in,' 'given to,' 'characterized by,' 'having,' 'of the nature of,' 'like,' etc., as in *glorious, joyous, mucous, nervous, sonorous, wondrous.* In chemical terms, as compared with *-ic, -ous* implies a larger proportion of the element indicated by the word, as (with reference to the element tin, L. *stannum*) in *stannous* chloride, $SnCl_2$, beside *stannic* chloride, $SnCl_4$; or, in other words, *-ous* implies a lower valence than in the case of a corresponding term in *-ic.*

ou-sel (ö′zl), *n.* See *ouzel.*

oust (oust), *v. t.* [AF. *ouster*, OF. *oster* (F. *ôter*), remove; origin uncertain.] In *law*, to put out of possession; eject; dispossess; also, to take away (a right, privilege, etc.); also, in general use, to eject or expel from a place or position occupied; fig., to put out of vogue, fashion, or notice (as, "The war problem . . . *ousted* for a time all other intellectual interests": H. G. Wells's "Soul of a Bishop," iii.).—**oust′er**[1], *n.* One who ousts.—**oust′er**[2], *n.* [AF. *ouster*, inf.] In *law*, a putting out of possession; ejection; dispossession.

out (out), *adv.* [AS. *ūt* = D. *uit* = OHG. *ūz*, G. *aus*, = Icel. and Goth. *ūt*, out; akin to Skt. *ud-*, up, out.] Forth from, away from, or not in a place, position, state, etc. (as, to rush *out*; to be *out* of doors, or *out* of town; *out* of joint; *out* of office; *out* of fashion); away from one's home, country, etc. (as, to set *out* on a journey; on the voyage *out*); away from one's work (as, to be *out* on account of illness); on strike (as, the miners are going *out*); from a number, stock, or store (as, to pick *out*; to deal *out*); from a source, ground or cause, material, etc. (with *of*: as, good *out* of evil; *out* of pity; made *out* of scraps); so as to project or extend (as, to stand *out*; to stretch *out*); removed from or not in effective operation, or play, a turn at bat, or the like, as in a game; from a state of composure, satisfaction, or harmony (as, to feel put *out*; to fall *out* with a friend); astray from what is correct (as, *out* in one's calculations); at a pecuniary loss (as, to be *out* ten dollars); so as to deprive or be deprived (with *of*: as, to cheat *out* of money); having used the last (with *of*: as, to be *out* of coal); to or at an end or conclusion (as, to fight it *out*; before the year is *out*); with completeness or effectiveness (as, to fit *out*); into or in existence, activity, or outward manifestation (as, fever broke *out*; the flowers are *out*); into or in public notice or knowledge (as, the book came *out* in May; the truth is *out*); into or in society (as, a young girl who came *out* last season); aloud or loudly (as, to speak or call *out*).—**out and out,** thoroughly; completely; entirely. Cf. *out-and-out.* —**out of hand.** See under *hand, n.*—**out of place.** See under *place, n.*—**out of the way.** See under *way*[2].—**out,** *prep.* Out or forth from (now used chiefly after *from* or in certain expressions, as 'out the door,' 'out the window'); outside of, on the exterior of, or beyond (now chiefly in certain expressions); also, out along, or out on (colloq.: as, *out* the road; *out* Broadway).—**out,** *interj.* Begone! away! (as, "*Out,* beast! . . . begone!" Tennyson's "Becket," i. 1. 130); sometimes (archaic or prov.), an exclamation of abhorrence, indignation, or reproach (as, *out* upon you!), or of grief.—**out.** **I.** *a.* External; exterior; outer; also, outlying; also, in *baseball,* etc., not having its inning (as, the *out* side). **II.** *n.* *Pl.*, those who are out, as the political party out of office; also, projections, or projecting corners (in 'ins and outs': see *in, n.*); *sing.*, an outing (colloq. or prov.: as, "Us London lawyers don't often get an *out,*" Dickens's "Bleak House," vii.); *pl.*, odds, or bad terms (colloq.: as, "You're at *outs* with yourself," Wister's "Virginian," xxvii.; on the *outs*); *sing.*, in *printing,* the omission of a word or words, or that which is omitted; in *baseball,* etc., a put-out.—**out,** *v.* [ME. *outen,* < AS. *ūtian,* < *ūt,* E. *out, adv.*] **I.** *tr.* To put out; expel; discharge; oust; also, to put forth† or issue†; also, to utter†, express†, or speak†. **II.** *intr.* To go or come out: as, "My frozen speech would not well *out*" (W. Morris's "Chapel in Lyoness," 19); murder will *out* (see under *murder, n.*).—**to out with,** to come out with; bring out; utter: as, "rather too prompt to *out with* poniard" (Scott's "Abbot," xix.); "He *outs wi'* his speech at last" (George Eliot's "Adam Bede," liii.).

out-. Prefixal use of *out, adv., prep.,* or *a.*, occurring in various senses in compounds, as in *outcast, outcome, outdoor, outgush, outhouse, outside,* and serving also to form many transitive verbs denoting a going beyond, surpassing, or outdoing in the particular action indicated, as in *outbid, outdo, outgeneral, outlast, outstay, outvote,* and many other words in which the meaning is readily perceived, the more important of these being entered below.

out-act (out-akt'), *v. t.* To surpass in acting.

out-age (out'āj), *n.* An outlet; also, a quantity lost or lacking, as from a container; in *elect.*, in a system of arc-lamps in series, the failure of a lamp to act when current is sent into the circuit.

out=and=out (out'ạnd-out'), *a.* Thoroughgoing; thorough; complete; unqualified: as, "ladies and gentlemen, claiming to be *out-and-out* Christians" (Dickens's "Oliver Twist," xviii.); an *out-and-out* swindle; *out-and-out* rebellion.—**out'=and=out'er,** *n.* A thoroughgoing person or thing; a perfect example of the kind. [Colloq.]

out-ar-gue (out-är'gū), *v. t.* To outdo or defeat in arguing.

out-bal-ance (out-bal'ạns), *v. t.* To outweigh.

out-bid (out-bid'), *v. t.*; pret. *-bid,* pp. *-bidden* or *-bid,* ppr. *-bidding.* To outdo in bidding.

out-bloom (out-blöm'), *v. t.* To surpass in bloom.

out-board (out'bōrd), *adv.* and *a.* *Naut.*, on the outside, or away from the center, of a ship or boat.

out-bound (out'bound), *a.* Outward bound: as, an *outbound* vessel.

out-brave (out-brāv'), *v. t.* To face bravely or defiantly; also, to surpass in bravery or daring (as, "I would . . . *Outbrave* the heart most daring on the earth . . . To win thee, lady": Shakspere's "Merchant of Venice," ii. 1. 28); also, to surpass in beauty, splendor, etc.

out-break (out-brāk'), *v. i.*; pret. *-broke,* pp. *-broken,* ppr. *-breaking.* To break out; burst forth: as, "The blare of horns *outbroke*" (W. Morris's "Jason," ix. 274).—**out'-break,** *n.* A breaking out; an outburst; a sudden and active manifestation; often, a public disturbance; a riot; an insurrection.

out-build-ing (out'bil"ding), *n.* A detached building subordinate to a main building; an outhouse.

out-burn (out-bėrn'), *v.* **I.** *intr.* To burn out, or until consumed: as, "She burn'd out love, as soon as straw *outburneth*" (Shakspere's "Passionate Pilgrim," 98). **II.** *tr.* To surpass in burning; burn brighter than: as, "We . . . lit Lamps which *out-burn'd* Canopus" (Tennyson's "Dream of Fair Women," 146).

out-burst (out-bėrst'), *v. i.*; *-burst, -bursting.* To burst forth.—**out'burst,** *n.* A bursting forth; a sudden and violent issue, outpouring, or burst of something (as, an *outburst* of smoke, sound, or words; an *outburst* of tears or anger; "A furious *outburst* of firing followed," Galsworthy's "Saint's Progress," ii. 1); an outbreak.

out-cast (out'kåst). **I.** *a.* Cast out, esp. from one's home or social circle or from society generally; being an outcast; pertaining to or characteristic of an outcast (as, an *outcast* state; *outcast* misery); also, less frequently, rejected or discarded, as things. **II.** *n.* A person who is cast out, as from home or society (as, "Pearl was a born *outcast* of the infantile world": Hawthorne's "Scarlet Letter," vi.); a pariah; also, rejected matter, or refuse; also, a falling out, or quarrel (Sc.).

out-caste (out'kåst), *n.* In India, one who has forfeited membership in his caste; also, a person of no caste.

out-class (out-klås'), *v. t.* To surpass in class or grade; be, or prove to be, of a distinctly higher class than (a competitor, etc.).

out-come (out'kum), *n.* That which comes out of or results from something; the result, consequence, or issue.

out-crop (out'krop), *n.* A cropping out, as of a stratum or vein at the surface of the earth; also, the emerging part.—**out'crop,** *v. i.*; *-cropped, -cropping.* To crop out, as strata.—**out'crop"ping,** *n.* The action or fact of cropping out; also, a part that crops out (as, "Its white houses look like the *outcroppings* of quartz on the mountain-side": Bret Harte's "Mliss," i.).

out-cry (out'krī), *n.*; pl. *-cries* (-krīz). A crying out; a cry of distress, indignation, or the like; loud clamor; also, an auction (as, "He . . . sold it [wine] at public *outcry,* at an enormous loss to himself": Thackeray's "Vanity Fair," xxxviii.).—**out-cry',** *v.*; *-cried, -crying.* **I.** *intr.* To cry out; cry aloud. **II.** *tr.* To outdo in crying; cry louder than.

out-curve (out'kėrv), *n.* That which curves out; in *baseball,* an outshoot.

out-dare (out-dãr'), *v. t.* To dare or meet defiantly, or outbrave (as, "And boldly did *outdare* The dangers of the time": Shakspere's "1 Henry IV.," v. 1. 40); also, to surpass in daring.

out-date (out-dāt'), *v. t.* To put out of date; render antiquated or obsolete.

out-dis-tance (out-dis'tạns), *v. t.* To distance completely; leave far behind; outstrip.

out-do (out-dö'), *v. t.*; pret. *-did,* pp. *-done,* ppr. *-doing.* To surpass (a person, etc.) in doing or performance (as, "They taught the savages to make wickerwork . . . but they soon *outdid* their masters": Defoe's "Robinson Crusoe," ii. 5); do more or better than; excel; also, to surpass (a deed, performance, etc.: as, "Every action admits of being *outdone,*" Emerson's "Essays," Circles); also, to overcome or defeat.—**out-do'er,** *n.*

out-door (out'dōr), *a.* Occurring or used out of doors; also, outside of a poorhouse, hospital, etc. (as, *outdoor* paupers or relief).—**out'doors'.** **I.** *adv.* Out of doors; in or into the open air. **II.** *n.* The world outside of houses; the open air: as, the great *outdoors.*

out-er (ou'tėr), *a.* [Compar. of *out.*] Further out; exterior; external; of or pertaining to the outside.—**out'er-most,** *a. superl.* Furthest out; remotest from the interior or center.

out-face (out-fās'), *v. t.* To face or confront boldly; defy; also, to face or stare down; put out of countenance.

out-fall (out'fâl), *n.* The outlet or place of discharge of a river, drain, sewer, etc.

out-field (out'fēld), *n.* The outlying land of a farm, esp. beyond the inclosed land; an outlying region or domain; in *baseball,* the part of the field beyond the diamond or infield; also, the players stationed in it; in *cricket,* the part of the field farthest from the batsman.—**out'field"er,** *n.* In *baseball* and *cricket,* one of the players stationed in the outfield.

out-fit (out'fit), *n.* The act of fitting out or equipping, as for a voyage, journey, or expedition, or for any purpose; also, an assemblage of articles for fitting out or equipping (as, a complete *outfit* for an expedition; an explorer's *outfit;* a bride's *outfit*); a set of articles for any purpose (as, a cooking *outfit;* a sewing *outfit*); fig., the mental or moral equipment; also, a body of persons traveling together or associated in any undertaking, as those carrying on the work of a ranch, or as a military body or force (colloq., U. S.); in general, a party, company, or set (colloq., U. S.).—**out'fit,**

v.; *-fitted, -fitting.* **I.** *tr.* To furnish with an outfit; fit out; equip. **II.** *intr.* To furnish one's self with an outfit.—**out'fit"ter,** *n.* One who furnishes or prepares outfits.

out-flank (out-flangk'), *v. t.* To go or extend beyond the flank of (an opposing army, etc.); turn the flank of; fig., to circumvent; get the better of.

out-flow (out'flō), *n.* The act of flowing out; also, that which flows out. Often fig.

out-fly (out-flī'), *v.*; pret. *-flew,* pp. *-flown,* ppr. *-flying.* **I.** *intr.* To fly out or forth. **II.** *tr.* To surpass or outstrip in flying.

out-foot (out-fůt'), *v. t.* To surpass in running, walking, dancing, etc.; of one boat, to excel (another) in speed.

out-frown (out-froun'), *v. t.* To outdo in frowning; frown down. See Shakspere's "King Lear," v. 3. 6.

out-gen-er-al (out-jen'ẹ-rạl), *v. t.*; *-aled* or *-alled, -aling* or *-alling.* To outdo in generalship; get the better of by superior strategy: as, "Coligny had to retire from the field—his rival had *out-generalled* him" (Besant's "Coligny," viii.).

out-giv-ing (out'giv"ing), *n.* The act of giving out something, or that which is given out; an utterance or statement; *pl.*, disbursements.

out-go (out-gō'), *v.*; pret. *-went,* pp. *-gone,* ppr. *-going.* **I.**† *intr.* To go out or forth. **II.** *tr.* To outstrip in going, or go faster than; hence, to surpass, excel, or outdo (as, "In worth and excellence he shall *outgo* them": Milton's "At a Vacation Exercise," 79); also, to go beyond or exceed.—**out'go,** *n.*; pl. *-goes* (-gōz). A going out, or that which goes out; outflow; esp., expenditure (cf. *income*).—**out'go"er,** *n.*—**out'go"ing,** *n.* A going out; also, that which goes out; an effluence; esp., an amount of money expended (usually in *pl.*); also, the extremity, or extreme limit, as of land† (as, "The *outgoings* of their border were at Jordan": Josh. xix. 22).—**out'go"ing,** *a.* Going out; departing: as, *outgoing* trains; the *outgoing* tenant.

out-grow (out-grō'), *v.*; pret. *-grew,* pp. *-grown,* ppr. *-growing.* **I.** *intr.* To grow out or forth; protrude. **II.** *tr.* To surpass in growing; grow faster or greater than; also, to grow out of, or beyond the limits of (as, "Till thou at length art free, Leaving thine *outgrown* shell by life's unresting sea!" Holmes's "Chambered Nautilus"); grow too large for (as, a child *outgrows* its clothes); grow out of fitness for or sympathy with (as, to *outgrow* early surroundings or friends); put off, leave behind, or lose in the changes incident to development or the passage of time (as, to *outgrow* opinions, habits, or weaknesses; to *outgrow* a bad reputation).—**out'growth,** *n.* A growing out or forth; also, that which grows out; an offshoot; an excrescence; fig., a natural development, product, or result.

out-guard (out'gärd), *n.* A guard at a distance from the main body of an army; an advanced guard; an outpost.

out-gun (out-gun'), *v. t.*; *-gunned, -gunning.* To surpass in guns or gunnery: as, "We *out-gun* you. We are piling up munitions now faster than you" (H. G. Wells's "Italy, France, and Britain at War," iii. 4).

out-gush (out-gush'), *v. i.* To gush out or forth.—**out'gush,** *n.* A gushing out; a sudden outflow (lit. or fig.): as, "A lovely, peaceful old lady . . . came to us with a perfect *outgush* of motherly kindness" (Mrs. Stowe's "Oldtown Folks," xxiv.).

out-haul (out'hâl), *n.* *Naut.*, a rope used for hauling out a sail on a boom, yard, etc.

out=her-od (out-her'ọd), *v. t.* [A Shaksperian word (see quotation from "Hamlet," below); from *Herod,* as represented in the old mystery-plays.] To surpass (Herod) in extravagance (orig. in blustering acting on the stage: as, "I would have such a fellow whipped for o'erdoing Termagant; it *out-herods* Herod," Shakspere's "Hamlet," iii. 2. 15; "The figure in question had *out-Heroded* Herod, and gone beyond the bounds of even the Prince's indefinite decorum," Poe's "Masque of the Red Death"); hence, to outdo (any person, etc.) in extravagance or excess.

out-house (out'hous), *n.* An outbuilding.

out-ing (ou'ting), *n.* An airing, excursion, or pleasure-trip (as, "He liked . . . *outings* into the country on a Sunday": S. Butler's "Way of All Flesh," lxxiii.); also, the part of the sea out from the shore; the offing.—**outing cloth, outing flannel,** a light cotton flannel with a short nap.

out-jock-ey (out-jok'i), *v. t.* To get the better of by adroitness or trickery; outwit; overreach.

out-land (out'lạnd or -land), *n.* [AS. *ūtland.*] **I.** *n.* A foreign land (archaic); also, outlying land, as of an estate. **II.** *a.* Foreign (archaic: as, "*outland* merchants," W. Morris's "Jason," xii. 372); also, outlying, as districts.—**out'land-er** (-lạn-dėr or -lan-dėr), *n.* A foreigner; an alien; also, an outsider (colloq.).—**out-land'ish** (-lan'dish), *a.* [AS. *ūtlendisc.*] Foreign (archaic: as, "*outlandish* women," Neh. xiii. 26); hence, foreign-looking, strange, or odd (as, "They were dressed in a quaint, *outlandish* fashion": Irving's "Sketch-Book," Rip Van Winkle); now, commonly, freakishly or grotesquely strange or odd, as appearance, dress, objects, ideas, practices, etc.; bizarre; barbarous; also, out-of-the-way, as places (now usually in disparagement).—**out-land'ish-ly,** *adv.*—**out-land'ish-ness,** *n.*

out-last (out-låst'), *v. t.* To last longer than; surpass in duration; outlive: as, "a work to *outlast* immortal Rome" (Pope's "Essay on Criticism," 131).

out-law (out'lâ), *n.* [AS. *ūtlaga;* from Scand.] One excluded from the benefits and protection of the law; one under sentence of outlawry; hence, a disorderly person living in defiant violation of the law; a habitual criminal; also, an untamed or untamable horse or other animal.—**out'law,** *v. t.* [AS. *ūtlagian.*] To deprive of the benefits and protection of the law, as a person; proscribe; also, to remove from legal jurisdiction, or deprive of legal force (as, "a debt . . . *outlawed* by the statute of limitations": Mark Twain's "Life on the Mississippi," xlii.).—**out'law-ry** (-ri), *n.*; pl. *-ries* (-riz). The act or process of outlawing, or the state of being outlawed; also, disregard or defiance of the law.

out-lay (out-lā'), *v. t.*; *-laid, -laying.* To lay or spread out (now rare); also, to expend, as money.—**out'lay,** *n.* A laying out or expending; an expenditure, as of money; also, an amount expended.

out-leap (out-lēp'), *v.* **I.** *intr.* To leap out or forth. **II.** *tr.* To leap over or beyond; also, to surpass in leaping.—**out'leap,** *n.* A leaping out; fig., a sally; an outburst.

out-let (out'let), *n.* A letting out or discharging; also, an opening or passage by which anything is let out; a place or channel of discharge or egress; a vent; an exit. Also fig.

out-lie[1] (out-lī'), *v.*; pret. *-lay,* pp. *-lain,* ppr. *-lying.* **I.** *intr.* To lie outside (see *outlying*); also, to camp out. **II.** *tr.* To lie outside of or beyond.

out-lie[2] (out-lī'), *v. t.*; *-lied, -lying.* To outdo in lying, or telling lies.

out-li-er (out'lī"ėr), *n.* One who or that which lies outside; one residing outside the place of his business, duty, etc.; an outlying part; in *geol.*, a part of a formation left detached through the removal of surrounding parts by denudation.

out-line (out'līn), *n.* The line, real or apparent, by which a figure or object is defined or bounded; the contour; also, a drawing or a style of drawing with merely lines of contour, without shading; hence, a general sketch, account, or report, indicating only the main features, as of a book, a subject, a project or work, facts, events, etc.—**out'line,** *v. t.* To draw the outline of, or draw in outline, as a figure or object; indicate the outline of (as, hills *outlined* against the sky; "Each rib and every bone in his [a dog's] frame were *outlined* cleanly through the loose hide," Jack London's "Call of the Wild," v.); also, to give an outline of (a subject, etc.); sketch the main features of.

out-live (out-liv'), *v. t.* To live longer than, or survive (a person, etc.); live beyond the period of, or after the end or cessation of (as, "This is old age; but then, thou must *outlive* Thy youth, thy strength, thy beauty," Milton's "Paradise Lost," xi. 538; to *outlive* one's usefulness); of things, to endure longer than, or outlast (as, "Why should honour *outlive* honesty?" Shakspere's "Othello," v. 2. 245); also, to live or last through (as, if we *outlive* these dangers; the ship *outlived* the storm).

out-look (out'lůk), *n.* A looking out; a watch kept; also, the place from which an observer looks out; a lookout; also, the view or prospect from a place (as, "It . . . was a back room, though it had a pleasant *outlook*": Howells's "Chance Acquaintance," iv.); fig., prospect of the future (as, the political *outlook;* a discouraging *outlook*); also, the mental view (as, one's *outlook* upon life; "The difficulties in explaining the changes of his *outlook* . . . had now increased enormously," H. G. Wells's "Soul of a Bishop," vi.).

out-ly-ing (out′lī″ing), *a.* Lying outside the boundary or limit; lying at a distance from the center or the main body; remote; out-of-the-way.

out-man (out-man′), *v. t.*; *-manned, -manning.* To surpass in man-power, or number of men; also, to surpass in manly qualities or achievements.

out-ma-neu-ver, out-ma-nœu-vre (out-mạ-nö′vėr), *v. t.* To outdo in or get the better of by maneuvering: as, "It is very difficult to *outmanœuvre* a Frenchman, as you know" (J. Conrad's "Rover," xvi.).

out-march (out-märch′), *v. t.* To outstrip or outdo in marching.

out-match (out-mach′), *v. t.* To overmatch; surpass; outdo.

out-most (out′mōst), *a. superl.* Furthest out; outermost.

out-ness (out′nes), *n.* The state of being out or external; externality.

out-num-ber (out-num′bėr), *v. t.* To exceed in number: as, "troops . . . *outnumbering* his own by nearly four to one" (Motley's "Dutch Republic," i. 2).

out=of=door (out′ọv-dōr′), *a.* Outdoor. Also **out′=of=doors′.**

out=of=the=way (out′ọv-ᴛʜė-wā′), *a.* Remote from much-traveled ways or frequented or populous regions (as, an *out-of-the-way* cottage; "in this *out-of-the-way* part of the world," H. James's "Europeans," vi.); unfrequented; secluded; also, seldom met with, or unusual (as, *out-of-the-way* bits of information); also, deviating from the proper course, or improper (as, an *out-of-the-way* performance).

out=of=town (out′ọv-toun′), *a.* Living or situated in, coming from, or pertaining to, territory outside the limits of a town or city specified or understood.

out=par-ish (out′par″ish), *n.* An outlying or rural parish; a parish lying outside the boundaries of a city or town with which it is in some way connected.

out=pa-tient (out′pā″shẹnt), *n.* A patient receiving treatment at a hospital but not being an inmate.

out=pen-sion (out′pen″shọn), *n.* A pension granted to one not required to reside in a particular charitable institution.—**out′=pen″sion,** *v. t.* To grant an out-pension to.—**out′=pen″sion-er,** *n.* One who receives an out-pension; a non-resident pensioner.

out-play (out-plā′), *v. t.* To play better than; surpass or defeat in playing.

out-point (out-point′), *v. t.* To excel in number of points, as in a competition or contest; *naut.*, to sail closer to the wind than (another vessel).

out-post (out′pōst), *n.* A post or station at a distance from the main body of an army; the detachment of soldiers stationed there. Also fig.

out-pour (out-pōr′), *v. t.* or *i.* To pour out.—**out′pour,** *n.* A pouring out; that which is poured out.

out-put (out′pu̇t), *n.* The act of putting or turning out; production; the quantity or amount produced, as in a given time; the product or yield, as of a mine, a mill, or a factory, or of any industry or exertion.

out-rage (out′rāj), *n.* [OF. F. *outrage,* < *outre,* beyond: see *outré.*] A passing beyond reasonable bounds†; excess†; extravagance†; also, a passionate or violent outbreak† (as, "I fear some *outrage,* and I'll follow her": Shakspere's "King John," iii. 4. 106); also, injurious or grievous violence, as toward persons (as, acts of *outrage*; "The noise Of riot ascends . . . And injury, and *outrage,*" Milton's "Paradise Lost," i. 500); gross and wanton injury or wrong; an act of wanton violence (as, "These fellows . . . had committed a dastardly *outrage* upon an emigrant party": Parkman's "Oregon Trail," vi.); any gross violation of law or decency; anything that outrages the feelings; also, the state or the feeling of having been outraged (as, "He tried to recall his fading sense of *outrage*": Howells's "Foregone Conclusion," xi.).—**out′rage,** *v. t.*; *-raged, -raging.* To subject to outrage, or grievous violence or indignity (as, "Gentleman and peasant . . . priest and layman, all were plundered, maltreated, *outraged*": Motley's "Dutch Republic," iv. 4); ravish (a woman); offend against (right, decency, principles, feelings, etc.) grossly or shamelessly; hence, to affect (a person) with a sense of offended right or decency, or shock (as, "Agnes . . . was *outraged* by what seemed to her Rose's callousness": Mrs. H. Ward's "Robert Elsmere," xxxi.).—**out-ra′geous** (-rā′jus), *a.* Passing reasonable bounds, or extravagant, now always to an intolerable or shocking degree (as, *outrageous* conceit; an *outrageous* price; to carry a joke to *outrageous* lengths); also, violent in action or temper (as, "At these words the squire grew still more *outrageous* than before": Fielding's "Tom Jones," vi. 9); also, of the nature of or involving outrage or gross injury or wrong (as, *outrageous* treatment; *outrageous* injustice; an *outrageous* slander or insult); atrocious; flagrant; grossly offensive to the sense of right or decency.—**out-ra′geous-ly,** *adv.*—**out-ra′geous-ness,** *n.*

ou-trance (F. ö-träṅs), *n.* [OF. F. *outrance,* < *outrer*: see *outré.*] The uttermost extremity, as in combat: formerly used in certain phrases, as 'to fight to (the) outrance' (that is, to the death), 'combat at outrance,' etc. [Now regarded as French.]

out-rank (out-rangk′), *v. t.* To rank above.

ou-tré (ö-trā), *a.* [F., pp. of *outrer,* push beyond bounds, carry to excess or extremes, < *outre,* beyond, < L. *ultra*: see *ultra.*] Passing the bounds of what is usual and considered proper; extravagant; eccentric; bizarre: as, "a desperately particular fellow, with . . . *outré* notions about people's duties and vocations" (Kingsley's "Alton Locke," xxiv.); "Ernest was always so *outré* and strange; there was never any knowing what he would do next, except that it would be something unusual and silly" (S. Butler's "Way of All Flesh," l.).

out-reach (out-rēch′), *v.* **I.** *tr.* To reach beyond; exceed; also, to reach out; extend. **II.** *intr.* To reach out.—**out′-reach,** *n.* A reaching out; also, length of reach.

ou-tre-cui-dance (ö-tėr-kwē′dạns, F. ö-trė-kwē-däṅs), *n.* [OF. F., < *outre* (< L. *ultra*), beyond, + *cuider* (< L. *cogitare*), think.] Excessive self-confidence; overweening conceit: as, "It is full time . . . that the *outrecuidance* of these peasants should be restrained" (Scott's "Ivanhoe," ix.). [Now only archaic or as French.]

ou-tre=mer (ö-trė-mãr), *adv.* [F., < *outre* (< L. *ultra*), beyond, + *mer* (< L. *mare*), sea.] Beyond the sea.

out-ride (out-rīd′), *v.*; pret. *-rode,* pp. *-ridden,* ppr. *-riding.* **I.** *intr.* To ride out. **II.** *tr.* To outdo or outstrip in riding; of a ship, to last through (a storm: as, "Was it possible for the Dolphin to *outride* such a storm?" Aldrich's "Story of a Bad Boy," xiv.).—**out′rid″er** (-rī″dėr), *n.* A mounted attendant riding before or beside a carriage: as, "a grand equipage, with four horses and *outriders*" (Galt's "Annals of the Parish," xxxix.).

out-rig-ger (out′rig″ėr), *n.* A spar rigged out from a mast or the like, as for extending a sail; also, any of various projecting frames or parts on an aëroplane, as for supporting a rudder, etc.; also, a bracket extending outward from the side of a boat, to support a rowlock; a boat equipped with such brackets; also, a framework terminating in a float, extended outward from the side of a canoe to prevent upsetting.—**out′rigged, out′rig″gered,** *a.*

Canoe with Outrigger.

out-right (out′rīt′), *adv.* Straight out or ahead, or directly onward (as, "I never travelled in this journey above two miles *outright* in a day": Defoe's "Robinson Crusoe," i. 8); also, forthwith; at once; also, completely, entirely, or altogether (as, to sell a thing *outright*); also, without restraint, reserve, or concealment (as, "I laughed *outright,*" Bulwer-Lytton's "Caxtons," iv. 4; to tell a thing *outright*); openly.—**out′right,** *a.* Directed straight out or on (as, "The river . . . glided seaward with an even, *outright,* but imperceptible speed": Stevenson's "Inland Voyage," xx.); also, complete or total (as, an *outright* loss; the *outright* cost); also, downright or unqualified (as, "an *outright* refusal": H. G. Wells's "Tono-Bungay," ii. 2. § 3).—**out′right-ness,** *n.*

out-ri-val (out-rī'val), *v. t.*; *-valed* or *-valled, -valing* or *-valling.* To outdo as a rival; surpass in competition: as, "Margaret soon *outrivalled* her instructress" (Motley's "Dutch Republic," ii. 1).

out-road (out'rōd), *n.* [Cf. *inroad.*] A hostile or predatory excursion; a raid. [Obs. or archaic.]

out-roar (out-rōr'), *v. t.* To outdo in roaring; roar louder than: as, "This animal — miscalled 'howler' . . . would *outroar* the mightiest lion that ever woke the echoes of an African wilderness" (W. H. Hudson's "Green Mansions," iii.).

out-root (out-röt'), *v. t.* To root out; extirpate.

out-row (out-rō'), *v. t.* To outdo in rowing.

out-run (out-run'), *v.*; pret. *-ran*, pp. *-run*, ppr. *-running.* **I.** *intr.* To run out. **II.** *tr.* To outdo or outstrip in running; hence, to escape by or as by running (as, "The gods are very swift; no man *outruns* them": Dunsany's "Laughter of the Gods," iii.); fig., to outstrip in any course of procedure; also, to run or go beyond, or exceed (as, "a boy whose tongue *outruns* his knowledge": M. Arnold's "Empedocles on Etna," i. 1).—**out'run''ner,** *n.* One who or that which runs out or outside; an attendant who runs before or beside a carriage; the leader of a team of dogs; fig., a forerunner.

out-rush (out-rush'), *v. i.* To rush out or forth.—**out'rush,** *n.* A rushing out; a rapid or violent outflow.

out-sail (out-sāl'), *v. t.* To outdo in sailing: as, "We were several times chased in our passage, but *outsailed* everything" (B. Franklin's "Autobiography," xiv.).

out-scorn (out-skôrn'), *v. t.* To overcome or defeat by scorn. See Shakspere's "King Lear," iii. 1. 10.

out-sell (out-sel'), *v. t.*; *-sold, -selling.* To outdo in selling; sell more than; also, to sell or be sold for more than; hence, to exceed in value†.

out-sen-try (out'sen''tri), *n.*; pl. *-tries* (-triz). A sentry placed considerably in advance; a picket.

out-set (out'set), *n.* A setting out or starting (as, "The *outset* of a band of adventurers on one of these expeditions is always animated": Irving's "Captain Bonneville," ii.); hence, the start or beginning of anything (as, "I hardly expect at the *outset* to number aristocrats in my little day-school": C. Brontë's "Villette," xli.).

out-shine (out-shīn'), *v.*; *-shone, -shining.* **I.** *intr.* To shine out or forth: as, "From the east faint yellow light *outshone*" (W. Morris's "Jason," ii. 909). **II.** *tr.* To surpass in shining; fig., to surpass in splendor, excellence, etc. (as, "For sheer splendor the newly built mansion . . . *outshone* them all": W. Churchill's "Coniston," i. 11).

out-shoot (out-shöt'), *v.*; *-shot, -shooting.* **I.** *intr.* To shoot out or forth; project. **II.** *tr.* To shoot or send forth; also, to shoot beyond; overshoot; also, to surpass or excel in shooting.—**out'shoot,** *n.* A shooting out; also, something that shoots out; a projection; an offshoot; in *baseball*, a curve which shoots or bends out away from the batter as it approaches the home base.

out-side (out'sīd' or out-sīd'), *n.* The outer side, surface, or part; the exterior; also, the external aspect or appearance (as, "O, what a goodly *outside* falsehood hath!" Shakspere's "Merchant of Venice," i. 3. 103); sometimes, something merely external; an externality; also, the space without or beyond an inclosure, boundary, etc. (as, "Can I open the door from the *outside*, I wonder": Dickens's "Martin Chuzzlewit," xxxvi.); also, an outside passenger or place on a coach, etc. (colloq.: as, "the four inside people . . . whose dignity would have been compromised by exchanging one word of civility with the three miserable . . . *outsides*," De Quincey's "English Mail-Coach," i.); also, with *the*; the utmost limit (colloq.: as, not more than ten, at the *outside*).—**out-side** (out'sīd' or out'sīd), *a.* Situated on or pertaining to the outside, or outer surface or part; exterior; external; also, being, acting, done, or originating without or beyond an inclosure, boundary, etc. (as, the *outside* world; *outside* work; *outside* noises); not belonging to or connected with an institution, society, etc. (as, *outside* influences); also, reaching the utmost limit, or extreme (colloq.: as, an *outside* estimate).—**out-side'.** **I.** *adv.* On or to the outside, exterior, or space without; also, with the exception (*of*: colloq.). **II.** *prep.* Outside of; also, except (colloq.).—**out-sid'er** (-sī'dėr), *n.* One outside; one not within an inclosure, boundary, etc.; often, one not belonging to a particular group, set, company, party, association, etc. (as, "What good did an *outsider* ever get by meddling in a love affair?" Mrs. H. Ward's "Robert Elsmere," viii.; "In no company had I ever felt so much an *outsider*," Wister's "Virginian," ii.); hence, one unconnected or unacquainted with the matter in question; also, a race-horse, etc., not included among the favorites.

out-sing (out-sing'), *v.*; pret. *-sang* or *-sung*, pp. *-sung*, ppr. *-singing.* **I.** *intr.* To sing out: as, "When once more . . . The meadow-lark *outsang*" (Whittier's "Witch of Wenham," ii.). **II.** *tr.* To surpass or excel in singing; sing better than; also, to sing louder than.

out-sit (out-sit'), *v. t.*; *-sat, -sitting.* To sit beyond the time of (as, to *outsit* the twilight); also, to sit longer than (another: as, "Dacier could allow Mr. Hepburn to *outsit* him," G. Meredith's "Diana of the Crossways," xxviii.).

out-skirt (out'skėrt), *n.* An outer or bordering part or district: often in *pl.*: as, "Every other part of the Five Towns was more impressive . . . than the poor little *outskirt*, Turnhill, of her birth" (Arnold Bennett's "Hilda Lessways," ii. 3); "to continue their walk to the *outskirts* of the village" (Marryat's "King's Own," xlii.).—**out-skirt',** *v. t.* To form an outskirt of; also, to pass along the outskirts of.

out-sleep (out-slēp'), *v. t.*; *-slept, -sleeping.* To sleep beyond; oversleep; also, to sleep longer than (another); also, to sleep to the end of.

out-soar (out-sōr'), *v. t.* To soar beyond.

out-span (out-span'), *v.*; *-spanned, -spanning.* [D. *uitspannen.*] **I.** *tr.* To unyoke or unhitch, as oxen from a wagon; unharness or unsaddle, as horses; unhitch animals from (a wagon). [South Africa.] **II.** *intr.* To remove the yoke, harness, etc., from animals; hence, to encamp. [South Africa.]—**out'span,** *n.* The act or the place of outspanning. [South Africa.]

out-spar-kle (out-spär'kl), *v. t.* To surpass in sparkling.

out-speak (out-spēk'), *v.*; pret. *-spoke*, pp. *-spoken*, ppr. *-speaking.* **I.** *tr.* To speak out; utter frankly or boldly; also, to say or express more than†; also, to outdo or excel in speaking. **II.** *intr.* To speak out.

out-speed (out-spēd'), *v. t.*; *-sped* or *-speeded, -speeding.* To surpass in speed.

out-spend (out-spend'), *v. t.*; *-spent, -spending.* To exceed or surpass in spending.—**out-spent',** *p. a.* Exhausted.

out-spok-en (out'spō'kn), *a.* Free or unreserved in speech (as, "She said the Quakers were rather *outspoken* people": Weir Mitchell's "Hugh Wynne," vi.); candid; frank; also, uttered or expressed with frankness or lack of reserve (as, "*outspoken* criticism": Bret Harte's "Fool of Five Forks").—**out'spok'en-ly,** *adv.*—**out'spok'en-ness,** *n.*

out-spread (out-spred'), *v. t.* or *i.*; *-spread, -spreading.* To spread out; extend.—**out'spread,** *n.* A spreading out; also, that which is spread out; an expanse.

out-stand (out-stand'), *v.*; *-stood, -standing.* **I.** *intr.* To stand out; be prominent; also, of a ship, to sail out to sea (as, "Many a keel shall seaward turn, And many a sail *outstand*": Whittier's "Dead Ship of Harpswell"). **II.** *tr.* To withstand; also, to stay or remain beyond. [Now rare.]—**out-stand'ing,** *p. a.* Standing out; projecting; detached; fig., prominent; conspicuous; striking; also, that continues in existence; that remains unsettled, unpaid, etc.

out-stare (out-stâr'), *v. t.* To outdo in staring; stare out of countenance.

out-stay (out-stā'), *v. t.*; *-stayed, -staying.* To stay beyond the time or duration of; overstay; also, to outdo in staying; stay longer than.

out-stretch (out-strech'), *v. t.* To stretch out in length or breadth; expand; also, to stretch forth; hold out; extend; also, to stretch to the limit; strain; also, to stretch beyond (a limit, etc.).

out-strip (out-strip'), *v. t.*; *-stripped, -stripping.* [From *out-* + *strip*[3].] To outdo or pass in running or swift travel; get ahead of or leave behind in a race or in any course of competition; in general, to outdo; surpass; excel.

out-stroke (out'strōk), *n.* A stroke in an outward direction; specif., in an engine, the stroke during which the piston-rod moves outward from the cylinder.

out-swear (out-swãr′), *v. t.*; pret. *-swore*, pp. *-sworn*, ppr. *-swearing.* To outdo in swearing; also, to overcome by swearing.
out=talk (out-tâk′), *v. t.* To outdo or overcome in talking.
out=tongue (out-tung′), *v. t.* To excel with the tongue; speak louder than; drown the sound of. See Shakspere's "Othello," i. 2. 19.
out=top (out-top′), *v. t.*; *-topped, -topping.* To overtop; rise above; surpass.
out=trump (out-trump′), *v. t.* To surpass in trumping at cards; hence, to get the better of.
out=turn (out′tėrn), *n.* The quantity turned out or produced; the output.
out-val-ue (out-val′ū), *v. t.* To exceed in value.
out-vote (out-vōt′), *v. t.* To outdo or defeat in voting.
out-walk (out-wâk′), *v. t.* To outdo in walking.
out-wall (out′wâl), *n.* The outer wall; fig., the exterior.
out-ward (out′wạrd), *adv.* [AS. *ūtweard, ūteweard,* < *ūt,* out, + *-weard*: see *-ward.*] Toward the outside; out; often, away from port (as, a ship bound *outward*); also, on the outside; without.—**out′ward.** [AS. *ūteweard.*] **I.** *a.* Proceeding or directed toward the outside or exterior; also, that lies toward the outside (as, "I heard a noise in my *outward* room": Addison and Steele, in "Tatler," 103); that is on the outer side; also, of or pertaining to the outside, outer surface, or exterior; pertaining to the outside of the body (as, a remedy for *outward* application); also, pertaining to the body as opposed to the mind or spirit (as, our *outward* eyes); also, being, or pertaining to, what is seen or apparent, as distinguished from the underlying nature, facts, etc., or from what is in the mind (as, the *outward* looks; an *outward* semblance of peace; *outward* civility; *outward* assent); also, belonging or pertaining to the external world as opposed to the mind or spirit (as, "Why idly seek from *outward* things The answer inward silence brings?" Whittier's "Questions of Life"); belonging or pertaining to what is external to one's self (as, a man's *outward* relations); also, external to a country†; foreign†. **II.** *n.* The outward part; the outside or exterior; outward appearance; also, that which is without; the external or material world.—**out′ward-ly,** *adv.* Toward the outside; also, on the outside or outer surface; also, as regards appearance or outward manifestation.—**out′ward-ness,** *n.* The state of being outward; externality; outward existence; also, occupation with outward things.—**out′wards,** *adv.* Outward.
out-watch (out-woch′), *v. t.* To outdo in watching, or watch longer than (see the quotation at *outweary*); also, to watch until the disappearance or end of.
out-wear (out-wãr′), *v. t.*; pret. *-wore*, pp. *-worn*, ppr. *-wearing.* To wear out, or to an end; consume by wearing; also, to exhaust in strength or endurance; also, to pass (time: as, "All that day she *outwore* in wandering," Spenser's "Faerie Queene," iii. 12. 29); also, to outlive or outgrow (as, to *outwear* sorrow; to *outwear* habits); also, to wear or last longer than, or outlast (as, "I have made a Calender for every yeare, That steele in strength, and time in durance, shall *outweare*": Spenser's "Shepheardes Calender," Epilogue).
out-wear-y (out-wēr′i), *v. t.* To weary to exhaustion; tire out: as, "He came prepared . . . to outwatch and *outweary* them in the game to which his impatient predecessor had fallen a baffled victim" (Motley's "Dutch Republic," vi. 1).
out-weigh (out-wā′), *v. t.* To exceed in weight; hence, to exceed in value, importance, influence, etc. (as, "a sufficient objection to *outweigh* every possible advantage," Jane Austen's "Sense and Sensibility," iv.; "Belarab, at the distance, could still *outweigh* the power on the spot of Tengga," J. Conrad's "Rescue," v. 2); also, to be too heavy or burdensome for (see Shakspere's "2 Henry IV.," i. 3. 45).
out-well (out-wel′), *v. i.* To well or gush out.
out-wit (out-wit′), *v. t.*; *-witted, -witting.* To surpass in wit or intelligence (now rare); also, to get the better of by superior ingenuity or craft (as, "The constant study of the rival bands is to forestall and *outwit* each other": Irving's "Captain Bonneville," i.); prove too clever for.—**out-wit′ter,** *n.*
out-work (out′wėrk), *n.* In *fort.*, a part of the fortifications of a place lying outside the main work; a minor defense beyond the main work.—**out-work′,** *v. t.*; *-worked* or *-wrought, -working.* To surpass in working; work harder or faster than; also, to surpass in workmanship†.—**out′work″-er,** *n.* One who works outside, as out of doors, or outside a factory, etc.
out-worn (out-wôrn′), *p. a.* Worn out, as clothes, etc.; consumed or wasted by wear or use; exhausted in strength or endurance, as persons, etc.; outgrown, as opinions, etc.; obsolete, or out of date.
ou-zel, ou-sel (ö′zl), *n.* [AS. *ōsle* = G. *amsel.*] The European blackbird, *Merula vulgaris,* a kind of thrush; also, an allied species, *M. torquata,* of Europe, having a white ring or bar on the breast ('ring-ouzel'); also, any of certain other birds, as the water-ouzels.

Ring-ouzel (*Merula torquata*).

o-va (ō′vạ), *n.* Plural of *ovum.*
o-val (ō′vạl). [= F. *ovale,* < L. *ovum,* egg: see *ovum.*] **I.** *a.* Having the general (solid) form or shape, or the longitudinal outline, of an egg (with one end broader than the other); egg-shaped; commonly, ellipsoidal or elliptical. **II.** *n.* A body or a plane figure oval in shape or outline (see *oval, a.*); any of various oval things; a football (colloq.); an elliptical field, or a field on which an elliptical track is laid out, as for athletic contests; a cartouche, as on ancient Egyptian monuments (as, "the royal *oval* in which the name of Cleopatra . . . is spelt": Amelia B. Edwards's "Thousand Miles up the Nile," vii.).—**o′val-ly,** *adv.*—**o′val-ness,** *n.*
o-va-ri-an (ọ-vā′ri-ạn), *a.* Of or pertaining to an ovary.
o-va-ri-ot-o-my (ọ-vā-ri-ot′ọ-mi), *n.* [See *-tomy.*] In *surg.*, incision into or removal of an ovary.—**o-va-ri-ot′o-mist,** *n.*
o-va-ri-tis (ō-vạ-rī′tis), *n.* [NL.] In *pathol.*, inflammation of an ovary.
o-va-ry (ō′vạ-ri), *n.*; pl. *-ries* (-riz). [NL. *ovarium,* < L. *ovum,* egg: see *ovum.*] In *anat.*, the female reproductive organ, in which the ova or eggs are produced; in *bot.*, the enlarged lower part of the pistil in angiospermous plants, inclosing the ovules or young seeds.

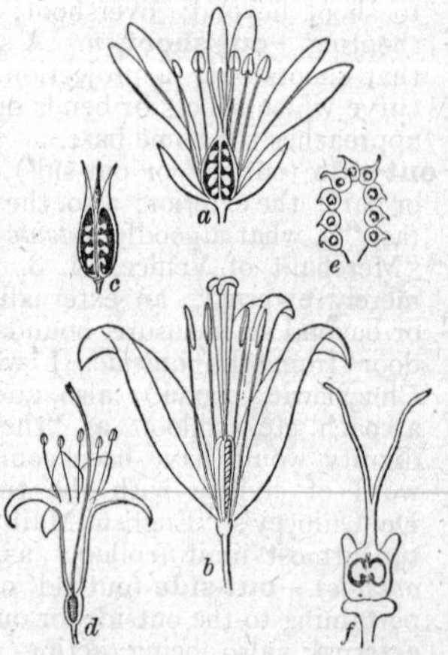

Ovaries, with the Ovules, of different Plants, shown in longitudinal section. — *a,* chickweed (*Alsine media*); *b,* lily (*Lilium superbum*); *c,* larkspur (*Delphinium consolida*); *d,* fuchsia (*Fuchsia coccinea*); *e,* buttercup (*Ranunculus bulbosus*); *f,* maple (*Acer rubrum*).

o-vate (ō′vāt), *a.* [L. *ovatus,* < *ovum,* egg: see *ovum.*] Egg-shaped; esp., having a plane figure like the longitudinal section of an egg; specif., having such a figure with the broader end at the base, as a leaf. Cf. *ovoid.*—**o′vate-ly,** *adv.*

Ovate Leaf.

o-va-tion (ọ-vā′shọn), *n.* [L. *ovatio(n-),* < *ovare,* exult, rejoice, hold a triumphal celebration.] A lesser form of triumph accorded to an ancient Roman commander; also, an enthusiastic public reception of a person; a burst of enthusiastic applause.
ov-en (uv′n), *n.* [AS. *ofen* = D. *oven* = G. *ofen* = Icel. *ofn* = Goth. *auhns,* oven.] A chamber or receptacle for baking or

heating, or for drying with the aid of heat.—**ov′en=bird,** *n.* Any of various birds which build oven-shaped or domed nests, as any of the South American passerine birds of the family *Furnariidæ*, or as an American warbler, *Seiurus auricapillus*, with a golden-brown crown.

Oven-bird (*Seiurus auricapillus*).

o-ver (ō′vėr), *prep.* [AS. *ofer* = D. *over* = G. *über* = Icel. *yfir* = Goth. *ufar*, over; akin to L. *super*, Gr. *ὑπέρ*, over, Skt. *upari*, above: see *hyper-* and *super-*.] Above in place or position (as, the roof *over* one's head; clouds hang *over* the lake; a shelter projecting *over* the sidewalk); higher up than; often, reaching higher than, so as to submerge (as, to be in water *over* one's shoes, head, etc.: hence, to be *over* one's shoes, head, etc., in water, etc.); also, above in authority, power, etc.; so as to govern, control, or conquer; also, above in degree, etc.; in preference to; in excess of, or more than (as, *over* a mile); also, on or upon; so as to rest on or cover; often, here and there on or in (as, at various places *over*, or all *over*, the country); to and fro on or in (as, to travel *over* Europe); through all parts of, or all through (as, to look *over* some papers; to go *over* a matter); also, above, and to the other side of (as, to leap *over* a wall; to fly *over* a lake); from side to side of, or to the other side of (as, to sail *over* a river; to go *over* a bridge); from end to end of (as, *over* the wire); also, on the other side of (as, lands *over* the sea); also, during the duration of (as, *over* a long term of years); until after the end of (as, to adjourn *over* the holidays; to stay *over* night, or *over* Sunday); also, while engaged on or concerned with (as, to fall asleep *over* one's work; to discuss a matter *over* a bottle of wine); also, in reference to, concerning, or about (as, to quarrel *over* a matter).—**over all,** from one extremity of a thing to the other.—**over and above,** in addition to; besides.—**over head and ears.** See under *head, n.*—**over one's head.** See under *head, n.*—**over the top,** over the top of the parapet before a trench, as in issuing to charge against the enemy. Also fig., as of entrance on any campaign or course of open and vigorous action.—**o′ver,** *adv.* Over the top or upper surface or edge of something; also, so as to bring the upper end or side down or under (as, to throw, or to turn, a thing *over*); with reversal of position; also, remaining beyond a certain amount (as, five goes into seven once, with two *over*); in excess or addition (as, to receive the full sum and something *over*); also, excessively or too (now usually in composition: as, *over*-burdensome; *over*nice); also, once more, or again (as, to do a thing *over*); in repetition (as, twenty times *over*); also, so as to cover the surface, or affect the whole surface (as, to paint, strew, or rub a thing *over*); also, through a region, area, etc. (as, to travel all *over*; black all *over*); also, from beginning to end, or all through (as, to read a thing *over*), also, from side to side, or to the other side (as, to sail *over*); across any intervening space (as, when are you coming *over* to see us?); also, from one person, party, etc., to another (as, to deliver *over*; to make property *over* to others); also, on the other side, as of a sea, a river, or any space (as, *over* in Europe); at some distance, as in a direction indicated (as, *over* by the hill); also, throughout or beyond a period of time (as, to stay *over* until Monday; let the matter stand *over* till then); also, at an end, done, or past (as, when the war was *over*).—**once over.** See under *once, adv.*—**over again,** once more; with repetition.—**over against,** opposite to; in front of.—**over and above,** in addition; besides; also, overmuch, too much, or too (colloq.: as, "Your mother . . . is not *over and above* hale and hearty," Malkin's tr. Le Sage's "Gil Blas," x. 2).—**over and over,** repeatedly: as, "He came out *over and over* with this cant phrase" (Maria Edgeworth's "Belinda," iii.).—**over there** (as used in the U. S. during the World War), over in Europe at the scene of war. [Colloq.]—**o′ver. I.** *a.* Upper; higher up; also, higher in authority, station, etc. (as, an *over*lord); also, that is in excess or addition; surplus; extra; also, too great; excessive; also, serving or intended as an outer covering, or outer (as, an *over*coat; an *over*garment). [Now chiefly in composition.] **II.** *n.* An amount in excess or addition; an extra; also, in *cricket*, the number of balls (now usually six) delivered between successive changes of bowlers; also, the part of the game played between such changes.—**maiden over.** See under *maiden, a.*—**o′ver,** *v.* **I.** *tr.* To go or get over; leap over. [Rare.] **II.** *intr.* To go or pass over: as, "I'll *over* then to England" (Shakspere's "I Henry VI.," v. 3. 167). [Rare.]

over-. Prefixal use of *over, prep., adv.*, or *a.*, occurring in various senses in compounds, as in *overboard, overcoat, overhang, overlap, overlord, overrun, overthrow*, and especially employed, with the sense of 'over the limit,' 'to excess,' 'too much,' 'too,' to form verbs, adjectives, adverbs, and nouns, as *overact, overcapitalize, overcrowd, overfull, overmuch, oversupply, overweight*, and many others, mostly self-explanatory: a hyphen, which is commonly absent from old or well-established formations, being often used in new coinages, or in any words whose component parts it may be desirable to set off distinctly (as in *over-burdensome*, from *over-* and *burdensome*, not from *overburden*). Cf. *under-*.

o-ver-a-bound (ō″vėr-ạ-bound′), *v. i.* To abound to excess.

o-ver-a-bun-dance (ō′vėr-ạ-bun′dạns), *n.* Excessive abundance; a too abundant supply.—**o′ver-a-bun′dant,** *a.* Too abundant; superabundant.—**o′ver-a-bun′dant-ly,** *adv.*

o-ver-act (ō-vėr-akt′), *v.* **I.** *intr.* To act to excess, or go too far in acting. **II.** *tr.* To overdo in acting; act (a part) in an exaggerated manner.—**o′ver-ac′tion** (-ak′shọn), *n.* Action carried to excess: as, "*overaction* and misapplication of the very noblest faculties" (Mrs. Stowe's "Oldtown Folks," xxix.).—**o′ver-ac′tive** (-tiv), *a.* Active to excess; too active.—**o′ver-ac-tiv′i-ty** (-tiv′i-ti), *n.*

o-ver-all (ō′vėr-âl). **I.** *a.* From one extreme limit of a thing to the other (as, the *overall* length of a bridge or a ship); in general, covering or including everything. **II.** *n.* An outer garment that covers or protects; *pl.*, loose, stout trousers, often with a part extending up over the breast and supported by straps passing over the shoulders, worn over the clothing to protect it, as by workmen and others; also, long waterproof leggings.

o-ver-anx-ious (ō′vėr-angk′shus), *a.* Unduly or unnecessarily anxious; too anxious.—**o′ver-anx-i′e-ty** (-ang-zī′ẹ-ti), *n.*

o-ver-arch (ō-vėr-ärch′), *v.* **I.** *tr.* To arch over, or span with or like an arch; also, to curve or dispose like an arch (as, "In Vallombrosa, where the Etrurian shades High *overarch'd* imbower": Milton's "Paradise Lost," i. 304). **II.** *intr.* To form an arch over something.—**o-ver-arch′,** *n.* An overarching extent of something.

o-ver-arm (ō′vėr-ärm), *a.* In *cricket*, etc., delivered or executed with the arm raised above the shoulder; overhand.

o-ver-awe (ō-vėr-â′), *v. t.*; *-awed, -awing.* To restrain or subdue by inspiring awe; cow: as, "I was irresolute, *overawed*, and abashed" (Godwin's "Caleb Williams," xx.).

o-ver-bal-ance (ō-vėr-bal′ạns), *v. t.* To do more than balance; outweigh (lit. or fig.: as, "One great disadvantage there was, amply to *overbalance* all other possible gain," De Quincey's "Revolt of the Tartars"); also, to cause to lose balance or to fall or turn over.—**o-ver-bal′ance,** *n.* Overbalancing weight or amount, or preponderance (as, "Those things . . . may be . . . productive of an *overbalance* of happiness": J. Butler's "Analogy of Religion," i. 7); also, something that more than balances or offsets.

o-ver-bear (ō-vėr-bãr′), *v. t.*; pret. *-bore*, pp. *-borne*, ppr. *-bearing.* To bear over or down by weight or force (as, "As a wild wave . . . *overbears* the bark . . . so they *overbore* Sir Lancelot and his charger": Tennyson's "Lancelot and Elaine," 483); overthrow; overwhelm; fig., to overcome or overpower (as, "The ecstasy hath so much *overborne* her": Shakspere's "Much Ado about Nothing," ii. 3. 157); prevail over or overrule (wishes, objections, etc., or a person); oppress (as, "I have . . . interfered to protect, not *overbear*, the sufferer": Godwin's "Caleb Williams," xxii.); treat in a domineering way.—**o-ver-bear′ing,** *p. a.* That overbears; domineering; dictatorial; haughtily or rudely arrogant: as, "I have seen him as much afraid of that *overbearing* Hector, as ever schoolboy was of his pedagogue" (Smollett's "Humphry Clinker," June 5).—**o-ver-bear′ing-ly,** *adv.* —**o-ver-bear′ing-ness,** *n.*

o-ver-bid (ō-vėr-bid′), *v. t.*; pret. *-bid*, pp. *-bidden* or *-bid*, ppr. *-bidding.* To outbid (a person, etc.); also, to bid more than the value of (a thing).

o-ver-blow (ō-vėr-blō′), *v.*; pret. *-blew*, pp. *-blown*, ppr. *-blowing.* **I.** *intr.* To blow over, or pass away, as a storm (also fig.); also, to blow violently, as the wind†. **II.** *tr.* To blow (clouds, etc.) over or away; also, to blow down, or overthrow by blowing; also, to blow over the surface of, as the wind, sand, or the like does.

o-ver-blown (ō′vėr-blōn′), *a.* More than full-blown, as a flower.

o-ver-board (ō′vėr-bōrd), *adv.* Over the side of a ship or boat, esp. into or in the water: as, to fall *overboard*; a cry of 'Man *overboard!*' to throw a thing *overboard* (often fig., to discard or renounce a thing).

o-ver-bod-ice (ō′vėr-bod″is), *n.* An outer bodice.

o-ver-bold (ō′vėr-bōld′), *a.* Unduly bold; audacious; impudent.—**o′ver-bold′ly,** *adv.*—**o′ver-bold′ness,** *n.*

o-ver-brim (ō-vėr-brim′), *v.*; *-brimmed, -brimming.* **I.** *intr.* To brim over; overflow at the brim. **II.** *tr.* To flow over the brim of.

o-ver-build (ō-vėr-bild′), *v. t.*; *-built, -building.* To cover or surmount with a building or structure; also, to erect too many buildings on (an area); also, to build (a structure) on too great or elaborate a scale.

o-ver-bur-den (ō-vėr-bėr′dn), *v. t.* To load with too great a burden; overload. Often fig.

o-ver=bur-den-some (ō′vėr-bėr′dn-sum), *a.* Excessively burdensome.

o-ver-bur-then (ō-vėr-bėr′ᴛʜn), *v. t.* Var. of *overburden.* [Archaic.]

o-ver-can-o-py (ō-vėr-kan′ọ-pi), *v. t.*; *-pied, -pying.* To cover over with or as with a canopy: as, "I know a bank where the wild thyme blows . . . Quite *over-canopied* with luscious woodbine" (Shakspere's "Midsummer Night's Dream," ii. 1. 251).

o-ver-cap-i-tal-ize (ō-vėr-kap′i-tạl-īz), *v. t.* To fix or estimate the capital of (a company, enterprise, etc.) at too high an amount.—**o-ver-cap″i-tal-i-za′tion** (-i-zā′shọn), *n.*

o-ver-care-ful (ō′vėr-kãr′fu̇l), *a.* Careful to excess; too careful.—**o′ver-care′ful-ly,** *adv.*—**o′ver-care′ful-ness,** *n.*

o-ver-cast (ō-vėr-kȧst′), *v.*; *-cast, -casting.* **I.** *tr.* To cast or throw over or down, or overthrow (obs. or prov.); also, to cast or throw (one thing) over another (now rare); also, to cover or overspread with something, now esp. with clouds; spread over, as clouds do (as, "The distress spread as wintry gray *overcasts* a sky": G. W. Cable's "Bonaventure," ii. 7); overcloud, darken, or make gloomy; also, to sew with stitches passing successively over an edge, esp. long stitches set at intervals and serving to prevent raveling. **II.** *intr.* To become cloudy or dark.—**o-ver-cast′,** *p. a.* Overspread with clouds, as the sky; cloudy (as, "It was a dull, close, *overcast* summer evening": Dickens's "Oliver Twist," xxxviii.); dark; gloomy.

o-ver-cau-tion (ō′vėr-kâ′shọn), *n.* Excessive caution.—**o′ver-cau′tious,** *a.* Cautious to excess; too cautious.

o-ver-charge (ō-vėr-chärj′), *v. t.* To charge or load to excess; overload; fill too full; also, to exaggerate; also, to charge (a person) too high a price; also, to charge (an amount) in excess of what is due.—**o′ver-charge,** *n.* An excessive charge or load; also, a charge in excess of a just price.

o-ver-check (ō′vėr-chek), *n.* A check-rein passed over a horse's head between the ears.

o-ver-cloud (ō-vėr-kloud′), *v.* **I.** *tr.* To cloud over; overspread with or as with clouds; spread over, as a cloud does; hence, to darken; obscure; make gloomy. **II.** *intr.* To become clouded over or overcast.

o-ver-coat (ō′vėr-kōt), *n.* A coat worn over the ordinary clothing, as for warmth in cold weather; a greatcoat.—**o′ver-coat″ing,** *n.* Cloth for making overcoats.

o-ver-col-or (ō-vėr-kul′ọr), *v. t.* To color too highly; fig., to exaggerate.

o-ver-come (ō-vėr-kum′), *v.*; pret. *-came*, pp. *-come*, ppr. *-coming.* [AS. *ofercuman.*] **I.** *tr.* To get the better of in a struggle or conflict (as, to *overcome* an adversary in wrestling; "Arthur . . . Fought, and in twelve great battles *overcame* The heathen hordes," Tennyson's "Coming of Arthur," 517); conquer; defeat; hence, to prevail over (opposition, objections, temptations, etc.); surmount (difficulties, etc.); also, to overpower (a person, etc.) in body or mind, or affect in an overpowering or paralyzing way, as liquor, a drug, excessive exertion, violent emotion, or the like does; overwhelm in feeling (as, "Mrs. Mackenzie was charmed and *overcome* at this novel compliment": Thackeray's "Newcomes," xliii.); also, to surpass, excel, or exceed (archaic); also, to overspread or overrun (archaic: as, "Trees . . . *O'ercome* with moss and baleful mistletoe," Shakspere's "Titus Andronicus," ii. 3. 95). **II.** *intr.* To gain the victory; conquer: as, "To him that *overcometh* will I grant to sit with me in my throne" (Rev. iii. 21).—**o-ver-com′er** (-kum′ėr), *n.*

o-ver-con-fi-dent (ō′vėr-kon′fi-dẹnt), *a.* Too confident.—**o′ver-con′fi-dence,** *n.*—**o′ver-con′fi-dent-ly,** *adv.*

o-ver-count (ō-vėr-kount′), *v. t.* To overestimate; also, to outnumber (see Shakspere's "Antony and Cleopatra," ii. 6. 26).

o-ver-cov-er (ō-vėr-kuv′ėr), *v. t.* To cover over; cover completely.

o-ver-crit-i-cal (ō′vėr-krit′i-kạl), *a.* Critical to excess; too critical; hypercritical.

o-ver-crop (ō-vėr-krop′), *v. t.*; *-cropped, -cropping.* To crop (land) to excess; exhaust the fertility of by continuous cropping.

o-ver-crow (ō-vėr-krō′), *v. t.* To crow or exult over; hence, to triumph over or overcome (see Shakspere's "Hamlet," v. 2. 364).

o-ver-crowd (ō-vėr-kroud′), *v. t.* or *i.* To crowd to excess.

o-ver-de-vel-op (ō″vėr-dẹ-vel′ọp), *v. t.* To develop to excess: specif. in *photog.*—**o″ver-de-vel′op-ment,** *n.* Development carried to excess: specif. in *photog.*

o-ver=dis-charge (ō′vėr-dis-chärj″), *n.* In *elect.*, the discharge of an accumulator or storage-battery beyond the usual limit.

o-ver-do (ō-vėr-dö′), *v.*; pret. *-did*, pp. *-done*, ppr. *-doing.* [AS. *oferdōn.*] **I.** *tr.* To do to excess (as, to *overdo* efforts or exercise; to *overdo* a piece of work); overact (a part); exaggerate (as, "The usual gaudy splendour of the heraldic attire was caricatured and *overdone*": Scott's "Quentin Durward," xxxiii.); carry to excess or beyond the proper limit (as, "Mrs. Stanhope *overdid* the business, I think," Maria Edgeworth's "Belinda," ii.; "He . . . was careful not to *overdo* the rack-and-gridiron dodge," J. H. Newman's "Callista," xxi.); cook (food, etc.) too much (chiefly in *overdone, pp.*); also, to overtax the strength of, fatigue, or exhaust (as, "It might be that she was a little *overdone* with work and anxiety": George Eliot's "Adam Bede," xxxv.); also, to surpass in doing, or outdo (archaic). **II.** *intr.* To do too much; go to excess in doing anything: as, "You needn't be afraid I shall *overdo*" (Howells's "Rise of Silas Lapham," i.).—**o-ver-do′er,** *n.*

o-ver-door (ō′vėr-dōr). **I.** *a.* Placed, or to be placed, over a door, as a decorative piece. **II.** *n.* A piece of decorative work surmounting a door.

o-ver-dose (ō′vėr-dōs), *n.* An excessive dose.—**o-ver-dose′,** *v. t.* To dose to excess.

o-ver-draft, o-ver-draught (ō′vėr-drȧft), *n.* A draft made to pass over a fire, as in a furnace; a draft passing downward through a kiln; also (in the spelling *overdraft*), the action of overdrawing an account, as at a bank; a draft in excess of one's credit, or the amount of the excess; an excess draft or demand made on anything.

o-ver-draw (ō-vėr-drâ′), *v.*; pret. *-drew*, pp. *-drawn*, ppr. *-drawing.* **I.** *tr.* To draw too far; strain, as a bow, by drawing; also, to exaggerate in drawing, depicting, or describing (as, features somewhat *overdrawn*; the writer has *overdrawn* the situation); also, to draw upon (an account, allowance, etc.) in excess of what is to one's credit or at one's disposal. **II.** *intr.* To overdraw an account or the like; make an overdraft.—**o′ver-draw,** *n.* An act of overdrawing; an overdraft.

o-ver-dress (ō-vėr-dres′), *v. t.* or *i.* To dress to excess or with too much display.—**o′ver-dress,** *n.* A dress or garment, as of lace, worn over the main dress or gown.

o-ver-drive (ō-vėr-drīv′), *v. t.*; pret. *-drove*, pp. *-driven*, ppr. *-driving.* To drive too hard (as, "If men should *overdrive* them one day, all the flock will die": Gen. xxxiii. 13); hence, to overwork; push or carry to excess (as, "periodical crises of reaction against an *overdriven* rationalism": Mrs. H. Ward's "Robert Elsmere," v.).—**o′ver-driv″en** (-driv″n), *a.* In *mach.*, noting or pertaining to a driving mechanism in which the power is applied above the place where the work is done (cf. *underdriven*); also, noting a machine or the like which is driven at a speed or power above that for which it is designed.

o-ver-due (ō′vėr-dū′), *a.* More than due, as a belated train or a bill not paid by the assigned date.

o-ver-dye (ō-vėr-dī′), *v. t.* To dye over with a second color.

o-ver-ea-ger (ō′vėr-ē′gėr), *a.* Too eager.—**o′ver-ea′ger-ly,** *adv.*—**o′ver-ea′ger-ness,** *n.*

o-ver-eat (ō-vėr-ēt′), *v.*; pret. *-ate* or *-eat*, pp. *-eaten*, ppr. *-eating* (see *eat*). **I.** *intr.* To eat too much. **II.** *tr.* To eat more than is good for (one's self): as, "Without doubt, the most of mankind grossly *overeat* themselves" (Stevenson's "Travels with a Donkey," iii. 2).

o-ver-e-lec-tri-fy (ō″vėr-ę-lek′tri-fī), *v. t.*; *-fied*, *-fying.* To electrify to excess, or beyond necessary or desirable limits.—**o″ver-e-lec″tri-fi-ca′tion** (-fi-kā′shǫn), *n.*

o-ver-es-ti-mate (ō-vėr-es′ti-māt), *v. t.* To estimate at too high a value, amount, rate, or the like: as, "Men often *overestimate* their capacity for evil" (Hawthorne's "Twice-Told Tales," Fancy's Show-Box).—**o-ver-es′ti-mate** (-mąt), *n.* An estimate that is too high.—**o″ver-es-ti-ma′tion** (-mā′shǫn), *n.*

o-ver-ex-cite (ō″vėr-ek-sīt′), *v. t.* To excite too much.—**o″ver-ex-cite′ment,** *n.*

o-ver-ex-ert (ō″vėr-eg-zėrt′), *v. t.* To exert too much.—**o″ver-ex-er′tion** (-eg-zėr′shǫn), *n.* Excessive exertion.

o-ver-ex-pose (ō″vėr-eks-pōz′), *v. t.* To expose too much; in *photog.*, to expose too long to light.—**o″ver-ex-po′sure** (-pō′zhųr), *n.*

o-ver-eye† (ō-vėr-ī′), *v. t.* To survey; oversee. See Shakspere's "Love's Labour's Lost," iv. 3. 80.

o-ver-fall (ō′vėr-fâl), *n.* A waterfall†; also, a turbulent extent of water caused by the meeting of currents or by a strong current running over a submerged ridge or shoal; hence, such a ridge or shoal; also, a sudden drop in the sea-bottom; also, a place for the overflow of water, as from a canal.

o-ver-feed (ō-vėr-fēd′), *v. t.* or *i.*; *-fed*, *-feeding.* To feed to excess.

o-ver-fill (ō-vėr-fil′), *v.* **I.** *tr.* To fill too full; fill so as to cause overflowing: as, "The heart is so full that a drop *overfills* it" (Lowell's "Vision of Sir Launfal," i., Prelude). **II.** *intr.* To become overfull, or so full as to overflow.

o-ver-fine (ō′vėr-fīn′), *a.* Too fine.—**o′ver-fine′ness,** *n.*

o-ver-flood (ō-vėr-flud′), *v. t.* To pour over in or as in a flood.

o-ver-flow (ō-vėr-flō′), *v.* [AS. *oferflōwan.*] **I.** *tr.* To flow over, or overspread or cover by flowing (as, "Waters rise up . . . and shall *overflow* the land, and all that is therein": Jer. xlvii. 2); flood, inundate, submerge, or overwhelm (often fig.); also, to flow over or beyond (the brim, banks, sides, borders, etc.); flow over the edge or brim of (a vessel, etc.); also, to fill to the point of running over. **II.** *intr.* To flow or run over, as rivers, water, etc.; fig., to pass from one place or part to another as if flowing from an overfull space (as, the population *overflowed* into the adjoining territory); also, to have the contents flowing over, as an overfull vessel; discharge a flow of something as from being overfull (followed by *with*: "The fats shall *overflow* with wine and oil," Joel, ii. 24; eyes *overflowing* with tears); fig., to be filled or supplied in overflowing measure (*with*: as, a heart *overflowing* with gratitude; "The house *overflowed* with newspapers of every kind," Howells's "Chance Acquaintance," ii.).—**o′ver-flow,** *n.* An overflowing (as, the annual *overflow* of the Nile); also, that which flows or runs over (as, to carry off the *overflow* from a fountain); a portion passing or crowded out from an overfilled place (as, an *overflow* of people from the cities; to house the *overflow* from a museum); an excess or superabundance; also, an outlet for excess liquid.—**o-ver-flow′ing,** *p. a.* That overflows; superabundant; lavish; exuberant.—**o-ver-flow′ing-ly,** *adv.*

o-ver-fly (ō-vėr-flī′), *v. t.*; pret. *-flew*, pp. *-flown*, ppr. *-flying.* To fly over or across; also, to surpass in flying; fly faster, farther, or higher than.

o-ver-fond (ō′vėr-fond′), *a.* Too fond.—**o′ver-fond′ly,** *adv.*—**o′ver-fond′ness,** *n.*

o-ver-fraught (ō-vėr-frât′), *a.* Fraught or laden too heavily; overladen.

o-ver-free (ō′vėr-frē′), *a.* Too free.—**o′ver-free′ly,** *adv.*

o-ver-full (ō′vėr-fůl′), *a.* Too full.—**o′ver-full′ness,** *n.*

o-ver-gar-ment (ō′vėr-gär″mẹnt), *n.* An outer garment.

o-ver-gild (ō-vėr-gild′), *v. t.* To cover with gilding.

o-ver-glance (ō-vėr-glȧns′), *v. t.* To glance over.

o-ver-glaze (ō′vėr-glāz), *n.* A glaze applied over another glaze on pottery.

o-ver-go (ō-vėr-gō′), *v. t.*; pret. *-went*, pp. *-gone*, ppr. *-going.* [AS. *ofergān.*] To go or pass over, traverse, or go through (a place, etc.); overrun or overspread; also, to pass over (a wall, bound, etc.); also, to go beyond, exceed, or surpass (as, "O, what cause have I . . . To *overgo* thy plaints and drown thy cries!" Shakspere's "Richard III.," ii. 2. 61); also, to overcome (as, "With his powre he all doth *overgo*": Spenser's "Faerie Queene," v. 2. 7); fig., to overwhelm, overburden, or oppress (as, "sad-hearted men, much *overgone* with care": Shakspere's "3 Henry VI.," ii. 5. 123). [Now prov. or archaic.]

o-ver-gorge (ō-vėr-gôrj′), *v. t.* To gorge to excess.

o-ver-great (ō′vėr-grāt′), *a.* Too great.

o-ver-ground (ō′vėr-ground), *a.* Above the ground: as, underground and *overground* railways.

o-ver-grow (ō-vėr-grō′), *v.*; pret. *-grew*, pp. *-grown*, ppr. *-growing.* **I.** *tr.* To grow over, or cover with a growth of something (as, ivy has *overgrown* the walls; bread *overgrown* with mold; "Hedges . . . Like prisoners wildly *overgrown* with hair," Shakspere's "Henry V.," v. 2. 43); also, to outdo in growing, or choke or supplant by a more exuberant growth (as, "seeds of a new and rampant quality, which were destined to *overgrow* them all": Mrs. Stowe's "Oldtown Folks," v.); also, to grow beyond, grow too large for, or outgrow (as, the vine has *overgrown* its support). **II.** *intr.* To grow to excess; grow too large.—**o′ver-grown′,** *p. a.* Covered with a growth of vegetation, etc.; also, grown too large, or beyond the due size or proportions (as, a great, *overgrown* boy; an *overgrown* village; *overgrown* self-esteem).—**o′ver-growth,** *n.* Excessive or too exuberant growth; also, a growth overspreading or covering something.

o-ver-hand (ō′vėr-hand). **I.** *adv.* With the hand over the object; with the knuckles upward; also, with the hand raised above the shoulder, as in pitching a ball; in *needle-work*, with stitches passing successively over an edge. **II.** *a.* Done or delivered overhand.—**o′ver-hand,** *v. t.* To sew overhand.—**o′ver-hand″ed,** *a.* Overhand.

o-ver-hang (ō-vėr-hang′), *v.*; *-hung*, *-hanging.* **I.** *tr.* To hang or be suspended over (as, "She pulled at the bell-rope that *overhung* the head of the bed": Arnold Bennett's "Hilda Lessways," vi. 3); extend, project, or jut over (as, a dark sky *overhangs* the earth; "Under the sycamore-tree were hives *overhung* by a penthouse," Longfellow's "Evangeline," i. 1); fig., to impend over, or threaten, as danger or evil; hang or rest over, as if ominously (as, "Quentin tried to dispel the sadness which *overhung* him": Scott's "Quentin Durward," xix.); also, to adorn with hangings. **II.** *intr.* To hang over; project or jut out over something below: as, "The granite walls, *overhanging*, bend forward above to meet one another, almost forming an arch" (H. Kingsley's "Geoffry Hamlyn," xliii.).—**o′ver-hang,** *n.* An overhanging; a projection; the extent of projection, as of the bow of a vessel; specif., in *aëronautics*, the amount by which an upper wing of a biplane projects laterally beyond the corresponding lower wing.

o-ver-hast-y (ō′vėr-hās′ti), *a.* Too hasty; precipitate.—**o′ver-hast′i-ly,** *adv.*—**o′ver-hast′i-ness,** *n.*

o-ver-haul (ō-vėr-hâl′), *v. t.* To haul or turn over for examination; investigate or examine thoroughly, as for repair or correction; also, to gain upon or overtake; also, *naut.*, to slacken (a rope) by hauling in the opposite direction to that in which it was drawn taut; release the blocks of (a tackle).—**o′ver-haul,** *n.* An overhauling; a thorough examination. Also **o-ver-haul′ing.**

o-ver-head (ō′vėr-hed′), *adv.* Over one's head, or aloft; up in the air or sky, esp. near the zenith (as, "*Overhead* was a gray expanse of cloud": Hawthorne's "Scarlet Letter," xvi.); on the floor above (as, "The Miss Prynnes were . . . inclined to . . . make complaint about Mr. Jerrythought's noises *overhead*": W. De Morgan's "Alice-for-Short," xviii.); also, so that the water or the like reaches higher than one's head; so as to be completely submerged or deeply involved (as, to plunge one *overhead* in the river; *overhead* in debt).—**o'ver-head,** *a.* Situated, operating, or passing overhead, aloft, or above; also, applicable to one and all; general; average.—**overhead charges, expenses,** etc., general charges, expenses, etc., of any business, such as are not chargeable entirely to any particular part of the work, the output, the goods, etc.—**o'ver-head,** *n.* Overhead charges or expenses.

o-ver-hear (ō-vėr-hēr'), *v. t.*; *-heard, -hearing.* To hear (speech, etc., or a speaker) without the speaker's intention or knowledge; also, to hear again†.—**o-ver-hear'er,** *n.*

o-ver-heat (ō-vėr-hēt'), *v. t.* To heat to excess.—**o'ver-heat',** *n.* Excessive heat; overheated condition.

o-ver-high (ō'vėr-hī'), *a.* and *adv.* Too high.

o-ver-hours (ō'vėr-ourz), *n. pl.* Excess hours of labor; overtime; also, spare or odd hours (as, "I only worked at it in *over-hours*—often late at night": George Eliot's "Adam Bede," xxi.).

o-ver-hung (ō'vėr-hung), *a.* Hung from above, as a door. Cf. *underhung.*

o-ver-in-dulge (ō"vėr-in-dulj'), *v. t.* or *i.* To indulge to excess.—**o"ver-in-dul'gent,** *a.* Too indulgent.—**o"ver-in-dul'gence,** *n.*

o-ver-is-sue (ō-vėr-ish'ö), *v. t.* To issue in excess of a proper or authorized amount: as, to *overissue* notes, bonds, or stock.—**o'ver-is"sue,** *n.* An excessive issue; an issue in excess, as of notes, bonds, or stock.

o-ver-joy (ō-vėr-joi'), *v. t.* To overcome with joy; make exceedingly joyful: now usually in *overjoyed, pp.*: as, "My sister . . . was *overjoyed* at the intelligence of my safe return" (Marryat's "Peter Simple," liii.).

o-ver-la-bor (ō-vėr-lā'bor), *v. t.* To force to or exhaust by excessive labor (as, "But they must pick me out, with shackles tired, And *over-labour'd* at their publick mill, To make them sport": Milton's "Samson Agonistes," 1327); overwork; also, to labor to excess over; elaborate to excess.

o-ver-lade (ō-vėr-lād'), *v. t.* To overload: now chiefly in *overladen, pp.*

o-ver-land (ō'vėr-land'), *adv.* Over or across the land; by land: as, to travel *overland* to the Pacific coast.—**o'ver-land,** *a.* Proceeding, performed, or carried on overland: as, "when the *overland* Indian trade fell off with the discovery of the Cape passage" (Motley's "Dutch Republic," Introd., vi.).

o-ver-lap (ō-vėr-lap'), *v.*; *-lapped, -lapping.* **I.** *tr.* To lap over (something else or each other); extend over and cover a part of; also, to cover and extend beyond (something else). **II.** *intr.* To lap over.—**o'ver-lap,** *n.* An overlapping; the place of overlapping; the extent or amount of overlapping; an overlapping part.

o-ver-lay (ō-vėr-lā'), *v. t.*; *-laid, -laying.* To lay or place (one thing) over or upon another; also, to cover, overspread, or surmount with something (as, "Or *overlay* With bridges rivers proud, as with a yoke": Milton's "Paradise Regained," iii. 333); esp., to finish with a layer or applied decoration of something (as, wood *overlaid* with gold; "bright ivory *overlaid* with sapphires," Cant. v. 14); also, to lie over or upon (something beneath); overlie (an infant); fig., to weigh down, overburden, or overwhelm (now rare: as, to be *overlaid* with business); also, to conceal or obscure as if by covering; in *printing,* to put an overlay upon.—**o'ver-lay,** *n.* Something laid over something else; a covering; a layer or decoration of something applied (as, an *overlay* of fine wood; an *overlay* of gold); also, a neck-cloth or cravat (Sc.); in *printing,* a shaped piece of paper, or a sheet of paper reinforced at the proper places by shaped pieces, put on the tympan of a press to increase or equalize the impression (cf. *make-ready*).

o-ver-leap (ō-vėr-lēp'), *v. t.* [AS. *oferhlēapan.*] To leap over or across; hence, to pass over or omit; also, to leap farther than, or outleap; hence, to overreach (one's self) by leaping too far (as, "vaulting ambition, which *o'erleaps* itself": Shakspere's "Macbeth," i. 7. 27).

o-ver-lie (ō-vėr-lī'), *v. t.*; pret. *-lay,* pp. *-lain,* ppr. *-lying.* To lie over or upon; rest upon, as a covering, layer, or stratum of something does; also, to smother (an infant) by lying upon it, as in sleep.

o-ver-ling (ō'vėr-ling), *n.* [See *-ling*[1], and cf. *underling.*] One who is over others in position or authority: now used in depreciation: as, "But the idle-minded *overlings* . . . Shall they thrust for high employments as of old?" (Kipling's "Mesopotamia").

o-ver-live (ō-vėr-liv'), *v.* **I.** *tr.* To live longer than; outlive; outlast: as, "The mighty Pyramids . . . have *overlived* The feeble generations of mankind" (Southey's "Thalaba," i. 29). **II.** *intr.* To survive; continue to live: as, "Why do I *overlive?* Why am I mock'd with death, and lengthen'd out To deathless pain?" (Milton's "Paradise Lost," x. 773).

o-ver-load (ō-vėr-lōd'), *v. t.* To load to excess; overburden.—**o'ver-load,** *n.* An excessive load.

o-ver-long (ō'vėr-lông'), *a.* and *adv.* Too long.

o-ver-look (ō-vėr-lůk'), *v. t.* To look over, as from a higher position; hence, to afford a view down over (as, a hill *overlooking* the sea); rise above, or overtop; also, to look over in inspection, examination, or perusal; look after, oversee, or supervise; look at, survey, or watch (as, "Utterly absorbed in her task, she had no suspicion that she was being *overlooked*": Arnold Bennett's "Helen with the High Hand," vii.); also, to look over and beyond (something) without seeing it; fail to notice, perceive, or consider (as, to *overlook* a misspelled word; to *overlook* the disadvantages of a plan); take no notice of, or ignore (as, "neglecting, and as it were, *overlooking* revelation, as of small importance, provided natural religion be kept to": J. Butler's "Analogy of Religion," ii. 1); often, to disregard or ignore indulgently, as faults, misconduct, etc.; forbear to censure or punish; also, to look upon with the evil eye, or bewitch (as, "I tell you she has *overlooked* me; and all this doctor's stuff is no use, unless you can say a charm as will undo her devil's work": H. Kingsley's "Geoffry Hamlyn," viii.).—**o-ver-look'er,** *n.*

o-ver-lord (ō'vėr-lôrd), *n.* One who is lord over another or over other lords.—**o'ver-lord-ship,** *n.*

o-ver-ly (ō'vėr-li), *adv.* Overmuch; excessively; too: as, "a voyage . . . not *overly* dangerous" (Galt's "Annals of the Parish," x.). [Now chiefly Sc. and U. S.]

o-ver-man (ō'vėr-man), *n.*; pl. *-men.* A man in authority over others, now esp. a foreman or overseer; also, an arbiter or umpire; also (pron. ō'vėr-man), same as *superman.*—**o-ver-man'** (-man'), *v. t.*; *-manned, -manning.* To oversupply with men, esp. for service.

o-ver-man-tel (ō'vėr-man"tl), *n.* A piece of decorative work placed above a mantelpiece, often a piece of ornamental cabinet-work with or without a mirror.

o-ver-mas-ter (ō-vėr-mås'tėr), *v. t.* To gain the mastery over; overcome; overpower.—**o-ver-mas'ter-ing-ly,** *adv.*

o-ver-match (ō-vėr-mach'), *v. t.* To be more than a match for; outmatch; surpass; outdo.—**o'ver-match,** *n.* One who or that which is more than a match, as for an opponent or an opposing force: as, "A very small force, skilfully and rapidly manœuvring . . . will be an *overmatch* for the much larger body of men" (Emerson's "Representative Men," vi.).

o-ver-much (ō'vėr-much'), *a., n.,* and *adv.* Too much.

o-ver-nice (ō'vėr-nīs'), *a.* Too nice or fastidious.

o-ver-night (ō'vėr-nīt'), *adv.* On the previous evening (as, preparations were made *overnight* for an early start; "He . . . posted the letter he had written . . . *overnight,*" H. G. Wells's "Men Like Gods," i. 1); also, during the night (as, to change one's mind *overnight*; to stay *overnight* with a friend).—**o'ver-night. I.** *n.* The previous evening. **II.** *a.* Of or pertaining to the previous evening; also, done, occurring, or continuing during the night (as, "He had invariably refused *overnight* hospitality whenever it was possible for him to get back to his home": H. G. Wells's "Soul of a Bishop," iv.).

o-ver-pass (ō-vėr-pås'), *v.*; *-passed* or *-past, -passing.* **I.** *tr.* To pass over or traverse (a region, space, etc.: as, "The next few miles would be no light thing for the whale-boats to *overpass,*" Kipling's "Light That Failed," ii.); hence, to pass through (time, experiences, etc.); also, to pass over (bounds, limits, etc.); get over (obstacles, difficulties, etc.);

also, to go beyond, exceed, or surpass (as, "Men Who *overpass* their kind": Browning's "Paracelsus," i.); also, to pass over indifferently or without notice (as, "All the beauties of the East He slightly view'd, and slightly *overpass'd*": Milton's "Paradise Regained," ii. 198); overlook, disregard, or omit. **II.** *intr.* To pass over or across; also, to pass by or away (now chiefly in *pp.*, often spelled *overpast*: as, "I view her . . . As a sweet sunset almost *overpast*," Henley's "In Hospital," x.).

o-ver-pay (ō-vėr-pā′), *v. t.*; *-paid, -paying.* To pay or recompense in excess; also, to pay more than (an amount due).—**o-ver-pay′ment,** *n.*

o-ver-peer (ō-vėr-pēr′), *v. t.* To peer over; look down over; hence, to rise or tower above, or overtop (as "The cedar . . . Whose top-branch *overpeer'd* Jove's spreading tree": Shakspere's "3 Henry VI.," v. 2. 14); fig., to excel.

o-ver-peo-ple (ō-vėr-pē′pl), *v. t.* To overstock with people: usually in *overpeopled, pp.*

o-ver-per-suade (ō″vėr-pėr-swād′), *v. t.* To bring over by persuasion; esp., to persuade (a person) against his inclination or intention (as, "I should have left you before now, if Mrs. Jakeman had not *over-persuaded* me": Godwin's "Caleb Williams," viii.).—**o″ver-per-sua′sion** (-swā′zhọn), *n.*

o-ver-plaid (ō′vėr-plad), *n.* A plaid pattern appearing over another pattern on woven fabrics; cloth with such a combination of patterns.

o-ver-play (ō-vėr-plā′), *v. t.* To play (a part, etc.) to excess, or in an exaggerated manner; also, to surpass or defeat in playing.

o-ver-please (ō-vėr-plēz′), *v. t.* To please excessively or beyond measure: now often with a negative: as, he was not *overpleased* with your reply.

o-ver-plus (ō′vėr-plus), *n.* An excess over a particular amount, or a surplus; also, an excessive amount, or superabundance (as, "He was ruined, morally, by an *overplus* of the very same ingredient [purpose]": Hawthorne's "Blithedale Romance," xxix.).

o-ver-pop-u-late (ō-vėr-pop′ū-lāt), *v. t.* To overpeople.—**o″ver-pop-u-la′tion** (-lā′shọn), *n.*

o-ver-pow-er (ō-vėr-pou′ėr), *v. t.* To overcome, master, or subdue by superior power or force (as, to *overpower* a resisting adversary; to *overpower* a maniac); fig., to prevail over by greater strength or effectiveness (as, "The thunder-claps for the time *overpowered* the noise of the wind": Marryat's "King's Own," li.); also, to overmaster the bodily powers or mental faculties of (as, "The troops of King Edward lay *overpowered* with wine," Jane Porter's "Scottish Chiefs," liv.; to be *overpowered* by gas, by fatigue, or by a mental shock); often, to overcome or overwhelm in feeling, or affect or impress excessively (as, "The thought of one man owning all those books *overpowered* him": W. Churchill's "Coniston," i. 15).—**o-ver-pow′er-ing,** *p. a.* That overpowers; overcoming any power of resistance; overwhelming; irresistible.—**o-ver-pow′er-ing-ly,** *adv.*

o-ver-praise (ō-vėr-prāz′), *v. t.* To praise to excess or too highly.—**o′ver-praise′,** *n.* Excessive praise.

o-ver-print (ō-vėr-print′), *v. t.* To print or stamp over with additional marks or matter (as, to *overprint* a postage-stamp with a special official mark: cf. *surcharge, v. t.*); in *textile printing*, to print (a fabric) with another color applied, as in a pattern, upon one already used; also, in *photog.*, to print (a positive) darker than is intended for the finished work.—**o′ver-print,** *n.* An offprint.

o-ver-prize (ō-vėr-prīz′), *v. t.* To prize too highly; overvalue; also, to surpass in value (obs. or archaic).

o-ver-pro-duce (ō″vėr-prọ-dūs′), *v. t.* To produce too much of, as a commodity; produce in excess of the demand.—**o″ver-pro-duc′tion** (-duk′shọn), *n.* Excessive production; production of commodities in excess of the demand for them.

o-ver-proof (ō′vėr-pröf), *a.* Containing a greater proportion of alcohol than proof-spirit does.

o-ver-proud (ō′vėr-proud′), *a.* Excessively or unduly proud.

o-ver-rate (ō-vėr-rāt′), *v. t.* To rate too highly; overestimate: as, his fortune has been greatly *overrated*; "I had . . . *overrated* my strength, and was no sooner left to myself than I reeled, and fell" (Godwin's "Caleb Williams," xxviii.).

o-ver-reach (ō-vėr-rēch′), *v.* **I.** *tr.* To reach or extend over or beyond; also, to overtake (now chiefly Sc.); also, to reach for or aim at but go beyond, as a thing sought, a mark, etc.; also, to get the better of (a person, etc.), now always by cunning or sharp practice (as, "Every person you deal with endeavours to *overreach* you in the way of business": Smollett's "Humphry Clinker," June 8); outwit in dealing, bargaining, etc.; cheat; also, to stretch (the arm, etc.) to excess, as by a straining effort; strain or exert (one's self) to the point of exceeding the purpose; defeat (one's self) by overdoing matters, often by excessive eagerness or cunning. **II.** *intr.* To reach or extend over something; also, to practise overreaching or cheating others; also, to reach too far; of horses, etc., to strike, or strike and injure, the fore foot with the hind foot in going.—**o-ver-reach′er,** *n.*

o-ver-re-fine (ō″vėr-rẹ-fīn′), *v. t.* or *i.* To refine to excess.—**o″ver-re-fine′ment,** *n.*

o-ver-ride (ō-vėr-rīd′), *v. t.*; pret. *-rode*, pp. *-ridden*, ppr. *-riding.* [AS. *oferrīdan.*] To ride over or across (a region, etc.); also, to drive over, or overthrow and trample, in riding (as, "The boy Paused not, but *overrode* him . . . and so left him bruised And batter'd": Tennyson's "Pelleas and Ettarre," 534); fig., to ride roughshod over, or trample roughly upon (as, "*overriding* another's happiness in pursuit of your own": G. W. Cable's "Bonaventure," i. 6); pursue one's course or purpose in arrogant, wilful, or open disregard of (as, to *override* one's advisers or instructions; to *override* the authority, objections, or opposition of another); prevail over (as, a decision that *overrides* all previous decisions); also, to overtake or pass in riding†; also, to ride too much, or exhaust by excessive riding, as a horse; also, to pass or extend over; in *surg.*, to overlap, as one piece of a fractured bone does another.

o-ver-ripe (ō′vėr-rīp′), *a.* Too ripe; more than ripe.—**o′ver-ripe′ness,** *n.*

o-ver-roast (ō-vėr-rōst′), *v. t.* To roast too much.

o-ver-roof (ō-vėr-röf′), *v. t.* To cover over with or as with a roof.

o-ver-rule (ō-vėr-röl′), *v. t.* To exercise rule or controlling influence over (now used chiefly of Providence or God); also, to prevail over so as to change the purpose or action (as, "My lord, you shall *o'er-rule* my mind for once": Shakspere's "Richard III.," iii. 1. 57); also, to rule or decide against (a plea, argument, objection, etc.); disallow; also, to rule against or disallow the arguments of (a person).—**o-ver-rul′ing-ly,** *adv.*

o-ver-run (ō-vėr-run′), *v.*; pret. *-ran*, pp. *-run*, ppr. *-running.* **I.** *tr.* To run over; overflow; also, to rove over (a country, etc.), as hostile or ravaging invaders; swarm over in great numbers, as animals, esp. vermin; spread or grow rapidly over, as plants, esp. vines, weeds, etc.; spread rapidly throughout, as a new idea, spirit, etc.; also, to run over so as to injure or overwhelm (as, "Like a gallant horse fall'n . . . *O'er-run* and trampled on": Shakspere's "Troilus and Cressida," iii. 3. 163); also, to outrun, or overtake in running (archaic: as, "Atalanta . . . *overran* A white high-crested bull," W. Morris's "Jason," xi. 138); run away from (now prov. Eng.); also, to run beyond; fig., to exceed; in *printing*, to carry over (letters, words, or lines) to the next line, column, or page; carry over words, etc., of. **II.** *intr.* To run over; overflow; extend beyond the proper or desired limit.—**o′ver-run,** *n.* An overrunning; also, an amount overrunning or carried over.—**o-ver-run′ner,** *n.*

o-ver-score (ō-vėr-skōr′), *v. t.* To score over, as with strokes or lines.

o-ver-sea, o-ver-seas (ō′vėr-sē′, -sēz′), *adv.* Over, across, or beyond the sea; on the other side of the sea: as, "to fly *over-sea* from Dover to Calais" (H. Brooke's "Fool of Quality," xvii.); "a French lord *overseas*" (Swinburne's "Chastelard," v. 1).—**o′ver-sea, o′ver-seas,** *a.* Of or pertaining to passage over the sea (as, *oversea* travel); also, situated beyond the sea (as, *oversea* lands); also, pertaining to or connected with countries beyond the sea, or foreign (as, *oversea* languages or customs); carried on, used, or serving in countries beyond the sea (as, *oversea* military service; an *overseas* cap for soldiers; *overseas* regiments).

o-ver-seam (ō′vėr-sēm), *n.* A seam made by oversewing edges.—**o-ver-seam′,** *v. t.* or *i.* To sew with an overseam.

o′ver-seas′, o′ver-seas. See *oversea, adv.* and *a.*
o-ver-see (ō-vėr-sē′), *v. t.*; pret. *-saw*, pp. *-seen*, ppr. *-seeing.* [AS. *oferseōn.*] To overlook, as from a higher position; survey; watch; also, to look over, inspect, or examine (obs. or archaic); now, esp., to look after and direct (work or workers); supervise; superintend; manage; also, to overlook, fail to notice, or disregard (obs. or prov.).—**o-ver-seer** (ō′vėr-sēr or ō-vėr-sē′ėr), *n.* One who oversees; a supervisor; a superintendent.—**o′ver-seer-ship,** *n.*
o-ver-sell (ō-vėr-sel′), *v. t.*; *-sold, -selling.* To sell for more than the actual value† (as, "The thing call'd life, with ease I can disclaim, And think it *over-sold* to purchase fame": Dryden's tr. Virgil's "Æneid," ix. 265); also, to sell to excess; sell more of (a stock, etc.) than can be delivered.
o-ver-set (ō-vėr-set′), *v.*; *-set, -setting.* **I.** *tr.* To upset or overturn (as, "The boat was *overset* by a sudden flurry from the north": Swift's "Gulliver's Travels," i. 1); hence, fig., to overthrow (as, to *overset* kingdoms or institutions); throw into confusion (as, to *overset* one's reckoning); disorder physically; disturb mentally (as, "So *overset* was she by the dramatic surprise of his challenging remark . . . that her manner changed in an instant": Arnold Bennett's "Hilda Lessways," i. 6); also, in *printing*, to set in or to excess, as type or copy; set too much type for, as space. **II.** *intr.* To become upset or overturned (as, "This raft . . . *overset*, and threw me . . . into the water": Defoe's "Robinson Crusoe," i. 4); fig., to become overthrown.—**o′ver-set,** *n.* The act or fact of oversetting; overturn; also, in *printing*, matter set up in excess of space.
o-ver-sew (ō′vėr-sō), *v. t.* To sew with stitches passing successively over an edge, esp. closely, so as to cover the edge or make a firm seam.
o-ver-shade (ō-vėr-shād′), *v. t.* To cast a shade over; render dark or gloomy.
o-ver-shad-ow (ō-vėr-shad′ō), *v. t.* To cast a shadow or shade over; make dark or gloomy; also, to shelter or protect (as, "The power of the Highest shall *overshadow* thee": Luke, i. 35); also, to tower over so as to cast a shadow over; hence, to diminish the importance of, or render insignificant in comparison (as, "Mr. Gamaliel Ives . . . would have been the first citizen if that other first citizen had not . . . so completely *overshadowed* him": W. Churchill's "Coniston," ii. 15).
o-ver-shine (ō-vėr-shīn′), *v. t.*; *-shone, -shining.* To shine over or upon; also, to outshine; fig., to surpass in splendor, excellence, etc.
o-ver-shoe (ō′vėr-shö), *n.* A shoe worn over another shoe for protection against wet, cold, etc.; esp., a waterproof outer shoe of india-rubber.
o-ver-shoot (ō-vėr-shöt′), *v. t.*; *-shot, -shooting.* To shoot or go over or above (something); also, to shoot or go beyond (a point, limit, etc.); also, to shoot a missile over or beyond (what is aimed at), thus missing (as, to *overshoot* the mark, fig., to go further in any course or matter than is intended or proper, or go too far); also, to force or drive (a thing) beyond the proper limit.—**to overshoot one's self,** to overshoot one's mark; go too far in any course or matter; defeat one's end by doing too much; overreach one's self.—**o′ver-shot,** *a.* Having the upper jaw projecting beyond the lower, as a dog; also, driven by water shot over from above, as a kind of vertical water-wheel.

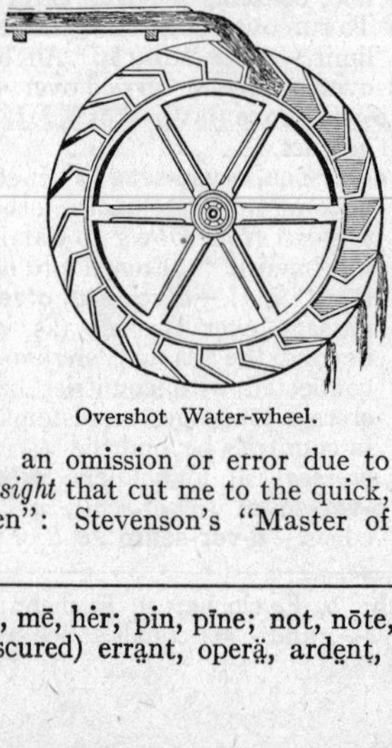
Overshot Water-wheel.

o-ver-side (ō′vėr-sīd′), *adv.* Over the side, as of a ship.—**o′ver-side,** *a.* Effected over the side of a ship (as, *overside* discharge of a cargo); also, unloading or unloaded over the side.
o-ver-sight (ō′vėr-sīt), *n.* Supervision; superintendence; inspection; watchful care; also, the act of overlooking, or failing to notice or consider; an omission or error due to inadvertence (as, "By an *oversight* that cut me to the quick, my place had been forgotten": Stevenson's "Master of Ballantrae," iv.).
o-ver-size[1] (ō′vėr-sīz). **I.** *a.* Of excessive size; of a size larger than is necessary or required. **II.** *n.* Something that is oversize; an oversize article or object; also, a size larger than the proper or usual size.
o-ver-size[2] (ō-vėr-sīz′), *v. t.* To cover over with or as with size (see Shakspere's "Hamlet," ii. 2. 484); also, to size too much.
o-ver-sized (ō′vėr-sīzd), *a.* Of excessive size; over the average size, or abnormally large.
o-ver-skirt (ō′vėr-skėrt), *n.* An outer skirt; also, a drapery arranged over or upon a dress-skirt.
o-ver-slaugh (ō-vėr-slâ′ or ō′vėr-slâ), *v. t.* [D. *overslaan,* < *over*, over, + *slaan*, strike, = E. *slay*[2].] To remit (a military duty), or excuse (a soldier or soldiers) from a duty, in consideration of some other duty; also, to pass over (a military officer) in favor of another, as in promotion; in general, to pass over or ignore; also, to hinder or obstruct.—**o′ver-slaugh,** *n.* A bar or sand-bank impeding navigation in a river (U. S.); also, *milit.*, an overslaughing.
o-ver-sleep (ō-vėr-slēp′), *v. t.*; *-slept, -sleeping.* To sleep beyond (a certain hour).—**to oversleep one's self,** to sleep beyond the time at which one should awake: as, "They were weary, and *overslept themselves*" (Defoe's "Robinson Crusoe," ii. 3).—**o-ver-sleep′,** *v. i.* To sleep beyond the proper time of waking.
o-ver-soul (ō′vėr-sōl), *n.* The Deity as the spiritual unity of all being: as, "that Unity, that *Over-soul*, within which every man's particular being is contained and made one with all other" (Emerson's "Essays," The Over-Soul).
o-ver-spread (ō-vėr-spred′), *v. t.*; *-spread, -spreading.* To spread (one thing) over another; also, to cover (a thing) with something else (as, "Dealers had erected booths . . . and *overspread* them with scanty awnings": Hawthorne's "Marble Faun," xxxiv.); of a thing, to be spread over (something else: as, "Soon the thick blackness *overspread* the whole sky," Parkman's "Oregon Trail," xiii.).
o-ver-state (ō-vėr-stāt′), *v. t.* To state too strongly; exaggerate in statement: as, to *overstate* one's case; "She was . . . anxious to *overstate* . . . her real social status" (H. G. Wells's "Tono-Bungay," ii. 1. § 4).—**o-ver-state′ment,** *n.*
o-ver-stay (ō-vėr-stā′), *v. t.*; *-stayed, -staying.* To stay beyond the time or duration of: as, "She had already *overstayed* her invitation" (H. James's "Portrait of a Lady," li.).
o-ver-step (ō-vėr-step′), *v. t.*; *-stepped, -stepping.* To step or pass over or beyond.
o-ver-stock (ō-vėr-stok′), *v. t.* To stock to excess; supply with more than is needed; glut.—**o′ver-stock,** *n.* A stock in excess of need or demand.
o-ver-strain (ō-vėr-strān′), *v. t.* or *i.* To strain to excess.—**o′ver-strain′,** *n.* An overstraining; excessive strain.
o-ver-stride (ō-vėr-strīd′), *v. t.*; pret. *-strode*, pp. *-stridden*, ppr. *-striding.* To stride or step over or across; also, to bestride; also, to stride beyond; fig., to surpass.
o-ver-strung (ō′vėr-strung′), *a.* Too highly strung: as, "nerves *o'erstrung*" (Scott's "Lady of the Lake," iii. 6).
o-ver-stud-y (ō-vėr-stud′i), *v. t.* or *i.*; *-studied, -studying.* To study too much or too hard.—**o′ver-stud′y,** *n.* Excessive study.
o-ver-sub-scribe (ō″vėr-sub-skrīb′), *v. t.* To subscribe for in excess of what is available or required.—**o″ver-sub-scrip′tion** (-skrip′shon), *n.* The act of oversubscribing; an amount subscribed for in excess.
o-ver-sub-tle (ō′vėr-sut′l), *a.* Subtle to excess; too subtle.—**o′ver-sub′tle-ty,** *n.*
o-ver-sup-ply (ō″vėr-su-plī′), *v. t.*; *-plied, -plying.* To supply in excess.—**o′ver-sup-ply′,** *n.* An excessive supply.
o-ver-swarm (ō-vėr-swârm′), *v. t.* To swarm over; spread over in swarms; also, to swarm in excess of.
o-ver-sway (ō-vėr-swā′), *v. t.* To sway over, or cause to incline to one side or fall over; also, to exercise sway or rule over†; prevail over by superior authority†; persuade, as to some course of action (as, "If he be so resolved, I can *o'ersway* him": Shakspere's "Julius Cæsar," ii. 1. 203).
o-ver-sweep (ō-vėr-swēp′), *v. t.*; *-swept, -sweeping.* To sweep over.
o-ver-swell (ō-vėr-swel′), *v.* **I.** *tr.* To swell so as to pass over or beyond; overflow. **II.** *intr.* To swell beyond the bounds or limits.

o-vert (ō′vėrt or o̤-vėrt′), *a.* [OF. *overt*, pp. of *ovrir* (F. *ouvrir*), open, appar. with sense < L. *aperire*, open, but with form < L. *operire*, cover, < *ob*, before + *-perire*, occurring also (with different prefix) in *aperire*: see *aperient.*] Open to view or knowledge (as, *overt* hostility; an *overt* attempt); evident, manifest, or outward; not concealed or secret; in *her.*, open, or not closed, as a purse; outspread, as a bird's wings.—**overt act,** in *criminal law*, an open or outward act from which criminal intent is inferred.

o-ver-take (ō-vėr-tāk′), *v. t.*; pret. *-took*, pp. *-taken*, ppr. *-taking*. To come up with in traveling in the same direction, or in pursuit (as, "They . . . went in and searched the house, and by that means missed *overtaking* the thief": Fielding's "Tom Jones," vi. 3); come up with in any course of action; sometimes, to get through (a task) when pressed for time, or within the time (Sc.: as, "It's a job you could doubtless *overtake* with the other," Stevenson's "David Balfour," ii.); also, to come upon suddenly or unexpectedly (said esp. of night, storm, misfortune, death, etc.: as, "Fearful was the fate that . . . *overtook* some of the members of that party," Parkman's "Oregon Trail," x.); also, to overcome the mind, senses, or feelings of, or overpower (obs. or prov.); intoxicate (now prov.: as, "I don't appear to carry drink the way I used to . . . I get *overtaken*," Stevenson's "Master of Ballantrae," xi.).

o-ver-task (ō-vėr-tȧsk′), *v. t.* To impose too heavy a task upon: as, "In those days children's brains were not *overtasked* as they now are" (S. Butler's "Way of All Flesh," ii.).

o-ver-tax (ō-vėr-taks′), *v. t.* To tax too heavily; overburden or oppress with taxes; hence, to make too great demands on (as, "I had *overtaxed* my strength," Mrs. Shelley's "Frankenstein," xxii.; "Our credulity is *overtaxed*," Dunsany's "Laughter of the Gods," ii.).—**o″ver-tax-a′tion** (-tak-sā′sho̤n), *n.*

o-ver-teem (ō-vėr-tēm′), *v.* **I.** *intr.* To teem, breed, or produce excessively. **II.** *tr.* To wear out or exhaust with excessive breeding or production.

o-ver-throw (ō-vėr-thrō′), *v. t.*; pret. *-threw*, pp. *-thrown*, ppr. *-throwing*. To throw over; upset; overturn; knock down and demolish; hence, fig., to cast down as from a position of power; overcome, defeat, or vanquish (as, "A fierce, bloody, and confused action succeeded, in which the patriots were completely *overthrown*": Motley's "Dutch Republic," iv. 1); reduce to powerlessness or impotence; also, to subvert, ruin, or destroy (as, "Here's Gloucester . . . That seeks to *overthrow* religion," Shakspere's "1 Henry VI.," i. 3. 65; a discovery that *overthrows* a theory); put an end to by force, as governments or institutions; destroy the sound condition of (the mind: as, "O, what a noble mind is here *o'erthrown!*" Shakspere's "Hamlet," iii. 1. 158).—**o′ver-throw,** *n.* The act of overthrowing, or the resulting state; overturn; deposition from power; defeat; destruction; ruin.—**o-ver-throw′er,** *n.*

o-ver-thrust (ō′vėr-thrust). In *geol.*: **I.** *n.* A fault in which the rocks on the upper side have been moved upward and lie above rocks of later formation, thus reversing the normal succession. **II.** *a.* Of the nature of or pertaining to an overthrust.

o-ver-thwart (ō-vėr-thwârt′), *adv.* and *prep.* Across; athwart. [Now prov.]—**o′ver-thwart,** *a.* Lying across; also, situated across or opposite; also, contrary, perverse, or cross. [Now prov.]

o-ver-time (ō′vėr-tīm), *n.* Time during which one works beyond the regular hours; extra time.—**o′ver-time′,** *adv.* During extra time: as, to work *overtime*.—**o-ver-time′,** *v. t.* To give or allow too much time to, as in photographic exposure.

o-ver-tire (ō-vėr-tīr′), *v. t.* To tire excessively.

o-vert-ly (ō′vėrt-li or o̤-vėrt′li), *adv.* In an overt manner; openly; publicly.—**o′vert-ness,** *n.*

o-ver-toil (ō-vėr-toil′), *v. t.* To weary or exhaust by too much toil: as, "*Overtoil'd* By that day's grief and travel" (Tennyson's "Geraint and Enid," 376).

o-ver-tone (ō′vėr-tōn), *n.* [= G. *oberton.*] In *acoustics*, a harmonic.

o-ver-top (ō-vėr-top′), *v. t.*; *-topped*, *-topping*. To rise over or above the top of (as, "One . . . building, in course of construction, had already far *overtopped* the highest of its neighbours": Arnold Bennett's "Hilda Lessways," iii. 3); surpass in height; tower above; fig., to rise above in authority; override (law, etc.); also, to surpass or excel.

o-ver-trade (ō-vėr-trād′), *v. i.* To trade in excess of one's capital or the requirements of the market.

o-ver-train (ō-vėr-trān′), *v. t.* To train to excess, or beyond the limits of safety.

o-ver-trump (ō-vėr-trump′), *v. t.* In *card-playing*, to trump with a higher trump than has already been played; surpass in trumping by playing a higher trump.

o-ver-ture (ō′vėr-t̤ūr), *n.* [OF. *overture* (F. *ouverture*), < *ovrir*, open: see *overt.*] An opening† or aperture†; also, a disclosure† (as, "It was he That made the *overture* of thy treasons to us": Shakspere's "King Lear," iii. 7. 89); also, an opening of negotiations, or a formal proposal or offer (as, "I hear there is an *overture* of peace," Shakspere's "All's Well," iv. 3. 46; "The first *overtures* . . . must come from them," Marryat's "Mr. Midshipman Easy," xiv.); also, an opening†, beginning†, or commencement†; in *music*, an orchestral composition forming the prelude or introduction to an opera, oratorio, etc.; an independent piece of similar character; hence, by transfer, an introductory part, as of a poem.—**o′ver-ture,** *v. t.*; *-tured*, *-turing*. To submit as an overture or proposal; also, to make an overture or proposal to.

o-ver-turn (ō-vėr-tėrn′), *v.* **I.** *tr.* To turn over on its side or face; throw over with violence; upset; hence, to overthrow; destroy the power of; defeat or vanquish; bring to destruction or ruin. **II.** *intr.* To turn over on its side or face; upset; capsize.—**o′ver-turn,** *n.* The act of overturning, or the state of being overturned; also, a turning over, as in the course of trade; a turnover.—**o-ver-turn′er,** *n.*

o-ver-use (ō-vėr-ūz′), *v. t.* To use too much; use too hard or too often.—**o′ver-use′** (-ūs′), *n.* Excessive use.

o-ver-val-ue (ō-vėr-val′ṳ̄), *v. t.* To value too highly; put too high a value on.—**o″ver-val-u-a′tion** (-ā′sho̤n), *n.*

o-ver-watch (ō-vėr-woch′), *v. t.* To watch over; also, to watch through† (see Shakspere's "Midsummer Night's Dream," v. 1. 373); also, to weary by watching (as, "Morning was well advanced, when Tressilian, fatigued and *overwatched*, came down to the hall": Scott's "Kenilworth," xv.).

o-ver-wear-y (ō-vėr-wēr′i), *v. t.* To weary to excess; overcome with weariness.—**o′ver-wear′y,** *a.* Excessively weary; tired out: as, "The little girl, *over-weary*, had . . . fallen asleep" (Mrs. Stowe's "Oldtown Folks," vii.).

o-ver-ween (ō-vėr-wēn′), *v. i.* [See *ween.*] To think too highly or too confidently, esp. of one's self; be conceited or arrogant; presume: now chiefly in *overweening*, *p. a.*—**o-ver-ween′ing,** *p. a.* That overweens; conceited, overconfident, or presumptuous, as a person, or as the opinion, expectations, pretensions, etc.: as, "*overweening* confidence in his own powers" (Prescott's "Conquest of Mexico," iv. 6).—**o-ver-ween′ing-ly,** *adv.*—**o-ver-ween′ing-ness,** *n.*

o-ver-weigh (ō-vėr-wā′), *v. t.* To exceed in weight; overbalance or outweigh (lit. or fig.: as, "My duty is imperative, and must *overweigh* my private feelings," Wiseman's "Fabiola," i. 10); also, to weigh down; oppress.

o-ver-weight (ō′vėr-wāt′), *n.* Extra weight; excess of weight; also, greater weight; preponderance; also, too great weight.—**o-ver-weight′,** *v. t.* To weight to excess; overburden.

o-ver-whelm (ō-vėr-hwelm′), *v. t.* [See *whelm.*] To overturn or overthrow (obs. or rare); also, to turn or throw (one thing) over something else†; also, to cover or bury beneath a mass of something, a flood, or the like, or cover as a mass or flood does (as, volcanic eruptions *overwhelming* great areas; "the ocean leaving one coast dry, and *overwhelming* another," Swift's "Gulliver's Travels," iii. 10); submerge; fig., to load, heap, treat, or address with an overpowering or excessive amount of anything (as, to *overwhelm* a person with gifts, favors, or insults; "He . . . *overwhelmed* her with a profusion of compliment," Smollett's "Humphry Clinker," May 6); come, rest, or weigh upon overpoweringly, overcome, or crush (as, misfortunes or sorrows *overwhelm* us; "small debts that were not so small but that finally they *overwhelmed* him," H. G. Wells's "Tono-Bungay," i. 2. § 1); overcome completely in mind or feeling (as,

"At this surprising change of my circumstances from a merchant to a miserable slave, I was perfectly *overwhelmed*": Defoe's "Robinson Crusoe," i. 2).—**o-ver-whelm′ing,** *p. a.* That overwhelms; covering, submerging, or bearing down like a flood; overcoming utterly; overpowering; sometimes, so great as to render resistance or opposition useless (as, an *overwhelming* majority).—**o-ver-whelm′ing-ly,** *adv.*

o-ver-wind (ō-vėr-wīnd′), *v. t.*; *-wound, -winding.* To wind beyond the proper limit; wind too far.

o-ver-wise (ō′vėr-wīz′), *a.* Too wise.—**o′ver-wise′ly,** *adv.*

o-ver-word (ō′vėr-wėrd), *n.* A word or phrase often repeated; esp., the burden of a song. [Chiefly Sc.]

o-ver-work (ō′vėr-wėrk′), *n.* Extra work; work done beyond the amount stipulated, or during overtime; also, work beyond one's strength or capacity.—**o-ver-work′,** *v.*; *-worked* or *-wrought, -working.* **I.** *tr.* To work or decorate all over; decorate the surface of (as, "Of Gothic structure was the Northern side, *O'erwrought* with ornaments of barbarous pride": Pope's "Temple of Fame," 120); also, to spend too much work upon, or elaborate to excess (chiefly in *overwrought, pp.*); also, to cause to work too hard or too long; weary or exhaust with work (often reflexively: as, "I know how busy you are; you mustn't *overwork* yourself," Chesterton's "Magic," i.); fill (time) too full of work; also, to work up, stir up, or excite excessively, as the mind, feelings, etc. (chiefly in *overwrought, pp.*). **II.** *intr.* To work too hard; work to excess.—**o-ver-wrought′** (-rôt′), *p. a.* Overworked; elaborated to excess; wearied or exhausted by overwork; worked up or excited excessively.

ovi-. Form of L. *ovum*, egg, used in combination. Cf. *ovo-*.

O-vid-i-an (ọ-vid′i-ạn), *a.* Pertaining to or characteristic of the Roman poet Ovid (43 B.C.—A.D. 17?) or his poetry.

o-vi-duct (ō′vi-dukt), *n.* [NL. *oviductus*, < L. *ovum*, egg, + *ductus*, E. *duct*.] In *anat.* and *zoöl.*, the duct or canal through which the ovum or egg passes from the ovary.

o-vif-er-ous (ọ-vif′ẹ-rus), *a.* [See *ovi-* and *-ferous*.] In *anat.* and *zoöl.*, bearing eggs; serving to contain or convey ova or eggs.

o-vi-form (ō′vi-fôrm), *a.* [See *ovi-* and *-form*.] Egg-shaped.

o-vine (ō′vin or ō′vīn), *a.* [LL. *ovinus*, < L. *ovis*, sheep: see *ewe*.] Pertaining to, of the nature of, or resembling sheep.

o-vip-a-rous (ọ-vip′ạ-rus), *a.* [L. *oviparus*, < *ovum*, egg, + *parere*, bring forth.] In *zoöl.*, producing ova or eggs which are matured or hatched after being expelled from the body, as birds, most reptiles and fishes, etc.—**o-vi-par-i-ty** (ō-vi-par′i-ti), *n.*

Field-cricket. — *o*, ovipositor.

o-vi-pos-it (ō-vi-poz′it), *v. i.* [L. *ovum*, egg, + *positus*, pp. of *ponere*, place, put.] To deposit or lay eggs, esp. by means of an ovipositor.—**o″vi-po-si′tion** (-pọ-zish′ọn), *n.* The act of ovipositing.—**o-vi-pos′i-tor,** *n.* In certain insects, an organ at the end of the abdomen, by which eggs are deposited. See cut above.

o-vi-sac (ō′vi-sak), *n.* [See *ovi-*.] In *zoöl.*, a sac or capsule containing an ovum or ova; in *anat.*, a Graafian follicle.

o-vism (ō′vizm), *n.* [L. *ovum*, egg.] In *biol.*, the old doctrine that the egg contains all the organs of the future animal.—**o′vist,** *n.*

O-vis po-li (ō′vis pō′lī or -lẹ̄). [NL., 'sheep of Polo.'] See *Tian-shan sheep*.

ovo-. Form of L. *ovum*, egg, used in combination. Cf. *ovi-*.

o-vo-gen-e-sis (ō-vọ-jen′e-sis), *n.* [See *ovo-*.] Same as *oögenesis*.—**o″vo-ge-net′ic** (-jẹ-net′ik), *a.*

o-void (ō′void). [L. *ovum*, egg: see *-oid*.] **I.** *a.* Egg-shaped; esp., having the solid form of an egg; specif., having such a form with the broader end at the base, as a fruit. Cf. *ovate*. **II.** *n.* An ovoid body.—**o-voi-dal** (ō′voi-dạl), *a.* Ovoid.—**o″voi-do-con′i-cal** (-dọ-kon′i-kạl), *a.* Conical but with a slightly convex profile, as the roofs of certain towers. See cut in preceding column.

Ovoidoconical Roof.

o-vo-lo (ō′vọ-lō), *n.*; pl. *-li* (-lē). [It., dim. < L. *ovum*, egg.] In *arch.*, a convex molding forming or approximating in section a quarter of a circle or ellipse.

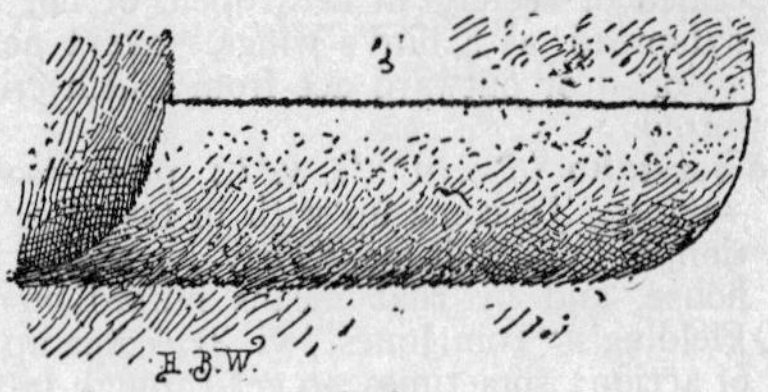

Ovolo.

o-vo-vi-tel-lin (ō″vọ-vi-tel′in or -vi-tel′in), *n.* [See *ovo-* and *vitellin*.] In *physiol. chem.*, a protein contained in the yolk of eggs.

o-vo-vi-vip-a-rous (ō″vọ-vī-vip′ạ-rus), *a.* [See *ovo-* and *viviparous*.] In *zoöl.*, producing eggs which are hatched within the body, so that the young are born alive but without placental attachment, as certain reptiles, fishes, etc.

o-vu-lar (ō′vụ-lär), *a.* Pertaining to or of the nature of an ovule.

o-vu-la-tion (ō-vụ-lā′shọn), *n.* In *biol.*, the formation of ovules or ova; the discharge of an ovum from the ovary.

o-vule (ō′vūl), *n.* [F. *ovule*, dim. < L. *ovum*, egg: see *ovum*.] In *biol.*, a little egg; an ovum, esp. when small, immature, or unfertilized; in *bot.*, a rudimentary seed; the body which contains the embryo-sac and hence the female germ-cell, and which after fertilization develops into a seed.—**o-vu-lif-er-ous** (ō-vụ-lif′ẹ-rus), *a.* [See *-ferous*.] Producing ovules.

o-vum (ō′vum), *n.*; pl. *ova* (ō′vạ̈) or *ovums*. [L., egg; akin to Gr. ᾠόν, egg: cf. *egg*[2].] In *biol.*, an egg, in a broad biological sense; the female reproductive cell of animals, which (usually only after fertilization) is capable of developing into a new individual; the female reproductive cell or gamete of plants; in *arch.*, an egg-shaped ornament.

owe (ō), *v.*; pret. *owed* (formerly *ought*), pp. *owed* (formerly *own*), ppr. *owing*. [AS. *āgan* = OHG. *eigan* = Icel. *eiga* = Goth. *aigan*, have, possess: cf. *own* and *ought*[2].] **I.** *tr.* To own† or possess†; also, to be under obligation to pay or repay, or to render (often with *to* or a simple dative: as, to *owe* interest on a mortgage; to *owe* $10 to a friend; to *owe* a person obedience or allegiance); sometimes (by omission of the ordinary direct object), to be in debt to (as, "He *owes* not any man," Longfellow's "Village Blacksmith"; to *owe* a grocer for supplies); also, to have or cherish (a certain feeling) toward a person (now only in 'to owe one a grudge'); also, to be indebted or beholden for (usually with *to*: as, "It is difficult to say whether England *owes* more to the Roman Catholic religion or to the Reformation," Macaulay's "Hist. of Eng.," i.). **II.** *intr.* To be in debt: as, to *owe* for the very clothes one wears.—**ow-ing** (ō′ing), *p. a.* That owes; indebted; also, owed or due (as, to pay what is *owing*).—**owing to,** owing existence to, due to, or attributable to (as, "Such false impressions are *owing to* the abandoned writings of men of wit": Steele, in "Spectator," 6); also, on account of, or because of (as, "I could not see many yards ahead *owing to* the bushes": W. H. Hudson's "Green Mansions," v.).

owl (oul), *n.* [AS. *ūle* = MLG. *ūle* = D. *uil* = G. *eule* = Icel. *ugla*, owl: cf. L. *ulula*, screech-owl; all imit., from the bird's cry.] Any member of the suborder or group *Striges*, comprising birds of prey, chiefly nocturnal, with a broad head and with large eyes which are usually set in disks of modified feathers (they feed on mice, small birds and reptiles, etc., and from their solemn appearance are taken as a type of gravity and wisdom: see cut on following page); also, one of a variety of domestic pigeons of owl-like appearance; also, in fig. use, a person of nocturnal habits; an owl-train; a person of owl-like solemnity of appearance; a solemn-looking wiseacre; a wise-looking but stupid person.

owl-et (ou′let), *n.* [Dim. of *owl*.] An owl, esp. when small or young; also, an owlet-moth.—**owl′et=moth,** *n.* Any noctuid moth.

owl=eyed (oul′īd), *a.* Having eyes like those of an owl; seeing best in the dark.

owl-ish (ou′lish), *a.* Owl-like; characteristic of or suggesting an owl: as, "round *owlish* eyes" (Parkman's "Oregon Trail," x.); an *owlish* air of wisdom; "the *owlish* pedantry which had so long flapped and hooted through mediæval cloisters" (Motley's "Dutch Republic," Introd., xii.).—**owl′ish-ly,** *adv.*—**owl′ish-ness,** *n.*

owl=light (oul′līt), *n.* Twilight; dusk.

owl=train (oul′trān), *n.* A railroad-train that makes its trip during the night.

Barred Owl (*Strix varia*).

own (ōn), *a.* [AS. *āgen*, orig. pp. of *āgan*, have, possess: see *owe*.] Belonging, pertaining, or relating to one's self or itself (used after a possessive to emphasize the idea of ownership, interest, or relation conveyed by the possessive: as, John's *own* book, his *own* money, its *own* characteristics; my *own* death; I am my *own* master, he does his *own* typewriting, a machine that furnishes its *own* power); also (without a possessive preceding), belonging to one's self or itself (as, "He does not see why each should not have an *own* name," W. D. Whitney's "Life and Growth of Language," ii.: how rare except with reference to relationship, as in 'an *own* brother,' that is, one not a half-brother, brother-in-law, etc., and '*own* cousins,' that is, first cousins). Also, absolutely, with a possessive preceding, own property, possessions, relatives, friends, etc.: as, to come into one's *own*; "The cup . . . from which our Lord Drank at the last sad supper with his *own*" (Tennyson's "Holy Grail," 47).—**of one's own,** that is one's own; belonging to one's self: as, "You have a good sword and a good mother-wit *of your own*" (Whyte-Melville's "Katerfelto," vii.). Cf. *of his, of hers*, etc., under *of*.—**on one's own,** on one's own account, responsibility, resources, etc.: as, "I might have had half a dozen situations as managing clerk . . . Only . . . I wanted to be *on my own*" (Arnold Bennett's "Hilda Lessways," iii. 2); "knocking about the world *on his own*" (J. Conrad's "Victory," iii. 10). [Colloq., orig. Eng.]—**to be one's own man,** to be independent; have full control of one's self: as, "Constance Neville may marry whom she pleases, and Tony Lumpkin *is his own man* again!" (Goldsmith's "She Stoops to Conquer," v. 3).—**to hold one's own.** See under *hold*², *v. t.*—**own,** *v.* [AS. *āgnian*, < *āgen*.] **I.** *tr.* To have or hold as one's own, or possess (as, "His lordship . . . *owned* now the major part of the parish": Galt's "Annals of the Parish," xiv.); also, to acknowledge as one's own (as, "Thy brat hath been cast out . . . No father *owning* it": Shakspere's "Winter's Tale," iii. 2. 89); also, to acknowledge or admit (as, to *own* a fault; "I *own* myself an ass," Stevenson's "Treasure Island," xii.; "The St. Lawrence was worthy to be seen, as even Mr. Arbuton *owned*," Howells's "Chance Acquaintance," i.). **II.** *intr.* To confess: as, to *own* to being uncertain; to *own* to doubts; to *own* up (to confess fully or unreservedly, as when questioned or pressed: colloq.).—**own′er,** *n.* One who owns; a proprietor.—**own′er-less,** *a.* Having no owner.—**own′ership,** *n.* The state or fact of being an owner; legal right of possession; proprietorship.

ow-sen (ou′sn), *n. pl.* Sc. and north. Eng. form of *oxen*.

ox (oks), *n.*; pl. *oxen* (ok′sn). [AS. *oxa* (pl. *oxan*) = OHG. *ohso* (G. *ochse*) = Icel. *uxi* = Goth. *auhsa*, ox.] A common domestic ruminant quadruped, *Bos taurus*, esp. the male or bull (the female being a *cow*); specif., the adult castrated male of this animal, used as a draft-animal and for food; also, any of various other ruminants of the same or an allied genus, as the buffalo, zebu, musk-ox, etc.

ox-a-late (ok′sa̤-lāt), *n.* In *chem.*, a salt of oxalic acid.

ox-al-ic (ok-sal′ik), *a.* [See *oxalis*.] In *chem.*, noting or pertaining to a white crystalline acid, $C_2H_2O_4$, first discovered in the juice of a species of oxalis (wood-sorrel).

ox-a-lis (ok′sa̤-lis), *n.* [L., < Gr. ὀξαλίς, sorrel, < ὀξύς, sharp, acid.] Any plant of the genus *Oxalis*, comprising species with a characteristic acid juice, leaves usually composed of three heart-shaped leaflets, and white, yellow, or pink flowers; wood-sorrel.—**ox-al-i-da-ceous** (ok-sal-i-dā′shius), *a.*

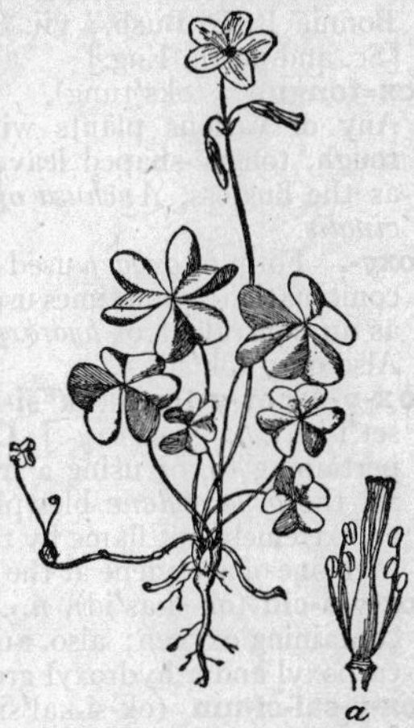

Flowering Plant of Oxalis (*O. violacea*).—*a*, pistil with some of the stamens.

ox=blood (oks′blud), *n.* A deep, dull red color.

ox=bow (oks′bō), *n.* A bow-shaped piece of wood placed under and around the neck of an ox, with its upper ends inserted in the bar of the yoke; also, a bow-shaped bend in a river, or the land embraced by it (U. S.: as, "The Connecticut . . . wantons in huge luxurious *oxbows* about the fair Northampton meadows," Holmes's "Autocrat of the Breakfast-Table," x.).

ox-en (ok′sn). Plural of *ox*.

ox-eye (oks′ī), *n.* Any of various plants with flowers composed of a disk with marginal rays, as the mayweed, the 'oxeye daisy' (see under *daisy*), and the false sunflower (*Heliopsis*); also, any of various birds, as the American dunlin.—**ox′=eyed,** *a.* Having large, full eyes like those of an ox.

ox=fly (oks′flī), *n.*; pl. *-flies* (-flīz). A fly, esp. *Hypoderma bovis*, troublesome to cattle.

ox-ford (oks′fo̤rd), *n.* Oxford gray; also, an Oxford shoe.

Ox-ford (oks′fo̤rd) **cor′ners.** [From *Oxford*, city (and seat of university) in England.] In *printing*, ruled border-lines about the text of a page, etc., that cross and project slightly at the corners.—**Ox′ford gray.** A very dark gray color in woolen and other fabrics, produced by combining black and gray or white threads in the yarn.—**Ox′ford move′ment.** A movement toward High-church principles in the Church of England, which originated at Oxford University about 1833.—**Ox′ford shoe.** A low shoe laced or buttoned over the instep.—**Ox′ford tie.** A laced Oxford shoe.

ox-heart (oks′härt), *n.* A large, heart-shaped variety of cherry.

ox-i-date (ok′si-dāt), *v. t.* or *i.*; *-dated, -dating.* [F. *oxider* (now *oxyder*), < *oxide*, E. *oxide*.] To oxidize.—**ox-i-da′tion** (-dā′sho̤n), *n.* The act or process of oxidizing, or the resulting state.

ox-ide, ox-id (ok′sīd or -sid, -sid), *n.* [F. *oxide*, now *oxyde*, < *ox*(*ygène*), oxygen, + (*ac*)*ide*, acid.] In *chem.*, a compound of oxygen with another element or a radical.

ox-id-iz-a-ble (ok′si-dī-za̤-bl), *a.* Capable of being oxidized.

ox-id-i-za-tion (ok″si-di-zā′sho̤n), *n.* Oxidation.

ox-id-ize (ok′si-dīz), *v.*; *-ized, -izing.* **I.** *tr.* To convert into an oxide; combine with oxygen or more oxygen; also, to cover with a coating of oxide, or rust; also, to take away hydrogen from, as by the action of oxygen; also, to change (a compound) so that the valence of the positive element is higher. **II.** *intr.* To become oxidized.—**ox′id-ized,** *p. a.* Affected by or as by oxidizing.—**oxidized silver,** silver which has been darkened by the formation of a coating of silver sulphide on its surface.—**ox-id-iz-er** (ok′si-dī-zėr), *n.*

ox-lip (ok′slip), *n.* [AS. *oxanslyppe*, < *oxan*, oxen, + *slyppe*, slime: see *slip*¹, and cf. *cowslip*.] A kind of hybrid primrose; also, a species of primrose, *Primula elatior*, with pale-yellow flowers.

Ox-o-ni-an (ok-sō′ni-a̤n). [ML. *Oxonia*, Oxford.] **I.** *a.* Of or pertaining to Oxford, England, or Oxford University. **II.** *n.* A native or inhabitant of Oxford; also, a member or graduate of Oxford University.

ox-peck-er (oks′pek″ėr), *n.* Either of two small African birds of the genus *Buphaga*, which feed on parasites infesting the hide of cattle and other animals.

Oxpecker (*Buphaga africana*).

ox-ter (oks′tėr), *n.* [AS. *ōxta.*] The armpit: as, "wi' his sleeves up tae his *oxters*" (Ian Maclaren's "Beside the Bonnie Brier Bush," vii. 3). [Sc. and north. Eng.]

ox=tongue (oks′tung), *n.* Any of various plants with rough, tongue-shaped leaves, as the bugloss, *Anchusa officinalis.*

oxy-. Form of *oxygen* used in combination: sometimes used as an equivalent of *hydroxy-.* Also **ox-y** (ok′si), *a.*

ox-y-a-cet-y-lene (ok″si-a-set′i-lēn), *a.* [See *oxy-.*] Of, pertaining to, or using a mixture of oxygen and acetylene: as, the *oxyacetylene* blowpipe (an apparatus for producing an extremely hot flame by the meeting of a stream of oxygen with one of acetylene at the moment of burning).

ox-y-a-cid (ok-si-as′id), *n.* [See *oxy-.*] In *chem.*, any acid containing oxygen; also, any organic acid containing both a carboxyl and a hydroxyl group.

ox-y-cal-ci-um (ok-si-kal′si-um), *a.* [See *oxy-.*] Pertaining to or produced by oxygen and calcium: as, the *oxycalcium* light (the calcium light).

ox-y-chlo-ride (ok-si-klō′rīd or -rid), *n.* [See *oxy-.*] In *chem.*, a compound of oxygen and chlorine with another element.

ox-y-gen (ok′si-jen), *n.* [F. *oxygène*, < Gr. ὀξύς, sharp, acid, + γεν-, bear, produce (from its being regarded as an acid-forming principle).] Chem. sym., O; at. wt., 16.0. A colorless, odorless gaseous element, constituting about one fifth of the volume of the atmosphere and present in a combined state throughout nature.—**ox′y-gen-ate** (-āt), *v. t.*; *-ated, -ating.* To treat or combine with oxygen; oxidize.—**ox″y-gen-a′tion** (-ā′shọn), *n.*—**ox-y-gen′ic,** *a.* Pertaining to, consisting of, or containing oxygen; oxygenous.—**ox′y-gen-ize** (-īz), *v. t.*; *-ized, -izing.* To oxygenate.—**ox′y-gen-iz-a-ble** (-ī-zạ-bl), *a.*—**ox-yg-e-nous** (ok-sij′e-nus), *a.* Consisting of or containing oxygen.

ox-y-hem-o-glo-bin (ok″si-hem-ọ-glō′bin), *n.* [See *oxy-.*] The substance formed when hemoglobin proper unites loosely with oxygen: present in arterial blood.

ox-y-hy-dro-gen (ok-si-hī′drọ-jen), *a.* [See *oxy-.*] Of, pertaining to, or using a mixture of oxygen and hydrogen: as, the *oxyhydrogen* blowpipe (an apparatus for producing an extremely hot flame by the meeting of a stream of oxygen with one of hydrogen at the moment of burning).

ox-y-mel (ok′si-mel), *n.* [L. *oxymeli*, < Gr. ὀξύμελι, < ὀξύς, sharp, acid, + μέλι, honey.] A mixture of acetic acid or vinegar with honey: used in pharmacy as a vehicle, etc.: as, "The patient took a draught made with *oxymel* of squills" (Smollett's "Humphry Clinker," Oct. 3).

ox-y-mo-ron (ok-si-mō′ron), *n.*; pl. *-ra* (-rạ̈). [NL., < Gr. ὀξύμωρον, < ὀξύς, sharp, + μωρός, foolish.] In *rhet.*, a figure employed in an expression or statement which is apparently self-contradictory but in which a point is involved, as in 'cruel kindness' or 'to make haste slowly.'

ox-y-salt (ok′si-sâlt), *n.* [See *oxy-.*] In *chem.*, a salt of an oxyacid.

ox-y-sul-phide (ok-si-sul′fīd or -fid), *n.* [See *oxy-.*] In *chem.*, a sulphide in which part of the sulphur is replaced by oxygen.

ox-y-to-cia (ok-si-tō′siạ̈), *n.* [NL., < Gr. ὀξύς, sharp, quick, + -τοκία, a bringing forth, as in δυστοκία, E. *dystocia.*] In *pathol.*, rapid parturition.—**ox-y-to′cic** (-tos′ik). In *med.*: **I.** *a.* Serving to promote or accelerate parturition. **II.** *n.* An oxytocic medicine or drug.

ox-y-tone (ok′si-tōn). [Gr. ὀξύτονος, < ὀξύς, sharp, acute, + τόνος, E. *tone.*] In *gram.*: **I.** *a.* Having an acute accent on the last syllable. **II.** *n.* An oxytone word.

o-yer (ō′yėr or oi′ėr), *n.* [AF. *oyer*, prop. inf., OF. *oir* (F. *ouïr*), < L. *audire*, hear.] In *law*, a hearing or trial of (criminal) causes (chiefly in the phrase 'oyer and terminer,' that is, hearing and determining, used in England of a commission or writ directing the holding of a court to try offenses, and hence used also of the court, and in the U. S. of various higher criminal courts); also, the hearing or viewing in court of some document pleaded by one party and demanded by the other.

o-yez, o-yes (ō′yes or ō-yes′). [AF. *oyez*, 'hear ye,' 2d pers. pl. impv. of *oyer*: see *oyer.*] **I.** *interj.* Hear! attend! a cry uttered, usually thrice, by a public or court crier to command silence and attention before a proclamation, etc., is made. **II.** *n.* A cry of 'oyez!'

oys-ter (ois′tėr), *n.* [OF. *oistre* (F. *huître*), < L. *ostrea*, *ostreum*, < Gr. ὄστρεον, oyster.] Any of various edible marine bivalve mollusks (family *Ostreidæ*), with irregularly shaped shell, found on the bottom or adhering to rocks, etc., in shallow water, some species being extensively cultivated for food; also, any of various similar bivalves; also, the oyster-shaped bit of dark meat in the front hollow of the side bone of a fowl; also, fig., something from which one may extract or derive advantage (from the use in Shakspere's "Merry Wives of Windsor," ii. 2. 2, "The world's mine *oyster*, Which I with sword will open").—**oys′ter,** *v. i.* To dredge for or otherwise take oysters; engage in gathering oysters.

oys-ter-age (ois′tėr-ạ̄j), *n.* An oyster-bed.

oys-ter=bed (ois′tėr-bed), *n.* A place where oysters breed or are cultivated.

oys-ter=catch-er (ois′tėr-kach″ėr), *n.* Any of the maritime wading birds constituting the genus *Hæmatopus*, with a plumage chiefly of black and white, as *H. palliatus*, the common American species.

American Oyster-catcher (*Hæmatopus palliatus*).

oys-ter=plant (ois′tėr-plant), *n.* The salsify, whose root has an oyster-like flavor; also, the sea-lungwort, whose leaves have a similar flavor.

oys-ter=rock (ois′tėr-rok), *n.* An oyster-bed, which often contains masses of old shells, etc.

oys-ter=tongs (ois′tėr-tôngz), *n. pl.* or *sing.* An implement for dredging up oysters.

Oyster-tongs.

oys-ter=white (ois′tėr-hwīt), *n.* White with a greenish-gray tinge.

o-zo-ce-rite (ō-zọ-sē′rīt or ọ-zos′ẹ-), *n.* [Gr. ὄζειν, smell, + κηρός, wax.] A waxy mixture of natural hydrocarbons, sometimes occurring in sandstones.

o-zone (ō′zōn), *n.* [F. *ozone*, < Gr. ὄζειν, smell.] A gas, a form of oxygen having three atoms to the molecule, with a peculiar odor suggesting that of weak chlorine, which is produced when an electric spark is passed through air, and in the electrolysis of water, and in other ways, and is found in the atmosphere in minute quantities, esp. after a thunderstorm: being a powerful oxidizing agent, and used for bleaching, sterilizing water, etc. Hence, popularly, a supposed especially bracing element in the air, as among the mountains or at the seaside.—**o-zon-ic** (ọ-zon′ik), *a.* Pertaining to, containing, or resembling ozone: as, *ozonic* ether (a solution of hydrogen dioxide in ether).—**o-zon-ize** (ō′zọn-īz), *v. t.*; *-ized, -izing.* To convert into ozone; also, to impregnate or treat with ozone.—**o″zon-i-za′tion** (-i-zā′shọn), *n.*—**o′zon-iz-er** (-ī-zėr), *n.*—**o-zo-nom-e-ter** (ō-zọ-nom′e-tėr), *n.* [See *-meter.*] A device for determining the relative amount of ozone in air, etc.—**o-zo-nom′e-try,** *n.*

P

P, p (pē); pl. *P's, p's* (pēz). A consonant, the 16th letter of the English alphabet.

pa (pä), *n.* Childish or colloquial form of *papa*[1].

paauw, pauw (päö), *n.* [D., peacock.] Any of several South African species of bustard.

pab-u-lum (pab′ū-lum), *n.* [L., akin to *pascere*, feed.] That which nourishes an animal or vegetable organism; food, aliment, or nutriment; by extension, fuel; fig., intellectual or spiritual nourishment; food for the mind.

pac-a (pak′ä), *n.* [Pg. and Sp.; from native name.] A large hystricomorphic rodent, *Cœlogenys paca*, of South and Central America; any rodent of this genus.

Paca (*Cœlogenys paca*).

pa-ca-ble (pā′-kạ-bl), *a.* [L. *pacare*, pacify, < *pax* (*pac-*), peace.] Capable of being pacified; placable.

Pac-chi-o-ni-an (pak-i-ō′ni-ạn), *a.* Of, pertaining to, or described by Antonio Pacchioni (1665–1726), an Italian anatomist: as, *Pacchionian* bodies or glands (certain small whitish patches, not glandular in character, found in clusters on the membranes enveloping the brain).

pa-ce[1] (pā′sē), *prep.* [L., abl. of *pax*, peace, grace, pardon, leave.] With the leave of: a courteous form used to introduce a mention of one who differs in opinion.

pace[2] (pās), *n.* [OF. F. *pas*, < L. *passus*, a step, pace, lit. 'a stretch' (of the leg), < *pandere* (pp. *passus*), spread, stretch, extend.] A single step, as in walking or running (as, "She made three *paces* thro' the room": Tennyson's "Lady of Shalott," iii.); also, the distance traversed in a step (as, "Lady Casterley . . . stood six *paces* inside the . . . gates": Galsworthy's "Patrician," i. 2); hence, a linear measure of varying length, representing this distance, commonly $2\frac{1}{2}$ feet (see also phrases below); also, manner of stepping in walking or running, or gait (as, "late to lag behind, with truant *pace*": Dryden's tr. Virgil's "Georgics," iii. 708); esp., any of the various gaits of a horse, etc. (also fig.: as, to put a person through his *paces*, to cause him to display his accomplishments, qualifications, or the like); specif., a gait of a horse, etc., in which the feet on the same side are lifted and put down together (also called *rack*); also, rate of stepping, or, fig., of movement or progress in general (as, "We soon begin to enter upon our natural *pace* of ten miles an hour," De Quincey's "English Mail-Coach," i.; to set the *pace*, to fix or regulate the speed, as in racing; to keep *pace*, to maintain the same rate of speed, movement, or progress); also, a raised step or platform.—**geometrical pace** or **great pace,** 5 feet, representing the distance from the place where either foot is taken up, in walking, to that where the same foot is set down.—**military pace,** the length of a step in marching, being, in the U. S. army, $2\frac{1}{2}$ feet for quick time and 3 feet for double time.—**Roman pace,** 5 Roman feet, or about 58.1 English inches (reckoned like the geometrical pace).—**pace**[2], *v.*; *paced, pacing.* **I.** *intr.* To move with paces or steps; walk with a slow, regular pace; esp., of a horse, etc., to go at a pace. **II.** *tr.* To traverse with paces or steps (as, "Then pale and worn, he *paced* his deck": Joaquin Miller's "Columbus"); hence, to measure by paces (as, to *pace* a piece of ground); also, to train to a certain pace, as a horse; regulate the pace of; exercise in pacing; also, to set the pace for, as in racing.—**paced,** *a.* Having a pace: as, slow-*paced*.—**pace′=mak″er** (-mā″kėr), *n.* One who sets the pace, as in racing.—**pace′=mak″ing,** *n.*—**pa-cer** (pā′sėr), *n.* One who paces; a horse that paces, or whose natural gait is a pace; a pace-maker.

pach-a (pȧsh′ạ̈ or pȧ-shä′), etc. See *pasha*, etc.

pa-chi-si (pạ-chē′si or -zi), *n.* [Hind. *pachīsī*, < *pachīs*, twenty-five (the highest throw in the game).] A game somewhat resembling backgammon, played in India; also, a simplified form of this, played elsewhere.

pach-ou-li (pach′ọ̈-li or pạ-chö′li), *n.* See *patchouli*.

pach-y-derm (pak′i-dėrm), *n.* [F. *pachyderme*, < Gr. παχύδερμος, thick-skinned, < παχύς, thick, + δέρμα, skin.] Any one of the *Pachydermata*, a former order of hoofed, non-ruminant quadrupeds, mostly thick-skinned, as the elephant, hippopotamus, and rhinoceros; hence, any thick-skinned animal; fig., a thick-skinned person; one who is not sensitive to criticism, ridicule, rebuff, etc.—**pach-y-der′-ma-tous** (-dėr′mạ-tus), *a.* Belonging or pertaining to the *Pachydermata*; thick-skinned; fig., insensitive to criticism, rebuff, etc.

pa-cif-ic (pạ-sif′ik). [L. *pacificus*, < *pax* (*pac-*), peace, + *facere*, make.] **I.** *a.* Making or tending to make peace, or conciliatory (as, "The policy of the Prince was *pacific* and temporizing": Motley's "Dutch Republic," iii. 1); also, peaceable, as in disposition or character, or not warlike (as, a *pacific* people; a *pacific* disposition); also, peaceful, or at peace (as, "Mr. Britling . . . marked the steady conversion of the old *pacific* countryside into an armed camp": H. G. Wells's "Mr. Britling," ii. 4. § 5); tranquil, calm, or quiet; [*cap.*] designating, or pertaining to, the ocean between America and Asia (named by Magellan from its calmness during his voyage of 1519–21); of or pertaining to the region bordering on that ocean (as, the *Pacific* States; *Pacific* time, see *standard time*, under *standard*, *a.*). **II.** *n.* [*cap.*] The Pacific Ocean.—**pa-cif′i-cal,** *a.* Pacific.—**pa-cif′i-cal-ly,** *adv.*

pa-cif-i-cate (pạ-sif′i-kāt), *v. t.*; *-cated, -cating.* [L. *pacificatus*, pp. of *pacificare*: see *pacify*.] To pacify; bring into a state of peace: as, "The remaining dominions . . . will doubtless by degrees be conquered and *pacificated*" (Carlyle's "Sartor Resartus," ii. 8).

pa-ci-fi-ca-tion (pas″i-fi-kā′shọn), *n.* [OF. F. *pacification*, < L. *pacificatio*(*n-*), < *pacificare*: see *pacify*.] The act of pacifying, or the state of being pacified; also, a compact or treaty establishing peace (as, "The *Pacification* had just been signed at Ghent": Motley's "Dutch Republic," v. 1).

pa-cif-i-ca-tor (pạ-sif′i-kā-tọr), *n.* [L., < *pacificare*: see *pacify*.] A peacemaker: as, the Great *Pacificator* (Henry Clay).—**pa-cif′i-ca-to-ry** (-kạ-tọ̄-ri), *a.* [L. *pacificatorius*.] Tending to make peace; conciliatory.

pa-cif-i-cism (pạ-sif′i-sizm), **pa-cif′i-cist** (-sist). Same as *pacifism, pacifist*.

pa-ci-fi-co (pä-sē′fẹ-kō), *n.*; pl. *-cos* (-kōz, Sp. -kōs). [Sp.] In Spanish America, the Philippines, etc., a peaceable person; a non-belligerent.

pa-ci-fi-er (pas′i-fī-ėr), *n.* One who or that which pacifies; specif., a rubber nipple given to a baby to suck.

pa-ci-fism (pas′i-fizm), *n.* [F. *pacifisme*, < *pacifique*, < L. *pacificus*, E. *pacific*. For *pacifism* as compared with *pacificism*, cf. *conservatism* (from *conservative*), *idly* (for *idlely*), *simply*, *mammalogy*, *symbology*, etc.: see def. of *haplology*.] The principle or policy of establishing and maintaining universal peace or such relations among all nations that all differences may be adjusted by peaceful means, or without recourse to war; sometimes, in a disparaging sense, the spirit, attitude, or procedure of those who insist on peace at any price.—**pa′ci-fist. I.** *n.* An advocate of pacifism; one who favors the policy of settling international differences by peaceful means; sometimes, one who insists on peace at any price (as, "a mere useless, gibbering, stop-the-war-at-any-price *pacifist*": H. G. Wells's "Italy, France, and Britain at War," iv. 1). **II.** *a.* Belonging or pertaining to pacifists; characteristic of a pacifist.—**pa-ci-fis′tic,** *a.*—**pa-ci-fis′ti-cal-ly,** *adv.*

pa-ci-fy (pas′i-fī), *v.*; *-fied, -fying.* [OF. F. *pacifier*, < L. *pacificare*, < *pax* (*pac-*), peace, + *facere*, make.] **I.** *tr.* To bring into a state of peace, or establish peace throughout (a country, etc.); quiet (strife, disorder, etc.); also, to calm or quiet (a person, etc.) in feeling; allay the anger, discontent, excitement, curiosity, etc., of (as, "The explanation . . . was merely an invention framed to *pacify* his guests": C. Brontë's "Jane Eyre," xx.); allay (anger, etc.); appease (curiosity, appetite, etc.). **II.** *intr.* To become peaceful or calm.—**pa′ci-fy-ing-ly,** *adv.*

Pa-cin-i-an (pạ-sin′i-ạn), *a.* Pertaining to or discovered or described by Filippo Pacini (1812–83), an Italian anatomist. —**Pacinian bodies** or **corpuscles,** in *anat.*, little bulb-like bodies attached to and inclosing nerve-endings in various parts of the body, esp. in the subcutaneous tissue of the fingers and toes.

pack[1] (pak), *v.* [Appar. connected with *pact.*] **I.**† *intr.* To conspire or plot: as, "Go *pack* with him, and give the mother gold" (Shakspere's "Titus Andronicus," iv. 2. 155). **II.** *tr.* To involve in a plot†; also, to make up (a jury, a parliament, etc.) corruptly, so as to further particular interests; also, to arrange (playing-cards) so as to cheat.—**pack**[1], *n.* A private or secret agreement; a plot. [Obs. or Sc.]

pack[2] (pak), *a.* [Cf. *pack*[1].] Intimate; friendly; of animals, tame. [Sc. and north. Eng.]

pack[3] (pak), *n.* [ME. *packe, pakke*; prob. from D. or LG.: cf. D. *pak*, MLG. *pak, packe*, G. *pack.*] A quantity of anything wrapped or tied up, as for carrying on the back of man or beast; a bundle, parcel, or bale, sometimes of fixed amount as a measure; a complete set, as of playing-cards; in general, a set, lot, or 'parcel' of things or persons (usually in contempt: as, a *pack* of nonsense, or of lies; "It's a wicked, thieving, lying, scheming lot you are, the *pack* of you," Synge's "Tinker's Wedding," ii.); a worthless person† (as, a naughty *pack*); a company of animals, as wolves or hounds; a considerable area of pieces of floating ice driven or packed together; also, the quantity of anything, as food, packed or put up at one time or in one season; also, in *med.*, a wrapping of the body in wet or dry cloths for therapeutic purposes, the state of being so wrapped, or the cloths used. —**pack**[3], *v.* **I.** *tr.* To make into a pack; put together compactly in a bundle, box, etc.; put up (meat, fish, eggs, etc.) in suitable form for the market or for preservation; hence, to press or crowd together, as into a compact mass or in close quarters (as, snow becomes *packed* underfoot; to *pack* three persons into the space intended for two; *packed* audiences); also, to fill (a box, trunk, etc.) with anything compactly arranged; cram or crowd (a place: as, "The air became stifling, for now the front of the gallery was *packed*," W. Churchill's "Coniston," i. 15); make close with something impervious to water, steam, air, etc. (cf. *packing*); also, to cover or envelop with something pressed closely around; treat with the therapeutic pack; also, to load (a horse, etc.) with a pack; also, to carry as a pack or load (as, "the rosewood cradle—*packed* eighty miles by mule": Bret Harte's "Luck of Roaring Camp"); hence, in general, to carry (western U. S.); also, to send off summarily (as, "I would *pack* you from the house like a dog," Stevenson's "Master of Ballantrae," viii.; "My mother . . . *packed* me off to bed," H. Melville's "Moby-Dick," iv.). **II.** *intr.* To pack goods, etc., in compact form, as for transportation or storage; pack possessions or necessaries with a view to removal or traveling (often with *up*: as, "I shall tell him to *pack* up and be off to his uncle's next week," Bulwer-Lytton's "Kenelm Chillingly," ii. 21); admit of compact storing or arrangement (as, goods or articles that *pack* well); also, to become compacted, as snow or ice; crowd together, as persons, etc.; collect into a pack or packs, as animals; also, to take one's self off, or be off, esp. in haste (as, "Out, I say; *pack* out this moment!" Goldsmith's "Vicar of Wakefield," xxi.; to send a person *packing*).

pack-age (pak′ạ̄j), *n.* The packing of goods, etc.; also, a quantity of anything packed together; a bundle or parcel; also, that in which anything is packed, as a case, crate, hogshead, or other container (as, goods in the original *package*).

pack=an-i-mal (pak′an″i-mạl), *n.* An animal used for carrying packs.

pack-er (pak′ėr), *n.* One who or that which packs; esp., one who packs provisions, as meat, for the market.—**pack′er-y** (-i), *n.*; pl. *-ies* (-iz). A packing-house.

pack-et (pak′et), *n.* [Dim. of *pack*[3].] A small pack or package of anything, orig. of letters (as, "a small *packet* of papers . . . tied up with silk, and addressed to the Prince of Saxe-Felstein," Conan Doyle's "Exploits of Brigadier Gerard," vi.; "several *packets* of seeds," J. Conrad's "Victory," iii. 1); a parcel or bundle (as, "The frock I made up into a small *packet*": Godwin's "Caleb Williams," xxxiv.); also, a packet-boat (as "I had agreed with Captain Morris, of the *packet* at New York, for my passage": B. Franklin's "Autobiography," xiv.).—**pack′et=boat,** *n.* A boat that carries mail, passengers, and goods regularly on a fixed route.

pack-horse (pak′hôrs), *n.* A horse used as a pack-animal; fig., a drudge.

pack-house (pak′hous), *n.* A warehouse.

pack-ing (pak′ing), *n.* The act or work of one who or that which packs; also, any material used for packing or making water-tight, steam-tight, etc., as a fibrous substance closing a joint, a metallic ring round a piston, etc.—**pack′ing=house,** *n.* An establishment in which provisions, esp. beef and pork, are packed for the market.

pack-man (pak′mạn), *n.*; pl. *-men.* A man who carries a pack of goods for sale; a peddler.

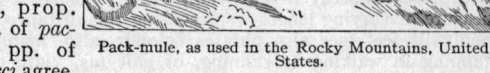

Pack-mule, as used in the Rocky Mountains, United States.

pack=mule (pak′mūl), *n.* A mule used for carrying packs.

pack=sad-dle (pak′sad″l), *n.* A saddle specially adapted for supporting the load on a pack-animal.

pack-thread (pak′thred), *n.* A strong thread or twine for sewing or tying up packages.

pact (pakt), *n.* [L. *pactum*, prop. neut. of *pactus*, pp. of *pacisci*, agree, akin to *pangere*, make fast, fasten, Gr. πηγνύναι, make fast, fix, Skt. *paç-*, fasten, bind.] An agreement; a compact.

pac-tion (pak′shọn), *n.* [L. *pactio(n-)*, < *pacisci*: see *pact.*] Agreement; also, an agreement, compact, or pact.—**pac′tion-al,** *a.*

Pac-to-li-an (pak-tō′li-ạn), *a.* Of or pertaining to the river Pactolus in ancient Lydia, Asia Minor, famed for its auriferous sands; hence, golden.

pad[1] (pad), *n.* [Orig. beggars' and thieves' slang: cf. D. *pad*, path, and E. *path*; in later use, associated with the sound.] A path or road (slang or prov.); also, a highwayman (as, "Four *pads* In ambush laid": Byron's "Don Juan," xi. 11); also, a road-horse (as, "an abbot on an ambling *pad*": Tennyson's "Lady of Shalott," ii.); also, a dull sound, as of footsteps on the ground (as, "'Tis the regular *pad* of the wolves in pursuit of the life in the sledge!" Browning's "Ivàn Ivànovitch").—**pad**[1], *v. t.*; *padded, padding.* To travel along (a road, etc.) on foot; also, to beat down by treading.—**to pad the hoof,** to go on foot; walk along on one's way: as, "Charley Bates expressed his opinion that it was time to *pad the hoof*" (Dickens's "Oliver Twist," ix.). [Slang.]—**pad**[1], *v. i.* To travel on foot; trudge; also, to go with a dull sound of footsteps (as, "My camel *padded* into their camp by moonlight": G. W. Steevens's "With Kitchener to Khartum," viii.).

pad[2] (pad), *n.* [Var. of *ped.*] An open pannier or basket. [Eng.]

pad[3] (pad), *n.* [Origin uncertain.] A cushion-like mass of some soft material, as for comfort or protection or for filling out or stuffing; specif., a cushion used as a saddle; also, one of the cushion-like protuberances on the under side of the feet of dogs, foxes, and some other animals; the pulvillus on an insect's foot; also, the foot of a fox or other beast of the chase; the footprint of such an animal; also, a number of sheets of paper held together at the edge to form a tablet; also, the large floating leaf of the water-lily; also, the socket of a brace, in which the bit is inserted; the handle of any of certain tools; a tool-handle for various sizes or kinds of tools. —**pad**[3], *v. t.*; *padded, padding.* To furnish, protect, fill out, or stuff with a pad or padding; also, to expand (writing or speech) with unnecessary words or matter.—**pad′der,** *n.* —**pad′ding,** *n.* The act of one who or that which pads; also, material, as cotton, hair, or straw, used to pad with; also, unnecessary matter used to expand a written article, a speech, etc. (as, "His letters were usually all common form and *padding*": S. Butler's "Way of All Flesh," l.).

pad-dle[1] (pad′l), *v.*; *-dled, -dling.* [Origin uncertain.] **I.** *intr.* To dabble or play in or as in shallow water; also, to toy with the fingers (see Shakspere's "Hamlet," iii. 4. 185); also, to toddle. **II.**† *tr.* To toy with; finger. See Shakspere's "Winter's Tale," i. 2. 115.

pad-dle[2] (pad′l), *n.* [ME. *padell*; origin uncertain.] A spade-like implement used for cleaning off a plowshare, digging up weeds, etc. (prov. Eng. and Sc.); any of various similar implements used in industrial processes; a kind of short oar with a broad blade at one or each end, used (without a rowlock) for propelling a canoe, etc.; also, one of the broad boards on the circumference of a paddle-wheel, by means of which a vessel is propelled, or one of the similar boards by means of which a water-wheel is turned; a paddle-wheel, or a vessel propelled by this means; any of various implements resembling such boards; also, a flipper or limb of a penguin, turtle, whale, etc.; also, the act of paddling.—**pad′dle**[2], *v.*; *-dled, -dling.* **I.** *intr.* To use a paddle to propel a canoe or the like (as, "being fatigued with rowing, or *paddling*, as it is called": Defoe's "Robinson Crusoe," i. 10); propel, or travel in, a canoe or the like by using a paddle; move by means of paddle-wheels, as a steamer; also, to row lightly or gently with oars. **II.** *tr.* To propel (a canoe, etc.) by paddling (as, to *paddle* one's own canoe, fig., to get on, or make one's way, by one's own unaided exertions); convey, as in a canoe, by paddling (as, "She would herself *paddle* me off to the ship": H. Melville's "Omoo," lxxxii.); make (one's way) over the water by paddling; also, to beat with or as with a paddle (colloq.).

pad-dle=box (pad′l-boks), *n.* A box or casing covering the upper part of the paddle-wheel of a vessel.

pad-dle=fish (pad′l-fish), *n.* A large ganoid fish, *Polyodon spathula,* allied to the sturgeons, with a long, flat, paddle-like projection of the snout: abundant in the Mississippi River and its larger tributaries. Also called *spoonbill.*

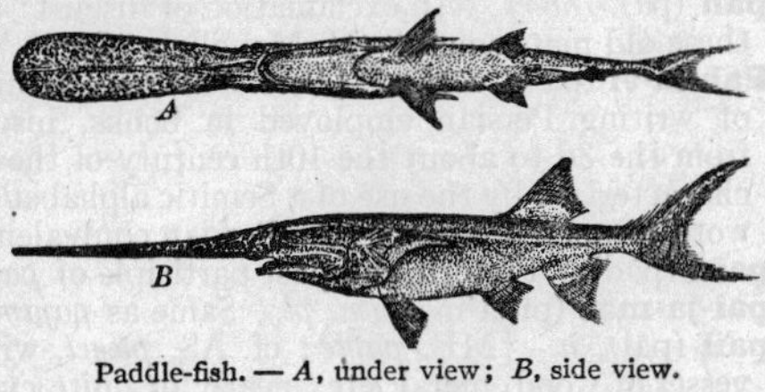

Paddle-fish. — *A*, under view; *B*, side view.

pad-dler[1] (pad′lėr), *n.* One who or that which paddles, as in water or mud.

pad-dler[2] (pad′lėr), *n.* One who paddles a canoe or the like; also, a paddle† (as, "All I could do with my *paddlers* [against a current] signified nothing": Defoe's "Robinson Crusoe," i. 10).

pad-dle=wheel (pad′l-hwēl), *n.* A steam-driven wheel with float-boards (paddles) on its circumference, for propelling a vessel over the water.

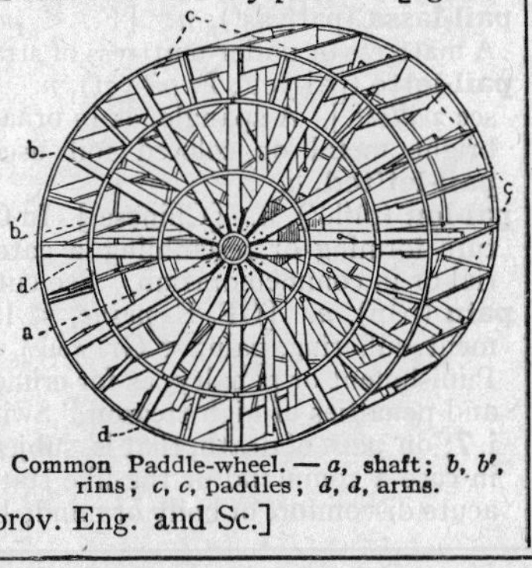

Common Paddle-wheel. — *a*, shaft; *b, b′*, rims; *c, c*, paddles; *d, d*, arms.

pad-dock[1] (pad′ǫk), *n.* [ME. *paddok*, dim. of *pade* = Icel. *padda* = D. *pad*, toad.] A frog or toad. [Now chiefly prov. Eng. and Sc.]

pad-dock[2] (pad′ǫk), *n.* [Var. of *parrock*.] A small field or inclosure, esp. one for pasture near a stable or house; a turfed inclosure for horses, esp. at a race-course; in Australia, any inclosed field or piece of land.—**pad′dock**[2], *v. t.* To confine in or as in a paddock; also, to inclose or fence (land) as a paddock (Australia).

Pad-dy[1] (pad′i), *n.*; pl. *Paddies* (-iz). [For *Patrick* (Ir. *Padraig*), man's name.] A familiar name for an Irishman.

pad-dy[2] (pad′i), *n.* [Malay *pādī*.] Rice in the husk, uncut or gathered; in general, rice: as, "The country, like most parts of India near to the coast, consisted of *paddy* or rice fields, under water" (Marryat's "King's Own," xliii.). [Orig. East Indian.]—**pad′dy=bird,** *n.* Any of various birds that frequent rice-fields, as the Java sparrow.

pad-e-mel-on, pad-dy-mel-on (pad′ẹ-mel″ǫn, pad′i-), *n.* [Native name.] A small Australian kangaroo or wallaby of the genus *Halmaturus.*

Pademelon.

pa-di-shah (pä′di-shä), *n.* [Pers. *pādshāh* (whence Turk. *pādishāh*), 'lord king': cf. *shah.*] [Usually *cap.*] Great king; emperor: a title applied esp. to the Shah of Persia, to the Sultan of Turkey, and, in India, to the British sovereign as emperor of India.

pad-lock (pad′lok), *n.* [ME. *padlokke*; first element uncertain.] A portable or detachable lock having a pivoted or sliding hasp which passes through a staple, ring, or the like and is then made fast.—**pad′lock,** *v. t.* To fasten with or as with a padlock.

pad=nag (pad′nag), *n.* [See *pad*[1].] An ambling nag; an easy-going road-horse.

pa-dre (pä′drā), *n.*; pl. *-dres* (-drāz). [Sp., Pg., and It., < L. *pater.*] Father (used esp. with reference to a priest); among soldiers and sailors, a chaplain.

pa-dro-ne (pä-drō′nā), *n.*; pl. *-nes* (-nāz), It. *-ni* (-nē). [It., < L. *patronus*, E. *patron.*] In Italian use, a master; specif., the master of a vessel; an innkeeper; one who controls and supplies Italian laborers, as in America.

pad-u-a-soy (pad̦′ū-a̦-soi), *n.* [Appar. a corruption of F. *pou-de-soie*, by association with *Padua*, city in Italy.] A smooth, strong, rich silk fabric, much worn by both men and women in the 18th century.

pæ-an (pē′a̦n), *n.* [L., < Gr. παιάν, pæan, Παιάν, Homer's name for the physician of the gods, later Apollo.] A hymn of invocation or thanksgiving to Apollo or some other Greek deity; hence, any song of praise, joy, or triumph (as, "Loud *pæans* chanted through the valley announced the approach of the victors": H. Melville's "Typee," xxxi.).

pæd-er-as-ty (ped′ẹ-ras-ti), etc. See *pederasty*, etc.

pæd-i-at-ric (ped-i-at′rik or pē-di-), etc. See *pediatric*, etc.

pædo-, etc. See *pedo-*, etc.

pæ-on (pē′ǫn), *n.* [L., < Gr. παιών, pæon, also hymn, pæan, = παιάν, E. *pæan.*] In *anc. pros.*, a foot of four syllables, one long (in any position) and three short: being distinguished as a first, second, third, or fourth pæon according to the position of the long syllable as the first, second, third, or fourth syllable in the foot.—**pæ-on-ic** (pẹ-on′ik), *a.* and *n.*

pæ-o-ny (pē′ǫ-ni), *n.* See *peony.*

pa-gan (pā′ga̦n). [LL. *paganus*, a pagan, L. countryman, citizen, civilian, orig. adj. < L. *pagus*, district, province, country (as opposed to city).] **I.** *n.* Orig., one of a people or community professing some other than the Christian religion (applied to the ancient Romans, Greeks, etc., and sometimes the Jews: as, "He [a Roman legionary] remained a *pagan*, though he could not shake off the impression which the martyrs had made upon him," J. H. Newman's "Callista," ii.); hence, in general, one who does not worship the one true God, or a heathen (as, "Till our good Arthur broke The *Pagan* yet once more on Badon hill": Tennyson's "Lancelot and Elaine," 279); an irreligious or heathenish person; sometimes, a person whose easy indifference to religious questions, often coupled with a high degree cf intellectual or esthetic culture, is suggestive of the ancient Greek and Roman world. **II.** *a.* Being a pagan or pagans; of, pertaining to, or characteristic of pagans; heathen; irreligious.—**pa'gan-dom** (-dọm), *n.* The pagan world; pagans collectively.—**pa'gan-ish,** *a.* Pagan-like; heathenish.—**pa'gan-ism,** *n.* [LL. *paganismus*: cf. *paynim.*] The state of being a pagan; the beliefs or practices of pagans; pagan spirit or attitude, as with respect to religious or moral questions.—**pa'gan-ize** (-īz), *v. t.* or *i.*; *-ized, -izing.* To render or become pagan.—**pa''gan-iz-a'tion** (-i-zā'shọn), *n.*

page[1] (pāj), *n.* [F. *page*, < L. *pagina*, page, < *pag-*, stem of *pangere*, make fast: see *pact.*] One side of a leaf of a book, manuscript, letter, or the like (as, "a beautiful quarto *page*, where a neat rivulet of text shall meander through a meadow of margin": Sheridan's "School for Scandal," i. 1); hence, a book or literary work, or any portion of it (as, "old Chaucer's merry *page*," Cowper's "Anti-Thelyphthora," 84; "The priest-like father reads the sacred *page*," Burns's "Cotter's Saturday Night," 118); fig., a record (as, deeds that brighten the *page* of history; memory's *page*); also, any proceeding or period regarded as a matter of history (as, the most glorious *page* in a nation's history); in *printing*, the type set and arranged for one side of a leaf of a book or the like.—**page**[1]; *v. t.*; *paged, paging.* To mark or number the pages of (a book, etc.); paginate; also, to make up (composed type) into pages.

page[2] (pāj), *n.* [OF. F. *page* = ML. *pagius*; origin uncertain.] A boy servant or attendant; specif., a youth in attendance on a person of rank, sometimes formerly in the course of training for knighthood; hence, a boy attendant on the bride at a wedding; also, a young male attendant, usually in uniform, in a legislative hall, a hotel or club, a household, etc.—**page**[2], *v. t.*; *paged, paging.* To attend as a page; also, to seek for (a person), as a hotel page does when sent for the purpose.

pag-eant (paj'ẹnt, also pā'jẹnt), *n.* [ME. *pagent, pagyn,* = AL. *pagina*, appar. the same word as L. *pagina*, page (of a book, etc.: see *page*[1]), also tablet, slab, whence possibly the sense 'platform,' 'stage.'] A platform or stage, usually moving on wheels, on which scenes from the medieval mystery-plays were presented†; a platform or structure, movable or fixed, bearing any kind of a show or spectacle, as in public or open-air festivities†; also, a scene from a mystery-play presented on a movable stage or otherwise, or any dramatic piece or play (hist. or archaic: as, "This wide and universal theatre Presents more woeful *pageants* than the scene Wherein we play in," Shakspere's "As You Like It," ii. 7. 138); later, a show or spectacle, as a costumed procession, a masque, an allegorical tableau, or the like, in public or social festivities (as, "Remembering how we three presented Maid, Or Nymph, or Goddess, at high tide of feast, In masque or *pageant* at my father's court," Tennyson's "Princess," i. 195; "A rumor was circulated among the company that some new spectacle or *pageant* was about to be exhibited," Hawthorne's "Twice-Told Tales," Howe's Masquerade); specif., in recent use, an elaborate public spectacle, whether processional or at some fitting spot or spots, illustrative of the history of a place, institution, or other subject, and employing costume and other artistic aids, dramatic action, speaking, music, dancing, etc.; also, any imposing, fine, or showy spectacle (as, the *pageant* of a coronation; the *pageant* of the sunset); often, a splendid or stately procession or parade (as, "Lead out the *pageant*: sad and slow . . . Let the long, long procession go": Tennyson's "Ode on the Death of the Duke of Wellington," iii.); sometimes, a specious but vain or empty show (as, "We love the man [the king]; the paltry *pageant* you": Cowper's "Task," v. 348).—**pag'eant,** *v. t.* To present or exhibit in or as in a pageant (obs. or rare); also, to honor with a pageant; celebrate with pageantry.—**pag'eant-ry** (-ri), *n.* Pageants collectively†; spectacular entertainment or festivity† (as, "There let Hymen oft appear . . . With mask, and antique *pageantry*": Milton's "L'Allegro," 128); hence, spectacular or splendid show, gorgeous display, or pomp (as, the *pageantry* of war); sometimes, mere show, or empty display.

pag-i-nal (paj'i-nạl), *a.* [LL. *paginalis*, < L. *pagina*, E. *page*[1].] Of or pertaining to a page or pages, as of a book; consisting of pages; page for page (as, a *paginal* reprint). Also **pag'i-na-ry** (-nạ-ri).

pag-i-nate (paj'i-nāt), *v. t.*; *-nated, -nating.* [F. *paginer*, < L. *pagina*, E. *page*[1].] To mark or number the pages of (a book, etc.).—**pag-i-na'tion** (-nā'shọn), *n.* The act of paginating; also, the figures with which pages are numbered.

Great Pagoda, Tanjore, Southern India.

pa-ging (pā'jing), *n.* The numbering of the pages of a book, or the figures used; pagination.

pag-od (pag'od), *n.* A pagoda; also, an idol. [Archaic.]

pa-go-da (pạ-gō'dạ), *n.* [Pg. *pagode*, perhaps < Pers. *butkadah*, idol-temple.] In India, Burma, China, etc., a temple or sacred building, usually more or less pyramidal or forming a tower of many stories; also, a small ornamental structure built to imitate such a temple; also, an idol†; also, a gold (or less often silver) coin formerly current in India, of several varieties, some worth about $1.70.—**pa-go'da=tree,** *n.* Any of several trees so called from their form or for some other reason, as the sophora, *Sophora japonica*, of Japan and China, or the banian of India; also, a mythical East Indian tree fabled to let fall pagodas (the coins) when shaken (archaic: as, to shake the *pagoda-tree*, fig., to make a fortune in India).—**pa-go'dite** (-dīt), *n.* Agalmatolite.

Obverse. Reverse.
Pagoda, in the British Museum.

pa-gu-ri-an (pạ-gū'ri-ạn). [NL. *Pagurus*, the typical genus, < L. *pagurus*, < Gr. πάγουρος, kind of crab.] **I.** *a.* Belonging or pertaining to the family *Paguridæ*, comprising the hermit-crabs, now specif. the aquatic hermit-crabs with short antennules. **II.** *n.* A pagurian crab.—**pa-gu'rid,** *n.* A pagurian crab.

pah (pä), *interj.* An exclamation of disgust: as, "*Pah!* how these old mats smell!" (H. Melville's "Omoo," lvi.).

Pah-la-vi (pä'lạ-vē), *n.* [Pers. *Pahlavī*, Parthian.] A mode of writing Persian employed in books, inscriptions, etc., from the 3d to about the 10th century of the Christian era, characterized by the use of a Semitic alphabet and of Semitic word-forms representing the Persian equivalents.

paid (pād). Preterit and past participle of *pay*[2].

pai-ja-mas (pī-jä'mạz), *n. pl.* Same as *pajamas.*

pail (pāl), *n.* [ME. *payle*; cf. AS. *pægel*, wine-vessel.] A vessel of wood, metal, etc., nearly or quite cylindrical, with a bail or handle, for holding liquids, etc.; also, a pailful.—**pail'ful** (-fůl), *n.*; pl. *-fuls.* A quantity sufficient to fill a pail.

pail-lasse (pal-yas'), *n.* [F., < *paille*, straw: see *pallet*[1].] A mattress or under-mattress of straw or the like.

pail-lette (pal-yet', F. pȧ-yet), *n.* [F., dim. of *paille*, straw: see *pallet*[1].] A spangle, as in ornamentation; also, a bit of bright metal or colored foil used in enamel-painting.—**pail-let'ted,** *a.*

pai-lou (pī'lö'), *n.* [Chinese.] In China, an elaborate structure forming or resembling a gateway, erected as a memorial or in commemoration. See cut on following page.

pain (pān), *n.* [OF. F. *peine*, < L. *pœna*, penalty, punishment, suffering, pain, < Gr. ποινή, fine, penalty: cf. *pine*[2].] Punishment or penalty, as for crime (as, "liable to the *pains* and penalties of high treason," Swift's "Gulliver's Travels," i. 7; on *pain* of death, that is, subject to the penalty of death in case a command or the like stated is not fulfilled); also, acute discomfort of body or mind; bodily or mental suffering or distress; a single feeling of this kind; esp., bodily suffering; a distressing sensation, as in a particular part of the body; specif., the suffering of childbirth (now only in *pl.*); also, trouble experienced or taken in doing something† (as, "The bow inflexible resists their *pain*": Pope's tr. Homer's "Odyssey," xxi.); *pl.*, laborious or careful efforts, or assiduous care (as, "You . . . are like to have nothing but your travel for your *pains*," Bunyan's "Pilgrim's Progress," i.; "Great . . . *pains* have been taken to inflame our minds," Burke's "American Taxation": sometimes with *pl.* form used as *sing.*, as, your *pains* is wasted).—**pain,** *v.* [OF. *pener* (F. *peiner*), < ML. *pœnare*, < L. *pœna*.] **I.** *tr.* To subject to a penalty†; also, to inflict pain on; affect with pain; hurt; distress; also, to exert (one's self) in taking pains (archaic: as, "She her *paynd* with womanish art To hide her wound," Spenser's "Faerie Queene," iv. 6. 40). **II.** *intr.* To cause pain or suffering (as, "a natural desire to *pain*": Kipling's "Light That Failed," i.); also, to suffer, or be affected with, pain.

Pailou.

pain-ful (pān′fụl), *a.* Full of, attended with, or causing pain (as, a *painful* operation; "*painful* thoughts," Southey's "Thalaba," iv. 4); affected with pain (as, *painful* eyes); also, troublesome or laborious (archaic: as, "a *painful* passage o'er a restless flood," Cowper's "Hope," 3); also, characterized by or performed with labor and care (archaic: as, "the *painful* chronicle of honest John Stowe," Southey's "Doctor," ch. vi.); of persons, painstaking (archaic).—**pain′ful-ly,** *adv.*—**pain′ful-ness,** *n.*

pain-less (pān′les), *a.* Devoid of pain; causing no pain.—**pain′less-ly,** *adv.*—**pain′less-ness,** *n.*

pains-tak-ing (pānz′tā″king). **I.** *n.* The taking of pains; careful and assiduous effort in doing anything: as, "I afterwards, with a little *painstaking*, acquired as much of the Spanish as to read their books" (B. Franklin's "Autobiography," vi.). **II.** *a.* Taking or showing pains; assiduously careful: as, a *painstaking* person; *painstaking* work.—**pains′tak″ing-ly,** *adv.*

paint (pānt), *v. t.* [OF. F. *peint*, pp. of *peindre*, < L. *pingere* (pp. *pictus*), represent pictorially, paint, adorn.] To represent (an object, etc.) or execute (a picture, design, etc.) in colors or pigments, usually on a prepared surface; hence, to depict as if by painting (as, "A lively surprise . . . was *painted* on his countenance": Mrs. Shelley's "Frankenstein," xxiii.); depict or describe vividly in words (as, "I shall . . . *paint* to you . . . something like the true form of the whale as he actually appears to the eye of the whaleman": H. Melville's "Moby-Dick," lv.); also, to coat, cover, or decorate (something) with color or pigment; hence, to color as if by painting; adorn or variegate; also, to coat with a liquid medicine, etc.; also, to give a false coloring or aspect to†; also, to flatter†; also, to apply like paint.—**to paint the town red,** to indulge publicly in boisterous or disorderly merrymaking; go on a boisterous spree. [Slang.]—**paint,** *v. i.* To paint pictures, etc.; also, to coat or cover anything with paint; also, to put or use artificial colors on the face in order to beautify it; also, to blush†.—**paint,** *n.* A substance composed of solid coloring matter intimately mixed with a liquid vehicle, and applied as a coating; also, the solid coloring matter alone; a pigment; also, color, as rouge, used on the face.

paint-a-ble (pān′tạ-bl), *a.* That may be painted; suitable for being painted: as, "It had never before occurred to him that she was *paintable*" (Mrs. Wharton's "Son at the Front," xix.).

paint-ed (pān′ted), *p. a.* Depicted or executed in colors; coated or decorated with paint; of bright or variegated coloring, as certain animals (as, the *painted* hyena: see under *hyena*); feigned, artificial, or insincere (archaic).—**Painted Porch.** See *porch*.—**paint′ed=cup′,** *n.* Any plant of the scrophulariaceous genus *Castilleja*, esp. *C. coccinea* ('scarlet painted-cup'): so called from the highly colored dilated bracts about the flowers.—**paint′ed=la′dy,** *n.* A handsome butterfly, *Vanessa* (or *Pyrameis*) *cardui*, of an orange-red color spotted with black and white.

Painted-lady.

paint-er[1] (pān′tėr), *n.* One who paints; an artist who paints pictures; a workman who coats surfaces with paint.

paint-er[2] (pān′tėr), *n.* [Origin uncertain.] A rope, usually at the bow, for fastening a boat to a ship, stake, etc.

paint-er[3] (pān′tėr), *n.* [Var. of *panther*.] The American panther, or cougar: as, "The *painters* (panthers) used to come round their log cabin at night" (Mrs. Stowe's "Oldtown Folks," xxviii.).

paint-ing (pān′ting), *n.* The act, art, or work of one who paints; also, something executed in paints or colors, as a picture or a decorative design.

paint-less (pānt′les), *a.* Without paint: as, "dead plants in *paintless* boxes" (Mrs. Wharton's "Son at the Front," xix.).

paint-ress (pān′tres), *n.* A female painter; a woman who paints; specif., a woman employed in painting pottery (as, "a *paintress* at Peel's great manufactory": Arnold Bennett's "Hilda Lessways," vi. 1).

paint-y (pān′ti), *a.* Of, pertaining to, or abounding in paint; overcharged with paint, as a picture.

pair (pãr), *n.*; pl. *pairs*, sometimes (as after a numeral: colloq.) *pair*. [OF. F. *paire*, < L. *paria*, neut. pl. of *par*, equal.] Two things of a kind, matched for use together (as, a *pair* of gloves); also, two persons or animals of opposite sexes mated together; a married or engaged couple; also, a set of two (as, a *pair* of pistols); a brace; specif., two members on opposite sides in a deliberative body who for convenience (as to permit absence) arrange together to forgo voting on a given occasion; the arrangement thus made; also, a combination of two parts joined together (as, a *pair* of scissors); also, a set or combination of more than two (archaic or prov.: as, "Serle lodges in Stall-street, up two *pair* of stairs," Smollett's "Humphry Clinker," May 10; a *pair* of beads); in *card-playing*, two cards of the same denomination, without regard to suit or color; in *mech.*, two parts or pieces so connected that they mutually constrain relative motion ('kinematic pair').—**pair,** *v.* **I.** *intr.* To form a pair or pairs; match; mate; also, to separate in a pair or pairs (with *off*); also, in a deliberative body, to form a pair to forgo voting. **II.** *tr.* To join in a pair; match; mate; couple; arrange in pairs.

pa-ja-mas, py-ja-mas (pạ-jä′mạz, pī-), *n. pl.* [Hind. *pāejāma*, lit. 'leg-garment.'] Loose drawers or trousers, usually of silk or cotton, worn by both sexes in India, etc., and adopted by Europeans, esp. for night wear; hence, night-clothes consisting of loose trousers and jacket.—**pa-ja′maed, py-ja′maed** (-mạd), *a.*

pak-tong (pak′tong), *n.* [Chinese.] A Chinese alloy having the same ingredients as German silver.

pal (pal), *n.* [Said to be of Gipsy origin.] A comrade, mate, or partner; a chum (as, "I miss you — I've no *pal* now": L. Merrick's "Conrad in Quest of His Youth," xiii.); an accomplice. [Slang.]—**pal,** *v. i.*; *palled, palling.* To associate as a pal or as pals. [Slang.]

pa-la-bra (pä-lä′brä), *n.* [Sp.: see *palaver.*] A word; hence, speech; talk.

pal-ace (pal′ās), *n.* [OF. F. *palais,* < L. *palatium,* palace, < *Palatium,* the Palatine Hill in Rome (on which Augustus had a residence).] The official residence of a sovereign, a bishop, or some other exalted personage; hence, a magnificent or stately mansion or building; also, a more or less imposing or pretentious place of entertainment, etc.—**pal′ace=car,** *n.* A luxuriously equipped passenger-car on a railroad.

pal-a-din (pal′ạ-din), *n.* [F. *paladin,* < It. *paladino,* < L. *palatinus:* see *palatine*[1].] One of the legendary twelve peers or knightly champions in attendance on Charlemagne; hence, any knightly or heroic champion.

Pa-læ-arc′tic, *a.* See *Palearctic.*

palæo-, etc. See *paleo-,* etc.

pa-læs′tra, *n.* See *palestra.*

pal-a-fitte (pal′ạ-fit), *n.* [F. *palafitte,* < It. *palafitta,* fence of piles, < *palo* (< L. *palus*), stake, + *fitto,* pp. of *figgere* (< L. *figere*), fix.] A prehistoric lake-dwelling supported on piles, esp. one of those of Switzerland or northern Italy.

pal-an-quin, pal-an-keen (pal-ạn-kēn′), *n.* [Pg. *palanquim,* < Skt. *palyanka, paryanka,* couch, bed.] In India and other Eastern countries, a covered or box-like litter borne by means of poles resting on men's shoulders.—**pal-an-quin′, pal-an-keen′,** *v. i.* To travel in a palanquin: as, "the land of slaves and *palankeening*" (Hood's "Lines to a Lady on Her Departure for India").

Palanquin.

pal-at-a-ble (pal′ā-tạ-bl), *a.* Agreeable to the palate or taste; savory; hence, fig., agreeable to the mind or feelings (as, "His eloquence was distinguished by a bold, uncompromising, truth-telling spirit, whether the words might prove *palatable* or bitter to his audience": Motley's "Dutch Republic," vi. 3).—**pal′at-a-ble-ness,** *n.*—**pal′at-a-bly,** *adv.*

pal-a-tal (pal′ā-tạl). [F. *palatal.*] **I.** *a.* Of or pertaining to the palate; in *phonetics,* of speech-sounds, uttered with the aid of the palate, as the German *ch* in *ich.* **II.** *n.* In *anat.,* a palatal bone; a palatine; in *phonetics,* a palatal sound.—**pal′a-tal-ize** (-īz), *v. t.; -ized, -izing.* In *phonetics,* to render palatal; change into a palatal.—**pal″a-tal-i-za′tion** (-i-zā′shọn), *n.*

pal-ate (pal′ạt), *n.* [L. *palatum.*] The roof of the mouth, consisting of bone ('hard palate') in front and of a fleshy structure ('soft palate') at the back; also, this part of the mouth popularly considered as the organ of taste; hence, the sense of taste; fig., mental taste or liking (as, "Any subject that was not to their *palate,* they . . . condemned": Milton's "Areopagitica").

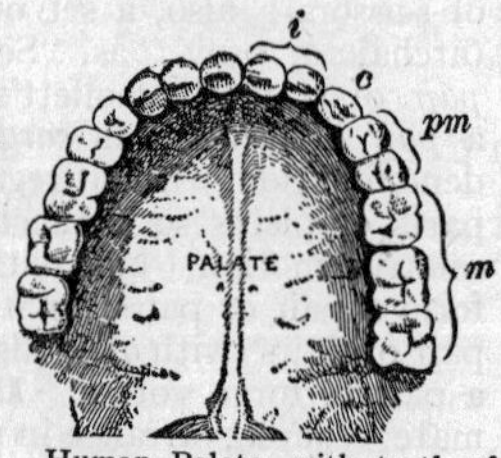

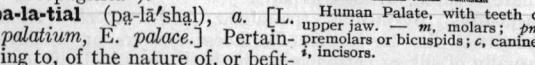

Human Palate, with teeth of upper jaw. — *m,* molars; *pm,* premolars or bicuspids; *c,* canine; *i,* incisors.

pa-la-tial (pạ-lā′shạl), *a.* [L. *palatium,* E. *palace.*] Pertaining to, of the nature of, or befitting a palace: as, "*palatial* establishments" (G. B. Shaw's "Arms and the Man," iii.); "*palatial* drawing-rooms" (J. Conrad's "Rescue," iii. 4).—**pa-la′tial-ly,** *adv.*

pa-lat-i-nate (pạ-lat′i-nạt), *n.* The territory under the jurisdiction of a palatine or count palatine; also [*cap.*], a native or inhabitant of the Palatinate.—**the Palatinate,** a district of Germany, lying west of the Rhine, which now forms an exclave province or governmental district of Bavaria, but which formerly, with portions of the neighboring territory both west and east of the Rhine, constituted a state and electorate of the Holy Roman Empire. Also called *the Rhine* (or *Lower*) *Palatinate,* in contradistinction to the Upper Palatinate.—**the Upper Palatinate,** a district of Germany, bordering on Bohemia, which now forms a province or governmental district of Bavaria, but which formerly, at times, was under the rule of the Palatinate.

pal-a-tine[1] (pal′ạ-tīn or -tin). [F. *palatin,* < L. *palatinus,* belonging to the palace, imperial (as n., an officer of the palace), < *palatium:* see *palace.*] **I.** *a.* Of or pertaining to a palace; palatial; also, possessing or characterized by royal privileges (as, a count or earl *palatine,* see under *count*[1]; a county *palatine*); pertaining to a count or earl palatine, or to a county palatine; also [*cap.*], of or pertaining to the Palatinate. **II.** *n.* An officer of an imperial palace; a high official of an empire; also, a vassal exercising royal privileges in a province; a count or earl palatine; also [*cap.*], a native or inhabitant of the Palatinate; also [*l. c.*], a fur tippet formerly worn by women.

pal-a-tine[2] (pal′ā-tin). [F. *palatin.*] **I.** *a.* Of or pertaining to the palate; palatal. **II.** *n.* In *anat.,* either of the two bones, right and left, that form the hard palate.

pa-lav-er (pạ-lav′ėr), *n.* [Pg. *palavra* = Sp. *palabra,* < L. *parabola:* see *parole* and *parable.*] A parley or conference, esp. with much talk, as between travelers and uncivilized natives; hence, profuse and plausible or cajoling talk (as, "smooth-tongued *palaver*": George Eliot's "Adam Bede," xxxii.).—**pa-lav′er,** *v.* **I.** *intr.* To indulge in palaver; talk profusely and plausibly or cajolingly: as, "Don't stand there *palavering* all day" (Mark Twain's "Huckleberry Finn," vii.). **II.** *tr.* To use palaver to; cajole.—**pa-lav′er-er,** *n.*

pale[1] (pāl), *n.* [OF. F. *pal,* < L. *palus,* stake, < *pag-,* stem of *pangere,* make fast: cf. *pole*[1].] A stake or picket, as of a fence (as, "stakes . . . stuck in one by another like *pales*": Defoe's "Captain Singleton," vii.); also, a fence made of stakes or pickets; a paling; any inclosing or confining barrier; also, an area inclosed by a fence (as, "I brought all my goods into this *pale*": Defoe's "Robinson Crusoe," i. 4); any inclosed area; a district or region within fixed bounds (as, the English *Pale* in Ireland, to which English jurisdiction was confined before the complete subjugation of the island by Oliver Cromwell; the Jewish *Pale* of Settlement in Russia, formerly marked off for the enforced residence of Jews); also, in fig. use, limits or bounds, or field or scope (as, "to leap the rotten *pales* of prejudice," Tennyson's "Princess," ii. 126; "men without the *pale* of public life," W. Churchill's "Coniston," ii. 1); in *her.,* a broad vertical stripe in the middle of an escutcheon.—**pale**[1], *v. t.; paled, paling.* [OF. *paler.*] To inclose with pales; fence; fig., to encircle or encompass.

Heraldic Pale.

pale[2] (pāl). [OF. *pale* (F. *pâle*), < L. *pallidus:* see *pallid.*] **I.** *a.;* compar. *paler,* superl. *palest.* Of a whitish appearance or hue, as a person, the complexion, etc.; pallid; wan; in general, of a shade of color approaching white; lacking intensity or depth of color (as, "the yellow cowslip and the *pale* primrose," Milton's "Song on May Morning"; *pale* blue); also, wanting in brightness, or dim (as, "Ere the moon grew *pale* they were woke by Desborough": H. Kingsley's "Geoffry Hamlyn," xli.); fig., faint; feeble; wanting vigor. **II.**† *n.* Pallor: as, "A sudden *pale* . . . Usurps her cheek" (Shakspere's "Venus and Adonis," 589).—**pale**[2], *v. i.* or *t.; paled, paling.* [OF. *palir* (F. *pâlir*).] To become or make pale: as, "Becky's face *paled*" (Mark Twain's "Tom Sawyer," xxxi.); "The glow-worm . . . 'gins to *pale* his uneffectual fire" (Shakspere's "Hamlet," i. 5. 90).

pale[3] (pāl), *n.* In *bot.,* same as *palea.*

pa-le-a (pā′lẹ-ä), *n.;* pl. *paleæ* (-ē). [L., chaff.] In *bot.,* a chaff-like scale or bract.—**pa-le-a′ceous** (-ā′shius), *a.* In *bot.,* chaff-like; chaffy; having paleæ.

Pa-le-arc-tic, Pa-læ-arc-tic (pā-lẹ-ärk′tik), *a.* [Gr. παλαιός, ancient, + ἀρκτικός, E. *arctic.*] In *zoögeog.,* belonging to the northern division of the Old World (Europe, Africa north of the tropic of Cancer, and Asia north of the Himalayas).

pa-le-ate (pā′lẹ-āt), *a.* In *bot.,* having paleæ.

pa-le-eth-nol-o-gy, pa-læ-eth-nol-o-gy (pā″lẹ-eth-nol′ọ-ji or pal″ẹ-), *n.* [See *paleo-.*] The branch of ethnology that treats of the earliest or most primitive races of mankind.

pale-face (pāl′fās), *n.* A name for a white person, attributed to the American Indians: as, "Where a *Pale-face* comes, a Red-man cannot stay" (Cooper's "Prairie," xxx.).—**pale′=faced,** *a.* Having a pale face; pale.

pa-le-ich-thy-ol-o-gy, pa-læ-ich-thy-ol-o-gy (pā″lē-ik-thi-ol′ǭ-ji or pal″ẹ-), *n.* [See *paleo-.*] The branch of ichthyology that treats of fossil fishes.

pale-ly (pāl′li), *adv.* In a pale manner; with a pale look or appearance.—**pale′ness,** *n.*

paleo-, palæo-, pale-, palæ-. Forms of Gr. παλαιός, old, ancient, used in combination.—**pa-le-o-bot-a-ny, pa-læ-o-bot-a-ny** (pā″lē-ǭ-bot′ạ-ni or pal″ẹ-), *n.* The branch of paleontology that treats of fossil plants.—**pa″le-o-bot′a-nist, pa″læ-o-bot′a-nist,** *n.*—**pa″le-o-cos′mic, pa″læ-o-cos′-mic** (-koz′mik), *a.* Belonging to the earliest period of the world characterized by human life. Cf. *neocosmic.*—**pa″le-o-crys′tic, pa″læ-o-crys′tic** (-kris′tik), *a.* [+ Gr. κρύσταλλος, ice.] Consisting of or containing ice supposed to have remained frozen since early ages.—**pa″le-o-fau′na, pa″læ-o-fau′na** (-fâ′nạ), *n.* The fossil fauna of a geological formation or period.—**pa″le-o-flo′ra, pa″læ-o-flo′ra** (-flō′-rạ), *n.* The fossil flora of a geological formation or period.

pa-le-og-ra-phy, pa-læ-og-ra-phy (pā-lē-og′rạ-fi or pal-ẹ-), *n.* [NL. *palæographia,* < Gr. παλαιός, ancient, + -γραφία, < γράφειν, write.] Ancient writing, or ancient forms of writing, as in documents and inscriptions; also, the study of ancient writing, including determination of origin and date, deciphering, etc.—**pa-le-og′ra-pher, pa-læ-og′ra-pher,** *n.*—**pa″le-o-graph′ic, pa″læ-o-graph′ic, pa″le-o-graph′i-cal, pa″læ-o-graph′i-cal** (-ǭ-graf′ik, -i-kạl), *a.*

pa-le-o-lith, pa-læ-o-lith (pā′lē-ǭ-lith or pal′ẹ-), *n.* [Gr. παλαιός, ancient, + λίθος, stone.] A paleolithic stone implement.—**pa″le-o-lith′ic, pa″læ-o-lith′ic,** *a.* Noting or pertaining to the earlier part of the stone age, characterized by the existence of primitive stone implements.

pa-le-ol-o-gy, pa-læ-ol-o-gy (pā-lē-ol′ǭ-ji or pal-ẹ-), *n.* [See *paleo-* and *-logy.*] The science of antiquities; archæology.—**pa-le-ol′o-gist, pa-læ-ol′o-gist,** *n.*

pa-le-on-tog-ra-phy, pa-læ-on-tog-ra-phy (pā″lē-on-tog′-rạ-fi or pal″ẹ-), *n.* [= F. *paléontographie,* < Gr. παλαιός, ancient, + ὄντα, neut. pl. of ὤν, being, + -γραφία, < γράφειν, write.] The description of fossils; descriptive paleontology.—**pa″le-on-to-graph′i-cal, pa″læ-on-to-graph′i-cal** (-tǭ-graf′i-kạl), *a.*

pa-le-on-tol-o-gy, pa-læ-on-tol-o-gy (pā″lē-on-tol′ǭ-ji or pal″ẹ-), *n.* [= F. *paléontologie,* < Gr. παλαιός, ancient, + ὄντα, neut. pl. of ὤν, being, + -λογία, < λέγειν, speak.] The science of the forms of life existing in former geological periods, as represented by fossil animals and plants.—**pa″le-on-to-log′ic, pa″læ-on-to-log′ic, pa″le-on-to-log′i-cal, pa″læ-on-to-log′i-cal** (-tǭ-loj′ik, -i-kạl), *a.*—**pa″le-on-tol′-o-gist, pa″læ-on-tol′o-gist,** *n.*

pa-le-o-phy-tol-o-gy, pa-læ-o-phy-tol-o-gy (pā″lē-ǭ-fī-tol′-ǭ-ji or pal″ẹ-), *n.* [See *paleo-* and *phytology.*] Paleobotany.

pa-le-or-ni-thol-o-gy, pa-læ-or-ni-thol-o-gy (pā″lē-ôr-ni-thol′ǭ-ji or pal″ẹ-), *n.* [See *paleo-.*] The branch of ornithology that treats of fossil birds.

Pa-le-o-trop-i-cal, Pa-læ-o-trop-i-cal (pā″lē-ǭ-trop′i-kạl or pal″ẹ-), *a.* [See *paleo-.*] In *zoögeog.*, belonging to the tropical (and sub-tropical) regions of the Old World or eastern hemisphere.

Pa-le-o-zo-ic, Pa-læ-o-zo-ic (pā″lē-ǭ-zō′ik or pal″ẹ-). [Gr. παλαιός, ancient, + ζωή, life.] **I.** *a.* Noting or pertaining to a geological era or a group of rocks whose fossils represent early forms of life. Cf. *Mesozoic, Cenozoic.* **II.** *n.* The Paleozoic era or group.

pa-le-o-zo-öl-o-gy, pa-læ-o-zo-öl-o-gy (pā″lē-ǭ-zǭ-ol′ǭ-ji or pal″ẹ-), *n.* [See *paleo-.*] The branch of paleontology that treats of fossil animals.

Pal-es-tin-i-an (pal-es-tin′i-ạn). [L. *Palæstina,* < Gr. Παλαιστίνη, Palestine, lit. 'Philistine (country).'] **I.** *a.* Of or pertaining to Palestine, or the Holy Land, a region in southwestern Syria. **II.** *n.* A native or inhabitant of Palestine.

pa-les-tra, pa-læs-tra (pạ-les′trạ), *n.*; pl. *-tras* or *-træ* (-trē). [L. *palæstra,* < Gr. παλαίστρα, < παλαίειν, wrestle.] In *Gr. antiq.*, a public place for training or exercise in wrestling or athletics.

pa-let (pā′let or pal′et), *n.* [Dim. of *pale*[3].] In *bot.*, a palea.

pal-e-tot (pal′e-tō, F. pàl-tō), *n.* [F.; origin uncertain.] A loose outer garment for men or women.

pal-ette (pal′et), *n.* [F. *palette,* palette, flat-bladed implement, dim. of *pale, pelle,* shovel, < L. *pala,* spade, shovel: cf. *peel*[3] and *pallet*[2].] A thin, usually oval or oblong board or tablet with a thumb-hole at one end, used by painters to lay and mix colors on; also, the set of colors on a palette; hence, a selection of colors, as those used by a particular artist; also, in *armor*, a small rounded plate formerly used to protect the armpit.—**pal′ette=knife,** *n.* A thin, flexible blade rounded at the end and set in a handle, used for mixing painters' colors, etc.

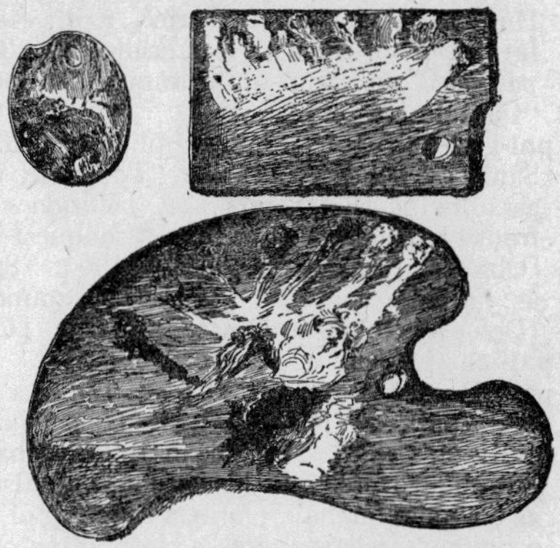

Painters' Palettes.

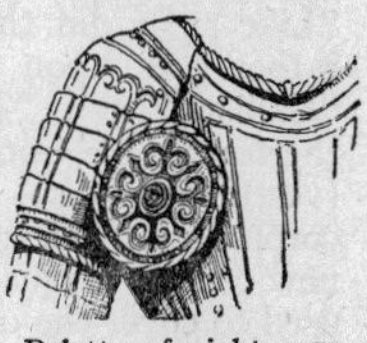

Palette of right arm; 15th century.

pale-wise (pāl′wīz), *adv.* [See *pale*[1].] In *her.*, in the manner or direction of a pale; vertically.

pal-frey (pâl′fri or pal′-), *n.*; pl. *-freys* (-friz). [OF. *palefrei* (F. *palefroi*), < LL. *paraveredus,* < Gr. παρά, beside, + L. *veredus,* light horse.] An ordinary riding-horse, as distinguished from a war-horse (as, "The Duke . . . threw himself from his noble charger . . . while Louis dismounted from his little ambling *palfrey*": Scott's "Quentin Durward," xxvi.); esp., a woman's saddle-horse (as, "He . . . shook his drowsy squire awake, and cried, 'My charger and her *palfrey*'": Tennyson's "Marriage of Geraint," 126). [Archaic or poetic.]

Pa-li (pä′lē), *n.* [Skt. *pāli,* line (of canonical text).] A later form of Sanskrit used in the sacred writings of the Buddhists, and still existing as a literary language in Ceylon and Farther India.

pal-imp-sest (pal′imp-sest), *n.* [L. *palimpsestus,* < Gr. παλίμψηστος, scraped again, < πάλιν, back, again, + ψῆν, rub.] A parchment or the like from which one writing has been erased to make room for another; a manuscript with one text written over another; also, a monumental brass turned and engraved anew on the reverse side.—**pal-imp-ses′tic,** *a.*

pal-in-drome (pal′in-drōm), *n.* [Gr. παλίνδρομος, running back, < πάλιν, back, + δραμεῖν, run.] A word, verse, or sentence whose letters are the same read backward as forward, as, "Madam, I'm Adam."—**pal-in-drom′ic** (-drom′ik), *a.*

pal-ing (pā′ling), *n.* The act of one who pales, or fences with pales; also, pales collectively; a fence of pales (as, "I had seen . . . a gap in the *paling*—one stake broken down": C. Brontë's "Villette," xxxviii.); a pale, as in a fence (as, "The *palings* round the little gardens were broken and ruinous": Mrs. H. Ward's "Robert Elsmere," xv.).

pal-in-gen-e-sis (pal-in-jen′e-sis), *n.* [Gr. πάλιν, back, again, + γένεσις, genesis.] Birth again or anew; rebirth; regeneration; reincarnation; in *biol.*, that development of an individual which reproduces the ancestral features without change (opposed to *cenogenesis*).

pal-i-node (pal′i-nōd), *n.* [LL. *palinodia,* < Gr. παλινῳδία, < πάλιν, back, + ἀείδειν, sing.] A poem in which the poet retracts something said in a former poem; in general, a recantation.

pal-i-sade (pal-i-sād′), *n.* [F. *palissade,* < *palisser,* furnish with a paling, < *palis,* paling, < L. *palus,* E. *pale*[1].] A fence of pales or stakes set firmly in the ground, as for inclosure or defense; also, a long, strong stake pointed at the top, for fixing firmly in the ground with others like it, in a close row, either vertical or inclined, for a defense, as in fortification; also, fig., something resembling a fence of stakes; *pl.*, a line of lofty cliffs (as, the *Palisades* of the Hudson River).—**pal-i-sade′**, *v. t.*; *-saded, -sading.* To furnish or fortify with a palisade: as, "Our carpenters . . . *palisaded* our camp quite round with long stakes" (Defoe's "Captain Singleton," vii.).

pal-i-sa-do (pal-i-sā′dō), *n.*; pl. *-does* (-dōz). [Sp. *palizada.*] Same as *palisade, n.*: as, "To guard against the sudden assaults of the Moors . . . *palisadoes* [were] erected in front of the camp" (Irving's "Conquest of Granada," lvii.). [Obs. or archaic.]—**pal-i-sa′do,** *v. t.* Same as *palisade, v.*: as, "a little house . . . *palisadoed* round with large canes" (Defoe's "Robinson Crusoe," ii. 13). [Obs. or archaic.]

pal-ish (pā′lish), *a.* Somewhat pale.

pal-ki (päl′kē), *n.* [Hind.] In India, a palanquin.

pall[1] (pâl), *n.* [AS. *pæll*, < L. *pallium*, cloak, covering, pall: cf. *palla.*] A cloak or robe (archaic); specif., a robe put on a sovereign at his coronation; also, fine or rich cloth, as for robes (archaic); also, a covering of rich cloth (archaic); a canopy (archaic); esp., a cloth, often of velvet, for spreading over a coffin, bier, or tomb; fig., something that covers, shrouds, or overspreads, esp. with darkness or gloom (as, "Like snow did they [locusts] descend, a living carpet, or rather *pall*, upon fields, crops, gardens," J. H. Newman's "Callista," xv.; "The sun had set behind the black *pall* of the forest," J. Conrad's "Rescue," v. 3); *eccles.*, a pallium (vestment); also, a cloth spread upon the altar, esp. a corporal (archaic); a frontal (archaic); a linen cloth, or now usually a square piece of cardboard covered with linen, used to cover the chalice; in *her.*, a bearing representing the front of an episcopal pall or pallium (vestment), and consisting of a Y-shaped form charged with crosses.—**pall**[1], *v. t.* To cover with or as with a pall: as, "The Holy Grail, All *pall'd* in crimson samite" (Tennyson's "Holy Grail," 844).

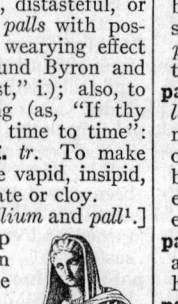

Heraldic Pall.

pall[2] (pâl), *v.* [Appar. a shortened form of *appal.*] **I.** *intr.* To become pale†; become faint†; become vapid or flat, as liquors (obs. or archaic); fig., to become insipid, distasteful, or wearisome (as, "Beauty is a thing which *palls* with possession": Steele, in "Tatler," 2); have a wearying effect (with *on* or *upon*: as, "Lancelot had found Byron and Shelley *pall* on his taste," Kingsley's "Yeast," i.); also, to become satiated or cloyed with something (as, "If thy stomach *palls* with it—discontinue it from time to time": Sterne's "Tristram Shandy," viii. 34). **II.** *tr.* To make pale†; make faint or weak†; daunt†; make vapid, insipid, or distasteful (obs. or archaic); also, to satiate or cloy.

pal-la (pal′ạ̈), *n.*; pl. *pallæ* (-ē). [L.: cf. *pallium* and *pall*[1].] In *Rom. antiq.*, a full outer robe or wrap worn out of doors by women; *eccles.*, an altar-cloth; a corporal; also, a pall for the chalice.

Roman Matron wearing the Palla. — From a statue found at Herculaneum.

Pal-la-di-an[1] (pạ-lā′di-ạn), *a.* [L. *Palladius*, < *Pallas* (*Pallad-*), Pallas.] Of or pertaining to Pallas Athene, the goddess of wisdom; hence, pertaining to wisdom, knowledge, or study.

Pal-la-di-an[2] (pạ-lā′di-ạn), *a.* Pertaining to, introduced by, or in the style of Andrea Palladio (1518–80), an Italian architect: as, *Palladian* architecture (a variety of neoclassic architecture in which the ancient Roman orders are employed rather as a decorative feature than as a constructive element, and applied without regard to classic precedent: see cut in next column); "a *Palladian* palace" (Disraeli's "Coningsby," i. 3).

pal-la-dic (pạ-lā′dik or -lad′ik), *a.* [See *palladium*[2].] Of or containing palladium. See *palladious.*—**pal-la′di-ous,** *a.* Containing palladium (in larger proportion than a corresponding palladic compound).

Pal-la-di-um[1] (pạ-lā′di-um), *n.*; pl. *-dia* (-di-ạ̈). [L., < Gr. Παλλάδιον, < Παλλάς (Παλλαδ-), Pallas.] A statue of Pallas Athene, esp., in classical legend, one in the citadel of Troy on which the safety of the city was supposed to depend (see cut below); hence [usually *l. c.*], anything believed to afford effectual defense, protection, or safety (as, "Trial by jury . . . is looked upon by all as the *Palladium* of our liberties": Disraeli's "Coningsby," iv. 13).

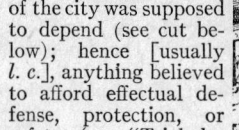

Palladian Architecture. — Teatro Olimpico, Vicenza, Italy.

pal-la-di-um[2] (pạ-lā′di-um), *n.* [NL.; named (1803) from the asteroid Pallas, then recently discovered.] Chem. sym., Pd; at. wt., 106.7; sp. gr., 11.4. A rare metallic element of the platinum group, silver-white, ductile and malleable, and harder than platinum and fusing more readily.

Pal-las (pal′ạs), *n.* [L., < Gr. Παλλάς.] An epithet or name of Athene (often *Pallas Athene*); in *astron.*, one of the asteroids.

pall=bear-er (pâl′bãr″ėr), *n.* [See *pall*[1].] One of those who attend the coffin at a funeral: so called from the old custom of holding up the corners or edges of the pall carried over the coffin.

pal-let[1] (pal′et), *n.* [ME. *pailet*, dim. < OF. F. *paille*, straw, < L. *palea*, chaff.] A bed or mattress of straw; a small or poor bed (as, "a *pallet* of mats": Irving's "Captain Bonneville," xxxiii.).

Ulysses carrying off the Palladium of Troy. — From a Greek vase.

pal-let[2] (pal′et), *n.* [F. *palette*: see *palette.*] An implement consisting of a flat blade or plate with a handle, used by potters, etc.; also, a painter's palette; also, a lip or projection on a pawl, that engages with the teeth of a ratchet-wheel.

pal-let[3] (pal′et), *n.* [Dim. of *pale*[1].] In *her.*, a bearing resembling the pale, but of only half its breadth.

Pallet. — *a, b,* pallets; *c,* pivot on which pawl oscillates.

pal-li-al (pal′i-ạl), *a.* In *zoöl.*, pertaining to a pallium, esp. of a mollusk.

pal-liard (pal′yạrd), *n.* [OF. *paillart* (F. *paillard*), orig. one who lies on straw, < *paille*, straw: see *pallet*[1].] A beggar or vagabond; also, a lewd fellow; a lecher. [Obs. or archaic.]

pal-li-asse (pal′i-as), *n.* Same as *paillasse.*

pal-li-ate (pal′i-āt), *v. t.*; *-ated, -ating.* [L. *palliatus*, pp. of *palliare*, cover with a cloak, < *pallium*, cloak: see *pallium* and *pall*[1].] To cloak†; also, to disguise or conceal (obs. or archaic); also, to cause (an offense, etc.) to appear less grave or heinous (as, "He was far from *palliating* the crime": Motley's "Dutch Republic," vi. 6); extenuate; excuse; also, to mitigate or alleviate (as, to *palliate* a disease; "His well-known financial ability made men turn to him in the hour of distress, as of all statesmen the most fitted to *palliate* it," Lecky's "Hist. of Eng. in the 18th Century," iii.).—**pal-li-a′tion** (-ā′shọn), *n.* [ML. *palliatio(n-).*] The act of palliating; extenuation; mitigation; also, something that palliates; an extenuation or excuse; a mitigation.—**pal′li-a-tive** (-ạ-tiv). **I.** *a.* Serving to palliate; extenuating; mitigating. **II.** *n.* Something that serves to palliate, extenuate, or mitigate.—**pal′li-a-tor** (-ā-tọr), *n.*

pal-lid (pal′id), *a.* [L. *pallidus*, < *pallere*, be pale: cf. *pale*[2] and *pallor*.] Pale; esp., unnaturally pale in complexion or hue, or wan (as, "Strange hardships . . . poor, emaciated, *pallid* wanderer!" C. Brontë's "Jane Eyre," xxix.); deficient in color.—**pal′lid-ly,** *adv.*—**pal′lid-ness,** *n.*

pal-li-um (pal′i-um), *n.*; pl. *palliums* or *pallia* (-ạ̈). [L., cloak, covering: see *pall*[1].] In *Rom. antiq.*, a voluminous rectangular mantle worn by men, and esp. by philosophers; *eccles.*, a woolen vestment worn by the Pope and conferred by him on archbishops, consisting, in its present form, of a narrow ring-like band, which rests upon the shoulders, with two dependent bands or lappets, one in front and one behind; also, an altar-cloth; a pall; in *zoöl.*, an outgrowth of the dorsal body-wall of many mollusks, forming folds or processes which represent the foot and other parts; a similar structure in brachiopods.

pall=mall (pel′mel′), *n.* [Obs. F. *pallemaille*, < It. *pallamaglio*, the game, < *palla*, ball (from Teut.; akin to E. *ball*[1]), + *maglio*, mallet, < L. *malleus*, E. *mall*.] A game formerly played in which a ball of boxwood was struck with a mallet, the object being to drive it through a raised iron ring at the end of an alley; an alley in which this game was played (whence the name of the London street *Pall Mall*).

pal-lo-graph (pal′ọ-gräf), *n.* [Gr. πάλλειν, sway, shake, + γράφειν, mark, write.] An instrument designed to record the vibrations of a ship or other structure exposed to the action of forces.

pal-lo-pho-to-phone (pal-ọ-fō′tọ-fōn), *n.* [Gr. πάλλειν, sway, shake, + φῶς (φωτ-), light, + φωνή, sound.] A device for making a photographic record of sound and for reproducing it, the process consisting essentially of photographing on a moving film the oscillations of a beam of light reflected from a minute mirror which is attached to a diaphragm vibrated by the sound-waves, and of subsequently reproducing the sound by moving the film past an electrical device sensitive to light and connected with telephonic and amplifying apparatus: used esp. to supplement moving pictures with the element of synchronized sound, as of speech, in which case the sound record is made along the edge of the moving-picture film.

pal-lor (pal′ọr), *n.* [L., < *pallere*, be pale: cf. *pallid*.] Pale color or appearance, as of the face or body; paleness, esp. unnatural paleness, as from fear, ill health, or death; wanness: as, "Though no faintest colour had come to the face, its *pallor* had lost something of its deathly waxen appearance" (W. H. Hudson's "Green Mansions," xvii.).

palm[1] (päm), *n.* [OF. *palme* (F. *paume*), < L. *palma*, palm, hand, also palm-tree (see *palm*[2]); akin to Gr. παλάμη, AS. *folm*, palm, hand, Skt. *pāni*, hand.] That part of the inner surface of the hand which extends from the wrist to the bases of the fingers; the corresponding part of the fore foot of an animal; also, the part of a glove covering the palm; also, an instrument worn over the palm of the hand by sailmakers to serve instead of a thimble; also, a flat, widened part at the end of an arm-like projection; the blade of an oar; the flat, expanded part of the horn or antler of some deer; the inner surface of the fluke of an anchor; also, a linear measure based on either the breadth of the hand (3 to 4 inches) or its length from wrist to finger-tips (7 to 9 inches).—**palm**[1], *v. t.* To touch or stroke with the palm or hand; handle; shake hands with; also, to conceal in the palm, as in cheating at cards or dice or in juggling; hence, to impose (something) fraudulently (*on* or *upon*: as, "She dared not *palm* a presumptuous fiction on herself," Kingsley's "Alton Locke," i.); pass (*off*) fraudulently or deceptively (as, to *palm* off spurious things as genuine; to *palm* off a borrowed witticism as one's own).

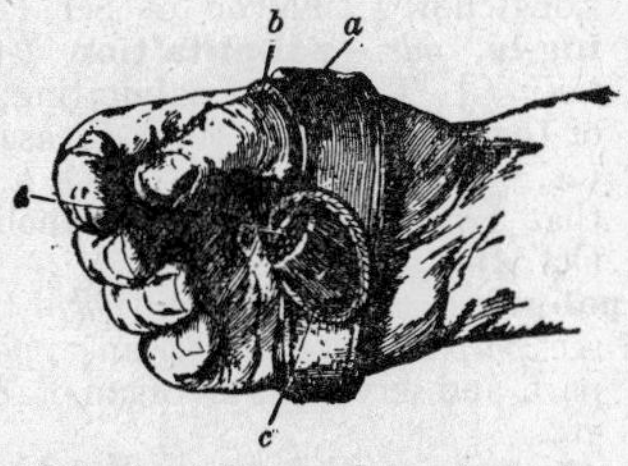

Sailmakers' Palm. — *a*, palm-leather; *b*, thumb-hole; *c*, metal shield fastened to palm-leather; *d*, small countersinks, into some one of which the butt of the needle enters in sewing to prevent the needle from slipping.

palm[2] (päm), *n.* [AS. *palm*, < L. *palma*, palm-tree, orig. palm of the hand (see *palm*[1]); from the resemblance of the leaf to the outspread hand.] Any of the tropical or subtropical plants constituting the large and important family *Phœnicaceæ*, remarkable for their varied usefulness, the majority of which are trees with a tall, usually unbranched stem surmounted by a crown of large pinnate or palmately cleft (fan-shaped) leaves (as, "tall *palms* balancing their feathery foliage on slender stems": W. H. Hudson's "Green Mansions," xiv.); also, a leaf or branch of a palm-tree, esp. as formerly borne for an emblem of victory or triumph or as used on festal occasions (as, "A great multitude . . . stood before the throne . . . clothed with white robes, and *palms* in their hands": Rev. vii. 9); a representation of such a leaf or branch, as on a decoration of honor, or as an addition of honor to a military decoration (as, "There are . . . many true stories of splendid acts . . . The V. C.'s and the *palms* do but indicate samples": H. G. Wells's "Italy, France, and Britain at War," i.); fig., the victor's reward of honor, or the honor of being victorious or of surpassing others (as, "Another race hath been, and other *palms* are won," Wordsworth's "Intimations of Immortality," xi.; "We carried off the *palm* from all the rival shows at country fairs," Irving's "Tales of a Traveler," ii. 10); also, any of various other trees or shrubs which resemble the palm, or which afford a substitute for it as in church use on Palm Sunday; a branch or twig of such a plant.—**Palm Sunday,** the Sunday next before Easter: so called from the custom in the Roman Catholic Church, and in some Anglican churches, of solemnly blessing and distributing palm or other branches and carrying them in procession, in commemoration of Christ's triumphal entry into Jerusalem, when he was met by a multitude of people bearing palm-branches (see John, xii. 13).

pal-ma-ceous (pal-mā′shius), *a.* Belonging to the palm family of plants; phœnicaceous.

pal-ma Chris-ti (pal′mạ̈ kris′ti). [ML., 'hand of Christ': with allusion to the shape of the leaf.] The castor-oil plant, *Ricinus communis*.

pal-mar (pal′mạ̈r), *a.* [L. *palmaris*.] Pertaining to the palm of the hand, or to the corresponding part of the fore foot of an animal.

pal-ma-ry (pal′mạ-ri), *a.* [L. *palmarius*.] Deserving the palm; preëminent; chief: as, "Such are the locusts,—whose existence the ancient heretics brought forward as their *palmary* proof that there was an evil creator" (J. H. Newman's "Callista," xv.).

pal-mate (pal′māt), *a.* [L. *palmatus*.] Shaped like an open palm, or like a hand with the fingers extended, as a leaf or an antler; of a bird's foot, webbed; of a bird, web-footed. Also **pal′-mat-ed** (-mā-ted).—**pal′-mate-ly,** *adv.*—**pal-ma′tion** (-mā′shọn), *n.* Palmate state or formation; also, a palmate structure; each of the divisions of a palmate structure.

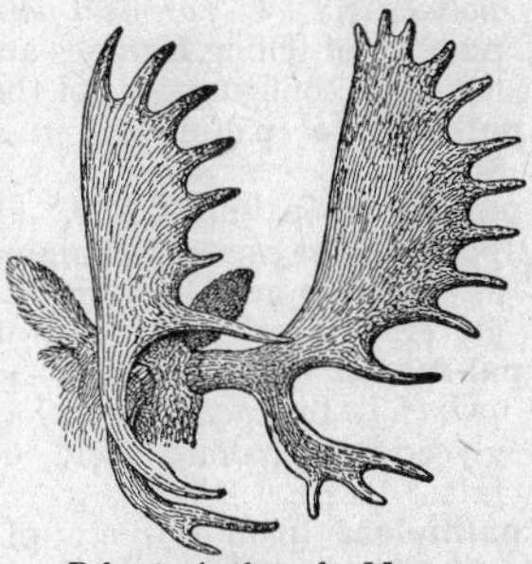
Palmate Antlers of a Moose.

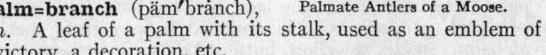

palm=branch (päm′brȧnch), *n.* A leaf of a palm with its stalk, used as an emblem of victory, a decoration, etc.

palm=cat, palm=civ-et (päm′kat, -siv″et), *n.* Any of various viverrine animals (genera *Paradoxurus*, *Arctogale*, etc.) of southeastern Asia, the East Indies, etc., chiefly arboreal in habit, about the size of the domestic cat, and having a spotted or striped fur and a long curled or revolute tail; a paradoxure.

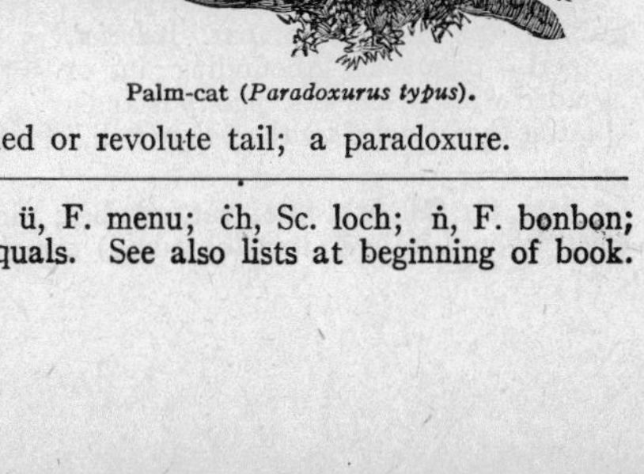
Palm-cat (*Paradoxurus typus*).

palm-er[1] (pä′mėr), *n.* One who palms something, or conceals it in the palm of the hand, as in cheating at cards or in juggling.

palm-er[2] (pä′mėr), *n.* [OF. *palmier*, *paumier*, < ML. *palmarius*, < L. *palma*, E. *palm*[2].] Formerly, a pilgrim who had returned from the Holy Land, in token of which he bore a palm-branch; also, an itinerant monk who went from shrine to shrine, under a perpetual vow of poverty; in general, a pilgrim; also, a palmer-worm; also, a kind of hairy artificial fly used in angling; a hackle.—**palm′er=worm,** *n.* Any of various caterpillars destructive to vegetation; esp., the larva of an American moth, *Ypsolophus ligulellus*, which is destructive to fruit-trees.

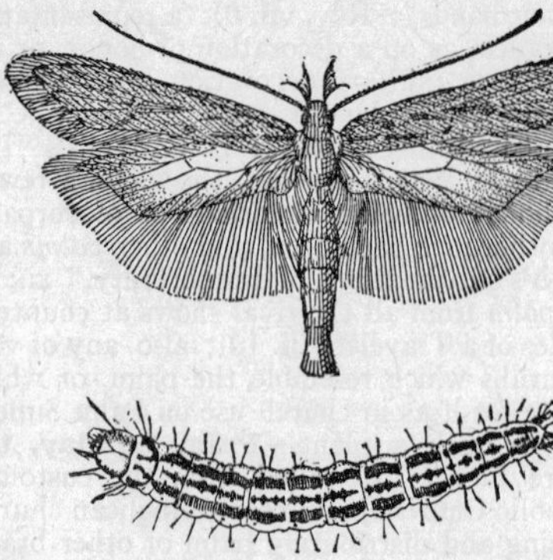

Palmer-worm (*Ypsolophus ligulellus*). — Moth above, larva below. (Much enlarged.)

pal-mette (pal-met′), *n.* [F., dim. of *palme*, < L. *palma*, E. *palm*[2].] In *archæol.*, an ornament, sculptured or painted, more or less resembling a palm-leaf.

pal-met-to (pal-met′ō), *n.*; pl. *palmettos* or *palmettoes* (-ōz). [Sp. *palmito*, dim. of *palma*, < L. *palma*, E. *palm*[2].] Any of various species of palm with fan-shaped leaves; esp., the tree *Inodes palmetto*, abounding on the southeast coast of the U. S. (the 'cabbage-palmetto': represented on the seal of South Carolina, the 'Palmetto State').

pal-mi-ped, pal-mi-pede (pal′mi-ped, -pēd). [L. *palmipes* (*palmiped-*), < *palma*, E. *palm*[1], + *pes* (*ped-*), foot.] **I.** *a.* Having palmate feet, as a bird; web-footed. **II.** *n.* A web-footed bird.

palm-ist (pä′mist or pal′mist), *n.* One who practises palmistry. Also **palm′ist-er.**

palm-is-try (pä′mis-tri or pal′mis-tri), *n.* [ME. *pawmestry*, *palmestrie*, < *paume*, *palme*, E. *palm*[1].] The art or practice of telling fortunes and interpreting character by the lines and configurations of the palm of the hand.

pal-mi-tate (pal′mi-tāt), *n.* In *chem.*, a salt of palmitic acid.

pal-mit-ic (pal-mit′ik), *a.* [F. *palmitique*, < L. *palma*, E. *palm*[2].] In *chem.*, pertaining to or derived from palm-oil: as, *palmitic* acid (a white crystalline acid occurring as a glyceride in palm-oil and in most solid fats).

pal-mi-tin (pal′mi-tin), *n.* [F. *palmitine*, < L. *palma*, E. *palm*[2].] In *chem.*, a colorless crystalline compound, a glyceride of palmitic acid, occurring in palm-oil and solid fats.

palm=leaf (päm′lēf), *n.*; pl. *-leaves* (-lēvz). A leaf of a palm-tree: used for making hats, baskets, fans, etc.

palm=oil (päm′oil), *n.* Oil obtained from various species of palm; specif., a yellow, butter-like oil from the fruit of *Elæis guineensis*, of western Africa, used by the natives as food, and employed also for making soap and candles, for lubricating machinery, etc.

Palm-oil Tree (*Elæis guineensis*).

palm=sug-ar (päm′shụg″ạr), *n.* Sugar obtained from the sap of certain palm-trees; jaggery.

palm=wax (päm′waks), *n.* A waxy substance secreted by certain palm-trees. See *wax-palm.*

palm=wine (päm′wīn), *n.* Wine made from the sap of certain palm-trees; toddy. Cf. *arrack.*

palm-y (pä′mi), *a.*; compar. *palmier*, superl. *palmiest.* Abounding in or shaded with palms (as, *palmy* islands; "fairer than Rachel by the *palmy* well," Tennyson's "Aylmer's Field," 679); pertaining to or derived from palms; palm-like; also, worthy of the palm, glorious, prosperous, or flourishing (as, "in the most high and *palmy* state of Rome," Shakspere's "Hamlet," i. 1. 113; his *palmy* days are over).

pal-my-ra (pal-mī′rạ), *n.* [Pg. *palmeira*, < L. *palma*, E. *palm*[2].] An East Indian palm, *Borassus flabelliformis*, with large fan-shaped leaves, notable for its great variety of uses: the fruit and young roots being used for food, the sap as a source of palm-sugar and palm-wine, the wood for timber, and the leaves for thatching, baskets, hats, paper, etc. Also **pal-my′ra=palm′.**

pa-lo-lo (pạ-lō′lō), *n.* [Native name in Pacific islands.] A marine worm, *Palolo viridis*, found in vast numbers in the Polynesian waters, and much used for food by the natives.

pa-lo=ver-de (pä″lō-vãr′dā), *n.* [Sp., < *palo*, stick, wood (< L. *palus*, E. *pale*[1]), + *verde* (< L. *viridis*), green.] Any of several cæsalpiniaceous trees of the arid regions of the southwestern U. S. and northern Mexico, as *Cercidium torreyanum* or *C. floridum*, characterized by a light-green bark, and by small pinnate leaves that fall off early.

palp (palp), *n.* Same as *palpus.*

pal-pa-ble (pal′pạ-bl), *a.* [LL. *palpabilis*, < L. *palpare*: see *palpate*[2].] That can be touched or felt, perceptible by the sense of touch, or tangible (as, "I felt as if my soul were grappling with a *palpable* enemy": Mrs. Shelley's "Frankenstein," iii.); of darkness, etc., thick or dense enough to be felt (from the use in Ex. x. 21); also, perceptible by some other sense, as the sight (as, "the clear and *palpable* impression of an Indian moccasin": Parkman's "Oregon Trail," xiii.); readily or plainly seen, heard, etc.; fig., readily perceived by the mind, obvious, or patent (as, a *palpable* lie; *palpable* ignorance; "The advantages Mr. Falkland possessed . . . are *palpable*," Godwin's "Caleb Williams," iii.); in *med.*, perceptible by palpation.—**pal-pa-bil′i-ty** (-bil′i-ti), **pal′pa-ble-ness,** *n.*—**pal′pa-bly,** *adv.*

pal-pal (pal′pạl), *a.* In *zoöl.*, pertaining to or of the nature of a palpus.

pal-pate[1] (pal′pāt), *a.* In *zoöl.*, having a palpus or palpi.

pal-pate[2] (pal′pāt), *v. t.*; *-pated*, *-pating.* [L. *palpatus*, pp. of *palpare*, touch, feel, stroke.] To examine by the sense of touch; in *med.*, to perform palpation upon.—**pal-pa′tion** (-pā′shọn), *n.* The act of touching; in *med.*, examination by touch or feeling, as with the hand.—**pal-pa′tor,** *n.*

pal-pe-bra (pal′pē-brạ), *n.*; pl. *-bræ* (-brē). [L.] In *anat.*, an eyelid.—**pal′pe-bral** (-brạl), *a.*

pal-pi (pal′pī), *n.* Plural of *palpus.*

pal-pi-tant (pal′pi-tạnt), *a.* Palpitating.

pal-pi-tate (pal′pi-tāt), *v. i.*; *-tated*, *-tating.* [L. *palpitatus*, pp. of *palpitare*, freq. of *palpare*: see *palpate*[2].] To pulsate with unnatural rapidity, as the heart, from exertion, emotion, disease, etc.; also, to quiver or tremble, as the body, a person, or anything else (as, "fountains *palpitating* in the heat": Longfellow's "Falcon of Ser Federigo," 87).—**pal′pi-tat-ing-ly,** *adv.*—**pal-pi-ta′tion** (-tā′shọn), *n.* [L. *palpitatio*(*n*-).] The act of palpitating; rapid or violent pulsation of the heart, specif. from disease; a quivering or trembling (as, "I was seized with such a *palpitation* and trembling that I could not stand": Smollett's "Humphry Clinker," Oct. 4).

pal-pus (pal′pus), *n.*; pl. *palpi* (-pī). [NL., < L. *palpare*: see *palpate*[2].] In *zoöl.*, an appendage attached to an oral part, and serving as an organ of sense, in insects, crustaceans, etc.

pals-grave (pâlz′grāv or palz′-), *n.* [MD. *paltsgrave* (D. *paltsgraaf*) = G. *pfalzgraf*, 'palace count.'] A German count palatine. See under *count*[1].—**pals′gra-vine** (-grạ-vēn), *n.* [D. *paltsgravin* = G. *pfalzgräfin.*] The wife or widow of a palsgrave.

pal-sied (pâl′zid), *p. a.* Affected with or as with palsy; paralyzed; impotent; shaking; trembling: as, "*palsied* eld" (Shakspere's "Measure for Measure," iii. 1. 36).

pal-stave, pal-staff (pâl′stāv, -stȧf), *n.*; pl. *-staves.* [Dan. *paalstav*, < Icel. *pālstafr*, 'pole-staff.'] In *archæol.*, a form of celt which resembles a chisel, having a tongue which fits into a handle instead of a socket to receive the handle.

pal-sy (pâl′zi), *n.*; pl. *-sies* (-ziz). [OF. *paralisie* (F. *paralysie*), < L. *paralysis*: see *paralysis.*] Paralysis; esp., a progressive form of paralysis occurring late in life, characterized esp. by tremors of the limbs, muscular weakness and rigidity, and a peculiar gait and attitude (often called 'shaking palsy'); fig., any condition in which the energies, sensibilities, powers of resolution, etc., are weakened seriously or overcome; any palsying or paralyzing influence. —**pal′sy,** *v.*; *-sied, -sying.* **I.** *tr.* To affect with or as with palsy; paralyze (esp. fig.); render powerless to act, think, resolve, etc.: as, "Disappointment *palsied* her heart" (Jane Porter's "Scottish Chiefs," lvi.); "I felt . . . *palsied* in mind, and compelled to sit in speechless expectation of the misery to which I was destined" (Godwin's "Caleb Williams," xviii.). **II.** *intr.* To suffer from palsy; become palsied: as, "pining and *palsying* faculties" (C. Brontë's "Shirley," x.).

pal-ter (pâl′tėr), *v. i.* [Origin obscure.] To babble† or chatter†; also, to talk or act insincerely, or trifle deceitfully in speech or dealings (as, "And be these juggling fiends no more believed, That *palter* with us in a double sense," Shakspere's "Macbeth," v. 8. 20; "He soon found himself watched, *paltered* with, suspected by the administration at Brussels," Motley's "Dutch Republic," ii. 8); equivocate; shuffle; deal crookedly; also, to use shifts in bargaining, or haggle (as, "Who never sold the truth to serve the hour, Nor *palter'd* with Eternal God for power": Tennyson's "Ode on the Death of the Duke of Wellington," vii.); also, to trifle, dilly-dally, or act carelessly (as, "Even in that haughty suburb there was none who dared *palter* with an invitation from Mrs. Prockter": Arnold Bennett's "Helen with the High Hand," v.).—**pal′ter-er,** *n.*

pal-try (pâl′tri), *a.*; compar. *paltrier*, superl. *paltriest.* [Cf. prov. Eng. *palt* and *paltry*, refuse, rubbish, LG. *paltrig*, ragged, G. dial. *palter*, rag, *palterig*, paltry.] Rubbishy, trashy, or worthless (as, *paltry* rags; *paltry* finery); hence, wretched, sorry, or poor (as, "Besides the miserable entrance, the house itself seemed *paltry* and half ruinous": Scott's "Guy Mannering," xxxvi.); mean or contemptible (as, a *paltry* trick; "a *paltry* coward," Marryat's "King's Own," xxxiv.); petty, insignificant, or of no consequence (as, "What is this *paltry* little Dog-cage of an Earth?" Carlyle's "Sartor Resartus," ii. 8; "What insults . . . had he received from this *paltry* girl!" Godwin's "Caleb Williams," x.); trifling (as, a *paltry* sum; "He . . . considered the prize too *paltry* for the lives it must cost," Motley's "Dutch Republic," iii. 8).—**pal′tri-ly,** *adv.*—**pal′tri-ness,** *n.*

pal-u-dal (pal′ū-dạl or pạ-lū′-), *a.* [L. *palus* (*palud-*), marsh.] Of or pertaining to marshes; produced by marshes, as miasma or disease.

pa-lu-da-ment (pạ-lū′dạ-mẹnt), *n.* [L. *paludamentum*: cf. *pallium.*] In *Rom. antiq.*, a kind of cloak or mantle worn by a general in war, but later reserved exclusively for the emperor as head of the army.

Paludament. — Statue of the Emperor Augustus, Villa Albani, Rome.

pa-lu-dic (pạ-lū′dik), *a.* Same as *paludal.*

pa-lu-di-cole (pạ-lū′di-kōl), *a.* [F. *paludicole*, < L. *palus* (*palud-*), marsh, + *colere*, inhabit.] Inhabiting or frequenting marshes: as, *paludicole* birds. Also **pal-u-dic-o-line, pal-u-dic-o-lous** (pal-ū-dik′ọ-lin, -lus).

pal-u-dine (pal′ū-din), *a.* [L. *palus* (*palud-*), marsh.] Of or pertaining to marshes; inhabiting marshes; paludose; palustral.

pal-u-dism (pal′ū-dizm), *n.* [L. *palus* (*palud-*), marsh.] In *pathol.*, malarial disease.

pal-u-dose (pal′ū-dōs), *a.* [L. *paludosus*, < *palus* (*palud-*), marsh.] Living or growing in marshes, as animals or plants; paludine.

pa-lus-tral (pạ-lus′trạl), *a.* [L. *paluster* (*palustr-*), < *palus*, marsh.] Of or pertaining to marshes; found in or inhabiting marshes; paludine. Also **pa-lus′trine** (-trin).

pal-y¹ (pā′li), *a.* [F. *palé*, < *pal*, E. *pale¹*.] In *her.*, divided palewise, or vertically, into four or more equal parts of alternating tinctures.

Paly.

pal-y² (pā′li), *a.* Palish; pale: as, "*paly* locks of gold" (Whittier's "Reformer"). [Chiefly poetic.]

pam (pam), *n.* [For F. *pamphile*, orig. (Greek) proper name, Pamphilus.] In *card-playing*, the knave of clubs, esp. in a form of loo in which it is the best trump; also, the game.

Pa-mir (pä-mēr′) **sheep.** See *Tian-shan sheep.*

pam-pa (pam′pạ), *n.*; pl. *-pas* (-pạz). [Sp.; from Peruvian.] One of the vast treeless plains lying south of the forest-covered belt of the Amazon basin, esp. in Argentina: commonly in *pl.*: as, "The *pampas* are, in most places, level as a billiard-table" (W. H. Hudson's "Far Away and Long Ago," i.).—**pam′pas-grass,** *n.* An ornamental grass, *Cortaderia argentea* (or *Gynerium argenteum*), native in South America but widely cultivated, having large, thick, feathery panicles of a silvery white, borne on stems which sometimes reach a height of 12 feet.—**pam-pe-an** (pam-pē′ạn or pam′-pẹ-ạn), *a.* Of or pertaining to the pampas.

Pampas-grass.

pam-per (pam′pėr), *v. t.* [ME. *pampren*: cf. G. *pampen*, cram.] To cram with food†, or feed to repletion†; also, to indulge with rich food, luxurious comforts, etc. (as, to *pamper* a household; a *pampered* menial); bring up (a child) with excessive indulgence; in general, to indulge (a person, etc.) to the full or to excess by gratifying tastes or desires; minister indulgently to (appetites, feelings, etc.: as, "He was *pampering* the poor girl's lust for singularity and self-glorification," Kingsley's "Yeast," x.; to *pamper* pride or vanity).—**pam′per-er,** *n.*

pam-pe-ro (pam-pā′rō), *n.*; pl. *-ros* (-rōz). [Sp.] A cold wind which blows from the Andes over the pampas of South America: as, "the sudden south-west wind called *pampero*, almost knocking the breath out of your body, then passing as suddenly away" (W. H. Hudson's "Purple Land," vii.).

pam-phlet (pam′flet), *n.* [ME. *pamflet, pamfilet*; of disputed origin.] A book of relatively few sheets, fastened together but not bound, and with or without a paper cover: usually dealing with some one subject, as of temporary interest, and often controversial in character: as, "The extraordinary multiplication of *pamphlets* published at a very low price, and industriously dispersed in the streets, was especially noticed" (Lecky's "Hist. of Eng. in the 18th Century," i.).—**pam′phlet-a-ry** (-ā-ri), *a.* Of the nature of a pamphlet; of or pertaining to pamphlets.—**pam-phlet-eer′** (-ēr′), *n.* A writer of pamphlets or a pamphlet: as, "these idle, lying words of a Whig *pamphleteer* declaiming against indulgency to Jacobites" (Stevenson's "Master of Ballantrae," x.).—**pam-phlet-eer′,** *v. i.* To write and issue pamphlets: chiefly in *pamphleteering*, *ppr.* and *n.*

pan¹ (pan), *n.* [AS. *panne* = D. *pan* = G. *pfanne*, pan.] A vessel, commonly of metal, usually broad and shallow and often open, used for domestic purposes (as, kitchen pots and *pans*; a frying-*pan*; a sauce*pan*; a warming-*pan*); any of various open or closed vessels used in industrial or mechanical processes; specif., a vessel in which gold is separated from gravel, etc., by agitation with water; also, any dish-like receptacle or part (as, the *pans*, or scales, of a balance); in general, anything suggesting a pan or hollow vessel; the brainpan or skull (obs. or Sc.); in old guns, the depressed part of the lock, which holds the priming (as, a flash in the *pan*; see under *flash, n.*); a depression in the ground, as a natural one containing water or mud, or an artificial one for evaporating salt water to make salt; also, a hard substratum underlying the soil; hard-pan.—**pan**[1], *v.*; *panned, panning.* **I.** *tr.* To cook (oysters, etc.) in a pan; also, to wash (auriferous gravel, sand, etc.) in a pan to separate the gold; separate by such washing; also, to yield or afford (with *out*: colloq.); also, to get or obtain (colloq.); also, to criticize or reprimand severely (slang). **II.** *intr.* To wash gravel, etc., in a pan in seeking for gold; yield gold, as gravel washed in a pan; hence, to yield results, or turn out with reference to results (with *out*: as, the scheme did not *pan* out very well; how has your trip *panned* out?).

Pan[2] (pan), *n.* [L., < Gr. Πάν: cf. *panic*[2].] In *Gr. myth.*, the god of forests, pastures, flocks, and shepherds, represented with the head, chest, and arms of a man, and the legs and sometimes the horns and ears of a goat.—**Pan's pipes,** a primitive wind-instrument consisting of a series of reeds or pipes of graduated length closed at the lower ends, the tones being produced by blowing with the breath across the upper ends.

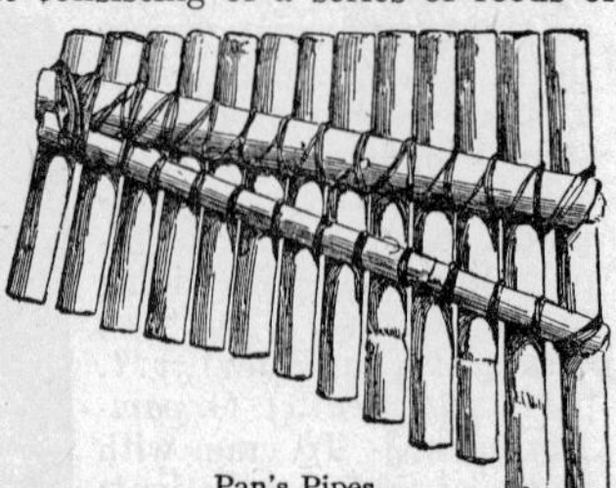

Pan's Pipes.

pan[3] (pän), *n.* [Hind. *pān.*] The betel-leaf, or the masticatory made with it. See *betel.*

pan-. [Gr. παν-, also παντο-, παντ-, repr. πᾶς (παντ-), neut. πᾶν, all.] A combining-form or prefix meaning 'all,' first occurring in words from the Greek, but now used freely as a general formative in English and other languages, esp. in terms implying the union, association, or consideration together, as forming a whole, of all the branches of a race, people, church, or other body, as in *Pan-Anglo-Saxon, Pan-Celtic, Pan-Christian, Pan-Presbyterian,* and other like words of obvious meaning, formed at will, and tending with longer use to lose the hyphen and the second capital, unless these are retained in order to set off clearly the component elements.

pan-a-ce-a (pan-ạ-sē'ä), *n.* [L., < Gr. πανάκεια, < παν-, all (see *pan-*), + ἀκεῖσθαι, heal, cure.] A remedy for all diseases or ills; a cure-all: as, "For my *panacea* . . . let me have a draught of undiluted morning air" (Thoreau's "Walden," v.). Often fig.—**pan-a-ce'an,** *a.*

pa-nache (pạ-nash'), *n.* [F., < It. *pennacchio*, < *penna*, < L. *penna*, feather.] An ornamental plume or tuft of feathers, esp. one worn on a helmet or on a cap or the head: as, "With him came a gallant train . . . decorated with rich surcoats and *panaches* of feathers" (Irving's "Conquest of Granada," xxxvi.).

pa-na-da (pạ-nä'dạ), *n.* [Sp. and Pr. *panada* (F. *panade*), < L. *panis*, bread.] A dish made of bread boiled to a pulp in water or milk, and variously seasoned or flavored. Also **pa-nade'** (-näd').

Pan-a-ma (pan-ạ-mä') **hat.** A fine plaited hat made of the young leaves of a palm-like plant, *Carludovica palmata*, of Central and South America.

Pan-a-man (pan-ạ-män'). **I.** *a.* Of or pertaining to Panama. **II.** *n.* A native or inhabitant of Panama.—**Pan-a-ma'ni-an** (-mä'ni-ạn), *a.* and *n.*

Pan=Amer-i-can (pan-ạ-mer'i-kạn), *a.* [See *pan-.*] Of, pertaining to, or embracing all the states of North and South America, or all Americans.—**Pan=A-mer'i-can-ism,** *n.* The idea or principle of a political alliance or union of all the states of North and South America; advocacy of this principle.

Pan=An-gli-can (pan-ang'gli-kạn), *a.* [See *pan-.*] Of, pertaining to, or embracing all the churches or Christians of the Anglican communion.

pan-a-tel-a (pan-ạ-tel'ä), *n.* See *panetela.*

Pan-ath-e-næ-a (pạn-ath-ẹ-nē'ä), *n. pl.* [NL., < Gr. Παναθήναια, < παν-, all (see *pan-*), + Ἀθήναια, games in honor of Athene.] The chief national festival of ancient Athens, held annually in honor of Athene, the patroness of the city, the celebration in the third year of each Olympiad being known, from its special solemnity and magnificence, as the *greater Panathenæa*, in contradistinction to the *lesser Panathenæa* of other years.—**Pan-ath-e-næ'an, Pan-ath-e-na'ic** (-nē'ạn, -nā'ik), *a.*

Pan=Bri-tan-nic (pan-bri-tan'ik), *a.* [See *pan-.*] Of, pertaining to, or embracing all the British dominions.

pan-cake (pan'kāk), *n.* A thin, flat cake of batter cooked in a pan or on a griddle; a griddle-cake; a flapjack; in *aëronautics*, a landing made by pancaking.—**pan'cake,** *v.*; *-caked, -caking.* In *aëronautics*: **I.** *intr.* Of an aëroplane, etc., to drop flat to the ground, or come abruptly down with little or no forward movement. **II.** *tr.* To cause (an aëroplane) to pancake.

pan-chro-mat-ic (pan-krọ-mat'ik), *a.* [Gr. παν-, all (see *pan-*), + χρῶμα (χρωματ-), color.] Sensitive to light of all colors, as a photographic plate.

pan-cra-ti-um (pan-krā'shi-um), *n.*; pl. *-tia* (-shi-ä). [L., < Gr. παγκράτιον, < παν-, all (see *pan-*), + κράτος, strength.] In *Gr. antiq.*, an athletic contest combining wrestling and boxing.—**pan-crat'ic** (-krat'ik), *a.*

pan-cre-as (pan'krẹ-as or pang'-), *n.* [NL., < Gr. πάγκρεας, < παν-, all (see *pan-*), + κρέας, flesh.] In *anat.* and *zoöl.*, a gland situated near the stomach, secreting an important digestive fluid (the pancreatic juice) which is discharged into the intestine by one or more ducts: when of an animal and used as food, called *sweetbread.*—**pan-cre-at'ic** (-at'ik), *a.*—**pan'cre-a-tin** (-ạ-tin), *n.* In *physiol. chem.*, any of the enzymes of the pancreatic juice; also, a preparation of the enzymes in the pancreas of animals, used in medicine as a digestive, etc.—**pan'cre-a-tize,** *v. t.*; *-tized, -tizing.* To treat with pancreatin.

pan-da (pan'dạ), *n.* [Native name.] A carnivorous quadruped, *Ælurus fulgens*, of the Himalayas, somewhat larger than a cat, and having reddish-brown fur darker beneath, face marked with white, and a long, bushy tail marked with pale rings.—**giant panda,** a large, bear-like quadruped, *Æluropus melanoleucus* (or *Æluropoda melanoleuca*), of Tibet and southern China, white or gray with black limbs, shoulders, and ears, and a black ring around each eye: little known in captivity before 1936.

Panda (*Ælurus fulgens*).

pan-da-na-ceous (pan-dạ-nā'shius), *a.* Belonging to the *Pandanaceæ*, or pandanus family of trees and shrubs.

pan-da-nus (pan-dā'nus), *n.* [NL., < Malay *pandan.*] Any plant of the genus *Pandanus*, comprising tropical trees or shrubs, esp. of the islands of the Malay Archipelago and the Indian Ocean and the Pacific Ocean, characterized by a palm-like or branched stem, a tuft or tufts of long, narrow, rigid, spirally arranged leaves, and aërial roots which prop up the stem or support the whole plant when the lower part of the stem is decayed, and bearing edible fruit occurring in large heads; a screw-pine.

pan-dar (pan'dặr), etc. See *pander*, etc.

Pan-de-an (pan-dē'ạn or pan'dẹ-), *a.* [Irreg. < *Pan*[2].] Of or pertaining to the god Pan: as, *Pandean* pipes (same as *Pan's pipes*, under *Pan*[2]).

pan-dect (pan'dekt), *n.* [L. *pandecta, pandectes*, < Gr. πανδέκτης, lit. 'all-receiver,' < παν-, all (see *pan-*), + δέχεσθαι, receive.] A comprehensive treatise or digest; also, a complete body or code of laws; *pl.* [*cap.*], a digest of Roman civil law, in fifty books, made by order of the emperor Justinian in the 6th century, systematizing the decisions and opinions of eminent jurists, to which the emperor gave the force of law (also called *the Digest*).

pan-dem-ic (pan-dem′ik). [= F. *pandémique*, < Gr. πάνδημος, public, common, < παν-, all (see *pan-*), + δῆμος, people.] **I.** *a.* General; universal; esp., of a disease, prevalent throughout an entire country or continent, or the whole world. **II.** *n.* A pandemic disease.

pan-de-mo-ni-um (pan-dē-mō′ni-um), *n.* [Orig. *Pandæmonium*, Milton's name for the capital of hell, < Gr. παν-, all (see *pan-*), + δαίμων, E. *demon*.] [*cap.*] The abode of all the demons, the capital of hell (see etym.: as, "*Pandæmonium*, the high capital Of Satan and his peers," Milton's "Paradise Lost," i. 756); hence, hell, or the infernal regions; also [*l. c.*], a den of wickedness or vice; a place of riotous disorder or lawless confusion (as, "What kind of a *pandemonium* that vessel was, I cannot describe, but she was commanded by a lunatic, and might be called a floating Bedlam": Stevenson's "Master of Ballantrae," iii.); any place of wild uproar or bewildering noise; also, wild lawlessness or uproar.—**pan-de-mo′ni-ac** (-ak), *a.*

pan-der (pan′dėr), *n.* [For *pandar*, from *Pandare* or *Pandarus*, who is described in medieval romance as lending his aid to bring together Troilus and Cressida. Cf. Shakspere's "Troilus and Cressida," iii. 2. 210.] A go-between, usually a man, in intrigues of love; one who caters to the lusts of others; a pimp; also, one who ministers to the baser passions of others.—**pan′der,** *v.* **I.** *tr.* To act as a pander for. **II.** *intr.* To act as a pander; minister with unprincipled complaisance (*to*); cater basely: as, "He . . . was much more prone to rebuke the vices than to *pander* to the passions of his hearers" (Motley's "Dutch Republic," vi. 7).—**pan′der-er,** *n.*—**pan′der-ess,** *n.*—**pan′der-ly,** *a.* Of the nature of or befitting a pander: as, "a *panderly* barber" (Scott's "Quentin Durward," xxvii.); *panderly* practices.

pan-dic-u-la-tion (pan-dik-ū̧-lā′shọn), *n.* [= F. *pandiculation*, < L. *pandiculari*, stretch one's self, < *pandere*, stretch.] An instinctive stretching of one's self, as on awakening from sleep or while yawning.

pan-door (pan′dör), *n.* See *pandour*.

Pan-do-ra[1] (pan-dō′rạ̈), *n.* [L., < Gr. Πανδώρα, < παν-, all (see *pan-*), + δῶρον, gift.] In *class. myth.*, the first mortal woman, on whom all the gods and goddesses bestowed gifts.—**Pandora's box,** in *class. myth.*, a box or jar, the gift of Zeus to Pandora, containing all human ills, which escaped when she opened it: according to a later version, the box contained all the blessings of the gods, which would have been preserved for the human race had not Pandora opened it, thus letting all the blessings escape, with the exception of hope. Also fig.

pan-do-ra[2], **pan-dore** (pan-dō′rạ̈, -dōr′), *n.* [It. *pandora* = F. *pandore*, < LL. *pandura*, < Gr. πανδοῦρα, musical instrument with three strings.] Same as *bandore*.

pan-dour (pan′dör), *n.* [F.; from Croatian.] One of a force of brutal, rapacious soldiers raised by Baron Franz von der Trenck (1711–49) in Croatia and later incorporated as a regiment in the Austrian army; hence, a brutal, marauding soldier; also, in Croatia, etc., an armed retainer; a guard.

pan-dow-dy (pan-dou′di), *n.*; pl. *-dies* (-diz). [Origin obscure.] A kind of pudding or deep pie made with apples, and usually sweetened with molasses: as, "Hollingsworth [would] fill my plate from the great dish of *pan-dowdy*" (Hawthorne's "Blithedale Romance," xxiv.). [U. S.]

pan-du-rate (pan′dū̧-rāt), *a.* [LL. *pandura*: see *pandora*[2].] Shaped like a fiddle, as a leaf. Also **pan-du′ri-form** (-dū′ri-fôrm).

Pandurate Leaf.

pane (pān), *n.* [OF. F. *pan*, < L. *pannus*, a cloth, rag.] A piece or strip of cloth†; also, a flat section, side, or surface, as one of the sides of a bolt-head, a dressed side of a stone, etc.; also, one of the compartments of a window, etc., consisting of a single plate of glass in a frame; a plate of glass for such a compartment; also, a panel, as of a wainscot, ceiling, door, etc.; also, a rectangular division of some surface.—**paned,** *a.* Having panes: as, a diamond-*paned* window.

pan-e-gyr-ic (pan-ẹ-jir′ik). [L. *panegyricus*, < Gr. πανηγυρικός, a festival oration, prop. adj. < πανήγυρις, a general assembly, < παν-, all (see *pan-*), + ἄγυρις, ἀγορά, assembly.] **I.** *n.* An oration, discourse, or writing in praise of a person or thing (as, "You have made a most admirable *panegyric* upon your country": Swift's "Gulliver's Travels," ii. 6); a eulogy; a formal or elaborate encomium; often, an enthusiastic or extravagant expression of praise; also, eulogistic speech or writing (as, an outburst of *panegyric*). **II.** *a.* Panegyrical.—**pan-e-gyr′i-cal,** *a.* Of the nature of a panegyric; eulogistic; highly laudatory.—**pan-e-gyr′i-cal-ly,** *adv.*—**pan′e-gyr-ist,** *n.* One who panegyrizes; a eulogist.—**pan′e-gy-rize** (-ji-rīz), *v. t.*; *-rized*, *-rizing*. [Gr. πανηγυρίζειν, < πανήγυρις.] To pronounce or write a panegyric upon; eulogize.

pan-el (pan′ẹl), *n.* [OF. *panel* (F. *panneau*), < ML. *pannellus*, dim. of L. *pannus*, E. *pane*.] A pad placed under a saddle, or a pad or the like serving as a saddle; formerly, a wooden saddle for an ass; also, a slip of parchment, esp. that on which the names of jurors were formerly entered; the list of persons summoned for service as jurors; the body of persons composing a jury; also, some other list or body of persons, as of those selected or employed for some purpose; the list or body of physicians of a district engaged in and available for the treatment of persons paying for health insurance, as in connection with the governmental system in Great Britain (also used attributively, as in 'panel doctor,' 'panel practice,' 'panel patient'); also, a distinct portion or compartment of a wainscot, ceiling, door, shutter, etc., or of any surface, sunk below or raised above the general level, or inclosed by a frame or border; such a compartment on the side or the back of the binding of a book; a broad strip of the same or another material set vertically, as for ornament, in or on a woman's skirt; also, a comparatively thin, flat piece of wood or the like; a thin, flat piece of wood used as a surface for a painting, or a picture painted on such a piece of wood; a large size of photograph of much greater height than width; also, in *Sc. law*, the person or persons indicted and brought to trial.—**pan′el,** *v. t.*; *-eled* or *-elled*, *-eling* or *-elling*. To put a panel on (an animal); also, to arrange in or divide into, or furnish with, panels (as, "Some one of its former occupants . . . had *paneled* the walls of this . . . apartment with a dark wood running half way to the low ceiling": F. H. Smith's "Colonel Carter of Cartersville," i.); ornament with a panel or panels; also, to set in a frame as a panel; also, in *Sc. law*, to bring to trial (as, "He was still in Carlisle Castle, and was soon to be *panelled* for his life": Scott's "Waverley," lxvi.).—**pan′el-ing, pan′el-ling,** *n.* The making of panels; also, wood or other material made into panels, or panels collectively (as, "Between the tapestries . . . there were breadths of carved *panelling*": Mrs. H. Ward's "Robert Elsmere," xiv.).—**pan′el=work,** *n.* The work of making panels; also, work, in wood or other material, consisting of or containing panels.

Panels. — Section of the south door of the Baptistery at Florence. (By Andrea Pisano.)

pan-e-tel-a (pan-ẹ-tel′ạ̈), *n.* [Sp.] A long, slender cigar pointed at the end intended for the mouth.

pan=fish (pan′fish), *n.* A fish suitable for frying whole in a pan; also, a king-crab.

pan-ful (pan′fůl), *n.*; pl. *-fuls*. A quantity sufficient to fill a pan.

pang (pang), *n.* [Origin uncertain.] A sudden, brief, sharp pain, or a spasm or severe twinge of pain (as, the *pangs* of death or of childbirth; gouty *pangs*); an acutely painful sensation (as, the *pangs* of hunger); fig., a sudden feeling of mental distress (as, "A stanch Dissenter himself, he saw with a slight *pang* his son Thomas turn Churchman": Kingsley's "Yeast," vi.); a sudden and distressing or disturbing feeling (*of*: as, *pangs* of grief or remorse; "Noel felt a real *pang* of compunction," Galsworthy's "Saint's Progress," iii. 3); also, a sudden, brief access of any feeling† (as, a *pang* of affection or devotion).—**pang,** *v. t.* To cause to suffer pangs (lit. or fig.): as, "I grieve myself To think . . . how thy memory Will then be *pang'd* by me" (Shakspere's "Cymbeline," iii. 4. 98).

pan-gen (pan′jen), *n.* [See *pan-* and *-gen.*] In *biol.*, one of the hypothetical primary constituent units of germ-plasm.

pan-gen-e-sis (pan-jen′e-sis), *n.* [See *pan-* and *genesis.*] In *biol.*, a theory advanced by Darwin, according to which a reproductive cell or body contains gemmules or invisible germs which were derived from the individual cells from every part of the organism, and which are the bearers of hereditary attributes.—**pan-ge-net′ic** (-jẹ-net′ik), *a.*

Pan=Ger-man (pan-jėr′mạn). [See *pan-.*] **I.** *a.* Pertaining to all Germans, or to Pan-Germanism. **II.** *n.* An advocate of Pan-Germanism.—**Pan=Ger-man′ic** (-man′ik), *a.* Pan-German.—**Pan=Ger′man-ism,** *n.* The idea or principle of a union of all the German peoples in one political organization or state; advocacy of this principle.—**Pan=Ger′man-ist,** *n.*—**Pan=Ger′man-y,** *n.* All the German peoples collectively, considered as constituting one political community.

pan-go-lin (pang-gō′lin), *n.* [Malay *penggōling*, roller.] Any of the scaly edentate quadrupeds constituting the genus *Manis* or family *Manidæ*, of tropical Asia and Africa, which have the habit of rolling themselves into a ball when in danger; a scaly ant-eater.

Long-tailed Pangolin (*Manis longicauda*).

pan-han-dle (pan′han″dl), *n.* The handle of a pan; hence (U. S.), a narrow projecting strip of land, esp. part of a State (as, the *Panhandle* of West Virginia, Texas, or Idaho).—**pan′han″dle,** *v. i.*; *-dled, -dling.* To beg as a panhandler. [Slang.]—**pan′han″dler,** *n.* One who accosts persons on the street to beg. [Slang.]

Pan-hel-len-ic (pan-he-len′ik), *a.* [See *pan-*, and cf. Gr. Πανέλληνες, pl., all the Hellenes.] Pertaining to all members of the Greek race, or to Panhellenism.—**Pan-hel′len-ism** (-hel′en-izm), *n.* The idea or principle of a union of all Greeks in one political body.—**Pan-hel′len-ist,** *n.*

pan-ic[1] (pan′ik), *n.* [L. *panicum.*] Orig., the grass *Chætochloa italica* (formerly *Panicum italicum*), Italian or foxtail millet, cultivated in southern Europe for its edible grain; hence, any grass of the genus *Panicum*, many species of which bear edible grain; also, the grain of any such grass.

pan-ic[2] (pan′ik). [F. *panique*, < Gr. Πανικός, pertaining to or caused by Pan, < Πάν, E. *Pan*[2].] **I.** *a.* Of fear, terror, etc., such as was anciently supposed to be caused by the god Pan (as by sounds heard at night in lonely places); suddenly destroying the self-control and impelling to flight or some precipitate or frantic procedure; of the nature of panic; also, due to or showing panic (as, *panic* haste). **II.** *n.* Panic fear, or demoralizing terror, with or without clear cause, often as affecting a body of persons or animals (as, to be seized with *panic*; grave danger of *panic*); an instance, outbreak, or period of such fear (as, "The grand move of the lurking savage is to cause a *panic* among the horses . . . one horse frightens another, until all are alarmed": Irving's "Captain Bonneville," xxxvii.); specif., an outbreak of widespread alarm, as in a community, over financial or commercial matters, which tends to demoralize the judgment and impel persons to hasty and ill-advised measures to avoid loss, thus often precipitating a real and general financial disaster.—**pan′ic**[2], *v. t.* or *i.*; *-icked, -icking.* To affect or be affected with panic.—**pan′i-cal,** *a.* Panic. [Obs. or rare.]—**pan′i-cal-ly,** *adv.*

pan-ic=grass (pan′ik-gràs), *n.* Any grass of the panic kind. See *panic*[1].

pan-ick-y (pan′i-ki), *a.* Of the nature of or characterized by panic (as, *panicky* feelings); due to or showing panic (as, *panicky* haste; *panicky* actions); inclined to or affected by panic (as, a *panicky* crowd; a *panicky* market).

pan-i-cle (pan′i-kl), *n.* [L. *panicula*, tuft on plants, dim. of *panus*, swelling, ear of millet.] In *bot.*, a compound raceme; hence, any loose, diversely branching flower-cluster.—**pan′i-cled,** *a.* Having or forming panicles.

Branch with Panicle.

pan-ic=mong-er (pan′ik-mung″gėr), *n.* One seeking or inclined to create panics.—**pan′ic=mong″er-ing,** *n.*

pan-ic=strick-en, pan-ic=struck (pan′ik-strik″n, -struk), *a.* Stricken with panic or demoralizing fear: as, "The Spaniards . . . became *panic-struck* at being thus enclosed between fire and water" (Motley's "Dutch Republic," iii. 6).

pa-nic-u-late (pạ-nik′ū-lāt), *a.* [NL. *paniculatus*, < L. *panicula*, E. *panicle.*] In *bot.*, arranged in panicles; panicled.—**pa-nic′u-late-ly,** *adv.*

pan-ier (pan′iėr), *n.* See *pannier.*

Pan=Is-lam (pan-is′lạm), *n.* [See *pan-.*] All Islam; all Mohammedan nations collectively, considered as constituting one political body.—**Pan=Is-lam′ic** (-lam′ik), *a.* Pertaining to all Islam, or to a union of all Mohammedan nations.—**Pan=Is′lam-ism,** *n.* The idea or principle of a union of all Mohammedan nations in one political body; advocacy of this principle.

Pan-ja-bi (pun-jä′bē), *n.* [Hind. *Panjābī.*] A native of the Panjab (Punjab, or Punjaub), a northern province of British India; also, the language of the Panjab, an Indo-European tongue related to Hindi, etc.

pan-jan-drum (pan-jan′drum), *n.* [A made word, with prefix *pan-* (see *pan-*) and termination simulating Latin: appar. first used by Samuel Foote (1720–77), the English dramatist and actor.] A mock title for an imaginary personage of great power or importance; hence, any pretentious personage or official.

pan-mix-i-a (pan-mik′si-ä), *n.* [NL., < Gr. παν-, all (see *pan-*), + μῖξις, a mixing.] Indiscriminate crossing of breeds without selection.

panne (pan, F. pȧn), *n.* [F.] A soft, lustrous, light-weight velvet with flattened pile. Also called *panne velvet.*

pan-nier (pan′iėr), *n.* [OF. F. *panier*, < L. *panarium*, bread-basket, < *panis*, bread.] A basket, esp. one of considerable size, for carrying provisions, etc.; esp., a basket for carrying on a person's back, or one of a pair to be slung across the back of a beast of burden; also, a framework formerly used for distending the skirt of a woman's dress at the hips; hence, a puffed arrangement of drapery about the hips.—**pan′niered,** *a.* Laden with a pannier or panniers: as, "*panniered* mules" (H. Melville's "Omoo," lix.).

pan-ni-kin (pan′i-kin), *n.* [Dim. of *pan*[1].] A small pan; hence, a small metal drinking-vessel.

pan-ning (pan′ing), *n.* [See *pan*[1], *v. t.*] A severe criticism or reprimand. [Slang.]

pa-no-cha (pạ-nō′chạ), *n.* [Mex. Sp.] A coarse grade of sugar made in Mexico; also, a candy made of brown sugar, butter, and milk, usually with nuts.

pan-o-ply (pan′ọ-pli), *n.*; pl. *-plies* (-pliz). [F. *panoplie*, < Gr. πανοπλία, < παν-, all (see *pan-*), + ὅπλον, tool, implement, pl. arms: cf. *hoplite.*] A complete suit of armor, or the full armor of a soldier, as in ancient and medieval times (as, "In arms they stood Of golden *panoply*, refulgent host": Milton's "Paradise Lost," vi. 527); hence, any complete equipment of war or defense (lit. or fig.: as, "an Indian warrior in a splendor of factitious savage *panoply*," Howells's "Chance Acquaintance," xiii.; armed in the *panoply* of innocence); a complete covering or array of something (as, fields clad in a *panoply* of snow).—**pan′o-ply,** *v. t.*; *-plied, -plying.* To furnish with or as with a panoply: chiefly in *panoplied, pp.*: as, "Armies all *panoplied* wheel into line" (Holmes's "Freedom, Our Queen").

pan-o-ra-ma (pan-ọ̄-rä′mạ̈), *n.* [Gr. παν-, all (see *pan-*), + ὅραμα, view.] An extended pictorial representation of a landscape or other scene, often as viewed from a central point, sometimes arranged circularly about the spectators' position (see *cyclorama*), and sometimes exhibited a part at a time and made to pass continuously before them; hence, a continuously passing or changing scene (lit. or fig.: as, the *panorama* of traffic in the streets; the *panorama* of memory); also, an unobstructed view or prospect over a wide area (as, "The scene was one of those splendid *panoramas* which are only to be gazed upon in tropical climes": Marryat's "King's Own," xxiv.); also, a comprehensive survey, as of a subject.—**pan-o-ram′ic** (-ram′ik), *a.* Of, pertaining to, or of the nature of a panorama: as, a *panoramic* view; a *panoramic* camera (any of various forms of photographic camera for taking panoramic views).—**pan-o-ram′i-cal-ly,** *adv.*—**pan-o-ra′mist** (-rä′mist or -ram′ist), *n.* A painter of panoramas.

Pan=pipe (pan′pīp), *n.* Pan's pipes. See under *Pan*[2].

pan-psy-chism (pan-sī′kizm), *n.* [Gr. παν-, all (see *pan-*), + ψυχή, soul, mind.] The doctrine that the entire universe, or any least particle of it, has a psychic or mental as well as a physical side or aspect.—**pan-psy′chist,** *n.*

Pan-slav, Pan-slav-ic (pan-släv′ or -slav′, -släv′ik or -slav′ik), *a.* [See *pan-*, and cf. F. *panslave.*] Of or pertaining to all the Slavic races; also, of or pertaining to Panslavism. Also **Pan-sla-von′ic** (-slạ-von′ik).—**Pan-slav′ism,** *n.* [Cf. G. *Panslawismus*, F. *panslavisme.*] The idea or principle of a union of all the Slavic races in one political body; advocacy of this principle.—**Pan-slav′ist,** *n.*—**Pan-sla-vis′tic** (-vis′tik), *a.*

pan-so-phy (pan′sọ̄-fi), *n.* [Gr. πάνσοφος, all-wise, < παν-, all (see *pan-*), + σοφός, wise.] Universal wisdom or knowledge; also, the claim or pretension to universal knowledge.—**pan-soph′ic, pan-soph′i-cal** (-sof′ik, -i-kạl), *a.*

pan-sper-ma-tism (pan-spėr′mạ-tizm), *n.* [Gr. παν-, all (see *pan-*), + σπέρμα (σπερματ-), seed.] The doctrine that the atmosphere is full of invisible germs ready for development under favorable conditions. Also **pan-sper′my** (-mi).

pan-sy (pan′zi), *n.*; pl. *-sies* (-ziz). [F. *pensée*, pansy, lit. 'thought,' < *penser*, think: see *pensive.*] The plant *Viola tricolor*, a species of violet having many cultivated varieties with large, richly and variously colored flowers: as, "There is *pansies*, that's for thoughts" (Shakspere's "Hamlet," iv. 5. 176). Cf. *heart's-ease* and *love-in-idleness.*

pant (pant), *v.* [ME. *panten*, appar. connected with OF. *pantaisier*, pant, prob. (with reference to the feeling of oppression in nightmare) < LL. *phantasia*, a phantasm, L. idea, fancy, E. *fantasy.*] **I.** *intr.* To breathe hard and quickly, as after exertion, as a person or an animal; hence, to emit steam or the like in loud puffs (as, "ships moving, tugs *panting*, hawsers taut": H. G. Wells's "Tono-Bungay," iv. 3. § 2); also, to gasp, as for air; hence, fig., to long with breathless or intense eagerness (as, "He had ever since *panted* for revenge," Irving's "Conquest of Granada," xxix.; "that lofty order of minds who *pant* after the ideal," George Eliot's "Adam Bede," xvii.); also, to throb or heave violently or rapidly, as the heart, the breast, etc.; palpitate. **II.** *tr.* To breathe or utter gaspingly: as, " 'He has come,' I *panted*" (Stevenson's "Master of Ballantrae," iv.).—**pant,** *n.* The act or an act of panting; a short, quick, labored effort of breathing; a gasp; a puff, as of an engine; a throb or heave, as of the breast.

panta-. Erroneous form of *panto-*.

Pan-ta-gru-el-i-an (pan″tạ-grö-el′i-ạn), *a.* Of, pertaining to, or befitting Pantagruel, one of the characters of Rabelais, represented as dealing with serious matters in a spirit of broad and somewhat cynical good humor; coarsely humorous, with satirical intent.—**Pan-ta-gru′el-ism** (-grö′ẹl-izm), *n.* Pantagruelian spirit, principles, or practice; coarse humor with satirical intent.—**Pan-ta-gru′el-ist,** *n.*

pan-ta-lets, pan-ta-lettes (pan-tạ-lets′), *n. pl.* [Dim. < *pantaloon.*] Long drawers with a frill or other finish at the bottom of each leg, and extending below the dress, formerly worn by women and girls; also, formerly, a pair of separate frilled or trimmed pieces for attaching to the legs of women's drawers; in more recent use, bloomers or knickerbockers worn by women.

pan-ta-loon (pan-tạ-lön′), *n.* [F. *pantalon*, < It. *pantalone*, buffoon, *Pantalone*, a Venetian, so called from St. *Pantaleone*, patron of Venice.] [*cap.* or *l. c.*] In the early Italian comedy, the Venetian character, represented as a lean and foolish old man wearing pantaloons and slippers; hence, in the modern pantomime, a character represented as a foolish, vicious old man, the butt and accomplice of the clown; also [*l. c.*], in general, a feeble or doting old man (as, "The lean and slipper'd *pantaloon*, With spectacles on nose": Shakspere's "As You Like It," ii. 7. 158); also, *pl.*, a man's more or less closely fitting garment for the hips and legs, varying in form at different periods; in the late 18th and the earlier 19th century, a tightly fitting garment fastened below the calf of the leg with ribbons or buttons, or, in a longer form, by straps passing under the boots; now, trousers.—**pan-ta-looned′,** *a.* Wearing pantaloons.

Early form of Pantaloons; Venetian, 16th century.

pan-tel-e-graph (pan-tel′ẹ̄-grȧf), *n.* [See *pan-*.] A facsimile telegraph.—**pan-te-leg′ra-phy** (-tẹ̄-leg′rạ-fi), *n.*

pan-tel-e-phone (pan-tel′ẹ̄-fōn), *n.* [See *pan-*.] A telephonic device for the reproduction at a distance of sounds of feeble intensity.

pant-er (pan′tėr), *n.* One who or that which pants.

pan-ter-er (pan′tėr-ėr), *n.* Same as *pantler.*

Pan=Teu-ton-ic (pan-tū̦-ton′ik), *a.* [See *pan-*.] Of, pertaining to, or embracing all the Teutonic peoples; also, of or pertaining to Pan-Teutonism.—**Pan=Teu′ton-ism** (-tū′tọn-izm), *n.* The idea or principle of a union of all Teutonic peoples in one political body; advocacy of this principle.

pan-the-ism (pan′thẹ̄-izm), *n.* [Gr. παν-, all (see *pan-*), + θεός, god.] The religious belief or philosophical doctrine which identifies the universe with God; also, the heathen worship of all the gods.—**pan′the-ist,** *n.* One who holds the doctrine of pantheism.—**pan-the-is′tic,** *a.*—**pan-the-is′ti-cal-ly,** *adv.*

pan-the-on (pan′thẹ̄-ọn or pan-thē′ọn), *n.* [L., < Gr. πάνθειον, prop. neut. of πάνθειος, of all gods, < παν-, all (see *pan-*), + θεός, god.] A temple dedicated to all the gods, esp. [*cap.*] that at Rome built by Agrippa about 25 B.C., now serving as a Christian church; also [*l. c.*], a public building containing tombs or memorials of the illustrious dead of a nation, esp. [*cap.*] that in Paris; also [*l. c.*], the deities of a people collectively.—**pan-the-on′ic** (-on′ik), *a.*

pan-ther (pan′thėr), *n.* [OF. *pantere* (F. *panthère*), < L. *panthera*, < Gr. πάνθηρ.] The leopard, *Felis pardus*; in America, the cougar or puma, *F. concolor*, also the jaguar, *F. onca.*—**pan′ther-ess,** *n.* A female panther.—**pan′ther-ine** (-in), *a.* [L. *pantherinus.*] Panther-like.

pan-tile (pan′tīl), *n.* [Cf. D. *pan*, pan, also tile, *dakpan*, pantile, lit. 'roof tile.'] A roofing-tile straight in its length but curved in its width (laid so that the joint of two concave tiles is overlapped by a convex tile), or both concave and convex in its width (and laid so that the convex portion overlaps the next tile).—**pan′til″ing** (-tī″ling), *n.* The covering of a roof with pantiles; also, pantiles collectively.

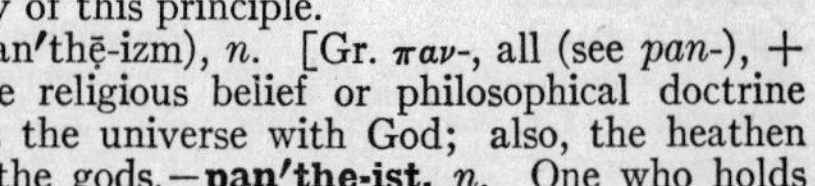
Pantiles of the compound form.

pant-ing (pan′ting), *p. a.* That pants; breathing hard and quickly; puffing; gasping; throbbing or heaving.—**pant′ing-ly,** *adv.*

pan-ti-soc-ra-cy (pan-tī-sok′rą-si or pan-ti-), *n.*; pl. *-cies* (-siz). [See *panto-* and *isocracy.*] A scheme of social organization in which all are equal in rank and social position; a Utopian community in which all the members are equal and all rule.—**pan″ti-so-crat′ic** (-sǫ-krat′ik), *a.*

pant-ler (pant′lėr), *n.* [Altered form (perhaps after *butler*) of earlier *panter*, < OF. F. *panetier*, < L. *panis*, bread.] Formerly, an officer in a great household who supplied the bread and had charge of the pantry: as, "A' would have made a good *pantler*, a' would ha' chipped bread well" (Shakspere's "2 Henry IV.," ii. 4. 258).

pan-to (pan′tō), *n.*; pl. *-tos* (-tōz). A pantomime: as, "'I once was in the chorus in a *panto* at Hanbridge,' she said" (Arnold Bennett's "The Old Adam," vi.). [Colloq., Eng.]

panto-, pant-. [Gr. παντο-, παντ-: see *pan-.*] Same as *pan-* ('all').

pan-to-fle (pan′tǫ-fl), *n.* [F. *pantoufle*; origin unknown.] A slipper: as, "pretty small feet . . . with . . . white *pantofles* with red heels" (Thackeray's "Henry Esmond," i. 3).

pan-to-graph (pan′tǫ-gråf), *n.* [See *panto-* and *-graph.*] An instrument for the mechanical copying of plans, diagrams, etc., upon the same or a reduced or enlarged scale.—**pan-to-graph′ic** (-graf′ik), *a.*

pan-tol-o-gy (pan-tol′ǭ-ji), *n.* [See *panto-* and *-logy.*] A systematic view of all branches of human knowledge; universal knowledge.—**pan-to-log′i-cal** (-tǭ-loj′i-kąl), *a.*

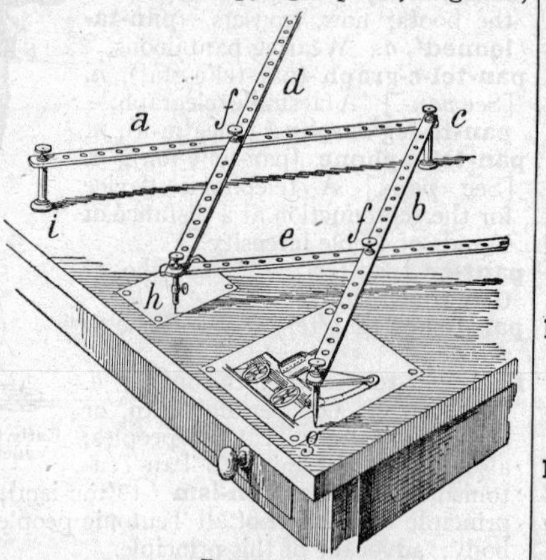

Pantograph.

a, b, d, and *e* are rules perforated with holes for adjustment to different scales for enlargement or reduction of the picture; *a* and *b* are permanently but movably jointed at *c* to a traversing support; *d* and *e* are similarly jointed at *h* to a pencil-holder or point-holder; *f, f,* are thumb-screws which act as pivots for joining *a* and *d* and *b* and *e*. The rule *a* is pivoted to a support *i* which is fixed to the drawing-table; *g* is a style attached to the end of the rule *b*. Lines traced by *g* will be also drawn by *h* on a larger or smaller scale corresponding to the adjustment.

pan-to-mime (pan′tǭ-mīm), *n.* [L. *pantomimus*, < Gr. παντόμιμος, < παντο-, all (see *pan-*), + μῖμος, imitator, E. *mime*.] An actor in dumb-show, as in ancient Rome and hence elsewhere (as, "In come troops of dancers from Lydia, or *pantomimes* from Alexandria," J. H. Newman's "Callista," v.; "Those *pantomimes*, Who vary action with the times," Butler's "Hudibras," iii. 2); also, a play or entertainment in which the performers express themselves by mute gestures, often to the accompaniment of music; also, a form of theatrical spectacle, common in England during the Christmas season, a feature of which is a harlequinade (now sometimes omitted) including pranks of the clown and pantaloon and dancing of the harlequin and columbine; also, significant gesture without speech, or dumb-show (as, "The old man accompanied his words with such admirable *pantomime* that translation was hardly necessary": Parkman's "Oregon Trail," xv.).—**pan′to-mime,** *v.*; *-mimed, -miming.* **I.** *intr.* To express one's self by pantomime or dumb-show. **II.** *tr.* To represent or express by pantomime or dumb-show: as, "Thomas *pantomimed* infinite perplexity" (H. G. Wells's "Realby," i.).—**pan-to-mim′ic** (-mim′ik), *a.* [L. *pantomimicus.*] Of, in, or like pantomime: as, "*pantomimic* gestures which . . . are substituted for intelligible words" (Macaulay's "Hist. of Eng.," i.).—**pan-to-mim′i-cal-ly,** *adv.*—**pan′to-mim-ist** (-mī-mist), *n.* One who acts in pantomime: as, "Owhhigh [an Indian] as a *pantomimist* would have commanded brilliant success on any stage" (T. Winthrop's "Canoe and the Saddle," iv.).

pan-to-prag-mat-ic (pan″tǭ-prag-mat′ik), *a.* [See *panto-* and *pragmatic.*] Concerned or busied with all things; universally meddlesome.

pan-to-scope (pan′tǭ-skōp), *n.* [See *panto-* and *-scope.*] A form of lens including a very wide angle, devised especially for photographic use; also, a panoramic camera.—**pan-to-scop′ic** (-skop′ik), *a.* Having or affording a wide range of vision or field of view.—**pantoscopic camera,** a panoramic camera.—**pantoscopic spectacles,** spectacles with lenses made up of two parts or segments, upper and lower, one for viewing objects at a distance and the other for those close at hand.

pan-toum (pan-töm′), *n.* [F., < Malay *pantun.*] A poem in a fixed form, based on the Malay pantun (see *pantun*), consisting of a number of stanzas of four lines, with lines riming alternately, the second and fourth lines of each stanza being repeated to form the first and third of the succeeding stanza, and the first and third lines of the first stanza forming the second and fourth of the last stanza.

pan-try (pan′tri), *n.*; pl. *-tries* (-triz). [OF. F. *paneterie*, < *panetier*, pantler: see *pantler.*] A room or closet in which bread and other provisions, or plate, dishes, linen, etc., for the table, are kept.—**pan′try-man** (-mąn), *n.*; pl. *-men.* A man employed in a pantry.

pants (pants), *n. pl.* Pantaloons; trousers. [Colloq.]

pan-tun (pan-tön′), *n.* [Malay.] A Malay verse-form, usually of four lines, the third riming with the first, and the fourth with the second: sometimes employed in contests in which the pantun last uttered serves to suggest a succeeding one. Cf. *pantoum.*

pan-zer (pän′tsėr), *a.* [G.] Armored: as, a German *panzer* division, one made up of tanks, etc.

pap[1] (pap), *n.* [ME. *pappe*; prob. from Scand.] A teat or nipple (archaic or prov.); hence, something resembling a teat or nipple; a conical peak of a hill (now only in names).

pap[2] (pap), *n.* [ME. *pap* = D. *pap* = G. *pappe.*] Soft food for infants or invalids, as bread soaked in water or milk; hence, any soft, semiliquid substance; a pulpy mass; also, profits or favors secured through public office or official patronage (slang).

pa-pa[1] (pą-pä′ or, esp. in U. S., pä′pą), *n.* [F. *papa*, redupl. of a syllable common in natural infantile utterance: see *papa*[2], and cf. *mamma*[1].] Father: used esp. by children or young people.

pa-pa[2] (pä′pä), *n.* [ML. *papa*, pope, LL. bishop, < Gr. πάππας, father (orig. in childish use): see *pope*, and cf. *papa*[1].] The Pope (of Rome; obs. or rare); also, in the *Gr. Ch.*, a parish priest, or pope (as, "the Greek '*Papa*' . . . that is, the Greek priest": Kinglake's "Eothen," xxv.).

pa-pa-cy (pā′pą-si), *n.* [ML. *papatia*, < *papa*, pope: see *papa*[2].] The office, dignity, or jurisdiction of the Pope (of Rome); also, the succession or line of the popes; also, the system of ecclesiastical government in which the Pope is recognized as the supreme head; the papal government.

pa-pa-in (pą-pā′in), *n.* [From *papaya.*] In *chem.*, a proteolytic enzyme contained in the milky juice of the unripe fruit of the papaw-tree, *Carica papaya*; also, a commercial preparation of this in the form of a grayish powder resembling pepsin, used as a digestant.

pa-pal (pā′pąl), *a.* [OF. F. *papal*, < ML. *papalis*, < *papa*, pope: see *papa*[2].] Of or pertaining to the Pope or the papacy.—**pa′pal-ism,** *n.* The papal system.—**pa′pal-ist,** *n.* An adherent of the papal system or the papacy.—**pa′pal-ize** (-īz), *v. i.* or *t.*; *-ized, -izing.* To become or render papal.—**pa″pal-i-za′tion** (-i-zā′shǫn), *n.*—**pa′pal-ly,** *adv.*

pa-pav-er-a-ceous (pą-pav-ẹ-rā′shius), *a.* [L. *papaver*, poppy.] Belonging to the *Papaveraceæ*, or poppy family of plants.

pa-paw (pą-pâ′ or pâ′pâ), *n.* [Sp. *papaya*, the fruit, *papayo*, the tree; from Carib.] The large yellow edible fruit of a papayaceous tree, *Carica papaya*, native in tropical America, oblong in form and having a pulpy flesh inclosed within a thick rind; the tree itself; also, a small North American anonaceous tree, *Asimina triloba*, bearing an oblong fruit with bean-like seeds embedded in a sweet pulp; the fruit of this tree.

pa-pa-ya (pą-pā′yä, Sp. pä-pä′yä), *n.* [Sp.: see *papaw.*] The fruit of the tropical American papaw-tree, *Carica papaya*, or the tree itself.—**pap-a-ya-ceous** (pap-ą-yā′shius), *a.* Belonging to the *Papayaceæ*, or papaya (papaw) family of trees of tropical and subtropical regions.

pa-per (pā′pėr), *n.* [OF. F. *papier,* < L. *papyrus,* the plant papyrus, also paper made from it: see *papyrus.*] A substance made from rags, straw, wood, or other fibrous material, usually in thin sheets, for writing or printing on, wrapping things in, decorating walls, etc.; something resembling this substance, as papyrus; also, a piece, sheet, or leaf of paper; such a piece or sheet used as a wrapper, receptacle, etc., sometimes including the contents (as, a *paper* of nuts); a sheet or card of paper with pins or needles stuck through it in rows (as, a *paper* of pins); a curl-paper; also, a sheet, leaf, or piece of paper bearing writing; a written or printed document or instrument; a document establishing identity, status, or the like (usually in *pl.*: as, a ship's *papers,* the documents required to be carried by a ship for the manifestation of her ownership, nationality, destination, etc.); a set of questions for an examination, or an individual set of written answers to them; an essay, article, or dissertation on a particular topic; a newspaper or journal (as, "the public *papers,*" Smollett's "Humphry Clinker," June 2; "to-morrow's *paper,*" Tarkington's "Gentleman from Indiana," xiv.); also, negotiable notes, bills, etc., collectively (as, commercial *paper*; mercantile *paper*); also, paper money; also, free passes of admission to a place of entertainment, or persons thus admitted (slang).—**scrap of paper.** See under *scrap*², *n.*—**pa′per,** *a.* Made or consisting of paper (as, a *paper* box; *paper* money); hence, paper-like, or thin, flimsy, or frail; also, pertaining to, or carried on by means of, letters, articles, books, etc. (as, a *paper* warfare); also, written or printed on paper; existing on paper only and not in reality (as, a *paper* blockade; *paper* profits).—**pa′per,** *v. t.* To write or set down on paper; describe in writing; also, to fold, inclose, or put up in paper; also, to cover or line with paper; decorate (a wall, room, etc.) with wall-paper; also, to supply with paper; also, to treat in any way by means of paper; smooth with sandpaper, etc.; also, to fill (a place of entertainment) with an audience mostly admitted by paper, or free passes (slang).

pa-per=chase (pā′pėr-chās), *n.* The sport of hare and hounds.

pa-per=cut-ter (pā′pėr-kut″ėr), *n.* A paper-knife; also, a machine for cutting paper in piles or trimming the edges of books, etc.

pa-per-er (pā′pėr-ėr), *n.* One who papers; esp., a paper-hanger.

pa-per=hang-er (pā′pėr-hang″ėr), *n.* One whose business it is to cover or decorate walls with wall-paper.—**pa′per=hang″ing,** *n.* The work or business of a paper-hanger; *pl.,* paper used for covering or decorating walls; wall-paper.

pa-per-ing (pā′pėr-ing), *n.* The act of one who papers; esp., the work of a paper-hanger; also, wall-paper (as, "a room . . . with such large-figured *papering* on the walls as inn rooms have": C. Brontë's "Jane Eyre," xi.).

pa-per=knife (pā′pėr-nīf), *n.*; pl. *-knives* (-nīvz). A knife-like instrument with a blade of metal, ivory, wood, or the like, for cutting open the leaves of books, folded papers, etc.

pa-per=nau-ti-lus (pā′pėr-nâ′ti-lus), *n.* The argonaut, a dibranchiate cephalopod of the genus *Argonauta*: so called from the delicate shell of the female.

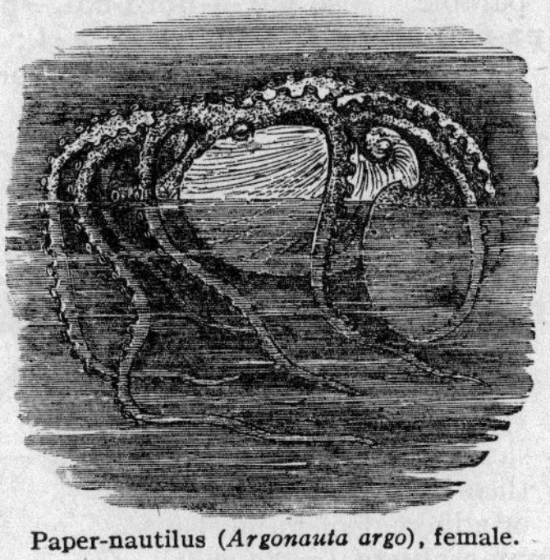

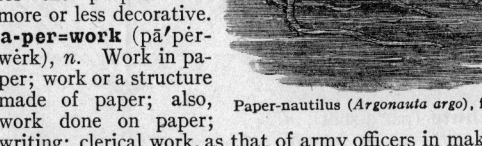

Paper-nautilus (*Argonauta argo*), female.

pa-per=weight (pā′pėr-wāt), *n.* A small heavy object used to lay on loose papers to keep them from being scattered, esp. one made for the purpose and more or less decorative.

pa-per=work (pā′pėr-wėrk), *n.* Work in paper; work or a structure made of paper; also, work done on paper; writing; clerical work, as that of army officers in making out reports, etc.; the written work of a student, etc., as in a class or an examination.

pa-per=works (pā′pėr-wėrks), *n. pl.* or *sing.* An establishment where paper is made.

pa-per-y (pā′pėr-i), *a.* Like paper; thin or flimsy.

pa-pete-rie (pȧ-pet-rē), *n.* [F., < *papetier,* one who makes or sells paper, < *papier,* E. *paper.*] A case or box of paper and other materials for writing.

Pa-phi-an (pā′fi-ạn), *a.* Of or pertaining to Paphos, an ancient city of Cyprus sacred to Aphrodite or Venus, and containing one of her most celebrated temples; hence, pertaining to love, esp. illicit love or sexual indulgence.

pa-pier=mâ-ché (pȧ-pyā-mä-shā), *n.* [F. *papier mâché,* 'chewed paper.'] A substance made of pulped paper or paper-pulp mixed with glue and other materials, or of layers of paper glued and pressed together, molded when moist to form various articles, and becoming hard and strong when dry.

pa-pil-i-o (pạ-pil′i-ō), *n.*; pl. *-os* (-ōz). [L.] A butterfly, esp. one of the genus *Papilio,* as *P. machaon,* the swallow-tailed butterfly of Europe.

pa-pil-i-o-na-ceous (pạ-pil″i-ọ-nā′shius), *a.* [NL. *papilionaceus,* < L. *papilio(n-),* butterfly.] Pertaining to or resembling a butterfly; in *bot.,* having an irregular corolla shaped somewhat like a butterfly, as the pea and other fabaceous plants; hence, belonging to the family *Fabaceæ,* or *Papilionaceæ*; fabaceous.

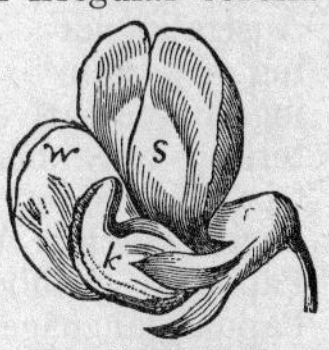

Papilionaceous Flower of Bean (*Phaseolus vulgaris*), with one of the wings removed.—*s,* standard; *w,* wing; *k,* keel or carina.

pa-pil-i-on-id (pạ-pil-i-on′id). [NL. *Papilionidæ,* pl., < L. *papilio(n-),* butterfly.] **I.** *n.* Any of the *Papilionidæ,* a family of butterflies including the swallow-tails and containing many beautiful species. **II.** *a.* Belonging or pertaining to the *Papilionidæ.*

pa-pil-la (pạ-pil′ạ̈), *n.*; pl. *papillæ* (-ē). [L., dim. of *papula,* E. *papule.*] The mammilla or nipple; also, any small nipple-like process or projection; one of certain small protuberances concerned with the senses of touch, taste, and smell (as, the *papillæ* of the finger-tips, tongue, etc.); a small vascular process at the root of a hair; a papule or pimple; a small nipple-like projection on a plant.—**pap-il-la-ry** (pap′i-lạ̄-ri), *a.* Of or pertaining to, or of the nature of, a papilla or papillæ; provided or furnished with papillæ.—**pap′il-late** (-lāt), *a.* Covered with papillæ.—**pap-il-lo′ma** (-lō′mạ̈), *n.*; pl. *-mas* or *-mata* (-mạ-tạ̈). [NL.: see *-oma.*] In *pathol.,* a tumor of the skin or of a mucous membrane, consisting of a hypertrophied papilla or group of papillæ, as a wart or a corn.—**pap′il-lose** (-lōs), *a.* Full of papillæ.

pap-il-lote (pap′i-lōt), *n.* [F., < *papillon,* < L. *papilio(n-),* butterfly.] A curl-paper; also, a buttered or oiled paper in which a cutlet or the like is cooked and sometimes served.

pa-pish (pā′pish). [Cf. *popish* and *papist.*] **I.** *a.* Same as *popish.* [Now prov.] **II.** *n.* Same as *papist.* [Now prov.]

pa-pism (pā′pizm), *n.* [F. *papisme,* < *pape,* < ML. *papa,* pope: see *papa*².] The papal system; popery; Roman Catholicism: usually in disparagement.

pa-pist (pā′pist), *n.* [F. *papiste,* < *pape,* pope: see *papism.*] An adherent of the Pope; a member of the Roman Catholic Church: usually in disparagement: as, "My man Friday was a Protestant, his father was a Pagan and a cannibal, and the Spaniard was a *Papist*" (Defoe's "Robinson Crusoe," i. 16).—**pa-pis-ti-cal, pa-pis-tic** (pā-pis′ti-kạl, -tik), *a.* Of, pertaining to, or characteristic of papists or papistry; popish: usually in disparagement.—**pa-pis′ti-cal-ly,** *adv.*—**pa′pis-try** (-tri), *n.* The system, doctrines, or practices of papists; popery: usually in disparagement.

pap-meat (pap′mēt), *n.* Pap or soft food, as for infants.

pa-poose, pap-poose (pạ-pös′), *n.* [Algonquian.] A North American Indian baby or young child. See cut on following page.

pap-pose, pap-pous (pap′ōs, -us), *a.* In *bot.,* having or forming a pappus; downy.

pap-pus (pap′us), *n.*; pl. *pappi* (-ī). [L., < Gr. πάππος, down, orig. grandfather.] In *bot.,* a downy, bristly, or other appendage of the seed of certain plants, as the dandelion and the thistle.

pap-py¹ (pap′i), *a.* Like pap; soft; mushy.

pap-py² (pap′i), *n.* [Childish dim. of *papa*¹.] Papa; father. [Now chiefly prov.]

pap-ri-ka (pap′ri-kạ̈), *n.* [Hung.] Hungarian pepper; the dried fruit of a cultivated form of *Capsicum annuum* (see *pepper* and *capsicum*), ground as a condiment: much less pungent than ordinary red pepper.

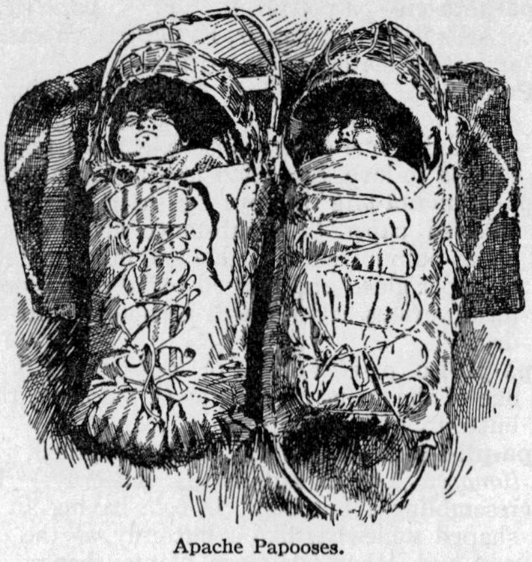

Apache Papooses.

Pap-u-an (pap′ṳ̄-ạn). **I.** *a.* Of or pertaining to Papua, or New Guinea, a large island north of Australia; noting or pertaining to the native negroid race of Papua, which is characterized by a black or sooty-brown complexion and crisp, frizzled hair, and which inhabits also many other islands of the Pacific north of Australia. **II.** *n.* A native or inhabitant of Papua; a member of the Papuan race; also, any of the Papuan languages or dialects.

pap-ule (pap′ūl), *n.* [L. *papula*, pustule, pimple.] In *pathol.*, a small, somewhat pointed elevation of the skin, usually inflammatory but not suppurative.—**pap′u-lar** (-ṳ̄-lạ̈r), *a.*

pap-y-ra-ceous (pap-i-rā′shius), *a.* [L. *papyraceus*, < *papyrus*: see *papyrus*.] Of the nature of paper; paper-like; papery.

pa-py-ro-graph (pạ-pī′rō̤-grȧf), *n.* [Gr. *πάπυρος*, papyrus (hence used to mean 'paper'), + *γράφειν*, write.] Any of various devices for producing copies of a writing, etc., esp. by a paper stencil.

pa-py-rus (pạ-pī′rus), *n.*; pl. *-ri* (-rī). [L., < Gr. *πάπυρος*, the plant papyrus, something made from papyrus: cf. *paper*.] A tall aquatic plant, *Cyperus papyrus*, of the sedge family, found in Abyssinia, Palestine, etc., and formerly abundant in Egypt; also, a material for writing on, prepared from thin strips of the pith of this plant laid together, soaked, pressed, and dried, used by the ancient Egyptians, Greeks, and Romans (as, "letters, written on *papyrus* in the hieratic character": Amelia B. Edwards's "Thousand Miles up the Nile," xv.); also, an ancient document or manuscript written on this material.

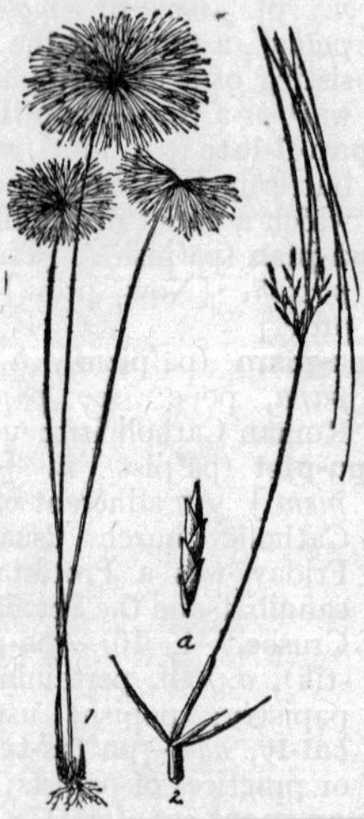

Papyrus. — 1, the plant; 2, the upper part of the culm, showing the involucre and one of the spike-bearing branches; *a*, a spike.

par[1] (pär), *n.* [L. *par*, equal.] An equality in value or standing, or a level of equality (as, the gains and the losses are about on a *par*; to put one person upon a *par* with another); also, an average or normal amount, degree, quality, condition, or the like (as, taking 70° as the *par* of temperature indoors); in *com.*, the established value of the monetary unit of one country in terms of that of another using the same metal as a standard of value ('par of exchange'); also, equality between the market value and the nominal (or face) value of stocks, bonds, etc. (as, a stock issued at *par*, that is, at a price equal to the face value; the bonds have risen to *par*); in *golf*, the number of strokes allowed to a hole or course as representing a score made by perfect playing. —**above par,** above the average or normal, as in amount, quality, etc.; in *com.*, at a price above the face value, as of a stock or bond; at a premium.—**below par,** below the average or normal, esp. in quality or condition (as, his last book is *below par*; to feel *below par*, as in health); in *com.*, at a price below the face value, as of a stock or bond; at a discount.—**par**[1], *a.* Average or normal (as, the *par* height of the barometric column at a particular level); in *com.*, at or pertaining to par (as, the *par* value of a bond).

par[2] (pär), *n.* See *parr*.

pa-ra (pä′rä), *n.*; pl. *paras* or *para*. [Turk.] Formerly, a small Turkish coin, orig. of silver, later of copper; now, a monetary unit of Turkey, equal to one fortieth of a piaster, or about .11 U. S. cent.

para-, par-. [Gr. *παρα-*, *παρ-*, repr. *παρά*, prep., beside, beyond, against.] A prefix meaning 'beside,' 'near,' 'beyond,' 'aside,' 'amiss,' and sometimes implying alteration or modification, occurring orig. in words from the Greek, but used also as a modern formative, chiefly in scientific words.

pa-rab-a-sis (pạ-rab′ạ-sis), *n.*; pl. *-ases* (-ạ-sēz). [Gr. *παράβασις*, < *παραβαίνειν*, come forward, < *παρά*, beside, + *βαίνειν*, go.] The chief of the choral parts in ancient Greek comedy, sung by the chorus during an intermission in the action, and consisting of an address from the poet to the audience.

par-a-blast (par′ạ-blast), *n.* [See *para-* and *-blast*.] In *biol.*, the nutritive yolk of an ovum or egg.

par-a-ble (par′ạ-bl), *n.* [OF. *parable*, *parabole* (F. *parabole*), < L. *parabola*, comparison, LL. parable, proverb, speech, ML. word, < Gr. *παραβολή*, a placing beside, comparison, parable, also parabola, < *παραβάλλειν*, throw beside, < *παρά*, beside, + *βάλλειν*, throw: cf. *parabola*, also *palaver* and *parole*.] A discourse or saying conveying the intended meaning by a comparison or under the likeness of something comparable or analogous (as, "Another *parable* spake he unto them; The kingdom of heaven is like unto leaven, which a woman took . . . ," Mat. xiii. 33; "He spake a *parable* unto them, Can the blind lead the blind?" Luke, vi. 39); specif., a short allegorical story, designed to convey some truth or moral lesson (frequent in the Bible: as, the *parable* of the poor man's one ewe lamb, see 2 Sam. xii. 1–10; the *parable* of the prodigal son, see Luke, xv. 11–32); also, any enigmatical, obscure, or dark saying (as, "He will seek out the secrets of grave sentences, and be conversant in dark *parables*," Ecclus. xxxix. 3: archaic, except as in 'to speak in parables'); also, speech or discourse (a Biblical use: as, to take up one's *parable*, to begin one's discourse; "Job continued his *parable*, and said . . . ," Job, xxvii. 1).—**par′a-ble,** *v. i.* or *t.*; *-bled*, *-bling*. To speak in or represent by a parable.

pa-rab-o-la (pạ-rab′ō̤-lạ̈), *n.*; pl. *-las* (-lạ̈z). [NL., < Gr. *παραβολή*: see *parable*.] In *geom.*, a plane curve formed by the intersection of a cone with a plane parallel to a side of the cone.—**par-a-bol-ic**[1] (par-ạ-bol′ik), *a.* Pertaining to, of the form of, or resembling a parabola: as, "He compelled the frothy liquor . . . to spout forth from one glass and descend into the other, in a great *parabolic* curve" (Hawthorne's "Blithedale Romance," xxi.).

par-a-bol-ic[2] (par-ạ-bol′ik), *a.* [Gr. *παραβολικός*, < *παραβολή*: see *parable*.] Of, pertaining to, or involving a parable. Also **par-a-bol′i-cal.**—**par-a-bol′i-cal-ly,** *adv.*

pa-rab-o-lize (pạ-rab′ō̤-līz), *v. t.*; *-lized*, *-lizing*. To give the form of a parabola or paraboloid to.—**pa-rab″o-li-za′tion** (-li-zā′shọn), *n.*

pa-rab-o-loid (pạ-rab′ō̤-loid), *n.* [See *-oid*.] In *geom.*, a solid or surface generated by the revolution of a parabola about its axis, or one some of whose plane sections are parabolas.—**pa-rab-o-loi′dal,** *a.*

Par-a-cel-si-an (par-ạ-sel′si-ạn). **I.** *a.* Of or pertaining to Paracelsus (1493?–1541), a Swiss-German physician and alchemist, or his theories. **II.** *n.* A follower or adherent of Paracelsus.

par-a-chute (par′ạ-shöt), *n.* [F., < *para-* (as in *parasol*: see *parasol*) + *chute*, a fall: see *chute*.] An apparatus used in descending safely through the air from a great

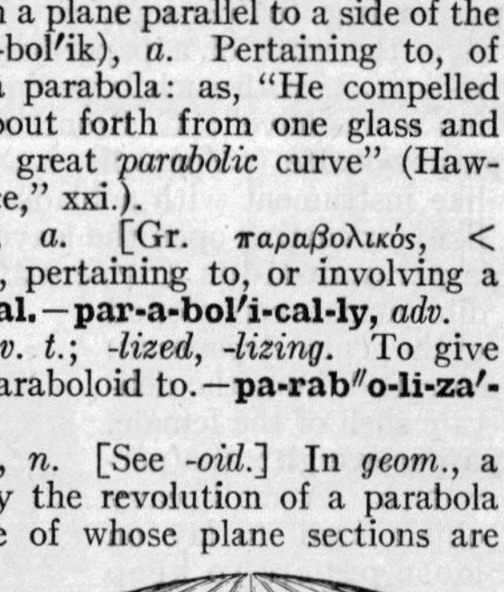

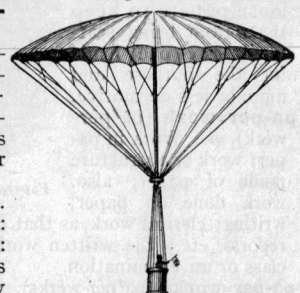

Garnerin's Parachute, descending.

height, esp. from a balloon, being umbrella-like in form and rendered effective by the resistance of the air, which expands it during the descent and then reduces the velocity of its motion; hence, something resembling or suggesting this, as the patagium of a flying mammal or reptile.—**par′a-chute,** *v. i.* or *t.*; *-chuted, -chuting.* To descend or convey through the air by, or as if by, the aid of a parachute.—**par′a-chut-ist** (-shö-tist), *n.* One who uses a parachute; one skilled in making descents with a parachute.

par-a-clete (par′ą-klēt), *n.* [LL. *paracletus,* < Gr. παράκλητος, < παρακαλεῖν, call to aid, < παρά, beside, + καλεῖν, call.] One called in to aid; an advocate or intercessor; esp. [*cap.*], the Holy Spirit, or Comforter (as, "the *Paraclete* [Authorized Version, *Comforter*], the Holy Ghost, whom the Father will send in my name," John (Douay Version), xiv. 26; "It was approaching the third hour, the hour at which the *Paraclete* originally descended upon the Apostles," J. H. Newman's "Callista," xxx.); rarely, Christ, the Advocate.

pa-rade (pą-rād′), *n.* [F. *parade,* < Sp. *parada,* < *parar,* < L. *parare,* prepare: cf. *pare.*] Show, display, or ostentation (as, "He loves to make *parade* of pain," Tennyson's "In Memoriam," xxi.; "The Cardinal left Brussels with . . . much *parade,*" Motley's "Dutch Republic," ii. 4); also, the orderly assembly or muster of troops for inspection or display; also, a public procession for display (as, a political *parade*); also, a place where troops regularly assemble for parade; the level space forming the interior or inclosed area of a fortification; also, a public walk or promenade (as, the Marine *Parade* at Brighton, England); a body of promenaders; also, in *fencing,* a parry (as, "He was an admirable swordsman. His *parade* and riposte were as quick as lightning": Conan Doyle's "Exploits of Brigadier Gerard," i.).—**pa-rade′,** *v.*; *-raded, -rading.* **I.** *tr.* To make parade of, or display ostentatiously (as, "He [Byron] early discovered that, by *parading* his unhappiness before the multitude, he produced an immense sensation": Macaulay's "Essays," Moore's Byron); also, to assemble and marshal, as troops for inspection; also, to cause to march or proceed for display; also, to march or proceed along or through (a place), as for display; walk up and down on or in (as, "the skipper *parading* his quarter-deck with an elated grandeur": H. Melville's "Moby-Dick," xxxiii.). **II.** *intr.* To assemble in military order for inspection or display; also, to march or proceed with display (as, "Bodies of men . . . *paraded* hourly with fife and drum before his windows": Motley's "Dutch Republic," iii. 2); promenade in a public place in order to show one's self.—**pa-rad′er** (-rā′dėr), *n.*—**pa-rade′=rest,** *n. Milit.,* a position of rest, esp. at parade, in which the soldier stands silent and motionless, with the right foot slightly to the rear and the left knee slightly bent.

par-a-digm (par′ą-dim or -dīm), *n.* [LL. *paradigma,* < Gr. παράδειγμα, < παραδεικνύναι, show side by side, < παρά, beside, + δεικνύναι, show.] A pattern; an example; in *gram.,* an example of a noun, verb, or other inflected part of speech, in all its inflections.—**par″a-dig-mat′ic** (-dig-mat′ik), *a.*

par-a-di-sa-ic, par-a-di-sa-i-cal (par″ą-di-sā′ik, -i-kąl), *a.* Same as *paradisiac, paradisiacal*: as, "*paradisaical* ecstasy" (Arnold Bennett's "Helen with the High Hand," viii.).

par-a-di-sal (par′ą-dī-sąl), *a.* Of or pertaining to paradise: as, "*paradisal* bliss" (Joaquin Miller's "Joaquin Murietta").

par-a-dise (par′ą-dīs), *n.* [OF. F. *paradis,* < LL. *paradisus,* < Gr. παράδεισος, park, < OPers. *pairidaēza,* inclosure.] The garden of Eden (as, "He . . . to the border comes Of Eden, where delicious *Paradise* . . . crowns with her enclosure green . . . the champain head Of a steep wilderness": Milton's "Paradise Lost," iv. 132); also, heaven, as the final abode of the righteous; the Mohammedan heaven (as, "The Moors imagined the *paradise* of their prophet to be situated in that part of the heaven which overhung the kingdom of Granada": Irving's "Conquest of Granada," i.); also, according to some, an intermediate place for the departed souls of the righteous awaiting resurrection; also, a place of extreme beauty or delight; a state of supreme felicity (as, "This state of things should have been to me a *paradise* of peace," C. Brontë's "Jane Eyre," iii.; a fool's *paradise,* see under *fool*[1], *n.*); also, an Oriental park or pleasure-ground, esp. one containing wild beasts of the chase; hence, a park in which foreign animals are kept.—**par′a-dise=fish,** *n.* A fish, *Macropodus viridiauratus,* of southeastern Asia, remarkable for the extension of its fins, and much admired for its beautiful coloration and preserved in aquariums, etc.—**par′a-dise=tree,** *n.* A tree, *Simaruba glauca,* ranging from southern Florida to Brazil, with panicles of pale-yellow flowers, and with a root whose bitter bark contains a tonic principle.

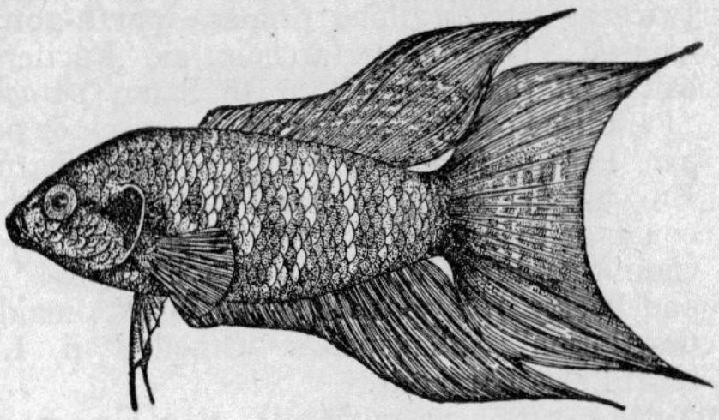
Paradise-fish.

par-a-dis-i-ac, par-a-di-si-a-cal (par-ą-dis′i-ak, par″ą-di-sī′ą-kąl), *a.* [LL. *paradisiacus.*] Of, like, or befitting paradise: as, "the *paradisiac* beauty and simplicity of tropic humanity" (Kingsley's "Alton Locke," xl.); "*paradisiacal* dreams of love and joy" (Mrs. Shelley's "Frankenstein," xxii.). Also **par-a-dis′i-al, par-a-dis′i-an** (-dis′i-ąl, -ąn).

par-a-dox (par′ą-doks), *n.* [L. *paradoxum,* < Gr. παράδοξον, neut. of παράδοξος, contrary to received opinion, incredible, < παρά, against, + δόξα, opinion.] An opinion or statement contrary to received opinion; also, a statement or proposition seemingly self-contradictory or absurd, and yet explicable as expressing a truth (see 2 Cor. vi. 9, 10); such statements collectively, or the making of them (as, to indulge in *paradox*; to be given to *paradox*); also, a self-contradictory and false proposition; also, any person or thing exhibiting apparent contradictions.—**par-a-dox′i-cal,** *a.* Of the nature of or involving a paradox (as, "Comedians, *paradoxical* as it may seem, may be too natural": Lamb's "Stage Illusion"); also, given to paradoxes (as, "He was an eternal talker—brilliant, various, *paradoxical,* florid": Bulwer-Lytton's "Caxtons," vii. 7).—**par-a-dox′i-cal-ly,** *adv.*—**par-a-dox′i-cal-ness,** *n.*—**par′a-dox-ist,** *n.* One given to paradoxes.

par-a-dox-ure (par-ą-dok′sūr), *n.* [NL. *Paradoxurus,* name of the typical genus, < Gr. παράδοξος, incredible, + οὐρά, tail.] A palm-cat or palm-civet.

par-æs-the-sia (par-es-thē′ziä), *n.* [NL.: see *para-* and *æsthesia.*] In *pathol.,* abnormal sensation, as prickling, itching, etc. Also **par-æs-the′sis** (-sis).

par-af-fin, par-af-fine (par′ą-fin, -fin or -fēn), *n.* [G. *paraffin,* < L. *parum,* too little, + *affinis,* related; from its want of affinity for other substances.] A white or colorless waxy substance (a mixture of hydrocarbons, chiefly the solid members of the methane series with a high boiling-point), not easily acted upon by reagents, obtained chiefly from crude petroleum, and used for making candles, forming preservative coatings, waterproofing paper, etc.; also, paraffin-oil; also, in *chem.,* any hydrocarbon of the methane series.—**par′af-fin, par′af-fine,** *v. t.*; *-fined, -fining.* To cover or impregnate with paraffin.—**par-af-fin′ic,** *a.*—**par′af-fin=oil′, par′af-fine=oil′,** *n.* Any of various oils associated with paraffin, as oils distilled from bituminous shale, oils obtained from petroleum (esp. heavy or lubricating oils), and oils from which paraffin may be made; specif., in British use, kerosene or some allied oil.

par-a-gen-e-sis (par-ą-jen′e-sis), *n.* [See *para-* and *genesis.*] In *geol.,* the formation of minerals in close contact, so that one affects another's development.—**par″a-ge-net′ic** (-ję-net′ik), *a.*

par-a-go-ge (par-ą-gō′jē), *n.* [LL., < Gr. παραγωγή, < παράγειν, lead beside, < παρά, beside, + ἄγειν, lead.] In *gram.,* the addition of a letter or syllable at the end of a word.—**par-a-gog′ic** (-goj′ik), *a.*

par-a-gon (par′ą-gon or -gǫn), *n.* [OF. *paragon* (F. *parangon*), < It. *paragone,* touchstone, comparison, paragon; origin uncertain.] A model or pattern of excellence, or of a particular excellence (as, "If that young man goes on as charmingly as he has begun . . . he will be a *paragon,*" Thackeray's "Newcomes," xviii.; a *paragon* of beauty);

the finest example of a particular class or kind (as, "This young lady . . . was the *paragon* of princesses": Motley's "Dutch Republic," ii. 5); also, a printing-type (20 point) twice as large as long primer.—**par'a-gon,** *v. t.*; *-goned, -goning.* To compare (archaic: as, "Lucifer; so by allusion call'd Of that bright star to Satan *paragon'd,*" Milton's "Paradise Lost," x. 426); also, to match or parallel (archaic: as, "Pass to join your peers, *paragon* charm with charm," Browning's "Fifine at the Fair," xxiii.); be a match for, equal, or rival (archaic: as, "Who could *paragon* The fervid choir that lifted up a noise Of harmony?" Keats's "Sleep and Poetry"); also, to surpass† (as, "A maid That *paragons* description": Shakspere's "Othello," ii. 1. 62); also, to regard as a paragon†.

pa-rag-o-nite (pạ-rag'ọ-nīt), *n.* [Gr. παράγων, ppr. of παράγειν, lead beside, mislead: see *paragoge.*] A kind of mica analogous to muscovite but containing sodium in place of potassium.

par-a-graph (par'ạ-gråf), *n.* [OF. F. *paragraphe,* < ML. *paragraphus,* < Gr. παράγραφος, a line or mark in the margin, < παρά, beside, + γράφειν, mark, write.] A character (now usually ¶) used to indicate the beginning of a distinct or separate portion of a text, or as a mark of reference; also, a distinct portion of written or printed matter dealing with a particular point, and usually beginning (commonly with indention) on a new line; also, a note, item, or brief article, as in a newspaper, usually forming a distinct, undivided whole (as, "She had been irritated by newspaper *paragraphs*—nobody could ever find out who wrote them": H. G. Wells's "Soul of a Bishop," vi.).—**par'a-graph,** *v. t.* To divide into paragraphs; also, to express in a paragraph; also, to mention in a paragraph; write or publish paragraphs about.—**par'a-graph-er,** *n.* One who writes paragraphs, as for a newspaper; a paragraphist.

par-a-graph-i-a (par-ạ-graf'i-ạ̈), *n.* [NL., < Gr. παρα-, amiss (see *para-*), + γράφειν, write.] In *pathol.*, a cerebral disorder marked by the writing of words or letters other than those intended.

par-a-graph-ic (par-ạ-graf'ik), *a.* Of, pertaining to, or forming a paragraph; divided into paragraphs; also, of or pertaining to paragraphia.—**par-a-graph'i-cal-ly,** *adv.*

par-a-graph-ist (par'ạ-gråf-ist), *n.* A paragrapher.

Par-a-guay (par'ạ-gwā) **tea.** Same as *mate*³.

par-a-keet (par'ạ-kēt), *n.* See *parrakeet.*

par-a-kite (par'ạ-kīt), *n.* [See *para-.*] A number of kites connected in series and flying tandem, used for sending up meteorological instruments, etc.

par-al-de-hyde (par-al'dẹ-hīd), *n.* [See *para-.*] In *chem.*, a colorless liquid, $C_6H_{12}O_3$, formed by the polymerization of ordinary aldehyde: used in medicine as a hypnotic.

par-a-leip-sis (par-ạ-līp'sis), *n.* See *paralipsis.*

par-a-li-pom-e-na (par"ạ-li-pom'e-nạ̈), *n. pl.* [LL., < Gr. παραλειπόμενα, neut. pl. ppr. pass. of παραλείπειν, leave out, < παρά, beside, + λείπειν, leave.] Things omitted; a supplement containing things omitted from a preceding work; [*cap.*] the two books of the Old Testament which are commonly known as Chronicles, so called as containing particulars omitted from the books of Kings (usually in the form *Paralipomenon,* representing the genitive plural, as used in the title in the Septuagint and the Vulgate).

par-a-lip-sis, par-a-leip-sis (par-ạ-lip'sis, -līp'sis), *n.*; pl. *-lipses* (-lip'sēz), *-leipses* (-līp'sēz). [NL., < Gr. παράλειψις, < παραλείπειν, leave out: see *paralipomena.*] In *rhet.*, a pretended ignoring, for rhetorical effect, of something actually spoken of, as, 'not to mention other faults.'

par-al-lax (par'ạ-laks), *n.* [Gr. παράλλαξις, < παραλλάσσειν, change, vary, deviate, < παρά, beside, + ἀλλάσσειν, change.] The apparent displacement of an object observed, esp. a heavenly body, due to a change or difference in the position of the observer; in *astron.*, the angular amount of such a displacement of a heavenly body as measured between lines drawn to it from the two different points of observation (as, diurnal or geocentric *parallax,* measured between the line drawn from the heavenly body to the observer and the line from the heavenly body to the center of the earth; annual or heliocentric *parallax,* measured between the line drawn from the heavenly body to the observer and the line from the heavenly body to the center of the sun).—**par-al-lac'tic** (-lak'tik), *a.*

par-al-lel (par'ạ-lel), *a.* [F. *parallèle,* < L. *parallelus,* < Gr. παράλληλος, < παρά, beside, + ἀλλήλων, of one another, < ἄλλος, other.] Of lines (straight or curved), planes, or curved surfaces, so placed one beside another as to be equidistant at all corresponding points; of a single such line, plane, etc., equidistant from another or others at all corresponding points (with *to* or *with*); of things, involving the relation of such lines, planes, etc.; specif., according to non-Euclidean theories, intersecting at infinity, as lines or planes; in fig. use, having the same direction, course, or tendency; corresponding, similar, or analogous (as, "There are *parallel* points in her history and yours": C. Brontë's "Jane Eyre," xxxiii.); in *music,* noting or pertaining to consecutive harmonic intervals which consist of the same number of degrees (as, *parallel* fifths); also, of a tonality or key, relative.—**parallel bars,** a pair of bars raised above the ground, used in gymnastics to develop the muscles of the arms, chest, etc.—**parallel file,** a file of uniform section, without taper from tang to point.—**parallel forces,** forces which act in directions parallel to each other.—**parallel motion,** a mechanism by which the end of a piston-rod is caused to move in a straight line in spite of deflecting effort.—**par'al-lel,** *n.* A parallel line or surface; fig., anything parallel in direction, course, or tendency; a match or counterpart (as, "Behold this ring, Whose high respect and rich validity Did lack a *parallel*": Shakspere's "All's Well," v. 3. 193); also, the position or relation of being parallel (as, in *parallel*: see phrase below); fig., correspondence or analogy (as, "There is no sort of *parallel* between the cases": J. Butler's "Analogy of Religion," ii. 6); also, a comparison of things as if regarded side by side (as, "He runs a laboured *parallel* between Schiller, Goethe, and Kotzebue; one is more this, the other more that": Carlyle's "Essays," Taylor's Historical Survey of German Poetry); specif., in *geog.*, any of the imaginary circles on the earth's surface, parallel to the equator, by which degrees of latitude are represented ('parallel of latitude'); *milit.*, a trench cut in the ground before a fortress, parallel to its defenses, for the purpose of covering a besieging force; in *printing,* a pair of vertical parallel lines (‖) used as a mark of reference.—**in parallel,** in *elect.*, with all the positive poles, terminals, etc., joined to one conductor and all the negative to the other: said of batteries, lamps, etc.—**par'al-lel,** *v. t.*; *-leled* or *-lelled, -leling* or *-lelling.* To make parallel; also, to furnish a parallel for; find or provide a match for; also, to form a parallel to; be equivalent to, or equal; also, to bring into comparison; compare.

par-al-lel-e-pip-ed (par"ạ-lel-e-pip'ed or -pī'ped), *n.* [Gr. παραλληλεπίπεδον, < παράλληλος, parallel, + ἐπίπεδον, plane surface, < ἐπί, on, + πέδον, ground.] A prism whose bases are parallelograms. Also **par"al-lel-e-pip'e-don** (-pip'e-don or -pī'pe-don).

par-al-lel-ism (par'ạ-lel-izm), *n.* The position or relation of parallels; agreement in direction, tendency, or character; correspondence or analogy; also, a parallel; also, a comparison; in *metaph.*, the doctrine that mental and bodily processes are concomitant, each varying with variation of the other, but that there is no causal relation or relation of interaction between the two series of changes.—**par'al-lel-ist,** *n.* One who draws a parallel or comparison; also, an adherent of the metaphysical doctrine of parallelism.—**par"al-lel-is'tic,** *a.*

par-al-lel-i-ty (par-ạ-lel'i-ti), *n.* Parallel arrangement, condition, or character.

par-al-lel-ize (par'ạ-lel-īz), *v. t.*; *-ized, -izing.* To make parallel; place so as to be parallel; esp., to place side by side for comparison; bring into comparison; compare; also, to furnish a parallel for, or form a parallel to; match.—**par"al-lel-i-za'tion** (-i-zā'shọn), *n.*

par-al-lel-ly (par'ạ-lel-li), *adv.* In a parallel manner.

par-al-lel-o-gram (par-ạ-lel'ọ-gram), *n.* [Gr. παραλληλόγραμμον, < παράλληλος, parallel, + γραμμή, line.] A quadrilateral whose opposite sides are parallel.

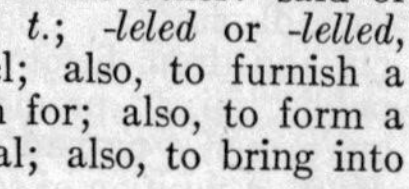

Parallelogram.

par"al-lel-o-pip'ed, etc. Same as *parallelepiped,* etc.

pa-ral-o-gism (pạ-ral′ọ-jizm), *n.* [F. *paralogisme*, < Gr. παραλογισμός, < παραλογίζεσθαι, reason falsely, < παρά, beside, + λογίζεσθαι, calculate, infer, < λόγος, reckoning, reason.] In *logic*, a piece of false or fallacious reasoning, esp. (as distinguished from *sophism*) one of whose falseness the reasoner himself is not conscious; also, reasoning of this kind.—**pa-ral′o-gist** (-jist), *n.* One who uses paralogisms; a false reasoner.—**pa-ral-o-gis′tic,** *a.*

par-a-lyse (par′ạ-līz), etc. See *paralyze*, etc.

pa-ral-y-sis (pạ-ral′i-sis), *n.*; pl. *-yses* (-i-sēz). [L., < Gr. παράλυσις, < παραλύειν, disable at the side, < παρά, beside, + λύειν, loose.] In *pathol.*, impairment or loss of the power of voluntary motion, or of sensation, in one or more parts of the body, or a disease characterized by this; hence, in fig. use, a more or less complete crippling, or arrest of powers and activities (as, a *paralysis* of trade, or of government); a condition of powerlessness or helpless inactivity; any paralyzing influence.—**general paralysis,** in *pathol.*, a progressive disease characterized by degeneration of the central nervous system, with impairment of motor functions and gradual mental enfeeblement; paresis.—**infantile paralysis.** See under *infantile*.

par-a-lyt-ic (par-ạ-lit′ik). [L. *paralyticus*, < Gr. παραλυτικός, < παραλύειν: see *paralysis*.] **I.** *a.* Pertaining to or of the nature of paralysis; affected with or subject to paralysis. **II.** *n.* One affected with paralysis; also, a stroke of paralysis (Sc.: as, "It was in this year that Patrick Dilworth . . . was disabled by a *paralytic*," Galt's "Annals of the Parish," ii.).—**par-a-lyt′i-cal-ly,** *adv.*

par-a-lyze (par′ạ-līz), *v. t.*; *-lyzed*, *-lyzing*. [F. *paralyser*, < L. *paralysis*: see *paralysis*.] To affect with paralysis; fig., to bring to a condition of helpless inactivity (as, "Longing *paralysed* their brains," Galsworthy's "Saint's Progress," i. 5; to *paralyze* the energies); render (a person, etc.) powerless to act, think, etc. (as, "I overcame the extreme shyness that had formerly *paralyzed* me in her presence": Irving's "Tales of a Traveler," i. 9).—**par″a-ly-za′tion** (-li-zā′shọn), *n.*—**par′a-lyz-er** (-lī-zėr), *n.*

par-a-mag-net (par-ạ-mag′net), *n.* [See *para-*.] A substance having paramagnetic properties.—**par″a-mag-net′ic,** *a.* Loosely, pertaining to ordinary magnetism (opposed to *diamagnetic*); specif., noting or pertaining to a class of substances (as liquid oxygen) which, like iron but in a much less degree, are magnetic in the usual way, and hence tend to take a position with the longer axis parallel to the lines of force (distinguished from *ferromagnetic*, and opposed to *diamagnetic*).—**par-a-mag′net-ism,** *n.* The quality of being paramagnetic; paramagnetic phenomena, or the science dealing with them.

par-a-mat-ta (par-ạ-mat′ạ), *n.* [From *Paramatta*, now *Parramatta*, town in Australia.] A light, twilled dress-fabric having a silk or cotton warp and a woolen weft.

pa-ra-mo (pä′rạ-mō), *n.*; pl. *-mos* (-mōz). [Sp. *páramo*.] A high plateau region in tropical South America, esp. one bare of trees.

par-a-morph (par′ạ-môrf), *n.* [Gr. παρα- (see *para-*) + μορφή, form.] In *mineral.*, a pseudomorph formed by a change in molecular structure without a change in chemical composition.—**par-a-mor′phic** (-môr′fik), *a.* Pertaining to a paramorph; characterized by paramorphism.—**par-a-mor′phism** (-fizm), *n.* The state of being a paramorph, or the process by which it is brought about.

par-a-mount (par′ạ-mount). [AF. *paramont*, above, < OF. *par* (< L. *per*), by, + *amont*, upward, up, < L. *ad*, to, + *mons* (*mont-*), mountain: cf. *amount*.] **I.** *a.* Above others in rank or authority, or superior in power or jurisdiction (as, "He was also feudal lord *paramount* of the whole soil of his kingdom": Macaulay's "Hist. of Eng.," i.); hence, in general, chief in importance (as, *paramount* claims or duties; "All circumstances of mere convenience were obliged to give way to a *paramount* sense of danger," Scott's "Castle Dangerous," i.); supreme; preëminent. **II.** *n.* A lord paramount; an overlord; a supreme ruler: as, "In order came the grand infernal peers: Midst came their mighty *paramount*" (Milton's "Paradise Lost," ii. 508).—**par′a-mount-cy** (-si), **par′a-mount-ship,** *n.* The condition or rank of being paramount.—**par′a-mount-ly,** *adv.*

par-a-mour (par′ạ-mör), *n.* [Orig. phrase, OF. *par amour*, 'by love,' by way of (sexual) love, < *par* (< L. *per*), by, + *amour* (< L. *amor*), love.] A lover, now usually an illicit lover, of either sex; one taking the place of a husband or wife without legal right.

par-a-neph-ros (par-ạ-nef′ros), *n.* [NL., < Gr. παρά, beside, + νεφρός, kidney.] In *anat.*, a suprarenal capsule. See *suprarenal*, *a.*—**par-a-neph′ric,** *a.*

pa-rang (pä′rang), *n.* [Malay.] A large, heavy knife used as a tool or a weapon by the Malays: as, "One of Lingard's seamen at once retaliated by striking at the . . . savage with his *parang* — three such choppers brought for the purpose of clearing the bush . . . being all the weapons the party . . . possessed" (J. Conrad's "Rescue," ii. 2).

par-a-noi-a, par-a-nœ-a (par-ạ-noi′ạ, -nē′ạ), *n.* [NL., < Gr. παράνοια, < παρά, beside, + νοῦς, mind.] In *pathol.*, mental derangement; esp., a chronic form of insanity characterized chiefly by systematic delusions.—**par-a-noi′ac, par-a-nœ′ac** (-ak). **I.** *a.* Pertaining to or affected with paranoia. **II.** *n.* A person affected with paranoia.

par-a-nu-cle-in (par-ạ-nū′klẹ-in), *n.* [See *para-*.] In *physiol. chem.*, any of a group of amorphous substances which, unlike true nucleins, do not yield nitrogenous bases on decomposition; a pseudonuclein.

par-a-nymph (par′ạ-nimf), *n.* [LL. *paranymphus* (fem. *paranympha*), < Gr. παράνυμφος, < παρά, beside, + νύμφη, bride.] In ancient Greece, a friend who accompanied the bridegroom when he went to bring home the bride; also, the bridesmaid who escorted the bride to the bridegroom; hence, in modern use, a groomsman or a bridesmaid; also, a person who speaks in behalf of another.

par-a-pet (par′ạ-pet), *n.* [It. *parapetto*, < *parare*, protect, ward off (see *parry*), + *petto*, < L. *pectus*, breast.] A defensive wall or elevation, as of earth or stone, in fortification; such an elevation raised above the main wall or rampart of a permanent fortification; also, a protective wall or barrier at the edge of a balcony, roof, bridge, or the like (as, "the *parapet* of the great dam": H. G. Wells's "Men Like Gods," ii. 1).—**par′a-pet-ed,** *a.* Furnished with a parapet: as, "a *parapeted* terrace" (M. Hewlett's "Open Country," iv.).

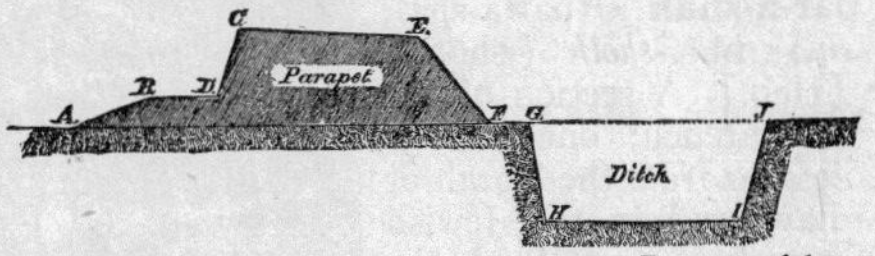

Parapet. — *A*, foot of banquette slope; *B*, crest of banquette; *C*, interior crest; *D*, foot of interior slope; *E*, exterior crest; *F*, foot of exterior slope; *G*, crest of scarp; *H*, foot of scarp; *I*, foot of counterscarp; *J*, crest of counterscarp; *AB*, banquette slope; *BD*, banquette tread; *CD*, interior slope; *CE*, superior slope; *EF*, exterior slope; *FG*, berm; *GH*, scarp; *HI*, bottom of ditch; *IJ*, counterscarp.

par-aph (par′ạf), *n.* [OF. F. *paraphe*, < ML. *paraphus*, for *paragraphus*, E. *paragraph*.] A paragraph†; also, a flourish made after a signature, as in a document, orig. as a precaution against forgery.—**par′aph,** *v. t.* To add a paraph to; hence, to sign, esp. with one's initials.

par-a-pher-na-li-a (par″ạ-fėr-nā′li-ạ), *n. pl.* [ML., < LL. *parapherna*, < Gr. παράφερνα, bride's belongings other than dowry, < παρά, beside, + φερνή, dowry, < φέρειν, bear.] The personal articles, apart from dower, reserved by law to a married woman; hence, personal belongings (as, "trunks containing . . . personal property — their sole chattels and *paraphernalia* on earth": Arnold Bennett's "Hilda Lessways," iii. 3); articles of personal adornment or attire (as, "These *paraphernalia* [of Indian dress] would not have been much admired by a modern fine lady": Smollett's "Humphry Clinker," July 13); trappings; equipments; in general, appurtenances (as, "the ample fireplace . . . garnished with a crane having various hooks and other *paraphernalia*": Mrs. Stowe's "Oldtown Folks," xv.); occasionally, as *sing.*, an outfit or apparatus (as, "There's a certain *paraphernalia* of dignity . . . The King comes down in a gilt coach . . . and wears long robes and a crown": H. G. Wells's "Tono-Bungay," iv. 3. § 2).

par-a-phrase (par′ạ-frāz). *n.* [F. *paraphrase*, < L. *paraphrasis*, < Gr. παράφρασις, < παραφράζειν, say in other words, < παρά, beside, + φράζειν, tell.] A statement of the sense of a text or passage in other words, as for clearness; a free rendering or translation, as of a passage; also, the act or process of paraphrasing.—**par′a-phrase,** *v. t.* or *i.*;

-*phrased*, -*phrasing*. To restate or render in, or to make, a paraphrase.—**par′a-phras-er** (-frā-zėr), *n.*

par-a-phrast (par′ạ-frast), *n.* [LL. *paraphrastes*, < Gr. παραφράστης, < παραφράζειν: see *paraphrase*.] One who paraphrases.—**par-a-phras′tic** (-fras′tik), *a.* [Gr. παραφραστικός.] Pertaining to or of the nature of a paraphrase.—**par-a-phras′ti-cal-ly,** *adv.*

pa-raph-y-sis (pạ-raf′i-sis), *n.*; pl. -*yses* (-i-sēz). [NL., < Gr. παράφυσις, offshoot, < παραφύεσθαι, grow at the side, < παρά, beside, + φύειν, produce.] In *bot.*, one of the sterile, usually filamentous outgrowths often occurring among the reproductive organs in many cryptogamous plants.

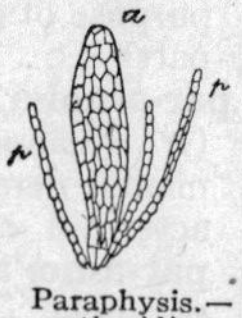

Paraphysis.—*a*, antheridium, with *p, p*, paraphyses, of a moss, *Polytrichum commune*.

par-a-ple-gi-a (par-ạ-plē′ji-ä), *n.* [NL., < Gr. παραπληγία, < παραπλήσσειν, strike on one side, < παρά, beside, + πλήσσειν, strike.] In *pathol.*, paralysis of both lower limbs with more or less of the trunk.—**par-a-pleg′ic** (-plej′ik or -plē′jik), *a.*

Pa-rá (pä-rä′) **rub′ber.** [From *Pará*, in Brazil.] The india-rubber obtained from the euphorbiaceous tree *Hevea brasiliensis* and other species of the same genus, natives of tropical South America.

par-a-sang (par′ạ-sang), *n.* [L. *parasanga*, < Gr. παρασάγγης; of Persian origin.] A Persian measure of length, of varying extent, anciently equal to about 3⅝ English miles.

par-a-se-le-ne (par″ạ-se-lē′nē), *n.*; pl. -*næ* (-nē). [NL., < Gr. παρά, beside, + σελήνη, moon.] A bright moon-like spot on a lunar halo; a mock moon. Cf. *parhelion*.—**par″a-se-len′ic** (-len′ik), *a.*

Paraselenæ.

par-a-shah (par′ạ-shä), *n.*; pl. -*shoth* (-shōth). [Heb.] A section of the Pentateuch; one of the lessons from the Torah or Law read in the Jewish synagogue on Sabbaths and festivals, or one of the subsections into which these lessons are divided. Cf. *haphtarah*.

par-a-site (par′ạ-sīt), *n.* [L. *parasitus*, < Gr. παράσιτος, one who eats at the table of another, < παρά, beside, + σῖτος, food.] One who lives on the hospitality or patronage of others (as, "He had daily guests . . . picked up . . . among the many *parasites* on the look-out for good fare": Wiseman's "Fabiola," i. 4); a hanger-on of the rich; hence, in general, one who lives on others or another without making any useful and fitting return; sometimes, a person considered as living on society without having any productive or useful function (as, "Nine people out of ten looked on him as something of a *parasite*, with no real work in the world": Galsworthy's "Saint's Progress," ii. 1); in *zoöl.* and *bot.*, an animal or plant which lives on or in another organism (the host), from which it obtains nutriment (cf. *louse*, *tapeworm*, *ectozoön*, *entozoön*, and *broom-rape*, *mistletoe*, *rafflesia*); sometimes, a commensal animal or plant.—**par-a-sit′ic, par-a-sit′i-cal** (-sit′ik, -i-kạl), *a.* [L. *parasiticus*, < Gr. παρασιτικός.] Of, pertaining to, or characteristic of parasites; living as or resembling a parasite; of diseases, due to parasites.—**par-a-sit′i-cal-ly,** *adv.*—**par-a-sit′i-cide** (-sīd), *n.* [See -*cide*.] An agent or preparation that destroys parasites.—**par′a-sit-ism** (-sī-tizm), *n.* Parasitic mode of life or existence; in *pathol.*, diseased condition due to parasites.—**par″a-si-tol′o-gy** (-sī-tol′ọ-ji), *n.* [See -*logy*.] The branch of science that treats of parasites.

par-a-sol (par′ạ-sol), *n.* [F. *parasol*, < It. *parasole*, < *parare*, ward off (see *parry*), + *sole*, < L. *sol*, sun.] A woman's small or light sun-umbrella; a sunshade.

pa-ras-ti-chy (pạ-ras′ti-ki), *n.*; pl. -*chies* (-kiz). [Gr. παρά, beside, + στίχος, row.] In *bot.*, in a spiral arrangement of leaves, scales, etc., where the internodes are short and the members closely crowded, as in the houseleek and the pine-cone, one of a number of secondary spirals or oblique ranks seen to wind around the stem or axis to the right and left, more or less concealing the genetic spiral.

par-a-syn-the-sis (par-ạ-sin′the-sis), *n.* [NL., < Gr. παρασύνθεσις, < παρά, beside, + σύνθεσις, composition, E. *synthesis*.] In *philol.*, derivation from a combination of two or more elements; a process of combination and derivation in the formation of words: illustrated by *great-hearted*, derived from the combination *great heart* by means of the suffix -*ed* (not from *great* and *hearted*), *free-trader*, from *free trade*, with suffix -*er*, and in French by many verbs derived from a preposition, or prepositional prefix, and a noun (see etymologies of *abut*, *aline*, *imprison*).—**par″a-syn-thet′ic** (-thet′ik), *a.* In *philol.*, pertaining to parasynthesis.

par-a-tax-is (par-ạ-tak′sis), *n.* [NL., < Gr. παράταξις, a placing side by side, < παρατάσσειν, place side by side, < παρά, beside, + τάσσειν, arrange.] In *gram.*, the ranging of propositions or clauses one after another without connectives showing the relation between them.—**par-a-tac′tic** (-tak′tik), *a.*

par-a-thy-roid (par-ạ-thī′roid). [See *para-*.] In *anat.*: **I.** *a.* Noting or pertaining to several small glands, or oval masses of epithelioid cells, lying near or embedded in the thyroid gland. **II.** *n.* A parathyroid gland.

par-a-troop-er (par′ạ-trö-pėr), *n.* A soldier who lands from a plane by parachute. Hence, **par′a-troop,** *n.*

par-a-ty-phoid (par-ạ-tī′foid). [See *para-*.] In *pathol.*: **I.** *a.* Noting or pertaining to a fever resembling typhoid fever but usually milder. **II.** *n.* Paratyphoid fever.

par-a-vane (par′ạ-vān), *n.* [From *para-* + *vane*.] (*a*) A device (invented by Lieutenant-Commander Charles Denistoun Burney of the British Navy, and extensively used in the World War) for protecting a ship against moored mines, consisting of a steel torpedo-shaped body towed from the bow of a ship by a steel towing-rope, the body being fitted with a plane, fins, and a rudder or rudders, which keep it at some distance from the ship and at the proper depth: used in pairs, one paravane on each side of the ship, the steel towing-ropes thus forming a taut V-shaped barrier which, when it comes in contact with the mooring-cable of a mine, deflects it toward one of the paravanes, which are fitted with sharp-toothed jaws by which the cable is cut, causing the mine to rise to the surface at a safe distance from the ship, where it is exploded or sunk by gun-fire. Also called *otter-gear* and *otter*. (*b*) An explosive form of this device, used in the World War, and towed from the stern of a vessel, usually one on each quarter, for attacking and destroying submerged submarines.

par-boil (pär′boil), *v. t.* [OF. *parbouillir*, < LL. *perbullire*, < L. *per*, through, + *bullire*, E. *boil*².] To boil thoroughly†; also, to boil partially, or for a short time. Also fig.

par-buck-le (pär′buk-l), *n.* [Earlier *parbunkel*; origin unknown.] A kind of purchase for raising or lowering a cask or similar object along an inclined plane or a vertical surface, consisting of a rope looped over a post or the like, with its two ends passing around the object to be moved; also, a kind of double sling made with a rope, as around a cask to be raised or lowered.—**par′buck-le,** *v. t.*; -*led*, -*ling*. To raise or lower with a parbuckle.

Parbuckle.—above, in 1st sense; *a*, in 2d sense.

Par-cæ (pär′sē), *n. pl.* [L., pl. of *Parca*.] In *Rom. myth.*, the Fates. See *fate*, *n.*

par-cel (pär′sẹl), *n.* [OF. F. *parcelle*, < ML. *particella*, dim. of L. *particula*, E. *particle*.] A part or portion of anything (chiefly archaic: cf. *part and parcel*, under *part*, *n.*); specif., a piece (of land, etc.); also, an item†, particular†, or detail† (as, "I sent your grace The *parcels* and particulars of our grief": Shakspere's "2 Henry IV.," iv. 2. 36); also, a number, group, or assemblage of persons or things (as, "This youthful *parcel* Of noble bachelors," Shakspere's "All's Well," ii. 3. 58: now prov., or as in next); contemptuously, a set, lot, or pack (as, "a *parcel* of sneaks," Thackeray's "Newcomes," xvii.; a *parcel* of lies); also, a quantity of something, as of a commodity for sale; a lot; also, a quantity of something wrapped or put up together; a package or bundle.—**parcel post,** a branch of a postal service charged with conveying parcels. Also called *parcels post.*—**par′cel,** *v. t.*; *-celed* or *-celled, -celing* or *-celling.* To divide into or distribute in parcels or portions (usually with *out*: as, "The pastures were *parcelled* out in divisions by new wire-fences," Bulwer-Lytton's "Caxtons," v. 1); also, to make into a parcel, or put up in parcels, as goods; *naut.*, to cover or wrap (a rope, etc.) with strips of canvas.—**par′cel. I.** *adv.* In part; partly; partially: as, "My grandame . . . is *parcel* blind by age" (Scott's "Kenilworth," x.). [Chiefly archaic.] **II.** *a.* Being in part, or to some extent (what is specified): as, "He was a jester and a *parcel* poet" (Scott's "Abbot," iv.). [Archaic.]—**par′cel=gilt,** *a.* Gilded in part, as on the inner surface only, as a silver cup or bowl.—**par′cel-ing, par′cel-ling,** *n.* *Naut.*, the process of covering or wrapping a rope, etc., with strips of canvas, usually tarred; also, strips of canvas for such use.

Parceling.

par-ce-na-ry (pär′sẹ-nā-ri), *n.* [AF. *parcenarie,* OF. *parçonerie,* < *parçonier*: see *parcener.*] In *law,* joint heirship.

par-ce-ner (pär′sẹ-nėr), *n.* [AF. *parcener,* OF. *parçonier,* < L. *partitio(n-),* E. *partition.*] In *law,* a joint heir; a coheir.

parch (pärch), *v.* [ME. *parchen, perchen*; origin uncertain.] **I.** *tr.* To dry (peas, beans, grain, etc.) by exposure to heat that expels moisture without burning; sometimes, to roast (as, "I made up the fire and *parched* an ear of maize for my dinner": W. H. Hudson's "Green Mansions," x.); also, to make dry, esp. to excess, or dry up, as heat, the sun, or a hot wind does (as, the sun's torrid rays *parch* the ground or the vegetation); scorch; make (a person, the lips, throat, etc.) dry and hot, or thirsty, as heat, fever, or thirst does; sometimes, of cold, etc., to dry or shrivel, like heat (archaic: as, "The *parching* air Burns frore, and cold performs the effect of fire," Milton's "Paradise Lost," ii. 594). **II.** *intr.* To become parched; undergo drying by heat; dry (*up*: as, "There is a fresh sweet growth of grass in the spring, but it . . . *parches* up in the course of the summer," Irving's "Captain Bonneville," iv.); suffer from heat or thirst (as, "We were better *parch* in Afric sun": Shakspere's "Troilus and Cressida," i. 3. 370).—**parched,** *p. a.* Dried by heat; roasted; also, dried up; scorched; also, dry or thirsty, as from heat.—**parch′ed-ness,** *n.*

par-che-si (pär-chē′si or -zi), *n.* See *pachisi.*

parch-ment (pärch′mẹnt), *n.* [OF. F. *parchemin,* < LL. *pergamena,* parchment, < *Pergamum,* the city of Pergamum in Mysia, Asia Minor, whence parchment was brought.] The skin of sheep, goats, etc., prepared for use as a writing-material, etc.; also, a manuscript or document on such material (as, "a *parchment* with the seal of Cæsar," Shakspere's "Julius Cæsar," iii. 2. 133; "I once requested your hands as witnesses to a certain *parchment,*" Congreve's "Way of the World," v.); also, a paper resembling this material; also, a skin or membrane resembling it; the husk of the coffee-bean.—**parch′ment-ize** (-īz), *v. t.*; *-ized, -izing.* To convert into parchment; render parchment-like.—**parch″ment-i-za′tion** (-i-zā′shọn), *n.*—**parch′ment-y,** *a.* Parchment-like.

pard (pärd), *n.* [L. *pardus,* < Gr. πάρδος, earlier πάρδαλις; of Eastern origin.] A leopard or panther: as, "A soldier, Full of strange oaths, and bearded like the *pard*" (Shakspere's "As You Like It," ii. 7. 150); "freckled like a *pard*" (Keats's "Lamia," i.). [Archaic.]

par-di, par-die (pär-dē′), *interj.* [OF. *par de,* 'by God.'] A form of oath formerly much used for emphasis, with the force of 'verily,' 'indeed.' [Archaic.]

par-don (pär′dọn), *v. t.* [OF. *pardoner* (F. *pardonner*), < ML. *perdonare,* < L. *per,* through, + *donare,* give: see *donate.*] To remit (a penalty, etc.)†; also, to remit the penalty of (an offense: as, "Provoke him not; for he will not *pardon* your transgressions," Ex. xxiii. 21); release (a person) from liability for an offense (as, "As you from crimes would *pardon'd* be, Let your indulgence set me free": Shakspere's "Tempest," Epilogue, 19); also, to make courteous allowance for, or excuse, as an action or circumstance, or a person (as, "if . . . you will *pardon* my negligence," Marryat's "King's Own," xlvii.; "Those . . . will easily *pardon* the length of my discourse," Addison, in "Spectator," 321; *pardon* me, a phrase much used in making apology, often in expressing dissent or objection).—**par′don,** *n.* A pardoning; a remission of penalty, as by an executive, or a warrant containing it; forgiveness of an offense or offender; an ecclesiastical indulgence; a church festival at which indulgences are granted; courteous indulgence or allowance, as in excusing fault or seeming rudeness (as, I beg your *pardon,* a conventional form of apology, as for something done or said, often used in expressing dissent or objection, interrupting a person, addressing a stranger, or requesting that a remark be repeated or explained).—**par′don-a-ble,** *a.* That may be pardoned: as, "It gives me a feeling of *pardonable* importance" (G. W. Curtis's "Prue and I," ii.); "I dare say your daughter is *pardonable*" (Jane Porter's "Thaddeus of Warsaw," xxxvi.).—**par′don-a-ble-ness,** *n.*—**par′don-a-bly,** *adv.*—**par′don-er,** *n.* One who pardons; also, formerly, an ecclesiastical official charged with the granting of indulgences (as, "A gentil *Pardoner* . . . That streight was comen fro the court of Rome": Chaucer's "Prologue to the Canterbury Tales," 669).

par-dy (pär-dē′), *interj.* See *pardi.*

pare (pãr), *v. t.*; *pared, paring.* [OF. F. *parer,* prepare, dress, trim, also adorn, < L. *parare,* make ready, prepare: cf. *parure, parade, parry, prepare,* and *apparatus.*] To cut off the outer coating, layer, or part of (as, to *pare* potatoes; to *pare* a horse's hoofs; to *pare* one's nails); trim by cutting; cut off the turf or vegetation from (the ground: as, to *pare* worn-out grassland); also, to reduce by or as if by cutting or shaving; diminish little by little (as, to *pare* down one's expenses); also, to remove (an outer coating, layer, or part) by cutting (often with *off* or *away*); remove as if by cutting (as, to *pare* away redundancies).

pa-re-cious (pa-rē′shus), etc. See *parœcious,* etc.

par-e-gor-ic (par-ẹ-gor′ik). [LL. *paregoricus,* < Gr. παρηγορικός, < παρήγορος, consoling, soothing, < παρά, beside, + -αγορος, akin to ἀγορεύειν, speak.] **I.** *a.* In *med.*, assuaging pain; soothing. **II.** *n.* A soothing medicine; an anodyne; esp., a camphorated tincture of opium.

pa-rei-a-sau-ri-an (pạ-rī-ạ-sâ′ri-ạn). [NL. *Pareiasauria,* pl., < Gr. παρειά, cheek, + σαῦρος, lizard.] **I.** *a.* Belonging or pertaining to the *Pareiasauria,* an order or group of extinct, heavily built reptiles of which the genus *Pareiasaurus* is the type, known by remains found in South Africa and elsewhere. **II.** *n.* One of the *Pareiasauria.*

Pareiasaurian (*Pareiasaurus baini*).

pa-rei-ra (pạ-rā′rạ), *n.* [Pg. *parreira,* vine.] Orig., a tropical climbing plant, *Cissampelos pareira,* or its medicinal root; now, the root of a South American vine, *Chondrodendron tomentosum,* used as a diuretic, etc.—**pa-rei′ra bra′va** (brä′vạ). [Pg. *parreira brava,* wild vine.] Same as *pareira.*

pa-ren-chy-ma (pạ-reng′ki-mạ), *n.* [NL., < Gr. παρέγχυμα, < παρεγχεῖν, pour in beside, < παρά, beside, + ἐν, in, + χεῖν, pour.] In *anat.* and *zoöl.*, the proper tissue of an animal organ as distinguished from its connective or supporting tissue; also, a soft, jelly-like connective tissue, as in the flatworms; also, the undifferentiated cell-substance in a protozoan; in *bot.*, the fundamental (soft) cellular tissue of plants, as in the softer parts of leaves, the pulp of fruits, the pith of stems, etc.—**pa-ren′chy-mal, par-en-chym-a-tous** (par-eng-kim′ạ-tus), *a.* Pertaining to or of the nature of parenchyma.

par-ent (pãr′ẹnt). [OF. F. *parent*, parent, relative, < L. *parens* (*parent-*), parent, < *parere*, bring forth.] **I.** *n.* A father or a mother; by extension, a progenitor; also, any organism that produces or generates another; in fig. use, an author or source (as, "These are thy glorious works, *Parent* of good," Milton's "Paradise Lost," v. 153; "Idleness . . . is the *parent* of vice," H. Melville's "Omoo," xlix.); a protector or guardian. **II.** *a.* Being a parent; having the relation of a parent, or, fig., of a source, or a protector or guardian; also, of or pertaining to a parent.—**par′ent-age** (-ẹn-tāj), *n.* [OF. F. *parentage.*] Derivation from parents; birth, lineage, or family; origin; also, the parental condition or relation.—**pa-ren-tal** (pạ-ren′tạl), *a.* [L. *parentalis.*] Of or pertaining to a parent (as, "the *parental* relation," Cooper's "Two Admirals," x.; "I fled from *parental* tyranny," Peacock's "Nightmare Abbey," xv.); proper to or characteristic of a parent (as, "*parental* feelings": Marryat's "King's Own," ii.); also, having the relation of a parent.

Par-en-ta-li-a (par-ẹn-tā′li-ạ̈), *n. pl.* [L., neut. pl. of *parentalis*, E. *parental.*] Among the ancient Romans, an annual festival in honor of deceased parents and relatives, held from the 13th to the 21st of February, and marked by the closing of the temples, the visiting of tombs, and the offering of oblations to the shades of the dead.

pa-ren-tal-ly (pạ-ren′tạl-i), *adv.* In a parental manner; as or like a parent.

pa-ren-the-sis (pạ-ren′the-sis), *n.*; pl. *-theses* (-the-sēz). [ML., < Gr. παρένθεσις, < παρεντιθέναι, put in beside, < παρά, beside, + ἐν, in, + τιθέναι, set, put.] A qualifying or explanatory word, phrase, sentence, etc., inserted, within the curved lines ( ), or brackets, dashes, or commas, in a passage to which it is not grammatically necessary; also, either or both of the curved lines so used; also, in fig. use, an interval.—**pa-ren′the-size** (-sīz), *v. t.*; *-sized, -sizing.* To insert as or in a parenthesis; put between marks of parenthesis; also, to interlard with parentheses.

par-en-thet-ic (par-ẹn-thet′ik), *a.* Of, pertaining to, or of the nature of a parenthesis; also, characterized by the use of parentheses. Also **par-en-thet′i-cal.—par-en-thet′i-cal-ly,** *adv.*

par-ent-hood (pãr′ẹnt-hůd), *n.* The position or relation of a parent: as, "the holy dignity of *parenthood*" (Miss Mulock's "John Halifax," xxv.).

par-ent-less (pãr′ẹnt-les), *a.* Without parents (as, "He was my own uncle . . . he had taken me when a *parentless* infant to his house": C. Brontë's "Jane Eyre," ii.); sometimes, without known parents, author, or source.

par-er (pãr′ėr), *n.* One who pares; an instrument for paring (as, an apple-*parer*).

par-e-sis (par′e-sis, often pạ-rē′sis), *n.* [NL., < Gr. πάρεσις, < παριέναι, let go, relax, < παρά, from, + ἱέναι, send.] In *pathol.*, incomplete paralysis, affecting motion but not sensation; also, a progressive cerebral disease, general paralysis (see under *paralysis*).

par-es-the-sia (par-es-thē′ziạ̈), etc. See *paræsthesia*, etc.

pa-ret-ic (pạ-ret′ik). **I.** *a.* Pertaining to or affected with paresis. **II.** *n.* One who has paresis.

par-fait (pär-fā), *n.* [F., lit. 'perfect.'] A frozen preparation of cream, variously flavored: as, a vanilla *parfait*; a café (coffee) *parfait.*

par-fi-lage (pär-fē-läzh), *n.* [F., < *parfiler*, unravel.] The unraveling of textile fabrics, galloons, etc., esp. those containing gold or silver threads, in vogue as a pastime in France and elsewhere in the latter part of the 18th century.

par-fleche (pär-flesh′), *n.* [Appar. Canadian F., from N. Amer. Ind.] A hide, esp. of a buffalo, deprived of hair by soaking in water mixed with wood-ashes, and then stretched on a frame and dried; an article made of such a hide.

par-get (pär′jet), *v. t.*; *-geted, -geting.* [Appar. < OF. *pargeter* (recorded in sense of 'cast or send forth'), for *pourgeter*, rough-cast, parget, lit. 'cast forward or forth' (F. *projeter*), < L. *pro*, before, + *jactare*, throw: cf. *jet*[1].] To cover with plaster or parget; decorate with plaster-work: as, "a room otherwise so handsome, with . . . the *pargeted* ceiling with pendants, and the carved chimney" (Stevenson's "Master of Ballantrae," ii.).—**par′get,** *n.* Plaster; plaster-work, esp. of an ornamental kind.—**par′get-ing,** *n.* The act of one who pargets; also, plaster or plaster-work, esp. when ornamental; parget.

Pargeting, at Wyvenhoe, Essex, England.

par-he-li-on (pär-hē′li-ọn), *n.*; pl. *-lia* (-li-ạ̈). [NL. *parhelion*, for L. *parelion*, < Gr. παρήλιον, παρήλιος, < παρά, beside, + ἥλιος, sun.] A bright circular spot on a solar halo; a mock sun: usually one of two or more such spots seen on opposite sides of the sun, and often accompanied by additional luminous arcs and bands. See cut below. Cf. *paraselene.*—**par-he-li′a-cal** (-hẹ-lī′ạ-kạl), **par-hel′ic** (-hel′ik), *a.*

Pa-ri-ah (pā′ri-ạ̈ or pä′ri-ạ̈), *n.* [Tamil *paraiyan* (pl. *paraiyar*), lit. 'drummer' (from a hereditary duty of the caste), < *parai*, a festival drum.] A member of a low caste in southern India; hence [*l. c.*], any person or animal generally despised, or an outcast (as, "the juvenile *pariah* of the village, Huckleberry Finn, son of the town drunkard": Mark Twain's "Tom Sawyer," vi.).

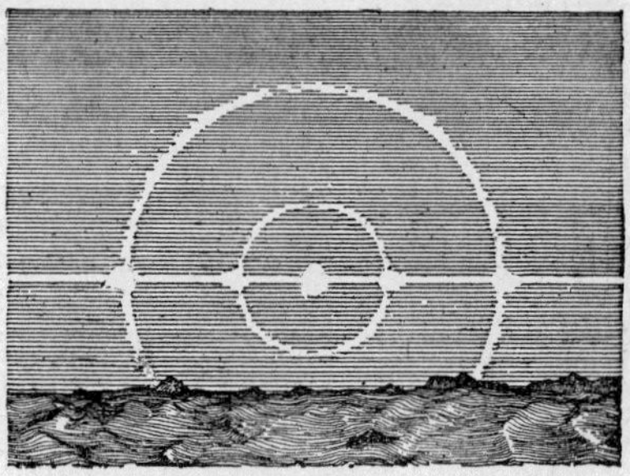
Parhelia.

Pa-ri-an (pā′ri-ạn). **I.** *a.* Of or pertaining to Paros, an island in the Ægean Sea noted for its white marble; also, noting or pertaining to a fine variety of porcelain resembling this marble. **II.** *n.* A native or inhabitant of Paros; also, Parian porcelain.

pa-ri-a-sau-ri-an (pạ-rī-ạ-sâ′ri-ạn), *a.* and *n.* See *pareiasaurian.*

pa-ri-es (pā′ri-ēz), *n.*; pl. *parietes* (pạ-rī′ẹ-tēz). [L., a wall.] In *biol.*, a wall, as of a hollow organ; an investing part: usually in *pl.*

pa-ri-e-tal (pạ-rī′ẹ-tạl). [LL. *parietalis*, < L. *paries*, a wall.] **I.** *a.* Of or pertaining to a wall; also, pertaining to, or having authority over, those within the walls or buildings of a college (U. S.: as, a *parietal* board); in *biol.*, of or pertaining to parietes or structural walls; in *anat.*, noting or pertaining to a pair of bones forming part of the top and sides of the skull. **II.** *n.* In *anat.*, a parietal bone.

pa-ril-lin (pạ-ril′in), *n.* [From (*sarsa*)*parilla.*] In *chem.*, a bitter, white crystalline principle obtained from the root of sarsaparilla, etc.

pa-ri mu-tuel (pȧ-rē mü-tüel); pl. *paris mutuels* (pȧ-rē mü-tüel). [F., 'mutual bet.'] A form of betting, as on horse-races, in which those who bet on the winners divide the bets or stakes, less a small percentage for the managers.

par-ing (pãr′ing), *n.* The act of one who or that which pares; also, a piece or part pared off; the rind or outermost crust.

par-i-pin-nate (par-i-pin′āt), *a.* [L. *par* (gen. *paris*), equal, + *pinna*, E. *pinna.*] In *bot.*, evenly pinnate; pinnate without an odd terminal leaflet.

Par-is (par′is) **dai′sy.** [From *Paris*, capital of France.] See under *daisy.*—**Par′is green.** An emerald-green pigment prepared from arsenic trioxide and acetate of copper, now used chiefly as an insecticide.

par-ish (par′ish). [OF. *paroche*, *parosse* (F. *paroisse*), < LL. *parochia*, for *parœcia*, < Gr. παροικία, a sojourning, an ecclesiastical district, < πάροικος, dwelling beside, < παρά, beside, + οἶκος, house.] **I.** *n.* An ecclesiastical district, having its own church and clergyman; a local church with its field of activity; also, a civil district or administrative division; in Louisiana, a county; also, the people of a parish (ecclesiastical or civil). **II.** *a.* Of or pertaining to a parish; parochial: as, "the *parish* church, known as the auld kirk"

(Barrie's "Auld Licht Idylls," ii.).—**pa-rish-ion-er** (pa-rish′-on-ėr), *n.* [Extended form of earlier *parishion, parishen*, < OF. *parochien, paroissien* (F. *paroissien*).] One of the community or inhabitants of a parish: as, "The church . . . was not large enough to hold all the *parishioners* of a parish which stretched over distant villages and hamlets" (George Eliot's "Felix Holt," iii.).

Pa-ri-sian (pa-riz′ian). [F. *parisien*, masc., *parisienne*, fem.] **I.** *a.* Of or pertaining to Paris, France. **II.** *n.* A native or inhabitant of Paris.

par-i-syl-lab-ic (par″i-si-lab′ik), *a.* [L. *par* (gen. *paris*), equal, + *syllaba*, syllable.] Having the same number of syllables, as a noun throughout its declensional forms.

par-i-ty[1] (par′i-ti), *n.* [LL. *paritas*, < L. *par*, equal.] Equality, as in amount, status, or character; equivalence; correspondence; similarity or analogy; in *finance*, equivalence in value in the currency of another country; also, equivalence in value at a fixed ratio between moneys of different metals.

par-i-ty[2] (par′i-ti), *n.* [L. *parere*, bring forth.] In *obstet.*, the condition or fact of having borne offspring.

park (pärk), *n.* [OF. F. *parc*; from Teut., and akin to G. *pferch*, fold, pen, and AS. *pearroc*, inclosure, E. *parrock, paddock*[2].] An inclosed tract of land privileged for wild beasts of the chase (Eng.); a considerable extent of land forming the grounds of a country-house (as, "the turrets of an ancient chateau rising out of the trees of its walled *park*": Irving's "Tales of a Traveler," i. 3); a tract of land set apart for recreation, sports, etc. (as, a baseball *park*); a tract of land set apart, as by a city or a nation, for the benefit of the public (as, Hyde *Park* in London; Central *Park* in New York City; Yellowstone National *Park* in Wyoming, Montana, and Idaho; Yosemite National *Park* in California); also, a high plateau-like valley (western U. S.); also, an inclosure for oyster-breeding; also, the space occupied by the assembled guns, wagons, animals, stores, etc., of a body of soldiers, or the assemblage formed; hence, a complete equipment, as of guns, tools, etc.; also, a space where vehicles, esp. automobiles, may be assembled or stationed, or the assembled vehicles themselves.—**park,** *v. t.* To inclose in or as in a park; also, to assemble (artillery, etc.) in compact arrangement; also, to station or leave (vehicles, esp. automobiles) in a park or reserved space; let (an automobile, etc.) stand for a time in a particular place, as on the street.

par-ka (pär′kạ), *n.* [Russ.] A fur coat, cut like a shirt, worn in northeastern Asia and in Alaska.

park-ing (pär′king), *n.* The act of one who parks something; esp., the act of leaving an automobile, etc., for a time in a reserved space or in any particular place; also, ground for or like a park; turf, with or without trees, in the middle or along the side of a street.

park-way (pärk′wā), *n.* A broad thoroughfare with spaces planted with grass, trees, etc.

parl, parle (pärl), *v. i.*; *parled, parling.* [OF. F. *parler*, < ML. *parabolare*, speak, talk, < L. *parabola*: see *parable*.] To speak; talk; parley. [Archaic or prov.]—**parl, parle,** *n.* Talk; discussion; parley. [Archaic or prov.]

par-lance (pär′lans), *n.* [OF. *parlance*, < *parler*, speak, E. *parl.*] Speech, talk, or parley (archaic); now, commonly, way of speaking, or language (as, " 'I'm satisfied where we be, Si,' said Mrs. Lapham, recurring to the *parlance* of her youth," Howells's "Rise of Silas Lapham," ii.; "In common *parlance*, she was inclined to hang about him," J. Conrad's "Rover," xiv.).

par-lan-do (pär-län′dō), *a.* [It., gerund of *parlare*, speak, = E. *parl.*] In *music*, rendered in a speaking or declamatory style; sometimes, noting an emphasized or leading voice-part or melody as distinguished from accompanying parts. Also **par-lan′te** (-tā).

parle, *v.* and *n.* See *parl.*

par-ley (pär′li), *v.*; *-leyed, -leying.* [Appar. a later form, beside *parl*, < OF. F. *parler*: see *parl.*] **I.** *intr.* To speak, talk, or confer (archaic: as, "The housemaids *parley* at the gate, The scullions on the stair," Holmes's "Agnes," iii.); now, commonly, to discuss terms; hold a parley with an opponent; specif., to hold an informal conference with an enemy, under a truce, as between active hostilities (as, "We . . . offered a truce to *parley*": Defoe's "Robinson Crusoe," ii. 11). **II.** *tr.* To speak (a language, etc.).—**par′ley,** *n.*; pl. *-leys* (-liz). Speech, talk, or discussion (as, "Mrs. Reed . . . thrust me back and locked me in, without further *parley*": C. Brontë's "Jane Eyre," ii.); also, a conference for discussing terms, or matters in dispute; specif., an informal conference with an enemy, under a truce, as concerning an exchange of prisoners or a cessation of hostilities (as, "Alva held no *parley* with rebels before a battle, nor gave quarter afterwards": Motley's "Dutch Republic," iii. 4).

par-lia-ment (pär′li-ment), *n.* [OF. F. *parlement*, < *parler*, speak, E. *parl.*] A conference†; also, a meeting or assembly for conference on public or national affairs; also, a legislative assembly or body; esp. [usually *cap.*], the legislature of Great Britain, the assembly of the three estates, composed of lords spiritual and lords temporal (forming together the House of Lords), and representatives of the counties, cities, boroughs, and universities (forming the House of Commons); also, the legislature of a self-governing British dominion or colony; also [*l. c.*], formerly, in France, a high court of justice.—**par″lia-men-ta′ri-an** (-men-tā′-ri-an), *n.* One skilled in parliamentary procedure or debate; also [*cap.*], in *Eng. hist.*, a partizan of the Parliament in opposition to Charles I.—**par-lia-men′ta-rism** (-ta-rizm), *n.* The parliamentary system of government.—**par-lia-men′-ta-rize** (-rīz), *v. t.*; *-rized, -rizing.* To render (a government) parliamentary; subject to the control of a parliament.—**par-lia-men″ta-ri-za′tion** (-ri-zā′shon), *n.*—**par-lia-men′ta-ry** (-ri), *a.* Of or pertaining to a parliament (as, *parliamentary* authority); enacted or established by a parliament (as, *parliamentary* statutes); characterized by the existence of a parliament (as, a *parliamentary* form of government); of the nature of a parliament (as, a *parliamentary* body); also, in accordance with the rules and usages of parliaments or deliberative bodies (as, *parliamentary* procedure); often, of language, etc., such as is allowed in legislative or deliberative bodies; hence, such as is permitted in polite discussion or speech, or civil or courteous (as, "The nomination-day was a great epoch of successful trickery, or, to speak in a more *parliamentary* manner, of war-stratagem": George Eliot's "Felix Holt," xxx.).

par-lor (pär′lor). [OF. *parleor* (F. *parloir*), < *parler*, speak, E. *parl.*] **I.** *n.* A room set apart for conversation or social intercourse; a sitting-room, reception-room, or drawing-room; also, a room more or less elegantly fitted up for the reception of business patrons or customers (U. S.: as, a tonsorial *parlor*). **II.** *a.* Pertaining to or characteristic of a parlor; esp., of socialists, radicals, etc., belonging to a class who advocate their views and proposed policies as if from the comfortable and safe remoteness of the parlor rather than from a situation of practical contact with the matters involved; of socialism, etc., such as is characteristic of this class of persons.—**par′lor=board′er,** *n.* A pupil in a boarding-school who lives with the principal's family and has privileges not granted to the ordinary pupils.—**par′lor=car,** *n.* A railroad passenger-car for day travel, fitted up more luxuriously than the ordinary cars.—**par′lor=maid,** *n.* A maid-servant employed to take care of a parlor, sitting-room, or the like, or perform other duties.—**par′lor=match,** *n.* A friction-match containing little or no sulphur.

par′lour, *n.* British preferred form of *parlor.*

par-lous (pär′lus). [Var. of *perilous.*] **I.** *a.* Perilous or dangerous (as, "Thou art in a *parlous* state, shepherd": Shakspere's "As You Like It," iii. 2. 45); hence, 'terrible,' 'awful,' or very great (as, a *parlous* deal of nonsense); also, clever or shrewd (as, "A *parlous* boy: go to, you are too shrewd": Shakspere's "Richard III.," ii. 4. 35). [Archaic or prov.] **II.** *adv.* 'Terribly'; 'awfully'; excessively: as, "You look *parlous* handsome when you smile" (Whyte-Melville's "Katerfelto," xxvi.). [Archaic or prov.]—**par′-lous-ly,** *adv.*

Par-me-san (pär-mē-zan′), *a.* Of or pertaining to the city, the province, or the former duchy of Parma in northern Italy: esp. applied to a hard, dry, fine-flavored variety of skim-milk cheese.

Par-nas-sian (pär-nas′ian). **I.** *a.* Pertaining to Parnassus, or to poetry; also, noting or pertaining to a school of French poets, of the latter half of the 19th century, characterized esp. by emphasis of form and by repression of emotion (so called from "Le Parnasse Contemporain," the title of their first collection of poems, published in 1866). **II.** *n.* A poet; also, a member of the Parnassian school of French poets.—**Par-nas′sian-ism,** *n.*

Par-nas-sus (pär-nas′us), *n.* [L. *Parnassus, Parnasus,* < Gr. Παρνασός, later Παρνασσός.] A mountain in central Greece, anciently sacred to Apollo and the Muses; the fabled mountain of poets, whose summit is their goal: sometimes used as a title for a collection of poems.

pa-ro-chi-al (pa̤-rō′ki-a̤l), *a.* [OF. *parochial,* < ML. *parochialis,* < LL. *parochia*: see *parish.*] Of or pertaining to a parish or parishes, ecclesiastical or civil (as, *parochial* clergy; a *parochial* school; *parochial* relief of the poor); hence, confined to or interested only in one's own parish, or some particular narrow district or field (as, "some pride or ambition, big or small, imperial or *parochial*," Kinglake's "Eothen," xvii.; too *parochial* in his ideas).—**pa-ro′chi-al-ism,** *n.* Parochial character, spirit, or tendency; narrowness of interests or view.—**pa-ro′chi-al-ize** (-īz), *v.*; *-ized, -izing.* **I.** *tr.* To render parochial. **II.** *intr.* To do parish work: as, "I must *parochialise* a bit" (Mrs. H. Ward's "Robert Elsmere," xiv.).—**pa-ro″chi-al-i-za′tion** (-i-zā′-sho̤n), *n.*—**pa-ro′chi-al-ly,** *adv.*

par-o-di-a-ble (par′o̤-di-a̤-bl), *a.* That may be parodied.

pa-rod-ic (pa-rod′ik), *a.* [Gr. παρῳδικός.] Pertaining to or of the nature of a parody. Also **pa-rod′i-cal.**

par-o-dist (par′o̤-dist), *n.* The author of a parody.—**par-o-dis′tic,** *a.*

par-o-dy (par′o̤-di), *n.*; pl. *-dies* (-diz). [L. *parodia,* < Gr. παρῳδία, < παρά, beside, + ἀείδειν, sing.] A humorous imitation of a serious piece of literature or writing (as, "satiric poems, full of *parodies*; that is, of verses patch'd up from great poets, and turn'd into another sense than their author intended them": Dryden's "Discourse concerning Satire"); the kind of literary composition represented by such imitations; sometimes, a burlesque imitation of a musical composition; also, fig., a poor imitation of something, or a travesty (as, "its old pavilion, a little wooden *parody* of the temple of Vesta at Tibur": H. G. Wells's "Tono-Bungay," i. 1. § 3).—**par′o-dy,** *v. t.*; *-died, -dying.* To turn into parody, or imitate in a parody (as, "All these peculiarities [of Johnson's literary style] have been imitated by his admirers and *parodied* by his assailants": Macaulay's "Essays," Boswell's Johnson); imitate (a composition, etc.) in such a way as to ridicule; also, to imitate in a way that is no better than a parody (as, "Behind him, strangely deformed and ink-black upon the frosty ground, the creature's shadow repeated and *parodied* his swift gesticulations": Stevenson's "Master of Ballantrae," xii.); imitate poorly or feebly.

pa-rœ-cious (pa-rē′shus), *a.* [Gr. πάροικος, dwelling beside, < παρά, beside, + οἶκος, house.] In *bot.,* having the male and female reproductive organs beside or near each other, as certain mosses.—**pa-rœ′cism** (-sizm), *n.*

pa-rœ-mi-og-ra-pher (pa-rē-mi-og′ra̤-fėr), *n.* [Gr. παροιμία, proverb, + γράφειν, write.] A writer or compiler of proverbs.—**pa-rœ-mi-og′ra-phy,** *n.*

pa-rol (pa̤-rōl′ or par′o̤l). [=*parole.*] In *law*: **I.** *n.* Word of mouth; oral statement; also, the pleadings in a suit. **II.** *a.* Oral; not written; also, not under seal.

pa-role (pa̤-rōl′), *n.* [OF. F. *parole,* < ML. *paraula,* for *parabola*: see *parable.*] Word of honor given or pledged; specif., *milit.,* the promise of a prisoner of war to refrain from trying to escape, or, if released, to return to custody or to forbear taking up arms against his captors (as, "If . . . I had given a *parole,* then I should have been an infamous wretch had I dreamed of escaping. But no *parole* had been asked of me": Conan Doyle's "Exploits of Brigadier Gerard," iii.); also, *milit.,* the password given to officers and inspectors of the guard.—**pa-role′,** *v. t.*; *-roled, -roling.* To put on parole; set at liberty in consideration of some promise given.

par-on-o-ma-sia (par″on-o̤-mā′zia̤), *n.* [L., < Gr. παρονομασία, < παρά, beside, + ὀνομάζειν, name, call, < ὄνομα, name.] In *rhet.,* a playing on words; punning; a pun.—**par″on-o-mas′tic** (-mas′tik), *a.*—**par″on-o-mas′ti-cal-ly,** *adv.*

par-o-nych-i-a (par-o̤-nik′i-a̤), *n.* [L., < Gr. παρωνυχία, < παρά, beside, + ὄνυξ (ὀνυχ-), nail.] In *pathol.,* an inflammation about the nail; a whitlow.—**par-o-nych′i-al,** *a.*

par-o-nym (par′o̤-nim), *n.* [F. *paronyme,* < Gr. παρώνυμος, derivative, < παρά, beside, + ὄνυμα, name.] A word derived from or related to another word; a derivative or cognate word; also, the form in one language for a word in another, as English *canal* for Latin *canalis.*—**pa-ron-y-mous** (pa-ron′-i-mus), *a.* [Gr. παρώνυμος.] Having the same derivation, as words; allied in origin; also, derived from a word in another language with little or no change in form.—**pa-ron′y-my** (-mi), *n.* Paronymous character; also, the transference of a word from one language to another with little or no change in form.

par-o-quet (par′o̤-ket), *n.* Same as *parrakeet.*

par-o-rex-i-a (par-o̤-rek′si-a̤), *n.* [NL., < Gr. παρά, beside, + ὄρεξις, appetite.] In *pathol.,* perversion of the appetite.

pa-ros-mi-a (pa-ros′mi-a̤ or pa-roz′-), *n.* [NL., < Gr. παρά, beside, + ὀσμή, smell.] In *pathol.,* perversion of the sense of smell.

pa-rot-ic (pa-rot′ik), *a.* [Gr. παρά, beside, + οὖς (ὠτ-), ear.] In *anat.* and *zoöl.,* situated about or near the ear.

pa-rot-id (pa-rot′id). [L. *parotis* (*parotid-*), < Gr. παρωτίς (παρωτιδ-), < παρά, beside, + οὖς (ὠτ-), ear.] In *anat.*: **I.** *n.* Either of two saliva-producing glands situated one in front of each ear. **II.** *a.* Noting, pertaining to, or situated near either parotid.—**pa-rot-i-di′tis** (-i-dī′tis), *n.* [NL.] In *pathol.,* inflammation of the parotid gland; mumps. Also **par-o-ti-tis** (par-o̤-tī′tis).—**pa-ro′toid** (-rō′toid). In *zoöl.*: **I.** *a.* Resembling a parotid gland: applied esp. to certain cutaneous glands forming warty masses or excrescences near the ear in certain batrachians, as toads. **II.** *n.* A parotoid gland.

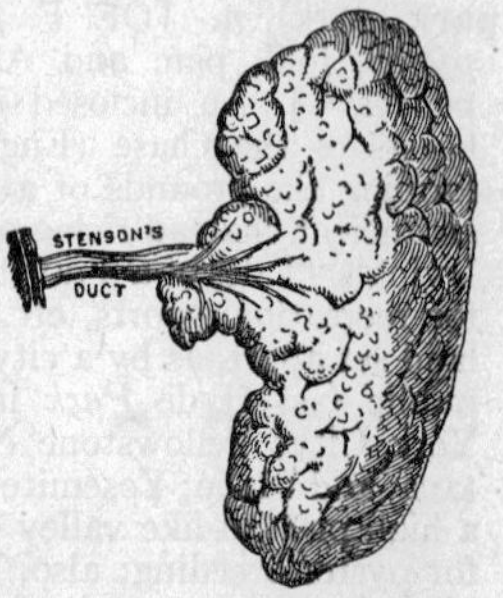

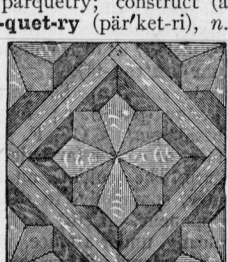

Parotid, or Parotid Gland, with Stenson's (or Steno's) Duct, opening into the mouth.

-parous. [L. *-parus,* fem. *-para,* < *parere,* bring forth.] An adjective termination meaning 'bringing forth,' 'bearing,' 'producing,' as in *biparous, oviparous, pupiparous, viviparous.*

par-ox-ysm (par′o̤k-sizm), *n.* [F. *paroxysme,* < ML. *paroxysmus,* < Gr. παροξυσμός, < παροξύνειν, stimulate, aggravate, < παρά, beside, beyond, + ὀξύνειν, sharpen, < ὀξύς, sharp.] A severe temporary attack, or increase in violence, of a disease, usually recurring periodically; hence, any sudden, violent outburst (as, "As I grew older, my feelings remained equally acute, and I was easily transported into *paroxysms* of pleasure or rage": Irving's "Tales of a Traveler," i. 9); a fit of violent action or emotion; a convulsion.—**par-ox-ys-mal, par-ox-ys-mic** (par-o̤k-siz′ma̤l, -mik), *a.*—**par-ox-ys′mal-ly,** *adv.*

par-ox-y-tone (par-ok′si-tōn). [Gr. παροξύτονος, < παρά, beside, + ὀξύτονος, E. *oxytone.*] In *gram.*: **I.** *a.* Having an acute accent on the next to the last syllable. **II.** *n.* A paroxytone word.

par-quet (pär-ket′ or -kā′), *n.* [F., part of a park, inclosure, flooring, dim. of *parc,* E. *park.*] The division of the main floor of a theater, etc., immediately behind the (musicians') orchestra and extending to the parterre or rear division, or comprising the entire floor space for spectators; also, a floor of parquetry.—**parquet circle,** a space with curving tiers of seats behind and around the parquet of a theater, etc.—**par-quet′,** *v. t.*; *-quetted* (-ket′ed) or *-queted* (-ket′ed or -kād′), *-quetting* (-ket′ing) or *-queting* (-ket′ing or -kā′ing). To furnish with a floor, etc., of parquetry; construct (a flooring, etc.) of parquetry.—**par-quet-ry** (pär′ket-ri), *n.* [F. *parqueterie.*] Mosaic work of wood used for floors, wainscoting, etc.

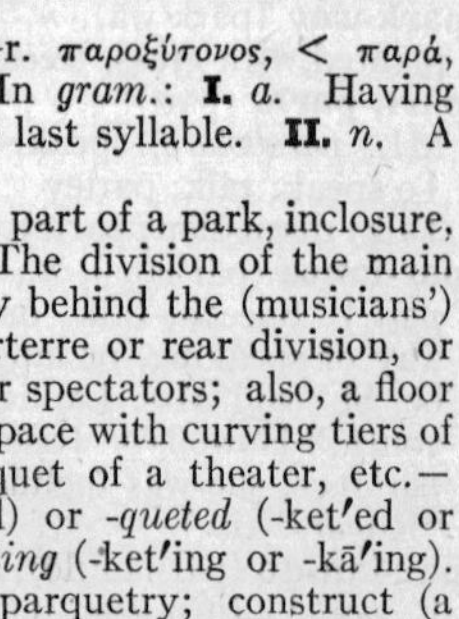
Parquetry.

parr, par² (pär), *n.* [Origin obscure.] A young salmon, having dark cross-bars on its sides, in the stage before it descends to the sea or becomes a smolt.

par-ra-keet (par′a̤-kēt), *n.* [OF. *paroquet* (F. *perroquet*), < It. *parrocchetto,* appar. dim. of *parroco,* parish priest, parson: cf. Sp. *peri-*

quito, perico.] A parrot, esp. a small one, or any of certain undersized, slender, long-tailed species.

par-rel, par-ral (par′e̤l, -a̤l), *n.* [For *apparel.*] *Naut.*, a sliding ring or collar of rope or iron, which confines a yard to the mast but allows of a vertical movement.

Carolina Parrakeet (*Conurus carolinensis*).

par-ri-cide (par′i-sīd), *n.* [L. *parricida, parricidium*, appar. < *pater*, father: see *-cide*, and cf. *patricide.*] One who kills his father, or either parent, or any one to whom he owes reverence; also, the act or crime of such killing.—**par′ri-ci-dal** (-sī-da̤l), *a.*

par-ri-er (par′i-ėr), *n.* One who parries.

par-rock (par′o̤k), *n.* [AS. *pearroc*: cf. *park.*] A small field or inclosure; a paddock. [Prov. Eng. and Sc.]

par-rot (par′o̤t), *n.* [Origin uncertain: cf. F. *Perrot, Pierrot*, dim. of *Pierre*, Peter, also E. *parrakeet.*] Broadly, any of the hook-billed, mostly tropical, often gaily-colored birds which constitute the order *Psittaci*, as the cockatoo, lory, macaw, and parrakeet; esp., any of certain larger old-world species with fleshy tongue and short, square tail, many of which are taught to articulate words; fig., a person who unintelligently repeats the words or imitates the actions of another.—**par′rot,** *v. t.* To repeat or imitate like a parrot; also, to teach to repeat or imitate thus.—**par′rot-er,** *n.*—**par′rot=fish,** *n.* Any of various marine fishes so called on account of their coloring or the shape of their jaws, as the species, mainly tropical, constituting the family *Scaridæ*, or certain species of the family *Labridæ*, esp. *Labrichthys psittacula* of Australasia and *Halichœres radiatus* of Florida.—**par′rot-ry** (-ri), *n.* Parroting; unintelligent repetition or imitation.

Gray Parrot (*Psittacus erithacus*), of Africa, common in domestication.

par-ry (par′i), *v.*; *-ried, -rying.* [Prob. < F. *parez*, impv. of *parer*, < It. *parare*, ward off, also dress, adorn, protect, < L. *parare*, make ready, prepare: cf. *pare.*] **I.** *tr.* To ward off (a thrust, stroke, weapon, etc.), as in fencing (as, "The Moor rushed upon Don Alonzo with his scimetar; but the latter was on the alert, and *parried* his blow": Irving's "Conquest of Granada," xvi.); in general, to turn aside, evade, or avoid (as, "He was wholly at a loss . . . how to *parry* her searching questions": W. Churchill's "Coniston," ii. 6). **II.** *intr.* To parry a thrust, etc.—**par′ry,** *n.*; pl. *parries* (-iz). An act or mode of parrying, as in fencing; a defensive movement or procedure.

parse (pärs, Brit. also pärz), *v. t.*; *parsed, parsing.* [L. *pars*, part, as in *pars orationis*, part of speech.] To describe (a word) grammatically, telling the part of speech, inflectional form, syntactic relations, etc.; analyze (a sentence, etc.) grammatically.

par-sec (pär′sek), *n.* [From *par*(*allax*) + *sec*(*ond*)².] In *astron.*, a unit of distance corresponding to a heliocentric parallax of one second of arc, being equal to about 206,000 times the distance of the earth from the sun (or about 3¼ light-years).

Par-see, Par-si (pär′sē or pär-sē′), *n.*; pl. *-sees, -sis* (-sēz). [Pers. and Hind. *Pārsī*, a Persian.] One of a Zoroastrian sect in India, descendants of the Persians who settled in India in the 8th century to escape Mohammedan persecution. See *Zoroastrian, n.*—**Par′see-ism, Par′si-ism,** *n.* The religion of the Parsees.

pars-er (pär′sėr), *n.* One who parses.

par-si-mo-ni-ous (pär-si-mō′ni-us), *a.* Characterized by or showing parsimony; sparing or frugal, esp. to excess.—**par-si-mo′ni-ous-ly,** *adv.*—**par-si-mo′ni-ous-ness,** *n.*

par-si-mo-ny (pär′si-mo̤-ni), *n.* [L. *parsimonia, parcimonia*, < *parcere*, spare.] Sparingness in the use or expenditure of means; esp., extreme or excessive economy or frugality; niggardliness.

pars-ley (pärs′li), *n.* [OF. *peresil* (F. *persil*), < L. *petroselinum*, < Gr. πετροσέλινον, < πέτρος, stone, + σέλινον, parsley.] An apiaceous garden herb, *Petroselinum petroselinum*, with aromatic leaves which are much used to garnish or season food; also, any of certain allied or similar plants.

pars-nip (pärs′nip), *n.* [ME. *pasnepe* (with modification due to ME. *nepe*, turnip, E. *neep*), < OF. *pasnaie* (F. *panais*), < L. *pastinaca*, parsnip.] An apiaceous plant, *Pastinaca sativa*, the cultivated varieties of which have a large whitish edible root; also, the root.

par-son (pär′so̤n or -sn), *n.* [OF. *persone*, parson, person, < ML. *persona*, parson, L. person: see *person.*] The holder or incumbent of a parochial benefice (as, "A *parson* . . . is one that hath full possession of all the rights of a parochial church . . . He is sometimes called the rector . . . of the church": Blackstone's "Commentaries," I. 384); in general, a clergyman, minister, or preacher (chiefly colloq.).—**par′son-age** (-ā̤j), *n.* [OF. *personnage.*] The benefice of a parson (obs. or legal); also, the residence of a parson or clergyman, as provided by the parish or church.—**par′son=bird,** *n.* A honey-eating bird, *Prosthemadera novæ-zealandiæ*, of New Zealand, having the plumage chiefly black with a tuft of white feathers at each side of the throat, and valued as a cage-bird for its song and its powers of mimicry.—**par′son-ess,** *n.* The wife of a parson.—**par-son′ic, par-son′i-cal** (-son′ik, -i-ka̤l), *a.* Of, like, or befitting a parson: as, "in these days of increased *parsonic* pretensions" (Mrs. H. Ward's "Robert Elsmere," iv.); "in a grey *parsonical* suit, on whose black kerseymere vest a little gold cross dangled" (Galsworthy's "Saint's Progress," i. 1).—**par-son′i-cal-ly,** *adv.*

Parson-bird.

part (pärt), *n.* [OF. F. *part*, < L. *pars* (*part-*), piece, portion, share, rôle, region, party.] A portion or division of a whole, separate in reality, or in thought only; a piece, fragment, fraction, or section; a constituent; often, an essential or integral portion (as, "The . . . rider sate as if he had been a *part* of the horse which he bestrode": Scott's "Black Dwarf," vi.); also, a portion, member, or organ of an animal body; also, one of the voices or instruments in harmonized music, or the melody or score for it; also, each of a number of equal portions composing a whole (as, a third *part*, or one third; the work is two *parts*, or nine *parts*, done, that is, two thirds, or nine tenths, done, such phrases implying that the number of parts stated is one less than the number composing the whole); an aliquot part or exact divisor; a partial fraction (see under *partial*); also, an allotted portion; a share; hence, participation, interest, or concern in something; also, one's share in some action; a duty, function, or office (as, "Accuse not nature; she hath done her *part*, Do thou but thine": Milton's

"Paradise Lost," viii. 561); also, a character sustained in a play or in real life (as, "All the world's a stage . . . And one man in his time plays many *parts*," Shakspere's "As You Like It," ii. 7. 142; "A *part* remained for him to play, which must be played with tact," Mrs. H. Ward's "Robert Elsmere," xxix.); a rôle; the words or lines assigned to an actor in such a character; also, a personal or mental quality or endowment (usually in *pl.*: as, "an exact description of my person and *parts*," Swift's "Gulliver's Travels," ii. 2; "The girl's *parts* are not despicable, and her education has not been neglected," Smollett's "Humphry Clinker," April 17; a man of good *parts*, or a man of *parts*, a man of intelligence or ability); also, a region, quarter, or district (chiefly in *pl.*: as, in foreign *parts*; a custom unknown in these *parts*); also, one of the sides to a contest, question, agreement, etc., or the cause or interest it represents (as, "What strength can help him, or what art, Or which of all the Gods be on his *part?*" W. Morris's "Jason," viii. 90; the party of the first *part* to a contract); also, the dividing line formed in parting the hair.—**for my (his,** etc.) **part,** so far as concerns me (him, etc.): as, "*For my* own *part*, I was indifferent which it might be" (Conan Doyle's "Exploits of Brigadier Gerard," v.).—**for the most part,** as concerns the greatest part; mostly: as, the attempts were *for the most part* unsuccessful.—**in good part,** with favor; without offense: as, "She took the appellation *in good part*" (Hawthorne's "Blithedale Romance," ii.).—**in ill part,** with displeasure or offense: as, he took the criticism *in ill part*.—**in part,** in some measure or degree; to some extent; partly: as, "For we know *in part*, and we prophesy *in part*" (1 Cor. xiii. 9). —**on the part of one,** or **on one's part,** as regards one's share in the matter; as far as one is concerned: as, "Foul distrust, and breach Disloyal *on the part of man*" (Milton's "Paradise Lost," ix. 7); there is no objection *on his part*. —**part and parcel,** an essential part; something forming an essential portion of a whole: as, "Every individual is *part and parcel* of a great picture of the society in which he lives and acts" (Mrs. Stowe's "Oldtown Folks," i.).—**part of speech,** in *gram.*, one of the kinds of words, classed according to their function or relations in a sentence, recognized as the constituents of speech: comprising the noun, adjective, pronoun, verb, adverb, preposition, conjunction, interjection, and article, the last being often classed with the adjective.—**principal parts.** See under *principal*, *a.*—**to take part,** to participate.—**to take part with,** to range one's self on the side of; side with: as, to *take part with* one party against another.—**to take the part of one,** or **to take one's part,** to espouse one's side or cause; support one; back one up: as, to *take the part of a person*; "Fear God, and *take your* own *part*" (Borrow's "Romany Rye," xvi.).—**part,** *adv.* In part; partly; in some measure: as, "He spoke in words *part* heard, in whispers *part*" (Tennyson's "Merlin and Vivien," 837).—**part,** *v.* [OF. F. *partir*, < L. *partire*, *partiri* (pp. *partitus*), < *pars*.] **I.** *tr.* To divide (a thing) into parts; break; cleave; divide; specif., to comb (the hair) away from a dividing line (as, "He went into good society sometimes, with . . . his hair *parted* in the middle!": Du Maurier's "Trilby," iii.); also, to dissolve (a connection, etc.) by separation of the parts, persons, or things involved (as, "She *parted* company with her sisters . . . and came up to London": S. Butler's "Way of All Flesh," xxxii.); also, to divide into shares; distribute in parts; apportion; also, to put or keep asunder (two or more parts, persons, etc., or one part, person, etc., from another); draw or hold apart; disunite; separate; also, to leave† or quit† (as, "Presently your souls must *part* your bodies": Shakspere's "Richard II.," iii. 1. 3). **II.** *intr.* To be or become divided into parts, break, or cleave (as, "The frigate *parted* amidships": Marryat's "King's Own," liv.); also, to go or come apart or asunder, or separate, as two or more things (as, "Her lips grew pale, *Parted*, and quivered": Shelley's "Revolt of Islam," i. 18); go apart from each other or one another, as persons (as, "We met to *part* no more": Tennyson's "Edwin Morris," 70); also, to be or become separated from something else (as, "Even thought meets thought ere from the lips it *part*": Pope's "Eloisa to Abelard," 95); also, to go away or depart (as, "But now he *parted* hence, to embark for Milan": Shakspere's "Two Gentlemen of Verona," i. 1. 71); sometimes, to die (see Shakspere's "Henry V.," ii. 3. 12).—**to part from,** to separate from, go away from, or leave (as, "This ring I gave him when he *parted from* me": Shakspere's "Two Gentlemen of Verona," iv. 4. 102); also, to part with (now rare: as, "This ring; Which when you *part from*, lose, or give away, Let it presage the ruin of your love," Shakspere's "Merchant of Venice," iii. 2. 174).—**to part with,** to part from (now rare: as, "How *parted* he *with* thee?" Shakspere's "As You Like It," iii. 2. 235); also, to give up, relinquish, or let go (as, "O, that I should *part with* so much gold!" Marlowe's "Jew of Malta," iv.).

par-take (pạr-tāk′ or pär-), *v.*; pret. *-took*, pp. *-taken*, ppr. *-taking*. [Back-formation from *partaking*, *partaker*, for *part-taking*, *part-taker*.] **I.** *intr.* To take or have a part or share in common with others (as, "Thou hast provided all things: but with me I see not who *partakes* . . . who can enjoy alone?" Milton's "Paradise Lost," viii. 364); participate (*in*); receive or have a share (*of*: as, "I come in for my share . . . and *partake* of many gifts of fortune and power that I was never born to," Addison, in "Tatler," 117); hence, to take a portion of something, esp. by eating or drinking (as, to *partake* of refreshments); also, fig., to have something of the nature or character (*of*: as, feelings *partaking* of both pleasure and regret; "Mr. Travers made an inarticulate noise *partaking* of a groan and a grunt," J. Conrad's "Rescue," v. 1). **II.** *tr.* To take or have a part in, or share (as, "The soul *partakes* the season's youth": Lowell's "Vision of Sir Launfal," i., Prelude); also, to impart† or communicate† (as, "Your exultation *Partake* to every one": Shakspere's "Winter's Tale," v. 3. 132).—**par-tak′er** (-tā′kėr), *n.*

par-tan (pär′tạn), *n.* [Gael.] A crab. [Sc.]

part-ed (pär′ted), *p. a.* Divided into parts; cleft; combed away from a dividing line, as the hair; also, put or kept apart; separated; also, departed (archaic); deceased (archaic); also, furnished with or having parts, or personal or mental qualities or endowments, as specified†; in *bot.*, of a leaf, separated into rather distinct portions by incisions which extend nearly to the midrib or the base; in *her.*, party, as a shield.

part-er (pär′tėr), *n.* One who or that which parts.

par-terre (pär-tãr′), *n.* [F., < *par* (< L. *per*), by, on, + *terre* (< L. *terra*), earth.] An ornamental arrangement of flower-beds of different shapes and sizes (as, "They [gardens of Damascus] are not the formal *parterres* which you might expect from the Oriental taste": Kinglake's "Eothen," xxvii.); also, a division of the main floor of a theater, etc., behind the (spectators') orchestra or under the galleries.

par-the-no-gen-e-sis (pär″the-nọ-jen′e-sis), *n.* [Gr. παρθένος, virgin, + γένεσις, genesis.] In *biol.*, reproduction from an ovum or ovule without fecundation by the male element, as in case of many insects, etc.—**par″the-no-ge-net′ic** (-jẹ-net′ik), *a.*—**par″the-no-ge-net′i-cal-ly,** *adv.*

Par-the-non (pär′the-non or -nọn), *n.* [L., < Gr. Παρθενών, < παρθένος, virgin (Ἀθήνη Παρθένος, Athene the Virgin).] The temple of Athene on the Acropolis of Athens, completed (structurally) about 438 B.C.: regarded as the finest example of Doric architecture.

Par-thi-an (pär′thi-ạn). **I.** *a.* Pertaining to Parthia, an ancient kingdom of western Asia southeast of the Caspian Sea, or to its inhabitants; of a kind attributed to or associated with the Parthians (as, "The Moors kept up a *Parthian* retreat; several times they turned to make

Parthenon, from the southwest.

battle," Irving's "Conquest of Granada," xvi.; a *Parthian* shot, a shot sent back at an adversary by one fleeing or pretending to flee, and hence, fig., any sharp parting remark or the like). **II.** *n.* A native or inhabitant of Parthia.

par-ti (pär-tē), *n.* [F., part, party, match: see *party*¹.] A person considered as a matrimonial match: as, "A girl in our society accepts the best *parti* which offers itself" (Thackeray's "Newcomes," xxx.).

par-tial (pär′shạl), *a.* [OF. *parcial* (F. *partial*), < ML. *partialis*, < L. *pars* (*part-*), E. *part*, *n.*] Pertaining to or affecting a part, or being such in part only (as, a *partial* eclipse of the sun; *partial* blindness; "He . . . gained many *partial* successes," De Quincey's "Revolt of the Tartars"); not total or general; incomplete; also, being a part; component or constituent; also, inclined to favor one party or side more than another, as in a controversy; biased in judgment; lacking dispassionate fairness; also, biased or prejudiced in favor of a person or thing (as, a *partial* parent or friend); fond; particularly inclined in fondness or liking (*to*: as, "Our English friend was by no means *partial* to us," Parkman's "Oregon Trail," viii.; "The lovely daughter asked him if he was *partial* to boiled chicken," Mallock's "New Republic," iii. 2); in *bot.*, secondary or subordinate (as, a *partial* umbel).—**partial fraction,** in *alg.*, one of the fractions into which a given fraction can be resolved, the sum of such simpler fractions being equal to the given fraction.—**partial tone** (in *music*). See *tone*, *n.*—**par-ti-al-i-ty** (pär-shi-al′i-ti), *n.*; pl. *-ties* (-tiz). The state or character of being partial; the favoring of one party or side more than another; favorable bias or prejudice (as, "Either I am blinded by the *partiality* of a parent, or he is a boy of a very amiable character": Smollett's "Humphry Clinker," Oct. 11); a particular fondness or liking (as, "He had always shown a *partiality* for my society": H. Melville's "Typee," iv.).—**par′tial-ly,** *adv.*—**par′tial-ness,** *n.*

par-ti-ble (pär′ti-bl), *a.* [LL. *partibilis*.] That may be parted or divided; divisible.—**par-ti-bil′i-ty** (-bil′i-ti), *n.*

par-ti-ci-pant (pạr-tis′i-pạnt or pär-). **I.** *a.* Participating; sharing. **II.** *n.* One who participates; a participator.

par-ti-ci-pate (pạr-tis′i-pāt or pär-), *v.*; *-pated*, *-pating*. [L. *participatus*, pp. of *participare*, < *particeps*, partaking, < *pars*, part, + *capere*, take.] **I.** *tr.* To take or have a part or share in; share: as, "When I am glowing with the enthusiasm of success, there will be none to *participate* my joy" (Mrs. Shelley's "Frankenstein," letter ii.). **II.** *intr.* To take or have a part or share, as with others; share (*in*: as, to *participate* in profits, advantages, danger, or sorrow); take part (*in*: as, to *participate* in a performance, attempt, or crime).—**par-ti-ci-pa′tion** (-pā′shọn), *n.* [LL. *participatio*(*n-*).] The act or fact of participating; a sharing, as in benefits or profits; a taking part, as in some action or attempt.—**par-ti′ci-pa-tive** (-pạ-tiv), *a.* Participating; characterized by participation.—**par-ti′ci-pa-tive-ly,** *adv.* —**par-ti′ci-pa-tor** (-pā-tọr), *n.*—**par-ti′ci-pa-to-ry** (-pạ-tọ-ri), *a.* Participative.

par-ti-cip-i-al (pär-ti-sip′i-ạl), *a.* [L. *participialis*.] Of or pertaining to a participle; of the nature of a participle, or being a participle in origin and form (as, a *participial* adjective, such as the adjectives in 'a *masked* man,' '*running* water,' 'a *sunken* ship').—**par-ti-cip′i-al-ly,** *adv.*

par-ti-ci-ple (pär′ti-si-pl), *n.* [OF. *participle* (F. *participe*), < L. *participium*, < *particeps*, partaking: see *participate*.] In *gram.*, a word partaking of the nature of both a verb and an adjective; a word forming a part of a verb, and having also the value of an adjective: in English, ending in *-ing*, as *cheering*, *shining* ('present participle'), or in *-ed*, *-d*, *-t*, *-en*, *-n*, etc., as *blunted*, *laid*, *burnt*, *beaten*, *mown* ('past participle' or 'passive participle').

par-ti-cle (pär′ti-kl), *n.* [L. *particula*, dim. of *pars* (*part-*), E. *part*, *n.*] A minute portion or piece of a material substance (as, a *particle* of dust; "an opaque stone, with *particles* of mica glittering on its surface," Hawthorne's "Twice-Told Tales," The Great Carbuncle); a very small bit; an atom; hence, a very small portion or amount of something immaterial (as, he has not a *particle* of pride; if you have the least *particle* of doubt, say so); also, a clause or article, as of a document; in the *Rom. Cath. Ch.*, a little piece or fragment of the host; also, the small host given to each lay communicant; in *gram.*, a minor part of speech, as a conjunction, a preposition, or a monosyllabic adverb; also, a prefix or a suffix; in *mech.*, a portion of matter so minute that, while it possesses mass, it may be treated as a geometrical point.

par-ti=col-ored (pär′ti-kul″ọrd), *a.* See *party-colored*.

par-tic-u-lar (pạr-tik′ụ̄-lạr). [OF. *particuler* (F. *particulier*), < L. *particularis*, < *particula*, E. *particle*.] **I.** *a.* Pertaining to or affecting a part†, or partial†; hence, pertaining to some one person, thing, group, class, occasion, etc., rather than to others or all (as, one's *particular* duty or interests; the *particular* advantages of this plan; "They long to . . . take the diversions of the metropolis, which they are not allowed to do without a *particular* licence from the King," Swift's "Gulliver's Travels," iii. 2); special; not general; also, belonging characteristically, or peculiar (as, the *particular* properties of a plant); also, personal† or private† (as, "these domestic and *particular* broils": Shakspere's "King Lear," v. 1. 30); also, being a definite one, individual, or single, or considered separately (as, take any *particular* instance; *particular* members raised objections; each *particular* part or item); also, distinguished or different from others or from the ordinary (as, "There was nothing at all *particular* about the knocker on the door, except that it was very large": Dickens's "Christmas Carol," i.); noteworthy, marked, or unusual; exceptional or especial (as, to take *particular* pains; of no *particular* use; "This was a *particular* satisfaction to us," Defoe's "Captain Singleton," vi.); being such in an exceptional degree (as, he is a *particular* friend of mine; a *particular* favorite in his circle); also, dealing with or giving details, as an account, description, etc., or a person; detailed, minute, or circumstantial; also, attentive to or exacting about details or small points (as, to be *particular* about one's work, food, or dress; "People . . . that were not *particular* as to morals, used to go out to visit them," Mrs. Stowe's "Oldtown Folks," vi.); careful; fastidious; scrupulous; also, pointedly or devotedly attentive, as to a person† (as, "I must tell you, in confidence, he was a little *particular*; but perhaps I mistake his complaisance": Smollett's "Humphry Clinker," May 31); in *logic*, not general; not referring to the whole extent of a class, but only to some individual or individuals in it (as, a *particular* proposition); in *law*, noting an estate precedent to a future or ultimate ownership, as where lands are devised to a widow during her lifetime, and after her death to her children; also, noting the tenant of such an estate. **II.** *n.* A part or division of a whole†; now, an individual or distinct part, as an item of a list or enumeration (as, "A tapster's arithmetic may soon bring his *particulars* therein to a total": Shakspere's "Troilus and Cressida," i. 2. 124); a point, detail, or circumstance (as, a work complete in every *particular*; the *particulars* of the accident are unknown; a bare statement of fact, without *particulars*); also, a particular case or instance (chiefly in *pl.*, and as opposed to *generals*, etc.).—**in particular,** individually or severally (obs. or archaic: as, "Now ye are the body of Christ, and members *in particular*," 1 Cor. xii. 27); also, particularly or especially (as, one book *in particular*; nowhere *in particular*).

par-tic-u-lar-ism (pạr-tik′ụ̄-lạr-izm), *n.* Exclusive attention or devotion to one's own particular interests, party, etc.; also, the principle of leaving each state of a federation free to retain its own laws and promote its own interests; also, in *theol.*, the doctrine that divine grace is provided only for the elect.—**par-tic′u-lar-ist,** *n.* An advocate or adherent of particularism.—**par-tic″u-lar-is′tic,** *a.*

par-tic-u-lar-i-ty (pạr-tik-ụ̄-lar′i-ti), *n.*; pl. *-ties* (-tiz). The quality or fact of being particular; special, peculiar, or individual character; detailed, minute, or circumstantial character, as of description or statement; attentiveness to details or small points, or special carefulness (as, "She had from time to time remarked the Chichester, but never with any *particularity*": Arnold Bennett's "Hilda Lessways," iv. 2); fastidiousness; scrupulousness; also, that which is particular, a particular or characteristic feature or trait, or a peculiarity (as, "He had a great many other *particularities* in his character, which I shall not mention": Fielding's "Tom Jones," viii. 4); a detail, circumstance, or particular, as of an affair (obs. or archaic).

par-tic-u-lar-ize (pär-tik′ū-lär-īz), *v.*; *-ized*, *-izing*. **I.** *tr.* To make particular (rather than general); also, to mention or indicate particularly; specify individually; state or treat in detail. **II.** *intr.* To speak or treat particularly or specifically; mention individuals; go into detail on any subject. —**par-tic″u-lar-i-za′tion** (-i-zā′shon), *n.*

par-tic-u-lar-ly (pär-tik′ū-lär-li), *adv.* In a particular manner; specially; individually; in detail, or minutely; also, in a particular or exceptional degree, or especially (as, "I scarcely think you'd like her *particularly*": Tarkington's "Alice Adams," xii.).—**par-tic′u-lar-ness,** *n.*

par-tic-u-late (pär-tik′ū-lāt), *a.* [L. *particula*, E. *particle*.] Consisting of or pertaining to separate particles.

part-ing (pär′ting), *n.* The act of one who or that which parts; division; separation; leave-taking; departure; death; also, a place of division or separation; a dividing line made in the hair by combing; a place where a road divides into two or more roads proceeding in different directions; also, something that serves to part or separate things.—**part′ing,** *p. a.* Dividing; separating; also, departing (as, "The curfew tolls the knell of *parting* day": Gray's "Elegy," i.); dying; also, of or pertaining to parting, leave-taking, departure, or death; given, taken, done, etc., at parting (as, a *parting* shot; a *parting* injunction).—**part′ing=cup,** *n.* A drinking-cup having two handles on opposite sides, used by two persons in taking a draft of liquor at parting. —**part′ing=strip,** *n.* A strip, as of wood, used to keep two parts separated, as a long vertical strip inserted in each side of the frame of a window to keep the upper and lower sashes apart when lowered or raised.

Parting-cup. — Old English pottery.

par′ti-san¹, par′ti-san². See *partizan¹*, *partizan²*.

par-tite (pär′tīt), *a.* [L. *partitus*, pp. of *partire*, E. *part*, *v.*] Divided into parts; in *entom.*, divided to the base, as a wing; in *bot.*, same as *parted.*

par-ti-tion (pär-tish′on or pär-), *n.* [F. *partition*, < L. *partitio*(*n*-), < *partire*, E. *part*, *v.*] The act of parting, or the fact of being parted; division into parts; division into or distribution in portions or shares; separation, as of two or more things; also, something that separates; that which separates one part of a space from another; an interior wall or barrier dividing a building, inclosure, etc. (as, "an oblong space about eight yards long, divided into two unequal portions by a lath and plaster *partition*": Mrs. H. Ward's "Robert Elsmere," xv.); a septum or dissepiment, as in a plant or animal structure; also, each of the parts into which a thing is divided, as by boundaries; a part, division, or section; a compartment; a panel; an apartment; in *law*, a division of property among joint owners, esp. a division of real property held jointly; in *logic*, the separation of a whole into its integrant parts; in *math.*, a mode of separating a positive whole number into a sum of positive whole numbers. —**par-ti′tion,** *v. t.* To make partition of; divide into parts or portions; dismember and distribute; also, to divide or separate by a partition (as, "a small room . . . *partitioned* off from the main apartment": Bret Harte's "How Santa Claus Came to Simpson's Bar").—**par-ti′tion-er,** *n.*—**par-ti′tion-ment,** *n.*

par-ti-tive (pär′ti-tiv). [= F. *partitif*, < L. *partire*, E. *part*, *v.*] **I.** *a.* Serving to divide into parts; in *gram.*, expressing the relation of a part to the whole. **II.** *n.* In *gram.*, a partitive word or phrase.—**par′ti-tive-ly,** *adv.*

par-ti-zan¹, par-ti-san¹ (pär′ti-zan), *n.* [OF. *partizane* (F. *pertuisane*),< It. *partigiana*; origin uncertain.] A halberd-like weapon formerly used by foot-soldiers and others (as, "Duke Charles, followed by a part of his train, armed with *partizans* and battle-axes, entered the hall": Scott's "Quentin Durward," xxxii.); also, a soldier, attendant, etc., armed with this weapon.

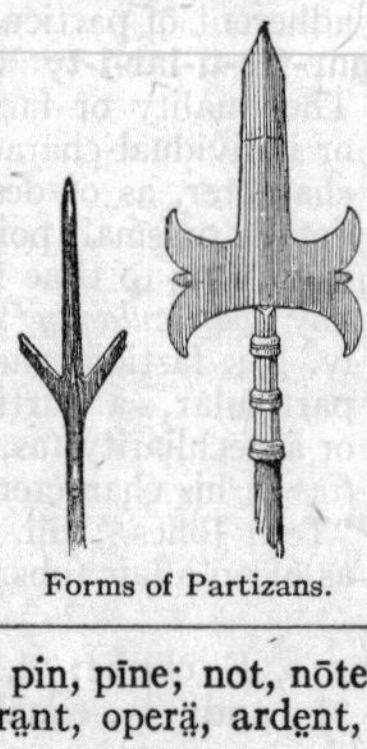

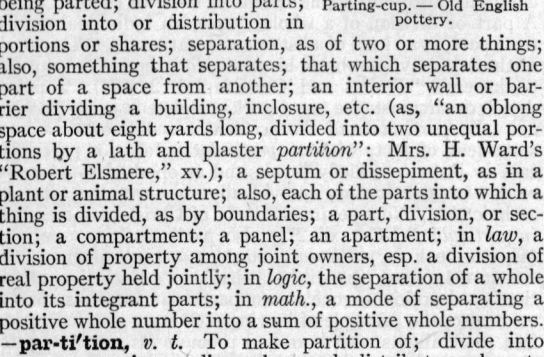

Forms of Partizans.

par-ti-zan², par-ti-san² (pär′ti-zan). [F. *partisan*, < It. *partigiano*, < L. *pars* (*part*-), E. *part*, *n.*] **I.** *n.* An adherent or supporter of a person, party, or cause, esp. a devoted or zealous supporter, and often, unfavorably, an unreasoning or fanatical one (as, "The Duke of Gloucester . . . had now placed himself at the head of the *partizans* of the war," Green's "Short Hist. of the Eng. People," vi. 1; "I became his zealous *partizan*, and contributed all I could to raise a party in his favor," B. Franklin's "Autobiography," vi.; "No one can be a right good *partisan*, who is not a thorough-going hater," Irving's "Knickerbocker's New York," iv. 8); *milit.*, a member of a party of light or irregular troops engaged in harassing the enemy; the leader of such a party; also, a guerrilla, or a guerrilla chief. **II.** *a.* Of, pertaining to, or characteristic of partizans; characteristic of or characterized by adherence to a party or cause, esp. zealous or unreasoning adherence (as, "a judgment . . . that is not a *partisan* judgment," W. Churchill's "Coniston," ii. 10; *partizan* malice); *milit.*, pertaining to or carried on by military partizans.—**par′ti-zan-ship, par′ti-san-ship,** *n.*

Part-let (pärt′let), *n.* [OF. *Pertelote*, woman's name.] A name for the hen (sometimes 'Dame Partlet'); [*l. c.*] a hen (as, "A fair, white *partlet* has torn his crest out, and he shall crow no more": Longfellow's "Hyperion," iv. 2).

part-ly (pärt′li), *adv.* In part; in some measure.

part=mu-sic (pärt′mū″zik), *n.* Music, esp. vocal music, with parts for two or more independent performers.

part-ner (pärt′nėr), *n.* [Var. of *parcener*, appar. by association with *part*.] A sharer or partaker; an associate; a husband or a wife; one's companion in a dance; a player on the same side with another in a game; in *com.*, one associated with another or others as a principal or a contributor of capital in a business or a joint adventure, usually sharing its risks and profits (as, a silent or sleeping *partner*, a partner taking no active part in the conduct of a business, or not openly announced as a partner); *pl.*, *naut.*, a framework of timber round a hole in a ship's deck, to support a mast, capstan, pump, etc.—**part′ner,** *v. t.* To associate as a partner or partners; also, to be, or act as, the partner of. —**part′ner-ship,** *n.* The state or condition of being a partner; participation; association; joint interest; in *com.*, the relation between partners in business; the contract creating this relation; an association of persons joined as partners in business; in *arith.*, same as *fellowship.*

par-took (pär-tůk′ or pär-). Preterit of *partake*.

par-tridge (pär′trij), *n.* [OF. *perdriz* (F. *perdrix*), < L. *perdix*, < Gr. πέρδιξ.] Any of various old-world gallinaceous game-birds of the genus *Perdix* and allied genera, esp. *P. cinerea* (the common 'gray partridge' of Europe); any of various similar birds, as the ruffed grouse, *Bonasa umbellus* (northeastern U. S.), or the common American quail, *Colinus virginianus* (southern U. S.); also, any of various South American tinamous. —**par′tridge=ber″ry,** *n.* An American trailing rubiaceous herb, *Mitchella repens*, having roundish evergreen leaves, fragrant white flowers, and scarlet berries (see cut on following page); also, the wintergreen, *Gaultheria procumbens.*—**par′tridge=wood,** *n.* A hard, beautifully marked wood of a reddish color, obtained from the West Indies from the tree *Vouacapoua americana* and perhaps other fabaceous trees: used for cabinet-work, walking-sticks, etc.

Common Gray Partridge (*Perdix cinerea*).

part=song (pärt′sông), *n.* A song with parts for several voices, esp. one meant to be sung without accompaniment.

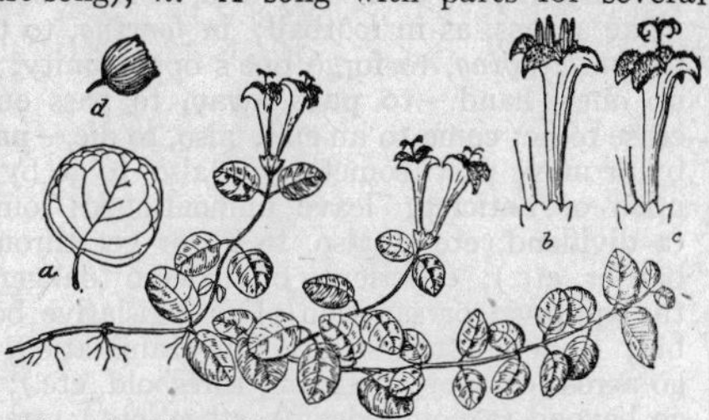

Flowering Plant of Partridge-berry (*Mitchella repens*).—*a*, a leaf, showing the nervation; *b*, a flower with long stamens; *c*, a flower with long style; *d*, the fruit.

par-tu-ri-ent (pär-tū′ri-ent), *a.* [L. *parturiens* (*-ent-*), ppr. of *parturire*, be in labor, < *parere*, bring forth.] Bringing forth or about to bring forth young; travailing; also, pertaining to parturition.—**par-tu′ri-en-cy,** *n.*

par-tu-ri-fa-cient (pär-tū-ri-fā′shent). [L. *parturire*, be in labor, + *faciens* (*facient-*), ppr. of *facere*, make.] In *med.*: **I.** *a.* Serving to promote or accelerate parturition. **II.** *n.* A parturifacient agent or medicine.

par-tu-ri-tion (pär-tū-rish′on), *n.* [LL. *parturitio*(*n-*), < L. *parturire*: see *parturient*.] The action of bringing forth young; childbirth.

par-ty[1] (pär′ti). [OF. F. *partie*, fem., *parti*, masc., < *partir*, E. *part*, *v.*] **I.** *n.*; pl. *-ties* (-tiz). A part†; also, a side or cause (obs. or rare); also, a number or body of persons ranged on one side, or united in purpose or opinion, in opposition to others, as in politics, etc. (as, the Republican *party* in U. S. politics; the Low-church *party* in the Church of England); a body of partizans; a faction; hence, the system of taking sides on public questions or the like; attachment or devotion to a side or faction; partizanship; also, a company collected or met together for some purpose; a number of persons who have come together for amusement or entertainment; a social gathering or entertainment, as of invited guests at a private house or elsewhere (as, to give a *party*); also, a detachment, as of troops, assigned to perform some particular service; also, each of the persons or bodies of persons concerned in a proceeding, as in a lawsuit or a contract; also, one who participates in some action or affair, or is concerned with it in some way (as, "Murder has been done, to which you were morally if not really a *party*," Dickens's "Oliver Twist," xlix.; "You have stained my honour by making me a *party* to your eavesdropping," G. B. Shaw's "Arms and the Man," ii.); a participator or an accessory; also, the person under consideration, or a person in general (now vulgar or humorous: as, "They were introduced to the *party* in question, a slight-made, well-looking young man," Marryat's "Mr. Midshipman Easy," xxviii.; a queer old *party*). **II.** *a.* Of or pertaining to a party or faction; partizan: as, *party* issues; *party* feeling.

par-ty[2] (pär′ti), *a.* [OF. F. *parti*, pp. of *partir*, E. *part*, *v.*] Variegated† or party-colored†; in *her.*, divided into parts, usually two parts, as of different tinctures, as a shield.

Party.

par-ty=col-ored (pär′ti-kul″ord), *a.* [See *party*[2].] Colored differently in different parts, or variegated (as, *party-colored* dress; *party-colored* flowers; a *party-colored* patch-work); wearing a dress combining various colors (as, "a *party-colored* Merry Andrew, jingling his cap and bells": Hawthorne's "Twice-Told Tales," Howe's Masquerade); fig., diversified in character, or presenting a variety of contrasting elements (as, "In a very sober mood . . . he resumed his *party-colored* narrative": Irving's "Tales of a Traveler," ii. 8).

par-ty=line (pär′ti-līn), *n.* A telephone line by which a number of subscribers are connected by one circuit with the exchange; also, the bounding line between adjoining premises.

par-ty=man (pär′ti-man), *n.*; pl. *-men.* A man belonging to a party, as in politics; often, a man who adheres strictly to the principles and policy of his party, regardless of any individual opinion.

par-ty=wall (pär′ti-wâl′), *n.* [See *party*[1].] A wall on the line between adjoining premises, in which each of the respective owners has certain rights.

par-u-la (par′ö-lä), *n.* [NL., dim. of L. *parus*, titmouse.] Any bird of the American genus *Parula* (or *Compsothlypis*), comprising small creeping warblers of variegated coloration; esp., *P. americana*, of eastern North America, with blue, golden-brown, yellow, and white coloration. Also called *parula warbler*.

pa-rure (pä-rür), *n.* [F., < *parer*, prepare, adorn: see *pare*.] A set of jewels or ornaments; sometimes, a set of articles or pieces of embroidery or lace to be worn together.

par-ve-nu (pär′ve-nū, F. pär-ve-nü). [F., prop. pp. of *parvenir*, < L. *pervenire*, arrive, < *per*, through, + *venire*, come.] **I.** *n.*; pl. *-nus* (-nūz, F. -nü). One who has risen above his class or to a position above his personal or social qualifications; an upstart: as, "She . . . is as hungry . . . for titles and big-wigs, as though she were the purest *parvenu*" (Mrs. H. Ward's "Robert Elsmere," xii.). **II.** *a.* Being or resembling a parvenu; characteristic of a parvenu. —**par-ve-nue** (pär′ve-nū, F. pär-ve-nü), *n.*; pl. *-nues* (-nūz, F. -nü). [F.] Fem. of *parvenu*.

par-vis (pär′vis), *n.* [OF. *parevis* (F. *parvis*), < LL. *paradisus*, E. *paradise*.] A vacant inclosed area in front of a church or other building, sometimes surrounded by a colonnade; hence, a colonnade or portico in front of a church, or a church porch, or (erroneously) a room over a church porch.

par-vo-line (pär′vo-lin), *n.* [L. *parvus*, small (with reference to its relatively small volatility).] In *chem.*, any of several isomeric organic bases of an oily nature, one occurring in coal-tar and another in decaying mackerel.

pas (pä), *n.* [F.: see *pace*[2].] A step or movement in dancing, or a kind of dance; also, precedence, or right of preceding (as, to take or have the *pas*; to give or yield the *pas*).

Pasch (pask), *n.* [OF. *pasche*, *pasque* (F. *pâque*), < LL. *pascha*, < Gr. πάσχα, < Heb. *pesakh*, Passover, < *pāsakh*, pass over.] The Jewish feast of the Passover; also, the Christian feast of Easter. [Archaic.]—**pas-chal** (pas′kal), *a.* [LL. *paschalis*.] Pertaining to the Passover, or to Easter. —**paschal candle,** or **paschal taper,** in the *Rom. Cath. Ch.*, a large wax candle blessed in the service of Holy Saturday (the day before Easter) and placed at the side of the altar, there to remain until Ascension Day.—**paschal controversy,** a controversy in the early church regarding the proper time for the celebration of Easter.—**paschal lamb,** among the Jews, the lamb slain and eaten at the Passover (see Ex. xii. 3–14); hence [*caps.*], Christ, of whom the lamb of the Jewish Passover is taken as a figure; also, any of various symbolical representations of Christ (cf. *Agnus Dei*).

pas-cu-al, pas-cu-ous (pas′kū-al, -us), *a.* [L. *pascuum*, pasture, < *pascere*, feed.] Pertaining to or growing in pastures.

pa-se-ar (pä-sā-är′), *n.* [Sp., inf., to walk, take a walk, < *paso*, < L. *passus*, E. *pace*[2].] A walk; a promenade; an airing: as, "'Whar's the boys?' . . . 'Gone up the cañon on a little *pasear*'" (Bret Harte's "How Santa Claus Came to Simpson's Bar"). [Southwestern U. S.]

pash[1] (pash), *v.* [Prob. imit.] **I.** *tr.* To hurl or dash; also, to smash or shatter; also, to strike with a smashing or violent blow (as, "With my armed fist I'll *pash* him o'er the face": Shakspere's "Troilus and Cressida," ii. 3. 213); dash (*out*) by a violent blow. [Now chiefly prov.] **II.** *intr.* To dash or strike violently, as waves or rain. [Now chiefly prov.]—**pash**[1], *n.* A smashing blow; also, a crashing fall; a crash. [Now prov.]

pash[2] (pash), *n.* [Origin unknown.] The head. See Shakspere's "Winter's Tale," i. 2. 128. [Now Sc.]

pash-a (pȧsh′ä or pa-shä′), *n.* [Turk. *pāshā*.] A title, placed after the name, borne by civil and military officials of high rank in Turkish dominions; also, a person bearing this title.—**pash′a-lik** (-lik), *n.* [Turk. *pāshālik*.] The jurisdiction of a pasha; the territory governed by a pasha.

Pash-to (push′tō), *n.* Same as *Pushtu*.

pa-sig-ra-phy (pa-sig′ra-fi), *n.* [Gr. πᾶσι, for all (dat. pl. of πᾶς, all), + -γραφία, < γράφειν, write.] Any of various systems of writing proposed for universal use, which employ characters representing ideas instead of words; a kind of writing that may be understood and used by all nations.—**pas-i-graph-ic, pas-i-graph-i-cal** (pas-i-graf′ik, -i-kal), *a.*

Pasque (pask), *n.* [OF.] Same as *Pasch.*

pasque=flow-er (pask′flou″ėr), *n.* [Altered (after *Pasque*) from earlier *passeflower*, < F. *passe-fleur*, < *passer*, E. *pass*, *v.*, + *fleur*, E. *flower*.] An old-world ranunculaceous plant, *Pulsatilla* (or *Anemone*) *pulsatilla*, with purple flowers having a hairy outer surface and blooming about Easter (cf. *Danes'-blood* and *pulsatilla*); also, some other plant of this genus, as an American species, *P. hirsutissima*, found from Illinois westward.

pas-quil (pas′kwil), *n.* [It. *pasquillo*.] A pasquinade: as, "The pamphlets, handbills, *pasquils*, and other popular productions were multiplied" (Motley's "Dutch Republic," ii. 5).

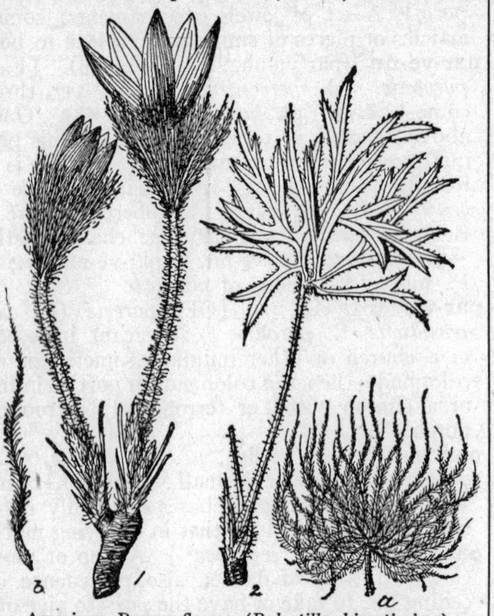

American Pasque-flower (*Pulsatilla hirsutissima*). — 1, flowering plant; 2, a leaf; *a*, the fruit; *b*, one of the nutlets with the long plumose style.

Pas-quin (pas′kwin), *n.* [It. *Pasquino*, said to be named from a man near whose house or shop the statue was found.] A mutilated statue found at Rome in 1501 and set up in a public place, on which anonymous satirical writings were posted; hence, an imaginary personage supposed to be the source of such writings; [*l. c.*] a pasquinade†.—**pas-quin-ade′** (-kwi-nād′), *n.* [F., < It. *pasquinata*.] A publicly posted satirical writing; a lampoon: as, "*Pasquinades* and pamphlets were already appearing daily, each more bitter than the other" (Motley's "Dutch Republic," ii. 4).—**pas-quin-ade′**, *v. t.*; *-aded*, *-ading*. To assail in a pasquinade or pasquinades: as, "a quondam cobbler . . . who, becoming stage-mad, had attempted the rôle of Xerxes . . . and been notoriously *pasquinaded*" (Poe's "Murders in the Rue Morgue").—**pas-quin-ad′er** (-kwi-nā′dėr), *n.*

pass (pȧs), *v. i.*; pret. *passed*, sometimes *past*, pp. *passed* or *past*, ppr. *passing*. [OF. F. *passer*, < ML. *passare*, < L. *passus*, a step: see *pace*[2].] To go, move onward, or proceed; make one's or its way; also, to go away or depart; sometimes, to die (as, "But our world is none the kinder Now Great-Heart hath *passed!*" Kipling's "Great-Heart: Theodore Roosevelt in 1919"); also, to go by or move past, as a procession; also, to elapse or be spent, as time; come to an end, as things in time (as, "realms that *pass* to rise no more": Tennyson's "To Virgil," vii.); also, to go on or take place (as, to learn what has *passed*); happen or occur; also, to go about or circulate; be current; be accepted or received (with *for* or *as*: as, "silk—or a material that *passed* for it," L. Merrick's "Conrad in Quest of His Youth," xiv.); also, to go from one to another; be transferred or conveyed (as, "Thou shalt cause the inheritance of their father to *pass* unto them": Num. xxvii. 7); be interchanged, as between two persons (as, "Sharp words *passed* between 'Miss Jo' and the old man": Bret Harte's "Romance of Madroño Hollow"); undergo transition or conversion (as, blue *passing* into green; to *pass* from a solid to a liquid state); also, to go or get through something, such as a channel or a barrier, or, fig., an investigation, test, or the like; be voided, as excrement; be ratified or enacted, as a bill or law; be successful in an examination, as a person; go unheeded, uncensured, or unchallenged (as, "It is something new . . . that a vassal should demand pledges from his sovereign; but let that *pass*": Scott's "Quentin Durward," xxx.); also, to go beyond bounds†, or go to excess†; be surpassing†, or excel†; also, to express or pronounce an opinion, judgment, verdict, etc. (usually with *on* or *upon*); also, to cause something to pass; make a pass, as in football; in *fencing*, to thrust or lunge; in *card-playing*, to forgo one's opportunity; also, to throw up one's hand.—**to pass away**, to pass out of existence; cease to be; come to an end; also, to die.—**pass**, *v. t.* To go by or move past (something); also, to go by without acting upon or noticing; leave unmentioned; omit payment of (a dividend, etc.); also, to go or get through (a channel, barrier, etc.); experience or undergo (dangers, etc.); obtain the approval or sanction of (a legislative body, etc.), as a bill; undergo successfully (an examination, etc.); also, to go across or over (a stream, threshold, etc.); cross; also, to go beyond (a point, degree, stage, etc.); transcend, exceed, or surpass; also, to cause to go, move onward, or proceed (as, to *pass* a rope about a thing); cause to go by or move past (as, to *pass* troops in review); also, to spend, as time; also, to cause to go about or circulate; give currency to; cause to be accepted or received; also, to cause to go from one to another; convey, transfer, or transmit; deliver; hand over; pledge, as one's word; also, to cause or allow to go through something, as through a channel or a barrier, or an investigation, test, or the like; discharge or void, as excrement; sanction or approve (as, to *pass* accounts as correct); ratify or enact, as a bill or law; also, to express or pronounce, as an opinion or judgment; also, to perform a pass on (a pack of cards, etc.).—**to pass muster**, to undergo inspection without censure, as troops; hence, to come up to a required standard; prove acceptable.—**to pass off**, to put into circulation, or dispose of, esp. deceptively or fraudulently (as, to *pass off* a bad dollar); cause to be accepted or received in a false character (as, "He *passed* himself *off* for my servant": Malkin's tr. Le Sage's "Gil Blas," v. 1).—**to pass the buck**. See under *buck*[7].—**pass**, *n.* [In part, < *pass*, *v.*, or OF. F. *passe*, < *passer*; in part, < OF. F. *pas*, step, passage: see *pace*[2].] The act of passing; passage; the passing of an examination, test, or the like; in a university, etc., the passing of an examination, but without honors; also, a causing to pass; a thrust or lunge, as in fencing; a sally of wit† (see Shakspere's "Tempest," iv. 1. 244); a passing of the hand over, along, or before anything, as by a mesmerist (as, "Alexis, after a few *passes* from Dr. Elliotson, despises pain, reads with the back of his head, sees miles off": Thackeray's "Vanity Fair," xxiii.); the transference or changing of objects by or as by sleight of hand; a manipulation, as of a juggler; a trick; the transference of a ball, etc., from one player to another, as in football; also, a permission or license to pass, or to go, come, or enter; often, a free ticket; also, a stage in procedure or experience; a particular stage or state of affairs (as, "Things have come to a pretty *pass* when such trifles are scrutinized," Motley's "Dutch Republic," ii. 9; "Things had got to a terrible *pass*," Du Maurier's "Trilby," vii.); also, a way affording passage, as through an obstructed region or any barrier (as, "They had reached one of those very narrow *passes* between two tall stones, which performed the office of a stile": George Eliot's "Adam Bede," iii.); a passage; a road or route; a navigable channel, as at the mouth or in the delta of a river; esp., a narrow passage through a mountainous region or across a mountain-range; a defile in mountains.

pass-a-ble (pȧs′a-bl), *a.* [OF. F. *passable*.] That may be passed; that may be proceeded through or over, or traversed, penetrated, crossed, etc., as a road, forest, or stream; that may be circulated, or has valid currency, as a coin; that may be ratified or enacted, as a bill; also, that can pass muster, or may be allowed to pass; admissible, tolerable, fair, or moderate (as, to have a *passable* knowledge of a subject).—**pass′a-ble-ness**, *n.*—**pass′a-bly**, *adv.* Tolerably; fairly; moderately: as, "*passably* well dressed for a provincial" (Arnold Bennett's "The Old Adam," iii.).

pas-sa-ca-glia (päs-ạ-käl′yä), *n.* [It., < Sp. *pasacalle*, < *pasar*, pass, + *calle*, street (appar. because played in the streets).] An old form of dance-tune of Spanish origin, constructed upon a recurring theme, usually a ground bass, in slow triple rhythm; also, the dance performed to this.

pas-sade (pạ-säd′), *n.* [F., < It. *passata*, < ML. *passare*, E. *pass*, *v.*] In the *manège*, a turn or course of a horse backward or forward on the same ground.

pas-sa-do (pạ-sä′dō), *n.*; pl. *-dos* or *-does* (-dōz). [It. *passata*: see *passade.*] In *fencing*, a forward thrust with the sword, one foot being advanced at the same time. See Shakspere's "Romeo and Juliet," iii. 1. 88. [Obs. or archaic.]

pas-sage[1] (pas′ạj), *v.*; *-saged, -saging.* [F. *passager, passéger*, < It. *passeggiare*, to pace, walk, < L. *passus*, E. *pace*[2].] In the *manège*: **I.** *intr.* Of a horse, to move sideways, in obedience to pressure by the rider's leg on the opposite side; of a rider, to cause a horse to do this. **II.** *tr.* To cause (a horse) to passage.—**pas′sage**[1], *n.* In the *manège*, the act of passaging.

pas-sage[2] (pas′ạj), *n.* [OF. F. *passage*, < *passer*, E. *pass, v.*] The act of passing; movement, transit, or transition, as from one place or state to another; a traveling from one place to another, esp. by sea, commonly a voyage across the sea from one port to another (as, "The Aspasia continued her *passage* with light but favourable winds," Marryat's "King's Own," xlv.; to have a rough *passage*); the privilege of conveyance as a passenger, esp. on a sea-going vessel (as, to secure *passage* for Europe); departure† or death†; lapse, as of time; progress or course, as of events; an occurrence, incident, or event (archaic: as, "Her life has lately met with *passages* very uncommon," Steele, in "Tatler," 198); an interchange of communications, confidences, etc., between persons; an exchange of blows, or an altercation or dispute (often 'a passage at arms' or 'a passage of arms'); an evacuation of the bowels; the passing into law of a legislative measure; also, the causing of something to pass; transference or transmission; also, liberty, leave, or right to pass (as, to grant, or to refuse, *passage* through a territory); also, that by which a person or thing passes; a means of passing; a way or route; an avenue; a channel; a pass; a thoroughfare for foot-passengers; a hall, corridor, or the like; also, an indefinite portion of a writing, speech, or the like, usually one of no great length; a paragraph, verse, etc. (as, a *passage* of Scripture); in *music*, a phrase or other division of a piece; also, a scale-like or arpeggio-like series of tones introduced as an embellishment; a run, roulade, or flourish.—**bird of passage.** See under *bird, n.*—**pas′sage**[2], *v. i.*; *-saged, -saging.* To make a passage; cross; pass; voyage; also, to have a passage at arms, or encounter; fence with words.—**pas′sage-way,** *n.* A way for passage, as in a building or among buildings, etc.; a passage.

pas-sant (pas′ạnt), *a.* [OF. F., ppr. of *passer*, E. *pass, v.*] Passing†; in *her.*, walking, and looking forward to the dexter side of the escutcheon (said of a beast used as a bearing).—**passant gardant,** in *her.*, walking, but with the head turned and looking out from the escutcheon.—**passant regardant,** in *her.*, walking, but with the head turned and looking backward.

pass=book (pȧs′bu̇k), *n.* A customer's book in which a merchant or trader makes entries of goods sold on credit; also, a bank-book.

pas-sé (pȧ-sā), *a.* [F., pp. of *passer*, E. *pass, v.*] Past; esp., past the prime; faded; also, antiquated, or out of date (as, "I can't conceive anything more *passé* than amateur pianoforte playing!" Mrs. H. Ward's "Robert Elsmere," xviii.).—**pas-sée** (pȧ-sā), *a.* [F.] Fem. of *passé*.

passed (pȧst), *p. a.* That has passed or has been passed; having passed an examination or test; esp., having passed an examination for promotion, and awaiting a vacancy in the senior grade (as, a *passed* assistant surgeon in the navy).—**passed ball,** in *baseball*, a pitched ball, not hit by the batsman, which the catcher fails to stop, though it is within his reach, his failure allowing a base-runner or base-runners to advance.—**passed′=mas′ter,** *n.* One who has passed as a master; an adept. Cf. *past-master.*

passe-ment (pas′mẹnt), *n.* [F., < *passer*, E. *pass, v.*] Lace (as of gold or silver), braid, or gimp for trimming. [Archaic.]—**passe′ment,** *v. t.* To trim with passement. [Archaic.]

passe-men-terie (pas-men′tri or -tẹ-ri), *n.* [F., < *passement*: see *passement.*] Trimming made of braid, cord, beads, etc., in various forms.

pas-sen-ger (pas′ẹn-jėr), *n.* [OF. *passagier* (F. *passager*), < *passage*, E. *passage*[2].] One who passes along on his way, or a wayfarer (as, "the *passengers* that pass through the land," Ezek. xxxix. 15: now chiefly in *foot-passenger*); also, one who has passage or is carried in traveling by some form of conveyance (as, *passengers* by ship, coach, or train; an aëroplane carrying a pilot and one *passenger*); also, a migratory bird (archaic or in certain bird-names: as, "It was as if a band of Italian days had come from the south, like a flock of glorious *passenger*-birds, and lighted to rest them on the cliffs of Albion," C. Brontë's "Jane Eyre," xxiii.; the *passenger* falcon, the peregrine falcon).—**pas′senger=mile,** *n.* A unit in railroad accounts, representing the transportation of one passenger for the distance of one mile.—**pas′sen-ger=pi″geon,** *n.* A wild pigeon, *Ectopistes migratorius*, formerly common in North America but now practically extinct: remarkable for great power of flight, and for extensive wanderings, in extraordinary numbers, in search of food.

Passenger-pigeon.

passe=par-tout (pas-pär-tö′), *n.* [F., lit. 'pass-everywhere.'] That which passes, or by means of which one can pass, everywhere; esp., a master-key; also, a kind of ornamental mat, or a frame with such a mat, to receive a photograph or the like; also, a picture-frame consisting of a piece of glass, under which the picture is placed, affixed to a backing by means of strips of paper or the like pasted over the edges; also, paper, etc., prepared for this purpose.

pass-er (pȧs′ėr), *n.* One that passes or causes something to pass; esp., one who passes or goes by, or a passer-by (as, "the black-robed priests, who mixed with the *passers* on the narrow wooden sidewalk": Howells's "Chance Acquaintance," iv.).—**pass′er=by′,** *n.*; pl. *passers-by.* One who passes by: as, "That cry is so common . . . that the *passers-by* never turned their heads" (Kipling's "Kim," xi.).

pas-ser-ine (pas′ẹ-rin). [L. *passerinus*, < *passer*, sparrow.] **I.** *a.* Belonging or pertaining to the *Passeres*, an order of birds, typically insessorial or perching, embracing more than half of all birds (including many song-birds), and containing the sparrows, thrushes, warblers, swallows, crows, jays, etc. (see *oscine* and *clamatorial*); also, of about the size of a sparrow (as, the *passerine* ground-dove, *Columbigallina passerina*: see cut at *ground-dove*). **II.** *n.* Any bird of the order *Passeres.*

pas-si-ble (pas′i-bl), *a.* [LL. *passibilis*, < L. *pati*, suffer.] Capable of suffering or feeling; susceptible of sensation or emotion.—**pas-si-bil′i-ty** (-bil′i-ti), *n.*

pas-si-flo-ra-ceous (pas″i-flọ-rā′shius), *a.* [NL. *Passiflora*, the typical genus, < L. *passio*, passion, + *flos* (*flor-*), flower.] Belonging to the *Passifloraceæ*, or passion-flower family of plants.

pas-sim (pas′im), *adv.* [L., < *passus*, pp. of *pandere*, spread.] Here and there, as in books or writings.

pass-ing (pȧs′ing), *n.* The act of one that passes or causes something to pass; passage; also, a means or place of passage (as, "A river Runs in three loops about her living-place; And o'er it are three *passings*": Tennyson's "Gareth and Lynette," 598); also, a gold or silver thread produced by twisting a thin, narrow band of the metal spirally about a silk thread.—**in passing,** in the course of passing, going on, or proceeding; as one proceeds, as in a narrative: as, "It may be remarked, *in passing*, that . . . " (C. Brontë's "Shirley," vi.).—**pass′ing,** *p. a.* That passes; going by; elapsing; that passes away; fleeting or transitory; that is now happening, or current; also, done, given, etc., in passing, or cursory (as, "Anne Rory, who deserves more than a *passing* mention": W. Churchill's "Modern Chronicle," i. 6); also, surpassing, preëminent, or extreme (obs. or archaic:

as, "'Tis a *passing* shame," Shakspere's "Two Gentlemen of Verona," i. 2. 17).—**pass′ing,** *adv.* Surpassingly; exceedingly; very: as, "A man he was . . . *passing* rich with forty pounds a year" (Goldsmith's "Deserted Village," 142). [Archaic.]—**pass′ing=bell,** *n.* Orig., a bell rung at the time of a person's death to summon Christians to pray for the passing soul; now, usually, a bell tolled to announce that a death has just occurred or that a funeral is taking place; fig., a portent or sign of the passing away of anything.—**pass′ing-ly,** *adv.*—**pass′ing=note,** *n.* In *music,* a note unessential to the harmony, introduced between two successive notes which are essential to it, in order to produce a melodic transition.

pas-sion (pash′ọn), *n.* [OF. F. *passion,* < L. *passio(n-),* < *pati,* suffer.] Suffering (now obs. in the general sense); the sufferings of a martyr, or martyrdom (archaic); specif. [often *cap.*], the sufferings of Christ on the cross, or his sufferings subsequent to the Last Supper; the gospel narrative of these sufferings, or a musical setting of it; a pictorial representation of Christ's sufferings; also [*l. c.*], a painful physical disorder (now only in certain phrases: as, the iliac *passion,* or ileus); also, the state or fact of being acted upon or affected by something external (opposed to *action*); a passive as opposed to an active state; also, any kind of feeling or emotion, as hope, fear, joy, grief, anger, love, desire, etc., esp. when vehement, overmastering, or of compelling force (as, "They seemed like ungoverned children inflamed with the fiercest *passions* of men": Parkman's "Oregon Trail," x.); vehement feeling or emotion (as, to sing with *passion*); often, esp., violent anger, or a fit of violent anger (as, to be wild with *passion*; "He flew into a violent *passion* and abused me mercilessly," H. G. Wells's "Tono-Bungay," iii. 1. § 4); also, strong amorous feeling or desire, or passionate sexual love, or an instance or experience of it (as, "I love thee so, that . . . Nor wit nor reason can my *passion* hide," Shakspere's "Twelfth Night," iii. 1. 164; "There was ever . . . consciousness that Time was after her, and this her last grand *passion,*" Galsworthy's "Saint's Progress," ii. 8); a person who is the object of such a feeling; also, a strong or extravagant fondness, enthusiasm, or desire for anything (as, a *passion* for books or music; "He now became troubled with the *passion* for reforming the world," Peacock's "Nightmare Abbey," ii.); the object of such a fondness or desire (as, music was his *passion*; accuracy became a *passion* with him); also, a passionate outburst (as, "She broke into a *passion* of tears and lamentations": Dickens's "Hard Times," iii. 6).—**Passion Sunday,** the fifth Sunday in Lent, being the second before Easter.—**Passion Week,** the week preceding Easter; Holy Week; sometimes, the week before Holy Week, beginning with Passion Sunday.—**pas′sion,** *v. t.* or *i.* [OF. F. *passionner.*] To affect or be affected with passion. [Chiefly poetic.]

pas-sion-al (pash′ọn-ạl). [LL. *passionalis,* adj. (as n., ML. *passionale*).] **I.** *a.* Of or pertaining to passion or the passions; due to passion (as, *passional* crimes). **II.** *n.* A book containing descriptions of the sufferings of saints and martyrs, for reading on their festivals.

pas-sion-a-ry (pash′ọn-ā-ri), *n.*; pl. *-ries* (-riz). Same as *passional, n.*

pas-sion-ate (pash′ọn-ạt), *a.* [ML. *passionatus.*] Affected with or dominated by passion or vehement emotion (as, a *passionate* advocate of a cause; "Decorous and self-poised, he was only *passionate* before the enemy," Motley's "Dutch Republic," vi. 1); characterized by, expressing, or showing vehement emotion, or impassioned (as, *passionate* language; "using the most *passionate* gestures of entreaty, affliction, and despair, even to a kind of extravagance," Defoe's "Robinson Crusoe," i. 17); vehement, as feelings or emotions (as, *passionate* grief, love, or longing); also, easily moved to passion or swayed by the passions or emotions (as, "The *passionate* heart of the poet is whirl'd into folly": Tennyson's "Maud," i. 4. 7); often, easily moved to anger, quick-tempered, or irascible (as, "My brother was *passionate,* and had often beaten me, which I took extremely amiss": B. Franklin's "Autobiography," i.); also, swayed by the passion of love†, or in love†; also, sorrowful†; also, compassionate (obs. or prov. Eng.).—**pas′sion-ate-ly,** *adv.*—**pas′sion-ate-ness,** *n.*

pas-sion=flow-er (pash′ọn-flou″ėr), *n.* Any plant of the genus *Passiflora,* which comprises climbing herbs or shrubs, mainly American, bearing showy flowers and a pulpy berry or fruit which in some species is edible: so called from a fancied resemblance or symbolical correspondence of its floral parts to the wounds, nails, crown of thorns, etc., of Christ's passion or crucifixion, the hands of his persecutors, the apostles present, etc.

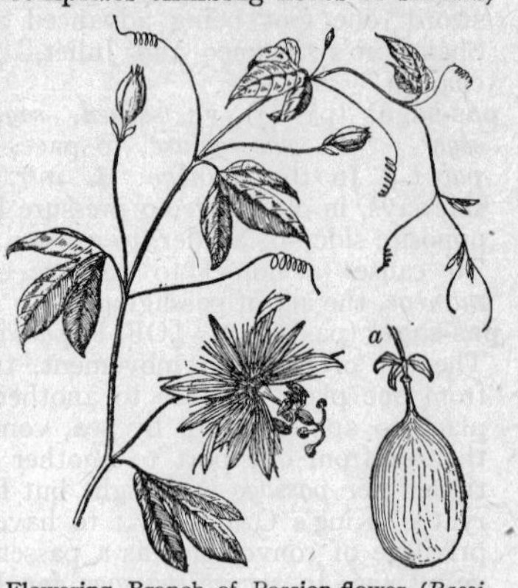

Flowering Branch of Passion-flower (*Passiflora incarnata*). — *a,* the fruit (may-pop).

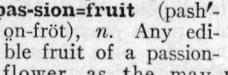

pas-sion=fruit (pash′ọn-fröt), *n.* Any edible fruit of a passion-flower, as the may-pop.

pas-sion-ful (pash′ọn-fůl), *a.* Full of or subject to passion; passionate.

Pas-sion-ist (pash′ọn-ist), *n.* A member of a Roman Catholic order, called in full "Congregation of Discalced Clerks of the Most Holy Cross and Passion of Our Lord Jesus Christ," founded by St. Paul of the Cross, in Italy, in 1720, the members of which are pledged to the utmost zeal in keeping fresh the memory of Christ's passion.

pas-sion-less (pash′ọn-les), *a.* Void of passion; not affected by or subject to passion; coldly calm; cold: as, "The Queen . . . thought him cold, High, self-contain'd, and *passionless*" (Tennyson's "Guinevere," 403).—**pas′sion-less-ly,** *adv.*—**pas′sion-less-ness,** *n.*

pas-sion=play (pash′ọn-plā), *n.* A dramatic representation of scenes in the passion of Christ: a notable example being that given periodically (ordinarily every tenth year) by the people of the village of Oberammergau in Bavaria, in pious fulfilment of a vow made by the inhabitants in 1633 in the hope of staying a plague then raging.

Pas-sion-tide (pash′ọn-tīd), *n.* The last two weeks of Lent.

pas-sion=vine (pash′ọn-vīn), *n.* The passion-flower.

pas-sive (pas′iv). [OF. F. *passif,* < L. *passivus,* < *pati,* suffer.] **I.** *a.* Suffering action, acted upon, or being the object of action (opposed to *active*); receiving, or characterized by the reception of, impressions from without (as, "That substances and modes . . . Are mere impressions on the *passive* mind," Cowper's "Anti-Thelyphthora," 43; "in an hour like this, when the mind has a *passive* sensibility, but no active strength," Hawthorne's "Twice-Told Tales," The Haunted Mind); produced by or due to external agency (as, *passive* impressions; *passive* movements); also, suffering, receiving, or submitting without resistance, or characterized by or involving doing this (as, to remain *passive* under provocation; *passive* fortitude; *passive* obedience); unresisting or submissive; also, not acting, or not attended with or manifested in open or positive action (as, a *passive* opponent; *passive* resistance; "The quarrel slowly crystallised into a permanent estrangement, a *passive* feud," Arnold Bennett's "Helen with the High Hand," ii.); inactive, quiescent, or inert; in *gram.,* representing the subject as acted upon (as, the *passive* voice, comprising those forms of transitive verbs which represent the subject as acted upon, as *was broken* in 'the window was broken by John'; a *passive* verb-form; a *passive* participle: opposed to *active*). **II.** *n.* In *gram.,* the passive voice, or a verb-form belonging to it.—**pas′sive-ly,** *adv.*—**pas′sive-ness, pas-siv-i-ty** (pa-siv′i-ti), *n.*

pass=key (pȧs′kē), *n.* A key for opening several locks; a master-key; also, a private key; also, a latch-key.

pass-less (pȧs′les), *a.* Impassable; also, without a pass, or license to pass.

Pass-o-ver (pȧs′ō″vėr), *n.* [Cf. *Pasch.*] An annual feast of the Jews, instituted to commemorate the passing over or sparing of the Hebrews in Egypt when God smote the first-born of the Egyptians (see Ex. xii.); also [*l. c.*], the lamb sacrificed at this feast; fig., Christ, the Paschal Lamb (as, "Christ our *passover* is sacrificed for us": 1 Cor. v. 7).

pass-port (pȧs′pōrt), *n.* [F. *passeport*, < *passer*, pass, + *port*, port, harbor.] Authorization to pass from a port or leave a country, or to enter or pass through a country†; also, a document granting this; esp., formerly, a safe-conduct; now, an official document granting permission to the person specified in it to travel, and authenticating his right to protection; also, a document issued to a ship, esp. to a neutral merchant vessel in time of war, granting or requesting permission to proceed without molestation in certain waters; also, in fig. use, an authorization to pass or go anywhere; a certificate intended to secure admission; anything that gives admission or acceptance (as, "The uniform of his corps was always a *passport* to the best tables": Cooper's "Spy," xiii.).—**pass′port,** *v. t.* To supply or provide with a passport.

pas-sus (pas′us), *n.*; L. pl. *passus.* [ML., in L. a step, pace: see *pace*[2].] A section or division of a story, poem, etc.; a canto.

pass-word (pȧs′wėrd), *n.* A secret word by which one having a right to pass is recognized; a watchword; a countersign.

past (pȧst). Past participle and occasional preterit of *pass.* —**past. I.** *p. a.* Gone by in time (as, "My day's delight is *past*": Shakspere's "Venus and Adonis," 380); belonging to, or having existed or occurred in, time previous to this (as, "*Past* indiscretion is a venial crime": Cowper's "Truth," 491); also, gone by just before the present time, or just passed (as, for some time *past*); foregoing or preceding (as, the *past* century; the *past* week); also, ago (as, "I . . . Never . . . reveal'd myself unto him, Until some half-hour *past*": Shakspere's "King Lear," v. 3. 193); also, having served a turn in an office (cf. *past-master*); in *gram.*, indicating time gone by, or former action or state (as, the *past* tense; the *past* participle of a verb). **II.** *n.* The time gone by (with *the*: as, far back in the *past*); the events of that time (with *the*: as, to forget the *past*); also, a past history, life, career, etc. (as, the *past* of a person or a thing; a city with a glorious *past*); sometimes, a past career which is kept concealed (as, a woman with a *past*); in *gram.*, the past tense, or a verb-form in it.—**past. I.** *prep.* Beyond in time, or after (as, *past* noon); beyond the time for (as, "We are *past* the hour of these civilities": Stevenson's "Master of Ballantrae," v.); beyond the age of (as, he is *past* seventy); also, beyond in position, or further on than (as, the next house *past* the church); by, in passing (as, "Crowds of persons were running *past* our shop": Marryat's "Japhet," vii.); also, beyond the reach, scope, influence, or power of (as, *past* compare; *past* belief; that is *past* my comprehension); no longer capable of (as, "I was almost *past* making any exertion": W. H. Hudson's "Green Mansions," i.); also, beyond in number or amount (obs. or rare); beyond in degree (as, "He set store on her *past* everything": C. Brontë's "Jane Eyre," xxxvi.). **II.** *adv.* So as to pass by or beyond; by: as, "The alarum of drums swept *past*" (Longfellow's "The Cumberland").

paste (pāst), *n.* [OF. *paste* (F. *pâte*), < LL. *pasta*, < Gr. πάστη, barley porridge, < πάσσειν, sprinkle (with salt).] Dough, esp. when prepared with shortening as for making pie-crust and other pastry (as, puff-*paste*); hence, any of various sweet confections of dough-like consistence (as, fig-*paste*); a preparation of fish, tomatoes, or some other article of food reduced to a smooth, soft mass, as for a relish or for seasoning; any of the various food-preparations, made from flour, of the macaroni and noodle kind; a mixture of flour and water, often with starch, etc., used for causing paper, etc., to adhere; in general, any material or preparation in a soft or plastic mass (as, to pound almonds to a *paste*; a polishing-*paste*; a tooth-*paste*); specif., a mixture of clay, water, etc., for making earthenware or porcelain; also, a kind of brilliant, heavy glass made by fusing silica, lead, potash, borax, etc., used for making artificial gems (as, "shoe buckles of the best *paste*, sparkling like real diamonds," Mrs. Stowe's "Oldtown Folks," v.: also called *strass*); an artificial gem of this material; also, a smart blow, esp. on the face (slang). —**paste,** *v. t.*; *pasted, pasting.* To fasten or stick with paste or the like (as, to *paste* a label on a box; "a white paper *pasted* on the wall," Mrs. Wharton's "Son at the Front," v.); cause to adhere by or as if by means of paste; also, to cover with something applied by means of paste (as, to *paste* a door over with notices); also, to strike with a smart blow, or beat soundly, as on the face or body (slang).

paste-board (pāst′bōrd). **I.** *n.* A stiff, firm material made of sheets of paper pasted together or of paper-pulp; also, a card, as a visiting-card or a playing-card (slang); a ticket, as for an entertainment (slang). **II.** *a.* Made of pasteboard; hence, fig., unsubstantial or flimsy; sham.

pas-tel[1] (pas′tel), *n.* [F., < Pr. *pastel*, dim. < LL. *pasta*, E. *paste.*] The plant woad, or the dye made from it.

pas-tel[2] (pas′tel or pas-tel′), *n.* [F., < It. *pastello*, dim. < LL. *pasta*, E. *paste.*] A kind of dried paste used for crayons, made of pigments ground with chalk and compounded with gum-water; a crayon made with such paste; also, the art of drawing, or a drawing made, with such crayons; also, a short, slight prose study or sketch; also, a soft, pale shade of some color (usually attributive: as, *pastel* pink; *pastel* tints).—**pas′tel-ist, pas′tel-list,** *n.* An artist who draws with pastels or colored crayons.

past-er (pās′tėr), *n.* One who or that which pastes; also, a slip of paper gummed on the back, to be pasted on or over something, as over a name on a ballot.

pas-tern (pas′tėrn), *n.* [OF. *pasturon* (F. *paturon*), < *pasture*, shackle for animal while pasturing, orig. pasture: see *pasture.*] A shackle placed on the foot of an animal at pasture†; also, that part of the foot of a horse, etc., between the fetlock and the hoof; either of two bones of this part, the upper or first phalanx ('great pastern-bone') and the lower or second phalanx ('small pastern-bone'), between which is a joint ('pastern-joint').

Pas-teur-ism (pas′tėr-izm), *n.* [From Louis *Pasteur* (1822–95), French scientist.] A treatment devised by Pasteur for preventing certain diseases, esp. hydrophobia, by inoculations with virus of gradually increasing strength; also, the act or process of pasteurizing milk, etc.—**pas′teur-ize** (-īz), *v. t.*; *-ized, -izing.* To expose (milk, etc.) to a high temperature, usually about 140° F., in order to destroy certain micro-organisms and prevent or arrest fermentation; also, to subject (a person or animal) to Pasteurism in order to prevent certain diseases, esp. hydrophobia.—**pas″teur-i-za′tion** (-i-zā′shọn), *n.*—**pas′teur-iz-er** (-ī-zėr), *n.* An apparatus for pasteurizing milk, etc.

pas-tic-cio (päs-tēt′chō), *n.*; pl. *pasticci* (-chē). [It., < *pasta*, < LL. *pasta*, E. *paste.*] A medley, hodgepodge, or farrago; an opera, cantata, etc., made up of pieces from various sources; a picture or design made up of fragments pieced together; a picture or design copied with modification from an original; any work of art, literature, or music in professed imitation of the work of another. Also (F.) **pas-tiche** (pȧs-tēsh).

pas-tille, pas-til (pas-tēl′, pas′til), *n.* [F. *pastille*, < L. *pastillus*, little loaf, lozenge, appar. dim. < *panis*, bread: cf. LL. *pasta*, E. *paste.*] A small roll or cone of paste containing aromatic substances, burned as a perfume, disinfectant, etc.; also, a flavored or medicated lozenge; also, pastel for crayons, or a crayon made of it.

pas-time (pȧs′tīm), *n.* [From *pass* + *time*: cf. F. *passetemps.*] That which serves to make time pass agreeably; diversion, amusement, or sport (as, to read fiction, or play cards, for *pastime*); also, a particular form of diversion or amusement; an amusement, recreation, game, or the like (as, "Having no better *pastime*, he fell to reading the Scriptures," Motley's "Dutch Republic," i. 2; the *pastimes* of a people).

past-i-ness (pās′ti-nes), *n.* Pasty quality.

past=mas-ter (pȧst′mȧs′tėr), *n.* One who has filled the office of master in a gild, lodge, etc.; also, one who has ripe experience in any profession, art, etc. (cf. *passed-master*).

pas-tor (pȧs′tọr), *n.* [OF. *pastor* (F. *pasteur*), < L. *pastor*, < *pascere*, feed.] A herdsman or shepherd (now rare); hence, one having spiritual care of a number of persons, esp. a minister or clergyman with reference to his flock or congregation; sometimes, one who exercises protecting care or guidance over any body of persons (as, "Pierced in the flank by Menelaus's steel, His people's *pastor*, Hyperenor fell": Pope's tr. Homer's "Iliad," xiv.); also, a starling, *Pastor roseus*, of Asia and Europe, whose plumage is partly rose-colored, or any bird of the same genus.

Pastor (*P. roseus*).

pas-tor-al (pȧs′tọr-ạl), *a.* [L. *pastoralis*, < *pastor*: see *pastor*.] Pertaining to shepherds, or to the care of flocks or herds; living as a shepherd or shepherds (as, a *pastoral* people); used for pasture, as land or country; having the simplicity or charm of such country, as scenery, etc.; pertaining to the country or life in the country, rustic, or rural; also, portraying the life of shepherds or of the country, as a work of literature, art, or music; in the form of or pertaining to a pastoral; also, pertaining to a pastor of souls, or a minister or clergyman, or to his labors, duties, etc. (as, "To eschew evil myself, and to teach others to do the same, I thought the main duties of the *pastoral* office," Galt's "Annals of the Parish," xix.; a *pastoral* visit).—**pastoral Epistles,** the two Epistles to Timothy and the Epistle to Titus, in the New Testament, so called because they deal largely with the work of a pastor.—**pastoral staff,** the crozier of a bishop or an abbot.—**pas′tor-al,** *n.* A poem, play, or the like, dealing with the life of shepherds, commonly in a conventional or artificial manner, or with simple rural life generally; a bucolic (as, "Theocritus, Bion, and Moschus are the most famous amongst the Greek writers of *pastorals*": Steele, in "Guardian," 28); pastoral poetry, drama, etc., as a form of literature (as, "There are some things of an established nature in *pastoral*, which are essential to it, such as a country scene, innocence, simplicity": Steele, in "Guardian," 30); also, a pastoral picture or work of art; also, a pastorale; also, a treatise on the duties of a pastor of souls, or minister or clergyman; a letter from a spiritual pastor to his people or flock, esp. one from a bishop to his clergy or people; *pl.*, the pastoral Epistles (see under *pastoral*, *a.*); also, *sing.*, a pastoral staff, or crozier.

pas-to-ra-le (päs-tō-rä′lā), *n.*; pl. *-les* (-lāz), It. *-li* (-lē). [It.] In *music*, an opera, cantata, or the like, with a pastoral subject; a piece of music suggestive of pastoral life.

pas-tor-al-ism (pȧs′tọr-ạl-izm), *n.* Pastoral quality or character.—**pas′tor-al-ist,** *n.* A keeper of flocks or herds; also, a writer of pastorals.

pas-tor-al-ly (pȧs′tọr-ạl-i), *adv.* In a pastoral or rustic manner; in a pastoral; also, in the manner of a pastor.

pas-tor-ate (pȧs′tọr-ạt), *n.* The office, or the term of office, of an ecclesiastical pastor; also, a body of pastors.

pas-to-ri-um (pȧs-tō′ri-um), *n.*; pl. *-riums*, L. *-ria* (-ri-ạ). [NL., < L. *pastor*: see *pastor*.] A parsonage. [Southern U. S.]

pas-tor-ship (pȧs′tọr-ship), *n.* The dignity or office of a pastor.

past=per-fect (pȧst′pėr′fekt), *a.* and *n.* In *gram.*, same as *pluperfect*.

pas-try (pās′tri), *n.*; pl. *-tries* (-triz). Food made of paste, esp. the shortened paste used for pie-crust, etc. (as, "tarts wherein the raspberry jam coyly withdrew itself . . . behind a lattice work of *pastry*": Dickens's "Martin Chuzzlewit," xii.); articles of food of which such paste forms an essential part, as pies, tarts, napoleons, etc.; a particular form or variety of such food (as, French *pastries*); also, a room or place where pies, etc., are made, as for a household† (as, "They call for dates and quinces in the *pastry*": Shakspere's "Romeo and Juliet," iv. 4. 2).—**pas′try=cook,** *n.* One who makes pastry; often, one who makes pastry for sale.

pas-tur-a-ble (pȧs′tūr-ạ-bl), *a.* Capable of affording pasture, as land.—**pas″tur-a-bil′i-ty** (-bil′i-ti), *n.*

pas-tur-age (pȧs′tūr-āj), *n.* [OF. *pasturage* (F. *pâturage*).] The act or business of pasturing cattle, etc.; also, growing grass or herbage for cattle, etc.; also, grazing-ground.

pas-tur-al (pȧs′tūr-ạl), *a.* Of or pertaining to pasture.

pas-ture (pȧs′tūr), *n.* [OF. *pasture* (F. *pâture*), < LL. *pastura*, < L. *pascere*, feed.] Feeding or grazing, as of cattle, etc.; also, growing grass or herbage for feeding cattle, etc.; also, ground covered with grass or herbage, appropriated to or suitable for the grazing of cattle, etc.; grassland; a piece of such ground (as, "To-morrow to fresh woods and *pastures* new": Milton's "Lycidas," 193).—**pas′ture,** *v.*; *-tured*, *-turing*. [OF. *pasturer* (F. *pâturer*).] **I.** *tr.* To feed (cattle, etc.) by putting them to graze on pasture; put to pasture; of land, to furnish pasturage for (cattle, etc.); also, of cattle, etc., to graze upon (herbage or grassland); of persons, to put cattle, etc., to graze upon (pasture). **II.** *intr.* Of cattle, etc., to graze: as, "There were smooth areas where sheep had *pastured*" (W. H. Hudson's "Far Away and Long Ago," v.).—**pas′tur-er,** *n.*

past-y[1] (pās′ti), *a.* Of the nature or consistence of paste; doughy, soft, or semisolid; also, having the appearance of paste; of persons, the face, etc., pallid, sallow, or flabby (as, "a little *pasty* woman with a pinched yellowish face": Galsworthy's "Saint's Progress," iii. 9).

pas-ty[2] (Brit. pȧs′ti or pās′ti, U. S. pās′ti), *n.*; pl. *-ties* (-tiz). [OF. *paste* (F. *pâté*), < *paste*, E. *paste*.] A pie filled with game, fish, or the like: as, a *venison* pasty.

pat (pat), *v. t.*; *patted*, *patting*. [Prob. imit.] To strike lightly with something flat, as an implement, the palm of the hand, or the foot (as, "Hetty tossed and *patted* her pound of butter," George Eliot's "Adam Bede," vii.; "his foot *patting* the ground," Stevenson's "Master of Ballantrae," xii.); often, to strike gently with the palm or fingers as an expression of affection, kindness, approbation, or the like (as, to *pat* a horse or a dog; "The old minister . . . *patted* my head and praised me," Kingsley's "Alton Locke," i.); also, to strike (the floor, etc.) with lightly sounding footsteps.—**to pat juba.** See *juba*.—**to pat on the back,** fig., to praise or compliment, often complaisantly or flatteringly.—**pat,** *v. i.* To strike lightly or gently; also, to walk or run with lightly sounding footsteps.—**pat,** *n.* A light stroke or blow with something flat, as an implement, the palm of the hand, etc.; often, a gentle stroke with the hand or fingers, given as in affection, kindness, or approbation (as, "a fatherly *pat* o' the cheek," Browning's "Ring and the Book," iv.: also fig.); also, a small mass of something, as butter, shaped by patting or other manipulation; a distinct mass of anything; also, the sound of a light stroke, or of light footsteps.—**pat,** *adv.* With an exact stroke or hit (as, to hit the nail *pat* on the head); hence, exactly (as, "You shall see, it will fall *pat* as I told you": Shakspere's "Midsummer Night's Dream," v. 1. 188); appositely or aptly; opportunely; readily or promptly.—**to stand pat,** in *poker*, to play a hand as dealt, without drawing other cards; fig., to hold to an existing order of things, or to a policy, etc., in force, as in politics (colloq.).—**pat,** *a.* Exactly to the point or purpose; apt; opportune; ready.

pat-a-gi-um (pat-ā-jī′um or pạ-tā′ji-um), *n.*; pl. *-gia* (-jī′ạ or -ji-ạ). [NL., in L. a gold border on a woman's tunic.] A wing-membrane, as of a bat; the extensible fold of skin of a flying mammal or reptile, as a flying-squirrel; the fold of skin between the humeral and the radial and ulnar parts of a bird's wing.—**pa-ta-gi-al** (pạ-tā′ji-ạl), *a.*

Pat-a-go-ni-an (pat-ạ-gō′ni-ạn). [From *Patagonia*, < Sp. *Patagón*, Patagonian, lit. 'large foot'; from the large footprints seen by the explorer Magellan.] **I.** *a.* Of or pertaining to Patagonia, a region at the southern extremity of South America, divided between Argentina and Chile. **II.** *n.* A native or inhabitant of Patagonia; esp., one of the aboriginal Indian race known as the Tehuelches, noted for their great stature.

pat-a-mar (pat′ạ-mär), *n.* [Pg.; from E. Ind.] A lateen-rigged vessel with an upward curving keel and considerable

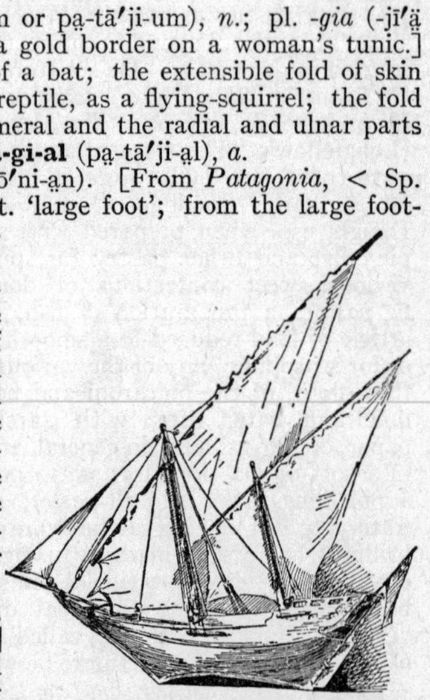
Patamar, Bombay. — From model in Victoria and Albert Museum, London.

overhang of stern and esp. stem, used in the coasting-trade of western India.

patch[1] (pach), *n.* [Said to be from the nickname of Cardinal Wolsey's jester.] A jester† or fool†; hence, a foolish or stupid person (obs. or archaic: as, "Coxcomb, idiot, *patch!*" Shakspere's "Comedy of Errors," iii. 1. 32); also, an ill-natured person, esp. a child (prov. or colloq.: cf. *cross-patch*).

patch[2] (pach), *n.* [ME. *pacche*; origin uncertain.] A piece of material used to mend a hole or break, or strengthen a weak place (as, "Many a *patch* of brown and grey variegated the faded scarlet of our uniform," Lever's "Harry Lorrequer," i.; a *patch* on a sail, a kettle, or a roadway); a piece of material used to cover or protect a wound, an injured part, etc. (as, to wear a *patch* over the eye); a piece of cloth or material applied for any purpose, as for a badge; specif., a small piece of black silk or court-plaster worn on the face or elsewhere to hide a defect or to heighten the complexion by contrast (much worn by women in the 17th and 18th centuries); also, any of the pieces of cloth sewed together to form patchwork; a small piece or scrap of anything; also, a relatively small part or area of a particular color, appearance, or character (as, a *patch* of white on a horse's face; *patches* of ice or snow; "*patches* of dim stars," Arnold Bennett's "Pretty Lady," xxxiii.); often, a piece or tract of land (as, "a *patch* of land known as the Spring Pasture," Mrs. Stowe's "Oldtown Folks," xlii.; "a very inviting *patch* of woodland covering five or six square miles," W. H. Hudson's "Green Mansions," ii.); a small piece of ground under cultivation, or the stretch of growing plants upon such a piece (as, a garden-*patch*; "There was little more left than a mere *patch* of Indian corn and potatoes," Irving's "Sketch-Book," Rip Van Winkle).—**not a patch on,** not to be compared with: as, "They . . . agreed that the show was *not a patch on* that in Hyde Park during the London season" (Du Maurier's "Trilby," vii.). [Colloq.]—**patch**[2], *v.* **I.** *tr.* To mend or strengthen with or as with a patch or patches (as, to *patch* clothes or boots; "The windows are *patched* with wooden panes," George Eliot's "Adam Bede," vi.); serve for mending (as, "O, that that earth . . . Should *patch* a wall to expel the winter's flaw!" Shakspere's "Hamlet," v. 1. 239); in general, to repair, restore, or bring back to a more or less satisfactory state, esp. in a hasty or makeshift way (usually with *up*: as, "The doctor . . . will *patch* up your arm in the twinkling of an eye," Cooper's "Spy," vii.; to *patch* up a quarrel); also, to adorn (the face, etc.) with a patch or patches; also, to put on or apply as or like a patch; join or piece together as or like patches; make by joining patches or pieces together (as, to *patch* a quilt); put (*together*) out of various pieces or elements (as, to *patch* together a complete history of an affair; "a miscellaneous old gentleman . . . *patched* together, too, of different epochs; an epitome of times and fashions," Hawthorne's "House of the Seven Gables," iv.); make (*up*) in a hasty or makeshift manner (as, to *patch* up a list of grievances; "An imperfect peace was *patched* up with the Italians," Froude's "Cæsar," vii.); also, to furnish or diversify with patches or areas of something (as, hills *patched* with snow); mark or spot with something. **II.** *intr.* To mend garments, etc., with patches; also, to use patches on the face, etc.; also, to form patches, as snow or vegetation.—**patch′=box,** *n.* A small box for holding patches for the face: used esp. in the 17th and 18th centuries.—**patch′er,** *n.*—**patch′er-y,** *n.*; pl. *-ies* (-iz). The act of patching; rough mending; hasty or clumsy patching together; botchery; also, something made by patching parts together.

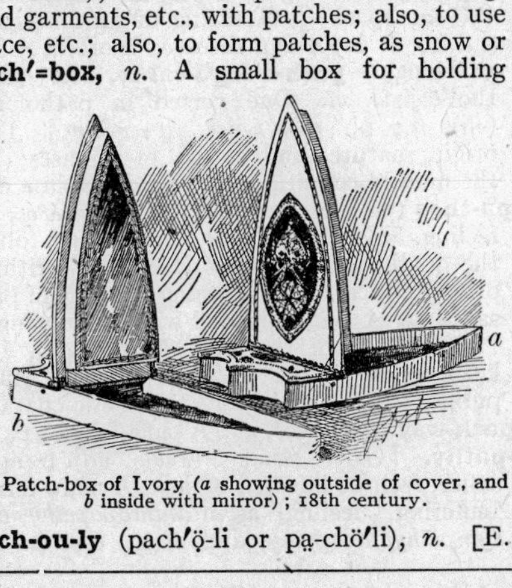

Patch-box of Ivory (*a* showing outside of cover, and *b* inside with mirror); 18th century.

patch-ou-li, patch-ou-ly (pach′ọ̈-li or pạ-chö′li), *n.* [E. Ind.] An East Indian menthaceous plant, *Pogostemon patchouli*, which yields a fragrant oil; also, a penetrating perfume derived from it.

patch=pock-et (pach′pok′et), *n.* A pocket formed by sewing a piece of the material on the outside of a garment.

patch-work (pach′wėrk), *n.* Work made of pieces of cloth of various colors or shapes sewed together, used esp. for covering quilts, cushions, etc. (as, "The counterpane was of *patchwork*, full of odd little parti-colored squares and triangles": H. Melville's "Moby-Dick," iv.); hence, work or a product of any kind made up of various pieces or parts put together (as, a *patchwork* of verses or reminiscences); any diversified area (as, a *patchwork* of fields and woods); sometimes, work or a thing made up of clumsily combined or ill-assorted parts.

patch-y (pach′i), *a.* Abounding in or characterized by patches; diversified like patchwork; also, occurring in, forming, or resembling patches.

pate (pāt), *n.* [ME. *pate*; origin uncertain.] The head (as, "Let him to the Tower, And chop away that factious *pate* of his": Shakspere's "2 Henry VI.," v. 1. 135); esp., the crown or top of the head (as, "with his bald *pate* uncovered": Smollett's "Humphry Clinker," April 24); also, the head as the seat of the intellect; hence, brains; sometimes, a person with brains (as specified: as, a shallow *pate*). [Now usually humorous.]

pâte (pät), *n.* [F.: see *paste*.] Paste; in *ceram.*, the paste for making earthenware or porcelain.

pâ-té (pä-tā), *n.* [F.: see *pasty*[2].] A case or form of pastry filled with chicken, sweetbreads, oysters, or the like.—**pâté de foie gras** (dė fwo grä). [F., 'pâté of fat liver.'] A pâté made with the livers of specially fattened geese; also, a preparation of the livers for such or other use.

pat-ed (pā′ted), *a.* Having a pate (of a kind specified): as, "a giddy-*pated* boy" (Scott's "Quentin Durward," xxv.).

pa-tel-la (pạ-tel′ạ̈), *n.*; pl. *patellas* or *patellæ* (-ē). [L., small pan, kneepan, dim. of *patina*: see *patina*.] In *archæol.*, a small pan or shallow vessel; in *bot.*, *zoöl.*, etc., a pan-like or cup-like formation; in *anat.*, the knee-cap.—**pa-tel′lar** (-tel′ạ̈r), *a.* Of or pertaining to the patella or knee-cap.—**pa-tel′late** (-tel′āt), *a.* Having a patella; also, patelliform.—**pa-tel′li-form** (-tel′i-fôrm), *a.* Having the form of a patella; shaped like a saucer, knee-cap, or limpet-shell.

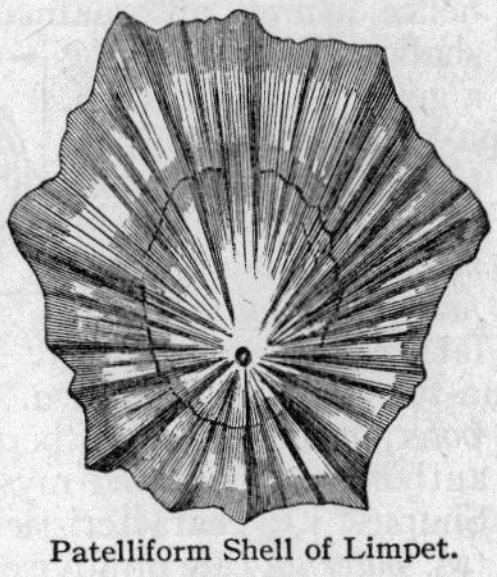
Patelliform Shell of Limpet.

pat-en (pat′ẹn), *n.* [Also *patine*; OF. *patene* (F. *patène*), < L. *patena*, *patina*: see *patina*.] A broad, shallow dish or plate (archaic); specif., the plate on which the bread is placed in the celebration of the eucharist; also, a plate or flat piece of metal, or something resembling or suggesting it (archaic: as, "Look how the floor of heaven Is thick inlaid with *patines* of bright gold," Shakspere's "Merchant of Venice," v. 1. 59).

pat-en-cy (pat′ẹn-si or pā′tẹn-si), *n.* The state of being patent.

pat-ent (pat′ẹnt or, esp. Brit., pā′tẹnt), *a.* [L. *patens* (*patent-*), ppr. of *patere*, lie open; in latter senses, through OF. F. *patent* (*lettres patentes*, letters patent).] (Often pā′tẹnt.) Open, as a door or a passage; also, lying open, or not shut in or inclosed, as a place; also, expanded or spreading (specif. in *bot.*); also, open to view or knowledge, or manifest, evident, or plain (as, "The deception of the Queen-mother was at last *patent* to him; all her lies and treacheries lay unrolled before him like a map": Besant's "Coligny," ix.); also (in U. S., usually pat′ẹnt), open to the perusal of all (as, letters *patent*, an official document issued by a sovereign, government, etc., for any of various purposes, commonly to grant some right, privilege, or the like, now esp. the exclusive rights to an invention for a certain term of years); hence, conferred by letters patent, as a right or privilege; made the subject of letters patent, as a commodity or article; endowed with letters patent, as persons; appointed by letters patent, as a person; esp., appropriated by letters patent to a person or persons for manufacture, sale, etc., during a certain term of years, as an invention; of a kind specially protected by a patent; by extension, belonging as if by a proprietary claim.—**patent insides,** newspaper sheets printed on the inside only, and thus sold to publishers, who fill the unprinted side with matter of their own selection.—**patent leather,** leather with a finely varnished glossy surface, commonly black, used for boots, shoes, harness, etc.—**patent medicine,** a medicine which is patented; any medicine whose manufacture and sale are restricted in any way, as by patent, registry of name as a trade-mark, etc.; any proprietary medicine.—**patent outsides,** newspaper sheets printed on the outside only, sold to publishers and filled up by them like patent insides.—**pat-ent** (pat′ẹnt or, esp. Brit., pā′tẹnt), *n.* Letters patent (see *patent, a.*); an official document conferring some right, privilege, or the like (as, "Alva . . . received an especial *patent* . . . by which Philip empowered him to proceed against all persons implicated in the troubles," Motley's "Dutch Republic," iii. 2; a *patent* of nobility); now, esp., a grant from a government, to a person or persons, conferring the exclusive rights to the manufacture, sale, etc., of a new invention for a certain term of years; also, an invention, process, etc., which has been patented; also, a tract of land granted by letters patent (archaic or hist., U. S.: as, "the *'Patent'* . . . the district . . . originally granted to old Major Effingham by the 'king's letters patent,' " Cooper's "Pioneers," viii.); also, fig., a token indicating a right to something; authority or leave to do something (see Shakspere's "Othello," iv. 1. 209).—**pat-ent** (pat′ẹnt or, esp. Brit., pā′tẹnt), *v. t.* To grant by letters patent; grant the exclusive rights to (an invention) by a patent; sometimes, to appoint by letters patent, as a person; also, to take out a patent on; obtain the exclusive rights to (an invention) by letters patent; hence, fig., to originate and establish as one's own.—**pat′ent-a-ble,** *a.* That may be patented.—**pat-ent-ee′,** *n.* One to whom a patent is granted.—**pat′ent-ly,** *adv.* —**pat′ent-or,** *n.* One who grants a patent; also, a patentee.

pa-ter (pā′tėr), *n.* [L.: see *father.*] Father; also, the paternoster or Lord's Prayer, or a recital of it.

pat-er-a (pat′ẹ-rạ̈), *n.*; pl. *pateræ* (-rē). [L., < *patere*, lie open.] In *Rom. antiq.*, a broad, shallow, saucer-like dish, used esp. in making libations; hence, in *arch.*, an ornament in bas-relief resembling a round, shallow dish, or having a generally round form.

Roman Patera.

Architectural Pateræ.

pa-ter-fa-mil-i-as (pā″-tėr-fạ-mil′i-as), *n.* [L., < *pater*, father, + *familias*, archaic gen. of *familia*, family.] The father of a family.

pa-ter-nal (pạ-tėr′nạl), *a.* [F. *paternel*, < L. *paternus*, < *pater*, father.] Of or pertaining to a father (as, *paternal* authority; "I quitted my *paternal* roof," Marryat's "Peter Simple," i.); characteristic of or befitting a father, or fatherly (as, *paternal* care or advice; to speak in a *paternal* manner); also, being a father (as, one's *paternal* parent); acting like a father (as, a *paternal* ruler); also, derived or inherited from a father (as, "a few *paternal* acres": Pope's "Ode on Solitude"); also, related on the father's side (as, one's *paternal* grandmother).—**pa-ter′nal-ism,** *n.* The principle or practice, on the part of a government or of any body or person in authority, of managing or regulating the affairs of a country or community, or of individuals, in the manner of a father dealing with his children.—**pa-ter-nal-is′tic,** *a.* Pertaining to or of the nature of paternalism.—**pa-ter′nal-ly,** *adv.*

pa-ter-ni-ty (pạ-tėr′ni-ti), *n.* [LL. *paternitas*, < L. *paternus*: see *paternal.*] The state of being a father, or fatherhood (as, the responsibilities of *paternity*); also, derivation from a father (as, the child's *paternity* is unknown); fig., origin or authorship (as, to dispute the *paternity* of an anonymous book).

pa-ter-nos-ter (pā′tėr-nos′tėr or pat′ėr-), *n.* [L. *pater noster*, our father: the first words of the prayer in the Latin version.] The Lord's Prayer, esp. in the Latin form; a recital of this prayer as an act of worship; hence, any form of words used as a prayer or charm, or as of special potency (as, "This is the Black *Pater-noster* . . . All the devils in the air The stronger be, that hear the Black Prayer!" Longfellow's "Golden Legend," ii. 558); also, one of certain beads in a rosary, regularly every eleventh bead, differing in size or material from the rest, and indicating that a paternoster is to be said; hence, the whole rosary; also, something resembling a rosary, as a fish-line with hooks and sinkers attached at intervals (as, "Here's your gudgeons and minnows, sir . . . and here's that *paternoster* as you gave me to rig up": Kingsley's "Yeast," iii.).

path (påth), *n.*; pl. *paths* (påᴛʜz). [AS. *pæth* = D. *pad* = G. *pfad*, path.] A way beaten or trodden by the feet of men or beasts (as, "He left the barren-beaten thoroughfare, Chose the green *path* that show'd the rarer foot": Tennyson's "Lancelot and Elaine," 161); a footway; often, a walk in a garden or through grounds; in general, a way, road, or route (as, "the fish . . . and whatsoever passeth through the *paths* of the seas": Ps. viii. 8); the way, course, or track in which something moves (as, the *path* of a planet); fig., a course of action, conduct, or procedure (as, "The *paths* of glory lead but to the grave": Gray's "Elegy," ix.).

Pa-than (pạ-thän′), *n.* An Afghan, esp. one of those dwelling in, or in the borderland of, India.

pa-thet-ic (pạ-thet′ik), *a.* [F. *pathétique*, < LL. *patheticus*, < Gr. παθητικός, < παθεῖν, suffer.] Affecting or moving the feelings; now, esp., exciting pity or sympathetic sadness (as, "Job's *pathetic* plaint, and wailing cry," Burns's "Cotter's Saturday Night," 124; "The old, rather shabby room struck her as extraordinarily *pathetic*," Galsworthy's "Saint's Progress," iii. 13); full of pathos; formerly, passionate† (as, "Thee too, enamour'd of the life I lov'd, *Pathetic* in its praise . . . Ingenious Cowley!" Cowper's "Task," iv. 719); also, pertaining or due to the feelings (as, "The active periods of the world were not really happy at all. We only fancy them to have been so by a *pathetic* fallacy": Mallock's "New Republic," iv. 1); in *anat.*, designating certain eye-muscles and their motor nerves, because regarded as enabling the eye to express the feelings or emotions.—**pa-thet′i-cal-ly,** *adv.*

path-find-er (påth′fīn″dėr), *n.* One who finds a path or way, as through a wilderness.

path-less (påth′les), *a.* Without paths; trackless: as, "There is a Power whose care Teaches thy way along that *pathless* coast" (Bryant's "To a Waterfowl").—**path′less-ness,** *n.*

patho-. Form of Gr. πάθος, suffering, disease, feeling, used in combination.—**path-o-gene** (path′ọ-jēn), *n.* A pathogenic or disease-producing organism.—**path-o-gen′e-sis** (-jen′e-sis), *n.* The production or development of disease; the mode of production or development of a disease.—**path″o-ge-net′ic** (-jẹ-net′ik), *a.*—**path-o-gen′ic,** *a.* [+ *-genic.*] Pertaining to pathogeny; producing disease.—**pa-thog-e-ny** (pạ-thoj′e-ni), *n.* [+ *-geny.*] Pathogenesis.—**pa-thog-no-mon-ic** (pạ-thog-nọ-mon′ik), *a.* [Gr. παθογνωμονικός, skilled in judging of diseases (γνώμων, a judge).] Indicative or characteristic of a particular disease.—**pa-thog′no-my** (-mi), *n.* [+ Gr. γνώμη, judgment.] The science of the signs or symptoms indicating particular diseases.—**path-o-log′ic, path-o-log′i-cal** (-loj′ik, -i-kạl), *a.* [Gr. παθολογικός (λέγειν, speak).] Treating of or concerned with diseases; due to or involving disease; morbid; of or pertaining to pathology.—**path-o-log′i-cal-ly,** *adv.*—**pa-thol-o-gist** (pạ-thol′ọ-jist), *n.* One versed in pathology.—**pa-thol′o-gy** (-ji), *n.*; pl. *-gies* (-jiz). [+ *-logy.*] The science of the origin, nature, and course of diseases; also, the sum of the morbid conditions and processes in a disease.

pa-thos (pā′thos), *n.* [LL., < Gr. πάθος, suffering, disease, feeling, < παθεῖν, suffer.] Suffering (obs. or rare); also, the quality or power, as in speech, writing, music, a scene or occurrence, etc., of rousing a feeling of pity or sympathetic sadness (as, "She pleaded with a touching *pathos*," Green's "Short Hist. of the Eng. People," vi. 1; "We are more keenly alive to the *pathos* of failure," Mallock's "New Republic," iv. 2); touching or pathetic character or effect.

path-way (påth′wā), *n.* A path; a foot-path; a way.

-pathy. [Gr. -πάθεια, < -παθής, adj. termination < παθεῖν, suffer, feel, be affected with.] A noun termination meaning 'suffering,' 'feeling,' as in *anthropopathy, antipathy, apathy, sympathy, telepathy*, and often, esp. in words of modern formation, 'morbid affection,' 'disease,' as in *arthropathy, deuteropathy, neuropathy, psychopathy,* and hence used also in names of systems or methods of treating disease, as in *allopathy, homeopathy, hydropathy, osteopathy.*

pa-tience (pā′shẹns), *n.* [OF. F. *patience,* < L. *patientia.*] The state or quality of being patient; calm and uncomplaining endurance, as under pain, affliction, injury, provocation, etc.; long-suffering, forbearance, or tolerance (as, a thing that tries one's *patience;* I have no *patience* with such folly); calmness in waiting, or patient willingness to wait (as, have *patience* just a little longer); quiet perseverance (as, to labor with *patience*); also, sufferance† or leave† (as, "I can go no further, sir . . . By your *patience,* I needs must rest me": Shakspere's "Tempest," iii. 3. 3); also, a kind of card-game, usually played by one person alone, and then also called *solitaire.*

pa-tient (pā′shẹnt). [OF. F. *patient,* < L. *patiens* (*patient-*), ppr. of *pati,* suffer.] **I.** *a.* Enduring pain, trouble, affliction, hardship, etc., with fortitude, calmness, or quiet submission, or marked by such endurance (as, "O suffering, sad humanity . . . *Patient,* though sorely tried!" Longfellow's "Goblet of Life"; *patient* suffering); also, quietly enduring injury, annoyance, etc., or disposed to or characterized by such endurance (as, "Beware the fury of a *patient* man," Dryden's "Absalom and Achitophel," i. 1005; *patient* tolerance); composed and uncomplaining under provocation; long-suffering, forbearing, or lenient; bearing indulgently (*with:* as, "I want you to be *patient* with me and hear me out," H. G. Wells's "Mr. Britling," iii. 2. § 5); also, enduring delay with calmness or equanimity, or marked by such endurance (as, be *patient,* and you shall hear all; *patient* waiting); not overeager or hasty; also, quietly persevering or diligent (as, *patient* workers; *patient* labor or efforts); also, having or showing the capacity for endurance (*of:* as, "They are incredibly abstemious, and *patient* of hunger and fatigue," Smollett's "Humphry Clinker," Sept. 6); tolerant (*of:* as, "The admirable woman is *patient* of my idiosyncrasies," G. W. Curtis's "Prue and I," i.); sometimes, susceptible (*of:* as, language *patient* of a particular interpretation); also, undergoing the action of another (opposed to *agent:* as, "Every creature is man agent or *patient,*" Emerson's "Essays," History: archaic). **II.** *n.* A sufferer (obs. or rare); hence, one who is under medical or surgical treatment; also, a person or thing that undergoes action (opposed to *agent*).—**pa′tient-ly,** *adv.*

pat-in (pat′in), *n.* See *paten.*

pat-i-na (pat′i-nạ), *n.*; pl. *patinas,* L. *patinæ* (-nē). [L., shallow dish, pan.] A kind of broad, shallow dish in use among the ancient Romans; also, a film or incrustation, usually green, produced by oxidation on the surface of old bronze, and esteemed as ornamental; hence, a similar film or coloring produced in the course of time on the surface of some other substance.—**pat′i-nat-ed** (-nā-ted), *a.* Covered with a patina.—**pat-i-na′tion** (-nā′shọn), *n.*

pat-ine (pat′in), *n.* See *paten.*

pa-ti-o (pä′tẹ-ō), *n.*; pl. *-os* (-ōz). [Sp.] In Spain and Spanish-American countries, a court, as of a house, esp. an inner court open to the sky.

Patio, with Stairway, of a Mexican House.

pâ-tisse-rie (pä-tēs-rē), *n.* [F.] Pastry; also, a shop for the sale of pastry.

pat-ly (pat′li), *adv.* In a pat manner.—**pat′ness,** *n.*

pa-tois (pȧ-two), *n.* [F.; origin uncertain.] A dialect, as of French, spoken by the common people of a district; any peasant or provincial form of speech.

pa-tri-al (pā′tri-ạl), *a.* [L. *patria,* fatherland, < *pater,* father.] Of or pertaining to one's native country; also, of nouns and adjectives (or their suffixes), indicating nationality or local extraction (as *Roman, Parisian*); gentile.

pa-tri-arch (pā′tri-ärk), *n.* [LL. *patriarcha,* < Gr. πατριάρχης, < πατριά, family (< πατήρ, father), + ἄρχειν, lead, rule.] The father and ruler of a family; the male head of a family or tribal line; specif., any of the earlier Biblical personages regarded as the fathers of the human race, comprising those from Adam to Noah ('antediluvian patriarchs') and those between the Deluge and the birth of Abraham; one of the three great progenitors of the Israelites—Abraham, Isaac, and Jacob; one of the sons of Jacob (the 'twelve patriarchs'), from whom the tribes of Israel were descended; also, a person regarded as the father or founder of an order, class, etc.; one of the elders or leading older members of a community (as, "He . . . was reverenced as one of the *patriarchs* of the village," Irving's "Sketch-Book," Rip Van Winkle: also fig., as of an animal or a tree); a venerable old man; in the early church, a bishop of high rank, esp. one with jurisdiction over metropolitans; in the Orthodox Eastern Church, the bishop of any of the ancient sees of Alexandria, Antioch, Constantinople, and Jerusalem, the bishop of Constantinople being the highest dignitary in the church and bearing the title of 'ecumenical patriarch'; a bishop of the highest rank or authority in any of the various non-Orthodox churches in the East; in the *Rom. Cath. Ch.,* the Pope ('Patriarch of Rome'); also, a bishop of the highest rank next after the Pope.

pa-tri-ar-chal (pā-tri-är′kạl), *a.* Of or pertaining to a patriarch, as of a family, tribe, or community; characteristic of, befitting, or suggesting a patriarch (as, "The governor . . . gave a short but truly *patriarchal* address to his citizens," Irving's "Knickerbocker's New York," vi. 6; a *patriarchal* beard); being or resembling a patriarch (as, "the Selectmen of Boston, plain, *patriarchal* fathers of the people": Hawthorne's "Twice-Told Tales," Edward Randolph's Portrait); also, of, pertaining to, or characteristic of the state of society under the headship of a patriarch (as, a *patriarchal* system or community; *patriarchal* life; "The whole family, in *patriarchal* fashion, master and mistress, children and servants, were assembled in that glorious kitchen," George Eliot's "Adam Bede," ix.); also, of, pertaining to, or subject to an ecclesiastical patriarch (as, a *patriarchal* church or see).—**patriarchal cross,** a cross with two transverse pieces, the upper being shorter than the lower. See cut at *cross, n.*—**pa-tri-ar′chal-ism,** *n.* The patriarchal form of society or government.—**pa-tri-ar′chal-ly,** *adv.*

pa-tri-ar-chate (pā-tri-är′kāt), *n.* [ML. *patriarchatus.*] The office, dignity, jurisdiction, province, or residence of an ecclesiastical patriarch; also, a patriarchy.

pa-tri-ar-chic (pā-tri-är′kik), *a.* Patriarchal.

pa-tri-ar-chy (pā′tri-är-ki), *n.*; pl. *-chies* (-kiz). [Gr. πατριαρχία.] The patriarchal system; a form of social organization in which the father is head of the family, and in which descent is reckoned in the male line, the children belonging to the father's clan; a family, community, or tribe governed by a patriarch or the eldest male; also, an ecclesiastical patriarchate†.

pa-tri-cian (pạ-trish′ạn). [L. *patricius,* < *patres,* senators, patricians, lit. 'fathers,' pl. of *pater,* father.] **I.** *a.* Of or belonging to the class of the senators or nobility of ancient Rome; hence, in general, of high social rank or noble family, noble, or aristocratic; proper to or befitting an aristocrat (as, *patrician* aloofness; a *patrician* air). **II.** *n.* A member of the patrician class in ancient Rome; hence, in general, a noble or aristocrat (as, "the Prince of Orange, Count Egmont, and many of the leading *patricians* of the Netherlands": Motley's "Dutch Republic," i. 3).—**pa-tri′cian-hood** (-hu̇d), *n.* Patrician rank or dignity; also, patricians collectively.—**pa-tri′cian-ism,** *n.* Patrician rank or spirit.—**pa-tri′cian-ly,** *adv.*

pa-tri-ci-ate (pạ-trish′i-āt), *n.* [L. *patriciatus*, < *patricius*: see *patrician*.] Patrician rank; also, the patrician class.

pat-ri-cide (pat′ri-sīd), *n.* [L. *pater* (*patr-*), father: see *-cide*, and cf. *parricide*.] One who kills his father; also, the act of killing one's father.—**pat′ri-ci-dal** (-sī-dạl), *a.*

pat-ri-mo-ni-al (pat-ri-mō′ni-ạl), *a.* Pertaining to or constituting a patrimony; inherited from one's father or ancestors.—**pat-ri-mo′ni-al-ly**, *adv.*

pat-ri-mo-ny (pat′ri-mọ-ni), *n.*; pl. *-nies* (-niz). [OF. F. *patrimoine*, < L. *patrimonium*, < *pater*, father.] An estate inherited from one's father or ancestors (as, "Denzil had a small *patrimony* . . . and that he dissipated before he left college": G. Meredith's "Ordeal of Richard Feverel," i.); a heritage; also, the estate or endowment of a church, religious house, etc.

pat-rin, pat-ter-an (pat′rin, pat′ėr-ạn), *n.* [Romany *patrin*, lit. 'leaf.'] Leaves, grass, etc., placed as a mark by Gipsies to indicate the course taken: as, "Follow the Romany *patteran* West to the sinking sun" (Kipling's "Gipsy Trail"). See Borrow's "Romany Rye," xi.

pa-tri-o-fe-lis (pā″tri-ọ-fē′lis or pat″ri-), *n.* [NL., < L. *patrius*, of one's father or forefathers, + *felis*, cat.] A creodont or primitive carnivorous mammal of the genus *Patriofelis*, about the size of a jaguar, of the Eocene deposits of Wyoming.

Patriofelis. — From a skeleton in the American Museum of Natural History, New York.

pa-tri-ot (pā′tri-ọt or pat′ri-ọt), *n.* [F. *patriote*, < LL. *patriota*, < Gr. πατριώτης, fellow-countryman, < πάτριος, of one's fathers (πατρίς, πάτρα, fatherland), < πατήρ, father.] A fellow countryman†; also, a person who loves his country and zealously supports and defends it and its interests (as, "Such is the *patriot's* boast, where'er we roam, His first, best country ever is at home": Goldsmith's "Traveller," 73).—**Patriots' Day,** the anniversary (April 19) of the battle of Lexington in 1775, observed as a legal holiday in Massachusetts and Maine.—**pa″tri-ot-eer′** (-ọ-tēr′), *n.* [Cf. *profiteer*.] One who makes a parade of his patriotic spirit or service, esp. in doing what is to his own profit.—**pa″tri-ot-eer′**, *v. i.* To act as a patrioteer; parade as patriotic what is done to one's own profit: chiefly in *patrioteering*, *n.* and *p. a.*—**pa-tri-ot′ic** (-ot′ik), *a.* Of, like, or befitting a patriot; inspired or dictated by love of country: as, "a *patriotic* mind anxious to be proud of its country even in little things" (H. G. Wells's "Italy, France, and Britain at War," iii. 3); *patriotic* zeal; a *patriotic* duty.—**pa-tri-ot′i-cal-ly**, *adv.*—**pa′tri-ot-ism**, *n.* The spirit or action of a patriot; ardent or zealous devotion to one's country: as, "Battalions sprung up in a night from spontaneous *patriotism*" (Bancroft's "Hist. of the U. S.," Amer. Revolution, i. 1).

pa-tris-tic (pạ-tris′tik), *a.* [= F. *patristique*, < Gr. πατήρ (πατρ-) or L. *pater* (*patr-*), father.] Of or pertaining to the fathers of the Christian church or their writings. Also **pa-tris′ti-cal.**—**pa-tris′tics**, *n.* The study of the doctrines, writings, and lives of the fathers of the Christian church.

pa-trol (pạ-trōl′), *v.*; *-trolled*, *-trolling*. [F. *patrouiller*, patrol, earlier paddle or dabble in mud, orig. paw over, < OF. *pate* (F. *patte*), paw.] **I.** *intr.* To go the rounds in a camp or garrison, as a guard does; traverse a particular district or beat on duty, as a policeman. **II.** *tr.* To go about in or traverse for the purpose of watching, guarding, or protecting (as, "The camp at night [was] sedulously chosen and *patrolled*": Stevenson's "Master of Ballantrae," xii.).—**pa-trol′**, *n.* The act of patrolling; also, a person or a body of persons charged with patrolling (as, "In the front of the palace a *patrol* of sixty men was established": Prescott's "Conquest of Mexico," iv. 3); also, a patrol-wagon.—**pa-trol′ler**, *n.*—**pa-trol′man** (-mạn), *n.*; pl. *-men*. A man who patrols; esp., a member of the police force of a city who patrols a certain district or beat.

pa-trol-o-gy (pạ-trol′ọ-ji), *n.*; pl. *-gies* (-jiz). [NL. *patrologia*, < Gr. πατήρ (πατρ-), father, + -λογία, < λέγειν, speak.] The study of the writings of the fathers of the Christian church; patristics; a treatise on these writings; also, a collection of the writings of the fathers and other early ecclesiastical writers.—**pat-ro-log-ic, pat-ro-log-i-cal** (pat-rọ-loj′ik, -i-kạl), *a.*—**pa-trol′o-gist**, *n.*

pa-trol=wag-on (pạ-trōl′wag″ọn), *n.* A wagon used by the police for the conveyance of prisoners and for other purposes; also, a wagon used by a fire-insurance patrol, etc., in hastening to fires to protect insured goods.

pa-tron (pā′trọn or pat′rọn), *n.* [OF. F. *patron*, patron, also pattern, < L. *patronus*, patron, ML. pattern, < L. *pater*, father.] In ancient Rome, the ex-master of a freedman, still retaining certain rights over him; the protector of a client (as, "Let him who works the client wrong beware the *patron's* ire!" Macaulay's "Virginia"); an advocate or pleader in law; hence, elsewhere and in general, a protector or supporter, as of a person, cause, institution, art, or enterprise (as, "a renowned *patron* of learning," Swift's "Gulliver's Travels," i. 1; a *patron* of a charitable enterprise); a saint regarded as the special guardian of a person, trade, place, etc. (now usually *patron saint*: as, St. Crispin, the *patron* of shoemakers; St. George, the *patron saint* of England); one who supports with his custom or patronage a shop, hotel, or the like (as, "The enormous demand for military boots was rendering it . . . difficult for him to give to old *patrons* that . . . attention which he would desire to give": Arnold Bennett's "Pretty Lady," viii.); *eccles.*, one who has the right of presenting a clergyman to a benefice.—**Patrons of Husbandry.** See *grange*.—**pat-ron-age** (pat′rọn-āj or pā′trọn-), *n.* [OF. F. *patronage*.] The position, countenance, or support of a patron (as, "Aided by their *patronage* and his own abilities, he had arrived at distinguished posts": Motley's "Dutch Republic," ii. 3); often, condescending favor (as, to assume an air of *patronage*); specif., the financial support afforded a shop, hotel, etc., by customers or patrons; business custom; also, the right of presentation to an ecclesiastical benefice; also, the control of appointments to the public service or of other political favors; offices or other favors so controlled.—**pa-tron-ess** (pā′trọn-es or pat′rọn-), *n.* A female patron.—**pat-ron-ize** (pat′rọn-īz or pā′trọn-), *v. t.*; *-ized*, *-izing*. To act as patron toward; support; countenance; specif., to favor (a shop, restaurant, etc.) with one's custom, patronage, or financial support (as, "the hotel which our friend Florac *patronised*": Thackeray's "Newcomes," lvii.); also, to assume the air of a patron toward; treat in a condescending way (as, "You've no right to *patronise* me! I only want what I have worked for so long": Kipling's "Light That Failed," vii.).—**pat′ron-iz-er** (-ī-zėr), *n.*—**pat′ron-iz-ing**, *p. a.* That patronizes; condescendingly kind or favorable.—**pat′ron-iz-ing-ly**, *adv.*

pat-ro-nym (pat′rọ-nim), *n.* A patronymic name.

pat-ro-nym-ic (pat-rọ-nim′ik). [LL. *patronymicus*, < Gr. πατρωνυμικός, < πατήρ, father, + ὄνυμα, name: cf. *metronymic*.] **I.** *a.* Of names, derived from the name of a father or ancestor, esp. by the addition of a suffix or prefix indicating descent; of a suffix or prefix, indicating such descent. **II.** *n.* A patronymic name, such as *Tydides* (son of Tydeus), *Williamson* (son of William), or *Macdonald* (son of Donald); a family name, or surname.—**pat-ro-nym′i-cal-ly**, *adv.*

pa-troon (pạ-trön′), *n.* [In part, F. *patron* or Sp. *patrón*; in part, D. *patroon*; all < L. *patronus*, E. *patron*.] A patron† or protector†; also, the officer in charge of a ship or boat (archaic: as, "The *patroon* of the boat scrupled at the risk," Stevenson's "David Balfour," xxii.); also, one who held an estate in land with certain manorial privileges and the right to entail, granted under the old Dutch governments of New York and New Jersey (as, "the *patroon* Killian Van Rensellaer, who had come out from Holland to found a colony or patroonship on a great tract of wild land": Irving's "Knickerbocker's New York," iii. 5).—**pa-troon′ship,** *n.* The position or estate of a patroon.

pat-ta-mar (pat′a̤-mär), *n.* See *patamar.*

pat-té, pat-tée (pat′ā, F. pȧ-tā), *a.* [F. *patté,* masc., *pattée,* fem., lit. 'having paws,' < *patte,* paw.] In *her.,* having arms which expand outward, in an approximately triangular form, as a cross.

Cross Patté.

pat-ten (pat′n), *n.* [OF. F. *patin,* perhaps < OF. *pate* (F. *patte*), paw, foot.] Any of various kinds of footwear, as a wooden shoe, a shoe with a wooden sole, a chopine, etc.; esp., a kind of wooden sandal or overshoe mounted on an iron ring, to raise the foot above wet ground (Great Britain: as, "Mrs. Peerybingle . . . clicking over the wet stones in a pair of *pattens*" Dickens's "Cricket on the Hearth," i.).—**pat′tened,** *a.* Wearing pattens: as, "Wherever they went, some *pattened* girl stopped to courtesy" (Jane Austen's "Northanger Abbey," xxiii.).

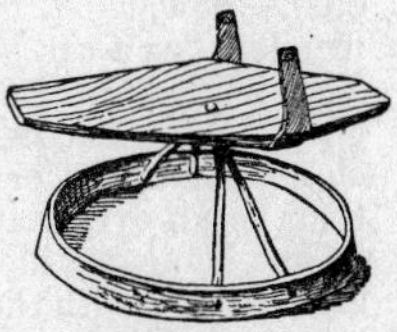
Form of Patten, used about 1830.

pat-ter[1] (pat′ėr), *v.* [Freq. of *pat.*] **I.** *intr.* To strike or move with a succession of slight tapping sounds: as, "He sat . . . listening to the rain *patter* on the shrubs" (L. Merrick's "Conrad in Quest of His Youth," iii.); "Bare feet began to *patter* all round Carter" (J. Conrad's "Rescue," iii. 9). **II.** *tr.* To cause to patter; also, to spatter with something (as, "The trees would *patter* me all over with big drops from the rain of the afternoon": Stevenson's "Travels with a Donkey," ii. 1).—**pat′ter**[1], *n.* The act of pattering; a pattering sound: as, "the heavy *patter* of the rain . . . upon the broad pavement" (Lever's "Harry Lorrequer," xxxv.); "the *patter* of the horsehoofs" (Kingsley's "Yeast," i.).

pat-ter[2] (pat′ėr), *v.* [From L. *pater,* father, the first word of the paternoster: see *paternoster.*] **I.** *intr.* To repeat the paternoster or any prayer, etc., in a rapid, mechanical way; in general, to talk rapidly, esp. with little regard to matter; chatter; often, to talk glibly as a faker in praising his wares or a conjurer in performing his tricks; also, to talk the cant of beggars, thieves, etc. **II.** *tr.* To recite or repeat (prayers, etc.) in a rapid, mechanical way (as, "to *patter* an Ave Mary": Scott's "Lay of the Last Minstrel," ii. 6); in general, to repeat or say rapidly or glibly; also, to talk (a language, etc.: as, "You all *patter* French more or less, and perhaps German," Hughes's "Tom Brown's School Days," i. 1).—**pat′ter**[2], *n.* Rapid speech; esp., mere rapid talk; chatter; gabble; often, the glib speech used by a faker to praise his wares, a conjurer to distract the attention of his audience while performing his tricks, or the like (as, "I have more respect for conjurer's *patter* than for doctor's *patter.* They are both meant to stupefy": Chesterton's "Magic," iii.); also, light, rapidly spoken words or talk in singing, theatrical performances, etc.; also, the cant of beggars, thieves, etc.; the jargon of any class, group, etc.; any particular speech or language (as, "They call me Fin Cooper . . . in the *patter* of the Gorgios": Whyte-Melville's "Katerfelto," xi.).

pat-ter-an (pat′ėr-a̤n), *n.* See *patrin.*

pat-tern (pat′ėrn). [Earlier *patron,* < OF. F. *patron,* pattern, also patron: see *patron.*] **I.** *n.* An original or model proposed for or deserving of imitation (as, "She shall be . . . A *pattern* to all princes": Shakspere's "Henry VIII.," v. 5. 23); an exemplar; a model of a specified excellence (as, "The Manlii and Valerii were *patterns* of courage, the Lucretias and Virginias of purity," Froude's "Cæsar," ii.; "My brother was always a *pattern* of solemnity," C. B. Brown's "Wieland," viii.); also, anything fashioned or designed to serve as a model or guide for something to be made (as, a paper *pattern* for use in cutting out a garment); also, a sample or specimen; an example or instance, esp. a typical instance; also, a precedent† (as, "A *pattern,* precedent, and lively warrant, For me . . . to perform the like": Shakspere's "Titus Andronicus," v. 3. 44); also, a copy†; also, a decorative design, as for china, wall-paper, textile fabrics, etc., or such a design carried out on something (as, "She wore a black-and-white frock, of a small check *pattern*": Arnold Bennett's "Helen with the High Hand," i.); sometimes, a style of marking of natural or chance origin (as, the *patterns* of frost on the windows); in general, style, type, or make; also, a sufficient quantity of material for making a garment (U. S.); also, the festival of a patron saint, or the festivities with which it is celebrated (Ir.: as, "the occasion of a fair, or a *pattern,* or market-day," Lover's "Handy Andy," viii.); also, specif., in *founding,* the counterpart, as in wood or metal, of a casting, from which the mold in sand is made; in *numis.,* a specimen model for a proposed coin not ultimately adopted for the currency; in *gun.,* the distribution of shot in a target at which a shot-gun or the like is fired; a diagram showing such distribution. **II.** *a.* Serving, or worthy to serve, as a pattern or model; model: as, "Ernest was not so careful about money as a *pattern* boy should be" (S. Butler's "Way of All Flesh," xlii.).—**pat′tern,** *v.* **I.** *tr.* To serve as a pattern for† (as, "*Pattern'd* by thy fault, foul sin may say, He learn'd to sin, and thou didst teach the way": Shakspere's "Lucrece," 629); also, to make after a pattern; model; also, to take as a pattern (rare); also, to match† or equal†; also, to cover or mark with a pattern or design (as, "The German anti-aircraft guns . . . begin to *pattern* the sky about them with little balls of black smoke": H. G. Wells's "Italy, France, and Britain at War," iii. 2). **II.** *intr.* To model one's conduct, etc. (*by* or *after*).—**pat′tern=mak″er,** *n.* One who makes patterns, esp. for castings.

pat-ty (pat′i), *n.*; pl. *patties* (-iz). [F. *pâté.*] A little pie; a pâté: as, oyster *patties.*—**pat′ty=pan,** *n.* A small pan for baking patties, little cakes, etc.

pat-u-lous (pat̤′ṳ̄-lus), *a.* [L. *patulus,* < *patere,* lie open.] Open; gaping; expanded; spreading, as a tree or its boughs; specif., in *bot.,* spreading slightly, as a calyx; bearing the flowers loose or dispersed, as a peduncle.—**pat′u-lous-ly,** *adv.*

pau-ci-ty (pâ′si-ti), *n.* [L. *paucitas,* < *paucus,* little, pl. few.] Smallness of number or quantity; fewness; scantiness: as, "the *paucity* of the troops" (Motley's "Dutch Republic," iv. 1); *paucity* of material.

pauk, pauk-y (pâk, pâ′ki). See *pawk, pawky.*

paul-dron (pâl′dro̤n), *n.* [OF. *espauleron,* < *espaule* (F. *épaule*), shoulder: see *epaule.*] A piece of armor for the shoulder.

A, Pauldron.

Paul-ine (pâ′līn or -lin), *a.* Of or pertaining to the apostle Paul, or his doctrines or writings.

Paul-ist (pâ′list), *n.* A member of the Missionary Society of St. Paul the Apostle, a community of Roman Catholic priests founded in New York in 1858.

pau-low-ni-a (pâ-lō′ni-ä̤), *n.* [NL.; named from Anna *Pavlovna,* daughter of the czar Paul I., of Russia.] A scrophulariaceous tree, *Paulownia tomentosa,* a native of Japan, bearing terminal panicles of showy pale-violet or blue flowers, which blossom in early spring: widely cultivated for ornament.

Branch of Paulownia, with the inflorescence and young leaves. — *a,* the fruit; *b,* the seed.

paunch (pânch or pänch), *n.* [OF. *panche, pance* (F. *panse*), < L. *pantex* (*pantic-*).] The belly or abdomen, or the stomach as the receptacle of food (as used to refer to a human being, now commonly derogatory, implying prominence of the belly, gluttony, etc.: as, "a short, rosy-cheeked, apoplectic-looking subject, with . . . a *paunch* like an alderman's," Lever's "Harry Lorrequer," xvii.); also, the rumen, or first stomach of a ruminant.—**paunch,** *v. t.* To stab in the paunch; also, to disembowel; also, to swallow greedily.—**paunch′y,** *a.* Having a large or prominent paunch.—**paunch′i-ness,** *n.*

pau-per (pâ′pėr), *n.* [L. *pauper,* poor, as n. a poor man: cf. *poor.*] A person in utter poverty or destitution; esp., one who, being without private means of support, lives as a charge upon the community.—**pau′-**

per-ism, *n.* The condition of a pauper; the existence of paupers; also, paupers collectively.—**pau′per-ize** (-īz), *v. t.*; *-ized, -izing.* To reduce to pauperism; make a pauper of.—**pau″per-i-za′tion** (-i-zā′shọn), *n.*—**pau′per-iz-er** (-ī-zėr), *n.*

pause (pâz), *n.* [OF. F. *pause,* < L. *pausa,* < Gr. παῦσις, cessation, < παύειν, cause to cease, stop.] A temporary stop or rest; an intermission of speech or action; often, a cessation proceeding from doubt or uncertainty; also, intermission; delay; hesitation; suspense; specif., a break or rest in speaking or reading as depending on sense, grammatical relations, metrical divisions, etc., or in writing or printing as marked by punctuation; in *music,* the symbol ◡ or ⌢ placed under or over a note or rest to indicate that it is to be prolonged.—**pause,** *v. i.*; *paused, pausing.* To make a pause; stop; wait; hesitate; dwell or linger (*upon*).—**pause′less,** *a.* Without pause; ceaseless.—**pause′less-ly,** *adv.*—**paus′er,** *n.*—**paus′ing-ly,** *adv.*

pauw (päö), *n.* See *paauw.*

pav-an (pav′ạn), *n.* [F. *pavane*; origin uncertain.] A stately dance in vogue in the 16th century, or the music for it.

pave (pāv), *v. t.*; pret. *paved,* pp. *paved* (archaic *paven*), ppr. *paving.* [OF. F. *paver,* < ML. *pavare,* for L. *pavire,* beat down.] To cover or lay (a road, walk, etc.) with stones, bricks, tiles, wood, concrete, etc., so as to make a firm, level surface; fig., to prepare (the way) for something (as, "Experience and practice must *pave* the way to excellent production": Godwin's "Caleb Williams," xxxiv.).—**pave,** *n.* A pavement.—**pa-vé** (pȧ-vā), *n.* [F., orig. pp. of *paver.*] A paved road, walk, etc.; a pavement (as, "Beneath a splendid dome were men of all nations, moving to and fro over the marble *pavé*": Mrs. Stowe's "Uncle Tom's Cabin," xxx.); also, a setting in which the jewels are placed close together so as to show no metal.—**pave′ment,** *n.* [OF. F. *pavement,* < L. *pavimentum,* < *pavire.*] A surface, ground-covering, or floor made by paving; a paved road, sidewalk, etc.; specif., the paved sidewalk, as distinct from the roadway; also, some structure or formation resembling a pavement; also, a material used for paving.—**pav-er** (pā′vėr), *n.*

pav-id (pav′id), *a.* [L. *pavidus,* < *pavere,* be struck with fear.] Frightened; fearful; timid.

pa-vil-ion (pạ-vil′yọn), *n.* [OF. F. *pavillon,* < L. *papilio(n-),* tent, orig. butterfly.] A tent, esp. a large tent raised on posts; also, a canopy (obs. or poetic); also, a light, more or less open structure for purposes of shelter, pleasure, etc., as in a park or at the seaside; also, a projecting division of a building, usually distinguished from the main structure by greater height or more elaborate decoration; also, one of a group of buildings forming a hospital; also, a French gold coin struck by Philip VI. (14th century), or a gold coin

Obverse. Reverse.
Pavilion of Edward, the Black Prince.—British Museum.

struck by Edward, the English Black Prince (14th century), for circulation in France; in *anat.,* the auricle of the ear; in *brilliant-cutting,* the sloping surfaces between the girdle and the culet, taken together; also, the whole lower part of the stone, taken from the girdle and including the culet.—**pa-vil′ion,** *v. t.* To shelter in or as in a pavilion; also, to furnish with pavilions.

pav-in (pav′in), *n.* See *pavan.*

pav-ing (pā′ving), *n.* The act or work of one who or that which paves; also, a pavement, or material for a pavement.

pav-ior, pav-iour (pāv′yọr), *n.* One who lays pavements.

pav-is, pav-ise (pav′is), *n.* [OF. *pavais* (F. *pavois*), < It. *pavese,* appar. named from *Pavia,* in Italy.] A large medieval shield, covering the whole body.—**pav′is-er, pav′is-or,** *n.* One armed with or bearing a pavis.

Pavis, 14th century.

pav-o-nine (pav′ọ-nīn or -nin), *a.* [L. *pavoninus,* < *pavo(n-),* peacock.] Of or like the peacock; resembling the peacock's feathers, as in coloring.

paw (pâ), *n.* [OF. *poe*: cf. D. *poot,* G. *pfote,* paw.] The foot of an animal with nails or claws; the foot of any animal; also, the human hand (humorous or contemptuous).—**paw,** *v.* **I.** *tr.* To strike or scrape with the paws or feet (as, "as a cat *paws* a soft hearth-rug," Kipling's "Light That Failed," iii.; "some proud, restrained horse *pawing* the grass," Weir Mitchell's "Hugh Wynne," ix.); also, to handle clumsily, rudely, or over-familiarly (colloq.: as, "They run their hands over your clothes—they *paw* you," H. G. Wells's "Tono-Bungay," iii. 2. § 5). **II.** *intr.* To beat or scrape the ground, etc., with the paws or feet (as, "Neighing steeds, tied to swinging limbs . . . *pawed,* wheeled, and gazed after their vanished riders": G. W. Cable's "John March, Southerner," xxiii.); also, to use the hands clumsily or rudely on something (colloq.: as, "Upstairs the hall was dark, but I found the duke's room, and started to *paw* around it," Mark Twain's "Huckleberry Finn," xxvi.).

pawk (pâk), *n.* [Origin obscure.] A trick or wile. [Sc. and north. Eng.]—**pawk′y,** *a.* Cunning; artful; sly; shrewd: as, "Benjamin Franklin at the court of Louis XVI, with his long hair, his plain clothes, and his *pawky* manner" (H. G. Wells's "Outline of History," xxxvii. § 6). [Chiefly Sc. and north. Eng.]—**pawk′i-ly,** *adv.*—**pawk′i-ness,** *n.*

pawl (pâl), *n.* [Cf. D. *pal,* pawl.] A short iron bar acting as a catch to prevent a windlass or capstan from turning back; a pivoted bar adapted to engage with the teeth of a ratchet-wheel or the like so as to prevent movement backward or to impart motion.—**pawl,** *v. t.* To secure or check with a pawl.

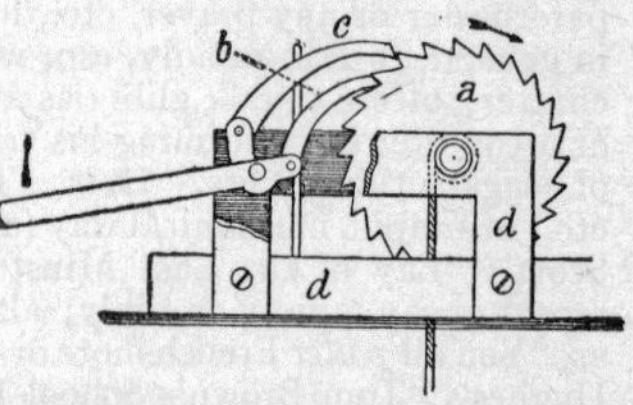

Pawl in Hoisting-apparatus.—*a,* ratchet-wheel; *b* and *c,* pawls, engaging with teeth by gravitation; *d, d,* frame; *f,* handle. The wheel is moved in the direction of the arrow by the pawl *c* when *f* is lifted, and by *b* when *f* is depressed.

pawn[1] (pân), *n.* [OF. *paon, peon* (F. *pion*), < ML. *pedo(n-),* foot-soldier, < L. *pes* (*ped-*), foot.] One of the 16 pieces of lowest value at chess. Also fig.: as, "We have got the poor *pawn* but the hand which plays the game is still out of our reach" (Conan Doyle's "Exploits of Brigadier Gerard," viii.).

pawn[2] (pân), *n.* [OF. *pan*: cf. D. *pand,* G. *pfand,* pawn, pledge.] Something given or deposited as security, as for money borrowed; any thing or person serving as security; a pledge; also, the state of being deposited or held as security (as, to put jewels in *pawn,* as to a pawnbroker); also, the act of pawning.—**pawn**[2], *v. t.* To deposit as security, as for money borrowed (as, to *pawn* a watch or a ring); put in pawn; in general, to pledge or stake (as, "Thereon I *pawn* my credit and mine honour": Shakspere's "3 Henry VI.," iii. 3. 116).—**pawn′bro″ker,** *n.* One whose business it is to lend money at interest on pledged personal property. —**pawn′bro″king,** *n.* and *a.*—**pawn-ee** (pâ-nē′), *n.* The person with whom something is deposited as a pawn or security.—**pawn′er, pawn′or,** *n.* One who pawns or deposits something as security.—**pawn′shop,** *n.* The shop of a pawnbroker.

Pax.—Brass of 15th century.

paw-paw (pâ′pâ), *n.* Same as *papaw.*

pax (paks), *n.* [L., peace.] In the

Rom. Cath. Ch., a small tablet bearing a representation of the Crucifixion or some other sacred subject, formerly kissed by the celebrating priest and the congregation at mass. See cut on preceding page.

pax-wax (paks′waks), *n.* [ME. *paxwax*, earlier *faxwax*, appar. < AS. *feax*, hair, + *weaxan*, grow.] In many mammals, the stout median ligament of the back of the neck, composed of yellow elastic fibrous tissue, and assisting in the support of the head.

pay[1] (pā), *v. t.*; *payed, paying.* [OF. *peier, poier*, < L. *picare*, < *pix*, pitch.] *Naut.*, to coat or cover (seams, a ship's bottom, etc.) with pitch, tar, or the like: as, "We had no tar or pitch to *pay* the seams and secure the bottom" (Defoe's "Captain Singleton," iii.).

pay[2] (pā), *v. t.*; *paid, paying.* [OF. *paier* (F. *payer*), < L. *pacare*, pacify: see *pacable.*] To appease†, satisfy†, or please†; also, to satisfy the claims of (a person, etc.), as by giving money due; compensate, as for goods supplied or services rendered; recompense or remunerate; fig., to requite, as for good, harm, offense, etc.; esp., to retaliate upon or punish (often with *off* or *out*: as, "She had been piqued . . . and . . . it had pleased her to *pay* me out in this manner," W. H. Hudson's "Green Mansions," v.); also, to yield a recompense or return to, or be profitable to (as, the investment has *paid* us very well; it will hardly *pay* you to go further); often, to yield as a return (as, the stock *pays* six per cent; the property has *paid* nothing for two years); also, to give compensation for, or meet the expense of (as, highly *paid* work; "He was welcomed like a brother by the Chevalier, who thence *paid* his way to France," Stevenson's "Master of Ballantrae," iii.); also, to discharge (a debt, obligation, etc.), as by giving or doing something; defray (cost or expense); also, to give (money, etc.) as in discharge of debt or obligation; hence, to give or render (attention, regard, court, compliments, etc.), as if due or fitting; make (a call, visit, etc.); also, *naut.*, etc., to let out (a rope, etc.) as by slackening (with *out* or *away*: as, "As they *paid* out chain, we swung clear of them," Dana's "Two Years before the Mast," xv.).—**to pay the piper,** to pay for one's good time; pay the cost or bear the consequences of anything: as, "He was invariably the best to come off; and his partners in mischief were usually alone to *pay the piper*" (Stevenson's "Master of Ballantrae," i.).—**pay**[2], *v. i.* To give money, etc., due (as, to *pay* for goods or work; to *pay* by instalments); discharge debt; give compensation, as for damage or loss sustained; fig., to make amends, or atone (as, "They shall . . . *pay* for their presumption": Shakspere's "3 Henry VI.," iv. 1. 114); suffer, or be punished, as for something; also, to yield a return or profit; be profitable or advantageous; be worth while; also, *naut.*, to fall (*off*) to leeward (as, "The little vessel '*paid off*' from the wind": Dana's "Two Years before the Mast," iv.).—**to pay through the nose,** to pay under improper exaction, as in case of overcharges, extortion, or blackmail; pay exorbitantly.—**pay**[2], *n.* [OF. *paie* (F. *paye, paie*).] Satisfaction†; also, payment, as of wages; paid employ (as, spies in the enemy's *pay*); also, wages, salary, or stipend; compensation (as, "Two good horses were very good *pay* for one bad wife": Irving's "Captain Bonneville," xlvii.); fig., requital; reward or punishment; also, a source of payment (as, a person, or a line of work, that is good *pay*, or bad *pay*).—**pay dirt,** earth, etc., containing a sufficient quantity of metal to be profitably worked by the miner.

pay-a-ble (pā′ạ-bl), *a.* That may be paid; also, that is to be paid; due; also, paying or profitable (as, *payable* ore-deposits).

pay=day (pā′dā), *n.* The day when payment is made, or to be made; the day on which wages are paid (as, "The following *payday* Bok found an increase in his weekly envelope": Bok's "Americanization of Edward Bok," xi.); in the stock-exchange, the day on which a transfer of stock must be completed and paid for.

pay-ee (pā-ē′), *n.* One to whom money is paid, or to be paid.

pay-er, pay-or (pā′ėr, pā′ọr), *n.* One who pays; esp., the person named in a bill or note who has to pay the holder.

pay-ing (pā′ing), *p. a.* That pays; giving money or compensation for what is received (as, a *paying* guest); yielding a return or profit, or remunerative (as, a *paying* business).

pay-mas-ter (pā′mȧs″tėr), *n.* An officer of an army or navy, or an official in any service, charged with the payment of wages or salaries.—**pay′mas″ter=gen′er-al,** *n.*; pl. *paymasters-.* The officer at the head of the pay department of an army or navy.

pay-ment (pā′mẹnt), *n.* [OF. F. *paiement.*] The act or an act of paying; also, that which is paid, esp. a sum of money; compensation; recompense; fig., requital.

pay-mis-tress (pā′mis″tres), *n.* A woman charged with the payment of wages or salaries.

pay-nim (pā′nim). [OF. *paienime, paienisme*, < LL. *paganismus*, E. *paganism.*] **I.** *n.* Pagan lands†; pagandom†; also, a pagan or heathen (archaic); esp., a Mohammedan (archaic: as, "the crusader, who had sunk thirty thousand *paynims* at a blow," Motley's "Dutch Republic," v. 1). **II.** *a.* Pagan or heathen (as, "A people . . . a remnant that were left *Paynim* amid their circles, and the stones They pitch up straight to heaven": Tennyson's "Holy Grail," 661); esp., Mohammedan (as, "*Paynim* sons of swarthy Spain": Scott's "Rob Roy," ii.). [Archaic.]

pay=roll (pā′rōl), *n.* A roll or list of persons to be paid, with the amounts due; also, the aggregate of these amounts.

pay-sage (pā-ē-zäzh), *n.* [F., < *pays*, country: see *peasant.*] A landscape.

pea (pē), *n.*; pl. *peas* (see *pease*). [Assumed sing. of *pease* (orig. sing., but later taken as pl.): see *pease.*] The round, highly nutritious seed of *Pisum sativum*, a hardy fabaceous vine in wide cultivation, or the plant; any of various related or similar plants, or the seed, as the field-pea (or 'gray pea'), the chick-pea, or the cow-pea; any plant of the fabaceous genus *Lathyrus*, as *L. odoratus* ('sweet pea'), a climbing annual esteemed for its sweet-scented, variously colored flowers.—**pea′ber″ry,** *n.* A coffee-berry with one of its two seeds aborted, the developed seed being round and pea-like, and not flattened on one side like the ordinary seed.

Pea-bod-y (pē′bod-i) **bird.** [From the *Peabody* Glen, White Mountains, N. H.] A large North American sparrow, *Zonotrichia albicollis*, with a white throat.

Peabody Bird.

peace (pēs), *n.* [OF. *pais* (F. *paix*), < L. *pax* (*pac-*), peace, akin to *pacisci*, agree: see *pact.*] Freedom from war or hostilities (as, "The king has . . . the sole prerogative of making war and *peace*," Blackstone's "Commentaries," I. 257; "to dream of *peace* amidst a world in arms," Whittier's "Peace Convention at Brussels"); also, an agreement between contending parties to abstain from further hostilities (as, "Catherine signed the *Peace* of Lonjumeau, and the Calvinists dispersed": Besant's "Coligny," ix.); also, freedom from strife or dissension; concord; also, freedom from disturbance; tranquillity; freedom from mental disturbance (as, "Returning health and *peace* of mind gave a new interest to everything around me": H. Melville's "Typee," xvii.); stillness or quiet; also, freedom from civil commotion; public order and security (as, to keep the *peace*; a justice of the *peace*).—**to hold,** or **keep, one's peace.** See under *hold*[2], *v. t.*—**to make one's peace,** to effect reconciliation for one's self, or for another person: as, "I have long *made my peace* with God and man" (Marryat's "King's Own," iv.); "I will *make your peace* with him" (Shakspere's "Twelfth Night," iii. 4. 295).

peace-a-ble (pē′sạ-bl), *a.* [OF. F. *paisible.*] Disposed to peace, or inclined to avoid strife or dissension (as, "They will not meddle with *peaceable* merchants," Defoe's "Robinson Crusoe," ii. 12; *peaceable* intentions); not quarrelsome or pugnacious; also, characterized by peace, or peaceful (as, a *peaceable* reign; a *peaceable* adjustment).—**peace′a-ble-ness,** *n.*—**peace′a-bly,** *adv.*

peace-ful (pēs′ful), *a.* Characterized by peace, or free from strife or commotion (as, a *peaceful* reign); untroubled; tranquil; quiet; pertaining to or characteristic of a state of peace (as, *peaceful* pursuits); also, disposed or inclined to peace, or peaceable (as, a *peaceful* creature; *peaceful* words).—**peace′ful-ly,** *adv.*—**peace′ful-ness,** *n.*

peace-less (pēs′les), *a.* Without peace; unquiet.—**peace′-less-ness,** *n.*

peace-mak-er (pēs′mā″kėr), *n.* One who makes peace, as by reconciling parties at variance: as, "Blessed are the *peace-makers*: for they shall be called the children of God" (Mat. v. 9).—**peace′mak″ing,** *n.* and *a.*

peace-mong-er (pēs′mung″gėr), *n.* One who persistently advocates peace: used in disparagement. Cf. *pacifist, n.*

peace=of-fer-ing (pēs′of″ėr-ing), *n.* An offering or sacrifice prescribed by the Levitical law (see Lev. iii., vii.) as an expression of thanksgiving to God; hence, any offering made to procure peace (as, "He was not to be sacrificed as a *peace-offering* to revengeful Rome": Motley's "Dutch Republic," Introd., iv.).

peace=of-fi-cer (pēs′of″i-sėr), *n.* A civil officer appointed to preserve the public peace, as a sheriff or a constable.

peace=pipe (pēs′pīp), *n.* The calumet or pipe smoked by the North American Indians in token or ratification of peace. See Longfellow's "Hiawatha," i. 30.

peach[1] (pēch), *v.* [For *appeach.*] **I.** *tr.* To impeach†; also, to inform against (now rare). **II.** *intr.* To inform against an accomplice or associate: as, "If I be ta'en, I'll *peach* for this" (Shakspere's "1 Henry IV.," ii. 2. 47); "No good was to be got by *peaching* on him" (H. Kingsley's "Geoffry Hamlyn," x.). [Now slang.]

peach[2] (pēch), *n.* [OF. *pesche* (F. *pêche*), < ML. *persica*, for L. *Persicum*, < Gr. Περσικόν, lit. 'Persian (apple).'] The subacid, juicy fruit of a tree, *Amygdalus persica*, of many varieties, widely cultivated in temperate climates; the tree itself; also, any of various similar fruits, or its plant; also, a person or thing especially admired or liked (slang); also, peach-color.—**peach′blow,** *n.* A purplish-pink color, esp. on Oriental porcelain.—**peach′=col″or,** *n.* A yellowish-pink color.—**peach′=col″ored,** *a.*—**peach′y,** *a.* Peach-like, as in color or appearance.—**peach′i-ness,** *n.*

pea-cock (pē′kok), *n.* [ME. *pecok*, < AS. *pēa* (< L. *pavo*), peacock, + *coc*, E. *cock*[1].] The male of the peafowl, esp. of the common peafowl, *Pavo cristatus*, a native of India but now widely domesticated, distinguished for its long, erectile, ocellated tail-coverts with rich iridescent coloring of green, blue, and gold, and taken as a proverbial type of vainglory; often, any peafowl (male or female).—**pea′-cock,** *v.* **I.** *tr.* To make like a peacock; render vainglorious. **II.** *intr.* To strut like a peacock; make a vainglorious display.—**pea′cock=blue′,** *n.* A deep, rich blue with a tinge of green.—**pea′cock=pheas′ant,** *n.* Any pheasant of the Asiatic genus *Polyplectron*, notable for the handsome ocellated plumage and the spurred legs of the male. See cut in next column.—**pea′cock-y,** *a.* Peacock-like; showy; vainglorious.

Peacock (*Pavo cristatus*).

pea-fowl (pē′foul), *n.* [With *pea-* as in *peacock.*] Any of the gallinaceous birds constituting the genus *Pavo*; a peacock or peahen.

peag (pēg), *n.* [See *wampumpeag.*] Strings of white or of black or dark-purple beads made from shells, used by North American Indians as money and for ornament. See *wampum.*

Peacock-pheasant (*Polyplectron bicalcaratum*).

pea=green (pē′-grēn′), *n.* A light green, not markedly yellowish or bluish.

pea-hen (pē′-hen), *n.* [ME. *pehen*: cf. *peacock.*] The female peafowl.

pea=jack-et (pē′jak″et), *n.* [Cf. D. *pijakker, pijekker*, pea-jacket, *pij*, coat of coarse woolen cloth.] A short coat of thick woolen cloth, worn by seamen: as, "*pea jackets* . . . very short great-coats" (Marryat's "Peter Simple," x.).

peak[1] (pēk). [Var. of *pike*[1].] **I.** *n.* A projecting point (as, the *peak* of a man's beard); also, a projecting front piece, or vizor, of a cap; also, the pointed top of a mountain; a mountain with a pointed summit; hence, the pointed top of anything (as, "There sat the dove again, on the *peak* of the same dormer-window!" Hawthorne's "Blithedale Romance," xviii.); fig., the highest point, or summit; the maximum point or degree of anything; *naut.*, the contracted part of a ship's hold at the bow or the stern (as, "The captain shut him down in the fore *peak*": Dana's "Two Years before the Mast," vi.); also, the upper after corner of a sail that is extended by a gaff; also, the outer extremity of a gaff (as, "a full-rigged brig, with the Yankee ensign at her *peak*": Dana's "Two Years before the Mast," xviii.); in *mech.* and *elect.*, the maximum of a curve showing the variation of the load of a power-station or the like during a certain period of time; a maximum or greatest load, esp. the load of a power-station or the like at the time of greatest demand. **II.** *a.* Being the peak, or highest point or degree; being the maximum (as, *peak* prices); also, pertaining to the peak or maximum (as, the *peak* hour, or hour of maximum load, of a power-station or the like).—**peak**[1], *v.* **I.** *intr.* To project in a peak. **II.** *tr.* *Naut.*, to raise (a yard, gaff, etc.) to or toward a vertical position; in *whaling*, of a whale, to raise (the flukes or tail) straight up in the air in diving perpendicularly (see H. Melville's "Moby-Dick," lxxxvi.).

peak[2] (pēk), *v. i.* [Origin uncertain.] To become thin or emaciated; waste; droop; mope: as, "*peaking* and pining over what people think of him" (Kingsley's "Two Years Ago," xiv.).

peaked[1] (pēkt or pē′ked), *a.* Having a peak; pointed: as, "He seems robed in a long cloak, with a *peaked* cap or hood like the elves in my nursery stories" (Chesterton's "Magic," i.); "His *peaked* beard was dishevelled" (Hawthorne's "House of the Seven Gables," i.).

peaked[2] (pēkt or pē′ked), *p. a.* Thin; emaciated: as, "a *peaked*, sharp, wiry-featured, virulent-tongued virago" (Mrs. Stowe's "Oldtown Folks," xxxix.).

peak-y (pē′ki), *a.* Peaked or pointed; peak-like; abounding in peaks.

peal (pēl), *n.* [ME. *pele*, appar. for *appele*, E. *appeal*, as if meaning orig. a summons or call by bell-ringing.] A loud, prolonged sound of bells, or of cannon, thunder, applause, laughter, etc.; specif., a series of changes rung on a set of bells; also, a set of bells tuned to one another.—**peal,** *v.* **I.** *intr.* To sound forth in a peal; resound: as, "A hundred bells began to *peal*": (Tennyson's "Epic," 352); "an outcry that went *pealing* through the night" (Hawthorne's "Scarlet Letter," xii.). **II.** *tr.* To assail with loud sounds†; also, to give forth loudly and sonorously: as, "Till from the trumpet's mouth is *pealed* The blast of triumph o'er thy grave" (Bryant's "Battle-Field")..

pe-an (pē′ạn), *n.* See *pæan.*

pea-nut (pē′nut), *n.* The fruit (pod) or the edible seed of *Arachis hypogæa*, a fabaceous plant in which the stipe of the ovary bends downward in growing and forces the pod underground, where it ripens; also, the plant.—**peanut butter,** a smooth paste made from finely ground roasted peanuts: used as a relish, etc.

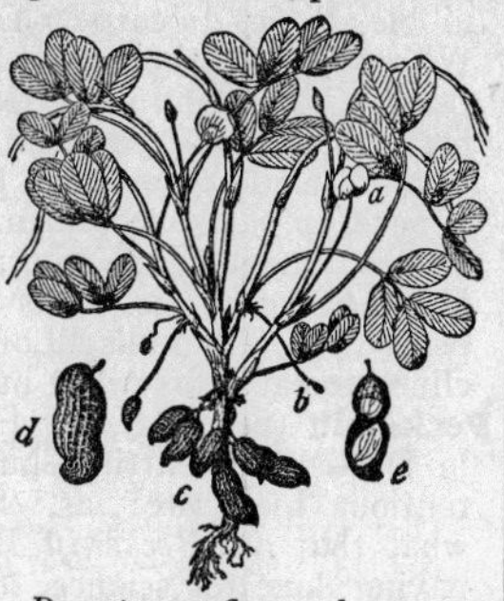

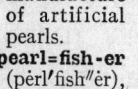

Peanut. — *a*, flower; *b*, ovary on lengthened stipe; *c*, fruit; *d*, ripe pod; *e*, pod opened, showing seeds.

pear (pãr), *n.* [AS. *peru*, < ML. *pira*, for L. *pirum*, pear.] The edible fruit, typically rounded but elongated and growing smaller toward the stem, of a malaceous tree, *Pyrus communis*, familiar in cultivation; the tree itself; also, some similar fruit, or its plant, as the alligator-pear or the prickly pear.

pearl[1] (pėrl), *n.* See *purl*[2].

pearl[2] (pėrl), *n.* [OF. F. *perle* = ML. *perla*, *perula*, perhaps dim. (with reference to shape) < L. *pirum*, pear.] A hard, smooth, often highly lustrous concretion, a mass of nacre, white or variously colored, and rounded, pear-shaped, or irregular (baroque) in form, secreted as a morbid product within the shell of various bivalve mollusks, and often valuable as a gem; also, something similar in form, luster, etc., as a dewdrop or a capsule of medicine; a cataract of the eye†; also, fig., something precious or choice; the finest example of anything; also, nacre, or mother-of-pearl; also, pearl-gray; also, a printing-type (5 point) of a size between diamond and agate (see *type*).—**pearl barley,** barley reduced by grinding to small rounded grains: used in soups, etc.—**pearl millet,** a tall grass, *Pennisetum typhoideum*, cultivated in Africa, the Orient, etc., for its edible seeds and as a forage-plant.—**pearl tapioca,** tapioca in the form of small, round grains.—**pearl**[2], *v.* **I.** *tr.* To adorn or stud with or as with pearls; also, to make like pearls, as in form or color. **II.** *intr.* To seek for pearls (as, "We've *pearled* on half-shares in the Bay": Kipling's "Lost Legion"); also, to take a pearl-like form or appearance.

pearl-ash (pėrl′ash), *n.* Commercial carbonate of potassium.

pearl=div-er (pėrl′dī″vėr), *n.* One who dives for pearl-oysters.—**pearl′=div″ing,** *n.*

pearl-er (pėr′lėr), *n.* A pearl-diver, or an employer of pearl-divers; also, a boat used by pearl-fishers.

pearl=farm-ing (pėrl′fär″ming), *n.* The act or business of cultivating pearl-oysters.

pearl=fish (pėrl′fish), *n.* Any of the small fishes of the family *Fierasferidæ*, which live in the shells of mollusks and in large holothurians; also, any of certain fishes, as a minnow, *Alburnus lucidus* (the bleak), whose scales are used in the manufacture of artificial pearls.

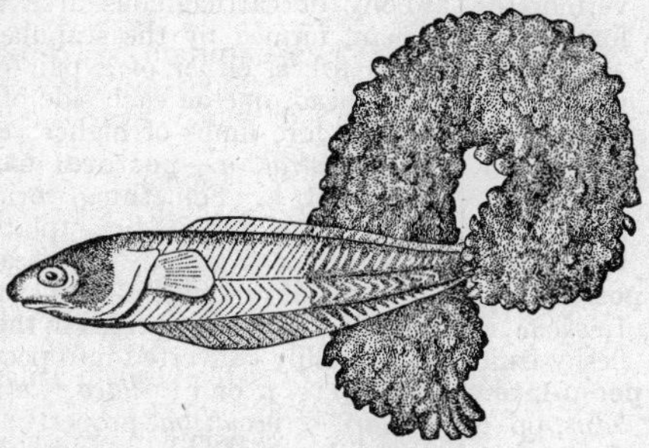
Pearl-fish (*Fierasfer acus*), issuing from a holothurian.

pearl=fish-er (pėrl′fish″ėr), *n.* One who fishes for pearls.—**pearl′=fish″er-y,** *n.*; pl. *-ies* (-iz). The occupation or industry of fishing for pearls; also, the place where this is carried on.—**pearl′=fish″ing,** *n.*

pearl=gray (pėrl′grā′), *n.* A very pale, clear, bluish gray approaching white.

pearl-ing (pėr′ling), *n.* The act or industry of seeking for pearls.

pearl-ite (pėr′līt), *n.* In *metal.*, an alloy of carbon and iron present in slowly cooled steels, constituting the whole substance of steels with 0.9 per cent of carbon, and forming an important constituent in other steels; in *petrog.*, perlite.

pearl=oys-ter (pėrl′ois″tėr), *n.* A pearl-bearing mollusk of the family *Aviculidæ*, as *Meleagrina margaritifera* of the Indian Ocean and the Pacific Ocean.

pearl-y (pėr′li), *a.* Like a pearl, or like pearl; of the color or luster of pearl; nacreous; also, adorned with or abounding in pearls or pearl.—**pearly nautilus.** See *nautilus*.

pear-main (pãr′mān), *n.* [OF. *parmain* (pear), F. *permaine* (apple); appar. named from *Parma*, in Italy.] A kind of pear†; also, a kind of apple, of several varieties.

pear=shaped (pãr′shāpt), *a.* Of an elongated, rounded form contracting toward one end.

peart (pērt), *a.* [Var. of *pert.*] Lively or brisk; cheerful; clever. [Now prov.]

peas-ant (pez′ạnt), *n.* [OF. *paisant* (F. *paysan*), < *pais* (F. *pays*), country, < ML. *pagensis*, adj. < L. *pagus*, district, country: cf. *pagan.*] A countryman or rustic; esp., one of a class of persons, as in European countries, of inferior social rank, living in the country and engaged usually in agricultural labor; also, a boor† or clown†; also, a knave† or rascal†.—**peas′ant-ry** (-ri), *n.* Peasants collectively (as, "the British *peasantry*": C. Brontë's "Jane Eyre," xxxiv.); also, the status or character of a peasant.

pease (pēz), *n.*; pl. *pease*, archaic or prov. *peasen*, *peason*, obs. *peases.* [AS. *pise* (pl. *pisan*), < LL. *pisa*, for L. *pisum*, < Gr. *πίσον*, pulse, pea.] A pea; *pl.*, peas collectively. [Archaic or prov.]—**pease′cod, peas′cod** (-kod), *n.* [See *cod*[1].] The pod of the pea.—**pease′cod=bel″lied,** *a.* Of a doublet, having the lower front part so shaped and quilted as to project from the body, in a fashion in vogue toward the end of the 16th century.

Peasecod-bellied Doublet.

peat[1] (pēt), *n.* [Origin uncertain: appar. not connected with *pet*[1].] A pet or darling: used of a woman or girl. [Archaic.]

peat[2] (pēt), *n.* [ME. *pete* (AL. *peta*); origin uncertain.] A block or piece of a kind of partially decomposed vegetable matter consisting esp. of certain mosses and occurring, often in extensive tracts, in marshy or damp regions, cut out and dried for use as fuel (as, "The fireplace . . . was fed in winter with the sticks and *peats* brought by the scholars": Ian Maclaren's "Beside the Bonnie Brier Bush," i. 1); also, such vegetable matter as a substance or fuel (as, "A few of the brethren were digging *peat* for our winter's fuel": Hawthorne's "Blithedale Romance," xii.).—**peat-er-y** (pē′tėr-i), *n.*; pl. *-ies* (-iz). A place from which peat is dug.—**peat′y,** *a.* Of, like, or abounding in peat.

peau=de=cygne (pō-dė-sēn-y′), *n.* [F., 'skin of swan.'] A soft, lustrous, satin-faced silk fabric.

peau=de=soie (pō-dė-swo), *n.* [F., 'skin of silk.'] A soft silk fabric with little luster, having a satin finish on both sides or on one only: often confused with *poult-de-soie.*

pea-vey, pea-vy (pē′vi), *n.*; pl. *-veys, -vies* (-viz). [From the name of the inventor.] A lumberman's cant-hook having a strong spike at the end.

Peavey.

pe-ba (pē′bạ̈), *n.* [Brazilian.] A small armadillo, *Tatusia novemcincta*, ranging from Paraguay to Texas.

Peba.

peb-ble (peb′l), *n.* [Found first in AS. *papolstān*, E. *pebble-stone*; origin unknown.] A small, rounded stone, esp. one worn by the action of water; also, a transparent, colorless rock-crystal used for the lenses of spectacles; a lens made of it; also, an agate or other like ornamental stone, esp. as used in jewelry (as, Scotch *pebble*: see under *Scotch*³, *a.*); also, pebbleware; also, pebble-leather, or its granulated surface.—**peb'ble,** *v. t.*; *-bled, -bling.* To pelt with or as with pebbles (as, "The peasants . . . betook themselves to stones, and . . . *pebbled* the priest": Scott's "Antiquary," xviii.); also, to prepare (leather, etc.) so as to have a granulated surface.—**peb'bled,** *a.* Abounding in pebbles; pebbly: as, "the *pebbled* shore" (Shakspere's "Sonnets," lx.).—**peb'ble=leath'er,** *n.* Pebbled leather; leather with a granulated surface.—**peb'ble=stone,** *n.* [AS. *papolstān.*] A pebble; also, pebbles collectively.—**peb'ble-ware** (-wãr), *n.* In *ceramics*, a variety of Wedgwood ware in which differently colored clays are intermingled in the body of the paste.—**peb'bly,** *a.* Abounding in or covered with pebbles: as, "a broad, *pebbly* path" (C. Brontë's "Jane Eyre," v.).

pé-brine (pā-brēn), *n.* [F., < Pr. *pebrino*, < *pebre*, pepper, < L. *piper*: see *pepper*.] An epidemic disease of silkworms, in which small black spots appear.

pe-can (pē-kan'), *n.* [N. Amer. Ind.] A tree, *Hicoria pecan*, a species of hickory, common in the Ohio and Mississippi valleys, valued for its olive-shaped, smooth-shelled nut with a sweet, oily, edible kernel; also, the nut ('pecan-nut').

Pecan.

pec-ca-ble (pek'ạ-bl), *a.* [F. *peccable*, < L. *peccare*, sin: see *peccant*.] Liable to sin or err.—**pec-ca-bil'i-ty** (-bil'i-ti), *n.*

pec-ca-dil-lo (pek-ạ-dil'ō), *n.*; pl. *-dilloes* or *-dillos* (-dil'ōz). [Sp. *pecadillo* or It. *peccadiglio*, both dim. < L. *peccatum*, a sin, < *peccare*: see *peccant*.] A petty sin or offense; a trifling fault: as, "My sins were all *peccadilloes*" (H. James's "Europeans," xii.).

pec-cant (pek'ạnt), *a.* [L. *peccans* (*peccant-*), ppr. of *peccare*, do amiss, transgress, sin.] Sinning or offending (as, "a *peccant* soul": Milton's "Areopagitica"); faulty; also, morbid, unhealthy, or corrupt (as, *peccant* humors); inducing disease.—**pec-can-cy** (pek'ạn-si), *n.*—**pec'cant-ly,** *adv.*

pec-ca-ry (pek'ạ-ri), *n.*; pl. *-ries* (-riz). [Carib.] A gregarious American quadruped related to the swine, ranging from Paraguay to Texas, and occurring in two species, *Dicotyles torquatus* ('collared peccary') and *D. labiatus* ('white-lipped peccary').

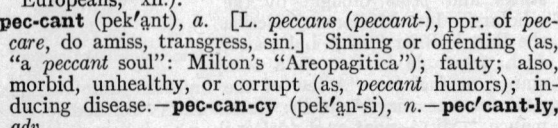

Collared Peccary (*Dicotyles torquatus*).

pec-ca-vi (pe-kā'vī). [L.] 'I have sinned': an expression forming a confession of guilt, and sometimes used as a noun.

peck¹ (pek), *n.* [OF. *pek*; origin unknown.] A dry measure of 8 quarts, the fourth part of a bushel; a vessel for measuring this quantity; also, a considerable quantity (as, "He had known . . . a *peck* of trouble": Dickens's "Hard Times," i. 10).

peck² (pek), *v.* [Var. of *pick*¹.] **I.** *tr.* To strike or indent with the beak, as a bird does, or with some pointed instrument, esp. with quick, repeated movements; also, to make (a hole, etc.) by such strokes; also, to take (food, etc.) bit by bit, with or as with the beak. **II.** *intr.* To make strokes with the beak or a pointed instrument; also, to pick or nibble at food.—**to peck at,** to strike at with the beak, as a bird does; nibble at; fig., to carp or nag at (as, "to . . . *peck at* flaws," Whittier's "Lines on a Fly-Leaf"; "Miss Watson . . . kept *pecking at* me, and it got tiresome," Mark Twain's "Huckleberry Finn," i.).—**peck**², *n.* A pecking stroke; also, a hole or mark made by or as by pecking; also, food (slang, Eng.).—**peck'er,** *n.* One who or that which pecks; a woodpecker; an instrument for pecking; also, courage or spirits (slang: as, "keeping up his *pecker* with such tonics as Mariani dispensed," J. Conrad's "Lord Jim," v.).—**peck'ish,** *a.* Inclined to eat; somewhat hungry. [Colloq.]

Peck-sniff (pek'snif), *n.* [From Mr. *Pecksniff*, a character in Dickens's "Martin Chuzzlewit."] An unctuous or pretentious hypocrite: as, "Someone should do for morals what that old *Pecksniff* Bacon has obtained the credit of having done for science" (S. Butler's "Way of All Flesh," ix.).—**Peck-sniff'i-an,** *a.* Resembling or suggesting Dickens's Mr. Pecksniff; making hypocritical parade of benevolence or high principle.

pec-tase (pek'tās), *n.* [From *pectic* + *-ase*.] In *chem.*, an enzyme found in various fruits, and concerned with the formation of jellies.

pec-tate (pek'tāt), *n.* In *chem.*, a salt of pectic acid.

pec-ten (pek'ten), *n.*; pl. *pectines* (-ti-nēz). [L. *pecten* (*pectin-*), a comb, < *pectere*, to comb.] In *zoöl.* and *anat.*, a comb-like part or process; esp., a pigmented vascular membrane with parallel folds suggesting the teeth of a comb, projecting into the vitreous humor of the eye in birds and reptiles.

pec-tic (pek'tik), *a.* [Gr. πηκτικός, congealing, curdling, < πηγνύναι, fix: see *pact*.] In *chem.*, noting or pertaining to an acid which is derived from pectin, and which in large part makes up the jellies of fruit; pertaining to pectin.

pec-tin (pek'tin), *n.* [From *pectic*.] In *chem.*, a substance (probably a mixture of compounds derived from pectose) which occurs in ripe fruits, esp. in apples, currants, etc., and which dissolves in boiling water, forming a jelly upon subsequent evaporation.—**pec-ti-na'ceous** (-ti-nā'shius), *a.* Of the nature of or containing pectin.

pec-ti-nate, pec-ti-nat-ed (pek'ti-nāt, -nā-ted), *a.* [L. *pectinatus*, < *pecten*: see *pecten*.] Comb-like; formed into or with teeth like a comb.—**pec-ti-na'tion** (-nā'shọn), *n.*

pec-to-ral (pek'tọ-rạl), *a.* [L. *pectoralis* (as n., *pectorale*), < *pectus* (*pector-*), breast.] Of or pertaining to the breast or chest; thoracic; also, good for disease of the chest (as, a *pectoral* medicine); also, worn on the breast or chest (as, the *pectoral* cross of a bishop); also, fig., proceeding from the heart or inner consciousness.—**pectoral arch** or **girdle,** in vertebrates, a bony or cartilaginous arch supporting the fore limbs: in man, formed by the scapulæ and clavicles.—**pectoral fin,** in fishes, either of a pair of fins situated usually behind the head, one on each side of the body, and corresponding to the fore limbs of higher vertebrates. Cf. *ventral fin*, under *ventral*, *a.*—**pectoral sandpiper.** See *sandpiper*.—**pec'to-ral,** *n.* Something worn on the breast, as for ornament or protection; a breastplate; also, a pectoral fin; also, a medicine or remedy for disease of the chest.

pec-tose (pek'tōs), *n.* [From *pectic* + *-ose* as in *cellulose*.] In *chem.*, a substance which is contained in the pulp of unripe fleshy fruit, and is readily converted into pectin.

pec-u-late (pek'ū-lāt), *v. t.* or *i.*; *-lated, -lating.* [L. *peculatus*, pp. of *peculari*, < *peculium*, property: see *peculium*.] To embezzle (public money); appropriate dishonestly (money or goods intrusted to one's care).—**pec-u-la'tion** (-lā'shọn), *n.*—**pec'u-la-tor,** *n.*

pe-cu-liar (pē-kū'lyạr). [L. *peculiaris*, < *peculium*, property: see *peculium*.] **I.** *a.* One's own (as, the Lord's *peculiar* people, the Jews: see Deut. xiv. 2); belonging exclusively to a person or thing (as, "luxurious lounges, among which one capacious chair was his *peculiar* seat": G. W. Curtis's "Prue and I," iv.); belonging characteristically, or proper (*to*: as, "the style and manner of expression *peculiar* to that people," Swift's "Gulliver's Travels," i. 3); also, particular or individual (obs. or rare: as, "The hand of Nature on *peculiar* minds Imprints a different bias," Akenside's "Pleasures of Imagination," i. 83); also, distinguished in nature or character from others (as, "Though the same sun brightens it every fair morning, yet the steeple has a *peculiar* robe of brightness for the Sabbath": Hawthorne's "Twice-Told Tales," Sunday at Home); singular, uncommon, or unusual (as, "Mr. Weller's knowledge of London was extensive and *peculiar*": Dickens's "Pickwick Papers," xx.); strange, odd, or queer (as, "The young man gazed for an instant hard at Hilda, with a *peculiar* expression," Arnold Bennett's "Hilda Lessways," iv. 2; "She knew that he was *peculiar* in many ways," Du Maurier's "Trilby," iii.). **II.** *n.* A peculiar property or privilege.—**pe-cu-li-ar′i-ty** (-li-ar′i-ti), *n.*; pl. *-ties* (-tiz). Peculiar or characteristic quality; a distinguishing quality or characteristic; also, singularity or oddity; an odd trait or characteristic (as, "They had been discussing our little *peculiarities*": Thackeray's "Newcomes," xxxiii.).—**pe-cu′liar-ly,** *adv.*

pe-cu-li-um (pē-kū′li-um), *n.* [L., property, orig. in cattle, < *pecu,* cattle: cf. *fee*[1].] Private property; a private possession or appurtenance; in *Rom. law,* that which was given by a father to his child or by a master to his slave to be the recipient's private property.

pe-cu-ni-a-ry (pē-kū′ni-ā-ri), *a.* [L. *pecuniarius,* < *pecunia,* money, orig. property in cattle, < *pecu*: see *peculium.*] Of or pertaining to money (as, *pecuniary* affairs or losses); consisting of or given or exacted in money (as, "a *pecuniary* compensation," Burke's "American Taxation"; "*pecuniary* penalties," B. Franklin's "Autobiography," iv.); of an offense, etc., entailing a money penalty.—**pe-cu′ni-a-ri-ly,** *adv.*

pe-cu-ni-ous (pē-kū′ni-us), *a.* [L. *pecuniosus,* < *pecunia,* money: see *pecuniary.*] Having much money; wealthy.—**pe-cu-ni-os′i-ty** (-os′i-ti), *n.*

ped (ped), *n.* [ME. *pedde*; origin unknown.] A pannier or basket. [Prov. Eng.]

-ped. A termination from L. *pes* (*ped-*), foot, serving to form adjectives and nouns, as *aliped, biped, breviped, pinnatiped, quadruped.*

ped-a-gog-ic (ped-ạ-goj′ik), *a.* [Gr. παιδαγωγικός, < παιδαγωγός, E. *pedagogue.*] Of or pertaining to a pedagogue or pedagogy. Also **ped-a-gog′i-cal.**—**ped-a-gog′i-cal-ly,** *adv.*—**ped-a-gog′ics,** *n.* The science or art of teaching or education; pedagogy.

ped-a-gog-ism (ped′ạ-gog-izm), *n.* See *pedagoguism.*

ped-a-go-gist (ped′ạ-gō-jist), *n.* One versed in pedagogy or pedagogics.

ped-a-gogue (ped′ạ-gog), *n.* [F. *pédagogue,* < L. *pædagogus,* < Gr. παιδαγωγός, < παῖς (παιδ-), child, + ἀγωγός, leading, < ἄγειν, lead.] A teacher of children; a schoolteacher: now usually implying pedantry, dogmatism, or narrow-mindedness.—**ped′a-go-guish** (-gog-ish), *a.* Like or befitting a pedagogue; pedantic.—**ped′a-go-guism** (-gog-izm), *n.* The occupation, character, or ways of a pedagogue; the system of pedagogy.—**ped′a-go-gy** (-gō-ji or -goj-i), *n.* [Gr. παιδαγωγία.] The function, work, or art of a teacher; teaching; pedagogics.

ped-al (ped′ạl or pē′dạl), *a.* [L. *pedalis,* < *pes* (*ped-*), foot.] Of or pertaining to a foot or the feet; also (pron. ped′ạl), of or pertaining to a pedal or pedals; consisting of pedals (as, a *pedal* keyboard).—**ped-al** (ped′ạl), *n.* [F. *pédale,* < It. *pedale,* < L. *pedalis.*] A lever worked by the foot, in various musical instruments, as the organ, pianoforte, and harp, and having various functions; also, a lever-like part worked by the foot, in various other mechanisms, as the sewing-machine and the bicycle; a treadle; in *music,* same as *pedal-point.*—**ped′al,** *v. i.* or *t.*; *-aled* or *-alled, -aling* or *-alling.* To work or use the pedals (of), as in playing an organ or propelling a bicycle.—**ped-a-lier′** (-ạ-lēr′), *n.* [F. *pédalier,* < *pédale,* E. *pedal, n.*] A pedal keyboard, as of an organ; also, a bass pianoforte played, in conjunction with an ordinary pianoforte, by means of a pedal keyboard.—**ped′al-ist,** *n.* A user of pedals, as in organ-playing or bicycling.—**ped′al=point,** *n.* In *music,* a single tone, usually the tonic or the dominant, held or sustained by one of the parts (in organ music usually by holding down a pedal) while the other parts progress without reference to the sustained tone, except at the beginning and end of the passage; also, the passage containing it.

ped-ant (ped′ạnt), *n.* [F. *pédant,* < It. *pedante,* teacher, pedant; origin uncertain: cf. *pedagogue.*] A schoolmaster† or teacher†; one who makes an excessive or tedious show of learning or learned precision; one who possesses mere book-learning without practical wisdom (as, "He [James I.] had the temper of a *pedant*; and with it a *pedant's* love of theories, and a *pedant's* inability to bring his theories into any relation with actual facts": Green's "Short Hist. of the Eng. People," viii. 2).—**pe-dan-tic** (pē-dan′tik), *a.* Pertaining to or characteristic of a pedant; exhibiting pedantry; resembling a pedant; tediously or absurdly learned: as, "There was nothing *pedantic* in their discourse" (Smollett's "Humphry Clinker," June 10); "They regulated verse by the most *pedantic* and minute laws" (Hallam's "Literature of Europe," i. 1. § 43); "He was often considered rather a *pedantic* than a practical commander, more capable to discourse of battles than to gain them" (Motley's "Dutch Republic," iii. 1). Also **pe-dan′ti-cal.**—**pe-dan′ti-cal-ly,** *adv.*—**pe-dan′ti-cism** (-sizm), *n.* A pedantic notion or expression; a piece of pedantry.—**ped′ant-ism,** *n.* Pedantry; a pedanticism.—**ped′ant-ize,** *v. i.*; *-ized, -izing.* To play the pedant; display pedantry.

ped-an-toc-ra-cy (ped-ạn-tok′rạ-si), *n.*; pl. *-cies* (-siz). [F. *pédantocratie*: see *pedant* and *-cracy.*] Government by pedants or a pedant; a system of government conducted by pedants.—**pe-dan-to-crat** (pē-dan′tō-krat), *n.*—**pe-dan-to-crat′ic,** *a.*

ped-ant-ry (ped′ạnt-ri), *n.*; pl. *-ries* (-riz). The character or practice of a pedant; an undue display of learning.

ped-ate (ped′āt), *a.* [L. *pedatus,* < *pes* (*ped-*), foot.] Having feet; also, foot-like; having divisions like toes; in *bot.,* of a leaf, palmately parted or divided with the lateral lobes or divisions cleft or divided.—**ped′ate-ly,** *adv.*—**pe-dat-i-fid** (pē-dat′i-fid), *a.* [See *-fid.*] In *bot.,* of a leaf, cleft in a pedate manner.—**pe-dat′i-nerved** (-nėrvd), *a.* In *bot.,* having the nerves or ribs arranged in a pedate manner, as a leaf.

Pedate Leaf of Stinking Hellebore (*Helleborus fœtidus*).

Pedate Leaf of Bird's-foot Violet (*Viola pedata*).

ped-der (ped′ėr), *n.* [ME. *pedder,* appar. < *pedde,* pannier, E. *ped*: cf. *peddler.*] A peddler. [Now Sc. and prov. Eng.]

ped-dle (ped′l), *v.*; *-dled, -dling.* [Appar. a back-formation from (earlier) *peddler,* and in part confused with *piddle.*] **I.** *intr.* To travel about retailing small wares; hence, to occupy one's self with trifles; trifle. **II.** *tr.* To carry about for sale at retail; hawk; hence, to deal out in small quantities.

ped-dler (ped′lėr), *n.* [ME. *pedlere,* perhaps for *pedder*: see *pedder.*] One who travels about with goods for sale at retail; an itinerant dealer in small wares.—**ped′dler-y** (-i), *n.*; pl. *-ies* (-iz). The business of a peddler; also, peddlers' wares; hence, trumpery.

ped-dling (ped′ling), *p. a.* Engaged in the trade of a peddler; also, trifling; paltry; piddling.

ped-er-as-ty (ped′ẹ-ras-ti or pē′dẹ-), *n.* [Gr. παιδεραστία, < παῖς (παιδ-), child, boy, + ἐρᾶν, love.] Unnatural sexual intercourse of a male with a male, orig. a boy.—**ped′er-ast** (-ẹ-rast), *n.*

ped-es-tal (ped′es-tạl), *n.* [F. *piédestal,* < It. *piedestallo, piedistallo,* < *piè* (< L. *pes*), foot, + *di* (< L. *de*), of, + *stallo* (from Teut.), = E. *stall*[2].] An architectural support for a column, statue, vase, or the like; in general, a supporting structure or piece; a base.—**ped′es-tal,** *v. t.*; *-taled* or *-talled, -taling* or *-talling.* To set on or supply with a pedestal.

Pedestal found near the Dionysiac Theater, Athens.

pe-des-tri-an (pē-des′tri-ạn). [L. *pedester* (*pedestr-*), on foot, < *pes* (*ped-*), foot.]

I. *a.* Going or performed on foot; walking; pertaining to walking; fig., commonplace; prosaic; dull. **II.** *n.* One who goes or travels on foot (as, "More than one *pedestrian* paused to look back": W. Churchill's "Modern Chronicle," i. 1); a walker; specif., one who walks for exercise or athletic performance.—**pe-des′tri-an-ism,** *n.* The exercise or practice of walking: as, "a large, cheerful street, in which . . . a great deal of *pedestrianism* went forward" (H. James's "Europeans," i.).

ped-i-at-ric (ped-i-at′rik or pē-di-), *a.* [Gr. παῖς (παιδ-), child, + ἰατρικός, E. *iatric.*] Of or pertaining to the medical and hygienic care of children.—**ped″i-a-tri′cian** (-ạ-trish′ạn), *n.* A pediatrist.—**ped-i-at′rics,** *n.* The science of the medical and hygienic care or of the diseases of children.—**ped-i-at′rist,** *n.* One versed in pediatrics; a physician who makes a specialty of treating the diseases of children.—**ped′i-at-ry** (-ri), *n.* Pediatrics.

ped-i-cel (ped′i-sel), *n.* [NL. *pedicellus*, dim. of L. *pediculus*, E. *pedicle.*] In *bot.*, a small stalk; an ultimate division of a common peduncle; one of the subordinate stalks in a branched inflorescence, bearing a single flower; in *zoöl.* and *anat.*, a small stalk or stalk-like part; a peduncle.—**ped′i-cel-late, ped′i-cel-lat-ed** (-se-lāt, -lā-ted), *a.* Having a pedicel or pedicels.—**ped″i-cel-la′tion** (-se-lā′shọn), *n.* Pedicellate condition.

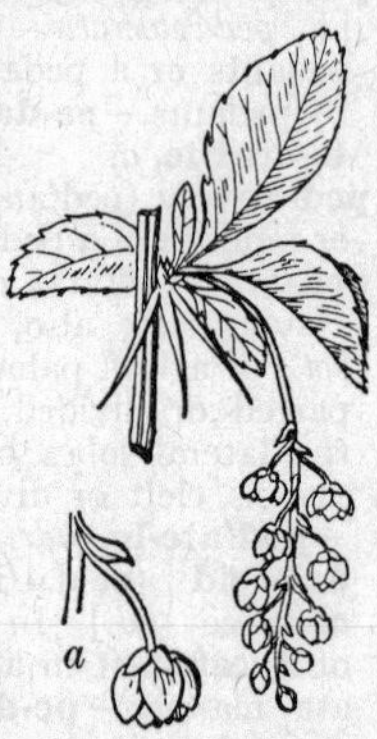

Raceme of Barberry (*Berberis vulgaris*), showing the Pedicels. — *a*, a flower, enlarged, showing the pedicel and a part of the rachis with the bract.

ped-i-cle (ped′i-kl), *n.* [L. *pediculus*, dim. of *pes* (*ped-*), foot.] In *bot.*, *zoöl.*, etc., a small stalk or stalk-like support; a pedicel or peduncle.

pe-dic-u-lar (pē-dik′ū-lạr), *a.* [L. *pedicularis*, < *pediculus*, louse, dim. of *pedis*, louse, < *pes* (*ped-*), foot.] Of or pertaining to lice.—**pe-dic-u-lo′-sis** (-lō′sis), *n.* [NL., < L. *pediculus.*] In *pathol.*, the state of being infested with lice; phthiriasis.—**pe-dic′u-lous,** *a.* [L. *pediculosus*, < *pediculus.*] Infested with lice; lousy.

ped-i-cure (ped′i-kūr), *n.* [F. *pédicure*, < L. *pes* (*ped-*), foot, + *curare*, care for: cf. *manicure.*] One who makes a business of caring for the feet; a chiropodist; also, professional care or treatment of the feet.—**ped′i-cure,** *v. t.*; *-cured, -curing.* To treat (the feet or the person) as a pedicure does.

ped-i-form (ped′i-fôrm), *a.* [L. *pes* (*ped-*), foot: see *-form.*] Having the form of a foot.

ped-i-gra-ic (ped-i-grā′ik), *a.* [Irreg. < *pedigree.*] Pertaining to or of the nature of a pedigree.

ped-i-gree (ped′i-grē), *n.* [ME. *pedegru*, < OF. *pied de grue*, 'foot of crane,' said to refer to a mark having three branching lines, used in old genealogical tables.] A genealogical table (as, to make a family *pedigree*); also, an ancestral line, or line of descent, esp. as recorded (as, "I can look but a very little way into my *pedigree*," Defoe's "Captain Singleton," i.; "The *pedigree* of the Dictator goes no further than to his grandfather, Caius Julius," Froude's "Cæsar," iv.); lineage, esp. when recorded or notable (as, noble by *pedigree*; to boast of, or to despise, *pedigree*); fig., derivation, as from a source (as, the *pedigree* of a word); also, a line, family, or race.—**ped′i-greed,** *a.* Having a recorded or notable pedigree: used esp. of domestic animals.

ped-i-ment (ped′i-mẹnt), *n.* [Earlier *periment*, perhaps a corruption of *pyramid.*] In *arch.*, a low triangular part resembling a gable, crowning the front of buildings in the Greek style, esp. over a portico; hence, any decorative member of similar outline and position, as over an opening.—**ped-i-men′tal** (-men′tạl), *a.* Of, on, or like a pediment.—**ped′i-ment-ed,** *a.* Having or resembling a pediment.

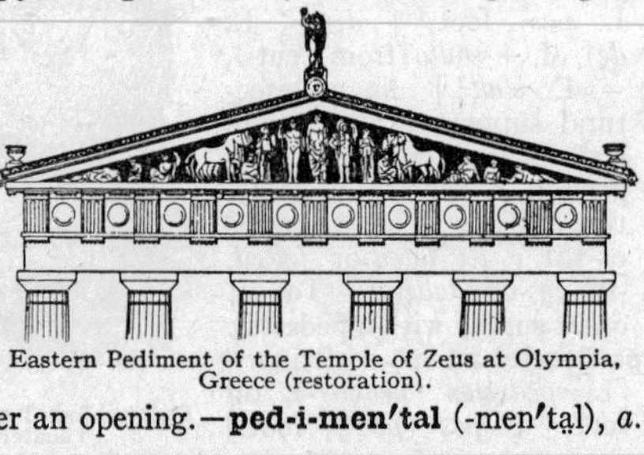
Eastern Pediment of the Temple of Zeus at Olympia, Greece (restoration).

ped-i-palp (ped′i-palp), *n.* [NL. *pedipalpus*, the appendage, *Pedipalpi*, pl., the order, < L. *pes* (*ped-*), foot, + NL. *palpus*: see *palpus.*] A pedipalpus; also, any of the *Pedipalpi*, an order of arachnids, including the whip-scorpions, distinguished by large palpi.—**ped-i-pal′pate** (-pal′-pāt), *a.* Having pedipalpi.—**ped-i-pal′pus** (-pus), *n.*; pl. *-pi* (-pī). [NL.] Either of a pair of palpi attached to the head of most arachnids, in front of the ambulatory limbs.

ped-lar, ped-ler (ped′lạr, -lėr), etc. See *peddler*, etc.

pedo-, pædo-. Forms of Gr. παῖς (παιδ-), child, used in combination.—**pe-do-bap-tism, pæ-do-bap-tism** (pē-dọ-bap′tizm), *n.* The baptism of infants.—**pe-do-bap′tist, pæ-do-bap′tist,** *n.*—**pe-do-gen′e-sis, pæ-do-gen′e-sis** (-jen′e-sis), *n.* Reproduction by animals in the larval state.—**pe-dol-o-gy, pæ-dol-o-gy** (pē-dol′ọ-ji), *n.* [+ *-logy.*] The scientific study of the nature and development of children; also, pediatrics.—**pe-dol′o-gist, pæ-dol′o-gist,** *n.*

pe-dom-e-ter (pē-dom′e-tėr), *n.* [F. *pédomètre*, < L. *pes* (*ped-*), foot, + Gr. μέτρον, measure.] An instrument for recording the number of steps taken in walking, and thus showing approximately the distance traveled.

ped-rail (ped′rāl), *n.* [L. *pes* (*ped-*), foot, + E. *rail*[1].] A wheel-like device (invented by B. J. Diplock) for use on a self-propelled vehicle, consisting of a series of foot-like supports on the periphery of a circular frame, these supports being laid down in front (and taken up behind) as the vehicle advances, and serving as a temporary rail enabling the vehicle to pass over rough ground, obstacles, etc.; a vehicle or traction-engine fitted with such devices: as, "The idea [of a 'land-ironclad'] was suggested to me by the contrivances of a certain Mr. Diplock, whose '*ped-rail*' notion, the notion of a wheel that was something more than a wheel, a wheel that would take locomotives up hill-sides and over ploughed fields, was public property nearly twenty years ago . . . To the *Ped-rail* also . . . Murray Sueter, one of the many experimentalists upon the early tanks, admits his indebtedness" (H. G. Wells's "Italy, France, and Britain at War" (1917), iii. 5). Cf. *caterpillar*, also *tank.*

pe-dro (pē′drō), *n.* [Sp. *Pedro*, man's name, Peter.] Any of several varieties of the card-game of seven-up in which the five of trumps (sometimes also the other five of the same color) counts at its face value; also, the five of trumps, or sometimes either the five of trumps ('right pedro') or the other five of the same color ('left pedro'), in these games.

pe-dun-cle (pē-dung′kl), *n.* [NL. *pedunculus*, dim. of L. *pes* (*ped-*), foot.] In *bot.*, a flower-stalk, supporting either a cluster or a solitary flower; in *zoöl.*, *anat.*, etc., a stalk or stem; a stalk-like part or structure.—**pe-dun′cled,** *a.* Pedunculate.—**pe-dun′cu-lar** (-kū-lạr), *a.* Of or pertaining to a peduncle.—**pe-dun′cu-late, pe-dun′cu-lat-ed** (-lāt, -lā-ted), *a.* Having a peduncle; growing on a peduncle.

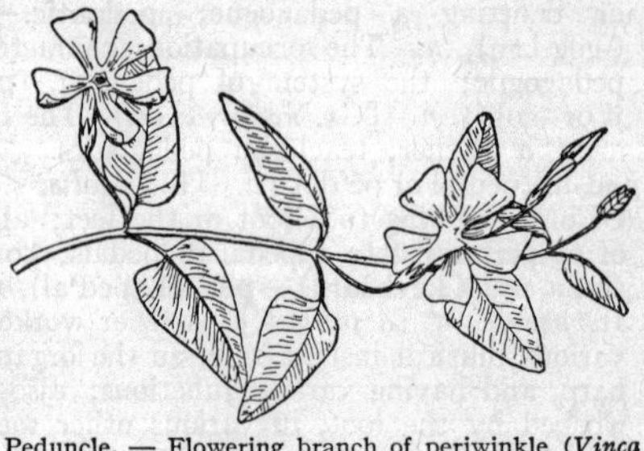
Peduncle. — Flowering branch of periwinkle (*Vinca minor*), showing the one-flowered peduncles.

peek (pēk), *v. i.* [ME. *piken*; origin uncertain.] To peep; peer.—**peek,** *n.* A peeking look; a peep.

peel[1] (pēl), *v. t.* [Var. of *pill*[1].] To plunder; despoil. [Archaic.]

peel[2] (pēl), *v.* [ME. *pelen*, also *pilen*, late AS. *pylian*, prob. < L. *pilare*, deprive of hair, < *pilus*, hair; prob. affected by OF. F. *peler*, strip of skin, peel, < L. *pellis*, skin.] **I.** *tr.* To deprive of hair†; also, to strip of the skin, rind, bark, etc.; decorticate; also, to strip off (skin, etc.). **II.** *intr.* To lose the skin, rind, bark, etc.; of skin, etc., to come off (as, "dingy wall-paper that had *peeled* in places": H. G. Wells's "Tono-Bungay," ii. 2. § 1); also, to take off one's clothes, or undress (slang).—**peel**[2], *n.* The skin or rind of a fruit, etc.

peel[3] (pēl), *n.* [OF. *pele* (F. *pelle*), shovel, < L. *pala*, spade, shovel.] A shovel-like implement for putting bread, pies, etc., into the oven or taking them out.

peel[4] (pēl), *n.* [OF. *pel* (F. *pieu*), stake, < L. *palus*, E. *pale*[1].] A stake†; also, a stockade†; also, one of a class of fortified towers for residence or safe resort, common in the border counties of England and Scotland in the 16th century, typically having the ground floor vaulted and used as a shelter for cattle, with access to the upper part by a door considerably raised above the ground and reached by a movable stair or the like.

Peel, Gilnockie, Dumfriesshire, Scotland.

peel-er[1] (pē′lėr), *n.* [See *peel*[2].] One who or that which peels.

peel-er[2] (pē′lėr), *n.* [From Sir Robert *Peel*, under whom as secretary for Ireland (1812–18) the Irish constabulary was founded: cf. *bobby*.] A policeman: as, "You'll hear me telling the *peelers* who it was stole the black ass belonging to Philly O'Cullen" (Synge's "Tinker's Wedding," ii.); "He's gone for a *peeler* and a search warrant" (Kingsley's "Alton Locke," xxxv.). [Slang, Ir. and Eng.]

peel-ing (pē′ling), *n.* The act of one who or that which peels; also, that which is peeled from something; a piece of the skin or rind of a fruit, etc., peeled off.

peen (pēn), *n.* [Cf. Norw. *pen*, *pænn*, F. *panne*, and G. *pinne*.] The sharp, spherical, or otherwise modified end of the head of a hammer, opposite to the face.—**peen,** *v. t.* To treat by striking regularly all over with the peen of a hammer.

Peens. — *a*, narrow peen for riveting; *b*, broad peen for machinists; *c*, peen for coopers; *d*, cone peen for chasing; *e*, ball peen, upsetting hammer for engravers.

peep[1] (pēp), *v. i.* [ME. *pepen*, also *pipen*: cf. OF. F. *piper*, L. *pipare*, D. and G. *piepen*, peep, all imit., also E. *pipe*, *n.*] To utter the shrill little cry of a young bird, a mouse, etc.; cheep; squeak; also, to speak in a thin, weak voice.—**peep**[1], *n.* A peeping cry or sound; also, any of various small sandpipers.

peep[2] (pēp), *v.* [Cf. *peek*.] **I.** *intr.* To look through or as through a small aperture (as, "I shall be up stairs in my room, *peeping* through the window-blinds": Howells's "Chance Acquaintance," xiii.); look slyly, pryingly, or furtively; peer, as from a hiding-place (as, "In the corn opposite to her a rabbit stole along, crouched, and *peeped*": Galsworthy's "Saint's Progress," iv. 4); also, to come partially into view (as, "He stood there . . . his bare feet *peeping* from the blanket": Bret Harte's "How Santa Claus Came to Simpson's Bar"); begin to appear (as, "The spring being early, all manner of green things were *peeping* forth": Weir Mitchell's "Hugh Wynne," xxiv.). **II.** *tr.* To show or protrude slightly; also, to direct (the eye) in peeping.—**peep**[2], *n.* A peeping look or glance (as, "Just step forward there, and take a *peep* over the weather-bow": H. Melville's "Moby-Dick," xvi.); also, the first appearance, as of dawn (as, "He arose with the first *peep* of day": Peacock's "Headlong Hall," ix.); also, an aperture for looking through.—**peep′er,** *n.* One who or that which peeps; a prying or spying person; also, an eye (slang: as, "a secret . . . invisible . . . to the stupid *peepers* of that young whiskered prig, Lieutenant Osborne," Thackeray's "Vanity Fair," xiv.).—**peep′=hole,** *n.* A hole through which one may peep.—**peep′ing,** *p. a.* That peeps.—**peeping Tom,** a prying observer: in allusion to the man in the legend who peeped at Lady Godiva riding naked through Coventry. Cf. Tennyson's "Godiva."—**peep′=show,** *n.* An exhibition of objects or pictures viewed through an aperture usually fitted with a magnifying lens: as, "the well-known Gubbins with his 'A' the World in a Box': a halfpenny *peepshow*" (Barrie's "Auld Licht Idylls," ii.).—**peep′=sight,** *n.* A plate containing a small hole through which the gunner peeps in sighting, attached to the breech of a cannon or small arm.

pee-pul (pē′pul), *n.* See *pipal*.

peer[1] (pēr), *v. i.* [Origin uncertain; prob. in part for *appear*.] To look narrowly, as in the effort to discern clearly (as, "I walked there, occasionally stopping to *peer* into some shadowy glade or opening": W. H. Hudson's "Green Mansions," xviii.); also, to peep out or appear slightly (as, "Streaks of blue *peer* through our clouds": Carlyle's "Sartor Resartus," iii. 11); come into view (as, "when daffodils begin to *peer*": Shakspere's "Winter's Tale," iv. 3. 1).

peer[2] (pēr), *n.* [OF. *per* (F. *pair*), < L. *par*, equal.] A person of the same civil rank or standing; an equal before the law; also, one who ranks with another in respect to endowments or other qualifications; an equal in any respect (as, "She hasn't a *peer* for courage": G. Meredith's "Diana of the Crossways," xxvi.); also, a companion or associate (archaic: as, "To stray away into these forests drear, Alone, without a *peer*," Keats's "Endymion," iv.); also, a nobleman; esp., a member of any of the five degrees of the nobility in Great Britain and Ireland, namely, duke, marquis, earl, viscount, and baron.—**peer of the realm,** any of a class of peers in Great Britain and Ireland entitled by hereditary right or by creation of the sovereign to sit in the House of Lords (the membership of the House of Lords including, in addition to this class of peers, certain elected representatives of the Scottish and Irish peerages as well as certain prelates of the Church of England).—**peer′age** (-āj), *n.* The body of peers of a country or state (as, the British *peerage*; "a West End solicitor with clients in the *peerage*," M. Hewlett's "Open Country," i.); also, the rank or dignity of a peer (as, "By aspiring higher, he might have got a *peerage*": Cooper's "Two Admirals," i.); also, a book giving a list of peers, with their genealogy, etc. (as, Burke's "*Peerage*"; Whitaker's "*Peerage*").—**peer′ess,** *n.* The wife of a peer; a woman having in her own right the rank of a peer.—**peer′less,** *a.* Having no peer or equal; matchless.—**peer′less-ly,** *adv.*—**peer′less-ness,** *n.*

peer-y (pēr′i), *a.* Peering; prying; suspicious.

peet-weet (pēt′wēt), *n.* [Imit.: cf. *pewit*.] The spotted sandpiper, *Tringoides macularius*, of North America.

peeve (pēv), *v. t.*; *peeved*, *peeving*. [Back-formation from *peevish*.] To render peevish. [Colloq.]

pee-vish (pē′vish), *a.* [ME. *pevysh*; origin unknown.] Foolish†; also, perverse† or froward†; also, querulous or fretful, as from vexation or discontent (as, "The jolting occasioned such pain to my uncle that he was become exceedingly *peevish* when we arrived at this place": Smollett's "Humphry Clinker," June 23); characterized by or showing querulous or fretful discontent (as, "*peevish* complaints": Howells's "Rise of Silas Lapham," iv.).—**pee′vish-ly,** *adv.*—**pee′vish-ness,** *n.*

pee-wit (pē′wit), *n.* See *pewit*.

peg (peg), *n.* [ME. *pegge*: cf. LG. *pigge*, peg, Sw. *pigg*, Dan. *pig*, point, spike.] A pin of wood or other material driven or fitted into something, as to fasten parts together, to hang things on, to make fast a rope or string on, to stop a hole, or to mark some point; a small pin of wood, metal, etc., used in shoemaking to secure the upper to the sole or to build up the heel; a pin of wood or metal to which one end of a string of a musical instrument is fastened, and which may be turned in its socket to adjust the string's tension; the metal pin on which a top spins; also, a degree (colloq.: as, to come down a *peg*; "As for heathen countries, they are a *peg* below those of Christianity," Mrs. Stowe's "Oldtown Folks," xxv.); a step (colloq.: as, "He would not move a *peg*," H. Melville's "Moby-Dick," xvii.); also, a leg, sometimes one of wood (colloq.: as, "You'll hear about the cannon-ball That carried off his *pegs*," Holmes's "Music-Grinders"); also, an implement having a pin or point at the end, as for harpooning; also, a drink made usually of brandy and soda-water (orig. Anglo-Ind.: as, "I suspected the old fellow was going to cool his wrath with a '*peg*,'" F. M. Crawford's "Mr. Isaacs," x.).—**peg,** *v.*; *pegged*, *pegging*. **I.** *tr.* To drive or insert a peg into; fasten with or as with pegs; mark with pegs; strike or pierce with or as with a peg; also, to aim or throw (colloq.). **II.** *intr.* To work persistently, or keep on energetically (with *away, along, on,* etc.: as, "The labor dragged a little, but still they made progress. They *pegged* away in silence for some time," Mark Twain's "Tom Sawyer," xxv.: colloq.); also, to make one's way (with *off,* etc.: colloq.); also, to aim or throw (colloq.).

Peg-a-sus (peg′ą-sus), *n.* [L., < Gr. Πήγασος, < πηγή, stream, spring.] In *class. myth.*, a winged horse, sprung from the blood of Medusa when slain by Perseus, that with a stroke of his hoof caused the spring Hippocrene to well forth on Mount Helicon (being the favorite steed of the Muses, and hence proverbially appropriated to poets); in *astron.*, a northern constellation represented as the forward half of a flying horse.

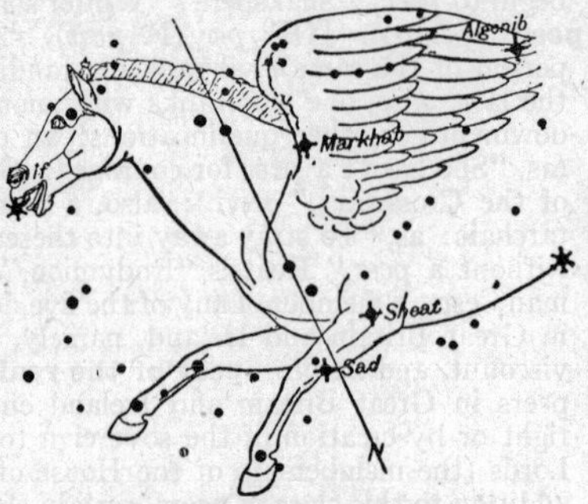

The Constellation Pegasus.

peg-ger (peg′ėr), *n.* One who or that which pegs; a machine for driving pegs in shoemaking.

peg=leg (peg′leg′), *n.* A wooden leg; also, one who has a wooden leg. [Colloq.]

peg-ma-tite (peg′-mą-tīt), *n.* [Gr. πῆγμα (πηγματ-), something fastened together, < πηγνύναι, make fast.] A coarsely crystalline granitic or other rock occurring in veins; specif., granite with a graphic texture. —**peg-ma-tit′ic** (-tit′ik), *a.*

peg=top (peg′top′). **I.** *n.* A child's wooden top spinning on a metal peg; *pl.*, peg-top trousers. **II.** *a.* Shaped like a peg-top, as a style of men's trousers wide at the hips and gradually narrowing to the ankle.

pei-gnoir (pe-nwor), *n.* [F., < *peigner*, < L. *pectinare*, to comb, < *pecten*, a comb.] A woman's loose sack for wearing while the hair is being combed; a dressing-gown.

peine (pān, F. pen), *n.* [F.: see *pain.*] A former method of punishment or torture, inflicted by putting heavy weights upon a prisoner's body, sometimes pressing him to death: usually called *peine forte et dure* (fōrt ā dür) (F., 'severe and hard punishment').

peise (pāz), *v. t.*; *peised, peising.* [= *poise.*] To weigh; press; force as by pressure. [Obs. or prov.]

pe-jo-rate (pē′jǫ-rāt), *v. t.*; *-rated, -rating.* [L. *pejoratus*, pp. of *pejorare*, < *pejor*, worse, compar. of *malus*, bad.] To make worse; deteriorate; depreciate.—**pe-jo-ra′tion** (-rā′shǫn), *n.*—**pe′jo-ra-tive** (-rą-tiv). **I.** *a.* Tending to make worse; depreciative; having a disparaging force, as certain derivative word-forms. **II.** *n.* A pejorative form or word, as *poetaster* (a petty or inferior *poet*).—**pe′jo-ra-tive-ly,** *adv.*

pek-an (pek′ąn), *n.* [Canadian F. *pêkan*; from N. Amer. Ind.] The fisher (marten), *Mustela pennanti.*

pe-kin (pē-kin′), *n.* [F. *pékin*; named from *Pekin, Peking*, capital of China.] A silk fabric with lengthwise stripes, usually of uniform width, of alternating colors, or of satin and plain finish alternately.—**pekin stripes,** lengthwise stripes, esp. of uniform width, in textile fabrics; also, fabrics with such stripes. Cf. *bayadere, a.*

Pe-king-ese (pē-king-ēs′ or -ēz′). **I.** *a.* Pertaining to Peking, in China; also, noting a breed of small, long-haired Chinese dogs prized as pets. **II.** *n.*; pl. *-ese.* A native of Peking; also, a Pekingese dog.

pe-koe (pē′kō or pek′ō), *n.* [Chinese *pak-hao*, 'white down' (that on the young leaves).] A superior kind of black tea.

pel-age (pel′āj), *n.* [F., < OF. *peil* (F. *poil*), < L. *pilus*, hair.] The hair, fur, wool, or other soft covering of a mammal.

pe-la-gi-an[1] (pe-lā′ji-ąn), *a.* Same as *pelagic.*

Pe-la-gi-an[2] (pe-lā′ji-ąn), *n.* A follower of Pelagius, a British monk (flourished about 400 to 418), who denied the doctrine of original sin and maintained the freedom of the will and its power, apart from divine grace, to attain righteousness.—**Pe-la′gi-an-ism,** *n.*

pe-lag-ic (pe-laj′ik), *a.* [L. *pelagicus*, < Gr. πελαγικός, < πέλαγος, the open sea.] Of or pertaining to the ocean or open sea; living at or near the surface of the ocean, at a distance from land, as certain animals and plants.

pe-lar-go-nate (pe-lär′gǫ-nāt), *n.* In *chem.*, a salt of pelargonic acid.

pel-ar-gon-ic (pel-ąr-gon′ik), *a.* In *chem.*, noting or pertaining to an oily organic acid occurring in a volatile oil in species of pelargonium.

pel-ar-go-ni-um (pel-ąr-gō′ni-um), *n.* [NL., < Gr. πελαργός, stork: cf. the names *geranium* and *crane's-bill.*] Any plant of the genus *Pelargonium*, the cultivated species of which are usually called *geranium.* See *geranium.*

Pe-las-gi-an (pe-las′ji-ąn or pe-laz′-). **I.** *a.* Of or pertaining to the Pelasgi, an ancient race inhabiting Greece and the islands and coasts of the Ægean Sea and the eastern Mediterranean in prehistoric times. **II.** *n.* One of the Pelasgi. —**Pe-las′gic** (-jik), *a.*

pel-er-ine (pel′ę-rin or pel-ę-rēn′), *n.* [F. *pèlerine*, < *pèlerin*, pilgrim: see *pilgrim.*] A woman's cape, esp. a narrow cape with long descending ends in front.

Pe-le's (pē′lēz) **hair.** [From *Pele*, goddess of the Hawaiian volcano of Kilauea.] A filamentous form of lava, often occurring in tow-like masses, and commonly supposed to have been formed from drops of lava by the wind.

pelf (pelf), *n.* [ME. *pelf*, < OF. *pelfre*, spoil, frippery; origin uncertain: cf. *pilfer.*] Spoil† or booty†; property†; money or riches (used in contempt: as, "The scholar whom the love of *pelf* Tempts from his books and from his nobler self," Longfellow's "Morituri Salutamus," 228); rubbish or refuse (now prov. Eng.).

pel-i-can (pel′i-kąn), *n.* [LL. *pelicanus, pelecanus*, < Gr. πελεκάν.] Any of various large natatorial fish-eating birds constituting the genus *Pelecanus*, having a large bill with a distensible pouch beneath used for storing food: as, "a top-heavy *pelican* balancing his huge yellow bill over the edge of the stream, and fishing for his dinner" (Amelia B. Edwards's "Thousand Miles up the Nile," vi.).

Brown Pelican (*Pelecanus fuscus*).

pe-lisse (pę-lēs′), *n.* [F., < ML. *pellicia*, fur garment, prop. fem. of LL. *pellicius*, made of skins, < L. *pellis*, skin.] An outer garment lined or trimmed with fur (as, a hussar's *pelisse*); also, a woman's long cloak with arm-openings or sleeves.

pel-lag-ra (pe-lag′rą or pe-lā′grą), *n.* [It. and NL., < L. *pellis*, skin, + Gr. ἄγρα, a catching.] In *pathol.*, a chronic disease endemic in Italy and elsewhere, characterized by eruption on the skin, severe functional disturbances, and finally mental derangement.—**pel-lag′rous,** *a.*

pel-let (pel′et), *n.* [OF. F. *pelote*, < L. *pila*, ball.] A round or spherical body, esp. one of small size; a little ball, as of food or medicine; a bolus; a pill; specif., a ball, usually of stone, formerly used as a missile; hence, a bullet; one of a charge of small shot, as for a sportsman's gun; an imitation bullet, as of wax or paper.—**pel′let,** *v. t.* To form into pellets; also, to hit with pellets.

pel-li-cle (pel′i-kl), *n.* [L. *pellicula*, dim. of *pellis*, skin.] A thin skin or membrane; a film; a scum.—**pel-lic-u-lar** (pe-lik′ū-ląr), *a.*

pel-li-to-ry (pel′i-tǫ-ri), *n.*; pl. *-ries* (-riz). [Partly by corruption < LL. *parietaria*, < L. *paries*, wall; partly for ME. *peletre* = Sp. *pelitre* = OF. *piretre*, < L. *pyrethrum*, pellitory of Spain.] A small, bushy, old-world urticaceous plant, *Parietaria officinalis*, growing on old walls, etc. ('wall-pellitory'); any species of the same genus; also, an asteraceous plant, *Anacyclus pyrethrum*, of Algeria, etc., whose root is used as a local irritant ('pellitory of Spain'); also, any of various other plants, as the feverfew, *Chrysanthemum parthenium*.

pell=mell (pel'mel'). [F. *pêle-mêle*, OF. *pesle mesle*, appar. a varied redupl. < *mesler*, mix: see *meddle*.] **I.** *adv.* In an indiscriminate medley; in a confused mass or crowd; also, in disorderly, headlong haste (as, "She had made her escape that way, and down after her they rushed, *pell-mell*": W. H. Hudson's "Green Mansions," xv.). **II.** *a.* Indiscriminate; disorderly; tumultuous. **III.** *n.* An indiscriminate medley; violent disorder; also, a mêlée.

pel-lu-cid (pe-lū'sid), *a.* [L. *pellucidus*, < *perlucere*, shine through, be transparent, < *per*, through, + *lucere*, shine.] Allowing the passage of light; transparent or translucent; clear or limpid, as water (as, "*pellucid* streams": Wordsworth's "Laodamia," 104); fig., clear to the mind; obvious in meaning.—**pel-lu-cid-i-ty** (pel-ū-sid'i-ti), **pel-lu'cid-ness**, *n.*—**pel-lu'cid-ly**, *adv.*

Pel-o-pon-ne-sian (pel″ō-pō-nē'shian or -zhian). **I.** *a.* Of or pertaining to the Peloponnesus, the southern peninsula of Greece: as, the *Peloponnesian* War (carried on between Athens and her allies on the one side and Sparta and her allies on the other, from 431 to 404 B.C., the result being the transference of the hegemony in Greece from Athens to Sparta). **II.** *n.* A native or inhabitant of the Peloponnesus.

pe-lo-ri-a (pē-lō'ri-ä), *n.* [NL., < Gr. πέλωρ, monster.] In *bot.*, regularity of structure occurring abnormally in flowers normally irregular.—**pe-lor'ic** (-lor'ik), *a.*—**pel-o-rize** (pel'ō-rīz), *v. t.*; *-rized*, *-rizing*. To affect with peloria. —**pel″o-ri-za'tion** (-ri-zā'shon), *n.*

pe-lo-ta (pe-lō'tä), *n.* [Sp., < L. *pila*, ball: cf. *pellet*.] A Basque, Spanish, and Spanish-American game played in a court with a ball which is struck with a kind of curved wicker racket fastened to a glove worn on the hand.

pelt[1] (pelt), *v.* [Origin uncertain.] **I.** *tr.* To assail with repeated blows or (now usually) with missiles (as, "They stood *pelting* us . . . with darts and arrows": Defoe's "Robinson Crusoe," ii. 9); fig., to assail with abuse (as, "an . . . old woman . . . whom the low comedian was to *pelt* with insults": L. Merrick's "Conrad in Quest of His Youth," xiii.); also, to drive, put, etc., by blows or missiles (as, "The storm *pelted* the sentinel from his post," Irving's "Conquest of Granada," iv.; "The young lords of Rome . . . had *pelted* them . . . to death with tiles," Froude's "Cæsar," xi.); also, to throw (missiles). **II.** *intr.* To strike blows; beat with force or violence (as, "The rain was still *pelting*": L. Merrick's "Conrad in Quest of His Youth," iii.); throw missiles; fig., to cast abuse; also, to go rapidly, or hurry (as, "The clerk . . . ran home to Camden Town as hard as he could *pelt*": Dickens's "Christmas Carol," i.).—**pelt**[1], *n.* The act or an act of pelting; a vigorous stroke (as, "The cripple . . . gave him . . . a good *pelt* on the head with his crutch": Smollett's "Humphry Clinker," July 4); a blow with something thrown; also, speed (as, "a horse that comes full *pelt*": Hood's "Tale of a Trumpet," 356).

pelt[2] (pelt), *n.* [Appar. a back-formation from *peltry*.] The skin of a beast with or without the hair on it; specif., an undressed fur-skin; also, the human skin, esp. when hairy (as, "his powerful arms folded on the grizzled *pelt* of his bare breast": J. Conrad's "Rover," ix.); also, the dead quarry of a hawk.

pel-tast (pel'tast), *n.* [L. *peltasta*, < Gr. πελταστής, < πέλτη, light shield.] An ancient Greek soldier armed with a light shield.

pel-tate (pel'tāt), *a.* [NL. *peltatus*, < L. *pelta*, < Gr. πέλτη, light shield.] Shield-shaped; in *bot.*, of a leaf, etc., having the stalk or support attached to the lower surface at a distance from the margin.—**pel'tate-ly**, *adv.*

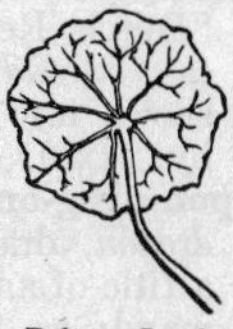

Peltate Leaf.

pelt-er (pel'tėr), *n.* One who or that which pelts; a pelting shower (colloq.).—**pelt'ing**[1], *p. a.* That pelts; assailing with or as with missiles; beating; driving; violent or furious (now prov.).

pelt-ing[2] (pel'ting), *a.* [Cf. *paltry*.] Paltry; petty; mean. [Archaic.]

Pel-ton (pel'ton) **wheel.** [Named from the inventor.] In *mach.*, a form of water-wheel or turbine having on its periphery cup-shaped buckets on which one or more tangential jets of water impinge with high velocity.

pel-try (pel'tri), *n.*; pl. *-tries* (-triz). [OF. *peleterie* (F. *pelleterie*), < *peletier*, a skinner, < *pel*, < L. *pellis*, skin.] Pelts collectively, esp. fur-skins (as, "the profits of a little traffic he drove in *peltry*": Smollett's "Humphry Clinker," Oct. 26); also, a pelt (as, "The traders Touching at times on the coast, to barter and chaffer for *peltries*": Longfellow's "Courtship of Miles Standish," vii.).

pe-lure (pę-lūr'), *n.* [F., lit. 'peeling,' < *peler*, peel: see *peel*[2], and cf. *onion-skin*.] A crisp, hard, thin paper.

pel-vic (pel'vik), *a.* Of or pertaining to the pelvis.—**pelvic girdle** or **arch,** in vertebrates, a bony or cartilaginous arch supporting the hind limbs or analogous parts: in man, formed by the two innominate bones.

pel-vis (pel'vis), *n.*; pl. *-ves* (-vēz). [L., basin.] In *anat.* and *zoöl.*, the basin-like cavity in the lower part of the trunk of many vertebrates, formed in man by the innominate bones, sacrum, etc.; the bones forming this cavity; also, the basin-like cavity into which the ureter expands at the hilum of the kidney.

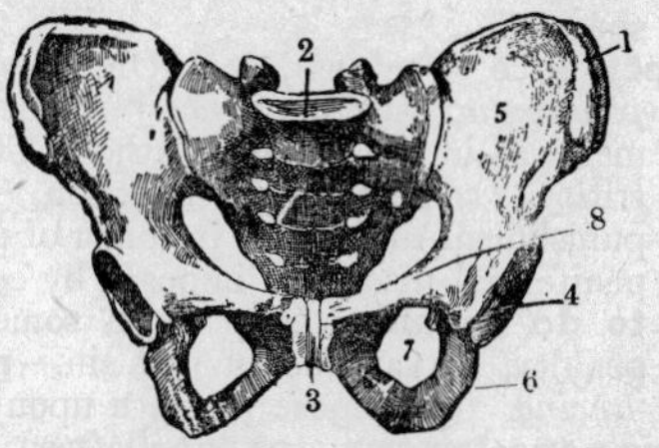

Human Pelvis, from the front. — 1, crest of ilium; 2, base (uppermost) of sacrum; 3, pubic symphysis; 4, acetabulum or socket of thigh-bone; 5, iliac fossa, a part of the false pelvis; 6, ischium; 7, foramen; 8, brim of true pelvis. (Coccyx, not shown, directly behind pubic symphysis.)

Pem-broke (pem'bruk) **ta'ble.** [From *Pembroke*, in Wales.] A table the top of which has hinged to it two side leaves that can be folded down when not in use.

pem-mi-can (pem'i-kan), *n.* [N. Amer. Ind.] Dried meat pounded into a paste with melted fat and pressed into cakes: orig. prepared by North American Indians.

pem-phi-gus (pem'fi-gus or pem-fī'-), *n.* [NL., < Gr. πέμφιξ (πεμφιγ-), bubble.] In *pathol.*, a disease of the skin and mucous membranes characterized by an eruption of blister-like vesicles.—**pem'phi-goid,** *a.*

pen[1] (pen), *n.* [AS. *penn*.] A small inclosure for domestic animals, as hogs, cows, sheep, or poultry; hence, any place of confinement or safe-keeping (as, a slave-*pen*).—**pen**[1], *v. t.*: *penned*, *penning*. To confine in or as in a pen; shut (*up* or *in*).

pen[2] (pen), *n.* [OF. F. *penne*, < L. *penna*, feather, LL. pen to write with: see *feather*.] A feather of a bird, esp. a large feather of the wing or tail; a quill-feather; a quill; also, *pl.*, wings (archaic); also, *sing.*, something resembling or suggesting a feather or quill; an internal, corneous or chitinous, feather-shaped structure in certain cephalopods, as the squid (see *calamary*); a snuff-spoon, orig. one made of a quill shaped like a spoon (Sc.); also, a quill pointed and split at the nib, used for writing with ink; in later use, a small instrument of steel or other metal, with a split point, used, when fitted into a penholder, for writing with ink; the pen and penholder together; any instrument for writing with ink (as, a fountain-*pen*); also, a stylus, graver, or the like†; also, the pen as the instrument of writing or authorship (as, "Beneath the rule of men entirely great The *pen* is mightier than the sword," Bulwer-Lytton's "Richelieu," ii. 2; "His [Cicero's] enemies' characters have been accepted from his *pen* as correct portraits," Froude's "Cæsar," xiii.); the practice of writing or literature (as, men of the *pen*); style or quality of writing (as, a writer who has a clever *pen*); a writer or author (as, the writings of a learned *pen*).—**pen**[2], *v. t.*; *penned*, *penning*. To write with a pen; set down in writing; compose and write.

pen-. See *pene-*.

pe-nal (pē'nal), *a.* [OF. *penal* (F. *pénal*), < L. *pœnalis*, < *pœna*, penalty, punishment: see *pain*.] Of or pertaining to punishment, as for offenses or crimes; prescribing punishment (as, *penal* laws; a *penal* code); constituting punishment (as, *penal* servitude); used as a place of punishment (as, a *penal* settlement); subject to or incurring punishment (as, *penal* neglect; a *penal* offense); payable or forfeitable as a punishment or penalty (as, a *penal* sum; a *penal* forfeit).—**pe′nal-ize** (-īz), *v. t.*; *-ized, -izing.* To declare penal, or punishable by law, as an action; also, to subject to a penalty, as a person; hence, to lay under a disadvantage.—**pe″nal-i-za′tion** (-i-zā′shọn), *n.*—**pe′nal-ly,** *adv.*

pen-al-ty (pen′ạl-ti), *n.*; pl. *-ties* (-tiz). [OF. *penalite* (F. *pénalité*), < ML. *pœnalitas*, < L. *pœnalis*, E. *penal.*] Penal retribution; a punishment imposed or incurred for a violation of law or rule; a loss or forfeiture to which one subjects himself by non-fulfilment of an obligation; that which is forfeited, as a sum of money; fig., painful consequences or any disadvantage attached to some procedure, condition, etc. (as, the *penalty* of carelessness, or of fame; "the *penalties* of old age," Galt's "Annals of the Parish," xxxvii.); specif., a disadvantage imposed upon a competitor or side in sports as punishment for infraction of the rules; also, a handicap imposed to equalize the chances.—**on, upon,** or **under penalty,** with the liability of incurring a penalty in case of non-fulfilment of an injunction, condition, etc., specified.

pen-ance (pen′ạns), *n.* [OF. *penance, peneance,* < L. *pœnitentia*: see *penitence.*] Penitence†; specif., a sacrament, as in the Roman Catholic Church, consisting in contrition, confession, satisfaction, and absolution; also, punishment undergone in token of penitence for sin; esp., a penitential discipline imposed by ecclesiastical authority.—**to do penance,** to perform some act, or undergo some penalty, in satisfaction for sin.—**pen′ance,** *v. t.*; *-anced, -ancing.* To impose penance upon; discipline by penance.

pe-nang=law-yer (pē-nang′lâ′yėr), *n.* [Prob. corruption of a native name: cf. Malay *pīnang*, areca.] A cane or walking-stick made from the stem of a small East Indian palm, *Licuala acutifida.*

pen-an-nu-lar (pē-nan′ū-lạr or pen-an′-), *a.* [See *pene-.*] Almost annular; forming an incomplete ring (with a small portion wanting).

pe-na-tes (pē-nā′tēz), *n. pl.* [L.: cf. *penetrate.*] [Also *cap.*] Among the ancient Romans, tutelary deities of the household and of the state, worshiped in close association with the lares; household gods. Also fig. Cf. *lar.*

pence (pens), *n.* Plural of *penny.*

pen-cel (pen′sẹl), *n.* [For *pennoncel.*] A small pennon or streamer, as at the head of a lance (archaic); also, a lady's favor worn or carried by a knight†.

pen-chant (poṅ-shäṅ), *n.* [F., orig. ppr. of *pencher*, incline, lean, < *pendere*, hang.] A strong inclination; a taste or liking for something: as, "my tender *penchant* for Miss Ingram" (C. Brontë's "Jane Eyre," xx.); "a most decided *penchant* for the ancient Greek music" (Longfellow's "Hyperion," iv. 4).

pen-cil (pen′sil), *n.* [OF. *pincel* (F. *pinceau*), < L. *penicillum*, dim. of *peniculus*, brush, dim. of *penis*, tail.] An artist's paint-brush, esp. for fine work (as, "Take your pallet . . . choose your most delicate camel-hair *pencils*": C. Brontë's "Jane Eyre," xvi.); hence, style or skill in painting or delineation; also, a slender, pointed piece of some marking substance; esp., a strip of chalk, graphite, or the like incased in wood, metal, etc., used for drawing or writing; sometimes, a stick of coloring material for use on the eyebrows, etc., for cosmetic or theatrical purposes; also, a similarly shaped piece of some other substance, as lunar caustic; also, a set of lines, light-rays, or the like diverging from or converging to a point.—**pen′cil,** *v. t.*; *-ciled* or *-cilled, -ciling* or *-cilling.* To use a pencil on; mark or color with or as with a pencil; also, to execute, draw, or write with or as with a pencil.—**pen′ciled, pen′cilled,** *p. a.* Marked with or as with a pencil (as, "her soft, *pencilled* eyebrows": Mrs. Stowe's "Oldtown Folks," viii.); also, executed, drawn, or written with or as with a pencil (as, *penciled* lines; a *penciled* note); also, formed into a pencil or pencils, as rays; radiated.—**pen′cil-er, pen′cil-ler,** *n.* —**pen′cil-ing, pen′cil-ling,** *n.* The act of one who pencils; also, marks made with or as with a pencil; marking in delicate lines, as on feathers (see cut in next column); a penciled drawing, note, etc.

pen-craft (pen′krȧft), *n.* Writing; penmanship; authorship.

pend (pend), *v. i.* [L. *pendere* (*pendēre*), hang, depend, be undecided, akin to *pendere* (*pendĕre*), weigh: cf. *pension* and *poise.*] To hang; also, to depend (obs. or rare); also, to remain undecided, as a case in court (esp. used in *pending, ppr.*).

Penciling on Feathers.

pend-ant (pen′dạnt). [OF. F. *pendant*, < L. *pendens* (*pendent-*), ppr.: see *pendent.*] **I.** *a.* See *pendent.* **II.** *n.* Something pendent or hanging; a hanging ornament, as of a necklace or earring or of a vaulted roof (see cut below); a chandelier; also, that by which something is suspended, as the ringed stem of a watch; also, something appended or conjoined; a match or parallel; also, *naut.*, a short rope with a thimble or block at one end; also, a pennant.

pende-loque (poṅd-lok), *n.* [F., < OF. *pendeler*, dangle, < *pendre*, < L. *pendere*, hang.] A pear-shaped pendant, as a diamond cut in this form.

pend-ent (pen′dẹnt). [L. *pendens* (*pendent-*), ppr. of *pendere*, hang: see *pend*, and cf. *pendant.*] **I.** *a.* Hanging or suspended; also, overhanging; jutting or leaning over; also, impending; also, pending or undecided. **II.** *n.* See *pendant.*—**pend′en-cy,** *n.*—**pend′ent-ly,** *adv.*

Pendant in the Choir of the Church of Eu, Seine Inférieure, France.

pen-den-tive (pen-den′tiv), *n.* [F. *pendentif*, < L. *pendens*, ppr.: see *pendent.*] In *arch.*, a triangular segment of the lower part of a hemispherical dome, between two adjacent penetrating arches (see cut below); also, a similar segment of a groined vault, constituting the part which rests on a single pier or corbel.

pen-di-cle (pen′di-kl), *n.* [A dim. form < L. *pendere*, hang.] A pendant; a hanging ornament; also, an adjunct or appendage; specif., a small piece of land, a cottage, or the like, attached to an estate (Sc.).

Domes resting on Pendentives. — Nave of the Cathedral of Angoulême, France.

pend-ing (pen′ding). **I.** *p. a.* That pends; hanging; impending; esp., remaining undecided; awaiting decision. **II.** *prep.* In the period before the decision or conclusion of, or during (as, "*Pending* the peace negotiations, Philip had been called upon to mourn for his wife and father": Motley's "Dutch Republic," i. 3); also, while awaiting, or until (as, "*Pending* his return, Kate and her mother were shown into a dining-room": Dickens's "Nicholas Nickleby," xxi.).

pen-drag-on (pen-drag′ọn), *n.* [W., < *pen*, head, + *dragon*, dragon (used as symbol), leader.] Chief leader: a title of ancient British chiefs invested with supreme command: as, "the dread *Pendragon*, Britain's King of kings" (Tennyson's "Lancelot and Elaine," 422).—**pen-drag′on-ship,** *n.*

pen-dụ-lous (pen′dụ̄-lus), *a.* [L. *pendulus*, hanging, swinging, < *pendere*, hang: cf. *pendulum.*] Hanging or pendent; hanging loosely; swinging freely; oscillating; fig., vacillating; also, overhanging†.—**pen′du-lous-ly,** *adv.*—**pen′du-lous-ness,** *n.*

pen-du-lum (pen′dụ̄-lum), *n.*; pl. *-lums.* [NL., prop. neut. of L. *pendulus*: see *pendulous.*] A body so suspended (as by a rod) from a fixed point that it can move to and fro by the alternate action of gravity and acquired momentum; esp., such a device used for controlling the movement of clockwork.

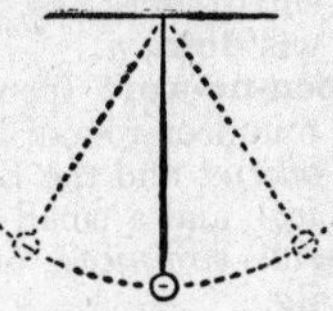

Pendulum.

pene-, pen-. [L. *pæne, pene,* adv., nearly, almost.] A prefix meaning 'nearly,' 'almost,' 'all but,' occurring in a few words from the Latin, as *peninsula, penult,* and occasionally used as an English formative, as in *penannular, peneplain.*

Pe-nel-o-pe (pẹ-nel′ọ-pẹ), *n.* [L., < Gr. Πηνελόπη.] The wife of Odysseus in ancient Greek legend, who, during her husband's long absence, remained faithful to him in spite of the importunities of numerous suitors; hence, allusively, a faithful wife.

pe-ne-plain (pē′nẹ-plān), *n.* [See *pene-.*] In *geol.*, an area reduced almost to a plain by erosion. —**pe′ne-plain,** *v. t.* To reduce by erosion to a peneplain.—**pe″ne-pla-na′tion** (-plạ-nā′shọn), *n.* The forming of a peneplain by erosion.

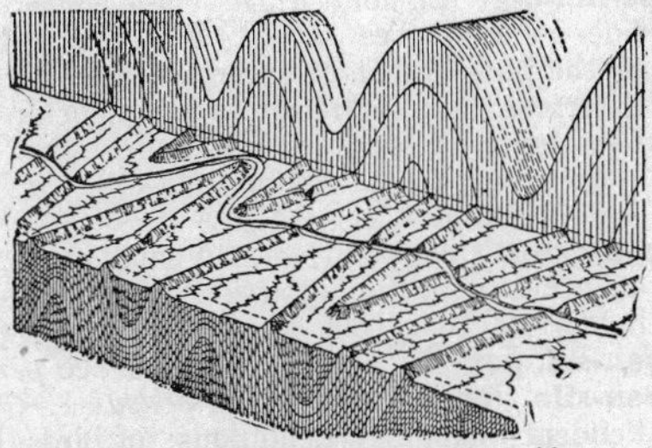

Diagram of Peneplain, with residual ridges.

pen-e-tra-ble (pen′ẹ-trạ-bl), *a.* [L. *penetrabilis.*] Capable of being penetrated; also, penetrating†.—**pen″e-tra-bil′i-ty** (-bil′i-ti), **pen′e-tra-ble-ness,** *n.*—**pen′e-tra-bly,** *adv.*

pen-e-tra-li-a (pen-ẹ-trā′li-ạ), *n. pl.* [L., prop. neut. pl. of *penetralis*, inner, orig. penetrating, < *penetrare*: see *penetrate.*] The innermost parts or recesses of a place or thing: as, "Mr. Campbell . . . is fain to . . . retire into the *penetralia* of his habitation, in order to avoid this diurnal annoyance" (Smollett's "Humphry Clinker," Sept. 3); "to disclose the very *penetralia* of my heart" (Lever's "Harry Lorrequer," xi.).

pen-e-trant (pen′ẹ-trạnt), *a.* Penetrating.

pen-e-trate (pen′ẹ-trāt), *v.*; *-trated, -trating.* [L. *penetratus*, pp. of *penetrare*, put within, enter, penetrate, akin to *penitus*, inward: cf. *penates.*] **I.** *tr.* To pierce into or through; enter into the interior of; also, to enter and diffuse itself through; permeate; also, to affect or impress deeply (as, to be *penetrated* with a sense of gratitude); also, to arrive at the meaning of; see through; discern; understand. **II.** *intr.* To enter or reach as by piercing (as, "Even where the trees were largest the sunshine *penetrated*": W. H. Hudson's "Green Mansions," ii.); make a way in or through something (as, "To reach this place, the visitor has to *penetrate* through a maze of close, narrow, and muddy streets": Dickens's "Oliver Twist," l.); pierce; also, to affect the feelings (as, "I advised him to give her music o' mornings; they say it will *penetrate*": Shakspere's "Cymbeline," ii. 3. 14); also, to gain insight (*into*, etc.: as, "Mrs. Rainscourt *penetrated* into the motives which had induced her husband to act," Marryat's "King's Own," xlvii.).—**pen′e-trat-ing** (-trā-ting), *p. a.* That penetrates; piercing; sharp; acute; discerning.—**pen′e-trat-ing-ly,** *adv.*—**pen-e-tra′tion** (-trā′shọn), *n.* [L. *penetratio(n-).*] The act or power of penetrating; mental acuteness, discernment, or insight (as, "Mrs. M'Elvina, with the usual *penetration* of her sex, discovered what was passing in the mind of Seymour": Marryat's "King's Own," lviii.); in *gun.*, the depth to which a projectile will pass in any material against which it is fired; in *optics*, of a microscope or its objective, the power of giving fairly distinct vision for points both inside and outside of the exact focus; of a telescope, the power of making distant objects distinct.—**pen′e-tra-tive** (-trạ-tiv), *a.* Tending to penetrate; piercing; acute; keen.—**pen′e-tra-tive-ly,** *adv.* —**pen′e-tra-tive-ness,** *n.*—**pen′e-tra-tor** (-trā-tọr), *n.*

pen-guin (pen′gwin or peng′-), *n.* [= F. *pingouin*, earlier *penguyn*, auk; of disputed origin.] Orig., the great auk†; later, any of various flightless aquatic birds (family *Spheniscidæ*) of the southern hemisphere, with webbed feet, and wings reduced to flippers; in *aëronautics*, a form of aëroplane which when operated merely rolls along the ground, thus enabling a beginner to learn certain manipulations in safety.

Emperor Penguin (*Aptenodytes imperator* or *forsteri*).

pen-hold-er (pen′hōl″dėr), *n.* A handle by which a steel or other pen is held in writing; also, a rack for a pen or pens.

pen-i-cil (pen′i-sil), *n.* [L. *penicillum*, painter's brush.] A small brush-like tuft of hairs, as on a caterpillar; in *surg.*, a tent or pledget.—**pen′i-cil-late** (-si-lāt), *a.* Having or forming a pencil.—**pen′i-cil-late-ly,** *adv.*—**pen″i-cil-la′tion,** *n.*

pen-i-cil-lin (pen-i-sil′in), *n.* A powerful bacteria-destroying drug made from molds of family *Penicillium.*

pe-nin-su-la (pẹ-nin′ṣụ̄-lạ), *n.*; pl. *-las.* [L. *pæninsula*, < *pæne*, almost, + *insula*, island.] A piece of land almost surrounded by water, esp. one connected with the mainland by only a narrow neck or isthmus; [*cap.*] with *the*, Spain and Portugal.—**pe-nin′su-lar** (-lạr), *a.* Of or pertaining to, or of the nature of, a peninsula: as, the *Peninsular* War (that carried on from 1808 to 1814 in Spain, Portugal, and southern France, by the British, Spanish, and Portuguese against the French, as the result of which the French were driven out of the Peninsula).—**pe-nin-su-lar′i-ty** (-lar′i-ti), *n.* The state of being a peninsula; also, the character or habit of mind attributed to those living in a peninsula and having little contact with other people; narrowness of mind; provincialism.—**pe-nin′su-late** (-lāt), *v. t.*; *-lated, -lating.* To form into a peninsula or peninsulas.

pe-nis (pē′nis), *n.*; pl. *penes* (-nēz). [L.] The male organ of copulation.

pen-i-tence (pen′i-tẹns), *n.* [OF. *penitence* (F. *pénitence*), < L. *pænitentia*, later *pœnitentia*, < *pænitens*: see *penitent*, and cf. *penance.*] The state of being penitent; repentance; contrition; also, penance (now rare).

pen-i-tent (pen′i-tẹnt). [OF. *penitent* (F. *pénitent*), < L. *pænitens* (*-ent-*), ppr. of *pænitere*, *pœnitere*, repent: cf. *repent*[2].] **I.** *a.* Repentant; contrite; sorry for sin or fault and disposed to atonement and amendment; also, doing penance† (as, "We that know what 'tis to fast and pray Are *penitent* for your default to-day": Shakspere's "Comedy of Errors," i. 2. 52). **II.** *n.* A penitent person; specif., one who confesses sin and submits to a penance imposed by ecclesiastical authority.

pen-i-ten-tial (pen-i-ten′shạl). [ML. *pœnitentialis.*] **I.** *a.* Of or pertaining to, proceeding from, or expressive of penitence or repentance (as, the *penitential* psalms, the 6th, 32d, 38th, 51st, 102d, 130th, and 143d psalms, which give expression to feelings of penitence); also, pertaining to or of the nature of penance. **II.** *n.* A penitent; also, a book or code of canons relating to penance, its imposition, etc.—**pen-i-ten′tial-ly,** *adv.*

pen-i-ten-tia-ry (pen-i-ten′shạ-ri). [ML. *pœnitentiarius.*] **I.** *a.* Of or pertaining to penance; penitential; also, pertaining to or intended for penal confinement and discipline; of an offense, punishable by imprisonment in a penitentiary. **II.** *n.*; pl. *-ries* (-riz). A penitent†; also, a place for penance†; a house of refuge for prostitutes (Eng.); a place for imprisonment and reformatory discipline; in the U. S., usually, a State prison; also, in the *Rom. Cath. Ch.*, an officer appointed to deal with cases of conscience reserved for the bishop of a diocese or for the papal court; also, an office of the papal court (presided over by the 'cardinal grand penitentiary') having jurisdiction over such cases.

pen-i-tent-ly (pen′i-tent-li), *adv.* In a penitent manner.

pen-knife (pen′nīf), *n.*; pl. *-knives* (-nīvz). A small pocket-knife, orig. one for making and mending quill pens.

pen-man (pen′man), *n.*; pl. *-men.* One who uses a pen, as in writing; one skilled in the use of the pen; also, a writer or author.—**pen′man-ship,** *n.*

pen-na (pen′ä), *n.*; pl. *pennæ* (-ē). [L., feather: see *pen*[2].] In *ornith.*, a contour-feather, as distinguished from a down-feather, plume, etc.

pen=name (pen′nām), *n.* A nom de plume. See *nom.*

pen-nant (pen′ant), *n.* [Var. of *pendant*, associated also with *pennon.*] A flag of distinctive form (as long and tapering, short and swallow-tailed, or triangular) and special significance, borne on naval or other vessels or used in signaling, etc.; any flag serving as an emblem, as of success in an athletic contest; also, in *music*, a hook (stroke attached to the stem of an eighth-note, etc.).

pen-nate (pen′āt), *a.* [L. *pennatus*, winged, < *penna*, feather.] Winged; feathered. Also **pen-nat-ed** (pen′ā-ted).

pen-nat-u-la (pe-nat′ū-lä), *n.*; pl. *-las* or *-læ* (-lē). [NL., prop. fem. of LL. *pennatulus*, dim. of L. *pennatus*, winged: see *pennate.*] A sea-pen (polyp) of the genus *Pennatula.*

pen-ner (pen′ėr), *n.* One who pens or writes something.

pen-ni-less (pen′i-les), *a.* Without a penny; destitute of money.—**pen′ni-less-ly,** *adv.*—**pen′ni-less-ness,** *n.*

pen-non (pen′on), *n.* [OF. F. *penon*, < *penne*, < L. *penna*, feather.] A distinctive flag in various forms (tapering, triangular, swallow-tailed, etc.), orig. one borne on the lance of a knight below the rank of banneret; a pennant; any flag or banner; also, a wing or pinion (poetic: as, "Fluttering his *pennons* vain, plumb down he drops Ten thousand fathom deep," Milton's "Paradise Lost," ii. 933).

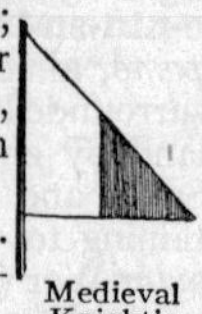

Medieval Knight's Pennon.

pen-non-cel (pen′on-sel), *n.* [OF. *penoncel*, dim. of *penon*, E. *pennon.*] A small pennon; a pencel. [Archaic.]

pen-noned (pen′ond), *a.* Bearing a pennon.

Penn-syl-va-ni-a (pen-sil-vā′ni-ä) **Dutch.** See under *Dutch, n.*

Penn-syl-va-ni-an (pen-sil-vā′ni-an). **I.** *a.* Of or pertaining to the State of Pennsylvania; in *geol.*, noting or pertaining to a geological period or a system of rocks which comprises the upper or later portion of the Carboniferous period or system in North America. **II.** *n.* A native or inhabitant of Pennsylvania; in *geol.*, the Pennsylvanian period or system.

pen-ny (pen′i), *n.*; pl. *pennies* (pen′iz) (individual coins) or *pence* (pens) (a sum or amount in this denomination). [AS. *penig, pening, pending,* = D. *penning* = G. *pfennig* = Icel. *peningr* = Sw. *penning*, penny.] An English bronze coin equal to one twelfth of a shilling, or about 2 U. S. cents; any of various coins of other countries, as the Roman denarius (see Luke, xx. 24) or the U. S. cent; in general, a coin; a piece of money; a sum of money (small or large: as, a pretty *penny*, that is, a considerable sum). Also used in composition to form adjectives denoting price or value, as in *fourpenny, fivepenny*, etc. (as used in *fourpenny nails, fivepenny nails*, etc., formerly meaning nails costing fourpence, fivepence, etc., a hundred, but now nails of certain arbitrary sizes).—**pen″ny=a=lin′er** (-a-lī′nėr), *n.* One who writes, as for a newspaper, at a penny a line or some low rate; a hack writer.—**pen′ny=an′te,** *n.* The game of poker when the amount of the ante is limited to one penny (one cent).

American Pennyroyal (*Hedeoma pulegioides*).

pen-ny-roy-al (pen-i-roi′al), *n.* [Appar. a corruption of obs. *puliol royal* (OF. *puliol*, dim. < L. *pulegium*, pennyroyal).] A low European mint, *Mentha pulegium*; also, an American menthaceous plant, *Hedeoma pulegioides*, used medicinally and yielding a pungently aromatic oil (see cut).

pen-ny-weight (pen′i-wāt), *n.* In troy weight, a weight of 24 grains or one twentieth of an ounce.

pen-ny=wise (pen′i-wīz′), *a.* Wise or saving in regard to small sums: as, *penny-wise* and pound-foolish.—**pen′ny=wis′dom,** *n.*

pen-ny-wort (pen′i-wėrt), *n.* Any of several plants with round or roundish leaves, as the navelwort, *Cotyledon umbilicus*, and the Kenilworth ivy, *Cymbalaria cymbalaria* (see *ivy*), and a small American plant, *Obolaria virginica*, of the gentian family.

Pennywort (*Obolaria virginica*).—*a*, a flower.

pen-ny-worth (pen′i-wėrth), *n.* As much as may be bought for a penny; hence, a small quantity or amount; also, value for the money given, or return for one's money or trouble (as, "Have once more with hail shot. I will have some *pennyworth*, I will not lese [lose] all": Udall's "Ralph Roister Doister," iv. 7); a bargain (good, bad, etc.).

pe-nol-o-gy (pē-nol′ō-ji), *n.* [Gr. ποινή, fine, penalty: see *-logy.*] The science of the punishment of crime, in both its deterrent and its reformatory aspects; the science of the management of prisons.—**pe-no-log-i-cal** (pē-nō-loj′i-kal), *a.*—**pe-nol′o-gist,** *n.*

pen=point (pen′point), *n.* A small steel or other pen, for insertion in a penholder. [Prov., Eng. and U. S.]

pen-sel, pen-sil (pen′sel, -sil), *n.* See *pencel.*

pen-sile (pen′sil), *a.* [L. *pensilis*, < *pendere*, hang.] Pendent; hanging; pendulous; of birds, building a hanging nest.

pen-sion (pen′shon), *n.* [OF. F. *pension*, < L. *pensio(n-)*, payment, < *pendere* (*pendĕre*), weigh, pay: cf. *pend.*] A payment made or exacted†; also, a fixed periodical payment made in consideration of past services, injury or loss sustained, merit, poverty, etc.; an allowance or annuity; also (F. poṅ-syôṅ), in France and elsewhere on the Continent, a boarding-house or boarding-school.—**pen′sion,** *v. t.* To grant a pension to; cause to retire on a pension (with *off*).—**pen′sion-a-ble,** *a.* Entitled or entitling to a pension.—**pen′sion-a-ry** (-ā-ri). [ML. *pensionarius.*] **I.** *a.* Of the nature of a pension; also, receiving a pension; hence, hireling. **II.** *n.*; pl. *-ries* (-riz). A pensioner; in the Netherlands, formerly, the chief magistrate of a city (as, "Jean Sersanders, the *pensionary* of Ghent": J. F. Kirk's "Charles the Bold," iii. 1); specif. (usually 'grand pensionary'), the chief minister of the state.—**pen′sion-er,** *n.* One who receives a pension; hence, a hireling; also, a member of a body-guard†; a gentleman-at-arms†; also, at Cambridge University, a student who pays for his commons, etc., and is not supported by any foundation.

pen-sive (pen′siv), *a.* [OF. F. *pensif*, < *penser*, think, < L. *pensare*, weigh, ponder, freq. of *pendere*, weigh: see *pension.*] Deeply, seriously, or sadly thoughtful (as, "Their hearts . . . with thoughts of vanished years Were *pensive*": W. Morris's "Jason," x. 555); grave; sober; melancholy; also, expressing or inducing thoughtfulness and sadness (as, "the *pensive* shade of the Italian ruins": G. W. Curtis's "Prue and I," ii.).—**pen′sive-ly,** *adv.*—**pen′sive-ness,** *n.*

pen=stab (pen′stab), *n.* An article for a writing-desk, commonly a small vessel containing a brush with the bristles turned upward, for thrusting a pen into after using. Also **pen′=stab″ber,** *n.*

pen-stock (pen′stok), *n.* [See *pen*[1].] A flood-gate; also, a channel or conduit for conveying water to a water-wheel or the like; also, the barrel of a pump.

pent[1] (pent), *p. a.* [Pp. of *pend*, obs. or prov. var. of *pen*[1].] Penned or shut in or up; closely confined: as, "as if he had in prison long bene *pent*" (Spenser's "Faerie Queene," iv. 5. 34); "His voice trembled with *pent* feeling" (G. W. Cable's "Bonaventure," ii. 10). Often with *up*: as, "ready to choke

with *pent-up* curiosity" (J. Conrad's "Rescue," iii. 9).
pent² (pent), *n.* Same as *penthouse.*
penta-, pent-. Forms of Gr. πέντε, five, used in combination. See *mono-.*—**pen-ta-ba-sic** (pen-tą-bā'sik), *a.* In *chem.*, of an acid, having five atoms of hydrogen replaceable by basic atoms or radicals.—**pen-ta-car'pel-la-ry** (-kär'pe-lą-ri), *a.* In *bot.*, having five carpels.—**pen'ta-chord** (-kôrd), *n.* [Gr. πεντάχορδος, five-stringed (χορδή, string).] In *music*, an instrument with five strings; also, a diatonic series of five tones.—**pen-ta'cid** (-tas'id), *a.* In *chem.*, capable of combining with five molecules of a monobasic acid.
pen-ta-cle (pen'tą-kl), *n.* [In form, a dim. (prob. through F. or ML.) < Gr. πέντε, five: cf. *pentangle.*] A pentagram, or five-pointed star-shaped figure of symbolical or mystic meaning (as, "He was tracing circles and *pentacles* in the grass and talking the language of the elves": Chesterton's "Magic," i.); an amulet or like object bearing this figure; loosely, some more or less similar figure, as a hexagram.
pen-tad (pen'tad), *n.* [Gr. πεντάς (πενταδ-), < πέντε, five.] The number five; a group or series of five; a period of five days or years; in *chem.*, a pentavalent element or radical.
pen-ta-gon (pen'tą-gon), *n.* [Gr. πεντάγωνον, < πέντε, five, + γωνία, angle.] A plane figure having five angles and five sides.—**pen-tag'o-nal** (-tag'ọ-nąl), *a.* Of, pertaining to, or having the form of a pentagon; having a pentagon as base or cross-section; divided into pentagons.—**pen-tag'o-nal-ly,** *adv.*

Regular Pentagon.

pen-ta-gram (pen'tą-gram), *n.* [Gr. πεντάγραμμον, < πέντε, five, + γραμμή, line.] A five-pointed star-shaped figure made by extending the sides of a regular pentagon until they meet (a symbolical figure used by the Pythagoreans and later philosophers, also by magicians and others); a pentacle, pentalpha, or pentangle.—**pen''ta-gram-mat'ic** (-grą-mat'ik), *a.*

Pentagram.

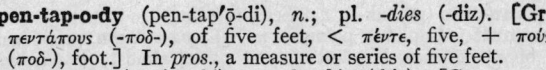

pen-ta-he-dron (pen-tą-hē'drọn), *n.*; pl. *-drons* or *-dra* (-drą). [See *penta-* and *-hedron.*] A solid figure having five faces.—**pen-ta-he'dral,** *a.*
pen-tail (pen'tāl), *n.* A small, squirrel-like, insectivorous animal, *Ptilocercus lowi*, of Borneo, Sumatra, etc., having a long tail naked toward the base but with the terminal portion fringed on opposite sides with long hairs so as to look somewhat like a quill pen.

Pentail.

pen-tal-pha (pen-tal'fą), *n.* [LGr. πεντάλφα, < Gr. πέντε, five, + ἄλφα, alpha; from the likeness to five alphas (Gr. A) combined.] A pentagram.
pen-tam-er-ous (pen-tam'ẹ-rus), *a.* [Gr. πενταμερής, < πέντε, five, + μέρος, part.] Consisting of or divided into five parts; in *bot.*, of flowers, having five members in each whorl.
pen-tam-e-ter (pen-tam'e-tėr). [L., < Gr. πεντάμετρος, < πέντε, five, + μέτρον, measure.] In *pros.*: **I.** *n.* A verse of five metrical feet; also, a verse consisting of two dactyls and one long syllable followed by two more dactyls and another single syllable ('elegiac pentameter': see *elegiac, a.*). **II.** *a.* Consisting of five metrical feet.
pen-tane (pen'tān), *n.* [Gr. πέντε, five (with reference to the atoms of carbon).] In *chem.*, a hydrocarbon, C_5H_{12}, of the methane series, existing in three isomeric forms.
pen-tan-gle (pen'tang-gl), *n.* [See *penta-.*] A pentagram; also, a pentagon.—**pen-tan'gu-lar** (-tang'gū-lär), *a.* Having five angles.

pen-tap-o-dy (pen-tap'ọ-di), *n.*; pl. *-dies* (-diz). [Gr. πεντάπους (-ποδ-), of five feet, < πέντε, five, + πούς (ποδ-), foot.] In *pros.*, a measure or series of five feet.
pen-tar-chy (pen'tär-ki), *n.*; pl. *-chies* (-kiz). [Gr. πενταρχία, < πέντε, five, + ἄρχειν, lead, rule.] A government by five persons; also, a group of five states or kingdoms, each under its own ruler; also, a governing body of five persons.
pen-ta-stich (pen'tą-stik), *n.* [Gr. πεντάστιχος, of five lines, < πέντε, five, + στίχος, row, line.] In *pros.*, a strophe, stanza, or poem consisting of five lines or verses.
pen-ta-style (pen'tą-stīl). [Gr. πέντε, five, + στῦλος, pillar, column.] **I.** *a.* Having five columns in front, as a temple or a portico. **II.** *n.* A pentastyle structure.
pen-ta-syl-la-ble (pen-tą-sil'ą-bl), *n.* [LL. *pentasyllabus*, < Gr. πεντασύλλαβος, of five syllables, < πέντε, five, + συλλαβή: see *syllable.*] A word of five syllables.—**pen''ta-syl-lab'ic** (-si-lab'ik), *a.*
Pen-ta-teuch (pen'tą-tūk), *n.* [LL. *Pentateuchus*, < Gr. πεντάτευχος, consisting of five books, < πέντε, five, + τεῦχος, book.] The first five books of the Old Testament (Genesis, Exodus, Leviticus, Numbers, and Deuteronomy), regarded as a connected group.—**Pen'ta-teuch-al,** *a.*
pen-tath-lete (pen-tath'lēt), *n.* [Gr. πενταθλητής.] A contestant in a pentathlon.
pen-tath-lon (pen-tath'lon), *n.* [Gr. πένταθλον, < πέντε, five, + ἆθλον, ἆθλος, contest.] An athletic contest comprising five different exercises or events, and won by the contestant having the highest total score.
pen-ta-tom-ic (pen-tą-tom'ik), *a.* [See *penta-.*] In *chem.*, having five atoms in the molecule; also, containing five replaceable atoms or groups.
pen-ta-va-lent (pen-tą-vā'lẹnt or pen-tav'ą-), *a.* [See *penta-* and *-valent.*] In *chem.*, having a valence of five.
Pen-te-cost (pen'tē-kost), *n.* [LL. *Pentecoste*, < Gr. πεντηκοστή, 'fiftieth (day),' < πεντηκοστός, fiftieth, < πεντήκοντα, fifty, < πέντε, five.] A Jewish harvest festival observed on the fiftieth day from the day (counted as the first) of the offering of the sheaf in the week following the Passover (see Lev. xxiii. 5–16); hence, a Christian festival commemorating the descent of the Holy Ghost upon the apostles on the day of the Jewish festival (see Acts, ii. 1–4); Whitsunday.—**pen'te-cos-tal,** *a.*
Pen-tel-ic (pen-tel'ik), *a.* Of or from Mount Pentelicus, near Athens: as, *Pentelic* marble (a fine-grained white marble much used in ancient Greek sculpture and architecture).
pent-house (pent'hous), *n.* [Corruption of earlier *pentise*, *pentice*, ME. *pentis*, < OF. *apentis* (F. *appentis*), < L. *appendere*, hang to or on, E. *append.*] A shed with a sloping roof, or a sloping roof, projecting from a wall or the side of a building, as to shelter a door; any roof-like shelter or overhanging part; a structure on a roof for housing elevator machinery, etc., or forming a separate apartment or dwelling.

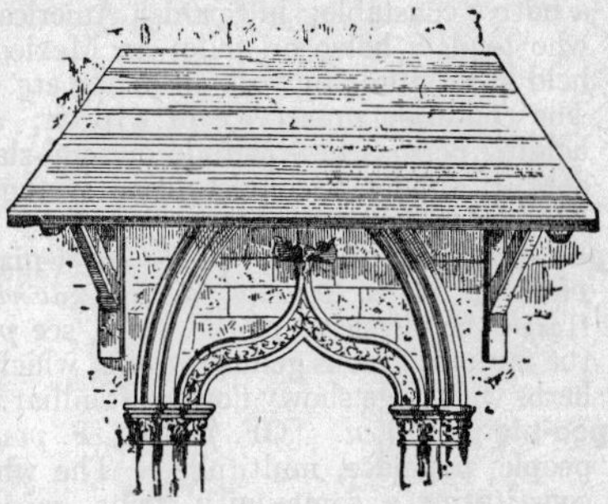
Penthouse.

pen-tice, pen-tise (pen'tis), *n.* Older forms of *penthouse.*
pen-to-san (pen'tọ-san), *n.* [From *pentose.*] In *chem.*, any of a class of complex carbohydrates which form pentoses upon hydrolysis, and occur in plants, humus, etc.
pen-tose (pen'tōs), *n.* [See *penta-* and *-ose².*] In *chem.*, any of a class of sugars containing five atoms of carbon, and produced from pentosans by hydrolysis.
pent=roof (pent'röf), *n.* [See *pent²*, for *penthouse.*] A roof like that of a penthouse, sloping in one direction only.
pent-ste-mon (pent-stē'mọn), *n.* [NL., < Gr. πέντε, five, + στήμων, warp, thread (with reference to the fifth stamen, usually rudimentary).] Any plant of the scrophulariaceous genus *Pentstemon*, chiefly of North America, including species cultivated for their variously colored flowers with long-tubed corolla; a beard-tongue.

pe-nuch-le (pē′nuk-l), *n.* See *pinochle.*

pe-nult (pẹ̄-nult′ or pē′nult), *n.* [L. *pænultima*, prop. fem. of *pænultimus*, last but one, < *pæne*, almost, + *ultimus*, last.] The last syllable but one in a word. Also **pe-nul-ti-ma** (pẹ̄-nul′ti-mạ̈).—**pe-nul′ti-mate** (-mạ̄t). **I.** *a.* Next to the last; the last but one; also, of or pertaining to the penult. **II.** *n.* The penult.—**pe-nul-ti-ma′tum** (-mā′-tum), *n.* A declaration, demand, or the like, that immediately precedes an ultimatum, or is all but an ultimatum.

pe-num-bra (pẹ̄-num′brạ̈), *n.*; pl. *-bras*, L. *-bræ* (-brē). [NL., < L. *pæne*, almost, + *umbra*, shade, shadow.] The partial or imperfect shadow outside of the complete shadow (umbra) of an opaque body, as a planet, where the light from the source of illumination is only partly cut off; also, the grayish marginal portion of a sun-spot; in general, a partial shadow.—**pe-num′bral,** *a.*

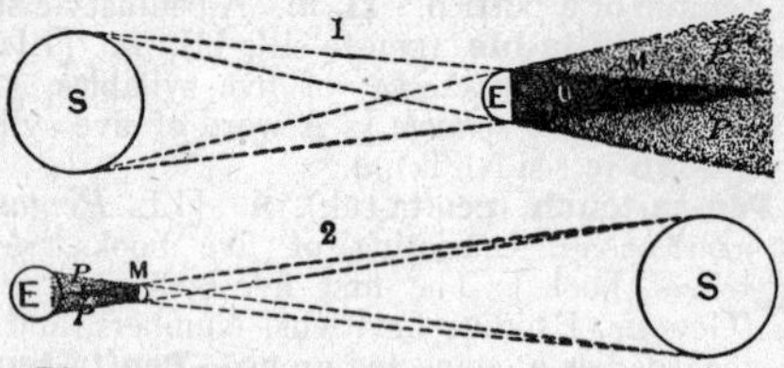

Diagrams of Umbra and Penumbra. — Fig. 1. Lunar eclipse. Fig. 2. Solar eclipse. *S*, sun; *E*, earth; *M*, moon; *P*, penumbra; *U*, umbra.

pe-nu-ri-ous (pẹ̄-nū′ri-us), *a.* In a condition of penury or want†; poverty-stricken†; also, scanty†; also, barren†; also, meanly parsimonious, or stingy (as, "a *penurious*, accumulating curmudgeon," Irving's "Tales of a Traveler," ii. 7; "He lived in the most *penurious* manner, and denied himself every indulgence," Godwin's "Caleb Williams," xxxvi.).—**pe-nu′ri-ous-ly,** *adv.*—**pe-nu′ri-ous-ness,** *n.*

pen-u-ry (pen′ụ̄-ri), *n.* [L. *penuria*, want, scarcity: cf. Gr. πενία, poverty, need.] Want or destitution (as, "My scanty purse was exhausted, and . . . I experienced the sordid distress of *penury*": Irving's "Tales of a Traveler," i. 9); extreme poverty; also, dearth or insufficiency; also, mean parsimony (as, "Her relatives considered that the *penury* of her table discredited the Mingott name": Mrs. Wharton's "Age of Innocence," ii.).

pen=wip-er (pen′wī″pėr), *n.* Something used or intended for wiping or cleaning pens.

pen-wom-an (pen′wụm″ạn), *n.*; pl. *-women* (-wim″en). A woman who uses, or is skilled in the use of, the pen; a female writer.

pe-on (pē′ọn), *n.* [Pg. *peão* and Sp. *peón*, foot-soldier, pedestrian, day-laborer, < ML. *pedo(n-)*, foot-soldier: see *pawn*[1].] In India, a foot-soldier; a messenger or attendant; a native constable; in Spanish America, a day-laborer; one who tends a horse or mule; in Mexico and elsewhere, one held in servitude to work off debts, etc.—**pe′on-age** (-ạ̄j), *n.* The condition or service of a peon; also, the practice of holding persons in servitude or semi-slavery, as to work off debt or (under a convict lease system) a penal sentence. Also **pe′on-ism.**

pe-o-ny (pē′ọ̄-ni), *n.*; pl. *-nies* (-niz). [OF. *peone* (F. *pivoine*), < L. *pæonia*, < Gr. παιωνία, peony, < Παιών, Παιάν, the physician of the gods: see *pæan.*] Any plant of the ranunculaceous genus *Pæonia*, which comprises perennial herbs with large showy flowers, familiar in gardens.

peo-ple (pē′pl), *n.* [OF. *pueple* (F. *peuple*), < L. *populus*, people, populace, multitude.] The whole body of persons constituting a community, tribe, race, or nation (as, the *people* of England; the Jewish *people*); a race or nation (as, all the *peoples* of the earth); also, the persons of any particular group, company, or number (as, the *people* of a parish; "I have arranged with the furniture *people* to take . . . things back that you do not like," W. Churchill's "Modern Chronicle," ii. 2); also, persons in relation to a superior, leader, etc. (as, the king and his *people*; a pastor and his *people*); a body of attendants, retainers, or the like; also, one's family or relatives (as, to visit one's *people*); the members of any group or number to which one belongs; also, the body of enfranchised citizens of a state (as, representatives chosen by the *people*); also, the commonalty or populace (as, "Our *people* and our peers are both misled," Shakspere's "3 Henry VI.," iii. 3. 35; a man of the *people*); also, persons indefinitely, whether men or women (as, *people* may say what they please; many *people* think so; there were not ten *people* present); sometimes, human beings as distinguished from animals; also, living creatures (chiefly poetic).—**People's party.** See *Populist.*—**peo′-ple,** *v. t.*; *-pled, -pling.* [OF. *puepler* (F. *peupler*).] To furnish with people; populate; hence, to stock with animals, etc. (as, "crystal pools, *peopled* with fish": Hood's "Midsummer Fairies," iv.); also, to occupy (a place, etc.) as inhabitants; inhabit.—**peo′pler,** *n.*

pep[1] (pep), *n.* [Short for *pepper.*] Spirit or animation; vigor, energy, or vim. [Slang.]

pep[2] (pep), *n.* [Var. of *pip*[3].] The pip or central part of an artificial flower.

pe-pi-no (pe-pē′nō), *n.* [Sp., < L. *pepo*: see *pepo.*] An evergreen shrub, *Philesia buxifolia*, a native of the extreme southern part of South America, bearing showy red flowers; also, a tropical American plant, *Solanum muricatum*, bearing an edible melon-like fruit.

pep-los, pep-lus (pep′los, -lus), *n.* [L. *peplus*, < Gr. πέπλος.] A voluminous outer garment worn draped in folds about the person by the ancient Greek women.

Athene wearing the Peplos. — Capitoline Museum, Rome.

pep-lum (pep′lum), *n.* [L. *peplum*, *peplus*: see *peplos.*] A peplos; in modern use, a woman's long overskirt; also, a short skirt attached to a bodice or coat.

pe-po (pē′pō), *n.* [L., melon, pumpkin, < Gr. πέπων, kind of gourd or melon eaten when ripe, orig. adj., ripe.] The characteristic fruit of cucurbitaceous plants, having a fleshy, many-seeded interior, and a hard or firm rind, as the gourd, melon, cucumber, etc.

pep-per (pep′ėr), *n.* [AS. *pipor*, < L. *piper*, < Gr. πίπερι, πέπερι, pepper; of Eastern origin.] A pungent condiment obtained from various plants of the genus *Piper*, esp. from the dried berries, either whole or ground (affording the 'black pepper' and 'white pepper' of commerce), of *P. nigrum*, a tropical climbing shrub; any plant of the genus *Piper* or family *Piperaceæ*; also, the condiment cayenne ('red pepper'), prepared from species of capsicum; any species of capsicum, esp. *Capsicum annuum* (the common pepper of the garden: see *capsicum*), or its fruit (green or red, hot or sweet). See *bell-pepper, chilli, paprika,* and *pimiento.*—**pep′per,** *v.* **I.** *tr.* To season with or as with pepper; also, to sprinkle as with pepper; dot; stud; also, to sprinkle like pepper; also, to pelt with shot or missiles; also, to inflict severe punishment upon; hence, to give a quietus to†, or do for† (as, "I am *peppered*, I warrant, for this world": Shakspere's "Romeo and Juliet," iii. 1. 102). **II.** *intr.* To discharge shot or missiles at something: as, "The Grangerfords . . . *peppered* away at him, and he *peppered* away at them" (Mark Twain's "Huckleberry Finn," xviii.).

Pepper (*Piper nigrum*).

pep-per=and=salt (pep′ėr-ạnd-sâlt′), *a.* Composed of a fine mixture of black or dark gray with white or light gray, as cloth.

pep-per=box (pep′ėr-boks), *n.* A box or vessel with a perforated lid, for sprinkling pulverized pepper on food.

pep-per-corn (pep′ėr-kôrn), *n.* [AS. *piporcorn.*] The dried berry of the pepper-plant, *Piper nigrum*; hence, anything very small, insignificant, or trifling.

pep-per-grass (pep′ėr-gràs), *n.* Any plant of the brassicaceous genus *Lepidium*, as *L. sativum*, which has a pungent flavor and is used as a cress.

pep-per-i-ness (pep′ėr-i-nes), *n.* Peppery quality.

pep-per-mint (pep′ėr-mint), *n.* A menthaceous herb, *Mentha piperita,* cultivated for its aromatic pungent oil; this oil, or some preparation of it; a lozenge or confection flavored with it.

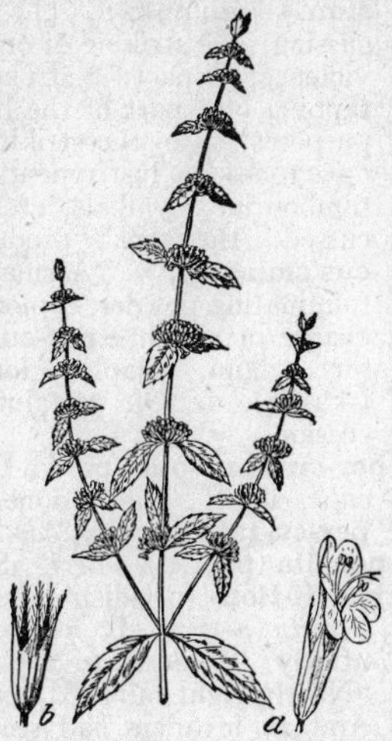

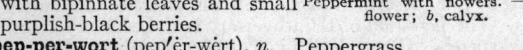

Peppermint with flowers. — *a,* flower; *b,* calyx.

pep-per=pot (pep′ėr-pot), *n.* A West Indian dish, the principal ingredient of which is cassareep, with meat or fish and vegetables; also, a kind of soup made of tripe and highly seasoned, and usually containing small balls of dough (chiefly Penn.).

pep-per=tree (pep′ėr-trē), *n.* An anacardiaceous evergreen tree, *Schinus molle,* with pungent red fruit, native in South America and cultivated elsewhere for ornament and shade.

pep-per=vine (pep′ėr-vīn), *n.* An upright, scarcely twining vitaceous shrub, *Ampelopsis arborea,* of the southern U. S., with bipinnate leaves and small purplish-black berries.

pep-per-wort (pep′ėr-wėrt), *n.* Peppergrass.

pep-per-y (pep′ėr-i), *a.* Of or pertaining to pepper; resembling pepper; full of pepper; pungent; fig., sharp or stinging, as speech (as, "a few *peppery* words and angry jerks of the head": Mrs. Gaskell's "Cranford," i.); irascible or irritable, as persons or their temper (as, "Pettingil, whose *peppery* temper was well known among the boys": Aldrich's "Story of a Bad Boy," viii.).

pep-sin (pep′sin), *n.* [G. *pepsin,* < Gr. πέψις, digestion, < πέπτειν: see *peptic.*] A proteolytic enzyme found in the gastric juice; also, a digestive preparation made from it.—**pep′sin-ate** (-si-nāt), *v. t.*; *-ated, -ating.* To treat, prepare, or mix with pepsin.

pep-tic (pep′tik). [L. *pepticus,* < Gr. πεπτικός, < πέπτειν, soften, cook, digest.] **I.** *a.* Pertaining to or concerned in digestion; digestive; promoting digestion; able to digest; also, of or pertaining to pepsin. **II.** *n.* A substance promoting digestion.

pep-to-gen (pep′tọ-jen), *n.* [See *peptone* and *-gen.*] A substance or preparation which facilitates peptic digestion.

pep-tone (pep′tōn), *n.* [G. *pepton,* < Gr. πέπτειν: see *peptic.*] Any of a class of diffusible and soluble substances into which proteids are converted by the action of pepsin or trypsin.—**pep-ton′ic** (-ton′ik), *a.*—**pep′ton-ize** (-tọ-nīz), *v. t.*; *-ized, -izing.* To convert into a peptone; esp., to subject (food) to an artificial partial digestion by means of pepsin or pancreatic extract, as an aid to digestion.—**pep″ton-i-za′tion** (-tọ-ni-zā′shọn), *n.*—**pep′ton-iz-er** (-tọ-nī-zėr), *n.*

per (pėr), *prep.* [L.: cf. *per-.*] Through; by; for each: used in many phrases, Latin and English, as *per annum* (by the year, annually), *per capita* ('by heads,' for each person), *per centum* (by the hundred), *per diem* (by the day, daily), *per se* (by or in itself, himself, herself, or themselves), *per day, mile,* or *yard* (for each day, mile, or yard), etc.

per-. [L. *per-,* repr. *per,* prep., through, by: see *per.*] A prefix meaning 'through,' 'thoroughly,' 'utterly,' 'very,' occurring orig. in words from the Latin, but used also as an English formative, esp. in chemical terms, in which it implies the maximum or a large amount of oxygen or some other element, as in *peroxide, perchloride.* Cf. *hyper-* and *super-.*

per-a-cute (pėr-ạ-kūt′), *a.* [L. *peracutus,* < *per-,* very, + *acutus,* E. *acute.*] Very acute or severe, as diseases.

per-ad-ven-ture (per-ạd-ven′tūr), *adv.* [OF. F. *par aventure,* < *par* (< L. *per*), by, and *aventure,* E. *adventure.*] By chance or accident, or perchance (as, if *peradventure* I should be delayed); also, it may be, maybe, or possibly (as, "*Peradventure* I may be an hour later": Fielding's "Joseph Andrews," iii. 12).—**per-ad-ven′ture,** *n.* Chance; uncertainty; hence, doubt or question (as, "It was affirmed — and the truth was certainly beyond *peradventure* — that religious liberty was dead": Motley's "Dutch Republic," vi. 6).

per-am-bu-late (pẹ-ram′bụ̄-lāt), *v.*; *-lated, -lating.* [L. *perambulatus,* pp. of *perambulare,* < *per,* through, + *ambulare,* walk.] **I.** *tr.* To walk through, about, or over (as, "Burgomaster Van der Werf . . . ordered the city musicians to *perambulate* the streets, playing lively melodies and martial airs": Motley's "Dutch Republic," iv. 2); travel through, or traverse; also, to traverse and examine or inspect. **II.** *intr.* To walk or travel about; stroll.—**per-am-bu-la′tion** (-lā′shọn), *n.* [ML. *perambulatio(n-).*] The act of perambulating; a journey on foot; a tour; a traversing for inspection; a survey.—**per-am′bu-la-tor,** *n.* One who perambulates; also, a form of hodometer; also, a small carriage for a child, pushed by hand from behind.—**per-am′bu-la-to-ry** (-lạ-tọ-ri), *a.* Perambulating; traveling.

per-cale (pėr-kāl′, F. per-kȧl), *n.* [F.; appar. of E. Ind. origin.] A closely woven, smooth-finished cambric, plain or printed.

per-ca-line (pėr-kạ-lēn′ or pėr′kạ-lēn), *n.* [F., < *percale:* see *percale.*] A fine, light-weight cotton fabric, usually finished with a gloss and dyed in one color, used esp. for linings.

per-ceiv-a-ble (pėr-sē′vạ-bl), *a.* Capable of being perceived; perceptible.—**per-ceiv′a-bly,** *adv.*

per-ceive (pėr-sēv′), *v. t.*; *-ceived, -ceiving.* [OF. *perceveir* (F. *percevoir*), < L. *percipere* (pp. *perceptus*), < *per,* through, + *capere,* take.] To apprehend with the mind (as, "I plainly *perceive* some objections remain": Burke's "Conciliation with the Colonies"); become aware of; understand; also, to gain knowledge of through one of the senses; discover by seeing, hearing, etc. (as, "We *perceived* a little girl coming towards us": Marryat's "Peter Simple," xxv.).—**per-ceiv′er,** *n.*

per cent (pėr sent). [Prop. *per cent.* (with period), abbr. of L. *per centum,* by the hundred.] By the hundred; for or in every hundred: used in expressing proportions, rates of interest, etc.: as, 25 *per cent* of a number; to get 6 *per cent* interest on money. Symbol, %.—**per-cen′tage** (-sen′tạ̄j), *n.* A rate or proportion per hundred (as, "The French were . . . suffering a lower *percentage* of casualties than the British": H. G. Wells's "Italy, France, and Britain at War," iii. 2); an allowance, duty, commission, discount, or rate of interest on a hundred; loosely, a proportion in general.

per-cept (pėr′sept), *n.* [L. *perceptum,* neut. of *perceptus,* pp. of *percipere,* E. *perceive.*] That which is perceived; the object of perception; also, the mental result or product of perceiving, as distinguished from the act of perceiving.

per-cep-ti-ble (pėr-sep′ti-bl), *a.* [LL. *perceptibilis,* < L. *percipere,* E. *perceive.*] Capable of being perceived; cognizable; discernible; appreciable (as, "quite a *perceptible* time": H. G. Wells's "Tono-Bungay," ii. 4. § 6).—**per-cep-ti-bil′i-ty** (-bil′i-ti), *n.*—**per-cep′ti-bly,** *adv.*

per-cep-tion (pėr-sep′shọn), *n.* [L. *perceptio(n-),* < *percipere,* E. *perceive.*] The act of perceiving; apprehension with the mind or the senses; cognition; a taking cognizance, as of a sensible object; an immediate or intuitive recognition, as of a moral or esthetic quality; also, the or a faculty of perceiving (as, "Defect in manners is usually the defect of fine *perceptions*": Emerson's "Essays," Manners); also, the result or product of perceiving, as distinguished from the act of perceiving; a percept.—**per-cep′tion-al,** *a.*

per-cep-tive (pėr-sep′tiv), *a.* [L. *percipere* (pp. *perceptus*), E. *perceive.*] Of or pertaining to perception; having the power or faculty of perceiving; sometimes, of ready or quick perception.—**per-cep′tive-ly,** *adv.*—**per-cep′tive-ness, per-cep-tiv′i-ty** (-tiv′i-ti), *n.*

per-cep-tu-al (pėr-sep′tụ̄-ạl), *a.* Pertaining to perception.

perch[1] (pėrch), *n.*; pl. *perches* or (esp. collectively) *perch.* [OF. F. *perche,* < L. *perca,* < Gr. πέρκη, perch.] A spiny-finned, fresh-water fish of the

American Yellow Perch (*Perca flavescens*).

genus *Perca* (family *Percidæ*), as *P. fluviatilis*, of Europe, or *P. flavescens* ('yellow perch'), of the U. S. (see cut on preceding page), used for food; any of various similar fishes of the same and other families, often marine.

perch² (pėrch), *n.* [OF. F. *perche*, < L. *pertica*, pole, measuring-rod, measure of land.] A pole, rod, or the like (now rare except as in senses following); a pole or staff set up in a shallow or other place in water, to serve as a mark for navigation; a pole in a carriage or other vehicle, connecting the fore and hind running parts; esp., a pole or rod fixed horizontally to serve as a roost for birds; hence, any thing or place serving for a bird, or for anything else, to alight or rest upon (as, "From my *perch* on the cross-trees I had nothing below me but the surface of the bay": Stevenson's "Treasure Island," xxvii.); an elevated position or station (as, "Not making his high place the lawless *perch* Of wing'd ambitions": Tennyson's "Idylls of the King," Dedication, 21); a small seat on a vehicle, for the driver or a servant; also, a rod, or linear measure of 5½ yards or 16½ feet; a square rod (30¼ square yards); a solid measure for stone, etc., commonly 16½ feet by 1½ feet by 1 foot.—**perch²**, *v.* [OF. F. *percher*.] **I.** *intr.* To alight or rest upon a perch, as a bird; hence, to settle or rest in some elevated position, as if on a perch (as, "The little village *perches* high among the hills": H. G. Wells's "Mr. Britling," ii. 3. § 5). **II.** *tr.* To set or place on a perch; set in some elevated position, as if on a perch (as, "some two dozen farm-houses, hid in green hollows, or *perched* on breezy hilltops": Mrs. Stowe's "Oldtown Folks," i.).

per-chance (pėr-chȧns′), *adv.* [OF. *par* (< L. *per*), by, + *cheance*, E. *chance*.] By chance or accident; by any chance (as, "I counsel thee to stand aloof . . . lest *perchance* He smite thee with his spear": Bryant's tr. Homer's "Iliad," iii. 534); also, it may be, maybe, or possibly (as, "E'en now *perchance* faint rumours reach Men's ears of this our victory," W. Morris's "Jason," xiv. 141; "The climax would be interesting, if *perchance* uncomfortable," W. Churchill's "Modern Chronicle," i. 10).

perch-er (pėr′chėr), *n.* One who or that which perches; specif., a bird whose feet are adapted for perching.

Per-che-ron (pėr′shẹ-ron, F. per-shė-rôṅ), *n.* [F.] One of a breed of horses combining strength, lightness, and speed, orig. raised in Perche, a district in northern France, west and southwest of Paris.

per-chlo-rate (pėr-klō′rāt), *n.* [See *per-*.] In *chem.*, a salt of perchloric acid.—**per-chlo′ric**, *a.* In *chem.*, noting or pertaining to an acid of chlorine, $HClO_4$, containing one more oxygen atom than chloric acid, and occurring as a colorless syrupy liquid.—**per-chlo′ride** (-rīd or -rid), *n.* In *chem.*, that chloride of any particular element or radical with maximum proportion of chlorine.

per-cip-i-ent (pėr-sip′i-ẹnt). [L. *percipiens* (*-ent-*), ppr. of *percipere*, E. *perceive*.] **I.** *a.* Perceiving; having perception: as, "the *percipient* thinking substance, the Ego" (Hallam's "Literature of Europe," iii. 3. § 99). **II.** *n.* One who or that which perceives.—**per-cip′i-ence, per-cip′i-en-cy,** *n.*

per-coid (pėr′koid). [L. *perca*, perch: see *-oid*.] **I.** *a.* Resembling a perch; belonging to the *Percoidea*, a group of acanthopterygian fishes comprising the true perches and related families, and constituting one of the largest natural groups of fishes. **II.** *n.* A percoid fish.—**per-coi′de-an** (-koi′dẹ-ạn), *a.* and *n.*

per-co-late (pėr′kọ-lāt), *v.*; *-lated, -lating.* [L. *percolatus*, pp. of *percolare*, < *per*, through, + *colare*, strain.] **I.** *tr.* To cause (a liquid) to pass through a porous body; filter; also, to sift, as meal; also, of a liquid, to filter through (something porous); permeate. **II.** *intr.* To pass through a porous substance; filter; ooze.—**per′co-late**, *n.* A liquid which has been percolated.—**per-co-la′tion** (-lā′shọn), *n.*—**per′co-la-tor**, *n.* One who or that which percolates; esp., a kind of coffee-pot in which boiling water filters through ground coffee.

per-cur-rent (pėr-kur′ẹnt), *a.* [L. *percurrens* (*-ent-*), ppr. of *percurrere*, run through, < *per*, through, + *currere*, run.] Running through the entire length, as the midrib of a leaf.

per-cuss (pėr-kus′), *v. t.* [L. *percussus*, pp. of *percutere*, < *per*, through, + *quatere*, shake, strike.] To strike (something) so as to shake or cause a shock to; in *med.*, to strike or tap for diagnostic or therapeutic purposes.—**per-cus′sion** (-kush′ọn), *n.* [L. *percussio*(*n-*).] The act of percussing; the striking of one body against another with some violence; impact; a stroke or blow; specif., the striking or tapping of a part of the body for diagnostic or therapeutic purposes; also, the striking of musical instruments to produce tones (as, instruments of *percussion*, the drum, triangle, tambourine, cymbals, etc.); also, the state of being percussed; the shock produced by violent collision.—**per-cus′sion=cap,** *n.* A small metallic cap or cup containing fulminating powder, exploded by percussion so as to fire the charge of a gun.—**per-cus′sion=lock,** *n.* A form of lock for a gun, adapted for percussion-caps.—**per-cus′sive** (-kus′iv), *a.* Of, pertaining to, or characterized by percussion.

per-cu-ta-ne-ous (pėr-kṳ̄-tā′nẹ-us), *a.* [L. *per*, through, + *cutis*, skin.] Made, done, or effected through the skin.—**per-cu-ta′ne-ous-ly,** *adv.*

per-die (pėr-dē′), *interj.* Same as *pardi.*

per-di-tion (pėr-dish′ọn), *n.* [OF. F. *perdition*, < LL. *perditio*(*n-*), < L. *perdere*, destroy, ruin, lose, < *per-*, utterly, + *dare*, give.] Utter destruction or ruin (as, "Nearly eight hundred years were past and gone, since the Arabian invaders had sealed the *perdition* of Spain": Irving's "Conquest of Granada," i.); also, loss† or diminution† (as, "The *perdition* of th' athversary hath been very great": Shakspere's "Henry V.," iii. 6. 103); also, a condition of final spiritual ruin or damnation; the future state of the wicked; the place of damnation, or hell.

per-du, per-due (pėr-dū′, F. per-dü). [F. *perdu* (fem. *perdue*), pp. of *perdre*, lose, < L. *perdere*: see *perdition*.] **I.** *a.* Lost to sight; hidden or concealed (as, "James . . . was lying *perdu* in the lobby": Scott's "Redgauntlet," letter viii.); also, placed as a sentinel, outpost, etc., in a dangerous position. **II.**† *n.* A soldier placed in a dangerous position or sent on a hazardous enterprise.

per-du-ra-ble (pėr-dū′rạ-bl or pėr′dṳ̄-), *a.* [LL. *perdurabilis*, < L. *perdurare*, E. *perdure*.] Enduring continuously; permanent; everlasting; imperishable: as, "cables of *perdurable* toughness" (Shakspere's "Othello," i. 3. 343); "leaving a name *perdurable* on earth" (Southey's "Roderick," xvi. 288).—**per-du-ra-bil′i-ty** (-bil′i-ti), *n.*—**per-du′ra-bly,** *adv.*

per-dure (pėr-dūr′), *v. i.*; *-dured, -during.* [L. *perdurare*, < *per*, through, + *durare*, endure, E. *dure²*.] To endure or continue long or forever.

père (pãr), *n.* [F., < L. *pater*.] Father: sometimes used after a name to distinguish father from son (*fils*), as in Dumas *père* (the French novelist and dramatist, 1802–70) and Dumas *fils* (the French dramatist and novelist, 1824–95).

per-e-gri-nate (per′ẹ-gri-nāt), *v.*; *-nated, -nating.* [L. *peregrinatus*, pp. of *peregrinari*, < *peregrinus*: see *peregrine*.] **I.** *intr.* To travel or journey. **II.** *tr.* To travel over; traverse.—**per′e-gri-nate,** *a.* Of foreign fashion; foreign: as, "I perceive . . . that there is something outlandish, *peregrinate*, and lawless about me" (Bulwer-Lytton's "Caxtons," xviii. 2). See Shakspere's "Love's Labour's Lost," v. 1. 15. [Obs. or archaic.]—**per″e-gri-na′tion** (-nā′shọn), *n.* [L. *peregrinatio*(*n-*).] The act of traveling in foreign countries, or from one country or place to another; also, a course of travel (as, "The gray-haired veteran retired, after a long *peregrination*, to his native town": Borrow's "Lavengro," iii.); a journey.—**per′e-gri-na-tor,** *n.*

per-e-grine, per-e-grin (per′ẹ-grin), *a.* [L. *peregrinus*, foreign, as n. a foreigner, < *pereger*, being on a journey, or abroad, < *per*, through, + *ager*, field, land: cf. *pilgrim*.] Foreign; alien; coming from abroad; also, being upon a pilgrimage†, or traveling abroad† (as, "the whole army of *peregrine* martyrs: more especially those travellers who set out upon their travels with the benefit of the clergy": Sterne's "Sentimental Journey," Preface, In the Desobligeant); also, in *astrol.*, of a planet, so situated in the zodiac that it has none of its essential dignities.—**peregrine falcon.** [= ML. *falco peregrinus*, F. *faucon pèlerin*, lit. 'pilgrim falcon.'] A large, spirited falcon, *Falco peregrinus*, formerly much used in Europe for hawking, of which there are several varieties, including the American duck-hawk.—**per′e-**

grine, per′e-grin, *n.* A foreign sojourner in a state; a resident not having the rights of citizenship; also, a peregrine falcon (as, "Out of the reeds, like an arrow, shot the *peregrine*": Kingsley's "Hereward," xx.).—**per-e-grin′i-ty** (-i-ti), *n.* The condition of a foreigner or alien.

per-emp-to-ry (per′emp-tō-ri or pe-remp′-), *a.* [L. *peremptorius,* destructive, decisive, < *perimere,* take away entirely, < *per-,* utterly, + *emere,* take, buy.] In legal use, that precludes or does not admit of debate, question, etc. (as, a *peremptory* edict or decree); in which a command is absolute and unconditional (as, a *peremptory* writ); decisive or final; in general, leaving no opportunity for denial or refusal; imperative (as, "A *peremptory* command would have compelled obedience": Johnson's "Rasselas," xxxiv.); positive or downright (as, "This demand of government was met by a *peremptory* refusal": Motley's "Dutch Republic," ii. 9); also, definitely or positively settled upon, as a date; also, fully resolved or determined, as a person†; hence, obstinate† or stubborn†; also, positive in speech, tone, manner, etc., as a person, or as the tone, manner, etc. (as, "He spoke in a loud and *peremptory* voice, using the tone of one in authority": Tarkington's "Magnificent Ambersons," xix.); insistent in requirement; imperious or dictatorial.—**per′emp-to-ri-ly,** *adv.*—**per′emp-to-ri-ness,** *n.*

per-en-dure (pėr-en-dūr′), *v. i.*; *-dured, -during.* [See *per-,* and cf. *perdure.*] To endure long or forever.

pe-ren-ni-al (pe-ren′i-al). [L. *perennis,* < *per,* through, + *annus,* year.] **I.** *a.* Lasting or continuing throughout the year, as a spring or stream; also, lasting through a succession of years, or for an indefinitely long time; enduring; perpetual; everlasting; specif., in *bot.,* continuing more than two years. **II.** *n.* In *bot.,* a perennial plant.—**pe-ren′ni-al-ly,** *adv.*

per-fect (pėr′fekt). [OF. *parfit* (F. *parfait*), < L. *perfectus,* pp. of *perficere,* perform, complete, finish, < *per,* through, + *facere,* do, make.] **I.** *a.* Carried through to completion in every detail; in a state proper to a thing when completed; having all essential elements, characteristics, etc.; lacking in no respect; complete; also, in a state of complete excellence; without blemish or defect; faultless; sometimes, of supreme moral excellence (as, "Mark the *perfect* man, and behold the upright: for the end of that man is peace": Ps. xxxvii. 37); also, completely skilled or versed (as, "Our battle is more full of names than yours, Our men more *perfect* in the use of arms": Shakspere's "2 Henry IV.," iv. 1. 155); having learned one's lesson or part thoroughly; thoroughly learned or acquired, as a lesson (as, "The lesson is but plain, And once made *perfect,* never lost again": Shakspere's "Venus and Adonis," 408); also, completely corresponding to a type or description; exact (as, a *perfect* sphere); correct in every detail (as, a *perfect* copy); entire or unqualified (as, "Both of them were *perfect* strangers to the rest of the company": Swift's "Gulliver's Travels," iii. 8); pure or unmixed (as, "your straw-coloured beard, your orange-tawny beard . . . your *perfect* yellow": Shakspere's "Midsummer Night's Dream," i. 2. 98); hence, unmitigated or utter (chiefly colloq.: as, "The Greenock ladies have a great name for beauty; but those that I have seen are *perfect* frights," Galt's "Ayrshire Legatees," i.); also, assured† or certain† (as, "Thou art *perfect* then, our ship hath touch'd upon The deserts of Bohemia?" Shakspere's "Winter's Tale," iii. 3. 1); also, satisfied† or contented† (as, "Might we but have that happiness . . . we should think ourselves for ever *perfect*": Shakspere's "Timon of Athens," i. 2. 90); in *bot.,* having all parts or members present; esp., monoclinous; in *gram.,* denoting an action or state completed at the present time (as, the *perfect* tense: cf. *pluperfect* and *future-perfect*); in *music,* noting the consonances of a normal unison, octave, fifth, and fourth, as distinguished from those of a third and sixth, which are called *imperfect;* noting the intervals, harmonic or melodic, of an octave, fifth, and fourth in their normal form, as opposed to *augmented* and *diminished;* noting a chord or triad involving a perfect fifth and having its fundamental tone in the bass; of a cadence or period, complete or fully satisfactory. **II.** *n.* In *gram.,* the perfect tense; a verb-form in this tense, as Latin *amavi,* 'I have loved.'—**per-fect** (pėr′fekt or pėr-fekt′), *v. t.* To bring to completion, complete, or finish (as, "The numerous vine-yards were patiently awaiting the suns of the next month slowly to *perfect* their present promise," J. H. Newman's "Callista," xiv.; "the system of religious persecution commenced by Charles, and *perfected* by Philip," Motley's "Dutch Republic," ii. 3); also, to make perfect or faultless; bring to perfection; hence, loosely, to bring nearer to perfection; improve; also, to make fully skilled or versed (as, to *perfect* one's self in an art).—**per-fect-er** (pėr′fek-tėr or pėr-fek′tėr), *n.*—**per-fect′i-ble,** *a.* Capable of becoming, or being made, perfect.—**per-fect-i-bil′i-ty** (-bil′i-ti), *n.*

per-fec-tion (pėr-fek′shon), *n.* [L. *perfectio(n-),* < *perficere:* see *perfect.*] The act or fact of perfecting, or bringing to completion; the completed state or full development of a thing (as, "They . . . bring no fruit to *perfection*": Luke, viii. 14); also, the state or quality of being perfect, or without blemish or defect; flawlessness; faultlessness; supreme excellence; specif., supreme moral excellence; holiness; also, the highest degree of proficiency, as in some art; often, loosely, comparative excellence (as, things displaying different degrees of *perfection;* to strive to attain greater moral *perfection*); also, a perfect embodiment of something (as, "The Umpire coach was the *perfection* of fast travelling": Lever's "Harry Lorrequer," x.); a perfect person or thing; also, a quality, trait, or feature of a high degree of excellence; also, the highest or most perfect degree of a quality or trait (as, the *perfection* of goodness, or of cruelty).—**to perfection,** completely; fully; perfectly.—**per-fec′tion,** *v. t.* To bring to perfection; perfect: as, "He only receives pupils for *perfectioning*" (Galt's "Ayrshire Legatees," vi.).—**per-fec′tion-ism,** *n.* Any of various doctrines maintaining that religious, moral, social, or political perfection is attainable.—**per-fec′tion-ist,** *n.*—**per-fec-tion-is′tic,** *a.*

per-fec-tive (pėr-fek′tiv), *a.* Tending to make perfect; conducive to perfection.—**per-fec′tive-ly,** *adv.*—**per-fec′tive-ness,** *n.*

per-fect-ly (pėr′fekt-li), *adv.* In a perfect manner or degree; completely or thoroughly; fully; faultlessly, or so as to leave nothing to be desired; with the utmost exactness, correctness, etc.; entirely or quite (as, *perfectly* new; *perfectly* clear or simple).—**per′fect-ness,** *n.*

per-fec-to (pėr-fek′tō), *n.*; pl. *-tos* (-tōz). [Sp., lit. 'perfect.'] A rather thick, medium-sized cigar tapering toward both ends.

per-fer-vid (pėr-fėr′vid), *a.* [NL. *perfervidus,* < L. *per-,* very, + *fervidus,* E. *fervid.*] Very fervid; very ardent: as, "She was moved by this *perfervid* letter . . . Its effect—the effect of its passionate flattery—was to lift her nobly to an eminence" (M. Hewlett's "Open Country," xix.).—**per-fer′vid-ness, per-fer′vor,** *n.*

per-fid-i-ous (pėr-fid′i-us), *a.* [L. *perfidiosus.*] Guilty of or characterized by perfidy; deliberately faithless; basely treacherous: as, "I am the victim of a *perfidious* woman" (Bulwer-Lytton's "Pelham," xvii.); "Compelled to parley, Bossu resorted to a *perfidious* stratagem" (Motley's "Dutch Republic," iii. 6).—**per-fid′i-ous-ly,** *adv.*—**per-fid′i-ous-ness,** *n.*

per-fi-dy (pėr′fi-di), *n.*; pl. *-dies* (-diz). [F. *perfidie,* < L. *perfidia,* < *perfidus,* breaking faith, < *per,* through, + *fides,* faith.] Base breach of faith or trust; deliberate faithlessness; base treachery: as, "a forsaken lady . . . bewailing the *perfidy* of her lover" (C. Brontë's "Jane Eyre," xi.).

per-fo-li-ate (pėr-fō′li-āt), *a.* [NL. *perfoliatus,* < L. *per,* through, + *folium,* leaf.] In *bot.,* having the stem apparently passing through the leaf, owing to congenital union of the basal edges of the leaf round the stem: as, a *perfoliate* leaf.—**per-fo-li-a′tion** (-ā′shon), *n.*

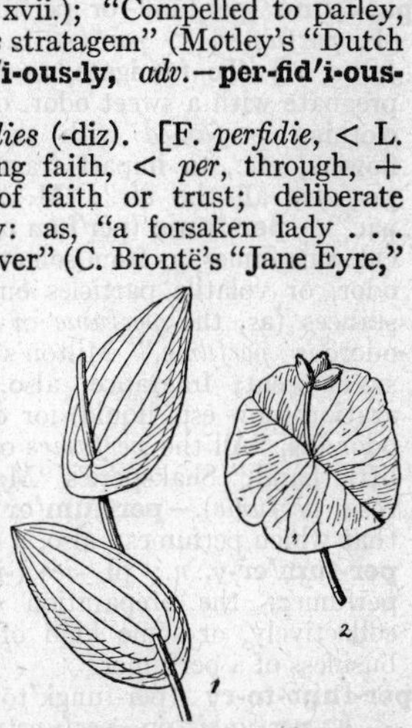

1. Perfoliate Leaves of Bellwort (*Uvularia perfoliata*). 2. Connate-perfoliate Leaf of Honeysuckle (*Lonicera sempervirens*).

per-fo-rate (pėr′fō-rāt), *v.*; *-rated, -rating.* [L. *perforatus,* pp. of *perforare,* < *per,* through, + *forare,* pierce, bore.] **I.** *tr.* To pierce through (as, to *perforate* a target with bullets; "a tall, steep roof, *perforated* with innumerable narrow windows," Lever's "Harry Lorrequer," xix.); esp., to make a hole or holes through by boring, punching, or other process (as, to *perforate* sheets of postage-stamps along the lines of division); sometimes, to pierce to the interior of, or penetrate. **II.** *intr.* To make its way through or into something; penetrate.—**per′fo-rate,** *a.* Pierced with a hole or holes: as, *perforate* corals.—**per-fo-ra′tion** (-rā′-shọn), *n.* [ML. *perforatio(n-).*] The act of perforating, or the state of being perforated; also, a hole made or passing through a thing; often, a hole, or one of a number of holes, bored or punched through something (as, the *perforations* of a colander; detach the check at the line of *perforations*). —**per′fo-ra-tive** (-rā-tiv), *a.* Perforating; tending to perforate.—**per′fo-ra-tor** (-rā-tọr), *n.* One who or that which perforates; esp., an instrument or machine for perforating.

per-force (pėr-fōrs′), *adv.* [OF. F. *par force,* < *par* (< L. *per*), by, and *force,* E. *force*[3].] By force or violence†; also, by the force of necessity, or of necessity (as, "The wind was foul and boisterous, so *perforce* There must they bide": W. Morris's "Jason," vi. 217).

per-form (pėr-fôrm′), *v.* [AF. *parfourmer,* appar. for OF. *parfournir,* complete, accomplish, < *par* (< L. *per*), through, + *fournir, furnir,* E. *furnish.*] **I.** *tr.* To complete†, or bring to completion†; also, to carry into effect, or fulfil (as, to *perform* a command, promise, or vow; "Every purpose of the Lord shall be *performed* against Babylon," Jer. li. 29); also, to carry out, go through, execute, or do (as, to *perform* work, operations, or acts; to *perform* miracles); esp., to go through or execute in due form (as, to *perform* a ceremony; "one Sunday forenoon, as Captain M—— was *performing* divine service," Marryat's "King's Own," xxx.); render (music), as by playing or singing; act (a play, a part, etc.), as on the stage. **II.** *intr.* To fulfil a command, promise, or undertaking (as, "Ithacus . . . Wise to resolve, and patient to *perform*": Pope's tr. Homer's "Odyssey," iv.); also, to execute or do something; perform music; act in a play; go through some performance.—**per-form′a-ble,** *a.* Capable of being performed.—**per-form′ance,** *n.* The act of performing, or the fact of being performed; fulfilment, as of a promise or undertaking; execution or doing, as of work, acts, or feats; the performing of ceremonies, or of music, or of a play, part, or the like; also, a particular action, deed, or proceeding (as, "Besides her walking and other actual *performances,* what . . . have you heard her say?" Shakspere's "Macbeth," v. 1. 13); esp., an action or proceeding of a more or less unusual or spectacular kind (as, have you heard of his latest *performance?*); an exploit; also, a musical, dramatic, or other entertainment; also, a production, esp. a piece of literary or artistic work.—**per-form′er,** *n.*

per-fume (pėr-fūm′ or pėr′fūm), *v. t.*; *-fumed, -fuming.* [F. *parfumer,* < *par* (< L. *per*), through, + *fumer,* E. *fume, v.*] To fumigate, as in disinfecting†; also, to impregnate with a sweet odor, or scent (as, to *perfume* soap; clothing *perfumed* with sachet-powder); of substances, flowers, etc., to impart fragrance to (as, "The blue-bells *perfume* all the air": M. Arnold's "Stanzas from Carnac").—**per-fume** (pėr′fūm or pėr-fūm′), *n.* [F. *parfum.*] Odorous fumes, as from something burned†; also, the scent, odor, or volatile particles emitted by sweet-smelling substances (as, the *perfume* of violets; "an amber scent of odorous *perfume,*" Milton's "Samson Agonistes," 720); sweet scent; fragrance; also, a substance, extract, or preparation (now esp. liquid) for diffusing or imparting a sweet odor (as, "All the *perfumes* of Arabia will not sweeten this little hand," Shakspere's "Macbeth," v. 1. 57; a bottle of rose *perfume*).—**per-fum′er** (-fū′mėr), *n.* One who or that which perfumes; also, a maker or seller of perfumes.—**per-fum′er-y,** *n.*; pl. *-ies* (-iz). The art or business of a perfumer; the preparation of perfumes; also, perfumes collectively, or some kind of perfume; also, the place of business of a perfumer.

per-func-to-ry (pėr-fungk′tō-ri), *a.* [LL. *perfunctorius,* < L. *perfungi* (pp. *perfunctus*), fulfil, < *per,* through, + *fungi,* perform.] Done in or suggestive of mere performance of an uninteresting duty or mere observance of routine or form (as, a *perfunctory* compliance or response; *perfunctory* courtesy; "He saw her . . . and raised his hat, but in a *perfunctory,* preoccupied manner," Arnold Bennett's "Hilda Lessways," iii. 2); mechanical or formal; indifferent, careless, or superficial; of persons, acting as if merely to get rid of a duty or matter.—**per-func′to-ri-ly,** *adv.*—**per-func′to-ri-ness,** *n.*

per-fuse (pėr-fūz′), *v. t.*; *-fused, -fusing.* [L. *perfusus,* pp. of *perfundere,* < *per,* through, + *fundere,* pour.] To overspread with moisture, color, etc.; also, to diffuse (a liquid, etc.) through or over something.—**per-fu′sion** (-fū′zhọn), *n.*

Per-ga-mene (pėr′gạ-mēn), *a.* [L. *Pergamenus,* < Gr. Περγαμηνός.] Pertaining to the ancient city of Pergamum in Mysia, Asia Minor, or to a notable school of sculpture which flourished there in the 3d and 2d centuries B.C.

Pergamene Sculpture. — Part of the Athene group from the frieze of the altar at Pergamum.

per-go-la (pėr′gō-lạ), *n.* [It., < L. *pergula,* shed, vine-arbor.] An arbor formed of horizontal trellis-work supported on columns or posts, over which vines or other plants are trained: as, "A trellised arbour (which some years later would have been called a *pergola*) led from the porch up the hill to an old-fashioned summer-house" (W. Churchill's "Modern Chronicle," i. 7).

per-haps (pėr-haps′, commonly praps), *adv.* [From *per-,* as in *perchance,* + *hap*[2].] Perchance, or by any chance (as, "Repent . . . and pray God, if *perhaps* the thought of thine heart may be forgiven thee": Acts, viii. 22); also, it may be, maybe, or possibly (as, *perhaps* he will come tonight; you may think, *perhaps,* that this is unnecessary).

pe-ri (pē′ri), *n.*; pl. *-ris* (-riz). [Pers. *parī.*] One of a race of beautiful fairy-like beings of Persian mythology, represented as descended from fallen angels and excluded from paradise till their penance is accomplished.

peri-. [Gr. περι-, repr. περί, prep. and adv., around, about, near, beyond.] A prefix meaning 'around,' 'about,' 'beyond,' or having an intensive force, occurring in words from the Greek, and used also as a modern formative, esp. in scientific terms.

per-i-a-gua (per-i-ä′gwạ), *n.* Same as *piragua.*

per-i-anth (per′i-anth), *n.* [NL. *perianthium,* < Gr. περί, around, + ἄνθος, flower.] In *bot.,* the envelop of a flower, whether calyx or corolla or both.

per-i-apt (per′i-apt), *n.* [F. *périapte,* < Gr. περίαπτον, < περί, around, + ἅπτειν, fasten.] Something worn around the neck or elsewhere on the person as a charm; an amulet: as, "It is a trafficking with the Evil One. Spells, *periapts,* and charms, are of his device" (Scott's "Guy Mannering," v.).

per-i-blast (per′i-blast), *n.* [Gr. περί, around, + βλαστός, sprout, germ.] In *biol.,* the protoplasm surrounding the nucleus of a cell or ovum; cytoplasm.

per-i-blem (per′i-blem), *n.* [G. *periblem,* < Gr. περίβλημα, a covering, < περί, around, + βάλλειν, throw.] In *bot.,* the portion of meristem lying outside of the plerome in the growing ends of stems and roots, giving rise to the cortex.

per-i-car-di-ac, per-i-car-di-al (per-i-kär′di-ak, -ạl), *a.* Of or pertaining to the pericardium.

per-i-car-di-tis (per″i-kär-dī′tis), *n.* [NL.] In *pathol.,* inflammation of the pericardium.

per-i-car-di-um (per-i-kär′di-um), *n.*; pl. *-dia* (-di-ạ). [NL., < Gr. περικάρδιον, < περί, around, + καρδία, heart.] In *anat.,* the membranous sac inclosing the heart.

per-i-carp (per′i-kärp), *n.* [NL. *pericarpium,* < Gr. περικάρπιον, < περί, around, + καρπός, fruit.] In *bot.,* the walls of a ripened ovary or fruit, sometimes consisting of three layers, the epicarp, mesocarp, and endocarp; a ripened ovary; a seed-vessel. —**per-i-car′pi-al** (-kär′-pi-ạl), *a.*

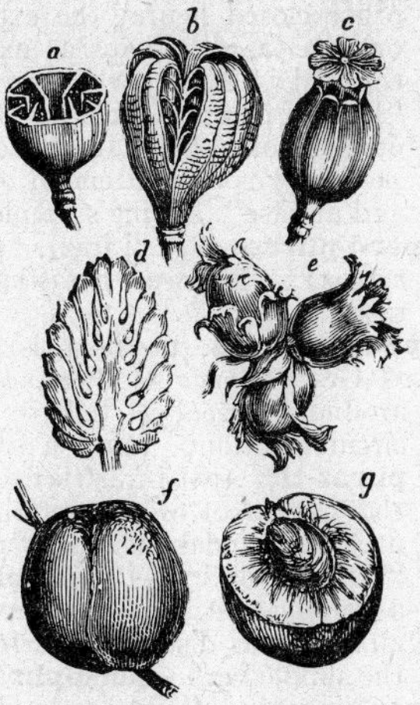

Pericarps. — *a* and *c*, capsules of poppy; *b*, capsule of birthwort; *d*, section of strobile (or cone) of pine; *e*, nuts of filbert; *f*, drupe of plum or peach; *g*, section of drupe.

per-i-chon-dri-um (per-i-kon′dri-um), *n.*; pl. *-dria* (-dri-ä̤). [NL., < Gr. περί, around, + χόνδρος, cartilage.] In *anat.*, the membrane of fibrous connective tissue covering the surface of cartilages except at the joints. —**per-i-chon′dri-al,** *a.*

Per-i-cle-an (per-i-klē′ạn), *a.* Of or pertaining to Pericles (about 490–429 B.C.) or his age, the period of the intellectual and material preëminence of Athens.

per-i-cline (per′i-klīn), *n.* [G. *periklin*, < Gr. περικλινής, sloping on all sides, < περί, around, + κλίνειν, incline.] A mineral, a variety of albite, occurring in large white opaque crystals.

per-i-cra-ni-um (per-i-krā′ni-um), *n.*; pl. *-nia* (-ni-ä̤). [NL., < Gr. περικράνιον, neut. of περικράνιος, around the skull, < περί, around, + κρανίον, skull.] In *anat.*, the external periosteum of the cranium; hence, in general, the skull; the brain (as, "various knotty points which had puzzled his *pericranium*": Peacock's "Headlong Hall," i.). —**per-i-cra′ni-al,** *a.*

per-i-cy-cle (per′i-sī-kl), *n.* [Gr. περί, around, + κύκλος, ring, circle.] In *bot.*, the mantle of parenchymatous cells surrounding the stele. —**per-i-cyc′lic** (-sik′lik), *a.*

per-i-derm (per′i-dėrm), *n.* [G. *peridermis*, < Gr. περί, around, + δέρμα, skin.] In *bot.*, the cork-producing tissue of stems together with the cork layers and other tissues derived from it. —**per-i-der′mal,** *a.*

pe-rid-i-um (pē-rid′i-um), *n.*; pl. *-ia* (-i-ä̤). [NL., < Gr. πηρίδιον, dim. of πήρα, leather pouch, wallet.] In *bot.*, the outer enveloping coat of the sporophore in many fungi. —**pe-rid′i-al,** *a.*

per-i-dot (per′i-dot), *n.* [F. *péridot*; origin unknown.] A green variety of chrysolite used as a gem. —**per′i-do-tite** (-dọ-tīt), *n.* Any of a group of igneous rocks of granitic structure, composed chiefly of olivine with an admixture of various other minerals, but nearly or wholly free from feldspar.

per-i-gee (per′i-jē), *n.* [NL. *perigeum*, < Gr. περίγειον, < περί, near, + γῆ, earth.] In *astron.*, the point in the orbit of a heavenly body, now usually of the moon, that is nearest to the earth: opposed to *apogee.* —**per-i-ge′al** (-jē′ạl), **per-i-ge′an,** *a.*

pe-rig-y-nous (pe-rij′i-nus), *a.* [Gr. περί, around, + γυνή, woman, female.] In *bot.*, situated around the pistil on the edge of a cup-like receptacle, as stamens, etc.; having stamens, etc., so arranged, as a flower. —**pe-rig′y-ny** (-ni), *n.*

per-i-he-li-on (per-i-hē′li-ọn), *n.*; pl. *-lia* (-li-ä̤). [NL., < Gr. περί, near, + ἥλιος, sun.] In *astron.*, the point of a planet's or comet's orbit nearest to the sun: opposed to *aphelion.*

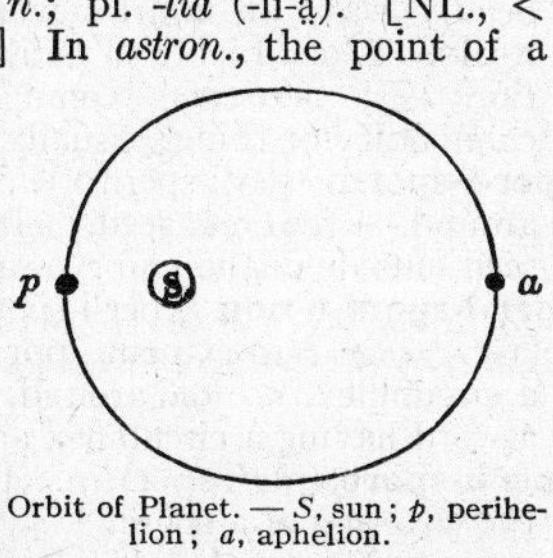

Orbit of Planet. — *S*, sun; *p*, perihelion; *a*, aphelion.

per-il (per′il), *n.* [OF. *peril* (F. *péril*), < L. *periculum*, trial, risk, danger, < *per-*, occurring also in *peritus*, experienced: see *experience* and *fare.*] Exposure to injury, loss, or destruction; risk; jeopardy; danger; also, a case of risk or danger (as, "to smile at scapes and *perils* overblown": Shakspere's "Taming of the Shrew," v. 2. 3); a source of risk or danger. —**per′il,** *v. t.*; *-iled* or *-illed*, *-iling* or *-illing.* To put in peril or danger; imperil: as, "Cæsar was *perilling* his own interest to remain in Asia to crush Pharnaces" (Froude's "Cæsar," xxiv.). —**per′il-ous,** *a.* [OF. *perillos* (F. *périlleux*), < L. *periculosus.*] Full of or attended with peril; hazardous; dangerous: as, "It is always *perilous* to adopt expediency as a guide" (Disraeli's "Coningsby," ii. 1). —**per′il-ous-ly,** *adv.* —**per′il-ous-ness,** *n.*

per-i-lymph (per′i-limf), *n.* [See *peri-* and *lymph.*] In *anat.*, the fluid contained within the osseous labyrinth of the internal ear and surrounding the membranous labyrinth.

pe-rim-e-ter (pe-rim′e-tėr), *n.* [L. *perimetros*, < Gr. περίμετρος, < περί, around, + μέτρον, measure.] The circumference, border, or outer boundary of a superficial figure; the measure of such a boundary; also, an instrument for determining the field of distinct vision. —**per-i-met-ric, per-i-met-ri-cal** (per-i-met′rik, -ri-kạl), *a.* —**per-i-met′ri-cal-ly,** *adv.*

per-i-morph (per′i-môrf), *n.* [Gr. περί, around, + μορφή, form.] A mineral inclosing another mineral: opposed to *endomorph.* —**per-i-mor′phic** (-môr′fik), *a.*

per-i-ne-al (per-i-nē′ạl), *a.* Of or pertaining to the perineum.

per-i-neph-ri-um (per-i-nef′ri-um), *n.* [NL., < Gr. περί, around, + νεφρός, kidney.] In *anat.*, the capsule of connective tissue which envelops the kidney.

per-i-ne-um, per-i-næ-um (per-i-nē′um), *n.*; pl. *-nea, -næa* (-nē′ä̤). [NL., < Gr. περίναιον, περίνεος.] In *anat.*, the (superficial) region between the anus and the genital organs; also, the region included by the outlet of the pelvis, containing the rectum, urethra, etc.

per-i-neu-ri-tis (per″i-nṳ̄-rī′tis), *n.* [NL.] In *pathol.*, inflammation of the perineurium.

per-i-neu-ri-um (per-i-nū′ri-um), *n.*; pl. *-ria* (-ri-ä̤). [NL., < Gr. περί, around, + νεῦρον, nerve.] In *anat.*, the sheath of connective tissue which incloses a funiculus, or bundle of nerve-fibers.

per-i-oc-u-lar (per-i-ok′ṳ̄-lär), *a.* [Gr. περί, around, + L. *oculus*, eye: cf. *periophthalmic.*] Situated about the eye or eyeball: as, the *periocular* space (the space between the eyeball and the orbit).

pe-ri-od (pē′ri-ọd), *n.* [OF. *periode* (F. *période*), < L. *periodus*, < Gr. περίοδος, a going around, circuit, cycle, period, < περί, around, + ὁδός, way.] A round of time marked by the recurrence of some phenomenon or occupied by some recurring process of action; the time in which a circuit or revolution, as of a heavenly body, is made; the time in which a planet or satellite revolves about its primary; a round of time or series of years by which time is measured; also, the time during which anything runs its course (as, "the short *period* of the life of man": Burke's "Conciliation with the Colonies"); also, an indefinite portion of time, or of history, life, etc., characterized by certain features or conditions; specif., one of the larger divisions of geological time, usually regarded as a subdivision of an era; in general, any specified division or portion of time; (with *the*) the time in question, esp. the present time (as, the young people of *the period*); also, the point of completion of a round of time or course of duration or action, or a conclusion or end (archaic: as, "The *period* of thy tyranny approacheth," Shakspere's "1 Henry VI.," iv. 2. 7; "when some well-contested and decisive victory had put a *period* to the war," Hawthorne's "Twice-Told Tales," Snow-Flakes); hence, the end to be attained†, or the goal† (as, "This is the *period* of my ambition": Shakspere's "Merry Wives of Windsor," iii. 3. 47); also, a complete sentence; esp., a rhetorically constructed sentence (as, "If sentiment were sacrific'd to sound, And truth cut short to make a *period* round": Cowper's "Table Talk," 517); *pl.*, rhetorical language (as, "This lady had composed a set of rules for the conduct of the children, in the most ornate and resounding *periods*": Mrs. Stowe's "Oldtown Folks," xxxiii.); also, *sing.*, a full pause such as is made at the end of a complete sentence; in *punctuation*, the point or character (.) used to mark the end of a complete declarative sentence, indicate an abbreviation, etc.; in *anc. pros.*, a group of two or more cola; in *music*, a division of a composition, usually a passage of eight or sixteen measures, which is complete and satisfactory in itself, commonly consisting of two or more contrasted or complementary phrases and involving a cadence at the end; in *physics*, the time of one complete oscillation or cycle of a periodic motion; the interval between a phase and its recurrence; the time required for an alternating current to pass through one cycle or double alternation.

per-i-o-date (pėr-ī'ǫ-dāt), *n.* In *chem.*, a salt of periodic acid.

per-i-od-ic[1] (pėr-ī-od'ik), *a.* [See *per-*.] In *chem.*, noting or pertaining to any of certain acids of iodine, next in series above iodic acid.

pe-ri-od-ic[2] (pē-ri-od'ik), *a.* [F. *périodique*, < L. *periodicus*, < Gr. περιοδικός, < περίοδος, E. *period.*] Of or pertaining to a period, as of the revolution of a heavenly body (as, the *periodic* time of a planet); characterized by a series of successive circuits or revolutions, as the motion of a planet or satellite; characterized by periods or rounds of recurrence, as the motion of a vibrating string; occurring or appearing at regular intervals, as events, etc.; loosely, recurring or reappearing from time to time; intermittent; also, pertaining to or characterized by rhetorical periods; of a sentence, having the sense incomplete or suspended until the end is reached.—**periodic law,** in *chem.*, the statement that the properties of the chemical elements are periodic functions of their atomic weights, that is, that the chemical and physical properties recur periodically when the elements are arranged in the order of their atomic weights.—**periodic system,** in *chem.*, a system of classification of the elements based on the periodic law.—**periodic table,** in *chem.*, a table illustrating the periodic system, in which the chemical elements, arranged in the order of their atomic weights, are shown in related groups.—**pe-ri-od'i-cal. I.** *a.* Periodic; esp., of magazines, etc., issued at regularly recurring intervals (of more than one day); of or pertaining to such publications. **II.** *n.* A periodical publication.—**pe-ri-od'i-cal-ism,** *n.* The work of writing for or conducting periodicals. Cf. *journalism.*—**pe-ri-od'i-cal-ist,** *n.*—**pe-ri-od'i-cal-ly,** *adv.*—**pe"ri-o-di'ci-ty** (-ǫ-dis'i-ti), *n.*; pl. *-ties* (-tiz). Periodic character; tendency to recur at regular intervals: as, "He would interest himself in the *periodicity* of the attacks, timing them by his watch" (Arnold Bennett's "Clayhanger," iii. 16).

per-i-o-dide (pėr-ī'ǫ-dīd or -did), *n.* [See *per-*.] In *chem.*, an iodide with the maximum proportion of iodine.

per-i-oph-thal-mic (per"i-of-thal'mik), *a.* [Gr. περί, around, + ὀφθαλμός, eye.] Situated about or surrounding the eye; periocular.

per-i-os-te-um (per-i-os'tẹ-um), *n.*; pl. *-tea* (-tẹ-ạ̈). [NL., < Gr. περιόστεος, around the bones, < περί, around, + ὀστέον, bone.] In *anat.*, the dense fibrous membrane covering the surface of bones except at their cartilaginous extremities.—**per-i-os'te-al,** *a.*—**per"i-os-ti'tis** (-tī'tis), *n.* [NL.] In *pathol.*, inflammation of the periosteum.—**per"i-os-tit'ic** (-tit'ik), *a.*

per-i-o-tic (per-i-ō'tik or -ot'ik), *a.* [Gr. περί, around, + οὖς (ὠτ-), ear.] In *anat.*, surrounding the ear; noting or pertaining to certain bones or bony elements which form or help to form a protective capsule for the internal ear, being usually confluent or fused, and in man constituting part of the temporal bone.

Per-i-pa-tet-ic (per"i-pạ-tet'ik). [L. *Peripateticus*, < Gr. περιπατητικός, walking about (with reference to the practice of Aristotle while teaching), < περιπατεῖν, walk about, < περί, about, + πατεῖν, tread, walk.] **I.** *a.* Of or pertaining to the philosophy or the followers of Aristotle, who taught while walking in the Lyceum of ancient Athens; hence [*l. c.*], walking about, perambulating, or itinerant (chiefly humorous). **II.** *n.* A member of the Aristotelian school of philosophers; [*l. c.*] one who walks or travels about (chiefly humorous: as, "The *peripatetic* who walked before her was a watchman in that neighbourhood," Steele, in "Spectator," 376).—**per"i-pa-tet'i-cal-ly,** *adv.*—**Per"i-pa-tet'i-cism** (-i-sizm), *n.* The Peripatetic system of philosophy; [*l. c.*] the practice of walking about (chiefly humorous).

pe-riph-er-al (pe-rif'ẹ-rạl), *a.* Pertaining to, situated in, or constituting the periphery, encompassing boundary, or external surface of something.—**peripheral nervous system.** See *nervous system.*—**pe-riph'er-al-ly,** *adv.*

pe-riph-er-y (pe-rif'ẹ-ri), *n.*; pl. *peripheries* (-riz). [LL. *peripheria*, < Gr. περιφέρεια, < περιφέρειν, carry around, < περί, around, + φέρειν, bear.] The circumference of a circle, or the line forming the boundary of any rounded or other closed figure; the external boundary of any surface or area (as, "Perhaps as many as thirty bonfires could be counted within the whole *periphery* of the district": Hardy's "Return of the Native," i. 3); also, the external surface, or outside, of a body (as, "Your round, sleek, fat, unwieldy *periphery* is ever attended by a mind . . . tranquil, torpid, and at ease": Irving's "Knickerbocker's New York," iii. 2).

per-i-phrase (per'i-frāz), *n.* Periphrasis.—**per'i-phrase,** *v. t.* or *i.*; *-phrased, -phrasing.* To express by or use periphrasis.

pe-riph-ra-sis (pe-rif'rạ-sis), *n.*; pl. *-rases* (-rạ-sēz). [L., < Gr. περίφρασις. < περιφράζειν, to periphrase, < περί, around, + φράζειν, tell.] A roundabout way of speaking; circumlocution; also, a roundabout expression.—**per-i-phras-tic** (per-i-fras'tik), *a.* [Gr. περιφραστικός.] Of the nature of or characterized by periphrasis; circumlocutory; roundabout: as, "*periphrastic* language" (Scott's "Woodstock," viii.).—**periphrastic conjugation,** in *gram.*, a conjugation formed by combining a simple verb and an auxiliary, as distinguished from one formed by inflection of the simple verb.—**per-i-phras'ti-cal-ly,** *adv.*

per-i-plus (per'i-plus), *n.* [L., < Gr. περίπλους, περίπλοος, < περί, around, + πλόος, voyage, < πλεῖν, sail.] A voyage around a body of land or water; also, an account of such a voyage.

pe-rip-ter-al (pe-rip'tẹ-rạl), *a.* [Gr. περίπτερος, < περί, about, + πτερόν, wing, row of columns.] In *arch.*, surrounded by a single row of columns, as a temple.

pe-rique (pẹ-rēk'), *n.* [Louisiana F.] A rich-flavored tobacco produced in Louisiana.

per-i-sarc (per'i-särk), *n.* [Gr. περί, around, + σάρξ (σαρκ-), flesh.] In *zoöl.*, the horny or chitinous outer case or covering with which the soft parts of hydrozoans are often protected.

per-i-scope (per'i-skōp), *n.* [Gr. περί, around, + σκοπεῖν, view.] An optical instrument consisting essentially of a tube with an arrangement of prisms or mirrors by which a view at the surface of water or land, the top of a parapet, etc., may be seen by observers below or behind.—**per-i-scop'ic** (-skop'ik), *a.* Giving distinct vision obliquely as well as in a direct line, as certain lenses.

per-ish (per'ish), *v.* [OF. *perir* (*periss-*) (F. *périr*), < L. *perire*, pass away, perish, < *per-*, utterly, + *ire*, go.] **I.** *intr.* To pass away, pass out of existence, or decay and disappear (as, "All things change—all things *perish*": De Quincey's "English Mail-Coach," i.); come to an end, or cease to be (as, fame and fortune *perish*; the art *perished* with them; *perish* the thought!); of material things, to suffer destruction (as, buildings *perish* in flames; whole cities *perish* in an earthquake); of living beings, to suffer death, or lose life, through violence, accident, exposure, privation, etc. (as, to *perish* in battle, by shipwreck, or from starvation; "I felt ready to *perish* with cold," C. Brontë's "Jane Eyre," vi.); fig., to suffer spiritual death or ruin (as, "Except ye repent, ye shall all likewise *perish*": Luke, xiii. 3). **II.** *tr.* To cause to perish, put an end to, destroy, or kill (archaic or prov.: as, "We charm man's life, and do not *perish* it," Hood's "Midsummer Fairies," lxviii.); also, to affect in a deadly way, or injure severely (chiefly prov.).—**per'ish-a-ble. I.** *a.* Liable to perish; subject to decay or destruction: as, *perishable* commodities. **II.** *n.* A perishable commodity or thing: usually in *pl.*—**per'ish-a-ble-ness,** *n.*

per-i-sperm (per'i-spėrm), *n.* [F. *périsperme*, < Gr. περί, around, + σπέρμα, seed.] In *bot.*, the nutritive tissue of a seed outside of the embryo-sac.

per-i-spom-e-non (per-i-spom'e-non), *n.*; pl. *-na* (-nạ̈). [Gr. περισπώμενον, neut. ppr. pass. of περισπᾶν, mark with a circumflex, < περί, around, + σπᾶν, draw.] In *Gr. gram.*, a word having a circumflex accent on the last syllable.

per-i-spore (per'i-spōr), *n.* [See *peri-* and *spore.*] In *bot.*, the covering of a spore.

pe-ris-sad (pe-ris'ad). [Gr. περισσός, odd, uneven.] In *chem.*: **I.** *n.* An atom or element whose valence is expressed by an odd number: opposed to *artiad.* **II.** *a.* Having the valence expressed by an odd number.

pe-ris-so-dac-tyl (pe-ris-ǫ-dak'til). [Gr. περισσός, odd, uneven, + δάκτυλος, finger or toe.] **I.** *a.* Having an uneven number of toes or digits on each foot; belonging to the *Perissodactyla*, a suborder of ungulate or hoofed mammals including the horse, tapir, and rhinoceros: opposed to *artiodactyl*. **II.** *n.* One of the *Perissodactyla*.—**pe-ris-so-dac′ty-lous** (-ti-lus), *a.*

per-i-stal-sis (per-i-stal′sis), *n.* [NL., < Gr. περιστέλλειν, wrap around (compress), < περί, around, + στέλλειν, set.] In *physiol.*, peristaltic movement.—**per-i-stal′tic,** *a.* [Gr. περισταλτικός, compressing, < περιστέλλειν.] In *physiol.*, noting or pertaining to the involuntary muscular movements of hollow organs by which their contents are propelled onward, as the wave-like circular contractions of the alimentary canal.—**per-i-stal′ti-cal-ly,** *adv.*

pe-ris-te-ron-ic (pe-ris-tę-ron′ik), *a.* [Gr. περιστερά, pigeon.] Of or pertaining to pigeons.

per-i-stome (per′i-stōm), *n.* [Gr. περί, around, + στόμα, mouth.] In *bot.*, the ring or fringe of small, pointed tooth-like appendages around the orifice of the capsule or theca in mosses; in *zoöl.*, any of various structures or sets of parts which surround, or form the walls, etc., of, a mouth or mouth-like opening.

per-i-style (per′i-stīl), *n.* [L. *peristylum*, < Gr. περίστυλον, neut. of περίστυλος, having columns all around, < περί, around, + στῦλος, pillar, column.] In *arch.*, a range or ranges of columns surrounding a building, court, or the like; also, a space or court so inclosed.

per-i-to-ne-um, per-i-to-næ-um (per″i-tǫ-nē′um), *n.*; pl. *-nea, -næa* (-nē′ą). [LL., < Gr. περιτόναιον, neut. of περιτόναιος, stretched over, < περί, around, + τείνειν, stretch.] In *anat.*, the serous membrane lining the abdominal cavity and investing its viscera.—**per″i-to-ne′al, per″i-to-næ′al,** *a.*

per-i-to-ni-tis (per″i-tǫ-nī′tis), *n.* [NL., < LL. *peritonæum*: see *peritoneum*.] In *pathol.*, inflammation of the peritoneum.—**per″i-to-nit′ic** (-nit′ik), *a.*

per-i-vis-ce-ral (per-i-vis′ę-rąl), *a.* [See *peri-*.] In *zoöl.*, surrounding and containing viscera: as, the *perivisceral* cavity (the general body-cavity in which are contained the alimentary canal and its appendages).

per-i-wig (per′i-wig), *n.* [By corruption < F. *perruque*, E. *peruke*.] A peruke or wig.—**per′i-wig,** *v. t.*; *-wigged, -wigging.* To dress or cover with or as with a periwig: as, "the *periwigged* . . . gentleman of the artist's legend" (Hawthorne's "House of the Seven Gables," xviii.).

per-i-win-kle[1] (per′i-wing-kl), *n.* [L. *pervinca*.] Any plant of the apocynaceous genus *Vinca*, as *V. minor* ('lesser periwinkle') or *V. major* ('greater periwinkle'), trailing evergreen plants native in Europe, with blue flowers, in *V. minor* varying to white, *V. minor* being familiar in cultivation in the U. S., where it is known also as *myrtle*.

per-i-win-kle[2] (per′i-wing-kl), *n.* [Origin obscure: cf. AS. *winewinclan*, or *pinewinclan*, pl., sea-snails, also E. *winkle*.] Any of various marine gastropods or sea-snails, esp. *Littorina littorea*, which is used for food in Europe.

per-jink (pėr-jingk′), *a.* [Origin uncertain.] Exact or precise; neat or trim: as, "All my things were kept by her in a most *perjink* and excellent order" (Galt's "Annals of the Parish," xxxvii.). [Sc.]

Periwinkle (*Littorina littorea*).

per-jure (pėr′jǫr), *v. t.*; *-jured, -juring.* [OF. F. *parjurer*, < L. *perjurare*, < *per*, through, + *jurare*, swear.] To render (one's self) guilty of swearing falsely, or of wilfully making a false statement under oath or solemn affirmation; forswear (one's self); show (one's self) false to an oath, vow, etc.; also, to prove false to (an oath, vow, etc., or a person)†; also, to render false to an oath or vow† (as, "Want will *perjure* The ne'er-touch'd vestal": Shakspere's "Antony and Cleopatra," iii. 12. 30).—**per′jured,** *p. a.* Having perjured one's self, or guilty of perjury (as, a *perjured* witness; a *perjured* villain); also, characterized by or involving perjury (as, *perjured* testimony; "Curse on his *perjur'd* arts, dissembling smooth!" Burns's "Cotter's Saturday Night," 86).—**per′jur-er,** *n.* One who commits perjury. —**per′ju-ry** (-jǫ-ri), *n.*; pl. *-ries* (-riz). [AF. *perjurie*, < L. *perjurium*.] The act of swearing falsely, as to a statement known to be untrue, or to a promise that one has no intention of keeping; also, wilful violation of an oath or vow, or an instance of it (as, "If thou swear'st, Thou mayst prove false; at lovers' *perjuries*, They say, Jove laughs": Shakspere's "Romeo and Juliet," ii. 2. 92); specif., in *law*, the wilful utterance of a false statement under oath or affirmation, before a competent tribunal, upon a point material to a legal inquiry.

perk (pėrk), *v.* [ME. *perken*; origin uncertain.] **I.** *intr.* To carry one's self, lift the head, or act in a jaunty or smart manner (also fig.: as, "The crocuses were *perking* behind the Park rails," L. Merrick's "Conrad in Quest of His Youth," i.); hence, to put one's self forward briskly or self-assertively; thrust one's self (*up*, etc.) presumptuously, or as an upstart; of things, to stick up or out with a smart appearance; also, to brighten up, or become lively or vigorous, as after depression or sickness (with *up*); also, to prink, as before the looking-glass (prov. Eng.: as, "You'd be *perking* at the glass the next minute," George Eliot's "Adam Bede," viii.). **II.** *tr.* To raise smartly or briskly (as, "The squirrel, flippant, pert . . . whisks his brush, And *perks* his ears," Cowper's "Task," vi. 318: often with *up*); thrust (out); also, to dress smartly, or deck (sometimes with *up* or *out*: as, " 'Tis better to be lowly born . . . Than to be *perk'd* up in a glistering grief, And wear a golden sorrow," Shakspere's "Henry VIII.," ii. 3. 21).—**perk,** *a.* Jaunty; smart; perky.—**perk′y,** *a.* Jaunty; smart; brisk; self-assertive; pert.—**perk′i-ly,** *adv.*—**perk′i-ness,** *n.*

per-lite (pėr′līt), *n.* [F. *perlite*, < *perle*, E. *pearl*.] In *petrog.*, a form of obsidian or other vitreous rock, usually appearing as a mass of enamel-like globules; in *metal.*, pearlite.—**per-lit′ic** (-lit′ik), *a.*

per-lus-trate (pėr-lus′trāt), *v. t.*; *-trated, -trating.* [L. *perlustratus*, pp. of *perlustrare*, < *per*, through, + *lustrare*, traverse, survey.] To travel through and view; survey or inspect thoroughly: as, "Mr. Asterias *perlustrated* the sea-coast for several days" (Peacock's "Nightmare Abbey," vii.). —**per-lus-tra′tion** (-trā′shǫn), *n.*

per-ma-nence (pėr′mą-nęns), *n.* The condition or quality of being permanent; continued existence; abidingness.—**per′ma-nen-cy** (-nęn-si), *n.*; pl. *-cies* (-siz). Permanence; also, a permanent person, thing, or position.

per-ma-nent (pėr′mą-nęnt), *a.* [L. *permanens* (*-ent-*), ppr. of *permanere*, remain throughout, < *per*, through, + *manere*, remain.] Lasting or intended to last indefinitely; enduring, or remaining unchanged, in character, condition, position, etc.; not temporary; abiding: as, *permanent* possession; a *permanent* structure or building; *permanent* colors; a *permanent* employee.—**permanent way,** the road-bed, track, etc., of a railroad, as distinguished from a temporary way used in construction, etc.—**per′ma-nent-ly,** *adv.*

per-man-ga-nate (pėr-mang′gą-nāt), *n.* In *chem.*, a salt of permanganic acid: as, potassium *permanganate* (a disinfectant).

per-man-gan-ic (pėr-mang-gan′ik), *a.* [See *per-*.] In *chem.*, noting or pertaining to an acid, $HMnO_4$, containing manganese.

per-me-a-bil-i-ty (pėr″mę-ą-bil′i-ti), *n.* The property or state of being permeable; in *physics*, specific permeance, the magnetic permeance of a material compared with that of air ('magnetic permeability').

per-me-a-ble (pėr′mę-ą-bl), *a.* [LL. *permeabilis*.] Capable of being permeated.—**per′me-a-bly,** *adv.*

per-me-ance (pėr′mę-ąns), *n.* The act of permeating; permeation; in *physics*, the conducting power of a magnetic circuit for magnetic flux, or the reciprocal of magnetic reluctance ('magnetic permeance').—**per′me-ant,** *a.* Permeating; passing through something; penetrating; pervading.

per-me-ate (pėr′mę-āt), *v.*; *-ated, -ating.* [L. *permeatus*, pp. of *permeare*, < *per*, through, + *meare*, go.] **I.** *tr.* To pass through the substance or mass of; penetrate through the pores, interstices, etc., of; be diffused through; pervade; saturate. **II.** *intr.* To penetrate; diffuse itself.—**per-me-a′tion** (-ā′shǫn), *n.*—**per′me-a-tive** (-ą-tiv), *a.* Tending to permeate.

Per-mi-an (pėr′mi-an). [From *Perm*, in eastern Russia.] **I.** *a.* Noting or pertaining to a geological period or a system of rocks which precedes the Triassic and succeeds the Carboniferous, and constitutes the latest principal division of the Paleozoic. **II.** *n.* The Permian period or system.

per-mis-si-ble (pėr-mis′i-bl), *a.* That may be permitted; allowable.—**per-mis-si-bil′i-ty** (-bil′i-ti), *n.*—**per-mis′si-bly,** *adv.*

per-mis-sion (pėr-mish′on), *n.* [= F. *permission*, < L. *permissio(n-)*.] The act of permitting; formal or express allowance or consent; liberty or license granted to do something; leave; specif., leave of absence, or furlough, as for a soldier (a French use).—**per-mis-sion-naire** (per-mē-syo-nãr), *n.* [F.] One who is on permission, or leave of absence, as a soldier.

per-mis-sive (pėr-mis′iv), *a.* Permitting or allowing; also, permitted or allowed; optional.—**per-mis′sive-ly,** *adv.*—**per-mis′sive-ness,** *n.*

per-mit (pėr-mit′), *v.*; *-mitted, -mitting.* [L. *permittere* (pp. *permissus*), let go through, let go, let, < *per*, through, + *mittere*, send.] **I.** *tr.* To let (something) be done or occur; allow (something), whether by giving express leave or by refraining from prohibiting or hindering (as, the law *permits* the sale of such drugs under special conditions; "It is not *permitted* unto them to speak," 1 Cor. xiv. 34; shall we *permit* such injustice?); suffer; tolerate; sometimes, to afford opportunity for, or admit of (as, vents *permitting* the escape of gases; conditions *permitting* no delay); also, to allow (a person, etc.) to do something; grant leave to (as, *permit* me to explain; "The law expressly *permitted* the inhabitants to seize . . . property . . . wrecked upon their coast," Lecky's "Hist. of Eng. in the 18th Century," iii.); leave at liberty to do something, as by refraining from prohibiting or hindering (as, "Ere we *permit* a foreign foe On British ground to rally": Burns's "Does Haughty Gaul"); sometimes, to afford opportunity to (as, the weather did not *permit* the boat to land; "Philip's deception *permitted* no man to be frank," Motley's "Dutch Republic," ii. 9); also, to commit† or leave† (*to*: as, "What thou livest Live well; how long or short *permit* to Heaven," Milton's "Paradise Lost," xi. 554). **II.** *intr.* To grant leave or permission; allow liberty to do something; afford opportunity or possibility (as, write when time *permits*; I will go on Monday, the weather *permitting*); allow or admit (*of*: as, a tool *permitting* of a variety of uses; statements that *permit* of no denial).—**per′mit,** *n.* A written order granting leave to do something; an authoritative or official certificate of permission; a license; also, permission or leave.—**per-mit-tee′** (-mi-tē′), *n.* One to whom a permit is granted.—**per-mit′ter,** *n.*

per-mu-ta-tion (pėr-mū-tā′shon), *n.* [L. *permutatio(n-)*, < *permutare*: see *permute*.] The act of permuting; alteration; in *math.*, the act of changing the order of a number of individuals arranged in a particular order (as *abc* into *acb, bac, bca, cab,* or *cba*), or of arranging a number of individuals in groups made up of equal numbers of the individuals taken in different orders (as *a, b,* and *c* into *ab, ba, ac, ca, bc,* and *cb*); also, any of the resulting arrangements or groups.

per-mute (pėr-mūt′), *v. t.*; *-muted, -muting.* [L. *permutare* (pp. *permutatus*), < *per*, through, + *mutare*, change.] To interchange†; also, to alter; in *math.*, to subject to permutation.—**per-mut′er** (-mū′tėr), *n.*

pern (pėrn), *n.* [NL. *Pernis.*] Any of the hawks of the old-world genus *Pernis*, of moderate size and chiefly insectivorous, as *P. apivorus*, the common European species. See cut in next column.

per-ni-cious[1] (pėr-nish′us), *a.* [L. *pernix* (*pernic-*), < *per*, through, + *niti*, strive.] Quick; swift: as, "Part incentive reed Provide, *pernicious* with one touch to fire" (Milton's "Paradise Lost," vi. 520). [Obs. or rare.]

per-ni-cious[2] (pėr-nish′us), *a.* [L. *perniciosus*, < *pernicies*, destruction, < *per*, through, + *necare*, kill: cf. *internecine*.] Destructive, deadly, or fatal (as, *pernicious* anemia); hence, ruinous, or highly mischievous or hurtful (as, "Such hasty inferences he reckoned still more *pernicious* to true knowledge": Hallam's "Literature of Europe," iii. 3. § 43); esp., highly injurious to character or moral well-being (as, *pernicious* teachings or influences); also, evil or wicked (obs. or archaic: as, "O most *pernicious* woman!" Shakspere's "Hamlet," i. 5. 105; "With his death, the kingdom fell even into more *pernicious* hands," Motley's "Dutch Republic," i. 3).—**per-ni′cious-ly,** *adv.*—**per-ni′cious-ness,** *n.*

Pern (*Pernis apivorus*).

per-nick-e-ty (pėr-nik′e-ti), *a.* [Origin obscure.] Precise about trifles; fastidious; fussy; also, full of petty details; requiring painstaking care; ticklish. [Colloq.]—**per-nick′e-ti-ness,** *n.*

per-o-ne (per′ō-nē), *n.* [NL., < Gr. περόνη, pin, brooch.] In *anat.*, the fibula.—**per-o-ne′al,** *a.*

per-o-rate (per′ō-rāt), *v. i.*; *-rated, -rating.* [L. *peroratus*, pp. of *perorare*, < *per*, through, + *orare*, speak.] To speak at length; make a speech; also, to bring a speech to a close with a formal conclusion.—**per-o-ra′tion** (-rā′shon), *n.* [L. *peroratio(n-)*.] The concluding part of a speech or discourse, in which the speaker or writer recapitulates the principal points he has presented and urges them with greater earnestness and force, with a view to making a deep impression; hence, any rhetorical conclusion; a rhetorical outburst (as, "a fiery *peroration*": Bret Harte's "Romance of Madroño Hollow"); a discourse.—**per-o-ra′tion-al,** *a.*

per-ox-ide (pėr-ok′sīd or -sid), *n.* [See *per-*.] In *chem.*, that oxide of a given element or radical which contains the greatest, or an unusual, amount of oxygen (as, hydrogen *peroxide*, hydrogen dioxide); specif., hydrogen dioxide or peroxide (see under *hydrogen*).

per-pend[1] (pėr-pend′), *v.* [L. *perpendere*, < *per*, through, + *pendere*, weigh.] **I.** *tr.* To weigh mentally; consider: as, "*Perpend* my words" (Shakspere's "Henry V.," iv. 4. 8). [Archaic.] **II.** *intr.* To ponder; deliberate: as, "Henry *perpended* legally on the form of agreement" (Arnold Bennett's "Great Man," xi.). [Archaic.]

per-pend[2] (pėr′pend), *n.* [OF. *perpain, parpain* (F. *parpaing*); origin uncertain.] In *masonry*, a large stone passing through the entire thickness of a wall so as to show on both sides, and forming a bonder.

per-pen-dic-u-lar (pėr-pen-dik′ū-lär). [L. *perpendicularis*, < *perpendiculum*, plumb-line, < *per*, through, + *pendere*, hang.] **I.** *a.* Being at right angles with the plane of the horizon; vertical; upright; in *geom.*, meeting a given line or surface at right angles; in *arch.*, noting or pertaining to a style of architecture, the last stage of English Gothic, in which a large proportion of the chief lines of the tracery intersect at right angles (see cut on following page). **II.** *n.* A perpendicular line or plane; hence, upright position (as, "springing to her accustomed *perpendicular* like a bowed sapling": Hardy's "Far from the Madding Crowd," iii.); fig., rectitude; also, an instrument for indicating the vertical line from any point; in *geom.*, a straight line meeting a given line or surface at right angles.—**per-pen-dic-u-lar′i-ty** (-lar′i-ti), *n.*—**per-pen-dic′u-lar-ly,** *adv.*

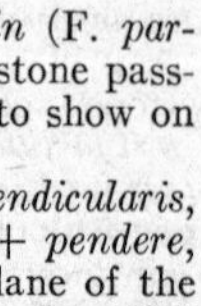

AB is perpendicular to *CD*.

per-pent (pėr′pent), *n.* Same as *perpend*[2].

per-pe-trate (pėr′pē-trāt), *v. t.*; *-trated, -trating.* [L. *perpetratus*, pp. of *perpetrare*, < *per*, through, + *patrare*, bring to pass.] To perform, execute, or commit (something bad: as, to *perpetrate* a crime, fraud, or folly; "I can only be dishonoured by *perpetrating* an unjust action," Godwin's

"Caleb Williams," xii.); often, humorously, to perform, do, or make (something implied to be bad or atrocious: as, "Sir Philip induced two of his sisters to *perpetrate* a duet," C. Brontë's "Shirley," xxxi.; to *perpetrate* a pun or a joke).—**per-pe-tra′tion** (-trā′shọn), *n.* [LL. *perpetratio(n-)*.] The act of perpetrating; also, that which is perpetrated; an evil action; an atrocity.—**per′pe-tra-tor,** *n.*

Perpendicular Style of Architecture. — The Abbey Church, Bath, England.

per-pet-u-a-ble (pėr-pet̤′ṳ̄-a̤-bl), *a.* That may be perpetuated.

per-pet-u-al (pėr-pet̤′ṳ̄-a̤l). [OF. *perpetuel* (F. *perpétuel*), < L. *perpetualis*, < *perpetuus*, continuing throughout, appar. < *per*, through, + *petere*, seek.] **I.** *a.* Continuing or enduring forever or indefinitely (as, "the Sierra Nevada crowned with *perpetual* snows," Irving's "Conquest of Granada," i.; *perpetual* youth; a *perpetual* covenant); eternal; permanent; also, continuing or continued without intermission or interruption (as, a *perpetual* struggle; a *perpetual* stream of visitors); uninterrupted; continuous; in *hort.*, blooming more or less continuously throughout the season or the year; also, perennial. **II.** *n.* In *hort.*, a plant that blooms more or less continuously throughout the season or the year; also, a perennial.—**per-pet′u-al-ly,** *adv.*—**per-pet′u-al-ness,** *n.*

per-pet-u-ance (pėr-pet̤′ṳ̄-a̤ns), *n.* Perpetuation.

per-pet-u-ate (pėr-pet̤′ṳ̄-āt), *v. t.*; *-ated, -ating.* [L. *perpetuatus*, pp. of *perpetuare*, < *perpetuus*: see *perpetual*.] To make perpetual; cause to continue or endure indefinitely: as, monuments for *perpetuating* the memory of the dead; to *perpetuate* an error by frequent repetition.—**per-pet-u-a′tion** (-ā′shọn), *n.* [ML. *perpetuatio(n-)*.] The act of perpetuating, or the state of being perpetuated.—**per-pet′u-a-tor,** *n.*

per-pe-tu-i-ty (pėr-pē̤-tū′i-ti), *n.*; pl. *-ties* (-tiz). [OF. *perpetuite* (F. *perpétuité*), < L. *perpetuitas*, < *perpetuus*: see *perpetual*.] The state or character of being perpetual (as, "A third attribute of the king's majesty is his *perpetuity* . . . The king never dies": Blackstone's "Commentaries," I. 249); endless or indefinitely long duration or existence; also, something that is perpetual; a perpetual annuity (as, "He settled a *perpetuity* of fourscore pounds on his parents, to be inherited by the other two sons after their decease": Smollett's "Humphry Clinker," Sept. 12); in *law*, of property, the condition of being inalienable perpetually, or for a period beyond certain limits fixed, or conceived as being fixed, by the general law; an estate, etc., in this condition.

per-plex (pėr-pleks′), *v. t.* [L. *perplexus*, entangled, confused, < *per*, through, + *plexus*, pp. of *plectere*, plait, interweave.] To bring into a tangled or confusingly involved condition (as, "The undergrowth Of shrubs and tangling bushes had *perplex'd* All path of man or beast": Milton's "Paradise Lost," iv. 176); fig., to render complicated or confused, as a matter, question, etc.; hamper with complications, confusion, or uncertainty (as, "difficulties that must have *perplexed* the engagement, and retarded the marriage," Jane Austen's "Sense and Sensibility," xxxv.; "Characteristic indecision *perplexed* their councils," Parkman's "Oregon Trail," xi.); also, to confuse mentally, bewilder, or puzzle over what is not understood or certain (as, "It is not worth while to *perplex* the reader with inquiries into the abstract nature of evidence": J. Butler's "Analogy of Religion," ii. 2); render at a loss what to think or do; trouble with uncertainty or doubt (as, "We are *perplexed*, but not in despair": 2 Cor. iv. 8).—**per-plexed′,** *p. a.* Tangled, involved, or confused (as, "He had engaged Dominie Sampson's assistance to disentangle some *perplexed* accounts": Scott's "Guy Mannering," xv.); also, bewildered or puzzled; at a loss what to think or do.—**per-plex′ed-ly** (-plek′sed-li), *adv.*—**per-plex′ing,** *p. a.* That perplexes; confusing; puzzling: as, "people to whom modern life was increasingly *perplexing*" (W. Churchill's "Inside of the Cup," iv.).—**per-plex′ing-ly,** *adv.*

per-plex-i-ty (pėr-plek′si-ti), *n.*; pl. *-ties* (-tiz). [LL. *perplexitas*, < L. *perplexus*: see *perplex*.] Tangled, involved, or confused condition; a tangle or complication (as, "the deity in the play, whose entrance was almost sufficient to bring its *perplexities* to a conclusion": Scott's "Castle Dangerous," xvi.); also, perplexed or puzzled condition, or uncertainty as to what to think or do (as, "The poor men were now in great *perplexity* whether they should stand . . . or fly": Defoe's "Robinson Crusoe," ii. 4); a feeling of perplexing uncertainty (as, "My mind is disturbed with a thousand *perplexities* of doubt": Johnson's "Rasselas," xxi.); also, something that perplexes; a perplexing matter or circumstance.

per-qui-site (pėr′kwi-zit), *n.* [ML. *perquisitum*, prop. neut. of L. *perquisitus*, pp. of *perquirere*, seek diligently for, < *per*, through, + *quærere*, seek.] An incidental emolument, fee, or profit over and above fixed income, salary, or wages (as, "the clerk's *perquisites* of office": Marryat's "King's Own," xl.); anything customarily supposed to be allowed or left to an employee or servant as an incidental advantage of the position held (as, "The wardrobe of her niece was the *perquisite* of her woman": Smollett's "Humphry Clinker," Oct. 26); fig., something advantageous specially belonging (as, "Saturday afternoon . . . was considered . . . as the children's *perquisite*": Mrs. Stowe's "Oldtown Folks," xxvi.).

per-qui-si-tion (pėr-kwi-zish′ọn), *n.* [ML. *perquisitio(n-)*, < L. *perquirere*: see *perquisite*.] A diligent or thorough search or inquiry.

per-ron (per′ọn, F. pe-rôṅ), *n.* [F., < L. *petra*, rock, stone.] In *arch.*, an outside platform upon which the entrance-door of a building opens, with a flight or flights of steps leading to it; also, the arrangement of steps or stairs leading to an entrance-door of a building or to a terrace or the like.

Perron. — Cour du Cheval Blanc, Palace of Fontainebleau, France.

per-ro-quet (per′ọ-ket), *n.* Same as *parrakeet*.

per-ry (per′i), *n.* [OF. *pere* (F. *poiré*), < ML. *pira*, E. *pear*.] A fermented beverage, similar to cider, made from the juice of pears.

per-salt (pėr′sâlt), *n.* [See *per-*.] In *chem.*, in a series of salts of a given metal or radical, that salt in which the metal or radical presents a high, or the highest, degree of apparent valence.

perse (pėrs), *a.* [OF. F. *pers*, < ML. *persus*; origin uncertain.] Of a dark or purplish blue color. [Archaic.]

per-se-cute (pėr′sē̤-kūt), *v. t.*; *-cuted, -cuting.* [OF. *persecuter* (F. *persécuter*), < L. *persequi* (pp. *persecutus*), pursue, < *per*, through, + *sequi*, follow.] To pursue†, chase†, or hunt†; hence, to pursue with harassing or oppressive treatment, or harass persistently; esp., to oppress with injury or punishment for adherence to principles or religious faith (as, "Blessed are they which are *persecuted* for righteousness' sake": Mat. v. 10); in general, to harass or torment (as, "We sat in the shade . . . *persecuted* by small stinging flies": W. H. Hudson's "Green Mansions," xv.); annoy by persistent attentions, importunities, or the like.

—**per-se-cu′tion** (-kū′shọn), *n.* [OF. *persecution* (F. *persécution*), < L. *persecutio(n-)*, < *persequi.*] The act of persecuting, or the state of being persecuted.—**per-se-cu′tion-al, per′se-cu-to-ry** (-kụ-tọ-ri), *a.*—**per′se-cu-tor** (-kū-tọr), *n.*

Per-se-id (pėr′sẹ̄-id), *n.* In *astron.*, any of a shower of meteors appearing in August, and radiating from a point in the constellation Perseus.

Per-seus (pėr′sūs), *n.* [L., < Gr. Περσεύς.] In *Gr. myth.*, a hero, the son of Zeus and Danaë, who slew the Gorgon Medusa (see *Gorgon*), and afterward saved Andromeda from a sea-monster; also, in *astron.*, one of the northern constellations.

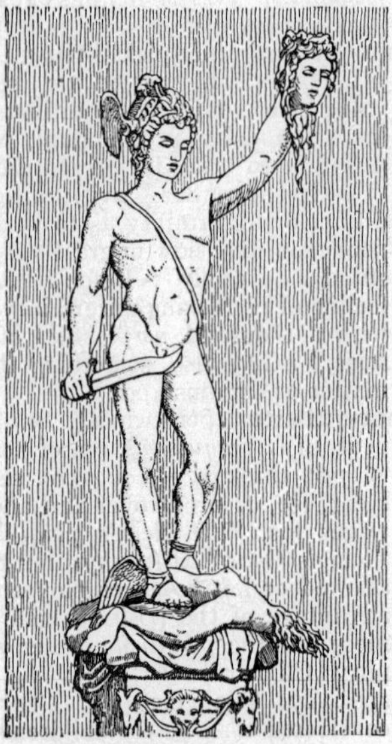

Perseus of Benvenuto Cellini, in the Loggia dei Lanzi, Florence.

per-se-ver-ance (pėr-sẹ̄-vēr′ạns), *n.* [OF. *perseverance* (F. *persévérance*), < L. *perseverantia.*] The act or quality of persevering; steady persistence in a course of action, a purpose, a state, etc. (as, "Great works are performed, not by strength, but *perseverance*," Johnson's "Rasselas," xiii.; "an obstinate *perseverance* in error," Burke's "Conciliation with the Colonies"); in *theol.*, continuance in a state of grace to the end, leading to eternal salvation (sometimes called *final perseverance*).—**perseverance of the saints,** in Calvinistic theology, the doctrine that "they whom God hath accepted in his Beloved, effectually called and sanctified by his Spirit, can neither totally nor finally fall away from the state of grace, but shall certainly persevere therein to the end, and be eternally saved" (Westminster Confession of Faith, xvii. § 1).

per-se-vere (pėr-sẹ̄-vēr′), *v. i.*; *-vered, -vering.* [OF. *perseverer* (F. *persévérer*), < L. *perseverare*, continue steadfastly, < *per*, through, + *severus*, serious, severe: cf. *asseverate.*] To persist in anything undertaken; maintain a purpose in spite of difficulty or obstacles; continue steadfastly.—**per-se-ver′ing-ly** (-vēr′ing-li), *adv.*

Per-sian (pėr′shạn or -zhạn), *a.* Of or pertaining to Persia, its people, or their language.—**Persian blinds.** Same as *persiennes.*—**Persian carpet,** a one-piece carpet made by twisting around the warp (of linen or hemp) tufts of colored wool, over each row of which a shoot of the weft is made. —**Persian cat.** Same as *Angora cat.*—**Persian lamb,** the lamb which furnishes caracul; also, its skin, caracul.—**Persian wheel,** a water-lifting wheel, as one with buckets at the rim, or one with radial or curved partitions for dipping the water near the rim and discharging it near the axle; a noria.—**Per′sian,** *n.* A member of the native race of Persia, now a mixed race descended in part from the ancient Iranians; also, the language spoken in Persia, in its oldest form (Old Persian) the principal member of the Iranian branch of the Aryan or Indo-European family (cf. *Avestan, Zend, Achæmenian*, and *Pahlavi*), but in its modern form containing a large admixture of Arabic, and employing the Arabic alphabet with certain additional characters; also, a thin silk fabric, formerly used for linings; also (usually in *pl.*), persiennes.

per-si-ennes (pėr-si-enz′, F. per-syen), *n. pl.* [F., 'Persian (blinds).'] Outside window-shutters made of thin, movable slats set horizontally in a frame.

per-si-flage (pėr′si-fläzh, F. per-sē-fläzh), *n.* [F., < *persifler*, banter lightly, < L. *per*, through, + *sifilare, sibilare*, hiss.] Light banter; idle, bantering talk; a frivolous style of treating a subject.

per-sim-mon (pėr-sim′ọn), *n.* [N. Amer. Ind. (Virginia).] Any of various trees of the genus *Diospyros*, esp. *D. virginiana* of North America, which has hard fine wood, small white flowers, and a plum-like fruit very astringent when green but sweet and edible when thoroughly ripe; also, the fruit.

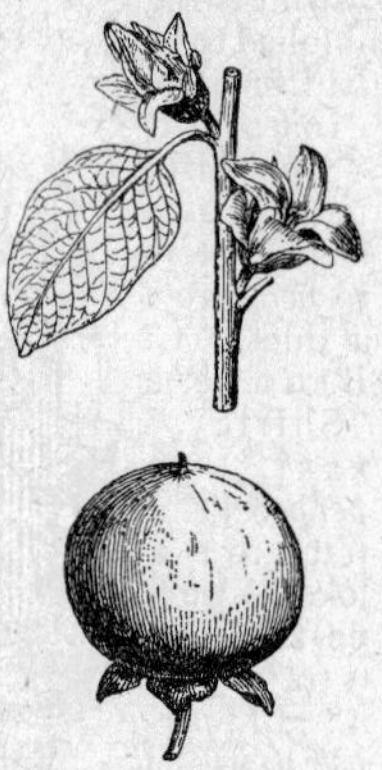

Flower and Fruit of Persimmon (*Diospyros virginiana*).

per-sist (pėr-sist′), *v.* [L. *persistere*, < *per*, through, + *sistere*, stand.] **I.** *intr.* To continue steadily or firmly in some state, purpose, course of action, or the like, esp. in spite of opposition, remonstrance, etc.; persevere, esp. with some degree of obstinacy; often, to be insistent in a statement or question; also, to last or endure (as, "Charnock had been kind, and a friendship had arisen and *persisted*": M. Hewlett's "Open Country," ii.). **II.** *tr.* To persist in saying; maintain insistently: as, "Gracchus *persisted* that the *ager publicus* belonged to the people" (Froude's "Cæsar," iii.).—**per-sist′ence,** *n.* The action or fact of persisting; the quality of being persistent; also, continued existence; continuous occurrence; specif., the continuance of an effect after the cause which first gave rise to it is removed. Also **per-sist′en-cy.**—**per-sist′ent,** *a.* Persisting, esp. in spite of opposition, etc.; persevering; also, lasting or enduring; also, continued; constantly repeated; in *biol.*, continuing or permanent.—**per-sist′ent-ly,** *adv.*

per-son (pėr′sọn or -sn), *n.* [OF. *persone* (F. *personne*), < L. *persona*, actor's mask, character acted, personage, person, ML. parson: cf. *parson.*] A character, part, or rôle sustained on the stage or in real life (as, "I must take upon me the *person* of a philosopher, and make them a present of my advice": Steele, in "Guardian," 141); hence, one of the characters in a play, story, etc. (as, the *persons* of the drama); also, a human being, whether man, woman, or child (as, four *persons* saw this; any *person* who wishes may come); sometimes, a human being as distinguished from an animal or a thing; also, esp. formerly, one of distinction or importance; a personage; also, one not entitled to social recognition, or one regarded as not entitled to a more respectful designation; specif., in philosophical use, a self-conscious or rational being; also, the actual self or individual personality of a human being (as, to assume a duty in one's own *person*); also, the living body of a human being (as, "The *persons* of Saturninus and Glaucia were doubly sacred, for one was tribune and the other prætor": Froude's "Cæsar," v.); often, the body in its external aspect (as, "the loveliest young woman for face and *person* that . . . I have beheld": De Quincey's "English Mail-Coach," i.); in *law*, an individual human being ('natural person') or a body corporate ('artificial person') having rights and duties before the law; in *theol.*, any of the three hypostases or modes of being in the Trinity (Father, Son, and Holy Ghost); in *gram.*, the property or form of pronouns indicating whether they refer to, or of verbs indicating whether their subject is, the speaker ('first person'), one spoken to ('second person'), or a person or thing spoken of ('third person'); a form of a pronoun or verb giving such indication.—**in person,** in one's own individual character, or with one's own bodily presence: as, to act *in person*; to apply *in person.*—**in the person of,** in the character of, or as representing (as, "which could not have been done, had I always written *in the person of* the Spectator": Addison, in "Spectator," 542); also, being, as to the person (as, "A new visitor arrived at the abbey, *in the person of* Mr. Asterias": Peacock's "Nightmare Abbey," vii.).

per-son-a-ble (pėr′sọn-ạ-bl), *a.* Having a well-formed person or body; of pleasing personal appearance; comely; presentable: as, "Miss Ingamells . . . a *personable* if somewhat heavy creature of twenty-eight" (Arnold Bennett's "Clayhanger," i. 8).—**per′son-a-ble-ness,** *n.*

per-son-age (pėr′sọn-āj), *n.* [OF. F. *personnage.*] A person or character in a play, story, etc.; also, a person, or man, woman, or child (as, "a stout, thickset *personage* in grey coat and red waistcoat," Marryat's "Mr. Midshipman

Easy," vi.; "a grandfatherly sort of *personage*," Hawthorne's "Scarlet Letter," viii.); often, a person of distinction or importance (as, "Who am I indeed? Perhaps a *personage* in disguise": C. Brontë's "Villette," xxvii.).

per-son-al (pėr′sọn-ąl), *a.* [OF. *personal* (F. *personnel*), < L. *personalis.*] Of or pertaining to a particular person (as, *personal* experiences or interests; a *personal* matter); individual; private; also, having an individual person as object; relating to, or directed to or aimed at, a particular person (as, a *personal* item or paragraph; a *personal* favor); often, referring or directed to a particular person in a disparaging or offensive sense or manner (as, *personal* remarks; *personal* abuse); hence, making personal remarks or attacks (as, to become *personal* in a dispute); also, done, effected, held, etc., in person; involving the actual action or presence of the person himself, as opposed to that of a deputy or representative (as, *personal* service; *personal* application); carried on or existing between persons directly (as, *personal* conference; *personal* relations); also, present in person† (as, "when he was *personal* in the Irish war": Shakspere's "1 Henry IV.," iv. 3. 88); also, pertaining to the person, body, or bodily aspect (as, *personal* cleanliness; *personal* ornaments; *personal* charms); also, pertaining to or characteristic of a person or self-conscious being (as, grief is a *personal* quality); of the nature of an individual rational being (as, a *personal* God); in *law*, noting or pertaining to estate or property consisting in general of things temporary and movable (opposed to *real*); in *gram.*, denoting person, or expressing the distinction as to the three persons (as, a *personal* pronoun).—**personal equation,** an allowance to be made, as in astronomical observations, to offset inaccuracy habitual to a particular observer; hence, personal tendency to deviation or error, for which allowance must be made.—**per′son-al,** *n.* A short paragraph in a newspaper, referring or addressed to a particular person or particular persons. —**per-son-a′li-a** (-ā′li-ạ), *n. pl.* [L., neut. pl. of *personalis.*] Personal items, anecdotes, etc.: as, "The . . . wife . . . talked . . . about people in the neighbourhood . . . My aunt received these *personalia* cheerfully" (H. G. Wells's "Tono-Bungay," iii. 2. § 6).—**per-son-al′i-ty** (-al′i-ti), *n.*; pl. *-ties* (-tiz). The quality of being personal, or of being a person; the essential character of a person as distinguished from a thing; existence as a self-conscious being; also, personal identity (as, one whose *personality* has not been determined); also, the qualities of a person, considered collectively; distinctive personal character (as, "I was lost in wonder and admiration at the change in her, and at her double *personality*": W. H. Hudson's "Green Mansions," vii.); often, marked or notable personal character (as, a man with *personality*); also, a person as an embodiment of an assemblage of qualities (as, "By its remoteness, it [a procession] melts all the petty *personalities*, of which it is made up, into one broad mass of existence": Hawthorne's "House of the Seven Gables," xi.); a personal being; also, application or reference to a particular person or particular persons; direct reference to a particular person, often in the way of disparagement or hostility (as, there was a degree of *personality* in his remarks); also, a remark or statement referring to or aimed at a particular person, often in a disparaging or offensive way (as, "He had . . . spoken of Dissenters as sneaks—a *personality* which could not be overlooked," George Eliot's "Felix Holt," xxiv.; to indulge in *personalities*); in *law*, personal estate or property; personalty.—**per′son-al-ize** (-ąl-īz), *v. t.*; *-ized, -izing.* To make personal; personify.—**per″son-al-i-za′tion** (-i-zā′-shọn), *n.*—**per′son-al-ly,** *adv.*—**per′son-al-ty** (-ti), *n.*; pl. *-ties* (-tiz). In *law*, personal estate or property.

per-son-ate (pėr′sọn-āt), *a.* [L. *personatus*, masked, < *persona*: see *person.*] Personated†, pretended†, or counterfeit†; in *bot.*, of a bilabiate corolla, mask-like; having the lower lip pushed upward so as to close the hiatus between the lips, as in the snapdragon; in *zoöl.*, having a masked or disguised form; larval, or not imaginal; also, having mask-like markings on the head.—**per′son-ate,** *v.*; *-ated, -ating.* **I.** *tr.* To act or play the part of (a character in a play, etc.); act or present (a play, etc.); also, to assume the character or appearance of; pass one's self off as (as, "To *personate* any other person (as bail) before any . . . commissioner authorized to take bail . . . is . . . felony": Blackstone's "Commentaries," IV. 128); also, to feign† or counterfeit† (as, "Did he *personate* remorse?" Godwin's "Caleb Williams," xxix.); also, to be a representative, an emblem, or an embodiment of (now rare); also, to represent or describe, as in writing†. **II.** *intr.* To act or play a part: as, "An actor . . . really *personates*, which your mere man of the stage never does" (Reade's "Peg Woffington," i.).—**per-son-a′tion** (-ā′shọn), *n.* The act of personating; dramatic representation, as of a character; the assuming of the character of another, as for the purpose of fraud; sometimes, the representation or embodiment of a quality, etc., as in a person; also, a person embodying a quality, etc. (as, "Mr. Pickwick was the very *personation* of kindness and humanity": Dickens's "Pickwick Papers," v.).—**per′son-a-tor,** *n.*

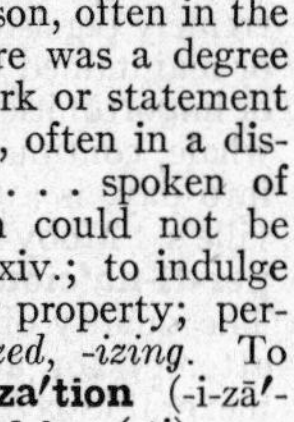

Personate Corolla of Snapdragon (*Antirrhinum majus*).

per-son-i-fi-ca-tion (pėr-son″i-fi-kā′shọn), *n.* The act of personifying; the attribution of personal nature or character to inanimate objects or abstract notions, esp. as a rhetorical figure; the representation of a thing or abstraction in the form of a person, as in art; hence, an imaginary person or creature conceived or figured to represent a thing or abstraction; also, the embodiment of a quality, idea, or other abstraction in a real person or a concrete thing; hence, the person or thing embodying a quality or the like; an embodiment; also, the representation of a character, as in a play.

Personification. — The "Church of Christ," from the west front of the Cathedral of Notre Dame, Paris (13th century sculpture).

per-son-i-fy (pėr-son′i-fī), *v. t.*; *-fied, -fying.* [= F. *personnifier*: see *person* and *-fy.*] To regard or represent as a person; attribute personal nature or character to (an inanimate object or an abstraction), as in speech or writing; represent (a thing or abstraction) in the form of a person, as in art; also, to embody (a quality, idea, etc.) in a real person or a concrete thing (as, "Mr. Bertram never embraced a general or abstract idea, and his notion of the revenue was *personified* in the commissioners, surveyors, comptrollers": Scott's "Guy Mannering," v.); be an embodiment of, or typify (as, he *personifies* all that is noble); also, to personate (a character or a person).—**per-son′i-fi-er** (-fī-ėr), *n.*

per-son-nel (pėr-sọ-nel′, F. per-so-nel), *n.* [F., orig. adj., lit. 'personal.'] The body of persons employed in any work, undertaking, or service: distinguished from *matériel*.

per-spec-tive (pėr-spek′tiv). [LL. *perspectivus*, adj. (as n., ML. *perspectiva*, 'perspective art,' optics), < L. *perspicere*, look through, look into, view, perceive, < *per*, through, + *specere*, look at.] **I.** *a.* Optical (obs. or rare: as, a *perspective* glass, a spy-glass or the like); also, of or pertaining to the art of perspective, or represented according to its laws. **II.** *n.* Optics†; also, an optical glass, as a spy-glass or telescope† (as, "a pair of spectacles . . . a pocket *perspective*, and several other little conveniences": Swift's "Gulliver's Travels," i. 2); also, the art of representing solid objects on a flat surface so as to give them the same appearance as in nature when viewed from a given point; commonly, linear perspective (see below); hence, the appearance of objects with reference to relative position, distance, etc.; fig., the relation of parts to one another and to the whole, in a mental view or prospect; also, a drawing or picture in perspective; specif., a painting or picture giving the effect of extension of the view or of distance; also, a visible scene, esp. one extending to a distance, or a vista (as, "The vastness of the thronged *perspectives* made promises to her romantic sense. The town seemed to be endless": Arnold Bennett's "Hilda Lessways," iii. 3); fig., a mental view or prospect (as, "Sleeping or waking, I beheld the same black *perspective* of approaching ruin": Stevenson's "Master of Ballantrae," ix.). —**aërial perspective,** that branch of perspective which considers the variations of light, shade, and color in objects delineated, according to their distances, the quantity of light falling on them, and the medium through which they are seen.—**linear perspective,** that branch of perspective which regards only the apparent positions, magnitudes, and forms of objects delineated.—**per-spec'tive-ly,** *adv.*—**per-spec'to-graph** (-tō-grȧf), *n.* [See *-graph.*] An instrument used in drawing objects in perspective.

per-spi-ca-cious (pėr-spi-kā'shus), *a.* [L. *perspicax* (*perspicac-*), < *perspicere*: see *perspective.*] Having keen sight (archaic); also, having keen mental perception, or discerning (as, "that acute and *perspicacious* lady": Galt's "Ayrshire Legatees," x.).—**per-spi-ca'cious-ly,** *adv.*—**per-spi-ca'ci-ty** (-kas'i-ti), *n.* The quality of being perspicacious; keenness of sight (archaic); keenness of mental perception; discernment; penetration.

per-spi-cu-i-ty (pėr-spi-kū'i-ti), *n.* The quality of being perspicuous; clearness, as of statement; lucidity; erroneously, perspicacity or discernment.

per-spic-u-ous (pėr-spik'ū-us), *a.* [L. *perspicuus,* < *perspicere*: see *perspective.*] Transparent, as crystal†; also, clear to the understanding; esp., clear in expression or statement, or lucid (as, "His manner of telling a story, or explaining his thoughts, was forcible, *perspicuous,* and original": Godwin's "Caleb Williams," xix.); also, erroneously, perspicacious or discerning (as, "It then became further obvious to the *perspicuous* Helen that Mrs. Prockter must have heard of her stepson's singular adventure": Arnold Bennett's "Helen with the High Hand," xxvii.).—**per-spic'u-ous-ly,** *adv.*—**per-spic'u-ous-ness,** *n.*

per-spir-a-ble (pėr-spīr'ạ-bl), *a.* Capable of perspiring or of being perspired.

per-spi-ra-tion (pėr-spi-rā'shọn), *n.* [F. *perspiration.*] The act or process of perspiring; also, that which is perspired; sweat.—**per-spir'a-to-ry** (-spīr'ạ-tō-ri), *a.*

per-spire (pėr-spīr'), *v.*; *-spired, -spiring.* [F. *perspirer,* exude, < L. *perspirare,* lit. 'breathe through,' < *per,* through, + *spirare,* breathe.] **I.** *intr.* To exude through pores†; also, to excrete watery fluid through the pores of the skin; sweat. **II.** *tr.* To emit through pores; exude: as, "They [firs] . . . continually *perspire* a fine balsam of turpentine" (Smollett's "Humphry Clinker," Aug. 8).—**per-spir-ing-ly** (pėr-spīr'ing-li), *adv.*

per-suade (pėr-swād'), *v.*; *-suaded, -suading.* [L. *persuadere* (pp. *persuasus*), < *per,* through, + *suadere,* advise, urge.] **I.** *tr.* To prevail on (a person, etc.), by advice, urging, reasons, inducements, etc., to do something (as, we could not *persuade* him to wait; he was *persuaded* to join them); induce; win over, influence, or bring by rendering willing (as, "We shall soon *persuade* . . . him . . . unto reason," Shakspere's "3 Henry VI.," iv. 7. 33; "All my retinue was that poor lad . . . whom I *persuaded* into my service," Swift's "Gulliver's Travels," iii. 9); also, to induce to believe, or convince (as, we *persuaded* him that he was mistaken; "The trader is firmly *persuaded* . . . that he himself was spared by favour," Stevenson's "Master of Ballantrae," xi.); also, sometimes, to seek to induce or convince (as, "Hearken not unto Hezekiah, when he *persuadeth* you, saying, The Lord will deliver us": 2 Kings, xviii. 32); urge to do or believe something; also, to induce the doing or practice of (something: archaic: as, to endeavor to *persuade* obedience); also, to induce belief in or acceptance of, as something asserted†; also, to urge (something) for doing, belief, etc.† (as, "Hadst thou thy wits, and didst *persuade* revenge, It could not move thus," Shakspere's "Hamlet," iv. 5. 168; "disputing and *persuading* the things concerning the kingdom of God," Acts, xix. 8). **II.** *intr.* To induce persons to do or believe something; also, to use persuasion, as in urging action or belief.—**per-suad'a-ble** (-swā'dạ-bl), *a.*—**per-suad'er,** *n.* One who or that which persuades; also, a spur, weapon, or other thing used to induce effort or obedience (slang: as, "He never appeared on deck without his '*persuader,*' which was three rattans twisted into one," Marryat's "Peter Simple," xii.).

per-sua-si-ble (pėr-swā'si-bl), *a.* [L. *persuasibilis.*] That may be persuaded; open to persuasion; also, persuasive†. —**per-sua-si-bil'i-ty** (-bil'i-ti), *n.*

per-sua-sion (pėr-swā'zhọn), *n.* [L. *persuasio(n-).*] The act or an act of persuading or seeking to persuade (as, to rely on *persuasion* rather than on force; to yield to the *persuasions* of friends); persuasive urging or speech; power of persuading, or persuasive force (as, "Is 't possible that my deserts to you Can lack *persuasion?*" Shakspere's "Twelfth Night," iii. 4. 382); also, something that serves or tends to persuade†, or an inducement†; also, the state or fact of being persuaded or convinced; a conviction or belief (as, "He had a strong *persuasion* that Likeman was wrong": H. G. Wells's "Soul of a Bishop," vi.); also, a form or system of belief, esp. religious belief, or the body of persons adhering to it (as, "a pious and pleasant young divine, though educated at Oxford for the Episcopalian *persuasion,*" Galt's "Annals of the Parish," xiv.; "most excellent discourses, which drew together considerable numbers of different *persuasions,*" B. Franklin's "Autobiography," vi.); sect or denomination; hence, kind or sort (humorous: as, an animal of the female *persuasion*).

per-sua-sive (pėr-swā'siv). **I.** *a.* Able, fitted, or intended to persuade: as, a *persuasive* speaker, voice, or manner; *persuasive* appeals. **II.** *n.* Something fitted or intended to persuade; a persuasive utterance: as, "Such *persuasives* at last prevailed with Bruce" (Jane Porter's "Scottish Chiefs," lvii.).—**per-sua'sive-ly,** *adv.*—**per-sua'sive-ness,** *n.*

pert (pėrt), *a.* [For *apert.*] Open† or unconcealed†; also, bold, forward, or impertinent in a smart or flippant way (as, "The boy was very *pert* and impudent," Smollett's "Humphry Clinker," Sept. 30; "She said it in very *pert* and airy accents," Arnold Bennett's "Helen with the High Hand," xxii.); saucy; also, lively, sprightly, or in good health and spirits (now prov.); also, smart or clever (obs. or prov.). Cf. *peart.*

per-tain (pėr-tān'), *v. i.* [OF. *partenir,* < L. *pertinere,* extend, reach, relate, < *per,* through, + *tenere,* hold.] To belong or be connected as a part, adjunct, possession, attribute, etc. (as, the house with the gardens *pertaining* to it; "All wide-stretched honours that *pertain* . . . Unto the crown of France," Shakspere's "Henry V.," ii. 4. 82); appertain; belong properly or fittingly, or be appropriate; also, to have reference or relation, or relate (as, documents *pertaining* to the case).

per-ti-na-cious (pėr-ti-nā'shus), *a.* [L. *pertinax* (*pertinac-*), < *per-,* very, + *tenax,* E. *tenacious.*] Holding tenaciously to a purpose, course of action, or opinion (as, to be *pertinacious* in pursuit or demands; a *pertinacious* beggar); extremely persistent, as in attempts or action characterized by or maintained with great persistence (as, *pertinacious* efforts or importunities; "This *pertinacious* pursuit of one particular whale, continued through day into night, and through night into day, is a thing by no means unprecedented," H. Melville's "Moby-Dick," cxxxiv.).—**per-ti-na'cious-ly,** *adv.*—**per-ti-na'cious-ness,** *n.*—**per-ti-na'ci-ty** (-nas'i-ti), *n.* The quality of being pertinacious; great persistence, as in attempts or action: as, "Again and again . . . with the inexorable *pertinacity* of a child intent upon some object important to itself, did he renew his efforts" (Hawthorne's "House of the Seven Gables," xix.).

per-ti-nence, per-ti-nen-cy (pėr'ti-nẹns, -nẹn-si), *n.* The character or fact of being pertinent; relevance; appositeness.

per-ti-nent (pėr'ti-nẹnt), *a.* [L. *pertinens* (*pertinent-*), ppr. of *pertinere*: see *pertain.*] Pertaining† or belonging†; appropriate†; also, pertaining or relating to the matter in hand, or having a bearing or application (as, a *pertinent* remark or suggestion; to adduce a *pertinent* case); to the point; relevant; apposite.—**per'ti-nent-ly,** *adv.*

pert-ly (pėrt'li), *adv.* In a pert manner.—**pert'ness,** *n.*

per-turb (pėr-tėrb'), *v. t.* [OF. *perturber,* < L. *perturbare* (pp. *perturbatus*), < *per,* through, + *turbare,* disturb, <

turba, disorder, tumult.] To disturb greatly, throw into disorder, or derange (as, to *perturb* the peace of a community); esp., to disturb or disquiet greatly in mind (as, "Highly *perturbed*, he wondered what was coming next": Arnold Bennett's "Helen with the High Hand," xxi.); render uneasy or troubled; agitate; in *astron.*, to cause irregularity of (planetary motion, planets, etc.); induce perturbation of. —**per-turb'a-ble,** *a.* That may be perturbed; liable to be disquieted or agitated.—**per-tur-ba'tion** (-tėr-bā'-shọn), *n.* [L. *perturbatio(n-).*] The act of perturbing, or the state of being perturbed; disturbance or disorder; mental disquiet or agitation; also, a cause of mental disquiet (as, "The crown . . . O polish'd *perturbation!* golden care!" Shakspere's "2 Henry IV.," iv. 5. 23); in *astron.*, a deviation of a heavenly body from its regular orbit.—**per'tur-ba-tor,** *n.* [LL.] One who perturbs; a disturber: as, "Such *perturbators* of the general quiet are to be executed" (Motley's "Dutch Republic," ii. 1).—**per-turb'ed-ly,** *adv.* —**per-turb'er,** *n.*

per-tuse (pėr-tūs'), *a.* [L. *pertusus*, pp. of *pertundere*, pierce, < *per*, through, + *tundere*, beat.] In *bot.*, having holes or slits, as a leaf.

per-tus-sis (pėr-tus'is), *n.* [NL., < L. *per-*, very, + *tussis*, cough.] In *pathol.*, whooping-cough.—**per-tus'sal,** *a.*

pe-ruke (pẹ-rök'), *n.* [F. *perruque*, < It. *perrucca*, *parrucca*; origin uncertain: cf. *periwig*.] A wig, esp. of the kind worn by men in the 17th and 18th centuries as the fashionable or customary head-covering; a periwig.—**pe-ruked',** *a.* Wearing a peruke.

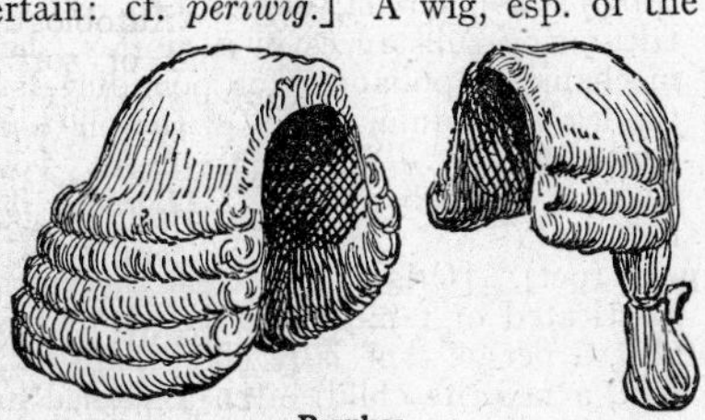

Perukes.

pe-ru-sal (pẹ-rö'-zạl), *n.* The act of perusing; survey or scrutiny (archaic: as, "He falls to such *perusal* of my face As he would draw it," Shakspere's "Hamlet," ii. 1. 90); reading (as, "deeply engaged in the *perusal* of a number of Pickwick": Mrs. Gaskell's "Cranford," ii.).

pe-ruse (pẹ-röz'), *v. t.*; *-rused, -rusing.* [OF. *paruser*, use wholly, finish, < *par* (< L. *per*), through, + *user*, E. *use, v.*] To use up†; also, to go through (a series, etc.) one by one†; hence, to survey or examine in detail (archaic); scrutinize (archaic: as, "The Stranger . . . with a curious eye *Perused* the Arab youth," Southey's "Thalaba," v. 14); now, usually, to read through, as with thoroughness or care, or, in general, to read (as, "The squire, having *perused* this letter, put it into my hand," Smollett's "Humphry Clinker," June 23; "This book I had again and again *perused* with delight," C. Brontë's "Jane Eyre," iii.).—**pe-rus'er** (-rö'zėr), *n.*

Pe-ru-vi-an (pẹ-rö'vi-ạn). **I.** *a.* Of or pertaining to Peru or its inhabitants: as, *Peruvian* bark (cinchona). **II.** *n.* A native or inhabitant of Peru; a member of the native Peruvian race under the Inca empire, or one of the people of Peru of later or modern times.

per-vade (pėr-vād'), *v. t.*; *-vaded, -vading.* [L. *pervadere* (pp. *pervasus*), < *per*, through, + *vadere*, go.] To go, pass, or spread through (now only as in following uses); go everywhere throughout (a place), as a person; extend one's presence, activities, influence, etc., throughout (as, "Eleanor, the cook, *pervaded* the house, doing the work of seven women": H. Kingsley's "Geoffry Hamlyn," xlii.); esp., of a fluid, or any subtle or immaterial agency, to diffuse itself throughout, or permeate (as, a tinge of pink *pervades* a cloud; "A drowsy springlike sultriness *pervaded* the air," Parkman's "Oregon Trail," ii.; "A broad generosity *pervaded* his life," Charnwood's "Theodore Roosevelt," iii.). —**per-vad'er** (-vā'dėr), *n.*—**per-vad'ing-ly,** *adv.*

per-va-sion (pėr-vā'zhọn), *n.* [LL. *pervasio(n-).*] The act of pervading, or the state of being pervaded; permeation. —**per-va'sive** (-siv), *a.* Tending, or having power, to pervade.—**per-va'sive-ly,** *adv.*—**per-va'sive-ness,** *n.*

per-verse (pėr-vėrs'), *a.* [OF. F. *pervers*, < L. *perversus*, turned the wrong way, awry, perverse, pp. of *pervertere*: see *pervert*.] Turned away from what is right, good, or proper; perverted or wicked (as, "blameless . . . in the midst of a crooked and *perverse* nation": Phil. ii. 15); incorrect or wrong (as, "trying to convince thee in spite of thine own *perverse* logic": Scott's "Castle Dangerous," xiii.); also, persistent or obstinate in what is wrong (as, "Hast thou, with heart *perverse* . . . still persever'd, And, having chosen evil . . . gloried in thy choice?" Cowper's "Expostulation," 396); also, wilfully determined or disposed to go counter to what is expected or desired, or contrary (as, "I'll frown and be *perverse* and say thee nay," Shakspere's "Romeo and Juliet," ii. 2. 96; "She refuses even to answer me;—so *perverse*, so foolish is she," W. H. Hudson's "Green Mansions," xiv.); characterized by or proceeding from such a determination (as, a *perverse* mood, impulse, or action; "There was something *perverse* in the inveteracy with which she avoided him," H. James's "Portrait of a Lady," xlviii.); wayward; cantankerous; also, untoward† or unfavorable† (as, "event *perverse!*" Milton's "Paradise Lost," ix. 405). —**per-verse'ly,** *adv.*—**per-verse'ness,** *n.*

per-ver-sion (pėr-vėr'shọn), *n.* [L. *perversio(n-)*, < *pervertere*: see *pervert*.] The act of perverting, or the state of being perverted; a turning or being turned to what is wrong; diversion to an improper use; distortion; vitiation; also, a perverted form of something; in *pathol.*, change to what is unnatural or abnormal (as, a *perversion* of function; *perversion* of appetite, or of a particular sense); specif., perverted or abnormal condition of the sexual instincts ('sexual perversion').

per-ver-si-ty (pėr-vėr'si-ti), *n.*; pl. *-ties* (-tiz). The quality of being perverse; perverse character or conduct, or an instance of it.

per-ver-sive (pėr-vėr'siv), *a.* Tending to pervert.

per-vert (pėr-vėrt'), *v. t.* [OF. F. *pervertir*, < L. *pervertere* (pp. *perversus*), turn about, overturn, corrupt, < *per*, through, + *vertere*, turn.] To turn away from the right course (as, "The Electress . . . entreated that he would not *pervert* her niece from the paths of the true religion": Motley's "Dutch Republic," ii. 2); bring over to a religious belief regarded as false or wrong (sometimes used in contrast to *convert*); lead astray morally, or corrupt; lead into mental error or false judgment; also, to turn from the proper to an improper use or purpose, or misapply (as, "The proscription . . . had been *perverted* to the license of avarice and private revenge," Froude's "Cæsar," xi.; to *pervert* one's talents or energies); wrest from the proper meaning or purport (as, "Ye have *perverted* the words of the living God": Jer. xxiii. 36); distort; also, to bring to a less excellent state, vitiate, or debase (as, "Luxury . . . while she polishes, *perverts* the taste": Cowper's "Retirement," 704); in *pathol.*, to change to what is unnatural or abnormal (see *perverted*); affect with perversion.—**per'vert,** *n.* One who has been perverted; one who has been brought over to a religious belief regarded as false or wrong (sometimes contrasted with *convert*: as, "In the end she died a *pervert* or convert, according to this or that person's point of view," W. H. Hudson's "Far Away and Long Ago," iii.); in *pathol.*, one affected with perversion.—**per-vert'ed,** *p. a.* Turned from what is right; wicked; misguided; misapplied; distorted; in *pathol.*, changed to or being of an unnatural or abnormal kind (as, a *perverted* appetite, see *pica*[1]; a *perverted* sense of smell, see *parosmia*); affected with or due to perversion.—**per-vert'ed-ly,** *adv.*—**per-vert'ed-ness,** *n.*—**per-vert'er,** *n.*—**per-vert'i-ble,** *a.* Capable of being perverted.

per-vi-ous (pėr'vi-us), *a.* [L. *pervius*, < *per*, through, + *via*, way.] Admitting of passage or entrance; esp., admitting of passage through the substance, or permeable (as, "light *pervious* soil": Kinglake's "Eothen," iv.); fig., penetrable by the mind; accessible to reason, feeling, etc. —**per'vi-ous-ness,** *n.*

pe-se-ta (pe-sā'tä), *n.*; pl. *-tas* (-täz). [Sp., dim. of *pesa*, weight: cf. *peso*.] The monetary unit of Spain, equiva-

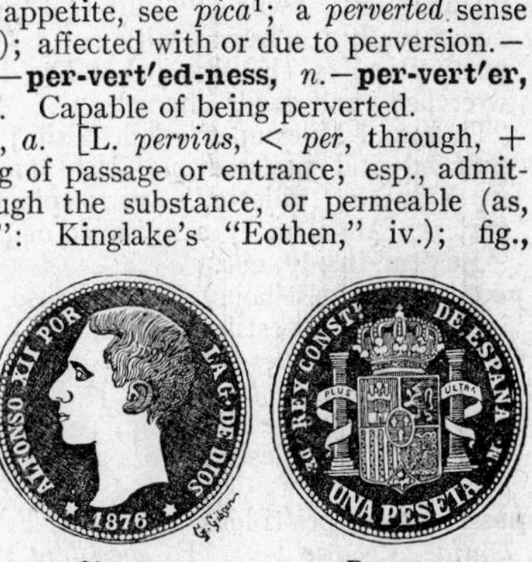

Obverse. Reverse.
Peseta of Alfonso XII. — British Museum.

lent to 19.3 U. S. cents; also, a silver coin nominally of this value (see cut on preceding page).

Pe-shit-ta, Pe-shit-to, Pe-shi-to (pe-shēt′tä, -tō, pe-shē′tō), *n.* [Syriac, lit. 'simple.'] The principal Syriac version of the Bible, the New Testament portion of which dates probably from the early part of the 5th century, while the Old Testament portion is much older.

pes-ky (pes′ki), *a.* [Origin uncertain: cf. *pest.*] Troublesome; annoying; plaguy: as, "I got caught in those *pesky* blackberry-bushes in the graveyard" (Mrs. Stowe's "Oldtown Folks," vi.). [Colloq., U. S.]

pe-so (pā′sō), *n.*; pl. *-sos* (-sōz). [Sp., lit. 'weight,' < L. *pensum*, pp. neut. of *pendere*, weigh.] A former Spanish gold or silver coin (dollar), equal to 8 reals; a modern Spanish gold or silver coin (5 pesetas), nominally worth 96.5 U. S. cents; the monetary unit and a silver coin of Mexico, equivalent to 49.8 U. S. cents; the monetary unit and a silver coin of the Philippine Islands, worth 50 U. S. cents; the monetary unit and a gold or silver coin of Cuba, equal to 100 centavos, or one U. S. dollar; any of various monetary units and coins of Central and South America.

pes-sa-ry (pes′ạ-ri), *n.*; pl. *-ries* (-riz). [LL. *pessarium*, < L. *pessum, pessus*, < Gr. πεσσός, pessary, orig. oval stone used in a game.] In *med.*, an instrument worn in the vagina to remedy uterine displacement; also, a medicated mass or the like for introduction into the vagina; a vaginal suppository.

pes-si-mism (pes′i-mizm), *n.* [L. *pessimus*, worst, superl. of *malus*, bad (compar. *pejor*): cf. *optimism.*] The doctrine that the existing world is the worst of all possible worlds, or that all things naturally tend to evịl; also, disposition to take the gloomiest or least hopeful view of circumstances; tendency to look on the dark side of things. Cf. *optimism.* —**pes′si-mist,** *n.* One who adheres to the doctrine of pessimism; also, one disposed to look on the dark side of things.—**pes-si-mis′tic,** *a.* Pertaining to or characterized by pessimism; disposed to take the least hopeful view of things.—**pes-si-mis′ti-cal-ly,** *adv.*—**pes′si-mize** (-mīz), *v.*; *-mized, -mizing.* **I.** *intr.* To hold or express pessimistic views. **II.** *tr.* To make the worst (rather than the best) of; take the least hopeful view of.

pest (pest), *n.* [F. *peste*, < L. *pestis*, plague, pestilence, bane.] A deadly epidemic disease; a pestilence; specif., the bubonic plague; also, a noxious, destructive, or troublesome thing or person (as, "those summer *pests*, the mosquitos," Weir Mitchell's "Hugh Wynne," xxiv.; "I was a nuisance, an incumbrance, and a *pest.* I know that very well," Dickens's "Hard Times," i. 4); a nuisance.

Pes-ta-loz-zi-an (pes-tạ-lot′sȩ̄-ạn), *a.* Of or pertaining to the Swiss educational reformer Johann Heinrich Pestalozzi (1746–1827), or his system of elementary instruction, in which teaching by object-lessons adapted to the ascertained capacity of each child was the principal feature.

pes-ter (pes′tėr), *v. t.* [Prob. for obs. *empester*, < F. *empestrer*, now *empêtrer*, hobble (a horse), hamper, entangle; in later use affected by *pest.*] To clog† or encumber†; obstruct† or overcrowd†; hence, to crowd or huddle together†; also, to infest (a place, etc.), as vermin, reptiles, or anything troublesome (as, "The kingdom is much *pestered* with flies in summer": Swift's "Gulliver's Travels," ii. 3); hence, now usually, to harass with petty annoyances, vexing importunities, or the like (as, "The boys *pester* us to buy wretched half-dead chameleons," Amelia B. Edwards's "Thousand Miles up the Nile," xiii.; "How she would have pursued and *pestered* me with questions and surmises," C. Brontë's "Villette," xxv.); plague or torment.—**pes′ter,** *n.* Annoyance; a nuisance or plague.—**pes′ter-er,** *n.* —**pes′ter-ing-ly,** *adv.*

pest=house (pest′hous), *n.* A house or hospital for persons infected with a pestilential disease.

pes-tif-er-ous (pes-tif′ẹ-rus), *a.* [L. *pestifer, pestiferus*, < *pestis*, pest, + *ferre*, bear.] Pest-bearing; of the nature of a pest; pestilential; fig., pernicious in any way; mischievous; troublesome or annoying.—**pes-tif′er-ous-ly,** *adv.*

pes-ti-lence (pes′ti-lẹns), *n.* [OF. F. *pestilence*, < L. *pestilentia*, < *pestilens*, E. *pestilent.*] A deadly epidemic disease (as, "a *pestilence* of small-pox or some other fever": W. H. Hudson's "Green Mansions," xiv.); specif., the bubonic plague; also, that which produces or tends to produce malignant disease (as, "The stench was frightful—the air heavy with *pestilence*": Kingsley's "Alton Locke," xxxv.); also, fig., that which is noxious in any respect; something morally pernicious.

pes-ti-lent (pes′ti-lẹnt), *a.* [L. *pestilens* (*pestilent-*), < *pestis*, E. *pest.*] Producing or tending to produce infectious disease; infectious, as a disease; pestilential; also, destructive to life; deadly; poisonous; fig., injurious to peace, morals, etc.; pernicious or mischievous (as, "a few *pestilent* agitators": Besant's "Coligny," v.); hence, troublesome or annoying (as, "a *pestilent* knave," Shakspere's "Romeo and Juliet," iv. 5. 147; "Look at the confusion your *pestilent* fowls are creating amongst my papers," W. H. Hudson's "Purple Land," x.).

pes-ti-len-tial (pes-ti-len′shạl), *a.* Producing or tending to produce pestilence (as, "*pestilential* vapors": Longfellow's "Hiawatha," ix. 37); also, pertaining to or of the nature of pestilence or infectious and deadly disease, specif. bubonic plague; fig., pernicious, harmful, or mischievous (as, "*pestilential* doctrines": Bulwer-Lytton's "Caxtons," xiii. 4). —**pes-ti-len′tial-ly,** *adv.*

pes-ti-lent-ly (pes′ti-lẹnt-li), *adv.* In a pestilent manner.

pes-tle (pes′l), *n.* [OF. *pestel*, < L. *pistillum*, < *pinsere* (pp. *pistus*), pound, bray.] An instrument for braying or triturating substances in a mortar; hence, any of various mechanical appliances for pounding, stamping, etc.; also, the leg of an animal, esp. of the pig (now only prov. Eng.). —**pes′tle,** *v.*; *-tled, -tling.* **I.** *tr.* To pound or triturate with or as with a pestle. **II.** *intr.* To work with a pestle.

pet[1] (pet). [Orig. Sc.; origin unknown.] **I.** *n.* Any domesticated or tamed animal that is fondled and indulged; also, a person especially cherished or indulged; a favorite; esp., a favorite child, often a spoiled one (as, "the spoiled *pet* of a wealthy family": C. Brontë's "Jane Eyre," xv.); also, sometimes, a thing particularly cherished. **II.** *a.* Treated as a pet, as an animal; especially cherished or indulged, as a child or other person; for which one has a particular fondness or weakness, or favorite, as a thing (as, a *pet* theory; a *pet* aversion, something that a person particularly dislikes); also, endearing, or manifesting affection (as, a *pet* name).—**pet**[1], *v.*; *petted, petting.* **I.** *tr.* To treat as a pet; fondle; indulge: as, "The master *petted* his pony" (Wister's "Virginian," xxv.); "She enjoyed being fêted and *petted* as much as a cat enjoys being stroked" (Mrs. Stowe's "Oldtown Folks," xxx.). **II.** *intr.* To fondle or caress one of the opposite sex; 'spoon.' [Slang.]

pet[2] (pet), *n.* [Origin uncertain.] A fit of peevishness or ill humor: as, "He tossed the titbit angrily into his cart, and drove off in a *pet*" (Hawthorne's "House of the Seven Gables," xix.).

pet-al (pet′ạl), *n.* [NL. *petalum*, petal, < Gr. πέταλον, leaf, < πεταννύναι, spread out.] In *bot.*, one of the leaves of a corolla.—**pet′aled, pet′alled,** *a.* Having petals: as, six-*petaled.*—**pet-al-if′er-ous** (-ạ-lif′ẹ-rus), *a.* [See *-ferous.*] Bearing petals.—**pet′al-ine** (-in), *a.* Pertaining to or resembling a petal.

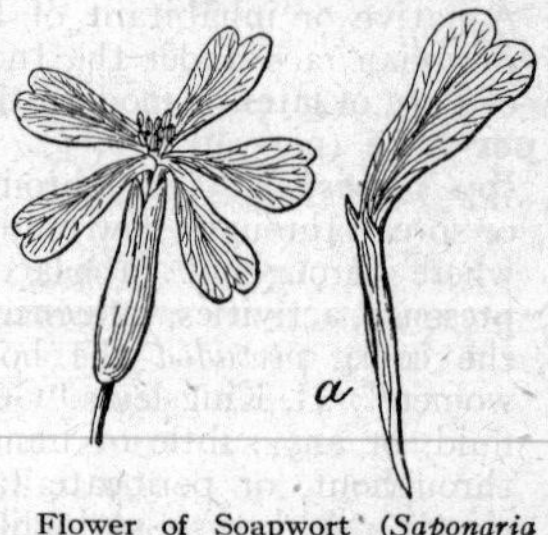

Flower of Soapwort (*Saponaria officinalis*), with (*a*) one of the Petals.

pet-a-lism (pet′ạ-lizm), *n.* [Gr. πεταλισμός, < πέταλον, leaf: see *petal.*] In ancient Syracuse, a mode of banishing citizens for five years by popular vote, with olive-leaves for ballots.

pet-a-lo-dy (pet′ạ-lō-di), *n.* [Gr. πεταλώδης, leaf-like, < πέταλον, leaf, + εἶδος, form.] In *bot.*, a condition frequent in flowers, in which certain organs, as the stamens in most double flowers, assume the appearance of or become metamorphosed into petals.

pet-a-loid (pet′ạ-loid), *a.* [See *-oid.*] Having the form or appearance of a petal.

pet-a-lous (pet′ạ-lus), *a.* Having petals.

pe-tard (pȩ̄-tärd′), *n.* [F. *pétard*, < *péter*, break wind, explode, < L. *pedere*, break wind.] An engine of war or explosive device used to blow in a door or gate, form a breach in a wall, etc.; also, a kind of fire-cracker.

Firing a Petard.

pet-a-sus (pet′ạ-sus), *n.* [L., < Gr. πέτασος, < πεταννύναι, spread out: cf. *petal.*] A low-crowned, broad-brimmed hat worn by ancient Greeks and Romans, often represented as worn by Hermes or Mercury; hence, the winged hat or cap which Mercury is represented as wearing in later art.

pe-tau-rist (pe-tâ′rist), *n.* [L. *petaurista*, < Gr. πεταυριστής, vaulter, tumbler, < πέταυρον, spring-board.] Any of the flying-phalangers of the genus *Petaurista* (or *Petaurus*).

Petaurist.

pet=cock (pet′kok), *n.* A small cock or faucet, as for draining off water from the cylinder of a steam-engine.

pe-tech-i-æ (pẹ-tek′i-ē or -tē′ki-ē), *n. pl.* [NL., < It. *petecchia*, purple spot in disease.] In *pathol.*, small purplish spots occurring on the skin in certain fevers, caused by hemorrhage into the cutaneous tissues.—**pe-tech′i-al,** *a.* Pertaining to or attended with petechiæ.—**petechial fever,** typhus fever; also, epidemic cerebrospinal meningitis.—**pe-tech′i-ate** (-āt), *a.* Having petechiæ.

pe-ter[1] (pē′tėr), *v. i.* [Origin unknown.] With *out*: To diminish gradually and then disappear or cease; give out by degrees. [Colloq.]

pe-ter[2] (pē′tėr), *n.* [Appar. < *Peter*, man's name.] A traveling-bag, trunk, parcel, or the like (thieves' slang); *naut.*, a flag hoisted as a signal of sailing (as, "We looked towards the Admiral, where high the *Peter* flew," H. Newbolt's "Old Superb": see *blue peter*, under *blue*, *a.*).—**pe′ter-man** (-mạn), *n.*; pl. *-men.* A thief who steals travelers' bags, etc.; also, a thief who uses knock-out drops as an aid to robbery; also, a safe-blower. [Thieves' slang.]

pe-ter-sham (pē′tėr-shạm), *n.* [From Viscount *Petersham* (early 19th cent.).] A kind of heavy overcoat formerly in fashion; also, a kind of heavy woolen cloth used for overcoats, etc.

Pe-ter's pence (pē′tėrz pens). [From St. *Peter*, as the first bishop of Rome.] An annual tax or tribute, orig. of a penny from each householder having land of a certain value, formerly paid by the people of certain countries to the papal see at Rome; now, a voluntary contribution to the Pope, made by Roman Catholics everywhere.

pet-i-ole (pet′i-ōl), *n.* [L. *petiolus*, little foot, stem, stalk, dim. < *pes* (*ped-*), foot.] In *bot.*, a leafstalk; the slender stalk by which a leaf is attached to the stem (see cut in next column); in *zoöl.*, a stalk or peduncle, as that connecting the abdomen and thorax in wasps, etc.—**pet′i-o-lar** (-ọ-lặr), *a.*—**pet′i-o-late** (-lāt), *a.*

pet-it (pet′i, F. pė-tē), *a.* [F.; perhaps from Celtic: cf. *petty.*] Small; petty; minor: now only in legal phrases.—**petit jury.** See under *jury*.—**petit larceny.** See *larceny*. —**pe-tite** (pẹ-tēt′, F. pė-tēt), *a.* [F., fem. of *petit.*] Little; of small size; tiny: esp. with reference to a woman or girl: as, "How very *petite* and compact she was in those old days" (W. De Morgan's "Alice-for-Short," xxix.).—**pe-tite′ness,** *n.*

pe-ti-tion (pẹ-tish′ọn), *n.* [OF. *peticion* (F. *pétition*), < L. *petitio(n-)*, < *petere*, seek.] Request made for something desired, esp. respectful or humble request, as to a superior or to one or those in authority (as, to make *petition* for aid or pardon); entreaty; a humble or earnest request (as, "if it please the king to grant my *petition*, and to perform my request": Esther, v. 8); a supplication or prayer, as to God; specif., a formally drawn-up request addressed to a person or a body of persons in authority or power, soliciting some favor, right, mercy, or other benefit (as, "They were about to present a monster *petition* in favour of the Charter; to accompany it . . . to the door of the House of Commons": Kingsley's "Alton Locke," xxxii.); a written application for an order of court or for some judicial action; also, that which is sought by request or entreaty (as, "All their *petitions* are as freely theirs As they themselves would owe them": Shakspere's "Measure for Measure," i. 4. 82).—**pe-ti′tion,** *v.* **I.** *tr.* To make petition to; entreat, supplicate, or beg, as for something desired; specif., to address a formal petition to (a sovereign, a legislative body, etc.); also, to make petition for (something); seek by entreaty; beg (*that*: as, "In vain Captain Bonneville . . . *petitioned* that his [a dog's] life might be spared," Irving's "Captain Bonneville," xxxiii.). **II.** *intr.* To make petition; specif., to address or present a formal petition.—**pe-ti′tion-a-ry** (-ạ-ri), *a.* Of the nature of or expressing a petition; also, petitioning or suppliant (obs. or archaic: as, "I . . . conjure thee to pardon Rome, and thy *petitionary* countrymen," Shakspere's "Coriolanus," v. 2. 82).—**pe-ti′tion-er,** *n.*

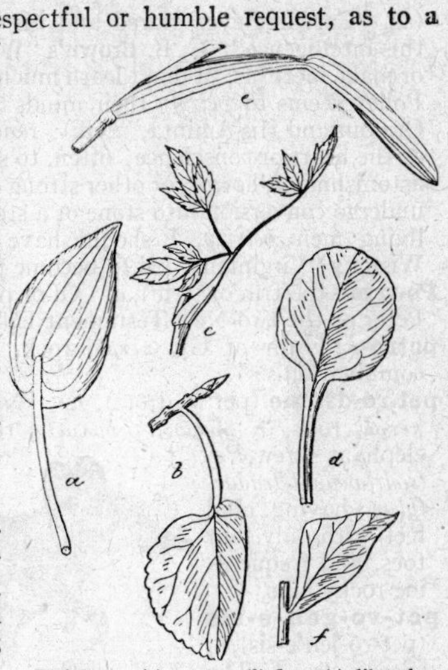

Petioles.—(*a*) terete; (*b*) flat; (*c*) dilated at the base; (*d*) winged; (*e*) forming a sheath; (*f*) leaf-like (the so-called phyllode).

pe-tit=maître (pė-tē-mātr), *n.* [F., 'little master.'] A dandy; an exquisite: as, "Every clerk, apprentice, and even waiter . . . assumes the air and apparel of a *petit maître*" (Smollett's "Humphry Clinker," May 29).

pet-rel (pet′rẹl), *n.* [Commonly associated with the apostle *Peter*, who "walked on the water" (Mat. xiv. 29).] Any of numerous sea-birds of the family *Procellariidæ*, esp. *Procellaria pelagica*, a small bird with black and white plumage and long, pointed wings.—**stormy petrel,** the petrel, *Procellaria pelagica*, or any of various other small, sooty, allied species, so called because popularly supposed to appear with or before a storm; a Mother Carey's chicken; fig., a person whose coming is supposed to portend trouble or strife.

Stormy Petrel (*Procellaria pelagica*).

pet-ri-fac-tion (pet-ri-fak′shọn), *n.* The act or process of petrifying, or the state of being petrified; also, something petrified.—**pet-ri-fac′tive** (-tiv), *a.* Causing petrifaction.

pet-ri-fi-ca-tion (pet″ri-fi-kā′shọn), *n.* Petrifaction.

pet-ri-fy (pet′ri-fī), *v.*; *-fied, -fying.* [F. *pétrifier*, < L. *petra*, rock, stone (< Gr. πέτρα, rock), + *facere*, make.] **I.** *tr.* To convert into stone or a stony substance (as, "The mortar which bound together the buildings was, by length of time, nearly *petrified*": Godwin's "Caleb Williams," xxvi.); fig., to change as if to stone; make rigid, stiffen, or benumb (as, "Carwin's eyes glared and his limbs were *petrified* at this intelligence": C. B. Brown's "Wieland," xxii.); deaden, or make inert (as, "I don't learn much from our senators . . . Policy seems to *petrify* their minds": G. Meredith's "Lord Ormont and His Aminta," xvii.); render hardened or callous, as the heart or conscience; often, to stupefy or paralyze with astonishment, horror, or other strong emotion. **II.** *intr.* To undergo conversion into stone or a stony substance (as, "Did living men *petrify*, I should have changed to mineral": Wister's "Virginian," xxi.); become petrified (lit. or fig.).

Pe-trine (pē′trīn or -trin), *a.* Of or pertaining to the apostle Peter or the two New Testament Epistles bearing his name.

petro-. Form of Gr. πέτρα, rock, πέτρος, stone, used in combination.

pet-ro-drome (pet′rō̤-drōm), *n.* [NL. *Petrodromus*, < Gr. πέτρα, rock, + -δρομος, < δραμεῖν, run.] An East African elephant-shrew, *Petrodromus tetradactylus*, having hind feet with only four toes, and frequenting rocky hills.

Petrodrome.

pet-ro-gen-e-sis (pet-rō̤-jen′e-sis), *n.* [See *petro-*.] The genesis or origination of rocks, esp. as a subject of scientific study. Also **pe-trog-e-ny** (pē̤-troj′e-ni).—**pet″-ro-ge-net′ic** (-jē̤-net′ik), **pet-ro-gen′ic,** *a.*

pet-ro-glyph (pet′rō̤-glif), *n.* [Gr. πέτρα, rock, + γλυφή, carving.] A carving on rock; esp., a prehistoric rock-carving.—**pet-ro-glyph′ic,** *a.*—**pe-trog-ly-phy** (pē̤-trog′-li-fi), *n.*

pe-trog-ra-pher (pē̤-trog′ra̤-fėr), *n.* One versed in petrography.

pe-trog-ra-phy (pē̤-trog′ra̤-fi), *n.* [See *petro-* and *-graphy.*] The scientific description and classification of rocks.—**pet-ro-graph-ic, pet-ro-graph-i-cal** (pet-rō̤-graf′ik, -i-ka̤l), *a.*

pet-rol (pet′rol or pe-trōl′), *n.* [F. *pétrole*, < ML. *petroleum*: see *petroleum.*] Petroleum (now rare); also, gasoline.—**pet′rol,** *v. t.*; *-rolled, -rolling.* To supply with petrol.

pet-ro-la-tum (pet-rō̤-lā′tum), *n.* [NL., < ML. *petroleum*: see *petroleum.*] A soft or semisolid unctuous substance obtained from petroleum, used as a basis for ointments and as a protective dressing; also, an oily liquid obtained from petroleum, used as a local application in inflammation of mucous membrane, as an intestinal lubricant, etc. ('liquid petrolatum').

pe-tro-le-um (pē̤-trō′lē̤-um), *n.* [ML., < L. *petra*, rock, + *oleum*, oil.] An oily, usually dark-colored liquid (a form of bitumen or mixture of various hydrocarbons), occurring naturally in the upper strata of the earth in various parts of the world, and commonly obtained by boring: used (in its natural state or after certain treatment) as a fuel, or separated by distillation into gasoline, naphtha, benzine, kerosene, paraffin, etc.

pé-tro-leur (pā-tro-lėr), *n.* [F.] An incendiary who uses petroleum; specif., one of those adherents of the Commune who set fire to public buildings in Paris, with the aid of petroleum, in May, 1871.—**pé-tro-leuse** (-lėz), *n.* [F.] Fem. of *pétroleur.*

pet-rol-ize (pet′rō̤-līz), *v. t.*; *-ized, -izing.* To treat with petroleum; spread petroleum on (water) to destroy mosquito larvæ; also, to set on fire by means of petroleum.—**pet″rol-i-za′tion** (-rō̤-li-zā′sho̤n), *n.*

pe-trol-o-gy (pē̤-trol′ō̤-ji), *n.* [See *petro-* and *-logy.*] The scientific study of rocks, including their origin, structure, changes, etc.—**pet-ro-log-ic, pet-ro-log-i-cal** (pet-rō̤-loj′ik, -i-ka̤l), *a.*—**pe-trol′o-gist,** *n.*

pet-ro-nel (pet′rō̤-ne̤l), *n.* [F. *pêtrinal*, < OF. *peitrine* (F. *poitrine*), breast, < L. *pectus* (*pector-*), breast; the stock of the weapon being held against the breast in firing.] An old hand-firearm, in size between the pistol and the harquebus, used esp. by horse-soldiers.

pe-tro-sal (pē̤-trō′sa̤l), *a.* [L. *petrosus*: see *petrous.*] In *anat.*, petrous; specif., noting or pertaining to the petrous portion of the temporal bone.

pet-rous (pet′rus or pē′trus), *a.* [L. *petrosus*, < *petra*, rock, stone, < Gr. πέτρα, rock.] Like stone in hardness; stony; rocky; in *anat.*, noting or pertaining to the hard and dense portion of the temporal bone, which contains the internal auditory organs; petrosal.

pet-ti-coat (pet′i-kōt). [From *petty* + *coat.*] **I.** *n.* A short inner coat worn by men†; later, a man's waistcoat (now prov. Eng.); also, a skirt, esp. an underskirt, worn by women and children; any similar garment, as the Scotch kilt or the Greek fustanella, worn by men (chiefly humorous); any skirt-like part or covering; also, a woman or girl (as, "There was nobody knew better how to make his way among the *petticoats* than my grandfather": Irving's "Tales of a Traveler," i. 5); the female sex. **II.** *a.* Of or pertaining to petticoats; wearing petticoats; female or feminine (as, "A kind of *petticoat* council was forthwith held . . . at which the governor's lady presided": Irving's "Knickerbocker's New York," iv. 4).—**petticoat government,** the government or rule of women; feminine control or management.—**pet′ti-coat=breech′es,** *n. pl.* A kind of loose breeches not gathered at the bottom of each leg but hanging somewhat like petticoats: worn by men about the middle of the 17th century.—**pet′ti-coat″ed,** *a.* Wearing petticoats.

Petticoat-breeches.

pet-ti-fog (pet′i-fog), *v. i.*; *-fogged, -fogging.* [Prob. a back-formation from *pettifogger.*] To act as a pettifogger; carry on a petty or shifty law business; practise chicanery.

pet-ti-fog-ger (pet′i-fog″ėr), *n.* [Appar. < *petty* + obs. *fogger*, pettifogger, of uncertain origin.] A petty legal practitioner; an inferior lawyer who employs mean shifts or petty trickery (as, "He carried home with him all the knavish chicanery of the lowest *pettifogger*": Smollett's "Humphry Clinker," June 26); hence, a petty, mean, or shifty practitioner in any field (as, "appointing as ambassador some political *pettifogger* skilled in delays, sophisms, and misapprehensions": Irving's "Knickerbocker's New York," v. 4).—**pet′ti-fog″ger-y,** *n.*; pl. *-ies* (-iz). The practice of a pettifogger; a proceeding characteristic of a pettifogger.

pet-ti-ly (pet′i-li), *adv.* In a petty manner.—**pet′ti-ness,** *n.*

pet-tish (pet′ish), *a.* [See *pet*².] Subject to pets, or fits of ill humor; in a pet, or impatiently displeased, now esp. over some trifling matter (as, "If she were a long while absent, he became *pettish* and nervously restless": Hawthorne's "House of the Seven Gables," ix.); characteristic of or due to a pet (as, *pettish* displeasure; a *pettish* refusal or frown).—**pet′tish-ly,** *adv.*—**pet′tish-ness,** *n.*

pet-ti-toes (pet′i-tōz), *n. pl.* [Appar. < *petty* + *toe.*] The feet of a pig, esp. as food (as, "a present of pigs' *pettitoes*": George Eliot's "Silas Marner," x.); also, the human feet, esp. those of a child.

pet-to (pet′tō), *n.* [It., < L. *pectus*, breast.] The breast: in the phrase *in petto* (in one's own breast or private thought): as, "I determined to try the poison of jealousy . . . I had long kept it *in petto* as my ultimate remedy" (Maria Edgeworth's "Belinda," iii.).

pet-ty (pet′i), *a.*; compar. *pettier*, superl. *pettiest.* [OF. F. *petit*: see *petit.*] Small in size†; also, of small importance, trifling, or trivial (as, *petty* gains; *petty* grievances; "Our knights are limited to *petty* enterprises," Scott's "Castle Dangerous," xi.); of no great dignity or power (as, a *petty* prince or chief; *petty* nobles); of no particular merit or note (as, a *petty* poet); on a small scale (as, *petty* traders); also, of lesser or secondary importance, minor, or inferior (as, *petty* larceny, as distinguished from grand larceny; a *petty* officer, see phrase following); also, having or showing a small mental range, or narrow ideas, interests, etc. (as, *petty* minds or thinkers; "A *petty* passion for contemptible details characterized him from his youth," Motley's "Dutch Republic,"

i. 2); often, mean or ungenerous in small or trifling things (as, to be *petty* in spirit or action; a *petty* spirit; a *petty* revenge).—**petty jury.** See under *jury.*—**petty larceny.** See *larceny.*—**petty officer,** an enlisted man in the navy holding an official rank corresponding to that of a non-commissioned officer in the army.

pet-u-lance (pet̹′ū̹-lạns), *n.* The state or quality of being petulant; petulant spirit or behavior; a petulant speech or action.—**pet′u-lan-cy** (-lạn-si), *n.*

pet-u-lant (pet̹′ū̹-lạnt), *a.* [F. *pétulant*, < L. *petulans* (*petulant-*), forward, pert, wanton, < *petere*, fall on, assail.] Forward or pert (now rare: as, "a young *petulant* jackanapes," Smollett's "Humphry Clinker," May 8); presuming or arrogant (now rare: as, "Mungo Argyle, the exciseman, waxing rich, grew proud and *petulant*," Galt's "Annals of the Parish," xxii.); also, quick to anger, or irritable (as, "The Southrons, inflammable, *petulant*, audacious, were the first to assault and to defy the imperial power," Motley's "Dutch Republic," Introd., iv.; "His temper was acid, *petulant*, and harsh," Godwin's "Caleb Williams," xix.); now, commonly, moved to, showing, or characterized by sudden, impatient irritation, esp. over some trifling or passing annoyance (as, to become *petulant* at a refusal; a *petulant* toss of the head; *petulant* dissatisfaction); fig., seeming to display or indicate irritation or petulance (as, "the hoarse murmuring of a *petulant* brook," Parkman's "Oregon Trail," xiii.; "the *petulant* abundance of mountain rain," Mrs. H. Ward's "Robert Elsmere," viii.).—**pet′u-lant-ly,** *adv.*

pe-tu-ni-a (pē̹-tū′ni-ạ̈), *n.* [NL., < F. *petun*, tobacco; of S. Amer. origin.] Any of the herbs constituting the solanaceous genus *Petunia*, native in tropical America but much cultivated elsewhere, bearing funnel-shaped flowers of various colors; also, a deep reddish-purple color.

pe-tun-tse, pe-tun-tze (pe-tun′tse), *n.* [Chinese, lit. 'white stone.'] A partially decomposed granitic rock containing some unaltered feldspar, used as one of the ingredients in making certain kinds of porcelain.

pew (pū), *n.* [OF. *puie*, balcony, < L. *podia*, pl. of *podium*, elevated place, balcony: see *podium.*] A raised standing-place, pulpit, or stall in a church, as for the preacher or reader†; a raised seat or inclosure in a public hall or place, as for judges or lawyers, persons doing business, or the like†; a box in a theater†; also, in a church, an inclosed seat, or an inclosure with seats, appropriated to the use of a family or other worshipers (as, "people of rank, who sat in *pews*, sumptuously lined and cushioned, furnished with richly gilded prayer-books, and decorated with their arms upon the *pew*-doors": Irving's "Sketch-Book," The Country Church); commonly, in modern churches, one of an assemblage of fixed bench-like seats (with backs), accessible by aisles, for the use of the congregation.—**pew′age** (-ạ̄j), *n.* The pews in a church collectively; the arrangement of pews; also, the rent paid for pews.

pe-wee (pē′wē), *n.* [Imit. of its note.] Any of certain small American birds, flycatchers of the genus *Contopus* (family *Tyrannidæ*), esp. *C. virens* (the common 'wood-pewee'); also, a pewit or phœbe.

pe-wit (pē′wit or pū′it), *n.* [Imit. of its note.] The lapwing, *Vanellus cristatus*; also, the European black-headed gull, *Larus ridibundus*; also, a phœbe.

pew-ter (pū′tėr). [OF. *peutre* (F. *peautre*) = Sp. *peltre* = It. *peltro*, pewter: cf. *spelter.*] **I.** *n.* Any of various alloys in which tin is the chief constituent, orig. one of tin and lead; a vessel or utensil made of such an alloy; such utensils collectively (as, "rows of resplendent *pewter*, ranged on a long dresser": Irving's "Sketch-Book," Sleepy Hollow). **II.** *a.* Consisting or made of pewter: as, *pewter* plates; a *pewter* mug.—**pew′ter-er,** *n.* A worker in pewter; a maker of pewter utensils.—**pew′ter-y,** *n.* Pewter utensils collectively; also, a room or place in which pewter utensils are kept.

-pexia, -pexy. Noun terminations from Gr. πῆξις, a making fast, fixing, used in surgical terms, as *hepatopexia* or *hepatopexy, hysteropexia, nephropexia.*

Pey-e-ri-an (pī-ē′ri-ạn), *a.* Pertaining to or named after Johann Konrad Peyer (1653-1712), a Swiss anatomist.—**Peyerian glands** or **patches,** patch-like aggregations of follicles composed of lymphoid tissue which are situated in the walls of the small intestine, and which undergo lesion in typhoid fever.

pe-yo-te (pā-yō′tā), *n.* [Sp.; from Mex.] A cactus of the genus *Lophophora*, the mescal of Mexico and Texas, which when dried (esp. the top, or mescal-button) is much used by the Indians of Mexico and the western U. S. for ceremonial and medicinal purposes, and as a stimulant and intoxicant producing illusions of beauty and happiness; the dried top of this plant, used as a drug.

pfen-nig (pfen′ig), *n.*; pl. *pfennigs*, G. *pfennige* (pfen′i-gė). [G.: see *penny.*] A small bronze coin and money of account of Germany, the hundredth part of a mark, normally equivalent to about one fourth of a U. S. cent.

Phæ-a-cian (fē̹-ā′shiạn). **I.** *a.* Of or pertaining to Phæacia, or Scheria, an island in the Ionian Sea (anciently identified with Córcyra, the modern Corfu), inhabited by the Phæaces, a fabulous people described by Homer in the "Odyssey," who led a life of undisturbed happiness, with feasting, etc. **II.** *n.* An inhabitant of Phæacia, or Scheria; fig., a gourmand.

phæ-no-gam, phe-no-gam (fē′nọ̄-gam), *n.* [NL. *phænogama*, < Gr. φαίνειν, show, + γάμος, marriage.] Same as *phanerogam.*—**phæ-nog-a-mous, phe-nog-a-mous** (fē̹-nog′ạ-mus), *a.*

pha-ë-ton (fā′ẹ-tọn), *n.* [F. *phaéton*, < L. *Phaëthon*, < Gr. Φαέθων, Phaëthon (lit. 'shining'), who once drove the chariot of his father, the sun-god Helios, and nearly set the world on fire.] A light four-wheeled carriage, with or without a top, having one or (more commonly) two seats facing forward, and made in various forms; also, an automobile of the touring-car type.

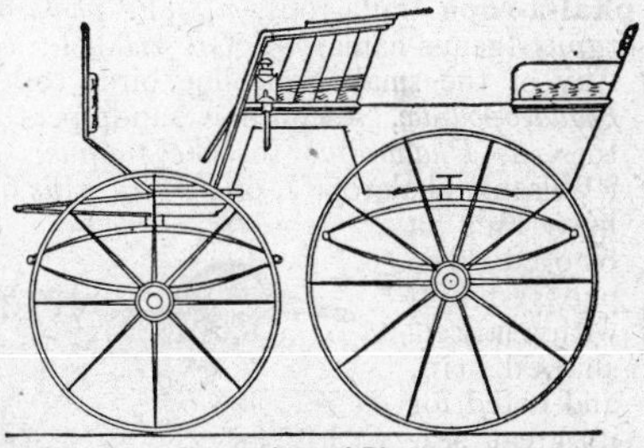

One variety of Phaëton.

phag-e-de-na, phag-e-dæ-na (faj-ẹ-dē′nạ̈), *n.* [L. *phagedæna*, < Gr. φαγέδαινα, < φαγεῖν, eat.] In *pathol.*, an obstinate spreading ulcer or ulceration; also, gangrene.—**phag-e-den′ic, phag-e-dæn′ic** (-den′ik), *a.*

phag-o-cyte (fag′ọ̄-sīt), *n.* [Gr. φαγεῖν, eat, + κύτος, a hollow.] In *physiol.*, a leucocyte or white blood-corpuscle capable of absorbing and destroying waste or harmful material, as pathogenic microbes.—**phag-o-cyt′ic** (-sit′ik), *a.* —**phag″o-cy-to′sis** (-sī-tō′sis), *n.* [NL.] The destruction of microbes, etc., by phagocytes.

-phagous. [Gr. -φάγος, < φαγεῖν, eat.] An adjective termination meaning 'eating,' 'feeding on,' 'devouring,' as in *creophagous, hylophagous, rhizophagous.*

-phagy. [Gr. -φαγία, < -φάγος, E. *-phagous.*] A noun termination meaning 'eating,' 'devouring,' esp. as a practice or habit, as in *allotriophagy, anthropophagy.*

phal-ange (fal′anj), *n.* In *anat.*, etc., a phalanx.

pha-lan-ge-al (fạ-lan′jē-ạl), *a.* In *anat.*, etc., pertaining to or of the nature of a phalanx or phalanges.

pha-lan-ger (fạ-lan′jėr), *n.* [NL., < Gr. φάλαγξ, bone of finger or toe; with reference to the webbed digits of the hind feet.] Any of numerous arboreal marsupials constituting the family *Phalangeridæ*, of the Australian region, esp. those of the genus *Phalanger* (or *Cuscus*), as *P. maculatus* ('spotted phalanger'). Cf. *flying-phalanger* and *petaurist.*

Spotted Phalanger (*P. maculatus*).

pha-lan-ges (fạ-lan′jēz), *n.* Pl. of *phalanx.*

phal-an-ste-ri-an (fal-ạn-stē′ri-ạn). [F. *phalanstérien.*] **I.** *a.* Of or pertaining to a phalanstery; also, of or pertaining to phalansterianism. **II.** *n.* A member of a phalanstery; also, an advocate of phalansterianism; a Fourierist. —**phal-an-ste′ri-an-ism, phal′an-ster-ism** (-stẹ-rizm), *n.* The system of phalansteries; Fourierism.

phal-an-ste-ry (fal′ạn-ste-ri), *n.*; pl. *-ries* (-riz). [F. *phalanstère,* < *phalange,* phalanx, + (*mona*)*stère,* monastery.] In Fourierism, the building or buildings occupied by a phalanx or socialistic community; also, the community itself; hence, any similar association of persons, or the building or buildings occupied by them.

pha-lanx (fā′langks or fal′angks), *n.*; pl. *phalanxes* or *phalanges* (fạ-lan′jēz). [L., < Gr. φάλαγξ, line of battle, phalanx (of troops), body, block, bone of finger or toe.] In ancient Greece, a body of heavy-armed infantry formed in ranks and files close and deep, with shields joined and long spears overlapping; hence, any body of troops in close array; also, a compact or closely massed body of persons, animals, or things (as, "The sheep . . . All huddling into *phalanx,* stood and gaz'd," Cowper's "Needless Alarm," 48; "a *phalanx* of carriages," Arnold Bennett's "Hilda Lessways," iii. 3); fig., a number of persons, etc., united or banded together, as for a common purpose; in Fourierism, a group of persons, numbering about 1,800, living together and holding their property in common; in *anat.* and *zoöl.,* any of the digital bones of the hand or foot; in *bot.,* a bundle of stamens, joined by their filaments.

phal-a-rope (fal′ạ-rōp), *n.* [F. *phalarope,* < NL. *Phalaropus* (genus-name), < Gr. φαλαρίς, coot, + πούς, foot.] Any of the small limicoline birds constituting the family *Phalaropodidæ,* resembling sandpipers but having lobate toes, as *Phalaropus* (or *Steganopus*) *wilsoni* of America ('Wilson's phalarope'), or *P. fulicarius* of both hemispheres, having a broad, depressed bill with a lancet-shaped tip, and noted for its great seasonal changes of plumage ('red phalarope' or 'gray phalarope').

Red Phalarope (*Phalaropus fulicarius*). — *a,* bill.

phal-lic (fal′ik), *a.* [Gr. φαλλικός.] Of or pertaining to the phallus or phallicism. —**phal-li-cism** (fal′i-sizm), *n.* Worship of the phallus. Also **phal′lism.** —**phal′li-cist** (-sist), *n.*

phal-lus (fal′us), *n.*; pl. *phalli* (-ī). [L., < Gr. φαλλός, penis.] An image of the male reproductive organ, symbolizing in certain religious systems the generative power in nature; esp., that carried in procession in ancient festivals of Dionysus or Bacchus.

Pha-nar-i-ot, Pha-nar-i-ote (fạ-nar′i-ot, -ōt). [NGr. Φαναριώτης; named from the *Phanar* (Turk. *Fanar*) quarter of Constantinople, so called from a lighthouse (Gr. φανάριον) on the Golden Horn.] **I.** *n.* One of a class of Greeks in Constantinople who, after the Turkish conquest, held important official positions under the Turks. **II.** *a.* Of, pertaining to, or characteristic of the Phanariots.

phan-e-ro-gam (fan′ẹ-rō-gam), *n.* [F. *phanérogame* = NL. *phanerogamus,* phanerogamous, < Gr. φανερός, visible, + γάμος, marriage.] In *bot.,* any of the *Phanerogamia,* an old primary division of plants comprising those having reproductive organs (stamens and pistils) developed and distinctly apparent; a flowering plant or seed-plant: opposed to *cryptogam.* —**phan″e-ro-gam′ic,** *a.* Of or pertaining to the phanerogams. —**phan-e-rog′a-mous** (-rog′ạ-mus), *a.* Having the characters of the phanerogams; having stamens and pistils; flowering.

phan-tasm (fan′tazm), *n.* [OF. F. *fantasme,* < L. *phantasma,* < Gr. φάντασμα, an appearance, phantasm, < φαντάζειν, present to the eye or mind, < φαίνειν, show.] Deceptive appearance (archaic); also, an illusion or deceptive appearance (as, "a *phantasm* bred by the fever which had then seized him": Milton's "Areopagitica"); an unreality; an illusive likeness of something (as, "Every *phantasm* of a hope was quickly nullified": George Eliot's "Daniel Deronda," lviii.); sometimes, an apparition or specter; a supposed appearance of an absent person, living or dead, at a place where his body is not at the time; also, a creation of the imagination or fancy; a fancy; a fantastic notion; also, in philosophical use, a mental image or representation of a real object. Also **phan-tas′ma** (-taz′mạ̈); pl. *-mata* (-mạ-tạ̈).

phan-tas-ma-go-ri-a (fan-taz-mạ-gō′ri-ạ̈), *n.* [NL., < Gr. φάντασμα, phantasm, + (appar.) ἀγορά, assembly.] An exhibition of optical illusions produced by a magic lantern or the like, as one in which figures increase or diminish in size, dissolve, pass into each other, etc.; hence, a shifting series of phantasms, illusions, or deceptive appearances, as in a dream or as created by the imagination; also, a changing scene made up of many elements (as, "to hang over Maule's well, and look at the constantly shifting *phantasmagoria* of figures produced by the agitation of the water over the mosaic work of colored pebbles at the bottom": Hawthorne's "House of the Seven Gables," x.). —**phan-tas-ma-go′ri-al, phan-tas-ma-gor′ic** (-gor′ik), *a.* —**phan-tas′ma-go-rist** (-gō-rist), *n.* One who exhibits or produces a phantasmagoria. —**phan-tas′ma-go-ry** (-ri), *n.*; pl. *-ries* (-riz). A phantasmagoria.

phan-tas-mal (fan-taz′mạl), *a.* Pertaining to or of the nature of a phantasm; unreal; illusive; spectral; imaginary. —**phan-tas′mal-ly,** *adv.*

phan-ta-sy (fan′tạ-si), *n.* See *fantasy.*

phan-tom (fan′tọm). [OF. *fantosme* (F. *fantôme*), var. of *fantasme*: see *phantasm.*] **I.** *n.* Deceptive appearance†; unreality†; falsity†; also, an appearance without material substance; an illusive likeness of something (as, "The forms Of which these are the *phantoms*": Shelley's "Prometheus Unbound," iii. 3. 52); an apparition or specter (as, "Did he really appear? or was it only a *phantom,* a pale spectre, to apprize me of his death?" Smollett's "Humphry Clinker," Oct. 4); also, fig., a thing or person that is little more than an appearance or show, or a mere semblance (as, "They annihilated the *phantom* of authority which still lingered with the name of khalif at Bagdad": Hallam's "Europe during the Middle Ages," vi.); also, an image appearing in a dream, or formed in the mind (as, "the *phantoms* of sleep," De Quincey's "English Mail-Coach," iii.; "She . . . looked at the man who stood beside her. At first she thought it was a *phantom* of her own brain," H. Kingsley's "Geoffry Hamlyn," xliv.); a creation of the imagination; also, a mental image of an external object. **II.** *a.* Of the nature of a phantom; merely apparent; unreal; illusive; spectral. —**phan-tom′ic** (-tom′ik), *a.*

-phany. [Gr. -φάνεια (sometimes -φάνια), < -φανής, shown, appearing, < φαίνειν, show, φαίνεσθαι, appear.] A noun termination meaning 'appearance,' 'manifestation,' as of a deity or a supernatural being, as in *angelophany, Christophany, epiphany, satanophany.*

Pha-raoh (fā′rō, also fā′rạ-ō), *n.* [LL. *Pharao,* < Gr. Φαραώ, < Heb. *Par'ōh,* < Egypt. *per-'o,* 'great house.'] A title of the ancient Egyptian kings; an Egyptian king: as, "Rameses the Second was the son of Seti I., the second *Pharaoh* of the XIXth Dynasty" (Amelia B. Edwards's "Thousand Miles up the Nile," xv.). —**Pharaoh's hen** or **chicken,** the Egyptian vulture, *Neophron percnopterus,* a species about two feet long, with mostly white plumage: frequently represented in ancient Egyptian art. —**Pha-**

Pharaoh's Hen.

raoh's rat, the ichneumon.—**Pha-ra-on-ic** (fā-rā-on'ik), *a.*

phare (fãr), *n.* Same as *pharos.* [Now rare.]

phar-i-sa-ic (far-i-sā'ik), *a.* [LL. *Pharisaicus,* < Gr. Φαρισαϊκός.] [*cap.*] Of or pertaining to the Pharisees; [*l. c.*] resembling or suggesting the Pharisees in strict observance of external forms and ceremonies of religion without regard to its spirit; laying great stress on the external observances of religion or an outward show of morality, and assuming superiority because of this, self-righteous, or hypocritical (as, "smug and *pharisaic* fools": Galsworthy's "Dark Flower," iii. 12). Also **phar-i-sa'i-cal.**—**phar-i-sa'i-cal-ly,** *adv.*

phar-i-sa-ism (far'i-sā-izm), *n.* [*cap.*] The doctrine and practice of the Pharisees; [*l. c.*] rigid observance of external forms of religion without genuine piety; hypocrisy.

Phar-i-see (far'i-sē), *n.* [OF. *pharisee,* < LL. *Pharisæus,* < Gr. Φαρισαῖος, Pharisee; from Aram. name meaning 'separated,' 'separatist.'] One of an ancient Jewish sect or party noted for strict interpretation and observance of the law and for pretensions to superior sanctity (cf. *Sadducee*); [*l. c.*] a pharisaic, self-righteous, or hypocritical person.—**phar'i-see-ism,** *n.*

phar-ma-cal (fär'mạ-kạl), *a.* Pertaining to pharmacy; pharmaceutic.

phar-ma-ceu-tic (fär-mạ-sū'tik), *a.* [LL. *pharmaceuticus,* < Gr. φαρμακευτικός, < φαρμακεύειν, administer drugs: see *pharmacy.*] Pertaining to pharmacy. Also **phar-ma-ceu'ti-cal.**—**phar-ma-ceu'ti-cal-ly,** *adv.*—**phar-ma-ceu'tics,** *n.* Pharmacy.—**phar-ma-ceu'tist,** *n.* A pharmacist.

phar-ma-cist (fär'mạ-sist), *n.* One skilled in pharmacy; a druggist or pharmaceutical chemist.

pharmaco-. Form of Gr. φάρμακον, drug, used in combination.

phar-ma-cog-no-sy (fär-mạ-kog'nọ-si), *n.* [See *pharmaco-* and *-gnosy.*] That branch of pharmacology which deals with medicinal substances in their natural or unprepared state.—**phar''ma-cog-nos'tic** (-nos'tik), *a.*

phar-ma-col-o-gy (fär-mạ-kol'ọ-ji), *n.* [See *pharmaco-* and *-logy.*] The science of drugs, their preparation, uses, and effects.—**phar''ma-co-log'i-cal** (-kọ-loj'i-kạl), *a.*—**phar-ma-col'o-gist,** *n.*

phar-ma-co-pœ-ia (fär''mạ-kọ-pē'iạ), *n.* [NL., < Gr. φαρμακοποιία, art of preparing drugs, < φάρμακον, drug, + ποιεῖν, make.] A book, esp. one published by authority, containing a list of drugs and medicines and describing their preparation, properties, uses, etc.; also, a stock of drugs (as, "The bishop . . . had but one medicine in his whole *pharmacopœia* strong enough to touch so grave a disorder": Trollope's "Warden," iii.).—**phar''ma-co-pœ'ial,** *a.*—**phar''-ma-co-pœ'ist,** *n.* A compiler of a pharmacopœia.

phar-ma-co-ther-a-py (fär''mạ-kọ-ther'ạ-pi), *n.* [See *pharmaco-* and *therapy.*] Treatment of disease by means of drugs.

phar-ma-cy (fär'mạ-si), *n.*; pl. *-cies* (-siz). [OF. *farmacie* (F. *pharmacie*), < LL. *pharmacia,* < Gr. φαρμακεία, < φαρμακεύειν, administer drugs, < φάρμακον, drug.] The art or practice of preparing and dispensing drugs and medicines; the occupation of a druggist; also, a drug-store.

Pharmacy Jars, 17th century.

pha-ros (fā'ros), *n.* [L., < Gr. φάρος, lighthouse, < Φάρος, the island of Pharos in the Bay of Alexandria, famous for its lighthouse.] A lighthouse or beacon to direct seamen: as, "a steep . . . mount, on the top of which . . . had been a *pharos* or lighthouse" (Irving's "Conquest of Granada," lii.).

pha-ryn-ge-al (fạ-rin'jē-ạl), *a.* Of, pertaining to, or connected with the pharynx.

phar-yn-gi-tis (far-in-jī'tis), *n.* [NL.] In *pathol.,* inflammation of the mucous membrane of the pharynx.

pharyngo-. Form of Gr. φάρυγξ (φαρυγγ-), throat, used in combination.—**phar-yn-gol-o-gy** (far-ing-gol'ọ-ji), *n.* [+ *-logy.*] The science of the pharynx and its diseases.—**pha-ryn-go-scope** (fạ-ring'gọ-skōp), *n.* [+ *-scope.*] An instrument for inspecting the pharynx.—**phar-yn-got'o-my** (-ing-got'ọ-mi), *n.* [+ *-tomy.*] Surgical incision into the pharynx.

phar-ynx (far'ingks), *n.*; pl. *pharynxes* or *pharynges* (fạ-rin'jēz). [NL., < Gr. φάρυγξ (φαρυγγ-), throat.] In *anat.,* the tube or cavity, with its surrounding membrane and muscles, which connects the mouth and nasal passages with the esophagus.

phase[1] (fāz), *v. t.* See *faze.*

phase[2] (fāz), *n.* [NL. *phasis,* < Gr. φάσις, appearance, phase, < φαίνειν, show.] Any of the appearances or aspects in which a thing of varying modes or conditions manifests itself to the eye or mind; a stage of change or development (as, "A *phase* of my life was closing to-night, a new one opening to-morrow": C. Brontë's "Jane Eyre," x.); in *astron.,* the particular appearance presented by a planet, etc., at a given time; specif., one of the recurring appearances or states of the moon or a planet in respect to the form, or the absence, of its illuminated disk (as, the most important *phases* of the moon are new moon, first quarter, full moon, and last quarter); in *physics,* a particular stage or point of advancement in a series of periodical changes or movements (as, the *phase* of an alternating current, the stage or point at which it reaches a given relative value).—**in phase,** in *physics,* in the same phase.—**out of phase,** in *physics,* in a different phase, or in different phases.

pheas-ant (fez'ạnt), *n.* [AF. *fesant,* OF. F. *faisan,* < L. *phasianus,* < Gr. φασιανός, pheasant, < Φᾶσις, the river Phasis in Colchis.] Any of various large, long-tailed gallinaceous birds of the genus *Phasianus* and allied genera, orig. natives of Asia, esp. *P. colchicus* (the common pheasant), a game-bird which, with other species, has been introduced into Europe and America; also, any of various similar birds, specif. the ruffed grouse (southern U. S.).—**pheas'ant-ry** (-ri), *n.*; pl. *-ries* (-riz). A place where pheasants are bred and kept.—**pheas'ant's-eye,** *n.* Any of certain plants, as a ranunculaceous herb, *Adonis autumnalis,* cultivated for its scarlet or crimson flowers, or a variety of the common garden pink, *Dianthus plumarius.*

Common Pheasant (*Phasianus colchicus*).

phe-be (fē'bē), *n.* See *phœbe*[2].

phello-. Form of Gr. φελλός, cork, used in combination.—**phel-lo-derm** (fel'ọ-dėrm), *n.* [+ *-derm.*] In *bot.,* a layer of tissue in certain plants, formed from the inner cells of phellogen, and consisting usually of green parenchyma.—**phel-lo-der'mal,** *a.*—**phel'lo-gen** (-jen), *n.* [+ *-gen.*] In *bot.,* cork cambium, a layer of tissue or secondary meristem external to the true cambium and giving rise to cork tissue on the outside and phelloderm on the inside.—**phel-lo-gen'ic, phel''lo-ge-net'ic** (-jē-net'ik), *a.*

phen-. [Gr. φαίνειν, show, give light, shine; with reference orig. to products from the manufacture of illuminating gas.] A formative element used in chemical terms to indicate derivation from benzene: sometimes used with particular reference to phenol.

phe-na-ce-tin (fē-nas'ē-tin), *n.* [From *phen(etidin)* + *acet(yl)* + *-in.*] A crystalline organic compound used as an antipyretic, etc. Also called *acetphenetidin.*

phen-a-cite (fen'ạ-sīt), *n.* [Gr. φέναξ (φενακ-), cheat, impostor.] A vitreous mineral consisting of a silicate of beryllium, resembling quartz and sometimes mistaken for it, and occurring in rhombohedral crystals: sometimes used as a gem.

phen-a-kis-to-scope (fen-ạ-kis′tō̤-skōp), *n.* [Gr. φενακιστής, cheater, + σκοπεῖν, view.] A device for producing the representation of actual motion, as in leaping, walking, etc., usually consisting of a disk on which a figure, as of a person running, is pictured in successive positions, the effect of motion being produced by rotating the disk and viewing, through a series of slits in the disk, the reflection of the figures in a mirror.

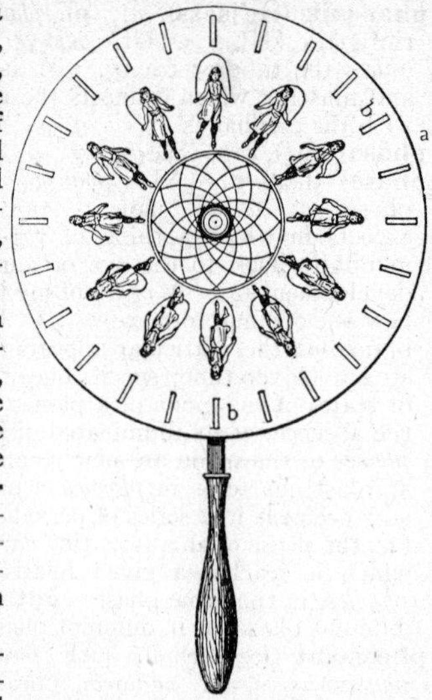

Phenakistoscope. — The disk *a* has drawn upon it the figures arranged in successive positions. It is rotated by spinning with the fingers applied to a small boss or nut in the rear (not shown in the cut). *b, b* are the slits through which the reflected images are viewed.

phe-na-zine (fē′nạ-zin or -zēn), *n.* [See *phen-* and *azote*.] In *chem.*, a yellowish crystalline organic compound, some derivatives of which are important dyes.—**phe′-na-zone** (-zōn), *n.* Antipyrine; also, a yellowish crystalline compound isomeric with phenazine.

phe-net-i-din (fē̤-net′i-din), *n.* [From *phenetol*.] In *chem.*, a liquid organic compound, a derivative of phenetol, used in making phenacetin, etc.

phe-ne-tol (fē′ne-tol or -tōl), *n.* [From *phen(yl)* + *et(hyl)* + *-ol*.] In *chem.*, the ethyl ether of phenol, a colorless volatile aromatic liquid.

Phe-ni-cian, Phœ-ni-cian (fē̤-nish′ạn). [L. *Phœnicia*, for *Phœnice*, < Gr. Φοινίκη, Phenicia, < Φοῖνιξ, a Phenician: cf. *Punic*.] **I.** *a.* Of or pertaining to Phenicia, an ancient country on the coast of Syria. **II.** *n.* A native or inhabitant of Phenicia; also, the ancient language of Phenicia, a Semitic tongue.

phe-nix, phœ-nix (fē′niks), *n.* [L. *phœnix*, < Gr. φοῖνιξ.] [Also *cap.*] A mythical bird of great beauty, the only one of its kind, fabled to live 500 or 600 years in the Arabian wilderness, to burn itself on a funeral pile, and to rise from its ashes in the freshness of youth and live through another cycle of years (often an emblem of immortality); hence [*l. c.*], a person or thing of peerless beauty or unique excellence; a paragon (as, "Picus of Mirandola . . . so justly called the *phœnix* of his age, and so extraordinarily gifted by nature": Hallam's "Literature of Europe," i. 3. § 96); also, something that rises from the ashes of its predecessor.

phe-no-cryst (fē′nō̤-krist), *n.* [Gr. φαίνειν, show, + κρύσταλλος, crystal.] Any of the conspicuous crystals in a porphyritic rock.

phe-no-gam (fē′nō̤-gam), etc. See *phænogam*, etc.

phe-nol (fē′nol or -nōl), *n.* [See *phen-*.] In *chem.*, carbolic acid, a hydroxyl derivative of benzene; also, any analogous hydroxyl derivative of benzene.—**phe-nol-ic** (fē̤-nol′ik), *a.* —**phe-nol-phthal′e-in** (-thal′ē̤-in), *n.* In *chem.*, a white crystalline compound formed by the interaction of phenol and phthalic anhydride: used to indicate the presence of alkalis, which turn it red, and also used medicinally as a purgative.

phe-nom-e-na (fē̤-nom′e-nặ), *n.* Plural of *phenomenon*.

phe-nom-e-nal (fē̤-nom′e-nạl), *a.* Of or pertaining to a phenomenon or phenomena; of the nature of a phenomenon; cognizable by the senses; often, extraordinary or prodigious (as, "Young Mr. Worthington stopped a ball flying at a *phenomenal* speed": W. Churchill's "Coniston," ii. 2).—**phe-nom′e-nal-ism,** *n.* The manner of thinking that considers things as phenomena only; also, the philosophical doctrine that phenomena are the only objects of knowledge, or that phenomena are the only realities.—**phe-nom′e-nal-ist,** *n.* An adherent of phenomenalism.—**phe-nom″e-nal-is′tic,** *a.*—**phe-nom′e-nal-ly,** *adv.*

phe-nom-e-nol-o-gy (fē̤-nom-e-nol′ō̤-ji), *n.* [See *phenomenon* and *-logy*.] The science of phenomena, as distinguished from ontology or the science of being; also, a description or history of phenomena.—**phe-nom″e-no-log′i-cal** (-nō̤-loj′i-kạl), *a.*

phe-nom-e-non (fē̤-nom′e-non), *n.*; pl. *-na* (-nặ). [LL. *phænomenon*, < Gr. φαινόμενον, neut. ppr. of φαίνεσθαι, appear, pass. of φαίνειν, show.] A thing that appears or is perceived; a fact, occurrence, or circumstance observed or observable (as, "a willingness to acquiesce in registering the *phenomena* of nature without seeking a revelation of her secrets," Hallam's "Literature of Europe," iii. 3. § 62; electrical *phenomena*; "These mutinies were of almost regular occurrence, and attended by as regular a series of *phenomena*," Motley's "Dutch Republic," iv. 1); also, something that impresses the observer as extraordinary; a remarkable thing or person (as, "You might have thought a goose the rarest of all birds — a feathered *phenomenon*," Dickens's "Christmas Carol," iii.; "This, sir . . . is the infant *phenomenon* — Miss Ninetta Crummles," Dickens's "Nicholas Nickleby," xxiii.); a prodigy; in *philos.*, an appearance or immediate object of experience; in the *Kantian philos.*, a thing as it appears to us, as distinguished from a noumenon, or thing in itself.

phe-nyl (fē′nil), *n.* [F. *phényle*, < Gr. φαίνειν, shine (see *phen-*), + ὕλη, matter.] In *chem.*, a univalent radical, C_6H_5, present in benzene, phenol, etc.—**phe′ny-lene** (-ni-lēn), *n.* In *chem.*, a bivalent organic radical, C_6H_4, which may be regarded as benzene with two of its hydrogen atoms removed.—**phe-nyl-ic** (fē̤-nil′ik), *a.*

Pher-e-cra-te-an (fer″e-krạ-tē′ạn). [From *Pherecrates* (5th century B.C.), Greek comic poet.] In *anc. pros.*: **I.** *a.* Noting or pertaining to a logaœdic tripody, catalectic or acatalectic, whose first or second foot is a dactyl, the others being trochees. **II.** *n.* A Pherecratean tripody or verse. —**Pher-e-crat′ic** (-krat′ik), *a.* and *n.*

phew (fū), *interj.* An exclamation of disgust, impatience, surprise, etc.: as, "*Phew!* . . . How close you womenfolks like to keep a room!" (Howells's "Rise of Silas Lapham," vii.).

phi (fī or fē), *n.* [Gr. φῖ.] The twenty-first letter (Φ, φ, = English ph) of the Greek alphabet.

phi-al (fī′ạl), *n.* and *v.* Same as *vial*.

Phid-i-an (fid′i-ạn), *a.* Of, pertaining to, or characteristic of Phidias (about 500 – about 432 B.C.), the celebrated Greek sculptor; associated with, or following the style of, Phidias (as, the *Phidian* school of sculpture, exemplified in the decorations of the Parthenon).

Phidian School of Sculpture. — From the eastern pediment of the Parthenon.

-phil, -phile. Termination from Greek φίλος, loving, friendly, also lover, friend, serving to form adjectives and nouns, as *Anglophil*, *bibliophile*, *demophil*, *Francophil*, *negrophil*.

phil-a-del-phi-an (fil-ạ-del′fi-ạn). [Gr. φιλαδελφία, brotherly love, < φιλάδελφος, having brotherly love, < φίλος, loving, + ἀδελφός, brother: cf. Gr. Φιλαδέλφεια, Philadelphia (name of cities in Asia Minor, so called from rulers surnamed *Philadelphus*).] **I.** *a.* Having or showing brotherly love, esp. for one's fellow-beings. **II.** *n.* One imbued with brotherly love, esp. for his fellow-beings.

Phi-lan-der (fi-lan′dėr), *n.* [Gr. φίλανδρος, loving men, < φιλεῖν, love, + ἀνήρ (ἀνδρ-), man.] A name given to a lover in old romance, poetry, etc.; [*l. c.*] a lover†, or a man given to making love†; also, a course of philandering.—**phi-lan′der,** *v. i.* Of a man, to make love, esp. without serious intentions; carry on a sentimental flirtation: as, "He had meant no harm, nothing worse than some pretty *philandering* with the loveliest woman of her time" (G. Meredith's "Diana of the Crossways," xiii.).—**phi-lan′der-er,** *n.*

phil-an-thrope (fil′ạn-thrōp), *n.* [F. *philanthrope*, < Gr. φιλάνθρωπος, loving mankind, < φιλεῖν, love, +

ἄνθρωπος, man.] One who loves mankind and seeks to promote their welfare; a philanthropist. Cf. *misanthrope.* —**phil-an-throp′ic** (-throp′ik), *a.* Of, pertaining to, or characterized by philanthropy; benevolent. Also **phil-an-throp′i-cal.**—**phil-an-throp′i-cal-ly,** *adv.*—**phi-lan-thro-pist** (fi-lan′thrō-pist), *n.* One who practises philanthropy. —**phi-lan′thro-py** (-pi), *n.*; pl. *-pies* (-piz). [Gr. φιλανθρωπία, < φιλάνθρωπος.] Love of mankind, esp. as manifested in deeds of practical beneficence; also, a philanthropic action, work, institution, or the like.

phi-lat-e-ly (fi-lat′ę-li), *n.* [F. *philatélie,* < Gr. φιλεῖν, love, + ἀτελής, free of tax (since a stamped letter is without further charge), < ἀ- priv. + τέλος, tax.] The collecting of postage-stamps, stamped envelops and post-cards, etc., as objects of interest and study; the pursuit of collecting postage-stamps.—**phil-a-tel-ic** (fil-ạ-tel′ik), *a.*—**phi-lat′e-list,** *n.*

-phile. See *-phil.*

phi-le-nor (fi-lē′nọr), *n.* [NL., < Gr. φιλήνωρ, loving one's husband, < φιλεῖν, love, + ἀνήρ, man.] A handsome North American swallow-tailed butterfly, *Papilio philenor,* having black fore wings and steel-blue hind wings, all with greenish reflections.

Philenor.

phil-har-mon-ic (fil-här-mon′ik), *a.* [See *philo-.*] Loving harmony; fond of music; music-loving: used esp. in the name of certain musical societies ('Philharmonic Society'), and hence applied to the concerts of such societies ('Philharmonic concerts').

Phil-hel-lene (fil-hel′ēn). [See *philo-,* and cf. Gr. φιλέλλην, adj.] **I.** *a.* Loving the Hellenes or Greeks; favoring or supporting the cause of the Greeks, as in their struggle against the Turks for independence. **II.** *n.* A friend or supporter of the Greeks.—**Phil-hel-len′ic** (-he-len′ik), *a.* —**Phil-hel′len-ism** (-hel′en-izm), *n.* Philhellene spirit or principles.—**Phil-hel′len-ist,** *n.*

phil-i-beg (fil′i-beg), *n.* See *filibeg.*

Phi-lip-pi-an (fi-lip′i-ạn). [L. *Philippianus.*] **I.** *a.* Of or pertaining to Philippi, a city of ancient Macedonia. **II.** *n.* A native or inhabitant of Philippi; *pl.,* the book of the New Testament called in full "The Epistle of Paul the Apostle to the Philippians."

Phi-lip-pic (fi-lip′ik), *n.* [L. *Philippicus,* < Gr. Φιλιππικός, pertaining to Philip.] Any of the orations delivered by Demosthenes, the Athenian orator, in the 4th century B.C., against Philip, king of Macedon; hence [*l. c.*], any discourse or speech of bitter denunciation (as, "With what satisfaction did I remember all Miss Debby Kittery's *philippics* against Ellery Davenport!" Mrs. Stowe's "Oldtown Folks," xxxvi.; "The scorn he put into those two words was more withering than a whole *philippic* against redemption by creature comforts," Galsworthy's "Patrician," ii. 7).

phil-ip-pi-na (fil-i-pē′nạ̈), *n.* Same as *philopena.*

Phil-ip-pine (fil′i-pēn). [Sp. *Filipino* (*Islas Filipinas,* Philippine Islands, named from Philip II. of Spain).] **I.** *a.* Of or pertaining to the Philippine Islands or their inhabitants. **II.** *n.* *Pl.,* the Philippine Islands.

Phi-lis-ti-a (fi-lis′ti-ạ̈), *n.* [ML.] The country occupied by the ancient Philistines, on the southwest coast of Palestine; the nation of the Philistines; also, the place or sphere of existence of Philistines, or uncultured, commonplace persons; the class or body of such Philistines.

Phi-lis-tine (fi-lis′tin or fil′is-, also, esp. Brit., fil′is-tīn). [LL. *Philistini,* pl.] **I.** *n.* One of a warlike ancient people inhabiting Philistia, and frequently at strife with the Israelites (as, "He shall begin to deliver Israel out of the hand of the *Philistines*": Judges, xiii. 5); hence, an enemy, or one regarded as an enemy (commonly in *pl.,* and often used of bailiffs, creditors, critics, etc.: as, "I must make an effort to advance what farther will be required to take my friend out of the hands of the *Philistines,*" Smollett's "Humphry Clinker," Oct. 26); also, one looked down upon as lacking in and indifferent to enlightenment, culture, esthetic refinement, etc., or contentedly commonplace in ideas and tastes (as, "anxious as I am to be a systematic *Philistine* . . . and generally to antagonise æsthetic prigs," H. G. Wells's "Italy, France, and Britain at War," ii. 2; "You are a *Philistine,* Henry: you have no romance in you," G. B. Shaw's "Man and Superman," iii.). **II.** *a.* Belonging or pertaining to the ancient Philistines (as, Goliath, the *Philistine* champion); also, belonging to or characteristic of the Philistines of the modern kind; lacking in culture; commonplace.—**Phi-lis′tin-ism,** *n.* The character or views of Philistines, or uncultured, commonplace persons.

philo-, phil-. Forms of Gr. φιλεῖν, love, or φίλος, loved. loving, used in combination.

phil-o-bib-lic (fil-ō-bib′lik), *a.* [Gr. φιλόβιβλος, < φιλεῖν, love, + βίβλος, book.] Fond of books; bibliophilous. —**phil-o-bib′list,** *n.* A lover of books; a bibliophile.

phi-log-y-nist (fi-loj′i-nist), *n.* [Gr. φιλογύνης, fond of women, < φιλεῖν, love, + γυνή, woman.] A lover or admirer of women. Cf. *misogynist.*—**phi-log′y-nous,** *a.* Loving women.—**phi-log′y-ny,** *n.* Love of women.

phi-lol-o-ger (fi-lol′ō-jėr), *n.* A philologist. [Archaic.]

phil-o-log-ic, phil-o-log-i-cal (fil-ō-loj′ik, -i-kạl), *a.* Of or pertaining to philology; concerned with the study of language.—**phil-o-log′i-cal-ly,** *adv.*

phi-lol-o-gist (fi-lol′ō-jist), *n.* One versed in philology.

phil-o-logue (fil′ō-log), *n.* [F.] A philologist.

phi-lol-o-gy (fi-lol′ō-ji), *n.* [L. *philologia,* < Gr. φιλολογία, love of learning and literature, study of language, < φιλεῖν, love, + λόγος, word, speech.] Literary scholarship†, or polite learning†; also, the study of literature, or of literary and other records (as, "how and for what purposes to investigate the literature of any people (*philology* in the more proper sense)": Encyc. Brit., 11th ed., XXI. 415); specif., the study or the science of language, its origin, development, laws, forms or branches, etc. (as, general or historical *philology*; Teutonic *philology*; English *philology*; comparative *philology,* which proceeds by comparison of different languages or tongues, in order to determine their common and their distinctive features, and hence their relations, classification, origins, etc.); linguistics.

phil-o-math (fil′ō-math), *n.* [Gr. φιλομαθής, fond of learning, < φιλεῖν, love, + μανθάνειν, learn.] A lover of learning; a student, esp. of mathematics or science; formerly, an astrologer†.—**phil-o-math′ic,** *a.*—**phi-lom-a-thy** (fi-lom′ạ-thi), *n.* Love of learning.

Phil-o-mel, Phil-o-me-la (fil′ō-mel, fil-ō-mē′lạ̈), *n.* [F. *philomèle,* L. *philomela,* < Gr. φιλομήλα, nightingale; associated with *Philomela,* daughter of King Pandion of Athens, who was fabled to have been turned into a nightingale.] The nightingale: used as a proper name: as, "All night long sweet *Philomel* pours forth her ravishing, delightful song" (Smollett's "Humphry Clinker," April 21). [Poetic.]

phil-o-pe-na (fil-ō-pē′nạ̈), *n.* [= F. *philippine,* appar. a corruption of G. *vielliebchen,* sweetheart, also philopena.] A friendly or playful practice by which when two persons have by agreement shared a nut with two kernels, or the like, the person who fails subsequently to meet certain conditions is bound to pay the other a forfeit; also, the thing shared, or the forfeit paid.

phil-o-pro-gen-i-tive-ness (fil″ō-prō-jen′i-tiv-nes), *n.* [See *philo-* and *progeny.*] In *phren.,* love of offspring; fondness for the young in general.

phi-los-o-pher (fi-los′ō-fėr), *n.* [OF. F. *philosophe,* < L. *philosophus,* < Gr. φιλόσοφος, lover of wisdom, philosopher, < φιλεῖν, love, + σοφός, wise.] A lover of wisdom, or one devoted to the search for fundamental truth; one versed in philosophy; formerly, an alchemist, or one versed in some other occult science (see *philosophers' stone,* following); also, a person who regulates his life, actions, judgments, utterances, etc., by the light of philosophy or reason (as, "He's . . . such a perfect *philosopher,* that he looks on all superfluities with the most sovereign contempt," Smollett's "Humphry Clinker," May 10; "I am naturally a *philosopher,* and no one can moralize better after a misfortune has taken place," Irving's "Tales of a Traveler," ii. 7); one who is philosophic, esp. under trying circumstances.—**philosophers' stone,** in *alchemy*, an imaginary solid substance or preparation believed to have the property of transmuting baser metals into gold or silver, and (by some) of prolonging life. Cf. *elixir*.

phil-o-soph-ic, phil-o-soph-i-cal (fil-ǫ-sof′ik, -i-kąl), *a.* [L. *philosophicus.*] Of or pertaining to philosophy (as, *philosophic*, or *philosophical*, studies or writings); sometimes, esp. formerly, of or pertaining to natural philosophy or physical science (as, "*Philosophic* tube, That brings the planets home into the eye Of observation," Cowper's "Task," iii. 229; a *philosophical* toy, such as the Cartesian devil); versed in or occupied with philosophy, as persons; also, proper to or befitting a philosopher, or showing the characteristics of a philosopher (as, "They were mostly scholarly, quiet men, of calm and *philosophic* temperament," Mrs. Stowe's "Oldtown Folks," i.; a *philosophical* historian); controlled by reason, as in action, thought, or speech; wise, dispassionate, or temperate; esp., rationally or sensibly calm under trying circumstances (as, to be *philosophic* in defeat; a *philosophical* acceptance of necessity).—**phil-o-soph′i-cal-ly,** *adv.*

phi-los-o-phism (fi-los′ǫ-fizm), *n.* Philosophizing; often, the affectation of philosophy; spurious philosophy.—**phi-los′o-phist** (-fist), *n.*

phi-los-o-phize (fi-los′ǫ-fīz), *v.*; *-phized, -phizing.* **I.** *intr.* To think or reason as a philosopher; speculate or theorize; moralize (as, "You are come . . . to *philosophize* to me, and to put me in the way of dying like Chione": J. H. Newman's "Callista," xi.). **II.** *tr.* To render philosophic; give a philosophic character to (doctrines, etc.); treat (a subject, etc.) in a philosophic manner.—**phi-los′o-phiz-er** (-fī-zėr), *n.*

phi-los-o-phy (fi-los′ǫ-fi), *n.*; pl. *-phies* (-fiz). [OF. F. *philosophie*, < L. *philosophia*, < Gr. φιλοσοφία, < φιλόσοφος: see *philosopher*.] The love or pursuit of wisdom; hence, the study or science of the truths or principles underlying all knowledge; any one of the three branches ('natural philosophy,' 'moral philosophy,' and 'metaphysical philosophy') accepted as composing this science; esp., metaphysical science; metaphysics; also, the study or science of the principles of a particular branch or subject of knowledge (as, the *philosophy* of history); also, a system of philosophical doctrine (as, the Stoic *philosophy*; the *philosophy* of Spinoza, Locke, or Kant); also, a system of principles for guidance in practical affairs (as, "Eat, drink, and be merry, that's my *philosophy*, that's my religion": J. H. Newman's "Callista," xxii.); also, philosophic spirit or attitude; wise composure throughout the vicissitudes of life.

-philous. Adjective termination from Gr. φίλος, loving, as in *anthophilous, dendrophilous, heliophilous*.

phil-ter, phil-tre (fil′tėr), *n.* [F. *philtre*, < L. *philtrum*, < Gr. φίλτρον, love-charm, < φιλεῖν, love.] A potion, drug, or the like, supposed to induce love; a love-potion; loosely, a magic potion for any purpose (as, "Tell me now, fairy . . . can't you give me a charm, or a *philtre*, or something of that sort, to make me a handsome man?" C. Brontë's "Jane Eyre," xxii.).—**phil′ter, phil′tre,** *v. t.*; *-tered, -tred, -tering, -tring.* To charm with a philter.

phiz (fiz), *n.* [Abbr. of *physiognomy*.] The face; the countenance: as, "There was no mistaking that tanned, genial *phiz* of his" (Aldrich's "Story of a Bad Boy," xx.). [Colloq.]

phle-bi-tis (flę-bī′tis), *n.* [NL., < Gr. φλέψ (φλεβ-), vein.] In *pathol.*, inflammation of a vein.—**phle-bit′ic** (-bit′ik), *a.*

phleb-o-scle-ro-sis (fleb″ǫ-sklę-rō′sis), *n.* [NL., < Gr. φλέψ (φλεβ-), vein, + σκλήρωσις, a hardening.] In *pathol.*, sclerosis or hardening of the walls of the veins, esp. of the intima.—**phleb″o-scle-rot′ic** (-rot′ik), *a.*

phle-bot-o-mize (flę-bot′ǫ-mīz), *v. t.*; *-mized, -mizing.* To subject to phlebotomy; bleed.—**phle-bot′o-mist,** *n.*

phle-bot-o-my (flę-bot′ǫ-mi), *n.* [OF. *flebothomie* (F. *phlébotomie*), < LL. *phlebotomia*, < Gr. φλεβοτομία, < φλέψ (φλεβ-), vein, + τέμνειν, cut.] In *med.*, the act or practice of opening a vein for letting blood; bleeding.

Phleg-e-thon (fleg′e-thon or flej′-), *n.* [L., < Gr. Φλεγέθων, prop. ppr. of φλεγέθειν, burn, blaze.] A fabled river of fire in Hades, the lower world of Greek mythology; hence [*cap.* or *l. c.*], a stream of fire or fiery light (as, "Heaven flows in a fierce *phlegethon* With the far-flashing wave for a brim": Eden Phillpotts's "Cherry-Stones," Sea Sunset).

phlegm (flem), *n.* [OF. *fleume, flemme* (F. *flegme*), < LL. *phlegma*, phlegm, < Gr. φλέγμα, flame, heat, inflammation, clammy humor, phlegm, < φλέγειν, burn.] The thick mucus secreted in the respiratory passages and discharged by coughing, etc., esp. that occurring in the lungs and throat passages during a cold, etc.; also, in the old physiology, that one of the four humors supposed when predominant to cause sluggishness or apathy; hence, phlegmatic temperament; sluggishness or apathy; coolness or self-possession.

phleg-mat-ic (fleg-mat′ik), *a.* [OF. *fleumatique* (F. *flegmatique*), < LL. *phlegmaticus*, < Gr. φλεγματικός.] Of the nature of or abounding in phlegm; also, having or showing the disposition or temperament supposed to result from predominance of the bodily humor 'phlegm'; not easily excited to action or feeling; sluggish or apathetic; cool or self-possessed.—**phleg-mat′i-cal-ly,** *adv.*

phleg-mon (fleg′mon), *n.* [L. *phlegmon, phlegmone*, < Gr. φλεγμονή, fiery heat, inflammation, boil, < φλέγειν, burn.] In *pathol.*, inflammation (usually suppurative) of the connective tissue, esp. the subcutaneous connective tissue.—**phleg′mo-nous** (-mǫ-nus), *a.*

phlegm-y (flem′i), *a.* Of the nature of or characterized by phlegm; also, phlegmatic.

phlob-a-phene (flob′ą-fēn), *n.* [Gr. φλόος, φλοιός, bark, + βαφή, dyeing, dye.] In *chem.*, any of various reddish-brown substances found in the bark of the oak, etc.

phlo-ëm (flō′em), *n.* [G., < Gr. φλόος, φλοιός, bark.] In *bot.*, that part of a vascular bundle not included in the xylem, usually comprising the softer and outer portion; bast tissue.

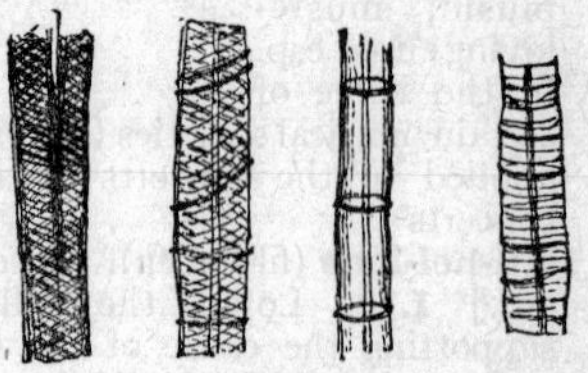
Portions of Phloëm, showing oblique and transverse striation of the cell-walls.

phlo-gis-tic (flǫ-jis′tik), *a.* In *old chem.*, pertaining to or consisting of phlogiston; in *pathol.*, inflammatory.

phlo-gis-ton (flǫ-jis′tǫn), *n.* [NL., < Gr. φλογιστόν, neut. of φλογιστός, inflammable, < φλογίζειν, set on fire, < φλόξ (φλογ-), flame: see *phlox*.] In *old chem.*, the principle of inflammability, a hypothetical substance formerly thought to exist in all combustible bodies.

phlog-o-pite (flog′ǫ-pīt), *n.* [G. *phlogopit*, < Gr. φλογωπός, fiery-looking, < φλόξ (φλογ-), flame, + ὤψ (ὠπ-), eye, face.] A kind of mica, usually of a yellowish-brown color, but sometimes reddish-brown or coppery.

phlo-go-sis (flǫ-gō′sis), *n.* [NL., < Gr. φλόγωσις, < φλόξ (φλογ-), flame: see *phlox*.] In *pathol.*, inflammation.—**phlo-got′ic** (-got′ik), *a.*

phlor-i-zin (flor′i-zin or flǫ-rī′zin), *n.* [Gr. φλόος, φλοιός, bark, + ῥίζα, root.] In *chem.*, a bitter crystalline glucoside obtained from the root-bark of the apple, pear, cherry, etc., and used as a tonic and antiperiodic and in testing the functional activity of the kidneys.

phlox (floks), *n.* [L., < Gr. φλόξ, kind of plant, orig. flame, < φλέγειν, burn.] Any of the herbs constituting the polemoniaceous genus *Phlox*, native in North America, many of which are cultivated for their cymes or panicles of showy flowers of various colors: as, "a cottage garden, gay with the pinks and carmines of the *phloxes*" (Mrs. H. Ward's "Robert Elsmere," xiii.).

Flowers of Phlox (*P. drummondii*).

phlox-in (flok′sin), *n.* [Gr. φλόξ, flame: see *phlox*.] A red coal-tar dye, resembling eosin.

phlyc-te-na, phlyc-tæ-na (flik-tē′nạ), *n.*; pl. *-næ* (-nē). [NL., < Gr. φλύκταινα, < φλύειν, bubble up.] In *pathol.*, a small vesicle, blister, or pustule.

-phobe. [Gr. -φόβος, fearing, < φέβεσθαι, flee in fear.] A noun termination meaning 'one who fears or dreads,' and often implying aversion or hatred, as in *Anglophobe, Gallophobe, negrophobe.*

pho-bi-a (fō′bi-ạ̈), *n.* [Noun use of *-phobia.*] Any obsessing or morbid fear or dread.

-phobia. [Gr. -φοβία, < -φόβος, fearing: see *-phobe.*] A noun termination meaning 'fear' or 'dread,' often of a morbid nature, or with implication of aversion or hatred, as in *ælurophobia, Anglophobia, hydrophobia, monophobia, negrophobia.*

pho-cine (fō′sin), *a.* [L. *phoca,* < Gr. φώκη, seal.] Of or pertaining to the seals; esp., belonging to the *Phocinæ,* a subfamily containing the typical seals.

Phœ-be[1] (fē′bẹ), *n.* [L., < Gr. Φοίβη, prop. fem. of φοῖβος, bright: cf. *Phœbus.*] Artemis (Diana) as goddess of the moon; hence, the moon personified (poetic).

phœ-be[2] (fē′bẹ), *n.* [Imit. of its note; with spelling conformed to *Phœbe*[1].] Any of certain small American birds, flycatchers of the genus *Sayornis* (family *Tyrannidæ*), esp. *Sayornis phœbe* of eastern North America. Also **phœ′be=bird.**

Phœbe (*Sayornis phœbe*).

Phœ-bus (fē′bus), *n.* [L., < Gr. Φοῖβος, < φοῖβος, bright: cf. *Phœbe*[1].] Apollo as the sun-god; hence, the sun personified (poetic: as, "Hark, hark! the lark at heaven's gate sings, And *Phœbus* 'gins arise," Shakspere's "Cymbeline," ii. 3. 22).—**Phœ-be′an,** *a.*

phœ-ni-ca-ceous (fē-ni-kā′shius), *a.* [NL. *Phœnix,* the date-palm genus, < Gr. φοῖνιξ, date-palm.] Belonging to the *Phœnicaceæ,* or palm family of plants.

Phœ-ni-cian (fẹ-nish′ạn), **phœ-nix** (fē′niks). See *Phenician, phenix.*

pho-nate (fō′nāt), *v. i.* or *t.*; *-nated, -nating.* [Gr. φωνή, sound, voice.] To utter (vocal sound).—**pho-na-tion** (fọ-nā′shọn), *n.*

pho-nau-to-graph (fọ-nâ′tọ-grȧf), *n.* [Gr. φωνή, sound, + αὐτός, self, + γράφειν, write.] An instrument, invented about 1855, for registering (in a zigzag line on a rotating and advancing horizontal cylinder) the vibrations of sound: a forerunner of the phonograph, the gramophone, etc.—**pho-nau-to-graph′ic** (-graf′ik), *a.*

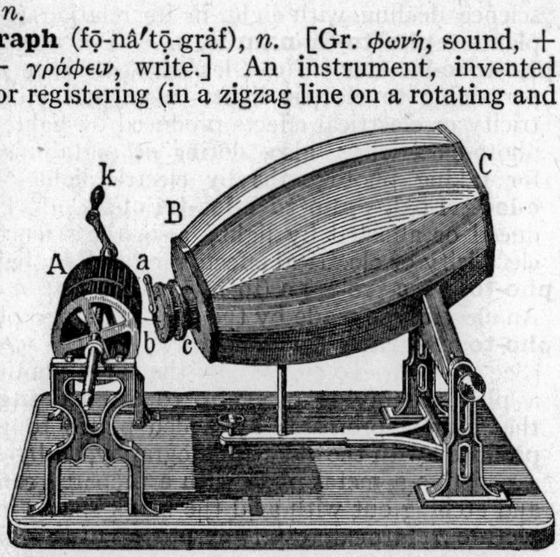

Phonautograph. — *BC,* barrel with opening at *C*; *c,* brass tube with membrane and style at *b,* and movable piece *a,* by which the position of the nodal points can be regulated; *k,* handle to turn cylinder (*A*) covered with paper coated with lampblack.

phone[1] (fōn), *n.* [Gr. φωνή, sound, voice.] In *phonetics,* a simple vocal sound; a primary element of speech.

phone[2] (fōn), *n.* and *v.* Shortened form of *telephone.* [Colloq.]

-phone. Noun termination from Gr. φωνή, sound, voice, as in *graphophone, megaphone, telephone.*

pho-net-ic (fọ-net′ik), *a.* [NL. *phoneticus,* < Gr. φωνητικός, < φωνεῖν, utter sound, < φωνή, sound, voice.] Pertaining to the human voice as used in speech, or to articulate sounds, their mode of production, relations, combinations, and changes (as, *phonetic* science); also, representing speech-sounds or the pronunciation of words, as signs or characters (as, a *phonetic* mode of writing, in contradistinction to an ideographic or pictorial one); specif., representing the individual elementary sounds of speech by letters or characters indicating always the same spoken sound (as, a *phonetic* mode of spelling the words of a language, in contradistinction to a traditional, historical, or etymological one).—**pho-net′i-cal-ly,** *adv.*—**pho-ne-ti-cian** (fō-ne-tish′ạn), *n.* One versed in phonetics.—**pho-net′ics,** *n.* Phonetic science; that division of language-study which deals with speech-sounds; phonology.—**pho-ne-tism** (fō′ne-tizm), *n.* The use of a phonetic system of writing or spelling.—**pho′ne-tist,** *n.* A phonetician; also, one who uses or advocates phonetic spelling.

pho′ney, *a.* See *phony.*

phon-ic (fon′ik), *a.* [Gr. φωνή, sound, voice.] Of or pertaining to sound; esp., pertaining to or of the nature of speech-sounds; phonetic.—**phon′ics,** *n.* The science of sound; esp., the science of speech-sounds; phonetics.

phono-. Form of Gr. φωνή, sound, voice, used in combination.

pho-no-film (fō′nọ-film), *n.* [See *phono-* and *film.*] A device (invented by Dr. Lee de Forest) for making a photographic record of sound and for reproducing it, sound waves being translated into electrical fluctuations, electrical fluctuations into light fluctuations, and the light fluctuations registered on a moving film, the order being reversed in reproducing the sound from the film: used esp. to supplement moving pictures with synchronized sound, as of speech, singing, etc., in which case the sound record is made on the edge of the moving-picture film. [Proprietary name.]—**pho′no-film,** *v. t.* To record, or record the speech, etc., of, by the phonofilm.

pho-no-gram (fō′nọ-gram), *n.* [See *phono-* and *-gram.*] A character or symbol representing a single speech-sound, a syllable, or a word; also, a phonograph record.

pho-no-graph (fō′nọ-grȧf), *n.* [See *phono-* and *-graph.*] An instrument invented in 1877 by Thomas A. Edison, for recording and reproducing speech, music, and other sounds, and consisting of a mechanism by which sound-vibrations produce characteristic indentations or (later) incisions of varying depth in a line of one direction in the impressible surface-covering (early of tin-foil, later of wax, etc.) of a rotating and advancing cylinder, and by which the record thus formed or a reproduction of it is subsequently employed to reproduce the sound-vibrations; in later use, any sound-reproducing machine employing for the record a rotating cylinder with indentations or incisions of varying depth; any talking-machine whatever, whether employing such a cylinder, a disk with such indentations or incisions, or the type of disk used in the gramophone. Cf. *phonautograph, graphophone,* and *gramophone.*

pho-no-graph-ic (fō-nọ-graf′ik), *a.* Of or pertaining to phonography (either phonetic spelling or phonetic shorthand); also, pertaining to the phonograph.—**pho-no-graph′i-cal-ly,** *adv.*

pho-nog-ra-phy (fọ-nog′rạ-fi), *n.* [See *phono-* and *-graphy.*] The art of writing according to sound; phonetic spelling; a system of phonetic shorthand invented by Sir Isaac Pitman in 1837; phonetic shorthand in general; also, the construction or use of phonographs.

pho-no-lite (fō′nọ-līt), *n.* [See *phono-* and *-lite.*] Any of a group of green, gray, or brown volcanic rocks containing much alkali feldspar and nepheline, and commonly splitting into pieces which ring on being struck. Cf. *clinkstone.*—**pho-no-lit′ic** (-lit′ik), *a.*

pho-nol-o-gy (fọ-nol′ọ̄-ji), *n.* [See *phono-* and *-logy.*] The science of speech-sounds; phonetics; esp., the study of the sounds of a particular language; also, the system of sounds used in a language.—**pho-no-log-ic, pho-no-log-i-cal** (fō-nọ-loj′ik, -i-kạl), *a.*—**pho-nol′o-gist,** *n.*

phon-o-ma-ni-a (fon-ọ-mā′ni-ạ̈), *n.* [NL., < Gr. φόνος, murder, slaughter, + μανία, E. *mania.*] In *pathol.,* a mania for murder or killing.

pho-nom-e-ter (fọ-nom′e-tėr), *n.* [See *phono-* and *-meter.*] An instrument for measuring the intensity of sound; also, an instrument for determining the number of vibrations of a sonorous body, as a tuning-fork, in a unit of time.—**pho-no-met-ric** (fō-nọ-met′rik), *a.*

pho-no-scope (fō′nọ-skōp), *n.* [See *phono-* and *-scope.*] Any of various devices by which sound is indicated by the optical phenomena it is made to produce; also, a device for testing the quality of strings for musical instruments; also, a microphone.

pho-no-type (fō'nọ-tīp), *n.* [See *phono-* and *type.*] A type bearing a phonetic character or symbol, as of a system of phonetic spelling or phonetic shorthand; also, phonetic type or print.—**pho-no-typ'ic** (-tip'ik), *a.*—**pho'no-ty-py** (-tī-pi), *n.*

pho-ny (fō'ni), *a.* [Origin uncertain.] Not genuine; spurious, counterfeit, or bogus; fraudulent. [Slang.]

-phore. [Gr. -φόρος, bearing: see *-phorous.*] A noun termination meaning 'bearer,' 'thing or part bearing (something),' as in *anthophore, gonophore, ommatophore.*

-phorous. [Gr. -φόρος, bearing, < φέρειν, bear.] An adjective termination meaning 'bearing,' 'having,' as in *anthophorous, rhynchophorous.*

phos-gene (fos'jēn), *n.* [Gr. φῶς, light, + -γενής, produced.] In *chem.*, carbonyl chloride; *milit.*, a dangerous poisonous gas used (first by the Germans) in shells; in *physiol.*, phosphene.—**phos'gen-ite** (-jẹ-nīt), *n.* A mineral consisting of chloride of lead and carbonate of lead, occurring in tetragonal crystals having an adamantine luster.

phos-phate (fos'fāt), *n.* [F. *phosphate,* < *phosphore,* phosphorus.] A salt of phosphoric acid; also, a fertilizing material containing such salts.—**phos-phat'ic** (-fat'ik), *a.* Pertaining to, of the nature of, or containing a phosphate or phosphates.—**phos'pha-tize** (-fạ-tīz), *v. t.*; *-tized, -tizing.* To change to the form of a phosphate; also, to treat with phosphates.—**phos-pha-tu'ri-a** (-tū'ri-ạ), *n.* [NL.: see *-uria.*] In *pathol.*, the presence of an excessive quantity of phosphates in the urine.

phos-phene (fos'fēn), *n.* [F. *phosphène,* < Gr. φῶς, light, + φαίνειν, show.] In *physiol.*, a luminous image produced by mechanical stimulation of the retina, as by pressing the eyeball with the finger when the lid is closed.

phos-phide (fos'fīd or -fid), *n.* In *chem.*, a compound of phosphorus with a basic element or radical.

phos-phine (fos'fin or -fēn), *n.* In *chem.*, phosphureted hydrogen, a colorless, poisonous, ill-smelling gas, PH_3, which when prepared in certain ways is spontaneously inflammable; hence, any of certain organic derivatives of this compound; in *dyeing*, a coal-tar coloring matter used chiefly for dyeing leather a reddish yellow.—**phos-phin'ic** (-fin'ik), *a.*

phos-phite (fos'fīt), *n.* [F. *phosphite,* < *phosphore,* phosphorus.] In *chem.*, a salt of phosphorous acid.

phos-pho-ni-um (fos-fō'ni-um), *n.* [NL., < *phosph(orus)* + *(amm)onium.*] In *chem.*, a univalent radical analogous to ammonium, composed of four atoms of hydrogen and one of phosphorus (PH_4).

Phos-phor (fos'fọr), *n.* [L. *Phosphorus*: see *phosphorus.*] The morning star, or Lucifer (poetic); [*l. c.*] any phosphorescent substance; specif. (in composition), phosphorus.

phos-pho-rate (fos'fọ-rāt), *v. t.*; *-rated, -rating.* In *chem.*, to combine or impregnate with phosphorus.

phos-pho-resce (fos-fọ-res'), *v. i.*; *-resced, -rescing.* [See *-esce.*] To be luminous without sensible heat, as phosphorus; exhibit phosphorescence.—**phos-pho-res'cence** (-res'ẹns), *n.* The property of being luminous at temperatures below incandescence, as from slow oxidation, as in the case of phosphorus, or after exposure to light or other radiation; also, the luminous appearance.—**phos-pho-res'cent,** *a.* Exhibiting phosphorescence.—**phos-pho-res'cent-ly,** *adv.*

phos-phor-ic (fos-for'ik), *a.* Phosphorescent; in *chem.*, pertaining to or containing the element phosphorus, esp. in its higher valence.

phos-pho-rite (fos'fọ-rīt), *n.* A massive form of the mineral apatite; also, any of various compact or earthy, more or less impure varieties of native calcium phosphate.

phos-pho-ro-scope (fos'fọ-rọ-skōp), *n.* [F., < NL. *phosphorus,* phosphorus, + Gr. σκοπεῖν, view.] An instrument for measuring the duration of evanescent phosphorescence in different substances.

phos-pho-rous (fos'fọ-rus), *a.* Phosphorescent; in *chem.*, pertaining to or containing the element phosphorus, esp. in its lower valence.

phos-pho-rus (fos'fọ-rus), *n.* [L. *Phosphorus,* Phosphor (NL. *phosphorus,* phosphorus), < Gr. Φωσφόρος, lit. 'light-bringer,' < φῶς, light, + φέρειν, bear.] [*cap.*] The morning star; Phosphor; [*l. c.*] any phosphorescent substance (now rare); in *chem.*, a solid non-metallic element (chem. sym., P; at. wt., 31.04), existing in at least two allotropic forms, one yellow, poisonous, and inflammable, and luminous in the dark, the other red, non-poisonous, and less inflammable.

phos-phu-ret† (fos'fū-ret), *n.* A phosphide.—**phos'phu-ret-ed, phos'phu-ret-ted,** *a.* In *chem.*, combined with phosphorus.—**phosphureted hydrogen,** phosphine.

-phote. Termination from Gr. φῶς (φωτ-), light, used to form nouns and adjectives, as *holophote, monophote, telephote.*

pho-tic (fō'tik), *a.* [Gr. φῶς (φωτ-), light.] Of or pertaining to light.—**pho'tics,** *n.* The science of light.

photo-. Form of Gr. φῶς (φωτ-), light, in combination: sometimes used to represent *photographic* or *photograph.*

pho-to (fō'tō), *n.*; pl. *photos* (-tōz). Shortened form of *photograph.* [Colloq.]

pho-to-chem-is-try (fō-tọ-kem'is-tri), *n.* [See *photo-.*] The branch of chemistry that deals with the chemical action of light.—**pho-to-chem'i-cal,** *a.*

pho-to-chrome (fō'tọ-krōm), *n.* [From *photo-* (for *photograph*) + Gr. χρῶμα, color.] A photograph in colors; a colored picture produced by photochromy.—**pho'to-chro-my** (-krō-mi), *n.* The art of producing photographs which show objects in their natural colors.

pho-to-chron-o-graph (fō-tọ-kron'ọ-gráf), *n.* [See *photo-.*] A device for taking instantaneous photographs at regular and generally short intervals of time, as of a bird, a horse, a projectile, etc., in motion; a picture taken by such a device; also, an instrument for recording the transit of a star by means of photography; also, a chronograph in which the tracing or record is made by the action of a pencil of light on a sensitized surface.

pho-to-dra-ma (fō'tọ-drä"mạ), *n.* [See *photo-.*] A drama presented, or arranged to be presented, in moving pictures; a photoplay.—**pho"to-dra-mat'ic** (-drạ-mat'ik), *a.*—**pho-to-dram'a-tist** (-dram'ạ-tist), *n.* A writer of photodramas.

pho-to-dy-nam-ics (fō"tọ-dī-nam'iks), *n.* [See *photo-.*] The science dealing with the energy of light; specif., the science dealing with light in its relation to movement in plants.—**pho"to-dy-nam'ic,** *a.*

pho-to=e-lec-tric (fō"tọ-ẹ-lek'trik), *a.* [See *photo-.*] Of or pertaining to electric light; also, pertaining to the electricity or electrical effects produced by light; pertaining to photo-electricity; also, noting or pertaining to apparatus for taking photographs by electric light. Also **pho"to=e-lec'tri-cal.**—**pho"to=e-lec-tri'ci-ty,** *n.* Electricity produced or affected by light; also, the science dealing with electricity or electrical effects produced by light.

pho-to=e-lec-tro-type (fō"tọ-ẹ-lek'trọ-tīp), *n.* [See *photo-.*] An electrotype made by the aid of photography.

pho-to=en-grave (fō"tọ-en-grāv'), *v. t.*; *-graved, -graving.* [See *photo-.*] To engrave by the aid of photography; make a photo-engraving of.—**pho"to=en-grav'ing,** *n.* Any of the various processes by which plates to print from are produced with the aid of photography, as by exposing under a negative a metal plate with a prepared sensitized surface and etching out with acid the blank spaces in the design or picture so formed; esp., any process of this kind by which a relief printing-surface is obtained; also, a plate so produced, or a print made from it.

pho-to=etch (fō"tọ-ech'), *v. t.* [See *photo-.*] To etch with the aid of photography; make a photo-etching of.—**pho"to=etch'ing,** *n.* Any process of photo-engraving in which the plate is etched by acid, etc.; a plate or print so produced.

pho-to-gen-ic (fō-tọ-jen'ik), *a.* [See *photo-* and *-genic.*] Produced by light (rare); in *biol.*, producing or emitting light, as certain bacteria; luminiferous; phosphorescent; in *photog.*, of a person, suitable for being photographed for artistic purposes, etc.—**pho-to-gen'i-cal-ly,** *adv.*

pho-to-graph (fō'tọ-gráf), *n.* [See *photo-* and *-graph.*] A picture produced by photography.—**pho'to-graph,** *v.* **I.** *tr.* To take a photograph of. **II.** *intr.* To practise photography.—**pho-tog-ra-pher** (fọ-tog'rạ-fėr), *n.* One who takes photographs or practises photography.—**pho-to-graph'ic** (-graf'ik), *a.* Of or pertaining to photography;

used in or produced by photography; fig., suggestive of photography or a photograph, or seeming as if produced by photography (as, *photographic* accuracy of portrayal; "The back of my mind took the *photographic* memory of it complete and vivid," H. G. Wells's "Tono-Bungay," iv. 3. § 2); representing or portraying nature or life with precise and minute detail, as a book or a writer; sometimes, in disparagement, mechanically imitative, with lack of artistic feeling.—**pho-to-graph′i-cal,** *a.*—**pho-to-graph′i-cal-ly,** *adv.*—**pho-tog′ra-phy,** *n.* [See *-graphy.*] The process or art of producing images of objects on sensitized surfaces by the chemical action of light.

pho-to-gra-vure (fō″tǫ-grą-vūr′ or fō-tǫ-grā′vūr), *n.* [F., < Gr. φῶς (φωτ-), light, + F. *gravure*, engraving.] Photo-engraving; esp., any of various processes, based on photography, by which an intaglio engraving is formed on a metal plate, from which ink reproductions are made; also, the plate, or a print made from it.

pho-to-he-li-o-graph (fō-tǫ-hē′li-ǫ-grȧf), *n.* [See *photo-.*] A telescope adapted for making photographs of the sun.

pho-to-lith-o-graph (fō-tǫ-lith′ǫ-grȧf), *n.* [See *photo-.*] A lithograph printed from a stone, etc., upon which the picture or design was formed by photography.—**pho-to-lith′o-graph,** *v. t.* To make a photolithograph of.—**pho″-to-lith-o-graph′ic** (-graf′ik), *a.*—**pho″to-li-thog′ra-phy** (-li-thog′rą-fi), *n.*

pho-tol-o-gy (fǫ-tol′ǫ-ji), *n.* [See *photo-* and *-logy.*] The science of light.—**pho-to-log-i-cal** (fō-tǫ-loj′i-kąl), *a.*—**pho-tol′o-gist,** *n.*

pho-to-mag-net-ism (fō-tǫ-mag′net-izm), *n.* [See *photo-.*] The science dealing with the relation of magnetism to light.—**pho″to-mag-net′ic,** *a.*

pho-to-me-chan-i-cal (fō″tǫ-mę-kan′i-kąl), *a.* [See *photo-.*] Noting or pertaining to any of various processes for printing in ink from plates or surfaces prepared by the aid of photography.—**pho″to-me-chan′i-cal-ly,** *adv.*

pho-tom-e-ter (fǫ-tom′e-tėr), *n.* [See *photo-* and *-meter.*] An instrument for measuring the intensity of light or the relative illuminating power of different lights.—**pho-to-met-ric, pho-to-met-ri-cal** (fō-tǫ-met′rik, -ri-kąl), *a.* Of or pertaining to photometry or the photometer.—**pho-to-met′ri-cal-ly,** *adv.*—**pho-tom′e-try,** *n.* [See *-metry.*] The measurement of the intensity of light or of relative illuminating power; the science dealing with this.

pho-to-mi-cro-graph (fō-tǫ-mī′krǫ-grȧf), *n.* [See *photo-* and *micrograph.*] An enlarged photograph of a microscopic object, taken through a microscope; also, a microphotograph.—**pho″to-mi-crog′ra-phy** (-krog′rą-fi), *n.*

pho-toph-i-lous (fǫ-tof′i-lus), *a.* [See *photo-* and *-philous.*] Light-loving; thriving in strong light, as a plant.

pho-to-pho-bi-a (fō-tǫ-fō′bi-ą), *n.* [NL.: see *photo-* and *-phobia.*] In *pathol.*, a morbid dread or intolerance of light, as in iritis.—**pho-to-pho′bic,** *a.*

pho-to-phone (fō′tǫ-fōn), *n.* [See *photo-* and *-phone.*] A form of telephone in which the vibrations set up in a diaphragm in the transmitter are conveyed to a distance by means of a beam of reflected light; also, the reproducing apparatus of the pallophotophone.

pho-to-play (fō′tǫ-plā), *n.* [See *photo-.*] A play presented, or arranged to be presented, in moving pictures.—**pho′to-play″er,** *n.* An actor or actress in photoplays.

pho-to-spec-tro-scope (fō-tǫ-spek′trǫ-skōp), *n.* [See *photo-.*] A spectroscope with an attachment for photographing spectra.—**pho″to-spec-tro-scop′ic** (-skop′ik), *a.*

pho-to-sphere (fō′tǫ-sfēr), *n.* [See *photo-.*] A sphere of light; esp., the luminous envelop surrounding the sun.—**pho-to-spher′ic** (-sfer′ik), *a.*

pho-to-stat (fō′tǫ-stat), *n.* [See *photo-* and *-stat.*] A special camera for making facsimile copies of maps, drawings, pages of books or manuscripts, documents, etc., which photographs directly on sensitized paper (instead of on a plate or film), has a lens fitted with a prism which inverts the image so that the copies are in correct position (with no right-and-left inversion as in an ordinary negative), and has attachments for holding the object to be photographed and for developing and fixing the print; also, a copy or photograph made with it. [Proprietary name.]—**pho′to-stat,** *v. t.*; *-stated, -stating.* To make a copy of (a drawing, page, document, or the like) with a photostat.—**pho′to-stat-er,** *n.*—**pho-to-stat′ic,** *a.*

pho-to-syn-the-sis (fō-tǫ-sin′the-sis), *n.* [See *photo-.*] In *bot.*, a form of anabolism in living plants by which carbohydrates are formed from the carbon dioxide and water of the air under the influence of light.—**pho″to-syn-thet′ic** (-thet′ik), *a.*

pho-to-tax-is (fō-tǫ-tak′sis), *n.* [NL.: see *photo-* and *-taxis.*] In *biol.*, the property of a cell or organism of exhibiting attraction or repulsion in relation to light.—**pho-to-tac′tic** (-tak′tik), *a.*

pho-to-te-leg-ra-phy (fō″tǫ-tę-leg′rą-fi), *n.* [See *photo-.*] Telegraphy by means of light, as with a heliograph; also, the electric transmission of facsimiles of photographs, etc.—**pho-to-tel′e-graph** (-tel′ę-grȧf), *n.*—**pho″to-tel-e-graph′-ic** (-graf′ik), *a.*

pho-to-tel-e-scope (fō-tǫ-tel′ę-skōp), *n.* [See *photo-.*] A telescope fitted with a photographing apparatus.—**pho″to-tel-e-scop′ic** (-skop′ik), *a.*

pho-to-the-od-o-lite (fō″tǫ-thę-od′ǫ-līt), *n.* [See *photo-* and *theodolite.*] In *surv.*, an instrument for the performance of triangulation by means of photographs.

pho-to-ther-a-peu-tics (fō″tǫ-ther-ą-pū′tiks), *n.* [See *photo-.*] That branch of therapeutics which deals with the curative use of light-rays.—**pho″to-ther-a-peu′tic,** *a.*—**pho-to-ther′a-py** (-pi), *n.* Treatment of disease by means of light-rays.

pho-to-ther-mic (fō-tǫ-thėr′mik), *a.* [See *photo-.*] Pertaining to the thermic effects of light; pertaining to or involving both light and heat.

pho-tot-o-nus (fǫ-tot′ǫ-nus), *n.* [NL., < *photo-* (see *photo-*) + Gr. τόνος, tension.] The normal condition of sensitiveness to light in leaves, etc.; also, the irritability exhibited by protoplasm when exposed to light of a certain intensity.—**pho-to-ton-ic** (fō-tǫ-ton′ik), *a.*

pho-to-trop-ic (fō-tǫ-trop′ik), *a.* [See *photo-* and *-tropic.*] In *bot.*, taking a particular direction under the influence of light; heliotropic.—**pho-to-trop′i-cal-ly,** *adv.*—**pho-tot-ro-pism** (fǫ-tot′rǫ-pizm), *n.* In *bot.*, phototropic tendency or growth.

pho-to-type (fō′tǫ-tīp), *n.* [See *photo-* and *type.*] A plate with a (relief) printing-surface produced by the aid of photography; also, any process for making such a plate, or a print made from it.—**pho″to-ty-pog′ra-phy** (-tī-pog′rą-fi), *n.* [See *typography.*] The art of making printing-surfaces by the aid of light or photography: a general term including a large number of processes.—**pho′to-ty-py** (-tī-pi), *n.* The art or process of producing phototypes.

phrag-mo-cone (frag′mǫ-kōn), *n.* [Gr. φραγμός, fence, + κῶνος, cone.] The conical, chambered or septate, internal skeleton of a belemnite.

phra-sal (frā′ząl), *a.* Of the nature of, or consisting of, a phrase.

phrase (frāz), *n.* [L. *phrasis*, < Gr. φράσις, speech, phraseology, expression, < φράζειν, tell.] Way of speaking, mode of expression, or phraseology (as, "the lady who was, in chivalrous *phrase*, empress of his thoughts and commander of his actions": Scott's "Castle Dangerous," xiii.); also, a particular form of words, or an expression, esp. a characteristic, current, or proverbial expression (as, "old English hospitality . . . this is a *phrase* very much used by the English themselves," Smollett's "Humphry Clinker," June 26; "In the old *phrase*, it is six of the one and half a dozen of the other," Stevenson's "Master of Ballantrae," x.); an effective, fine, or high-sounding expression (as, "I am a maker of war, and not a maker of *phrases*": Longfellow's "Courtship of Miles Standish," ii.); sometimes, a mere expression, without real meaning or force (as, "Authority is a *phrase* . . . we must look to time . . . to discover the truth": Disraeli's "Coningsby," i. 1); also, a brief utterance or remark (as, "I addressed some *phrases* to her in her own tongue": C. Brontë's "Jane Eyre," xi.); in *gram.*, a group of two or more words (not including a predicate verb) expressing practically a single notion or entering with a certain degree of unity into the structure of a sentence (cf. *clause*); in *music*, a division of a composition, commonly a passage of four or eight measures, forming part of a period.—**phrase,** *v.*; *phrased, phrasing.* **I.** *tr.* To express by a particular way of speaking (as, "Roland still continued to mend, as the surgeon *phrased* it": Bulwer-Lytton's "Caxtons," viii. 3); word in a particular manner; also, to describe by a phrase or in express terms; term, call, or style (as, "These suns – For so they *phrase* 'em": Shakspere's "Henry VIII.," i. 1. 34); also, to express or convey in words (as, "A man of the world! He could *phrase* his politeness": Arnold Bennett's "Pretty Lady," ii.); in *music*, to mark off or bring out the phrases of (a piece), esp. in execution; also, to group (notes) into a phrase. **II.** *intr.* To use a phrase or phrases; in *music*, to indicate or render phrases.—**phrase′mong″er** (-mung″gėr), *n.* One who deals in phrases; one given to fine (but often empty) phrases.

phra-se-o-gram (frā′zē-ō-gram), *n.* [Gr. φράσις (gen. φράσεως), E. *phrase*, + γράμμα, character, letter.] A written character or symbol representing a phrase, esp. in shorthand.—**phra′se-o-graph** (-gråf), *n.* [Gr. φράσις + γράφειν, write.] A phraseogram.—**phra″se-o-graph′ic** (-graf′ik), *a.*—**phra-se-og′ra-phy** (-og′ra-fi), *n.* The representation of phrases or sentences by abbreviated written characters or symbols, esp. in shorthand; the use of phraseograms; also, written phraseology.

phra-se-o-log-i-cal (frā″zē-ō-loj′i-kal), *a.* Of or pertaining to phraseology; characterized by a particular phraseology, or by the use of phrases or peculiar expressions.—**phra″se-o-log′i-cal-ly,** *adv.*

phra-se-ol-o-gist (frā-zē-ol′ō-jist), *n.* One who treats of phraseology; also, one who affects a particular phraseology, or is given to using phrases; a phrasemonger.

phra-se-ol-o-gy (frā-zē-ol′ō-ji), *n.* [NL. *phraseologia*, < NGr. φρασεολογία, < Gr. φράσις (gen. φράσεως), E. *phrase*, + -λογία, < λέγειν, speak.] A collection or book of phrases†; also, manner or style of verbal expression, or characteristic language (as, "the dogmatic *phraseology* of the pulpit," Kingsley's "Alton Locke," xxx.; "to bid a final adieu to the frontier: or in the *phraseology* of the region, to 'jump off!'" Parkman's "Oregon Trail," ii.); also, phrases or expressions (as, "He was . . . very fond of interlarding his conversation with high-sounding *phraseology*, without much regard as to the context": Marryat's "King's Own," xix.).

phras-er (frā′zėr), *n.* One who uses or makes phrases; one given to fine phrases; a phrasemonger.

phras-ing (frā′zing), *n.* The act of one who phrases; manner of expression; wording; phraseology; in *music*, the rendering of musical phrases.

phra-try (frā′tri), *n.*; pl. *-tries* (-triz). [Gr. φρατρία, < φράτηρ, clansman: see *brother*.] In ancient Greece, a division of the people, orig. based on kinship; a subdivision of a phyle; also, any analogous group among primitive races, as the aborigines of Australia or America.—**phra′-tric,** *a.*

phre-net-ic (frē-net′ik), etc. See *frenetic*, etc.

phren-ic (fren′ik), *a.* [NL. *phrenicus*, < Gr. φρήν (φρεν-), diaphragm: cf. *phrenitis*.] In *anat.*, of or pertaining to the diaphragm.

phre-ni-tis (frē-nī′tis), *n.* [NL., < Gr. φρενῖτις, < φρήν (φρεν-), mind, orig. diaphragm: cf. *phrenic* and *frenzy*.] In *pathol.*, inflammation of the brain or its meninges, attended with fever and delirium.

phre-nol-o-gy (frē-nol′ō-ji), *n.* [Gr. φρήν (φρεν-), mind: see *-logy*.] The theory that the mental powers of the individual consist of independent faculties, each of which has its seat in a definite brain-region whose size (supposed to be indicated by the shape of the skull over it) is commensurate with the development of the particular faculty; the system based on this theory.—**phren-o-log-i-cal** (fren-ō-loj′i-kal), *a.*—**phre-nol′o-gist,** *n.*

phren-zy (fren′zi), etc. See *frenzy*, etc.

Phryg-i-an (frij′i-an), *a.* Of or pertaining to Phrygia, an ancient country in Asia Minor, or its people.—**Phrygian cap,** a conical cap with its apex turned over toward the front, worn by the ancient Phrygians and in modern times adopted as a symbol of liberty. See cut in next column. Cf. *liberty-cap*.—**Phryg′i-an,** *n.* A native or inhabitant of Phrygia.

phthal-e-in (thal′ē-in or fthal′-), *n.* [See *phthalic*.] In *chem.*, any of a group of compounds (certain of whose derivatives are important dyestuffs) formed by treating phthalic anhydride with phenols.

phthal-ic (thal′ik or fthal′-), *a.* [From (*na*)*phthal*(*ene*).] In *chem.*, noting or pertaining to any of three isomeric acids derived from benzene, esp. that one which is prepared by oxidizing naphthalene and which readily forms an anhydride; noting this anhydride.—**phthal′in,** *n.* In *chem.*, any of a group of compounds obtained by the reduction of the phthaleins.

Phrygian Cap.—Statue of Paris, Vatican Museum, Rome.

phthi-ri-a-sis (thi-rī′a-sis or fthi-), *n.* [L., < Gr. φθειρίασις, < φθειριᾶν, be lousy, < φθείρ, louse.] In *pathol.*, the state of being infested with lice, with the resulting irritation or other effects; pediculosis.

phthis-ic (tiz′ik), *n.* [OF. *ptisique*, < L. *phthisica*, fem. of *phthisicus*, < Gr. φθισικός, consumptive, < φθίσις, E. *phthisis*.] In *pathol.*, a wasting disease of the lungs; phthisis.—**phthis′i-cal,** *a.* Pertaining to, of the nature of, or affected by phthisis. Also **phthis′ick-y.**

phthi-sis (thī′sis or fthī′-), *n.* [L., < Gr. φθίσις, < φθίειν, decay, waste.] In *pathol.*, a wasting away; esp., tuberculosis of the lungs; consumption.

phy-col-o-gy (fī-kol′ō-ji), *n.* [Gr. φῦκος, seaweed: see *-logy*.] The branch of botany that deals with algæ or seaweeds.—**phy-col′o-gist,** *n.*

phy-co-my-ce-tous (fī″kō-mī-sē′tus), *a.* [NL. *Phycomycetes*, pl., < Gr. φῦκος, seaweed, + μύκης (μυκητ-), fungus.] In *bot.*, belonging or pertaining to the *Phycomycetes*, a group or class of fungi the members of which are parasitic or saprophytic and resemble algæ.

-phyl, -phyll. Noun termination from Gr. φύλλον, leaf, as in *chlorophyl* or *chlorophyll*, *cladophyl*, *lithophyl*.

phy-la (fī′lä), *n.* Plural of *phylum*.

phy-lac-te-ry (fi-lak′tē-ri), *n.*; pl. *-ries* (-riz). [LL. *phylacterium*, < Gr. φυλακτήριον, outpost, safeguard, amulet, < φυλάσσειν, guard.] Either of two small leather cases containing slips inscribed with certain texts from the Pentateuch, worn by Jews during prayer to remind them to keep the law (cf. Deut. vi. 8, xi. 18); fig., a reminder; sometimes, an ostentatious display of righteousness; also, an amulet worn on the person; fig., a charm or safeguard (as, "some very good books, left as a never-failing *phylactery* against the blue devils": Malkin's tr. Le Sage's "Gil Blas," x. 7); also, a receptacle containing a holy relic.

phy-le (fī′lē), *n.*; pl. *phylæ* (-lē). [NL., < Gr. φυλή, < φύειν, produce: cf. *phylum*.] In ancient Greece, a tribe or clan, based on supposed kinship; in Attica, the largest political division of the people.

phy-let-ic (fī-let′ik), *a.* [Gr. φυλή, tribe, clan, or φῦλον, race, tribe: see *phyle* and *phylum*.] In *biol.*, pertaining to race or kind; phylogenic; racial.

-phyll. See *-phyl*.

Phyl-lis (fil′is), *n.* [L., < Gr. Φυλλίς.] A name, orig. in pastoral literature, for a country girl or a sweetheart.

phyllo-, phyll-. Forms of Gr. φύλλον, leaf, used in combination.—**phyl-lo-clade** (fil′ō-klād), *n.* [+ Gr. κλάδος, branch.] In *bot.*, a flattened stem or branch having the function of a leaf.—**phyl-lode** (fil′ōd), *n.* [Gr. φυλλώδης, leaf-like: see *-ode*[2].] In *bot.*, an expanded petiole resembling, and having the function of, a leaf.—**phyl-loid** (fil′oid), *a.* [+ *-oid*.] Leaf-like.—**phyl-lome** (fil′ōm), *n.* [+ *-ome* as in *caulome*, *rhizome*.] In *bot.*, a leaf of a plant, or a structure morphologically corresponding to it.—**phyl-lo-mic** (fi-lō′mik), *a.*—**phyl-loph-a-gous** (fi-lof′a-gus), *a.* [+ *-phagous*.] Leaf-eating, as certain beetles.—**phyl′lo-phore** (-fōr), *n.* [Gr. φυλλοφόρος, leaf-bearing: see *-phore*.] In *bot.*, the termi-

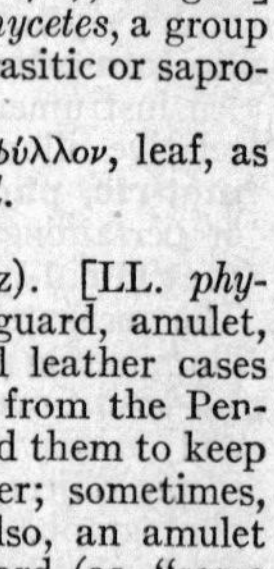

Phyllode (*a*) of Acacia (*A. heterophylla*).

nal leaf-producing bud or growing-point of a stem: used esp. with reference to palms.—**phyl-loph′o-rous** (-ọ̄-rus), *a.* Bearing leaves or leaf-like parts.

phyl-lo-pod (fil′ọ̄-pod). [NL. *Phyllopoda*, pl., < Gr. φύλλον, leaf, + πούς (ποδ-), foot.] **I.** *n.* Any of the *Phyllopoda*, an order of crustaceans characterized by leaf-like swimming feet. **II.** *a.* Pertaining to the phyllopods; belonging to the *Phyllopoda*.

phyl-lo-tax-is (fil-ọ̄-tak′sis), *n.* [NL.: see *phyllo-* and *-taxis*.] In *bot.*, the arrangement of leaves on a stem or axis; the principles governing such arrangement.

-phyllous. [Gr. -φυλλος, < φύλλον, leaf.] An adjective termination meaning 'having leaves,' 'leaved,' or implying some connection with a leaf, as in *diphyllous, epiphyllous, monophyllous, polyphyllous*.

phyl-lox-e-ra (fil-ok-sē′rạ̈), *n.*; pl. *-ræ* (-rē). [NL., < Gr. φύλλον, leaf, + ξηρός, dry.] Any of the plant-lice constituting the genus *Phylloxera*, esp. *P. vastatrix*, which has proved very destructive to European grape-vines.—**phyl-lox-e′ral** (-rạl), **phyl-lox-er-ic** (fil-ok-ser′ik), *a.* Of or pertaining to the phylloxera.—**phyl-lox-e-rat-ed** (fi-lok′-sẹ̄-rā-ted), **phyl-lox′-e-rized** (-rīzd), *a.* Infested with phylloxeræ.

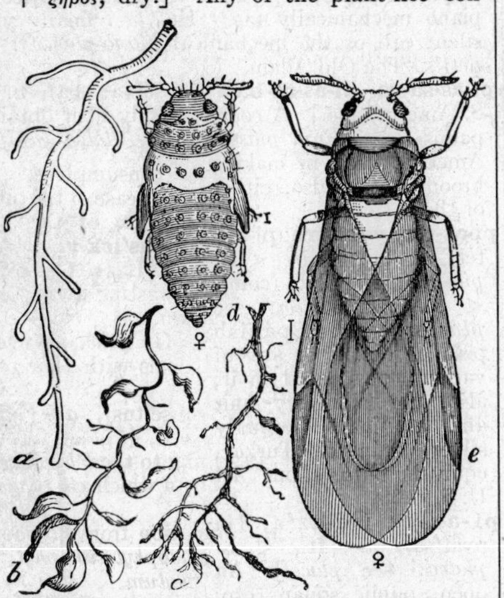

Phylloxera (*P. vastatrix*). — *a*, healthy vine rootlet; *b*, rootlet showing nodosities; *c*, rootlet in decay (natural size); *d*, female pupa; *e*, winged female, or migrant. (Short lines show natural sizes.)

phylo-. Form of Gr. φῦλον, race, tribe, used in combination.—**phy-lo-gen-e-sis** (fī-lọ̄-jen′e-sis), *n.* Phylogeny.—**phy″lo-ge-net′ic** (-jẹ̄-net′ik), *a.*—**phy-log′e-ny** (-loj′e-ni), *n.* [+ *-geny*.] In *biol.*, the development or evolution of a kind or type of animal or plant; racial history. Cf. *ontogeny*.—**phy-lo-gen′ic**, *a.*

phy-lum (fī′lum), *n.*; pl. *-la* (-lạ̈). [NL., < Gr. φῦλον, race, tribe, akin to φυλή: see *phyle*.] A primary division of the animal or vegetable kingdom: usually equivalent to *sub-kingdom*.

-phyre. [F. *-phyre*, < *porphyre*, porphyry; or G. *-phyr*, < *porphyr*, porphyry.] A termination used to form names of porphyritic rocks, as *granophyre, melaphyre, orthophyre*.

phys-ic (fiz′ik), *n.* [OF. *fisique* (F. *physique*), < L. *physica*, natural science (ML. science of medicine), < Gr. φυσική, science of nature, prop. fem. of φυσικός, pertaining to nature, < φύσις, nature, < φύειν, produce.] Natural science (obs. or rare); also, medical science (archaic); the medical art; the medical profession; also, medicine (as, "Throw *physic* to the dogs; I'll none of it": Shakspere's "Macbeth," v. 3. 47); a drug or medicament; specif., a medicine that purges; a cathartic.—**phys′ic**, *v. t.*; *-icked, -icking*. To treat with physic or medicine; also, to work upon as a medicine does; relieve or cure; specif., to treat with, or to act upon as, a cathartic; purge.

phys-i-cal (fiz′i-kạl), *a.* [ML. *physicalis*, < L. and ML. *physica*: see *physic*.] Of or pertaining to material nature; material; also, pertaining to the processes, laws, or science of nature, or to physics; specif., noting or pertaining to properties of a body other than those which are chemical, esp. when obvious to the senses; pertaining to or effected by natural forces or means that are not chemical; also, pertaining to the body, or bodily (as, a man of great *physical* strength; *physical* exercise; "courage, whether it be *physical* or mental," Marryat's "King's Own," xli.); also, medical†; medicinal†; curative† or remedial†.—**physical geography,** a branch of geography treating of the natural features and phenomena of the earth's surface, as land-forms, climate, winds, ocean-currents, etc.—**phys′i-cal-ly,** *adv.*

phy-si-cian (fi-zish′ạn), *n.* [OF. *fisicien*, physician (F. *physicien*, physicist), < L. and ML. *physica*: see *physic*.] One who is skilled in the art of healing; esp., one legally qualified to practise medicine; often, specif., one engaged in general medical practice as distinguished from one specializing in surgery.

phys-i-cist (fiz′i-sist), *n.* One versed in physics; also, one who seeks to explain the fundamental phenomena of life upon purely physical and chemical principles.

phys-ics (fiz′iks), *n.* Orig., the science of nature in general; natural science; now, the science dealing with the physical properties of matter and energy, and embracing the sciences of mechanics, heat, light, electricity, etc.

physio-. Form of Gr. φύσις, nature, used in combination.

phys-i-oc-ra-cy (fiz-i-ok′rạ-si), *n.* [F. *physiocratie*, < Gr. φύσις, nature, + -κρατία, < κρατεῖν, rule.] Government by, or in accordance with, nature; specif., the doctrine or system of the physiocrats.—**phys′i-o-crat** (-ọ̄-krat), *n.* [F. *physiocrate*.] One of a school of political economists, followers of the French economist François Quesnay (1694–1774), who recognized an inherent natural order as properly governing society, regarded land as the basis of wealth and taxation, and advocated freedom of industry and trade.—**phys″i-o-crat′ic**, *a.*

phys-i-og-no-my (fiz-i-og′nọ̄-mi), *n.*; pl. *-mies* (-miz). [OF. *phisonomie* (F. *physionomie*), < ML. *phisonomia*, ult. < Gr. φυσιογνωμονία, < φύσις, nature, + γνώμων, a judge.] The art of determining character or personal characteristics from the features of the face or the form of the body; also, the face or countenance considered as an index to the character (as, "His *physiognomy* indicated the inanity of character which pervaded his life": Scott's "Guy Mannering," ii.); particular cast or type of countenance (as, "the serious, even sad expression characteristic of the national *physiognomy*": Prescott's "Conquest of Mexico," iv. 2); hence, the face or visage (as, "Turning suddenly, he caught my gaze fastened on his *physiognomy*": C. Brontë's "Jane Eyre," xiv.); also, the general appearance of anything material (as, "Little details gave each field a particular *physiognomy*": George Eliot's "Middlemarch," xii.); the characteristic aspect of anything.—**phys″i-og-nom′ic, phys″i-og-nom′i-cal** (-nom′ik, -i-kạl), *a.*—**phys-i-og′no-mist,** *n.*

phys-i-og-ra-phy (fiz-i-og′rạ-fi), *n.* [See *physio-* and *-graphy*.] The science of nature in general; esp., physical geography.—**phys-i-og′ra-pher,** *n.*—**phys″i-o-graph′ic, phys″i-o-graph′i-cal** (-ọ̄-graf′ik, -i-kạl), *a.*

phys-i-ol-a-try (fiz-i-ol′ạ-tri), *n.* [See *physio-* and *-latry*.] The worship of nature.—**phys-i-ol′a-ter,** *n.*

phys-i-ol-o-gy (fiz-i-ol′ọ̄-ji), *n.* [L. *physiologia*, < Gr. φυσιολογία, natural philosophy, < φύσις, nature, + λέγειν, speak.] The science dealing with the normal functions of living organisms or their organs (as, animal *physiology*; human *physiology*; vegetable *physiology*); esp., this science as concerned with human beings; also, a treatise on this science.—**phys″i-o-log′ic, phys″i-o-log′i-cal** (-ọ̄-loj′ik, -i-kạl), *a.*—**phys″i-o-log′i-cal-ly,** *adv.*—**phys-i-ol′o-gist,** *n.*

phys-i-o-ther-a-py (fiz″i-ọ̄-ther′ạ-pi), *n.* [See *physio-* and *therapy*.] The treatment of disease or bodily weaknesses or defects by physical remedies, such as massage, gymnastics, etc. (rather than by drugs).

phy-sique (fi-zēk′), *n.* [F., prop. adj., physical, < L. *physicus*, < Gr. φυσικός: see *physic*.] Physical or bodily structure, organization, or development: as, "My exceptional *physique* protected me from the disease and exhaustion of which not a few of our number died" (F. M. Crawford's "Mr. Isaacs," i.); "Robespierre . . . was a man of poor *physique*" (H. G. Wells's "Outline of History," xxxvii. § 11).

phy-so-stig-mine (fī-sọ̄-stig′min), *n.* [NL. *Physostigma*, < Gr. φῦσα, bellows, + στίγμα, E. *stigma*.] In *chem.*, a poisonous alkaloid constituting the active principle of the Calabar bean, used in medicine as a myotic, etc.

-phyte. Noun termination from Gr. φυτόν, a growth, plant, as in *epiphyte, halophyte, lithophyte, osteophyte.*

phy-tin (fī′tin), *n.* [Gr. φυτόν, plant.] An organic compound containing phosphorus found in seeds, tubers, and rhizomes, where it serves as a reserve material.

phyto-, phyt-. Forms of Gr. φυτόν, plant, used in combination.—**phy-to-bi-ol-o-gy** (fī″tọ-bī-ol′ọ-ji), *n.* That branch of biology which deals with plants.—**phy-to-chem′is-try** (-kem′is-tri), *n.* The chemistry of plants.—**phy-to-gen′e-sis** (-jen′e-sis), *n.* The origin and development of plants. Also **phy-tog′e-ny** (-toj′e-ni).—**phy″to-ge-net′ic** (-jẹ-net′ik), **phy-to-gen′ic,** *a.*—**phy″to-ge-og′ra-phy** (-og′rạ-fi), *n.* The science treating of the geographical distribution of plants.—**phy-tog′ra-phy** (-tog′rạ-fi), *n.* [+ *-graphy.*] That branch of botany which deals with the description of plants.—**phy′toid** (-toid), *a.* [+ *-oid.*] Plant-like.

phy-to-lac-ca-ceous (fī″tọ-la-kā′shius), *a.* [NL. *Phytolacca*, the typical genus, < Gr. φυτόν, plant, + NL. *lacca*, lake (with reference to the red juice of the berries).] Belonging to the *Phytolaccaceæ*, a family of chiefly tropical trees, shrubs, and herbs, including the pokeweed, etc.

phy-tol-o-gy (fī-tol′ọ-ji), *n.* [See *phyto-* and *-logy.*] Botany. —**phy-tol′o-gist,** *n.*

phy-to-pa-thol-o-gy (fī″tọ-pạ-thol′ọ-ji), *n.* [See *phyto-.*] The science treating of the diseases of plants; in *med.*, the study of morbid conditions induced by plant growths.—**phy″to-pa-thol′o-gist,** *n.*

phy-toph-a-gous (fī-tof′ạ-gus), *a.* [See *phyto-* and *-phagous.*] Plant-eating; herbivorous.

pi[1] (pī or pē), *n.* [Gr. πῖ (the initial letter of περιφέρεια, circumference, E. *periphery*).] The sixteenth letter (Π, π, = English P, p) of the Greek alphabet; in *math.*, the letter Π, π, used as the symbol for the ratio (3.141592+) of the circumference of a circle to its diameter; also, the ratio itself.

pi[2], **pie**[3] (pī), *n.* [Origin uncertain.] Printing-types mixed together indiscriminately.—**pi**[2], **pie**[3], *v. t.*; *pied, piing, pieing.* To reduce (printing-types) to a state of pi.

pi-a[1] (pī′ạ), *n.* Same as *pia mater.*

pi-a[2] (pē′ạ), *n.* [Polynesian.] A perennial herb, *Tacca pinnatifida*, of Polynesia, the East Indies, etc., with a tuberous root which yields a nutritious starch, the so-called South Sea arrowroot.

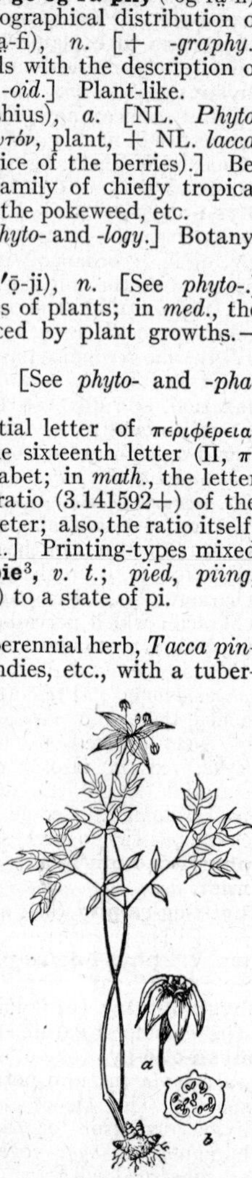

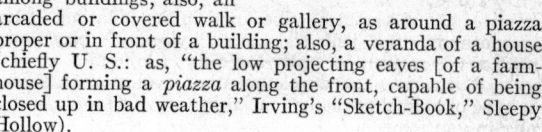

Pia.—*a*, a flower; *b*, transverse section of the fruit.

pi-ac-u-lar (pī-ak′ụ-lạr), *a.* [L. *piacularis*, < *piaculum*, expiatory offering, < *piare*, appease, < *pius*, devout, E. *pious.*] Making expiation; expiatory; also, requiring expiation; sinful; wicked.

piaffe (piaf), *v. i.*; *piaffed, piaffing.* [F. *piaffer*, make a show, strut, piaffe; origin uncertain.] In the *manège*, of a horse, to lift each pair of diagonally opposite legs in succession, as in the trot, but without going forward, backward, or sideways; loosely, to move slowly forward, backward, or sideways by lifting the legs in this manner. —**piaf-fer** (piaf′ėr), *n.* [F., inf.] In the *manège*, the act of piaffing.

pi-a ma-ter (pī′ạ mā′tėr). [ML., 'tender mother': cf. *dura mater.*] In *anat.*, the delicate, fibrous, and highly vascular membrane forming the innermost of the three meninges enveloping the brain and spinal cord. Cf. *arachnoid* and *dura mater.*

pi-a-nette (pē-ạ-net′), *n.* [Dim. of *piano*[2].] A small upright piano; also, a street-piano. [Eng.]

pi-an-ism (pi-an′izm or pē′ạ-nizm), *n.* Playing or execution on the pianoforte; the technique of the pianoforte.

pi-a-nis-si-mo (pē-ạ-nis′i-mō, It. pyä-nēs′sē-mō). [It., superl. of *piano*: see *piano*[1].] In *music*: **I.** *a.* Very soft. **II.** *adv.* Very softly.

pi-an-ist (pi-an′ist or pē′ạ-nist), *n.* A performer on the pianoforte. Also (F.) **pia-niste** (pyȧ-nēst).

pia-no[1] (pyä′nō). [It., < L. *planus*, E. *plain*[2].] In *music*: **I.** *a.* Soft; low. **II.** *adv.* Softly; in a low tone or voice.

pi-an-o[2] (pi-an′ō), *n.*; pl. *-os* (-ōz). [It.] The pianoforte. —**grand piano,** a pianoforte with a harp-shaped body supported horizontally and strings placed at right angles to the keyboard: in the largest size, called *concert grand piano.*—**square piano,** a pianoforte with a rectangular body supported horizontally and strings placed parallel with the keyboard.—**upright piano,** a pianoforte with a rectangular body placed vertically, and hence having the strings vertical.

pi-an-o-for-te (pi-an-ọ-fôr′tā or pi-an′ọ-fôrt), *n.* [It., < *piano*, soft (see *piano*[1]), + *forte*, loud (see *forte*[2]).] A musical instrument of the percussion type in which the tones are produced by hammers, operated by levers from a keyboard, striking upon stretched metal strings. See *piano*[2], *n.* —**pi-an-o-for′tist,** *n.*

pi-an-o=play-er (pi-an′ọ-plā″ėr), *n.* One who or that which plays the piano; esp., an instrument or device for playing a piano mechanically (as, "He . . . finally yielded to the silent call of the mechanical *piano-player*": Arnold Bennett's "The Old Adam," i.).

pi-as-sa-va, pi-as-sa-ba (pē-ạ-sä′vạ, -bạ), *n.* [Pg.; from S. Amer. name.] A coarse, woody fiber obtained from the palms *Leopoldinia piassaba* and *Attalea funifera* of South America, used in making brooms, etc.; also, either of these trees.

Piassava (*Attalea funifera*).—*a*, the upper part of the stem with the fibers.

pi-as-ter, pi-as-tre (pi-as′tėr), *n.* [F. *piastre*, < It. *piastra*, metal plate (coin), < L. *emplastrum*: see *plaster.*] The Spanish peso or dollar, or any of various coins based on it; also, the monetary unit and a nickel (formerly silver) coin of Turkey, equivalent to about 4.4 U. S. cents.

pi-az-za (pi-az′ạ, It. pyät′sä), *n.* [It., < L. *platea*: see *place.*] An open, public square, esp. in an Italian town; any open square or space, as among buildings; also, an arcaded or covered walk or gallery, as around a piazza proper or in front of a building; also, a veranda of a house (chiefly U. S.: as, "the low projecting eaves [of a farmhouse] forming a *piazza* along the front, capable of being closed up in bad weather," Irving's "Sketch-Book," Sleepy Hollow).

pi-broch (pē′broch), *n.* [Gael. *piobaireachd*, pipe-music, ult. < E. *pipe.*] In the Scottish Highlands, a kind of musical piece performed on the bagpipe, comprising a series of variations on a ground-theme, usually martial in character, but sometimes used as a dirge or otherwise: as, "Some pipe of war Sends the bold *pibroch* from afar" (Scott's "Lady of the Lake," ii. 15); "The body was committed to the earth, the pipers playing a *pibroch* all the time" (Smollett's "Humphry Clinker," Sept. 3).

pi-ca[1] (pī′kạ), *n.* [NL., < L. *pica*, magpie (with reference to its omnivorous feeding).] In *pathol.*, depraved or perverted appetite, or craving for unnatural food, as chalk, clay, etc., common in chlorosis, pregnancy, etc.

pi-ca[2] (pī′kạ), *n.* [Supposed to be < AL. *pica*, book of rules for church services, appar. the same word as L. *pica*, magpie: see *pie*[4], and cf. *pica*[1].] A printing-type (12 point) of a size between small pica and English (see *type*); also, the depth of this type-size (about one sixth of an inch) as a unit of measurement for type, etc.—**small pica,** a printing-type (11 point) of a size between long primer and pica. See *type.*

pic-a-dor (pik-ạ-dôr′ or pik′ạ-dôr), *n.* [Sp., < *picar*, prick, pierce.] One of the horsemen who open a bull-fight by irritating and enraging the bull with pricks of their lances, but purposely avoid disabling him.

pic-a-resque (pik-ạ-resk′), *a.* [F., < Sp. *picaresco*, < *picaro*, rogue.] Of or pertaining to rogues: applied to a type of fiction, of Spanish origin, with a rogue or adventurer for hero.

pic-a-roon (pik-ạ-rön′), *n.* [Sp. *picarón*, aug. of *pícaro*, rogue.] A rogue, thief, or brigand; also, a pirate or corsair (as, "He was somewhat of a trader, something more of a smuggler, with a considerable dash of the *picaroon*": Irving's "Tales of a Traveler," iv. 2); also, a piratical or privateering vessel (as, "Kennelled in the *picaroon* a weary band were we": Kipling's "Last Chantey").—**pic-a-roon′**, *v. i.* To act or cruise as a brigand or pirate.

pic-a-yune (pik-ạ-yön′). [F. *picaillon*, < Pr. *picaioun*, old copper coin of Piedmont.] **I.** *n.* Formerly, in Florida, Louisiana, etc., the Spanish half-real, equal to about 6¼ U. S. cents; hence, later, any small coin, as a five-cent piece; also, an insignificant person or thing (colloq.). **II.** *a.* Of little value or account; small; petty; mean. [Colloq.] —**pic-a-yun′ish** (-yö′nish), *a.*

pic-ca-lil-li (pik′ạ-lil″i), *n.* [Origin unknown.] A highly seasoned pickle, of East Indian origin, made of chopped vegetables.

pic-ca-nin-ny (pik′ạ-nin″i), *n.* See *pickaninny*.

pic-co-lo (pik′ọ-lō), *n.*; pl. *-los* (-lōz). [It., 'small.'] A small flute, sounding an octave higher than the ordinary flute; also, in some European (esp. Austrian) restaurants, an assistant waiter, usually a boy, who attends to the liquors.—**pic′co-lo-ist**, *n.* A player on the piccolo.

pice (pīs), *n.*; pl. *pice*. [Hind. *paisā*.] An East Indian bronze coin and money of account, equal to one fourth of an anna, and equivalent to about one half of a cent in U. S. money.

pi-ce-ous (pis′ẹ-us), *a.* [L. *piceus*, < *pix* (*pic-*), pitch.] Of, pertaining to, or resembling pitch; inflammable or combustible; of the color of pitch; pitch-black.

pi-ces-cent (pi-ses′ẹnt), *a.* [See *piceous* and *-escent*.] Approaching a piceous or pitch-black color.

pich-i-ci-a-go (pich″i-si-ā′gō), *n.*; pl. *-gos* (-gōz). [S. Amer. Sp., < *pichey*, small armadillo, + Sp. *ciego*, blind.] A small armadillo, *Chlamydophorus truncatus*, of South America, having the head and back protected by a continuous shield attached only along the middle line of the back, and having the hinder end of the body abruptly truncated and covered by a vertical shield.

Pichiciago.

pich-u-rim (pich′ụ-rim), *n.* [S. Amer.] A South American lauraceous tree, *Nectandra puchury*, with seeds having thick aromatic cotyledons ('pichurim beans') which are used medicinally and as a substitute for nutmegs.

pi-cine (pī′sin), *a.* [L. *picus*, woodpecker.] Belonging, allied, or pertaining to the woodpeckers.

pick[1] (pik), *v. t.* [ME. *piken*, *picken*, from an AS. verb represented in *pīcung*, pricking, and akin to *pīc*, pickax: see *pike*[1], and cf. *peck*[2] and *pique*, *v.*] To pierce, indent, dig into, or break up (something) with a pointed instrument; form (a hole, etc.) by such action; also, to use a pointed instrument, the fingers, the teeth, the beak, etc., on (a thing), in order to remove something; clear (a thing) of something by such action (as, to *pick* one's teeth; to *pick* a bone); prepare for use by removing feathers, hulls, or other parts (as, to *pick* a fowl; to *pick* berries for the table); also, to detach or remove with the fingers, the beak, or the like, esp. with the fingers; pluck or gather (as, to *pick* fruit or flowers); often, of birds or other animals, to take up (small bits of food) with the bill or teeth; hence, of persons, to eat in small morsels or daintily (as, "I *picked* a meal in fear and trembling": Stevenson's "Travels with a Donkey," v. 3); also, to choose or select (as, "Geraint, dismounting, *pick'd* the lance That pleased him best": Tennyson's "Geraint and Enid," 179); select carefully; sometimes, to choose (one's way or steps), as over rough ground or through a crowd; also, to seek and find occasion for (as, to *pick* a quarrel); also, to seek or find (flaws), in a spirit of faultfinding (as, "Whatever she had, she seemed to survey only to *pick* flaws in it": Mrs. Stowe's "Uncle Tom's Cabin," xxvii.); also, to steal†; rob†; now, to steal the contents of (a person's pocket, purse, etc.); also, to open (a lock) with a pointed instrument, a wire, or the like, esp. secretly, as for the purpose of robbery; also, to separate, pull apart, or pull to pieces (fibers, etc.: as, to *pick* oakum); also, to pluck (the strings of a musical instrument), or play (a stringed instrument) by plucking with the fingers; use the fingers on (a thing) with a plucking motion (as, the patient is *picking* the bedclothes).—**to pick a thank** (or **thanks**)†, to curry favor by sycophancy, talebearing, or the like. Cf. *pickthank*.—**to pick off**, to single out and shoot; shoot one by one: as, the riflemen *picked off* the enemy.—**to pick out**, to extract by picking; also, to choose; select carefully; also, to distinguish (a thing) from surrounding or accompanying things; also, to make out (sense or meaning); discover by combining separate fragments of information; also, to mark out or adorn as with lines or touches of color (as, "tall, dark houses, with window-frames of stone, or *picked out* of a lighter red": Thackeray's "Vanity Fair," xlvii.); relieve the general color of (a thing) by lines or touches of another color, as along outlines, etc.—**to pick up**, to take up, as with the fingers (as, to *pick up* a stone); also, to pluck up, recover, or regain (courage, etc.); also, to get casually; acquire or obtain as chance or opportunity offers (as, "a bargain which he had *picked up* for a mere song": Du Maurier's "Trilby," i.); gain by occasional opportunity (as, to *pick up* a livelihood); learn by occasional opportunity or without special teaching (as, "He had *picked up* the game with characteristic aptitude": W. Churchill's "Modern Chronicle," ii. 6); also, to take up into a vehicle or vessel, or along with one, as a person or thing come upon or overtaken (as, "They wandered alone, undergoing extraordinary sufferings; until first one and then the other was *picked up* by a party from Fort St. Frederick": Stevenson's "Master of Ballantrae," iii.).—**pick**[1], *v. i.* To strike with or use a pointed instrument or the like on something; also, to eat with small bites, or daintily; also, to choose; make careful or fastidious selection; also, to pilfer (as, to *pick* and steal). —**to pick at**, to nag at; worry by repeated faultfinding. [Colloq.]—**to pick on**, to pick at; tease; worry. [Colloq.] —**to pick up**, to recover; improve. [Colloq.]—**pick**[1], *n.* [Appar. partly < *pick*[1], *v.*, and partly < *pike*[1].] A tool consisting of an iron bar, usually curved, tapering to a point at one or both ends, wielded by means of a wooden handle inserted (on the concave side) in an eye between the ends, and used for loosening and breaking up soil, rock, etc.; any pointed or other tool or instrument for picking (as, an ice-*pick*; a tooth*pick*); also, a spike† or sharp point†; also, an act of picking; a stroke with something pointed; also, the quantity of a crop picked at a particular time; also, choice or selection; the right of selection; that which is selected; hence, the choicest or most desirable part, example, or examples (as, "Lady Dunstane's ponies were a present from Redworth, who always chose the *pick* of the land for his gifts": G. Meredith's "Diana of the Crossways," xix.); also, in *printing*, a speck of dirt, hardened ink, or extra metal on set type or a plate.

pick[2] (pik), *v. t.* or *i.* [Var. of *pitch*[1].] To pitch or throw. [Now prov. Eng.]—**pick**[2], *n.* A cast or throw (now prov. Eng.); in *weaving*, a cast or throw of the shuttle; also, a single weft-thread in cloth.

pick-a-back, pick-back (pik′ạ-bak, pik′bak), *adv.* [Origin uncertain.] On the back or shoulders like a pack: as, "the little lad whom I used to carry *pickaback*" (H. Kingsley's "Geoffry Hamlyn," xxv.).

pick-a-nin-ny (pik′ạ-nin″i), *n.*; pl. *-ninnies* (-iz). [Dim. < Sp. *pequeño* or Pg. *pequeno*, little.] A small child, esp. a negro or colored child: as, "A pleasant-faced negro woman . . . was polishing the parlor floor with a long brush, her little *pickaninny* astraddle on the broom end" (F. H. Smith's "Colonel Carter of Cartersville," xi.).

pick-a-pack, pick-pack (pik′ạ-pak, pik′pak), *adv.* Same as *pickaback*.

pick-ax, pick-axe (pik′aks), *n.* [Corruption of ME. *pikeys*, *pikoys*, < OF. F. *picois*, < *pic*, a pick: see *pike*[1].] A pick, esp. one with the iron bar tapering to a point at one end and having a chisel-like blade of equal length at the other.

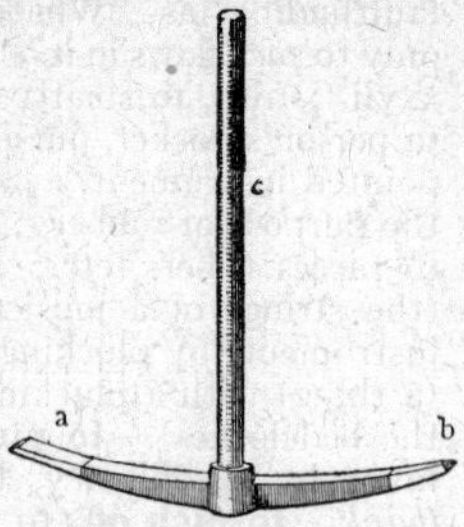

Pickax. — *a* and *b*, steel extremities welded to the iron; *c*, handle.

pick′back, *adv.* See *pickaback.*

picked¹ (pikt), *p. a.* [See *pick*¹, *v.*] Cleared or cleaned, as of refuse parts, by picking; also, specially chosen or selected, as for excellence or efficiency, or for a particular purpose (as, "the crew of the lugger . . . all of whom were *picked* men, remarkable for their strength and activity": Marryat's "King's Own," xiii.).

picked² (pikt), *a.* [See *pick*¹, *n.*, and cf. *piked.*] Having a spike or sharp point, spiked, or pointed (archaic or prov.); also, covered with sharp points; prickly.

pick-eer (pi-kēr′), *v. i.* [Appar. < F. *picorer*, maraud, orig. steal cattle, through Sp. < L. *pecus*, cattle.] To maraud†; skirmish†; reconnoiter or scout (archaic).

pick-el-hau-be (pik′ẹl-hou″bė), *n.* [G.] The spiked helmet worn by German soldiers.

pick-er¹ (pik′ėr), *n.* One who picks, esp. one who plucks or gathers fruit, flowers, etc.; a tool or instrument for picking.

pick-er² (pik′ėr), *n.* In *weaving*, the piece that throws the shuttle of the loom through the warp.

pick-er-el (pik′ẹ-rel), *n.*; pl. *pickerels* or (esp. collectively) *pickerel.* [Dim. of *pike*².] A young pike; in the U. S. and Canada, any of various species of pike, esp. one of the smaller species, as *Esox reticulatus*; also, the pike-perch.—**pick′er-el=weed,** *n.* Any plant of the American genus *Pontederia*, esp. *P. cordata*, a blue-flowered herb common in shallow fresh water; also, any of various other plants growing in still water.

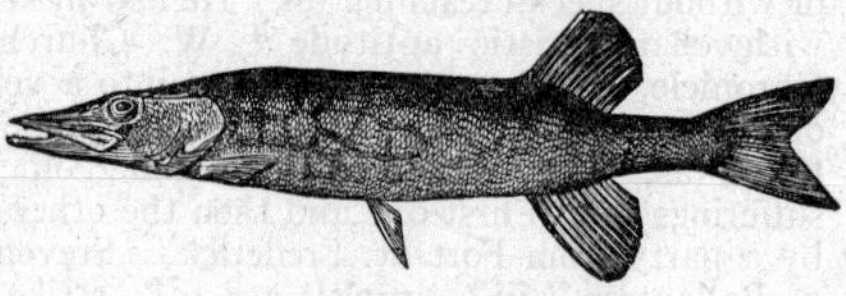
Pickerel (*Esox reticulatus*).

pick-et (pik′et), *n.* [F. *piquet*, pointed stake, military picket, dim. connected with *pic*, a pick, and *pique*, a pike: see *pike*¹ and *pike*³.] A pointed post, stake, pale, or peg, as for driving into the ground in making a stockade, for placing vertically to form the main part of a fence, for driving into the ground to fasten something to, etc.; also, a small detached body of troops, or a single soldier, posted in front of an army to warn against an enemy's approach or held in camp in readiness for such service; also, a person or a body of persons stationed by a trade-union or the like, as to watch persons going to work, or to dissuade or prevent them from doing so, during a strike.—**pick′et,** *v.* **I.** *tr.* To inclose, fence, or make secure with pickets; also, to fasten or tether to a picket (as, "There was a stake driven down where an animal had been *picketed* for the night": Wister's "Virginian," xxxii.); also, to guard, as a camp, by or as pickets; post as a picket; also, to place pickets at or near, as during a strike. **II.** *intr.* To act as a picket.—**pick′et-er,** *n.*

pick-ing (pik′ing), *n.* The act of one who or that which picks; also, that which is or may be picked or picked up; the amount picked; a scrap; *pl.*, things, portions, or scraps remaining and worth picking up or appropriating (as, "Take what you want, and leave us Romanies the *pickings*": Whyte-Melville's "Katerfelto," x.); also, *pl.*, pilferings, or perquisites gotten by means not strictly honest.

pick-le¹ (pik′l), *n.* [Origin uncertain.] A single grain of wheat, etc.; also, a small quantity; a little; a few. [Sc. and north. Eng.]

pick-le² (pik′l), *n.* [ME. *pekille*, *pykyl*, = D. *pekel* = G. *pökel*, pickle, brine.] A liquid prepared with salt or vinegar for preserving or flavoring fish, meat, vegetables, etc.; also, something thus preserved, esp. (often in *pl.*) vegetables, as cucumbers, cauliflower, etc., preserved in vinegar and eaten as a relish; specif., a pickled cucumber; also, an acid or other chemical solution for cleansing metal castings, etc.; also, fig., a condition or situation, esp. a disagreeable one (colloq.: as, "Chowder [a dog] has had the misfortune to be worried by a butcher's dog, and came home in a terrible *pickle*," Smollett's "Humphry Clinker," April 2; "I could see no way out of the *pickle* I was in," Stevenson's "David Balfour," xxiv.); an intoxicated condition (slang); also, a troublesome person, esp. a mischievous child (colloq.: as, "They observed that Shakespeare himself had been a mere *pickle* in his youth," Irving's "Tales of a Traveler," ii. 7).—**in pickle,** fig., kept prepared for use: as, to have a rod *in pickle* for a person (that is, to have punishment in reserve for him).—**pick′le**², *v. t.*; *-led, -ling.* To preserve or steep in pickle; also, to treat with a chemical pickle; also, fig., to intoxicate (slang); *naut.*, to rub salt or vinegar on the back of, after whipping, as a punishment (as, "They were taken on board, and . . . soundly whipped and *pickled*, after which they proved very honest and quiet fellows": Defoe's "Robinson Crusoe," i. 18).—**pick′led,** *p. a.* Preserved in or treated with a pickle; fig., intoxicated (slang).—**pick′ler,** *n.*—**pick′le=worm,** *n.* The larva of an American pyralid moth, *Diaphania nitidalis*, which lays its eggs on young cucumbers and other cucurbitaceous plants, the larva boring into the vegetable and spoiling it.

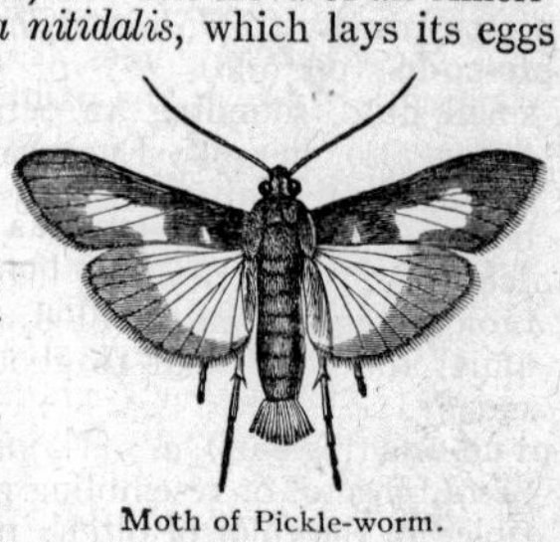
Moth of Pickle-worm.

pick-lock (pik′lok), *n.* A person who picks locks, esp. a thief; also, an instrument for picking locks.

pick=me=up (pik′mē-up), *n.* A stimulating or bracing drink or medicinal preparation: as, "Ribot came and sat by his bedside, and . . . got him a *pick-me-up* from the chemist's" (Du Maurier's "Trilby," iv.). [Colloq.]

pick′pack, *adv.* See *pickapack, pickaback.*

pick-pock-et (pik′pok″et), *n.* One who picks, or steals from, the pockets of others.

pick-purse (pik′pėrs), *n.* One who steals purses or from them.

pick-some (pik′sum), *a.* Given to picking and choosing; fastidious; particular.—**pick′some-ness,** *n.*

pick-thank (pik′thangk), *n.* One who seeks to win thanks or favor by sycophancy, talebearing, etc. [Archaic or prov.]

pick′=up, *n.* A receiving or recording device.

Pick-wick-i-an (pik-wik′i-ạn), *a.* Of, pertaining to, or characteristic of Mr. Pickwick (the hero of Dickens's "Pickwick Papers") or the club (Pickwick Club) founded by him.—**Pickwickian sense,** a sense that is attached to words merely for the occasion, regardless of their actual or literal sense. See Dickens's "Pickwick Papers," i. [Humorous.]

pic-nic (pik′nik), *n.* [F. *pique-nique*; origin obscure.] Orig., a social entertainment in which each participant contributed a share to a repast; now, a pleasure-party or excursion in which those taking part, commonly carrying their provisions with them, share a repast in the open air; also, fig., an enjoyable experience or time (often ironical: slang).—**pic′nic,** *v. i.*; *-nicked, -nicking.* To hold, or take part in, a picnic.—**pic′nick-er,** *n.*

pic-o-line (pik′ọ-lin), *n.* [L. *pix* (*pic-*), pitch, + *oleum*, oil.] In *chem.*, any of three isomeric derivatives of pyridine, obtained from coal-tar, etc., as colorless oily liquids with a strong odor.

pi-cot (pē′kō, F. pē-kō), *n.* [F., dim. of *pic*, a pick, something pointed: see *pike*¹.] One of a number of ornamental loops in embroidery, tatting, etc., or along the edge of lace, ribbon, etc.

pic-o-tee (pik-ọ-tē′), *n.* [F. *picoté*, pp. of *picoter*, mark with pricks or spots, < *picot*: see *picot.*] A florists' variety of carnation having petals with a white or yellow ground marked at the outer margin with another color, usually red.

pic-rate (pik′rāt), *n.* In *chem.*, a salt of picric acid.

pic-ric (pik′rik), *a.* [Gr. πικρός, bitter.] In *chem.*, designating or pertaining to an intensely bitter yellow acid used as a dye and in explosives.

pic-rite (pik′rīt), *n.* [Gr. πικρός, bitter.] Any of a group of igneous rocks of granular texture, composed chiefly of olivine and augite, often with hornblende, biotite, etc.

picro-. Form of Gr. πικρός, bitter, used in combination:

sometimes used to represent *picric.*—**pic-rol** (pik′rol or -rōl), *n.* [See *-ol.*] A bitter, odorless crystalline antiseptic, used as a substitute for iodoform, etc.—**pic-ro-ni-trate** (pik-rọ̄-nī′trāt), *n.* Same as *picrate.*—**pic-ro-tox′in** (-tok′-sin), *n.* [Cf. *toxin.*] In *chem.*, a bitter, highly poisonous, crystalline principle, obtained from cocculus indicus.—**pic-ro-tox′ic,** *a.*

Pict (pikt), *n.* [LL. *Picti*, pl.] One of a race of people of disputed origin who formerly inhabited parts of northern Britain, and in the 9th century became united with the Scots.—**Pict′ish,** *a.*

pic-to-gram (pik′tọ̄-gram), *n.* Same as *pictograph.*

pic-to-graph (pik′tọ̄-gráf), *n.* [L. *pictus*, pp. of *pingere*, represent pictorially, paint: see *-graph.*] A pictorial sign or symbol, or a record consisting of pictorial symbols: as, the *pictographs* of the American Indians.—**pic-to-graph′ic** (-graf′ik), *a.*—**pic-tog′ra-phy** (-tog′rạ-fi), *n.* [See *-graphy.*] The use of pictographs; picture-writing.

pic-to-ri-al (pik-tō′ri-ạl). [LL. *pictorius*, < L. *pictor*, painter, < *pingere*: see *picture.*] **I.** *a.* Of or pertaining to a painter or maker of pictures (as, "the *pictorial* calling," Thackeray's "Newcomes," xii.; "*Pictorial* skill being so rare in the colonies, the painter became an object of general curiosity," Hawthorne's "Twice-Told Tales," The Prophetic Pictures); also, pertaining to, expressed in, or of the nature of a picture or pictures (as, records in a *pictorial* form; *pictorial* writing or symbols; *pictorial* representations); illustrated by or containing pictures (as, a *pictorial* history or periodical); also, suggestive of, or representing as if by, a picture; picturesque; graphic. **II.** *n.* A periodical in which pictures are an important feature.—**pic-to′ri-al-ly,** *adv.*

pic-tur-a-ble (pik′ṭụ̄r-ạ-bl), *a.* Capable of or suitable for being pictured.

pic-tur-al (pik′ṭụ̄r-ạl), *a.* Pertaining to or of the nature of a picture or pictures; pictorial: as, "*pictural* incarnations of the fiend" (Poe's "Man of the Crowd").

pic-ture (pik′ṭụ̄r), *n.* [L. *pictura*, < *pingere* (pp. *pictus*), represent pictorially, paint: cf. *paint.*] Painting†, or pictorial representation†; also, a painting, drawing, photograph, or other representation, as of a person, object, or scene, executed on a surface; such a representation having sufficient merit to rank as a work of art (as, an exhibition of *pictures*; a *picture*-gallery); a portrait or likeness, as of a person (as, to have one's *picture* taken; that is a good *picture* of him); a moving picture; a tableau, as in theatrical representation ('living picture'); also, any visible image, however produced (as, the *picture* in a mirror; to see *pictures* in the fire); a prospect or scene presented to the eye (as, "The whale [with its widely separated eyes] . . . must see one distinct *picture* on this side, and another distinct *picture* on that side": H. Melville's "Moby-Dick," lxxiv.); fig., a mental image (as, memory's *pictures*); also, a description (written or spoken) calling up a mental image of something (as, Gibbon's *picture* of the latter days of ancient Rome); a graphic or vivid description or account; also, a person, thing, group, or scene regarded as resembling a work of pictorial art (as, "What a *picture* you are in those furs!" W. Churchill's "Coniston," ii. 10); also, one who presents the very appearance of another, or the image or counterpart (as, he is the *picture* of his father); a truly representative example of something (as, "Old Baltus Van Tassel was a perfect *picture* of a thriving, contented, liberal-hearted farmer": Irving's "Sketch-Book," Sleepy Hollow); a visible or concrete embodiment of some quality or the like (as, he is the *picture* of health); a type; in *med.*, the assemblage of conditions presented in a case of disease.—**pic′ture,** *v. t.*; *-tured, -turing.* To represent in a picture or pictorially; present to the eye as in a picture (as, "The whole scene at her feet lay *pictured* in the softest colors": Cooper's "Spy," xxx.); also, to form a mental picture of, or imagine (as, "He was older than she had been *picturing* him": Arnold Bennett's "Helen with the High Hand," ii.); also, to depict in words, or describe graphically (as, "Just such an open place as the Indian had *pictured* to me was here": W. H. Hudson's "Green Mansions," xxi.).—**pic′tured,** *a.* Illustrated or adorned with pictures; represented in or as in a picture; having the appearance of something in a picture (as, the *Pictured* Rocks, sandstone cliffs presenting a great variety of colors and worn into striking forms, extending for five miles along the Michigan shore of Lake Superior, east of Marquette).

pic-tu-resque (pik-ṭụ̄-resk′), *a.* [F. *pittoresque*, < It. *pittoresco*, lit. 'in the style of a painter,' < *pittore*, < L. *pictor*, painter: cf. *pictorial.*] Such as would make a striking or effective picture (as, "The appearance of the two was so *picturesque*, that I would give twenty guineas to have them tolerably represented on canvas," Smollett's "Humphry Clinker," July 15; "They [Indians] made a very striking and *picturesque* feature in the forest landscape," Parkman's "Oregon Trail," i.); having pleasing or interesting pictorial qualities (rather than the highest beauty or sublimity); strikingly effective in appearance; fig., of a character to suggest a picture; strikingly interesting, or colorful (as, "This theatrical recognition of imperial descent was one among the many romantic incidents of Don John's *picturesque* career": Motley's "Dutch Republic," v. 1); of language, etc., strikingly graphic or vivid.—**pic-tu-resque′ly,** *adv.*—**pic-tu-resque′ness,** *n.*

pic-ture=writ-ing (pik′ṭụ̄r-rī″ting), *n.* The art of recording events or expressing ideas by pictures, or pictorial symbols, as practised by the ancient Egyptians, the American Indians, etc.; also, pictorial symbols forming a record or communication (as, "All the various receipts and disbursements were set down in the *picture-writing* of the country": Prescott's "Conquest of Mexico," iv. 1).

pic-tur-i-za-tion (pik″ṭụ̄r-i-zā′shọn), *n.* The act of picturizing, or the state of being picturized; also, a picturized form of a novel or the like.

pic-tur-ize (pik′ṭụ̄r-īz), *v. t.*; *-ized, -izing.* To represent in a picture or pictures; put (a novel, drama, etc.) into the form of a moving picture.

pic-ul (pik′ul), *n.* [Malay.] In China and elsewhere in the East, a weight equal to 100 catties, or from about 133 to about 140 pounds avoirdupois.

pic-u-let (pik′ụ̄-let), *n.* [Dim. < L. *picus*, woodpecker.] Any of the small, soft-tailed woodpeckers of the subfamily *Picumninæ*, of tropical regions, as *Picumnus lepidotus*, an American species.

Piculet (*Picumnus lepidotus*).

pid-dle (pid′l), *v. i.*; *-dled, -dling.* [Origin obscure.] To do anything in a trifling or ineffective way; trifle at work (as, "I have discovered a manufacture to a great extent, of what you only *piddle* at": Boswell's "Johnson," April 18, 1783); toy with or pick at one's food.—**pid′dler,** *n.*—**pid′dling,** *p. a.* Trifling; petty.

pid-dock (pid′ọk), *n.* [Origin obscure.] Any of the bivalve mollusks of the genus *Pholas* or the family *Pholadidæ*, mostly marine, with long ovate shell, and burrowing in soft rock, wood, etc.

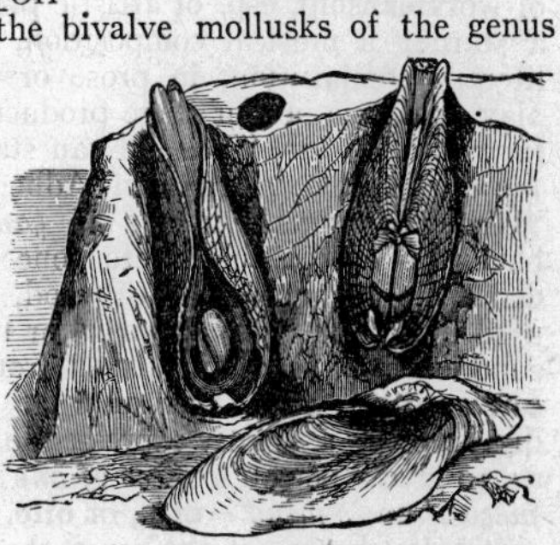

Piddocks (*Pholas dactylus*) in their holes.

Pidg-in=Eng-lish (pij′-in-ing′glish), *n.* [From *pidgin*, Chinese corruption of E. *business*, + *English.*] A jargon consisting chiefly of corrupted English words arranged according to the Chinese idiom, used in the East between Chinese and foreigners in business transactions and other dealings.

pie[1] (pī), *n.* [OF. F. *pie*, < L. *pica*, magpie.] A magpie; hence, any of various related or similar birds; fig., a chattering person.

pie[2] (pī), *n.* [ME. *pie, pye*; origin uncertain.] A dish consisting of meat, oysters, fruit, or the like, with an under or an upper layer or crust of pastry, or with both, cooked by baking; also, a layer-cake with a filling of cream, jelly, or the like (cf. *Washington pie*).

pie[3], *n.* and *v.* See *pi*[2].

pie[4], **pye** (pī), *n.* [Perhaps another use of *pie*[1] (magpie), from the black and white of the printed page: cf. *pica*[2].] *Eccles.*, in England before the Reformation, a book of rules for finding the particulars of the service for the day.

pie[5] (pī), *n.* [Hind. *pā'ī.*] An East Indian bronze coin, equal to one twelfth of an anna, and equivalent to about one sixth of a U. S. cent.

pie-bald (pī'bâld). [From *pie*[1] + *bald.*] **I.** *a.* Having patches of black and white (like a magpie) or of other colors (as, a *piebald* horse; "a *piebald* cat," Eden Phillpotts's "Cherry-Stones," Eviction); pied; party-colored; fig., mixed or mongrel (as, "Here we are, a society, and a nation . . . a vast and *piebald* congregation": M. Hewlett's "Open Country," xiv.). **II.** *n.* A piebald animal, esp. a horse: as, "*Piebalds* were not so popular as horses of a more normal colouring" (W. H. Hudson's "Far Away and Long Ago," xi.).

piece (pēs), *n.* [OF. *piece* (F. *pièce*), < ML. *pecia*, *petia*, piece; origin obscure.] One of the parts into which a thing is divided or broken (as, a *piece* of pie; *pieces* of broken glass; to tear a letter into *pieces*); a separate portion or part; a bit, fragment, or shred; also, a limited portion or quantity of something (as, a *piece* of land); a quantity of some substance or material forming a single mass or body (as, a *piece* of wood, ice, or chalk; a *piece* of rope); a more or less definite quantity, esp. a particular length, of some goods as put up for the market (as, cloth, ribbon, lace, or wall-paper sold only by the *piece*); a cask of wine or brandy, of varying capacity; an amount of work forming a single job (as, to work by the *piece*: cf. *piece-work*); sometimes, a portion of time, or a while, or a portion of space or distance, or a short distance (now prov.: as, "There's a man a *piece* down here that's going over . . . this evening," Mrs. Stowe's "Uncle Tom's Cabin," vii.); also, one of the parts which, assembled together, form a combined whole (as, the *pieces* of a machine or a harness; the sleeve-*pieces* of a garment); also, an individual article of a set or collection (as, a set of dishes of 100 *pieces*); also, an individual thing of a particular class or kind (as, a *piece* of furniture; a *piece* of jewelry or of finery); an example, specimen, or instance of something (as, a fine *piece* of work; a *piece* of news; a *piece* of impertinence); a specimen of humanity, or an individual or person (now prov. or archaic, usually disparaging, and chiefly used of a woman or girl: as, a dainty *piece*; a saucy *piece*); an article or thing of the artillery or firearm kind, as a cannon, gun, or pistol (as, a field-*piece*; a fowling-*piece*; "The patriot cavalry, mostly carabineers . . . retired to reload their *pieces*," Motley's "Dutch Republic," iv. 1); a coin (as, a five-cent *piece*; *piece* of eight, the old Spanish dollar or peso, of the value of 8 reals); a specimen of workmanship, esp. of artistic production, as a picture or a statue; a musical composition, usually a short one; a literary composition, in prose or verse, usually short; a play or drama, as for stage production; a literary selection for recitation (as, "The kid can stay up if she will say her *piece* . . . Her 'Abou Ben Adhem' ": Arnold Bennett's "Hilda Lessways," ii. 4); in *games*, as chess, checkers, backgammon, dominoes, etc., one of the 'men,' or figures, disks, blocks, or the like, of wood, ivory, or other material, used in playing, as on a board or table; in chess, specif., a superior man as distinguished from a pawn.—**a piece of one's mind,** something of what one is thinking, esp. in disapproval; a bluntly expressed, uncomplimentary opinion: as, to give a person *a piece of one's mind*; to get or hear *a piece of one's mind*.—**of a,** or **one, piece,** of the same piece or whole; hence, of the same character or kind (as, their excuses were all *of a piece*); in agreement or keeping (*with*: as, "His rusty and worn suit of black was *of a piece* with his uncarpeted room," Reade's "Peg Woffington," i.; "To discuss medicine before the ignorant is *of one piece* with teaching the peacock to sing," Kipling's "Kim," xii.).—**to pieces,** to bits or fragments (as, to break a dish *to pieces*); fig., to a shattered condition of health, fortunes, or the like (as, to go completely *to pieces*); also, to a state of separation of the constituent parts, or apart (as, to take a clock *to pieces*).—**piece,** *v. t.*; *pieced, piecing.* To mend (a garment, etc.) by applying a piece or pieces; patch; also, to complete, enlarge, or extend by an added piece or something additional (as, "*piecing* his own imperfect recollections with the narratives of Mannering and Pleydell": Scott's "Guy Mannering," liv.); eke (*out*) with something added; also, to make by joining pieces together (as, to *piece* a patchwork quilt); also, to join together, as pieces or parts; join as a piece or addition to something.—**piece'=dyed,** *a.* Of cloth, dyed in the piece, or after weaving.—**piece'=goods,** *n. pl.* Goods or fabrics which are woven in lengths suitable for retail sale by the usual linear measure.—**piece'meal** (-mēl). [With *-meal* as in *limbmeal.*] **I.** *adv.* Piece by piece; little by little; gradually; also, piece from piece, or into pieces or fragments (as, to be torn *piecemeal*). **II.** *a.* Done piece by piece; fragmentary; disconnected.—**pie-cer** (pē'sėr), *n.*—**piece'=work,** *n.* Work done and paid for by the piece.—**piece'=work''er,** *n.*

pie=crust (pī'krust), *n.* The crust of shortened paste with which pies are made.

pied (pīd), *a.* [From *pie*[1] (in allusion to the black and white plumage of the magpie).] Having patches of two or more colors, as various birds and other animals; party-colored, or wearing a party-colored dress (as, "The *Pied* Piper of Hamelin," title of a poem by Robert Browning, based on a medieval legend); diversified with color, or variegated, as flowers, meadows, etc.

pied=à=terre (pyā-tä-tãr), *n.* [F., lit. 'foot (footing) on ground.'] A lodging for temporary or occasional use; in general, a place or location serving as a foothold.

pied-mont (pēd'mont). [From *Piedmont*, It. *Piemonte*, division of northwestern Italy, < L. *pes* (*ped-*), foot, + *mons* (*mont-*), mountain.] In *phys. geog.*: **I.** *n.* A district lying along or near the foot of a mountain-range. **II.** *a.* Lying along or near the foot of a mountain-range: as, a *piedmont* plain; a *piedmont* glacier.

pie=plant (pī'plant), *n.* The common garden rhubarb, *Rheum rhaponticum*: so called from its use in pies. [U. S.]

pier (pēr), *n.* [ME. *per*; origin uncertain.] One of the supports of the spans of a bridge; also, a breakwater, mole, or jetty; also, a projecting quay or wharf; also, a structure supported on columns or piles, extending into a body of water, to serve as a landing-place, promenade, etc.; in *arch.* or *building*, a solid support of masonry or the like for sustaining vertical pressure; specif., a square pillar; a supporting structure from which an arch springs; a portion of wall between doors, windows, etc.; a pillar or post on which a gate or door is hung.

Pier in Cloister of Ste. Elne, near Perpignan, France; 12th century.

pierce (pērs), *v.*; *pierced, piercing.* [OF. *percier* (F. *percer*), perhaps ult. < L. *pertundere* (pp. *pertusus*), pierce: see *pertuse.*] **I.** *tr.* To penetrate or run into or through (something), as a sharp-pointed instrument, a jag of rock, a missile, or the like does; puncture or stab with a sharp instrument or the like (as, "One of the soldiers with a spear *pierced* his side": John, xix. 34); also, to make a hole or opening in; bore into or through; tunnel; perforate; make (a hole, etc.) by or as by boring or perforating; also, to force or make a way into or through (as, to *pierce* the enemy's center; to *pierce* a wilderness; "when sea-winds *pierced* our solitudes," Emerson's "Rhodora"); penetrate into or through (lit. or fig.); sound sharply through (the air, stillness, etc.), as a cry; often, to penetrate with the eye or mind (as, "Mr. Wharton had in vain endeavored to *pierce* the disguise of his guest's political feelings": Cooper's "Spy," i.); see into or through; also, to affect sharply with some sensation or emotion, as of cold, pain, grief, etc. **II.** *intr.* To force or make a way into or through something; penetrate: as, "a chill that *pierced* into the marrow" (Stevenson's "Treasure Island," xx.).—**pierce'a-ble,** *a.* Capable of being pierced.—**pier-cer** (pēr'sėr), *n.*—**pier'cing,** *p. a.* That pierces; penetrating; sharp; keen.—**pier'cing-ly,** *adv.*—**pier'cing-ness,** *n.*

pier=glass (pēr′glȧs), *n.* A tall mirror, such as is used to fill the pier or space between two windows.

Pi-e-ri-an (pī-ē′ri-ạn), *a.* Of or pertaining to Pieria, a district in ancient Thessaly, the fabled home of the Muses (hence called *Pierides*); of or pertaining to the Muses: as, "A little learning is a dangerous thing; Drink deep, or taste not the *Pierian* spring" (Pope's "Essay on Criticism," 216).

pi-er-i-dine (pī-er′i-din), *a.* [NL. *Pieridinæ*, pl., < *Pieris*, the typical genus, < Gr. Πιερίς, a Muse.] In *entom.*, belonging to the *Pieridinæ*, a subfamily of butterflies which includes various rather small whitish or yellowish North American species whose larvæ are injurious to the cabbage and other cruciferous plants.

Pieridine Butterfly. — Southern cabbage-butterfly (*Pieris protodice*), female.

Pier-rette (pye-ret), *n.* [F., fem. dim. < *Pierre*: see *Pierrot*.] A female character corresponding to Pierrot. Also [*l. c.*] *pierrette*.

Pier-rot (pye-rō), *n.* [F., dim. < *Pierre*, man's name, Peter.] A typical male character in French pantomime, having a whitened face and wearing a loose white fancy costume; [*l. c.*] a masquerader or buffoon so made up.

pier=ta-ble (pēr′tā″bl), *n.* A table or low bracket for occupying the space against a pier between two windows, often used under a pier-glass.

pi-et, py-et (pī′ẹt), *n.* [From *pie*[1].] A magpie. [Now only Sc. and north. Eng.]

pie-tà (pyā-tä′), *n.* [It., piety, pity, sorrow, < L. *pietas*: see *piety*.] A representation in painting or sculpture of the Virgin Mary seated and supporting the dead body of Christ in her arms or on her knees.

Pietà, by Michelangelo. — In St. Peter's, Rome.

Pi-e-tism (pī′ẹ-tizm), *n.* [NL. *Pietismus*, < L. *pietas*: see *piety*.] A movement inaugurated during the latter part of the 17th century for the revival and advancement of piety in the Lutheran churches in Germany; the principles and practices of the Pietists; [*l. c.*] depth of religious feeling; godliness of life; often, exaggeration or affectation of piety.—**Pi′e-tist**, *n.* An adherent of Pietism; [*l. c.*] one conspicuous for pietism. —**pi-e-tis′tic**, *a.*—**pi-e-tis′ti-cal-ly**, *adv.*

pi-e-ty (pī′ẹ-ti), *n.*; pl. *-ties* (-tiz). [OF. *piete* (F. *piété*), < L. *pietas*, piety, dutifulness, tenderness, pity, < *pius*, E. *pious*: cf. *pietà* and *pity*.] The quality or fact of being pious; pious character or spirit; reverence for God, or regard for religious obligations; dutiful respect or regard for parents or others; pious conduct; a pious act, remark, belief, or the like (as, "the small *pieties* with which they larded their discourse," S. Butler's "Way of All Flesh," xlvii.; "It was as though all the *pieties* of life, all the sacred assumptions . . . were shaken, outraged," Mrs. H. Ward's "Robert Elsmere," xv.).

pi-e-zo=e-lec-tri-ci-ty (pī″e-zọ̄-ē-lek-tris′i-ti), *n.* [Gr. πιέζειν, press.] Electricity produced by pressure, as that appearing in a crystal subjected to compression along a certain axis.

pi-e-zom-e-ter (pī-e-zom′e-tėr), *n.* [Gr. πιέζειν, press, + μέτρον, measure.] Any of various instruments for measuring pressure or something depending on pressure; a device for showing the pressure in a water-main; an instrument for testing the pressure of gas in a gun; an instrument for showing the compressibility of a liquid under varying pressure; a sounding-apparatus whose working depends on the pressures produced at different depths.—**pi″e-zo-met′ric** (-zọ̄-met′rik), *a.*—**pi-e-zom′e-try**, *n.* The measurement of pressure or compressibility; the use of the piezometer.

pif-fle (pif′l), *v. i.*; *-fled*, *-fling*. [Origin uncertain.] To talk or act in a weakly or foolishly ineffective manner: as, "They piddled and *piffled* with iron. I'd given my orders for steel!" (Kipling's "The 'Mary Gloster'"). [Prov. or slang.]—**pif′fle**, *n.* Piffling talk or action; twaddle; nonsense. [Prov. or slang.]—**pif′fler**, *n.*—**pif′fling**, *p. a.* That piffles; weakly ineffective; trifling. [Prov. or slang.]

pig[1] (pig), *n.* [ME. *pigge*: cf. D. *big*, young pig.] A young swine of either sex; also, a swine or hog in general; also, the flesh of swine; pork; also, a person or animal of piggish character or habits (colloq.); in *metal.*, an oblong mass of metal that has been run while still molten into a mold of sand or the like, esp. such a mass of iron from a blast-furnace (see *pig-iron*); also, one of the molds for such masses of metal; also, metal in the form of such masses, esp. pig-iron. —**pig**[1], *v. i.*; *pigged*, *pigging*. To bring forth pigs, as a sow; also, to huddle, lodge, or sleep together like pigs (as, "a dozen felons, *pigging* together on bare bricks in a hole fifteen feet square": Macaulay's "Essays," Sir William Temple); live, lie, etc., as if in a pigsty.

pig[2] (pig), *n.* [Origin unknown: cf. *piggin*.] An earthenware pot, jug, jar, or the like. [Sc.]

pig=deer (pig′dēr), *n.* The babirusa.

pi-geon (pij′ọn), *n.* [OF. *pijon* (F. *pigeon*), < LL. *pipio(n-)*, squab, < *pipire*, peep, chirp.] Any member of the family *Columbidæ*, comprising birds characterized by a compact body and short legs, and existing in several hundred species widely distributed throughout the world; a dove; esp., a domesticated member of this family, as one of the varieties of the rock-dove or rock-pigeon, *Columba livia*; fig., a simpleton, dupe, or gull (slang: as, "A flatterer may play what game he likes against the *pigeons* of high life!" Malkin's tr. Le Sage's "Gil Blas," iv. 7). —**pi′geon=breast**, *n.* Same as *chicken-breast*.—**pi′-geon=breast″ed**, *a.*

Domestic Pigeon, homing variety.

Pi′geon=Eng′lish, *n.* See *Pidgin-English*.

pi-geon=hawk (pij′ọn-hâk), *n.* A small North American true falcon, *Falco columbarius*, or any of certain other small hawks.

pi-geon-hole (pij′ọn-hōl), *n.* A hole for pigeons to pass in and out; a hole or recess, or one of a series of recesses, for pigeons to nest in; hence, any similar small hole or recess; esp., one of a series of small compartments in a desk, cabinet, or the like, open in front, and used for papers, etc.—**pi′geon-hole**, *v. t.*; *-holed*, *-holing*. To place in a pigeonhole or pigeonholes; put away in the proper place for later reference; assign to a definite place in some orderly system; put aside for the present, esp. with the intention of ignoring or forgetting; also, to furnish with pigeonholes.

pi-geon-ry (pij′ọn-ri), *n.*; pl. *-ries* (-riz). A place where pigeons are kept.

pi-geon's=blood (pij′ọnz-blud), *n.* A deep-red color, being the color most esteemed in the ruby.

pi-geon=toed (pij′ọn-tōd), *a.* Having the toes or feet turned inward.

pi-geon-wing (pij′ọn-wing), *n.* A kind of fancy step or evolution in dancing; also, a particular figure in skating.

pig=fish (pig′fish), *n.* Any of various fishes, as a grunt, *Orthopristis chrysopterus*, a food-fish of the southern Atlantic coast of the U. S.

pig-ger-y (pig′ėr-i), *n.*; pl. *piggeries* (-iz). A place where pigs are kept.

pig-gin (pig′in), *n.* [Appar. < *pig*[2].] A small pail or tub, esp. a wooden one with a handle formed by continuing one of the staves above the rim.

pig-gish (pig′ish), *a.* Like or befitting a pig; hoggish; greedy; selfish; unclean or filthy.—**pig′gish-ly,** *adv.*—**pig′-gish-ness,** *n.*

pig=head-ed (pig′hed′ed), *a.* Stupidly obstinate; perverse; unreasonable: as, "It's a pity pious folks are so apt to be *pig-headed*" (Mrs. Stowe's "Oldtown Folks," xxv.).—**pig′=head′ed-ly,** *adv.*—**pig′=head′ed-ness,** *n.*

pight (pīt). Old pret. and pp. of *pitch*[1].

pig=i-ron (pig′ī′ėrn), *n.* Crude impure iron in the form of pigs or oblong ingots, obtained by smelting iron ore, as with coke and limestone, in a blast-furnace, and letting the molten metal run into trough-like molds; such iron as a material, whether molten or in pigs.

pig-let (pig′let), *n.* A little pig: as, "the squealing of many little *piglets*" (W. H. Hudson's "Far Away and Long Ago," xii.).

pig-ment (pig′mẹnt), *n.* [L. *pigmentum*, < *pingere*, paint.] A coloring matter or substance; specif., a dry substance, usually pulverized, which when mixed with a liquid vehicle in which it is insoluble becomes a paint; in *biol.*, any substance whose presence in the tissues or cells of animals or plants colors them.—**pig-men′tal** (-men′tạl), **pig′men-ta-ry** (-mẹn-tạ-ri), *a.*—**pig-men-ta′tion** (-tā′-shọn), *n.* In *biol.*, coloration with or deposition of pigment; esp., excessive deposition of pigment.—**pig′ment-ed,** *a.* Charged with pigment; colored.

pig-my (pig′mi), etc. See *pygmy*, etc.

pig-no-rate (pig′nọ-rāt), *v. t.*; *-rated, -rating.* [Also *pignerate*; L. *pigneratus*, pp. of *pignerare* (ML. *pignorare*), < *pignus*, a pledge.] To pledge or pawn; also, to take in pawn.—**pig-no-ra′tion** (-rā′shọn), *n.*

pig-nut (pig′nut), *n.* The tuber of a European plant, *Conopodium denudatum*, a kind of earthnut; also, the nut of the brown hickory, *Hicoria glabra*, of North America, or the tree itself.

pig-skin (pig′skin), *n.* The skin of a pig or hog; leather made from it; also, a saddle (colloq.); also, a football (colloq.).

pig-stick-ing (pig′stik″ing), *n.* The sport of hunting the wild boar with a spear, the huntsman usually being mounted.

pig-sty (pig′stī), *n.*; pl. *-sties* (-stīz). A sty or pen for pigs.

pig-tail (pig′tāl), *n.* Tobacco in a thin twisted rope or roll; also, a plait or queue of hair, worn esp. by soldiers, sailors, and others in former times, and still sometimes by young girls, and long customarily by the Chinese (as, "Marley in his *pig-tail*, usual waistcoat, tights, and boots," Dickens's "Christmas Carol," i.; "Her abundant hair hung over her shoulders in two tight *pigtails*," Arnold Bennett's "Clayhanger," i. 6); also, a Chinaman (as, "She had been in the China passenger trade and her lower decks had bunks for two thousand *pigtails*": Kipling's "Light That Failed," viii.).—**pig′tailed** (-tāld), *a.*

pig-weed (pig′wēd), *n.* Any of the goosefoots of the genus *Chenopodium*, esp. *C. album* ('white pigweed'); also, any of certain amaranths, as the species *Amarantus retroflexus*.

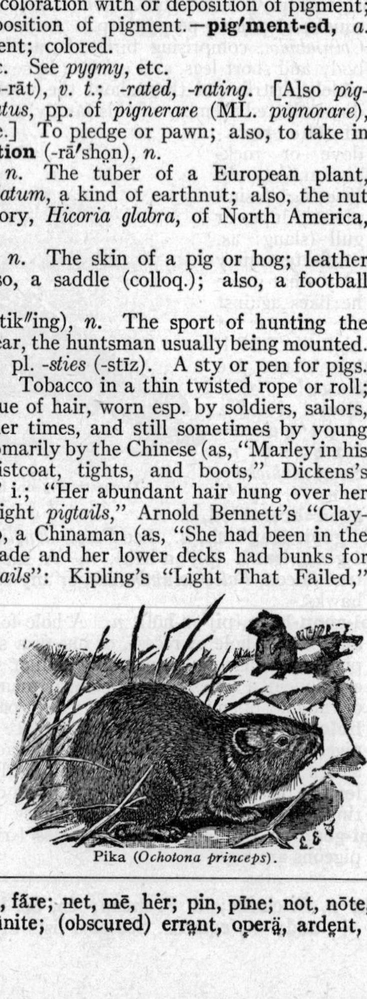
Pika (*Ochotona princeps*).

pi-ka (pī′kạ), *n.* [Native Siberian.] Any of various small rodent quadrupeds allied to the rabbits and inhabiting alpine regions of the northern hemisphere, as *Ochotona princeps* of North America. See cut in preceding column.

pike[1] (pīk), *n.* [AS. *pīc*, a pick or pickax: cf. OF. F. *pic*, a pick, F. also peak, Sp. *pico*, beak, pick, peak, also E. *peak*[1], *pick*[1], *pickax*, *picket*, and *pique*, *v.*] A pick or pickax (now prov. Eng.); also, a sharp point; a spike; the pointed end of anything, as of an arrow or a spear; also, the pointed summit of a hill or mountain, or a hill or mountain with such a summit (north. Eng.: as, "*Pikes*, of darkness named and fear and storms, Uplift in quiet their illumined forms," Wordsworth's "Descriptive Sketches," 472).

pike[2] (pīk), *n.*; pl. *pikes* or (esp. collectively) *pike*. [Prob. another use of *pike*[1], from the pointed snout.] Any of various large, slender, voracious fresh-water fishes of the genus *Esox*, having a long snout, esp. *E. lucius*, of the northern hemisphere; a luce; also, any of various similar fishes, as *Stizostedion vitreum* ('wall-eyed pike': see *pike-perch*).

Pike (*Esox lucius*).

pike[3] (pīk), *n.* [F. *pique*, akin to *pic*, a pick (see *pike*[1]), and *piquer*, prick (see *pique*, *v.*).] A long staff having a pointed head of iron or steel, in later times sometimes with a lateral beak or hook, or an ax-blade on one side and a beak or hook on the other, formerly much used as a weapon of infantry.—**pike**[3], *v. t.*; *piked, piking.* To pierce, wound, or kill with or as with a pike.

pike[4] (pīk), *n.* [Abbr. of *turnpike*.] A turnpike or toll-gate; also, the toll paid at a toll-gate; also, a turnpike road, or country highway (as, "The road . . . was an old one . . . abandoned . . . after the laying of the new *pike*," Mrs. Stowe's "Uncle Tom's Cabin," vii.; "The road . . . left the town and became . . . a country highway—called the *pike*—rather than a proud city boulevard," Tarkington's "Gentleman from Indiana," v.).

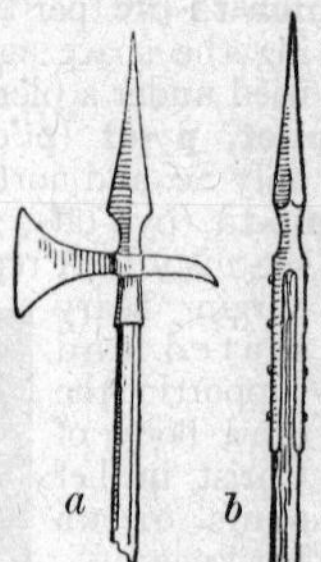

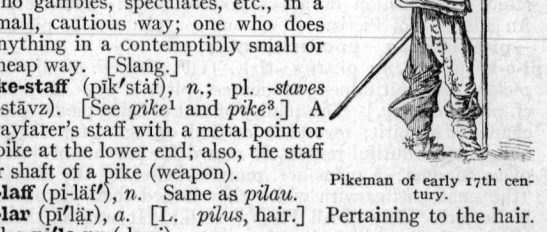

Pikes. — *a*, pike with ax-blade and beak; *b*, ordinary infantry pike, 17th century.

pike[5] (pīk), *v. i.*; *piked, piking.* [Origin uncertain.] To go, esp. quickly: often with *off*. [Now prov. or slang.]

pike[6] (pīk), *v. i.*; *piked, piking.* [Origin uncertain.] To gamble, speculate, etc., or do anything, in a small, cautious way; be a piker. [Slang.]

pik-ed (pī′ked or pīkt), *a.* [See *pike*[1].] Pointed; spiked; peaked.

pike-man (pīk′mạn), *n.*; pl. *-men.* [See *pike*[3].] A soldier armed with a pike.

pike=perch (pīk′pėrch), *n.* [See *pike*[2].] Any of several pike-like fishes of the perch family, as *Stizostedion vitreum* ('wall-eyed pike-perch') of North America, or *S. canadense*, the sauger. See cut on following page.

pik-er (pī′kėr), *n.* [See *pike*[6].] One who gambles, speculates, etc., in a small, cautious way; one who does anything in a contemptibly small or cheap way. [Slang.]

pike-staff (pīk′ståf), *n.*; pl. *-staves* (-stāvz). [See *pike*[1] and *pike*[3].] A wayfarer's staff with a metal point or spike at the lower end; also, the staff or shaft of a pike (weapon).

Pikeman of early 17th century.

pi-laff (pi-läf′), *n.* Same as *pilau*.

pi-lar (pī′lạr), *a.* [L. *pilus*, hair.] Pertaining to the hair. Also **pi′la-ry** (-lạ-ri).

pi-las-ter (pi-las′tėr), *n.* [F. *pilastre*, < It. *pilastro*, < ML. *pilastrum*, < L. *pila*, pillar: cf. *pile*[2].] In *arch.*, a square

United States
U. S. Union Jack
U. S. Revenue Flag
Canada
Mexico
Cuba
Haiti
Dominican Republic
Honduras
Guatemala
Salvador
Nicaragua
Costa Rica
Panama
Colombia
Venezuela
Ecuador
Peru
Bolivia
Brazil
Chile
Argentina
Paraguay
Uruguay
Zanzibar
Hungary
Czechoslovakia
Yugoslavia
Rumania
Lithuania
Soviet Russia
Finland
Latvia
Estonia
Bulgaria

NATIONAL FLAGS

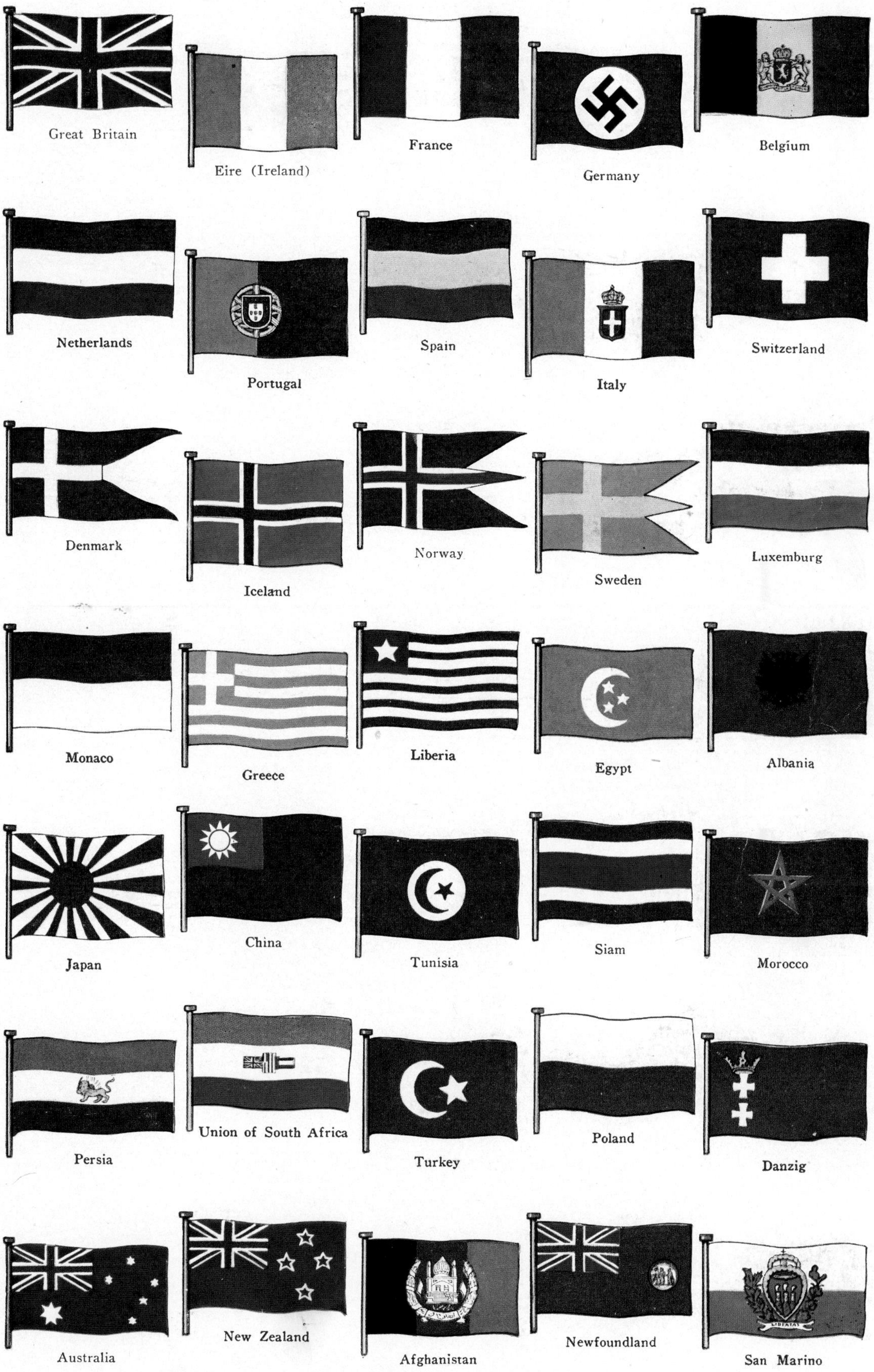
Great Britain
Eire (Ireland)
France
Germany
Belgium
Netherlands
Portugal
Spain
Italy
Switzerland
Denmark
Iceland
Norway
Sweden
Luxemburg
Monaco
Greece
Liberia
Egypt
Albania
Japan
China
Tunisia
Siam
Morocco
Persia
Union of South Africa
Turkey
Poland
Danzig
Australia
New Zealand
Afghanistan
Newfoundland
San Marino

NATIONAL FLAGS

or rectangular pillar, with capital and base, engaged in a wall from which it projects; an engaged rectangular pillar.—**pi-las'tered,** *a.* Furnished with pilasters.—**pil-as-trade** (pil-a̤s trād'), *n.* [It. *pilastrata.*] In *arch.*, a row of pilasters.—**pil-as-trad'ed** (-trā'ded), *a.*

Pike-perch (*Stizostedion vitreum*).

Pilaster.—Grand Trianon, Versailles, France.

pi-lau, pi-law (pi-lou', -lâ'), *n.* [Pers. and Turk. *pilāw.*] An Oriental dish consisting of rice boiled with mutton, fowl, or the like, and flavored with spices, raisins, etc.

pil-chard (pil'cha̤rd), *n.* [Origin uncertain.] A small European marine fish, the sardine, *Sardinella pilchardus*, allied to the herring but smaller and rounder; also, any of several related fishes. See cut below.

pile[1] (pīl), *n.* [AS. *pīl*, shaft, stake, < L. *pīlum*, javelin.] The heavy javelin of the ancient Roman infantry; also, a heavy stake or beam of timber, usually pointed at the lower end, driven vertically into the ground or the bed of a river, etc., to support a superstructure or form part of a wall (as, "He could see on the shore . . . bamboo huts perched upon *piles*": J. Conrad's "Rescue," ii. 3); any pillar or upright member, as of iron or concrete, similarly used; in *her.*, a bearing in the form of a wedge (assumed to represent an arrow-head), usually extending from the top of the escutcheon with its point downward.—**pile**[1], *v. t.*; *piled, piling.* To furnish, strengthen, or support with piles; drive piles into.

Pilchard (*Sardinella pilchardus*).

pile[2] (pīl), *n.* [OF. F. *pile*, < L. *pila*, pillar, pier, mole: cf. *pilaster.*] A pillar†; a pier, as of a bridge†; also, a mole, as in a harbor†; also, an assemblage of things laid or lying one upon another in a more or less orderly fashion (as, a *pile* of boxes, plates, or papers; a wood*pile*); a mass of any matter rising to some height (as, a *pile* of earth; "The clouds were like light *piles* of cotton," Parkman's "Oregon Trail," v.); a heap; specif., a heap of wood or other combustible material on which a dead body, a living person, or a sacrifice is burned; also, a lofty or large structure, building, or mass of buildings (as, "The cathedral is a huge, gloomy *pile*," Smollett's "Humphry Clinker," July 15; "high Whitby's cloister'd *pile*," Scott's "Marmion," ii. 1); also, a large number, quantity, or amount of anything (colloq.: as, he has a *pile*, or *piles*, of books; a *pile* of good sense); a large accumulation of money (colloq.: esp. used in 'to make one's pile'); in *elect.*, a series of plates of two dissimilar metals, as copper and zinc, arranged alternately with layers of cloth or paper, moistened with an acid solution, placed between them, for producing an electric current ('galvanic pile' or 'voltaic pile'); also, any similar arrangement for producing an electric current; a battery.—**funeral pile.** See under *funeral, a.*—**pile**[2], *v.*; *piled, piling.* **I.** *tr.* To lay or dispose in a pile (as, to *pile* wood or stones: often with *up*); heap; also, to place on or raise above something else, in or as if in a pile (as, "To fling Ossa upon Olympus, and to *pile* Pelion . . . On Ossa," Bryant's tr. Homer's "Odyssey," xi. 390; "huge dusky mountains, *piled* one over another," Smollett's "Humphry Clinker," Sept. 3); fig., to add as if to a pile (with *on*: as, to *pile* on details or ornaments; "Life *piled* on life Were all too little," Tennyson's "Ulysses," 24); also, to raise or erect (a pile, structure, etc.: with *up*: as, "that . . . a mighty race, now extinct, had *piled* up buildings which would never be dissolved till the judgment day," Macaulay's "Hist. of Eng.," i.); fig., to accumulate or amass (with *up*: as, to *pile* up a fortune); also, to cover or load with a pile or piles (as, to *pile* a plate with food; a counter *piled* with parcels); of things or matter, to form a pile or piles on (as, "The white drift *piled* the window-frame": Whittier's "Snow-Bound"). **II.** *intr.* To gather or rise in a pile or piles, as snow, etc. (as, "Chill o'er his slumbers *piles* the drifty heap!" Burns's "Winter Night," 80); fig., to accumulate, or mount up, as money, interest, debts, evidence, etc. (with *up*); also, to get (*in, into, out, off, down*, etc.) in a body and more or less confusedly (said of a number, or sometimes loosely of one: colloq.: as, "They all *piled* into it [a railroad-train]," Kipling's "Kim," xi.; "A lot of men begun to *pile* down off of the benches and swarm towards the ring," Mark Twain's "Huckleberry Finn," xxii.).

pile[3] (pīl), *n.* [L. *pilus*, a hair, the hair.] Hair, esp. soft, fine hair or down; wool, fur, or pelage; also, the nap of a fabric, esp. a soft, thick nap such as that on velvet, plush, many carpets, etc.; hence, a piled fabric, carpet, or the like (as, "The floor was covered with a rich soft *pile*": F. M. Crawford's "Mr. Isaacs," i.).

pile[4] (pīl), *n.* [Cf. L. *pila*, ball.] A swelling, often inflamed or bleeding, at the anus, formed by the dilatation of a blood-vessel; a hemorrhoid: usually in *pl.*

pil-e-ate (pil'ẹ-āt or pī'lẹ-), *a.* [L. *pileatus*, < *pileus*, felt cap: see *pileus.*] Capped; in *bot.*, having a pileus, as certain fungi.—**pil'e-at-ed** (-ā-ted), *a.* Capped; in *bot.*, pileate; in *ornith.*, crested (as, the *pileated* woodpecker, *Hylotomus* (or *Phlœotomus*) *pileatus*, a large North American woodpecker having a black plumage with streaks of white and a red crest).

Pileated Woodpecker.

piled (pīld), *a.* Having a pile or nap, as velvet and other fabrics.

pile=driv-er (pīl'drī"vėr), *n.* A machine for driving down piles, usually a tall framework in which a heavy weight of iron is raised between guides to a height, as by steam, and then allowed to fall upon the head of the pile.

pi-le-ous (pī'lẹ-us), *a.* [L. *pilus*, hair.] Of or pertaining to hair; hairy.

pil-er (pī'lėr), *n.* One who piles or heaps.

piles (pīlz), *n. pl.* See *pile*[4].

pil-e-um (pil'ẹ-um or pī'lẹ-), *n.*; pl. *pilea* (-ạ̈). [NL., < L. *pileum, pilleum*: see *pileus.*] In *ornith.*, the whole top of the head of a bird, from the base of the bill to the nape.

pil-e-us (pil'ẹ-us or pī'lẹ-), *n.*; pl. *pilei* (-ī). [L. *pileus*, better *pilleus*, also *pilleum*, felt cap, akin to *pilus*, hair, and Gr. πῖλος, felt, felt cap.] A kind of skullcap of felt worn by the ancient Romans and Greeks; in *bot.*, a cap or cap-like part, as of a mushroom.

pile-wort (pīl'wėrt), *n.* [So called from its reputed efficacy against *piles.*] The lesser celandine (plant).

pil-fer (pil'fėr), *v. t.* or *i.* [OF. *pelfrer*, pillage, rob: cf. *pelf.*] To steal, esp. in small quantities; obtain by, or practise, petty theft.—**pil'fer-age** (-ạ̄j), *n.* The act or practice of pilfering; petty theft; also, what is pilfered.—**pil'fer-er,** *n.*—**pil'fer-ing,** *n.* The act of one who pilfers; also, something pilfered.

pil-gar-lic (pil-gär'lik), *n.* [For *pilled* (peeled) *garlic.*] Orig., a bald head or bald-headed man; later, a poor creature, or wretch. [Now prov. or colloq.]

pil-grim (pil'grim), *n.* [OF. *peligrin, pellegrin* (F. *pèlerin*), < ML. *peregrinus*, pilgrim, L. foreigner: see *peregrine.*] A traveler or wanderer (now poetic or rhetorical); specif., one who journeys, esp. a long distance, to some sacred place, as an act of devotion (see cut on following page); one who makes a pilgrimage; also, *pl.* [*cap.*], in *U. S. hist.*, the English Puritans who founded the colony of Plymouth, Massachusetts, in 1620 (also called *Pilgrim Fathers*); also, *sing.* [*l. c.*], an original settler in a region (British colonies: as, "A few sheds received the '*Pilgrims*,' as the first comers are always called," Lady Barker's "Station Life in New

Zealand," iii.); a new-comer (person or animal) in a region (western U. S.).—**pil′grim,** *v. i.* To journey as a pilgrim.—**pil′grim-age** (-gri-māj), *n.* [OF. *peligrinage* (F. *pèlerinage*).] A journey undertaken or made by a pilgrim; a journey, esp. a long one, made to some sacred place, as an act of devotion; a journey undertaken for some pious purpose, or to visit a place held in honor (as, "The library, the museum, the aviary, and the botanical garden of Sir Thomas Browne, were thought . . . well worthy of a long *pilgrimage*": Macaulay's "Hist. of Eng.," iii.); a long journey; fig., the course of mortal life regarded as a journey (as, "And Jacob said unto Pharaoh, The days of the years of my *pilgrimage* are an hundred and thirty years": Gen. xlvii. 9).—**pil′grim-age,** *v. i.*; *-aged, -aging.* To go on a pilgrimage.—**pil′grim=bot″tle,** *n.* A flat bottle having rings for the insertion of a cord by which it may be carried; a costrel.

Pilgrim, in the recognized dress worn at Rome in the 18th century.

pi-lif-er-ous (pī-lif′ẹ-rus), *a.* [L. *pilus,* hair, + *ferre,* bear.] Bearing or having hair.

pi-li-form (pī′li-fôrm), *a.* [L. *pilus,* hair, + *forma,* form.] Having the form of a hair.

pil-ing (pī′ling), *n.* [See *pile*[1].] Piles collectively; a structure composed of piles.

pill[1] (pil), *v. t.* [OF. F. *piller,* < L. *pilare,* plunder, pillage: cf. *compile.*] To rob, plunder, or pillage. [Archaic.]

pill[2] (pil), *v. t.* or *i.* [Var. of *peel*[2].] To peel. [Archaic or prov.]

pill[3] (pil), *n.* [Prob. < OF. *pile,* pill, < L. *pila,* ball.] A small globular or rounded mass of medicinal substance, to be swallowed whole; hence, any small globular or pill-like body; a pellet; sometimes, a shot, bullet, or cannon-ball (colloq.); also, in fig. use, something unpleasant that has to be accepted or endured (as, "It had been a bitter *pill* to Theobald to lose his power of plaguing his first-born": S. Butler's "Way of All Flesh," lxxxii.); also, a person who is not liked or willingly endured (slang).—**pill**[3], *v. t.* To dose with pills; also, to blackball (slang).

pil-lage (pil′āj), *n.* [OF. F. *pillage,* < *piller,* E. *pill*[1].] The act of plundering, esp. in war; also, booty or spoil. —**pil′lage,** *v.*; *-laged, -laging.* **I.** *tr.* To strip of money or goods by open violence, as in war; plunder; also, to take as booty. **II.** *intr.* To rob with open violence; take booty. —**pil-lag-er** (pil′ā-jėr), *n.*

pil-lar (pil′ạr), *n.* [OF. *piler* (F. *pilier*), < ML. *pilare,* < L. *pila,* pillar, E. *pile*[2].] An upright shaft or structure, as of stone, brick, or other material, relatively slender in proportion to its height, and of any shape in section, used as a support, or standing alone, as for a monument; a column, pier, or the like; hence, in general, an upright supporting part; a post; a shaft-like part; a shaft-like or columnar mass (as, "The Lord went before them by day in a *pillar* of a cloud . . . and by night in a *pillar* of fire": Ex. xiii. 21); sometimes, a pillar-box (Eng.: as, "Will you just run out with this [letter] to the *pillar,* Miss Dadd?" Arnold Bennett's "Old Wives' Tale," ii. 1); also, fig., a person who is a chief supporter of a state, institution, etc. (as, "He . . . was a deacon and a *pillar* of the church": W. Churchill's "Coniston," i. 8); a principle, fact, or the like, that is a main support or stay of something (as, "Humanity . . . is the great *pillar* of my management": Mrs. Stowe's "Uncle Tom's Cabin," i.).—**from pillar to post,** from one place to another, orig. like a ball tossed at tennis; from one position, resort, resource, or the like, to another, as a person driven by persecution or by the harassing force of circumstances; in general, hither and thither.—**Pillars of Hercules,** two promontories on opposite sides of the Strait of Gibraltar, fabled to have been raised by Hercules.—**pil′lar,** *v. t.* To provide or support with pillars; also, to form into or like a pillar.—**pil′lar=box,** *n.* A short, hollow pillar set up in a public place, containing a receptacle for letters, etc., to be collected by postmen: as, "She wrote her letter and dropped it in the *pillar-box*" (M. Hewlett's "Open Country," ix.). [Eng.]

Pillar. — Cathedral of Tours, France, 13th century.

pill=box (pil′boks), *n.* A box, usually shallow and often round, for holding pills; also, something suggesting such a box; esp., a small, low structure of reinforced concrete, with very thick walls and roof, inclosing machine-guns, and employed as a minor fortress in warfare (colloq.).

pill=bug (pil′bug), *n.* Any of various small terrestrial isopods, esp. of the genus *Armadillo,* which can roll themselves up into a ball like a pill.

pil-lion (pil′yọn), *n.* [Gael. *pillean, pillin,* or Ir. *pillin,* prob. ult. < L. *pellis,* skin.] A kind of light saddle†; also, a pad or cushion attached behind a saddle, esp. as a seat for a woman (as, "I proposed that Jack . . . should ride my Aunt Gainor's horse, with Miss Peniston on the *pillion* behind him": Weir Mitchell's "Hugh Wynne," xi.).

pil-lo-ry (pil′ọ-ri), *n.*; pl. *-ries* (-riz). [OF. *pilori, pellori* (F. *pilori*); origin uncertain.] A wooden framework erected on a post, with holes for securing the head and hands, used to expose an offender to public derision.—**pil′lo-ry,** *v. t.*; *-ried, -rying.* To set in the pillory; punish by exposure in the pillory; fig., to expose to public ridicule or abuse (as, "a private person . . . *pilloried* in print": Mark Twain's "Life on the Mississippi," l.).

Pillory.

pil-low (pil′ō), *n.* [AS. *pyle, pylu,* < L. *pulvinus,* pillow, cushion.] A support for the head during sleep or rest, specif. a bag or case filled with feathers, down, or other soft material, and commonly forming part of a bed; also, a cushion or pad, as the cushion on which pillow-lace is made; also, a supporting piece or part, as the block on which the inner end of a bowsprit rests.—**pil′low,** *v.* **I.** *tr.* To rest on or as on a pillow; support with pillows; also, to serve as a pillow for. **II.** *intr.* To rest as on a pillow: as, "Thou shalt *pillow* on my breast" (J. R. Drake's "Culprit Fay," xxxii.).—**pil′low=bar,** *n.* One of the bars or brides connecting parts of the pattern of pillow-lace; the ground or filling formed by such threads.

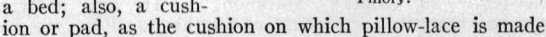

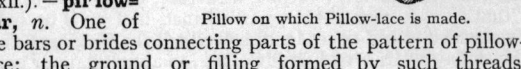

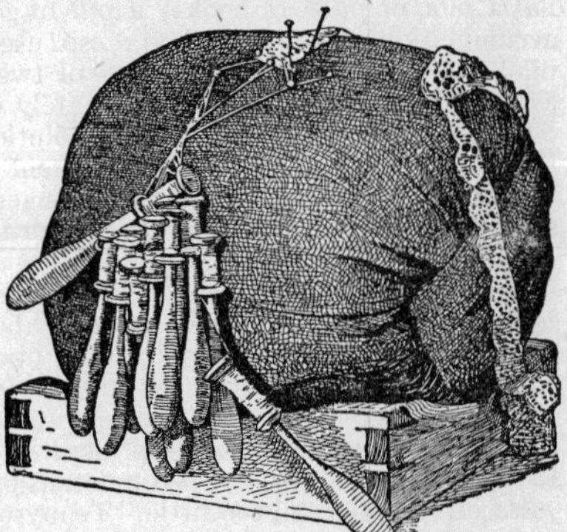
Pillow on which Pillow-lace is made.

—**pil′low=bere, pil′low=beer** (-bēr), *n.* [ME. *bere*, covering, case: cf. G. *bühre.*] A pillow-case. [Archaic or prov.] —**pil′low=case,** *n.* A removable case, usually of white cotton or linen, drawn over a pillow.—**pil′lowed,** *a.* Furnished with a pillow or pillows: as, "The Squire sat propped in a *pillowed* chair" (H. Newbolt's "Fidele's Grassy Tomb").—**pil′low=lace,** *n.* Lace made on a pillow with threads wound on bobbins.—**pil′low=sham,** *n.* An ornamental cover laid over a pillow on a bed when not in use.—**pil′low=slip,** *n.* A pillow-case.—**pil′low-y,** *a.* Pillow-like; soft; yielding.

pi-lo-car-pine (pī-lọ̄-kär′pin), *n.* [NL. *Pilocarpus*, < Gr. πῖλος, cap, + καρπός, fruit.] In *chem.*, an alkaloid obtained from the leaflets of species of *Pilocarpus* (jaborandi), used in medicine as a diaphoretic and diuretic.

pi-lose (pī′lōs), *a.* [L. *pilosus*, < *pilus*, hair.] Covered with hair, esp. soft hair; hairy; furry.—**pi-los′i-ty** (-los′-i-ti), *n.*

pi-lot (pī′lọt), *n.* [F. *pilote*, < It. *piloto*, *pilota*, appar. for earlier *pedotta*, pilot, perhaps < Gr. πηδόν, oar, πηδά, pl., rudder.] The steersman of a ship; specif., one duly qualified to steer ships into or out of a harbor or through certain difficult waters; hence, in general, a guide or leader; also, a cow-catcher; in *aëronautics*, one duly qualified to operate a balloon, airship, or flying-machine.—**pi′lot,** *v. t.* To act as pilot of, or direct the course of (as, to *pilot* a ship or an aircraft); steer; hence, to guide or conduct, as through unknown places, intricate affairs, etc.; also, to act as pilot on, in, or over (as, "Mentor, captain of the lordly crew . . . *Pilots* the course," Pope's tr. Homer's "Odyssey," iv.; "Morn and eve, night and day, Have I *piloted* your bay," Browning's "Hervé Riel," vi.).—**pi′lot-age** (-ạ̄j), *n.* [F. *pilotage.*] The act or practice of piloting; the function of a pilot; also, the fee paid to a pilot for his services.—**pi′lot=bal-loon″,** *n.* A small balloon sent up to ascertain the direction or force of air-currents.—**pi′lot=bis″cuit, pi′lot=bread,** *n.* Ship-biscuit.—**pi′lot=cloth,** *n.* A heavy woolen cloth used for pea-jackets, etc.—**pi′lot=coat,** *n.* A pea-jacket: as, "my travelling wear of country velveteen, *pilot-coat*, and knitted spencer" (Stevenson's "Travels with a Donkey," i. 1).—**pi′lot=en″gine,** *n.* A locomotive engine sent on ahead of a railroad-train to see that the way is clear. —**pi′lot=fish,** *n.* A small fish, *Naucrates ductor*, of bluish color with dark vertical bars, found in warm seas, often accompanying sharks.—**pi′lot=house,** *n.* An inclosed place or house on the deck of a vessel, sheltering the steering-gear and the pilot or helmsman.—**pi′lot=jack,** *n.* A flag hoisted by a vessel as a signal for a pilot.—**pi′lot-less,** *a.* Without a pilot.—**pi′lot=light,** *n.* A small light kept burning continuously, as beside a large gas-burner, to relight a main light whenever desired.—**pi′lot=whale,** *n.* A cetacean of the genus *Globicephalus*, of the dolphin family, as *G. melas*, the caaing-whale.

Pilot-fish.

pi-lous (pī′lus), *a.* [See *pilose.*] Covered with or abounding in hair; hairy; also, consisting of hair; hair-like.

Pilt-down (pilt′doun) **man.** A very early type of man (believed to belong to an earlier period than the Neanderthaloid type), whose existence is inferred from fragments of a skull discovered at Piltdown, in Sussex, England, in 1912.

pil-ule (pil′ūl), *n.* [F. *pilule*, < L. *pilula*, pill, dim. of *pila*, ball.] A pill; a little pill.—**pil′u-lar, pil′u-lous** (-ụ̄-lạ̈r, -lus), *a.*

pi-men-to (pi-men′tō), *n.*; pl. *-tos* (-tōz). [Sp. *pimienta*, pepper, *pimiento*, capsicum, < ML. *pigmentum*, spice, L. pigment: see *pigment.*] Allspice; the West Indian tree, *Pimenta pimenta*, yielding it (see cut in next column); the wood of this tree; also, the pimiento, or sweet pepper.

pi-mien-to (pē-myen′tō), *n.*; pl. *-tos* (-tōz, Sp. -tōs). [Sp.: see *pimento.*] Any plant of the genus *Capsicum*, or its fruit; esp., one of the so-called sweet peppers, which are used as a vegetable, a relish, etc.

pim-o-la (pim-ō′lạ̈), *n.* [See *pimento* and *olive.*] An olive stuffed with red sweet pepper.

pimp (pimp), *n.* [Origin uncertain.] One who provides means and opportunities for gratifying lust; a pander; hence, in general, one who ministers to base appetites, vices, or anything evil. —**pimp,** *v. i.* To act as a pimp; pander.

Pimento (*Pimenta pimenta*). — *a*, flower; *b*, flower in longitudinal section, the stamens removed; *c*, fruit.

pim-per-nel (pim′-pėr-nel), *n.* [OF. *pimprenele* (F. *pimprenelle*); origin uncertain.] A primulaceous herb of the genus *Anagallis*, esp. *A. arvensis*, a species with scarlet, purplish, or white flowers that close at the approach of bad weather.

pimp-ing (pim′ping), *a.* [Origin uncertain.] Little; insignificant; petty; also, weak; sickly.

pim-ple (pim′pl), *n.* [ME. *pinple*; origin uncertain.] A small, usually inflammatory swelling or elevation of the skin; a papule or pustule.—**pim′pled, pim′ply,** *a.*

pin (pin), *n.* [AS. *pinn*, appar. < L. *pinna*, pinnacle: see *pinnacle.*] A small, slender, commonly cylindrical, often pointed or tapering piece of wood, metal, or other material, used, as by fitting or driving into something, to hold things together or in place, to serve as a point of support or attachment, or to answer some other purpose; a peg, bolt, or the like; specif., a linch-pin, serving to keep a wheel on its axle; the projecting part, or tenon, of a dovetail-joint; a thole-pin, or peg fixed in the side of a boat to keep the oar in place; one of the pegs in a musical instrument, to which the strings are fastened at one end; a belaying-pin, to which rigging is secured; the peg stuck in the ground, at which quoits are thrown; a peg, nail, or stud marking the center of a target; also, a clothes-pin; a rolling-pin; one of the bottle-shaped pieces of wood knocked down in ninepins, tenpins, etc.; a leg (colloq.: as, "He was not quite so active on his *pins* as formerly," H. Kingsley's "Geoffry Hamlyn," xxii.); also, a short, slender piece of wire with a point at one end and a head at the other, for fastening things together; hence, such an implement as a type of smallness, slight value, or insignificance; a very small amount, or a trifle (as, "This day fortnight you'll hardly be a *pin* the worse of it": C. Brontë's "Jane Eyre," xx.); also, any of various forms of fastening or ornament consisting essentially or in part of a pointed penetrating bar (as, a hat-*pin*, scarf-*pin*, breast*pin*, safety-*pin*, or hair-*pin*); a badge having a pointed bar or pin attached, by which it is fastened to the clothing; also, mood, humor, or frame of mind (archaic or prov.: as, to be on a merry *pin*, or on the peevish *pin*; "Right glad to find His friend in merry *pin*," Cowper's "John Gilpin," 178).—**pin,** *v. t.*; *pinned, pinning.* To fasten or secure with one or more pins, pegs, or bolts; also, to fasten or attach with a pin (short piece of wire) or pins, or a hat-pin, hair-pin, or the like; transfix with a pin or the like; hence, to fasten or attach as if with a pin (as, to *pin* one's faith on a person or thing); hold fast in a spot or position (as, "rescued from the débris that had *pinned* her down," H. G. Wells's "Mr. Britling," ii. 3. § 11; to *pin* a man's arms to his sides); bind or hold to a course of action, a promise, etc. (often with *down*: as, "Mr. Britling's fluttering, unwilling mind was *pinned* down . . . to a definite belief," H. G. Wells's "Mr. Britling," ii. 3. § 2); also, to seize or nab (slang); also, to confine within a space or inclosure (as, "The legions at Alesia held twice their number *pinned* within their works": Froude's "Cæsar," xxviii.).

pi-na-ceous (pī-nā′shius), *a.* [L. *pinus*, pine.] Belonging to the *Pinaceæ*, or pine family of trees and shrubs, which includes the pine, spruce, fir, hemlock-spruce, etc.

pi-ña=cloth (pē'nyạ̈-klôth), *n.* [Sp. *piña*, pine-cone, pineapple.] A fine, sheer fabric made in the Philippines and elsewhere from the fiber of pineapple leaves.

pin-a-coid (pin'ạ-koid), *n.* [Gr. πινακοειδής, like a tablet, < πίναξ (πινακ-), tablet, + εἶδος, form.] In *crystal.*, a form consisting of two parallel faces.—**pin-a-coi'dal,** *a.*

pin-a-co-the-ca (pin''ạ-kọ̄-thē'kạ̈), *n.*; pl. *-cas* (-kạ̈z), L. *-cæ* (-sē). [L., < Gr. πινακοθήκη, < πίναξ (πινακ-), tablet, picture, + θήκη, case, repository.] A picture-gallery; an art-gallery. Also (G.) **pi-na-ko-thek** (pē-nä-kō-tāk').

pin-a-fore (pin'ạ-fōr), *n.* [From *pin*, *v.*, + *afore*, *adv.*] A child's apron, usually one large enough to cover most of the dress.—**pin'a-fored,** *a.* Wearing a pinafore.

pi-nas-ter (pī-nas'tėr), *n.* [L., < *pinus*, pine.] A pine, *Pinus pinaster*, of southern Europe, having the cones arranged around the branches in radiating clusters.

pin=bor-er (pin'bōr''ėr), *n.* Any of various small beetles of the family *Scolytidæ* that make minute holes through the bark of infested trees, as *Xyleborus dispar*, of Europe and North America.

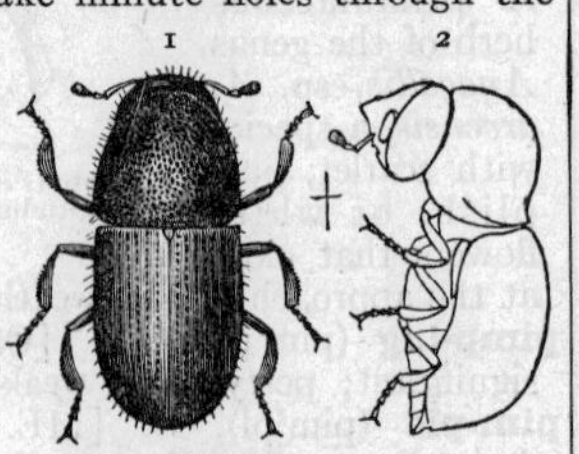

Pin-borer (*Xyleborus dispar*). — 1, female; 2, female in lateral outline. (Cross shows natural size.)

pince=nez (pans-nā), *n.* [F., 'pinch-nose.'] A pair of eyeglasses kept in place by a spring which pinches the nose.

pin-cers (pin'sėrz), *n. pl.* or *sing.* [ME. *pynceours*, *pinsers*, < OF. *pincier*: see *pinch*.] A gripping tool consisting of two pivoted limbs forming a pair of jaws and a pair of handles (often called a *pair of pincers*); in *zoöl.*, a grasping organ or pair of organs resembling this.

pinch (pinch), *v.* [OF. *pincier* (F. *pincer*), pinch: cf. It. *pizzicare*, pinch, pick.] **I.** *tr.* To compress between the finger and thumb, the teeth, the claws, the jaws of an instrument, or the like (as, to *pinch* a child's cheek playfully; "He was *pinched* with red-hot pincers, and racked," Besant's "Coligny," viii.); take or nip off (a bud, etc.) by sharp compression between the finger and thumb, or prune (a shoot, etc.) thus; also, to compress, constrict, or squeeze painfully, as a tight shoe or garment does; hence, to cramp within narrow bounds or quarters (as, "Who would not be a little *pinched* in his chamber, if his windows looked upon the sea?" G. W. Curtis's "Prue and I," iii.); render (the face, etc.) unnaturally contracted, shrunken, or thin and drawn, as pain or distress does; nip (plants) injuriously, as frost does; affect with sharp discomfort or distress, as cold, hunger, or want does; often, to straiten in means or circumstances; stint in allowance of money, food, or the like (as, "They had to *pinch* themselves in order to give us what they did": H. Melville's "Omoo," xxxiv.); hamper or inconvenience by want of something specified (as, to be *pinched* for time); stint the supply or amount of (a thing: now prov.); also, to put a pinch or small quantity of (a powder, etc.) into something (as, "to . . . *pinch* a murderous dust into her drink": Tennyson's "Merlin and Vivien," 608); also, to steal (slang); also, to arrest, or take into custody (slang); also, to move (a heavy object) by means of a pinch or pinch-bar; *naut.*, to sail (a vessel) close-hauled. **II.** *intr.* To exert a sharp or painful compressing force (as, to know where the shoe *pinches*, often fig., to know where the real trouble lies); hence, to cause sharp discomfort or distress (as, when hunger *pinches*; "Here's the pang that *pinches*," Shakspere's "Henry VIII.," ii. 3. 1); also, to stint one's self, or economize unduly (as, "Her father and sister were obliged to *pinch*, in order to allow her the small luxuries": Mrs. Gaskell's "Cranford," ii.); be parsimonious or niggardly; in *mining*, of a vein of ore, etc., to become narrower or smaller, or to give (*out*) altogether.—**pinch,** *n.* The act or an act of pinching; a nip or squeeze; sharp or painful stress, as of hunger, want, or any trying circumstances; also, a situation or time of special stress, a strait, or an emergency (as, "I will not fail him at this *pinch*": Scott's "Quentin Durward," xxvii.); also, as much of anything as can be taken up between the finger and thumb (as, a *pinch* of salt; a *pinch* of snuff); hence, a very small quantity of anything; also, a pinch-bar.—**at a pinch,** in an emergency: as, "I am not a bad cook *at a pinch*" (F. M. Crawford's "Mr. Isaacs," xii.).

pinch=bar (pinch'bär), *n.* A kind of crowbar or lever with a projection which serves as a fulcrum.

pinch-beck (pinch'bek). [From the inventor, Christopher *Pinchbeck* (died 1732), a London clock-maker.] **I.** *n.* An alloy of copper and zinc, used in imitation of gold; hence, something spurious. **II.** *a.* Made of pinchbeck; hence, sham or spurious (as, *pinchbeck* patriotism; *pinchbeck* heroism).

pinch=cock (pinch'kok), *n.* A clamp for compressing a flexible pipe, as an india-rubber tube, in order to regulate or stop the flow of a fluid.

pinched (pincht), *p. a.* Compressed, as between the finger and thumb; hence, contracted, as if by pinching; shrunken, or thin and drawn, as the face or features (as, "In the biting easterly wind her face looked small, and *pinched*, and cold": Galsworthy's "Dark Flower," iii. 14); distressed; straitened; narrow or scanty.—**pinched'ness,** *n.*

pinch-er (pin'chėr), *n.* One who or that which pinches.

pinch-ers (pin'chėrz), *n. pl.* or *sing.* Same as *pincers*.

pinch=hit-ter (pinch'hit'ėr), *n.* In *baseball*, one who hits or bats in a pinch or emergency; esp., a substitute who, at some critical moment of the game, takes the turn at bat of a weaker or less reliable batsman.

pinch-ing (pin'ching), *p. a.* That pinches; nipping; sharp; distressing; causing straits; also, sparing, parsimonious, or niggardly.—**pinch'ing-ly,** *adv.*

pinc=pinc (pingk'pingk), *n.* [Imit. of its note.] A South African warbler, *Cisticola* (or *Drymœca*) *textrix*, or some other species of the same genus.

Pinc-pinc (*Cisticola textrix*).

pin-cush-ion (pin'kůsh''ọn), *n.* A small cushion in which pins are stuck, in readiness for use.

Pin-dar-ic (pin-dar'ik). **I.** *a.* Of, pertaining to, or after the manner of Pindar (about 522—about 443 B.C.), the Greek lyric poet; hence, of elaborate or irregular metrical structure, as an ode or verse. **II.** *n.* A Pindaric ode or verse.

pin-dling (pin'dling), *a.* [Origin uncertain.] Fretful (prov. Eng.); also, puny, sickly, or delicate (local, U. S.).

pine[1] (pīn), *n.* [AS. *pīn*, < L. *pinus*, pine.] Any member of the genus *Pinus*, comprising evergreen coniferous trees varying greatly in size, with needle-shaped leaves, and including many species which are of the highest economic importance for their timber and as a source of turpentine, tar, pitch, etc.; any of various allied trees; the wood of any such tree; also, the pineapple.

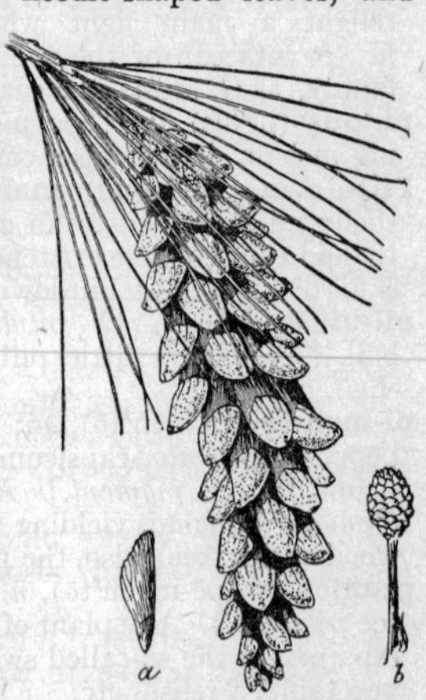

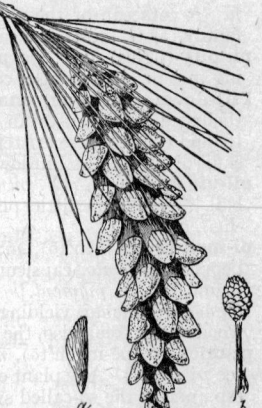

Branch with Cone of White Pine (*Pinus strobus*). — *a*, the seed; *b*, a very young cone.

pine[2] (pīn), *v.*; *pined*, *pining*. [AS. *pīnian*, torment, afflict, < L. *pœna*, punishment, suffering, pain: see *pain*.] **I.** *tr.* To torment†; afflict with pain or suffering†; also, to cause to languish or waste with suffering, hunger, etc. (archaic or prov.); also, to suffer grief or regret over, or repine at (archaic: as, "Abash'd the devil stood . . . and *pined* His loss," Milton's "Paradise Lost," iv. 848). **II.** *intr.* To languish, droop, or waste with suffering (of body or mind), want of food or favorable conditions, or the like (as, "remitted to the county bridewell, where, secluded from free air and sunshine . . . he *pined* and died," Scott's "Guy Mannering," vi.: often with *away*); often, to fail gradually in health or vitality from grief, regret, or longing (as, "Thro' her love her life Wasted and *pined*, desiring him in vain": Tennyson's "Pelleas and Ettarre," 486); suffer with longing, or long painfully (*for*: as, "Like all sailors ashore, I at last *pined* for the billows," H. Melville's "Omoo," lxxxii.); also, to repine or fret.—**pine**[2], *n.* Painful punishment†, or torment†; also, pain, suffering, or misery (archaic or Sc.: as, "heavy-dragg'd wi' *pine* an' grievin'," Burns's "Scotch Drink," 27); painful longing (obs. or archaic).

pin-e-al (pin'ē-a̤l), *a.* [F. *pinéal*, < L. *pinea*, pine-cone, < *pinus*, pine.] Resembling a pine-cone in shape (as, the *pineal* body or gland, a body of unknown function present in the brain of all vertebrates having a cranium, believed to be a vestigial sense-organ); also, pertaining to the pineal body.

pine-ap-ple (pīn'ap″l), *n.* [ME. *pinappel*, pine-cone.] A pine-cone (obs. or prov. Eng.); also, the edible juicy fruit (somewhat resembling a pine-cone) of a tropical bromeliaceous plant, *Ananas ananas*, being a large collective fruit developed from a spike or head of flowers, and surmounted by a crown of leaves; the plant itself, a native of tropical South America, now widely cultivated throughout the tropics, having a short stem and rigid, spiny-margined, recurved leaves; also, some other bromeliaceous plant, as *Bromelia pinguin* ('wild pineapple').—**pine'ap″ple=cloth,** *n.* Piña-cloth.

Pineapple (*Ananas ananas*).

pine=bar-ren (pīn'bar″e̤n), *n.* A level sandy tract covered sparsely with pine-trees. [Chiefly southern U. S.]

pine=cone (pīn'kōn), *n.* The cone or strobile of a pine-tree.

pine=drops (pīn'drops), *n.* A slender, leafless North American herb *Pterospora andromedea*, with nodding white flowers, found growing under pines.

pine=finch (pīn'finch), *n.* A small North American finch, *Chrysomitris* (or *Spinus*) *pinus*, with streaked plumage; also, the pine-grosbeak.

pine=gros-beak (pīn'grōs'bēk), *n.* A large finch, *Pinicola enucleator*, of North America, Europe, and Asia, found chiefly in coniferous woods.

Pine-grosbeak.

pine=mar-ten (pīn'mär″ten), *n.* A European marten, *Mustela martes*; also, an American marten, *M. americana*, the American sable.

pi-nene (pī'nēn), *n.* [L. *pinus*, pine.] In *chem.*, a terpene forming the principal constituent of oil of turpentine and occurring also in other essential oils.

pine=nee-dle (pīn'nē″dl), *n.* The acicular leaf of the pine-tree.

pin-er-y (pī'nėr-i), *n.*; pl. *pineries* (-iz). A place in which pineapples are grown; also, a forest, grove, or plantation of pine-trees.

pine=sap (pīn'sap), *n.* A leafless plant, *Hypopitys hypopitys*, of the north temperate zone, having yellowish or reddish flowers in a nodding raceme, and resembling the Indian-pipe: so called as being parasitic on the roots of pines. See cut in next column.

pine=sis-kin (pīn'sis'kin), *n.* The pine-finch, *Chrysomitris* (or *Spinus*) *pinus*.

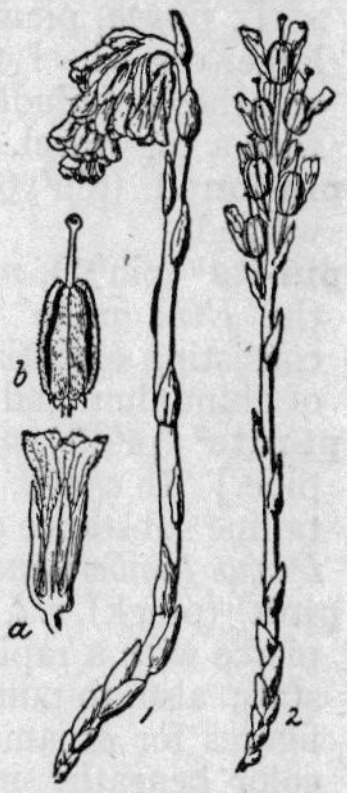

Pine-sap. — 1, flowering plant; 2, plant with fruits; *a*, a flower; *b*, the fruit.

pi-ne-tum (pī-nē'tum), *n.*; pl. *-tums* or *-ta* (-tä). [L., < *pinus*, pine.] A plantation or collection of growing pine-trees of different kinds, as for ornamental or scientific purposes; also, a treatise on pines.

pin-ey (pī'ni), *a.* See *piny*.

pin=feath-er (pin'feᴛʜ″ėr), *n.* An undeveloped feather, before the web portions have expanded.

pin=fire (pin'fīr), *a.* Noting an early type of cartridge fitted with a pin which, when struck by the hammer of the fire-arm, is driven into and explodes a percussion-cap in the cartridge; also, noting a firearm in which such a cartridge is used.

pin-fish (pin'fish), *n.* Either of two sparoid fishes, *Diplodus holbrooki* and *Lagodon rhomboides*, of the southern Atlantic coast of the U. S.; also, any of various other fishes.

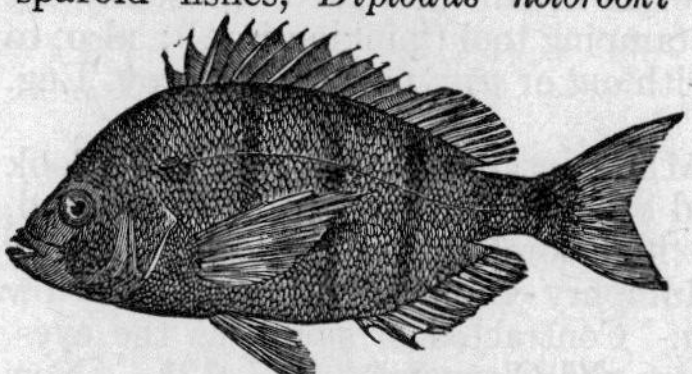
Pinfish (*Lagodon rhomboides*).

pin-fold (pin'fōld), *n.* [ME. *pynfold*, for earlier *pundfald*, 'pound-fold': see *pound*[1].] A pound for stray or distrained animals; also, a fold, as for sheep or cattle; hence, any place of confinement (as, "men . . . pester'd in this *pinfold* here": Milton's "Comus," 7).—**pin'fold,** *v. t.* To confine in or as in a pinfold.

ping (ping), *v. i.* [Imit.] To produce a sound like that of a rifle-bullet whistling through the air or striking an object.—**ping,** *n.* A pinging sound.

ping=pong (ping'pong'), *n.* [Varied redupl. of *ping*.] A variety of tennis played on a table with small rackets and a hollow celluloid ball.

pin=grass (pin'gràs), *n.* The plant alfileria.

pin-guid (ping'gwid), *a.* [L. *pinguis*.] Fat; oily; unctuous.—**pin-guid'i-ty** (-i-ti), *n.*

pin-head (pin'hed), *n.* The head of a pin; hence, something very small or insignificant; also, a person having little brain or intelligence (slang).—**pin'=head″ed,** *a.* Having a head like that of a pin; hence, having little brain or intelligence (slang).

pin-hole (pin'hōl), *n.* A hole for a pin or peg; also, a small hole or perforation made by or as by a pin.

pin-ing (pī'ning), *p. a.* That pines; languishing; wasting; failing with grief or longing.—**pin'ing-ly,** *adv.*

pin-ion[1] (pin'yo̤n), *n.* [OF. *pignon*, feather, = *penon*, E. *pennon*.] The distal or terminal segment of a bird's wing (in scientific use, the carpus, metacarpus, and phalanges); hence, the wing of a bird, or the flight-feathers collectively (chiefly poetic: as, "First a speck, and then a vulture, Till the air is dark with *pinions*," Longfellow's "Hiawatha," xix. 10); also, a feather, esp. a flight-feather (as, "He is pluck'd, when hither He sends so poor a *pinion* of his wing": Shakspere's "Antony and Cleopatra," iii. 12. 4).—**pin'ion**[1], *v. t.* To cut off the pinion of (a wing) or bind (the wings), as in order to prevent a bird from flying; disable or restrain (a bird) thus; also, to bind (a person's arms or hands), so as to deprive him of the use of them (as, "All their hands he *pinioned* behind With their own girdles": Chapman's tr. Homer's "Iliad," xxi.); disable thus, or shackle, as a person (as, "Finding us all prostrate upon our faces . . . they *pinioned* us with strong ropes," Swift's "Gulliver's Travels," iii. 1; "The captain of the vessel . . . lay *pinioned* against the gun," Marryat's "Mr. Midshipman Easy," xiii.); hence, in general, to bind or hold fast, as to a thing (as, "Some slave of mine be *pinioned* to their side," Pope's "Dunciad," iv. 134; "The speaker's victim writhed, but the riveted gaze and an uplifted finger *pinioned* him," G. W. Cable's "Bonaventure," iii. 3).

pin-ion[2] (pin′yọn), *n.* [F. *pignon*, pinion, OF. battlement, < L. *pinna*, pinnacle.] A small cog-wheel engaging with a larger cog-wheel or with a rack; sometimes, an arbor or spindle with teeth which engage with a cog-wheel.

Cog-wheel, with Pinion (*a*).

pin-ioned (pin′yọnd), *a.* Having pinions; winged.

pin-ite[1] (pin′īt), *n.* [G. *pinit*; named from the *Pini* mine in Saxony.] A mineral consisting essentially of a hydrous silicate of aluminium and potassium.

pi-nite[2] (pī′nīt), *n.* [F. *pinite*, < L. *pinus*, pine.] In *chem.*, a colorless, sweetish, crystalline substance obtained from the gum exuded by the pine *Pinus lambertiana*, and also from certain other plants.

pink[1] (pingk), *v. t.* [Perhaps a nasalized form of *pick*[1].] To pierce with a rapier or the like (as, to be *pinked* in a duel); stab; also, to punch (cloth, leather, etc.) with small holes or figures for ornament, often in order to show a material or color beneath; now, specif., to finish at the edge with a scalloped, notched, or other ornamental pattern, usually cut by means of a special stamping tool ('pinking-iron'); also, to deck or adorn (often with *out* or *up*: now chiefly prov. Eng. and Sc.).

pink[2] (pingk), *v. i.* [MD. *pincken* (D. *pinken*).] To look or peer with contracted eyes; of the eyes, to be contracted, narrow, or small (as, "high forehead, sandy locks, *pinking* eyes": Smollett's "Humphry Clinker," May 24). [Now prov. Eng.]—**pink**[2], *a.* Contracted or small, as the eyes. See Shakspere's "Antony and Cleopatra," ii. 7. 121. [Now prov. Eng.]

pink[3] (pingk), *n.* [MD. *pinck* (D. *pink*).] A kind of vessel or boat with a narrow stern.

pink[4] (pingk), *n.* [Origin uncertain: cf. *pink*[1], also *lake*[1] (orig. red).] Any plant of the silenaceous genus *Dianthus*, as *D. plumarius* (the common garden pink), *D. chinensis* ('China pink'), or *D. caryophyllus* ('clove-pink,' or carnation), or any of various related or similar plants; the flower of such a plant; fig., the flower, or highest type or example of excellence (as, "He had been to her the very *pink* of courtesy," Mrs. H. Ward's "Robert Elsmere," viii.; "Her kitchen always looked the *pink* of cleanliness," George Eliot's "Adam Bede," iv.); the highest form or degree, or the height (as, "You've had him [a fighter] at his best, too—in the *pink* of condition": Conan Doyle's "Exploits of Brigadier Gerard," iv.); also, a light reddish color of various shades or varieties (as, rose-*pink*; shell-*pink*); also, scarlet, or scarlet cloth, as worn by fox-hunters (as, "an English country gentleman, hunting in *pink*": F. M. Crawford's "Mr. Isaacs," ii.); a scarlet hunting-coat; a fox-hunter; also, any of various yellow or greenish-yellow lakes or pigments prepared by treating a white base, such as chalk, with certain vegetable juices.—**in the pink,** in the best of condition. [Colloq.]—**pink**[4], *a.* Of the color pink: as, a *pink* carnation; *pink* ribbon; *pink* cheeks.—**pink**[4], *v. i.* To turn pink; flush; blush: often with *up*. [Colloq. or prov.]

pink-er (ping′kėr), *n.* One who or that which pinks; a pinking-iron.

pink=eye (pingk′ī), *n.* In *pathol.*, a contagious form of conjunctivitis: so called from the color of the inflamed eye.

pink-ing=i-ron (ping′king-ī″ėrn), *n.* A tool of iron or steel with a specially shaped end for pinking cloth, etc., being driven through the material by blows of a hammer on the other end. See *pink*[1].

pink-ish (ping′kish), *a.* Somewhat pink; tending to pink: as, a *pinkish* white.

pink-ly (pingk′li), *adv.* With a pink color.—**pink′ness,** *n.*

pink-root (pingk′röt), *n.* The root of any of various plants of the loganiaceous genus *Spigelia*, esp. that of *S. marilandica* of the U. S., which is used as a vermifuge; also, any of these plants.

pink-ster=flow-er (pingk′stėr-flou″ėr), *n.* [D. *Pinkster*, Pentecost, Whitsuntide, ult. < Gr. πεντηκοστή, E. *Pentecost*.] A wild azalea, *Azalea nudiflora*, of the U. S., with pink or purplish flowers. See cut in next column.

pink-y (ping′ki), *a.* Somewhat pink; pinkish.

pin=mon-ey (pin′mun″i), *n.* An allowance of money made by a husband to his wife for her private expenditure on articles of dress or otherwise; hence, any similar allowance, as to a daughter.

pin-na (pin′ạ̈), *n.*; pl. *pinnæ* (-ē). [L., feather (pl. wing), also fin, = *penna*: cf. *penna* and *pen*[2].] A feather, wing, or wing-like part; a fin or flipper; the auricle of the ear; in *bot.*, one of the primary divisions of a pinnate leaf.

Flowering Branch of Pinkster-flower.

pin-nace (pin′ạ̄s), *n.* [F. *pinace*, *pinasse*, OF. *espinace*; origin uncertain.] A kind of light sailing-vessel, sometimes propelled also by oars, formerly in use, often in attendance on a larger vessel; hence, any light sailing-vessel (poetic: as, "The winged *pinnace* shot along the sea," Pope's tr. Homer's "Odyssey," xiii.); also, any of various kinds of ship's boat (as, "He used . . . to take the ship's *pinnace*, and go out into the road a-fishing": Defoe's "Robinson Crusoe," i. 2).

pin-na-cle (pin′ạ-kl), *n.* [OF. F. *pinacle*, < LL. *pinnaculum*, dim. of L. *pinna*, pinnacle, usually identified with *pinna*, feather: see *pinna*.] A relatively small upright structure, commonly terminating in a pyramid or cone, rising above the roof or coping of a building or capping a buttress or other projecting architectural member; hence, any pointed, towering part or formation, as of rock; a lofty peak (as, "Far off, three mountain-tops, Three silent *pinnacles* of aged snow, Stood sunset-flush'd": Tennyson's "Lotos-Eaters"); fig., a lofty eminence or position, or height (as, "to place Aristophanes on as high a literary *pinnacle* as any ancient writer," S. Butler's "Way of All Flesh," xlvi.; "the opportunity which had raised him to this *pinnacle* of wealth," Smollett's "Humphry Clinker," May 10); the highest or culminating point (as, to reach the *pinnacle* of one's fame).—**pin′na-cle,** *v. t.*; *-cled*, *-cling*. To furnish with a pinnacle or pinnacles; also, to place on or as on a pinnacle.

Pinnacle of Buttress, York Minster, England.

pin-nate (pin′āt), *a.* [L. *pinnatus*, feathered, pinnate, < *pinna*: see *pinna*.] Resembling a feather; having parts arranged on each side of a common axis; in *bot.*, of a leaf, having leaflets or primary divisions arranged on each side of a common petiole (cf. *paripinnate*, *imparipinnate*, and *odd-pinnate*). Also **pin-nat-ed** (pin′ā-ted).—**pin′nate-ly,** *adv.*—**pin-nat-i-fid** (pi-nat′i-fid), *a.* [See *-fid*.] In *bot.*, of a leaf, pinnately cleft, with clefts reaching half-way or more to the midrib.—**pin-nat-i-lo′bate** (-lō′bāt), *a.* In *bot.*, of a leaf, pinnately lobed, with the divisions extending less than half-way to the midrib. Also **pin-nat′i-lobed** (-lōbd).—**pin-na′tion** (-nā′shọn), *n.* In *bot.*, pinnate condition or formation.—**pin-nat-i-par′tite** (-pär′tīt), *a.* In *bot.*, of a leaf, parted in a pinnate manner. See *parted*.—**pin-nat′i-ped** (-ped), *a.* [+ L. *pes* (*ped-*), foot.] In *ornith.*, having lobate feet.—**pin-nat′i-sect** (-sekt), *a.* [+ L. *sectus*, pp. of *secare*, cut.] In *bot.*, of a leaf, divided in a pinnate manner; cut down quite to the midrib, but with the divisions not articulated so as to form separate leaflets.

Pinnatifid Leaf.

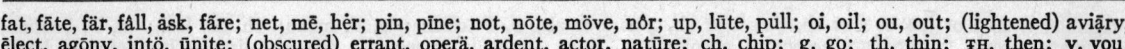

pin-ner (pin′ėr), *n.* One who or that which pins; also, a head-dress with a long hanging flap pinned on at each side, formerly worn by women; sometimes, one of the flaps (as, "the mistress of the family . . . dressed in her coif and *pinners*": Scott's "Black Dwarf," iii.); also, an apron with a bib, or a pinafore (prov. Eng.).

Pinner.

pin-ni-grade (pin′i-grād). [L. *pinna*, feather, fin, + *gradi*, walk.] **I.** *a.* Moving by means of fin-like parts or flippers, as the seals and walruses. **II.** *n.* A pinnigrade animal.

pin-ni-ped (pin′i-ped). [L. *pinna*, feather, fin, + *pes* (*ped-*), foot.] **I.** *a.* Having feet like fins; fin-footed; specif., belonging to the *Pinnipedia*, a suborder of carnivorous mammals with limbs adapted to an aquatic life, including the seals and walruses. **II.** *n.* A pinniped animal; specif., one of the *Pinnipedia*.

pin-nu-la (pin′ū-lạ̈), *n.*; pl. *-læ* (-lē). [L., dim. of *pinna*, feather, fin.] A pinnule; in *ornith.*, a barb of a feather.—**pin′nu-lar** (-lạ̈r), *a.* Of or pertaining to a pinnule.—**pin′nu-late, pin′nu-lat-ed** (-lāt, -lā-ted), *a.* Having pinnules.—**pin-nule** (pin′ūl), *n.* In *zoöl.*, a part or organ resembling a barb of a feather, or a fin or the like; one of the lateral branchlets of the arms of a crinoid; a small detached fin-like appendage in certain fishes, as the mackerel; in *bot.*, a secondary pinna; one of the pinnately disposed divisions of a pinna of a bipinnate leaf.

pi-noch-le (pē′nuk-l), *n.* [G. *pinochel*, *binochel*; origin uncertain.] A card-game played by two, three, or four persons, with two packs of 24 cards each; also, the combination of the queen of spades and the jack of diamonds in this game.

pi-no-le (pē-nō′lạ̈), *n.* [Sp.; from Mex.] Maize (or wheat) dried, ground, and sweetened (usually with the flour of mesquite-beans).

pi-ñon (pē-nyōn′), *n.* [Sp. *piñón*, < *piña*, < L. *pinea*, pine-cone, < *pinus*, pine.] Any of various pines, esp. of the Rocky Mountain region, producing large edible seeds; also, the seed.

pint (pīnt), *n.* [OF. F. *pinte*; origin uncertain.] A dry and also liquid measure of capacity, equal to one half of a quart or one eighth of a gallon: of varying content in different systems, places, and times. See *dry measure*, under *dry*, *a.*; *liquid measure*, under *liquid*, *a.*; and *apothecaries' measure*, under *apothecary*.

pin-ta (pin′tạ̈), *n.* [Sp., 'spot.'] In *pathol.*, a disease prevalent in Mexico and elsewhere, characterized by spots of various colors on the skin.

pin-ta-do (pin-tä′dō), *n.*; pl. *-dos* (-dōz). [Sp. and Pg., 'painted.'] A large scombroid food-fish, *Scomberomorus regalis*, of the West Indies, etc.

pin-tail (pin′tāl), *n.* Any of several birds having the middle tail-feathers elongated, as a widely distributed duck, *Dafila acuta*, or the American ruddy duck, *Erismatura rubida* (or *jamaicensis*), or an American grouse, *Pediœcetes phasianellus*.—**pin′=tailed,** *a.*

Pintail (*Dafila acuta*).

pin-tle (pin′tl), *n.* [AS. *pintel*, penis.] A pin or bolt, esp. one upon which something turns, as in a hinge.

pin-to (pin′tō). [Sp., 'painted.'] **I.** *a.* Piebald; mottled; spotted: as, a *pinto* horse (a calico horse); the *pinto* bean (a variety of the common bean, *Phaseolus vulgaris*, having mottled or spotted seeds). **II.** *n.*; pl. *-tos* (-tōz). A pinto horse.

pin=tuck (pin′tuk), *n.* A very narrow tuck, as made in cloth by sewing.

pin-weed (pin′wēd), *n.* Any plant of the cistaceous genus *Lechea*, so called from the slender stems and leaves; also, the alfileria, *Erodium cicutarium*.

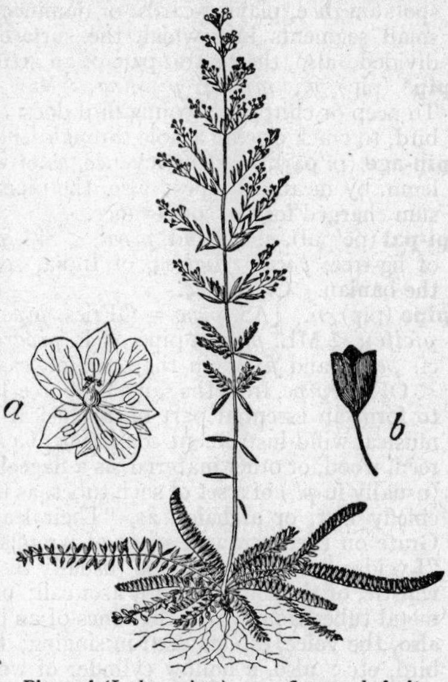

Pinweed (*Lechea minor*). — *a*, flower; *b*, fruit.

pin-wheel (pin′hwēl), *n.* A wheel with pins on the periphery for cogs, or one in which pins for cogs are set into the disk, at right angles to the plane of the wheel; also, a revolving circular box with wooden pins on the inner surface, in which hides are washed; also, a kind of firework supported on a pin and revolving rapidly when ignited; also, a child's toy consisting of a paper wheel fixed by a pin to a stick so as to revolve in the wind.

pin-worm (pin′wėrm), *n.* A small nematoid worm, *Oxyuris vermicularis*, infesting the rectum, esp. of children.

pinx-it (pingk′sit). [L.] '(The person specified) painted it': used in giving the artist's name or signature on a picture.

pin-y (pī′ni), *a.* Abounding in or covered with pine-trees (as, "*piny* mountains": Mrs. Shelley's "Frankenstein," ix.); consisting of pine-trees (as, *piny* woods); pertaining to or suggestive of pine-trees (as, "the *piny* odors in the night air": Longfellow's "Kavanagh," xxix.).

pi-o-neer (pī-ọ-nēr′), *n.* [F. *pionnier*, pioneer, OF. *peonier*, foot-soldier, < *peon*, foot-soldier: see *pawn*[1].] One of a body of foot-soldiers detailed to make or repair roads, dig intrenchments, etc., in advance of the main body; hence, one who goes before to prepare the way for others; esp., one of those who first enter, or settle in, a region, thus opening it for occupation and development by others (as, "restless and intrepid *pioneers* whose axes and rifles have opened a path from the Alleghanies to the western prairies": Parkman's "Oregon Trail," i.); fig., one of those who are first or earliest in any field of inquiry, enterprise, or progress (as, *pioneers* in electrical science, or in aëronautics; *pioneers* of prison reform).—**pi-o-neer′,** *v.* **I.** *intr.* To act as a pioneer; open or prepare a way. **II.** *tr.* To open or prepare (a way, etc.), as a pioneer does (as, "I will *pioneer* a new way, explore unknown powers": Mrs. Shelley's "Frankenstein," iii.); also, to open a way for (as, "It seems as if I had been *pioneered* invisibly, as if some dissolving force had gone before me": C. Brontë's "Villette," xxxviii.); loosely, to lead or guide; also, to be a pioneer in, or lead the way in (a movement, etc.).

piou-piou (pyö-pyö), *n.* [F.] A French common soldier. [Colloq.]

pi-ous (pī′us), *a.* [L. *pius*, dutiful, devout, tender, kind: cf. *piety* and *pity*.] Having or showing a dutiful spirit of reverence for God or an earnest regard for religious obligations, as persons, the heart, actions, observances, etc.; devout; religious; godly; also, practised or used from religious motives (real or pretended), or for some good object (as, a *pious* fraud; a *pious* deception or subterfuge); also, having or showing due respect or regard for parents or others (archaic).—**pi′ous-ly,** *adv.*—**pi′ous-ness,** *n.*

pip[1] (pip), *n.* [ME. *pippe*, appar. < MD. *pippe* (D. *pip*), < LL. *pipita*, for L. *pituita*, phlegm, also the pip.] A contagious disease of birds, esp. poultry, characterized by the secretion of a thick mucus in the mouth and throat.

pip[2] (pip), *n.* [Short for *pippin*.] The seed of fleshy fruits, as of an apple or orange.

pip[3] (pip), *n.* [Earlier *peep*; origin unknown.] One of the spots on dice, playing-cards, or dominoes; also, each of the small segments into which the surface of a pineapple is divided; also, the central part of an artificial flower.

pip[4] (pip), *v.*; *pipped, pipping.* [Var. of *peep*[1].] **I.** *intr.* To peep or chirp, as a young bird does. **II.** *tr.* Of a young bird, to crack or chip a hole through (the shell).

pip-age (pī'pạj), *n.* Conveyance, as of water, gas, or petroleum, by means of pipes; also, the pipes so used; also, the sum charged for the conveyance.

pi-pal (pē'pul), *n.* [Hind. *pīpal*, < Skt. *pippala.*] A species of fig-tree, *Ficus religiosa*, of India, somewhat resembling the banian. Cf. *bo-tree.*

pipe (pīp), *n.* [AS. *pīpe* = OFries. *pīpe* = OHG. *pfīfa* (G. *pfeife*), < ML. *pipa*, a pipe, < L. *pipare*, peep, chirp (imit.: cf. *peep*[1] and *fife*); in the sense of 'cask' (tubular vessel), < OF. F. *pipe*, from the same L. source.] A tube used as, or to form an essential part of, a musical wind-instrument; a musical wind-instrument consisting of a single tube of straw, reed, wood, or other material, as a flageolet, flute, or oboe, or (usually in *pl.*) of a set of such tubes, as the Pan's pipes (now chiefly hist. or archaic: as, "Their lean and flashy songs Grate on their scrannel *pipes* of wretched straw," Milton's "Lycidas," 124); a bagpipe (usually in *pl.*); a boatswain's whistle, or the sounding of it as a call; one of the wooden or metal tubes from which the tones of an organ are produced; also, the voice, esp. as used in singing; the note or call of a bird, etc.; also, a hollow cylinder of wood, metal, or other material, for the conveyance of water, gas, steam, etc., or for some other purpose; a tube; sometimes, material formed into a tube or tubes; piping or tubing; also, any of various tubular or cylindrical objects, parts, or formations; the tubular part of a key; a tubular organ or passage in an animal body, esp., in *pl.*, the respiratory passages; the stem of a plant; a cylindrical vein of ore; one of the vertical cylindrical masses of bluish rock (or 'blue ground'), of eruptive origin, in which diamonds are found embedded in South Africa; also, a tube of clay, wood, hard rubber, or other material, with a small bowl at one end, used for smoking tobacco or, sometimes, some other substance, such as opium; a quantity, as of tobacco, that fills the bowl and is smoked at one time (as, "Sir Jeoffery . . . gave me a *pipe* of his own tobacco": Steele, in "Tatler," 132); also, a large cask, of varying capacity, for wine, etc.; such a cask with its contents; esp., such a cask as a measure of capacity for wine, etc., equal to 4 barrels, 2 hogsheads, or half a tun, and containing 126 wine-gallons.—**pipe,** *v.*; *piped, piping.* **I.** *intr.* To play on a pipe; also, to make or utter a shrill sound like that of a pipe; whistle, as the wind (as, "No more they . . . heard the steady wind *pipe* boisterously Through the strained rigging": W. Morris's "Jason," x. 180); sing, as a bird (as, "In the thickets and the meadows *Piped* the bluebird": Longfellow's "Hiawatha," xxi. 125); speak shrilly; weep or cry (colloq.). **II.** *tr.* To play (music) on a pipe; also, to sing, as a bird (as, "I hear the wood-thrush *piping* one mellow descant more": Bryant's "Waiting by the Gate"); utter in a shrill tone (as, "'Oh!' *piped* Alicia from the window": Arnold Bennett's "Hilda Lessways," iii. 1); also, to bring, lead, etc., by playing on a pipe; summon, order, etc., by sounding the boatswain's pipe or whistle (as, "All hands were *piped* on deck," Stevenson's "Treasure Island," xii.; "The hammocks were *piped* down," Marryat's "Peter Simple," xi.); also, to supply with pipes; also, to convey by means of pipes; also, to trim or finish (a garment, etc.) with piping.—**to pipe one's** (or **the**) **eye** (or **eyes**), to shed tears; weep; cry: as, "He was very frail and tearful . . . his own peculiar mission was to *pipe his eye*" (Dickens's "Martin Chuzzlewit," xxxii.); "The rest [of the smoke] eddied about the house, and kept us coughing and *piping the eye*" (Stevenson's "Treasure Island," xix.). [Orig. nautical slang.]

pipe=clay (pīp'klā), *n.* A fine white clay used for making tobacco-pipes, whitening parts of military or other dress, etc.—**pipe'=clay,** *v. t.* To whiten with pipe-clay: as, "*pipe-clayed* white shoes" (J. Conrad's "Victory," ii. 4).

pipe=dream (pīp'drēm), *n.* A dream produced by smoking opium; fig., any fantastic or absurd notion, story, etc. (slang).

pipe=fish (pīp'fish), *n.* Any of the *Syngnathidæ*, a family of lophobranch fishes with an elongated tubular snout and a slender body of angular section.

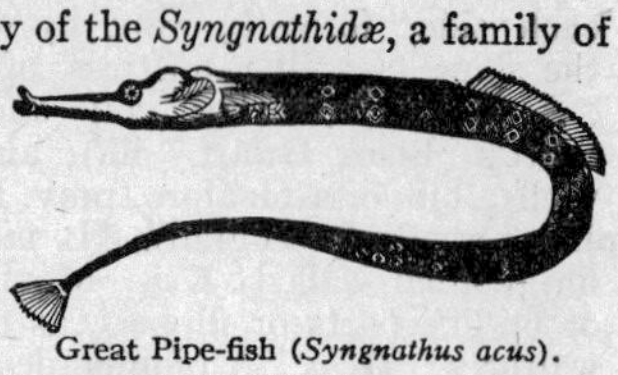

Great Pipe-fish (*Syngnathus acus*).

pipe-ful (pīp'fůl), *n.*; pl. *-fuls.* A quantity sufficient to fill the bowl of a pipe: as, "a *pipeful* of tobacco" (Kinglake's "Eothen," xiv.).

pipe=lay-er (pīp'lā"ėr), *n.* One who lays pipes for the conveyance of water, gas, etc.; fig., a person, esp. a politician, who lays plans for the promotion of some scheme or purpose; a political intriguer.—**pipe'=lay"ing,** *n.*

pipe=line (pīp'līn), *n.* A continuous line of pipes, as with pumping machinery, etc.; a conduit of pipe through which oil is forced by pumping from an oil-region to the market or refinery.—**pipe'=line,** *v. t.* To convey by a pipe-line; provide with a pipe-line.

pipe=or-gan (pīp'ôr"gạn), *n.* An organ with pipes, as distinguished from a reed-organ. See *organ.*

pip-er (pī'pėr), *n.* One who or that which pipes; one who plays on a pipe; often, a bagpiper.—**to pay the piper.** See under *pay*[2], *v. t.*

pip-er-a-ceous (pip-ẹ-rā'shius), *a.* [L. *piper*, pepper.] Belonging to the *Piperaceæ*, or pepper family of plants, which includes the spice-bearing pepper (*Piper nigrum*), the betel and cubeb plants, etc.

pi-per-a-zine (pi-per'ạ-zin), *n.* [From *piper*(*idine*) + *az*(*ote*) + *-ine*[2].] In *chem.*, a deliquescent crystalline compound obtained by the action of ammonia on ethylene bromide or chloride: used in medicine as a solvent for uric acid.

pi-per-i-dine (pi-per'i-din), *n.* [From *piperine.*] In *chem.*, a volatile liquid alkaloid with a strong pepper-like odor, obtained from piperine.

pip-er-ine (pip'ẹ-rin), *n.* [L. *piper*, pepper.] In *chem.*, a white crystalline alkaloid obtained from pepper and other piperaceous plants, and also prepared synthetically.

pip-er-o-nal (pip'ẹ-rọ-nal), *n.* [G., < *piperin*, piperine.] In *chem.*, a white crystalline aldehyde, a benzene derivative, with an odor resembling that of heliotrope: used in perfumery.

pipe=stem (pīp'stem), *n.* The stem of a tobacco-pipe.

pipe=stone (pīp'stōn), *n.* A reddish argillaceous stone, used by North American Indians for making tobacco-pipes.

pi-pette (pi-pet'), *n.* [F., dim. of *pipe*, pipe.] A slender pipe or tube, as for transferring liquids from one vessel to another.

pipe-wort (pīp'wėrt), *n.* Any plant of the genus *Eriocaulon* or the family *Eriocaulaceæ*, widely distributed, mostly in warm regions, and comprising aquatic or marsh herbs, stemless or nearly so, with fibrous roots, linear leaves, and naked scapes bearing dense heads of minute flowers.

Pipewort (*Eriocaulon*).

pip-ing (pī'ping), *n.* The act of one who or that which pipes; also, the sound of this; music of pipes; shrill sound; also, material formed into a pipe or pipes; pipes collectively; also, a kind of tubular band of material, sometimes containing a cord, used for trimming garments, etc., as along edges and seams; also, a cord-like ornamentation made of icing, used on pastry; in *hort.*, a mode of propagating jointed plants, as pinks, by cuttings taken off at a joint; also, one of the cuttings.—**pip'ing,** *p. a.* That pipes; playing on a musical pipe; characterized by the music of the peaceful pipe (rather than the martial fife or trumpet: in the Shaksperian phrase *piping time*, or *times, of peace*: see Shakspere's "Richard III.," i. 1. 24); emitting a shrill sound (as, a *piping* breeze; a *piping* voice).—**piping hot,** so hot as to hiss; very hot.—**pip'ing=crow',** *n.* Any bird of the genus *Gymnorhina*, belonging to the shrike family and found in the Australian region, as *G. tibicen*, a species with black and white plumage, which is often domesticated and can be taught to speak words. See cut on following page.

pip-it (pip′it), *n.* [Imit. of its note.] Any of various small lark-like birds of the genus *Anthus* and allied genera; a titlark.

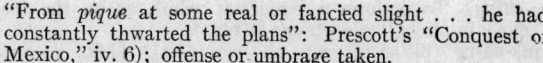

Black-backed Piping-crow (*Gymnorhina tibicen*).

pip-kin (pip′kin), *n.* [Origin uncertain: cf. *pipe.*] A small earthen pot; also, a piggin.

pip-less (pip′les), *a.* Without pips or seeds, as an orange.

pip-pin (pip′in), *n.* [OF. *pepin* (F. *pépin*), fruit-seed, pip; origin uncertain.] A pip or seed (obs. or prov.); also, any of numerous varieties of apple.

pip-sis-se-wa (pip-sis′ẹ-wạ̈), *n.* [N. Amer. Ind.] An evergreen herb of the genus *Chimaphila*, esp. *C. umbellata*, the leaves of which are used medicinally for their tonic, diuretic, and astringent properties.

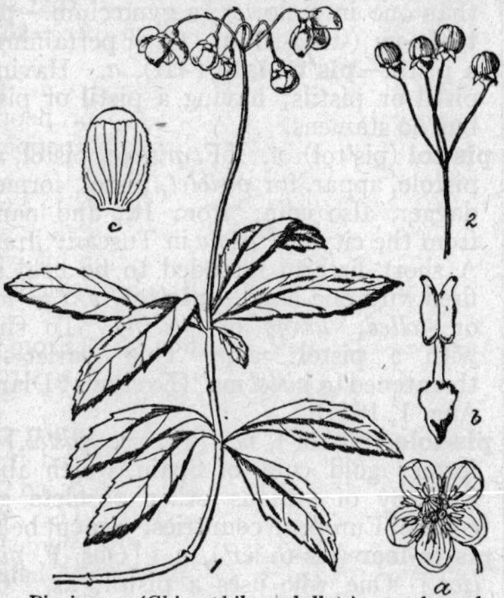

Pipsissewa (*Chimaphila umbellata*). — 1, branch; 2, stem with fruits; *a*, a flower; *b*, a stamen, exterior face; *c*, one of the petals.

pi-pul (pē′pul), *n.* See *pipal.*

pip-y (pī′pi), *a.* Pipe-like; tubular; also, piping; shrill.

pi-quant (pē′kạnt), *a.* [F., pricking, pungent, ppr. of *piquer*: see *pique, v.*] Sharp or stinging, esp. to the feelings (archaic); also, agreeably pungent or sharp in taste or flavor (as, "My appetite stood in need of some *piquant* stimulant to excite its activity": H. Melville's "Typee," xiv.); biting; tart; fig., appealing in an agreeably pungent manner to the mind, interest, esthetic sense, etc.; divertingly interesting (as, a *piquant* experience; "The eccentricity of the proceeding was *piquant*," C. Brontë's "Jane Eyre," xiii.); of a smart or racy character (as, *piquant* wit; a *piquant* anecdote); interestingly attractive (as, *piquant* beauty; "I stood feasting my sight on her bright, *piquant* face," W. H. Hudson's "Green Mansions," vi.).—**pi′quan-cy** (-kạn-si), **pi′quant-ness,** *n.*—**pi-quante** (pē-känt), *a.* [F., fem. of *piquant.*] Piquant, as a woman; of a sauce, tart or acid, as from seasoning with vinegar.—**pi′quant-ly,** *adv.*

pique (pēk), *v. t.*; *piqued, piquing.* [F. *piquer*, prick, sting, excite, also stitch, quilt, < *pic*, a pick, something pointed: see *pike*[1].] To sting mentally, or affect with sharp irritation and resentment, esp. by some wound to pride or self-esteem (as, to be *piqued* at a refusal; to be *piqued* by a person's indifference); nettle; wound (the pride, vanity, etc.: as, "The pride of Ferdinand had been *piqued* by being obliged . . . to recede from his plan," Irving's "Conquest of Granada," xliii.); provoke (*to, into*, etc.) by wounding the pride, etc.; also, to affect with a lively interest or curiosity (as, "She saw that he was puzzled, interested, and *piqued*, and that he was examining her quite afresh": Arnold Bennett's "Hilda Lessways," i. 6); excite (interest, curiosity, etc.); also, to pride or plume (one's self: as, "Captain Bradshaw . . . *piqued* himself upon keeping a good table," Marryat's "King's Own," xxxiv.).—**pique,** *n.* [F., < *piquer.*] A state of irritated feeling between persons (as, "Her sudden freak . . . must have been caused by some little *pique* or misunderstanding between them": George Eliot's "Adam Bede," xxxiii.); also, a feeling of sharp irritation and resentment, esp. from some wound to pride or self-esteem (as, "From *pique* at some real or fancied slight . . . he had constantly thwarted the plans": Prescott's "Conquest of Mexico," iv. 6); offense or umbrage taken.

pi-qué (pẹ-kā′). [F., stitched, quilted, pp. of *piquer*: see *pique, v.*] **I.** *a.* Of glove-seams and gloves, stitched through lapping edges. **II.** *n.* A thick cotton fabric woven with a quilted effect, commonly with narrow transverse ribs or raised stripes.

pi-quet (pẹ-ket′), *n.* [F.; origin uncertain: cf. *picket.*] A card-game played by two persons with a pack of 32 cards, the cards from deuces to sixes being excluded.

pi-ra-cy (pī′rạ-si), *n.*; pl. *-cies* (-siz). [ML. *piratia*, < Gr. πειρατεία.] The action or practice of a pirate; robbery on the sea, or on the coast by descent from the sea; an act or crime of this kind; often, the unauthorized appropriation and reproduction of the work or invention of another, esp. of literary work; something that is pirated, as a book (as, "Snyder fingered the *piracies*": Arnold Bennett's "Great Man," xiv.).

pi-ra-gua (pi-rä′gwạ̈), *n.* [Sp.; from Carib: cf. *pirogue.*] A canoe hollowed from the trunk of a tree, orig. as used by the natives of the West Indies, etc., at the time of the coming of the early Spanish explorers; hence, any of various modifications of such a canoe; a pirogue. See *pirogue.*

pi-rate (pī′rạt), *n.* [L. *pirata*, < Gr. πειρατής, pirate, < πειρᾶν, attempt.] One who robs on the sea, or by descent from the sea on the coast; one habitually engaged in such robbery; a sea-robber, buccaneer, freebooter, or corsair; a vessel employed by sea-robbers (as, "Squadrons of *pirates* hung yet about the smaller islands": Froude's "Cæsar," ix.); in general, any person or animal that acts like a sea-robber; a marauder; a plunderer; esp., one who appropriates and reproduces, without authorization, as for his own profit, the literary, artistic, or other work or any invention of another; sometimes, specif., one who infringes on the copyright of another.—**pi′rate,** *v.*; *-rated, -rating.* **I.** *tr.* To commit piracy upon; rob or plunder as a pirate does; also, to take by piracy; esp., to appropriate and reproduce (literary work, etc.) without authorization or legal right; publish or issue by piracy (as, "See this—and this . . . They're *pirated* editions of 'Love in Babylon' ": Arnold Bennett's "Great Man," xiv.). **II.** *intr.* To commit or practise piracy: as, "if we resolved to . . . give over our trade of *pirating*" (Defoe's "Captain Singleton," xiii.).—**pi′rate=perch,** *n.* A small, voracious fish, *Aphredoderus sayanus*, of a dark-olive color profusely dotted with black, found in sluggish waters of the eastern U. S. and the Mississippi basin.—**pi′-rate-ry** (-ri), *n.* [Also *piratry*: cf. F. *piraterie.*] Piracy; piratical depredation: as, "Ere rivers league against the land In *piratry* of flood" (Kipling's "Before a Midnight Breaks in Storm").—**pi-rat′i-cal, pi-rat′ic** (-rat′i-kạl, -ik), *a.* [L. *piraticus*, < Gr. πειρατικός.] Of or befitting pirates; of the nature of piracy; engaged in piracy.—**pi-rat′i-cal-ly,** *adv.*

Pirate-perch.

pirn (pėrn), *n.* [ME. *pyrne*; origin obscure.] A bobbin, spool, or reel: as, "a contrivance with *pirns* in it that was climbing up and down the whirring mill" (Barrie's "Sentimental Tommy," xi.). [Now Sc., Ir., and prov. Eng.]

pi-rogue (pi-rōg′), *n.* [F.; from Carib: cf. *piragua.*] A canoe hollowed from the trunk of a tree, orig. a native West Indian canoe, and later esp. one used in parts of America visited or settled by the French (cf. *piragua*); a dugout; a canoe of any kind; also, any of various modifications of the canoe or dugout; esp., a boat made from or resembling a dugout split lengthwise and widened by inserting planks; also, a two-masted, flat-bottomed boat having a lee-board, and decked at the end or ends but open in the middle.

pir-ou-ette (pir-ọ̈-et′), *n.* [F., top, whirligig, whirl: cf. It. *pirolo*, peg.] A whirling about on one foot or on the points of the toes, as in dancing; in the *manège*, a quick, short turn or whirl of a horse.—**pir-ou-ette′,** *v. i.*; *-etted,*

-*etting.* To perform a pirouette; whirl, as on the toes; move in pirouettes.—**pir-ou-et′ter,** *n.*

pis-ca-ry (pis′ka̤-ri), *n.*; pl. *-ries* (-riz). [ML. *piscaria,* prop. fem. of L. *piscarius,* pertaining to fish, < *piscis,* fish.] A place where fish may be caught; a fishing-ground; in *law,* the right or privilege of fishing in particular waters.

pis-ca-tol-o-gy (pis-ka̤-tol′ǭ-ji), *n.* [L. *piscatus,* n., a fishing, fishes: see *-logy.*] The scientific study of fishes; ichthyology.

pis-ca-tor (pis-kā′tọr), *n.* [L., < *piscari,* to fish, < *piscis,* fish.] A fisherman; an angler.—**pis-ca-to′ri-al** (-ka̤-tō′ri-a̤l), *a.* Pertaining to fishermen or fishing.—**pis-ca-to′ri-al-ly,** *adv.* —**pis′ca-to-ry** (-tǭ-ri), *a.* [L. *piscatorius.*] Of or pertaining to fishermen or fishing; given or devoted to fishing.

Pis-ces (pis′ēz), *n. pl.* [L., pl. of *piscis,* fish.] The Fishes, a zodiacal constellation; also, as *sing.,* the twelfth sign of the zodiac. See *zodiac.*

pis-ci-cap-ture (pis′i-kap-ţūr), *n.* [L. *piscis,* fish, + *captura,* capture.] The catching of fish.

pis-ci-cul-ture (pis′i-kul-ţūr), *n.* [L. *piscis,* fish, + *cultura,* culture.] The breeding, rearing, and preservation of fish by artificial means; fish-culture.—**pis-ci-cul′tur-al,** *a.*—**pis-ci-cul′tur-ist,** *n.*

pis-ci-form (pis′i-fôrm), *a.* [L. *piscis,* fish, + *forma,* form.] Having the form of a fish; fish-like.

pis-ci-na (pi-sī′nä̤ or pi-sē′-), *n.*; pl. *-næ* (-nē). [L., orig. fish-pond, < *piscis,* fish.] *Eccles.,* a basin with a drain, in old churches usually in a niche in the wall on the south side of the altar, used for certain ablutions, etc.—**pis-ci-nal** (pis′i-na̤l), *a.*

Piscina in Morning Chapel, Lincoln Cathedral, England.

pis-cine (pis′in), *a.* [L. *piscis,* fish.] Of or pertaining to fishes.

pis-civ-o-rous (pi-siv′ǭ-rus), *a.* [L. *piscis,* fish, + *vorare,* devour.] Fish-eating; feeding on fish.

Pis-gah (piz′gä̤), *n.* [Heb.] A mountain northeast of the Dead Sea, from which Moses viewed the promised land of Canaan. See Deut. iii. 27. Also fig.

pish (pish). **I.** *interj.* An exclamation of contempt or impatience. **II.** *n.* An exclamation of 'pish!'—**pish,** *v.* **I.** *intr.* To say 'pish': as, "The Captain kept *Pishing* and Tushing, and presently . . . swearing" (H. G. Wells's "Bealby," v.). **II.** *tr.* To say 'pish' at or to.

pi-si-form (pī′si-fôrm), *a.* [NL. *pisiformis,* < L. *pisum,* pea, + *forma,* form.] Having the form of a pea (as, a *pisiform* bone); also, composed of small, rounded masses like peas (as, *pisiform* iron ore).

pis-mire (pis′mīr), *n.* [ME., < *pisse,* piss, + *mire,* ant.] An ant: as, "The spider's skill,—The *pismire's* care to garner up his wheat" (Hood's "Midsummer Fairies," lv.). [Archaic or prov. Eng. and Sc.]

pi-so-lite (pī′sǭ-līt), *n.* [Gr. πῖσος, pea, + λίθος, stone.] Limestone composed of rounded concretions about the size of a pea. Cf. *oölite.*—**pi-so-lit′ic** (-lit′ik), *a.* Pertaining to, characteristic of, or having the structure of, pisolite: as, *pisolitic* structure.

Pisolitic Structure.

piss (pis), *v. i.* [OF. *pissier.*] To urinate. [Now vulgar.]—**piss,** *n.* Urine. [Now vulgar.]

pis-tache (pis-tàsh′), *n.* [F.] Same as *pistachio.*

pis-ta-chio (pis-tä′shiō or -tā′shiō), *n.*; pl. *-chios* (-shiōz). [It. *pistacchio,* < L. *pistacium,* < Gr. πιστάκιον, the nut, < πιστάκη, the tree; from Pers.] The seed or nut of a small anacardiaceous tree, *Pistacia vera,* of southern Europe and Asia Minor; its edible greenish kernel, much used for flavoring; the tree itself; also, a light-green color.

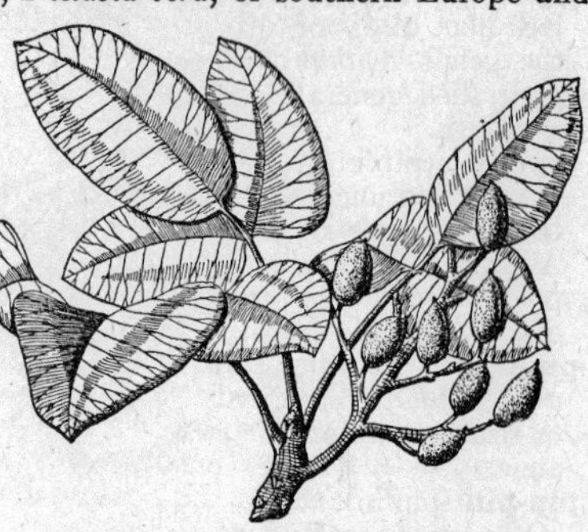

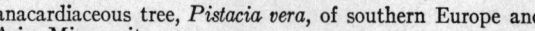

Branch of Pistachio-tree, with fruits.

pis-ta-reen (pis-ta̤-rēn′), *n.* [Cf. *peseta.*] In Spanish America, the old Spanish peseta.

pis-til (pis′til), *n.* [NL. *pistillum,* pistil, L. pestle: see *pestle.*] In *bot.,* the ovule-bearing or seed-bearing organ (the so-called female organ) of a flower, consisting when complete of ovary, style, and stigma; also, such organs collectively, when there are more than one in a flower; a gynœcium.—**pis′til-la-ry** (-ti-lā̤-ri), *a.* Of or pertaining to a pistil.—**pis′til-late** (-lāt), *a.* Having a pistil or pistils; having a pistil or pistils but no stamens.

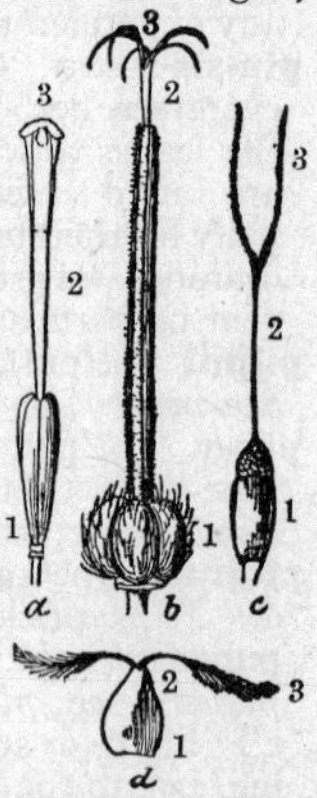

Pistils. — *a,* lily (*Lilium*); *b,* geranium (*Geranium*); *c,* spike-rush (*Eleocharis*); *d,* rice (*Oryza*). 1, ovary; 2, style; 3, stigma.

pis-tol (pis′tọl), *n.* [F. *pistole,* pistol, also pistole, appar. for *pistolet,* pistol, formerly dagger, also coin; from It., and named from the city of *Pistoia* in Tuscany, Italy.] A short firearm intended to be held and fired with one hand.—**pis′tol,** *v. t.*; *-toled* or *-tolled, -toling* or *-tolling.* To shoot with a pistol: as, "This varlet . . . threatened to *pistol* me" (Evelyn's "Diary," Aug. 1, 1644).

pis-tole (pis-tōl′), *n.* [F.: see *pistol.*] A former gold coin of Spain, worth about $4; any of various other obsolete gold coins of European countries. See cut below.

pis-to-leer (pis-tǭ-lēr′), *n.* [Obs. F. *pistolier.*] One who uses a pistol: as, "One homely piece of advice to the *pistoleer* was that he should not discharge his weapon until he could press the barrel close upon the body of his enemy" (Morley's "Oliver Cromwell," ii. 1).

Obverse. Reverse.

Pistole of Charles IV. of Spain, 1790. — British Museum.

pis-tol-grip (pis′tọl-grip), *n.* A grip or handle resembling the butt of a pistol, on the under side of the stock of a rifle or gun, to afford a better hold for the hand.

pis-ton (pis′tọn), *n.* [F. *piston,* < It. *pistone,* piston, var. of *pestone,* large pestle, ult. < L. *pinsere* (pp. *pistus*), pound, bray.] A movable disk or short cylinder fitting closely within a tube or hollow cylinder, and capable of being driven alternately forward and backward in the tube by pressure, as in a steam-engine, thus imparting reciprocatory motion to a rod ('piston-rod') attached to it on one side, or of being driven thus by the rod, as in a pump; also, a sliding valve used to change the pitch in a cornet or the like.—**pis′ton-head,** *n.* The movable disk or cylinder (the piston proper) to which the piston-rod is attached.—**pis′ton-ring,** *n.* A metallic ring, usually one of a series, and split so as to be expansible, placed around a piston in order to maintain a

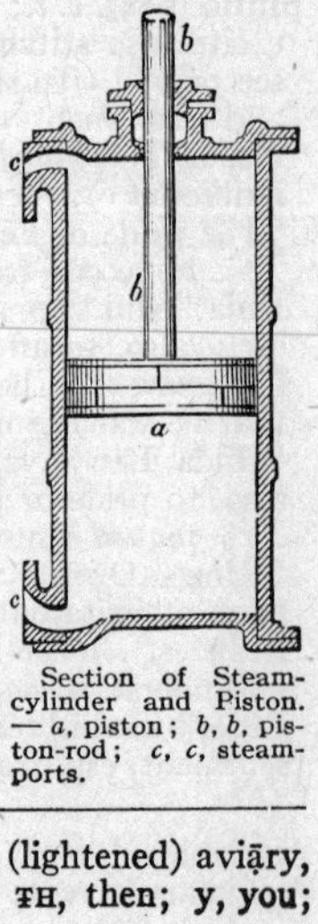

Section of Steam-cylinder and Piston. — *a,* piston; *b, b,* piston-rod; *c, c,* steam-ports.

tight fit, as inside the cylinder of an internal-combustion engine.—**pis'ton=rod,** *n.* The rod attached to a piston or piston-head. See *piston.*

pit[1] (pit), *n.* [AS. *pytt*, pit, hole, < L. *puteus*, well, pit, shaft.] A hole or cavity in the ground, whether natural or made by digging; an excavation made in digging for some mineral deposit; the shaft of a coal-mine, or the mine itself; a pitfall, or covered or concealed excavation in the ground to serve as a trap for animals or men; a grave, or hole dug in the ground to receive a dead body; also, the abode of evil spirits and lost souls; hell, or a part of it; also, in general, a hollow or indentation in a surface; a natural hollow or depression in the body (as, the arm*pits*; the *pit* of the stomach, the slight depression in the surface of the body below the lower end of the breast-bone); a small depressed scar such as those left on the skin after smallpox; also, an inclosure for combats, as of dogs or cocks; also, a section of a theater, orig. all that part on the floor of the house behind the musicians, but now usually (as in Great Britain) the parterre; the persons occupying this section; also, that part of the floor of an exchange devoted to a special kind of business (as, the grain-*pit*).—**pit**[1], *v.*; *pitted, pitting.* **I.** *tr.* To place or bury in a pit; also, to set (animals) in a pit or inclosure to fight; hence, to set in active opposition, as one against another (lit. or fig.: as, "She had *pitted* herself against Fate," Galsworthy's "Saint's Progress," iv. 1); match in a conflict or contest; also, to mark with pits or depressions (as, "a little swarthy young man . . . much *pitted* with the smallpox": Du Maurier's "Trilby," i.). **II.** *intr.* To become marked with pits or depressions; in *pathol.*, to retain for a time the mark of pressure by the finger, etc., as the skin.

pit[2] (pit), *n.* [Cf. D. *pit*, kernel.] The stone of a fruit, as of a cherry, peach, or plum. [U. S.]

pi-ta (pē'tạ̈), *n.* [Sp.; from Peruvian.] A fiber obtained from species of agave, as *Agave americana*, the century-plant, used for making cordage, etc.; the plant itself; also, istle; also, any of various similar fibers from other plants, or one of these plants.

pit-a-pat (pit'ạ-pat). [Varied redupl. of *pat.*] **I.** *adv.* With a quick succession of beats or taps: said esp. with reference to the heart's action, or to pattering footsteps. **II.** *n.* The movement or the sound of something going pitapat.—**pit'a-pat,** *v. i.*; *-patted, -patting.* To go pitapat.

pitch[1] (pich), *v.* [ME. *picchen*; origin uncertain; perhaps related to *pick*[1].] **I.** *tr.* To fix firmly, as in the ground (as, "In this half-circle I *pitched* two rows of strong stakes, driving them into the ground till they stood very firm like piles," Defoe's "Robinson Crusoe," i. 4; to *pitch* the wickets in cricket); now, esp., to set up or erect (a tent, camp, or the like); in general, to put, set, or plant in a fixed or definite place or position (as, "Here is a place to build a breastwork; here can ye *pitch* a fort," Kipling's "Kim," xii.; a roof having rafters *pitched* against an adjoining building); also, to set in order, or arrange, as a field of battle; also, to set at a certain point, degree, level, etc. (as, "He bade himself a hundred times *pitch* his expectations low": Mrs. H. Ward's "Robert Elsmere," xvii.); specif., to set at a particular pitch, or determine the key or key-note of (a tune, etc.: as, "He . . . *pitched* the tunes with his pitch-pipe," Mrs. Stowe's "Oldtown Folks," v.); also, in certain card-games, to lead (a card of a particular suit), thereby fixing that suit as trump; determine (the trump) in this way; also, to throw, fling, hurl, or toss (as, "to *pitch* a harpoon down a live whale's throat," H. Melville's "Moby-Dick," xvi.; "a special basket in my study . . . into which I *pitch* letters, circulars, pamphlets and so forth," H. G. Wells's "Italy, France, and Britain at War," iv. 5); in *baseball*, to deliver or serve (the ball) to the batter; in *golf*, to loft (the ball) so that it alights with little roll; also, in *mech.*, to engage; interlock. **II.** *intr.* To fix a tent or temporary habitation; encamp; also, to take up a position; settle; also, to fix or decide (*on* or *upon*), often casually or without particular consideration (as, "The young lady, in a hurry, *pitches* upon the very ugliest and worst thing that she has seen": Maria Edgeworth's "Belinda," iii.); also, to throw or toss; also, to plunge or fall forward or headlong; specif., to plunge with alternate fall and rise of bow and stern, as a ship (opposed to *roll*); in general, to lurch (as, "The huge green fragment of ice on which she alighted *pitched* and creaked": Mrs. Stowe's "Uncle Tom's Cabin," vii.); also, to slope downward, or dip; in *baseball*, to deliver or serve the ball to the batter; fill the position of pitcher; in *mech.*, to engage; interlock.—**to pitch in,** to set to work with promptness or energy: as, "I took hold with Dan and *pitched* right *in*" (Kipling's "Captains Courageous," ix.). [Colloq.]—**to pitch into,** to attack vigorously, as with blows, words, or otherwise. [Colloq.]—**pitch**[1], *n.* The act or manner of pitching; a throw or toss (as, "It's more than one maybe will get a bloody head on him with the *pitch* of my stone": Synge's "Well of the Saints," iii.); a plunge forward or headlong, or a lurch; the pitching movement, or a plunge forward, of a ship or the like; also, a card-game, a variety of seven-up, in which the trump suit for a deal is determined by the first card led; also, something that is pitched; a quantity of something pitched or placed somewhere; also, a place of pitching, encamping, or taking up a position (as, "It was a pleasant little island of green they chose for their midday *pitch*, a little patch of emerald turf": H. G. Wells's "Bealby," iii.); a spot where a person or thing is placed or stationed; also, point, position, or degree, as in a scale (as, "The chief actor . . . falls from some eminent *pitch* of honour and prosperity, into misery and disgrace," Addison, in "Spectator," 297; "To lowest *pitch* of abject fortune thou art fallen," Milton's "Samson Agonistes," 169; "happy to the *pitch* of ecstasy," H. G. Wells's "Bealby," iii.); specif., degree of highness (acuteness) or lowness (graveness) of a tone or of sound, depending upon the relative rapidity of the vibrations by which it is produced; also, a particular tonal standard with which given tones may be compared in respect to their relative height (as, concert *pitch*; French *pitch*); also, height in general (now chiefly in certain specific uses: as, the *pitch* of an arch, that is, its perpendicular height from the springing-line to the vertex); sometimes, the height to which a falcon or other bird of prey rises before swooping down on its prey; the height to which any bird rises in the air; also, the highest point or greatest height (lit. or fig.: as, "Down they fell Driven headlong from the *pitch* of heaven, down Into this deep," Milton's "Paradise Lost," ii. 772; "At the *pitch* of his voice, Mr. Sullivan Smith denounced Mr. Malkin," G. Meredith's "Diana of the Crossways," iii.); also, downward inclination or slope; a sloping part or place; the inclination of a bed or vein, as of ore, from the horizontal; the slope or steepness of a roof; also, in *mech.*, the distance between two things, esp. in a series; the distance between the centers of two adjacent teeth in a toothed wheel or rack, measured on the pitch-circle or pitch-line.

pitch[2] (pich), *n.* [AS. *pic*, < L. *pix* (*pic-*), akin to Gr. πίσσα, pitch.] Any of various dark-colored tenacious or viscous substances used for covering the seams of vessels after calking, for making pavements, etc., as the residuum ('coal-tar pitch') left after the distillation of coal-tar, or a product ('wood-pitch') derived similarly from wood-tar; also, any of certain bitumens (as, mineral *pitch*, asphaltum); also, any of various resins; the sap or crude turpentine which exudes from the bark of pines.—**pitch**[2], *v. t.* To smear or cover over with or as with pitch.—**pitch'=black', pitch'=dark',** *a.* Black or dark as pitch: as, "He groped along the *pitch-black* street for the remembered outline of the house" (Mrs. Wharton's "Son at the Front," x.).—**pitch'blende** (-blend), *n.* [= G. *pechblende.*] A mineral consisting largely of uranium oxide, occurring in black pitch-like masses: a source of uranium and radium.

pitch=cir-cle (pich'sėr″kl), *n.* An imaginary circle concentric with the axis of a toothed wheel, at such a distance from the base of the teeth that it is in contact with and rolls upon a similar circle of another toothed wheel engaging with the first.

pitched (picht), *a.* Prepared with due array of troops, as a battle; also, having a specified musical or vocal pitch (as, a high-*pitched* voice); also, having a specified pitch or slope (as, a single-*pitched* roof).

pitch-er[1] (pich'ėr), *n.* One who pitches; in *baseball*, the player who delivers or serves the ball to the batter.

pitch-er[2] (pich'ėr), *n.* [OF. *pichier*, < ML. *picarium*, *bicarium*; perhaps akin to E. *beaker.*] A vessel in various forms and sizes, usually with a handle or ear and a spout or lip, for holding and pouring liquids (as, "The water in the *pitchers* was frozen": C. Brontë's "Jane Eyre," vi.); a jug or ewer; also, the contents of such a vessel (as, a *pitcher* of milk or cream); in *bot.*, a pitcher-like modification of the leaf of certain plants; an ascidium.—

Washington Pitcher, supposed to have been made at Liverpool, England, in 1800. — Pennsylvania Museum, Philadelphia.

pitch'er-ful (-fůl), *n.*; pl. *-fuls.* A quantity sufficient to fill a pitcher.—**pitch'er=plant,** *n.* Any of various plants with leaves modified into a pitcher-like receptacle, or ascidium, as the plants of the American genus *Sarracenia* (see *sarracenia*) or of the East Indian *Nepenthes* (see *nepenthes*), or the Australian species *Cephalotus follicularis*, or *Chrysamphora* (or *Darlingtonia*) *californica*, of the mountains of northern California.

pitch-fork (pich'fôrk), *n.* A fork for lifting and pitching hay or the like.—**pitch'-fork,** *v. t.* To pitch or throw with or as with a pitchfork; cast or thrust roughly or unceremoniously (*in, into, out,* etc.: as, "Here he was . . . *pitch-forked* into a coil of scandal," Mrs. Wharton's "Age of Innocence," vi.).

pitch-i-ness (pich'i-nes), *n.* The state or quality of being pitchy; blackness or darkness.

pitch=line (pich'līn), *n.* A pitch-circle, or a corresponding straight line on a toothed rack.

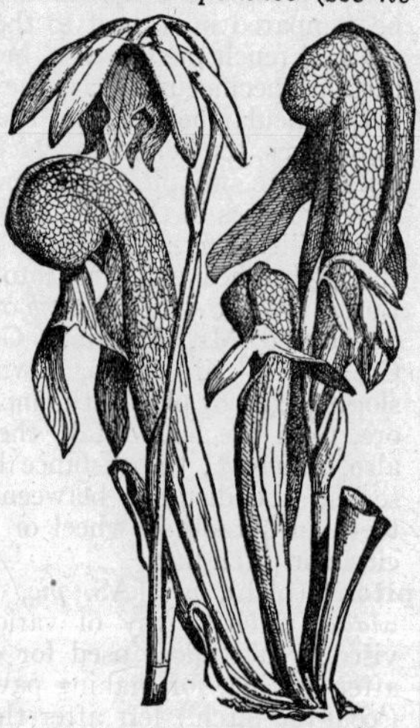

Pitcher-plant (*Chrysamphora californica*).

pitch=pine (pich'pīn), *n.* Any of several species of pine from which pitch or turpentine is obtained.

pitch=pipe (pich'pīp), *n.* A small musical pipe sounded with the breath to give the pitch for singing or for tuning an instrument.

pitch-stone (pich'stōn), *n.* A glassy igneous rock having a resinous luster and in appearance resembling hardened pitch.

pitch-y (pich'i), *a.* Full of or abounding in pitch; smeared with pitch; also, of the nature of pitch; resembling pitch; esp., black; dark as pitch (as, "thick *pitchy* smoke": Wiseman's "Fabiola," ii. 16).

pit-e-ous (pit'ē-us), *a.* [OF. *pitos, piteus* (F. *piteux*), < ML. *pietosus*, pitiful, < L. *pietas*: see *pity*.] Full of pity or compassion, or compassionate (archaic); also, such as to excite or deserve pity, or appealing strongly for pity (as, "They . . . made *piteous* lamentation to us to save them," Defoe's "Robinson Crusoe," ii. 9; "His end was *piteous*, but scarcely tragic," Froude's "Cæsar," xxiii.); pathetic; pitiful; pitiable.—**pit'e-ous-ly,** *adv.*—**pit'e-ous-ness,** *n.*

pit-fall (pit'fâl), *n.* A concealed pit prepared as a trap for animals or men to fall into; hence, any trap or danger for the unwary (as, "He beheld a dupe trotting into a carefully-laid *pitfall*": G. Meredith's "Diana of the Crossways," xxxv.).

pith (pith), *n.* [AS. *pitha*, pith: cf. D. *pit*, pith, marrow, kernel.] The central cylinder of spongy cellular tissue in the stems of dicotyledonous plants; hence, any soft, spongy tissue or substance (as, the *pith* of an orange); the spinal cord; the soft inner part of a feather, a hair, etc.; fig., the important inner part, or the essential part (as, "These passages were the very *pith* and marrow of the poems": Kingsley's "Alton Locke," xviii.); the essence, substance, or gist (as, "It's his abominable pride, that's the *pith* of the matter": J. H. Newman's "Callista," ix.); also, substantial quality, or force or meaning, as in speech or writing; weight or importance (as, "enterprises of great *pith* [var. *pitch*] and moment": Shakspere's "Hamlet," iii. 1. 86); also, strength, force, or vigor, physical or moral (as, "his look of native *pith* and genuine power": C. Brontë's "Jane Eyre," xvii.).—**pith,** *v. t.* To take the pith from (plants, etc.); also, to pierce, sever, or destroy the spinal cord of (an animal); slaughter, as cattle, by severing the spinal cord.

pith-e-can-thrope (pith-ē-kan'thrōp), *n.* Same as *pithecanthropus*.

pith-e-can-thro-pus (pith"ē-kan-thrō'pus), *n.*; pl. *-pi* (-pī). [NL., < Gr. πίθηκος, ape, + ἄνθρωπος, man.] A member of the hypothetical genus *Pithecanthropus*, of ape-like men or man-like apes, proposed by Haeckel as a link between the anthropoid apes and man; also, an extinct animal, *Pithecanthropus erectus*, approaching the present human type more closely than any of the anthropoid apes do (and taken to be the 'missing link'), the existence of which is assumed from late Pliocene or early Pleistocene remains, all apparently belonging to a single individual (the 'Java man'), found in Java in 1891–92 (which remains, however, adverse opinion has regarded as human, and as belonging to a very early type of man).—**pith-e-can'thro-poid** (-thrō-poid), *a.*

pi-the-coid (pi-thē'koid), *a.* [Gr. πιθηκοειδής, < πίθηκος, ape, + εἶδος, form.] Resembling, or pertaining to, the apes, esp. the anthropoid apes; simian.

pi-thi-a-tism (pi-thī'ą-tizm), *n.* [Gr. πείθειν, persuade, + ἰατός, curable; implying a state curable by persuasion.] In *pathol.*, hysteria.

pith-i-ly (pith'i-li), *adv.* In a pithy manner; tersely and forcibly.—**pith'i-ness,** *n.*

pith-less (pith'les), *a.* Without pith; wanting strength; weak.—**pith'less-ly,** *adv.*

pith-os (pith'os), *n.* [Gr. πίθος.] In *Gr. antiq.*, a very large earthenware jar of spheroidal form, with a wide mouth, used for storing wine, oil, grain, etc. It was in a pithos, commonly spoken of as a tub, that Diogenes, the Cynic philosopher, is said to have taken up his abode.

Pithos.

pith-y (pith'i), *a.*; compar. *pithier*, superl. *pithiest.* Abounding in pith or spongy substance, as a plant-stem, an orange, etc.; of the nature of or resembling pith, as a substance; fig., full of pith, substance, or meaning, as speech, writing, etc.; terse and forcible; speaking or writing tersely and forcibly, as a person.

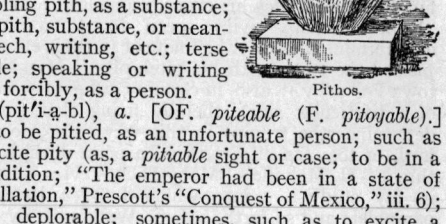

pit-i-a-ble (pit'i-ą-bl), *a.* [OF. *piteable* (F. *pitoyable*).] Deserving to be pitied, as an unfortunate person; such as justly to excite pity (as, a *pitiable* sight or case; to be in a *pitiable* condition; "The emperor had been in a state of *pitiable* vacillation," Prescott's "Conquest of Mexico," iii. 6); lamentable; deplorable; sometimes, such as to excite a contemptuous pity; pitiful, miserable, or contemptible.—**pit'i-a-ble-ness,** *n.*—**pit'i-a-bly,** *adv.*

pit-i-er (pit'i-ėr), *n.* One who pities.

pit-i-ful (pit'i-fůl), *a.* Full of pity or compassion, or compassionate (as, "The Lord is very *pitiful*, and of tender mercy": Jas. v. 11); also, such as to excite or deserve pity (as, a *pitiful* sight; "She told a most *pitiful* story," S. Butler's "Way of All Flesh," lxxvii.; "I should think him a *pitiful* little creature and be extremely sorry for him," H. G. Wells's "Tono-Bungay," i. 2. § 1); pathetic; touchingly sad or unhappy; sometimes, such as to excite pity by smallness, inadequacy, poor quality, etc. (as, a *pitiful* income; *pitiful* attempts; a *pitiful* showing); hence, miserable, sorry, or contemptible (as, "a *pitiful* scoundrel," Godwin's "Caleb Williams," iv.; "playing such *pitiful* tricks, and imposing so grossly on a poor ignorant boy," B. Franklin's "Autobiography," iii.).—**pit′i-ful-ly,** *adv.*—**pit′i-ful-ness,** *n.*

pit-i-less (pit′i-les), *a.* Without pity; feeling or showing no pity; merciless: as, "O, art thou *pitiless?* Wilt thou not note our measureless distress?" (W. Morris's "Jason," xvi. 37).—**pit′i-less-ly,** *adv.*—**pit′i-less-ness,** *n.*

pit-man (pit′mạn), *n.*; pl. *-men.* One who works in a pit, as in coal-mining or in sawing timber (see *pit-saw*); in *mach.*, a rod connecting a rotating with a reciprocating part.

Pi-tot (pē-tō) **tube.** [From Henri *Pitot* (1695–1771), French physicist and engineer.] In *hydraulics*, a device for ascertaining the velocity of water in rivers, etc., consisting, in its simplest form, of a vertical glass tube with a horizontal bend at the lower end, whose opening is held against the flow of water, thus causing water to rise in the vertical part of the tube in proportion to the velocity; in *aëronautics*, an analogous device forming a part of apparatuses for determining the velocity of a current of air, an aircraft, or the like.

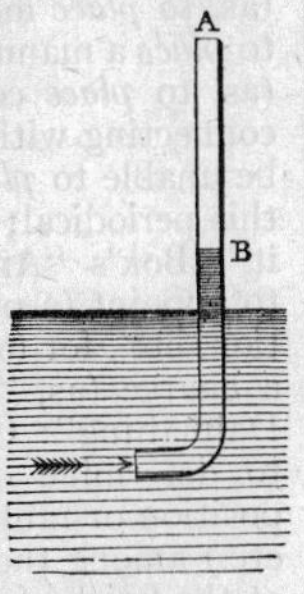

Pitot Tube. — *A*, tube; *B*, line to which water is raised by the force of the current.

pit-pat (pit′pat), *adv.*, *n.*, and *v.* Same as *pitapat.*

pit=saw (pit′sâ), *n.* A saw operated by two men, one on the log (top-sawyer) and the other below it, often in a pit (pit-sawyer).

pit-ta (pit′ạ̈), *n.* [NL.; from Telugu.] Any of the brightly colored passerine birds constituting the genus *Pitta*, chiefly of southeastern Asia, Australia, etc., including most of the old-world ant-thrushes. See cut below.

pit-tance (pit′ạns), *n.* [OF. F. *pitance*, prob. < L. *pietas*, E. *piety, pity.*] A donation or bequest to a religious house to provide an extra allowance of food, wine, etc., on special occasions, or the allowance itself (obs. or hist.); hence, a charitable gift, as of money, food, or clothing; also, a small allowance or portion of food, or a scanty meal (as, "From my hand he took His *pittance* ev'ry night": Cowper's "Epitaph on a Hare," 10); also, a small allowance or sum for living expenses, or a scanty income or remuneration (as, "She . . . contrived to earn a *pittance* scarcely sufficient to support life": Mrs. Shelley's "Frankenstein," i.); in general, a small allowance, portion, or share of anything (as, "a sort of animals to whose share . . . some small *pittance* of reason had fallen": Swift's "Gulliver's Travels," iv. 7); a small amount or quantity.

Pitta.

pit-ter=pat-ter (pit′ėr-pat′ėr). [Varied redupl. of *patter*[1].] **I.** *adv.* With a rapid succession of light beats or taps, as of rain. **II.** *n.* A rapid succession of light beats or taps, as of rain.

pi-tu-i-ta-ry (pi-tū′i-tạ̄-ri), *a.* [L. *pituita*, phlegm.] Of, pertaining to, or secreting mucus; also, pertaining to the pituitary body.—**pituitary body,** in *anat.*, a small, oval, gland-like body in the brain (situated in a depression of the sphenoid bone), to which various functions have been assigned: formerly supposed to secrete mucus.

pi-tu-i-tous (pi-tū′i-tus), *a.* [L. *pituitosus*, < *pituita*, phlegm.] Full of, resembling, or pertaining to mucus; characterized or caused by excess of mucus.

pi-tu-i-trin (pi-tū′i-trin), *n.* [See *pituitary.*] A preparation or extract from the pituitary body, used in medicine.

pit=vi-per (pit′vī″pėr), *n.* Any of the venomous serpents constituting the family *Crotalidæ* (the rattlesnake family), of America and southern Asia, characterized by a pit or depression between the eye and the nostril: as, "a *pit-viper* of the same family as the fer-de-lance, the bushmaster, and the rattlesnake" (W. H. Hudson's "Far Away and Long Ago," iv.).

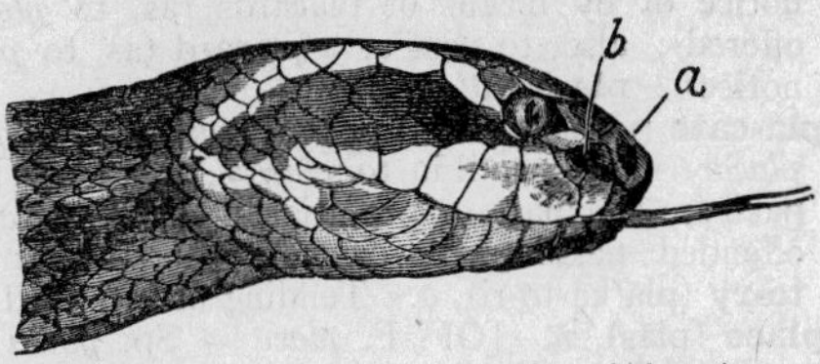

A Pit-viper, the Moccasin (*Ancistrodon piscivorus*). — *a*, nostril; *b*, pit.

pit-y (pit′i), *n.*; pl. *pities* (-iz). [OF. *pite* (F. *pitié*), < L. *pietas*, piety, also pity: see *piety.*] Sympathetic or kindly sorrow excited by the suffering or misfortune of another, or compassion (as, to weep from *pity*; "A beggar that is dumb . . . May challenge double *pity*," Raleigh's "Silent Lover"); often, such a feeling leading one to give relief or aid or to show mercy (as, to have or take *pity* on a person, esp., to show pity for him by some kindly act; "Him . . . thou didst not doom So strictly; but much more to *pity* incline," Milton's "Paradise Lost," iii. 402); also, a cause or reason for pity, sorrow, or regret (as, what a *pity* you could not go! "It's a thousand *pities* he ever lost his wife," Galsworthy's "Saint's Progress," ii. 10); ground for regret, or regrettable character (as, "O Iago, the *pity* of it, Iago!" Shakspere's "Othello," iv. 1. 207).—**pit′y,** *v.*; *pitied, pitying.* **I.** *tr.* To feel pity or compassion for; be sorry for; commiserate. **II.** *intr.* To feel pity; have compassion.—**pit′y-ing-ly,** *adv.*

pit-y-ri-a-sis (pit-i-rī′ạ-sis), *n.* [NL., < Gr. πιτυρίασις, < πίτυρον, bran.] In *pathol.*, any of various skin-diseases marked by the shedding of bran-like scales of epidermis.

piv-ot (piv′ọt), *n.* [F. *pivot*; origin uncertain.] A pin or short shaft, as of metal, on the end of which something rests and turns, or upon and about which something rotates or oscillates; the end of a shaft or arbor, resting and turning in a bearing; a pin serving for attachment, as a dowel-pin for fixing an artificial crown to the root of a natural tooth; also, the person upon whom a line, as of troops, wheels about; also, fig., that on which something turns, hinges, or depends (as, "The *pivot* of the whole affair was the stupidity of some admiral . . . Everything turned on that," J. Conrad's "Lord Jim," xv.; "The editor is the *pivot* of a magazine. On him everything turns," Bok's "Americanization of Edward Bok," xv.).—**piv′ot,** *v.* **I.** *tr.* To mount on, attach by, or provide with a pivot or pivots. **II.** *intr.* To turn on or as on a pivot: as, "There is a recess, and the board at the back *pivots*; a very simple hiding-place" (J. Conrad's "Victory," iii. 9).—**piv′ot-al,** *a.* Of, pertaining to, or serving as a pivot; being that on which something turns, hinges, or depends; of critical importance: as, a *pivotal* State in an election.—**piv′ot-al-ly,** *adv.*—**piv′ot=gun,** *n.* A gun mounted on a pivot or a rotating carriage, which makes it possible to point the gun in any direction.

pix-y, pix-ie (pik′si), *n.*; pl. *pixies* (-siz). [Origin obscure.] A fairy or sprite. [Orig. southwestern Eng.]—**pix′y=led,** *a.* Led astray by pixies; hence, lost; bewildered.

piz-zi-ca-to (pēt-sē-kä′tō). [It., pp. of *pizzicare*, pinch, pick.] In *music*: **I.** *a.* Played by plucking the strings with the finger instead of using the bow, as on a violin. **II.** *n.* A note or passage so played.

pla-ca-ble (plā′kạ-bl), *a.* [L. *placabilis.*] Capable of being placated or appeased; forgiving; pacific: as, "a *placable* enemy" (Macaulay's "Hist. of Eng.," i.); "the tone of philosophy proper to a *placable* country gentleman obedient to government on foreign affairs" (G. Meredith's "Lord Ormont and His Aminta," xiii.).—**pla-ca-bil′i-ty** (-bil′i-ti), **pla′ca-ble-ness,** *n.*—**pla′ca-bly,** *adv.*

plac-ard (plak′ạ̈rd or plạ-kärd′), *n.* [OF. F. *placard*, < OF. *plaquier* (F. *plaquer*), affix, apply: cf. D. *plakken*, paste on.] An official document with a seal affixed†; a license†; an edict† or proclamation†; also, a written or printed notice to be posted in a public place (as, "There were also *placards* calling for men on nearly all the taxicabs": H. G. Wells's "Mr. Britling," ii. 2. § 1); a poster; also, an additional or reinforcing plate of armor for the breast or back†.—**pla-card** (plạ-kärd′ or plak′ạ̈rd), *v. t.* To post placards on or in (as, to *placard* a wall; to *placard* a street or town); also, to give notice of by means of placards (as, to *placard* a reward offered); also, to post as a placard (as, to *placard* a bill or notice).—**pla-card′er,** *n.*

pla-cate (plā′kāt), *v. t.*; *-cated, -cating.* [L. *placatus*, pp. of *placare*, appease, akin to *placere*, E. *please.*] To appease; pacify; conciliate or propitiate: as, to *placate* an angry or offended person.—**pla-ca-tion** (plạ̄-kā′shọn), *n.*—**pla-ca-to-ry** (plā′kạ-tọ̄-ri), *a.* Tending or intended to placate.

place (plās), *n.* [OF. F. *place* = Sp. *plaza* = It. *piazza*, < L. *platea*, street, open space, area, < Gr. πλατεῖα, broad way, street, prop. fem. of πλατύς, broad.] An open space, or square, in a city or town (sometimes used to render F. *place* and its equivalents in other languages, referring to such spaces in foreign towns); a short street, a court, or a part of a street with the houses along it, in a city or town; also, space in general, or extension in space (chiefly in connection with *time*: as, "Tho' from out our bourne of Time and *Place* The flood may bear me far," Tennyson's "Crossing the Bar"); space or room (archaic, or in certain phrases: as, "*Place*, nobles, for the Falcon-Knight! Room, room, ye gentles gay," Scott's "Marmion," i. 12; to find *place*, to give *place*, to have *place*, see phrases below); also, a particular portion of space, of definite or indefinite extent; a region; the portion of space occupied by anything, or a thing's position, locality, or situation (as, "In the world I fill up a *place*, which may be better supplied when I have made it empty," Shakspere's "As You Like It," i. 2. 204; "Though you change your *place*, you need not change your trade," Shakspere's "Measure for Measure," i. 2. 110); a portion of space used for habitation, as a city, town, or village; also, a residence, dwelling, or house; a mansion or palace; a manor-house; a residence with its adjoining grounds, etc.; also, a building, a part of a building, or a space or spot, set apart or used for a particular purpose (as, a *place* of worship; a *place* of business; a *place* of amusement; a *place* of resort); also, any part or spot in a body or surface (as, a decayed *place* in a tooth; a sore *place* on one's foot); a particular passage in a book or writing; also, a proper or appropriate location or position (as, "The country is not a *place* for a person of my temper": Addison, in "Spectator," 131); fig., a fitting opportunity; a reasonable ground or occasion; also, a portion of space occupied, as by a person, by right, allotment, or the like; a space or seat for a person, as in a public hall or a conveyance; often, the space or position customarily or previously occupied by a person or thing, with reference to its being occupied by a successor or substitute (as, "Their *places* were supplied by men who had no recommendation but their religion": Macaulay's "Hist. of Eng.," vi.); room, stead, or lieu (as, to use water in the *place* of milk; to receive extra pay in *place* of a vacation); sometimes, position, situation, or circumstances (as, if I were in your *place*); also, a situation, post, or office (as, "Good servants need not want *places*": Fielding's "Tom Jones," vii. 8); an office in the service of the government; official employment or position, or office (as, to seek *place*; "'Twas his fate, unemploy'd, or in *place*," Goldsmith's "Retaliation," 41); function or duty (as, "It did not seem quite his *place* to tell her of her mistake": Howells's "Chance Acquaintance," i.); also, position or standing in the social scale, or in any order of merit, estimation, etc. (as, "I hold to being kind to servants . . . but you must make 'em know their *place*," Mrs. Stowe's "Uncle Tom's Cabin," xvi.; a writer holding a high *place* in the literature of his country, or the affections of his countrymen; to win fifth *place* in a competition); sometimes, high position or rank (as, to rise to *place*); also, a position among the leading competitors, usually the first three, at the finish of a race, esp. the position of the second as opposed to that of the winner; also, a step or point in order of proceeding (as, in the first *place*; in the next *place*); in *astron.*, the position of a heavenly body at any instant; in *falconry*, the pitch of a falcon or other bird, or the greatest elevation which it attains in its flight (archaic: as, "a falcon, towering in her pride of *place*," Shakspere's "Macbeth," ii. 4. 12); in *arith.*, the position of a figure in a series, as in decimal notation; *pl.*, the figures of the series.—**a place in the sun,** fig., a share of a good thing which is the right of all, or, more commonly, a position as favorable for advancement as any occupied by others.—**in place,** in the proper or usual place; also, in its original place; in situ; also, fig., in a fitting or suitable position; fitting or appropriate; timely.—**out of place,** not in the proper or usual place; misplaced; fig., not in a suitable place; inappropriate; ill-timed.—**to find place,** to find room; have being.—**to give place,** to make room or way (archaic); with *to*, to give way to, yield to, or be succeeded by (as, "The stern expression of his eye gradually *gave place to* a look of softness": Cooper's "Spy," viii.).—**to have place,** to have room, as in a place or situation; be present; exist.—**to take place,** to take precedence† (as, "Though Miss Crawford is in a manner at home at the Parsonage, you are not to be *taking place* of her": Jane Austen's "Mansfield Park," xxiii.); also, to happen; occur.—**place,** *v. t.*; *placed, placing.* To put or set in a particular place, position, situation, or relation; also, to put in the proper position or order; arrange; dispose; also, to put in a certain or suitable place, or into particular or proper hands, for some purpose (as, to *place* money in a bank; to *place* an order for goods; to *place* a manuscript with a publisher); also, to set or repose (as, to *place* confidence in a person); also, to identify by connecting with the proper place, circumstances, etc. (as, to be unable to *place* a person; "Edward could not quite *place* this periodical; he had never seen it, he had never heard of it," Bok's "Americanization of Edward Bok," ii.); also, to appoint (a person) to a post or office; find a place, situation, etc., for (a person); specif., to induct (a clergyman) to a charge (as, "I was *placed* and settled as the minister of Dalmailing": Galt's "Annals of the Parish," Introd.); also, to determine or indicate the place of; assign a certain position or rank to; specif., to assign a position to (a horse, etc.) among the leading competitors, usually the first three, at the finish of a race; also, to attribute or ascribe (as, "She . . . *places* her disappointment . . . to her being . . . less affluent than many of her acquaintance": Jane Austen's "Mansfield Park," xliv.).

place-a-ble (plā′sạ-bl), *a.* That may be placed.

pla-ce-bo (plạ-sē′bō), *n.*; pl. *-bos* (-bōz). [L., 'I shall be pleasing (or acceptable).'] In the *Rom. Cath. Ch.*, the vespers of the office for the dead, so called from the initial word of the first antiphon, taken from Ps. cxiv. 9 of the Vulgate (cxvi. 9 of the Authorized Version); in *med.*, a medicine given merely to please the patient.

place=kick (plās′kik), *n.* In *football*, a kick given the ball after it has been placed on the ground. Cf. *drop-kick* and *punt*[1].

place-less (plās′les), *a.* Having no place or locality; not local; also, having no situation or office.

place-man (plās′mạn), *n.*; pl. *-men.* One who holds a place or office, esp. under a government: often depreciatory: as, "a Cabinet which contains, not *placemen* alone, but independent and popular noblemen and gentlemen" (Macaulay's "Essays," Sir William Temple).

place-ment (plās′mẹnt), *n.* The act of placing, or the state of being placed; location; arrangement; specif., in *football*, the placing of the ball on the ground in attempting to kick a goal from the field of play (not after a touchdown) by means of a place-kick.

place=name (plās′nām), *n.* A name of a place or locality; any geographical name, as Athens, Asia, Samoa, Land's End, Pike's Peak, Brünig Pass, Niagara Falls, Rio Grande, Black Sea, Arctic Ocean.

pla-cen-ta (plạ-sen′tạ̈), *n.*; pl. *-tas*, L. *-tæ* (-tē). [L., a cake, = Gr. πλακοῦς (πλακουντ-), flat cake, contr. < πλακόεις (πλακοεντ-), flat.] In *zoöl.* and *anat.*, the organ by which in most mammals the fetus is attached to the wall of the uterus and nourished; in *bot.*, that part of the ovary of flowering plants which bears the ovules; also, in ferns, etc., the tissue giving rise to sporangia.—**pla-cen′tal** (-tạl). [NL. *placentalis.*] **I.** *a.* In *zoöl.* and *anat.*, of or pertaining to the placenta; having a placenta; in *bot.*, of or pertaining to the placenta of a plant. **II.** *n.* In *zoöl.*, a placental

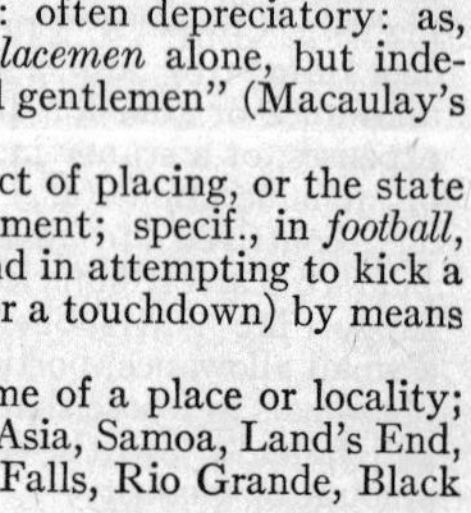

Human Placenta (unattached surface), with umbilical cord.

mammal.—**pla-cen-ta-tion** (plas-ẹn-tā'shọn), *n.* In *zoöl.*, the attachment of a fetus to the wall of the uterus by means of a placenta, or the mode of this attachment; also, the manner of the disposition or construction of a placenta; in *bot.*, the disposition or arrangement of a placenta.—**pla-cen'ti-form** (-ti-fôrm), *a.* Having the form of a placenta.

pla-cer[1] (plā'sėr), *n.* One who places.

pla-cer[2] (plas'ėr, Amer. Sp. plä-ser'), *n.* [Sp., sand-bank, akin to *plaza*: see *plaza* and *place.*] In *mining*, a superficial deposit containing particles of gold or other valuable minerals; a place where such a deposit is washed for gold, etc.

pla-cet (plā'set), *n.* [L.] An expression of assent or sanction by means of the Latin word *placet*, 'it pleases,' as in old university and other specific use (the negative being expressed by *non placet*, 'it does not please'); a vote of assent.

pla-cid (plas'id), *a.* [L. *placidus*, < *placere*, E. *please.*] Pleasantly calm or peaceful, or unaffected by disturbing emotions, as persons, the disposition, face, air, manner, etc.; also, undisturbed by tumult or disorder (as, a *placid* old town); of the sea, etc., undisturbed by storms; in general, calm, unruffled, tranquil, or serene.—**pla-cid-i-ty** (plạ-sid'i-ti), **pla'cid-ness**, *n.*—**pla'cid-ly**, *adv.*

plack (plak), *n.* [Cf. MD. and Flem. *placke*, a coin, OF. *plaque*, a coin, F. plate of metal, plaque: cf. *plaque.*] A small coin formerly current in Scotland; hence, the least bit of money (used in certain phrases: as, not worth a *plack*: Sc. and north. Eng.).

Obverse. Reverse.
Plack of Mary, Queen of Scots. — British Museum.

plack-et (plak'et), *n.* [Cf. *placard*, in sense of 'plate of armor.'] A petticoat or, fig., a woman (obs. or archaic); also, the opening or slit from the top of a petticoat or skirt, to facilitate putting it on and taking it off (also called *placket-hole*); also, a pocket, esp. one in a woman's skirt (archaic or prov. Eng.).

plack-less (plak'les), *a.* Without a plack; penniless: as, "poor *plackless* devils like mysel'" (Burns's "Scotch Drink," 93). [Sc.]

plac-oid (plak'oid). [Gr. πλάξ (πλακ-), something flat, tablet: see *-oid.*] **I.** *a.* Plate-like, as the scales or dermal investments of sharks; having such scales, as a fish. **II.** *n.* A fish with placoid scales.

Placoid Scales of a Shark.

pla-fond (plạ-fond', F. plȧ-fôṅ), *n.* [F., < *plat*, flat, + *fond*, bottom: see *plate* and *fund.*] In *arch.*, a ceiling, whether flat or arched, esp. one of decorative character.

pla-gal (plā'gạl), *a.* [ML. *plagalis*, < *plaga*, plagal mode, < Gr. πλάγιος, oblique, < πλάγος, side.] In *Gregorian music*, having the final tone or key-note in the middle of the compass, as a mode; in *modern music*, noting a cadence in which the chord of the tonic is preceded by that of the subdominant.

pla-gi-a-rism (plā'ji-ạ-rizm), *n.* [L. *plagiarius*, plunderer, later kidnapper, plagiarist, perhaps < *plaga*, net, snare.] The appropriating and putting forth as one's own of the ideas, designs, writings, etc., of another; esp., literary theft, as in reproducing (more or less exactly) passages from another writer as professedly original work; also, something appropriated and put forth in this manner.—**pla'gi-a-rist**, *n.* One guilty of plagiarism.—**pla''gi-a-ris'tic**, *a.*—**pla'gi-a-rize**, *v.*; *-rized*, *-rizing*. **I.** *tr.* To appropriate by plagiarism (as, "I could not help *plagiarizing* Miss Hannah More's first line": Mrs. Stowe's "Oldtown Folks," xxxix.); also, to appropriate ideas, passages, etc., from by plagiarism. **II.** *intr.* To commit plagiarism; appropriate ideas, passages, etc., for presentation as one's own: as, "He even had doubts whether in 'The Silent Places,' he had been *plagiarising*, more or less unconsciously, from Henry James's 'Great Good Place'" (H. G. Wells's "Mr. Britling," i. 5. § 6).—**pla'gi-a-ry** (-ạ-ri), *n.*; pl. *-ries* (-riz). [L. *plagiarius.*] A kidnapper†; also, a plagiarist; also, plagiarism.

pla-gi-o-clase (plā'ji-ọ-klās), *n.* [G. *plagioklas*, < Gr. πλάγιος, oblique, + κλάσις, fracture.] Triclinic feldspar of the soda-lime class, with two prominent cleavage-directions at oblique angles.

pla-gi-o-clas-tic (plā''ji-ọ-klas'tik), *a.* [Gr. πλάγιος, oblique: see *clastic.*] In *mineral.*, characterized by two different cleavage-directions oblique to each other, as certain feldspars (see *plagioclase*).

pla-gi-o-trop-ic (plā''ji-ọ-trop'ik), *a.* [Gr. πλάγιος, oblique, + -τροπος, < τρέπειν, turn.] In *bot.*, noting, pertaining to, or exhibiting a mode of growth which is more or less divergent from the vertical.—**pla-gi-ot'ro-pism** (-ot'rọ-pizm), *n.* In *bot.*, plagiotropic tendency or growth.

plague (plāg), *n.* [OF. *plague*, *plage*, < L. *plaga*, blow, stroke, wound, LL. affliction, pestilence; akin to L. *plangere*, beat, strike, Gr. πλήσσειν, strike, and πληγή, stroke.] A blow† or wound†; hence, an affliction, calamity, or evil, esp. one regarded as a visitation from God (as, the ten *plagues* of Egypt, see Ex. vii.–xii.); any general or public evil (as, a *plague* of army-worms; a *plague* of counterfeit money); any cause of trouble or vexation (as, "As the *plague* of happy life, I turn away from party-strife," M. Green's "The Spleen"; that child is the *plague* of our lives); a nuisance; a torment; also, an epidemic disease of high mortality; a pestilence or pest; specif., a malignant, infectious, epidemic disease occurring in several forms (bubonic, pneumonic, and septicemic), and prevalent at various periods under different names (as the 'black death' of the 14th century, the 'great plague of London' in 1664–65, and the 'Oriental plague'). —**plague on**, or **plague take**, may a plague, or mischief of some kind, befall (a thing, person, etc.): used in imprecation, often vaguely, in mere expressions of impatience: as, "*Plague on* my tongue! what have I done?" (Bulwer-Lytton's "Caxtons," xiii. 1); *plague take* the fellow!—**plague**, *v. t.*; *plagued*, *plaguing*. To smite with a plague or calamity (as, "The Lord *plagued* Pharaoh and his house with great plagues": Gen. xii. 17); afflict with any evil; trouble or torment in any manner (as, "God save thee, ancient Mariner! From the fiends, that *plague* thee thus!" Coleridge's "Ancient Mariner," i.); in a milder sense, to annoy, bother, or pester (as, "As I have no estate, I am *plagued* with no tenants or stewards": Fielding's "Tom Jones," viii. 15); urge or persuade by annoying importunities (as, "Here was his mother *plaguing* him to ask Towneley to come down to Battersby": S. Butler's "Way of All Flesh," xlviii.); also, to infect with a plague or pestilence.—**pla-guer** (plā'gėr), *n.* —**plague'=spot**, *n.* A spot on the body due to a plague or pestilence; also, a spot or locality where a plague prevails; fig., a seat of some grave or foul evil (as, the town was a *plague-spot* of rebellion; a *plague-spot* of vice).—**plague'=strick''en**, *a.* Stricken with a plague or pestilence: as, a *plague-stricken* city; "I did not hear of any instance in which a *plague-stricken* patient had recovered" (Kinglake's "Eothen," xviii.).—**pla'guy** (-gi), *a.* Plague-like or pestilential (obs. or rare); also, plague-stricken†; also, such as to plague, torment, or annoy, or vexatious (now colloq.); hence, excessive, or very great (colloq.).—**pla'gui-ly** (-gi-li), *adv.*—**pla'guy**, *adv.* Vexatiously or excessively: as, "It was *plaguy* hard on a fellow . . . to be gulled that way" (Mrs. Stowe's "Uncle Tom's Cabin," vi.). [Colloq.]

plaice (plās), *n.*; pl. *plaice*, occasionally *plaices*. [OF. *plais*, < LL. *platessa*, flatfish, prob. < Gr. πλατύς, broad, flat.] A European flatfish, *Pleuronectes platessa*, an important food-fish sometimes weighing more than 10 pounds; also, any of various American flatfishes or flounders.

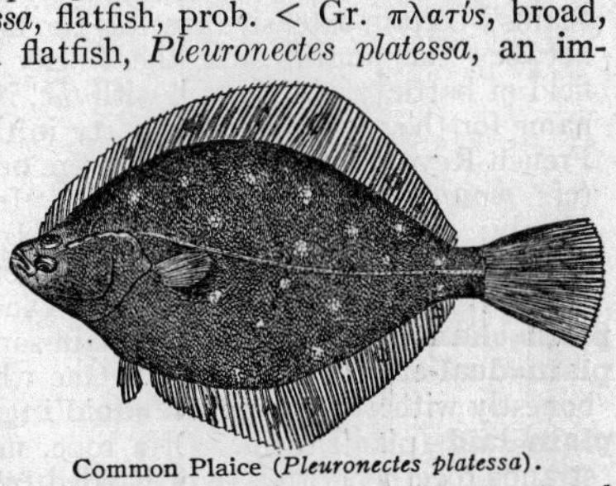

Common Plaice (*Pleuronectes platessa*).

plaid (plad, Sc. plād). [Gael. *plaide*, blanket, plaid.] **I.** *n.* A long, rectangular piece of woolen cloth, usually having a pattern of colored bars or stripes crossing at right angles, worn about the shoulders by the Scottish Highlanders (as, "The Gael around him threw His graceful *plaid* of varied hue," Scott's "Lady of the Lake," v. 2: cf. *maud*); the cloth of which this is made; hence, any fabric with a similar cross-barred pattern; a pattern of this kind. **II.** *a.* Having the pattern of a plaid: as, *plaid* silk.—**plaid'ed,** *a.* Made of plaid, or having a similar pattern; also, wearing a plaid.

Highlander wearing modern Kilt and separate Plaid.

plain[1] (plān), *v.* [OF. F. *plaindre,* < L. *plangere,* beat (the breast, etc.), lament: see *plague.*] **I.** *intr.* To lament; mourn; complain. [Archaic or prov.] **II.** *tr.* To lament over; complain of. [Archaic or prov.]

plain[2] (plān), *a.* [OF. F. *plain* (as n., OF. *plain,* masc., OF. F. *plaine,* fem.) = Sp. *llano* = It. *piano,* < L. *planus,* flat, even, level, plane (as n., L. *planum,* neut., a plain, NL. a plane): cf. *plane*[2].] Flat or level (as, "We met with . . . people in the *plain* country before we came to those hills": Defoe's "Captain Singleton," vi.); also, unobstructed, clear, or open, as ground, a space, etc. (obs. or prov. Eng.); hence, clear or distinct to the eye or ear (as, a *plain* trail; voices or sounds become *plainer* as one approaches; persons in *plain* sight and hearing); clear to the mind, evident, manifest, or obvious (as, to make one's meaning *plain*; "It's *plain* enough, I hope, that you can't want things which you've got already," M. Hewlett's "Open Country," xii.); being clearly such, unmistakable, downright, or sheer (as, *plain* stealing; *plain* folly); conveying the meaning clearly or simply, or easily understood, as words, explanations, a speaker or writer, etc.; without intricacies or difficulties, or simple, as work; also, free from ambiguity, evasion, or reserve, candid, frank, or outspoken (as, *plain* talk; I will be perfectly *plain* with you); free from dissimulation or duplicity, straightforward, honest, or sincere (as, "An honest mind and *plain,* he must speak truth!" Shakspere's "King Lear," ii. 2. 105); also, without special pretensions, advantages, superiority, elegance, etc. (as, a *plain* man; the *plain* people; *plain* manners or living); common or ordinary; homely or unaffected; simple, unostentatious, or frugal; also, with little or no embellishment, decoration, or enhancing elaboration (as, a *plain* cloak, ring, house, or monumental stone; to wear the hair *plain*); without pattern, device, or coloring; esp., without figured pattern, variegated coloring, specially varied weave, etc., as fabrics; not rich, highly seasoned, or elaborately prepared, as food; without relishing or customary accompaniments (as, *plain* bread); also, without pretensions to beauty, or homely (as, a *plain* face; "Eliza and Maria . . . were neither exactly pretty nor exactly *plain,*" S. Butler's "Way of All Flesh," vii.); in *card-playing,* not a court-card; also, not a trump.—**plain clothes,** the ordinary dress of civil life; non-official dress: opposed to *uniform*: as, a soldier or a policeman in *plain clothes.* Often used attributively (with hyphen): as, a *plain-clothes* man (a member of a police force assigned to special duties and wearing ordinary civilian dress).—**plain**[2], *n.* A tract of level or nearly level land, as ('the Great Plains') certain extensive treeless tracts of the western U. S. between the prairies and the Rocky Mountains; also, a field of battle†; also [*cap.*], with *the,* in *Fr. hist.,* a popular name for the more moderate party in the legislatures of the French Revolution, whose seats were on the floor of the hall (cf. *mountain, n.*).—**plain**[2], *adv.* In a plain manner; plainly; clearly or intelligibly (as, "My Poll . . . talked so articulately and *plain,* that it was very pleasant to me": Defoe's "Robinson Crusoe," i. 13); candidly or frankly.

plain=chant (plān'chȧnt), *n.* Plain-song.

plain=deal-er (plān'dē'lėr), *n.* One who deals frankly and honestly with others.—**plain'=deal'ing,** *n.* and *a.*

plain=laid (plān'lād), *a.* Of a rope, made by laying three strands together with a right-handed twist.

plain-ly (plān'li), *adv.* In a plain manner; clearly; manifestly; frankly; simply.—**plain'ness,** *n.*

plains-man (plānz'man), *n.*; pl. *-men.* A man or inhabitant of the plains: as, "The coolies . . . fled up the hill as fast as *plainsmen* run across the level" (Kipling's "Kim," xiii.).

plain=song (plān'sông), *n.* The unisonous vocal music used in the Christian church from the earliest times; also, a melody taken as the theme for contrapuntal treatment; any simple melody or theme.

plain=spok-en (plān'spō'kn), *a.* Plain or frank in speech, or as speech; candid; blunt; outspoken: as, a *plain-spoken* man; a *plain-spoken* rebuke.—**plain'=spok'en-ness,** *n.*

plaint (plānt), *n.* [OF. *plaint,* < L. *planctus,* lamentation, < *plangere*: see *plain*[1].] Lamentation, or a lament (archaic); also, a complaint, as of injury suffered; in *law,* a statement of grievance made to a court for the purpose of asking redress.

plain-tiff (plān'tif), *n.* [OF. *plaintif,* one who complains, noun use of *plaintif,* adj.: see *plaintive.*] In *law,* one who begins a suit before a tribunal to obtain a remedy for an injury to his rights: opposed to *defendant.*

plain-tive (plān'tiv), *a.* [OF. F. *plaintif,* < OF. *plaint*: see *plaint.*] Lamenting or complaining, now esp. in a subdued or weak way, as a person; conveying complaint, or expressing sorrow or melancholy discontent, as utterances, the voice, tone, air, etc.; suggestive of lamenting or complaining, or mournful (as, *plaintive* music; the *plaintive* cry of a bird).—**plain'tive-ly,** *adv.*—**plain'tive-ness,** *n.*

plain=wov-en (plān'wō'vn), *a.* Woven with a plain or simple weave (without twill, figure, or the like).

plai-sance (plā-zäns', F. ple-zäṅs), *n.* [F., pleasure: see *pleasance.*] A pleasure-ground, or place of amusements: as, the Midway *Plaisance* at Chicago in 1893 (see *midway, n.*).

plait (plāt), *n.* [OF. *pleit,* < L. *plicitum,* pp. neut. of *plicare,* fold: see *ply.*] A pleat or fold, as of cloth; also, a braid, as of hair or straw; a plat.—**plait,** *v. t.* To pleat (cloth, etc.); also, to braid or plat (hair, etc.); make (a mat, etc.) by braiding.

plan (plan), *n.* [F. *plan,* noun use of *plan,* flat, plane, < L. *planus,* E. *plane*[2], *plain*[2].] A representation of a thing drawn on a plane, as a map or diagram; esp., a drawing of a building or other structure in horizontal section, showing the arrangement and proportions of parts; also, a table, program, or the like; also, a scheme of arrangement (as, "A mighty maze! but not without a *plan*": Pope's "Essay on Man," i. 6); a design according to which things are arranged or to be arranged; hence, disposition of parts; type of structure; also, a scheme of action or procedure (as, to form, develop, or carry out a *plan* of operations; a *plan* of reorganization); a formulated method of proceeding; in general, a way of doing (as, "The good old rule . . . the simple *plan,* That they should take, who have the power, And they should keep who can": Wordsworth's "Rob Roy's Grave," 38); sometimes, a project or definite purpose of doing something (as, we have no *plans* for the future; "May such success attend the pious *plan,*" Cowper's "Conversation," 837).—**plan,** *v.*; *planned, planning.* **I.** *tr.* To draw or make a plan of (a building, etc.); also, to arrange a plan or scheme for (any work, enterprise, or proceeding); design, devise, or contrive; also, to form a plan, project, or purpose of (as, to *plan* a visit at the first opportunity; I had *planned* to refuse the offer). **II.** *intr.* To make plans.

pla-na-ri-an (plą-nā'ri-ąn). [NL. *Planaria,* the typical genus, prop. fem. of LL. *planarius,* level (flat), < L. *planus,* E. *plane*[2], *plain*[2].] **I.** *a.* Belonging to a group (*Planarida*) of turbellarians (flatworms), mostly oval or elliptical in form, and mostly aquatic, moving by means of vibratile cilia; turbellarian. **II.** *n.* A planarian flatworm; a turbellarian.

pla-na-tion (plą-nā'shǫn), *n.* [LL. *planare* (pp. *planatus*), make level: see *plane*[3], *v.*] In *geol.,* the process of erosion and deposit by which a stream produces a nearly level land-surface.

planch (planch), *n.* [OF. F. *planche,* = E. *plank.*] A plank, or a planking or floor (now prov. Eng.); also, a flat piece, plate, or slab, as of metal, stone, or baked clay (now technical).—**planch,** *v. t.* To lay or floor with planks; make of planks (as, "a *planched* gate": Shakspere's "Measure for Measure," iv. 1. 30). [Now prov. Eng.]

plan-chet (plan'chet), *n.* [Dim. of *planch.*] A flat piece of metal for stamping as a coin; a coin-blank.

plan-chette (plan-shet′, F. plän-shet), *n.* [F., dim. of *planche*, E. *planch.*] A small heart-shaped or triangular board supported on two casters and a vertical pencil, which is said to trace lines, words, or sentences without conscious effort on the part of persons whose fingers are lightly resting on the board. Cf. *ouija.*

plane[1] (plān), *n.* [OF. F. *plane,* < L. *platanus,* < Gr. πλάτανος, < πλατύς, broad (with reference to the broad leaves).] A plane-tree.

plane[2] (plān), *a.* [A later form, with differentiated sense, beside *plain*[2], < L. *planus,* flat, level, plane (as n., NL. *planum,* neut.): see *plain*[2], and cf. F. *plain* and *plan.*] Flat or level, as a surface; being wholly within a plane, as geometrical figures of two dimensions (length and breadth, but not thickness: cf. *solid, a.*); of or pertaining to such figures (as, *plane* geometry).—**plane sailing.** See under *sailing.*—**plane**[2], *n.* A flat or level surface; a surface such that a straight line joining any two of its points lies wholly within that surface; often, an imaginary plane surface or superficies conceived for some purpose, as one supposed to pass through a body, or to contain given points, or to form a level of elevation; fig., a level of dignity, character, existence, development, or the like (as, a high or a low moral *plane;* to be on a *plane* of equality with one's neighbors; to be on a *plane* with the savages); in *aëronautics,* a thin, flat or curved, extended member of an aëroplane or a hydroplane, affording a supporting surface (cf. *monoplane, biplane, triplane*); also, an aëroplane or a hydroplane.—**inclined plane.** See under *inclined.*—**plane of polarization** (of light). See under *polarization.*—**plane**[2], *v. i.*; *planed, planing.* To travel in an aëroplane or the like.

plane[3] (plān), *v.*; *planed, planing.* [OF. F. *planer,* < LL. *planare,* make flat or level, < L. *planus,* flat, level (see *plain*[2]); now associated with *plane*[3], *n.*] **I.** *tr.* To make flat, level, or smooth (archaic, and now chiefly fig.: as, to *plane* the way; "What student came but that you *planed* her path To Lady Psyche?" Tennyson's "Princess," iv. 296); also, to smooth or dress with or as with a plane or a planer; remove by or as by means of a plane (with *away* or *off*). **II.** *intr.* To work with a plane: as, "a rosy-cheeked Englishman . . . up to his knees in shavings, and *planing* away at a bench" (H. Melville's "Omoo," lxxvi.).—**plane**[3], *n.* [OF. F. *plane,* < LL. *plana,* < *planare.*] A tool with a blade for paring, truing, smoothing, or finishing the surface of wood, etc.: as, "Men . . . shaved the oars With sharpened *planes*" (W. Morris's "Jason," iii. 282).

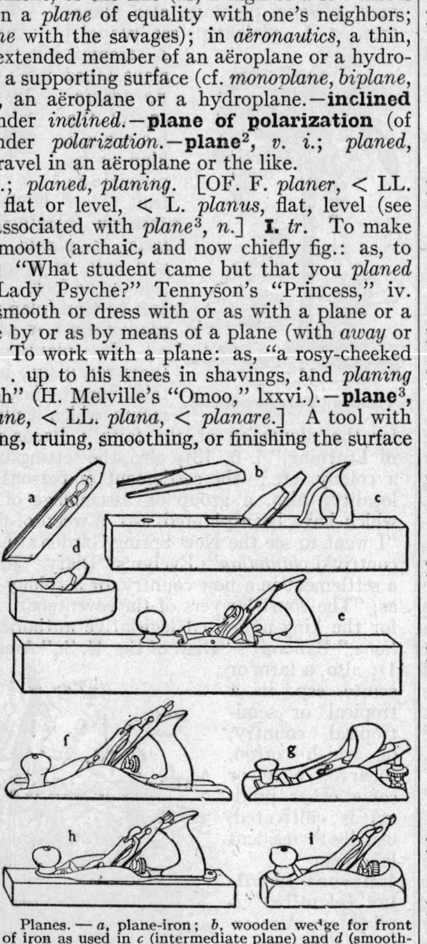

Planes. — *a,* plane-iron; *b,* wooden wedge for front of iron as used in *c* (intermediate plane) and *d* (smoothing-plane); *e,* jointing-plane; *f, h,* iron and wooden jack-planes; *g, i,* iron and wooden planes for use across the grain of wood.

plane-ness (plān′nes), *n.* The condition of being plane, or of having a plane surface.

plane=post (plān′pōst), *n.* A postal service conducted by aëroplane; an air-post.—**plane′=post,** *v. t.* To send or convey (letters, etc.) by plane-post.

plan-er (plā′nėr), *n.* One who or that which planes; a machine for planing wood; a machine for cutting or finishing flat surfaces on metal.

plan-er=tree (plan′ėr-trē), *n.* [From J. J. *Planer* (1743–89), German botanist.] A small ulmaceous tree, *Planera aquatica,* growing in moist ground in the southern U. S., bearing a small, ovoid, nut-like fruit and affording a compact light-brown wood.

plan-et (plan′et), *n.* [OF. *planete* (F. *planète*), < LL. *planeta,* < Gr. πλανήτης, planet, lit. 'wanderer,' < πλανᾶν, cause to wander.] Orig., a star moving in an orbit, as distinguished from a fixed star (formerly applied also to the sun); in modern use, any one of the heavenly bodies revolving about the sun (see note below); in *astrol.,* a heavenly body regarded as exerting influence on mankind and events. ⁂The planets consist of (1) the *primary planets,* which revolve directly round the sun as a center, including (*a*) the 'major planets,' Mercury, Venus, the earth, Mars, Jupiter, Saturn, Uranus, Neptune, and Pluto, so placed in order from the sun, and (*b*) the 'minor planets,' or asteroids, of which hundreds are known, whose orbits for the most part lie between those of Mars and Jupiter; and (2) the *secondary planets,* or satellites, which revolve round the primary planets. Those planets nearer to the sun than the earth is (Mercury and Venus) are known as *inferior planets;* those farther from the sun than the earth is (as Mars, Jupiter, Saturn, Uranus, Neptune, and Pluto) are known as *superior planets.*

plan-e-ta-ri-um (plan-e-tā′ri-um), *n.*; pl. *-riums* or *-ria* (-ri-ạ̈). [NL.] An apparatus or model representing the planetary system.

plan-e-ta-ry (plan′e-tạ-ri), *a.* [Cf. LL. *planetarius,* an astrologer.] Of, pertaining to, of the nature of, or resembling a planet or the planets; also, terrestrial or mundane; fig., wandering or erratic; in *astrol.,* pertaining to a planet or the planets as exerting influence on mankind and events; in *mach.,* noting or pertaining to a form of transmission (consisting of an epicyclic train of gears) for varying the speed in automobiles.

plan-e-tes-i-mal (plan-e-tes′i-mạl). [From *planet,* with *-esimal* as in *infinitesimal.*] **I.** *a.* Of or pertaining to minute bodies in space which, according to a certain hypothesis ('planetesimal hypothesis'), move in planetary orbits and gradually unite to form the planets of a given planetary system. **II.** *n.* One of the minute bodies of the planetesimal hypothesis.

plan-e-toid (plan′e-toid), *n.* [See *-oid.*] A minor planet (see *planet*); an asteroid.—**plan-e-toi′dal,** *a.*

plane=tree (plān′trē), *n.* [See *plane*[1].] Any tree of the genus *Platanus,* esp. *P. orientalis,* which is found wild from Italy to Persia and is much used in Europe for ornament, or *P. occidentalis,* the buttonwood or sycamore of North America.

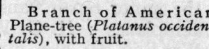

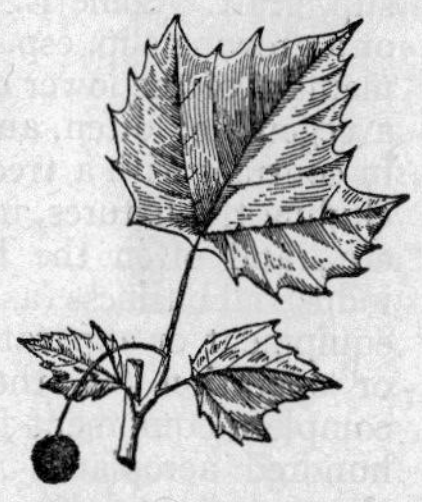
Branch of American Plane-tree (*Platanus occidentalis*), with fruit.

plan-et=strick-en, plan-et=struck (plan′et-strik″n, -struk), *a.* Stricken by the supposed influence of a planet; blasted; sometimes, panic-stricken.

plan-et=wheel (plan′et-hwēl), *n.* Any of the wheels in an epicyclic train, whose axes revolve around the common center.

plan-gent (plan′jẹnt), *a.* [L. *plangens* (*plangent-*), ppr. of *plangere,* beat, lament: see *plain*[1] and *plague.*] Beating or dashing, as waves (as, "the weltering of the *plangent* wave": Sir H. Taylor's "Philip van Artevelde," i. 1. 10); also, resounding loudly (as, "St. Margaret's bells . . . Hark! how those *plangent* comforters call and cry!" Henley's "London Voluntaries," i.).—**plan′gen-cy** (-jẹn-si), *n.*

plan-gor-ous (plang′gọr-us), *a.* [L. *plangor,* loud lamentation, < *plangere:* see *plangent.*] Characterized by loud lamentation; wailing.

plani-. Form of L. *planus,* flat, plane, used in combination. Cf. *plano-*[1].—**pla-nim-e-ter** (plạ-nim′e-tėr), *n.* [+ *-meter.*] An instrument for measuring mechanically the area of plane figures.—**pla-nim′e-try,** *n.* [+ *-metry.*] The mensuration of plane surfaces; plane geometry.—**plan-i-met-ric, plan-i-met-ri-cal** (plan-i-met′rik, -ri-kạl), *a.*—**pla-ni-ros-tral** (plā-ni-ros′trạl), *a.* [+ L. *rostrum,* beak.] Having a broad, flat beak.

plan-ish (plan′ish), *v. t.* [Obs. F. *planir* (*planiss-*), for *planer,* E. *plane*[3], *v.*] To flatten or smooth (metal) by hammering, rolling, etc.; finish off (metal, paper, etc.) with a polished surface.

plan-i-sphere (plan′i-sfēr), *n.* [= F. *planisphère,* < L.

planus, flat, plane, + *sphæra*, E. *sphere*.] A projection or representation of the whole or a part of a sphere on a plane, esp. a map of half or more of the celestial sphere with a device for indicating the part of the heavens visible at a given time.

plank (plangk), *n.* [OF. *planke*, var. of *planche* (F. *planche*), < L. *planca*, plank, board, slab: cf. *planch*.] A long, flat piece of timber thicker than a board; also, timber in such pieces; fig., something to stand on or to cling to for support; also, an article of a platform of political or other principles.—**to walk the plank.** See under *walk*, *v. t.*—**plank,** *v. t.* To lay, cover, or furnish with planks; also, to lay, put, or pay (*down*, etc.: colloq.: as, "He finished the glass, and *planked* it down firmly on the table," Arnold Bennett's "The Old Adam," iv.; "I *plank* out your share of the dollars," Mark Twain's "Life on the Mississippi," xxxvi.); also, to cook (shad, etc.) on a board.—**plank′ing,** *n.* The act of laying or covering with planks; also, planks collectively, as in a floor.

plank-ton (plangk′ton), *n.* [G., < Gr. πλαγκτόν, neut. of πλαγκτός, wandering, < πλάζειν, cause to wander.] The minor animal and plant organisms that float or drift in the water, esp. at or near the surface (cf. *nekton* and *benthos*); an aquatic vegetation of freely floating microscopic algæ.—**plank-ton′ic,** *a.*

plan-less (plan′les), *a.* Without a plan; lacking plan or method: as, "She made me feel more *planless* and incidental than ever" (H. G. Wells's "Tono-Bungay," iii. 3. § 3).—**plan′less-ly,** *adv.*—**plan′less-ness,** *n.*

plan-ner (plan′ėr), *n.* One who plans.

plano-¹. Form of L. *planus*, flat, plane, used in combination. Cf. *plani-*.

plano-². Form of Gr. πλάνος, wandering, used in combination.—**plan-o-blast** (plan′ǫ-blast), *n.* [+ *-blast*.] In *zoöl.*, the medusa form of a hydrozoan.

pla-no=con-cave (plā″nō-kon′kāv), *a.* [See *plano-*¹.] Plane on one side and concave on the other, as a lens.—**pla″no=con′vex,** *a.* Plane on one side and convex on the other.—**pla″no=cy-lin′dri-cal,** *a.* Plane on one side and cylindrical on the other.

pla-nom-e-ter (plạ-nom′e-tėr), *n.* [See *plano-*¹ and *-meter*.] A flat plate, usually of cast-iron, used as a gage for plane surfaces.

plant (plant), *n.* [AS. *plante*, < L. *planta*, sprout, shoot, slip, graft. Some E. senses are from *plant*, *v.*] A seedling or a growing slip, esp. one ready for transplanting; also, any member of the lower or vegetable group of living organisms; a vegetable; often, an herb or other small vegetable growth, in contrast with a tree or a shrub; also, the equipment, including the fixtures, machinery, tools, apparatus, appliances, etc., and often the buildings, necessary to carry on any industrial business (as, a manufacturing *plant*); the complete equipment or apparatus for a particular mechanical process or operation (as, the power-*plant* of an automobile); a complete equipment for any purpose (as, "a *plant* of a few hundred aeroplanes . . . armed with machine guns, and the motor repair vans and so forth needed to go with the aeroplanes": H. G. Wells's "Italy, France, and Britain at War," iii. 4); also, a collection of stolen goods, or the place where they are stored (thieves' slang); a scheme to trap, trick, swindle, or defraud (slang: as, "'It's a conspiracy,' said Ben Allen. 'A regular *plant*,' added Mr. Bob Sawyer," Dickens's "Pickwick Papers," xlviii.).—**plant,** *v. t.* [AS. *plantian*, < L. *plantare*, < *planta*.] To put or set in the ground for growth, as seeds, young trees, etc.; also, to introduce (a breed of animals) into a country; deposit (young fish, or spawn) in a river, lake, etc.; bed (oysters); also, to insert or set firmly in or on the ground or some other body or surface; fix in position; put or place; post or station; locate or situate; also, to establish or set up (a colony, city, etc.); found; settle (persons), as in a colony; also, fig., to implant (ideas, sentiments, etc.); introduce and establish (principles, doctrines, etc.: as, to *plant* Christianity among the heathen); also, to furnish or stock (land) with plants; furnish with a number of things disposed over a surface (as, "a vast ocean *planted* with innumerable islands": Addison, in "Spectator," 159); settle or colonize (a region); also, to deliver (a blow, etc.: slang); hide or conceal, as stolen goods (thieves' slang); put (gold-dust, ore, etc.) in a mine or the like so as to create a false impression of the value of the property.

Plan-tag-e-net (plan-taj′ẹ-net), *a.* [Ult. < L. *planta*, sprout, sprig, + *genesta*, *genista* (F. *genêt*), broom-plant.] Of or pertaining to the line of English sovereigns (Henry II., Richard I., John, Henry III., Edward I., Edward II., Edward III., and Richard II.), which reigned from 1154 to 1399, and which was descended from Geoffrey, count of Anjou, and Matilda, daughter of Henry I., father and mother of Henry II.: the word being a personal nickname of Geoffrey, who is said to have been in the habit of wearing a sprig of broom (see etym.) in his cap. Cf. *Lancastrian* and *Yorkist*.

plan-ta-gi-na-ceous (plan″tạ-ji-nā′shius), *a.* [L. *plantago* (*plantagin-*), plantain.] Belonging to the *Plantaginaceæ*, or plantain family of plants. See *plantain*¹.

plan-tain¹ (plan′tạn), *n.* [OF. F. *plantain*, < L. *plantago* (*plantagin-*), plantain.] Any plant of the widespread genus *Plantago*, esp. *P. major*, a common weed with large, spreading leaves close to the ground and long, slender spikes of small flowers.

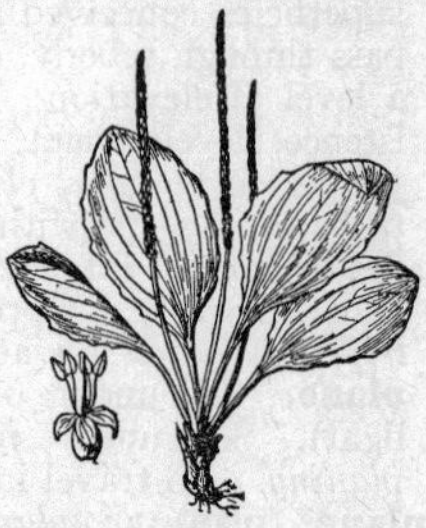

Plantain (*Plantago major*).

plan-tain² (plan′tạn), *n.* [Sp. *plántano*, *plátano*, plantain, also plane-tree, < L. *platanus*: see *plane*¹.] A tropical plant, *Musa paradisiaca*, of the banana kind, or its nutritious fruit.

Plantain (*Musa paradisiaca*).

plan-tar (plan′tạr), *a.* [L. *plantaris*, < *planta*, sole.] In *anat.* and *zoöl.*, of or pertaining to the sole of the foot.

plan-ta-tion (plan-tā′shọn), *n.* [L. *plantatio*(*n-*), < *plantare*, E. *plant*, *v.*] The planting of seeds, etc. (now rare); fig., implantation; establishment (as, "those instruments, which it pleased God to use for the *plantation* of the faith": Bacon's "Advancement of Learning," i. 6. 13); also, the setting up or planting of a colony, etc.; the settlement of persons in a region or locality; also, a group or assemblage of growing plants which have been planted, esp. a wood of planted trees (as, "I went to see the New Spring Garden at Lambeth, a pretty contriv'd *plantation*": Evelyn's "Diary," July 2, 1661); also, a settlement in a new country, or a colony (now only hist.: as, "The court lawyers of the seventeenth century asserted for the king unlimited legislative authority in the *plantations*," Bancroft's "Hist. of the U. S.," Amer. Revolution, i. 1); also, a farm or estate, esp. in a tropical or semi-tropical country, on which cotton, tobacco, coffee, or some other product is cultivated, usually by resident laborers.

plant=cat-er-pil-lar (plant′kat″ėr-pil-ạr), *n.* A caterpillar, the larva of any of several Australasian moths, within which a parasitic fungus (esp. of the genus *Cordyceps*) is growing, killing the caterpillar and sending up a long shoot from the head.

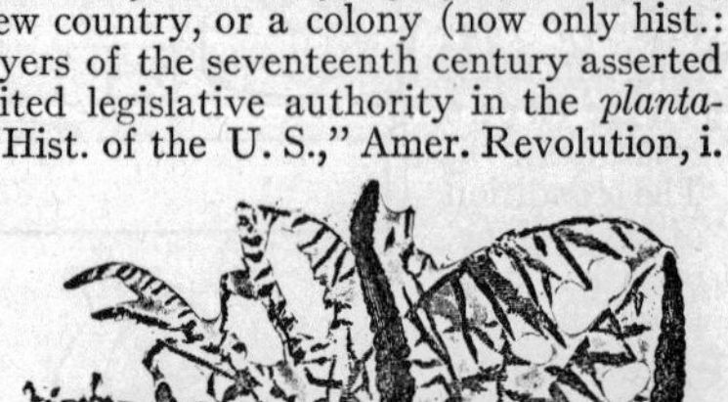

Plant-caterpillar.

plant-er (plan′tėr), *n.* One who plants (lit. or fig.); often, formerly, an early settler in a region, or a colonist (now only hist.); also, the owner or occupant of a plantation in a tropical or semitropical country (as, "one of the most considerable *planters* in the Brazils": Defoe's "Robinson Crusoe," i. 14); also, an implement or machine for planting seeds; also, a tree-trunk with one end firmly fixed in the bed of a stream and the other rising toward the surface of the water (U. S.).

plan-ti-grade (plan′ti-grād). [L. *planta*, sole, + *gradi*, walk.] **I.** *a.* Walking on the whole sole of the foot, as man, the bears, etc. **II.** *n.* A plantigrade animal.

Leg of a Plantigrade Animal (Polar Bear). — *a*, femur; *b*, tibia; *c*, tarsus and metatarsus, or foot; *d*, heel; *e*, sole; *f*, digits or toes.

plant-let (plant′let), *n.* A small plant; an undeveloped or rudimentary plant.

plant=louse (plant′lous), *n.*; pl. *-lice* (-līs). Any one of certain small insects that live on plants and suck their juices; an aphid.

plan-u-la (plan′ū-lạ̈), *n.*; pl. *-læ* (-lē). [NL., dim. < L. *planus*, flat, plane.] In *zoöl.*, the ciliated, free-swimming embryonic form of cœlenterates.—**plan′u-lar,** *a.*

plap (plap), *v. i.*; *plapped, plapping.* [Imit.] To plop.

plaque (plak), *n.* [F.: see *plack.*] A thin, flat plate or tablet of metal, porcelain, etc., intended for ornament, as on a wall, or set in a piece of furniture; sometimes, a plate-like brooch or ornament, esp. one worn as the badge of an honorary order; in *anat.* and *zoöl.*, a small, flat, rounded formation or area.

Plaque in Relief of Enameled Pottery, by Bernard Palissy; 16th century.

pla-quette (pla-ket′), *n.* [F., dim. of *plaque.*] A small plaque.

plash[1] (plash), *v. t.* [OF. *plaissier* (F. *plesser*), < L. *plectere*, plait: cf. *pleach.*] To interweave (branches, etc., bent over and often cut partly through), as for a hedge or an arbor; make or renew (a hedge, etc.) by such interweaving; pleach.

plash[2] (plash), *n.* [AS. *plæsc* = D. *plas.*] A small collection of standing water; a pool or puddle: as, "As he that leaves A shallow *plash* to plunge him in the deep" (Shakspere's "Taming of the Shrew," i. 1. 23).

plash[3] (plash), *v.* [Cf. D. *plassen*, MLG. *plasken*, G. *platschen*, splash, dabble, also E. *plash*[2] and *splash.*] **I.** *tr.* To splash. **II.** *intr.* To splash, or move with a splash, in water or the like, as oars, fish, etc.; of water, etc., to dash, fall, or strike with a sound of splashing (as, "Snake River . . . lulling the ear with the soft tumult of *plashing* waters": Irving's "Captain Bonneville," xxix.).—**plash**[3], *n.* The act or sound of plashing (as, "the *plash* and murmur of the waves": Hawthorne's "Scarlet Letter," ix.); a splash; also, a heavy fall of rain (Sc. and north. Eng.).

plash-y[1] (plash′i), *a.* Abounding in pools of water; marshy; wet: as, "As Governor Sonoy had opened many of the dykes, the land . . . was becoming *plashy*" (Motley's "Dutch Republic," iii. 9); "Seek'st thou the *plashy* brink Of weedy lake?" (Bryant's "To a Waterfowl").

plash-y[2] (plash′i), *a.* Plashing or splashing; also, marked as if splashed with color (as, "a serpent's *plashy* neck": Keats's "Hyperion," ii.).

plasm (plazm), *n.* In *anat.*, etc., same as *plasma.*

-plasm. Noun termination from Gr. πλάσμα, something formed or molded (see *plasma*), in biological and other scientific terms, as *bioplasm, metaplasm, neoplasm, protoplasm.*

plas-ma (plaz′mạ̈), *n.* [LL., < Gr. πλάσμα, something formed or molded, < πλάσσειν, form, mold.] A green, faintly translucent variety of quartz; in *anat.* and *physiol.*, the liquid part of blood or lymph, as distinguished from the corpuscles; the watery part of milk, as distinguished from the fat-globules; the juice that can be expressed from fresh muscle; in *biol.*, protoplasm.—**plas-mat′ic** (-mat′ik), **plas′mic,** *a.*

plasmo-. Form of Gr. πλάσμα, something formed or molded, E. *plasma*, used in combination.

plas-mo-di-um (plaz-mō′di-um), *n.*; pl. *-dia* (-di-ạ̈). [NL., < Gr. πλάσμα, E. *plasma*, + εἶδος, form.] In *biol.*, a mass or sheet of protoplasm formed by the fusion or contact of a number of amœboid bodies and exhibiting amœboid movement; in *zoöl.*, a parasitic protozoan organism of the genus *Plasmodium*, esp. *P. malariæ*, causing the quartan form of malaria, and *P. vivax*, causing the tertian form.

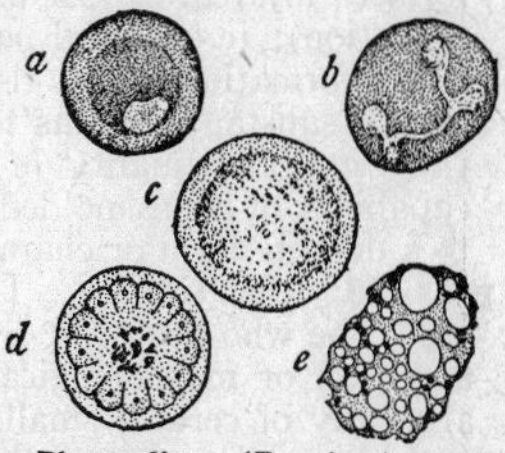

Plasmodium (*P. vivax*). — *a*, young form within a red blood-corpuscle; *b*, developing pigmented form within the corpuscle; *c*, full-grown body; *d*, segmenting body; *e*, degenerating form undergoing vacuolation.

plas-mo-gen (plaz′mō-jen), *n.* [See *plasmo-* and *-gen.*] In *biol.*, true or formative protoplasm.

plas-mol-y-sis (plaz-mol′i-sis), *n.* [See *plasmo-* and *-lysis.*] In *bot.*, contraction of the protoplasm in a living cell, when a certain amount of water is removed by exosmosis.—**plas-mo-lyt′ic** (-mō-lit′ik), *a.*

plas-mon (plaz′mon), *n.* [See *plasma.*] An almost odorless and tasteless flour-like food-preparation obtained from milk, consisting essentially of the proteid of milk.

plas-mo-some (plaz′mō-sōm), *n.* [NL. *plasmosoma*, < Gr. πλάσμα, E. *plasma*, + σῶμα, body.] In *biol.*, a true nucleolus of a cell, as distinguished from a karyosome (a nuclear body which is less properly called a nucleolus).

plas-ome (plas′ōm), *n.* [G. *plasom*, for earlier *plasmatosom*, < Gr. πλάσμα (πλασματ-), E. *plasma*, + σῶμα, body.] In *biol.*, one of the smallest theoretical units of living substance: a term practically equivalent to *biophore.*

-plast. Noun termination from Gr. πλαστός, formed, molded, esp. in biological and botanical terms, as *bioplast, chloroplast, mesoplast, protoplast.*

plas-ter (plȧs′tėr), *n.* [In first sense, AS. *plaster*, < L. *emplastrum*, < Gr. ἔμπλαστρον, a plaster, < ἐμπλάσσειν, daub on or over, < ἐν, in, on, + πλάσσειν, form, mold; in later senses, OF. *plastre* (F. *plâtre*), < L. *emplastrum.*] A solid or semisolid preparation for spreading upon cloth or the like and applying to the body for some remedial or other purpose; also, a pasty composition, as of lime, sand, water, and often hair, used for covering walls, ceilings, etc., where it hardens in drying; also, gypsum powdered but not calcined; also, calcined gypsum ('plaster of Paris'), a white powdery material which swells when mixed with water and sets rapidly, used for making casts, molds, etc.—**plas′ter,** *v. t.* To apply a plaster to (the body, etc.); also, to cover (walls, etc.) with plaster; daub or fill with plaster or something similar (as, "We adjusted a slab of sandstone to the opening . . . *plastered* up the crevices with clay": W. H. Hudson's "Green Mansions," xv.); hence, to overspread with anything, esp. thickly or to excess (as, to *plaster* the face with powder; a wall *plastered* with posters; a woman *plastered* with jewels); subject to a heavy application of anything (as, "Smee *plastered* his sitters with adulation as methodically as he covered his canvas," Thackeray's "Newcomes," xvii.; "They [guns] started in *plastering* the Germans overnight," H. G. Wells's "Mr. Britling," ii. 4. § 18); also, to apply in the manner of a plaster or of plaster (as, to *plaster* posters all over a wall); lay flat like a layer of plaster (as, to *plaster* the hair down over the forehead); also, to treat with gypsum or plaster of Paris.—**plas′ter-er,** *n.* One who plasters; esp., one who plasters walls, etc.; also, one who casts plaster figures, etc.—**plas′ter-ing,** *n.* The act of one who plasters;

also, a covering of plaster, as on walls, etc.—**plas′ter=work,** *n.* Work done with or in plaster; esp., the plastering, or work of plaster, on walls, ceilings, etc.—**plas′ter-y,** *a.* Of the nature of or resembling plaster.

plas-tic (plas′tik). [L. *plasticus*, < Gr. πλαστικός, < πλάσσειν, form, mold.] **I.** *a.* Having the power of molding or shaping formless or yielding material (as, "that divine *plastic* force which is for ever moulding human society": Mrs. H. Ward's "Robert Elsmere," xxxii.); concerned with or pertaining to molding or modeling (as, *plastic* arts, such as sculpture and ceramics); produced by molding (as, *plastic* figures); also, capable of being molded or of receiving form (as, *plastic* substances, such as clay, wax, or plaster); fig., capable of being brought to a definite condition or character (as, "The world is *plastic* for men to do what they will with it," H. G. Wells's "Mr. Britling," ii. 1 § 6; the *plastic* mind of youth); pliable; impressionable; in *surg.*, concerned with or pertaining to the remedying or restoring of malformed, injured, or lost parts (as, *plastic* surgery; a *plastic* operation); in *biol.* and *pathol.*, concerned with or pertaining to the formation of new tissue in the living body. **II.** *n.* A plastic substance.—**plas′ti-cal-ly,** *adv.*—**plas-ti′ci-ty** (-tis′-i-ti), *n.* The quality or property of being plastic; esp., capability of being molded, receiving shape, or being brought to a definite form or character.

plas-tid (plas′tid), *n.* [G., < Gr. πλάστις (πλαστιδ-), fem., one who forms, < πλάσσειν, form, mold.] In *biol.*, a morphon or morphological unit consisting of a single cell; also, any of certain small specialized masses of protoplasm (as chloroplasts, chromoplasts, etc.) occurring in certain cells.

plas-tron (plas′trọn), *n.* [F., < It. *piastrone*, aug. of *piastra*, metal plate, < L. *emplastrum*: see *plaster*, and cf. *piaster*.] A medieval metal breastplate worn under the hauberk; also, a protective shield of leather for the breast of a fencer; also, an ornamental front piece on a woman's bodice; in *zoöl.*, the ventral part of the shell of a turtle or tortoise.

-plasty. [Gr. -πλαστία, < -πλαστος, formed, < πλάσσειν, form, mold.] A noun termination meaning 'formation,' used in the names of processes of plastic surgery, as *autoplasty*, *cranioplasty*, *dermatoplasty*, *neoplasty*, *rhinoplasty*, and occasionally in other words, as *galvanoplasty*.

plat[1] (plat), *n.* [Var. of *plot*.] A plot of ground, usually of small extent, or a patch (as, "smooth *plats* of fruitful ground": Tennyson's "Blackbird"); also, a plan or map, as of land (now U. S.).—**plat**[1], *v. t.*; *platted, platting.* To make a plat or plan of; plot. [Now U. S.]

plat[2] (plat), *n.* [Var. of *plait*.] A plait or braid, as of hair or straw.—**plat**[2], *v. t.*; *platted, platting.* To plait or braid (hair, straw, etc.); make by plaiting (as, "They . . . *platted* a crown of thorns," Mark, xv. 17; "a fan *platted* from the young leaflets," H. Melville's "Omoo," lxix.).

plat[3] (plä), *n.* [F., noun use of *plat*, flat: see *plate*.] A plate or dish; a dish of food as served at table.

plat-an, plat-ane (plat′ạn, plat′ạn), *n.* [L. *platanus*: see *plane*[1].] A plane-tree: as, "thick-leaved *platans*" (Tennyson's "Princess," iii. 159); "three tall *platanes* . . . very poor as to foliage" (J. Conrad's "Rover," ii.).

plat-a-na-ceous (plat-ạ-nā′shius), *a.* [L. *platanus*: see *plane*[1].] Belonging or pertaining to the *Platanaceæ*, or plane-tree family of plants.

plat-band (plat′band), *n.* [F. *plate-bande*, 'flat band.'] In *arch.*, a flat rectangular molding the projection of which is much less than the width; also, a fillet between the flutings of a column.

plate (plāt), *n.* [OF. *plate*, flat piece, plate, prop. fem. of OF. F. *plat*, flat, akin to It. *piatto* and G. *platt*, flat; from LL., and perhaps ult. from Gr. πλατύς, broad, flat.] A thin, flat sheet or piece of metal or other material, esp. of uniform thickness; as a material, metal in such sheets; sometimes, plate-glass; also, a flat piece of metal used in making armor; armor composed of such pieces; also, a flat, polished piece of metal on which something may be or is engraved (as, a door-*plate*); also, such a piece engraved to print from; a printed impression from such a piece, or from some similar piece, as a woodcut; a full-page inserted illustration forming part of a book; also, a sheet of metal for printing from, formed by stereotyping or electrotyping a page of type; also, a flat strip of metal with a projecting flange, forming part of the track of a railway, or, sometimes, a rail of an ordinary railroad (chiefly Eng.); a kind of light horseshoe worn by race-horses; a thin piece or cut of beef at the lower end of the ribs; also, a coin, esp. of silver†; also, domestic vessels, utensils, etc., of gold or silver; hence, plated metallic ware; also, a gold or silver cup or the like awarded as a prize in horse-racing, etc.; hence, a horse-race or other contest for such a prize; also, a shallow, usually circular vessel, now usually of earthenware or porcelain, from which food is eaten; the contents of such a vessel; a service of food for one person at table; also, a vessel, as of metal or wood, resembling a plate for food, used for collecting offerings, as in a church; in *anat.*, *zoöl.*, etc., a plate-like part, structure, or organ; in *dentistry*, a piece of metal or other firm substance, with artificial teeth attached, worn in the mouth after the loss of natural teeth; in *photog.*, a sensitized sheet of glass, metal, etc., on which to take a photograph (see *dry plate*, under *dry*, *a.*, and *wet plate*, under *wet*, *a.*); in *wireless teleg.* and *teleph.*, one of the interior elements of a vacuum-tube (see *vacuum-tube*); in *arch.*, a timber laid horizontally, as in a wall, to receive the ends of other timbers; in *baseball*, the home base, at which the batter stands, and which he must return to and touch, after running around the bases, in order to score a run; in *mining*, shale.—**plate,** *v. t.*; *plated, plating.* To cover or overlay with metal plates for protection, etc.; cover (a ship, etc.) with armor-plates; also, to coat (metal) with a thin film of gold, silver, nickel, etc., by mechanical or chemical means; in *paper-making*, to give a high gloss to (paper), as by supercalendering; in *printing*, to make a stereotype or electrotype plate from (type).

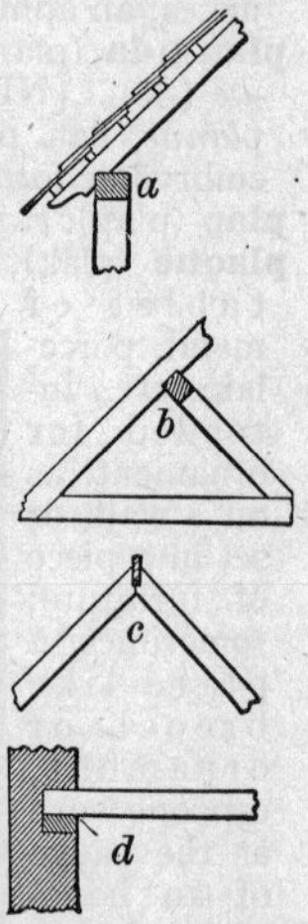

Architectural Plates. — *a*, rafter-plate; *b*, purlin-plate; *c*, crown-plate; *d*, wall-plate.

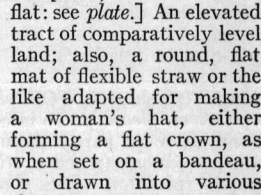

plate=ar-mor (plāt′är″mọr), *n.* Armor composed of plates of metal.

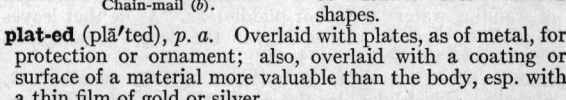

Plate-armor (*a*), as distinguished from Chain-mail (*b*).

pla-teau (pla-tō′), *n.*; pl. *-teaus* or *-teaux* (-tōz′). [F., dim. < *plat*, flat: see *plate*.] An elevated tract of comparatively level land; also, a round, flat mat of flexible straw or the like adapted for making a woman's hat, either forming a flat crown, as when set on a bandeau, or drawn into various shapes.

plat-ed (plā′ted), *p. a.* Overlaid with plates, as of metal, for protection or ornament; also, overlaid with a coating or surface of a material more valuable than the body, esp. with a thin film of gold or silver.

plate-ful (plāt′fụl), *n.*; pl. *-fuls.* As much as a plate will hold.

plate=glass (plāt′glȧs′), *n.* A fine kind of glass, cast in thick plates, used for mirrors, large window-panes, etc.

plate=hold-er (plāt′hōl″dėr), *n.* In *photog.*, a receptacle impervious to light, for holding a sensitized plate, used for exposing the plate within the camera by the removal of a slide, and for carrying the plate before and after using.

plate-let (plāt′let), *n.* A little or minute plate or plate-like body.

plat-en (plat′ẹn), *n.* [F. *platine*, < *plat*, flat: see *plate*.] A flat metal plate in a printing-press, which presses the paper against the inked type, thus securing an impression; a rotating cylinder used for the same purpose; also, the roller of a typewriter, against which the paper rests while receiving an impression.

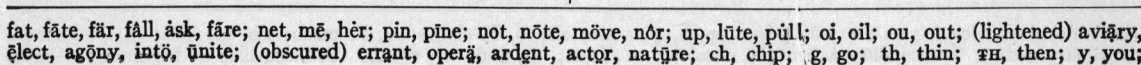

plate=pa-per (plāt′pā″pėr), *n.* A heavy, spongy, unsized paper with a smooth, dull finish, used for taking impressions from engraved plates; a similar heavy paper, as for books; also, a paper finished with a high gloss, as by supercalendering.

plat-er (plā′tėr), *n.* One who or that which plates; one engaged in the application or manufacture of metal plates; one who coats articles with a film of gold, silver, etc.; also, a horse that competes mostly in races for plates; an inferior race-horse.

plate=rail (plāt′rāl), *n.* A rail or narrow shelf placed along a wall to hold plates, etc.

plate=tra-cer-y (plāt′trā″sėr-i), *n.* In *arch.*, tracery formed by cutting openings through stone (rather than by assembling pieces): as, "Perhaps the finest examples of *plate-tracery* were produced in the rose windows of the 13th century" (Encyc. Brit., 11th ed., XXVII. 115).

Plate-tracery. — Head of a clearstory window, Cathedral of Chartres, France; 13th century.

plat-form (plat′fôrm). [F. *plate-forme*, lit. 'flat form,' plan, flat area: cf. *plate.*] **I.** *n.* A plane surface†; a plan†, chart†, or map†; also, a plan†, design†, or scheme†; specif., a plan of church government, or a scheme of religious principles or doctrines (now rare); also, a raised level surface or area; a level place for mounting guns, as in a fort; a flat elevated piece of ground; commonly, a raised level surface of boards, etc.; a raised walk or structure beside a railroad-track, as at a station, for passengers or freight (as, "At the station . . . Hilda . . . followed her trunk to the bleak *platform*": Arnold Bennett's "Hilda Lessways," i. 14); a projecting floor or landing at the end of a railroad-car or street-car; specif., a raised flooring or structure, as in a hall or meeting-place, for use by public speakers, performers, etc.; hence (with *the*), public speaking or discussion on the platform; public speakers collectively; often, the field of public lectures, the lyceum, and chautauquas (as distinguished from the stage or the dramatic field: cf. *lyceum, n.*, also *Chautauqua, n.*); also, a body of principles on which a party or the like takes its stand in appealing to the public; a public statement of the principles and policy of a political party, esp. as put forth by the representatives of the party assembled in convention to nominate candidates for an election. **II.** *a.* Of or pertaining to a platform used by public speakers (as, *platform* oratory); of or pertaining to the platform or field of public lectures, etc.—**plat′form,** *v. t.* To plan†; also, to furnish with or as with a platform; place on or as on a platform.—**plat′form=car,** *n.* An open railroad-car having no inclosing sides, or surrounded merely by low ledges.

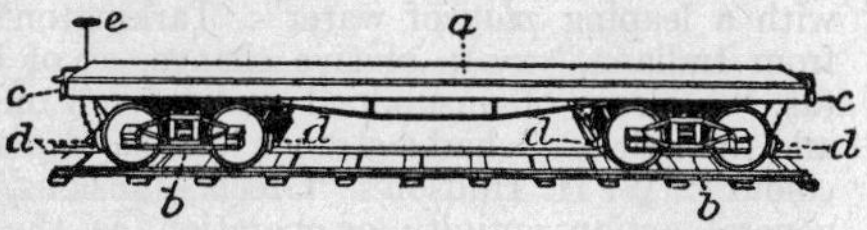

Platform-car. — *a*, platform; *b,b*, truck-frames; *c,c*, buffers; *d,d*, brake-shoes; *e*, brake-wheel.

plat-i-na (plat′i-nạ or plạ-tē′nạ), *n.* [NL. or Sp.: see *platinum.*] A native alloy of platinum with palladium, iridium, osmium, etc.

plat-i-nate (plat′i-nāt), *n.* In *chem.*, a salt of platinic acid.

plat-ing (plā′ting), *n.* The action of one who or that which plates; also, an external layer of metal plates; a thin coating of gold, silver, etc.

pla-tin-ic (plạ-tin′ik), *a.* Of or containing platinum. See *platinous.*—**platinic acid,** platinic hydroxide, $Pt(OH)_4$, which acts as a weak acid.

plat-i-nif-er-ous (plat-i-nif′ẹ-rus), *a.* [See *-ferous.*] Bearing or yielding platinum, as certain sands.

plat-i-ni-rid-i-um (plat″i-nī-rid′i-um), *n.* A natural alloy composed chiefly of platinum and iridium.

platino-. Form of *platinum* used in combination.—**plat-i-no-cy-an-ic** (plat″i-nō-sī-an′ik), *a.* In *chem.*, noting or pertaining to an acid containing platinum and the radical cyanogen.—**plat″i-no-cy′a-nide** (-sī′ạ-nīd or -nid), *n.* In *chem.*, a salt of platinocyanic acid.—**plat′i-noid.** [See *-oid.*] **I.** *a.* Resembling platinum. **II.** *n.* Any of the metals (palladium, rhodium, iridium, etc.) with which platinum is usually associated; also, an alloy (used in electrical work, etc.) resembling platinum, a compound of copper, nickel, zinc, and tungsten.—**plat′i-no-type** (-nō-tīp), *n.* [+ *-type.*] A process of photographic printing in which a platinum salt is employed, yielding prints which are more permanent and richer in tone than those obtainable with silver salts; also, a print made by such a process.

plat-i-nous (plat′i-nus), *a.* Containing platinum (in larger proportion than a corresponding platinic compound).

plat-i-num (plat′i-num), *n.* [NL., earlier *platina*, < Sp. *platina*, < *plata*, silver, = E. *plate.*] Chem. sym., Pt; at. wt., 195.2; sp. gr., 21.5. A heavy, grayish-white, highly malleable and ductile metal, resistant to most chemicals, practically unoxidizable, and fusible only at extremely high temperatures, used esp. for making chemical and scientific apparatus, and also jewelry.—**plat′i-num=black′,** *n.* A black powder consisting of very finely divided metallic platinum: used as an oxidizing agent because of its condensing large amounts of oxygen upon its surface.

plat-i-tude (plat′i-tūd), *n.* [F. *platitude*, < *plat*, flat: see *plate.*] Flatness, dullness, or triteness, as of speech or utterances; also, a flat, dull, or trite remark, esp. one uttered as if it were fresh and profound (as, " 'Nothing will be the same after the war.' This is one of the consoling *platitudes* with which people cover over voids of thought": H. G. Wells's "Italy, France, and Britain at War," iv. 5).—**plat″i-tu-di-na′ri-an** (-tū-di-nā′ri-ạn), *n.* One given to platitudes.—**plat-i-tu′di-nize,** *v. i.*; *-nized, -nizing.* To utter platitudes.—**plat-i-tu′di-nous,** *a.* Characterized by or given to platitudes; of the nature of a platitude.—**plat-i-tu′di-nous-ly,** *adv.*—**plat-i-tu′di-nous-ness,** *n.*

Pla-ton-ic (plạ-ton′ik), *a.* Of or pertaining to the Greek philosopher Plato (about 427–347 B.C.) or his doctrines (as, the *Platonic* philosophy; the *Platonic* ideas, see *idea*); hence [*l. c.* or *cap.*], as applied to love, affection, or friendship for one of the opposite sex, or between persons of opposite sex, purely spiritual, or free from sensual desire (as, "without admission that their love could not remain *platonic*": Galsworthy's "Dark Flower," ii. 9); of persons, feeling or professing such love.—**pla-ton′i-cal-ly,** *adv.*—**Pla-to-nism** (plā′tō-nizm), *n.* The philosophy or doctrines of Plato or his followers; also, a Platonic doctrine or saying; also [*l. c.* or *cap.*], the doctrine or the practice of platonic love.—**Pla′to-nist,** *n.* A follower of Plato, or of his doctrines.—**Pla-to-nis′tic,** *a.*—**Pla′to-nize,** *v.*; *-nized, -nizing.* **I.** *intr.* To follow the opinions or doctrines of Plato; reason like Plato. **II.** *tr.* To render Platonic; give a Platonic character to; explain in accordance with Platonic principles.

pla-toon (plạ-tön′), *n.* [F. *peloton*, ball, group, platoon, dim. of *pelote*, ball: see *pellet.*] A small body of soldiers, esp. a division of a company, operating as a unit; hence, in general, a company or set of persons.

Platt-deutsch (plät′doich), *n.* [G., < *platt*, flat, + *deutsch*, German: see *plate* and *Dutch.*] Low German, as the popular speech of northern Germany. See under *German*[2], *n.*

plat-ter[1] (plat′ėr), *n.* [AF. *plater*, < OF. F. *plat*, plate, dish: see *plat*[3].] A large, shallow dish, commonly oval, for holding or serving meat, etc.

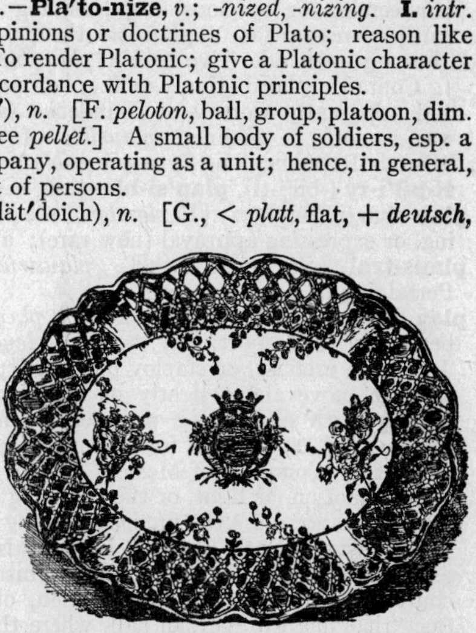

Platter, with openwork border; 18th century; from Strasburg. — Pennsylvania Museum, Philadelphia.

plat-ter² (plat′ėr), *n.* One who plats or plaits.—**plat′-ting,** *n.* The act or work of one who plats; also, straw, grass, or the like, platted into braid, or into some other form, as for hats, etc.

plat-y (plā′ti), *a.* Plate-like; consisting of plates.

platy-. Form of Gr. πλατύς, broad, flat, used in combination.

plat-y-hel-minth (plat-i-hel′minth), *n.* [NL. *Platyhelminthes,* n. pl., < Gr. πλατύς, broad, flat, + ἕλμινς (ἑλμινθ-), worm.] Any of the *Platyhelminthes,* a phylum or group of worms having a bilateral symmetry and a soft, usually flattened body, including the trematodes, cestodes, etc.

plat-y-pus (plat′i-pus), *n.*; pl. *-puses.* [NL., < Gr. πλατύπους, flat-footed, < πλατύς, broad, flat, + πούς, foot.] The duckbill. Also called *duck-billed platypus.*

plat-y-rhyn-chous (plat-i-ring′kus), *a.* [Gr. πλατύς, broad, flat, + ῥύγχος, snout, beak.] Having a broad, flat bill, as the flycatchers of the American genus *Platyrhynchus.*

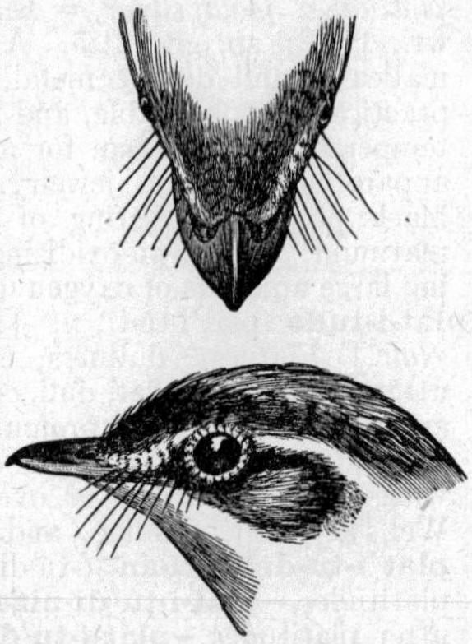

Platyrhynchous Flycatcher (*Platyrhynchus*). — Top and side views of head.

plat-yr-rhine, plat-y-rhine (plat′i-rin). [Gr. πλατύρρις (πλατυρριν-), broad-nosed, < πλατύς, broad, flat, + ῥίς (ῥιν-), nose.] **I.** *a.* Broad-nosed, as certain monkeys; in *anthropol.,* having a flat nose. **II.** *n.* A platyrrhine monkey; in *anthropol.,* a platyrrhine person or skull.

plau-dit (plâ′dit), *n.* [L. *plaudite,* 'applaud!' (said by Roman actors to the audience at the close of a play), 2d pers. pl. impv. of *plaudere* (pp. *plausus*), clap, applaud.] A demonstration or round of applause, as for some approved or admired performance (as, "The Colonel [after singing] bowed and smiled with very pleasant good nature at our *plaudits*": Thackeray's "Newcomes," i.); hence, any enthusiastic expression of approval.—**plau′di-to-ry** (-di-tō-ri), *a.* Applauding; laudatory.

plau-si-ble (plâ′zi-bl), *a.* [L. *plausibilis,* < *plaudere*: see *plaudit.*] Deserving of applause or approval†; commendable† or acceptable† (as, "Projects deep Of . . . leagues, *Plausible* to the world, to me worth naught": Milton's "Paradise Regained," iii. 393); agreeable† or pleasing†; in present use, seemingly worthy of approval or acceptance; fair-seeming or specious; esp., having an appearance of truth or reason (as, a *plausible* theory, story, or pretext; "For my own sake I've told a *plausible* lie at the club," J. Conrad's "Lord Jim," xviii.); of persons, fair-spoken and apparently worthy of confidence (as, "The Cardinal was smooth in manner, *plausible* of speech," Motley's "Dutch Republic," ii. 2; a *plausible* adventurer).—**plau-si-bil′i-ty** (-bil′i-ti), **plau′si-ble-ness,** *n.*—**plau′si-bly,** *adv.*

plau-sive (plâ′siv), *a.* [L. *plaudere*: see *plaudit.*] Applauding, or expressing approval (now rare); also, plausible†.

plaus-tral (plâs′tral), *a.* [L. *plaustrum,* wagon, cart.] Pertaining to a wagon or cart.

play (plā), *v. i.* [AS. *plegan, plegian, plægian,* move briskly, bestir one's self, sport, play, = MD. *pleyen,* dance, rejoice.] To bestir, exercise, or employ one's self†; act† or operate†; also, to move about lightly or quickly; move lightly or quickly with alternating or irregular motion, as flames, waves, wind, etc. (as, "A fresh breeze *played* on the waters": Prescott's "Conquest of Mexico," iv. 4); present the effect of such motion, as light, or the changing colors of an iridescent substance (as, "the firelight *playing* on her red frock": Galsworthy's "Dark Flower," iii. 8); also, to move freely, as within a space, as a part of a mechanism; also, to operate continuously or with repeated action, often on something (as, "that fine Elizabethan hall, where the fountain *plays,*" Lamb's "Old Benchers of the Inner Temple"; cannon *play* on the enemy's lines); also, to exercise or employ one's self in diversion, amusement, or recreation; sport; frolic; hence, to do something only in sport, which is not to be taken seriously; often, to amuse one's self or toy (*with*: as, "He *played* with his watch-chain wearily," Dickens's "Hard Times," ii. 1); trifle (*with*); also, to take part or engage in a game (as, "Her husband had been a cricketer, and *played* for his county": G. Meredith's "Lord Ormont and His Aminta," xx.); specif., to take part in a game for stakes; gamble; also, to act, or conduct one's self, in a specified way (as, to *play* fair; to *play* false); also, to exercise one's self or contend with weapons†; fence†; also, to perform on a musical instrument; of the instrument or the music, to sound in performance; also, to act on or as on the stage; perform.—**to play into a person's hands,** to act in such a way as to give him an advantage.—**to play on** or **upon,** to work on (the feelings, weaknesses, etc., of another) for one's own purposes: as, "He allowed men more cunning than himself to *play upon* his vanity" (Froude's "Cæsar," xxiii.).—**to play on a word** or **words,** to bring out playfully or ingeniously differences of meaning in a word, or in words of like sound.—**to play to the gallery.** See under *gallery, n.*—**play,** *v. t.* To cause to move or change lightly or quickly (as, to *play* colored lights on a fountain); specif., to allow (a hooked fish) to exhaust itself by pulling on the line; also, to operate, or cause to operate, esp. continuously or with repeated action (as, to *play* a hose on a fire, or guns on the enemy's position); also, to do, perform, or execute (as, to *play* tricks); also, to engage in (a game, pastime, etc.); represent or imitate in sport (as, to *play* school); also, to stake or wager, as in playing; waste or squander (*away*), as in gambling; lay a wager or wagers on (something); also, to contend against in a game; also, to employ (a player, etc.) in a game; also, to put forward, move, strike, drive, etc., in playing a game; fig., to use as if in playing a game, as for one's own advantage (as, to *play,* or *play* off, one person or thing against another); also, to perform (music) on an instrument; perform on (a musical instrument); also, to perform (a drama, etc.) on or as on the stage; act or sustain (a part) in a dramatic performance or in real life; act the part of (a person or character) in a dramatic performance (as, to *play* Malvolio in Shakspere's "Twelfth Night"); sustain the part or character of in real life (as, to *play* the tyrant; to *play* the fool; "He had yet a life before him wherein to *play* the man," Kingsley's "Yeast," xvi.); also, to give performances in, as a theatrical company does (as, to *play* the larger cities).—**to play off,** to play an extra game or round in order to settle (a tie).—**to play out,** to play or perform (a drama, etc.) to the end; hence, in general, to bring to an end, or finish; use up: chiefly in *played out* (performed to the end; finished, or over and done with; used up; worn out; physically exhausted).—**to play the game,** to play the game through, in accordance with the rules; hence, to play one's part, in any undertaking, or in life, without faltering or shirking. [Colloq.]—**play,** *n.* [AS. *plega.*] Brisk movement or action (as, sword-*play*); light and quick alternating or irregular motion (as, "On the lawn, there was a fountain with a leaping *play* of water": Tarkington's "Gentleman from Indiana," xv.); elusive change, as of light or colors (as, "A gleam of unsubdued sunlight fell on her hair . . . and the hair . . . had a strange lustre and *play* of iridescent colour": W. H. Hudson's "Green Mansions," v.); also, in general, action, activity, or operation (as, the *play* of fancy; to come into *play*; to bring into *play*; "I, with two more to help me, Will hold the foe in *play,*" Macaulay's "Horatius," xxix.); also, freedom of movement, as within a space, as of a part of a mechanism; a space in which a thing, as such a part, can move; hence, in general, freedom for action, or scope for activity (as, "periods when the imaginative faculty . . . was given full *play*": W. Churchill's "Modern Chronicle," i. 2); also, exercise or action by way of amusement or recreation; diversion; sport; hence, fun, jest, or trifling, as opposed to earnest (as, he said it merely in *play*); often, a sportive or playful use of a word or words, as to bring out differences of meaning occurring with likeness of sound (see *to play on a word,* under *play, v. i.*: cf. the B. Franklin quotation at *to hang together*); also, the playing, or carrying on, of a game; manner or style of playing; an act or performance in playing (as, a stupid *play*); turn to play (as, it's your *play*); the state, as of a ball, of being played with or in use in the active playing of a game (as, in *play*; out of *play*); also, specif., a playing for stakes (as, to lose money at *play*); gambling; also, a particular amusement, game, or sport (as, "The *plays* of children are nonsense, but very educative nonsense": Emerson's "Essays," Experience); also, action, conduct, or dealing of a specified kind (as, fair *play*; foul *play*); also, performance, or method of performing, on a musical instrument; also, a dramatic performance, as on the stage; also, a dramatic composition or piece; a drama.

pla-ya (plä′yạ), *n.* [Sp., shore, beach, < L. *plaga*, region, tract.] In the western U. S., a plain of silt or mud, covered with water during the wet season.

play-a-ble (plā′ạ-bl), *a.* Capable of or suitable for being played; of ground, fit to be played on.

play=act-ing (plā′ak″ting), *n.* The acting of plays; dramatic performance.—**play′=ac″tor,** *n.* An actor of plays; a dramatic performer.—**play′=ac″tress,** *n.* A female actor of plays; an actress.

play-bill (plā′bil), *n.* A bill or placard announcing a play (as, "a framed *play-bill* in a confectioner's window": L. Merrick's "Conrad in Quest of His Youth," iii.); a program of a play.

play-day (plā′dā), *n.* A day given to pastime or diversion; a holiday.

play-er (plā′ėr), *n.* [AS. *plegere.*] One who or that which plays; one who takes part or is skilled in some game; a person engaged in playing a game professionally (Great Britain); one who plays for stakes, or a gambler; a performer on a musical instrument; a mechanical device by which a musical instrument, esp. a pianoforte, is played automatically (as, "His musical education had . . . begun . . . with the advertisement of the 'Pianisto' mechanical *player*": Arnold Bennett's "The Old Adam," i.); one who plays parts on the stage, or an actor (as, "All the world's a stage, And all the men and women merely *players*": Shakspere's "As You Like It," ii. 7. 140).—**play′er=pi-an″o,** *n.* A type of pianoforte which may be played without manipulation of the keys, by means of a mechanical device contained within the case.

play-fel-low (plā′fel″ō), *n.* A playmate.

play-ful (plā′fůl), *a.* Full of play, sportive, or frolicsome (as, "the *playful* children just let loose from school": Goldsmith's "Deserted Village," 120); also, showing a sportive fancy or sprightly humor (as, a *playful* remark); pleasantly humorous.—**play′ful-ly,** *adv.*—**play′ful-ness,** *n.*

play-go-er (plā′gō″ėr), *n.* One who goes often or habitually to see plays at the theater.—**play′go″ing,** *n.* and *a.*

play-ground (plā′ground), *n.* A piece of ground used for open-air recreation, as one attached to a school; any place of open-air recreation.

play-house (plā′hous), *n.* [AS. *pleghūs.*] A theater; also, a house to play in (as, a child's *playhouse*; the *playhouse* of a gardener-bird); a toy house.

play-ing=card (plā′ing-kärd), *n.* Literally, one of a set or pack of cards for use in playing games; historically, and in actual use, one of the well-known set of 52 cards, in 4 suits (diamonds, hearts, spades, and clubs), marked with spots and figures (king, queen, and knave), used in playing various games of chance and skill.

play-let (plā′let), *n.* A short dramatic play.

play-mate (plā′māt), *n.* A companion in play, amusement, or sport.

play=off (plā′ôf″), *n.* The playing off of a tie, as in games or sports.

play-some (plā′sum), *a.* Playful. [Now prov.]

play-thing (plā′thing), *n.* A thing to play with; a toy; fig., something treated as a thing to be played with (as, "the toy and *plaything* of circumstance": Mrs. H. Ward's "Robert Elsmere," xix.).

play-time (plā′tīm), *n.* Time for play or recreation.

play-wright (plā′rīt), *n.* A writer of plays; a dramatist.

pla-za (plä′zạ), *n.* [Sp., < L. *platea*: see *place.*] A public square or open space in a city or town.

plea (plē), *n.* [OF. *plaid, plait,* < ML. *placitum*, assembly, court, plea, L. opinion, decision, prop. pp. neut. of L. *placere*, please, seem good, E. *please.*] A suit or action at law (now chiefly hist. or Sc., or in certain phrases: as, to hold *pleas*, to try actions at law: see also phrases below); also, an allegation made by, or on behalf of, a party to a legal suit, in support of his claim or defense; esp., a defendant's answer to a legal declaration or charge; in general, that which is alleged, urged, or pleaded in defense or justification (as, "The fiend . . . with necessity, The tyrant's *plea*, excused his devilish deeds": Milton's "Paradise Lost," iv. 394); an excuse; a pretext; also, an appeal or entreaty (as, a *plea* for mercy, for reform, or for a cause; "deaf to Nature's tend'rest *plea*," Cowper's "Tirocinium," 867).—**common pleas,** orig., in England, pleas or legal actions over which the crown did not claim exclusive jurisdiction (cf. *pleas of the crown*, below); later, civil actions brought by one subject against another; also [*caps.*], the (or a) Court of Common Pleas.—**Court of Common Pleas,** formerly, in England, a court for the trial of 'common pleas,' or civil actions (see the preceding phrase), one of the three superior courts of common law; also, in some States of the United States, a more or less similar common-law court.—**pleas of the crown,** orig., in England, pleas or legal actions over which the crown claimed exclusive jurisdiction (cf. *common pleas*, above); later, in England, all criminal actions or proceedings; in Scotland, the actions for robbery, rape, murder, and arson.

pleach (plēch), *v. t.* [ME. *plechen*, from a var. form (cf. F. dial. *plècher*) of OF. *plaissier*, E. *plash*[1].] To plash or interweave (growing branches, vines, etc.), as for a hedge or arbor; make or renew (a hedge, etc.) thus; cover, shade, or fence with interwoven branches, etc. (as, "walking in a thick-*pleached* alley in mine orchard": Shakspere's "Much Ado about Nothing," i. 2. 10); also, in general, to interweave, interlace, or entwine.

plead (plēd), *v.*; *pleaded* or *plead* (pled), archaic *pled*, *pleading*. [OF. *plaidier* (F. *plaider*), < *plaid*: see *plea.*] **I.** *intr.* To prosecute a suit or action at law†; also, to address a court as an advocate; put forward any allegation or plea in an action at law; put forward an answer on the part of a defendant to a legal declaration or charge; in general, to use arguments or persuasions, as with a person, or for or against something (as, to *plead* with a creditor for time; to *plead* against ill-advised leniency); make earnest appeal or entreaty; fig., to afford an argument or appeal (as, his youth *pleads* for him). **II.** *tr.* To maintain (a cause, etc.) by argument before a court (also fig.); also, to allege or set forth (something) formally in an action at law; esp., to allege formally as a legal plea or answer (as, to *plead* not guilty); allege or cite in legal defense (as, to *plead* a statute of limitations); in general, to allege or urge in defense, justification, or excuse (as, to *plead* ignorance or necessity; "Brown . . . declined all further conviviality for that evening, *pleading* his own weariness," Scott's "Guy Mannering," xxiv.); also, to plead for†, or entreat† (as, "When good will is show'd . . . The actor may *plead* pardon": Shakspere's "Antony and Cleopatra," ii. 5. 9).—**plead′a-ble,** *a.* Capable of being pleaded.—**plead′er,** *n.* One who pleads, esp. in a court of law; an advocate.—**plead′ing,** *n.* The act of one who pleads; specif., the advocating of a cause in a court of law; the art of setting forth or drawing pleas in legal causes; also, a formal statement (now usually written) setting forth the cause of action or the defense of a case at law; *pl.*, the successive statements delivered alternately by plaintiff and defendant until issue is joined.—**special pleading.** See under *special*, *a.*—**plead′ing-ly,** *adv.*

pleas-ance (plez′ạns), *n.* [OF. F. *plaisance*, < *plaisant*, E. *pleasant.*] Pleasure or enjoyment (archaic: as, "a feeling of solace and *pleasance*," Scott's "Castle Dangerous," x.); also, pleasurable or agreeable character (archaic: as, "Thence thro' the garden I was drawn—A realm of *pleasance*," Tennyson's "Recollections of the Arabian Nights," 101); also, a source of pleasure (obs. or archaic); also, a pleasure-ground, or space laid out with trees and shrubbery, pleasant walks, and sometimes fountains, statues, etc., esp. one attached to an old-time mansion.

pleas-ant (plez′ạnt), *a.* [OF. F. *plaisant*, ppr. of OF. *plaisir*, E. *please.*] Pleasing, agreeable, or affording enjoyment (as, a *pleasant* valley; *pleasant* news; a *pleasant* sight or taste; "Full rich I was, and led a *pleasant* life," W. Morris's "Jason," iv. 251); pleasurable; to one's liking; of persons, or the manners, disposition, etc., agreeable socially or in intercourse or personal relations; of weather, etc., fair, or not stormy; also, gay, sprightly, or merry (as, "Now Gilpin had a *pleasant* wit, And lov'd a timely joke": Cowper's "John Gilpin," 169); jocular or facetious (as, "Can a ghost laugh . . . when you are *pleasant* with him?" Lamb's "New Year's Eve"); also, amusing† or funny†.—**pleas'ant-ly,** *adv.*—**pleas'ant-ness,** *n.*—**pleas'an-try** (-ạn-tri), *n.*; pl. *-tries* (-triz). [F. *plaisanterie.*] Pleasant sprightliness or humor in conversation; hence, good-humored raillery (as, "Here commenced a running fire of *pleasantry* at the expense of my poor steed": Lever's "Harry Lorrequer," xxxiv.); also, a humorous or jesting speech (as, "He . . . made him the butt of his *pleasantries*": Irving's "Captain Bonneville," xxxv.); sometimes, a humorous action (as, "It was thought an ingenious *pleasantry* to hang the Reformers upon the beams under which they had hoped to worship God": Motley's "Dutch Republic," ii. 10).

please (plēz), *v. i.*; *pleased, pleasing.* [OF. *plaisir,* < L. *placere,* please, be pleasing, seem good: cf. *plea, placid,* and *placate.*] To be agreeable, or give pleasure or satisfaction (as, "Though every prospect *pleases,* And only man is vile": Heber's "From Greenland's Icy Mountains"); also, to find something agreeable, like, wish, or choose (as, go when and where you *please*; he may do so if he *pleases*; "He silently went on thinking and doing exactly as he *pleased,*" Mrs. Stowe's "Oldtown Folks," v.); be pleased or willing, consent, or have the goodness (to do something: as, "if his Majesty . . . would *please* to spare your life," Swift's "Gulliver's Travels," i. 7; "You must *please* to take my word for it," S. Butler's "Way of All Flesh," xv.). *Please,* as a polite addition to requests, etc. (as, come here, *please*; *please* come), and now seemingly an imperative or optative, apparently represents a reduction of some longer expression of an earlier date, as 'please you,' for 'may it please you': for example, "*Please you,* draw near" (Shakspere's "Tempest," v. 1. 318); "*Please you* repeat their names" (Shakspere's "Two Gentlemen of Verona," i. 2. 7).—**if you please,** if you like, or if it be your pleasure; by your leave: much used as a polite addition to a request, acceptance, statement of intentions, or the like (as, wait a moment, *if you please*; yes, *if you please*; I will take this one, *if you please*), or sometimes in stating, as if with the hearer's kindly allowance, some surprising fact (as, in his pocket, *if you please,* was the lost letter!).—**please,** *v. t.* To be agreeable or give pleasure to, gratify, or delight (as, colors that *please* the eye; the news *pleases* everybody; to be much *pleased* with one's self; "*Pleased* with his daily task, or, if not *pleased,* Contented," Wordsworth's "Prelude," vi. 511); act to the pleasure or satisfaction of (as, to seek to *please* customers or the public; you may *please* yourself about it, that is, you may do as you please); also, in impersonal uses (often reduced elliptically), to be the pleasure or will of, or seem good to (as, "Let it *please* thee to bless the house of thy servant," 1 Chron. xvii. 27; if it *please* your honor, or, elliptically, *please* your honor; may it *please* God, or *please* God).—**to be pleased,** to be moved to pleasure, as by something agreeable; also, to find it agreeable, be disposed, like, or choose (to do, be, etc.: as, "He administers what he *is pleased* to call spiritual consolation," S. Butler's "Way of All Flesh," xv.; "You *are pleased* to be facetious," Peacock's "Nightmare Abbey," vi.); also, to be willing, consent, or have the goodness (to do, etc.: as, "I request that two of you will *be pleased* to stand sentries at the door," Marryat's "King's Own," xl.).—**pleas-er** (plē'zėr), *n.*—**pleas'ing,** *p. a.* That pleases; giving pleasure; agreeable; gratifying; likable.—**pleas'ing-ly,** *adv.*—**pleas'ing-ness,** *n.*

pleas-ur-a-ble (plezh'ūr-ạ-bl), *a.* Such as to give pleasure; agreeable; pleasant: as, "the *pleasurable* excitement of reading what is new" (J. H. Newman's "Idea of a University," ii. 4).—**pleas'ur-a-ble-ness,** *n.*—**pleas'ur-a-bly,** *adv.*

pleas-ure (plezh'ūr), *n.* [OF. F. *plaisir,* noun use of OF. *plaisir,* inf., E. *please.*] The state or feeling of being pleased; enjoyment or satisfaction derived from what is to one's liking; gratification; delight; often, enjoyment as the sole end in view (as, to walk or to write for *pleasure*; a *pleasure-ground*; "Though on *pleasure* she was bent, She had a frugal mind," Cowper's "John Gilpin," 31); worldly or frivolous enjoyment (as, the pursuit of *pleasure*; the giddy round of *pleasure*); sensual gratification; also, one's will, desire, or choice (as, to make known one's *pleasure* in a matter; "The captain left the deck, in order to ascertain his superior's *pleasure,*" Cooper's "Two Admirals," xix.); also, something that pleases, or a cause or source of enjoyment or delight (as, the garden is a constant *pleasure*; your letter was a great *pleasure*); also, pleasurable quality.—**at pleasure,** as or whenever one pleases.—**pleas'ure,** *v.*; *-ured, -uring.* **I.** *tr.* To give pleasure to; gratify; please: as, "Thou art ever prompt to *pleasure* us poor women" (Scott's "Talisman," xxv.). **II.** *intr.* To take pleasure, or delight, as in something; also, to seek pleasure, as by taking a holiday (colloq.).—**pleas'ure=ground,** *n.* A piece of ground or land appropriated to pleasure or enjoyment.—**pleas'ure=house,** *n.* A house for purposes of pleasure or enjoyment: as, "He built this *pleasure-house* here in the woods, and hither he rode . . . to enjoy himself in the chase" (Howells's "Chance Acquaintance," xii.).—**pleas'ure-less,** *a.* Devoid of pleasure; joyless.

pleat (plēt), *n.* [Var. of *plait.*] A fold of definite, even width made by doubling cloth or the like upon itself, and pressing, stitching, or otherwise fastening in place.—**pleat,** *v. t.* To fold or arrange in pleats.—**pleat'ing,** *n.* Arrangement in pleats; also, pleated material, or a piece of it.

pleb (pleb), *n.* [Short for *plebeian.*] A plebeian or commoner.

plebe (plēb), *n.* [Cf. *pleb.*] At the U. S. military and naval academies at West Point and Annapolis, a member of the lowest class. [Colloq.]

ple-be-ian (plẹ-bē'ạn). [L. *plebeius,* < *plebs* (*pleb-*): see *plebs.*] **I.** *a.* Belonging or pertaining to the Roman plebs; in general, belonging or pertaining to the common people (as, "the craftsmen and other *plebeian* inhabitants of the town": Hawthorne's "Scarlet Letter," xxi.); hence, common, commonplace, or vulgar; coarse; mean; base. **II.** *n.* A member of the Roman plebs (as, "the struggles between *plebeians* and patricians": Froude's "Cæsar," i.); in general, one of the common people; a plebeian person; a person with plebeian ideas or tastes.—**ple-be'ian-ism,** *n.* Plebeian character or ways.

pleb-is-cite (pleb'i-sit), *n.* [F. *plébiscite,* < L. *plebiscitum*: see *plebiscitum.*] A plebiscitum; also, a direct vote of the qualified electors of a state in regard to some important public question.—**ple-bis-ci-ta-ry** (plẹ-bis'i-tā-ri), *a.*

pleb-is-ci-tum (pleb-i-sī'tum), *n.*; pl. *-ta* (-tạ). [L., < *plebis,* gen. of *plebs* (see *plebs*), + *scitum,* ordinance, < *sciscere,* approve.] A law enacted by the ancient Roman plebs; also, a plebiscite.

plebs (plebz), *n.* [L.] The lower class of the people of ancient Rome; in general, the common people; the populace.

plec-tog-nath (plek'tọg-nath), *n.* [NL. *Plectognathi,* pl., < Gr. πλεκτός, plaited, twisted, + γνάθος, jaw.] Any of the *Plectognathi,* a group of teleostean fishes having the jaws extensively ankylosed and including the file-fishes, globe-fishes, etc.—**plec-tog'na-thous** (-tog'nạ-thus), *a.*

plec-trop-ter-us (plek-trop'tẹ-rus), *n.* [NL., < Gr. πλῆκτρον, cock's spur, orig. plectrum, + πτερόν, wing.] Any of the spur-winged geese of the African genus *Plectropterus.*

plec-trum (plek'trum), *n.*; pl. *-trums* or *-tra* (-trạ). [L., < Gr. πλῆκτρον, < πλήσσειν, strike.] A small instrument of ivory, horn, metal, etc., used for plucking the strings of a lyre, mandolin, etc.

Plectropterus (*P. gambensis*).

pled (pled). Archaic preterit and past participle of *plead.*

pledge (plej), *n.* [OF. *plege* (F. *pleige*), < ML. *plevium, plebium*, appar. < *plevire, plebire*, to pledge; prob. from Teut.] One who becomes bail or surety for another†; also, a hostage†; also, a piece of personal property delivered as security for the payment of a debt or the discharge of some obligation, and liable to forfeiture; a thing put in pawn; also, a bailment of personal property as security; also, in general, anything given or regarded as a security, gage, or earnest of something (as, "Bear her this jewel, *pledge* of my affection," Shakspere's "1 Henry VI.," v. 1. 47; his past is the best *pledge* of his future): sometimes, a child as an evidence of the union or mutual love of the parents (as, "the unexpected hope of once more seeing my beloved country, and the dear *pledges* I had left in it": Swift's "Gulliver's Travels," i. 8); also, an assurance of support or good-will conveyed by drinking a person's health; the drinking of a health; a toast; also, a solemn promise of something, or to do or refrain from doing something (as, a *pledge* of aid; a *pledge* to support a candidate; "Pompey gave a definite *pledge*, which was afterwards broken," Froude's "Cæsar," xviii.); an engagement or vow; specif., with *the*, the solemn, formal engagement to abstain from intoxicating drink (as, to take the *pledge*); also, the state of being given or held as security (as, to put or to hold a thing in *pledge*); guaranty or assurance (*of*: as, "I answer for your safety. There is my hand in *pledge* of it," G. B. Shaw's "Arms and the Man," i.).—**pledge,** *v. t.*; *pledged, pledging.* To give or deposit as a pledge or pawn; pawn; fig., to plight or stake, as one's honor, word, etc.; also, to bind by or as by a pledge (as, to *pledge* one's self to observe a rule; to *pledge* hearers to secrecy); also, to secure by a pledge, or give a pledge for (as, "And here, to *pledge* my vow, I give my hand": Shakspere's "3 Henry VI.," iii. 3. 250); also, to give assurance of good-will or friendship to by drinking, or drink a health or toast to (as, "We did but talk you over, *pledge* you all In wassail": Tennyson's "Princess," Prologue, 183); also, to promise solemnly, or engage to give, maintain, etc. (as, to *pledge* one's support; to *pledge* secrecy).—**pledge′a-ble,** *a.* That may be pledged.—**pledg-ee** (ple-jē′), *n.* The person with whom something is deposited as a pledge. —**pledge-or** (plej′o̧r or ple-jôr′), *n.* In *law*, one who deposits something as a pledge.—**pledg′er,** *n.* One who pledges.

pledg-et (plej′et), *n.* [Origin uncertain.] A small, flat mass of lint, absorbent cotton, or the like, for using on a wound, sore, etc.

-plegia. [Gr. -πληγία, < πλήσσειν, strike: see *plague.*] A noun termination in pathological terms denoting forms of paralysis, as *hemiplegia, monoplegia, ophthalmoplegia, paraplegia.*

Plei-ad (plī′a̧d or plē′a̧d), *n.*; pl. *-ads.* [= F. *Pléiade*, < L. *Pleias* (*Pleiad-*): see *Pleiades.*] Any of the Pleiades; also, fig., a brilliant group of persons or things, esp. of seven; esp., the famous group of poets (called in French *La Pléiade*) of the French Renaissance, consisting of Ronsard, Du Bellay, Belleau, Jodelle, Dorat (Daurat), Baïf, and Pontus de Thiard (Tyard).

Plei-a-des (plī′a̧-dēz or plē′-), *n. pl.* [L. (sing. *Pleias*), < Gr. Πλειάδες (sing. Πλειάς).] In *class. myth.*, the seven daughters of Atlas and the nymph Pleione, transformed into the group of stars bearing their name (one star, missing, being the traditional 'lost Pleiad'); in *astron.*, a conspicuous group or cluster of stars in the constellation Taurus, commonly spoken of as seven, though only six are plain to the average naked eye.

plein=air (pla-nãr′), *a.* [F. *plein air*, 'full air,' open air.] In *painting*, pertaining to, or working or done in, the open air; concerned with rendering the effects of atmosphere and light in nature, as seen out of doors, rather than the artificial effects of the studio, as a school or style of painting that originated in France about 1870.—**plein=air′ism,** *n.* The principles or methods of the plein-air painters.—**plein=air′ist,** *n.*

Plei-o-cene (plī′ǫ-sēn), *a.* and *n.* See *Pliocene.*

Pleis-to-cene (plīs′tǫ-sēn). [Gr. πλεῖστος, most (superl. of πολύς, much), + καινός, new.] In *geol.*: **I.** *a.* Noting or pertaining to the earlier division of the Quaternary period or system, preceding the recent deposits. **II.** *n.* The Pleistocene division of the Quaternary.

ple-na-ry (plē′na̧-ri or plen′a̧-ri), *a.* [LL. *plenarius*, < L. *plenus*, full: see *plenum.*] Full, complete, or entire; absolute or unqualified; also, attended by all of its qualified members, as a council or assembly; fully constituted; also, having full power.—**ple′na-ri-ly,** *adv.*

ple-nip-o-tent (plē-nip′ǫ-tent), *a.* [LL. *plenipotens* (*-ent-*), < L. *plenus*, full, + *potens*, E. *potent.*] Invested with or possessing full power.—**ple-nip′o-tence,** *n.*

plen-i-po-ten-ti-a-ry (plen″i-pǫ-ten′shi-a̧-ri). [ML. *plenipotentiarius*, < LL. *plenipotens*, E. *plenipotent.*] **I.** *a.* Invested with full power or authority, as a diplomatic agent; also, bestowing full power, as a commission; also, absolute or full, as power. **II.** *n.*; pl. *-ries* (-riz). A person, esp. a diplomatic agent, invested with full power or authority to transact some particular business, or business in general: as, "Each municipality was, as it were, a little sovereign, sending envoys to a congress to vote and to sign as *plenipotentiaries*" (Motley's "Dutch Republic," iv. 4).

plen-ish (plen′ish), *v. t.* [OF. *plenir* (*pleniss-*), fill, < L. *plenus*, full: cf. *replenish.*] To fill up; stock; furnish. [Chiefly Sc.]—**plen′ish-ing,** *n.* The act of filling up or furnishing; also, that with which anything is furnished; household furniture; the outfit contributed by a bride for setting up housekeeping. [Chiefly Sc.]

ple-nism (plē′nizm), *n.* [See *plenum.*] The theory that all space is a plenum, and that there is no such thing as a vacuum.—**ple′nist,** *n.*

plen-i-tude (plen′i-tūd), *n.* [L. *plenitudo* (*plenitudin-*), < *plenus*, full: see *plenum.*] Fullness in quantity, measure, or degree (as, "kings in the *plenitude* of power": Scott's "Quentin Durward," xxix.); completeness; abundance; also, sometimes, the condition of being fully occupied, or full of something.—**plen-i-tu′di-nous** (-tū′di-nus), *a.*

plen-te-ous (plen′tē-us), *a.* [ME. *plentivous*, < OF. *plentivous*, < *plentif*, plenteous, < *plente*, E. *plenty.*] Existing in plenty; plentiful, copious, or abundant (as, "a *plenteous* supply of corn in a time of famine," Galt's "Annals of the Parish," xxxix.; "rich, *plenteous* tresses," C. Brontë's "Jane Eyre," xxxi.); also, abundantly supplied with something (as, "The *plenteous* horn Of autumn, filled and running o'er With fruit, and flower, and golden corn": Whittier's "For an Autumn Festival"); also, yielding abundantly (as, "The seasons had been *plenteous* in corn": George Eliot's "Romola," xxi.); also, giving abundantly†; bountiful in giving†.—**plen′te-ous-ly,** *adv.*—**plen′te-ous-ness,** *n.*

plen-ti-ful (plen′ti-fu̇l), *a.* Existing in great plenty; copious, abundant, or ample (as, "a *plentiful* fortune": Steele, in "Spectator," 79); also, amply supplied with something (as, "fair forests, *plentiful* of beasts": W. Morris's "Jason," x. 119); yielding abundantly; also, giving abundantly†; lavish†.—**plen′ti-ful-ly,** *adv.*—**plen′ti-ful-ness,** *n.*

plen-ty (plen′ti). [OF. *plente, plentet*, < L. *plenitas*, fullness, abundance, < *plenus*, full: see *plenum.*] **I.** *n.*; pl. *-ties* (-tiz). Abundance (as, to have resources or reasons in *plenty*); a full or abundant supply; as much or as many as one could desire (as, there is *plenty* of time; "He . . . had *plenty* of scholars, but very few fees," Scott's "Guy Mannering," ii.; "Of books there are a *plenty*," H. Melville's "Moby-Dick," xxxii.); also, abundance of the necessaries and comforts of life (as, "sixteen years of peace and *plenty*," H. Kingsley's "Geoffry Hamlyn," xxiv.; the horn of *plenty*, the cornucopia); a time of abundance; also, *pl.*, the necessaries and comforts of life†. **II.** *a.*; compar. *plentier*, superl. *plentiest.* Existing in ample quantity or number; plentiful; abundant: usually in the predicate: as, "if reasons were as *plenty* [var. *plentiful*] as blackberries" (Shakspere's "1 Henry IV.," ii. 4. 265). [Now chiefly colloq.]—**plen′ty,** *adv.* Abundantly; amply; fully: as, *plenty* good enough. [Colloq.]

ple-num (plē′num), *n.* [L., prop. neut. of *plenus*, full, filled, complete, abundant: see *full*[1].] A space that is filled, or conceived as being filled, with matter (opposed to a *vacuum*); the whole of space regarded as being filled with matter; also, a full assembly, as a joint legislative assembly. —**plenum method** (or **system**) **of ventilation,** a system in which fresh air is forced by artificial means into a space to be ventilated, vitiated air being driven out by displacement.

ple-och-ro-ism (plē-ok′rǫ-izm), *n.* [Gr. πλέων, πλείων, more (compar. of πολύς, much), + χρόα, color.] In *crystal.*, the property of exhibiting different colors in two or more different directions when viewed by transmitted light: a term including both *dichroism* and *trichroism.*—**ple-o-chro-ic** (plē-ǫ-krō′ik), *a.*

ple-o-chro-ma-tism (plē-ǫ-krō′mą-tizm), *n.* Pleochroism.

ple-o-mor-phism (plē-ǫ-môr′fizm), *n.* [Gr. πλέων, πλείων, more, + μορφή, form.] The property of existing in different forms; in *crystal.*, crystallization in two or more fundamental forms; in *biol.*, the existence of different forms or types in a species, genus, etc.; also, the occurrence of more than one independent stage or form in the life-cycle of a species.—**ple-o-mor′phic,** *a.*

ple-o-nasm (plē′ǫ-nazm), *n.* [LL. *pleonasmus*, < Gr. πλεονασμός, < πλεονάζειν, be redundant, < πλέων, πλείων, more, compar. of πολύς, much: cf. *poly-*.] The use of more words than are necessary to express an idea; redundancy of language; also, an instance of this, or the redundant word, phrase, or expression.—**ple-o-nas′tic** (-nas′tik), *a.* Characterized by or of the nature of pleonasm; redundant.—**ple-o-nas′ti-cal-ly,** *adv.*

ple-o-nex-i-a (plē-ǫ-nek′si-ä), *n.* [NL., < Gr. πλεονεξία, < πλεονέκτης, greedy person, < πλέων, πλείων, more, + ἔχειν, have.] Greed or grasping selfishness, esp. as an indication of disease.—**ple-o-nec′tic** (-nek′tik), *a.*

ple-rome (plē′rōm), *n.* [G. *plerom*, < Gr. πλήρωμα, a filling, < πληροῦν, fill, < πλήρης, full: see *full*[1].] In *bot.*, the portion of meristem in the growing ends of stems and roots which gives rise to the stele.—**ple-ro-mat′ic** (-rǫ-mat′ik), *a.*

ple-si-o-saur (plē′si-ǫ-sâr), *n.* [NL. *plesiosaurus*, < Gr. πλησίος, near, + σαῦρος, lizard.] Any member of the extinct genus *Plesiosaurus*, comprising marine reptiles with small head, very long neck, short tail, and four large paddles. Also **ple″si-o-sau′rus** (-sâ′rus).

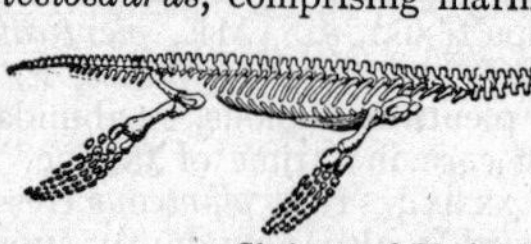

Skeleton of Plesiosaur.

ples-sor (ples′ǫr), *n.* Same as *plexor.*

pleth-o-ra (pleth′ǫ-rä), *n.* [NL., < Gr. πληθώρη, < πλήθειν, be full.] In *pathol.*, a morbid condition due to excess of red corpuscles in the blood or increase in the quantity of blood; hence, fig., overfullness in any respect; superabundance.—**ple-thor-ic** (plē-thor′ik or pleth′ǫ-rik), *a.* Characterized by plethora; hence, fig., overfull; turgid; inflated.—**ple-thor′i-cal-ly,** *adv.*

pleu-ra (plö′rä), *n.*; pl. *-ræ* (-rē). [NL., < Gr. πλευρά, rib, side.] A delicate serous membrane investing each lung in mammals and folded back to form a lining of the corresponding side of the thorax.—**pleu′ral,** *a.* Of or pertaining to the pleura: as, the *pleural* cavity (the space between the two layers of the pleura).

pleu-ri-sy (plö′ri-si), *n.* [OF. *pleurisie* (F. *pleurésie*), < LL. *pleurisis*, for L. *pleuritis*: see *pleuritis.*] In *pathol.*, inflammation of the pleura, with or without a liquid effusion.—**pleu′ri-sy=root,** *n.* A milkweed, *Asclepias tuberosa*, whose root is used as a popular remedy for pleurisy; also, the root.

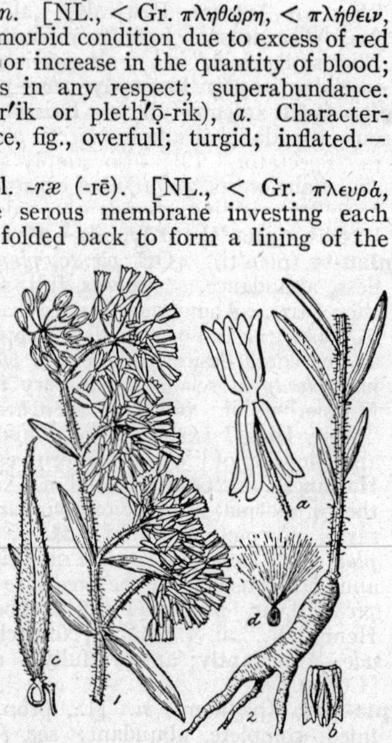

Pleurisy-root. — 1, part of the inflorescence; 2, the root and the lower part of the stem; *a*, a flower; *b*, the anthers and the stigma; *c*, the fruit; *d*, a seed.

pleu-ri-tis (plǫ-rī′tis), *n.* [L., < Gr. πλευρῖτις, < πλευρά, side, E. *pleura.*] Pleurisy.—**pleu-rit′ic** (-rit′ik), *a.*

pleuro-, pleur-. Forms of Gr. πλευρόν, or πλευρά, rib, side, or E. *pleura*, used in combination.—**pleu-ro-dont** (plö′rǫ-dont). [+ *-odont.*] In *zoöl.*: **I.** *a.* Ankylosed or attached to the inner edge of the jaw, as a tooth; having teeth so ankylosed, as certain lizards. **II.** *n.* A pleurodont animal.—**pleu-ro-dyn′i-a** (-din′i-ä), *n.* [NL. (Gr. ὀδύνη, pain).] In *pathol.*, pain in the side due to rheumatism in the muscles of the chest.—**pleu-ro-dyn′ic,** *a.*

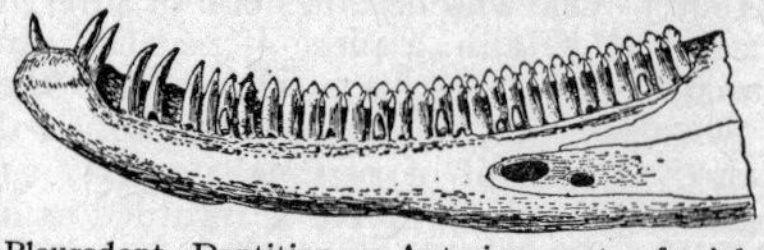

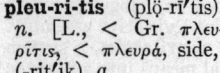

Pleurodont Dentition. — Anterior part of right ramus of lower jaw of an iguana.

pleu-ron (plö′ron), *n.*; pl. *-ra* (-rä). [NL., < Gr. πλευρόν, rib, side.] In *zoöl.*, one of the lateral parts of the body-wall of an animal; esp., one of the sides of a thoracic segment of an insect.

pleu-ro-pneu-mo-ni-a (plö″rǫ-nū-mō′ni-ä), *n.* [See *pleuro-*.] In *pathol.*, pleurisy conjoined with pneumonia.

pleu-rot-o-my (plǫ-rot′ǫ-mi), *n.* [See *pleuro-* and *-tomy.*] In *surg.*, the operation of cutting into the pleura.

plex-i-form (plek′si-fôrm), *a.* In the form of a plexus.

plex-im-e-ter (plek-sim′e-tėr), *n.* [Gr. πλῆξις, stroke, percussion, + μέτρον, measure.] In *med.*, a small, thin plate, as of ivory, placed in contact with the body and struck with the plexor in percussion for diagnostic purposes.

plex-or (plek′sǫr), *n.* [Irreg. < Gr. πλῆξις, stroke, percussion, < πλήσσειν, strike.] In *med.*, a small hammer or the like, used in percussion for diagnostic purposes.

plex-us (plek′sus), *n.*; pl. *plexuses* or *plexus.* [L., < *plectere*, plait, interweave: see *ply.*] A network, as of nerves or blood-vessels.—**solar plexus.** See under *solar.*

pli-a-ble (plī′ą-bl), *a.* [OF. F. *pliable*, < *plier*, fold, bend: see *ply.*] Easily bent; flexible; supple; hence, fig., easily influenced; yielding; adaptable.—**pli-a-bil′i-ty** (-bil′i-ti), **pli′a-ble-ness,** *n.*—**pli′a-bly,** *adv.*

pli-ant (plī′ąnt), *a.* [OF. F. *pliant*, ppr. of *plier*, fold, bend: see *ply.*] Bending readily (as, "*pliant* as a wand of willow": Longfellow's "Hiawatha," vi. 24); flexible; supple; hence, fig., easily inclined or influenced; yielding; compliant.—**pli′an-cy** (-ąn-si), **pli′ant-ness,** *n.*—**pli′ant-ly,** *adv.*

pli-ca (plī′kä), *n.*; pl. *-cæ* (-sē). [ML., a fold, < L. *plicare*, fold.] In *pathol.*, a matted, filthy condition of the hair caused by disease, etc.; in *zoöl.* and *anat.*, a fold or folding, as of the skin.

pli-cate (plī′kāt), *a.* [L. *plicatus*, pp. of *plicare*, fold: see *ply.*] Folded like a fan; pleated. Also **pli′cat-ed** (-kā-ted).—**pli′cate-ly,** *adv.*—**pli-ca′tion** (-kā′shǫn), *n.* A folding or fold; plicate form or condition. Also **plic-a-ture** (plik′ą-tūr).

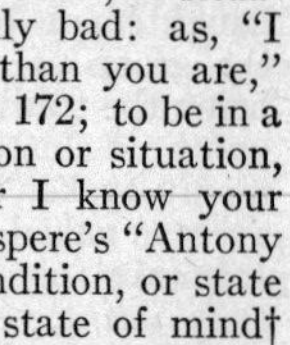

Plicate Leaf.

plied (plīd). Preterit and past participle of *ply.*

pli-er (plī′ėr), *n.* [See *ply.*] One who or that which plies; *pl.* (and construed as *pl.* or, sometimes, *sing.*), small pincers with long jaws, for bending wire, holding small objects, etc. (often called a *pair of pliers*).

plight[1] (plīt), *n.* [AF. *plit*, for OF. *pleit*, *ploit*, fold, manner of folding, condition: see *plait.*] Condition, state, or situation (good, bad, or as specified, now usually bad: as, "I think myself in better *plight* for a lender than you are," Shakspere's "Merry Wives of Windsor," ii. 2. 172; to be in a sorry *plight*); a bad or unfortunate condition or situation, or a predicament (as, "Have comfort, for I know your *plight* is pitied Of him that caused it": Shakspere's "Antony and Cleopatra," v. 2. 33); also, physical condition, or state of health (now esp. of cattle, etc.); also, state of mind† (as, "Thus they, in lowliest *plight*, repentant stood": Milton's "Paradise Lost," xi. 1).

plight[2] (plīt), *n.* [AS. *pliht*, danger, risk, akin to D. *plicht*, G. *pflicht*, duty, obligation.] Peril†; risk†; also, pledge or solemn engagement (as, "These young hearts, not knowing that they loved . . . nor by *plight* or broken ring Bound": Tennyson's "Aylmer's Field," 135).—**plight**[2], *v. t.* To give in pledge; pledge (one's faith, honor, etc.); often, to pledge (one's troth) in engagement to marry (as, "These two young people loved, and *plighted* their troth": Marryat's

"King's Own," v.); also, to bind by a pledge or engagement, now esp. of marriage (as, "He was half engaged . . . However, he was not absolutely *plighted*": G. Meredith's "Diana of the Crossways," xvi.); betroth.—**plight'er,** *n.*

Plim-soll (plim'sọl) **line.** [From Samuel *Plimsoll* (1824–98), member of Parliament, who urged shipping reforms.] A line or mark required to be placed on the hull of all British merchant vessels, showing the depth to which they may be submerged through loading. Also **Plim'soll's mark.**

plinth (plinth), *n.* [L. *plinthus*, plinth, < Gr. πλίνθος, brick, squared stone, plinth.] The lower square part of the base of a column; a square base or a lower block, as of a pedestal; a course of stones, as at the base of a wall, forming a continuous plinth-like projection; also, a gymnastic apparatus, used in vaulting, consisting of several wooden sections placed one on top of another, so as to permit of variations in height.

Gymnastic Plinth.

Pli-o-cene (plī'ọ-sēn). [Gr. πλείων, more (compar. of πολύς, much), + καινός, new.] In *geol.*: **I.** *a.* Noting or pertaining to the latest principal division of the Tertiary period or system. **II.** *n.* The Pliocene division of the Tertiary.

pli-o-tron (plī'ọ-tron), *n.* [Gr. πλείων, more: cf. *kenotron* and *electron.*] In *elect.*, a type of vacuum-tube used in wireless apparatus, etc., with an exceptionally high degree of vacuum, and containing a filament, plate, and grid. [Proprietary name.]

plis-ky (plis'ki), *n.*; pl. *-kies* (-kiz). [Origin obscure.] A mischievous trick; also, a plight or unfortunate condition. [Sc. and north. Eng.]

plod (plod), *v.*; *plodded, plodding.* [Perhaps imit.] **I.** *intr.* To walk heavily, or trudge (as, "Barefoot *plod* I the cold ground upon," Shakspere's "All's Well," iii. 4. 6; "We heard a great rhino *plodding* along the track in our direction," J. H. Patterson's "Man-Eaters of Tsavo," xv.); move laboriously (as, "In ten minutes the coach we are both looking for will be *plodding* up the hill": Whyte-Melville's "Kater-felto," x.); fig., to proceed in a heavy or dull, humdrum way (as, "an old, wary, taciturn, *plodding*, unobtrusive, and moderate man": Lecky's "Hist. of Eng. in the 18th Century," i.); work with dull perseverance (as, "I at your age was *plodding* away behind a desk": S. Butler's "Way of All Flesh," vi.); drudge. **II.** *tr.* To walk heavily over or along; make (one's way) by so doing (as, "The plowman homeward *plods* his weary way": Gray's "Elegy," i.).—**plod,** *n.* The act or a course of plodding; also, a sound of or as of a heavy tread.—**plod'der,** *n.*—**plod'ding-ly,** *adv.*

plop (plop), *v. i.*; *plopped, plopping.* [Imit.] To make a sound like that of a flat object striking water without a splash; fall plump with such a sound (as, "The released lead *plopped* into the sea": Kipling's "Captains Courageous," iii.).—**plop,** *adv.* With a plop: as, "The old ship went down all on a sudden with a lurch to starboard—*plop*" (J. Conrad's "Lord Jim," xiii.).—**plop,** *n.* A plopping sound or fall; the act of plopping.

plot (plot), *n.* [AS. *plot*, piece of ground; origin uncertain. Later E. senses are prob. due in part to *complot.*] A small piece or area of ground (as, a garden *plot*; "persuading the purchaser that . . . he must put on the *plot* a house worthy of the *plot*," Arnold Bennett's "Clayhanger," ii. 3); also, a plan, map, or diagram, as of land, a building, etc. (now chiefly U. S.); also, the plan, scheme, or main story of a play, novel, poem, or the like; also, a plan, design, or purpose to be carried out†; now, commonly, a secret plan or scheme, on the part of one person or of a number, to accomplish some purpose, esp. a hostile, unlawful, or evil purpose (as, "a *plot* for the subversion of Protestantism and the death of the King": Green's "Short Hist. of the Eng. People," ix. 4); a conspiracy.—**Gunpowder Plot.** See under *gunpowder.* —**plot,** *v.*; *plotted, plotting.* **I.** *tr.* To divide (land) into plots; also, to make a plot, plan, or map of, as a tract of land, a building, etc.; mark on a plan, map, or chart, as a position, a ship's course, etc.; specif., to determine and mark (points), as on plotting-paper, by means of measurements or coördinates; draw (a curve) by means of points so marked; represent by means of such a curve; also, to devise the plot of (a play, etc.); also, to form plans for† (as, "the good man and woman . . . who used to sit and *plot* the welfare of us their children": Steele, in "Spectator," 263); also, to plan secretly (something hostile or evil: as, to *plot* mischief or revenge; to *plot* mutiny, treason, or murder). **II.** *intr.* To make plots, plans, or maps (as, "They will *plot* and survey and map of course": Kipling's "Kim," xii.); plot positions, points, curves, etc.; also, to form secret plots, as of mischief or evil (as, "The wicked *plotteth* against the just": Ps. xxxvii. 12); conspire.—**plot'ter,** *n.*—**plot'ting-ly,** *adv.*—**plot'ting=pa''per,** *n.* Paper ruled with precision into small squares or spaces, used in plotting points, curves, etc.

plough, etc. See *plow*, etc.

plov-er (pluv'ėr), *n.*; pl. *plovers* or (esp. collectively) *plover.* [OF. *plovier* (F. *pluvier*), < L. *pluvia*, rain (see *pluvial*); the connection of the bird with rain being variously explained.] Any of various limicoline birds of the family *Charadriidæ*, esp. those with a short tail and a bill like that of a pigeon, as *Charadrius pluvialis* (or *apricarius*) of Europe and *C. dominicus* of America (both called 'golden plover': as, "Immense numbers of golden *plover* had appeared [in Argentina] and were in large flocks on the plain," W. H. Hudson's "Far Away and Long Ago," v.); also, any of various sandpipers.

Golden Plover (*Charadrius pluvialis*), in autumn plumage.

plow, plough (plou), *n.* [Late AS. *plōh*, a plowland, = Icel. *plōgr* = D. *ploeg* = G. *pflug*, plow.] An agricultural implement for cutting furrows in and turning up the soil, as for sowing or planting; also, any of various implements resembling or suggesting this, as a kind of plane for cutting grooves or a contrivance for clearing away snow from a road or track; [*cap.*] in *astron.*, Charles's Wain, or the Dipper; also, the whole constellation Ursa Major.—**plow, plough,** *v.* **I.** *tr.* To make furrows in or turn up (the soil) with a plow; make (a furrow, etc.) with a plow; also, to furrow, remove, etc., or make (a furrow, groove, etc.), as if with a plow; fig., to furrow (the face, etc.) with wrinkles; make (wrinkles) on the face, etc.; of a ship, etc., to cleave the surface of (the water); make (a way) or follow (a course) thus. **II.** *intr.* To till the soil with a plow; work with a plow; also, to move through anything in the manner of a plow (as, "the . . . horse-dealer whose caravans *ploughed* through their fastnesses belly deep in snow": Kipling's "Kim," i.); move through water by cleaving the surface.—**plow'a-ble, plough'a-ble,** *a.* Capable of being plowed.—**plow'boy, plough'boy,** *n.* A boy who leads or guides a team drawing a plow; hence, a country boy.—**plow'er, plough'er,** *n.*—**plow'land, plough'land** (-land), *n.* An old English measure of land, usually 120 acres, considered as the area capable of being tilled with one plow-team of eight oxen (cf. *carucate* and *hide*[2]); also, arable land.—**plow'man, plough'man** (-mạn), *n.*; pl. *-men.* A man who plows; hence, a farm-laborer or a rustic.—**plow'share, plough'share,** *n.* [See *share*[1].] The share of a plow, or that part which cuts the slice of earth and raises it to the mold-board.—**plow'=tail, plough'=tail,** *n.* The handle or handles of a plow.—**plow'wright, plough'-wright** (-rīt), *n.* One who makes and repairs plows.

ploy[1] (ploi), *n.* [Origin uncertain.] A performance or proceeding; a frolic; a trick. [Sc. and north. Eng.]

ploy[2] (ploi), *v. t.* or *i.* [Back-formation from *deploy.*] *Milit.*, to move from line into column.

pluck (pluk), *v. t.* [AS. *pluccian, ploccian,* = MLG. *plucken* = Icel. *plukka, plokka,* pluck: cf. OF. *peluchier, pelukier,* pick, peck, It. *piluccare*, pluck.] To pull off or out from the place of growth, as fruit, flowers, feathers, etc.; pick; cull; gather; also, to pull by force (with *away*, *off*, *out*, etc.: as, "The false Christianity . . . when it is at last *plucked* rudely away from us . . . will carry away a part of the true with it," Mallock's "New Republic," ii. 1); snatch; drag; draw; also, to give a pull at (as, "Children . . . *pluck'd* his gown": Goldsmith's "Deserted Village," 184); pull with sudden force or with a jerk; sound (the strings of a musical instrument) by doing this with the fingers or a plectrum; also, to pull off the feathers, hair, etc., from; strip (a bird) of feathers; fig., to rob, plunder, or fleece; also, to reject, as after an examination, as not coming up to the required standard (colloq.: as, "He went to college, and he got — *plucked*, I think they call it," C. Brontë's "Jane Eyre," x.).—**to pluck up,** to pull up, as out of the ground; uproot; eradicate; also, to summon up, or rouse (courage, spirit, etc.: as, "The Blackfeet were defeated; and from that time the Crows *plucked up* fresh heart, and were frequently successful," Irving's "Captain Bonneville," xlix.).—**pluck,** *v. i.* To pull sharply; tug (*at*); also, to snatch (*at*).—**pluck,** *n.* An act of plucking; a pull, tug, or jerk; a snatch; also, something plucked; also, the heart, liver, and lungs, esp. of an animal used for food; fig., courage, spirit, or resolution in the face of difficulties (colloq.: as, "the *pluck*, daring, and admirable work of our aviators," H. G. Wells's "Italy, France, and Britain at War," iii. 3); also, boldness, or striking effect, as of a photographic print, of color, of words, etc. (colloq.).—**pluck'er,** *n.*—**pluck'y,** *a.*; compar. *pluckier*, superl. *pluckiest.* Having or showing pluck or courage (as, "Everybody was . . . anxious to show these Belgians what England thought of their *plucky* little country": H. G. Wells's "Mr. Britling," ii. 2. § 8); also, bold or striking in effect, as a photographic print, etc. [Colloq.]—**pluck'i-ly,** *adv.*—**pluck'i-ness,** *n.*

plug (plug), *n.* [MD. *plugge* (D. *plug*), plug, peg, akin to G. *pflock.*] A piece of wood or other material used to stop up a hole or aperture, to fill a gap, or to act as a wedge; specif., a tapering piece of conducting material inserted between two electrical conductors to form a connection; any similar electrical connecting device, as one for screwing into a socket; also, a spark-plug; also, a hydrant for supplying water to a fire-engine and for other purposes ('fire-plug'); also, a cake of pressed tobacco, or a piece of tobacco cut off for chewing, etc.; also, a man's tall silk hat ('plug-hat': slang); also, a worn-out or inferior horse (colloq.); also, a shop-worn or unsalable article (colloq.); also, a punch or blow (slang).—**plug,** *v.*; *plugged*, *plugging.* **I.** *tr.* To stop or fill with or as with a plug; insert or drive a plug into; also, to secure by a plug; also, to insert (something) as a plug; also, to cut a small tapering piece from (a watermelon) in testing ripeness; also, to punch or hit (slang); shoot (slang). **II.** *intr.* To work steadily or doggedly; plod; also, to strike; shoot. [Slang.]—**plug'ger,** *n.*

plug=ug-ly (plug'ug'li), *n.*; pl. *-lies* (-liz). [Cf. *plug*.] A city ruffian; a rowdy; a tough. [Slang.]

plum[1] (plum), *n.* [AS. *plūme*, < ML. *pruna*, plum: see *prune*[1].] The drupaceous fruit of any of various trees of the amygdalaceous genus *Prunus*; a tree bearing such fruit; any of various other trees with a plum-like fruit, or the fruit itself; also, a raisin as in a cake or pudding; also, a sugar-plum; also, fig., a good or choice thing, as one of the best parts of anything, a fine situation or appointment, etc.; also, the sum of £100,000 sterling (colloq., Eng.: as, "a stock-broker in the city, who died worth a *plum*," Marryat's "King's Own," xlvii.); also, plum-color.

plum[2] (plum), *a.* and *adv.* See *plumb*.

plu-mage (plö'māj), *n.* [OF. F. *plumage*, < *plume*, feather, E. *plume.*] Feathers collectively; the entire feathery covering of a bird. Also fig.—**plu'maged,** *a.* Furnished with or having plumage: as, "some common dull-*plumaged* little bird" (W. H. Hudson's "Green Mansions," vii.).

plu-mate (plö'māt), *a.* [L. *plumatus*, pp. of *plumare*, cover with feathers, < *pluma*, feather, E. *plume.*] In *zoöl.*, resembling a feather, as a hair or bristle which bears smaller hairs.

plumb (plum), *n.* [OF. F. *plomb*, < L. *plumbum*, lead.] A small mass of lead or heavy material, used for various purposes; esp., a weight or bob attached to a line, used in testing the perpendicularity of walls, etc., or in sounding; a plummet; also, the position of a plumb-line when freely suspended, or the perpendicular (as, out of *plumb*).—**plumb. I.** *a.* True according to a plumb-line; perpendicular; vertical; also, downright or absolute (colloq.: as, "This was their home, called by every mountaineer neighbor 'a *plumb* palace,'" G. W. Cable's "John March, Southerner," ii.). **II.** *adv.* In a perpendicular or vertical direction; perpendicularly; also, exactly, precisely, or directly; also, completely or absolutely (colloq.: as, "You'll have me *plumb* scared," Wister's "Virginian," xxxv.; "They . . . *plumb* lost their senses," W. Churchill's "Coniston," ii. 16).—**plumb,** *v.* **I.** *tr.* To test or adjust by a plumb-line; make vertical; also, to sound (the ocean, etc.) with or as with a plumb-line; measure (depth) by sounding; fig., to sound the depths of, or penetrate to the bottom of (as, "The mind of that deep and truly knowing man was not to be *plumbed* by a chit of my age," Bulwer-Lytton's "Caxtons," ii. 4; "*plumbing* a deeper deep of woe," H. G. Wells's "Bealby," iv.); also, to weight with lead; also, to seal with lead; also, to supply with plumbing, as a building (colloq.). **II.** *intr.* To be perpendicular or vertical; hang vertically; also, to work as a plumber (colloq.)—**plumb'a-ble,** *a.* Capable of being plumbed.

plum-bag-i-na-ceous (plum-baj-i-nā'shius), *a.* [See *plumbago.*] Belonging to the *Plumbaginaceæ*, or leadwort family of plants.

plum-ba-go (plum-bā'gō), *n.* [L. *plumbago* (*plumbagin-*), lead ore, leadwort, < *plumbum*, lead.] Any of certain oxides or ores of lead†; also, graphite, a form of carbon; also, any of the herbaceous plants, chiefly with light-blue or whitish flowers, of the genus *Plumbago*, certain species of which are cultivated; a leadwort.—**plum-bag'i-nous** (-baj'i-nus), *a.*

plumb=bob (plum'bob), *n.* The bob or weight of a plumb-line.

plum-be-ous (plum'bē-us), *a.* [L. *plumbeus*, < *plumbum*, lead.] Leaden; lead-colored.

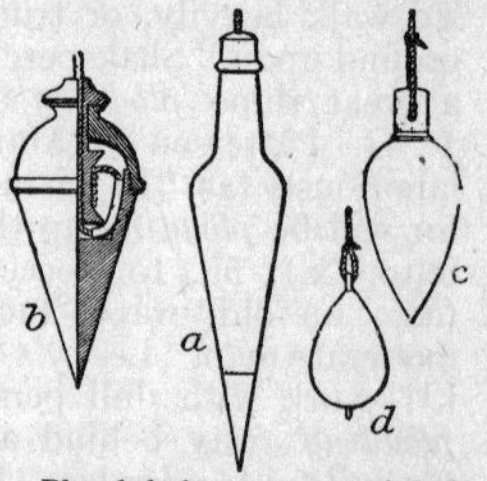

Plumb-bobs. — *a*, plumb-bob made of brass, with cap to attach cord, and steel point at bottom; *b*, plumb-bob with reel inclosed; *c*, cast-iron plumb-bob; *d*, lead plumb-bob with wire core.

plumb-er (plum'ėr), *n.* [OF. *plommier* (F. *plombier*), < LL. *plumbarius*, < L. *plumbum*, lead.] Orig., a worker in lead or similar metals; later, one who fits and repairs pipes and other apparatus for water, drainage, gas, and the like, in buildings, etc.; now, commonly, a worker in water and drainage apparatus, as distinguished from a gas-fitter, steam-fitter, etc.—**plumb'er-y,** *n.*; pl. *-ies* (-iz). [OF. *plommerie* (F. *plomberie*).] Working in lead; plumbers' work; plumbing; also, the workshop of a plumber.

plum-bic (plum'bik), *a.* [L. *plumbum*, lead.] Of or containing lead. See *plumbous*.

plum-bif-er-ous (plum-bif'ẹ-rus), *a.* [L. *plumbum*, lead, + *ferre*, bear.] Yielding or containing lead.

plumb-ing (plum'ing), *n.* The act of one who plumbs, as in ascertaining depth; also, the work or trade of a plumber; the system of pipes and other apparatus for conveying water, etc., as in a building.

plum-bism (plum'bizm), *n.* [L. *plumbum*, lead.] In *pathol.*, chronic lead-poisoning.

plumb-less (plum'les), *a.* That cannot be plumbed or sounded; unfathomable: as, "the *plumbless* depths of the past" (Dickens's "Hard Times," i. 15).

plumb=line (plum'līn), *n.* A line or cord to one end of which is attached a metal plumb or bob, used to determine perpendicularity, find the depth of water, etc.; also, sometimes, a plumb-rule.

plumb-ness (plum'nes), *n.* The state of being plumb, perpendicular, or vertical.

plum-bous (plum'bus), *a.* [L. *plumbosus*, < *plumbum*, lead.] Containing lead (in larger proportion than a corresponding plumbic compound).

plumb=rule (plum'röl), *n.* A device used by builders, etc., for determining perpendicularity, consisting of a narrow board fitted with a plumb-line and bob.

plum-bum (plum'bum), *n.* [L.] Lead: in *chem.*, abbreviated *Pb* (without period).

plum=cake (plum'kāk), *n.* A cake containing raisins, currants, and often other fruits.

plum=col-or (plum'kul"ọr), *n.* A dark bluish-purple color. —**plum'=col"ored,** *a.*

plum-cot (plum'kot), *n.* [From *plum* + (*apri*)*cot*.] In *hort.*, a hybrid between the plum and the apricot.

plum=duff (plum'duf'), *n.* [See *duff*[1].] A kind of flour pudding containing raisins or currants and boiled in a cloth or bag.

plume (plöm), *n.* [OF. F. *plume*, < L. *pluma*, feather.] A feather, esp. a large, long, or conspicuous feather (as, the *plumes* of an ostrich, or of a bird of paradise); hence, plumage (now chiefly poetic: as, "Like some full-breasted swan That . . . Ruffles her pure cold *plume*, and takes the flood," Tennyson's "Passing of Arthur," 436); also, a feather, or a tuft or bunch of feathers (or some substitute, as hair), worn on the head, hat, helmet, etc., or borne on a hearse, etc. (as, "Her photograph . . . showed her stiff in her glories of *plumes* and satin," M. Hewlett's "Open Country," xv.; "Press where ye see my white *plume* shine, amidst the ranks of war," Macaulay's "Ivry"); fig., an ornament, or a token of honor or distinction; also, something resembling a feather, as a pinnate leaf (as, "the slender coco's drooping crown of *plumes*": Tennyson's "Enoch Arden," 570); any plumose part or formation.—**plume,** *v. t.*; *plumed, pluming.* To strip (a bird) of feathers; pluck; also, to furnish, cover, or adorn with plumes or feathers; also, of a bird, to preen (itself or its feathers); hence, fig., to display or feel satisfaction with or pride in (one's self), esp. on a particular score; pride (one's self) complacently (*on* or *upon*: as, "I was . . . *pluming* myself on having made an heroic proposal," Barrie's "Tommy and Grizel," xxxi.).—**plume'=bird,** *n.* Any bird of the genus *Epimachus* or the subfamily *Epimachinæ* (family *Paradiseidæ*), of New Guinea, notable for the luxuriance and brilliance of their plumage.—**plumed,** *a.* Having plumes or plume-like parts; adorned with or as with a plume or plumes (as, "*plumed* steeds gorgeously caparisoned": Amelia B. Edwards's "Thousand Miles up the Nile," xvi.).—**plume'less,** *a.* Without plumes or feathers.—**plume'let,** *n.* A small plume.

Plume, as worn at tourneys and ceremonials, 16th century.

Plume-bird (*Epimachus speciosus*).

plu-mi-corn (plö'mi-kôrn), *n.* [L. *pluma*, feather, + *cornu*, horn.] One of a pair of horn-like or ear-like tufts of feathers on the head of certain owls, as the horned owls.

plum-met (plum'et), *n.* [OF. *plommet, plombet*, dim. of *plomb*, E. *plumb*.] A piece of lead or some other weight attached to a line, used for determining perpendicularity, for sounding, etc.; the bob of a plumb-line; also, a plumb-rule; also, fig., something that weighs down or depresses.

plum-my (plum'i), *a.* Full of or resembling plums; also, of the nature of a plum or choice thing (colloq.); good or desirable (colloq.).

plu-mose (plö'mōs or plọ-mōs'), *a.* [L. *plumosus*, < *pluma*, feather.] Having feathers or plumes; feathered; also, feathery or plume-like.

plump[1] (plump), *n.* [ME. *plumpe, plompe*; origin uncertain.] A compact group of persons, animals, or things; a company, flock, cluster, or clump. [Archaic or prov.]

plump[2] (plump), *a.* [ME. *plompe*, dull, rude, = MLG. *plump* = D. *plomp*, blunt, thick, rude.] Dull†; blunt†; also, well filled out or rounded in form, as a person or animal, the body or a part of it, etc.; somewhat fleshy or fat; chubby; hence, filled out or developed well, as a seed or fruit; filled to roundness, as a cushion, a purse, etc.—**plump**[2], *v.* **I.** *tr.* To make plump; fatten; distend; swell (*up* or *out*). **II.** *intr.* To become plump, fat, or distended: often with *up* or *out*: as, "The little man *plumped* up very considerably" (H. G. Wells's "Tono-Bungay," iii. 1. § 1).

plump[3] (plump), *v.* [ME. *plumpen* = D. *plompen*; prob. imit.] **I.** *intr.* To fall heavily or suddenly and directly (as, "The branch . . . broke, and the poor lad *plumped* over head and ears into the water": Fielding's "Tom Jones," iv. 3); drop, sink, or come abruptly, or with direct impact; run plump (*into*); also, to vote exclusively for one candidate, at an election, instead of distributing or splitting one's votes among a number (Eng.: as, "enormous red posters exhorting the shrewd common sense potter not to be misled by paid agitators, but to *plump* for his true friend," Arnold Bennett's "Clayhanger," iii. 17). **II.** *tr.* To drop or throw heavily or suddenly (as, "I could hear . . . Israel Hands, *plumping* down a round-shot on the deck": Stevenson's "Treasure Island," xvii.); also, to utter or say bluntly (often with *out*: as, "If it ain't a liberty to *plump* it out . . . what do you do for your living?" Dickens's "Our Mutual Friend," i. 8).—**plump**[3]. **I.** *adv.* With a heavy or sudden fall or drop; with direct impact; with sudden encounter (as, "At the corner . . . they come *plump* against the old merchant": Hawthorne's "Twice-Told Tales," Sights from a Steeple); also, directly or straight (as, "I fired *plump* at the side of his [a lion's] head": J. H. Patterson's "Man-Eaters of Tsavo," xx.); right; also, directly or bluntly, as in speaking. **II.** *a.* Direct; downright; blunt: as, "I hate qualifying arguers—*plump* assertion or *plump* denial for me" (Maria Edgeworth's "Belinda," xvii.).—**plump**[3], *n.* A heavy or sudden fall; also, a sudden downpour of rain (Sc.).

plump-er[1] (plum'pėr), *n.* Something that plumps, or makes plump; esp., something carried in the mouth to fill out hollow cheeks.

plump-er[2] (plum'pėr), *n.* A plumping or falling heavily; also, the vote of one who plumps, or a voter who plumps (Eng.).

plump-ly (plump'li), *adv.* In a plump manner.—**plump'ness,** *n.*

plum=pud-ding (plum'pu̇d'ing), *n.* A rich boiled pudding containing raisins, currants, citron, spices, etc.

plump-y (plum'pi), *a.* Plump, as in body or form: as, "*plumpy* Bacchus" (Shakspere's "Antony and Cleopatra," ii. 7. 121).

plu-mule (plö'mūl), *n.* [L. *plumula*, dim. of *pluma*, feather.] In *ornith.*, a down-feather; in *bot.*, the bud of the ascending axis of a plant while still in the embryo.

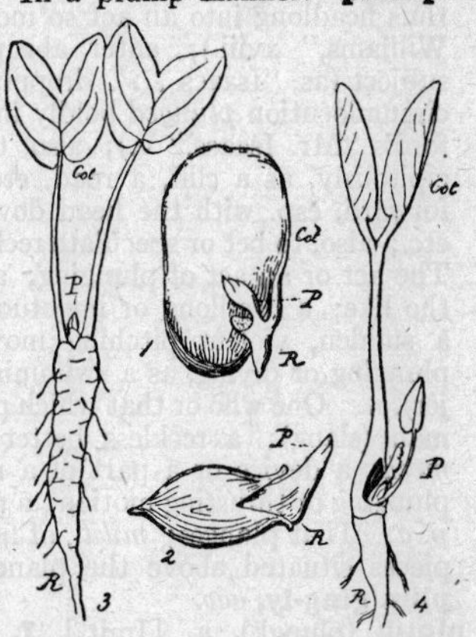

Plumules. — 1, seed of bean (*Vicia faba*), one cotyledon detached; 2, germinating plantlet of sedge (*Cyperus*); 3, germinating plantlet of ipomœa (*Ipomœa*); 4, germinating plantlet of rhubarb (*Rheum*), showing the plumule breaking through the tubular base of the petioles of the cotyledons: — *Cot*, cotyledon; *P*, plumule; *R*, root.

plum-y (plö'mi), *a.* Having plumes or feathers (as, "a flock of white *plumy* birds": C. Brontë's "Jane Eyre," xvii.); adorned with a plume or plumes (as, a *plumy* helmet); also, plume-like or feathery (as, "the *plumy* palms of Memphis": Amelia B. Edwards's "Thousand Miles up the Nile," xxii.).

plun-der (plun′dėr), *v.* [G. *plündern*, < *plunder*, household effects, lumber, stuff, trash.] **I.** *tr.* To rob of goods or valuables by open force, as in war, hostile raids, brigandage, etc. (as, to *plunder* a town or its inhabitants; to *plunder* a caravan); pillage; in general, to rob, despoil, or fleece (as, to *plunder* the public treasury; to *plunder* an orchard; "The man wouldn't be above *plundering* the natives," J. Conrad's "Rescue," v. 1); also, to take by pillage or robbery (as, "The law of self-preservation had now obliged the fugitive Tartars to *plunder* provisions": De Quincey's "Revolt of the Tartars"); steal. **II.** *intr.* To take plunder; pillage; commit depredations.—**plun′der,** *n.* Plundering, pillage, or spoliation (as, "some expedition of war or *plunder*," H. Melville's "Typee," iii.; "Cordova was given up to *plunder* and massacre," Froude's "Cæsar," xxv.); also, that which is taken in plundering, or spoil, booty, or loot (as, "The gold, silver, and precious jewelry . . . brocades, laces, and similar . . . portable *plunder*, were rapidly appropriated": Motley's "Dutch Republic," iv. 5); anything taken by robbery, theft, or fraud; also, household goods, personal effects, or baggage (local, U. S.).—**plun′der-age** (-ạj), *n.* The act of plundering; pillage; spoliation; in *maritime law*, the embezzlement of goods on board a ship; also, the goods embezzled.—**plun′der-bund** (-bund or -bu̇nt), *n.* [See *bund*².] A league or organized body of plunderers, esp. plunderers of the public. [Colloq., U. S.]—**plun′der-er,** *n.*—**plun′der-ous,** *a.* Given to plundering.

plunge (plunj), *v.*; *plunged, plunging.* [OF. *plungier, plongier* (F. *plonger*), < L. *plumbum*, lead.] **I.** *tr.* To cast or thrust forcibly or suddenly into a liquid, a penetrable substance, a place, etc. (as, to *plunge* the hand into water; to *plunge* a dagger into one's heart; "Yet shalt thou *plunge* me in the ditch," Job, ix. 31); immerse or submerge; pitch or send with a sudden, violent movement (as, "The least irregularity of the sea might *plunge* you overboard": Stevenson's "Master of Ballantrae," ix.); fig., to throw or bring into some state, condition, situation, course of activities, etc. (as, to *plunge* a country into anarchy or war; "Instead of escaping the catastrophe, he found himself *plunged* into the heart of it," Froude's "Cæsar," xx.); immerse mentally, as in thought or some subject of thought. **II.** *intr.* To cast one's self, or fall as if cast, into water, a deep place, etc. (as, "A stone dropped . . . *plunges* into water deep enough to float a skiff": Scott's "Guy Mannering," xvii.); rush or dash with headlong haste (as, to *plunge* into or through a burning building; to *plunge* through a doorway); pass or go impetuously or abruptly; fig., to throw one's self impetuously or abruptly into some state, condition, situation, course, etc. (as, to *plunge* into debt, excesses, or war; "having *plunged* thus headlong into an act so monstrous," Godwin's "Caleb Williams," xviii.); enter abruptly into some matter or subject (as, "Isaacs . . . dropping all forms of ceremony or circumlocution *plunged* boldly into business": F. M. Crawford's "Mr. Isaacs," v.); also, to descend abruptly or precipitously, as a cliff, a road, etc.; also, to pitch violently forward, esp. with the head downward, as a horse, a ship, etc.; also, to bet or speculate recklessly (slang).—**plunge,** *n.* The act or an act of plunging; a leap or dive into water or the like; a headlong or impetuous rush or dash (also fig.); a sudden, violent pitching movement; also, a place for plunging or diving, as a swimming-tank.—**plun-ger** (plun′jėr), *n.* One who or that which plunges; a diver; a cavalryman (slang); a reckless better or speculator (slang); in *mech.*, a device or a part of a machine which acts with a plunging or thrusting motion; a piston; a ram.—**plun′ging,** *p. a.* That plunges; *milit.*, of fire, directed downward from pieces situated above the plane of the object fired at.—**plun′ging-ly,** *adv.*

plunk (plungk), *v.* [Imit.] **I.** *tr.* To pluck (a stringed instrument or its strings); twang; also, to throw, push, put, etc., heavily or suddenly; also, to strike or hit. [Colloq.] **II.** *intr.* To give forth a twanging sound; also, to drop down heavily or suddenly; plump. [Colloq.]—**plunk,** *n.* The act or sound of plunking (colloq.: as, "They played in such magnificent time that every high-stepping foot in all the line came down with the same jubilant *plunk*," Tarkington's "Gentleman from Indiana," xix.); a direct, forcible blow (colloq.); also, a dollar (slang, U. S.: as, "I'll sell you the Candersen place for three thousand *plunks*," Sinclair Lewis's "Main Street," iii.).—**plunk,** *adv.* With a plunking sound; also, plump. [Colloq.]

plu-per-fect (plö′pėr′fekt). [Contr. < LL. *plus quam perfectum*, 'more than perfect': cf. F. *plus-que-parfait.*] In *gram.*: **I.** *a.* Denoting an action or state completed before a given past time (as, the *pluperfect* tense); past-perfect. **II.** *n.* The pluperfect tense; a verb-form in this tense, as Latin *amaveram*, 'I had loved.'

plu-ral (plö′rạl), *a.* [L. *pluralis*, < *plus* (*plur-*), more: see *plus.*] Consisting of, containing, or pertaining to more than one; pertaining to or involving a plurality of persons or things; also, being one of such a plurality (as, a *plural* wife: see phrase below); in *gram.*, signifying or implying more than one person or thing (as, the *plural* number; a *plural* verb-form: cf. *singular*, *a.*, and *dual*, *a.*).—**plural livings,** two or more ecclesiastical benefices held by one person at the same time.—**plural marriage,** the marriage of a man to two or more women at the same time; polygamy: so called esp. with reference to the Mormons.—**plural wife,** any of the wives of a polygamist, or in a plural marriage.—**plu′ral,** *n.* In *gram.*, the plural number; a noun, verb, or other word in this number. Examples of plurals of English nouns are *books* (plural of *book*), *mosses* (plural of *moss*), *foxes* (plural of *fox*), *dishes* (plural of *dish*), *mosquitoes* or *mosquitos* (plural of *mosquito*), *jellies* (plural of *jelly*), and *knives* (plural of *knife*); *M. D.'s*, *a's*, and *9's* (plurals of *M. D.*, *a*, and *9*: see *apostrophe*²); *men* (plural of *man*), and *teeth* (plural of *tooth*); *Chinese* and *Portuguese* (plurals of *Chinese* and *Portuguese*); *fathoms* or *fathom*, and *hundreds* or *hundred* (plurals of *fathom* and *hundred*, the second form being used esp. after a numeral); *elks* or *elk*, and *herrings* or *herring* (plurals of *elk* and *herring*, the second form being used esp. in a collective sense); *deer* or *deers*, and *mackerel* or *mackerels* (plural of *deer* and *mackerel*, the second form being used esp. with reference to different species).—**plu′ral-ism,** *n.* The character of being plural; also, the holding by one person of two or more offices, esp. ecclesiastical benefices, at the same time; in *philos.*, a theory or system that recognizes more than one ultimate substance or principle (cf. *monism* and *dualism*).—**plu′ral-ist,** *n.* One who holds two or more offices, esp. ecclesiastical benefices, at the same time; in *philos.*, an adherent of pluralism.—**plu-ral-is′tic,** *a.*—**plu-ral-i-ty** (plọ̈-ral′i-ti), *n.*; pl. *-ties* (-tiz). The state or fact of being plural; a number greater than unity; also, the fact of being numerous; a large number, or a multitude; also, pluralism, or the simultaneous holding of two or more offices or benefices; any of the offices or benefices so held; also, the greater number or part; more than half of the whole; the majority; in *U. S. politics*, an excess of votes received by one candidate in an election over those received by any other candidate for the same office; commonly, when there are three or more candidates, the excess of votes received by the leading candidate over those received by the next candidate (esp. in distinction from a *majority*, or an excess over the combined votes received by all the other candidates).—**plu′ral-ize,** *v. t.*; *-ized, -izing.* To make plural; express in the plural form.—**plu′ral-ly,** *adv.*

pluri-. Form of L. *plus* (*plur-*), more, *pl.* many, used in combination.—**plu-ri-ax-i-al** (plö-ri-ak′si-ạl), *a.* Having more than one axis.—**plu-ri-cel′lu-lar** (-sel′ū-lạr), *a.* Having several cells; multicellular.—**plu-ri-lit′er-al** (-lit′ẹ-rạl), *a.* [+ L. *litera*, letter.] Consisting of more than three letters, as a Hebrew root.—**plu-ri-se′ri-al** (-sē′ri-ạl), *a.* Consisting of several series.

plus (plus). [L., more (used as compar. of *multus*, much, many), akin to Gr. πολύς, much, many (see *poly-*), compar. πλείων, and ult. to E. *full*¹.] **I.** *a.* More (by a certain amount: a quasi-prepositional use: see *plus*, *prep.*); also, involving or denoting addition (as, a *plus* quantity; the *plus* sign, +); positive; also, with something in addition (colloq.). **II.** *n.* The plus sign; also, a plus quantity; also, something additional; a surplus or gain.—**plus,** *prep.* More by the addition of, or increased by (as, 10 *plus* 3); hence, with the addition of; with.—**plus′=fours′,** *n. pl.* [From *plus four*, the handicap of a first-rate British golfer.] Baggy, hanging knickerbockers, as for sports wear.

plush (plush), *n.* [F. *pluche, peluche,* ult. < L. *pilus,* hair.] A fabric of silk, cotton, wool, etc., having a softer and longer nap than that of velvet.—**plush'y,** *a.* Of or like plush.

Plu-to (plö'tō), *n.* [L., < Gr. Πλούτων, < πλοῦτος, wealth.] In *Gr. myth.,* Hades, the lord of the lower world, esp. in the aspect of a beneficent god and the bestower of blessings produced in the earth; in *astron.,* a major planet, the ninth and outermost from the sun (beyond Neptune), discovered in 1930.

Pluto, enthroned, with Proserpine. (From a vase-painting.)

plu-toc-ra-cy (plö-tok'rạ-si), *n.*; pl. *-cies* (-siz). [Gr. πλουτοκρατία, < πλοῦτος, wealth, + κρατεῖν, rule.] The rule or power of wealth or of the wealthy; a government or state in which the wealthy class rules (as, "Public spirit in the masses was dead or sleeping; the Commonwealth was a *plutocracy*": Froude's "Cæsar," ii.); also, a class or group ruling, or exercising power or influence, by virtue of its wealth (as, "He [Gibbon] idealized the crude and gross *plutocracy* of Rome into a world of fine gentlemen": H. G. Wells's "Outline of History," xxxvi. § 11).—**plu-to-crat** (plö'tọ-krat), *n.* A member of a plutocracy; a person exercising power or influence by virtue of his wealth.—**plu-to-crat'ic,** *a.*

plu-tol-a-try (plö-tol'ạ-tri), *n.* [Gr. πλοῦτος, wealth, + λατρεία, worship.] The worship of wealth.

plu-tol-o-gy (plö-tol'ọ-ji), *n.* [Gr. πλοῦτος, wealth: see *-logy.*] The science of wealth; political economy; economics.—**plu-tol'o-gist,** *n.*

Plu-to-ni-an (plö-tō'ni-ạn), *a.* Of or pertaining to Pluto, the god of the lower world; infernal; in *geol.,* Plutonic.—**Plu-ton'ic** (-ton'ik), *a.* Plutonian; [*cap.* or *l. c.*] in *geol.,* noting or pertaining to the theory that the present condition of the earth's crust is mainly due to igneous action; also [now usually *l. c.*], noting a class of igneous rocks which have solidified far below the earth's surface.—**Plu-to-nism** (plö'tọ-nizm), *n.* The Plutonic theory.—**Plu'to-nist,** *n.* An adherent of the Plutonic theory.

plu-ton-o-my (plö-ton'ọ-mi), *n.* [Gr. πλοῦτος, wealth, + -νομία, < νέμειν, deal out, manage.] The science of wealth; political economy; economics.—**plu-to-nom-ic** (plö-tọ-nom'ik), *a.*—**plu-ton'o-mist,** *n.*

plu-vi-al (plö'vi-ạl), *a.* [L. *pluvialis,* < *pluvia,* rain, prop. fem. of *pluvius,* rainy, < *pluere,* to rain.] Of or pertaining to rain; rainy; in *geol.,* due to rain.

plu-vi-o-graph (plö'vi-ọ-gräf), *n.* [L. *pluvia,* rain, + Gr. γράφειν, write.] A self-recording rain-gage.—**plu"vi-o-graph'ic** (-graf'ik), *a.*—**plu-vi-og'ra-phy** (-og'rạ-fi), *n.*

plu-vi-om-e-ter (plö-vi-om'e-tėr), *n.* [L. *pluvia,* rain, + Gr. μέτρον, measure.] An instrument for measuring rainfall.—**plu"vi-o-met'ric** (-ọ-met'rik), *a.*—**plu-vi-om'e-try,** *n.*

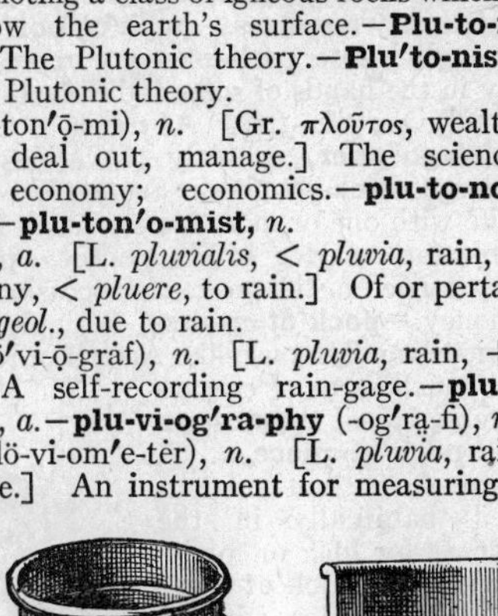

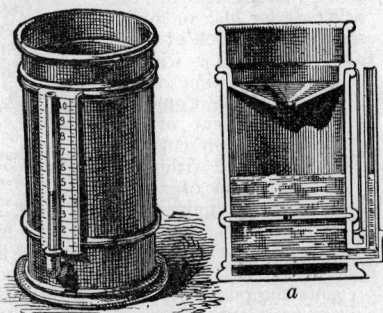

Pluviometer. — *a,* vertical section.

Plu-viôse (plü-vyōz), *n.* [F. *pluviôse,* < L. *pluviosus,* rainy, E. *pluvious.*] In the calendar of the first French republic, the fifth month of the year, extending from Jan. 20 to Feb. 18.

plu-vi-ous (plö'vi-us), *a.* [L. *pluviosus,* < *pluvia,* rain: see *pluvial.*] Abounding in rain; rainy; pertaining to rain

ply (plī), *v.*; *plied, plying.* [In part, < OF. F. *plier,* fold, bend, < L. *plicare,* fold, akin to *plectere,* plait, interweave, and Gr. πλέκειν, plait, twine, weave; in part, a reduced form of E. *apply* (OF. *aplier,* L. *applicare*).] **I.** *tr.* To bend, fold, or mold (now chiefly prov.); also, to use or employ busily, or work with or at (as, to *ply* the needle, the pen, the knife and fork, or the oars; "The smith still *plies* his anvil," Johnson's "Rasselas," xxviii.); exercise or exert (faculties, powers, energies, etc.); also, to carry on, practise, or pursue (as, to *ply* a trade, art, or task; "Busy trade his labours *plies,*" Burns's "Address to Edinburgh," 10); also, to treat with something repeatedly applied (as, "I *plied* the fire with fresh fuel round the outside": Defoe's "Robinson Crusoe," i. 9); hence, to keep up work or efforts upon, or assail persistently (as, to *ply* the water with oars; to *ply* horses with a whip; to *ply* the enemy with artillery fire); work, or seek to work, upon (a person) with something steadily supplied or offered (as, to *ply* a person with bribes, drink, or flattery; "Jack Wilson had resolved to execute some jokes on Lismahago, and . . . began to *ply* him with bumpers," Smollett's "Humphry Clinker," Nov. 8); supply with something pressingly offered (as, to *ply* a guest with food); address persistently or importunately, as with questions, solicitations, etc.; importune; also, to traverse (a river, etc.), esp. on regular trips. **II.** *intr.* To bend, incline, or yield (obs. or prov.); also, to perform one's or its work or office busily or steadily (as, to *ply* with the oars; "Soon all the boats . . . were dropped . . . all the paddles *plying,*" H. Melville's "Moby-Dick," cxxxiii.); pursue a trade or profession, or wait in readiness for employment (as, "The famous Dr. L——n . . . is come to *ply* at the Well for patients": Smollett's "Humphry Clinker," April 18); also, to work or make the way, as with effort, on the water (as, "The foremost ship gained upon us, especially upon one tack, for we *plied* away from them to windward": Defoe's "Captain Singleton," xi.); pursue or direct the course, on the water or otherwise (as, "Thither he *plies*": Milton's "Paradise Lost," ii. 954); esp., to travel or run regularly over a fixed course or between certain places, as a boat, a stage, etc. (as, "Aldea Gallega, between which place and Lisbon the boats *ply*": Borrow's "Bible in Spain," ii.).—**ply,** *n.*; pl. *plies* (plīz). A fold; a thickness; a strand, as of yarn or rope; also, bent, bias, or inclination —**ply'er,** *n.* See *plier.*

Plym-outh (plim'uth) **Rock.** [From the rock at *Plymouth,* Mass., on which the Pilgrims are said to have landed.] One of an American breed of domestic fowls, usually having pearl-gray plumage barred transversely with bluish black.

ply-wood (plī'wůd), *n.* A material consisting of two or more thin sheets or strips of wood glued together: used in aëroplane construction.

pneu-mat-ic (nū-mat'ik). [L. *pneumaticus,* < Gr. πνευματικός, < πνεῦμα, wind, air, breath, spirit, < πνεῖν, blow, breathe.] **I.** *a.* Of or pertaining to air, or gases in general; pertaining to pneumatics; also, operated by air, or by pressure or exhaustion of air; also, containing air; filled with compressed air, as a tire; in *zoöl.,* containing air or air-cavities; in *theol.,* of or pertaining to the spirit; spiritual. **II.** *n.* A pneumatic tire; also, a vehicle having wheels with such tires.—**pneu-mat'i-cal-ly,** *adv.*—**pneu-mat'ics,** *n.* That branch of physics which deals with the mechanical properties (pressure, elasticity, etc.) of air and other gases.

pneumato-. Form of Gr. πνεῦμα (πνευματ-), wind, air, breath, spirit, used in combination.—**pneu-ma-to-cyst** (nū'mạ-tọ-sist), *n.* [See *cyst.*] An air-sac, as in a hydrozoan.—**pneu-ma-tol'o-gy** (-tol'ọ-ji), *n.* [+ *-logy.*] The science of air and other gases; pneumatics; also, the doctrine or theory of spiritual beings; also, the science treating of the mind; psychology; in *theol.,* the doctrine of the Holy Spirit.—**pneu-ma-tol'y-sis** (-i-sis), *n.* [+ *-lysis.*] In *geol.,* the process by which minerals and ores are formed by the action of vapors given off from igneous magmas.—**pneu"ma-to-lyt'ic** (-lit'ik), *a.* In *geol.,* pertaining to or formed by pneumatolysis.—**pneu-ma-tom'e-ter** (-tom'e-tėr), *n.* [+ *-meter.*] An instrument for measuring the quantity of air inhaled or exhaled during a single inspiration or expiration, or the force of inspiration or expiration.—**pneu′ma-to-phore** (-fōr), *n.* [+ *-phore.*] In *zoöl.*, the air-sac of a siphonophore, serving as a float, or the structure supporting it; in *bot.*, a specialized structure developed from the root in certain plants growing in swamps and marshes, and serving as a respiratory organ.

pneumo-. Form of Gr. *πνεύμων*, lung, or, less often, of *πνεῦμα*, wind, air, breath (cf. *pneumato-*), used in combination.—**pneu-mo-coc-cus** (nū-mō-kok′us), *n.*; pl. *-cocci* (-kok′sī). [NL.: see *coccus.*] A bacterium, *Micrococcus lanceolatus*, regarded as causing croupous pneumonia.—**pneu″mo-dy-nam′ics** (-dī-nam′iks), *n.* The dynamics of air or gases; pneumatics.—**pneu-mo-gas′tric** (-gas′trik). In *anat.*: **I.** *a.* Pertaining to the lungs and the stomach or abdomen (as, the *pneumogastric* nerve, either of the vagus nerves, a pair of cranial nerves which supply the respiratory organs, the stomach, etc.); pertaining to the pneumogastric nerve. **II.** *n.* The pneumogastric nerve.

pneu-mo-ni-a (nū-mō′ni-ạ̈), *n.* [NL., < Gr. *πνευμονία*, < *πνεύμων*, lung: see *pneumonic.*] In *pathol.*, inflammation of the lungs; esp., an acute affection of the lungs ('croupous pneumonia' or 'lobar pneumonia') regarded as due to the pneumococcus.

pneu-mon-ic (nū-mon′ik), *a.* [Gr. *πνευμονικός*, < *πνεύμων*, earlier *πλεύμων*, lung, akin to L. *pulmo(n-)*, lung: see *pulmonary.*] Of, pertaining to, or affecting the lungs; pulmonary; also, pertaining to or affected with pneumonia.—**pneumonic plague.** See *plague.*

pneu-mo-noph-thi-sis (nū″mō-nof-thī′sis), *n.* [NL., < Gr. *πνεύμων*, lung, + *φθίσις*, E. *phthisis.*] In *pathol.*, pulmonary phthisis; tuberculosis of the lungs.

pneu-mo-tho-rax (nū-mō-thō′raks), *n.* [NL., < Gr. *πνεῦμα*, wind, air, + *θώραξ*, chest.] In *pathol.*, the presence of air or gas in the pleural cavity.

po-a-ceous (pō-ā′shius), *a.* [NL. *Poa*, the typical genus, < Gr. *πόα*, grass.] Belonging to the *Poaceæ* (or *Gramineæ*), the grass family of plants.

Poaceous Plant (Kentucky blue-grass, *Poa pratensis*).—*a*, a spikelet; *b*, the empty glumes; *c*, flowering glume, palet, and perfect flower.

poach[1] (pōch), *v. t.* [OF. *pochier* (F. *pocher*), lit. 'put into a bag' (with reference to the white becoming set about the yolk in cooking), < *poche*, bag: see *pouch.*] To cook (an egg) by dropping it whole (without the shell) into boiling water.

poach[2] (pōch), *v.* [Cf. OF. *pocher*, thrust or put out (eyes), dig out with the fingers, prob. from Teut., from the same source as E. *poke*[3].] **I.** *tr.* To poke, push, or stir (now prov.); also, to trample; break up or render slushy by trampling; also, to mix with water and reduce to a uniform consistency, as clay. **II.** *intr.* To tramp or plod heavily, as through mud; also, of land, to become broken up or slushy by being trampled.—**poach′er**[1], *n.*

poach[3] (pōch), *v.* [Perhaps the same word as *poach*[2].] **I.** *intr.* To trespass on another's land, etc., esp. in order to steal game; hence, to take game or fish illegally. **II.** *tr.* To trespass on (land or water), esp. in order to steal game; also, to take (game or fish) illegally (as, "imperial property, and *poached* from a preserve": J. H. Newman's "Callista," v.).—**poach′er**[2], *n.*

po-chard (pō′chạ̈rd), *n.* [Origin uncertain.] An old-world duck, *Æthyia* (or *Aythya*) *ferina*, with a chestnut-red head; any of various related ducks, as the American redhead, *Æ. americana*, or the old-world *Nyroca leucophthalma* (commonly called 'white-eyed pochard'). See cut in next column.

pock (pok), *n.* [AS. *poc* = MLG. *pocke* = D. *pok.*] A pustule on the surface of the body in an eruptive disease, as smallpox; a mark or spot left by or resembling such a pustule.—**pocked,** *a.* Marked with pocks, as from smallpox, or with any disfiguring spots.

pock-et (pok′et), *n.* [OF. *pokete*, *pouquette*, dim. of *poke*, *pouque*, var. of *poche*, bag: see *poke*[2] and *pouch.*] A bag or pouch; esp., a small one inserted in a garment, for carrying a purse or other small articles; hence, that which is carried in such a receptacle; money, means, or financial resources; also, any pouch-like receptacle, hollow, or cavity; a small bag or net at the corner or side of a billiard-table; a cavity in the earth, esp. one containing gold or other ore; also, a small isolated mass of ore; in *racing*, a position in which a contestant is so hemmed in by others that his progress is impeded; in *aëronautics*, an air-pocket.—**to be in pocket,** to have gain or profit; be a gainer by a transaction.—**to be out of pocket,** to expend or lose money; be a loser by a transaction.—**pock′et,** *a.* Suitable for carrying in the pocket; small enough to go in the pocket; diminutive.—**pock′et,** *v. t.* To put into one's pocket (as, "He *pocketed* the letter," Hardy's "Return of the Native," ii. 7; "He wished me good luck, and *pocketed* my shilling," Weir Mitchell's "Hugh Wynne," xvi.); also, to take possession of as one's own, often dishonestly (as, "There was neither law nor justice . . . if Hunks . . . were permitted to *pocket* the cash": Godwin's "Caleb Williams," xxxvii.); also, fig., to submit to or endure without protest or open resentment (as, to *pocket* an affront); conceal or suppress (as, to *pocket* one's pride); specif., in the U. S., of the President or a legislative executive, to retain (a bill) without action on it and thus prevent it from becoming a law (see *pocket veto*, below); also, to inclose or confine as in a pocket; drive (a ball) into a pocket, as in billiards; hem in (a contestant) so as to impede progress, as in racing; also, to furnish with pockets; also, to form into a pocket or the like.—**pock′et bat′tle=ship.** A German war-ship of moderate tonnage but heavily armed.—**pock′et=book,** *n.* A book small enough for the pocket; also, a note-book to be carried in the pocket; also, a small case or receptacle, as of leather, for papers, money, etc., intended to be carried in the pocket; fig., pecuniary resources.—**pock′et bor′ough.** In England, a borough whose parliamentary representation was practically in the hands of some individual or family.—**pock′et-ful** (-fu̇l), *n.*; pl. *-fuls.* As much as a pocket will hold.—**pock′et=go″pher,** *n.* Any of various burrowing rodents with large cheek-pouches. See *gopher.*—**pock′et=knife,** *n.* A knife with one or more blades which fold into the handle, suitable for carrying in the pocket.—**pock′et=mon″ey,** *n.* Money carried in the pocket for occasional expenses; spending-money.—**pock′et=mouse,** *n.*; pl. *-mice* (-mīs). Any of various small, mouse-like American rodents with external cheek-pouches, as *Perognathus fasciatus*, of the western U. S.—**pock′et=piece,** *n.* A coin, often one not current, carried habitually in the pocket, as for luck or for its associations.—**pock′et ve′to.** The retaining without action past the time of the adjournment of Congress, by the President of the U. S., of a bill presented to him for signature within ten days of the end of a session: which is equivalent to a veto, since by law he is allowed ten days for acting upon the bill, and if Congress adjourns within these ten days and the bill is not yet acted upon by him, it fails to become a law, and which, moreover, prevents the possible passing of the bill by Congress over a direct presidential veto. Also applied to similar action on the part of any legislative executive.

White-eyed Pochard (*Nyroca leucophthalma*).

Pocket-mouse (*Perognathus fasciatus*). (Lower figure shows external cheek-pouches.)